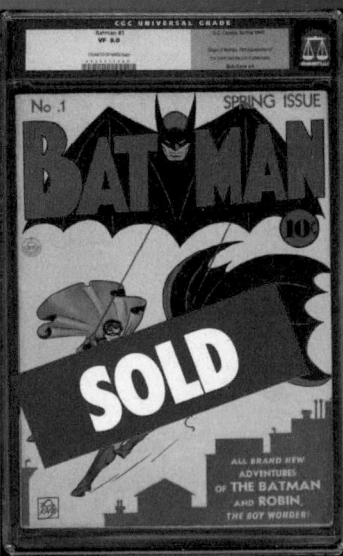

COMICS • PRICING • HISTORY

THE OFFICIAL OVERSTREET® COMIC BOOK PRICE GUIDE

39th Edition

COMICS FROM THE 1500s–PRESENT INCLUDED
FULLY ILLUSTRATED CATALOGUE & EVALUATION GUIDE

by ROBERT M. OVERSTREET

GEMSTONE PUBLISHING

J.C. Vaughn, Executive Editor & Associate Publisher
Brenda Busick, Creative Director
Lindsay Dunn, Editor • **Jenna Handy**, Marketing Manager
Mark Huesman, Production Coordinator • **Diana Hundt**, Advertising Assistant
Amanda Sheriff, Editorial Coordinator • **Heather Winter**, Office Manager

SPECIAL CONTRIBUTORS TO THIS EDITION

Robert Beerbohm • Dr. Arnold T. Blumburg • Eric C. Caren • Brandon G. DeStefano • Steve Geppi • Gene Gonzales • Ted Hake
Rob Hughes • Richard D. Olson, Ph.D. • John Seals • Jim Shooter • Billy Tucci • J.C. Vaughn • Richard Samuel West

SENIOR OVERSTREET ADVISORS FOR OVER 25 YEARS

Dave Alexander • Gary M. Carter • Bill Cole • Steve Geppi • Stan Gold • M. Thomas Inge • Phil Levine • Paul Levitz • Michelle Nolan
Richard D. Olson, Ph.D. • Ron Pussell • Gene Seger • Rick Sloane • David R. Smith • John K. Snyder Jr. • Doug Sulipa • Harry B. Thomas
Raymond S. True • Frank Verzyl • John Verzyl

SENIOR OVERSTREET ADVISORS FOR OVER 20 YEARS

Jon Berk • Gary Colabuono • Stephen Fishler • James Payette • Joe Vereneault • Jerry Weist

SPECIAL ADVISORS

Weldon Adams • David Alexander • Tyler Alexander • Lon Allen • Dave Anderson • David J. Anderson, DDS • Matt Ballesteros • Stephen Barrington
Lauren Becker • Robert L. Beerbohm • Jon Berk • Peter J. Bilelis • Brian Block • Dr. Arnold T. Blumberg • Steve Borock • Kevin Boyd • Mike Broder
Michael Browning • Michael Carbonaro • Gary M. Carter • John Chruscinski • Russ Cochran • Gary Colabuono • Bill Cole • Tim Collins • Jack Copley
Dan Cusimano • Frank Cwiklik • Carl De La Cruz • Peter Dixon • Gary Dolgoff • Joe Duncan • Walter Durajlija • Bruce Ellsworth • Conrad Eschenberg
Michael Eury • Richard Evans • D'Arcy Farrell • Stephen Fishler • Dan Fogel • Chris Foss • Philip J. Gaudino • Steven Gentner • Steve Geppi
Stan Gold • Michael Goldman • Tom Gordon III • Jamie Graham • Daniel Greenhalgh • Eric Groves • Gary Guzzo • John Grasse • John Haines
Jim Halperin • Mark Haspel • John Hauser • Jef Hinds • Greg Holland • John Hone • George Huang • Bill Hughes • Rob Hughes
M. Thomas Inge • William Insignares • Ed Jaster • Brian Ketterer • Dennis Keum • Phil Levine • Paul Levitz • Paul Litch • Larry Lowery
Joe Mannarino • Nadia Mannarino • Rick Manzella • Harry Matetsky • Dave Matteini • Jon McClure • Todd McDevitt • Michael McKenzie
Fred McSurley • Pete Merolo • John Jackson Miller • Steve Mortensen • Michael Naiman • Marc Nathan • Josh Nathanson • Matt Nelson
Jamie Newbold • Michelle Nolan • Charlie Novinski • Richard D. Olsen, Ph.D. • Terry O'Neill • George Pantela • James Payette • Chris Pedrin
John Petty • Jim Pitts • Bill Ponseti • Ron Pussell • Yolanda Ramirez • Jo Ann Reisler • Stephen Ritter • Dave Robie • "Doc" Robinson
Israel Rodriguez • Robert Rogovin • Marnin Rosenberg • Chuck Rozanski • Barry Sandoval • Gene Seger • Matt Schiffman • Doug Schmell
Rich Slone • Ben Smith • David R. Smith • John K. Snyder, Jr. • Laura Sperber • Tony Starks • West Stephan • Al Stoltz
Bob Storms • Ken Stribling • Doug Sulipa • Joel Thingvall • Harry B. Thomas • Maggie Thompson • Michael Tierney • Raymond S. True
Ted Van Liew • Joe Verenault • Frank Verzyl • John Verzyl • Rose Verzyl • Bob Wayne • Lon Webb • Jerry Weist • Rick Whitelock
Mark Wilson • Alex Winter • Anthony Yamada • Harley Yee • Mark Zaid • Vincent Zurzolo, Jr.

House of Collectibles
New York

Gemstone Publishing

NOTICE: Values for items pictured in this book are based on author's experience, consultations with a network of advisors including collectors specializing in various categories, and actual prices realized for specific items sold through private sales and auctions. The values offered in this book are approximations influences by many factors including condition, rarity and demand, and they should serve as only guidelines, presenting an average range of what one might expect to pay for the items. In the marketplace, knowledge and opinions held by both sellers and buyers determine prices asked and prices paid. This is not a price list of items for sale or items wanted by the author or publisher. The author and the publisher shall not be held responsible for losses that may occur in the purchase, sale or other transaction of property because of information contained herein. Efforts have been made to present accurate information, but the possibility of error exists. Readers who believe that have discovered an error are invited to mail corrective information to the author, Robert M. Overstreet, Gemstone Publishing, at P.O. Box 12001, York, PA 17402. Verified corrections will be incorporated into future editions of this book.

www.houseofcollectibles.com

ISBN: 978-0-375-72311-7
ISSN: 0891-8872

Printed in China

10 9 8 7 6 5 4 3 2 1

Thirty-Ninth Edition: April 2009

www.CollectorsAssemble.com
for high grade quality rare vintage comic books!!!
COLLECTORS ASSEMBLE!

www.ComicCollectors.net
for high grade quality rare vintage comic books!!!
DEFENDERS OF FREEDOM

ENHANCEMENT FREE

NETWORK OF DISCLOSURE

PROFESSIONALLY PRESSED

Table of Contents

Acknowledgements

Lon Allen (Golden Age data); Mark Arnold (Harvey data); Larry Bigman (Frazetta-Williamson data); Glenn Bray (Kurtzman data); Gary Carter (DC data); J. B. Clifford Jr. (EC data); Gary Coddington (Superman data); Gary Colabuono (Golden Age ash-can data); Wilt Conine (Fawcett data); Chris Cormier (Miracleman data); Dr. S. M. Davidson (Cupples & Leon data); Al Dellinges (Kubert data); Chris Friesen (Glossary additions); David Gerstein (Walt Disney Comics data); Gene Gonzales (introduction illustrations); Kevin Hancer (Tarzan data); Charles Heffelfinger and Jim Ivey (March of Comics listing); R. C. Holland and Ron Pussell (Seduction and Parade of Pleasure data); Grant Irwin (Quality data); Richard Kravitz (Kelly data); Phil Levine (giveaway data); Paul Litch (Copper & Modern Age data); Dan Malan & Charles Heffelfinger (Classic Comics data); Jon McClure (Whitman data); Fred Nardelli (Frazetta data); Michelle Nolan (love comics); Mike Nolan (MLJ, Timely, Nedor data); George Olshevsky (Timely data); Chris Pedrin (DC War data); Scott Pell ('50s data); Greg Robertson (National data); Don Rosa (Late 1940s to 1950s data); Matt Schiffman (Bronze Age data); Frank Scigliano (Little Lulu data); Gene Seger (Buck Rogers data); Rick Sloane (Archie data); David R. Smith, Archivist, Walt Disney Productions (Disney data); Tony Starks (Silver and Bronze Age data); Al Stoltz (Golden Age & Promo data); Don and Maggie Thompson (Four Color listing); Mike Tiefenbacher & Jerry Sinkovec (Atlas and National data); Raymond True & Philip J. Gaudino (Classic Comics data); Jim Vadeboncoeur Jr. (Williamson and Atlas data); Kim Weston (Disney and Barks data); Cat Yronwode (Spirit data); Andrew Zerbe and Gary Behymer (M. E. data).

Many thanks to John K. Snyder III for his *Avengers* #1 recreation, the great Murphy Anderson for his wonderful *All-Select Comics* #1 recreation, and Sheldon Moldoff for his *All Star Comics* #3 recreation featured on the traditional book market version of this edition. Credit is due my two grading advisors, Steve Borock and Mark Haspel for their ongoing input on grading.

Thanks again to Doug Sulipa, Jon McClure, Fred McSurley and Tony Starks for continuing to provide detailed Bronze Age data. To Dave Alexander, Tyler Alexander, Lon Allen, Dave Anderson (Oklahoma), Dave Anderson (Virginia), Matt Ballesteros, Stephen Barrington, Lauren Becker, Peter J. Bilelis, Kevin Boyd, Michael Browning, Dan Cusimano, Frank Cwiklik, Peter Dixon, Gary Dolgoff, Walter Durajlija, Conrad Eschenberg, D'Arcy Farrell, Dan Fogel, Stephen Gentner, Jamie Graham, Dan Greenhalgh, Eric Groves, John Haines, John Hauser, Jef Hinds, Greg Holland, Bill Hughes, Brian Ketterer, Dennis Keum, Nadia Mannarino, Joe Mannarino, Dave Matteini, Todd McDevitt, Steve Mortensen, Josh Nathanson, Matt Nelson, Jamie Newbold, Terry O'Neill, Jim Payette, John Petty, Jim Pitts, Ron Pussell, Stephen Ritter, Rob Rogovin, Marnin Rosenberg, Chuck Rozanski, Barry Sandoval, Matt Schiffman, Doug Schmell, Doug Simpson, Ben Smith, West Stephan, Al Stoltz, Harry B. Thomas, Maggie Thompson, Michael Tierney, John Verzyl, Frank Verzyl, Lon Webb, Eddie Wendt, Rick Whitelock, Alex Winter, Harley Yee, Mark Zaid and Vincent Zurzolo Jr., who supplied detailed pricing data, market reports or other material in this edition.

My gratitude is given to Chris Pedrin for his advice on DC war comics data; to Stephen Fishler for inspiring and helping develop the 10-point grading system adopted in the 30th Edition; to Dr. Richard Olson for grading and Yellow Kid information; to Dr. Arnold T. Blumberg for his introduction to the Promotional Comics section; to Bill Blackbeard of the San Francisco Academy of Comic Art for his Platinum Age cover photos; to Bill Spicer and Zetta DeVoe (Western Publishing Co.) for their contribution of data; to Ted Hake for pricing the Big Little Book section; and especially to Bill for his kind permission to reprint portions of his and Jerry Bails' America's Four Color Pastime.

Special recognition is due Bob Beerbohm, Richard Samuel West and Richard Olson for researching the Victorian and Platinum sections. Thanks to Eric C. Caren for providing the Pioneer Age article, Rob Hughes for the *Batman* article, Brandon DeStefano for his article on comics at the movies, John Seals for the article on The Hero Initiative, and the CGC Grading Team for the feature on third-party grading.

Acknowledgement is also due to the following people who generously contributed much needed data for this edition, including but not limited to Ron Almaria, Mark Arnold, Stephen Baer, Ron Ballard, Jonathan Bennett, Jonathan Calure, Monte Hall, Lawrence Kaufman, Jason Latko, Jason Lohr, Rod Matlack, Bob Morello, Stephen O'Day, Bill Parker, Dan Paulin, James Pender, Dennis Petilli, Mark Squirek, Tom Trombley, Ryan Wagman, Jeff Walker and Mike Wilbur.

Finally, special credit is due our talented production staff for their assistance with this edition: Mark Huesman (Production Coordinator), Brenda Busick (Creative Director), Lindsay Dunn (Editor), Jenna Hardy (Marketing Manager), Diana Hundt (Advertising Assistant), Amanda Sheriff (Editorial Coordinator), and Heather Winter (Office Manager), and J.C. Vaughn (Executive Editor and Associate Publisher). Thanks to my wife, Caroline, for her encouragement and support on such a tremendous project, and to all who placed ads in this edition.

webuy
comics.com

GREEN
...IS ALL YOU WILL SEE WHEN YOU
BRING YOUR COMICS TO YEE!
• Over 15 years of Experience as One of the Top Dealers in the Industry.
• Senior Advisor to the Overstreet Comic Book Price Guide.
• We will Travel Anywhere to view your comics.
• No Collection is too Small or too Large for Our Attention.
• Highest Prices Paid and Immediate Cash Available.
• Courteous, Prompt and Professional Service.
• Complete Customer Satisfaction.
• Accurate Grading and Competitive Pricing.
© Marvel
HARLEY YEE
P.O. Box #51758
Livonia, MI
48151-5758 USA
(800) 731-1029 or
(734) 421-7921
(734) 421-7928 Fax
Cash in the Hand is Quite Grand
www.HarleyYeeComics.com • HarleyComx@aol.com
Call, email or write us for a Free Catalog

PEANUTS
$41,264
$151,534
$11,550
AMAZING! STARTLING!
SUPERMAN
IS HERE!
TECHNICOLOR
AMERICANA & HAKE'S COLLECTIBLES
$19,898
Fantastic Four
THE GOERKE CO.
WELCOME
$10,350

CGC 9.8 Gaines
CGC 9.0 Rockford
CGC 9.0
CGC 8.0
CGC 8.5
CGC 9.2
CGC 9.2
CGC 4.5
MAD
Leading COMICS
GREEN LANTERN
ALL STAR Comics
COMIC CAVALCADE
BATMAN
ALL-AMERICAN COMICS
THE OVERSTREET COMIC BOOK ADVISOR
NETWORK OF DISCLOSURE
© DC COMICS

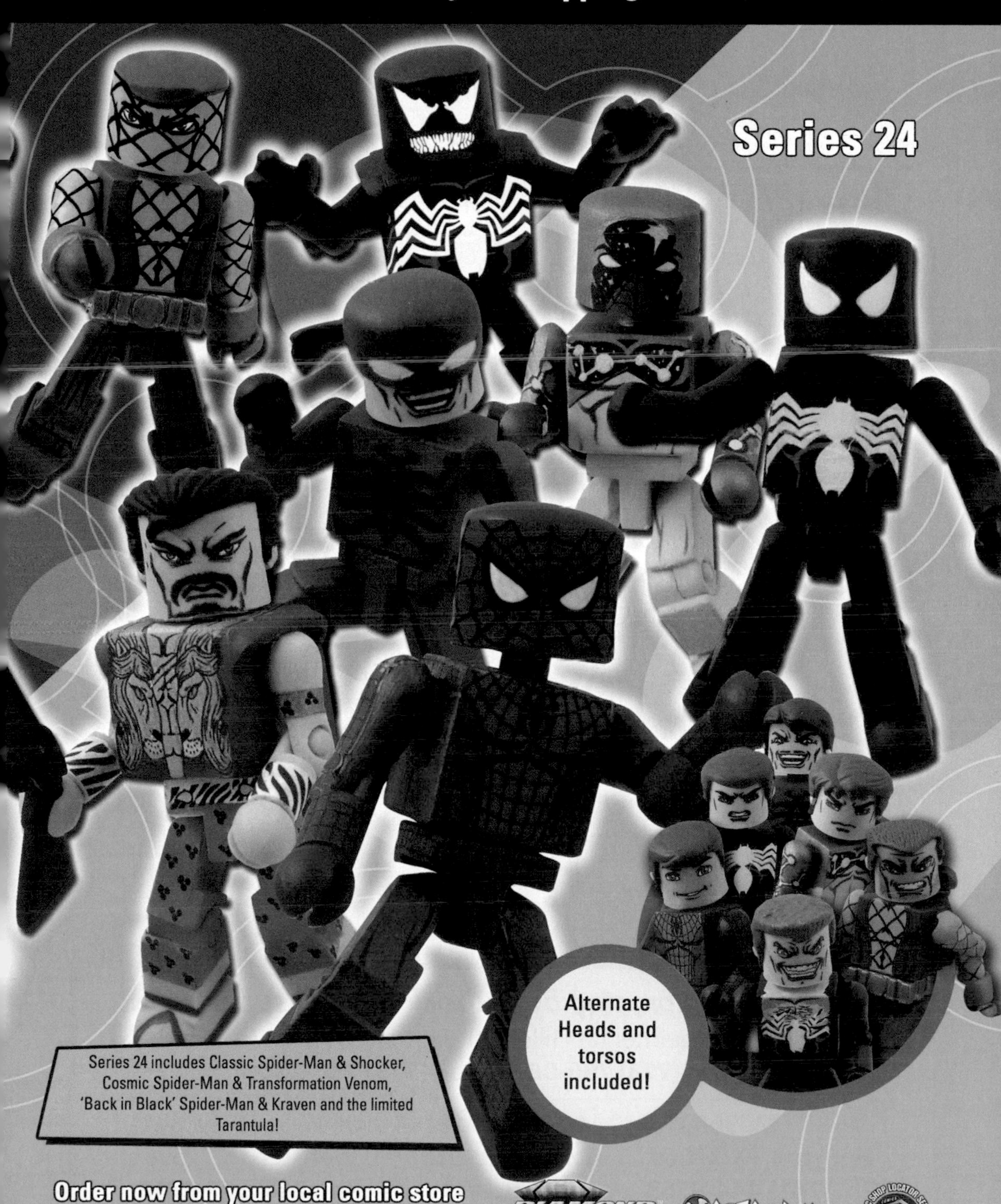
Get ready for a fantastic voyage through the Marvel Universe with these all-new jaw-dropping Marvel Minimates!
Series 24
Alternate Heads and torsos included!
Series 24 includes Classic Spider-Man & Shocker, Cosmic Spider-Man & Transformation Venom, 'Back in Black' Spider-Man & Kraven and the limited Tarantula!
Order now from your local comic store or www.diamondselecttoys.com
DIAMOND SELECT TOYS
www.diamondselecttoys.com
ArtAsylum
www.artasylum.com
COMIC SHOP LOCATOR SERVICE
888-COMIC-BOOK
comicshoplocator.com

Presenting the key to the city
www.bedrockcity.com
BEDROCK CITY
COMIC COMPANY
TM
Hey, cyber surfers! The ultimate comic book shop is now a comic book galaxy online.
G.I. COMB
Archie's Girls
Betty and Veronica
Fantastic Four
"MEET... DOCTOR DOOM!"
When in Houston, stop by Bedrock's stellar superstore.
6517 Westheimer (at Hillcroft) Houston, Texas 77057
Phone (713) 780-0675 Fax (713) 780-2366
4683 FM 1960 W.
Houston, TX 77069
Ph. (281) 444-9763
or our other two celestial locations
106 W. Bay Area Blvd.
Webster, TX 77598
Ph. (281) 557-2748

GEMSTONE PUBLISHING
presents
DISNEY
COMICS
www.gemstonepub.com/disney
or toll free 1-800-322-7978
Subscribe Today
NEW AND PREVIOUSLY RELEASED ISSUES AVAILABLE!
© 2009 Disney Enterprises Inc
Each month Gemstone Publishing brings you fun, action, adventure, and your favorite Disney characters in two comic collections: *Walt Disney's Comics & Stories* and *Walt Disney's Uncle Scrooge*. Both are available at your local comic shop, online, or by mail.
Are you missing issues in your collection? Back issues are available for the following books: *Walt Disney's Comics and Stories* #635-current, *Walt Disney's Uncle Scrooge* #320-current, *Mickey Mouse Adventures* #1-12, *Donald Duck Adventures* #1-21.
MAIL THIS COUPON TO:
Gemstone Publishing • P.O. Box 469 • West Plains, Missouri 65775
☐ Walt Disney's Comics & Stories: $83.40 for 12 issues, 64 pages ($90.00 Canada, payable in US funds) .... $ ______
☐ Walt Disney's Uncle Scrooge: $83.40 for 12 issues, 64 pages ($90.00 Canada, payable in US funds) .... $ ______
Back Issues
☐ Walt Disney's Comics & Stories: Indicate issue # ______ Quantity _____ ($8.00 each) .... $ ______
☐ Walt Disney's Uncle Scrooge: Indicate issue # ______ Quantity _____ ($8.00 each) .... $ ______
☐ Walt Disney's Mickey Mouse Adventures: Indicate issue # ______ Quantity _____ ($8.50 each) .... $ ______
☐ Walt Disney's Donald Duck Adventures: Indicate issue # ______ Quantity _____ ($8.50 each) .... $ ______
SUBTOTAL: $ ______
SALES TAX (MO residents add 6.975%; MD add 6%; MS add 7%; AZ add 8.35%; PA add 6%): $ ______
TOTAL: $ ______
Name:
E-mail:
Address:
CREDIT CARD:
☐ Visa ☐ MasterCard ☐ Discover
City: State: Zip:
Card #:
Phone:
Exp. Date:

pop culture with character
GEPPI'S
entertainment
MUSEUM

WWW.GEPPISMUSEUM.COM

WHAT'S online @ PREVIEWS world.com

diamondcomics.com | Home | Video Vault | Toychest | Bookshelf | Retailers | Vendors

PREMIER

- Dark Horse
- DC Comics
- Image
- Marvel
- Wizard

SECTIONS

- Comics & Graphic Novels
- Magazines
- Books
- Calendars
- International
- Trading Cards
- Apparel
- Toys & Models
- Designer Toy Collectibles
- Import Toys
- Collectibles & Novelties
- Games
- DVDs & Digital Media
- PREVIEWS UK
- PREVIEWS Plus

DEPARTMENTS

- Splash Page News
- Staff Picks
- Burning Questions
- Indie Edge
- Certified Cool
- Be FANtastic!

RESOURCES

- Order Forms
- Users Guide
- Convention Calendar

NEW RELEASES

- New Releases
- Upcoming Releases
- Shipping Updates
- Product Changes

PREVIEWS Publications

UPDATED EVERY MONDAY:

- **NEW RELEASES:** Find out what's coming to your comic shop on Wednesday!
- **UPCOMING RELEASES:** See what's available in two weeks!
- **WEEKLY NEWS:** Stay up-to-date with the latest on comics, upcoming products, and more!
- **PRODUCT & RELEASE DATE UPDATES:** Creator changes, new covers, updated release date, and more!
- **NEW PRINTINGS & VARIANTS:** The latest comics you didn't see coming!

SNEAK PEEK PREVIEWS:

Visit us to view sneak peeks from the hottest, soon-to-be released comics!

enter ZIP GO!

Click here for Marvel Previews

• SOLID GRADING, SOLID REPUTATION, COMPETITIVE PRICING •

CGC AND NON-CGC GOLDEN AGE, SILVER AGE AND BRONZE AGE. ALL GENRES

Have you been to large comic shows and only purchased 1 or 2 books?

Do you wish that all of a dealer's high grade selection could be in just one location?

Are you having difficulty in locating that hard-to-find issue?

Are you looking to upgrade from VF (8.0) to NM- (9.2) or NM (9.4)?

Large selection of CGC and non-CGC issues covering multiple genres.

All characters ©2009 respective copyright holders.

WELCOME TO THE WEB SITE DEDICATED TO THE BUYING AND SELLING OF CGC AND NON-CGC GOLDEN AGE, SILVER AGE AND BRONZE AGE COLLECTIBLES!

HighGradeComics.com

WILL BATTLE FOR YOUR BUSINESS!

I understand the emotional attachment involved when selling your collection.

I pay very fairly and the most important thing will happen: the check will clear.

ROBERT C. STORMS
17 Bethany Drive, Commack, NY 11725
Tel # 631-543-1917 Fax # 631-864-1921
Email: BobStorms@Highgradecomics.com

Want lists accepted and actually looked at.

• SOLID GRADING, SOLID REPUTATION, COMPETITIVE PRICING •

ABOUT THIS BOOK
BY
J.C. VAUGHN
ILLUSTRATED BY
GENE GONZALES
HI THERE!
WELCOME TO THE 39TH EDITION OF THE OFFICIAL OVERSTREET COMIC BOOK PRICE GUIDE.

SINCE THE PRICE GUIDE DEBUTED IN 1970, A LOT HAS CHANGED. COVER PRICES FOR NEW ISSUES HAVE GONE UP...
CHARACTERS AND EVEN PUBLISHERS HAVE COME AND GONE. . .
AND THE BACK ISSUE MARKET HAS HAD ITS UPS AND DOWNS. . . MOSTLY UPS, OF COURSE.

BUT SOME THINGS HAVEN'T CHANGED AT ALL.
NO MATTER HOW MUCH MONEY WE'RE TALKING ABOUT. . .
MOST OF US ARE STILL COLLECTING COMICS FOR FUN.

BUT "FUN" ALSO MEANS WE'D LIKE TO KNOW WHAT THEY'RE REALISTICALLY SELLING FOR, RIGHT?

THAT'S WHAT THIS BOOK IS ABOUT.
AND WE'RE GLAD YOU ARE HERE.

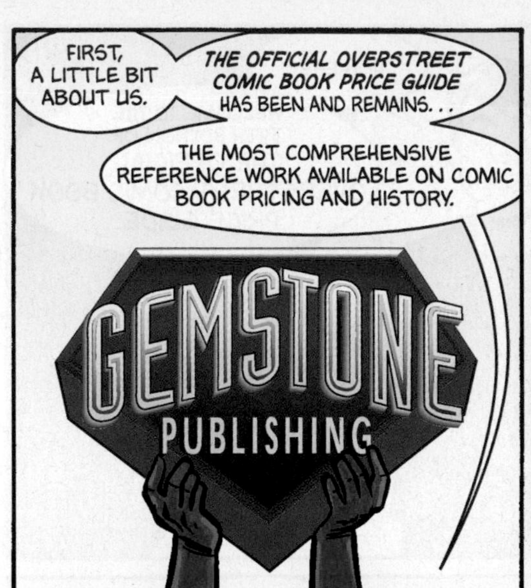

FIRST, A LITTLE BIT ABOUT US.
THE OFFICIAL OVERSTREET COMIC BOOK PRICE GUIDE HAS BEEN AND REMAINS. . .
THE MOST COMPREHENSIVE REFERENCE WORK AVAILABLE ON COMIC BOOK PRICING AND HISTORY.
GEMSTONE PUBLISHING

IT'S RESPECTED AND USED BY DEALERS AND COLLECTORS EVERYWHERE.
OVERSTREET PRICING AND GRADING STANDARDS ARE THE ACCEPTED FOUNDATIONS OF THE COMIC BOOK MARKETPLACE AROUND THE WORLD.
THROUGH HARD WORK, DILIGENCE AND CONSTANT CONTACT WITH THE MARKET FOR DECADES, OVERSTREET HAS BECOME THE MOST TRUSTED NAME IN COMICS.

OUR BOOK IS A DETAILED ALPHABETICAL LIST OF COMIC BOOKS AND THEIR MARKET VALUES.

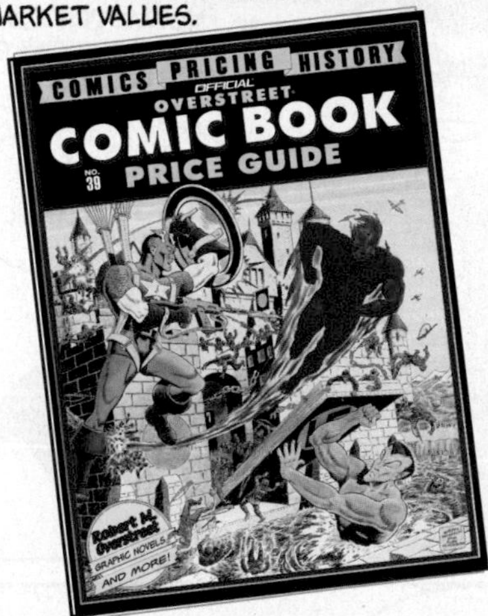

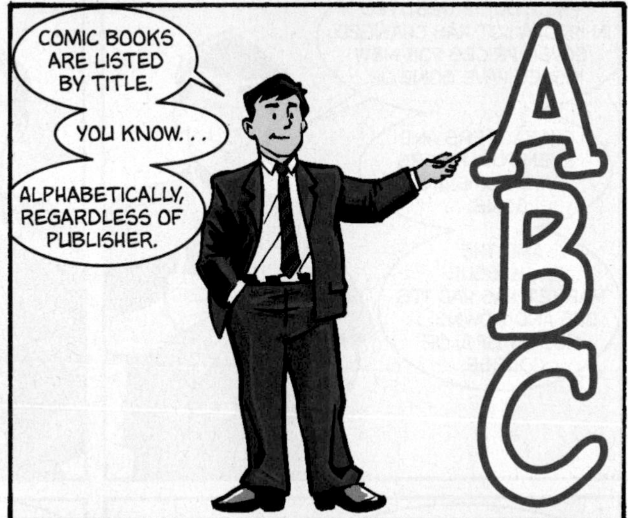

COMIC BOOKS ARE LISTED BY TITLE.
YOU KNOW. . .
ALPHABETICALLY, REGARDLESS OF PUBLISHER.
A
B
C

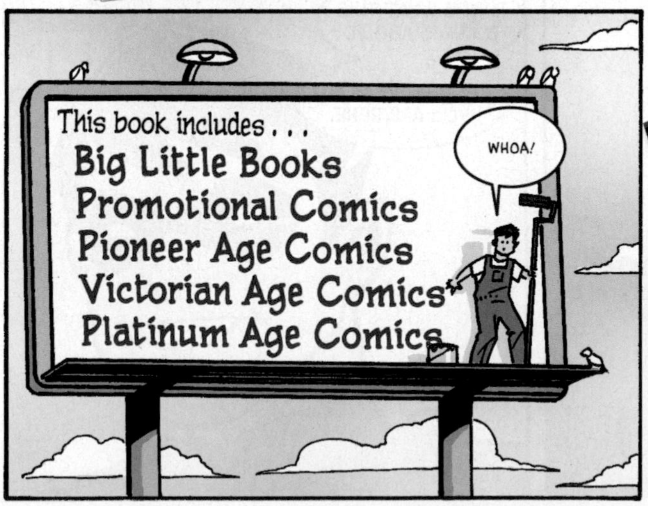

This book includes . . .
Big Little Books
Promotional Comics
Pioneer Age Comics
Victorian Age Comics
Platinum Age Comics
WHOA!

THE MAIN PRICING SECTION FEATURES COMICS FROM 1938 THROUGH THE PRESENT!

AMAZING SPIDER-MAN, THE
Marvel Comics Group: March, 1963 - No. 441, Nov, 1998

1-Retells origin by Steve Ditko; 1st Fantastic Four x-over (ties with F.F. #12 as first Marvel x-over); intro. John Jameson & The Chameleon; Spider-Man's 2nd app.; Kirby/Ditko-c; Ditko-c/a #1-38	1250	2500	3750	11,000	25,500	40,000
1-Reprint from the Golden Record Comic set	14	28	42	102	181	260
With record (1966)	22	44	66	155	258	360
2-1st app. the Vulture & the Terrible Tinkerer	340	680	1020	3060	5780	8500
3-1st app. Doc Octopus; 1st full-length story; Human Torch cameo; Spider-Man pin-up by Ditko	267	534	801	2336	4368	6400
4-Origin & 1st app. The Sandman (see Strange Tales #115 for 2nd app.); 1st monthly issue; intro. Betty Brant & Liz Allen	208	416	624	1820	3410	5000
5-Dr. Doom app.	171	342	513	1496	2798	4100
6-1st app. Lizard	156	312	468	1365	2558	3750
7-Vs. The Vulture	109	218	327	927	1714	2500
8-Fantastic Four app. in back up story by Kirby & Ditko	98	196	294	833	1442	2050
9-Origin & 1st app. Electro (2/64)	117	234	351	995	1723	2450
10-1st app. Big Man & The Enforcers	100	200	300	850	1575	2300
11,12: 11-1st app. Bennett Brant. 12-Doc Octopus unmasks Spider-Man-c/story			216	612	1131	1650

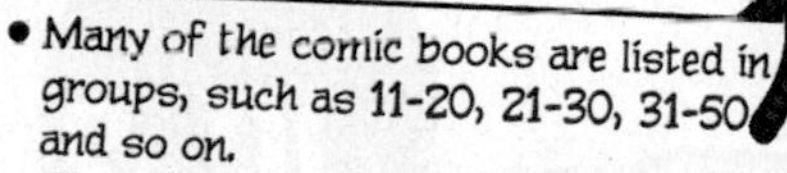

LIKE ANY OTHER PART OF LIFE, IN COMICS INFORMATION IS KING. THERE ARE ALL SORTS OF PUBLICATIONS ABOUT COLLECTING.

THEY COVER WHAT'S GOING ON IN THE BUSINESS NOW AS WELL AS WHAT HAPPENED IN THE PAST AND WHAT'S COMING UP IN THE FUTURE.

DISNEY COLLECTIBLES

150 YEARS OF CHARACTER TOYS & COLLECTIBLES

THERE ARE LOTS OF INTERESTING WEBSITES AND CHATROOMS DEVOTED TO COMIC BOOKS, TOO.

OUR OWN FREE WEEKLY NEWSLETTER, SCOOP, COVERS COMICS AND COMIC CHARACTERS.

FROM THE LATEST AUCTION RESULTS TO THE UNEXPLORED HISTORY OF THE MEDIUM, SCOOP'S WEEKLY UPDATES ARE IMPORTANT SUPPLEMENTS TO THIS BOOK.

JUST VISIT HTTP://SCOOP.DIAMONDGALLERIES.COM TO CHECK IT OUT.
SCOOP

WHAT'S THE FIRST APPEARANCE OF WOLVERINE?
I THINK IT WAS INCREDIBLE HULK #181, BUT LET'S LOOK IT UP IN OVERSTREET.
COMIC BOOK

DID ROBERT KIRKMAN OR GRANT MORRISON WRITE IT?
NO, THAT WAS BEFORE THEY WROTE EVERYTHING.
HERE IT IS. WOLVERINE HAD A BRIEF APPEARANCE AT THE END OF #180 AND SHOWED UP FOR REAL IN #181.

MANY FIRST APPEARANCES AND OTHER IMPORTANT ISSUES ARE NOTED.

WHAT ABOUT THE 34TH APPEARANCE OF GOAT RIDER?
UH, NO.
COMIC BOOK

IT IS IMPORTANT TO UNDERSTAND THAT VALUES LISTED IN THIS BOOK ARE APPROXIMATIONS OR GUIDELINES, PRESENTING AN AVERAGE RANGE OF WHAT ONE MIGHT EXPECT TO PAY FOR THE CORRESPONDING ITEMS.

THAT'S A COMPLICATED WAY OF SAYING "IT'S A GUIDE, NOT A PRICE LIST." IN THE MARKETPLACE, BUYERS AND SELLERS DETERMINE PRICES ASKED AND PRICES PAID.

WITH INPUT FROM A NETWORK OF EXPERIENCED ADVISORS INCLUDING WELL ESTABLISHED COLLECTORS, DEALERS AND HISTORIANS OF POPULAR CULTURE, WE HAVE UNDERTAKEN SIGNIFICANT EFFORT TO ASSEMBLE THIS PRICING INFORMATION.

THE RESULTING LISTINGS COME THROUGH THE OBSERVATION AND DOCUMENTATION OF PRICES REALIZED THROUGH HOBBY AND TRADE SHOWS, CATALOG SALES, RETAIL SALES, AND INTERNET, LIVE AND MAIL-IN AUCTIONS. DOCUMENTED PERSONAL SALES MAY ALSO BE INCLUDED.

WE HAVE EARNED OUR REPUTATION FOR OUR CAUTIOUS, CONSERVATIVE APPROACH TO PRICING.

WE ACTIVELY ENCOURAGE READERS WHO BELIEVE THEY HAVE DISCOVERED AN ERROR TO MAIL RELATED INFORMATION TO THE AUTHOR.
WRITE TO: ROBERT M. OVERSTREET GEMSTONE PUBLISHING, INC. 3679 CONCORD ROAD YORK, PA 17402
OR EMAIL FEEDBACK@GEMSTONEPUB.COM
VERIFIED CORRECTIONS WILL BE INCORPORATED INTO FUTURE EDITIONS OF THIS BOOK.
Editor's note: More information about this Guide is available online at www.gemstonepub.com

GOOD NEWS IN BAD TIMES! 2008 IN REVIEW

by Robert M. Overstreet

This was the cover art for *Adventures with the DC Super-Heroes*, a giveaway comic offered at Oriole Park celebrating Geppi's Entertainment Museum. Its interior was the *Batman and Cal Ripken, Jr.* comic found inserted in many DC titles in 2007.

Economic issues were at the forefront throughout the year as the world banking system suffered from bad loans made during the real estate boom. As housing values dropped, tens of billions of dollars were lost in banking last year, due to foreclosures. Loans, then, became very difficult, further exacerbating economic decline. It was reported over 60% of these loans were held by the mega-financial institutions, Fannie Mae and Freddie Mac. As their stock plummeted to junk status, the U.S. Government finally took them over in September as an attempt to save these institutions and restore confidence. The housing decline coupled with high gas prices that exceeded $4.00 per gallon and unemployment passing 6% became the daily headlines.

However, in spite of all the bad news, the comic book market kept rolling right along. Harley Yee wrote, "The 2008 market was one of the strongest in many years and saw many new trends." He also stated, "*Amazing Fantasy* #15 in Fine jumped from $5500 in 2007 to $9000 in 2008."

In July, Heritage Auctions announced that they had sold over $100,000,000 in comics since they began in 2001. Additionally CGC is beyond 1,000,000 books certified.

As we noted last year with ComicLink's recording-smashing *Amazing Fantasy* #15 and *Amazing Spider-Man* #1 sales, among other offerings, the market is neither shying away from previously undreamed of prices nor making them look like oddities.

Movies of comic heroes always influence sales. As Lauren Becker of Warp 9 Comics noted, "The one surprise that came with the *Iron Man* movie success was the amount of *Invincible Iron Man* #1's that we sold. We had ordered 10 times our normal (regular) *Iron Man* title....and the book did much better than expected." The first Iron Man appearance book, *Tales of Suspense* #39 soared with record sales occurring from $725 in Good to $2,629 in VG/FN to

$10,755-$18,000 in Very Fine. Batman was also in demand with *The Dark Knight* movie release with Heath Ledger as The Joker. Mid-range numbers were selling for multiples in *Guide* in high grade, and the *Incredible Hulk* movie increased demand for *Incredible Hulk* comics. As future movies are released, Maggie Thompson advised, "Plenty of people who would be part of theater audiences had never read (the comics). It's a good idea for would-be investors to keep that sort of trend in mind when they plan their strategies–while being aware that prices often peak just before a film's release." Look out in 2009 as several comic related movies are being planned.

Throughout 2008, thousands of comic book sales were observed resulting in price changes in this volume. Certain issues and titles have enjoyed increased demand with a decrease in supply forcing prices higher. Other issues have experienced a lower demand or increased supply which is reflected in lower prices.

Platinum Age: Many of the titles in this period remained scarce for the most part with mixed reports on sales from below *Guide* list to above *Guide*.

Golden Age: Early issues of *Action Comics* remained scarce with a CGC-certified #7 in 8.0 selling for a record $143,400! This issue is the second cover appearance of Superman making it a very important book. An *Action* #1 coverless sold for $22,250 and another copy in VF+(restored) brought $116,512! A CGC-certified *Adventure* #40 in 7.0 went for $35,850, the highest graded copy as reported by Peter J. Bilelis. A *Batman* #1 sold for $18,000 in VG, $80,000 in VF and a record $280,000 in 9.0. A CGC-certified *Detective Comics* #35 sold for $17,925 in 5.5. Another favorite book is *More Fun* #52, which sold in 6.0 for $65,725! *Wonder Woman* issues between #61 and #120 sold for over *Guide* list in all grades. A *Wonder Woman* #1 in 8.0 sold for $19,120!

An **Action Comics** #7 CGC-certified 8.0 sold for $143,000, a record for the second cover appearance of Superman.

Continuing to be equally as hot from the year before were the Timelys with *Captain America* in the highest demand. A CGC-certified *Captain America* #1 in 9.0 sold for $150,000 with all other issues of this title going for over-*Guide* list in all grades. The same is true for *Marvel Mystery, Human Torch* and *Sub-Mariner*. An *All Winners* #1 certified at 9.6 got $83,650; a *Daring Mystery* #1 in 9.4 brought $62,439 and a *Human* Torch #2 in 9.4 sold for $74,750! A *Marvel Mystery* #9 in VG/FN sold for $20,315!

Fawcetts from the Davis Crippen and other pedigree collections sold during the year at and around *Guide* prices. A *Captain Marvel Adventures* #1 in VG/FN brought $10,755. A remarkable CGC-certified *Special Edition Comics* #1 in 9.8 sold for $37,375! The Holyoke title *Catman Comics* remained hot with a #1 in 9.4 selling for $12,362, a #27 in 9.0 going for $1,610 and many other issues selling at over *Guide* in all grades.

Disney Duck one-shots were selling at *Guide* levels in the lower grades and over *Guide* in 9.0 and higher. A *Four Color* #4 brought $5,975 in VG and $3,585 in FN (restored). *Four Color* #178 in 9.0 got $2,629 while *Four Color* #189 in VF+ brought in $3,107! An *Uncle Scrooge* #1 (*Four Color* #386) in CGC 9.4 sold for $28,680! *Walt Disney's Comics & Stories* sales: #16 in 9.4 for $8,365; #19 in 9.4 for $15,535; #104 in 9.4 for $3,884 and #143 in 9.4 for $1,912.

Spirit Sections remained hot from 2007 with the first issue in VG- selling for $1,852 and another copy in GD+ getting $448! A copy of one of the rare Wood issues in VF sold for $2,868 and another copy in FN brought $507. The rare *Double Action* #2 sold in FN/VF (restored) for $16,730.

Schomburg cover books put out by Nedor were popular, especially the World War II cover issues. *Startling* #12 with the Hitler cover in VG/FN sold for $896. #49 with the classic robot cover in 9.4 sold for $9,560! A *Fighting Yank* #12 with the Hirohito cover in CGC 9.2 brought $2,012. *America's Best* #10 with the flag cover in 9.2 went for $1,673 and #11 with the Hirohito cover sold for $478 in Fine.

The Mile High pedigree books seem to be as popular as ever. David J. Anderson, DDS noted, "Comics from the Edgar Church Mile High Collection continue to sell well. The multiples of *Guide* values that these books are selling for continue to increase." A run of Mile High *Flash Comics*, all certified, sold last year at high multiples of *Guide*. A few prices realized were: #1 in 9.6 for $273,125; #2 in 9.4 for $53,775; #3 in 9.6 for $41,825; #6 in 9.6 for $65,725; #10 in 9.4 for $38,837; #14 in 9.6 for $35,850. As the years have rolled by since their discovery, these books are proving to be, in many cases, the best surviving copies of Golden Age books known that they represent.

One of our advisors, Ron Pussell, noted that early issues of *Action Comics* #1-20, *Detective Comics* #27-60 and *Superman* #1-20 were not at the conventions for sale. Also, the supply of Golden Age Key first issues and origin issues has dried up.

Restored books: We are seeing that more and more sales of Golden Age keys are restored copies as original, unrestored copies are becoming impossible to find. In today's market, key, important issues with light to moderate restoration could prove to be good investments for the future since they usually can be acquired at prices as low as 25% of the listed grade value. As Harley Yee noted, "Collectors have begun to realize with key books and rarer books that a lightly or moderately restored book is still highly desirable, and more importantly, highly collectible." Obviously, as supplies continue to dry up, restored copies of the keys will be the only copies available, especially at reasonable prices, affordable by more collectors.

Atom Age: Another hot area worth mentioning are the Matt

Baker art books such as *Diary Secrets, Teen Age Temptations, True Love Pictorial, Giant Comics Edition* #12 and others which brought multiples of *Guide* list. As Matt Schiffman wrote, "Fiction House and St. John are the Publishers of the Year for collectors. Matt Baker covers showed strength and then skyrocketed in '08 and Lubber's *Wings* covers finally popped in the marketplace."

The Harvey warehouse books were auctioned off during the year with many copies graded at 9.4 and higher and most were mid to higher range numbers. A *Little Dot* #1 in FN/VF sold for $3,585 with many above-*Guide* sales occurring for the run. A *Little Dot's Uncles & Aunts* went for $311 in 9.4 and a *Little Dot Dotland* #2 sold for $263 in 9.4. A *Little Lotta* #1 in 9.0 went for $1,315 and a *Stumbo Tinytown* #1 in 9.2 sold for $538 and another copy went for $388. *Harvey Hits* #3 in VF sold for $1,673 and $2,868 in VF+ and #9 in VF+ brought $1,912.

A CGC-certified copy of the scarce *All Negro* #1 sold for $10,062 in 7.5, $3,720 in GD+ and $4,481 in GD/VG. A *Reform School Girl* nn in VF sold for $8,962 & $3,107 in VG/FN. *Untamed Love* #1 in 9.4 brought $1,434.

EC horror and science fiction sold at and above *Guide* list with Gaines EC file copies continuing to sell well at multiples of *Guide*: *Haunt of Fear* #18 in 9.4 got $2,250 or 3.75x *Guide*; #10 in 9.4 got $2,400 or 3.27x list.

Other horror titles that were in demand with a few reported sales (all above *Guide* list): *Beware Terror Tales* #1 in 9.0 for $816; *Chilling Tales* #13(#1) in 9.0 for $862; *Dark Mysteries* #19 in 9.0 for $956; *Earth Man On Venus* in 9.2 for $2,760; *Eerie* #3 in 9.0 for $1,553; *Forbidden Love* #1 VF+ for $2,151; *Weird Tales of the Future* #3VF+ for $3,000 (White Mountain); #5 VF- for $2,850 (River City); *Horrific* #3 VG for $263, #6 in 9.0 for $777; *Menace* #5 VG/FN for $262; *Weird Mysteries* #7 in 9.0 for $1,195, #4 VF- for $1,912.

Terry O'Neill reported buying a large group of Atlas Horror and War comics. "These books were in an average grade of very good to fine and sold well at above-*Guide* prices."

In contrast, many Western titles continued to sell at below *Guide* list during the year.

Silver Age: Early issues of Marvel and DC titles were again the most popular. The Silver Age keys such as *Amazing Fantasy* #15, *Amazing Spider-Man* #1, *Fantastic Four* #1, *Tales Of Suspense* #39, *Incredible Hulk* #1, *Showcase* #4, and *Brave & the Bold* #28 were in high demand in all grades. *Amazing Fantasy* #15 (first Spider-Man) sales: $139,000 in VF, $42,700 in FN/VF; $13,145 in FN & $3,585 in GD+. *Adventure* #247 in VF+ sold for $10,157! *Amazing Spider-Man* #1 in 9.0 brought $31,070. *Brave & the Bold* #28 in 9.2 sold for $35,850; #29 in 9.0 for $7,767 and #30 in 9.2 for $9,560. *Justice League* issues sold for over *Guide* in high grade. A CGC-certified copy of #1 in 9.4 brought $35,850. *Iron Man* #1 in 9.2 sold for $896 and an *Iron Man & Sub-Mariner* #1 in 9.4 brought $777. A *Fantastic Four* #1 in VG/FN sold for $6,572!

DC war titles such as *All-American Men of War, G.I. Combat, Our Army At War* and *Our Fighting Forces* enjoyed strong sales at and over *Guide* list levels. *G.I. Combat* #68 sold for $1,673 in FN/VF and $1,075 in FN respectively. A 9.0 copy of #44 (the 1st DC issue) brought $2,629! *Our Army At War* sales: #1VF/NM for $3107; #2 FN/VF for $777; $81 FN- for $1195; $83 FN+ for $1912; 91 VF+ for $4,780. An *Our Fighting Forces* #1 in VF sold at $2,270 and a #45 in VG brought $956.

Silver Age keys like Iron Man's debut in ***Tales of Suspense*** *#39 continued to be in high demand.*

Stephen Barrington reminded us that 2008 was the 50th anniversary of The Legion of Super-Heroes who first appeared in *Adventure Comics* #247, a very popular Silver Age Key. A VF+ copy sold for $10,157 in 2008!

Bronze Age: Condition is the key for this period. Jon McClure reported that a 9.4 *Star Wars* #1 variant sold for $10,500! The *Iron Fist* #14 variant sold in CGC 8.5 for $2,200! Jon further stated, "DC War is this year's hot genre, although War titles from all publishers sold well in all grades, with key issues sometimes bringing double *Guide*." He also added, "*Green Lantern* #76, *All Star Western* #10, and *Weird War Tales* #1 remain elusive and continue to jump in high grade." *Green Lantern* #76 sales, all in CGC 9.2: $1,903, $1,899, $2,031 & $1,917! *Amazing Spider-Man* #129 selling in high grade for $1,000 was still in demand along with *Werewolf By Night* #32. A CGC-certified 9.6 copy of *Incredible Hulk* #181 brought $5,400 sold by Big B Comics.

Al Stoltz, who has an eBay store reported, "Huge increase in sales of comics to out of country buyers due to a plunging dollar."

In summary, as Peter Bilelis wrote, "2008 can be summarized as a year of continued growth and interest in the hobby. Top books and titles continue to excel."

It is amazing that the top movies for 2008 were based on comic book characters. Today, the general public has accepted the idea of "super heroes" that years ago were looked down upon by adults as trash literature. With future technology, we will see comic books mined for even more spectacular movies to come.

The top conventions had strong attendance in 2008. San Diego had over 130,000 attending with over 9,000 exhibitors and New York keeps growing, becoming a very strong supported con for the East Coast, as it used to be back in the Seuling days.

The following market reports were submitted from some of our many advisors and are published here for your information only. The opinions in these reports belong to each contributor and do not necessarily reflect the views of the publisher or the staff of *The Official Overstreet Comic Book Price Guide* or Gemstone Publishing. Have a wonderful and profitable 2009 everyone!

David T. Alexander, Tyler Alexander and Eddie Wendt
David T. Alexander Collectibles

This year marks our 40th year of continuous operations in the field of Popular Culture Collectibles. There was a time a couple of decades ago we thought we had seen and owned every comic book and pulp magazine ever published, but in the last few years we have unearthed several "one of a kind" issues that have made us realize that there are probably more treasures to be discovered. Nothing in comic collecting can compare with the thrill of the treasure hunt.

As was the case in 2007, the largest collections that we acquired in 2008 came from the estates of deceased collectors. Many big collections came our way and in several cases we had to bring in extra staff to move and process them. Penske Truck Rental Co. should be giving us a large discount! Our second warehouse is now loaded with material that we literally have not had time to sort; the majority pre-1975 publications. We have come to the realization that we will never be able to research, organize and sell quantities of items published after 1975. All of our comments will pertain to material published prior to 1975 back to the early 1900s. If we do take in later material, we wholesale it out to those who deal in it. Our system dictates that we research, grade, price and scan every item prior to placement on our web site.

The Economy: The subject daily on every news broadcast - The economy is up or mostly that the economy is down; stocks, bonds, real estate are taking a nosedive. One thing that stands out to us over the last 40 years is that comic book and collector's item sales are strong when the economy is weak. Sales are good when the economy is strong but impressive when the economy is weak. Maybe investors want to move funds into tangible assets when things go downhill or maybe it is because collectors love their comics and their attention is diverted from problem areas. Whether it is a change in investment strategies or just escapism, comics and the collectibles market still hold fast in these turbulent times.

Internet Sales: Website and eBay sales have become the foundation of our comic collectible business. Their volume is neck and neck with our call-in and want-list sales. In a way, we are a bit sad that catalogs are a thing of the past, as we always got a kick out of producing them. One smaller dealer recently told us that he still does catalogs but admitted that he printed only 10 copies at a time for old time customers who do not use computers. Every year we hear from a few more past catalog customers who are now computer literate, but the volume of new customers generated by the internet is amazing. Again in 2008 we had many buyers that were not familiar with the organized hobby and did not know about Price Guides or conventions.

Website: Our website has turned into a lifetime project. This site has become an archive for collectors and researchers and we welcome inquiries from those with a historical interest in paper popular culture. Our goal is to get every item in our warehouses on the site, scanned and described. There are many publications that have a relation to comic books that receive little or no mention, and we want to share this knowledge with others. Many of these are not easy to describe, but being able to provide a scan allows collectors and researchers to get a more detailed concept of some more elusive and esoteric items. Everything on the site is for sale and while it is heartbreaking to see rare items being packed up and shipped out, we need the funding to continue the Treasure Hunt. If you have not checked our site please do so. We have just completed the first part of our "About Us" page. Several collectors have told us that they found it informative and humorous.

*Pre-superhero DC issues were on fire all year long. (**New Adventure Comics** #26 shown)*

Golden Age Comics: Our most popular seller has been *Action Comics*. We have had more demand for *Action Comics* #1 this year than in the past several years. More collectors requested it than either *Detective* #27 or *Captain America* #1. Oddly enough *Superman* comics were not nearly as popular as *Action Comics*. *Batman* and *Detective Comics* were in second place followed by *Captain America*. The pre-superhero DC issues were on fire all year long. We could come nowhere near meeting the demand and had to beat the bushes for old time collectors who would part with some of their collections. We were successful in turning up many ultra-rare issues. One highlight sale was the highest CGC-graded copy of *New Adventure Comics* #26, which has the first full-page ad for *Action Comics* #1 featuring Superman. We are always looking for the pre-superhero DC issues.

All the Timely superhero titles sell well and this is no surprise to anyone. The big push in Timely this year is the Teen-Age and Good Girl Art titles. Among the favorites are *Millie the Model*, *Patsy Walker*, *Tessie The Typist*, *Gay* and *Comedy Comics*. Paper Doll issues have a crossover demand, as do those with Basil Wolverton and Harvey Kurtzman art. The Timely Westerns had an increased demand in 2008; most of these were actually published when the company adopted the Atlas Globe trademark. *Rawhide Kid*, *Ringo Kid*, *Kid Colt*, *Western Kid*, *Two-Gun Kid*, *Apache Kid* (Atlas was loaded with "Kids"), *Black Rider* and *Wyatt Earp* all drew lots of interest. The generic Atlas Western titles were more popular if they featured the continuing characters. For several years, we have felt that the Atlas Western demand was somewhat fueled by their fantastic line up of artists. Who would not want to read and collect comics with art by John Severin, Jack Kirby, Jack Keller, Jack Davis (Atlas also had a lot of "Jacks"), John Romita, Russ Heath, Gene Colan, Mort Drucker, Doug Wildey, and Joe Maneely?

While we are on the subject of Atlas/Timely, lets mention the Joke Books and Cartoon Magazines that were printed from the early 1950s thru the late 1960s. Most of these were digest-sized and featured pin-up photos and cartoons. Bettie Page, Tempest Storm and Dianne Webber all appeared in many of these issues. Comic collectors have long sought them as many feature art by Dan DeCarlo and Bill Ward. However the most popular issues seem to be the ones with Powerhouse Pepper comic strips by Basil Wolverton. Titles like *Stare*, *Gee Whiz*, *Romp*, *Comedy*, *Gaze*, *Snappy*, *Cartoon Parade*, *Jest*, *Joker* (which was also a comic book title) and *Laugh* are among the most in demand. Depending on contents these are available at prices between $15 and $50.

Star Spangled Comics was the surprise of the DC line in 2008. We had huge and frequent requests for all issues of this title. There were many character changes during the 130-issue run that was highlighted by several Batman appearances near the end of the series and some Jack Kirby art in the early issues. One key here is that this is an affordable run that can actually be completed without a major cash outlay. We had a lot of requests for *World's Finest Comics*, which is another secondary DC title, but the demand was nowhere near as intense as the excitement *Star Spangled* created. Here is a tip for bargain hunters: look for titles and issues that have something good about them but have no current demand. You will do best to buy books not while they are going up but while no one else wants them.

Fawcett comics are still consistent sellers. They do not have spectacular price increases from year to year, but if you examine their performance, you can see steady advances. Captain Marvel, who was created by Jack Kirby and expertly rendered by CC Beck, is one of the icons of the Golden Age. Even non-collectors still use the word Shazam. Many collectors buy these because it is still possible to complete runs of the major titles like *Whiz*, *Master*, *Wow*, *Captain Marvel Adventures*, *Marvel Family* and *Bulletman*. A few of the Fawcett titles will bring over *Guide* prices but most can be located easily at *Guide* values, but do not expect this to continue. If you have an interest in these characters get them now. Fiction House titles have been steady sellers for years and the trend was similar in 2008. Top sellers are *Jumbo*, *Planet*, *Sheena*, *Rangers*, *Jungle*, and *Fight* in that order. MLJ super hero titles had a decreasing interest during the year. Maybe collectors are frustrated in not finding copies and have turned to other titles. Golden Age Archie issues are strong sellers and have a big following. It does not hurt that the Archie characters are still on the newsstands and currently entertain legions of kids. Centaur Comics remain popular to a small group of serious collectors. Not enough of these issues turn up and several collectors call us frequently with almost impossible to fill want lists. We are still searching.

Many Golden Age comics sell above *Guide* levels. When you consider that the information in the *Price Guide* is about 2 years old it is easy to understand that items sell higher than *Guide* values. *The Guide* is charting past sales history and not giving future predictions.

1950s Comics: EC is the highlight of this era. All the titles sell and are led in popularity by *Tales From the Crypt*, *Vault of Horror*, *Haunt of Fear*, *Mad*, *Weird Science* and *Weird Fantasy* in that order. How long has it been since you have seen *Modern Love* or *A Moon, A Girl..Romance* issues for sale? We have seen increased requests for the various EC reprint comic books; various publishers including East Coast Comix, Russ Cochran and Gladstone have printed these. We have been selling these in the $15.00 to $25.00 range. The East Coast editions are from the '70s and had smaller print runs. Other EC items including books, portfolios and art have been strong sellers.

Good Girl Art issues generally have a short shelf life at our warehouse. Matt Baker action and romance titles move very rapidly. How often do you see copies of *Teen-Age Temptations* or *Wartime Romances* for sale? We search conventions for St. John and Avon titles and rarely find any. Even the major national dealers have a shortage of comics from these publishers.

Western comics have been steady sellers in 2008. The exception has been comics with secret identity characters such as *Tim Holt*, *Lone Ranger*, *Masked Ranger*, *Ghost Rider*, *Straight Arrow*, *Two-Gun Kid*, *Vigilante*, *Nighthawk* & *Trigger Twins* issues, and *Durango Kid*. There has been a very noticeable increase in demand for secret identity westerns from the 1950s.

Disney and DC and non-Dell funny animal comics have been surprisingly popular. Carl Barks leads the way followed by small publisher pre-code issues. Archie humor titles are consistent sellers with *Katy Keene*, *Betty & Veronica* and the 1960s sci-fi cover issues being the most requested. *Richie Rich*, *Casper*, *Hot Stuff* and *Baby Huey* are the most popular Harvey humor titles in that order.

War comics have been a consistent seller all year. DC is the most popular with *Star Spangled War Stories* out-selling *Our Army At War* for the first time ever. Atlas is the next most popular publisher for War title collectors. Some of the Atlas titles are a bit repetitive, but they feature the same great line up of artists that we detailed in the Golden Age section and they did span a wide range of wars in their stories. Many requests have been fielded by those with an interest in Korean War material.

Dell Comics: Dell probably printed more copies of every issue than any other publisher and every original collection that we bought in 2008 had some Dell issues in it. We have witnessed an increase in demand for photo cover Movie and TV comics. Many of these requests came from fans that were not in the comic book hobby. Several collectors admitted that they are trying to complete the *Four Color* run. We have not experienced this before.

Marvel & DC Silver Age Comics: The Marvel titles with the largest percentage of increased interest have been *Tales To Astonish*, *Tales Of Suspense* and *Journey Into Mystery*. The *Iron Man* movie certainly had a positive effect on *Tales Of Suspense*. Issue #39 has skyrocketed and we have had problems buying CGC-certified 9.2 copies at multiples of *Guide*. These three titles have always had a lower demand than *Amazing Spider-Man*, *Fantastic Four* and *X-Men* but currently appear to have been bargains. Our suggestion is to grab these titles before it is too late! The early '70s Marvel 20-cent cover price issues have become high priority items on our want lists. The issues with the framed covers are getting a lot of respect and they are not plentiful in high grades. If you have a chance to grab any of the issues with Steranko covers you should jump on them. Some of the Steranko issues are relatively scarce even in lower grades. Marvel Horror comics from this era are good long-term investments and they are fun to read. The big Marvel Silver Age question is - will *Amazing Fantasy* #15 become the most valuable comic book? This concept would not even be considered five years ago, but look at the way high-grade CGC copies have climbed in value and interest.

DC Silver Age closely followed the trends of DC Golden Age comics with Superman and Batman titles being the most popular. Most impressive in DC Silver has been *House of Mystery*. This early Silver title really picks up steam with issue #174 when the format changes from horror to mystery. Many issues between #180 and #200 have Neal Adams or Berni Wrightson art. Other issues in the Silver/Bronze era with these artists have become hard to keep in stock.

Original Art: Man, the art is popular. One of a kind items demand the respect of seasoned collectors and are always in high demand. Among our art selection, we were pleased to obtain and sell several pieces by Leo O'Mealia. Leo did the covers to *Action Comics* #2-6, and is a highly stylized Golden Age artist who went on to do sports cartoons for *The Sporting News*.

Pulp Magazines: Top selling titles are: *Doc Savage*, *Black Mask* and *Weird Tales*. *The Shadow* took a back seat to *Doc Savage* for the first time since 2001. *Black Mask* is the premier detective title and is credited with first publishing the "hard-boiled" detective story. Over the years we have provided lots of information about the virtues of pulp collection and their close connections to comic books. Those concepts have not changed, but we want to expand the horizons for those who want new areas to consider. When the pulps began to die out at the end of WWII, two formats stepped in to take up the gap. The Men's Adventure genre had its foundations in the pulps and went on to become hardboiled and lurid publications aimed at older readers, many of which were returning from military service in WWII. These "slick" magazines carried on the traditions of the wild pulp covers and bizarre features under the guise of "true" stories. Many of the top comic and pulp artists, such as Norman Saunders, George Gross and Rafael deSoto, contributed to these publications that were geared to a more adult audience. Today these are mostly collected for their cover art, which in many cases is spectacular. Check titles such as *New Men*, *Men Today*, *Rage*, *Fury* and *Man's Action*. These range in price from $10.00 to $150.00.

The other genre of consideration is paperback books. These have long been collected as they continued to offer pulp fiction when the larger sized pulps were no longer viable. Many of these have a comic book orientation as both authors and artists crossed over to both formats. Frank Frazetta, Neal Adams, Ray Bradbury, Gardner Fox, Graham Ingles, Wally Wood, John Wayne, Robert E. Howard, Edgar Rice Burroughs, Ian Fleming and Jeff Jones all appear in comics and paperbacks. Many paperbacks are well worth owning and high-grade examples are beginning to disappear.

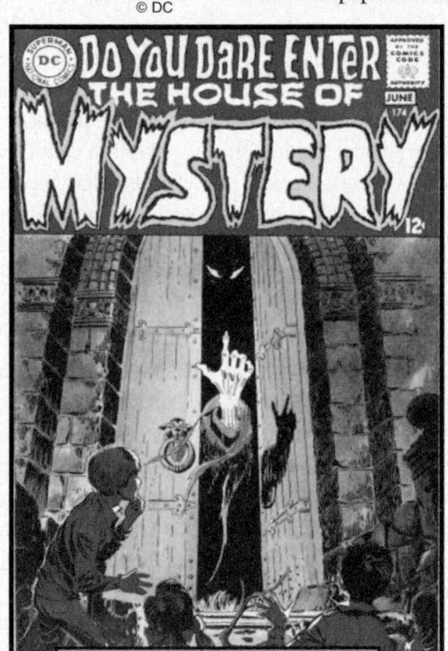

Sales of **House of Mystery,** DC's most impressive Silver Age title, really pick up steam with issue #174's switch to horror.

Foreign Collectors: Over the years we have shipped comics all over the world. When we printed mail order catalogs from the late 1960s up to the early 2000s we always encouraged orders from foreign collectors. With the advent of the Internet we have had a massive increase in orders from outside the US and Canada. We have spent considerable time trying to determine how to best serve collectors outside the US. In order to further research the situation and provide more immediate service to those who are located outside the US and who want to buy or sell, we have opened an office in Hanover, Germany. Tyler Alexander, our Chief Operations Officer has relocated and is staffing our European operation and can be reached through our website at talexander@cultureandthrills.com. During our years in the business we have always looked for new ways to serve collectors worldwide.

Conventions: The San Diego Comic-Con International gets an unprecedented amount of media attention. We saw it publicized on about half a dozen national TV talk shows for several weeks before the show opened. The crowds were massive, tickets were sold out in advance and for the first time ever tickets were offered by scalpers. The only downside to this multimedia event is that the comic collectors and dealers are now in the minority. Publishers of new comic books and Hollywood's many TV and Movie production companies have taken over. Year after year we hear collectors and dealers vowing not to return. Unfortunately they are serious and do not return. The show can be a lot of fun, but if it is old comics that you want, it can be disappointing. The Chicago and New York shows could become the places for old comic hunting. We still fondly remember the early 1970s when a convention table was $25.00 and a collector could afford to set up and sell his own collection. When was the last time you saw a collector take a space and set up at a comic book show? We have probably attended and set up at over 1000 shows since the first San Diego Comic Con in 1970. Currently it seems that the best chances of locating fresh material is at some on the one day shows that take place around the country during the year. The best one day show we have been to for the last few years is the Tampa Comic & Toy Show which takes place about 3-4 times a year near the Tampa airport. Dealers from around the country have sold there and chances are good that someone will be selling their own collection. I used to think that there were no comics in Florida but this show has proved me wrong. Conventions will always provide an element of fun that is missing from internet transactions. Everybody wants to meet other collectors, hang out and talk about comics once in a while.

Lon Allen and Barry Sandoval
Heritage Auction Galleries

This year we once again had the privilege to introduce several "fresh" personal collections to the market, and none caused more hubbub than the David N. Toth collection of Silver Age DC. As of this writing we aren't quite finished selling Dr. Toth's collection, but we've sold $757,000 worth so far. Leading the way was his *Brave and the Bold* #28 (CGC NM- 9.2) and *Justice League of America* #1 (CGC 9.4) which each fetched $35,850. Also, many of his copies are now the highest-graded on CGC's census report.

Some other staggering results from the David N. Toth collection include CGC-certified comics such as *Flash* #129 (9.6) $7,170 or 13 times *Guide*, *Action Comics* #252 (9.0) $7,170 or 2.9 times *Guide*, *Batman* #121 (9.2) $5,550 or 7 times *Guide*, *Adventure Comics* #290 (9.8) $5,375 or 16 times *Guide*, and *Detective Comics* #327 (9.4) $3,100 which is 15 times the *Guide* price, just to name a few!

The larger point is that DC Silver Age books are much tougher to find in high grade than their Marvel counterparts. This is true for the NM 9.4 level in particular - Marvels in this grade, with some exceptions, can be readily found in this condition, while DC 9.4s can fetch 5x to 10x *Guide* with regularity, as a copy in this grade is often tied for the highest assigned.

We were also very proud to be able to present the Rich Kylberg collection. It was an extremely impressive collection of virtually all the field's top comics, including *Action Comics* #1, which realized $116,512 - making it the first restored book ever to exceed $100,000 - and *Detective Comics* #27, that brought $65,725, as well as *Tales of Suspense* #39, which sold for $10,755, a record price for the grade and more than double *Guide*. The price realized for the entire collection - nearly $700,000, an average of about $8,000 per book - exceeded everyone's expectations, including those of Mr. Kylberg, the Denver media executive who assembled the collection.

One ashcan in the Kylberg collection is worthy of note for the hobbyist: a Fawcett *Flash Comics* ashcan edition with no cover art, but with Golden Arrow mentioned on the cover. This probably preceded the one with Captain Marvel on the cover (called Captain Thunder)... after all, if the more polished-looking Captain Thunder version had been first, whether it had succeeded or failed, there would scarcely have been any reason to follow up with this rougher-looking version later.

Walt Disney's Comics and Stories: Most everyone knows how high the print runs for this series were and how plentiful every later issue is... but while we think the *Guide* price in Good and Very Good should go down for this series (at least for #150-up), "top of *Guide*" is too low when you are talking about a strict NM- or NM copy. Just to take a random example of a non-key issue, we sold a CGC-certified *WDC&S* #156 in 9.4 for $657. Here's how tough the first 50 issues are in grade: as we write this, CGC has certified a total of nine NM 9.4 copies, two NM+ 9.6 copies, and not one NM/MT 9.8 copy. As for issues #1-20, these are tough even in mid-grade, try finding them in strict FN at last year's *Guide* prices!

Marvel Silver Age: The demand for *Amazing Fantasy* #15 and *Amazing Spider-Man* #1 seems unquenchable no matter what the grade, in fact several collectors who bought their copies in one of our auctions a couple of years ago have since re-consigned for a tidy profit.

Meanwhile, *Iron Man* #1 sells above last year's *Guide* price in every grade from Good up, but curiously, the rest of the Silver Age run from #2-up isn't in any higher demand than it was before.

Forgive us for saying this every year, but: almost every Marvel key is in high demand. Even the "second tier" keys, such as *Avengers* #1 and *Daredevil* #1 are strong sellers regardless of grade. Low grade copies sell for full *Guide* easily, as there are many collectors looking to fill those holes in their collection, and only have $500 to spend on one book.

Marvel Bronze Age: It seems we seldom encounter a collector who isn't trying to complete the run of *Amazing Spider-Man* #100-200. We were all set to anoint #188 (an almost all-black cover featuring Jigsaw) as the toughest issue of this run to find in high grade, and to dub it the Bronze Age counterpart to the 1960s Molten Man issue (#28)... but upon closer inspection, the toughest issue is actually #160 with the Spider-Mobile cover (and a black border)! We look forward to offering a 9.8 copy to our frantic bidders if a copy ever receives that grade! A very high-demand issue right now is #194, the first appearance of the Black Cat.

One interesting aspect of Bronze Age collecting is watching titles and issues heat up that were not hot in anyone's book not too long ago. One of the more gratifying examples is *The Invaders*. For those who can't afford to collect Timelys (which, let's face it, is almost everyone), this Bronze Age run has similar appeal with its great World War II covers, many by Kirby. Note #19 and #32, which even have the nefarious Hitler himself!

Ice-cold: Any 1955-present funny animal book in low grade. Also, any and all Platinum Age.

Scarce Issues: With each passing year we get a better handle on which books are truly scarce. We would urge the *Guide* to give the "scarce" designation to *Pep Comics* #22 (Archie's first appearance has incredible demand and almost no supply). *New Fun Comics* #6 is just about impossible (even compared to the other five *New Funs*, which we've been fortunate enough to offer now and then). As for Fawcett's *Wow Comics* #nn .... wow, where are all the copies? Someone give us a call to at least sum up the high points of Mr. Scarlet's origin (just kidding... do call us if you have this comic, though).

We can't wait to find the next David Toth or Rich Kylberg collection, and we look forward to helping collectors maximize the value of their four-color treasures.

Some titles/issues overvalued in the Guide:

Marvel Comics #1 (Still very, very desirable... just not a half-million-dollar comic.)

All Star Comics #4-7

Star-Spangled Comics all issues. Very expensive in the *Guide*, but has been a low-demand title for years.

Kamandi (nothing against Kirby's great stories and art, but you could argue that there is no key issue other than #1), *Sandman* #1 (1974), and *Omac*. These were all hoarded in such large quantities when they came out, that they are just never going to be tough to find in high grade.

House of Secrets #61-80 (this is the Eclipso run - it seems even the most avid DC horror completist treats these issues as if they contained Kryptonite)

Pizzazz

Crisis on Infinite Earths (more like Crisis of Infinite High-Grade Copies!)

Some titles/issues undervalued in the Guide:

Motion Picture Funnies (we auctioned a restored VG with brittle pages for $11,352)

Great Comics #3 (CGC FN 6.0 sold for $4,481)

Startling Comics #12 (Hitler, Hirohito, and Mussolini - we auctioned a VG+ copy for $896, and CGC has only certified one copy)

Captain Marvel Adventures #20, 21, 23 with miniature comic attached (good luck finding some, but when we finally did they fetched 2-3 times *Guide* at auction)

Superman #11 (as an aside, it will be interesting to see if the comics that were used on U.S. postage stamps gain any additional value in years to come).

David J. Anderson, DDS
Collector

At the midway point of the year and on the eve of the San Diego Comic-Con, I have noticed some obvious trends that have been present for some time in the comic book market, yet they seem to be particularly obvious at the time of this writing. First, despite a troubled economy, desirable titles of Golden and Silver Age comics continue to sell for hefty prices especially in high grades. This does not always apply to less desirable titles so these lofty prices are fueled by collector interest in specific titles in specific grades. It is also becoming obvious as more time passes and more guides are published that certain comics are rarer than others, so when these particular comics become available, they are something new and different and interest levels are high. These types of books will sell for over *Guide* values whereas common, often seen comics many times fail to reach *Guide* values when sold. Stating the obvious, but condition is important: A low grade mid-number *Walt Disney's Comics & Stories* may not sell for half of *Guide*, but the same book in CGC 9.6 or better may sell for ten times *Guide* or more. Comics from the Edgar Church Mile High Collection continue to sell well. More and more collectors are appreciating these books and interest levels are high. The multiples of *Guide* values that these books are selling for continue to increase. As I worked through the pricing that all advisors are asked to do, I couldn't help but notice that the 9.2 listing of most key books is more representative of the 9.0 price. It would make sense to consider making the top listed price in the *Guide* 9.0 for most major key books from the Golden and Silver Age, which would help make the *Guide* reflect the very high values obtained for these books when in 9.2 and higher. Select other books could qualify for a 9.0 top price, but not all. The reality is that only a very small number of key Golden Age books are better than 9.0, so to list values for 9.2 on these books when they are virtually non-existent is not truly reflective of the overall market. The same formula should apply to most early Marvel comics which consistently bring values over *Guide*. A few years ago, *The Overstreet Comic Book Price Guide* recognized the need to change the top

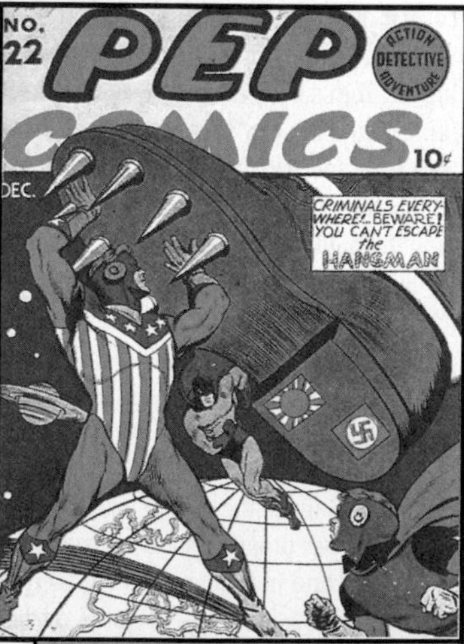

Archie's first appearance in **Pep Comics** #22 has incredible demand and almost no supply.

listed grade from 9.4 to its current 9.2, so another change to 9.0 should be considered.

Matt Ballesteros Collector

The War Report: This is the first of what we hope will be many dispatches on the "War Comic" genre. Our goal is to highlight and educate ourselves and others on what has become one of the more elusive and coveted categories in the comic book world. In this and in future reports we not only aim to focus on noteworthy or influential books but we also intend on sharing our findings regarding actual characters, title runs, trends and pricing.

In this first report we tackle one of the larger undertakings of creating a definitive "ranking" for the most significant issues of the war genre; something that we found to be an arduous and time-consuming task to say the least. But the results were well worth the effort.

News from the Front: As an avid collector of war-themed comic books, I both enjoyed and was frustrated by the niche's anonymity in the '80s, '90s and beyond. Have you ever noticed that published "genre" lists include top books for Superhero, Crime, Horror, Romance, Sci-Fi and Western... but never War. I honestly believe that most of us who collect war books secretly wanted people to pay heed to what we know to be a pedigree category of the comic collecting hobby. There was, of course, an advantageous element to this anonymity, in that my cohorts and I could gain from astute purchases on (what we considered) highly underappreciated and undervalued books. For instance, although there might be a notion about the scarcity or noteworthiness of a particular war comic, where it really stood in the annals of the genre was unknown but to a few ardent collectors and dealers. Conversely, we could also find ourselves facing overpriced titles for almost the identical reason I just mentioned, as there were instances where portions of the industry were uneducated as to significance and true value of these war books.

Well, as nice as our sentiments were about possibly sharing our passion, there was no real reason to run around and call attention to us, was there? Actually there was. And there are two enormous factors that make it unequivocally essential to continue to talk, share and spotlight the war comic genre. First, and most importantly, being the artists and creators who were behind it all. Although they need no advocacy from us, their contribution to the genre and to the comic industry should be continuously praised in the highest and most public manner possible-period. Second, Sgt. Rock celebrates his 50th Anniversary in 2009. Wow. This is pretty monumental in ways we do not have time to cover in this report, but a critical milestone in the war comic genre to say the least; and, whether certain collectors and buyers are on board or not, war books may soon find themselves center stage along with a few other highly desired and popular categories.

Base Intel: I think it is important to note that regardless of my beliefs regarding the shift in attention toward war comics, there have been a series of noteworthy events in the last few years that have lead to the recent fervor for this sector of the hobby. The first worth mentioning was the release of Chris Pedrin's *magna carta* published in 1994 and entitled "Chris Pedrin's Big Five" (a tip of the hat to you sir). His comprehensive look at the DC War category helped generate some general interest in the genre. The ensuing formation of the Big Five enthusiasts club may have also helped perpetuate war book fandom. Hollywood's modern romance with the subject of 20th century warfare with releases such as *Band of Brothers*, *Saving Private Ryan*, *The Thin Red Line*, *Enemy at the Gates* and so many more likewise may have whet the appetites of some for the war comic genre. The release of comic book titles by publishers in this new millennium chronicling original battle tales of *Sgt. Rock*, *Enemy Ace* and *The Unknown Soldier* along with recent releases such as *Battler Britton*, *War Heroes* and William Tucci's latest Sgt. Rock stories have likewise sparked increased interest. Most recently, the flurry of high dollar purchases both online and at auction houses whose origins (from my point of view) can be traced and attributed to the release and auctioning of Keith Marlow's renowned war book collection which primarily hit auction blocks at Heritage Auctions in 2007, kicked off what has been a continued feeding frenzy for high quality war books. These and other factors have made it fairly clear to me and fellow enthusiasts that the genre is now appreciated and highly sought after at an entirely new level.

That said, there is a lot of clarification that needs to happen for both veteran and incoming collectors that could help answer questions and even pave the way in the years to come for the niche hobby. We aim to help.

Orders from HQ and Some Reinforcements: When J.C. Vaughn at Gemstone invited me to develop a comprehensive list of the top 10 war books, I was both honored and daunted. As big of a fan as I might be, there are so many facts, details, titles and even characters that were unknown to me that span 70+ years of comic book publishing. Although I pride myself in my understanding of the category, I could not, in good conscience, produce a bona-fide report merely on the laurels of my general, and at times, limited knowledge of the subject. It became obvious to me that I needed to enlist the help of expert enthusiasts who could aid in creating a conclusive report and ranking. Within days I had assembled a small team of war comic hobbyists from coast to coast that I not only hold in the highest esteem, but whom I consider to be better versed in the matter of war comic specifics, lore and history. I now affably refer to them as "The War Correspondents."

Battle Plans: Although there were several different models we could have implemented in developing this first ranking list, the following is an explanation of how we generated, refined and finalized what is now listed in this issue of the *Guide*.

The first thing we did was to go through *The Overstreet Comic Book Price Guide* and record every instance of a title or issue that was either a war comic, or that had war subject matter, or that contained the appearance of a war-related character or, simply, just smacked of war. After we reached well beyond our 1,000th line listing, with no end in sight, we truly realized what a laborious campaign we had embarked on. From Don Winslow's first appearance in *Popular Comics* #1 to Vertigo's *Weird War Tales,* there were scores and scores of war-related stories and characters saturating the archives of the comic book publishing field. We did our best to chronicle every single one of them and even used resource material outside the *Guide* to fill in holes or corroborate specific findings.

It is important to state here that regardless of the countless hours of research - we are decidedly certain that we have missed characters, issues and even entire title runs that may have qualified as war material. Whether they are simply no longer listed in any resource publication or that our team was wholly unaware of a particular issue's importance to the genre, there is no way to guarantee that our oversized net captured every significant title out there. That said, please understand that the list published in this issue of the *Guide*, although quite comprehensive, will in fact evolve and morph from year to year to reflect new evidence discovered, hopefully to include feedback from experts and enthusiasts, and, of course, to adjust to price fluctuations in the market.

On the Attack!: After developing our massive "master list," our second task was to determine what truly constituted a "war comic." This became an almost equally daunting undertaking and engendered multiple conference calls and heavy discourse and debate between our team at all hours of the night. Our burden was to classify the difference between books and even characters that spoke of or appeared to be in a war-based environment. The first and most obvious course of action was to define war itself. So we set parameters that narrowed the field by characterizing war comics as "stories centered on the military, which is involved in armed conflicts" and, as such, needed to be relegated to those wars "categorized as a major conflict." Although some titles still persevered through this elimination process, it did help purge many comics that were centered on themes such as the Cold War, police actions, spy-centric, etc.

The next monumental task was to tackle actual characters in war-related stories. It goes without saying that during World War II there was an onslaught of comics created by a large number of comic book publishers that took on the subject of war. Particularly after Pearl Harbor, whereby everything from funny animals to costumed heroes bore arms against the Axis. Thus there exist numerous issues within originally "non-war" titles that were dedicated to fighting battles against the Germans, Italians and Japanese. Needless to say, we were able to easily eliminate a good deal of these candidates by employing the notion that "Any war story blended with a superhero is by definition a 'fantasy' story and would not be a war story. Schomburg covers featuring the Timely heroes taking on Hitler and 3,000 Germans do not qualify." OK, tights and fur aside, we still faced the prospect of determining where characters like Blackhawk or Joe Palooka stood, how about the Boy Commandos or Canteen Kate? And you would not believe the large number of Golden Age heroes that existed in a very large grey area like protagonists The Phantom Eagle or Captain Valor.

Another Tactical Objective: It became evident to us that as holistic and thorough as we wanted our coverage to be, we needed to create another classification within our own war book genre in order to formulate a concise final report. This classification consisted of defining what type of war themes actually existed. Therefore a class order began to emerge that, as of today, is still being refined. Either way, its implementation was of tremendous help in developing the list you see in this publication. The classifications roughly took shape as follows:

War Battle Tales - Stories that were predominantly centered on characters engulfed in battle. *Frontline Combat*, *All-American Men of War* and *Sgt. Fury* are good examples.

Military Life - Stories that encompass all aspects of being a member of the armed forces. *Beetle Bailey*, *Sgt Barney Barker*, *Canteen Kate* and *Sad Sack* are military stories that are generally set outside of battles.

War Adventure - Stories or characters that may have launched from a major conflict or may be military centric, yet whose storylines do not focus on battles in the trenches. *Blackhawk* and Modern *G.I. Joe* are such examples.

War Propaganda - Stories or accounts specifically developed to promote and justify military action and/or for real life recruitment. *Design for Survival*, *The Red Iceberg*, *Adventure is My Career*, to name a few.

Lifetime During War - Stories about life during wartime. *Joe Palooka* fits here.

Tragedy in Wartime - Stories or accounts of the holocaust or of human tragedy during war. *Maus* and *Fax from Sarajevo* are key examples of this.

Anti-War - Stories or accounts specifically developed to propagate the philosophy of ending wars altogether. *I Saw It* and *Maus* (again). There was even discussion amongst us about the fact that many war titles may actually be anti-war, such as most of Kurtzman's war battle tales.

There are even more categorizations, including romance, horror, sci-fi and fantasy (DC War's dinosaur stories) to name a few. The above classifications we developed allowed us to narrow the field to a digestible size, at which point we were able to definitively choose our path for developing our War Book List. We obviously picked "War Battle Tales" as our specific criteria and concluded that, over the ensuing years, we may (and hope) be able to develop a grander and wider-ranging "Master" list that includes all or some of the other categories detailed above. But for now, War Battle Tales has become our category of choice-a refined list that, interestingly enough, still boasts over 700 listings.

Assessments after Battle: Finally, we came to the conclusion that there were clearly defined and separate ages for the war book genre. For us, they are currently the Golden Age, the Atom/Silver Age and the Modern Age. Although there are certainly countless titles launched during the Atom and Silver age respectively, the two ages are intrinsically meshed. Many

© DC

***Our Army at War** #83*
introduced the most definitive Sgt. Rock in June 1959.

Silver Age mammoths got their start in the Atom Age and blossommed into and through the lifespan of the Silver Age. Consequently, our report here only focuses on two, the Golden and Atom/Silver Ages as the Modern Age does not have any title or issue with the caliber to even attain a ranking in the top 50+ books. That said, please be aware that the Golden Age in particular is so vast and undocumented (unlike the subsequent Silver Age) that the list developed for this year's *Guide* should only serve as a "go-by" until we can do further research, receive feedback and substantiate our initial findings.

Gaining Rank: After reducing our total listings by way of adhering to the criteria I have elaborated on, the War Correspondent team was each handed a digital file with the final remaining titles to consider. At which point each member separated and voted autonomously, dispensing our individual votes on each war book in order to create an absolute ranking. Criteria used during our considerations included factors such as significance of book, appearances, art and storyline, rarity, and so on. Each participant placed a number next to each book which they felt represented its ranking; for instance, a #1 for the top book of their choice, a #2 for the next book and so on, until 40 or so books were picked in each category. Of course #40, although being noteworthy in the genre, still represented the bottom of the list.

Victory!: The result came as we combined our scoring to ascertain a comprehensive and, at least for us, conclusive ranking of war comic books. We hope that these lists, accepted or not, will do their small part for the hobby in eventually formalizing a foundation for the genre. And we also hope that the lists can be used as tools in perpetuating interest in war comics, highlighting deserving titles, characters and creators while carefully moderating their value accordingly. Enjoy!

In closing, I would like to reiterate that although the lists contain titles that we avid enthusiasts canonize and admire, these lists are by no means the final say on how and where these comic books rank. It needs to be understood by collectors and dealers alike that the process to truly finalize these particular rankings and the subsequent course of determining accurate values will take years to accomplish. Use these lists to your advantage, but be aware that there may be notable changes in the short term as we get feedback, see how the market responds and reassess our initial findings.

Top 10 Golden Age War Comic Nominees

1) *Wings Comics* #1 - Fundamental war & adventure title launch
2) *War Comics* #1 - 1st comic completely dedicated to war
3) *Real Life Comics* #3 - "Emperor of Hate"-- infamous Hitler war cover
4) *Contact Comics* #1 - LB Cole aviation war covers begin
5) *Real Life Comics* #1 - Historic war depictions begin -- Uncle Sam cover
6) *Wings Comics* #2 - Air war adventures continue
7) *Bill Barnes Comics* #1 - 1st comic book app. of Bill Barnes
8) *Rangers Comics* #8 - U.S. Rangers begin
9) *Remember Pearl Harbor* nn - Tribute to Pearl Harbor
10) *United States Marines* #2 Classic cover -- Mart Bailey art

Other Notable Golden Age War Comics

Don Winslow of the Navy V1 #1 - Early app of Don Winslow
American Library nn (#1) - Thirty Seconds Over Tokyo -- Classic title and cover

Top 20 Atom & Silver Age War Comics

1) *Our Army at War* #83 - Most definitive 1st Sgt. Rock
2) *G.I. Combat* #87 - 1st Haunted Tank and 1st Jeb Stuart -- Classic Heath washtone
3) *G.I. Combat* #68 1st in trio to Sgt. Rock lead-up by Kanigher and Kubert
4) *Our Army at War* #81 - 2nd in trio to Sgt. Rock lead-up by Haney and Andru/Esposito
5) *Our Army at War* #82 - 3rd in trio to Sgt. Rock lead-up by Haney/Drucker
6) *Our Army at War* #1 - 1st DC War title -- tied with *Star Spangled War Stories* #131
7) *Two Fisted Tales* #18 - 1st classic Kurtzman war title
8) *Frontline Combat* #1 - 2nd classic Kurtzman war title
9) *Our Army at War* #90 - 1st origin of Sgt. Rock -- "How Rock Got His Stripes"
10) *Sgt. Fury* #1 - 1st Sgt Fury -- Major Marvel war title
11) *G.I. Combat* #44 - DC takes over classic war title -- washtone cover
12) *Our Army at War* #88 - 1st Sgt. Rock cover -- Kubert
13) *Our Fighting Forces* #1 - Launch of fourth DC Big Five war title
14) *Our Fighting Forces* #45 - Gunner and Sarge begin; 1st Grandenetti
15) *Our Army at War* #91 - 1st all Sgt. Rock issue
16) *All-American Men of War* #28 - 1st Sgt. Rock prototype by Heron and Kubert
17) *All-American Men of War* #127(#1) - Tied with *Our Army at War* #1 for 1st DC war title
18) *Star Spangled War Stories* #131 - Launch of 3rd DC Big Five war title
19) *Our Army at War* #151 - 1st Enemy Ace -- Kanigher & Kubert -- black cover
20) *Star Spangled War Stories* #84 - 1st Mlle. Marie

Thanks to the Troops: I would like to give a gigantic thank you to the following people who were instrumental in developing this report and the lists; Alan Bartholomew, Keith Marlow and Mick Rabin. Their time and hours of dedication are what made this tremendous task possible. Of course, our team would like to extend our gratitude to J.C. Vaughn and Bob Overstreet for entrusting us with such an important endeavor. And, I also want to give quick thanks to Richard Evans from Bedrock City Comics for his insight and for keeping my war book collecting habit at an unquestionably unhealthy level.

Stephen Barrington
Flea Market Comics

The local comic market on the Alabama Gulf Coast (Mobile) took a downturn in 2007 with the main store enjoying success only as a part-time entity for a metropolitan area of over 400,000.

The sluggish economy had flat sales during the summer months, including new and back issues. The few exceptions have been DC's weekly titles (*Countdown* and *Trinity*) and Marvel's *Secret Invasion* titles. DC's *Final Crisis* line sales have been strong. Image sales have been weak but Dark Horse's *Star Wars* titles have been strong, especially with *Legacy*. Back issues are hard to keep in stock. Batman's new sales have also been strong as well as Marvel's two main X-Men titles.

Vertigo imprints seem to appeal to a very limited market while Marvel's Max titles aren't much better. Basically it's DC versus Marvel for the new comics while Dark Horse is a distant third and Image bringing up the rear.

Silver Age DC's sell in spurts with Batman titles staying strong as always. Superman doesn't seem to be a consistent seller for 1960s and back. Occasionally someone will come in a buy a handful. *World's Finest Comics* doesn't do well, with *Adventure Comics* in the same boat. DC digests don't show up in the shop but that's just as well since we don't have anyone asking for them. *Green Lantern*, *Flash*, *The Atom* and *Justice League of America* are steady sellers when priced right. Key issues for these titles rarely show up for sale.

Adventure Comics #247 (first Legion of Super-Heroes) has become a tough book to find in any grade and will sell over *Guide* easily. The Legion celebrated its 50th anniversary in 2008. It's hard to believe this book listed for $2.00 in 1974. Their second appearance in *Adventure* #267 in 1959 is also a red-hot item.

We receive a lot of calls from people wanting to sell their collections, but most of the time the issues are in rough shape and the sellers having too high of expectations as to what they are worth. Many think just because it's an old comic or that it's 10 years or older, that it must be valuable. Golden Age comics don't show up at all but they are hard to sell anyway with the exception of *Batman* and *Detective*.

Marvel's variant covers sell steady but not above the $10 or $15 mark. *Amazing Spider-Man* sells well for issues below #105; *Fantastic Four* issues #100 and under sell radically. The *Incredible Hulk* section just gathers dust with a few exceptions.

The *Iron Man* and *Incredible Hulk* movies did little to spur sales of these titles. All it did was increase demand for $1.00 issues since it was kids looking for bargains..

The main books collectors are always looking for are predictable: *Incredible Hulk* #180, 181 and 182 and *Giant-Size X-Men* #1 and *X-Men* #94. These issues never seem to stay in the shop in any grade. For those who can afford them, *Amazing Fantasy* #15, *X-Men* #1, *Amazing Spider-Man* #1 seem to be the goals for older collectors with *Fantastic Four* #1 a distant fourth. These issues rarely show up for sale. *Strange Tales*, *Tales To Astonish* and *Tales Of Suspense*, despite Iron Man stories, don't cause much of a ripple in the market. Our half-price section of these titles in low grade do well, though.

CGC-certified issues don't seem to interest many in this area but occasionally someone will come in to have us send off comics to be graded. They're usually happy with the results. The main complaint about CGC books is why bother to have a brand new comic graded even if it does come back a 9.6 or 9.8. By the same token, why bother getting mid-grade non-key Silver Age comics graded when they come back 6.0 or 5.5?

Comics from the 1950s form a strange market. Decent condition comics from the many areas sell at half-price. Dell humor titles, including *Donald Duck*, *Uncle Scrooge* and *Bugs Bunny* are extremely slow sellers. Harvey and Archie titles from the 1960s do a little better. Pulps and Big Little book sales are non-existent. Comic book collector supplies sell very well with emphasis on Mylars, full and regular backing boards and boxes heading the list.

Quarter comics move very well as do $1.00 issues. The ever increasing prices on new comics probably has something to do with it. Quarter comics sometimes create a shortage until another collection comes in with a lot of so-so demand books.

eBay sales are deplorable with listed items not even garnering close to 50% of *Guide*. Many bargains can be found through eBay which in turn sell in the shop because they can be heavily discounted. Everyone loves a bargain.

The Guide helps sales on almost all books since collectors can get an idea as to how comics sell in other parts of the country or world. The reference material in *The Overstreet Comic Book Price Guide* is one of its greatest assets.

With Wizard World Chicago being held before Comic Con International: San Diego last year, it seemed to be a big boost to this three-day convention. The attendance was incredible with Saturday being jam-packed. The total number of comics there was massive and sales seemed to be brisk. The convention featured many artists from fan favorites Alex Ross and Todd McFarlane to dozens and dozens of up and coming artists. Many familiar dealers were in attendance including Graham Crackers, Harley Yee, JHV Associates, Crazy Ed, Terry's Comics, Super World and many others.

Lauren Becker
Warp 9 Comics

With a troubling economy and gas prices soaring to a new high ($4.10 a gallon as of this writing), how is the comic collectibles business surviving? Pretty well actually. Now don't get me wrong…it's pretty brutal right now…we did lose some customers, however, there are *still* new customers coming in every month. This is especially true due to the high profile movies and special projects that capture the common person's attention…

Case in point? *Iron Man*. This is the one movie that, even though we knew it would do well, no one expected it to do *this* well! And let me tell you, did this movie bring in the people (of course, the movie came out the same weekend as Free Comic Book Day, but that is besides the point). The one surprise that came with the *Iron Man* movie success was the amount of *Invincible Iron Man* #1's that we sold. We had ordered 10 times our normal (regular) *Iron Man* title, mainly due to the variants, and the book did *much* better than expected. A title that I thought we might have to blow out in a convention $1 box later on, is already commanding $4-5 each in the back issues. The hype machine on this title also helped back issues. We sold a copy of *Tales of Suspense* #39 (1st app.) that we graded at Good for $725.00 online (eBay)- almost 2x the *Guide* price!

And lets not forget the long awaited *Dark Knight* movie. It's been suggested that Heath Ledger will be getting an Oscar nomination (just saw the movie, and yes, he is *that* good). If Ledger does get a posthumous Oscar nod, you will see more studios looking at comic properties. If he *wins*, you will see studios grabbing *everything*…and I do mean *everything*. Seriously…*Strangers in Paradise*, *Bone*, *Rasl*, *Echo*, *Cerebus*, any Vertigo title (although, I think Warner Bros. has those locked up). Marvel will be putting out movies based on B-list characters like Hawkeye, Spider-Woman, Cloak & Dagger (which was already rumored anyway). Ready to see a Power Pack film?

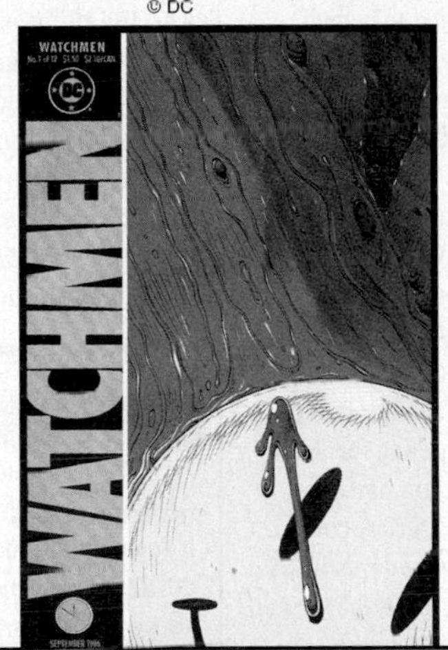

The **Watchmen** movie trailer generated huge hype and increased sales of back issues and trade paperbacks. (**Watchmen** #1 shown)

Speaking of the *Dark Knight*, kudos to DC for making the *Watchmen* TP available on a consignment level in July. I could not figure out why they did this so early, considering the movie does not come out until March. I guess someone was paying attention in upper management, because the *Watchmen* trailer (which came on right before *The Dark Knight* started) generated huge hype! People were coming in the next day asking for the trade…which we sold out of within 48 hours (20 copies…*gone*). We had also sold our 9.4 CGC-graded first issue for $99.99 that week also.

Let's talk about the 2008 convention circuit. Let me tell ya…it was pretty rough out there this year. While some shows were pleasant surprises (Motor City Comic Con), others were surprisingly disappointments (NYCC). There was a *lot* of dumping at the shows this year. I saw many $1.00 boxes and even 25¢ boxes. The biggest surprise to see this at was Wizard World Chicago. On opening preview night (Thursday), one of the bigger dealers there started his boxes at 25 cents. Think about that for a moment…25 cents a book with approximately 300 books in a box, multiplied by 100 boxes (approximately). If that person had sold everything, that would be roughly $7500…Sounds great to see that, but you have to factor in: 1) booth cost (and for WWChicago, for that person's space, approximately $3500), 2) travel expense (U-Hauls ain't free), and 3) employee costs. However, this is a trend I keep seeing with many larger (convention) retailers…just "blow it out" and replace it later. Good philosophy if you can afford to do it. The way the economy is affecting all aspects of the collecting community, many shops are ordering the bare minimum, with maybe a few left over for the shelf or back issues.

But not everything was doom and gloom with the industry this year, let's start with…

Marvel: Have you counted how many Marvel titles come out in a month? With the July catalog, I am counting 130 different titles, not including variants. Granted, some are just shelf filler (*Spider-Man Family*, *World War Hulk, Damage Control*, etc), there have been some exciting titles that sell very well. Marvel's best and most consistent seller has been *Captain America*. Brubaker just knocks it out of the park every month. We have a 90% sell through within 5 weeks. The back issues are impossible to keep in stock, as #14 (1st meeting of Cap and Winter Soldier) is the highest so far at $40.00!!! #1-13 range from $10-15.00 each! The new *Hulk* series is just *red* hot (no joke intended). #1 1st print goes for $8.00. A big surprise considering that the story line, while probably pitched well, lacks any kind of direction or focus. Jeph Loeb has great ideas, but can not execute them very well…must be Ed McGuinness' art work that keeps them in. While not a very strong seller, *Thunderbolts* had a strong cult following when Warren Ellis took over the title. Now that he is gone (I still cry a little inside) from the book, I predict that it will not last too much longer, unless a competent writer takes over. Anything Mark Millar writes is an instant seller! His run on *Wolverine* just started and we are selling 2x the normal amount! *Kick-Ass* (which has now been optioned as a movie) has been very strong. #1 1st prints are $20.00 if I can get any in stock.

Amazing Spider-Man has slowed a bit in sales, now that the "Brand New Day" arc is not so "New" any longer…I have never had so many people drop a title, and so many others pick up a title, all at the same time. So many angry collectors...but the new ones are actually appreciating this story arc. They are the ones who did *not* know Spider-Man had a life *before* marriage! Just a little FYI...Spidey got married in 1986. One of my employees was born in 1985...he was *one* when this book came out, and did not start reading Spider-Man until the late 1990s. I think this is what Quesada was trying to do to attract new readers... 'cause the older readers hate this approach to Spidey, even though this was exactly how Spidey was before he got married (down on his luck with no $$$ or chicks). Personally, I kinda think it's getting trite right now, but I don't think I was the target audience Quesada had in mind.

Last year, I was talking about Marvel's licensing of other properties and how well that was...boy, did *that* come back to slap me in the face. The sequel to *Dark Tower* was met with a ho-hum reaction, and after a five month delay between issues #6 and #7 of *Anita Blake: Guilty Pleasures*, what was once a powerful seller has dwindled to a shelf warmer. Our orders for the last issue of the series was 25% of #1's initial orders. And do not get me started with *Halo Uprising*. Every week, Marvel has it on it's final order cut off list...this book is officially 1 year late. How embarassing!

DC: Weird...DC is the exact opposite of Marvel, as DC is doing very well with the licensing of other properties, but failing with their own. *World of Warcraft* was a *huge* seller (especially for us since we sell the *World of Warcraft* card game), with 1st print #1 going for $12.00 and #2-3 at $10.00 each. *Freddy vs. Jason vs. Ash* was another good seller, with the variant 2nd print covers outselling the 1st print covers (ie: a set of 1-6 2nd prints sold on line for $25.00). *Chuck* however, based on the NBC series, could have sold much better if they had used a photo cover instead of a drawn one (even if Phil Noto had done it). If they would have used the photo cover that they had shown in the *Previews* catalog, I would have sold 3x the amount. Despite that, the book still sold in solid numbers.

DC properties however...how can I put this...bleeech! *Superman*? Pathetic (even with James Robinson doing it *and* with Alex Ross covers, people don't care.) *Wonder Woman*? Pitiful. *Justice League*? Once the staple of DC's sales, now a "Oh? This came out? Eh...maybe next time." Same can be said of *Teen Titans*, *Supergirl*, *Nightwing*, *Green Lantern*, and even *Justice Society*...once a solid seller, now maybe half of what I used to sell.

Final Crisis? Aptly put, as if this book doesn't see a sales spike soon, could quite possibly be the last DC x-over for awhile. Is there an editor on this book? Grant Morrison's writing on this makes his former mini series *The Filth* read like a copy of *The Batman Strikes*. The book has sold less that half of Marvel's *Secret Invasion* mini series, which is 3 times more enjoyable and *easier* to follow. Speaking of Morrison, his Batman R.I.P. storyline is generating a huge buzz, with speculation of Bruce Wayne's demise. However, R.I.P. could stand for something else (retire in peace?), and to be honest, I have no idea what this story is about. It's not stopping collectors however, as first print copies of #676 have gone for $10.00 with a third print being solicitated. If something major does happen in this book, $10.00 might be a steal for this issue. And the R.I.P. x-overs in *Detective*, *Nightwing*, et al., will be sleeper hits as well.

Where is DC's silver lining? Their Johnny DC properties. Seriously. *Tiny Titans* has made Art Baltazar a *huge* comic star, and as of this writing, *Billy Batson and the Magic of Shazam* #1 has sold half its ordered copies. Mike Kunkel's take on this book is nothing short of spectacular! If you missed his *Herobear and the Kid* series, you *must* pick up this book! Seriously! Mark my words...$10.00 by next year.

Independents: Dark Horse's *Buffy* and IDW's *Angel* still lead the pack. IDW's *Angel* #1, $10.00, #2 $15, #3 $10 (all 1st prints by the way). *Spike* is hotly anticipated, and *Serenity* did VERY well! We ordered 1-1/2 times Buffy numbers on this and as of now have sold out of all issues! Other well-to-do indies are Terry Moore's *Echo*, Jeff Smith's *Rasl*, and DDP's *Hack/Slash*. The break-out star however is IDW's *Locke & Key*! This took even us by surprise, as, I had no idea who Joe Hill was (hey...I know who Brad Metzler is though) or how important his books are (or who his daddy is). *Completely* blindsided, #1 1st print goes for $50.00, and will soon be going for more...guaranteed! Dabel Bros.' *Dresden Files* is a big hit, as the 1st issue has sold out and we get $10.00 for 1st prints (when we have them). Dave Sim's *Glamourpuss* has done well also, as our orders on this title are better than *Cerebus*.

Peter J. Bilelis, Esq.
Collector

I suspect much of my report, which focuses primarily on Golden Age (GA), will be different from many of the others. It seems that much of the *Guide*'s Market Report section has evolved into dealers telling us, "everything is selling at or above *Guide*" or "this was my best year ever in the hobby." While this might testify to an individual dealer's experience, frankly, I don't see how it helps anyone understand the state of the market. I try to focus on trends and their drivers in order to assess where the market may be going. I find value in this type of data reporting, as it helps me determine whether I am making smart choices. I hope you do too.

San Diego Comic-Con has just concluded as I write this. From all accounts, it was a good all-around show. I am of the opinion, however, that this year's New York Comic-Con was at least as good for comic book aficionados. This is good news, as it means there is enough demand to, once again, support such gala events on both coasts. With that said, the availability of top GA material could have been better. Like last year, the explosion of internet-based sales venues fostered a glut of average books. True "A" books (like unrestored F/VF or better copies of *Action Comics* (#1 - 40), pre-Robin *Detective Comics*, Spectre cover *More Fun Comics*, early *Marvel Mystery Comics*, *Captain America Comics*, etc.), however, were in very limited supply while demand continued to escalate. Similarly, other highly sought after books, such as many DC and Timely keys, *Master Comics* that feature Mac Raboy artwork, books that feature Lou Fine cover art, most Centaurs, *Pep Comics* #22 - 34,

Wow #1- 4, etc., were all very, very tough to locate (especially in nice shape) and commanded big money when they surfaced.

Myriad other books, however, continue to remain flat or are very slow movers when priced at, or even below, *Guide*. Many argue the economy is the culprit, however, based on the continuing polarization in sale prices for various books, I believe this argument fails. My suspicion is that calculated opportunism is driving the wild swing on some books and prudence is driving the price resistance on a multitude of others. Clearly, prices are becoming increasingly prohibitive on high-grade books and on many other books regardless of their condition. Additionally, with many of the hobby elephants getting closer to retirement age and some starting to sell off their collections, many people believe the GA segment might have crested several years ago. This combination results in a diminishing number of people that can afford very expensive books, and those that can, becoming much more selective as they ponder eventual resale audience/yield.

This could explain why many hobbyists tend to be sporty when purchasing blue chip books ("blue chip books" means: (a) Superman, Batman and Spider-Man books (pop culture icons with appeal that transcends the hobby); (b) many CGC 9.4 (or better) Edgar Church copies; and (c) books with truly classic covers) and conservative when buying other books. Of course, many other books do well, but pound-for-pound, those I've mentioned consistently (typically) outperform the others. With this premise, seeing a CGC-certified 8.0 *Action Comics* #7 sell for $143,400 (or 6X *Guide*) and a CGC 7.0 *Action* #9 sell for $19,120 (or 3.6X *Guide*) makes sense. And it could explain why the highest graded copy of *Adventure Comics* #40 (CGC 7.0) sold for $35,850 (or only 1.3X *Guide*). While many would like to own the *Action* #9 and *Adventure* #40, purchasing the always in-demand blue chip book might be a better idea than putting that same money into a DC "key" that has the mystique of being rare, especially when that "key" isn't really a key (Sandman first appeared in *New York World's Fair* 1939) and doesn't have mass appeal, as it features a "B" character.

If calculated opportunism and prudence are the reasons for what we're seeing, it could mean a paradigm shift. In conjunction with encapsulation, which arguably subverts the essence of collecting (i.e. buying back issues to enjoy more of our favorite stories and artwork), this would suggest some are moving toward a commodity mindset. A commodity mindset means the primary driver for purchasing comic books is not buying what we like but buying what we think has the best chance of doing well in the future.

Obviously, a death knell is unwarranted. The hobby is enjoying much popularity, the number of collectors (both casual and serious) seems to be growing, and many books continue to excel. With respect to Golden Age, a lot of this is driven by the richness of this hobby segment. It offers spectacular WWII covers and stories, the first artwork of many hobby giants, the first appearances of many superheroes that are still popular today, and the thrill of the hunt to locate something that only a relatively few others own. Naturally, the Silver Age offers many of these benefits too, as well as the added benefit of less prohibitive prices (on a relative scale). Additionally, those with means continue to buy what they like without much regard to eventual resale yield. What will keep the hobby strong in the long run is informed hobbyists and keeping comic books relevant, which fosters continued interest. Hollywood has helped in this regard with films like *Fantastic Four*, *X-Men*, *Hulk*, *Iron Man*, *Dark Knight*, *Watchmen*, etc. And, making new comic books widely available, affordable, and interesting also helps. So, while commoditization continues (over one million books now encapsulated by CGC) and has infused the hobby with money and interest, keeping the hobby relevant to collectors will help ensure future stability, as, unlike speculators and investors, collectors typically do not trend in and out of a hobby based on rate of return.

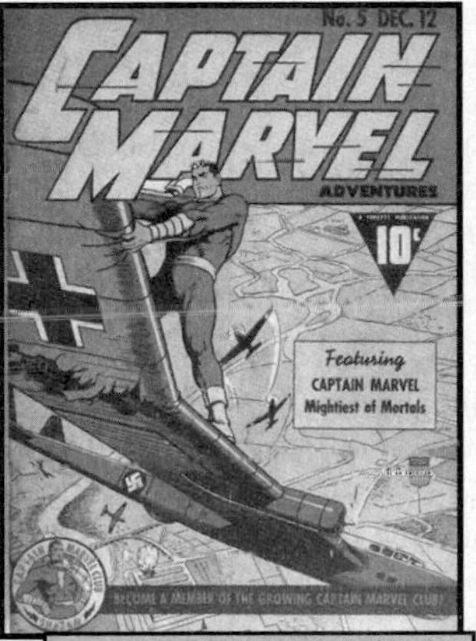

No. 5 DEC. 12
CAPTAIN MARVEL
ADVENTURES
10¢
Featuring
CAPTAIN MARVEL
Mightiest of Mortals
BECOME A MEMBER OF THE GROWING CAPTAIN MARVEL CLUB!

Spectacular World War II covers are part of the richness of the Golden Age. (**Captain Marvel Adventures** #5 shown)

Based on the foregoing, 2008 can be summarized as a year of continued growth and interest in the hobby. Top books and titles continued to excel. The stability and success of the hobby continued to reinforce that there are investment opportunities that appeal to a more mainstream audience. Hollywood continued to validate the source of our hobby. And, market corrections continued as many people responded to increasing prices with a more surgical approach to spending. Good luck hunting in 2009.

Steve Borock
Steveborockcollectibles.com
Hobbyist/Collector/Dealer

Hi! Welcome to my first *Overstreet* market report as a "Non" CGC employee! This is a bit weird for me as I have just gotten back into the market after a ten year stint at CGC where I did not buy, sell, or collect vintage comic books. I had given up all comic book collecting to make sure that, while I was heading CGC, there would never seem to be any conflict of interest whatsoever. CGC needed to be seen as a totally independent third party certification service if it was to be accepted in our hobby, and luckily for all of us, it is not only seen that way, but CGC is so entrenched in our hobby, most high dollar or high grade comic books do not change hands without the great and impartial eyes of people like Mark Haspel, Paul Litch, Shawn Caffrey, Chris Friesen, West Stephan, and the other graders, seeing those books first.

It is probably my greatest honor in this hobby that I was

able to help create and then helm CGC for so many years! I know I have left it in the best of hands.

As I mentioned, I have just got back into buying and selling comic books, and the hobby has really changed in the last ten years. For the last few months, I have attended as a hobbyist, the San Diego, Baltimore, and the Mid-Ohio Comic cons and I have to say, I am having the time of my life! Vintage comic books seem to be even more popular now than ten years ago! I am sure the "good" movies based on comic books (something for everyone from *Ghost World*, to *Sin City*, to *Iron Man*, to *American Splendor*), Geppi's Entertainment Museum, CGC, the internet (especially the CGC message boards) all have something to do with this. I really don't care about the "whys," I am just extremely happy that our hobby seems to thrive even in these "uncertain" economic times. That said, who knows what the future holds? I sure don't. Before I talk about the comic books themselves, I would like to touch on a few things.

© MAR

The John Romita, Sr. cover for the Hero Initiative **Ultimate Spider-Man** #100 edition set.

First is Geppi's Entertainment Museum. This place is *fantastic*! Not only should it be seen by every comic book fan, but a fan of any kind of pop culture and everyone else in the world as well. It will make you feel like a kid again. What Steve Geppi has done by putting this unbelievably enormous and extremely expensive tribute to Americana and our hobby shows his love for comic books, our hobby, and the people in it. Thanks should also go to some of the people "behind-the -scenes" who helped put this together such as John Snyder, Tom Gordon, J.C. Vaughn, Joe McGuckin, and Curator Arnold Blumberg.

Next, I would like to say a bit about my favorite place in cyberspace: the CGC Message boards. This is a place that has a sense of family to it while being the "new" collectors best friend. If you are new to collecting and want to learn about comic books and our hobby, this place is a "must visit" for you. The topics on the boards is anything from the newest Vertigo title and how cool it is, to restoration detection, to showing off a high grade *Action Comics* #7, to learning how to bid at auctions, and even friends and family. I am on these boards almost every day and always seem to learn something new about our hobby or the people in it. It is very common to see a thread where someone who collects only modern comic books and/or does not spend much money can be seen chatting with some of the most knowledgeable people in our hobby or, even a person who spends two hundred thousand dollars on a single comic book. It is the same at the dinners that are put together by all of us on the boards when a convention is in town. Sometimes the dinners are small with only ten people and sometimes it is so large that 50 people show up. Most everyone at these dinners is super friendly, and now, even significant others look forward to going. There have been lunches and dinners that don't even happen during a con! If we are visiting a different city, some of us mention it on the boards and an impromptu lunch or dinner gets put together with less than a week's notice. Some of the best friends I have ever made and some of the best nights I have ever enjoyed in this hobby in the last 35 years have been at these dinners and on these boards.

Many people do not know about The Hero Initiative. The H.I. is a not-for-profit charity that helps us give back to the professional people from our hobby who cannot afford things like health care, housing, or even, food. Remember, "back in the day," most people involved with comic books did not get paid like some of our "superstars" today and their original art was destroyed, kept, or given away so they could not sell it then and cannot sell it now when they really need the money. As a matter of fact, some got paid what most of us would consider a very small amount of money with no retirement or health care plans at all. I am on the fund-raising board of the Hero Initiative and have seen first hand how we can make a difference in someone's life who is in need. Please check out www.heroinitiative.org when you get a chance and give something back to the people who have helped create the comic book medium that we all love so much.

The final thing I would like to mention before I go on to write about the market is Mr. Robert M. Overstreet. Without Bob, I truly believe the comic collecting community would not be as fun or our market, as I write this, as stable as it is. At the beginning, as it is today, putting out a price guide was a labor of love for Bob, not a way to make money and he has been doing this for going on forty years. Bob loves comics as much as anyone in the hobby I have ever met. He does not go after the "limelight" doing interviews, writing columns, and being a special guest at conventions. No, Bob does this because he is one of us; a true comic book collector and reader. He does not get the credit on the internet or in our hobby's news magazines as he should deserve. During my many years at CGC, Bob, with his knowledge, honesty, trust, and friendship, had helped me to become the hobbyist I am today. Thanks Bob!

As far as the market goes, it still seems to be the same as when I left it in as far as trends go. What people call "Blue Chip" comic books with characters such as Superman, Spider-Man, Captain America, Batman, Wonder Woman, Wolverine and all the other "big hitters," over all, trade and are asked for more often than other comic books.

There are also the titles or characters that get "hot." These comics, whether from 1938 or last year, are hard to keep a handle on. Some will rise quickly in price and then drop like a stone (mostly very modern ones) once it is common or no longer "hot." Writers and artists play a big part in this, sometimes even artist/writer teams. We fans love a good comic book first and foremost, but we are also very fickle if what we loved about the way that artist draws or the writer explores changes, or sometimes if they do not change at all, or if that artist/writer team no longer works together. We are a hard crowd to please. What can I say, we have great taste and, heck, I still love getting and reading new comics every week! I want them to be worth the money I spend on them. Some comic books will rise in price slowly and steadily, and then, only drop a little in price, if at all. This is because the title or character, or, once again the writer and/or artist are deemed "worthy" by the collecting community. Again this happens with both the very modern and the very vintage markets and everything in between.

Buying and selling the "hot" books has and always will remain risky. Investor/collectors play "Hot Potato" with these kinds of books. Once the music stops, you are the one who gets burned. This happens much less on a more "proven" book, and by "proven," I mean those "Blue Chip" books I mentioned earlier.

Another risk is buying a restored book as unrestored. Happens everyday. If you want the best insurance policy in our hobby today, use CGC. I wish they were around when I first started collecting. Boy, would I have saved a small fortune by not buying over-graded comics or ones with undisclosed restoration.

I want to make something very clear about putting your hard-earned money into comic books. Even though I believe in this market, there is no such thing as a free lunch! If you are going to invest in comic books, you had better love them. If the economy ever gets really bad, just like if you owned stocks, you will not be able to sell them at a high price quickly and you certainly cannot use them to house or feed yourself and your family. The best advice I can give anyone, and have been doing so since I can remember, is: buy what you love. It really is that simple. Enjoy collecting and reading comic books, enjoy the friendships we make in the wonderful hobby, look at all the cool stuff around us, from original comic book art to comic book memorabilia, and it will all seem worth while in the end.

Thanks for taking the time to read my ramblings as I hope they helped you in some way. Happy Collecting!

Kevin A. Boyd
Collector/Dealer
& CGC Signature Series Director

As I always point out at the start of each of my market reports, I am not a dealer, although I do dabble in some online sales. I am a collector and fan, one who has been trying, through different avenues, to promote comics books to new audiences. That promotion has included running and working on Toronto area comic book conventions, working on the Canadian Comic Book Creator Awards Association's annual Joe Shuster Awards and going to a lot of different conventions across North America working for CGC as their Signature Series Director.

2008 was a sad year for comics as we saw the passing of many comics creators, including the tragic passing of two younger creators: Michael Turner and Dave Stevens. They will be missed.

Toronto Conventions: 2008 was definitely a much quieter year for conventions in Toronto than 2007 was. So far we've seen only a handful of events: two local 2-day shows -- April's Toronto Comicon Fan Appreciation Show (HobbyStar) and the Paradise Comics Toronto Comicon in July. Also there's August's significantly larger 3-day multi-genre event, Fan Expo Canada. Each show had different purposes, and each saw differing levels of success. Fan Expo Canada showed significant growth in 2008 in advance ticket sales, and guests like Alex Ross, Brian Bolland, J. Scott Campbell, Peter David, Mark Bagley, Adam Hughes and many other superstar creators have made this the country's biggest comic book event.

There were also a couple of one-day events: one day (HobbyStar) Toronto Comicons in February and November, and the CCBCAA's own Sequential Arts Symposium, held in June and preceding the presentation of the Joe Shuster Awards.

The Joe Shuster Awards: The fourth edition of the annual comic book creator awards took place at a special ceremony held after the aforementioned Sequential Arts Symposium on June 14, 2008 in Toronto's Lillian H. Smith Library Auditorium. The preparation for the annual awards ceremony begins about two days after the last ones were handed out, and in 2007-8 a number of changes were made to ensure that Canada's only national comic book award solidified its rules and regulations. The biggest change was the elimination of popular vote in almost all categories in favor of Jury selection. Nominating committees across the country were given more time to finalize their ballot selections and the choices for the Hall of Fame awards. The only new category in 2008 was the edition of the Outstanding Canadian Colorist Award.

The purpose of the Joe Shuster Awards, named in honor of the Canadian born co-creator of Superman, is to raise the visibility of, and excellence in creativity and craftsmanship among our many Canadian creators, retailers and publishers. As a national award, the Joe Shuster Awards recognize creators and publishers that create original works in either of our official languages - English and French. The winners this year included: Outstanding Canadian Comic Book Artist – Dale Eaglesham, *Justice Society of America;* Outstanding International Comic Book – Ed Brubaker, *Captain America*, *Criminal*, *Daredevil*, *Immortal Iron Fist*, *Uncanny X-Men*; The Harry Kremer Award for Outstanding Canadian Comic Book Retailer – Big B Comics, Hamilton, Ontario. The four inductees into the Canadian Comic Book Creator Hall of Fame were: Stanley Berneche, John Byrne, Pierre Fournier, Edwin R. "Ted" McCall.

Congratulations to all the nominees and winners, and thanks to everyone who participated this year – from the nomination committees, to the administrative committee, to the jury, to our sponsors (CGC, Lionshead, Diamond Comic Distributors, Sips Publishing and Quebecor World), to Tom Grummett and Paul Rivoche for their stunning poster design, to the amazing Canadian artists that contributed to our *Visions of an Icon: Superman* art exhibit, and lastly, to my associates on the Executive Committee: James Waley, Peter

Fisico and Robert Haines.

CGC Signature Series: CGC's prestigious Signature Series service continued to expand in 2008. The service was offered to fans and collectors and almost every major convention or comics related event in 2008, including some new ones.

The prestigious CGC Signature Series label (yellow) is applied to comic books that have been signed by someone of significance to the comic, under the direct observation of a CGC employee or select CGC authorized Witness. The signatures are then authenticated by CGC with the labels indicating who signed the book, the date it was signed, and in some cases the location of where it was signed. The Signature Series service is the hobby's only 100% Authenticated Signature service.

In 2008 I attended the following events for CGC: New York Comic Con, WonderCon, Wizard World Los Angeles, the Pittsburgh Comicon, Wizard World Philadelphia, San Diego Comic-Con International, Wizard World Chicago, the Baltimore Comicon, Mid-Ohio Con. The remaining cons: MegaCon, Emerald City Comicon, Wizard World Dallas, Fan Expo Canada, the Paradise Toronto Comicon, Florida SuperCon, San Jose Super-Con, HeroesCon and The NY Big Apple National were covered by other CGC employees. 2008 was the year when our Signature Series Witnesses and collectors started looking to obtain more autographs from creators who rarely make public appearances. Two limited signings with the legendary Frank Frazetta definitely set the bar higher, and limited signing with Stan Lee, such as those arranged by Desert Wind Comics and Paradise Comics, continued to be successful.

2008 did not have a "champ" for Signature Series requests, but creators in high demand at public events in 2008 were Alex Ross, Joe Hill, Geoff Johns, Robert Kirkman, Joe Simon, Charlie Adlard, Ed Brubaker, Steve Epting, David Michelinie, Brian Michael Bendis, Mark Millar, Joe Quesada, Todd McFarlane, Jim Lee, the Romitas (Sr, and Jr.), the Kuberts (Joe, Adam, Andy), Peter David, Jerry Robinson, Dave Gibbons, Bruce Timm, David Finch, and Grant Morrison. Neil Gaiman, Frank Miller and Joss Whedon would be in there as well if they did more public appearances!

The Dark Knight saw an increase in Batman related Signature Series this summer, especially Joker and Harley Quinn related items such as *Batman: The Man Who Laughs* (Brubaker), *The Killing Joke* (Bolland), *Batman Adventures: Mad Love* (Timm), and *Batman: Harley Quinn* (Alex Ross).

The *Watchmen* film has already increased interest in back issues of *Watchmen*, and Signature Series books signed by co-creator Dave Gibbons will be books to watch.

There continues to be rising demand for CGC Signature Series graded and encapsulated comics with sketch covers – such as last years *Fallen Son* #3 and 2008's *Secret Invasion* #1, along with Dynamite's sketch covers for *Battlestar Galactica*, *Red Sonja* and *Avengers/Invaders*. Also, sales of the Hero Initiative's *Ultimate 100 Spider-Man* covers exceeded many estimates and this success has continued with the *Hulk 100* covers project. Fans can't get enough of unique sketches on these comics and these items straddle the line between collectibles and original art – appealing to both types of collectors. If you have any questions about Signature Series, you can e-mail us at signature@cgc-comics.com.

General Observations: Comic book conventions continue to evolve along different paths. Multi-genre conventions continued to see growth; comic book focused events seemed to stagnate, with rare exceptions. Part of that problem is that as with last year, too many events took place between April and late July's San Diego Comic-Con. Local customers will usually attend, but traveling to these events has become a much more selective process, and I think the smaller shows have been losing out to the larger ones. Shows continue gravitating in different directions – art collectors have their favorites, back issue collectors have theirs, and everyone else falls somewhere in between.

Marvel Comics: General observations: *Secret Invasion* dominates the sales charts, while printing quality seems to be suffering in general on Marvel titles. Brand New Day succeeded in reviving *Spider-Man* sales but does seem to be running out of steam. *Captain America* continues to be a popular read. The *Hulk* reboot was not as strong as hoped, nor was *Ultimates 3*. Millar and Romita Jr's *Kick-Ass* was a hit, and a movie is already been greenlit. Marvel continues to do an excellent job with keeping their older material out there in many different formats such as Masterworks, Omnibuses and Essentials.

DC Comics: General observations: *Final Crisis* was a non-starter as comic readers were fed up with more "Crisis" stories and the lead-ins directly contradicted the very confusing Morrison written series. *Final Crisis: Legion of 3 Worlds* (starring Superman) should do well as Johns' "Superman and the Legion of Super-Heroes arc" was a hit with fans. "New Krypton" should also see some interest. *Green Lantern* continues to be a hit with fans, as do *Justice Society of America* and *Justice League of America*. The upcoming *Flash: Rebirth* should be a hit. *Y: the Last Man* ended this year, but *Fables* and *Ex Machina* continue to roll along for Vertigo and Wildstorm, respectively.

In many ways, DC seems to have unraveled over the last two years, so I hope that *Final Crisis* will succeed in doing something that DC has been unable to do over the past two years – end with a cohesive and stable group of titles and characters produced by strong creative visions.

Image Comics: Image seems poised to make some headway into the future as the home of creator-owned projects, so let's hope that the hype generated this year in San Diego translates into actuality. The making of Kirkman into an Image partner and writer of the first crossover arc in quite some time was a smart move as *Invincible*, *The Walking Dead* and *The Astounding Wolf-Man* are strong titles with loyal audiences.

Dark Horse Comics: *Buffy* continues to score for Dark Horse. *The Umbrella Academy* was a hit and fans can't wait for more. *Star Wars*, *Conan*, *Fear Agent*, and *Indiana Jones* continue to hold their audiences. *Hellboy* returned in 2008 to much acclaim and with another movie, but the real gem is the ongoing series of *B.P.R.D.* mini-series and these books are well worth looking into.

Other: The *other* part of the catalogue is a diverse and often daunting place to look! There is a lot of product out there and it is not easy to discern good from okay. Petersen's *Mouse Guard*, Moore's *Echo*, Smith's *Rasl* and Sim's *Glamourpuss* are worth looking into. Top Shelf, Dynamite, SLG, Drawn & Quarterly, Fantagraphics… I've sampled many different titles and graphic novels from these companies, and I highly recommend Jeff Lemire's *Essex County Trilogy: Tales from the Farm*, *Ghost Stories* and *The Country Nurse*.

Closing Remarks: 2008 continues to see the comics market in transition. New comic sales are down, while graphic novel sales are stable and in some areas growing. Traditional comics people tend to dismiss the continued interest of young people in Manga as a fad, and booksellers and educators continue to look to sequential art in all of its many glorious formats as a means to reach and create new readers. Movies continue to mine the best in comics and graphic novels for new material – and in turn, comic book movies dominate at the box office while the source material fluctuates in interest or sales depending on the content. High grade back issue sales are still up, while back issue sales in general are not as strong as they could be. Original art prices continue to rise for now, as more collectors transition towards original art for fun and potential investment.

Michael Browning
Collector

I've said it for years: Trade paperbacks will be collectible one of these days. Well, it appears that day is finally here. Several out of print trade paperbacks are selling at premium prices as collectors look to complete their collections. This year, in southern West Virginia, southwestern Virginia, east Tennessee and eastern Kentucky, trade paperback sales have increased and back issue sales have leveled out.

© VAL

*Valiants were more popular this past year then they've been since their heyday in the 1990s. (**Harbinger** #1 shown)*

One of the questions I've been asked by collectors is: Why buy back issues these days when nearly everything is being reprinted in trade paperbacks? You can find so much in trade paperbacks these days (DC crossover events like *Millennium* and *Invasion* have been reprinted, along with a lot of other stuff -- like the New Universe comics -- many collectors never imagined seeing in the trades).

Cavalier Comics in Wise, Va., stocks a full line of trade paperbacks, including Marvel, DC, Dark Horse, Dynamite, Vertigo and other companies' trades, along with hardcovers and archive-style editions. Page 3's Comics and Gamezone in Pikeville, Ky., also stocks a good number of trade paperbacks and phone book-style reprint editions and sales remain good on all of the volumes they sell. Good selling trade paperbacks for the Pikeville shop have been trades featuring Robin, Batman, Superman, Starman, X-Men, *Civil War*, Captain America, Hulk, Flash, Green Lantern and Spider-Man. The DC *Showcase Presents* line and the Marvel *Essentials* are always good sellers in the shops I visited.

The Dynamite *Red Sonja* trades are tough to find here, as they are almost always snatched up as collectors have enjoyed the new stories and the reprints of the old Marvel series. This is a quality series and the trade paperbacks sell out as quickly as they hit the shelves. *The Lone Ranger* trade paperback and hardcover reprinting the Dynamite series are good sellers. The first issue of *The Lone Ranger* series from Dynamite with John Cassaday covers sold for awhile at $10 and the early variants sold for around $20 each. *Red Sonja* cover variants were hot for awhile, but have cooled off over the last six months.

The Omnibus hardcover reprints from DC and Marvel have done well. DC's *Jack Kirby Omnibus* series sold out at several of the stores I visited.

Page 3 keeps the Marvel Omnibus editions of *Amazing Spider-Man* and *Uncanny X-Men* in stock and the store has sold out of copies of all the other omnibus editions like *Devil Dinosaur*, *Fantastic Four*, *Howard the Duck*, *Iron Man*, *Captain America*, *Incredible Hulk* and *The Death and Return of Superman*.

Online and in shops, the first (and only) prints of some omnibus editions like Jack Kirby's *Eternals* and Grant Morrison's *New X-Men* have doubled in value. The *Eternals Omnibus* with a $75 cover price has sold for as high as $150, while I've seen copies of the *New X-Men Omnibus* selling for nearly $200. These quickly going out of print probably has something to do with the price increases.

The *New X-Men* hardcover volumes 2-3 have been good sellers, with copies of Volume 3 hitting prices as high as $100. But, of the shops I surveyed, many are still seeing healthy back issue sales.

I've seen increases in sales of *Superman* #75 which features the death of Superman that so many people bought with hopes of putting their kids through college by selling. I've seen copies selling for as high as $25 each for the regular editions and $100-$150 for the Platinum *Superman* #75s. This was an event that defined the 1990s and it's nice to see it selling for more than cover price or in quarter bins.

Valiants were more popular this year than they've been since their heyday in the 1990s. It was no surprise to me when the CGC-certified *Harbinger* #1 in 9.8 sold for $2,025. I've said it for years that Valiant Comics were quality comics – especially those early Jim Shooter issues – and people who have fond memories of those great stories are now trying to put together sets of these and the prices continue to rise. I hardly ever see a copy of the *Magnus Robot Fighter Steel*

Nation trade paperback sell for under $50. It's rare that I ever see one for sale, but they're never cheap.

Harbinger is one of the more fondly remembered Valiant series and prices increased even higher when the hardcover reprint issued this year was delayed, then sold only through special orders, then finally released after all the court battles over who owned the reprint rights were resolved. The hardcover, reprinting *Harbinger* #0-6, was tough to find in our area and I had to special order my copy from an online shop. The *Harbinger* #0 Pink edition still sells for more than $100 and the Valiant Validated Signature Series rares sell well whenever they are available. Many shops I visit don't have a whole lot of Valiant back issues. Many of them sold the Valiant back issues in fifty-cent boxes a few years back.

Surprisingly, I've seen sales on the old *Marvel Graphic Novel* series increasing. The *Squadron Supreme: Death of a Universe* and *Conan: The Rogue* (by John Buscema) graphic novels regularly sell for around $50-$75 each. These are good, quality stories and have been long out of print and long overlooked. The *Hercules* graphic novel by Bob Layton, which continued the Hercules stories he started with the two miniseries in the mid-1980s is a good seller with sales of $20 for VF copies. *Groo* trade paperbacks from Epic which reprint the Epic series sell well at $25-$50 each and the last issue of the Marvel/Epic *Groo The Wanderer*, #120, sells for $20-$25.

Hitman trade paperbacks, which have now gone out of print, are increasing in value. The *Hitman: Local Heroes* trade paperback has sold for around $35. Cavalier Comics had a full line of *Hitman* trade paperbacks in stock, but as prices increased on eBay, the store's stock quickly sold out. The *Walter Simonson Visionaries* Vol. 2 and 3 trade paperbacks were in high demand as these two were tough to find and sold for around $35-$40 each.

In many of the shops, last issues still reign supreme and in many shops I visited, those final issues are in short supply but always in high demand. Near mint copies of *G.I. Joe, A Real American Hero* #155 sold for upwards of $80. High grade copies of *G.I. Joe* #1 and #21 also continue to sell well. At one shop, the owner was selling last issues for $5-$10 each. The tougher-to-find last issues reached as high as $20, as he, himself, is a last issue collector and knows the lower print runs cause these issues to be in high demand.

Jonah Hex back issues have seen an increase this year. The last issue, #92, regularly sells for $25 in VF (I've not seen a NM copy in my area in many years) and I've never seen an issue from the first series sell for less than $10 each. The *All-Star Western* and *Weird Western Tales* appearances of Jonah Hex are always good sellers, but are rarely found at any of the shops in my region. A big shocker was seeing a copy of the Vertigo *Jonah Hex: Two-Gun Mojo* trade paperback priced at $100. Wow! I don't think it sold for that, but someone definitely had confidence that they could get that for a copy. I've not seen sales on eBay or in any online shop going this high, but I know it's out of print and, due to the legal problems DC had with the *Jonah Hex: Riders of the Worm and Such*, I doubt this or any of the other Vertigo Jonah Hexes will ever be reprinted again. Even the futuristic *Hex* series from the 1980s which has been maligned by Jonah Hex fans for years has seen an increase in its price. One Tennessee shop had a set for $70 and I saw sets in other stores going for nearly as much. The current ongoing *Jonah Hex* series written by Justin Gray and Jimmy Palmiotti sells well in our area and the first issue sold as high as $10 at one shop. There's talk of a movie, so expect *All-Star Western* #10 and #11 to continue to increase and the *DC Special Series* #16 issue with the death of Jonah Hex to get hotter and hotter as more news is released on the upcoming film. A copy of *The Comics Journal* #56 from 1979 with an interview with Jonah Hex writer Michael Fleisher and a painted Jonah Hex cover by Luis Dominguez sold for $25. That's not bad for a fanzine. A water-soaked copy of *The Amazing World of DC Comics* Vol. 2 No. 6, featuring a John Albano-written and Tony DeZuniga-drawn Jonah Hex parody sold for $10. The *Jonah Hex* trade paperbacks reprinting the current series have sold well in local shops and bookstores.

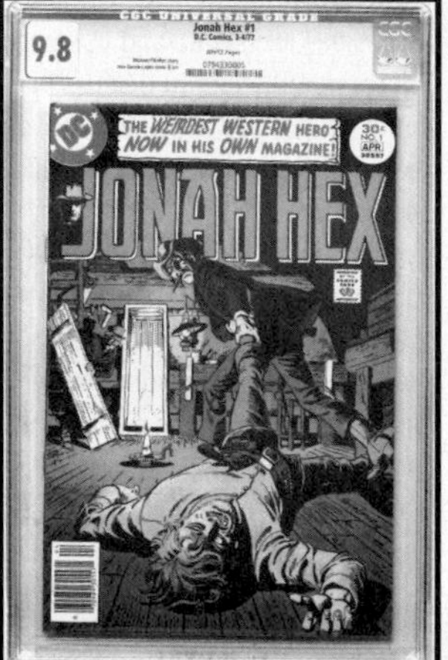

© DC

***Jonah Hex** #1 and other early issues have seen an increase in sales.*

Variant sales have declined over the last year in my area. So many titles now have a 1:10 variant or a 1:25 special cover, and I see those sitting on shelves at all of the stores I visit. Does every issue published by Marvel and DC have a variant edition? Many collectors don't have the cash to put into multiple covers, what with gas prices hitting more than $4 for a gallon of regular unleaded. The cash they used to have available for variant editions is now being spent on gasoline to get to the shops. One collector told me he just didn't see the need to get every variant cover sold each week (and there are plenty) because the money could be spent on other comics he'd enjoy reading. As gas prices increased each week, many regular comics readers and back issue collectors had to cut down on their purchases in my area. Gas prices were higher in our region than in most other areas of the country and the comic shops are so far away for many collectors, which made weekly trips to comic shops turn into monthly trips and pull lists were trimmed to bare minimum. So, when a comic had a variant cover, many collectors were forced to pass it by in favor of the much cheaper regular cover. One store discounted the variant cover comics at around $5 each, but still had trouble finding buyers for these supposedly rare issues.

Are collectors tiring of the variant covers? That seems to be the case here. One shop has an entire wall dedicated to variants and still sitting there are *Civil War* variant covers, as well as early *Justice League of America*, *Red Sonja* and

Action Comics variants, among many others. Sales have definitely cooled off on variant covers at all of the shops I visited. The *Dark Tower* variants were quickly snatched up by comic collectors and Steven King fans alike at one store in Charleston, W.Va. One Steven King fan asked me at a restaurant if I could direct him to a store that carried *Dark Tower* from Marvel, because he wanted to buy one of each issue. I directed him to Cheryl's Comics in Kanawha City, W.Va., and he bought nearly $100 of variants and regular covers for issues 1 and 2.

Buffy the Vampire Slayer #1 was a good seller here, reaching $15 a copy before leveling out at $10 a copy. The numerous Indiana Jones miniseries produced by Dark Horse in the 1990s have been hot all year. The stories in these comics were always entertaining. The art was solid, and some of the print runs were tiny. *Indiana Jones and the Spear of Destiny* sets sold for around $100, while other Indiana Jones sets sold for double cover price in many instances. The latest installment of the Indiana Jones movie series helped sales on back issues of the Dark Horse minis and the *Indiana Jones Omnibus* Volumes 1-2 sell well in comic shops and bookstores here.

The Dark Knight blockbuster movie starring Christian Bale and the late Heath Ledger caused Batman books like *The Dark Knight Returns* and *The Killing Joke* to see a price hike. First prints of *The Killing Joke* were selling for around $40, fueled by Ledger's riveting performance and, sadly, his tragic death at such a young age.

We only had one comic convention locally this year and it was held in Ashland, Ky., about 150 miles from where I live. West Virginia hasn't hosted a comic convention in many years, so this was the closest we've come to a comic show in a long, long time. Only a handful of dealers set up at the show, but there were nearly 100 collectors who showed up to look for bargains. Dollar boxes were big at the show, with many collectors filling bags with bargains.

Several of the shops I visited are seeing good sales on comics-related toys, including the Marvel Legends line of action figures and the DC Direct figures and sets. The build-a-figure action figures sell well to collectors trying to get a full set so they can put each piece found inside the packs together to make an exclusive figure, like the Metamorpho figure or the Fin Fang Foom.

Original art continues to sell well online as many comic readers discover the joy of collecting unique pages and covers. It seems once a comics reader learns all about original art and gets his or her first piece, they get hooked. One page leads to another and that leads to a splash page and, in turn, that leads to the desire to own a cover.

Dan Cusimano
Flying Donut Trading Company

eBay continues to dominate the market, as the reports of eBay's demise continue to be greatly exaggerated. The jump in eBay fees was supposed to push sellers away from eBay toward other venues, but this migration (which has been predicted before) just isn't happening. eBay continues to have the overwhelming market share and continues to be the driving force in the back issue market.

Sales remain strong on most market areas online, with prices remaining at approximately 50% of *Guide* on almost all comics between VG and VF. *Guide* prices are simply too high for the vast majority of titles published since 1965 in mid-grade, as supply of mid-grade books vastly exceeds demand. *Guide* prices are too low for most Marvel keys in low grade, and prices for pre-1964 DCs are too low in all grades. Demand for these books, especially in higher grade, continues to be strong.

I am concerned for the future of the *Guide*, as there seems to be no push towards an electronic outlet. As all media transfers towards electronic outlets, with instant updating of data, the *Guide*, in static paper form, runs the risk of becoming an anachronism. It is nearly imperative for the *Guide* to move towards an electronic release - a PDF through Heritage simply does not count - as other outlets will fill the space.

Gary Dolgoff
Gary Dolgoff Comics

2008... 'Yes, they still want the comics'!...
...Although the 'general economy' is 'dodgy' these days... comic-selling is still 'holding up well'...

Golden Age: This year, I bought (with another guy) a large Golden Age collection out of Utah, for 80% of *Guide*. The main strength of the collection consisted of large runs (almost complete sets) of Fiction House comics (*Jumbo* #1-up, *Jungle* #1-up, *Planet* #1-up, etc.) Also, in the collection was a stack of Fox (late-40s, 'good girl' art) comics (*Phantom Lady*, *Rulah*, *Zoot*, etc.) Rounding out the collection was a stack of *Captain Marvel Jr.*s and *Marvel Family*s (some cool-covers there.) I've been selling many of the early '40s *Planet*s and *Jumbo*s for well over *Guide*,ditto for the *Phantom Lady*s, of course. I also offered 110% of *Guide* for a stack of 1940s *Captain America*s, and *Marvel Mystery Comics* (didn't get those unfortunately.) I love Golden Age Timelys. When I get 'em, I often put them in my "keepsies" collection!

Much of the "better" Golden Age still sells very well... in fact, I find that I must pony-up high paying prices if I want to get "the goodies" (as I did when buying that Utah Fiction House collection).

Gone are the days when I could get the "glorious Golden Age" for 50% of *Guide.* Now I find myself compelled to pay 80%-110% of *Guide* for Timelys, 70%-100% for late '30s-early '40s DCs, 60%-70% (and more) for mid/late '40s DCs, 70%-100% of *Guide* for early '40s Centaurs, Fiction House, etc., and full *Guide* for those cool *Hangman* comics #2-8.

I also noticed Donald Duck *Four Color*s selling well, and in general, almost anything pre-1943 makes for "compelling selling," regardless of title. Late '40s and early 1950s Superhero and Horror (plus most ECs, and all Atlas comics) sold very well.

Silver Age (1960s-1971, plus later 1950s) and **Bronze Age** ('72-'81, or so): I enjoy buying and accumulating books from this era – though I have about 50,000 comics from the Silver Age and 200,000+ Bronze Age comics - "I want more!"

Silver Age is, to my mind, the "bread and butter" of the comics' industry. I have, for instance, an overseas buyer who purchases runs of 1960s and 1970s comics (about 20,000 pieces a year) – and then sells them to his customers, throughout the year.

I can't keep *Iron Man* in stock, they sell so fast (ever since the publicity of the movie "hit the presses") – particularly #s 1-70 (especially #1!) plus the "alcoholic Tony Stark" #128. *Batmans* are a solid seller through #400 or so and *X-Men* sell great, through the Byrne run (#s 1-140 sell nicely). In general, the top Marvel titles (plus *Batman*) and 10¢ cover superhero DCs, most all titles, are the most consistent Silver Age sellers. It definitely helps to have a well-rounded Silver and Bronze Age stock. Another thing: early '70s keys sell great, even for 20% (or so) over-*Guide* and sometimes more! The Keys: *Amazing Spider-Man* #121,122,129; *Batman* #232; *Daredevil* #158,168; *Marvel Spotlight* #5 (first Ghost Rider); *Werewolf by Night* #32 (first appearance of Moon Knight); and of course *Incredible Hulk* #181, in all grades. I'm ashamed to say – but I recently sold on eBay auction (a CGC-certified 9.8) *Marvel Spotlight* #32 (first appearance of Spider-Woman), for $958! (that is close to 40x *Guide*, folks!) In the same week, we sold a CGC-certified 9.8 *Star Wars* #1 for $640.

1980s – 2000s: I'm starting to like buying these more these days. I bought 365 boxes of comics from a lady in Long Island (who owned stores with her late husband). In the store-stocks were batches of '60s and '70s books which were cool. However, the vast majority of the comics were from the 1980s-2000s and I've been finding out that more of the "later books" from these eras have nicer value than I've thought!

For instance, a warehouse customer/dealer went through the pallets from this deal (before I got to sort 'em) and pulled out 9 copies of *G.I. Joe Special* from the 2000s. He happily paid me $250 for them, for resale! I separated the other 1980s-2000s comics into 3 main categories:

1. Lesser titles: I pulled out approximately 60,000 comics that I'm "bulking-out" for 8¢ each.

2. Mainline titles: Mostly long-running titles/characters (Spider-Man, X-Men, Batman, Superman, Flash, Avengers, Captain America, Daredevil, Fantastic Four, Hulk, Iron Man, Swamp Thing, Thor, etc.) – I sell these to folks for 50¢-90¢ each, depending upon how much they buy, etc.

3) Better stuff: Comics that are mainly $5 - $25 in Near Mint *Price Guide* (NMPG) I usually sell these (in batches, etc.) for 1/3 to 1/2 of NMPG, in nice shape. (McFarlane *Amazing Spider-Man*, *X-Men* between #150-275, *Punisher* #1-10, *Wolverine* #1-10, etc.)

Original Art: I love this stuff! It's getting much harder to buy at reasonable prices, though I did get in a stack of lesser-known newspaper stories and Sundays. I've been offering out small batches of *Winnie Winkle* and *Juliet Jones* dailies for $10 each and less; Sundays at $30-$40 each. I also sold an early *Krazy Kat* daily for $4,000 and some early '70s *Avengers* pages for $200-$300 each.

eBay vs. Website vs. Print Catalog: For the past couple of years or so, me and "the crew" have been putting in way too much time listing stuff on eBay, especially our eBay store. eBay always intrigues me. There always seems to be so much potential there. I figure, "once they see my grading, they'll just keep on buying." However, eBay is very labor intensive, so much so, that it has kept our crew from listing on our website (www.gdcomics.com) and me from grading. Truly, I've been buying, and continue to buy, much faster than I can process the funny books.

Now, eBay has implemented new "draconian" rules. The most absurd is telling sellers that they cannot accept checks or money-orders! Because my listings were done before these new rules were implemented, eBay has removed my 2,000-3,000 store listings! I will continue to list (as "gdcomics") on eBay, but by the time you read this, I will have graded many boxes of oldies for the website.

Admittedly, I've neglected my website for too long. Now it's been revamped to make it more user-friendly, and easier on the eyes. Plus, "me and the crew" are listing a lot more on the website, (so buyers can have a consistent "strict grader" as supplier).

With over 800,000 comics and comic magazines in my inventory, it's insane not to grade them, and put 'em up for sale. I notice that when I list Silver Age as sets (i.e. *Fantastic Four* #48-100, *Atom* #1-12, *Justice League of America* #1-8 (missing #2, etc.), they sell really well.

One more thing: Last year Bob Overstreet, whom I like and respect, reduced prices on a lot of '50s and '60s comics in the Good to Fine categories. To my mind, the problem with this was that I think he used "too broad a brush" in this reduction. I can understand reducing the GD to FN prices on, say, *Tales to Astonish* above #70, as they don't move well at the "old prices." Why reduce prices of (just to give a few examples) GD to FN Atlas '50s *Marvel Tales*, 1960s *Munsters*, *Creepy* (Warren) #1, and many mid 1960s *Amazing Spider-Man*, *Fantastic Four*, and *X-Men* issues?

Anyways – Have a "Happy Comic Book Year!"

Walter Durajlija
Big B Comics

In 2008, the market here in southern Ontario was strong for both back issues and new comics. First let's talk back issues. Our purchases exceeded $100,000 in 2007. Most of this went to three large collections. We knew the back issue market was strong going into the year so we bought with some degree of aggression and confidence. Every era and every grade were represented in these collections. This gave us a great opportunity to look at the whole cross section of the market and gauge how each area performed.

Golden Age: Timely and DC heroes sold within days and at above *Guide*. We sold a raw *Batman* #47 that I graded a 6.0 for $1100.00, a *Captain America Comics* #66 I graded 5.0 for $600.00 and a *Classics Illustrated* #43 I graded a 5.5 for $275.00. Heroes rule the roost, especially if they're still alive and kicking in today's comics. Horror titles do well if they're EC or if they have any of the classic covers. Otherwise, run of the mill Horror books are slow. Westerns are slow in lower grades but sell quickly in high grade. We sold a *Lash Larue* #1 at *Guide* and we somehow acquired 2 *Roy Rogers Annuals* (which the *Guide* lists as less than 5 known copies) and they both sold quickly. For us the most in-demand Westerns are nicer grades of *Rawhide Kid* #17 and #23. In general, the supply of Golden Age is dwindling more and more each year while demand for the good books remains about the same.

Silver Age: High grade Silver Age comics were the hottest ticket in town. For anything 9.0 or higher we have buyers lining up at the door. Same goes for almost all key issues. We sold a *Journey into Mystery* #112 that I graded an 8.5 for $750.00, a *Wonder Woman* #105 at a 4.0 for $300.00 and a *Tales of Suspense* #39 VG 4.0 for $1200.00. The hottest parts of the Silver Age market though are the big Marvel Keys. *Amazing Fantasy* #15 and *Incredible Hulk* #1 are impossible to find close to *Guide*. We sold a CGC 3.5 *Incredible Hulk* #1 for $2200.00 and this was before the *Overstreet Guide* #38 came out. We sold 3 low grade copies of *Amazing Spider-Man* #1 and all went for about 20% over *Guide*. High grade DCs from the '50s are very scarce and also sell briskly at over *Guide*.

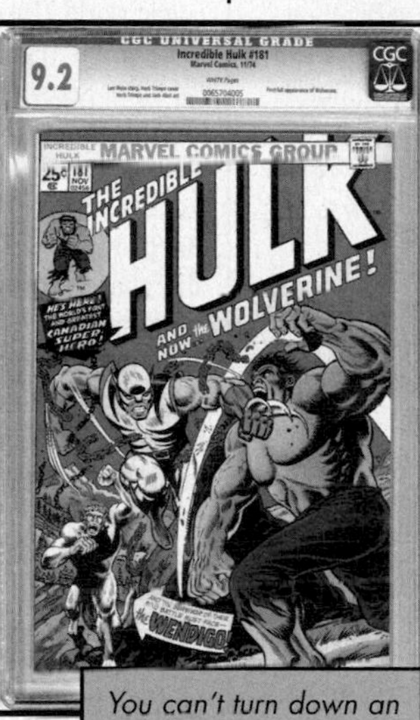

©MAR

You can't turn down an offer of $5,400 for a CGC-certified 9.6 **Incredible Hulk** #181.

The weak spot for us has been the mid- to lower grade Silver Age run books. Mid '60s issues of all the major Marvel and DC titles are worth a considerable amount in the *Guide*, but we're having trouble selling these at *Guide*. Examples of this would be G/VG copies of books like *Amazing Spider-Man* from the #20s-50s (excluding the keys). Ditto for *Fantastic Four* or *JLA*. For us, these books and books like them are currently tough sells at *Guide*, but they are selling well in the 50% off bins. The fact that they are selling however tells me the supply will eventually dry up and these books too will realize prices closer to *Guide* value. I must add that the slowest Silver Age Marvel title for us (that's still going strong today) is *Daredevil*. DCs like *Metamorpho*, *Metal Men*, *Sea Devils*, etc. are dead in the water in mid-grade. They may *Guide* at $10-20 but this is not realistic. They sell quickly at $1.99 though.

The large majority of non-superhero books from this era are relatively slow and only sell in super high grade or at heavily discounted prices. Archies, Funny Animal, Dells, Gold Keys, Westerns, etc - they all end up in our $1.99 bins if they are in mid-grade or less. New buyers coming into the market don't care about John Wayne photo covers because they've never seen a John Wayne movie. This is an exaggeration obviously, but the point is that these types of comics are selling to the same people they were selling to 10 years ago. This is a trend that can only result in decreased demand as time goes by and people finish their runs or fall out of collecting.

Bronze Age: Bronze is a heavily speculated area. We sold a bunch of high grade Bronze at multiples of *Guide* to buyers who openly told us they would get the books pressed and then send them to CGC. Prices realized for high grade Bronze (all very high grade and raw) include *Incredible Hulk* #162 $165.00, *Amazing Spider-Man* #88 $275.00, *Daredevil* #131 $450.00, *Batman* #232 $475.00 and an *Amazing Spider-Man* #129 $1,000.00. We don't do a lot of CGC sales but we were offered $5,400 for an *Incredible Hulk* #181 9.6 and couldn't turn that down. Most of the Bronze Age sales are Marvels. DC sales are heavily grouped around Batman, Adams art and Wrightson horror stuff. Once again, non Marvel/DC books are fairly slow.

The nicest thing about Bronze is that this is where we have seen the largest influx of new collectors. Young people with money to spend on back issues are driving prices up on in demand titles.

Copper/Modern Age: For people who just want to read the stories, we have found that there is heavy competition with graphic novels for comics from this era. Back issues of series like *Sandman* or *Preacher*, which were hot when they were ongoing, now have difficulty selling anywhere except in the bargain bins. In the meantime, we turn full sets of the graphic novels around 30 times a year. Most people, especially those new to the hobby, prefer the ease and convenience of the collected edition. For the diehards who want the actual comics to fill in runs, we mostly sell comics from this era in two ways: individually in the $1.99 bargain bins or as bundled together sets of story arcs, full runs, etc. Pricing on sets will depend on quality, but they also tend to hover around $2 an issue.

Books from this era in high demand include *Walking Dead* #1-4 (#1 easily sells for over $100 and should hold its value considering the low print run), *New Mutants* #98 ($20 easy), *New Teen Titans* #2 ($50 easy), and *Amazing Spider-Man* v2 #36 (raw 9.4s get $40 easy).

Now let's talk current retail. Sales at our comic shop have been increasing nicely over the last few years and 2008 was no exception. Sales of graphic novels have shown the largest increase. Our store now does as much business with graphic novels as it does with new monthly comics. Popular movies like *Iron Man* and *The Dark Knight* were boons because they brought huge amounts of new people into the shop. Interestingly, we sold 100+ copies of *Watchmen* within the first month of the *Dark Knight* release just on the power of the *Watchmen* trailer. Movies and other publicity bring people in but it is quality that keeps them coming back. We saw lots of new faces after *Iron Man,* but the poor selection and quality of *Iron Man* graphic novels available didn't exactly impress. Fast forward to *Dark Knight* and we were selling tons of *Killing Joke*, *Year One*, *Dark Knight Returns*, *Long Halloween*, etc. Now these people loved the stuff and came back in greater numbers than did our *Iron Man* visitors. Many of these new comers were at one time into comics and just needed the spark to return. We've had a nice group of these returnees begin buying up the collectible back issues again. Many are amazed at how valuable old comics have become.

The good news is that the majority of people buying new comics today are buying for pleasure. Few collect in the classic sense. I say that's good news because this was the way things were more or less before the speculative collecting that began in the early '80s. There are so many quality products on the stands now and comics are becoming more and more mainstream. This gives me confidence that our industry will enjoy an even more prosperous future.

I'd like to close by thanking everyone here at Big B on our award winning year. Big B Comics won the Harry Kremer Outstanding Retailer Award at the 2008 Joe Shuster Awards ceremony. The Shusters are an annual award honoring the best of the best in the Canadian comic book industry (our Eisner Awards) and the Harry Kremer award is given to the best comic shop in Canada!

D'Arcy Farrell
Pendragon Comics

Comic fandom had a glorious year mainly for 3 reasons. The movies, all 3 of them. There were others, but you know the 3 that have made collecting comics a pleasure and appreciated by non-collectors. If the studios do their movies with the same attitude and quality as *The Dark Knight*, *Iron Man* (or *Incredible Hulk*), and avoid the *X-Men* trilogy (though the first movie was alright), the whole industry will shine, with fans all the happier. No one wants to go to work/school, be known as a "comic-guy," have a favorite character in a movie trashed to bits in a production, and be teased all year. Instead, it helps to have a well made movie, to help justify the comic-geekness in all of us. A little silly, but true when you think about it. It confirms our hobby is not for old guys still pretending to be teens, but that actually comics/trades are good reads, good art, somewhat thought provoking (*Fables*, *Sandman*, *DMZ*). Oh yea, not all comics are about guys in tights!

The big Fan Expo comic convention in August was amazing. Again, Hobbystar put on a great mass-media show. Over 50,000 attendees from all over come to see many guests of the sci-fi, TV, movie and of course comic world. I'm glad to see less complaining of lineups, and a better orchestrated convention as a whole. We always do quite well there. As per sales, we saw an increase year over year. Highlights we sold... *Amazing Fantasy* #15 in low and mid grade, various Golden Age *Supermans*, our few Timelys went first day, and a *Batman* #5 in higher grade. No interest in CGC material. Most collectors were running around trying to find higher level keys like *Amazing Spider-Man* #1-14, *Fantastic Four* #1-5 and the like. This show is awesome since it transcends all media forms/genres, though segregated to avoid confusing overlapping of various functions and dealers. The fans can still browse anywhere and see items (such as comics) they would not normally bother to see. This helps introduce our industry to everyone. Less dumping of run-of-the-mill books, and a better informed collector seemed the norm. That is refreshing. We noticed an increase in trades/hardcover dealers as well, and more local stores are partaking in the event. Again, very good for business and fandom.

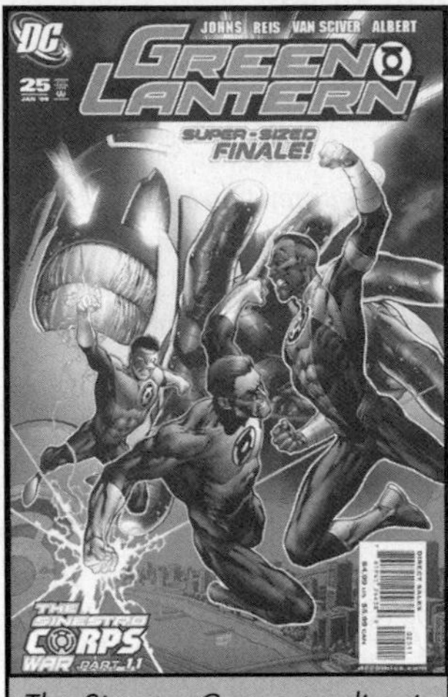

The Sinestro Corps storyline in the Green Lantern titles was a highlight of 2008. (**Green Lantern** #25 shown)

Heath, we all applaud your *Dark Knight* performance, and appreciate your obvious effort to bring a mainstay in the comic world (Joker) to it's proper light on the Silver Screen. You'll be missed.

Trades, Graphic Novels, and Hardcovers: We are allocating more space to this section in both our stores year after year. DC still rules, but Marvel is doing better. We like the Omnibus books of Marvel and Absolute Editions of DC. The art is clearer and better defined due to larger size format. Buy *Crisis* by Pérez in Absolute, or *Hush*...amazing! We rid ourselves of our Manga selection for a few reasons as well. One... need space for DC/Marvel trades, which grow daily in number. Two... selling to teens/adolescents can be worrysome as the age recommendation is so-so at best. Three... our sales have slowed. *True Naruto* always flies, but the rest are lagging for us.

Current Comics This Year: These are the main highlights of 09/2007-09/2008....*Northlanders*, Planet Hulk, World War Hulk, Sinestro Corps War, *Countdown*, The Initiative, Death of Capt. America, *Marvel Zombies 2*, Resurrection Of R'as Al Ghul, new *Thor*, new volume of *JSA*, *Titans* (new title, old team), *The Programme*, *Walking Dead*, *Ultimates 3*, *Annihilation: Conquest*, *X-Men* Messiah Complex, *X-Men* Divided We Stand, *Rann-Thanagar Holy War*, death of young Bart Allen (Impulse - Flash), Stephen King's *Dark Tower*, *Buffy* Season 8, *Marvel: 1985*, *Secret Invasion*, *Secret Invasion*: the Infiltration, *Incredible Hercules*, Old man Logan arc in *Wolverine*, *X-Force* new series, *Cable* new series, *Kick-Ass*, *Salvation Run*, *Justice*, new *Hulk* (red) series, *Ultimate Human*, ... I'm sure I missed something, but I tried. Out of above, these I thought were excellent buys and you should consider in trade form: *Northlander*, Sinestro Corps War, Ra's Al Ghul, Batman R.I.P., *Thor*, *Programme*, *Walking Dead*, *Wolverine*, *Kick-Ass*. All were quite good. The rest are up to you, most are fine reads.

These were all our top sellers as well.

Overall, you may notice every year, most advisors mention some Vertigo titles. These books are always a breath of fresh air. Getting a bit tired of hero stuff? Go get a trade of vol. 1 of either *DMZ*, *Programme*, *Fables*, *Sandman*, *Northlanders* and more. Of course DC doesn't have everything awesome like that. Try some indy titles like *Grimm Fairy Tales*, *Walking Dead*, various Boom titles. A new company, Radical, seems to good to me. Art is ok, story fine, and quantity of pages for your buck is good. If you trust your local store owner, tell him what you usually read and like, then ask for a suggestion. I personally make an attempt to explain a trade or story with some background. If that gets the interest of the collector, I suggest it in an affordable format (softcover trade beginning at vol.1). I almost always mention the best trades of all time, *Batman Dark Knight Returns*, *Watchmen*, and *Kingdom Come*.

The lows this year... *Spawn*, most Image, especially Top Cow(what is going on here?) Too many *Secret Invasion* crossovers. *Amazing Spider-Man* Brand New Day (wow, I can go on all day about this...it's like turning a light switch off and on again 100 times by a naughty child. Good, then bad, then good, then bad, then worse, then silly, and so on). Watch out as it will end up being a nightmare or dream or a Skrull! Oh yea, too many Skrulls. Also, *Marvel Apes* (what in the world??). Wally, please go away and bring back Impulse. The other decent mentionables... Barry is coming back! *JSA* Gog/Magog stuff. *G.I. Joe* finale at DDP. *Trinity* keeps increasing in sales week after week due to decent art/story, very underrated.

Recap... excellent year in sales. DC will be going strong by the time this report is being read. Movies fuel sales and interest everywhere when well done. After DC is done, I expect a dip to follow in sales for 1-2 years. Consumers are a bit tired of constant crossovers. As with *Secret Invasion* and *Civil War*, Marvel is way overdoing it again. Can't once a company just put the crossovers *directly* into a long running weekly title? I do not mean like *52* or *Trinity*, but perhaps skip the issue of *Ms. Marvel* that month if she's involved that month and just make it in the run. That would be not bad. It's annoying to collect, and people tire after months/years. Obviously I'm not Quésada or an editor, but something along those lines, tweaked with the right timing, with a great story, could do quite well, and fans may appreciate the effort. Mass crossovers beware, collectors do remember!

Modern Back Issue Sales (1986-2004): We are selling more complete sets and runs than back issues singlely. Back issues, even at dumping prices, add up to more than trades or sets. The sets tend to be the best price for your buck, trades for the space with some money savings, and single books for the die-hard collector. With so many trades available, it also makes it pointless to attempt starting a long run such as *Nightwing* or *Robin*....or an expensive modern run like *Sandman*. Except of course for the (again) die-hard collector. We have begun putting mid-grade copies into our modern bins, and have noticed better awareness and sales, but we will never see the glory days of the 1980s for bin sales. Of course, we also never saw the great sales in trades/hardcovers back then either. Either way, it's all good reading.

Copper Age - Late Bronze Age Back Issues (1976-1985): Marvel is finally selling well and gaining value. DC is still lower printed and a better investment to me, but those pesky Marvel icons have a huge following. The excellent Marvel movies this year helped fuel the fire. *Thor* from #190-280 for example, is very brisk and cheap. All other titles in the same timeframe do just as well. *Incredible Hulk*, *Iron Man* lead the charge (decent movies, and bravo to Downey Jr.) as did the sales. Rumors abound for G.I. Joe, Avengers, Thor, and of course Captain America to shine on the Silver Screen soon.

So to recap, DC still rules due to scarcity, but Marvel is picking up on the better main titles like *Incredible Hulk*, *Thor* and so on. Sales are lower as well, and getting more main titles than oddballs. Scarce indies are starting to move as well. *TMNT* first printings are extremely hot!

Early Bronze Age Back Issues (1970-1975): Oh, what to say? As always, cheaper than Silver Age, much less available compared to 1975-1985, fantastic art (Steranko, Adams, Wrightson, Starlin, Byrne and on!), many firsts and origins. What more do you want for investing, reading, or art appreciation? The early 1970s was different from the 1960s Silver Age in this way to me... Experimentation. The '60s were the renaissance for comics (or rebirth). But the early 1970s were vivid in change in our hobby and thinking. Just look at Steranko's *Nick Fury*, or Wrightson's *Swamp Thing*? Ever see a movie-western with a dude like Jonah Hex for its hero? Awesome stuff. If you skip *Sgt. Fury*, and those Marvel horror reprints, it's almost all good. I like even Charlton stuff at this stage (not reprint). Sales are abundant at all stages and companies. You name it, we sold it. Gold Key, DC, Marvel, Warrens, all of it!

1960s Marvel: Well, Marvel always rules this time. Too many firsts to ignore. After all, DC was already old news, though still good. Every year, *Amazing Spider-Man*, *X-Men*, *Fantastic Four* all take top spots. Rarely have I seen otherwise. But as you've noticed, I try to inform readers on the not-as-obvious. Point said, pay attention to those much much less expensive 1966-1969 issues of Marvel main titles. You can get many in high grade for still under $50, even $30. Now maybe not a CGC copy in 9.4, but a naked 8.5 is nothing to sneer at? It's still around half the price of a 9.2, and you can read it, too! *Tales To Astonish* and *Tales Of Suspense* should be sky-rocketing as well. Too many Keys to ignore. The only title I usually steer you from is *Sgt.Fury*. Why do I always say that? Because no war title compares to the Rock. *Our Army At War* is number one, and always will be. Nail-biting, realistic, Kubert's art on these should be on *Time* or *Life* mags. Always in demand.

Recap.... buy less expensive, end of Silver Age titles like *Amazing Spider-Man*, *Fantastic Four*, *X-Men*, *Tales To Astonish*, *Tales Of Suspense*, *Daredevil*, *Avengers*, *Journey Into Mystery* and the like. They're underpriced, always CGC'd in high grade, and they always sell.

1960s DC: The beginning of Neal Adams at DC is always the best to buy. The best to sell. The best to collect. Neal Adams did *X-Men* and *Avengers* as well, but it's *Batman* and *Detective Comics* that collectors strive to attain. Comics' #1 character with one of (if not *the*) best human physique pencillers of our comicdom-time. Anyhow, sales about the same as last year with *Batman*, *Detective Comics*, and *Action Comics* reigning supreme. Our war books did really well, with *Star Spangled* coming in 2nd to *Our Army at War*. In the summer of 2008, the JLA really picked up, selling *Brave and the Bold* #28-30, and *JLA* #1-up in most grades. A movie may still be in the works, but my sales were to collectors, not investors. Anyhow, a great title. Big excitement is coming on Barry Allen's return, and that is helping *Flash* sales, but to be truthful, Barry sells 3rd best in DC after Bats and Supes (Hal is 4th).

Recap.... watch out Marvel, DC movies will be coming forth in waves, and if anything like the *Batman* sequels success happens, sales in this period will sway a bit to DC as it is more affordable than the Marvel Keys with the exception of *Showcase* 1st appearances like Barry in #4,#8 and Hal in #22, Lois Lane in #9.

1960s Other: Gold Key is my best in sales with *Solar*, *Magnus* and *Star Trek* tops. Charlton has picked up due to Ditko and very affordable prices. Romance for me is dead. Harvey is *hot*! The Warren mags, except *Vampirella*, slowed. One thing I did notice. A revival for the Dell classics followed up by Gold Keys like *Tarzan* (especially photo covers) and *Lone Ranger*. Affordable *Classics Illustrated* sold well (especially first editions). Some Gold Key ducks moved as well.

Recap... Gold Key does best. I sold runs and complete sets of *Star Trek* and *Dark Shadows* easily. Still nowhere near the sales and demand of DC and Marvel, but increased year over year for me. Considering I specialize in high grade Gold Keys, that made a good year for me. Almost no one buys these books slabbed as a note.

Golden Age - Atomic Age (1939-1955): ECs have slowed greatly, but DCs have exploded. Timelys I never have enough stock, but we all know they sell fast in all grades, and over *Guide* usually, especially *Capt. America*, *Human Torch* and *Marvel Mystery*. I always sell DCs, but this year was a record. I had about 10 *Detective*s from #40-59, mid to high grade ranges, and they all went like lightning.

Not much happened for Dell, but again, I sold some early *Tarzan*, *Lone Ranger*, *Walt Disney's Comics & Stories* and *Uncle Scrooge*. Horror from the Atomic age sold OK, as most are really cool but cheap! The small amount of Timelys I had sold out except for a few.

Recap.... *Detective* and *Action* reign supreme as unlike Timelys, they have the same demand, but at least the supply is not as scarce. My *Superman* issues sold well too, but at or near *Guide*.

Pendragon Comics Store News: We are pleased to announce our Markham store's opening on Main Street North. It's mainly a used book store, but with renovating, we have expanded the store sections to include comics. We noticed immediately a positive response from teens and adults alike. Comics can be sold anywhere under proper conditions to those never living near a comic store before. Most new collectors are rash with questions and have a genuine desire to read these great books. With the success of this summer's movies, and future ones, it has greatly sparked an interest in those not currently collecting. With DC and Marvel's increased lineup of comics geared towards under-12 year olds (all ages books), I don't have to turn away disappointed youngsters, and instead, can show an impressive rack loaded with non-manga books. This helps my new store (there are many young ones in an area surrounded by grade schools), and everyone alike. DC and Marvel are also keeping the costs down to around $2.25 per issue, which helps young ones on a small weekly allowance. I would suggest a decrease in cost for the digest books. If Archie can charge $2.50-$3.50 per digest, why not do so for DC/Marvel digests(currently $7 up). I'd say $4.95 for a digest would be excellent. The paper quality is greater, and the print runs I'm sure are not near Archie levels, but adjust it for the kids and make it happen. They do grow up eventually and buy the bigger books in the end!

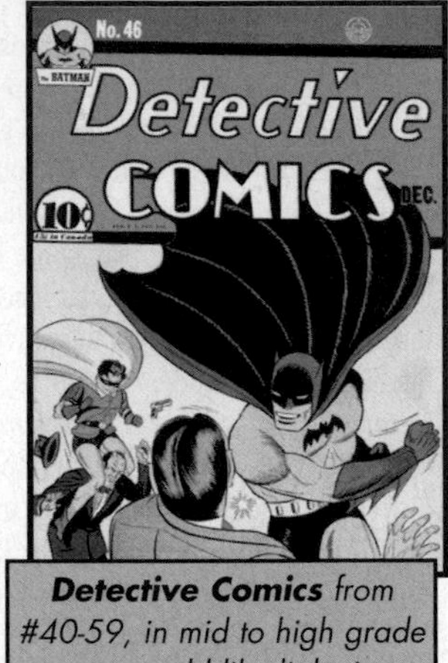

Detective Comics *from #40-59, in mid to high grade ranges, sold like lightning.* ***(Detective Comics** #46 shown)*

Conclusion: Movies, well made, really do attract new blood into the market of all ages. The *Iron Man* movie made believers out of everyone. *Incredible Hulk* was decent, but nowhere near the other two. Ledger and Downey deserve some recognition for sure. No one else could have filled their shoes in those roles with the same passion and impact.

As per comic business, Marvel ruled current sales with *Civil War* and *Secret Invasion*, and all but Golden Age (DC) for vintage back issues. A big turnaround since year 2000. DC still does well in all ages. Online sales and interest on eBay are waning. I personally don't much care to buy/sell on that system myself, and most of my customers don't bother much either. The cost of gas has affected shipping, so if you buy something in another city/country/state, the cost on smaller purchases to ship seems crazy to do so. Auction sites have it made, making percentages at both ends, but at least it's better and safer than eBay(what isn't?). But it will cost you more, especially in shipping. You also can't really get those smaller valued issues to fill in those pesky holes in your runs. So as always, I end up saying.... buy in person, whether at a store or a con! It's the safest, cheapest (shipping at least) way to do it. You can still trade or sell or "make a deal" in person at a store. We even do layaway as do others! Of course, you can always check out an advisor or advertiser in this honorable publication! Fly-by-nighters are not usually found here, but they are on eBay!

Dan Fogel
Hippy Comix, Inc.

Three decades of comics and collectibles retailing have rendered me unfit for life in the real world, but given me a unique and ever developing skill-set in our shared comics universe. Fair trade or not, I'm gonna stick with it!

As the author of *Fogel's Underground Comix Price Guide*, and its long-awaited First Supplement, my focus is mainly on the esoteric, small press, adult, and alternative titles that are mostly not listed in this fine publication. That being said, there are increasing numbers of retailers, investors, collectors and auction companies dipping their toes in these offbeat waters, with record prices being set every year. Underground print runs are fractions of the mainstream, with truly high-grade items scarcer as a result. Multiple print runs and bizarre printing variations add to the unique challenge of collecting in this genre. There are also many points of crossover of creative talent working both "Over(street)ground" and Underground, a tradition begun by such masters as Will Eisner, Harvey Kurtzman, Bill Ward and Wally Wood, continued by the next generation of luminaries including Howard Chaykin, Richard Corben, and Frank Brunner, and embodied today by The Hernandez Brothers, Peter Bagge, Kieron Dwyer, Chuck Austen, Rick Remender, Ed Brubaker, among others. Readers and collectors today are more faithful to their favorite creators and are inclined to follow them to less familiar publishers, formats, and subject matter.

I do keep my "mainstream" chops honed by scouting and brokering deals across the country for all varieties of comics and collectibles. It is getting harder to stumble across new caches of decent Golden and Atomic Age books, while the more plentiful Silver and Bronze Age collections I see are mostly bereft of Keys and higher grades. And to repeat my earlier market reports, 1980-2000 era books flow like the mighty Mississippi and are mainly suitable for landfill, to mix unflattering metaphors. Recent back issues have more modest print runs compared to the excesses of yore and can be surprisingly collectible and hold their value, assuming the titles are still running or the creators still "hot."

My main focus this year is on the directly related but little understood Original Art market. These are items that are truly unique and one of a kind embodiments of collectors' emotional attachments to characters and creators. They are also sought after as the most tangible appreciation of an artist's skill. As such, the right piece presented to the right buyer can be a windfall to the lucky artist or canny dealer who sells it.

When I started out in the 1970s, there were few original art dealers and most comics retailers, if they had any, stockpiled it in the back of the store and mainly traded and sold pieces back and forth with other dealers. The best source at the time (and still a good one today!) was to buy the art directly from the artists at conventions. Most Golden and early-to-mid Silver Age artwork had been little valued and actually destroyed or thrown away by the publishers, making them scarce. The few creators lucky enough to have their pages returned stuck them in file drawers or traded with their peers. Gradually, great strides were made in creator's rights, which included ownership and return of artwork. By the mid-1980s there were many pages coming to market, and it was not uncommon to see stacks of $10 or $15 pages. The higher end was slowly growing, dominated by Frank Frazetta and Carl Barks' drawings and paintings.

The original art market began taking off in the early 1990s. The big money that swiftly inflated Golden and Silver Age books migrated into this arena and never left. Pieces that sold for hundreds only a few years before now changed hands for thousands. Auction house Sothebys, advised by the top level collector-dealers of the time, began offering comic art consignments and realized record sales. The advent of the Internet democratized the market, as more experienced buyers and sellers were joined by new blood throughout the country, and with the shrinking dollar, the world.

What are the different types of art and what makes them collectible? Like a comic book, we start with the cover. These can be symbolic images demonstrating the iconic appeal of the character, a dramatic excerpt luring you to read the story within, or a (sometimes intentionally) goofy or downright weird tableau. Covers are the most valuable type of art, as a rule. However, tears, coffee rings, or mystery stains drive down the value of any piece. It is also not uncommon to find an older cover without the title logo or other trade dress, as these were pasted-on photostats often peeled off and reused for next month's issue. Naturally, these specimens are less aesthetically or financially desirable.

The meat of the book is the pages. Most are panel pages showing the story progressing in little boxes. Splashes, usually but not always the first page, are a full-size image taking up the page. A double-page splash is two facing pages with a really big image. Any type of splash tends to be pricier, a fact not unnoticed by the artist! A panel page is more desirable if it contains the main character, the more times the better. For superhero books, you want him (or her) in costume, preferably in action or displaying superpowers. For collectors of comics writers, having a page or consecutive pages of a cherished story is a treasured goal. Of course, the aforementioned tears and stains drive down values, as do tape, excessive whiteout, production notes (unless by Stan Lee!), and cut-and-pasted or photostatted panels.

Other varieties of comic art include: pin-up pages, sketches, newspaper strips, and magazine, book, trading card, advertising, or record cover illustration. Animation art is a whole other subject and market, but there is some crossover.

There can be no complete discussion of this subject without tackling the main component: the artists. Whoever is hot and collectible on the stands or historically revered is echoed in the art world. You can't go wrong with buying, in rough chronological order: Outcoult, McKay, Herriman, Raymond, Foster, Hogarth, Caniff, Shuster, (Bob or Gil) Kane, Fine, Crandall, Beck, Simon and/or Kirby, Feldstein, Davis, Wood, Schulz, Ditko, Kubert, Swan, DeCarlo, Infantino, Romita, Buscema, Crumb, Shelton, Bode, Wilson,

Spain, Adams, Kaluta, Wrightson, Byrne, Perez, and Ross. There are hundreds of other artists as well whose work sells frequently to fans, investors, and collectors.

I've been fortunate recently to work with powerhouse dealer and all around nice guy Bechara Maalouf, who has recently expanded his Nostalgic Investments brand into 100Auctions.com, focusing on high-end and collectible original art. The market is booming and constantly evolving, and I'm thrilled as always to be a part of it!

Before I go I'd like to thank my fellow dealers and collectors who actually read these market reports and give me positive feedback throughout the year, and as always Bob Overstreet, Steve Geppi, and Mark Huesman of Gemstone Publishing, for providing me the opportunity. There have been a lot of changes in comics since I began these reports in 1987, and as always, I look forward to seeing what's ahead!

Stephen H. Gentner
Collector

I have found the market to be in very healthy shape this year. Prices in Golden Age high grade, slabbed in particular, have been firm and strong. Unslabbed high grade and lower grades appear healthy as well. The appreciation of certain titles and artists has been very strong; such as *Batman*, Timely titles, Good Girl, and Standard Nedor. Artists like Alex Schomberg, Matt Baker, Jack Kamen, and Bob Lubbers show strength and durability. Fiction House titles like *Fight*, *Wings*, *Rangers*, and *Planet* are also strong. *Jumbo* and *Jungle*, depending upon cover graphics are also doing OK, albeit less than the other Fiction House stable. My experience with Fawcett, Centaur, Four Color, etc. has been minimal, and less impressive than the above referenced material.

In Silver, high grade slabbed Marvel, especially Keys, still defy gravity!! What more can I say? DC is strong also, but not to the levels of Marvels save some super Keys such as *Showcase* #4, 8, 22, 34, early *Flash*, etc. From a purely "appreciation" viewpoint, parking your money in a *Tales of Suspense* #39 in high grade, or a *Fantastic Four* #1 would seem pretty good, especially with the stock market and the price of oil. Speculation in the right books in CGC high grade can be lucrative. As a collecting objective, speculation is enticing. Yet, I believe the true collector who loves and appreciates the stories and characters is rewarded many times over beyond lucre.

It's nice to have our books worth more, but I can't look at my collection in only those terms. The affection for stories I read as a kid and adolescent has deeply shaped my collecting interests. It is a worn idea, but the comics I read back in the late 1950s and early 1960s still today transport me back to a simpler time. My priorities were to make sure I got the current issue of *Adventure Comics* for the Legion, or *Flash*, *Dr. Strange*, Ant-Man, or Adam Strange. Heck, even *Turok* and *The Fly* were essential! Those stories and characters were (and are) my friends. Few things are as personal as the relationship between the reader and art/stories. There is a physical reaction in me to the trials, tribulations, and triumphs of my characters. It is for those early revelations in comic books so long ago which has given me the drive and appreciation for earlier heroes in the Golden Age, and those on the newsstands today.

As I am a collector and not a dealer, I thought I would share some of the purchases I made this year. With the new *Iron Man* movie, which was so good, I put together a nice run of the Obediah Stane story arc in *Iron Man*. Issues #162-200 are a great read, and only $4-6 each in NM-!

I also finally put together McFarlane's *Amazing Spider-Man* run #298-350. I'm ashamed to say I had never read them, but what a neat run–(at or below *Guide* $20-$25).

With the very sad passing of Dave Stevens, I chased all the covers of his I could find, i.e., *Cheval Noir*, *3-D Seduction of the Innocent*, *Planet Comics* (1988), *Airboy*, *Jonny Quest*, etc., and of course, Rocketeer material I was missing.

In Silver, I nailed down *Showcase*, *Star Spangled War Stories*, and other Enemy Ace appearances in high grade (well over *Guide* in high grade.) I love Kubert's work on this character! I am still chasing some, but have filled in most of the *Mystery in Space* Adam Strange issues. These are really tough to find in grade or even nice! Prices were over *Guide* in FN/VF/VF-. On the modern side, I have nailed down Hellboy appearances, *B.P.R.D.*, and *Usagi Yojimbo* from Fantagraphics, Mirage, and Dark Horse.

I look forward to another good year coming up!

Eric J. Groves
The Comic Art Foundation

As this is written, the American economy, if not in the tank, is deeply disturbed. Disposable income is limited, we are told, eroded by inflated prices for gas, food and other necessities. Yet the market for old comic books thrives in 2008. Go figure.

There are two lines of thought explaining this. First, that the collectibles market operates independently of the general economy, fueled by the passion and determination of collectors. Second, that when other investment opportunities are volatile and uncertain, collectibles are sure and steady. Either way, comics continue to attract new collectors and new capital.

Golden Age: Collectors continue to acquire a broad array of GA titles in all grades. Condition is important, of course, but a solid VG is entirely acceptable to most. Timelys are highly desirable, especially *Captain America*. DC's hold their own, with *Batman*, *Superman*, *Green Lantern*, *All-American*, *Star Spangled* and *Wonder Woman* more popular than ever. Fawcetts are in third place, with titles like *Captain Marvel* and *Whiz* finding new homes, and at very reasonable prices.

This takes nothing away from other eagerly sought after GA titles. Comic fans want Quality's *Plastic Man* by Jack Cole as well as early issues of *Uncle Sam*, *National*, *Military* and *Police*. MLJ titles are harder to locate than in previous times, so *Jackpot*, *Black Hood* and *Pep* don't stay around very long. Fans are still chasing low numbers of Fiction House titles, especially *Planet*, *Jumbo* and *Wings*. Fox titles are a bit slower, as are Lev Gleasons, but early wartime covers of *Daredevil* and *Boy* are quite attractive. Nedor comics like *Black Terror* with Schomberg covers enjoy a faithful following and are bargains.

Early Dell *Four Colors*, particularly when in condition, picked up in 2008. Some of them offer spectacular cover art, such as the Walt Kelly issues. Many of those *Four Colors* are, of course, newspaper strip reprints, but provide great reading at bargain prices. Regrettably, other reprint titles like *Ace*, *King*, *Super*, *Popular*, *Crackajack* and *Famous Funnies* sell very slowly to a limited collector base. Some other non-superhero GA titles sell briskly, however, especially earlier Archie comics and related titles.

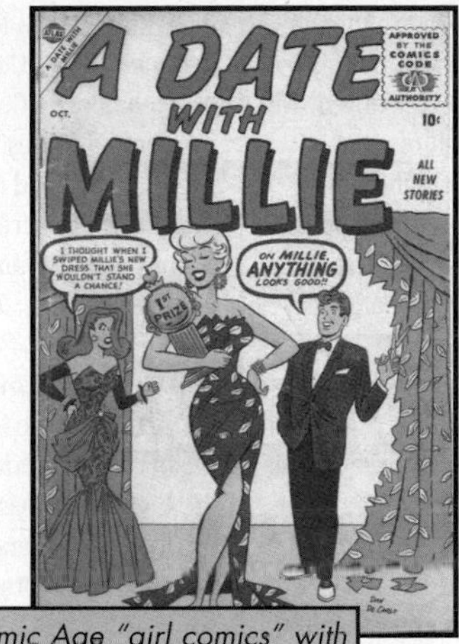

© MAR

Atomic Age "girl comics" with Dan DeCarlo art are in demand. (**A Date With Millie** #1 shown)

Atomic Age: Year by year, collector appreciation of this marvelous era of comic publishing expands. From 1946 to 1956, experimentation and title proliferation produced a fascinating array of comic books. Timely and Atlas are among those most in demand, particularly the girl comics with Dan DeCarlo art, such as *Millie the Model*, *Tessie the Typist*, *Nellie the Nurse*, *Patsy Walker* and *My Friend Irma*. Pre-Code Atlas horror comics are also delicious, especially early issues. War and crime titles in general are slow but steady and probably underpriced.

EC comics are enjoying a resurgence, having slowed somewhat in view of the many less expensive reprints available to fan-addicts. Superhero titles from this period do very well, especially later issues of *Flash* with Kubert art. Also, the several off-beat DC efforts of the early 1950s, like *Danger Trail*, attract collector interest.

Silver Age: Condition is king in the quest for Silver Age books, especially Marvels. Many fans are satisfied with copies in Fine or better, but advanced collectors want the highest grade they can find, slabbed or not. Then there are the speculators, who buy only for condition, not to complete a run of anything in particular.

With Marvels, *Amazing Spider-Man* remains number one, but interest has broadened widely. Marvel's exploitation of its characters in film has probably contributed to this. Thus, almost all titles move out briskly, including *Fantastic Four*, *Tales of Suspense*, *X-Men*, *Avengers*, *Daredevil*, and most recently, *Iron Man*. We observe very little price resistance at current levels, but this is not to say book values should be increased.

There is a resurgence of interest in Silver Age DCs. Classic superhero titles like *Batman*, and *Superman* lead the way, followed by *Flash*, *Green Lantern*, *JLA* and *Wonder Woman*. In particular, early SA issues published in the late 1950s command special attention because of condition problems inherent in the way the books were printed. They deserve the prices they bring, especially when in grade.

Buying and Selling: eBay fundamentally changed the hobby, as everyone knows. Nonetheless, there is much business to be done at conventions where collectors and dealers can inspect unslabbed books first hand and haggle over prices.

Regrettably, the largest convention, in San Diego, appears to be largely focused on the motion picture industry, quite a departure from its long and storied tradition. The second largest convention is Wizard World in Chicago, which, despite some persistent problems, still manages to attract a great deal of material and lots of buyers. There are several other, smaller conventions scattered about the country where comics can be bought and sold in a less frenctic atmosphere. These gatherings deserve fan attendance and support.

Here in Oklahoma City, long time fans Bart Bush and Robert Brown have reinvigorated a non-profit fan club formed in the late 1960s, known as the Oklahoma Alliance of Fandom ("OAF"). We are staging an intimate two-day gathering here in which only genuinely older material will be available: comics, pulps, Big Little Books, movie posters, vintage paperbacks, even old radio shows. We think these back-to-basics conventions on a very local level are healthy for our hobby. And yes, there will be bargains.

We continue to unearth collections of GA books from attics and basements, but nowhere near as often as back in the day. Sometimes we buy comics from the estates of people in their eighties who have kept them since childhood. The treasure hunt is challenging. But it can be enormously rewarding when you know you are bringing a rare comic to market for the very first time. It's a pleasure to say: "I am the second owner of this book."

John Haines
John Haines Rare Comics

The vintage market continues to evolve with two distinct venues for comics solidifying their positions: internet and conventions. For us, the larger conventions are becoming dicey - almost all of the big shows are raising booth prices to dealers while continuing to focus on attracting autograph hounds instead of comic book collectors. In response to this, we changed our game plan this year, deciding to skip the Wizard shows entirely. And you know what? We didn't miss them any more than they missed us. Instead, we chose to focus on smaller shows in areas that we hadn't been to before - the reception we received from vintage collectors in these areas was overwhelming. It really reminded us of the 1980s when the convention circuit was just beginning to boom - really enthusiastic collectors giddy to come across a wide inventory of comics they like - quite nostalgic really.

On the other hand, we have upped our focus on internet

sales as it seems that vintage collectors have migrated there as well as going to shows. We can't believe the number of new friends we make every month through the internet - and most are 30-somethings - this influx of new blood is an event that hasn't happened in years. We have seen more Golden Age collections and collectors come our way this year than any year we can remember. We hope this continues!

Our traditional catalog sales continue to grow, although at a much slower pace than internet sales mostly due to a policy change on our part. Because of the effort involved, we are only issuing our catalog once a year, which of course disappoints the faithful. The old adage "out of sight, out of mind" is appropriate. What do they buy out of the catalog? Atom Age and Golden Age mostly - which illustrates the lack of availability of decent books from the 1940s at the local level.

Restoration: We continue to have solid sales of restored books. Our customers seem to like them when we price them at what we determine would be their unrestored grade. That way they get a pretty nice copy at a fraction of the price - and they feel comfortable that we will always buy their restored copies back. Of course, this does not include CGC purple labels - if you want to sell a restored book, it cannot be in a CGC holder.

Bronze Age: Can't keep key issues. We've had several *Hulk* #181s over the year, and none lasted more than 48 hours with some selling only minutes after we acquired them. In general, this area remains the hottest for us. Low grade sells just below *Guide*, mid-grade issues sell right around *Guide*, and high grade copies sell well above *Guide* regardless of genre. Above NM- 9.2 multiples of *Guide* prices are common. At the high-end, Romance sells as well as Superhero as well as Horror as well as esoteric. It really doesn't matter - if it was made during the 1970s, someone is looking for it: *Ms. Marvel*, *Savage Sword of Conan*, *House of Mystery*, *House of Secrets*, Neal Adams' *Green Lantern/Detective*, Marvel Romance, DC Digest issues, Movie/TV issues like *Funky Phantom*, *Chan Clan*, *Scooby-Doo*, *Wacky Races*, *Lancelot Link*, etc. All black and white magazines are selling fast. Collectors are always looking to fill in runs of *Captain America* and *Iron Man*. Barry Smith *Conan* issues blaze away while issues after #24 end up in the dollar boxes - go figure. *X-Men* under #125 continue to grind away and *Giant-Size X-Men* #1 is always in demand. Treasury Editions sell steadily day after day with the *Superman Vs. Muhammad Ali* issue most in demand.

Silver Age: Didn't think we'd ever say this, but Silver Age sales have plateaued for us with no significant change from the previous year. We believe that there are two reasons for this: First, Silver Age is plentiful with collectors having no problem locating common issues and second, most local dealers of vintage comics focus on Silver Age so they are abundant. We'll leave the superhero news to others since it's always the same - but we will tell you we had strong interest in teen/hippy comics like Harvey's *Bunny* and Charton's *GoGo*. Collectors continued to search out those elusive DC war comics issues that they still need - especially anything with Sgt. Rock. Movie/TV slowed down somewhat in lower grades but continued to move in fine or better condition with *The Munsters* being most sought after. And it never seems like we never have enough Tower comics to satisfy demand - ditto *Turok* #1 - #10.

Atom Age: Smoking hot - as we continue to find more oddities we haven't encountered before our collector friends just gobble them up. Even Gleason titles (yes, Gleason!) are moving with requests for *Crime Does Not Pay*, *Boy*, and *Daredevil*. All DC titles from 1947 through 1953 sell incredibly well above VG. We think that this is due to the very poor production values that DC employed during this period - cheap paper lead to high destruction rates for DCs from this period. We're sure you've noticed that 80% of DC material from this time frame is shattered. Always hot are classic cover issues like: *The Saint* #6, *Teenage Dope Slaves*, *Crime Does Not Pay* #47, and later issues of *Super-Mystery*. *Strange Adventures* issues from the 1950s are selling above *Guide* across the board regardless of grade with the highest increases in the lower numbers. Collectors also crave good-girl issues - any title will do - they want classic Matt Baker issues just as much as they want a nice copy of *Dogface Dooley* or *Mopsy* - yeah, just try to pick up a decent copy of *Mopsy* for anywhere near *Guide*.

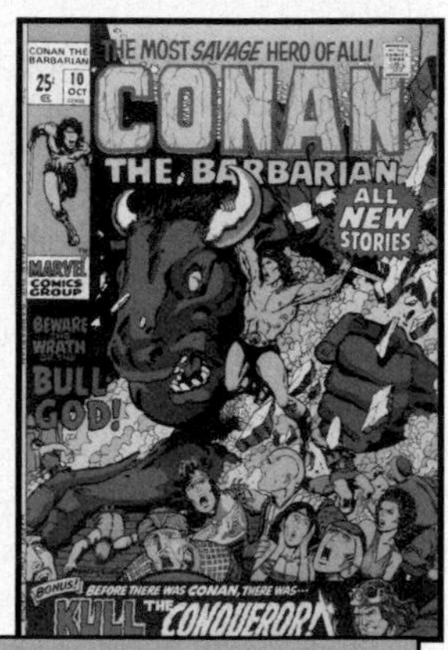

Barry Smith **Conan** issues blaze away. (**Conan the Barbarian** #10 shown)

The amazing thing is that throughout it all, year after year, pre-code Horror rules the Atom Age! The more bizarre the cover, the better - collectors want Atlas titles like *Adventures into Terror* and *Journey into Mystery* - also EC goodies, and off-brand titles like *Beware*, *Weird Chills*, and *Strange Mysteries*. We struggle to keep one magazine box full of pre-code horror for our collectors. The Atlas teen titles have been building and now are hot hot hot with *Millie the Model* Dan DeCarlo issues just on fire - just make sure that the paper dolls have not been clipped from these, as is common. Finally, Harvey #1 issues have taken off. We have sold issues like *Richie Rich* #1 and *Hot Stuff* #1 at full *Guide* to other dealers! Imagine what their customers were willing to pay.

Golden Age: We have seen steady growth in Quality titles like *Plastic Man*, *Police* (with classic Spirit stories), *Military*, *Modern*, and *Smash*. As soon as we get any of these titles, our collectors thin them right out. The exception seems to be the *Blackhawk* title. For some reason this has cooled over the past few years - bargains abound and sooner or later *Blackhawk* will take off again. Once again, Dells are doing great for us with *Four Colors*, *Walt Disney's Comics and Stories*, and *Looney Tunes* out in front - Barks issues always seem to sell first, but eventually everything goes. We constantly hear other dealers poo-poo Dells, but if they are in nice shape, we pick them up whenever we can. What is the bottom line in Golden Age? Well Timely rules the roost with *Captain America Comics* as the King of them all - a fact that hasn't changed in twenty years. Can't find or afford those early *Marvel Mystery* issues? Well then, Nedor titles like *America's Best* and *Black Terror* may be the cure. Westerns have slowed down, but *Tarzans* have sped up - call it a wash. DC titles have picked up for us over the year as we had built up a nice back stock of them. Luckily we have been able to replace what we've sold. As always, we have seen no letup in demand for Golden Age.

John Hauser
JMHComics

Comics are finally out of the back alleys and closets. We no longer have to collect in secret and be closet readers. The success of comics in the movies is bringing knowledge of comics to the average person. They now know the DC and Marvel Universes and have seen how entertaining they can be. This can only bode well for the future of comics. Two-Face is now a household word!

This year has been one of my best years for selling comics at shows. Every show has been well attended with lots of buyers showing up to spend money. Even the Emerald City Convention held in Seattle on the busy Mothers Day weekend had bigger crowds than ever. I can't wait to see it back to its April schedule. Planet Comicon in Kansas City was busier than ever this spring.

The summer Chicago Comicon was perhaps my best one ever! Amidst all the talk of doom and gloom for the economy comic sales have been stronger than ever. Perhaps the economy is not as bad as its made out to be. Since you can't eat comics (though I've tried!). They tend to come out of your budget for fun.

My only complaint with shows is they tend to be grouped together so it is feast or famine. If show promoters paid more attention to other's show schedules we might not see three large shows in a given area all on the same bloody weekend. A good example is the Mid-Ohio Convention moving its schedule to conflict with the long standing MCBA show in Minneapolis. This definitely cuts into my opportunities to sell comics and make the fans happy!

eBay sales continue to be steady in spite of their every attempt to drive us sellers away. It's to bad we have no good alternatives. My feeling is that the door is now open for competition. eBay's changes are a constant source of worry as we sellers seem to be at their mercy.

Sales of comics graded by CGC continue to do well in grade. I've been very happy with the results on everything I've sent their way. This continues to be the best way to realize high dollars on your precious comics. This price guide continues to be a great source of pricing data and reference data. I couldn't manage without my copy in hand. And I'm sure you've all seen me carrying my copy around at shows!

Golden Age: I've had strong sales on Golden Age comics all year long. Strip reprint and funny animal comics are the worst selling Golden Age comics. The collectors for many of these are aging, and I don't see many young collectors stepping up to the plate. Low grade Horror, DC and Fawcetts have been my market leaders this year.

Silver Age: Nice clean Silver Age sells very well. Marvel always sell the best. DCs are selling in every grade but not as fast as Marvels. Oddball Silver Age sells if the price is right. DC war sales have slowed a bit for me, but DC superhero is picking up steam. Anything Joker has been great this year. It seems I am always looking for more Marvel comics to buy.

Bronze Age: Continues to be one of the best selling time periods of comics. Prices are still relatively low on this kind of material. There seems to be plenty of collectors trying to fill in their runs. Almost anything will sell given some exposure and time.

Copper/Modern Age: 1980s comics are finally picking up some steam. *The Killing Joke* and *Watchmen* comics are the market leaders this year. They are proof that all those '80s comics may develop a strong following. I am guessing many of these have been destroyed in floods, natural disasters and uncaring collectors.

This has been a great year for comics and comic collectors

Jef Hinds
Jef Hinds Comics

The sub-prime crisis and dramatic oil price increases created a general economic downturn in 2008. Like everything else, the comic industry was affected. Despite the challenges of the past year, I am optimistic about the future.

The first part of 2007 was going well but sales took an abrupt downturn that August. Monthly totals were significantly less than those of August 2006. This weakness persisted thought the holiday selling season and aggressive discounting was necessary to achieve an average December profit.

January 2008 saw sales improving but not quite to levels of previous years. Since then, I am seeing gradual monthly gains which leads to my optimism. I have observed over many years that variations in comic sales can foretell by several months changes in overall economic vitality. Perhaps sales of comic books (or collectibles overall) are a gauge of diposable income or consumer confidence. For example, when the media were still touting a strong US economy in fall of 2007, I and many other dealers I had spoken with, were already sensing the slowdown.

My own business has been strengthened by numerous collections which have surfaced since January. I was able to acquire in the first half of 2008 as much as I ordinarily find in an entire year. A highlight was a large Silver Age collection with every Marvel and DC Key except *Showcase* #4. Other items include early Golden Age titles, a complete *Walt Disney's Comics & Stories* set, a nearly-complete *Four Color* series #1 and complete *Classics* first editions. This represents the greatest volume of new collections I have seen in many years.

Gold and Silver Age: High end investment copies and low end reader/filler copies continue to dominate the market.

Middle grade Gold and Silver Age titles are slow at *Guide* prices, perhaps being seen as merely expensive reader copies. Thus, the percentage of *Guide* I would pay for a collection of G or VF comics is substantially greater than for a collection in FN condition. The *Guide* began to reflect this a few years back but will likely need to go further to accurately portray the market. The split should be around 1.0 for GD, 1.75 for VG and 2.5 for FN.

The number of original-owner Gold and Silver Age collections coming up for sale continues to wind down. To use an oil analogy, we have certainly passed "Peak Golden Age" and we may be nearing "Peak Silver Age" soon. Prices will continue their upward trend.

Bronze Age: Condition is paramount. Only high grades (VF or greater) are sellable at *Guide* or above. Others are slow sellers at *Guide*. Bronze Age collections will continue to surface for some time. It is recommended that NM or better books from this period should be certified to achieve their maximum value.

International Sales: Sales have been strong for several years and remain robust with the UK, Canada and Australia leading the pack. They see our prices in dollars as bargains. The continued weaker dollar will no doubt foster this ongoing trend.

eBay: Sales growth in this venue seems to have peaked; overall customer traffic on eBay is down from past years. The continuous series of changes eBay imposes on sellers can be tiresome, like last spring when they raised final value fees and changed feedback rules to advantage buyers. Time will tell if these changes can reverse the flat growth in this marketplace. In my ten years selling on eBay, I have needed to monitor and adjust sales strategies frequently in response to their procedural changes in order to maintain positive sales. Currently, unless a book has at least $150.00 *Guide* value, I will not do a $.99 no-reserve auction anymore. Middle grade books at $100.00 or less at no-reserve auction only sell for 40-50% of *Guide*. I do more fixed-priced listings now, placing books that don't get adequate offers in my eBay store to avoid excess listing fees.

Part of the fun of being a back issue comic dealer is that there is an element of luck involved. And, of course, the thrill of the hunt. You never know what you might find the next time the phone rings or the next time you get your mail. Keep at it and sooner or later a Green River or White Mountain may come your way.....

Brian Ketterer
Collector

With the rest of 2007 and a little over half of 2008 (including 2008's San Diego and Chicago shows) now concluded since last year's *Guide* report, the market remains healthy and vibrant. From a consumer standpoint, the amount of quality material being offered from a variety of outlets continues to amaze. Auction houses such as Comiclink and Heritage are listing incredible high grade material (including comic books and original comic book art) including impressive collections from Heritage such as the Toth early DC collection and Comiclink offering up high grade original owner *Amazing Spider-Man* and record prices for other keys. Some of the highest prices that have been obtained for books and some of the highest prices I have paid over the course of the past year have come through bids on auction sites. It is impossible to ignore the incredible listings from both of these sites. In addition, competitors such as Doug Schmell of Pedigree Comics, Steve Fishler/Vincent Zurzolo of Metropolis (with their auction site ComicConnect) and Brent Moeshlin of Quality Comix have all recently added auctions to their websites. All have offered very high quality material.

During the course of the last year, Marvel and DC keys in high grade have both experienced continued and rapid growth. *Amazing Fantasy* #15 has seen especially rapid growth. Unrestored copies of this book have seen aggressive price increases with prices in low, mid and high grade all receiving large upward movement. However, *Fantastic Four* #1, *Tales of Suspense* #39, *Journey Into Mystery* #83 and most of the early Marvel keys have seen steady, impressive price gains. This year, Marvel movies helped books such as *Iron Man* #1 achieve extremely high prices for this very common book. Many collectors are either unaware or do not care about how common books like *Iron Man* #1, *Incredible Hulk* #181 and other later Marvels are to obtain, even in high grade. In low and mid grade, these books are plentiful, but nevertheless, because of the movie speculation, these books have continued to experience a continued growth.

Speculation is now driving keys like *Avengers* #4, *Captain America* #100 and other Avengers-related keys because of the announcement of the *Avengers* movie. *Incredible Hulk* #181, which was hovering around the $2,000-$2,200 level for CGC-graded 9.4 copies, has started to move up. More surprising are the increases in low grade copies with some incomplete (missing Marvel value stamp) copies going for around $200 on eBay in otherwise VG shape. Again, hunger for Wolverine and the bounce from his upcoming movie are making demand skyrocket. Currently, I have noticed an even higher interest in Marvel keys than ever before, and I have been aggressively buying these books from all available outlets.

While it should be no surprise to tell anyone reading this that Marvel keys are hot, their DC counterparts are beginning to receive increased attention in high grade. Top graded early Silver Age *Flash* books are hitting the market and obtaining strong prices in high grade. *Green Lantern* #76 is continuing its rapid ascent in price as CGC graded 9.0s are escalating in price to well over $1,000. Similar record prices are being seen 8.5, 9.2, 9.4 and other grades. With few high grade CGC copies available, prices are strong when top graded copies reach the market. Similarly, even ungraded copies of *Green Lantern* #76 continue to obtain strong prices in low, mid and high grades. Is this book destined to become DC's equivalent to *Incredible Hulk* #181? While not a first appearance of a major character, it is fast approaching those levels. In fact 9.4 copies of *Green Lantern* #76 sell at multiples of what an *Incredible Hulk* #181 sells at due to the scarcity of *Green Lantern* #76 in high grade. All Neal Adams covers seem to be on the rise. Even lesser titles such as *Tomahawk* with Neal Adams drawn covers are showing incredibly strong prices in high grade. Neal Adams' *Batman* work continues to draw attention and focus in all grades and prices remain healthy and constant. Demand is also increasing as many collectors are drawn to Adams' groundbreaking rendition of one of DC's most popular characters.

Early DC keys such as *Action Comics* #252 (first Supergirl) and *Action Comics* #242 (first Brainiac) remain in demand and elusive to obtain in all grades. *Action Comics* #242 specifically remains tough to obtain in any grade as many dealers don't have a copy above Good in their inventory, if they have one at all. Early ten cent DCs in high grade are also receiving increased competition and attention as early *Supermans* (such as *Superman* #144, 146, 147 as well as many others) with ten cent covers reach incredible multiples of *Guide* prices when CGC-graded 9.0 and above. *Mystery in Space* is also a title well sought after and receiving a great deal of attention for high grade (9.0 and up) copies of Carmine Infantino Adam Strange covers. DC war, especially early ten cent and grey tone covers on such titles as *Our Army at War* and Sgt. Rock are solid sellers. Over the past year, I have concentrated on early 10 cent DCs and found them next to impossible to obtain in high grade. As other collectors discover these, I expect interest to increase and other high grade DC collections to hit the market due to increased demand.

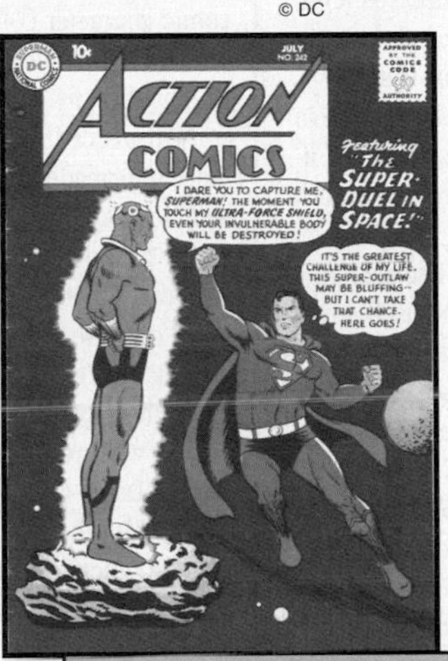

Early DC Silver Age keys, like **Action Comics** #242, remain in demand and elusive in all grades.

While keys remain steady and strong, common run books in mid grade and low grade, even for popular titles like *Action Comics*, *Batman*, *Amazing Spider-Man*, *Avengers*, etc. are sellable primarily at a discount to *Guide* prices. There is a wealth of material in low and mid grade with almost all major dealers and many collectors sitting on a plentiful supply of such comics. These books routinely sell at the 40-50% off *Guide* range and remain available at such prices through a variety of online outlets and even at local/national conventions.

Niche books such as romance, crime and horror all remain strong. During this past year, I have discovered some wonderful titles and some very cool artwork (especially John Romita's romance work) on titles such as *Our Love Story* and others. What I continually find interesting about comics is that areas that I once ignored have so much to offer. EC science fiction, Fiction House, Charlton, pre-code horror are all genres which I have been buying in chunks and enjoying immensely. One of the great things about comic books in general is just the incredible variety to satisfy a myriad of tastes.

Finally, I need to make my annual push for the local comic book shop, which to me is still an incredibly important facet of the hobby. While the internet does provide an outlet to buy discounted new books and trades, it is an impersonal way to shop and provides little remedy when there are problems. More importantly, the brick and mortar stores are still a great way to introduce new fans to the medium and provide the lifeblood of the new book market. Retailers can be great ambassadors for our hobby and continue to promote it. As part of my job, I usually have to travel all parts of the country. In doing so, it gives me a chance to visit a number of different comic book shops to see how they operate. Each one is unique and provides a wonderful resource for their local collectors. I have to single out the following shops and owners who provide incredible customer service for new books and provide an extensive line of vintage comics. I would also highly recommend them for their honesty and integrity: Ben Lichtenstein of Zapp Comics in Wayne and Manalapan, New Jersey, Joe and Jeff Conzolo of JC Comics in North Plainfield, New Jersey, and Mike Pfieffer of Main Street Comics and Hobbies in Milltown, New Jersey.

Let me single out Frank Link owner of Comic Universe in Folsom, PA. Frank is celebrating his 30th anniversary as a comic book retailer and the doors of his shop being open. Through that time, he has generated a loyal following among his customers, sold many vintage books, and survived some of the down turns in the industry. Every time I go into Comic Universe, Frank is there with a smile on his face and an enthusiasm, even after all these years, for comic books. If you are in the area, you should stop by and say hello. Better yet, utilize him as a resource for new and vintage books. After 30 years, Frank continues to be one of the best examples in the industry of what is right with comic book retailers and why they deserve to be supported.

Finally, there are many fantastic advertisers for vintage books in the *Guide*, and the *Guide* remains the number one research/pricing source in the hobby. Many of the advertisers in this *Guide* are some of the top retailers in the industry. Even in this day and age, there are still many charlatans in our hobby. From a consumer standpoint, I have found that for honesty, integrity and an easy transaction, I recommend to all of you fellow collectors the following dealers: Robert C. Storms owner of www.highgradecomics.com, Joe Verenault of JHV Associates, Steve Ritter of World Wide Comics, Ted VanLiew of Superworld, Vincent Zurzolo of Metropolis Collectibles, Dale Roberts and Dave Reynolds/Terry O'Neill of Nationwide Comics. There are plenty of other fabulous dealers, but these to me are the standouts.

The hobby remains strong and there is no reason to see an immediate downturn even in the face of the fairly deep economic troubles in the United States. While I would expect some softening of the market the longer the overall economy stumbles as people tend to pull back on luxury items, I still believe the highest end of the market and the key books will continue their growth.

Dennis Keum
Fantasy-Comics

Demand for comic books has been tremendous over the past year. Despite the slow economy, rising commodity prices, and stagnant income growth, it is clear the comic book market is as strong as ever. As we continue to see more mainstream media coverage, there an increased level of general public awareness of comic characters and comic books as financial investments. Not only can this trend be seen within the U.S. but we can also see marked increase in demand for comic books globally. As we look around us, it appears we are living in another Golden Age era in comic books.

Our sales continue to grow with Silver and Bronze Age Marvels still dominating sales volume. Marvels outsell any other comics 10 to 1. In addition to usual strong demand for *Amazing Spider-Man* and X-Men titles, there was notable increase in customers seeking *Avengers* and *Iron Man* comics this past year. DCs are still solid sellers with titles such as *House of Mystery*, *House of Secrets*, *Ghosts*, and *Weird War Tales* continuing to show strong interest. Most high grade Bronze and Copper Age comics are still relatively inexpensive and represent great buying opportunities.

As we look ahead, it is clear the comic book market will be stronger than ever with continued growth. I am honored to be contributing to this hobby and being able to do what I love everyday. As of this writing, we are hard at work cataloging our entire inventory of 100,000+ books in an effort to make them available through our eBay store and website over the upcoming year.

Nadia Mannarino
All Star Auctions

The trend of museum shows continued into 2008 with more thematic exhibits highlighting the best of comic art and newspaper strip art. The Montclair Museum September opening at the Montclair Art Museum was one of their most popular exhibits (www.montclairartmuseum.org). The four exhibits, Reflecting Culture: The Evolution of American Comic Book Superheroes, Comic Book Legends: Joe, Adam and Andy Kubert, Dulce Pinzon: The Real Story of The Superheroes, and Greg Hildebrandt: Golden and Silver Age Superheroes, drew crowds with over 3,000 attendees on the last weekend alone!

It is extremely important that this type of exposure continue as it elevates the medium to a new level. For the past several years, attention has been paid to our industry as Hollywood adapted comic books and their heroes for movies, now with all this increased attention in the form of museum opening and showings, we are even further poised for takeoff!

As a result of this heightened awareness, prices have risen sharply, and we have been approached for interviews by various publications to explain the continued rise in popularity as well as the steady growth and increase in prices seen in the comic character collectibles arena. Easy enough to cite Hollywood's influence but there are other factors contributing as well.

Historically, in uncertain times, collectibles do enjoy resurgence. There is a need for a comfort zone which these items provide, bringing us back to our childhood and simpler times, many of these items are "feel good" purchases. We have seen the resurrection of the toy market, the animation market and the premium market and the other areas of comic character collectibles are still extremely solid, with the original comic book and newspaper strip art market leading the way.

With record prices being established, a need arises for more information about caring for, storing and insuring collectibles. Appraisals are becoming a necessity rather than a luxury as most insurance companies will not insure items valued at $5,000 or above without proof of authenticity and proof of ownership. Mark your calendars, review your collection and remember it is our responsibility to be caretakers of these precious items! Let your motto be: "Collect and protect what you like!"

San Diego Comic-Con 2008 was yet another incredible event! With the final attendance numbers coming in at over 130,000 attendees, plus 9,000 exhibitors and their staff, this has become the "must exhibit" and "must attend" show of the year. The Con has become a launching pad for TV and movie projects, and with so many stars in attendance, the media once again covered the con throughout the country. Here are some of the highlights of sales at the convention:

Frank Frazetta's *Escape from Venus* realizes $251,000 – a world record price for the artist. A second Frazetta oil, *King Kong* realized over $200,000.

George Herriman's rare hand-colored 1922 *Krazy Kat* realizes $75,000 – a world record price for the artist; far exceeding the previous record of $50,000.

Neal Adams/Bernie Wrightson collaboration on the full issue of *Green Lantern* #84 realizes a price exceeding $115,000 – a world record price for Adams' art.

Winsor McCay *In The Land Of Wonderful Dreams* April 13, 1913 partially hand colored Sunday $70,000 – a world record price for the artist.

Joe Kubert's *Star Spangled War Stories* #38 undersized cover realizes $38,000 – a world record price for the artist.

Also, a seminal feature in the history of illustrative narrative: a Dave Gibbons original from *Watchmen* was purchased for over $6,000. Preparatory art from Will Eisner's ground breaking *A Contract With God* was also sold along with numerous originals from major artists including: Jack Kirby, Steve Ditko, Curt Swan, Charles Schulz, Milton Caniff, Chester Gould, John Buscema, Carmine Infantino, Frank Miller (*Sin City* and *The Spirit*), Alex Toth, Bob Oksner, Jim Lee to name but a few. All Star Auctions concluded the San Diego Comic-Con having realized over $1.2 million in direct (non-Auction) sales. Our re-cap: "This unprecedented series of direct sales by All Star illustrates a continued confidence at every level of the global art market, and highlights San

Diego's prominence as a leading international sale site. For the last two weeks, international collectors from all over the world have turned their attention to San Diego Comic Con in San Diego, California and competed for exceptional works which were fresh to the market and offered with impressive provenances and appealing estimates. Comic Con 2008 follows recent successful sales by All Star which have demonstrated the continued strength, depth and breadth of the global art market, and which have seen a consistency in the number and commitment of international buyers at every level."

We ran thousands of eBay and internet sales as well as catalogue sales throughout 2008 and we noticed the increased demand for CGC-graded comic books from the Silver and Bronze Age. We also noticed that in the arena of comic and newspaper strip art, European buyers are certainly impacting prices once again, with their currency enjoying a healthy run against the dollar.

2009 promises to be another banner year as far as comic character themed movies are concerned, with many movies scheduled for release.

Following are some highlights and results from 2008.

Golden Age: CGC-certified Golden Age comic books in the 8.0 to 9.0 range continue their upward climb, with copies graded higher obviously realizing higher prices. It seems selling Golden Age comic books is not the problem, but securing these individual books and collections is certainly the issue. Another area within Golden Age comics is the bound volume, these are copies bound by the publisher (publisher file copies) and in some instances by collectors. These bound volumes are such a great resource and the books can be read and enjoyed and still maintain their condition. Dell bound volumes, Harvey bound volumes, Timely bound volumes etc., exist and we are seeing an increased interest.

Silver Age: CGC-graded Silver Age comics in the 9.4 to 9.8 ranges continue to exceed expectations. The frenzy for high grade Silver Age books seems to have subsided a bit, but for the high grade (9.6 to 9.8) key Silver Age issues, demand is still strong.

Newspaper strip art: This uniquely American art form continues to gain in popularity. Europeans appreciate this art form and continue their unabashed enthusiasm. The seminal artists: Raymond, Herriman, McCay, Foster, Frazetta, Caniff, Gould, Sickles, Capp, Schulz, Kelly, etc. remain sought after and prices certainly reflect that. We are also seeing a rising trend in the "newer" comic strip artists: Jim Davis (*Garfield*), Russell Myers (*Broom Hilda*), Scott Adams (*Dilbert*), etc. While these artists have been toiling and producing their dailies and Sundays for years, we are seeing more demand for their art.

During 2008, we sold many examples of Winsor McCay's art, including, *Little Nemo In Slumberland*, *Sammy Sneeze*, as well as editorial cartoons and the very popular feature, *Dreams of the Rarebit Fiend*. We also sold examples of Herriman, Schulz, Raymond, Capp, Caniff and Frazetta newspaper strip art.

Original Comic art: Covers and splash pages, whether DC or Marvel, still continue to be the items of interest to most collectors. Throughout 2008 we offered and sold many DC splash pages by the masters: Carmine Infantino and Murphy Anderson. Other examples of DC art covers and splashes, included *Justice League of America*, *Brave and the Bold*, *The Flash* and *Mystery in Space*. As always, the mainstay artists: Kirby, Ditko, Steranko, Wood, Infantino, etc. continue in popularity with prices reflecting this.

Animation Art: This market is enjoying resurgence and with proper guidance and nurturing should once again become a dominant market. With the majority of studios going to computer generated animation, these hand drawn examples by the masters should once again gain strength. Look to this market to continue to rebound in 2008 due to increased attention.

Toys and premiums: Another area of comic ccharacter collectibles that seems to be enjoying a comeback. A great and educational way to link with the past while building a collection.

For all prices realized for 2008 events and earlier, please visit our web site at: http://allstarauc.com/asonline/realized.htm These are very exciting times to be in our business, increased awareness along with integrity should be the focus in 2009!

David Matteini Collector

Greetings comic collectors! This year I wanted to comment on three key themes. First would be the state of the economy, the second would be blockbuster comic movies (which keep getting bigger and better), and the third is a few thoughts on the future of the hobby.

To not mention the economy would be to ignore the elephant in the room. There is considerable stress in financial institutions and more generally, in the overall US economy. Falling home prices, rising unemployment and a restriction of consumer credit are all reasons for concern. While in the past everyone had a job, it was easy to borrow and home prices continued to swell net worths, it was much easier to expect that comic prices would go up. Given the current environment, the all-time high levels that many high grade keys are currently sold for and the abundant competition for the marginal dollar, I expect a tentative comic environment.

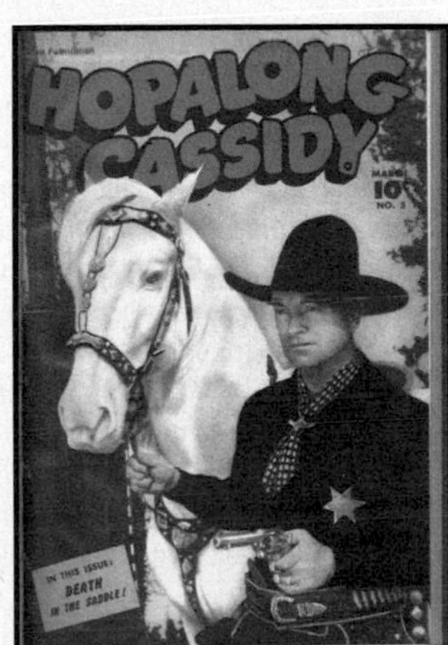

© FAW

For collectors and readers, bound volumes are a great resource.

This past year, it does appear that comic prices have remained very strong, particularly at the high end. There has been no dearth of very public high end sales. Heritage brought to market the David N. Toth and Kylberg collections in May (as well as several other collections throughout the year), ComicConnect ran a massive sale with several keys in September and ComicLink has been hot all year. The quality of the auctions has been amazing - there have been numerous keys and deep runs of books. In this May Heritage auction, I was amazed to see a CGC-certified *Batman* #121 9.2 OW go for $5,557. While I have never seen this book's peer, it went for 7.2x *Guide* and further, for that kind of money, you could have had your pick of many single digit *Batman* books (albeit not in that grade). This is the first year where I was able to really see abundant high quality material in a long time.

Perhaps some of these sales were inspired by a blockbuster year for comic movies! The best (in my humble opinion) had to be *The Dark Knight*. I am one of the many people who saw it numerous times in the theater and loved every moment. I appreciate how the movie really did a "Dark Knight" and gave Batman and the Joker a lot of edge and grittiness. Catering to a more mature, adult audience certainly paid off for Warner Brothers and was a great flick for moviegoers. I do want to express that my thoughts and prayers go out to the family and friends of Heath Ledger.

The other two movies I would like to mention are *Iron Man* and *The Incredible Hulk*. *Iron Man* was a great movie. I think I liked the *Iron Man* movie more than any Iron Man comic I have ever read (except maybe for the Armor Wars). Robert Downey Jr. *is* Tony Stark. The casting was great, I loved how they modernized the story as to how he becomes Iron Man and loved the end. It was just a really fun, uplifting movie and I am looking forward to the sequel.

I give Marvel a lot of credit for trying again with *Incredible Hulk*. I thought that Edward Norton was great and I really enjoyed that movie. The first *Hulk* was just horrible and to start over again was exactly the right thing to do.

The question becomes how can we as a hobby translate these great movies and exposure to the characters and the medium into the next generation of comic book collectors. This brings up the final point that I would like to address, which is the future of the hobby. I think it is a non-trivial question to ask ourselves where the next generation of collectors will come from. In today's day and age, where there are abundant opportunities for the marginal dollar of entertainment, comics need to find a way to stay relevant and exciting to the next generation. I don't have any easy answers, but I do sincerely hope that the industry is able to find a way to promote comic book collecting in a sustainable and meaningful way.

In some parting words, I would like to give another "congratulations" to the organizers of the New York Comic Con which was held at the Jacob Javits Center this past April. While this past year I wasn't able to attend as many shows as I would like, this show continues to build and become a true East Coast equivalent to San Diego. I would also like to recognize the Baltimore Comic-Con which is always a great time and found the magic formula to make a show a wild success by focusing on the books.

Looking ahead to next year, I am very excited for the *Watchmen* movie. It's great to see in the trailer they make specific mention of the graphic novel. I said it last year, but it's worth repeating: in terms of new offerings, I hope that DC and Marvel continue to bulk up their Archives and Masterworks series, which are the best value in the hobby.

Happy Collecting!

Jon McClure
Dealer/Collector

2008 was an amazing year for Marvel 35¢ price variants! A CGC-certified 9.4 *Star Wars* #1 variant sold for $10,500, which is a first for Bronze Age books. The *Iron Fist* #14 variant had several sales, including a CGC-certified 8.5 for $2,200. This makes the sale from last year of $5,200 for a certified 9.4 seem like a real bargain. It remains my opinion that these two comics are, or ought to be, ranked as the top two Bronze Age comics, and collectors and investors are shelling out the cash to prove it.

DC War is this year's hot genre, although War titles from all publishers sold well in all grades, with key issues sometimes bringing double *Guide*. With high quality films like *The Incredible Hulk*, *Iron Man* and most notably *The Dark Knight* setting box office records, back issue sales for these characters did well regardless of era. *Green Lantern* #76, *All Star Western* #10, and *Weird War Tales* #1 remain elusive and continue to jump in high grade.

Todd McDevitt
New Dimension Comics

First, some insight on me. I started New Dimension Comics in 1986 while still in high school. I have grown to 5 stores surrounding the Pittsburgh, PA area. I have been blessed with many adventures, some of which I have chronicled in my own comic, which I will be happy to send to any curious reader—please just contact me and ask. I buy everything. From a small handful of books (offered $2,500 for 8 comics just the other day) to giant warehouses of store overstock (bought 150,000+ comics from 1 store this year, had the same offered to me yesterday again!).

Golden Age: I'm starting to think I'm the luckiest guy in this business. I have had about 4 to 5 "once-in-a-lifetime" collections come my way. This past year was a great one that included a *Detective Comics* #27. I was warned early on that this isn't a comic book, it's a relic. As such, there are Indiana Jones-style rivals chasing it down too. And just like the movies, it brings out the best and worst in people. My purchase of it garnered attention from Fox News, *Jimmy Kimmel Live*, *The New York Times*, and even made the ticker on CNN. For now, I'm keeping it. It's become clear that so few of these come up for sale, especially in the well-preserved shape that this one is in. When it is offered for sale, it will be very interesting.

Silver Age: I was blessed this past year with a *huge* (15,000 books) Silver Age collection purchase from a man who accumulated it over 38 years. Many hearty runs of desirable titles. I spent a month of my life, with lots of superb help from my staff, getting it graded/priced. After all that, I gave it a big premiere in one of my main store locations. While I sold a good bit of it, it didn't blow me away. It got me wondering.... Here I have the best Silver Age stock I have ever had, so where is the feeding frenzy? Well, I took it shortly after to the Pittsburgh Comicon and that was better, but still not gangbusters. I guess I wonder why my region isn't hungry for this material. So... I'm doing what the rest of the industry is doing and posting my stuff online (eBay user ID ndcauctions) and hoping that the obscure books I have will find some matches with collectors. Of note, I sold an *Amazing Spider-Man* #129 (9.6) for $810, #194 (9.2) for $50, and *Ghost Rider* #81 (9.6) for $91.

Modern Age: I'm not sure exactly *how* rare *San Diego Comic Con Comics* #2, featuring the first appearance of Hellboy, is, but I managed to sell two copies at $175.00 each. These were slightly unique in that they had also inserted with them the original backing boards with the Comic Defense System logo and booth # printed on them. These boards were apparently how they got distributed when the book was passed out to attendees. *Miracleman* is still hot. After buying all the remaining inventory from Eclipse years ago, several foil editions have still been selling for high premiums for us, many for $200-250 each with limited print runs of 25-250. Variant and exclusive covers on new releases are hit and miss. Some do great (like *Angel: After The Fall* #1) and others are duds (like *JSA* and most other DC titles). The rarity might be in the condition on these since many arrive with printing or packaging errors, making nice ones even harder to come by. *Watchmen* is selling great, if I have them in stock, for $8-12 each. And the trade paperback is flying off our shelves. Hasn't everyone read it by now? I guess not. Skrulls are keeping fans guessing, but *Final Crisis* is turning out to be one too many trips to the well for DC.

CGC-certified 9.8 issues of **Simpsons Comics #1** have sold very well.

Thoughts on Buying and Selling: Buying collections has gotten harder and easier. Harder since people try so many other ways to sell them and after selling some of their good stuff, "give up" and bring the dregs into stores. They seem to waste a lot of their time trying to figure out how to do what we do. It's not easy! I've dabbled in other things myself and seen the light. Let the experts do their job. I sell comics. Let me be the comic book guy. When I'm offered records, I call the record guy. I think specializing and recognizing that niche is important on both sides. So easier? I guess it's gotten easier since many people seem to realize the value of their own time. Screwing around online and trying to get an extra dollar doesn't make sense for busy folks. Also, I think there is a lot more stuff out there that's getting parted with today. There were a lot of people collecting 15-25 years ago who aren't now. Heck, I had a call this morning offering me the books if I would just come and haul them away! I have about 300,000 comics in my Ellwood City store that are for sale for $1.00 each everyday. And lots of good stuff, not all crap. You'd think I'd be swamped with buyers. I have some busy days, but not crazy ones like I would expect when selling $3-7 items at $1.00 each.

Steve Mortensen
Colossus Comics

The modern CGC market has reached a plateau, and most CGC books sell for the cost of grading, except for key issues that remain in high demand. This year, I ended my CGC subscription service for new comics. I had a great run, but in the end it was not very profitable because there was too much competition from eBay dealers selling their modern books at very low margins. Many of my customers were sorry to see my service go and were still willing to pay the $37.50 price for the books that they wanted. Generally these collectors were completists who didn't want to take the time to have their books graded themselves. These collectors were not interested in selling their comics - just collecting them. I think, in the end, a long, complete series may be worth more than the sum of its parts. I continue to track the CGC high-grade modern market, write my "I've Been Slabbed" column for *Comic Buyer's Guide* and maintain my own collection of graded and non-graded comics. Here's a summary of my picks and predictions over the past year:

I noticed a spike in the price of *Watchmen* back issues. One CGC copy of #1 in 9.8 sold above $900. Currently the book sells in the $400 range and the other issues sell for about $100-200 in 9.8. I expect the prices will remain solid until after the movie comes out.

CGC-certified *Simpsons Comics* have sold very well in 9.8. I sold a few #1s for $200 each and other early back issues showed some interest. It's a very hard series to complete in 9.8 due to shipping/handling issues and bindery flaws. I've started to collect the series myself – not just because I love the characters but because of the potential of future appreciation of the issues.

Towards the end of 2007, I noticed a slowdown in the CGC modern market, perhaps because there hasn't been a big book to hit the market since *Captain America* #25 and collectors were waiting to see which issue would reveal the new Captain America. The variant cover market also did poorly at this time. There was a time when dealers could buy extra copies of regular covers, grade the variant and pay for the entire lot with its sale. But demand is not like it used to be, partly due to the fact that there's so many that are produced now - several or more a month. In addition, Marvel actually flooded the market with *Dark Tower* sketch covers and the prices dropped considerably.

On a positive note, *Astonishing X-Men* back issues sold very well for me at this time, with most selling in the $30 range, which is twice the cost of grading.

In January 2008, I noticed the price differences between some *Ultimate Spider-Man* issues. Some issues sell for the cost of CGC grading in 9.8 and some sell for much more. Issues #64, #70 and #93 remain a few of the toughest books to find in 9.8. *Ultimate Spider-Man* #64 sells for around $75 and #70 sells for around $50 although it used to sell above $150 in 2006; one of three known copies of #93 sold for $61 this month, which I think is very low.

In February, after Bucky was announced as the new Captain America, *Captain America* #6 saw a spike in value. Sales shot up to $228 an issue for a CGC-certified 9.8 but have now settled to $75 as of August 2008.

In March, Marvel and DC both began epic mini-series, *Secret Invasion* and *Final Crisis*. On the secondary CGC market both have fallen flat in value. As of August 2008, *Secret Invasion* #1 sells for around $17 and *Final Crisis* #1 sells for around $15 in 9.8. I wish I had better news for the modern CGC market. For the speculator, the best years may be behind us, although for the collector CGC still offers a great way to protect and guarantee grades of your favorite comics.

In April, the death of Dave Stevens was a real blow to the comics industry. He helped spur the independent movement in the '80s with his great covers. I personally love his work and I collect CGC 9.8 copies of his covers. Most are very affordable, selling for around $30 each.

I researched *Amazing Spider-Man* #238, seeing prices fluctuating greatly in the past several years. As mentioned in my *Comics Buyer's Guide* column in June 2008: "In November 2007 it reached a record price of $1,500 and in May of 2008 it reached a 6 month low of $511. The book has had some fluctuation since July 2002 beginning with a price of $430 and then a low that was reached in December of 2002 of $234. Some months the price of the book doubled from a previous sale, or was cut in half from a previous sale as in the case of October of 2004 when it sold for $305 October 4, then $677 October 21, then $316 October 23. The book shows an overall upward trend, but be careful what you buy it for - another one will be just around the corner. It appears the best time to buy is the auction right after the one where a high price was achieved."

Michael Turner died this past June and will be sorely missed. Like Dave Stevens, I think his back issues will increase in the coming years, especially Signature Series comics.

Deadpool has become a more popular character due to his new series coming out and his appearance in the upcoming *Wolverine* movie. CGC sales have been strong for this character and I'm guessing will continue to progress until the movie comes out. *Deadpool* #1 (1997) sells for about $100 in CGC 9.8.

Following Heath Ledger's tragic death, *The Dark Knight* came out and there was an increased interest in Joker comics. *Batman: the Killing Joke* increased to $173 just after the movie debut. The price in August 2008 has settled in the $90 range.

There continues to be a pipeline of comic book-based movies in the works. I'm especially looking forward to *G.I. Joe* as CGC-graded *G.I. Joe* comics are particularly strong. *G.I. Joe* #1 has been increasing in value. It currently sells for around $400. #2 has progressed to more than $500 for a CGC-certified 9.8. Issue #21 sells for more than $800 and many of the issues in the #20s sell in the $150-300 range. I remember buying this series off the shelves and trading with friends. I'm so happy to see these books selling so well and I expect the market for *G.I. Joe* to continue to increase in value as the movie gets closer.

Josh Nathanson
ComicLink.com

ComicLink buyers are snapping up key and high-grade Silver and Bronze Age Marvels and DCs like never before and setting records I would not have even thought possible just a year ago. We have also seen incredible record prices realized for ComicLink sellers of quality Golden Age, especially those books from popular titles and ones with stand-out covers. Even post-1980 books have been moving well in the highest CGC grades.

I know it sounds like a broken record because I say the same thing every year but it is true -- as of the date of this report (9/25/2008) the vintage comic book market is stronger than ever before. That may seem strange, as banks have failed, real estate is stagnant, the stock market is volatile, interest rates are low, and the dollar has devalued significantly against foreign currencies. Some readers without the inside track are probably saying to themselves, "why on earth are vintage comic books and original comic book art at an all-time high?" The answer is for all of these reasons and then some!

The "flight to quality" into investments perceived as secure, such as gold, has spread out to include collectible investments such as comic books, where there is an intrinsic value, established sales histories, a long-time and growing collector-investor base, established grading standards, and market liquidity. The devaluation of the dollar means that overseas and Canadian buyers can buy more than ever before. And, of course superheroes continue to be featured prominently in the movies and box office records are broken by blockbusters such as 2008's *Dark Knight*, and the quality of the scripts, actors and special effects in movies from *Dark Knight* to *Iron Man* to *The Incredible Hulk* continues to be stellar. All of this fuels demand, and demand continues to greatly outpace supply (which has been the case for as long as I can remember). This leads to more and more record breaking prices.

What follows is a sample of some of the higher dollar comic book sales made by ComicLink sellers, via both the Comic Book Exchange and ComicLink Auctions (though sellers can sell comic books on ComicLink individually at much lower price points than you see below, and can also sell original comic book art). Many of these price results are record setters for the particular issue in the condition represented at the time this report is written, but as is the nature of the beast, by the time this price guide comes out, ComicLink buyers and sellers will probably have seen many of these records broken.

Golden Age Comics: *Action Comics* #1 CGC (0.5)(coverless) $22,250, #3 (4.0) $10,378, #10 (5.5) $17,509, #23 (6.5) $7,000, *All-American Comics* #16 (6.0) $85,500, (5.5) $60,000, #17 (7.0) $7,500, #61 (9.0) $7,900, *Batman* #1 (9.0) $280,000, #1 (8.0, extensive restoration) $9,001, #6 (9.4) $16,000, #16 (9.0) $10,764, #20 (9.4) $21,361, #62 (9.4) $6,766, *Captain America Comics* #1 (9.0) $150,000, #1 (8.0) $50,000, #77 (7.5) $5,000, *Detective Comics* #7 (6.5) $7,600, #11 (6.0) $7,300, #19 (8.5) $7,600, #27 (0.5, front cover missing) $10,500, #35 (5.0) $17,100, (5.5, extensive restoration) $8,000, #69 (8.5) $5,250, #71 (8.5) $4,950, #120 (9.4, Mile High pedigree) $13,000, #140 (7.5) $5,300, *Exciting Comics* #28 (7.0) $4,050, *Flash Comics* #57 (9.8) $9,401, *Four Color* #27 (9.4) $5,000, #108 (9.2) $9,400, #386 (9.2) $9,600, *Green Hornet Comics* #1 (8.5) $5,500, *Green Lantern* #1 (9.0) $40,000, *Horrific* #3 (8.0) $1,950, *Marvel Comics* #1 (4.5, extensive restoration) $21,500, *Marvel Mystery Comics* #4 (9.0) $50,000, #24 (9.2) $5,100, *More Fun Comics* #64 (9.6, Mile High Pedigree) $22,000, *New Adventure Comics* #24 (8.5) $4,900, #27 (8.5) $11,400, *New Comics* #11 (7.5) $7,000, *Pep Comics* #50 (8.0, Mile High Pedigree) $3,311, *Shock Illustrated* #1 (9.0, Gaines File Copy) $7,208, *Sub-Mariner Comics* #1 (5.0) $5,050, #32 (7.5) $7,800, *Superman* #1 (5.0) $121,000, (1.0) $20,001, #3 (8.0) $9,088, #76 (9.6) $20,000, *Suspense Comics* #3 (5.0, extensive restoration) $5,000, *Terry-Toons* #7 (7.0) $2,500, *Weird Fantasy* #14 (9.8, Gaines File Copy) $5,299, *World's Finest Comics* #18 (9.6) $7,100

Silver/Bronze Age Comics: *Action Comics* #248 (9.2) $2,164, *Amazing Fantasy* #15 (9.4, White Mountain Pedigree) $227,000, (9.0) $139,000, (8.0) $66,000, (7.5) $42,500, (7.0) $34,611, *Amazing Spider-Man* #1 (9.6) $150,000, (8.5) $26,000, #4 (9.2) $7,000, #9 (9.6) $16,550, #12 (9.6) $13,050, #13 (9.4) $11,361, #18 (9.6) $7,600, #19 (9.8) $7,600, #24 (9.4) $5,200, #25 (9.4) $5,350, #31 (9.8) $21,961, #32 (9.6) $5,600, #35 (9.6) $5,600, #37 (9.6) $13,583, #39 (9.6) $8,100, #42 (9.6) $5,300, #50 (9.8) $32,500, *Avengers* #2 (9.4) $5,600, #4 (9.2) $6,301, #5 (9.2) $4,100, #9 (9.2) $5,600, *Brave and the Bold* #93 (9.8) $3,676, *Captain America* #100 (9.6) $3,250, #117 (9.6) $4,000, *Daredevil* #1 (9.2) $10,000, #7 (9.4, Western Penn pedigree) $16,500, *Detective Comics* #405 (9.8) $3,250, *Fantastic Four* #1 (8.5) $52,000, #1 (6.0) $15,250, #2 (9.4) $33,000, #12 (9.0) $11,600, #18 (9.4) $10,927, #25 (9.4) $6,800, #50 (9.4) $6,600, #55 (9.4) $3,979, *Flash* #106 (9.0) $7,901, #107 (9.0) $6,260, #112 (9.0) $6,105, #115 (9.2) $5,477, #121 (9.4) $7,270, #127 (9.4) $6,600, *Green Lantern* #76 (9.2) $9,030, *Incredible Hulk* #1 (9.2) $117,500, (8.5) $61,000, #103 (9.6) $2,221, #115 (9.8) $2,217, *Iron Man* #1 (9.4) $1,900, #9 (9.8) $2,800, *Journey Into Mystery* #83 (9.2) $45,000, *Justice League of America* #1 (8.5) $6,250, #4 (9.4) $6,802, #14 (9.6) $4,100, *Showcase* #13 (9.0) $6,655, *Silver Surfer* #15 (9.6) $2,815, *Star Wars* #1 35¢-c variant (9.4) $12,019, *Superman* #151 (9.8) $4,900, #156 (9.6) $2,099, *Tales of Suspense* #11 (9.4) $4,950, #39 (9.0) $25,000, #65 (9.4, Overstreet Collection) $2,751, #79 (9.6) $2,300, *Tales to Astonish* #27 (8.0) $7,322, #35 (9.0) $6,300, *X-Men* #4 (9.4, Pacific Coast Pedigree) $8,300, #7 (9.4) $4,795, #94 (9.6) $6,300.

Jamie Newbold
Southern California Comics

Greetings from San Diego! Gino Siragusa and I operate a store in a warehouse here in town. Our store concept is different in structure and content from most other comic book stores.

Contemporary comic book retailing has evolved into certain retail constants. One such constant is the nature of comic book stores. Most comic book stores are merchandise heavy and comic book light. Back issues are difficult to find at just about every comic book store I have ever visited. However, exceptions do occur. It takes confident store owner nerve to cast his lot with comic books as his or her sales lead, maybe the only product they offer. Currently, there are two such stores in the city and county of San Diego. Travel outside town, north through Los Angeles and the odds remain the same. Maybe one out of ten stores allow new and old comic books to dominate their displays. We offer little merchandise. Bowen statues (love em!) and t-shirts are about the only things not printed on paper that we retail. New comics and trade paper backs are our dominant source of weekly material from Diamond. We are also back issue strong and are sensitive to any decline in the comic book market.

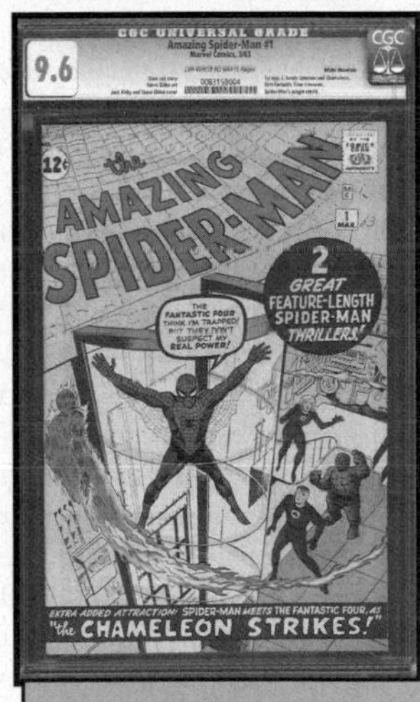

A CGC-certified 9.6 copy of **Amazing Spider-Man** #1 sold for $150,000.

San Diego is a city with a population constantly in flux. Changing economics, a transitory military, and San Diego's atypical cost-of-living contribute to the rise and fall of its comic book buying population. We began our store in 1998 in a warehouse. The idea being we could succeed or fail with minimal overhead. We succeeded and watched business grow and flourish right up to the fall Of 2007. As the mortgage crisis, gas crisis, and war competed for headline dominance, we began to see a decline in customers buying new comics. Slowly but steadily we watched the decline continue through March 2008. Some customers melted away. Others saw fit to say goodbye as they pulled up stakes and moved out of California. Still, others were resolute in dropping titles from their pull lists to save money. It is tougher than ever for comic book publishers - big and small - to succeed. The lackluster economy is cutting the chaff from the wheat...

Independent comics sell slowly for us and in single-digit numbers. Devil's Due Publishing and Dark Horse have stood their ground on the sales of *GI Joe*, *Hack/Slash*, *Star Wars*, and *Hellboy*, respectively. Dynamite Entertainment, with its acquisition of *The Boys* and its adaptations of established characters (Red Sonja, etc.), has pulled its sales up to Image and Dark Horse standards. Boom Studios has yet to achieve equal numbers. Zenescope is seeing a growing hit from its *Grimm's Fairy Tales* stories. Avatar keeps buyers active with offerings penned by Warren Ellis. Image just seems to be tagging along working the titles penned by Robert Kirkman. We all know what a phenom *The Walking Dead* is. But can anyone explain why *Invincible* sells great as a trade but less so as a monthly comic? Image's *Spawn* leveled off long ago at about 10-13 copies per month and could use a spark of creativity to regain its former sales glory. Other indies struggle under the weight of $3.50-$3.99 cover prices and a lack of reader interest. One exceptional note: IDW continues to attract readers at my store. *30 Days Of Night* introduced this company to the world and *Transformers*, Steve Niles and Ashley Wood have continued to create titles that lure in readers not daunted by the cover prices (love Bernie Wrightson's return to monthlies in *Dead, She Said*).

DC and Marvel have met their own challenges. Marvel continues to run the tables as their titles dominate our readership. $2.99 an issue used to be a luxury for our readers. It's been the norm now for a couple of years so our customers don't balk at the prices. They do hold up at $3.99 and up for one-shots and annuals. I wish they would drop the annual concept and go back to a thirteenth issue each year. Also, enough with the $4.99 Giant-Size titles! My readers overwhelmingly stay away from those because they don't want reprints. Stuffing new material into a comic that's filled with reprints is cheating our buyers. Enough already. Solicit reprints separately so our customers don't feel ripped off. Please consider dropping the more exotic card-stock cover paper in favor of standard cover paper if that is what it takes to keep cover prices at parity with other comics.

The story events of the past two years have clearly been a plus for Marvel. *Civil War* and the Skrull invasion have kept Marvel sales at a peak. The X-Men's *Divided We Stand* and such have not done so well. I think the X-Men overkill has begun (shades of the 1990s!) Marvel sales at my store are roughly 60-70% of our new comics sales. DC has never been equal in overall sales to Marvel at our store. Now, they have lost a little more ground, tackling about 30-40% of our market with the indie sales squeezed somewhere within.

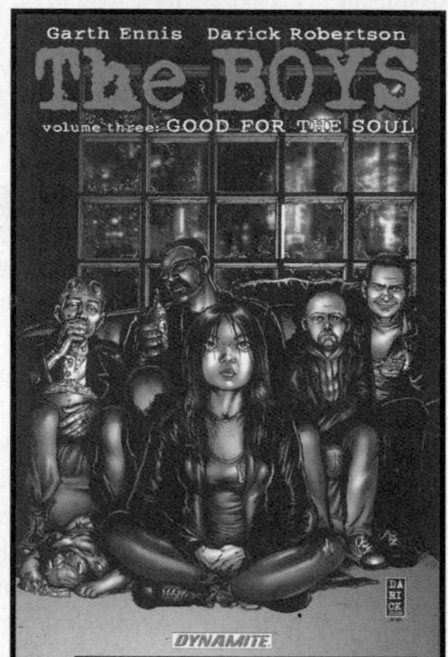

Garth Ennis Darick Robertson
The BOYS
volume three: GOOD FOR THE SOUL
DYNAMITE

Trade paperback sales have steadily risen for titles like **The Boys**. (Volume 3 shown)

Marvel's comprehensive writing, plotlines reaching two to three years into the future and hot artists have held the attention of many of my customers. DC has reduced a number of their titles through *Previews* and should cancel a few other non-starters. They have run some interesting story events. "Batman R.I.P." has retained Batman readers. Superman has continued to mope along in sales. Fortunately, this long-revered character shines in both content and sales in *All-Star Superman*. The surprise story event of the year was the Sinestro Corps Wars. Sales of the Green Lantern comics tripled and have retained some of that extra readership since the arc ended (I enjoyed them too). I think the team-up of villains outside of their normal story contexts helped carry the stories.

DC has top grade talent. Talent that is often harnessed for Vertigo titles. Our customers miss the story-power of its leading hit: *Y: The Last Man*. Finishing strong, it continues to slaughter other titles in trade paperback sales. *Fables* sells well in trade form. Subsequent Vertigo titles, like *Exterminators*, *Army@Love*, and *House Of Mystery* have yet to catch up. DC's hot stable of artists based in Brazil has registered with our customers. Joe Prado and Renato Guedes have done some great covers for DC.

New comic books and trades account for about 50-75% of our weekly store sales. Near-new back issues account for another 25%. Trade paperback book sales have steadily risen. *Y: The Last Man*, *The Boys*, *The Walking Dead*, *Fables*, *Punisher*, *Astonishing X-Men*, *Civil War*, Ultimate titles, a selection of Batman trades and *Star Wars* trades are frequent sellers. At least these figures were true until the end of 2007. As new comics sales dropped about 10% our back issues seemingly picked up steam.

We've been eBay sellers for almost eleven years. We utilize eBay to off-load non-sellers at the store, website or conventions. Occasionally we will use eBay to pony up some quick cash by offering more expensive stuff like CGC'd comics or older comic books. eBay as a retail tool fulfills some of our requirements annually. eBay and PayPal fees are steep but unavoidable in a market where daily options for cash are just not there. Fortunately, eBay was there for my business when sales dropped through the Fall and early Spring. Back issues in general helped make my monthly overhead and eBay remained consistent. We sold a lot of Gold, Silver, and Bronze Age comics in tandem with store merchandise that had been on the shelves for too long. We take the acknowledged hit in value on things like common Silver Age Marvels and Bowen statues . Reduced profits are constants to selling on eBay. We accept that we are freeing up money for other things. Old comic books will not go out of fashion in the next 20 years. The average age of the back issue buyers at my store and online is thirty. Those customers have bridged the period in their lives where they were out of comics and subsequently returned. If history is an indicator, they will continue to collect twenty years from now. Our collector forebears are still at it and so are fifty-two year olds like me.

Covering the collector spread means constant acquisitions of back issue collections. Having a store and selling at conventions guarantees access to a fair share of those collections. With luck we seem to nail down a couple of really good Gold-Bronze Age collections every year. Three years ago we purchased a collection of 350 high-grade and white paged Golden Age comics containing low number *Batman*s and *Superman*s. Two tears ago we picked up a high-grade Silver Age collection we named the Hollywood Hills Collection. Last year we picked up *Batman* #1-100 with 80% of the books CGC'd. We also bought out a local man looking to reduce his personal debt. He sold us 500 CGC Bronze to Modern Age books. Grades were in the 9.6 to 9.8 range. We purchased a collection with *Amazing Fantasy* #15 and *Amazing Spider-Man* #1-200, annuals and other comics just as I'm writing this report. Many of the best aspects of these purchases were submitted to CGC and subsequently sold. After several years of CGC'd books, we've drawn some conclusions about their marketability.

CGC Comics: CGC books sell well for us. They sell all the time on eBay. They sell on their own merit on our website. It's just a matter of who is shopping and pricing. Strangely, we sell fewer CGC books through the store than we anticipate. We get a lot of customers that buy CGC books and at prices similar to ours. They are just not the first thing back issue buyers will buy at our store. We also see fewer CGC buyers at the San Diego Comic Con. Key books will attract buyers. Dealers will buy them from us for resale elsewhere. But mostly the buyers prefer to buy raw.

Our store tries to reflect the CGC market by submitting a sampling of books to CGC periodically. These submissions might include recent purchases or books that have been in inventory awhile and will move better (on eBay). We examine GPA, *Overstreet* pricing and our own experiences to predict which books submitted should come back at grades we will profit from. I also believe that CGC's grading is generally accurate. We pre-grade our stuff before submission. Our grades and their grades have averaged out over the years. In the beginning, I used to groan under the weight of early submissions I did not agree with. Now, I'm more apt to support their standards. I fear that rising shipping/business costs may increase their submission prices. Against the narrow margin of prices obtained from CGC'd Modern comics sales, I think any increase could kill that side of business.

We do what every other dealer does or should do. Prices for CGC books are a blend of the knowledge gained from CGC's census numbers, GPAnalysis stats, eBay's history, Heritage stats, *Overstreet*, our own previous sales history, and gut feelings (with a little greed thrown in). Not one of the listed can be applied as sales verbatim. We utilized GPA extensively for the 750+ CGC books we've sold in the past year. Prices for older non-key books hover at within 20% of GPA for the highest grade stuff (9.4-9.6). *Overstreet* does not apply and eBay does not offer examples of enough books to offer much help. Heritage and GPA demonstrate the best a sale can be but not necessarily what a little business like ours will achieve. The more Modern books we sold range in grade from 9.4-9.8. Unfortunately, we relied on GPA's yearly or overall average to set the original purchase prices for many of those books post-CGC. The retail on eBay was not consistent with GPA. We are talking runs on 1980s to present *Uncanny X-Men*, *Amazing Spider-Man*, *Wolverine* and a smattering of DCs and other Marvels. We found that the actual sales prices were often lower than GPA's overall or yearly averages. Lower to the tune of 20-30%. These are generally $15-50 books. But it cuts nervously into our profit. Key older books are closer to GPA. Closer to *Overstreet*, too, in lower grades. High grade older Keys are hard to come by for resale. We practically name our own prices for those and often get those prices or slightly discounted numbers. Key Modern books are closer to GPA sales prices. We hold the line on those prices and usually get them.

Buying collections, especially at the San Diego Con is more problematic then ever. Owners within this city have a lot of publicity about comic values to sway their judgments on their collection's value. We are finding increased reliance on eBay to unload their comic books. We've competed with others for certain collections and lost. We've seen owners refuse my offers and bring the books to eBay. We've had these opportunities to see what happened to those collections on eBay, as well. In the cases where the books were purchased by competitors at public auction we've watched dealers lose money on eBay. We've watched owners put their books on eBay and not sustain enough high-dollar bids to make the effort worthwhile. Some owners are simply not quick to trust comic book dealers with evaluating their collections. They would rather take their chances with the internet. Post-San Diego Comic Con (Comic Con International ain't for me!) brings local collections forward for us to view each year. Disclosure of the evaluation and pricing process to the owner (how we do what we do) comforts the owners. All they want is a working knowledge of the process and we usually conclude the deal successfully.

Which prices should go up?: Marvel keys in all grades. Few customers, shoppers or collectors attach any *Guide* value to the key Marvels they desire so strongly. Purchases of those books seem to be made on an instinctual level. Some buy for investment but mainly the popular reason is, "I just want to own one." High-grade comics still have no peak. Just when we thought we reached too high for a sale, a buyer meets our price.

Which prices should go down?: A downward price trend creates a conundrum. All sellers want top price. All buyers want discounts or free. The dealers can sell more with discounts. The dealers have much invested in their inventories.

Some dealers reduce price for certain occasions or as a norm (we do). If formally accepted that it was time to cut huge swaths across the retail price market, we would need to be prepared for our own loss of money. Spot-reducing particular titles or issues was done long ago by the buyers. We just accept the lack of interest in our westerns and funny animal comics. I suppose it would be up to committee to formalize the realistic, achievable prices for long-ignored genres and titles. For now, it seems the only people paying attention to *Guide* prices of comics not usually sought after are the owners that have them and want to unload them on dealers.

Personally, I'd like to see *Overstreet* pricing reflect the price-per-pound mentality of the 1980s-90s market. We have thousands of comics from the '80s and '90s sitting in our one dollar bins and many will continue to sit there; proving that many comics from that period (especially early Image Comics) are not worth more than a dollar. By marking entire series as one dollar an issue (*Justice League Europe*, *Cybernary*, *Dark Horse Presents* etc.), one could devote the saved space to more detailed information on other titles. The information provided through price guides everywhere has more resonance than any prices attached to them. I'd be content if the prices for the majority of the books from that period simply identified the non-CGC value as cover price. Perhaps *Overstreet* could then include more creator information, or pertinent story lines, character appearances, and less-recorded information in place of exhaustive pricing.

The economic struggles nationwide have had seemingly little effect on the back issue market. 2007 ended for us with some worry. As we reach August I'm excited about the amount of business we've done in back issue sales at the store, online, and at conventions. 2008 has proven to me that old comic books still have a market. A market that actually may be getting stronger against a struggling US dollar and fears of recession.

Terry O'Neill
Terry's Comics/Nationwide Comics

Sales from 2007 to 2008 have been very good in spite of the high gas prices and economic slowdown. All conventions appeared to have good attendance, with corresponding sales. Catalog orders are a little less than last year but the orders have been steady. We continue to be able to purchase quality collections and groups of books. We have been paying higher percentages on Marvel keys and most Atomic Age comics to have a good selection on hand.

Golden Age: We are noticing a slight decrease in sales of this material; many people have completed their collections and there is no one new to take their place. The exceptions to this are DC titles like *Action Comics*, *Adventure Comics* and *Detective Comics*. Centaurs are still always in demand because they are so scarce. Restored Golden Age books, when reasonably priced, are starting to sell again, especially ones with color touch and tear seals only. Many of these books had been doctored to improve their appearance by older collectors. Major Timely titles like *Captain America*, *Marvel Mystery*, *Human Torch* and *Sub-Mariner* continue to sell above *Guide* in solid middle grades. I was able to pick up some early Disney *Four Color* and *Walt Disney's Comics & Stories*. They all sold well at slightly over *Guide*.

Atom Age: We acquired a great collection of DC comics from the late 1940s through the end of their runs in the 1970s. There were near-complete runs of DC War, Romance, Mystery, Humor and Western titles. I've never seen such complete runs of titles like *Adventures of Rex the Wonder Dog*, *Young Romance*, *All-American Men of War*, *G.I Combat*, *Western Comics*, *House of Mystery* and *Leave it to Binky*. Some of the best selling titles were *Our Army at War*, *Rex the Wonder Dog* and *G.I. Combat*. *Tarzan* and *Walt Disney's Comics and Stories* have been selling again as well. We also purchased a large group of Atlas Horror and War comics at about 70% of *Guide*. These books were in an average grade of Very Good to Fine and sold well at above-*Guide* prices.

Silver Age: Early Marvel Keys sell best for us. *Amazing Fantasy* #15, *Fantastic Four* #1, *Incredible Hulk* #1 , *Journey into Mystery* #83 and *Tales of Suspense* #39 are all in demand in any grade and are selling above *Guide*. For DC Silver Age, Batman is selling well, especially books with appearances by the Riddler, Joker and Catwoman. DC keys are still selling but often need to be discounted if below fine condition. *Iron Man* and *Incredible Hulk* have had really good sales due to their characters' successful movies. *Kid Colt*, *Rawhide Kid* and *Two-Gun Kid* are back in demand along with other Silver Age Western titles. The surprise title that has been selling is *Strange Tales* superhero comic, which had been cool for some time. TV and Movie titles are still selling well with *Dark Shadows* and *Bewitched* asked for often.

Bronze Age: Once a plentiful commodity in high grade but now not as common. We have purchased quite a few collections with Bronze Age, but seldom are we finding them in high grade. Few comics from this era are hard to find although there are some Monster and Mystery titles that a lot of people are looking for. *Werewolf by Night* #32 is harder to find and often sought after. *Giant-Sized Chillers* #1 (35¢ edition) is often asked for and sells quickly. *Incredible Hulk* #181 and *Amazing Spider-Man* #129 are two of the best selling Marvel keys from this era. *Weird War Tales*, *Ghosts* and *Witching Hour* are some better selling DC titles from this era. Charlton Comics with artists such as Sutton, Newton and Ditko are also in demand.

Magazines: Sales of magazines were slower this year, possibly because we have not purchased a lot of new inventory. The sales we had were all through the mail or at my local comic show CalComicCon in Yorba Linda, CA. Some of the titles we sold were *Deadly Hands of Kung Fu*, *Famous Monsters* and some Skywald magazines like *Scream* and *Nightmare*. We even sold some *Heavy Metal* magazines with wonderful Bernie Wrightson art in them.

Modern Age & Independents: We only stock the titles that collectors of vintage books seem to ask about. High grade *X-Men* and *Amazing Spider-Man* sell well, but most other titles go to the dollar box. We did purchase a large DC collection that had full runs of War and Mystery titles (such as *Ghosts* and *Weird War Tales*) all the way to their ends in the Modern Age. These comics are hard to find in high grade due to their low *Guide* value (many years in dollar boxes); they have been selling steady at above *Guide*, especially when CGC graded at 9.6 or better.

Graded books: This is where we make a lot of our sales lately. We often get high grade and high dollar books graded to protect them and ensure they have no restoration. Graded books are selling well and they often get a premium price in high grade. They are the best way to sell comics on auction sites.

Internet Sales: Website sales are up despite the fact that our sites were having hosting problems for a good part of the year. Many people want scans of listed items but with over 50,000 items in our inventory, it is not possible to scan all of them. We will send scans for items over $100 and offer a 30-day unconditional return on all sales. Our eBay store has been producing steady sales of un-graded Timelys, Marvel Keys and CGC books.

In summary, while the economy is currently in a lull, it appears there is no shortage of demand for the comics that remind us of better days. Sales for the first two quarters of 2008 have been at an all time high for us. As a side note, I had several unexpected sales due to customers receiving their stimulus checks from the federal government. I love when the government supplements comic book collecting.

Jim Pitts
Surf City Comix

Has another year come and gone already?!? Is it time for my 23rd market report for the *Guide*? It's hard to believe but San Diego is past, and WonderCon is just a blip on the horizon. So lets take a look at what sold, or didn't, in the last year.

Platinum Age: Always in demand in almost any grade, and almost impossible in high grade! Here's a few of the books I had this year: *Bringing Up Father* #3 FN $125, *Bringing Up Father* #5 GD $40, *Foxy Grandpa and Mother Goose* (1908) FN $400, and *Smitty at the Ball Game* FN $300.

Golden Age: A crazy year where many books sold for record prices at major auction houses, and my table. While #1's topped many peoples lists, first cover apps. were snapped up as well as last issues. Archie titles heated up as their scarcity is finally getting recognized. Hitler covers also stayed hot this year. While Funny Animal books got hot that contained Walt Kelly's Pogo or Hoppy the Marvel Bunny, many similar titles slowed. Some of my sales included: *Action Comics* #42 GD+ $275, *Action Comics* #57 VG $320, *Action Comics* #101 VG $300, *Adventure Comics* #77 VG/FN $450, *Amazing Man* #21 VG $200, *Archie* #33 FN/VF $175, *Archie Annual* #3 FN $200, *Archie's Pal Jughead* #2 VG $175, *Boy Commandos* #3 VG/FN $325, *Captain Marvel Adventures* #11 FN $300, *Captain Marvel Adventures* #29 FN $200, *Captain Marvel Jr.* #3 GD $125, *Captain Marvel Jr.* #4 VG $250, *Dell Giant Christmas Parade* #1 FN $200, *Detective Comics* #99 VG $250, *Hit Comics* #32 FN $100, *Jumbo Comics* #14 VG $300, *Kid Eternity* #3 FN $135, *Minute Man* #1 VG/FN $500, *National Comics* #24 VG $150, *National Comics* #25 FN $150, *National Comics* #38 FN $200, *National Comics* #39 FN $200, *Plastic Man* #3 VG/FN $300, *Slam Bang Comics* #1 GD $250, *Smash Comics* #38 FN $300, *Startling Comics* #9 FN $175, *Startling Comics* #10 VG/FN $1000, *Superboy* #8 VG $250, *Superboy* #10 VG/FN $300, *Superman* #30 VG/FN $600, *Superman* #36 VG $250, *Superman* #40 FN $350, just to name a few.

Silver Age: Since I don't deal in "slabbed" books, I didn't have too many sales of note in Silver, outside of "Keys." Of interesting note, I had bought many of the "Collectors Bookstore Archives" Disney comics, signed by Carl Barks. Many of these high grade books were snapped up at San Diego. Books I did sell included: *Adventure Comics* #247 GD $400, *Amazing Spider-Man* #5 VG $350, *Brave and the Bold* #29 VG/FN $400, *Brave and the Bold* #34 VG/FN(r) $300, *Fantastic Four* #2 GD $400, *Incredible Hulk* #4 GD/VG $200, *Incredible Hulk* #6 GD $180, *Sgt. Fury* #1 GD $175, *Showcase* #30 VG/FN $180, *Tales of Suspense* #1 VG+ $300, #2 VG/FN $150, #3 VG $125, #7 FN $125, #9 FN $150, #39 VG- $1050.

Early **Mad** magazines continue to be monster sellers. (**Mad** #29 shown)

Bronze Age: A hotbed of activity for those dealing in slabbed books. Since I don't sell those, I've concentrated more on oddball items from the era. Last issues of Disney books, Whitman Pre-Pack books, price variants, and odd firsts are what move for me here. Sales include *Howard the Duck* #12 (1st app. Kiss) NM $40 each for 11 copies, #13 (1st full app. Kiss) NM $45 each for 10 copies, #13 35-cent variant NM $150.

Pulps: An overlooked, and underappreciated area of collecting. While I didn't sell too many Pulps for over $100 this year, it is worth noting that many of these from the '20s to '40s have some great bondage covers and Fu Manchu covers, while many pulps from the '50s and '60s feature covers by Alex Schomburg, L.B. Cole, Kelly Freas, Virgil Finlay, and Vaughn Bode.

Magazines: Monster sellers here! Many Marvel/Curtis mags from the '70s and '80s are just starting to heat up. As more people get turned on to these titles, expect to see the prices go up! *Mad Magazine* continues to be my big seller, along with any Warren title. Skywald titles have started to slow as prices on these books climb. A couple sales of note in this area include: *Mad* #29 FN $120, #35 VF $150, #60 FN $60, #166 (finger cover) FN $25.

Big Little Books: Another area that I made a lot of sales in. Activity seems to stay towards the Disney BLBs and Sports BLBs. Collectors don't seem to be as picky about condition as long as the book is complete.

Underground Comics: They have virtually "blown up" in the last couple of years. Early printings of *Freak Brothers* and Crumb books just keep selling. The other big thing that people have been digging for is color variants, books with missing colors from the covers. A few sales of note in the area include: *Zap* #2 (1st) VG $250, *Zap* #4 color variant VF $175, *Cherry Poptart* #1 (1st) VF/NM $125, *Armadillotoons* #1 VG $150, *Works of Art Comics* (AP edition, signed to Carl Barks. From the Barks Estate) NM $150, *Gory Stories* #2 1/2 (yellow cover file copies) NM $30 each for 21 copies.

Golden Age Timelys do very well in all grades. (***Marvel Mystery Comics*** *#29 shown)*

Rock and Roll: It's amazing how many comic book collectors have started collecting rock and roll memorabilia. With a combination of scarcity in print runs and fantastic art, it's no wonder that the market for items from the 1950s to the present has blown up in recent years! Always in demand are the following performers: Grateful Dead, Janis Joplin, Jimi Hendrix, Bob Dylan, Neil Young, Bruce Springsteen, and The Doors. Artists that command attention include: Rick Griffin, Gilbert Shelton, Victor Moscoso, newcomers Mark Armanski, Chris Shaw, and EMEK.

So that's a look at just some of the things that sold, or were hot this year for me. Hope to see you all at the shows this year!

Bill Ponseti
Collector

Again we have enjoyed a year of record prices. Each month a new mind-blowing price is realized for a Silver Age or Golden Age key. High grade CGC books continue to set the pace.

Lower grade Marvel Silver Age keys sell very briskly at or even up to 20% over *Guide*. Mid-grade copies of these books are tougher to sell.

Golden Age Timely and most Batman and Superman-related titles do very well in all grades. The one exception is *World's Finest*, which does not sell very well at all. Pre-Robin *Detectives*, early *Marvel Mystery* and all *Captain America Comics* sell above *Guide* on a consistent basis.

The time for the $1,000,000 *Guide* price is upon us. *Action Comics* #1 should list for $1,000,000 in 9.2, and that is conservative. Doing so will add credibility to the hobby and to the *Guide*.

Marnin Rosenberg
NOD Chief Executive Officer
NetworkOfDisclosure.com

This has been a joyful year for all lovers of the comic book medium. We have seen our favorite childhood heroes vaulted into mainstream popularity in a multitude of motion pictures. We are also seeing more and more comic book inspired television shows that reflect the genre without showcasing a known super hero. These forays into a larger audience's purview have had wonderful effects on our hobby.

First and most importantly, the new material produced by all major houses is more sophisticated and engrossing –therefore imminently collectable. Second, the over-sizing and popularizing of existing stalwarts has made books long thought static into hot items. However, and there always has to be a however, this has led to a few nuances in our hobby that need to be controlled and curtailed.

Demand is a great thing if the supply can match it. We are seeing record five and six figure prices being paid for books that grade out extremely high. How do we escape the pitfalls that have plagued other assets that appreciated quickly? How many customers do we encourage to buy a book for a huge price and when they turn around and need to sell it find that they can only get a percentage of their purchase price? What potential damage will this reap on our hobby. You don't need to look any further than what's currently happening in the housing market.

My impassioned plea to all serious collectors and dealers is adhere to practices that will create a sustainable hobby. Ultimately, it will only be one deadly sin that can hurt all of us: Greed. If we all adhere to a uniform set of conduct and proactively disclosed restoration/enhancement, report our sales prices to GPAnalysis and above all, educate our customers, we will have a thriving trade for many years to come.

Matt Schiffman
Collector

Platinum Age: I can only really speak for the Northwestern U.S. in regards to the supply and sales for these books. I used to see plenty of them in Fair to VG sitting around in just about every antique or vintage bookshop. Of course they always were asking way too much for them, but curiously, over the past two years they've sold. Some of the sellers report that they often go to eBay retailers that look to flip them, but just as often they go to collectors. Where the *Guide* used to be too high in regards to Northwestern area books, it seems to be more and more reflective of the local sales.

Golden Age: In the past two years, the market has not seen this much Golden Age come up for sale in quite a long time. All grades could be found, and it gave a true gauge of the market's acceptance of these individual grades. Good continues to sell well and even fairly priced VG issues, but that

VG/FN to VF- (non-key) range still sits. They are expensive and wait a bit longer to find a home. I'm afraid that VF or better need to be professionally graded these days. With so many things to go wrong with these books and the history of rampant restoration on even the highest graded keys, one must protect themselves. It is a sad thing to see, but there it is. Perhaps we'll all pick up our graded high-grade book and then a reading copy to accompany it. Maybe that is why the GD grade does so well.

Atomic Age: Fiction House and St. John are the publishers of the year for collectors in this genre. Matt Baker covers showed strength and then skyrocketed in '08 and Lubber's *Wings* covers finally popped in the marketplace. Although these new prices would bring out the really good and hidden stuff, that didn't happen. So after a short leveling, they took off again to new heights. There was a slight slowdown in the EC issues below 9.0, but then again, they were getting quite expensive. Oddball Horror and War still moves quite well, but nothing excited the market more than Romance. Love - who doesn't love it? We might profess to all want Schomburg Timely War covers, but auction and sales records for Romance begs to differ. The prices are not that high yet, but steadily climb each and every year.

Silver Age: Silver Keys hitting six figures is no longer a surprise, especially when those books do not feature Spider-Man. But what is really surprising is that lower grade DC and Marvel are showing signs of life and that collectors are willing to put together runs of lower grade material again. It isn't always about investment and resale value, but the joy of having an original run - in any grade. Prices did pull back a bit over the past two years and coupled with new exposure to the mainstream populace, these GD to FN books are finding success where previously there wasn't much. DC War plugs right along in just about any grade and shows a resiliency that trumps the rest of the Marvel or DC titles.

Bronze Age: If we ever thought that enough was enough, we can just put that to rest. The rules continue to be broken time and time again. *Amazing Spider-Man* #129 takes a breather and then continues upward. Has *Werewolf by Night* #32 reached its peak? Doesn't seem so. Was the *Hero For Hire* run-up over the past three years just a fad? Appears not. Do that many people really collect the first appearance of Jonah Hex? The numbers say they do. Even books that seem to have no shortage of 9.4 and 9.6 certifications keep climbing upward. Sitting on the sidelines was not and still is not an option if you want to collect Bronze. Still, discoveries continue to be made and revelations hike prices overnight. A great segment to keep collecting because the adventure continues.

Copper Age: More and more activity is happening in this genre and it continues to be the most active and broad based for collectors discovering what is out there. First, Comico, Capitol, Kitchen Sink, Dark Horse, and Eclipse all have hidden gems buried deep in their runs. Finding those are part of the fun, trying to locate print numbers, last issue documentation, and first appearances can be more than rewarding. Many of the great artists and writers over the past 30 years got their start in the back-up stories, and obscure titles from these non-mainstream publishers. Look for the depth and breadth to further expand as collectors are able to pick up small, and yet to be documented, titles in nice shape and at reasonable prices.

Doug Simpson and Peter Dixon Paradise Comics

What can be said about 2008, except that it was a phenomenal year for Paradise Comics. Our sales continued to increase throughout the year and our customer base grew by 15%. Our Internet sales also continued to grow and our new website contributed to an 11% increase in sales over last year. The greatest area of growth in-store continues to be our sales of graphic novels; this format is definitely the direction the hobby is going, and I hope that the major companies start to take more notice. Customers are continuing to change their collecting habits, from picking up the regular monthly issues to graphic novels.

Key issues from the Silver and Bronze Age are consistently selling well and don't seem to be slowing down at all. I simply can't keep up with the demand for high-grade Silver and Bronze Age books – from *Action* to *X-Men*, people want them in the highest grades and as fast as possible. The usual suspects are always involved: *Amazing Fantasy* #15, *Fantastic Four* #1, *Daredevil* #1, *Giant-Size X-Men* #1, *Incredible Hulk* #181, and *X-Men* #94. But I'm also seeing some new ones: *Incredible Hulk* #1, *Tales of Suspense* #39, *Avengers* #4, *Batman* #171, #181 & #234, and *Marvel Spotlight* #32 are just a few examples.

Golden Age sales are very sluggish, and with so many collectors only pursuing Timely issues and high-grade Silver Age, sales have continued to be exceptionally slow. There is always a market for Golden Age hero comics, but never at *Guide*, and usually well below. The increase in the Golden Age reprint market has also contributed to the slowdown.

Silver Age sales are without a doubt incredible, with any high-grade copies selling out as fast as I can get them in. For DC Silver Age, hero and horror comics have seen the greatest growth in sales, especially the horror tandem of *House of Mystery* and *House of Secrets*. The one book that deserves special mention here is *Green Lantern* #7, the first Sinestro appearance – I can't keep them in stock and it seems to be on every want list.

Marvel Silver Age is selling very well, with *Amazing Spider-Man* and *X-Men* leading the way, and demand for *Avengers* and *Thor* is increasing. The Marvel Silver Age market is always strong and doesn't look to be slowing down anytime soon.

It could just be the value, but Silver Age DC bin stock sells way more in volume than its Marvel counterparts.

Bronze Age comic sales are through the roof in high grade, and demand for mid-grade copies has increased as well. Marvel leads the way in this category with Byrne *X-Men* (#108-143) and all *Amazing Spider-Man* issues between #100 and #200. These issues are on almost everyone's list and, if I had an entire box of each, they would be gone within a week. I have also noticed an increase in demand for

Avengers and *Incredible Hulk*. It goes without saying that *Incredible Hulk* #181 is the most in-demand Bronze Age book out there today. DC titles, including *Batman* and *Justice League of America*, are always in demand and *Green Lantern* is seeing incredible growth thanks to the Sinestro Corps War storyline.

Sales of modern books have continued to fall in 2008, with the only bright spots being DC's *Final Crisis*, and Marvel's *Mighty Avengers*, *New Avengers* and *Secret Invasion*.

2008 saw the beginning of the end of the variant craze. Whether it was 10 to 1 or 75 to 1, the demand was down and we started selling them at a discounted rate. I feel that the future of the medium is with the graphic novel, and the increased output by all publishers will continue this trend.

As mentioned earlier, our on-line sales were sensational and continued to grow all year. Our eBay store has been a wonderful addition to our business. Our new website will continue to provide a consistent source of Silver Age and graphic novels in 2009. (www.paradisecomics.com)

CGC continues to be the standard in independent third-party grading. I would like to mention that CGC is the exclusive grading company for Paradise Comics and Paradise Conventions. Some recent CGC sales include:
Amazing Spider-Man #122 (7.0) Signature Series (Stan Lee & John Romita) $270;
Amazing Spider-Man #129 (6.5) Sig. Series (Stan Lee) $305;
Journey Into Mystery #85 (7.5) Sig. Series (Stan Lee) $739;
Sub-Mariner #1 (9.0) Sig. Series (Stan Lee) $358;
X-Men #14 (9.0) Sig. Series (Stan Lee) $424.99;
X-Men #27 (9.0) Sig. Series (Stan Lee) $199.99;
Amazing Spider-Man #129 (9.0) $496.00;
Fantastic Four #3 (6.5 UK Edition) $999.99;
Green Lantern #76 (8.5) $629.99;
Incredible Hulk #1 (1.5) $1,476.71;
Uncle Scrooge #66 (9.8) $1,250;
Uncle Scrooge #70 (9.6) $750.

I would like to finish by mentioning our sixth annual Paradise Toronto Comicon, held July 12-13, 2008. With the show evolving over the past year, including the change in location and, more importantly, with management, things went very smoothly and, from the feedback we have received, the general opinion was that it was another success. We would like to extend a special thank you to our Guests of Honour Herb Trimpe, Joseph Michael Linsner, and Greg Land for going above and beyond for the fans. We would also like to thank all our guests for understanding that a great show starts with great people, and we could not have asked for a friendlier and more outgoing group of creators. For more information, visit (www.torontocomicon.com)

Al Stoltz
Basement Comics

While the year is not yet over and many more crazy sales can happen before December comes to a close, we still have had a great selling year at both conventions and thru our eBay store. Huge increase in sales of comics to out of country buyers due to a plunging dollar, which in a interesting move made my year better than ever and reached many new buyers, just not in my country. New York Comic Con was a very crowded affair and lots of buyers were buying Marvel Silver Age and Bronze Age keys. If I could only find a case of *Incredible Hulk* #181s to meet the need at every show that we set up! San Diego Comic-Con was more crowded than ever, but with more people through the door, does that translate to more comic back issue buyers also fighting the lines to get in? I do not think so, and have decided after eight years to call it quits setting up at this particular convention. I now feel that I can fly out and spend the money that went into doing the convention, well over $11,000, and just spend that on inventory to add to our E-Store and eventual new web site. New day, new approach to trying to make money out of this hobby for us. Wizard World Chicago I feel is still the show to buy and sell comics at and feel like you are at a large comic convention. While Baltimore Comic-Con is smaller, it also still is a real comic show and we do rather well at. Nice to have that thirty five minute ride to a Con for change.

Maybe the one thing I would hope to point out in this year's report would be that I hope for 2009 that *The Overstreet Comic Book Price Guide* finally goes online and can be searched from my iPhone when I am at a convention or at an Antique store looking at comics. I am getting older and cannot remember all the price breaks, so having it at my finger tips would be a great thing and a tool I am sure many other comic fans would love to access. I enjoy being able to use many of the other searchable data base systems that are offered and think that the *Overstreet* would be a great thing to use as well. This is my second year of mentioning this topic and hope that I am not alone in asking the Powers in Charge to push hard for this change.

eBay: We start with eBay sales because that is where we are selling like crazy! List 15,000 items and the crowds searching always finds something they have to have. We sell a little of everything offline including *Famous Monsters of Filmland*, *Fangoria*, Marvel magazines, *Cracked*, *Mad*, lots of Silver Age comics and Bronze Age comics. Middle of the year saw a demand for lots of art such as original *Dick Tracy* Harvey pages. Original art of all types was mailed to Europe. We listed a huge collection of Harvey Digests and Archie Digests and were stunned by the large orders of issues that followed. Same thing happened with a high grade group of Treasury Editions and Marvel paperbacks that sold very quickly. Seems that buyers still are looking for oddball items that dealers are hesitant to list or bring to shows and jump at the chance to buy them if they come up for sale. CGC comics have taken off and here are some that have sold recently: *Avengers* #32 (9.2) $115.00, *Teen Titans* #50 (9.6) $80.00, *Batman* #314 (9.8) $140.00, *Uncanny X-Men* #119 (9.6) $120.00, *Thor* #337 (9.8) $300.00, *Amazing Spider-Man* #299 (9.8) $125.00, *Gorgo* #1 (9.2) $550.00, *Tales Of Suspense* #30 (7.0) $5,700, *Werewolf By*

Night #33 (9.6) $400.00, *Startling Comics* #12 (6.5) $650.00, *Justice League Of America* #185 (9.8) $135.00. Some non-certified items that come to mind that sold thru eBay are *Teen-age Dope Slaves* (G-VG) $360.00, *Amazing Spider-Man* #1 (GD-) $900.00, *America's Best Comics* #1 (VG+) $650.00, *Sun Fun Komics* $500.00, *Daring Love* #1 $550.00, *Four Color* #386 (GD) $150.00.

©MAR

Convention buyers were on a mission this year to buy Marvel keys like **Werewolf By Night** #32.

As of this letter being written, eBay has made drastic changes to listing formats so we will see how that changes listing patterns by sellers on that platform. In the end, offering a wide variety and being well known in the Internet buying world will still enable us to continue to list and sell lots of off-the-wall items worldwide.

Comic Conventions: Convention buyers were on a mission this year to buy keys and Marvel Comics keys lead in sales for us. Very hard to keep a copy of *Fantastic Four* #1 or *Amazing Fantasy* #15 or *Tales of Suspense* #39 in stock. *Hulk* #181 just continues to stun me, not rare in any grade but still out-strips all other Bronze keys as the demand issue at shows. *Amazing Spider-Man* #129 and *Werewolf by Night* #32 also are two issues that seem to be asked for many times a day at conventions this year. High-grade hawks still want to score the best comic in the world, but I love the box pickers that pour through and fill holes in the collection with mid-grade and lower copies. And we did see many customers taking the time to look through our inventory at NY, Chicago and San Diego this Summer. Just a side mention here, the craziest and funniest buyers at conventions including myself are comic dealers during the set up hours of a show. My favorite dealer at controlling the mad crowds of other comic dealers is Gary Colabuono at Wizard World Chicago.

It seemed to me that more customers at shows were looking for harder to find Dell comics, Charlton horror in high grade, especially with Steve Ditko art. Looking for items that are off the radar of those who are slabbing and high grade hunters will hopefully keep collectors in the market and actually make going to shows and hunting online fun again. What did we sell at shows? Matt Baker comics were sought after and we sold two of the beautiful St. John Giant comics that feature nice Baker covers at the San Diego Con. Two *Incredible Hulk* #181s in GD- condition for $300.00, *Blazing Combat* #1 (FN+) $220.00, *Detective Comics* #9 (GD-) $700.00, *Batman* #100 (VG+) $350.00, *X-Men* #1 (VG+) $1150.00, *Showcase* #7 (VG+) $350.00, *Strange Suspense Stories* #19 (VF) $750.00. *Pep* #8 (VG+) $320.00, and a coverless *Tales Of Suspense* #39 for $250.00.

Buying at shows seems to have gotten better this year as well. We purchased what we hope is part one of a great original owner Bronze Age collection and many other bits and small piles of weird and wonderful comics to add to our ever growing inventory. Books are coming out of the woodwork and it seems as fast as they enter the market, they are swallowed up. A good sign is that back issues are still strong sellers and collectors are still out there in force to keep the hobby alive. Hollywood's use of comics for screenplays has also had a positive impact on back issue sales as well. Can we get a producer to look at old *Marvel Two-in-One* issues or *Omac* comics? I have a few sitting around here.

Season starts early in 2009 with New York Comic Con in February and it will be interesting to see if collectors will come out and spend during a New York winter. Maybe a little global warming on just that one weekend will warm up the spenders and start the year out with a great start.

Doug Sulipa
Doug Sulipa's Comic World

My 8,000 square foot warehouse is bursting at the seams with over 600,000 pounds (by weight) of inventory. I needed to make the choice between building an expensive addition to my warehouse, or beginning the huge process of clearing out overstocked items. I decided on the latter. Since the great majority of my overstock is 1975-1995 Marvels & DC in middle grades (VG-VF), I started with those, making up 50 to 150 issue sets, moving them at a Blow Out Sale on my website and on eBay. Although I barely made a dent in the 200,000+ issues I want to clear out, I did manage to clear out over 10,000 comics in the 40-65% off *Guide* price ranges. The big surprise was that, even though I had *Spider-Man*, *X-Men* and *Ghost Rider* sets, the #1 most popular was *Rom* #1-75, Annual #1-4 (15 VF sets sold @ $99 ea), followed by *Micronauts* #1-59, Ann #1-2 (11 VF sets @ $75 ea) and *Defenders* #31-152 (9 VF sets @ $125 ea) and strangely enough, no one wanted *Wolverine* #1-74.

When we next get some downtime, I am hoping to get to clearing out some overstocked VG sets of 1970s Archies, Charltons and Gold Keys. To my delight, as a side-effect of clearance sales, I found that low grade, hard-to-put-together, uncommon 25-100 issue sets of 1950s & 1960s comics, would bring 100-125% *Guide* (especially Dell, Disney, Harvey and Gold Key cartoons, *Tarzan*, TV and other popular culture titles.)

Demand for popular Key issues was huge as usual. Most rarely remained in stock for long in VF/NM or better. The twist this year is that many fans feel that most of the major Marvel and DC key issues of the 1966-1980 era are undervalued in G-FN grades, and we started selling out of a lot of them. Thus I started to buy many of these G-FN issues at 60-90% *Guide* and flip them swiftly at 135-200% *Guide*. High grade Marvel and DC comics were the most requested, but my selection of 1974 and earlier issues in VF/NM or higher continues to dwindle. I did offer a huge selection of 15,000+ raw comics (90% from 1975 thru 1987 era) in high grades on my website (most from the Manitoba collection) in the 9.0 thru 9.8 grades and sold over 2,000 of them (at 135-300% *Guide*) with nearly zero returns, due to my strict grading.

Even though I do well with the above mentioned high grade comics, what I have become the best known for among my clients over the last 38 years is having the biggest selection on the planet of affordable "different comics" from the 1950s thru the Present. I mostly stock comics in the $2-$100 price range (but I do have a decent selection of over-$100 comics). I do not normally carry higher grade Silver Age in the $200-$10,000+ price range. Collectors from around the world come to us to complete their sets of comics that the majority of dealers do not bother with (Archie, ACG, Charlton, Classics, Dell, digests, Dennis the Menace, fanzines, Gold Key, Harvey, magazines, religious, Treasuries, Walt Disney and more). Oddball comics have become my #1 specialty and it is commonplace for collectors to buy 50, 100 or even 300 comics at a time at full retail, as they are so very happy to find them all in one place. They save time and postage, while also having the satisfaction of crossing most numbers off want lists. Naturally many of these comics are uncommon-to-scarce, so GD-FN copies are all I am able to re-stock on many, many titles, but that is OK, as they are also the most popular and requested grades for us. For example, it is commonplace for us to get 5 want lists in a row, all asking for the lowest graded available, complete Reading copies in stock. Reading copies are so popular on some titles, that I sometimes only have FN and VF copies left in stock. I often find myself buying GD-FN copies uncommon-to-scarce high demand comics that *Guide* under $10, at 60-100% *Guide*, and pricing them at 135%-200% *Guide*. When I list them on my site, many resell swiftly within a few weeks to months.

*Reading copies of all 1950s ACG titles were in high demand. (**Cookie** #1 shown)*

ACG Comics: We sold a bunch of hero issues (Magicman, Nemesis, Magic Agent) of *Adventures into the Unknown* and *Forbidden Worlds*, mainly to fans trying to complete runs (GD-FN=120-140% *Guide*; VF& up=110-120% *Guide*.) The Pre-Hero issues were in high demand (GD-FN=135-150% *Guide*; VF& up=120-130% *Guide*.) *Herbie* comics are a fondly remembered cult favorite and sold well, as did *Gasp*, *Magic Agent* and *Midnight Mystery* (GD-FN=120-140% *Guide*; VF& up=110-120% *Guide*). The Herbie one-page original material (all different?) comic strips and cartoon ads were great sellers to completionists, as I have them all identified on my website (*Forbidden Worlds* #125, 126, *Unknown Worlds* #20, 31-39, etc.; GD-FN=135-150% *Guide*; VF& up=120-130% *Guide*). There was resistance on most VF or better copies, especially on the pricier 1950s issues.

Reading copies of all 1950s titles were in high demand, as many collectors were filling in gaps in their sets. There is strong demand for everything printed by this publisher, including: *Blazing West*, *Commander Battle and the Atomic Sub*, *Cookie*, *Funny Films*, *Giggle*, *Ha Ha*, *Hooded Horseman*, *Kilroys*, *Lovelorn*, *Romantic Adventures*, *Operation Peril*, *Out of the Night*, *Soldiers of Fortune*, *Spy Hunters* and *Young Heroes* (GD-FN= 125-150% *Guide*; VF & up=110-125% Guide).

Archie Comics: About 30 years ago, I discovered there are many thousands of Archie collectors around the world, that are unknown to most other dealers. This inspired me to specialize in them, and to go out to buy all the Archie collections I could find. I ended up with our current inventory of 35,000+ Archie comics and 10,000+ digests, and they are by far some of our bestsellers, with a turnover rate that is about 500% better than Marvel or DC comics. Most pre-1988 Archies are scarce in VF and rare in VF/NM. About 15% of my clients are looking for VF or better copies, but usually only under 10% of my pre-1988 Archies attain this lofty grade.

The most requested in VF or better (with most tough to locate) include: All Dan DeCarlo art issues, *Betty & Veronica*, *Josie*, *Red Circle Horror*, Neal Adams art issues, Cheryl Blossom issues, Giants, monster covers, *Sabrina*, 1974-1985 digests; #1, #100 and final issues; and all other Key issues (bringing 120-135% *Guide*).

The 1990s Hanna-Barbera titles bring 200% *Guide* on average and continue to get scarcer, with *Scooby-Doo* the most requested. *TMNT Adventures* #50-72, *Specials* #6-10, *Sourcebook* #1-2, and digests, plus *Mighty Mutant Animals* #5-9, are low-print items, hard to find in any grade. Almost all dealers everywhere are sold out, but I managed to buy a couple collections at over 100% *Guide* and sell them at 200-400% *Guide* in VF thru VF/NM average grades. Most of the 1980s Cheryl Blossom appearance stories sell for 200% *Guide* in any grade.

Over 90% of our Archie back issue sales are for Fair and GD-FN condition copies, as condition is not a big factor for most buyers. There were not actually a lot of different 1941-1950 Archies published as they only had a handful of titles in this period, thus demand usually outstrips supply by 2-1 to 3-1 depending on the issue, and most easily sell at 120-150% *Guide*, especially if they are lower graded Reading copies. 1951-1960 Archies are also in lower supply, as most are locked away in permanent collections, and it can often take collectors years to complete their runs of titles from these years (most Fair and GD-FN copies we sell at 120-150% *Guide*). I have seen many buyers get into real battles in eBay auctions, often paying 200-400% *Guide* for over-graded copies. Most 1960s Archies are uncommon, and completing sets can still be quite a challenge. Issues from the 1970s seem to be the most plentiful. From about 1978-1984, Archie had an implosion similalr to that at DC, cancelling about half of their titles, and cutting back others from monthly to bi-monthly or quarterly. In this same era, the digests started to rival and then surpass the sales of the standard comics. I surmize that they realized that they would eventually run out of material to reprint, thus from 1987-1990 and on, they started to publish regular format comics once again. However, the print runs of the regular sized comics never got large again as the digests became their eternal bestsellers. The comics presumably were meant for collectors, and the digests became the inexpensive compact trade paperback reprints for the general public and readers worldwide. I have found that re-stocking 1983-2008 Archies missing in our inventory is much tougher than re-stocking most issues of the 1965-1982 era. Most buyers are not too concerned about condition on comics that value out at $7 or less. *Guide* value becomes irrelavant in this range, thus I find almost no price resistance when pricing GD-FN copies at 135-175% *Guide*, as is needed to keep many of these items in stock.

Atlas/Marvel: We have in stock a decent selection of about 1000 Atlas/Marvel comics, and as always, they were very popular. When compared to 1961-1965 Marvel comics, this much scarcer 1950s selection still seems a relative bargain and many Marvel fans find themselves dabbling with these highly collectible comics. This year the bestsellers were the Western and teenage titles. We could have sold a lot of Horror and SF titles, but are currently low in stock. Many fans grew up on the 1970s Marvel reprints (*Dead of Night*, *Monsters on the Prowl*, *Where Monsters Dwell*, etc.) and now want the originals, especially the issues that have not been reprinted. Alan Class of the UK reprinted a lot more Atlas/Marvel Horror/SF comics than US Marvel ever did, and readers are advised to pick some up. Most sell for only $6-12 each. Joe Maneely started at Timely in 1949 and became Atlas' main workhorse by the mid-1950s (in the period when Timely was transforming into Atlas) until his tragic death in June 1958. He is fondly remembered for his hundreds of dramatic covers. After his passing, Jack Kirby came along and more than filled that void, transforming most of the horror comics into the tongue-in-cheek, "Big-Lumbering-Monster"-type stories, as did Steve Ditko, who rendered many memorable fantasy stories. Stan Lee, along with the dynamo team of Kirby and Ditko, led to the creation of the Marvel superheroes and that changed comics forever. I sometimes wonder what direction comics would have gone if Joe Maneely had remained among Atlas' chief artists. Many Joe Maneely covers and art are still not listed in the *Guide*, but I have noted a growing number of collectors are more likely to buy comics that I list as having his artwork. Any and every Atlas with art by Dan DeCarlo is Red Hot (selling at 125-150% *Guide.*) DeCarlo's *Millie the Model* #18-93 are the most requested of all Atlas comics (FA, and GD-FN copies=150-200% *Guide*; VF or better copies=125-150% *Guide.*) The crime/mystery, funny animal, sports, and spy titles were slower sellers, but still uncommon (selling at 110-120% *Guide.*) Horror/SF, humor/parody, romance and war titles were also good solid sellers (GD-FN= 120-140% *Guide*; VF up =110-120% *Guide*).

Charlton: In the 1970s when some of the Comic Code restrictions were lifted on horror comics (allowing vampires, werewolves etc.), Marvel and DC led the way to a boom in the sale of Horror comics and magazines (*Tomb of Dracula*, *Werewolf by Night*, *House of Mystery*, *Swamp Thing*, and others). Naturally both were already publishing horror/mystery/ SF titles, as was Charlton, but they were suddenly less bland. A lot of top art talent migrated to these titles and fans started buying horror comics in droves. Warren and others were already publishing great horror, but in much higher priced and less accessable B&W magazine formats. Charlton gladly jumped on the bandwagon and produced hundreds of Horror comics under many titles. They had smaller print runs than most of the other major publishers and an even lower survival rate. Collectors of that period still considered anything published by Charlton to be "junk," judging that Marvel and DC were the most collectible comics. Those that did not bother to check them out missed a lot, especially since most of the artwork of Tom Sutton and Steve Ditko appeared in Charltons through all these years. While most fans say that the 1970s Ditko art just does not compare to his '50s classics, an amazing amount of fans now collect all these comics. Perhaps most of Tom Sutton's best art appeared in his Charlton years and many fans consider him one of the top 10 horror comics artists of all-time, and most certainly of the Bronze Age. Since I have had a comic shop in Winnipeg through most of the 1970s, I lived through this "horror boom" period and it was because of this I got heavily involved in stocking all Charlton comics. I now have the world's biggest selection of Charltons, with over 35,000 in stock. Usually I have in stock 90% of all 1961-1986 issues ever printed and about 35% of the 1946-1960 issues printed, and because I specialize in them, our turnover rate is excellent and I always do well with them.

Charlton did manage to publish a lot of comics with poor art and stories, so many dismiss them without looking closer. But for those that take the time to look, they turn out to be one of the most fascinating publishers of all time. Of all the major publishers, they offer one of the widest varieties of genres: cartoon, ccrime, history, horror, humor/parody, licensed characters, monsters, movie, hot rod, jungle, martial arts, mythology, mystery, newspaper comic strip, pirates, pop music stars, radio, romance, science, SF, soap opera, superhero, teenage, TV, war and western. They published comics, digests, magazines and non-comic mags (adult cartoon, crossword and puzzle mags, horror film mags, kung-fu and karate mags, *Sick* mag, *True Romance* mags, *True*

Western mags). With minimal control by editors, many creators did a lot of experimenting and produced a lot of great and often overlooked classics. Charlton had a lot of painted covers through the 1970s, whereas most other publishers dropped them. These artists produced a lot of great work at Charlton: Aparo, Boyette, Buscema, Byrne, Cuti, Ditko, Giordano, Glanzman, Himes, Wayne Howard, Sanho Kim, Larson, Lopez, Rocke Mastroserio, Morisi, Don Newton, Severin, Staton, Tom Sutton, Wildman, Williamson, Wood, and Mike Zeck.

The Charlton bestsellers were *Gorgo*, *Konga*, *Flash Gordon*, *Phantom*, *Blue Beetle*, *Judomaster*, and TV titles like *Emergency*, *Six Million Dollar Man* and *Space 1999.* They were the most requested in high grades, although moving well in all grades (GD-FN= 125-150% *Guide*; VF-NM+ =120-300% *Guide*). We sold about 150 high grade and Manitoba Collection Charltons in 9.0-9.6 grades at 125-300%+ *Guide*. Charltons are all good steady sellers in all grades, but 90% of our non-Horror/Superhero sales were in the FA/GD to FN/VF condition ranges, and most are scarce in VF or better (GD-FN= 120-150% *Guide*; VF or better =110-125% *Guide*). The Hanna-Barbera titles are eternal bestsellers, especially in the more affordable mid- to lower grades. There is a lot of demand for all Hanna-Barbera issue #1s in VF or better conditions to key issue collectors. *Phantom* comics are popular among American buyers, but are among the most requested Charltons to overseas buyers. The Phantom has a huge cult following in Europe, the British Colonies and Australia. The Western and war titles have a rather large following, with many fans trying to complete their sets. Sam Glanzman is a big favorite among the war comics fans, and he did much of his best work at Charlton.

Classics Illustrated & Related: We had a *boom* year for *Classics* comics, selling hundreds of issues mainly in the $15 to $200 each price ranges. We have perhaps about 5,000 *Classics* in stock and they are among our best turnover items in stock, and naturally, selection makes all the difference. The biggest single factor that made buyers come to us is our big selection, including examples of all the various covers and art variants for each issue. Several of the buyers already had complete sets of all the cheaper painted cover and later interor art issues, but now wanted to add examples of the line drawn covers and original interior art to their collections, resulting in several orders for 50-100+ books. We also had several buyers who had complete sets of originals, or editons with original covers and art, but now wanted examples of second and third covers and art printings. There are 199 interior art variations in the set and 272 different covers in a complete set. Obtaining all these variations is now the major goal of many collectors. The most serious collectors, who had nearly complete to complete sets of originals, wanted only the first printings of the painted covers for #1-80 and the 1st prints of second and third cover and interior art printings, as they are widely viewed as a new type of "original". Most "First new cover and art" issues are uncommon to scarce and most are tough to find in even FN or better. Since we get a lot of action on these, I bought up a lot of them at 75-100% *Guide* from other dealers to boost our inventory selection and priced them in the 150-200% *Guide* range. The result was a nearly 90% sellout in a 6 month period (over 200 issues), with no price resistance. Canadian variant editions (not in *Guide*) of #1-74 are still in high demand, especially those with new illustrated text stories that do not appear in U.S. editions and many have HRN numbers that do not exist on U.S. printings. For printings with HRN #s within 5 digits of the issue number, I usually price at 50% of the price of the U.S. Original. Other Canadian variants I price at 150-300% U.S. Prices. The rarest Canadian variants are #17-20 (blank inside covers = VG @ $100+ ea), and issue #11.

There is a definite shortage of most issues of *Classics Illustrated* #109-169 in the marketplace, because 49 of these 61 issues had 5 or fewer printings. There is an overabundance of issues #1-50, as most issues had 10-20+ Printings (15 printings average). Most people who collect *Classics* have the long term goal of completeing the set. Yet the common editions of low # issues value out at almost the same prices as the scarcer high numbers, thus there is a permanent marketplace shorage of most issues from #109-169. To solve this problem in my own inventory, I price the cheaper Reading copies of my #109-169's in stock, at 50-100% Higher than my #1-50 Reading copies. As they are difficult to restock, I usually need to buy my #109-169 issues at 75-100% *Guide* from other dealers, but I am well rewarded by having many buyers who order 50-100 books at a time from us, because we have 'em and most other sellers do not.

Classics Illustrated issues that had only one or just a few printings are *always* in big demand (any printing and all grades = 120-150% *Guide*) including #14,20,21,33,40,43, 44,53,66,71,73,74,84,110,113-118,129,161-169. Scarcer *Classics Juniors* include; #506, 514, 525-529, 532-534, 537,540,542,543,547,553,555, 556,558-565,568,571-573, 575-577 (FA-VG = 200-300% *Guide*; FN-VF = 150-200% *Guide*). About 1/3 of all *Junior*s are common (in ANY printing), another 1/3 are uncommon, and about 1/3 are scarce, and there is a permanent shortage of most issues from #553-577 (because they had less printings). The UK British *Classics* #143, 146-150, 156, 157, 159,162 with all-new stories never seen in USA are in very high demand (VG/FN = $100+ each) (#158A James Bond Dr. No =$500; #161 Aeneid = $200+; #163 Argonauts = $300+); We sold a lot of *Classics* related items, mainly to collectors that had almost everything else. These items included: *Acclaim*, *Amar Chitra Katha* (India Mythology and Legend), *Berkley/First*, *Boys Life*, *British Classic Editions*, Dell (related *Four Color* and Movie classics), *Dell Junior Treasury*, *Famous Authors*, Gold Key (related *Movie Classics*), *Golden Legacy* (history of black people), *Golden Picture Classics*, *King Classics* (a tough series to complete), *Marvel Classics*, Marvel-UK Classic Graphic Novels and Digests, Mexican *Junior* series, Moby Books (Big Little Book format #4501-4536) , Pendulum, *Pocket Classics*, *Power Records*, *Tele-Guide*

(Graphic Novels), *World Illustrated* and all others.

There are still quite a few *Classics* completionists looking to get one copy each of every printing of #1-169 (nearly 1400 variations). Most of the second Printings (1943 up) through to reprints with HRN #161(3/1961) are undervalued, especially those that *Guide* for nearly the same value as the more common HRN#164-169 printings. Completionists constantly tell me that many HRN#(161 and earlier)reprint printings are very tough to find in even strict VG or FN, thus I have gone out of my way to stock some of these, priced at a still inexpensive 150-200% *Guide* and have done quite well with them. There is a glut on the market of multiple copies of common HRN#164-169 printings (especially of issues #1-50), that fosters the illusion that *Classics Comics* are common, when that is only true for perhaps less than 1/3 of the various 1400 printings.

Comic Digests: We sold nearly 1000 comic digests this year, with nearly 90% in the FA/GD through FN/VF condition ranges and mostly to customers buying near-complete sets, or filling in numbers off their want lists. When I had my retail stores in Winnipeg (1974-1996) I always carried all the various comics digests and always did well with them. I had saved a few copies each for back issue inventory through all these years and bought all the collections in sight. I literally sold perhaps 30,000 digests over the last 35 years, and I have a current inventory of 10,000 Archie digests and 5,000 other comics digests. High grade pre-1995 comic digests in VF to VF/NM are uncommon to scarce, with 9.2 to 9.6 copies being rare. Very few have yet been graded by CGC. We located perhaps the highest graded existing set of *Mystery Comics Digest* #1-26 and sold 85% of them as Raw copies in the 200-350% *Guide* range. There are high grade collectors for virtually all pre-1995 digests, (Archie, Charlton, *Classics* related, DC, *Dennis the Menace*, Gold Key, Harvey, Marvel, Skylark and Walt Disney related) but not many high grade copies exist to satisfy demand. Luckily, most collectors are happy with average mid-grade copies. There are 16 different titles known (plus at least 7 different cover price variants) for the rare Charlton related Xerox / Now Age Comic Digests, and these are our minimum selling prices (VF/NM=$50; VF=$40; FN=$30; VG=$20; GD=$14). The Harvey 1986-1994 digests are by far the toughest sets to complete, with most issue #1-5s being uncommon, but with #6-up and the latter half of each larger set being scarce to rare.

DC Comics: Batman has been hot for many years now, but the film *Dark Knight* has fueled the fire. With *Dark Knight* now entrenched as the #2 Box Office Hit of all-time, there is no doubt that he is one of the most recognized fictional characters in history. Superman historically is recognized as DC's main character. In the Golden Age, Batman and Superman sell equally well. From 1955-1962, Batman sells about 50-100% faster than Superman. But from 1963 to the present, Batman titles rule, selling 300-400% of the quantities of Superman titles. This explains why Batman prices are so much higher. Yet, when compared to Spider-Man comics of the same vintage, Batman comics remain a bargain. 1963-1986 Batman titles are in the most demand and sell in all grades, but there is a notable shortage of high grade copies, as they simply were not hoarded in quantities as Marvel comics were. All Batman key issues from 1950 through early 1990s are in demand, with scarcer, uncommon and high demand issues easily bringing 135-165% *Guide* in all grades. By far the most requested Batmans are those with Neal Adams covers and art. Many fans already have all the issues with interior art and thus there has been even higher demand for all the Adams cover issues. Demand is so high for high grade copies and supply so low, that collectors who really want them, have found themselves buying VF copies and even FN/VF copies. *Batman* #263-403 should be considered the "Slump" era with lower sales, and these issues are all still very undervalued. Frank Miller's *Dark Knight Returns* from 1986 revitalized the franchise and the Miller mini-series in *Batman* #404-407 made the title hot once again. We have all forgotten that Batman was actually slow seller in the 1976-1985 era, when it was competing against *New Teen Titans*, Spider-Man, the new X-Men and the prolific Direct Market-only titles. Superman was also slower in this period and was resurrected by John Byrne and *Crisis*. *Batman* #331-400 had perhaps the title's lowest print run in its first 48 years. After Miller, came *Crisis*, "A Death in the Family", the Movies, Tim Drake, "Knightfall" (Azrael and Bane) and more, and thus the title has been a top seller in the subsequent 22 years. A *Detective Comics* #405 (Adams-c) CGC 9.8 sold for $3,250.00 at auction = over 54 Times *Guide*. Joker #1-9 (1975-1976) became red hot for the first time in years, due to Heath Ledger in the 2008 film. One of the big secrets to Batman's success is that he boasts the greatest stable of cool villains in all of comics (followed in a close 2nd with Spider-Man). Great villains make a superhero great. Flash has some great villains too, thus his popularity has risen above other characters such as Hawkman. The Bronze Age bestsellers for us this year (at 110% to 135% *Guide*) included: *All-New Collectors' Edition*, *All-Out War*, *All Star Comics*, *Amazing World of DC*, all Batman titles, *Batman Family* #11-20; *Best of DC Digest*, *Binky*, *Black Magic*, *Blitzkreig*, *Brave and*

Due to Heath Ledger's movie portrayal, **The Joker** series became red hot for the first time in years. (#1 shown)

the Bold, Crisis, DC Comics Presents, DC 100 Page Super Spectacular, DC Special, DC Special Series, DC Special Blue Ribbon Digest, Detective, Doorway to Nightmare, Flash, Freedom Fighters, Ghosts, G.I. Combat, Girls' Love, Girls' Romances, Heart Throbs, House of Mystery, House of Secrets, Isis, Joker, Jonah Hex, JLA, Limited Collectors' Edition, Men of War, New Teen Titans, Our Army at War, Our Fighting Forces, Phantom Stranger, Rima, Secret Society of Super-Villains, Secrets of Haunted House, Sgt. Rock, Shazam, Showcase, Sinister House, Star Spangled War, Super DC Giant, Super Friends, Supergirl (1972), *Lois Lane, Jimmy Olsen, Superman Family, Swamp Thing* (1982), *Tarzan, Tarzan Family, Time Warp, Tomahawk, Unexpected, Unknown Soldier, V for Vendetta, Watchmen, Warlord, Weird Mystery, Weird War, Weird Western, Witching Hour, Wonder Woman, World's Finest, Young Love* and *Young Romance*.

Superman has some good villains, but those do not compare to Batman's. However, Superman has one of the greatest mythos, with all the colorful Superman Family characters, Krypton tie-ins, various kryptonites, the Fortress, the Superboy years, Legion crossovers, JLA membership, movies, memorabilia and huge worldwide recognition.

Starting with *Crisis of Infinite Earths* #1 in 1985, a new era began for DC Comics. They realized that Superman, Batman and Wonder Woman needed to be the foundation on which the strength of the company needed to be built. Wonder Woman is the most important female superhero of all time, with no close second. Demand is relentless for first series *Wonder Woman* #51-220. They were not going to become #1 with titles like *Arak, Arion, Amethyst*. They needed to revitalize their core characters. Add in improvements to their other long-running series, *Flash, Green Lantern, JLA* and JSA in *All-Star Squadron, Swamp Thing, Legion* and you had a formula for success. Demand for JLA and JSA just continues to grow, but especially the JSA appearnces in the original JLA title. *Justice League of America* #100-263 are all in high demand and still undervalued, especially the issues over #200 and the Pérez and JSA issues. *All-Star* #58-74 (esp #58, 69) and *All-Star Squadron* continue to be bestsellers. *DC Special* #29 and *DC Super-Stars* #17 are Red Hot. All pre-1970 comics with the main DC female characters (Batgirl, Batwoman, Catwoman, Supergirl and Wonder Woman) sell 150-300% faster than the ordinary issues that surround them, and many need to show higher premiums. Many fans are now on a quest to own all vintage comics with Neal Adams art. Most seem to have the majority of the interior art issues and are now chasing the more elusive issues with his cover art, thus demand continues to grow for his covers on *Tomahawk*, Love, Sci Fi, horror, humor and other odd titles. *Tomahawk* #116 and *Batman* #227(classic Gothic cover) are the 2 most requested Adams cover and continue to get harder to find, now even in strict FN or better. Nick Cardy covers of the 1960s through mid-1970s continue to appear on want list, especially on *Aquaman*, *Teen Titans* and Romance comics. *Aquaman* #53-56 ('71) should be the same value as #41-49, yet list at 75% lower in the *Guide*, quite a bargain if you can find a dealer who is not sold out. These 1960s strong DC characters were surprisingly slower sellers this year: Aquaman, Atom, Blackhawk, Hawkman, Green Lantern, Metal Men, Plastic Man, Rip Hunter, and Superboy (non-Legion). Note that the *Green Lantern* #76-89 with Green Arrow by Adams are eternal bestsellers, with high grade #76s continuing to bring record prices. These titles remained in moderate to good demand: *Adventure* (Legion and Supergirl), *Capt. Action, Creeper, Deadman, Doom Patrol, Flash, JLA, Legion, Mystery in Space, Spectre, Strange Adventures, Superboy* (with Legion), and Superman (all titles). *Bob Hope* and *Jerry Lewis* are strong sellers, with issues #1-75 being hard to keep in stock in any grades. Many buyers have been picking up a lot more of both *Brave and the Bold*, and *DC Comics Presents*, specifically looking for key crossover issues with the high-demand characters. *DC Special Series* is a hot title, as many fans are intrigued that this is a mostly new-material series of Annual Giants that match other titles and offers a variety of formats (comics, digests and Treasuries) with high grade copies being red hot and getting harder to find (only the *Swamp Thing* reprint issues are slower). #16 is one of the most fondly remembered comics of the entire Bronze Age with that shock ending in the "Death of Jonah Hex" story. Kubert's *Tarzan* was in moderate demand through the year, but was a bestseller in strict VF/NM or better ranges, and demand tagged along for the related titles (*Tarzan Family* and *Korak*). All 100 Page Giants and the "Dollar" Giants of the late 1970s are considered to be Key issues by fans, and they sold about 200% better than surrounding regular-sized issues. Most remained elusive in higher grades. The Kirby 4th World titles were moderate to slow sellers, unless in strict VF/NM or better, with the *Jimmy Olsen* titles easily the toughest.

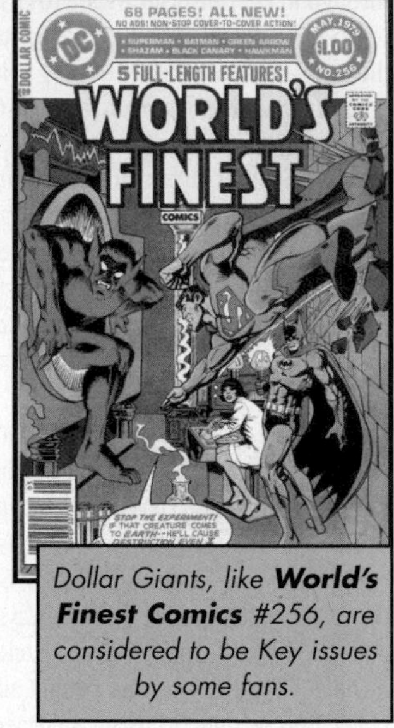

Dollar Giants, like **World's Finest Comics** *#256*, are considered to be Key issues by some fans.

From about 1964-1986, Marvel was #1 in the Marketplace. By the 1990s, DC sales started to rival those of Marvel and by the late 1990s, many outsold Marvel. For us, modern DC back issues have been outselling modern Marvel back issues for over a decade. *New Teen Titans* broke new ground for DC in 1980 and led the way for updating all their main characters. *Titans* established George Pérez as a comics superstar and only the large print runs of the Pérez issues hold back prices from skyrocketing. *New Teen Titans* #1-40 are actually uncommon in strict VF/NM or better, as they have been well handled for 25-28+ years, and 9.4 or better copies should be a good long term investment. 1950s DC Super-hero comics sold moderately well in all grades. 1960s DC Super-hero comics were slower, with the exception of Batman and anything in strict VF or better. 1970-1987 DC Super-hero comics were moderate to good sellers through the year, with strict VF/NM or better copies selling excellent to hot.

This was our best year ever for DC Big 5 War Comics: *All-American Men of War*, *G.I. Combat*, *Our Army at War*, *Our Fighting Forces* and *Star Spangled War Stories*). They sold well in all grades. Just a few years back we had near complete runs of all titles in stock, but we are now sold out of 75% of the 1950s titles. High grade collectors, who actually want to complete these runs, have decided to start buying them at the point at which they start getting scarce in grade, thus 1950s (FN or better), 1960s (FN/VF or better), 1970s (VF or better), 1980s (VF/NM or better) and any books we had that met these standards sold very well at 120-135% *Guide*. *Our Army at War* #83 is the new Holy Grail of DC War, with #81s now slow sellers. *G.I. Combat* #68 and *Our Army at War* #83 are near impossible to find and both bring 200%+ of *Guide* in any grade. The Hot Key issues (at 120-150% *Guide* in all grades) include: *All-American Men of War* #127(#1; 1952), 17,18,21,28,39,42,48,57,63,64,67-69,82,89,112, *G.I. Combat* #44,55-58,66,67, 83,87-100, 108,114,138,144-150, 193, 200-202,288, *Our Army at War* #67, 83-120, 127,128,140,151-155, 158,162-164,168,177, 182,183,186,190,200,203,216,220,229,235-246,269,275, 280-300; *Our Fighting Forces* #41,45,123-137, *Star Spangled War Stories* #131(#1; 1952), 53,64,67,84-100, 134,138-163,181-183,200; ** FA/GD through VG Reading copies of *Our Army at War* #83-260 are in very high demand and usually bring 135-160% *Guide*. The other DC War titles also have a strong following (*All-Out War*, *Blitzkreig*, *Capt. Storm*, *Men of War*, *Weird War*, etc.) *Sgt. Rock* and *Unknown Soldier* comics from the 1980s are among our best selling DC comics in all grades, with stirct VF/NM or better copies flying out the door. The low print *Sgt. Rock* #400-422 are notably scarcer, with most major dealers sold out in all grades. Those issues are overdue for a 50-100% price jump in the *Guide*. *Weird War* #37-124 are also very undervalued and need to see a similar price hike, to encourage more copies to come back onto the market. The Enemy Ace issues of *Unknown Soldier* (#251-up) are in bigger demand, especially in strict VF/NM or better.

1968 through 1980s DC horror comics are still in very high demand and continue to sell well in all grades. (1950-1967 issues are moderate to slow sellers, except in higher grades.) The 1968-1974 issues are especially tough in high grades and many fans are now happy finding a nice VF, or even a FN/VF. Neal Adams and Wrightson issues, including all covers only and one page art issues are all in the highest demand, at 125-150% *Guide*. *Swamp Thing* (1972-1976), although one of DC's all-time most important titles, remain rather common and slow selling. However, the *Swamp Thing* (1982-1996) #20-64 classics by Alan Moore are highly collected and a lot tougher in strict VF/NM or better than one would think. 1975-1983 DC horror issues in strict VF/NM are still among our top sellers. *Dark Mansion* and *Sinister House* continue to have strong demand, especially the scarce early Gothic issues. In the last 12 months we sold nearly 1,000 raw high grade and Manitoba Collection DC comics of all types, in the 9.0 to 9.8 range, mainly from the 1974-1987 era at 125-300% *Guide*, with the affordable 1980s titles being the bestsellers.

DC is perhaps the most prolific comics publisher of all-time (Ian Levine, who completed the entire DC set, says over 32,000 different issues exist) and they had a huge selection of non-superhero genre titles (cartoon, horror, humor and parody, love, SF, sword and sorcery, teenage, toy-related, TV/movie, war, Western, etc.) Fans of these oddball comics typically prefer them in affordable GD-FN grades (which is a good thing, as most would be rare in high grades). This year, we sold an unusual amount of DC cartoon comics, with *Fox and the Crow* and Sheldon Mayer titles being in the most demand. *Binky* and the other teenage titles, as well as all the Romance titles, sold very well to many collectors who were filling in their runs. Many DC Oddball comics sold at 120-135% *Guide*, (mostly in G-FN grades). The Western titles were only moderate sellers, except for the good selling *Bat Lash*, *Jonah Hex*, *All-Star Western* and *Weird Western*. Since we have a big selection, we always manage to sell a lot of *Amazing World of DC*, digests, fanzines, *Fireside Books*, giveaways, magazines, paperbacks, posters, promo items, and Treasuries, to anxious buyers who want them in any grade (most at 120-135 *Guide*).

Dell: Dell comics feature more photo and painted covers than any other publisher. They specialized in licensing popular characters from other media, including newspaper comic strips, movies, TV series, cartoons, kids shows, novels and Pulp series adaptations, radio stars, and Westerns. They captured the essense and images of two generations of popular media, and thus they have many of the bestselling comics of all time. Many of these characters are still popular today and most still have followings around the world, as the nostalgic images continue to resonate in the minds on fans. Larger print runs have kept most titles affordable, with most series relatively easy to complete given an adequate amount of searching, so they remain among the most collectible comics of all time. They are especially popular with the many thousands of collectors around the world, and large amounts back issues continue to disappear into permanent foreign collections each and every year. Price seems to be the most important factor to most of these buyers, thus low grade complete Reading copies (FA and GD) are always in extremely high demand. Next most popular is the mid-grade (VG and FN) presentable copies, for those who want nicer looking collectible copies. Of all the major publishers, Dell might well be the least popular in higher (VF-NM) grades, especially due to the excessively widening price spreads between GD and NM. Most of our hundreds of regular Dell buyers are NOT willing to pay 100%, 200% or even 300% more for a VF copy over a FN copy. If the VF copies were priced at only 50% more than FN copies, then VF would once again become popular. The major exceptions are Carl Barks comics, major Key and first issues, *Tarzan*, *Turok*, the better Hanna-Barbera titles and the most popular TV/movie comics, which have a good following for VF or better copies. Over 90% of Dells we sell are FA or GD-FN copies, and turnover is well above average, as compared to almost all other publishers. I often buy missing issues to restock the gaps in our inventory of our better selling titles at 65-80% *Guide*, if in FA, or GD-FN and then ask 125-150% *Guide* when resellling them. Most FN/VF, VF, VF/NM copies met price resistance and were are slow sellers (with the above listed exceptions) when priced at *Guide* and if I really wanted to move them, I would need to discount them. When *Guide* #38 came out, there were widespread price reductions of 5-15% (perhaps 10% average drops) as compared to *Guide* #37 on most GD-FN Dell comics, when there should have been 20-35% price increases. Ironically, most of the VF-NM Dells had modest price increases. Rather than think negative of this, I have begun to take advantage. I have been buying up hundreds of undervalued Dells in FA and GD-FN from eBay and other dealers to restock my best selling titles. I am still using the *Guide* #37 GD-FN prices and still adding premiums to those prices. Thus I was able to get many complete runs back in stock. Many of my regular buyers were very happy to see my selection get much better and I found that I managed to sell over 15 near complete runs of titles with 50 or more issues to collectors who were ecstatic to see them all in one place at one time. In addition, I also sold many complete smaller runs, with affordable FA/GD through GD/VG copies by far the most popular (at 135%-165% *Guide*, with no resistance). Collectors should take advantage of the low prices on Reading copies while they can. Many major dealer inventories that once had near complete selections of the many long runs are quickly getting depleted, and selections are dropping to 10-35% of all existing issues. This year we found that Western comics were the most requested, followed by *Tarzan*, TV comics, *Turok*, *Four Colors* and Cartoon titles.

Gold Key (Non-Disney): Demand for high grade copies was up for the titles that investors judged as high demand items with good "Long Term Investment Potential." When one compares equivalent prices to Marvel comics of the same vintage, some of these books seem incredibly low. When you factor in that most are 10-100 times scarcer in high grade, they seem even more attractive. Raw copies of these titles sold well at 125-140% *Guide* for VF, VF+ and VF/NM copies; and at 150-160% *Guide* for 9.2 copies: *Boris Karloff*, *Dark Shadows*, *Dr. Solar*, *Grimm's Ghost*, Hanna-Barbera (all #1 and key issues), *Korak*, *John Carter*, *Magnus Robot Fighter*, *M.A.R.S. Patrol*, *Mighty Samson*, *Munsters*, *Occult Files of Dr. Spector*, *Phantom*, *Ripley's Believe it or Not*, *Scooby Doo*, *Space Family Robinson*, *Spine Tingling Tales*, *Star Trek* #1-10, *Tarzan*, *Turok*, *Twilight Zone* and *Wild Wild West*. Whitman variants of the Gold Key comics (11/1971 through 3/1980) continue to bring 125-200% of GK issue values. Canadian newsstand variant cover price issues (5-8/1968, and 4/1972-4/1973 sell at 125-150% *Guide*). Most of the other GK titles sell moderately well in VF, VF+ and VF/NM and the prices are mostly pretty accurate in the *Guide*. Since most are scarce in these grades, we usually ask and get 110-120% *Guide* for them. Except for about 5% of the different existing issues that hit the marketplace as high grade File copies, most Gold Keys remain scarce in even strict VF or better.

Despite that fact that high grade collectors hunted the above titles, the majority (80%+) of our Gold Key sales are for afforable copies in the GD-FN condition ranges. Most are currently undervalued in these grades and all the uncommon to scarce issues tend to be sold out in most dealer inventories. Many are so low that I am able to pay 75-100% *Guide* to restock Reading copies and have found that many buyers are more than willing to pay 150-200% *Guide* in these grades. For example, many of the Cartoon title series can be extremely challenging to complete, and since most only sell for $2-$5, fans try their best to avoid having to buy them on eBay and have to add $5-7 postage for *each* single comic. Low *Guide* values for most Uncommon to Scarce that price out at under $7 are often irrelevant to collectors who need them, and sellers often have a hard time stocking them without extra efforts. Healthy premiums are easily justifiable, to once again make these titles available to our many happy buyers. They are more than happy to pay $3 for a book that lists at $2, or $5 for one that lists at $3, thus we sell literally thousands of comics like this. In fact, buyer orders with 200-600 comics in one shipment are getting more and more common for us. All the titles above also sold extremely well in lower grades.

The next most popular sellers were most of the Hanna-Barbera titles and TV-related titles. Since we always have in stock 35,000+ Gold Key comics, about 95% of all they ever published, we continue to sell many hundreds of other misc. Cartoon comics too, with many fans always telling us they are not able to complete all these titles with any other dealers.

Harvey: Investors have decided that high grade pre-1975 Harveys are very desirable (whereas cartoon comics from Archie, Dell, GK, etc., are much less coveted) and record prices continue to be set on CGC-graded copies. Unfortuantely, other than the 1980s File Copies find, not a lot of high grade copies survived. Most 1950s Harveys in the Marketplace are in in the FA/GD through GD/VG condition range, with most 1960s in VG average, 1970-1985 in VG/FN average and 1986-1993 in FN/VF average. The 1988-1994 Harvey comics including Hanna-Barbera and other Harvey Cartoon titles, all had low print runs (#1-5= VF $4-$8 ea; scarcer #6-up issues = VF $6-10 ea.) Scooby-Doo is hot from all publishers (Harvey issues sell at 200% *Guide*.) It is commonplace for collectors to buy 25-100 or more comics at a time.

1950s and 1960s Harvey Cartoon comics are among our bestsellers in any grade, with 1970s through 1990s issues also good solid sellers. As per usual, our biggest problem is trying to restock them once sold. About 95% of the issues we sell are graded in the FA/GD through FN/VF condition ranges. Most pre-1976 issues are undervalued in *Guide* in all grades, but especially in the GD-FN ranges. Values of uncommon and scarce copies that *Guide* at under $10 in GD-FN are often so low they are irrelevant. To restock many of these issues sold out in our inventory, I have resorted to paying 75-100% *Guide* for GD-FN copies and buying from other dealers, pricing them at the required 150-200% *Guide* when necessary. Many of my efforts have been well rewarded, with a good number of orders for 50-100 comics at a time from happy collectors. Richie Rich, Sad Sack and Casper issues from the 1977-1984 period are the most plentiful Cartoon Harveys in the Marketplace. Virtually everything else is uncommon to scarce.

© Paramount

1950s and 1960s Harvey Cartoon comics are among the bestsellers in any grade. **(Casper, the Friendly Ghost** *#8 shown)*

We have in stock about 20,000 Richie Rich comics and about 10,000 other assorted Harvey comics. I have so many Richie Rich comics, as there was a boom in Richie collecting in the 1974-1984 period. Richie Rich is one of the very few characters to boast having over 50 titles (including digests) and has become Harvey's most important character. Casper originally was Harvey's most important character and is still a very highly collected character. There were a lot of Sad Sack comics published and there are many collectors, yet prices lag far behind the values of Richie and Casper, most remaining quite undervalued.

Low Grade vs. High Grade comics: High grade comics continue to break records and dominate the headlines in our hobby. As per usual I sold a lot of "Investment Grade" comics, mainly from the Manitoba Collecton. Since my biggest selection of high grade is in the 1976-1986 era, those are the books that flew out the door in large numbers to collectors. Almost all were Raw (non-CGC Graded) copies, yet due to my strict grading, many of my 9.0 to 9.8 comics sold for 125% to 400% of *Guide* with almost NO resistance. There is a HUGE segment of the Marketplace looking to fill in runs of 1976-1986 comics with values in the $2 to $20 price range (by *Guide* NM- 9.2 prices). These "Low End" priced comics normally do NOT show up in large numbers graded by CGC. Yet, many collectors feel that these books are still very undervalued and want to scoop them up while still affordable. Usually, it is easier for a $5 to rise to $20 in the *Guide*, than for a $50 comic to rise to $200, thus greater percentage increases are predicted for these 23-33 year old comics.

The great majority of the strong demand for high grade is for Marvel and DC Superhero comics, which are the most plentiful of all comics in the post-1964 era. Most 1966-1970 Marvel Superhero comics have have 50-100 graded 9.0 or better at CGC, with perhaps 500-2000 copies existing (including Raw examples) in VF or better. But, comics from the other misc. major publishers of the era (ACG, Archie, Classics, Charlton, comic digests, comic magazines, Dell, Gold Key, Harvey, oddball Golden Age and Silver Age, etc.) exist in quantities of perhaps 1% to 10% of the Marvels from said era. Many oddball comics of the era have only 1-10 copies graded by CGC in 9.0 or better. In addition, misc. major publishers exist in much smaller quantities in all grades, as compared to Marvel. Logic would seem to dictate that the oddball comics should bring very high premiums, but the opposite is the case. The high grade and CGC Marvel superhero comics bring high premiums, but the scarce-to-rare Oddball comics bring small premiums. The reason is supply and demand. There are probably 100 times as many buyers for *Avengers* #57 in 9.4 as there are for *Time Tunnel* #1 in same grade.

Our turnover rate is very high for 9.0 and better Marvel and DC Superhero comics of the 1960-1986 era. We have a large inventory of the same in GD to VF condition ranges, as do hundreds of other dealers worldwide, thus there is heavy competition and a GLUT on the Market. Many dealers resort to discounting and sales on these. This has caused the large price spread in the *Guide* between GD to NM-. Normally I have no problem getting the current *Guide* prices on most of these comics, as GD-FN comics are now real bargains in most cases. But, on comic where I am overstocked with excess copies, I do sometimes discount at 25-60% Off *Guide*, just as everyone else does.

I believe many of the Key issues and lesser Keys are too low in the *Guide* in GD-FN Grades, and thus are getting hard to keep in stock and harder yet to re-stock. To streamline prices, the *Guide* has dropped premiums on GD-FN copies of many minor Keys. For example, *World's Finest* #241-246 are all priced at $2-6 in G-FN, but #241-243 are $8-12 in VF-NM, while #244-246 are $11-$20 in VF-NM. My 38 years of experience show that this is a big mistake, as demand does not drop for minor Keys issues, just because they are in lower grades. The opposite is in fact true. Demand increases as the Keys and minor Keys always sell faster.

There is now a big shortage of many Key issues in GD-FN. These easily bring 125%-200% *Guide* in G-FN: *All-Star*

Comics #58, 69, *All-Star Western* #10, *Amazing Adventures* #11, *Amazing Spider-Man* #121, 122, 129, *Avengers* #57, 100, *Batman* by Neal Adams, *Conan* #1,3, *Dark Mansion* #1-4, DC 100 Pagers (many), *Deadly Hands* #28, *Defenders* #1, *Detective* by Neal Adams, *Fantastic Four* #112, *Ghost Rider* #1-5, *Gothic Romances* #1, *Green Lantern* #76, *Incredible Hulk* #180, 181, *Iron Fist* #14, *Iron Man* #1, 55, *Marvel Spotlight* #5, *My Love* #1-39, *Our Army at War* #83-200, *Our Love Story* #1-38, *Phantom Stranger* #1-4, *Savage Sword* #1, *Silver Surfer* #1,4, *Tomb of Dracula* #1-10, *Weird War* #1-5, *Wonder Woman* #100-200 and many others. A small "cottage industry" has started of basement dealers buying up these affordable GD-FN copies of Key issues from bigger dealers at full *Guide* and re-selling them at 150%-250% *Guide*, often loosening the graded condition, for great profits.

An anomaly has occured in the *Guide*, due to the large price spread in the *Guide* between GD and NM-. The misc. publishers comics and all TNC (traditionally non-collected) comics (cartoon, crime, humor, jungle, love, movie, SF, teen, TV, war, etc), have had the wide price-to-condition spreads that correctly apply to superhero comics, also creep into these uncommon to scarcer comics. Unfortunately, the reality of the marketplace is that there is big demand for affordable GD-FN copies and with many too cheap in low grades. The great majority of dealer inventories of these comics are typically GD-FN condition copies. For Marvel and DC Superhero comics, many dealers have deep near complete runs in many grades, but this is certainly not the case for Oddball comics. In fact collectors have to look far and wide to fill in runs of many series, such as *Nancy*, *Red Ryder*, *Millie the Model*, *Betty & Veronica*, *Wild Western* and many many others. Most sellers have selections of only 5%-25% of all issues of such series. Demand in affordable grades is often bigger than supply. Thus when I go out of my way to re-stock such series (at high cost), I find no problem and no resistance to selling at over *Guide* prices.

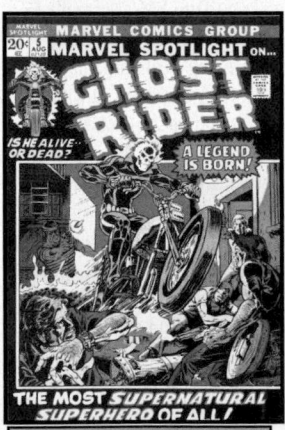

There is a big shortage in Key issues like **Marvel Spotlight** #5.

For us, for the last 39 years and still today, there is lower demand for VF-NM copies on most of these titles and this is the area in which I find price resistance. Strangely enough, *Guide* #38 chose to raise VF-NM prices and drop thousands of GD-FN prices on vintage comics. My turnover rate for oddball comics is much much higher than the common Marvel and DC superhero comics. Naturally if a dealer specializes in Marvel Comics and has a small selection of a hundred or fewer Harvey comics, they are not going to sell well for them. But dealers who do specialize in comics like Archies, Dell, GK, and Harvey, and have a great selection, will find they do very well and have a great turnover rate. As I attempt to fill out client wantlists (something I do often), I sometimes check 20 or more dealer inventories and would gladly pay 100% *Guide* to buy for resale, but often end up filling in only 10-35% of these extensive want lists, as almost everybody is sold out. It was strange to seem widespread price drops in *Guide* #38 for GD-FN comics that actually needed significant price increases. The effect is that the supply of vintage oddball comics will become even smaller and they will be even more difficult to find in affordable conditions. Although about 30% of my entire sales revenue in a year is higher graded comics, still the great majority (perhaps 90%) of the sheer volume of back issues that I ship out throughout the year are ordinary GD-FN comics, as they are "the bread and butter" backbone of my entire market. Here is a quick random list of great selling back issues that should have gone up in price, yet dropped in the last *Guide*: *Archie Comics* #81-93, 95-99 (14.3% price drop), *Batman* #182 Giant Joker-c/s (10%), *Batman* #222 Beatles-c/s (16.6%), *Brave and the Bold* #34 - 1st SA Hawkman (6%), *Doctor Solar* (GK) #1 (14.3%), *Iron Man* #1 (8.5%), *John Wayne Adventure Comics* #31 Williamson/ Frazetta (5%), *Journey into Mystery* #41-44,46,48 (9.5%), *Looney Tunes* #20-25 (8.5%), *MAD* magazine #71-75, 77-80 (16.7%), *Magnus Robot Fighter* (GK) #1 (12%), *Maverick* FC #892 (15.5%), *Munsters* #1 (15%), *Mystery in Space* #5 (8.3%), *Our Army at War* (Sgt. Rock) #121-125,130-133,135-139,141-150 (10%), *Red Ryder* #11-20 (12.5%), *Space Family Robinson* (GK) #1 (12.5%), *Superman* #150 (9.1%), *Tarzan* (Dell) #6-10 (10.4%) and *Turok* (Dell) #3 (13%).

Proper grading is still a big problem within our hobby. Most small shops, flea market dealers, eBay sellers and convention sellers routinely price (for example) VF 8.0 comics at NM-, 9.2 prices, many actually believing they have actual 9.2 copies, while other do not actually grade the items at all and leave it to the buyers to figure out. I would estimate, it is likely that over 80% of the raw comics sold by dealers would not attain the grade described if the item where submitted to CGC. Similarily, I see many sellers grade an item VF, when the actual strict grade would be FN, so naturally, educated buyers would avoid these as that would make many such items price out at 200% *Guide* in actual strict grade. When this type of seller complains that the items are not selling and offers a 25% discount, he often finds collectors who only buy discounted items, but sadly the misinformed buyer is still paying 50% over *Guide* as if he bought the item from a strict grading seller who graded it FN and sold it at *Guide*. The average inexpensive 1980s comic sitting in dealer inventories would grade out strictly to be in the FN/VF to VF range, but sellers routinely grade them as NM, and because they are low priced, most buyers are not really concerned if they receive an actual NM. The hard facts are, that only about 10% of these 1980s comics would grade out a strict VF/NM or better, if submitted to CGC. Most fans do not recall that in the late 1990s, the *Guide* once stereotypically stated that all 1970s (Bronze Age) comics are *common* in Near Mint and thus have low values, yet about a dozen years later, we certainly know that is not true. In fact, for those that do not bother to hand-select their own brand new comics off the store shelves and just grab the top copy, you should know that the average new comic that has had minor handling would grade out as a strict 9.0 to 9.2 (NOT 9.4 to 9.8 as many fans assume). In fact, probably under 2% of 1970s comics would grade a strict 9.4 or better.

Now that Bronze Age prices are getting increasingly higher, it seems a sure thing to predict that Copper Age comics are due next for big price hikes in scarcer high grades. Collectors need to educate themselves, to see what strictly graded 8.0, 9.0 and 9.4 comics actually look like, and the best way to be sure is to closely examine a few CGC copies of each different grade.

Marvel Comics: For over 40 years, Marvel comics have formed the backbone of the entire vintage comics industry, and they are a substantial part of most dealers' inventories, with the exception of dealers who deal mainly in Silver and Golden Age comics. There are over 1,000 comic shops, plus probably over 2,000 mail order and eBay dealers, ranging in size from small to large. I estimate that 90% of these dealers make most of their back issue money from vintage Marvel comics, mainly those of the 1961-1986 era. (DC comics from 1987 to the present sell perhaps equally well, if not better than Marvel in this Modern era.) In the 1960s, Marvel comics started and ruled the market. The continuous stream of Marvel movies continues to fuel demand for these classic back issues. Among the characters slated for the big screen are Luke Cage, the Avengers, Ant-Man, and Captain America. All will be *hot* in back issue sales in near future. The majority of 1961-1975 Marvels are in Good through Fine conditions in most dealer inventories (with most 1976-1986 in VG-VF average). Marvels are by far the most collected comics in high grades, and they also boast the most slabbed comics by CGC. Luckily 1,000-5,000+ copies each exist for most 1960s Marvels, with perhaps 5K-50K Marvels each existing from 1970s issues, as they are the most hoarded comics of the era. There are usually plenty of copies to meet most demand on the market. However, when everyone suddenly wants higher graded copies (viewed as better investments), suddenly supply is low on anything that would grade among the 1-10% best existing copies. Surely this trend will continue and perhaps strenghten even more as time goes on. CGC has brought out most of the best existing copies over the last 8+ years or so, and most have sold, returning to private collections. There seems to be a "Lull" in new high grade vintage Marvel finds and a bit of a shortage as compared to demand, thus many collectors have been forced to lower their minimum grade requirements. 1961-1964 Marvel Superhero comics were still top sellers in every grade. 1965-1969 era Marvels sold best in FA/GD-VG and VF or better. The smaller print run 1970-1974 era Marvels were our top sellers in all grades and are in especially huge demand in strict VF/NM or better. The 1975-1980 era comics were in high demand, especially in VF or better. The 1981-1987 late Bronze to Copper Age comics were in *very high* demand in strict VF/NM 9.0 or better grades, but only in moderate demand in low to middle grades. 1988-1995 Marvels were the slowest sellers, but when they did sell, condition was not important. 1996-2008 Marvels had smaller print runs and continue to boast moderate to semi-hot demand, with condition typically not important and many issues being hard to restock once sold. Most dealer inventories have far less copies per issue in stock for 1996-2008 Marvels, as compared to the much more common 1976-1995 issues. Many popular modern Marvels have average print runs under 40,000 copies, as compared to 200,000+ copies for 1970s print runs. Many modern Marvels have a good resale value as sets on eBay and many should be a good long term investment.

All good Bronze Age Key issues were selling in all grades, with shortages of affordable GD-FN copies becoming a lot more common, as many are undervalued in the *Guide*. Bronze Age Keys in G-FN and 9.2 brought 135-175% *Guide*; VF through VF/NM copies brought 120-135% *Guide*. Many GD-FN Key issues now bring much higher premiums than semi-high grade (VF,VF+,VF/NM copies). We sold about 1500+ Raw Bronze and Copper Age issues in 9.0 through 9.8 (mostly from the "Manitoba" collection) at 120-300%+ of *Guide*, with almost no resistance and must again report that high grade 1980-1987 Marvels continue to be in big demand. As always, many collectors come to us for our big selection of Marvel fanzines, giveaway/promo items, memorabilia, posters, Slurpee cups, calendars, portfolios, etc. For these items, condition is usually not important. Just locating these collectibles at all seems to be the hardest task. Many items sell as fast as I can find them.

Of special note is that demand has increased twofold average for these still undervalued 1970s and 1980s era comics in strict VF/NM or better Investment grades: *Avengers* #101-250, *Capt. America* #131-300, *Conan the Barbarian* #25-200, *Incredible Hulk* #140-300, *Iron Man* #21-200, *Jungle Action* #5-23, *Luke Cage* #1-50, *Marvel Team-Up* #21-150, *Marvel Two-in-One* #1-100 and *Thor* #191-350.

We sold a lot of Oddball comics and other format items, mainly because of our giant selection, including: cartoon, humor and parody, TV/movie, romance, teenage, toy-related, TV, war, Western, etc., at 125-200% *Guide*, with G-FN the most requested. *Night Nurse* seems extra tough to keep in stock, even at 150% *Guide*. Digests, Treasuries, paperbacks and magazines sold in all Grades, but with G-FN copies selling best (at 125-175% *Guide*). *My Love* and *Our Love Story* easily bring 50% over *Guide* in all grades, as many collectors are filling in runs and almost all dealers are sold out. The 1970s Atlas horror reprint titles (*Beware*, *Chamber of Chills*, *Vault of Evil*, etc.) were in huge demand in all grades, with demand over double supply, thus we sold out of about 20% of the numbers for the first time ever. I located only one *Gothic Tales of Love* (#1) in any grade this year, and sold it swiftly for $725.00 (CGC 9.0). The shortage of *Planet of the Apes* mags #21-29 continues, with all bringing

150% *Guide* in any grade (#29 brings 200% *Guide*). All Moebius comics and especially graphic novels are blazing hot, with almost every mail order and internet dealer in North America sold out, as the overseas collectors consider them some of the greatest comics of all time. Condition is not important on Moebius items and most bring 200-500% *Guide* in any grade. We sold *Moebius* (Epic GN 1987) #5 in near FN for $20; #7 in VF/NM for $75; #8 in FN+ for $35; *Lieutenant Blueberry* #2 *Steelfingers* (Epic GN) in VG/FN for $44. Treasuries and Marvel Horror Mags were top sellers, with notable shortages of Reading copies (GD-FN, 9.2=135-165% *Guide*; VF-VF/NM=120-135% *Guide*). The 1960s Marvel paperbacks are scarce in higher grades and sold moderately well. Average prices: VF/NM=$50; VF=$36; FN=$24; VG=$16; G=$8. 1976-1986 Marvel paperbacks average prices: VF/NM=$20; VF=$15; FN=$10; VG=$7; G=$4, with the #1-11 Novel Series at 150%+ higher.

Savage Sword of Conan is an eternal bestseller in all grades, with high grade collectors mainly after #1-100. *Savage Sword* #200-235 are low print and bring 150-200% *Guide* and the scarce #235 at 400% *Guide*. *Transformers* #71-80 and *G.I. Joe* #150-155 are very hard to stock and bring 150-200% *Guide*. *Ghost Rider* #93 (2/98) is an instant seller at $25 for VF or better. Many more high numbered comics and especially LAST issues of the 1990s had lower print runs. Many were already scarcer, and I expect they will gain value in the years to come as collectors find this to be true. These include: *Akira* #31-38, *Amazing Spider-Man* #421-441, *Avengers* #350-402, *Conan* #250-275, *Conan the King* #50-55, *Conan Saga* #90-96, *Conan* (1996-2000 titles), *Daredevil* #350-380; *Fantastic Four* #381-416, *Ghost Rider* #61-93, *Iron Man* #300-332; *Savage Sword* #200-235, *Thor* #460-502 and *What If* #81-114.

1970s and '80s *Electric Company* magazines are in bigger demand than supply, due to the *Spidey Super-Stories* comic strips, with #1-40 and #100 up being the scarcest issues. Average Retail: VF/NM=$16; VF=$12; FN=$9; VG=$6. A few notable sales: *Film International* (1975 Marvel Mag) #1-4 (VG/FN $30 each); *Photo News Feature* (1975 Marvel Mag) #1 (Hitler app.; VF $30); #2 (FDR; VF $24); *You Don't Say* (1973 Marvel Mag) #1 (VF $79); many 1970s Adult Cartoon mags (*Best Cartoons*; *Popular Cartoons*, etc.; with Pussycat-s in VG average for $15 ea; NO Pussycat in VG = $10 ea.). The Marvel Western and War titles were moderate to slow sellers in GD-VF, but have picked up in demand for the scarce VF/NM or better copies. The Marvel Anti-Hero Horror titles (*Death*, *Dracula*, *Frankenstein*, *Ghost Rider*, *Man-Thing*, *Morbius*, *Mummy*, *Scarecrow*, *Satana*, *Werewolf*, *Zombie*) in both color comics and B&W mags are all still top sellers (with all Key issues being Red-Hot) in all grades, with a lower supply than demand on high grade copies.

Treasury Editions: We usually manage to keep about 95% of all the large oversized Treasury format comics in stock at all times, where most of our competing sellers are typically 50-90% sold out. Thus they are always strong sellers for us and there are always a few issues we need to scramble to restock.

The rarest issues (bringing 200%+ *Guide*) include: *Rudolph* #NN(1972), *Christmas and Archie*, *Superman vs. Muhammad Ali* (Whitman variant). Also rare (bringing 150% *Guide*) is *Golden Picture Story Book* (1961) ST#1-4 and *Famous First Edition* (Silver Stone Graphics Pub) C-61 S&N Signature Edition. The scarce titles (bringing 150-175% *Guide*) include: *Annie*, *G.I. Joe*, F*untastic World of Hanna-Barbera* #1-3, *Smurfs*, *Star Wars* #3, *Empire Strikes Back*, *Modern Promotions* (1972/73; *Beetle Bailey*, *Flash Gordon*, *Katzenjammer Kids*, *Mandrake*) and *Walt Disney Paint Book* series (six different circa 1975). *Superman vs. Muhammad Ali* is by far the all-time bestseller treasury (we had 200 copies in 2001 and are now down to under 25 copies.) Rounding out the Top Six Bestsellers are: *Superman vs. Spider-Man* #1, *Captain America's Bicentennial Battles* (Kirby/Smith-a), *DC Special Series* #27(Batman vs. Hulk), C-54 (Superman vs. Wonder Woman), and C-55 (Legion marriage issue). All Batman and Spider-Man Treasuries are always in strong demand. Most of the DC and Marvel Treasuries with new material are in high demand and are still undervalued, as they continue to get scarcer. Most buyers are happy with middle grade VG through VF copies.

Traditionally, Treasuries never had plastic bags readily availiable for protection. Factor in the cumbersome size and format, with too much handling. Add to this the fact that they have stiff cardboard covers that easily show a lot of stress marks when handled. And finally take note that handling easily causes rubbing wear and scuffing to the originally glossy covers. It readily becomes obvious why Treasuries are now scarce in strict VF/NM 9.0 or better grades. We again sold about 50+ high grade and Manitoba collection copies in 9.0-9.6 range copies (at 125-300% *Guide*).

Variants & Premium Editions: The Marvel 30¢ and 35¢ variants are now among the hottest of all Bronze Age comics. The 30¢ variants sell at 350% the price of the regular 25¢ editions at minimum, and up to 1000% more. The 35¢ variants sell at 700% the price of the regular 30¢ editions at minimum, and up to 2000% more. The rare Western, war, horror and reprint title variants sell at even higher prices in any grade, as only a handful of each exist (VG-FN copies of 30¢ variants $50-$200; and 35¢ variants in the $100-$800 range.)

1979 Marvel Direct Market editions are often mistakenly sold as "Whitman Variants of Marvel" comics. Only a few Treasuries were actual Whitman printings. Otherwise only the plastic bags were actually "Whitman". (See *Guide* #36 on page 125 for full details, or email me.) Early Marvel Direct Market editions can be identified with a Black Diamond on cover, or with no "cc" on cover, or with no UPC or obscured UPC Codes, or blank white UPC Codes. 1977 Marvel Direct Market editions sell at 120-150% *Guide* to variant collectors. For the 2 months 7/1978 and 3-4/1979, only newsstand editions were published, (exceptions are *Micronauts* and *Shogun Warriors*, often mistaken as reprints, but actually just Direct first printings). These are only on the ground floor as collectibles, as a lot is not yet known or documented.

This was again another record year for sales of the Canadian newsstand cover price variant editions. They are not listed in the *Guide*, because it involves perhaps over 5,000 comics. Character completionists and variant collectors alike have been very actively seeking these out and we are starting to sell out on about 20% of existing issues. We sell these variants at 150-200% *Guide* as most of these comics were bought by the general public and not collectors. Most existing copies, perhaps 90%, are in lower grades (GD through FN), with FN/VF to VF copies being uncommon, VF+ to VF/NM copies are scarce, and NM- or better copies being rare. VF/NM copies occasionally sell at auction for 300-500% of *Guide*. Sometimes these are sold on eBay as "Rare Variants" by sellers who do not know what they are and buyers that do not know either, thus occasionally have been known to pay 10-50 times *Guide*, when they should not have paid over 2 times. Only a handful of these variants have even been graded by CGC, perhaps because they have not yet realized some of them are variants yet. They are about 50-100 times scarcer than U.S. Direct Market edition Printings. Dates for Canadian newsstand cover price variants existing include: Archie comics and digests (1/1984-12/1997), Charlton (2/1983-8/1984), DC (all Newsstand comics, magazines and digests from 10/1982-9/1988), Dell (random 1960-1962, plus back cover variants and assorted 1950s cover price variants, as well as regular issues with 15¢ covers and Giants with 30¢ covers), Gold Key (5-8/1968, and 4/1972-4/1973), Harvey (1960s Giants with 35¢ cover prices), *Mad* (some 1964 and 7/1978-7/1979), Marvel (all Newsstand comics, magazines and digests from 10/1982-8/1986), Warren (3/1977-3/1983), Whitman (mainly early 1981, and 1983-1984). The most requested issues have been comics that feature Spider-Man. I have so far sold 4 near complete sets. Over 300 different Spider-Man related comics exist in the period.

Walt Disney: There has been a notable increase in demand for strict VF or better pre-1976 titles. Pre-1966 Carl Barks comics in VF/NM or better are hot, especially if CGC graded, especially *Four Colors* and 1940s issues, with even 9.0 copies bringing 400-800% of *Guide*. I had several high grade collectors purchase quantities of VF or better Oddball Cartoon titles, focusing on titles that did not see much reprints, including: *Beagle Boys*, *Chip 'N Dale*, *Mickey Mouse*, *Scamp*, *Super Goof*, *Winnie the Pooh* (VF-VF/NM= 125% *Guide*; 9.2=150% *Guide*; 9.4=200% *Guide*).

1950s and older issues were in strong demand, in all grades. 1951-1970s issues were all steady sellers and continue to grow stronger, and they are especially popular to our European customers, with over 35% of our sales headed overseas. Reading copies were very popular, as many readers tried to complete their sets. When Gold Key changes to Whitman in 1980, the Pre-Pack only issues become an obstacle to many fans trying to complete collections, but I have managed to keep most of these in stock and our clients are always greatful. Strangely, most of the inexpensive 1986-1995 Gladstone and Disney Pub comics are slow sellers, even though they are loaded with great content. I suppose most have been reprinted too many times, but they are loaded with great new Don Rosa art, plus English reprints of foreign Disneys not seen over here before. The Don Rosa Classic "Life and Times of Scrooge McDuck" issues serialized in *Uncle Scrooge* #285-296 are in high demand and getting hard to find. It is with these issues that demand for modern Disneys once again gets strong. The high cover priced *Uncle Scrooge* #309-318 and *WDC&S* #601-633 had smaller print runs and are now sold out with most back issue dealers, some already bring high premiums on eBay. *Uncle Scrooge* #309, 311-320= $15-20 ea; #310 (scarce) = $50+. Two recent eBay sales of #310 were at $119 and $179. The majority of 1995-2008 Walt Disney comics are uncommon to scarce (bringing 150-400% *Guide*). All of the better live action TV and movie classic comics showed a resurgence in demand, with Nature and Science titles very slow. Most Dell *Four Color* Disneys were popular sellers, except a few that were reprinted too often by Gold Key. We sold 3-5 copies each of the unusual *Walt Disney Paint Books Series* (circa 1975, Treasury-sized) to curious collectors who had never heard of or seen them before.

Walt Disney's
Donald Duck
in
"Sheriff of Bullet Valley"

Pre-1966 Carl Barks comics in VF/NM or better are hot. (**Donald Duck Four Color** #199 shown)

Warren, Skywald & Misc. Horror Comic Mags: Demand for Warren mags has been strong and still growing for over 8 years, with no end in sight. The more afforable GD-FN copies are by far the most requested, and we sold over 1500 of them this year. On about 15% of the issues, we have nothing left in stock in less than FN/VF Grades, especially on *Vampirella* #91-112 and *Creepy/Eerie* #35-70 and #130 up. On most GD and VG Warrens that *Guide* under $10, we ask and get 135-150% of *Guide*. For a client, I managed to put together complete sets of *Creepy*, *Eerie* and *Vampirella* in GD/VG average conditions and sold thus at over *Guide* for the VG prices as sets (approx. 150% *Guide*). This was actually quite a difficult task, because each set has about a dozen scarcer issues, like *Eerie* #17, *Creepy* #32 and *Vampi* #112, and many issues were hard to restock as Reading copies. About 70% of all our Warren sales is for these 3 strong titles, about 10% of sales are for *Famous Monsters*, with the remaining 20% for the other 25-plus titles. There are quite a few Warren completionists out to get everything, but there are quite a number of scarce to rare issues that make it very difficult quest. *Blazing Combat* #1 and the Anthology are listed below wholesale in the *Guide*. They are instant sellers: G-FN=400%

Guide; 8.0-9.2=200% *Guide*. *Eerie* #17 is on everyone's want list and sells at 400% of *Guide* in any grade.

On the flip side, Warren mags are also highly collectible in high grades, especially in VF/NM or better. But since most collectors of high grade actually want to be able to complete their sets, most have decided to buy VF or better copies (often on my recommendation), and thus the complete sets become attainable. It should be noted than many Warrens still have only 2-10 copies so far graded. Thus, so far, CGC 9.4 sets of *Creepy*, *Eerie* and *Vampirella* are virtually unattainable. We sold a about 200 high grade and Manitoba Collection copies of Warren mags from the 1975-1983 era (VF/NM to NM+ copies at 125-300% *Guide*).

Skywald magazines like *Nightmare*, *Psycho* and *Scream* are not as popular as Warren, but the demand is typically double that of supply, so our turnover is always high. These are excellent mags, and those who have not looked closely at them should take another look to see what they are missing. The "Horror-Mood" issues, Werewolf, Vampires/Dracula, Heap, Frankenstein, Nosferatu, Lady Satan, Human Gargoyles, Lovecraft, Poe, decapitatation issues, Al Hewetson stories and many others are fondly remembers by fans. There was art by Wrightson, Boris Vallejo, Segrelles, Everett, Jeff Jones, Bruce Jones, Kaluta, Marcos, John Byrne and others. The "Horror-Mood" issues are said to be credited as an inspiration to Stephen King. They are very hard to restock once sold, with VF or better copies especially difficult, thus I usually buy them at 65-80% *Guide* and resell them at 140-160% *Guide*. Strict graded VF/NM or better copies are very hard to find. When I find them, I sell them instantly at 9.0=150% *Guide*; 9.2=165%; 9.4=225% *Guide*.

The Horror comic mags published by Eerie Pub, Modern Day, and Stanley are in very high demand in GD-FN, especially in lowest graded Reading copies. About 75% of the copies we get in stock in FA/GD through VG sell within just a few weeks, and usually most of what we have in stock is in about FN/VF to VF average. The lurid violence and gore on the covers and inside made them very memorable to many fans. Most of the titles have scarcer issues, and thus most of the sets are quite difficult to complete. Examples in FN/VF, VF and VF+ are all slow sellers, as most collectors want either Reading copies, or Investment copies. Strict graded VF/NM copies are more popular, with 9.2-9.4 copies in better demand. We sell them at these rates: GD-FN=140-160%; FN/VF, VF,VF+=100-115%; VF/NM=120-130%; 9.2=150%. *Weird Vampire Tales* and *Terrors of Dracula* list the publisher as Modern Day, which is a pseudonym for Eerie Pun and they are perhaps their scarcest titles and among our fastest sellers. The Stanley Pub mags have a lot of Pre-Code Horror reprints and are about 50% scarcer than Eerie Pub mags, thus are also in higher demand.

Whitman Comics: There exists six scarce Whitman Error variant cover price editions (all dated 1/1981 with incorrect 40 Cent cover prices: *Bugs Bunny* #223, *Donald Duck* #225, *Little Lulu* #262, *Pink Panther* #78, *Super Goof* #63 and *Walt Disney's Comics and Stories* #484), all existing with more common correctly priced copies bearing 50¢ cover prices. The 40¢ variants are worth about double the value of the corrected editions. All other 1/1981 Whitmans carry the 50¢ cover prices. The Pre-Pack only Whitman comics from 8-12/1980 are all scarce and now have a large following of collectors and a few completionists (they sell at 150-400% *Guide*). The No-Date, no Date Code Whitman comics of 1983-1984 issues are uncommon and sell well at 135-200% *Guide*. These variants make it tough on many collectors attempting to finish these many series that start as Gold Key and end up as Whitmans. Now that prices have risen, they are much more readily availiable than when they were mysteriously scarce and not yet listed as thus in the *Guide*. Uncommon to scarce Whitman variant editions exist for about 50% of all the Gold Keys published from 11/1971 through 2/1980. Not yet catalogued in the *Guide*, they sell for 125-200% of Gold Key issue values. Marvel Whitman variants *do not* exist (see my Variant report).

© Skywald

Demand is typically double that of supply for magazines like ***Psycho****. (#2 shown)*

Approximately 160 different Whitman Variants of DC comics were published in the 3/1978 - 8/1980 time period, with most being 20 to 50 times scarcer than standard DC printings. This was our best year ever for these Variants, as we sold almost 50% of all the issues we had in stock in any grades that were availiable. Previously collectors wanted VF or better, then FN or better, but now have begun to buy whatever they can find, as copies are disappearing from the market in most dealer inventories. Our minimum prices for DC Whitmans are VF/NM=$18; VF+=$15; VF=$12; FN=$9; VG=$6; and G=$4.

Maggie Thompson
Comic Buyer's Guide

2008 seemed to be the breakout year with regard to comics' place in public consciousness. With Comic-Con International: San Diego sold out in its entirety, people repeatedly commented to me something along the lines of, "We've made it at last!" and "Geeks are in." While booth prices, placement, and traffic affected individual dealers' decisions concerning next year's event, wild enthusiasm on the part of attendees was visible.

Moreover, I'm seeing full families at all the shows I attend, with kids interested in what the field has to offer. That makes me more confident about the field's ability to retain customers over the long haul, as long as we maintain something (even if it's beat-up 1950s funny-animal issues) to entertain them till they begin to explore fare for older readers.

All this is helped along by the fact that 2008 was the year of the comics blockbuster movie. *Iron Man*, *Incredible Hulk*, *Wanted*, *The Dark Knight*, *Hellboy II*: None hid its comics connections, and each provided extra fun for comics fans. The post-credits scene in *Iron Man*, for example, started discussions between fans and other members of the audience as to what was going on — and what the implications were. Thanks, movie-makers!

When stores were able to put together promotions with their local theaters, it pulled more potential fans of the future into those stores. Guerilla marketing techniques, such as providing costumed characters and flyer handouts to theaters, buying a slide for pre-show advertising, and discounts at stores for show attendees raised consciousnesses that could pay off for years to come.

Aside from that, a speculator frenzy was sparked the way Tim Burton's 1989 *Batman* film sparked it then. Joker material, including DC's fresh edition of *The Greatest Joker Stories Ever Told*, introduced — and reintroduced — enough to lead buyers to find more. And buyers were on the lookout for the first appearances of such Bat-Trinkets as the Batmobile. Oddly, there didn't seem to be as much of a spike of interest in Two-Face.

Similarly, the new Hulk movie seemed to provoke more interest in issues that featured the adapted story than in earlier, key issues. Dealers and fans might want to consider this in case it's a trend: stocking up now on the more recent (and affordable) back issues.

Iron Man's first appearance drew more collector attention, and *Wanted* gained higher back-issue prices (though special collections of the mini-series may have kept prices lower than they could have gone).

It seems hard for comics buffs to believe, but, by late 2008, there were still folks in the mainstream who had no idea that either *The Spirit* or *Watchmen* had comic-book connections. There was buzz about both, but plenty of people who would be part of theater audiences had never read either. It's a good idea for would-be investors to keep that sort of trend in mind when they plan their strategies — while being aware that prices often peak just before a film's release.

Aside from Hollywood, there are obviously other pressures at work in the back-issue market. People who need money will be looking to cash in on decades of investment, pulling back issues from basements and attics in order to pay bills. On the other hand, collectibles are often the focus of investors, when normal stocks and bonds look chancy. (Remember: A decade ago, we were figuring a NM *Action Comics* #1 would bring $185,000 and an *Amazing Fantasy* #15 would be worth $27,000 in NM.) And collectors who do have funds will look to upgrade issues they have that are in bad shape. The flip side of that is that beat-up copies of non-key comics of long ago can sometimes be found for about the price of current comics.

Michael Tierney
Collector's Edition/The Comic Book Store

2008 was a banner year for comics-related movies, what with the success of *Iron Man* and the return of the Hulk and Batman. The demand created by previews for *Watchmen* made it the top selling graphic novel of the year. As a result of this exposure, *Invincible Iron Man* #1 sold very good numbers, and the "Batman R.I.P". storyline that crossed through all the Bat-related titles did extremely well. Joker action figures had the dust knocked off them and vanished all at the same time.

But the increase in interest that these movies created was offset by economic concerns over spiraling gas prices that soared to record levels. Operating in a rural area where most of my traffic is destination based, my sales were especially hurt when customers had to make budgetary decisions to adjust for the increases in the cost of living. Many customers cut their titles back, and some had to drop the hobby altogether.

Despite the influx of new customers, when compared to the year before, except for a handful of months, the 2008 sales results showed declines. One of the industry mainstays that was hardest hit was the X-Men. When I started my first store in 1982, the X-Men were far away the best selling comics title, and it remained that way for a long time. Now the X-Men have fallen from heights back into the pack.

That wasn't the only big change in mainstream of Marvel and DC sales. The once mighty "Crossover Effect" was the least effective that I've ever seen for the year's big events; Marvel's *Secret Invasion* and DC's *Final Crisis*. *Final Crisis* started slow and then built interest, whereas *Secret Invasion* started big and then slowed. Spin-off mini-series connected to those two events performed based strictly on the popularity of the characters involved, and in the case of *Final Crisis*, sales were limited by the $3.99 cover prices. But crossovers seem to be a sales gimmick that has lost much of its glamour.

Another gimmick that no longer works is the magic of a "#1 Issue." In the early days of the Direct Market, first issues were uncommon and a #1 on the cover guaranteed a sales boost. They were considered a good investment.

Relaunchs of once popular characters like Venom saw extrememly disappointing demand. Even subsequent series of widely recognized poperties such as Stephen King's *Dark Tower* saw huge declines with each new #1. Nowadays first issues have become an inordinate amount of the monthly selection, and a #1 on the cover has almost become a detriment. Customers no longer look for the latest fad. They're looking for solid entertainment, and a high number count series has an appearance that's become uncommon in the marketplace.

While, strangely, there were no adaptions for any of this year's major comics-related movies, adaptations of video games increased. Marvel's *Halo* was the best received, with sellout reprints of the first couple of issues. But a long delay in the middle of the run killed demand.

Overall, the lateness bug bit less in '08 than it has in

recent years. Another big improvement was the massive number of reprints done for hot-selling titles. Once, some publishers tried to manipulate the back issue market by intentionally under printing with hopes of creating immediate collectors' demand. Instead, they choked the sales on later issues. Nowadays publishers have realized that their primary job is to satisfy consumer demand. These subsequent printings of early issues have fueled sales throughout the run of series, which, given that the majority of publications these days are new launches with no sales history, has been a huge help for new comics retailers.

Graphic novel reprints are starting to impact back issue sales, as collectors no longer need to refer to the original material in order to read the story. As a result, the majority of my key sales in the last year were books not currently in print. Superbaby was popular as *Superboy* #8, featuring the Tyke of Steel's first appearance, sold in VG for $165.00, and his second appearance in *Superman* #66 went for $60.00 in Good. Other key *Superboy* sales included Lana Lang's second appearance in #15 for $170.00 in VG, and her subsequent appearance in #21 went for $90.00 in VG. In fact, I sold quite a few Superboy comics, including his appearances in *Adventure Comics* and from the Golden Age, with all of them in and around the Fine category at current *Guide*. It seems strange to say, but Superboy had far greater demand than the often reprinted Superman.

The hottest DC back issues for me were *House of Mystery* and *House of Secrets*. Lex Luthor's crossover appearance in *Batman* #130 went for $80.00 in Fine. I also sold a number of Golden Age *World's Finest* at *Guide* or above.

Marvel Key books had the lowest demand that I've seen in my 26 years of comics retailing. The only Key books of interest that moved were the Punisher's first appearance in *Amazing Spider-Man* #129 in Fine Minus for $95.00, Venom's first full appearance in *Amazing Spider-Man* #300 for $75.00 in VF+, and (Uncanny) *X-Men* #94 in Fine for $150.00. Otherwise, key Marvels sat in my display cases like lonesome puppies looking to catch a passerby's eye. One exception was the suddenly hot *Iron Man* #1. Thanks to the interest generated by the movie, copies sold above *Guide* regardless of grade as fast as I could get them. Another exception was *Wolverine* Volume One featuring art by Frank Miller, which still moves well at *Guide* values. Volumes Two and Three of *Wolverine* are another story, and were sluggish.

Westerns classics have consistently become harder and harder to sell, with only a smattering of sales connected to still recognizable characters like The Lone Ranger and Roy Rogers. War comics were likewise down in local demand. Science Fiction seems to be on the rebound, especially when they have a fantasy flair, such as in the *House of Secrets* and *House of Mystery*.

Overall, the sluggishness of Silver and Bronze Age Marvels was more than offset by high demand for Golden and Silver Age DCs. If it hadn't been for the harpooning of new comic sales by high gas prices, this could have been another banner year.

Rick Whitelock
New Force Comics

2008 has been an outstanding year for comic collecting, both for buying and selling. Our sales and purchases are primarily within the Golden Age of comics, with our primary focus on several publishers from the time period: Centaur, DC, and Timely. We found that demand for quality books, whether restored or unrestored, low grade to mid grade to high grade, as long as priced fairly, sold quickly. We have made some incredible friends this year, bought and sold some truly fantastic books, and hope to continue with an even better 2009.

Centaur: This small publisher of the late '30s and early '40s produced some of the era's most compelling artists and writers. Regular contributors that helped to shape the early Golden Age of comics can be found in a myriad of Centaur books and should not be overlooked or forgotten. Greats of the era like Bill Everett, Paul Gustavson, Tarpe Mills, Charles Biro, Frank Thomas, Carl Burgos etc., produced some wonderful art and stories that transcend the medium, even today. Some notable sales and acquisitions of Centaurs in the last year include: *Amazing-Man* #5 CGC (3.5) for $3,850, #6 CGC (7.0)(Rockford) for $1,800, #9 CGC (3.5) for $500, #22 CGC (3.5)(Cosmic Aeroplane) for $3,000, #22 in CGC (4.0) for $3,000, #22 in CGC (4.5)(mod. restored) for $2,500. *Amazing Mystery Funnies* v1, #1 , CGC (7.0)(Larson) for $3,200, v1 #2 in CGC (7.0)(Mile High) for $5,000, v1 #3 in CGC (4.0) for $750, v2 #3 CGC (9.0)(Lloyd Jacquet) for $2,850, v2 #6 CGC (5.0)(Twilight) for $500, v2 #7 CGC (8.0) (Cosmic Aeroplane) for $3,450, v2 #9 CGC (7.0)(Larson) for $1,928, v2 #8 CGC (6.5)(Twilight) for $800, #18 CGC (9.2) (San Francisco) for $2,750. *The Comics Magazine* (all Lost Valley) #2 CGC (7.0) for $2,600, #3 CGC (8.0) for $2,800, #4 CGC (6.0) for $1,500, #5 CGC (8.0) for $2,800. *Funny Pages* v2 #10 (1st app. Arrow) in CGC (4.5) for $1,500, v2 #12 in CGC (6.5)(Larson) for $2,000, v3 #4 (Mile High) in FN/VF for $1,350, #35 in CGC (8.0) for $1,900, #37 CGC (8.5)(Larson) for $2,200. *Keen Detective Funnies* #20 in VG for $600. *Star Ranger* #6 in VG for $1,200.

DC Comics: It was a fantastic year for the DC Superhero. Demand for early *Action Comics*, pre-Robin *Detectives* and *Wonder Woman* was unrelenting! *More Fun Comics* (the Spectre and Dr. Fate issues, particularly #52-67) seemed to experience very high demand. Demand for 1950s *World's Finest* and Wonder Woman comics continues to be very strong, with higher grade examples selling for many times *Guide* (2-4x when you can find them). Early *Sensations* (#2-12) are very difficult to find, as are the later end of the run (#80-106). *Green Lantern* and *Flash* seemed to remain undervalued and under appreciated in 2008, but I suspect that won't last long. Some notable sales and acquisitions: *Action Comics* #2, app FN for $4750, #5 CGC (4.5)(mod. rest.) for $1,900, #10 app FN/VF for $2,500, *Adventure* #40 app FN/VF for $8,000, *All-American Comics* #61, CGC (5.5) for $2,250, *All Star Comics* #8, CGC (5.5) for $8,000, #33 FN for $1,000, *Batman* #1, CGC (5.0) for $30,000, #1, CGC

(8.0)(ext. rest.) for $13,000, #18, CGC (8.5) for $3,400, #47, CGC (7.0) for $2250. *Detective Comics* #1, CGC (6.0)(ext. rest.) for $14,750, #8, CGC (1.5) for $2,000, #18, CGC (4.0) for $3,000, #27, CGC (8.5) (ext. rest.) for $85,000, #27, app FN- for $45,000, #29, CGC (3.5) for $16,000, #31, CGC (8.0)(mod. rest.) for $9,000, #31, CGC (5.0) for $13,150, #31, CGC (5.0) for $18,000 (cash and trade), #35, CGC (5.0) for $15,000, #36, CGC (8.5)(slight rest. Cosmic Aeroplane) $4,000, #36, CGC (4.5)(Crippen) for $4,000. *Flash Comics* #1, CGC (3.5) for $13,500. *More Fun Comics* #54, CGC (5.5) for $5,800, #67 CGC (5.0)(Detroit Trolley) for $3,000. *Superman* #1, CGC (3.0) for $38,000, #1, CGC (7.5)(ext. rest.) for $32,000, #14, CGC (3.0) for $750, #17, CGC (4.5) for $1,100.

Timely Comics: Wow!, is all I can say. Incredible demand, especially for early Simon/Kirby and of course, Schomburg! We were able to buy and sell virtually all issues of *Captain America Comics*, *Marvel Mystery Comics*, *Daring Mystery Comics*, *Mystic Comics*, *All-Select* and *All Winners*. Some notable sales and acquisitions: *All-Select* #1, CGC (8.0) for $10,250, #2, CGC (8.0) for $3,400. *All Winners* #11, CGC (7.5) for $1,400, #12, CGC (6.5) for $1,500. *Captain America Comics* #1, CGC (3.5) for $12,500, #13, CGC (7.0) for $4,000, #16, CGC (7.0) for $3,650, #36, CGC (7.5) for $3,800, #46, CGC (6.5)(ext. rest.) for $2,500, #46, CGC (3.0) for $3,500, #46, CGC (7.0) for $7,000. *Daring Mystery Comics* #1, CGC (3.0) for $2,900. *Marvel Comics* #1 CGC (7.0)(slight rest.) (Kansas City) for $36,000. *Marvel Mystery Comics* #2, CGC (5.5)(slight rest.) for $5,000, #9, CGC (1.8) for $5,800, #9, CGC (5.0) for $20,300, #46, CGC (5.0)(slight rest.) for $2,500. *Human Torch* #1 in CGC (7.5) for $17,500, #1 in CGC (8.0) for $22,000, *Mystic Comics* #1 in CGC (7.0) for $7,500, #4, CGC (4.5) for $1,250, #5, CGC (8.5) for $3,000, #10, CGC (8.0) for $3,100. *USA Comics* #7, CGC (3.5) for $2,000, #11, FR/GD for $400.

Harley Yee
Harley Yee Rare Comics

The 2008 market was one of the strongest in many years and saw many new trends. The market was strong for key Marvels, pre-hero and early DC, high grade Silver Age DC, Timely, Canadian comic books, early Fawcett, Fiction House and EC.

One of the trends that continues is that present and future movies impact on the key Marvel market. They are nearly impossible to keep in stock, and the prices have nearly doubled on some of the books. *Amazing Fantasy* #15 in FN- jumped from $5,500 in 2007 to $9,000 in 2008. The other hot ones are *Journey Into Mystery* #83, *Incredible Hulk* #1, *Avengers* #1 and *Fantastic Four* #1, but all the other keys are not that far behind.

Another trend is the increase in the Golden Age market with younger collectors. Across many of the important markets, early DC, Timely, Centaur, *Silver Streak*, Fiction House, and Fawcett are all very strong. Without a doubt, it has been the internet forums that have sparked this renewed interest, just like the *Gerber Photo-Journals* did.

The third trend is the increasing acceptance of professionally restored comic books. Collectors have begun to realize with key books and rarer books that a lightly or moderately restored book is still highly desirable, and more importantly, highly collectible.

Even with all the talk of the economic downturn of 2007-2008, the comic book market has remained strong. For some reason, when the stock market is down, comic book sales stay strong. It must be the enduring love affair with owning a piece of American history.

Mark S. Zaid, Esq.
Esquire Comics

As the U.S. economy continued in its downward spiral from 2007, and the country's jitters concerning the next presidential election increased, the comic book market appeared to remain essentially unaffected. Sales remained strong across most genres, and that included both online venues and conventions. Though no doubt there are collectors, and perhaps even dealers, who were selling off inventory to offset stock market losses and balance mortgage concerns, there were just as many, and likely more, collectors and dealers waiting with baited breath to snatch up those collections, and many at record level prices. The fact that other currencies, particularly in Europe and Asia, continued to strengthen against the American dollar contributed to the positive impact on sales as many books were very clearly traveling to overseas purchasers.

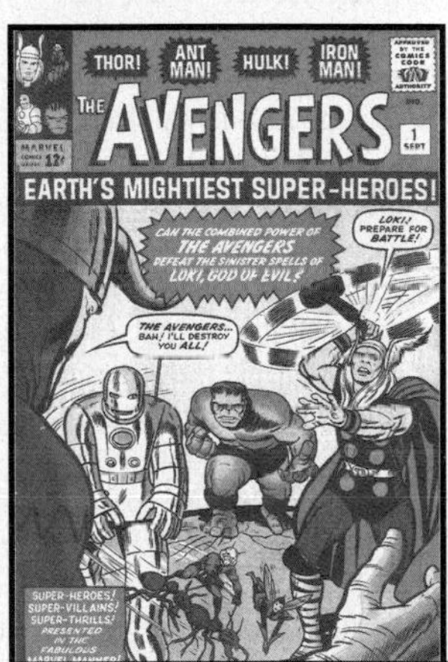

Present and future movies impact on the key Marvel market. ***The Avengers*** *(#1 shown) may hit theaters in 2011.*

I spent much of my time in 2007 acquiring original owner collections with books from the Golden Age to Bronze Age. It does not take a rocket scientist to accurately predict that the coming years will offer a treasure trove of comics, particularly due to the ever increasing daily deaths of the "Greatest Generation" of WW II veterans and the retirement of the baby boomers. What we cannot predict, absent some prescient uncanny ability, is how this will impact the marketplace. While I doubt we will likely, if ever, witness anything that parallels the Edgar Church "Mile High" collection, there are many desirable and respected pedigree collections that I daresay will be surpassed in the coming years. When these collections surface, and in what frequency, will probably determine the ultimate impact upon the community.

A particular focus of mine continues to be rare and esoteric comics. There has been no shortage, to be quite candid, of books previously believed to have less than 20 copies existing suddenly appearing for sale at a rate not seen before. Some books are simply becoming more available due to the nature of the Internet, while others - such as several notable ashcans (rare comics used by publishers primarily in the 1930s and 1940s to trademark titles) - just happened to come on the open market and will no doubt disappear back into private collections for years to come. I am presently engaged in an effort to re-evaluate the esteemed Gerber scarcity index (as well as those books listed in the *Guide* as "scarce" or "rare") to truly ascertain the availability of these books. Hopefully this effort will be reported in a future *CBPG* article, as well as a history of political and ideological promotional comic books, which is another avocation of mine and a topic that has not been particularly documented yet and has played a significant social and historical role in the United States. I encourage anyone who has an interest in rare and unusual comics to check out my website's "Special Collections" section (www.EsquireComics.com) which features hundreds of fascinating books from my personal collection. Indeed, I was pleased to contribute images of some valuable rare ashcans to *The DC Vault: A Museum-in-a-Book with Rare Collectibles from the DC Universe* (Running Press, 2008).

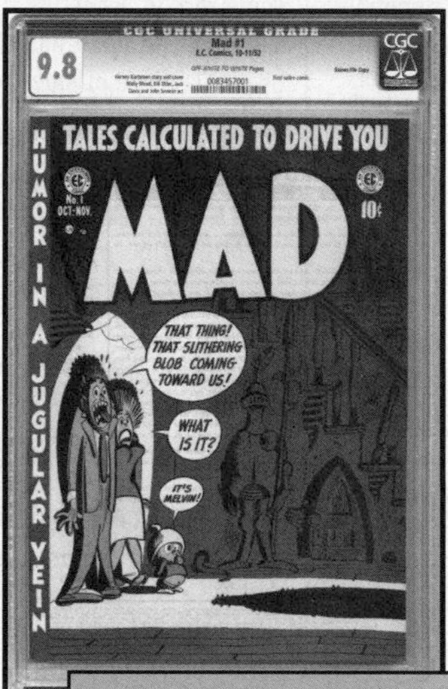

*Notable sales from 2008 include a CGC-certified 9.8 Gaines file copy of **Mad** #1 for $24,500.*

Some notable sales/purchases during the last year (all CGC-certified): *Mad* #1 9.8 Gaines - $24,500.00; *Fantastic Four* #1 8.0 - $22,000.00; *Double Action* #2 5.5 (SP) - $16,730.00; *Action* #2 7.0 (SP, Court exhibit copy) - $14,340.00; *Four Color* #9 8.5 - $7,500.00; *Superman* #48 9.4 Toledo - $5,100.00; *Silver Streak* #6 4.5 - $3,000.00; *Mad* #17 9.6 Gaines - $2,900.00; *Tales of Suspense* #39 4.5 - $1,300.00; and the following raw or uncertified comics: *Amazing Fantasy* #15 VG-/VG - $3,600.00; *Cancelled Comic Cavalcade* #1 and #2 - $2,629.00; *Amazing Spider-Man* #1 VG+ - $2,350.00; and *Motion Picture Funnies* #2 - #4 (covers only) - $1,200.00.

While I remain confident that the sky is not falling with respect to the health of the comic book community, I am very concerned with the increasing amount of fraudulent activity that is occurring, especially on eBay. As a practicing attorney I am often contacted and even retained by collectors and dealers who have suffered losses at the hands of criminal activity (I also use my legal skills to offer expert estate valuations for charitable tax purposes). Our hobby, as many are, is very susceptible to fraudulent behavior and the existence of online entities, such as eBay, with little to no oversight offers ample feeding grounds for those who wish to take advantage of unsuspecting individuals. Amazingly, and sadly, an unintended consequence of becoming a comic book dealer has been to generate legal work to recover financial losses and persuade law enforcement agencies to investigate suspicious activity. Even more depressing is the fact that there are recognized dealers and longtime collectors who apparently have no ethical qualms about associating with suspected or even known fraudulent characters simply to generate additional revenue for their business. My prediction for these individuals is that their long term adverse consequences will outweigh their short term gains. I will not hesitate to assist, as best I can, any individual who has become a victim of fraudulent behavior stemming from a comic book transaction. Those who potentially require assistance can contact me at EsquireComics@aol.com.

Notwithstanding the negative perception noted above, there continues to be positive trends in the community that seek to further balance the tilting of power between buyers and sellers. The Network of Disclosure (www.networkofdisclosure.org), of which I was a founder, has progressed into its third year of existence and has started to embark upon a dedicated educational approach while still maintaining its strong ethical principles. The NOD, in fact, sponsored a well-attended panel discussion at the 2008 San Diego Comic Con featuring the son of Malcolm Wheeler-Nicholson, the founder of DC Comics. The coming year should be an exciting time for the NOD and I strongly encourage collectors and dealers to consider becoming members and participating in the many discussions that occur on the NOD's internal message board. I also continue to freely supply market data to GPAnalysis.com, a fantastic internet resource from "down under" that provides actual CGC sales information that can be used by buyers and sellers alike to consider when negotiating sales and purchases. Allowing the community to possess this information, in my opinion, only benefits the entire market place and it is regrettable that certain mainstream dealers take the view that their sales data constitutes proprietary secrets that can only be selectively shared for their own self-interests. Finally, I am pleased to have joined the ranks of a member dealer with CGC and offer my customers, and anyone else for that matter, an opportunity to have their books graded at a discount.

Vincent Zurzolo, Frank Cwiklik & Ben Smith Metropolis/ComicCollect.com

Vincent Zurzolo - Metropolis Comics

The stock market fell over 777 points in one day. Lehman Brothers is going bankrupt. Companies like Freddie

Mac, Fannie Mae, Bear Sterns and AIG are being bailed out by the Federal government. The real estate boom has gone bust and the repercussions are being felt throughout the world. Gas prices are through the roof and our country's gross national debt hovers around $9 trillion dollars. On the day I am writing this market report, these are the headlines. [Publisher's note: Since the time this report was written, the market's volatility has continued. - RMO]

Earlier in 2008, I was invited by the Fox Business Channel to speak about investing in comic books. I was told I would be asked a few questions and then placed in a round table discussion afterward. I asked who would be on the round table. Would they be other collectibles dealers? I was given a very vague answer and assured it would be a very friendly discussion. I knew at this point I should be on my guard. When I got to the studio, I was seated next to two gentlemen and we went live. The host of the show asked me questions about investing in comics, what's hot, what's not, those types of questions. It was fun. Next, the host brought the two other gentlemen on to the show. Apparently they were finance guys, brought on to tell people why comics are not such a good investment. They questioned how you could invest in comics if you had to compete against someone like me, where you would get your information and how you could liquidate your comics quickly without taking a hit. I didn't get to give all my rebuttal answers (yes, I loved to debate back in junior and high school) as the host cut me off, apparently we ran out of time. But, I first said that someone interested in buying comics as an investment should do their own market research, talk to experts, read *The Overstreet Comic Book Price Guide*, use online pricing guides, just like you would with stocks. By their own argument, in that case, how could you ever buy a stock if you have to compete against large finance firms, who have way more info than you or I could ever hope to gather. I think I defended investing in comics pretty well. Unfortunately, I didn't get a chance to explain how easy it is to sell high grade comics in the marketplace. I would have also liked to have explained how my company, aside from buying comics, also takes consignments from sellers and works on as little as a 10% commission, leaving an investor with the lion's share of the sale.

If you'd like to watch the interview in its entirety, it's viewable at metropoliscomics.com, click on "Market Info" at the top of the home page, which will bring you a drop down menu, then click on the "In The Press Section" and you'll see the two Fox Business segments.

In short, what I am getting at is this: comics are an amazing American art form to be appreciated for the illustrations and stories. They are collectible escapist pleasures of recapturing one's youth, and they are an alternative form of investment. As mentioned in my opening, the stock market dropped over 777 points in one day. I don't remember the last time period an *Amazing Fantasy* #15 dropped even $5.00 in price. Do you? Comics have come into their own with the tremendous success of a myriad number of movie franchises like *Batman* and *Spider-Man*. The advent of the Internet provides buyers and sellers market information and a wealth of resources to buy and sell, and 3rd party grading services can provide their opinion about a grade of a comic if you don't have grading knowledge but want to get started. The days of being scoffed at by more "traditional investments" are gone. You can collect something you really love and can believe in and invest as well. Are there any guarantees? Of course not, go into this realistically. But by researching and looking at the history of the comic market, you can see that comics are very stable… you do have to pick the right ones.

Iron Man & Batman: Last year I wrote about how well the origin issue of Iron Man in *Tales of Suspense* #39 was doing and recommended it wholeheartedly. The movie was well received, and collector/investor interest has not waned. That comic has skyrocketed and anybody who bought a copy did very well. Average prices for a NM- 9.2 copy increased from $25,000 in 2007 to $35,000 in 2008. VG 4.0 copies went from $850 in 2007 to $1,400 in 2008. Altogether, Metropolis Collectibles sold 21 copies in the past year. I feel very strongly that high grade copies of this book will continue to see very healthy increases.

The Dark Knight was an amazing movie. Not just an amazing superhero movie, it was simply an amazing movie. It raked in over $500 million in the U.S. and over $850 million worldwide, truly a herculean effort by any standard. What was also incredible to see was the massive demand for *Batman* #1 and *Detective Comics* #27 leading up to the premiere, and even after the film had been in the theaters for months. While Batman is a perennial favorite, demand has definitely increased. In the last 12 months, Metropolis has sold 5 copies of *Detective* #27 and 10 copies of *Batman* #1. In fact, we sold our last 3 copies during the week of San Diego Comic Con; a low grade copy for $7,500, a CGC-graded VG 4.0 for $18,000 and a CGC-graded restored NM- 9.2 for $33,000. In the 9 years Stephen and I have been partners, it was the only time I can remember being sold out of *Batman* #1. I do believe *Batman* and *Detective* will continue to appreciate, though I think it will be slower than *Tales of Suspense*. My reasons are the following: The Bats are more expensive books even at lower grades, they are not as common and they don't sell as often.

If you want to find a niche in which to invest, follow the movie trends, Hollywood buzz and feedback from the San Diego Comic Con trailers. Watch for upcoming green lit projects and capitalize early. I think *Captain America*, *Thor*, *Avengers* and *Watchmen* all have the potential to explode in price.

Super Heroes: Fashion & Fantasy at Metropolitan Museum of Art Exhibit: In the spring of 2008, along with a friend, I was able to convince the curators at the Metropolitan Museum of Art to include comic books in their exhibit "Super Heroes: Fashion & Fantasy." Yes, that is correct. Comic books hung in the most famous museum in North America. I was so proud to see comics in The MET and to see the "from the collection of Metropolis Collectibles" sign below each book. This was a professional and personal achievement, and it helps move the art form one step closer to its place of respect and appreciation as one of the great American Art forms. I count this as one of my proudest achievements in my career. Personally, it was validation of what I already knew: a comic is real art and should be respected as such. Most of you reading this are saying "Of course a comic is art! Who doesn't know that?" But this is not how it is viewed by most. That way of thinking is changing, and I am happy to help push it along.

In closing, 2008 has been a record year for Metropolis. Our orders increased by an average of 100 a month more than the previous year, and sales have never been higher. With over 150,000 comic books in stock, and a friendly staff always willing to lend their expert advice, I hope you check us out online or give us a call. A special thanks to all of you who helped to make 2008 a great year.

Frank Cwiklik - Metropolis Collectibles

Compared with being a collector, it's a very different experience being down "in the trenches" as the head of Sales for Metropolis Collectibles. From this vantage point, I can see how the comic collectibles market ebbs and flows, I see the trends in both buying and grading, how books can go from hot to not overnight, and how quickly prices can shoot up. It's been a great lesson in market mentalities, human nature, and fandom. Sometimes I feel like part of my job description should involve "cultural anthropologist".

NEW X MEN

GRANT MORRISON

© MAR

It's a thrill to see so many old and new classic comics available in reprint form. (**New X-Men Omnibus** shown)

I think the first book I ever read was a Batman comic. When I discovered, in a tiny classified ad in a comic, that there were people who *actually sold old comic books*, I nearly fell over. From then on, every birthday, every holiday, every Christmas, every good report card, I would plead for $30 (a small fortune at the time!) and a car ride to the local comic shop, where I would snap up beaten Golden and Silver Age comics and walk out loaded down with piles of four-color magic. I still remember the first Golden Age comic I bought, and still have it, a battered *Sensation Comics* #27 with a split spine. It's no better than a Fair (1.0), but I still have it, love it, and still treasure the memory of showing it off to my comic-collecting pals after buying it.

Times changed, I stopped reading comics in the early '90s (can you blame me?), sold off almost all of my vintage stuff and pretty much forgot about comics entirely. I didn't start collecting seriously again until around 2002. Whoa. What happened? Gone were the days of comic shops wallpapered with *Black Mask* and *All Star Comics* covers, Romita posters, *Amazing Spider-Man* #121, and other vintage goodies. Now, stores were crammed stem to stern with reprints, manga, graphic novels, hardbacks, variant this and that. I was thrilled to see that so many classic comics were finally available in reprint form, but the joy of digging through musty old boxes for hidden treasure was long gone, and, worse, none of the new readers seemed to care. It seemed that a hobby based on remembering and arguing over the smallest minutiae of comics history was now populated with readers who believed that anything published before 1995 was passé or campy or out of style. It was disorienting and a little upsetting.

I'd been working in retail for years, plugging away in managerial positions while running a theater company at nights with my wife. I was burnt out and needed to find something more rewarding when my wife lucked across an ad for Metropolis. They were looking for a new stock clerk. It seemed like a fun gig, and I was getting back into comics anyway, so I figured I'd give it a shot. After I made the appointment, I looked them up online to see what I was getting into... Holy cow! This was more like it. I was looking forward to the interview just to check the place out, and was not disappointed. And upon starting at Metropolis, I was delighted to discover that the network of fans, collectors, scholars, and packrats who I so loved hanging around with in my childhood had not actually vanished, but instead had coalesced into a small but vibrant community based around conventions, exciting deals, incredible collections, and a deep and abiding love of the history of comics and the importance of their contributions to pop culture history. Upon being promoted to Sales Executive not long after starting , it has been my joy and privilege to not only meet so many like-minded collectors, but to introduce new and younger collectors and fans to this wonderful hobby, both in person at conventions, and over the phone and Internet. And now, Holy Cow! Look at me. I'm in the *Overstreet Guide*!

As I said earlier, my experience at Metropolis has allowed me to notice trends and buying patterns from a unique vantage point. I get to experience the visceral excitement of a collector discovering lost treasures, as well as the dealer and seller perspective of following what's hot and what's a good investment buy. This unique position has led me to conclude that, despite the wobbly economy and the seismic shift in how vintage comics are bought and sold (thanks, internet!), the long term picture for the vintage comics market is very good and has a firm foundation that can be used to bring even greater respect, marketability, stability and growth to this very unique market.

In recent years, orders that came in were predictable -- High-grade Spidey, Golden Age keys, Silver Age Marvel, etc. Business was very strong, but it was largely the same group of sellers chasing the same hot books. Recently, however, that's been changing. What I find encouraging for the long term prospects for both Metropolis as a company and the comics business in general has been the diversification of interest in terms of genre, titles and condition. Lower-grade copies of obscure books that we've had sitting around for years are now selling respectably - Westerns, Disneys, Dells, Charltons, obscure series and genres of all types. I have a rabid Katy Keene collector who contacts me once a month, several overseas collectors who love Quality titles, and, of course, Disney sells like gangbusters in all grades to our European clients.

I'm also encouraged by the number of new collectors who are just now coming into the market. Some are fans of the art and stories, like the retired priest from California who's a big Dick Tracy and Charles Biro fan, or the French Canadian collector who's crazy about Joe Palooka. Some are drawn by the investment potential, like the local collector I've just started working with who loves high-grade Silver Age DC and Golden Age Superman War covers, and has shrewdly amassed an impressive and valuable collection in a short amount of time. Plus, the phone now rings off the hook with requests from people who want to stop by on their trip to NYC to pick up a key book or a run of Golden Age treasures - one Italian couple showed us their itinerary last year, with the Metropolis Gallery at the top of their NYC must-see list!

The thing they all have in common is that they've heard the good buzz coming from our business. Comics are great investments, long term and short term, and there are books for every budget and taste. Plus, the exploding popularity of the San Diego Con and New York Comic Con is whetting the average, non-comic collecting person's appetite. Whereas a few years ago, new comics collectors would pass our booth at shows and wonder whether we were selling reprints, now even younger readers know both the financial and historical worth of the books we're offering - when 10-year old boys are rattling off key issue numbers at conventions without being prompted, it's a sign that the hobby is healthy. At least once a week I hear a story from a new client about how excited they are about getting into the hobby, about their grail books, and, best of all, how their families are just as excited as they are! In short, rare comics collecting is now gaining the acceptance and gravitas that is afforded rare books, furniture, Americana, or other respected antiques, and the number of new clients we sign up every day attests to this growth of interest.

This, of course, is all spurred on by huge sales and record-breaking prices. *Amazing Fantasy* #15 has become the Silver Age equivalent of *Action Comics* #1, and sells at top prices in all grades. We sold all of our copies at this year's San Diego show without breaking a sweat - it's the single hottest, best investment book on today's market, and I get calls asking for it all day, every day. Marvel keys in general are doing killer business. The biggest growth has been in *Avengers* #1 and 4, which were unjustly neglected books only a couple of years ago, and now, with Marvel's aggressive and clever movie-making strategy, interest in these books has exploded. If you see an *Avengers* #4, buy it; it's the next big Marvel key.

We've also been doing very well with a variety of keys and rarities: in just the past six months, we've sold *Marvel Comics* #1 and *Captain America* #1, along with other Timelys (which are selling briskly), an *All Star Comics* #8, a *Superman* #1, a gorgeous *More Fun* #54 in 8.0, and all of our copies of *Batman* #1, which show that DC Golden Age books are still attracting investors and collectors. In addition, we recently sold the Mile High copies of both *Exciting Comics* #9 and 11, a Gaines file copy of *Tales From the Crypt* #20, and even the Mile High *Captain Midnight* #9. Looking at our recent sales list is fascinating, as the range and variation of the types makes it look like a history of comics in general, rather than a laundry list of the same big keys. It seems all sectors of the market are growing, not just one or two specific niche markets or a handful of key books.

© DC

***Wonder Woman** #1 (shown) and **Sensation Comics** #1 have seen a rise in collectability.*

In more unusual sales, a handsome copy of the exceedingly rare *Great Comics* #3 arrived in our offices earlier this year and sold to a long-time client who specializes in rare comics such as these, which I think of as "caviar" comics - the sort of stuff not everyone knows about, but hard-core comic collectors drool over. It was a pleasure to finally have a chance to see the book in person and find it a good home. It was also gratifying to see the unjustly neglected but very important *Funny Picture Stories* #1 sell in a Mile High pedigree, as did the Mile High copy of *Roly Poly Comics* #1. As a Wonder Woman fan, I've been personally pleased to see her collectability rise this year, with strong sales for both *Wonder Woman* #1 and *Sensation Comics* #1, and for us to obtain a number of scarce issues from her late Golden Age period, some of which we hadn't had in years, if ever! And, of course, Chris Nolan's astoundingly good *The Dark Knight* spurred renewed interest in Batman, which led to terrific sales of Silver Age Batman key issues that had plateaued for some time and are now desirable again. In fact, any comic property that's been optioned for movies or TV seems to experience an interest spike, however brief, so keep an eye on the industry trades! Finally, if there's a Neal Adams cover on a comic, and it's VF+ or better, there's not even a point in putting it into our stockroom as it will be sold the minute it hits the site.

Trends to watch: We've recently been doing very well with Copper and late Bronze books. Comics we would have blown out in wholesale lots are now selling briskly, sometimes above *Guide*. Claremont-Byrne *Uncanny X-Men*, Miller *Batman*, any *Spider-Man* (especially McFarlane), Wolfman-

Pérez *New Teen Titans*, Miller *Daredevil*, even *Captain America*, *Avengers* and *Defenders* have all been growing in demand. *Iron Man*'s been good, too, though it remains to be seen whether this is a short-term trend from the movie's popularity. (I have a sense his popularity is going to continue for some time). I also believe that seminal and popular DC and Marvel titles from between 1978 and 1985 are sleepers and have great growth potential. Keep in mind, they're very common books, so they've got to be 9.0 or better (unless they're Spidey or X-Men, which sell in any grade), but bearing that in mind, this may just be the next growth market.

In conclusion, it's been really enjoyable meeting so many of you at conventions, and starting up correspondences through email and over the phone. The vintage comics market has changed drastically over the past 15 years, and is undergoing another transition now, but the explosion of online selling and the new influx of fans driven by movies, conventions, and TV series hints at a new and exciting future for the market. Numerous museum retrospectives and scholarly tomes on comics history are giving a new and very real respect for the history of the medium. It's an awesome time to be a vintage comics collector. If you've been around for awhile, fear not, the best is yet to come, and if you're new to the hobby, I envy you the excitement and joy you're sure to get in your journey through comics collecting.

© MAR

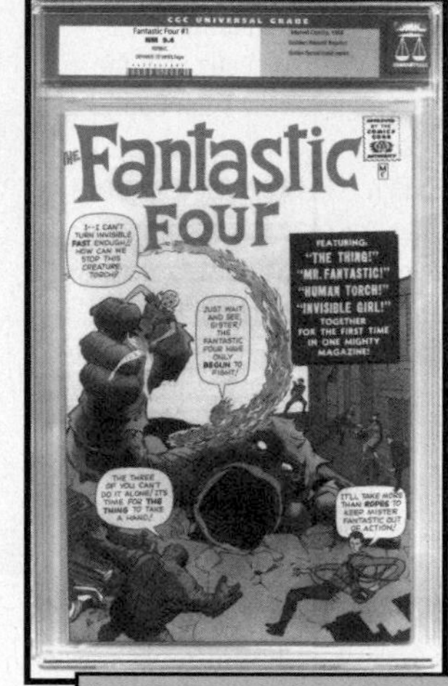

A CGC-certified 9.4 ***Fantastic Four* #1** brought in $47,977.

Ben Smith - ComicConnect.com

During 2008, ComicConnect.com continued to see enormous growth in both the comic book market and transactions among buyers and sellers on the website. At the time this report is written, world financial markets are slumping, and the Dow just dropped below 10,000 for the first time since 2004. On Monday, September 29th, Keith Olberman on MSNBC's *Countdown* even mused, "What happens next? Should you be running to the bank in the morning? Move all your money into vintage comic books?"

We certainly would not recommend that anyone move their family's entire life savings into comic books, but Mr. Olberman does raise an interesting subject close to the heart of many collectors in the hobby. Just how will the status of the economy impact the comic market, and will its effects be adverse or positive?

In 2001-2002, during the aftermath of the dotcom bubble burst, vintage comic books did become popular counter-cyclical investments to safe-house money, that is, investments that thrive during the time of a weak economy. Historically, the vintage comic market as a whole has achieved steady compound annual growth and consistent returns. One positive indication ComicConnect.com saw recently was that collectors did not flinch when bidding during the second session of our September Event Auction -- the same day the Dow dropped a record-setting 777 points.

2008 saw some record-breaking sales for sellers on ComicConnect. Our first Event Auction in March brought in $47,977 for a CGC-certified *Fantastic Four* #1 CGC 9.4, and $42,700 realized for an *Amazing Fantasy* #15 7.5. Shortly thereafter, the underbidder obtained another copy in the same grade from ComicConnect, which was sold for $40,000. ComicConnect's September's Event Auction saw $160,200 for a *Showcase* #4 9.4, $25,000 for a *Detective Comics* #29 6.0, $118,977 for an *Amazing Fantasy* #15 8.5, and $24,766 for an *Amazing Fantasy* #15 6.5, all CGC-certified.

Golden Age keys in all grades continue to do well on ComicConnect, including the sale of a couple copies of *Detective Comics* #27, *Batman* #1, *Superman* #1, three copies of *Captain America Comics* #1 and so forth. Early *Action Comics*, *Detective Comics*, *Batman* and *Superman* all continue to sell well, as collectors completing runs seem to start from the top and work their way down. Marvel Silver and Bronze Age keys sell well in any grade, and *Incredible Hulk* #1 and #181, *Tales of Suspense* #39, *Tales to Astonish* #27, *Journey into Mystery* #83, *Fantastic Four* #1, *Amazing Spider-Man* #1 and #129, and *Giant-Size X-Men* #1 continue to march through our doors at great prices.

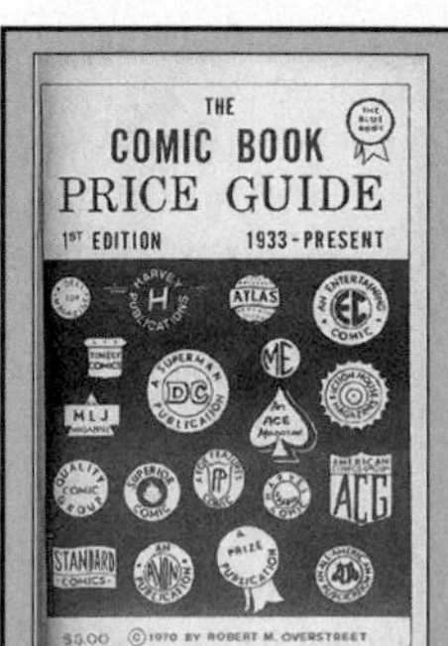

In the inaugural edition of *The Overstreet Comic Book Price Guide* in 1970, the top five Golden Age keys were valued at the following.

	Mint 1970	9.2 2009
Action Comics #1	$300	$750,000
Detective Comics #27	$275	$575,000
Marvel Comics #1	$250	$460,000
Superman #1	$250	$440,000
All-American Comics #16	$50	$280,000

Key Sales from 2008

The following lists of sales were reported to Gemstone during the year and represent only a small portion of the total amount of important books that have sold.

PLATINUM AGE SALES

Banana Oil (1924) GD/VG $295.55
Bringing Up Father #3 FN $125
Bringing Up Father #5 GD $40
Bunny's Red Book FN/VF $115
Buster Brown and His Pets $93
Charlie Chaplin In The Movies #316 FR $50
Chasing the Blues (1912) VG $221.38
Foxy Grandpa, Adventures of (1900) VG $632.50
Foxy Grandpa and Mother Goose (1908) FN $400
Foxy Grandpa's Triumphs GD $159.50
Little Orphan Annie Bucking The World VF+ $24.10
Mickey Mouse Book (1st printing) FN/VF (7.0) $5,676.25
Smitty at the Ball Game nn FN $300
Yellow Kid in McFadden's Flats app. VF $12,200.00

GOLDEN AGE - ATOM AGE SALES

Action Comics #42 GD+ $275
Action Comics #43 VF $1,075
Action Comics #79 VF $925
Action Comics #90 GD/VG $129
Action Comics #101 VG $300
Action Comics #158 VG+ $160
Action Comics #175 VG+ $112.50
Action Comics #181 VG $100
Adventure Comics #53 VG/FN $550
Adventure Comics #77 VG/FN $450
Adventure Comics #97 VF $625
Adventure Comics #100 FN $360
Adventure Comics #103 FN/VF $1,000
Adventure Comics #115 FN- $200
Adventure Comics #170 FN $170
Adventure Comics #185 FN+ $175
Adventure Comics #192 FN $115
All American Comics #59 VG+ $249
All-Flash #1 VF- $10,000
All-Flash #30 app FN+ $143
All Select #2 VG/FN $1,200
All Select #3 VG $750
All Select #11 VG/FN $700
All Winners Comics #10 VG- $550
All Winners Comics #14 VG $450
All Winners Comics #14 VG/FN $600
Amazing Man #21 VG $200
Archie Annual #3 FN $200
Archie Comics #10 G- $175
Archie Comics #33 FN/VF $175
Archie's Pal Jughead #2 VG $175
Batman #1 VF $16,000 light rest.
Batman #1 VF+ $18,000 light rest.
Batman #19 VG/FN $500
Batman #24 VG+ $262.90
Batman #29 VF $2,500
Batman #38 VG $160
Batman #47 FN $1,100
Batman #50 GD $90.82
Batman #56 FN $365
Big All-American Book Of Comics #nn GD/VG $800
Bingo Comics #1 VG $126
Blackhawk #108 VG $80
Black Magic Vol. 3 #2 GD- $16.50
Black Terror #2 FN $600
Black Terror #6 VG $10
Black Terror #24 VF $350
Boy Commandos #3 VG/FN $325
Boy Explorers #1 VF+ $435
Brave and the Bold #4 FN/VF $500
Bulletman #16 VG/FN $155
Captain America Comics #3 GD/VG $1,508
Captain America Comics #3 VG $2,300
Captain America Comics #5 GD $800
Captain America Comics #7 G/VG $790
Captain America Comics #8 VG $800
Captain America Comics #8 VG/FN $1,300
Captain America Comics #14 VG- $550
Captain America Comics #15 FR/GD $500
Captain America Comics #16 GD- $700
Captain America Comics #16 VG $750
Captain America Comics #17 FN $1,700
Captain America Comics #17 G/VG $600
Captain America Comics #29 VG $1,000
Captain America Comics #62 F/VF $1,200
Captain America Comics #66 VG/FN $750
Captain America Comics #69 FN $500
Captain Marvel Adventures #11 FN $300
Captain Marvel Adventures #29 FN $200
Captain Marvel Jr. #3 GD $125
Captain Marvel Jr. #4 VG $250
Captain Marvel Jr. #9 FN- $167.30

Classics Illustrated #43 FN- $275
Crimes By Women # GD- $25
Dell Giant Christmas Parade #1 FN $200
Detective Comics #19 VG $900
Detective Comics #27 FN/VF $65,000 (restored)
Detective Comics #45 FN- $925
Detective Comics #47 VG $465
Detective Comics #65 G $300
Detective Comics #99 VG $250
Detective Comics #111 VF $500
Detective Comics #140 FN $300
Dick Tracy Four Color #21 VF $490
Dick Tracy Four Color #34 VF- $280
Donald Duck FC #189 # GD $922 Carl Barks File Copy
Double Action Comics #2 VF/NM $16,730
E.C. Pictofiction: Crime Illustrated #1 VG $35
5 Cent Comics Ashcan #1 NM $3,050
5 Cent Comics Ashcan #1 NM $3,050
Flash Comics #10 F/VF $2,000
Flash Comics #74 VF/NM $1,000
Flash Comics #76 VG/FN $147
Flash Comics #97 VG $265
Four Color #16 FN $5,000
Four Color #33 G/VG $350
Four Color #48 VG/FN $400
Four Color Comics #12 VG/FN $90.82
Fox and Crow #108 FN- $8
Gene Autry #5 GD- $13.50
Ghost #10 FN/VF $130
Girls' Romances #105 FN $9
Green Hornet Comics #17 FN $190
Green Hornet Comics #24 FN $150
Green Hornet Comics #26 F/VF $200
Green Hornet Comics #27 VF $300
Henry #1 VF $65
Henry #2 VF/NM $100
Henry #3 NM- $100
Henry #4 NM- $100
Henry #6 NM- $85
Henry #7 NM $150
Henry #8 NM+ $225
Henry #10 NM $150
Hit Comics #10 FN $900
Hit Comics #25 FN- $800
Hopalong Cassidy #23 GD $17
Human Torch #1 VG/FN $5,000 (restored)
Human Torch Comics #27 FN+ $500
Indian Chief #7 VG+ $12.50
Invisible Scarlet O'Neil #3 VF $50
Jackpot Comics #5 VG $310
Jumbo Comics #14 VG $300
Jumbo Comics #89 VF/NM $195
Keen Detective Funnies #22 G/VG $250
Keen Detective Funnies Vol. 2 #6 VG $300
Keen Detective Funnies Vol. 3 #1 VG $250
Kid Eternity #3 FN $135
Kid Komics #5 FN/VF $630
Little Beaver Four Color #294 VG- $11.25
Little Orphan Annie FC #12 FN $170
Looney Tunes #87 VF- $50
Mad #1 VG/FN $1,100
Marvel Comics #1 FN $100,000
Marvel Mystery Comics #11 VG/FN $1,000
Marvel Mystery Comics #62 FN+ $500
Marvel Mystery Comics #71 FN+ $550
Marvel Mystery Comics #84 VG $350
Mary Marvel #27 FN $55
Mask of Fu Manchu # FN $280
Master Comics #40 VF- $600 Crowley copy
Master Comics #42 VF $450
Master Comics #48 VF- $330
Mickey Mouse Magazine #1 VG/FN $2,270.50
Mickey Mouse Magazine Vol 5 #12 G/VG $800
Minute Man #1 VG/FN $500
More Fun Comics #27 VG $550
More Fun Comics #47 VG+ $475
More Fun Comics #65 G/VG $1,200
Mystic Comics #7 VG- $1,200
National Comics #24 VG $150
Our Army at War #1 VG $300
Our Fighting Forces #1 VG $200
Panic #9 VF/NM $77.68
Perfect Crime #3 NM- $300
Plastic Man #3 VG/FN $300
Plastic Man (Qua) #1 GD/VG $500
Pogo #5 VG- $21
Police Action #4 GD+ $11.50
Police Comics #1 VG $1,200
Popular Comics #3 VG $400
Popular Comics #4 FN $350
Popular Comics #5 VG $300
Popular Comics #6 VG+ $500
Popular Comics #7 VG $225
Popular Comics #8 FN $300
Porky Pig #284 VF- $60
Porky Pig Four Color #342 NM+ $50
Prince Valiant Feature Books #26 VG/FN $245
Rangers Comics #35 VG $60
Real Screen Comics #15 FN+ $34.75
Rocky Lane Western #17 GD- $12.50
Roy Rogers #1 FN/VF $450
Saint #6 VG $160 (restored)
Shadow Comics #3 VG $350
Shadow Vol. 2 #12 VG $100
Sheena #7 GD $44
Silver Streak Comics #2 GD/VG $600
Slam Bang Comics #1 GD $250
Smash Comics #38 FN $300
Sparkle #31 FN- $14
Speed Comics #40 VG $84
Star Spangled Comics #1 VG- $650
Star Spangled Comics #7 G- $590
Star Spangled War Stories #130 FN+ $39
Startling Comics #9 FN $175

Startling Comics #10 VG/FN $1,000
Straight Arrow #1 VG- $19
Strange Tales #42 VG- $17.50
Sub-Mariner Comics #3 GD $800
Sub-Mariner Comics #34 VF+ $699
Sub-Mariner Comics #37 VG $200
Sugar and Spike #1 VG- $700
Super Comics #119 FN $27
Super Western Comics #1 GD+ $14.50
Superboy #8 VG $250
Superboy #8 VG $165
Superboy #10 VG/FN $300
Superboy #15 VG $170
Superboy #36 VF $85
Superman #2 VF- $12,000
Superman #6 GD+ $325
Superman #18 GD+ $325
Superman #21 VG/FN $400
Superman #30 VG/FN $600
Superman #36 VG $250
Superman #40 FN $350
Superman #81 VF $500
Superman #90 FN- $270
Tailspin Tommy #1 VF $80
Tarzan #1 VF $1,000
Teenage Dope Slaves # VG- $800
Top Notch #30 VG+ $175
USA Comics #1 VG $3,000
Walt Disney's C&S #9 VG $275
Walt Disney's Comics and Stories #15 FN $400
Walt Disney's Comics and Stories #32 VG/FN $500
Walt Disney's Comics and Stories #35 FN/VF $500
Walt Disney's Comics and Stories #40 FN/VF $450
Web of Mystery #22 VG- $38.50
Weird #6 VG- $180
Western Comics #17 GD- $13
Whiz Comics #3 VG $700
Wonder Comics #5 VG/FN $150
Wonder Woman #28 GD- $75
Wonder Woman #79 FN $93
World's Finest Comics #6 FN $550
World's Finest Comics #25 VG/FN $220
World's Finest Comics #39 VG+ $200
World's Finest Comics #44 FN+ $203
World's Finest Comics #69 VG $120
Young Allies Comics #1 VG $2,500 (restored)

SILVER AGE SALES

Action Comics #110 VG+ $175
Action Comics #284 FN+ $45
Action Comics #290 FN/VF $50
Adventure Comics #247 GD $400
Amazing Fantasy #15 FN- $9,000
Amazing Fantasy #15 GD+ $2,000 Signed By Stan Lee
Amazing Fantasy #15 VG $3,100
Amazing Spider-Man #1 FN $5,500
Amazing Spider-Man #1 GD $1,000
Amazing Spider-Man #1 GD $765
Amazing Spider-Man #1 GD $1,250
Amazing Spider-Man #1 GD+ $1,500 Signed By Stan Lee
Amazing Spider-Man #1 VF+ $32,000
Amazing Spider-Man #1 VG- $2,000
Amazing Spider-Man #1 VG- $2,350
Amazing Spider-Man #1 VG/FN $2,900
Amazing Spider-Man #2 FN+ $1,750
Amazing Spider-Man #2 GD+ $599
Amazing Spider-Man #5 VG $350
Amazing Spider-Man #15 VF $800
Amazing Spider-Man #20 VF $575
Amazing Spider-Man #39 FN/VF $165
Amazing Spider-Man #40 FN/VF $205
Anthro #1 VG+ $14.25
Aquaman #1 VG $110
Aquaman #6 FN/VF $65
Atom #13 FN/VF $48
Avengers #1 FN $800
Avengers #1 FN- $850
Avengers #1 VG $500
Avengers #4 FN- $600
Avengers #16 VF $200
Batman #121 F/VF $300
Batman #130 FN $80
Batman #155 VF/NM $500
Batman #171 VF $250
Batman #171 VG $76
Batman #173 VF- $56
Batman Annual #7 VG+ $15
Batman Prell Shampoo premium FN $4142.73
Brave and the Bold #29 VG/FN $400
Brave and the Bold #34 VG/FN $300 (restored)
Brave and the Bold #50 VG+ $40
Captain America #100 FN+ $20
Challengers of the Unknown #9 FN+ $117
Daniel Boone #3 FN+ $18
Daredevil #1 FN- $500
Daredevil #8 VF $100
Daredevil #131 VG+ $160
Dark Shadows (v1) #4 FN $16
Deputy Dawg Four Color #1238 GD+ $12.50
Detective Comics #297 VF- $95
Doom Patrol #87 VF $45
Dracula (Dell) #1 VG+ $15
Fantastic Four #1 app VF/NM $2,400
Fantastic Four #1 FN- $6,000
Fantastic Four #1 FR $602
Fantastic Four #1 GD $1,200

Fantastic Four #2 GD $400
Fantastic Four #7 FN/VF $750
Fantastic Four #48 VG $90
Fantastic Four Annual #3 VF $135
Fantastic Four Annual #4 VF+ $160
Flash #109 GD- $24
Flash #110 FN $400
Flash #134 VF $99
Flash Annual #1 VG/FN $85
G.I. Combat #76 VG $32
G.I. Combat #98 VG $22
G.I. Combat #108 FN $30
G.I. Combat #111 FN $24
G.I. Combat #114 VG/FN $38
Green Lantern #1 GD+ $350
Green Lantern #1 VG+ $800
Green Lantern #12 FN/VF $100
Green Lantern #21 VF- $80
Green Lantern #34 NM- $180
Green Lantern #38 VF- $68
Green Lantern #40 VF/NM $600
Hanna Barbara Super Heroes #3 FN+ $20
Hawkman #1 GD- $28
Hot Stuff #1 VG/FN $150
Hot Wheels #1 VG+ $13
House of Mystery #129 VG+ $19
House of Mystery #131 FN $24
House of Secrets #40 VG+ $21.50
Incredible Hulk #1 FN+ $9,500
Incredible Hulk #1 GD $1,200
Incredible Hulk #1 VF $3,500 (restored)
Incredible Hulk #1 VF+ $24,000
Incredible Hulk #2 FN/VF $1,350
Incredible Hulk #4 GD/VG $200
Iron Man #1 VF $280
Iron Man #1 VF $260
Iron Man #1 VG $75
Iron Man #1 VG $70
Iron Man #1 VG- $40
John Carter of Mars (Gold Key) #1 VG $13
Journey Into Mystery #83 G/VG $500
Journey Into Mystery #83 GD $500
Journey Into Mystery #112 VF+ $750
Justice League of America #1 F/VF $3,000
Justice League of America #2 VF $850
Justice League of America #3 VF $750
Justice League of America #11 VF/NM $400
Justice League of America #18 FN $60
Justice League of America #21 NM- $750
Justice League of America #50 FN- $35
Lone Ranger #116 GD+ $13.50
Marvel Tales #1 VG- $46
Metal Men #17 FN/VF $38
Munsters #2 VG/FN $23
My Greatest Adventure #31 FN+ $47
Nick Fury, Agent of S.H.I.E.L.D. #4 VF $22
Our Army at War #81 VG/FN $500
Our Army at War #83 FA/GD $250
Our Army at War #86 VG+ $60
Our Army at War #87 VG $55
Our Army at War #92 FN/VF $685
Our Fighting Forces #68 FN $20
Richie Rich #1 FN $700
Sea Devils #3 VG- $33
Sgt. Fury #1 GD $175
Showcase #6 VG/FN $600
Showcase #24 GD+ $140
Showcase #30 VG/FN $180
Silver Surfer (v1) #1 GD $27.50
Spectre #1 VG+ $29
Strange Adventures #1 GD/VG $197.18
Strange Tales #110 VG $300
Strange Tales #110 VG/FN $350
Sub-Mariner #1 FN $50
Sub-Mariner #1 VF+ $145
Sugar and Spike #3 FN- $350
Superboy #68 GD+ $32.50
Superman #129 FN/VF $138
Superman #199 VG+ $60
Superman's GF Lois Lane #40 VF $58
Tales of Suspense #1 VG+ $300
Tales of Suspense #2 VG/FN $150
Tales of Suspense #39 G- $435
Tales of Suspense #39 GD $725
Tales of Suspense #39 VG- $1,050
Tales of Suspense #48 VG $90
Tales of the Unexpected #73 FN/VF $41
Tales To Astonish #27 GD/VG $500
Tales to Astonish #35 FN/VF $300
Teen Titans #9 FN/VF $30
Teen Titans #10 FN+ $25
Tom & Jerry #213 VG $12
Tom Thumb (Four Color) #972 VG+ $15
Tomahawk #31 FN $36
Wonder Woman #105 FN+ $875
Wonder Woman #105 VG $300
World of Fantasy #18 GD+ $29.50
World's Finest Comics #112 FN/VF $60
World's Finest Comics #113 FN $28
World's Finest Comics #116 FN+ $40
World's Finest Comics #124 VF $55
World's Finest Comics #148 VF- $40
World's Finest Comics #168 FN $12
X-Men #1 FN+ $2,000
X-Men #1 G/VG $700
X-Men #1 GD+ $1,099
X-Men #1 VG $1,100
X-Men #1 VG- $1,100
X-Men #1 VG- $800
X-Men #2 VF/NM $2,200
X-Men #2 VG $350
Yak Yak #1 Four Color #1186 FN+ $40
Young Men #24 G- $300
Zorro (Four Color) #920 GD- $12.00

Bronze Age Sales:

Amazing Adventures #11 VF/NM $250
Amazing Adventures #11 VG $45
Amazing Spider-Man #129 FN- $95
Amazing Spider-Man #178 VF- $14.25
Amazing Spider-Man #200 VF+ $39
Amazing Spider-Man King Size Special #5 VG $33
Archie at Riverdale High #89 VF+ $39
Archie's Pals 'n' Gals #161 FN/VF $29
Archie's Roller Coaster nn NM+ $54
Avengers #92 VF/NM $40
Batman #227 VF+ $175
Batman #232 VF/NM $300
Batman #232 FN/VF $110
Beetle Bailey #112 (Byrne-a) VF/NM $45
Bugaloos #1 GD/VG $20
Conan (Marvel) #23 FN+ $19.50
Conan the Barbarian #23 FN+ $15
Conan the Barbarian #24 FN $15
Dracula Lives! #1 VF/NM $99
Dudley Do-Right #1 FN/VF $59
Eerie (Magazine) #17 FN $225
Fantastic Four #112 VF $31
Giant-Size X-Men #1 FN/VF $395
Green Lantern #76 VF $300
Green Lantern #76 VG $95
Green Lantern #87 FN $18
Hero For Hire #1 VF $99
House of Secrets #92 VF/NM $800
Howard the Duck #12 NM $40 (11 copies)
Howard the Duck #12 VF+ $24.50
Howard the Duck #13 NM $45 (10 copies)
Howard the Duck #13 NM $150 35¢-c variant
Howard the Duck #13 VF+ $27.25
Hulk King-Size Special #1 FN- $30
Hulk Special #3 VG+ $25
Incredible Hulk #181 FN/VF $450
Incredible Hulk #181 NM+ $7,000
Incredible Hulk #181 VF- $750
Incredible Hulk #181 VF- $500
Incredible Hulk #181 VG $239
Invaders #1 GD- $23.75
Iron Fist #14 (35¢ variant) GD/VG $205
Iron Man #55 GD $26
Justice League of America #111 VG+ $30
Marvel Feature #1 VG $22
Marvel Spotlight #5 VG $22.50
Mister Miracle #1 FN $18
Mister Miracle #7 VG+ $12
New Gods #1 FN $25
New Teen Titans #1 NM- $15.50
New Teen Titans #2 VF $19.99
Sandman #1 (Kirby) NM $14.99
Star Wars #1 VG+ $19
Superman #233 FN $21.50
Superman #238 FN+ $17.50
Tomb of Dracula #1 VG- $25
Tomb of Dracula #2 FN- $11
Tomb of Dracula #7 VG- $11
Tomb of Dracula #10 FN $50
Warlock #1 VG+ $12.50
Wolverine (v1) #1 VF+ $34
Wolverine (v1) #2 VF $25
Wolverine (v1) #2 VF+ $31.50
Wolverine (v1) #3 VF+ $32.50
Wolverine (v1) #4 VF+ $25.50
X-Men #69 VG+ $19
X-Men #94 FN $150
X-Men #95 GD+ $12.50
X-Men #95 VG- $24.50
X-Men #100 GD $11.50

Copper Age Sales:

Amazing Spider-Man #300 VF+ $75
Amazing Spider-Man #300 FN/VF $59
Batman #400 VG $19
Batman #407 NM $14
Marvel Super Heroes Secret Wars #8 VF $18
Miracleman #15 FN $65
Sandman #1 NM $24.88
Star Wars (Marvel) #107 NM $22
Uncanny X-Men #266 VF $22.50
Uncanny X-Men #266 VF+ $28.75
Watchmen #1 NM/MT $102.50
Watchmen #1 NM $45
Watchmen #1 VF/NM $25
Watchmen #1-12 set VF/NM $120
Watchmen #2 NM $12
Wolverine #10 VF+ $21.00

Modern Age Sales:

All Star Batman and Robin #10 NM $159.95 (recalled edition, Quitely variant cover)
All Star Batman and Robin #10 NM $150 (recalled edition, Jim Lee regular cover)
Amazing Spider-Man (v2) #36 NM $10 2 copies
Amazing Spider-Man #529 NM- $20
Captain America (2008) #25 NM- $25
Eternals Omnibus NM $118.50
Invincible #1 NM $64.99
New X-Men Omnibus NM $160.01
San Diego Comic Con Comics #2 VF $61
Savage Sword of Conan #235 NM- $125
Spawn #1 MT $19.99
Spawn #1 (B&W variant-c) NM/MT $95
Ultimate Spider-Man #1 (White cover) FN/VF $260
Walking Dead #1 NM $163.50
Walt Disney's Uncle Scrooge #310 NM $75.00

BIG LITTLE BOOK SALES

Brave Little Tailor VF $31
Buck Rogers and the Planetoid Plot FN+ $125
Buck Rogers in the City of Floating Globes VF/NM $286.80
Buck Rogers in the 25th Century A.D. nn VF/NM $131.45
Buck Rogers in the 25th Century A.D. nn VF $143.40
Captain Midnight and the Secret Squadron FN $31
Ceiling Zero VF+ $35
Chester Gump at Silver Creek Ranch VF/NM $51
Dick Tracy on the High Seas FN+ $39
Dick Tracy Out West GD $36.55
Dick Tracy the Detective and Dick Tracy, Jr. nn VF/NM $173.50
Fighting President, The VG $34.34
Flash Gordon in the Forest Kingdom of Mongo VF/NM $203.15
Flash Gordon in the Forest Kingdom of Mongo FN+ $55
G-Man on the Crime Trail NM- $89.63
John Carter of Mars #1402 FN/VF $98
Little Orphan Annie and Chizzler GD $30.99
Lone Ranger and the Red Renegades NM- $143.40
Mickey Mouse and the 'Lectro Box VF- $77.68
Mickey Mouse Presents Silly Symphonies Stories VF $101.58
Mickey Mouse the Mail Pilot nn FN/VF $71.70
Mickey Mouse the Mail Pilot nn VG $48
Mickey Mouse Runs His Own Newspaper VF $113.53
Mickey Rooney Himself FN $35
Phantom and the Sign of the Skull VF $113.53
Phantom and the Sign of the Skull VG $49
Robin Hood (EVW #10) VG- $25.49
Shadow and The Master of Evil FN/VF $191.20
Shadow and The Master of Evil VG/FN $65.73
Spy, The NM- $89.63
Tailspin Tommy The Pay-Roll Mystery nn NM- $119.50
Tarzan, The Son of VF- $83.65
Tarzan Escapes FN/VF $107.55
Tarzan the Terrible VF $51
Tarzan Twins, The (1935) #770 VG $41
Tom Swift and His Electric Silencer VF $48
Walt Disney's Story of Dippy the Goof FN- $34.71
Walt Disney's Story of Minnie Mouse GD/VG $15.39

GOLDEN AGE - SALES OF CGC-CERTIFIED COMICS

Action Comics #1 VF+ (8.5) $116,512 Mod (P)
Action Comics #1 PR (0.5) $22,250.00(coverless)
Action Comics #2 FN- (5.5) $16,730 Rockford
Action Comics #7 VF (8.0) $143,400
Action Comics #9 FN/VF (7.0) $19,120
Action Comics #10 FR/GD (1.5) $2,500 (restored)
Action Comics #31 VF (8.0) $2,600
Action Comics #222 NM (9.4) $2,270
Adventure Comics #40 FN+ (6.5) $8,365
Adventure Comics #40 FN/VF (7.0) $35,850
Adventure Comics #51 NM/MT (9.8) $44,812.50 Mile High
Adventure Comics #67 NM/MT (9.8) $44,812.50 Mile High
Adventure Comics #72 VG- (3.5) $1,399.99
Adventure Comics #72 NM/MT (9.8) $50,787.50 Mile High
All-American Comics #1 VF (8.0) $3,107 Larson
All-American Comics #16 VF+ (8.5) $28,680 Mod (P)
All-American Comics #16 FN (6.0) $85,500
All-American Comics #16 FN- (5.5) $60,000
All-American Men of War #128 VF- (7.5) $1,016
All-Flash #1 NM (9.4) $29,875 Denver
All-Flash #1 GD/VG (3.0) $1,300
All-Flash #8 NM+ (9.6) $4,500 San Francisco
All-Negro Comics #1 FN- (5.5) $3,107
All Star Comics #3 FN- (5.5) $7,250
All Star Comics #3 VG (4.0) $5,825
All Star Comics #8 VF/NM (9.0) $8,365
All Star Comics #33 VF/NM (9.0) $3,883.75
All Star Comics #36 VF (8.0) $2,237.99
All Star Comics #36 NM+ (9.6) $9,560
All Winners Comics #1 VF- (7.5) $9,560
All Winners Comics #1 VF+ (8.5) $14,340
All Winners Comics #1 NM+ (9.6) $83,650 Chicago
All Winners Comics #16 VF (8.0) $1,300
Batman #1 NM- (9.2) $33,000 (restored)
Batman #1 VF/NM (9.0) $280,000
Batman #1 VF (8.0) $9,001 (restored)
Batman #1 VF- (7.5) $15,535 Mod (P)
Batman #1 FN/VF (7.0) $10,000 (restored)
Batman #1 FN+ (6.5) $10,755 (restored)
Batman #1 VG/FN (5.0) $37,000
Batman #1 VG (4.0) $18,000
Batman #1 FR/GD (1.5) $8,365
Batman #2 VG/FN (5.0) $3,000
Batman #4 VG/FN (5.0) $1,600
Batman #8 FN/VF (7.0) $1,650
Batman Annual #1 NM (9.4) $4,780 Mohawk Valley
Black Terror #1 FN (6.0) $1,100
Brave and the Bold #1 FN- (5.5) $645
Captain America Comics #1 VF/NM (9.0) $150,000
Captain America Comics #1 VF/NM (9.0) $23,000 (rest.)
Captain America Comics #1 VF (8.0) $50,000
Captain America Comics #1 VF (8.0) $14,340 Slight (P)
Captain America Comics #1 VF- (7.5) $15,535 Mod (P)
Captain America Comics #1 FN+ (6.5) $11,000 (rest.)

Captain America Comics #46 FN/VF (7.0) $6,572.50
Captain Marvel Adventures #1 VG/FN (5.0) $10,755
Captain Midnight #14 NM- (9.2) $360 Crowley copy
Captain Midnight #14 NM (9.4) $956
Colossus Comics #1 NM (9.4) $17,000 Mile High
Crackajack Funnies #1 VF/NM (9.0) $17,000 Mile High
Crime Patrol #15 NM/MT (9.8) $9,560 Gaines File copy
Crime Patrol #16 NM (9.4) $4,481.25
Daredevil Comics #1 VF+ (8.5) $14,340 Rockford
Daredevil Comics #1 NM (9.4) $21,510
Daring Mystery Comics #1 FN- (5.5) $8,365 Kansas City
Detective Comics #1 FN (6.0) $13,145 Mod (P)
Detective Comics #1 FN/VF (7.0) $10,000 (restored)
Detective Comics #1 app 4.0 $10,000
Detective Comics #18 VG (4.0) $6,572.55
Detective Comics #27 VF- (7.5) $65,725 Mod (P)
Detective Comics #27 app 7.0 $50,787 Extensive (P)
Detective Comics #27 VG/FN (5.0) $40,000 (restored)
Detective Comics #27 GD/VG (3.0) $35,850 Slight (A)
Detective Comics #27 PR (0.5) $10,500 (Front-c missing)
Detective Comics #29 VG/FN (5.0) $19,120
Detective Comics #29 FN/VF (7.0) $5,500 (restored)
Detective Comics #30 FN- (5.5) $2,600
Detective Comics #30 VF/NM (9.0) $2,500 (restored)
Detective Comics #31 FN (6.0) $7,300 (restored)
Detective Comics #34 GD/VG (3.0) $1,500
Detective Comics #34 VG- (3.5) $1,549
Detective Comics #35 GD- (1.8) $2,208 (restored)
Detective Comics #35 GD/VG (3.0) $8,365 Slight (A)
Detective Comics #35 VG/FN (5.0) $17,100
Detective Comics #71 VF+ (8.5) $4,950
Detective Comics #112 VF/NM (9.0) $596.63
Fantastic Comics #1 NM- (9.2) $7,767.50
Feature Funnies #1 NM+ (9.6) $14,000 Mile High
Fighting Yank #1 VF/NM (9.0) $8,000 Mile High
Flash Comics #1 FN+ (6.5) $38,837
Flash Comics #1 FN/VF (7.0) $8,000 (restored)
Flash Comics #2 NM (9.4) $53,775 Mile High
Flash Comics #3 NM+ (9.6) $41,825 Mile High
Flash Comics #10 NM (9.4) $38,837 Mile High
Flash Comics #14 NM+ (9.6) $35,850 Mile High
Flash Comics #92 NM- (9.2) $17,327.50 Mile High
Flash Comics #104 NM (9.4) $47,800 Mile High
Flash Comics (Ashcan) #1 NM (9.4) $14,340
Flying Saucers #1 VF/NM (9.0) $900 Bethlehem copy
Four Color Comics #16 GD (2.0) $1,015.75
Four Color Comics #422 NM (9.4) $3,883.75 Donald Duck
Funnies on Parade #nn GD (2.0) $1,314
Green Hornet Comics #1 VF+ (8.5) $5,500
Green Lantern #1 VF/NM (9.0) $40,000
Green Lantern #1 FN- (5.5) $3,500 (restored)
Haunt of Fear #16 #(#2) NM+ (9.6) $3,346
Hit Comics #1 VF+ (8.5) $4,780
Hopalong Cassidy #1 NM- (9.2) $6,572.50 Vancouver
Horrific #3 VF (8.0) $1,950
Human Torch Comics #1 VF (8.0) $20,000
Jackpot Comics #4 NM- (9.2) $20,000
Lone Ranger Comics #1 VG (4.0) $1,081
Marvel Comics #1 VF- (7.5) $31,070 Mod (P)
Marvel Comics #1 VG+ (4.5) $21,500 (extensive rest.)
Marvel Mystery Comics #9 VG+ (4.5) $4,000 (restored)
Marvel Mystery Comics #9 VG/FN (5.0) $20,315
Marvel Mystery Comics #13 VG/FN (5.0) $1,380
Marvel Mystery Comics #13 VG/FN (5.0) $1,380
Marvel Mystery Comics #13 FN+ (6.5) $2,000
Marvel Mystery Comics #92 FN/VF (7.0) $2,000
Master Comics #39 VF/NM (9.0) $2,400 Edgar Church
Mickey Mouse #197 NM+ (9.6) $145 Whitman Comic
More Fun Comics #52 VG/FN (5.0) $8,365
More Fun Comics #52 FN (6.0) $65,725
More Fun Comics #52 FN+ (6.5) $7,000 (restored)
More Fun Comics #64 VF- (7.5) $2,500
More Fun Comics #73 VF (8.0) $10,157.50
Motion Picture Funnies Weekly #1 VG (4.0) $11,352.50
Movie Comics #1 NM+ (9.6) $17,000 Carson City
New Comics #1 FN/VF (7.0) $3,500 (restored)
New Comics #11 VF- (7.5) $7,000
Rangers Comics #15 FN/VF (7.0) $575 Rockford
Sensation Comics #1 VF (8.0) $3,107
Shock Illustrated #1 VF/NM (9.0) $7,208 (Gaines File)
Silver Streak Comics #7 FN (6.0) $1,226.89
Skippy's Own Book of Comics #nn GD+ (2.5) $695
Special Edition Comics #1 FN/VF (7.0) $3,346
Speed Comics #1 VF+ (8.5) $4,481.25
Star Spangled Comics #7 VF+ (8.5) $4,182.50
Sub-Mariner Comics #1 FN/VF (7.0) $10,755
Sub-Mariner Comics #1 VG/FN (5.0) $5,050
Sun Girl #1 VF- (7.5) $975.65
Super Comics #1 NM+ (9.6) $14,000 Mile High
Superman #1 VF- (7.5) $28,680 Mod (P)
Superman #1 VG/FN (5.0) $121,000
Superman #2 FN/VF (7.0) $9,560
Superman #5 VF (8.0) $3,346
Superman #11 FN (6.0) $735
Superman Annual #4 NM+ (9.6) $4,481.25
Tales From The Crypt #20 NM/MT (9.8) $6,572.50 Gaines
Target Comics #4 NM+ (9.6) $4,182.50
Thrill Comics (Ashcan) #1 VF/NM (9.0) $20,315
Walt Disney's C&S #19 NM (9.4) $15,535
Walt Disney's C&S #47 NM (9.4) $6,572.50
Whiz Comics #1 #2 VG/FN (5.0) $5,300 (restored)
Witness, The #1 NM (9.4) $6,400 Vancouver
Wonder Woman #1 FN/VF (7.0) $10,157.50
Wonder Woman #1 VF (8.0) $19,120
Wonder Woman #4 NM (9.4) $7,000
Wonder Woman #96 VF+ (8.5) $956
Wonder Woman #98 VG+ (4.5) $295
World's Best Comics #1 FN+ (6.5) $4,182.50
World's Finest Comics #18 NM+ (9.6) $7,100
Yellow Claw #1 FN+ (6.5) $500.00

SILVER AGE - SALES OF CGC-CERTIFIED COMICS

Action Comics #248 NM- (9.2) $2,164
Action Comics #252 VF/NM (9.0) $7,170
Action Comics #285 NM+ (9.6) $3,107
Adventure Comics #247 VF+ (8.5) $10,157.50
Adventure Comics #247 VG (4.0) $537.75 Slight (A)
Adventure Comics #248 VF+ (8.5) $1,434
Adventure Comics #290 NM/MT (9.8) $5,375
Adventure Comics #307 NM+ (9.6) $1,792.50
All-American Men of War #67 VF (8.0) $971
Amazing Fantasy #15 NM+ (9.6) $50,300 (restored)
Amazing Fantasy #15 NM (9.4) $227,000 (White Mountain)
Amazing Fantasy #15 VF/NM (9.0) $139,000
Amazing Fantasy #15 VF (8.0) $66,000
Amazing Fantasy #15 VF- (7.5) $42,500
Amazing Fantasy #15 FN (6.0) $13,145
Amazing Fantasy #15 VG/FN (5.0) $11,352.50
Amazing Fantasy #15 GD+ (2.5) $3,951.01
Amazing Spider-Man #1 NM+(9.6) $150,000
Amazing Spider-Man #1 VF+ (8.5) $26,000
Amazing Spider-Man #1 FN/VF (7.0) $8,365
Amazing Spider-Man #1 VG/FN (5.0) $3,800
Amazing Spider-Man #1 GD (2.0) $1,500
Amazing Spider-Man #2 VG (4.0) $1,912
Amazing Spider-Man #6 VF+ (8.5) $2,390
Amazing Spider-Man #14 VF+ (8.5) $2,025
Amazing Spider-Man #14 FR (1.0) $130
Amazing Spider-Man #19 NM/MT (9.8) $10,000
Amazing Spider Man #19 FN+ (6.5) $250
Amazing Spider-Man #32 NM- (9.2) $550
Amazing Spider-Man #34 NM (9.4) $1,500
Amazing Spider-Man #39 VF+ (8.5) $400
Amazing Spider-Man #43 NM (9.4) $1,100
Amazing Spider-Man #44 NM- (9.2) $300
Amazing Spider-Man #47 NM (9.4) $400
Amazing Spider-Man #50 NM/MT (9.8) $32,500
Amazing Spider-Man #50 VF (8.0) $500
Amazing Spider-Man #52 NM (9.4) $900
Amazing Spider-Man #54 VF/NM (9.0) $250
Amazing Spider-Man #65 NM- (9.2) $125
Amazing Spider-Man #67 NM (9.4) $400
Amazing Spider-Man #75 NM- (9.2) $180
Amazing Spider-Man #77 NM (9.4) $350
Amazing Spider-Man #91 NM+ (9.6) $776.75
Avengers #1 FN/VF (7.0) $1,800
Avengers #1 GD/VG (3.0) $388.38
Avengers #2 NM (9.4) $5,600
Avengers #4 NM- (9.2) $6,301
Avengers #4 VF (8.0) $1,195
Avengers #4 VF- (7.5) $1,250
Avengers #21 VF+ (8.5) $85
Avengers #22 VF (8.0) $90
Avengers #22 NM+ (9.6) $625
Avengers #42 NM (9.4) $225
Avengers #57 NM+ (9.6) $3,346
Batman #121 NM- (9.2) $5,550
Batman #148 NM (9.4) $1,673
Batman #181 NM+ (9.6) $4,481.25
Batman #200 NM (9.4) $400
Brave and the Bold #28 NM- (9.2) $35,850
Brave and the Bold #28 NM- (9.2) $35,850
Brave and the Bold #30 NM- (9.2) $9,560
Brave and the Bold #34 VF/NM (9.0) $1,912
Brave and the Bold #50 NM+ (9.6) $1,673 Pacific Coast
Brave and the Bold #54 NM+ (9.6) $7,170 Western Penn
Brave and the Bold #60 NM+ (9.6) $8,365 Pacific Coast
Captain America #100 NM+ (9.6) $3,250
Daredevil #1 NM- (9.2) $10,000
Daredevil #1 VF/NM (9,0) $4,182.50
Daredevil #13 NM+ (9.6) $1,000
Daredevil #26 NM+ (9.6) $600
Dell Giant Comics Tom and Jerry Winter Fun #6 NM (9.4) $155.35 File Copy
Detective Comics #327 NM (9.4) $3,100
Detective Comics #359 NM (9.4) $3,107
Eighty Page Giant #1 (Superman Annual) NM+ (9.6) $3,107
Fantastic Four #1 VF+ (8.5) $52,000
Fantastic Four #1 FN (6.0) $15,200
Fantastic Four #1 FN- (5.5) $5,975
Fantastic Four #1 VG (4.0) $2,600
Fantastic Four #1 GD (2.0) $1,500
Fantastic Four #2 NM- (9.2) $9,560
Fantastic Four #4 NM- (9.2) $8,365
Fantastic Four #12 VF/NM (9.0) $11,600
Fantastic Four #20 NM- (9.2) $1,500
Fantastic Four #48 VF/NM (9.0) $1,314.50
Fantastic Four #55 NM (9.4) $3,979
Fantastic Four #55 NM+ (9.6) $2,000
Flash #105 FN (6.0) $1,286
Flash #105 FN/VF (7.0) $2,390
Flash #123 NM (9.4) $19,120
Flash #129 NM+ (9.6) $7,170
Flash #136 NM (9.4) $3,107
Flash #139 NM (9.4) $3,883.75
Flash #175 NM (9.4) $597.50
G.I. Combat #68 FN (6.0) $1,075
G.I. Combat #68 FN (6.0) $1,076
G.I. Combat #87 VG/FN (5.0) $522
G.I. Combat #117 NM (9.4) $427
Ghost Rider #81 NM+ (9.6) $91
Green Lantern #13 NM- (9.2) $776.75
Green Lantern #13 NM- (9.2) $776.75
Green Lantern #18 NM (9.4) $1,434
Hawkman #1 VF/NM (9.0) $650
If The Devil Could Talk (1958) NM (9.4) $537.75
I Love Lucy #10 VF/NM (9.0) $123.09
Incredible Hulk #1 NM- (9.2) $117,500
Incredible Hulk #1 VF+ (8.5) $61,000
Incredible Hulk #1 FN/VF (7.0) $12,082

Incredible Hulk #1 FN+ (6.5) $8,500
Incredible Hulk #1 FN+ (6.5) $7,000
Incredible Hulk #1 FN+ (6.5) $7,250
Incredible Hulk #1 FN+ (6.5) $5,975
Incredible Hulk #1 VG- (3.5) $1,500
Incredible Hulk #1 FR/GD (1.5) $1,476.71
Incredible Hulk #2 VF- (7.5) $2,238
Incredible Hulk #6 FN+ (6.5) $587.89
Incredible Hulk #102 NM+ (9.6) $2,151
Iron Man #1 NM+ (9.6) $3,500
Iron Man #1 NM+ (9.6) $2,868
Iron Man #1 NM (9.4) $2,400
Iron Man #1 NM (9.4) $1,900
Iron Man #1 NM (9.4) $1,500
Iron Man #2 NM/MT (9.8) $1,300
Iron Man #6 NM+ (9.6) $410
Iron Man #10 NM (9.4) $200
Iron Man #55 NM (9.4) $657.25
Iron Man #55 NM (9.4) $640
Journey Into Mystery #83 NM- (9.2) $45,000
Journey Into Mystery #83 VG/FN (5.0) $2,629
Journey Into Mystery #97 NM- (9.2) $1,797
Journey Into Mystery #112 NM (9.4) $2,629
Journey Into Mystery #125 NM+ (9.6) $1,500
Justice League of America #1 NM (9.4) $35,850
Justice League of America #1 VF+ (8.5) $6,250
Justice League of America #1 FN/VF (7.0) $1,912
Justice League of America #2 FN+ (6.5) $278.30
Justice League of America #9 NM+ (9.6) $9,560
Justice League of America #12 NM (9.4) $1,673
Justice League of America #21 NM- (9.2) $1,015.75
Justice League of America #38 VF/NM (9.0) $158.13
Our Army at War #81 VF (8.0) $5,000
Our Army at War #81 VF+ (8.5) $6,596
Our Army at War #82 VF/NM (9.0) $5,000
Our Army at War #83 FN/VF (7.0) $5,000
Our Army at War #84 VF (8.0) $717
Our Army at War #88 FN/VF (7.0) $657.25
Our Army at War #91 VF+ (8.5) $4,780
Our Army at War #155 NM (9.4) $900
Our Army at War #156 NM+ (9.6) $1,375
Our Fighting Forces #1 VF (8.0) $2,271
Richie Rich #1 NM+ (9.6) $26,290
Richie Rich #1 NM (9.4) $8,365
Richie Rich #1 FN- (5.5) $625
Richie Rich #38 VF/NM (9.0) $67.66 File copy
Sgt. Fury #1 FN/VF (7.0) $800
Sgt. Fury #2 VF (8.0) $300
Showcase #4 FN/VF (7.0) $2,250 (restored)
Showcase #4 FN/VF (7.0) $10,755
Showcase #4 VG- (3.5) $2,629
Showcase #7 VF+ (8.5) $2,868
Showcase #8 FN+ (6.5) $1,374.25
Showcase #12 VF+ (8.5) $2,868
Showcase #22 VG (4.0) $567.63
Showcase #34 FN/VF (7.0) $537.75
Silver Surfer #3 VF/NM (9.0) $200
Silver Surfer #6 NM+ (9.6) $1,450
Silver Surfer #13 NM- (9.2) $225
Space Mouse Four Color #1244 NM+ (9.6) $191.20
Star Spangled War Stories #53 VF- (7.5) $318
Star Spangled War Stories #142 NM/MT (9.8) $596
Strange Adventures #117 VF (8.0) $523
Strange Tales #12 NM- (9.2) $1,050
Sub-Mariner #1 VF/NM (9.0) $358 Signature series Stan Lee
Sub-Mariner #1 VF/NM (9.0) $200
Sub-Mariner #6 NM (9.4) $120
Sub-Mariner #7 NM+ (9.6) $350
Sub-Mariner #8 NM- (9.2) $200
Sub-Mariner #8 NM (9.4) $525
Sub-Mariner #8 NM+ (9.6) $1,600
Sub-Mariner #9 NM+ (9.6) $365
Sub-Mariner #10 NM+ (9.6) $350
Sub-Mariner #15 NM/MT (9.8) $375
Superman #149 NM (9.4) $1,792.50
Superman #199 NM- (9.2) $1,075.50
Tales of Suspense #39 NM- (9.2) $35,000
Tales of Suspense #39 VF/NM (9.0) $23,250
Tales of Suspense #39 VF (8.0) $10,755
Tales of Suspense #39 FN/VF (7.0) $2,500
Tales of Suspense #39 FN/VF (7.0) $4,250
Tales of Suspense #39 FN (6.0) $2,800
Tales of Suspense #39 VG/FN (5.0) $2,800 Signature series Stan Lee
Tales of Suspense #39 VG/FN (5.0) $5,377.50 Stan Lee File
Tales of Suspense #39 VG (4.0) $1,500
Tales of Suspense #39 VG (4.0) $1,400
Tales of Suspense #45 FN/VF (7.0) $450
Tales of Suspense #57 VF/NM (9.0) $1,018
Tales of Suspense #59 VF/NM (9.0) $500
Tales of Suspense #59 NM (9.4) $1,673
Tales of Suspense #87 NM+ (9.6) $600
Tales To Astonish #92 NM+ (9.6) $900
Tales To Astonish #93 NM+ (9.6) $2,500
Tastee-Freez Comics #1 VF/NM (9.0) $200 File copy
Tastee-Freez Comics #1 NM (9.4) $400 File copy
Thor #126 NM (9.4) $2,400
Thor #133 NM+ (9.6) $600
Thor Annual #2 NM (9.4) $454.10
Thunder Agents #8 NM/MT (9.8) $450
Uncle Scrooge #66 NM/MT (9.8) $1,250
Uncle Scrooge #66 NM/MT (9.8) $1,250
Uncle Scrooge #70 NM+ (9.6) $750
Weird Fantasy #14 NM/MT (9.8) $5,299
World's Finest Comics #113 NM (9.4) $717
X-Men #1 VF+ (8.5) $14,340
X-Men #1 VF+ (8.5) $15,361
X-Men #1 VF+ (8.5) $14,340
X-Men #1 FN/VF (7.0) $4,545
X-Men #4 NM (9.4) $8,300 Pacific Coast
X-Men #13 VF/NM (9.0) $900
X-Men #14 VF/NM (9.0) $424.99 Sig. series Stan Lee
X-Men #27 VF/NM (9.0) $199.99 Sig. series Stan Lee

BRONZE AGE - SALES OF CGC-CERTIFIED COMICS

Alpha Flight #1 NM/MT (9.8) $65.73
Amazing Adventures #11 NM (9.4) $657.25
Amazing Spider-Man #100 NM+ (9.6) $956
Amazing Spider-Man #100 NM/MT (9.8) $3,000.65
Amazing Spider-Man #121 NM+ (9.6) $1,434
Amazing Spider-Man #121 NM+ (9.6) $1,912
Amazing Spider-Man #122 FN/VF (7.0) $270 Sig. series Stan Lee & John Romita
Amazing Spider-Man #122 NM+ (9.6) $1,100
Amazing Spider-Man #129 FN+ (6.5) $305 Sig. series Stan Lee
Amazing Spider-Man #129 VF/NM (9.0) $496
Amazing Spider-Man #129 NM- (9.2) $717
Amazing Spider-Man #129 NM+ (9.6) $1,915
Amazing Spider-Man #129 NM+ (9.6) $810
Amazing Spider-Man #129 NM/MT (9.8) $9,560
Amazing Spider-Man #194 NM- (9.2) $50
Avengers #193 NM/MT (9.8) $154
Avengers #196 NM/MT (9.8) $545
Batman #220 NM/MT (9.8) $1,314.50
Batman #232 NM+ (9.6) $1,314.50
Cerebus #1 VF/NM (9.0) $1,853.45 Dave Sim signed file copy
Cerebus #2 NM/MT (9.8) $896.25 Dave Sim signed file copy
Cerebus #3 NM/MT (9.8) $1,912 Dave Sim signed file copy
Conan the Barbarian #3 NM+ (9.6) $478
Daredevil #158 NM+ (9.6) $160
Daredevil #158 NM/MT (9.8) $1,075.50
Daredevil #158 NM/MT (9.8) $956
Daredevil #168 NM (9.4) $143.40
Daredevil #168 NM+ (9.6) $320
Daredevil #168 NM/MT (9.8) $1,553.50
Daredevil #186 MT (9.9) $170
DC Comics Presents #1 NM (9.4) $31
DC Comics Presents #26 NM (9.4) $56.89
DC 100-Pg Super Spect. #5 VF (8.0) $507.88
Demon #12 NM+ (9.6) $75
Detective Comics #402 NM (9.4) $488
Detective Comics #405 NM/MT (9.8) $3,250
Detective Comics #431 NM+ (9.6) $79.95
Fantastic Four #100 NM/MT (9.8) $1,934
Fantastic Four #233 NM/MT (9.8) $120
Fantastic Four #235 NM/MT (9.8) $120
Fantastic Four #236 NM/MT (9.8) $250
Fantastic Four #241 MT (9.9) $295
Fantastic Four #250 NM/MT (9.8) $135
Fantastic Four #257 MT (9.9) $300
Giant-Size X-Men #1 NM+ (9.6) $3,400
Giant-Size X-Men #1 NM+ (9.6) $2,390
Giant-Size X-Men #1 NM/MT (9.8) $12,500
Gothic Romances #1 NM (9.4) $1,800
Gothic Romances #1 VF/NM (9.0) $725
Green Lantern #76 NM- (9.2) $9,030
Green Lantern #76 NM- (9.2) $1,900
Green Lantern #76 VF+ (8.5) $629.99
Green Lantern #79 NM (9.4) $1,050
Incredible Hulk #181 VF/NM (9.0) $1,130
Incredible Hulk #181 NM (9.4) $1,800
Incredible Hulk #181 NM+ (9.6) $5,400
Iron Fist #14 VF (8.0) $2,025 35¢-c variant
Iron Fist #14 VF+ (8.5) $2,200 35¢-c variant
Iron Fist #14 VF/NM (9.0) $2,000 35¢-c variant
Iron Fist #14 NM+ (9.6) $567.63
Iron Man #128 NM/MT (9.8) $2,025
Iron Man #170 NM/MT (9.8) $100
Jonah Hex #1 NM/MT (9.8) $567.63
Justice League of America #100 NM (9.4) $107.50
Justice League of America #166 NM (9.4) $39
Marvel Spotlight #12 NM (9.4) $200
Marvel Team-Up #64 NM/MT (9.8) $149.95
Marvel Team-Up #69 NM/MT (9.8) $109.99
Marvel Zombies #1 NM/MT (9.8) $384
Mister Miracle #2 VF/NM (9.0) $22.50
New Gods #1 NM+ (9.6) $179.25
Primer #2 NM/MT (9.8) $1,125
Ronin #6 NM/MT (9.8) $305
Star Wars #1 NM (9.4) $12,019 35¢-c variant
Star Wars #1 NM (9.4) $10,500 35¢-c variant
Star Wars #1 NM- (9.2) $4,950 35¢-c variant
Star Wars #1 VF (8.0) $1,700 35¢-c variant
Star Wars #1 FN- (5.5) $700 35¢-c variant
Sub-Mariner #34 NM+ (9.6) $875 Don Rosa
Sub-Mariner #37 NM/MT (9.8) $500 Oakland
Superman #300 NM/MT (9.8) $388.38
Thing, The #1 NM/MT (9.8) $62.14
Tomb Of Dracula #12 NM+ (9.6) $100
Tomb Of Dracula #19 NM+ (9.6) $100
Tomb Of Dracula #70 NM+ (9.6) $65
Weird War Tales #1 NM (9.4) $597.50
Weird War Tales #9 NM (9.4) $150
Weird War Tales #11 NM- (9.2) $60
Weird War Tales #32 NM+ (9.6) $150
Werewolf By Night #1 NM (9.4) $310.70
Werewolf By Night #1 NM+ (9.6) $819.09
Witching Hour #28 NM (9.4) $120
Wolverine (1982 mini) #1 NM/MT (9.8) $657.25 Signed by Stan Lee
X-Men #94 NM+ (9.6) $6,300
X-Men #94 NM (9.4) $2,025
X-Men #94 VF/NM (9.0) $700
X-Men #96 NM/MT (9.8) $1,792.50
X-Men #100 NM/MT (9.8) $1,673
X-Men #100 NM/MT (9.8) $2,151
X-Men #101 NM/MT (9.8) $3,585
X-Men #140 NM/MT (9.8) $205
X-Men (Uncanny) #157 NM/MT (9.8) $95.60
X-Men (Uncanny) #160 MT (9.9) $617.00

COPPER AGE - SALES OF CGC-CERTIFIED COMICS

Amazing Spider-Man #238 NM (9.4) $89.63
Amazing Spider-Man #238 NM/MT (9.8) $899.95
Amazing Spider-Man #252 NM (9.4) $40
Amazing Spider-Man #252 NM/MT (9.8) $717 Sig. series
Amazing Spider-Man #300 NM- (9.2) $89.63
Amazing Spider-Man #300 NM+ (9.6) $227.05
Amazing Spider-Man #300 NM+ (9.6) $275
Amazing Spider-Man #300 NM/MT (9.8) $956
Amazing Spider-Man #333 NM/MT (9.8) $62.97
Amazing Spider-Man Annual #21 NM/MT (9.8) $65.73
Batman #428 VF/NM (9.0) $661
Batman: The Cult #1 GM (10) $142
Batman: The Killing Joke # NM/MT (9.8) $131.45
G.I. Joe, A Real American Hero #1 NM (9.4) $45
G.I. Joe, A Real American Hero #154 NM/MT (9.8) $860
G.I. Joe A Real American Hero #1 NM/MT (9.8) $400
Incredible Hulk #300 NM+ (9.6) $25
Justice League (1987) #3 NM- (9.2) $44 Variant Cover
Marvel Super Heroes Secret Wars #1 NM/MT (9.8) $135
Marvel Super Heroes Secret Wars #3 NM/MT (9.8) $91
Marvel Super Heroes Secret Wars #3 MT (9.9) $435
Marvel Super Heroes Secret Wars #4 NM/MT (9.8) $178
Marvel Super Heroes Secret Wars #5 NM/MT (9.8) $91
Marvel Super Heroes Secret Wars #5 MT (9.9) $407
Punisher (Lim series) #2 NM/MT (9.8) $203.15
Sandman #1 NM/MT (9.8) $720 Sig series
Sandman #8 NM/MT (9.8) $299
Spider-Man #1 NM/MT (9.8) $25 Silver ed.
Superman #423 NM+ (9.6) $29
Teenage Mutant Ninja Turtles #1 VF+ (8.5) $1,195
Thor #338 NM/MT (9.8) $213
Thor #339 NM/MT (9.8) $155
Thor #366 NM/MT (9.8) $48
Transformers #1 NM+ (9.6) $70
Transformers #1 NM/MT (9.8) $400
Transformers #4 NM/MT (9.8) $80
Transformers #5 NM/MT (9.8) $80
Transformers #9 NM/MT (9.8) $125
Transformers #32 NM/MT (9.8) $99.95
Watchmen #1 NM/MT (9.8) $510
Watchmen #1 NM (9.4) $99.99
Watchmen #1 NM- (9.2) $71.70
Watchmen #2 NM+ (9.6) $31
Watchmen #12 NM/MT (9.8) $204

MODERN AGE - SALES OF CGC-CERTIFIED COMICS

Action Comics #812 MT (9.9) $87.47 2nd Print Sketch Turner
Amazing Spider-Man #529 NM/MT (9.8) $160 Signed Garney
Amazing Spider-Man #533 MT (9.9) $279.97
Amazing Spider-Man #538 NM/MT (9.8) $174.97 Signed Garney Variant
Batman #608 RRP NM/MT (9.8) $1,500
Conan #24 NM/MT (9.8) $102 Variant Cover
Daredevil Vol. 2 #1 NM/MT (9.8) $115
Dark Tower: Gunslinger Born #2 NM/MT (9.8) $135 Sketch
Ghost Rider #1 NM/MT (9.8) $90 Sketch Cover
Harbinger #1 NM/MT (9.8) $2,550
Harbinger #1 NM+ (9.6) $162.50
Infinite Crisis #1 NM/MT (9.8) $11.49
Invincible #1 NM/MT (9.8) $35.99
John Byrne's Next Men #21 NM+ (9.6) $70
Justice League Of America #0 NM/MT (9.8) $24.51 Campbell variant cover
Justice Society Of America #1 MT (9.9) $150
Kingdom Come #1 NM+ (9.6) $29
League of Extr. Gentlemen Vol. 1 #5 NM- (9.2) $280 Recalled issue
League of Extr. Gentlemen Vol. 1 #5 VF- (7.5) $112.50 Recalled issue
Marvel Knights Spider-Man #20 NM/MT (9.8) $64 Variant Cover
Marvel Zombies #3 NM/MT (9.8) $259.90 Suydam Signed
Marvel Zombies #3 NM/MT (9.8) $104.97 Suydam Signed
Marvel Zombies #3 NM/MT (9.8) $149.95 Suydam Signed
New Avengers #27 NM/MT (9.8) $200 Variant 1 In 100
Secret Invasion #1 NM/MT (9.8) $15
Simpsons Comics #1 NM/MT (9.8) $199.95
Solar, Man of the Atom #10 NM/MT (9.8) $1,125
Spawn #1 NM+ (9.6) $15.50
Spider-Woman #1 NM/MT (9.8) $140
Strangers in Paradise #1 (1993) VF+ (8.5) $105
Superman/Batman #1 NM+ (9.6) $101.58 RRP
Ultimate Fantastic Four #21 NM/MT (9.8) $125
Ultimates #5 NM/MT (9.8) $139.97
Ultimate Spider-Man #1 NM/MT (9.6) $549.99 White Var-c
Ultimate Spider-Man #1 VF (8.0) $71.70 White Var-c
Ultimate Spider-Man #70 NM/MT (9.8) $104.97
Ultimate Spider-Man #74 NM/MT (9.8) $139.97
Ultimate Spider-Man #104 NM+ (9.6) $50 White Variant
Ultimate Spider-Man #104 NM/MT (9.8) $209.97 White Variant-c
Ultimate X-Men #1 NM/MT (9.8) $76.01
Walking Dead #1 NM/MT (9.8) $355.87
Walking Dead #32 MT (9.9) $114.95
Walking Dead #34 MT (9.9) $114.95
Wolverine: Origins #2 NM/MT (9.8) $200 Canada Variant Signed
Wonder Woman #219 NM/MT (9.8) $69.95

Top Books

The following tables denote the rate of appreciation of the top Golden Age, Platinum Age, Silver Age and Bronze Age books, as well as selected genres over the past year. The retail value for a Near Mint- copy of each book (or VF where a Near Mint- copy is not known to exist) in 2009 is compared to its Near Mint- value in 2008. The rate of return for 2009 over 2008 is given. The place in rank is given for each comic by year, with its corresponding value in highest known grade. These tables can be very useful in forecasting trends in the market place. For instance, the investor might want to know which book is yielding the best dividend from one year to the next, or one might just be interested in seeing how the popularity of books changes from year to year. For instance, *Action Comics* #7 was in 25th place in 2008 and has increased to 17th place in 2009. Premium books are also included in these tables and are denoted with an asterisk(*).

The following tables are meant as a guide to the investor. However, it should be pointed out that trends may change at anytime and that some books can meet market resistance with a slowdown in price increases, while others can develop into real comers from a presently dormant state. In the long run, if the investor sticks to the books that are appreciating steadily each year, he shouldn't go very far wrong.

Top 100 Golden Age Books

TITLE/ISSUE#	2009 RANK	2009 NM- PRICE	2008 RANK	2008 NM- PRICE	$ INCR.	% INCR.
Action Comics #1	1	$750,000	1	$675,000	$75,000	11%
Detective Comics #27	2	$575,000	2	$525,000	$50,000	10%
Marvel Comics #1	3	$460,000	3	$440,000	$20,000	5%
Superman #1	4	$440,000	4	$400,000	$40,000	10%
All-American Comics #16	5	$280,000	5	$245,000	$35,000	14%
Batman #1	6	$215,000	6	$185,000	$30,000	16%
Captain America Comics #1	7	$190,000	7	$175,000	$15,000	9%
Flash Comics #1	8	$135,000	8	$130,000	$5,000	4%
More Fun Comics #52	9	$125,000	9	$115,000	$10,000	9%
Adventure Comics #40	10	$105,000	10	$95,000	$10,000	11%
Whiz Comics #2 (#1)	11	$95,000	10	$95,000	$0	0%
Detective Comics #33	12	$85,000	12	$80,000	$5,000	6%
All Star Comics #3	13	$80,000	13	$75,000	$5,000	7%
Detective Comics #38	13	$80,000	13	$75,000	$5,000	7%
Detective Comics #31	15	$78,000	15	$70,000	$8,000	11%
Action Comics #2	16	$75,000	17	$66,000	$9,000	14%
Action Comics #7	17	$72,000	25	$57,000	$15,000	26%
Detective Comics #29	17	$72,000	17	$66,000	$6,000	9%
Detective Comics #1	19	VF $70,000	16	VF $68,000	$2,000	3%
All Star Comics #8	20	$65,000	19	$60,000	$5,000	8%
More Fun Comics #53	20	$65,000	19	$60,000	$5,000	8%
Sensation Comics #1	20	$65,000	19	$60,000	$5,000	8%
Human Torch #2 (#1)	23	$62,000	19	$60,000	$2,000	3%
Sub-Mariner Comics #1	23	$62,000	19	$60,000	$2,000	3%
Green Lantern #1	25	$61,000	19	$60,000	$1,000	2%
Marvel Mystery Comics #2	26	$60,000	26	$55,000	$5,000	9%
Marvel Mystery Comics #9	27	$58,000	27	$52,000	$6,000	12%
Captain Marvel Adventures #1	28	$51,000	28	$50,000	$1,000	2%
Adventure Comics #48	29	$50,000	30	$47,500	$2,500	5%
Marvel Mystery Comics #5	29	$50,000	32	$46,000	$4,000	9%
New Fun Comics #1	29	VF $50,000	29	VF $49,000	$1,000	2%
Wonder Woman #1	29	$50,000	31	$47,000	$3,000	6%
Action Comics #3	33	$48,000	33	$44,000	$4,000	9%
Detective Comics #28	34	$44,000	34	$40,000	$4,000	10%
Action Comics #10	35	$42,000	36	$36,000	$6,000	17%
All Winners Comics #1	36	$40,000	34	$40,000	$0	0%
Archie Comics #1	37	$38,000	38	$34,200	$3,800	11%
Pep Comics #22	37	$38,000	39	$33,000	$5,000	15%
Daring Mystery Comics #1	39	$37,000	36	$36,000	$1,000	3%
Suspense Comics #3	40	$36,000	43	$30,000	$6,000	20%
Walt Disney's Comics & Stories #1	40	$36,000	39	$33,000	$3,000	9%

TITLE/ISSUE#	2009 RANK	2009 NM- PRICE	2008 RANK	2008 NM- PRICE	$ INCR.	% INCR.
All-American Comics #19	42	$34,000	41	$31,000	$3,000	10%
Marvel Mystery Comics #3	43	$33,000	43	$30,000	$3,000	10%
*Marvel Mystery Comics 132 pg.	44	VF $32,000	43	VF $30,000	$2,000	7%
Superman #2	45	$31,000	50	$27,000	$4,000	15%
Batman #2	46	$30,000	50	$27,000	$3,000	11%
Captain America Comics 132 pg.	46	VF $30,000	49	VF $28,000	$2,000	7%
Detective Comics #35	46	$30,000	67	$24,000	$6,000	25%
*Motion Picture Funnies Wkly #1	46	$30,000	46	$29,000	$1,000	3%
New Book of Comics #1	46	VF $30,000	46	VF $29,000	$1,000	3%
Captain America Comics #2	51	$29,000	50	$27,000	$2,000	7%
Famous Funnies-Series 1	51	VF $29,000	46	VF $29,000	$0	0%
More Fun Comics #54	51	$29,000	56	$26,000	$3,000	12%
More Fun Comics #55	51	$29,000	50	$27,000	$2,000	7%
New York World's Fair 1939	51	VF/NM $29,000	41	VF/NM $31,000	-$2,000	-6%
Action Comics #4	56	$28,000	63	$25,000	$3,000	12%
Action Comics #5	56	$28,000	63	$25,000	$3,000	12%
Action Comics #6	56	$28,000	63	$25,000	$3,000	12%
Amazing Man Comics #5	56	$28,000	50	$27,000	$1,000	4%
More Fun Comics #73	56	$28,000	56	$26,000	$2,000	8%
All-American Comics #17	61	$27,500	56	$26,000	$1,500	6%
All Flash #1	62	$27,000	55	$26,500	$500	2%
Wonder Comics #1	62	$27,000	56	$26,000	$1,000	4%
Wow Comics (FAW) #1	62	$27,000	56	$26,000	$1,000	4%
All-Select Comics #1	65	$26,000	67	$24,000	$2,000	8%
Marvel Mystery Comics #4	65	$26,000	67	$24,000	$2,000	8%
Mystic Comics #1	65	$26,000	61	$25,500	$500	2%
Young Allies Comics #1	65	$26,000	61	$25,500	$500	2%
*Century of Comics	69	VF $25,000	63	VF $25,000	$0	0%
World's Best Comics #1	69	$25,000	67	$24,000	$1,000	4%
Silver Streak Comics #6	69	$25,000	67	$24,000	$1,000	4%
Adventure Comics #73	72	$24,500	67	$24,000	$500	2%
Captain America Comics #3	73	$24,000	75	$22,000	$2,000	9%
New Fun Comics #6	74	VF $23,500	73	VF $23,000	$500	2%
Adventure Comics #61	75	$23,000	75	$22,000	$1,000	5%
Four Color Ser. 1 (Donald Duck) #4	75	$23,000	82	$21,500	$1,500	7%
Planet Comics #1	75	$23,000	75	$22,000	$1,000	5%
All Star Comics #1	78	$22,500	75	$22,000	$500	2%
Daredevil #1	78	$22,500	74	$22,500	$0	0%
Red Raven Comics #1	80	$22,500	75	$22,000	$500	2%
USA Comics #1	80	$22,500	75	$22,000	$500	2%
Famous Funnies #1	82	VF $22,000	75	VF $22,000	$0	0%
Marvel Mystery Comics #8	82	$22,000	85	$20,000	$2,000	10%
Jumbo Comics #1	84	VF $21,500	82	VF $21,500	$0	0%
New Fun Comics #2	84	VF $21,500	84	VF $21,000	$500	2%
Green Giant Comics #1	86	$21,000	87	$19,000	$2,000	11%
Looney Tunes and Merrie Melodies #1	86	$21,000	85	$20,000	$1,000	5%
Action Comics #13	88	$20,000	93	$18,000	$2,000	11%
All-American Comics #18	88	$20,000	91	$18,500	$1,500	8%
Detective Comics #2	88	VF $20,000	87	VF $19,000	$1,000	5%
Double Action Comics #2	91	$19,500	91	$18,500	$1,000	5%
New Comics #1	91	VF $19,500	87	VF $19,000	$500	3%
Adventure Comics #72	93	$19,000	87	$19,000	$0	0%
All-American Comics #25	93	$19,000	98	$17,000	$2,000	12%
Daring Mystery Comics #2	93	$19,000	93	$18,000	$1,000	6%
Mickey Mouse Magazine - 1935 #1	96	VF/NM $18,500	93	VF/NM $18,000	$500	3%
Silver Streak Comics #1	96	$18,500	93	$18,000	$500	3%
Comics Magazine #1	98	VF $18,000	103	VF $16,500	$1,500	9%
Four Color Ser. 2 (Donald Duck) #9	98	$18,000	98	$17,000	$1,000	6%
Mystery Men Comics #1	98	$18,000	97	$17,500	$500	3%

Top 20 Silver Age Books

TITLE/ISSUE#	2009 RANK	2009 NM- PRICE	2008 RANK	2008 NM- PRICE	$ INCR.	% INCR.
Amazing Fantasy #15	1	$65,000	1	$50,000	$15,000	30%
Fantastic Four #1	2	$52,000	3	$41,000	$11,000	27%
Showcase #4 (The Flash)	3	$48,000	2	$45,000	$3,000	7%
Amazing Spider-Man #1	4	$44,000	4	$40,000	$4,000	10%
Incredible Hulk #1	5	$40,000	5	$32,000	$8,000	25%
X-Men #1	6	$22,000	6	$19,000	$3,000	16%
Journey Into Mystery #83 (Thor)	7	$18,000	8	$15,000	$3,000	20%
Showcase #8 (The Flash)	7	$18,000	7	$18,000	$0	0%
Tales of Suspense #39 (Iron Man)	9	$15,000	10	$12,500	$2,500	20%
The Flash #105	10	$14,000	10	$12,500	$1,500	12%
Showcase #9 (Lois Lane)	11	$13,500	9	$13,000	$500	4%
Brave and the Bold #28	12	$13,000	12	$11,500	$1,500	13%
Adventure Comics #247 (Legion)	13	$12,000	13	$10,000	$2,000	20%
Justice League of America #1	13	$12,000	13	$10,000	$2,000	20%
Fantastic Four #5	15	$10,000	16	$9,200	$800	9%
Showcase #22 (Green Lantern)	15	$10,000	15	$9,300	$700	8%
Tales To Astonish #27 (Ant-Man)	15	$10,000	16	$9,200	$800	9%
Fantastic Four #2	18	$9,500	18	$9,000	$500	6%
Green Lantern #1	18	$9,500	19	$8,700	$800	9%
Avengers #1	20	$9,200	-	$8,000	$1,200	15%

Top 10 Bronze Age Books

TITLE/ISSUE#	2009 RANK	2009 NM- PRICE	2008 RANK	2008 NM- PRICE	$ INCR.	% INCR.
Star Wars #1 (35¢ price variant)	1	$2,300	1	$2,000	$300	15%
Iron Fist #14 (35¢ price variant)	2	$1,600	3	$1,200	$400	33%
Incredible Hulk #181	3	$1,550	2	$1,450	$100	7%
Giant-Size X-Men #1	4	$1,250	3	$1,200	$50	4%
Green Lantern #76	5	$1,200	10	$700	$500	71%
X-Men #94	6	$1,150	5	$1,150	$0	0%
House of Secrets #92	7	$1,050	6	$1,000	$50	5%
Cerebus #1	8	$1,000	8	$900	$100	11%
DC 100 Page Super Spectacular #5	9	$975	7	$925	$50	5%
Amazing Spider-Man #129	10	$800	10	$700	$100	14%

Top 10 Copper Age Books

TITLE/ISSUE#	2009 RANK	2009 NM- PRICE	2008 RANK	2008 NM- PRICE	$ INCR.	% INCR.
Miracleman #1 Gold Edition	1	$1,500	1	$1,500	$0	0%
Gobbledygook #1	2	$1,100	2	$1,000	$100	10%
Miracleman #1 Blue Edition	3	$800	3	$800	$0	0%
Gobbledygook #2	4	$700	4	$650	$50	8%
Albedo #2	5	$650	5	$550	$100	18%
Vampirella #113	6	$510	6	$485	$25	5%
Grendel #1	7	$180	7	$175	$5	3%
Primer #2	8	$140	8	$130	$10	8%
Spider-Man #1 (Platinum)	9	$130	9	$130	$0	0%
Spider-Man #1 (2nd pr. w/Gold UPC)	10	$120	10	$120	$0	0%

***Teenage Mutant Ninja Turtles #1** - Recent sales of this book include a CGC 8.5 for $1,195

Top 20 Big Little Books

BOOK #	TITLE	2009 RANK	2009 VF/NM PRICE	2008 RANK	2008 VF/NM PRICE	$ INCR.	% INCR.
731	**Mickey Mouse the Mail Pilot** (variant version of Mickey Mouse #717) (Fine copy sold at auction for $5,090)						
nn	**Mickey Mouse and Minnie Mouse at Macy's**	2	$3,500	2	$3,200	$300	9%
717	**Mickey Mouse** (skinny Mickey on-c)	3	$3,135	3	$2,850	$285	10%
nn	**Mickey Mouse and Minnie March to Macy's**	4	$2,400	4	$2,200	$200	9%
W-707	**Dick Tracy The Detective**	5	$2,310	5	$2,100	$210	10%
725	**Big Little Mother Goose** HC	6	$2,035	6	$1,850	$185	10%
717	**Mickey Mouse** (reg. Mickey on-c)	7	$1,650	7	$1,500	$150	10%
4063	**Popeye Thimble Theater Starring...** (2nd printing)	8	$1,620	8	$1,470	$150	10%
721	**Big Little Paint Book**	9	$1,540	9	$1,400	$140	10%
725	**Big Little Mother Goose** SC	10	$1,495	10	$1,350	$145	11%
nn	**Mickey Mouse** (Great Big Midget Book)	10	$1,485	10	$1,350	$135	10%
4062	**Mickey Mouse and the Smugglers**	12	$1,430	12	$1,300	$130	10%
2070	**Big Big Paint Book**	13	$1,400	13	$1,275	$125	10%
4063	**Popeye Thimble Theater Starring...**(1st pr.)	14	$1,385	14	$1,260	$125	10%
nn	**Buck Rogers**	15	$1,320	15	$1,200	$120	10%
nn	**Mickey Mouse Silly Symphonies**	15	$1,320	15	$1,200	$120	10%
4062	**Mickey Mouse, The Story of...**	17	$1,210	17	$1,100	$110	10%
nn	**Mickey Mouse Sails For Treasure Island** (Great Big Midget Book)	18	$1,150	18	$1,050	$100	10%
nn	**Mickey Mouse and the Magic Carpet**	19	$1,050	-	$800	$250	31%
4057	**Buck Rogers, The Adventures of...**	20	$1,045	20	$975	$70	7%
4071	**Dick Tracy and the Mystery of the Purple Cross**	20	$1,045	-	$945	$100	10%
nn	**Tarzan**	20	$1,045	19	$980	$65	7%

Top 10 Platinum Age Books

TITLE/ISSUE#	2009 RANK	2009 PRICE	2008 RANK	2008 PRICE	$ INCR.	% INCR.
Yellow Kid in McFadden Flats	1	FN $14,000	1	FN $13,000	$1,000	8%
Mickey Mouse Book (2nd printing)-variant	2	FN $12,000	2	FN $12,000	$0	0%
Mickey Mouse Book (1st printing)	2	VF $12,000	2	VF $12,000	$0	0%
Mickey Mouse Book (2nd printing)	4	VF $10,000	4	VF $10,000	$0	0%
Little Sammy Sneeze	5	FN $6,000	7	FN $5,000	$1,000	20%
Pore Li'l Mose	6	FN $5,775	5	FN $5,500	$225	4%
Buster Brown and His Resolutions 1903	7	FN $5,500	5	FN $5,500	$0	0%
Little Nemo 1906	8	FN $5,000	8	FN $4,500	$500	11%
Little Nemo 1909	9	FN $4,000	9	FN $3,500	$500	14%
Yellow Kid #1	10	FN $3,500	9	FN $3,500	$0	0%

Top 10 Crime Books

TITLE/ISSUE#	2009 RANK	2009 NM- PRICE	2008 RANK	2008 NM- PRICE	$ INCR.	% INCR.
Crime Does Not Pay #22	1	$4,800	1	$4,500	$300	7%
Crime Does Not Pay #23	2	$2,600	2	$2,400	$200	8%
Crime Does Not Pay #24	3	$2,500	4	$2,000	$500	25%
True Crime Comics #2	4	$2,400	3	$2,300	$100	4%
Crimes By Women #1	5	$1,825	5	$1,750	$75	4%
The Killers #1	6	$1,750	6	$1,650	$100	6%
True Crime Comics #3	7	$1,725	6	$1,650	$75	5%
True Crime Comics #4	8	$1,475	8	$1,425	$50	4%
The Killers #2	9	$1,425	9	$1,350	$75	6%
True Crime Comics V2 #1	10	$1,350	10	$1,300	$50	4%

Top 10 Horror Books

TITLE/ISSUE#	2009 RANK	2009 NM- PRICE	2008 RANK	2008 NM- PRICE	$ INCR.	% INCR.
Vault of Horror #12	1	$8,300	1	$8,000	$300	4%
Eerie #1	2	$7,800	2	$7,300	$500	7%
Tales of Terror Annual #1	3	VF $6,000	3	VF $5,200	$800	15%
Journey into Mystery #1	4	$5,300	4	$5,000	$300	6%
Strange Tales #1	5	$5,100	5	$4,800	$300	6%
Crypt of Terror #17	5	$5,000	5	$4,800	$200	4%
Haunt of Fear #15	7	$5,000	7	$4,750	$250	5%
Crime Patrol #15	8	$4,600	8	$4,400	$200	5%
House of Mystery #1	9	$3,650	9	$3,500	$150	4%
Tales to Astonish #1	10	$3,600	10	$3,300	$300	9%

Top 10 Romance Books

TITLE/ISSUE#	2009 RANK	2009 NM- PRICE	2008 RANK	2008 NM- PRICE	$ INCR.	% INCR.
Giant Comics Edition #12	1	$2,800	1	$2,500	$300	12%
Intimate Confessions #1	2	$1,300	2	$1,250	$50	4%
Modern Love #1	3	$1,175	5	$1,075	$100	9%
A Moon, A Girl...Romance #9	3	$1,175	3	$1,100	$75	7%
A Moon, A Girl...Romance #12	3	$1,175	3	$1,100	$75	7%
Giant Comics Edition #9	6	$1,000	6	$950	$50	5%
DC 100 Page Super Spectacular #5	7	$975	7	$925	$50	5%
A Moon, A Girl...Romance #10	7	$975	8	$900	$75	8%
A Moon, A Girl...Romance #11	7	$975	8	$900	$75	8%
Giant Comics Edition #15	10	$950	8	$900	$50	6%

Top 10 Sci-Fi Books

TITLE/ISSUE#	2009 RANK	2009 NM- PRICE	2008 RANK	2008 NM- PRICE	$ INCR.	% INCR.
Mystery In Space #1	1	$6,000	1	$5,700	$300	5%
Strange Adventures #1	2	$5,700	2	$5,400	$300	6%
Showcase #17 (Adam Strange)	3	$4,700	3	$4,400	$300	7%
Weird Science-Fantasy Annual 1952	4	$4,000	4	$3,700	$300	8%
Journey Into Unknown Worlds #36	5	$3,850	4	$3,700	$150	4%
Showcase #15 (Space Ranger)	6	$3,750	6	$3,600	$150	4%
Fawcett Movie #15 (Man From Planet X)	7	$3,600	7	$3,500	$100	3%
Weird Fantasy #13 (#1)	8	$3,500	8	$3,350	$150	4%
Weird Science #12 (#1)	8	$3,500	8	$3,350	$150	4%
Strange Adventures #9	10	$3,400	10	$3,250	$150	5%

Top 10 Western Books

TITLE/ISSUE#	2009 RANK	2009 NM- PRICE	2008 RANK	2008 NM- PRICE	$ INCR.	% INCR.
Gene Autry Comics #1	1	$11,000	1	$12,000	-$1,000	-8%
Hopalong Cassidy #1	2	$8,400	2	$8,300	$100	1%
*Lone Ranger Ice Cream 1939 2nd	3	VF $6,500	3	VF $7,000	-$500	-7%
*Lone Ranger Ice Cream 1939	4	VF $6,000	4	VF $6,400	-$400	-6%
*Red Ryder Victory Patrol '42	5	$4,500	5	$4,800	-$300	-6%
Red Ryder Comics #1	6	$4,000	8	$4,000	$0	0%
*Red Ryder Victory Patrol '43	6	$4,000	6	$4,400	-$400	-9%
*Red Ryder Victory Patrol '44	6	$4,000	6	$4,400	-$400	-9%
Roy Rogers Four Color #38	6	$4,000	8	$4,000	$0	0%
*Tom Mix Ralston #1	10	$3,800	8	$4,000	-$200	-5%

Grading Definitions

10.0 GEM MINT (GM): This is an exceptional example of a given book - the best ever seen. The slightest bindery defects and/or printing flaws may be seen only upon very close inspection. The overall look is "as if it has never been handled or released for purchase." Only the slightest bindery or printing defects are allowed, and these would be imperceptible on first viewing. No bindery tears. Cover is flat with no surface wear. Inks are bright with high reflectivity. Well centered and firmly secured to interior pages. Corners are cut square and sharp. No creases. No dates or stamped markings allowed. No soiling, staining or other discoloration. Spine is tight and flat. No spine roll or split allowed. Staples must be original, centered and clean with no rust. No staple tears or stress lines. Paper is white, supple and fresh. No hint of acidity in the odor of the newsprint. No interior autographs or owner signatures. Centerfold is firmly secure. No interior tears.

9.9 MINT (MT): Near perfect in every way. Only subtle bindery or printing defects are allowed. No bindery tears. Cover is flat with no surface wear. Inks are bright with high reflectivity. Generally well centered and firmly secured to interior pages. Corners are cut square and sharp. No creases. Small, inconspicuous, lightly penciled, stamped or inked arrival dates are acceptable as long as they are in an unobtrusive location. No soiling, staining or other discoloration. Spine is tight and flat. No spine roll or split allowed. Staples must be original, generally centered and clean with no rust. No staple tears or stress lines. Paper is white, supple and fresh. No hint of acidity in the odor of the newsprint. Centerfold is firmly secure. No interior tears.

9.8 NEAR MINT/MINT (NM/MT): Nearly perfect in every way with only minor imperfections that keep it from the next higher grade. Only subtle bindery or printing defects are allowed. No bindery tears. Cover is flat with no surface wear. Inks are bright with high reflectivity. Generally well centered and firmly secured to interior pages. Corners are cut square and sharp. No creases. Small, inconspicuous, lightly penciled, stamped or inked arrival dates are acceptable as long as they are in an unobtrusive location. No soiling, staining or other discoloration. Spine is tight and flat. No spine roll or split allowed. Staples must be original, generally centered and clean with no rust. No staple tears or stress lines. Paper is off-white to white, supple and fresh. No hint of acidity in the odor of the newsprint. Centerfold is firmly secure. Only the slightest interior tears are allowed.

9.6 NEAR MINT+ (NM+): Nearly perfect with a minor additional virtue or virtues that raise it from Near Mint. The overall look is "as if it was just purchased and read once or twice." Only subtle bindery or printing defects are allowed. No bindery tears are allowed, although on Golden Age books bindery tears of up to 1/8" have been noted. Cover is flat with no surface wear. Inks are bright with high reflectivity. Well centered and firmly secured to interior pages. One corner may be almost imperceptibly blunted, but still almost sharp and cut square. Almost imperceptible indentations are permissible, but no creases, bends, or color break. Small, inconspicuous, lightly penciled, stamped or inked arrival dates are acceptable as long as they are in an unobtrusive location. No soiling, staining or other discoloration. Spine is tight and flat. No spine roll or split allowed. Staples must be original, generally centered, with only the slightest discoloration. No staple tears, stress lines, or rust migration. Paper is off-white, supple and fresh. No hint of acidity in the odor of the newsprint. Centerfold is firmly secure. Only the slightest interior tears are allowed.

9.4 NEAR MINT (NM): Nearly perfect with only minor imperfections that keep it from the next higher grade. The overall look is "as if it was just purchased and read once or twice." Subtle bindery defects are allowed. Bindery tears must be less than 1/16" on Silver Age and later books, although on Golden Age books bindery tears of up to 1/4" have been noted. Cover is flat with no surface wear. Inks are bright with high reflectivity. Generally well centered and secured to interior pages. Corners are cut square and sharp with ever-so-slight blunting permitted. A 1/16" bend is permitted with no color break. No creases. Small, inconspicuous, lightly penciled, stamped or inked arrival dates are acceptable as long as they are in an unobtrusive location. No soiling, staining or other discoloration apart from slight foxing. Spine is tight and flat. No spine roll or split allowed. Staples are generally centered; may have slight discoloration. No staple tears are allowed; almost no stress lines. No rust migration. In rare cases, a comic was not stapled at the bindery and therefore has a missing staple; this is not considered a defect. Any staple can be replaced on books up to Fine, but only vintage staples can be used on books from Very Fine to Near Mint. Mint books must have original staples. Paper is cream to off-white, supple and fresh. No hint of acidity in the odor of the newsprint. Centerfold is secure. Slight interior tears are allowed.

9.2 NEAR MINT– (NM–): Nearly perfect with only a minor additional defect or defects that keep it from Near Mint. A limited number of minor bindery defects are allowed. Cover is flat with no surface wear. Inks are bright with only the slightest dimming of reflectivity. Generally well centered and secured to interior pages. Corners are cut square and sharp with ever-so-slight blunting permitted. A 1/16"-1/8" bend is permitted with no color break. No creases. Small, inconspicuous, lightly penciled, stamped or inked arrival dates are acceptable as long as they are in an unobtrusive location. No soiling, staining or other discoloration apart from slight foxing. Spine is tight and flat. No spine roll or split allowed. Staples may show some discoloration. No staple tears are allowed; almost no stress lines. No rust migration. In rare cases, a comic was not stapled at the bindery and therefore has a missing staple; this is not considered a defect. Any staple can be replaced on books up to Fine, but only vintage staples can be used on books from Very Fine to Near Mint. Mint books must have original staples. Paper is cream to off-white, supple and fresh. No hint of acidity in the odor of the newsprint. Centerfold is secure. Slight interior tears are allowed.

9.0 VERY FINE/NEAR MINT (VF/NM): Nearly perfect with outstanding eye appeal. A limited number of bindery defects are allowed. Almost flat cover with almost imperceptible wear. Inks are bright with slightly diminished reflectivity. An 1/8" bend is allowed if color is not broken. Corners are cut square and sharp with ever-so-slight blunting permitted but no creases. Several lightly penciled, stamped or inked arrival dates are acceptable. No obvious soiling, staining or other discoloration, except for very minor foxing. Spine is tight and flat. No spine roll or split allowed. Staples may show some discoloration. Only the slightest staple tears are allowed. A very minor accumulation of stress lines may be present if they are nearly imperceptible. No rust migration. In rare cases, a comic was not stapled at the bindery and therefore has a missing staple; this is not considered a defect. Any staple can be replaced on books up to Fine, but only vintage staples can be used on books from Very Fine to Near Mint. Mint books must have original staples. Paper is cream to off-white and supple. No hint of acidity in the odor of the newsprint. Centerfold is secure. Very minor interior tears may be present.

8.5 VERY FINE+ (VF+): Fits the criteria for Very Fine but with an additional virtue or small accumulation of virtues that improves the book's appearance by a perceptible amount.

8.0 VERY FINE (VF): An excellent copy with outstanding eye appeal. Sharp, bright and clean with supple pages. A comic book in this grade has the appearance of having been carefully handled. A limited accumulation of minor bindery defects is allowed. Cover is relatively flat with minimal surface wear beginning to show, possibly including some minute wear at corners. Inks are generally bright with moderate to high reflectivity. A 1/4" crease is acceptable if color is not broken. Stamped or inked arrival dates may be present. No obvious soiling, staining or other discoloration, except for minor foxing. Spine is almost flat with no roll. Possible minor color break allowed. Staples may show some discoloration. Very slight staple tears and a few almost very minor to minor stress lines may be present. No rust migration. In rare cases, a comic was not stapled at the bindery and therefore has a missing staple; this is not considered a defect. Any staple can be replaced on books up to Fine, but only vintage staples can be used on books from Very Fine to Near Mint. Mint books must have original staples. Paper is tan to cream and supple. No hint of acidity in the odor of the newsprint. Centerfold is mostly secure. Minor interior tears at the margin may be present.

7.5 VERY FINE– (VF–): Fits the criteria for Very Fine but with an additional defect or small accumulation of defects that detracts from the book's appearance by a perceptible amount.

7.0 FINE/VERY FINE (FN/VF): An above-average copy that shows minor wear but is still relatively flat and clean with outstanding eye appeal. A small accumulation of minor bindery defects is allowed. Minor cover wear beginning to show with interior yellowing or tanning allowed, possibly including minor creases. Corners may be blunted or abraded. Inks are generally bright with a moderate reduction in reflectivity. Stamped or inked arrival dates may be present. No obvious soiling, staining or other discoloration, except for minor foxing. The slightest spine roll may be present, as well as a possible moderate color break. Staples may show some discoloration. Slight staple tears and a slight accumulation of light stress lines may be present. Slight rust migration. In rare cases, a comic was not stapled at the bindery and therefore has a missing staple; this is not considered a defect. Any staple can be replaced on books up to Fine, but only vintage staples can be used on books from Very Fine to Near Mint. Mint books must have original staples. Paper is tan to cream, but not brown. No hint of acidity in the odor of the newsprint. Centerfold is mostly secure. Minor interior tears at the margin may be present.

6.5 FINE+ (FN+): Fits the criteria for Fine but with an additional virtue or small accumulation of virtues that improves the book's appearance by a perceptible amount.

6.0 FINE (FN): An above-average copy that shows minor wear but is still relatively flat and clean with no significant creasing or other serious defects. Eye appeal is somewhat reduced because of slight surface wear and the accumulation of small defects, especially on the spine and edges. A FINE condition comic book appears to have been read a few times and has been handled with moderate care. Some accumulation of minor bindery defects is allowed. Minor cover wear apparent, with minor to moderate creases. Inks show a major reduction in reflectivity. Blunted or abraded corners are more common, as is minor staining, soiling, discoloration, and/or foxing. Stamped or inked arrival dates may be present. A minor spine roll is allowed. There can also be a 1/4" spine split or severe color break. Staples show minor discoloration. Minor staple tears and an accumulation of stress lines may be present, as well as minor rust migration. In rare cases, a comic was not stapled at the bindery and therefore has a missing staple; this is not considered a defect. Any staple can be replaced on books up to Fine, but only vintage staples can be used on books from Very Fine to Near Mint. Mint books must have original staples. Paper is brown to tan and fairly supple with no signs of brittleness. No hint of acidity in the odor of the newsprint. Minor interior tears at the margin may be present. Centerfold may be loose but not detached.

5.5 FINE– (FN–): Fits the criteria for Fine but with an additional defect or small accumulation of defects that detracts from the book's appearance by a perceptible amount.

5.0 VERY GOOD/FINE (VG/FN): An above-average but well-used comic book. A comic in this grade shows some moderate wear; eye appeal is somewhat reduced because of the accumulation of defects. Still a desirable copy that has been handled with some care. An accumulation of bindery defects is allowed. Minor to moderate cover wear apparent, with minor to moderate creases and/or dimples. Inks have major to extreme reduction in reflectivity. Blunted or abraded corners are increasingly common, as is minor to moderate staining, discoloration, and/or foxing. Stamped or inked arrival dates may be present. A minor to moderate spine roll is allowed. A spine split of up to 1/2" may be present. Staples show minor discoloration. A slight accumulation of minor staple tears and an accumulation of minor stress lines may also be present, as well as minor rust migration. In rare cases, a comic was not stapled at the bindery and therefore has a missing staple; this is not considered a defect. Any staple can be replaced on books up to Fine, but only vintage staples can be used on books from Very Fine to Near Mint. Mint books must have original staples. Paper is brown to tan with no signs of brittleness. May have the faintest trace of an acidic odor. Centerfold may be loose but not detached. Minor tears may also be present.

4.5 VERY GOOD+ (VG+): Fits the criteria for Very Good but with an additional virtue or small accumulation of virtues that improves the book's appearance by a perceptible amount.

4.0 VERY GOOD (VG): The average used comic book. A comic in this grade shows some significant moderate wear, but still has not accumulated enough total defects to reduce eye appeal to the point that it is not a desirable copy. Cover shows moderate to significant wear, and may be loose but not completely detached. Moderate to extreme reduction in reflectivity. Can have an accumulation of creases or dimples. Corners may be blunted or abraded. Store stamps, name stamps, arrival dates, initials, etc. have no effect on this grade. Some discoloration, fading, foxing, and even minor soiling is allowed. As much as a 1/4" triangle can be missing out of the corner or edge; a missing 1/8" square is also acceptable. Only minor unobtrusive tape and other amateur repair allowed on otherwise high grade copies. Moderate spine roll may be present and/or a 1" spine split. Staples discolored. Minor to moderate staple tears and stress lines may be present, as well as some rust migration. Paper is brown but not brittle. A minor acidic odor can be detectable. Minor to moderate tears may be present. Centerfold may be loose or detached at one staple.

3.5 VERY GOOD– (VG–): Fits the criteria for Very Good but with an additional defect or small accumulation of defects that detracts from the book's appearance by a perceptible amount.

3.0 GOOD/VERY GOOD (GD/VG): A used comic book showing some substantial wear. Cover shows significant wear, and may be loose or even detached at one staple. Cover reflectivity is very low. Can have a book-length crease and/or dimples. Corners may be blunted or even rounded. Discoloration, fading, foxing, and even minor to moderate soiling is allowed. A triangle from 1/4" to 1/2" can be missing out of the corner or edge; a missing 1/8" to 1/4" square is also acceptable. Tape and other amateur repair may be present. Moderate spine roll likely. May have a spine split of anywhere from 1" to 1-1/2". Staples may be rusted or replaced. Minor to moderate staple tears and moderate stress lines may be present, as well as some rust migration. Paper is brown but not brittle. Centerfold may be loose or detached at one staple. Minor to moderate interior tears may be present.

2.5 GOOD+ (GD+): Fits the criteria for Good but with an additional virtue or small accumulation of virtues that improves the book's appearance by a perceptible amount.

2.0 GOOD (GD): Shows substantial wear; often considered a "reading copy." Cover shows significant wear and may even be detached. Cover reflectivity is low and in some cases completely absent. Book-length creases and dimples may be present. Rounded corners are more common. Moderate soiling, staining, discoloration and foxing may be present. The largest piece allowed missing from the front or back cover is usually a 1/2" triangle or a 1/4" square, although some Silver Age books such as 1960s Marvels have had the price corner box clipped from the top left front cover and may be considered Good if they would otherwise have graded higher. Tape and other forms of amateur repair are common in Silver Age and older books. Spine roll is likely. May have up to a 2" spine split. Staples may be degraded, replaced or missing. Moderate staple tears and stress lines may be present, as well as rust migration. Paper is brown but not brittle. Centerfold may be loose or detached. Moderate interior tears may be present.

1.8 GOOD– (GD–): Fits the criteria for Good but with an additional defect or small accumulation of defects that detracts from the book's appearance by a perceptible amount.

1.5 FAIR/GOOD (FR/GD): A comic showing substantial to heavy wear. A copy in this grade still has all pages and covers, although there may be pieces missing. Books in this grade are commonly creased, scuffed, abraded, soiled, and possibly unattractive, but still generally readable. Cover shows considerable wear and may be detached. Nearly no reflectivity to no reflectivity remaining. Store stamp, name stamp, arrival date and initials are permitted. Book-length creases, tears and folds may be present. Rounded corners are increasingly common. Soiling, staining, discoloration and foxing is generally present. Up to 1/10 of the back cover may be missing. Tape and other forms of amateur repair are increasingly common in Silver Age and older books. Spine roll is common. May have a spine split between 2" and 2/3 the length of the book. Staples may be degraded, replaced or missing. Staple tears and stress lines are common, as well as rust migration. Paper is brown and may show brittleness around the edges. Acidic odor may be present. Centerfold may be loose or detached. Interior tears are common.

1.0 FAIR (FR): A copy in this grade shows heavy wear. Some collectors consider this the lowest collectible grade because comic books in lesser condition are usually incomplete and/or brittle. Comics in this grade are usually soiled, faded, ragged and possibly unattractive. This is the last grade in which a comic remains generally readable. Cover may be detached, and inks have lost all reflectivity. Creases, tears and/or folds are prevalent. Corners are commonly rounded or absent. Soiling and staining is present. Books in this condition generally have all pages and most of the covers, although there may be up to 1/4 of the front cover missing or no back cover, but not both. Tape and other forms of amateur repair are more common. Spine roll is more common; spine split can extend up to 2/3 the length of the book. Staples may be missing or show rust and discoloration. An accumulation of staple tears and stress lines may be present, as well as rust migration. Paper is brown and may show brittleness around the edges but not in the central portion of the pages. Acidic odor may be present. Accumulation of interior tears. Chunks may be missing. The centerfold may be missing if readability is generally preserved (although there may be difficulty). Coupons may be cut.

0.5 POOR (PR): Most comic books in this grade have been sufficiently degraded to the point where there is little or no collector value; they are easily identified by a complete absence of eye appeal. Comics in this grade are brittle almost to the point of turning to dust with a touch, and are usually incomplete. Extreme cover fading may render the cover almost indiscernible. May have extremely severe stains, mildew or heavy cover abrasion to the point that some cover inks are indistinct/absent. Covers may be detached with large chunks missing. Can have extremely ragged edges and extensive creasing. Corners are rounded or virtually absent. Covers may have been defaced with paints, varnishes, glues, oil, indelible markers or dyes, and may have suffered heavy water damage. Can also have extensive amateur repairs such as laminated covers. Extreme spine roll present; can have extremely ragged spines or a complete, book-length split. Staples can be missing or show extreme rust and discoloration. Extensive staple tears and stress lines may be present, as well as extreme rust migration. Paper exhibits moderate to severe brittleness (where the comic book literally falls apart when examined). Extreme acidic odor may be present. Extensive interior tears. Multiple pages, including the centerfold, may be missing that affect readability. Coupons may be cut.

Publishers' Codes

The following abbreviations are used with cover reproductions throughout the book for copyright purposes:

ABC-America's Best Comics
AC-AC Comics
ACE-Ace Periodicals
ACG-American Comics Group
AJAX-Ajax-Farrell
AP-Archie Publications
ATLAS-Atlas Comics (see below)
AVON-Avon Periodicals
BP-Better Publications
C & L-Cupples & Leon
CC-Charlton Comics
CEN-Centaur Publications
CCG-Columbia Comics Group
CG-Catechetical Guild
CHES-Harry 'A' Chesler
CLDS-Classic Det. Stories
CM-Comics Magazine
CN-Condé Nast
DC-DC Comics, Inc.
DEF-Defiant Comics
DELL-Dell Publishing Co.
DH-Dark Horse
DIS-Disney Enterprises, Inc.
DMP-David McKay Publishing
DS-D. S. Publishing Co.
EAS-Eastern Color Printing Co.
EC-E. C. Comics
ECL-Eclipse Comics
ENWIL-Enwil Associates
EP-Elliott Publications
ERB-Edgar Rice Burroughs
FAW-Fawcett Publications
FC-First Comics
FF-Famous Funnies
FH-Fiction House Magazines
FOX-Fox Features Syndicate
GIL-Gilberton
GK-Gold Key
GP-Great Publications
HARV-Harvey Publications
H-B-Hanna-Barbera
HILL-Hillman Periodicals
HOKE-Holyoke Publishing Co.
IM-Image Comics
KING-King Features Syndicate
LEV-Lev Gleason Publications
MAL-Malibu Comics
MAR-Marvel Characters, Inc.
ME-Magazine Enterprises
MLJ-MLJ Magazines
MS-Mirage Studios
NOVP-Novelty Press
NYNS-New York News Syndicate
PG-Premier Group
PINE-Pines
PMI-Parents' Magazine Institute
PRIZE-Prize Publications
QUA-Quality Comics Group
REAL-Realistic Comics
RH-Rural Home
S & S-Street and Smith Publishers
SKY-Skywald Publications
STAR-Star Publications
STD-Standard Comics
STJ-St. John Publishing Co.
SUPR-Superior Comics
TC-Tower Comics
TM-Trojan Magazines
TMP-Todd McFarlane Prods.
TOBY-Toby Press
TOPS-Tops Comics
UFS-United Features Syndicate
VAL-Valiant
VITL-Vital Publications
WB-Warner Brothers.
WEST-Western Publishing Co.
WHIT-Whitman Publishing Co.
WHW-William H. Wise
WMG-William M. Gaines (E. C.)
WP-Warren Publishing Co.
YM-Youthful Magazines
Z-D-Ziff-Davis Publishing Co.

Overstreet Advisors

Even before the first edition of *The Official Overstreet Comic Book Price Guide* was printed, author Robert M. Overstreet solicited pricing data, historical notations, and general information from a variety of sources. What was initially an informal group offering input quickly became an organized field of comic book collectors, dealers and historians whose opinions are actively solicited in advance of each edition of this book. Some of these Overstreet Advisors are specialists who deal in particular niches within the comic book world, while others are generalists who are interested in commenting on the broader marketplace. Each advisor provides information from their respective areas of interest and expertise, spanning the history of American comics.

While some choose to offer pricing and historical information in the form of annotated sales catalogs, auction catalogs, or documented private sales, assistance from others comes in the form of the market reports such as those beginning on page 75 in this book. In addition to those who have served as Overstreet Advisors almost since *The Guide*'s inception, each year new contributors are sought.

With that in mind, we are pleased to present our newest Overstreet Advisors:

THE CLASS OF 2009

MATT BALLESTEROS
Collector
Houston, TX

FRANK CWIKLIK
Dealer
New York, NY

WALTER DURAJLIJA
Dealer
Hamilton, ONT

JEF HINDS
Dealer
Madison, WI

JAMIE NEWBOLD
Dealer
San Diego, CA

BARRY SANDOVAL
Auction Sales
Dallas, TX

BEN SMITH
Auction Sales
New York, NY

RICK WHITELOCK
Dealer
Lynn Haven, FL

A complete listing of our Overstreet Advisors can be found on our title page and beginning on page 1,104.

Bill Hughes
Paid You How Much?

CALL NOW FOR IMMEDIATE PAYMENT!!

ALWAYS SEEKING:

Golden-Age, Silver-Age & Bronze-Age Comics
Vintage Original Comic & Collector Card Art
Vintage Baseball Cards & Uncut Sheets
Movie Posters & Stills
Western, Sci-Fi and Comedy Collectibles
Vintage Toys in Original Boxes
Vintage Disneyana & Other Animation

William Hughes' Vintage Collectables
P.O. Box 270244
Flower Mound, Texas 75027
Office: 972-539-9190
Mobile: 973-432-4070
Fax: 972-691-8837
www.VintageCollectables.net
Email: whughes199@yahoo.com

Senior Advisor Overstreet Price Guide

Chicago Daily Tribune
THE WORLD'S GREATEST NEWSPAPER
HOME

DEWEY DEFEATS TRUMAN

G.O.P. Sweep Indicated in State; Boyle Leads in City

REPUBLICAN TICKET AHEAD OF 1944 VOTE
Town Balloting Gives Trend

Tops Coghlan in Hot Race for Attorney

RECORD CITY VOTE SEEN IN LATE TALLIES
Suburban Ballot Near 375,000

BULLETINS ON ELECTIONS

Early Count Gives G.O.P. Senate Edge

PUTS G.O.P. BACK IN THE WHITE HOUSE
Sizable Electoral Margin Seen

RARE AND HISTORICAL NEWSPAPERS BOUGHT AND SOLD

(16th Century-20th Century)

BUYING:

Bound Volumes and Rare Individual Issues of Newspapers, Harper's Weekly, Leslie's, Gentleman's Magazine (18th century), Police Gazettes (19th century only), The Daily Graphic, etc.

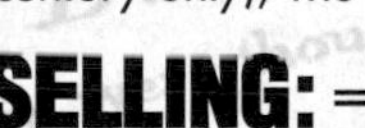

SELLING:

Major Events in U.S. and World History, European 16th-17th century, Colonial and Rev. War, Civil War, Wild West, 20th century big headlines, etc.

Contact Eric C. Caren 914-248-8038 or
Stephen A. Goldman toll free at 888-228-8755
or in PA. 717-846-5120

OldNews, Inc. The Caren Archive and
Stephen A. Goldman Historical Newspapers
P.O. Box 359, Parkton, MD 21120

CREDENTIALS:

Both Members- American Antiquarian Society, Consultants- The Freedom Forum Newseum, etc.
Author, *Pioneer Age*

We'll pay
TOP DOLLAR
for your
collection!

SILVER
Presenting THE FLASH
File Edit View Go Bookmarks Options Directory
Netscape: four color comics
Back Forward Home Reload Images Open Print Find Stop
FAN FORUM
FOUR COLOR COMICS
SEARCH COMICS!
COMPANY INFO.
1000's of comics on-line!
SEARCH-ABLE
www.fourcolorcomics.com
the AMAZING SPIDER-MAN
the CHAMELEON STRIKES!
AMAZING FANTASY
SPIDER MAN
Fantastic Four
The FLASH
MASTER OF MIRRORS!
THE INCREDIBLE HULK
THE STRANGEST MAN OF ALL TIME!!
IS HE MAN OR MONSTER OR... IS HE BOTH?
JUSTICE LEAGUE of AMERICA
"STARRO THE CONQUEROR!"
WHY YOU SHOULD CALL US BEFORE YOU SELL YOUR COLLECTION OF COMICS, ARTWORK OR MEMORABILIA:
We make it easy! No waiting for payment, No song and dance about grading. We'll come to you; anywhere, anytime! Four Color Comics takes the risk out of selling. Treat yourself to an honest, straight-forward experience—Sell your collection to us and walk away with more money in your pocket and a smile on your face!
FOUR COLOR
COMICS
P.O. BOX 1399, Scarsdale, NY 10583
TEL: (914) 722-4696, FAX (914) 722-7656

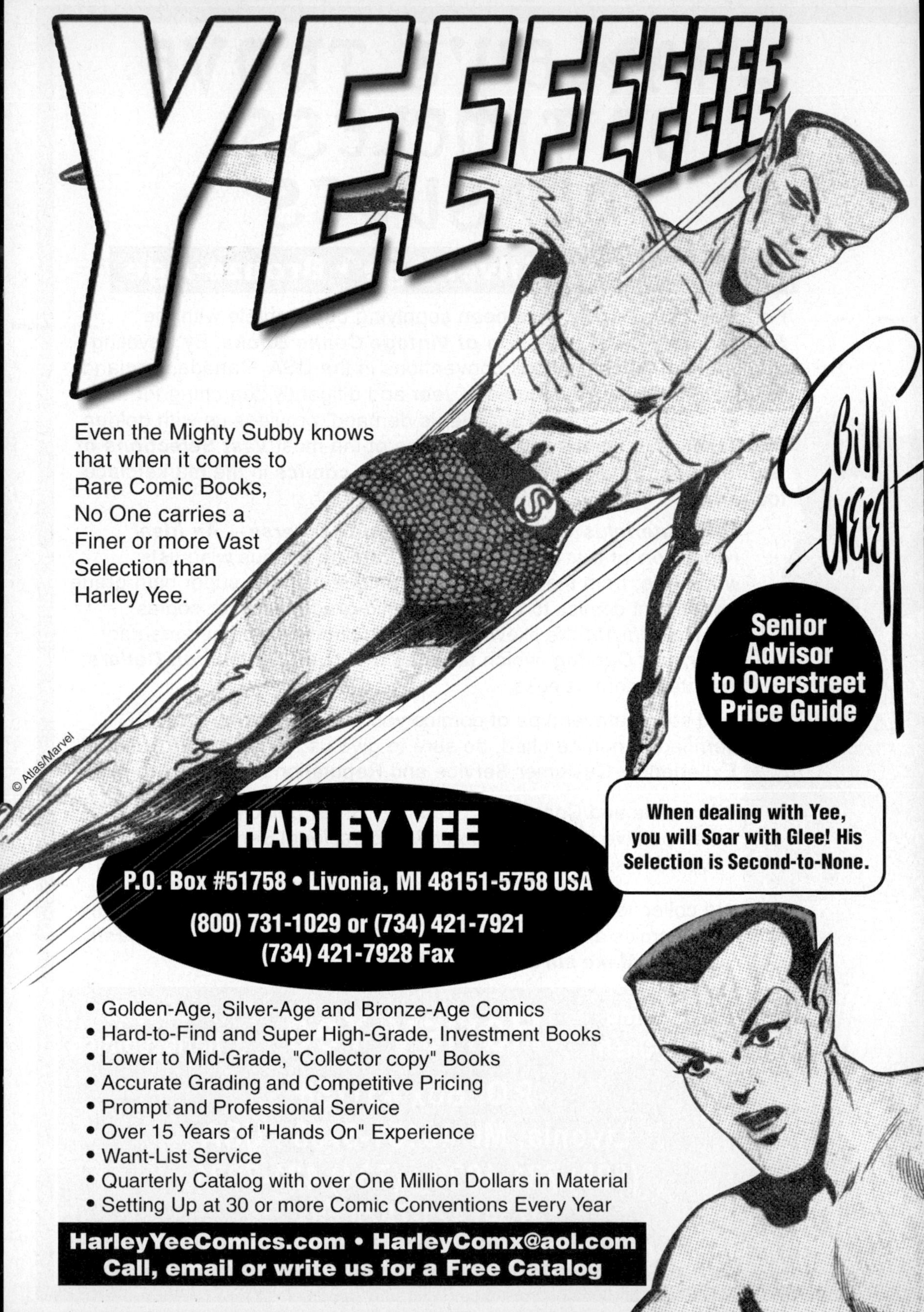
YEEEEEEEE
Bill Everett
Even the Mighty Subby knows that when it comes to Rare Comic Books, No One carries a Finer or more Vast Selection than Harley Yee.
Senior Advisor to Overstreet Price Guide
© Atlas/Marvel
HARLEY YEE
P.O. Box #51758 • Livonia, MI 48151-5758 USA
(800) 731-1029 or (734) 421-7921
(734) 421-7928 Fax
When dealing with Yee, you will Soar with Glee! His Selection is Second-to-None.
• Golden-Age, Silver-Age and Bronze-Age Comics
• Hard-to-Find and Super High-Grade, Investment Books
• Lower to Mid-Grade, "Collector copy" Books
• Accurate Grading and Competitive Pricing
• Prompt and Professional Service
• Over 15 Years of "Hands On" Experience
• Want-List Service
• Quarterly Catalog with over One Million Dollars in Material
• Setting Up at 30 or more Comic Conventions Every Year
HarleyYeeComics.com • HarleyComx@aol.com
Call, email or write us for a Free Catalog

THE SELLER'S GUIDE

Yes, here are the pages you're looking for. These percentages will help you determine the sale value of your collection. If you do not find your title, call with any questions. We have purchased many of the major well-known collections. We are serious about buying your comics and paying you the most for them.

If you have comics or related items for sale call or send your list for a quote. No collection is too large or small. Immediate funds available of 500K and beyond.

These are some of the high prices we will pay. Percentages stated will be paid for any grade unless otherwise noted. All percentages based on this Overstreet Guide.

—*JAMES PAYETTE*

We are paying 100% of Guide for the following:

All Select	1-up
All Winners	6-up
America's Best	1-up
Black Terror	1-25
Captain Aero	3-25
Captain America	11-up
Catman	1-up
Dynamic	2-15
Exciting	3-50
Human Torch	6-35
Marvel Mystery	11-up
Pep	22-45
Prize	2-50
Reform School Girl	1
Speed	10-30
Startling	2-up
Sub-Mariner	3-32
Thrilling	2-52
U.S.A.	6-up
Wonder (Nedor)	1-up

We are paying 75% of Guide for the following:

- Action 1-15
- Adventure 247
- All New 2-13
- All Winners 1-5
- Amazing Man all
- Amazing Mystery Funnies all
- Andy Devine
- Arrow all
- Captain America 1-10
- Daredevil (2nd) 1
- Detective 2-26
- Detective Eye all
- Detective Picture Stories all
- Fantastic Four 1-2
- Four Favorites 3-27
- Funny Pages all
- Funny Picture Stories all
- Hangman all
- Jumbo 1-10
- Journey into Mystery 83
- Keen Detective Funnies all
- Marvel Mystery 1-10
- Mystery Men all
- Showcase 4
- Spiderman 1-2
- Superman 1
- Superman's Pal 1
- Tim McCoy all
- Wonder (Fox)
- Young Allies all

BUYING & SELLING GOLDEN & SILVER AGE COMICS SINCE 1975

SILVER AGE
12¢
BUYING
ALL COMICS, ALL GRADES
• WILL TRAVEL TO YOU!
• WILL PAY MORE!
• WILL PAY CASH!
COMICS
107 APR.
SELLING
the LARGEST SELECTION of SILVER AGE in N.Y.C. WITHOUT APPOINTMENT
• COMPETITIVE PRICING!
• STRICT GRADING!
• MAIL ORDER ANYWHERE
• WANT LIST SERVICE
• FREE CATALOGUE
• OPEN 7 DAYS
©MARVEL COMICS

DON'T BUY OR SELL ANOTHER

This X-men #66 had previously graded CGC 9.2. Utilizing the **pressing service**, the book obtained a CGC 9.6 grade upon resubmission. Cost for pressing: $25.

A Batman #1 with an ugly sticker on the front cover, dying to be removed using the **conservation service**. Cost for conservation: $125.

WHAT WE DO

For over a decade, Classics Incorporated has been helping collectors preserve their treasures. Given the advanced state of the hobby these days, it's imperative that you make the right decisions whether you're buying or selling one comic, or an entire collection. Classics Incorporated is an expert in all aspects of the marketplace, from third-party grading and auctions, to pedigreed comics, restoration, and investment consulting. Our accuracy in CGC grading, pressing and valuation is unparalleled. Using our unique combination of services and advice will ensure that you make the best decision for your comics.

The process is easy. Our website classicsincorporated.com will answer any questions you have about our services, and guide you through the easy process of submission. In addition, the website offers many insights into the marketplace, including published articles, comic valuation tables, before and after pictures of our work, and links to helpful sites that delve deeper into the nuances of comic collecting. You will not find such a complete accumulation of crucial information anywhere else.

A quick look at a few of the many services we offer:

PRESSING

One of the most popular services used by our clients today, pressing is best utilized for **high grade, unrestored comics**. Pressing is not considered restoration, and is used to remove light defects to make a high grade even higher (for example, pressing a Spider-man #20 from CGC 9.0 to 9.2). The age of the comic does not matter, and because of the low cost of pressing (as low as $12 per book), the comic's value does not have to be high for the service to be beneficial. But it takes practice to find the right candidates for pressing. Many factors must be considered for each book, such as how to spot "bad" and "good" defects. Guidelines are set forth on classicsincorporated.com so you can make informed decisions before sending us your books for review.

CONSERVATION

Another low-cost service, conservation best suits **lower to mid grade comics in the GD to VF range**. Its main goal is to rid a comic book of harmful agents (tape, glue, stains, mold), and/or improve the appearance and

(972) 980-8040 • 1440 Halsey Way, Suite 114 • Carrollton, TX 75007 • www.classicsincorporated.com

COMIC UNTIL YOU CALL US!

desirability through light restorative techniques. Comics older than 1964 are the best candidates for conservation, although there are exceptions. Value is not a significant factor due to the low cost of conservation, which starts at $30. Conservation can include water, dry, and solvent cleaning, tear seals, support, staple cleaning/replacement and pressing. A breakdown of costs can be found on classicsincorporated.com.

This Amazing Fantasy #15 is a prime **restoration** candidate. Other than the torn off logo area, the book is in VF. Current value is $750.

RESTORATION

The eldest of the services offered, restoration targets **low grade comics in the FA to GD+ range**. It utilizes every weapon in our arsenal to maximize the grade of a comic, including piece replacement, grafting and color matching. The best candidates for restoration are pre-1960 comics with a current value of $1000 or more. The truth is as many as 50% of comics submitted to us for restoration are turned down because the work is either unnecessary or detrimental to its value. But restoring the right candidates can produce eye-popping results. Classicsincorporated.com offers guidelines that will aid you in finding the right books for this service. We also offer free appraisals on emailed scans and online auctions.

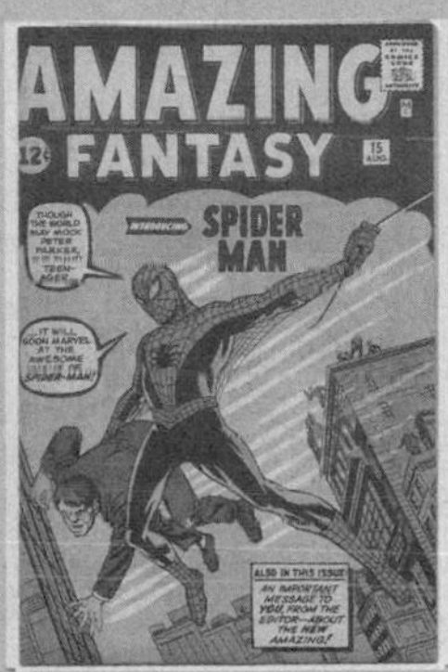

The same Amazing Fantasy #15 after restoration. Its new grade is VF, with a value of $2000. Cost of restoration: $650

RE-CREATION

This service is strictly for coverless comics, particularly the key issues like Spider-man #1, Superman #1, and Marvel Comics #1. We attach exact replicas of covers onto these **coverless comics**, each cut to fit the comic perfectly. Many collectors purchase coverless key issues because of their affordability. This service allows the comic to appear complete without the collector having to pay thousands of dollars more for a real cover. Cost is $150 per cover, and includes any necessary interior support, tear seals, assembly and pressing. Check classicsincorporated.com for more information and a complete list of available covers.

RESTORATION REMOVAL

On occasion, you may find minor unnecessary restoration on one of your books. Is removal feasible? Minor professional restoration, such as tear seals and support using rice paper and water-soluble adhesive, and acrylic and water-based color touch are the safest to remove. In some cases a book's value can significantly increase with this service, but great care must be taken in choosing the right candidates. Check classicsincorporated.com if you think you have a book that can benefit from restoration removal.

Gold • Silver • Bronze

Big Little Books

Pulps

Comic Art

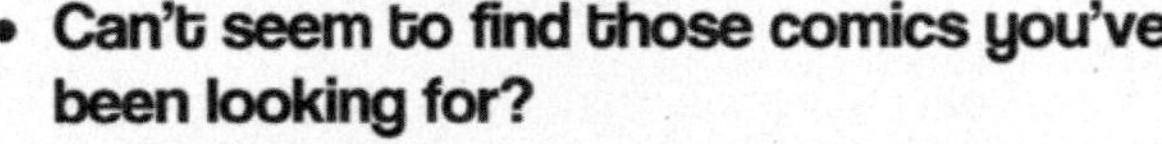

- Can't seem to find those comics you've been looking for?
- Local store just not interested in buying your collection?
- Getting unreasonably low offers?

Located in northeast Ohio, John Haines Rare Comics has been serving the collector community for nearly thirty years - Buying and supplying the best in comics and related collectibles.

Contact us now to receive a copy of our free catalog

216-390-0129 jhrc@roadrunner.com

References available

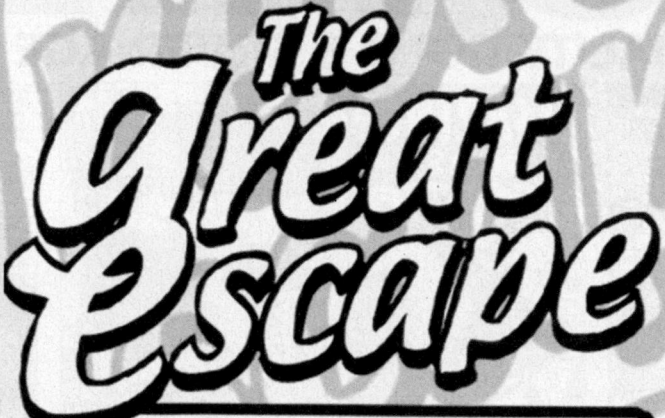

9400 SNOWDEN RIVER PKWY
COLUMBIA, MD 21045
MONDAY-SATURDAY 12-8PM
410-381-2732
COMICS TO ASTONISH
WE BUY!
-ALL COMICS 30'S TO 80'S!
-ENTIRE COLLECTIONS!
-BRONZE TO GOLDEN AGE!
-GRADED BOOKS!
-ORIGINAL COMIC ART AND COVERS!
CONTACT:
KEEGAN F. CONRAD
410-381-2732
COMICS2U@AOL.COM
MIKEY LIKES IT
THERE'S ALWAYS ROOM FOR TELLO
RIFF RAPH
KISS ME, I'M A LEO
WE HAVE OVER 80,000 BACK ISSUES!
CHECK OUT OUR WEB COMIC AT:
WWW.FATGUYBLACKGUYBALDGUY.COM
WWW.COMICSTOASTONISH.COM

©2009 Marvel Comics.

©2009 DC Comics.

©2009 Marvel Comics.

©2009 DC Comics.

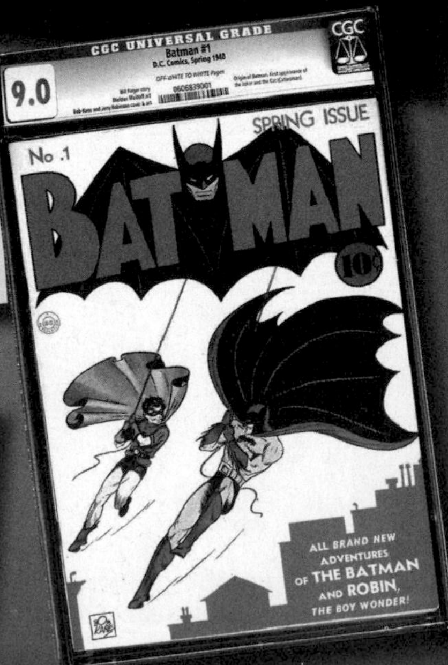

CGC UNIVERSAL GRADE
9.0
SPRING ISSUE
No. 1
BATMAN
10¢
ALL BRAND NEW ADVENTURES OF THE BATMAN AND ROBIN, THE BOY WONDER!

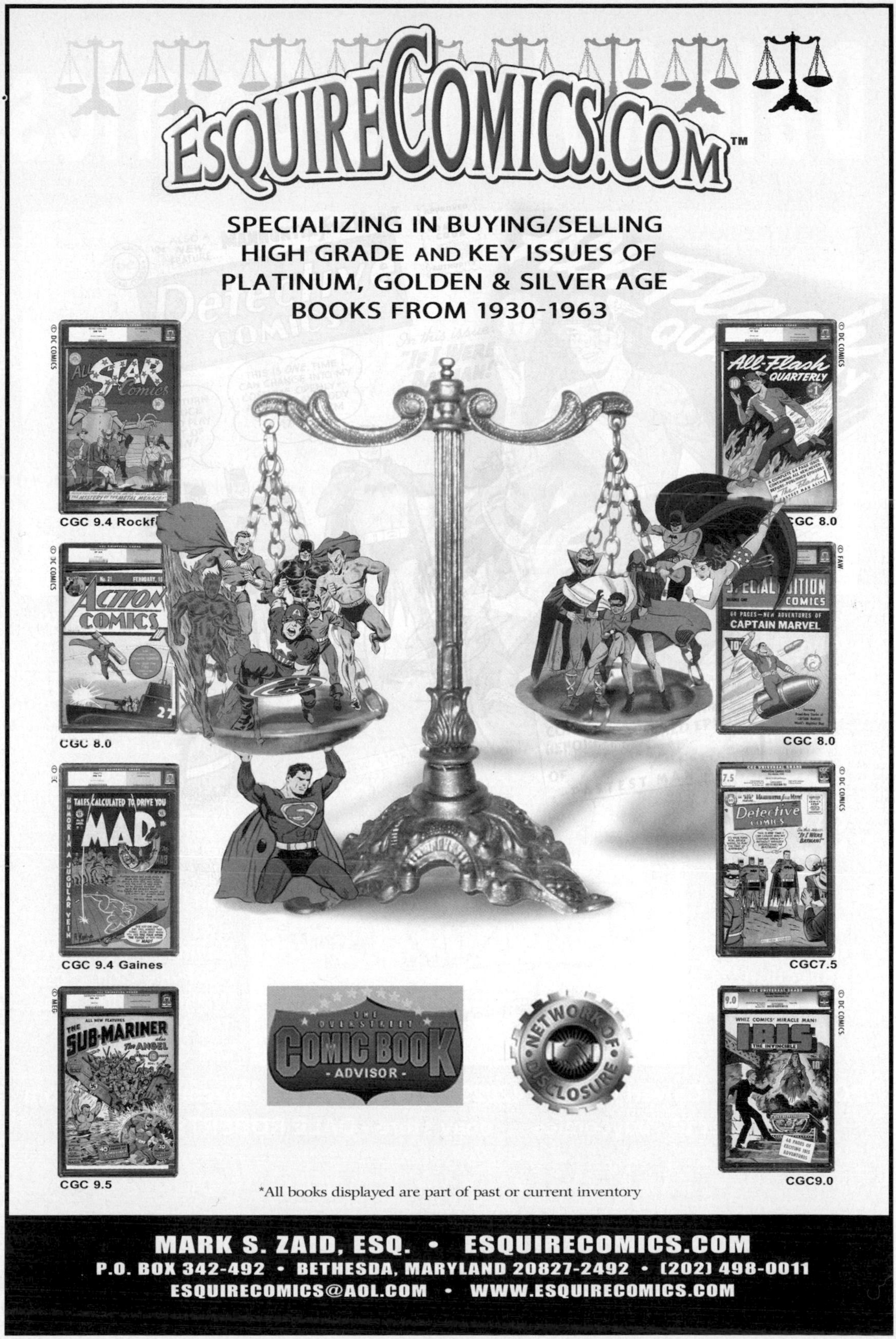

MIDTOWN COMICS GROUP
MIDTOWN COMICS NYC
BACK ISSUES ONLINE!
NYC
#1
SPECIAL SAVINGS!
SUBSCRIBE TO MIDTOWN'S NEWSLETTER FOR EXCITING WEEKLY CODEWORD SALES!

THE COMIC STORES THAT YOU
ILLI

MY HISTORY IN COMICS:

If you are about to sell your Comic Book or Comic Art collection, above everything else seek an *experienced dealer whom you can trust.* I began with comics in the early 1960s, eventually publishing the EC fanzine *Squa Tront*. I attended conventions (even before there was *The Overstreet Comic Book Price Guide*), introducing people like Bruce Hamilton to fandom and becoming friends with *MAD Magazine* publisher Bill Gaines. By 1974 I had opened one of the first specialty comic stores in America, *The Million Year Picnic*.

Two partnerships and twenty years later, I inaugurated the first *Sotheby's Comic Book and Comic Art Auctions* in the fall of 1991. The auctions set the tone for the comics market with $12 million in sales and brought national press coverage and respect that comics had never before experienced. I recently have moved onto ***eBay*** with special "event" auctions that have sold over $1.5 million during the past two years and made me one of the leading *PowerSellers* in America for rare *Comic Art and Comic Books*.

I am also the author of *The Comic Art Price Guide*, 1st and 2nd editions, have recently finished Bradbury: An Illustrated Life for William Morrow, and also wrote The 100 Greatest Comic Books, just out this year from Whitman Press.

MY PROMISE TO YOU:

What all this means to you the seller is that in Jerry Weist you have one of the most experienced and capable people in comics at your disposal.

** Do you want to sell your comics?
I can give you the best price, and honestly appraise your collection before you sell.

** Do you want to bring your collection to auction, and possibly gain a better percentage of Guide value?
I have been bringing people to auction for the past fifteen years – with outstanding results!

** Do you want to consider a private sale of important comic artwork?

I have been working with the top buyers and VIP clients for over twenty years, and I wrote the book on comic art prices. My promise to you is that with my years of experience, I can honestly evaluate your collectibles and give you the assurance that you can choose the option that best fits your needs — Private Sales, Auction Sales or Individual Purchase. I have the flexibility to act as a consult, helping you decide how to best sell your collection and gain top dollar.

Jerry Weist, Ray Bradbury and Al Feldstein during filming for Tales From The Crypt: From Comic Books To Television, produced by Chip Selby in the fall of 2003. This photo was taken during the filming for the special DVD release interview where Bradbury and Feldstein met for the first time on film to discuss their experiences working together on EC's Bradbury adaptations.

You may contact me at jerryweist@comcast.net, my home phone (978) 283-1419, or my home office at Jerry Weist, 18 Edgemoor Road, Gloucester, Massachusetts, 10930, USA.

Senior Overstreet Advisor since the 1970s, Charter CGC Member, Sotheby's Comic Art and Comic Book Consultant, eBay seller of the month and Power Seller with over 400 100% positive feedbacks, author of *The Comic Art Price Guide*, with over 40 years experience in the comic field.

JOHN VERZYL AND DAUGHTER ROSE, "HARD AT WORK."

John Verzyl started collecting comic books in 1965, and within ten years he had amassed thousands of Golden and Silver Age comic books. In 1979, with his wife Nanette, he opened "COMIC HEAVEN," a retail store devoted entirely to the buying and selling of comic books.

Over the years, John Verzyl has come to be recognized as an authority in the field of comic books. He has served as a special advisor to the "Overstreet Comic Book Price Guide" for the last 25 years. Thousands of his "mint" comics were photographed for Ernst Gerber's "Photo-Journal Guide to Comic Books." His tables and displays at the annual San Diego Comic Convention and the Chicago Comic Convention draw customers from all over the country.

The first COMIC HEAVEN AUCTION was held in 1987, and today his Auction Catalogs are mailed out to more than ten thousand interested collectors and dealers.

Comic Heaven
John and Nanette Verzyl
P.O. Box 900
Big Sandy, TX 75755
www.comicheaven.net
1-903-636-5555

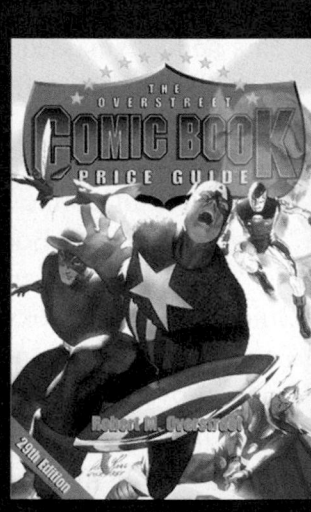

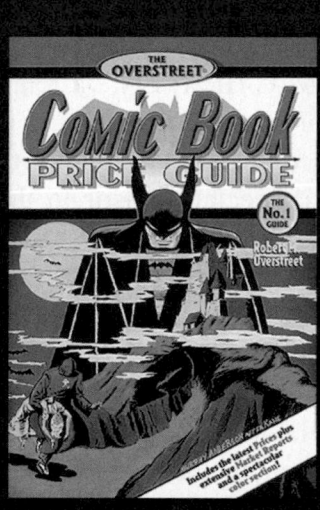

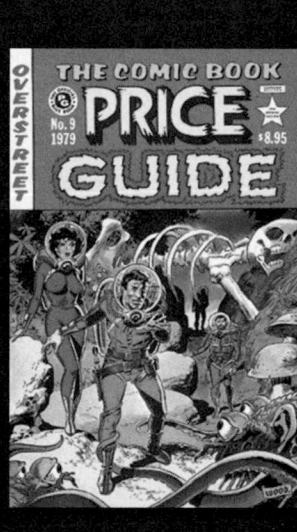

Big Little Books

INTRODUCTION

In 1932, at the depths of the Great Depression, comic books were not selling despite their successes in the previous two decades. Desperate publishers had already reduced prices to 25¢, but this was still too much for many people to spend on entertainment.

Comic books quickly evolved into two newer formats, the comics magazine and the Big Little Book. Both types retailed for 10¢.

Big Little Books began by reprinting the art (and adapting the stories) from newspaper comics. As their success grew and publishers began commissioning original material, movie adaptations and other entertainment-derived stories became commonplace.

GRADING

Before a Big Little Book's value can he assessed, its condition or state of preservation must be determined. A book in **Near Mint** condition will bring many times the price of the same book in **Poor** condition. Many variables influence the grading of a Big Little Book and all must be considered in the final evaluation. Due to the way they are constructed, damage occurs with very little use - usually to the spine, book edges and binding. More important defects that affect grading are: Split spines, pages missing, page browning or brittleness, writing, crayoning, loose pages, color fading, chunks missing, and rolling or out of square. The following grading guide is given to aid the novice:

9.4 Near Mint: The overall look is as if it was just purchased and maybe opened once; only subtle defects are allowed; paper is cream to off-white, supple and fresh; cover is flat with no surface wear or creases; inks and colors are bright; small penciled or inked arrival dates are acceptable; very slight blunting of corners at top and bottom of spine are common; outside corners are cut square and sharp. Books in this grade could bring prices of guide and a half or more.

9.0 Very Fine/Near Mint: Limited number of defects; full cover gloss with only very slight wear on book corners and edges; very minor foxing; very minor tears allowed, binding still square and tight with no pages missing; paper quality still fresh from cream to off-white. Dates, stamps or initials allowed on cover or inside.

8.0 Very Fine: Most of the cover gloss retained with minor wear appearing at corners and around edges; spine tight with no pages missing; cream/tan paper allowed if still supple; up to 1/4" bend allowed on covers with no color break; cover relatively flat; minor tears allowed.

6.0 Fine: Slight wear beginning to show; cover gloss reduced but still clean, pages tan/brown but still supple (not brittle); up to 1/4" split or color break allowed; minor discoloration and/or foxing allowed.

4.0 Very Good: Obviously a read copy with original printing luster almost gone; some fading and discoloration, but not soiled; some signs of wear such as corner splits and spine rolling; paper can be brown but not brittle; a few pages can be loose but not missing; no chunks missing; blunted corners acceptable.

2.0 Good: An average used copy complete with only minor pieces missing from the spine, which may be partially split; slightly soiled or marked with spine rolling; color flaking and wear around edges, but perfectly sound and legible; could have minor tape repairs but otherwise complete.

1.0 Fair: Very heavily read and soiled with small chunks missing from cover; most or all of spine could be missing; multiple splits in spine and loose pages, but still sound and legible, bringing 50 to 70 percent of good price.

0.5 Poor: Damaged, heavily weathered, soiled or otherwise unsuited for collecting purposes.

IMPORTANT

Most BLBs on the market today will fall in the **Good** to **Fine** grade category. When **Very Fine** to **Near Mint** BLBs are offered for sale, they usually bring premium prices.

A WORD ON PRICING

The prices are given for **Good**, **Fine** and **Very Fine/ Near Mint** condition. A book in **Fair** would be 50-70% of the **Good** price. **Very Good** would be halfway between the **Good** and **Fine** price, and **Very Fine** would be halfway between the **Fine** and **Very Fine/**

Near Mint price. The prices listed were averaged from convention sales, dealers' lists, adzines, auctions, and by special contact with dealers and collectors from coast to coast. The prices and the spreads were determined from sales of copies in available condition or the highest grade known. Since most available copies are in the **Good** to **Fine** range, neither dealers nor collectors should let the **Very Fine/Near Mint** column influence the prices they are willing to charge or pay for books in less than near perfect condition.

The prices listed reflect a six times spread from **Good** to **Very Fine/ Near Mint** (1 - 2.5 - 6.5). We feel this spread accurately reflects the current market, especially when you consider the scarcity of books in **Very Fine/Near Mint** condition. When one or both end sheets are missing, the book's value would drop about a half grade.

Books with movie scenes are of double importance due to the high crossover demand by movie collectors.

Abbreviations: a-art; c-cover; nn-no number; p-pages; r-reprint.

Publisher Codes: BRP-Blue Ribbon Press; **ERB**-Edgar Rice Burroughs; **EVW**-Engel van Wiseman; **FAW**-Fawcett Publishing Co.; **Gold**-Goldsmith Publishing Co.; **Lynn**-Lynn Publishing Co.; **McKay**-David McKay Co.; **Whit**-Whitman Publishing Co.; **World**-World Syndicate Publishing Co.

Terminology: *All Pictures Comics*-no text, all drawings; *Fast-Action*-A special series of Dell books highly collected; *Flip Pictures*-upper right corner of interior pages contain drawings that are put into motion when rifled; *Movie Scenes*-book illustrated with scenes from the movie. *Soft Cover*-A thin single sheet of cardboard used in binding most of the giveaway versions.

"Big Little Book" and "Better Little Book" are registered trademarks of Whitman Publishing Co. "Little Big Book" is a registered trademark of the Saalfield Publishing Co.

"Pop-Up" is a registered trademark of Blue Ribbon Press. "Little Big Book" is a registered trademark of the Saalfield Co.

Top 20 Big Little Books and related size books*

Issue#	Rank	Title	Price
731	1	Mickey Mouse the Mail Pilot (variant version of Mickey Mouse #717)	(Fine copy sold at auction for $5,090)
nn	2	Mickey Mouse and Minnie Mouse at Macy's	$3,500
717	3	Mickey Mouse (skinny Mickey on-c)	$3,135
nn	4	Mickey Mouse and Minnie March to Macy's	$2,400
W-707	5	Dick Tracy The Detective	$2,310
725	6	Big Little Mother Goose HC	$2,035
717	7	Mickey Mouse (reg. Mickey on-c)	$1,650
4063	8	Popeye Thimble Theater Starring... (2nd printing)	$1,620
721	9	Big Little Paint Book	$1,540
725	10	Big Little Mother Goose SC	$1,495
nn	10	Mickey Mouse (Great Big Midget Book)	$1,485
4062	12	Mickey Mouse and the Smugglers	$1,430
2070	13	Big Big Paint Book	$1,400
4063	14	Popeye Thimble Theater Starring... (1st printing)	$1,385
nn	15	Buck Rogers	$1,320
nn	15	Mickey Mouse Silly Symphonies	$1,320
4062	17	Mickey Mouse, The Story of...	$1,210
nn	18	Mickey Mouse Sails For Treasure Island (Great Big Midget Book)	$1,150
nn	19	Mickey Mouse and the Magic Carpet	$1,050
4057	20	Buck Rogers, The Adventures of...	$1,045
4071	20	Dick Tracy and the Mystery of the Purple Cross	$1,045
nn	20	Tarzan	$1,045

*Includes only the various sized BLBs; no premiums, giveaways or other divergent forms are included.

1422 - The Adventures of Huckleberry Finn © WHIT

707-10 - Andy Panda and Presto the Pup © Walter Lantz

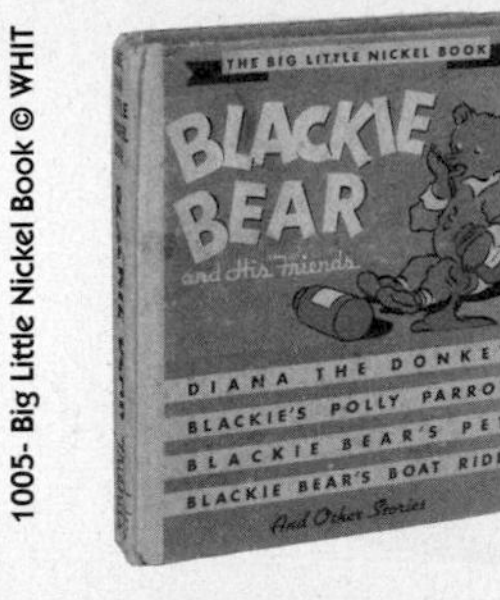
1005- Big Little Nickel Book © WHIT

	GD	FN	VF/NM
1175-0- **Abbie an' Slats**, 1940, Saalfield, 400 pgs.	12.00	30.00	80.00
1182- **Abbie an' Slats-and Becky**, 1940, Saalfield, 400 pgs.	12.00	30.00	80.00
1177- **Ace Drummond**, 1935, Whitman, 432 pgs.	12.00	30.00	85.00
Admiral Byrd (See Paramount Newsreel ...)			
nn- **Adventures of Charlie McCarthy and Edgar Bergen, The**, 1938, Dell, 194 pgs., Fast-Action Story, soft-c	26.00	65.00	185.00
1422- **Adventures of Huckleberry Finn, The**, 1939, Whitman, 432 pgs., Henry E. Vallely-a	12.00	30.00	75.00
1648- **Adventures of Jim Bowie** (TV Series), 1958, Whitman, 280 pgs.	5.00	12.50	33.00
1056- **Adventures of Krazy Kat and Ignatz Mouse in Koko Land**, 1934, Saalfield, 160 pgs., oblong size, hard-c, Herriman-c/a	72.00	180.00	505.00
1306- **Adventures of Krazy Kat and Ignatz Mouse in Koko Land**, 1934, Saalfield, 164 pgs., oblong size, soft-c, Herriman-c/a	72.00	180.00	505.00
1082- **Adventures of Pete the Tramp, The**, 1935, Saalfield, hard-c, by C. D. Russell	12.00	30.00	75.00
1312- **Adventures of Pete the Tramp, The**, 1935, Saalfield, soft-c, by C. D. Russell	12.00	30.00	75.00
1053- **Adventures of Tim Tyler**, 1934, Saalfield, hard-c, oblong size, by Lyman Young	26.00	65.00	180.00
1303- **Adventures of Tim Tyler**, 1934, Saalfield, soft-c, oblong size, by Lyman Young	26.00	65.00	180.00
1058- **Adventures of Tom Sawyer, The**, 1934, Saalfield, 160 pgs., hard-c, Park Sumner-a	12.00	30.00	75.00
1308- **Adventures of Tom Sawyer, The**, 1934, Saalfield, 160 pgs., soft-c, Park Sumner-a	12.00	30.00	75.00
1448- **Air Fighters of America**, 1941, Whitman, 432 pgs., flip picture	12.00	30.00	85.00
Alexander Smart, ESQ. (See Top Line Comics)			
759- **Alice in Wonderland**, 1933, Whitman, 160 pgs., hard-c, photo-c, movie scenes	30.00	75.00	210.00
1481- **Allen Pike of the Parachute Squad U.S.A.**, 1941, Whitman, 432 pgs.	12.00	30.00	85.00
763- **Alley Oop and Dinny**, 1935, Whitman, 384 pgs., V. T. Hamlin-a	21.00	52.50	145.00
1473- **Alley Oop and Dinny in the Jungles of Moo**, 1938, Whitman, 432 pgs., V. T. Hamlin-a	21.00	52.50	145.00
nn- **Alley Oop and the Missing King of Moo**, 1938, Whitman, 36 pgs., 2 1/2" x 3 1/2", Penny Book	12.00	30.00	85.00
nn- **Alley Oop in the Kingdom of Foo**, 1938, Whitman, 68 pgs., 3 1/4" x 3 1/2", Pan-Am premium	29.00	73.00	200.00
nn- **"Alley Oop the Invasion of Moo,"** 1935, Whitman, 260 pgs., Cocomalt premium, soft-c; V. T. Hamlin-a	22.00	52.50	155.00
Andy Burnette (See Walt Disney's...)			
Andy Panda (Also see Walter Lantz ...)			
531- **Andy Panda**, 1943, Whitman, 3 3/4x8 3/4", Tall Comic Book, All Pictures Comics	26.00	65.00	180.00
1425- **Andy Panda and Tiny Tom**, 1944, Whitman, All Pictures Comics	12.00	30.00	85.00
1431- **Andy Panda and the Mad Dog Mystery**, 1947, Whitman, 288 pgs., by Walter Lantz	12.00	30.00	80.00
1441- **Andy Panda in the City of Ice**, 1948, Whitman, All Picture Comics, by Walter Lantz	12.00	30.00	85.00
1459- **Andy Panda and the Pirate Ghosts**, 1949, Whitman, 88 pgs., by Walter Lantz	12.00	30.00	80.00
1485- **Andy Panda's Vacation**, 1946, Whitman, All Pictures Comics, by Walter Lantz	12.00	30.00	85.00
15- **Andy Panda (The Adventures of)**, 1942, Dell, Fast-Action Story	26.00	65.00	180.00
707-10 - **Andy Panda and Presto the Pup**, 1949, Whitman	12.00	30.00	80.00
1130- **Apple Mary and Dennie Foil the Swindlers**, 1936, Whitman, 432 pgs. (Forerunner to Mary Worth)	12.00	30.00	80.00
1403- **Apple Mary and Dennie's Lucky Apples**, 1939, Whitman, 432 pgs.	12.00	30.00	80.00
2017- **(#17)-Aquaman-Scourge of the Sea**, 1968, Whitman, 260 pgs., 39 cents, hard-c, color illos	4.00	10.00	27.00

	GD	FN	VF/NM
1192- **Arizona Kid on the Bandit Trail, The**, 1936, Whitman, 432 pgs.	11.00	27.50	70.00
1469- **Bambi** (Walt Disney's), 1942, Whitman, 432 pgs.	26.00	65.00	180.00
1497- **Bambi's Children** (Disney), 1943, Whitman, 432 pgs., Disney Studios-a	26.00	65.00	180.00
1138- **Bandits at Bay**, 1938, Saalfield, 400 pgs.	10.00	25.00	65.00
1459- **Barney Baxter in the Air with the Eagle Squadron**, 1938, Whitman, 432 pgs.	12.00	30.00	80.00
1083- **Barney Google**, 1935, Saalfield, hard-c	21.00	52.50	145.00
1313- **Barney Google**, 1935, Saalfield, soft-c	21.00	52.50	145.00
2031-(#31)- **Batman and Robin in the Cheetah Caper**, 1969, Whitman, 258 pgs.	4.00	10.00	27.00
5771- **Batman and Robin in the Cheetah Caper**, 1974, Whitman, 258 pgs., 49 cents	2.00	5.00	11.00
5771-1- **Batman and Robin in the Cheetah Caper**, 1974, Whitman, 258 pgs., 69 cents	2.00	5.00	11.00
5771-2- **Batman and Robin in the Cheetah Caper**, 1975?, Whitman, 258 pgs.	2.00	5.00	11.00
nn- **Beauty and the Beast**, nd (1930s), np (Whitman), 36 pgs., 3" x 3 1/2" Penny Book	4.00	10.00	27.00
760- **Believe It or Not!**, 1933, Whitman, 160 pgs., by Ripley (c. 1931)	12.00	30.00	80.00
Betty Bear's Lesson (See Wee Little Books)			
1119- **Betty Boop in Snow White**, 1934, Whitman, 240 pgs., hard-c; adapted from Max Fleischer Paramount Talkartoon	68.00	170.00	480.00
1119- **Betty Boop in Snow White**, 1934, Whitman, 240 pgs., soft-c; same contents as hard-c	54.00	135.00	385.00
1158- **Betty Boop in "Miss Gullivers Travels,"** 1935, Whitman, 288 pgs., hard-c	58.00	145.00	410.00
2070- **Big Big Paint Book**, 1936, Whitman, 432 pgs., 8 1/2" x 11 3/8", B&W pages to color	175.00	438.00	1400.00
1432- **Big Chief Wahoo and the Lost Pioneers**, 1942, Whitman, 432 pgs., Elmer Woggon-a	12.00	30.00	80.00
1443- **Big Chief Wahoo and the Great Gusto**, 1938, Whitman, 432 pgs., Elmer Woggon-a	12.00	30.00	80.00
1483- **Big Chief Wahoo and the Magic Lamp**, 1940, Whitman, 432 pgs., flip pictures, Woggon c/a	12.00	30.00	80.00
725- **Big Little Mother Goose, The**, 1934, Whitman, 580 pgs. (Rare) Hardcover	254.00	635.00	2035.00
725- **Big Little Mother Goose, The**, 1934, Whitman, 580 pgs. (Rare) Softcover	186.00	467.00	1495.00
1005- **Big Little Nickel Book**, 1935, Whitman, 144 pgs., Blackie Bear stories and Donna the Donkey	11.00	27.50	70.00
1006- **Big Little Nickel Book**, 1935, Whitman, 144 pgs., Blackie Bear stories, folk tales in primer style	11.00	27.50	70.00
1007- **Big Little Nickel Book**, 1935, Whitman, 144 pgs., Wee Wee Woman, etc.	11.00	27.50	70.00
1008- **Big Little Nickel Book**, 1935, Whitman, 144 pgs., Peter Rabbit, etc.	11.00	27.50	70.00
721- **Big Little Paint Book**, The, 1933, Whitman, 336 pgs., 3 3/4" x 8 1/2", for crayoning (Rare)	192.00	481.00	1540.00
1178- **Billy of Bar-Zero**, 1940, Saalfield, 400 pgs.	11.00	27.50	70.00
773- **Billy the Kid**, 1935, Whitman, 432 pgs., Hal Arbo-a	12.00	30.00	80.00
1159- **Billy the Kid on Tall Butte**, 1939, Saalfield, 400 pgs.	11.00	27.50	70.00
1174- **Billy the Kid's Pledge**, 1940, Saalfield, 400 pgs.	11.00	27.50	70.00
nn- **Billy the Kid, Western Outlaw**, 1935, Whitman, 260 pgs., Cocomalt premium, Hal Arbo-a, soft-c	12.00	30.00	85.00
1057- **Black Beauty**, 1934, Saalfield, hard-c	10.00	25.00	65.00
1307- **Black Beauty**, 1934, Saalfield, soft-c	10.00	25.00	65.00
1414- **Black Silver and His Pirate Crew**, 1937, Whitman, 300 pgs.	12.00	30.00	75.00
1447- **Blaze Brandon with the Foreign Legion**, 1938, Whitman, 432 pgs.	12.00	30.00	75.00
1410- **Blondie and Dagwood in Hot Water**, 1946, Whitman, 352 pgs., by Chic Young	12.00	30.00	80.00

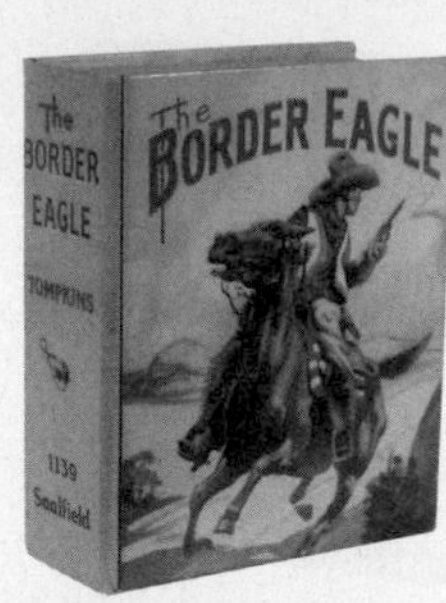

1139 - The Border Eagle © Saalfield

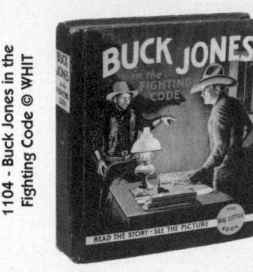

1104 - Buck Jones in the Fighting Code © WHIT

1437 - Buck Rogers in the War with the Planet Venus © KING

	GD	FN	VF/NM
1415- **Blondie and Baby Dumpling**, 1937, Whitman, 432 pgs., by Chic Young	12.00	30.00	85.00
1419- **Oh, Blondie the Bumsteads Carry On**, 1941, Whitman, 432 pgs., flip pictures, by Chic Young	12.00	30.00	85.00
1423- **Blondie Who's Boss?**, 1942, Whitman, 432 pgs., flip pictures, by Chic Young	12.00	30.00	85.00
1429- **Blondie with Baby Dumpling and Daisy**, 1939, Whitman, 432 pgs., by Chic Young	12.00	30.00	85.00
1430- **Blondie Count Cookie in Too!**, 1947, Whitman, 288 pgs., by Chic Young	12.00	30.00	80.00
1438- **Blondie and Dagwood Everybody's Happy**, 1948, Whitman, 288 pgs., by Chic Young	12.00	30.00	80.00
1450- **Blondie No Dull Moments**, 1948, Whitman, 288 pgs., by Chic Young	12.00	30.00	80.00
1463- **Blondie Fun For All**, 1949, Whitman, 288 pgs., by Chic Young	12.00	30.00	80.00
1466- **Blondie or Life Among the Bumsteads**, 1944, Whitman, 352 pgs., by Chic Young	12.00	30.00	85.00
1476- **Blondie and Bouncing Baby Dumpling**, 1940, Whitman, 432 pgs., by Chic Young	12.00	30.00	85.00
1487- **Blondie Baby Dumpling and All!**, 1941, Whitman, 432 pgs. flip pictures, by Chic Young	12.00	30.00	85.00
1490- **Blondie Papa Knows Best**, 1945, Whitman, 352 pgs., by Chic Young	12.00	30.00	80.00
1491- **Blondie-Cookie and Daisy's Pups**, 1943, Whitman, 1st printing, 432 pgs.	12.00	30.00	85.00
1491- **Blondie-Cookie and Daisy's Pups**, 1943, Whitman,. 2nd printing with different back-c & 352 pgs.	12.00	30.00	75.00
703-10- **Blondie and Dagwood Some Fun!**, 1949, Whitman, by Chic Young	10.00	25.00	65.00
21- **Blondie and Dagwood**, 1936, Lynn, by Chic Young	21.00	52.50	145.00
1108- **Bobby Benson on the H-Bar-O Ranch**, 1934, Whitman, 300 pgs., based on radio serial	13.00	32.50	90.00
Bobby Thatcher and the Samarang Emerald (See Top-Line Comics)			
1432- **Bob Stone the Young Detective**, 1937, Whitman, 240 pgs., movie scenes	12.00	30.00	85.00
2002- **(#2)-Bonanza-The Bubble Gum Kid**, 1967, Whitman, 260 pgs., 39 cents, hard-c, color illos	4.00	10.00	27.00
1139- **Border Eagle, The**, 1938, Saalfield, 400 pgs.	10.00	25.00	65.00
1153- **Boss of the Chisholm Trail**, 1939, Saalfield, 400 pgs.	10.00	25.00	65.00
1425- **Brad Turner in Transatlantic Flight**, 1939, Whitman, 432 pgs.	11.00	27.50	70.00
1058- **Brave Little Tailor, The** (Disney), 1939, Whitman, 5" x 5 1/2", 68 pgs., hard-c (Mickey Mouse)	16.00	40.00	115.00
1427- **Brenda Starr and the Masked Impostor**, 1943, Whitman, 352 pgs., Dale Messick-a	15.00	37.50	105.00
1426- **Brer Rabbit** (Walt Disney's ...), 1947, Whitman, All Picture Comics, from "Song Of The South" movie	22.00	52.50	155.00
704-10- **Brer Rabbit**, 1949, Whitman	19.00	47.50	135.00
1059- **Brick Bradford in the City Beneath the Sea**, 1934, Saalfield, hard-c, by William Ritt & Clarence Gray	18.00	45.00	125.00
1309- **Brick Bradford in the City Beneath the Sea**, 1934, Saalfield, soft-c, by Ritt & Gray	18.00	45.00	125.00
1468- **Brick Bradford with Brocco the Modern Buccaneer**, 1938, Whitman, 432 pgs., by Wm. Ritt & Clarence Gray	12.00	30.00	80.00
1133- **Bringing Up Father**, 1936, Whitman, 432 pgs., by George McManus	16.00	40.00	115.00
1100- **Broadway Bill**, 1935, Saalfield, photo-c, 4 1/2" x 5 1/4", movie scenes (Columbia Pictures, horse racing)	12.00	30.00	85.00
1580- **Broadway Bill**, 1935, Saalfield, soft-c, photo-c, movie scenes	12.00	30.00	85.00
1181- **Broncho Bill**, 1940, Saalfield, 400 pgs.	11.00	27.50	70.00
nn- **Broncho Bill**, 1935, Whitman, 148 pgs., 3 1/2" x 4", Tarzan Ice Cream cup lid premium	36.00	90.00	255.00
nn- **Broncho Bill in Suicide Canyon** (See Top-Line Comics)			
1417- **Bronc Peeler the Lone Cowboy**, 1937, Whitman, 432 pgs., by Fred Harman, forerunner of Red Ryder (also see Red Death on the Range)	12.00	30.00	80.00
nn- **Brownies' Merry Adventures, The**, 1993, Barefoot Books, 202 pgs., reprints from Palmer Cox's late 1800s books	3.00	7.50	18.00
1470- **Buccaneer, The**, 1938, Whitman, 240 pgs., photo-c, movie scenes	13.00	32.50	90.00
1646- **Buccaneers, The** (TV Series), 1958, Whitman, 4 1/2" x 5 1/4", 280 pgs., Russ Manning-a	5.00	12.50	33.00
1104- **Buck Jones in the Fighting Code**, 1934, Whitman, 160 pgs., hard-c, movie scenes	19.00	47.50	135.00
1116- **Buck Jones in Ride 'Em Cowboy** (Universal Presents), 1935, Whitman, 240 pgs., photo-c, movie scenes	19.00	47.50	135.00
1174- **Buck Jones in the Roaring West** (Universal Presents), 1935, Whitman, 240 pgs., movie scenes	19.00	47.50	135.00
1188- **Buck Jones in the Fighting Rangers** (Universal Presents), 1936, Whitman, 240 pgs., photo-c, movie scenes	19.00	47.50	135.00
1404- **Buck Jones and the Two-Gun Kid**, 1937, Whitman, 432 pgs.	13.00	32.50	90.00
1451- **Buck Jones and the Killers of Crooked Butte**, 1940, Whitman, 432 pgs.	13.00	32.50	90.00
1461- **Buck Jones and the Rock Creek Cattle War**, 1938, Whitman, 432 pgs.	13.00	32.50	90.00
1486- **Buck Jones and the Rough Riders in Forbidden Trails**, 1943, Whitman, flip pictures, based on movie; Tim McCoy app.	18.00	45.00	125.00
3- **Buck Jones in the Red Ryder**, 1934, EVW, 160 pgs., movie scenes	24.00	60.00	165.00
8- **Buck Jones Cowboy Masquerade**, 1938, Whitman, 132 pgs., soft-c, 3 3/4" x 3 1/2", Buddy Book premium	43.00	108.00	300.00
15- **Buck Jones in Rocky Rhodes**, 1935, EVW, 160 pgs., photo-c, movie scenes	24.00	60.00	165.00
4069- **Buck Jones and the Night Riders**, 1937, Whitman, 7" x 9", 320 pgs., Big Big Book	79.00	198.00	550.00
nn- **Buck Jones on the Six-Gun Trail**, 1939, Whitman, 36 pgs., 2 1/2" x 3 1/2", Penny Book	12.00	30.00	80.00
nn- **Buck Jones Big Thrill Chewing Gum**, 1934, Whitman, 8 pgs., 2 1/2" x 3 1/2" (6 diff.) each...	20.00	50.00	140.00
742- **Buck Rogers in the 25th Century A.D.**, 1933, Whitman, 320 pgs., Dick Calkins-a	47.00	118.00	330.00
nn- **Buck Rogers in the 25th Century A.D.**, 1933, Whitman, 204 pgs.,Cocomalt premium, Calkins-a	30.00	75.00	210.00
765- **Buck Rogers in the City Below the Sea**, 1934, Whitman, 320 pgs., Dick Calkins-a	36.00	90.00	255.00
765- **Buck Rogers in the City Below the Sea**, 1934, Whitman, 324 pgs., soft-c, Dick Calkins-c/a	64.00	160.00	450.00
1143- **Buck Rogers on the Moons of Saturn**, 1934, Whitman, 320 pgs., Dick Calkins-a	38.00	95.00	255.00
nn- **Buck Rogers on the Moons of Saturn**, 1934, Whitman, 324 pgs., premium w/no ads, soft 3-color-c, Dick Calkins-a	64.00	160.00	450.00
1169- **Buck Rogers and the Depth Men of Jupiter**, 1935, Whitman, 432 pgs., Calkins-a	36.00	90.00	255.00
1178- **Buck Rogers and the Doom Comet**, 1935, Whitman, 432 pgs., Calkins-a	34.00	85.00	240.00
1197- **Buck Rogers and the Planetoid Plot**, 1936, Whitman, 432 pgs., Calkins-a	34.00	85.00	240.00
1409- **Buck Rogers Vs. the Fiend of Space**, 1940, Whitman, 432 pgs., Calkins-a	45.00	113.00	315.00
1437- **Buck Rogers in the War with the Planet Venus**, 1938, Whitman, 432 pgs., Calkins-a	34.00	85.00	240.00
1474- **Buck Rogers and the Overturned World**, 1941, Whitman, 432 pgs., flip pictures, Calkins-a	36.00	90.00	250.00
1490- **Buck Rogers and the Super-Dwarf of Space**, 1943, Whitman, 11 Pictures Comics, Calkins-a	34.00	85.00	240.00
4057- **Buck Rogers, The Adventures of**, 1934, Whitman, 7" x 9 1/2", 320 pgs., Big Big Book, "The Story of Buck Rogers on the Planet Eros," Calkins-c/a	130.00	327.00	1045.00
nn- **Buck Rogers**, 1935, Whitman, 4" x 3 1/2", Tarzan Ice Cream cup premium (Rare)	165.00	412.00	1320.00
nn- **Buck Rogers in the City of Floating Globes**, 1935, Whitman, 258 pgs., Cocomalt premium, soft-c, Dick Calkins-a			

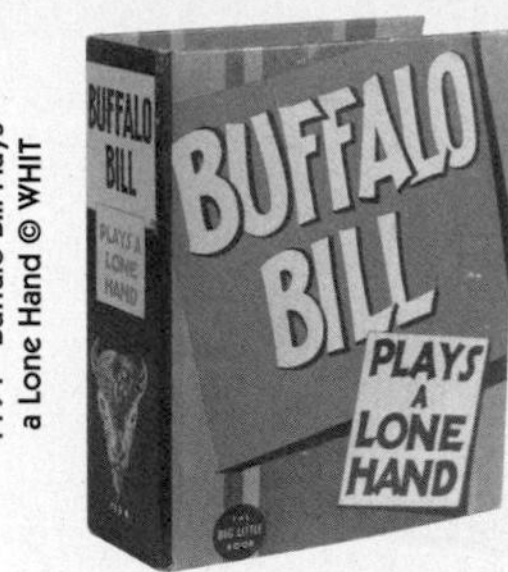
1194 - Buffalo Bill Plays a Lone Hand © WHIT

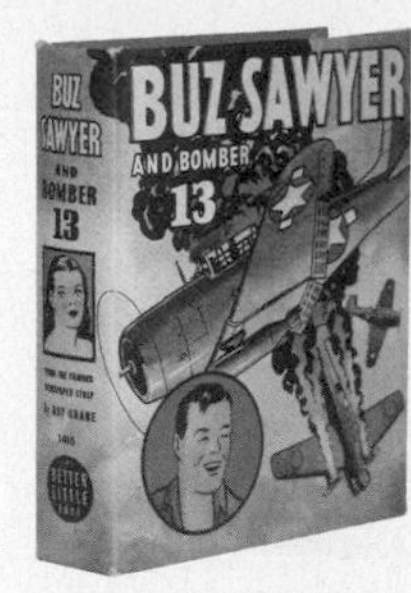
1415 - Buz Sawyer and Bomber 13 © Saalfield

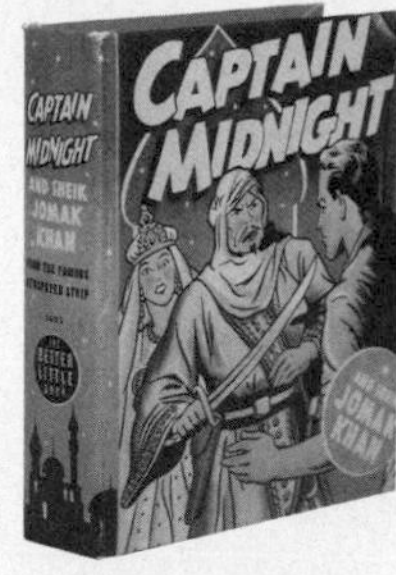
1402 - Captain Midnight and Sheik Jomak Khan © FAW

	GD	FN	VF/NM
	115.00	287.00	810.00
nn- **Buck Rogers Big Thrill Chewing Gum**, 1934, Whitman, 8 pgs., 2 1/2" x 3 " (6 diff.) each...	29.00	73.00	200.00
1135- **Buckskin and Bullets**, 1938, Saalfield, 400 pgs.	11.00	27.50	70.00
Buffalo Bill (See Wild West Adventures of ...)			
nn- **Buffalo Bill**, 1934, World Syndicate, All pictures, by J. Carroll Mansfield	11.00	27.50	70.00
713- **Buffalo Bill and the Pony Express**, 1934, Whitman, hard-c, 384 pgs., Hal Arbo-a	12.00	30.00	80.00
nn- **Buffalo Bill and the Pony Express**, 1934, Whitman, soft-c, 384 pgs., Hal Arbo-a; three-color premium	36.00	90.00	255.00
1194- **Buffalo Bill Plays a Lone Hand**, 1936, Whitman, 432 pgs., Hal Arbo-a	11.00	27.50	70.00
530- **Bugs Bunny**, 1943, Whitman, All Pictures Comics, Tall Comic Book, 3 1/4" x 8 1/4", reprints/Looney Tunes 1 & 5	31.00	78.00	215.00
1403- **Bugs Bunny and the Pirate Loot**, 1947, Whitman, All Pictures Comics	12.00	30.00	80.00
1435- **Bugs Bunny**, 1944, Whitman, All Pictures Comics	12.00	30.00	85.00
1440- **Bugs Bunny in Risky Business**, 1948, Whitman, All Pictures & Comics	12.00	30.00	80.00
1455- **Bugs Bunny and Klondike Gold**, 1948, Whitman, 288 pgs.	12.00	30.00	80.00
1465- **Bugs Bunny The Masked Marvel**, 1949, Whitman, 288 pgs.	12.00	30.00	80.00
1496- **Bugs Bunny and His Pals,** 1945, Whitman, All Pictures Comics; r/Four Color Comics #33	12.00	30.00	80.00
13- **Bugs Bunny and the Secret of Storm Island**, 1942, Dell,194 pgs., Fast-Action Story	36.00	90.00	255.00
706-10- **Bugs Bunny and the Giant Brothers**, 1949, Whitman	11.00	27.50	70.00
2007- **(#7)-Bugs Bunny-Double Trouble on Diamond Island**, 1967, Whitman, 260 pgs., 39 cents, hard-c, color illos	5.00	12.50	33.00
2029-**(#29)- Bugs Bunny, Accidental Adventure**, 1969, Whitman, 256 pgs., hard-c, color illos.	4.00	10.00	22.00
2952- **Bugs Bunny's Mistake**, 1949, Whitman, 3 1/4" x 4", 24 pgs., Tiny Tales, full color (5 cents) (1030-5 on back-c)	11.00	27.50	70.00
5757-2- **Bugs Bunny in Double Trouble on Diamond Island**,1967, (1980-reprints #2007), Whitman, 260 pgs., soft-c, 79 cents, B&W	2.00	5.00	12.00
5758- **Bugs Bunny, Accidental Adventure**, 1973, Whitman, 256 pgs., soft-c, B&W illos.	2.00	5.00	12.00
5758-1- **Bugs Bunny, Accidental Adventure**, 1973, Whitman, 256 pgs., soft-c, B&W illos.	2.00	5.00	12.00
5772- **Bugs Bunny the Last Crusader**, 1975, Whitman, 49 cents, flip-it book	2.00	5.00	12.00
5772-2- **Bugs Bunny the Last Crusader**, 1975, Whitman, $1.50, flip-it book	1.00	2.50	6.00
1169- **Bullet Benton**, 1939, Saalfield, 400 pgs.	11.00	27.50	70.00
nn- **Bulletman and the Return of Mr. Murder**, 1941, Fawcett, 196 pgs., Dime Action Book	54.00	135.00	375.00
1142- **Bullets Across the Border** (A Billy The Kid story), 1938, Saalfield, 400 pgs.	11.00	27.50	70.00
Bunky (See Top-Line Comics)			
837- **Bunty** (Punch and Judy), 1935, Whitman, 28 pgs., Magic-Action with 3 pop-ups	16.00	40.00	115.00
1091- **Burn 'Em Up Barnes**, 1935, Saalfield, hard-c, movie scenes	15.00	37.50	105.00
1321- **Burn 'Em Up Barnes**, 1935, Saalfield, soft-c, movie scenes	15.00	37.50	105.00
1415- **Buz Sawyer and Bomber 13**,1946, Whitman, 352 pgs., Roy Crane-a	15.00	37.50	105.00
1412- **Calling W-1-X-Y-Z, Jimmy Kean and the Radio Spies**, 1939, Whitman, 300 pgs.	12.00	30.00	80.00
Call of the Wild (See Jack London's...)			
1107- **Camels are Coming**, 1935, Saalfield, movie scenes	12.00	30.00	75.00
1587- **Camels are Coming**, 1935, Saalfield, movie scenes	12.00	30.00	75.00
nn- **Captain and the Kids, Boys Vill Be Boys, The**, 1938, 68 pgs., Pan-Am Oil premium, soft-c	15.00	37.50	105.00
1128- **Captain Easy Soldier of Fortune**, 1934, Whitman, 432 pgs., Roy Crane-a	15.00	37.50	105.00
nn- **Captain Easy Soldier of Fortune**, 1934, Whitman, 436 pgs., Premium, no ads, soft 3-color-c, Roy Crane-a	26.00	65.00	180.00
1474- **Captain Easy Behind Enemy Lines**, 1943, Whitman, 352 pgs., Roy Crane-a	13.00	32.50	90.00
nn- **Captain Easy and Wash Tubbs**, 1935, 260 pgs., Cocomalt premium, Roy Crane-a	13.00	32.50	90.00
1444- **Captain Frank Hawks Air Ace and the League of Twelve**, 1938, Whitman, 432 pgs.	12.00	30.00	80.00
nn- **Captain Marvel**, 1941, Fawcett, 196 pgs., Dime Action Book	65.00	163.00	460.00
1402- **Captain Midnight and Sheik Jomak Khan**, 1946, Whitman, 352 pgs.	26.00	65.00	180.00
1452- **Captain Midnight and the Moon Woman**, 1943, Whitman, 352 pgs	28.00	70.00	195.00
1458- **Captain Midnight Vs. The Terror of the Orient**, 1942, Whitman, 432 pgs., flip pictures, Hess-a	28.00	70.00	195.00
1488- **Captain Midnight and the Secret Squadron**, 1941, Whitman, 432 pgs.	28.00	70.00	195.00
Captain Robb of.. (See Dirigible ZR90 ...)			
nn- **Cauliflower Catnip Pearls of Peril**, 1981, Teacup Tales, 290 pgs., Joe Wehrle Jr.-s/a; deliberately printed on aged-looking paper to look like an old BLB	4.00	10.00	27.00
20- **Ceiling Zero**, 1936, Lynn, 128 pgs., 7 1/2" x 5", hard-c, James Cagney, Pat O'Brien photos on-c, movie scenes, Warner Bros. Pictures	12.00	30.00	80.00
1093- **Chandu the Magician**, 1935, Saalfield, 5" x 5 1/4", 160 pgs., hard-c, Bela Lugosi photo-c, movie scenes	16.00	40.00	115.00
1323- **Chandu the Magician**, 1935, Saalfield, 5" x 5 1/4", 160 pgs., soft-c, Bela Lugosi photo-c	18.00	45.00	125.00
Charlie Chan (See Inspector ...)			
1459- **Charlie Chan Solves a New Mystery** (See Inspector..), 1940, Whitman, 432 pgs., Alfred Andriola-a	16.00	40.00	110.00
1478- **Charlie Chan of the Honolulu Police, Inspector**, 1939, Whitman, 432 pgs., Andriola-a	16.00	40.00	110.00
Charlie McCarthy (See Story Of ...)			
734- **Chester Gump at Silver Creek Ranch**, 1933, Whitman, 320 pgs., Sidney Smith-a	15.00	37.50	105.00
nn- **Chester Gump at Silver Creek Ranch**, 1933, Whitman, 204 pgs., Cocomalt premium, soft-c, Sidney Smith-a	18.00	45.00	125.00
nn- **Chester Gump at Silver Creek Ranch**, 1933, Whitman, 52 pgs., 4" x 5 1/2", premium-no ads, soft-c, Sidney Smith-a	26.00	65.00	180.00
766- **Chester Gump Finds the Hidden Treasure**, 1934, Whitman, 320 pgs., Sidney Smith-a	15.00	37.50	105.00
nn- **Chester Gump Finds the Hidden Treasure**, 1934, Whitman, 52 pgs., 3 1/2" x 5 3/4", premium-no ads, soft-c, Sidney Smith-a	26.00	65.00	180.00
nn- **Chester Gump Finds the Hidden Treasure**, 1934, Whitman, 52 pgs., 4" x 5 1/2", premium-no ads, Sidney Smith-a	26.00	65.00	180.00
1146- **Chester Gump in the City Of Gold**, 1935, Whitman, 432 pgs., Sidney Smith-a	15.00	37.50	105.00
nn- **Chester Gump in the City Of Gold**, 1935, Whitman, 436 pgs., premium-no ads, 3-color, soft-c, Sidney Smith-a	30.00	75.00	210.00
1402- **Chester Gump in the Pole to Pole Flight**, 1937, Whitman, 432 pgs.	13.00	32.50	90.00
5- **Chester Gump and His Friends**, 1934, Whitman, 132 pgs., 3 1/2" x 3 1/2", soft-c, Tarzan Ice Cream cup lid premium	29.00	73.00	200.00
nn- **Chester Gump at the North Pole**, 1938, Whitman, 68 pgs. soft-c, 3 3/4" x 3 1/2", Pan-Am giveaway	29.00	73.00	200.00
nn- **Chicken Greedy**, nd(1930s), np (Whitman), 36 pgs., 3" x 2 1/2", Penny Book	4.00	10.00	22.00
nn- **Chicken Licken**, nd (1930s), np (Whitman), 36 pgs., 3" x 2 1/2",			

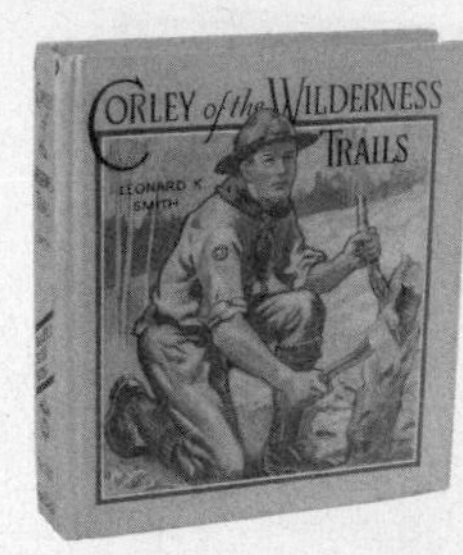
1127 - Corley of the Wilderness Trail © Saalfield

1160 - Dan of the Lazy L © Saalfield

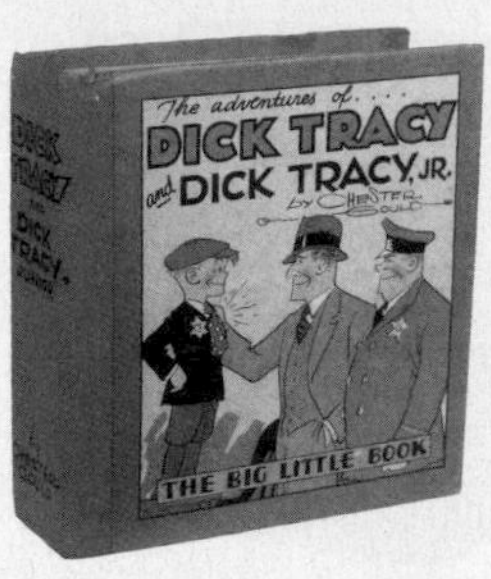

710 - Dick Tracy and Dick Tracy Jr. © NYNS

GD FN VF/NM

Penny Book 4.00 10.00 22.00
1101- **Chief of the Rangers**, 1935, Saalfield, hard-c, Tom Mix photo-c, movie scenes from "The Miracle Rider" 21.00 52.50 145.00
1581- **Chief of the Rangers**, 1935, Saalfield, soft-c, Tom Mix photo-c, movie scenes 21.00 52.50 145.00
Child's Garden of Verses (See Wee Little Books)
L14- **Chip Collins' Adventures on Bat Island**, 1935, Lynn, 192 pgs. 12.00 30.00 85.00
2025- **Chitty Chitty Bang Bang**, 1968, Whitman, movie photos 4.00 10.00 27.00
Chubby Little Books, 1935, Whitman, 3" x 2 1/2", 200 pgs.
W803- **Golden Hours Story Book, The** 7.00 17.50 40.00
W803- **Story Hours Story Book, The** 7.00 17.50 40.00
W804- **Gay Book of Little Stories, The** 7.00 17.50 40.00
W804- **Glad Book of Little Stories, The** 7.00 17.50 40.00
W804- **Joy Book of Little Stories, The** 7.00 17.50 40.00
W804- **Sunny Book of Little Stories, The** 7.00 17.50 40.00
1453- **Chuck Malloy Railroad Detective on the Streamliner**, 1938, Whitman, 300 pgs. 12.00 30.00 75.00
Cinderella (See Walt Disney's...)
Clyde Beatty (See The Steel Arena)
1410- **Clyde Beatty Daredevil Lion and Tiger Tamer**, 1939, Whitman, 300 pgs. 14.00 35.00 95.00
1480- **Coach Bernie Bierman's Brick Barton and the Winning Eleven**, 1938, 300 pgs. 11.00 27.50 70.00
1446- **Convoy Patrol** (A Thrilling U.S. Navy Story), 1942, Whitman, 432 pgs., flip pictures 11.00 27.50 70.00
1127- **Corley of the Wilderness Trail**, 1937, Saalfield, hard-c 11.00 27.50 70.00
1607- **Corley of the Wilderness Trail**, 1937, Saalfield, soft-c 11.00 27.50 70.00
1- **Count of Monte Cristo**, 1934, EVW, 160 pgs., (Five Star Library), movie scenes, hard-c 20.00 50.00 140.00
1457- **Cowboy Lingo Boys' Book of Western Facts**, 1938, Whitman, 300 pgs., Fred Harman-a 12.00 30.00 75.00
1171- **Cowboy Malloy**, 1940, Saalfield, 400 pgs. 10.00 25.00 65.00
1106- **Cowboy Millionaire**, 1935, Saalfield, movie scenes with George O'Brien, photo-c, hard-c 15.00 37.50 105.00
1586- **Cowboy Millionaire**, 1935, Saalfield, movie scenes with George O'Brien, photo-c, soft-c 15.00 37.50 105.00
724- **Cowboy Stories**, 1933, Whitman, 300 pgs., Hal Arbo-a 12.00 30.00 85.00
nn- **Cowboy Stories**, 1933, Whitman, 52 pgs., soft-c, premium-no ads, 4" x 5 1/2" Hal Arbo-a 15.00 37.50 105.00
1161- **Crimson Cloak, The**, 1939, Saalfield, 400 pgs. 11.00 27.50 70.00
L19- **Curley Harper at Lakespur**, 1935, Lynn, 192 pgs. 11.00 27.50 70.00
5785-2- **Daffy Duck in Twice the Trouble**, 1980, Whitman, 260 pgs., 79 cents soft-c 1.00 2.50 6.00
2018-(#18)-**Daktari-Night of Terror**, 1968, Whitman, 260 pgs., 39 cents, hard-c, color illos 4.00 10.00 27.00
1010- **Dan Dunn And The Gangsters' Frame-Up**, 1937, Whitman, 7 1/4" x 5 1/2", 64 pgs., Nickel Book 45.00 114.00 320.00
1116- **Dan Dunn "Crime Never Pays,"** 1934, Whitman, 320 pgs., by Norman Marsh 14.00 35.00 95.00
1125- **Dan Dunn on the Trail of the Counterfeiters**, 1936, Whitman, 432 pgs., by Norman Marsh 14.00 35.00 95.00
1171- **Dan Dunn and the Crime Master**, 1937, Whitman, 432 pgs., by Norman Marsh 14.00 35.00 95.00
1417- **Dan Dunn and the Underworld Gorillas**, 1941, Whitman, All Pictures Comics, flip pictures, by Norman Marsh 14.00 35.00 95.00
1454- **Dan Dunn on the Trail of Wu Fang**, 1938, Whitman, 432 pgs., by Norman Marsh 16.00 40.00 115.00
1481- **Dan Dunn and the Border Smugglers**, 1938, Whitman, 432 pgs., by Norman Marsh 13.00 32.50 90.00
1492- **Dan Dunn and the Dope Ring**, 1940, Whitman, 432 pgs., by Norman Marsh 12.00 30.00 85.00
nn- **Dan Dunn and the Bank Hold-Up**, 1938, Whitman, 36 pgs.,

GD FN VF/NM

2 1/2" x 3 1/2", Penny Book 11.00 27.50 70.00
nn- **Dan Dunn and the Zeppelin Of Doom**, 1938, Dell, 196 pgs., Fast-Action Story, soft-c 33.00 83.00 230.00
nn- **Dan Dunn Meets Chang Loo**, 1938, Whitman, 66 pgs., Pan-Am premium, by Norman Marsh 29.00 73.00 200.00
nn- **Dan Dunn Plays a Lone Hand**, 1938, Whitman, 36 pgs.,
2 1/2" x 3 1/2", Penny Book 11.00 27.50 70.00
3 3/4" x 3 1/2", Buddy book 39.00 98.00 275.00
6- **Dan Dunn Secret Operative 48 and the Counterfeiter Ring**, 1938, Whitman, 132 pgs., soft-c, 3 3/4" x 3 1/2", Buddy Book premium 39.00 98.00 275.00
9- **Dan Dunn's Mysterious Ruse**, 1936, Whitman, 132 pgs., soft-c, 3 1/2" x 3 1/2", Tarzan Ice Cream cup lid premium 39.00 98.00 275.00
1177- **Danger Trail North**, 1940, Saalfield, 400 pgs. 11.00 27.50 70.00
1151- **Danger Trails in Africa**, 1935, Whitman, 432 pgs. 18.00 45.00 125.00
nn- **Daniel Boone**, 1934, World Syndicate, High Lights of History Series, hard-c, All in Pictures 11.00 27.50 70.00
1160- **Dan of the Lazy L**, 1939, Saalfield, 400 pgs. 11.00 27.50 70.00
1148- **David Copperfield**, 1934, Whitman, hard-c, 160 pgs., photo-c, movie scenes (W. C. Fields) 20.00 50.00 140.00
nn- **David Copperfield**, 1934, Whitman, soft-c, 164 pgs., movie scenes 20.00 50.00 140.00
1151- **Death by Short Wave**, 1938, Saalfield 12.00 30.00 75.00
1156- **Denny the Ace Detective**, 1938, Saalfield, 400 pgs. 10.00 25.00 65.00
1431- **Desert Eagle and the Hidden Fortress, The**, 1941, Whitman, 432 pgs., flip pictures 12.00 30.00 75.00
1458- **Desert Eagle Rides Again, The**, 1939, Whitman, 300 pgs. 12.00 30.00 75.00
1136- **Desert Justice**, 1938, Saalfield, 400 pgs. 10.00 25.00 65.00
1484- **Detective Higgins of the Racket Squad**, 1938, Whitman, 432 pgs. 12.00 30.00 75.00
1124- **Dickie Moore in the Little Red School House**, 1936, Whitman, 240 pgs., photo-c, movie scenes (Chesterfield Motion Picts. Corp) 13.00 32.50 90.00
W-707- **Dick Tracy the Detective, The Adventures of**, 1933, Whitman, 320 pgs. (The 1st Big Little Book), by Chester Gould (Scarce) 289.00 722.00 2310.00
nn- **Dick Tracy Detective, The Adventures of**, 1933, Whitman, 52 pgs., 4" x 5 1/2", premium-no ads, soft-c, by Chester Gould 100.00 250.00 695.00
nn- **Dick Tracy Detective, The Adventures of**, 1933, Whitman, 52 pgs., 4" x 5 1/2", inside back-c & back-c ads for Sundial Shoes, soft-c, by Chester Gould 107.00 268.00 750.00
710- **Dick Tracy and Dick Tracy, Jr.** (The Advs. of ...), 1933, Whitman, 320 pgs., by Chester Gould 79.00 198.00 550.00
nn- **Dick Tracy and Dick Tracy, Jr.** (The Advs. of ...), 1933, Whitman, 52 pgs., premium-no ads, soft-c, 4" x 5 1/2", by Chester Gould 79.00 198.00 550.00
nn- **Dick Tracy the Detective and Dick Tracy, Jr.**, 1933, Whitman, 52 pgs., premium-no ads, 3 1/2"x 5 1/4", soft-c, by Chester Gould 79.00 198.00 550.00
723- **Dick Tracy Out West**, 1933, Whitman, 300 pgs., by Chester Gould 49.00 122.00 345.00
749- **Dick Tracy from Colorado to Nova Scotia**, 1933, Whitman, 320 pgs., by Chester Gould 45.00 113.00 315.00
nn- **Dick Tracy from Colorado to Nova Scotia**, 1933, Whitman, 204 pgs., premium-no ads, soft-c, by Chester Gould 49.00 122.00 345.00
1105- **Dick Tracy and the Stolen Bonds**, 1934, Whitman, 320 pgs., by Chester Gould 26.00 65.00 185.00
1112- **Dick Tracy and the Racketeer Gang**, 1936, Whitman, 432 pgs., by Chester Gould 21.00 52.50 145.00
1137- **Dick Tracy Solves the Penfield Mystery**, 1934, Whitman, 320 pgs., by Chester Gould 26.00 65.00 185.00
nn- **Dick Tracy Solves the Penfield Mystery**, 1934, Whitman, 324 pgs., premium-no ads, 3-color, soft-c, by Chester Gould 54.00 135.00 375.00
1163- **Dick Tracy and the Boris Arson Gang**, 1935, Whitman,

1488 - Dick Tracy the Super-Detective © NYNS

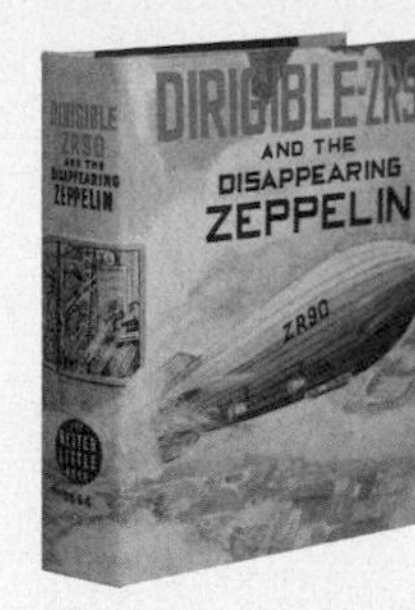

1464 - Dirigible ZR90 and the Disappearing Zeppelin © WHIT

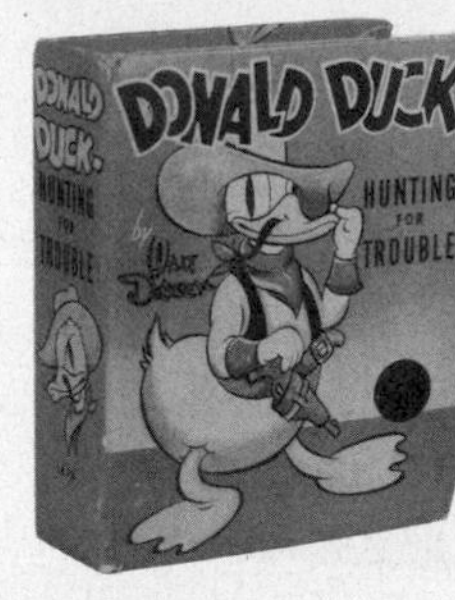

1478 - Donald Duck-Hunting For Trouble © DIS

	GD	FN	VF/NM
432 pgs., by Chester Gould	24.00	60.00	165.00
1170- **Dick Tracy on the Trail of Larceny Lu**, 1935, Whitman, 432 pgs., by Chester Gould	21.00	52.50	145.00
1185- **Dick Tracy in Chains of Crime**, 1936, Whitman, 432 pgs., by Chester Gould	24.00	60.00	165.00
1412- **Dick Tracy and Yogee Yamma**, 1946, Whitman, 352 pgs., by Chester Gould	21.00	52.50	145.00
1420- **Dick Tracy and the Hotel Murders**, 1937, Whitman, 432 pgs., by Chester Gould	24.00	60.00	165.00
1434- **Dick Tracy and the Phantom Ship**, 1940, Whitman, 432 pgs., by Chester Gould	24.00	60.00	165.00
1436- **Dick Tracy and the Mad Killer**, 1947, Whitman, 288 pgs., by Chester Gould	18.00	45.00	125.00
1439- **Dick Tracy and His G-Men**, 1941, Whitman, 432 pgs., flip pictures, by Chester Gould	24.00	60.00	165.00
1445- **Dick Tracy and the Bicycle Gang**, 1948, Whitman, 288 pgs., by Chester Gould	18.00	45.00	125.00
1446- **Detective Dick Tracy and the Spider Gang**, 1937, Whitman, 240 pgs., movie scenes from "Adventures of Dick Tracy" (Republic serial)	29.00	73.00	200.00
1449- **Dick Tracy Special F.B.I. Operative**, 1943, Whitman, 432 pgs. by Chester Gould	24.00	60.00	165.00
1454- **Dick Tracy on the High Seas**, 1939, Whitman, 432 pgs., by Chester Gould	24.00	60.00	165.00
1460- **Dick Tracy and the Tiger Lilly Gang**, 1949, Whitman, 288 pgs., by Chester Gould	18.00	45.00	125.00
1478- **Dick Tracy on Voodoo Island**, 1944, Whitman, 352 pgs., by Chester Gould	18.00	45.00	125.00
1479- **Detective Dick Tracy Vs. Crooks in Disguise**, 1939, Whitman, 432 pgs., flip pictures, by Chester Gould	24.00	60.00	165.00
1482- **Dick Tracy and the Wreath Kidnapping Case**, 1945, Whitman, 352 pgs.	20.00	50.00	140.00
1488- **Dick Tracy the Super-Detective**, 1939, Whitman, 432 pgs., by Chester Gould	24.00	60.00	165.00
1491- **Dick Tracy the Man with No Face**, 1938, Whitman, 432 pgs.	24.00	60.00	165.00
1495- **Dick Tracy Returns,** 1939, Whitman, 432 pgs., based on Republic Motion Picture serial, Chester Gould-a	24.00	60.00	165.00
2001- **(#1)-Dick Tracy-Encounters Facey,** 1967, Whitman, 260 pgs., 39 cents, hard-c, color illos	4.00	10.00	27.00
4055- **Dick Tracy, The Adventures of**, 1934, Whitman, 7" x 9 1/2", 320 pgs., Big Big Book, by Chester Gould	107.00	268.00	750.00
4071- **Dick Tracy and the Mystery of the Purple Cross**, 1938, 7" x 9 1/2", 320 pgs., Big Big Book, by Chester Gould (Scarce)	130.00	327.00	1045.00
nn- **Dick Tracy and the Invisible Man**, 1939, Whitman, 3 1/4" x 3 3/4", 132 pgs., stapled, soft-c, Quaker Oats premium; NBC radio play script, Chester Gould-a	41.00	103.00	285.00
Vol. 2- **Dick Tracy's Ghost Ship**, 1939, Whitman, 3 1/2" x 3 1/2", 132 pgs., soft-c, stapled, Quaker Oats premium; NBC radio play script episode from actual radio show; Gould-a	41.00	103.00	285.00
3- **Dick Tracy Meets a New Gang**, 1934, Whitman, 3" x 3 1/2", 132 pgs., soft-c, Tarzan Ice Cream cup lid premium	70.00	175.00	490.00
11- **Dick Tracy in Smashing the Famon Racket**, 1938, Whitman, 3 3/4" x 3 1/2", Buddy Book-ice cream premium, by Chester Gould	70.00	175.00	490.00
nn- **Dick Tracy Gets His Man**, 1938, Whitman, 36 pgs., 2 1/2" x 3 1/2", Penny Book	12.00	30.00	75.00
nn- **Dick Tracy the Detective**, 1938, Whitman, 36 pgs., 2 1/2" x 3 1/2", Penny Book	12.00	30.00	75.00
9- **Dick Tracy and the Frozen Bullet Murders**, 1941, Dell, 196 pgs., Fast-Action Story, soft-c, by Gould	41.00	103.00	285.00
6833- **Dick Tracy Detective and Federal Agent**, 1936, Dell, 244 pgs., Cartoon Story Books, hard-c, by Gould	49.00	122.00	345.00
nn- **Dick Tracy Detective and Federal Agent**, 1936, Dell, 244 pgs., Fast-Action Story, soft-c, by Gould	46.00	115.00	320.00
nn- **Dick Tracy and the Blackmailers**, 1939, Dell, 196 pgs., Fast-Action Story, soft-c, by Gould	46.00	115.00	320.00
nn- **Dick Tracy and the Chain of Evidence, Detective**, 1938, Dell, 196 pgs., Fast-Action Story, soft-c, by Chester Gould	46.00	115.00	320.00
nn- **Dick Tracy and the Crook Without a Face**, 1938, Whitman, 68 pgs., 3 1/4" x 3 1/2", Pan-Am giveaway, Gould-c/a	49.00	122.00	345.00
nn- **Dick Tracy and the Maroon Mask Gang**, 1938, Dell, 196 pgs., Fast-Action Story, soft-c, by Gould	46.00	115.00	320.00
nn- **Dick Tracy Cross-Country Race**, 1934, Whitman, 8 pgs., 2 1/2" x 3", Big Thrill chewing gum premium (6 diff.)	18.00	45.00	125.00
nn- **Dick Whittington and his Cat**, nd(1930s), np(Whitman), 36 pgs., Penny Book	5.00	12.50	33.00
Dinglehoofer und His Dog Adolph (See Top-Line Comics)			
Dinky (See Jackie Cooper in ...)			
1464- **Dirigible ZR90 and the Disappearing Zeppelin** (Captain Robb of ...), 1941, Whitman, 300 pgs., Al Lewin-a	20.00	50.00	140.00
1167- **Dixie Dugan Among the Cowboys**, 1939, Saalfield, 400 pgs.	12.00	30.00	85.00
1188- **Dixie Dugan and Cuddles**, 1940, Saalfield, 400 pgs., by Striebel & McEvoy	12.00	30.00	85.00
Doctor Doom (See Foreign Spies... & International Spy...)			
Dog of Flanders, A (See Frankie Thomas in ...)			
1114- **Dog Stars of Hollywood**, 1936, Saalfield, photo-c, photo-illos	16.00	40.00	115.00
1594- **Dog Stars of Hollywood**, 1936, Saalfield, photo-c, soft-c, photo-illos	16.00	40.00	115.00
Donald Duck (See Silly Symphony... & Walt Disney's ...)			
800- **Donald Duck in Bringing Up the Boys**, 1948, Whitman, hard-c, Story Hour series	12.00	30.00	85.00
1404- **Donald Duck (Says Such a Life)** (Disney), 1939, Whitman, 432 pgs., Taliaferro-a	31.00	78.00	220.00
1411- **Donald Duck and Ghost Morgan's Treasure** (Disney), 1946, Whitman, All Pictures Comics, Barks-a; reprints Four Color #9	38.00	95.00	255.00
1422- **Donald Duck Sees Stars** (Disney), 1941, Whitman, 432 pgs., flip pictures, Taliaferro-a	31.00	78.00	215.00
1424- **Donald Duck Says Such Luck** (Disney), 1941, Whitman, 432 pgs., flip pictures, Taliaferro-a	31.00	78.00	215.00
1430- **Donald Duck Headed For Trouble** (Disney), 1942, Whitman, 432 pgs., flip pictures, Taliaferro-a	31.00	78.00	215.00
1432- **Donald Duck and the Green Serpent** (Disney), 1947, Whitman, All Pictures Comics, Barks-a; reprints Four Color #108	34.00	85.00	240.00
1434- **Donald Duck Forgets To Duck** (Disney), 1939, Whitman, 432 pgs., Taliaferro-a	31.00	78.00	215.00
1438- **Donald Duck Off the Beam** (Disney), 1943, Whitman, 352 pgs., flip pictures, Taliaferro-a	31.00	78.00	215.00
1438- **Donald Duck Off the Beam** (Disney), 1943, Whitman, 432 pgs., flip pictures, Taliaferro-a	31.00	78.00	215.00
1449- **Donald Duck Lays Down the Law**, 1948, Whitman, 288 pgs.,	31.00	78.00	215.00
1457- **Donald Duck in Volcano Valley** (Disney), 1949, Whitman, 288 pgs., Barks-a	31.00	78.00	215.00
1462- **Donald Duck Gets Fed Up** (Disney), 1940, Whitman, 432 pgs.,Taliaferro-a	31.00	78.00	215.00
1478- **Donald Duck-Hunting For Trouble** (Disney), 1938, Whitman, 432 pgs., Taliaferro-a	31.00	78.00	215.00
1484- **Donald Duck is Here Again!**, 1944, Whitman, All Pictures Comics, Taliaferro-a	31.00	78.00	215.00
1486- **Donald Duck Up in the Air** (Disney), 1945, Whitman, 352 pgs., Barks-a	34.00	85.00	240.00
705-10- **Donald Duck and the Mystery of the Double X**, (Disney), 1949, Whitman, Barks-a	16.00	40.00	115.00
2033-(#33)- **Donald Duck, Luck of the Ducks,** 1969, Whitman, 256 pgs., hard-c, 39 cents, color illos.	4.00	10.00	22.00
2009-(#9)-**Donald Duck-The Fabulous Diamond Fountain,** (Walt Disney), 1967, Whitman, 260 pgs., 39 cents, hard-c, color illos	4.00	10.00	27.00
5756- **Donald Duck-The Fabulous Diamond Fountain,** (Walt Disney), 1973, Whitman, 260 pgs., 79 cents, soft-c, color illos	3.00	7.50	20.00
5756-1- **Donald Duck-The Fabulous Diamond Fountain,** (Walt Disney), 1973, Whitman, 260 pgs., 79 cents, soft-c,			

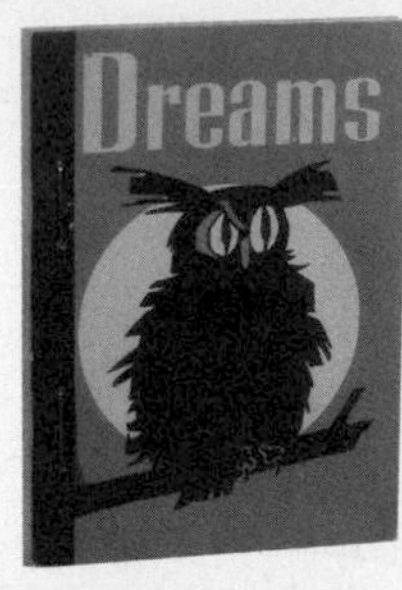

1100B - Dreams © WHIT

Eddie Cantor in Laughland © Goldsmith

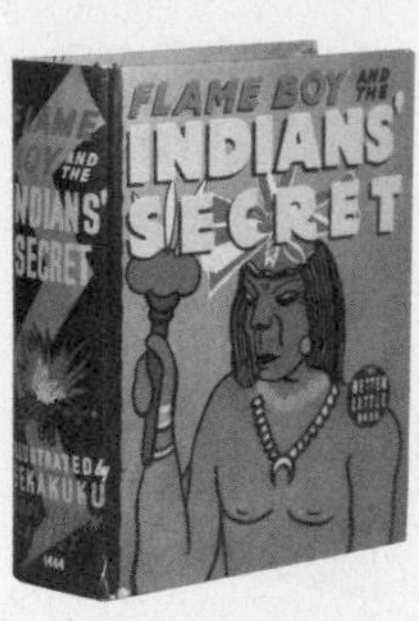

1464 - Flame Boy and the Indians' Secret © WHIT

GD FN VF/NM

color illos 3.00 7.50 20.00
5756-2- Donald Duck-The Fabulous Diamond Fountain, (Walt Disney), 1973, Whitman, 260 pgs., 79 cents, soft-c, color illos 3.00 7.50 20.00
5760- Donald Duck in Volcano Valley (Disney), 1973, Whitman, 39 cents, flip-it book 3.00 7.50 20.00
5760-2- Donald Duck in Volcano Valley (Disney), 1973, Whitman, 79 cents, flip-it book 2.00 5.00 14.00
5764- Donald Duck, Luck of the Ducks, 1969, Whitman, 256 pgs., soft-c, 49 cents, color illos. 3.00 7.50 20.00
5773- Donald Duck - The Lost Jungle City, 1975, Whitman, 49 cents, flip-it book; 6 printings through 1980 2.00 5.00 14.00
nn- Donald Duck and the Ducklings, 1938, Dell, 194 pgs., Fast-Action Story, soft-c, Taliaferro-a 58.00 146.00 410.00
nn- Donald Duck Out of Luck (Disney), 1940, Dell, 196 pgs., Fast-Action Story, has Four Color #4 on back-c, Taliaferro-a 58.00 146.00 410.00
8- Donald Duck Takes It on the Chin (Disney), 1941, Dell, 196 pgs., Fast-Action Story, soft-c, Taliaferro-a 58.00 146.00 410.00
L13- Donnie and the Pirates, 1935, Lynn, 192 pgs. 12.00 30.00 85.00
1438- Don O'Dare Finds War, 1940, Whitman, 432 pgs. 11.00 27.50 70.00
1107- Don Winslow, U.S.N., 1935, Whitman, 432 pgs. 20.00 50.00 140.00
nn- Don Winslow, U.S.N., 1935, Whitman, 436 pgs., premium-no ads, 3-color, soft-c 31.00 78.00 220.00
1408- Don Winslow and the Giant Girl Spy, 1946, Whitman, 352 pgs. 13.00 32.50 90.00
1418- Don Winslow Navy Intelligence Ace, 1942, Whitman, 432 pgs., flip pictures 18.00 45.00 125.00
1419- Don Winslow of the Navy Vs. the Scorpion Gang, 1938, Whitman, 432 pgs. 18.00 45.00 125.00
1453- Don Winslow of the Navy and the Secret Enemy Base, 1943, Whitman, 352 pgs. 18.00 45.00 125.00
1489- Don Winslow of the Navy and the Great War Plot, 1940, Whitman, 432 pgs. 18.00 45.00 125.00
nn- Don Winslow U.S. Navy and the Missing Admiral, 1938, Whitman, 36 pgs., 2 1/2" x 3 1/2", Penny Book 11.00 27.50 70.00
1137- Doomed To Die, 1938, Saalfield, 400 pgs. 11.00 27.50 70.00
1140- Down Cartridge Creek, 1938, Saalfield, 400 pgs. 11.00 27.50 70.00
1416- Draftie of the U.S. Army, 1943, Whitman, All Pictures Comics 12.00 30.00 75.00
1100B- Dreams (Your dreams & what they mean), 1938, Whitman, 36 pgs., 2 1/2" x 3 1/2", Penny Book 4.00 10.00 27.00
24- Dumb Dora and Bing Brown, 1936, Lynn 14.00 35.00 95.00
1400- Dumbo, of the Circus - Only His Ears Grew! (Disney), 1941, Whitman, 432 pgs., based on Disney movie 28.00 70.00 195.00
10- Dumbo the Flying Elephant (Disney), 1944, Dell, 194 pgs., Fast-Action Story, soft-c 46.00 115.00 320.00
nn- East O' the Sun and West O' the Moon, nd (1930s), np (Whitman), 36 pgs., 3" x 2 1/2", Penny Book 4.00 10.00 27.00
774- Eddie Cantor in an Hour with You, 1934, Whitman, 154 pgs., 4 1/4" x 5 1/4", photo-c, movie scenes 16.00 40.00 115.00
nn- Eddie Cantor in Laughland, 1934, Goldsmith, 132 pgs., soft-c, photo-c, Vallely-a 16.00 40.00 115.00
1106- Ella Cinders and the Mysterious House, 1934, Whitman, 432 pgs. 15.00 37.50 105.00
nn- Ella Cinders and the Mysterious House, 1934, Whitman, 52 pgs., premium-no ads, soft-c, 3 1/2" x 5 3/4" 22.00 52.50 155.00
nn- Ella Cinders, 1935, Whitman, 148 pgs., 3 1/4" x 4", Tarzan Ice Cream cup lid premium 36.00 90.00 255.00
nn- Ella Cinders Plays Duchess, 1938, Whitman, 68 pgs., 3 3/4" x 3 1/2", Pan-Am Oil premium 16.00 40.00 115.00
nn- Ella Cinders Solves a Mystery, 1938, Whitman, 68 pgs., Pan-Am Oil premium, soft-c 16.00 40.00 115.00
11- Ella Cinders' Exciting Experience, 1934, Whitman, 3 1/2" x 3 1/2", 132 pgs., Tarzan Ice Cream cup lid giveaway 36.00 90.00 255.00

GD FN VF/NM

1406- Ellery Queen the Adventure of the Last Man Club, 1940, Whitman, 432 pgs. 15.00 37.50 105.00
1472- Ellery Queen the Master Detective, 1942, Whitman, 432 pgs., flip pictures 15.00 37.50 105.00
1081- Elmer and his Dog Spot, 1935, Saalfield, hard-c 11.00 27.50 70.00
1311- Elmer and his Dog Spot, 1935, Saalfield, soft-c 11.00 27.50 70.00
722- Erik Noble and the Forty-Niners, 1934, Whitman, 384 pgs. 11.00 27.50 70.00
nn- Erik Noble and the Forty-Niners, 1934, Whitman, 386 pgs., 3-color, soft-c 16.00 40.00 115.00
2019-(#19)- Fantastic Four in the House of Horrors, 1968, Whitman, 256 pgs., hard-c, color illos. 4.00 10.00 27.00
5775 - Fantastic Four in the House of Horrors, 1976, Whitman, 256 pgs., soft-c, color illos. 3.00 7.50 20.00
5775-1 - Fantastic Four in the House of Horrors, 1976, Whitman, 256 pgs., soft-c, color illos. 3.00 7.50 20.00
1058- Farmyard Symphony, The (Disney), 1939, 5" X 5 1/2", 68 pgs., hard-c 15.00 37.50 105.00
1129- Felix the Cat, 1936, Whitman, 432 pgs., Messmer-a 33.00 83.00 230.00
1439- Felix the Cat, 1943, Whitman, All Pictures Comics, Messmer-a 28.00 70.00 195.00
1465- Felix the Cat, 1945, Whitman, All Pictures Comics, Messmer-a 24.00 60.00 165.00
nn- Felix (Flip book), 1967, World Retrospective of Animation Cinema, 188 pgs., 2 1/2" x 4" by Otto Messmer 4.00 10.00 27.00
nn- Fighting Cowboy of Nugget Gulch, The, 1939, Whitman, 2 1/2" x 3 1/2", Penny Book 7.00 17.50 45.00
1401- Fighting Heroes Battle for Freedom, 1943, Whitman, All Pictures Comics, from "Heroes of Democracy" strip, by Stookie Allen 11.00 27.50 70.00
6- Fighting President, The, 1934, EVW (Five Star Library), 160 pgs., photo-c, photo ill., F. D. Roosevelt 12.00 30.00 85.00
nn- Fire Chief Ed Wynn and "His Old Fire Horse," 1934, Goldsmith, 132 pgs., H. Vallely-a, photo, soft-c 12.00 30.00 85.00
1464- Flame Boy and the Indians' Secret, 1938, Whitman, 300 pgs., Sekakuku-a (Hopi Indian) 11.00 27.50 70.00
22- Flaming Guns, 1935, EVW, with Tom Mix, movie scenes 20.00 50.00 140.00
1110- Flash Gordon on the Planet Mongo, 1934, Whitman, 320 pgs., by Alex Raymond 49.00 122.00 345.00
1166- Flash Gordon and the Monsters of Mongo, 1935, Whitman, 432 pgs., by Alex Raymond 41.00 103.00 290.00
nn- Flash Gordon and the Monsters of Mongo, 1935, Whitman, 436 pgs., premium-no ads, 3-color, soft-c, by Alex Raymond 61.00 153.00 430.00
1171- Flash Gordon and the Tournaments of Mongo, 1935, Whitman, 432 pgs., by Alex Raymond 43.00 108.00 300.00
1190- Flash Gordon and the Witch Queen of Mongo, 1936, Whitman, 432 pgs., by Alex Raymond 43.00 108.00 300.00
1407- Flash Gordon in the Water World of Mongo, 1937, Whitman, 432 pgs., by Alex Raymond 38.00 95.00 255.00
1423- Flash Gordon and the Perils of Mongo, 1940, Whitman, 432 pgs., by Alex Raymond 33.00 83.00 230.00
1424- Flash Gordon in the Jungles of Mongo, 1947, Whitman, 352 pgs., by Alex Raymond 24.00 60.00 170.00
1443- Flash Gordon in the Ice World of Mongo, 1942, Whitman, 432 pgs., flip pictures, by Alex Raymond 36.00 90.00 250.00
1447- Flash Gordon and the Fiery Desert of Mongo, 1948, Whitman, 288 pgs., Raymond-a 24.00 60.00 170.00
1469- Flash Gordon and the Power Men of Mongo, 1943, Whitman, 352 pgs., by Alex Raymond 36.00 90.00 250.00
1479- Flash Gordon and the Red Sword Invaders, 1945, Whitman, 352 pgs., by Alex Raymond 34.00 85.00 240.00
1484- Flash Gordon and the Tyrant of Mongo, 1941, Whitman, 432 pgs., flip pictures, by Alex Raymond 36.00 90.00 250.00
1492- Flash Gordon in the Forest Kingdom of Mongo, 1938, Whitman, 432 pgs., by Alex Raymond 46.00 115.00 320.00

2003 - Flipper - Killer Whale Trouble © WHIT

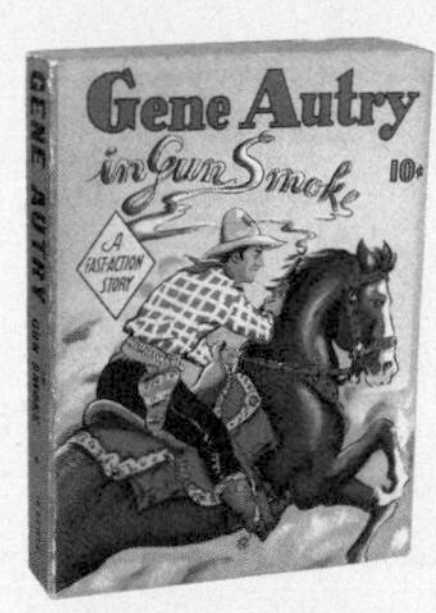

Gene Autry in Gun-Smoke © DELL

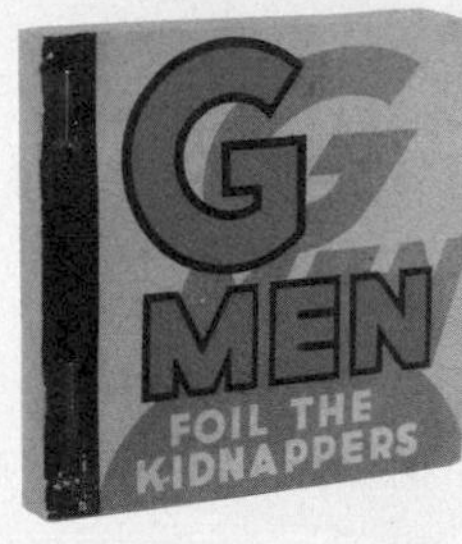

4 - G-Men Foil the Kidnappers © WHIT

GD FN VF/NM

12- **Flash Gordon and the Ape Men of Mor**, 1942, Dell, 196 pgs., Fast-Action Story, by Alex Raymond 64.00 160.00 450.00

6833- **Flash Gordon Vs. the Emperor of Mongo**, 1936, Dell, 244 pgs., Cartoon Story Books, hard-c, Alex Raymond-c/a 79.00 198.00 550.00

nn- **Flash Gordon Vs. the Emperor of Mongo**, 1936, Dell, 244 pgs., Fast-Action Story, soft-c, Alex Raymond-c/a 62.00 155.00 440.00

1467- **Flint Roper and the Six-Gun Showdown**, 1941, Whitman, 300 pgs. 11.00 27.50 70.00

2014-(#14)- **Flintstones-The Case of the Many Missing Things**, 1968, Whitman, 260 pgs., 39 cents, hard-c, color illos 4.00 10.00 27.00

nn- **Flintstones: A Friend From the Past**, 1977, Modern Promotions, 244 pgs., 49 cents, soft-c, flip pictures 2.00 5.00 11.00

nn- **Flintstones: It's About Time**, 1977, Modern Promotions, 244 pgs., 49 cents, soft-c, flip pictures 2.00 5.00 11.00

nn- **Flintstones: Pebbles & Bamm-Bamm Meet Santa Claus**, 1977, Modern Promotions, 244 pgs., 49 cents, soft-c, flip pictures 2.00 5.00 11.00

nn- **Flintstones: The Great Balloon Race**, 1977, Modern Promotions, 244 pgs., 49 cents, soft-c, flip pictures 2.00 5.00 11.00

nn- **Flintstones: The Mystery of the Many Missing Things**, 1977, Modern Promotions, 244 pgs., 49 cents, soft-c, flip pictures 2.00 5.00 11.00

2003-(#3)- **Flipper-Killer Whale Trouble**, 1967, Whitman, 260 pgs., hard-c, 39 cents, color illos 3.00 7.50 20.00

2032-(#32)- **Flipper, Deep-Sea Photographer,** 1969, Whitman, 256 pgs., hard-c, color illos. 3.00 7.50 20.00

1108- **Flying the Sky Clipper with Winsie Atkins**, 1936, Whitman, 432 pgs. 11.00 27.50 70.00

1460- **Foreign Spies Doctor Doom and the Ghost Submarine**, 1939, Whitman, 432 pgs., Al McWilliams-a 13.00 32.50 90.00

1100B- **Fortune Teller**, 1938, Whitman, 36 pgs., 2 1/2" x 3 1/2", Penny Book 5.00 12.50 33.00

1175- **Frank Buck Presents Ted Towers Animal Master**, 1935, Whitman, 432 pgs. 12.00 30.00 80.00

2015-(#15)-**Frankenstein, Jr. - The Menace of the Heartless Monster**, 1968, Whitman, 260 pgs., 39 cents, hard-c, color illos. 4.00 10.00 27.00

16- **Frankie Thomas In A Dog of Flanders**, 1935, EVW, movie scenes 15.00 37.50 105.00

1121- **Frank Merriwell at Yale**, 1935, 432 pgs. 11.00 27.50 70.00

Freckles and His Friends in the North Woods (See Top-Line Comics)

nn- **Freckles and His Friends Stage a Play**, 1938, Whitman, 36 pgs., 2 1/2" x 3 1/2", Penny Book 11.00 27.50 70.00

1164- **Freckles and the Lost Diamond Mine**, 1937, Whitman, 432 pgs., Merrill Blosser-a 12.00 30.00 85.00

nn- **Freckles and the Mystery Ship**, 1935, Whitman, 66 pgs., Pan-Am premium 16.00 40.00 115.00

1100B- **Fun, Puzzles, Riddles**, 1938, Whitman, 36 pgs., 2 1/2" x 3 1/2", Penny Book 4.00 10.00 27.00

1433- **Gang Busters Step In**, 1939, Whitman, 432 pgs., Henry E. Vallely-a 13.00 32.50 90.00

1437- **Gang Busters Smash Through**, 1942, Whitman, 432 pgs. 13.00 32.50 90.00

1451- **Gang Busters in Action!**, 1938, Whitman, 432 pgs. 13.00 32.50 90.00

nn- **Gang Busters and Guns of the Law**, 1940, Dell, 4" x 5", 194 pgs., Fast-Action Story, soft-c 41.00 103.00 285.00

nn- **Gang Busters and the Radio Clues**, 1938, Whitman, 36 pgs., 2 1/2" x 3 1/2", Penny Book 11.00 27.50 70.00

1409- **Gene Autry and Raiders of the Range**, 1946, Whitman, 352 pgs. 15.00 37.50 105.00

1425- **Gene Autry and the Mystery of Paint Rock Canyon**, 1947, Whitman, 288 pgs. 15.00 37.50 105.00

1428- **Gene Autry Special Ranger**, 1941, Whitman, 432 pgs., Erwin Hess-a 20.00 50.00 140.00

1433- **Gene Autry in Public Cowboy No. 1**, 1938, Whitman, 240 pgs., photo-c, movie scenes (1st Autry BLB) 38.00 95.00 255.00

1434- **Gene Autry and the Gun-Smoke Reckoning**, 1943, Whitman, 352 pgs. 19.00 47.50 135.00

GD FN VF/NM

1439- **Gene Autry and the Land Grab Mystery**, 1948, Whitman, 290 pgs. 14.00 35.00 95.00

1456- **Gene Autry in Special Ranger Rule**, 1945, Whitman, 352 pgs., Henry E. Vallely-a 19.00 47.50 135.00

1461- **Gene Autry and the Red Bandit's Ghost**, 1949, Whitman, 288 pgs. 13.00 32.50 90.00

1483- **Gene Autry in Law of the Range**, 1939, Whitman, 432 pgs. 19.00 47.50 135.00

1493- **Gene Autry and the Hawk of the Hills**, 1942, Whitman, 428 pgs., flip pictures, Vallely-a 19.00 47.50 135.00

1494- **Gene Autry Cowboy Detective**, 1940, Whitman, 432 pgs., Erwin Hess-a 19.00 47.50 135.00

700-10- **Gene Autry and the Bandits of Silver Tip**, 1949, Whitman 12.00 30.00 80.00

714-10- **Gene Autry and the Range War**, 1950, Whitman 12.00 30.00 80.00

nn- **Gene Autry in Gun-Smoke**, 1938, Dell, 196 pgs., Fast-Action story, soft-c 46.00 115.00 320.00

2035-(#35)- **Gentle Ben, Mystery of the Everglades**, 1969, Whitman, 256 pgs., hard-c, color illos. 3.00 7.50 20.00

1176- **Gentleman Joe Palooka**, 1940, Saalfield, 400 pgs. 16.00 40.00 115.00

George O'Brien (See The Cowboy Millionaire)

1101- **George O'Brien and the Arizona Badman**, 1936?, Whitman 15.00 37.50 105.00

1418- **George O'Brien in Gun Law**, 1938, Whitman, 240 pgs., photo-c, movie scenes, RKO Radio Pictures 15.00 37.50 105.00

1457- **George O'Brien and the Hooded Riders**, 1940, Whitman, 432 pgs., Erwin Hess-a 11.00 27.50 70.00

nn- **George O'Brien and the Arizona Bad Man**, 1939, Whitman, 36 pgs., 2 1/2" x 3 1/2", Penny Book 11.00 27.50 70.00

1462 **Ghost Avenger**, 1943, Whitman, 432 pgs., flip pictures, Henry Vallely-a 11.00 27.50 70.00

nn- **Ghost Gun Gang Meet Their Match, The**, 1939. Whitman, 2 1/2" x 3 1/2", Penny Book 10.00 25.00 65.00

nn- **Gingerbread Boy, The**, nd(1930s), np(Whitman), 36 pgs., Penny Book 4.00 10.00 22.00

1118- **G-Man on the Crime Trail**, 1936, Whitman, 432 pgs. 12.00 30.00 80.00

1147- **G-Man Vs. the Red X**, 1936, Whitman, 432 pgs. 14.00 35.00 95.00

1162- **G-Man Allen**, 1939, Saalfield, 400 pgs. 11.00 27.50 70.00

1173- **G-Man in Action, A**, 1940, Saalfield, 400 pgs., J.R. White-a 11.00 27.50 70.00

1434- **G-Man and the Radio Bank Robberies**, 1937, Whitman, 432 pgs. 13.00 32.50 90.00

1469- **G-Man and the Gun Runners, The**, 1940, Whitman, 432 pgs. 13.00 32.50 90.00

1470- **G-Man vs. the Fifth Column**, 1941, Whitman, 432 pgs., flip pictures 13.00 32.50 90.00

1493- **G-Man Breaking the Gambling Ring**, 1938, Whitman, 432 pgs., James Gary-a 13.00 32.50 90.00

4- **G-Men Foil the Kidnappers**, 1936, Whitman, 132 pgs., 3 1/2" x 3 1/2", soft-c, Tarzan Ice Cream cup lid premium 36.00 90.00 255.00

nn- **G-Man on Lightning Island**, 1936, Dell, 244 pgs., Fast-Action Story, soft-c, Henry E. Vallely-a 33.00 83.00 230.00

6833- **G-Man on Lightning Island**, 1936, Dell, 244 pgs., Cartoon Story Book, hard-c, Henry E. Vallely-a 29.00 73.00 200.00

1157- **G-Men on the Trail**, 1938, Saalfield, 400 pgs. 11.00 27.50 70.00

1168- **G Men on the Job**, 1935, Whitman, 432 pgs. 12.00 30.00 85.00

nn- **G-Men on the Job Again**, 1938, Whitman, 36 pgs., 2 1/2" x 3 1/2", Penny Book 11.00 27.50 70.00

nn- **G-Men and Kidnap Justice**, 1938, Whitman, 68 pgs., Pan-Am premium, soft-c 12.00 30.00 85.00

nn- **G-Men and the Missing Clues**, 1938, Whitman, 36 pgs., 2 1/2"x 3 1/2", Penny Book 11.00 27.50 70.00

1097- **Go Into Your Dance**, 1935, Saalfield, 160 pgs.. photo-c, movie scenes with Al Jolson & Ruby Keeler 15.00 37.50 105.00

1577- **Go Into Your Dance**, 1935, Saalfield, 160 pgs., photo-c, movie scenes, soft-c 15.00 37.50 105.00

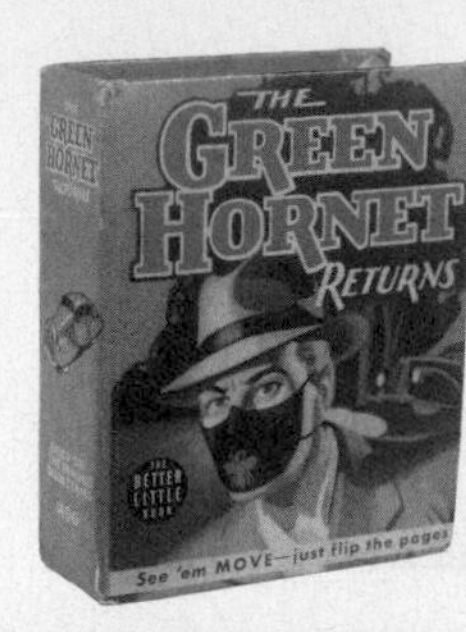

1496 - The Green Hornet Returns © WHIT

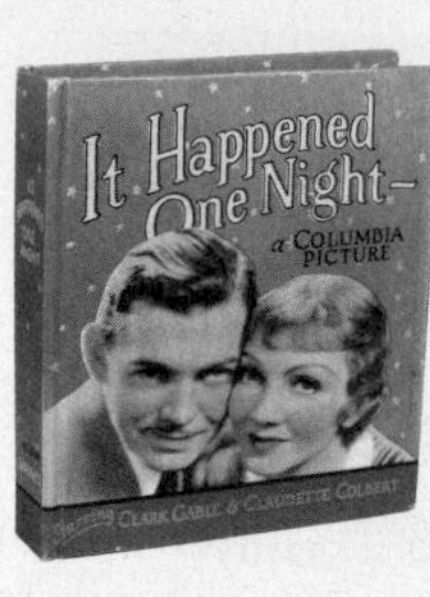

1098 - It Happened One Night © Columbia

27 - Jimmy Allen in The Sky Parade © WHIT

	GD	FN	VF/NM
2021- Goofy in Giant Trouble (Walt Disney's ...), 1968, Whitman, hard-c, 260 pgs., 39 cents, color illos.	3.00	7.50	20.00
5751- Goofy in Giant Trouble (Walt Disney's ...), 1968, Whitman, soft-c, 260 pgs., 39 cents, color illos.	3.00	7.50	20.00
5751-2- Goofy in Giant Trouble, 1968 (1980-reprint of '67 version), Whitman, soft-c, 260 pgs., 79 cents, B&W	1.00	2.50	6.00
8- Great Expectations, 1934, EVW, (Five Star Library), 160 pgs., photo-c, movie scenes	20.00	50.00	140.00
1453- Green Hornet Strikes!, The, 1940, Whitman, 432 pgs., Robert Weisman-a	49.00	122.00	345.00
1480- Green Hornet Cracks Down, The, 1942, Whitman, 432 pgs., flip pictures, Henry Vallely-a	46.00	115.00	320.00
1496- Green Hornet Returns, The, 1941, Whitman, 432 pgs., flip pictures	49.00	122.00	345.00
5778- Grimm's Ghost Stories, 1976, Whitman, 256 pgs., Laura French-s adapted from fairy tales; blue spine & back-c	2.00	5.00	13.00
5778-1- Grimm's Ghost Stories, 1976, Whitman, 256 pgs., reprint of #5778; yellow spine & back-c	2.00	5.00	13.00
1172- Gullivers' Travels, 1939, Saalfield, 320 pgs., adapted from Paramount Pict. Cartoons	20.00	50.00	140.00
nn- Gumps In Radio Land, The (Andy Gump and the Chest of Gold), 1937, Lehn & Fink Prod. Corp., 100 pgs., 3 1/4" x 5 1/2", Pebeco Tooth Paste giveaway, by Gus Edson	24.00	60.00	165.00
nn- Gunmen of Rustlers' Gulch, The, 1939, Whitman, 36 pgs., 2 1/2" x 3 1/2", Penny Book	11.00	27.50	70.00
1426- Guns in the Roaring West, 1937, Whitman, 300 pgs.	11.00	27.50	70.00
1647- Gunsmoke (TV Series), 1958, Whitman, 280 pgs., 4 1/2" x 5 3/4"	7.00	17.50	44.00
1101- Hairbreath Harry in Department QT, 1935, Whitman, 384 pgs., by J. M. Alexander	12.00	30.00	85.00
1413- Hal Hardy in the Lost Land of Giants, 1938, Whitman, 300 pgs., "The World 1,000,000 Years Ago"	12.00	30.00	85.00
1159- Hall of Fame of the Air, 1936, Whitman, 432 pgs., by Capt. Eddie Rickenbacker	11.00	27.50	70.00
nn- Hansel and Grethel, The Story of, nd (1930s), no publ., 36 pgs., Penny Book	4.00	10.00	22.00
1145- Hap Lee's Selection of Movie Gags, 1935, Whitman, 160 pgs., photos of stars	15.00	37.50	105.00
Happy Prince, The (See Wee Little Books)			
1111- Hard Rock Harrigan-A Story of Boulder Dam, 1935, Saalfield, hard-c, photo-c, photo illos.	11.00	27.50	70.00
1591- Hard Rock Harrigan-A Story of Boulder Dam, 1935, Saalfield, soft-c, photo-c, photo illos.	11.00	27.50	70.00
1418- Harold Teen Swinging at the Sugar Bowl, 1939, Whitman, 432 pgs., by Carl Ed	12.00	30.00	80.00
nn- Hercules - The Legendary Journeys, 1998, Chronicle Books, 310 pgs., based on TV series, 1-color (brown) illos	1.00	2.50	9.00
1100B- Hobbies, 1938, Whitman, 36 pgs., 2 1/2" x 3 1/2", Penny Book	4.00	10.00	22.00
1125- Hockey Spare, The, 1937, Saalfield, sports book	8.00	20.00	50.00
1605- Hockey Spare, The, 1937, Saalfield, soft-c	8.00	20.00	50.00
728- Homeless Homer, 1934, Whitman, by Dee Dobbin, for young kids	5.00	12.50	33.00
17- Hoosier Schoolmaster, The, 1935, EVW, movie scenes	15.00	37.50	105.00
715- Houdini's Big Little Book of Magic, 1927 (1933), 300 pgs.	16.00	40.00	115.00
nn- Houdini's Big Little Book of Magic, 1927 (1933), 196 pgs., American Oil Co. premium, soft-c	16.00	40.00	115.00
nn- Houdini's Big Little Book of Magic, 1927 (1933), 204 pgs., Cocomalt premium, soft-c	16.00	40.00	115.00
Huckleberry Finn (See The Adventures of...)			
nn- Huckleberry Hound Newspaper Reporter, 1977, Modern Promotions, 244 pgs., 49 cents, soft-c, flip pictures	2.00	5.00	13.00
1644- Hugh O'Brian TV's Wyatt Earp (TV Series), 1958, Whitman, 280 pgs.	7.00	17.50	44.00
5782-2- Incredible Hulk Lost in Time, 1980, 260 pgs., 79¢-c, soft-c, B&W	2.00	5.00	10.00

	GD	FN	VF/NM
1424- Inspector Charlie Chan Villainy on the High Seas, 1942, Whitman, 432 pgs., flip pictures	16.00	40.00	115.00
1186- Inspector Wade of Scotland Yard, 1940, Saalfield, 400 pgs.	11.00	27.50	70.00
1448- Inspector Wade and The Feathered Serpent, 1939, Saalfield, 400 pgs.	11.00	27.50	70.00
1448- Inspector Wade Solves the Mystery of the Red Aces, 1937, Whitman, 432 pgs.	11.00	27.50	70.00
1148- International Spy Doctor Doom Faces Death at Dawn, 1937, Whitman, 432 pgs., Arbo-a	12.00	30.00	85.00
1155- In the Name of the Law, 1937, Whitman, 432 pgs., Henry E. Vallely-a	11.00	27.50	70.00
2012-(#12)-Invaders, The-Alien Missile Threat (TV Series), 1967, Whitman, 260 pgs., hard-c, 39 cents, color illos.	4.00	10.00	27.00
1403- Invisible Scarlet O'Neil, 1942, Whitman, All Pictures Comics, flip pictures	12.00	30.00	85.00
1406- Invisible Scarlet O'Neil Versus the King of the Slums, 1946, Whitman, 352 pgs.	11.00	27.50	70.00
1098- It Happened One Night, 1935, Saalfield, 160 pgs., Little Big Book, Clark Gable, Claudette Colbert photo-c, movie scenes from Academy Award winner	21.00	52.50	145.00
1578- It Happened One Night, 1935, Saalfield, 160 pgs., soft-c	21.00	52.50	145.00
Jack and Jill (See Wee Little Books)			
1432- Jack Armstrong and the Mystery of the Iron Key, 1939, Whitman, 432 pgs., Henry E. Vallely-a	12.00	30.00	85.00
1435- Jack Armstrong and the Ivory Treasure, 1937, Whitman, 432 pgs., Henry Vallely-a	12.00	30.00	85.00
Jackie Cooper (See Story Of..)			
1084- Jackie Cooper in Peck's Bad Boy, 1934, Saalfield, 160 pgs., hard, photo-c, movie scenes	15.00	37.50	105.00
1314- Jackie Cooper in Peck's Bad Boy, 1934, Saalfield, 160 pgs., soft, photo-c, movie scenes	15.00	37.50	105.00
1402- Jackie Cooper in "Gangster's Boy," 1939, Whitman, 240 pgs., photo-c, movie scenes	15.00	37.50	105.00
13- Jackie Cooper in Dinky, 1935, EVW, 160 pgs., movie scenes	15.00	37.50	105.00
nn- Jack King of the Secret Service and the Counterfeiters, 1939, Whitman, 36 pgs., 2 1/2" x 3 1/2", Penny Book, by John G. Gray	11.00	27.50	70.00
L11- Jack London's Call of the Wild, 1935, Lynn, 20th Cent. Pic., movie scenes with Clark Gable	15.00	37.50	105.00
nn- Jack Pearl as Detective Baron Munchausen, 1934, Goldsmith, 132 pgs., soft-c	12.00	30.00	85.00
1102- Jack Swift and His Rocket Ship, 1934, Whitman, 320 pgs.	24.00	60.00	165.00
1498- Jane Arden the Vanished Princess, Whitman, 300 pgs.	11.00	27.50	70.00
1179- Jane Withers in This is the Life (20th Century-Fox Presents...), 1935, Whitman, 240 pgs., photo-c, movie scenes	15.00	37.50	105.00
1463- Jane Withers in Keep Smiling, 1938, Whitman, 240 pgs., photo-c, movie scenes	15.00	37.50	105.00
Jaragu of the Jungle (See Rex Beach's ...)			
1447- Jerry Parker Police Reporter and the Candid Camera Clue, 1941, Whitman, 300 pgs.	11.00	27.50	70.00
Jim Bowie (See Adventures of ...)			
nn- Jim Brant of the Highway Patrol and the Mysterious Accident, 1939, Whitman, 36 pgs., 2 1/2" x 3 1/2", Penny Book	10.00	25.00	65.00
1466- Jim Craig State Trooper and the Kidnapped Governor, 1938, Whitman, 432 pgs.	11.00	27.50	70.00
nn- Jim Doyle Private Detective and the Train Hold-Up, 1939, Whitman, 36 pgs., 2 1/2" x 3 1/2", Penny Book	12.00	30.00	75.00
1180- Jim Hardy Ace Reporter, 1940, Saalfield, 400 pgs., Dick Moores-a	12.00	30.00	75.00
1143- Jimmy Allen in the Air Mail Robbery, 1936, Whitman, 432 pgs.	12.00	30.00	75.00
27- Jimmy Allen in The Sky Parade, 1936, Lynn, 130 pgs., 5 x 7 1/2", Paramount Pictures, movie scenes	13.00	32.50	90.00
L15- Jimmy and the Tiger, 1935, Lynn, 192 pgs.	12.00	30.00	75.00

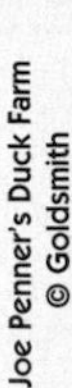
Joe Penner's Duck Farm © Goldsmith

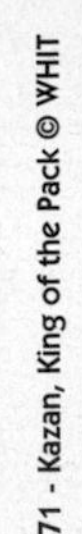
1471 - Kazan, King of the Pack © WHIT

1149 - Lee Brady Range Detective © Saalfield

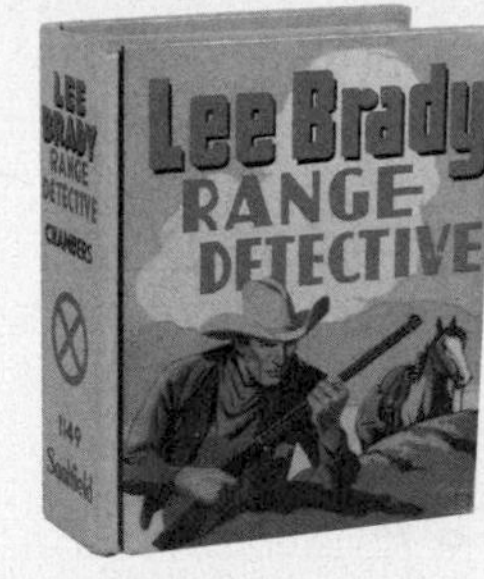

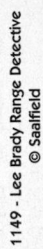

GD FN VF/NM

1428- Jim Starr of the Border Patrol, 1937, Whitman, 432 pgs. 12.00 30.00 75.00

Joan of Arc (See Wee Little Books)

1105- Joe Louis the Brown Bomber, 1936, Whitman, 240 pgs., photo-c, photo-illos. 24.00 60.00 170.00

Joe Palooka (See Gentleman ...)

1123- Joe Palooka the Heavyweight Boxing Champ, 1934, Whitman, 320 pgs., Ham Fisher-a 22.00 52.50 155.00

1168- Joe Palooka's Great Adventure, 1939, Saalfield 18.00 45.00 125.00

nn- Joe Penner's Duck Farm, 1935, Goldsmith, Henry Vallely-a 12.00 30.00 85.00

1402- John Carter of Mars, 1940, Whitman, 432 pgs., John Coleman Burroughs-a 84.00 210.00 585.00

nn- John Carter of Mars, 1940, Dell, 194 pgs., Fast-Action Story, soft-c 84.00 210.00 585.00

1164- Johnny Forty Five, 1938, Saalfield, 400 pgs. 11.00 27.50 70.00

John Wayne (See Westward Ho!)

1100B- Jokes (A book of laughs galore), 1938, Whitman, 36 pgs., 2 1/2" x 3 1/2", Penny Book, laughing guy-c 4.00 10.00 22.00

1100B- Jokes (A book of side-splitting funny stories), 1938, Whitman, 36 pgs., 2 1/2" x 3 1/2", Penny Book, clowns on-c 4.00 10.00 22.00

2026-(#26)- Journey to the Center of the Earth, The Fiery Foe, 1968, Whitman 4.00 10.00 27.00

Jungle Jim (See Top-Line Comics)

1138- Jungle Jim, 1936, Whitman, 432 pgs., Alex Raymond-a 22.00 52.50 155.00

1139- Jungle Jim and the Vampire Woman, 1937, Whitman, 432 pgs., Alex Raymond-a 22.00 52.50 155.00

1442- Junior G-Men, 1937, Whitman, 432 pgs., Henry E. Vallely-a 12.00 30.00 80.00

nn- Junior G-Men Solve a Crime, 1939, Whitman, 36 pgs., 2 1/2" x 3 1/2", Penny Book 12.00 30.00 80.00

1422- Junior Nebb on the Diamond Bar Ranch, 1938, Whitman, 300 pgs., by Sol Hess 12.00 30.00 80.00

1470- Junior Nebb Joins the Circus, 1939, Whitman, 300 pgs. by Sol Hess 12.00 30.00 80.00

nn- Junior Nebb Elephant Trainer, 1939, Whitman, 68 pgs., Pan-Am Oil premium, soft-c 15.00 37.50 105.00

1052- "Just Kids" (Adventures of ...), 1934, Saalfield, oblong size, by Ad Carter 22.00 52.50 155.00

1094- Just Kids and the Mysterious Stranger, 1935, Saalfield, 160 pgs., by Ad Carter 15.00 37.50 105.00

1184- Just Kids and Deep-Sea Dan, 1940, Saalfield, 400 pgs., by Ad Carter 12.00 30.00 85.00

1302- Just Kids, The Adventures of, 1934, Saalfield, oblong size, soft-c, by Ad Carter 22.00 52.50 155.00

1324- Just Kids and the Mysterious Stranger, 1935, Saalfield, 160 pgs., soft-c, by Ad Carter , 15.00 37.50 105.00

1401- Just Kids, 1937, Whitman, 432 pgs., by Ad Carter 15.00 37.50 105.00

1055- Katzenjammer Kids in the Mountains, 1934, Saalfield, hard-c, oblong, H. H. Knerr-a 21.00 52.50 145.00

1305- Katzenjammer Kids in the Mountains, 1934, Saalfield, soft-c, oblong, H. H. Knerr-a 21.00 52.50 145.00

14- Katzenjammer Kids, The, 1942, Dell, 194 pgs., Fast-Action Story, H. H. Knerr-a 24.00 60.00 165.00

1411- Kay Darcy and the Mystery Hideout, 1937, Whitman, 300 pgs., Charles Mueller-a 13.00 32.50 90.00

1180- Kayo in the Land of Sunshine (With Moon Mullins), 1937, Whitman, 432 pgs., by Willard 15.00 37.50 105.00

1415- Kayo and Moon Mullins and the One Man Gang, 1939, Whitman, 432 pgs., by Frank Willard 12.00 30.00 85.00

7- Kayo and Moon Mullins 'Way Down South, 1938, Whitman, 132 pgs., 3 1/2" x 3 1/2", Buddy Book 31.00 78.00 220.00

1105- Kazan in Revenge of the North (James Oliver Curwood's...), 1937, Whitman, 432 pgs., Henry E. Vallely-a 11.00 27.50 70.00

1471- Kazan, King of the Pack (James Oliver Curwood's...), 1940, Whitman, 432 pgs. 10.00 25.00 65.00

1420- Keep 'Em Flying! U.S.A. for America's Defense, 1943, Whitman, 432 pgs., Henry E. Vallely-a, flip pictures 11.00 27.50 70.00

1133- Kelly King at Yale Hall, 1937, Saalfield 10.00 25.00 65.00

Ken Maynard (See Strawberry Roan, Western Frontier & Wheels of Destiny)

776- Ken Maynard in "Gun Justice," 1934, Whitman, 160 pgs., hard-c, movie scenes (Universal Pic.) 21.00 52.50 145.00

776- Ken Maynard in "Gun Justice," 1934, Whitman, 160 pgs., soft-c, movie scenes (Universal Pic.) 21.00 52.50 145.00

1430- Ken Maynard in Western Justice, 1938, Whitman, 432 pgs., Irwin Myers-a 12.00 30.00 85.00

1442- Ken Maynard and the Gun Wolves of the Gila, 1939, Whitman, 432 pgs. 12.00 30.00 85.00

nn- Ken Maynard in Six-Gun Law, 1938, Whitman, 36 pgs., 2 1/2" x 3 1/2", Penny Book 10.00 25.00 65.00

1134- King of Crime, 1938, Saalfield, 400 pgs. 11.00 27.50 70.00

King of the Royal Mounted (See Zane Grey)

nn- Kit Carson, 1933, World Syndicate, by J. Carroll Mansfield, High Lights Of History Series, hard-c 11.00 27.50 70.00

nn- Kit Carson, 1933, World Syndicate, same as hard-c above but with a black cloth-c 11.00 27.50 70.00

1105- Kit Carson and the Mystery Riders, 1935, Saalfield, hard-c, Johnny Mack Brown photo-c, movie scenes 18.00 45.00 125.00

1585- Kit Carson and the Mystery Riders, 1935, Saalfield, soft-c, Johnny Mack Brown photo-c, movie scenes 18.00 45.00 125.00

Krazy Kat (See Adventures of...)

2004- (#4)-Lassie-Adventure in Alaska (TV Series), 1967, Whitman, hard-c, 260 pgs., 39 cents, color illos 4.00 10.00 27.00

5754- Lassie-Adventure in Alaska (TV Series), 1973, Whitman, soft-c, 260 pgs., 49 cents, color illos 2.00 5.00 13.00

2027- Lassie and the Shabby Sheik (TV Series), 1968, Whitman, hard-c, 260 pgs., 39 cents 4.00 10.00 25.00

5702- Lassie and the Shabby Sheik (TV Series), 1972, Whitman, soft-c, 260 pgs., 39 cents 2.00 5.00 13.00

5769- Lassie, Old One-Eye (TV Series), 1975, Whitman, soft-c, 260 pgs., 49 cents, three printings 2.00 5.00 13.00

1132- Last Days of Pompeii, The, 1935, Whitman, 5 1/4" x 6 1/4", 260 pgs., photo-c, movie scenes 15.00 37.50 105.00

1128- Last Man Out (Baseball), 1937, Saalfield, hard-c 11.00 27.50 70.00

L30- Last of the Mohicans, The, 1936, Lynn, 192 pgs., movie scenes with Randolph Scott, United Artists Pictures 16.00 40.00 115.00

1126- Laughing Dragon of Oz, The, 1934, Whitman 432 pgs., by Frank Baum (scarce) 102.00 256.00 715.00

1086- Laurel and Hardy, 1934, Saalfield, 160 pgs., hard-c, photo-c, movie scenes 21.00 52.50 145.00

1316- Laurel and Hardy, 1934, Saalfield, 160 pgs. soft-c, photo-c, movie scenes 21.00 52.50 145.00

1092- Law of the Wild, The, 1935, Saalfield, 160 pgs., photo-c, movie scenes of Rex, The Wild Horse & Rin-Tin-Tin Jr. 12.00 30.00 85.00

1322- Law of the Wild, The, 1935, Saalfield, 160 pgs., photo-c, movie scenes, soft-c 12.00 30.00 85.00

1100B- Learn to be a Ventriloquist, 1938, Whitman, 36 pgs. 2 1/2" x 3 1/2", Penny Book 4.00 10.00 22.00

1149- Lee Brady Range Detective, 1938, Saalfield, 400 pgs. 10.00 25.00 65.00

L10- Les Miserables (Victor Hugo's ...), 1935, Lynn, 192 pgs., movie scenes 15.00 37.50 105.00

1441- Lightning Jim U.S. Marshal Brings Law to the West, 1940, Whitman, 432 pgs., based on radio program 12.00 30.00 85.00

nn- Lightning Jim Whipple U.S. Marshal in Indian Territory, 1939, Whitman, 36 pgs., 2 1/2" x 3 1/2", Penny Book 11.00 27.50 70.00

653- Lions and Tigers (With Clyde Beatty), 1934, Whitman, 160 pgs., photo-c movie scenes 15.00 37.50 105.00

1187- Li'l Abner and the Ratfields, 1940, Saalfield, 400 pgs., by Al Capp 19.00 47.50 135.00

1193- Li'l Abner and Sadie Hawkins Day, 1940, Saalfield, 400 pgs., by Al Capp 19.00 47.50 135.00

1198- Li'l Abner in New York, 1936, Whitman, 432 pgs., by Al Capp 21.00 52.50 145.00

1401- Li'l Abner Among the Millionaires, 1939, Whitman, 432 pgs., by Al Capp 21.00 52.50 145.00

1112 - Little Hollywood Stars © Saalfield

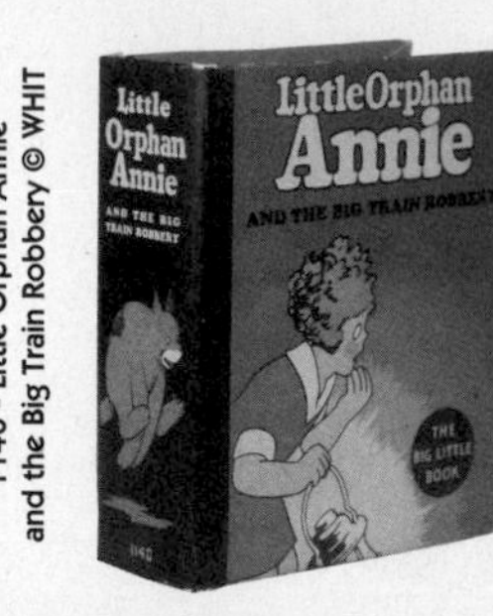

1140 - Little Orphan Annie and the Big Train Robbery © WHIT

1181 - Lone Ranger and his Horse Silver © Lone Ranger Inc.

GD FN VF/NM

1054- Little Annie Rooney, 1934, Saalfield, oblong - 4" x 8", All Pictures Comics, hard-c 20.00 50.00 140.00

1304- Little Annie Rooney, 1934, Saalfield, oblong - 4" x 8", All Pictures, soft-c 20.00 50.00 140.00

1117- Little Annie Rooney and the Orphan House, 1936, Whitman, 432 pgs. 12.00 30.00 80.00

1406- Little Annie Rooney on the Highway to Adventure, 1938, Whitman, 432 pgs. 12.00 30.00 80.00

1149- Little Big Shot (With Sybil Jason), 1935, Whitman, 240 pgs., photo-c, movie scenes 15.00 37.50 105.00

nn- Little Black Sambo, nd (1930s), np (Whitman), 36 pgs., 3" x 2 1/2", Penny Book 12.00 30.00 85.00

Little Bo-Peep (See Wee Little Books)

Little Colonel, The (See Shirley Temple)

1148- Little Green Door, The, 1938, Saalfield, 400 pgs. 11.00 27.50 70.00

1112- Little Hollywood Stars, 1935, Saalfield, movie scenes (Little Rascals, etc.), hard-c 15.00 37.50 105.00

1592- Little Hollywood Stars, 1935, Saalfield, movie scenes, soft-c 15.00 37.50 105.00

1087- Little Jimmy's Gold Hunt, 1935, Saalfield, 160 pgs., hard-c, Little Big Book, by Swinnerton 20.00 50.00 140.00

1317- Little Jimmy's Gold Hunt, 1935, Saalfield, 160 pgs., 4 1/4" x 5 3/4", soft-c, by Swinnerton 20.00 50.00 140.00

Little Joe and the City Gangsters (See Top-Line Comics)

Little Joe Otter's Slide (See Wee Little Books)

1118- Little Lord Fauntleroy, 1936, Saalfield, movie scenes, photo-c, 4 1/2" x 5 1/4", starring Mickey Rooney & Freddie Bartholomew, hard-c 12.00 30.00 85.00

1598- Little Lord Fauntleroy, 1936, Saalfield, photo-c, movie scenes, soft-c 12.00 30.00 85.00

1192- Little Mary Mixup and the Grocery Robberies, 1940, Saalfield 11.00 27.50 70.00

8- Little Mary Mixup Wins A Prize, 1936, Whitman, 132 pgs., 3 1/2" x 3 1/2", soft-c, Tarzan Ice Cream cup lid premium 36.00 90.00 255.00

1150- Little Men, 1934, Whitman, 4 3/4" x 5 1/4", movie scenes (Mascot Prod.), photo-c, hard-c 12.00 30.00 80.00

9- Little Minister, The,-Katharine Hepburn, 1935, 160 pgs., 4 1/4" x 5 1/2", EVW (Five Star Library), movie scenes (RKO) 16.00 40.00 115.00

1120- Little Miss Muffet, 1936, Whitman, 432 pgs., by Fanny Y. Cory 12.00 30.00 80.00

708- Little Orphan Annie, 1933, Whitman, 320 pgs., by Harold Gray, the 2nd Big Little Book 70.00 175.00 495.00

nn- Little Orphan Annie, 1928('33), Whitman, 52 pgs., 4" x 5 1/2", premium-no ads, soft-c, by Harold Gray 39.00 98.00 275.00

716- Little Orphan Annie and Sandy, 1933, Whitman, 320 pgs., by Harold Gray 33.00 83.00 230.00

716- Little Orphan Annie and Sandy, 1933, Whitman, 300 pgs., by Harold Gray 33.00 83.00 230.00

nn- Little Orphan Annie and Sandy, 1933, Whitman, 52 pgs., premium-no ads, 4" x 5 1/2", soft-c by Harold Gray 39.00 98.00 275.00

748- Little Orphan Annie and Chizzler, 1933, Whitman, 320 pgs., by Harold Gray 26.00 65.00 185.00

1010- Little Orphan Annie and the Big Town Gunmen, 1937, 7 1/4" x 5 1/2", 64 pgs., Nickel Book 15.00 37.50 105.00

nn- Little Orphan Annie with the Circus, 1934, Whitman, 320 pgs., same cover as L.O.A. 708 but with blue background, Ovaltine giveaway stamp inside front-c, by Harold Gray 58.00 146.00 410.00

1140- Little Orphan Annie and the Big Train Robbery, 1934, Whitman, 300 pgs., by Gray 20.00 50.00 140.00

1140- Little Orphan Annie and the Big Train Robbery, 1934, Whitman, 300 pgs., premium-no ads, soft-c, by Harold Gray 36.00 90.00 255.00

1154- Little Orphan Annie and the Ghost Gang, 1935, Whitman, 432 pgs. by Harold Gray 20.00 50.00 140.00

nn- Little Orphan Annie and the Ghost Gang, 1935, Whitman, 436 pgs., premium-no ads, 3-color, soft-c, by Harold Gray 36.00 90.00 255.00

1162- Little Orphan Annie and Punjab the Wizard, 1935, Whitman, 432 pgs., by Harold Gray 20.00 50.00 140.00

1186- Little Orphan Annie and the $1,000,000 Formula, 1936, Whitman, 432 pgs., by Gray 18.00 45.00 125.00

1414- Little Orphan Annie and the Ancient Treasure of Am, 1939, Whitman, 432 pgs., by Gray 16.00 40.00 115.00

1416- Little Orphan Annie in the Movies, 1937, Whitman, 432 pgs., by Harold Gray 16.00 40.00 115.00

1417- Little Orphan Annie and the Secret of the Well, 1947,Whitman, 352 pgs., by Gray 12.00 30.00 85.00

1435- Little Orphan Annie and the Gooneyville Mystery, 1947, Whitman, 288 pgs., by Gray 13.00 32.50 90.00

1446- Little Orphan Annie in the Thieves' Den, 1949, Whitman, 288 pgs., by Harold Gray 13.00 32.50 90.00

1449- Little Orphan Annie and the Mysterious Shoemaker, 1938, Whitman, 432 pgs., by Harold Gray 15.00 37.50 105.00

1457- Little Orphan Annie and Her Junior Commandos, 1943, Whitman, 352 pgs., by H. Gray 12.00 30.00 85.00

1461- Little Orphan Annie and the Underground Hide-Out, 1945, Whitman, 352 pgs., by Gray 12.00 30.00 85.00

1468- Little Orphan Annie and the Ancient Treasure of Am, 1949 (Misdated 1939), 288 pgs., by Gray 12.00 30.00 85.00

1482- Little Orphan Annie and the Haunted Mansion, 1941, Whitman, 432 pgs., flip pictures, by Harold Gray 16.00 40.00 115.00

3048- Little Orphan Annie and Her Big Little Kit, 1937, Whitman, 384 pgs., 4 1/2" x 6 1/2" box, includes miniature box of 4 crayons-red, yellow, blue and green 94.00 235.00 660.00

4054- Little Orphan Annie, The Story of, 1934, Whitman, 7" x 9 1/2", 320 pgs., Big Big Book, Harold Gray-c/a 102.00 255.00 715.00

nn- Little Orphan Annie Gets into Trouble, 1938, Whitman, 36 pgs., 2 1/2" x 3 1/2", Penny Book 11.00 27.50 70.00

nn- Little Orphan Annie in Hollywood, 1937, Whitman, 3 1/2" x 3 1/4", Pan-Am premium, soft c 29.00 73.00 200.00

nn- Little Orphan Annie in Rags to Riches, 1939, Dell, 194 pgs., Fast-Action Story, soft-c 39.00 98.00 275.00

nn- Little Orphan Annie Saves Sandy, 1938, Whitman, 36 pgs., 2 1/2" x 3 1/2", Penny Book 11.00 27.50 70.00

nn- Little Orphan Annie Under the Big Top, 1938, Dell, 194 pgs., Fast-Action Story, soft-c 39.00 98.00 270.00

nn- Little Orphan Annie Wee Little Books (In open box) nn, 1934, Whitman, 44 pgs., by H. Gray

L.O.A. And Daddy Warbucks 9.00 22.50 55.00
L.O.A. And Her Dog Sandy 9.00 22.50 55.00
L.O.A. And The Lucky Knife 9.00 22.50 55.00
L.O.A. And The Pinch-Pennys 9.00 22.50 55.00
L.O.A. At Happy Home 9.00 22.50 55.00
L.O.A. Finds Mickey 9.00 22.50 55.00
Complete set with box 57.00 143.00 400.00

nn- Little Polly Flinders, The Story of, nd (1930s), no publ., 36 pgs., 2 1/2" x 3", Penny Book 4.00 10.00 22.00

nn- Little Red Hen, The, nd(1930s), np(Whitman), 36 pgs., Penny Book 4.00 10.00 22.00

nn- Little Red Riding Hood, nd(1930s), np(Whitman), 36 pgs., 3" x 2 1/2", Penny Book 4.00 10.00 22.00

nn- Little Red Riding Hood and the Big Bad Wolf (Disney), 1934, McKay, 36 pgs., stiff-c, Disney Studio-a 33.00 83.00 230.00

757- Little Women, 1934, Whitman, 4 3/4" x 5 1/4", 160 pgs., photo-c, movie scenes, starring Katharine Hepburn 21.00 52.50 145.00

Littlest Rebel, The (See Shirley Temple)

1181- Lone Ranger and his Horse Silver, 1935, Whitman, 432 pgs., Hal Arbo-a 29.00 73.00 200.00

1196- Lone Ranger and the Vanishing Herd, 1936, Whitman, 432 pgs. 24.00 60.00 165.00

1407- Lone Ranger and Dead Men's Mine, The, 1939, Whitman, 432 pgs. 22.00 52.50 155.00

1421- Lone Ranger on the Barbary Coast, The, 1944, Whitman, 352 pgs., Henry Vallely-a 19.00 47.50 135.00

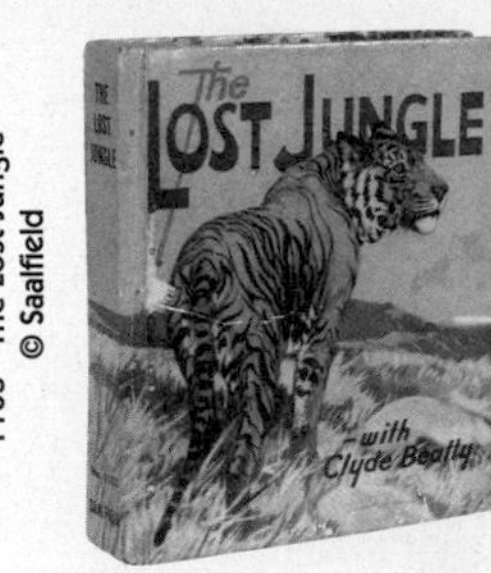

1103 - The Lost Jungle © Saalfield

2022 - Major Matt Mason, Moon Mission © WHIT

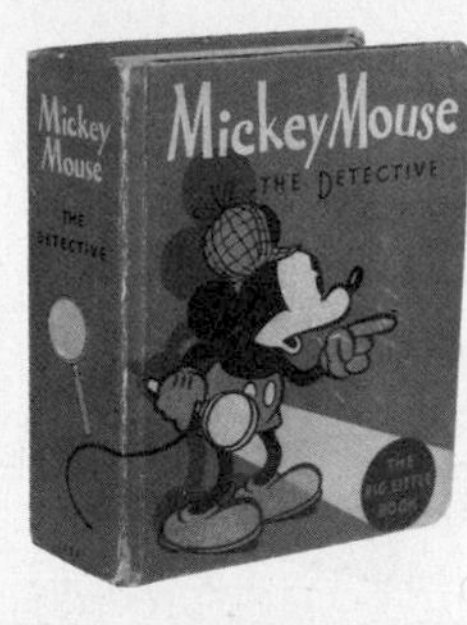

1139 - Mickey Mouse the Detective © WDC

GD FN VF/NM

1428- Lone Ranger and the Secret Weapon, The, 1943, Whitman, 19.00 47.50 135.00

1431- Lone Ranger and the Secret Killer, The, 1937, Whitman 432 pgs., H. Anderson-a 24.00 60.00 165.00

1450- Lone Ranger and the Black Shirt Highwayman, The, 1939, Whitman, 432 pgs. 22.00 52.50 155.00

1465- Lone Ranger and the Menace of Murder Valley, The, 1938, Whitman, 432 pgs., Robert Wiseman-a 21.00 52.50 145.00

1468- Lone Ranger Follows Through, The, 1941, Whitman, 432 pgs., H.E. Vallely-a 21.00 52.50 145.00

1477- Lone Ranger and the Great Western Span, The, 1942, Whitman, 424 pgs., H. E. Vallely-a 19.00 47.50 135.00

1489- Lone Ranger and the Red Renegades, The, 1939, Whitman, 432 pgs. 24.00 60.00 165.00

1498- Lone Ranger and the Silver Bullets, 1946, Whitman, 352 pgs., Henry E. Vallely-a 19.00 47.50 135.00

712-10- Lone Ranger and the Secret of Somber Cavern, The, 1950, Whitman 12.00 30.00 80.00

2013- (#13)-Lone Ranger Outwits Crazy Cougar, The, 1968, Whitman, 260 pgs., 39 cents, hard-c, color illos 4.00 10.00 27.00

5774- Lone Ranger Outwits Crazy Cougar, The, 1976, Whitman, 260 pgs., 49 cents, soft-c, color illos 4.00 10.00 22.00

5774-1- Lone Ranger Outwits Crazy Cougar, The, 1979, Whitman, 260 pgs., 69 cents, soft-c, color illos 4.00 10.00 22.00

nn- Lone Ranger and the Lost Valley, The, 1938, Dell, 196 pgs., Fast-Action Story, soft-c 43.00 108.00 300.00

1405- Lone Star Martin of the Texas Rangers, 1939, Whitman, 432 pgs. 18.00 45.00 125.00

19- Lost City, The, 1935, EVW, movie scenes 16.00 40.00 115.00

1103- Lost Jungle, The (With Clyde Beatty), 1936, Saalfield, movie scenes, hard-c 16.00 40.00 115.00

1583- Lost Jungle, The (With Clyde Beatty), 1936, Saalfield, movie scenes, soft -c 13.00 32.50 90.00

753- Lost Patrol, The, 1934, Whitman, 160 pgs., photo-c, movie scenes with Boris Karloff 15.00 37.50 105.00

nn- Lost World, The - Jurassic Park 2, 1997, Chronicle Books, 312 pgs., adapts movie, 1-color (green) illos 3.00 7.50 20.00

1189- Mac of the Marines in Africa, 1936, Whitman, 432 pgs. 12.00 30.00 80.00

1400- Mac of the Marines in China, 1938, Whitman, 432 pgs. 12.00 30.00 80.00

1100B- Magic Tricks (With explanations), 1938, Whitman, 36 pgs., 2 1/2" x 3 1/2", Penny Book, rabbit in hat-c 4.00 10.00 22.00

1100B- Magic Tricks (How to do them), 1938, Whitman, 36 pgs., 2 1/2" x 3 1/2", Penny Book, genie-c 4.00 10.00 22.00

Major Hoople (See Our Boarding House)

2022-(#22)- Major Matt Mason, Moon Mission, 1968, Whitman, 256 pgs., hard-c, color illos. 4.00 10.00 27.00

1167- Mandrake the Magician, 1935, Whitman, 432 pgs., by Lee Falk & Phil Davis 24.00 60.00 170.00

1418- Mandrake the Magician and the Flame Pearls, 1946, Whitman, 352 pgs., by Lee Falk & Phil Davis 15.00 37.50 105.00

1431- Mandrake the Magician and the Midnight Monster, 1939, Whitman, 432 pgs., by Lee Falk & Phil Davis 16.00 40.00 115.00

1454- Mandrake the Magician Mighty Solver of Mysteries, 1941, Whitman, 432 pgs., by Lee Falk & Phil Davis, flip pictures 16.00 40.00 115.00

2011-(#11)-Man From U.N.C.L.E., The-The Calcutta Affair (TV Series), 1967, Whitman, 260 pgs., 39 cents, hard-c, color illos 4.00 10.00 27.00

1429- Marge's Little Lulu Alvin and Tubby, 1947, Whitman, All Pictures Comics, Stanley-a 31.00 78.00 215.00

1438- Mary Lee and the Mystery of the Indian Beads, 1937, Whitman, 300 pgs. 11.00 27.50 70.00

1165- Masked Man of the Mesa, The, 1939, Saalfield, 400 pgs. 10.00 25.00 65.00

nn- Mask of Zorro, The, 1998, Chronicle Books, 312 pgs., adapts movie, 1-color (yellow-green) illos 1.00 2.50 9.00

1436- Maximo the Amazing Superman, 1940, Whitman, 432 pgs., Henry E. Vallely-a 15.00 37.50 105.00

1444- Maximo the Amazing Superman and the Crystals of Doom, 1941, Whitman,432 pgs., Henry E. Vallely-a 15.00 37.50 105.00

1445- Maximo the Amazing Superman and the Supermachine, 1941, Whitman, 432 pgs. 15.00 37.50 105.00

755- Men of the Mounted, 1934, Whitman, 320 pgs. 15.00 37.50 105.00

nn- Men of the Mounted, 1933, Whitman, 52 pgs., 3 1/2" x 5 3/4", premium-no ads; other versions with Poll Parrot & Perkins ad; soft-c 21.00 52.50 145.00

nn- Men of the Mounted, 1934, Whitman, Cocomalt premium, soft-c, by Ted McCall 12.00 30.00 85.00

1475- Men With Wings, 1938, Whitman, 240 pgs., photo-c, movie scenes (Paramount Pics.) 12.00 30.00 85.00

1170- Mickey Finn, 1940, Saalfield, 400 pgs., by Frank Leonard 12.00 30.00 85.00

717- Mickey Mouse (Disney), (1st printing) 1933, Whitman, 320 pgs., Gottfredson-a, skinny Mickey on cover 392.00 980.00 3135.00

717- Mickey Mouse (Disney), (2nd printing)1933, Whitman, 320 pgs., Gottfredson-a, regular Mickey on cover 206.00 515.00 1650.00

nn- Mickey Mouse (Disney), 1933, Dean & Son, Great Big Midget Book, 320 pgs. 186.00 464.00 1485.00

731- Mickey Mouse the Mail Pilot (Disney), 1933, Whitman, (This is the same book as the 1st Mickey Mouse BLB #717(2nd printing) but with "The Mail Pilot" printed on the front. Lower left of back cover has a small box printed over the existing "No. 717." "No. 731" is printed next to it.) (sold at auction in 2001 in Fine condition for $5,090)

726- Mickey Mouse in Blaggard Castle (Disney), 1934, Whitman, 320 pgs., Gottfredson-a 47.00 118.00 330.00

731- Mickey Mouse the Mail Pilot (Disney), 1933, Whitman, 300 pgs., Gottfredson-a 47.00 118.00 330.00

nn Mickey Mouse the Mail Pilot (Disney), 1933, Whitman, 292 pgs., American Oil Co. premium, soft-c, Gottfredson-a; another version 3 1/2" x 4 3/4" 47.00 118.00 330.00

750- Mickey Mouse Sails for Treasure Island (Disney), 1933, Whitman, 320 pgs., Gottfredson-a 47.00 118.00 330.00

nn- Mickey Mouse Sails for Treasure Island (Disney), 1935, Whitman, 196 pgs., premium-no ads, soft-c, Gottfredson-a (Scarce) 56.00 140.00 395.00

nn- Mickey Mouse Sails for Treasure Island (Disney), 1935, Whitman, 196 pgs., Kolynos Dental Cream premium (Scarce) 56.00 140.00 395.00

nn- Mickey Mouse Sails for Treasure Island (Disney), 1933, Dean & Son, Great Big Midget Book, 320 pgs. 144.00 360.00 1150.00

756- Mickey Mouse Presents a Walt Disney Silly Symphony (Disney), 1934, Whitman, 240 pgs., Bucky Bug app. 43.00 108.00 300.00

801- Mickey Mouse's Summer Vacation, 1948, Whitman, hard-c, Story Hour series 12.00 30.00 85.00

1111- Mickey Mouse Presents Walt Disney's Silly Symphonies Stories, 1936, Whitman, 432 pgs., Donald Duck app. 43.00 108.00 300.00

1128- Mickey Mouse and Pluto the Racer (Disney), 1936, Whitman, 432 pgs., Gottfredson-a 38.00 95.00 255.00

1139- Mickey Mouse the Detective (Disney), 1934, Whitman, 300 pgs., Gottfredson-a 43.00 108.00 300.00

1139- Mickey Mouse the Detective (Disney), 1934, Whitman, 304 pgs., premium-no ads, soft-c, Gottfredson-a (Scarce) 64.00 160.00 450.00

1153- Mickey Mouse and the Bat Bandit (Disney), 1935, Whitman, 432 pgs., Gottfredson-a 39.00 98.00 275.00

nn- Mickey Mouse and the Bat Bandit (Disney), 1935, Whitman, 436 pgs., premium-no ads, 3-color, soft-c, Gottfredson-a (Scarce) 64.00 160.00 450.00

1160- Mickey Mouse and Bobo the Elephant (Disney), 1935, Whitman, 432 pgs., Gottfredson-a 39.00 98.00 275.00

1187- Mickey Mouse and the Sacred Jewel (Disney), 1936, Whitman, 432 pgs., Gottfredson-a 36.00 90.00 255.00

1401- Mickey Mouse in the Treasure Hunt (Disney), 1941, Whitman, 430 pgs., flip pictures of Pluto, Gottfredson-a 34.00 85.00 240.00

1409- Mickey Mouse Runs His Own Newspaper (Disney), 1937, Whitman, 432 pgs., Gottfredson-a 34.00 85.00 240.00

1413- Mickey Mouse and the 'Lectro Box (Disney), 1946,

1464 - Mickey Mouse and the Stolen Jewels © DIS

746 - Moon Mullins and Kayo © WHIT

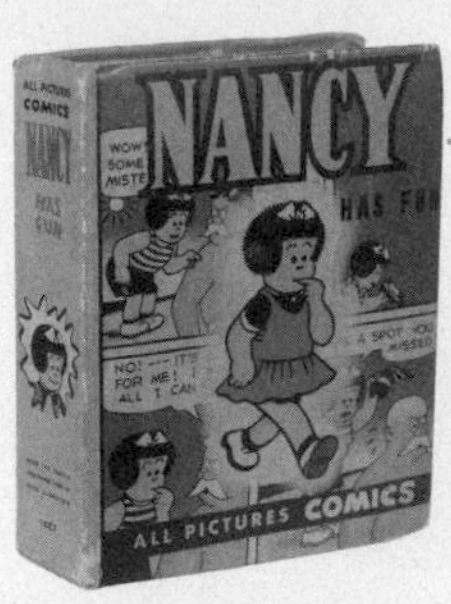

1487 - Nancy Has Fun © UFS

GD FN VF/NM

Whitman, 352 pgs., Gottfredson-a 24.00 60.00 165.00
1417- Mickey Mouse on Sky Island (Disney), 1941, Whitman, 432 pgs., flip pictures, Gottfredson-a; considered by Gottfredson to be his best Mickey story 34.00 85.00 240.00
1428- Mickey Mouse in the Foreign Legion (Disney), 1940, Whitman, 432 pgs., Gottfredson-a 34.00 85.00 240.00
1429- Mickey Mouse and the Magic Lamp (Disney), 1942, Whitman, 432 pgs., flip pictures 34.00 85.00 240.00
1433- Mickey Mouse and the Lazy Daisy Mystery (Disney), 1947, Whitman, 288 pgs. 24.00 60.00 165.00
1444- Mickey Mouse in the World of Tomorrow (Disney), 1948, Whitman, 288 pgs., Gottfredson-a 36.00 90.00 255.00
1451- Mickey Mouse and the Desert Palace (Disney), 1948, Whitman, 288 pgs. 24.00 60.00 165.00
1463- Mickey Mouse and the Pirate Submarine (Disney), 1939, Whitman, 432 pgs., Gottfredson-a 34.00 85.00 240.00
1464- Mickey Mouse and the Stolen Jewels (Disney), 1949, Whitman, 288 pgs. 33.00 83.00 230.00
1471- Mickey Mouse and the Dude Ranch Bandit (Disney), 1943, Whitman, 432 pgs., flip pictures 34.00 85.00 240.00
1475- Mickey Mouse and the 7 Ghosts (Disney), 1940, Whitman, 432 pgs., Gottfredson-a 34.00 85.00 240.00
1476- Mickey Mouse in the Race for Riches (Disney), 1938, Whitman, 432 pgs., Gottfredson-a 34.00 85.00 240.00
1483- Mickey Mouse Bell Boy Detective (Disney), 1945, Whitman, 352 pgs. 33.00 83.00 230.00
1499- Mickey Mouse on the Cave-Man Island (Disney), 1944, Whitman, 352 pgs. 33.00 83.00 230.00
2004- Mickey Mouse, Here Comes (Disney), 1936, Whitman, (Very Rare), 224 pgs., 12" x 8 1/4" box, with red, yellow and blue crayons, contains 224 loose pages to color, reprinted from early Mickey Mouse related movie and strip reprints 475.00 1187.00 3800.00
2020-(#20)- Mickey Mouse, Adventure in Outer Space, 1968, Whitman, 256 pgs.,hard-c, color illos. 4.00 10.00 27.00
5750- Mickey Mouse, Adventure in Outer Space, 1973, Whitman, 256 pgs.,soft-c, 39 cents, color illos. 2.00 5.00 13.00
3049- Mickey Mouse and His Big Little Kit (Disney), 1937, Whitman, 384 pgs., 4 1/2" x 6 1/2" box, includes miniature box of 4 crayons-red, yellow, blue and green 150.00 375.00 1210.00
3061- Mickey Mouse to Draw and Color (The Big Little Set), nd (early 1930s), Whitman, with crayons; box contains 320 loose pages to color, reprinted from early Mickey Mouse BLBs 123.00 308.00 880.00
4062- Mickey Mouse, The Story Of, 1935, Whitman, 7" x 9 1/2", 320 pgs., Big Big Book, Gottfredson-a 150.00 375.00 1210.00
4062- Mickey Mouse and the Smugglers, The Story Of, 1935, Whitman, (Scarce), 7" x 9 1/2", 320 pgs., Big Big Book, same contents as above version; Gottfredson-a 179.00 447.00 1430.00
708-10- Mickey Mouse on the Haunted Island (Disney), 1950, Whitman, Gottfredson-a 15.00 37.50 105.00
nn- Mickey Mouse and Minnie at Macy's, 1934 Whitman, 148 pgs., 3 1/4" x 3 1/2", soft-c, R. H. Macy & Co. Christmas giveaway (Rare, less than 20 known copies) 438.00 1095.00 3500.00
nn- Mickey Mouse and Minnie March to Macy's, 1935, Whitman, 148 pgs., 3 1/2" x 3 1/2", soft-c, R. H. Macy & Co. Christmas giveaway (scarce) 300.00 750.00 2400.00
nn- Mickey Mouse and the Magic Carpet, 1935, Whitman, 148 pgs., 3 1/2"x 4", soft-c, giveaway, Gottfredson-a, Donald Duck app. 131.00 328.00 1050.00
nn- Mickey Mouse Silly Symphonies, 1934, Dean & Son, Ltd (England), 48 pgs., with 4 pop-ups, Babes In The Woods, King Neptune
With dust jacket 165.00 412.00 1320.00
Without dust jacket 119.00 298.00 835.00
nn- Mickey Mouse the Sheriff of Nugget Gulch (Disney) 1938, Dell, 196 pgs., Fast-Action Story, soft-c, Gottfredson-a 56.00 140.00 395.00
nn- Mickey Mouse Waddle Book, 1934, BRP, 20 pgs., 7 1/2" x 10", forerunner of the Blue Ribbon Pop-Up books; with 4 removable articulated cardboard characters Book Only 100.00 200.00 500.00

GD FN VF/NM

Near Mint Complete $19,000
nn- Mickey Mouse with Goofy and Mickey's Nephews, 1938, Dell, Fast-Action Story, Gottfredson-a 56.00 140.00 395.00
16- Mickey Mouse and Pluto (Disney), 1942, Dell, 196 pgs., Fast-Action Story 56.00 140.00 395.00
512- Mickey Mouse Wee Little Books (In open box), nn, 1934, Whitman, 44 pgs., small size, soft-c
Mickey Mouse and Tanglefoot 13.00 32.50 90.00
Mickey Mouse at the Carnival 13.00 32.50 90.00
Mickey Mouse Will Not Quit! 13.00 32.50 90.00
Mickey Mouse Wins the Race! 13.00 32.50 90.00
Mickey Mouse's Misfortune 13.00 32.50 90.00
Mickey Mouse's Uphill Fight 13.00 32.50 90.00
Complete set with box 93.00 233.00 650.00
1493- Mickey Rooney and Judy Garland and How They Got into the Movies, 1941, Whitman, 432 pgs., photo-c 15.00 37.50 105.00
1427- Mickey Rooney Himself, 1939, Whitman, 240 pgs., photo-c, movie scenes, life story 15.00 37.50 105.00
532- Mickey's Dog Pluto (Disney), 1943, Whitman, All Picture Comics, A Tall Comic Book , 3 3/4" x 8 3/4" 41.00 103.00 285.00
2113- Midget Jumbo Coloring Book, 1935, Saalfield 41.00 103.00 285.00
21- Midsummer Night's Dream, 1935, EVW, movie scenes 15.00 37.50 105.00
nn- Minute-Man (Mystery of the Spy Ring), 1941, Fawcett, Dime Action Book 57.00 143.00 400.00
710- Moby Dick the Great White Whale, The Story of, 1934, Whitman, 160 pgs., photo-c, movie scenes from "The Sea Beast" 15.00 37.50 105.00
746- Moon Mullins and Kayo (Kayo and Moon Mullins-inside), 1933, Whitman, 320 pgs., Frank Willard-c/a 16.00 40.00 115.00
nn- Moon Mullins and Kayo, 1933, Whitman, Cocomalt premium, soft-c, by Willard 16.00 40.00 115.00
1134- Moon Mullins and the Plushbottom Twins, 1935, Whitman, 432 pgs., Willard-c/a 16.00 40.00 115.00
nn- Moon Mullins and the Plushbottom Twins, 1935, Whitman, 436 pgs., premium-no ads, 3-color, soft-c, by Willard 29.00 73.00 200.00
1058- Mother Pluto (Disney), 1939, Whitman, 68 pgs., hard-c 13.00 32.50 90.00
1100B- Movie Jokes (From the talkies), 1938, Whitman, 36 pgs., 2 1/2" x 3 1/2", Ponny Book 4.00 10.00 22.00
1408- Mr. District Attorney on the Job, 1941, Whitman, 432 pgs., flip pictures 12.00 30.00 75.00
nn- Musicians of Bremen, The, nd (1930s), np (Whitman), 36 pgs., 3" x 2 1/2", Penny Book 4.00 10.00 22.00
1113- Mutt and Jeff, 1936, Whitman, 300 pgs., by Bud Fisher 26.00 65.00 180.00
1116- My Life and Times (By Shirley Temple), 1936, Saalfield, Little Big Book, hard-c, photo-c/illos 16.00 40.00 115.00
1596- My Life and Times (By Shirley Temple), 1936, Saalfield, Little Big Book, soft-c, photo-c/illos 16.00 40.00 115.00
1497- Myra North Special Nurse and Foreign Spies, 1938, Whitman, 432 pgs. 12.00 30.00 85.00
1400- Nancy and Sluggo, 1946, Whitman, All Pictures Comics, Ernie Bushmiller-a 13.00 32.50 90.00
1487- Nancy Has Fun, 1946, Whitman, All Pictures Comics 13.00 32.50 90.00
1150- Napoleon and Uncle Elby, 1938, Saalfield, 400 pgs., by Clifford McBride 12.00 30.00 85.00
1166- Napoleon Uncle Elby And Little Mary, 1939, Saalfield, 400 pgs., by Clifford McBride 12.00 30.00 85.00
1179- Ned Brant Adventure Bound, 1940, Saalfield, 400 pgs. 11.00 27.50 70.00
1146- Nevada Rides The Danger Trail, 1938, Saalfield, 400 pgs., J.R. White-a 11.00 27.50 70.00
1147- Nevada Whalen, Avenger, 1938, Saalfield, 400 pgs. 11.00 27.50 70.00
Nicodemus O'Malley (See Top-Line Comics)
1115- Og Son of Fire, 1936, Whitman, 432 pgs. 16.00 40.00 115.00

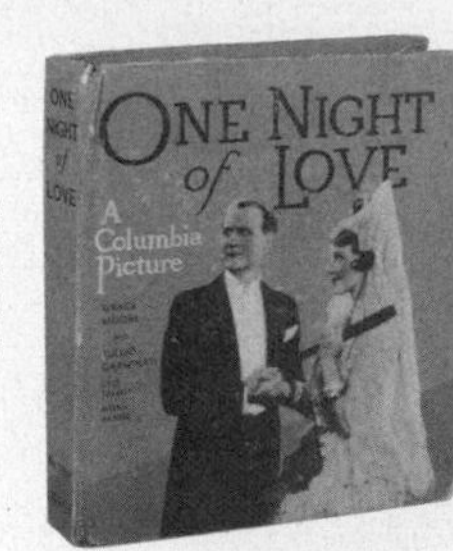
1099 - One Night of Love © Columbia

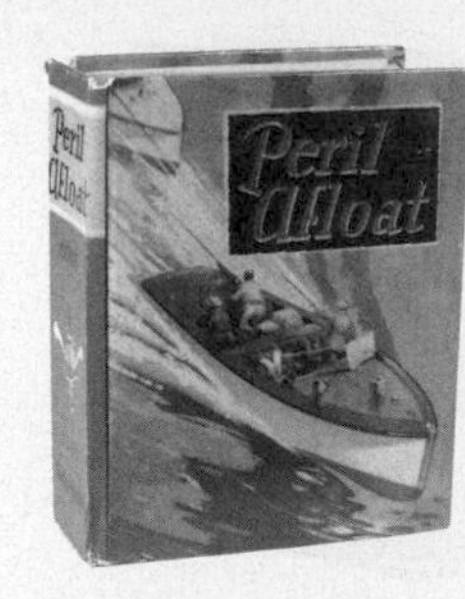
1143 - Peril Afloat © Saalfield

1497 - Popeye and Caster Oyl © KING

GD FN VF/NM

1419- **Oh, Blondie the Bumsteads** (See Blondie)

11- **Oliver Twist**, 1935, EVW (Five Star Library), movie scenes, starring Dickie Moore (Monogram Pictures) 15.00 37.50 105.00

718- **Once Upon a Time**, 1933, Whitman, 364 pgs., soft-c 15.00 37.50 105.00

712- **100 Fairy Tales for Children, The**, 1933, Whitman, 288 pgs., Circle Library 11.00 27.50 70.00

1099- **One Night of Love**, 1935, Saalfield, 160 pgs., hard-c, photo-c, movie scenes, Columbia Pictures, starring Grace Moore 15.00 37.50 105.00

1579- **One Night of Love**, 1935, Sat, 160 pgs., soft-c, photo-c, movie scenes, Columbia Pictures, starring Grace Moore 15.00 37.50 105.00

1155- **$1000 Reward**, 1930, Saalfield, 400 pgs. 11.00 27.50 70.00

Orphan Annie (See Little Orphan ...)

L17- **O'Shaughnessy's Boy**, 1935, Lynn, 192 pgs., movie scenes, w/Wallace Beery & Jackie Cooper (Metro-Goldwyn-Mayer) 12.00 30.00 85.00

1109- **Oswald the Lucky Rabbit**, 1934, Whitman, 288 pgs. 21.00 52.50 145.00

1403- **Oswald Rabbit Plays G-Man**, 1937, Whitman, 240 pgs., movie scenes by Walter Lantz 22.00 52.50 155.00

1190- **Our Boarding House, Major Hoople and his Horse**, 1940, Saalfield, 400 pgs. 12.00 30.00 85.00

1085- **Our Gang**, 1934, Saalfield, 160 pgs., photo-c, movie scenes, hard-c 15.00 37.50 105.00

1315- **Our Gang**, 1934, Saalfield, 160 pgs., photo-c, movie scenes, soft-c 15.00 37.50 105.00

1451- **"Our Gang" on the March**, 1942, Whitman, 432 pgs., flip pictures, Vallely-a 15.00 37.50 105.00

1456- **Our Gang Adventures**, 1948, Whitman, 288 pgs. 12.00 30.00 85.00

nn- **Paramount Newsreel Men with Admiral Byrd in Little America**, 1934, Whitman, 96 pgs., 6 1/4" x 6 1/4", photo-c, photo ill. 16.00 40.00 115.00

nn- **Patch**, nd (1930s), np (Whitman), 36 pgs., 3" x 2 1/2", Penny Book 4.00 10.00 22.00

1445- **Pat Nelson Ace of Test Pilots**, 1937, Whitman, 432 pgs. 11.00 27.50 70.00

1411- **Peggy Brown and the Mystery Basket**, 1941, Whitman, 432 pgs., flip pictures, Henry E. Vallely-a 12.00 30.00 75.00

1423- **Peggy Brown and the Secret Treasure**, 1947, Whitman, 288 pgs., Henry E. Vallely-a 12.00 30.00 75.00

1427- **Peggy Brown and the Runaway Auto Trailer**, 1937, Whitman, 300 pgs., Henry E. Vallely-a 12.00 30.00 75.00

1463- **Peggy Brown and the Jewel of Fire**, 1943, Whitman, 352 pgs., Henry E. Vallely-a 12.00 30.00 75.00

1491- **Peggy Brown in the Big Haunted House**, 1940, Whitman, 432 pgs., Vallely-a 12.00 30.00 75.00

1143- **Peril Afloat**, 1938, Saalfield, 400 pgs. 11.00 27.50 70.00

1199- **Perry Winkle and the Rinkeydinks**, 1937, Whitman, 432 pgs., by Martin Branner 15.00 37.50 105.00

1487- **Perry Winkle and the Rinkeydinks get a Horse**, 1938, Whitman, 432 pgs., by Martin Branner 15.00 37.50 105.00

Peter Pan (See Wee Little Books)

nn- **Peter Rabbit**, nd(1930s), np(Whitman), 36 pgs., Penny Book, 3" x 2 1/2" 5.00 12.50 33.00

Peter Rabbit's Carrots (See Wee Little Books)

1100- **Phantom, The**, 1936, Whitman, 432 pgs., by Lee Falk & Ray Moore 47.00 118.00 330.00

1416- **Phantom and the Girl of Mystery, The**, 1947, Whitman, 352 pgs. by Falk & Moore 21.00 52.50 145.00

1421- **Phantom and Desert Justice, The**, 1941, Whitman, 432 pgs., flip pictures, by Falk & Moore 28.00 70.00 195.00

1468- **Phantom and the Sky Pirates, The**, 1945, Whitman, 352 pgs., by Falk & Moore 24.00 60.00 170.00

1474- **Phantom and the Sign of the Skull, The**, 1939, Whitman, 432 pgs., by Falk & Moore 29.00 73.00 205.00

1489- **Phantom, Return of the...**, 1942, Whitman, 432 pgs., flip pictures, by Falk & Moore 28.00 70.00 195.00

GD FN VF/NM

1130- **Phil Barton, Sleuth** (Scout Book), 1937, Saalfield, hard-c 9.00 22.50 55.00

Pied Piper of Hamlin (See Wee Little Books)

1466- **Pilot Pete Dive Bomber**, 1941, Whitman, 432 pgs., flip pictures 11.00 27.50 70.00

5776- **Pink Panther Adventures in Z-Land, The**, 1976, Whitman, 260 pgs., soft-c, 49 cents, B&W 1.00 2.50 8.00

5776-2- **Pink Panther Adventures in Z-Land, The**, 1980, Whitman, 260 pgs., soft-c, 79 cents, B&W 1.00 2.50 8.00

5783-2- **Pink Panther at Castle Kreep, The**, 1980, Whitman, 260 pgs., soft-c, 79 cents, B&W 1.00 2.50 8.00

Pinocchio and Jiminy Cricket (See Walt Disney's ...)

nn- **Pioneers of the Wild West** (Blue-c), 1933, World Syndicate, High Lights of History Series 10.00 25.00 65.00

nn- **Pioneers of the Wild West** (Red-c), 1933, World Syndicate, High Lights of History Series 10.00 25.00 65.00

1123- **Plainsman, The**, 1936, Whitman, 240 pgs., photo-c, movie scenes with Gary Cooper (Paramount Pics.) 26.00 65.00 180.00

Pluto (See Mickey's Dog ... & Walt Disney's ...)

2114- **Pocket Coloring Book**, 1935, Saalfield 39.00 98.00 270.00

1060- **Polly and Her Pals on the Farm**, 1934, Saalfield, 164 pgs., hard-c, by Cliff Sterrett 15.00 37.50 105.00

1310- **Polly and Her Pals on the Farm**, 1934, Saalfield, soft-c 15.00 37.50 105.00

1051- **Popeye, Adventures of...**, 1934, Saalfield, oblong-size, E.C. Segar-a, hard-c 58.00 146.00 410.00

1088- **Popeye in Puddleburg**, 1934, Saalfield, 160 pgs., hard-c, E. C. Segar-a 22.00 52.50 155.00

1113- **Popeye Starring in Choose Your Weppins**, 1936, Saalfield, 160 pgs., hard-c, Segar-a 46.00 115.00 320.00

1117- **Popeye's Ark**, 1936, Saalfield, 4 1/2" x 5 1/2", hard-c, Segar-a 24.00 60.00 165.00

1163- **Popeye Sees the Sea**, 1936, Whitman, 432 pgs., Segar-a 24.00 60.00 170.00

1301- **Popeye, Adventures of...**, 1934, Saalfield, oblong-size, Segar-a 58.00 146.00 410.00

1318- **Popeye in Puddleburg**, 1934, Saalfield, 160 pgs., soft-c, Segar-a 24.00 60.00 165.00

1405- **Popeye and the Jeep**, 1937, Whitman, 432 pgs., Segar-a 24.00 60.00 170.00

1406- **Popeye the Super-Fighter**, 1939, Whitman, All Pictures Comics, flip pictures, Segar-a 24.00 60.00 165.00

1422- **Popeye the Sailor Man**, 1947, Whitman, All Pictures Comics 16.00 40.00 115.00

1450- **Popeye in Quest of His Poopdeck Pappy**, 1937, Whitman, 432 pgs., Segar-c/a 24.00 60.00 170.00

1458- **Popeye and Queen Olive Oyl**, 1949, Whitman, 288 pgs., Sagendorf-a 16.00 40.00 115.00

1459- **Popeye and the Quest for the Rainbird**, 1943, Whitman, Winner & Zaboly-a 18.00 45.00 125.00

1480- **Popeye the Spinach Eater**, 1945, Whitman, All Pictures Comics 16.00 40.00 115.00

1485- **Popeye in a Sock for Susan's Sake**, 1940, Whitman, 432 pgs., flip pictures 18.00 45.00 125.00

1497- **Popeye and Caster Oyl the Detective**, 1941, Whitman, 432 pgs. flip pictures, Segar-a 21.00 52.50 145.00

1499- **Popeye and the Deep Sea Mystery**, 1939, Whitman, 432 pgs., Segar-c/a 21.00 52.50 145.00

1593- **Popeye Starring in Choose Your Weppins**, 1936, Saalfield, 160 pgs., soft-c, Segar-a 21.00 52.50 145.00

1597- **Popeye's Ark**, 1936, Saalfield, 4 1/2" x 5 1/2", soft-c, Segar-a 21.00 52.50 145.00

2008-(#8)- **Popeye-Ghost Ship to Treasure Island**, 1967, Whitman, 260 pgs., 39 cents, hard-c, color illos 4.00 10.00 27.00

5755- **Popeye-Ghost Ship to Treasure Island**, 1973, Whitman, 260 pgs., soft-c, color illos 2.00 5.00 11.00

2034-(#34)- **Popeye, Danger Ahoy!**, 1969, Whitman, 256 pgs., hard-c, color illos. 4.00 10.00 25.00

5768- **Popeye, Danger Ahoy!**, 1975, Whitman, 256 pgs.,

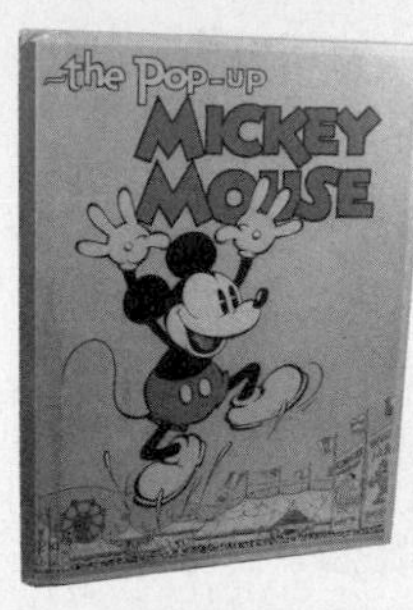

The Pop-Up Mickey Mouse © DIS

1440 - Punch Davis of the U.S. Aircraft Carrier © WHIT

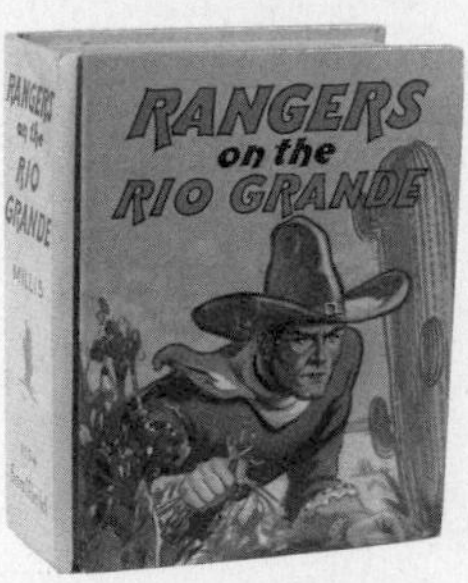

1154 - Rangers on the Rio Grande © Saalfield

GD FN VF/NM

soft-c, color illos. 2.00 5.00 11.00
4063- Popeye, Thimble Theatre Starring, 1935, Whitman, 7" x 9 1/2", 320 pgs., Big Big Book, Segar-c/a; (Cactus cover w/yellow logo) 173.00 433.00 1385.00
4063- Popeye, Thimble Theatre Starring, 1935, Whitman, 7" x 9 1/2", 320 pgs., Big Big Book, Segar-c/a; (Big Balloon-c with red logo), (2nd printing w/same contents as above) 202.00 506.00 1620.00
5761- Popeye and Queen Olive Oyl, 1973, 260 pgs., B&W, soft-c 4.00 10.00 27.00
5761-2- Popeye and Queen Olive Oyl, 1973 (1980-reprint of 1973 version), 260 pgs., 79 cents, B&W, soft-c 2.00 5.00 11.00
103- "Pop-Up" Buck Rogers in the Dangerous Mission (with Pop-Up picture), 1934, BRP, 62 pgs., The Midget Pop-Up Book w/Pop-Up in center of book, Calkins-a 173.00 433.00 1385.00
206- "Pop-Up" Buck Rogers - Strange Adventures in the Spider Ship, The, 1935, BRP, 24 pgs., 8" x 9", 3 Pop-Ups, hard-c, by Dick Calkins 173.00 433.00 1385.00
nn- "Pop-Up" Cinderella, 1933, BRP, 7 1/2" x 9 3/4", 4 Pop-Ups, hard-c
With dustjacket ($2.00) 118.00 295.00 825.00
Without dustjacket 90.00 225.00 630.00
207- "Pop-Up" Dick Tracy-Capture of Boris Arson, 1935, BRP, 24 pgs., 8" x 9", 3 Pop-Ups, hard-c, by Gould 116.00 290.00 810.00
210- "Pop-Up" Flash Gordon Tournament of Death, The, 1935, BRP, 24 pgs., 8" x 9", 3 Pop-Ups, hard-c, by Alex Raymond 173.00 433.00 1385.00
202- "Pop-Up" Goldilocks and the Three Bears, The, 1934, BRP, 24 pgs., 8" x 9", 3 Pop-Ups, hard-c 45.00 113.00 315.00
nn- "Pop-Up" Jack and the Beanstalk, 1933, BRP, hard-c (50 cents), 1 Pop-Up 45.00 113.00 315.00
nn- "Pop-Up" Jack the Giant Killer, 1933, BRP, hard-c (50 cents), 1 Pop-Up 45.00 113.00 315.00
nn- "Pop-Up" Jack the Giant Killer, 1933, BRP, 4 Pop-Ups, hard-c
With dustjacket ($2.00) 118.00 295.00 825.00
Without dust jacket 90.00 225.00 630.00
nn- "Pop-Up" Little Black Sambo, (with Pop-Up picture), 1934, BRP, 62 pgs., The Midget Pop-Up Book, one Pop-Up in center of book 73.00 182.00 515.00
208- "Pop-Up" Little Orphan Annie and Jumbo the Circus Elephant, 1935, BRP, 24 pgs., 8" x 9 1/2", 3 Pop-Ups, hard-c, by H. Gray 119.00 298.00 835.00
nn- "Pop-Up" Little Red Ridinghood, 1933, BRP, hard-c (50 cents), 1 Pop-Up 57.00 143.00 400.00
nn- "Pop-Up" Mickey Mouse, The, 1933, BRP, 34 pgs., 6 1/2" x 9", 3 Pop-Ups, hard-c, Gottfredson-a (75 cents) 110.00 275.00 775.00
nn- "Pop-Up" Mickey Mouse in King Arthur's Court, The,1933, BRP, 56 pgs., 7 1/2" x 9 1/4", 4 Pop-Ups, hard-c, Gottfredson-a
With dust jacket ($2.00) 302.00 756.00 2420.00
Without dustjacket 188.00 470.00 1500.00
101- "Pop-Up" Mickey Mouse in "Ye Olden Days" (with Pop-Up picture), 1934, 62 pgs., BRP, The Midget Pop-Up Book, one Pop-Up in center of book, Gottfredson-a 130.00 327.00 1045.00
nn- "Pop-Up" Minnie Mouse, The, 1933, BRP, 36 pgs., 6 1/2" x 9", 3 Pop-Ups, hard-c (75 cents), Gottfredson-a 110.00 275.00 775.00
203- "Pop-Up" Mother Goose, The, 1934, BRP, 24 pgs., 8" x 9 1/4", 3 Pop-Ups, hard-c 79.00 198.00 550.00
nn- "Pop-Up" Mother Goose Rhymes, The, 1933, BRP, 96 pgs., 7 1/2" x 9 1/4", 4 Pop-Ups, hard-c
With dustjacket ($2.00) 107.00 268.00 750.00
Without dustjacket 84.00 210.00 580.00
209- "Pop-Up" New Adventures of Tarzan, 1935, BRP, 24 pgs., 8" x 9", 3 Pop-Ups, hard-c 130.00 327.00 1045.00
104- "Pop-Up" Peter Rabbit, The (with Pop-Up picture), 1934, BRP, 62 pgs., The Midget Pop-Up Book, one Pop-Up in center of book 73.00 182.00 515.00
nn- "Pop-Up" Pinocchio, 1933, BRP, 7 1/2" x 9 3/4", 4 Pop-Ups, hard-c
With dustjacket ($2.00) 118.00 295.00 825.00
Without dust jacket 90.00 225.00 630.00
102- "Pop-Up" Popeye among the White Savages (with Pop-Up picture), 1934, BRP, 62 pgs., The Midget Pop-Up Book, one Pop-Up in center of book, E. C. Segar-a 116.00 290.00 810.00
205- "Pop-Up" Popeye with the Hag of the Seven Seas, The, 1935, BRP, 24 pgs., 8" x 9", 3 Pop-Ups, hard-c, Segar-a 124.00 310.00 955.00
201- "Pop-Up" Puss In Boots, The, 1934, BRP, 24 pgs., 3 Pop-Ups, hard-c 46.00 115.00 320.00
nn- "Pop-Up" Silly Symphonies, The (Mickey Mouse Presents His ...), 1933, BRP, 56 pgs., 9 3/4" x 7 1/2", 4 Pop-Ups, hard-c
With dust jacket ($2.00) 172.00 430.00 1375.00
Without dust jacket 121.00 304.00 865.00
nn- "Pop-Up" Sleeping Beauty, 1933, BRP, hard-c, (50 cents), 1 Pop-up 53.00 132.00 370.00
212- "Pop-Up" Terry and the Pirates in Shipwrecked, The, 1935, BRP, 24 pgs., 8" x 9", 3 Pop-Ups, hard-c 110.00 275.00 775.00
211- "Pop-Up" Tim Tyler in the Jungle, The, 1935, BRP, 24 pgs., 8" x 9", 3 Pop-Ups, hard-c 84.00 210.00 580.00
1404- Porky Pig and His Gang, 1946, Whitman, All Pictures Comics, Barks-a, reprints Four Color #48 24.00 60.00 165.00
1408- Porky Pig and Petunia, 1942, Whitman, All Pictures Comics, flip pictures, reprints Four Color #16 & Famous Gang Book of Comics 16.00 40.00 115.00
1176- Powder Smoke Range, 1935, Whitman, 240 pgs., photo-c, movie scenes, Hoot Gibson, Harey Carey app. (RKO Radio Pict.) 14.00 35.00 95.00
1058- Practical Pig!, The (Disney), 1939, Whitman, 68 pgs., 5" x 5 1/2", hard-c 12.00 30.00 85.00
758- Prairie Bill and the Covered Wagon, 1934, Whitman, 384 pgs., Hal Arbo-a 12.00 30.00 85.00
nn- Prairie Bill and the Covered Wagon, 1934, Whitman, 390 pgs., premium-no ads, 3-color, soft-c, Hal Arbo-a 18.00 45.00 125.00
1440- Punch Davis of the U.S. Aircraft Carrier, 1945, Whitman, 352 pgs. 10.00 25.00 65.00
nn- Puss in Boots, nd(1930s), np(Whitman), 36 pgs., Penny Book 4.00 10.00 22.00
1100B- Puzzle Book, 1938, Whitman, 36 pgs., 2 1/2" x 3 1/2", Penny Book 4.00 10.00 27.00
1100B- Puzzles, 1938, Whitman, 36 pgs., 2 1/2" x 3 1/2", Penny Book 4.00 10.00 27.00
1100B- Quiz Book, The, 1938, Whitman, 36 pgs., 2 1/2" x 3 1/2", Penny Book 4.00 10.00 27.00
1142- Radio Patrol, 1935, Whitman, 432 pgs., by Eddie Sullivan & Charlie Schmidt (#1) 12.00 30.00 85.00
1173- Radio Patrol Trailing the Safeblowers, 1937, Whitman, 432 pgs. 11.00 27.50 70.00
1496- Radio Patrol Outwitting the Gang Chief, 1939, Whitman, 432 pgs. 11.00 27.50 70.00
1498- Radio Patrol and Big Dan's Mobsters, 1937, Whitman, 432 pgs. 11.00 27.50 70.00
nn- Raiders of the Lost Ark, 1998, Chronicle Books, 304 pgs., adapts movie, 1-color (green) illos 4.00 10.00 22.00
1441- Range Busters, The, 1942, Whitman, 432 pgs., Henry E. Vallely-a 11.00 27.50 70.00
1163- Ranger and the Cowboy, The, 1939, Saalfield, 400 pgs. 11.00 27.50 70.00
1154- Rangers on the Rio Grande, 1938, Saalfield, 400 pgs. 11.00 27.50 70.00
1447- Ray Land of the Tank Corps, U.S.A., 1942, Whitman, 432 pgs., flip pictures, Hess-a 11.00 27.50 70.00
1157- Red Barry Ace-Detective, 1935, Whitman, 432 pgs., by Will Gould 15.00 37.50 105.00
1426- Red Barry Undercover Man, 1939, Whitman, 432 pgs., by Will Gould 13.00 32.50 90.00
20- Red Davis, 1935, EVW, 160 pgs. 12.00 30.00 85.00
1449- Red Death on the Range, The, 1940, Whitman, 432 pgs., Fred Harman-a (Bronc Peeler) 12.00 30.00 85.00
nn- Red Falcon Adventures, The, 1937, Seal Right Ice Cream, 8 pgs., set of 50 books, circular in shape
Issue #1 87.00 218.00 605.00
Issue #2-5 60.00 150.00 420.00
Issue #6-10 49.00 122.00 345.00

702-10 - Red Ryder Acting Sheriff © WHIT

1448 - Roy Rogers and the Mystery of the Howling Mesa © Roy Roges

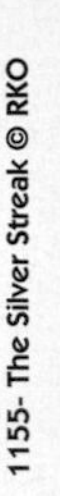
1155- The Silver Streak © RKO

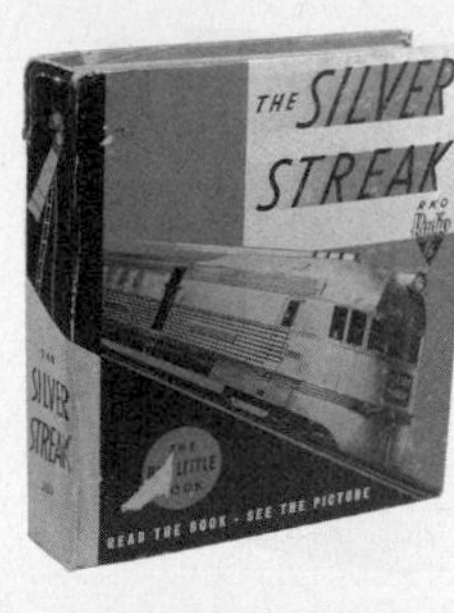

GD FN VF/NM

Issue #11-50 31.00 78.00 220.00

nn- Red Hen and the Fox, The, nd(1930s), np(Whitman), 36 pgs., 3" x 2 1/2", Penny Book 4.00 10.00 22.00

1145- Red-Hot Holsters, 1938, Saalfield, 400 pgs. 11.00 27.50 70.00

1400- Red Ryder and Little Beaver on Hoofs of Thunder, 1939, Whitman, 432 pgs., Harman-c/a 20.00 50.00 140.00

1414- Red Ryder and the Squaw-Tooth Rustlers, 1946, Whitman, 352 pgs., Fred Harman-a 15.00 37.50 105.00

1427- Red Ryder and the Code of the West, 1941, Whitman, 432 pgs., flip pictures, by Harman 19.00 47.50 135.00

1440- Red Ryder the Fighting Westerner, 1940, Whitman, Harman-a 19.00 47.50 135.00

1443- Red Ryder and the Rimrock Killer, 1948, Whitman, 288 pgs., Harman-a 14.00 35.00 95.00

1450- Red Ryder and Western Border Guns, 1942, Whitman, 432 pgs., flip pictures, by Harman 19.00 47.50 135.00

1454- Red Ryder and the Secret Canyon, 1948, Whitman, 288 pgs., Harman-a 14.00 35.00 95.00

1466- Red Ryder and Circus Luck, 1947, Whitman, 288 pgs., by Fred Harman 14.00 35.00 95.00

1473- Red Ryder in War on the Range, 1945, Whitman, 352 pgs., by Fred Harman 15.00 37.50 105.00

1475- Red Ryder and the Outlaw of Painted Valley, 1943, Whitman, 352 pgs., by Harman 14.00 35.00 95.00

702-10- Red Ryder Acting Sheriff, 1949, Whitman, by Fred Hannan 12.00 30.00 85.00

nn- Red Ryder Brings Law to Devil's Hole, 1939, Dell, 196 pgs., Fast-Action Story, Harman-c/a 44.00 110.00 310.00

nn- Red Ryder and the Highway Robbers, 1938, Whitman, 36 pgs., 2 1/2" x 3 1/2", Penny Book 12.00 30.00 85.00

754- Reg'lar Fellers, 1933, Whitman, 320 pgs., by Gene Byrnes 13.00 32.50 90.00

nn- Reg'lar Fellers, 1933, Whitman, 202 pgs., Cocomalt premium, by Gene Byrnes 13.00 32.50 90.00

1424- Rex Beach's Jaragu of the Jungle, 1937, Whitman, 432 pgs. 11.00 27.50 70.00

12- Rex, King of Wild Horses in "Stampede," 1935, EVW, 160 pgs., movie scenes, Columbia Pictures 12.00 30.00 75.00

1100B- Riddles for Fun, 1938, Whitman, 36 pgs., 2 1/2" x 3 1/2", Penny Book 4.00 10.00 27.00

1100B- Riddles to Guess, 1938, Whitman, 36 pgs., 2 1/2" x 3 1/2", Penny Book 4.00 10.00 27.00

1425- Riders of Lone Trails, 1937, Whitman, 300 pgs. 12.00 30.00 75.00

1141- Rio Raiders (A Billy The Kid Story), 1938, Saalfield, 400 pgs. 12.00 30.00 75.00

2023-(#23)- The Road Runner, The Super Beep Catcher, 1968, Whitman, 256 pgs., hard-c, color illos. 1.00 2.50 9.00

5759- The Road Runner, The Super Beep Catcher, 1973, Whitman, 256 pgs., soft-c, 39 cents, B&W illos., and flip pictures 1.00 2.50 6.00

5767-2- Road Runner, The Lost Road Runner Mine, The, 1974 (1980), 260 pgs., 79 cents, B&W, soft-c 1.00 2.50 6.00

5784- The Road Runner and the Unidentified Coyote, 1974, Whitman, 260 pgs., soft-c, flip pictures 1.00 2.50 6.00

5784-2- The Road Runner and the Unidentified Coyote, 1980, Whitman, 260 pgs., soft-c, flip pictures 1.00 2.50 6.00

nn- Road To Perdition, 2002, Dreamworks, screenplay from movie, hard-c (Dreamworks and 20th Century Fox) 1.00 2.50 9.00

Robin Hood (See Wee Little Books)

10- Robin Hood, 1935, EVW, 160 pgs., movie scenes w/Douglas Fairbanks (United Artists), hard-c 18.00 45.00 125.00

719- Robinson Crusoe (The Story of...), nd (1933), Whitman, 364 pgs., soft-c 13.00 32.50 90.00

1421- Roy Rogers and the Dwarf-Cattle Ranch, 1947, Whitman, 352 pgs., Henry E. Vallely-a 18.00 45.00 125.00

1437- Roy Rogers and the Deadly Treasure, 1947, Whitman, 288 pgs. 18.00 45.00 125.00

1448- Roy Rogers and the Mystery of the Howling Mesa, 1948, Whitman, 288 pgs. 18.00 45.00 125.00

GD FN VF/NM

1452- Roy Rogers in Robbers' Roost, 1948, Whitman, 288 pgs. 18.00 45.00 125.00

1460- Roy Rogers Robinhood of the Range, 1942, Whitman, 432 pgs., Hess-a (1st) 21.00 52.50 145.00

1462- Roy Rogers and the Mystery of the Lazy M, 1949, Whitman 15.00 37.50 105.00

1476- Roy Rogers King of the Cowboys, 1943, Whitman, 352 pgs., Irwin Myers-a, based on movie 22.00 52.50 155.00

1494- Roy Rogers at Crossed Feathers Ranch, 1945, Whitman, 320 pgs., Erwin Hess-a , 3 1/4" x 5 1/2" 18.00 45.00 125.00

701-10- Roy Rogers and the Snowbound Outlaws, 1949, 3 1/4" x 5 1/2" 12.00 30.00 85.00

715-10- Roy Rogers Range Detective, 1950, Whitman, 2 1/2" x 5" 12.00 30.00 85.00

nn- Sandy Gregg Federal Agent on Special Assignment, 1939, Whitman, 36 pgs., 2 1/2" x 3 1/2", Penny Book 11.00 27.50 70.00

Sappo (See Top-Line Comics)

1122- Scrappy, 1934, Whitman, 288 pgs. 20.00 50.00 140.00

L12- Scrappy (The Adventures of...), 1935, Lynn, 192 pgs., movie scenes 20.00 50.00 140.00

1191- Secret Agent K-7,1940, Saalfield, 400 pgs., based on radio show 11.00 27.50 70.00

1144- Secret Agent X-9, 1936, Whitman, 432 pgs., Charles Flanders-a 15.00 37.50 105.00

1472- Secret Agent X-9 and the Mad Assassin, 1938, Whitman, 432 pgs., Charles Flanders-a 15.00 37.50 105.00

1161- Sequoia, 1935, Whitman, 160 pgs., photo-c, movie scenes 12.00 30.00 85.00

1430- Shadow and the Living Death, The, 1940, Whitman, 432 pgs., Erwin Hess-a 65.00 163.00 460.00

1443- Shadow and the Master of Evil, The, 1941, Whitman, 432 pgs., flip pictures, Hess-a 65.00 163.00 460.00

1495- Shadow and the Ghost Makers, The, 1942, Whitman, 432 pgs., John Coleman Burroughs-c 65.00 163.00 460.00

2024- Shazzan, The Glass Princess, 1968, Whitman 4.00 10.00 27.00

Shirley Temple (See My Life and Times & Story of..)

1095- Shirley Temple and Lionel Barrymore Starring In "The Little Colonel," 1935, Saalfield, photo hard-c, movie scenes 20.00 50.00 140.00

1115- Shirley Temple in "The Littlest Rebel," 1935, Saalfield, photo-c, movie scenes, hard-c 20.00 50.00 140.00

1575- Shirley Temple and Lionel Barrymore Starring In "The Little Colonel," 1935, Saalfield, photo soft-c, movie scenes 20.00 50.00 140.00

1595- Shirley Temple in "The Littlest Rebel," 1935, Saalfield, photo-c, movie scenes, soft-c 20.00 50.00 140.00

1195- Shooting Sheriffs of the Wild West, 1936, Whitman, 432 pgs. 11.00 27.50 70.00

1169- Silly Symphony Featuring Donald Duck (Disney), 1937, Whitman, 432 pgs., Taliaferro-a 38.00 95.00 255.00

1441- Silly Symphony Featuring Donald Duck and His (MIS) Adventures (Disney), 1937, Whitman, 432 pgs., Taliaferro-a 38.00 95.00 255.00

1155- Silver Streak, The, 1935, Whitman, 160 pgs., photo-c, movie scenes (RKO Radio Pict.) 12.00 30.00 75.00

Simple Simon (See Wee Little Books)

1649- Sir Lancelot (TV Series), 1958, Whitman, 280 pgs. 7.00 17.50 44.00

1112- Skeezix in Africa, 1934, Whitman, 300 pgs., Frank King-a 14.00 35.00 95.00

1408- Skeezix at the Military Academy, 1938, Whitman, 432 pgs., Frank King-a 14.00 35.00 95.00

1414- Skeezix Goes to War, 1944, Whitman, 352 pgs., Frank King-a 14.00 35.00 95.00

1419- Skeezix on His Own in the Big City, 1941, Whitman, All Pictures Comics, flip pictures, Frank King-a 14.00 35.00 95.00

761- Skippy, 1934, Whitman, 320 pgs., by Percy Crosby 14.00 35.00 95.00

4056- Skippy, The Story of, 1934, Whitman, 320 pgs., 7" x 9 1/2", Big Big Book, Percy Crosby-a 70.00 175.00 490.00

1477 - Smitty in Going Native © WHIT

1104 - The Steel Arena © Saalfield

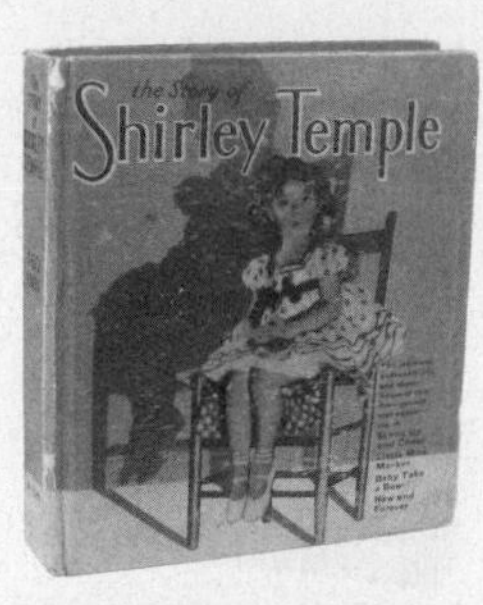

1089 - The Story of Shirley Temple © Saalfield

		GD	FN	VF/NM
nn-	**Skippy, The Story of**, 1934, Whitman, Phillips Dental Magnesia premium, soft-c, by Percy Crosby	14.00	35.00	95.00
1439-	**Skyroads with Clipper Williams of the Flying Legion**, 1938, Whitman, 432 pgs., by Lt. Dick Calkins, Russell Keaton-a	12.00	30.00	85.00
1127-	**Skyroads with Hurricane Hawk**, 1936, Whitman, 432 pgs., by Lt. Dick Calkins, Russell Keaton-a	12.00	30.00	80.00
	Smilin' Jack and his Flivver Plane (See Top-Line Comics)			
1152-	**Smilin' Jack and the Stratosphere Ascent**, 1937, Whitman, 432 pgs., Zack Mosley-a	16.00	40.00	115.00
1412-	**Smilin' Jack Flying High with "Downwind,"** 1942, Whitman, 432 pgs., Zack Mosley-a	15.00	37.50	105.00
1416-	**Smilin' Jack in Wings over the Pacific**, 1939, Whitman, 432 pgs., Zack Mosley-a	15.00	37.50	105.00
1419-	**Smilin' Jack and the Jungle Pipe Line**, 1947, Whitman, 352 pgs., Zack Mosley-a	12.00	30.00	85.00
1445-	**Smilin' Jack and the Escape from Death Rock**, 1943, Whitman, 352 pgs., Mosley-a	12.00	30.00	85.00
1464-	**Smilin' Jack and the Coral Princess**, 1945, Whitman, 352 pgs., Zack Mosley-a	12.00	30.00	85.00
1473-	**Smilin' Jack Speed Pilot**, 1941, Whitman, 432 pgs., Zack Mosley-a	16.00	40.00	115.00
2-	**Smilin' Jack and his Stratosphere Plane**, 1938, Whitman, 132 pgs., Buddy Book, soft-c, Zack Mosley-a	39.00	98.00	275.00
nn-	**Smilin' Jack Grounded on a Tropical Shore**, 1938, Whitman, 36 pgs., 2 1/2" x 3 1/2", Penny Book	11.00	27.50	70.00
11-	**Smilin' Jack and the Border Bandits**, 1941, Dell, 196 pgs., Fast-Action Story, soft-c, Zack Mosley-a	36.00	90.00	255.00
745-	**Smitty Golden Gloves Tournament**, 1934, Whitman, 320 pgs., Walter Berndt-a	15.00	37.50	105.00
nn-	**Smitty Golden Gloves Tournament**, 1934, Whitman, 204 pgs., Cocomalt premium, soft-c, Walter Berndt-a	16.00	40.00	115.00
1404-	**Smitty and Herby Lost Among the Indians**, 1941, Whitman, All Pictures Comics	11.00	27.50	70.00
1477-	**Smitty in Going Native**, 1938, Whitman, 300 pgs., Walter Berndt-a	11.00	27.50	70.00
2-	**Smitty and Herby**, 1936, Whitman, 132 pgs., 3 1/2" x 3 1/2", soft-c, Tarzan Ice Cream cup lid premium	36.00	90.00	255.00
9-	**Smitty's Brother Herby and the Police Horse**, 1938, Whitman, 132 pgs., 3 1/4" x 3 1/2", Buddy Book-ice cream premium, by Walter Berndt	36.00	90.00	255.00
1010-	**Smokey Stover Firefighter of Foo**, 1937, Whitman, 7 1/4" x 5 1/2", 64 pgs., Nickel Book, Bill Holman-a	16.00	40.00	115.00
1413-	**Smokey Stover**, 1942, Whitman, All Pictures Comics, flip pictures, Bill Holman-a	14.00	35.00	95.00
1421-	**Smokey Stover the Foo Fighter**, 1938, Whitman, 432 pgs., Bill Holman-a	14.00	35.00	95.00
1481-	**Smokey Stover the Foolish Foo Fighter**, 1942, Whitman, All Pictures Comics	14.00	35.00	95.00
1-	**Smokey Stover the Fireman of Foo**, 1938, Whitman, 3 3/4" x 3 1/2", 132 pgs., Buddy Book-ice cream premium, by Bill Holman	41.00	103.00	285.00
1100A-	**Smokey Stover**, 1938, Whitman, 36 pgs., 2 1/2" x 3 1/2", Penny Book	12.00	30.00	80.00
nn-	**Smokey Stover and the Fire Chief of Foo**, 1938, Whitman, 36 pgs., 2 1/2" x 3 1/2", Penny Book, yellow shirt on-c	12.00	30.00	80.00
nn-	**Smokey Stover and the Fire Chief of Foo**, 1938, Whitman, 36 pgs., Penny Book, green shirt on-c	12.00	30.00	80.00
1460-	**Snow White and the Seven Dwarfs** (The Story of Walt Disney's ...), 1938, Whitman, 288 pgs.	29.00	73.00	200.00
1136-	**Sombrero Pete**, 1936, Whitman, 432 pgs.	11.00	27.50	70.00
1152-	**Son of Mystery**, 1939, Saalfield, 400 pgs.	11.00	27.50	70.00
1191-	**SOS Coast Guard**, 1936, Whitman, 432 pgs., Henry E. Vallely-a	12.00	30.00	75.00
2016-(#16)-	**Space Ghost-The Sorceress of Cyba-3** (TV Cartoon), 1968, Whitman, 260 pgs., 39¢-c, hard-c, color illos	10.00	25.00	60.00
1455-	**Speed Douglas and the Mole Gang-The Great Sabotage Plot**, 1941, Whitman, 432 pgs., flip pictures	11.00	27.50	70.00
5779-	**Spider-Man Zaps Mr. Zodiac**, 1976, 260 pgs., soft-c, B&W	1.00	2.50	9.00
5779-2-	**Spider-Man Zaps Mr. Zodiac**, 1980, 260 pgs., 79¢-c, soft-c, B&W	1.00	2.50	6.00
1467-	**Spike Kelly of the Commandos**, 1943, Whitman, 352 pgs.	11.00	27.50	70.00
1144-	**Spook Riders on the Overland**, 1938, Saalfield, 400 pgs.	11.00	27.50	70.00
768-	**Spy, The**, 1936, Whitman, 300 pgs.	13.00	32.50	90.00
nn-	**Spy Smasher and the Red Death**, 1941, Fawcett, 4" x 5 1/2", Dime Action Book	58.00	146.00	410.00
1120-	**Stan Kent Freshman Fullback**, 1936, Saalfield, 148 pgs., hard-c	9.00	22.50	55.00
1132-	**Stan Kent, Captain**, 1937, Saalfield	9.00	22.50	55.00
1600-	**Stan Kent Freshman Fullback**, 1936, Saalfield, 148 pgs., soft-c	9.00	22.50	55.00
1123-	**Stan Kent Varsity Man**, 1936, Saalfield, 160 pgs., hard-c	9.00	22.50	55.00
1603-	**Stan Kent Varsity Man**, 1936, Saalfield, 160 pgs., soft-c	9.00	22.50	55.00
nn-	**Star Wars - A New Hope**, 1997, Chronicle Books, 320 pgs., adapts movie, 1-color (blue) illos	3.00	7.50	20.00
nn-	**Star Wars - Empire Strikes Back, The**, 1997, Chronicle Books, 296 pgs., adapts movie, 1-color (blue) illos	3.00	7.50	20.00
nn-	**Star Wars - Episode 1 - The Phantom Menace**, 1999, Chronicle Books, 344 pgs., adapts movie, 1-color (blue) illos	1.00	2.50	9.00
nn-	**Star Wars - Episode 2 - Attack of the Clones**, 2002, Chronicle Books, 340 pgs., adapts movie, 1-color (blue) illos	1.00	2.50	9.00
nn-	**Star Wars - Return of the Jedi**, 1997, Chronicle Books, 312 pgs., adapts movie, 1-color (blue) illos	3.00	7.50	20.00
1104-	**Steel Arena, The** (With Clyde Beatty), 1936, Saalfield, hard-c, movie scenes adapted from "The Lost Jungle"	12.00	30.00	85.00
1584-	**Steel Arena, The** (With Clyde Beatty), 1936, Saalfield, soft-c, movie scenes	12.00	30.00	85.00
1426-	**Steve Hunter of the U.S. Coast Guard Under Secret Orders**, 1942, Whitman, 432 pgs.	11.00	27.50	70.00
1456-	**Story of Charlie McCarthy and Edgar Bergen, The**, 1938, Whitman, 288 pgs.	15.00	37.50	105.00
	Story of Daniel, The (See Wee Little Books)			
	Story of David, The (See Wee Little Books)			
1110-	**Story of Freddie Bartholomew, The**, 1935, Saalfield, 4 1/2" x 5 1/4", hard-c, movie scenes (MGM)	12.00	30.00	75.00
1590-	**Story of Freddie Bartholomew, The**, 1935, Saalfield, 4 1/2" x 5 1/4", soft-c, movie scenes (MGM)	12.00	30.00	75.00
	Story of Gideon, The (See Wee Little Books)			
W714-	**Story of Jackie Cooper, The**, 1933, Whitman, 240 pgs., photo-c, movie scenes, "Skippy" & "Sooky" movie	15.00	37.50	105.00
	Story of Joseph, The (See Wee Little Books)			
	Story of Moses, The (See Wee Little Books)			
	Story of Ruth and Naomi (See Wee Little Books)			
1089-	**Story of Shirley Temple, The**, 1934, Saalfield, 160 pgs., hard-c, photo-c, movie scenes	13.00	32.50	90.00
1319-	**Story of Shirley Temple, The**, 1934, Saalfield, 160 pgs., soft-c, photo-c, movie scenes	13.00	32.50	90.00
1090-	**Strawberry-Roan**, 1934, Saalfield, 160 pgs., hard-c, Ken Maynard photo-c, movie scenes	13.00	32.50	90.00
1320-	**Strawberry-Roan**, 1934, Saalfield, 160 pgs., soft-c, Ken Maynard photo-c, movie scenes	13.00	32.50	90.00
	Streaky and the Football Signals (See Top-Line Comics)			
5780-2-	**Superman in the Phantom Zone Connection**, 1980, 260 pgs., 79¢-c, soft-c, B&W	1.00	2.50	9.00
582-	**"Swap It" Book, The**, 1949, Samuel Lowe Co., 260 pgs., 3 1/2" x 4 1/2"			
	1. Little Tex in the Midst of Trouble	7.00	17.50	44.00
	2. Little Tex's Escape	7.00	17.50	44.00
	3. Little Tex Comes to the XY Ranch	7.00	17.50	44.00
	4. Get Them Cowboy	7.00	17.50	44.00
	5. The Mail Must Go Through! A Story of the Pony Express	7.00	17.50	44.00
	6. Nevada Jones, Trouble Shooter	7.00	17.50	44.00
	7. Danny Meets the Cowboys	7.00	17.50	44.00

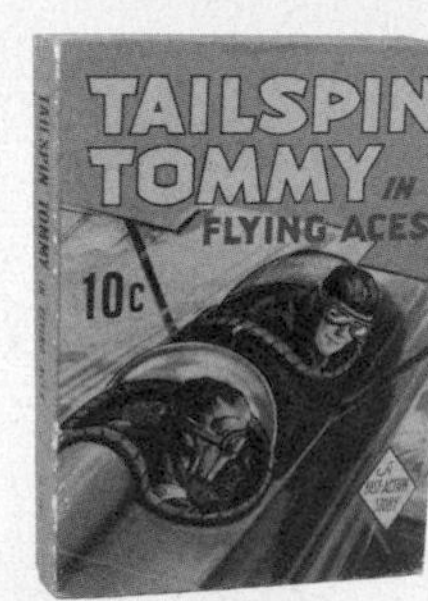

Tailspin Tommy in Flying Aces © DELL

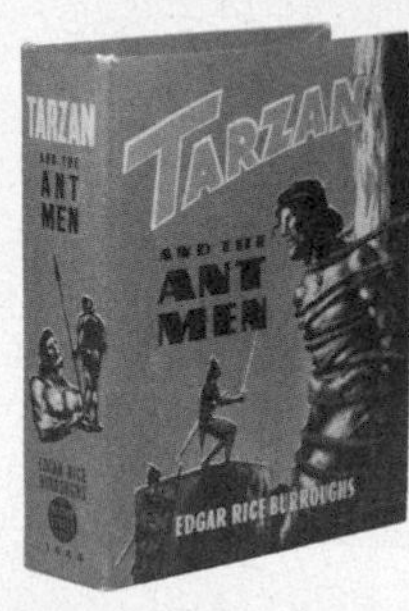

1444 - Tarzan and the Ant Men © ERB

1436 - Terry and the Pirates The Plantation Mystery © WHIT

GD FN VF/NM

8. Flint Adams and the Stage Coach 7.00 17.50 44.00

9. Bud Shinners and the Oregon Trail 7.00 17.50 44.00

10. The Outlaws' Last Ride 7.00 17.50 44.00

Sybil Jason (See Little Big Shot)

747- Tailspin Tommy in the Famous Pay-Roll Mystery, 1933, Whitman, hard-c, 320 pgs., Hal Forrest-a (# 1) 15.00 37.50 105.00

747- Tailspin Tommy in the Famous Pay-Roll Mystery, 1933, Whitman, soft-c, 320 pgs., Hal Forrest-a (# 1) 15.00 37.50 105.00

nn- Tailspin Tommy the Pay-Roll Mystery, 1934, Whitman, 52 pgs., 3 1/2" x 5 1/4", premium-no ads, soft-c; another version with Perkins ad, Hal Forrest-a 26.00 65.00 185.00

1110- Tailspin Tommy and the Island in the Sky, 1936, Whitman, 432 pgs., Hal Forrest-a 13.00 32.50 90.00

1124- Tailspin Tommy the Dirigible Flight to the North Pole, 1934, Whitman, 432 pgs., H. Forrest-a 15.00 37.50 105.00

nn- Tailspin Tommy the Dirigible Flight to the North Pole, 1934, Whitman, 436 pgs., 3-color, soft-c, premium-no ads, Hal Forrest-a 36.00 90.00 255.00

1172- Tailspin Tommy Hunting for Pirate Gold, 1935, Whitman, 432 pgs., Hal Forrest-a 13.00 32.50 90.00

1183- Tailspin Tommy Air Racer, 1940, Saalfield, 400 pgs., hard-c 13.00 32.50 90.00

1184- Tailspin Tommy in the Great Air Mystery, 1936, Whitman, 240 pgs., photo-c, movie scenes 15.00 37.50 105.00

1410- Tailspin Tommy the Weasel and His "Skywaymen," 1941, Whitman, All Pictures Comics, flip pictures 12.00 30.00 80.00

1413- Tailspin Tommy and the Lost Transport, 1940, Whitman, 432 pgs., Hal Forrest-a 12.00 30.00 80.00

1423- Tailspin Tommy and the Hooded Flyer, 1937, Whitman, 432 pgs., Hal Forrest-a 13.00 32.50 90.00

1494- Tailspin Tommy and the Sky Bandits, 1938, Whitman 432 pgs., Hal Forrest-a 13.00 32.50 90.00

nn- Tailspin Tommy and the Airliner Mystery, 1938, Dell, 196 pgs., Fast-Action Story, soft-c, Hal Forrest-a 47.00 118.00 330.00

nn- Tailspin Tommy in Flying Aces, 1938, Dell, 196 pgs., Fast-Action Story, soft-c, Hal Forrest-a 47.00 118.00 330.00

nn- Tailspin Tommy in Wings Over the Arctic, 1934, Whitman, Cocomalt premium, Forrest-a 20.00 50.00 140.00

nn- Tailspin Tommy Big Thrill Chewing Gum, 1934, Whitman, 8 pgs., 2 1/2" x 3 " (6 diff.) each.. 13.00 32.50 90.00

3- Tailspin Tommy on the Mountain of Human Sacrifice, 1938, Whitman, soft-c, Buddy Book 43.00 108.00 300.00

7- Tailspin Tommy's Perilous Adventure, 1934, Whitman, 132 pgs., 3 1/2" x 3 1/2" soft-c, Tarzan Ice Cream cup premium 43.00 108.00 300.00

nn- Tailspin Tommy, 1935, Whitman, 148 pgs., 3 1/2" x 4", Tarzan Ice Cream cup premium 54.00 135.00 385.00

L16- Tale of Two Cities, A, 1935, Lynn, movie scenes 15.00 37.50 105.00

744- Tarzan of the Apes, 1933, Whitman, 320 pgs., by Edgar Rice Burroughs (1st) 46.00 115.00 325.00

nn- Tarzan of the Apes, 1935, Whitman, 52 pgs., 3 1/2" x 5 1/4", soft-c, stapled, premium, no ad; another version with a Perkins ad 58.00 146.00 410.00

769- Tarzan the Fearless, 1934, Whitman, 240 pgs., Buster Crabbe photo-c, movie scenes, ERB 33.00 83.00 230.00

770- Tarzan Twins, The, 1934, Whitman, 432 pgs., ERB 118.00 295.00 825.00

770- Tarzan Twins, The, 1935, Whitman, 432 pgs., ERB 58.00 146.00 410.00

nn- Tarzan Twins, The, 1935, Whitman, 52 pgs., 3 1/2" x 5 3/4", premium-no ads, soft-c, ERB 79.00 198.00 550.00

nn- Tarzan Twins, The, 1935, Whitman, 436 pgs., 3-color, soft-c, premium-no ads, ERB 84.00 210.00 580.00

778- Tarzan of the Screen (The Story of Johnny Weissmuller), 1934, Whitman, 240 pgs., photo-c, movie scenes, ERB 34.00 85.00 240.00

1102- Tarzan, The Return of, 1936, Whitman, 432 pgs., Edgar Rice Burroughs 24.00 60.00 170.00

GD FN VF/NM

1180- Tarzan, The New Adventures of, 1935, Whitman, 160 pgs., Herman Brix photo-c, movie scenes, ERB 28.00 70.00 195.00

1182- Tarzan Escapes, 1936, Whitman, 240 pgs., Johnny Weissmuller photo-c, movie scenes, ERB 34.00 85.00 240.00

1407- Tarzan Lord of the Jungle, 1946, Whitman, 352 pgs., ERB 18.00 45.00 125.00

1410- Tarzan, The Beasts of, 1937, Whitman, 432 pgs., Edgar Rice Burroughs 21.00 52.50 145.00

1442- Tarzan and the Lost Empire, 1948, Whitman, 288 pgs., ERB 18.00 45.00 125.00

1444- Tarzan and the Ant Men, 1945, Whitman, 352 pgs., ERB 18.00 45.00 125.00

1448- Tarzan and the Golden Lion, 1943, Whitman, 432 pgs., ERB 22.00 52.50 155.00

1452- Tarzan the Untamed, 1941, Whitman, 432 pgs., flip pictures, ERB 22.00 52.50 155.00

1453- Tarzan the Terrible, 1942, Whitman, 432 pgs., flip pictures, ERB 22.00 52.50 155.00

1467- Tarzan in the Land of the Giant Apes, 1949, Whitman, ERB 18.00 45.00 125.00

1477- Tarzan, The Son of, 1939, Whitman, 432 pgs., ERB 22.00 52.50 155.00

1488- Tarzan's Revenge, 1938, Whitman, 432 pgs., ERB 22.00 52.50 155.00

1495- Tarzan and the Jewels of Opar, 1940, Whitman, 432 pgs. 22.00 52.50 155.00

4056- Tarzan and the Tarzan Twins with Jad-Bal-Ja the Golden Lion, 1936, Whitman, 7" x 9 1/2", 320 pgs., Big Big Book 115.00 288.00 810.00

709-10- Tarzan and the Journey of Terror, 1950, Whitman, 2 1/2" x 5", ERB, Marsh-a 12.00 30.00 75.00

2005- (#5)-Tarzan: The Mark of the Red Hyena, 1967, Whitman, 260 pgs., 39 cents, hard-c, color illos 4.00 10.00 27.00

nn- Tarzan, 1935, Whitman, 148 pgs., soft-c, 3 1/2" x 4", Tarzan Ice Cream cup premium, ERB (scarce) 130.00 327.00 1045.00

nn- Tarzan and a Daring Rescue, 1938, Whitman, 68 pgs., Pan-Am premium, soft-c, ERB (blank back-c version also exists) 47.00 118.00 330.00

nn- Tarzan and his Jungle Friends, 1936, Whitman, 132 pgs., soft-c, 3 1/2" x 3 1/2", Tarzan Ice Cream cup premium, ERB (scarce) 112.00 280.00 785.00

nn- Tarzan in the Golden City, 1938, Whitman, 68 pgs., Pan-Am premium, soft-c, ERB 33.00 83.00 230.00

nn- Tarzan The Avenger, 1939, Dell, 194 pgs., Fast-Action Story, ERB, soft-c 47.00 118.00 330.00

nn- Tarzan with the Tarzan Twins in the Jungle, 1938, Dell, 194 pgs., Fast-Action Story, ERB 47.00 118.00 330.00

1100B- Tell Your Fortune, 1938, Whitman, 36 pgs., 2 1/2" x 3 1/2", Penny Book 5.00 12.50 33.00

nn- Terminator 2: Judgment Day, 1998, Chronicle Books, 310 pgs., adapts movie, 1-color (blue-gray) illos 1.00 2.50 9.00

1156- Terry and the Pirates, 1935, Whitman, 432 pgs., Milton Caniff-a (#1) 18.00 45.00 125.00

nn- Terry and the Pirates, 1935, Whitman, 52 pgs., 3 1/2" x 5 1/4", soft-c, premium, Milton Caniff-a; 3 versions: No ad, Sears ad & Perkins ad 31.00 78.00 220.00

1412- Terry and the Pirates Shipwrecked on a Desert Island, 1938, Whitman, 432 pgs., Milton Caniff-a 15.00 37.50 105.00

1420- Terry and War in the Jungle, 1946, Whitman, 352 pgs., Milton Caniff-a 13.00 32.50 90.00

1436- Terry and the Pirates The Plantation Mystery, 1942, Whitman, 432 pgs., flip pictures, Milton Caniff-a 15.00 37.50 105.00

1446- Terry and the Pirates and the Giant's Vengeance, 1939, Whitman, 432 pgs., Caniff-a 15.00 37.50 105.00

1499- Terry and the Pirates in the Mountain Stronghold, 1941, Whitman, 432 pgs., Caniff-a 15.00 37.50 105.00

4073- Terry and the Pirates, The Adventures of, 1938, Whitman, 7" x 9 1/2" 320 pgs., Big Big Book, Milton Caniff-a 87.00 218.00 605.0

4- Terry and the Pirates Ashore in Singapore, 1938, Whitman, 132 pg

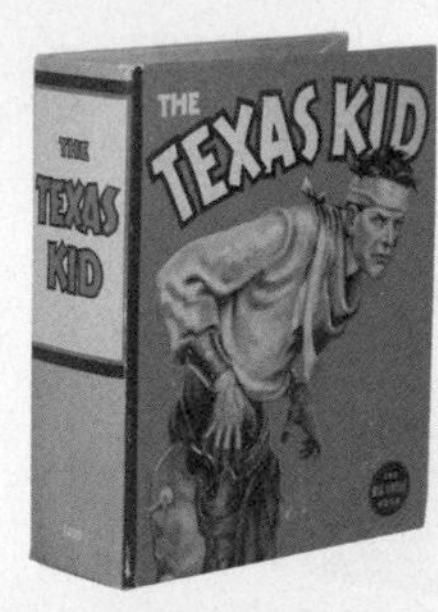

1429 - The Texas Kid © WHIT

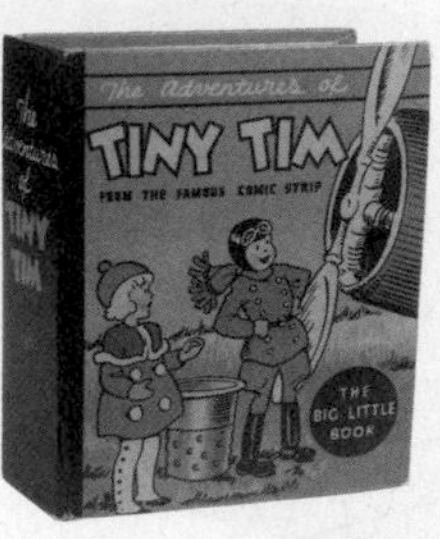

767 - Tiny Tim, The Adventures of... © WHIT

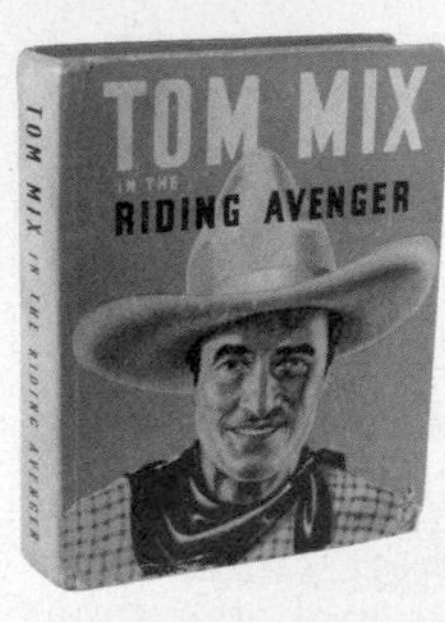

6833 - Tom Mix in the Riding Avenger © WHIT

GD FN VF/NM

3 1/2" x 3 3/4", soft-c, Buddy Book premium 38.00 95.00 255.00
10- Terry and the Pirates Meet Again, 1936, Whitman, 132 pgs., 3 1/2" x 3 1/2", soft-c, Tarzan Ice Cream cup lid premium 58.00 146.00 410.00
nn- Terry and the Pirates, Adventures of, 1938, 36 pgs., 2 1/2" x 3 1/2", Penny Book, Caniff-a 11.00 27.50 70.00
nn- Terry and the Pirates and the Island Rescue, 1938, Whitman, 68 pgs., 3 1/4" x 3 1/2", Pan-Am premium 29.00 73.00 200.00
nn- Terry and the Pirates on Their Travels, 1938, 36 pgs., 2 1/2" x 3 1/2", Penny Book, Caniff-a 11.00 27.50 70.00
nn- Terry and the Pirates and the Mystery Ship, 1938, Dell, 194 pgs., Fast-Action Story, soft-c 39.00 98.00 275.00
1492- Terry Lee Flight Officer U.S.A., 1944, Whitman, 352 pgs., Milton Caniff-a 12.00 30.00 85.00
7- Texas Bad Man, The (Tom Mix), 1934, EVW, 160 pgs., (Five Star Library), movie scenes 24.00 60.00 165.00
1429- Texas Kid, The, 1937, Whitman, 432 pgs. 11.00 27.50 70.00
1135- Texas Ranger, The, 1936, Whitman, 432 pgs., Hal Arbo-a 11.00 27.50 70.00
nn- Texas Ranger, The, 1935, Whitman, 260 pgs., Cocomalt premium, soft-c, Hal Arbo-a 12.00 30.00 85.00
nn- Texas Ranger and the Rustler Gang, The, 1936, Whitman, Pan-Am giveaway 29.00 73.00 200.00
nn- Texas Ranger in the West, The, 1938, Whitman, 36 pgs., 2 1/2" x 3 1/2", Penny Book 10.00 25.00 65.00
nn- Texas Ranger to the Rescue, The, 1938, Whitman, 36 pgs., 2 1/2" x 3 1/2", Penny Book 10.00 25.00 65.00
12- Texas Ranger in Rustler Strategy, The, 1936, Whitman, 132 pgs., 3 1/2" x 3 1/2", soft-c, Tarzan Ice Cream cup lid premium 36.00 90.00 255.00
Tex Thorne (See Zane Grey)
Thimble Theatre (See Popeye)
26- 13 Hours By Air, 1936, Lynn, 128 pgs., 5" x 7 1/2", photo-c, movie scenes (Paramount Pictures) 14.00 35.00 95.00
nn- Three Bears, The, nd (1930s), np (Whitman), 36 pgs., 3" x 2 1/2", Penny Book 4.00 10.00 22.00
1129- Three Finger Joe (Baseball), 1937, Saalfield, Robert A. Graef-a 10.00 25.00 65.00
nn- Three Little Pigs, The, nd (1930s), np (Whitman), 36 pgs., 3" x 2 1/2", Penny Book 4.00 10.00 22.00
1131- Three Musketeers, 1935, Whitman, 182 pgs., 5 1/4" x 6 1/4", photo-c, movie scenes 18.00 45.00 125.00
1409- Thumper and the Seven Dwarfs (Disney), 1944, Whitman, All Pictures Comics 24.00 60.00 165.00
1108- Tiger Lady, The (The life of Mabel Stark, animal trainer), 1935, Saalfield, photo-c, movie scenes, hard-c 11.00 27.50 70.00
1588- Tiger Lady, The, 1935, Saalfield, photo-c, movie scenes, soft-c 11.00 27.50 70.00
1442- Tillie the Toiler and the Wild Man of Desert Island, 1941, Whitman, 432 pgs., Russ Westover-a 12.00 30.00 85.00
1058- "Timid Elmer" (Disney), 1939, Whitman, 5" x 5 1/2", 68 pgs., hard-c 12.00 30.00 85.00
1152- Tim McCoy in the Prescott Kid, 1935, Whitman, 160 pgs., hard-c, photo-c, movie scenes 20.00 50.00 140.00
1193- Tim McCoy in the Westerner, 1936, Whitman, 240 pgs., photo-c, movie scenes 18.00 45.00 125.00
1436- Tim McCoy on the Tomahawk Trail, 1937, Whitman, 432 pgs., Robert Weisman-a 12.00 30.00 85.00
1490- Tim McCoy and the Sandy Gulch Stampede, 1939, Whitman, 424 pgs. 12.00 30.00 75.00
2- Tim McCoy in Beyond the Law, 1934, EVW, Five Star Library, photo-c, movie scenes (Columbia Pictures) 21.00 52.50 145.00
10- Tim McCoy in Fighting the Redskins, 1938, Whitman, 130 pgs., Buddy Book, soft-c 34.00 85.00 240.00
14- Tim McCoy in Speedwings, 1935, EVW, Five Star Library, 160 pgs., photo-c, movie scenes (Columbia Pictures) 24.00 60.00 165.00
nn- Tim the Builder, nd (1930s), np (Whitman), 36 pgs., 3" x 2 1/2", Penny Book 4.00 10.00 22.00
Tim Tyler (Also see Adventures of ...)

GD FN VF/NM

1140- Tim Tyler's Luck Adventures in the Ivory Patrol, 1937, Whitman, 432 pgs., by Lyman Young 13.00 32.50 90.00
1479- Tim Tyler's Luck and the Plot of the Exiled King, 1939, Whitman, 432 pgs., by Lyman Young 12.00 30.00 80.00
767- Tiny Tim, The Adventures of, 1935, Whitman, 384 pgs., by Stanley Link 15.00 37.50 105.00
1172- Tiny Tim and the Mechanical Men, 1937, Whitman, 432 pgs., by Stanley Link 13.00 32.50 90.00
1472- Tiny Tim in the Big, Big World, 1945, Whitman, 352 pgs., by Stanley Link 13.00 32.50 90.00
2006- (#6)-Tom and Jerry Meet Mr. Fingers, 1967, Whitman, 39¢-c 260 pgs., hard-c, color illos. 4.00 10.00 27.00
5752- Tom and Jerry Meet Mr. Fingers, 1973, Whitman, 39¢-c 260 pgs., soft-c, color illos., 5 printings 2.00 5.00 11.00
2030-(#30)- Tom and Jerry, The Astro-Nots, 1969, Whitman, 256 pgs., hard-c, color illos. 3.00 7.50 20.00
5765- Tom and Jerry, The Astro-Nots, 1974, Whitman, 256 pgs., soft-c, color illos. 2.00 5.00 11.00
5787-2- Tom and Jerry Under the Big Top, 1980, Whitman, 79¢-c, 260 pgs., soft-c, B&W 2.00 5.00 11.00
723- Tom Beatty Ace of the Service, 1934, Whitman, 256 pgs., George Taylor-a 13.00 32.50 90.00
nn- Tom Beatty Ace of the Service, 1934, Whitman, 260 pgs., soft-c 13.00 32.50 90.00
1165- Tom Beatty Ace of the Service Scores Again, 1937, Whitman, 432 pgs., Weisman-a 12.00 30.00 80.00
1420- Tom Beatty Ace of the Service and the Big Brain Gang, 1939, Whitman, 432 pgs. 12.00 30.00 80.00
nn- Tom Beatty Ace Detective and the Gorgon Gang, 1938?, Whitman, 36 pgs., 2 1/2" x 3 1/2", Penny Book 11.00 27.50 70.00
nn- Tom Beatty Ace of the Service and the Kidnapers, 1938?, Whitman, 36 pgs., 2 1/2" x 3 1/2", Penny Book 11.00 27.50 70.00
1102- Tom Mason on Top, 1935, Saalfield, 160 pgs., Tom Mix photo-c, from Mascot serial "The Miracle Rider," movie scenes, hard-c 20.00 50.00 140.00
1582- Tom Mason on Top, 1935, Saalfield, 160 pgs., Tom Mix photo-c, movie scenes, soft-c 20.00 50.00 140.00
Tom Mix (See Chief of the Rangers, Flaming Guns & Texas Bad Man)
762- Tom Mix and Tony Jr. in "Terror Trail," 1934, Whitman, 160 pgs., movie scenes 20.00 50.00 140.00
1144- Tom Mix in the Fighting Cowboy, 1935, Whitman, 432 pgs., Hal Arbo-a 15.00 37.50 105.00
nn- Tom Mix in the Fighting Cowboy, 1935, Whitman, 436 pgs., premium-no ads, 3 color, soft-c, Hal Arbo-a 29.00 73.00 200.00
1166- Tom Mix in the Range War, 1937, Whitman, 432 pgs., Hal Arbo-a 12.00 30.00 85.00
1173- Tom Mix Plays a Lone Hand, 1935, Whitman, 288 pgs., hard-c, Hal Arbo-a 12.00 30.00 85.00
1183- Tom Mix and the Stranger from the South, 1936, Whitman, 432 pgs. 12.00 30.00 85.00
1462- Tom Mix and the Hoard of Montezuma, 1937, Whitman, H. E. Vallely-a 12.00 30.00 85.00
1482- Tom Mix and His Circus on the Barbary Coast, 1940, Whitman, 432 pgs., James Gary-a 12.00 30.00 85.00
3047- Tom Mix and His Big Little Kit, 1937, Whitman, 384 pgs., 4 1/2" x 6 1/2" box, includes miniature box of 4 crayons-red, yellow, blue and green 100.00 250.00 700.00
4068- Tom Mix and the Scourge of Paradise Valley, 1937, Whitman, 7" x 9 1/2", 320 pgs., Big Big Book, Vallely-a 70.00 175.00 490.00
6833- Tom Mix in the Riding Avenger, 1936, Dell, 244 pgs., Cartoon Story Book, hard-c 31.00 78.00 220.00
nn- Tom Mix Rides to the Rescue, 1939, 36 pgs., 2 1/2" x 3", Penny Book 11.00 27.50 70.00
nn- Tom Mix Avenges the Dry Gulched Range King, 1939, Dell, 196 pgs., Fast-Action Story, soft-c 33.00 83.00 230.00
nn- Tom Mix in the Riding Avenger, 1936, Dell, 244 pgs., Fast-Action Story 33.00 83.00 230.00
nn- Tom Mix the Trail of the Terrible 6, 1935, Ralston Purina Co., 84 pgs., 3" x 3 1/2", premium 24.00 60.00 170.00

25 - Trail of the Lonesome Pine © Lynn

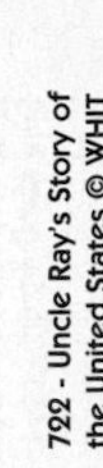
722 - Uncle Ray's Story of the United States © WHIT

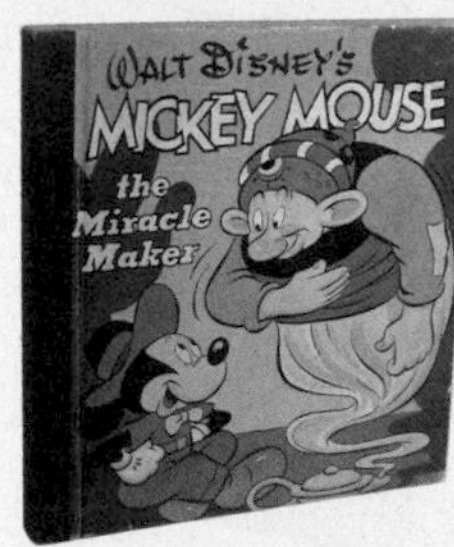

845 - Walt Disney's Mickey Mouse the Miracle Maker © DIS

	GD	FN	VF/NM
4- Tom Mix and Tony in the Rider of Death Valley, 1934, EVW, Five Star Library, 160 pgs., movie scenes (Universal Pictures), hard-c	24.00	60.00	165.00
7- Tom Mix in the Texas Bad Man, 1934, EVW, Five Star Library, 160 pgs., movie scenes	24.00	60.00	165.00
10- Tom Mix in the Tepee Ranch Mystery, 1938, Whitman, 132 pgs., Buddy Book, soft-c	34.00	85.00	240.00
1126- Tommy of Troop Six (Scout Book), 1937, Saalfield, hard-c	10.00	25.00	65.00
1606- Tommy of Troop Six (Scout Book), 1937, Saalfield, soft-c	10.00	25.00	65.00
Tom Sawyer (See Adventures of ...)			
1437- Tom Swift and His Magnetic Silencer, 1941, Whitman, 432 pgs., flip pictures	20.00	50.00	140.00
1485- Tom Swift and His Giant Telescope, 1939, Whitman, 432 pgs., James Gary-a	20.00	50.00	140.00
540- Top-Line Comics (In Open Box), 1935, Whitman, 164 pgs., 3 1/2" x 3 1/2", 3 books in set, all soft-c:			
Bobby Thatcher and the Samarang Emerald	18.00	45.00	125.00
Broncho Bill in Suicide Canyon	18.00	45.00	125.00
Freckles and His Friends in the North Woods	18.00	45.00	125.00
Complete set with box	62.00	155.00	440.00
541- Top-Line Comics (In Open Box), 1935, Whitman, 164 pgs., 3 1/2" x 3 1/2", 3 books in set; all soft-c:			
Little Joe and the City Gangsters	18.00	45.00	125.00
Smilin' Jack and His Flivver Plane	18.00	45.00	125.00
Streaky and the Football Signals	18.00	45.00	125.00
Complete set with box	62.00	155.00	440.00
542- Top Line Comics (In Open Box), 1935, Whitman, 164 pgs., 3 1/2" x 3 1/2", 3 books in set; all soft-c:			
Dinglehoofer Und His Dog Adolph by Knerr	18.00	45.00	125.00
Jungle Jim by Alex Raymond	22.00	52.50	155.00
Sappo by Segar	22.00	52.50	155.00
Complete set with box	79.00	198.00	550.00
543- Top-Line Comics (In Open Box), 1935, Whitman, 164 pgs., 3 1/2" x 3 1/2", 3 books in set; all soft-c:			
Alexander Smart, ESQ by Winner	18.00	45.00	125.00
Bunky by Billy de Beck	18.00	45.00	125.00
Nicodemus O'Malley by Carter	18.00	45.00	125.00
Complete set with box	62.00	155.00	440.00
1158- Tracked by a G-Man, 1939, Saalfield, 400 pgs.	10.00	25.00	65.00
25- Trail of the Lonesome Pine, The, 1936, Lynn, movie scenes	16.00	40.00	115.00
nn- Trail of the Terrible 6 (See Tom Mix ...)			
1185- Trail to Squaw Gulch, The, 1940, Saalfield, 400 pgs.	11.00	27.50	70.00
720- Treasure Island, 1933, Whitman, 362 pgs.	21.00	52.50	145.00
1141- Treasure Island, 1934, Whitman, 164 pgs., hard-c, 4 1/4" x 5 1/4", Jackie Cooper photo-c, movie scenes	16.00	40.00	115.00
1141- Treasure Island, 1934, Whitman, 164 pgs., soft-c, 4 1/4" x 5 1/4", Jackie Cooper photo-c, movie scenes	16.00	40.00	115.00
1018- Trick and Puzzle Book, 1939, Whitman, 100 pgs., soft-c	4.00	10.00	22.00
1100B- Tricks Easy to Do (Slight of hand & magic), 1938, Whitman, 36 pgs., 2 1/2" x 3 1/2", Penny Book	4.00	10.00	22.00
1100B- Tricks You Can Do, 1938, Whitman, 36 pgs., 2 1/2" x 3 1/2", Penny Book	4.00	10.00	22.00
5777- Tweety and Sylvester, The Magic Voice, 1976, Whitman, 260 pgs., soft-c, flip-it feature; 5 printings	2.00	5.00	11.00
1104- Two-Gun Montana, 1936, Whitman, 432 pgs., Henry E. Vallely-a	11.00	27.50	70.00
nn- Two-Gun Montana Shoots it Out, 1939, Whitman, 36 pgs., 2 1/2" x 3 1/2", Penny Book	11.00	27.50	70.00
1058- Ugly Duckling, The (Disney), 1939, Whitman, 68 pgs., 5" x 5 1/2", hard-c	14.00	35.00	95.00
nn- Ugly Duckling, The, nd (1930s), np (Whitman), 36 pgs., 3" x 2 1/2", Penny Book	4.00	10.00	22.00
Unc' Billy Gets Even (See Wee Little Books)			
1114- Uncle Don's Strange Adventures, 1935, Whitman, 300 pgs., radio star-Uncle Don Carney	12.00	30.00	75.00
722- Uncle Ray's Story of the United States, 1934, Whitman, 300 pgs.	12.00	30.00	75.00
1461- Uncle Sam's Sky Defenders, 1941, Whitman, 432 pgs., flip pictures	11.00	27.50	70.00
1405- Uncle Wiggily's Adventures, 1946, Whitman, All Pictures Comics	16.00	40.00	115.00
1411- Union Pacific, 1939, Whitman, 240 pgs., photo-c, movie scenes	12.00	30.00	85.00
1189- Up Dead Horse Canyon, 1940, Saalfield, 400 pgs.	10.00	25.00	65.00
1455- Vic Sands of the U.S. Flying Fortress Bomber Squadron, 1944, Whitman, 352 pgs.	12.00	30.00	85.00
1645- Walt Disney's Andy Burnett on the Trail (TV Series), 1958, Whitman, 280 pgs.	4.00	10.00	27.00
803- Walt Disney's Bongo, 1948, Whitman, hard-c, Story Hour Series	12.00	30.00	85.00
711-10-Walt Disney's Cinderella and the Magic Wand, 1950, Whitman, 2 1/2" x 5", based on Disney movie	12.00	30.00	75.00
845- Walt Disney's Donald Duck and his Cat Troubles (Disney), 1948, Whitman, 100 pgs., 5" x 5 1/2", hard-c	12.00	30.00	85.00
845- Walt Disney's Donald Duck and the Boys, 1948, Whitman, 100 pgs., 5" x 5 1/2", hard-c, Barks-a	28.00	70.00	195.00
2952- Walt Disney's Donald Duck in the Great Kite Maker, 1949, Whitman, 24 pgs., 3 1/4" x 4", Tiny Tales, full color (5 cents)	11.00	27.50	70.00
804- Walt Disney's Mickey and the Beanstalk, 1948, Whitman, hard-c, Story Hour Series	12.00	30.00	85.00
845- Walt Disney's Mickey Mouse and the Boy Thursday, 194 pgs., Whitman, 5" x 5 1/2", 100 pgs.	12.00	30.00	85.00
845- Walt Disney's Mickey Mouse the Miracle Maker, 1948, Whitman, 5" x 5 1/2", 100 pgs.	12.00	30.00	85.00
2952- Walt Disney's Mickey Mouse and the Night Prowlers, Whitman, 1949, 24 pgs., 3 1/4" x 4", Tiny Tales, full color (5 ¢)	11.00	27.50	70.00
5770- Walt Disney's Mickey Mouse - Mystery at Disneyland, Whitman, 1975, 260 pgs., four printings	2.00	5.00	13.00
5781-2- Walt Disney's Mickey Mouse - Mystery at Dead Man's Cove, Whitman, 1980, 260 pgs., two printings	2.00	5.00	11.00
845- Walt Disney's Minnie Mouse and the Antique Chair, 1948, Whitman, 5" x 5 1/2", 100 pgs.	12.00	30.00	85.00
1435- Walt Disney's Pinocchio and Jiminy Cricket, 1940, Whitman, 432 pgs.	21.00	52.50	145.00
845- Walt Disney's Poor Pluto, 1948, Whitman, 5" x 5 1/2", 100 pgs., hard-c	12.00	30.00	85.00
1467- Walt Disney's Pluto the Pup (Disney), 1938, Whitman, 432 pgs., Gottfredson-a	18.00	45.00	125.00
1066- Walt Disney's Story of Clarabelle Cow (Disney), 1938, Whitman, 100 pgs.	12.00	30.00	85.00
66- Walt Disney's Story of Dippy the Goof (Disney), 1938, Whitman, 100 pgs.	12.00	30.00	85.00
1066- Walt Disney's Story of Donald Duck (Disney), 1938, Whitman, 100 pgs., hard-c, Taliaferro-a	12.00	30.00	85.00
1066- Walt Disney's Story of Mickey Mouse (Disney), 1938, Whitman, 100 pgs., hard-c, Gottfredson-a, Donald Duck app.	12.00	30.00	85.00
1066- Walt Disney's Story of Minnie Mouse (Disney), 1938, Whitman, 100 pgs., hard-c	12.00	30.00	85.00
1066- Walt Disney's Story of Pluto the Pup, (Disney), 1938, Whitman, 100 pgs., hard-c	12.00	30.00	85.00
2952- Walter Lantz Presents Andy Panda's Rescue, 1949, Whitman, Tiny Tales, full color (5 cents) (1030-5 on back-c)	11.00	27.50	70.00
751- Wash Tubbs in Pandemonia, 1934, Whitman, 320 pgs., Roy Crane-a	12.00	30.00	85.00
nn- Wash Tubbs in Pandemonia, 1934, Whitman, 52 pgs., 4" x 5 1/2", premium-no ads, soft-c, Roy Crane-a	20.00	50.00	140.00
1455- Wash Tubbs and Captain Easy Hunting For Whales, 1938, Whitman, 432 pgs., Roy Crane-a	12.00	30.00	85.00
6- Wash Tubbs in Foreign Travel, 1934, Whitman, soft-c, 3 1/2" x 3 1/2",			

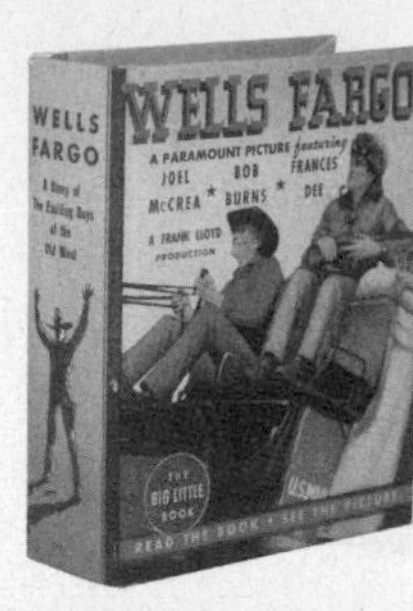

1471 - Wells Fargo © WHIT

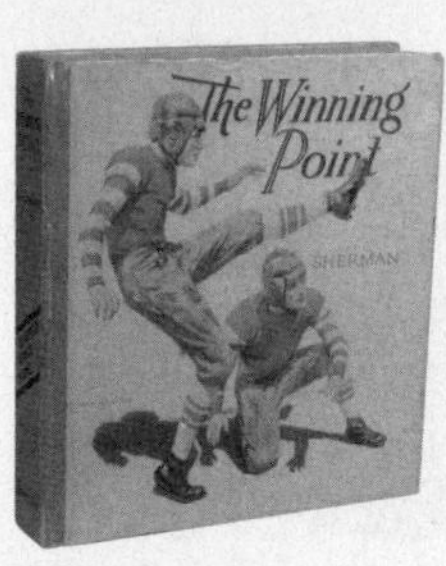

1122 - The Winning Point © Saalfield

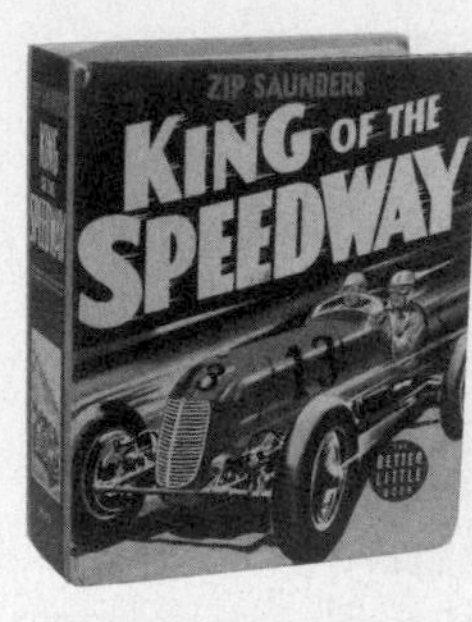

1465 - Zip Saunders King of the Speedway © WHIT

	GD	FN	VF/NM
Tarzan Ice Cream cup premium	34.00	85.00	240.00
513- **Wee Little Books** (In Open Box), 1934, Whitman, 44 pgs., small size, 6 books in set			
Child's Garden of Verses	5.00	12.50	30.00
The Happy Prince (The Story of)	5.00	12.50	30.00
Joan of Arc (The Story of)	5.00	12.50	30.00
Peter Pan (The Story of)	5.00	12.50	30.00
Pied Piper Of Hamlin	5.00	12.50	30.00
Robin Hood (A Story of...)	5.00	12.50	30.00
Complete set with box	31.00	78.00	220.00
514- **Wee Little Books** (In Open Box), 1934, Whitman, 44 pgs., small size, 6 books in set			
Jack And Jill	5.00	12.50	30.00
Little Bo-Peep	5.00	12.50	30.00
Little Tommy Tucker	5.00	12.50	30.00
Mother Goose	5.00	12.50	30.00
Old King Cole	5.00	12.50	30.00
Simple Simon	5.00	12.50	30.00
Complete set with box	33.00	83.00	230.00
518- **Wee Little Books** (In Open Box), 1933, Whitman, 44 pgs., small size, 6 books in set, written by Thornton Burgess			
Betty Bear's Lesson-1930	5.00	12.50	30.00
Jimmy Skunk's Justice-1933	5.00	12.50	30.00
Little Joe Otter's Slide-1929	5.00	12.50	30.00
Peter Rabbit's Carrots-1933	5.00	12.50	30.00
Unc' Billy Gets Even-1930	5.00	12.50	30.00
Whitefoot's Secret-1933	5.00	12.50	30.00
Complete set with box	33.00	83.00	230.00
519- **Wee Little Books** (In Open Box) (Bible Stories), 1934, Whitman, 44 pgs., small size, 6 books in set, Helen Janes-a			
The Story of David	5.00	12.50	30.00
The Story of Gideon	5.00	12.50	30.00
The Story of Daniel	5.00	12.50	30.00
The Story of Joseph	5.00	12.50	30.00
The Story of Ruth and Naomi	5.00	12.50	30.00
The Story of Moses	5.00	12.50	30.00
Complete set with box	33.00	83.00	230.00
1471- **Wells Fargo**, 1938, Whitman, 240 pgs., photo-c, movie scenes	14.00	35.00	95.00
L18- **Western Frontier**, 1935, Lynn, 192 pgs., starring Ken Maynard, movie scenes	21.00	52.50	145.00
1121- **West Pointers on the Gridiron**, 1936, Saalfield, 148 pgs., hard-c, sports book	10.00	25.00	65.00
1601- **West Pointers on the Gridiron**, 1936, Saalfield, 148 pgs., soft-c, sports book	10.00	25.00	65.00
1124- **West Point Five, The**, 1937, Saalfield, 4 3/4" x 5 1/4", sports book, hard-c	10.00	25.00	65.00
1604- **West Point Five, The**, 1937, Saalfield, 4 1/4" x 5 1/4", sports book, soft-c	10.00	25.00	65.00
1164- **West Point of the Air**, 1935, Whitman, 160 pgs., photo-c, movie scenes	12.00	30.00	85.00
18- **Westward Ho!**, 1935, EVW, 160 pgs., movie scenes, starring John Wayne (Scarce)	49.00	122.00	345.00
1109- **We Three**, 1935, Saalfield, 160 pgs., photo-c, movie scenes, by John Barrymore, hard-c	11.00	27.50	70.00
1589- **We Three**, 1935, Saalfield, 160 pgs., photo-c, movie scenes, by John Barrymore, soft-c	11.00	27.50	70.00
5- **Wheels of Destiny**, 1934, EVW, 160 pgs., movie scenes, starring Ken Maynard	21.00	52.50	145.00
Whitefoot's Secret (See Wee Little Books)			
nn- **Who's Afraid of the Big Bad Wolf**, "Three Little Pigs" (Disney), 1933, McKay, 36 pgs., 6" x 8 1/2", stiff-c, Disney studio-a	39.00	98.00	275.00
nn- **Wild West Adventures of Buffalo Bill**, 1935, Whitman, 260 pgs., Cocomalt premium, soft-c, Hal Arbo-a	15.00	37.50	105.00
1096- **Will Rogers, The Story of**, 1935, Saalfield, photo-hard-c	12.00	30.00	75.00
1576- **Will Rogers, The Story of**, 1935, Saalfield, photo-soft-c	12.00	30.00	75.00

	GD	FN	VF/NM
1458- **Wimpy the Hamburger Eater**, 1938, Whitman, 432 pgs., E.C. Segar-a	24.00	60.00	165.00
1433- **Windy Wayne and His Flying Wing**, 1942, Whitman, 432 pgs., flip pictures	11.00	27.50	70.00
1131- **Winged Four, The**, 1937, Saalfield, sports book, hard-c	11.00	27.50	70.00
1407- **Wings of the U.S.A.**, 1940, Whitman, 432 pgs., Thomas Hickey-a	11.00	27.50	70.00
nn- **Winning of the Old Northwest, The**, 1934, World Syndicate, High Lights of History Series, full color-c	11.00	27.50	70.00
nn- **Winning of the Old Northwest, The**, 1934, World Syndicate, High Lights of History Series; red & silver-c	11.00	27.50	70.00
1122- **Winning Point, The**, 1936, Saalfield, (Football), hard-c	9.00	22.50	58.00
1602- **Winning Point, The**, 1936, Saalfield, soft-c	9.00	22.50	58.00
nn- **Wizard of Oz Waddle Book**, 1934, BRP, 20 pgs., 7 1/2" x 10", forerunner of the Blue Ribbon Pop-Up books; with 6 removable articulated cardboard characters. Book only	54.00	135.00	375.00
Dust jacket only	61.00	153.00	490.00
Near Mint Complete - $12,500			
710-10-**Woody Woodpecker Big Game Hunter**, 1950, Whitman, by Walter Lantz	10.00	25.00	65.00
2010-(#10)-**Woody Woodpecker-The Meteor Menace**, 1967, Whitman, 260 pgs., 39¢-c, hard-c, color illos.	4.00	10.00	27.00
5753- **Woody Woodpecker-The Meteor Menace**, 1973, Whitman, 260 pgs., no price, soft-c, color illos.	1.00	2.50	6.00
2028- **Woody Woodpecker-The Sinister Signal**, 1969, Whitman	4.00	10.00	22.00
5763- **Woody Woodpecker-The Sinister Signal**, 1974, Whitman, 1st printing-no price; 2nd printing-39¢-c	1.00	2.50	6.00
23- **World of Monsters, The**, 1935, EVW, Five Star Library, movie scenes	16.00	40.00	115.00
779- **World War in Photographs, The**, 1934, Whitman, photo-c, photo illus.	11.00	27.50	70.00
Wyatt Earp (See Hugh O'Brian ...)			
nn- **Xena - Warrior Princess**, 1998, Chronicle Books, 310 pgs., based on TV series, 1-color (purple) illos	1.00	2.50	9.00
nn- **Yogi Bear Goes Country & Western**, 1977, Modern Promotions, 244 pgs., 49 cents, soft-c, flip pictures	2.00	5.00	13.00
nn- **Yogi Bear Saves Jellystone Park**, 1977, Modern Promotions, 244 pgs., 49 cents, soft-c, flip pictures	2.00	5.00	13.00
nn- **Zane Grey's Cowboys of the West**, 1935, Whitman, 148 pgs., 3 3/4" x 4", Tarzan Ice Cream Cup premium, soft-c, Arbo-a	39.00	98.00	275.00
Zane Grey's King of the Royal Mounted (See Men of the Mounted)			
1010- **Zane Grey's King of the Royal Mounted in Arctic Law**, 1937, Whitman, 7 1/4" x 5 1/2", 64 pgs., Nickel Book	15.00	37.50	105.00
1103- **Zane Grey's King of the Royal Mounted**, 1936, Whitman, 432 pgs.	14.00	35.00	95.00
nn- **Zane Grey's King of the Royal Mounted**, 1935, Whitman, 260 pgs., Cocomalt premium, soft-c	18.00	45.00	125.00
1179- **Zane Grey's King of the Royal Mounted and the Northern Treasure**, 1937, Whitman, 432 pgs.	14.00	35.00	95.00
1405- **Zane Grey's King of the Royal Mounted the Long Arm of the Law**, 1942, Whitman, All Pictures Comics	14.00	35.00	95.00
1452- **Zane Grey's King of the Royal Mounted Gets His Man**, 1938, Whitman, 432 pgs.	14.00	35.00	95.00
1486- **Zane Grey's King of the Royal Mounted and the Great Jewel Mystery**, 1939, Whitman, 432 pgs.	14.00	35.00	95.00
5- **Zane Grey's King of the Royal Mounted in the Far North**, 1938, Whitman, 132 pgs., Buddy Book, soft-c	36.00	90.00	255.00
nn- **Zane Grey's King of the Royal Mounted in Law of the North**, 1939, Whitman, 36 pgs., 2 1/2" x 3 1/2", Penny Book	9.00	22.50	58.00
nn- **Zane Grey's King of the Royal Mounted Policing the Frozen North**, 1938, Dell, 196 pgs., Fast-Action Story, soft-c	26.00	65.00	180.00
1440- **Zane Grey's Tex Thorne Comes Out of the West**, 1937, Whitman, 432 pgs.	11.00	27.50	70.00
1465- **Zip Saunders King of the Speedway**, 1939, 432 pgs., Weisman-a	11.00	27.50	70.00

Promotional Comics

THE MARKETING OF A MEDIUM

by Dr. Arnold T. Blumberg, DCD

with new material and additional research by Sol M. Davidson, PhD, and Robert L. Beerbohm

Everyone wants something for free. It's in our nature to look for the quick fix, the good deal, the complimentary gift. We long to hit the lottery and quit our job, to win the trip around the world, or find that pot of gold at the end of the proverbial rainbow. Collectors in particular are certainly built to appreciate the notion of the "free gift," since it not only means a new item to collect and enjoy, but no risk or obligation in order to acquire it.

Ah, but there's the rub. Because things are not always what they seem, and "free gifts" usually come with a price. As the saying goes, "there's no such thing as a free lunch," so if it seems too good to be true, it probably is. This is the case even in the world of comics, where premiums and giveaways have a familiar agenda hidden behind the bright colors and fanciful stories. But where did it all begin?

Some of the earliest characters that were used as successful tools in promotional comics were Palmer Cox's creation "The Brownies." The illustration shown here showcases them drinking and endorsing Seal Brand Coffee.

EXTRA EXTRA

As we learn more about the early history of the comic book industry through continual investigation and the publishing of articles like those regularly featured in this book, we gain a much greater understanding of the financial and creative forces at work in shaping the medium, but perhaps one of the most intriguing and least recognized factors that influenced the dawn of comics is the concept of the premium or giveaway. (Note: Some of the historical information referenced in this article is derived from material also presented in Robert L. Beerbohm's introductory articles to the Platinum Age and Modern Age sections.)

The birth of the comic book as we know it today is intimately connected with the development of the comic strip in American newspapers and their use as an advertising and marketing tool for staple products such as bread, milk, and cereal. From the very beginning, comic characters have played several roles in pop culture, entertaining the youth of the country while also (sometimes none too subtly) acting as hucksters for whatever corporation foots the bill. From important staples to frivolous material produced simply to make a buck, these products have utilized the comics medium to sell, sell, sell. And what better way to hook a prospective customer than to give them "something for nothing?"

Starting in the 1850s, comics were being used in free almanacs such as **Elton's**, **Hostetter's** and **Wright's** to lure readers for the little booklets to sell patent medicine, farm products, tobacco, shoe polish, etc. Most of these are exceedingly rare today, hence it is difficult to compile an accurate history. More mention of these early precursors can be found in the Victorian Comics Era essay following this one. But although comic characters themselves were already being aggressively merchandised all around the world by the mid-1890s--as with, for example, Palmer Cox's **The Brownies**--the real starting point for the success of comics as a giveaway marketing mechanism can be traced to the introduction of **The Yellow Kid**, Richard Outcault's now legendary newspaper strip.

Newspaper publishers had already recognized that comic strips could boost circulation as well as please sponsors and advertisers by drawing more eyes to the page, so Sunday "supplements" were introduced to entice fans. Outcault's creation cemented the theory with proof of comic characters' marketing and merchandising power.

This unused cover was designed as the second cover for "Motion Picture Funnies Weekly." While the concept for this promotional comic title never caught on, the inaugural issue did feature the origin and first printed appearance of the Sub-Mariner.

Soon after, Outcault (who had most likely been inspired by Cox's merchandising success with **The Brownies** in the first place) caught lightning in a bottle once more with **Buster Brown**, who has the distinction of being America's first nationally licensed comic strip character. Soon, comic strips proliferated throughout the nation's newspapers as tycoons like Hearst and Pulitzer recognized the drawing power of the new medium and fought circulation wars to capture the pennies of the nouveau readership. They paid exorbitant salaries to comic strip artists such as Rudolph Dirks (**Katzenjammer Kids**), and used the funnies as newspaper supplements and as premiums to attract readers. Corporations soon had the chance to license recognizable personas as their own personal pitchmen (or women or animals...). Comic character merchandise wasn't far behind, resulting in a boom of future collectibles now catalogued in volumes like **Hake's Price Guide to Character Toys**.

TWO BIRTHS FOR THE PRICE OF ONE

Comic books themselves were at the heart of this movement, and giveaway and premium collections of comic strips not only appealed to children and adults alike, but provided the impetus for the birth of the modern comic book format itself. It could be said that without the concept of the giveaway comic or the marketing push behind it, there would be no comic book industry as we have it today. Well-known now is the story of how in spring 1933 Harry Wildenberg of Eastern Color Printing Company convinced Proctor & Gamble to sponsor the first modern comic book, **Funnies on Parade**, as a premium. Its success led to the first continuing comic book, **Famous Funnies**, and the rest, as they say, is history.

In 1935, while working on the printing presses of Eastern Color developing how modern comic books get printed, Juliun J. Proskauer came up with an idea for printing "Comic-Books-For-Industry." In July 1936 he made his first sale through his newly formed William C. Popper & Co. to David M. Davies, then advertising manager for Seagram's Distillers Corp. for three million copies of **Seagram's Merrymakers** in time for the 1936-37 Christmas season. "Thus was a new industry born," wrote **Printing News** in August 1945.

Even a casual perusal of the listings in this section of the Guide will dazzle the reader with the endless variety of purposes that this medium has served. Yes, promos have been used to hawk products from athletic equipment to zithers and zip codes, but comics are too versatile an art form to be confined to a few uses. They've swayed elections in cities (**The O'Dwyer Story**, 1949), in states (**Giant for a Day**: Jacob Javits, 1946) and nationwide (**The Story of Harry Truman**, 1948); solicited for charities (**Donald Duck and the Red Feather**, 1948); addressed health issues (**Blondie**, 1949, mental hygiene); discouraged kids from smoking (**Captain America Meets the Asthma Monster**, 1987); coached youngsters in sports skills (**Circling the Bases**, 1947, A.G. Spaulding); explained scientific complexities (**Adventures in Science**, 1946-61, GE); pleaded for social justice (**Consumer Comics**, 1975); espoused religious causes (**Oral Roberts' True Stories**, 1950s); protected the environment (**Our Spaceship Earth**, 1947); encouraged tourism (**Wyoming, The Cowboy State**, 1954); conveyed a sense of history (**Louisiana Purchase**, 1953); taught about computers (**Superman Radio Shack Giveaway**, 1980); trained employees (**Dial Finance Dialogues**, 1961-70) and executives (**Beneficial Finance System, Managing New Employees**, 1950s); cautioned safety (**Willy Wing Flap**, 1944(?)); announced corporate annual results (**Motorola Annual Report**, 1952); defended free enterprise (**Steve Merritt**, 1949); hammered communism (**How Stalin Hopes to Destroy America**, 1951); fought discrimination (**Mammy Yokum & the Great Dogpatch Mystery**, 1956, B'nai Brith); aided young workers in job-hunting (**The Job Scene**, 1969); battled the scourge of sickle cell anemia (**Where's Herbie**, 1972, U.S. H.E.W.); inspired the overcoming of adversity (**Al Capp by Li'l Abner**, 1946); fostered reading (**Linus Gets a Library Card**, 1960); recruited for the armed forces (**Li'l Abner Joins the Navy**, 1950); beguiled readers into

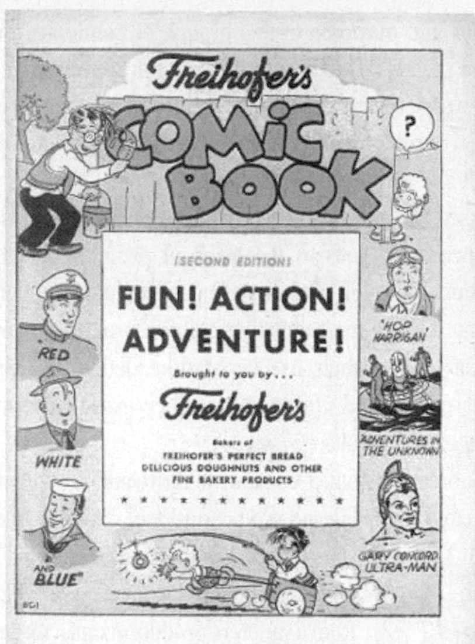

Every market and product has been on the promotional comic book bandwagon. Freihofer's Baking Company distributed a comic in the 1940s that featured reprinted pages from "All-American Comics."

learning languages (**Blondie**, 1949, Philadelphia public schools); and even instructed in such delicate matters as birth control (**Escape from Fear**, 1950 (revised 1959, etc.), for Planned Parenthood).

READ ALL ABOUT IT

The impact of this new approach to advertising was not lost on the business world. Contrary to modern belief, comic books were hardly discounted by the adults of the time...at least not those who had the marketing savvy to recognize an opportunity - or a threat - when they saw one. In the April 1933 issue of **Fortune** magazine, an article titled "The Funny Papers" trumpeted the arrival of comics as a force to be reckoned with in the world of advertising and business, and what's more, a force to fear as well. At first providing a brief survey of the newspaper comic strip business (which for many of the magazine's readers must have seemed a foreign topic for serious discussion), the article goes on to examine the incredible financial draw of comics and their characters:

"Between 70 and 75 per cent {sic} of the readers of any newspaper follow its comic sections regularly...Even the advertiser has succumbed to the comic, and in 1932 spent well over $1,000,000 for comic-paper space."

"**Comic Weekly** is the comic section of seventeen Hearst Sunday papers...Advertisers who market their wares through balloon-speaking manikins {sic} may enjoy the proximity of Jiggs, Maggie, Barney Google, and other funny Hearst headliners."

Although the article continues to cast the notion of relying on comic strip material to sell product in a negative light, actually suggesting that advertisers who utilize comics are violating unspoken rules of "advertising decorum" and bringing themselves "down to the level" of comics (and since when have advertisers been stalwart preservers of good taste and high moral standards), there is no doubt that they are viewing comics in a new light. The comic characters have arrived by 1933...and they're ready to help sell your merchandise too.

Fortune wasn't the only one to take notice as World War II came and went. In 1948, Louis P. Birk, the head of Brevity, Inc., an important promotional comics publisher said, "Comics are serious business." In an article in **Printers' Ink** magazine, he estimated that more than 80 different "comic booklets" had been produced and more than 45,000,000 million copies distributed in the five years before 1948. But of course, comics were serious business long before businessman/historian Birk noted the fact for posterity.

THE MARCH OF WAR AND BEYOND

Through the relentless currents of time, comic strips, books, and the characters that starred in them became more and more an intrinsic part of American culture. During the turmoil of the Great Depression and World War II, comic characters in print and celluloid form entertained while informing and selling at the same time, and premium and giveaway comics came well and truly into their own, pushing everything from loaves of bread to war bonds.

In the 1950s and '60s, there was a shift in focus as the power of giveaway and premium comics was applied to more altruistic endeavors than simply selling something. Comic book format pamphlets, fully illustrated and often inventively written, taught children about banking, money, the dangers of poison and other household products, and even chronicled moments in

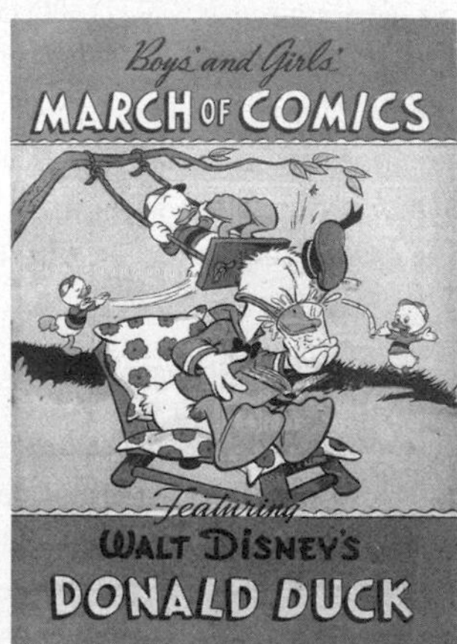

The promotional title "March of Comics" was a prolific comic that ran for 36 years and 488 issues featuring a variety of subjects and characters. (#20 shown)

American history. The comic book as giveaway was now not only a marketing gimmick--it was a tool for educating as well.

The 1970s and '80s saw another boom in premium and giveaway comics. Every product imaginable seemed to have a licensing deal with a comic book character, usually one of the prominent flag bearers of the Big Two, Marvel or DC. Spider-Man fought bravely against the Beetle for the benefit of All Detergent; Captain America allied himself with the Campbell Kids; and Superman helped a class of computer students beat a disaster-conjuring foe at his own game with the help of Radio Shack Tandy computers.

Newspapers rediscovered the power of comics, not just with enlarged strip supplements but with actual comic books. Spider-Man, the Hulk, and others turned up as giveaway comic extras in various American newspapers (including Chicago and Dallas publications), while a whole series of public information comics like those produced decades earlier used superheroes to caution children about the dangers of smoking, drugs, and child abuse.

Comics also turned up in a plethora of other toy products as the 1980s introduced kids to the joy of electronic games and action figures. Supplementary comics provided "free" with action figure and video game packages told the backstory about the product, adding depth to the play experience while providing an extra incentive to buy. Comics became an intrinsic part of the Atari line of video cartridges, for example, eventually spawning its own full-blown newsstand series as well.

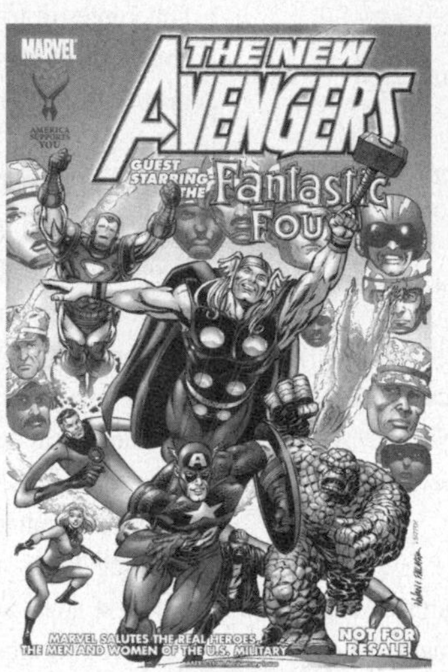

Today, promotional comics continue to be used as a marketing tool to reach both children and adults alike. This 2005 comic was produced by Marvel Comics as a salute to the men and women of the armed forces.

As the twentieth century gave way to the twenty-first, giveaway comics were still being produced for inclusion in action figure and video game packages, as well as in conjunction with countless consumer items and corporations. It seems that the medium still has a lot to offer for all those companies desperate to make the most of their market share.

A COMIC BY ANY OTHER NAME

One of the earliest names for promotional comics was "special purpose comics." In their pursuit of superheroes, collectors have allowed promotional comics to lie fallow - underappreciated and uncollected. Without a legitimate name, these products were given sundry other appellations - industrial comics, promos, giveaways, premiums, promics - each accurate but only for a small segment of the unorganized but lusty and lively medium. Perhaps no one name can cover all the variations and purposes of this branch of comic art, but for practical reasons if we accept the general premise that these comics were created to promote an idea, a product or a person, then "Promotional Comics" is probably as convenient a catch-all title as we can come up with.

We used the phrase "for practical reasons" because the word "practical" goes to the heart of promotional comics more than it does for any other comics product. What greater testimony is there to the medium's impact on American culture than to note their use by hard-headed, profit-minded business people and corporations? They invest their money and they expect results.

Today, premium comics continue to thrive and are still utilized as a valuable marketing and promotional tool. "Free" comics are still packaged with action figures and video games, and offered as mail-away premiums from a variety of product manufacturers. The comic industry itself has expanded its use of giveaway comics to self-promote as well, with "ashcan" and other giveaway editions turning up at conventions and comic shops to advertise upcoming series and special events. Many of these function as old-fashioned premiums, with a coupon or other response required from the reader to receive the comic.

As for the supplements and giveaways printed all those years ago, they have spawned a collectible fervor all their own, thanks to their atypical distribution and frequent rarity. For that and the desire to delve deeper into comics history, we hope that by focusing more directly on this genre, we can enhance our understanding of this vital component in the development and history of the modern comic book.

Whether you're a collector or not, we're all motivated by that desire to get something for nothing. For as long as consumers are enticed by the notion of the "free gift," promotional comics will remain a vital marketing component in many business models, but they will also continue to fight the stigma that has long been associated with the industry as a whole. "Respectable" sources like **Fortune** may have taken notice of the power of comic-related advertising 71 years ago, but after all this time comics still fight an uphill battle to establish some measure of dignity for the medium. Perhaps the higher visibility of promotional comics will eventually prove to be a deciding factor in that intellectual war.

See ya in the funny papers.

Adventures @ eBay #1 © eBay

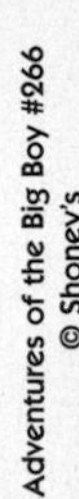
Adventures of the Big Boy #266 © Shoney's

Alaska Bush Pilot #1 © Jan Enterprises

	GD 2.0	VG 4.0	FN 6.0	VF 8.0	VF/NM 9.0	NM- 9.2

ACTION COMICS
DC Comics: 1947 - 1998 (Giveaway)

1 (1976) paper cover w/10¢ price, 16 pgs. in color; reprints complete Superman story from #1 ('38)	3	6	9	19	29	38
1 (1976) Safeguard Giveaway; paper cover w/"free", 16 pgs. in color; reprints complete Superman story from #1 ('38)	3	6	9	19	29	38
1 (1983) paper cover w/10¢ price, 16 pgs. in color; reprints complete Superman story from #1 ('38)	3	6	9	15	20	25
1 (1987 Nestle Quik; 1988, 50¢)	1	2	3	5	7	9
1 (1993)-Came w/Reign of Superman packs						4.00
1 (1998 U.S. Postal Service, $7.95) Reprints entire issue; extra outer half-cover contains First Day Issuance of 32¢ Superman stamp with Sept. 10, 1998 Cleveland, OH postmark	1	2	3	5	6	8
Theater (1947, 32 pgs., 5" x 7", nn)-Vigilante story based on Columbia Vigilante serial; no Superman-c or story	65	130	195	410	693	975

ACTION ZONE
CBS Television: 1994 (Promotes CBS Saturday morning cartoons)

1-WildC.A.T.s, T.M.N.Turtles, Skeleton Warriors stories; Jim Lee-c 2.50

ADVENTURE COMICS
IGA: No date (early 1940s) (Paper-c, 32 pgs.)

Two diff. issues; Super-Mystery-r from 1941	22	44	66	129	207	285

ADVENTURE IN DISNEYLAND
Walt Disney Productions (Dist. by Richfield Oil): May, 1955 (Giveaway, soft-c., 16 pgs)

nn	10	20	30	56	76	95

ADVENTURES @ EBAY
eBay: 2000 (6 3/4" x 4 1/2", 16 pgs.)

1-Judd Winick-a/Rucka & Van Meter-s; intro to eBay comic buying 2.50

ADVENTURES OF BARRY WEEN, BOY GENIUS, THE
Oni Press: July, 2004 (Free Comic Book Day giveaway)

...Secret Crisis Origin Files -Judd Winick-s/a 2.50

ADVENTURES OF BIG BOY (Also titled Adventures of the Big Boy)
Timely Comics/Webs Adv. Corp./Illus. Features: 1956 - Present (Giveaway) (East & West editions of early issues)

1-Everett-c/a	100	200	300	630	1065	1500
2-Everett-c/a	37	74	111	215	345	475
3-5: 4-Robot-c	18	36	54	105	165	225
6-10: 6-Sci/fic issue	10	20	30	73	129	180
11-20: 11,13-DeCarlo-a	6	12	18	43	69	95
21-30	4	8	12	24	37	50
31-50	3	6	9	17	25	32
51-100	2	4	6	9	13	16
101-150	2	4	6	8	10	12
151-240	1	2	3	5	7	9
241-265,267-269,271-300:						6.00
266-Superman x-over	3	6	9	18	27	35
270-TV's Buck Rogers-c/s	3	6	9	14	20	25
301-400						4.00
401-500						3.00
1-(2nd series - '76-'84,Paragon Prod.) (...Shoney's Big Boy)	1	3	4	6	8	10
2-20						5.00
21-50						3.00
Summer, 1959 issue, large size	7	14	21	49	80	110

ADVENTURES OF G. I. JOE
1969 (3-1/4x7") (20 & 16 pgs.)

First Series: 1-Danger of the Depths. 2-Perilous Rescue. 3-Secret Mission to Spy Island. 4-Mysterious Explosion. 5-Fantastic Free Fall. 6-Eight Ropes of Danger. 7-Mouth of Doom. 8-Hidden Missile Discovery. 9-Space Walk Mystery. 10-Fight for Survival. 11-The Shark's Surprise.
Second Series: 2-Flying Space Adventure. 4-White Tiger Hunt. 7-Capture of the Pygmy Gorilla. 12-Secret of the Mummy's Tomb.
Third Series: Reprinted surviving titles of First Series. Fourth Series: 13-Adventure Team Headquarters. 14-Search For the Stolen Idol.

each....	3	6	9	16	22	28

ADVENTURES OF JELL-O MAN AND WOBBLY, THE
Welsh Publishing Group: 1991 ($1.25)

1 3.00

ADVENTURES OF KOOL-AID MAN
Marvel Comics: 1983 - No. 3, 1985 (Mail order giveaway)

1-3	1	2	3	4	5	7

ADVENTURES OF MARGARET O'BRIEN, THE
Bambury Fashions (Clothes): 1947 (20 pgs. in color, slick-c, regular size) (Premium)

In "The Big City" movie adaptation (scarce)	19	38	57	112	176	240

ADVENTURES OF QUIK BUNNY
Nestle's Quik: 1984 (Giveaway, 32 pgs.)

nn-Spider-Man app.	2	4	6	8	11	14

ADVENTURES OF STUBBY, SANTA'S SMALLEST REINDEER, THE
W. T. Grant Co.: nd (early 1940s) (Giveaway, 12 pgs.)

nn	7	14	21	37	46	55

ADVENTURES OF VOTEMAN, THE
Foundation For Citizen Education Inc.: 1968

nn	4	8	12	28	44	60

ADVENTURES WITH SANTA CLAUS
Promotional Publ. Co. (Murphy's Store): No date (early 50's) (9-3/4x 6-3/4", 24 pgs., giveaway, paper-c)

nn-Contains 8 pgs. ads	6	12	18	29	36	42
16 pg. version	6	12	18	33	41	48

ADVENTURES WITH THE DC SUPER HEROES (Interior also inserted into some DC issues)
DC Comics/Geppi's Entertainment Museum: 2007 Free Comic Book Day giveaway

"The Batman and Cal Ripken, Jr. Hall of Fame Edition "A Rare Catch" " in indicia 2.25

AIR POWER (CBS TV & the U.S. Air Force Presents)
Prudential Insurance Co.: 1956 (5-1/4x7-1/4", 32 pgs., giveaway, soft-c)

nn-Toth-a? Based on 'You Are There' TV program by Walter Cronkite	10	20	30	56	76	95

ALASKA BUSH PILOT
Jan Enterprises: 1959 (Paper cover)

1-Promotes Bush Pilot Club (Value will be based on sale)
NOTE: *A CGC certified 9.9 Mint sold for $632.50 in 2005.*

ALICE IN BLUNDERLAND
Industrial Services: 1952 (Paper cover, 16 pgs. in color)

nn-Facts about government waste and inefficiency	14	28	42	76	108	140

ALICE IN WONDERLAND
Western Printing Company/Whitman Publ. Co.: 1965; 1969; 1982

Meets Santa Claus(1950s), nd, 16 pgs.	6	12	18	28	34	40
Rexall Giveaway(1965, 16 pgs., 5x7-1/4) Western Printing (TV, Hanna-Barbera)	3	6	9	16	23	30
Wonder Bakery Giveaway(1969, 16 pgs, color, nn, nd) (Continental Baking Company)	3	6	9	16	22	28

ALICE IN WONDERLAND MEETS SANTA
No publisher: nd (6-5/8x9-11/16", 16 pgs., giveaway, paper-c)

nn	9	18	27	50	65	80

ALL ABOARD, MR. LINCOLN
Assoc. of American Railroads: Jan, 1959 (16 pgs.)

nn-Abraham Lincoln and the Railroads	6	12	18	28	34	40

ALL NEW COMICS
Harvey Comics: Oct, 1993 (Giveaway, no cover price, 16 pgs.)(Hanna-Barbera)

1-Flintstones, Scooby Doo, Jetsons, Yogi Bear & Wacky Races previews for upcoming Harvey's new Hanna-Barbera line-up 5.00
NOTE: *Material previewed in Harvey giveaway was eventually published by Archie.*

AMAZING SPIDER-MAN, THE
Marvel Comics Group

Acme & Dingo Children's Boots (1980)-Spider-Woman app.	2	4	6	10	14	18
Adventures in Reading Starring... (1990,1991) Bogdanove & Romita-c/a						4.00
Aim Toothpaste Giveaway (36 pgs., reg. size)-1 pg. origin recap; Green Goblin-c/story	2	4	6	8	11	14
Aim Toothpaste Giveaway (16 pgs., reg. size)-Dr. Octopus app.	2	4	6	9	12	15
All Detergent Giveaway (1979, 36 pgs.), nn-Origin-r	2	4	6	9	13	16
Amazing Fantasy #15 (8/02) reprint included in Spider-Man DVD Collector's Gift Set						3.00
Amazing Fantasy #15 (2006) News America Marketing newspaper giveaway						2.50
Amazing Spider-Man nn (1990, 6-1/8x9", 28 pgs.)-Shan-Lon giveaway; reprints Amazing Spider-Man #303 w/McFarlane-c/a	1	2	3	5	7	9
Amazing Spider-Man #1 Reprint (1990, 4-1/4x6-1/4", 28 pgs.)-Packaged with the book "Start Collecting Comic Books" from Running Press						4.00
Amazing Spider-Man #3 Reprint (2004)-Best Buy/Sony giveaway						2.50
Amazing Spider-Man #50 (Sony Pictures Edition) (8/04)-mini-comic included in Spider-Man 2 movie DVD Collector's Gift Set; r/#50 & various ASM covers with Dr. Octopus						2.50
Amazing Spider-Man #129 (Lion Gate Films) (6/04)-promotional comic given away at movie theaters on opening night for The Punisher						2.50

...& Power Pack (1984, nn)(Nat'l Committee for Prevention of Child Abuse) (two versions, mail offer & store giveaway)-Mooney-a; Byrne-c

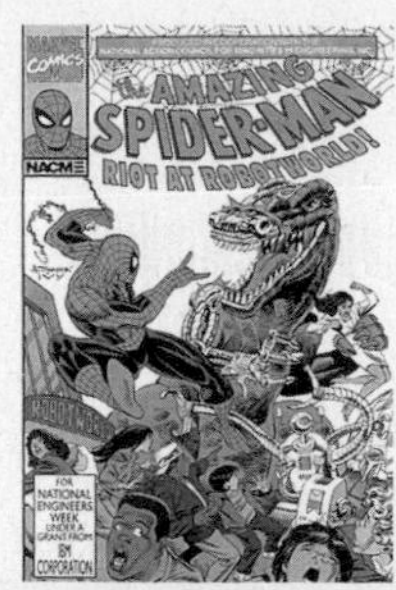

Amazing Spider-Man: Riot at Robotworld © MAR

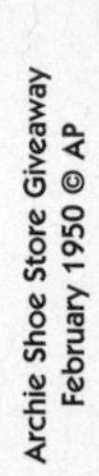
Archie Shoe Store Giveaway February 1950 © AP

Atari Force #5 © Atari

GD VG FN VF VF/NM NM-
2.0 4.0 6.0 8.0 9.0 9.2

Mail offer 2 4 6 8 10 12
Store giveaway 4.00
...& The Hulk (Special Edition)(6/8/80; 20 pgs.)-Supplement to Chicago Tribune
2 4 6 9 13 16
...& The Incredible Hulk (1981, 1982; 36 pgs.)-Sanger Harris or May D&F supplement to Dallas Times, Dallas Herald, Denver Post, Kansas City Star, Tulsa World; Foley's supplement to Houston Chronicle (1982, 16 pgs.)- "Great Rodeo Robbery"; The Jones Store-giveaway (1983, 16 pgs.) 2 4 6 11 16 20
...and the New Mutants Featuring Skids nn (National Committee for Prevention of Child Abuse/K-Mart giveaway)-Williams-c(i) 5.00
... Battles Ignorance (1992)(Sylvan Learning Systems) giveaway; Mad Thinker app. Kupperberg-a 1 2 3 5 6 8
...Captain America, The Incredible Hulk, & Spider-Woman (1981) (7-11 Stores giveaway; 36 pgs.) 2 4 6 9 12 15
...: Christmas in Dallas (1983) (Supplement to Dallas Times Herald) giveaway 2 4 6 9 12 15
...: Danger in Dallas (1983) (Supplement to Dallas Times Herald) giveaway 2 4 6 9 12 15
...: Danger in Denver (1983) (Supplement to Denver Post) giveaway for May D&F stores 2 4 6 9 12 15
..., Fire-Star, And Ice-Man at the Dallas Ballet Nutcracker (1983; supplement to Dallas Times Herald)-Mooney-p 2 4 6 9 12 15
Giveaway-Esquire Magazine (2/69)-Miniature-Still attached (scarce)
12 24 36 86 153 220
Giveaway-Eye Magazine (2/69)-Miniature-Still attached
9 18 27 61 103 145
...: Riot at Robotworld (1991; 16 pgs.)(National Action Council for Minorities in Engineering, Inc.) giveaway; Saviuk-c 6.00
..., Storm & Powerman (1982; 20 pgs.)(American Cancer Society) giveaway; also a 1991 2nd printing and a 1994 printing 1 2 3 5 6 8
...: Swing Shift (2007 FCBD Edition) Jimenez-c/a; Slott-s 2.25
...Vs. The Hulk (Special Edition; 1979, 20 pgs.)(Supplement to Columbus Dispatch)
2 4 6 11 16 20
...Vs. The Prodigy (Giveaway, 16 pgs. in color (1976, 5x6-1/2")-Sex education; (1 million printed; 35-50¢) 2 4 6 10 14 18
Spidey & The Mini-Marvels Halloween 2003 Ashcan (12/03, 8 1/2"x 5 1/2") Giarusso-s/a; Venom and Green Goblin app. 2.00

AMERICA MENACED!
Vital Publications: 1950 (Paper-c)

nn Anti-communism 33 66 99 192 309 425

AMERICAN COMICS
Theatre Giveaways (Liberty Theatre, Grand Rapids, Mich. known): 1940's

Many possible combinations. "Golden Age" superhero comics with new cover added and given away at theaters. Following known: Superman #59, Capt. Marvel #20, Capt. Marvel Jr. #5, Action #33, Classics Comics #8, Whiz #39. Value would vary with book and should be 70-80 percent of the original.

ANDY HARDY COMICS
Western Printing Co.:

...& the New Automatic Gas Clothes Dryer (1952, 5x7-1/4", 16 pgs.) Bendix Giveaway (soft-c) 6 12 18 31 38 45

ANIMANIACS EMERGENCY WORLD
DC Comics: 1995

nn-American Red Cross 4.00

APACHE HUNTER
Creative Pictorials: 1954 (18 pgs. in color) (promo copy) (saddle stitched)

nn-Severin, Heath stories 15 30 45 85 130 175

AQUATEERS MEET THE SUPER FRIENDS
DC Comics: 1979

nn 2 4 6 9 12 15

ARCHIE AND HIS GANG (Zeta Beta Tau Presents...)
Archie Publications: Dec. 1950 (St. Louis National Convention giveaway)

nn-Contains new cover stapled over Archie Comics #47 (11-12/50) on inside; produced for Zeta Beta Tau 15 30 45 88 137 185

ARCHIE COMICS (Also see Sabrina)
Archie Publications

... And Friends and the Shield (10/02, 8 1/2"x 5 1/2") Diamond Comic Dist. 3.00
... And Friends - A Halloween Tale (10/98, 8 1/2"x 5 1/2") Diamond Comic Dist.; Sabrina and Sonic app.; Dan DeCarlo-a 3.00
... And Friends - A Timely Tale (10/01, 8 1/2"x 5 1/2") Diamond Comic Dist. 3.00
... And Friends Monster Bash 2003 (8 1/2"x 5 1/2") Diamond Comic Dist. Halloween 3.00
...And His Friends Help Raise Literacy Awareness In Mississippi nn (3/94) 6.00
...And His Friends Vs. The Household Toxic Wastes nn (1993, 16 pgs.) produced for the San Diego Regional Household Hazardous Materials Program 6.00
...And His Pals in the Peer Helping Program nn (2/91, 7"x4 1/2") produced by the FBI 6.00
...And the History of Electronics nn (5/90, 36 pgs.)-Radio Shack giveaway; Bender-c/a 6.00

GD VG FN VF VF/NM NM-
2.0 4.0 6.0 8.0 9.0 9.2

Fairmont Potato Chips Giveaway-Mini comics 1970 (6 issues-nn's.,6 7/8" x 2 1/4", 8 pgs. each)
3 6 9 16 22 28
Fairmont Potato Chips Giveaway-Mini comics 1971 (4 issues-nn's.,6 7/8" x 5", 8 pgs. each)
3 6 9 16 22 28
... Free Comic Book Day Edition 1,2: 1-(7/03). 2-(9/04) 2.50
Little Archie "The Legend of the Lost Lagoon FCBD Edition (5/07) Bolling-s/a 2.25
Official Boy Scout Outfitter (1946, 9-1/2x6-1/2, 16 pgs.)-B. R. Baker Co. (Scarce) 47 92 141 291 483 675
...'s Ham Radio Adventure (1997) Morse code instruction; Goldberg-a 5.00
...'s 65th Anniversary Bash ('06) Free Comic Book Day giveaway 2.50
...'s Weird Mysteries (9/99, 8 1/2"x 5 1/2") Diamond Comic Dist. Halloween giveaway 2.50
Tales From Riverdale (2006, 8 1/2"x 5 1/2") Diamond Comic Dist. Halloween giveaway 2.50

ARCHIE SHOE-STORE GIVEAWAY
Archie Publications: 1944-50 (12-15 pgs. of games, puzzles, stories like Superman-Tim books, No nos. - came out monthly)

(1944-47)-issues 15 30 45 84 127 170
2/48-Peggy Lee photo-c 15 30 45 84 127 170
3/48-Marylee Robb photo-c 14 28 42 80 115 150
4/48-Gloria De Haven photo-c 15 30 45 84 127 170
5/48,6/48,7/48 14 28 42 80 115 150
8/48-Story on Shirley Temple 15 30 45 85 130 175
10/48-Archie as Wolf on cover 14 28 42 82 121 160
5/49-Kathleen Hughes photo-c 13 26 39 72 101 130
7/49 12 24 36 69 97 125
8/49-Archie photo-c from radio show 15 30 45 94 147 200
10/49-Gloria Mann photo-c from radio show 14 28 42 82 121 160
11/49,12/49, 2/50 12 24 36 69 97 125

ARCHIE'S JOKE BOOK MAGAZINE (See Joke Book ...)
Archie Publications

Drug Store Giveaway (No. 39 w/new-c) 7 14 21 35 43 50

ARCHIE'S TEN ISSUE COLLECTOR'S SET (Title inside of cover only)
Archie Publications: June, 1997 - No. 10, June, 1997 ($1.50, 20 pgs.)

1-10: 1,7-Archie. 2,8-Betty & Veronica. 3,9-Veronica. 4-Betty. 5-World of Archie. 6-Jughead. 10-Archie and Friends each... 4.00

ASTRO COMICS
American Airlines (Harvey): 1968 - 1979 (Giveaway)(Reprints of Harvey comics)

1908-Richie Rich, Hot Stuff, Casper, Wendy on-c only; Spooky and Nightmare app. inside
4 8 12 22 34 45
1970-Casper, Spooky, Hot Stuff, Stumbo the Giant, Little Audrey, Little Lotta, & Richie Rich reprints. Five different versions 3 6 9 19 29 38
1973,1975,1976: 1973-Three different versions 3 6 9 16 23 30
1977-r/Richie Rich & Casper #20. 1978-r/Richie Rich & Casper #25. 1979-r/Richie Rich & Casper #30 (scarce) 3 6 9 16 22 28

ATARI FORCE
DC Comics: 1982 - No. 5, 1983

1-3 (1982, 5X7", 52 pgs.)-Given away with Atari games
1 2 3 4 5 7
4,5 (1982-1983, 52 pgs.)-Given away with Atari games (scarcer)
2 4 6 8 10 12

AURORA COMIC SCENES INSTRUCTION BOOKLET (Included with superhero model kits)
Aurora Plastics Co.: 1974 (6-1/4x9-3/4," 8 pgs., slick paper)

181-140-Tarzan; Neal Adams-a 3 6 9 18 27 36
182-140-Spider-Man. 4 8 12 24 37 50
183-140-Tonto(Gil Kane art). 184-140-Hulk. 185-140-Superman. 186-140-Superboy. 187-140-Batman. 188-140-The Lone Ranger(1974-by Gil Kane). 192-140-Captain America(1975). 193-140-Robin 3 6 9 16 23 30

BACK TO THE FUTURE
Harvey Comics

Special nn (1991, 20 pgs.)-Brunner-c; given away at Universal Studios in Florida 5.00

BALTIMORE COLTS
American Visuals Corp.: 1950 (Giveaway)

nn-Eisner-c 45 90 135 279 465 650

BAMBI (Disney)
K. K. Publications (Giveaways): 1941, 1942

1941-Horlick's Malted Milk & various toy stores; text & pictures; most copies mailed out with store stickers on-c 41 82 123 250 413 575
1942-Same as 4-Color #12, but no price (Same as '41 issue?) (Scarce)
67 134 201 422 711 1000

BATMAN
DC Comics: 1966 - Present

Act II Popcorn mini-comic(1998) 3.00
Batman #121 Toys R Us edition (1997) r/1st Mr. Freeze 3.00

Batman #121 Toys R Us Ed. © DC

Bionicle #9 © LEGO Toys

Bongo Comics Free-For-All 2006 © Bongo

GD 2.0 | VG 4.0 | FN 6.0 | VF 8.0 | VF/NM 9.0 | NM- 9.2

Batman #362 Mervyn's edition (1989) 4.00
Batman #608 New York Post edition (2002) 3.00
Batman Adventures #1 Free Comic Book Day edition (6/03) Timm-c 3.00
Batman Adventures #25 Best Western edition (1997) 3.00
Batman and Other DC Classics 1 (1989, giveaway)-DC Comics/Diamond Comic Distributors; Batman origin-r/Batman #47, Camelot 3000-r, Justice League-r('87), New Teen Titans-r 4.00
Batman and Robin movie preview (1997, 8 pgs.) Kellogg's Cereal promo 2.50
Batman Beyond Six Flags edition 6.00
Batman: Canadian Multiculturalism Custom (1992) 4.00
Batman Claritan edition (1999) 2.50
Kellogg's Poptarts comics (1966, Set of 6, 16 pgs.); All were folded and placed in Poptarts boxes. Infantino art on Catwoman and Joker issues.
"The Man in the Iron Mask", "The Penguin's Fowl Play", "The Joker's Happy Victims", "The Catwoman's Catnapping Caper", "The Mad Hatter's Hat Crimes", "The Case of the Batman II"
each.... 4 8 12 28 44 60
Mask of the Phantasm (1993) Mini-comic released w/video
1 2 3 4 5 7
Onstar - Auto Show Special Edition (OnStar Corp., 2001, 8 pgs.) Riddler app. 2.50
Pizza Hut giveaway (12/77)-exact-r of #122,123; Joker-c/story
2 4 6 8 10 12
Prell Shampoo giveaway (1966, 16 pgs.)- "The Joker's Practical Jokes" (6-7/8x3-3/8") 6 12 18 37 59 80
Revell in pack (1995) 3.00
The Batman Strikes #1 Free Comic Book Day edition (6/05) Penguin app. 2.50
...: The 10-Cent Adventure (3/02, 10¢) intro. to the "Bruce Wayne: Murderer" x-over; Rucka-s/Burchett & Janson-a/Dave Johnson-c; these are alternate copies with special outer half-covers (at least 10 different) promoting comics, toys and games shops 2.50

BATMAN RECORD COMIC
National Periodical Publications: 1966 (one-shot)
1-With record (still sealed) 14 28 42 102 181 260
Comic only 8 16 24 58 97 135

BATTLESTAR GALACTICA SEASON ZERO/THE LONE RANGER #0
Dynamite Entertainment: 2007 Free Comic Book Day Edition
nn-Flip book with Cassaday Lone Ranger-c 2.25

BEETLE BAILEY
Charlton Comics: 1969-1970 (Giveaways)
Armed Forces ('69)-same as regular issue (#68) 2 4 6 10 14 18
Bold Detergent ('69)-same as regular issue (#67) 2 4 6 10 14 18
Cerebral Palsy Assn. V2#71('69) - V2#73(#1,1/70) 2 4 6 10 14 18
Red Cross (1969, 5x7", 16 pgs., paper-c) 2 4 6 10 14 18

BEST WESTERN GIVEAWAY
DC Comics: 1999
nn-Best Western hotels 2.50

BETTER LIFE FOR YOU, A
Harvey Publications Inc.: (16 pgs., paper cover)
nn-Better living through higher productivity 3 6 9 16 22 28

BETTY AND VERONICA
Archie Comic Publications: 2005
... Free Comic Book Day Edition #1 (6/05) Katy Keene-c/app.; Cheryl Blossom app. 2.50

BEWARE THE BOOBY TRAP
Malcolm Alter: 1970 (5" x 7")
nn-Deals with drug abuse 4 8 12 24 37 50

B-FORCE (Milwaukee Brewers and Wisconsin Dental Asso.)
Dark Horse Comics: 2001 (School and stadium giveaway)
nn-Brewers players combat the evils of smokeless tobacco 3.00

BIG BOY (see Adventures of...)

BIG JIM'S P.A.C.K.
Mattel, Inc. (Marvel Comics): No date (1975) (16 pgs.)
nn-Giveaway with Big Jim doll; Buscema/Sinnott-c/a 4 8 12 22 34 45

"BILL AND TED'S EXCELLENT ADVENTURE" MOVIE ADAPTATION
DC Comics: 1989 (No cover price)
nn-Torres-a 4.00

BIONICLE (LEGO robot toys)
DC Comics: Jun, 2001 - No. 27, Nov, 2005 ($2.25/$3.25, 16 pages, available to LEGO club members)
1 1 2 3 5 6 8
2-5 6.00
6-13 4.00
14-27 3.00
The Legend of Bionicle (McDonald's Mini-comic, 4-1/4 x 7") 4.00
Special Edition #0 (Six Heroes...One Destiny) '03 San Diego Comic Con; Ashley Wood-c 6.00

BLACK GOLD
Esso Service Station (Giveaway): 1945? (8 pgs. in color)
nn-Reprints from True Comics 6 12 18 27 33 38

BLAZING FOREST, THE (See Forest Fire and Smokey Bear)
Western Printing: 1962 (20 pgs., 5x7", slick-c)
nn-Smokey The Bear fire prevention 2 4 6 12 16 20

BLESSED PIUS X
Catechetical Guild (Giveaway): No date (Text/comics, 32 pgs., paper-c)
nn 6 12 18 29 36 42

BLIND JUSTICE (Also see Batman: Blind Justice)
DC Comics/Diamond Comic Distributors: 1989 (Giveaway, squarebound)
nn-Contains Detective #598-600 by Batman movie writer Sam Hamm, w/covers; published same time as originals? 6.00

BLONDIE COMICS
Harvey Publications: 1950-1964
1950 Giveaway 7 14 21 37 46 55
1962,1964 Giveaway 3 6 9 16 22 28
N. Y. State Dept. of Mental Hygiene Giveaway-(1950) Regular size; 16 pgs.; no # 4 8 12 22 34 45
N. Y. State Dept. of Mental Hygiene Giveaway-(1956) Regular size; 16 pgs.; no # 3 6 9 16 23 30
N. Y. State Dept. of Mental Hygiene Giveaway-(1961) Regular size; 16 pgs.; no # 3 6 9 15 21 26

BLOOD IS THE HARVEST
Catechetical Guild: 1950 (32 pgs., paper-c)
(Scarce)-Anti-communism (13 known copies) 167 334 501 1052 1776 2500
Black & white version (5 known copies), saddle stitched
87 174 261 548 924 1300
Untrimmed version (only one known copy); estimated value - $1000
NOTE: *In 1979 nine copies of the color version surfaced from the old Guild's files plus the five black & white copies.*

BLUE BIRD CHILDREN'S MAGAZINE, THE
Graphic Information Service: V1#2, 1957 - No. 10 1958 (16 pgs., soft-c, regular size)
V1#2-10: Pat, Pete & Blue Bird app. 2 4 6 8 11 14

BLUE BIRD COMICS
Various Shoe Stores/Charlton Comics: Late 1940's - 1964 (Giveaway)
nn(1947-50)(36 pgs.)-Several issues; Human Torch, Sub-Mariner app. in some
18 36 54 103 162 220
1959-Li'l Genius, Timmy the Timid Ghost, Wild Bill Hickok (All #1)
3 6 9 16 21 26
1959-(6 titles; all #2) Black Fury #1,4,5, Freddy #4, Li'l Genius, Timmy the Timid Ghost #4, Masked Raider #4, Wild Bill Hickok (Charlton) 3 6 9 14 20 25
1959-(#5) Masked Raider #21 3 6 9 16 22 28
1960-(6 titles)(All #4) Black Fury #6,8,9, Masked Raider #6, Freddy #8,9, Timmy the Timid Ghost #6,9, Li'l Genius #7,9 (Charlt.) 3 6 9 14 19 24
1961,1962-(All #10's) Atomic Mouse #12,13,16, Black Fury #11,12, Freddy, Li'l Genius, Masked Raider, Six Gun Heroes, Texas Rangers in Action, Timmy the Ghost, Wild Bill Hickok, Wyatt Earp #3,11-13,16-18 (Charlton) 2 4 6 13 18 22
1963-Texas Rangers #17 (Charlton) 2 4 6 9 13 16
1964-Mysteries of Unexplored Worlds #18, Teenage Hotrodders #18, War Heroes #18 (Charlton) 2 4 6 9 13 16
1965-War Heroes #18 2 4 6 8 10 12
NOTE: *More than one issue of each character could have been published each year. Numbering is sporadic.*

BOB & BETTY & SANTA'S WISHING WHISTLE
Sears Roebuck & Co.: 1941 (Christmas giveaway, 12 pgs.)
nn 12 24 36 69 97 125

BOBBY BENSON'S B-BAR-B RIDERS (Radio)
Magazine Enterprises/AC Comics
...in the Tunnel of Gold-(1936, 5-1/4x8"; 100 pgs.) Radio giveaway by Hecker-H.O. Company (H.O. Oats); contains 22 color pgs. of comics, rest in novel form
11 22 33 62 86 110
...And The Lost Herd-same as above 11 22 33 62 86 110

BOBBY SHELBY COMICS
Shelby Cycle Co./Harvey Publications: 1949
nn 5 10 14 20 24 28

BONGO COMICS ...
Bongo Comics: 2005; 2006; 2007 (Free Comic Book Day giveaways)
Gimme Gimme Giveaway! (2005) - Short stories from Simpsons Comics, Futurama Comics and Radioactive Man 2.50
Free-For-All! (2006, 2007) - Short stories in each 2.50

BOY SCOUT ADVENTURE

Bozo the Clown © DELL

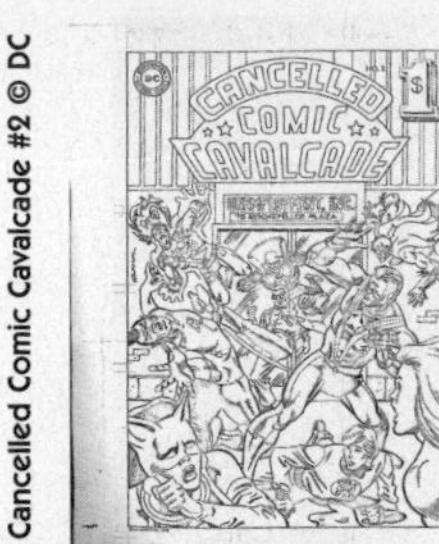

Cancelled Comic Cavalcade #2 © DC

Captain America and the Campbell Kids © MAR

	GD 2.0	VG 4.0	FN 6.0	VF 8.0	VF/NM 9.0	NM- 9.2

Boy Scouts of America: 1954 (16 pgs., paper cover)
nn 5 10 14 20 24 28

BOYS' RANCH
Harvey Publications: 1951
Shoe Store Giveaway #5,6 (Identical to regular issues except Simon & Kirby centerfold replaced with ad) 14 28 42 76 108 140

BOZO THE CLOWN (TV)
Dell Publishing Co.: 1961
Giveaway-1961, 16 pgs., 3-1/2x7-1/4", Apsco Products
5 10 15 32 51 70

BRER RABBIT IN "ICE CREAM FOR THE PARTY"
American Dairy Association: 1955 (5x7-1/4", 16 pgs., soft-c) (Walt Disney) (Premium)
nn-(Scarce) 38 76 114 226 363 500

BUCK ROGERS (In the 25th Century)
Kelloggs Corn Flakes Giveaway: 1933 (6x8", 36 pgs)
370A-By Phil Nowlan & Dick Calkins; 1st Buck Rogers radio premium & 1st app. in comics (tells origin) (Reissued in 1995) 95 190 285 700 - -
with envelope 115 230 345 850 - -

BUGS BUNNY (Puffed Rice Giveaway)
Quaker Cereals: 1949 (32 pgs. each, 3-1/8x6-7/8")
A1-Traps the Counterfeiters, A2-Aboard Mystery Submarine, A3- Rocket to the Moon, A4-Lion Tamer, A5-Rescues the Beautiful Princess, B1-Buried Treasure, B2-Outwits the Smugglers, B3-Joins the Marines, B4-Meets the Dwarf Ghost, B5-Finds Aladdin's Lamp, C1-Lost in the Frozen North, C2-Secret Agent, C3-Captured by Cannibals, C4-Fights the Man from Mars, C5-And the Haunted Cave
each.... 9 18 27 52 69 85
Mailing Envelope (has illo of Bugs on front)(Each envelope designates what set it contains, A,B or C on front) 9 18 27 52 69 85

BUGS BUNNY (3-D)
Cheerios Giveaway: 1953 (Pocket size) (15 titles)
each.... 11 22 33 62 86 110
Mailing Envelope (has Bugs drawn on front) 11 22 33 62 86 110

BUGS BUNNY
DC Comics: May, 1997 ($4.95, 24 pgs., comic-sized)
1-Numbered ed. of 100,000; "1st Day of Issue" stamp cancellation on-c 6.00

BUGS BUNNY POSTAL COMIC
DC Comics: 1997 (64 pgs., 7.5" x 5")
nn -Mail Fan; Daffy Duck app. 4.50

BULLETMAN
Fawcett Publications
Well Known Comics (1942)-Paper-c, glued binding; printed in red (Bestmaid/Samuel Lowe giveaway) 15 30 45 85 130 175

BULLS-EYE (Cody of The Pony Express No. 8 on)
Charlton: 1955
Great Scott Shoe Store giveaway-Reprints #2 with new cover
18 36 54 103 162 220

BUSTER BROWN COMICS (Radio)(Also see My Dog Tige in Promotional sec.)
Brown Shoe Co: 1945 - No. 43, 1959 (No. 5: paper-c)
nn, nd (#1,scarce)-Featuring Smilin' Ed McConnell & the Buster Brown gang "Midnight" the cat, "Squeaky" the mouse & "Froggy" the Gremlin; covers mention diff. shoe stores. Contains adventure stories 60 120 180 378 639 900
2 19 38 57 109 172 235
3,5-10 13 26 39 72 101 130
4 (Rare)-Low print run due to paper shortage 15 30 45 94 147 200
11-20 9 18 27 47 61 75
21-24,26-28 6 12 18 31 38 45
25,33-37,40,41-Crandall-a in all 10 20 30 56 76 95
29-32-"Interplanetary Police Vs. the Space Siren" by Crandall (pencils only #29)
10 20 30 58 79 100
38,39,42,43 6 12 18 31 38 45

BUSTER BROWN COMICS (Radio)
Brown Shoe Co: 1950s
...Goes to Mars (2/58-Western Printing), slick-c, 20 pgs., reg. size
12 24 36 67 94 120
...In "Buster Makes the Team!" (1959-Custom Comics)
8 16 24 44 57 70
...In The Jet Age ('50s), slick-c, 20 pgs., 5x7-1/4" 10 20 30 58 79 100
...Of the Safety Patrol ('60-Custom Comics) 3 6 9 18 27 35
...Out of This World ('59-Custom Comics) 7 14 21 35 43 50
...Safety Coloring Book ('58, 16 pgs.)-Slick paper 7 14 21 35 43 50

CALL FROM CHRIST
Catechetical Educational Society: 1952 (Giveaway, 36 pgs.)
nn 6 12 18 29 36 42

CANCELLED COMIC CAVALCADE
DC Comics, Inc.: Summer, 1978 - No. 2, Fall, 1978 (8-1/2x11", B&W)
(Xeroxed pgs. on one side only w/blue cover and taped spine)(Only 35 sets produced)
1-(412 pgs.) Contains xeroxed copies of art for: Black Lightning #12, cover to #13; Claw #13,14; The Deserter #1; Doorway to Nightmare #6; Firestorm #6; The Green Team #2,3.
2-(532 pgs.) Contains xeroxed copies of art for: Kamandi #60 (including Omac), #61; Prez #5; Shade #9 (including The Odd Man); Showcase #105 (Deadman), 106 (The Creeper); Secret Society of Super Villains #16 & 17; The Vixen #1; and covers to Army at War #2, Battle Classics #3, Demand Classics #1 & 2, Dynamic Classics #3, Mr. Miracle #26, Ragman #6, Weird Mystery #25 & 26, & Western Classics #1 & 2.
(A FN set of Number 1 & 2 was sold in 2005 for $3680; a VG set sold in 2007 for $2629)
NOTE: *In June, 1978, DC cancelled several of their titles. For copyright purposes, the unpublished original art for these titles was xeroxed, bound in the above books, published and distributed. Only 35 copies were made. Beware of bootleg copies.*

CAP'N CRUNCH COMICS (See Quaker Oats)
Quaker Oats Co.: 1963; 1965 (16 pgs.; miniature giveaways; 2-1/2x6-1/2")
(1963 titles)- "The Picture Pirates", "The Fountain of Youth", "I'm Dreaming of a Wide Isthmus". (1965 titles)- "Bewitched, Betwitched, & Betweaked", "Seadog Meets the Witch Doctor", "A Witch in Time" 5 10 15 34 55 75

CAPTAIN ACTION (Toy)
National Periodical Publications
...& Action Boy('67)-Ideal Toy Co. giveaway (1st app. Captain Action)
11 22 33 74 145 215

CAPTAIN AMERICA
Marvel Comics Group
...& The Campbell Kids (1980, 36pg. giveaway, Campbell's Soup/U.S. Dept. of Energy)
2 4 6 8 10 12
...Goes To War Against Drugs(1990, no #, giveaway)-Distributed to direct sales shops; 2nd printing exists 6.00
...Meets The Asthma Monster (1987, no #, giveaway, Your Physician and Glaxo, Inc.) 6.00
Return of The Asthma Monster Vol. 1 #2 (1992, giveaway, Your Physician & Allen & Hanbury's) 6.00
...Vs. Asthma Monster (1990, no #, giveaway, Your Physician & Allen & Hanbury's) 6.00

CAPTAIN AMERICA COMICS
Timely/Marvel Comics: 1954
Shoestore Giveaway #77 70 140 210 441 746 1050

CAPTAIN ATOM
Nationwide Publishers
...- Secret of the Columbian Jungle (16 pgs. in color, paper-c, 3-3/4x5-1/8")-Fireside Marshmallow giveaway 6 12 18 28 34 40

CAPTAIN BEN DIX
Bendix Aviation Corporation: 1943 (Small size)
nn 8 16 24 42 54 65

CAPTAIN BEN DIX IN ACTION WITH THE INVISIBLE CREW
Bendix Aviation Corp.: 1940s (nd), (20 pgs, 8-1/4"x11", heavy paper)
nn-WWII bomber-c; Japanese app. 7 14 21 35 43 50

CAPTAIN BEN DIX IN SECRETS OF THE INVISIBLE CREW
Bendix Aviation Corp.: 1940s (nd), (32 pgs, soft-c)
nn 6 12 18 31 38 45

CAPTAIN FORTUNE PRESENTS
Vital Publications: 1955 - 1959 (Giveaway, 3-1/4x6-7/8", 16 pgs.)
"Davy Crockett in Episodes of the Creek War", "Davy Crockett at the Alamo", "In Sherwood Forest Tells Strange Tales of Robin Hood" ('57), "Meets Bolivar the Liberator" ('59), "Tells How Buffalo Bill Fights the Dog Soldiers" ('57), "Young Davy Crockett"
4 7 9 14 17 20

CAPTAIN GALLANT (...of the Foreign Legion) (TV)
Charlton Comics
Heinz Foods Premium (#1?)(1955; regular size)-U.S. Pictorial; contains Buster Crabbe photos; Don Heck-a 1 3 4 6 8 10
Mailing Envelope 20.00

CAPTAIN MARVEL ADVENTURES
Fawcett Publications
Bond Bread Giveaways-(24 pgs.; pocket size-7-1/4x3-1/2"; paper cover): "...& the Stolen City" ('48), "The Boy Who Never Heard of Capt. Marvel", "Meets the Weatherman" (1950) (reprint) each.... 22 44 66 131 211 290
...Well Known Comics (1944; 12 pgs.; 8-1/2x10-1/2")-printed in red & in blue; soft-c; glued binding - (Bestmaid/Samuel Lowe Co. giveaway) 15 30 45 94 147 200

CAPTAIN MARVEL ADVENTURES (Also see Flash and Funny Stuff)
Fawcett Publications (Wheaties Giveaway): 1945 (6x8", full color, paper-c)

Captain Marvel and the Lts. of Safety #3 © FAW

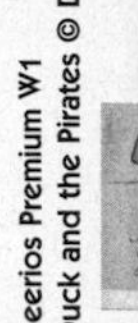
Cheerios Premium W1 Donald Duck and the Pirates © DIS

Cheerios 3-D Giveaways Set 2 #6 Mickey Mouse, Phantom Sheriff © DIS

	GD 2.0	VG 4.0	FN 6.0	VF 8.0	VF/NM 9.0	NM- 9.2
nn- "Captain Marvel & the Threads of Life" plus 2 other stories (32 pgs.)	100	200	450	750	-	-

NOTE: *All copies were taped at each corner to a box of Wheaties and are never found in Fine or Mint condition. Prices listed for each grade include tape.*

CAPTAIN MARVEL AND THE LTS. OF SAFETY
Ebasco Services/Fawcett Publications: 1950 - 1951 (3 issues - no No.'s)

	GD	VG	FN	VF	VF/NM	NM-
nn (#1) "Danger Flies a Kite" ('50, scarce),	107	214	321	674	1137	1600
nn (#2)"Danger Takes to Climbing" ('50),	83	166	249	523	887	1250
nn (#3)"Danger Smashes Street Lights" ('51)	83	166	249	523	887	1250

CAPTAIN MARVEL, JR.
Fawcett Publications: (1944; 12 pgs.; 8-1/2x10-1/2")

	GD	VG	FN	VF	VF/NM	NM-
...Well Known Comics (Printed in blue; paper-c, glued binding)-Bestmaid/Samuel Lowe Co. giveaway	14	28	42	76	108	140

CARDINAL MINDSZENTY (The Truth Behind the Trial of...)
Catechetical Guild Education Society: 1949 (24 pgs., paper cover)

	GD	VG	FN	VF	VF/NM	NM-
nn-Anti-communism	10	20	30	56	76	95
Press Proof-(Very Rare)-(Full color, 7-1/2x11-3/4", untrimmed) Only two known copies						290.00
Preview Copy (B&W, stapled), 18 pgs.; contains first 10 pgs. of Cardinal Mindszenty and was sent out as an advance promotion. Only one known copy						300.00 - 400.00

NOTE: *Regular edition also printed in French. There was also a movie released in 1949 called "Guilty of Treason" which is a fact-based account of the trial and imprisonment of Cardinal Mindszenty by the Communist regime in Hungary.*

CARNIVAL OF COMICS
Fleet-Air Shoes: 1954 (Giveaway)

	GD	VG	FN	VF	VF/NM	NM-
nn-Contains a comic bound with new cover; several combinations possible; Charlton's Eh! known	5	10	15	24	30	35

CARTOON NETWORK
DC Comics: 1997 (Giveaway)

	GD	VG	FN	VF	VF/NM	NM-
nn-reprints Cow and Chicken, Scooby-Doo, & Flintstones stories						4.00

CARVEL COMICS (Amazing Advs. of Capt. Carvel)
Carvel Corp. (Ice Cream): 1975 - No. 5, 1976 (25¢; #3-5: 35¢) (#4,5: 3-1/4x5")

	GD	VG	FN	VF	VF/NM	NM-
1-3	1	2	3	5	6	8
4,5(1976)-Baseball theme	2	4	6	8	10	12

CASE OF THE WASTED WATER, THE
Rheem Water Heating: 1972? (Giveaway)

	GD	VG	FN	VF	VF/NM	NM-
nn-Neal Adams-a	4	8	12	28	44	60

CASPER SPECIAL
Target Stores (Harvey): nd (Dec, 1990) (Giveaway with $1.00 cover)

	GD	VG	FN	VF	VF/NM	NM-
Three issues-Given away with Casper video						6.00

CASPER, THE FRIENDLY GHOST (Paramount Picture Star...)(2nd Series)
Harvey Publications

	GD	VG	FN	VF	VF/NM	NM-
American Dental Association (Giveaways):						
...'s Dental Health Activity Book-1977	2	4	6	8	10	12
...Presents Space Age Dentistry-1972	2	4	6	8	11	14
..., His Den, & Their Dentist Fight the Tooth Demons-1974	2	4	6	8	11	14
Casper Rides the School Bus (1960, 7x3.5", 16 pgs.)	2	4	6	8	11	14

CELEBRATE THE CENTURY SUPERHEROES STAMP ALBUM
DC Comics: 1998 - No. 5, 2000 (32 pgs.)

	GD	VG	FN	VF	VF/NM	NM-
1-5: Historical stories hosted by DC heroes						3.00

CENTIPEDE
DC Comics: 1983

	GD	VG	FN	VF	VF/NM	NM-
1-Based on Atari video game	1	3	4	6	8	10

CENTURY OF COMICS
Eastern Color Printing Co.: 1933 (100 pgs.)
Bought by Wheatena, Malt-O-Milk, John Wanamaker, Kinney Shoe Stores, & others to be used as premiums and radio giveaways. No publisher listed.

	GD	VG	FN	VF	VF/NM	NM-
nn-Mutt & Jeff, Joe Palooka, etc. reprints	3670	7335	11,000	25,000	-	-

CHEERIOS PREMIUMS (Disney)
Walt Disney Productions: 1947 (16 titles, pocket size, 32 pgs.)

	GD	VG	FN	VF	VF/NM	NM-
Mailing Envelope for each set "W,X,Y & Z" (has Mickey illo on front)(each envelope designates the set it contains on the front)	11	22	33	60	83	105
Set "W"						
W1-Donald Duck & the Pirates	11	22	33	60	83	105
W2-Bucky Bug & the Cannibal King	7	14	21	37	46	55
W3-Pluto Joins the F.B.I.	7	14	21	37	46	55
W4-Mickey Mouse & the Haunted House	8	16	24	42	54	65
Set "X"						
X1-Donald Duck, Counter Spy	11	22	33	60	83	105
X2-Goofy Lost in the Desert	7	14	21	37	46	55
X3-Br'er Rabbit Outwits Br'er Fox	7	14	21	37	46	55
X4-Mickey Mouse at the Rodeo	8	16	24	42	54	65
Set "Y"						
Y1-Donald Duck's Atom Bomb by Carl Barks. Disney has banned reprinting this book	85	170	255	536	906	1275
Y2-Br'er Rabbit's Secret	7	14	21	37	46	55
Y3-Dumbo & the Circus Mystery	7	14	21	37	46	55
Y4-Mickey Mouse Meets the Wizard	8	16	24	42	54	65
Set "Z"						
Z1-Donald Duck Pilots a Jet Plane (not by Barks)	11	22	33	60	83	105
Z2-Pluto Turns Sleuth Hound	7	14	21	37	46	55
Z3-The Seven Dwarfs & the Enchanted Mtn.	8	16	24	42	54	65
Z4-Mickey Mouse's Secret Room	8	16	24	42	54	65

CHEERIOS 3-D GIVEAWAYS (Disney)
Walt Disney Productions: 1954 (24 titles, pocket size) (Glasses came in envelopes)

	GD	VG	FN	VF	VF/NM	NM-
Glasses only...	8	16	24	40	50	60
Mailing Envelope (no art on front)	9	18	27	47	61	75
(Set 1)						
1-Donald Duck & Uncle Scrooge, the Firefighters	9	18	27	52	69	85
2-Mickey Mouse & Goofy, Pirate Plunder	9	18	27	47	61	75
3-Donald Duck's Nephews, the Fabulous Inventors	9	18	27	52	69	85
4-Mickey Mouse, Secret of the Ming Vase	9	18	27	47	61	75
5-Donald Duck with Huey, Dewey, & Louie; ...the Seafarers (title on 2nd page)	9	18	27	52	69	85
6-Mickey Mouse, Moaning Mountain	9	18	27	47	61	75
7-Donald Duck, Apache Gold	9	18	27	52	69	85
8-Mickey Mouse, Flight to Nowhere	9	18	27	47	61	75
(Set 2)						
1-Donald Duck, Treasure of Timbuktu	9	18	27	52	69	85
2-Mickey Mouse & Pluto, Operation China	9	18	27	47	61	75
3-Donald Duck and the Magic Cows	9	18	27	52	69	85
4-Mickey Mouse & Goofy, Kid Kokonut	9	18	27	47	61	75
5-Donald Duck, Mystery Ship	9	18	27	52	69	85
6-Mickey Mouse, Phantom Sheriff	9	18	27	47	61	75
7-Donald Duck, Circus Adventures	9	18	27	52	69	85
8-Mickey Mouse, Arctic Explorers	9	18	27	47	61	75
(Set 3)						
1-Donald Duck & Witch Hazel	9	18	27	52	69	85
2-Mickey Mouse in Darkest Africa	9	18	27	47	61	75
3-Donald Duck & Uncle Scrooge, Timber Trouble	9	18	27	52	69	85
4-Mickey Mouse, Rajah's Rescue	9	18	27	47	61	75
5-Donald Duck in Robot Reporter	9	18	27	52	69	85
6-Mickey Mouse, Slumbering Sleuth	9	18	27	47	61	75
7-Donald Duck in the Foreign Legion	9	18	27	52	69	85
8-Mickey Mouse, Airwalking Wonder	9	18	27	47	61	75

CHESTY AND COPTIE (Disney)
Los Angeles Community Chest: 1946 (Giveaway, 4pgs.)

	GD	VG	FN	VF	VF/NM	NM-
nn-(One known copy) by Floyd Gottfredson	80	160	240	504	852	1200

CHESTY AND HIS HELPERS (Disney)
Los Angeles War Chest: 1943 (Giveaway, 12 pgs., 5-1/2x7-1/4")

	GD	VG	FN	VF	VF/NM	NM-
nn-Chesty & Coptie	52	104	156	322	536	750

CHOCOLATE THE FLAVOR OF FRIENDSHIP AROUND THE WORLD
The Nestle Company: 1955

	GD	VG	FN	VF	VF/NM	NM-
nn	4	8	12	21	30	40

CHRISTMAS ADVENTURE, THE
S. Rose (H. L. Green Giveaway): 1963 (16 pgs.)

	GD	VG	FN	VF	VF/NM	NM-
nn	2	4	6	10	13	16

CHRISTMAS AT THE ROTUNDA (Titled Ford Rotunda Christmas Book 1957 on) (Regular size)
Ford Motor Co. (Western Printing): 1954 - 1961 (Given away every Christmas at one location)

	GD	VG	FN	VF	VF/NM	NM-
1954-56 issues (nn's)	7	14	21	35	43	50
1957-61 issues (nn's)	6	12	18	28	34	40

CHRISTMAS CAROL, A
Sears Roebuck & Co.: No date (1942-43) (Giveaway, 32 pgs., 8-1/4x10-3/4", paper cover)

	GD	VG	FN	VF	VF/NM	NM-
nn-Comics & coloring book	18	36	54	103	162	220

CHRISTMAS CAROL, A
Sears Roebuck & Co.: 1940s ? (Christmas giveaway, 20 pgs.)

	GD	VG	FN	VF	VF/NM	NM-
nn-Comic book & animated coloring book	15	30	45	94	147	200

CHRISTMAS CAROLS
Hot Shoppes Giveaway: 1959? (16 pgs.)

	GD	VG	FN	VF	VF/NM	NM-
nn	4	8	11	16	19	22

CHRISTMAS COLORING FUN

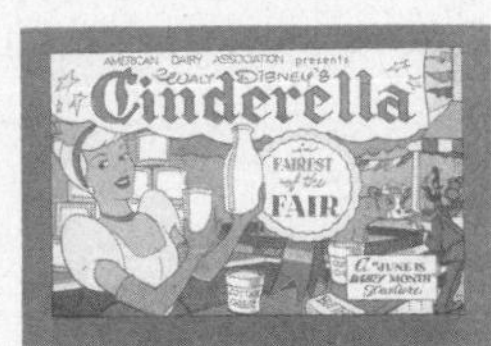

Cinderella in "Fairest of the Fair" © DIS

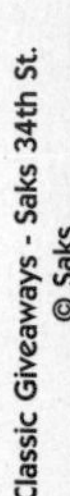
Classic Giveaways - Saks 34th St. © Saks

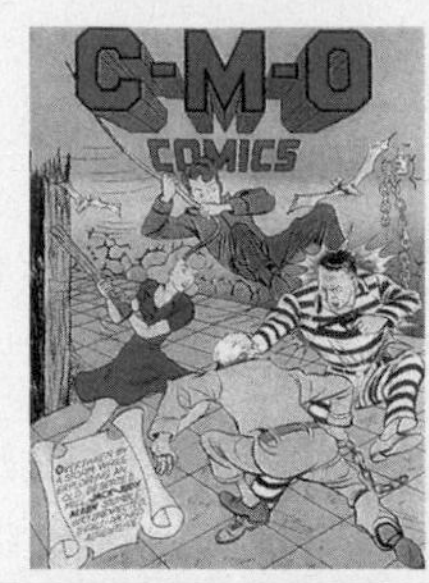

C-M-O Comics #1 © CEN

GD 2.0 | VG 4.0 | FN 6.0 | VF 8.0 | VF/NM 9.0 | NM- 9.2

H. Burnside: 1964 (20 pgs., slick-c, B&W)
nn 2 4 6 11 16 20

CHRISTMAS DREAM, A
Promotional Publishing Co.: 1950 (Kinney Shoe Store Giveaway, 16 pgs.)
nn 5 10 15 23 28 32

CHRISTMAS DREAM, A
J. J. Newberry Co.: 1952? (Giveaway, paper cover, 16 pgs.)
nn 4 8 12 18 22 25

CHRISTMAS DREAM, A
Promotional Publ. Co.: 1952 (Giveaway, 16 pgs., paper cover)
nn 4 8 12 18 22 25

CHRISTMAS FUN AROUND THE WORLD
No publisher: No date (early 50's) (16 pgs., paper cover)
nn 5 10 15 22 26 30

CHRISTMAS FUN BOOK
G. C. Murphy Co.: 1950 (Giveaway, paper cover)
nn-Contains paper dolls 6 12 18 28 34 40

CHRISTMAS IS COMING!
No publisher: No date (early 50's?) (Store giveaway, 16 pgs.)
nn 4 8 12 18 22 25

CHRISTMAS JOURNEY THROUGH SPACE
Promotional Publishing Co.: 1960
nn-Reprints 1954 issue Jolly Christmas Book with new slick cover
3 6 9 16 23 30

CHRISTMAS ON THE MOON
W. T. Grant Co.: 1958 (Giveaway, 20 pgs., slick cover)
nn 8 16 24 44 57 70

CHRISTMAS PLAY BOOK
Gould-Stoner Co.: 1946 (Giveaway, 16 pgs., paper cover)
nn 8 16 24 44 57 70

CHRISTMAS ROUNDUP
Promotional Publishing Co.: 1960
nn-Marv Levy-c/a 2 4 6 9 13 16

CHRISTMAS STORY CUT-OUT BOOK, THE
Catechetical Guild: No. 393, 1951 (15¢, 36 pgs.)
393-Half text & half comics 8 16 24 42 54 65

CHRISTMAS USA (Through 300 Years) (Also see Uncle Sam's...)
Promotional Publ. Co.: 1956 (Giveaway)
nn-Marv Levy-c/a 4 7 9 14 16 18

CHRISTMAS WITH SNOW WHITE AND THE SEVEN DWARFS
Kobackers Giftstore of Buffalo, N.Y.: 1953 (16 pgs., paper-c)
nn 8 16 24 42 54 65

CHRISTOPHERS, THE
Catechetical Guild: 1951 (Giveaway, 36 pgs.) (Some copies have 15¢ sticker)
nn-Stalin as Satan in Hell 22 44 66 129 207 280

CINDERELLA IN "FAIREST OF THE FAIR"
American Dairy Association (Premium): 1955 (5x7-1/4", 16 pgs., soft-c) (Walt Disney)
nn 10 20 30 56 76 95

CINEMA COMICS HERALD
Paramount Pictures/Universal/RKO/20th Century Fox/Republic:
1941 - 1943 (4-pg. movie "trailers", paper-c, 7-1/2x10-1/2")(Giveaway)
"Mr. Bug Goes to Town" (1941) 15 30 45 86 133 180
"Bedtime Story" 11 22 33 62 86 110
"Lady For A Night", John Wayne, Joan Blondell ('42) 18 36 54 103 162 220
"Reap The Wild Wind" (1942) 12 24 36 67 94 120
"Thunder Birds" (1942) 11 22 33 62 86 110
"They All Kissed the Bride" 11 22 33 62 86 110
"Arabian Nights" (nd) 12 24 36 67 94 120
"Bombardie" (1943) 11 22 33 62 86 110
"Crash Dive" (1943)-Tyrone Power 12 24 36 67 94 120
NOTE: *The 1941-42 issues contain line art with color photos. 1943 issues are line art.*

CLASSICS GIVEAWAYS (Classic Comics reprints)
12/41–Walter Theatre Enterprises (Huntington, WV) giveaway containing #2 (orig.) w/new generic-c (only 1 known copy) 80 160 240 504 852 1200
1942–Double Comics containing CC#1 (orig.) (diff. cover) (not actually a giveaway) (very rare) (also see Double Comics) (only one known copy)
147 294 441 926 1563 2200
12/42–Saks 34th St. Giveaway containing CC#7 (orig.) (diff. cover) (very rare; only 6 known copies) 300 600 900 2010 3505 5000
2/43–American Comics containing CC#8 (orig.) (Liberty Theatre giveaway) (different cover) (only one known copy) (see American Comics) 100 200 300 630 1065 1500
12/44–Robin Hood Flour Co. Giveaway - #7-CC(R) (diff. cover) (rare) (edition probably 5 [22]) 160 320 480 1008 1704 2400
NOTE: How are above editions determined without CC covers? 1942 is dated 1942, and CC#1-first reprint did not come out until 5/43. 12/42 and 2/43 are determined by blue note at bottom of first text page only in original edition. 12/44 is estimated from page width each reprint edition had progressively slightly smaller page width.
1951–Shelter Thru the Ages (C.I. Educational Series) (actually Giveaway by the Ruberoid Co.) (16 pgs.) (contains original artwork by H. C. Kiefer) (there are 5 diff. back cover ad variations: "Ranch" house ad, "Igloo" ad, "Doll House" ad, "Tree House" ad & blank) (scarce) 53 106 159 334 567 800
1952–George Daynor Biography Giveaway (CC logo) (partly comic book/pictures/newspaper articles) (story of man who built Palace Depression out of junkyard swamp in NJ) (64 pgs.) (very rare; only 3 known copies, one missing back-c)
371 742 1113 2523 4412 6300
1953–Westinghouse/Dreams of a Man (C.I. Educational Series) (Westinghousebio./Westinghouse Co. giveaway) (contains original artwork by H. C. Kiefer) (16 pgs.) (also French/Spanish/Italian versions) (scarce) 48 96 144 298 499 700
NOTE: Reproductions of 1951, 1952, and 1953 exist with color photocopy covers and black & white photocopy interior ("W.C.N. Reprint") 2 4 5 7 8 10
1951-53–Coward Shoe Giveaways (all editions very rare); 2 variations of back-c ad exist:
With back-c photo ad: 5 (87), 12 (89), 22 (85), 32 (85), 49 (85), 69 (87), 72 (no HRN), 80 (0), 91 (0), 92 (0), 96 (0), 98 (0), 100 (0), 101 (0), 103-105 (all Os)
30 60 90 174 280 385
With back-c cartoon ad: 106-109 (all 0s), 110 (111), 112 (0)
32 64 96 190 305 420
1956–Ben Franklin 5-10 Store Giveaway (#65-PC with back cover ad) (scarce) 25 50 75 147 236 325
1956–Ben Franklin Insurance Co. Giveaway (#65-PC with diff. back cover ad) (very rare) 48 96 144 298 499 700
11/56–Sealtest Co. Edition - #4 (135) (identical to regular edition except for Sealtest logo printed, not stamped, on front cover) (only two copies known to exist)
29 58 87 169 272 375
1958–Get-Well Giveaway containing #15-CI (new cartoon-type cover) (Pressman Pharmacy) (only one copy known to exist) 28 56 84 166 268 370
1967-68–Twin Circle Giveaway Editions - all HRN 166, with back cover ad for National Catholic Press.
2(R68), 4(R67), 10(R68), 13(R68) 3 6 9 19 29 38
48(R67), 128(R68), 535(576-R68) 3 6 9 21 32 42
16(R68), 68(R67) 4 8 12 28 44 60
12/69–Christmas Giveaway ("A Christmas Adventure") (reprints Picture Parade #4-1953, new cover) (4 ad variations)
Stacey's Dept. Store 3 6 9 19 29 38
Anne & Hope Store 5 10 15 30 48 65
Gibson's Dept. Store (rare) 5 10 15 30 48 65
"Merry Christmas" & blank ad space 3 6 9 19 29 38

CLIFF MERRITT SETS THE RECORD STRAIGHT
Brotherhood of Railroad Trainsmen: Giveaway (2 different issues)
...and the Very Candid Candidate by Al Williamson 1 3 4 6 8 10
...Sets the Record Straight by Al Williamson (2 different-c: one by Williamson, the other by McWilliams) 1 3 4 6 8 10

CLYDE BEATTY COMICS (Also see Crackajack Funnies)
Commodore Productions & Artists, Inc.
...African Jungle Book('56)-Richfield Oil Co. 16 pg. giveaway, soft-c
10 20 30 54 72 90

C-M-O COMICS
Chicago Mail Order Co.(Centaur): 1942 - No. 2, 1942 (68 pgs., full color)
1-Invisible Terror, Super Ann, & Plymo the Rubber Man app. (all Centaur costume heroes)
87 174 261 548 924 1300
2-Invisible Terror, Super Ann app. 52 104 156 322 536 750

COCOMALT BIG BOOK OF COMICS
Harry 'A' Chesler (Cocomalt Premium): 1938 (Reg. size, full color, 52 pgs.)
1-(Scarce)-Biro-c/a; Little Nemo by Winsor McCay Jr., Dan Hastings; Jack Cole, Guardineer, Gustavson, Bob Wood-a 213 426 639 1342 2271 3200

COMIC BOOK (Also see Comics From Weatherbird)
American Juniors Shoe: 1954 (Giveaway)
Contains a comic rebound with new cover. Several combinations possible. Contents determine price.

COMIC BOOK MAGAZINE
Chicago Tribune & other newspapers: 1940 - 1943 (Similar to Spirit sections) (7-3/4x10-3/4"; full color; 16-24 pgs. ea.)
1940 issues 7 14 21 37 46 55
1941, 1942 issues 6 12 18 28 34 40
1943 issues 5 10 15 24 30 35

Comic Books #1 Talullah © Met. Printing Co.

Dan Curtis Giveaway #1 Dark Shadows © Dan Curtis

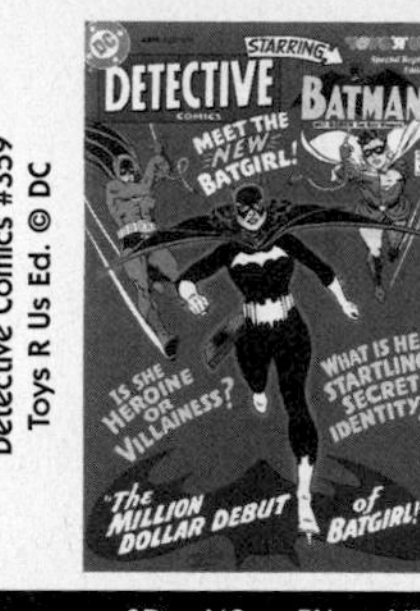

Detective Comics #359 Toys R Us Ed. © DC

	GD	VG	FN	VF	VF/NM	NM-
	2.0	4.0	6.0	8.0	9.0	9.2

NOTE: *Published weekly. Texas Slim, Kit Carson, Spooky, Josie, Nuts & Jolts, Lew Loyal, Brenda Starr, Daniel Boone, Captain Storm, Rocky, Smokey Stover, Tiny Tim, Little Joe, Fu Manchu appear among others. Early issues had photo stories with pictures from the movies; later issues had comic art.*

COMIC BOOKS (Series 1)
Metropolitan Printing Co. (Giveaway): 1950 (16 pgs.; 5-1/4x8-1/2"; full color; bound at top; paper cover)

	GD	VG	FN	VF	VF/NM	NM-
1-Boots and Saddles; intro The Masked Marshal	6	12	18	31	38	45
1-The Green Jet, Green Lama by Raboy	23	46	69	135	218	300
1-My Pal Dizzy (Teen-age)	5	10	15	22	26	30
1-New World; origin Atomaster (costumed hero)	10	20	30	56	76	95
1-Talullah (Teen-age)	5	10	15	22	26	30

COMIC CAVALCADE
All-American/National Periodical Publications

	GD	VG	FN	VF	VF/NM	NM-
Giveaway (1944, 8 pgs., paper-c, in color)-One Hundred Years of Co-operation-r/Comic Cavalcade #9	57	114	171	359	605	850
Giveaway (1945, 16 pgs., paper-c, in color)-Movie "Tomorrow The World" (Nazi theme); r/Comic Cavalcade #10	73	146	219	460	780	1100
Giveaway (c. 1944-45; 8 pgs, paper-c, in color)-The Twain Shall Meet-r/Comic Cavalcade #8	57	114	171	359	605	850

COMIC SELECTIONS (Shoe store giveaway)
Parents' Magazine Press: 1944-46 (Reprints from Calling All Girls, True Comics, True Aviation, & Real Heroes)

	GD	VG	FN	VF	VF/NM	NM-
1	5	10	15	22	26	30
2-6	4	8	11	16	19	22

COMICS FROM WEATHER BIRD (Also see Comic Book, Edward's Shoes, Free Comics to You & Weather Bird)
Weather Bird Shoes: 1954 - 1957 (Giveaway)
Contains a comic bound with new cover. Many combinations possible. Contents would determine price. Some issues do not contain complete comics, but only parts of comics. Value equals 40 to 60 percent of contents.

COMICS READING LIBRARIES (Educational Series)
King Features (Charlton Publ.): 1973, 1977, 1979 (36 pgs. in color) (Giveaways)

	GD	VG	FN	VF	VF/NM	NM-
R-01-Tiger, Quincy	2	4	6	8	10	12
R-02-Beetle Bailey, Blondie & Popeye	2	4	6	9	13	16
R-03-Blondie, Beetle Bailey	2	4	6	8	10	12
R-04-Tim Tyler's Luck, Felix the Cat	3	6	9	16	22	28
R-05-Quincy, Henry	2	4	6	8	10	12
R-06-The Phantom, Mandrake	3	6	9	16	22	28
1977 reprint(R-04)	2	4	6	9	11	14
R-07-Popeye, Little King	2	4	6	11	16	20
R-08-Prince Valiant (Foster), Flash Gordon	3	6	9	17	26	34
1977 reprint	2	4	6	10	14	18
R-09-Hagar the Horrible, Boner's Ark	2	4	6	9	13	16
R-10-Redeye, Tiger	2	4	6	8	10	12
R-11-Blondie, Hi & Lois	2	4	6	8	10	12
R-12-Popeye-Swee'pea, Brutus	2	4	6	11	16	20
R-13-Beetle Bailey, Little King	2	4	6	8	10	12
R-14-Quincy-Hamlet	2	4	6	8	10	12
R-15-The Phantom, The Genius	2	4	6	11	16	20
R-16-Flash Gordon, Mandrake	3	6	9	17	26	34
1977 reprint	2	4	6	9	13	16
Other 1977 editions....	1	2	3	5	7	9
1979 editions (68 pgs.)	1	2	3	5	7	9

NOTE: *Above giveaways available with purchase of $45.00 in merchandise. Used as a reading skills aid for small children.*

COMMANDMENTS OF GOD
Catechetical Guild: 1954, 1958

	GD	VG	FN	VF	VF/NM	NM-
300-Same contents in both editions; diff-c	5	10	15	24	30	34

COMPLIMENTARY COMICS
Sales Promotion Publ.: No date (1950's) (Giveaway)

	GD	VG	FN	VF	VF/NM	NM-
1-Strongman by Powell, 3 stories	8	16	24	40	50	60

CONAN
Dark Horse Comics: May, 2006 (Free Comic Book Day giveaway)

	GD	VG	FN	VF	VF/NM	NM-
...: FCBD 2006 Special (5/06) Paul Lee-a; flip book with Star Wars FCBD 2006 Special						2.50

COURTNEY CRUMRIN & THE NIGHT THINGS
Oni Press: 2003

	GD	VG	FN	VF	VF/NM	NM-
Free Comic Book Day Edition (5/03) Naifeh-s/a						2.50

CRACKAJACK FUNNIES (Giveaway)
Malto-Meal: 1937 (Full size, soft-c, full color, 32 pgs.)(Before No. 1?)

	GD	VG	FN	VF	VF/NM	NM-
nn-Features Dan Dunn, G-Man, Speed Bolton, Buck Jones, The Nebbs, Clyde Beatty, Freckles, Major Hoople, Wash Tubbs	83	166	249	523	887	1250

CROSLEY'S HOUSE OF FUN (Also see Tee and Vee Crosley...)
Crosley Div. AVCO Mfg. Corp.: 1950 (Giveaway, paper cover, 32 pgs.)

	GD	VG	FN	VF	VF/NM	NM-
nn-Strips revolve around Crosley appliances	5	10	15	22	26	30

CSI: CRIME SCENE INVESTIGATION
IDW Publishing: July, 2004 (Free Comic Book Day edition)

	GD	VG	FN	VF	VF/NM	NM-
Previews CSI: Bad Rap; The Shield: Spotlight; 24: One Shot; and 30 Days of Night						2.50

DAGWOOD SPLITS THE ATOM (Also see Topix V8#4)
King Features Syndicate: 1949 (Science comic with King Features characters) (Giveaway)

	GD	VG	FN	VF	VF/NM	NM-
nn-Half comic, half text; Popeye, Olive Oyl, Henry, Mandrake, Little King, Katzenjammer Kids app.	9	18	27	50	65	80

DAISY COMICS (Daisy Air Rifles)
Eastern Color Printing Co.: Dec, 1936 (5-1/4x7-1/2")

	GD	VG	FN	VF	VF/NM	NM-
nn-Joe Palooka, Buck Rogers (2 pgs. from Famous Funnies No. 18, 1st full cover app.), Napoleon Flying to Fame, Butty & Fally	33	66	99	192	309	425

DAISY LOW OF THE GIRL SCOUTS
Girl Scouts of America: 1954, 1965 (16 pgs., paper-c)

	GD	VG	FN	VF	VF/NM	NM-
1954-Story of Juliette Gordon Low	5	10	15	22	26	30
1965	2	4	6	9	12	15

DAN CURTIS GIVEAWAYS
Western Publishing Co.:1974 (3x6", 24 pgs., reprints)

	GD	VG	FN	VF	VF/NM	NM-
1-Dark Shadows	3	6	9	16	22	28
2,6-Star Trek	3	6	9	16	22	28
3,4,7-9: 3-The Twilight Zone. 4-Ripley's Believe It or Not! 7-The Occult Files of Dr. Spektor. 8-Dagar the Invincible. 9-Grimm's Ghost Stories	2	4	6	10	14	18
5-Turok, Son of Stone (partial-r/Turok #78)	3	6	9	16	22	28

DANNY KAYE'S BAND FUN BOOK
H & A Selmer: 1959 (Giveaway)

	GD	VG	FN	VF	VF/NM	NM-
nn	7	14	21	35	43	50

DAREDEVIL
Marvel Comics Group: 1993

	GD	VG	FN	VF	VF/NM	NM-
...Vs. Vapora 1 (Engineering Show Giveaway, 16 pg.) - Intro Vapora						6.00

DAVY CROCKETT (TV)
Dell Publishing Co.

	GD	VG	FN	VF	VF/NM	NM-
...Christmas Book (no date, 16 pgs., paper-c)-Sears giveaway	6	12	18	31	38	45
...Safety Trails (1955, 16pgs, 3-1/4x7")-Cities Service giveaway	8	16	24	40	50	60

DAVY CROCKETT
Charlton Comics

	GD	VG	FN	VF	VF/NM	NM-
Hunting With... nn ('55, 16 pgs.)-Ben Franklin Store giveaway (Publ.-S. Rose)	5	10	15	24	30	35

DAVY CROCKETT
Walt Disney Prod.: (1955, 16 pgs., 5x7-1/4", slick, photo-c)

	GD	VG	FN	VF	VF/NM	NM-
...In the Raid at Piney Creek-American Motors giveaway	8	16	24	40	50	60

DC SAMPLER
DC Comics: nn (#1) 1983 - No. 3, 1984 (36 pgs.; 6 1/2" x 10", giveaway)

	GD	VG	FN	VF	VF/NM	NM-
nn(#1) -3: nn-Wraparound-c, previews upcoming issues. 3-Kirby-a						6.00

DC SPOTLIGHT
DC Comics: 1985 (50th anniversary special) (giveaway)

	GD	VG	FN	VF	VF/NM	NM-
1-Includes profiles on Batman:The Dark Knight & Watchmen						5.00

DEATH JR. HALLOWEEN SPECIAL
Image Comics: Oct, 2006 (8-1/2"x 5-1/2", Halloween giveaway)

	GD	VG	FN	VF	VF/NM	NM-
nn-Guy Davis-a/Joe Morrisey-s; wraparound-c						2.50

DENNIS THE MENACE
Hallden (Fawcett)

	GD	VG	FN	VF	VF/NM	NM-
...& Dirt ('59)-Soil Conservation giveaway; r-# 36; Wiseman-c/a	2	4	6	13	18	22
...& Dirt ('68)-reprints '59 edition	2	4	6	8	10	12
...Away We Go('70)-Caladryl giveaway	1	3	4	6	8	10
...Coping with Family Stress-giveaway	1	3	4	6	8	10
...Takes a Poke at Poison('61)-Food & Drug Admin. giveaway; Wiseman-c/a	2	4	6	8	10	12
...Takes a Poke at Poison-Revised 1/66, 11/70	1	2	3	5	6	8
...Takes a Poke at Poison-Revised 1972, 1974, 1977, 1981	1	2	3	4	5	7

DESERT DAWN
E.C./American Museum of Natural History: 1935 (paper-c)
nn-Johnny Jackrabbit stars. Three known copies: A Fair copy (brittle) sold for $657 in 2007. A GD+ copy (brittle) sold for $2300 in 2005. Another Fair copy (brittle) sold for $690 in 2004

DETECTIVE COMICS (Also see other Batman titles)
National Periodical Publications/DC Comics

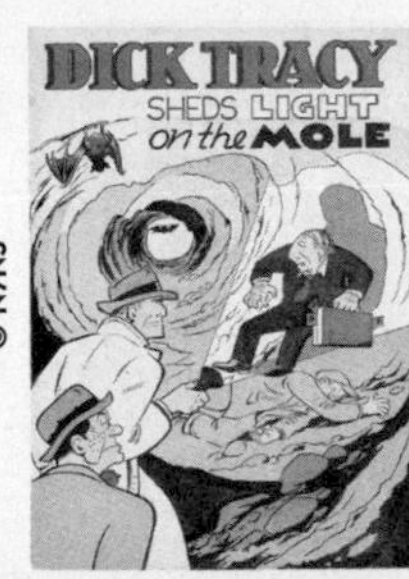

Dick Tracy Sheds Light on the Mole © NYNS

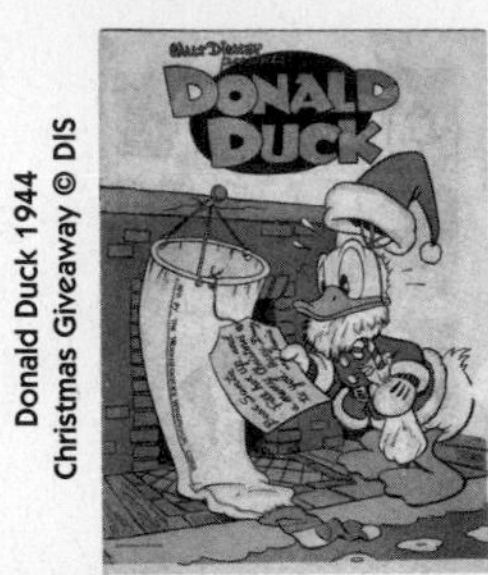

Donald Duck 1944 Christmas Giveaway © DIS

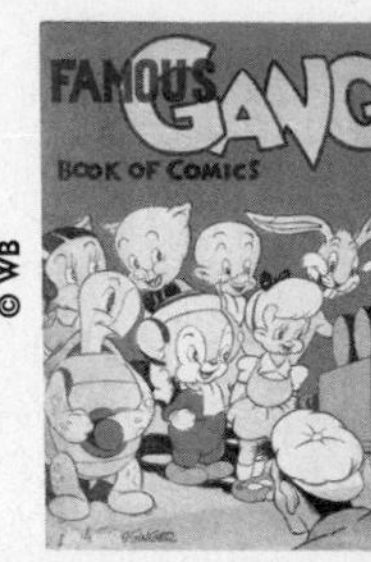

Famous Gang Book of Comics © WB

GD 2.0 | VG 4.0 | FN 6.0 | VF 8.0 | VF/NM 9.0 | NM- 9.2

27 (1984)-Oreo Cookies giveaway (32 pgs., paper-c) r-/Det. #27,#38 & Batman #1 (1st Joker) 5 10 15 30 48 65
38 (1995) Blockbuster Video edition; reprints 1st Robin app. 3.00
38 (1997) Toys R Us edition 3.00
359 (1997) Toys R Us edition; reprints 1st Batgirl app. 3.00
373 (1997, 6 1/4" x 4") Warner Brothers Home Video 3.00

DEVIL'S DUE FREE COMIC BOOK DAY
Devil's Due Publ.: May, 2005 (Free Comic Book Day giveaway)
nn-Short stories of G.I. Joe, Defex and Darkstalkers; Darkstalkers flip cover 2.50

DICK TRACY GIVEAWAYS
1939 - 1958; 1990
Buster Brown Shoes Giveaway (1940s?, 36 pgs. in color); 1938-39-r by Gould 30 60 90 174 280 385
Gillmore Giveaway (See Superbook)
...Hatful of Fun (No date, 1950-52, 32pgs.; 8-1/2x10")-Dick Tracy hat promotion; Dick Tracy games, magic tricks. Miller Bros. premium 15 30 45 90 140 190
Motorola Giveaway (1953)-Reprints Harvey Comics Library #2; "The Case of the Sparkle Plenty TV Mystery" 7 14 21 37 46 55
Original Dick Tracy by Chester Gould, The (Aug, 1990, 16 pgs., 5-1/2x8-1/2")-Gladstone Publ.; Bread Giveaway 1 3 4 6 8 10
Popped Wheat Giveaway (1947, 16 pgs. in color)-1940-r; Sig Feuchtwanger Publ.; Gould-a 4 8 12 18 22 25
...Presents the Family Fun Book; Tip Top Bread Giveaway, no date or number (1940, Fawcett Publ., 16 pgs. in color)-Spy Smasher, Ibis, Lance O'Casey app. 45 90 135 279 465 650
Same as above but without app. of heroes & Dick Tracy on cover only 14 28 42 82 121 160
Service Station Giveaway (1958, 16 pgs. in color)(regular size, slick cover)-Harvey Info. Press 5 10 14 20 24 28
Shoe Store Giveaway (Weatherbird and Triangle Stores)(1939, 16 pgs.)-Gould-a 14 28 42 76 108 140

DICK TRACY SHEDS LIGHT ON THE MOLE
Western Printing Co.: 1949 (16 pgs.) (Ray-O-Vac Flashlights giveaway)
nn-Not by Gould 8 16 24 40 50 60

DICK WINGATE OF THE U.S. NAVY
Superior Publ./Toby Press: 1951; 1953 (no month)
nn-U.S. Navy giveaway 5 10 15 24 30 35
1(1953, Toby)-Reprints nn issue? (same-c) 5 10 14 20 24 28

DIG 'EM
Kellogg's Sugar Smacks Giveaway: 1973 (2-3/8x6", 16 pgs.)
nn-4 different issues 1 3 4 6 8 10

DOC CARTER VD COMICS
Health Publications Institute, Raleigh, N. C. (Giveaway): 1949 (16 pgs. in color) (Paper-c)
nn 18 36 54 107 169 230

DONALD AND MICKEY MERRY CHRISTMAS (Formerly Famous Gang Book Of Comics)
K. K. Publ./Firestone Tire & Rubber Co.: 1943 - 1949 (Giveaway, 20 pgs.)
Put out each Christmas; 1943 issue titled "Firestone Presents Comics" (Disney)
1943-Donald Duck-r/WDC&S #32 by Carl Barks 77 154 231 481 816 1150
1944-Donald Duck-r/WDC&S #35 by Barks 73 146 219 460 780 1100
1945- "Donald Duck's Best Christmas", 8 pgs. Carl Barks; intro. & 1st app. Grandma Duck in comic books 110 220 330 693 1172 1650
1946-Donald Duck in "Santa's Stormy Visit", 8 pgs. Carl Barks 75 150 225 473 799 1125
1947-Donald Duck in "Three Good Little Ducks", 8 pgs. Carl Barks 75 150 225 473 799 1125
1948-Donald Duck in "Toyland", 8 pgs. Carl Barks 75 150 225 473 799 1125
1949-Donald Duck in "New Toys", 8 pgs. Barks 70 140 210 441 746 1050

DONALD DUCK
K. K. Publications: 1944 (Christmas giveaway, paper-c, 16 pgs.)(2 versions)
nn-Kelly cover reprint 93 186 279 586 993 1400

DONALD DUCK AND THE RED FEATHER
Red Feather Giveaway: 1948 (8-1/2x11", 4 pgs., B&W)
nn 19 38 57 112 176 240

DONALD DUCK IN "THE LITTERBUG"
Keep America Beautiful: 1963 (5x7-1/4", 16 pgs., soft-c) (Disney giveaway)
nn 5 10 15 30 48 65

DONALD DUCK "PLOTTING PICNICKERS" (See Frito-Lay Giveaway)

DONALD DUCK'S SURPRISE PARTY
Walt Disney Productions: 1948 (16 pgs.) (Giveaway for Icy Frost Twins Ice Cream Bars)
nn-(Rare)-Kelly-c/a 253 506 759 1594 2697 3800

DOT AND DASH AND THE LUCKY JINGLE PIGGIE
Sears Roebuck Co.: 1942 (Christmas giveaway, 12 pgs.)
nn-Contains a war stamp album and a punch out Jingle Piggie bank 11 22 33 64 90 115

DOUBLE TALK (Also see Two-Faces)
Feature Publications: No date (1962?) (32 pgs., full color, slick-c)
Christian Anti-Communism Crusade (Giveaway)
nn-Sickle with blood-c 15 30 45 90 140 190

DRUMMER BOY AT GETTYSBURG
Eastern National Park & Monument Association: 1976
nn-Fred Ray-a 3 6 9 14 20 25

DUMBO (Walt Disney's..., The Flying Elephant)
Weatherbird Shoes/Ernest Kern Co.(Detroit)/ Wieboldt's (Chicago): 1941 (K.K. Publ. Giveaway)
nn-16 pgs., 9x10" (Rare) 43 86 129 267 446 625
nn-52 pgs., 5-1/2x8-1/2", slick cover in color; B&W interior; half text, half reprints 4-Color No. 17 (Dept. store) 23 46 69 137 221 300

DUMBO WEEKLY
Walt Disney Prod.: 1942 (Premium supplied by Diamond D-X Gas Stations)
1 48 96 144 298 499 700
2-16 15 30 45 90 140 190
Binder only 300
NOTE: *A cover and binder came separate at gas stations. Came with membership card.*

EAT RIGHT TO WORK AND WIN
Swift & Company: 1942 (16 pgs.) (Giveaway)
Blondie, Henry, Flash Gordon by Alex Raymond, Toots & Casper, Thimble Theatre(Popeye), Tillie the Toiler, The Phantom, The Little King, & Bringing up Father - original strips just for this book -(in daily strip form which shows what foods we should eat and why) 35 70 105 200 325 450

EC SAMPLER - FREE COMIC BOOK DAY
Gemstone Publishing: May, 2008
Reprinted stories with restored color from Weird Science #6, Two-Fisted Tales #22, Crypt of Terror #17, Shock Suspenstories #6 2.50

EDWARD'S SHOES GIVEAWAY
Edward's Shoe Store: 1954 (Has clown on cover)
Contains comic with new cover. Many combinations possible. Contents determines price, 50-60 percent of original. (Similar to Comics From Weatherbird & Free Comics to You)

ELSIE THE COW
D. S. Publishing Co.
Borden's cheese comic picture bk ("40, giveaway) 19 38 57 109 180 250
Borden Milk Giveaway-(16 pgs., nn) (3 ishs, 1957) 14 28 42 81 118 155
Elsie's Fun Book(1950; Borden Milk) 14 28 42 81 118 155
Everyday Birthday Fun With... (1957; 20 pgs.)(100th Anniversary); Kubert-a 14 28 42 81 118 155

ESCAPE FROM FEAR
Planned Parenthood of America: 1956, 1962, 1969 (Giveaway, 8 pgs., color) (On birth control)
1956 edition 11 22 33 60 83 105
1962 edition 4 8 12 24 37 50
1969 edition 3 6 9 14 20 25

EVEL KNIEVEL
Marvel Comics Group (Ideal Toy Corp.): 1974 (Giveaway, 20 pgs.)
nn-Contains photo on inside back-c 4 8 12 24 37 50

FAMOUS COMICS (Also see Favorite Comics)
Zain-Eppy/United Features Syndicate: No date; Mid 1930's (24 pgs., paper-c)
nn-Reprinted from 1933 & 1934 newspaper strips in color; Joe Palooka, Hairbreadth Harry, Napoleon, The Nebbs, etc. (Many different versions known) 63 126 189 397 674 950

FAMOUS FAIRY TALES
K. K. Publ. Co.: 1942; 1943 (32 pgs.); 1944 (16 pgs.) (Giveaway, soft-c)
1942-Kelly-a 40 80 120 237 384 530
1943-r-/Fairy Tale Parade No. 2,3; Kelly-a 26 52 78 154 247 340
1944-Kelly-a 23 46 69 135 218 300

FAMOUS FUNNIES -A CARNIVAL OF COMICS
Eastern Color: 1933
36 pgs., no date given, no publisher, no number; contains strip reprints of The Bungle Family, Dixie Dugan, Hairbreadth Harry, Joe Palooka, Keeping Up With the Jones, Mutt & Jeff, Reg'lar Fellers, S'Matter Pop, Strange As It Seems, and others. This book was sold by M. C. Gaines to Wheatena, Malt-O-Milk, John Wanamaker, Kinney Shoe Stores, & others to be given away as premiums and radio giveaways (1933). Originally came with a mailing envelope. 800 1600 2400 4800 8900 13,000

FAMOUS GANG BOOK OF COMICS (Becomes Donald & Mickey Merry Christmas 1943 on)
Firestone Tire & Rubber Co.: Dec, 1942 (Christmas giveaway, 32 pgs., paper-c)
nn-(Rare)-Porky Pig, Bugs Bunny, Mary Jane & Sniffles, Elmer Fudd; r/Looney Tunes

Fawcett Miniatures - Delecta of the Planets © FAW

Forest Fire © Commercial Comics

Frito-Lay Giveaways © DIS

GD 2.0 VG 4.0 FN 6.0 VF 8.0 VF/NM 9.0 NM- 9.2

70 140 210 441 746 1050

FANTASTIC FOUR
Marvel Comics
nn (1981, 32 pgs.) Young Model Builders Club 2 4 6 8 10 12
Vol. 3 #60 Baltimore Comic Book Show (10/02, newspaper supplement) 200,000 copies were distributed to Baltimore Sun home subscribers to promote Baltimore Comic Con 3.00

FATHER OF CHARITY
Catechetical Guild Giveaway: No date (32 pgs.; paper cover)
nn 5 10 15 24 29 34

FAVORITE COMICS (Also see Famous Comics)
Grocery Store Giveaway (Diff. Corp.) (detergent): 1934 (36 pgs.)
Book 1-The Nebbs, Strange As It Seems, Napoleon, Joe Palooka, Dixie Dugan, S'Matter Pop, Hairbreadth Harry, etc. reprints 100 200 300 630 1065 1500
Book 2,3 62 124 186 391 658 925

FAWCETT MINIATURES (See Mighty Midget)
Fawcett Publications: 1946 (3-3/4x5", 12-24 pgs.) (Wheaties giveaways)
Captain Marvel "And the Horn of Plenty"; Bulletman story 16 32 48 94 147 200
Captain Marvel "& the Raiders From Space"; Golden Arrow story 16 32 48 94 147 200
Captain Marvel Jr. "The Case of the Poison Press!" Bulletman story 16 32 48 94 147 200
Delecta of the Planets; C. C. Beck art; B&W inside; 12 pgs.; 3 printing variations (coloring) exist 21 42 63 125 200 275

FEARLESS FOSDICK
Capp Enterprises Inc.: 1951
...& The Case of The Red Feather 6 12 18 27 33 38

FIGHT FOR FREEDOM
National Assoc. of Mfgrs./General Comics: 1949, 1951 (Giveaway, 16 pgs.)
nn-Dan Barry-c/a; used in POP, pg. 102 6 12 18 31 38 45

FIRE AND BLAST
National Fire Protection Assoc.: 1952 (Giveaway, 16 pgs., paper-c)
nn-Mart Baily A-Bomb-c; about fire prevention 15 30 45 84 127 170

FIRE CHIEF AND THE SAFE OL' FIREFLY, THE
National Board of Fire Underwriters: 1952 (16 pgs.) (Safety brochure given away at schools) (produced by American Visuals Corp.)(Eisner)
nn-(Rare) Eisner-c/a 41 82 123 256 428 600

FLASH, THE
DC Comics
nn-(1990) Brochure for CBS TV series 4.00
The Flash Comes to a Standstill (1981, General Foods giveaway, 8 pages, 3-1/2 x 6-3/4", oblong) 2 4 6 9 12 15

FLASH COMICS (Also see Captain Marvel and Funny Stuff)
National Periodical Publications: 1946 (6-1/2x8-1/4", 32 pgs.) (Wheaties Giveaway)
nn-Johnny Thunder, Ghost Patrol, The Flash & Kubert Hawkman app.; Irwin Hasen-c/a 260 520 1200 - - -
NOTE: *All known copies were taped to Wheaties boxes and are never found in mint condition. Copies with light tape residue bring the listed prices in all grades*

FLASH FORCE 2000
DC Comics: 1984
1-5 5.00

FLASH GORDON
Dell Publishing Co.: 1943 (20 pgs.)
Macy's Giveaway-(Rare); not by Raymond 60 120 180 378 639 900

FLASH GORDON
Harvey Comics: 1951 (16 pgs. in color, regular size, paper-c) (Gordon Bread giveaway)
1,2: 1-r/strips 10/24/37 - 2/6/38. 2-r/strips 7/14/40 - 10/6/40; Reprints by Raymond each.... 2 4 6 10 14 18
NOTE: *Most copies have brittle edges.*

FLOOD RELIEF
Malibu Comics (Ultraverse): Jan, 1994 (36 pgs.)(Ordered thru mail w/$5.00 to Red Cross)
1-Hardcase, Prime & Prototype app. 6.00

FOREST FIRE (Also see The Blazing Forest and Smokey Bear)
American Forestry Assn.(Commerical Comics): 1949 (dated-1950) (16 pgs., paper-c)
nn-Intro/1st app. Smokey The Forest Fire Preventing Bear; created by Rudy Wendelein; Wendelein/Sparling-a; 'Carter Oil Co.' on back-c of original 17 34 51 100 158 215

FOREST RANGER HANDBOOK
Wrather Corp.: 1967 (5x7", 20 pgs., slick-c)
nn-With Corey Stuart & Lassie photo-c 2 4 6 13 18 22

FORGOTTEN STORY BEHIND NORTH BEACH, THE
Catechetical Guild: No date (8 pgs., paper-c)
nn 5 10 15 23 28 32

FORK IN THE ROAD
U.S. Army Recruiting Service: 1961 (16 pgs., paper-c)
nn 2 4 6 11 16 20

48 FAMOUS AMERICANS
J. C. Penney Co. (Cpr. Edwin H. Stroh): 1947 (Giveaway) (Half-size in color)
nn - Simon & Kirby-a 10 20 30 58 79 100

FOXHOLE ON YOUR LAWN
No Publisher: No date
nn-Charles Biro art 4 7 10 14 17 20

FRANKIE LUER'S SPACE ADVENTURES
Luer Packing Co.: 1955 (5x7", 36 pgs., slick-c)
nn - With Davey Rocket 4 8 12 17 21 24

FREDDY
Charlton Comics
Schiff's Shoes Presents... #1 (1959)-Giveaway 4 7 10 14 17 20

FREE COMICS TO YOU FROM... (name of shoe store) (Has clown on cover & another with a rabbit) (Like comics from Weather Bird & Edward's Shoes)
Shoe Store Giveaway: Circa 1956, 1960-61
Contains a comic bound with new cover - several combinations possible; some Harvey titles known. Contents determine price.

FREEDOM TRAIN
Street & Smith Publications: 1948 (Giveaway)
nn-Powell-c w/mailer 18 36 54 103 162 220

FREIHOFER'S COMIC BOOK
All-American Comics: 1940s (7 1/2 x 10 1/4")
2nd edition-(Scarce) Cover features All-American Comics characters Ultra-Man, Hop Harrigan, Red, White and Blue and others 57 114 171 359 605 850

FRIENDLY GHOST, CASPER, THE
Harvey Publications: 1967 (16 pgs.)
American Dental Assoc. giveaway-Small size 3 6 9 17 25 32

FRITO-LAY GIVEAWAY
Frito-Lay: 1962 (3-1/4x7", soft-c, 16 pgs.) (Disney)
nn-Donald Duck "Plotting Picnickers" 5 10 15 32 51 70
nn-Ludwig Von Drake "Fish Stampede" 3 6 9 20 30 40
nn- Mickey Mouse & Goofy "Bicep Bungle" 4 8 12 22 34 45

FRONTIER DAYS
Robin Hood Shoe Store (Brown Shoe): 1956 (Giveaway)
1 4 7 10 14 17 20

FRONTIERS OF FREEDOM
Institute of Life Insurance: 1950 (Giveaway, paper cover)
nn-Dan Barry-a 8 16 24 44 57 70

FUNNIES ON PARADE (Premium)(See Toy World Funnies)
Eastern Color Printing Co.: 1933 (36 pgs., slick cover)
No date or publisher listed
nn-Contains Sunday page reprints of Mutt & Jeff, Joe Palooka, Hairbreadth Harry, Reg'lar Fellers, Skippy, & others (10,000 print run). This book was printed for Proctor & Gamble to be given away & came out before Famous Funnies or Century of Comics. 1000 2000 3000 6000 10,500 15,000

FUNNY PICTURE STORIES (Comic Pages V3#4 on)
Comics Magazine Co./Centaur Publications
Laundry giveaway (16-20 pgs., 1930s)-slick-c 25 50 75 149 240 330

FUNNY STUFF (Also see Captain Marvel & Flash Comics)
National Periodical Publications (Wheaties Giveaway): 1946 (6-1/2x8-1/4")
nn-(Scarce)-Dodo & the Frog, Three Mouseketeers, etc.; came taped to Wheaties box; never found in better than fine 170 340 520 – – –

FUTURE COP: L.A.P.D. (Electronic Arts video game)
DC Comics (WildStorm): 1998
nn-Ron Lim-a/Dave Johnson-c 2.50

FUTURE SHOCK
Image Comics: 2006 (Free Comic Book Day giveaway)
...: FCBD 2006 Edition; Spawn, Invincible, Savage Dragon & others short stories 2.50

GABBY HAYES WESTERN (Movie star)

Gulf Funny Weekly #356 © Gulf Oil Co.

Hellboy: Free Comic Book Day © Mike Mignola

If The Devil Would Talk © CG

	GD 2.0	VG 4.0	FN 6.0	VF 8.0	VF/NM 9.0	NM- 9.2

Fawcett Publications
Quaker Oats Giveaway nn's(#1-5, 1951, 2-1/2x7") (Kagran Corp.)-...In Tracks of Guilt, ...In the Fence Post Mystery, ...In the Accidental Sherlock, ...In the Frame-Up, ...In the Double Cross Brand known 10 20 30 54 72 90
Mailing Envelope (has illo of Gabby on front) 10 20 30 54 72 90

GARY GIBSON COMICS (Donut club membership)
National Dunking Association: 1950 (Included in donut box with pin and card)
1-Western soft-c, 16 pgs.; folded into the box 5 10 14 20 24 28

GENE AUTRY COMICS
Dell Publishing Co.
...Adventure Comics And Play-Fun Book ('47)-32 pgs., 8x6-1/2"; games, comics, magic (Pillsbury premium) 35 70 105 208 334 460
Quaker Oats Giveaway(1950)-2-1/2x6-3/4"; 5 different versions; "Death Card Gang", "Phantoms of the Cave", "Riddle of Laughing Mtn.", "Secret of Lost Valley", "Bond of the Broken Arrow" (came in wrapper) each... 14 28 42 82 121 160
Mailing Envelope (has illo. of Gene on front) 14 28 42 82 121 160
3-D Giveaway(1953)-Pocket-size; 5 different 14 28 42 82 121 160
Mailing Envelope (no art on front) 10 20 30 58 79 100

GENE AUTRY TIM (Formerly Tim) (Becomes Tim in Space)
Tim Stores: 1950 (Half-size) (B&W Giveaway)
nn-Several issues (All Scarce) 19 38 57 109 172 235

GENERAL FOODS SUPER-HEROES
DC Comics: 1979, 1980
1-4 (1979), 1-4 (1980) each... 12.00

G. I. COMICS (Also see Jeep & Overseas Comics)
Giveaways: 1945 - No. 73?, 1946 (Distributed to U. S. Armed Forces)
1-73-Contains Prince Valiant by Foster, Blondie, Smilin' Jack, Mickey Finn, Terry & the Pirates, Donald Duck, Alley Oop, Moon Mullins & Capt. Easy strip reprints (at least 73 issues known to exist) 8 16 24 42 54 65

GOLDEN ARROW
Fawcett Publications
...Well Known Comics (1944; 12 pgs.; 8-1/2x10-1/2"; paper-c; glued binding)- Bestmaid/ Samuel Lowe giveaway; printed in green 10 20 30 54 72 90

GOLDILOCKS & THE THREE BEARS
K. K. Publications: 1943 (Giveaway)
nn 13 26 39 74 105 135

GREAT PEOPLE OF GENESIS, THE
David C. Cook Publ. Co.: No date (Religious giveaway, 64 pgs.)
nn-Reprint/Sunday Pix Weekly 5 10 15 23 28 32

GREAT SACRAMENT, THE
Catechetical Guild: 1953 (Giveaway, 36 pgs.)
nn 5 10 15 22 26 30

GRENADA
Commercial Comics Co.: 1983 (Giveaway produced by the CIA)
1-Air dropped over Grenada during the 1983 invasion 30.00

GRIT (YOU'VE GOT TO HAVE...)
GRIT Publishing Co.: 1959
nn-GRIT newspaper sales recruitment comic; Schaffenberger-a. Later version has altered artwork 5 10 15 22 26 30

GULF FUNNY WEEKLY (Gulf Comic Weekly No. 1-4)(See Standard Oil Comics)
Gulf Oil Company (Giveaway): 1933 - No. 422, 5/23/41 (in full color; 4 pgs.; tabloid size to 2/3/39; 2/10/39 on, regular comic book size)(early issues undated)
1 60 120 180 378 639 900
2-5 27 54 81 158 254 350
6-30 15 30 45 94 147 200
31-100 14 28 42 76 108 140
101-196 9 18 27 52 69 85
197-Wings Winfair begins(1/29/37); by Fred Meagher beginning in 1938 22 44 66 129 207 285
198-300 (Last tabloid size) 14 28 42 80 115 150
301-350 (Regular size) 9 18 27 50 65 80
351-422 8 16 24 40 50 60

GULLIVER'S TRAVELS
Macy's Department Store: 1939, small size
nn-Christmas giveaway 14 28 42 76 108 140

GUN THAT WON THE WEST, THE
Winchester-Western Division & Olin Mathieson Chemical Corp.: 1956 (Giveaway, 24 pgs.)
nn-Painted-c 5 10 15 24 30 35

HAPPINESS AND HEALING FOR YOU (Also see Oral Roberts'...)
Commercial Comics: 1955 (36 pgs., slick cover) (Oral Roberts Giveaway)
nn 9 18 27 52 69 85
NOTE: *The success of this book prompted Oral Roberts to go into the publishing business himself to produce his own material.*

HAPPY TOOTH
DC Comics: 1996
1 3.00

HAWKMAN - THE SKY'S THE LIMIT
DC Comics: 1981 (General Foods giveaway, 8 pages, 3-1/2 x 6-3/4", oblong)
nn 2 4 6 9 12 15

HAWTHORN-MELODY FARMS DAIRY COMICS
Everybody's Publishing Co.: No date (1950's) (Giveaway)
nn-Cheerie Chick, Tuffy Turtle, Robin Koo Koo, Donald & Longhorn Legends 2 4 6 8 11 14

HELLBOY
Dark Horse Comics: Apr, 2008
... : Free Comic Book Day; Three short stories; Mignola-c; art by Fegredo, Davis, Azaceta 2.50

HENRY ALDRICH COMICS (TV)
Dell Publishing Co.
Giveaway (16 pgs., soft-c, 1951)-Capehart radio 3 6 9 17 25 32

HERE IS SANTA CLAUS
Goldsmith Publishing Co. (Kann's in Washington, D.C.): 1930s (16 pgs., 8 in color) (stiff paper covers)
nn 12 24 36 69 97 125

HERE'S HOW AMERICA'S CARTOONISTS HELP TO SELL U.S. SAVINGS BONDS
Harvey Comics: 1950? (16 pgs., giveaway, paper cover)
Contains: Joe Palooka, Donald Duck, Archie, Kerry Drake, Red Ryder, Blondie & Steve Canyon 20 40 60 115 183 250

HISTORY OF GAS
American Gas Assoc.: Mar, 1947 (Giveaway, 16 pgs.)
nn-Miss Flame narrates 6 12 18 29 36 42

HOME DEPOT, SAFETY HEROES
Marvel Comics.: Oct, 2005 (Giveaway)
nn-Spider-Man and the Fantastic Four on the cover; Olliffe-a/c; Roseman-s 2.50

HONEYBEE BIRDWHISTLE AND HER PET PEPI (Introducing...)
Newspaper Enterprise Assoc.: 1969 (Giveaway, 24 pgs., B&W, slick cover)
nn-Contains Freckles newspaper strips with a short biography of Henry Fornhals (artist) & Fred Fox (writer) of the strip 4 8 12 28 44 60

HOODS UP
Fram Corp.: 1953 (15¢, distributed to service station owners, 16 pgs.)
1-(Very Rare; only 2 known); Eisner-c/a in all (a CGC 9.0 copy sold for $1840 in 2006)
2-6-(Very Rare; only 1 known of #3, 2 known of #2,4) 48 96 144 298 499 700
NOTE: *Convertible Connie gives tips for service stations, selling Fram oil filters.*

HOPALONG CASSIDY
Fawcett Publications
Grape Nuts Flakes giveaway (1950,9x6") 14 28 42 82 121 160
...& the Mad Barber (1951 Bond Bread giveaway)-7x5"; used in **SOTI**, pgs. 308,309 19 38 57 112 176 240
...Meets the Brend Brothers Bandits (1951 Bond Bread giveaway, color, paper-c, 16 pgs., 3-1/2x7")- Fawcett Publ. 10 20 30 54 72 90
...Strange Legacy (1951 Bond Bread giveaway) 10 20 30 54 72 90
White Tower Giveaway (1946, 16pgs., paper-c) 10 20 30 58 79 100

HOPELESS SAVAGES
Oni Press: May, 2002 (B&W)
Free Comic Book Day giveaway-Reprints #1 with "Free Comic Book Day" banner on-c 2.50

HOPPY THE MARVEL BUNNY (WELL KNOWN COMICS)
Fawcett Publications: 1944 (8-1/2x10-1/2", paper-c)
Bestmaid/Samuel Lowe (printed in red or blue) 10 20 30 56 76 95

HOT STUFF, THE LITTLE DEVIL
Harvey Publications (Illustrated Humor):1963
Shoestore Giveaway 4 8 12 22 34 45

HOW KIDS ENJOY NEW YORK
American Airlines: 1966 (Giveaway, 40 pgs., 4x9")
nn-Includes 8 color pages by Bob Kane featuring a tour of New York and his studio (a VG copy sold for $180 and a FN+ sold for $250 in 2004)

HOW STALIN HOPES WE WILL DESTROY AMERICA
Joe Lowe Co. (Pictorial Media): 1951 (Giveaway, 16 pgs.)

In The Good Hands of the Rockefeller Team © Country Art Studios

Jughead Comics - Night at Geppi's Entertainment Museum FCBD Ed. © AP

Justice League Unlimited FCBD Ed. © DC

	GD 2.0	VG 4.0	FN 6.0	VF 8.0	VF/NM 9.0	NM- 9.2

nn 45 90 135 279 465 650

HURRICANE KIDS, THE (Also See Magic Morro, The Owl, Popular Comics #45)
R.S. Callender: 1941 (Giveaway, 7-1/2x5-1/4", soft-c)
nn-Will Ely-a. 10 20 30 56 76 95

IF THE DEVIL WOULD TALK
Roman Catholic Catechetical Guild/Impact Publ.: 1950; 1958 (32 pgs.; paper cover; in full color)
nn-(Scarce)-About secularism (20-30 copies known to exist); very low distribution
80 160 240 504 852 1200
1958 Edition-(Impact Publ.); art & script changed to meet church criticism of earlier edition; 80 plus copies known to exist 26 52 78 154 247 340
Black & White version of nn edition; small size; only 4 known copies exist
32 64 96 186 298 410
NOTE: *The original edition of this book was printed and killed by the Guild's board of directors. It is believed that a very limited number of copies were distributed. The 1958 version was a complete bomb with very limited, if any, circulation. In 1979, 11 original, 4 1958 reprints, and 4 B&W's surfaced from the Guild's old files in St. Paul, Minnesota.*

IMAGE COMICS SUMMER SPECIAL
Image Comics: July, 2004 (Free Comic Book Day giveaway)
1-New short stories of Spawn, Invincible, Savage Dragon and Witchblade 2.50

IN LOVE WITH JESUS
Catechetical Educational Society: 1952 (Giveaway, 36 pgs.)
nn 7 14 21 37 46 55

INTERSTATE THEATRES' FUN CLUB COMICS
Interstate Theatres: Mid 1940's (10¢ on cover) (B&W cover) (Premium)
Cover features MLJ characters looking at a copy of Top-Notch Comics, but contains an early Detective Comic on inside; many combinations possible
10 20 30 58 79 100

IN THE GOOD HANDS OF THE ROCKEFELLER TEAM
Country Art Studios: No date (paper cover, 8 pgs.)
nn-Joe Simon-a 8 16 24 42 54 65

IRON GIANT
DC Comics: 1999 (4 pages, theater giveaway)
1-Previews movie 3.00

IRON HORSE GOES TO WAR, THE
Association of American Railroads: 1960 (Giveaway, 16 pgs.)
nn-Civil War & railroads 3 6 9 14 20 25

IS THIS TOMORROW?
Catechetical Guild: 1947 (One Shot) (3 editions) (52 pgs.)
1-Theme of communists taking over the USA; (no price on cover) Used in **POP**, pg. 102 21 42 63 125 200 275
1-(10¢ on cover) 25 50 75 147 236 325
1-Has blank circle with no price on cover 27 54 81 158 254 350
Black & White advance copy titled "Confidential" (52 pgs.)-Contains script and art edited out of the color edition, including one page of extreme violence showing mob nailing a Cardinal to a door; (only two known copies). A VF+ sold in 2/08 for $3346. A NM 9.6 sold in 1/07 for $5975
NOTE: *The original color version first sold for 10 cents. Since sales were good, it was later printed as a giveaway. Approximately four million in total were printed. The two black and white copies listed plus two other versions as well as a full color untrimmed version surfaced in 1979 from the Guild's old files in St. Paul, Minnesota.*

IT'S FUN TO STAY ALIVE
National Automobile Dealers Association: 1948 (Giveaway, 16 pgs., heavy stock paper)
Featuring: Bugs Bunny, The Berrys, Dixie Dugan, Elmer, Henry, Tim Tyler, Bruce Gentry, Abbie & Slats, Joe Jinks, The Toodles, & Cokey; all art copyright 1946-48 drawn especially for this book 17 34 51 98 154 210

JACK & JILL VISIT TOYTOWN WITH ELMER THE ELF
Butler Brothers (Toytown Stores): 1949 (Giveaway, 16 pgs., paper cover)
nn 5 10 15 22 26 30

JACK ARMSTRONG (Radio)(See True Comics)
Parents' Institute: 1949
12-Premium version (distr. in Chicago only); Free printed on upper right-c; no price (Rare) 18 36 54 103 162 220

JACKIE JOYNER KERSEE IN HIGH HURDLES (Kellogg's Tony's Sports Comics)
DC Comics: 1992 (Sports Illustrated)
nn 3.00

JACKPOT OF FUN COMIC BOOK
DCA Food Ind.: 1957, giveaway
nn-Features Howdy Doody 11 22 33 64 90 115

JEEP COMICS
R. B. Leffingwell & Co.: 1945 - 1946
1-46 (Giveaways)-Strip reprints in all; Tarzan, Flash Gordon, Blondie, The Nebbs, Little Iodine, Red Ryder, Don Winslow, The Phantom, Johnny Hazard, Katzenjammer Kids; distr. to U.S. Armed Forces from 1945-1946 6 12 18 31 38 45

JINGLE BELLS CHRISTMAS BOOK
Montgomery Ward (Giveaway): 1971 (20 pgs., B&W inside, slick-c)
nn 6.00

JOAN OF ARC
Catechetical Guild (Topix) (Giveaway): No date (28 pgs., blank back-c)
nn-Ingrid Bergman photo-c; Addison Burbank-a 12 24 36 67 94 120
NOTE: *Unpublished version exists which came from the Guild's files.*

JOE PALOOKA (2nd Series)
Harvey Publications
...Body Building Instruction Book (1958 B&M Sports Toy giveaway, 16pgs., 5-1/4x7")-Origin
9 18 27 47 61 75
...Fights His Way Back (1945 Giveaway, 24 pgs.) Family Comics
15 30 45 85 130 175
...in Hi There! (1949 Red Cross giveaway, 12 pgs., 4-3/4x6")
9 18 27 50 65 80
...in It's All in the Family (1945 Red Cross giveaway, 16 pgs., regular size)
11 22 33 60 83 105

JOE THE GENIE OF STEEL
U.S. Steel Corp., Pittsburgh, PA: 1950 (16 pgs.)
nn 5 10 15 22 26 30

JOHNNY JINGLE'S LUCKY DAY
American Dairy Assoc.: 1956 (16 pgs.; 7-1/4x5-1/8") (Giveaway) (Disney)
nn 5 10 15 24 30 35

JO-JOY (The Adventures of...)
W. T. Grant Dept. Stores: 1945 - 1953 (Christmas gift comic, 16 pgs., 7-1/16x10-1/4")
1945-53 issues 6 12 18 29 36 42

JOLLY CHRISTMAS BOOK (See Christmas Journey Through Space)
Promotional Publ. Co.: 1951; 1954; 1955 (36 pgs.; 24 pgs.)
1951-(Woolworth giveaway)-slightly oversized; no slick cover; Marv Levy-c/a
7 14 21 37 46 55
1954-(Hot Shoppes giveaway)-regular size-reprints 1951 issue; slick cover added; 24 pgs.; no ads 6 12 18 31 38 45
1955-(J. M. McDonald Co. giveaway)-reg. size 6 12 18 28 34 40

JOURNEY OF DISCOVERY WITH MARK STEEL (See Mark Steel)

JUGHEAD COMICS. NIGHT AT GEPPI'S ENTERTAINMENT MUSEUM
Archie Comic Publ. Inc: 2008
Free Comic Book Day giveaway - New story; Archie gang visits GEM; Steve Geppi app. 2.50

JUMPING JACKS PRESENTS THE WHIZ KIDS
Jumping Jacks Stores giveaway: 1978 (In 3-D) with glasses (4 pgs.)
nn 6.00

JUNGLE BOOK FUN BOOK, THE (Disney)
Baskin Robbins: 1978
nn-Ice Cream giveaway 2 4 6 9 12 15

JUSTICE LEAGUE ADVENTURES (Based on Cartoon Network series)
DC Comics: May, 2002
Free Comic Book Day giveaway-Reprints #1 with "Free Comic Book Day" banner on-c 2.50

JUSTICE LEAGUE OF AMERICA
DC Comics: 1999 (included in Justice League of America Monopoly game); 2007
nn - Reprints 1st app. in Brave and the Bold #28 2.50
Free Comic Book Day giveaway-Reprints #0 with "Free Comic Book Day" banner on-c 2.50

JUSTICE LEAGUE UNLIMITED (Based on Cartoon Network series)
DC Comics: May, 2006
Free Comic Book Day giveaway-Reprints #1 with "Free Comic Book Day" banner on-c 2.25

KASCO KOMICS
Kasko Grainfeed (Giveaway): 1945; No. 2, 1949 (Regular size, paper-c)
1(1945)-Similar to Katy Keene; Bill Woggon-a; 28 pgs.; 6-7/8x9-7/8"
17 34 51 98 154 210
2(1949)-Woggon-c/a 13 26 39 74 105 135

KATY AND KEN VISIT SANTA WITH MISTER WISH
S. S. Kresge Co. : 1948 (Giveaway, 16 pgs., paper-c)
nn 6 12 18 29 36 42

KELLOGG'S CINNAMON MINI-BUNS SUPER-HEROES
DC Comics: 1993 (4 1/4" x 2 3/4")
4 editions: Flash, Justice League America, Superman, Wonder Woman and the Star Riders each..... 4.00

KERRY DRAKE DETECTIVE CASES

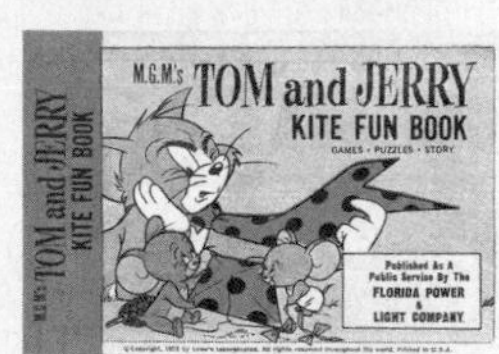

Kite Fun Book 1958 © H-B

Labor Is A Partner © CG

Little Klinker © Little Klinker Ventures

GD VG FN VF VF/NM NM-
2.0 4.0 6.0 8.0 9.0 9.2

Publisher's Syndicate
...in the Case of the Sleeping City-(1951)-16 pg. giveaway for armed forces; paper cover 6 12 18 29 36 42

KEY COMICS
Key Clothing Co./Peterson Clothing: 1951 - 1956 (32 pgs.) (Giveaway)
Contains a comic from different publishers bound with new cover. Cover changed each year. Many combinations possible. Distributed in Nebraska, Iowa, & Kansas. Contents would determine price, 40-60 percent of original.

KING JAMES "THE KING OF BASKETBALL"
DC Comics: 2004 (Promo comic for LeBron James and Powerade Flava23 sports drink)
nn - Ten different covers by various artists; 4 covers for retail, 4 for mail-in, 1 for military commissaries, and 1 general market; Damion Scott-a/Gary Phillips-s 2.50

KIRBY'S SHOES COMICS
Kirby's Shoes: 1959 (8 pgs., soft-c)
nn-Features Kirby the Golden Bear 3 5 7 10 12 14

KITE FUN BOOK
Pacific, Gas & Electric/Sou. California Edison/Florida Power & Light/ Missouri Public Service Co.: 1952 - 1998 (16 pgs, 5x7-1/4", soft-c)
1952-Having Fun With Kites (P.G.&E.) 12 24 36 69 97 125
1953-Pinocchio Learns About Kites (Disney) 43 86 129 267 446 625
1954-Donald Duck Tells About Kites-Fla. Power, S.C.E. & version with label issues -Barks pencils-8 pgs.; inks-7 pgs. (Rare) 280 560 840 1764 2982 4200
1954-Donald Duck Tells About Kites-P.G.&E. issue -7th page redrawn changing middle 3 panels to show P.G.&E. in story line; (All Barks-a) Scarce 227 454 681 1430 2415 3400
1955-Brer Rabbit in "A Kite Tail" (Disney) 28 56 84 162 261 360
1956-Woody Woodpecker (Lantz) 14 28 42 80 115 150
1957-Ruff and Reddy (exist?)
1958-Tom And Jerry (M.G.M.) 10 20 30 54 72 90
1959-Bugs Bunny (Warner Bros.) 5 10 15 30 48 65
1960-Porky Pig (Warner Bros.) 5 10 15 32 51 70
1960-Bugs Bunny (Warner Bros.) 5 10 15 32 51 70
1961-Huckleberry Hound (Hanna-Barbera) 6 12 18 37 59 80
1962-Yogi Bear (Hanna-Barbera) 4 8 12 28 44 60
1963-Rocky and Bullwinkle (TV)(Jay Ward) 8 16 24 52 86 120
1963-Top Cat (TV)(Hanna-Barbera) 4 8 12 28 44 60
1964-Magilla Gorilla (TV)(Hanna-Barbera) 4 8 12 26 41 55
1965-Jinks, Pixie and Dixie (TV)(Hanna-Barbera) 3 6 9 20 30 40
1965-Tweety and Sylvester (Warner); S.C.E. version with Reddy Kilowatt app. 3 6 9 14 20 25
1966-Secret Squirrel (Hanna-Barbera); S.C.E. version with Reddy Kilowatt app. 6 12 18 41 66 90
1967-Beep! Beep! The Road Runner (TV)(Warner) 3 6 9 16 23 30
1968-Bugs Bunny (Warner Bros.) 3 6 9 17 25 32
1969-Dastardly and Muttley (TV)(Hanna-Barbera) 4 8 12 26 41 55
1970-Rocky and Bullwinkle (TV)(Jay Ward) 6 12 18 37 59 80
1971-Beep! Beep! The Road Runner (TV)(Warner) 3 6 9 16 22 28
1972-The Pink Panther (TV) 3 6 9 14 19 24
1973-Lassie (TV) 3 6 9 20 30 40
1974-Underdog (TV) 3 6 9 16 23 30
1975-Ben Franklin 2 4 6 10 14 18
1976-The Brady Bunch (TV) 3 6 9 20 30 40
1977-Ben Franklin (exist?) 2 4 6 10 14 18
1977-Popeye 3 6 9 14 20 25
1978-Happy Days (TV) 3 6 9 16 23 30
1979-Eight is Enough (TV) 3 6 9 14 20 25
1980-The Waltons (TV, released in 1981) 3 6 9 14 20 25
1982-Tweety and Sylvester 2 4 6 11 16 20
1984-Smokey Bear 2 4 6 9 13 16
1986-Road Runner 2 4 6 8 11 14
1997-Thomas Edison 4.00
1998-Edison Field (Anaheim Stadium) 3.00

KNOW YOUR MASS
Catechetical Guild: No. 303, 1958 (35¢, 100 Pg. Giant) (Square binding)
303-In color 7 14 21 35 43 50

KOLYNOS PRESENTS THE WHITE GUARD
Whitehall Pharmacal Co.: 1949 (paper cover, 8 pgs.)
nn 6 12 18 27 33 38

K. O. PUNCH, THE (Also see Lucky Fights It Through)
E. C. Comics: 1948 (Educational giveaway)
nn-Feldstein-splash; Kamen-a 83 166 249 523 887 1250

KOREA MY HOME (Also see Yalta to Korea)
Johnstone and Cushing: nd (1950s)
nn-Anti-communist; Korean War 20 40 60 120 193 265

KRIM-KO KOMICS
Krim-ko Chocolate Drink: 5/18/35 - No. 6, 6/22/35; 1936 - 1939 (weekly)
1-(16 pgs., soft-c, Dairy giveaways)-Tom, Mary & Sparky Advs. by Russell Keaton, Jim Hawkins by Dick Moores, Mystery Island! by Rick Yager begin 14 28 42 76 108 140
2-6 (6/22/35) 10 20 30 56 76 95
Lola, Secret Agent; 184 issues, 4 pg. giveaways - all original stories each.... 7 14 21 37 46 55

LABOR IS A PARTNER
Catechetical Guild Educational Society: 1949 (32 pgs., paper-c)
nn-Anti-communism 20 40 60 120 193 265
Confidential Preview-(8-1/2x11", B&W, saddle stitched)-only one known copy; text varies from color version, advertises next book on secularism (If the Devil Would Talk) 25 50 75 147 236 325

LADY AND THE TRAMP IN "BUTTER LATE THAN NEVER"
American Dairy Assoc. (Premium): 1955 (16 pgs., 5x7-1/4", soft-c) (Disney)
nn 8 16 24 44 57 70

LASSIE (TV)
Dell Publ. Co
The Adventures of... nn-(Red Heart Dog Food giveaway, 1949)-16 pgs, soft-c; 1st app. Lassie in comics 32 64 96 190 305 420

LEAVE IT TO CHANCE
Image Comics: 2003
Free Comic Book Day Edition - James Robinson-s/Paul Smith-a 2.50

LEGION OF SUPER-HEROES IN THE 31ST CENTURY
DC Comics: June, 2007 (Free Comic Book Day giveaway)
1-Reprints #1 2.50

LIFE OF THE BLESSED VIRGIN
Catechetical Guild (Giveaway): 1950 (68pgs.) (square binding)
nn-Contains "The Woman of the Promise" & "Mother of Us All" rebound 7 14 21 35 43 50

LIGHTNING RACERS
DC Comics: 1989
1 4.50

LI'L ABNER (Al Capp's) (Also see Natural Disasters!)
Harvey Publ./Toby Press
...& the Creatures from Drop-Outer Space-nn (Job Corps giveaway; 36 pgs., in color) (entire book by Frank Frazetta) 22 44 66 127 204 280
...Joins the Navy (1950) (Toby Press Premium) 11 22 33 62 86 110
Al Capp by Li'l Abner (Circa 1946, nd, giveaway) Al Capp bio and his life as an amputee 11 22 33 62 86 110

LITTLE ALONZO
Macy's Dept. Store: 1938 (B&W, 5-1/2x8-1/2")(Christmas giveaway)
nn-By Ferdinand the Bull's Munro Leaf 9 18 27 50 65 80

LITTLE ARCHIE (See Archie Comics)

LITTLE DOT
Harvey Publications
Shoe store giveaway 2 4 8 12 26 41 55

LITTLE FIR TREE, THE
W. T. Grant Co. : nd (1942) (8-1/2x11") (12 pgs. with cover, color & B&W, heavy paper) (Christmas giveaway)
nn-Story by Hans Christian Anderson; 8 pg. Kelly-r/Santa Claus Funnies (not signed); X-Mas-c 90 180 270 563 957 1350

LITTLE KLINKER
Little Klinker Ventures: Nov, 1960 (20 pgs.) (slick cover) (Montgomery Ward Giveaway)
nn 2 4 6 9 13 16

LITTLE MISS SUNBEAM COMICS
Magazine Enterprises/Quality Bakers of America
Bread Giveaway 1-4(Quality Bakers, 1949-50)-14 pgs. each 6 12 18 31 38 45
Bread Giveaway (1957,61; 16pgs, reg. size) 5 10 15 24 30 35

LITTLE ORPHAN ANNIE
David McKay Publ./Dell Publishing Co.
Junior Commandos Giveaway (same-c as 4-Color #18, K.K. Publ.)(Big Shoe Store); same back cover as '47 Popped Wheat giveaway; 16 pgs; flag-c; r/strips 9/7/42-10/10/42 27 54 81 158 254 350
Popped Wheat Giveaway ('47)-16 pgs. full color; reprints strips from 5/3/40 to 6/20/40 4 8 12 18 22 25
Quaker Sparkies Giveaway (1940) 18 36 54 103 162 220

Lone Ranger in "Milk For Big Mike" © L.R. Ents.

March of Comics #8 © DIS

March of Comics #19 © K.K. Publ.

GD VG FN VF VF/NM NM-
2.0 4.0 6.0 8.0 9.0 9.2

Quaker Sparkies Giveaway (1941, full color, 20 pgs.); "LOA and the Rescue"; r/strips 4/13/39-6/21/39 & 7/6/39-7/17/39. "LOA and the Kidnappers"; r/strips 11/28/38-1/28/39 15 30 45 94 147 200
Quaker Sparkies Giveaway (1942, full color, 20 pgs.); "LOA and Mr. Gudge"; r/strips 2/13/38-3/21/38 & 4/18/37-5/30/37. "LOA and the Great Am" 15 30 45 88 137 185

LITTLE TREE THAT WASN'T WANTED, THE
W. T. Grant Co. (Giveaway): 1960, (Color, 28 pgs.)
nn-Christmas story, puzzles and games 4 8 12 22 34 45

LOADED (Also see Re-Loaded)
DC Comics: 1995 (Interplay Productions)
1-Garth Ennis-s; promotes video game 4.00

LONE RANGER, THE
Dell Publishing Co.
Cheerios Giveaways (1954, 16 pgs., 2-1/2x7", soft-c) #1- "The Lone Ranger, His Mask & How He Met Tonto". #2- "The Lone Ranger & the Story of Silver" each.... 15 30 45 85 130 175
Doll Giveaways (Gabriel Ind.)(1973, 3-1/4x5")- "The Story of The Lone Ranger," "The Carson City Bank Robbery" & "The Apache Buffalo Hunt" 2 4 6 12 16 20
How the Lone Ranger Captured Silver Book(1936)-Silvercup Bread giveaway 57 114 171 359 605 850
...In Milk for Big Mike (1955, Dairy Association giveaway), soft-c; 5x7-1/4", 16 pgs. 14 28 42 80 115 150
Legend of The Lone Ranger (1969, 16 pgs., giveaway)-Origin The Lone Ranger 4 8 12 22 34 45
Merita Bread giveaway (1954, 16 pgs., 5x7-1/4")- "How to Be a Lone Ranger Health & Safety Scout" 18 36 54 103 162 220

LONE RANGER COMICS, THE
Lone Ranger, Inc. : Book 1, 1939(inside) (shows 1938 on-c) (52 pgs. in color; regular size) (Ice cream mail order)
Book 1-(Scarce)-The first western comic devoted to a single character; not by Vallely 850 1700 2550 6000 - -
2nd version w/large full color promo poster pasted over centerfold & a smaller poster pasted over back cover; includes new additional premiums not originally offered (Rare) 928 1856 2784 6500 - -

LOONEY TUNES
DC Comics: 1991, 1998
Claritin promotional issue (1998) 2.50
Colgate mini-comic (1998) 2.50
Tyson's 1-10 (1991) 4.00

LOVE FIGHTS
Oni Press: July, 2004 (Free Comic Book Day giveaway)
1-Flip book with r/Love Fights #1 and preview of Everest Facing the Goddess 2.50

LUCKY FIGHTS IT THROUGH (Also see The K. O. Punch)
Educational Comics: 1949 (Giveaway, 16 pgs. in color, paper-c)
nn-(Very Rare)-1st Kurtzman work for E. C.; V.D. prevention 122 244 366 769 1297 1825
nn-Reprint in color (1977) 7.00
NOTE: *Subtitled "The Story of That Ignorant, Ignorant Cowboy". Prepared for Communications Materials Center, Columbia University.*

LUDWIG VON DRAKE (See Frito-Lay Giveaway)

MACO TOYS COMIC
Maco Toys/Charlton Comics: 1959 (Giveaway, 36 pgs.)
1-All military stories featuring Maco Toys 2 4 6 11 16 20

MAD MAGAZINE
DC Comics: 1997, 1999, 2008
Special Edition (1997, Tang giveaway) 2.50
Stocking Stuffer (1999) 2.50
San Diego Comic-Con Edition (2008) Watchmen parody with Fabry-a; Aragonés cartoons 2.50

MAGAZINELAND
DC Comics: 1977
nn-Kubert-c/a 3 6 9 14 19 24

MAGIC MORRO (Also see Super Comics #21, The Owl, & The Hurricane Kids)
K. K. Publications: 1941 (7-1/2 x 5-1/4", giveaway, soft-c)
nn-Ken Ernst-a. 10 20 30 58 79 100

MAGIC OF CHRISTMAS AT NEWBERRYS, THE
E. S. London: 1967 (Giveaway) (B&W, slick-c, 20 pgs.)
nn 1 3 4 6 8 10

MAJOR INAPAK THE SPACE ACE
Magazine Enterprises (Inapac Foods): 1951 (20 pgs.) (Giveaway)
1-Bob Powell-c/a 6.00
NOTE: *Many warehouse copies surfaced in 1973.*

MAMMY YOKUM & THE GREAT DOGPATCH MYSTERY
Toby Press: 1951 (Giveaway)
nn-Li'l Abner 15 30 45 88 137 185
nn-Reprint (1956) 5 10 15 22 26 30

MAN NAMED STEVENSON, A
Democratic National Committee: 1952 (20 pgs., 5 1/4 x 7")
nn 9 18 27 47 61 75

MAN OF PEACE, POPE PIUS XII
Catechetical Guild: 1950 (See Pope Pius XII... & To V2#8)
nn-All Powell-a 6 12 18 31 38 45

MAN OF STEEL BEST WESTERN
DC Comics: 1997 (Best Western hotels promo)
3-Reprints Superman's first post-Crisis meeting with Batman 4.00

MAN WHO WOULDN'T QUIT, THE
Harvey Publications Inc.: 1952 (16 pgs., paper cover)
nn-The value of voting 4 8 12 18 22 25

MARCH OF COMICS (Boys' and Girls'...#3-353)
K. K. Publications/Western Publishing Co.: 1946 - No. 488, April, 1982 (#1-4 are not numbered) (K.K. Giveaway) (Founded by Sig Feuchtwanger)
Early issues were full size, 32 pages, and were printed with and without an extra cover of slick stock, just for the advertiser. The binding was stapled if the slick cover was added; otherwise, the pages were glued together at the spine. Most 1948 - 1951 issues were full size,24 pages, pulp covers. Starting in 1952 they were half-size (with a few exceptions) and 32 pages with slick covers.1959 and later issues had only 16 pages plus covers. 1952 -1959 issues read oblong; 1960 and later issues read upright. All have new stories except where noted.
nn (#1, 1946)-Goldilocks; Kelly back-c (16 pgs., stapled) 48 96 144 298 499 700
nn (#2, 1946)-How Santa Got His Red Suit; Kelly-a (11 pgs., r/4-Color #61 from 1944) (16pgs., stapled) 31 62 93 181 291 400
nn (#3, 1947)-Our Gang (Walt Kelly) 40 80 120 235 380 525
nn (#4)-Donald Duck by Carl Barks, "Maharajah Donald", 28 pgs.; Kelly-c? (Disney) 722 1444 2166 5198 9099 13,000
5-Andy Panda (Walter Lantz) 19 38 57 109 180 250
6-Popular Fairy Tales; Kelly-c; Noonan-a(2) 22 44 66 123 202 280
7-Oswald the Rabbit 20 40 60 113 187 260
8-Mickey Mouse, 32 pgs. (Disney) 47 94 141 291 483 675
9(nn)-The Story of the Gloomy Bunny 14 28 42 76 108 140
10-Out of Santa's Bag 13 26 39 72 101 130
11-Fun With Santa Claus 11 22 33 64 90 115
12-Santa's Toys 11 22 33 64 90 115
13-Santa's Surprise 11 22 33 64 90 115
14-Santa's Candy Kitchen 11 22 33 64 90 115
15-Hip-It-Ty Hop & the Big Bass Viol 11 22 33 60 83 105
16-Woody Woodpecker (1947)(Walter Lantz) 14 28 42 82 121 160
17-Roy Rogers (1948) 24 48 72 143 229 315
18-Popular Fairy Tales 13 26 39 74 105 135
19-Uncle Wiggily 12 24 36 67 94 120
20-Donald Duck by Carl Barks, "Darkest Africa", 22 pgs.; Kelly-c (Disney) 318 636 954 2163 3782 5400
21-Tom and Jerry 13 26 39 72 101 130
22-Andy Panda (Lantz) 11 22 33 64 90 115
23-Raggedy Ann & Andy; Kerr-a 14 28 42 81 118 155
24-Felix the Cat, 1932 daily strip reprints by Otto Messmer 20 40 60 120 193 265
25-Gene Autry 20 40 60 120 193 265
26-Our Gang; Walt Kelly 19 38 57 112 176 240
27-Mickey Mouse; r/in M. M. #240 (Disney) 35 70 105 208 334 460
28-Gene Autry 20 40 60 117 186 255
29-Easter Bonnet Shop 8 16 24 44 57 70
30-Here Comes Santa 8 16 24 42 54 65
31-Santa's Busy Corner 8 16 24 42 54 65
32-No book produced
33-A Christmas Carol (12/48) 8 16 24 44 57 70
34-Woody Woodpecker 13 26 39 72 101 130
35-Roy Rogers (1948) 22 44 66 125 205 285
36-Felix the Cat(1949); by Messmer; '34 strip-r 18 36 54 103 162 220
37-Popeye 15 30 45 84 127 170
38-Oswald the Rabbit 10 20 30 56 76 95
39-Gene Autry 20 40 60 115 183 250
40-Andy and Woody 10 20 30 56 76 95
41-Donald Duck by Carl Barks, "Race to the South Seas", 22 pgs.; Kelly-c 306 612 918 2081 3641 5200
42-Porky Pig 10 20 30 58 79 100

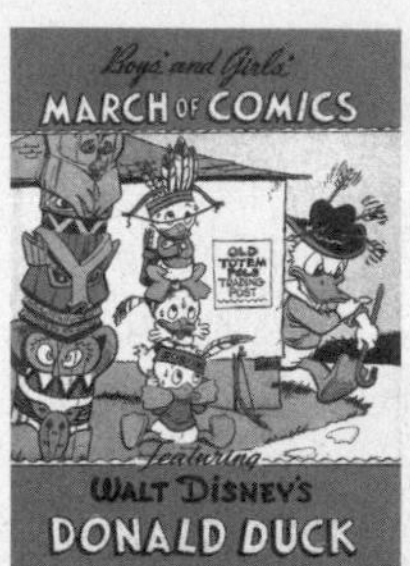

March of Comics #69 © DIS

March of Comics #115 © WB

March of Comics #174 © L.R. Ents.

	GD 2.0	VG 4.0	FN 6.0	VF 8.0	VF/NM 9.0	NM- 9.2
43-Henry	10	20	30	54	72	90
44-Bugs Bunny	11	22	33	62	86	110
45-Mickey Mouse (Disney)	27	54	81	158	254	350
46-Tom and Jerry	11	22	33	62	86	110
47-Roy Rogers	19	38	57	112	176	240
48-Greetings from Santa	6	12	18	31	38	45
49-Santa Is Here	6	12	18	31	38	45
50-Santa Claus' Workshop (1949)	6	12	18	31	38	45
51-Felix the Cat (1950) by Messmer	15	30	45	92	144	195
52-Popeye	14	28	42	76	108	140
53-Oswald the Rabbit	10	20	30	54	72	90
54-Gene Autry	17	34	51	100	158	215
55-Andy and Woody	9	18	27	52	69	85
56-Donald Duck; not by Barks; Barks art on back-c (Disney)	29	58	87	169	272	375
57-Porky Pig	10	20	30	54	72	90
58-Henry	8	16	24	44	57	70
59-Bugs Bunny	10	20	30	58	79	100
60-Mickey Mouse (Disney)	26	52	78	154	247	340
61-Tom and Jerry	10	20	30	54	72	90
62-Roy Rogers	19	38	57	109	172	235
63-Welcome Santa (1/2-size, oblong)	6	12	18	31	38	45
64(nn)-Santa's Helpers (1/2-size, oblong)	6	12	18	31	38	45
65(nn)-Jingle Bells (1950) (1/2-size, oblong)	6	12	18	31	38	45
66-Popeye (1951)	12	24	36	69	97	125
67-Oswald the Rabbit	9	18	27	52	69	85
68-Roy Rogers	18	36	54	105	165	225
69-Donald Duck; Barks-a on back-c (Disney)	25	50	75	147	236	325
70-Tom and Jerry	9	18	27	50	65	80
71-Porky Pig	9	18	27	52	69	85
72-Krazy Kat	10	20	30	58	79	100
73-Roy Rogers	16	32	48	96	151	205
74-Mickey Mouse (1951)(Disney)	20	40	60	118	189	260
75-Bugs Bunny	9	18	27	52	69	85
76-Andy and Woody	9	18	27	50	65	80
77-Roy Rogers	15	30	45	90	140	190
78-Gene Autry (1951); last regular size issue	15	30	45	86	133	180

Note: All pre #79 issues came with or without a slick protective wrap-around cover over the regular cover which advertised Poll Parrot Shoes, Sears, etc. This outer cover protects the inside pages making them in nicer condition.
Issues with the outer cover are worth 15-25% more

	GD 2.0	VG 4.0	FN 6.0	VF 8.0	VF/NM 9.0	NM- 9.2
79-Andy Panda (1952, 5x7" size)	7	14	21	35	43	50
80-Popeye	10	20	30	58	79	100
81-Oswald the Rabbit	6	12	18	29	36	42
82-Tarzan; Lex Barker photo-c	15	30	45	90	140	190
83-Bugs Bunny	7	14	21	37	46	55
84-Henry	6	12	18	29	36	42
85-Woody Woodpecker	6	12	18	29	36	42
86-Roy Rogers	14	28	42	76	108	140
87-Krazy Kat	8	16	24	44	57	70
88-Tom and Jerry	6	12	18	31	38	45
89-Porky Pig	6	12	18	29	36	42
90-Gene Autry	12	24	36	69	97	125
91-Roy Rogers & Santa	13	26	39	74	105	135
92-Christmas with Santa	5	10	15	24	30	35
93-Woody Woodpecker (1953)	5	10	15	23	28	32
94-Indian Chief	10	20	30	54	72	90
95-Oswald the Rabbit	5	10	15	23	28	32
96-Popeye	10	20	30	54	72	90
97-Bugs Bunny	7	14	21	35	43	50
98-Tarzan; Lex Barker photo-c	15	30	45	86	133	180
99-Porky Pig	5	10	15	23	28	32
100-Roy Rogers	11	22	33	62	86	110
101-Henry	5	10	15	22	26	30
102-Tom Corbett (TV)('53, early app).; painted-c	14	28	42	76	108	140
103-Tom and Jerry	5	10	15	23	28	32
104-Gene Autry	11	22	33	60	83	105
105-Roy Rogers	11	22	33	60	83	105
106-Santa's Helpers	5	10	15	24	30	35
107-Santa's Christmas Book - not published						
108-Fun with Santa (1953)	5	10	15	24	30	35
109-Woody Woodpecker (1954)	5	10	15	24	30	35
110-Indian Chief	6	12	18	31	38	45
111-Oswald the Rabbit	5	10	15	22	26	30
112-Henry	4	9	13	18	22	26
113-Porky Pig	5	10	15	22	26	30
114-Tarzan; Russ Manning-a	15	30	45	86	133	180
115-Bugs Bunny	6	12	18	27	33	38
116-Roy Rogers	11	22	33	60	83	105

	GD 2.0	VG 4.0	FN 6.0	VF 8.0	VF/NM 9.0	NM- 9.2
117-Popeye	10	20	30	54	72	90
118-Flash Gordon; painted-c	12	24	36	67	94	120
119-Tom and Jerry	5	10	15	22	26	30
120-Gene Autry	11	22	33	60	83	105
121-Roy Rogers	11	22	33	60	83	105
122-Santa's Surprise (1954)	5	10	15	22	26	30
123-Santa's Christmas Book	5	10	15	22	26	30
124-Woody Woodpecker (1955)	4	9	13	18	22	26
125-Tarzan; Lex Barker photo-c	15	30	45	83	124	165
126-Oswald the Rabbit	4	9	13	18	22	26
127-Indian Chief	7	14	21	35	43	50
128-Tom and Jerry	4	9	13	18	22	26
129-Henry	4	8	12	17	21	24
130-Porky Pig	4	9	13	18	22	26
131-Roy Rogers	11	22	33	60	83	105
132-Bugs Bunny	5	10	15	23	28	32
133-Flash Gordon; painted-c	11	22	33	60	83	105
134-Popeye	8	16	24	42	54	65
135-Gene Autry	10	20	30	56	76	95
136-Roy Rogers	10	20	30	56	76	95
137-Gifts from Santa	4	7	10	14	17	20
138-Fun at Christmas (1955)	4	7	10	14	17	20
139-Woody Woodpecker (1956)	4	9	13	18	22	26
140-Indian Chief	7	14	21	35	43	50
141-Oswald the Rabbit	4	9	13	18	22	26
142-Flash Gordon	11	22	33	60	83	105
143-Porky Pig	4	9	13	18	22	26
144-Tarzan; Russ Manning-a; painted-c	14	28	42	80	115	150
145-Tom and Jerry	4	9	13	18	22	26
146-Roy Rogers; photo-c	10	20	30	56	76	95
147-Henry	4	8	11	16	19	22
148-Popeye	8	16	24	42	54	65
149-Bugs Bunny	5	10	15	22	26	30
150-Gene Autry	10	20	30	56	76	95
151-Roy Rogers	10	20	30	56	76	95
152-The Night Before Christmas	4	8	11	16	19	22
153-Merry Christmas (1956)	4	9	13	18	22	26
154-Tom and Jerry (1957)	4	9	13	18	22	26
155-Tarzan; photo-c	14	28	42	78	112	145
156-Oswald the Rabbit	4	9	13	18	22	26
157-Popeye	7	14	21	35	43	50
158-Woody Woodpecker	4	9	13	18	22	26
159-Indian Chief	7	14	21	35	43	50
160-Bugs Bunny	5	10	15	22	26	30
161-Roy Rogers	9	18	27	52	69	85
162-Henry	4	8	11	16	19	22
163-Rin Tin Tin (TV)	8	16	24	42	54	65
164-Porky Pig	4	9	13	18	22	26
165-The Lone Ranger	10	20	30	54	72	90
166-Santa and His Reindeer	4	7	10	14	17	20
167-Roy Rogers and Santa	9	18	27	52	69	85
168-Santa Claus' Workshop (1957, full size)	4	8	11	16	19	22
169-Popeye (1958)	7	14	21	35	43	50
170-Indian Chief	7	14	21	35	43	50
171-Oswald the Rabbit	4	8	12	17	21	24
172-Tarzan	11	22	33	64	90	115
173-Tom and Jerry	4	8	12	17	21	24
174-The Lone Ranger	10	20	30	54	72	90
175-Porky Pig	4	8	12	17	21	24
176-Roy Rogers	9	18	27	47	61	75
177-Woody Woodpecker	4	8	12	17	21	24
178-Henry	4	8	11	16	19	22
179-Bugs Bunny	4	8	12	17	21	24
180-Rin Tin Tin (TV)	7	14	21	37	46	55
181-Happy Holiday	4	7	9	14	16	18
182-Happi Tim	4	8	11	16	19	22
183-Welcome Santa (1958, full size)	4	7	9	14	16	18
184-Woody Woodpecker (1959)	4	8	11	16	19	22
185-Tarzan; photo-c	11	22	33	60	83	110
186-Oswald the Rabbit	4	8	11	16	19	22
187-Indian Chief	6	12	18	28	34	40
188-Bugs Bunny	4	8	11	16	19	22
189-Henry	4	7	10	14	17	20
190-Tom and Jerry	4	8	11	16	19	22
191-Roy Rogers	8	16	24	44	57	70
192-Porky Pig	4	8	11	16	19	22
193-The Lone Ranger	9	18	27	52	69	85
194-Popeye	6	12	18	31	38	45
195-Rin Tin Tin (TV)	7	14	21	35	43	50

March of Comics #271 © H-B

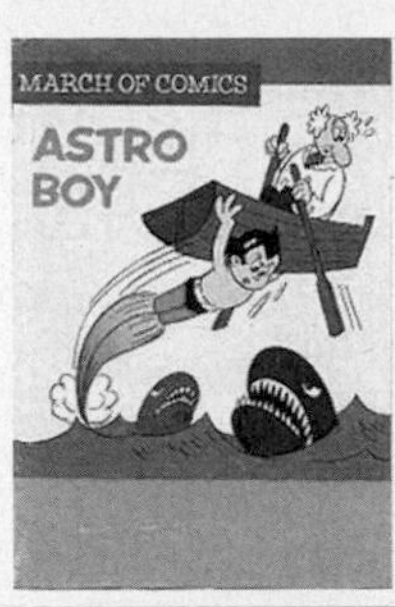

March of Comics #285 © Osamu Tezuka

march of comics
LASSIE
Sears
SEARS HAS EVERYTHING FOR CHILDREN

March of Comics #334 © CBS

	GD 2.0	VG 4.0	FN 6.0	VF 8.0	VF/NM 9.0	NM- 9.2
196-Sears Special - not published						
197-Santa Is Coming	4	7	10	14	17	20
198-Santa's Helpers (1959)	4	7	10	14	17	20
199-Huckleberry Hound (TV)(1960, early app.)	8	16	24	42	54	65
200-Fury (TV)	6	12	18	28	34	40
201-Bugs Bunny	4	8	11	16	19	22
202 Space Explorer	8	16	24	42	54	65
203-Woody Woodpecker	4	7	10	14	17	20
204-Tarzan	9	18	27	52	69	85
205-Mighty Mouse	6	12	18	33	41	48
206-Roy Rogers; photo-c	8	16	24	42	54	65
207-Tom and Jerry	4	7	10	14	17	20
208-The Lone Ranger; Clayton Moore photo-c	11	22	33	62	86	110
209-Porky Pig	4	7	10	14	17	20
210-Lassie (TV)	6	12	18	33	41	48
211-Sears Special - not published						
212-Christmas Eve	4	7	10	14	17	20
213-Here Comes Santa (1960)	4	7	10	14	17	20
214-Huckleberry Hound (TV)(1961)	7	14	21	35	43	50
215-Hi Yo Silver	8	16	24	40	50	60
216-Rocky & His Friends (TV)(1961); predates Rocky and His Fiendish Friends #1 (see Four Color #1128)	10	20	30	58	79	100
217-Lassie (TV)	6	12	18	31	38	45
218-Porky Pig	4	7	10	14	17	20
219-Journey to the Sun	5	10	15	24	30	35
220-Bugs Bunny	4	8	11	16	19	22
221-Roy and Dale; photo-c	8	16	24	42	54	65
222-Woody Woodpecker	4	7	10	14	17	20
223-Tarzan	9	18	27	52	69	85
224-Tom and Jerry	4	7	10	14	17	20
225-The Lone Ranger	8	16	24	40	50	60
226-Christmas Treasury (1961)	4	7	10	14	17	20
227-Letters to Santa (1961)	4	7	10	14	17	20
228-Sears Special - not published?						
229-The Flintstones (TV)(1962); early app.; predates 1st Flintstones Gold Key issue (#7)	11	22	33	60	83	105
230-Lassie (TV)	6	12	18	27	33	38
231-Bugs Bunny	4	8	11	16	19	22
232-The Three Stooges	10	20	30	54	72	90
233-Bullwinkle (TV) (1962, very early app.)	10	20	30	58	79	100
234-Smokey the Bear	5	10	15	23	28	32
235-Huckleberry Hound (TV)	7	14	21	35	43	50
236-Roy and Dale	7	14	21	35	43	50
237-Mighty Mouse	6	12	18	27	33	38
238-The Lone Ranger	8	16	24	40	50	60
239-Woody Woodpecker	4	7	10	14	17	20
240-Tarzan	8	16	24	44	57	70
241-Santa Claus Around the World	4	7	9	14	16	18
242-Santa's Toyland (1962)	4	7	9	14	16	18
243-The Flintstones (TV)(1963)	8	16	24	44	57	70
244-Mister Ed (TV); early app.; photo-c	7	14	21	35	43	50
245-Bugs Bunny	4	8	11	16	19	22
246-Popeye	6	12	18	27	33	38
247-Mighty Mouse	6	12	18	27	33	38
248-The Three Stooges	10	20	30	54	72	90
249-Woody Woodpecker	4	7	10	14	17	20
250-Roy and Dale	7	14	21	35	43	50
251-Little Lulu & Witch Hazel	12	24	36	67	94	120
252-Tarzan; painted-c	8	16	24	42	54	65
253-Yogi Bear (TV)	8	16	24	40	50	60
254-Lassie (TV)	6	12	18	27	33	38
255-Santa's Christmas List	4	7	10	14	17	20
256-Christmas Party (1963)	4	7	10	14	17	20
257-Mighty Mouse	6	12	18	27	33	38
258-The Sword in the Stone (Disney)	8	16	24	42	54	65
259-Bugs Bunny	4	8	11	16	19	22
260-Mister Ed (TV)	6	12	18	31	38	45
261-Woody Woodpecker	4	7	10	14	17	20
262-Tarzan	8	16	24	40	50	60
263-Donald Duck; not by Barks (Disney)	9	18	27	52	69	85
264-Popeye	6	12	18	27	33	38
265-Yogi Bear (TV)	6	12	18	31	38	45
266-Lassie (TV)	5	10	15	23	28	32
267-Little Lulu; Irving Tripp-a	10	20	30	56	76	95
268-The Three Stooges	9	18	27	47	61	75
269-A Jolly Christmas	3	6	8	12	14	16
270-Santa's Little Helpers	3	6	8	12	14	16
271-The Flintstones (TV)(1965)	8	16	24	44	57	70
272-Tarzan	8	16	24	40	50	60
273-Bugs Bunny	4	8	11	16	19	22
274-Popeye	6	12	18	27	33	38
275-Little Lulu; Irving Tripp-a	9	18	27	50	65	80
276-The Jetsons (TV)	14	28	42	76	108	140
277-Daffy Duck	4	8	11	16	19	22
278-Lassie (TV)	5	10	15	23	28	32
279-Yogi Bear (TV)	6	12	18	31	38	45
280-The Three Stooges; photo-c	9	18	27	47	61	75
281-Tom and Jerry	4	7	9	14	16	18
282-Mister Ed (TV)	6	12	18	31	38	45
283-Santa's Visit	4	7	9	14	16	18
284-Christmas Parade (1965)	4	7	9	14	16	18
285-Astro Boy (TV); 2nd app. Astro Boy	29	58	87	169	272	375
286-Tarzan	7	14	21	37	46	55
287-Bugs Bunny	4	8	11	16	19	22
288-Daffy Duck	4	7	10	14	17	20
289-The Flintstones (TV)	8	16	24	44	57	70
290-Mister Ed (TV); photo-c	5	10	15	24	30	35
291-Yogi Bear (TV)	6	12	18	27	33	38
292-The Three Stooges; photo-c	9	18	27	47	61	75
293-Little Lulu; Irving Tripp-a	8	16	24	42	54	65
294-Popeye	5	10	15	24	30	35
295-Tom and Jerry	4	7	9	14	16	18
296-Lassie (TV); photo-c	5	10	15	22	26	30
297-Christmas Bells	3	6	8	12	14	16
298-Santa's Sleigh (1966)	3	6	8	12	14	16
299-The Flintstones (TV)(1967)	8	16	24	44	57	70
300-Tarzan	7	14	21	37	46	55
301-Bugs Bunny	4	7	10	14	17	20
302-Laurel and Hardy (TV); photo-c	6	12	18	28	34	40
303-Daffy Duck	3	6	8	12	14	16
304-The Three Stooges; photo-c	8	16	24	44	57	70
305-Tom and Jerry	3	6	8	12	14	16
306-Daniel Boone (TV); Fess Parker photo-c	7	14	21	35	43	50
307-Little Lulu; Irving Tripp-a	7	14	21	37	46	55
308-Lassie (TV); photo-c	5	10	15	22	26	30
309-Yogi Bear (TV)	5	10	15	24	30	35
310-The Lone Ranger; Clayton Moore photo-c	11	22	33	62	86	110
311-Santa's Show	4	7	9	14	16	18
312-Christmas Album (1967)	4	7	9	14	16	18
313-Daffy Duck (1968)	3	6	8	12	14	16
314-Laurel and Hardy (TV)	6	12	18	27	33	38
315-Bugs Bunny	4	7	10	14	17	20
316-The Three Stooges	8	16	24	40	50	60
317-The Flintstones (TV)	8	16	24	42	54	65
318-Tarzan	7	14	21	35	43	50
319-Yogi Bear (TV)	5	10	15	24	30	35
320-Space Family Robinson (TV); Spiegle-a	12	24	36	69	97	125
321-Tom and Jerry	3	6	8	12	14	16
322-The Lone Ranger	7	14	21	37	46	55
323-Little Lulu; not by Stanley	5	10	15	24	30	35
324-Lassie (TV); photo-c	5	10	15	22	26	30
325-Fun with Santa	4	7	9	14	16	18
326-Christmas Story (1968)	4	7	9	14	16	18
327-The Flintstones (TV)(1969)	8	16	24	42	54	65
328 Space Family Robinson (TV); Spiegle-a	12	24	36	69	97	125
329-Bugs Bunny	4	7	10	14	17	20
330-The Jetsons (TV)	10	20	30	56	76	95
331-Daffy Duck	3	6	8	12	14	16
332-Tarzan	6	12	18	28	34	40
333-Tom and Jerry	3	6	8	12	14	16
334-Lassie (TV)	4	9	13	18	22	26
335-Little Lulu	5	10	15	24	30	35
336-The Three Stooges	8	16	24	40	50	60
337-Yogi Bear (TV)	5	10	15	24	30	35
338-The Lone Ranger	7	14	21	37	46	55
339-(Was not published)						
340-Here Comes Santa (1969)	3	6	8	12	14	16
341-The Flintstones (TV)	8	16	24	42	54	65
342-Tarzan	3	6	9	20	30	40
343-Bugs Bunny	2	4	6	10	14	18
344-Yogi Bear (TV)	3	6	9	16	23	30
345-Tom and Jerry	2	4	6	9	13	16
346-Lassie (TV)	3	6	9	15	21	26
347-Daffy Duck	2	4	6	9	13	16
348-The Jetsons (TV)	6	12	18	39	62	85
349-Little Lulu; not by Stanley	3	6	9	16	23	30
350-The Lone Ranger	3	6	9	18	27	35
351-Beep-Beep, the Road Runner (TV)	2	4	6	11	16	20

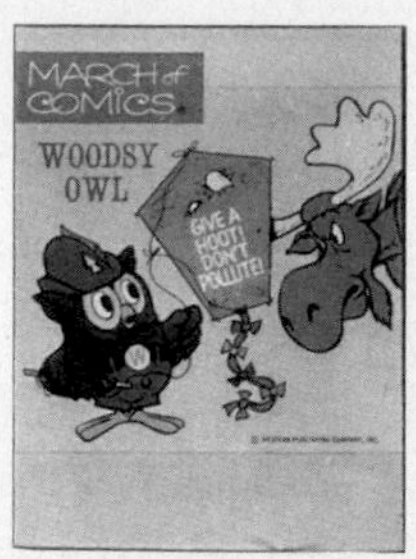

March of Comics #395 © USFS

March of Comics #468 © Marjorie Buell

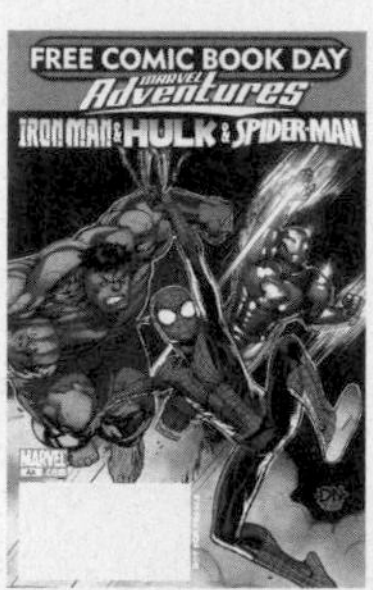

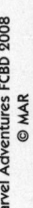

Marvel Adventures FCBD 2008 © MAR

	GD 2.0	VG 4.0	FN 6.0	VF 8.0	VF/NM 9.0	NM- 9.2
352-Space Family Robinson (TV); Spiegle-a	8	16	24	54	90	125
353-Beep-Beep, the Road Runner (1971) (TV)	2	4	6	11	16	20
354-Tarzan (1971)	3	6	9	18	27	35
355-Little Lulu; not by Stanley	3	6	9	16	23	30
356-Scooby Doo, Where Are You? (TV)	6	12	18	43	69	95
357-Daffy Duck & Porky Pig	2	4	6	8	11	14
358-Lassie (TV)	3	6	9	14	19	24
359-Baby Snoots	2	4	6	10	14	18
360-H. R. Pufnstuf (TV); photo-c	6	12	18	43	69	95
361-Tom and Jerry	2	4	6	8	11	14
362-Smokey Bear (TV)	2	4	6	8	11	14
363-Bugs Bunny & Yosemite Sam	2	4	6	9	13	16
364-The Banana Splits (TV); photo-c	6	12	18	37	59	80
365-Tom and Jerry (1972)	2	4	6	8	11	14
366-Tarzan	3	6	9	18	27	35
367-Bugs Bunny & Porky Pig	2	4	6	9	13	16
368-Scooby Doo (TV)(4/72)	6	12	18	37	59	80
369-Little Lulu; not by Stanley	3	6	9	14	19	24
370-Lassie (TV); photo-c	3	6	9	14	19	24
371-Baby Snoots	2	4	6	9	13	16
372-Smokey the Bear (TV)	2	4	6	8	11	14
373-The Three Stooges	4	8	12	24	37	50
374-Wacky Witch	2	4	6	8	11	14
375-Beep-Beep & Daffy Duck (TV)	2	4	6	8	11	14
376-The Pink Panther (1972) (TV)	2	4	6	10	14	18
377-Baby Snoots (1973)	2	4	6	9	13	16
378-Turok, Son of Stone; new-a	8	16	24	56	93	130
379-Heckle & Jeckle New Terrytoons (TV)	2	4	6	8	11	14
380-Bugs Bunny & Yosemite Sam	2	4	6	8	11	14
381-Lassie (TV)	2	4	6	11	16	20
382-Scooby Doo, Where Are You? (TV)	5	10	15	32	51	70
383-Smokey the Bear (TV)	2	4	6	8	11	14
384-Pink Panther (TV)	2	4	6	8	11	14
385-Little Lulu	2	4	6	13	18	22
386-Wacky Witch	2	4	6	8	11	14
387-Beep-Beep & Daffy Duck (TV)	2	4	6	8	11	14
388-Tom and Jerry (1973)	2	4	6	8	11	14
389-Little Lulu; not by Stanley	2	4	6	13	18	22
390-Pink Panther (TV)	2	4	6	8	11	14
391-Scooby Doo (TV)	4	8	12	26	41	55
392-Bugs Bunny & Yosemite Sam	2	4	6	8	10	12
393-New Terrytoons (Heckle & Jeckle) (TV)	2	4	6	8	10	12
394-Lassie (TV)	2	4	6	9	13	16
395-Woodsy Owl	2	4	6	8	10	12
396-Baby Snoots	2	4	6	8	11	14
397-Beep-Beep & Daffy Duck (TV)	2	4	6	8	10	12
398-Wacky Witch	2	4	6	8	10	12
399-Turok, Son of Stone; new-a	7	14	21	50	83	115
400-Tom and Jerry	2	4	6	8	10	12
401-Baby Snoots (1975) (r/#371)	2	4	6	8	11	14
402-Daffy Duck (r/#313)	1	3	4	6	8	10
403-Bugs Bunny (r/#343)	2	4	6	8	10	12
404-Space Family Robinson (TV)(r/#328)	6	12	18	41	66	90
405-Cracky	1	3	4	6	8	10
406-Little Lulu (r/#355)	2	4	6	10	14	18
407-Smokey the Bear (TV)(r/#362)	2	4	6	8	10	12
408-Turok, Son of Stone; c-r/Turok #20 w/changes; new-a	6	12	18	39	62	85
409-Pink Panther (TV)	1	3	4	6	8	10
410-Wacky Witch	1	2	3	5	6	8
411-Lassie (TV)(r/#324)	2	4	6	9	13	16
412-New Terrytoons (1975) (TV)	1	2	3	5	6	8
413-Daffy Duck (1976)(r/#331)	1	2	3	5	6	8
414-Space Family Robinson (r/#328)	6	12	18	39	62	85
415-Bugs Bunny (r/#329)	1	2	3	5	6	8
416-Beep-Beep, the Road Runner (r/#353)(TV)	1	2	3	5	6	8
417-Little Lulu (r/#323)	2	4	6	10	14	18
418-Pink Panther (r/#384) (TV)	1	2	3	5	6	8
419-Baby Snoots (r/#377)	1	3	4	6	8	10
420-Woody Woodpecker	1	2	3	5	6	8
421-Tweety & Sylvester	1	2	3	5	6	8
422-Wacky Witch (r/#386)	1	2	3	5	6	8
423-Little Monsters	1	3	4	6	8	10
424-Cracky (12/76)	1	2	3	5	6	8
425-Daffy Duck	1	2	3	5	6	8
426-Underdog (TV)	4	8	12	22	34	45
427-Little Lulu (r/#335)	2	4	6	8	11	14
428-Bugs Bunny	1	2	3	4	5	7
429-The Pink Panther (TV)	1	2	3	4	5	7

	GD 2.0	VG 4.0	FN 6.0	VF 8.0	VF/NM 9.0	NM- 9.2
430-Beep-Beep, the Road Runner (TV)	1	2	3	4	5	7
431-Baby Snoots	1	2	3	5	6	8
432-Lassie (TV)	2	4	6	8	10	12
433-437: 433-Tweety & Sylvester. 434-Wacky Witch. 435-New Terrytoons (TV). 436-Wacky Advs. of Cracky. 437-Daffy Duck	1	2	3	4	5	7
438-Underdog (TV)	3	6	9	20	30	40
439-Little Lulu (r/#349)	2	4	6	8	11	14
440-442,444-446: 440-Bugs Bunny. 441-The Pink Panther (TV). 442-Beep-Beep, the Road Runner (TV). 444-Tom and Jerry. 445-Tweety and Sylvester. 446-Wacky Witch	1	2	3	5	6	8
443-Baby Snoots	1	2	3	5	6	8
447-Mighty Mouse	2	4	6	8	10	12
448-455,457,458: 448-Cracky. 449-Pink Panther (TV). 450-Baby Snoots. 451-Tom and Jerry. 452-Bugs Bunny. 453-Popeye. 454-Woody Woodpecker. 455-Beep-Beep, the Road Runner (TV). 457-Tweety & Sylvester. 458-Wacky Witch	1	2	3	5	6	8
456-Little Lulu (r/#369)	2	4	6	8	10	12
459-Mighty Mouse	2	4	6	8	10	12
460-466: 460-Daffy Duck. 461-The Pink Panther (TV). 462-Baby Snoots. 463-Tom and Jerry. 464-Bugs Bunny. 465-Popeye. 466-Woody Woodpecker	1	2	3	5	6	8
467-Underdog (TV)	3	6	9	18	27	35
468-Little Lulu (r/#385)	1	2	3	5	6	8
469-Tweety & Sylvester	1	2	3	5	6	8
470-Wacky Witch	1	2	3	5	6	8
471-Mighty Mouse	1	3	4	6	8	10
472-474,476-478: 472-Heckle & Jeckle(12/80). 473-Pink Panther(1/81)(TV). 474-Baby Snoots. 476-Bugs Bunny. 477-Popeye. 478-Woody Woodpecker	1	2	3	5	6	8
475-Little Lulu (r/#323)	1	3	4	6	8	10
479-Underdog (TV)	3	6	9	16	23	30
480-482: 480-Tom and Jerry. 481-Tweety and Sylvester. 482-Wacky Witch	1	2	3	4	5	8
483-Mighty Mouse	1	3	4	6	8	10
484-487: 484-Heckle & Jeckle. 485-Baby Snoots. 486-The Pink Panther (TV). 487-Bugs Bunny	1	2	3	4	5	8
488-Little Lulu (4/82) (r/#335) (Last issue)	2	4	6	10	14	18

MARGARET O'BRIEN (See The Adventures of...)

MARK STEEL
American Iron & Steel Institute: 1967, 1968, 1972 (Giveaway) (24 pgs.)

1967,1968- "Journey of Discovery with..."; Neal Adams art	4	8	12	28	44	60
1972- "...Fights Pollution"; N. Adams-a	3	6	9	16	23	30

MARTIN LUTHER KING AND THE MONTGOMERY STORY
Fellowship Reconciliation: 1956 (Giveaway, 16 pgs.) (A Spanish edition also exists)

nn-In color with paper-c (a CGC 9.2 copy sold for $350 and a FN+ sold for $200 in 2004)

MARVEL ADVENTURES...
Marvel Comics: 2007, 2008 (Free Comic Book Day giveaway)

... Free Comic Book Day 2008 - Iron Man, Hulk, Ant-Man and Spider-Man app. 2.50
... Three-In-One (2007) 1-Iron Man, Incredible Hulk and Franklin Richards app. 2.50

MARVEL AGE SPIDER-MAN
Marvel Comics: Aug, 2004 (Free Comic Book Day giveaway)

1-Spider-Man vs. The Vulture; Brooks-a 2.50

MARVEL AGE SPIDER-MAN TEAM-UP (Marvel Adventures on cover)
Marvel Comics: June, 2005 (Free Comic Book Day giveaway)

1-Spider-Man meets the Fantastic Four 2.50

MARVEL COLLECTOR'S EDITION: X-MEN
Marvel Comics: 1993 (3-3/4x6-1/2")

1-4-Pizza Hut giveaways 5.00

MARVEL COMICS PRESENTS
Marvel Comics: 1987, 1988 (4 1/4 x 6 1/4, 20 pgs.)

...Mini Comic Giveaway

nn-(1988) Alf	1	2	3	5	6	8
nn-(1987) Captain America r/ #250	1	2	3	4	5	7
nn-(1987) Care Bears (Star Comics...)	1	2	3	4	5	7
nn-(1988) Flintstone Kids	1	2	3	5	6	8
nn-(1987) Heathcliffe (Star Comics...)	1	2	3	4	5	7
nn-(1987) Spider-Man-r/Spect. Spider-Man #21	1	2	3	4	5	7
nn-(1988) Spider-Man-r/Amazing Spider-Man #1	1	2	3	4	5	7
nn-(1988) X-Men-reprints X-Men #53; B. Smith-a	1	2	3	4	5	7

MARVEL GUIDE TO COLLECTING COMICS, THE
Marvel Comics: 1982 (16 pgs., newsprint pages and cover)

1-Simonson-c	1	2	3	4	5	7

MARVEL HALLOWEEN ASHCAN 2006

The Masked Pilot © R.S. Callender

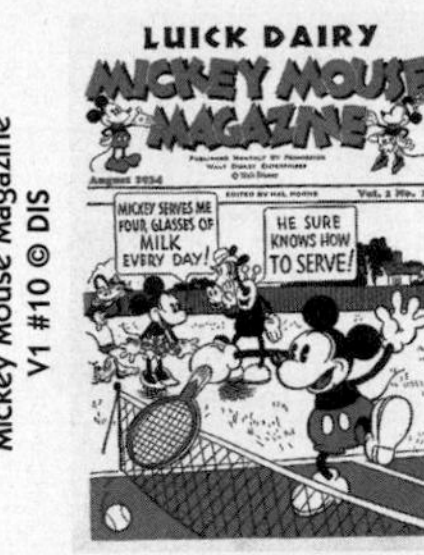

Mickey Mouse Magazine V1 #10 © DIS

Mr. Peanut, The Personal Story of... © Planters

	GD 2.0	VG 4.0	FN 6.0	VF 8.0	VF/NM 9.0	NM- 9.2

Marvel Comics: 2006 (8-1/2"x 5-1/2", Halloween giveaway)
nn-r/Marvel Adventures The Avengers #1 — 2.00

MARVEL MINI-BOOKS
Marvel Comics Group: 1966 (50 pgs., B&W; 5/8x7/8") (6 different issues) (Smallest comics ever published) (Marvel Mania Giveaways)

	GD	VG	FN	VF	VF/NM	NM-
Captain America, Millie the Model, Sgt. Fury, Hulk, Thor each...	3	6	9	20	30	40
Spider-Man	4	8	12	24	37	50

NOTE: *Each came in six different color covers, usually one color: Pink, yellow, green, etc.*

MARVEL SUPER-HERO ISLAND ADVENTURES
Marvel Comics: 1999 (Sold at the park polybagged with Captain America V3 #19, one other comic, 5 trading cards and a cloisonné pin)
1-Promotes Universal Studios Islands of Adventures theme park — 2.50

MARY'S GREATEST APOSTLE (St. Louis Grignion de Montfort)
Catechetical Guild (Topix) (Giveaway): No date (16 pgs.; paper cover)
nn — 5, 10, 15, 23, 28, 32

MASK
DC Comics: 1985
1-3 — 5.00

MASKED PILOT, THE (See Popular Comics #43)
R.S. Callender: 1939 (7-1/2x5-1/4", 16 pgs., premium, non-slick-c)
nn-Bob Jenney-a — 8, 16, 24, 44, 57, 70

MASTERS OF THE UNIVERSE (He-Man)
DC Comics: 1982 (giveaways with action figures, at least 35 different issues, unnumbered)
nn — 6.00

MATRIX, THE (1999 movie)
Warner Brothers: 1999 (Recalled by Warner Bros. over questionable content)
nn-Paul Chadwick c/a (16 pgs.); Geof Darrow-c — 1, 2, 3, 5, 6, 8

McCRORY'S CHRISTMAS BOOK
Western Printing Co: 1955 (36 pgs., slick-c) (McCrory Stores Corp. giveaway)
nn-Painted-c — 4, 8, 12, 18, 22, 25

McCRORY'S TOYLAND BRINGS YOU SANTA'S PRIVATE EYES
Promotional Publ. Co.: 1956 (16 pgs.) (Giveaway)
nn-Has 9 pg. story plus 7 pgs. toy ads — 4, 8, 11, 16, 19, 22

McCRORY'S WONDERFUL CHRISTMAS
Promotional Publ. Co.: 1954 (20 pgs., slick-c) (Giveaway)
nn — 4, 8, 12, 18, 22, 25

McDONALDS COMMANDRONS
DC Comics: 1985
nn-Four editions — 5.00

MEET HIYA A FRIEND OF SANTA CLAUS
Julian J. Proskauer/Sundial Shoe Stores, etc.: 1949 (18 pgs.?, paper-c)(Giveaway)
nn — 6, 12, 18, 31, 38, 45

MEET THE NEW POST-GAZETTE SUNDAY FUNNIES
Pittsburgh Post Gazette: 3/12/49 (7-1/4x10-1/4", 16 pgs., paper-c)
Commercial Comics (insert in newspaper) (Rare)
Dick Tracy by Gould, Gasoline Alley, Terry & the Pirates, Brenda Starr, Buck Rogers by Yager, The Gumps, Peter Rabbit by Fago, Superman, Funnyman by Siegel & Shuster, The Saint, Archie, & others done especially for this book. A fine copy sold at auction in 1985 for $276.00.
— 385, 770, 1155, 2500, -, -

MEN OF COURAGE
Catechetical Guild: 1949
Bound Topix comics-V7#2,4,6,8,10,16,18,20 — 6, 12, 18, 31, 38, 45

MEN WHO MOVE THE NATION
Publisher unknown: (Giveaway) (B&W)
nn-Neal Adams-a — 6, 12, 18, 31, 38, 45

MERRY CHRISTMAS, A
K. K. Publications (Child Life Shoes): 1948 (Giveaway)
nn — 6, 12, 18, 33, 41, 48

MERRY CHRISTMAS
K. K. Publications (Blue Bird Shoes Giveaway): 1956 (7-1/4x5-1/4")
nn — 4, 8, 12, 18, 22, 25

MERRY CHRISTMAS FROM MICKEY MOUSE
K. K. Publications: 1939 (16 pgs.) (Color & B&W) (Shoe store giveaway)
nn-Donald Duck & Pluto app.; text with art (Rare); c-reprint/Mickey Mouse Mag. V3#3 (12/37)(Rare) — 253, 506, 759, 1594, 2697, 3800

MERRY CHRISTMAS FROM SEARS TOYLAND (See Santa's Christmas Comic)

Sears Roebuck Giveaway: 1939 (16 pgs.) (Color)
nn-Dick Tracy, Little Orphan Annie, The Gumps, Terry & the Pirates — 107, 214, 321, 674, 1137, 1600

MICKEY MOUSE (Also see Frito-Lay Giveaway)
Dell Publ. Co

	GD	VG	FN	VF	VF/NM	NM-
...& Goofy Explore Business(1978)	1	3	4	6	8	10
...& Goofy Explore Energy(1976-1978, 36 pgs.); Exxon giveaway in color; regular size	1	3	4	6	8	10
...& Goofy Explore Energy Conservation(1976-1978)-Exxon	1	3	4	6	8	10
...& Goofy Explore The Universe of Energy(1985, 20 pgs.); Exxon giveaway in color; regular size	1	2	3	4	5	7

The Perils of Mickey nn (1993, 5-1/4x7-1/4", 16 pgs.)-Nabisco giveaway w/ games, Nabisco coupons & 6 pgs. of stories; Phantom Blot app. — 5.00

MICKEY MOUSE MAGAZINE
Walt Disney Productions: V1#1, Jan, 1933 - V1#9, Sept, 1933 (5-1/4x7-1/4")
No. 1-3 published by Kamen-Blair (Kay Kamen, Inc.)
(Scarce)-Distributed by dairies and leading stores through their local theatres. First few issues had 5¢ listed on cover, later ones had no price.

	GD	VG	FN	VF	VF/NM	NM-
V1#1	540	1080	2160	6500	-	-
2-4	225	450	900	1750	-	-
5-9	175	350	700	1350	-	-

MICKEY MOUSE MAGAZINE
Walt Disney Productions: V1#1, 11/33 - V2#12, 10/35 (Mills giveaways issued by different dairies)

	GD	VG	FN	VF	VF/NM	NM-
V1#1	240	600	960	1350	2025	2700
2-12: 2-X-Mas issue	80	200	320	475	688	900
V2#1-4,6-12: 2-X-Mas issue. 4-St. Valentine-c	55	124	192	310	455	600
V2#5 (3/35) 1st app. Donald Duck in sailor outfit on-c	96	192	288	600	975	1350

MICKEY MOUSE MAGAZINE
K.K. Publications: V4#1, Oct, 1938 (Giveaway)
V4#1 — 41, 82, 123, 256, 428, 600

MIGHTY ATOM, THE
Whitman

	GD	VG	FN	VF	VF/NM	NM-
Giveaway (1959, '63, Whitman)-Evans-a	3	6	9	14	19	24
Giveaway ('64r, '65r, '66r, '67r, '68r)-Evans-r?	2	4	6	8	11	14
Giveaway ('73r, '76r)	1	3	4	6	8	10

MILES THE MONSTER (Initially sold only at the Dover Speedway track)
Dover International Speedway, Inc.: 2006 ($3.00)
1,2-Allan Gross & Mark Wheatley-s/Wheatley-a — 3.00

MILITARY COURTESY
Harvey Publications: (16 pgs.)
nn-Regulations and saluting instructions — 5, 10, 14, 20, 24, 28

MINUTE MAN
Sovereign Service Station giveaway: No date (16 pgs., B&W, paper-c blue & red)
nn-American history — 3, 6, 8, 12, 14, 16

MINUTE MAN ANSWERS THE CALL, THE
By M. C. Gaines: 1942,1943,1944,1945 (4 pgs.) (Giveaway inserted in Jr. JSA Membership Kit)
nn-Sheldon Moldoff-a — 22, 44, 66, 127, 204, 280

MIRACLE ON BROADWAY
Broadway Comics: Dec, 1995 (Giveaway)
1-Ernie Colon-c/a; Jim Shooter & Co. story; 1st known digitally printed comic book; 1st app. Spire & Knights on Broadway (1150 print run) — 20.00
NOTE: *Miracle on Broadway was a limited edition comic given to 1100 VIPs in the entertainment industry for the 1995 Holiday Season.*

MISS SUNBEAM (See Little Miss Sunbeam Comics)

MR. BUG GOES TO TOWN (See Cinema Comics Herald)
K.K. Publications: 1941 (Giveaway, 52 pgs.)
nn-Cartoon movie (scarce) — 70, 140, 210, 441, 746, 1050

MR. PEANUT, THE PERSONAL STORY OF
Planters Nut & Chocolate Co.: 1956
nn — 4, 8, 12, 22, 34, 45

MOTH, THE
Rude Dude Productions: May 2008 (Free Comic Book Day giveaway)
... Special Edition - Steve Rude-s/a; sketch pages — 2.50

MOTHER OF US ALL
Catechetical Guild Giveaway: 1950? (32 pgs.)
nn — 5, 10, 15, 23, 28, 32

MOTION PICTURE FUNNIES WEEKLY (Amazing Man #5 on?)

Natural Disasters! © GIS

The Owl © WEST

Peter Wheat, Advs. of ... #58 © Bakers Assocs.

	GD 2.0	VG 4.0	FN 6.0	VF 8.0	VF/NM 9.0	NM- 9.2

First Funnies, Inc.: 1939 (Giveaway)(B&W, 36 pgs.) No month given; last panel in Sub-Mariner story dated 4/39 (Also see Colossus, Green Giant & Invaders No. 20)

1-Origin & 1st printed app. Sub-Mariner by Bill Everett (8 pgs.); Fred Schwab-c; reprinted in Marvel Mystery #1 with color added over the craft tint which was used to shade the black & white version; Spy Ring, American Ace (reprinted in Marvel Mystery #3) app. (Rare)-only eight known copies, one near mint with white pages, the rest with brown pages.
4400 8800 13,200 18,000 30,000 -

Covers only to #2-4 (set) 900

NOTE: Eight copies (plus one coverless) were discovered in 1974 in the estate of the deceased publisher. Covers only to issues No. 2-4 were also found which evidently were printed in advance along with #1. #1 was to be distributed only through motion picture movie houses. However, it is believed that only advanced copies were sent out and the motion picture houses not going for the idea. Possible distribution at local theaters in Boston suspected. The "pay" copy (graded at 9.0) was discovered after 1974, bringing the total known to nine. The last panel of Sub-Mariner contains a rectangular box with "Continued Next Week" printed in it. When reprinted in Marvel Mystery, the box was left in with lettering omitted.

MY DOG TIGE (Buster Brown's Dog)
Buster Brown Shoes: 1957 (Giveaway)

nn 5 10 15 24 30 35

MY GREATEST THRILLS IN BASEBALL
Mission of California: Date? (16 pg. Giveaway)

nn-By Mickey Mantle 55 110 165 347 586 825

MYSTERIOUS ADVENTURES WITH SANTA CLAUS
Lansburgh's: 1948 (paper cover)

nn 13 26 39 72 101 130

NASCAR HEROES
Starbridge Media Group: 2008 (Free Comic Book Day giveaway)

nn-The Mystery of Driver Z 2.50

NATURAL DISASTERS!
Graphic Information Service/ Civil Defense: 1956 (16 pgs., soft-c)

nn-Al Capp Li'l Abner-c; Li'l Abner cameo (1 panel); narrated by Mr. Civil Defense
10 20 30 54 72 90

NAVY: HISTORY & TRADITION
Stokes Walesby Co./Dept. of Navy: 1958 - 1961 (nn) (Giveaway)

1772-1778, 1778-1782, 1782-1817, 1817-1865, 1865-1936, 1940-1945:
1772-1778-16 pg. in color 5 10 15 22 26 30
1861: Naval Actions of the Civil War: 1865-36 pg. in color; flag-c
5 10 15 22 26 30

NEW ADVENTURE OF WALT DISNEY'S SNOW WHITE AND THE SEVEN DWARFS, A
(See Snow White Bendix Giveaway)

NEW ADVENTURES OF PETER PAN (Disney)
Western Publishing Co.: 1953 (5x7-1/4", 36 pgs.) (Admiral giveaway)

nn 14 28 42 76 108 140

NEW AVENGERS...
Marvel Comics: 2005 (Giveaway for U.S Military personnel)

... Guest Starring the Fantastic Four (4/05) Bendis-s/Jurgens-a/c 3.00
...: Pot of Gold (AAFES 110th Anniversary Issue) (10/05) Jenkins-s/Nolan-a/c 3.00

NEW FRONTIERS
Harvey Information Press (United States Steel Corp.) : 1958 (16 pgs., paper-c)

nn-History of barbed wire 2 4 6 14 18 22

NEW TEEN TITANS, THE
DC Comics: Nov. 1983

nn(11/83-Keebler Co. Giveaway)-In cooperation with "The President's Drug Awareness Campaign"; came in Presidential envelope w/letter from White House (Nancy Reagan)
1 2 3 4 5 7
nn-(re-issue of above on Mando paper for direct sales market); American Soft Drink Industry version; I.B.M. Corp. version 5.00

NOLAN RYAN IN THE WINNING PITCH (Kellogg's Tony's Sports Comics)
DC Comics: 1992 (Sports Illustrated)

nn 4.00

OLD GLORY COMICS
Chesapeake & Ohio Railway: 1944 (Giveaway)

nn-Capt. Fearless reprint 8 16 24 40 50 60

ON THE AIR
NBC Network Comic: 1947 (Giveaway, paper-c)

nn-(Rare) 20 40 60 115 183 250

OUT OF THE PAST A CLUE TO THE FUTURE
E. C. Comics (Public Affairs Comm.): 1946? (16 pgs.) (paper cover)

nn-Based on public affairs pamphlet "What Foreign Trade Means to You"
20 40 60 120 193 265

OUTSTANDING AMERICAN WAR HEROES
The Parents' Institute: 1944 (16 pgs., paper-c)

nn-Reprints from True Comics 5 10 15 22 26 30

OVERSEAS COMICS (Also see G.I. Comics & Jeep Comics)
Giveaway (Distributed to U.S. Armed Forces): 1944 - No. 105?, 1946 (7-1/4x10-1/4"; 16 pgs. in color)

23-105-Bringing Up Father (by McManus), Popeye, Joe Palooka, Dick Tracy, Superman, Gasoline Alley, Buz Sawyer, Li'l Abner, Blondie, Terry & the Pirates, Out Our Way
7 14 21 35 43 50

OWL, THE (See Crackajack Funnies #25 & Popular Comics #72)(Also see The Hurricane Kids & Magic Morro)
Western Pub. Co./R.S. Callender: 1940 (Giveaway)(7-1/2x5-1/4")(Soft-c, color)

nn-Frank Thomas-a 15 30 45 94 147 200

OXYDOL-DREFT
Toby Press:1950 (Set of 6 pocket-size giveaways; distributed through the mail as a set) (Scarce)

1-3: 1-Li'l Abner. 2-Daisy Mae. 3-Shmoo 10 20 30 58 79 100
4-John Wayne; Williamson/Frazetta-c from John Wayne #3
14 28 42 80 115 150
5-Archie 14 28 42 76 108 140
6-Terrytoons Mighty Mouse 10 20 30 58 79 100
Mailing Envelope (has All Capp's Shmoo on front) 11 22 33 62 86 110

OZZIE SMITH IN THE KID WHO COULD (Kellogg's Tony's Sports Comics)
DC Comics: 1992 (Sports Illustrated)

nn-Ozzie Smith app. 5.00

PADRE OF THE POOR
Catechetical Guild: nd (Giveaway) (16 pgs., paper-c)

nn 5 10 15 24 30 35

PAUL TERRY'S HOW TO DRAW FUNNY CARTOONS
Terrytoons, Inc. (Giveaway): 1940's (14 pgs.) (Black & White)

nn-Heckle & Jeckle, Mighty Mouse, etc. 13 26 39 72 101 130

PETER PAN (See New Adventures of Peter Pan)

PETER PENNY AND HIS MAGIC DOLLAR
American Bankers Association, N. Y. (Giveaway): 1947 (16 pgs., paper-c; regular size)

nn-(Scarce)-Used in **SOTI**, pg. 310, 311 15 30 45 88 137 185
Diff. version (7-1/4x11")-redrawn, 16 pgs., paper-c 10 20 30 56 76 95

PETER WHEAT (The Adventures of...)
Bakers Associates Giveaway: 1948 - 1957? (16 pgs. in color) (paper covers)

nn(No.1)-States on last page, end of 1st Adventure of...; Kelly-a
28 56 84 162 261 360
nn(4 issues)-Kelly-a 15 30 45 84 127 170
6-10-All Kelly-a 10 20 30 58 79 100
11-20-All Kelly-a 10 20 30 54 72 90
21-35-All Kelly-a 8 16 24 44 57 70
36-66 7 14 21 35 43 50
...Artist's Workbook ('54, digest size) 7 14 21 35 43 50
...Four-In-One Fun Pack (Vol. 2, '54), oblong, comics w/puzzles
8 16 24 40 50 60
...Fun Book ('52, 32 pgs., paper-c, B&W & color, 8-1/2x10-3/4")-Contains cut-outs, puzzles, games, magic & pages to color 9 18 27 50 65 80

NOTE: *Al Hubbard art #36 on; written by Del Connell.*

PETER WHEAT NEWS
Bakers Associates: 1948 - No. 30, 1950 (4 pgs. in color)

Vol. 1-All have 2 pgs. Peter Wheat by Kelly 23 46 69 132 214 295
2-10 14 28 42 76 108 140
11-20 8 16 24 44 57 70
21-30 7 14 21 35 43 50

NOTE: *Early issues have no date & **Kelly** art.*

PINOCCHIO
Cocomalt/Montgomery Ward Co.: 1940 (10 pgs.; giveaway, linen-like paper)

nn-Cocomalt edition 44 88 132 273 457 640
nn-store edition 37 74 111 218 352 485

PIUS XII MAN OF PEACE
Catechetical Guild: No date (12 pgs.; 5-1/2x8-1/2") (B&W)

nn-Catechetical Guild Giveaway 6 12 18 31 38 45

PLOT TO STEAL THE WORLD, THE
Work & Unity Group: 1948, 16pgs., paper-c

nn-Anti commumism 18 36 54 103 162 220

POCAHONTAS
Pocahontas Fuel Company (Coal): 1941 - No. 2, 1942

nn(#1), 2-Feat. life story of Indian princess Pocahontas & facts about Pocahontas coal,

Real Hit Comics #1 © FOX

Reddy Kilowatt #3 (1960) © EC

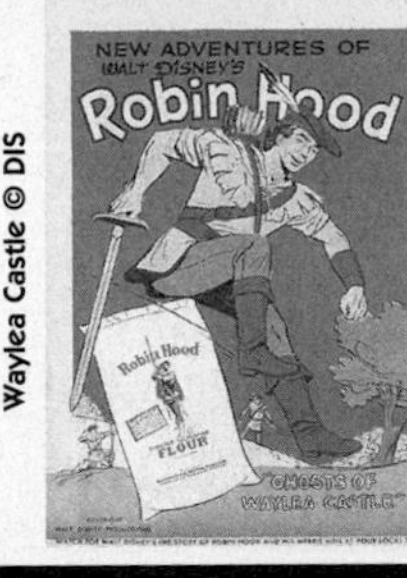

Robin Hood - Ghosts of Waylea Castle © DIS

	GD 2.0	VG 4.0	FN 6.0	VF 8.0	VF/NM 9.0	NM- 9.2
Pocahontas, VA.	15	30	45	85	130	175

POLL PARROT
Poll Parrot Shoe Store/International Shoe
K. K. Publications (Giveaway): 1950 - No. 4, 1951; No. 2, 1959 - No. 16, 1962

1 ('50)-Howdy Doody; small size 18 36 54 107 169 230
2-4('51)-Howdy Doody 15 30 45 88 137 185
2('59)-16('62): 2-The Secret of Crumbley Castle. 5-Bandit Busters. 7-The Make-Believe Mummy. 8-Mixed Up Mission('60). 10-The Frightful Flight. 11-Showdown at Sunup. 12-Maniac at Mubu Island. 13-...and the Runaway Genie. 14-Bully for You. 15-Trapped In Tall Timber. 16-...& the Rajah's Ruby('62) 3 6 9 16 22 28

POPEYE
Whitman
Bold Detergent giveaway (Same as regular issue #94) 2 4 6 8 11 14
Quaker Cereal premium (1989, 16pp, small size,4 diff.)(Popeye & the Time Machine, --On Safari, --& Big Foot, --vs. Bluto) 1 3 4 6 8 10

POPEYE
Charlton (King Features) (Giveaway): 1972 - 1974 (36 pgs. in color)
E-1 to E-15 (Educational comics) 2 4 6 8 11 14
nn-Popeye Gettin' Better Grades-4 pgs. used as intro. to above giveaways (in color) 2 4 6 8 11 14

POPSICLE PETE FUN BOOK (See All-American Comics #6)
Joe Lowe Corp.: 1947, 1948
nn-36 pgs. in color; Sammy 'n' Claras, The King Who Couldn't Sleep & Popsicle Pete stories, games, cut-outs 11 22 33 64 90 115
Adventure Book ('48)-Has Classics ad with checklist to HRN #343 (Great Expectations #43) 10 20 30 56 76 95

PORKY'S BOOK OF TRICKS
K. K. Publications (Giveaway): 1942 (8-1/2x5-1/2", 48 pgs.)
nn-7 pg. comic story, text stories, plus games & puzzles 47 94 141 291 483 675

POST GAZETTE (See Meet the New...)

PUNISHER: COUNTDOWN (Movie)
Marvel Comics: 2004 (7 1/4" X 4 3/4" mini-comic packaged with Punisher DVD)
nn Prequel to 2004 movie; Ennis-s/Dillon-a/Bradstreet-c 2.50

PURE OIL COMICS (Also see Salerno Carnival of Comics, 24 Pages of Comics, & Vicks Comics)
Pure Oil Giveaway: Late 1930's (24 pgs., regular size, paper-c)
nn-Contains 1-2 pg. strips; i.e., Hairbreadth Harry, Skyroads, Buck Rogers by Calkins & Yager, Olly of the Movies, Napoleon, S'Matter Pop, etc. Also a 16 pg. 1938 giveaway with Buck Rogers 35 70 105 208 334 460

QUAKER OATS (Also see Cap'n Crunch)
Quaker Oats Co.: 1965 (Giveaway) (2-1/2x5-1/2") (16 pgs.)
"Plenty of Glutton", starring Quake & Quisp; 3 6 9 14 19 24
"Lava Come-Back", "Kite Tale" 1 3 4 6 8 10

RAILROADS DELIVER THE GOODS!
Assoc. of American Railroads: Dec, 1954; Sept, 1957 (16 pgs.)
nn-The story of railway freight 6 12 18 28 34 40

RAILS ACROSS AMERICA!
Assoc. of American Railroads: nd (16 pgs.)
nn 6 12 18 28 34 40

REAL FUN OF DRIVING!!, THE
Chrysler Corp.: 1965, 1966, 1967 (Regular size, 16 pgs.)
nn-Schaffenberger-a (12 pgs.) 1 2 3 5 6 8

REAL HIT
Fox Features Publications: 1944 (Savings Bond premium)
1-Blue Beetle-r; Blue Beetle on-c 15 30 45 90 140 190
NOTE: *Two versions exist, with and without covers. The coverless version has the title, No. 1 and price printed at top of splash page.*

RED BALL COMIC BOOK
Parents' Magazine Institute: 1947 (Red Ball Shoes giveaway)
nn-Reprints from True Comics 4 8 11 16 19 22

REDDY GOOSE
International Shoe Co. (Western Printing): No number, 1958?; No. 2, Jan, 1959 - No. 16, July, 1962 (Giveaway)
nn (#1) 5 10 15 30 48 65
2-16 3 6 9 18 27 35

REDDY KILOWATT (5¢) (Also see Story of Edison)
Educational Comics (E. C.): 1946 - No. 2, 1947; 1956 - 1965 (no month) (16 pgs., paper-c)
nn-A Visit With Reddy (1948-1954?) 9 18 27 50 65 80
nn-Reddy Made Magic (1946, 5¢) 13 26 39 72 101 130
nn-Reddy Made Magic (1958) 9 18 27 50 65 80
2-Edison, the Man Who Changed the World (3/4" smaller than #1) (1947, 5¢) 13 26 39 72 101 130
...Comic Book 2 (1954)- "Light's Diamond Jubilee" 9 18 27 54 72 90
...Comic Book 2 (1958, 16 pgs.)- "Wizard of Light" 9 18 27 50 65 78
...Comic Book 2 (1965, 16 pgs.)- "Wizard of Light" 4 8 12 28 44 60
...Comic Book 3 (1956, 8 pgs.)- "The Space Kite"; Orlando story; regular size 9 18 27 47 61 75
...Comic Book 3 (1960, 8 pgs.)- "The Space Kite"; Orlando story; regular size 4 8 12 28 44 60
NOTE: *Several copies surfaced in 1979.*

REDDY MADE MAGIC
Educational Comics (E. C.): 1956, 1958 (16 pgs., paper-c)
1-Reddy Kilowatt-r (splash panel changed) 11 22 33 60 83 105
1 (1958 edition) 6 12 18 31 38 45

RED ICEBERG, THE
Impact Publ. (Catechetical Guild): 1960 (10¢, 16 pgs., Communist propaganda)
nn-(Rare)- "We The People" back-c 30 60 90 222 411 600
2nd version- "Impact Press" back-c 25 50 75 185 343 500
3rd version- "Explains comic" back-c 25 50 75 185 343 500
4th version- "Impact Press w/World Wide Secret Heart Program ad" 25 50 75 185 343 500
5th version- "Chicago Inter-Student Catholic Action" back-c 25 50 75 185 343 500
NOTE: *This book was the Guild's last anti-communist propaganda book and had very limited circulation. 3 - 4 copies surfaced in 1979 from the defunct publisher's files. Other copies do turn up.*

RED RYDER COMICS
Dell Publ. Co.
Buster Brown Shoes Giveaway (1941, color, soft-c, 32 pgs.) 23 46 69 135 218 300
Red Ryder Super Book of Comics (1944, paper-c, 32 pgs.; blank back-c) Magic Morro app. 25 50 75 149 240 330
Red Ryder Victory Patrol-nn(1942, 32 pgs.)(Langendorf bread; includes cut-out membership card and certificate, order blank and "Slide-Up" decoder, and a Super Book of Comics in color (same content as Super Book #4 w/diff. cover (Pan-Am)) (Rare) 300 600 900 1890 3195 4500
Red Ryder Victory Patrol-nn(1943, 32 pgs.)(Langendorf bread; includes cut-out "Rodeomatic" radio decoder, order coupon for "Magic V-Badge", cut-out membership card and certificate and a full color Super Book of comics comic book) (Rare) 267 534 801 1682 2841 4000
Red Ryder Victory Patrol-nn(1944, 32 pgs.)-r-/#43,44; comic has a paper-c & is stapled inside a triple cardboard fold-out-c; contains membership card, decoder, map of R.R. home range, etc. Herky app. (Langendorf Bread giveaway; sub-titled 'Super Book of Comics') (Rare) 267 534 801 1682 2841 4000
Wells Lamont Corp. giveaway (1950)-16 pgs. in color; regular size; paper-c; 1941-r 15 30 45 94 147 200

RICHIE RICH, CASPER & WENDY NATIONAL LEAGUE
Harvey Publications: June, 1976 (52 pgs.) (newsstand edition also exists)
1 (Released-3/76 with 6/76 date) 3 6 9 14 19 24
1 (6/76)-2nd version w/San Francisco Giants & KTVU 2 logos; has "Compliments of Giants and Straw Hat Pizza" on-c 3 6 9 14 19 24
1-Variants for other 11 NL teams, similar to Giants version but with different ad on inside front-c 3 6 9 14 19 24

RIDE THE HIGH IRON!
Assoc. of American Railroads: Jan, 1957 (16 pgs.)
nn-The Story of modern passenger trains 6 12 18 28 34 40

RIPLEY'S BELIEVE IT OR NOT!
Harvey Publications
J. C. Penney giveaway (1948) 9 18 27 50 65 80

ROBIN HOOD (New Adventures of...)
Walt Disney Productions: 1952 (Flour giveaways, 5x7-1/4", 36 pgs.)
"New Adventures of Robin Hood", "Ghosts of Waylea Castle", & "The Miller's Ransom" each.... 5 10 15 24 30 35

ROBIN HOOD'S FRONTIER DAYS (...Western Tales, Adventures of... #1)
Shoe Store Giveaway (Robin Hood Stores): 1956 (20 pgs., slick-c)(7 issues?)
nn 5 10 15 25 31 36
nn-Issues with Crandall-a 8 16 24 40 50 60

ROBOCOP (FRANK MILLER'S...)
Avatar Press: Apr, 2003
Free Comic Book Day Edition - Previews Robocop & Stargate SG-1; Busch-c 2.50

ROCKET COMICS: IGNITE
Dark Horse Comics: Apr, 2003 (Free Comic Book Day giveaway)
1-Previews Dark Horse series Syn, Lone, and Go Boy 7 2.50

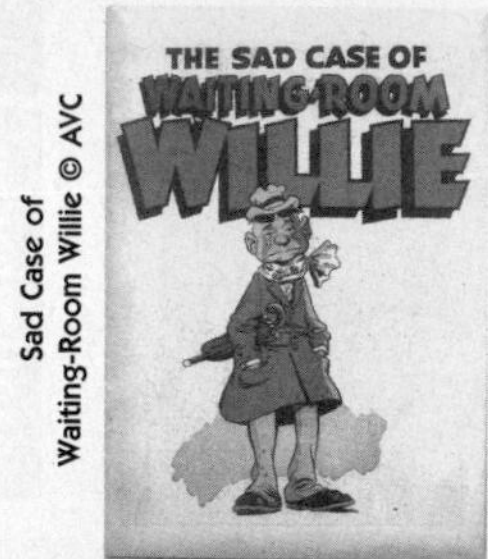

Sad Case of Waiting-Room Willie © AVC

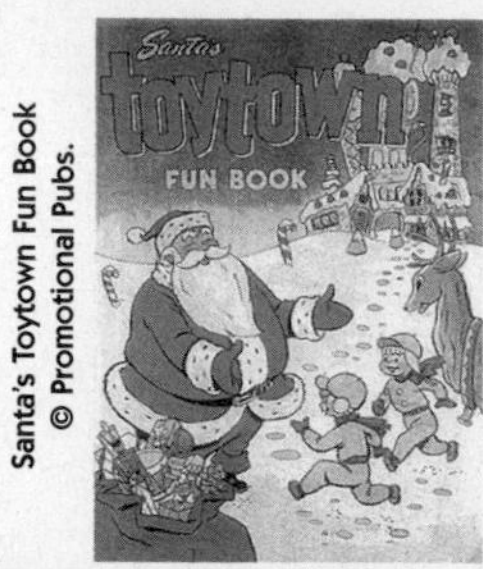

Santa's Toytown Fun Book © Promotional Pubs.

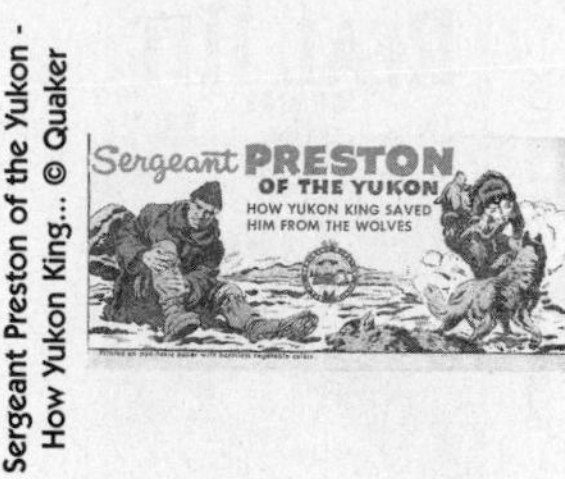

Sergeant Preston of the Yukon - How Yukon King... © Quaker

	GD	VG	FN	VF	VF/NM	NM-
	2.0	4.0	6.0	8.0	9.0	9.2

ROCKETS AND RANGE RIDERS
Richfield Oil Corp.: May, 1957 (Giveaway, 16 pgs., soft-c)
nn-Toth-a 14 28 42 82 121 160

ROUND THE WORLD GIFT
National War Fund (Giveaway): No date (mid 1940's) (4 pgs.)
nn 11 22 33 64 90 115

ROY ROGERS COMICS
Dell Publishing Co.
...& the Man From Dodge City (Dodge giveaway, 16 pgs., 1954)-Frontier, Inc. (5x7-1/4") 14 28 42 76 108 140
Official Roy Rogers Riders Club Comics (1952; 16 pgs., reg. size, paper-c) 25 50 75 147 236 325

RUDOLPH, THE RED-NOSED REINDEER
Montgomery Ward: 1939 (2,400,000 copies printed); Dec, 1951 (Giveaway)
Paper cover-1st app. in print; written by Robert May; ill. by Denver Gillen 15 30 45 83 124 165
Hardcover version 19 38 57 109 172 235
1951 Edition (Has 1939 date)-36 pgs., slick-c printed in red & brown; pulp interior printed in four mixed-ink colors: red, green, blue & brown 11 22 33 62 86 110
1951 Edition with red-spiral promotional booklet printed on high quality stock, 8-1/2"x11", in red & brown, 25 pages composed of 4 fold outs, single sheets and the Rudolph comic book inserted (rare) 47 94 141 291 483 675

SABRINA THE TEENAGE WITCH
Archie Comic Publications: (8 1/2"x 5 1/2", Diamond Comic Dist. Halloween giveaway)
... And The Archies (2004)-Tania Del Rio-s/a; manga-style; Josie and the Pussycats app. 2.50

SAD CASE OF WAITING ROOM WILLIE, THE
American Visuals Corp. (For Baltimore Medical Society): (nd, 1950?) (14 pgs. in color; paper covers; regular size)
nn-By Will Eisner (Rare) 44 88 132 273 457 640

SAD SACK COMICS
Harvey Publications: 1957-1962
Armed Forces Complimentary copies, HD #1-40 (1957-1962) 3 6 9 14 19 24

SALERNO CARNIVAL OF COMICS (Also see Pure Oil Comics, 24 Pages of Comics, & Vicks Comics)
Salerno Cookie Co.: Late 1930s (Giveaway, 16 pgs, paper-c)
nn-Color reprints of Calkins' Buck Rogers & Skyroads, plus other strips from Famous Funnies 43 86 129 267 446 625

SALUTE TO THE BOY SCOUTS
Association of American Railroads: 1960 (16 pgs.)
nn-History of scouting and the railroad 3 6 9 14 19 24

SANTA AND POLLYANNA PLAY THE GLAD GAME
Sales Promotion: Aug, 1960 (16 pgs.) (Disney giveaway)
nn 2 4 6 13 18 22

SANTA & THE BUCCANEERS
Promotional Publ. Co.: 1959 (Giveaway)
nn-Reprints 1952 Santa & the Pirates 2 4 6 11 16 20

SANTA & THE CHRISTMAS CHICKADEE
Murphy's: 1974 (Giveaway, 20 pgs.)
nn 2 4 6 8 10 12

SANTA & THE PIRATES
Promotional Publ. Co.: 1952 (Giveaway)
nn-Marv Levy-c/a 4 8 11 16 19 22

SANTA CLAUS FUNNIES (Also see The Little Fir Tree)
W. T. Grant Co./Whitman Publishing: nd; 1940 (Giveaway, 8x10"; 12 pgs., color & B&W, heavy paper)
nn-(2 versions- no date and 1940) 14 28 42 76 108 140

SANTA ON THE JOLLY ROGER
Promotional Publ. Co. (Giveaway): 1965
nn-Marv Levy-c/a 2 4 6 8 10 12

SANTA! SANTA!
R. Jackson: 1974 (20 pgs.) (Montgomery Ward giveaway)
nn 1 3 4 6 8 10

SANTA'S BUNDLE OF FUN
Gimbels: 1969 (Giveaway, B&W, 20 pgs.)
nn-Coloring book & games 2 4 6 8 10 12

SANTA'S CHRISTMAS COMIC VARIETY SHOW (See Merry Christmas From Sears Toyland)
Sears Roebuck & Co.: 1943 (24 pgs.)
Contains puzzles & new comics of Dick Tracy, Little Orphan Annie, Moon Mullins, Terry & the Pirates, etc. 53 106 159 331 558 785

	GD	VG	FN	VF	VF/NM	NM-
	2.0	4.0	6.0	8.0	9.0	9.2

SANTA'S CHRISTMAS TIME STORIES
Premium Sales, Inc.: nd (Late 1940s) (16 pgs., paper-c) (Giveaway)
nn 6 12 18 31 38 45

SANTA'S CIRCUS
Promotional Publ. Co.: 1964 (Giveaway, half-size)
nn-Marv Levy-c/a 2 4 6 8 11 14

SANTA'S FUN BOOK
Promotional Publ. Co.: 1951, 1952 (Regular size, 16 pgs., paper-c) (Murphy's giveaway)
nn 5 10 15 23 28 32

SANTA'S GIFT BOOK
No Publisher: No date (16 pgs.)
nn-Puzzles, games only 4 8 11 16 19 22

SANTA'S NEW STORY BOOK
Wallace Hamilton Campbell: 1949 (16 pgs., paper-c) (Giveaway)
nn 6 12 18 31 38 45

SANTA'S REAL STORY BOOK
Wallace Hamilton Campbell/W. W. Orris: 1948, 1952 (Giveaway, 16 pgs.)
nn 6 12 18 31 38 45

SANTA'S RIDE
W. T. Grant Co.: 1959 (Giveaway)
nn 3 6 9 14 19 24

SANTA'S RODEO
Promotional Publ. Co.: 1964 (Giveaway, half-size)
nn-Marv Levy-a 2 4 6 8 11 14

SANTA'S SECRET CAVE
W.T. Grant Co.: 1960 (Giveaway, half-size)
nn 2 4 6 11 16 20

SANTA'S SECRETS
Sam B. Anson Christmas giveaway: 1951, 1952? (16 pgs., paper-c)
nn-Has games, stories & pictures to color 4 8 12 17 21 24

SANTA'S STORIES
K. K. Publications (Klines Dept. Store): 1953 (Regular size, paper-c)
nn-Kelly-a 15 30 45 88 137 185
nn-Another version (1953, glossy-c, half-size, 7-1/4x5-1/4")-Kelly-a 11 22 33 62 86 110

SANTA'S SURPRISE
K. K. Publications: 1947 (Giveaway, 36 pgs., slick-c)
nn 8 16 24 40 50 60

SANTA'S TOYTOWN FUN BOOK
Promotional Publ. Co.: 1953 (Giveaway)
nn-Marv Levy-c 4 8 11 16 19 22

SANTA TAKES A TRIP TO MARS
Bradshaw-Diehl Co., Huntington, W.VA.: 1950s (nd) (Giveaway, 16 pgs.)
nn 4 8 11 16 19 22

SCIENCE FAIR STORY OF ELECTRONICS
Radio Shack/Tandy Corp.: 1975 - 1987 (Giveaway)
11 different issues (approx. 1 per year) each.... 3.00

SCOOBY-DOO!
DC Comics.: 2002 (Burger King/Cartoon Network giveaway)
1 2.50

SERGEANT PRESTON OF THE YUKON
Quaker Cereals: 1956 (4 comic booklets) (Soft-c, 16 pgs., 7x2-1/2" & 5x2-1/2") Giveaways
"How He Found Yukon King", "The Case That Made Him A Sergeant", "How Yukon King Saved Him From The Wolves", "How He Became A Mountie" each... 8 16 24 44 57 70

SHAZAM! (Visits Portland Oregon in 1943)
DC Comics: 1989 (69¢ cover)
nn-Promotes Super-Heroes exhibit at Oregon Museum of Science and Industry; reprints Golden Age Captain Marvel story 2 4 6 8 10 12

SHERIFF OF COCHISE, THE (TV)
Mobil: 1957 (16 pgs.) Giveaway
nn-Schaffenberger-a 4 8 12 17 21 24

SILLY PUTTY MAN

Snow White and the Seven Dwarfs (Bendix) © DIS

The Spirit (12/21/41) © Will Eisner

The Spirit (6/21/42) © Will Eisner

	GD 2.0	VG 4.0	FN 6.0	VF 8.0	VF/NM 9.0	NM- 9.2

DC Comics: 1978

1	2	4	6	8	11	14

SKATING SKILLS
Custom Comics, Inc./Chicago Roller Skates: 1957 (36 & 12 pgs.; 5x7", two versions) (10¢)

nn-Resembles old ACG cover plus interior art	4	7	10	14	17	20

SKIPPY'S OWN BOOK OF COMICS (See Popular Comics)
No publisher listed: 1934 (Giveaway, 52 pgs., strip reprints)

nn-(Scarce)-By Percy Crosby	365	730	1095	2482	4341	6200

Published by Max C. Gaines for Phillip's Dental Magnesia to be advertised on the Skippy Radio Show and given away with the purchase of a tube of Phillip's Tooth Paste. This is the first four-color comic book of reprints about one character.

SKY KING "RUNAWAY TRAIN" (TV)
National Biscuit Co.: 1964 (Regular size, 16 pgs.)

nn	6	12	18	39	65	90

SLAM BANG COMICS
Post Cereal Giveaway: No. 9, No date

9-Dynamo Man, Echo, Mr. E, Yankee Boy app.	9	18	27	50	65	80

SLAVE LABOR STORIES
SLG Publishing: May, 2003 (Giveaway, B&W)

1-Free Comic Book Day Edition; short stories by various; Dorkin Milk & Cheese-c 2.50

SMILIN' JACK
Dell Publishing Co.

Popped Wheat Giveaway (1947)-1938 strip reprints; 16 pgs. in full color	2	4	6	8	11	14
Shoe Store Giveaway-1938 strip reprints; 16 pgs.	5	10	15	24	30	35
Sparked Wheat Giveaway (1942)-16 pgs. in full color	5	10	15	24	30	35

SMOKEY BEAR (See Forest Fire for 1st app.)
Dell Publ. Co.: 1959,1960

True Story of..., The -U.S. Forest Service giveaway Publ. by Western Printing Co.; reprints 1st 16 pgs. of Four Color #932. Inside front-c differs slightly in 1959 & 1960 editions	5	10	15	22	26	30
1964,1969 reprints	2	4	6	11	16	20

SMOKEY STOVER
Dell Publishing Co.

General Motors giveaway (1953)	8	16	24	40	50	60
National Fire Protection giveaway(1953 & 1954)-16 pgs., paper-c	8	16	24	40	50	60

SNOW FOR CHRISTMAS
W. T. Grant Co.: 1957 (16 pgs.) (Giveaway)

nn	4	8	12	18	22	25

SNOW WHITE AND THE SEVEN DWARFS
Bendix Washing Machines: 1952 (32 pgs., 5x7-1/4", soft-c) (Disney)

nn	11	22	33	62	86	110

SNOW WHITE AND THE SEVEN DWARFS
Promotional Publ. Co.: 1957 (Small size)

nn	6	12	18	28	34	40

SNOW WHITE AND THE SEVEN DWARFS
Western Printing Co.: 1958 (16 pgs, 5x7-1/4", soft-c) (Disney promium)

nn- "Mystery of the Missing Magic"	7	14	21	35	43	50

SNOW WHITE AND THE 7 DWARFS IN "MILKY WAY"
American Dairy Assoc.: 1955 (16 pgs., soft-c, 5x7-1/4") (Disney premium)

nn	8	16	24	40	50	60

SONIC THE HEDGEHOG
Archie Comic Publications: 2008 (Free Comic Book Day giveaway)

Free Comic Book Day Edition 1 - Reprints Sonic the Hedgehog #1 from July 1993 2.50

SPACE GHOST COAST TO COAST
Cartoon Network: Apr, 1994 (giveaway to Turner Broadcasting employees)

1-(8 pgs.); origin of Space Ghost 6.00

SPACE PATROL (TV)
Ziff-Davis Publishing Co. (Approved Comics)

...'s Special Mission (8 pgs., B&W, Giveaway)	47	94	141	291	483	675

SPECIAL AGENT
Assoc. of American Railroads: Oct, 1959 (16 pgs.)

nn-The Story of the railroad police	8	16	24	40	50	60

SPECIAL DELIVERY
Post Hall Synd.: 1951 (32 pgs.; B&W) (Giveaway)

nn-Origin of Pogo, Swamp, etc.; 2 pg. biog. on Walt Kelly

(One copy sold in 1980 for $150.00)

SPECIAL EDITION (U. S. Navy Giveaways)
National Periodical Publications: 1944 - 1945 (Regular comic format with wording simplified, 52 pgs.)

1-Action (1944)-Reprints Action #80	53	106	159	330	553	775
2-Action (1944)-Reprints Action #81	53	106	159	330	553	775
3-Superman (1944)-Reprints Superman #33	53	106	159	330	553	775
4-Detective (1944)-Reprints Detective #97	53	106	159	330	553	775
5-Superman (1945)-Reprints Superman #34	53	106	159	330	553	775
6-Action (1945)-Reprints Action #84	53	106	159	330	553	775

NOTE: ***Wayne Boring** c-1, 2, 6. **Dick Sprang** c-4.*

SPIDER-MAN (See Amazing Spider-Man, The)

SPIRIT, THE (Weekly Comic Book)
Will Eisner: 6/2/40 - 10/5/52 (16 pgs.; 8 pgs.) (no cover) (in color)
(Distributed through various newspapers and other sources)
NOTE: **Eisner** script, pencils/inks for the most part from 6/2/40-4/26/42; a few stories assisted by Jack Cole, Fine, Powell and Kotsky.

6/2/40(#1)-Origin/1st app. The Spirit; reprinted in Police #11; Lady Luck (Brenda Banks) (1st app.) by Chuck Mazoujian & Mr. Mystic (1st. app.) by S. R. (Bob) Powell begin (rare)	150	300	450	945	1598	2250
6/9/40(#2)	37	74	111	215	345	475
6/16/40(#3)-Black Queen app. in Spirit	24	48	72	143	229	315
6/23/40(#4)-Mr. Mystic receives magical necklace	19	38	57	109	172	235
6/30/40(#5)	19	38	57	109	172	235
7/7/40(#6)-1st app. Spirit carplane; Black Queen app. in Spirit	20	40	60	115	183	250
7/14/40(#7)-8/4/40(#10): 7/21/40-Spirit becomes fugitive wanted for murder	15	30	45	94	147	200
8/11/40-9/22/40	15	30	45	90	140	190
9/29/40-Ellen drops engagement with Homer Creep	15	30	45	85	130	175
10/6/40-11/3/40	15	30	45	85	130	175
11/10/40-The Black Queen app.	15	30	45	85	130	175
11/17/40, 11/24/40	15	30	45	85	130	175
12/1/40-Ellen spanking by Spirit on cover & inside; Eisner-1st 3 pgs., J. Cole rest	19	38	57	109	172	235
12/8/40-3/9/41	14	28	42	80	115	150
3/16/41-Intro. & 1st app. Silk Satin	15	30	45	94	147	200
3/23/41-6/1/41: 5/11/41-Last Lady Luck by Mazoujian; 5/18/41-Lady Luck by Nick Viscardi begins, ends 2/22/42	14	28	42	76	108	140
6/8/41-2nd app. Satin; Spirit learns Satin is also a British agent	15	30	45	83	124	165
6/15/41-1st app. Twilight	14	28	42	80	115	150
6/22/41-Hitler app. in Spirit	14	28	42	80	115	150
6/29/41-1/25/42,2/8/42	12	24	36	67	94	120
2/1/42-1st app. Duchess	14	28	42	80	115	150
2/15/42-4/26/42-Lady Luck by Klaus Nordling begins 3/1/42	13	26	39	74	105	135
5/3/42-8/16/42-Eisner/Fine/Quality staff assists on Spirit	10	20	30	58	79	100
8/23/42-Satin cover splash; Spirit by Eisner/Fine although signed by Fine	15	30	45	84	127	170
8/30/42,9/27/42-10/11/42,10/25/42-11/8/42-Eisner/Fine/Quality staff assists on Spirit	10	20	30	56	76	95
9/6/42-9/20/42,10/18/42-Fine/Belfi art on Spirit; scripts by Manly Wade Wellman	8	16	24	42	54	65
11/15/42-12/6/42,12/20/42,12/27/42,1/17/43-4/18/43,5/9/43-8/8/43-Wellman/Woolfolk scripts, Fine pencils, Quality staff inks	8	16	24	42	54	65
12/13/42,1/3/43,1/10/43,4/25/43,5/2/43-Eisner scripts/layouts; Fine pencils, Quality staff inks	9	18	27	47	61	75
8/15/43-Eisner script/layout; pencils/inks by Quality staff; Jack Cole-a	7	14	21	37	46	55
8/22/43-12/12/43-Wellman/Woolfolk scripts, Fine pencils, Quality staff inks; Mr. Mystic by Guardineer-10/10/43-10/24/43	7	14	21	37	46	55
12/19/43-8/13/44-Wellman/Woolfolk/Jack Cole scripts; Cole, Fine & Robin King-a; Last Mr. Mystic-5/14/44	7	14	21	35	44	52
8/20/44-12/16/45-Wellman/Woolfolk scripts; Fine art with unknown staff assists	7	14	21	35	44	52

NOTE: *Scripts/layouts by Eisner, or Eisner/Nordling, Eisner/Mercer or Spranger/Eisner; inks by Eisner or Eisner/Spranger in issues 12/23/45-2/2/47.*

12/23/45-1/6/46: 12/23/45-Christmas-c	8	16	24	44	57	70
1/13/46-Origin Spirit retold	11	22	33	64	90	115
1/20/46-1st postwar Satin app.	10	20	30	56	76	95
1/27/46-3/10/46: 3/3/46-Last Lady Luck by Nordling	8	16	24	44	57	70
3/17/46-Intro. & 1st app. Nylon	10	20	30	56	76	95
3/24/46,3/31/46,4/14/46	8	16	24	44	57	70
4/7/46-2nd app. Nylon	9	18	27	50	65	80
4/21/46-Intro. & 1st app. Mr. Carrion & His Pet Buzzard Julia	11	22	33	62	86	110

The Spirit (9/07/52) © Will Eisner

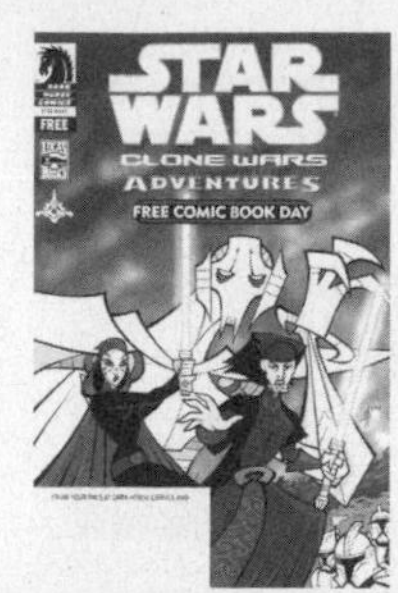

Star Wars Clone Wars Advs. © LucasFilm

Steve Canyon's Secret Mission © HARV

	GD 2.0	VG 4.0	FN 6.0	VF 8.0	VF/NM 9.0	NM- 9.2
4/28/46-5/12/46,5/26/46-6/30/46: Lady Luck by Fred Schwab in issues						
5/5/46-11/3/46	8	16	24	44	57	70
5/19/46-2nd app. Mr. Carrion	9	18	27	50	65	80
7/7/46-Intro. & 1st app. Dulcet Tone & Skinny	10	20	30	56	76	95
7/14/46-9/29/46	8	16	24	44	57	70
10/6/46-Intro. & 1st app. P'Gell	11	22	33	64	90	115
10/13/46-11/3/46,11/16/46-11/24/46	8	16	24	44	57	70
11/10/46-2nd app. P'Gell	10	20	30	54	72	90
12/1/46-3rd app. P'Gell	9	18	27	47	61	75
12/8/46-2/2/47	8	16	24	42	54	65

NOTE: *Scripts, pencils/inks by Eisner except where noted in issues 2/9/47-12/19/48.*

	GD 2.0	VG 4.0	FN 6.0	VF 8.0	VF/NM 9.0	NM- 9.2
2/9/47-7/6/47: 6/8/47-Eisner self satire	8	16	24	42	54	65
7/13/47- "Hansel & Gretel" fairy tales	10	20	30	56	76	95
7/20/47-Li'L Abner, Daddy Warbucks, Dick Tracy, Fearless Fosdick parody; A-Bomb blast-c	11	22	33	62	86	110
7/27/47-9/14/47	8	16	24	42	54	65
9/21/47-Pearl Harbor flashback	9	18	27	47	61	75
9/28/47-1st mention of Flying Saucers in comics-3 months after 1st sighting in Idaho on 6/25/47	15	30	45	85	130	175
10/5/47- "Cinderella" fairy tales	10	20	30	56	76	95
10/12/47-11/30/47	8	16	24	42	54	65
12/7/47-Intro. & 1st app. Powder Pouf	11	22	33	62	86	110
12/14/47-12/28/47	8	16	24	42	54	65
1/4/48-2nd app. Powder Pouf	9	18	27	47	61	75
1/11/48-1st app. Sparrow Fallon; Powder Pouf app.	9	18	27	47	61	75
1/18/48-He-Man ad cover; satire issue	9	18	27	47	61	75
1/25/48-Intro. & 1st app. Castanet	11	22	33	62	86	110
2/1/48-2nd app. Castanet	8	16	24	44	57	70
2/8/48-3/7/48	8	16	24	42	54	65
3/14/48-Only app. Kretchma	8	16	24	44	57	70
3/21/48,3/28/48,4/11/48-4/25/48	8	16	24	42	54	65
4/4/48-Only app. Wild Rice	8	16	24	44	57	70
5/2/48-2nd app. Sparrow	8	16	24	42	54	65
5/9/48-6/27/48,7/11/48,7/18/48: 6/13/48-TV issue	8	16	24	42	54	65
7/4/48-Spirit by Andre Le Blanc	7	14	21	35	44	52
7/25/48-Ambrose Bierce's "The Thing" adaptation classic by Eisner/Grandenetti	14	28	42	81	118	155
8/1/48-8/15/48,8/29/48-9/12/48	8	16	24	42	54	65
8/22/48-Poe's "Fall of the House of Usher" classic by Eisner/Grandenetti	14	28	42	81	118	155
9/19/48-Only app. Lorelei	9	18	27	47	61	75
9/26/48-10/31/48	8	16	24	42	54	65
11/7/48-Only app. Plaster of Paris	10	20	30	56	76	95
11/14/48-12/19/48	8	16	24	42	54	65

NOTE: *Scripts by Eisner or Feiffer or Eisner/Feiffer or Nordling. Art by Eisner with backgrounds by Eisner, Grandenetti, Le Blanc, Stallman, Nordling, Dixon and/or others in issues 12/26/48-4/1/51 except where noted.*

	GD 2.0	VG 4.0	FN 6.0	VF 8.0	VF/NM 9.0	NM- 9.2
12/26/48-Reprints some covers of 1948 with flashbacks	8	16	24	42	54	65
1/2/49-1/16/49	8	16	24	42	54	65
1/23/49,1/30/49-1st & 2nd app. Thorne	9	18	27	47	61	75
2/6/49-8/14/49	8	16	24	42	54	65
8/21/49,8/28/49-1st & 2nd app. Monica Veto	9	18	27	47	61	75
9/4/49,9/11/49	8	16	24	42	54	65
9/18/49-Love comic cover; has gag love comic ads on inside	9	18	27	47	61	75
9/25/49-Only app. Ice	8	16	24	44	57	70
10/2/49,10/9/49-Autumn News appears & dies in 10/9 issue	8	16	24	44	57	70
10/16/49-11/27/49,12/18/49,12/25/49	8	16	24	42	54	65
12/4/49,12/11/49-1st & 2nd app. Flaxen	8	16	24	44	57	70
1/1/50-Flashbacks to all of the Spirit girls-Thorne, Ellen, Satin, & Monica	12	24	36	67	94	120
1/8/50-Intro. & 1st app. Sand Saref	14	28	42	80	115	150
1/15/50-2nd app. Saref	11	22	33	62	86	110
1/22/50-2/5/50	8	16	24	42	54	65
2/12/50-Roller Derby issue	9	18	27	47	61	75
2/19/50-Half Dead Mr. Lox - Classic horror	10	20	30	56	76	95
2/26/50-4/23/50,5/14/50,5/28/50,7/23/50-9/3/50	8	16	24	42	54	65
4/30/50-Script/art by Le Blanc with Eisner framing	6	12	18	33	41	48
5/7/50,6/4/50-7/16/50-Abe Kanegson-a	6	12	18	33	41	48
5/21/50-Script by Feiffer/Eisner, art by Blaisdell, Eisner framing	6	12	18	33	41	48
9/10/50-P'Gell returns	9	18	27	47	61	75
9/17/50-1/7/51	8	16	24	42	54	65
1/14/51-Life Magazine cover; brief biography of Comm. Dolan, Sand Saref, Silk Satin, P'Gell, Sammy & Willum, Darling O'Shea, & Mr. Carrion & His Pet Buzzard Julia, with pin-ups by Eisner	10	20	30	56	76	95
1/21/51,2/4/51-4/1/51	8	16	24	42	54	65
1/28/51- "The Meanest Man in the World" by Eisner	10	20	30	56	76	95
4/8/51-7/29/51,8/12/51-Last Eisner issue	8	16	24	42	54	65
8/5/51,8/19/51-7/20/52-Not Eisner	6	12	18	31	38	45
7/27/52-(Rare)-Denny Colt in Outer Space by Wally Wood; 7 pg. S/F story of E.C. vintage	33	66	99	192	309	425
8/3/52-(Rare)- "Mission...The Moon" by Wood	33	66	99	192	309	425
8/10/52-(Rare)- "A DP On The Moon" by Wood	33	66	99	192	309	425
8/17/52-(Rare)- "Heart" by Wood/Eisner	28	56	84	162	261	360
8/24/52-(Rare)- "Rescue" by Wood	33	66	99	192	309	425
8/31/52-(Rare)- "The Last Man" by Wood	33	66	99	192	309	425
9/7/52-(Rare)- "The Man in The Moon" by Wood	33	66	99	192	309	425
9/14/52-(Rare)-Eisner/Wenzel-a	15	30	45	90	140	190
9/21/52-(Rare)- "Denny Colt, Alias The Spirit/Space Report" by Eisner/Wenzel	16	32	48	92	151	210
9/28/52-(Rare)- "Return From The Moon" by Wood	32	64	96	186	298	410
10/5/52-(Rare)- "The Last Story" by Eisner	15	30	45	88	137	185

Large Tabloid pages from 1946 on (Eisner) - Price 200 percent over listed prices.

NOTE: *Spirit sections came out in both large and small format. Some newspapers went to the 8-pg. format months before others. Some printed the pages so they cannot be folded into a small comic book section; these are worth less. (Also see Three Comics & Spiritman).*

SPY SMASHER
Fawcett Publications

	GD 2.0	VG 4.0	FN 6.0	VF 8.0	VF/NM 9.0	NM- 9.2
Well Known Comics (1944, 12 pgs., 8-1/2x10-1/2"), paper-c, glued binding, printed in green; Bestmaid/Samuel Lowe giveaway	15	30	45	83	124	165

STANDARD OIL COMICS (Also see Gulf Funny Weekly)
Standard Oil Co.: 1932-1934 (Giveaway, tabloid size, 4 pgs. in color)

	GD 2.0	VG 4.0	FN 6.0	VF 8.0	VF/NM 9.0	NM- 9.2
nn (Dec. 1932)	53	106	159	334	567	800
1-Series has original art	47	94	141	291	483	675
2-5	20	40	60	120	193	265
6-14: 14-Fred Opper strip, 1 pg.	14	28	42	76	108	140
1A (Jan 1933)	48	96	144	298	499	700
2A-14A (1933)	31	62	93	181	291	400
1B (1934)	38	76	114	226	363	500
2B-?B (1934)	31	62	93	181	291	400

NOTE: *Series A contains Frederick Opper's Si & Mirandi; Series B contains Goofus: He's From The Big City; McVittle by Walter O'Ehrle; interior strips include Pesty And His Pop & Smiling Slim by Sid Hicks.*

STAR TEAM
Marvel Comics Group: 1977 (6-1/2x5", 20 pgs.) (Ideal Toy Giveaway)

	GD 2.0	VG 4.0	FN 6.0	VF 8.0	VF/NM 9.0	NM- 9.2
nn	2	4	6	11	16	20

STAR WARS
Dark Horse Comics: May, 2002; July, 2004 (Free Comic Book Day giveaways)

	GD 2.0	VG 4.0	FN 6.0	VF 8.0	VF/NM 9.0	NM- 9.2
...: Clone Wars Adventures (7/04) based on Cartoon Network series; Fillbach Bros. -a						2.50
...: FCBD 2005 Special (5/05) Anakin & Obi-Wan during Clone Wars						2.50
...: FCBD 2006 Special (5/06) Clone Wars story; flip book with Conan FCBD Special						2.50
...: Tales - A Jedi's Weapon (5/02, 16 pgs.) Anakin Skywalker Episode 2 photo-c						2.50

STEVE CANYON COMICS
Harvey Publications

	GD 2.0	VG 4.0	FN 6.0	VF 8.0	VF/NM 9.0	NM- 9.2
Dept. Store giveaway #3(6/48, 36pp)	10	20	30	54	72	90
...'s Secret Mission (1951, 16 pgs., Armed Forces giveaway); Caniff-a	9	18	27	47	61	75
Strictly for the Smart Birds (1951, 16 pgs.)-Information Comics Div. (Harvey) Premium	8	16	24	40	50	60

STORIES OF CHRISTMAS
K. K. Publications: 1942 (Giveaway, 32 pgs., paper cover)

	GD 2.0	VG 4.0	FN 6.0	VF 8.0	VF/NM 9.0	NM- 9.2
nn-Adaptation of "A Christmas Carol"; Kelly story "The Fir Tree"; Infinity-c	30	60	90	176	283	390

STORY HOUR SERIES (Disney)
Whitman Publ. Co.: 1948, 1949; 1951-1953 (36 pgs., paper-c) (4-3/4x6-1/2")
Given away with subscription to Walt Disney's Comics & Stories

	GD 2.0	VG 4.0	FN 6.0	VF 8.0	VF/NM 9.0	NM- 9.2
nn(1948)-Mickey Mouse and the Boy Thursday	12	24	36	67	94	120
nn(1948)-Mickey Mouse the Miracle Master	12	24	36	67	94	120
nn(1948)-Minnie Mouse and Antique Chair	12	24	36	67	94	120
nn(1949)-The Three Orphan Kittens(B&W & color)	9	18	27	47	61	75
nn(1949)-Danny-The Little Black Lamb	9	18	27	47	61	75
800(1948)-Donald Duck in "Bringing Up the Boys"	15	30	45	88	137	185
1953 edition	11	22	33	64	90	115
801(1948)-Mickey Mouse's Summer Vacation	10	20	30	56	76	95
1951, 1952 editions	7	14	21	35	43	50
802(1948)-Bugs Bunny's Adventures	9	18	27	50	65	80
803(1948)-Bongo	8	16	24	40	50	60
804(1948)-Mickey and the Beanstalk	9	18	27	47	61	75
805-15(1949)-Andy Panda and His Friends	8	16	24	40	50	60
806-15(1949)-Tom and Jerry	8	16	24	44	57	70
808-15(1949)-Johnny Appleseed	8	16	24	40	50	60

1948, 1949 Hard Cover Edition of each....30% - 40% more.

STORY OF EDISON, THE

Story of Harry S. Truman © DNC

Super-Book of Comics (Omar) #25 © NYNS

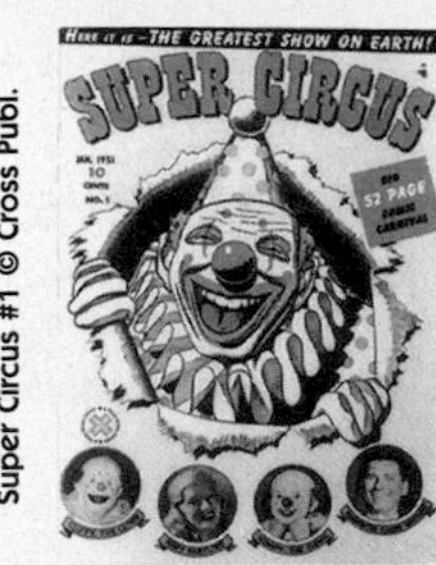

Super Circus #1 © Cross Publ.

GD VG FN VF VF/NM NM-
2.0 4.0 6.0 8.0 9.0 9.2

Educational Comics: 1956 (16 pgs.) (Reddy Killowatt)
nn-Reprint of Reddy Kilowatt #2(1947) 7 14 21 35 43 50

STORY OF HARRY S. TRUMAN, THE
Democratic National Committee: 1948 (Giveaway, regular size, soft-c, 16 pg.)
nn-Gives biography on career of Truman; used in **SOTI**, pg. 311 14 28 42 76 108 140

STORY OF THE BALLET, THE
Selva and Sons, Inc.: 1954 (16 pgs., paper cover)
nn 4 8 11 16 19 22

STRANGE AS IT SEEMS
McNaught Syndicate: 1936 (B&W, 5" x 7", 24 pgs.)
nn-Ex-Lax giveaway 8 16 24 44 57 70

STRAY
Dark Horse Comics: 2004 (8 1/2"x 5 1/2", Diamond Comic Dist. Halloween giveaway)
nn-Reprint from The Dark Horse Book of Hauntings; Evan Dorkin-s/Jill Thompson-a 2.50

STRAY BULLETS
El Capitan Books: May, 2002 (48 pgs., B&W, flip book)
Free Comic Book Day giveaway-Reprints #2 with "Free Comic Book Day" banner on-c; flip book with The Matrix (printing of internet comic) 2.50

SUGAR BEAR
Post Cereal Giveaway: No date, circa 1975? (2 1/2" x 4 1/2", 16 pgs.)
"The Almost Take Over of the Post Office", "The Race Across the Atlantic", "The Zoo Goes Wild" each... 1 2 3 5 6 8

SUNDAY WORLD'S EASTER EGG FULL OF EASTER MEAT FOR LITTLE PEOPLE
Supplement to the New York World: 3/27/1898 (soft-c, 16pg, 4"x8" approx., opens at top, color & B&W)(Giveaway)(shaped like an Easter egg)
nn-By R.F. Outcault 18 36 54 103 162 220

SUPER BOOK OF COMICS
Western Publishing Co.: nd (1942-1943?) (Soft-c, 32 pgs.) (Pan-Am/Gilmore Oil/Kelloggs premiums)
nn-Dick Tracy (Gilmore)-Magic Morro app. (2 versions: Dick Tracy Jr. on cover and a filing cabinet cover) 32 64 96 190 305 420
1-Dick Tracy & The Smuggling Ring; Stratosphere Jim app. (Rare) (Pan-Am) 32 64 96 190 305 420
1-Smilin' Jack, Magic Morro (Pan-Am) 13 26 39 74 105 135
2-Smilin' Jack, Stratosphere Jim (Pan-Am) 13 26 39 74 105 135
2-Smitty, Magic Morro (Pan-Am) 13 26 39 74 105 135
3-Captain Midnight, Magic Morro (Pan-Am) 23 46 69 135 218 300
3-Moon Mullins? 13 26 39 74 105 135
4-Red Ryder, Magic Morro (Pan-Am). Same content as Red Ryder Victory Patrol comic w/diff. cover 15 30 45 85 130 175
4-Smitty, Stratosphere Jim (Pan-Am) 13 26 39 74 105 135
5-Don Winslow, Magic Morro (Gilmore) 15 30 45 85 130 175
5-Don Winslow, Stratosphere Jim (Pan-Am) 15 30 45 85 130 175
5-Terry & the Pirates 16 32 48 92 151 210
6-Don Winslow, Stratosphere Jim (Pan-Am)-McWilliams-a 15 30 45 85 130 175
6-King of the Royal Mounted, Magic Morro (Pan-Am) 15 30 45 85 130 175
7-Dick Tracy, Magic Morro (Pan-Am) 19 38 57 107 176 245
7-Little Orphan Annie 11 22 33 64 90 115
8-Dick Tracy, Stratosphere Jim (Pan-Am) 16 32 48 92 151 210
8-Dan Dunn, Magic Morro (Pan-Am) 11 22 33 64 90 115
9-Terry & the Pirates, Magic Morro (Pan-Am) 16 32 48 92 151 210
10-Red Ryder, Magic Morro (Pan-Am) 15 30 45 85 130 175

SUPER-BOOK OF COMICS
Western Publishing Co.: (Omar Bread & Hancock Oil Co. giveaways) 1944 - No. 30, 1947 (Omar); 1947 - 1948 (Hancock) (16 pgs.)
NOTE: The Hancock issues are all exact reprints of the earlier Omar issues. The issue numbers were removed in some of the reprints.
1-Dick Tracy (Omar, 1944) 15 30 45 94 147 200
1-Dick Tracy (Hancock, 1947) 14 28 42 78 112 145
2-Bugs Bunny (Omar, 1944) 8 16 24 40 50 60
2-Bugs Bunny (Hancock, 1947) 6 12 18 32 39 46
3-Terry & the Pirates (Omar, 1944) 11 22 33 60 83 105
3-Terry & the Pirates (Hancock, 1947) 10 20 30 54 72 90
4-Andy Panda (Omar, 1944) 8 16 24 40 50 60
4-Andy Panda (Hancock, 1947) 6 12 18 32 39 46
5-Smokey Stover (Omar, 1945) 6 12 18 32 39 46
5-Smokey Stover (Hancock, 1947) 5 10 15 24 30 35
6-Porky Pig (Omar, 1945) 8 16 24 40 50 60
6-Porky Pig (Hancock, 1947) 6 12 18 32 39 46
7-Smilin' Jack (Omar, 1945) 8 16 24 40 50 60
7-Smilin' Jack (Hancock, 1947) 6 12 18 32 39 46
8-Oswald the Rabbit (Omar, 1945) 6 12 18 32 39 46
8-Oswald the Rabbit (Hancock, 1947) 5 10 15 24 30 35
9-Alley Oop (Omar, 1945) 11 22 33 64 90 115
9-Alley Oop (Hancock, 1947) 11 22 33 60 83 105
10-Elmer Fudd (Omar, 1945) 6 12 18 32 39 46
10-Elmer Fudd (Hancock, 1947) 5 10 15 24 30 35
11-Little Orphan Annie (Omar, 1945) 8 16 24 42 53 64
11-Little Orphan Annie (Hancock, 1947) 7 14 21 36 45 54
12-Woody Woodpecker (Omar, 1945) 6 12 18 32 39 46
12-Woody Woodpecker (Hancock, 1947) 5 10 15 24 30 35
13-Dick Tracy (Omar, 1945) 11 22 33 64 90 115
13-Dick Tracy (Hancock, 1947) 11 22 33 60 83 105
14-Bugs Bunny (Omar, 1946) 6 12 18 32 39 46
14-Bugs Bunny (Hancock, 1947) 5 10 15 24 30 35
15-Andy Panda (Omar, 1945) 6 12 18 28 34 40
15-Andy Panda (Hancock, 1947) 5 10 15 24 30 35
16-Terry & the Pirates (Omar, 1945) 11 22 33 60 83 105
16-Terry & the Pirates (Hancock, 1947) 9 18 27 47 61 75
17-Smokey Stover (Omar, 1946) 6 12 18 32 39 46
17-Smokey Stover (Hancock, 1948?) 5 10 15 24 30 35
18-Porky Pig (Omar, 1946) 6 12 18 28 34 40
18-Porky Pig (Hancock, 1948?) 5 10 15 24 30 35
19-Smilin' Jack (Omar, 1946) 6 12 18 32 39 46
nn-Smilin' Jack (Hancock, 1948) 5 10 15 24 30 35
20-Oswald the Rabbit (Omar, 1946) 6 12 18 28 34 40
nn-Oswald the Rabbit (Hancock, 1948) 5 10 15 24 30 35
21-Gasoline Alley (Omar, 1946) 8 16 24 42 53 64
nn-Gasoline Alley (Hancock, 1948) 7 14 21 36 45 54
22-Elmer Fudd (Omar, 1946) 6 12 18 28 34 40
nn-Elmer Fudd (Hancock, 1948) 5 10 15 24 30 35
23-Little Orphan Annie (Omar, 1946) 8 16 24 40 50 60
nn-Little Orphan Annie (Hancock, 1948) 6 12 18 32 39 46
24-Woody Woodpecker (Omar, 1946) 6 12 18 28 34 40
nn-Woody Woodpecker (Hancock, 1948) 5 10 15 24 30 35
25-Dick Tracy (Omar, 1946) 11 22 33 60 83 105
nn-Dick Tracy (Hancock, 1948) 9 18 27 50 65 80
26-Bugs Bunny (Omar, 1946)) 6 12 18 28 34 40
nn-Bugs Bunny (Hancock, 1948) 5 10 15 24 30 35
27-Andy Panda (Omar, 1946) 6 12 18 28 34 40
27-Andy Panda (Hancock, 1948) 5 10 15 24 30 35
28-Terry & the Pirates (Omar, 1946) 11 22 33 60 83 105
28-Terry & the Pirates (Hancock, 1948) 9 18 27 47 61 75
29-Smokey Stover (Omar, 1947) 6 12 18 28 34 40
29-Smokey Stover (Hancock, 1948) 5 10 15 24 30 35
30-Porky Pig (Omar, 1947) 6 12 18 28 34 40
30-Porky Pig (Hancock, 1948) 5 10 15 24 30 35
nn-Bugs Bunny (Hancock, 1948)-Does not match any Omar book 6 12 18 28 34 40

SUPER CIRCUS (TV)
Cross Publishing Co.
1-(1951, Weather Bird Shoes giveaway) 8 16 24 40 50 60

SUPER FRIENDS
DC Comics: 1981 (Giveaway, no ads, no code or price)
...Special 1 -r/Super Friends #19 & 36 2 4 6 8 10 12

SUPERGEAR COMICS
Jacobs Corp.: 1976 (Giveaway, 4 pgs. in color, slick paper)
nn-(Rare)-Superman, Lois Lane; Steve Lombard app. (500 copies printed, over half destroyed?) 20 40 60 143 264 385

SUPERGIRL
DC Comics: 1984, 1986 (Giveaway, Baxter paper)
nn-(American Honda/U.S. Dept. Transportation) Torres-c/a 2 4 6 8 10 12

SUPER HEROES PUZZLES AND GAMES
General Mills Giveaway (Marvel Comics Group): 1979 (32 pgs., regular size)
nn-Four 2-pg. origin stories of Spider-Man, Captain America, The Hulk, & Spider-Woman 3 6 9 14 19 24

SUPERMAN
National Periodical Publ./DC Comics
72-Giveaway(9-10/51)-(Rare)-Price blackened out; came with banner wrapped around book; without banner 72 144 216 454 765 1075
72-Giveaway with banner 107 214 321 674 1137 1600
Bradman birthday custom (1988)(extremely limited distribution) - no reported sales for 2008
... For the Animals (2000, Doris Day Animal Foundation, 30 pgs.) polybagged with Gotham

Superman (miniature) #1B © DC

Superman-Tim, May 1946 © DC

Tastee-Freez Comics #6 © Chicago Trib.

GD VG FN VF VF/NM NM-
2.0 4.0 6.0 8.0 9.0 9.2

Adventures #22, Hourman #12, Impulse #58, Looney Tunes #62, Stars and S.T.R.I.P.E. #8 and Superman Adventures #41 2.50
Kelloggs Giveaway-(2/3 normal size, 1954)-r-two stories/Superman #55
29 58 87 169 272 375
Kenner: Man of Steel (Doomsday is Coming) (1995, 16 pgs.) packaged with set of Superman and Doomsday action figures 3.50
...Meets the Quik Bunny (1987, Nestles Quik premium, 36 pgs.)
1 2 3 5 6 8
Pizza Hut Premiums (12/77)-Exact reprints of 1950s comics except for paid ads (set of 6 exist?); Vol. 1-r#97 (#113-r also known) 1 3 4 6 8 10
Radio Shack Giveaway-36 pgs. (7/80) "The Computers That Saved Metropolis", Starlin/Giordano-a; advertising insert in Action #509, New Advs. of Superboy #7, Legion of Super-Heroes #265, & House of Mystery #282. (All comics were 68 pgs.) Cover of inserts printed on newsprint. Giveaway contains 4 extra pgs. of Radio Shack advertising that inserts do not have 1 2 3 4 5 7
Radio Shack Giveaway-(7/81) "Victory by Computer" 1 2 3 4 5 7
Radio Shack Giveaway-(7/82) "Computer Masters of Metropolis"
1 2 3 4 5 7

SUPERMAN ADVENTURES, THE (TV)
DC Comics: 1996 (Based on animated series)

1-(1996) Preview issue distributed at Warner Bros. stores 4.00
Titus Game Edition (1998) 2.50

SUPERMAN AND THE GREAT CLEVELAND FIRE
National Periodical Publ.: 1948 (Giveaway, 4 pgs., no cover) (Hospital Fund)

nn-In full color 55 110 165 347 586 825

SUPERMAN AT THE GILBERT HALL OF SCIENCE
National Periodical Publ.: 1948 (Giveaway) (Gilbert Chemistry Sets / A.C. Gilbert Co.)

nn 31 62 93 176 288 400

SUPERMAN/BATMAN
DC Comics: June, 2006 (Free Comic Book Day giveaway)

1-Reprints #1 2.50

SUPERMAN (Miniature)
National Periodical Publ.: 1942; 1955 - 1956 (3 issues, no #'s, 32 pgs.)
The pages are numbered in the 1st issue: 1-32; 2nd: 1A-32A, and 3rd: 1B-32B

No date-Py-Co-Pay Tooth Powder giveaway (8 pgs.; circa 1942)
48 96 144 298 499 700
1-The Superman Time Capsule (Kellogg's Sugar Smacks)(1955)
29 58 87 172 276 380
1A-Duel in Space (1955) 27 54 81 158 254 350
1B-The Super Show of Metropolis (also #1-32, no B)(1955)
27 54 81 158 254 350

NOTE: *Numbering variations exist. Each title could have any combination-#1, 1A, or 1B.*

SUPERMAN RECORD COMIC
National Periodical Publications: 1966 (Golden Records)

(With record)-Record reads origin of Superman from comic; came with iron-on patch, decoder, membership card & button; comic-r/Superman #125,146
14 28 42 99 175 250
Comic only 7 14 21 45 73 100

SUPERMAN'S BUDDY (Costume Comic)
National Periodical Publications: 1954 (4 pgs., slick paper-c; one-shot)
(Came in box w/costume)

1-With box & costume 127 254 381 800 1350 1900
Comic only 57 114 171 359 605 850
1-(1958 edition)-Printed in 2 colors 17 34 51 98 154 210

SUPERMAN'S CHRISTMAS ADVENTURE
National Periodical Publications: 1940, 1944 (Giveaway, 16 pgs.)
Distributed by Nehi drinks, Bailey Store, Ivey-Keith Co., Kennedy's Boys Shop, Macy's Store, Boston Store

1(1940)-Burnley-a; F. Ray-c/r from Superman #6 (Scarce)-Superman saves Santa Claus. Santa makes real Superman Toys offered in 1940. 1st merchandising story; versions with Royal Crown Cola ad on front-c & Boston Store ad on front-c; cover art on each has the same layout but different art 371 742 1113 2523 4412 6300
nn(1944) w/Santa Claus & X-mas tree-c 100 200 300 630 1065 1500
nn(1944) w/Candy cane & Superman-c 93 186 279 586 993 1400

SUPERMAN-TIM (Becomes Tim)
Superman-Tim Stores/National Periodical Publ.: Aug, 1942 - May, 1950 (Half size)
(B&W Giveaway w/2 color covers) (Publ. monthly 2/43 on)

8/42 (#1)-All have Superman illos. 117 234 351 737 1244 1750
1/43 (#2) 40 80 120 235 380 525
2/43 (#3) 38 76 114 226 363 500
3/43 (#4) 38 76 114 226 363 500
4/43, 5/43, 6/43, 7/43, 8/43 35 70 105 203 327 450
9/43, 10/43, 11/43, 12/43 29 58 87 169 272 375

GD VG FN VF VF/NM NM-
2.0 4.0 6.0 8.0 9.0 9.2

1/44-12/44 25 50 75 145 233 320
1/45-5/45, 10-12/45, 1/46-8/46 22 44 66 131 211 290
6/45-Classic Superman-c 24 48 72 143 229 315
7/45-Classic Superman flag-c 24 48 72 143 229 315
9/45-1st stamp album issue 49 98 147 304 510 715
9/46-2nd stamp album issue 41 82 123 256 428 600
10/46-1st Superman story 30 60 90 174 280 385
11/46, 12/46, 1/47-8/47 issues-Superman story in each; 2/47-Infinity-c.
All 36 pgs. 30 60 90 174 280 385
9/47-Stamp album issue & Superman story 41 82 123 250 413 575
10/47, 11/47, 12/47-Superman stories (24 pgs.) 30 60 90 174 280 385
1/48-7/48,10/48, 11/48, 2/49, 4/49-11/49 24 48 72 143 229 315
8/48-Contains full page ad for Superman-Tim watch giveaway
24 48 72 143 229 315
9/48-Stamp album issue 32 64 96 190 305 425
1/49-Full page Superman bank cut-out 24 48 72 143 229 315
3/49-Full page Superman boxing game cut-out 24 48 72 143 229 315
12/49-3/50, 5/50-Superman stories 26 52 78 154 247 340
4/50-Superman story, baseball stories; photo-c without Superman
30 60 90 174 280 385

NOTE: *All issues have Superman illustrations throughout. The page count varies depending on whether a Superman-Tim comic story is inserted. If it is, the page count is either 36 or 24 pages. Otherwise all issues are 16 pages. Each issue has a special place for inserting a full color Superman stamp. The stamp album issues had spaces for the stamps given away the past year. The books were mailed as a subscription premium. The stamps were given away free (or when you made a purchase) only when you physically came into the store.*

SUPER SEAMAN SLOPPY
Allied Pristine Union Council, Buffalo, NY: 1940s, 8pg., reg. size (Soft-c)

nn 4 8 12 17 21 24

SWAMP FOX, THE
Walt Disney Productions: 1960 (14 pgs, small size) (Canada Dry Premiums)

Titles: (A)-Tory Masquerade, (B)-Turnabout Tactics, (C)-Rindau Rampage; each came in paper sleeve, books 1,2 & 3;
Set with sleeves 5 10 15 34 55 75
Comic only 2 4 6 13 18 22

SWORDQUEST
DC Comics/Atari Pub.: 1982, 52pg., 5"x7" (Giveaway with video games)

1,2-Roy Thomas & Gerry Conway-s; George Pérez & Dick Giordano-c/a in all
2 4 6 9 13 16
3-Low print 3 6 9 14 20 25

SYNDICATE FEATURES (Sci/fi)
Harry A. Chesler Syndicate: V1#3, 11/15/37 (Tabloid size, 3 colors, 4 pgs.) (Editors premium) (Came folded)

V1#3-Dan Hastings daily strips-Guardineer-a 173 346 519 1090 1845 2600

TALES FROM RIVERDALE (See Archie Comics)

TASTEE-FREEZ COMICS (Also see Harvey Hits and Richie Rich)
Harvey Comics: 1957 (10¢, 36 pgs.)(6 different issues given away)

1-Little Dot on cover; Richie Rich "Ride 'Em Cowboy" story published one year prior to being printed in Harvey Hits #9. 18 36 54 130 240 350
2,4,5: 2-Rags Rabbit. 4-Sad Sack. 5-Mazie 4 8 12 24 37 50
3-Casper 5 10 15 32 51 70
6-Dick Tracy 5 10 15 32 51 70

TAYLOR'S CHRISTMAS TABLOID
Dept. Store Giveaway: Mid 1930s, Cleveland, Ohio (Tabloid size; in color)

nn-(Very Rare)-Among the earliest pro work of Siegel & Shuster; one full color page called "The Battle in the Stratosphere", with a pre-Superman look; Shuster art thoughout. (Only 1 known copy) Estimated value... 4000.00

TAZ'S 40TH BIRTHDAY BLOWOUT
DC Comics: 1994 (K-Mart giveaway, 16 pgs.)

nn-Six pg. story, games and puzzles 4.00

TEE AND VEE CROSLEY IN TELEVISION LAND COMICS (Also see Crosley's House of Fun)
Crosley Division, Avco Mfg. Corp. : 1951 (52 pgs.; 8x11"; paper cover; in color) (Giveaway)

Many stories, puzzles, cut-outs, games, etc. 7 14 21 35 43 50

TEEN TITANS GO!
DC Comics: Sept, 2004 (Free Comic Book Day giveaway)

1-Reprints Teen Titans Go! #1; 2 bound-in Wacky Packages stickers 2.25

TENNESSEE JED (Radio)
Fox Syndicate? (Wm. C. Popper & Co.): nd (1945) (16 pgs.; paper-c; reg. size; giveaway)

nn 19 38 57 114 180 245

TENNIS (...For Speed, Stamina, Strength, Skill)
Tennis Educational Foundation: 1956 (16 pgs.; soft cover; 10¢)

Book 1-Endorsed by Gene Tunney, Ralph Kiner, etc. showing how tennis has helped them
6 12 18 28 34 40

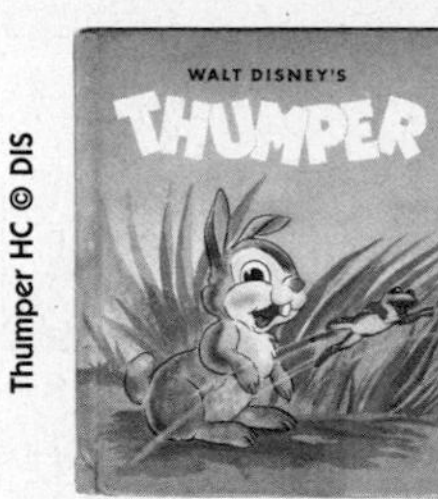

Thumper HC © DIS

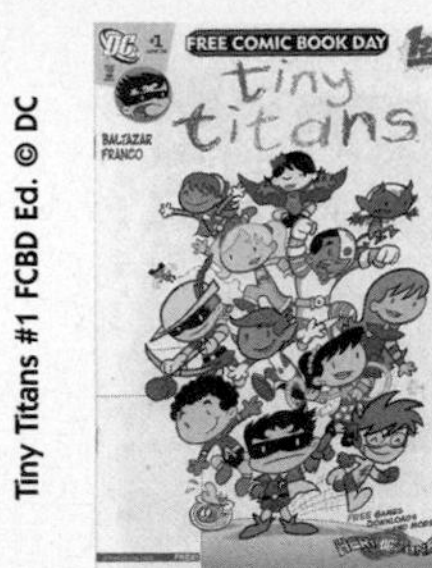

Tiny Titans #1 FCBD Ed. © DC

Triple-A Baseball Heroes (Omaha Royals) © MAR

GD 2.0 | VG 4.0 | FN 6.0 | VF 8.0 | VF/NM 9.0 | NM- 9.2

TERRY AND THE PIRATES
Dell Publishing Co.: 1939 - 1953 (By Milton Caniff)

Buster Brown Shoes giveaway(1938)-32 pgs.; in color 21 42 63 125 200 275
Canada Dry Premiums-Books #1-3(1953, 36 pgs.; 2x5")-Harvey; #1-Hot Shot Charlie Flies Again; 2-In Forced Landing; 3-Dragon Lady in Distress) 15 30 45 83 124 165
Gambles Giveaway (1938, 16 pgs.) 10 20 30 54 72 90
Gillmore Giveaway (1938, 24 pgs.) 10 20 30 56 76 95
Popped Wheat Giveaway(1938)-Strip reprints in full color; Caniff-a 2 4 6 8 10 12
Shoe Store giveaway (Weatherbird & Poll-Parrot)(1938, 16 pgs., soft-c)(2-diff.) 10 20 30 56 76 95
Sparked Wheat Giveaway(1942, 16 pgs.)-In color 10 20 30 56 70 95

TERRY AND THE PIRATES
Libby's Radio Premium: 1941 (16 pgs.; reg. size)(shipped folded in the mail)

"Adventure of the Ruby of Genghis Khan" - Each pg. is a puzzle that must be completed to read the story 400 800 1200 2600 - -

THAT THE WORLD MAY BELIEVE
Catechetical Guild Giveaway: No date (16 pgs.) (Graymoor Friars distr.)

nn 4 8 12 18 22 25

30 DAYS OF NIGHT
IDW Publishing: July, 2004 (Free Comic Book Day edition)

Previews CSI: Bad Rap; The Shield: Spotlight; 24: One Shot; and 30 Days of Night 2.50

3-D COLOR CLASSICS (Wendy's Kid's Club)
Wendy's Int'l Inc.: 1995 (5 1/2" x 8", comes with 3-D glasses)

The Elephant's Child, Gulliver's Travels, Peter Pan, The Time Machine, 20,000 Leagues Under the Sea: Neal Adams-a in all each.... 3.50

350 YEARS OF AMERICAN DAIRY FOODS
American Dairy Assoc.: 1957 (5x7", 16 pgs.)

nn-History of milk 3 6 8 12 14 16

THUMPER (Disney)
Grosset & Dunlap: 1942 (50¢, 32pgs., hardcover book, 7"x8-1/2" w/dust jacket)

nn-Given away (along with a copy of Bambi) for a $2.00, 2-year subscription to WDC&S in 1942. (Xmas offer). Book only 15 30 45 90 140 190
Dust jacket only 10 20 30 56 76 95

TILLY AND TED-TINKERTOTLAND
W. T. Grant Co.: 1945 (Giveaway, 20 pgs.)

nn-Christmas comic 7 14 21 37 46 55

TIM (Formerly Superman-Tim; becomes Gene Autry-Tim)
Tim Stores: June, 1950 - Oct, 1950 (B&W, half-size)

4 issues; 6/50, 9/50, 10/50 known 17 34 51 98 154 210

TIM AND SALLY'S ADVENTURES AT MARINELAND
Marineland Restaurant & Bar, Marineland, CA: 1957 (5x7", 16 pgs., soft-c)

nn-copyright Oceanarium, Inc. 2 4 6 8 10 12

TIME MACHINE, THE
DC Comics: 2002 (10 pgs.)

nn-Promotes the 2002 DreamWorks movie 5.00

TIME OF DECISION
Harvey Publications Inc.: (16 pgs., paper cover)

nn-ROTC recruitment 4 7 10 14 17 20

TIM IN SPACE (Formerly Gene Autry Tim; becomes Tim Tomorrow)
Tim Stores: 1950 (1/2 size giveaway) (B&W)

nn 14 28 42 78 112 145

TIM TOMORROW (Formerly Tim In Space)
Tim Stores: 8/51, 9/51, 10/51, Christmas, 1951 (5x7-3/4")

nn-Prof. Fumble & Captain Kit Comet in all 14 28 42 78 112 145

TINY TITANS (All ages stories of Teen Titans in Elementary school)
DC Comics: June, 2008 (Free Comic Book Day giveaway)

1-Reprints Tiny Titans #1; Baltazar & Franco-s/a 2.25

TITANS BEAT (Teen Titans)
DC Comics: Aug, 1996 (16 pgs., paper-c)

1-Intro./preview new Teen Titans members; Pérez-a 4.00

TOMB RAIDER: THE SERIES (Also see Witchblade/Tomb Raider)
Image Comics (Top Cow Prod.): May, 2002

Free Comic Book Day giveaway-Reprints #1 with "Free Comic Book Day" banner on-c 2.50

TOM MIX (...Commandos Comics #10-12)

GD 2.0 | VG 4.0 | FN 6.0 | VF 8.0 | VF/NM 9.0 | NM- 9.2

Ralston-Purina Co.: Sept, 1940 - No. 12, Nov, 1942 (36 pgs.); 1983 (one-shot)
Given away for two Ralston box-tops; 1983 came in cereal box

1-Origin (life) Tom Mix; Fred Meagher-a 253 506 759 1594 2697 3800
2 60 120 180 378 639 900
3-9 41 82 123 256 428 600
10-12: 10-Origin Tom Mix Commando Unit; Speed O'Dare begins; Japanese sub-c. 12-Sci/fi-c 38 76 14 226 363 500
1983- "Taking of Grizzly Grebb", Toth-a; 16 pg. miniature 2 4 6 9 12 15

TOM SAWYER COMICS
Giveaway: 1951? (Paper cover)

nn-Contains a coverless Hopalong Cassidy from 1951; other combinations known 3 6 9 14 20 25

TOP-NOTCH COMICS
MLJ Magazines/Rex Theater: 1940s (theater giveaway)

1-Black Hood-c; content & covers can vary 41 82 123 250 413 575

TOPPS COMICS PRESENTS
Topps Comics: No. 0, 1993 (Giveaway, B&W, 36 pgs.)

0-Dracula vs. Zorro, Teenagents, Silver Star, & Bill the Galactic Hero 2.50

TOWN THAT FORGOT SANTA, THE
W. T. Grant Co.: 1961 (Giveaway, 24 pgs.)

nn 3 6 9 16 23 30

TOY LAND FUNNIES (See Funnies On Parade)
Eastern Color Printing Co.: 1934 (32 pgs., Hecht Co. store giveaway)

nn-Reprints Buck Rogers Sunday pages #199-201 from Famous Funnies #5. A rare variation of Funnies On Parado; same format, similar contents, same cover except for large Santa placed in center (value will be based on sale)

TOY WORLD FUNNIES (See Funnies On Parade)
Eastern Color Printing Co.: 1933 (36 pgs., slick cover, Golden Eagle and Wanamaker giveaway)

nn-Contains contents from Funnies On Parade/Century Of Comics. A rare variation of Funnies On Parade, same format, similar contents, same cover except for large Santa placed in center (value will be based on sale)

TRANSFORMERS
Dreamwave Productions/IDW Publishing: May, 2003; 2006

... Armada (Dreamwave Prods., 5/03) Free Comic Book Day Edition 3.00
.../Beast Wars Special (IDW, 2006) Free Comic Book Day Edition; flip book 3.00

TRAPPED
Harvey Publications (Columbia Univ. Press): 1951 (Giveaway, soft-c, 16 pgs)

nn-Drug education comic (30,000 printed?) distributed to schools.; mentioned in **SOTI**, pgs. 256,350 2 4 6 8 10 12

NOTE: *Many copies surfaced in 1979 causing a setback in price; beware of trimmed edges, because many copies have a brittle edge.*

TRIPLE-A BASEBALL HEROES
Marvel Comics: 2007 (Minor league baseball stadium giveaway)

1-Special John Watson painted-c for Memphis, Durham and Buffalo; generic cover with team logos for each of the other 27 teams; Spider-Man, Iron Man, FF app. 3.00

TRIP TO OUTER SPACE WITH SANTA
Sales Promotions, Inc/Peoria Dry Goods: 1950s (paper-c)

nn-Comics, games & puzzles 5 10 15 22 26 30

TRIP WITH SANTA ON CHRISTMAS EVE, A
Rockford Dry Goods Co.: No date (Early 1950s) (Giveaway, 16 pgs., paper-c)

nn 5 10 15 22 26 30

TRUE BLOOD: THE GREAT REVELATION (Prequel to the 2008 HBO vampire series)
HBO/Top Cow: July, 2008 (no cover price, one shot continued on HBO website)

1-David Wohl-s/Jason Badower-a/c 2.25

TRUTH BEHIND THE TRIAL OF CARDINAL MINDSZENTY, THE (See Cardinal Mindszenty)

24 PAGES OF COMICS (No title) (Also see Pure Oil Comics, Salerno Carnival of Comics, & Vicks Comics)
Giveaway by various outlets including Sears: Late 1930s

nn-Contains strip reprints-Buck Rogers, Napoleon, Sky Roads, War on Crime 32 64 96 190 305 420

TWISTED METAL (Video game)
DC Comics: 1996

nn 3.00

TWO FACES OF COMMUNISM (Also see Double Talk)
Christian Anti-Communism Crusade, Houston, Texas: 1961 (Giveaway, paper-c, 36 pgs.)

nn 15 30 45 88 137 185

2001, A SPACE ODYSSEY (Movie)

Vicks Comics (16-pg. giveaway) © EAS

Walt Disney's Gyro Gearloose FCBD Ed. © DIS

Wheaties A-3 © DIS

Marvel Comics Group
Howard Johnson giveaway (1968, 8pp); 6 pg. movie adaptation, 2 pg. games, puzzles; McWilliams-a 2 4 6 9 12 15

ULTIMATE SPIDER-MAN
Marvel Comics: May, 2002
Free Comic Book Day giveaway - reprints #1 with "Free Comic Book Day" banner on-c 2.50
1-Kay Bee Toys variant edition 2 4 6 9 12 15

ULTIMATE X-MEN
Marvel Comics: July, 2003
1-Free Comic Book Day Edition - reprints #1 with "Free Comic Book Day" banner on-c 2.50

UMBRELLA ACADEMY (Zero Killer & Pantheon City on back-c)
Dark Horse Comics: Apr, 2007
1-Free Comic Book Day Edition - previews of the upcoming series; James Jean-c 10.00

UNCLE SAM'S CHRISTMAS STORY
Promotional Publ. Co.: 1958 (Giveaway)
nn-Reprints 1956 Christmas USA 2 4 6 10 13 16

UNCLE WIGGILY COMICS
Herberger's Clothing Store: 1942 (32 pgs., paper cover)
nn-Comic panels with 6 pages of puzzles 12 24 36 69 97 125

UNKEPT PROMISE
Legion of Truth: 1949 (Giveaway, 24 pgs.)
nn-Anti-alcohol 10 20 30 58 79 100

UNTOLD LEGEND OF THE BATMAN, THE
DC Comics: 1989 (28 pgs., 6X9", limited series of cereal premiums)
1-1st & 2nd printings known; Byrne-a 1 2 3 5 7 9
2,3: 1st & 2nd printings known 1 2 3 4 5 7

UNTOUCHABLES, THE (TV)
Leaf Brands, Inc.
Topps Bubblegum premiums produced by Leaf Brands, Inc.-2-1/2x4-1/2", 8 pgs. (3 diff. issues) "The Organization, Jamaica Ginger, The Otto Frick Story (drug), 3000 Suspects, The Antidote, Mexican Stakeout, Little Egypt, Purple Gang, Bugs Moran Story, & Lily Dallas Story" 3 6 9 16 23 30

VICKS COMICS (See Pure Oil Comics, Salerno Carnival of Comics & 24 Pages of Comics)
Eastern Color Printing Co. (Vicks Chemical Co.): nd (circa 1938) (Giveaway, 68 pgs. in color)
nn-Famous Funnies-r (before #40); contains 5 pgs. Buck Rogers (4 pgs. from F.F. #15, & 1 pg. from #16) Joe Palooka, Napoleon, etc. app. 56 112 168 353 597 840
nn-16 loose, untrimmed page giveaway; paper-c; r/Famous Funnies #14; Buck Rogers, Joe Palooka app. Has either "Vicks Comics" printed on cover or only a local store name as the logo. 22 44 66 127 204 280

WALT DISNEY'S COMICS & STORIES
K.K. Publications: 1942-1963 known (7-1/3"x10-1/4", 4 pgs. in color, slick paper) (folded horizontally once or twice as mailers) (Xmas subscription offer)
1942 mailer-r/Kelly cover to WDC&S 25; 2-year subscription + two Grosset & Dunlap hardcover books (32-pages each), of Bambi and of Thumper, offered for $2.00; came in an illustrated C&S envelope with an enclosed postage paid envelope
(Rare) Mailer only 22 44 66 129 207 285
with envelopes 28 56 84 162 261 360
1947,1948 mailer 17 34 51 98 154 210
1949 mailer-A rare Barks item: Same WDC&S cover as 1942 mailer, but with art changed so that nephew is handing teacher Donald a comic book rather than an apple, as originally drawn by Kelly. The tiny, 7/8"x1-1/4" cover shown was a rejected cover by Barks that was intended for C&S 110, but was redrawn by Kelly for C&S 111. The original art has been lost and this is its only app. (Rare) 40 80 120 236 378 520
1950 mailer-P.1 r/Kelly cover to Dell Xmas Parade 1 (without title); p.2 r/Kelly cover to C&S 101 (w/o title), but with the art altered to show Donald reading C&S 122 (by Kelly); hardcover book, "Donald Duck in Bringing Up the Boys" given with a $1.00 one-year subscription; P.4 r/full Kelly Xmas cover to C&S 99 (Rare) 17 34 51 98 154 210
1952 mailer-P1 r/cover WDC&S #88 14 28 42 80 115 150
1953 mailer-P.1 r/cover Dell Xmas Parade 4 (w/o title); insides offer "Donald Duck Full Speed Ahead," a 28-page, color, 5-5/8"x6-5/8" book, not of the Story Hour series; P.4 r/full Barks C&S 148 cover (Rare) 14 28 42 80 115 150
1963 mailer-Pgs. 1,2 & 4 r/GK Xmas art; P.3 r/a 1963 C&S cover (Scarce) 11 22 33 60 83 105
NOTE: *It is assumed a different mailer was printed each Xmas for at least twenty years.*

WALT DISNEY'S COMICS & STORIES
Walt Disney Productions: 1943 (36 pgs.) (Dept. store Xmas giveaway)
nn-X-Mas-c with Donald & the Boys; Donald Duck by Jack Hannah; Thumper by Ken Hultgren 45 90 135 279 465 650

WALT DISNEY'S DONALD DUCK
Gemstone Publishing: 2006
... Free Comic Book Day (5/06) r/WDC&S #531; Rosa-s/a; P&S. Block-s/a; Van Horn-s/a 2.50
nn-(8-1/2"x 5-1/2", Halloween giveaway) r/"A Prank Above" -Barks-s/a; Rosa-s/a 2.50

WALT DISNEY'S DONALD DUCK ADVENTURES
Gemstone Publishing: May, 2003 (giveaway promoting 2003 return of Disney Comics)
...Free Comic Book Day Edition - cover logo on red background; reprints "Maharajah Donald" & "The Peaceful Hills" from March of Comics #4; Barks-s/a; Kelly original-c on back-c 2.50
...San Diego Comic-Con 2003 Edition - cover logo on gold background 2.50
...ANA World's Fair of Money Baltimore Edition - cover logo on green background 2.50
...WizardWorld Chicago 2003 Edition - cover logo on blue background 2.50

WALT DISNEY'S GYRO GEARLOOSE
Gemstone Publishing: May, 2008
... Free Comic Book Day (5/08) short stories by Barks, Rosa, Van Horn, Gerstein 2.50

WALT DISNEY'S MICKEY MOUSE
Gemstone Publishing: May, 2007
... Free Comic Book Day (5/07) Floyd Gottfredson-s/a 2.50

WALT DISNEY'S MICKEY MOUSE AND UNCLE SCROOGE
Gemstone Publishing: June, 2004 (Free Comic Book Day giveaway)
nn-Flip book with r/Uncle Scrooge #15 and r/Mickey Mouse Four Color #79 (only Barks drawn Mickey Mouse story) 2.50

WALT DISNEY'S UNCLE SCROOGE
Gemstone Publishing: May, 2005 (Free Comic Book Day giveaway)
nn-Reprints Uncle Scrooge's debut in Four Color Comics #386; Barks-s/a 2.50

WATCH OUT FOR BIG TALK
Giveaway: 1950
nn-Dan Barry-a; about crooked politicians 7 14 21 37 46 55

WEATHER-BIRD (See Comics From..., Dick Tracy, Free Comics to You..., Super Circus & Terry and the Pirates)
International Shoe Co./Western Printing Co.: 1958 - No. 16, July, 1962 (Shoe store giveaway)
1 4 8 12 24 37 50
2-16 2 4 6 13 18 22
NOTE: *The numbers are located in the lower bottom panel, pg. 1. All feature a character called Weather-Bird.*

WEATHER BIRD COMICS (See Comics From Weather Bird)
Weather Bird Shoes: 1957 (Giveaway)
nn-Contains a comic bound with new cover. Several combinations possible; contents determine price (40 - 60 percent of contents).

WEEKLY COMIC MAGAZINE
Fox Publications: May 12, 1940 (16 pgs.) (Others exist w/o super-heroes)
(1st Version)-8 pg. Blue Beetle story, 7 pg. Patty O'Day story; two copies known to exist. (a VF copy sold in 5/07 for $1553)
(2nd Version)-7 two-pg. adventures of Blue Beetle, Patty O'Day, Yarko, Dr. Fung, Green Mask, Spark Stevens, & Rex Dexter (only one known copy, in FN; it sold in May 2007 for $1912)
(3rd version)-Captain Valor (only one known copy, in VG+; it sold in 2005 for $480)
Discovered with business papers, letters and exploitation material promoting **Weekly Comic Magazine** for use by newspapers in the same manner of **The Spirit** weeklies. Interesting note: these are dated three weeks before the first Spirit comic. Letters indicate that samples may have been sent to a few newspapers. These sections were actually 15-1/2x22" pages which will fold down to an approximate 8x10" comic booklet. Other various comic sections were found with the above, but were more like the Sunday comic sections in format.

WHAT DO YOU KNOW ABOUT THIS COMICS SEAL OF APPROVAL?
No publisher listed (DC Comics Giveaway): nd (1955) (4 pgs., slick paper-c)
nn-(Rare) 80 160 240 504 852 1200

WHAT'S BEHIND THESE HEADLINES
William C. Popper Co.: 1948 (16 pgs.)
nn-Comic insert "The Plot to Steal the World" 6 12 18 31 38 45

WHAT'S IN IT FOR YOU?
Harvey Publications Inc.: (16 pgs., paper cover)
nn-National Guard recruitment 4 7 10 14 17 20

WHEATIES (Premiums)
Walt Disney Productions: 1950 & 1951 (32 titles, pocket-size, 32 pgs.)
Mailing Envelope (no art on front)(Designates sets A,B,C or D on front) 8 16 24 42 54 65
(Set A-1 to A-8, 1950)
A-1-Mickey Mouse & the Disappearing Island, A-5-Mickey Mouse, Roving Reporter each... 6 12 18 31 38 45
A-2-Grandma Duck, Homespun Detective, A-6-Li'l Bad Wolf, Forest Ranger, A-7-Goofy, Tightrope Acrobat, A-8-Pluto & the Bogus Money each... 6 12 18 28 34 40
A-3-Donald Duck & the Haunted Jewels, A-4-Donald Duck & the Giant Ape each... 9 18 27 47 61 75
(Set B-1 to B-8, 1950)
B-1-Mickey Mouse & the Pharoah's Curse, B-4-Mickey Mouse & the Mystery Sea Monster each... 7 14 21 35 43 50
B-2-Pluto, Canine Cowpoke, B-5-Li'l Bad Wolf in the Hollow Tree Hideout,

Wisco/Klarer - Blaze Carson © FAW

Worlds of Aspen #3 © Aspen MLT

X-Men The Movie © MAR

	GD 2.0	VG 4.0	FN 6.0	VF 8.0	VF/NM 9.0	NM- 9.2

B-7-Goofy & the Gangsters each... 6 12 18 28 34 40
B-3-Donald Duck & the Buccaneers, B-6-Donald Duck,Trail Blazer, B-8 Donald Duck, Klondike Kid each... 9 18 27 47 61 75
(Set C-1 to C-8, 1951)
C-1-Donald Duck & the Inca Idol, C-5-Donald Duck in the Lost Lakes, C-8-Donald Duck Deep-Sea Diver each... 9 18 27 47 61 75
C 2-Mickey Mouse & the Magic Mountain, C-6-Mickey Mouse & the Stagecoach Bandits each... 7 14 21 35 43 50
C-3-Li'l Bad Wolf, Fire Fighter, C-4-Gus & Jaq Save the Ship, C-7-Goofy, Big Game Hunter each... 6 12 18 28 34 40
(Set D-1 to D-8, 1951)
D-1-Donald Duck in Indian Country, D-5-Donald Duck, Mighty Mystic each... 9 18 27 47 61 75
D-2-Mickey Mouse and the Abandoned Mine, D-6-Mickey Mouse & the Medicine Man each... 7 14 21 35 43 50
D-3-Pluto & the Mysterious Package, D-4-Bre'r Rabbit's Sunken Treasure, D-7-Li'l Bad Wolf and the Secret of the Woods, D-8-Minnie Mouse, Girl Explorer each... 6 12 18 28 34 40
NOTE: Some copies lack the Wheaties ad.

WHIZ COMICS (Formerly Flash Comics & Thrill Comics #1)
Fawcett Publications
Wheaties Giveaway(1946, Miniature, 6-1/2x8-1/4", 32 pgs.); all copies were taped at each corner to a box of Wheaties and are never found in very fine or mint condition; "Capt. Marvel & the Water Thieves", plus Golden Arrow, Ibis, Crime Smasher stories 100 200 450 - - -

WILD KINGDOM (TV) (Mutual of Omaha's...)
Western Printing Co.: 1965, 1966 (Giveaway, regular size, slick-c, 16 pgs.)
nn-Front & back-c are different on 1966 edition 2 4 6 9 12 15

WISCO/KLARER COMIC BOOK (Miniature)
Marvel Comics/Vital Publ./Fawcett Publ.: 1948 - 1964 (3-1/2x6-3/4", 24 pgs.)
Given away by Wisco "99" Service Stations, Carnation Malted Milk, Klarer Health Wieners, Fleers Dubble Bubble Gum, Rodeo All-Meat Wieners, Perfect Potato Chips, & others; see ad in Tom Mix #21
Blackstone & the Gold Medal Mystery (1948) 8 16 24 44 57 70
Blackstone "Solves the Sealed Vault Mystery" (1950) 8 16 24 44 57 70
Blaze Carson in "The Sheriff Shoots It Out" (1950) 8 16 24 44 57 70
Captain Marvel & Billy's Big Game (r/Capt. Marvel Adv. #76) 25 50 75 140 240 330
(Prices vary widely on this book)
China Boy in "A Trip to the Zoo" #10 (1948) 6 12 18 28 34 40
Indoors-Outdoors Game Book 4 8 12 17 21 24
Jim Solar Space Sheriff in "Battle for Mars", "Between Two Worlds", "Conquers Outer Space", "The Creatures on the Comet", "Defeats the Moon Missile Men", "Encounter Creatures on Comet", "Meet the Jupiter Jumpers", "Meets the Man From Mars", "On Traffic Duty", "Outlaws of the Spaceways", "Pirates of the Planet X", "Protects Space Lanes", "Raiders From the Sun", "Ring Around Saturn", "Robots of Rhea", "The Sky Ruby", "Spacetts of the Sky", "Spidermen of Venus", "Trouble on Mercury" 8 16 24 40 50 60
Johnny Starboard & the Underseas Pirates (1948) 5 10 15 24 30 35
Kid Colt in "He Lived by His Guns" (1950) 9 18 27 50 65 80
Little Aspirin as the "Crook Catcher" #2 (1950) 4 8 12 18 22 25
Little Aspirin in "Naughty But Nice" #6 (1950) 4 8 12 18 22 25
Return of the Black Phantom (not M.E. character)(Roy Dare)(1948) 7 14 21 35 43 50
Secrets of Magic 4 9 13 18 22 26
Slim Morgan "Brings Justice to Mesa City" #3 4 9 13 18 22 26
Super Rabbit(1950)-Cuts Red Tape, Stops Crime Wave! 10 20 30 54 72 90
Tex Farnum, Frontiersman (1948) 5 10 15 24 30 35
Tex Taylor in "Draw or Die, Cowpoke!" (1950) 7 14 21 37 46 55
Tex Taylor in "An Exciting Adventure at the Gold Mine" (1950) 7 14 21 35 43 50
Wacky Quacky in "All-Aboard" 4 7 9 14 16 18
When School Is Out 4 7 9 14 16 18
Willie in a "Comic-Comic Book Fall" #1 4 8 12 17 21 24
Wonder Duck "An Adventure at the Rodeo of the Fearless Quacker!" (1950) 9 18 27 50 65 80
Rare uncut version of three; includes Capt. Marvel, Tex Farnum, Black Phantom Estimated value... 700.00
Rare uncut version of three; includes China Boy, Blackstone, Johnny Starboard & the Underseas Pirates Estimated value... 250.00
Rare uncut version of three; includes Willie in a "Comic-Comic Book Fall", Little Aspirin #2, Slim Morgan Brings Justice to Mesa City (a VF/FN copy sold for $54 in Nov. 2007)

WOLVERINE
Marvel Comics
145-(1999 Nabisco mail-in offer) Sienkiewicz-c 8 16 24 50 88 125
...Son of Canada (4/01, ed. of 65,000) Spider-Man & The Hulk app.; Lim-a 3.00

WOMAN OF THE PROMISE, THE
Catechetical Guild: 1950 (General Distr.) (Paper cover, 32 pgs.)
nn 6 12 18 28 34 40

WONDERFUL WORLD OF DUCKS (See Golden Picture Story Book)
Colgate Palmolive Co.: 1975
1-Mostly-r 1 3 4 6 8 10

WONDER WOMAN
DC Comics: 1977
Pizza Hut Giveaways (12/77)-Reprints #60,62 2 4 6 10 12 15
... - The Minotaur (1981, General Foods giveaway, 8 pages, 3-1/2 x 6-3/4", oblong) 2 4 6 11 16 20

WONDER WORKER OF PERU
Catechetical Guild: No date (5x7", 16 pgs., B&W, giveaway)
nn 5 10 15 27 33 38

WOODY WOODPECKER
Dell Publishing Co.
Clover Stamp-Newspaper Boy Contest('56)-9 pg. story-(Giveaway) 7 14 21 37 46 55
In Chevrolet Wonderland(1954-Giveaway)(Western Publ.)-20 pgs., full story line; Chilly Willy app. 18 36 54 103 162 220
...Meets Scotty MacTape(1953-Scotch Tape giveaway)-16 pgs., full size 18 36 54 103 162 220

WOOLWORTH'S CHRISTMAS STORY BOOK
Promotional Publ. Co.(Western Printing Co.): 1952 - 1954 (16 pgs., paper-c) (See Jolly Christmas Book)
nn: 1952 issue-Marv Levy c/a 6 12 18 33 41 48

WOOLWORTH'S HAPPY TIME CHRISTMAS BOOK
F. W. Woolworth Co. (Western Printing Co.): 1952 (Christmas giveaway)
nn-36 pgs. 6 12 18 31 38 45

WORLD'S FINEST COMICS
National Periodical Publ./DC Comics
Giveaway (c. 1944-45, 8 pgs., in color, paper-c)-Johnny Everyman-r/World's Finest 21 42 63 123 197 270
Giveaway (c. 1949, 8 pgs., in color, paper-c)- "Make Way For Youth" r/World's Finest; based on film of same name 18 36 54 107 169 230
#176, #179- Best Western reprint edition (1997) 3.00

WORLD'S GREATEST SUPER HEROES
DC Comics (Nutra Comics) (Child Vitamins, Inc.): 1977 (Giveaway, 3-3/4x3-3/4", 24 pgs.)
nn-Batman & Robin app.; health tips 2 4 6 9 13 16

WORLDS OF ASPEN
Aspen MLT, Inc.: 2006 - No. 3, 2008 (Free Comic Book Day giveaways)
...: FCBD 2006, 2007, #3 Editions; Fathom, Soulfire, Shrugged short stories; Turner-c 2.50

XMAS FUNNIES
Kinney Shoes: No date (Giveaway, paper cover, 36 pgs.?)
Contains 1933 color strip-r; Mutt & Jeff, etc. 30 60 90 176 283 390

X-MEN / RUNAWAYS
Marvel Comics: 2006 (Free Comic Book Day giveaway)
...: FCBD 2006 Edition; new x-over story; Mighty Avengers preview; Jo Chen-c 2.50

X-MEN THE MOVIE
Marvel Comics/Toys R' Us: 2000
Special Movie Prequel Edition 5.00

X2 PRESENTS THE ULTIMATE X-MEN #2
Marvel Comics/New York Post: July, 2003
Reprint distributed inside issue of the New York Post 2.50

YALTA TO KOREA (Also see Korea My Home)
M. Phillip Corp. (Republican National Committee): 1952 (Giveaway, paper-c)
nn-(8 pgs.)-Anti-communist propaganda book 18 36 54 103 162 220

YOGI BEAR (TV)
Dell Publishing Co.
Giveaway ('84, '86)-City of Los Angeles, "Creative First Aid" & "Earthquake Preparedness for Children" 1 2 3 4 5 7

YOUR TRIP TO NEWSPAPERLAND
Philadelphia Evening Bulletin (Printed by Harvey Press): June, 1955 (14x11-1/2", 12 pgs.)
nn-Joe Palooka takes kids on newspaper tour 5 10 15 24 30 35

YOUR VOTE IS VITAL!
Harvey Publications Inc.: 1952 (5" x 7", 16 pgs., paper cover)
nn-The importance of voting 4 8 12 18 22 25

The Pioneer Age

The American Comic Book: 1500s-1828

by Eric C. Caren ©2009

Want to avoid an argument in social discourse? Steer clear of politics and religion. In the latter category, the most controversial subject is human evolution. Collectors can become just as squeamish when you start messing with the evolution of a particular collectible. In most cases, the origin of a particular comic character will be universally agreed upon, but try tackling the origin of printed comics and you are asking for trouble. Perhaps I will make more friends than enemies amongst comic collectors if I first admit that in my own field of expertise, rare newspapers and other news forms – broadsides, tracts, newsletters, periodicals, etc. – 35 years of experience has left me somewhat at a loss to tell you what the first newspaper was. Actually, to be fair to myself, I could give you a list of at least a dozen good candidates and then it would be subjective as to which item on the list qualified as the godfather. It so happens that journalism and comics are not such distant cousins, and because a picture paints a thousand words, I have provided you with a number of pictorial exhibits to accompany this treatise. First printed comic? Ancestors of my Silver Age companions growing up in the 1960s? Yes, centuries before there was a Spider-Man, an Incredible Hulk, and the Fantastic Four, there were comics and cartoons!

My friend and fellow newspaper collector, Dr. Stephen A. Goldman, has always lived by the old maxim, "Knowledge is Power," and to that end he keeps an enormous personal library of books relating to journalism, history, and collectibles. Many years ago, I was perusing through the spines of a myriad of reference books in his print library (pre-Internet) and hit upon a title that really intrigued me – *The Early Comic Strip* by David Kunzle, published by The University of California Press in 1973. The subtitle of the tome is *Narrative Strips and Picture Stories in the European Broadsheet from c. 1450 to 1825*. Kunzle gets down to business in the flap copy. He states that "because the 'comic strip' has never been adequately defined, no one has known where to look for its ancestors...In this book the 'comic strip' is defined as a mass produced series of narrative images printed either on a single sheet, or else strung across several sheets..." The Kunzle book opened a whole new world for me, and I started adding many early items to my news archive. These would share space in the comics division of the archive with more familiar friends like the Yellow Kid, Little Nemo, and the Brownies.

In this article, I would like to share some of our mutual cousins with you in the hopes that you will be inspired to

Figure 1. German broadsheet, dated 1569.

look back at what I am calling "The Pioneer Age" of comics. There are many things out there from the 16th to the 19th centuries that would be interesting for comic connoisseurs to collect. While some items illustrated within this article are virtually unobtainable, others *can* be found, and many other similar items are out there just waiting for inspired collectors to seek them out. All of the items pictured are taken from originals in my personal collection, with the exception of the Franklin snake cartoon which is proudly owned by Dr. Goldman. As far as I know, his example is the only one in private hands.

Figure 2. The Murder of King Henry III (1589).

Before we begin, a bit of terminology is imperative. The terms 'broadsheet' and 'broadside' regarding works of the 16th and 17th centuries are fairly interchangeable and they essentially refer to the modern equivalent of a poster. Today, technically speaking, a broadside is a single sheet of paper printed only on the recto and a broadsheet is a piece of paper with printing on both sides. The earliest comic item illustrated in Kunzle is a ten-panel religious broadside probably printed in Strasburg (then Germany) circa 1460. Ten panels, biblical – hmm, what could it possibly depict? Guttenberg had invented moveable type only a few years earlier and used his printing press to print a now famous bible in Mainz, Germany, so it is no surprise that this early comic would be religious in nature. Non-secular matter would dominate the printing arts for well over a century to come. However, Kunzle does present us with a satirical and rather racy comic broadsheet done by one Casper of Regensburg, with a title that roughly translates to "My Heart doth Smart." This piece is replete with a picture of an alluring half-clothed maiden just out of her German bathing-house being admired by a kneeling young male observer. Kunzle dates this piece to circa 1485.

The earliest comic piece in my archive is a German broadside dated 1569 [Figure 1]. It is an illustrated attack on the Spanish Catholics led by the notoriously cruel Duke of Alva (center) who had recently occupied the Low Countries (Belgium and The Netherlands) and committed atrocities on the resident Protestant populace. It is half-allegorical, with the foreground consisting of the Devil and a nun blowing ill wind into the ear of the Duke of Alva who has in turn chained up the women of the Low Countries, and half-journalistic, with the upper half depicting the execution of Egmont and Horn in Antwerp.

The next two exhibits are particularly interesting to me. They are the work of the Hogenberg family of Cologne, Germany. Franz Hogenberg, and later his son Abraham, issued approximately 500 current event illustrated news broadsides starting in the 1560s and ending around 1620. The father had already become famous for his extremely detailed and accurate city and town views that he had published with a partner named George Braun in atlas format. With correspondents all over Europe sending the Hogenberg family news and the city views already compiled, the Hogenbergs were able to have their news broadsides on the streets for sale within weeks of political and military events taking place in England and on the European Continent. In some cases, the news sheets were out of their print shop within days of the actual event, particularly when the event occurred in Germany. These sheets were of uniform size, approximately 10" x 13", sometimes numbered and interesting in that the graphics were always the dominant part of the broadside. Usually, text was relegated to a few lines of rhyming verse beneath the copperplate engravings. As literacy in this period was primarily confined to the nobility, this was a most pragmatic vehicle for dissemination of news – and often propaganda – to the populace at large. The picture told the story and the text could be read to groups of people who might remember it due to its catchy rhyming format.

A fair percentage of these news sheets were composed as strip narratives. One example of this is from 1589 [Figure 2] and shows the murder of King Henry III of France by the monk Jacques Clement near Paris. This four-panel broadside includes the stabbing of the king and concludes with Mr. Clement being drawn and quartered by four horses. The next work illustrated here is a 6-panel narrative strip with no text dating from 1617 [Figure 3]. The first panel depicts the shooting in Paris of the Italian Concini, who had ruled France while Louis XIII was still a young boy. The second panel shows the release of the birds from their cages to symbolize the new independence of the young King Louis, and the rest of the panels involve the common people attacking the corpse of Concini in various vicious ways.

The next piece is also the earliest English language piece in

Figure 3. The shooting of the Italian Concini (1617).

my collection to employ word balloons. It is a trompe l'oeil, or collage, caricature satirizing the catastrophic South Sea Bubble, which ruined many investors in a manner similar to our own Tech Stock "New Economy" bubble of the 1990s. It is titled "The Bubblers Medley, or a Sketch of the Times/Being Europe's Memorial from the Year 1720" [Figure 4]. The most interesting scene to comic historians would have to be the one in the upper right corner depicting a number of men in a London coffeehouse – where merchants would regularly gather to read and discuss the latest news – speaking with word balloons. One of the gentlemen seated at a table sarcastically announces "I was to have took S. Sea [stock] at 2000 but chose rather to live here like a Knave than go to Jayl [sic] like a Fool."

The first successful American newspaper was the *Boston News-Letter* begun in 1704. From that point until the French and Indian War, there were precious few illustrations in any colonial newspaper. Some of the best information on early illustration in colonial newspapers can be found in the book *Journals and Journeymen* by Clarence Brigham, author of the most important bibliography of colonial newspapers. In a chapter simply entitled "Illustration," Brigham points out that the first illustration in an American newspaper was a simple woodcut of a flag in an issue of the *Boston News-Letter* from January 26, 1708. Except for advertisements and title devices, Brigham could not find another illustration until 1733, when John Peter Zenger inserted a crude map of Louisburg into his *New York Weekly Journal*. Then, after perhaps one more map of Louisburg in 1745 came something in 1754 that was to have a lasting effect in the hearts and souls of the colonials right through the fight for independence.

Brigham tells us "Benjamin Franklin, in the *Pennsylvania Gazette* of May 9, 1754, published what may well be called the earliest American newspaper cartoon. That year, at a time when the prospect of a war with the French was imminent, a congress of the colonies was called at Albany to be held in June. Franklin, in a plea for united action, published an article on the situation on May 9. Accompanying the article was a cartoon woodcut engraving of a snake divided in eight parts [Figure 5]... Under the snake was the motto 'Join, Or Die...' The segmented snake device was of great importance in call-

Figure 4. "The Bubblers Medley" (1720).

Figure 5. "Join, or Die" from the Pennsylvania Gazette, May 9, 1754.

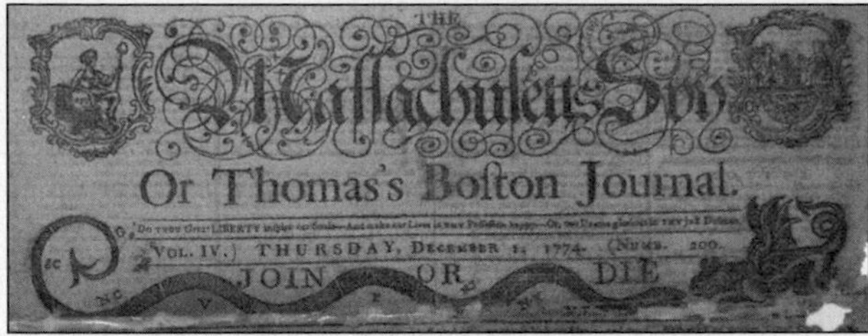

Figure 6. The snake meets a dragon in the Massachusetts Spy *(1774).*

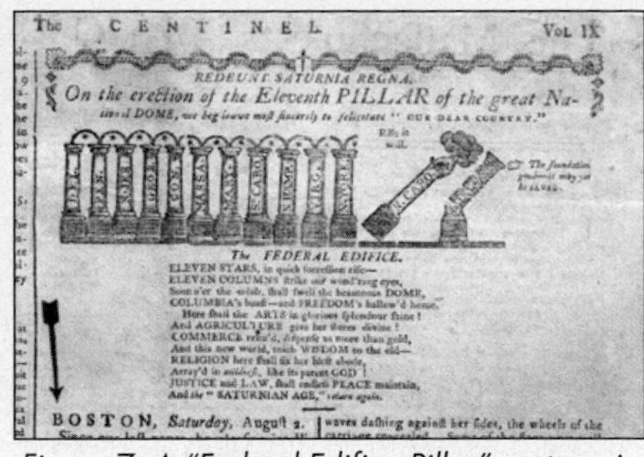

Figure 7. A "Federal Edifice Pillar" cartoon in the Massachusetts Centinel *(1788).*

ing the attention of the colonists to the necessity of union, and was revived at the time of the Stamp Act controversy in 1765 and again during the movement toward independence in 1774. That year, Isaiah Thomas used the snake cartoon device the full width of the first page in his *Massachusetts Spy*, and added a dragon, representing Great Britain, facing the snake…" [Figure 6]

The next time I find illustration in an American newspaper is at the time of our ratification process for the U.S. Constitution. *The Massachusetts Centinel* in 1787-1788 offered a series of what I call 'Federal Edifice Pillar' cartoons. Each time a state would ratify the Constitution, a new pillar would be added to the latest edifice cartoon. In Figure 7, we see the August 1788 cartoon with a headline reading "On the erection of the Eleventh Pillar of the great National Dome, we beg leave most sincerely to felicitate 'Our Dear Country.'" The cartoon thus shows that New York has ratified the Constitution. North Carolina's pillar is about to join New York according to the headline, which reads "Rise it Will," and lastly a fragmented Rhode Island Pillar is followed by a pointing hand which in turn is followed by the caption "The foundation Good it may yet be SAVED." Under the cartoon can be found a dozen lines of verse called "The Federal Edifice." I have never seen any other illustrations in American newspapers dated before 1800. Therefore, it is safe to conclude that of the very few illustrations that were produced in American newspapers during the 18th century, the majority of them are cartoons!

Magazines of the 18th century offered more illustrations, perhaps because most of them were printed monthly, thereby giving the printer more time to produce an engraved plate or portrait to accompany the text of the periodical. Most of the illustrated magazines offered little in the way of cartoons; a notable exception was the *Royal American Magazine* printed in Boston. The famous silversmith and patriot, Paul Revere, produced the most famous cartoon of the era for this Boston magazine in June 1774 when he satirized the tea taxes and the closing down of Boston Harbor with a full page engraved cartoon entitled "The able Doctor or America Swallowing the Bitter Draught." This allegorical piece shows an Indian woman (representing colonials) having a pot of tea forced down her unwilling throat; a document labeled "Boston Port Bill" is thrown down at her simultaneously. The engraved cartoon was boldly signed in the lower right corner "P. Revere Sculp."

Much has been written about the icon "Bloody [Boston] Massacre..." by Paul Revere. It is claimed as an ancestor by

Figure 8. "Florizel granting Independency to Perdita" from The Ramblers Magazine *(1783).*

Figure 9. "Amusement for John Bull..." from The European Magazine *(1783).*

Figure 10. From The Anti-Jacobin Review and Magazine, January 1799.

collectors of newspapers, broadsides, printed Americana and, alas, comic/cartoon aficionados. I would add that nostalgia played a factor in my getting one for the collection many years ago (remembering it from history books as a young student). My friend Dr. Stephen A. Goldman says of Paul Revere's 1770 engraving of the Boston Massacre that it "has various elements common to early political cartoons. The piece has a distinct comic-like appearance, contains descriptive text (in verse), and is partly news, opinion, and propaganda. Revere in this work reveals himself to have much in common with later political cartoonists such as *Harper's Weekly*'s Thomas Nast (19th Century) and the *Washington Post*'s Herb Block (20th Century)" (for the image, see the color gallery later in this book).

I have the first volume of a bawdy London monthly entitled *The Ramblers Magazine* that dates from the year that the American Revolution was officially ended by the Treaty of

Figure 11. "The Whiskers" in The New Wits Magazine (1805), annotated by the son of the illlustrator, George Cruikshank.

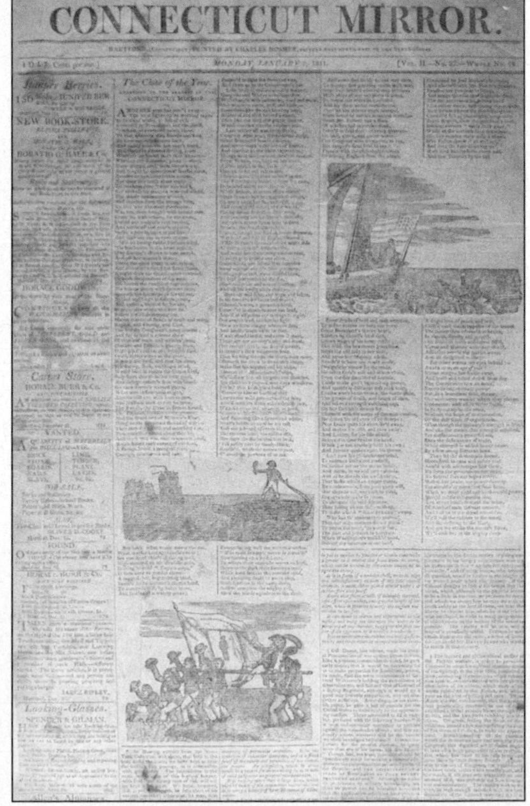
CONNECTICUT MIRROR.

Figure 12. Cartoons satirizing Napoleon on the front page of the Connecticut Mirror, dated January 7, 1811.

Figure 13. Another Napoleon cartoon, this time dubbing him "The Corsican Munchausen, from the London Strand*, December 4, 1813.*

Paris (1783). The full title page contends that the magazine will be filled "With a Most Delicious Banquet of Amorous, Bacchanalian, Whimsical, Humorous, Theatrical and Polite [Not!] Entertainment." Almost every issue of this magazine contains a cartoon including word balloons. I have chosen one that is particularly delightful [Figure 8]. This is the first issue of the magazine, and it contains a plate entitled "Florizel granting Independency to Perdita." In it, a British aristocrat grabs the arm of a young maiden and his word balloon reads "Submit to my Royal Will." Seated on a sofa, the maiden responds "Declare me Independent and Then -----."

Another London periodical from April 1783, *The European Magazine*, contains a cartoon including a buffalo. It is believed that this is the first time that the buffalo was used to symbolize the young American nation. The plate is headed "Amusement for John Bull and his Cousin Paddy or, the Gambols of the American Buffalo, in St. James Street" [Figure 9]. An enormous 12" x 20" fold-out political cartoon was included in the January 1799 issue of *The Anti-Jacobin Review and Magazine* [Figure 10]. I am not familiar enough with the politics of the day to interpret the cartoon, but it is notable for its size and its extensive use of word balloons.

The earliest English language periodical identifying itself as a "Comic Work" which I have come across is *The New Wits Magazine* [Figure 11], printed in London. The printing on the very top of the outer wrapper reads "This Comic Work (which will be completed in Twenty-four Numbers, making three Volumes) may be had of every liberal bookseller in the United Kingdom – It is published regularly every fortnight without any interruption whatever." The comic plate inside the issue is entitled "The Whiskers" and is dated December 1805. This is a remarkable issue in many ways; first of all, the pages are uncut, the original outer wrapper is present, and best of all, the plate is annotated in pencil and signed by the

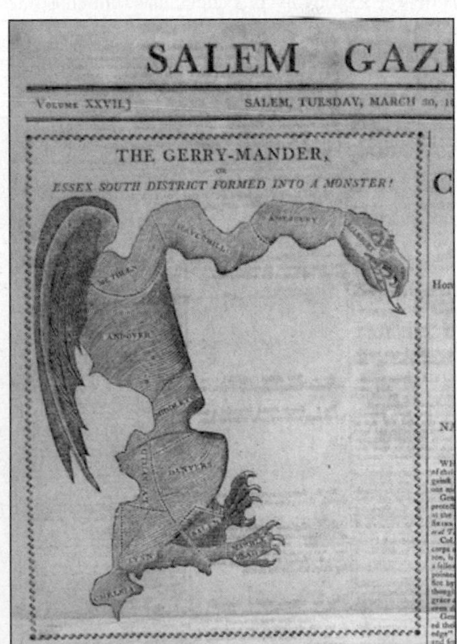

SALEM GAZ

VOLUME XXVII.] SALEM, TUESDAY, MARCH 30,

THE GERRY-MANDER,

OR

ESSEX SOUTH DISTRICT FORMED INTO A MONSTER!

Figure 14. "The Gerry-Mander" as seen in the Salem Gazette, dated March 30, 1813.

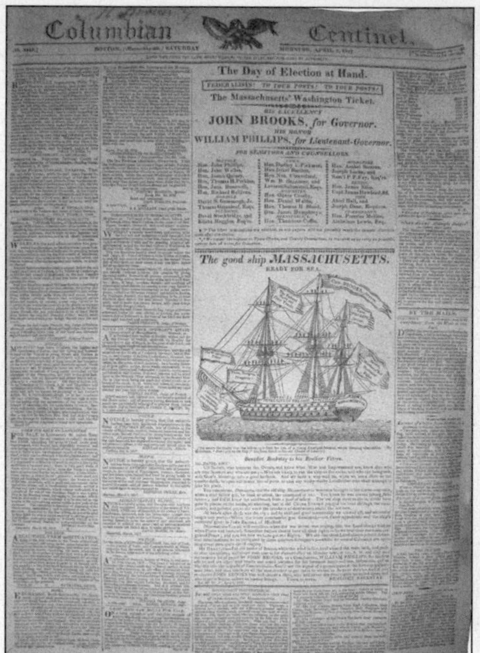

Columbian Centinel.

The Day of Election at Hand.

The Massachusetts' Washington Ticket.

JOHN BROOKS, for Governor.

WILLIAM PHILLIPS, for Lieutenant-Governor.

The good ship MASSACHUSETTS. READY FOR SEA.

Figure 15. "The Good Ship Massachusetts Ready for Sea" in the Columbian Centinel (1817).

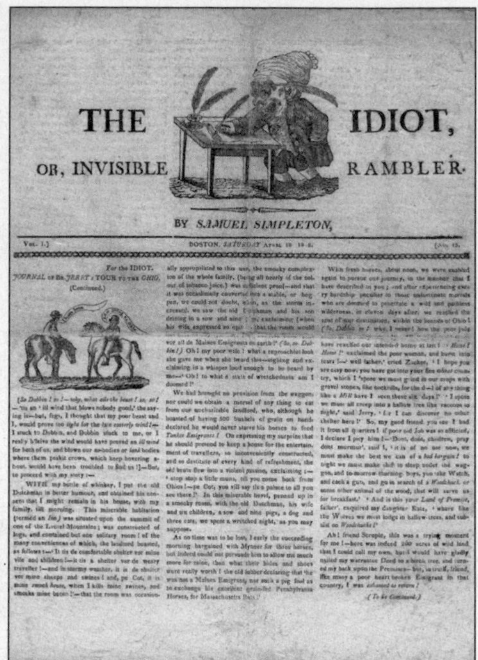

THE IDIOT, OR, INVISIBLE RAMBLER.

BY SAMUEL SIMPLETON,

BOSTON, SATURDAY

Figure 16. The comic paper, "The Idiot," printed in Boston in 1818.

most famous British illustrator of the 19th century – the illustrator for many of Charles Dickens' first editions, George Cruikshank. The blank space above the "Whisker" cartoon is filled with a pencil notation reading "engraved from a drawing by my father I. Cruikshank" and is signed in the same pencil with the initials "GCk." Isaac Cruikshank (c.1756-1811), father of George, was also a noted caricaturist. This then is George's own copy of a comic magazine illustrated by his father!

I have an issue of a Hartford, Connecticut newspaper entitled the *Connecticut Mirror* dated January 7, 1811. The front page contains what is known as a carrier's address. Newsboys would deliver a special issue either at Christmas or New Years, as in this case, with verse that would be specially prepared for that edition; to solicit tips, the newsboys used these carrier address issues. This particular title chose to grace the front page not only with verse but also three crude comic illustrations [Figure 12]. I am almost certain that the cartoons satirize Napoleon, as here is a sample of the accompanying comic verse: "...From deeds of bold and rash

Figure 17. "A Consultation at the Medical Board" from The Pasquin or General Satirist (1821).

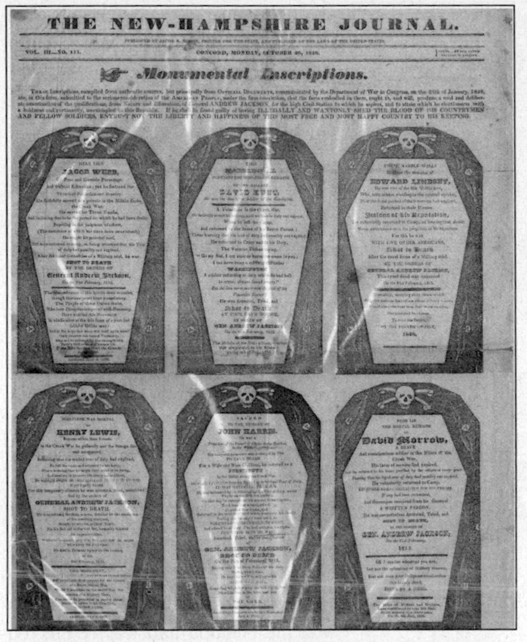

THE NEW-HAMPSHIRE JOURNAL.

Monumental Inscriptions.

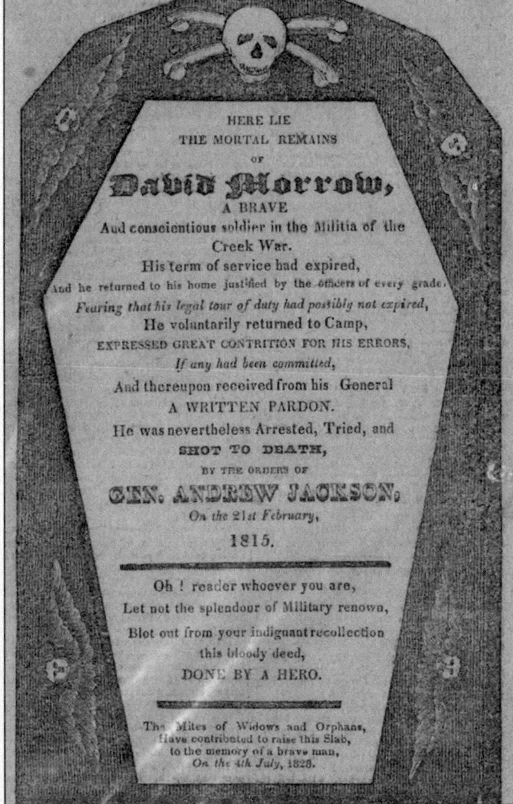

HERE LIE
THE MORTAL REMAINS
OF
David Morrow,
A BRAVE
And conscientious soldier in the Militia of the
Creek War.
His term of service had expired,
And he returned to his home justified by the officers of every grade.
Fearing that his legal tour of duty had possibly not expired,
He voluntarily returned to Camp,
EXPRESSED GREAT CONTRITION FOR HIS ERRORS,
If any had been committed,
And thereupon received from his General
A WRITTEN PARDON.
He was nevertheless Arrested, Tried, and
SHOT TO DEATH,
BY THE ORDERS OF
GEN. ANDREW JACKSON,
On the 21st February,
1815.

Oh ! reader whoever you are,
Let not the splendour of Military renown,
Blot out from your indignant recollection
this bloody deed,
DONE BY A HERO.

The Mites of Widows and Orphans,
Have contributed to raise this Slab,
to the memory of a brave man,
On the 4th July, 1828.

Figure 18. Above, the front page of The New Hampshire Journal, *dated October 20, 1828, with multiple tombstone "panels." Immediately above is a detail of the bottom right tombstone.*

emprize, to softer scenes we turn our eyes. Great Bonaparte's tender heart, Grows weary of his home-made queen, the mild, the beauteous Josephine..." It was not unusual to lampoon Napoleon, especially in Britain. "The Corsican Munchausen---Humming the Lads of Paris" [Figure 13] is a delightful hand-colored engraved cartoon "Published December 4, 1813" in the London *Strand*. Little Napoleon is spewing a multitude of word balloons ending with a particularly biting one that reads "Did I not burn Moscow – and leave 400,000 brave Soldiers to perish in the snow for the good of the French Nation?"

One of the most famous political cartoons in American history was first published in the *Salem Gazette* in Massachusetts on March 30, 1813. The front page contains "The Gerry-Mander, Essex South District Formed into a Monster!" [Figure 14] The expression gerrymandering has become famous when a geographical area is re-districted for the benefit of one political party over another. Elbridge Gerry, then Governor of Massachusetts, re-districted the state to get more Republican state senators than they otherwise would have netted. The cartoon puts the new district and the towns involved in a picture to resemble a winged dragon-like monster. Another Massachusetts newspaper called the *Columbian Centinel* issued a front-page endorsement in 1817 for John Brooks for Governor. Underneath this unabashed partisan endorsement is a cartoon of "The Good Ship Massachusetts Ready for Sea" [Figure 15] with all of the sails featuring either political slogans or the names of the candidates – Brooks, and his running mate for Lieutenant Governor, William Phillips.

Up until this point all of the American illustrations that I have discussed have been political cartoons of one sort or another. This would all change with the introduction of a comic paper called *The Idiot, or Invisible Rambler,* published under a pseudonym, "Samuel Simpleton." Printed in Boston in 1818, this publication was the earliest to present a recurring comic character that spoke with word balloons. This then is my choice for the 'Grandfather of all American Comics.' The comic is titled "Journal of Br. Jerry's Tour to the Ohio, (Continued)" [Figure 16]. The April 18, 1818 issue features the comic at the top of the first of the three columns on the front page of this four-page publication. It depicts two men on horses; one says to the other, "I am Going to Ohio." The other responds, "I have been." Ohio in 1818 was the Western frontier; it should be remembered that Lewis and Clark made their overland venture to the Pacific only about a dozen years earlier. Here, for the first time in American periodical publishing, do we encounter a secular and non-partisan comic of fictitious characters who speak with word balloons. Many of the elements that would later lead to familiar comic strip and comic book stylistic conventions are first found here.

Another really special publication in my holdings is an 1821 weekly British humor magazine in original green outer wrapper called *The Pasquin or General Satirist* [Figure 17]. I own issue #4, which has inserted into it a hand-colored word balloon cartoon relating to 'medical quackery.' One

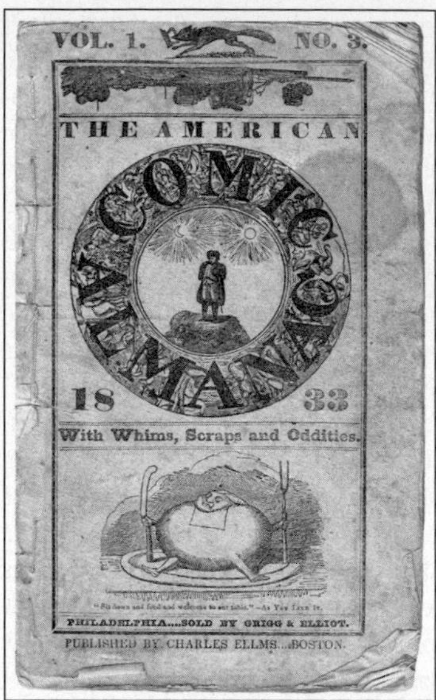

Figure 19. Front and back views of "The American Comic Almanac" (1833).

can only imagine the work that went into issuing a magazine with a hand-colored engraved cartoon. A poor patient stands before a doctor who is consulting with a mechanical robot made up of medical devices and tools. The consensus seems to be to "Bleed Him." The colored cartoon is titled "A Consultation at the Medical Board."

Did you know that the first full front-page illustration in an American newspaper was a cartoon? On Oct. 20, 1828, *The New Hampshire Journal* depicted a series of six coffins headed with skulls and bones. Each coffin has a biography describing various poor sods supposed to have been killed by General Andrew Jackson in duels, etc. Titled "Monumental Inscriptions" [Figure 18], who knows if it helped or hurt Jackson in his run for President. At any rate, he won the election and was re-elected President four years later.

PRICE THREE PENCE.

THE GALLERY OF 140 COMICALITIES,

Which has appeard from time to time, in that most Popular Sporting Sunday Paper, "Bell's Life in London,"

PRINTED AND PUBLISHED BY GEORGE GOODGER, 169, STRAND, LONDON.

Figure 20. The Gallery of 140 Comicalities, *a one-shot released by the newspaper* Bell's Life in London *on June 24, 1831.*

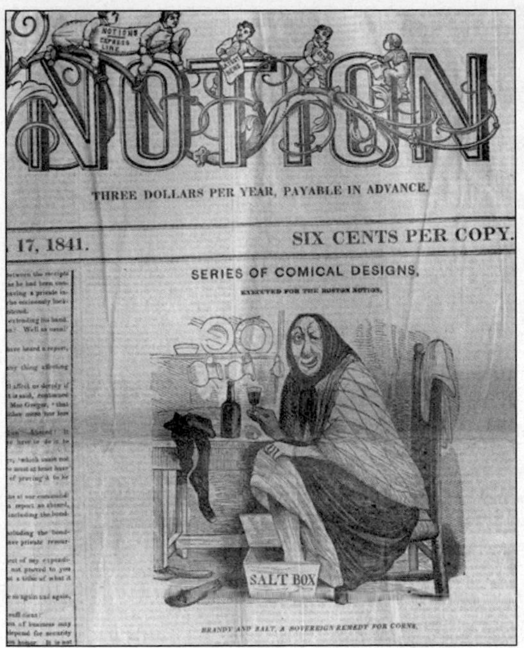
NOTION

THREE DOLLARS PER YEAR, PAYABLE IN ADVANCE.

17, 1841. SIX CENTS PER COPY.

SERIES OF COMICAL DESIGNS,

Figure 21. One of the "Series of Comical Designs" regularly featured on the front page of The Boston Notion (1841).

An interesting sidelight to the history of comics as they relate to newspapers and periodicals would be something that we might consider a distant cousin of everything in this *Guide*. I have the third issue of a series called "The American Comic Almanac" [Figure 19], dated 1833 and published in Philadelphia "With Whims, Scraps and Oddities," and of course lots of comics.

Bell's Life in London, a popular British newspaper in the first half of the 19th century, issued a one-shot on June 24, 1831 called *The Gallery of 140 Comicalities* [Figure 20]. It is subtitled "Which has appeared from time to time, in the most Popular Sporting Sunday Paper, 'Bell's Life in London'." The first British comic book? Let the Brits fight that one out!

The Boston Notion of 1841 not only had a comic nameplate, called a masthead by some, but some front pages of this title carried a column headed "Series of Comical Designs, Executed for The Boston Notion" [Figure 21]. Later in the 1840s, we start to see the advent of comic magazines in America styled after the successful British humor magazine *Punch*. The Victorian Age of comics dawned with titles such as *Yankee Doodle,* and *John Donkey*. Books composed of comics like Obadiah Oldbuck have previously been discussed in articles on the Victorian Age like the one featured in this edition of the *Guide*. One last note: It has previously been asserted, quite correctly, that *Harper's Monthly Magazine* started reprinting British comics in the back pages of its magazines in the early 1850s. But what about a regular comic feature in an American newspaper? Take a look at the May 31, 1856 issue of *Frank Leslie's Illustrated Newspaper* and you will find a page titled "Comic Department" [Figure 22]!

Eric C. Caren was born (a collector) in 1959. By the age of 5 he had collected stamps, coins and baseball cards. He started collecting rare newspapers at the age of 11, after stumbling upon an abandoned house full of them in Rockland County, NY where he lived. In high school in the mid-1970s he apprenticed with a rare book dealer in Connecticut and actually set up as a dealer at a comic book convention in NYC sometime around 1975. He graduated from the University of Maryland with a Business degree in 1981. His first job was director of a gallery that dealt in rare newspapers in London in Covent Garden Market soon after it opened. He established The Caren Archive, a full-time business selling historical collectibles in 1983. He co-founded HCA Auctions with Dennis Holzman. He is a former Director of The Ephemera Society of America, a Member of The American Antiquarian Society, a Member of the Antiquarian Booksellers Association of America, and a Consultant to The Newseum, which will re-open in Washington DC on Pennsylvania Avenue in several years (his first newspaper collection will be the most substantial part of their permanent collection). He is a partner with Stephen A. Goldman in the business that bears his name as well as in OldNews, Inc. He has authored nine books using rare newspapers – The "Extra" series with Castle Books – and has recently co-authored his 10th book, "The Civil War" Smithsonian Institution Headliners Series with Dr. Stephen A. Goldman. Reprints of papers from his and Dr. Goldman's archive are sold at The Smithsonian Institution and The Holocaust Memorial Museum.

FRANK LESLIE'S ILLUSTRATED NEWSPAPER.

COMIC DEPARTMENT.

Figure 22. The "Comic Department" from the May 31, 1856 issue of Frank Leslie's Illustrated Newspaper.

The Victorian Age

Comic Strips and Books: 1646-1900

A Concise History & Price Index Of The Field As Of 2008

ORIGINS OF EARLY AMERICAN COMIC STRIPS BEFORE THE YELLOW KID

by Robert Lee Beerbohm, Richard Samuel West & Richard D. Olson, PhD ©2009

(This article was originally created by Doug Wheeler, Robert Beerbohm and Richard D. Olson, PhD for CBPG #32 and continues to be revised annually by the current authors.) We welcome any and all corrections and additions. Special Thanks This Installment To Leonardo De Sa, Terrence Keegen, Gabriel Laderman and Joe Rainone.

Left: "The Burning of Mr. John Rogers," 1646 is the earliest known North American cartoon printed on paper printed in the earliest children's primer in America.

OUR COMICS HISTORY IS BEING RE-WRITTEN RIGHT HERE, FOLKS!

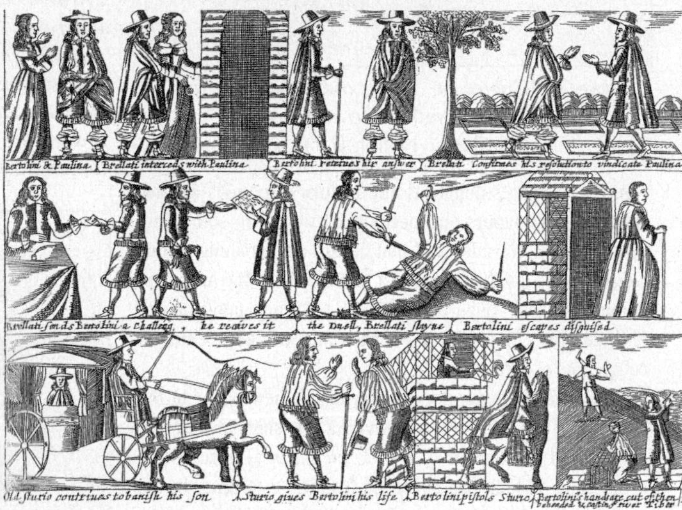

"God's Revenge For Murder" By John Reynolds, unknown artist, 1656. Earliest-known sequential comic "panel" strip created in the English language.

Left: From his pamphlet Plain Truth 1747 containing Ben Franklin's earliest-known cartoon titled "Heaven Helps Only Those Who Help Themselves" depicting ancient "super hero" Hercules in the upper right corner. Middle: "A Warm Place - Hell", one of two images definitely known to be drawn and engraved by Paul Revere, 1768. Word balloons had wide-spread usage in many cartoons in the 1700s. Right: The Tables Turned by James Gillray, 1797 commenting on an "invasion" of England by 1400 French convicts. The use of word balloons was wide spread in many parts of the world long before the Yellow Kid's parrot uttered a few words in 1896.

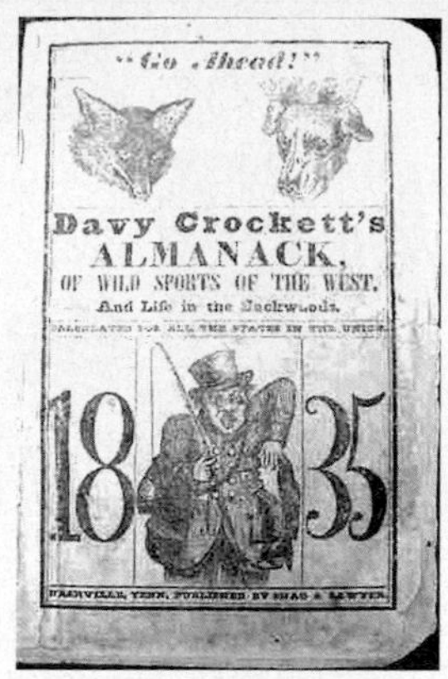

The Comic Almanac(k) debuted in America in 1831 with the earliest-known titles starting heavy with humor and sporting crude woodcut single panel cartoons. Ellm's American Comic Almanac was one of the first. By 1835 Davy Crockett, one of the nation's earliest national folk heroes, began issuing his own version. In the late 1840s the Comic Almanac(k)s began to offer tall-tale sequential comic strips which became somewhat commonplace in the 1850s, fueled by the advent of the California Gold Rush. They were instrumental in the development of the American comic strip and we will be reporting more new finds next year after more research into American folklore.

We have a lot of new discoveries to share with you again this year as amply evident in the price index which follows this year's history lesson. A quantum leap has finally been achieved in the area of introducing the comic book collecting world to *American Comic Almanac(k)s* as well as a huge multitude of American humor periodicals, many of which contained sequential comic strips.

This Victorian Era section is devoted to comic strips and books published during the years the United States expanded across the North American continent, fought a Civil War, shifted from an agrarian to an industrial society, "welcomed" waves of immigrants, and struggled over race, class, religion, temperance, and suffrage - and all of it depicted and satirized by generations of mostly now long-forgotten cartoonists. The social attitudes, beliefs, and conventions of 19th century America, the good as well as the bad, are to be found in abundance. Perhaps the first question to pop into most readers' minds will be, "What, beyond the happenstance of publication date, are Victorian Era comics?"

There has been a long slow-motion evolution of the comic strip which was not invented in America, contrary to many previous history books on the subject. One must examine many aspects of concurrent popular culture. The main aspect that we believe most distinguishes Victorian Era comic strips from those of later eras was the extremely rare use of word balloons within sequential (multi-picture) comic stories. When word balloons were used, it was nearly always within single-panel cartoons. On the occasions when they appeared inside a strip, with very few exceptions, the ballooned dialogue was inconsequential. Nineteenth-century comics tended to place both narration and dialogue beneath comic panels rather than within the panel's borders as they were thought by many to interfere with the art. Many of these comics are to the word balloon-strewn post-Yellow Kid comics of the 20th Century as silent movies are to the later "talkies." Just as sound changed how stories were structured on film, so too did comic strips change when the words were moved from beneath panels to inside them, and dialogue rather than narration drove the story in conjunction with the pictures.

The Victorian Era of actual comic strip books began on different dates in different nations, depending on when the first publication of a sequential comic book on their soil is known to have occurred. For the U.S. this happened when the American literary periodical *Brother Jonathan* printed the 40-page, 195-panel graphic novel *The Adventures of Mr. Obadiah Oldbuck* as a special extra dated September 14, 1842. Almost six decades later, America's Victorian comics came to their end, replaced by the onslaught of Platinum Age books reprinting newspaper strips from Bennett, Hearst, and Pulitzer Sunday comic sections, among many others.

There is considerable overlap between Victorian Era and Platinum Age comic books and strips. Those publications that continued from one century into the next, such as *Puck*, *Judge*, and *Life*, have their pre-1900 issues listed within the Victorian Age section, while their post-1899 issues can be found inside the Platinum Age. Some non-sequential (i.e., single-panel) American comic items existing prior to 1842 are also listed herein, going back to 1795. These belong to what could tentatively be called the Age of Caricature (1770s through 1830s). This was a fertile period for the art in England, when Gillray and Rowlandson, and, later, Cruikshank, Heath, and Seymour were that nation's top cartoonists. During the same period in the U.S., there were no artists who made their living as caricaturists, though William Charles, printer and engraver, did produce about two dozen spirited cartoon broadsides from 1805 to 1820, the most important ones concerning events of the War of 1812.

In addition, one can trace origins of American comic books to the humorous Comic Almanacs which began in earnest in the early 1830s.

The earliest known cartoon-like woodcut printed on paper

The Comus Offering, 1830 sample page of single panel cartoons using word balloons in every panel. Very Rare.

*Outlines Illustrative of the Journal of F****** A*** K******
Plate #6 By D.C. Johnston, 1835
Parodying a passage from the Journal of Fanny (Frances) A. Kemble, a British woman who wrote a highly negative book about American Culture after returning from the U.S. Word balloon use abounds.

in North America was in a Puritan children's book first published in 1646. Titled simply *The Burning of Mr. John Rogers*, it showed in flaming graphic detail what happens to those who stray from the flock and have to be burned at the stake. Dr. Wertham would have had a field day with that one!

Cartoon broadsides and other single panel images, often using word balloons, appeared from pre-Revolution days through the end of the 19th Century. The earliest known attributed cartoon, designed by the ubiquitous Benjamin Franklin, was "Heaven Helps Only Those Who Help Themselves," which first appeared in his pamphlet *Plain Truth* in 1747.

The most popularly remembered 18th-Century American cartoons are likely Franklin's *"Join or Die"* in 1754, representing the American Colonies as severed snake parts, and *"The Bloody Massacre Perpetrated in King Street"* -- Paul Revere's 1770 depiction of the Boston Massacre, which he pirated from the earlier Henry Pelham broadsheet cartoon *"The Fruits of Arbitrary Power."*

In September 1826, John Warner Barber, New Haven, Ct. (1798-1885) designed and self-published the broadside *The Drunkard's Progress, Or The Direct Road to Poverty, Wretchedness and Ruin* showing in four stages sequentially "The Morning Dram" which is "The Beginning of Sorrow, " "The Grog Shop" with its "Bad Company," "The Confirmed Drunkard" in a state of "Beastly Intoxication," and the "Concluding Scene" with the family being driven off to the alms house. It is an interesting set of cuts, faintly reminiscent of Hogarth. Barber began his career in 1819, age 21, engraving on wood. He devoted most of his career to the multitude of art chores associated with book production. As late as 1870 he was issuing *Barber's Temperance Tracts,* which built upon his 1826 original plus four panels showing the positive effects of living without alcohol.

The first American whose fame was based primarily on his cartoons appears to be David Claypoole Johnston (1798-1865). Johnston provided illustrations for various almanacs, books, and periodicals, including the masthead for *Brother Jonathans*. Most notable of Johnston's comics work was his nine-issue series *Scraps*, which he self-published from 1828 to 1849. This series was highly influenced by George Cruikshank's series *Scraps and Sketches*, which first appeared in 1827. Because of the resemblance, Johnston became known in his day as "the American Cruikshank." Each issue of Johnston's *Scraps* consists of four large folio-sized pages, printed on one side, with nine to twelve single-panel cartoons per page, and each page often organized around a theme. Also popular was his comic album Outlines Illustrative of the Journal of F****** A*** K***** (1835), which parodied passages from the journal of recently published observations on America by British actress Fanny Kemble.

Johnston, himself a failed

Adventures & Achievements of the Renowned Don Quixote & his Doughty Squire Sancho Panza by D.C. Johnston, 1837, America's earliest-known sequential comic broadside.

Left: Cover to the subscriber version of the earliest-known sequential comic book published in America, The Adventures of Mr. Obadiah Oldbuck, Sept. 1842, Wilson & Co. New York, originally conceived in 1828 in Geneva Switzerland by creator Rodolphe Töpffer. Right: Pages 28 from this 40-page 1842 graphic novel which launched the comic book business in America....

actor, had an interest in the theater his entire career. In addition to producing a number of prints depicting American actors in famous roles, he collaborated with actor Henry J. Finn to produce the 1831 *(American) Comic Annual*, with Finn as Editor and Johnston as artist, published by Richardson, Lord and Holbrook, Boston. It featured almost 30 full-page Johnston-designed copper engravings and woodcuts. Also that year, Finn solo produced *Finn's Comic Sketch Book*, a twelve-page album similar to Johnston's *Scraps* with upwards of half a dozen single-panel cartoons per page. It was published by Peabody and Co, of New York in business from 1831-1843. (Finn died tragically in a steamboat accident Jan. 13, 1840.)

Perhaps Johnston's most interesting contribution to the history of the comic strip in American came in 1837, when he produced the sequential comic broadside, *Illustrations of the Adventures & Achievements of the Renowned Don Quixote & his Doughty Squire Sancho Panza* (27.4 x 30.4 cm). This blank-reverse engraved print was an elaborate twelve-panel satire of the Andrew Jackson-Van Buren administration. It likely sold for 25 cents, seeing distribution in Boston, New York and Philadelphia. Much later, in 1863, Johnston drew another sequential comic broadside, *The House the Jeff Built* (27.5 x 36.7 cm), a bitter indictment of Jefferson Davis and the Southern slavocracy.

In July 1839, Wilson and Company, a newly formed New York printing firm, began publishing a mammoth newspaper by the name of *Brother Jonathan*. The publisher, J. Gregg Wilson had employed the newspaper format for *Brother Jonathan* to circumvent the higher postage rates imposed on magazines, but *Brother Jonathan* was a newspaper in format only -- it contained not a shred of news, instead specializing in serialized fiction, some of it written by Americans but most of it pirated from foreign sources. Despite the cost savings, the mammoth format had its limitations; when opened it measured a whopping three feet by four feet. So, once *Brother Jonathan* was an established success, Wilson and Day began in January 1841 the simultaneous publication of a magazine-sized quarto edition of *Brother Jonathan* that reprinted the contents of the mammoth edition.

Later that same year, to capitalize on the name recognition of their successful twin publications, Wilson and Company started issuing book-length *Brother Jonathan Extras* in the same format as the quarto magazine. These reprints are counted among the earliest paperback books in America. Most of the *Extra* numbers were pirated European novels. For example their eighth extra was the first American printing of a Charles Dickens

EXPLOITS OF PETER PIPER. 21

But is fortunately rescued from immediate peril by the faithful elephant.

LIST of BOOKS for sale at the Brother Jonathan Office.

THE ADVENTURES OF OBADIAH OLDBUCK.—A Book of Pictures, which set forth, in a laughable manner, the Curious, Comical, Cunning, Extraordinary, Extravagant, Funny, Farcical, Lively, Pathetic, Perplexing, Quizzical, and Wonderful Incidents which attended the Courtship and Marriage of that unfortunate and perplexed old gentleman—showing likewise how he attempted to commit suicide on five different occasions, and each time was saved by "invidious fate." The story of Mr. Oldbuck's Love, as set forth by these pictures, is one of the most admirable satires and caricatures of a lovesick old bachelor that can be imagined. It is full of genuine, original, sparkling wit—nothing old or borrowed. It will amuse the most refined person, and cannot fail to please everybody. This book comprises 80 pages of pictures, well printed on fine hot-pressed paper. It is one of the cheapest pictorial works ever published. We send it free of postage for 25 cents per copy.

A DAY'S SPORT—Or, Hunting Adventures of S. Winks Wattles, a shopkeeper, Thomas Titt. Esq., a "lega' gent.," and Major Nicholas Noggin, a jolly good fellow generally. This story is told by Pictures, and is really a witty and amusing book—the drawings by Henry L. Stevens of Philadelphia. It will make you laugh out loud to look over this book. It is handsomely printed, and put up in an illustrated cover, suitable for the centre table. We send it free of postage for 12½ cents per copy.

THE SEA-WITCH—A Story of Life and Adventure on board an African Slaver, and on the Coast. One of the best novels we have issued in a long time. Sent free of postage for 25 cents.

Send cash for the above books to B. H. Day, 48 Beekman-st., New York.

B. H. Day's Brother Jonathan Cheap Book Establishment 1855 catalog with 32-panel comic strip "Peter Piper in Bengal'" by John Tenniel (later Alice of Wonderland fame) with two comic books for sale on the above page: Obadiah Oldbuck by Töpffer and A Day's Sport by Henry L. Stephens of Philadelphia, a scarce newly-rediscovered original American comic book.

novel. But for their ninth *Extra*, they did something no American publisher had ever done before -- they pirated a graphic novel, Rodolphe Töpffer's *The Adventures of Mr. Obadiah Oldbuck*. By reformatting *Oldbuck* from its original small oblong strip design to fit *Brother Jonathan's* standard quarto format Wilson and Company inadvertently made this edition (alone) of *Obadiah Oldbuck* resemble a modern comic book. *Oldbuck's* arrival on the shores of the New World would directly inspire a wave of American imitators. [*This first Wilson printing of Oldbuck from 1842 was reprinted in same-size limited edition facsimile by the Naples Comicon in 2003. An English translation by Leonardo De Sá of Töpffer's original draft is at leonardo desa.interdinamica.net/comics/lds/*]

Even though in 1904 (in its September 3 edition), *The New York Times* accurately identified the *Brother Jonathan Extra* as the first American comic book as well as Wilson & Co. utilizing Tilt & Bougue's original printing plates as well as still being in print for sale in New York at such a late date, Töpffer has already been largely forgotten in the New World. It is high time Töpffer received credit long overdue as the inventor of the modern comic strip, laying previously long-held myths to rest.

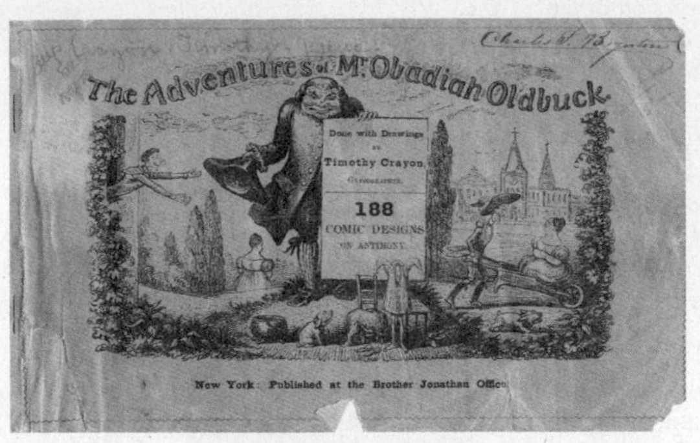

The Adventures of Mr. Obadiah Oldbuck
Done with Drawings by Timothy Crayon
188 COMIC DESIGNS
New York: Published at the Brother Jonathan Office

The Adventures of Obadiah Oldbuck, rare newly discovered 4th ediiton from mid 1850s. Says now "Published at Brother Jonathan Offices." Art & Story now accredited to the pseudonym "Timothy Crayon" - see Peter Piper ad previous page.

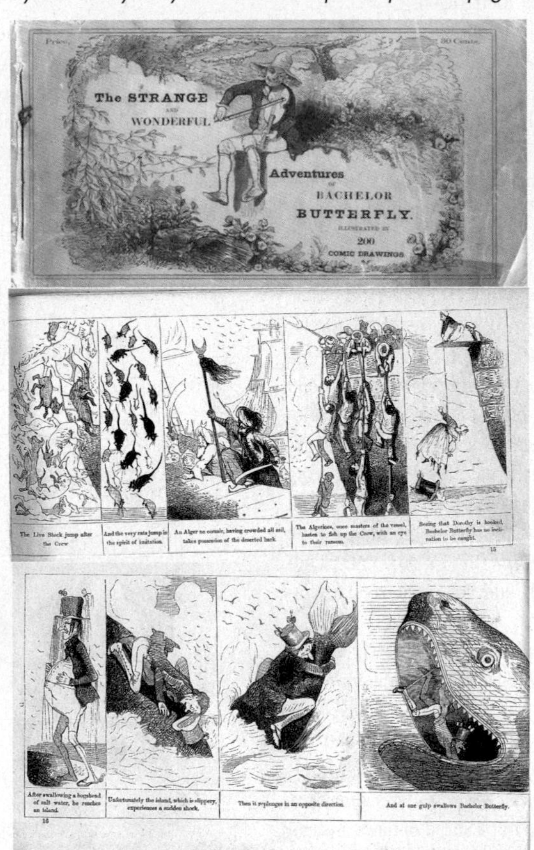

The Strange and Wonderful Adventures of Bachelor Butterfly by Rodolphe Töpffer (New York, 1846) was America's 3rd comic book; Wilson & Company's second comic book, this time out staying with the original European format. Below: sample pages 15 & 16.

Freydig, Frutiger (1830s) and Schmidt (1840s). These first sequential comic books, scripted in Töpffer's native French language, found their way to Paris and became an instant hit. According to Gombrich in *Art and Illusion* (1960), "Töpffer recognized that he could rely on the reader to supplement from their own lives what was omitted between the panels. This is crucial in the development of the sequential comic strip."

The demand for his comic books soon outstripped the supply, and pirated editions, redrawn by others, were created by Parisian publisher Aubert to capitalize on this. In a world where international copyright conventions did not exist, this was perfectly legal, if morally questionable. Thus, in 1841, London publisher Tilt and Bogue commissioned George Cruikshank to create an English version of Töpffer's *Les Amours de M. Vieux Bois* by pirating Aubert's pirated edition of the Geneva original.

This English translation, co-financed by George Cruikshank himself, sported a new cover page by George's brother Robert, based on a montage of Töpffer's scenes. Confirmation of this fact came when George Cruikshank's personal copy surfaced in auction recently with the inscription "Copied from a French book by my Brother Robert" above the title page with the same scene. This is

Töpffer (1799-1846) was a playwright, novelist, artist, and teacher from Geneva, Switzerland, who in 1827 had begun producing what he called "picture novels," sharing them with his friends and students. His earliest editions were self-published via lithography on transfer paper as they use the word "autographie" in their imprints. The earliest printers were J.

the translation that was reprinted by America's Wilson and Company as *The Adventures of Mr. Obadiah Oldbuck* utilizing the original Tilt and Bogue printing plates.

Tilt and Bogue followed up their success by translating into English two additional stories of Töpffer's seven published graphic novels: *Beau Ogleby*, circa 1843 (originally Histoire de M. Jabot), and *Bachelor Butterfly* two years later (from *Histoire de M. Cryptogame)*. David Bogue also published picture-story strip books by John Leighton using the pseudonym Luke Limner. He wrote and drew beautiful comic books titled *London Out of Town or The Adventures of the Browns At The Seaside; Comic Art-Manufactures; and The Ancient Story of the Old Dame and Her Pig* starting in 1847, but none of these seem to have ever been republished in America. They follow a definite Töpffer influence. This growing body of comic book production was made easier by the spreading understanding of transfer paper lithography, otherwise the panels would have had to have been drawn and lettered mirror reverse. Gombrich referred to Töpffer's comic books as "the innocent ancestors of today's manufactured dreams... everywhere in these countless episodes of almost surrealist inconsequence we find a mastery of physiognomic characterization which sets the standard for such influential humorous draftsmen in the 19th century as Wilhelm Busch in Germany."

A Register of The New York City Book Trades 1821-1842 by Sidney F. & Elizabeth Stege12, Huttner (The Bibliographical Society of America, NYC, 1993) mentions Benjamin H. Day bought into *Brother Jonathan*'s publisher, Wilson and Company, in this year, becoming at some point an equal partner with owner J. Gregg Wilson. The Register lists them both as publishers of *Brother Jonathan* at the same address of 162 Nassau Street. Other historical artifacts state Day eventually became sole-owner and publisher. Exactly when has not yet been determined, though we have figured out with certainly before 1850 .

This is the same Benjamin H. Day who started the first successful penny newspaper in 1833, *The (New York) Sun*, transforming it in four short years into the largest circulation daily in the world at that time. He sold out his ownership of the Sun to his brother-in-law during the financial "panic" of 1837, a mistake he regretted the rest of his life. He re-emerged heavily involved in *Brother Jonathan* definitely by 1840 and as a partner by 1841. *Brother Jonathan's* offices were right next door to Tamany Hall. (See the first 20 minutes of the 2002 movie *Gangs of New York* to visualize the period atmosphere and their customer base.) According to *The Brothers Harper* by Eugene Exmen (Harper & Row, 1965), on page 125, "*Brother Jonathan...* offered in its weekly edition and also in special supplements very cheap reprints of English novels. In effect, it began a price-cutting war against the older established 'pirates' among the book publishers..." Day, it appears, had found the perfect project on which to build a new empire.

Desirous of repeating the success they had with *Obadiah Oldbuck*, Wilson and Company published the first American edition of *Bachelor Butterfly* in 1846. Three years later, they reformatted *Obadiah Oldbuck* back into its original British shape using lithography, dropping a handful of comic panels and altering the text to hide these deletions. Soon thereafter, they published other comic books for a steadily growing market that they had helped to stimulate. In recognition of their significant role in the dissemination of sequential comics, Wilson and Company deserve to be remembered as the first comic book publisher in America.

Fisher's Comic Almanac, 1844, used a word balloon on its cover.

Back in Europe, perhaps inspired by his involvement with Töpffer's *Obadiah Oldbuck*, George Cruikshank soon created several sequential comic books of his own. These too found their way to America. *The Bachelor's Own Book*, published first in Britain in 1844, became the second known U.S. published sequential comic book when it was reprinted by Burgess, Stringer and Company the following year. Next was Cruikshank's masterpiece *The Bottle*, the Hogarthian-style tale of a man whose addiction to alcohol brings himself and his family to ruin. After debuting in London in 1847, it was reprinted the same year in a British-American co-publication between David Bogue and Americans Wiley and Putnam. Both printings were in huge folio form, available in either black and white or professionally hand-tinted versions. In 1848, the story saw American print again, this time in smaller form, placed at the front of the otherwise prose volume *Temperance Tales; Or, Six Nights with the Washing-tonians*. It continued to be reprinted by a variety of publishers into the early 20th Century. *The Bottle* was even reproduced onto painted glass slides and then projected by magic lantern onto a screen for the moral edification of temperance audiences. *The Drunkard's Children, Cruikshank's sequel to The Bottle*, was issued July 1, 1848 as a British-American-

The Bachelor's Own Book by George Cruikshank, published by Burgess, Stringer and Company, 1845, America's 2nd comic book, was also still a European reprint.

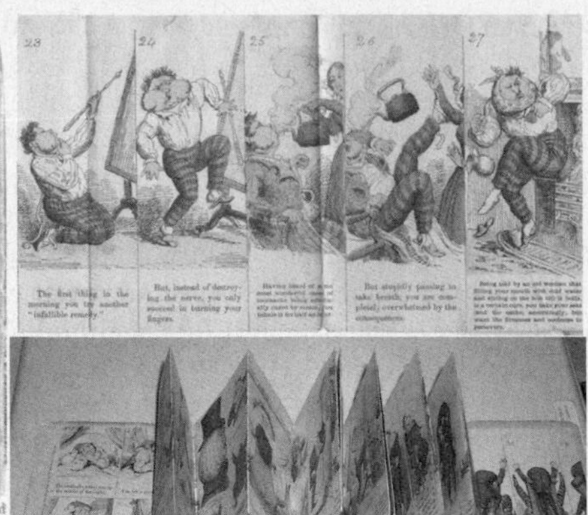

The Tooth-Ache by George Cruickshank 1849 © J. L. Smith, Philadelphia, PA. First American edition opens up accordian-like into a single continuous paper strip 7 feet, 3 inches long!

Thanks to Töpffer, Cruikshank, and a handful of enterprising American publishers, the 1840s should be remembered as the decade when America first fell in love with the comics. It had seen the U. S. publication of six sequential comic books, as well as the importation of other comics with foreign imprints. America's growing interest in graphic humor was further stimulated by the growth of two other fields: the cartoon broadside and the humor magazine.

Australian co-publishing venture, but was less successful, and had not nearly as many reprints.

The most clearly sequential, as well as fun, of George Cruikshank's comic books was *The Tooth-Ache*, first issued in London in 1849. It was reprinted in America later that same year by Philadelphia map maker J.L. Smith. An additional concurrent version was also issued from Boston.

When closed, this booklet appears an unassuming 5-1/4 inches tall by 3-1/4 inches wide. Its striking feature is that the book folds open accordion style, stretching the entire 43-panel story along one single strip of paper, which when fully extended is seven feet, three inches long! *The Tooth-Ache* was issued in both black and white and professionally hand-colored editions. Abridged editions of the story, printed in black and white and with a "normal" page-turning rather than foldout presentation, appeared inside promotional give-away comics issued by American companies in the 1880s.

As mentioned before, the cartoon broadside had been a part of the American scene since pre-Revolution days, but it did not flourish until stone lithography (introduced in 1818 and in wide use by the 1830s) made the reproduction of images relatively fast and cheap. From the early 1830s into the mid 1840s, the leading producer of cartoon broadsides in America was New York printer H. R. Robinson, who either drew his own cartoons or employed others, especially E. W. Clay, to do it. Clay is notable for having produced the first sequential comic broadside in America. Published in 1834 and entitled, "This Is the House that Jack Built" (50 x 32 cm), the nine-panel parody of the classic nursery rhyme was an attack on the Jackson Administration. The dominant theme of American cartoon broadsides was political, as befitted a nation where politics was the leading spectator sport. As the American electorate grew increasingly educated and prosperous, the demand for cartoon broadside also increased. During the 1840s, lithographers in New York, Boston, and Philadelphia, entered the field to satisfy that demand. The best known of these, Nathaniel Currier, later Currier and Ives, joined the fray in 1848. The firm employed

A few samples of the many humor magazines of the mid-1800s which ran cartoons. Wide-spread acceptance of the comic srtip slowly evolved over the decades. Right: Yankee Doodle #30, this title was the first American comic weekly which ran Oct 1846-Oct 1847; Second: Judy #1 ran Nov 28-Feb 20, 1847; Third: The John-Donkey #4 ran January-October 1848. Fourth: The Lantern #21, May 29, 1851 title ran Jan. 10, 1852-July 1853.

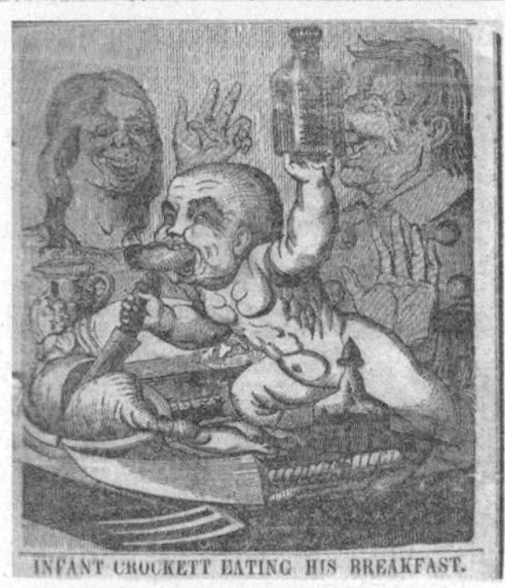

many artists, but its chief political cartoonist was Louis Maurer and its chief comic artist was Thomas Worth.

Except for the three previously cited sequential cartoon broadsides, nearly all of the cartoon broadsides published in America from 1832 to 1876, its dominant era, were single panels. From the 1860s onward, broadside series on a single comic theme became common, the most famous being Thomas Worth's *Darktown* series. These can be loosely categorized as sequential comics since they employed the same characters and formed a story of sorts when hung together on a wall, as was the publisher's expectation. Sequential art or not, the cartoon broadsides nearly always employed the speech balloons that later became one of the defining characteristic of the American comic strip.

Davy Crockett's Alamnac #14, 1848, contains a 17 panel comic strip detailing tall tales of his life culminating with Crockett's death in The Alamo in 1836.

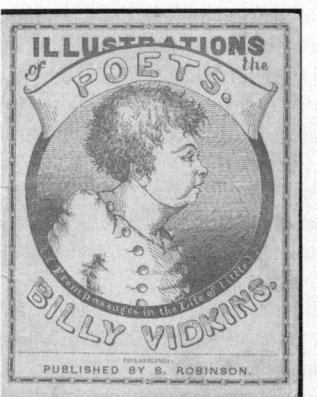

During the same decade that sequential comics and cartoon broadsides were growing in popularity, the illustrated American humor magazine made its debut. The British comic weekly *Punch*, founded in 1841, was an immediate success, both in England and the United States. It was a handsomely printed quarto, initially twelve pages and later sixteen, with a repeating cover design, backed by a page of small advertisements, humorous text interspersed with comic spot art, and a single panel full-page cartoon. A significant subset of *Punch*'s subscriber base was located in the U.S., to which thousands of copies were exported on an ongoing trans-Atlantic basis. Inevitably, enterprising American publishers attempted to repulse this invader with a home-grown comic weekly. The first, *Yankee Doodle*, came to town (New York, that is) on October 10, 1846, for one year. *Judy* (November 28, 1846 to February 20, 1847), *The John-Donkey* (January 1 to October 21, 1848), and *The Elephant* (January 22 to February 19, 1848) soon followed. None of them was successful, but all of them continued to feed the growing American interest in comic art.

Journey to the Gold Diggins By Jeremiah Saddlebags, June 1849, so far the earliest known sequential comic book by American creators, J.A. and D.F. Read. Below: a couple sample pages. Note similarity to Töpffer's comics especially Bachelor Butterfly

By the late 1840s, comic art was flourishing in America.

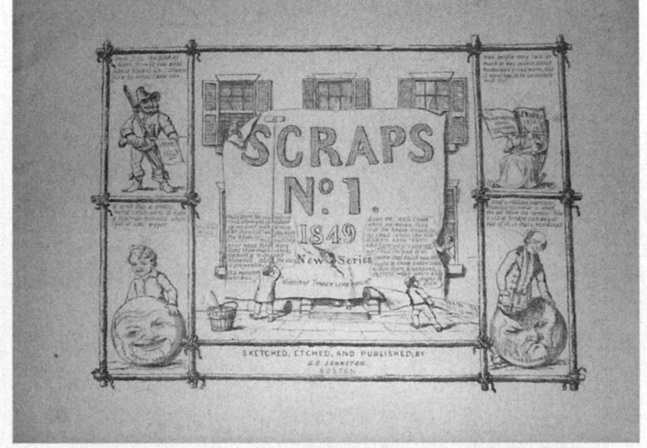

Illustrations of the Poets: From Passages in the Life of Little Billy Vidkins by Henry Stephens, S. Robinson, Phila, January, 1849, is an early American proto-comic book story told in poetry and reprinted several times. The Ohio State University Cartoon Research Library, Richard Samuel West Collection. RIGHT: In 1849 D.C. Johnston published his final issue of Scraps, nine years after the first series of eight issues. Mostly single panel cartoons all using word balloons.

Yankee Notions #1, January, 1852. This title began the first sequential comic strips in an American humor magazine, The Adventures of Jerimiah Old-Pot.

The conditions were right for the production of the earliest known American-created sequential comic book. Brothers James and Donald Read, who had worked for a time as cartoonists on *Yankee Doodle*, were the creators of *Journey to the Gold Diggins by Jeremiah Saddlebags*. This spirited send-up of the California gold rush craze was published in June 1849 by Stringer and Townsend, the late publishers of *Judy*, and, soon after, by U. P. James of Cincinnati. This Töpffer-influenced comic book chronicles the adventures of its hero *Jeremiah Saddlebags* in his get-rich-quick quest for gold in California. It is highly sought by collectors of Western Americana. Interestingly, the back cover of the Stringer and Townsend edition carries an advertisement for *Rose and Gertrude* - a Genevese Story, one of Rodolphe Töpffer's non-comics prose novels.

Stringer and Townsend was making something of a name for itself as a publisher of comic art. It will be remembered that it was one of the 1845 participants in the American publication of *The Bachelor's Own Book*. And, then, in 1846-47, it published *Judy*. Its decision to issue *Jeremiah Saddlebags* was all in due course.

The Gold Rush proved to be a gold mine for American comic artists. Aside from being a featured topic in the 1849 edition of David Claypool Johnston's *Scraps*, in comic almanacs, and in Currier cartoon prints, it was the subject of several other significant sequential series. The first, *The Adventures of Mr. Tom Plump* (a fat man who nearly starves to death in his failed attempt at California Gold riches), saw print in 1850. The second, *The Adventures of Jeremiah Old-Pot* (a twelve-part burlesque narrative of a New York businessman who attempts to get rich selling tin in price-inflated California), ran throughout 1852 in *Yankee Notions*. Though the narrative was distinctly American in its humor, the artwork was probably German in origin. *Yankee Notions*' Publisher, T. W. Strong, built his business on recycling old woodcuts with new captions attached. It should be noted that the *Old-Pot* series, borrowed or otherwise, was the first sequential art to appear in an American humor magazine. *Yankee Notions*, published from 1852 to 1875, also has the distinction of being the first comic monthly published in America.

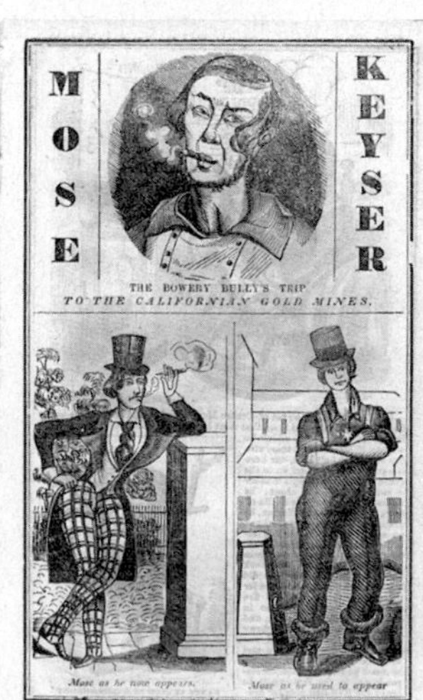

"Moses Keyser the Bowery Bully's Trip to the California Gold Mines," was a 13-page comic story that appeared in *Elton's Californian Comic All-My-Nack* for 1850. It was reprinted at least twice in the circa 1850-51 booklet *The Clown, Or The Banquet of Wit* and later again in *Sam Slick's Comic Almanac* in 1857. *The Clown* is also notable as the earliest known anthology of sequential comics, with the bonus that each multi-panel story is by a different artist. Many of the artists are as yet unidentified, and how much of it is original American material versus that reprinted from Europe is presently unknown. But verified are cartoons by George Cruikshank, Elton (American), the Read brothers, Grandville (French), and Richard Doyle (British). The Doyle contribution reprints the comics story "Brown, Jones and Robinson and How They Went to a Ball," which originally saw print in the August 24, 1850 issue of *Punch*. This is the first known American appearance of these Doyle characters, and was almost certainly pirated.

Richard Doyle's *The Foreign Tour of Messrs. Brown, Jones, and Robinson* is basically a travelogue in illustrated form, told via humorous episodes, part sequential cartoon sequences, and part snapshots of moments jumping forward in time. This halfway sequential format was ideal for most 19th Century cartoonists, who, with rare exception, had not quite grasped how to maintain a single sequential story for much longer than two dozen successive panels. Doyle had simplified Töpffer's formula in a manner most artists could attempt to emulate. Episodes of "*Brown, Jones, and Robinson*" originally appeared in *Punch* in 1850, until a dispute between the Roman Catholic Doyle and Punch's editors over an anti-Papal joke ended with Doyle's resignation. Doyle redrew and expanded the story into a single album, first seeing print in 1854 from British publisher Bradbury and Evans.

New York Publisher D. Appleton brought the album to America, reprinting it in 1860, 1871, and 1877. Next, Dick and Fitzgerald of New York pirated Doyle's story sometime in

"Moses Keyser the Bowery Bully's Trip to the California Gold Mines" first appeared Elton's in 1850 ;was reprinted at least twice

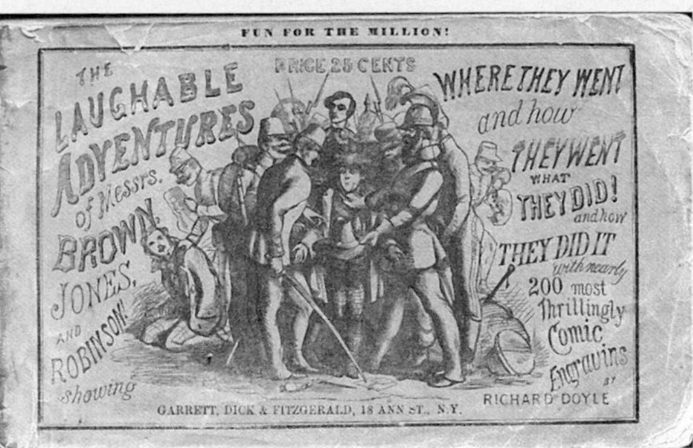

The Laughable Adventures of Messrs. Brown, Jones and Robinson by Richard Doyle published by Garrett, Dick & Fitzgerald, circa 1856.

the early 1870s. Doyle's format from *Foreign Tour* was emulated again and again. Examples include: the 1857 *Mr. Hardy Lee, His Yacht*, by Charles Stedman; the 1860s-1870s G. W. Carleton-published *Our Artist In...* series, set in various Latin American countries; the Augustus Hoppin 1870s sketch novels *On the Nile, Crossing the Atlantic*, and *Ups and Downs on Land and Water*; and *Life* founder John Ames Mitchell's 1881 (pre-Life) *The Summer School of Philosophy at Mt. Desert*. D. Appleton, the official, authorized American publisher of *Foreign Tour*, even commissioned an American artist - Toby - to create a sequel comic album involving Doyle's characters visiting the U.S. and Canada, published in 1872 as *The American Tour of Messrs Brown, Jones and Robinson*. In terms of influencing the development of mid-19th Century American comics, Doyle's *Foreign Tour* ranks with the works of Töpffer, Cruikshank, and Busch.

Doyle was also the author of an equally popular earlier cartoon series for Punch, entitled, *In Manners and Customs of Ye Englyshe, Mr. Pips Hys Diary*, which was reprinted in 1849. In this work, Doyle told his story using a deliberately primitive almost stick-figure art style, combined with the Hogarthian structure of large single panel cartoons leaping forward in time with each picture.

Manners and Customs of Ye Harvard Studente, which ran in the first year of the *Harvard Lampoon* (1876-current), shows the clearest influence. The series by then student Francis Gilbert Attwood was collected in 1877 by Houghton Mifflin. Attwood followed it up with *Manners and Customs of Ye Bostonians*, again in the pages of the *Harvard Lampoon*, but it is unknown whether that series was ever reprinted in book form. Attwood later became one of the regular artists in *Life*.

The Extraordinary and Mirth-provoking Adventures by Sea and Land of Oscar Shanghai, inspired by Bachelor Butterfly, was issued May 1855 by Garrett and Company, Publishers, No. 18 Ann Street, New York. Oscar Shanghai has many misadventures including being swallowed by a whale, making a trip in a flying machine to Africa, where he is shot out of a huge bow by a "Black Prince" for refusing to marry a local princess of color. After more adventures, he makes it back home.

Oscar Shanghai's first publisher was confirmed in 2002 with the discovery of a very rare 36-page catalog from 1856 of books, pamphlets and prints handled by B.H. Day (successor to Wilson and Company) who was by this time publishing *Brother Jonathan* as a twice-a-year holiday pictorial only. The catalog has a few crossover advertisement pages from an associate publisher, Garrett and Company. This rediscovered treasure, which sold for $750 in 2002, contains within a sequential strip of one panel per page over 32 of those pages titled *"Peter Piper in Bengal,"* by John Tenniel, reprinted from four 1853 issues of *Punch*. In the narrative, Peter Piper tries his hand hunting all different kinds of wild game with many misadventures.

Amongst the many varied type of "Cheap Books" for sale in this rare catalog are the comic books *The Adventures of Obadiah Oldbuck, Bachelor Butterfly's Queer Love Adventures and Misfortunes*, and *The Fortunes of Ferdinand Flipper*, plus the aforementioned *Oscar Shanghai*. All were priced at "25¢ per copy, postage free, refunds paid out in stamps." There is also an advertisement for a comic book entitled *A Day's Sport - Or, Hunting Adventures of S. Winks Wattles, a Shopkeeper, Thomas Titt, a "legal gent," and Major Nicholas Noggin, a Jolly Good Fellow Generally* by Henry L. Stephens (1824-1882)

TOP: The Sad Tale of the Courtship of Chevalier Slyfox-Wikof, Garrett & Co, New York, c1855.
BOTTOM: The Wonderful and Amusing Doings of Oscar Shanghai, first published circa 1855 by Garrett; here is a later Dick & Fitzgerald 1870's edition.

of Philadelphia.

Stephens, later the political cartoonist for *Vanity Fair* (New York, 1859-1863) and a leading children's book illustrator, produced his first work, *Illustrations of the Poets: From Passages in the Life of Little Billy Vidkins*, a small wrappered album of 32 comic woodcuts, in 1849. It was first published by S. Robinson, of Philadelphia, and reprinted with variant titles several times in the 1850s including *Yankee Notions*. It is likely that Little *Billy Vidkins* was printed before *Jeremiah Saddlebags*, though more research is needed before making this claim.

THE NEW YORK PICAYUNE.
VOL. VI.—NO. 46. NEW YORK: FOR THE WEEK ENDING SATURDAY, NOVEMBER 10, 1855. THREE CENTS.
THE SAD STORY OF THE LOVE AND DEATH OF VILLIKINS AND HIS DINAH.

The New York Picayune v6 #46, Nov 10, 1855, later edited by Frank Bellew, regularly ran comic strips, this one right on the cover.

Garrett and Company was also responsible for the 1856 publication of *The Sad Tale of the Courtship of Chevalier Slyfox-Wikof, Showing His Heart-Rending Astounding and Most Wonderful Love Adventures with Fanny Elssler and Miss Gambol*. This book parodied the very public relationship between the then-famous wealthy American aristocrat Henry Wikoff, and the even more famous European actress/dancer Fanny Elssler. It is dated thusly because Wikoff's memoir is pictured in the comic book.

Apparently in late 1854 Garrett and Company formed a brief two-year partnership with Dick and Fitzgerald, officially becoming Garrett, Dick and Fitzgerald in November 1856, while continuing to operate out of the same 18 Ann Street address in New York. One month later they issued Richard Doyle's British published graphic novel *The Foreign Tour of Messrs. Brown, Jones, and Robinson,* reformatting it into the same oblong shape as Garrett's two prior comic books (which in turn were formatted in imitation of Töpffer's albums). This information came to light just this year. The interested scholar is encouraged to check out the new listings for Garrett's The Home Circle in the index.

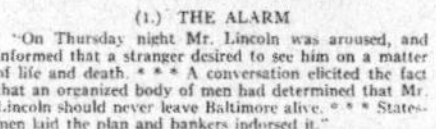

"The Flight of Abraham Lincoln," first appeared in Harper's Weekly, March 9, 1861.

In 1858, Garrett appears to have dropped out, leaving Dick and Fitzgerald alone with the former's book stock, his place of business, and most importantly, the printing plates for his comic books. For reasons unknown, Dick and Fitzgerald steered away from reprinting Garrett's comic books for more than a decade. But in the 1870s they resumed publication - not only of the three albums published by Garrett, but also of *Obadiah Oldbuck and Bachelor Butterfly* from Wilson and Company, and *Ferdinand Flipper* from *Brother Jonathan* - all of them also making use of the original printing plates. The inclusion of books from *Brother Jonathan*, Wilson and Company, and Garrett and Company all within the same promotional Peter Piper catalog from B.H. Day suggests that these early publishers of comic books had many over-lapping fields of interest,, and that Dick and Fitzgerald became the inheritor/acquirer of all of it. Dick and Fitzgerald also reprinted in the 1870s the earlier William T. Peter published *Ichabod Academicus* (how that title might have connected, if at all, with B.H. Day's business remains unclear). We can now say, though, that an evolving group of a handful of publishers was responsible, over a span of 46 years, beginning with the very first graphic novel published in America in 1842, for keeping in print in America a cluster of slightly over half a dozen graphic novels.

Tebbel's *History of Book Publishing* in the US (vol. 1, pages 351-2) states that Burgess and Stringer was dissolved in late 1840s and became two firms, Stringer and Townsend, and Burgess and Garrett. Burgess retired in 1850 and his nephew William Brisbane Dick stepped into the partnership, whereupon the new company was renamed Garrett, Dick and Fitzgerald. Garrett retired in 1851 and the firm became Dick and Fitzgerald. The firm persisted under that name until 1917.

Collections reprinting cartoons from Punch saw print in the U.S., such as *Merry Pictures by the Comic Hands*, imported for the 1859 Christmas Season, plus various John Leech, George Du Maurier, and Phil May books which appeared from the 1850s through 1910s. Finally, many American weekly newspapers and weekly and monthly magazines, humorous and non-humorous, reprinted cartoons from Punch. Such inclusions often became a prelude to switching to original material by American artists, if that publication find's cartoon section find American cartoonists of sufficient talent.

Harper's Monthly, the leading American monthly, was a prime example. Soon after it commenced publication in November 1850, it began to carry a few pages of single panel cartoons reprinted from *Punch* at the rear of each issue. This evolved into reprinting sequential comic pages from the British periodical *Town Talk*, and then, starting December 1853, original sequential comics by the great Frank Bellew.

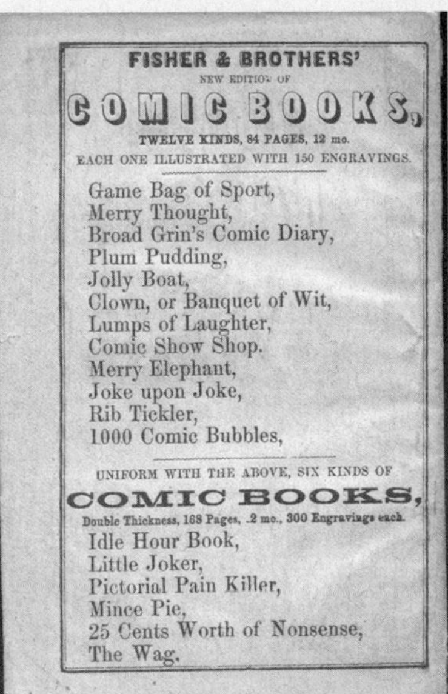
FISHER & BROTHERS'
NEW EDITION OF
COMIC BOOKS,
TWELVE KINDS, 84 PAGES, 12 mo.
EACH ONE ILLUSTRATED WITH 150 ENGRAVINGS.

Game Bag of Sport,
Merry Thought,
Broad Grin's Comic Diary,
Plum Pudding,
Jolly Boat,
Clown, or Banquet of Wit,
Lumps of Laughter,
Comic Show Shop.
Merry Elephant,
Joke upon Joke,
Rib Tickler,
1000 Comic Bubbles,

UNIFORM WITH THE ABOVE, SIX KINDS OF
COMIC BOOKS,
Double Thickness, 168 Pages, 12 mo., 300 Engravings each.
Idle Hour Book,
Little Joker,
Pictorial Pain Killer,
Mince Pie,
25 Cents Worth of Nonsense,
The Wag.

Earliest-known use of the description COMIC BOOKS dates from the early 1850s.

random samplings of highlights from issues from 1860:

- February: "A Day of Humiliation, Fasting, Supplica-tion, and Prayer (four panels, unsigned), "New Year Calls under the Influence of Hard Times" (twelve panels, unsigned), "Young Trouble-some; or, Master Jacky's Holidays" (nineteen panels covering three and half pages, unsigned);
- April: "Four Years After Marriage" (sixteen panels, unsigned), "Our Masked Ball" (twelve panel center-spread, Bellew), "Trials of a Witness" (eight panels, Bellew);
- May: "Precocities of Young Springles" (seven panels, unsigned), "The Fight for the Championship" (twenty-four panel centerspread, Bellew), "Steam Applied to Music" (three panels, unsigned), "The Course of True Love" (four panels, Bellew);
- June: "Further Particulars of the Fight" (nine panel cover, Bellew), "The Man Who Went to See the Fight" (twelve panels, unsigned);
- July: "Explaining American Politics to an Intelligent Foreigner" (twelve panels, unsigned), "The Meerschaum Mania" (two panels, Bellew), "The Art of Stump Speaking" (ten panels, unsigned), "Our Little Friend, Tom Noddy" (three panels, unsigned); "The Japanese in New York" (twelve panel centerspread, Bellew), "The Observant Child" (three panels, unsigned), "Mr. Dibbs Goes to Pike's Peak and Comes Back Again" (fourteen panel back cover, unsigned);
- September: "The Zouave Fever" (four panel cover, unsigned), "Mr. Lupell" (two panels, Bellew), "The Prince of Wales in America" (twenty-four panel centerspread, J. H. Howard), "D'ye Think It's True?" (three panels, Bellew);
- October: "The Duties of the Wide Awake" (four panels, Bellew), "Our Charley (two panels, unsigned), "The Three Young Friends" (eighteen panel back cover, unsigned);
- November: "The Hanlon's (sic) At Home" (nine panel back cover, unsigned);
- December: "The Target Excursion" (seventeen panel centerspread, signed with an unidentifiable monogram); "The Sporting Critic" two panels, Bellew).

Bellew (1828 1888) should be regarded as the "Father of American Sequential Comics." Born in India, educated in France and England, he emigrated to America in 1850. His earliest work shows an influence from Doyle, but he rapidly developed his own unique art style. Bellew's comics, both sequential and single panel, graced nearly every American comic periodical published from the 1850s into the 1870s.

A month after the publication of the anonymous first installment of *Jeremiah Old-Pot* in *Yankee Notions*, Bellew began contributing his six-part, 18-panel comic series, *"Mr. Blobb in Search of a Physician"* to *The Lantern*, a New York comic weekly published from January 10, 1852 to July 2, 1853. The series ran in six of the nine issues published from January 31 through March 27, 1852. This was followed in April and May by the 16-panel, three-issue comic sequence *"Mr. Bulbear's Dream"*, which concluded with the main character awakened from his dream by falling out of bed, exactly like *Little Nemo* would do five decades later.

These two series were just the beginning for Bellew, who contributed a voluminous amount of work to the *New York Picayune* (1850-1860) (which he also edited for a time in 1857-58), *The Comic Monthly* (1859-1881), *Momus*, an 1860 comic daily, *The Phunniest of Awl* (1864-1867) (which he also edited), *Punchinello* (1870), and *Wild Oats* (1870-1881), to name the most prominent.

The Comic Monthly deserves special mention. Started in March 1859 and published by J. C. Haney and Company, of 119 Nassau Street, New York, *The Comic Monthly* was a profusely illustrated 16-page folio, the same size as *Harper's Weekly*. It focused its graphic satire on politics, the theater, and the comedy of everyday life. A preponderance of the purely comic satire took the form of sequential art. Here are

The Comic Monthly also published many multi-panel cartoons grouped under a single heading, which were not strictly sequential in nature. Bellew was the monthly's chief artist, assisted by Thomas Nast, A. R Waud, and others. Some of the unsigned art was certainly by Bellew, some by journeymen artists, and some of it pirated from European journals.

The Comic Monthly was not the first folio-sized humor magazine. Those laurels go to *The New York Picayune*, which began as a newspaper, switched to a folio in 1856, adopted *Punch's* format for thirty-five issues in 1857-58, and returned to a folio for the remainder of its run.

FRANK LESLIE'S BUDGET OF FUN

NEW YORK, JUNE, 1860.

THE VERY LATEST FASHIONABLE AMUSEMENT, OR THE RULING FASHION.

TOP: Frank Leslie's Budget of Fun#19 June 1860 sports a comic strip on its front cover.
BOTTOM: Likewise Comic Monthly v2#4 June 1860.

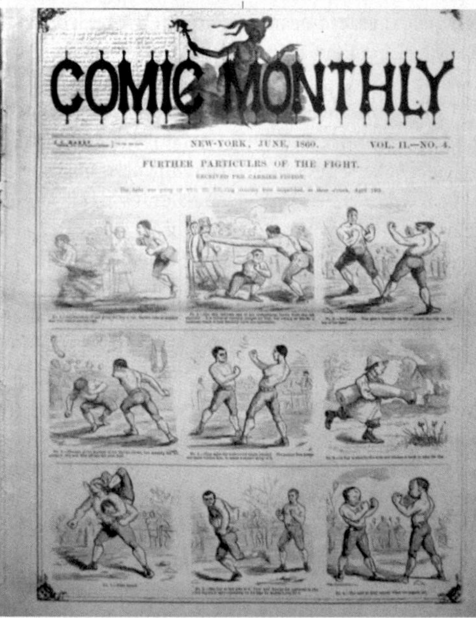
COMIC MONTHLY

NEW-YORK, JUNE, 1860. VOL. II.—NO. 4.

FURTHER PARTICULARS OF THE FIGHT.

Frank Leslie's *Budget of Fun*, the greatest of the folio monthlies, began in January 1859 and was published until June 1878. Its star cartoonist during the sixties was William Newman (c. 1817-1870), one of the founding artists of Punch. As we have noted, *The Comic Monthly* began two months later.

Frank Leslie was born Henry Cart in Ipswich, England in 1821. He became a very skilled engraver before coming over to America in 1948. He first worked as manager for P.T. Barnum's *New York Illustrated News* for several years. in 1850 he legally had his name changed to Frank Leslie. He died in 1880 and his wife continued the numerous publications he was publishing. Many of Frank Leslie's periodicals had a lot of sequental comic art.

Quarto-sized monthlies to compete with the successful *Yankee Notions* were also proliferating. *Nick-Nax* was the first (May 1856 to December 1875), followed by *Phunny Phellow* (October 1859- 1876) and *Merryman's Comic Monthly* (January 1863 to December 1875), to name the most prominent.

Enterprising publishers continued to attempt an American comic weekly in the style of *Punch*. The most notable efforts, *Vanity Fair* (1859-1863), *Mrs. Grundy* (1865), and *Punchinello* (1870), were distinguished but unsuccessful.

Nearly all of them, weeklies and monthlies, to varying degrees, featured sequential comic art. By the time of the American Civil War, sequential comic art was a part of the American graphic landscape.

While Bellew stood out for his sequential comics, Thomas Nast (1840-1902) brought a new style to American political cartoons, of which he is regarded the father. Even though he created several sequential strips early in his career (especially for Nick-Nax in 1859), Nast made his name in the pages of the national news periodical, *Harper's Weekly*, for which he worked from 1862 until 1886. Nast was influenced more by the dark wood engravings of Franco-German illustrator Gustave Dore than by the cartoonists of *Punch*. His somber cartoons were a novelty in American cartooning. Nast in the pages of *Harper's Weekly* (and Newman in the pages of the *Budget of Fun*) popularized the extravagant double-page folio-sized cartoon, which had no precedent in European or American cartooning, save for the separately published cartoon broadsides. This format would come to full maturity after 1876 in the pages of *Puck* (1876-1918) and then *Judge* (1881-1947).

As Nast grew in prominence and success, American cartoonists increasingly emulated him. U.S. humor publications evolved towards an amalgamation of Nast and Punch, rather than sheer imitation of the latter. After the War, with Nast's style of cartoons more entrenched in American readers' minds, efforts to launch *Punch*-like American periodicals floundered quickly. *Mrs. Grundy*, ironically most famous for its cover design by Nast, died after a mere twelve issues (running July 8 to September 23, 1865). *Punchinello* (April 2 to December 24, 1870) struggled nine months before its backers gave up. *Punchinello* had been financed by Tammany Hall politicians Tweed and Sweeney, as counter-propaganda against Nast's ongoing assault upon their corruption. They attempted to buy and threaten Nast into silence, to no avail.

American comics continued their pull away from Anglo-Franco imitation with the infusion of a third major European influence – the German humor magazine. The German-American community swelled significantly after the failed revolution of 1848. These émigrés brought with them a culture of humor, expressed most flamboyantly in their native humor magazines, the most famous being *Kladderadatsch, Fliegende Blätter*, and *Münchener Bilderbogen*. As high in quality, as were the graphic artists who contributed to them, one German comic artist in particular excelled beyond the rest, his stories breaking out and crossing over into English language translations, the demand for which resulted in numerous printings. This artist, of course, was Heinrich Christian Wilhelm Busch (1832-1908).

Sample panels from Frank Bellew Sr's The Flying Machine; And Professor High's Adventure therein in a Trip across the Ocean, Merryman's Monthly V3#5, May 1865.

Flag of Our Union, July 23, 1870, sample panels from Pt 1 of a 3 part comic strip depicting early baseball game.

Busch's work appeared in English in the 1860s in both British and American periodicals, often uncredited. For example, four of Busch's strips appeared in English in the pages of *Merryman's Monthly* in 1864, while in 1879 his graphic story "Fipps der Affe" was serialized across a 10-issue run of Puck as "Troddledums the Simian." The earliest known English language appearance of Busch in book form was *The Flying Dutchman, or The Wrath of Herr von Stoppelnoze*, in 1862, from New York publisher G. W. Carleton. Carleton not only pirated Busch's strip, but went so far as to credit the entire story to American poet John G. Saxe, with Busch's cartoons mere illustrations accompanying Saxe's prose!

Sample comics panels by Wilhelm Busch circa 1870.

The next known English language Busch book was **A** *Bushel of Merry Thoughts*, an 1868 London-published anthology collecting various Busch strips. Some of these same stories later appeared in the U.S.-published *The Mischief Book* (1880), newly translated and with a few more Busch tales added. One of these additions was "Hans Huckebein," a tale of a mischievous pet raven who in the end gets drunk and accidentally hangs himself. It became, at least in the States, Busch's second most popular sequential comic story. The unrepentant bird was promoted to title character in two later collections: the rare *Hookeybeak the Raven and Other Tales* in 1878 and *Jack Huckaback, the Scapegrace Raven*, circa 1888. There were also at least three trade card series in the 1870s and 1880s that reprinted the ending sequence, as *Fritz Spindle-Shanks, The Raven Black*.

The most popular Busch tale, though, was easily Max und Moritz, which in the U.S. saw print as *Max and Maurice - A Juvenile History in Seven Tricks*. Published in Boston in 1871, this English language version saw at minimum of 60 reprintings by the century's end, plus countless more printings thereafter. A separate British translation debuted in 1874, under the title *Max and Moritz*. It is well known that the later Rudolph Dirks comic strip series, Katzenjammer Kids, beginning in late 1897, was based on *Max und Moritz*.

According to documents found by comics historian Alfredo Castelli, *Katzenjammer Kids* may not have been pirated as has been assumed but was licensed by William Randolph Hearst instead. Hearst's *New York Journal* was published in different language editions for New York City's immigrant communities. In the German edition, the strip was published under its original name, *Max und Moritz*. Numerous other translations of Busch were published in America - too many to name in this article. Several can be found in the Victorian Age Price Index.

Britain's famous Alley Sloper created by Marie Duvall made an early appearance in Day's Doings #168, August, 1871

The most significant humor magazine of the 1870s, prior to the founding of the German-language *Puck* in 1876, was *Wild Oats* (1870-1881), which for part of its run also published a German-language edition, *Schnedereddeng*. In terms of the quality of its cartoons and comics, this New York City publication was in 1872 at an artistic level *Puck* would not achieve until 1880. Published by Winchell and Small (later Collin and Small) and distributed through the New York News Company, *Wild Oats* carried a cross-section of old and new generation comic artists, from the more established W. M. Avery, Frank Beard, Frank Bellew, E.S. Bisbee, Michael Angelo Woolf, and Thomas Worth, to up-and-comers such as Livingston Hopkins, Frederick Burr Opper, Palmer Cox, and James A. Wales.

Wild Oats began carrying sequential comic strips as early as #26, dated March 14, 1872, with the Livingston Hopkins strip pictured on the next page (we do not know anything yet about the first 25 issues). The very next issue has a Worth double-page spread titled "The Political Humpty Dumpty... Horace Greeley" told in eleven panels plus the sequential fictional "Graphic Account of the Assassination of Queen Victoria" and "Love As the Angels Love." "The Doings of the Japanese Embassy At Washington" related in twelve panels by W. M. Avery follows up in #28 April 11, 1872. An unknown hand drew "The Physiology of Moving" in six panels in #30. Hopkins returns with a beautiful intense 28-panel double-page spread in #31 May 23. Hopkins and Worth alternated for many issues with sequential comic strips on baseball, horse racing and other pertinent subjects of the day. In #45 December 5, 1872, E.S. Bisbee contributed his first sequential in seventeen panels and Worth showed up in "Humor and Pathos of a New England Thanksgiving" in eleven panels. Issue 47 expands the concept with a twelve-panel job by Bisbee, twenty-panel effort on one page by Hopkins and a three-panel effort by Worth. And on it goes through 1873 as well - comic strip after comic strip. Issue 58 June 5, 1873, includes a particularly humorous nineteen-panel double-pager drawn by someone still unknown titled "The Terrible Adventures of Messrs. Buster and Stumps, with the Indians" which begins with two white men heading out west in an effort to exterminate Indians - and their misadventures of not quite getting the job done. It reads across both pages in a unique evolution similar to Popeye #2052 (found in the Platinum listings). Issue 65 contains two nine-panel Thomas Worth strips "Only a Mad Dog Scare - Another Lesson For Nervous People" and "Only a Cholera Scare - Something For Nervous People to Read and Ponder Over." Issue 66 Sept 18, 1873, has the very funny Hopkins twelve-panel strip as well as two more ten-panel Worth strips on the

WILD OATS. 13

Wild Oats #26, 14 March 1872 Livingston Hopkins sequential comic strip. Hopkins later moved to Australia and became its premiere political cartoonist.

Wild Oats #163, Feb 9, 1876 last six panels by Palmer Cox who began doing sequential comic strips some years before he created The Brownies.

delights of Hunting and Fishing plus one by Hopkins titled "The Adventures of Mr Old Party with Jersey Mosquitoes" in twelve-panels. All told, four comic strips in this issue. They obviously liked what they were doing, judging from the exuberance of the work.

The next issue has Worth's nine-panel report on "The Adventures of Young Muttonhead among the Free Lovers" which was all about the "free sex" convention recently held in Chicago. Issue 68 has a nine-panel "An Adventure with a New Jersey Mosquito" which smacks of Winsor McCay in subject and even art style. Maybe McCay was inspired by this for his later animated cartoon as well as earlier Rarebit Fiend. We'll never know for sure. On through 1875, *Wild Oats* presented sequential comic strips issue after issue. With #148, October 27, 1875, Frederick Opper contributes his very first Wild Oats cover, a political cartoon on inflation then rampant in the US. He does covers through at least #161 before a short break and then comes back with many more. In #158, January 5, 1876, Palmer Cox - some five years before inventing The Brownies - begins a wonderful series of 24-panel double page spread comic strips, with a couple sample titles being "The Adventures of Mr. and Mrs. Sprowl And Their Christmas Turkey-A Crashing Chasing Tearful Tragedy But Happily Ending Well" and "Bachelor Broke and Widow Snuggi: A Pictorial Account of Their Sleigh Ride and What Became of It."

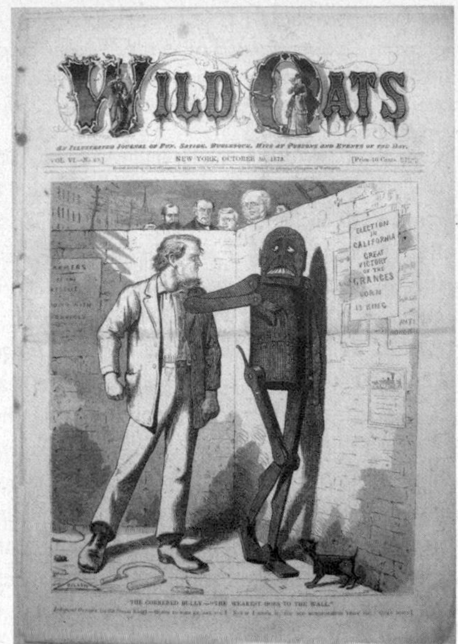

Wild Oats #69, Oct 30, 1873 Frank Bellew early robot cover. The zine presented many 100s of sequential comic strips over its life time. Today loose issues remain rare to very rare.

Even though he had been contributing many covers and interior single panel jobs to *Wild Oats* for years, Frank Bellew does not show up with his first comic strip until #190, August 16, 1876, with a nine-panel effort he titled, "Rodger's Patent Mosquito Armour." By this time America's "Father of the sequential comic strip" had inspired many other cartoonists to try their hand telling stories with words and pictures.

Wild Oats #190 August 16, 1876 by Frank Bellew Sr., Father of American Comic Strips. This one titled "Rodger's Patent Mosquito Armor."

Another highly desirable American graphic novel, sought especially by collectors of Western lore, is *Quiddities of an Alaskan Trip* by William H. Bell which debuted in 1873. Bell was Timothy O'Sullivan's assistant photographer on the 1871-74 expeditions of Lt. George Wheeler, surveying and mapping the western territories for the U.S. government. The story panels are laid out within ornate frames like those of stereograph cards, such as Bell was involved in creating on the expedition. It involves a parody of a trip from Washington, D.C., to survey the newly purchased territory of Alaska, which at the time was derisively referred to as "Seward's Folly." Bell published *Quiddities* in Portland, Oregon, in 1873, meaning that he drew it while he was on just such an expedition.

The seemingly disparate influences of Thomas Nast and German comics came together in the work of Austrian immigrant Joseph Keppler (1838-1894). Like many cartoonists in America, Keppler desired to rival Nast. Unlike most, he possessed the talent and drive to accomplish it. Keppler, trained as an artist but working as an actor, began contributing comic art to *Kikeriki* (1861-1923) in his native Vienna. He emigrated to St. Louis in 1868, where he took his first stab at starting a comic weekly, the German language *Die Vehme* (Aug 28, 1869 - Aug. 20, 1870). Seven months later, still in St. Louis, he tried again, launching another German language humor periodical, titled *Puck*. This German *Puck* began on March 18, 1871, joined by an English language version one year later, but both ended on Aug. 24, 1872.

Keppler moved to New York City and began working for Frank Leslie. His cartoons appeared in *Frank Leslie's Illustrated Newspaper*, Frank Leslie's *Budget of Fun*, and the Leslie-owned *Jolly Joker* and *Day's Doings*. (To capitalize on the 1876 Centennial Exposition in Philadelphia, Leslie published in that year a paperback collection of Centennial-related humor, *Centennial Fun*, most of which was Keppler's work.) Four years after

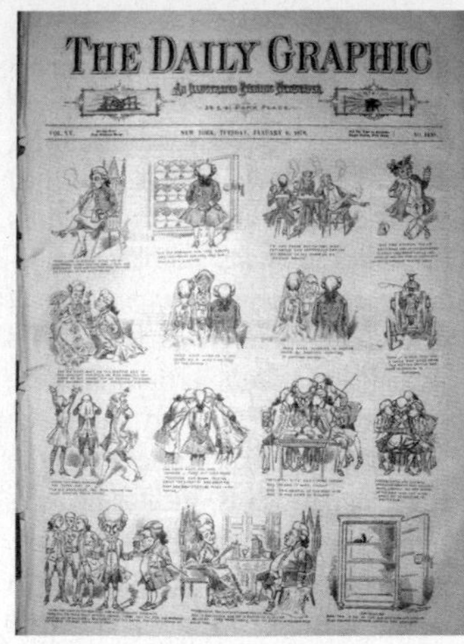
THE DAILY GRAPHIC

The Daily Graphic #1498, Jan 8, 1878, New York. Artist: Gray Parkxxx. This innovative paper carried all kinds of comic strips beginning more than 20 years before both Pulitzer and then Hearst got into the comic strip business. Largely overlooked by later historians, it is only recently being sought after once again.

the first *Puck* died, Keppler was ready to try again. He re-launched the German language edition of *Puck* in New York City on September 27, 1876.

This *Puck* was both familiar and exotic. Its format of an extravagant centerspread cartoon sandwiched between front and back cover cartoons had by this time become something of a comic periodical standard, certainly for the monthlies. But *Puck* was different from what had come before. The cartoons were lithographed, not engraved, which lent to them a softer, more pleasing quality, and they were in color, something virtually without precedent in American comic periodical literature.

Initially, the magazine's cartoons were tinted in just one color, but *Puck* appeared, ambitiously, every week, and the coloring set it apart from anything else on American stands. The parallel English language edition of *Puck* was launched six months after the German version, on March 14, 1877. This English edition of *Puck* was a money-loser for several years, kept afloat by the German edition's profits and the determination of the English edition's literary editor, H.C. Bunner, not to give up. By 1880, *Puck* was a huge success. It became the new model for American humor publications. In time, Keppler hired other artists, most notably Frederick Burr Opper, Eugene Zimmerman ("Zim") and F. M. Howarth, and added black and white sequential comics to the magazine's interior and then, with increasing frequency in the early 1890s to the magazine's back cover. *Funny Folks* by F. M. Howarth, 1899, collected many early sequential comics from *Puck;* one of the titles many consider bridges the Victorian and Platinum Ages of comics. *Puck* was the model that inspired William Randolph Hearst to add a color comics section to his Sunday Journal in 1895.

With the first issue dated October 29, 1881, *Puck's* chief rival, *Judge*, was born. Founded by *Puck* artist James A. Wales, it also featured the work of Thomas Worth and Livingston Hopkins. *Judge* made several forays into *Puck*'s talent pool over the years. Its best capture was Eugene Zimmerman ("Zim"), who became for Judge the star artist that Frederick Burr Opper was for Puck.

Judge struggled financially for several years, and likely would have ceased publication had it not been for Puck's powerful performance during the 1884 election. *Puck*'s success galvanized Republican powerbrokers into recognizing the importance of the political cartoon weekly. They financed newspaperman W. J. Arkell's purchase of *Judge* in 1886 to turn it into a reliable Republican house organ.

Numerous other Puck imitators emerged in the 1880s but quickly died. Note should be made of two that did not: the *Puck*-like *San Francisco Wasp*, which debuted August 5, 1876 (too early for it to be considered a *Puck* knockoff), and the black and white *Texas Siftings*, which debuted on May 9, 1881. Though neither was as successful as *Puck* or *Judge*, both cut their own paths, managing to survive as cartoon humor magazines into the 1890s.

Also worthy of mention is the New York City newspaper *The Daily Graphic* (March 4, 1873 to Sept 23, 1889), which claims the distinction of being the first regularly illustrated daily newspaper in the world, published every day except Sundays and holidays. The majority of its illustrations were portraits or depictions of news events, but nearly every issue contained some comic drawing, many of them gracing the front cover.

With so many pages to fill on a daily basis, *The Daily Graphic* became a rotating door for many young American cartoonists in the early stages of their careers (making one suspect that it was not the best paying gig in town). Within its pages, like needles to be found in the haystack of its more than 4800 issues, is early work by Livingston Hopkins (who mysteriously appears, vanishes, reappears, etc., for months to whole years at a time, right up to his 1884 departure to Australia), pre-*Life* work by Kemble, pre-*Harper*'s appearances by A.B. Frost and W.A. Rogers, pre-Puck and Judge Opper, C.J. Taylor, Hamilton, and Gillam. Old hats, too, appear at times, such as Michael Woolf and Frank Bellew, Sr.

Further, *The Daily Graphic* regularly plundered British periodicals for its back and sometimes center pages, not only

Leslie's Young America ran comic strips during its two year run 1881-82. Many are quite good. This example from #15 (10/15/81) reminds us of Zim.

The Daily Graphic - In 1873 this newspaper began running comic strips for 15 years, and there are other places comic strips keep cropping up; sample comic strip thought to be by Marie Duval of Alley Sloper fame.

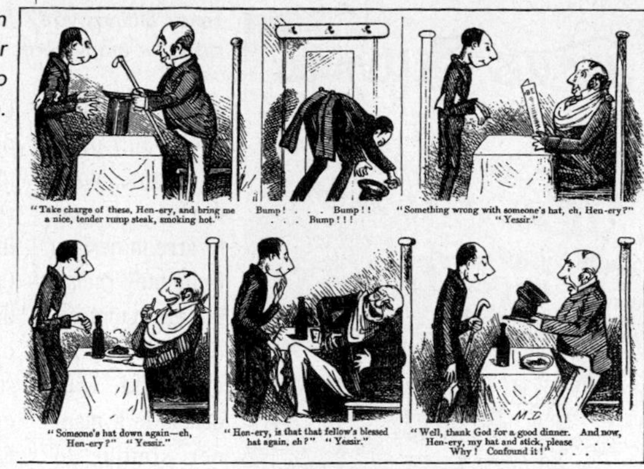

"Take charge of these, Hen-ery, and bring me a nice, tender rump steak, smoking hot."
Bump! . . . Bump!! . . . Bump!!!
"Something wrong with someone's hat, eh, Hen-ery?" "Yessir."
"Someone's hat down again—eh, Hen-ery?" "Yessir."
"Hen-ery, is that that fellow's blessed hat again, eh?" "Yessir."
"Well, thank God for a good dinner. And now, Hen-ery, my hat and stick, please . . . Why! Confound it!" . . .
M.D

A HAT OFF A PEG.

perpetrating the usual swipes of single-panel *Punch* cartoons, but also stealing sequential strips from Punch's two main rival publications, *Judy* and *Fun*. This included occasionally reprinting (albeit at random) episodes of continuing British strips "The British Workman" by James Sullivan, and "McNab of that Ilk" by James Brown, though, strangely enough, not Marie Duval's *Ally Sloper*, despite the fact that *The Daily Graphic* did reprint some of Duval's non-"Sloper" strips. ("Ally Sloper" was a continuing sequential strip character who debuted in 1867, lasting into the 1920s, and had very successful solo British book collections of his strip appearances published as early as 1873, more than two decades prior to *Yellow Kid In McFadden*'s Flats).

Livingston Hopkins, whose art style changed like a chameleon from one year to the next, exhibited a definite Duval influence in his work within a year following the publication of the first *Ally Sloper* collection. Given that Hopkins worked for *The Daily Graphic* during the same period in which this newspaper was stealing cartoons from *Sloper*'s home publication, *Judy*, this can hardly be considered coincidental. Hopkins contributed a daily comic strip to *The Daily Graphic* in 1874-75, complete with word balloons. By the time Hopkins was preparing to emigrate to Australia to become lead cartoonist for the Sydney Bulletin, his art style was an imitation of Kemble's, who was also working at *The Daily Graphic*.

Life debuted on January 4, 1883, founded by J.A. Mitchell, and modeled after the Harvard Lampoon. It quickly rose to become the third main pillar of late 1800s American humor periodicals. Smaller in size, black and white, and priced the same as *Puck* and *Judge*, it nevertheless succeeded by appealing to a more genteel audience. Its earliest artists included Kemble and Palmer Cox, but its foremost artist was Charles Dana Gibson, becoming world renowned as the hand behind the graceful, aristocratic "Gibson Girls."

Sequence by A.B. Frost, from the MidSummer Puck 1887.

Unlike *Judge*, which had to become a low-brow imitation of *Life* to survive in the next century, and *Puck*, which attempted but failed to become an American version of the highbrow European humor magazines, Life transitioned into the 20th century virtually unaltered, and thrived. By the mid-1880s, with *Puck, Judge*, and *Life* all solidly in place, American comics and cartoon humor had come very much into their own, no longer looking first at Europe to take their cues.

Almanacs began to appear in America starting in 1639. Humor was introduced as early as 1647 by Samuel Danforth. A very important one was *Leed Almanac* beginning in 1687. John Tulley produced the first humorous almanac in 1688. James Franklin, brother of Ben, began the *Rhode Island Almanac* in 1728 using the name "Poor Robin" and his younger brother began *Poor Richard's Almanac* in 1732. Farmer's Almanac began in 1792 and used some humor.

The first comic almanac totally devoted to humor was published by Charles Ellm in Boston in 1831 and featured the artwork of D.C. Johnston. Perhaps the most famous comic almanacs (certainly the most valuable) are the *Davy Crockett* series (1835-1856) which began in Nashville, Tennessee. The comic periodicals all ended up issuing comic almanacs beginning with *Yankee Notions* in 1856 and continuing into the 1890s with a one-shot comic almanac published by *Judge* for the year 1894.

Beginning in the 1850s, a new breed of almanacs appeared. Usually created by medicine and farm product companies, they were distributed for free to promote the company's product. Competition amongst companies, whose goal was to get customers to read the almanacs and the advertisements contained therein again and again, meant that attention-getting humorous cartoons soon found their way back into these giveaway pamphlets. Initially their cartoons were done cheap, either poorly drawn or pirated from elsewhere, such as those found in the Hostetter's and Wright's almanac series. More elaborate promotional almanacs eventually did evolve, though, and amongst the best of these was *Barker's Illustrated Almanac*, first produced for the year 1878, and annually into the 1930s. Each *Barker's Almanac*

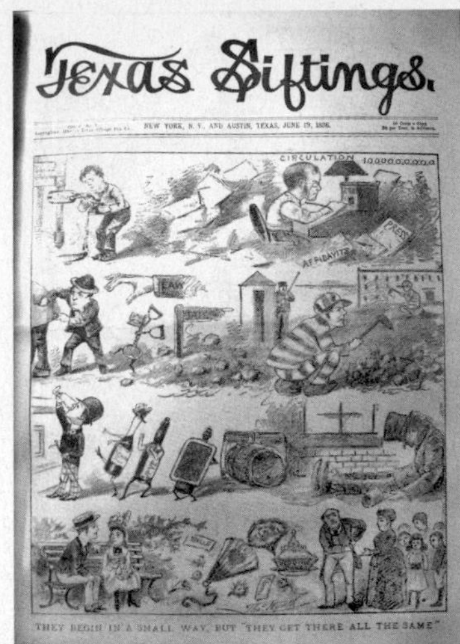

Texas Siftings v6#7 June 19, 1886 ran a whole slew of sequential comic strips for many years and is yet another sleeper for collectors to hunt.

contained ten to twelve full page cartoons, wonderful and bizarre in design, frequently racist, but also comically manic and crammed with details in a manner similar to Outcault's much later *Yellow Kid* pages. The cartoons in *Barker's Almanac* were so popular that in 1892, The Barker, Moore, and Mein Medicine Company published their first edition of *Barker's Komic Picture Souvenir*, reprinting nearly 150 pages of cartoons from their almanacs.

This first *Barker's Souvenir* features a wraparound color cover depicting people headed towards the Columbian World's Fair Exposition, which was to be held in Chicago the next year. It is the earliest confirmed "premium" comic book, sent to customers who mailed in a box label and outside wrapper from two different Barker's products. The *Souvenir* album was *Barker's* most in-demand premium. It was reprinted as a thick unnumbered booklet three more times in the 1890s, with the contents reorganized each time. Later, between 1901 and 1903, *Barker's* broke the album into three separate "Parts," each of which required still more box labels and wrappers to obtain. The 3-part series of reprint albums expanded to four parts circa 1906 or 1907. Both the 3 and 4-part album series had multiple printings.

Also very American in character were the country's promotional comics, which flourished throughout the latter half of the 19th century. They trace their beginnings to Comic Almanacs, which flourished in England and the United States since they first appeared in the 1830s. The first promotional comics which did not double as almanacs began to appear in the 1870s. They included the aforementioned reprints of Cruikshank and Busch strips, reprints of strips lifted from American sources (A.B. Frost's strip "The Bull Calf" was a particular favorite), and original material placing the product being promoted as the focus of the story. These original short cartoon dramas were in many ways similar in storyline to those found in modern television advertisements, except that the clothing is Victorian, and the claims, pre-F.D.A. and F.C.C., were unabashedly wild, over-the-top, and blunt. Chewing tobacco and snuff saved romances, calmed crying babies, and made the sick well. Stove polish that propelled you to wealth and power. Corsets that brought you a husband. The objective, of course, in an era before TV or radio, was to make each comic handout so entertaining that customers would want to keep and read the advertisement again and again.

The more wonderful graphics and outrageous claims tended to come from tobacco companies, who were using comic books and strips to sell their products more than a century before cries against "Joe Camel." The most elaborate of these were printed full color, and unfolded into a single long strip, just like Cruikshank's *The Tooth-Ache* from the 1840s, though usually limited to just the cover plus seven panels.

Examples are the Jackson Chewing Tobacco comics *How Adolphus Slim-Jim Used Jackson's Best and Ye Veracious Chronicle of Gruff and Pompey, and Durham Smoking Tobacco's Home Made Happy - A Romance for Married Men*. The artists of these comics are mostly unidentified, but their level of skill was equal to anything in *Puck* and *Judge*. *The Home Made Happy Comic*, in fact, was produced for Durham by The Graphic Company -- the publisher of *The Daily Graphic*, the aforementioned 1870s illustrated newspaper which included cartoons.

The earliest known anthology devoted to collecting the comic strips of a single American artist was A.B. Frost's *Stuff and Nonsense* in 1884. The next known American collection came in 1888, the very rare Frederick Burr Opper anthology, *Puck's Opper Book*. Both proved popular, so more Frost and Opper collections followed, to be joined within a few years by reprints collecting the cartoons and strips of Keppler, Kemble, Zim, Gibson, Mayer, Taylor, Frank Bellew's son "Chip," Howarth, Woolf, etc.

Puck, Judge, and *Texas Siftings* all began monthly Library series - 8-1/2" x 11" magazines, mostly black and white, which organized previously published material around one theme or one artist. For example, the first *Puck's Library* (July 1887) was titled "The National Game," and gathered

Young Men of America #527, Oct 13, 1887, by Frank Bellew towards the end of his illustrious career. By this time, he had the sequential comic art form down in most aspects, having published hundreds of them.

beneath one cover *Puck* material poking fun at the game of baseball. The third (March 1888) and ninth (November 1889) issues of *Judge's Serial (later named Judge's Library)* were devoted entirely to the work of Zim.

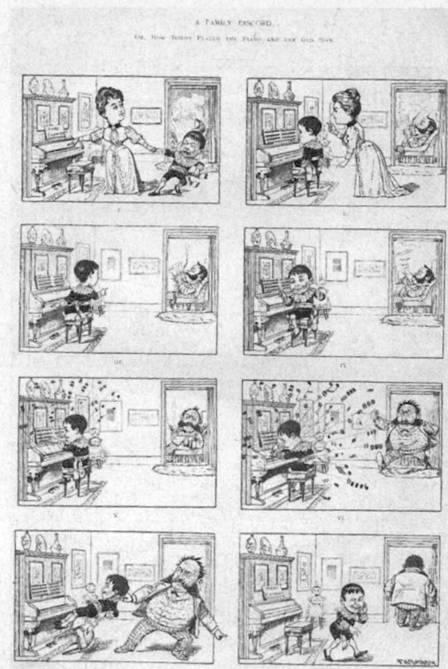

"A Family Discord" - One of many F.M. Howarth Puck back covers, this one later reprinted in Pickings From Puck #18 Dec 1895.

Life tended more towards hardcover collections, such as its annual ten-issue series *The Good Things of Life* (1884-1893), which included cartoons and strips by Palmer Cox, T.S. Sullivant, Hy Mayer, and others. *The Good Things of Life* was published initially by the firm of White, Stokes, and Allen, but which by the fourth book, had become simply Frederick A. Stokes. Stokes published a number of other cartoon books in the 1880s and 1890s, the majority of them reprint collections. The experience he gained at this time with these reprint albums placed Stokes in the perfect position to pick up the wealth of material about to be created for the comics supplements of William R. Hearst's newspapers, making Stokes the first major publisher of the coming Platinum Age.

In 1892, Charles Scribner's Sons published A. B. Frost's *Bull Calf and Other Tales*. It contains sequential comic strip art on quite a few pages as well as single panel cartoons. By 1898, Charles Scribner's Sons also issued Kemble's *The Billy Goat and Other Comicalities* as a 112-page hardcover, which also has sequential comic strips.

In the early 1890s, the slum children cartoons of artist Michael Woolf (many of which were reprinted in the 1896 collection *99 Woolfs from Truth* and in the posthumous 1899 collection *Sketches of Lowly Life in a Great City*) were popular. *Truth* magazine, which followed Puck's format of color front cover, back cover and centerspread cartoons, but in style was more akin to the aristocratic Life, was initially unable to secure Woolf's services, creating an opportunity for the young cartoonist Richard F. Outcault, who desired to break into one of the weekly comic periodicals.

It was in his Woolf-inspired slum children cartoons for *Truth* that Outcault's prototype of the *Yellow Kid* first emerged. The bald, sack-clothed youngster made four appearances in *Truth*, starting with #372 on June 2, 1894, prior to his newspaper debut.

During the rise of Yellow Kid's popularity, he appeared in American comic magazines in parodies drawn by others, with politicians, even Hearst and Pulitzer, dressed up as the *Yellow Kid*. Such cartoons are known to have appeared in *Judge, Life, The Bee*, and *Vim* plus various newspapers across the country. More about the *Yellow Kid's* importance can be found in the Platinum Age section of this book.

While comics definitely have their roots in Europe, and the earliest American comic books either reprinted or emulated those of Europe, the direction of influence was by no means one way. By at least the 1870s, American cartoons were being published and seen in the Old World, as evidenced by the arrest in Spain of the on-the-lamb corrupt Tammany Hall politician Boss Tweed by Spanish police who recognized Tweed from a Nast cartoon.

European piracy of American cartoons was just as lucrative as the American piracy of Europeans. In the 1880s and '90s, the comics of Zim, Chip Bellew, and Charles Dana Gibson all saw reprint in Europe. In April 1899, *Pictorial Comedy*, a monthly magazine destined for a ten-year run, commenced publication in London. It was made up entirely of cartoons reprinted with permission from *Puck* and *Life*. F.M. Howarth's domestic comedies from *Puck* were favorites in France. American Hy Mayer was commissioned to create original comics work for *Black and White* (Britain), *Le Rire* (France), and *Fliegende Blätter*. Michael Woolf's slum children cartoons saw print in the British periodical *Pick-Me-Up*, during the same years that top British artist Phil May's first published work debuted in that publication. May later became famous for his Woolf-inspired street children cartoons as well as his influence on the development of comics in Australia.

As the 19th Century ended, American comics were coming to the fore worldwide, soon to explode into a position of dominance with the Platinum Age revolution brought about by the emergence of the color comic supplement in America's newspapers and the arrival of Richard F. Outcault's *Yellow Kid.*

END NOTE: Victorian Era comics were issued in many relatively obscure

Judge 1896 Eugene "ZIM" Zimmerman "A Sagacious Animal" is but one of hundreds by mostly forgotten comics legend Zim who went on to run an early cartoonist training school.

Time, One Minute by Hy Mayer, Truth, 1896
"Our artist-draws-a picture-before the kinetscope"
The last panel in this cinematic wonder says
"Thoz. A. Edizon," inventor of movies.
At the turn of the 19th Century, comic strips and movies intersected on many levels.

formats compared to what most of us are used to today. The Victorian Era section can only grow as there are many more heretofore undiscovered comics from the 1800s which have fallen off the radar of history. Some may wonder why some of the earlier items listed contain as of yet no prices. The reason is simple. These books are part of a relatively "new" market which is still establishing itself.

High-grade copies are almost unheard of in almost all instances. Some books may truly have only a handful left in existence. We are sure there are some known to have been published which no (as of yet) known copies have survived the ravages of time and neglect.

Each year expect another quantum leap in our ever-expanding knowledge of the fascinating earliest origins of the comic strip as it relates to North America. Your input in helping this section of the Guide grow and mature is most welcome!

Judge
POLITICAL "KIDS" OUT IN THE COLD.

Judge #791, Dec 12, 1896, depicting Tammany Hall politicians as RFO's Yellow Kid & Cox's Brownies. Art by Hamilton.

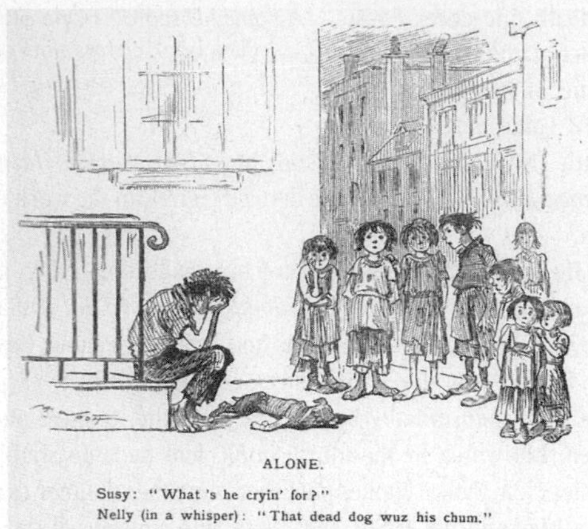

ALONE.
Susy: "What 's he cryin' for?"
Nelly (in a whisper): "That dead dog wuz his chum."

Michael Angelo Woolf cartoon from 99 Truths From Woolf. His many scenes from slum life in New York City was a major influence on Outcault's formulation of the Yellow Kid. Titled "Alone," The caption reads Susy: "What's he cryin' for?" Nelly (in a whisper): "That dog was his chum."

Robert Lee Beerbohm first sold comics through the legendary RBCC beginning in 1966, set up at his first comicon in 1967, helped found the northern California Comics & Comix chain of stores in August 1972, co-hosted Berkeleycon 1973, the first UG creator-owned comix con and operated comic book stores from 1972-1994. He now owns Robert Beerbohm Comic Art that specializes in buying and selling scarce comics and related material from the 1840s-1980s. He has been compiling a detailed history book of the business of the American comic book for some time now and hopes to complete it soon.

Contact Robert directly at www.BLBComics.com

Richard Olson is an Research Professor Emeritus at the University of New Orleans. He published the Richard Outcault Collector for years. Reach Richard directly at: rolsonredoak@bellsouth.net

Richard Samuel West is the author of Satire on Stone: The Political Cartoons of Joseph Keppler (University of Illinois, 1988) and The San Francisco Wasp: An Illustrate History (Periodyssey Press, 2004) and editor of several cartoon collections. He is the owner of Periodyssey, a business that specializes in buying and selling significant and unusual American magazines. Richard can be reached at:

www.oldmagazines.com

All three are life-long collectors and students of all forms of the comics who welcome corrections and additions to this concise compilation of our earliest American comics heritage dating back almost two centuries. Happy Hunting!

The American Comic Almanac #5
1835 © Charles Ellms, NYC

The Strange and Wonderful Adventures
of Bachelor Butterfly by Rodolphe Töpffer
1870s © Dick & Fitzgerald, NYC

Barker's "Komic" Picture Souvenir, 3rd Edition
1894 © Barker, Moore & Klein Medicine Co.

COLLECTOR'S NOTE: Most of the books listed in this section were published well over a century before organized comics fandom began archiving and helping to preserve these fragile popular culture artifacts. With some of these comics now over 160 years old, they almost never surface in Fine+ or better shape. Be happy when you simply find a copy.

This year has seen price growth in quite a few comic books in this era. Since this section began growing almost a decade now, comic books from Wilson, Brother Jonathan, Huestis & Cozans, Garrett, Dick & Fitzgerald, Frank Leslie, Street & Smith and others continue to be recognized by the more savvy in this fine hobby as legitimate comic book collectors' items. We had been more concerned with simply establishing what is known to exist. For the most part, that work is now a *fait accompli* in this section compiled, revised, and expanded by Robert Beerbohm with special thanks this year to Terrance Keegan plus acknowledgment to Bill Blackbeard, Chris Brown, Alfredo Castelli, Darrell Coons, Leonardo De Sá, Scott Deschaine, Joe Evans, Ron Friggle, Tom Gordon III, Michel Kempeneers, Andy Konkykru, Don Kurtz, Richard Olson, Robert Quesinberry, Joseph Rainone, Steve Rowe, Randy Scott, John Snyder, Art Spiegelman, Steve Thompson, Richard Samuel West, Doug Wheeler and Richard Wright. Special kudos to long-time collector and scholar Gabriel Laderman.

The prices given for Fair, Good and Fine categories are for strictly graded editions. If you need help grading your item, we refer you to the grading section in this book or contact the authors of this essay. Items marked Scarce, Rare or Very Rare we are still trying to figure out how many copies might still be in existence. We welcome additions and corrections from any interested collectors and scholars at robert@BLBcomics.com

For ease ascertaining the contents of each item of this listing and the Platinum index list, we offer the following list of categories found immediately following most of the titles:

E - EUROPEAN ORIGINAL COMICS MATERIAL; Printed in Europe or reprinted in USA
G - GRAPHIC NOVEL (LONGER FORMAT COMIC TELLING A SINGLE STORY)
H - "HOW TO DRAW CARTOONS" BOOKS
I - ILLUSTRATED BOOKS NOTABLE FOR THE ARTIST, BUT NOT A COMIC.
M - MAGAZINE / PERIODICAL COMICS MATERIAL REPRINTS
N - NEWSPAPER COMICS MATERIAL REPRINTS
O - ORIGINAL COMIC MATERIAL NOT REPRINTED FROM ANOTHER SOURCE
P - PROMOTIONAL COMIC, EITHER GIVEN AWAY FOR FREE, OR A PREMIUM GIVEN IN CONJUNCTION WITH THE PURCHASE OF A PRODUCT.
S - SINGLE PANEL / NON-SEQUENTIAL CARTOONS

Measurements are in inches. The first dimension given is Height and the second is Width. Some original British editions are included in the section, so as to better explain and differentiate their American counterparts.

ACROBATIC ANIMALS
R.H. Russell: 1899 (9x11-7/8", 72 pgs, B&W, hard-c)

nn (Scarce) 150.00 300.00 600.00
NOTE: *Animal strips by Gustave Verbeck, presented 1 panel per page.*

ALMY'S SANTA CLAUS (P,E)
Edward C. Almy & Co., Providence, R.I.: nd (1880's) (5-3/4x4-5/8", 20 pgs, B&W, paper-c

nn - (Rare) 12.50 40.00 80.00
NOTE: *Department store Christmas giveaway containing an abbreviated 28-panel reprinting of George Cruikshank's **The Tooth-ache**. Santa Claus cover.*

AMERICAN COMIC ALMANAC, THE (OLD AMERICAN COMIC ALMANAC 1839-1846)
Charles Ellms: 1831-1846 (5x8, 52 pgs, B&W)

1 first American comic almanac ever prrinted 500.00 1000.00 2000.00
2-16 100.00 200.00 400.00
NOTE:#1 from 1831 is the First American Comic Almanac

AMERICAN PUNCH
American Punch Publishing Co: Jan 1879-March 1881, J.A. Cummings Engraving Co (last 3 issues) (Quarto Monthly)

Most issues 25.00 50.00 150.00

THE AMERICAN WIT
Richardson & Collins, NY: 1867-68 (18-1/2x13. 8 pgs, B&W)
2/3 Frank Bellew single panels 50.00 100.00 200.00

AMERICAN WIT AND HUMOR
Harper & Bros, NY: 1859 (

nn - numerous McLenan sequential comic strips 100.00 200.00 400.00

ATTWOOD'S PICTURES - AN ARTIST'S HISTORY OF THE LAST TEN YEARS OF THE NINETEENTH CENTURY (M,S)
Life Publishing Company, New York: 1900 (11-1/4x9-1/8", 156 pgs, B&W, gilted blue hard-c)

nn - By Attwood 40.00 80.00 160.00
NOTE: *Reprints monthly calendar cartoons which appeared in **LIFE**, for 1887 through 1899.*

BACHELOR BUTTERFLY, THE VERITABLE HISTORY OF MR. (E,G)
D. Bogue, London: 1845 (5-1/2x10-1/4", 74 pgs, B&W, gilted hardcover)

nn - By Rodolphe Töpffer (Scarce) 500.00 1250.00 2500.00
nn - Hand colored edition (Very Rare) (no known sales)
NOTE: *This is the British Edition, translated from the re-engraved by Cham serialization found in **L'Illustration** - a periodical from Paris publisher Dubochet. Predates the first French collected edition. Third Töpffer comic book published in English. The first story page is numbered Page 3. Page 17 shows Bachelor Butterfly being swallowed by a whale.*

BACHELOR BUTTERFLY, THE STRANGE ADVENTURES OF (E,G)
Wilson & Co., New York: 1846 (5-3/8x10-1/8", 68 pgs, B&W, soft-c)

nn - By Rodolphe Töpffer (Very Rare) 600.00 1500.00 3000.00
nn - At least one hand colored copy exists (Very Rare) (no known sales)
NOTE: *2nd Töpffer comic book printed in the U.S., 3rd earliest known sequential comic book in the USA. Reprinted from the British D. Bogue 1845 edition, itself from the earlier French language **Histoire de Mr. Cryptogame**. Released the same year as the French Dubochet edition. Two variations known, the earlier printing with Page number 17 placed on the inside (left) bottom corner in error, with slightly later printings corrected to place page number 17 on the outside (right) bottom corner of that page. Another first printing indicator is pages 17 and 20 are printed on the wrong side of the page. For both printings: the first story page is numbered 2. Page 17 shows Bachelor Butterfly already in the whale. In most panels with 3 lines of text, the third line is indented further than the second, which is in turn indented further than the first.*

BACHELOR BUTTERFLY, THE STRANGE ADVENTURES
Brother Jonathan Press, NY: 1854 (5-1/2x10-5/8", 68 pgs, paper-c, B&W) (Very Rare)

nn - By Rodolphe Töpffer 250.00 500.00 1000.00

BACHELOR BUTTERFLY,THE STRANGE & WONDERFUL ADVENTURES OF
Dick & Fitzgerald, New York: 1870s-1888 (various printings 30 Cent cover price, 68 pgs, B&W, paper cover) (all versions Rare) (E,G)

nn - Black print on blue cover (5-1/2x10-1/2"); string bound 112.00 225.00 450.00
nn - Black print on green cover (5-1/2x10-1/2"); string bound 100.00 200.00 400.00
NOTE: *Reprints the earlier Wilson & Co. edition. Page 2 is the first story page. Page 17 shows Bachelor Butterfly already in the whale. In most panels with 3 lines of text, the second and third lines are equally indented in from the first. Unknown which cover (blue or green) is earlier*

BACHELOR'S OWN BOOK. BEING THE PROGRESS OF MR. LAMBKIN, (GENT.) IN THE PURSUIT OF PLEASURE AND AMUSEMENT (E,O,G)
(See also PROGRESS OF MR. LAMBKIN)
D. Bogue, London: August 1, 1844 (5x8-1/4", 28 pgs printed one side only, cardboard cover & interior) (all versions Rare)

nn - First printing hand colored 200.00 400.00 800.00
nn - First printing black & white 200.00 400.00 800.00
NOTE: *First printing has misspellings in the title. "PURSUIT" is spelled "PERSUIT", and "AMUSEMENT" is spelled "AMUSEMEMT".*
nn - Second printing hand colored 200.00 400.00 800.00
nn - Second printing black & white 200.00 400.00 800.00
NOTE: Second printing. The misspelling of "PURSUIT" has been corrected, but "AMUSEMEMT" error is still present.
nn - Third printing hand colored No misspellings 200.00 400.00 800.00
nn - Third printing black & white 200.00 400.00 800.00
NOTE: *By George Cruikshank. This is the British Edition. Issued both in black & white, and professionally hand-colored editions. Hand-colored editions have survived in higher quantities than uncolored. Originally made with thin paper sheets covering the plates.*

BACHELOR'S OWN BOOK; OR, THE PROGRESS OF MR. LAMBKIN, (GENT.), IN THE PURSUIT OF PLEASURE AND AMUSEMENT, AND ALSO IN SEARCH OF HEALTH AND HAPPINESS, THE (E,O,G)
David Bryce & Son: Glasgow: 1884 (one shilling; 7-5/8 x5-7/8", 62 pgs printed one side only, illustrated hardcover, page edges guilt

nn - Reprints the 1844 edition with altered title 17.50 35.00 70.00
nn - soft cover edition exists 15.00 30.00 60.00

BACHELOR'S OWN BOOK. BEIN-G TWENTY-FOUR PASSAGES IN THE LIFE OF MR. LAMBKIN, GENT. (E,G)
Burgess, Stringer & Co., New York on cover; Carey & Hart, Philadelphia on title page: 1845 (31-1/4 cents, 7-1/2x4-5/8", 52 pgs, B&W, paper cover)

nn - By George Cruikshank (Very Rare) (no known sales)
NOTE: *This is the second known sequential comic book story published in America. Reprints the earlier British edition. Pages printed on one side only. New cover art by an unknown artist.*

BAD BOY'S FIRST READER (O,S)
G.W. Carleton & Co.: 1881 (5-3/4 x 4-1/8", 44 pgs, B&W, paper cover)

nn - By Frank Bellew (Senior) 50.00 100.00 200.00
NOTE: *Parody of a children's ABC primer, one cartoon illustration plus text per page. Includes one panel of Boss Tweed. Frank Bellew is considered the "Father of the American Sequential Comics."*

BALL OF YARN OR, QUEER, QUIANT & QUIZZICAL STORIES, UNRAVELED WITH NEARLY 200 COMIC ENGRAVINGS OF FREAKS, FOLLIES & FOIBLES OF QUEER FOLKS BY THAT PRINCE OF COMICS, ELTON, THE (M)
Philip. J. Cozans, 116 Nassau St, NY: early 1850s (7-1/4x3-1/2", 76 pgs, yellow-wraps)

nn - sequential comic strips plus singles (no known sales)
NOTE: Mose Keyser-r, Jones, Smith & Robinson Goes To A Ball-r; The Adventures of Mr Goliah Starvemouse-r are all sequential comic strips printed in a number of sources

BARKER'S ILLUSTRATED ALMANAC (O,P,S)
Barker, Moore & Mein Medicine Co: 1878-1932+ (36 pgs, B&W, color paper-cr)

1878-1879 (Rare) 40.00 80.00 160.00
NOTE: *Not known yet what the cover art is.*
1880 Farmer Plowing Field-c 30.00 60.00 120.00
1881-1883 (Scarce,7-3/4x6-1/8") *4-mast ships & lighthouse-c* 30.00 60.00 120.00
1884-1889 (8x6-1/4") *Horse & Rider jumping picket fence-c* 20.00 40.00 80.00
1890-1897 (8-1/8x6-1/4") 20.00 40.00 80.00
1898-1899 (7-3/8x5-7/8") 20.00 40.00 80.00
1900+: see the Platinum Age Comics section (7x5-7/8")
NOTE: *Barker's Almanacs were actually issued in November of the year preceding the year which appears on the almanac. For example, the 1878 dated almanac was issued November 1877. They were given away to retailers of Barker's farm animal medicinal products, to in turn be given away to customers. Each Barker's Almanac contains 10 full page cartoons. These frequently included racist stereotypes of blacks. Each cartoon*

The Comical Adventures of Beau Ogleby
1843 © Tlit & Bogue, London

The Story of The Man of Humanity
and The Bull Calf by A. B. Frost
1890 © C.H. Fargo & Co.

Buzz A Buzz Or The Bees By Wilhelm Busch
1873 © Henry Holt And Company, New York

FR1.0 GD2.0 FN6.0

contained advertisements for Barker's products. It is unknown whether the cartoons appeared only in the almanacs, or if they also ran as newspaper ads or flyers. Originally issued with a metal hook attached in the upper left hand corner, which could be used to hang the almanac.

BARKER'S "KOMIC" PICTURE SOUVENIR (P,S)
Barker, Moore & Mein Medicine Co: nd (1892-94) (color cardboard cover, B&W interior) (all unnumbered editions Very Rare)

nn - (1892) (1st edition, 6-7/8x10-1/2, 150 pgs) wraparound cover showing people headed towards Chicago for the 1893 World's Fair 150.00 300.00 650.00
nn - (1893) (2nd edition, ??? pgs) same cover as 1st edition 150.00 300.00 650.00
nn - (1894) (3rd edition, 180 pgs, 6-3/4x10-3/8") 150.00 300.00 650.00
NOTE: *New cover art showing crowd of people laughing with a copy of Barker's Almanac.The crowd picture is flanked on both sides by picture of a tall thin person.*
nn - (1894) (4th edition, 124 pgs, 6-3/8x9-3/8") same-c as 3rd edition 150.00 300.00 650.00
NOTE: *Essentially same-c as 3rd edition, except flanking picture on left edge is now gone. The 2nd through 4th editions state their printing on the first interior page, in the paragraph beneath the picture of the Barker's Building. These have been confirmed as premium comic books, predating the Buster Brown premiums. They reprint advertising cartoons from Barker's Illustrated Almanac. For the 50 page booklets by this same name, numbered as "Part"s, see the PLATINUM AGE SECTION. All "Editions in Parts", without exception, were published after 1900.*

BEAU OGLEBY, THE COMICAL ADVENTURES OF (E,G)
Tilt & Bogue: nd (c1843) (5-7/8x9-1/8", 72 pgs, printed one side only, green gilted hard-c, B&W)

nn - By Rodolphe Töpffer (Rare) 300.00 600.00 1500.00
nn - Hand coloured edition (Very Rare) (no known sales)
NOTE: *British Edition; no known American Edition. 2nd Töpffer comic book published in English. Translated from Paris publisher Aubert's unauthorized redrawn 1839 bootleg edition of Töpffer's* ***Histoire de Mr. Jabot****. The back most interior page is an advertisement for* ***Obadiah Oldbuck****, showing its comic book cover*

BEE, THE
Bee Publishing Co: May 16 1898-Aug 2 1898 (Chromolithographic Weekly)

most issues 50.00 100.00 200.00
8 June Yellow Kid Hearst cover issue 150.00 300.00 650.00

BEFORE AND AFTER. A LOCOFOCO CHRISTMAS PRESENT. (O, C)
D.C. Johnston, Boston: 1837 (4-3/4x3", 1 page, hand colored cardboard)

nn - (Very Rare) by David Claypoole Johnston (sold at auction for $400 in GD)
NOTE: *Pull-tab cartoon envelope, parodying the 1836 New York City mayoral election, picturing the candidate of the Locofoco Party smiling "Before the N.York election", then, when the tab is pulled, picturing him with an angry sneer "After the N.York election".*

BILLY GOAT AND OTHER COMICALITIES, THE (M)
Charles Scribner's Sons: 1898 (6-3/4x8-1/2", 116 pgs., B&W, Hardcover)

nn - By E. W. Kemble 125.00 250.00 600.00

BLACKBERRIES, THE (N.S) (see Coontown's 400)
R. H. Russell: 1897 (9"x12", 76 pgs, hard-c, every other page in color, every other page in one color sepia tone)

nn - By E. W. Kemble 162.00 325.00 1300.00
NOTE: *Tastefully done comics about Black Americana during the USA's Jim Crow days.*

BOOK OF BUBBLES, YE (S)
Endicott & Co., New York: March 1864 (6-1/4 x 9-7/8",160 pgs, guilt-illus. hard-c, B&W

nn - By unknown 150.00 300.00 600.00
NOTE: *Subtitle: A contribution to the New York Fair in aid of the Sanitary Commission; 68 single-sided pages of B&W cartoons, each with an accompanying limerick. A few are sequential.*

BOOK OF DRAWINGS BY FRED RICHARDSON (N,S)
Lakeside Press, Chicago: 1899 (13-5/8x10-1/2", 116 pgs, B&W, hard-c)

nn - 80.00 160.00 320.00
NOTE: *Reprinted from the* ***Chicago Daily News****. Mostly single panel. Includes one* ***Yellow Kid*** *parody, some Spanish-American War cartoons.*

BOTTLE, THE (E,O) (see also THE DRUNKARD'S CHILDREN, and TEA GARDEN TO TEA POT, and TEMPERANCE TALES; OR, SIX NIGHTS WITH THE WASHINGTONIANS)
D. Bogue, London, with others in later editions: nd (1846) (16-1/2x11-1/2", 16 pgs, printed one side only, paper cover)

D. Bogue, London (nd; 1846): first edition:
nn - Black & white (Scarce) 200.00 400.00 900.00
nn - Hand colored (Rare) (no known sales)
D. Bogue, London, and Wiley and Putnam, New York (nd; 1847) : second edition, misspells American publisher "Putnam" as "Putman":
nn - Black & white (Scarce) 150.00 300.00 600.00
nn - Hand colored (Rare) (no known sales)
D. Bogue, London, and Wiley and Putnam, New York (nd; 1847) : third edition has "Putnam" spelled correctly.
nn - Black & white (Scarce) 150.00 300.00 600.00
nn - Hand colored (Rare) (no known sales)
D. Bogue, London, Wiley and Putnam, New York, and J. Sands, Sydney, New South Wales: (nd; 1847) : fourth edition with no misspellings
nn - Black & white (Scarce) 150.00 300.00 600.00
nn - Hand colored (Rare) (no known sales)
NOTE: *By George Cruikshank. Temperance/anti-alcohol story. All editions are in precisely identical format. The only difference is to be found on the cover, where it lists who published it. Cover is text only - no cover art.*

BOTTLE, THE HISTORY OF THE
J.C. Becket, 22 Grea St James St, Montreal, Canada: 1851 (9-1/8x6", B&W)

nn - From Engravings by Cruikshank 150.00 300.00 650.00
NOTE: *As published in The Canada Temperance Advocate.*

BOTTLE, THE (E)
W. Tweedie, London: nd (1862) (11-1/2x17-1/3", 16 pgs, printed one side only, paper cover)

nn - Black & white; By George Cruikshank (Scarce) 100.00 200.00 400.00
nn - Hand colored (Scarce) (no known sales)

BOTTLE, THE (E)
Geo. Gebbie, Philadelphia: nd (c.1871) (11-3/8x17-1/8", 42 pgs, tinted interior, hard-c)

nn - By George Cruikshank 100.00 200.00 400.00
NOTE: *New cover art (cover not by Cruikshank).*

BOTTLE, THE (E)
National Temperance, London: nd (1881) (11-1/2x16-1/2", 16 pgs, printed one side only, paper-c, color)

nn - By George Cruikshank 100.00 200.00 400.00
NOTE: *See Platinum Age section for 1900s printings.*

BOTTLE, THE (E)
Marques, Pittsburgh, PA: 1884/85 (6x8", 8 plates, full color, illustrated envelope)
nn - art not by Cruickshank; New Art 50.00 100.00 200.00
NOTE: Says Presented by J.M. Gusky, Dealer in Boots and Shoes

BROAD GRINS OF THE LAUGHING PHILOSOPHER
Dick & Fitzgerald,NY: 1870s
nn - (4) panel sequential strip 25.00 50.00 150.00

BROTHER JONATHAN
Wilson & Co/Benj H Day, 48 Beekman, NYC: 1839-???

July 4 1846 - ads for Obadiah & Butterfly 50.00 100.00 200.00
July 4 1856 catalog list - front cover comic strip 100.00 200.00 400.00
Xmas/New Years 1856 75.00 150.00 300.00
average large size issues 25.00 50.00 100.00
NOTE: has full page advert for Fredinand Flipper comic book**116**

BULL CALF, THE (P,M)
Various: nd (c1890's) (3-7/8x4-1/8", 16 pgs, B&W, paper-c)

nn - By A.B. Frost Creme Oatmeal Toilet Soap 25.00 50.00 150.00
nn - By A.B. Frost Thompson & Taylor Spice Co, Chicago 25.00 50.00 150.00
NOTE: *Reprints the popular strip story by Frost, with the art modified to place a sign for Creme Oatmeal Soap within each panel. The back cover advertises the specific merchant who gave this booklet away - multiple variations exist.*

BULL CALF AND OTHER TALES, THE (M)
Charles Scribner's Sons: 1892 (120 pgs., 6-3/4x8-7/8", B&W, illus. hard cover)

nn - By Arthur Burdett Frost 50.00 150.00 500.00
NOTE: *Blue, grey, tan hard covers known to exist.*

BULL CALF, THE STORY OF THE MAN OF HUMANITY AND THE (P,M)
C.H. Fargo & Co.: 1890 (5-1/4x6-1/4", 24 pgs, B&W, color paper-c)

nn - By A.B. Frost 42.50 85.00 185.00
NOTE: *Fargo shoe company giveaway; pages alternate between shoe advertisements and the strip story.*

BUSHEL OF MERRY THOUGHTS, A (see Mischief Book, The) (E)
Sampson Low Son & Marsten: 1868 (68 pgs, handcolored hardcover, B&W)

nn - (6-1/4 x 9-7/8", 138 pgs) red binding, publisher's name on title page only 200.00 400.00 800.00
nn - (6-1/2 x 10", 134 pgs) green binding, publisher's name on cover & title page 200.00 400.00 800.00
NOTE: *Cover plus story title pages designed by Leighton Brothers, based on Busch art. Translated by Harry Rogers (who is credited instead of Busch). This is a British publication, notable as the earliest known English language anthology collection of Wilhelm Busch comic strips. Page 13 of second story missing from all editions (panel dropped). Unknown which of the two editions was published first. A modern reprint, by Dover in 1971.*

BUTTON BURSTER, THE (M) (says on cover "ten cents hard cash")
M.J. Ivers & Co., 86 Nassau St., New York: 1873 (11x8-1/8", soft paper, B&W)

By various cartoonists (Very Rare) 125.00 250.00 500.00
NOTE: *Reprints from various 1873 issues of Wild Oats; has (5) different sequential comic strips: (3) by Livingston Hopkins, (1) by Thomas Worth, other one creator presently unknown; Bellew, Sr. single panel cartoons.*

BUZZ A BUZZ OR THE BEES (E)
Griffith & Farran, London: September 1872 (8-1/2x5-1/2", 168 pgs, printed one side only, orange, black & white hardcover, B&W interior)

nn - By Wilhelm Busch (Scarce) 112.00 225.00 450.00
NOTE: *Reprint published by Phillipson & Golder, Chester; text written by English to accompany Busch art.*

BUZZ A BUZZ OR THE BEES (E)
Henry Holt & Company, New York: 1873 (9x6", 96 pgs, gilted hardcover, hand colored)

nn - By Wilhelm Busch (Scarce) 100.00 200.00 450.00
NOTE: *Completely different translation than the Griffith & Farran version. Also, contains 28 additional illustrations by Park Benjamin. The lower page count is because the Henry Holt edition prints on both sides of each page, and the Griffith & Farran edition is printed one side only.*

CALENDAR FOR THE MONTH; YE PICTORIAL LYSTE OF YE MATTERS OF

The Carpet Bag #14
1851 © Snow & Wilder

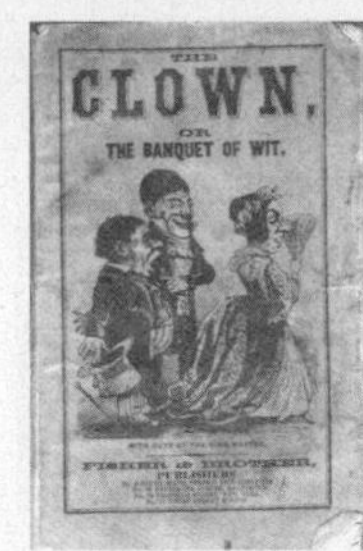

The Clown, or The Banquet of Wit
1851 © Fisher & Brother

Comic Monthly v2 #7
Sept. 1860 © J.C. Haney, NY

FR1.0 GD2.0 FN6.0

INTEREST FOR SUMMER READING (P,M)
S.E. Bridgman & Company, Northampton, Mass: nd (c. late 1880's-1890's) (5-5/8x7-1/4", 64 pgs, paper-c, B&W)

nn - (Very Rare) T.S. Sullivant-c/a 100.00 200.00 400.00

NOTE: *Book seller's catalog, with every other page reprinting cartoons and strips (from Life??). Art by: Chips Bellew, Gibson, Howarth, Kemble, Sullivant, Townsend, Woolf.*

CARICATURE AND OTHER COMIC ART
Harper & Brothers, NY: 1877 (9-5/16x7-1/8", 360 pgs, B&W, green hard-c)

nn - By James Parton (over 200 illustrations) 30.00 60.00 200.00

NOTE: *This is the earliest known serious history of comics & related genre from around the world produced by an American. Parton was a cousin of Thomas Nast's wife Sarah. A large portion of this book was first serialized in* ***Harper's Monthly*** *in 1875.*

CARPET BAG, THE
Snow & Wilder, later Wilder & Pickard, Boston: March 21 1851-March 26 1853

Each average issue 25.00 50.00 100.00
Samuel "Mark Twain" Clemmons issues (first app in print) 500.00 1000.00 2000.00

NOTE: *Many issues contain cartoons by DC Johnston, Frank Bellew, others; literature includes Artemus Ward's Miss Partington who had a mischevious little Katzenjammer Kids-like brat. Carpet Bag was not considered derogatory pre-Civil War.*

CARROT-POMADE (O,G)
James G. Gregory, Publisher, New York: 1864 (9x6-7/8", 36 pgs, B&W)

nn - By Augustus Hoppin 70.00 140.00 280.00

NOTE: *The story of a quack remedy for baldness, sequentially told in the format parodying ABC primers. Has protective tissue pages (not part of page count).*

CARTOONS BY HOMER C. DAVENPORT (M,N,S)
De Witt Publishing House: 1898 (16-1/8x12", 102 pgs, hard-c, B&W)

nn 100.00 200.00 400.00

NOTE: *Reprinted from Harper's Weekly and the New York Journal. Includes cartoons about the Spanish-American War. Title page reads "Davenport's Cartoons".*

CARTOONS BY WILL E. CHAPIN (P,N,S)
The Times-Mirror Printing and Binding House, Los Angeles: 1899 (15-1/4x12", 98 pgs, hard-c, B&W)

nn - scarce 100.00 200.00 400.00

NOTE: *Premium item for subscribing to the Los-Angeles Times-Mirror newspaper, from which these cartoons were reprinted. Includes cartoons about the Spanish-American War.*

CARTOONS OF OUR WAR WITH SPAIN (N,S)
Frederick A. Stokes Company: 1898 (11-1/2x10", 72 pgs, hardcover, B&W)

nn - By Charles Nelan (r-New York Herald) 40.00 100.00 200.00
nn - 2nd printing noted on copy right page 30.00 60.00 120.00

CARTOONS OF THE WAR OF 1898 (E,M,N,S)
Belford, Middlebrook & Co., Chicago: 1898 (7x10-3/8",190 pgs, B&W, hard-c)

nn 50.00 100.00 200.00

NOTE: *Reprints single panel editorial cartoons on the Spanish-American War, from American, Spanish, Latino, and European newspapers and magazines, at rate of 2 to 6 cartoons per page. Art by Bart, Berryman, Bowman, Bradley, Chapin, Gillam, Nelan, Tenniel, others.*

CENTENNIAL FUN (O,S) (Rare)
Frank Leslie, Philadelphia: (July) 1876 (25¢, 11x8", 32 pgs, paper cover, B&W)

nn - By Joseph Keppler-c/a;Thomas Worth-a 150.00 300.00 600.00

NOTE: *Issued for the 1876 Centennial Exposition in Philadelphia. Exists with both black & white, and orange, black & white covers. One copy of the latter had an embossed newstand label from Partland, Maine, implying that the orange cover version, at least, was distributed and sold outside of Philadelphia.*

CHAMPAIGNE
Frank Leslie: June-Dec 1871

1-7 scarce 150.00 225.00 350.00

CHIC
Chic Publishing Co: 1880-81 (Chromolithographic Weekly)

1-38 Livingston Hopkins, Charles Kendrick, CW Weldon 75.00 150.00 300.00

CHILDREN'S CHRISTMAS BOOK, THE
The New York Sunday World: 1897 (10-1/4x8-3/4", 16 pgs, full color)

Dec 12, 1897 - By George Luks, G.H. Grant, Will Crawford, others) (Rare) 50.00 100.00 280.00

CHIP'S DOGS (M)
R.H. Russell and Son Publishers: 1895 hardcover, B&W)

nn - By Frank P. W. "Chip" Bellew 25.00 50.00 100.00
Early printing 80 pgs, 8-7/8x11-7/8"; dark green border of hardcover surrounds all four sides of pasted on cover image; pages arranged in error -- see NOTE below. (more scarce)
nn - By Frank P. W. "Chip" Bellew 12.50 25.00 50.00
Later printing 72 pgs, 8-7/8x11-3/4";green border only on the binding side (one side) of the cover image.

NOTE: *Both are strip reprints from* ***LIFE***. *The difference in page count is due to more blank pages in the first printing -- all printings have the same comics contents, but with the pages in the first printing arranged differently. This is noticeable particularly in the 2-page strip "Getting a Pointer", which appears on the 2nd & 3rd to last pages of the later printings, but in the early printing the first half of this strip is near the middle of the book, while the last half appears on the 2nd to last story page.*

CHIP'S OLD WOOD CUTS (M,S)
R.H. Russell & Son: 1895 (8-7/8x11-3/4", 72 pgs, hardcover, B&W)

nn - By Frank P. W. ("Chip") Bellew 25.00 50.00 100.00

nn - 1897 reprint 15.00 30.00 60.00

CHIP'S UN-NATURAL HISTORY (O,S)
Frederick A. Stokes & Brother: 1888 (7x5-1/4", 64 pgs, hardcover, B&W)

nn - By Frank P. W. ("Chip") Bellew 12.50 25.00 50.00

NOTE: *Title page lists publisher as "Successors to White, Stokes & Allen."*

CLOWN, OR THE BANQUET OF WIT, THE (E,M,O)
Fisher & Brother, Philadelphia, Baltimore, New York, Boston: nd (c.1851) (7-3/8x4-1/2", 88 pgs, paper cover, B&W)

nn - (Very Rare; 3 known copies) 400.00 800.00 1500.00

NOTE: *Earliest known multi-artist anthology of sequential comics; contains multiple sequential comics, plus numerous single panel cartoons. A mixture of reprinted and original material, involving both European and American artists. "Jones, Smith, and Robinson Goes to a Ball" by Richard Doyle (1st app. of Doyle's "Foreign Tour" in America, reprinted from PUNCH, August 24, 1850); "Moses Keyser The Bowery Bully's Trip to the Californian Gold Mines", by John H. Manning; "The Adventures of Mr. Gulp" (by the Read brothers?); more comics by artists unknown; cartoons by George Cruikshank, Grandville, Elton.*

COLD CUTS AND PICKLED EELS' FEET; DONE BROWN BY JOHN BROWN
P.J. Cozans, New York: nd (c1855-60) (B&W)

nn (Very Rare) 100.00 200.00 300.00

NOTE: *Mostly a children's book. But, pages 87 to 110, and 111 to 122, contain narrative sequential stories.*

COLLEGE SCENES (O,G)
N. Hayward, Boston: 1850 (5x6-3/4", 72 pgs, printed one side only, B&W lithography)

nn - (Rare) by Nathan Hayward 200.00 400.00 600.00

NOTE: *This is the 2nd such production for an American University; the first issued at Yale circa 1845, decent funny art of story about life of a Harvard student from his entrance thru graduation entirely in caricature. Has art on back cover as well.*

COLLEGE CUTS Chosen From The Columbia Spectator 1880-81-82 (S)
White & Stokes, NY: 1882 (8x9-5/8", 92 pgs, B&W)

By F. Benedict Herzog, H. McVickar, W. Bard McVickar, others 20.00 40.00 80.00
nn - 2nd edition reprint (1888) (8-1/4x10-3/8) 10.00 20.00 40.00

COMICAL COONS (M)
R.H. Russell: 1898 (8-7/8 x 11-7/8", 68 pgs, hardcover, B&W)

nn - By E. W. Kemble 300.00 600.00 1200.00

NOTE: *Black Americana collection of 2-panel stories.*

COMICAL ALMANAC
Anton Bicker, Cinncinati, OH: 1885 (9x6, 260 pgs, B&W, illustrated-c)

nn - two (12) page sequential Busch comic strips 50.00 100.00 200.00

COMIC ALMANAC, THE
John Berger. Baltimore: 1854-? (7-1/2x6-1/4, 36 pgs, B&W)

nn - 60.00 120.00 240.00

COMIC ANNUAL, AMERICAN (O,I)
Richardson, Lord, & Holbrook, Boston: 1831 (6-7/8x4-3/8", 268 pgs, B&W, hard-c)

nn - (Scarce) 150.00 300.00 600.00

NOTE: *Mostly text; front & back cover illustrations, 13 full page, and scattered smaller illustrations by David Claypoole Johnston; edited by Henry J. Finn.*

COMIC HISTORY OF THE UNITED STATES, (I)
Carleton & Co., NY: 1876 (6-7/8x5-1/8", 336 pgs, hardcover, B&W)

nn - By Livingston Hopkins. 12.50 25.00 50.00
2nd printing: Cassell, Petter, Galpin & Co.: 1880 (6-7/8x5-1/8", 336 pgs, hardcover, B&W)
nn - By Livingston Hopkins. 12.50 25.00 50.00

NOTE: *Text with many B&W illustrations; some are multi-panel comics. Not to beconfused with* ***Bill Nye's Comic History Of The U.S.*** *which contains Frederick Opper illustrations.*

COMIC MONTHLY, THE
J.C. Haney, N.Y.: March 1859-1880 (16 x 11-1/2", 30 pgs average, B&W)

Certain average issues with sequential comics 50.00 100.00 200.00
11 (Jan 1860) Bellew-c 25.00 50.00 100.00
v2#2 (Apr 1860) Bellew-c 25.00 50.00 100.00
v2#3 (May 1860) Bellew-c 25.00 50.00 100.00
v2#4 (June 1860) Comic Strip Cover 50.00 100.00 200.00
v2#5 (July 1860) Bellew-c; (12) panel Explaining American Politics To An Intelligent Foreigner; (10) panel The Art of Stump Speaking; (15) panel Mr. Dibbs Goes to Pike's Peak and Comes Back Again 100.00 200.00 400.00
v2#7 (Sept 1860) Comic Strip Cover; (24) panel double page spread The Prince of Wales In America 50.00 100.00 200.00
v2#8 (18) panel The Three Young Friends Sillouette Strip 25.00 50.00 100.00
v2#9 (Nov 1860) (9) panel sequential 25.00 50.00 100.00
v2#10 11 not indexed 25.00 50.00 100.00
v2#12 (Jan 1861) (12) panel double page spread 25.00 50.00 100.00

COMIC TOKEN FOR 1836, A COMPANION TO THE COMIC ALMANAC, THE
Charles Ellms, Boston: 1836 (8x5', 48 pgs, B&W)

nn - 50.00 100.00 200.00

COMIC WEEKLY, THE
???, NYC: 1881-???

issues with comic strips (Chips, etc) 60.00 125.00 250.00

The Comus Offering
1830-31 © B. Franklin Edmands

The Daily Graphic #158 Frank Bellew-c
Sept 4, 1873 © The Graphic Company, NY

Elton's Californian Comic All-My-Nack #17
1850 © Elton's, NY

FR1.0 GD2.0 FN6.0

COMIC WORLD
???: 1876-1879 (Quarto Monthly)
issues with comic strips 37.50 75.00 150.00

COMICS FROM SCRIBNER'S MAGAZINE (M)
Scribner's: nd (1891) (10 cents, 9-1/2x6-5/8", 24 pgs, paper cover, side stapled, B&W)
nn - (Rare) F.M.Howarth C&A 100.00 200.00 400.00
NOTE: *Advertised in SCRIBNER'S MAGAZINE in the June 1891 issue, page 793, as available by mail order for 10 cents. Collects together comics material which ran in the back pages of Scribner's Magazine. Art by Attwood, "Chip" Bellew, Dões, Frost, Gibson, Zim.*

COMUS OFFERING CONTAINING HUMOROUS SCRAPS OF DIVERTING COMICALITIES, THE (O, S)
B. Franklin Edmands, 25 Court St, Boston: c1830-31 (8-7/8x10-3/4", 16 pgs, thin brown paper-c, blank on backs,
nn - (William F Straton, Engraver, 15 Water St, Boston) (no known sales)
NOTE: All hand-colored single panel cartoons format definitely inspired by D.C. Johnston's Scraps with every panel character using well-defined word balloons. Might become a seminal step in the evolution of the American comic book. More research is needed.

CONTRASTS AND CONCEITS FOR CONTEMPLATION BY LUKE LIMNER (O)
Ackerman & Co, 96 Strand, London: c1848 (9-3/4x6-1/4, 48 pgs, B&W)
nn - By John Leighton 50.00 100.00 200.00

COONTOWN'S 400 (M) (see **Blackberries**) (M)
The Life (Magazine) Co.: 1899 (10-15/16x8-7/8, 68 pgs, cloth light-brown hard-c, B&W
nn - By E.W. Kemble (scarce) 250.00 500.00 1500.00
NOTE: *Tastefully drawn depictions of Black Americana over one hundred years ago during Jim Crow days.*

CROSSING THE ATLANTIC (O,G)
James R. Osgood & Co., Boston: 1872 (10-7/8x16", 68 pgs, hardcover, B&W);
Houghton, Osgood & Co., Boston: 1880
1st printing - by Augustus Hoppin 50.00 100.00 200.00
2nd printing (1880; 66 pgs; 8-1/8x11-1/8") 32.50 65.00 150.00

C.R. PITT'S COMIC ALMANAC
C.R. Pitt: 1880 (7-1/2x4-5/8", 28 pgs)
nn - contains (8) panel sequential 50.00 100.00 200.00

CRUIKSHANK'S OMNIBUS: A VEHICLE FOR FUN AND FROLIC (E,S)
E. Ferrett & Co., Philadelphia: 1845 (25 cents, 7-1/2" x 4-5/8", 96 pgs, B&W, paper-c)
nn - By George Cruikshank c/a (Very Rare) 150.00 300.00 600.00
NOTE: *Mostly prose, with 10 plates of cartoons printed on one-side (about half the plates with multiple cartoons), plus illustrated cover, all by George Cruikshank. First (perhaps only) American printing of Cruikshank's Omnibus, which was published first in Britain. It is only a partial reprinting.*

CYCLISTS' DICTIONARY (S)
Morgan & Wright, Chicago: 1894 (5 x3-3/4, 80 pgs, soft-c, B&W
nn - By Unknown 37.50 75.00 150.00

THE DAILY GRAPHIC
The Graphic Company, 39 Park Place, NY: 1873-Sept 23, 1889 (14x20-1/2, 8 pgs, B&W)
Average issues with comic strips 7.50 15.00 30.00
Average issues without comic strips 5.00 10.00 20.00
NOTE:

DAVY CROCKETT'S COMIC ALMANACK
???, Nashville, TN, then elsewhere: 1835-end (32 pages plus wraps)
1 500.00 1000.00 2000.00
2-13 15 end 250.00 500.00 1000.00
14 contains (17) panel Crocket comic strip bio 1848 1000.00 1500.00 3000.00

DAY'S DOINGS (was The Last Sensation) (Becomes New York Illustrated Times)
James Watts, NYC: #1 June 6 1868-early 1876 (11x16, 16 pgs, B&W)
average issue with comic strips 10.00 15.00 25.00
Paul Pry & Alley Sloper character issues 25.00 50.00 100.00
Aug 19 1871 - First Alley Sloper in America?? 50.00 100.00 200.00
NOTE: *James Watts was a shadow company for Frank Leslie; outright sold to Frank Leslie in 1873. There are a lot of issues with comic strips from 1868 up.*

DAY'S SPORT - OR, HUNTING ADVENTURES OF S. WINKS WATTLES, A SHOPKEEPER, THOMAS TITT, A "LEGAL GENT," AND MAJOR NICHOLAS NOGGIN, A JOLLY GOOD FELLOW GENERALLY, A (O)
Brother Jonathan, NY: c1850s (5-7/8x8-1/4, 44 pgs)
nn - By Henry L. Stephens, Philadelphia (Very Rare) (no known sales)

DEVIL'S COMICAL OLDMANICK WITH COMIC ENGRAVINGS OF THE PRINCIPAL EVENTS OF TEXAS, THE
Turner & Fisher, NY & Philadelphia: 1837 (7-7/8x5", 24 pgs)
nn - many single panel cartoons 100.00 200.00 400.00

DIE VEHME, ILLUSTRIRTES WOCHENBLATT FUR SCHERZ UND ERNEST (M,O)
Heinrich Binder, St. Louis: No.1 Aug 28, 1869 - No.?? Aug 20, 1870 (10 cents, 8 pgs, B&W, paper-c) (see also PUCK)
1-?? (Very Rare) by Joseph Keppler 100.00 200.00 400.00
NOTE: *Joseph Keppler's first attempt at a weekly American humor periodical. Entirely in German. The title translates into: "The Star Chamber: An Illustrated Weekly Paper in Fun and Ernest".*

DOMESTIC MANNERS OF THE AMERICANS
The Imprint Society, Barre, Mass: 1969 (9-3/4 x 7-1/4", 390 pgs, hard-c in slipcase, B&W)
nn - 10.00 20.00 40.00
NOTE: *Reprints the 1882 edition of this book by Mrs. Trollope with an added insert. The 28-page insert is what is of primary interest to us -- it reproduces SCRAPS No. 4 (1833) by D.C. Johnston.*

DRUNKARD'S CHILDREN, THE (see also THE BOTTLE) (E,O)
David Bogue, London; John Wiley and G.P. Putnam, New York; J. Sands, Sydney, New South Wales: July 1, 1848 (16x11", 16 pgs, printed on one side only, paper-c)
nn - Black & white edition (Scarce) 300.00 600.00 950.00
nn - Hand colored edition (Rare) (no known sales)
NOTE: *Sequel story to THE BOTTLE, by George Cruikshank. Temperance/anti-alcohol story. British-American-Australian co-publication. Cover is text only - no cover art.*

DRUNKARD'S PROGRESS, OR THE DIRECT ROAD TO POVERTY, WRETCHEDNESS & RUIN, THE
J. W. Barber, New Haven, Conn.: Sept 1826 (single sheet)
nn - By John Warner Barber (Very Rare) (no known sales)
NOTE: *Broadside designed and printed by barber contains four large wood engravings showing "The Morning Dram" which is "The Beginning of Sorrow"; "The Grog Shop" with its "Bad Company"; "The Confirmed Drunkard" in a state of "Beastly Intoxication"; and the "Concluding Scene" with the family being drive off to the alms house. It is an interesting set of cuts, faintly reminiscent of Hogarth. Many modern reprints exist.*

DUEL FOR LOVE, A (O,P)
E.C. DeWitt & Co., Chicago: nd (c1880's) (3-3/8" x 2-5/8", 12 pgs, B&W, paper-c)
nn - Art by F.M. Howarth (Rare) 25.00 50.00 100.00
NOTE: *Advertising giveaway for DeWitt's Little Early Risers, featuring an 8-panel strip story, spread out 1 panel per page.*

DURHAM WHIFFS (O, P)
Blackwells Durham Tobacco Co: Jan 8 1878 (9x6.5", 8 pgs, color-c, B&W)
v1 #1 w/Trade Card Insert 37.50 75.00 150.00
NOTE: Sold in 2008 CGC 9.4 $1250

DYNALENE LAFLETS (P)
The Dynalene Company: nd (3 x 3-1/2", 16 pgs, B&W, paper cover)
nn - Dynalene Dyes promo (9) panel comic strip 25.00 50.00 75.00

ELEPHANT, THE
William H Graham, Tribune Building, NYC: Jan 22 1848-Feb 19 1848 (11x8.5", B&W)
1-5 Rare - single panel cartoons 150.00 300.00 600.00

ELTON'S COMIC ALL-MY-NACK (E,O.S)
Elton, Publisher, 18 Division & 98 Nassau St, NY: 1833-1852 (7 1/2x4 1/2", 36pgs, D&W
1-5 99% single panel cartoons 100.00 200.00 400.00
6 (1839) 100.00 200.00 400.00
NOTE: Two different covers & different interiors exist for this title and number
7-15 - 99% single panel cartoons 100.00 200.00 400.00
16 - contains 6 panel "A Tales of A Tayl-or" 1848-49 200.00 400.00 600.00
17 - contains "Moses Keyser, The Bowery Bully's Trip To the California Gold Mines" 1850
By John H. Manning, early comics creator, told in 15 panels 200.00 400.00 600.00
18-19 presently unknown contents 100.00 200.00 400.00
NOTE: *Contains both original American, and pirated European, cartoons. All single panel material, except where noted. Almanacs are published near the end of the year prior to that for which they are printed -- like calendars today. Thus, the 1833 No. 1 issue was really published in the last months of 1832. #17 has Elton's Californian Comic-All-My-Nack on the cover.*

ELTON'S COMIC ALMANAC (Publsiher change)
GW Cottrell & Co, Publishers & C Cornhill, Boston, Mass: 1853 (7-7/8x4-5/8,36pgs,B&W
20 - (2) sequential comic strips (9) panel "Jones, Smith and Robinson Goes To A Ball; (21) panel "The Adventures of Mr. Gulp" Rare 300.00 600.00 1200.00
NOTE: *Both strips appear in* The Clown, Or The Banquet of Wit

ELTON'S FUNNY ALMANACK (title change to Almanac)
Elton Publisher and Engraver, New York: 1846 (8x6-1/2", 36 pgs)
1 1846 50.00 100.00 200.00

ELTON'S FUNNY ALMANAC (#1 titled Almanack)
Elton & Co, New York: 1847-1853 (8x6-1/4, 36 pgs, B&W)
2 (1847) #3 (1848) 50.00 100.00 200.00
nn 1853 (8-1/8x4-7/8"; (5) panel comic strip "The Adventures of Mr. Goliah Starvemouse"

ELTON'S RIPSNORTER COMIC ALMANAC
Elton, 90 Nassau St, NY: 1850 (8x5, 24 pgs, B&W, paper-c)
nn - scarce 50.00 100.00 200.00

ENGLISH SOCIETY (S)
Harper & Brothers, Publishers, New York: 1897 (9-5/8x12-1/4", 206 pgs, B&W)
nn - by George Du Maurier 25.00 50.00 75.00

ENGLISH SOCIETY AT HOME (S)
James R. Osgood and Company: 1881 (10-7/8x8-5/8, 182 pgss, protective sheets on some pages - not included in pages count, hard-c, B&W 25.00 50.00 75.00
nn - by George Du Maurier

ENTER: THE COMICS (E,G)
University of Nebraska Press: 1965 (6-7/8x9-1/4", 120 pgs, hard-c)

The Evolution Of A Democrat
1888 © Paquet & Co, NY

Flying Leaves
1880s © E.R. Herrick & Company, New York

Frank Leslie's Boys & Girls Sample Comic Strip Page
1870s © Frank Leslie

FR1.0 GD2.0 FN6.0

nn - By Ellen Weisse 25.00 50.00 100.00
NOTE: *Contains overview of Töpffer's life and career plus only published English translation of Töpffer's Monsieur Crepin (1837); appears to have been re-drawn by Weisse in the days before xerox machines.*

ESQUIRE BROWN AND HIS MULE, STORY OF
A.C. Meyer, Baltimore, Maryland: 1880s (5x3/7/8", 28 pgs, B&W)

Booklet (9 panel story plus cough remedies catalog) 25.00 50.00 100.00
Fold-Out of Booklet (9 panel version) 25.00 50.00 100.00

"EVENTS OF THE WEEK" REPRINTED FROM THE CHICAGO TRIBUNE
Henry O. Shepard Co, Chicago: 1894 (5-3/8x15-7/8", 110 pg, B&W, hard-c)

First Series, Second Series - By HR Heaton 37.50 75.00 150.00

EVERYBODY'S COMICK ALMANACK
Turner & Fisher, NY & Philadelphia: 1837 (7-7/8x5", 36 pgs, B&W)

nn 50.00 100.00 200.00

EVOLUTION OF A DEMOCRAT - A DARWINIAN TALE, THE (O,G)
Paquet & Co., New York: 1888 (25 cents, 7-7/8x5-1/2", 100 pgs, printed one side only, orange paper cover, B&W) (Very Rare)

nn - Written by Henry Liddoll, art by G. Roberty 300.00 600.00 1200.00
NOTE: *Political parody about the rise of an Irishman through Tammany Hall. Grover Cleveland appears as linked with Tammany. Ireland becomes the next state in the USA.*

FABLES FOR THE TIMES (S, I)
R.H. Russell & Son, New York: 1896 (9-1/8x12-1/8", 52 pgs, yellow hard-c)

nn - By H.W. Phillips and T.S. Sullivant Scarce 75.00 150.00 300.00

FERDINAND FLIPPER, ESQ., THE FORTUNES OF (O,G)
Brother Jonathan, Publisher, NY: nd (1851) (5-3/4 x 9-3/8", 84 pgs, B&W, printed both sides)

nn - By Various (Very Rare) 500.00 1000.00 2500.00
NOTE: *Extended title: "...Commencing With A Period of Four Months And Anterior To His Birth Going Thru The Various Stages of His Infancy, Childhood, Verdant Years, Manhood, Middle Life, and Green and Ripe Old Age, And Ending A Short Time Subsequent to His Sudden Decease With His Final Exit, Funeral And Burial." Extremely unique comic book, put together by gathering 145 independent single illustrations and cartoons, by various artists, and stringing them together into a sequential story. The majority of panels are by Grandville. Also included are at least 10 signed Charles Martin, reprinted from 1847 issues of Yankee Doodle, 5 panels from D.C. Johnston, plus other panels by F.O.C. Darley, T.H. Matheson, and others. The story also contains several panels of Gold Rush content . Printed by E.A. Alverds. The 1851 date is derived from an advertisement found in the Oct-Dec 1851 issue of the Brother Jonathan newspaper. It ispossible, however, that it actually came out even earlier.*

FERDINAND FLIPPER, ESQ., THE FORTUNES OF (G)
Dick & Fitzgerald, New York: nd (1870's to 1888) (30 Cents, 84 pgs, B&W, paper cover)

nn - (Very Rare reprint - several editions possible) 375.00 750.00 1500.00

FINN'S COMIC ALMANAC
Marsh, Capen, & Lyon; Boston: 1835-??? (4.5x7.5, 36 pgs, B&W)

nn 100.00 200.00 400.00

FINN'S COMIC SKETCHBOOK (S)
Peabody & Co., 223 Broadway, NY: 1831 (10-1/2x16", 12 pgs, B&W)

nn - By Henry J. Finn (Very Rare) (no known sales)
NOTE: *Designs on copper plates; etched by J. Harris, NY; should have tissue paper in front of each plate.*

50 GREAT CARTOONS (M,P,S)
Ram's Horn Press: 1899 (14x10-3/4, 112 pgs, hard-c)

nn - By Frank Beard 30.00 60.00 120.00
NOTE: *Premium in return for a subscription to **The Ram's Horn** magazine.*

FISHER'S COMIC ALMANAC
Ames Fisher and Brother, No 12 North Sixth St, Philadelphia , Charles Small in NYC, Also in Boston: 1841-1868 (4-1/2 x 7-1/4, 36 pgs, B&W)

1-7 (1841-1847) 100.00 200.00 400.00
12 reprints mermaid-c with word balloon (1868) 100.00 200.00 400.00

F**** A*** K*****, OUTLINES ILLUSTRATIVE OF THE JOURNAL OF** (O,S)
D.C. Johnston, Boston: 1835 (9-5/16 x 6", 12 pgs, printed one side only, blue paper cover, B&W interior) (see also **SCRAPS**)

nn - by David Claypoole Johnston (Scarce) 600.00 1000.00 1600.00
NOTE: *This is a series of 8 plates parodying passages from the Journal of Fanny (Frances) A. Kemble, a British woman who wrote a highly negative book about American Culture after returning from the U.S. Though remembered now for her campaign against slavery, she was prejudiced against most everything American culture, thus inspiring Johnston's satire. Contains 4 protective sheets (not part of page count.)*

FLYING DUTCHMAN; OR, THE WRATH OF HERR VONSTOPPELNOZE, THE (E)
Carleton Publishing, New York: 1862 (7-5/8x5-1/4", 84 pgs, printed on one side only, gilted hardcover, B&W)

nn - By Wilhelm Busch (Scarce) 35.00 70.00 160.00
nn - 1975 Scarce 100 copy-r 74 pgs Visual Studies Workshop 5.00 10.00 20.00
NOTE: *This is the earliest known English language book publication of a Wilhelm Busch work. The story is plagiarized by American poet John G. Saxe, who is credited with the text, while the uncredited Busch cartoons are described merely as accompanying illustrations.*

FLYING LEAVES (E)
E.R. Herrick & Company, New York: nd (c1889/1890's) (8-1/4" x 11-1/2", 76 pgs, B&W interior, orange, b&w hard-c)

nn- (Scarce) 85.00 175.00 260.00

FR1.0 GD2.0 FN6.0

NOTE: *Reprints strips and single panel cartoons from 1888 Fliegende Blatter issues, translated into English. Various artists, including Bechstein, Adolf Hengeler, Lothar Meggendorfer, Emil Reinicke.*

FOOLS PARADISE WITH THE MANY ADVENTURES THERE AS SEEN IN THE STRANGE SURPRISING PEEP SHOW OF PROFESSOR WOLLEY COBBLE, THE (E)
(see also THE COMICAL PEEP SHOW)
John Camden Hotten, London: Nov 1871 (1 crown, 9-7/8x7-3/8", 172 pgs, printed one side only, gilted green hardcover, hand colored interior)

nn - By Wilhelm Busch (Rare) 400.00 800.00 1750.00
NOTE: *Title on cover is: **WALK IN! WALK IN!! JUST ABOUT TO BEGIN!!! the FOOLS PARADISE**; below the above title page. Anthology of Wilhelm Busch comics, translated into English.*

FOOLS PARADISE WITH THE MANY WONDERFUL SIGHTS AS SEEN IN THE STRANGE SURPRISING PEEP SHOW OF PROFESSOR WOLLEY COBBLE, FURTHER ADVENTURES IN (E)
Chatto & Windus, London: 1873 (10x7-3/8", 128 pgs, printed one side only, brown hardcover, hand colored interior)

nn - By Wilhelm Busch (Rare) 300.00 600.00 1320.00
NOTE: *Sequel to the 1871 **FOOLS PARADISE**, containing a completely different set of Busch stories, translated into English.*

FOOLS PARADISE MIRTH AND FUN FOR THE OLD & YOUNG (E)
Griffith & Farran, London: May 1883 (9-3/4x7-5/8", 78 pgs, color cover, color interior)

nn - By Wilhelm Busch (Rare) 100.00 200.00 420.00
NOTE: *Collection of selected stories reprinted from both the 1871 & 1873 **FOOLS PARADISE**.*

FOOLS PARADISE - MIRTH AND FUN FOR THE OLD & YOUNG (E)
E.P. Dutton and Co., NY: May 1883 (9-3/4x7-5/8", 78 pgs, color cover, color interior)

nn - By Wilhelm Busch (Rare) 100.00 200.00 420.00
NOTE: *Collection of selected stories reprinted from both the 1871 & 1873 **FOOLS PARADISE.***

FOREIGN TOUR OFMESSRS. BROWN, JONES, AND ROBINSON, THE (see Messrs...,)

FRANK LESLIE'S BOYS AND GIRLS
Frank Leslie, NYC: Oct 13 1866-#905 Feb 9 1884

average issue with comic strip 10.00 20.00 40.00

FRANK LESLIE'S BUDGET OF FUN
Frank Leslie, Ross & Tousey, 121 Nassau St, NYC: Jan 1859 1878 (newspaper size)

1-5 no comic strips 50.00 100.00 200.00
6 June 1859 (9) panel "The Wonderful Hunting Tour of Mr Borridge After the Deer" 75.00 150.00 300.00
7-9 no comic strips 25.00 50.00 100.00
10 Sept 1859 sequential comic strip 50.00 100.00 200.00
11 (8) panel sequential "Apropos of the Great Eastern" 50.00 100.00 200.00
12-14 25.00 50.00 100.00
15 Feb 1860 (12) panel "The Ballet Girl" strip 50.00 100.00 200.00
16-18 25.00 50.00 100.00
19 June 1860 comic strip front cover 100.00 200.00 300.00
NOTE: *Cover is (11) panel "The Very Latest Fashionable Amusement..."; Back cover comic strip "Mr Jogg's Reasons For Preferring to Board to Keeping House" (7) panels using word balloons. Plus centerfold double page (18) panel spread "The New York May, Moving in General, and Mrs. Grundy's In Particular."*
20 24 25 no comic strips 25.00 50.00 100.00
21 (7/15/60) (8) panel Mr Septimus Verdilater Visits the Baltimore Convention" 50.00 100.00 200.00
22 (8/1/60) (3) panel 25.00 50.00 100.00
23 (8/15/60) (12) panel "Superb Scheme For Perfecting of Dramatic Entertainment" 50.00 100.00 200.00
25 (9/15/60 (9) panel sequential 25.00 50.00 100.00
27 AbrahamLincoln Word Balloon cover 50.00 100.00 200.00
28 Wilhelm Busch sequential strip-r begin 50.00 100.00 200.00
29, 31-51 to be indexed next year 25.00 50.00 100.00
30 (12/15/60) (3) panel sequential strip 25.00 50.00 100.00
31 (Jan 1861) (12) panel The Boarding School Miss 25.00 50.00 100.00
32 (Feb 1861) (10) panel Telegraphic Horrors; Or, Mr Buchanan Undergoing A Series of Electric Shocks 50.00 100.00 200.00
35 (4/1/61) Abraham Lincoln Word Balloon cover 50.00 100.00 200.00
43 44 no sequential comic strips 25.00 50.00 100.00
45 (Nov 1861) (6) panel sequential; (11) panel The Budget Army and Infantry Tactics; First Bellew here? - Many Bellew full pagers begin 50.00 100.00 200.00
48 (Feb 1862) Bellew-c; (2) panel Bellew strip plus singles 50.00 100.00 200.00
49 (Mar 1862) Bellew-c; (16) panel Wilhelm Busch "The Fly Or The Disturbed Duchman A Story without Words" 50.00 100.00 200.00
50 (April 1862) Bellew-c "Succession Bath" plus singles 25.00 50.00 100.00
51 (May 1862) Bellew-c; (25) panel Busch The Toothache (6) panel Definitions of the Day 50.00 100.00 200.00
52 (June 1862) Bellew-c; (9) panel A Cock & A Bull Expedition; (6) panel Bellew The First Campaign of the Home Guard 50.00 100.00 200.00
NOTE: Johnny Bull & Louis Napolean with Brother Jonathan
53-67 To Be Indexed in the Future 25.00 50.00 100.00
68 (11/18//63) (6) panel Bellew strip "Cuts On Cowards" 25.00 50.00 100.00
NOTE: contains (1) panel William Newman 1817-1870, mentor to Thomas Nast
71 (Feb 1864) Wiord Balloon Jefferson Davis-c 25.00 50.00 100.00
72 (Mar 1864) Word Balloon-c 25.00 50.00 100.00

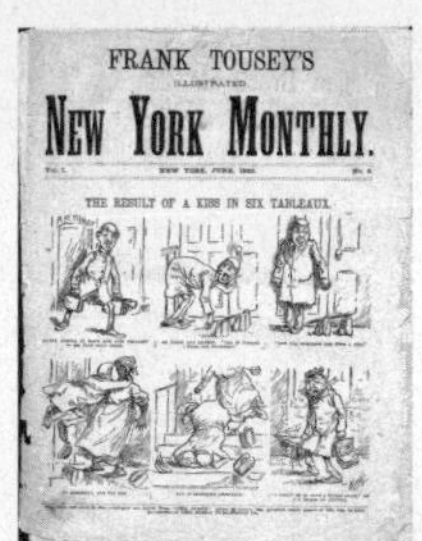

Frank Tousey's Illustrated New York Monthly #9
June 1882 © Frank Tousey

Funny Fellow's Own Book
1852 © Philip Cozans

Funny Folk by F.M. Howarth
1899© E.P. Dutton

FR1.0 GD2.0 FN6.0

73 (April 1864) Word Balloon-c in (6) panels 25.00 50.00 100.00
74 (May 1864) Newman Word Balloon-c 25.00 50.00 100.00
75 77 78 no sequentials 25.00 50.00 100.00
76 (July 1864) Newman Word Balloon-c 25.00 50.00 100.00
79 (Oct 1864) Word Balloon-c 25.00 50.00 100.00
80 (Nov 1864) Robt E Lee & JeffDavis-c; no sequentials 25.00 50.00 100.00
81 (Dec 1864) Word Balloon "Abyss of War"-c 25.00 50.00 100.00
83 (2/18/65) Back-c (6) panel "Petroleum" 25.00 50.00 100.00
84 (Mar 1865) (6) panel sequential 25.00 50.00 100.00
85 (Apr 1865) Word Balloon-c 25.00 50.00 100.00
86 89 90 92 no sequentials 25.00 50.00 100.00
88 (7/6/65) (6) panel "Marriage" 25.00 50.00 100.00
91 (Oct 1865) (6) panel "Brief Confab At The Corner 25.00 50.00 100.00
93-98 yet to be indexed 25.00 50.00 100.00
99 (June 1866) (18) panel Mr Paul Peters Adventures
While Trout-Fishing In The Adirondacks 50.00 100.00 200.00
100 (July 1866) (4) panel sequential comic strip 25.00 50.00 100.00
102 (Sept 1866) (6) panel sequential comic strip 25.00 50.00 100.00
103 (Oct 1866) (9) panel strip; (12) pane;l back cover
Adventures of McTiffin At Long Branch 50.00 100.00 200.00
104 (Nov 1866) (4) panel; (23) panel "The Budget Rebuses; (2) panel
Glut On Treason Market;back-c; (6) sequential strip 25.00 50.00 100.00
105 (12/18/66) Word Balloon-c; (20) panel sequential back-c 37.50 65.00 130.00
NOTE: Artists include William Newman (1863-1868), William Henry Shelton, Joseph Keppler (1873-1876), James A. Wales (1876-1878), Frederick Burr Opper (1878)

FRANK LESLIE'S LADY'S MAGAZINE
Frank Leslie, NYC: Feb 1863-Dec 1882 (8.5x12", typically 152 pgs)
issues with comic strips 10.00 20.00 40.00

FRANK LESLIE'S PICTORIAL WEEKLY
Frank Leslie, Ross & Tousey, 121 Nassau St, NYC:
average issue (Very Rare) 50.00 100.00 200.00

FRANK TOUSEY'S NEW YORK COMIC MONTHLY
Frank Tousey, NYC: (no known sales)

FREAKS
???, Philadelphia: Jan 8, 1881-April? 1881 (Chromolithographic Weekly)
(Very Rare) 50.00 100.00 300.00

FREELANCE, THE
A.M. Soteldo Jr, Edito, 292 Broadway, NYC: 1874-75 (Folio Weekly)
(Rare) 25.00 50.00 100.00

FREE MASONRY EXPOSED
Winchell & Small, 113 Fulton, NY: 1871 (7-5/8x10-1/2", 36pgs, blue paper-c, B&W)
nn- Thomas Worth Scarce 100.00 200.00 400.00
NOTE: Scathing satircal look at Free Masons thru many cartoons, their power waning by the 1870s

FREETHINKERS' PICTORIAL TEXT-BOOK, THE (S,O)
The Truth Seeker Company, New York: 1890, 1896, 1898 (9x12, hard-c, B&W)
1 (1890 edition) - Scarce 382 pgs By Watson Heston 200.00 400.00 800.00
1 (1896 edition) - Scarce 378 pgs By Watson Heston (1890-r)100.00 200.00 450.00
2 (1898 edition) - Scarce 408 pgs By Watson Heston 125.00 250.00 450.00
NOTE: *Sought after by collectors of Freethought/Atheism material. There is also 200 copy Modern Reprint.*

FRITZ SPINDLE-SHANKS, THE RAVEN BLACK
Cosack & C o, Buffalo, NY: 1870/80s (4-3/8x2-3/4", color)
(10) card comic strip set by Wilhelm Busch 25.00 50.00 100.00

FUN BY RALL
Unknown: circa 1865 (11x7-7/8", 68 pgs, soft-c, B&W)
nn - By presently unknown (Very Rare) 100.00 200.00 350.00
NOTE: *Wraparound soft cover like modern comic book; yellow paper cover with red & black ink.*

FUN FOR THE FAMILY IN PICTURES
D. Lothrop and Company: 1886 (4 x 7", 48 pgs, Silver & Red stiff-c; interior pages have various single color inks)
nn - By unknown hand 50.00 100.00 200.00
NOTE: *Single panel cartoons and sequential stories.*

FUN FROM LIFE
Frederick A Stokes & Brother, New York: 1889 (9 1/8 by 7 1/8, 72 pages, hard-c)
nn - Mostly by Frank "Chips" Bellew Jr 62.50 125.00 250.00
NOTE: *Contains both single panel and many sequential comics reprints from Life.*

FUNNYEST OF AWL AND THE FUNNIEST SORT OF PHUN, THE
AT Bellew Or W. Jennings Demorest, 121 Nassau St, NY : 1865-67 (30 issues, 16x11 tabloid 16 pgs B&W Monthly, 1-8 © American News; 9-on © A.T. Bellews)
1 (April 1864) Bellew-c 50.00 100.00 200.00
4 (1865) Bellew-c 50.00 100.00 200.00
5 (1865) Busch (20) panel comic srtip The Toothache 75.00 150.00 300.00
7 (1865) Bellew-c 50.00 100.00 200.00
8 (1865) Special Petroleum oil issue - much cartoon art 100.00 200.00 400.00
9 (July 1865) Bellew Bullfrog-c; centerfold double page spread hanging
many Confederates; (6) panel strip hanging Jeff Davis 100.00 200.00 400.00
10 (Aug 1865) Bellew-c (13) panel Busch strip with two ducks, a frog
and a butcher who gets the ducks in the end 100.00 200.00 400.00
11 (Sept 1865) Bellew Bull Frog Anti-French-c 50.00 100.00 200.00
13 14 15 (12/65-1/66) Bellew-c no sequential comic strips 50.00 100.00 200.00
16 (March 1866) address change to 39 Park Ave 50.00 100.00 200.00
22 (Sept 1866) 133 Nassau St 50.00 100.00 200.00
34 (Oct 1867) 133 Nassau St (7) panel Baseball comic strip;
Last Known Issue - were there more? 100.00 200.00 400.00
NOTE: *Radical Republican politics distributed by Great American News Company; owned by Frank Bellew's wife as a front for her husband. When the Civil War ended, the brutal anti-Confederate comic strips and jokes switched to frogs and began attacking France. Funny thing, history says without France's help in the 1700s, there just might not have been a United States.*

FUNNY ALMANAC
Elton & Co., NY: 1853 (8-1/8x4-7/8, 36 pgs)
nn - sequential comic strip 50.00 100.00 200.00
NOTE: (5) panel strip "The Adventures of Mr. Goliah Starvemouse"

FUNNY FELLOWS OWN BOOK, A COMPANION FOR THE LOVERS OF FROLIC AND GLEE, THE (M,N)
Philip. J. Cozans, 116 Nassau ST, NY: 1852 (4-1/2x7-1/2", 196 pgs, burnt orange paper-c)
nn - contains many sequential comic strips (Very Rare) (no known sales)
NOTE: Collected from many different Comic Alamac(k)s including Mose Keyser (Calif Gold Rush); Jones, Smith and Robinson Goes To A Ball; Adventures of Mr. Gulp, Or the Effects of A Dinner Party; The Bowery Bully's Trip To The California Gold Mines plus lots more. This one is a sleeper so far.

FUNNY FOLK (M)
E. P. Dutton: 1899 (12x16-1/2", 90 pgs,14 strips in color-rest in b&w, hard-c)
nn - By Franklin Morris Howarth 162.50 325.00 1500.00
nn - London: J.M. Dent, 1899 embossed-c; same interior 200.00 450.00 900.00
NOTE: *Reprints many sequential strips & single panel cartoons from* ***Puck****. This is considered by many to be yet another "missing link" between Victorian & Platinum Age comic books. Most comic books 1900-1917 reprinting Sunday newspaper comic strips follow this size format, except using cardboard-c rather than hard-c.*

FUNNY SKETCHES...Also Embracing Comic Illustrations
Frank Harrison, New York: 1881 (6-5/8x5", 68 pgs, B&W, Color-c)
nn - contains (3) sequential comic strips; one strip is (6) pages long;
plus one (3) pages; one more (2) pager 75.00 150.00 300.00

GIBSON BOOK, THE (M,S)
Charles Scribner's Sons & R.H. Russell, New York: 1906 (11-3/8x17 5/8", gilted red hard-c, B&W)
Book I 50.00 100.00 200.00
NOTE: *Reprints in whole the books: Drawings, Pictures of People, London,Sketches and Cartoons, Education of Mr. Pipp, Americans. 414 pgs. 1907 2nd editions exist same value.*
Book II 50.00 100.00 200.00
NOTE: *Reprints in whole the books: A Widow and Her Friends, The Weaker Sex, Everyday People, Our Neighbors. 314 pgs 1907 second edition for both also exists. Same value.*

GIBSON'S PUBLISHED DRAWINGS, MR. (M,S) (see Plat index for later issues post 1900)
R.H. Russell, New York: No.1 1894 - No. 9 1904 (11x17-3/4", hard-c, B&W)
nn (No.1; 1894) Drawings 96 pgs 30.00 60.00 120.00
nn (No.2; 1896) Pictures of People 92 pgs 30.00 60.00 120.00
nn (No.3; 1898) Sketches and Cartoons 94 pgs 30.00 60.00 120.00
nn (No.4; 1899) The Education of Mr. Pipp 88 pgs 30.00 60.00 120.00
nn (No.5; 1900) Americans 30.00 60.00 120.00
NOTE: *By Charles Dana Gibson cartoons, reprinted from magazines, primarily* ***LIFE****. The Education of Mr. Pipp tells a story. Series continues how long after 1904? Each of these books originally came in a boxx and are worth more with the box.*

GIRL WHO WOULDN'T MIND GETTING MARRIED, THE (O)
Frederick Warne & Co., London & New York: nd (c1870's) (9-1/2x11-1/2", 28 pgs, printed 1 side, paper-c, B&W)
nn - By Harry Parkes 62.50 125.00 250.00
NOTE: *Published simultaneously with its companion volume,* ***The Man Who Would Like to Marry****.*

GOBLIN SNOB, THE (O)
DeWitt & Davenport, New York: nd (c1853-56) (24 x 17 cm, 96 pgs, B&W, color hard-c)
nn - (Rare) by H.L. Stephens 250.00 500.00 1000.00

GOLDEN ARGOSY
Frank A. Munsey, 81 Warren St, NYC: 1880s (10-1/2x12, 16 pgs, B&W)
issues with full page comic strips by Chips and Bisbee 12.50 25.00 50.00

GOLDEN DAYS, THE
James Elverson, Publisher, NYC: March 6 1880-May 11 1907 weekly, 16 pgs
issues with comic strips 4.00 7.50 15.00
Horatio Alger issues 10.00 20.00 40.00
v10 #49-v11#1 1889 first Stratemeyer story 25.00 50.00 100.00

GOLDEN WEEKLY, THE
Frank Tousey, NYC: #1 Sept 25 1889-#145 Aug 18 1892 (10-3/4x14-1/2, 16 pgs, B&W)
average issue with comic striips 15.00 25.00 50.00

GREAT LOCOFOCO JUGGERNAUT, THE (S)
publisher unknown: Fall/Winter 1837 (7-5/8x3-1/4, handbill single page)

The Story of Han's The Swapper Cover & First Two Panels
1865 © L. Pranc & Co, Boston

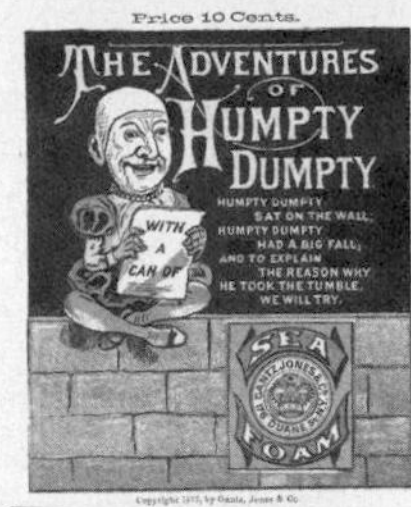

Humpty Dumpty, The Adventures of...
© Gantz, Jones and Co.

Imagerie d'Epinal
1888 © Mumoristic Publishing Co.

FR1.0 GD2.0 FN6.0

nn - By David Claypoole Johnston (a VG copy sold for $2000 in 2005)
nn - **Imprint Society:** 1971 (reprint) 6.00 12.00 25.00

HALF A CENTURY OF ENGLISH HISTORY (S. M)
G.P. Putnam's Sons - The Knickerbocker Press, New York and London: 1884 (7-3/4 x 5-3/4", 316 pgs., illustrated hard-c)
nn - By Various 25.00 50.00 175.00
NOTE: *Subtitle: Pictorially Presented in a Series of Cartoons from the Collection of Mr. Punch. Comprising 150 plates by Doyle, Leech, Tenniel, and others, in which are portrayed the political careers of Peel, Palmerston, Russell, Cobden, Bright, Beaconsfield, Derby, Salisbury, Gladstone and other English statesmen.*

HAIL COLUMBIA! HISTORICAL, COMICAL, AND CENTENNIAL (O,S)
The Graphic Co., New York & Walter F. Brown, Providence, RI: 1876 (10x11-3/8", 60 pgs, red gilted hard-c, B&W)
nn - by Walter F. Brown (Scarce) 100.00 200.00 450.00

HANS HUCKEBEIN'S BATCH OF ODD STORIES ODDLY ILLUSTRATEDED
McLoughlin Bros., New York: 1880s (9-3/4x7-3/8, 36?? pg?
nn - By Wilhelm Busch (Rare) 75.00 150.00 300.00

HANS THE SWAPPER, THE STORY OF (O)
L. Pranc & Co., 159 Washington St, Boston: 1865 (33 inch long fold out in colors)
nn - unique fold out comic book on one long piece of paper 75.00 150.00 300.00

HARPER'S NEW MONTHLY MAGAZINE
Harper & Brothers, Franklin Square, NY: 1850-1870s (6-3/4x10, 140 pgs, paper-c, B&W)
1850s issues with comic strips in back advert section 10.00 20.00 40.00

HEALTH GUYED (I)
Frederick A. Stokes Company: 1890 (5-3/8 x 8-3/8, 56 pgs, hardcover, B&W)
nn - By Frank P.W. ("Chip") Bellew (Junior) 25.00 50.00 175.00
NOTE: *Text & cartoon illustration parody of a health guide.*

HEATHEN CHINEE, THE (O)
Western News Co.: 1870 (5-1/32x7-1/4, B&W, paper)
nn - 10 sheets printed on one side came in envelope 75.00 150.00 300.00

HITS AT POLITICS (M,S)
R.H. Russell, New York: 1899 (15" x 12", 166 pgs, B&W, hard-c)
nn - W.A. Rogers c/a 100.00 200.00 300.00
NOTE: *Collection of W.A. Rogers cartoons, all reprinted from Harper's Weekly. Includes Spanish-American War cartoons.*

THE HOME CIRCLE
Garrett & Co, NY: 1854-56 (26x19", 4 pgs, B&W)
1 (1/54) beautiful ad of Garrett Building 100.00 200.00 400.00
2/4 (4/66) Cover ad for Yale College Scraps 100.00 200.00 400.00
2/5 (5/55) First ad for Oscas Shanghai 75.00 150.00 300.00
2/6 (6/55) another ad forOscas Snanghai 75.00 150.00 300.00
2/8 (#20) (8/55) Oscar Shanghai comic book cover repro 200.00 400.00 800.00
3/1 (#25) (1/56) 200.00 400.00 800.00
NOTE: Garrett's 2nd comic book Courtship of Chavalier Slyfox-Wikoff
3/8 (#32) (8/56) 50.00 100.00 200.00
NOTE: First print ad for Foreign Tour of Messrs. Brown, Jones, and Robinson
35 (11/56) first official Garrett, Dick & Fitzgerald issue 50.00 100.00 200.00
37 (1/57) 100.00 200.00 400.00
NOTE: Front page comic strip repro ad for Messrs. Brown, Jones, and Robinson's Foreign Tour; Back cover full of short sequentials, singles panel

HOME MADE HAPPY. A ROMANCE FOR MARRIED MEN IN SEVEN CHAPTERS (O,P)
Genuine Durham Smoking Tobacco & The Graphic Co.: nd (c1870's) (5-1/4 tall x 3-3/8" wide folded, 27" wide unfolded, color cardboard)
nn - With all 8 panels attached (Scarce) 30.00 60.00 200.00
nn - Individual panels/cards 5.00 10.00 25.00
NOTE: *Consists of 8 attached cards, printed on one side, which unfold into a strip story of title card & 7 panels. Scrapbook hobbyists in the 19th Century tended to pull the panels apart to paste into their scrapbooks, making copies with all panels still attached scarce.*

HOME PICTURE BOOK FOR LITTLE CHILDREN (E,P)
Home Insurance Company, New York: July 1887 (8 x 6-1/8", 36 pgs, b&w, color paper-c)
nn (Scarce) 40.00 80.00 160.00
NOTE: *Contains an abbreviated 32-panel reprinting of "The Toothache" by George Cruikshank. Remainder of booklet does not contain comics. Some copies known to exist do not contain The Toothache - buyer beware!*

HOOD'S COMICALITIES. COMICAL PICTURES FROM HIS WORKS (E,S)
Porter & Coates: 1880 (8-1/2x10-3/8", 104 pgs, printed one side, hard-c, B&W)
nn 20.00 40.00 80.00
NOTE: *Reprints 4 cartoon illustrations per page from the British Hood's Comic Annuals, which were poetry books by Thomas Hood.*

HOOKEYBEAK THE RAVEN, AND OTHER TALES (see also JACK HUCKABACK, THE SCAPEGRACE RAVEN) (E)
George Routledge and Sons, London & New York: nd (1878) (7-1/4x5-5/8", 104 pgs, hardcover, B&W)
nn - By Wilhelm Busch (Rare) 100.00 200.00 400.00

HOW ADOLPHUS SLIM-JIM USED JACKSON'S BEST, AND WAS HAPPY. A LENGTHY TALE IN 7 ACTS. (O,P)
Jackson's Best Chewing Tobacco & Donaldson Brothers: nd(c1870's) (5-1/8 tall x 3-3/8" wide folded, 27" wide unfolded, color cardboard)
nn - With all 8 panels attached (Scarce) 30.00 60.00 200.00
nn - Individual panels/cards 5.00 10.00 25.00
NOTE: *Consists of 8 attached cards, printed on one side, which unfold into a strip story of title card & 7 panels. Scrapbook hobbyists in the 19th Century tended to pull the panels apart topaste into their scrapbooks, making copies with all panels still attached scarce.*

HOW DAYS' DURHAM STANDARD OF THE WORLD SMOKING TOBACCO MADE TWO PAIRS OF TWINS HAPPY (O,P)
J.R. Day & Bro. Standard Durham Smoking Tobacco, Durham, NC: nd (c late 1870's/early 1880's) (3-5/8" x 5-1/2", folded, 21-3/4" tall unfolded, color cardboard)
nn- With all 6 panels attached (Scarce) 120.00 240.00 480.00
nn- Individual panels/cards 20.00 40.00 60.00
NOTE: *Highly sought by both Black Americana and Tobacciana collectors. Recurring mid-19th Century story about two African-American twin brothers who romance and marry a pair of African-American twin sisters. Although the text is racist at points, the art is not. Consists of 6 attached cards, printed on one side, which unfold downwards into a strip story of title card & 5 panels. Scrapbook hobbyists in the 19th Century tended to pull the panels apart and paste into their scrapbooks, making copies with all panels attached scarce. Note, there are numerous cartoon tellings of this same story, including several card series versions (with different art, and story variations, each time). But, the above is the only version which unfolds as a strip of attached cards. The cards from all the unattached versions are smaller sized, and thus distinguishable.*

HUGGINIANA; OR, HUGGINS' FANTASY, BEING A COLLECTION OF THE MOST ESTEEMED MODERN LITERARY PRODUCTIONS (I,S,P)
H.C. Southwick, New York: 1808 (296 pgs, printed one side, B&W, hard-c)
nn - (Very Rare)) (no known sales)
NOTE: *The earliest known surviving collected promotional cartoons in America. This is a booklet collecting 7 folded plus 1 full page flyer advertisements for barber John Richard Desborus Huggins, who hired American artists Elkanah Tisdale and William S. Leney to modify previously published illustrations into cartoons referring to his barber shop.*

HUMOROUS MASTERPIECES - PICTURES BY JOHN LEECH (E,M)
Frederick A. Stokes: nd (late 1900's - early 1910's) No.1-2 (5-5/8x3-7/8", 68 pgs, cardboard covers, B&W)
1- John Leech (single panel cartoon-r from **Punch**) 17.50 35.00 70.00
2- John Leech (single panel cartoon-r from **Punch**) 17.50 35.00 70.00

HUMOURIST, THE (E,I,S)
C.V. Nickerson and Lucas and Deaver, Baltimore: No.1 Jan 1829 - No.12 Dec 1829 (5-3/4x3-1/2", B&W text w/hand colored cartoon pg.)
Bound volume No.1-12 (Very Rare; copies in libraries 270 pgs) (no known sales)
NOTE: *Earliest known American published periodical to contain a cartoon every issue. Surviving individual issues currently unknown -- all information comes from 1 surviving bound volume. Each issue is mostly text, with one full page hand-colored cartoon. Bound volume contains an additional hand colored cartoons at front of each six month set (total of 14 cartoons in volume). Cartoons appear to be of British origin, possibly by George Cruikshank.*

HUMPTY DUMPTY, ADVENTURES OF...(I,P)
1877 (Promotional 4x3-1/2", 12 page chapbook from Gantz, Jones & Co, 10¢-c.)
nn-Promotes Gantz Sea Foam Baking Powder; early app. of a costumed character, dressed as Humpty Dumpty 50.00 100.00 350.00

HUSBAND AND WIFE, OR THE STORY OF A HAIR. (O,P)
Garland Stoves and Ranges, Michigan Stove Co.: 1883 (4-3/16 tall x 2-11/16" wide folded, 16" wide unfolded, color cardboard)
nn - With all 6 panels attached (Scarce) 25.00 50.00 125.00
nn - Individual panels/cards 5.00 10.00 25.00
NOTE: *Consists of 6 attached cards, printed on one side, which unfold into a strip story of title card & 5 panels. Scrapbook hobbyists in the 19th Century tended to pull the panels apart topaste into their scrapbooks, making copies with all panels still attached scarce.*

ICHABOD ACADEMICUS, THE COLLEGE EXPERIENCES OF (O,G)
William T. Peters, New Haven, CT: 1850 (5-1/2x9-3/4",108 pgs, B&W)
nn - By William T. Peters (Rare) 1000.00 2000.00 4000.00
NOTE: *Pages are not uniform in size. Also, a copy showed up on eBay with misspelled Academicus. Has "n" instead of "m" - not known yet which printing is earliest version.*

ICHABOD ACADEMICUS, THE COLLEGE EXPERIENCES OF (O,G)
Dick & Fitzgerald, New York: nd (1870s-1888) (paper-c, B&W)
nn - By William T. Peters (Very Rare) 250.00 500.00 1000.00
NOTE: *Pages are uniform in size.*

ILLUSTRATED SCRAP-BOOK OF HUMOR AND INTELLIGENCE (M)
John J. Dyer & Co.: nd (c1859-1860)
nn - Very Rare 200.00 400.00 800.00
NOTE: *A "printed scrapbook" of images culled from some unidentified periodical. About half of it is illustrations that would have accompanied prose pieces. There are pages of single panel cartoons (multiple per page). And there are roughly 8 to 12 pages of sequential comics (all different stories, but appears to all be by the same presently unidentified artist).*

THE ILLUSTRATED WEEKLY
Chars C Lucas & Co, 11 Dey St, NY: 1876 (15x18", 8pgs, 8¢ per issue)
2/8 (2/19/76) back-c all sequential comic strips 100.00 200.00 400.00
2/12 (3/18/76) full page of British-r sequentials 100.00 200.00 400.00
2/14 (4/1/76) April Fool Issue - (6) panel center; plus more 100.00 200.00 400.00
2/15 (4/8/76) (6) panel sequential 100.00 200.00 400.00
issues without comic strips 12.50 25.00 50.00

Jingo No. 3, Sept 24
1884 © Art Newspaper Co, Boston & NYC

Journey To The Gold Diggings By Jeremiah Saddlebags
1849 © Various - First Original USA Comic Book

The Lantern Dec 18
1852 © Stringer & Townsend

FR1.0 GD2.0 FN6.0

ILLUSTRATIONS OF THE POETS: FROM PASSAGES IN THE LIFE OF LITTLE BILLY VIDKINS (See A Day's Sport...)
S. Robinson, Philadelphia: May 1849 (14.7 cm x 11.3 cm, 32 pgs, B&W)
nn - by Henry Stephens (very rare) (no known sales)
NOTE: *Predates Journey to the Gold Diggins By Jeremiah Saddlebags by a few months and is an original American proto-comic strip book. More research needs to be done. A later edition brought $800 in G/VG 2007*

IMAGERIE d'EPINAL (untrimmed individual sheets) (E)
Pellerin for Humoristic Publishing Co, Kansas City, Mo.: nd (1888) No.1-60 (15-7/8x11-3/4",single sheets, hand colored) (All are Rare)
1-14, 21, 22, 25-46, 49-60 - in the Album d'Images 17.50 35.00 70.00
15-20, 23,24, 47, 48 - not in the Album d'Images 30.00 60.00 120.00
NOTE: *Printed and hand colored in France expressly for the Humoristic Publishing Company . Printed on one side only. These are single sheets, sold separately. Reprints and translates the sheets from their original French.*

IMAGERIE d'EPINAL ALBUM d'IMAGES (E)
Pellerin for Humoristic Publishing Co., Kansas City. Mo: nd (1888) (15-1/2x11-1/2",108 pgs plus full color hard-c, hand colored interior)
nn - Various French artists (Rare) 300.00 600.00 1800.00
NOTE: *Printed and hand colored in France expressly for the Humoristic Publishing Company . Printed on one side only. This is supposedly a collection of sixty broadsheets, originally sold separately. All copies known only have fifty of the sixty known of these broadsheets (slightly bigger, before binding, trimming the margins in the process, down to 15-1/4x11-3/8".). Three slightly different covers known to exist, with or without the indication in French "Textes en Anglais" ("Texts in Englishi), with or without the general title "Contes de FEes" ("Fairy Tales"). All known copies were collected with sheets 15-20, 23,24, 47, and 48 missing.*

IN LAUGHLAND (M)
R.H. Russell, New York: 1899 (14-9/16x12", 72 pgs, hard-c)
nn - By Henry "Hy" Mayer (scarce) 150.00 300.00 600.00
NOTE: *Mostly strips plus single panel cartoon-r from various magazines. The majority are reprinted from Life, with the rest from: Truth, Dramatic Mirror, Black and White, Figaro Illustre, Le Rire, and Fliegende Blatter.*

IN THE "400" AND OUT (M,S) (see also **THE TAILOR-MADE GIRL**)
Keppler & Schwarzmann, New York: 1888 (8-1/4x12", 64 pgs, hardc, B&W)
nn - By C.J. Taylor 42.50 85.00 170.00
NOTE: *Cartoons reprinted from **Puck**. The "400" is a reference to New York City's aristocratic elite.*

IN VANITY FAIR (M,S)
R.H.Russell & Son, New York: 1896 (11-7/8x17-7/8", 80 pgs, hard-c, B&W)
nn - By A.B.Wenzell, r-LIFE and HARPER'S 45.00 90.00 180.00

JACK HUCKABACK, THE SCAPEGRACE RAVEN (see also HOOKEYBEAK THE RAVEN) (E)
Stroefer & Kirchner, New York: nd (c1877) (9-3/8x6-3/8", 56 pgs, printed one side only, hand colored hardcover, B&W interior)
nn - By Wilhelm Busch (Rare) 75.00 150.00 350.00
NOTE: *The 1877 date is derived from a gift signature on one known copy. The publication date might in truth be earlier. There are also professionally hand colored copies known to exist which would be worth more.*

JEFF PETTICOATS
American News Company, NY: July 1865 (23 inches folded out; 6-1/4x8 folded,, B&W)
nn - Very Rare Frank Bellew (6) panel sequential foldout (10¢) (no known sales)
NOTE: printed also in **FUNNYEST OF AWL AND THE FUNNIEST SORT OF PHUN** #9 (July 1865) (6) panel strip hanging Jeff Davis; This sold hundreds of thousand of copies in its day

JINGO (M,O)
Art Newspaper Co., Boston & New York: No.1 Sept 10, 1884 - No.11 Nov 19, 1884 (10 cents, 13-7/8" x 10-1/4",16 pgs, color front/back-c and center, remainder B&W, paper-c)
1-11(Rare) 50.00 100.00 200.00
NOTE: *Satirical Republican propaganda magazine, modeled after **Puck** and **Judge**, which was published during the last couple months of the 1884 Presidential Election campaign. The Republicans lost, **Jingo** ceased publication, and Republican backers soon after purchased **Judge** magazine.*

JOHN-DONKEY, THE (O, S)
George Dexter, Burgess, Stringer & Co., NYC: 1848 (10x7.5",16 pgs,B&W, 6¢
1 Jan 1 1848 75.00 150.00 300.00
2-end (last issue Aug 12 1848) 50.00 100.00 200.00

JOLLY JOKER
Frank Leslie, NY: 1862-1878 (B&W, 10¢)
20/6 (July 1877) (Bellew Opper cover & single panels 150.00 300.00 600.00

JOLLY JOKER, OR LAUGH ALL-ROUND
Dick & Fitzgerald, NY: 1870s? (8-1/4x4-7/8", 148, B&W, illustrated green cover)
nn - cartoons on every page 100.00 200.00 400.00

JONATHAN'S WHITTLINGS OF THE WAR (O, S)
T.W. Strong, 98 Nassau St, NYC: April 1854-July 8 1854 (11.5x8.5", 16 pgs, B&W)
1 April 1854 100.00 200.00 400.00
NOTE: *Begins Frank Bellew's sequential comic strip* "Mr. Hookemcumsnivey, A Russian Gentleman, Hears That His Country Is In A State of War"
2-12 (July 8 1854) Many Bellew & Hopkins 100.00 200.00 400.00

JOURNAL CARRIER'S GREETING
???, Minn, Minn: 1897-98? (giveaway promo, 10-1/8x8-1/4, 36, B&W, paper-c)
nn - rare 50.00 100.00 200.00

JOURNEY TO THE GOLD DIGGINS BY JEREMIAH SADDLEBAGS (O,G)

FR1.0 GD2.0 FN6.0

Various publishers: 1849 (25 cents, 5-5/8 x 8-3/4", 68 pgs, green & black paper cover, B&W interior)
nn -- New York edition, Stringer & Townsend, Publishers
(Very Rare) By J.A. and D.F. Read. 4500.00 7500.00 12000.00
nn -- Cincinnati, Ohio edition, published by U.P. James
(Very Rare) By J.A. and D.F. Read. 4500.00 7500.00 12000.00
nn -- 1950 reprint, with introduction, published by William P. Wreden, Burlingame, California: 1950 (5-7/8 x 9", 92 pgs, hardcover, color interior)
(390 copies printed) By J.A. and D.F. Read. 67.50 125.00 250.00
NOTE: *Earliest known original sequential comic book by an American creator; directly inspired by Töpffer's **Obadiah Oldbuck** and **Bachelor Butterfly** The New York and Cincinnati editions were both published in 1849, one soon after the other. Antiquarian Book sources have traditionally cited that the Cincinnati edition preceded the New York, but without referencing their evidence. Conflicting with this, the Cincinnati edition lists the New York publishers' 1849 copyright, while the New York edition makes no reference to the Cincinnati publishers. Such would indicate that the New York edition was first. Both are very rare, and until resolved both will be regarded as published simultaneously. A New York copy with missing back cover, detached front cover, and G/VG interior sold for $2000 in 2000. Two copies sold at auction in 2006 for $11,500 and 12,000. (Prices vary widely.)*

JUDGE (M,O)
Judge Publishing, New York: No.1 Oct 29, 1881 - No. 950, Dec ??, 1899 (10 cents, color front/back c and centerspread, remainder B&W, paper-c)
1 (Scarce) (no known sales)
2-26 (Volume 1; Scarce) 20.00 40.00 80.00
27-790,792-950 12.50 25.00 50.00
791 (12/12/1896; Vol.31) - classic satirical-c depicting Tammany Hall politicians as the Yellow Kid & Cox's Brownies 50.00 150.00 350.00
Bound Volumes (six month, 26 issue run each):
Vol. 1 (Scarce) (no known sales)
Vol. 2-30,32-37 140.00 280.00 600.00
Vol. 31 - includes issue 791 **YK/Brownies** parody 165.00 230.00 725.00
NOTE: *Rival publication to Puck. Purchased by Republican Party backers, following their loss in the 1884 Presidential Election, to become a Republican propaganda satire magazine.*

JUDGE, GOOD THINGS FROM
Judge Publishing Co., NY: 1887 (13-3/4x10.5", 68 pgs, color paper-c)
1 first printing 50.00 100.00 200.00
NOTE: Zimmerman, Hamilton, Victor, Woolf, Beard, Ehrhart, De Meza, Howarth, Smith, Alfred Mitchell

JUDGE'S LIBRARY (M)
Judge Publishing, New York: No.1, April 1890 - No. 141, Dec 1899 (10 cents, 11x8-1/8", 36 pgs, color paper-c, B&W)
1 10.00 20.00 40.00
2-141 10.00 20.00 40.00
151-??? (post-1900 issues; see Platinum Age section)
NOTE: ***Judge's Library** was a monthly magazine reprinting cartoons & prose from **Judge**, with each issue's material organized around the same subject. The cover art was often original. All issues were kept in print for the duration of the series, so later issues are more scarce than earlier ones.*

JUDGE'S QUARTERLY (M)
Judge Publishing Company/Arkell Publishing Company, New York: No.1 April 1892 - 31 Oct 1899 (25¢, 13-3/4x10-1/4", 64 pgs, color paper-c, B&W)
1-11 13-31 contents presently unknown to us 15.00 30.00 60.00
12 ZIM Sketches From Judge Jan 1895 100.00 200.00 400.00
NOTE: *Similar to **Judge's Library**, except larger in size, and issued quarterly. All reprint material, except for the cover art.*

JUDGE'S SERIALS (M,S)
Judge Publishing, New York: March 1888 (10x7.5", 36 pgs)
#3 - Eugene Zimmerman 100.00 200.00 400.00
NOTE: *A bit of sequential comic strips; mostly single panel cartoons. This series runs to at least #8.*

JUDY
Burgess, Stringer & Co., 17 Ann St, NYC: Nov 28 1846-Feb 20 47 (11x8.5",12 pgs,B&W)
1 Nov 28 1846 67.50 125.00 250.00
2-13 50.00 100.00 200.00

JUVENILE GEM, THE (see also THE ADVENTURES OF MR. TOM PLUMP, and OLD MOTHER MITTEN) (O,I)
Huestis & Cozans: nd (1850-1852) (6x3-7/8", 64 pgs, hand colored paper-c, B&W) (all versions Very Rare)
nn - First printing(s) publisher's address is 104 Nassau Street (1850-1851) (1 copy sold for $800.00 in Fair)
nn - 2nd printing(s) publisher's address is 116 Nassau Street (1851-1852) (no known sales)
nn - 3rd printing(s) publisher's address is 107 Nassau Street (1852+) (no known sales)
NOTE: *The JUVENILE GEM is a gathering of multiple booklets under a single, hand colored cover (none of the interior booklets have the covers which they were given when sold separately). The publisher appears to have gathered whichever printings of each booklet were available when copies of THE JUVENILE GEM was assembled, so that the booklets within, and the conglomerate cover, may be from a mixture of printings. Contains two sequential comic booklets: THE ADVENTURES OF MR. TOM PLUMP, and OLD MOTHER MITTEN AND HER FUNNY KITTEN, plus five heavily illustrated children's booklets - **The Pretty Primer**, **The Funny Book**, **The Picture Book**, **The Two Sisters**, and **Story Of The Little Drummer**. Six of these -- including the two comic books -- were reprinted in the 1960's by Americana Review as a set of individual booklets, and included in a folder collectively titled "Six Children's Books of the 1850's".*

LANTERN, THE
Stringer & Townsend:1852-1853 (11x8-3/8", 12 pgs, soft paper, 6 ¢)

Leslie's Young America #1
1881 © Leslie & Company, NYC

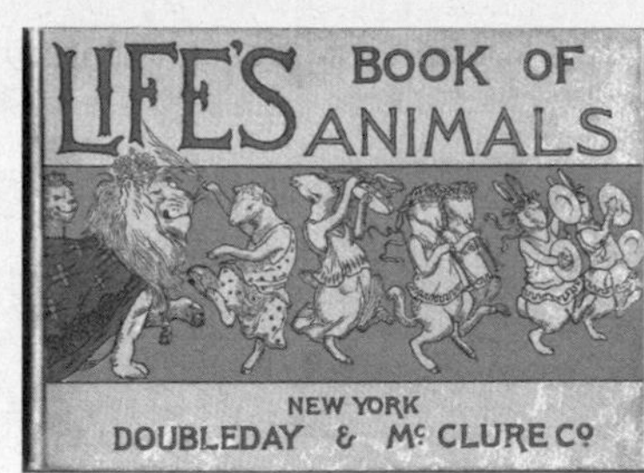

Life's Book of Animals
1888 © Doubleday & McClure Co.

Max and Maurice by Wilhelm Busch
1871 © Roberts Bros, Boston

	FR1.0	GD2.0	FN6.0
1 Jan 10, 1852	37.50	75.00	150.00
2	25.00	50.00	100.00
3 First Frank Bellew cartoons onwards each issue	37.50	75.00	150.00
4 Bellew 's Mr Blobb begins 1/31/52	50.00	100.00	200.00

NOTE: *Bellew serial sequential comic strip "Mr Blobb In Search Of A Physician" becomes 2nd earliest known recurring character in American comic strips plus full page single panel Bellew cartoon "The Modern Frankenstein" take-off on Shelly's story.*

	FR1.0	GD2.0	FN6.0
5 Hunsdale 2-panel "The Horrors of Slavery"; Mr Blobb	50.00	100.00	200.00
6 DF Read 15 panel "A Volley of Valentines"; Mr Blobb	50.00	100.00	200.00
7-8 10 Bellew's Mr Blobb continues	25.00	50.00	100.00
9 (4) panel "The Perils of Leap Year" MrBlobb	50.00	100.00	200.00
11 no Mr Blobb	20.00	40.00	80.00
12 Bellew's Mr Blobb continues 3/27/52	50.00	100.00	200.00
13 Bellew (10) panel sequential "Stump Speaking Studied"	50.00	100.00	200.00
14 no comic strips	20.00	40.00	80.00
15 Bellew's Mr Blobb ends (5) panel 4/17/52	50.00	100.00	200.00
16 Bellew begins new comic strip serial, "Mr. Bulbear, A Stockbroker, After having Supped at Delmonicos, Has A Dream", Part One, (6) panels	50.00	100.00	200.00
17 Bellew's Mr Bulbear continues	25.00	50.00	100.00
18 Bellew (8) panel "Trials of a Witness"	50.00	100.00	200.00
19 Bellew's Mr Bulbear's Dream continues	25.00	50.00	100.00
20-23 no comic strips	20.00	40.00	80.00
24 Bellew "Trials of a Publisher" (6) panel	50.00	100.00	200.00
25 comic strip "Travels of Jonathan Verdant"recurring character	25.00	50.00	100.00
26-49 contents to be indexed soon			
50 (12/18/52) (2) panel Impertinent Smile	25.00	50.00	100.00
58 (2/12/53) (6) panel Trip to California	25.00	50.00	100.00
66 (4/9/53) (3) panel sequential strip	25.00	50.00	100.00

LAST SENSATION, THE (Becomes Day's Doings)
James Watts, NYC: Dec 27 1867-May 30 1868 (11x16 folio-size, 16 pgs, B&W)

	FR1.0	GD2.0	FN6.0
issues with comic strips	50.00	100.00	200.00

LAUGH AND GROW FAT COMIC ALMANAC
Fisher & Brother, Philadelphia, New York & Boston: 1860-? (36 pgs)

	FR1.0	GD2.0	FN6.0
nn	60.00	120.00	240.00

LEGEND OF SAM'L OF POSEN (O)
M.B. Curtis Company: 1884-85 (8x3-3/8", 44 pgs, Color-c, B&W interior)

	FR1.0	GD2.0	FN6.0
nn - By M.B. Curtis	50.00	100.00	200.00

NOTE: Cover blurb says: From Early Days in Fatherland to affluence And Success in the Land of His Adoption, America

LESLIE'S YOUNG AMERICA (O. S)
Leslie & Co, 98 Chamber St, NY: 1881-82 (11-1/2x8", 5¢, B&W)

	FR1.0	GD2.0	FN6.0
1 (7/9/81) back cover (6) panel strip	125.00	250.00	500.00
2 (7/16/81) back cover (9) panel strip	50.00	100.00	200.00
3 (7/23/81) back cover (16) panel Busch strip	67.50	125.00	250.00
9 (9/3/81) sequentials; Hopkins singles	50.00	100.00	200.00
15 (10/15/81) Zim or Frost? (6) panel strip	50.00	100.00	200.00
19 (11/12/81) (9) panel back-c strip	50.00	100.00	200.00
24 (4) panel strip 25 (2) panel back-c strip	50.00	100.00	200.00
26 27 (6) panel back-c strip	50.00	100.00	200.00
29 31 (12) panel strip	50.00	100.00	200.00
32 (2/11/82) (8) panel strip	50.00	100.00	200.00
issues without comic strips or Jules Verne	25.00	50.00	100.00

NOTE: Jules Verne stories begin with #1 and run thru at least #42

LIFE (M,O) (continues with Vol.35 No. 894+ in the Platinum Age section)
J.A.Mitchell: Vol.1 No.1 Jan. 4, 1883 - Vol.1 No.26 June 29, 1883 (10-1/4x8", 16 pgs, B&W, paper cover); J.A. Mitchell: Vol. 2 No. 27, July 5, 1883 - Vol. 6 No.148, Oct 29, 1885 (10-1/4x8-1/4", 16 pgs., B&W, paper cover); Mitchell & Miller: Vol.6 No.149, Nov. 5, 1885 - Vol. 31, No. 796, March 17, 1898 (10-3/8x8-3/8", 16 pgs., B&W, paper cover); Life Publishing Company: Vol. 31 No. 797, March 24, 1898 - Vol. 34 No. 893, Dec 28, 1899 (10-3/8 x 8-1/2", 20 pgs., B&W, paper cover)

	FR1.0	GD2.0	FN6.0
1-26 (Scarce)	(no known sales)		
27-799	5.00	10.00	20.00
800 (4/7/1898) parody Yellow Kid / Spanish-American War cover (not by Outcault)	67.50	125.00	250.00
801-893	5.00	10.00	20.00

NOTE: *All covers for issues 1 - 26 are identical, apart from issue number & date.*

Hard bound collected volumes:

	FR1.0	GD2.0	FN6.0
V. 1 (No.1-26) (Scarce)	67.50	125.00	250.00
V. 2-34	45.00	90.00	180.00
V. 31 YK #800 parody-c not by RFO	70.00	140.00	280.00

NOTE: *Because the covers of all issues in Volume 1 are identical, it was common practice to remove the covers before binding the issues together. This is not true of later volumes, though, in all volumes it was common to drop the advertising pages which appeared at the rear of each issue. Information on many more individual issues will expand next Guide.*

LIFE AND ADVENTURES OF JEFF DAVIS (I)
J.C. Haney & Co., NY: 1865 (10 cents, 7-1/2" x 4", 36 pgs, B&W, paper-c)

	FR1.0	GD2.0	FN6.0
nn - By McArone (Scarce)	150.00	300.00	650.00
nn - 1974 Reprint (350) copies 6-3/4x4-3/8	50.00	10.00	20.00
nn - 1997 Reprint (7th Fla. Sutler, Clearwater, 6-3/4x4-1/4")	–	–	2.00

NOTE: *Humorous telling of the capture of Confederate President Jeff Davis in women's clothing, from the publisher of Merryman's Monthly. It contains an ad page for that publication; the material is perhaps reprinted from it. J.C. Haney licensed it to local printers, and so various publishers are found -- all printings currently regarded as simultaneous. (The Geo. H. Hees printing, Oswego, NY, contains an ad for the upcoming October 1865 issue of Merryman's Monthly, thus placing that printing in September 1865). Modern facsimile editions have been produced.*

LIFE IN PHILADELPHIA
W. Simpson, 66 Chestnut, Philadelphia; Siltart, No. 65 South Third St, Philadelphia: 1830 (7-3/4x6-7/8", 15 loose plates, hand colored copies exist, maybe B&W also)

	FR1.0	GD2.0	FN6.0
nn - By Edward Williams Clay (1799-1857) (Very Rare)		(no known sales)	

NOTE: *First 13 plates etched, with many word balloons; scenes of exaggerated Black Americana in Philadelphia viewed one by one as broadsides. Had several publishers over the years. Was also eventually collected into a book of same name but only with the first 13 plates used; the last two not used in book. Collected book not yet viewed to share info.*

LIFE'S BOOK OF ANIMALS (M.S)
Doubleday & McClure Co.: 1898 (7-1/4x10-1/8", 88 pgs, color hardcover, B&W)

	FR1.0	GD2.0	FN6.0
nn	25.00	50.00	100.00

NOTE: *Reprints funny animal single panel and strip cartoons reprinted from LIFE. Art by Blaisdell, Chip Bellew, Kemble, Hy Mayer, Sullivant, Woolf.*

LIFE'S COMEDY (M,S)
Charles Scribner's Sons: Series 1 1897 - Series 3 1898 (12x9-3/8", hardcover, B&W)

	FR1.0	GD2.0	FN6.0
1 (142 pgs). 2, 3 (138 pgs)	60.00	120.00	240.00

NOTE: *Gibson a-1-3; c-3. Hy Mayer a-1-3. Rose O'Neill a-2-3. Stanlaws a-2-3. Sullivant a-1-2. Verbeek a-2. Wenzell a-1-3; c(painted)-2.*

LIFE, THE GOOD THINGS OF (M,S)
White, Stokes, & Allen, NY: 1884 - No.3 1886 ; Frederick A. Stokes, NY: No.4 1887; Frederick Stokes & Brother, NY: No.5 1888 - No.6 1889; Frederick A. Stokes Company, NY: No. 7 1890 - No.10 1893 (8-3/8x10-1/2", 74 pgs, gilted hardcover, B&W)

	FR1.0	GD2.0	FN6.0
nn - 1884 (most common issue)	32.50	65.00	130.00
2 - 1885	32.50	65.00	130.00
3 - 1886 (76 pgs)	32.50	65.00	130.00
4 - 1887 (76 pgs)	32.50	65.00	130.00
5 - 1888	32.50	65.00	130.00
6 - 1889	32.50	65.00	130.00
7 - 1890	32.50	65.00	130.00
8 - 1891 (scarce)	50.00	100.00	200.00
9 - 1892	32.50	65.00	130.00
10 - 1893	32.50	65.00	130.00

NOTE: *Contains mostly single panel, and some sequential, comics reprinted from LIFE. Allwood a-1-4,10. Roswell Bacon a-5. Chip Bellew a-4-6. Frank Bellew a-4,6. Palmer Cox a-1. H. E. Dey a-5. C. D. Gibson a-4-10. F.M. Howarth a-5-6. Kemble a-1-3. Klapp a-5. Walt McDougall a-1-2. H. McVickar a-5; J. A. Mitchell a-5. Peter Newell a-2-3. Gray Parker a-4-5,7. J. Smith a-5. Albert E. Steiner a-5; T. S. Sullivant a-7-9. Wenzell a-8-10. Wilder a-3. Woolf a-3-6.)*

LIFE, THE SPICE OF (E,M,)
White and Allen: NY & London: 1888 (8-3/8x10-1/2",76 pgs, hard-c, B&W)

	FR1.0	GD2.0	FN6.0
nn	50.00	100.00	200.00

NOTE: *Resembles* ***THE GOOD THINGS OF LIFE*** *in layout and format, and appears to be an attempt to compete with their former partner Frederick A. Stokes. However, the material is not from* ***LIFE****, but rather is reprinted and translated German sequential and single panel comics.*

LIFE'S PICTURE GALLERY (becomes LIFE'S PRINTS) (M,S,P)
Life Publishing Company, New York: nd (1898-1899) (paper cover, B&W) (all are scarce)

	FR1.0	GD2.0	FN6.0
nn - (nd; 1898, 100 pgs, 5-1/4x8-1/2") Gibson-c of a woman with closed umbrella; 1st interior page announcing that after January 1, 1899 Gibson will draw exclusively for LIFE; the word "SPECIMEN" is printed in red, diagonally, across every print; a-Gibson, Rose O'Neill, Sullivant	37.50	75.00	150.00
nn - (nd; 1899, 128 pgs, 4-7/8x7-3/8") Gibson-c of a woman golfer; 1st interior page announcing that Gibson & Hanna, Jr. draw exclusively for LIFE; the word "SPECIMEN" is printed in red, horizontally, across every print. Includes prints from Gibson's **THE EDUCATION OF MR. PIPP**; a-Gibson, Sullivant	37.50	75.00	150.00

NOTE: *Catalog of prints reprinted from* ***LIFE*** *covers & centerspreads. The first catalog was given away free to anyone requesting it, but after many people got the catalog without ordering anything, subsequent catalogs were sold at 10 cents.*

LITTLE SICK BEAR, THE
Edwin W. Joy Co, San Francisco, CA: 1897 (6-1/4x5", 20 pgs, B&W, Scarce)

	FR1.0	GD2.0	FN6.0
nn - By James Swinnerton one long sequential comic strip	200.00	400.00	800.00

LIGHT AND SHADE
William Drey Doppel Soap: 1892 (3-3/4x5-3/8", 20 pgs, B&W, color cover)

	FR1.0	GD2.0	FN6.0
nn - By J.C.	50.00	100.00	200.00

NOTE: Contains (8) panel comic strip of black boy whose skin turns white using this soap.

LONDON OUT OF TOWN, OR THE ADVENTURES OF THE BROWNS AT THE SEA SIDE BY LUKE LIMNER, ESQ. (O)
David Bogue, 86 Fleet St, London: c1847 (5-1/2x4-1/4, 32 pgs, yellow paper hard-c, B&W

	FR1.0	GD2.0	FN6.0
nn - By John Leighton	150.00	300.00	600.00

NOTE: one long sequential comic strip multiple-panel per page story; each page crammed with panels inspired by the Töpffer comic books Bogue began several years earlier.

LORGNETTE, THE (S)

Max and Maurice by Wilhelm Busch
1871 © Roberts Brothers, Boston

Merryman's Monthly v3#5 with Bellew strip
May 1865 © J. C. Haney & Co., New York

Minneapolis Journal Cartoons Second Series
1895 © Minneapolis Journal

FR1.0 GD2.0 FN6.0

George J Coombes, New York: 1886 (6-1/2x8-3/4, 38 pgs, hard-c, B&W)

nn - By J.K. Bangs 50.00 100.00 200.00

LOVING BALLAD OF LORD BATEMAN, THE (E,I)
G.W. Carleton & Co., Publishers, Madison Square, NY: 1871 (9x5-7/8",16 pgs, soft-c, 6¢)

nn - By George Cruikshank 50.00 100.00 200.00

MADISON'S EXPOSITION OF THE AWFUL & TERRIFYING CEREMONIES OF THE ODD FELLOWS
T.E. Peterson & Brothers, 306 Chestnut St, Phila: 1870s? (5-3/4x9-1/4, 68 pgs, B&W)
nn - single panel cartoons 50.00 100.00 200.00

MANNERS AND CUSTOMS OF YE HARVARD STUDENTE (M,S)
Houghton Mifflin & Co., Boston & Moses King, Cambridge: 1877 (7-7/8x11", 72 pgs, printed one side, hardc, B&W)

nn - by F.G. Attwood 75.00 150.00 300.00
NOTE: *Collection of cartoons originally serialized in the **Harvard Lampoon**. Attwood later became a major cartoonist for **Life**.*

MAN WHO WOULD LIKE TO MARRY, THE (O)
Frederick Warne & Co., London & New York: nd (c 1880's) (9-1/2x11-1/2", 28 pgs, printed 1 side, paper-c, B&W)

nn - By Harry Parkes 62.50 125.00 250.00
NOTE: *Published simultaneously with its companion volume, **The Girl Who Wouldn't Mind Getting Married**.*

MAX AND MAURICE: A JUVENILE HISTORY IN SEVEN TRICKS (E)
(see also Teasing Tom and Naughty Ned)
Roberts Brothers, Boston: 1871 first edition (8-1/8 x 5-1/2", 76 pgs, hard & soft-c B&W)

nn - By Wilhelm Busch (green or brown cloth hardbound) 275.00 550.00 1000.00
nn - exactly the same, but soft paper cover 162.00 325.00 650.00
NOTE: *Page count includes 56 pgs of art, two blank endpapers at the front (one colored), 8 pgs of ads at the back, two blank endpapers at the end (one colored), and the covers. Green or brown illustrated hardcover. The name of the author is given on the title page as "William Busch." We assume this to be the 1st edition. Back side of title page states: Entered according to Act of Congress, in the year 1870, by Roberts Brothers, In the office of the Librarian of Congress at Washington.*

nn - By Wilhelm Busch (1872 edition) 225.00 470.00 900.00
nn - 1875 reprint 100.00 200.00 450.00
nn - 1882 reprint (76 pgs, hand colored- c/a, 75¢) 100.00 200.00 400.00
nn- 1889 reprint with new art on cover printed in full color 100.00 200.00 400.00
NOTE: *Each of the above contains 56 pages of art and text in a transitional format between a regular children's book and a comic book (the page count difference is ad pages in back). Seminal inspiration for William Randolph Hearst to acquire as a "new comic" (following the wild success of Outcault's Yellow Kid) to license M&M from Busch and hire Rudolph Dirks in late 1897 to create a New York American newspaper incarnation. In Hearst's English language newspapers it was called The Katzenjammer Kids and in his German language NYC newspaper it was titled Max & Moritz, Busch's original title. At least 50 other reprints versions are reputed to exist printed thru 1900. Translated from the 1865 German original. We are still sorting out the edition confusion.*

MAX AND MAURICE: A JUVENILE HISTORY IN SEVEN TRICKS (E)
(see also Teasing Tom and Naughty Ned)
Little, Brown, and Company, Boston: 1898-1902 (8-1/8 x 5-3/4", 72 pgs, hardcover, black ink on orange paper) (various early reprints)

nn - 1898 , 1899 By Wilhelm Busch 50.00 100.00 200.00
nn - 1902 (64 pages, B&W) 10.00 30.00 90.00

MERRY MAPLE LEAVES Or A Summer In The Country (S)
E.P. Dutton And Company, New York: 1872 (9-3/8x7-3/8", 90 and 86 pgs pgs, hard-c)

nn - By Abner Perk 25.00 50.00 150.00
NOTE: *Each drawing contained in a maple leaf motif by Livingston Hopkins and others.*

MERRYMAN'S MONTHLY A COMIC MAGAZINE FOR THE FAMILY (M,O,E)
J.C. Haney & Co, NY: 1863-1875 (10-7/8x7-13/16", 30 pgs average, B&W)

Certain issues with sequential comics 100.00 200.00 400.00
NOTE: *Sequential strips by Frank Bellew Sr, Wilhelm Busch found so far; others?*

MERRYTHOUGHT, OR LAUGHTER FROM YEAR TO YEAR, THE
Fisher & Brother, Phila, Baltimore: early 1850s (4-1/2x7", B&W)
nn - many singles, some sequential (Very Rare) (no known sales)
NOTE: See Vict article for back cover pic which is earliest known use of the term Comic Book

MESSRS. BROWN, JONES, AND ROBINSON, THE FOREIGN TOUR OF
(see also **THE CLOWN, OR THE BANQUET OF WIT**) (E,M,O,G)
Bradbury & Evans, London: 1854 (11-5/8x9-1/2", 196 pgs, gilted hard-c, B&W)

nn - By Richard Doyle 35.00 70.00 200.00
nn - Bradbury & Evans 1900 reprint 20.00 40.00 80.00
NOTE: *Protective sheets between each page (not part of page count). Expanded and redrawn sequential comics story from the serialized episodes originally published in PUNCH. Also comes in a 174 pg 8-3/4x11" version.*

MESSRS. BROWN, JONES, AND ROBINSON, THE LAUGHABLE ADVENTURES OF (E,M,G)
Garrett, Dick & Fitzgerald, NY: nd (1856 or 1857) (5-3/4x9-1/4", 100 pgs, printed one side only, paper-c, B&W)

nn - (Very Rare) by Richard Doyle c/a 300.00 500.00 1000.00
NOTE: *1st American reprinting of the "Foreign Tour"; reformatted into a small oblong format. Links the earlier Garrett & Co. to the later Dick & Fitzgerald. Back cover reprints full size the Garrett & Co. version cover for Oscar Shanghai. Interior front cover reprints full size the Garrett & Co. version cover for Slyfox-Wikof. Issued without a title page.*

FR1.0 GD2.0 FN6.0

MESSRS. BROWN, JONES, AND ROBINSON, THE FOREIGN TOUR OF (E,M,G)
D. Appleton & Co., New York: 1860 & 1877 (11-5/8x9-1/2", 196 pgs, gilted hard-c, B&W)

nn - (1860 printing) by Richard Doyle 30.00 60.00 200.00
nn - (1871 printing) by Richard Doyle 30.00 60.00 150.00
nn - (1877 printing) by Richard Doyle 30.00 60.00 150.00
NOTE: *Protective sheets between each page (not part of page count). Reprints the Bradbury & Evans edition.*

MESSRS BROWN JONES AND ROBINSON, THE AMERICAN TOUR OF (O,G)
D. Appleton & Co., New York: 1872 (11-5/8x9-1/2", 158 pgs, printed one side only, B&W, green gilted hard-c)

nn - By Toby 70.00 140.00 400.00
NOTE: *Original American graphic novel sequel to Richard Doyle's Foreign Tour of Brown, Jones, and Robinson, with the same characters visiting New York, Canada, and Cuba. Protective sheets between each page (not part of page count).*

MESSRS. BROWN, JONES, AND ROBINSON, THE LAUGHABLE ADVEN. OF (E,M,G)
Dick & Fitzgerald, NY: nd (late 1870's - 1888) (5-3/4x9-1/4", 100 pgs, printed one side only, green paper-c, B&W)

nn - (Scarce) by Richard Doyle 100.00 200.00 450.00
NOTE: *Reprints the Garrett, Dick & Fitzgerald printing, with the following changes: Takes what had been page 12 in the Garrett, D&F printing (art by M.H. Henry), and makes it a title page, which is numbered page 1. The first story page, "Go to the Races", is numbered 2 (whereas it is numbered 1 in the Garrett, Dick & Fitzgerald version). Numbering stays ahead of the G,D&F edition by 1 page up through page 12, after which the page numbering becomes identical.*

MINNEAPOLIS JOURNAL CARTOONS (N,S)
Minneapolis Journal: nn 1894 - No.2 1895 (7-3/4" x 10-7/8", 76 pgs, B&W, paper-c)

nn (1894) (Rare) 50.00 100.00 200.00
Second Series (1895) (Rare) 50.00 100.00 200.00
nn- "War Cartoons" Jan 1899 (9x8", 160 pgs, paperback, punched & string bound) (Scarce) 24.00 96.00 170.00

NOTE: *Reprints single panel cartoons from the prior year, by Charles "Bart" L. Bartholomew.*

MISCHIEF BOOK, THE (E)
R. Worthington, New York: 1880 (7-1/8 x 10-3/4", 176 pgs, hard-c, B&W)

nn - Green cloth binding; green on brown cover; cover art by R. Lewis based on Busch art by Wilhelm Busch 175.00 350.00 735.00
nn - Blue cloth binding; hand colored cover; completely different cover art based on Busch by Wilhelm Busch 175.00 350.00 735.00
NOTE: *Translated by Abby Langdon Alger. American published anthology collection of Wilhelm Busch comic strips. Includes two of the strips found in the British "Bushel of Merry-Thoughts" collection, translated better, and with the dropped panel restored. Unknown which cover version was first.*

MISSES BROWN, JONES AND ROBINSON, THE FOREIGN TOUR OF THE (E,O,G)
Bickers & Sons, London: nd (c1850's) (12-1/4" x 9-7/8", 108 pgs, printed on one side, B&W, hard-c)

nn- "by Miss Brown" (Rare) 100.00 200.00 400.00
NOTE: *A female take on Doyle's Foreign Tour, by an unknown woman artist, using the pseudonym "Miss Brown."*

MISS MILLY MILLEFLEUR'S CAREER (S)
Sheldon & Co., NY: 1869 (10-3/4x9-7/8", 74 pgs, purple hard-c)

nn - Artist unknown (Rare) 75.00 150.00 300.00

MR PODGER AT COUP'S GREATEST SHOW ON EARTH HIS HAPS AND MISHAPS, THE ADVENTURES OF (O,S)
W.C. Coup, New York: 1884 (5-5/8x4-1/4", 20 pgs, color-c, B&W)

nn - Circus Themes; Similar to Barker's Comic Almanacs 20.00 40.00 80.00

MR. TOODLES' GREAT ELEPHANT HUNT (See Peter Piper in Bengal)
Brother Jonathan, NYC: 1850s (4-1/4x7-7/8", page count presently unknown)

nn - catalog contains comic strip (Very Rare) (no known sales)

MR. TOODLES' TERRIFIC ELEPHANT HUNT
Dick & Fitzgerald, NYC: 1860s (5-3/4x9-1/4", 32 pgs, paper-c, B&W) (Very Rare)

nn - catalog reprint contains 28 panel comic strip 150.00 300.00 600.00

MRS GRUNDY
Mrs Grundy Publishing Co, NYC: July 8 1865-Sept 30 1865 (weekly)

1-13 Thomas Nast, Hoppin, Stephens, 50.00 100.00 200.00

MUSEUM OF WONDERS, A (O,I)
Routledge & Sons: 1894 (13x10", 64 pgs, color-c, color thru out)

nn - By Frederick Opper 100.00 200.00 450.00

MY FRIEND WRIGGLES, A (Laughter) Moving Panorama, of His Fortunes And Misfortunes, Illustrated With Over 200 Engravings, of Most Comic Catastrophes And Side-Splitting Merriment) (O,G)
Stearn & Co, 202 Williams St, NY: 1850s (5-7/8x9-3/4", 100 pgs, B&W)

nn - By S. P. Avery (also the engraver) (Very Rare) 200.00 400.00 800.00

MY SKETCHBOOK (E,S)
Dana Estes & Charles E. Lauriat, Boston; J. Sabins & Sons, New York: circa 1880s (9-3/8x12", brown hard-c)

nn - By George Cruikshank 25.00 50.00 150.00
NOTE: *Reprints British editions 1834-36; extensive usage of word balloons.*

Nasby's Life Of Andy Jonson
1866 © Jesse Haney Company

99 "Woolf's" from Truth
1896 © Truth Company

The Adventures of Obadiah Oldbuck 4th printing
mid-1850s © Brother Jonathan Offices, NY

FR1.0 GD2.0 FN6.0

NASBY'S LIFE OF ANDY JONSON (O, M)
Jesse Haney Co., Publishers No. 119 Nassau St, NY: 1866 (4-1/2x7-1/2, 48 pgs, B&W)
nn - President Andrew Johnson satire — 100.00 — 200.00 — 450.00
NOTE: Blurb further reads: With a True Pictorial History of His STumping Tour Out West By Petroleum V. Nasby, A Dimmicrat of Thirty Years Standing, And Who Allus Tuk His Licker Straight. Front of book has long sequential comic strip satire on President Andrew Johnson, misspelling his name on the cover on purpose.

NAST'S ILLUSTRATED ALMANAC
Harper & Brothers, Franklin Square, NYC: 1872-1874 (8x5.5", 80 pgs, B&W, 35¢)
nn — 60.00 — 120.00 — 240.00

NAST'S WEEKLY (O,S)
???: 1892-93 (Quarto Weekly)
all issues scarce — 50.00 — 100.00 — 200.00

NATIONAL COMIC ALMANAC
An Association of Gentlemen, Boston: 1838-?? (8.25x4.75", 34 pgs, B&W)
nn — 60.00 — 120.00 — 240.00

NEW AMERICAN COMIC ALL-IMAKE (ELTON'S BASKET OF COMICAL SCRAPS), THE
Elton, Publisher, New York: 1839 (7-1/2x4-5/8, 24 pgs)
1 — 100.00 — 200.00 — 400.00

NEW BOOK OF NONSENSE, THE: A Contribution To The Great Central Fair In Aid of the Sanitary Commission (O,S)
Ashmead & Evans, No. 724 Chestnut St, Philadelphia: June 1864 (red hard-c)
nn - Artists unknown (Scarce) — 50.00 — 150.00 — 300.00

NEW YORK ILLUSTRATED NEWS
Frank Leslie, NYC: 10/14/76-June 1884
average issues with comic strips — 10.00 — 20.00 — 40.00

NEW YORK PICAYUNE (see PHUN FOTOCRAFT)
Woodward & Hutchings: 1850-1855 newspaper-size weekly; 1856-1857 Folio Monthly 16x10.5; 1857-1858 Quarto Weekly; 1858-1860 Quarto Weekly
Average Issue With Comic Strips — 50.00 — 100.00 — 200.00
Issues with Full Front Page Comic Strip — 100.00 — 200.00 — 400.00
NOTE: *Many Issues contain Frank Bellew sequential comic strips & single panel cartoons. Later issues published by Woodward, Levison & Robert Gun (1853-1857) ; Levison & Thompson (1857-1860)*

NICK-NAX
Levison & Haney, NY: 1857-1858? (11x7-3/4", 32 pgs, B&W, paper-c)
v2 #10 Feb 1858 has many single panel cartoons — 50.00 — 100.00 — 200.00

99 "WOOLFS" FROM TRUTH (see Sketches of Lowly Life in a Great City, Truth)
Truth Company, NY: 1896 (9x5-1/2", 72 pgs, varnished paper-like cloth hard-c, 25 cents)
nn - By Michael Angelo Woolf (Rare) — 150.00 — 300.00 — 600.00
NOTE: *Woolf's cartoons are regarded as a primary influence on R.F. Outcault in the later development of The Yellow Kid newspaper strip. Copy sold in 2002 on eBay for $800.00.*

NONSENSE OR, THE TREASURE BOX OF UNCONSIDERED TRIFLES
Fisher & Brother, 12 North Sixth St, Phila, PA, 64 Baltimore St, Baltimore, MD: early 1850s (4-1/2x7", 128 pgs, B&W)
nn - much Davy Crocket sequential story-telling comic strips — 250.00 — 500.00 — 1000.00

OBADIAH OLDBUCK, THE ADVENTURES OF MR. (E,G)
Tilt & Bogue, London: nd (1840-41) (5-15/16x9-3/16", 176 pgs,B&W, gilted hard-c)
nn - By Rodolphe Töpffer — 700.00 — 1200.00 — 2800.00
nn - Hand coloured edition (Very Rare) — (no known sales)
NOTE: *This is the British edition, translating the unauthorized redrawn 1839 edition from Parisian publisher Aubert, adapted from Töpffer's "Les Amours de Mr. Vieux Bois" (aka "Histoire de Mr. Vieux Bois"), originally published in French in Switzerland, in 1837 (2nd ed. 1839). Early 19th century books are often found rebound, with original cover and/or title page gone. To distinguish editions having no cover or title page: the British oblong editions (published by Tilt & Bogue) use Roman Numerals to number pages. American oblong shaped editions use Arabic Numerals. British are printed on one side only. This is the earliest known English language sequential comic book. Has a new title page with art by Robert Cruikshank.*

OBADIAH OLDBUCK, THE ADVENTURES OF MR. (E,G)
Wilson and Company, New York: September 14, 1842 (11-3/4x9", 44 pgs, B&W, yellow paper-c on bookstand editions, hemp paper interior)
Brother Jonathan Extra No. IX - Rare bookstand edition — 2500.00 — 5000.00 — 10000.00
Brother Jonathan Extra No. IX Very Rare subscriber/mailorder — 2500.00 — 5000.00 — 10000.00
NOTE: *By Rodolphe Töpffer. Earliest known sequential American comic book, reprinting the 1841 British edition. Pages are numbered via Roman numerals. States "BROTHER JONATHAN EXTRA - ADVENTURES OF MR. OBADIAH OLDBUCK." at the top of each page. Prints 2 to 3 tiers of panels on both sides of each page. Copies could be had for ten cents according to adverts in* ***Brother Jonathan****. By Rodolphe Töpffer with cover masthead design by David Claypool Johnston, and cover art beneath the masthead reprinting Robert Cruikshank's title page art from the Tilt & Bogue edition. A special, additional cover was added for copies sold on stands (it was not issued with mail order or subscriber copies). Only 1 known copy possesses (partially) this very thin outer yellow cover. A decent (subscriber) copy sold on eBay in later October 2002 for over $3500.00. In 2005, a FR copy sold for $10,000; a G/VG for $20,000; and a VG for $20,000. A copy GVG sold in auction in 2007 for $9500. (Prices vary widely.)*

OBADIAH OLDBUCK, THE ADVENTURES OF MR. (E,G)
Wilson & Co, New York: nd (1849) (5-11/16x8-3/8", 84 pgs, B&W,paper-c)
nn - by Rodolphe Töpffer; title page by Robert Cruikshank (Very Rare) — 500.00 — 1200.00 — 4000.00
NOTE: *2nd Wilson & Co printing, reformatted into a small oblong format, with nine panels edited out, and text modified to smooth out this removal. Results in four less printed tiers/strips. Pages are numbered via Arabic numerals. Every panel on Pages 11, 14, 19, 21, 24, 34, 35 has one line of text. Reformatted to conform with British first edition.*

OBADIAH OLDBUCK, THE ADVENTURES OF MR. (E,G)
Wilson & Co, 162 Nassau, NY: nd (early-1850s) (5-11/16x8-3/8", 84 pgs, B&W, yellow-c
nn - 3rd USA Printing by Rodolphe Töpffer; title page by Robert Cruikshank (Very Rare) Says By Timothy Crayon, an obvious pseudonym — 800.00 — 1600.00 — 4500.00
NOTE: *Front cover banner the giant is holding says "Done With Drawings By Timothy Crayon, Gypsographer, 188 Comic Etchings On Antimony" Title page changes address to No. 15 Spruce-Street. (Late 162 Nassau Street.)*

OBADIAH OLDBUCK, THE ADVENTURES OF MR..
Brother Jonathan Offices: ND (mid-1850s) (5-11/16x8-3/8", 84 pages, B&W, oblong)
nn - 4th printing; Originally by Rodolphe Töpffer (Very Rare) — 500.00 — 1200.00 — 4000.00
NOTE: *Cover States: "New York: Published at the Brother Jonathan Office". Front cover banner the giant is holding says "Done With Drawings By Timothy Crayon, Gypsographer, 188 Comic Designs On Antimony."*

OBADIAH OLDBUCK, THE ADVENTURES OF MR. (E,G)
Dick & Fitzgerald, New York: nd (various printings; est. 1870s to 1888) (Thirty Cents, 84 pgs, B&W, paper-c) (all versions scarce)
nn - Black print on green cover(5-11/16x8-15/16"); string bound — 200.00 — 400.00 — 800.00
nn - Black print on blue cover; same format as green-c — 200.00 — 400.00 — 800.00
nn - Black print on white cover(5-13/16x9-3/16"); staple bound beneath cover); this is a later printing than the blue or green-c — 200.00 — 400.00 — 800.00
NOTE: *Reprints the abbreviated 1849 Wilson & Co. 2nd printing. Pages are numbered via Arabic numerals. Many of the panels on Pages 11, 14, 19, 21, 24, 34, 35 take two lines to print the same words found in the Wilson & Co version, which used only one text line for the same panels. Unknown whether the blue or green cover is earlier. White cover version has "thirty cents" line blackened out on the two copies known to exist. Robert Cruikshank's title page has been made the cover in the D&F editions.*

OLD FOGY'S COMIC ALMANAC
Philip J. Cozans, NY: 1858 (4-7/8x7-1/4, 48 pgs)
nn - sequential comic strip told one panel per page — 50.00 — 100.00 — 200.00
NOTE: Contains (12) panel "Fourth of July in New York" sequential

OLD MOTHER MITTEN AND HER FUNNY KITTEN (see also **The Juvenile Gem**) (O)
Huestis & Cozans: nd(1850-1852) (6x3-7/8"12pgs, hand colored paper-c, B&W)
nn - first printing(s) publisher's address is 104 Nassau Street (1850-1851) (Very Rare) — (no known sales)
NOTE: *A hand colored outer cover is highly rare, with only 1 recorded copy possessing it. Front cover image and text is repeated precisely on page 3 (albeit b&w), and only interior pages are numbered, together leading owners of coverless copies to believe they have the cover. The true back cover has ads for the publisher. Cover was issued only with copies which were sold separately books which were bound together as part of THE JUVENILE GEM never had such covers.*

OLD MOTHER MITTEN AND HER FUNNY KITTEN (see JUVENILE GEM) (O)
Philip J. Cozans: nd (1850-1852) (6x3-7/8",12 pgs, hand colored paper-c, B&W)
nn - Second printing(s) publisher's address is 116 Nassau Street (1851-1852) (Very Rare) — (no known sales)
nn - Third printing(s) publisher's address is 107 Nassau Street (1852+) (Very Rare) — (no known sales)

OLD MOTHER MITTEN AND HER FUNNY KITTEN
Americana Review, Scotia, NY: nd (1960's) (6-1/4x4-1/8", 8 pgs, side-stapled, cardboard, B&W)
nn - Modern reprint — 2.50 — 5.00 — 10.00
NOTE: *Issued within a folder titled SIX CHILDREN'S BOOKS OF THE 1850'S. States "Reprinted by American Review" at bottom of front cover. Reprints the 104 Nassau Street address.*

ON THE NILE (O,G)
James R. Osgood & Co., Boston: 1874 ; **Houghton, Osgood & Co., Boston:** 1880 (112 pgs, gilted green hardcover, B&W)
1st printing (1874; 10-3/4x16") - by Augustus Hoppin — 45.00 — 90.00 — 180.00
2nd printing (1880; smaller sized) — 32.50 — 65.00 — 130.00

OSCAR SHANGHAI, THE EXTRAORDINARY AND MIRTH-PROVKING ADVENTURES BY SEA & LAND OF (O, G)
Garrett & Co., Publishers, No. 18 Ann Street, New York: May 1855 (5-3/4x9-1/4", 100 pgs, printed one side only, paper-c, 25¢, B&W)
nn - Samuel Avery-c; interior by ALC Very Rare) — 1000.00 — 2000.00 — 4000.00
NOTE: *Not much is known of this first edition as the data comes from a recently rediscovered* ***Brother Jonathan*** *catalog issued circa 1853-55. No original known yet to exist.*

OSCAR SHANGHAI, THE WONDERFUL AND AMUSING DOINGS BY SEA AND LAND OF (G)
Dick & Fitzgerald, 10 Ann St, NY: nd (1870s-1888) (25 ¢, 5-3/4x9-1/4", 100 pgs, printed one side only, green paper c, B&W)
nn - Cover by Samuel Avery; interior by ALC (Rare) — 300.00 — 500.00 — 1000.00
NOTE: *Exact reprint of Garrett & Co original.*

OUR ARTIST IN CUBA (O)
Carleton, New York: 1865 (6-5/8x4-3/8", 120 pgs, printed one side only, gilted hard-c, B&W)
nn - By Geo. W. Carleton — 37.50 — 75.00 — 150.00

OUR ARTIST IN CUBA, PERU, SPAIN, AND ALGIERS (O)
Carleton: 1877 (6-1/2x5-1/8", 156 pgs, hard-c, B&W)
nn - By Geo. W. Carleton — 50.00 — 100.00 — 200.00
nn - By Geo. W. Carleton (wraps paper cover) (Rare) — 45.00 — 90.00 — 180.00

The Wonderful and Amusing Doings by Sea & Land of Oscar Shanghai
1870s © Dick & Fitzgerald, New York

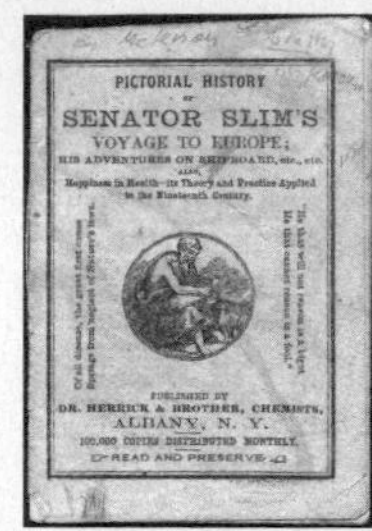

Pictorial History of Senator Slim's Voyage To Europe
1860 © Dr. Herrick & Brother, Albany, NY

Puck #1
1877 © Keppler & Schwarzman, NY

FR1.0 GD2.0 FN6.0

NOTE: *Reprints OUR ARTIST IN CUBA and OUR ARTIST IN PERU, then adds new section on Spain and Algiers.*

OUR ARTIST IN PERU (O)
Carleton, New York: 1866 (7-3/4x5-7/8", 68 pgs, gilted hardcover, B&W)

nn- By Geo. W. Carleton 37.50 75.00 150.00
NOTE: *Contains advertisement for the upcoming books* ***OUR ARTIST IN ITALY*** *and* ***OUR ARTIST IN FRANCE****, but no such publications have been found to date.*

PARSON SOURBALL'S EUROPEAN TOUR (O)
Duff and Ashmead: 1867 (6x7-1/2", 76 pgs, blue embossed title hard-c)
nn - By Horace Cope 100.00 200.00 400.00
NOTE: see **REV. MR. SOURBALL'S EUROPEAN TOUR, THE** for the soft paper cover version

PEN AND INK SKETCHES OF YALE NOTABLES (O,S)
Soule, Thomas and Winsor, St. Louis: 1872 (12-1/4x9-3/4", B&W)

By Squills 25.00 50.00 100.00
NOTE: *Printed by Steamlith Press, The R.P. Studley Company, St Louis.*

PETER PIPER IN BENGAL
Bengamin H Day.Publisher, Brother Jonathan Cheap Book Establishment, 48 Beekman, NY: 1953-55 (6-5/8x4-1/4, 36 pgs, yellow paper-c, B&W, 3 cents - two dollars per hundred) (Very Rare)

nn - By John Tenniel - 32 panel comic strip Punch-r 500.00 1000.00 2000.00
NOTE: *Actually also a catalog of inexpensive books, prints, maps and half a dozen comic books for sale on separate pages from publishers Day and Garrett - see full story of this brand new find in the Victorian Era essay. A complete copy with split spine sold in November 2002 for $750.00. Published date most likely 1855.*

THE PHILADELPHIA COMIC ALMANAC (S)
G. Strong, 44 Strawberry St, NYC: 1835 (8-1/2x5", 36 pgs)
nn - 100.00 200.00 600.00
NOTE: 77 engravings full of recurring cartoon characters but not sequential; early use of recurring characters.

PHIL MAY'S SKETCH BOOK (E,S,M)
R.H. Russell, New York: 1899 (14-5/8x10", 64 pgs, brown hard-c, B&W)

nn - By Phil May 32.50 65.00 130.00
NOTE: *American reprint of the British edition.*

PHUNNY PHELLOW, THE
Oakie, Dayton & Jones: Oct 1859-1876; **Street & Smith** 1876: (Folio Monthly)

average issue with Thomas Nast 50.00 100.00 200.00

PHUN FOTOCRAFT, KEWREUS KONSEETS KOMICALLY ILLUSTRATED BY A KWEER FELLER (N) (see **NEW YORK PICAYUNE**)
The New York Picayune, NY: 1850s (104 pgs)

nn - Mostly Frank Bellew, some John Leach 250.00 500.00 1000.00
NOTE: Many sequential comic strips as well as single cartoons all collected from The New York Picayune. Ross & Tousey, Agents, 121 Nassau St, NY. The Picayune ran many sequential comic strips in its decade.

PICTORIAL HISTORY OF SENATOR SLIM'S VOYAGE TO EUROPE
Dr. Herrick & Brother, Chemists, Albany, NY: 1860 (3-1/4x4-3/4", 32 pgs, B&W)

nn - By John McLenan Very Rare 150.00 300.00 600.00

PICTURES OF ENGLISH SOCIETY (Parchment-Paper Series, No.4) (M,S,E)
D. Appleton & Co., New York: 1884 (5-5/8x4-3/8", 108 pgs, paper-c, B&W)

4 - By George du Maurier; Punch-r 15.00 30.00 60.00
NOTE: *Every other page is a full page cartoon, with the opposite page containing the cartoon's caption.*

PICTURES OF LIFE AND CHARACTER (M,S,E)
Bradbury and Evans, London: No.1 1855 - No.5 c1864 (12-1/2x18", 100 pgs, illustrated hard-c, B&W)

nn (No.1) (1855) 32.50 65.00 130.00
2 (1858), 3 (1860) 32.50 65.00 130.00
4 (nd; c1862) 5 (nd; c1864) 32.50 65.00 130.00
nn (nd (late 1860's) 32.50 65.00 130.00
NOTE: 2-1/2x18-1/4", 494 pgs, green gilted-c) reprints 1-5 in one book
1-3 John Leech's... (nd; 12-3/8x10", ? pgs, red gilted-c). 25.00 50.00 100.00
NOTE: *Reprints John Leech cartoons from* ***Punch****. note that the Volume Number is mentioned only on the last page of these versions.*

PICTURES OF LIFE AND CHARACTER (E,M,S)
G.P. Putnam's Sons: 1880's (8-5/8x6-1/4", 218 pgs, hardcover, color-cr, B&W)

nn - John Leech (single panel **Punch** cartoon-r) 20.00 40.00 160.00
NOTE: *Leech reprints which extend back to the 1850s.*

PICTURES OF LIFE AND CHARACTER (Parchment-Paper Series) (E,M,S)
(see also Humerous Masterpieces)
D. Appleton & Co., NY: 1884 (30¢, 5-3/4 x 4-1/2", 104 pgs, paper-c, B&W)

nn - John Leech (single panel **Punch** cartoon-r) 20.00 40.00 160.00
NOTE: *An advertisment in the back refers to a cloth-bound edition for 50 cents.*

PIPPIN AMONG THE WIDE-AWAKES (O,S)
Werill & Chapin, 113 Nassau St, NYC, NY): 1860 (6x4-1/2", 36 pgs, 6 cents)

nn - Artist unknown (Very Rare) 100.00 200.00 400.00

PLISH AND PLUM (E.G)
Roberts Brothers, Boston: 1883 (8-1/8x5-3/4", 80 pgs, hardcover, B&W)

nn - By Wilhelm Busch 40.00 80.00 200.00
nn - Reprint (Roberts Brothers, 1895) 40.00 80.00 200.00
nn - Reprint (Little, Brown & Co., 1899) 40.00 80.00 200.00
NOTE: *The adventures of two dogs.*

POUNDS OF FUN
Frank Tousey, 34 North Moore St, NY: 1881 (6-1/2x9-1/2", 68pgs, B&W)
nn - Bellew, Worth, Woolf, Chips 40.00 80.00 200.00

PRESIDENTS MESSAGE, THE
G.P. Putnam's Sons, NY: 1887 (5-3/4x7-5/8, 44 pgs)
nn - (19) Thomas Nast single panel full page cartoons 40.00 80.00 200.00

PROTECT THE U.S. FROM JOHN BULL - PROTECTION PICTURES FROM JUDGE
Judge Publishing, New York: 1888 ((10 cents, 6-7/8x10-3/8", 36 pgs, paper-c, B&W)

nn - (Scarce) 25.00 50.00 100.00
NOTE: *Reprints both cartoons and commentary from* ***Puck****, concerning the issue of tariffs which were then being debated in Congress. Art by Gillam, Hamilton, Victor.*

PUCK (German language edition, St. Louis) (M,O) (see also Die Vehme)
Publisher unknown, St. Louis: No.1, March 18, 1871 - No. ??, Aug. 24, 1872 (B&W, paper-c)

1-?? (Very Rare) by Joseph Keppler (no known sales)
NOTE: *Joseph Keppler's second attempt at a weekly humor periodical, following* ***Die Vehme*** *one year earlier. This was his first attempt to launch using the title* ***Puck****. This German language version ran for a full year before being joined by an English language version.*

PUCK (English language edition, St. Louis) (M,O)
Publisher unknown, St. Louis: No.1, March ?? 1872 - No. ??, Aug. 24, 1872 (B&W, paper c)

1-?? (Very Rare) by Joseph Keppler (no known sales)
NOTE: *Same material as in the German language edition, but in English.*

PUCK, ILLUSTRIRTES HUMORISTISCHES WOCHENBLATT (German language edition, NYC) (M,O)
Keppler & Schwarzmann, New York: No.1 Sept (27) 1876 - 1164 Dec ?? 1899 (10 cents, color front/back-c and centerspread, remainder B&W, paper-c)

1-26 (Volume 1; Rare) by Joseph Keppler - these issues precede the English language version, and contain cartoons not found in them. Includes cartoons on the controversial Tilden-Hayes 1876 Presidential Election debacle. (no known sales)
27-52 (Volume 2; Rare) by Joseph Keppler - contains some cartoon material not found in the English language editions. Particularly in the earlier issues. (no known sales)
53-1164 7.50 15.00 30.00
Bound Volumes (six month, 26 issue run each):
Vol. 1 (Rare) (no known sales)
Vol. 2-4 (Rare) (no known sales)
Vol. 5-47 62.50 125.00 250.00
NOTE: *Joseph Keppler's second, and successful, attempt to launch* ***Puck****. In German. The first six months precede the launch of the English language edition. Soon after (but not immediately after) the launch of the English edition, both editions began sharing the same cartoons, but, their prose material always remained different. The German language edition ceased publication at the end of 1899, while the English language edition continued into the early 20th Century. First American periodical to feature printed color every issue.*

PUCK (English language edition, NYC) (M,O)
Keppler & Schwarzmann, New York: No.1 March (14) 1877 - 1190 Dec ?? 1899 (10 cents, color front/back-c and centerspread, remainder B&W, paper-c)

1 (Rare) by Joseph Keppler (no known sales)
2-26 (Rare) by Joseph Keppler (no known sales)
27-1190 12.50 25.00 50.00
(see Platinum Age section for year 1900+ issues)
Bound volumes (six month, 26 issue run each):
Vol. 1 (Rare) (one set sold on eBay for $2300.00)
Vol. 2 (Scarce) (one set sold on eBay for $1500.00)
Vol. 3-6 (pre-1880 issues) 175.00 375.00 750.00
Vol. 7-46 140.00 300.00 600.00
NOTE: *The English language editions began six months after the German editions, and so the English edition numbering is always one volume number, and 26 issue numbers, behind its parallel German language edition. Pre-1880 & post-1900 issues are more scarce than 1880's & 1890's.*

PUCK (miniature) (M,P,I)
Keppler & Schwarzmann, New York: nd (c1895) (7x5-1/8", 12 pgs, color front & back paper-c, B&W interior)

nn - Scarce 25.00 50.00 110.00
NOTE: *C.J.Taylor-c; F.M.Howarth-a; F.Opper-a; giveaway item promoting* ***Puck's*** *various publications. Mostly text, with art reprinted from* ***Puck****.*

PUCK, CARTOONS FROM (M,S)
Keppler & Schwarzmann, New York: 1893 (14-1/4x11-1/2", 244 pgs, hard-c, mostly B&W)

nn - by Joseph Keppler (Signed and Numbered) 100.00 200.00 400.00
NOTE: *Reprints Keppler cartoons from 1877 to 1893, mostly in B&W, though a few in color, with a text opposite each cartoon explaining the situation then being satirized. Issued only in an edition of 300 numbered issues, signed by Keppler. Only 1/4 of the pages are cartoons.*

PUCK'S LIBRARY (M)
Keppler & Schwarzmann, New York: No.1, July, 1887 - No. 174, Dec, 1899 (10 cents, 11-1/2x8-1/4", 36 pgs, color paper-c, B&W)

1- "The National Game" (Baseball) 50.00 100.00 200.00
2-149 10.00 20.00 40.00
NOTE: ***Puck's Library*** *was a monthly magazine reprinting cartoons & prose from* ***Puck****, with each issue's*

Rays of Light
1886 © Morse Bros., Canton, Mass.

Scraps, New Series #1 by D.C. Johnston
1849 © D.C. Johnston, Boston

Shakespeare Would Ride A Bicycle If Alive Today
1896 © Cleveland Bicycles, Toledo, OH.

FR1.0 GD2.0 FN6.0

material organized around the same subject. The cover art was often original. All issues were kept in print for the duration of the series, so later issues are more scarce than earlier ones.

PUCK, PICKINGS FROM (M)
Keppler & Schwarzmann, New York: No.1, Sept, 1891 - No. 34, Dec, 1899 (25 cents, 13-1/4x10-1/4", 68 pgs, color paper-c, B&W)

1-34 Scarce 15.00 30.00 60.00
NOTE: *Similar to* ***Puck's Library****, except larger in size, and issued quarterly. All reprint material, except for the cover art. There also exist variations with "RAILROAD EDITION 30 CENTS" printed on the cover in place of the standard 25 cent price.*

PUCK'S OPPER BOOK (M)
Keppler & Schwarzmann, New York: 1888 (11-3/4x13-7/8", color paper-c, 68 pgs,interior B&W, 30¢)

nn - (Very Rare) by F. Opper 225.00 450.00 750.00
NOTE: *Puck's first book collecting work by a single artist.; mostly sequential comic strips.*

PUCK'S PRINTING BOOK FOR CHILDREN (S,O,I)
Keppler & Schwarzman, Pubs, NY: 1891 (10-3/8x7-7/8", 52 pgs, color-c, B&W and color)

nn - Frederick B Opper (Very Rare) (no known sales)
NOTE: *Left side printed in color; Right side B&W to be colored in.*

PUCK PROOFS (M,P,S)
Keppler & Schwarzmann, New York: nd (1906-1909) (74 pgs, paper cover; B&W) (all are Scarce)

nn - (c.1906, no price, 4-1/8x5-1/4") B&W painted -c of couple kissing over a chess board; 1905 & 1906-r 25.00 50.00 100.00
nn- (c.1909, 10 cents, 4-3/8x5-3/8") plain green paper-c; 76 pgs 1905-1909-r 25.00 50.00 100.00
NOTE: *Catalog of prints available from* ***Puck****, reprinting mostly cover & centerspread art from* ***Puck****. There likely exist more as yet unreported* ***Puck Proofs*** *catalogs. Art by Rose O'Neill.*

PUCK, THE TARIFF ?, CARTOONS AND COMMENTS FROM (M,S)
Keppler & Schwarzmann, New York: 1888 (10 cents, 6-7/8x10-3/8", 36 pgs, paper-c, B&W)

nn - (Scarce) 37.50 75.00 200.00
NOTE: *Reprints both cartoons and commentary from* ***Puck****, concerning the issue of tariffs which were then being debated in Congress. Art by Gillam, Keppler, Opper, Taylor*

PUCK, WORLD'S FAIR
Keppler & Schwarzmann, PUCK BUILDING, World's Fair Grounds, Chicago: No.1 May 1, 1893 - No.26 Oct 30, 1893 (10 cents, 11-1/4x8-3/4, 14 pgs, paper-c, color front/back/center pages, rest B&W)(All issues Scarce to Rare)

1-26 30.00 60.00 130.00
1-26 bound volume: 500.00 1100.00 2200.00
NOTE: *Art by Joseph Keppler, F. Opper, F.M. Howarth, C.J. Taylor, W.A. Rogers. This was a separate, parallel run of* ***Puck****, published during the 1893 Chicago World's Fair from within the fairgrounds, and containing all new and different material than the regular weekly* ***Puck****. Smaller sized and priced the same, this originally sold poorly, and had not as wide distribution as* ***Puck****, and so consequently issues are much more rare than regular* ***Puck*** *issues from the same period. Not to be confused with the larger sized regular* ***Puck*** *issues from 1893 which sometimes also contained World's Fair related material, and sometimes had the words "World's Fair" appear on the cover. Can also be distinguished by the fact that* ***Puck's*** *issue numbering was in the 800's in 1893, while these issue number 1 through 26.*

PUNCHINELLO
Punchinello Publishing Co, NYC: April 2-Dec 24 1870 (weekly)

1-39 Henry L. Stephens, Frank Bellew, Bowlend 12.50 25.00 50.00
NOTE: *Funded by the Tweed Ring, mild politics attacking Grant Admin & other NYC newspapers. Bound copies exist.*

QUIDDITIES OF AN ALASKAN TRIP (O,G)
G.A. Steel & Co., Portland, OR: 1873 (6-3/4x10-1/2", 80 pgs, gilted hard-c, Red-c and Blue-c exist, B&W)

nn - By William H. Bell (Scarce) 350.00 750.00 1500.00
NOTE: *Highly sought Western Americana collectors. Parody of a trip from Washington DC to Alaska, by a member of the team which went to survey Alaska, purchase commonly known then as "Seward's Folly".*

"RAG TAGS" AND THEIR ADVENTURES, THE (N,S)
A. M. Robertson, San Francisco: 1899 (10-1/4x13-7/8, 84 pgs, color hard-c, B&W inside)

nn - By Arthur M. Lewis (SF Chronicle newspaper-r) (Scarce) 60.00 120.00 240.00

RAYS OF LIGHT (O,P)
Morse Bros., Canton, Mass.: No.1 1886 (7-1/8x5-1/8", 8 pgs, color paper-c, B&W)

1- (Rare) 50.00 100.00 200.00
NOTE: *Giveaway pamphlet in guise of an educational publication, consisting entirely of a sequential story in which a teacher instructs her classroom of young girls in the use of Rising Sun Stove Polish. Color front & back covers.*

RELIC OF THE ITALIAN REVOLUTION OF 1849, A
Gabici's Music Stores, New Orleans: 1849 (10-1/8x12-3/4", 144 pgs, hardcover)

nn - By G. Daelli (Scarce) 100.00 200.00 400.00
NOTE: *From the title page: "Album of fifty line engravings, executed on copper, by the most eminent artists at Rome in 1849; secreted from the papal police after the 'Restoration of Order,' And just imported into America."*

REMARKS ON THE JACOBINIAD (I,S)
E.W. Weld & W. Greenough, Boston: 1795-98 (8-1/4x5-1/8", 72 pgs, a number of B&W plates with text)

nn - Written by Rev. James Sylvester Gardner,artist unknown (Rare) (no known sales)
NOTE: *Early comics-type characters. Not sequential comics, but uses word balloons. Satire directed against "The Jacobin Club," supporters of the French Revolution and Radical Republicans. Gardner came to America from England in 1783, was minister of Trinity Church, Boston. There appears to be some reprints of this done as late as 1798.*

FR1.0 GD2.0 FN6.0

REV. MR. SOURBALL'S EUROPEAN TOUR, THE RECREATION OF A CITY, THE
Duffield Ashmead, Philadelphia: 1867 (7-5/8x6-1/4", 72 pgs, turquoise blue soft wrappers)

By Horace Cope (Rare) 50.00 100.00 200.00
NOTE: see **PARSON SOURBALL'S EUROPEAN TOUR** for the hard cover version.

RHYMES OF NONSENSE TRUTH & FICTION (S)
G.W. Carleton & Co, Publishers, NY: 1874 (10x7-3/4", 44 pgs, hard-c, B&W) (Very Rare)

nn - By Chaucer Jones and Michael Angelo Raphael Smith 100.00 200.00 400.00
NOTE: *Creator names obviously pseudonyms; looks like weak A.B. Frost.*

ROMANCE OF A HAMMOCK, THE - AS RECITED BY MR. GUS WILLIAMS IN "ONE OF THE FINEST" (O,P)
Unknown: 1880s (5-1/2x3-5/8" folded, 7 attached cardboard cards which fold out into a strip, color)

nn - By presently unknown Scarce 75.00 150.00 300.00
NOTE: *12-panel story, which one begins reading on one side of the folded-out strip, then flip to the other side to continue -- unlike the vast majority of folded strips, which are printed on only one side. This was a promotional handout, for a play titled "One of the Finest". The story pictured comes from a poem read in the play by then famous New York stage actor Gus Williams, who is pictured on the "cover"/title card."*

SAD TALE OF THE COURTSHIP OF CHEVALIER SLYFOX-WIKOF, SHOWING HIS HEART-RENDING ASTOUNDING & MOST WONDERFUL LOVE ADVENTURES WITH FANNY ELSSLER AND MISS GAMBOL, THE (O,G)
Garrett & Co., NY: Jan 1856 (25 ¢, 5-3/4x9-1/4", 100 pages, paper-c, B&W)

nn - By T.C. Bond ?? (Very Rare) 500.00 1000.00 2000.00
NOTE: *No surviving copies yet reported -- known via ads in Home Circle published by Garrett. Cover art by John McLenan and Samuel Avery. Graphic novel parodying the real-life romance between European actress/dancer Fanny Elssler and American aristocrat Henry Wikoff. The entire graphic novel is reprinted in the 1976 book "Fanny Elssler in America."*

SAD TALE OF THE COURTSHIP OF CHEVALIER SLYFOX-WIKOF, SHOWING HIS HEART-RENDING ASTOUNDING & MOST WONDERFUL LOVE ADVENTURES WITH FANNY ELSSLER AND MISS GUMBEL, THE (G) (25 cents printed on cover)
Dick And Fitzgerald, NY: 1870s-1888 (5-3/4x9-1/4", ??? pages, soft paper-c, B&W)

nn - By T.C. Bond ?? (Very Rare) 250.00 500.00 1000.00
NOTE: *Reprint of Garrett original printing before G,D&F partnership begins.*

SALT RIVER GUIDE FOR DISAPPOINTED POLITICIANS
Winchell, Small & Co., 113 Fulton St, NY: 1870s (16 pgs, 10¢)

nn - single panel cartoons from Wild Oats (Rare) 75.00 150.00 300.00

SAM SLICK'S COMIC ALMANAC
Philip J. Cozans, NYC: 1857 (7.5x4.5, 48 pgs, B&W) 100.00 200.00 400.00
NOTE: *Contains reprint of "Mose Keyser the Bowery Bully's Trip to the California Gold Mines" from Elton's Comic Almanac #17 1850.*

SCRAPS (O,S) (see also **F****** A*** K*******)
D.C. Johnston, Boston: 1828 - No.8 1840; New Series No.1 1849 (12 pgs, printed one side only, paper-c, B&W)

1 - 1828 (9-1/4 x 11-3/4") (Very Rare) (no known sales)
2 - 1830 (9-3/4 x 12-3/4") (Very Rare) (no known sales)
3 - 1832 (10-7/8 x 13-1/8") (Very Rare) (no known sales)
4 - 1833 (11 x 13-5/8") (Very Rare) (no known sales)
5- 1834 (10-3/8 x 13-3/8") (Very Rare) (no known sales)
6 - 1835 (10-3/8 x 13-1/4") red lettering in title SCRAPS (Very Rare) 250.00 500.00 1000.00
6 - 1835 (10-3/8 x 13-1/4") no red lettering in title (Rare) 200.00 400.00 880.00
7 - 1837 (10-3/4 x 13-7/8") 1st Edition (Very Rare) 200.00 400.00 880.00
7 - 1837 (10-3/4 x 13-3/4") 2nd Edition (so stated) 100.00 175.00 375.00
NOTE: *20 pgs. of text (double-sided), 4 pgs. of art (single-sided), plus the covers. There are no protective sheets between the art pages.*
8 - 1840 (10-1/2 x 13-7/8") (Rare) 200.00 400.00 880.00
New Series 1- 1849 (10-7/8 x 13-3/4") 125.00 250.00 475.00
NOTE: *By David Claypoole Johnston. All issues consist of four one-sided sheets with 9 to 12 single panel cartoons per sheet. The other pages are blank or text. With #1-5 the size of the pages can vary up to an inch. Contains 4 protective sheets (not part of page count) Only 1 3 4 and the 1849 New Series Number 1 has cover art along with 4 art pgs. (single sided) with 4 protective sheets and no text pages.New Series Number 1, as well as #6 with bo red lettering and the second printing of issue 7, have survived in higher numbers due to a 1940s warehouse discovery.*

THE SETTLEMENT OF RHODE ISLAND (O)
The Graphic Co. Photo-Lith 39 & 41, Park Place, New York: 1874 (11-3/8x10, 40 pgs, gilted blue hard-c

nn - Charles T. Miller & Walter F. Brown 50.00 100.00 250.00
NOTE: *This is also the Same Walter F. Brown that did "Hail Columbia".*

SHAKESPEARE WOULD RIDE THE BICYCLE IF ALIVE TODAY. "THE REASON WHY" (O,P,S)
Cleveland Bicycles H.A. Lozier & Co., Toledo, OH: 1896 (5-1/2x4",16 pgs, paper-c, color)

nn - By F. Opper (Rare) 70.00 140 .00 300.00
NOTE: *Original cartoons of Shakespearian characters riding bicycles; also popular amongst collectors of bicycle ephemera.*

Stuff and Nonsense by A.B. Frost
1884 © Charles Scribner's Sons

Texas Siftings v6 #2 May 15
1886 ©Texas Siftings Publishing Co.

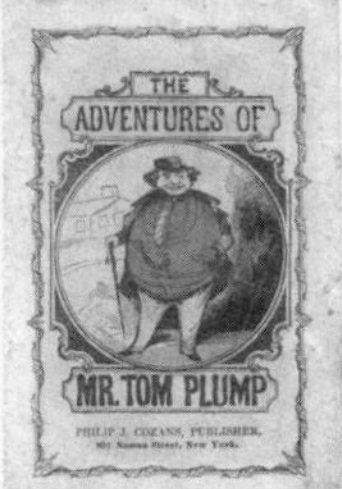

The Adventures Of Mr. Tom Plump
1851 © Huestis & Cozans, NY

FR1.0 GD2.0 FN6.0

SHAKINGS - ETCHINGS FROM THE NAVAL ACADEMY BY A MEMBER OF THE CLASS OF '67 (O,S)
Lee & Shepard, Boston: 1867 (7-7/8x10", 132 pages, blue hard-c)

By: Park Benjamin 38.00 75.00 150.00
NOTE: *Park Benjamin later became editor of Harper's Bazaar magazine.*

SHOO FLY PICTORIAL (S)
John Stetson, Chestnut sT Theatre, Phila, PA: June 1870 (15-1/2x11-1/2", 8 pgs, B&W)

1 67.50 125.00 250.00

SHYS AT SHAKSPEARE
J.P. and T.C.P., Philadelphia: 1869 (9-1/4x6", 52 pgs)

nn - Artist unknown 75.00 150.00 300.00

SKETCHES OF LOWLY LIFE IN A GREAT CITY (M,S) (See 99 "Woolfs" From Truth)
G. P. Puntam's Sons: 1899 (8-5/8x11-1/4", 200 pgs, hard-c, B&W)
(reprints from Life and Judge of Woolf's cartoons of NYC slum children)

nn - By Michael Angelo Woolf 75.00 150.00 350.00
NOTE: *Woolf's cartoons are regarded as a primary influence on R.F. Outcault in the later development of The Yellow Kid newspaper strip.*

SNAP (O,S)
Valentine & Townsend, Tribune Bldg, NYC: March 13,1885 (17x11, 8 pgs, B&W)

1-Contains a sequential comic strip 50.00 100.00 150.00

SOCIETY PICTURES (M,S,E)
Charles H. Sergel Company, Chicago: 1895 (5-1/4x7-3/4", 168 pgs, printed 1 side, paper-c, B&W)

nn - By George du Maurier; reprints from **Punch**. 12.50 25.00 50.00

SOLDIERS AND SAILORS HALF DIME TALES OF THE LATE REBELLION
Soldiers & Sailors Publishing Co: 1868 (5-1/4x7-7/8", 32 pgs)

v1#1-#16 v2#1-#10 10.00 20.00 40.00
v2 #11 contains (5) page comic strip 20.00 40.00 80.00
NOTE: *Changes to Soldiers & Sailors Half Dime Magazine with v2 #1.*

SOUVENIR CONTAINING CARTOONS ISSUED BY THE PRESS BUREAU OF THE OHIO STATE REPUBLICAN EXECUTIVE COMMITTEE, A (S)
Ohio State Republican Executive Committee, Columbus, OH: 1899 (10-3/8x13-1/2, 248 pgs, Hard-c, B&W)

nn - By William L. Bloomer (Scarce) 100.00 200.00 400.00

SOUVENIR OF SOHMER CARTOONS FROM PUCK, JUDGE, AND FRANK LESLIE'S (M,S,P)
Sohmer Piano Co.: nd(c.1893) (6x4-3/4", 16 pgs, paper-c, B&W)

nn 20.00 40.00 80.00
NOTE: *Reprints painted "cartoon" Sohmer Piano advertisements which appeared in the above publications. Artists include Keppler, Gillam, others.*

SPORTING NEW YORKER, THE
Ornum & Co, Beekman ST, NYC: 1870s

issues with sequential comic strips (Rare) 50.00 100.00 200.00

STORY OF THE MAN OF HUMANITY AND THE BULL CALF, THE
(see Bull Calf, The Story of The Man Of Humanity And The)
NOTE: *Reprints of two of A. B. Frost's mostfamous sequential comic strips.*

STREET & SMITH'S LITERARY ALBUM
Street & Smith, NY: #1 Dec 23 1865-#225 Apr 9 1870 (11-3/4x16-3/4", 16 pgs, B&W)

1 (23 Dec 1865) 10.00 30.00 50.00
2-129 131-225 (issues with short sequential strips) 7.50 15.00 30.00
130 (Steam Man satire parody) 100.00 200.00 300.00

STUFF AND NONSENSE (Harper's Monthly strip-r) (M)
Charles Scribner's Sons: 1884 (10-1/4x7-3/4", 100 pgs, hardcover, B&W)

nn - By Arthur Burdett Frost 100.00 185.00 375.00
nn - By A.B. Frost (1888 reprint, 104 pgs) 40.00 80.00 180.00
NOTE: *Earliest known anthology devoted to collecting the comic strips of a single American artist. 1888 2nd printing has a different cover and is layed out somewhat differently inside with a new title page, 3 added pages of cartoons, and a couple more illustrations. For more Frost, the 2nd is worth checki ng out also.*

STUMPING IT (LAUGHING SERIES BRICKTOP STORIES #8) (O,S)
Collin & Small, NY: 1876 (6-5/8x9-1/4, 68 pgs, perfect bound, B&W)

nn - Thomas Worth art abounds (some sequentials) 75.00 150.00 300.00
NOTE: Mainly single panel cartoons w/text; however, some sequential comic strips inside worth picking up

SUMMER SCHOOL OF PHILOSOPHY AT MT. DESERT, THE
Henry Holt & Co.: 1881 (10-3/8x8-5/8", 60 pgs, illus. gilt hard-c, B&W)

nn - By J. A. Mitchell 60.00 120.00 240.00
NOTE: *J.A.Mitchell went on to found **LIFE** two years later in 1883. Also, the long-running mascot for **LIFE** was Cupid - which you see multitudes of Cupids flying around in this story.*

SURE WATER CURE, THE
Carey Grey & Hart, Phila, PA: c1841-43 (8-/2x5, 32 pgs, B&W

nn - proto-comic-strip Very Rare 150.00 300.00 600.00

TAILOR-MADE GIRL, HER FRIENDS, HER FASHIONS, AND HER FOLLIES, THE
(see also IN THE "400" AND OUT) (M)

FR1.0 GD2.0 FN6.0

Charles Scribner's Sons, New York: 1888 (8-3/8x10-1/2", 68 pgs, hard-c, B&W)

nn - Art by C.J. Taylor 17.50 35.00 70.00
NOTE: *Format is a full page cartoon on every other page, with a script style vignette, written by Philip H. Welch, on every page opposite the art.*

TALL STUDENT, THE
Roberts Brothers, Boston: 1873 (7x5", 48 pgs, printed one side only, gilted hard-c, B&W)

nn - By Wilhelm Busch (Scarce) 37.50 75.00 150.00

TARIFF ?, CARTOONS AND COMMENTS FROM PUCK, THE (see Puck, The Tariff...)

TEASING TOM AND NAUGHTY NED WITH A SPOOL OF CLARK'S COTTON, THE ADVENTURES OF (O,P)
Clark's O.N.T. Spool Cotton: 1879 (4-1/4x3", 12 pgs, B&W, paper-c)

nn 17.50 35.00 70.00
NOTE: *Knock-off of the "First Trick" in Wilhelm Busch's **Max and Maurice**, modified to involve Clark's Spool Cotton in the story, with similar but new art by an artist identified as "HB". The back cover advertises the specific merchant who gave this booklet away -- multiple variations of back cover suspected.*

TEMPERANCE TALES; OR, SIX NIGHTS WITH THE WASHINGTONIANS, VOL I & II
W.A. Leary & Co., Philadelphia: 1848 (50¢, 6-1/8x4", 328 pgs, B&W, hard-c)

nn 100.00 200.00 400.00
NOTE: *Mostly text. This edition gathers Volume I & II together. The first 8 pages reprints George Cruikshank's **THE BOTTLE**, re-drawn & re-engraved by Phil A. Pilliner. Later editions of this book do not include **THE BOTTLE** reprint and are therefore of little interest to comics collectors.*

TEXAS SIFTINGS
Texas Siftings Publishing Co, Austin, Texas (1881-1887), **NYC** (1887-1897): 1881-1885 newspaper-size weekly; 1886-1897 folio weekly (15x10-3/4", 16 pgs, B&W 10¢

1881-1885 issues 25.00 50.00 100.00
v6#1 (5/8/86) (8) panel strip Afterwhich He Emigrated;
(16) panel The Tenor's Triumph Veni Vidi Vici 12.50 25.00 50.00
v6#2 (5/16/86 (5) panel sewuential 12.50 25.00 50.00
v6#3 no sequentials 12.50 25.00 50.00
v6#4 (5/29/86) Worth-c (4) panel Worth strip; (2) panel 12.50 25.00 50.00
v6#5 no sequentials 12.50 25.00 50.00
v6#6 (6/12/86) Comic Strip Cover (11) panels The Rise of a Great Artist
(5) panel sequential 50.00 100.00 200.00
v6#7 (6/19/86) Worth-c (2) panel Wiorth;
(10) panel Ha! Ha! The Honest Youth & the Lordly Villain 25.00 50.00 100.00
v6#8 (6/26/86) Worth-c; (15) panel The Kangaroo Hunter 25.00 50.00 100.00
v6#9 (7/3/86) Worth-c; Bellew (2) panel How Wives Get What They Want
12.50 25.00 50.00
v6#10 ((7/10/86) Baseball-c; (3) panel;
(5) panel A Story Without Words from Fliegende Blätter 12.50 25.00 50.00
v6 #11 12 13 Worth-c no sequentials 12.50 25.00 50.00
v6#14 (8/7/86) Wiorth-c; (7) panel Mrs Cleveland Presents
The President With A New Rocking Chair 12.50 25.00 50.00
v6#15 (8/14/86) Worth-c; (6) panel Worth strip 12.50 25.00 50.00
v6#16 (8/21/86) Worth-c Asleep At Post USA/Mexico Border
(6) panel sequential 12.50 25.00 50.00
v6#17 no sequrntials 12.50 25.00 50.00
v6#18 (9/4/86) Worth-c; (3) panel from Fliegende 12.50 25.00 50.00
v6#19 (9/11/86) Worth Anarchist & Uncle Sam-c;
(5) panel Duel of the Dudes 12.50 25.00 50.00
v6#20 (9/18/86) Worth-c (6) panel sequential 12.50 25.00 50.00
v6#21 (9/25/86) Worth-c; Verbeck single panel; (9) panel 12.50 25.00 50.00
v6#22 (10/2/86) Verbeck-c plus interiors 12.50 25.00 50.00
v6#23 (10/9/86) Worth-c Geronimo & Devil cover;
Verbeck and Chips singles 25.00 50.00 100.00
v6#24 (10/16/86) Worth-c Verbeck strip "Evolution" 12.50 25.00 50.00
v6#25 no sequential strips 12.50 25.00 50.00
v6#26 (10/30/86) Worth-c; (6) panel Verbeck "A Warning To Smokers"
12.50 25.00 50.00
NOTE: *Many Thomas Worth sequential comic strips. Frank Bellew and Dan McCarthy appear. Wilhelm Busch-r from German Fligende Blaetter. Later issues in 1890s comics become sporadic*

THAT COMIC PRIMER (S)
G.W. Carleton & Co., Publishers: 1877 (6-5/8x5", 52 pgs, paper soft-c, B&W)

nn - By Frank Bellew 75.00 150.00 300.00
NOTE: *Premium for the United States Life Insurance Company, New York.*

TIGER, THE LEFTENANT AND THE BOSUN, THE
Prudential Insurance Home Office, 878 & 880 Broad St, Newark, NJ: 1889 (4.5x3.25", 12 pgs) (Scarce)

nn - 8 panel sequential story in color 50.00 100.00 200.00

TOM PLUMP, THE ADVENTURES OF MR. (see also The Juvenile Gem) (O)
Huestis & Cozans, New York: nd (c1850-1851) (6x3-7/8", 12 pgs, hand colored paper-c, B&W)

nn- First printing(s) publisher's address is 104 Nassau Street (1850-1851)
(Very Rare) 625.00 1250.00 2500.00
NOTE: *California Gold Rush story. The hand colored outer cover is highly rare, with only 1 recorded copy possessing it. The front cover image and text is repeated precisely on page 3 (albeit b&w), and only interior pages are numbered, together leading owners of coverless copies to believe they have the cover. The true back*

The Tooth-Ache by George Cruickshank
1849 © J. L. Smith, Philadelphia, PA

Uncle Josh's Trunk Full Of Fun
1870s © Dick & Fitzgerald

Wild Oats #115 March 10
1875 © Winchell & Small, NYC

FR1.0 GD2.0 FN6.0

cover contains ads for the publisher. The cover was issued only with copies which were sold separately - booklets which were bound together as part of ***THE JUVENILE GEM*** *never had such covers.*

TOM PLUMP, THE ADVENTURES OF MR. (see also The Juvenile Gem) (O)
Philip J. Cozans: nd (1851-1852) (6x3-7/8", 12 pgs, hand colored paper-c, B&W)
nn- Second printing(s) publisher's address is 116 Nassau Street (1851-1852) (Very Rare) 400.00 800.00 1600.00
nn- Third printing(s) publisher's address is 107 Nassau Street (1852+) (Very Rare) 400.00 800.00 1600.00

TOM PLUMP, THE ADVENTURES OF MR.
Americana Review, Scotia, NY: nd(1960's) (6-1/4x4-1/8", 8 pgs, side-stapled, cardboard-c, B&W)
nn - Modern reprint - 12.00 24.00
NOTE: *Issued within a folder titled SIX CHILDREN'S BOOKS OF THE 1850'S. States "Reprinted by American Review" at bottom of front cover. Reprints the 104 Nassau Street address.)*
nn - Modern reprint (Scarce 1980s) (6 1/2x4-1/4", 8 pgs, side-stapled) - 5.00 10.00
NOTE: *Photocopy reprint by a comix zine publisher, from an Americana Review cop; vailable by mail order*

TOOTH-ACHE, THE (E,O)
D. Bogue, London: 1849 (5-1/4x3-3/4)
nn - By Cruikshank, B&W (Very Rare) 250.00 500.00 1000.00
nn - By Cruikshank, hand colored (Rare) (no known sales)
NOTE: *Scripted by Horace Mayhew, art by George Cruikshank. This is the British edition. Price 1/6 b&w, 3 hand colored. In British editions, the panels are not numbered. Publisher's name appears on cover. Booklet's "pages" unfold into a single, long, strip.*
J.L. Smith, Philadelphia, PA: nd (1849) (5-1/8"x 3-3/4" folded, 86-7/8" wide unfolded, 26 pgs, cardboard-c, color, 15¢)
nn - By Cruikshank, hand colored (Very Rare) 400.00 800.00 1600.00
NOTE: *Reprints the D. Bogue edition. In American editions, the panels are numbered (43 panels, not counting front & back cover). Publisher's name stamped on inside front cover, plus printed along left-hand side of first interior page. Page 1 is pasted to inside back cover, and unfolds from there. Front cover not attached to back cover by design. Booklet's "pages" unfold into a single, long, strip (made from four individual strips pasted together on the blank back side). There is a fairly common1974 British Arts Council reprint.*

TRAMP, THE: His Tricks, Tallies, and Tell-Tales, with His Signs, Countersigns, Grips, Passwords and Villainies Exposed (O,S)
Dick & Fitzgerald, New York: 1878 (11-3/8x8, 36 pgs, paper-c, B&W, 25¢) (Rare)
1 Frank Bellew 150.00 300.00 600.00
NOTE: *Edited by Frank Bellew, A Bee And A Chip (Bellew's daughter and son Frank).*

TRUTH (See Platinum Age section for 1900-1906 issues)
Truth Company, NY: 1886-1906? (13-11/16x10-5/16", 16 pgs, process color-c & center-folds, rest B&W)
1886-1887 issues 20.00 40.00 100.00
1888-1895 issues non Outcault issues 15.00 30.00 80.00
Mar 10 1894 - precursor Yellow Kid RFO 60.00 180.00 400.00
#372 June 2 1894 - first app Yellow Kid RFO 215.00 650.00 1300.00
June 23 1894 - precursor Yellow Kid R. F. Outcault 60.00 180.00 400.00
July 14 1894 -2nd app Yellow Kid RFO 110.00 330.00 700.00
Sept 15 1894 - (2) 3rd app YK RFO plus YK precursor 110.00 330.00 700.00
Feb 9 1895 - 4th app Yellow Kid RFO 110.00 330.00 700.00
1896-1899 issues 10.00 20.00 55.00
NOTE: *This magazine contains the earliest known appearances of* ***The Yellow Kid*** *by Richard Felton Outcault. Feb 9 1895 issue's YK cartoon was reprinted one week later in the* ***New York World*** *Feb 17 1895 edition. We are still sorting out further Outcault appearances. Truth also contained full color sequential strips by Hy Mayer on the back plus Woolf, Verbeek, etc.*

TRUTH, SELECTIONS FROM
Truth Company, NY: 1894-Spr 1897 (13-11/16x10-1/4, color-c, quarterly)
1-4 25.00 50.00 100.00
5-Outcault's early Yellow Kid 100.00 200.00 400.00
6-13 20.00 40.00 80.00
NOTE: *#5 reprints all early Outcault Yellow Kid appearances*

TURNER'S COMIC ALMANAC
Charles Strong, 298 Pearl St, NYC: ???-1843 (7.25x4.5", 36 pgs, B&W)
nn 60.00 120.00 240.00

TURNER'S COMICK ALMA-NACK
Turner & Fisher, NYC: 1844-?? (7.25x4.5", 36 pgs, B&W)
nn 60.00 120.00 240.00

TWO HUNDRED SKETCHES, HUMOROUS AND GROTESQUE, BY GUSTAVE DORE (E)
Frederick Warne & Co, London: 1867 (13-3/4x11-3/8, 94 pgs, hard-c, B&W)
nn - (1867) by Gustave Dore 100.00 200.00 500.00
nn - (Second Edition; 1871)- by Gustave Dore 50.00 100.00 240.00
nn - (Third Edition; 1870's)- by Gustave Dore 50.00 100.00 240.00
nn - (Fourth Edition; 1870's- by Gustave Dore 50.00 100.00 240.00
NOTE: *Contains sequential comics stories, single panel cartoons, and sketches. Reprints and translates material which originally appeared in the French publications "Le Journal pour Rire", circa 1848-49. Although dated 1867, it was likely published & available for the 1866 Christmas Season, as has been confirmed for the American edition. Printed by Dalziel. The American & first British editions were printed simultaneously, the American edition is not a reprint of the British.*

TWO HUNDRED SKETCHES, HUMOROUS AND GROTESQUE, BY GUSTAVE DORE (E)
Roberts Brothers, Boston: 1867 (13-3/4x11-3/8", 96 pgs, hard-c, B&W)

FR1.0 GD2.0 FN6.0

nn - By Gustave Dore 100.00 200.00 500.00
NOTE: *Although dated 1867, it was published & available for the 1866 Christmas Season. Printed by Dalziel, in England, and imported to the USA expressly for a USA publisher.*

UNCLE JOSH'S TRUNK-FUL OF FUN
Dick & Fitzgerald, 18 Ann St, NY: 1870s (5-3/4x9", 68 pgs, B&W & Red-c, B&W inside)
nn - Rare 75.00 125.00 200.00
NOTE: *Many single panel cartoons; (2) pages of early boxing sequential strip*

UNCLE SAM'S COMIC ALMANAC
M.J. Meyers, NY: 1879 (11x8", 32 pgs)
nn - 50.00 100.00200.00

UNDER THE GASLIGHT
Gaslight Publishing Co (Frank Tousey): Oct 13 1878-Apr 12 1879 (Folio, 16pgs)
1-27 75.00 125.00 200.00

UNITED STATES COMIC ALMANAC
King & Baird, Philadelphia: 1851-?? (7.5x4.5", 36 pgs, B&W)
nn 60.00 120.00 240.00

UPS AND DOWNS ON LAND AND WATER (O.G)
James R. Osgood & Co., Boston: 1871 ; **Houghton, Osgood & Co., Boston:** 1880 (108 pgs, gilted hard-c, B&W)
1st printing (1871; 10-3/4x16") - By Augustus Hoppin 45.00 90.00 180.00
2nd printing (1880; smaller sized) 32.50 65.00 130.00
NOTE: *Exists as blue or orange hard covers.*

VANITY FAIR
William A. Stephens (for Thompson & Camac): Dec 29 1859-July 4 1863 Quarto Weekly
average issues with comic strips 12.50 25.00 50.00

VERDICT, THE
Verdict Publishing Co: Dec 19 1898-Nov 12 1900 (Chromolithographic Weekly)
Average Issues 50.00 100.00 200.00
NOTE: *Artists included George B. Luks, Horace Taylor, MIRS. Striking anti-Republican weekly full o fsome of the most savage political cartoons of the era. The last brilliant burst of energy for the political cartoon weekly*

VERY VERY FUNNY (M,S)
Dick & Fitzgerald, New York: nd(c1880's) (10¢, 7-1/2x5", 68 pgs, paper-c, B&W)
nn - (Rare) 75.00 150.00 300.00
NOTE: *Unauthorized reprints of prose and cartoons extracted from Puck, Texas Siftings, and other publications. Includes art by Chips Bellew, Bisbee, Graetz, Oppor, Waloc, Zim.*

VIM
H. Wimmel, NYC: June 22-Aug 24 1898 (Chromolithographic Weekly)
average issue 50.00 100.00 200.00
Yellow Kid by Leon Barritt issues 75.00 150.00 300.00

WAR IN THE MIDST OF AMERICA. FROM A NEW POINT OF VIEW. (E,O,G)
Ackermann & Co., London: 1864 (4-3/8" x 5-7/8", folded, 36 feet wide unfolded, 80 pgs, hard-c, B&W)
nn- by Charles Dryden (rare) 375.00 750.00 1500.00
NOTE: *British graphic novel about the American Civil War, with a pro-Confederate bent. Adventures of a British artist who decides to visually summarize the American Civil War for his countrymen, from newspaper accounts. Reaching current events, he finds he can not finish the story until the War ends, and so he travels to America, to end it. Book unfolds into a single long strip (binding was issued split, to enable the unfolding).*

WASP, THE ILLUSTRATED SAN FRANCISCO
F. Korbel & Bros and Numerous Others: August 5 1876-April 25 1941 (Chromolithographic Weekly)
average 1800s issues with comic strips 50.00 100.00 200.00

WHAT I KNOW OF FARMING: Founded On The Experience of Horace Greeley (S)
The American News Company, New York: 1871 (7-1/4x4-1/2", paper-c, B&W)
nn - By Joseph Hull (Scarce) 35.00 70.00 140.00
NOTE: *Pay & Cox, Printers & Engravers, NY; political tract regarding Presidential elections.*

WILD FIRE
Wild Fire Co, NYC: Nov 30 1877-at least#16 Mar 1878 (Folio, 16 pgs)
1-16 12.50 25.00 50.00

WILD OATS, An Illustrated Weekly Journal of Fun, Satire, Burlesque, and Nits at Persons and Events of the Day (O)
Winchell & Small, 113 Fulton St /48 Ann St, NYC: Feb 1870-1881 (16-1/4x11", generally 16 pages, B&W, began as monthly, then bi-weekly, then weekly) All loose issues Very Rare (See *The Overstreet Price Guide* #35 2005 for a detailed index of single issue contents)
1-25 Very Rare - contents to be indexed next year 50.00 100.00 200.00
26-28 30 32 35 36 39 40 41 43-46 1872 (sequential strips) 50.00 100.00 200.00
29 33 37 42 no sequential strips 40.00 80.00 160.00
31 34 38 47 Hopkins sequential comic strips 50.00 100.00 200.00
48 (1/16/73) Worth 13 panel sequential; first Woolf-c 50.00 100.00 200.00
49 51 53 54 60 62 61 64 65 66 67 69 1873 sequential strips 50.00 100.00 200.00
50 52 56 59 63 71 no sequential strips 40.00 80.00 160.00
51 (Worth 18 panel double page spread, Woolf 9 panel 50.00 100.00 200.00
55 Hopkins 22 panel double page spread; Bellew-c 50.00 150.00 300.00
57 intense unknown 6 panel "Two Relics of Barbarism, or A Few Contrasted Pictures,

War in the Midst of America
1864 © Ackerman & Co., London

Wild Oats #139 August 25
1875 © Winchell & Small, NY

Yankee Notions #7 (v2#1)
July 1852 © T.W. Strong, NY

FR1.0 GD2.0 FN6.0

Showing the origin of the North American Indian 50.00 100.00 200.00
58 (6/5/73) unknown 19 panel double pager "The Terrible Adventures of Messrs Buster & Stumps, About Exterminating the Indians" reads across both pages like Popeye #2095 (1933); Woolf-c 100.00 200.00 400.00
68 (10/16/73) unknown 9 panel "Adv of New jersey Mosquito" looks like Winsor McCay type style: early inspiration for McCay's animated cartoon? 50.00 100.00 200.00
70 unknown 6 panel; Hopkins 6 panel "Hopkins novel: A Tale of True Love, with all the variations"; Bellew-c 50.00 100.00 200.00
72 (12/11/73) Worth 11 panel; Wales President Grant war-c 50.00 100.00 200.00
73 74 75 Hopkins sequential comic strip 75.00 150.00 300.00
76 77 sequential strips 50.00 100.00 200.00
78 Bellew 5 panel double pager 50.00 100.00 200.00
79-105 (March 1874-Dec 1874) contents presently unknown 50.00 100.00 200.00
106 107 111 no sequentials;Bellew-c #106 110;Wales-c #107 50.00 100.00 200.00
108 (1/20/75) Wales 12 panel double pg spread; Bellew-c 50.00 100.00 200.00
109 (1/27/75) unknown 6 panel; Wales-c 50.00 100.00 200.00
111 Busch 13 panel "The Conundrum of the Day - Is Lager Beer Intoxicating?"; Bellew-c 50.00 100.00 200.00
112 116 sequential comic strips 50.00 100.00 200.00
113 114 115 no sequentials Worth-c #114 40.00 80.00 160.00
117 intense Wales 6 panel "One of the Oppresions of the Civil Rights Laws"' Bellew-c 75.00 150.00 300.00
118-137 (3/31/75-8/4/75) no sequential comic strips 40.00 80.00 160.00
138 (8/18/75) Bellew Sr & Bellew "Chips" Jr singles appear 50.00 100.00 200.00
139-143 145-147 154-157 159 no sequentials 40.00 80.00 160.00
144 (9/29/75) Hopkins 8 panel sequential; Wales-c 50.00 100.00 200.00
148 (10/27/75) Opper's first cover; many Opper singles 75.00 150.00 300.00
149 150 151 152 153 all Opper-c and much interior work 50.00 100.00 200.00
158 (1/5/76) Palmer Cox 1rst comic strip 24 panel double page spread "The Adv of Mr & Mrs Sprowl And Their Christmas Turkey - A Crashing Chasing Tearful Tragedy But Happily Ending Well"; Opper-c 100.00 200.00 400.00
159 160 162 165 167 169-173 no sequentials 40.00 80.00 160.00
161 163 164 166 168 179 182 Palmer Cox sequential strips 100.00 200.00 400.00
174 (4/26/76) Cox 24 panel double pager "The Tramp's Progress; A Story of the West And the Union Pacific Railroad" 100.00 200.00 400.00
175-178 183-189 no sequentials 40.00 80.00 160.00
180 (6/7/76) Beard & Opper jam; Woolf, Bellew singles 50.00 100.00 200.00
181 more Mann two panel jobs; Opper-c 50.00 100.00 200.00
190 Bellew 9 panel "Rodger's Patent Mosquito Armour" 75.00 150.00 300.00
191-end contents to be indexed in the near future 40.00 80.00 160.00
NOTE: *There are very few lknown oose issues. All loose issues are Very Rare. Prices vary widely on this magazine. Issues with sequential comic strips would be in higher demand than issues with no comic strips. We present this index from the Library of Congress and New York Historical Society bound sets. We would love to hear from any one who turns up loose copies. This scarce humor bi-weekly contains easily a couple hundred original first-time published sequential comic strips found in most issues plus innumerable single panel cartoons in every issue*

WYMAN'S COMIC ALMANAC FOR THE TIMES
T.W.Strong, NY: 1854 (8x5", 24 pgs)
nn - 50.00 100.00 200.00

WOMAN IN SEARCH OF HER RIGHTS, THE ADVENTURES OF (G)
Lee & Shepard, Boston And New York: early 1870s (8-3/8x13", 40 pgs, hard-c)
By Florence Claxton (Very Rare) 400.00 800.00 1600.00
NOTE: *Earliest known original comic book sequential story by a woman; contains "nearly 100 original drawings by the author, which have been reproduced in fac-simile by the graphotype process of engraving." Tinted two color lithography; orange tint printed first, then printed 2nd time with black ink; early women's sufferage.*

WORLD OVER, THE (I)
G. W. Dillingham Company, New York: 1897 (192 pgs, hard-c)
nn - By Joe Kerr; 80 illustrations by R.F. Outcault (Rare) 250.00 500.00 1000.00
NOTE: soft cover editions also exist

WRECK-ELECTIONS OF BUSY LIFE (S)
Kellogg & Bulkeley: 1867 (9-1/4x11-3/4", ??? pages, soft-c)
nn - By J. Bowker (Rare) 100.00 200.00 400.00
NOTE: *Says "Sold by American News Company, New York" on cover.*

YANKEE DOODLE
W.H. Graham, Tribune Building, NYC: Oct 10 1846-Oct 2 1847 (Quarto weekly)
average issue 50.00 100.00 200.00

YANKEE NOTIONS, OR WHITTLINGS OF JONATHAN'S JACK-KNIFE
T.W. Strong, 98 Nassau St, NYC: Jan. 1852-1875 (11x8, 32 pgs, paper-c, 12.5¢, monthly)
1 Brother Jonathan character single panel cartoons 50.00 100.00 200.00
NOTE: *Begins continuing character sequential comic strip, "The Adventures of Jeremiah Oldpot" in "A Bird in the Hand Is Worth Two in The Bush"*
2-4 25.00 50.00 100.00
5 British X-Over 25.00 50.00 100.00
NOTE: *Single panel of John Bull & Brother Jonathan exchanging civilities (issues of* Punch & Yankee Notions)
6 end of Jeremiah Oldpot continued strip 25.00 50.00 100.00
v2#1 begin "Hoosier Bragg" sequential strip - six issue serial 25.00 50.00 100.00
v2#2 Feb 1853 two pg 12 panel sequential "Mr Vanity's Exploits, Arising Out Of A Valentine" 37.50 75.00 150.00
v2#3-v2#5 continues Hoosier Bragg 25.00 50.00 100.00
v2#6 Juen 1853 Lion Eats Hoosier Bragg, end of story 25.00 50.00 100.00
v3#1 begins referring to its cartoons as "Comic Art" 37.50 75.00 150.00

FR1.0 GD2.0 FN6.0

v4#1-V4#6 v5#1-v5#2 no sequential comic strips 20.00 40.00 80.00
v5#3 two sequential comic strips 37.50 75.00 150.00
NOTE: *Mr Take-A-Drop And The Maine Law (5) panels and The First Segar (7) panels (about smoking tobacco)*
v5#4 April 1856 begin Billy Vidkins 37.50 75.00 150.00
NOTE: *Begins reprinting "From Passages in the Life of Little Billy Vidkins, first issued as a stand alone proto-comic book in 1849 Illustrations of the Poets*
v5#5 The McBargem Guards (9) panel sequential; Vidkins 25.00 50.00 100.00
v5#6 v5 #9 no comics 20.00 40.00 80.00
v5#7 Billy Vidkins continues 25.00 50.00 100.00
v5#8 end of Vidkins By HL Stephens, Esq. 25.00 50.00 100.00
v5#10 (6) panel "How We Learn To Ride"; Timber is hero 25.00 50.00 100.00
v5#11 (7) panel "How Mr. Green Sparrowgrass Voted-A Warning For the Benefit of Quiet Citizens About To Excercize the Elective Franchise" plus Pt Two "How We Learn to Ride" 37.50 75.00 150.00
v5#12 (6) panel "How Mr Pipp Got Struck"; "The Eclipse" featuring Mr Phips; Pt 3 "How We Learn to Ride" 25.00 50.00 100.00
v6#1 (Jan 1857) (12) panel "A Tale of An Umbrella; (4) panel begins a serial "The Man Who Bought The Elephant; (8) panel How Our Young New Yorkers Celebrate New Years Day 25.00 50.00 100.00
v6#2 (Feb 1857) Pt 2 (4) panels The Man Who Bought the Elephant; (7) panel A Game of All Fours 25.00 50.00 100.00
v6#3 (Mar 1857) Pt 3 (4) panels The Man Who Bought the Elephant ending; (4) panel Ye Great Crinoline Monopoly 25.00 50.00 100.00
v6#4 no comic strips 25.00 50.00 100.00
v6#5 (May 1850) (3) panel A Short Trip to Mr Bumps, And How It Ended; (2) panel How mr Trembles Was Garrotted 25.00 50.00 100.00
v6#6 no comic strips 25.00 50.00 100.00
v6#7 (July 1857) (5) panel Alma Mater; (3) panel Three Tableaux In the Life of A Broadway Swell 25.00 50.00 100.00
v6 #8 9 no comic strips 25.00 50.00 100.00
v6#10 (Oct 1857) (3) panel Adv of Mr Near-Sight 25.00 50.00 100.00
v6#11 (Nov 1857) (11) panel Mrs Champignon's Dinner Party And the Way She Arranged Her Guests; (4) panel A Stroll in August 25.00 50.00 100.00
v6#12 (Dec 1857) (8) panel strip; (12) panel Young Fitz At A Blow Out in the Fifth Ave 25.00 50.00 100.00
v10#1 (Jan 1860) comic strip Bibbs at Central Park Skating Pond using word balloons 25.00 50.00 100.00

YE TRUE ACCOUNTE OF YE VISIT TO SPRINGFIELDE BY YE CONSTABEL HIS SPECIAL REPORTER
Frank Leslie: 1861 (5-1/8 x 5-1/4 or 93 inches when folded out, paper-c, B&W)
nn - Very Rare fold-out of 18 comic strip panels plus covers - -
NOTE: *8 panels contain word balloons (Very Rare - only one copy known to exist.) First printed in Frank Leslie's Budget of Fun Jan 1 1861 issue. Abraham Lincoln Biography.*

YE VERACIOUS CHRONICLE OF GRUFF & POMPEY IN 7 TABLEAUX. (O,P)
Jackson's Best Chewing Tobacco & Donaldson Brothers: nd (c1870's) (5-1/8 tall x 3-3/8" wide folded, 27" wide unfolded, color cardboard)
nn - With all 8 panels attached (Scarce) 40.00 80.00 160.00
nn - Individual panels/cards 6.00 12.00 24.00
NOTE: *Black Americana interest. Consists of 8 attached cards, printed on one side, which unfold into a strip story of title card & 7 panels. Scrapbook hobbyists in the 19th Century tended to pull the panels apart and paste into their scrapbooks, making copies with all panels attached scarce.*

YOUNG AMERICA (continues as Yankee Doodle)
T.W. Strong, NYC: 1856
1-30 John McLennon 50.00 100.00 200.00

YOUNG AMERICA'S COMIC ALMANAC
T.W. Strong, NY: 1857 (7-1/2x5", 24 pgs)
nn 50.00 100.00 200.00

THE YOUNG MEN OF AMERICA (becomes Golden Weekly) (S)
Frank Tousey, NYC: 1887-88 (14x10-1/4", 16 pgs, B&W)
527 (10/13/87) Bellew strip "Story of A Black Eye" 25.00 50.00 100.00
530 (11/3/87) Thomas Worth (6) panel strip 125
531 (11/10/87) Thomas Worth(3) panel strip
537 (12/22/87) H.E. Patterson (3) panel strip
544 (2/9/88) Caran s'Ache (6) panel strip-r 37.50 75.00 100.00
555 (4/26/88) Thomas Worth (3) panel strip
556 (5/3/88) Thomas Worth (6) panel strip; Kit Carson-c 75.00 150.00 300.00
569 (8/21/88) Frank Bellew (2) panel strip
570 (8/9/88) Kemble (2) panel strip
571 (8/16/88) Kemble (2) panel strip; first Davy Crockett 75.00 150.00 300.00
Issues with just single panel cartoons 10.00 20.00 40.00

ZIM'S QUARTERLY (M)
(13-13/16x10-1/4", 60 pgs, color-c; most;y B&W, some interior color)
1 - Eugene Zimmerman 112.50 225.00 450.00
NOTE: *Approx. half sequential comic strips, other half single panel cartoons.*

For a free, lively e-mail discussion group of Victorian & Platinum Age comics collectors, fans, dealers, enthusiasts, and scholars you can join to look, listen, learn, and share at **PlatinumAgeComics@Yahoogroups.com/subscribe**.
Any additions or corrections to this section are always welcome, very much encouraged and can be sent to **robert@BLBcomics.com** to be processed for next year's Guide.

The Platinum Age

The American Comic Book: 1883-1938

Further Concise History & Price Index Of The Field As Of 2008

NEWSPAPERS HARNESS COMICS POWER MYRIAD FORMATS COMPETE

by Robert Lee Beerbohm and Richard D. Olson, PhD ©2009

(This article was originally created by Robert L. Beerbohm and Richard D. Olson beginning in CBPG #27 1997 and is revised annually as new information comes to light.)

The story of the success of the modern comic strip as we know it today is tied closely to the companies who sponsored and bought licenses from the copyright holder for the purpose of advertising products. Platinum Age comic books have come back into their own after languishing mostly forgotten for a few decades. With this series of comics history research updates now marking its first decade, these historically important books are seem by many now as very collectible. Online sources such as eBay and bookfinder.com have demonstrate that many of these Platinum books are actually not scarce at all as previously thought, though they are in any type of higher-grade condition. Even so, most Platinum Age books are much rarer than so-called Golden Age comic books, yet despite this scarcity, *Mutt & Jeff, Bringing Up Father, The Katzenjammer Kids*, and many more were more popular than say Superman and Batman when they were introduced. Recent research has come up with some more amazing rediscoveries. There is much that can be learned and applied to today's comics market by a simple historical examination of the medium's evolution over more than 160 years.

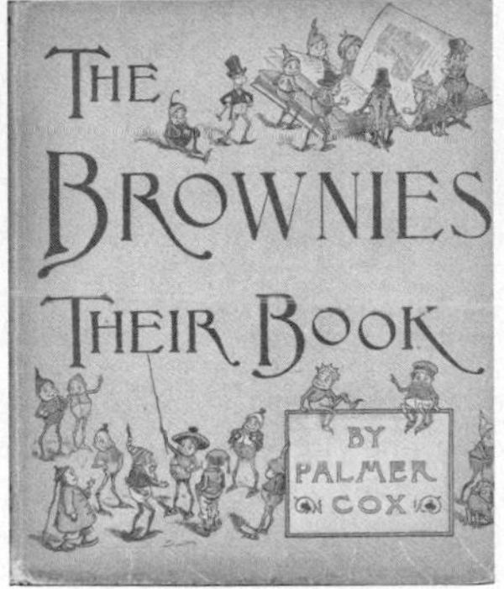

The Brownies' first book, 1887 by Palmer Cox, set a precedent for the Platinum Age, collecting and reprinting previously published material.

It should be noted that "ages" are applied to historical periods in the history of comics for convenience. In fact, ages typically overlap and there is no discrete beginning or ending for any given "age." This is the case with the Platinum Age, which clearly began with Palmer Cox's creation of *The Brownies* in 1883 even though it overlaps with the Victorian Age which ran through the end of the 19th Century. Cox introduced a qualitative change to the field, not an incremental quantitative change. Specifically, he produced art and verse for children in children's magazines and then merchandised those characters. He published work for children not only in books but in magazines and newspapers, and he merchandised his creations to an extent that had never been done previously.

Palmer Cox was born in 1840 near Granby, Quebec. He journeyed to Oakland, California in 1863, and began publishing cartoon, prose and poems in the local press and media outlets such as *The San Francisco Examiner* wherein by 1867 it has been reported he also began creating sequential comic strips, though none have yet surfaced.

His first book, *Squibs of California*, was published in 1874. He subsequently moved to New York in 1875 and almost immediately began working for the magazine *Wild Oats*, of which more is written about in the preceding Victorian Age history introduction as well as a sample of his sequential work. He drew dozens of sequential comic strips for *Wild Oats*, a humor magazine so scarce only one issue has been offered on eBay in the past six years.

Soon thereafter he became a major contributor to the Scribner publications, including *The St. Nicholas*, an illustrated magazine for young folk. His first cartoon for them was "The Wasp And The Bee," published in the March 1879 cover-date issue. While it is now clear that Cox used elves and

The Brownies in the Philippines by Palmer Cox, Oct 1904 - scarce original art from the book. President Roosevelt is pictured within these multitudes of Brownie madness, a Cox "signature trademark." Cox's stories are comic strip-oriented in nature of time sequence as he boldly took his Brownies around the world.

brownie-like characters in his art for several different magazines as early as 1877 in *Harper's Young People* magazine as well as using Brownies-type characters beginning in the Feb 1881 issue of *Wide Awake*, the first true appearance of the Brownies in their own story using that title, a combination of art and verse was February, 1883, in *St. Nicholas*. Palmer Cox's *The Brownies* were the first North American comics-type characters to be internationally merchandised. Even though Cox was continuously doing sequential comic strips in magazines like *Wild Oats*, he left the popular medium of comics when he hit paydirt with *The Brownies*. For over a quarter of a century, Cox deftly combined the popular advertising motifs of animals and fairies into a wonderful, whimsical world of society at its best and worst.

The Inter Ocean Jr.

(Supplement to The Sunday Inter Ocean.)

VOL. XXIII., SUNDAY MAY 27, 1894. NO. 64.

Copyright, 1894, by C. W. Saalburg.

THE TING-LINGS LISTEN TO THE PHONOGRAPH.

Chicago Inter Ocean Jr., May 27, 1894 Cover of The Ting-Lings by Charles W. Saalsburg, was inspired by Palmer Cox's The Brownies and later provided inspiration for Outcault's Yellow Kid.

The Brownies' first book was issued in 1887, titled *The Brownies: Their Book*; many more followed. Cox also added a run of his hugely popular characters in *Ladies Home Journal* from October 1891 through February 1895, as well as a special for December 1910. With the 1892-93 World's Fair, the merchandising exploded with a host of products, including pianos, paper dolls and other figurines, chairs, stoves, puzzles, cough drops, coffee, soap, boots, candy, and many more. *Brownies* material was being produced in Europe as well as the United States of America.

Cox tried out *The Brownies* as a newspaper strip in the *San Francisco Examiner* during 1898, where he had begun his newspaper career over 30 years before, and then in the *New York World* in 1900. It was then syndicated from 1903 through 1907. He seems to have retired from regularly drawing *The Brownies* with the January 1914 issue of *St. Nicholas* when he was 74. A wealthy man, he lived to the ripe old age of 84, spending his last decade in his home he affectionately called Brownie Castle, back in Granby, Quebec.

By the mid-1890s, while keeping careful track of steadily rising circulations of magazines with graphic humor such as *Harper's, Puck, St. Nicholas, Judge, Life* and *Truth*, New York based newspaper publishers began to recognize that illustrated humor would sell extra papers. This is what *The Yellow Kid* taught these publishers. Thus was born the Sunday "comic supplement." Most of the super star favorites were under contract with these magazines. However, there was an artist working for *Truth* who wasn't. Roy L McCardell, then a staffer at *Puck*, informed Morrill Goddard, Sunday Editor of *The New York World*, that he knew someone who could fit what was needed at the then-largest newspaper in America.

Richard F. Outcault (1863-1928) first introduced his street children strip in *Truth* #372, June 2, 1894, somewhat inspired by Michael Angelo Woolf's slum kids single panel cartoons in **Life** which had begun in the mid 1880s. The interested collector should seek out a copy of Woolf's *Sketches of Lowly Life In A Great City* (1899) listed in the *Guide* for comparison study. Edward Harrigan's play "O'Reilly and the Four Hundred," which had a song beginning with the words "Down in Hogan's Alley..." also likely provided direct inspiration.

It's also probable that Outcault's *Hogan's Alley* cast, including the *Yellow Kid*, was inspired by Charles W. Saalburg's *The Ting Lings*, which began in the *Chicago Inter Ocean Jr* supplement post-dated May 1, 1894 in the April 29, 1894 edition of Chicago Inter Ocean. That first episode is titled: "The Brownies Welcome The Ting-Lings."

There is also a definite similarity in Mickey Dugan's appearance and clothing style to Saalburg's creation which we will now examine in more detail thanks to welcome, on-going research by long time comics historian Allan Holtz supplemented by living comics history legend Bill Blackbeard .

Charles Saalzburg was an artist who was also the genius behind color printing in newspapers. He seems to have pioneered the concept from whom all others learned their craft.

On June 23, 1892 the *Chicago Inter Ocean* introduced a section with mostly editorial cartoons titled the *Illustrated Supplement*, commemorating the Democratic National Convention held in that city. Early regulars included Thomas Nast and Art Young. Starting June 26, the *Inter Ocean* began steadily issuing this weekly four page supplement, typically featuring full page editorial cartoons on its front and back covers. In May 1893 the supplement began coming out twice a week, and even greater frequency to daily during the *World Columbian Exposition* held in Chicago later that same year as it was used as a wrapper to attract sales from fair goers. Art Young did some of the color cover art and comic strips for the early Fair supplements, printing them right at the Fair to goggle-eyed fair tourists. Thomas Nast did some art as well during a visit he made to the Fair.

By September 10, 1893 the *Inter Ocean* introduced color, a multi-panel editorial comic strip by Charles Saalsburg. The supplement used yellow ink, a further nail in the coffin of various Yellow Kid myths which had clouded serious comics scholarship in earlier decades before being proven wrong.

On October 1, Tom E. Powers introduced their first sequential non-political comic strip in color, a humorous pantomime.

As the Exposition ended in November, the contents were soon aimed more at children, enhanced with color added to the center as well by December 24, 1893, then changing its title to *Inter Ocean Jr* in January 1894. This was accomplished easily by folding the single four page sheet into eight pages.

In the January 1894 Saalsburg began using Brownies-inspired characters in his color comic strips. The present theory is the *Ting-Ling* characters took over solo five months later in response to a presumed cease and desist letter which inevitably must have been issued from Palmer Cox to the *Inter Ocean.*

However, on July 8 1894, the *Inter Ocean Jr* stopped color and full page comics-type work in this supplement, devolving back to simple small spot art works. By mid-1894, color comics printing genius Saalburg had been lured to Pulitzer's New York World, becoming Art Director in charge of coloring for the new color printing press at the *New York World.* The color supplement was soon to be unleashed in the largest city in America.

By the November 18, 1894 issue of the *World*, Outcault was working for Goddard and Saalburg. Outcault produced a successful Sunday newspaper sequential comic strip in color with "The Origin of a New Species" on the back page in the World's first colored Sunday supplement. Long time pro Walt McDougall, a famous cartoonist reputed to have turned the 1884 Presidential race with a single cartoon that ran in the *World*, handled the cartoon art on the front page. Earlier, *The World* began running full page color single panels on May 21, 1893. McDougall did various other page panels during 1893, but it was Jan. 28, 1894 when the first sequence of comic pictures in a New York World newspaper appeared in panels in the same format as our comic strips today. It was a full page cut up into nine panels. This historic sequence was drawn entirely in pantomime, with no words, by Mark Fenderson.

The second page to appear in panels was an eight panel strip from February 4, 1894, also lacking words except for the title. This page was a collaboration between Walt McDougall and Mark Fenderson titled "The Unfortunate Fate of a Well-Intentioned Dog." From then on, many full page color strips by McDougall and Fenderson appeared; they were the first cartoonists to draw for the Sunday newspaper comic section. It was Outcault, however, who soon became the most famous cartoonist featured. After first appearing in black and white in Pulitzer's *The New York World* on Feb-ruary 17, 1895 and again on March 10, 1895, *The Yellow Kid* was introduced to the public in color on May 5, 1895.

Some have erroneously reported in scholarly journals that perhaps it was Frank Ladendorf's "Uncle Reuben," first introduced May 26, 1895, which became the first regularly recur-

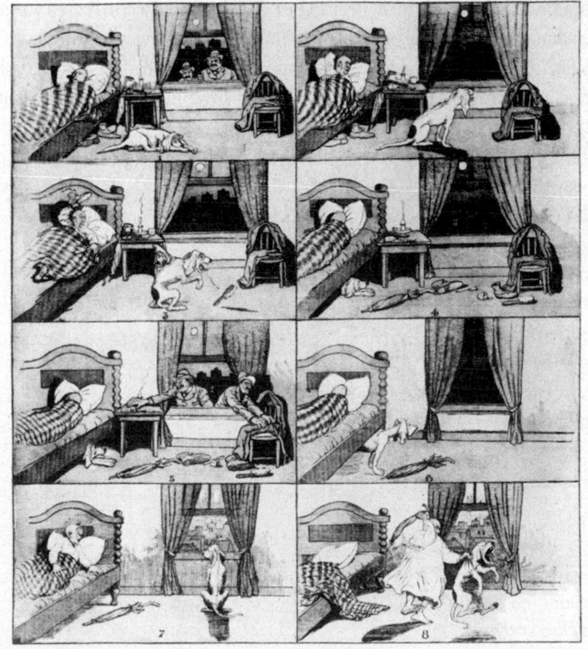

Left: Walt McDougall & Mark Fenderson, the 2nd sequential comic strip in New York World, February 4, 1894, predates Yellow Kid in The World by over a year. Mark Fenderson drew the first NY World newspaper comic strip and we are still hunting down an example to display here in future editions.
Right: New York World, Nov. 18, 1894 predates YK "Origin of A New Species," Richard F. Outcault.

R.F. Outcault
A FAIR CHAMPION.
LORRENNA LAFFERTY (as a parting shot)—Remember dis, Issy Silberman may be a motzer. But de day will come when as a millionaire banker, an' me his bride, de dust his carriage wheels makes t'roo Forsythe street will not be able den to blind yours to his good qualities.

"A Fair Champion" artwork by Richard F. Outcault, Truth, July 14, 1894 (2nd Yellow Kid app.). Many of RFO's comics were fully integrated down around the corner of Hogan's Alley and Ryan's Arcade.

"Fourth Ward Brownies," artwork by Richard F. Outcault, Feb. 17, 1895, the 4th Yellow Kid app. and 1st in Pulitzer's New York World. Note the Kid, second from left. This panel first saw print in Truth, Feb 9, 1895.

ring comics character in newspapers. This is wrong, as even Outcault's "Yellow Kid" began in Pulitzer's paper a good three months before *Uncle Reuben*. Until firm evidence to the contrary comes to light, that honor will forever be enshrined with Jimmy Swinnerton's *Little Bears* cartoon characters, found all over inside Hearst's *San Francisco Examiner* beginning October 14, 1893 with the first one called "Baby Monarch. Though never actually a comic strip, they nonetheless were the earliest presently-known recurring comics-type characters in American newspapers. In June 1895, a semi-regular "Little Bears" feature began. On January 26, 1896, children were introduced, the title eventually changed to "Little Bears and Tykes," forever confusing some scholars decades later. There never was a strip titled *Little Bears and Tigers,* as the *Tigers* were strictly for New York consumption when Hearst ordered Swinnerton to move to the Big Apple to compete better in the brewing comic strip wars.

The Yellow Kid'**s** importance is widely recognized today as the first newspaper comic strip to demonstrate without a doubt that the general public was ready for full color comics. *The Yellow Kid* was the first in the USA to show that comics could increase newspaper sales, and that comic characters could be merchandised. *The Yellow Kid* was the headlining spark of what was soon dubbed by Hearst as "eight pages of polychromatic effulgence that makes the rainbow look like a lead pipe."

Ongoing research suggests that Palmer Cox's fabulous success with *The Brownies* was a direct inspiration for Richard Outcault's future merchandising work. The ultimate proof lies in the fourth Yellow Kid cartoon, which appeared in the February 9, 1895 issue of *Truth*. It was reprinted in the *New York World* eight days later on February 17, 1895, becoming the first Yellow Kid cartoon in the newspapers. The caption read "FOURTH WARD BROWNIES. MICKEY, THE ARTIST (adding a finishing touch) Dere, Chimmy! If Palmer Cox wuz t' see yer, he'd git yer copyrighted in a minute." The Yellow Kid was widely licensed in the greater New York area for all kinds of products, including gum and cigarette cards, toys, pinbacks, cookies, postcards, tobacco products, and appliances. There was also a short-lived humor magazine from

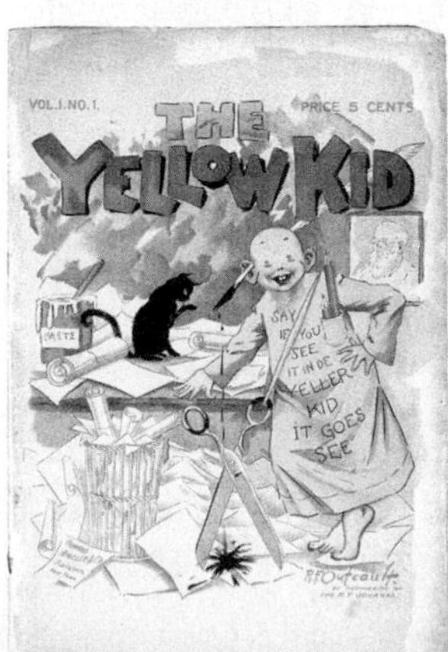

Left: The Yellow Kid #1, March 20, 1897, Street & Smith as Howard Ainslee, NY.
Right: A rare full color "The Yellow Kid in McFadden Flats" advertising sign promoting the first comic book featuring the Yellow Kid. The sign is from 1896 and measures 12x18".

The Adventures of Foxy Grandpa, late 1900, cover for the rare earliest known first edition of Carl "Bunny" Schultze's famous creation. He was one of the newspaper comics' first superstars.

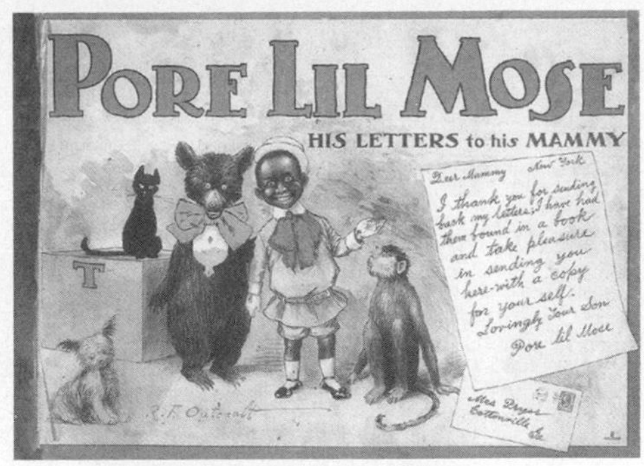

Pore Li'l Mose by Richard Outcault, 1901. Bridges in between Yellow Kid and Buster Brown. Becoming scarce because many copies have been cut up.

Street & Smith named *The Yellow Kid*, featuring exquisite Outcault covers, plus a 196-page comic book from Dilling-ham & Co. known as *The Yellow Kid in McFadden's Flats,* dated to early 1897. Check out the covers in "The Platinum Age" three-page comic strip elsewhere in this Guide. In addition, there were several Yellow Kid plays produced, spawning other collectibles like show posters, programs and illustrated sheet music. (For those interested in more information regarding the Yellow Kid, it is available on the Internet at www.neponset.com/yellowkid.)

Mickey Dugan burned brightly for a few years as Outcault secured a copyright on the character with the United States Government by September 1896. By the time he completed the necessary paperwork, however, hundreds of business people nationwide had pirated the image of The Yellow Kid and plastered it all over every product imaginable; mothers were even dressing their newborns to look like Dugan. Outcault, however, kept regularly utilizing images of *The Yellow Kid* in his comics style advertising work confirmed as late as 1915. Outcault soon found himself in a maelstrom not of his choosing, which probably pushed him to eventually drop the character. Outcault's creation went back and forth between newspaper giants Pulitzer and Hearst until Bennett's New York Herald mercifully snatched the cartoonist away in 1900 to do what amounted to a few relatively short-run strips. Later, he did one particular strip for a year–a satire of rural Black America titled *Pore Li'l Mose His Letters to his Mammy*, and then his newer creation, *Buster Brown*, debuted May 4, 1902. *Mose* had a very rare comic book collection published in 1902 by Cupples & Leon, now highly sought after by today's savvy collectors. Outcault continued drawing him in the background of occasional *Buster Brown* strips for many years to come.

William Randolph Hearst loved the comic strip medium ever since he was a little boy growing up on *Max & Moritz* by Wilhelm Busch in American collected book editions translated from the original German (these collections were first published in book form in 1871, serving as the influence for *The Katzenjammer Kids*). One of the ways Hearst responded to losing Outcault in 1900 was by purchasing the highly successful 23-year-old humor magazine *Puck* from the heirs of founder Joseph Keppler. With *Puck* and its exclusive cartoonist contracts, he commanded, among others, the very popular F. M. Howarth and Frederick Burr Opper's undivided attention. Opper first burst upon the comics scene in America back in 1880. Within a year Hearst had expanded this *National Lampoon* of its day into the colored Sunday comics section, *Puck-The Comic Weekly*. At first featuring Rudolph Dirk's *The Katzenjammer Kids* (1897), *Happy Hooligan* and other fine strips by the wildly popular Opper and a few others including Rudolph's brother Gus Dirks, the Hearst comic section steadily added more strips. For decades to come, there wasn't anything else that could compete with *Puck*. Hearst hired the best of the best and transformed *Puck* into the most popular comics section anywhere.

Outcault, meanwhile, followed in Palmer Cox's footprints a decade later by using the nexus of a World's Fair as a jumping off venue. *Buster Brown* was an instant sensation when he debuted as the new merchandising mascot of the Brown Shoe Company at the 1904 St. Louis World's Fair in a special Buster Brown Shoes pavilion. The character has the honor of being the first nationally licensed comic strip character in America with this time Outcault in almost full control. Many hundreds of different *Buster Brown* premiums have been issued. Comic books by Frederick A. Stokes Company featuring *Buster Brown & His Dog Tige* began as early as 1903 with *Buster Brown and His Resolutions*, simultaneously published in several different languages throughout the world.

After a few years,

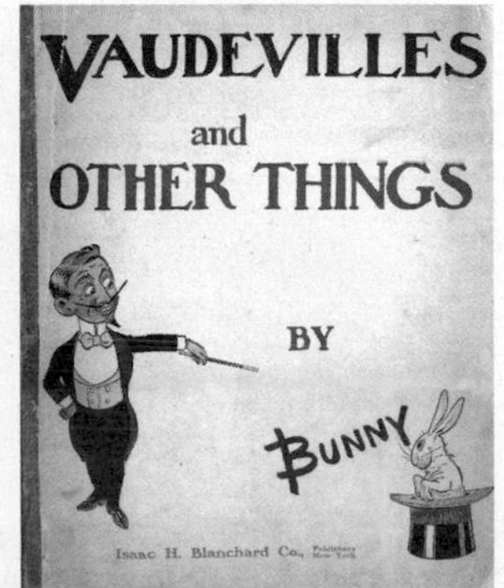

Vaudevilles And Other Things, 1900, first printing. Carl Schultze later became famous for creating Foxy Grandpa.

The Chicago Tribune introduced a straight super hero with obvious super strength called "Hugo Hercules" by the unknown artist J. Koerner. This Sunday strip ran September 7, 1902 through January 11, 1903 and ran only in this one paper. It is entirely possible a very young Chicago-resident named Philip Wylie read "Hugo" since that was the same name he gave his super-heroic main character in his much-later book The Gladiator (1930). Other appearances have Hugo running with almost super speed.

Buster and Outcault returned to Hearst in late 1905, joining what soon became the flagship of the comics world. Buster's popularity quickly spread all over the United States and then the world as he single-handedly spawned the first great comic strip licensing dynasty. For years, there were little people traveling from town to town performing as *Buster Brown* and selling shoes while accompanied by small dogs named Tige. Many other highly competitive licensed strips would soon follow. We suggest getting *Hake's Price Guide to Character Toys* for info on several hundred *Buster Brown* competitors, as well as several pages of the more fascinating *Buster Brown* material.

Soon there were many comic strip syndicates not only offering hundreds of various comic strips but also offering to license the characters for any company interested in paying the fee. The history of the comic strip with wide popularity since *The Yellow Kid* has been intertwined with giveaway premiums and character-based, store-bought merchandise of all kinds. Since its infancy as a profitable art form unto itself with *The Yellow Kid*, the comic strip world has profited from selling all sorts of "stuff" to the public featuring their favorite character or strip as its motif. American business gladly responded to the desire for comic character memorabilia with thousands of fun items to enjoy and collect. Most of the early comics were not aimed specifically at kids, though children understandably enjoyed them as well.

Comic books have generally been associated with almost all of the licensed merchandise in this century. In the Platinum Age section beginning right after this essay, you will find a great many comic books in varied formats and sizes pub-

Katzenjammer Kids #1, 1902, by Rudolph Dirks was inspired by Wilhelm Busch.

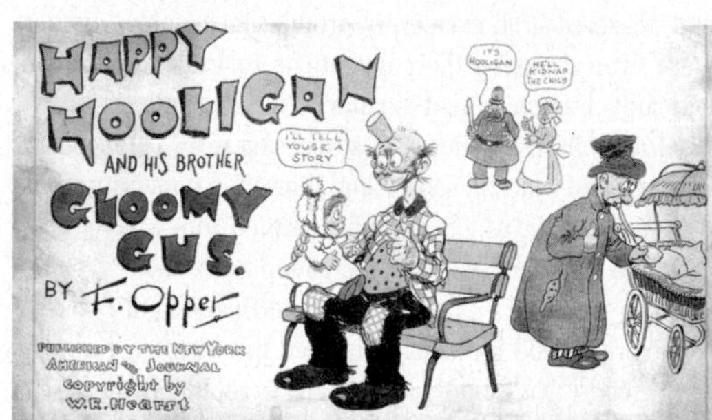

Happy Hooligan Book #1, 1902, by Frederick Opper, was wildly popular.

Katzenjammer Kids #2 by Rudolph Dirks. These Katz Kids have the longest running strip in America.

The second Happy Hooligan comic book, 1903, by Frederick Opper set a high standard.

Originally discovered listed for sale in a 1906 Lockwood Art School brochure, the existences of The Naughty Adventures of Vivacious Mr. Jack and Alphonse and Gaston New Edition 1903 were recently verified. Several copies of each are known to exist.

lished before the advent of the first successful monthly newsstand comic magazine, *Famous Funnies*. What drove each of these evolutionary format changes was the need by their producers to make money so more books could be issued.

A very significant format was F. M. Howarth's *Funny Folks*, published in 1899 by E. P. Dutton and drawn from color as well as black and white pages of *Puck*. This rather large hardcover volume measured 16 1/2" wide by 12" tall. It contains numerous sequential comic strip pages as well as single gag illustrations. Howarth's art was a joy to behold and deserves wider recognition.

By Oct. 1900, Hearst had already caused Opper's *Folks In Funnyville* to be collected by publisher R. H. Russell, NY in a 12x9 hard cover format from his *New York Journal American Humorist* section. At the end of 1900, Carl Shultze had a first edition of *Vaudevilles and Other Things* published by Isaac H. Blanchard Co., NY. It measures 10 1/2" wide by 13" tall with 22 pages including covers. Each interior page is a 2 to 7 panel comic strip with lots of color.

There were also recently unearthed format variation second and third printings of *Vaudevilles* with the inscription "From the Originator of the 'Foxy Grandpa' Series" at the bottom of its front cover of the third printing. This note is lacking on the earlier first two editions, and it also switches format size to 11" tall by 13" wide. Discovered last year was a heretofore undocumented *The Adventures of Foxy Grandpa* - also issued in 1900 - new to the Platinum listings. The second number dated 1901 drops the words "The Adventures of..." from the title.

E. W. Kemble's *The Blackberries* had a color collection by 1901, also published by R. H. Russell, NY, as well as a few other comic-related volumes by Kemble still to be unearthed and properly identified. An earlier one was titled *Coontown's 400* (1899) newly listed this year. While the title is definitely not "PC" by today's standards, Kemble's drawings are excellent slices of African-American life in the USA with some humor injected. Kemble did a good job documenting aspects of life.

Confirmed is the exact format of Hearst's 1902 *The Katzenjammer Kids and Happy Hooligan And His Brother Gloomy Gus*. They both measure 15 5/16" wide by 10" tall and contain 88 pages including covers. Confirmed also is the fact that there are two separate editions with different covers for the pictured 1902 first edition and a 1903 Frederick Stokes edition of *Katzenjammer Kids* and *Happy Hooligan* with differing contents. They both are two different books entirely, and what confuses many collectors is that they have identical indicia title pages, but so does an entirely different *KK* from 1905.

Settling on a popular size of 17" wide by 11" tall, comic books were soon available that featured Charles "Bunny" Schultze's *Foxy Grandpa*, Rudolph Dirk's *The Katzenjammer Kids*, Winsor McCay's *Little Sammy Sneeze, Rarebit Fiend* and *Little Nemo*, and Fred Opper's *Happy Hooligan* and *Maud*, in addition to dozens of *Buster Brown* comic books.

Little Sammy Sneeze, 1905, by Winsor McCay.

The Three FunMakers, 1908, the first anthology Platinum Age comic book.

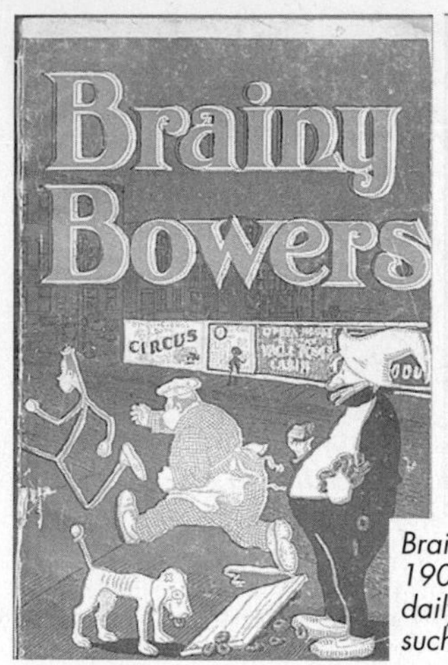

Brainy Bowers and Drowsy Duggan by R.W. Taylor 1905 © Star Publishing Co - appears to be the first daily newspaper reprint comic book compilation ever. As such, this is a sleeper investment comic book.

were reprinted over and over as demand warranted. Note the number of titles in the advertisement pulled from the back of *The Three Fun Makers* shown below.

With the ever-increasing popularity of Bud Fisher's new daily strip sensation, *Mutt & Jeff*, a new format was created for reprinting daily strips in black and white, a hardcover book about 15" wide by 5" tall, published by Ball starting in 1910 for five volumes. In 1912, Ball also branched out with at least the now-obscure *Doings of the Van Loons* by Fred I. Leipziger, a rare comic book in the same format as the *Mutt & Jeffs*.

For well over a decade, these large-size, full-color volumes were the norm, retailing for 60¢. These collections offered full-size Sunday comics with the back side blank per page.

Though not the first daily newspaper strip, the very rare *Brainy Bowers and Drowsy Dugan* by R. W. Taylor is now crowned the first collection of strip reprints from a daily newspaper published in America. There are now four different collections of Brainy Bower known to exist.

The Outbursts of Everett True by A. D. Condo and J. W. Raper was first published by Saalfield in 1907 in an 88-page hardcover collection. It qualifies as the second daily comic strip collection as it predates the first *Mutt & Jeff* collection from Ball by three years. Condo & Raper's creation began its regular run several times a week in 1905 daily newspapers and lasted until 1927, when Condo became too sick to continue. This same *Everett True* collection was later truncated a bit by Saalfield in 1921 to 56 strips in just 32 pages measuring the standard 10"x10" Cupples & Leon size.

By 1908 Stokes had a large backlist of full color comic books for sale at 60¢ each. Some of these titles date back to 1903 and

Cartoons Magazine also began in 1912 and ran through 1921 before undergoing a radical format change. It is notable as a wonderful source for information on early comics and their creators. See also the Platinum index.

The next significant evolutionary change occurred in 1919, when Cupples & Leon began issuing their black and white daily strip reprint books in a new aforementioned format, about 10" wide by 10" tall, with four panels reprinted per page in a two by two matrix. These books were 52 pages for 25¢. The first ones featured *Bringing Up Father* and *Mutt & Jeff;* there were about 100 others.

By 1921, the last of the oblong (11"x15") color comic books were issued, with Cupples & Leon's *Jimmie Dugan* and *The Reg'lar Fellers* by Gene Byrne, and EmBee's *The Trouble Of Bringing Up Father* by self publisher George McManus. Of special historical interest, Embee issued the first 10¢ monthly comic book, *Comic Monthly,* with the first

Left, The Outbursts of Everett True. 2nd daily strip collection, published 1907 Right: The earliest known comic book display ad, from in the back of1908 Stokes comic books, 27 titles then in print. Cover prices are 60¢.

issue dated January 1922. A dozen 8-1/2"x9" issues were published, each featuring solo adventures of popular King Features strips. The monthly 10¢ comic book concept had finally arrived, though it would be more than a decade before it became truly successful.

Above, Mutt & Jeff #5 by Bud Fisher, 1916, is fairly scarce as there was only one printing. Below, Reg'lar Fellers by Gene Byrne, 1921, one of the very last large oblong comics.

Skippy by Percy Crosby debuted in the long-running humor magazine *Life* in the March 22, 1923 issue. By 1924 the first hard cover collection, *Life Presents Skippy*, was published. The newspaper comic strip debuted June 23, 1925 with the McClure syndicate. Hearst soon picked up a Sunday page a year later in mid-1926, then added a daily strip in 1929. By the 1930s it was red hot - think *Calvin & Hobbes or Peanuts* in popularity. In its day, it was one of the most popular comic strips ever created. Read the Modern era essay for more on *Skippy's* immense popularity.

In 1926, Cupples & Leon added a new 7" wide by 9" tall format with *Little Orphan Annie, Smitty,* and others. These were issued in both softcover and hardcover editions with dust jackets, and became extremely popular at 60¢ per copy.

Dell began publishing all original material in *The Funnies* in late 1929 in a larger tabloid format. At least three dozen issues were published before Delacorte threw in the towel. Even the extremely popular *Big Little Book*, introduced in 1932, can be viewed as a smaller version of the existing formats. The competition amongst publishers now included Dell, McKay, Sonnet, Saalfield and Whitman. The 1930s saw a definite shift in merchandising comic strip material from adults to children. This was the decade when Kellogg's placed *Buck Rogers* on the map, when Ovaltine issued tons of *Little Orphan Annie* material. Merchandising from such pioneers as Sam Gold and Kay Kamen spearheaded this next transformation of the comics biz beginning in the early 1930s.

Upwards of a thousand of these *Funnies On Parade* precursors, in all formats, were published through 1935 and were very popular. Towards the end of this era of once-popular comic book formats, beautiful collections of *Popeye, Mickey Mouse, Dick Tracy*, and many others were published which today command ever higher prices on the open market as they are rediscovered by the advanced collector who appreciates and enjoys truly great classic comics.

END NOTE: Each year we strive to add to the many 1930s variant formats. This Platinum Age section has grown as a result of advanced collectors who continue to report in with new finds. We encourage interested collectors and scholars to help with this section of the book, as each new data entry is very important for recovering our history. For corrections and additions to next year's next edition of *The Overstreet Guide* of some treasures you may have uncovered, please feel free to contact Gemstone Publishing at feedback@gemstonepub.com.

For further information on this era of American comic books, check out the previous evolving comics history essays in Guides #27,29-#37. Happy Hunting!

Comic Monthly #11 1922 (top), the first 10¢ monthly newsstand comic book title.

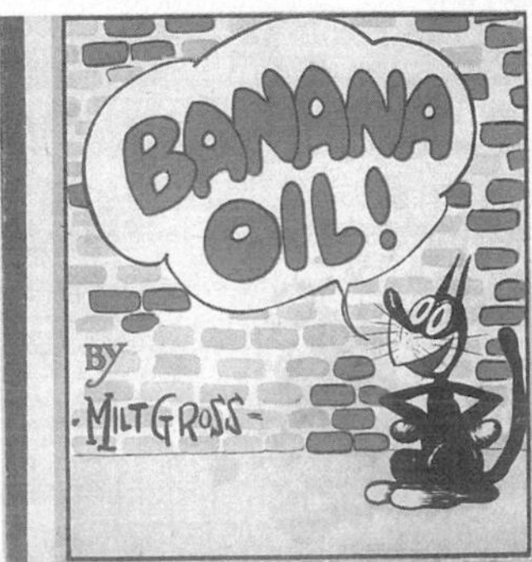

Banana Oil, a 1924 example of Cupples & Leon's then-revolutionary format from M.S. Publishers

Tillie the Toiler #8 1933 from Cupples & Leon, another scarce number at the end of this once popular format.

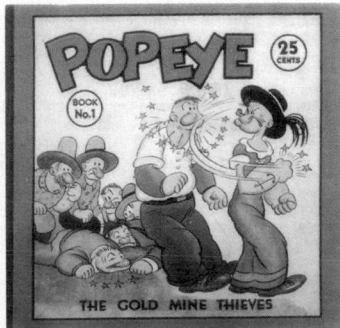

David McKay published the last of the 10x10 comic books in 1935 as Famous Funnies grew in popularity.

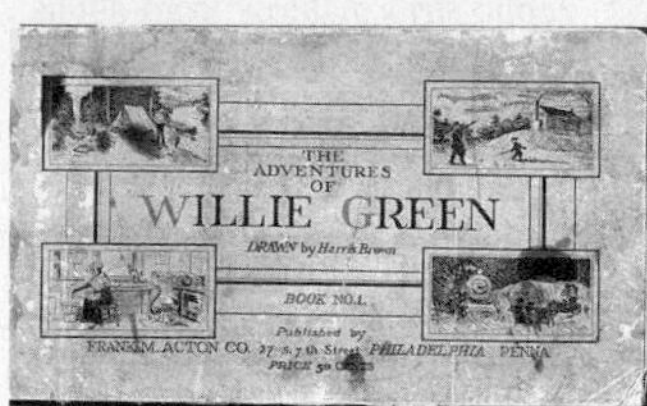

The Adventures of Willie Green
© Frank M. Acton

American-Journal-Examiner Joke Book
Special Suuplement #12
1912 © New York American-Examiner

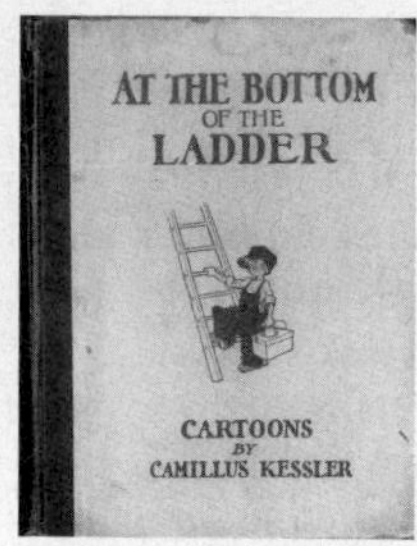

At The Bottom Of The Ladder
1926 © J.P. Lippincott Company

GD2.0 FN6.0 VF8.0

COLLECTOR'S NOTE: The books listed in this section were published many decades before organized comics fandom began archiving and helping to preserve these fragile popular culture artifacts. Consequently, copies of most all of these comics do not often surface in Fine+ or better shape. eBay has proven after more than a decade that many items once considered rare actually are not, though they almost always are in higher grades. For items marked scarce, we are trying to ascertain how many copies might still be in existence. Your input is always welcome.

Most Platinum Age comic books are in the Fair to VG range. If you want to collect these only in high grade, your collection will be extremely small. The prices given for Good, Fine and Very Fine categories are for strictly graded editions. If you need help grading your item, we refer you to the grading section in the front of this price guide or contact the authors of the Platinum essay. Most measurements are in inches. A few measurements are in centimeters. The first dimension given is Height and the second is Width.

For ease of ascertaining the contents of each item of this listing, there is a code letter or two following most titles we have been adding in over the years to aid you. A helpful list of categories pertaining to these codes can be found at the beginning of the Victorian Age pricing sections.This section created, revised, and expanded by Robert Beerbohm and Richard Olson with able assistance from Ray Agricola, Jon Berk, Bill Blackbeard, Roy Bonario, Ray Bottorff Jr., Chris Brown, Alfredo Castelli, Darrell Coons, Sol Davidson, Leonardo De Sá, Scott Deschaine, Mitchell Duval, Joe Evans, Tom Gordon III, Bruce Hamilton, Andy Konkykru, Don Kurtz, Gabriel Laderman, Bruce Mason, Donald Puff, Robert Quesinberry, Steve Rowe, Randy Scott, John Snyder, Art Spiegelman, Steve Thompson, Joan Crosby Tibbets, Richard Samuel West, Doug Wheeler, Richard Wright and Craig Yoe.

ADVENTURES OF EVA, PORA AND TED (M)
Evaporated Milk Association: 1932 (5x15", 16 pgs, B&W)

nn - By Steve 10.00 30.00 70.00
NOTE: *Appears to have had green, blue or white paper cover versions.*

ADVENTURES OF HAWKSHAW (N) (See Hawkshaw The Detective)
The Saalfield Publishing Co.: 1917 (9-3/4x13-1/2", 48 pgs., color & two-tone)

nn - By Gus Mager (only 24 pgs. of strips, reverse of each pg. is blank) 50.00 175.00 300.00
nn - 1927 Reprints 1917 issue 30.00 150.00 260.00
NOTE: *Started Feb 23, 1913-Sept 4, 1922, then begins again Dec 13, 1931-Feb 11, 1952.*

ADVENTURES OF SLIM AND SPUD, THE (M)
Prairie Farmer Publ. Co.: 1924 (3-3/4x 9-3/4", 104 pgs., B&W strip reprints)

nn 21.00 84.00 150.00
NOTE: *Illustrated mailing envelope exists postmarked out of Chicago, add 50%.*

ADVENTURES OF WILLIE WINTERS, THE (O,P)
Kelloggs Toasted Corn Flake Co.: 1912 (6-7/8x9-1/2", 20 pgs, full color)

nn - By Byron Williams & Dearborn Melvill 54.00 189.00 350.00

ADVENTURES OF WILLIE GREEN, THE (N) (see The Willie Green Comics)
Frank M. Acton Co.: 1915 (50¢, 52 pgs, 8-1/2X16", B&W, soft-c)

Book 1 - By Harris Brown; strip-r 54.00 189.00 350.00

A. E. F. IN CARTOONS BY WALLY, THE (N)
Don Sowers & Co.: 1933 (12x10-1/8", 88 pgs, hardcover B&W)

nn - By Wally Wallgren (WW One Stars & Stripes-r) 25.00 90.00 150.00

AFTER THE TOWN GOES DRY (I)
The Howell Publishing Co, Chicago: 1919 (48 pgs, 6-1/2x4", hardbound two color-c)

nn - By Henry C. Taylor; illus by Frank King 25.00 75.00 150.00

AIN'T IT A GRAND & GLORIOUS FEELING? (N) (Also see Mr. & Mrs.)
Whitman Publishing Co.: 1922 (9x9-3/4", 52 pgs., stiff cardboard-c)

nn - 1921 daily strip-r; B&W, color-c; Briggs-a 36.00 143.00 250.00
nn -(9x9-1/2", 28pgs., stiff cardboard-c)-Sunday strip-r in color (inside front-c says "More of the Married Life of Mr. & Mrs".) 36.00 143.00 250.00
NOTE: *Strip started in 1917; This is the 2nd Whitman comic book, after Brigg's MR. & MRS.*

ALL THE FUNNY FOLKS (I)
World Press Today, Inc.: 1926 (11-1/2x8-1/2", 112 pgs., color, hard-c)

nn-Barney Google, Spark Plug, Jiggs & Maggie, Tillie The Toiler, Happy Hooligan, Hans & Fritz, Toots & Casper, etc. 100.00 400.00 700.00
With Dust Jacket By Louis Biedermann 200.00 800.00 1600.00
NOTE: *Booklength race horse story masterfully enveloping all major King Features characters.*

ALPHONSE AND GASTON AND THEIR FRIEND LEON (N)
Hearst's New York American & Journal: 1902,1903 (10x15-1/4", Sunday strip reprints in color)

nn - (1902) - By Frederick Opper (scarce) 500.00 1800.00 -
nn - (1903) - By Frederick Opper (scarce) (72 pages) 500.00 1800.00 -
NOTE: *Strip ran Sept 22, 1901to at least July 17, 1904.*

ALWAYS BELITTLIN' (see Skippy; That Rookie From the 13th Squad; Between Shots)
Henry Holt & Co.: 1927 (6x8", hard-c with DJ,

nn -By Percy Crosby (text with cartoons) 43.00 172.00 300.00

ALWAYS BELITTLIN' (I) (see Skippy; That Rookie From the 13th Squad, Between Shots)
Percy Crosby, Publisher: 1933 (14 1/4 x 11", 72 pgs, hard-c, B&W)

nn - By Percy Crosby 43.00 172.00 300.00
NOTE: *Self-published; primarily political cartoons with text pages denouncing prohibition's gang warfare effects and cuts in the national defense budget as Crosby saw war looming in Europe and with Japan.*

AMERICAN-JOURNAL-EXAMINER JOKE BOOK SPECIAL SUPPLEMENT (O)
New York American: 1911-12 (12 x 9 3/4", 16 pgs) (known issues) (Very Rare)

1 Tom Powers Joke Book(12/10/11) 80.00 280.00 -
2 Mutt & Jeff Joke Book (Bud Fisher 12/17/11) 100.00 350.00 -
3 TAD's Joke Book (Thomas Dorgan 12/24/11) 80.00 300.00 -
4 F. Opper's Joke Book (Frederick Burr Opper 12/31/11) (contains Happy Hooligan) 100.00 350.00 -
5 not known to exist
6 Swinnerton's Joke Book (Jimmy Swinnerton 01/14/12) (contains Mr. Jack) 100.00 350.00 -
7 The Monkey's Joke Book (Gus Mager 01/21/12) (contains Sherlocko the Monk) 100.00 350.00 -
8 Joys And Glooms Joke Book (T. E. Powers 01/28/12) 80.00 280.00 -
9 The Dingbat Family's Joke Book (George Herriman 02/04/12) (contains early Krazy Kat & Ignatz) 200.00 700.00 -
10 Valentine Joke Book, A (Opper, Howarth, Mager, T. E. Powers 02/11/12) 80.00 280.00 -
11 Little Hatchet Joke Book (T. E. Powers 02/18/12) 80.00 280.00 -
12 Jungle Joke Book (Dirks, McCay 02/25/12) 100.00 400.00 -
13 The Hayseeds Joke Book (03/03/12) 80.00 280.00 -
14 Married Life Joke Book (T.E. Powers 03/10/12) 80.00 280.00 -
NOTE: *These were insert newspaper supplements similar to Eisner's later Spirit sections. A Valentine Joke Book recently surfaced from Hearst's Boston Sunday American proving that other cities besides New York City had these special supplements. Each issue also contains work by other cartoonists besides the cover featured creator and those already listed above such as Sidney Smith, Winsor McCay, Hy Mayer, Grace Weiderseim (later Drayton), others.*

AMERICA'S BLACK & WHITE BOOK 100 Pictured Reasons Why We Are At War (N,S)
Cupples & Leon: 1917 (10 3/4 x 8", 216 pgs)

nn - W. A. Rogers (New York Herald-r) 32.00 114.00 195.00

AMONG THE FOLKS IN HISTORY
Rand McNally Print Guild: 1935 (192 pgs, 8-1/2x9-1/2", hard-c, B&W)

nn - By Gaar Williams 21.00 84.00 150.00

AMONG THE FOLKS IN HISTORY
The Book and Print Guild: 1935 (200 pgs, 8-1/2x9-1/2:,

nn - By Gaar Williams 21.00 84.00 150.00
NOTE: *Both the above are evidently different editions and contain largely full-page, single panel cartoons similar to Briggs' work of that sort. 8 or 10 pages are broken into panels, usually with a this is how it was in the old days, this is how it is today theme.*

ANGELIC ANGELINA (N)
Cupples & Leon Company: 1909 (11-1/2x17", 56 pgs., 2 colors)

nn - By Munson Paddock 67.00 233.00 400.00
NOTE: *Strip ran March 22, 1908-Feb 7, 1909.*

ANDY GUMP, HIS LIFE STORY (I)
The Reilly & Lee Co, Chicago: 1924 (192 pgs, hardbound)

nn - By Sidney Smith (over 100 illustrations) 20.00 80.00 150.00

ANIMAL CIRCUS, THE (from Puggery Wee)
Rand McNally + Company: 1908 (48 pgs, 11x8-1/2", color-c, 3-color insides)

nn - By unknown 20.00 80.00 150.00
NOTE: *Illustrated verse, many pages with multiple illustrations.*

ANIMAL SERIALS
T. Y. Crowell: 1906 (9x6-7/8", 214 pgs, hard-c, B&W)

nn - By E Warde Blaisdell 20.00 80.00 150.00
NOTE: *Multi-page comic strip stories. Reprints of Sunday strip "Bunny Bright He's All-Right".*

A NOBODY'S SCRAP BOOK
Frederik A. Stokes Co., New York: 1900 (11" x 8-5/8", hard-c, color)

nn- (Scarce) 67.00 233.00 400.00
NOTE: *Designed in England, printed in Holland, on English paper -- which likely explains the mispelling of Frederick Stokes' name. Highly fragile paper. Strips and cartoons, all by the same unidentified artist, "A Nobody", almost certainly reprinted from somewhere, as they are very professional.*

AT THE BOTTOM OF THE LADDER (M)
J.P. Lippincott Company: 1926 (11x8-1/4", 296 pgs, hardcover, B&W)

nn - By Camillus Kessler 45.00 157.50 300.00
NOTE: *Hilarious single panel cartoons showing first jobs of then important "captains of industry."*

AUTO FUN, PICTURES AND COMMENTS FROM "LIFE"
Thomas Y. Crowell & Co.: 1905 (152 pgs, 9x7", hard-c, B&W)

nn -By various 45.00 157.00 300.00
NOTE: *The cover just has "Auto Fun" but the title page also has the subheading listed here. This is similar to other reprint books of Life cartoons printed in the guide. Largely single panel cartoons but also several sequential. One or more cartoons by Kemble, Levering, Dirks, Flagg, Sullivant. Sequential cartoons by Kemble, Levering, Sullivant, and the highpoint, a 2 pg 6 panel piece by Winsor McCay.*

BANANA OIL (N) (see also HE DONE HER WRONG)

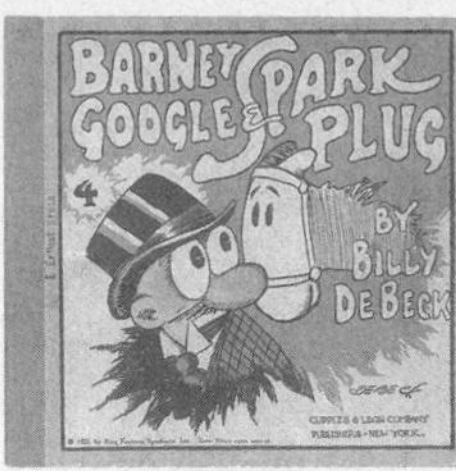

Barney Google and Spark Plug #4
1926 © Cupples & Leon

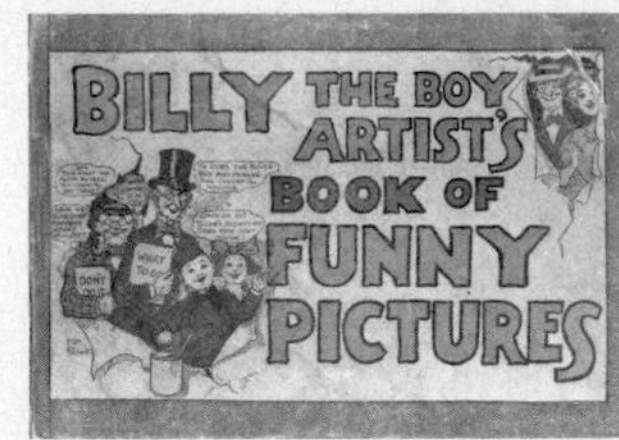

Bill the Boy Artist's Book by Ed Payne
1910 © C.M. Clark Publishing Co

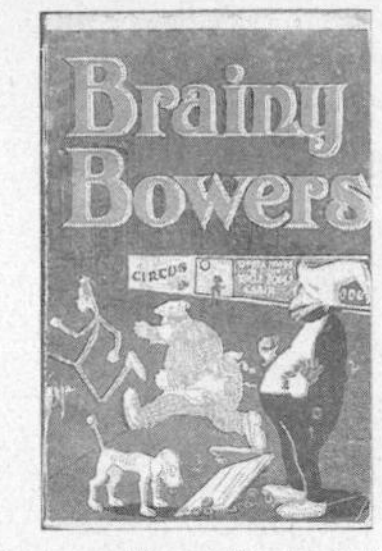

Brainy Bowers and Drowsy Duggan by R.W. Taylor
1905 © Star Publishing Co. - the first daily reprints

GD2.0 FN6.0 VF8.0

MS Publ. Co.: 1924 (9-7/8x10", 52 pgs., B&W)
nn - Milt Gross comic strips; not reprints 150.00 450.00 750.00

BARKER'S ILLUSTRATED ALMANAC (O,P,S) (See Barkers in Victorian Era section)
Barker, Moore & Mein Medicine Co: 1900-1932+ (36 pgs, B&W, color paper-c)
1900-1932+ (7x5-7/8") 20.00 70.00 125.00

BARKER'S "KOMIC" PICTURE SOUVENIR (P,S) (see Barker's in Victorian)
Barker, Moore & Mein Medicine Co: nd (Parts 1-3, 1901-1903; Parts 1-4, 1906+) (color cardboard-c, B&W interior, 50 pages)
Parts 1-3 (Rare, earliest printing, nd (1901)) 60.00 300.00 600.00
NOTE: *Same cover as 4th edition in Victorian Age Section, except has "Part 1", "Part 2", or "Part 3" printed in the blank space beneath the crate on which central figure is sitting. States "Edition in 3 Parts" on the first interior page, beneath the picture of the Barker's Building.*
Parts 1-3 (nd, c1901-1903) 40.00 200.00 400.00
NOTE: *New cover art on all Parts. States "Edition in 3 Parts" on the first interior page.*
Parts 1-4 (nd, c1906+) 25.00 100.00 300.00
NOTE: *States "Edition in 4 Parts" on the first interior page. Various printings known.These have been confirmed as premium comic books, predating the Buster Brown premiums. They reprint advertising cartoons from Barker's Illustrated Almanac. For the 50 page booklets by this same name, numbered as "Part"s, without exception, were published after 1900. Some editions are found to have 54 pages.*

BARNEY GOOGLE AND SPARK PLUG (N) (See **Comic Monthly**)
Cupples & Leon Co.: 1923 - No.6, 1928 (9-7/8x9-3/4"; 52 pgs., B&W, daily-r)
1 (nn)-By Billy DeBeck 60.00 240.00 450.00
2-4 (#5 & #6 do not exist) 46.00 186.00 350.00
NOTE: *Started June 17, 1919 as newspaper strip; Spark Plug introduced July 17, 1922; strip still running making it one of the oldest still in existence.*

BART'S CARTOONS FOR 1902 FROM THE MINNEAPOLIS JOURNAL (N,S)
Minneapolis Journal: 1903 (11x9", 102 pgs, paperback, B&W)
nn - By Charles L. Bartholomew 28.00 99.00 170.00

BELIEVE IT OR NOT! by Ripley (N,S)
Simon & Schuster: 1929 (8x 5-1/4", 68 pgs, red, B&W cover, B&W interior)
nn - By Robert Ripley (strip-r text & art) 40.00 120.00 240.00
NOTE: *1929 was the first printing of many reprintings . Strip began Dec 19, 1918 and is still running.*

BEN WEBSTER (N)
Standard Printing Company: 1928-1931 (13-3/4x4-7/16", 768 pgs, soft-c)
1 - "Bound to Win" 40.00 120.00 280.00
2 - "...in old Mexico 40.00 120.00 280.00
3 - "...At Wilderness Lake 40.00 120.00 280.00
4 - "...in the Oil Fields 40.00 120.00 280.00
NOTE: *Self Published by Edwin Alger, also contains fan's letter pages.*

BIG SMOKER
W.T. Blackwell & Co.: 1908 (16 pgs, 5-1/2x3-1/2", color-c & interior)
nn - By unknown 12.00 48.00 80.00
NOTE: *Stated reprint of 1878 version. no known copies yet of original printing.*

BILLY BOUNCE (I)
Donohue & Co.: 1906 (288 pgs, hardbound)
nn - By W.W. Denslow & Dudley Bragdon 150.00 525.00 900.00
NOTE: *Billy Bounce was created in 1901 as a comic strip by W. W. Denslow (strip ran from 1901 NOV 11 to 1905 DEC 3), but the series is best remembered in the C. W. Kahles version (from 1902 SEP 28). Denslow resumed his character in the above illustrated book.*

BILLY HON'S FAMOUS CARTOON BOOK (H)
Wasley Publishing Co.: 1927 (7-1/2x10", 68 pgs, softbound wraparound)
nn - By Billy Hon 12.00 48.00 80.00

BILLY THE BOY ARTIST'S BOOK OF FUNNY PICTURES (N)
C.M.Clark Publishing Co.: 1910 (9x12", hardcover-c, Boston Globe strip-r)
nn - By Ed Payne 125.00 400.00 750.00
NOTE: *This long lived strip ran in* ***The Boston Globe*** *from Nov 5 1899-Jan 7 1955; one of the longer run strips.*

BILLY THE BOY ARTIST'S PAINTING BOOK OF FUNNY PICTURES
(known to exist; more data required) - - -

BIRD CENTER CARTOONS: A Chronicle of Social Happenings (N,S)
A. C. McClurg & Co.: 1904 (12-3/8x9-1/2", 216 pgs, hardcover, B&W, single panels)
nn - By John McCutcheon 40.00 140.00 260.00
NOTE: *Strip began in* ***The Chicago Tribune*** *in 1903. Satirical cartoons and text concerning a mythical town.*

BLASTS FROM THE RAM'S HORN
The Rams Horn Company: 1902 (330 pgs, 7x9", B&W)
nn - By various 20.00 70.00 120.00
NOTE: *Cartoons reprinted from what was, apparently, a religious newspaper. Many cartoons by Frank Beard. Mostly single panel but occasionally sequential. Allegorical cartoons similar to the Christian Cartoons book. This book mixes cartoons and text sort of like the Caricature books. One or more cartoons on every page.*

BOBBY THATCHER & TREASURE CAVE (N)
Altemus Co.: 1932 (9x7", 86 pgs., B&W, hard-c)
nn - Reprints; Storm-a 54.00 189.00 400.00

BOBBY THATCHER'S ROMANCE (N)
The Bell Syndicate/Henry Altemus Co.: 1931 (8-3/4x7", color cover, B&W)
nn - By Storm 54.00 189.00 400.00

BOOK OF CARTOONS, A (M,S)
Edward T. Miller: 1903 (12-1/4x9-1/4", 120 pgs, hardcover, B&W)
nn - By Harry J. Westerman (Ohio State Journal-r) 20.00 70.00 120.00

BOOK OF DRAWINGS BY A.B. FROST, A (M,S)
P.F. Collier & Son: 1904 (15-3/8 x 11", 96 pgs, B&W)
nn - A.B. Frost 50.00 100.00 300.00
NOTE: *Pages alternate verses by Wallace Irwin and full-page plated by A.B.Frost. 39 plates.*

BOTTLE, THE (E) (see Victorian Age section for earlier printings)
Gowans & Gray, London & Glasgow: June 1905 (3-3/4x6", 72 pgs, printed one side only, paper cover, B&W)
nn - 1st printing (June 1905) 17.50 35.00 70.00
nn - 2nd printing (March 1906) 17.50 35.00 70.00
nn - 3rd printing (January 1911) 17.50 35.00 70.00
NOTE: *By George Cruikshank. Reprints both THE BOTTLE and THE DRUNKARD'S CHILDREN. Cover is text only - no cover art.*

BOTTLE, THE (E)
Frederick A. Stokes: nd (c1906) (3-3/4x6", 72 pgs, printed one side only, paper-c, B&W)
nn- by George Cruikchank 17.50 35.00 70.00
NOTE: *Reprint of the Gowans & Gray edition. Reprints both THE BOTTLE and THE DRUNKARD'S CHILDREN. Cover is text only - no cover art.*

BOYS AND FOLKS (N).
George H. Dornan Company: 1917 (10-1/4 x 8-1/4", 232 pgs. (single-sided), B&W strip-r.
nn - By Webster 21.00 64.00 150.00
NOTE: *Four sections: Life's Darkest Moments, Mostly About Folks, The Thrill That Comes Once in a Lifetime, and Our Boyhood Ambitions. Most are single-panel cartoons, but there are some sequential comic strips.*

BOY'S & GIRLS' BIG PAINTING BOOK OF INTERESTING COMIC PICTURES (N)
M. A. Donohue & Co.: 1914-16 (9x15, 70 pgs)
nn - By Carl "Bunny" Schultze (Foxy Grandpa-r) 81.00 284.00 -
#2 (1914) 81.00 284.00 -
#337 (1914) (sez "Big Painting & Drawing Book") 81.00 284.00 -
nn - (1916) (sez "Big Painting Book")(9 1/4x15") 81.00 284.00 -
NOTE: *These are all* ***Foxy Grandpa*** *items.*

BRAIN LEAKS: Dialogues of Mutt & Flea (N)
O. K. Printing Co. (Rochester Evening Times): 1911 (76 pgs, 6-5/8x4-5/8, hard-c, B&W)
nn - By Leo Edward O'Melia; newspaper strip-r 29.00 100.00 171.00

BRAINY BOWERS AND DROWSY DUGGAN (N)
Star Publishing: 1905 (7-1/4 x 4-9/16", 98 pgs., blue, brown & white color cover, B&W interior, 25¢) (daily strip-r 1902-04 Chicago Daily News)
#74 - By R. W. Taylor (Scarce) 500.00 1700.00 -
NOTE: *Part of a series of Atlantic Library Heart Series. Strip begins in 1901 and runs thru 1915. Taylor also created Yen the Janitor for the* ***New York World.***

BRAIN BOWERS AND DROWSY DUGAN (N)
Max Stein Pub. House, Chicago: 1905 (6-3/16x4-3/8", 64 pgs, B&W)
nn - By R.W. Taylor (Scarce) 500.00 1700.00 -
NOTE: *A coverless copy of this surfaced on eBay in 2002 selling for $700.00.;*

BRAINY BOWERS AND DROWSY DUGGAN GETTING ON IN THE WORLD WITH NO VISIBLE MEANS OF SUPPORT (STORIES TOLD IN PICTURES TO MAKE THEIR TELLING SHORT) (N)
Max Stein/Star Publishing: 1905 (7-3/8x5 1/8", 164 pgs, slick black, red & tan color cover, interior newsprint) (daily strip-r 1902-04 Chicago Daily News)
nn - By R. W. Taylor (Scarce) 500.00 1700.00 -
nn - Possible hard cover edition also? - - -
NOTE: *These Brainy Bowers editions are the earliest known daily newspaper strip reprint books.*

BRINGING UP FATHER (N)
Star Co. (King Features): 1917 (5-1/2x16-1/2", 100 pgs., B&W, cardboard-c)
nn - (Scarcer)-Daily strip- by George McManus 158.00 553.00 950.00

BRINGING UP FATHER (N)
Cupples & Leon Co.: 1919 - No. 26, 1934 (10x10", 52 pgs., B&W, stiff cardboard-c) (No. 22 is 9-1/4x9-1/2")
1-Daily strip-r by George McManus in all 25.00 100.00 260.00
2-10 25.00 100.00 250.00
11-20 40.00 200.00 375.00
21-26 (Scarcer) 60.00 300.00 550.00
The Big Book 1 (1926)-Thick book (hardcover, 142 pgs.) 127.00 508.00 1000.00
w/dust jacket (rare) 183.00 732.00 1325.00
The Big Book 2 (1929) 96.00 384.00 700.00
w/dust jacket (rare) 183.00 732.00 1325.00
NOTE: *The Big Books contain 3 regular issues rebound.* Strip began Jan 2 1913-May 28 2000

BRINGING UP FATHER, THE TROUBLE OF (N)
Embee Publ. Co.: 1921 (9-3/4x15-3/4", 46 pgs, Sunday-r in color)
nn - (Rare) 100.00 350.00 600.00
NOTE: *Ties with Mutt & Jeff (EmBee) and Jimmie Dugan And The Reg'lar Fellers (C&L) as the last of the*

Bringing Up Father #2
© C&L

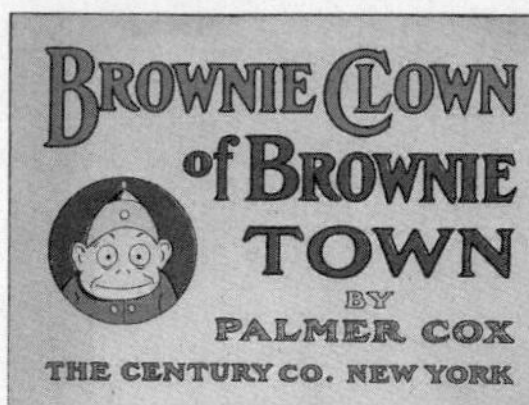

Brownie Clown of Brownie Town
© The Century Co.

Buster Brown His Dog Tige And Their Jolly Times
1906 © Cupples & Leon

GD2.0 FN6.0 VF8.0

oblong size era. This was self published by George McManus.

BRINGING UP FATHER (N) (see SAGARA'S ENGLISH CARTOONS
Publisher unknown (actually, unreadable), Tokyo: October 1924 (9-7/8" x 7-1/2", 90 pgs, color hard-c, B&W)
nn- (Scarce) by George McManus C&A (no known sales)
NOTE: *Published in Tokyo, Japan, with all strips in both English and Japanese, to facilitate learning English. Introduction by George McManus. Scarce in USA.*

BRONX BALLADS (I)
Simon & Schuster, NY: 1927 (9-1/2x7-1/4", hard-c, B&W)
nn - By Robert Simon and Harry Hershfield 36.00 143.00 250.00

BROWNIES, THE (not sequential comic strips)
The Century Co.: 1887 - 1914 (all came with dust jackets; add $100-150 to value if original dust jacket is included and intact)

	GD2.0	FN6.0	VF8.0
Book 1 - The Brownies: Their Book (1887)	200.00	850.00	1320.00
Book 2 - Another Brownies Book (1890)	150.00	635.00	1000.00
Book 3 - The Brownies at Home (1893)	125.00	530.00	825.00
Book 4 - The Brownies Around the World (1894)	100.00	425.00	660.00
Book 5 - The Brownies Through the Union (1895)	100.00	425.00	660.00
Book 6 - The Brownies Abroad (1899)	100.00	425.00	660.00
Book 7 - The Brownies in the Philippines (1904)	100.00	425.00	660.00
Book 8 - The Brownies' Latest Adventures (1910)	100.00	425.00	660.00
Book 9 - The Brownies Many More Nights (1914)	100.00	425.00	660.00

...Raid on Kleinmaier Bros. (c. 1910, 16 pages) Kleinmaier Bros. Clothing, Marion, Ohio (no known sales)

BROWNIE CLOWN OF BROWNIE TOWN (N)
The Century Co.: 1908 (6-7/8 x 9-3/8", 112 pgs, color hardcover & interior)
nn - By Palmer Cox (rare; 1907 newspaper comic strip-r) 250.00 800.00 1400.00
NOTE: *The Brownies created 1883 in* ***St Nicholas Magazine.***

BUDDY TUCKER & HIS FRIENDS (N) (Also see **Buster Brown Nuggets**)
Cupples & Leon Co.: 1906 (11-5/8 x17", 58 pgs, color) (Scarce)
nn - 1905 Sunday strip-r by R. F. Outcault 500.00 1500.00 2500.00
NOTE: *Strip began Apr 30, 1905 thru at least Oct 1905.*

BUFFALO BILL'S PICTURE STORIES
Street & Smith Publications: 1909 (Soft cardboard cover)
nn - Very rare 67.00 233.00 400.00

BUGHOUSE FABLES (N) (see also **Comic Monthly**)
Embee Distributing Co. (King Features): 1921 (10¢, 4x4-1/2", 48 pgs.)
1-By Barney Google (Billy DeBeck) 46.00 186.00 350.00

BUG MOVIES (O) (Also see Clancy The Cop & Deadwood Gulch)
Dell Publishing Co.: 1931 (9-13/16x9-7/8", 52 pgs., B&W)
nn - Original material; Stookie Allen-a 150.00 300.00 500.00

BULL
Bull Publishing Company, New York: No.1, March, 1916 - No.12, Feb, 1917 (10 cents, 10-3/4x8-3/4", 24 pgs, color paper-c, B&W)
1-12 (Very Rare) – – –
NOTE: *Pro-German, Anti-British cartoon/humor monthly, whose goal was to keep the U.S. neutral and out of World War I. We know of no copies which have sold in the past few years.*

BUNNY'S BLUE BOOK (see also Foxy Grandpa) (N)
Frederick A. Stokes Co.: 1911 (10x15, 60¢)
nn - By Carl "Bunny" Schultze strip-r 100.00 350.00 –

BUNNY'S RED BOOK (see also Foxy Grandpa) (N)
Frederick A. Stokes Co.: 1912 (10-1/4x15-3/4", 64 pgs.)
nn - By Carl "Bunny" Schultze strip-r 100.00 350.00 –

BUNNY'S GREEN BOOK (see also Foxy Grandpa) (N)
Frederick A. Stokes Co.: 1913 (10x15")
nn - By Carl "Bunny" Schultze 100.00 350.00 –

BUSTER BROWN (C) (Also see Brown's Blue Ribbon Book of Jokes and Jingles & Buddy Tucker & His Friends)
Frederick A. Stokes Co.: 1903 - 1916 (Daily strip-r in color)
1903...& His Resolutions (11-1/4x16", 66 pgs.) by R. F. Outcault (Rare)-1st nationally distributed comic. Distr. through Sears & Roebuck 1600.00 5500.00 –
1904...His Dog Tige & Their Troubles (11-1/4x16-1/4", 66 pgs.)(Rare) 600.00 1875.00 –
1905...Pranks (11-1/4x16-3/8", 66 pgs.) 400.00 1450.00 –
1906...Antics (11x16-3/8", 66 pgs.) 400.00 1450.00 –
1906...And Company (11x16-1/2", 66 pgs.) 300.00 1050.00 –
1906...Mary Jane & Tige (11-1/4x16, 66 pgs.) 300.00 1050.00 –
NOTE: ***Yellow Kid*** *pictured on two pages.*
1908 Collection of Buster Brown Comics 250.00 835.00 –
1909 Outcault's Real Buster and The Only Mary Jane (11x16, 66 pgs, Stokes) 250.00 835.00 –

GD2.0 FN6.0 VF8.0

1910...Up to Date (10-1/8x15-3/4", 66 pgs.) 208.00 729.00 1315.00
1911...Fun And Nonsense (10-1/8x15-3/4", 66 pgs.) 183.00 642.00 1150.00
1912...The Fun Maker (10-1/8x15-3/4", 66 pgs.) -Yellow Kid (4 pgs.) 183.00 642.00 1150.00
1913...At Home (10-1/8x15-3/4", 56 pgs.) 167.00 583.00 1050.00
1914...And Tige Here Again (10x16, 62 pgs, Stokes) 153.00 535.00 1000.00
1915...And His Chum Tige (10x16, Stokes) 153.00 535.00 1000.00
1916...The Little Rogue (10-1/8x15-3/4", 62 pgs.) 162.00 567.00 1025.00
1917...And the Cat (5-1/2x 6-1/2, 26 pgs, Stokes) 115.00 402.00 750.00
1917...Disturbs the Family (5-1/2x 6 1/2, 26 pgs, Stokes
NOTE: *Story featuring statue of "the Chinese Yellow Kid"* 115.00 402.00 750.00
1917...The Real Buster Brown (5-1/2x 6 -/2, 26 pgs, Stokes 115.00 402.00 750.00

Frederick A. Stokes Co. Hard Cover Series (I)
...Abroad (1904, 10-1/4x8", 86 pgs., B&W, hard-c)-R. F. Outcault-a (Rare) 200.00 700.00 1260.00
...Abroad (1904, B&W, 67 pgs.)-R. F. Outcault-a 200.00 700.00 1260.00
NOTE: *Buster Brown Abroad is not an actual comic book, but prose with illustrations.*
..."Tige" His Story 1905 (10x8", 63 pgs., B&W) (63 illos.)
nn-By RF Outcault 143.00 500.00 –
...My Resolutions 1906 (10x8", B&W, 68 pgs.)-R.F. Outcault-a (Rare) 233.00 817.00 1475.00
...Autobiography 1907 (10x8", B&W, 71 pgs.) (16 color plates & 36 B&W illos) 67.00 233.00 440.00
...And Mary Jane's Painting Book 1907 (10x13-1/4", 60 pgs, both card & hardcover versions exist
nn-RFO (first printing blank on top of cover) 67.00 233.00 440.00
First Series- this is a reprint if it says First Series 67.00 233.00 440.00
Volume Two - By RFO 67.00 233.00 440.00
... My Resolutions by Buster Brown (1907, 68 pgs, small size, cardboard covers) scarce 43.00 150.00 285.00
NOTE: *Not actual comic book per se, but a compilation of the Resolutions panels found at the end of Outcault's Buster Brown newspaper strips.*

BUSTER BROWN (N)
Cupples & Leon Co./N. Y. Herald Co.: 1906 - 1917 (11x17", color, strip-r)
NOTE: *Early issues by R. F. Outcault; most C&L editions are not by Outcault.*
1906...His Dog Tige And Their Jolly Times (11-3/8x16-5/8", 68 pgs.) 300.00 1100.00 1900.00
1906...His Dog Tige & Their Jolly Times (11x16, 46 pgs.) 163.00 600.00 1025.00
1907...Latest Frolics (11-3/8x16-5/8", 66 pgs., r/'05-06 strips) 163.00 600.00 1025.00
1908...Amusing Capers (58 pgs.) 129.00 475.00 815.00
1909...The Busy Body (11-3/8x16-5/8", 62 pgs.) 129.00 475.00 815.00
1910...On His Travels (11x16", 58 pgs.) 115.00 402.00 750.00
1911...Happy Days (11-3/8x16-5/8", 58 pgs.) 115.00 402.00 750.00
1912...In Foreign Lands (10x16", 58 pgs) 115.00 402.00 750.00
1913...And His Pets (11x16", 58 pgs.) STOKES???? 115.00 402.00 750.00
1913...And His Pets (26 pg partial reprint) – – –
1914...Funny Tricks (11-3/8x16-5/8", 58 pgs.) 115.00 402.00 750.00
1916...At Play (10x16, 58 pgs) 115.00 402.00 750.00

BUSTER BROWN NUGGETS (N)
Cupples & Leon Co./N.Y.Herald Co.: 1907 (1905, 7-1/2x6-1/2", 36 pgs., color, strip-r, hard-c)(By R. F. Outcault) (NOTE: books are all unnumbered)
Buster Brown Goes Fishing, Goes Swimming, Plays Indian, Goes Shooting, Plays Cowboy, On Uncle Jack's Farm, Tige And the Bull, And Uncle Buster 39.00 137.00 275.00
Buddy Tucker Meets Alice in Wonderland 56.00 200.00 400.00
Buddy Tucker Visits The House That Jack Built 39.00 137.00 275.00

BUSTER BROWN MUSLIN SERIES (N)
Saalfield: 1907 (also contain copyright Cupples & Leon)
...Goes Fishing, Plays Indian, And the Donkey
(1907, 6-7/8x6-1/8", 24 pgs., color)-r/1905 Sunday comics page by Outcault (Rare) 50.00 175.00 315.00
...Plays Cowboy (1907, 6-3/4x6", 10 pgs., color)-r/1905 Sunday comics page by Outcault (Rare) 50.00 175.00 315.00
NOTE: *These are muslin versions of the C&L BB Nugget series. Muslin books are all cloth books, made to be washable so as not easily stained/destroyed by very young children. The Muslin books contain one strip each (the title strip), to the more common NUGGET's three strips.*

BUSTER BROWN PREMIUMS (Advertising premium booklets)
Various Publishers: 1904 - 1912 (3x5" to 5x7"; sizes vary)

American Fruit Product Company, Rochester, NY
Buster Brown Duffy's 1842 Cider (1904, 7x5". 12 pgs, C.E. Sherin Co, NYC)
nn - By R. F. Outcault (scarce) 100.00 350.00 600.00

The Brown Shoe Company, St. Louis, USA
Set of five books (5x7", 16 pgs., color)
Brown's Blue Ribbon Book of Jokes and Jingles Book 1 (nn, 1904)-By R. F. Outcault; Buster Brown & Tige, Little Tommy Tucker, Jack & Jill, Little Boy Blue, Dainty Jane; The Yellow Kid app. on back-c (1st BB comic book premium) 300.00 1050.00 1900.00

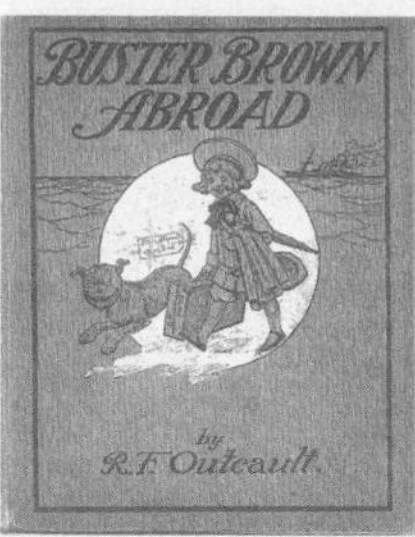

Buster Brown Abroad
1904 © Frederick A. Stokes Co.

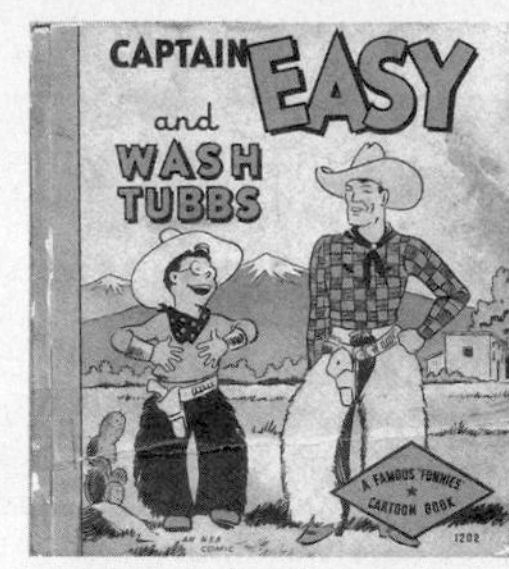

Captain Easy and Wash Tubbs by Roy Crane
1934 © Whitman Famous Comics Cartoon Book

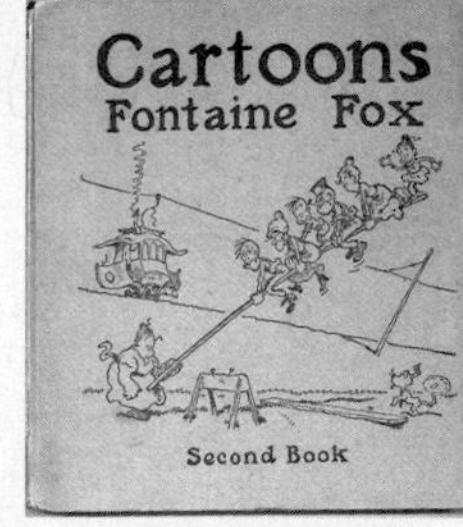

Cartoons Fontaine Fox Second Book
early 1920s © Harper & Bros, NY

GD2.0 FN6.0 VF8.0

Buster Brown's Blue Ribbon Book of Jokes and Jingles Book 2 (1905)-
Original color art by Outcault 200.00 600.00 1260.00
Buster's Book of Jokes & Jingles Book 3 (1909)
not by R.F. Outcault 150.00 400.00 840.00
NOTE: *Reprinted from the Blue Ribbon post cards with advert jingles added.*
Buster's Book of Instructive Jokes and Jingles Book 4 (1910)-Original color art
not by R.F. Outcault 150.00 585.00 1050.00
...Book of Travels nn (1912, 3x5")-Original color art not signed by Outcault
117.00 408.00 735.00
NOTE: *Estimated 5 or 6 known copies exist of books #1-4.*

The Buster Brown Bread Company

"Buster Brown" Bread Book of Rhymes, The (1904, 4x6", 12 pgs., half color, half
B&W)- Original color art not signed by RFO 158.00 553.00 1000.00

Buster Brown's Hosiery Mills

"How Buster Brown Got The Pie" nn (nd, 7x5-1/4". 16 pgs, color paper cover and
color interior By R.F. Outcault 83.00 292.00 525.00
"The Autobiography of Buster Brown" nn (nd,9x6-1/8", 36 pgs, text story & art by
R.F. Outcault 83.00 292.00 525.00
NOTE: *Similar to, but a distinctly different item than "Buster Brown's Autobiography."*

The Buster Brown Stocking Company

Buster Brown Drawing Book, The nn (nd, 5x6", 20 pgs.)-B&W reproductions of 1903
R.F. Outcault art to trace 50.00 150.00 315.00
NOTE: *Reprints a comic strip from Burr McIntosh Magazine, which includes Buster, Yellow Kid, and Poro Li'l Mose (only known story involving all three.)*
Buster Brown Stocking Magazine nn (Jan. 1906, 7-3/4x5-3/8", 36 pgs.) R.F. Outcault
50.00 100.00 200.00
NOTE: *This was actually a store bought item selling for 5 cents per copy.*

Collins Baking Company

Buster Brown Drawing Book nn (1904, 5x3", 12 pgs.)-Original B&W art to trace,
not signed by R.F. Outcault 50.00 150.00 315.00

C. H. Morton, St. Albans, VT

Merry Antics of Buster Brown, Buddy Tucker & Tige nn (nd, 3-1/2x5-1/2", 16 pgs.)
-Original B&W art by R.F. Outcault 83.00 292.00 525.00

Ivan Frank & Company

Buster Brown nn (1904, 3x5", 12 pgs.)-B&W repros of R. F. Outcault Sunday pages
(First premium to actually reproduce Sunday comic pages – may be first premium
comic strip-r book?) 125.00 438.00 785.00
Buster Brown's Pranks (1904, 3-1/2x5-1/8", 12 pgs.)-reprints intro of Buddy Tucker into
the BB newspaper strip before he was spun off into his own short lived newspaper strip
125.00 438.00 785.00

Kaufmann & Strauss

Buster Brown Drawing Book (1906, 28 pages, 5x3-1/2") Color Cover, B+W original story
signed by Outcault, tracing paper inserted as alternate pages. Back cover imprinted for
Nox' Em All Shoes 50.00 150.00 315.00

Pond's Extract

Buster Brown's Experiences With Pond's Extract nn (1904, 6-3/4x4-1/2", 28 pgs.)
Original color art by R.F. Outcault (may be the first BB premium comic book with
original art) 100.00 250.00 525.00

C. A. Cross & Co.

Red Cross Drawing Book nn (1906, 4-7/8x3-1/2", color paper -c, B&W interior, 12 pgs.)
50.00 150.00 315.00
NOTE: *This is for Red Cross coffee; not the health organization.*

Ringen Stove Company

Quick Meal Steel Ranges nn (nd, 5x3", 16 pgs.)-Original B&W art not signed
by R.F. Outcault 50.00 150.00 315.00

Steinwender Stoffregen Coffee Co.

"Buster Brown Coffee" (1905, 4-7/8x3", color paper cover, B&W interior, 12 printed pages,
plus 1 tracing paper page above each interior image (total of 8 sheets) (Very Rare)
83.00 292.00 525.00
NOTE: *Part of a BB drawing contest. If instructions had been followed, most copies would have ended up destroyed.*

U. S. Playing Card Company

Buster Brown - My Own Playing Cards (1906, 2-1/2x1-3/4", full color)
nn - By R. F. Outcault 42.00 147.00 250.00
NOTE: *Series of full color panels tell stories, average about 5 cards per story.*

Publisher Unknown

The Drawing Book nn (1906, 3-9/16x5", 8 pgs.)-Original B&W art to trace
not by R.F. Outcault 50.00 150.00 300.00

BUTLER BOOK A Series of Clever Cartoons of Yale Undergraduate Life
Yale Record: June 16, 1913 (10-3/4 x 17", 34 pgs, paper cover B&W)
nn - By Alban Bernard Butler 21.00 73.00 130.00
NOTE: *Cartoons and strips reprinted from The Yale Record student newspaper.*

BUTTONS & FATTY IN THE FUNNIES
Whitman Publishing Co.: nd 1927 (10-1/4x15-1/2", 28pg., color)
W936 - Signed "M.E.B.", probably M.E. Brady; strips in color copyright The Brooklyn
Daily Eagle; (very rare) 61.00 244.00 425.00

BY BRIGGS (M,N,P) (see also OLD GOLD THE SMOOTHER AND BETTER CIGARETTE)
Old Gold Cigarettes: nd (c1920's) (11" x 9-11/16", 44 pgs, cardboard-c, B&W)
nn- (Scarce) 20.00 70.00 130.00
NOTE: *Collection reprinting strip cartoons by Clare Briggs, advertising Old Gold Cigarettes. These strips originally appeared in various magazines, play program booklets, newspapers, etc. Some of the strips involve regular Briggs strip series. Contains all of the strips in the smaller, color "OLD GOLD" giveaways, plus more.*

CAMION CARTOONS
Marshall Jones Company: 1919 (7-1/2x5", 136 pgs, B&W)
nn - By Kirkland H. Day (W.W.One occupation) 20.00 70.00 120.00

CANYON COUNTRY KIDDIES (M)
Doubleday, Page & Co: 1923 (8x10-1/4", 88 pgs, hard-c, B&W)
nn - By James Swinnerton 39.00 137.00 260.00

CARLO (H)
Doubleday, Page & Co.: 1913 (8 x 9-5/8, 120 pgs, hardcover, B&W)
nn - By A.B. Frost 40.00 140.00 300.00
NOTE: *Original sequential strips about a dog. Became short lived newspaper comic strip in 1914. Originally published with a dust jacket which increases value 50%.*

CARTOON BOOK, THE
Bureau of Publicity, War Loan Organization, Treasury Department, Washington, D.C.:
1918 (6-1/2x4-7/8", 48 pgs, paper cover, B&W)
nn - By various artists 31.00 108.00 185.00
NOTE: *U.S. government issued booklet of WW I propaganda cartoons by 40 artists promoting the third sale of Liberty Loan bonds. The artists include: Berryman, Clare Briggs, Cesare, J. N. "Ding" Darling, Rube Goldberg, Kemble, McCutcheon, George McManus, F. Opper, T. E. Powers, Ripley, Satterfield, H. T. Webster, Gaar Williams.*

CARTOON CATALOGUE (S)
The Lockwood Art School, Kalamazoo, Mich.: 1919 (11-5/8x9, 52 pgs, B&W)
nn - Edited by Mr. Lockwood 20.00 60.00 140.00
NOTE: *Jammed with 100s of single panel cartoons and some sequential comics; Mr Lockwood began the very first cartoonist school back in 1892. Clare Briggs was one of his students.*

CARTOON COMICS
Lasco Publications, Detroit, Mich: #1, April 1930 - #2, May 1930 (8-3/6x5-1/5")
1, 2 - By Lu Harris 20.00 60.00 100.00
NOTE: *Contains recurring characters Hollywood Horace, Campus Charlie, Pair-A-Dice Alley and Jocko Monkey. Not much is presently known about the creator(s) or publisher.*

CARTOON HISTORY OF ROOSEVELT'S CAREER, A
The Review of Reviews Company: 1910 (276 pgs, 8-1/4x11",
nn - By various 43.00 129.00 325.00
NOTE: *Reprints editorial cartoons about Teddy Roosevelt from U.S. and international newspapers and cartoons from the humor magazines (Puck, Judge, etc.). A few cartoonists whose work is included are Dalrymple, Opper, McDougall, McCutcheon, Remington, Rogers, Kemble. Mostly single panel but 10 or so are sequential strips.*

CARTOON HUMOR
Collegian Press: 1938 (102 pgs, squarebound, B&W)
nn 20.00 70.00 120.00
NOTE: *Contains cartoons & strips by Otto Soglow, Syd Hoff, Peter Arno, Abner Dean, others.*

CARTOONIST'S PHILOSOPHY, A
Percy Crosby: 1931, HC, 252 pgs, 5-1/2x7-1/2", hard-c, celluloid dust wrapper
nn - By Percy Crosby (10 plates, 6 are of Skippy) 20.00 60.00 130.00
NOTE: *Crosby's partial autobiography regarding his return to France in 1929, and portrayals of Normandy, the "cliff dwellers" on Normandy cliffs (destroyed in WWII), his visit to London, comments on art, philosophy, several poems, and political dialogue. His description of his Cockney driver, " Harold" is amusing. Also describes his experience visiting Chicago to speak out against Capone, his concerns over the evils of Prohibition, and the economy prior to the 1929 crash. This book reveals he was aware of the dangers of his outspoken views, and is prophetic, re: his later years as political prisoner. Also reveals his religious beliefs.*

CARTOONS BY BRADLEY: CARTOONIST OF THE CHICAGO DAILY NEWS
Rand McNally & Company: 1917 (11-1/4x8-3/4", 112 pgs, hardcover, B&W)
nn - By Luther D. Bradley (editorial) 20.00 70.00 120.00

CARTOONS BY FONTAINE FOX (Toonerville Trolley) (S)
Harper & Brothers Publishers: nd early '20s (9x7-7/8",102 pgs., hard-c, B&W)
Second Book- By Fontaine Fox (Toonerville-r) 150.00 300.00 500.00

CARTOONS BY HALLADAY (N,S)
Providence Journal Co., Rhode Island: Dec 1914 (116 pgs, 10-1/2x 7-3/4", hard-c, B&W)
nn- (Scarce) 50.00 125.00 250.00
NOTE: *Cartoons on Rhode Island politics, plus some Teddy Roosevelt & WW I cartoons.*

CARTOONS BY McCUTCHEON (S)
A. C. McClurg & Co.: 1903 (12-3/8x9-3/4", 212 pgs., hardcover, B&W)
nn - By John McCutcheon 20.00 70.00 120.00

CARTOONS BY W. A. IRELAND (S)
The Columbus-Evening Dispatch: 1907 (13-3/4 x 10-1/2", 66 pgs, hardcover)
nn - By W. A. Ireland (strip-r) 20.00 70.00 120.00

CARTOONS MAGAZINE (I,N,S)
H. H. Windsor, Publisher: Jan 1912-June 1921; July 1921-1923; 1923-1924; 1924-1927
(1912-July 1913 issues 12x9-1/4", 68-76 pgs; 1913-1921 issues 10x7", average 112 to 188
pgs, color covers)
1912-Jan-Dec 30.00 75.00 125.00

Cartoons Magazine Sept, 1917
by various creators © H. H. Windsor, Chicago

Charlie Chaplin in the Movies by Segar
1917 © Essaney

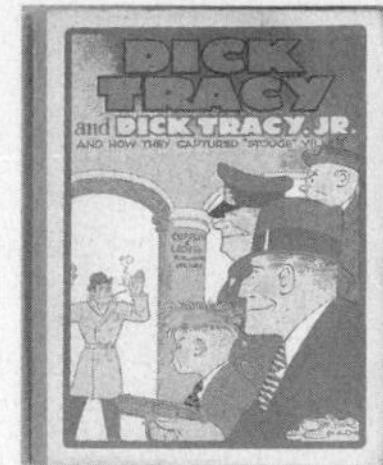

How Dick Tracy and Dick Tracy, Jr. And How
They Captured Stooge Villar by Chester Gould
1933 © Cupples & Leon

	GD2.0	FN6.0	VF8.0
1913-1917	30.00	75.00	125.00
1917-(Apr) "How Comickers Regard Their Characters"	30.00	105.00	150.00
1917-(June) "A Genius of the Comic Page" - long article on George Herriman, Krazy Kat, etc with lots of Herriman art; "Cartoonists and Their Cars"	125.00	250.00	500.00
1918-1919	30.00	75.00	125.00
1920-June 1921	30.00	75.00	125.00
July 1921-1923 titled Wayside Tales & Cartoons Magazine	30.00	75.00	125.00
1923-1924 becomes Cartoons Magazine again	30.00	75.00	125.00
1924-1927 becomes Cartoons & Movie Magazine	30.00	75.00	125.00

NOTE: *Many issues contain a wealth of historical background on then current cartoonists of the day with an international slant; each issue profusely illustrated with many cartoons. We are unsure if this magazine continued after 1927.*

CARTOONS BY J. N. DARLING (S,N - some sequential strips)
The Register & Tribune Co., Des Moines, Iowa: 1909?-1920 (12x8-7/8",B&W)

	GD2.0	FN6.0	VF8.0
Book 1	15.00	51.00	90.00
Book 2 Education of Alonzo Applegate (1910)	15.00	51.00	90.00
2nd printing	10.00	30.00	90.00
Book 3 Cartoons From The Files (1911)	15.00	51.00	90.00
Book 4	15.00	51.00	90.00
Book 5 In Peace And War (1916)	15.00	51.00	90.00
Book 6 Aces & Kings War Cartoons (Dec 1, 1918)	15.00	51.00	90.00
Book 7 The Jazz Era (Dec 1920)	15.00	51.00	90.00
Book 8 Our Own Outlines of History (1922)	15.00	51.00	90.00

NOTE: *Some of the most inspired hard hitting cartoons ever printed. Are there more?*

CARTOONS THAT MADE PRINCE HENRY FAMOUS, THE (N,S)
The Chicago Record-Herald: Feb/March 1902 (12-1/8" x 9", 32 pgs, paper-c, B&W)

	GD2.0	FN6.0	VF8.0
nn- (Scarce) by McCutcheon	15.00	51.00	90.00

NOTE: *Cartoons about the visit of the British Prince Henry to the U.S.*

CAVALRY CARTOONS (O)
R. Montalboddi: nd (c1918) (14-1/4" x 11", 30 pgs, printed on one side, olive & black construction paper-c, B&W interior)

	GD2.0	FN6.0	VF8.0
nn - By R.Montalboddi	15.00	51.00	90.00

NOTE: *Comics about life in the U.S.Cavalry during World War I, by a soldier who was in the 1st Cavalry.*

CHARLIE CHAPLIN (N)
Essanay/M. A. Donohue & Co.: 1917 (9x16", B&W, large size soft-c)

	GD2.0	FN6.0	VF8.0
Series 1, #315-Comic Capers (9-3/4x15-3/4")-20 pgs. by Segar; Series 1, #316-In the Movies	165.00	525.00	1200.00
#317-Up in the Air (20 pgs), #318-In the Army	165.00	525.00	1400.00
Funny Stunts-(12-1/2x16-3/8",16 color pgs)	165.00	525.00	1400.00

NOTE: *All contain pre-Thimble Theatre Segar art. The thin paper used makes high grade copies very scarce.*

CHASING THE BLUES
Doubleday Page: 1912 (7-1/2x10", 108 pgs., B&W, hard-c)

	GD2.0	FN6.0	VF8.0
nn - By Rube Goldberg	150.00	525.00	900.00

NOTE: *Contains a dozen Foolish Questions, baseball, a few Goldberg poems and lots of sequential strips.*

CHRISTIAN CARTOONS (N,S)
The Sunday School Times Company: 1922 (7-1/4 x 6-1/8,104 pgs, brown hard-c, B&W)

	GD2.0	FN6.0	VF8.0
nn - E.J. Pace	15.00	51.00	90.00

NOTE: *Religious cartoons reprinted from The Sunday School Times.*

CLANCY THE COP (O))
Dell Publishing Co.: 1930 - No. 2, 1931 (10x10", 52 pgs., B&W, cardboard-c)
(Also see Bug Movies & Deadwood Gulch)

	GD2.0	FN6.0	VF8.0
1, 2-By VEP Victor Pazimino (original material; not reprints)	10000	250.00	500.00

CLIFFORD MCBRIDE'S IMMORTAL NAPOLEON & UNCLE ELBY (N)
The Castle Press: 1932 (12x17"; soft-c cartoon book)

	GD2.0	FN6.0	VF8.0
nn - Intro. by Don Herod	36.00	144.00	250.00

COLLECTED DRAWINGS OF BRUCE BAIRNSFATHER, THE
W. Colston Leigh: 1931 (11-1/4x8-1/4 ", 168 pages, hardcover, B&W)

	GD2.0	FN6.0	VF8.0
nn - By Bruce Bairnsfather	24.00	96.00	165.00

COMICAL PEEP SHOW
McLoughlin Bros: 1902 (36 pgs, B&W)

	GD2.0	FN6.0	VF8.0
nn	24.00	96.00	165.00

NOTE: *Comic stories of Wilhelm Busch redrawn; two versions with green or gold front cover logos; back covers different.*

COMIC ANIMALS (I)
Charles E. Graham & Co.: 1903 (9-3/4x7-1/4", 90 pgs, color cover)

	GD2.0	FN6.0	VF8.0
nn - By Walt McDougall (not comic strips)	43.00	150.00	260.00

COMIC CUTS (O)
H. L. Baker Co., Inc.: 5/19/34-7/28/34 (Tabloid size 10-1/2x15-1/2", 24 pgs., 5¢)
(full color, not reprints; published weekly; created for news stand sales)

	GD2.0	FN6.0	VF8.0
V1#1 - V1#7(6/30/34), V1#8(7/14/34), V1#9(7/28/34)-Idle Jack strips	200.00	400.00	800.00

NOTE: *According to a 1958 Lloyd Jacquet interview, this short-lived comics mag was the direct inspiration for Major Malcolm Wheeler-Nicholson's* ***New Fun Comics****, not* ***Famous Funnies****.*

COMIC MONTHLY (N)
Embee Dist. Co.: Jan, 1922 - No. 12, Dec, 1922 (10¢, 8-1/2"x9", 28 pgs., 2-color covers)
(1st monthly newsstand comic publication) (Reprints 1921 B&W dailies)

	GD2.0	FN6.0	VF8.0
1-Polly & Her Pals by Cliff Sterrett	375.00	1125.00	2225.00
2-Mike & Ike by Rube Goldberg	140.00	490.00	1000.00
3-S'Matter, Pop?	140.00	490.00	1000.00
4-Barney Google by Billy DeBeck	140.00	490.00	1000.00
5-Tillie the Toiler by Russ Westover	140.00	490.00	1000.00
6-Indoor Sports by Tad Dorgan	140.00	490.00	1000.00

NOTE: *#6 contains more Judge Rummy than Indoor Sports.*

	GD2.0	FN6.0	VF8.0
7-Little Jimmy by James Swinnerton	140.00	490.00	1000.00
8-Toots and Casper b y Jimmy Murphy	140.00	490.00	1000.00
9-New Bughouse Fables by Barney Google	140.00	490.00	1000.00
10-Foolish Questions by Rube Goldberg	140.00	490.00	1000.00
11-Barney Google & Spark Plug by Billy DeBeck	140.00	490.00	1000.00
12-Polly & Her Pals by Cliff Sterrett	214.00	752.00	1500.00

NOTE: *This series was published by George McManus (Bringing Up Father) as Em & Rudolph Block, Jr., son of Hearst's cartoon editor for many years, as "Bee." One would have thought this series would have done very well considering the tremendous amount of talent assembled. All issues are extremely hard to find these days and rarely show up in any type of higher grade.*

COMIC PAINTING AND CRAYONING BOOK (H)
Saalfield Publ. Co.: 1917 (13-1/2x10", 32 pgs.) (No price on-c)

	GD2.0	FN6.0	VF8.0
nn - Tidy Teddy by F. M. Follett, Clarence the Cop, Mr. & Mrs. Butt-In; regular comic stories to read or color	50.00	175.00	300.00

COMPLETE TRIBUNE PRIMER, THE (I)
Mutual Book Company: 1901 (7 1/4 x 5", 152 pgs, red hard-c)

	GD2.0	FN6.0	VF8.0
nn - By Frederick Opper; has 75 Opper cartoons	25.00	88.00	150.00

COURTSHIP OF TAGS, THE (N)
McCormick Press: pre-1910 (9x4", 88 pgs, red & B&W-c, B&W interior)

	GD2.0	FN6.0	VF8.0
nn - By O. E. Wertz (strip-r Wichita Daily Beacon)	25.00	88.00	150.00

DAFFYDILS (N)
Cupples & Leon Co.: 1911 (5-3/4x7-7/8", 52 pgs., B&W, hard-c)

	GD2.0	FN6.0	VF8.0
nn - By "Tad" Dorgan	58.00	204.00	350.00

NOTE: *Also exists in self-published TAD edition: The T.A. Dorgan Company; unknown which is first printing.*

DAN DUNN SECRET OPERATIVE 48 (Also See Detective Dan) (N)
Whitman Publishing: 1937 ((5 1/2 x 7 1/4", 68pgs., color cardboard-c, B&W)

	GD2.0	FN6.0	VF8.0
1010 And The Gangsters' Frame-Up	50.00	150.00	300.00

NOTE: *There are two versions of the book the later printing has a 5 cent cover price. Dick Tracy look-alike character by Norman Marsh.*

DANGERS OF DOLLY DIMPLE, THE (N)
Penn Tobacco Co.: nd (1930's) (9-3/8x7-7/8", 28 pgs, red cardboard-c, B&W)

	GD2.0	FN6.0	VF8.0
nn - (Rare) by Walter Enright	25.00	88.00	150.00

NOTE: *Reprints newspaper comic strip advertisements, in which in every episode, Dolly Dimple's life is saved by Penn's Smoking Tobacco. - how very un-P.C. by today's standards.*

DEADWOOD GULCH (O) (See The Funnies 1929)(also see Bug Movies & Clancy The Cop)
Dell Publishing Co.: 1931 (10x10", 52 pgs., B&W, color covers, B&W interior)

	GD2.0	FN6.0	VF8.0
nn - By Charles "Boody" Rogers (original material)	150.00	300.00	600.00

DESTINY A Novel In Pictures (O)
Farrar & Rinehart: 1930 (8x7", 424 pgs, B&W, hard-c, dust jacket?)

	GD2.0	FN6.0	VF8.0
nn - By Otto Nuckel (original graphic novel)	25.00	100.00	175.00

DICK TRACY & DICK TRACY JR. CAUGHT THE RACKETEERS, HOW
Cupples & Leon Co.: 1933 (8-1/2x7", 88 pgs., hard-c) (See Treasure Box of Famous Comics) (N)

	GD2.0	FN6.0	VF8.0
2-(Numbered on pg. 84)-Continuation of Stooge Viller book (daily strip reprints from 8/3/33 thru 11/8/33)(Rarer than #1)	94.00	376.00	750.00
With dust jacket...	175.00	500.00	1000.00

DICK TRACY & DICK TRACY JR. AND HOW THEY CAPTURED "STOOGE" VILLER (N)
Cupples & Leon Co.: 1933 (8-1/2x7", 100 pgs., hard-c, one-shot)
Reprints 1932 & 1933 Dick Tracy daily strips

	GD2.0	FN6.0	VF8.0
nn(No.1)-1st app. of "Stooge" Viller	94.00	376.00	750.00
With dust jacket...	175.00	500.00	1000.00

DIMPLES By Grace Drayton (N) (See Dolly Dimples)
Hearst's International Library Co.: 1915 (6 1/4 x 5 1/4, 12 pgs) (5 known)

	GD2.0	FN6.0	VF8.0
nn-Puppy and Pussy; nn-She Goes For a Walk; nn-She Had A Sneeze; nn-She Has a Naughty Play Husband; nn-Wait Till Fido Comes Home	21.00	74.00	150.00

DOINGS OF THE DOO DADS, THE (N)
Detroit News (Universal Feat. & Specialty Co.): 1922 (50¢, 7-3/4x7-3/4", 34 pgs, B&W, red & white-c, square binding)

	GD2.0	FN6.0	VF8.0
nn-Reprints 1921 newspaper strip "Text & Pictures" given away as prize in the Detroit News Doo Dads contest; by Arch Dale	43.00	173.00	360.00

DOING THE GRAND CANYON
Fred Harvey: 1922 (7 x 4-3/4", 24 pgs, B&W, paper cover)

'Erbie And 'Is Playmates By F. Opper
1932 © Democratic National Committee

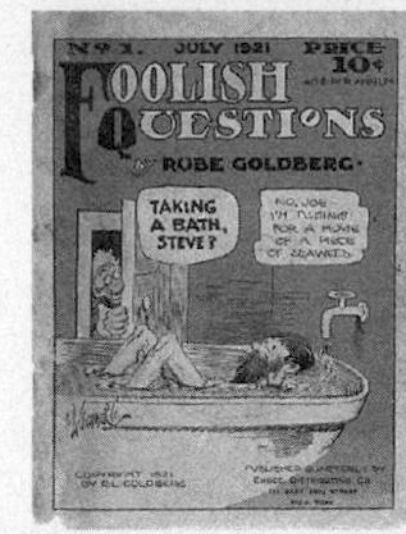

Foolish Questions by Rube Goldberg
1921 © EmBee Distributing Co., NY.

The Latest Adventures of Foxy Grandpa 1905
© Bunny Publ.

GD2.0 FN6.0 VF8.0

nn - John McCutcheon 20.00 40.00 100.00
NOTE: *Text & 8 cartoons about visiting the Grand Canyon.*

DOINGS OF THE VAN-LOONS (N) (from same company as Mutt & Jeff #1-#5)
Ball Publications: 1912 (5-3/4X15-1/2", 68pg., B&W, hard-c)
nn - By Fred I. Leipziger (scarce) 72.00 252.00 600.00

DOLLY DIMPLES & BOBBY BOUNCE (See Dimples)
Cupples & Leon Co.: 1933 (8-3/4x7", color hardcover, B&W)
nn - Grace Drayton-a 24.00 96.00 165.00

DOO DADS, THE (Sleepy Sam and Tiny the Elephant)
Universal Feature * Specialty Co: 1922 (5-1/4x14", 36 pgs.,B&W, R&W-c,square binding)
nn - By Arch Dale 35.00 125.00 250.00

DRAWINGS BY HOWARD CHANDLER CHRISTIE (S, M)
Moffat, Yard & Company, NY: 1905 (11-7/8x16-1/2", 68 pgs, hard-c, B&W)
nn - Howard C. Christie 30.00 60.00 120.00
NOTE: *Reprints1898-1905 from Hapner & Bros, Ch. Scribners Sons, Leslie's, MacMillians, McLurg, Russell.*

DREAMS OF THE RAREBIT FIEND (N)
Frederick A. Stokes Co.:1905 (10-1/4x7-1/2", 68 pgs, thin paper cover all B&W)
newspaper reprints from the New York Evening Telegram printed on yellow paper
nn-By Winsor "Silas" McCay (Very Rare) (Five copies known to exist)
Estimated value.... 750.00 2500.00 –
NOTE: *A G/VG copy sold for $2,045 in May 2004. This item usually turns up with fragile paper.*

DRISCOLL'S BOOK OF PIRATES (O)
David McKay Publ.: 1934 (9x7", 124 pgs, B&W, hardcover)
nn - By Montford Amory ("Pieces of Eight strip-r) 21.00 64.00 150.00

DUCKY DADDLES
Frederick A. Stokes Co: July 1911 (15x10")
nn - By Grace Weiderseim (later Drayton) strip-r 50.00 175.00 300.00

DUMBUNNIES AND THEIR FRIENDS IN RABBITBORO, THE (O)
Albertine Randall Wheelan: 1931 (8-3/4x7-1/8", 82 pgs, color hardcover, B&W)
nn - By Albertine Randall Wheelan (self-pub) 34.00 103.00 240.00

EDISON - INSPIRATION TO YOUTH (N)(Also see Life of Thomas---)
Thomas A. Edison, Incorporated: 1939 (9-1/2 x 6-1/2, paper cover, B&W)
nn - Photo-c 46.00 138.00 275.00
NOTE: *Reprints strip material found in the 1928 Life of Thomas A. Edison in Word and Picture.*

'ERBIE AND 'IS PLAYMATES
Democratic National Committee: 1932 (8x9-1/2, 16 pgs, B&W)
nn - By Frederick Opper (Rare) 100.00 200.00 400.00
NOTE: *Anti-Hoover/Pro-Roosevelt political comics.*

EXPANSION BEING BART'S BEST CARTOONS FOR 1899
Minneapolis Journal: 1900 (10-1/4x8-1/4", 124 pgs, paperback, B&W)
v2#1 - By Charles L. Bartholomew 24.00 84.00 145.00

FAMOUS COMICS (N)
King Features Synd. (Whitman Pub. Co.): 1934 (100 pgs., daily newspaper-r)
(3-1/2x8-1/2"; paper cover)(came in an illustrated box)
684 (#1) - Little Jimmy, Katz Kids & Barney Google 34.00 103.00 240.00
684 (#2) - Polly, Little Jimmy, Katzenjammer Kids 34.00 103.00 240.00
684 (#3) - Little Annie Rooney, Polly and Her Pals, Katzenjammer Kids
34.00 103.00 240.00
Box price... 75.00 150.00 375.00

FAMOUS COMICS CARTOON BOOKS (N)
Whitman Publishing Co.: 1934 (8x7-1/4", 72 pgs, B&W hard-c, daily strip-r)
1200-The Captain & the Kids; Dirks reprints credited to Bernard
Dibble 29.00 86.00 200.00
1202-Captain Easy & Wash Tubbs by Roy Crane; 2 slightly different
versions of cover exist 34.00 103.00 240.00
1203-Ella Cinders By Conselman & Plumb 28.00 84.00 195.00
1204-Freckles & His Friends 25.00 75.00 175.00
NOTE: *Called Famous Funnies Cartoon Books inside back area sales advertisement.*

FANTASIES IN HA-HA (M)
Meyer Bros & Co.: 1900 (14 x 11-7/8", 64 pgs, color cover hardcover, B&W)
nn - By Hy Mayer 50.00 150.00 300.00

FELIX (N)
Henry Altemus Company: 1931 (6-1/2"x8-1/4", 52 pgs., color, hard-c w/dust jacket)
1-3-Sunday strip reprints of Felix the Cat by Otto Messmer. Book No. 2 r/1931 Sunday panels mostly two to a page in a continuity format oddly arranged so each tier of panels reads across two pages, then drops to the next tier. (Books 1 & 3 have not been documented.)(Rare)
Each 104.00 416.00 900.00
With dust jacket 250.00 750.00 1200.00

FELIX THE CAT BOOK (N)

GD2.0 FN6.0 VF8.0

McLoughlin Bros.: 1927 (8"x15-3/4", 52 pgs, half in color-half in B&W)
nn - Reprints 23 Sunday strips by Otto Messmer from 1926 & 1927, every other one in color, two pages per strip. (Rare) 200.00 800.00 1550.00
260-Reissued (1931), reformatted to 9-1/2"x10-1/4" (same color plates, but one strip per every three pages), retitled ("Book" dropped from title) and abridged (only eight strips repeated from first issue, 28 pgs.).(Rare) 79.00 316.00 600.00

F. FOX'S FUNNY FOLK (see Toonerville Trolley; Cartoons by Fontaine Fox) (C)
George H. Doran Company: 1917 (10-1/4x8-1/4", 228 pgs, red, B&W cover, B&W interior, hardcover; dust jacket?)
nn - By Fontaine Fox (Toonerville Trolley strip-r) 150.00 450.00 750.00

52 CAREY CARTOONS (O,S)
Carey Cartoon Service, NY: 1915 (25 cents, 6-3/4" x 10-1/2", 118 pgs, printed on one side, color cardboard-c, B&W)
nn - (1915) War – – –
NOTE: *The Carey Cartoon Service supplied a weekly, hand-colored single panel cartoon broadsheet, on current news events, starting in 1906 or 1907, for window display in Carey Fountain Pen chain stores. These broadsheets were 22-1/2" x 33" in size. Starting circa 1915, Carey Fountain Pens began offering subscriptions for the broadsheets to other merchants, for window display in their stores as well. This collects, in B&W, the cartoons for 1915. An "Edition Deluxe" was also advertised, with all cartoons hand colored. It is currently unknown whether a reprint collection was only issued in 1915, or if other editions exist.*

52 LETTERS TO SALESMEN
Steven-Davis Company: 1927 (???)
nn - (Rare) 23.00 92.00 140.00
NOTE: *52 motivational letters to salesmen, with page of comics for each week, bound into embossed leather binder.*

FOLKS IN FUNNYVILLE (S)
R.H. Russell: 1900 (12"x9-1/4", 48 pgs.)(cardboard-c)
nn - By Frederick Opper 271.00 950.00 –
NOTE: *Reprinted from Hearst's NY Journal American Humorist supplements.*

FOOLISH QUESTIONS (S)
Small, Maynard & Co.: 1909 (6-7/8 x 5-1/2", 174 pgs, hardcover, B&W)
nn - By Rube Goldberg (first Goldberg item) 100.00 300.00 500.00
NOTE: *Comic strip began Oct 23, 1908 running thru 1941. Also drawn by George Frink in 1909*

FOOLISH QUESTIONS THAT ARE ASKED BY ALL
Levi Strauss & Co./Small, Maynard & Co.: 1909 (5-1/2x5-3/4", 24 pgs, paper-c, B&W)
nn- (Rare) by Rube Goldberg 65.00 175.00 350.00

FOOLISH QUESTIONS (Boxed card set) (S)
Wallie Dorr Co., N.Y.: 1919 (5-1/4x3-3/4")(box & card backs are red)
nn - Boxed set w/52 B&W comics on cards; each a single panel gag complete set w/box
75.00 263.00 450.00
NOTE: *There are two diff sets put out simultaneously with the first set, by the same company. One set continues/picks up the numbering of the cards from the other set.*

FOOLISH QUESTIONS (S)
EmBee Distributing Co.: 1921 (10¢, 4x5 1/2; 52 pgs, 3 color covers; B&W)
1-By Rube Goldberg 46.00 160.00 300.00

FOXY GRANDPA
Foxy Grandpa Company, 33 Wall St, NY : 1900 (9x15", 84 pgs, full color, cardboard-c)
nn - By Carl Schultze (By Permission of New York Herald) 271.00 1200.00 –
NOTE: *This seminal comic strip began Jan 7, 1900 and was collected later that same year.*

FOXY GRANDPA (Also see The Funnies, 1st series) (N)
N. Y. Herald/Frederick A. Stokes Co./M. A. Donahue & Co./Bunny Publ.
(L. R. Hammersly Co.): 1901 - 1916 (Strip-r in color, hard-c)
1901- 9x15" in color-N. Y. Herald 313.00 1100.00 –
1902- "Latest Larks of...", 32 pgs., 9-1/2x15-1/2" 164.00 575.00 –
1902- "The Many Advs. of...", 9x12", 148 pgs., Hammersly Co.
179.00 625.00 –
1903- "Latest Advs.", 9x15", 24 pgs., Hammersly Co. 164.00 575.00 –
1903- "...'s New Advs.", 11x15", 66 pgs., Stokes 164.00 575.00 –
1904- "Up to Date", 10x15", 66 pgs., Stokes 146.00 510.00 950.00
1904- "The Many Adventures of...", 9x15, 144pgs, Donohue 146.00 510.00 950.00
1905- "& Flip-Flaps", 9-1/2x15-1/2", 52 pgs. 146.00 510.00 950.00
1905- "The Latest Advs. of...", 9x15", 28, 52, & 68 pgs, M.A. Donohue Co.; re-issue of 1902 issue 104.00 365.00 700.00
1905- "Latest Larks of...", 9-1/2x15-1/2", 52 pgs., Donahue; re-issue of 1902 issue with more pages added 104.00 365.00 700.00
1905- "Latest Larks of...", 9-1/2x15-1/2", 24 pgs. edition, Donahue; re-issue of 1902 issue 104.00 365.00 700.00
1905- "Merry Pranks of...", 9-1/2x15-1/2", 28, 52 & 62 pgs., Donahue
104.00 365.00 700.00
1905-"...Surprises",10x15", color, 64 pg,Stokes, 60¢ 104.00 365.00 700.00
1906- "Frolics", 10x15", 30 pgs., Stokes 104.00 365.00 700.00
1907?-"...& His Boys",10x15", 64 color pgs, Stokes 104.00 365.00 700.00
1907- "Triumphs", 10x15", 62 pgs, Stokes 104.00 365.00 700.00
1908-"...Mother Goose", Stokes 104.00 365.00 700.00

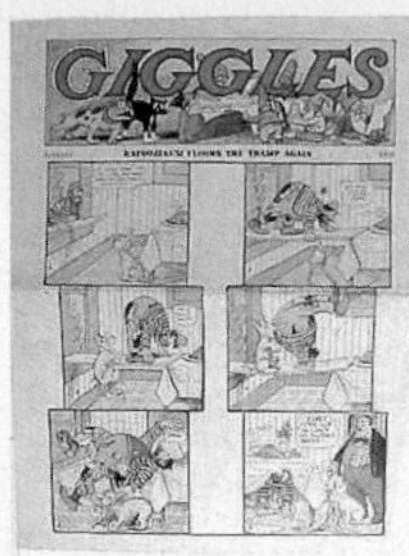
Giggles
© Pratt Food Co.

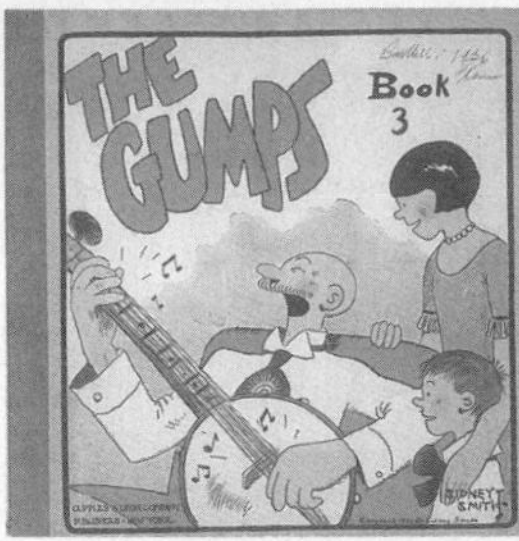

The Gumps #3 by Sidney Smith
1926 © Cupples & Leon

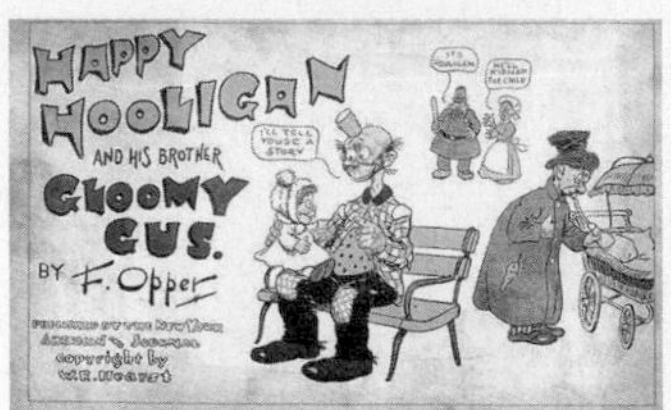

Happy Hooligan Book 1 1902
© Frederick A. Stokes

	GD2.0	FN6.0	VF8.0
1909- "...& Little Brother", 10x15, 58 pgs, Stokes	104.00	365.00	700.00
1911- "Latest Tricks", r-1910,1911 Sundays-Stokes Co.	104.00	365.00	700.00
1914-(9-1/2x15-1/2", 24 pgs.)-6 color cartoons/page, Bunny Publ. Co.	88.00	306.00	575.00
1915 - ...Always Jolly (10x16, Stokes)	88.00	306.00	575.00
1916- "Merry Book", (10x15", 64 pgs, Stokes)	88.00	306.00	575.00
1917-"...Adventures (5 1/2 x 6 1/2, 26 pgs, Stokes)	57.00	200.00	400.00
1917-"...Frolics (5 1/2 x 6 1/2, 26 pgs, Stokes)	57.00	200.00	400.00
1917-"...Triumphs (5 1/2 x 6 1/2, 26 pgs, Stokes)	57.00	200.00	400.00

FOXY GRANDPA, FUNNY TRICKS OF (The Stump Books)
M.A. Donahue Co, Chicago: approx 1903 (1-7/8x6-3/8", 44 pgs, blue hardcover)

nn - By Carl Schultze	54.00	189.00	325.00

NOTE: *One of a series of ten "stump" books; the only comics one.*

FOXY GRANDPA'S MOTHER GOOSE (I)
Stokes: October 1903 (10-11/16x8-1/2", 86 pgs, hard-c)

nn - By Carl Schultze (not comics - illustrated book)	54.00	189.00	325.00

FOXY GRANDPA SPARKLETS SERIES (N)
M. A. Donahue & Co.: 1908 (7-3/4x6-1/2"; 24 pgs., color)

"... Rides the Goat", "...& His Boys", "...Playing Ball", "...Fun on the Farm", "...Fancy Shooting", "...Show His Boys Up-To-Date Sports", "...Plays Santa Claus" each....	88.00	306.00	525.00
900- "Playing Ball"; Bunny illos; 8 pgs., linen like pgs., no date	73.00	254.00	435.00

FOXY GRANDPA VISITS RICHMOND (O,P)
Dietz Printing Co., Richmond, VA / Hotel Rueger: nd (c1920's) (5-7/8" x 4-1/2", 16 pgs, paper-c, B&W)

nn - (Scarce) By Bunny	25.00	88.00	175.00

NOTE: *Promotional comic given away to its guests by the Hotel Rueger, about Foxy Grandpa visiting and enjoying the Hotel. Originally came in an envelope, with the words "Foxy Grandpa Visits Richmond -- and Rueger's" printed on it.*

FOXY GRANDPA VISITS WASHINGTON, D.C. (P)
Dietz Printing Co., Richmond, VA / Hamilton Hotel: nd (c1920's) (5-7/8" x 4-1/2", 16 pgs, paper-c, B&W)

nn - (Scarce) By Bunny	25.00	88.00	150.00

NOTE: *Mostly reprints "... Visits Richmond", changing all references to Hotel Rueger, to Hamilton Hotel instead. Also, changes depictions of a waiter and a cook from black to white, plus incompletely erases the cover art on a book Foxy Grandpa falls asleep with (the latter is how we know that the Richmond version was first).*

FRAGMENTS FROM FRANCE (S)
G. P. Putnam & Sons: 1917 (9x6-1/4", 168 pgs, hardcover, $1.75)

nn - By Bruce Bairnsfather	25.00	88.00	150.00

NOTE: *WW1 trench warfare cartoons; color dust jacket.*

FUNNIES, THE (H) (See Clancy the Cop, Deadwood Gulch, Bug Movies)
Dell Publishing Co.: 1929 - No. 36, 10/18/30 (10¢; 5¢ No. 22 on) (16 pgs.)
Full tabloid size in color; not reprints; published every Saturday

1-My Big Brudder, Jonathan, Jazzbo & Jim, Foxy Grandpa, Sniffy, Jimmy Jams & other strips begin; first four-color comic newsstand publication; also contains magic, puzzles & stories	200.00	700.00	1500.00
2-21 (1930, 10¢)	150.00	300.00	600.00
22(nn-7/12/30-5¢)	150.00	300.00	600.00
23(nn-7/19/30-5¢), 24(nn-7/26/30-5¢), 25(nn-8/2/30), 26(nn-8/9/30), 27(nn-8/16/30), 28(nn-8/23/30), 29(nn-8/30/30), 30(nn-9/6/30), 31(nn-9/13/30), 32(nn-9/20/30), 33(nn-9/27/30), 34(nn-10/4/30), 35(nn-10/11/30), 36(nn, no date-10/18/30) each....	150.00	300.00	600.00

GASOLINE ALLEY (Also see Popular Comics & Super Comics) (N)
Reilly & Lee Publishers: 1929 (8-3/4x7", B&W daily strip-r, hard-c)

nn - By King (96 pgs.)	125.00	300.00	600.00
with scarce Dust Wrapper	250.00	500.00	900.00

NOTE: *Of all the Frank King reprint books, this is the only one to reprint actual complete newspaper strips - all others are illustrated prose text stories.*

GIBSON'S PUBLISHED DRAWINGS, MR. (M,S) (see Victorian index for earlier issues)
R.H. Russell, New York: No.1 1894 - No. 9 1904 (11x17-3/4", hard-c, B&W)

nn (No.6; 1901) A Widow and her Friends (90 pgs.)	30.00	60.00	120.00
nn (No.7; 1902) The Social Ladder (88 pgs.)	30.00	60.00	120.00
8 - 1903 The Weaker Sex (88 pgs.)	30.00	60.00	120.00
9 - 1904 Everyday People (88 pgs.)	30.00	60.00	120.00

NOTE: *By Charles Dana Gibson cartoons, reprinted from magazines, primarily LIFE. The Education of Mr. Pipp tells a story. Series continues how long after 1904?*

GIGGLES
Pratt Food Co., Philadelphia, PA: 1908-09? (12x9", 8 pgs, color, 5 cents-c)

1-8: By Walt McDougall (#8 dated March 1909)	40.00	175.00	–

NOTE: *Appears to be monthly; almost tabloid size; yearly subscriptions was 25 cents.*

GOD'S MAN (H)
Jonathan Cape and Harrison Smith Inc.: 1929 (8-1/4x6", 298 pgs, B&W hardcover w/dust jacket) (original graphic novel in wood cuts)

	GD2.0	FN6.0	VF8.0
nn - By Lynd Ward	43.00	171.00	300.00

GOLD DUST TWINS
N. K. Fairbank Co.: 1904 (4-5/8x6-3/4", 18 pgs, color and B&W)

nn - By E. W. Kemble (Rare)	30.00	60.00	130.00

NOTE: *Promo comic for Gold DustWashing Powder; includes page of watercolor paints.*

GOLF
Volland Co.: 1916 (9x12-3/4", 132 pgs, hard-c, B&W)

nn - By Clair Briggs	100.00	200.00	400.00

GUMPS, THE (N)
Landfield-Kupfer: No. 1, 1918 - No. 6, 1921; (B&W Daily strip-r)

Book No. 1(1918)(scarce)-cardboard-c, 5-1/4x13-1/3", 64 pgs., daily strip-r by Sidney Smith	75.00	250.00	500.00
Book No.2(1918)-(scarce); 5-1/4x13-1/3"; paper cover; 36 pgs. daily strip reprints by Sidney Smith	75.00	250.00	500.00
Book No. 3	100.00	350.00	700.00
Book No. 4 (1918) 5-3/8x13-7/8", 20 pgs. Color card-c	100.00	350.00	700.00
Book No. 5 10-1/4x13-1/2", 20 pgs. Color paper-c	100.00	350.00	700.00
Book No. 6 (Rare, 20 pgs, 8x13-3/8, strip-r 1920-21)	121.00	423.00	725.00

GUMPS, ANDY AND MIN, THE (N)
Landfield-Kupfer Printing Co., Chicago/Morrison Hotel: nd (1920s) (Giveaway, 5-1/2"x14", 20 pgs., B&W, soft-c)

nn - Strip-r by Sidney Smith; art & logo embossed on cover w/hotel restaurant menu on back-c or a hotel promo ad; 4 different contents of issues known	50.00	175.00	300.00

GUMPS, THE (N)
Cupples & Leon: 1924-1930 (10x10, 52 pgs, B&W)

1 - By Sidney Smith	61.00	244.00	450.00
2-7	39.00	154.00	300.00

THE GUMPS (P)
Cupples & Leon Company: 1924 (9 x 7-1/2", 28 pgs, paper cover)

nn (1924)	50.00	175.00	300.00

NOTE: *Promotional comic for Sunshine Andy Gump Biscuits. Daily strip-r from 1922-24.*

GUMP'S CARTOON BOOK, THE (N)
The National Arts Company: 1931 (13-7/8x10", 36 pgs, color covers, B&W)

nn - By Sidney Smith	57.00	228.00	450.00

GUMPS PAINTING BOOK, THE (N)
The National Arts Company: 1931 (11 x 15 1/4", 20 pgs, half in full color)

nn - By Sidney Smith	57.00	228.00	450.00

HALT FRIENDS! (see also **HELLO BUDDY**)
???: 1918? (4-3/8x5-3/4", 36 pgs, color-c, B&W, no cover price listed)

nn - Unknown	10.00	30.00	70.00

NOTE: *Says on front cover: "Comics of War Facts of Service Sold on its merits by Unemployed or Disabled Ex-Service Men. Credentials Shown On Request. Price - Pay What You Please." These are very common; contents vary widely.*

HAMBONE'S MEDITATIONS
Jahl & Co.: no date 1920 (6-1/8 x 7-1/2, 108 pgs, paper cover, B&W)

nn - By J. P. Alley	33.00	132.00	250.00

NOTE: *Reprint of racist single panel newspaper series, 2 cartoons per page.*

HAN OLA OG PER (N)
Anundsen Publishing Co, Decorah, Iowa: 1927 (10-3/8 x 15-3/4", 54 pgs, paper-c, B&W)

nn - American origin Norwegian language strips-r	33.00	131.00	230.00

NOTE: *1940s and modern reprints exist.*

HANS UND FRITZ (N)
The Saalfield Publishing Co.: 1917, 1927-29 (10x13-1/2", 28 pgs., B&W)

nn - By R. Dirks (1917, r-1916 strips)	96.00	335.00	600.00
nn - By R. Dirks (1923 edition- reprint of 1917 edition)	58.00	204.00	350.00
nn - By R. Dirks (1926 edition- reprint of 1917 edition)	58.00	204.00	350.00
The Funny Larks Of... By R. Dirks (©1917 outside cover; ©1916 inside indicia)	96.00	335.00	600.00
The Funny Larks Of... (1927) reprints 1917 edition of 1916 strips Halloween-c	58.00	204.00	350.00
The Funny Larks Of... 2 (1929)	58.00	204.00	350.00
193 - By R. Dirks; contains 1916 Sunday strip reprints of Katzenjammer Kids & Hawkshaw the Detective - reprint of 1917 nn edition (1929) this edition is not rare	58.00	204.00	350.00

HAPPY DAYS (S)
Coward-McCann Inc.: 1929 (12-1/2x9-5/8", 110 pgs, hardcover B&W)

nn - By Alban Butler (WW 1 cartoons)	20.00	60.00	120.00

HAPPY HOOLIGAN (See Alphonse...) (N)
Hearst's New York American & Journal: 1902,1903
Book 1-(1902)-"And His Brother Gloomy Gus", By Fred Opper; has 1901-02-r;

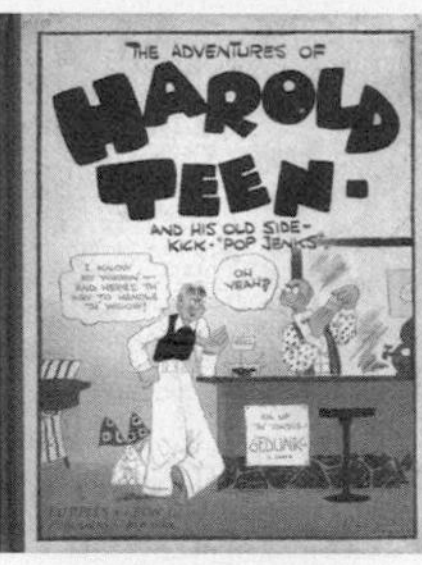

Harold Teen #2 by Carl Ed
1931 © Cupples & Leon

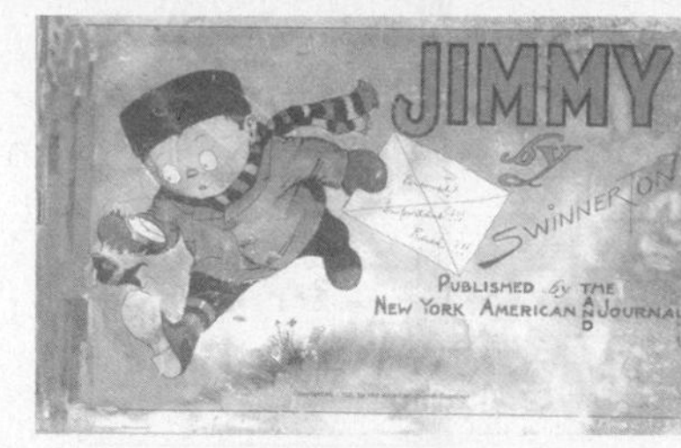

Jimmy By Jimmy Swinnerton
1905 © Frederick A. Stokes

Joys & Glooms By T.E. Powers
1912 © Reilly & Britton Co.

	GD2.0	FN6.0	VF8.0
(yellow & black)(86 pgs.)(10x15-1/4")	600.00	1800.00	3000.00
New Edition, 1903 -10x15" 82 pgs. in color	350.00	1400.00	–

NOTE: *Strip ran March 26, 1900-Aug 14, 1932 and is widely recognized as setting the format standard for all newspaper comic strips which came after it. Opper (1857-1937) was going blind towards the end.*

HAPPY HOOLIGAN (N) (By Fredrick Opper)
Frederick A. Stokes Co.: 1906-08 (10-1/4x15-3/4", cardboard color-c)

	GD2.0	FN6.0	VF8.0
1906 - :Travels of...), 68 pgs,10-1/4x15-3/4", 1905-r	300.00	900.00	–
1907 - "--Home Again", 68 pgs., 10x15-3/4", 60¢; full color-c	300.00	900.00	–
1908 - "Handy--", 68 pgs, color	300.00	900.00	–

HAPPY HOOLIGAN, THE STORY OF (G)
McLoughlin Bros.: No. 281, 1932 (12x9-1/2", 20 pgs., soft-c)

	GD2.0	FN6.0	VF8.0
281-Three-color text, pictures on heavy paper	57.00	228.00	400.00

NOTE: *An homage to Opper's creation on its 30th Anniversary in 1932.*

HAROLD HARDHIKE'S REJUVENATION
O'Sullivan Rubber: 1917 (6-1/4x3-1/2, 16 pgs, B&W)

	GD2.0	FN6.0	VF8.0
nn	25.00	100.00	175.00

NOTE: *Comic book to promote rubber shoe heels.*

HAROLD TEEN (N)
Cupples & Leon Co.: 1929 (9-7/8x9-7/8", 52 pgs, cardboard covers)

	GD2.0	FN6.0	VF8.0
1 - By Carl Ed	50.00	200.00	500.00
nn - (1931, 8-11/16x6-7/8", 96 pgs, hardcover w/dj)	41.00	164.00	290.00

NOTE: *Title 2nd book:* ***HAROLD TEEN AND HIS OLD SIDE-KICK- POP JENKINS,*** *(Adv. of...). Precursor for Archie Andrews & crew; strip began May 4, 1919 running into 1959.*

HAROLD TEEN PAINT AND COLOR BOOK (N)
McLoughlin Bros Inc.: 1932 (13x9-3/4, 28 pgs, B&W and color)

	GD2.0	FN6.0	VF8.0
#2054	25.00	100.00	175.00

HAWKSHAW THE DETECTIVE (See Advs. of..., Hans Und Fritz & Okay) (N)
The Saalfield Publishing Co.: 1917 (10-1/2x13-1/2", 24 pgs., B&W)

	GD2.0	FN6.0	VF8.0
nn - By Gus Mager (Sunday strip-r)	54.00	190.00	350.00
nn - By Gus Mager (1923 reprint of 1917 edition)	25.00	100.00	175.00
nn - By Gus Mager (1926 reprint of 1917 edition)	25.00	100.00	175.00

NOTE: *Runs Feb 23, 1913-Sept 4, 1922, starts again from Dec 13, 1931-Feb 11, 1952; Sherlock Holmes spoof.*

HEALTH IN PICTURES
American Public Health Association, NYC: 1930 (6-1/2" x 5-3/16", 76 pgs, green & black paper-c, B&W interior)

	GD2.0	FN6.0	VF8.0
nn - By various	15.00	51.00	90.00

NOTE: *Collection of strips and cartoons put out by the Public Health Association, on topics ranging from boating and food safety, to small pox and typhoid prevention.*

HE DONE HER WRONG (O) (see also BANANA OIL)
Doubleday, Doran & Company: 1930 (8-1/4x 7-1/4", 276pgs, hard-c with dust jacket, B&W interiors)

	GD2.0	FN6.0	VF8.0
nn - By Milt Gross	75.00	225.00	400.00

NOTE: *A seminal original-material wordless graphic novel, not reprints. Several modern reprints.*

HELLO BUDDY (see also **HALT FRIENDS**)
???: 1919? (4-3/8x5-3/4", 36 pgs, color-c, B&W, 15¢)

	GD2.0	FN6.0	VF8.0
nn - Unknown	10.00	30.00	70.00

NOTE: *Says on front cover: "Comics of War Facts of Service Sold on its merits by Unemployed or Disabled Ex-Service Men." These are very common; contents vary widely.*

HENRY (N)
David McKay Co.: 1935 (25¢, soft-c)

	GD2.0	FN6.0	VF8.0
Book 1 - By Carl Anderson	57.00	200.00	400.00

NOTE: *Strip began March 19 1932; this book ties with Popeye (David McKay) and Little Annie Rooney (David McKay) as the last of the 10x10" Platinum Age comic books.*

HENRY (M)
Greenberg Publishers Inc.: 1935 (11-1/4x 8-5/8", 72 pgs, red & blue color hard-c, dust jacket, B&W interiors) (strip-r from Saturday Evening Post)

	GD2.0	FN6.0	VF8.0
nn - By Carl Anderson	57.00	200.00	400.00

HIGH KICKING KELLYS, THE (M)
Vaudeville News Corporation, NY: 1926 (5x11", B&W, two color soft-c)

	GD2.0	FN6.0	VF8.0
nn - By Jack A. Ward (scarce)	40.00	160.00	280.00

HIGHLIGHTS OF HISTORY (N)
World Syndicate Publishing Co.: 1933-34 (4-1/2x4", 288 pgs)

	GD2.0	FN6.0	VF8.0
nn - 5 different unnumbered issues; daily strip-r	10.00	40.00	70.00

NOTE: *Titles include Buffalo Bill, Daniel Boone, Kit Carson, Pioneers of the Old West, Winning of the Old Northwest. There are line drawing color covers and embossed hardcover versions. It is unknown which came out first.*

HOMER HOLCOMB AND MAY (N)
no publisher listed: 1920s (4 x 9-1/2", 40 pgs, paper cover, B&W)

	GD2.0	FN6.0	VF8.0
nn - By Doc Bird Finch (strip-r)	10.00	40.00	70.00

HOME, SWEET HOME (N)
M.S. Publishing Co.: 1925 (10-1/4x10")

	GD2.0	FN6.0	VF8.0
nn - By Tuthill	33.00	134.00	235.00

HOW THEY DRAW PROHIBITION (S)
Association Against Prohibition: 1930 (10x9", 100 pgs.)

	GD2.0	FN6.0	VF8.0
nn - Single panel and multi-panel comics (rare)	71.00	285.00	500.00

NOTE: *Contains art by J.N. "Ding" Darling, James Flagg, Rollin Kirby, Winsor McCay, T.E. Powers, H.T. Webster, others. Also comes with a loose sheet listing all the newspapers where the cartoons originally appeared.*

HOW TO BE A CARTOONIST (H)
Saalfield Pub. Co: 1936 (10-3/8x12-1/2", 16 pgs, color-c, B&W)

	GD2.0	FN6.0	VF8.0
nn - By Chas. H. Kuhn	10.00	40.00	70.00

HOW TO DRAW: A PRACTICAL BOOK OF INSTRUCTION (H)
Harper & Brothers: 1904 (9-1/4x12-3/8", 128 pgs, hardcover, B&W)

	GD2.0	FN6.0	VF8.0
nn - Edited By Leon Barritt	57.00	228.00	400.00

NOTE: *Strips reprinted include: "Buster Brown" by Outcault, "Foxy Grandpa" by Bunny, "Happy Hooligan" by Opper, "Katzenjammer Kids" by Dirks, "Lady Bountiful" by Gene Carr, "Mr. Jack" by Swinnerton, "Panhandle Pete" by George McManus, "Mr E.Z. Mark" by F.M. Howarth others; non-character strips by Hy Mayer, Winsor McCay, T.E. Powers, others; single panel cartoons by Davenport, Frost, McDougall, Nast, W.A. Rogers, Sullivant, others.*

HOW TO DRAW CARTOONS (H)
Garden City Publishing Co.: 1926, 1937 (10 1/4 x 7 1/2, 150 pgs)

	GD2.0	FN6.0	VF8.0
1926 first edition By Clare Briggs	25.00	75.00	150.00
1937 2nd edition By Clare Briggs	20.00	60.00	120.00

NOTE: *Seminal "how to" break into the comics syndicates with art by Briggs, Fisher, Goldberg, King, Webster, Opper, Tad, Hershfield, McCay, Ding, others. Came with Dust Jacket -add 50%.*

HOW TO DRAW FUNNY PICTURES: A Complete Course in Cartooning (H)
Frederick J. Drake & Co., Chicago: 1936 (10-3/8x6-7/8", 168 pgs, hardcover, B&W)

	GD2.0	FN6.0	VF8.0
nn - By E.C. Matthews (200 illus by Eugene Zimmerman)	20.00	60.00	120.00

HY MAYER (M)
Puck Publishing: 1915 (13-1/2 x 20-3/4", 52 pgs, hardcover cover, color & B&W interiors)

	GD2.0	FN6.0	VF8.0
nn - By Hy Mayer(strip reprints from Puck)	40.00	140.00	300.00

HYSTERICAL HISTORY OF THE CIVILIAN CONSERVATION CORPS
Peerless Engraving: 1934 (10-3/4x7-1/2", 104 pgs, soft-c, B&W)

	GD2.0	FN6.0	VF8.0
nn - By various	20.00	60.00	120.00

NOTE: *Comics about CCC life, includes two color insert postcards in back.*

INDOOR SPORTS (N,S)
National Specials Co., New York: nd circa 1912 (25 cents, 6 x 9", 68 pgs, B&W)

	GD2.0	FN6.0	VF8.0
nn - Tad	35.00	125.00	225.00

NOTE: *Cartoons reprinted from Hearst papers.*

IT HAPPENS IN THE BEST FAMILIES (N)
Powers Photo Engraving Co.: 1920 (52 pgs.)(9-1/2x10-3/4")

	GD2.0	FN6.0	VF8.0
nn - By Briggs; B&W Sunday strips-r	29.00	114.00	200.00
Special Railroad Edition (30¢)-r/strips from 1914-1920	26.00	103.00	180.00

JIMMIE DUGAN AND THE REG'LAR FELLERS (N)
Cupples & Leon: 1921, 46 pgs. (11"x16")

	GD2.0	FN6.0	VF8.0
nn - By Gene Byrne	71.00	284.00	500.00

NOTE: *Ties with EmBee's Mutt & Jeff and Trouble of Bringing Up Father as the last of this size.*

JIMMY (N) (see Little Jimmy Picture & Story Book)
N. Y. American & Journal: 1905 (10x15", 84 pgs., color)

	GD2.0	FN6.0	VF8.0
nn - By Jimmy Swinnerton (scarce)	300.00	800.00	1500.00

NOTE: *James Swinnerton was one of the original first pioneers of the American newspaper comic strip.*

JIMMY AND HIS SCRAPES (N)
Frederick A. Stokes: 1906, (10-1/4x15-1/4", 66 pgs, cardboard-c, color)

	GD2.0	FN6.0	VF8.0
nn - By Jimmy Swinnerton (scarce)	300.00	800.00	1500.00

JOE PALOOKA (N)
Cupples & Leon Co.: 1933 (9-13/16x10", 52 pgs., B&W daily strip-r)

	GD2.0	FN6.0	VF8.0
nn - By Ham Fisher (scarce)	114.00	456.00	800.00

JOHN, JONATHAN AND MR. OPPER BY F. OPPER (S,I,N)
Grant, Richards, 48 Leicester Square, W.C.: 1903 (9-5/8x8-3/8", 108 pgs, hard-c B&W)

	GD2.0	FN6.0	VF8.0
nn - Opper (Scarce)	50.00	200.00	380.00

NOTE: *British precursor-type companion to* Willie And His Poppa *reprints from Hearst's* NY American & Journal *Opper cartoons interfacing* Uncle Sam *precursor* Brother Jonathan, John Bull. *Uses name* Happy Hooligan *in one cartoon, has* John Bull *smoking opium in another.*

JOLLY POLLY'S BOOK OF ENGLISH AND ETIQUETTE (S)
Jos. J. Frisch: 1931 (60 cents, 8 x 5-1/8, 88 pgs, paper-c, B&W)

	GD2.0	FN6.0	VF8.0
nn - By Jos. J. Frisch	20.00	60.00	120.00

NOTE: *Reprint of single panel newspaper series, 4 per page, of English and etiquette lessons taught by a flapper.*

JOYS AND GLOOMS (N)
Reilly & Britton Co.: 1912 (11x8", 72 pgs, hard-c, B&W interior)

	GD2.0	FN6.0	VF8.0
nn - By T. E. Powers (newspaper strip-r)	39.00	156.00	325.00

JUDGE - yet to be indexed

The Cruise of the Katzenjammer Kids
© NY American & Journal

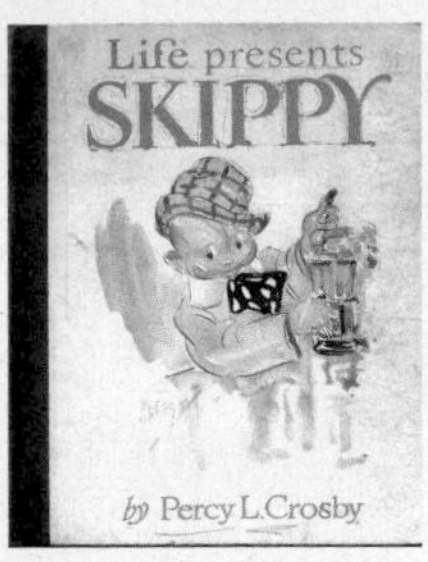

Life Presents Skippy by Percy L. Crosby
1924 © Life Publishing Company

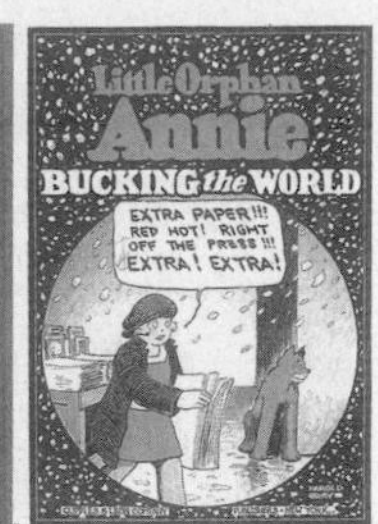

Little Orphan Annie by Harold Gray #2
1927 © Cupples & Leon

GD2.0 FN6.0 VF8.0 GD2.0 FN6.0 VF8.0

JUDGE'S LIBRARY - yet to be indexed

JUST KIDS COMICS FOR CRAYON COLORING
King Features. NYC: 1928 (11x8-1/2, 16 pgs, soft-c)
nn - By Ad Carter 33.00 100.00 200.00
NOTE: *Porous better grade paper; top pics printed in color; lower in b&w to color.*

JUST KIDS, THE STORY OF (I)
McLoughlin Bros.: 1932 (12x9-1/2", 20 pgs., paper-c)
283-Three-color text, pictures on heavy paper 39.00 156.00 275.00

KAPTIN KIDDO AND PUPPO (N)
Frederick A. Stokes Co.: 1910-1913 (11x16-1/2", 62 pgs)
1910-By Grace Wiederseim (later Drayton) 40.00 140.00 240.00
1910-Turr-ble Tales of... By Grace Wiederseim (Edward Stern & Co., 11x16-1/2", 64 pgs.) 40.00 140.00 240.00
1913- ...'Speriences By Grace Drayton 40.00 140.00 240.00
NOTE: *Strip ran approx. 1909-1912.*

KATZENJAMMER KIDS, THE (Also see Hans Und Fritz) (N)
New York American & Journal: 1902,1903 (10x15-1/4", 86 pgs., color)
(By Rudolph Dirks; strip first appeared in 1897) © W.R. Hearst
NOTE: *All KK books 1902-1905 all have the same exact title page with a 1902 copyright by W.R. Hearst; almost always look instead on the front cover.*
1902 (Rare) (red & black); has 1901-02 strips 1000.00 2400.00 –
1903- **A New Edition** (Rare), 86 pgs 750.00 2000.00 –
1904- 10x15", 84 pgs 250.00 900.00 –
1905?-The Cruise of the, 10x15", 60¢, in color 250.00 900.00 –
1905-A Series of Comic Pictures, 10x15", 84 pgs. in color, possible reprint of 1904 edition 250.00 800.00 –
1905-Tricks of... (10x15", 66 pgs, Stokes) 250.00 800.00 –
1906-Stokes (10x16", 32 pgs. in color) 186.00 800.00 –
1907- The Cruise of the, 10x15", 62 pgs 1905-r? 186.00 800.00 –
1910-The Komical...(10x15) 150.00 450.00 800.00
1921-Embee Dist. Co., 10x16", 20 pgs. in color 150.00 450.00 800.00

KATZENJAMMER KIDS MAGIC DRAWING AND COLORING BOOK (N)
Sam L Gabriel Sons And Company: 1931 (8 1/2 x 12", 36 pages, stiff-c
838-By Knerr 50.00 200.00 350.00

KEEPING UP WITH THE JONESES (N)
Cupples & Leon Co.: 1920 - No. 2, 1921 (9-1/4x9-1/4",52 pgs.,B&W daily strip-r)
1,2-By Pop Momand 39.00 154.00 270.00

KID KARTOONS (N,S)
The Century Co.: 1922 (232 pgs, printed 1 side, 9-3/4 x 7-3/4", hard-c, B&W)
nn - By Gene Carr (Metropolitan Movies strip-r) 60.00 240.00 –

KING OF THE ROYAL MOUNTED (Also See Dan Dunn) (N)
Whitman Publishing: 1937 (5 1/2 x 7 1/4", 68 pgs., color cardboard-c, B&W)
1010 36.00 144.00 250.00

LADY BOUNTIFUL (N)
Saalfield Publ. Co./Press Publ. Co.: 1917 (13-3/8x10", 36 pgs, color cardboard-c, B&W interiors)
nn - By Gene Carr; 2 panels per page 50.00 175.00 300.00
193S - 2nd printing (13-1/8x10",28 pgs color-c, B&W) 33.00 117.00 200.00

LAUGHS YOU MIGHT HAVE HAD From The Comic Pages of Six Week Day Issues of the Post-Dispatch (N)
St. Louis Post-Dispatch: 1921 (9 x 10 1/2", 28 pgs, B&W, red ink cover)
nn - Various comic strips 39.00 154.00 270.00

LIFE, DOGS FROM (M)
Doubleday, Page & Company: nn 1920 - No.2 1926 (130 pgs, 11-1/4 x 9", color painted-c, hard-c, B&W)
nn (No.1) 120.00 360.00 –
Second Litter 80.00 320.00 –
NOTE: *Reprints strips & cartoons featuring dogs, from Life Magazine. Editted by Thomas L. Masson. Highly sought by collectors of dog ephemera. Art in both books is mostly by Robert L. Dickey. Other art: Carl Anderson-1,2; Barbes-1; Chip Bellew-1; Lang Campbell-1,2; Percy Crosby-1,2; Edwina-2; Frueh-2; R.B. Fuller-1; Gibson-1,2; Don Herold-2; Gus Mager-2; Orr-1; J.R. Shaver-1,2; T.S. Sullivant-2; Russ Westover-1,2; Crawford Young-1.*

LIFE OF DAVY CROCKETT IN PICTURE AND STORY, THE
Cupples & Leon: 1935 (8-3/4x7", 64 pgs, B&W hard-c, dust jacket?)
nn - By C. Richard Schaare 29.00 116.00 200.00

LIFE OF THOMAS A. EDISON IN WORD AND PICTURE, THE (N)(Also see Edison...)
Thomas A. Edison Industries: 1928 (10x8", 56 pgs, paper cover, B&W)
nn - Photo-c 100.00 250.00 400.00
NOTE: *Reprints newspaper strip which ran August to November 1927.*

LIFE'S LITTLE JOKES (S)
M.S. Publ. Co.: No date (1924)(10-1/16x10", 52 pgs., B&W)
nn - By Rube Goldberg 64.00 257.00 525.00

LIFE, MINIATURE (see also LIFE (miniature reprint of of issue No. 1)) (M,P,S)
Life Publishing Co.: No. 1 - No. 4 1913, 1916, 1919 (5-3/4x4-5/8", 20 pgs, color paper-c
1- 3 (1913) 4 (1916) 5 (1919) (no known sales)
NOTE: *Giveaway item from Life, to promote subscriptions. All reprint material. No.2: James Montgomery Flagg-c; a-Chip Bellew, Gus Dirks, Gibson, F.M.Howarth, Art Young.*

LIFE'S PRINTS (was **LIFE'S PICTURE GALLERY** - See Victorian Age section) (M,S,P)
Life Publishing Company, New York: nd (c1907) (7x4-1/2", 132 pgs, paper cover, B&W)
nn - (nd; c1907) unillustrated black construction paper cover; reprints art from 1895-1907; art by J.M.Flagg, A.B.Frost, Gibson (Scarce) – – –
nn - (nd; c1908) b&w cardboard painted cover by Gibson, showing angel raising a champagne glass; reprints art from 1901-1908; art by J.M.Flagg, A.B.Frost, Gibson, Walt Kuhn, Art Young (Scarce) – – –
NOTE: *Catalog of prints reprinted from LIFE covers & centerspreads. There are likely more as yet unreported catalogs.*

LIFE, THE COMEDY OF LIFE
Life Publishing Company: 1907 (130 pgs, 11-3/4x9-1/4",embossed printed cloth covered board-c, B+W
nn - By various 20.00 80.00 120.00
NOTE: *Single cartoons and some sequential cartoons). Artists include Charles Dana Gibson, Harrison Cady, E.W. Kemble, James Montgomery Flagg.*

LILY OF THE ALLEY IN THE FUNNIES
Whitman Publishing Co.: No date (1927) (10-1/4x15-1/2"; 28 pgs., color)
W936 - By T. Burke (Rare) 57.00 228.00 400.00

LITTLE ANNIE ROONEY (N)
David McKay Co.: 1935 (25¢, soft-c)
Book 1 43.00 172.00 340.00
NOTE: *Ties with Henry & Popeye (David McKay) as the last of the 10x10" size Plat comic books.*

LITTLE ANNIE ROONEY WISHING BOOK (G) (See Happy Hooligan, Story of #281)
McLoughlin Bros.: 1932 (12x9-1/2", 16 pgs., soft-c, 3-color text, heavier paper)
282 - By Darrell McClure 41.00 144.00 250.00

LITTLE BIRD TOLD ME, A (E)
Life Publishing Co.: 1905? (96 pgs, hardbound)
nn - By Walt Kuhn (Life-r) 41.00 144.00 250.00

LITTLE FOLKS PAINTING BOOK (N)
The National Arts Company: 1931 (10-7/8 x 15-1/4", 20 pgs, half in full color)
nn - By "Tack" Knight (strip-r) 41.00 144.00 250.00

LITTLE JIMMY PICTURE AND STORY BOOK (I) (see Jimmy)
McLaughlin Bros., Inc.: 1932 (13-1/4 x 9-3/4", 20 pgs, cardstock color cover)
284 Text by Marion Kincaird; illus by Swinnerton 57.00 228.00 400.00

LITTLE JOHNNY & THE TEDDY BEARS (Judge-r) (M) (see Teddy Bear Books)
Reilly & Britton Co.: 1907 (10x14".; 68 pgs, green, red, black interior color)
nn - By J. R. Bray-a/Robert D. Towne-s 67.00 233.00 400.00

LITTLE JOURNEY TO THE HOME OF BRIGGS THE SKY-ROCKET, THE
Lockhart Art School: 1917 (10-3/4x7-7/8", 20 pgs, B&W) (I)
nn - About Clare Briggs (bio & lots of early art) 41.00 144.00 250.00

LITTLE KING, THE (see New Yorker Cartoon Albums for 1st appearance) (M)
Farrar & Reinhart, Inc: 1933 (10-1/4 x 8-3/4, 80 pgs, hardcover w/dust jacket
nn - By Otto Soglow (strip-r The New Yorker) 125.00 250.00 450.00
NOTE: *Copies with dust jacket are worth 50% more. Also exists in a 12x8-3/4 edition.*

LITTLE LULU BY MARGE (M)
Rand McNally & Company, Chicago: 1936 (6-9/16x6", 68 pgs, yellow hard-c, B&W)
nn - By Marjorie Henderson Buell 25.00 100.00 250.00
NOTE: *Begins reprinting single panel Little Lulu cartoons which began with Saturday Evening Post Feb. 23, 1935. This book was reprinted several times as late as 1940.*

LITTLE NAPOLEON
No publisher listed: 1924 , 50 pages, 10" by 10"; Color cardstock-c, B&W
nn - By Bud Counihan (Cupples &Leon format) 25.00 100.00 240.00

LITTLE NEMO (...in Slumberland) (N) (see also Little Sammy Sneeze, Dreams...Rarebit F)
Doffield & Co.(1906)/Cupples & Leon Co.(1909): 1906, 1909 (Sunday strip-r in color, cardboard covers)
1906-11x16-1/2" by Winsor McCay; 30 pgs. (scarce) 1500.00 5000.00 –
1909-10x14" by Winsor McCay (scarce) 1300.00 4000.00 –

LITTLE ORPHAN ANNIE (See Treasure Box of Famous Comics) (N)
Cupples & Leon Co.: 1926 - 1934 (8-3/4x7", 100 pgs., B&W daily strip-r, hard-c)
1 (1926)-Little Orphan Annie (softback see Treasure Box) 50.00 200.00 375.00
2 (1927)-In the Circus (softback see Wonder Box...) 36.00 144.00 275.00
3 (1928)-The Haunted House (softback see Wonder Box...) 36.00 144.00 275.00
4 (1929)-Bucking the World 36.00 144.00 275.00

The Trials of Lulu and Leander by Howarth
1906 © NY American & Journal

Maud the Mirthful Mule by Opper
1908 © Frederick A. Stokes

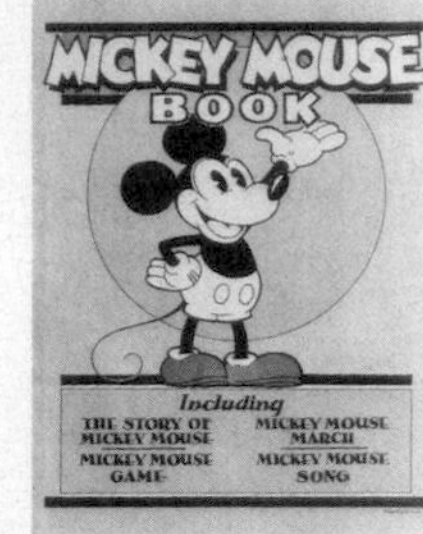

Mickey Mouse Book
1930 © Bibo & Lang

GD2.0 FN6.0 VF8.0

5 (1930)-Never Say Die 30.00 120.00 225.00
6 (1931)-Shipwrecked 30.00 120.00 225.00
7 (1932)-A Willing Helper 25.00 100.00 200.00
8 (1933)-In Cosmic City 25.00 100.00 200.00
9 (1934)-Uncle Dan (not rare) 25.00 100.00 200.00
NOTE: *Each book reprints dailies from the previous year. Each hardcover came with a dust jacket. Books without dust jackets are worth 50% less. Many of copies of #9 Uncle Dan have been turning up on eBay recently.*

LITTLE ORPHAN ANNIE RUMMY CARDS (N)
Whitman Publishing Co., Racine: 1935 (box: 5 x 6 1/2" Cards: 3 1/2 x 2 1/4")
nn-Harold Gray 20.00 60.00 120.00
NOTE: *36 cards, including 1 instruction card, 5 character cards and 30 cards forming 5 sequential stories (6 cards each).*

LITTLE SAMMY SNEEZE (N) (see also Little Nemo, Dreams of A Rarebit Fiend)
New York Herald Co.: Dec 1905 (11x16-1/2", 72 pgs., color)
nn - By Winsor McCay (Very Rare) 2500.00 6000.00 –
NOTE: *Rarely found in fine to mint condition.*

LIVE AND LET LIVE
Travelers Insurance Co.: 1936 (5-3/4x7/3/4", 16 pgs. color and B&W)
nn - Bill Holman, Carl Anderson, etc 20.00 60.00 120.00

LULU AND LEANDER (N) (see also Funny Folk, 1899, in Victorian section)
New York American & Journal: 1904 (76 pgs); **William A Stokes & Co:** 1906
nn - By F.M. Howarth 300.00 750.00 1500.00
nn - The Trials of...(1906, 10x16", 68 pgs. in color) 300.00 750.00 1500.00
NOTE: *F. M. Howarth helped pioneer the American comic strip in the pages of PUCK magazine in the early 1890s before the Yellow Kid.*

MADMAN'S DRUM (O)
Jonathan Cape and Harrison Smith Inc.: 1930 (8-1/4x6", 274 pgs, B&W hardcover w/dust jacket) (original graphic novel in wood cuts)
nn - By Lynd Ward 50.00 175.00 300.00

MAMA'S ANGEL CHILD IN TOYLAND (I)
Rand McNally, Chicago: 1915 (120 pgs, hardbound)
nn - By M.T. "Penny" Ross & Marie C, Sadler 40.00 140.00 240.00
NOTE: *Mamma's Angel Child published as a comic strip by the "Chicago Tribune" 1908 Mar 1 to 1920 Oct 17.This novel dedicated to Esther Starring Richartz, "the original Mamma's Angel Kid."*

MAUD (N) (see also **Happy Hooligan**)
Frederick A. Stokes Co.: 1906 - 1908? (10x15-1/2", cardboard-c)
1906-By Fred Opper (Scarce), 66 pgs. color 400.00 1200.00 –
1907-The Matchless, 10x15" 70 pgs in color 300.00 900.00 –
1908-The Mirthful Mule, 10x15", 64 pgs. in color 300.00 900.00 –
NOTE: *First run of strip began July 24, 1904 to at least Oct 6, 1907, spun out of* ***Happy Hooligan.***

MEMORIAL EDITION The Drawings of Clare Briggs (S)
Wm H. Wise & Company: 1930 (7-1/2x8-3/4", 284 pgs, pebbled false black leather, B&W) (posthumous boxed set of 7 books by Clare Briggs)
nn - The Days of Real Sport; nn-Golf; nn-Real Folks at Home; nn-Ain't it a Grand and Glorious Feeling?; nn-That Guiltiest Feeling; nn-Somebody's Always Taking the Joy Out of Life; nn-When a Feller Needs a Friend
Each book... 30.00 120.00 210.00
NOTE: *Also exists in a whitish cream colored paper back edition; first edition unknown presently.*

MENACE CARTOONS (M, S)
Menace Publishing Company, Aurora, Missouri: 1914 (10-3/8x8", 80 pgs, cardboard-c, B&W)
nn - (Rare) 50.00 150.00 450.00
NOTE: *Reprints anti-Catholic cartoons from K.K.K. related publication* ***The Menace.***

MEN OF DARING (N)
Cupples & Leon Co.: 1933 (8-3/4x7", 100 pgs)
nn - By Stookie Allen, intro by Lowell Thomas 30.00 90.00 200.00

MICKEY MOUSE BOOK
Bibo & Lang: 1930-1931 (12x9", stapled-c, 20 pgs., 4 printings)
nn - First Disney licensed publication (a magazine, not a book–see first book, Adventures of Mickey Mouse). Contains story of how Mickey met Walt and got his name; games, cartoons & song "Mickey Mouse (You Cute Little Feller)," written by Irving Bibo; Minnie, Clarabelle Cow, Horace Horsecollar & caricature of Walt shaking hands with Mickey. The changes made with the 2nd printing have been verified by billing affidavits in the Walt Disney Archives and include:Two Win Smith Mickey strips from 4/15/30 and 4/17/30 added to page 8 & back-c; "Printed in U.S.A." added to front cover; Bobette Bibo's age of 11 years added to title page; faulty type on the word "tail" corrected top of page 3; the word "start" added to bottom of page 7, removing the words "start 1 2 3 4" from the top of page 7; music and lyrics were rewritten on pages 12-14. A green ink border was added beginning with 2nd printing and some covers have inking variations. Art by Albert Barbelle, drawn in an Ub Iwerks style. Total circulation : 97,938 copies varying from 21,000 to 26,000 per printing.
1st printing. Contains the song lyrics **censored** in later printings, "When little Minnie's pursued by a big bad villain we feel so bad then we're glad when you up and kill him." Attached to the Nov. 15, 1930 issue of the Official Bulletin of the Mickey Mouse Club notes: "Attached to this Bulletin is a new Mickey Mouse Book that has just been published." This is thought to be the reason why a slightly disproportionate larger number of copies of the first printing still exist 1200.00 6000.00 12,000.00
2nd printing with a theater/advertising. Christmas greeting added to inside front cover (1 copy known with Dec. 27, 1930 date) – 12,000.00 –
2nd-4th printings 1050.00 5000.00 10,000.00
NOTE: *Theater/advertising copies do not qualify as separate printings. Most copies are missing pages 9 & 10 which had a puzzle to be cut out. Puzzle (pages 9 and 10) cut out or missing, subtract 60% to 75%.*

MICKEY MOUSE COLORING BOOK (S)
Saalfield Publishing Company:1931 (15-1/4x10-3/4", 32 pgs, color soft cover, half printed in full color interior, rest B&W
871 - By Ub Iwerks & Floyd Gottfredson (rare) 400.00 1200.00 2520.00
NOTE: *Contains reprints of first MM daily strip ever, including the "missing" speck the chicken is after found only on the original daily strip art by Iwerks plus other very early MM art. There were several other Saalfield Mickey Mouse coloring books manufactured around the same time.*

MICKEY MOUSE, THE ADVENTURES OF (I)
David McKay Co., Inc.: Book I, 1931 - Book II, 1932 (5-1/2"x8-1/2", 32 pgs.)
Book I-First Disney book, by strict definition (1st printing-50,000 copies)(see Mickey Mouse Book by Bibo & Lang). Illustrated text refers to Clarabelle Cow as "Carolyn" and Horace Horsecollar as "Henry". The name "Donald Duck" appears with a non-costumed generic duck on back cover & inside, not in the context of the character that later debuted in the Wise Little Hen.
Hardback w/characters on back-c 75.00 300.00 650.00
Softcover w/characters on back-c 38.00 151.00 350.00
Version without characters on back-c 45.00 180.00 400.00
Book II-Less common than Book I. Character development brought into conformity with the Mickey Mouse cartoon shorts and syndicated strips. Captain Church Mouse, Tanglefoot, Pog-Leg Pete and Pluto appear with Mickey & Minnie 46.00 186.00 400.00

MICKEY MOUSE COMIC (N)
David McKay Co.: 1931 - No. 4, 1934 (10"x9-3/4", 52 pgs., card board-c) (Later reprints exist)
1 (1931)-Reprints Floyd Gottfredson daily strips in black & white from 1930 & 1931, including the famous two week sequence in which Mickey tries to commit suicide 229.00 914.00 1680.00
2 (1932)-1st app. of Pluto reprinted from 7/8/31 daily. All pgs. from 1931 164.00 656.00 1200.00
3 (1933)-Reprints 1932 & 1933 Sunday pages in color, one strip per page, including the "Lair of Wolf Barker" continuity pencilled by Gottfredson and inked by Al Taliaferro & Ted Thwaites. First app. Mickey's nephews, Morty & Ferdie, one identified by name of Mortimer Fieldmouse, not to be confused with Uncle Mortimer Mouse who is introduced in the Wolf Barker story 214.00 856.00 1600.00
4 (1934)-1931 dailies, include the only known reprint of the infamous strip of 2/4/31 where the villainous Kat Nipp snips off the end of Mickey's tail with a pair of scissors 140.00 560.00 1050.00

MICKEY MOUSE (N)
Whitman Publishing Co.: 1933-34 (10x8-3/4", 34 pgs, cardboard-c)
948-1932 & 1933 Sunday strips in color, printed from the same plates as Mickey Mouse Book #3 by David McKay, but only pages 5-17 & 32-48 (including all of the "Wolf Barker" continuity) 157.00 629.00 1100.00
NOTE: *Some copies bound with back cover upside down. Variance doesn't affect value. Same art appears on front and back covers of all copies. Height of Whitman reissue trimmed 1/2 inch.*

MILITARY WILLIE
J. I. Austen Co.: 1907 (7x9-1/2", 12 pgs., every other page in color, stapled)
nn - By F. R. Morgan 70.00 245.00 400.00

MINNEAPOLIS TRIBUNE CARTOON BOOK (S)
Minneapolis Tribune: 1899-1903 (11-3/8x9-3/8", B&W, paper cover)
nn (#1) (1899) 28.00 99.00 170.00
nn (#2) (1900) 28.00 99.00 170.00
nn (#3) (1901) (published Jan 01, 1901) 28.00 99.00 170.00
nn (#4) (1902) (114 pgs) 28.00 99.00 170.00
nn (#5) (1903) (9x10-3/4",110 pgs, B&W; color-c) 28.00 99.00 170.00
NOTE: *All by Roland C. Bowman (editorial-r).*

MINUTE BIOGRAPHIES: INTIMATE GLIMPSES INTO THE LIVES OF 150 FAMOUS MEN AND WOMEN
Grossett & Dunlap: 1931, 1933 (10-1/4x7-3/4", 168 pgs, hardcover, B&W)
nn - By Nisenson (art) & Parker(text) 21.00 63.00 125.00
More.... (1933) 21.00 63.00 125.00

MISCHIEVOUS MONKS OF CROCODILE ISLE, THE (N)
J. I. Austen Co., Chicago: 1908 (8-1/2x11-1/2", 12 pgs., 4 pgs. in color)
nn - By F. R. Morgan; reads longwise 125.00 375.00 600.00

MR. & MRS. (Also see Ain't It A Grand and Glorious Feeling?) (N)
Whitman Publishing Co.: 1922 (9x9-1/2", 52 & 28 pgs., cardboard-c)
nn - By Briggs (B&W, 52 pgs.) 37.00 149.00 260.00
nn - 28 pgs.-(9x9-1/2")-Sunday strips-r in color 41.00 163.00 285.00

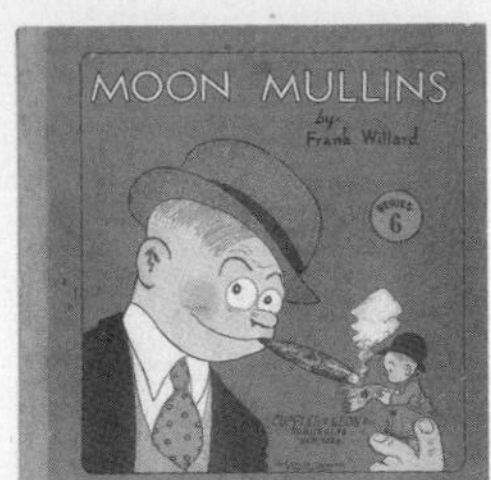

Moon Mullins #6 by Frank Willard
1932 @ Cupples & Leon

The Nebbs
© C&L

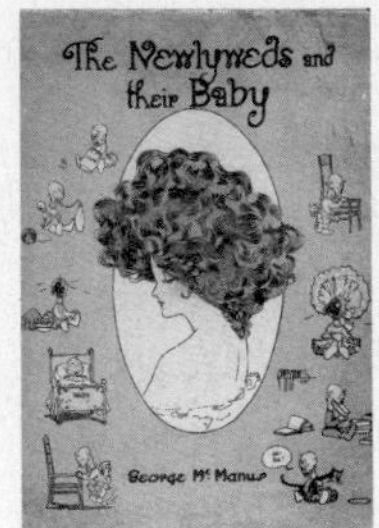

The Newlyweds by George McManus
1907 © Saalfield Publishing Co.

GD2.0 FN6.0 VF8.0

NOTE: *The earliest presently-known Whitman comic books*

MR. BLOCK (N)
Industrial Workers of the World (IWW): 1913, 1919
nn - By Ernest Riebe (C) 50.00 150.00 –
...And The Profiteers (original material) (H) 50.00 150.00 –
NOTE: *Mr Block was a daily strip published from 1912 NOV 7 to 1913 SEP ? by the socialist newspaper "Industrial Worker"; Mr Block was a "square" guy (his head was in fact a block) who enthusiastically supported the same system that exploited him. The noted Joe Hill wrote a song about him (Mr Block,1913, on the air of "It loooks me like a big time tonight") for the "Industrial Worker Songbook".*

MR. TWEE-DEEDLE (N)
Cupples & Leon: 1913, 1917 (11-3/8 x 16-3/4" color strips-r from NY Herald)
nn - By John B. Gruelle (later of Raggedy Ann fame) 350.00 900.00 1800.00
nn - "Further Adventures of..." By Gruelle 350.00 900.00 1800.00
NOTE: *Strip ran Feb 5, 1911-March 10, 1918.*

MONKEY SHINES OF MARSELEEN AND SOME OF HIS ADVENTURES (C)
McLaughlin Bros. New York: 1906 (10 x 12-3/8", 36 pgs, full color hardcover)
nn - By Norman E. Jennett strip-r NY Evening Telegram 100.00 250.00 450.00
NOTE: *Strip began in 1906 until at least March 13, 1910.*

MONKEY SHINES OF MARSELEEN (N)
Cupples & Leon Co.: 1909 (11-1/2 x 17", 58 pgs. in two colors)
nn - By Norman E. Jennett (strip-r New York Herald) 100.00 250.00 450.00

MOON MULLINS (N)
Cupples & Leon Co.: 1927 - 1933 (52 pgs., B&W daily strip-r)
Series 1 ('27)-By Willard 63.00 250.00 500.00
Series 2 ('28), Series 3 ('29), Series 4 ('30) 39.00 156.00 300.00
Series 5 ('31), 6 ('32), 7 ('33) 39.00 156.00 300.00
Big Book 1 ('30)-B&W (scarce) 100.00 400.00 750.00
w/dust jacket (rare) 183.00 732.00 1300.00

MOVING PICTURE FUNNIES
Saml Gabriel Sons & Company: 1918 (5-1/4 x 10-1/4", 52 pgs, B&W, illustrated hard-c)
nn 20.00 40.00 80.00
NOTE: *823 Comical illustrations that show a different scene when folded.*

MUTT & JEFF (...Cartoon, The) (N)
Ball Publications: 1911 - No. 5, 1916 (5-3/4 x 15-1/2", 72 pgs, B&W, hard-c)
1 (1910)(50¢) very common 71.00 286.00 500.00
2,3: 2 (1911)-Opium den panels; Jeff smokes opium (pipe dreams)
3 (1912) both very common 71.00 286.00 500.00
2-(1913) Reprint of 1911 edition with black ink cover 50.00 175.00 300.00
4 (1915) (50¢) (Scarce) 150.00 350.00 650.00
5 (1916) (Rare) -Photos of Fisher, 1st pg. (68 pages) 200.00 480.00 900.00
5-Scarce 84 page reprint edition 150.00 450.00 800.00
NOTE: *Mutt & Jeff first appeared in newspapers in 1907. Cover variations exist showing Mutt & Jeff reading various newspapers; i.e., The Oregon Journal, The American, and The Detroit News. Reprinting of each issue began soon after publication. No. 4 and 5 may not have been reprinted. Values listed include the reprints. Mutt & Jeff was the first successful American daily newspaper comic strip and as such remains one of the seminal strips of all time.*

MUTT & JEFF (N)
Cupples & Leon Co.: No. 6, 1919 - No. 22, 1934? (9-1/2x9-1/2", 52 pgs., B&W dailies, stiff-c)
6, 7 - By Bud Fisher (very common) 32.00 128.00 225.00
8-10 46.00 186.00 325.00
11-18 (Somewhat Scarcer) (#19-#22 do not exist) 60.00 â240.00 420.00
nn (1920) (Advs. of...) 11x16"; 44 pgs.; full color reprints of 1919 Sunday strips 93.00 372.00 650.00
Big Book nn (1926, 144 pgs., hardcovers) 114.00 456.00 800.00
w/dust jacket 193.00 772.00 1350.00
Big Book 1 (1928) - Thick book (hardcovers) 114.00 456.00 800.00
w/dust jacket (rare) 182.00 729.00 1275.00
Big Book 2 (1929) - Thick book (hardcovers) 114.00 456.00 800.00
w/dust jacket (rare) 182.00 729.00 1275.00
NOTE: *The Big Books contain three previous issues rebound.*

MUTT & JEFF (N)
Embee Publ. Co.: 1921 (9x15", color cardboard-c & interior)
nn - Sunday strips in color (Rare)- BY Bud Fisher 143.00 572.00 1000.00
NOTE: *Ties with The Trouble of Bringing Up Father (EmBee) and Jimmie Dugan & The Reg'lar Fellers (C&L) as the last of this size.*

MYSTERIOUS STRANGER AND OTHER CARTOONS, THE
McClure, Phillips & Co.: 1905 (12-3/8x9-3/4", 338 pgs, hardcover, B&W)
nn - By John McCutcheon 32.00 128.00 225.00

MY WAR - Szeged (Szuts)
Wm. Morrow Co.: 1932 (7x10-1/2", 210 pgs, hard-c, B&W)
nn - (All story panels, no words - powerful) 32.00 128.00 225.00

NAUGHTY ADVENTURES OF VIVACIOUS MR. JACK, THE
New York American & Journal: 1904 (15x10", color strips)
nn - By James Swinnerton; (Very Rare - 3 known copies) 800.00 1500.00 2000.00

GD2.0 FN6.0 VF8.0

NEBBS, THE (N)
Cupples & Leon Co.: 1928 (52 pgs., B&W daily strip-r)
nn - By Sol Hess; Carlson-a 40.00 160.00 280.00

NERVY NAT'S ADVENTURES (E)
Leslie-Judge Co.: 1911 (90 pgs, 85¢, 1903 strip reprints from **Judge**)
nn - By James Montgomery Flagg 75.00 263.00 450.00

THE NEWLYWEDS AND THEIR BABY (N)
Saalfield Publ. Co.: 1907 (13x10", 52 pgs., hardcover)
...& Their Baby' by McManus; daily strips 50% color 300.00 900.00 –
NOTE: *Strip ran Apr 10, 1904 thru Jan 14, 1906 and then May 19, 1907-Dec 5, 1916; was a huge success with Baby Snookums long before McManus invented Bringing Up Father; Snookums brought back as a topper strip over BUF Nov 19, 1944-Dec 30, 1956.*

THE NEWLYWEDS AND THEIR BABY'S COMIC PICTURES FOR PAINTING AND CRAYONING (N)
Saalfield Publishign Company: 1916 (10-1/4x14-3/4", 52 pgs. Cardboard-c)
nn - 44 B&W pages, covers, and one color wrap glued to B&W title page.
Color wrap: color title pg. & 3 pgs of color strips 83.00 290.00 500.00
nn - (1917, 10x14", 20 pgs, oblong, cardboard-c) partial reprint of 1916 edition 31.00 124.00 275.00

THE NEWLYWEDS AND THEIR BABY (N)
Saalfield Publishing Company: 1917 (10-1/8x13-9/16 ", 52 pgs, full color cardstock-c, some pages full color, others two color (orange, blue))
nn 83.00 290.00 500.00

NEW YORKER CARTOON ALBUM, THE (M)
Doubleday, Doran & Company Inc.: (1928-1931); **Harper & Brothers.:** (1931-1933); **Random House** (1935-1937), 12x9", various pg counts, hardcovers w/dust jackets)
1928: nn-114 pgs Arno, Held, Soglow, Williams, etc 20.00 60.00 120.00
1928: SECOND-114 pgs Arno, Bairnsfather, Gross, Held, Soglow, Williams 10.00 30.00 60.00
1930: THIRD-172 pgs Arno, Bairnsfather, Held, Soglow, Art Young 10.00 30.00 60.00
1931: FOURTH-154 pgs Arno, Held, Soglow, Steig, Thurber, Williams, Art Young, "Little King" by Soglow begins 10.00 30.00 60.00
1932: FIFTH-156 pgs Arno, Bairnsfather, Held, Hoff, Soglow, Steig, Thurber, Williams 10.00 30.00 60.00
1933: SIXTH 156 pgs same as above 10.00 30.00 60.00
1935: SEVENTH-164 pgs 10.00 30.00 60.00
1937: 168 pgs; Charles Addams plus same as above but no Little King, two page "Gone With The Wind" parody strip 10.00 30.00 60.00
NOTE: *Some sequential strips but mostly single panel cartoons.*

NIPPY'S POP (N)
The Saalfield Publishing Co.: 1917 (10-1/2x13-1/2", 36 pgs., B&W, Sunday strip r)
nn - Charles M Payne (better known as S'Matter Pop) 43.00 152.00 260.00

OH, MAN (A Bully Collection of Those Inimitable Humor Cartoons) (S)
P.F. Volland & Co.: 1919 (8-1/2x13"; 136 pgs.)
nn - By Briggs 43.00 152.00 260.00
NOTE: *Originally came in illustrated box with Briggs art (box is Rare - worth 50% more with box).*

OH SKIN-NAY! (S)
P.F. Volland & Co.: 1913 (8-1/2x13", 136 pgs.)
nn - The Days Of Real Sport by Briggs 43.00 152.00 260.00
NOTE: *Originally came in illustrated box with Briggs art (box is Rare - worth 50% more with box).*

OLD GOLD THE SMOOTHER AND BETTER CIGARETTE...NOT A COUGH IN A CARLOAD (M,N,P) (see also BY BRIGGS)
Old Gold Cigarettes: nd (c1920's) (16 pgs, paper-c, color) (both Scarce)
nn- (4-1/4" x 3-7/8") cover strip is "Oh, Man!"; also contains: "Real Folks at Home", "Ain't It a Grand and Glorious Feelin?", "It Happens in the Best Regulated Families", and "Mr. and Mrs." (no known sales)
1440- (5-9/16" x 5-1/4") cover strip is "Frank and Ernest"; also contains: "That Guiltiest Feeling", "Real Folks at Home", "Oh, Man!", "When a Feller Needs a Friend". (no known sales)
NOTE: *Collection reprinting strip cartoons by Clare Briggs, advertising Old Gold Cigarettes. These strips originally appeared in various magazines, play program booklets, newspapers, etc. Some of the strips involve regular Briggs strip series. The two booklets contain a completely different set of comics.*

ON AND OFF MOUNT ARARAT (also see **Tigers**) (N)
Hearst's New York American & Journal: 1902, 86pgs. 10x15-1/4"
nn - Rare Noah's Ark satire by Jimmy Swinnerton (rare) 450.00 1500.00 –

ON THE LINKS (N)
Associated Feature Service: Dec, 1926 (9x10", 48 pgs.)
nn - Daily strip-r 25.00 100.00 175.00

ONE HUNDRED WAR CARTOONS (S)
Idaho Daily Statesman: 1918 (7-3/4x10", 102 pgs, paperback, B&W)
nn - By Villeneuve (WW I cartoons) 20.00 60.00 120.00

OUR ANTEDILUVIAN ANCESTORS (N,S)

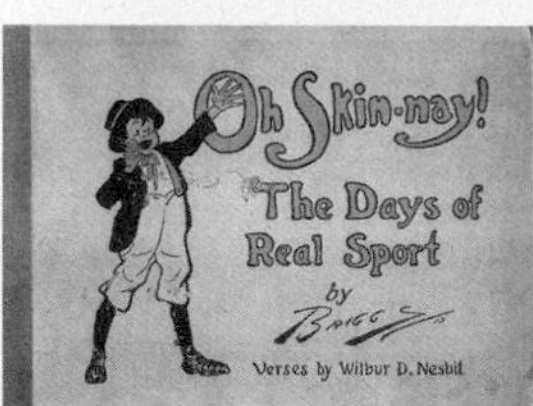

Oh Skin-nay! by Claire Briggs
1913 © P.F. Volland

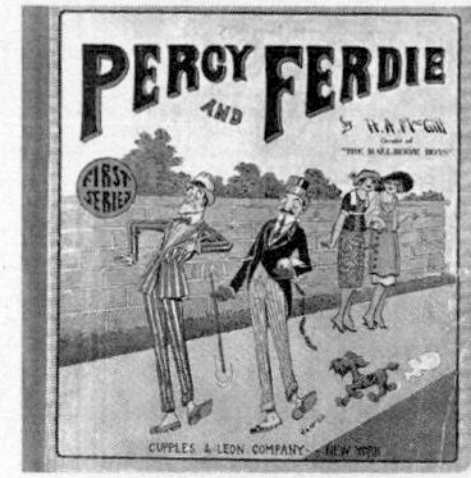

Percy and Ferdie
1921 © Cupples & Leon

Roger Bean, R.G. #4
© C&L

GD2.0 FN6.0 VF8.0

New York Evening Journal, NY: 1903 (11-3/8x8-7/8", hardcover)

nn - By F Opper 75.00 200.00 400.00
NOTE: *There is a simultaneously published British edition, identical size and contents, from C. Arthur Pearson Ltd, London. A collection of single panel cartoons about cavemen. Similar to an earlier British cartoon book "Prehistoric Peeps from Punch", by E.T. Reed.*

OUTBURSTS OF EVERETT TRUE, THE (N)
Saalfield Publ. Co.(Werner Co.): 1907 (92 pgs, 9-7/16x5-1/4")

1907 (2-4 panel strips-r)-By Condo & Raper 125.00 350.00 675.00
1921-Full color-c; reprints 56 of 88 cartoons from 1907 ed. (10x10", 32 pgs B&W) 125.00 225.00 350.00

OVER THERE COMEDY FROM FRANCE
Observer House Printing: nd (WW 1 era) (6x14", 60 pgs, paper cover)

nn - Artist(s) unknown 15.00 53.00 90.00

OWN YOUR OWN HOME (I)
Bobbs-Merrill Company, Indianapolis: 1919 (7-7/16x5-1/4")

nn - By Fontaine Fox – – –

PECKS BAD BOY (N)
Charles C. Thompson Co, Chicago (by Walt McDougal): 1906-1908 (strip-r)

The Adventures of... (1906) 11-1/2x16-1/4", 68 pgs 100.00 400.00 800.00
...& His Country Cousin Cynthia (1907) 12x16-1/2," 34 pgs In color 100.00 400.00 800.00
Advs. of...And His Country Cousins (1907) 5-1/2x10 1/2", 18 pgs In color 50.00 175.00 300.00
Advs. of...And His Country Cousins (1907) 11-1/2x16-1/4", 36 pgs 50.00 175.00 300.00
...& Their Advs With The Teddy Bear (1907) 5-1/2x10-1/2", 18 pgs in color 50.00 175.00 300.00
...& Their Balloon Trip To the Country (1907) 5-1/2x 10-1/2, 18 pgs in color 50.00 175.00 300.00
...With the Teddy Bear Show (1907) 5-1/2x 10-1/2 50.00 175.00 300.00
...With The Billy Whiskers Goats (1907) 5-1/2 x 10-1/2, 18 pgs in color 50.00 175.00 300.00
...& His Chums (1908) - 11x16-3/8", 36 pgs. Stanton & Van Vliet Co 100.00 400.00 750.00
...& His Chums (1908)-Hardcover; full color;16 pgs. 100.00 350.00 600.00
Advs. of...in Pictures (1908) (11x17, 36 pgs)-In color; Stanton & Van V. Liet Co. 100.00 400.00 700.00

PERCY & FERDIE (N)
Cupples & Leon Co.: 1921 (10x10", 52 pgs., B&W dailies, cardboard-c)

nn - By H. A. MacGill (Rare) 61.00 244.00 450.00

PETER RABBIT (N)
John H. Eggers Co. The House of Little Books Publishers: 1922 - 1923

B1-B4-(Rare)-(Set of 4 books which came in a cardboard box)-Each book reprints half of a Sunday page per page and contains 8 B&W and 2 color pages; by Harrison Cady (9-1/4x6-1/4", paper-c) each.... 43.00 172.00 300.00
Box only 57.00 228.00 400.00

PHILATELIC CARTOONS (M)
Essex Publishing Company, Lynn, Mass.: 1916 (8-11/16" x 5-7/8", 40 pgs, light blue construction paper-c, B&W interior)

nn - By Leroy S. Bartlett 25.00 75.00 175.00
NOTE: *Comics reprinted from The New England Philatelist.*

PICTORIAL HISTORY OF THE DEPARTMENT OF COMMERCE UNDER HERBERT HOOVER (see Picture Life of a Great American) (O)
Hoover-Curtis Campaign Committee of New York State: no date, 1928 (3-1/4 x 5-1/4, 32 pgs, paper cover, B&W)

nn - By Satterfield (scarce) 50.00 140.00 260.00
NOTE: *1928 Presidential Campaign giveaway. Original material, contents completely different from Picture Life of a Great American.*

PICTURE LIFE OF A GREAT AMERICAN (see Pictorial History of the Department of Commerce under Herbert Hoover) (O)
Hoover-Curtis Campaign Committee of New York State: no date, 1928 (paper cover, B&W)

nn - (8-3/4 x 7, 20 pgs) Text cover, 2 page text introduction, 18 pgs of comics (scarcer first print) 43.00 129.00 260.00
nn - (9 x 6-3/4,24 pgs) Illustrated cover,5 page text introduction, 18 pgs of comics (scarce) 43.00 129.00 260.00
NOTE: *1928 Presidential Campaign giveaway. Unknown which above version was published first. Both contain the same original comics material by Satterfield.*

PINK LAFFIN (I)
Whitman Publishing Co.: 1922 (9x12")(Strip-r; some of these actually text joke books)

...the Lighter Side of Life, ...He Tells 'Em, ...and His Family, ...Knockouts; Ray Gleason-a (All rare) each... 26.00 104.00 185.00

POLLY (AND HER PALS) - (N)

GD2.0 FN6.0 VF8.0

Newspaper Feature Service: 1916 (3x2-1/2", color)

Altogether: Three Rahs and a Tiger! by Cliff Sterrett 21.00 63.00 130.00
There Is A Limit To Pa's Patience by Cliff Sterrett 21.00 63.00 130.00
Pa's Lil Book Has Some Uncut Pages by Sterrett 21.00 63.00 130.00
NOTE: *Single newsprint sheet printed in full color on both sides, unfolds to show 12 panel story.*

POPEYE PAINT BOOK (N)
McLaughlin Bros, Inc., Springfield, Mass.: 1932 (9-7/8x13", 28 pgs, color-c)

2052 - By E. C. Segar 90.00 300.00 600.00
NOTE: *Contains a full color panel above and the exact same art in below panel n B&W which one was to color in; strip-r panels.*

POPEYE CARTOON BOOK (N)
The Saalfield Co.: 1934 (8-1/2x13", 40 pgs, cardboard-c)

2095-(scarce)-1933 strip reprints in color by Segar. Each page contains a vertical half of a Sunday strip, so the continuity reads row by row completely across each double page spread. If each page is read by itself, the continuity makes no sense. Each double page spread reprints one complete Sunday page from 1933 300.00 900.00 2700.00
12 Page Version 100.00 300.00 900.00

POPEYE (See **Thimble Theatre** for earlier Popeye-r from Sonnett) (N)
David McKay Publications: 1935 (25¢; 52 pgs, B&W) (By Segar)

1-Daily strip reprints- "The Gold Mine Thieves" 200.00 400.00 800.00
2-Daily strip-r (scarce) 200.00 400.00 900.00
NOTE: *Ties with Henry & Little Annie Rooney (David McKay) as the last of the 10x10" size books.*

PORE LI'L MOSE (N)
New York Herald Publ. by Grand Union Tea
Cupples & Leon Co.: 1902 (10-1/2x15", 78 pgs., color)

nn - By R. F. Outcault; Earliest known C&L comic book (scarce in high grade - very high demand) 1750.00 5775.00 –
NOTE: *Black Americana one page newspaper strips; falls in between Yellow Kid & Buster Brown. Complete copies have become scarce. Some have cut this book apart thinking that reselling individual pages will bring them more money.*

PRETTY PICTURES (M)
Farrar & Rinehart: 1931 (12 x 8-7/8", 104 pgs, color hardcover w/dust jacket, B&W; reprints from New Yorker, Judge, Life, Collier's Weekly)

nn - By Otto Soglow (contains "The Little King") 33.00 134.00 235.00

QUAINT OLD NEW ENGLAND (S)
Triton Syndicate: 1936 (5-1/4x6-1/4", 100 pgs, soft-c squarebound, B&W)

nn - By Jack Withycomb 36.00 144.00 250.00
NOTE: *Comics about weird doings in Old New England.*

RED CARTOONS (S)
Daily Worker Publishing Company: 1926 (12 x 9", 68 pgs,cardboard cover, B&W)

nn - By Various (scarce) 40.00 160.00 280.00
NOTE: *Reprint of American Communist Party editorial cartoons, from The Daily Worker, The Workers Monthly, and the Liberator. Art by Fred Ellis, William Gropper, Clive Weed, Art Young.*

REG'LAR FELLERS (See All-American Comics, Jimmie Dugan & The..., Popular Comics & Treasure Box of Famous Comics) (N)
Cupples & Leon Co./MS Publishing Co.: 1921-1929

1 (1921)-52 pgs. B&W dailies (Cupples & Leon, 10x10") 43.00 171.00 300.00
1925, 48 pgs. B&W dailies (MS Publ.) 39.00 157.00 275.00
Hardcover (1929, 8-3/4x7-1/2"; 96 pgs.)-B&W-r 54.00 214.00 375.00

REG'LAR FELLERS STORY PAINT BOOK
Whitman, Racine, Wisc.: 1932 (8-3/4x12-1/8", 132 pgs, red soft-c)

By Gene Byrnes 25.00 75.00 150.00

ROGER BEAN, R. G. (Regular Guy) (N)
The Indiana News Co, Distributers.: 1915 - No. 2, 1915 (5-3/8x17", 68 pgs., B&W, hardcovers); #3-#5 published by **Chas. B. Jackson:** 1916-1919
(No. 1 2 4 & 5 bound on side, No. 3 bound at top)

1-By Chas B. Jackson (68pgs.)(Scarce) 60.00 210.00 360.00
2- 5-5/8x17-1/8", 66 pgs (says 1913 inside - an obvious printing error) (red or green binding) 60.00 210.00 360.00
3-Along the Firing Line... (1916; 68 pgs, 6x17") 60.00 210.00 360.00
3-Along the Firing Line side-bound version 60.00 210.00 360.00
4-Into the Trenches and Out Again with... (1917, 68 pgs) 60.00 210.00 360.00
5 ...And The Reconstruction Period (1919, 5-3/8x15-1/2", 84 pgs) (Scarce) (has $1 printed on cover) 60.00 210.00 360.00
Baby Grand Editions 1-5 (10x10", cardboard-c) 60.00 210.00 360.00
NOTE: *No. 1 & 2 of the Twin Baby Grands (nd) 8-1/4x10-7/8", 52 pgs. #3 & #4 9x10-7/8" Cardboard cover. B&W strip reprints. Cover also says "Politics Pickles People Police."*
nn - 9x11, 68 pgs 60.00 210.00 360.00
NOTE: Has picture of Chic Jackson and a posthumous dedication from his three children. strip-r 1931-32

ROGER BEAN PHILOSOPHER
Schnull & Co: 1917 (5-1/2x17", 36 pgs., B&W, brown & black paper-c, square binding)

nn - By Chic Jackson (no known sales)

ROOKIE FROM THE 13TH SQUAD, THAT (N) (also Between Shots; Always Belittlin';Skippy)

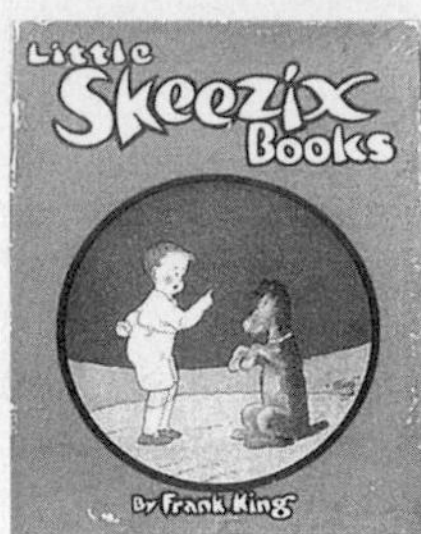

Little Skeezix Books by Frank King
1929 © Reilly & Lee

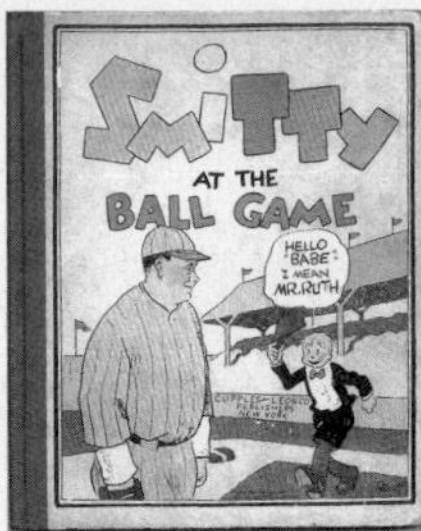

Smitty #2 By Walter Berndt
1929 © Cupples & Leon

Tailspin Tommy Story & Paint Book
By Hal Forest and Glenn Chappin
1932 © Cupples & Leon

GD2.0 FN6.0 VF8.0

Harper & Brothers Publishers: Feb. 1918 (8x9-1/4", 72 pgs, hardcover, B&W)
nn - By Lieut. P(ercy) L. Crosby 75.00 225.00 400.00
NOTE: *Strip began in 1917 at an Army base during basic training.*

ROUND THE WORLD WITH THE DOO-DADS (see Doings of the Doo-Dads, Doo Dads)
Universal Feature And Specialty Co, Chicago: 1922 (12x10-1/2", 52 pgs, B&W, red & light blue-c, square binding)
nn - By Arch Dale newspaper strip-r 43.00 173.00 300.00
NOTE: *Intermixed single panel and sequential comic strips with scenes from Scotland, Ireland, England, Holland, Italy, Spain, Egypt, Africa, and Lions & Elephants along the Nile River, China, Australia & back home.*

RUBAIYKT OF THE EGG
The John C Winston Co, Philadelphia: 1905 (7x5/12", 64 pgs, purple-c, B&W)
nn - By Clare Victor Dwiggins 20.00 60.00 125.00
NOTE: *Book is printed & cut into the shape of an egg.*

RULING CLAWSS, THE (N,S)
The Daily Worker: 1935 (192 pgs, 10-1/4 x 7-3/8", hard-c, B&W)
nn - By Redfield 60.00 240.00 –
NOTE: *Reprints cartoons from the American Communist Party newspaper The Daily Worker.*

SAGARA'S ENGLISH CARTOONS AND CARTOON STORIES (N)
Bunkosha, Tokyo: nd (c1925) (6-5/8" x 4-1/4", 272 pgs, hard-c, B&W)
nn- (Scarce) – – –
NOTE: *Published in Tokyo, Japan, with all strips in both English and Japanese, to facilitate learning English. Majority of book is Bringing Up Father by George McManus. Also contains Japanese strip Father Takes it Easy, by T. Sagara, reprinted from the Kokusai News Agency.*

SAM AND HIS LAUGH (N)
Frederick A. Stokes: 1906 (10x15", cardboard-c, Sunday strip-r in color)
nn - By Jimmy Swinnerton (Extremely Rare) 600.00 1200.00 2400.00
NOTE: *Strip ran July 24, 1904-Dec 26 1906; its ethnic humor might be considered racist by today's standards.*

SCHOOL DAYS (N)
Harper & Bros.: 1919 (9x8", 104 pgs.)
nn - By Clare Victor Dwiggins 75.00 150.00 300.00

SEAMAN SI - A Book of Cartoons About the Funniest "Gob" in the Navy (N)
Pierce Publishing Co.: 1916 (4x8-1/2, 200 pgs, hardcover, B&W); 1918 (4-1/8x8-1/4, 104 pgs, hardcover, B&W)
nn - By Perce Pearce (1916) 50.00 150.00 300.00
nn - 1918 - (Reilly & Britton Co.) 30.00 125.00 200.00
NOTE: *There exists two different covers for the 1918 reprints. The earlier edition was self published by the artist. The newspaper strip is sometimes also known as "The American Sailor."*

SECRET AGENT X-9 (N)
David McKay Pbll.: 1934 (Book 1: 84 pgs; Book 2: 124 pgs.) (8x7-1/2")
Book 1-Contains reprints of the first 13 weeks of the strip by Dashiell Hammett & Alex Raymond, complete except for 2 dailies 100.00 300.00 750.00
Book 2-Contains reprints immediately following contents of Book 1, for 20 weeks by Dashiell Hammett & Alex Raymond; complete except for two dailies. Last 5 strips misdated from 6/34, continuity correct 100.00 300.00 750.00

SILK HAT HARRY'S DIVORCE SUIT (N)
M. A. Donoghue & Co.: 1912 (5-3/4x15-1/2", oblong, B&W)
nn - Newspaper-r by Tad (Thomas A. Dorgan) 33.00 117.00 400.00

SINBAD A DOG'S LIFE (M)
Coward - McCann, Inc.: 1930 (11x 8-3/4", 104 pgs., single-sided, illustrated hard-c, B&W
nn - By Edwina 11.00 33.00 100.00
Sinbad...Again (1932, 10-15/16x 8-9/16", 104 pgs.) 11.00 33.00 100.00
NOTE: *Wordless comic strips from LIFE.*

SIS HOPKINS OWN BOOK AND MAGAZINE OF FUN
Leslie-Judge Co.: 1899-July 1911 (36 pgs, color-c, B&W) (merged into Judge's Library, later titled Film Fun)
any issue - By various 11.00 33.00 100.00
NOTE: *Zim, Flagg, Young, Newell, Adams, etc.*

SKEEZIX (Also see Gasoline Alley & Little Skeezix Books listed below) (I)
Reilly & Lee Co.: 1925 - 1928 (Strip-r, soft covers) (pictures & text)
...and Uncle Walt (1924)-Origin 26.00 104.00 180.00
...and Pal (1925), ...at the Circus (1926) 21.00 84.00 160.00
...& Uncle Walt (1927) (does this actually exist? reprint? never seen one yet)
...Out West (1928) 30.00 100.00 200.00
Hardback Editions... 34.00 136.00 235.00

SKEEZIX BOOKS, LITTLE (Also see Skeezix, Gasoline Alley) (G)
Reilly & Lee Co.: No date (1928, 1929) (Boxed set of three Skeezix books)
nn - Box with 3 issues of Skeezix. Skeezix & Pal, Skeezix at the Circus, Skeezix & Uncle Walt known. 1928 Set... 60.00 180.00 360.00
nn - Box with 4 issues of (3) above Skeezix plus "Out West" 80.00 330.00 550.00

SKEEZIX COLOR BOOK (N)
McLaughlin Bros. Inc, Springfield, Mass: 1929 (9-1/2x10-1/4", 28 pgs, one third in full color, rest in B&W)

GD2.0 FN6.0 VF8.0

2023 - By Frank King; strip-r to color 20.00 75.00 135.00

SKIPPY (see also Life Presents Skippy, Always Belittlin', That Rookie From 13th Squad)
No publisher listed: Circa 1920s (10x8", 16 pgs., color/B&W cartoons)
nn - By Percy Crosby 20.00 84.00 150.00

SKIPPY, LIFE PRESENTS (M)
Life Publishing Company & Henry Holt, NY: nd 1924 (134 pgs, 10-13/16x8-3/4", color hard-c, B&W
nn - By Percy L Crosby 100.00 300.00 500.00
NOTE: *Many sequential & single panel reprints from Skippy's earliest appearances in Life Magazine.*

SKIPPY
Greenberg, Publisher, Inc, NY: 1925. (11-14x8-5/8, 72 pgs, hard-c, B&W and color
nn - By Percy L. Crosby 50.00 150.00 300.00
NOTE: *Some but not all of these comics were also in Life Presents Skippy; issued with dust wrapper.*

SKIPPY AND OTHER HUMOR
Greenberg: Publisher, NY: 1929 (11-1/4x8-1/2",72 pgs,tan hard-c, B&W and color)
nn - By Percy L. Crosby 25.00 75.00 150.00
NOTE: *Came with a dust jacket.*

SKIPPY (I)
Grossett & Dunlap: 1929 (7-3/8x6, 370 pgs, hardcover text with some art)
nn - By Percy Crosby (issued with a dust jacket) 23.00 92.00 160.00
NOTE: *This is worth very little without the dust wrapper; very common without athe dust jacket.*

SKIPPY
Greenberg Press: 1930 (soft cover, ca. 16 pp.,
nn - By Percy Crosby (scarce) 50.00 175.00 300.00
NOTE: *Reprints from LIFE cartoons, color, b/w. Crosby told Greenberg to withdraw from the market as it cheapened the hard cover prior editions. Greenberg then stopped publishing per agreement, and sent Crosby all the copper & zinc bookplates, which were in Crosby estate until 1996.*

SKIPPY CRAYON AND COLORING BOOK (N)
McLoughlin Bros, Inc., Springfield, MA: 1931 (13x9-3/4", 28 pgs, color-c, color & B&W)
2050 - By Percy Crosby 28.00 84.00 195.00
NOTE: *This item says on the front cover: "Licensed by Percy Crosby" because he owned his creation. About half the pages have one panel pre-printed in full color with same one b&w below for person to copy the colors.*

SKIPPY RAMBLES (I)
G.P. Putnam's Sons: 1932 (7 1/8 x 5 1/8, 202 pgs)
nn - By Percy Crosby 21.00 84.00 150.00
NOTE: *Issued with a dustjacket. Has Skippy plates by Crosby every 4 or 5 pages.*

SKUDDABUD STARRY STORY SERIES - FOLK FROM THE FUTURE (O,G)
no publisher listed: 1936 (9" x 11-7/8", 48 pgs, cardboard-c, B&W)
Book One (Rare) "Parachuting" 21.00 84.00 150.00
NOTE: *By Columba Krebs. Top half of each page is a continuing strip story, while bottom half are different stories, in prose, about the same characters -- a race of aliens who have migrated to Earth, from their dying world.*

S'MATTER POP? (N)
Saalfield Publ. Co.: 1917 (10x14", 44 pgs., B&W, cardboard-c,)
nn - By Charlie Payne; in full color; pages printed on one side 48.00 169.00 290.00

S'MATTER POP? (N) (25 ¢ cover price)
E.I. Company, New York: 1927 (8-15/16x7-1/8", 52 pgs, yellow soft-c perfect bound
nn - By C.M. Payne (scarce) 24.00 84.00 145.00
NOTE: *First comic book published by Hugo Gernsback, noted for inventing Amazing Stories among other memorable science fiction pulps. The World Science Fiction Convention Award, The Hugo, is named for him.*

SMITTY (See Treasure Box of Famous Comics) (N)
Cupples & Leon Co.: 1928 - 1933 (9x7", 96 pgs., B&W strip-r, hardcover)
1928-(96 pgs. 7x8-3/4") By Walter Berndt 43.00 172.00 300.00
1929-At the Ball Game (Babe Ruth on cover) 57.00 229.00 450.00
1930-The Flying Office Boy, 1931-The Jockey, 1932-In the North Woods each... 31.00 126.00 250.00
1933-At Military School 31.00 126.00 250.00
NOTE: *Each hardbound was published with a dust jacket; worth 50% more with dust jacket. The 1929 edition is very popular with baseball collectors. Strip debuted Nov 27, 1922.*

SMOKEY STOVER (See Dan Dunn & King of the Royal Mounted) (N)
Whitman Publishing: 1937 (5 1/2 x 7 1/4", 68pgs., color cardboard-c, B&W)
1010 36.00 144.00 250.00

SOCIAL COMEDY (M)
Life Publishing Company: 1902 (11-3/4 x 9-1/2", 128 pgs, B&W, illustrated hardcover)
nn - Artists include C.D. Gibson & Kemble. 20.00 70.00 120.00
NOTE: *Reprints cartoons and a few sequential comics from LIFE. Came in unmarked slipcase.*

SOCIAL HELL, THE (O)
Rich Hill: 1902
nn - By Ryan Walker 21.00 74.00 130.00
NOTE: *"The conditions of workers and the corruption of a political system beholden to corporate interests have been a major focus of human rights concerns since the 19th century. This early graphic novel depicts the social evils of unreformed capitalism. Ryan Walker was a syndicate cartoonist for many mainstream newspapers as well as for the communist Daily Worker." This description comes from http://www.lib.uconn.edu/DoddCenter/ascexh3.html, where*

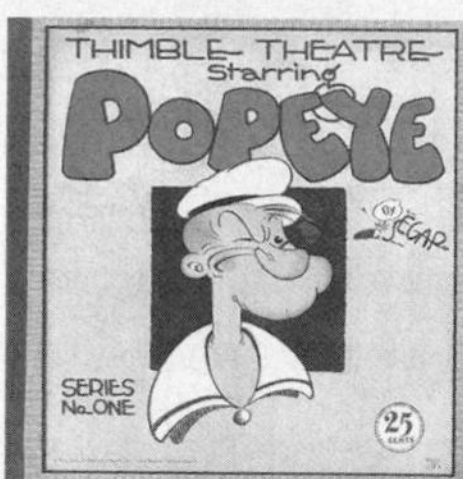

Thimble Theater #1 by E.C. Segar
1931 © Sonnet Publishing Co.

Tillie the Toiler #3 by Russ Westover
1927 © Cupples & Leon

Tim McCoy, Police Car 17
© Whitman Publ. Co.

GD2.0 FN6.0 VF8.0

you can find also a reproduction of the cover. I add that Ryan Walker was the editor of "The Saint Louis Republic" comic section since its inception in 1897; the supplement published "Alma and Oliver", George McManus's first series.

SPORT AND THE KID (see The Umbrella Man) (N)
Lowman & Hanford Co.: 1913 (6-1/4x6-5/8",114 pgs, hardcover, B&W&orange)
nn - By J.R. "Dok" Hager 20.00 70.00 120.00

STORY OF CONNECTICUT (N)
The Hartford Times: Vol.1 1935 - Vol.3 1936 (10-1/2" x 7-3/8",304 pgs,color hard-c, B&W)
Vol.1 - 3 20.00 70.00 120.00
NOTE: *Collects a newspaper strip on Connecticut State history, which ran in the Hartford Times. Strip is in a similar format to "Texas History Movies". Also published in a plain, blue hardcover.*

STORY OF JAPAN IN CHINA, THE (N,S)
Trans-Pacific News Service, NYC: Vol. 3, No.1 March 10, 1938 (9" x 6", 36 pgs, construction paper-c, B&W)
Vol.3 No.1 21.00 64.00 150.00
NOTE: *Part of the "China Reference Series" of booklets, detailing the Japanese occupation and brutalization of China. Consists entirely of cartoons. The other booklets in the series have no cartoons. Art by: Ding, Fitzpatrick, Herblock, Herman, Rollin Kirby, Knox, Low, Manning, Orr, Shoemaker, Talburt.*

STRANGE AS IT SEEMS (S)
Blue-Star Publishing Co.: 1932 (64 pgs., B&W, square binding)
1-Newspaper-r (*Published with & without No. 1 and price on cover.*) 32.00 128.00 225.00
Ex-Lax giveaway (1936, B&W, 24 pgs., 5x7") - McNaught Synd. 13.00 52.00 90.00

SULLIVANT'S ABC ZOO (I)
The Old Wine Press: 1946 (11-3/4x9-3/8", hardcover)
nn - By T.S. Sullivant (Rare) – – –
NOTE: *Reprints Mitchell & Miller material 1895-1898 and Life Publishing 1898-1926.*

TAILSPIN TOMMY STORY & PICTURE BOOK (N)
McLoughlin Bros.: No. 266, 1931? (nd) (10x10-1/2", color strip-r)
266 - By Forrest 43.00 172.00 300.00

TAILSPIN TOMMY (Also see Famous Feature Stories & The Funnies)(N)
Cupples & Leon Co.: 1932 (100 pgs., hard-c) (B&W 1930 strip reprints)
nn - (Scarce)- by Hal Forrest & Glenn Chaffin 50.00 150.00 375.00

TALES OF DEMON DICK AND BUNKER BILL (O)
Whitman Publishing Co.: 1934 (5-1/4x10-1/2", 80 pgs, color hardcover, B&W)
793 - By Spencer 33.00 100.00 300.00

TARZAN BOOK (The Illustrated...) (N)
Grosset & Dunlap: 1929 (9x7", 80 pgs.)
1(Rare)-Contains 1st B&W Tarzan newspaper comics from 1929. By Hal Foster Cloth reinforced spine & dust jacket (50¢); Foster-c
With dust jacket... 86.00 344.00 630.00
Without dust jacket... 43.00 172.00 315.00
2nd Printing(1934, 25¢, 76 pgs.)-4 Foster pgs. dropped; paper spine, circle in lower right cover with 25¢ price. The 25¢ is barely visible on some copies 34.00 136.00 250.00
1967-House of Greystoke reprint-7x10", using the complete 300 illustrations/text from the 1929 edition minus the original indicia, foreword, etc. Initial version bound in gold paper & sold for $5.00. Officially titled **Burroughs Bibliophile #2**. A very few additional copies were bound in heavier blue paper. Gold binding... 2.25 6.75 20.00
Blue binding... 2.50 7.50 27.00

TARZAN OF THE APES TO COLOR (N)
Saalfield Publishing Co.: No. 988, 1933 (15-1/4x10-3/4", 24 pgs)
(Coloring book)
988-(Very Rare)-Contains 1929 daily reprints with some new art by Hal Foster. Two panels blown up large on each page with one at the top of opposing pages on every other double-page spread. Believed to be the only time these panels appeared in color. Most color panels are reproduced a second time in B&W to be colored 271.00 1084.00 2000.00

TARZAN OF THE APES The Big Little Cartoon Book (N)
Whitman Publishing Company: 1933 (4-1/2x3 5/8", 320 pgs, color-c, B&W)
744 - By Hal Foster (comic strips on every page) 60.00 175.00 325.00

TECK HASKINS AT OHIO STATE (S)
Lea-Mar Press: 1908 (7-1/4x5-3/8", 84 pgs, B&W hardcover)
nn - By W.A. Ireland; football cartoons-r from Columbus Ohio Evening Dispatch 28.00 99.00 170.00
NOTE: *Small blue & white patch of cover art pasted atop a color cloth quilt patter; pasted patch can easily peel off some copies.*

TECK 1909 (S)
Lea-Mar Press: 1909 (8-5/8 x 8-1/8", 124 pgs., B&W hardcover, 25¢)
nn - By W.A. Ireland; Ohio State University baseball cartoons-r from Columbus Evening Dispatch 28.00 99.00 170.00

TEDDY BEAR BOOKS, THE (M) (see also LITTLE JOHNNY AND THE TEDDY BEARS)
Reilly & Britton Co., Chicago: 1907 (7-1/16" x 5-3/8", 24 pgs, hard-c, color
The Teddy Bears Come to Life, The Teddy Bears at the Circus, The Teddy Bears in a Smashup, The Teddy Bears on a Lark, The Teddy Bears on a Toboggan, The Teddy Bears at School, The Teddy Bears Go Fishing, The Teddy Bears in Hot Water 21.00 63.00 130.00
NOTE: *Books are all unnumbered. C & A by J.R. Bray; s-Robert D. Towne. Reprints "Little Johnny & the Teddy Bears" strips, from Judge Magazine. Similar in format to the Buster Brown Nuggets series. All eight books debuted simultaneously.*

TEDDY BEARS IN FUN AND FROLIC (M) (see LITTLE JOHNNY & THE TEDDY BEARS)
Reilly & Britton Co., Chicago: 1908 (8-3/4" x 8-3/4", 50 pgs, cardboard-c, color)
nn - (Rare) by J.R. Bray-a; Robert D. Towne-s 100.00 400.00 700.00
NOTE: *Reprints "Little Johnny & the Teddy Bears" strips, from Judge Magazine. Unknown if there were any other "Teddy Bear" titles published in this format.*

THE TEENIE WEENIES
Reilly & Britton, Chicago: 1916 (16-3/8x10-1/2", 52 pgs, cardboard-c, full color)
nn - By Wm. Donahey (Chicago Tribune-r) 200.00 550.00 900.00

TERROR OF THE TINY TADS (see also UPSIDE DOWNS OF LITTLE LADY LOVEKINS AND OLD MAN MUFFAROO)
Cupples & Leon: 1909 (11x17, 26 Sunday strips in Black & Red, Stiff cardboard-c)
nn - By Gustave Verbeek (Very Rare) (no known sales)

TEXAS HISTORY MOVIES (N)
Various editions, 1928 to 1986 (B&W)
Book I -1928 Southwest Press (7-1/4 x 5-3/8, 56 pgs, cardboard cover) for the Magnolia Petroleum Company 50.00 125.00 250.00
nn - 1928 Southwest Press (12-3/8 x 9-1/4, 232 pgs, HC) 75.00 200.00 400.00
nn - 1935 Magnolia Petroleum Company (6 x 9, 132 pgs, paper cover) 21.00 63.00 130.00
NOTE: *Exists with either Wagon Train or Texas Flag & Lafitte/pirate covers.*
nn - 1943 Magnolia Petroleum Company (132 pgs, paper cover) 16.00 48.00 100.00
nn - 1963 Graphic Ideas Inc (11 x 8-1/2, softcover) 12.00 37.00 75.00
NOTE: *Reprints daily newspaper strips from the Dallas News, on Texas history. 1935 editions onward distributed within the Texas Public School System. Prior to that they appear to be giveaway comic books for the Magnolia Petroleum Company. There are many more editions than the ones pointed out above.*

THAT SON-IN-LAW OF PA'S! (N)
Newspaper Feature Service: 1914 (2-1/2 by 3", color)
nn - imprinted on back for THE LESTER SHOE STORE 15.00 25.00 50.00
NOTE: *Single sheet printed in full color on both sides, unfolds to show 12 panel story.*

THIMBLE THEATRE STARRING POPEYE (See also Popeye) (N)
Sonnet Publishing Co.: 1931 - No. 2, 1932 (25¢, B&W, 52 pgs.)(Rare)
1-Daily strip serial-r in both by Segar 157.00 650.00 1300.00
2 136.00 544.00 1100.00
NOTE: *The very first Popeye reprint book. The first Thimble Theatre Sunday page appeared Dec 19, 1919. Popeye first entered Thimble Theatre on Jan 17, 1929.*

THREE FUN MAKERS, THE (N)
Stokes and Company: 1908 (10x15", 64 pgs., color) (1904-06 Sunday strip-r)
nn - Maud, Katzenjammer Kids, Happy Hooligan 800.00 2000.00 -
NOTE: *This is the first comic book to compile more than one newspaper strip together.*

TIGERS (Also see On and Off Mount Ararat) (N)
Hearst's New York American & Journal: 1902, 86 pgs. 10x15-1/4"
nn - Funny animal strip-r by Jimmy Swinnerton 600.00 1600.00 -
NOTE: *The strip began as The Journal Tigers in The New York Journal Dec 12, 1897-Sept 28 1903*

TILLIE THE TOILER (N)
Cupples & Leon Co.: 1925 - No. 8, 1933 (52 pgs., B&W, daily strip-r)
nn (#1) By Russ Westover 54.00 216.00 450.00
2-8 50.00 175.00 360.00
NOTE: *First newspaper strip appearance was in January, 1921.*

TILLIE THE TOILER MAGIC DRAWING AND COLORING BOOK
Sam L Gabriel Sons And Company: 1931 (8-1/2 x 12", 36 pages, stiff-c)
838-By Russ Westover 39.00 156.00 275.00

TIMID SOUL, THE (N)
Simon & Schuster: 1931 (12-1/4x9", 136 pgs, B&W hardcover, dust jacket?)
nn - By H. T. Webster (newspaper strip-r) 40.00 120.00 260.00

TIM McCOY, POLICE CAR 17 (O)
Whitman Publishing Co.: 1934 (14-3/4x11", 32 pgs, stiff color covers)
674-1933 original material 75.00 300.00 600.00
NOTE: *Historically important as first movie adaptation in comic books.*

TOAST BOOK
John C. Winston Co: 1905 (7-1/4 x 6,104 pgs, skull-shaped book, feltcover, B&W)
nn - By Clare Dwiggins 50.00 175.00 300.00
NOTE: *Cartoon illustrations accompanying toasts/poems, most involving alcohol.*

TOM SAWYER & HUCK FINN (N)
Stoll & Edwards Co.:1925 (10x10-3/4", 52 pgs, stiff covers)
nn - By "Dwig" Dwiggins; 1923, 1924-r color Sunday strips 5000 200.00 350.00

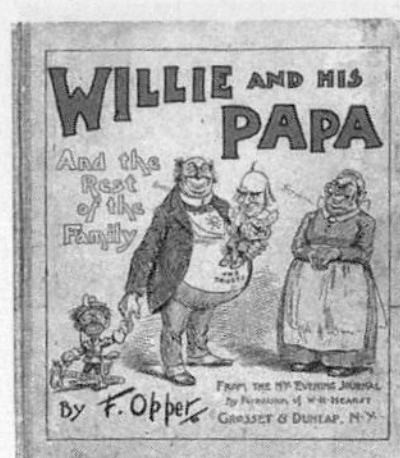

Willie and His Papa & the Rest of the Family by Opper
1901 © Grossett & Dunlap

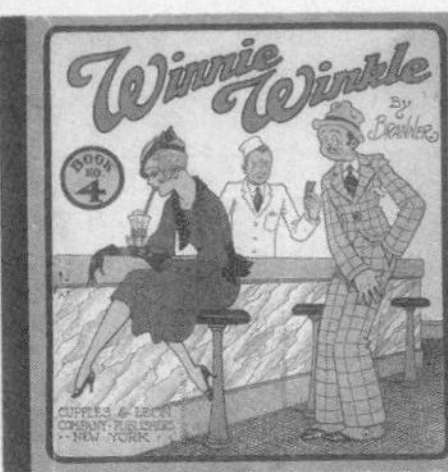

Winnie Winkle #4 by Branner
1933 © Cupples & Leon

The Yellow Kid #4 cover by Outcault
1897 © Howard Ainslee & Co.

GD2.0 FN6.0 VF8.0

NOTE: *By Permission of the Estate of Samuel L. Clemons and the Mark Twain Company.*

TOONERVILLE TROLLEY AND OTHER CARTOONS (N) (See Cartoons by Fontaine Fox)
Cupples & Leon Co.: 1921 (10 x10", 52 pgs., B&W, daily strip-r)
1 - By Fontaine Fox 100.00 350.00 600.00

TRAINING FOR THE TRENCHES (M)
Palmer Publishing Company: 1917 (5-3/8 x 7", 20 pgs., paper-c, 10¢)
nn - By Lieut. Alban B. Butler, Jr. 21.00 84.00 150.00
NOTE: *Subtitle: "A book of humorous cartoons on a serious subject." Single-panels about military training.*

TREASURE BOX OF FAMOUS COMICS (N) (see Wonder Chest of Famous Comics)
Cupples & Leon Co.: 1934 8-1/2x(6-7/8", 36 pgs, soft covers) (Boxed set of 5 books)

	GD2.0	FN6.0	VF8.0
Little Orphan Annie (1926)	21.00	84.00	165.00
Reg'lar Fellers (1928)	19.00	76.00	145.00
Smitty (1928)	19.00	76.00	145.00
Harold Teen (1931)	19.00	76.00	145.00
How Dick Tracy & Dick Tracy Jr. Caught The Racketeers (1933)	26.00	104.00	205.00
Softcover set of five books in box	160.00	640.00	1250.00
Box only	57.00	228.00	450.00

NOTE: *Dates shown are copyright dates; all books actually came out in 1934 or later. The softcovers are abbreviated versions of the hardcover editions listed under each character.*

T.R. IN CARTOONS (N)
A.C. McClurg & Co., Chicago: June 13, 1910 (10-5/8" x 8", 104? pgs, paper-c, B&W)
nn - By McCutcheon about Teddy Roosevelt - - -

TRUTH (See Victorian section for earlier issues including the first Yellow Kid appearances)
Truth Company, NY: 1886-1906? (13-11/16x10-5/16", 16 pgs, process color-c & center-folds, rest B&W)
1900-1906 issues 10.00 20.00 50.00

TRUTH SAVE IT FROM ABUSE & OVERWORK BEING THE EPISODE OF THE HIRED HAND & MRS. STIX PLASTER, CONCERTIST (N)
Radio Truth Society of WBAP: no date, 1924 (6-3/8 x 4-7/8, 40 pgs, paper cover, B&W)
nn - By V.T. Hamlin (Very Rare) 100.00 400.00 700.00
NOTE: *Radio station WBAP giveaway reprints strips from the Ft. Worth Texas Star-Telegram set at local radio station. 1st collected work by V.T. Hamlin, pre-Alley Oop.*

TWENTY FIVE YEARS AGO (see At The Bottom Of The Ladder) (M,S)
Coward-McCann: 1931 (5-3/4x8-1/4, 328 pgs, hardcover, B&W)
nn - By Camillus Kessler 32.00 128.00 225.00
NOTE: *Multi-image panel cartoons showing historical events for dates during the year.*

UMBRELLA MAN, THE (N) (See Sport And The Kid)
Lowman & Hanford Co.: 1911 (8-7/8x5-7/8",112 pgs, hard-c, B&W & orange)
nn - By J.R. "Dok" Hager (Seattle Times-r) 20.00 70.00 120.00

UNCLE REMUS AND BRER RABBIT (N)
Frederick A. Stokes Co.: 1907 (64 pgs, hardbound, color)
nn - By Joel C Harris & J.M. Conde 50.00 175.00 300.00

UPSIDE DOWNS OF LITTLE LADY LOVEKINS AND OLD MAN MUFFAROO
(see also TERROR OF THE TINY TADS)
New York Herald: 1905 (?) (N)
nn - By Gustav Verbeck 150.00 450.00 750.00

VAUDEVILLES AND OTHER THINGS (N)
Isaac H. Blandiard Co.: 1900 (13x10-1/2", 22 pgs., color) plus two reprints
nn - By Bunny (Scarce) 400.00 1200.00 -
nn - 2nd print "By the Creator of Foxy Grandpa" on-c but only has copyright info of 1900 (10-1/2x15 1/2, 28 pgs, color) 450.00 900.00 -
nn - 3rd print. "By the creator of Foxy Grandpa" on-c; has both 1900 and 1901 copyright info (11x13") 350.00 700.00 -

WALLY - HIS CARTOONS OF THE A.E.F. (N)
Stars & Stripes: 1917 (96 and 108 pgs, B&W)
nn - By Abian A "Wally" Wallgren (7x18; 96 pgs) 25.00 75.00 150.00
nn - another edition (108 pgs, 7x17-1/2) 25.00 75.00 150.00
NOTE: *World War One cartoons reprints from Stars & Stripes; sold to U.S. servicemen with profits to go to French War Orphans Fund. various editions from 1917-1920; there might be more than what we list here.*

WAR CARTOONS (S)
Dallas News: 1918 (11x9", 112 pgs, hardcover, B&W)
nn - By John Knott (WWOne cartoons) 20.00 70.00 125.00

WAR CARTOONS FROM THE CHICAGO DAILY NEWS (N,S)
Chicago Daily News: 1914 (10 cents, 7-3/4x10-3/4", 68 pgs, paper-c, B&W)
nn - By L.D. Bradley 20.00 70.00 125.00

WEBER & FIELD'S FUNNYISMS (S,M,O)
Arkell Comoany, NY: 1904 (10-7/8x8", 112 pgs, color-c, B&W)
1 - By various (only issue?) 20.00 70.00 150.00
NOTE: *Contains some sequential & many single panel strips by Outcault, George Luks, CA David, Houston, L Smith, Hy Mayer, Verbeck, Woolf, Sydney Adams, Frank "Chip" Bellew, Eugene "ZIM" Zimmerman, Phil May, FT Richards, Billy Marriner, Grosvenor and many others.*

WE'RE NOT HEROES (O,S)
E.C. Wells and J.W. Moss: 1933 (8-11/16" x 5-7/8", 52 pgs, B&W interior)
nn - By Eddie Wells; red & black paper-c 10.00 30.00 60.00
NOTE: *Amateurish cartoons about World War I vets in the Walter Reed Veteran's Hospital.*

WHEN A FELLER NEEDS A FRIEND (S)
P. F. Volland & Co.: 1914 (11-11/16x8-7/8)
nn - By Clare Briggs 37.00 131.00 225.00
NOTE: *Originally came in box with Briggs art (box is Rare); also numerous more modern reprints)*

WILD PILGRIMAGE (O)
Harrison Smith & Robert Haas: 1932 (9-7/8x7", 210 pgs, B&W hardcover w/dust jacket) (original wordless graphic novel in woodcuts)
nn - By Lynd Ward 50.00 175.00 300.00

WILLIE AND HIS PAPA AND THE REST OF THE FAMILY (I)
Grossett & Dunlap: 1901 (9-1/2x8", 200 pgs, hardcover from N.Y. Evening Journal by Permission of W. R. Hearst) (pictures & text)
nn - By Frederick Opper 100.00 260.00 450.00
NOTE: *Political satire series of single panel cartoons, involving whiny child Willie (President William McKinley), his rambunctious and uncontrollable cousin Teddy (Vice President Roosevelt), and Willie's Papa (trusts/monopolies) and their Maid (Senator) Hanna.*

WILLIE GREEN COMICS, THE (N) (see Adventures of Willie Green)
Frank M. Acton Co./Harris Brown: 1915 (8x15, 36 pgs); 1921 (6x10-1/8", 52 pgs, color paper cover, B&W interior, 25¢)
Book No. 1 By Harris Brown 45.00 158.00 270.00
Book 2 (*#2 sold via mail order directly from the artist)(very rare)* 45.00 172.00 300.00
NOTE: *Book No. 1 possible reprint of Adv. of Willie Green; definitely two different editions.*

WILLIE WESTINGHOUSE EDISON SMITH THE BOY INVENTOR (N)
William A. Stokes Co.: 1906 (10x16", 36 pgs. in color)
nn - By Frank Crane (Scarce) 350.00 850.00 1500.00
NOTE: *Comic strip began May 27, 1900 and ran thru 1914. Parody of inventors Westinghouse and Edison.*

WINNIE WINKLE (N)*Strip began as a daily Sept 20, 1920.*
Cupples & Leon Co.: 1930 - No. 4, 1933 (52 pgs., B&W daily strip-r)
1 43.00 172.00 400.00
2-4 29.00 116.00 300.00

WISDOM OF CHING CHOW, THE (see also The Gumps)
R. J. Jefferson Printing Co.: 1928 (4x3", 100 pgs, red & B&W cardboard cover) (newspaper strip-r The Chicago Tribune)
nn - By Sidney Smith (scarce) 30.00 90.00 150.00

WONDER CHEST OF FAMOUS COMICS (N) see Treasure Chest of Famous Comics)
Cupples & Leon Co.: 1935? 8-1/2x(6-7/8", 36 pgs, soft covers) (Boxed set of 5 books)

	GD2.0	FN6.0	VF8.0
Little Orphan Annie #2 (1927) (Haunted House)	21.00	84.00	130.00
Little Orphan Annie #3 (1928) (in the Circus)	19.00	76.00	130.00
Smitty #2 (1929) (Babe Ruth app.)	19.00	76.00	130.00
Dolly Dimples and Bobby Bounce (1933) by Grace Drayton	19.00	76.00	130.00
How Dick Tracy & Dick Tracy Jr. Caught The Racketeers (1933)	26.00	104.00	185.00
Softcover set of five books in box	160.00	640.00	1125.00
Box only	57.00	228.00	400.00

NOTE: *Dates shown are original copyright dates of the first printings; all actually came out in 1934 or later. Extremely abbreviated versions of the hardcover editions listed under each character. It is suspected this came out the Christmas season following Teasure Chest of Famous Comics. which contains earlier editions.*

WORLD OF TROUBLE, A (S)
Minneapolis Journal: 1901 (10x8-3/4", 100 pgs, 40 pgs full color)
v3#1 - By Charles L. Bartholomew (editorial-r) 28.00 99.00 170.00

WRIGLEY'S "MOTHER GOOSE"
Wm. Wrigley Jr. Company, Chicago: 1915 (6" x 4", 28 pgs, full color)
nn - *Promotional comics for Wrigley's gum. Intro Wrigley's "Spearmen* 20.00 70.00 120.00
Book No. 2 20.00 70.00 120.00

YELLOW KID, THE (Magazine)(I) (becomes **The Yellow Book** #10 on)
Howard Ainslee & Co., N.Y.: Mar. 20, 1897 - #9, July 17, 1897
(5¢, B&W w/color covers, 52p., stapled) (not a comic book)
1-R.F. Outcault Yellow kid on-c only #1-6. The same Yellow Kid color ad app. on back-c #1-6 (advertising the New York Sunday Journal) 857.00 3500.00 -
2-6 (#2 4/3/97, #5 5/22/97, #6, 6/5/97) 743.00 2800.00 -
7-9 (Yellow Kid not on-c) 121.00 425.00 -
NOTE: *Richard Outcault's Yellow Kid from the Hearst New York American represents the very first successful newspaper comic strip in America. Listed here due to historical importance.*

YELLOW KID IN MCFADDEN'S FLATS, THE (N)
G. W. Dillingham Co., New York: 1897 (50¢, 7-1/2x5-1/2", 196 pgs., B&W, squarebound)
nn - The first "comic" book featuring The Yellow Kid; E. W. Townsend narrative w/R. F. Outcault Sunday comic page art-r & some original drawings 7000.00 14000.00 -
NOTE: *A Fair condition copy sold for $2,901 in August 2004.; restored app VF sold for $10,500 in 2005. A copy in Fine+ (spine intact) and loose bacl cover sold for $17,000 in 2006.*

YESTERDAYS (S)
The Reilly & Lee Co.: 1930 (8-3/4 x 7-1/2", 128 pgs, illustrated hard-c with dust jacket
nn - Text and cartoons about Victorian times by Frank Wing 20.00 40.00 80.00

Any addititions or corrections to this section are always welcome, very much encouraged and can be sent to **feedback@gemstonepub.com** to be processed for next year's Guide.

The American Comic Book: 1929-Present
A Concise History Of The Field As Of 2009
THE MODERN COMICS MAGAZINE SUPPLANTS THE EARLIER FORMATS

by Robert Lee Beerbohm & Richard D. Olson, PhD ©2009

(This article was originally created by Robert Beerbohm and Richard Olson for CBPG #27 1997.)

Although somewhat similar in appearance to comic books of the Golden Age of the superhero, the varied formats that comic publishing pioneers Stokes, Cupples & Leon and others popularized beginning in 1899 are quite different in appearance from today's comics. Even so, those many formats were consistently successful until the early 1930s, when they then had to compete against The Great Depression; the Depression eventually won. One major reason for a format change was that at a cost of 25¢ per book for the 10" x 10" cardboard style and 60¢ for the 7" x 8 1/2" dustjacketed hardcovers, the price became increasingly prohibitive for most consumers already stifled by the crushed economy. As a result, all Cupples & Leon style books published between 1929-1935 are much rarer than their earlier counterparts because most Americans had little money to spend after paying for necessities like food and shelter.

By the early 1930s, the era of the Prestige Format black & white reprint comic book was over. In 1932-33 a lot of format variations arose, collecting such newspaper strips as *Bobby Thatcher, Bringing Up Father, Buck Rogers, Dick Tracy, Happy Hooligan, Joe Palooka, The Little King, Little Orphan Annie, Mickey Mouse, Moon Mullins, Mutt & Jeff, Smitty, Tailspin Tommy, Tarzan, Thimble Theater starring Popeye, Tillie the Toiler, Winnie Winkle, and the Highlights of History.*

There had been Embee's *Comic Monthly's* dozen issues a decade earlier in 1922, and several dozen of Dell & Eastern's *The Funnies* tabloid in 1929-30. It contained only original material, went from a dime to a nickel and still it failed to catch a decent circulation.

A couple years ago it was discovered that Eastern Color and Dell were also co-partners in *The Funnies*. It is possible that Eastern came up with the idea and Delecorte agreed to publish it for general stand-alone distribution. Similar format Sunday sections of the same material have been discovered by comics historian Ken Barker to be published at the same time in the *Montreal Standard*, a Canadian newspaper; it appears to have been an effort to get a new comics syndicate off the ground. The effort was not too successful as *The Standard* dropped the sections after just a few months. Allan Holtz went through the *E&P* yearbooks and found that this section (presumably a preprint) was advertised from 1930-34 by Eastern Color Printing out of New York City.

The Funnies #1, early 1929, Dell Publishing Company and Eastern Color. This was the very first original material newsstand comic book!

This is a re-discovery of important magnitude as it pushes back the time known for Eastern Color Printing Company and Dell Publishing Company to be partners by four years into late 1928. They had almost discovered the winning formula which has ruled the format of comic books in America for the last 70 years. Unfortunately, it would be another four years before they successfully figured it out.

With another format change including four colors, page counts beginning at 32 (soon hitting a whopping 68), and a hefty price reduction (starting for free as promotional premiums due to the nationwide numbing effects of worldwide deflation), the birthing pangs of the modern American comic book occurred in late 1932. Created out of desperation, to keep the printing presses rolling, the modern American comic book was born when a 45-year-old sales manager for Eastern Color Printing Company of New York reinvented the format from the failed tabloid *The Funnies.*

Harry I. Wildenberg's job was to come up with ideas that would sell color printing for Eastern, a company which also printed the comic sections for a score of newspapers along the eastern seaboard, including the *Boston Globe, the Brooklyn Times, the Providence Journal, and the Newark Ledger.* Down-time meant less take-home pay, so Wildenberg was always racking his brains to keep the color presses running. He was fascinated by the miles of funny sheets which rolled off Eastern's presses each week, and he constantly sought new ways to exploit their commercial possibilities. If the funny papers were this popular, he reasoned, they should prove a good advertising medium. He decided to pitch a comics tabloid to various oil company clients.

Brand new research conducted late in December 2005 has discovered the existence of a no number introduction issue of *Standard Oil Comics* dated to December 1932. Evidently it was Rockefeller's Standard Oil which decided before Gulf Oil to entice customers with a comics giveaway.

There are at least 14 issues each of at least a 1933 A and a 1934 B series of a four page tabloid-size full color comics giveaway titled *Standard Oil Comics*. The A issues all contain Fred Opper's *Si & Mirandi*, an older couple who interact with perennial favorites, *Happy Hooligan & Maud the Mule*, drawn by the grand old master himself, Frederick Opper, who had been a professional cartoonist for over 60 years by this time. This new "no number" 1932 precursor instructed readers to listen to the Si & Miandi radio show, come in regularly to Standard Oil stations and pick up *Standard Oil Comics*.

The 1934 B series front Goofus "He's From The Big City" McVittle by Walter O'Ehrle, set in humorous farming scenarios. Interior strips include *Pesty And His Pop & Smiling Slim* by Sid Hicks. Considering the concept of *Gulf Funny Weekly* has been well known for decades while *Standard Oil Comics* remains virtually unknown, what we now know is Gulf copied Standard in almost all respects.

Gulf Oil Company also liked the idea and hired a few artists to create an original comic called *Gulf Comic Weekly*. Their first issue was dated April 1933 and was 10 1/2" x 15". Gulf copied Standard Oil by advertising their giveaway nationally on the radio beginning April 30th. Its first artists were Stan Schendel doing *The Uncovered Wagon*, Victor doing *Curly and the Kids*, and Svess on a strip named *Smileage*. All were full page, full color comic strips. Wildenberg promptly had Eastern print this four page comic, making it probably the first tabloid newsprint comic published for American distribution outside of a newspaper in the 20th Century. Wildenberg and Gulf were astonished when the tabloids were grabbed up as fast as Gulf service stations could offer them. Distribution shot up to 3,000,000 copies a week after Gulf changed the name to *Gulf Funny Weekly* with its 5th issue. It remained a tabloid until early 1939 & ran for 422 issues until May 23, 1941.

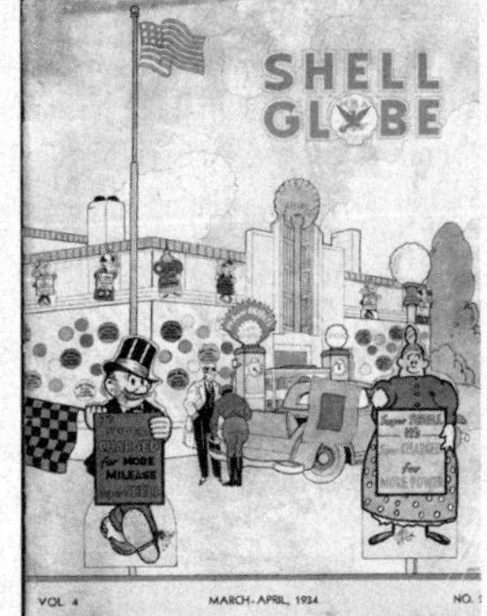

Top: Newly discovered Standard Oil Comics from Dec 1932. One copy presently known to exist. This rare give-away ended in late in 1934. Standard Oil was the first to issue a regular give-away using comics to bring in customers; Middle: Gulf Comic Weekly #1, April, 1933, copied what Standard Oil began. Gulf's weekly changed its name to Gulf Funny Weekly with #5; Bottom: Not to be outdone, by March 1934, Shell Oil began a huge comics promotion to compete with Standard and Gulf.

Recent research has also turned up "new" rediscovered comics material from other oil companies from this same time span of 1933-34. Perhaps spurred by the runaway success of first *Standard Oil Comics, then Gulf Funny Weekly*, these other oil companies found they had to compete with licensed comic strip material of their own in order to remain profitable.

Beginning with the March-April 1934 issue of *Shell Globe* (V4 #2), characters from Bud Fisher (*Mutt & Jeff*) and Fontaine Fox (*Toonerville Folks*) were licensed to sell gas & oil for this company. 52,000 eight foot standees were made for Fisher's *Mutt and Jeff* and Fox's *Powerful Katrinka* and *The Skipper* for placement around 13,000 Shell gas stations. Augmenting them was an army of 250,000 miniature figures of the same characters. In addition, more than 1,000,000 play masks were given away to children along with more than 285,000 window stickers. If that wasn't enough, hundreds of thousands of 3x5 foot posters featuring these characters were released in conjunction with twenty-four sheet outdoor billboards. Radio announcements of this promotion began running April 7th, 1934. It is presently unknown if Shell had a comics tabloid created to give away to customers.

In addition, new research has uncovered the Gilmore Oil Company issuing an eight page giveaway titled *The Gilmore Cub*. It appears to have carried "Starnge As It Seems" among other cartoon features by John Hix. At least one issue, v4 #2, May, 1938, is known to exist.

The authors of this essay are actively soliciting help in uncovering more information regarding these and potentially other oil comics giveaways.

With the 1933 newsstand appearance of Humor's *Detective Dan, Adventures of Detective Ace King, Bob Scully, Two Fisted Hick Detective*, and possibly the still unrediscovered, but definitely advertised, *Happy Mulligan*, these little understood original-material comic books from Humor were the direct inspiration for Jerry Siegel and Joe Shuster to transform their fanzine's evil character The Superman from *Science Fiction* #3 (January 1933) into a comic strip that would stand as a watershed heroic mark in American pop culture. The stage was set for a new frontier. The idea for creating an actual comic book as we know it today, however, did not occur to Wildenberg until later in 1933, when he said he was idly folding a newspaper in halves, then in quarters. As he looked at the twice-folded paper, it occurred to him that it was a convenient book size (actually it was late stage Dime Novel size, which companies like Street & Smith were pumping out). The format had its heyday from the 1880s through the 1910s, having been invented by the firm of Beadle and Adam in 1860 in more of a digest format. According to a 1942 article by Max Gaines (née Ginzberg), another contributing factor in the development of the format was an inspection of a promotional folder published by the Ledger Syndicate, in which four-color Sunday comic pages were printed in 7"x9".

According to a 1949 interview with Wildenberg, he thought "why not a comic book? It would have 32 or 64 pages and make a fine item for concerns which distribute premiums." All they did at Eastern Color that one fateful day is fold a tabloid newspaper format down to "dime novel" size running full color throughout on most of the comic strips, then staple it, and they hit upon their winning formula.

But they did not yet know this...as we will find out.

Working for Eastern Color at this same time were quite a few future legends of the comics business, such as Max Gaines, Lev Gleason and a fellow named Harold Moore (all sales staff directly underneath the supervision of Wilden-berg), Sol Harrison as a color separator, and George Dougherty Sr. as a printer.

Janosik, Wildenberg, Gaines, Gleason and crew obtained publishing rights to certain Associated, Bell, Fisher, McNaught and Public Ledger Syndicate comics, had an artist make up a few dummies by hand. The sales staff then walked them around to their biggest prospects. Wildenberg received a telegram from Proctor & Gamble for an order of a million copies for a 32-page color comic magazine called **Funnies on Parade**. The entire print run was given away in just a few weeks

The Adventures of Detective Ace King, Bob Scully The Two Fisted Hick Detective & Detective Dan Secret Op. #48, early 1933, Humor Publishing Co. All issues Very Rare from the 2nd original newsstand comic book publisher; the direct inspiration for Jerry Siegel & Joe Shuster's 1933 conversion of The Superman into a comic book due to a promise of publication. This earliest Superman was never published.

in the Spring of 1933. Most copies no longer exist and it is now hard to find. All of them worked on the *Funnies on Parade* project. Morris Margolis was brought in from Charlton in Derby, Connecticut to solve binding problems centered on getting the pages in proper numerical sequence on that last fold to "modern" comic book size. Most of them were infected with the comics bug for most of the rest of their lives.

The success of *Funnies on Parade* quickly led to Eastern publishing additional giveaway books in the same format by late 1933, including the 32-page *Famous Funnies A Carnival of Comics*, the 100-page *A Century of Comics* and the 52-page *Skippy's Own Book of Comics*.

The latter became the first "new" format comic book about a single character. Out of all the comic strips on the market in 1933, Eastern Color's growing comics market as devised by Harry Wildenberg, M.C. Gaines and Lev Gleason chose the Percy Crosby creation in *Skippy's Own Book of Comics* to be its first standalone title. This first solo effort in their new 52-page newsprint *Funnies On Parade* format had an initial print run of half a million, as did their 100-pager.

The idea that anyone would pay for them seemed fantastic to Wildenberg, so Max Gaines stickered ten cents on several dozen of the latest premium, *Famous Funnies A Carnival of Comics*, as a test, and talked a couple newsstands into participating in this experiment. The copies sold out over the weekend and newsies asked for more.

Eastern sales staffers then approached Woolworth's. The late Oscar Fitz-Alan Douglas, sales brains of Woolworth, showed some interest, but after several months of deliberation decided the book would not give enough value for ten cents. Kress, Kresge, McCrory, and several other dime stores turned them down even more abruptly. Wildenberg next went to George Hecht, editor of *Parents Magazine*, and tried to persuade him to run a comic supplement or publish a "higher level" comic magazine. Hecht also frowned on the idea.

In Wildenberg's 1949 interview, he noted that "even the comic syndicates couldn't see it. 'Who's going to read old comics?' they asked." With the failures of EmBee's *Comic Monthly* (1922) and Dell's *The Funnies* (1929) still fresh in some minds, no one could see why children would pay ten cents for a comic magazine when they could get all they wanted for free in a Sunday newspaper. But Wildenberg had become convinced that children as well as grown-ups were not getting all the comics they wanted in the Sunday papers; otherwise, *Standard Oil Comics, Gulf Comic Weekly* and the premium comics would not have met with such success. Wildenberg said, "I decided that if boys and girls were willing to work for premium coupons to obtain comic books, they might be willing to pay ten cents on the newsstands." This conviction was also strengthened by Max Gaines' ten cent sticker experiment.

Funnies on Parade, 1933 - what we recognize today as the first "modern" comic book with its slick cover.

George Janosik, the president of Eastern Color, then called on George Delacorte to form another 50-50 joint venture to publish and market a comic book "magazine" for retail sales as they did with *The Funnies* just a few years previously, but this time American News turned them down cold. The magazine monopoly remembered the abortive *The Funnies* from just a few years before. After much discussion on how to proceed, Delacorte finally agreed to publish it and a partnership was formed. Feeling cautious, they printed 40,000 copies for distribution to a few chain stores who agreed to try it out. Known today as *Famous Funnies Series One*, it clocks in at 68 pages, with half its pages coming from reprints of the reprints in *Funnies on Parade* and half from *Famous Funnies A Carnival of Comics*. It is the scarcest issue.

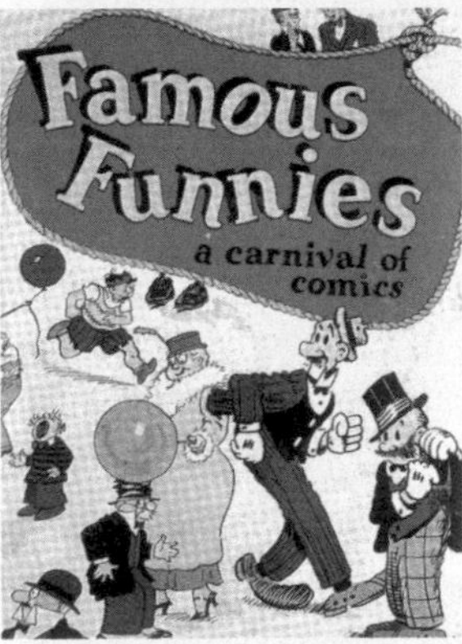

The fateful version Charlie Gaines stickered 10¢ a copy one weekend in late '33 which sold out over a weekend.

With 68 full-color pages at only ten cents a piece, it sold out in thirty days with not a single returned copy. Delacorte refused to print a second edition. "Advertisers won't use it," he complained. "They say it's not dignified enough." The profit, however, was approximately $2,000. This particular edition is the rarest of all these early Eastern comic book experiments.

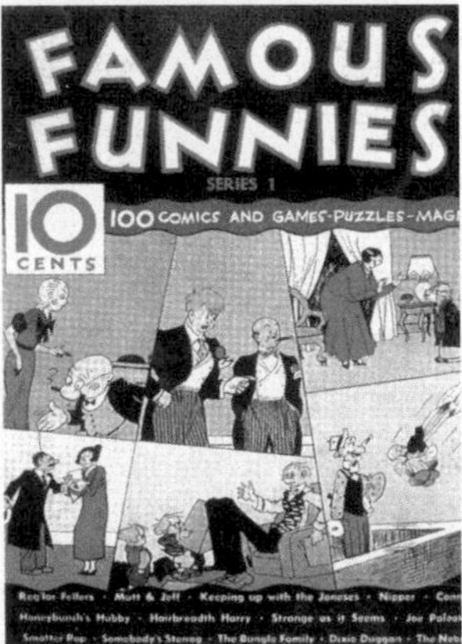

Famous Funnies Series One is the rare one, only 40,000 copies were printed.

In early 1934, while riding the train, another Eastern Color employee named Harold A. Moore read an account from a prominent New York newspaper that indicated they owed much of their circulation success to their comics section. Mr. Moore went back to Harry Gold, President of American News, with the article in hand. He succeeded in acquiring a print order for 250,000 copies for a proposed monthly comics magazine. In May 1934, *Famous Funnies* #1 (with a July cover date) hit the newsstands with Steven O. Douglass as its only editor (even though Harold Moore was listed as such in #1) until it ceased publication some twenty years later. It was a 64-page version of the 32-page giveaways, and more importantly, it still sold for a dime! The first issue lost $4,150.60. Ninety percent of the copies sold out and a second issue dated September debuted in July. From then on, the comic book was published monthly. *Famous Funnies* also began carrying original material, apparently as early as the second issue. With #3, Buck Rogers took center stage and stayed there for the next twenty years, with covers by Frank Frazetta towards the end of the run–some of his best comics work ever.

Delacorte got cold feet and sold back his interest to Eastern, even though the seventh issue cleared a profit of $2,664.25. Wildenberg emphasized that Eastern could make a manufacturer's profit by printing its own books as well as the publishing profits once it was distributed. Every issue showed greater sales than the preceding one, until within a year, close to a million 64-page books were being sold monthly at ten cents apiece; Eastern received the lion's share of the receipts, and soon found it was netting $30,000 per issue. The comic syndicates received $640 ($10 a page) for publishing rights. Original material could be obtained from budding professionals for just $5 a page. According to Will Eisner in R. C. Harvey's *The Art of the Comic Book*, the prices then paid for original material had a long range effect of keeping creator wages low for years.

Initially, Eastern's experiment was eyed with skepticism by the publishing world, but within a year or so after *Famous Funnies* was nonchalantly placed on sale alongside slicker magazines like *Atlantic Monthly* or *Harper's*, at least five other competitors tried this brand new format.

However, one other abortive periodical comics experiment was launched cover dated a full two months before the highly successful newsstand *Famous Funnies* format would have an important influence on a chain of events which led ultimately to *Superman* being published.

Comic Cuts #1, May 19, 1934, debuted published by H.L. Baker Co., Inc., 195 Main St, Buffalo, New York with editorial

Famous Funnies #1, July 1934, was the first successful newsstand comic book, lasting until 1955.

and executive offices at 381 Fourth St, NYC, same address as ULTEM (Centaur) would use just a couple years later - this address housed a number of publishers fighting to exist during the Great Depression. The indica says H. L. Baker was President & Treasurer and J. D. Geller was Vice President and Secretary. It lasted nine issues with the final one cover-dated July 28. It appears Jake Geller, Windsor, Ontario, Canada, acquired American rights to a number of comic strips from the publisher Amalgamated Press, publisher of *Comic Cuts* in England. He partnered in the publishing with H. L. Baker and they acquired the backing of S-M News Co., Inc. as their distributor. Most distributors back then functioned on many important levels. It was common practice for the distributor back then to front the funds to pay the paper company and the printer, collecting the revenue from the 900 I.D. distributors located around the country after months of on-sale time, then paying the publisher.

In late 1934, army officer/diplomat turned pulp writer turned publisher Major Wheeler-Nicholson (1890-1968) formed the under-funded National Allied Publishing which introduced *New Fun #1* (Feb 1935) at almost tabloid-size. *New Fun* was also distributed by S-M News. It is entirely possible Wheeler-Nicholson somehow convinced them he could produce a superior "home-grown" package as the imported strips were not selling well. *New Fun* was basically the same as *Comic Cuts* while also containing all original USA material such as carried in *The Funnies* (1929-30) from Dell/Eastern. With *New Fun*, what S-M News offered was more familiar American home grown. Coulton

Comic Cuts #8, July 14, 1934, issued weekly by H.L. Baker Co. Inc., Buffalo, New York; editorial offices at 381 Fourth Ave, NYC; co-owner Jake D. Geller was Canadian. Title provided inspiration for New Fun.

Skippy's Own Book of Comics, 1934, had half a million issues printed. It was the very first single character comic book in this "new" format.

Waugh speculated in his 1947 history book *The Comics* on page 342: "...The Major had gone back to the 1929 idea of *The Funnies*, for the contents of *New Fun* were original material. (It should be recorded here that original art work had appeared in a one-color book called *Detective Dan*."

However, Lloyd Jacquet, a person definitely in a position to know better, wrote as Chapter One of a proposed "History of the Comic Book" in 1957, "When Major Malcolm Wheeler-Nicholson set up his card table and chair in an eleventh floor office of the Hatha-way Building in New York that Fall of 1934, these most modest beginnings sparked off what can rightly be called the 'comic book era.' When he came back to the U.S. after his last stay abroad, he looked over the American newsstand, and thought that the European juvenile weekly papers, with their picture-story continuities, their colorful illustrations, and their low price would appeal to the American boys and girls in the same way. He knew that those European publications were made up of new material, specially drawn and produced for each little magazine. He also knew that the American presentation of such material would have to be different, and merely importing, or translating European produced features for republication here was not the answer. This was about the time I joined with him in his project. It was still embryonic, but beginning to take form under Nicholson's direction. We were in the depression then, & it was not too difficult to secure writers and artists - but it was a task to instruct them as to exactly what was wanted. We finally rounded up a small but gifted group of creative people, and we produced our first issue of a monthly magazine composed of original features and material, and which was called,

New Fun #1, Feb 1935. According to first-employee Lloyd Jacquet, the format Major Malcolm Wheeler-Nicholson used was directly inspired by Comic Cuts. Many of the non-comics features were the same.

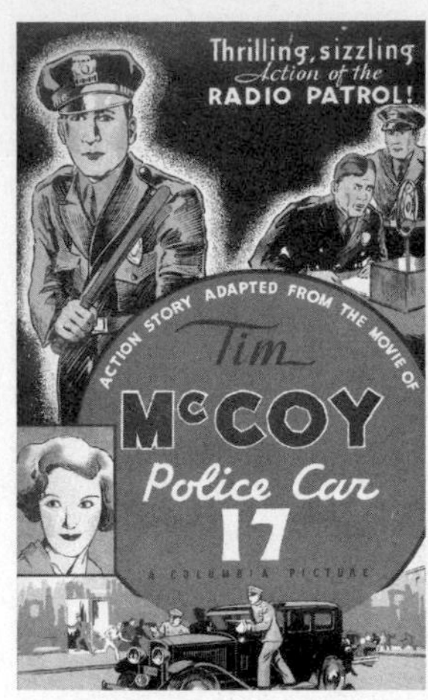

Tim McCoy Police Car #17, Whitman's first 1930s comic book (1934); the first movie adaptation

simply, "*FUN*."

Around this same time in late 1934, M.C. Gaines left Eastern Color moving over to the McClure Newspaper Syndicate to become their manager of their Color Printing Department He immediately went to work convincing clients to issue promotional comics. Also, long-time comics publisher Whitman brought out the first original material movie adaptation, Tim McCoy Police Car 17, in the tabloid New Fun format with stiff card covers. A few years before, they had introduced the new comics formats known as the Big Little Book and the Big Big Book. The BLB and BBB formats would go toe-to-toe with Eastern's creation throughout the 1930s, but Eastern would win out with their new comics magazine format.

The very last 10" x 10" comic books pioneered by Cupples & Leon were published by the David McKay Publishing Company around mid-1935. Around this same time the Major published his 2nd comic book in which the editorial mentions amongst other exciting stories they were going to be showcasing the adventures of "hero supermen of the days to come."

By late 1935, Max Gaines (with his youthful assistant Sheldon Mayer) reached a business agreement with George Delacorte (who was re-entering the comic book business a third time) and McClure Syndicate (a growing newspaper comic strip enterprise) to be come editor of reprint newspaper comic strips in *Popular Comics.*

New Comics #1, Dec. 1935, was the Major's second entry into comic books, re-emphasizing the concept of "New!"

Also by late '35, Lev Gleason, another pioneer who participated in mercantiling *Funnies on Parade* and the early *Famous Funnies*, had become the first editor of United Feature's own *Tip Top Comics* with its first issue cover dated April 1936. In 1939 he would begin publishing his own titles starting with *Silver Streak*, created by the comics genius, Jack Cole, best known for Plastic Man. Gleason later created the crime comic book as a separate popular genre by 1942 with *Crime Does Not Pay* with a long run until 1955.

Wheeler-Nicholson introduced the concept of "the annual" into this new format with *Big Book of Fun Comics* #1 cover dated March 1936. It featured reprints from his earlier efforts in *New Fun* #1-5 as he struggled to make a go of it.

Industry giant King Features introduced *King Comics* #1 cover dated April 1936 through publisher David McKay, with Ruth Plumly Thompson as editor. McKay had already been issuing various format comic books with King Feature characters for a few years, including Mickey Mouse, Henry, Popeye and Secret Agent X-9, wherein Dashiell Hammett received cover billing and Alex Raymond was listed inside simply as "illustrator." McKay readily adapted to trying several formats. Soon many young comic book illustrators were copying Raymond.

The next month, William Cook & John Mahon, former disgruntled employees of Major Wheeler-Nicholson, issued their first issue of *Comics Magazine* #1 in May 1936.

Left, Charlie Gaines & Sheldon Mayer packaged Popular Comics #1, Feb. 1936, for George Delecorte in late 1935 after the former left Eastern Color. Middle, King Comics #1, April 1936, marked King Features Syndicate's entry into the new 64-page color comic market with their new heavyweights, Flash Gordon and Popeye. By this point, Hearst had been involved in publishing comic books for close to 40 years. Right, Lev Gleason left Eastern & Wildenberg about the same time as Gaines to edit Tip Top Comics #1, April 1936, for United Features.

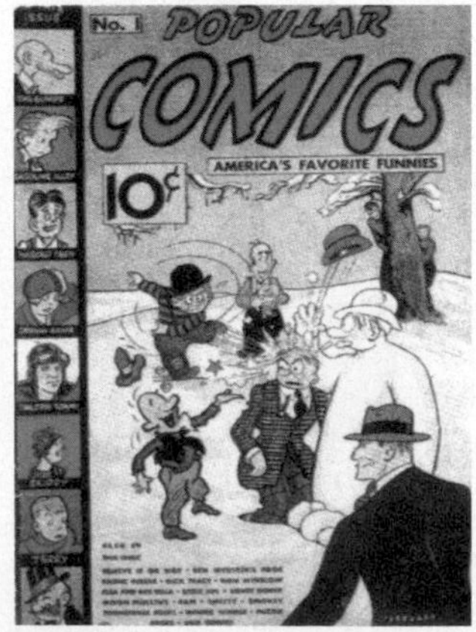

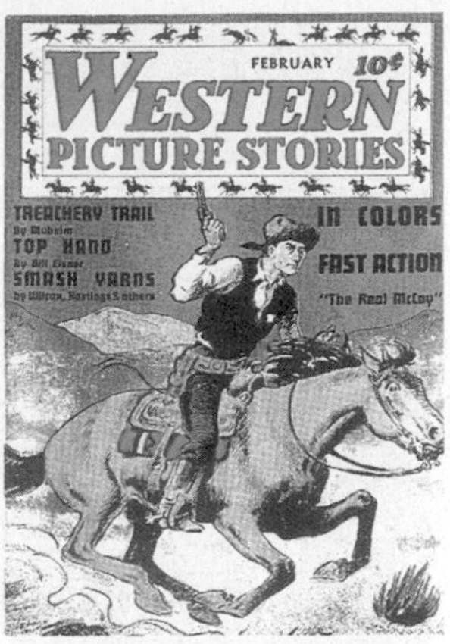

Left, The Comics Magazine #2, June 1936, was the first title of what later became Centaur. Soon it had a name change and quickly made history. Middle, Wow What A Magazine is a rare title which ran four issues beginning in June 1936 with the first published work by youthful, eager Bernard Baily, Dick Briefer, Will Eisner & Bob Kane. Painted cover by Will Eisner. Western Picture Stories #1, Feb. 1937 has more art by Eisner, ties with Star Ranger Funnies #1 as first western comic book. Centaur also introduced the earliest crime comic book, Detective Picture Stories #1 dated December 1936.

This was followed by Henle Publishing issuing *Wow What A Magazine*, which contained the earliest comic work of Will Eisner, Bob Kane, Dick Briefer & others. By the end of 1936, Cook and Mahon pioneered the first single theme comic books: *Funny Picture Stories* #1 in Nov. 1936 (adventure), *Detective Picture Stories* #1 in Feb. 1937 (crime), as well as *Western Picture Stories* #1 in Feb. 1937 (the Western). The company would eventually be known historically as Centaur Comics, and serve as the subject of endless debate among fan historians regarding their earliest origins as to who the owners were, where they came from and where they went.

Dell issued the second western genre comic book titled *Western Action Thrillers* #1 in April 1937. It was ten cents for one hundred pages as well as *100 Pages of Comics 101*, containing Big Little Book art reworked back into sequential comics

Harry 'A' Chesler jumped ship from the Major, issuing his first comic books with **Star Comics** and **Star Ranger Funnies**, dated Feb 1937. Later that year, he sold these two titles to Ultem while remaining editor, and his newly set up art shop supplied contents. He then began **Feature Funnies** #1 in Oct. 1937, headlining Joe Palooka, at one time the #1 newspaper comic strip in America. Issue #2 sported a Rube Goldberg cover while #3 contains "Hawk of the Sea," Will Eisner's first work for what would soon become the Quality Comics Group when Everett "Busy" Arnold bought the company. **Feature Funnies** #3 also contains the first appearance of The Clock by George Brenner - the first costumed comic book hero.

Almost forty years after the first newspaper strip comic book compilations were issued at the dawn of international

Left, Feature Funnies #3, Dec. 1937, contains George Brenner's The Clock, the first comic book costumed hero plus Eisner's first work for Quality Comics, when still owned by Chesler. Circus the Comic Riot #1, June 1938, contains Basil Wolverton's earliest professional comic book work plus more Will Eisner and Bob Kane. Right, Action Comics #1, June 1938, began revolutionizing the industry when Superman by Jerome Siegel & Joseph Shuster debuted. The publishers did not understand what they had at first as Superman does not appear on a cover again until #7. Nobody knew at first, it seemed, except book-keeper Victor Fox counting copies sold, who quit and formed his own comic book company.

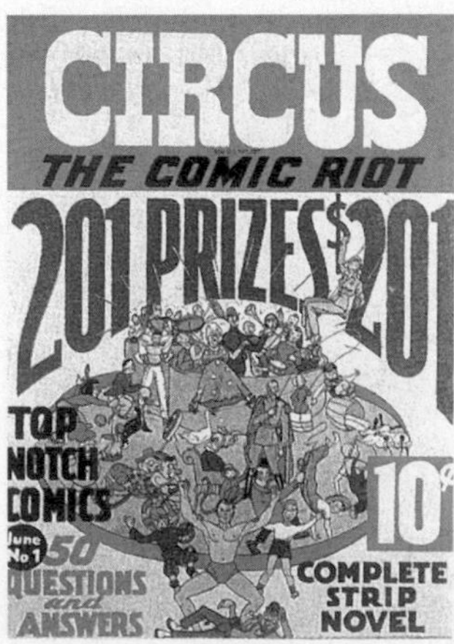

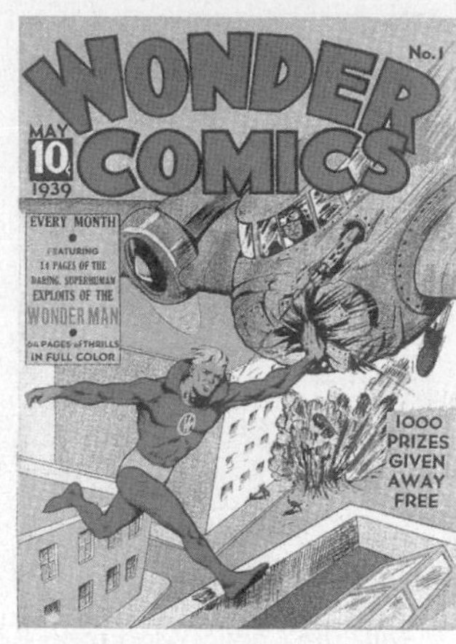

Left, Jumbo Comics #1, Sept. 1938, debuts pulp publisher Fiction House's entry into the growing comic book industry. Middle, Detective Comics #27 introduced Batman created by Bob Kane and Bill Finger - need we say more? Right, Wonder Comics #1, May 1939, became Victor Fox's first entry into the comics biz when he fast-talked a youthful Will Eisner into creating a near-exact clone of the creation of Siegel & Shuster's brainchild, Superman. There was a quick lawsuit and #2 featured Yarko The Great instead. Bob Kane was busy that May as he is also in Wonder #1.

popularity for American comic strips, the race was on to get titles out of the starting block. In late 1937 the Major began stumbling when he couldn't pay his printing bill to Harry Donenfeld. In recent interviews, Harry's son, Irwin, who as a 12-year old read the original art to the first issue of *Action Comics* #1 and *Detective Comics* #27 said "in 1932 my father and Paul Sampliner started Independent News with Liebowitz as the accountant. The company was begun with Paul Sampliner's mother's money. If it hadn't been for her investments into building the distribution as well as purchasing color printing presses, there might never have been a DC Comics. My father took over Wheeler-Nicholson's company with the Major's books literally on the printing presses. Harry had to absorb debt that could not otherwise be paid." Irwin told this writer "my dad did not originally willingly enter the comics business"

Soon after the Major lost control of his company, *Action Comics* #1 was published with a cover date of June 1938, and the first Golden Age of superhero comics had begun. Early in 1938 at McClure Syndicate, Max Gaines and Shelly Mayer showed editor Vin Sullivan a many times rejected sample strip. Sullivan then talked Donenfeld, Paul Sampliner and Jack Liebowitz into publishing Jerry Siegel & Joe Shuster's creation of "The Last Son of Krypton." This was followed in 1939 by a lucrative partnership for Gaines beginning with Harry Donenfeld as the All-American Comics Group.

While there's a great deal of controversy surrounding such labeling, the "Golden Age" is viewed by many these days as beginning with *Action Comics* #1 and continuing through the end of World War II. There was a time not that long ago that the newspaper reprint comic book was collected with more fervor than the heroic comics of the '40s. *Prince Valiant FB*

Left, Marvel Comics #1, Oct. 1939, was the first Martin Goodman comic book, introducing Human Torch by Carl Burgos and Sub-Mariner by Bill Everett. Middle, Silver Streak #1, Dec. 1939, Lev Gleason's first published comic book, introduced Jack Cole's classic, The Claw, running until #24, when the title changed to Crime Does Not Pay. Right, Whiz Comics #2 (#1), Feb. 1940, ushered Fawcett onto the comic book scene with yet another Superman clone - Captain Marvel, who was successful from the get-go. At one time his main title was issued every three weeks.

Left, Crime Does Not Pay #43, Nov. 1945. Lev Gleason instigated a popular new genre which brought the industry unfairly under heavy fire from church and state. Middle, My Date #1, July 1947. Joe Simon and Jack Kirby created the romance genre when they developed the older female audience which lasted into the '70s. Right, Atomic War #1, Nov. 1952. Nuclear obliteration was heavy on the minds of most Americans. Due to the Korean War, there was a plethora of war titles and the genre survived well into the 1970s before being eventually marginalized by the super hero revival.

#26, *Flash Gordon 4C* #10 and *Tarzan SS* #20 were some of the highest Holy Grails of collecting, but no more even though they contain fantastic art & story.

Today's marketplace dictates super heroes command the highest prices and are seemingly the most desirable. Maybe one day that pendulum will swing once again as there have been many years since they were introduced when super heroes almost disappeared completely from the racks.

The Atomic/Romance Age debuted with a bang by early 1946, revamping the industry once again as circulations soon hit their all-time highs with well over 1.3 billion periodical issues sold a year by the consignment honor system. By the early 1950s one in three periodicals sold in the USA was a comic book. 90% of all children admitted they read and enjoyed comics. There were dozens of genres being published. There were comic books for every taste and style. Hundreds of titles were being issued every month.

For many readers, the pinnacle was reached with the "New Trend" Entertaining Comics (E.C.) began delivering to the newsstands in 1950. The company still has a large following even today - a testament to its emphasis on quality art & story.

Comic book publishers glutted the market place by 1952-53. The attacks on comics begun the late 1940s came back anew in 1954 brought on by over-zealous church people and district attorneys with an agenda.

This continued until the advent of the self-censoring, industry-stifling Comics Code, created in response to a public outcry spearheaded by Dr. Frederic Wertham's tirade against

Left, Crime Detective #9, July 1948. Some say the tied-up figure represents Dr. Fredric Wertham following his earliest attacks on the crime comic book. Hillman joined the first Code. Middle, Justice Traps the Guilty #56, Nov. 1953. The S&K studio placed themselves in the spotlight, with a pretty mother pointing out Joe Simon as the tall, dastardly ringleader. Jack Kirby is on the right end. Right, Thing #15, Apr. 1954. Ditko wreaks havoc on a world rising against comics as a giant worm eats Brooklyn in one of the most gruesome titles created. His early work is intense.

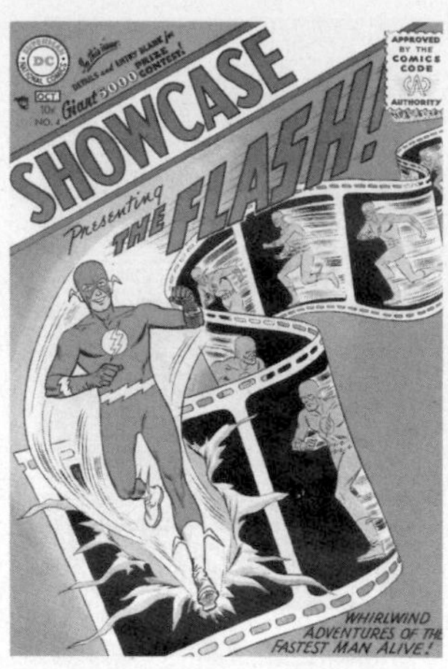

Left, By the early 1950s, Carl Barks increased the circulation of Walt Disney's C&S to over 4 million per issue & in 1952 his creation, Uncle Scrooge, got his own book, selling over a million an issue through the '50s while superheroes slumbered. Middle, Harvey Kurtzman created Mad Comics #1, 1952, as the comics industry went in an entirely "New" Direction and has directly inspired countless comics creators for years. Right, Showcase #4, Sept. 1956, the superhero revival starts a year after the Code, though it was three years before the Flash earned his own title once again.

the American comics industry, published as a book titled *Seduction of the Innocent*, which removed crime and horror comic books from the marketplace. Some of them were quite gruesome; however in his last book, *The World of Fanzines*, Wertham exhonerated comics fans for misinterpreting his data more than 20 years previous.

It took a year or two to recover from that moralistic assault, with many historians speculating the Silver Age of Superheroes began with the publication of *Showcase* #4 in 1956. Others point to the 1952 successful releases of Kurtzman's *MAD* #1 and Bark's *Uncle Scrooge Four Color* #386 as true Silver, since those titles soon broke the "million sold per issue" mark when the rest of the comic book industry was reeling from the effects of the public uproar fueled by Wertham. Within the Silver Era the term Bronze Age has been stated by some to begin when the Code approved newsstand comic book industry raised its standard cover price from 12 to 15 cents and Jack Kirby left Marvel for DC. As circulations plummeted after the Batman TV craze wore off by 1968 and the ensuing superhero glut withered on the stands, out in the Bay Area cartoonist Robert Crumb's creator-owned *Zap Comics* #1 appeared in Feb 1968, printed by Charles Plymell & Don Donahue on a small printing press. Soon after in Chicago, Jay Lynch and Skip Williamson brought out *Bijou Funnies*, Gilbert Shelton self-published *Feds 'N' Heads* while still in Austin, Texas, with Print Mint reprinting it almost immediately & Crumb let S. Clay Wilson, Victor Moscoso & Rick Griffin into Zap #2.

As originally published by the Print Mint beginning with #2 in 1968, *Zap Comics* almost single-handedly spawned an industry with tremendous growth in alternative comix run-

Left, Brave & Bold #28, Feb/Mar. 1960, gathered together the revived DC heroes, further expanding the resurging superhero market DC Comics ushered in. Middle, Fantastic Four #1, Nov. 1961, began the revitalization of Martin Goodman's moribund Marvel Comics Group, directly inspired by the success of the JLA's own regular series begun 2 years earlier in late 1960. Right, Amazing Fantasy #15, Aug. 1962, introduced the Amazing Spider-Man, created almost completely by Steve Ditko with some assists from Stan Lee and Jack Kirby, which revolutionized the way comic book stories could be told.

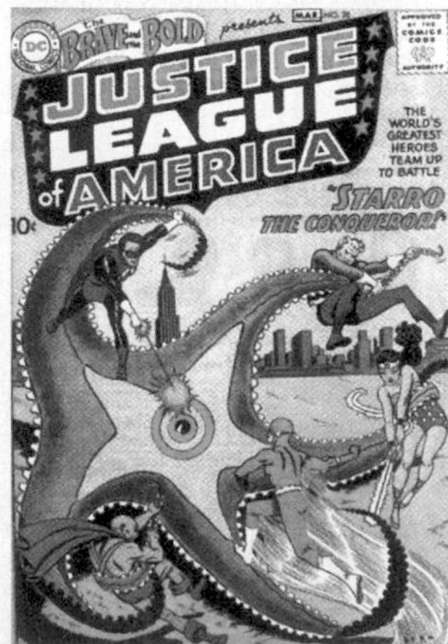

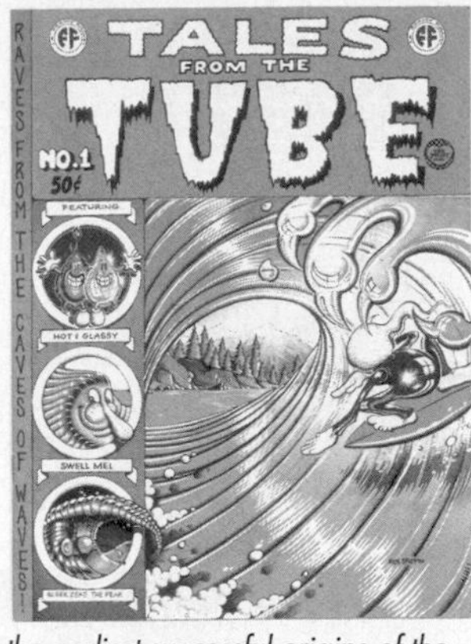

Left, Zap Comics #1, Plymell first printing, Feb. 1968, was the "direct" inspiration for the earliest successful origins of the Direct Market and has sold over a million copies. Most issues have been continuously in print for over 30 years. High grade first printings have sold for over $4500. Middle, soon afterwards Gilbert Shelton brought Feds 'N' Heads to Print Mint and later joined Zap. It has sold for $1000. Right, famed poster artist Rick Griffin edited his own comic book, Tales From the Tube in 1973, with most of the Zap crew joining him. It currently brings over $200 in NM high grade.

ning through the 1970s. During this decade the San Francisco Bay Area was an intense hotbed of comix being issued without a comics code "seal of approval" from companies such as Rip Off Press, Last Gasp, San Francisco Comic Book Company, Company & Sons, Weirdom Publications, Star*Reach, and Comics & Comix. Kitchen Sink prospered for many years in Wisconsin and many small press comix publishers scattered across the USA and Canada - all of whom created the Direct Sales Market. There were hundreds of people involved with an independent mind producing & distributing alternative underground comix, creating the direct market. Phil Seuling introduced DC, Marvel and Warren to this already developed for five years, San Francisco Bay Area-based, comix business system as a "new" way of selling comics in late 1973, acknowedged by Phil himself in his last interview in *Will Eisner's Quarterly* #3, Summer 1984.

After DC and Marvel joined the DM in a serious way in 1979, the last 20 years have generally been called the "Modern Age", although there are hints of a new age emerging since the mid-'90s. The jury is still out on naming it.

The comic book store as an industry came into its own in the 1980s. Thousands of fans & entrepreneurs opened stores, fulfilling a life's dream for many of them - fueled by a vibrant speculator's market which lasted until the early 1990s, its last hurrah being when DC "killed" Superman in 1992. The comic book marketplace has been rebuilding ever since. Much of that growth has been outside the super hero genre.

In each of the preceding eras, however, the secret for collectors has remained the same: buy what you enjoy. We did, and we are still collectors today! *Portions excerpted from* **Comics Archeology 101** *© 2006 Robert L. Beerbohm, a detailed, heavily researched book in progress covering the more than 160 year history of the American comic book business. You may contact him thru his web site at* www.BLBComics.com

Left, Conan #1, Oct. 1970, by Roy Thomas and Barry Windsor-Smith intro'd the sword & sorcery genre. Middle, StarReach #1, April 1974, published by Mike Friedrich, was the first comic book directed specifically at comic book stores. Right, Giant-Size X-Men #1, Summer, 1975, introduced the new X-team, which later on revolutionized the comic book store system with its phenomenal sales once Chris Claremont and John Byrne teamed up on the title.

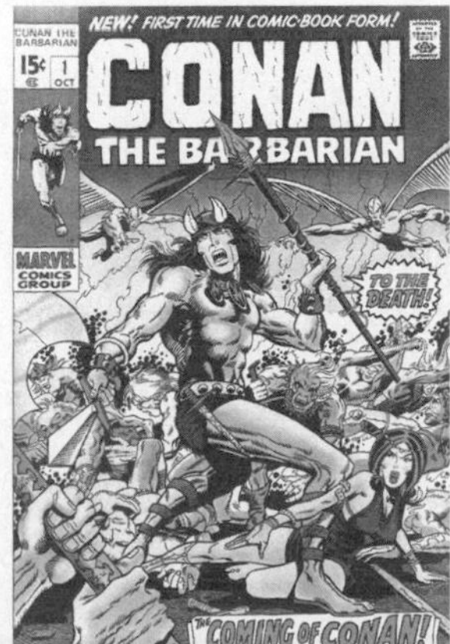

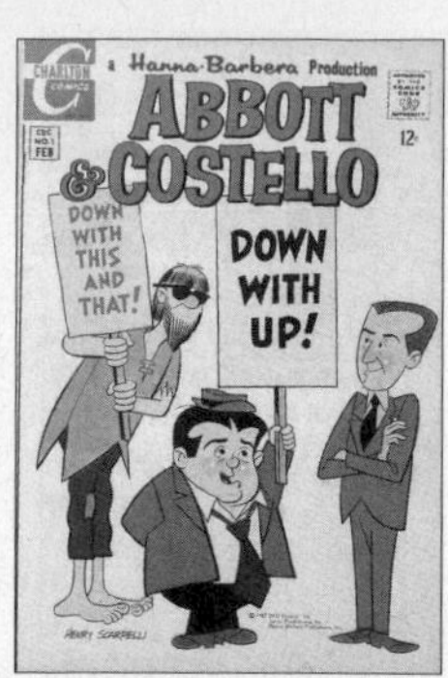

Abbott & Costello #1 © RKO & H-B

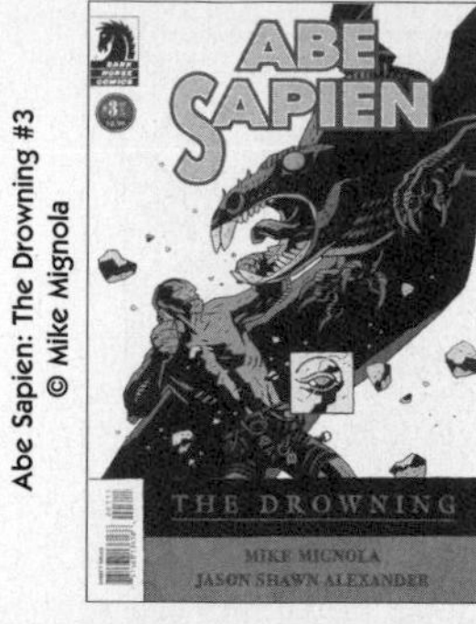

Abe Sapien: The Drowning #3 © Mike Mignola

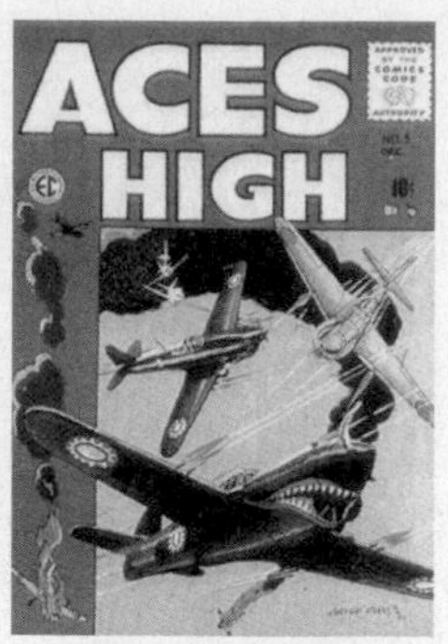

Aces High #5 © WMG

	GD 2.0	VG 4.0	FN 6.0	VF 8.0	VF/NM 9.0	NM- 9.2

The correct title listing for each comic book can be determined by consulting the indicia (publication data) on the beginning interior pages of the comic. The official title is determined by those words of the title in capital letters only, and not by what is on the cover. Titles are listed in this book as if they were one word, ignoring spaces, hyphens, and apostrophes, to make finding titles easier. Exceptions are made in rare cases. Comic books listed should be assumed to be in color unless noted "B&W".

Comic publishers are invited to send us sample copies for possible inclusion in future guides.

PRICING IN THIS GUIDE: Prices for **GD 2.0** (Good), **VG 4.0** (Very Good), **FN 6.0** (Fine), **VF 8.0** (Very Fine), **VF/NM 9.0** (Very Fine/Near Mint),and **NM– 9.2** (Near Mint–) are listed in whole U.S. dollars except for prices below $7 which show dollars and cents. **The minimum price listed is $2.25**, the cover price for current new comics. Many books listed at this price can be found in $1.00 boxes at conventions and dealers stores.

A-1 (See A-One)

ABADAZAD
CrossGen (Code 6): Mar, 2004 - No. 3, May, 2004 ($2.95)

	GD	VG	FN	VF	VF/NM	NM-
1-3-Ploog-a/c; DeMatteis-s						3.00
1-2nd printing with new cover						3.00

ABBIE AN' SLATS (...With Becky No. 1-4) (See Comics On Parade, Fight for Love, Giant Comics Edition 2, Giant Comics Editions #1, Sparkler Comics, Tip Topper, Treasury of Comics, & United Comics)
United Features Syndicate: 1940; March, 1948 - No. 4, Aug, 1948 (Reprints)

	GD	VG	FN	VF	VF/NM	NM-
Single Series 25 ('40)	40	80	120	240	390	540
Single Series 28	34	68	102	198	319	440
1 (1948)	17	34	51	98	154	210
2-4: 3-r/Sparkler #68-72	10	20	30	58	79	100

ABBOTT AND COSTELLO (...Comics)(See Giant Comics Editions #1 & Treasury of Comics)
St. John Publishing Co.: Feb, 1948 - No. 40, Sept, 1956 (Mort Drucker-a in most issues)

	GD	VG	FN	VF	VF/NM	NM-
1	60	120	180	378	639	900
2	35	70	105	203	327	450
3-9 (#8, 8/49; #9, 2/50)	22	44	66	129	207	285
10-Son of Sinbad story by Kubert (new)	26	52	78	154	247	340
11,13-20 (#11, 10/50; #13, 8/51; #15, 12/52)	15	30	45	94	147	200
12-Movie issue	17	34	51	98	154	215
21-30: 28-r/#8. 29,30-Painted-c	13	26	39	74	105	135
31-40: 33,38-Reprints	10	20	30	56	76	95
3-D #1 (11/53, 25¢)-Infinity-c	32	64	96	186	298	410

ABBOTT AND COSTELLO (TV)
Charlton Comics: Feb, 1968 - No. 22, Aug, 1971 (Hanna-Barbera)

	GD	VG	FN	VF	VF/NM	NM-
1	8	16	24	54	90	125
2	4	8	12	28	44	60
3-10	4	8	12	22	34	45
11-22	3	6	9	18	27	35

ABC (See America's Best TV Comics)

ABC: A-Z (one-shots)
America's Best Comics: Nov, 2005 - Present ($3.99, one-shots)

	GD	VG	FN	VF	VF/NM	NM-
... Greyshirt and Cobweb (1/06) character bios; Veitch-s/a; Gebbie-a; Dodson-c						4.00
... Terra Obscura and Splash Brannigan (3/06) character bios; Barta-a; Dodson-c						4.00
... Tom Strong and Jack B. Quick (11/05) character bios; Sprouse-a; Nowlan-a; Dodson-c						4.00
... Top Ten and Teams (7/06) character bios; Ha & Cannon-a; Veitch-a; Dodson-c						4.00

ABE SAPIEN... (Hellboy character)
Dark Horse Comics

	GD	VG	FN	VF	VF/NM	NM-
...: Drums of the Dead (3/98, $2.95) 1-Thompson-a. Hellboy back-up; Mignola-s/a/c						3.00
...: The Drowning (2/08 - No. 5, 6/08, $2.99) 1-5-Mignola-s/c; Alexander-a						3.00

A. BIZARRO
DC Comics: Jul, 1999 - No. 4, Oct, 1999 (2.50, limited series)

	GD	VG	FN	VF	VF/NM	NM-
1-4-Gerber-s/Bright-a						2.50

ABOMINATIONS (See Hulk)
Marvel Comics: Dec, 1996 - No. 3, Feb, 1997 (1.50, limited series)

	GD	VG	FN	VF	VF/NM	NM-
1-3-Future Hulk storyline						2.50

ABRAHAM LINCOLN LIFE STORY (See Dell Giants)

ABRAHAM STONE
Marvel Comics (Epic): July, 1995 - No. 2, Aug, 1995 ($6.95, limited series)

	GD	VG	FN	VF	VF/NM	NM-
1,2-Joe Kubert-s/a						7.00

ABSENT-MINDED PROFESSOR, THE
Dell Publishing Co.: Apr, 1961 (Disney)

	GD	VG	FN	VF	VF/NM	NM-
Four Color #1199-Movie, photo-c	8	16	24	56	93	130

ABSOLUTE VERTIGO
DC Comics (Vertigo): Winter, 1995 (99¢, mature)

	GD	VG	FN	VF	VF/NM	NM-
nn-1st app. Preacher. Previews upcoming titles including Jonah Hex: Riders of the Worm, The Invisibles (King Mob), The Eaters, Ghostdancing & Preacher	1	2	3	5	7	9

ABYSS, THE (Movie)
Dark Horse Comics: June, 1989 - No. 2, July, 1989 ($2.25, limited series)

	GD	VG	FN	VF	VF/NM	NM-
1,2-Adaptation of film; Kaluta & Moebius-a						3.00

ACCELERATE
DC Comics (Vertigo): Aug, 2000 - No. 4, Nov, 2000 ($2.95, limited series)

	GD	VG	FN	VF	VF/NM	NM-
1-4-Pander Bros.-a/Kadrey-s						3.00

ACCLAIM ADVENTURE ZONE
Acclaim Books: 1997 ($4.50, digest size)

	GD	VG	FN	VF	VF/NM	NM-
1-Short stories of Turok, Troublemakers, Ninjak and others						4.50

ACE COMICS
David McKay Publications: Apr, 1937 - No. 151, Oct-Nov, 1949 (All contain some newspaper strip reprints)

	GD	VG	FN	VF	VF/NM	NM-
1-Jungle Jim by Alex Raymond, Blondie, Ripley's Believe It Or Not, Krazy Kat begin (1st app. of each)	324	648	972	2203	3852	5500
2	95	190	285	599	1012	1425
3-5	63	126	189	397	674	950
6-10	47	94	141	291	486	680
11-The Phantom begins (1st app., 2/38) (in brown costume)	82	164	246	517	871	1225
12-20	40	80	120	235	380	525
21-25,27-30	35	70	105	203	327	450
26-Origin & 1st app. Prince Valiant (5/39); begins series?	103	206	309	649	1100	1550
31-40: 37-Krazy Kat ends	26	50	75	147	236	325
41-60	19	38	57	109	172	235
61-64,66-76-(7/43; last 68 pgs.)	15	30	45	94	147	200
65-(8/42)-Flag-c	19	38	57	109	172	235
77-84 (3/44; all 60 pgs.)	14	28	42	80	115	150
85-99 (52 pgs.)	12	24	36	69	97	125
100 (7/45; last 52 pgs.)	14	28	42	80	115	150
101-134: 128-(11/47)-Brick Bradford begins. 134-Last Prince Valiant (all 36 pgs.)	10	20	30	56	76	95
135-151: 135-(6/48)-Lone Ranger begins	9	18	27	52	69	85

ACE KELLY (See Tops Comics & Tops In Humor)

ACE KING (See Adventures of Detective...)

ACES
Acme Press (Eclipse): Apr, 1988 - No. 5, Dec, 1988 ($2.95, B&W, magazine)

	GD	VG	FN	VF	VF/NM	NM-
1-5						3.00

ACES HIGH
E.C. Comics: Mar-Apr, 1955 - No. 5, Nov-Dec, 1955

	GD	VG	FN	VF	VF/NM	NM-
1-Not approved by code	22	44	66	176	281	385
2	13	26	39	104	162	220
3-5	11	22	33	88	144	200

NOTE: *All have stories by* ***Davis, Evans, Krigstein,*** *and* ***Wood. Evans*** *c-1-5.*

ACES HIGH
Gemstone Publishing: Apr, 1999 - No. 5, Aug, 1999 ($2.50)

	GD	VG	FN	VF	VF/NM	NM-
1-5-Reprints E.C. issues						2.50
Annual 1 ($13.50) r/#1-5						13.50

ACME NOVELTY LIBRARY, THE
Fantagraphics Books: Winter 1993-94 - Present (quarterly, various sizes)

	GD	VG	FN	VF	VF/NM	NM-
1-Introduces Jimmy Corrigan; Chris Ware-s/a in all	1	3	4	6	8	10
1-2nd and later printings						4.00
2,3: 2-Quimby						6.00
4-Sparky's Best Comics & Stories	1	2	3	4	5	7
5-12: Jimmy Corrigan in all						5.00
13,15-($10.95-c)						11.00
14-($12.95-c) Concludes Jimmy Corrigan saga						13.00
16-($15.95, hardcover) Rusty Brown						16.00
17-($16.95, hardcover) Rusty Brown						17.00

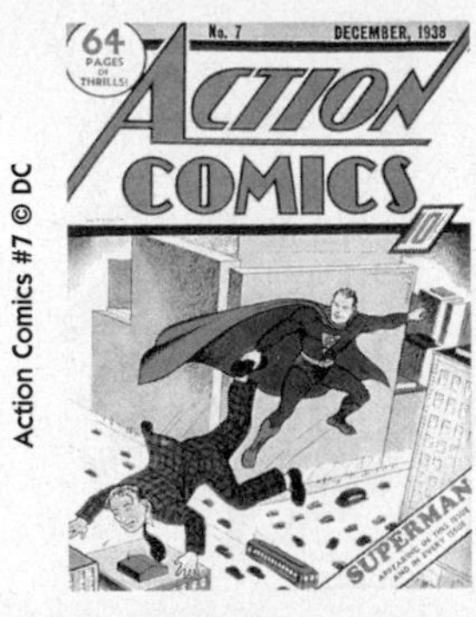

Action Comics #7 © DC

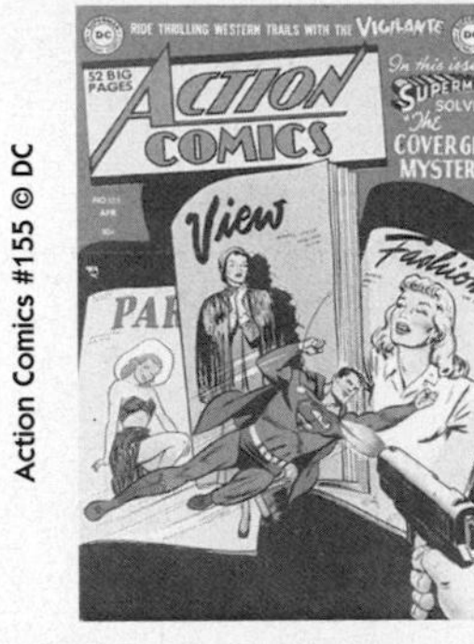

Action Comics #155 © DC

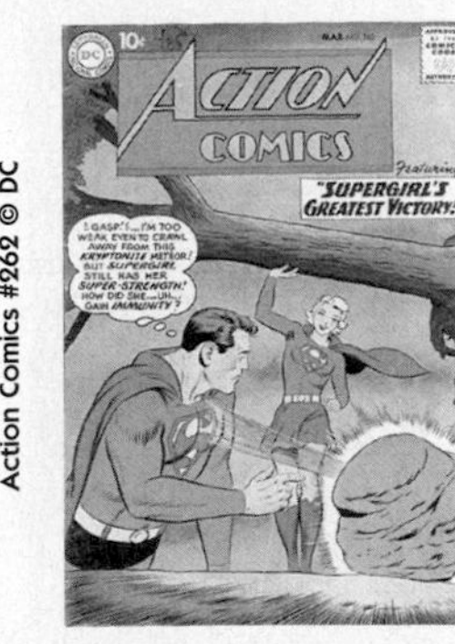

Action Comics #262 © DC

GD VG FN VF VF/NM NM-
2.0 4.0 6.0 8.0 9.0 9.2

18-($17.95, hardcover) 18.00
Jimmy Corrigan, The Smartest Kid on Earth (2000, Pantheon Books, Hardcover, $27.50, 380 pgs.) Collects Jimmy Corrigan stories; folded dust jacket 27.50
Jimmy Corrigan, The Smartest Kid on Earth (2003, Softcover, $17.95) 18.00
NOTE: *Multiple printings exist for most issues.*

ACROSS THE UNIVERSE: THE DC UNIVERSE STORIES OF ALAN MOORE (Also see DC Universe: The Stories of Alan Moore)
DC Comics: 2003 ($19.95, TPB)
nn Reprints selected Moore stories from '85-'87; Superman, Batman, Swamp Thing app. 20.00

ACTION ADVENTURE (War) (Formerly Real Adventure)
Gillmor Magazines: V1#2, June, 1955 - No. 4, Oct, 1955
V1#2-4 6 12 18 29 36 42

ACTION COMICS (...Weekly #601-642) (Also see The Comics Magazine #1, More Fun #14-17 & Special Edition) (Also see Promotional Comics section)
National Periodical Publ./Detective Comics/DC Comics: 6/38 - No. 583, 9/86; No. 584, 1/87 - Present

1-Origin & 1st app. Superman by Siegel & Shuster, Marco Polo, Tex Thompson, Pep Morgan, Chuck Dawson & Scoop Scanlon; 1st app. Zatara & Lois Lane; Superman story missing 4 pgs. which were included when reprinted in Superman #1; Clark Kent works for Daily Star; story continued in #2 45,000 90,000 135,000 300,000 525,000 750,000
1-Reprint, Oversize 13-1/2x10". **WARNING:** This comic is an exact reprint of the original except for its size. DC published it in 1974 with a second cover titling it as a Famous First Edition. There have been many reported cases of the outer cover being removed and the interior sold as the original edition. The reprint with the new outer cover removed is practically worthless. See Famous First Edition for value.
2-O'Mealia non-Superman covers thru #6 4400 8800 13,200 32,500 53,750 75,000
3 (Scarce)-Superman apps. in costume in only one panel 2824 5648 8472 20,898 34,449 48,000
4-6: 6-1st Jimmy Olsen (called office boy) 1647 3294 4941 12,188 19,971 28,000
7-2nd Superman cover 4235 8470 12,705 31,339 51,070 72,000
8,9 1059 2118 3177 7937 12,919 18,000
10-3rd Superman cover by Siegel & Shuster; splash panel used as cover art for Superman #1 2470 4940 7410 18,278 30,139 42,000
11,14: 1st X-Ray Vision? 14-Clip Carson begins, ends #41; Zatara-c 539 1078 1617 3881 6791 9700
12-Has 1 panel Batman ad for Det. #27 (5/39); Zatara sci-fi cover 583 1166 1749 4198 7349 10,500
13-Shuster Superman-c; last Scoop Scanlon 1025 2050 3075 7700 13,850 20,000
15-Guardineer Superman-c; has ad for Detective Comics #27 778 1556 2334 5602 9801 14,000
16 411 822 1233 2795 4898 7000
17-Superman cover; last Marco Polo 639 1278 1917 4601 8051 11,500
18-Origin 3 Aces; has a 1 panel ad for New York World's Fair 1939 at the end of the Superman story (ad also in #19) 411 822 1223 2795 4898 7000
19-Superman covers begin 600 1200 1800 4320 7560 10,800
20-The 'S' left off Superman's chest; Clark Kent works at 'Daily Star' 572 1144 1716 4118 7209 10,300
21-Has 2 ads for More Fun #52 (1st Spectre) 359 718 1077 2441 4271 6100
22,24,25: 24-Kent at Daily Planet. 25-Last app. Gargantua T. Potts, Tex Thompson's sidekick 353 706 1059 2400 4200 6000
23-1st app. Luthor (w/red hair) & Black Pirate; Black Pirate by Moldoff; 1st mention of The Daily Planet (4/40)-Has 1 panel ad for Spectre in More Fun 806 1612 2418 5803 10,152 14,500
26-28,30 306 612 918 2081 3641 5200
29-1st Lois Lane-c (10/40) 341 682 1023 2319 4060 5800
31,32: 32-Intro/1st app. Krypto Ray Gun in Superman story by Burnley 213 426 639 1342 2271 3200
33-Origin Mr. America; Superman by Burnley; has half page ad for All Star Comics #3 220 440 660 1386 2343 3300
34,35,38,39 207 414 621 1304 2202 3100
36, 40: 36-Classic robot-c. 40-(9/41)-Intro/1st app. Star Spangled Kid & Stripesy; Jerry Siegel photo 215 430 645 1355 2290 3225
37-Origin Congo Bill 210 420 630 1323 227 3150
41 187 374 561 1178 1989 2800
42-1st app./origin Vigilante; Bob Daley becomes Fat Man; origin Mr. America's magic flying carpet; The Queen Bee & Luthor app; Black Pirate ends; not in #41 213 426 639 1342 2271 3200
43-46,48-50: 44-Fat Man's i.d. revealed to Mr. America. 45-1st app. Stuff (Vigilante's oriental sidekick) 173 346 519 1090 1845 2600
47-1st Luthor cover in comics (4/42) 253 506 759 1594 2697 3800
51-1st app. The Prankster 183 366 549 1153 1952 2750
52-Fat Man & Mr. America become the Ameri-commandos; origin Vigilante retold; classic Superman and back-ups-c 200 400 600 1260 2130 3000
53-56,59,60: 56-Last Fat Man. 59-Kubert Vigilante begins?, ends #70. 60-First app. Lois Lane as Super-woman 140 280 420 882 1491 2100
57-2nd Lois Lane-c in Action (3rd anywhere, 2/43) 160 320 480 1008 1704 2400
58-"Slap a Jap-c" 160 320 480 1008 1704 2400
61-Historic Atomic Radiation-c (6/43) 147 294 441 926 1563 2200
62,63-Japan war-c. 63-Last 3 Aces 140 280 420 882 1491 2100
64-Intro Toyman 147 294 441 926 1563 2200
65-70 117 234 351 737 1244 1750
71-79: 74-Last Mr. America 93 186 279 586 993 1400
80-2nd app. & 1st Mr. Mxyztplk-c (1/45) 123 246 369 775 1313 1850
81-88,90: 83-Intro Hocus & Pocus 83 166 249 523 887 1250
89-Classic rainbow cover 87 174 261 548 924 1300
91-99: 93-X-Mas-c. 99-1st small logo (8/46) 77 154 231 481 816 1150
100 113 226 339 712 1206 1700
101-Nuclear explosion-c (10/46) 147 294 441 926 1563 2200
102-107,109-120: 102-Mxyztplk-c. 105,117-X-Mas-c 70 140 210 441 746 1050
108-Classic molten metal-c 78 156 234 491 833 1175
121,122,124-126,128-140: 135,136,138-Zatara by Kubert 65 130 195 410 693 975
123-(8/48) 1st time Superman flies, not leaps 66 132 198 416 701 985
127-Vigilante by Kubert; Tommy Tomorrow begins (12/48, see Real Fact #6) 67 134 201 422 711 1000
141-157,159-161: 151-Luthor/Mr. Mxyztplk/Prankster team-up. 156-Lois as Super Woman. 161- Last 52 pgs. 62 124 186 391 658 925
158-Origin Superman retold 127 254 381 800 1350 1900
162-180: 168,176-Used in **POP**, pg. 90. 173-Robot-c 58 116 174 365 620 875
181-201: 191-Intro. Janu in Congo Bill. 198-Last Vigilante. 201-Last pre-code issue 55 110 165 347 586 825
202-220,232: 212-(1/56)-Includes 1956 Superman calendar that is part of story. 232-1st Curt Swan-c in Action 50 100 150 310 518 725
221-231,233-240: 221-1st S.A. issue. 224-1st Golden Gorilla story. 228-(5/57)-Kongorilla in Congo Bill story (Congorilla try-out) 41 82 123 266 428 600
241,243-251: 241-Batman x-over. 248-Origin/1st app. Congorilla; Congo Bill renamed Congorilla. 251-Last Tommy Tomorrow 38 76 114 226 363 500
242-Origin & 1st app. Brainiac (7/58); 1st mention of Shrunken City of Kandor 160 320 480 1400 2700 4000
252-Origin & 1st app. Supergirl (5/59); 1st app. Metallo 180 360 540 1575 3038 4500
253-2nd app. Supergirl 57 114 171 359 605 850
254-1st meeting of Bizarro & Superman-c/story 41 82 123 253 419 585
255-1st Bizarro Lois Lane-c/story & both Bizarros leave Earth to make Bizarro World; 3rd app. Supergirl 37 74 111 218 352 485
256-260: 259-Red Kryptonite used 25 50 75 147 236 325
261-1st X-Kryptonite which gave Streaky his powers; last Congorilla in Action; origin & 1st app. Streaky The Super Cat 28 56 84 162 261 360
262,264-266,268-270 22 44 66 127 204 280
263-Origin Bizarro World (continues in #264) 28 56 84 162 261 360
267(8/60)-3rd Legion app; 1st app. Chameleon Boy, Colossal Boy, & Invisible Kid, 1st app. of Supergirl as Superwoman. 50 100 150 310 518 725
271-275,277-282: 274-Lois Lane as Superwoman; 282-Last 10¢ issue 19 38 57 112 176 240
276(5/61)-6th Legion app; 1st app. Brainiac 5, Phantom Girl, Triplicate Girl, Bouncing Boy, Sun Boy, & Shrinking Violet; Supergirl joins Legion 33 66 99 196 316 435
283(12/61)-Legion of Super-Villains app. 1st 12¢ 13 26 39 97 171 245
284(1/62)-Mon-el app. 13 26 39 97 171 245
285(2/62)-12th Legion app; Brainiac 5 cameo; Supergirl's existence revealed to world; JFK & Jackie cameos 18 36 54 130 240 350
286-287,289-292,294-299: 286(3/62)-Legion of Super Villains app. 287(4/62)-15th Legion app. (cameo). 289(6/62)-16th Legion app. (Adult); Lightning Man & Saturn Woman's marriage 1st revealed. 290(7/62)-Legion app. (cameo); Phantom Girl app. 1st Supergirl emergency squad. 291-1st meeting Supergirl & Mr. Mxyzptlk. 292-2nd app. Superhorse (see Adv.#293). 297-Mon-el app. 298-Legion cameo 11 22 33 79 140 200
288-Mon-el app.; r-origin Supergirl 12 24 36 82 146 210
293-Origin Comet (Superhorse) 14 28 42 99 175 250
300-(5/63) 13 26 39 90 160 230
301-303,305,307,308,310-312,315-320: 307-Saturn Girl app. 317-Death of Nor-Kan of Kandor. 319-Shrinking Violet app. 8 16 24 58 97 135
304,306,313: 304-Origin/1st app. Black Flame (9/63). 306-Brainiac 5, Mon-el app. 313-Batman app. 9 18 27 60 100 140
309-(2/64)-Legion app.; Batman & Robin-c & cameo; JFK app. (he died 11/22/63; on stands last week of Dec, 1963) 9 18 27 61 103 145
314-Retells origin Supergirl; J.L.A. x-over 9 18 27 60 100 140
321-333,335-339: 336-Origin Akvar (Flamebird) 7 14 21 47 76 105
334-Giant G-20; origin Supergirl, Streaky, Superhorse & Legion (all-r)

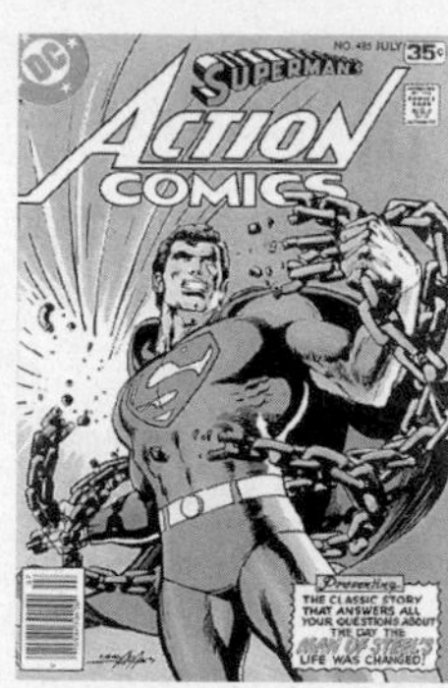

Action Comics #485 © DC

Action Comics #812 (sketch variant) © DC

Action Comics #863 © DC

	GD	VG	FN	VF	VF/NM	NM-
	2.0	4.0	6.0	8.0	9.0	9.2

11 22 33 79 140 200
340-Origin, 1st app. of the Parasite; 2 pg. pin-up 7 14 21 50 83 115
341,344,350,358: 341-Batman app. in Supergirl back-up story. 344-Batman x-over. 350-Batman, Green Arrow & Green Lantern app. in Supergirl back-up story. 358-Superboy meets Supergirl 6 12 18 41 66 90
342,343,345,346,348,349,351-357,359: 342-UFO story. 345-Allen Funt/Candid Camera story. 6 12 18 39 62 85
347,360-Giant Supergirl G-33,G-45; 347-Origin Comet-r plus Bizarro story. 360-Legion app.-r; r/origin Supergirl 8 16 24 56 93 130
361-364,367-372,374-378: 361-2nd app. Parasite. 362-366-Leper/Death story. 370-New facts about Superman's origin. 376-Last Supergirl in Action; last 12¢-c. 377-Legion begins (thru #392) 5 10 15 32 51 70
365,366: 365-JLA & Legion app. 366-JLA app. 5 10 15 34 55 75
373-Giant Supergirl G-57; Legion-r 8 16 24 52 86 120
379-399,401: 388-Sgt. Rock app. 392-Batman-c/app.; last Legion in Action; Saturn Girl gets new costume. 393-401-All Superman issues 3 6 9 19 29 38
400 4 8 12 22 34 45
402-Last 15¢ issue; Superman vs. Supergirl duel 3 6 9 19 29 38
403-413: All 52 pg. issues. 411-Origin Eclipso-(r). 413-Metamorpho begins, ends #418 3 6 9 19 29 38
414-424: 419-Intro. Human Target. 421-Intro Capt. Strong; Green Arrow begins. 422,423-Origin Human Target 2 4 6 9 13 16
425-Neal Adams-a(p); The Atom begins 3 6 9 14 19 24
426-431,433-436,438,439 2 4 6 8 10 12
432-1st Bronze Age Toyman app. (2/74) 2 4 6 13 18 22
437,443-(100 pg. Giants) 4 8 12 24 37 50
440-1st Grell-a on Green Arrow 2 4 6 9 13 16
441,442,444-448: 441-Grell-a on Green Arrow continues 1 3 4 6 8 10
449-(68 pgs.) 2 4 6 9 13 16
450-465,467-483,486,489-499: 454-Last Atom. 456-Grell Jaws-c. 458-Last Green Arrow. 1 2 3 4 5 7
466,485,487,488: 466-Batman, Flash app. 485-Adams-c. 487,488-(44 pgs.). 487-Origin & 1st app. Microwave Man; origin Atom retold 1 2 3 5 7 9
481-483,485-492,495-499,501-505,507,508-Whitman variants (low print run; none show issue # on cover) 1 3 4 6 8 10
484-Earth II Superman & Lois Lane wed; 40th anniversary issue(6/78) 1 3 4 6 8 10
484-Variant includes 3-D Superman punchout doll in cello. pack; 4 different inserts; Canadian promo?) 3 6 9 14 20 25
500-($1.00, 68 pgs.)-Infinity-c; Superman life story retold; shows Legion statues in museum 1 3 4 6 8 10
501-543,545,547-551: 511-514-Airwave II solo stories. 513-The Atom begins. 517-Aquaman begins; ends #541. 521-1st app. The Vixen. 532,536-New Teen Titans cameo. 535,536-Omega Men app. 551-Starfire becomes Red-Star 4.00
504,505,507,508-Whitman variants (no cover price) 1 3 4 6 8 10
544-(6/83, Mando paper, 68 pgs.)-45th Anniversary issue; origins new Luthor & Brainiac; Omega Men cameo; Shuster-a (pin-up); article by Siegel 1 2 3 4 5 7
546-J.L.A., New Teen Titans app. 1 2 3 5 6 8
552,553-Animal Man-c & app. (2/84 & 3/84) 5.00
554-582 3.00
583-Alan Moore scripts; last Earth 1 Superman story (cont'd from Superman #423) 2 4 6 8 10 12
584-Byrne-a begins; New Teen Titans app. 6.00
585-599: 586-Legends x-over. 596-Millennium x-over; Spectre app. 598-1st Checkmate 3.00
600-($2.50, 84 pgs., 5/88) 6.00
601-610,619-642: (#601-642 are weekly issues) ($1.50, 52 pgs.) 601-Re-intro The Secret Six; death of Katma Tui 3.00
611-618: 611-614-Catwoman stories (new costume in #611). 613-618-Nightwing stories 3.00
643-Superman & monthly issues begin again; Perez-c/a/scripts begin; swipes cover to Superman #1 4.00
644-649,651-661,663-673,675-683: 645-1st app. Maxima. 654-Part 3 of Batman storyline. 655-Free extra 8 pgs. 660-Death of Lex Luthor. 661-Begin $1.00-c. 667-($1.75, 52 pgs.). 675-Deathstroke cameo. 679-Last $1.00 issue. 683-Doomsday cameo 2.50
650-($1.50, 52 pgs.)-Lobo cameo (last panel) 3.00
662-Clark Kent reveals i.d. to Lois Lane; story cont'd in Superman #53 4.00
674-Supergirl logo & c/story (reintro) 6.00
683-685-2nd & 3rd printings 2.50
684-Doomsday battle issue 3.00
685,686-Funeral for a Friend issues; Supergirl app. 3.00
687-($1.95)-Collector's Ed.w/die-cut-c 3.00
687-($1.50)-Newsstand Edition with mini-poster 2.50

	GD	VG	FN	VF	VF/NM	NM-
	2.0	4.0	6.0	8.0	9.0	9.2

688-699,701-703-($1.50): 688-Guy Gardner-c/story. 697-Bizarro-c/story. 703-(9/94)-Zero Hour 2.50
695-($2.50)-Collector's Edition w/embossed foil-c 3.00
700-($2.95, 68 pgs.)-Fall of Metropolis Pt 1, Guice-a; Pete Ross marries Lana Lang and Smallville flashbacks with Curt Swan art & Murphy Anderson inks 3.00
700-Platinum 15.00
700-Gold 18.00
0(10/94), 704(11/94)-710-719,721-731: 710-Begin $1.95-c. 714-Joker app. 719-Batman-c/app. 721-Mr. Mxyzptlk app. 723-Dave Johnson-c. 727-Final Night x-over. 2.50
720-Lois breaks off engagement w/Clark 3.00
720-2nd print. 2.50
732-749,751-767: 732-New powers. 733-New costume, Ray app. 738-Immonen-s/a(p) begins. 741-Legion app. 744-Millennium Giants x-over. 745-747-70's-style Superman vs. Prankster. 753-JLA-c/app. 757-Hawkman-c. 760-1st Encantadora. 761-Wonder Woman app. 765-Joker & Harley-c/app. 766-Batman-c/app. 2.50
750-($2.95) 3.00
768,769,771-774: 768-Begin $2.25-c; Marvel Family-c/app. 771-Nightwing-c/app. 772,773-Ra's al Ghul app. 774-Martian Manhunter-c/app. 2.50
770-($3.50) Conclusion of Emperor Joker x-over 3.50
775-($3.75) Bradstreet-c; intro. The Elite 3.75
776-799: 776-Farewell to Krypton; Rivoche-c. 780-782-Our Worlds at War x-over. 781-Hippolyta and Major Lane killed. 782-War ends. 784-Joker: Last Laugh; Batman & Green Lantern app. 793-Return to Krypton. 795-The Elite app. 798-Van Fleet-c 2.50
800-(4/03, $3.95) Struzan painted-c; guest artists include Ross, Jim Lee, Jurgens, Sale 4.00
801-811: 801-Raney-a. 809-The Creeper app. 811-Mr. Majestic app. 2.50
812-Godfall part 1; Turner-c; Caldwell-a(p) 4.00
812-2nd printing; B&W sketch-c by Turner 3.00
813-Godfall pt. 4; Turner-c; Caldwell-a(p) 3.00
814-824, 826-828,830-836: 814-Reis-a/Art Adams-c; Darkseid app.; begin $2.50-c. 815,816-Teen Titans-c/app. 820-Doomsday app. 826-Capt. Marvel app. 827-Byrne-c/a begin. 831-Villains United tie-in. 835-Livewire app. 836-Infinite Crisis; revised origin 2.50
825-($2.99, 40 pgs.) Doomsday app. 3.00
829-Omac Project x-over Sacrifice pt. 2 5.00
829-(2nd printing) red tone cover 2.50
837-843-One Year Later; powers return after Infinite Crisis; Johns & Busiek-s 3.00
844-Donner & Johns-s/Adam Kubert-a/c begin; brown-toned cover 4.00
844-Andy Kubert variant-c 5.00
844-2nd printing with red-toned Adam Kubert cover 3.00
845-849,851-857: 845-Bizarro-c/app.; re-intro. General Zod, Ursa & Non. 846-Jax-Ur app. 847-849-No Kubert-a. 851-Kubert-a/c. 855-857-Bizarro app.; Powell-a/c 3.00
850-($3.99) Supergirl and LSH app., origin re-told; Guedes-a/c 4.00
858-($3.50) Legion of Super-Heroes app.; 1st meeting re-told; Johns-s/Frank-a/c 4.00
858-Variant-c (Superman & giant Brainiac robot) by Frank 5.00
858-Second printing with regular cover with red background instead of yellow 3.00
859-867: 859-863-Legion of Super-Heroes app.; var-c on each (859-Andy Kubert. 860-Lightle. 861-Grell. 862-Giffen. 863-Frank) 864-Batman and Lightning Lad app. 866-Brainiac returns 3.00
#1,000,000 (11/98) Gene Ha-c; 853rd Century x-over 2.50
Annual 1-6 ('87-'94, $2.95)-1-Art Adams-c/a(p); Batman app. 2-Perez-c/a(i). 3-Armageddon 2001. 4-Eclipso vs. Shazam. 5-Bloodlines; 1st app. Loose Cannon. 6-Elseworlds story 3.00
Annual 7,9 ('95, '97, $3.95) 7-Year One story. 9-Pulp Heroes sty 4.00
Annual 8 (1996, $2.95) Legends of the Dead Earth story 3.00
Annual 10 ('07, $3.99) Short stories by Johns & Donner and various incl. A. Adams, J. Kubert, Wight, Morales; origin of Phantom Zone, Mon-El; Metallo app.; Adam & Joe Kubert-c 4.00
Annual 11 (7/08, $4.99) Conclusion to General Zod story continued from #851; Kubert-a 5.00

NOTE:***Supergirl's** origin in 262, 280, 285, 291, 305, 309.* **N. Adams** *c-356, 358, 359, 361-364, 366, 367, 370-374, 377-379i, 398-400, 402, 404,405, 419p, 466, 468, 469, 473i, 485.* **Aparo** *a-642.* **Austin** *c/a-682i.* **Baily** *a-24, 25.* **Boring** *a-164, 194, 211, 223, 233, 241, 250, 261, 266-268, 346, 348, 352, 356, 357.* **Burnley** *a-28-33; c-48?, 53-55, 58, 59?, 60-63, 65, 66p, 67p, 70p, 71p, 79p, 82p, 84-86p, 90-92p, 93p?, 94p, 107p, 108p.* **Byrne** *a-584-598p, 599i, 600p; c-584-591, 596-600.* **Ditko** *a-642.* **Giffen** *a-560, 563, 565, 577, 579; c-539, 560, 563, 565, 577, 579.* **Grell** *a-440-442, 444-446, 450-452, 456-458; c-456.* **Guardineer** *a-24, 25; c-8, 11, 12, 14-16, 18. 25.* **Guice** *a(p)-676-681, 683-698, 700; c-683, 685, 686, 687(direct), 688-693i, 694-696, 697i, 698-700.* **Infantino** *a-642.* **Kaluta** *c-613.* **Bob Kane's** *Clip Carson-14-41.* **Gil Kane** *a-443r, 493r, 539-541, 544-546, 551-554, 601-605, 642; c-535p, 540, 541, 544p, 545-549, 551-554, 580, 627.* **Kirby** *c-638.* **Meskin** *a-42-121(most).* **Mignola** *a-600, Annual 2; c-c-614.* **Moldoff** *a-23-25, 443r.* **Mooney** *a-667p.* **Mortimer** *c-153, 154, 159-172, 174, 178-181, 184, 186-189, 191-193, 196, 200, 206.* **Orlando** *a-617p; c-621.* **Perez** *a-600i, 643-652p, Annual 2p; c-529p, 602, 643-651, Annual 2p.* **Quesada** *c-Annual 4p.* **Fred Ray** *c-34, 36-46, 50-52.* **Siegel & Shuster** *a-1-27.* **Paul Smith** *c-608.* **Starlin** *a-509; c-631.* **Leonard Starr** *a-597i(part),* **Staton** *a-525p, 526p, 531p, 535p, 536p.* **Swan/Moldoff** *c-281, 286, 287, 293, 298, 334.* **Thibert** *c-676, 677p, 678-681, 684.* **Toth** *a-406, 407, 413, 431; c-616.* **Tuska** *a-486p, 550.* **Williamson** *a-568i.* **Zeck** *c-Annual 5*

ACTION COMICS
DC Comics: (no date)

1-Ashcan comic, not distributed to newsstands, only for in-house use. Cover art is the rejected art to Detective Comics #2 and interior from Detective Comics #1.
A CGC certified 9.0 copy sold for $17,825 in 2002 and for $29,000 in 2008.

ACTION FORCE (Also see G.I. Joe European Missions)

Adam-12 #9 © GK

Adventure Comics #72 © DC

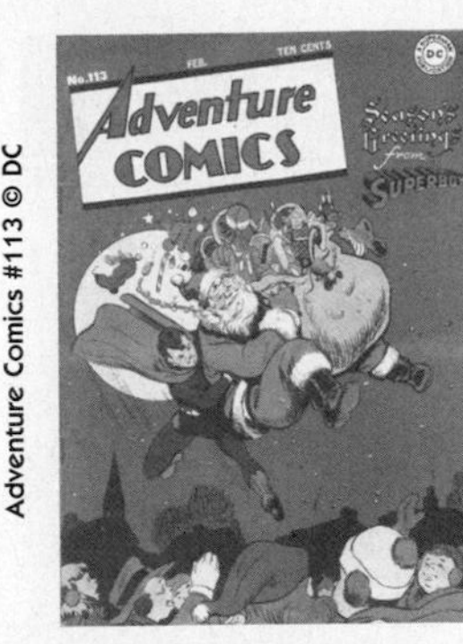

Adventure Comics #113 © DC

GD 2.0 | VG 4.0 | FN 6.0 | VF 8.0 | VF/NM 9.0 | NM- 9.2

Marvel Comics Ltd. (British): Mar, 1987 - No. 50, 1988 ($1.00, weekly, magazine)

1,3: British G.I. Joe series. 3-w/poster insert 1 2 3 5 6 8
2,4 6.00
5-10 4.00
11-50 2.50
...Special 1 (7/87) Summer holiday special; Snake Eyes-c/app. 1 2 3 5 6 8
...Special 2 (10/87) Winter special; 5.00

ACTION FUNNIES
DC Comics: 1938

nn - Ashcan comic, not distributed to newsstands, only for in house use. Cover art is Action Comics #3 and interior from Detective Comics #10. The Mallette/Brown copy in VG+ condition sold for $15,000 in 2005.

ACTION GIRL
Slave Labor Graphics: Oct, 1994 - Present ($2.50/$2.75/$2.95, B&W)

1-19: 4-Begin $2.75-c. 19-Begin $2.95-c 3.00
1-6 ($2.75, 2nd printings): All read 2nd Print in indicia. 1-(2/96). 2-(10/95). 3-(2/96). 4-(7/96). 5-(2/97). 6-(9/97) 2.75
1-4 ($2.75, 3rd printings): All read 3rd Print in indicia. 2.75

ACTION PLANET COMICS
Action Planet: 1996 - No. 3, Sept, 1997 ($3.95, B&W, 44 pgs.)

1-3: 1-Intro Monster Man by Mike Manley & other stories 4.00
Giant Size Action Planet Halloween Special (1998, $5.95, oversized) 6.00

ACTUAL CONFESSIONS (Formerly Love Adventures)
Atlas Comics (MPI): No. 13, Oct, 1952 - No. 14, Dec, 1952

13,14 9 18 27 47 61 75

ACTUAL ROMANCES (Becomes True Secrets #3 on?)
Marvel Comics (IPS): Oct, 1949 - No. 2, Jan, 1950 (52 pgs.)

1 14 28 42 80 115 150
2-Photo-c 10 20 30 54 72 90

ADAM AND EVE
Spire Christian Comics (Fleming H. Revell Co.): 1975,1978 (35¢/39¢/49¢)

nn-By Al Hartley 2 4 6 9 13 16

ADAM STRANGE (Also see Green Lantern #132, Mystery In Space #53 & Showcase #17)
DC Comics: 1990 - No. 3, 1990 ($3.95, 52 pgs, limited series, squarebound)

Book One - Three: Andy & Adam Kubert-c/a 4.00
...: The Man of Two Worlds (2003, $19.95, TPB) r/#1-3; sketch pages by Andy Kubert 20.00

ADAM STRANGE (Leads into the Rann/Thanagar War mini-series)
DC Comics: Nov, 2004 - No. 8, June, 2005 ($2.95, limited series)

1-8-Andy Diggle-s/Pascal Ferry-a/c. 1-Superman app. 3.00
...: Planet Heist TPB (2005, $19.99) r/series; sketch pages 20.00

ADAM-12 (TV)
Gold Key: Dec, 1973 - No. 10, Feb, 1976 (Photo-c)

1 6 12 18 43 69 95
2-10 4 8 12 22 34 45

ADDAMS FAMILY (TV cartoon)
Gold Key: Oct, 1974 - No. 3, Apr, 1975 (Hanna-Barbera)

1 8 16 24 54 90 125
2,3 6 12 18 37 59 80

ADLAI STEVENSON
Dell Publishing Co.: Dec, 1966

12-007-612-Life story; photo-c 4 8 12 22 34 45

ADOLESCENT RADIOACTIVE BLACK BELT HAMSTERS (See Clint)
Comic Castle/Eclipse Comics: 1986 - No. 9, Jan, 1988 ($1.50, B&W)

1-9: 1st & 2nd printings exist 2.50
1-Limited Edition 6.00
1-In 3-D (7/86), 2-4 ($2.50) 2.50
Massacre The Japanese Invasion #1 (8/89, $2.00) 2.50

ADOLESCENT RADIOACTIVE BLACK BELT HAMSTERS
Dynamite Entertainment: 2008 - No. 4, 2008 ($3.50, limited series)

1-4-Tom Nguyen-a/Keith Champagne-s; 2 covers by Nguyen and Oeming 3.50

ADRENALYNN (See The Tenth)
Image Comics: Aug, 1999 - No. 4, Feb, 2000 ($2.50)

1-4-Tony Daniel-s/Marty Egeland-a; origin of Adrenalynn 2.50

ADULT TALES OF TERROR ILLUSTRATED (See Terror Illustrated)

ADVANCED DUNGEONS & DRAGONS (Also see TSR Worlds)
DC Comics: Dec, 1988 - No. 36, Dec, 1991 (Newsstand #1 is Holiday, 1988-89) ($1.25-$1.75)

1-Based on TSR role playing game 4.00
2-36: 25-$1.75-c begins 2.50
Annual 1 (1990, $3.95, 68 pgs.) 4.00

ADVENTURE BOUND
Dell Publishing Co.: Aug, 1949

Four Color 239 6 12 18 39 62 85

ADVENTURE COMICS (Formerly New Adventure)(...Presents Dial H For Hero #479-490)
National Periodical Publications/DC Comics: No. 32, 11/38 - No. 490, 2/82; No. 491, 9/82 - No. 503, 9/83

32-Anchors Aweigh (ends #52), Barry O'Neil (ends #60, not in #33), Captain Desmo (ends #47), Dale Daring (ends #47), Federal Men (ends #70), The Golden Dragon (ends #36), Rusty & His Pals (ends #52) by Bob Kane, Todd Hunter (ends #38) and Tom Brent (ends #39) begin 430 860 1290 2408 3404 4400
33-38: 37-Cover used on Double Action #2 210 420 630 1176 1663 2150
39(6/39)- Jack Wood begins, ends #42; 1st mention of Marijuana in comics 210 420 630 1176 1663 2150
40-(Rare, 7/39, on stands 6/10/39)-The Sandman begins by Bert Christman (who died in WWII); believed to be 1st conceived story (see N.Y. World's Fair for 1st published app.); Socko Strong begins, ends #54 5450 10,800 16,200 40,500 72,750 105,000
41-O'Mealia shark-c 583 1166 1749 4198 7349 10,500
42,44-Sandman-c by Flessel. 44-Opium story 722 1444 2166 5198 9099 13,000
43,45: 45-Full page ad for Flash Comics #1 329 658 987 2237 3919 5600
46,47-Sandman covers by Flessel. 47-Steve Conrad Adventurer begins, ends #76 511 1022 1533 3679 6440 9200
48-Intro & 1st app. The Hourman by Bernard Baily; Baily-c (Hourman c-48,50,52-59) 2567 5134 7700 19,250 34,625 50,000
49,50: 50-Cotton Carver by Jack Lehti begins, ends #64 280 560 840 1764 2982 4200
51,60-Sandman-c: 51-Sandman-c by Flessel. 353 706 159 2400 4200 6000
52-59: 53-1st app. Jimmy "Minuteman" Martin & the Minutemen of America in Hourman; ends #78. 58-Paul Kirk Manhunter begins (1st app.), ends #72 243 486 729 1531 2591 3650
61-1st app. Starman by Jack Burnley (4/41); Starman c-61-72; Starman by Burnley in #61-80 1180 2360 3540 8850 15,925 23,000
62-65,67,68,70: 67-Origin & 1st app. The Mist; classic Burnley-c. 70-Last Federal Men 203 406 609 1279 2165 3050
66-Origin/1st app. Shining Knight (9/41) 247 494 741 1556 2628 3700
69-1st app. Sandy the Golden Boy (Sandman's sidekick) by Paul Norris (in a Bob Kane style); Sandman dons new costume 213 426 639 1342 2271 3200
71-Jimmy Martin becomes costumed aide to the Hourman; 1st app. Hourman's Miracle Ray machine 197 394 591 1241 2096 2950
72-1st Simon & Kirby Sandman (3/42, 1st DC work) 1000 2000 3000 7400 13,200 19,000
73-Origin Manhunter by Simon & Kirby; begin new series; Manhunter-c (scarce) 1267 2534 3800 9500 17,000 24,500
74-78,80: 74-Thorndyke replaces Jimmy, Hourman's assistant; new Sandman-c begin by S&K. 75-Thor app. by Kirby; 1st Kirby Thor (see Tales of the Unexpected #16). 77-Origin Genius Jones; Mist story. 80-Last S&K Manhunter & Burnley Starman 187 374 561 1178 1989 2800
79-Classic Manhunter-c 260 520 780 1638 2769 3900
81-90: 83-Last Hourman. 84-Mike Gibbs begins, ends #102 119 238 357 750 1268 1785
91-Last Simon & Kirby Sandman 110 220 330 693 1172 1650
92-99,101,102: 92-Last Manhunter. 101-Shining Knight origin retold. 102-Last Starman, Sandman, & Genius Jones; most-S&K-c (Genius Jones cont'd in More Fun #108) 97 194 291 611 1036 1460
100-S&K-c 132 264 396 832 1404 1975
103-Aquaman, Green Arrow, Johnny Quick & Superboy all move over from More Fun Comics #107; 8th app. Superboy; Superboy-c begin; 1st small logo (4/46) 317 634 951 1981 3391 4800
104 108 216 324 680 1153 1625
105-110 78 156 234 491 833 1175
111-120: 113-X-Mas-c 69 138 207 435 738 1040
121,122-126,128-130: 128-1st meeting Superboy & Lois Lane 62 124 186 391 658 925
127-Brief origin Shining Knight retold 63 126 189 397 669 940
131-141,143-149: 132-Shining Knight 1st return to King Arthur time; origin aide Sir Butch 53 106 159 330 553 775
142-Origin Shining Knight & Johnny Quick retold 55 110 165 347 586 825

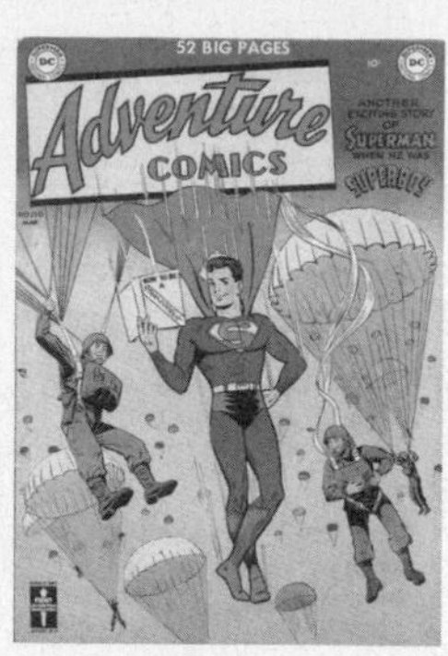

Adventure Comics #150 © DC

Adventure Comics #293 © DC

Adventure Comics #452 © DC

GD VG FN VF VF/NM NM-
2.0 4.0 6.0 8.0 9.0 9.2

150,151,153,155,157,159,161,163-All have 6 pg. Shining Knight stories by Frank Frazetta. 159-Origin Johnny Quick. 161-1st Lana Lang app. in this title 66 132 198 416 701 985
152,154,156,158,160,162,164-169: 166-Last Shining Knight. 168-Last 52 pg. issue 47 94 141 291 483 675
170-180 44 88 132 273 454 635
181-199: 189-B&W and color illo in **POP** 42 84 126 260 435 610
200 (5/54) 55 110 165 347 584 820
201-208: 207-Last Johnny Quick (not in 205) 40 80 120 244 397 550
209-Last pre-code issue; origin Speedy 41 82 123 249 410 570
210-1st app. Krypto (Superdog)-c/story (3/55) 310 620 930 2400 4450 6500
211-213,215-219 38 76 114 226 363 500
214-2nd app. Krypto 63 126 189 397 674 950
220-Krypto-c/sty 41 82 123 256 428 600
221-246: 229-1st S.A. issue. 237-1st Intergalactic Vigilante Squadron (6/57). 239-Krypto-c 32 64 96 190 305 420
247(4/58)-1st Legion of Super Heroes app.; 1st app. Cosmic Boy, Saturn Girl & Lightning Boy (later Lightning Lad in #267) (origin) 480 960 1440 4320 8160 12,000
248-252,254,255-Green Arrow in all: 255-Intro. Red Kryptonite in Superboy (used in #252 but with no effect) 27 54 81 158 254 350
253-1st meeting of Superboy & Robin; Green Arrow by Kirby in #250-255 (also see World's Finest #96-99) 32 64 96 186 298 410
256-Origin Green Arrow by Kirby 66 132 198 416 701 985
257-259: 258-Green Arrow x-over in Superboy 23 46 69 135 218 300
260-1st Silver-Age origin Aquaman (5/59) 76 152 228 479 810 1140
261-265,268,270: 262-Origin Speedy in Green Arrow. 270-Congorilla begins, ends #281,283 19 38 57 112 176 240
266-(11/59)-Origin & 1st app. Aquagirl (tryout, not same as later character) 20 40 60 115 183 250
267(12/59)-2nd Legion of Super Heroes; Lightning Boy now called Lightning Lad; new costumes for Legion 97 194 291 611 1031 1450
269-Intro. Aqualad (2/60); last Green Arrow (not in #206) 31 62 93 181 291 400
271-Origin Luthor retold 35 70 105 203 327 450
272-274,277-280: 279-Intro White Kryptonite in Superboy. 280-1st meeting Superboy & Lori Lemaris 18 36 54 103 162 220
275-Origin Superman-Batman team retold (see World's Finest #94) 24 48 72 140 225 310
276-(9/60) Robinson Crusoe-like story 18 36 54 107 169 230
281,284,287-289: 281-Last Congorilla. 284-Last Aquaman in Adv.; Mooney-a. 287,288-Intro Dev-Em, the Knave from Krypton. 287-1st Bizarro Perry White & Jimmy Olsen. 288-Bizarro-c. 289-Legion cameo (statues) 15 30 45 94 147 200
282(3/61)-5th Legion app; intro/origin Star Boy 31 62 93 181 291 400
283-Intro. The Phantom Zone 26 52 78 154 247 340
285-1st Tales of the Bizarro World-c/story (ends #299) in Adv. (see Action #255) 22 44 66 127 204 280
286-1st Bizarro Mxyzptlk; Bizarro-c 21 42 63 123 197 270
290(11/61)-9th Legion app; origin Sunboy in Legion (last 10¢ issue) 28 56 84 162 261 360
291,292,295-298: 291-1st 12¢ ish, (12/61). 292-1st Bizarro Lana Lang & Lucy Lane. 295-Bizarro-c; 1st Bizarro Titano 11 22 33 75 133 190
293(2/62)-13th Legion app; Mon-el & Legion of Super Pets (1st app./origin) app. (1st Superhorse). 1st Bizarro Luthor & Kandor 16 32 48 114 212 310
294-1st Bizarro Marilyn Monroe, Pres. Kennedy. 13 26 39 90 160 230
299-1st Gold Kryptonite (8/62) 11 22 33 77 136 195
300-Tales of the Legion of Super-Heroes series begins (9/62); Mon-el leaves Phantom Zone (temporarily), joins Legion 38 76 114 293 547 800
301-Origin Bouncing Boy 14 28 42 103 184 265
302-305: 303-1st app. Matter-Eater Lad. 304-Death of Lightning Lad in Legion 11 22 33 77 136 195
306-310: 306-Intro. Legion of Substitute Heroes. 307-1st app. Element Lad in Legion. 308-1st app. Lightning Lass in Legion 10 20 30 71 126 180
311-320: 312-Lightning Lad back in Legion. 315-Last new Superboy story; Colossal Boy app. 316-Origins & powers of Legion given. 317-Intro. Dream Girl in Legion; Lightning Lass becomes Light Lass; Hall of Fame series begins. 320-Dev-Em 2nd app. 9 18 27 61 103 145
321-Intro. Time Trapper 8 16 24 56 93 130
322-330: 327-Intro/1st app. Lone Wolf in Legion. 329-Intro The Bizarro Legionnaires; intro. Legion flight rings 7 14 21 50 83 115
331-340: 337-Chlorophyll Kid & Night Girl app. 340-Intro Computo in Legion 7 14 21 47 76 105
341-Triplicate Girl becomes Duo Damsel 6 12 18 43 69 95
342-345,347-351: 345-Last Hall of Fame; returns in 356,371. 348-Origin Sunboy; intro Dr. Regulus in Legion. 349-Intro Universo & Rond Vidar. 351-1st app. White Witch 6 12 18 41 66 90

GD VG FN VF VF/NM NM-
2.0 4.0 6.0 8.0 9.0 9.2

346-1st app. Karate Kid, Princess Projectra, Ferro Lad, & Nemesis Kid. 8 16 24 52 86 120
352,354-360: 354,355-Superman meets the Adult Legion. 355-Insect Queen joins Legion (4/67) 6 12 18 39 62 85
353-Death of Ferro Lad in Legion 7 14 21 49 80 110
361-364,366,368-370: 369-Intro Mordru in Legion 5 10 15 34 55 75
365,367: 365-Intro Shadow Lass (memorial to Shadow Woman app. in #354's Adult Legion-s); lists origins & powers of L.S.H. 367-New Legion headquarters 6 12 18 37 59 80
371,372: 371-Intro. Chemical King (mentioned in #354's Adult Legion-s). 372-Timber Wolf & Chemical King join 6 12 18 37 59 80
373,374,376-380: 373-Intro. Tornado Twins (Barry Allen Flash descendants). 374-Article on comics fandom. 380-Last Legion in Adventure; last 12¢-c 5 10 15 32 51 70
375-Intro Quantum Queen & The Wanderers 6 12 18 37 59 80
381-Supergirl begins; 1st full length Supergirl story & her 1st solo book (6/69) 11 22 33 75 133 190
382-389 4 8 12 28 44 60
390-Giant Supergirl G-69 6 12 18 43 69 95
391-396,398 4 8 12 22 34 45
397-1st app. new Supergirl 5 10 15 30 48 65
399-Unpubbed G.A. Black Canary story 4 8 12 24 37 50
400-New costume for Supergirl (12/70) 5 10 15 30 48 65
401,402,404-408-(15¢-c) 3 6 9 17 25 32
403-68 pg. Giant G-81; Legion-r/#304,305,308,312 6 12 18 43 69 95
409-411,413-415,417-420-(52 pgs.): 413-Hawkman by Kubert r/B&B #44; G.A. Robotman-r/Det. #178; Zatanna by Morrow. 414-r-2nd Animal Man/Str. Advs. #184. 415-Animal Man-r/Str. Adv.#190 (origin recap). 417-Morrow Vigilante; Frazetta Shining Knight-r/Adv. #161; origin The Enchantress; no Zatanna. 418-Prev. unpub. Dr. Mid-Nite story from 1948; no Zatanna. 420-Animal Man-r/Str. Adv. #195 3 6 9 18 27 35
412-(52 pgs.) Reprints origin & 1st app. of Animal Man from Strange Adventures #180 3 6 9 18 27 35
416-Also listed as DC 100 Pg. Super Spectacular #10; Golden Age-r; r/1st app. Black Canary from Flash #86; no Zatanna
(see DC 100 Pg. Super Spectacular #10 for price)
421-424: 424-Last Supergirl in Adventure 2 4 6 11 16 20
425-New look, content change to adventure; Kaluta-c; Toth-a, origin Capt. Fear 3 6 9 16 23 30
426,427: 426-1st Adventurers Club. 427-Last Vigilante 2 4 6 9 12 15
428-Origin/1st app. Black Orchid (c/story, 6-7/73) 6 12 18 37 59 80
429,430-Black Orchid-c/stories 3 6 9 21 32 42
431-Spectre by Aparo begins, ends #440. 6 12 18 41 66 90
432-439-Spectre app. 433-437-Cover title is Weird Adventure Comics. 436-Last 20¢ issue 4 8 12 22 34 45
440-New Spectre origin. 4 8 12 28 44 60
441-458: 441-452-Aquaman app. 443-Fisherman app. 445-447-The Creeper app. 446-Flag-c. 449-451-Martian Manhunter app. 450-Weather Wizard app. in Aquaman story. 453-458-Superboy app. 453-Intro. Mighty Girl. 457,458-Eclipso app. 1 3 4 6 8 10
459,460 (68 pgs.): 459-New Gods/Darkseid storyline concludes from New Gods #19 (#459 is dated 9-10/78) without missing a month. 459-Flash (ends #466), Deadman (ends #466), Wonder Woman (ends #464), Green Lantern (ends #460). 460-Aquaman (ends #478) 3 6 9 14 20 26
461,462 ($1.00, 68 pgs.): 461-Justice Society begins; ends 466. 461,462-Death Earth II Batman 4 8 12 24 37 50
463-466 ($1.00 size, 68 pgs.) 2 4 6 10 14 18
467-Starman by Ditko & Plastic Man begins; 1st app. Prince Gavyn (Starman). 2 4 6 8 10 13
468-490: 470-Origin Starman. 479-Dial 'H' For Hero begins, ends #490. 478-Last Starman & Plastic Man. 480-490: Dial 'H' For Hero 5.00
491-503: 491-100pg. Digest size begins; r/Legion of Super Heroes/Adv. #247, 267; Spectre, Aquaman, Superboy, S&K Sandman, Black Canary-r & new Shazam by Newton begin. 492,495,496,499-S&K Sandman-r/Adventure in all. 493-Challengers of the Unknown begins by Tuska w/brief origin. 493-495,497-499-G.A. Captain Marvel-r. 494-499-Spectre-r/Spectre 1-3, 5-7. 496-Capt. Marvel Jr. new-s, Cockrum-a. 498-Mary Marvel new-s; Plastic Man-r begin; origin Bouncing Boy-r/ #301. 500-Legion-r (Digest size, 148 pgs.).
501-503: G.A.-r 2 4 6 9 13 16
... 80 Page Giant (10/98, $4.95) Wonder Woman, Shazam, Superboy, Supergirl, Green Arrow, Legion, Bizarro World stories 5.00

NOTE: *Bizarro covers-285, 286, 288, 294, 295, 329. Vigilante app.-420, 426, 427.* **N. Adams** *a(r)-495i-498i; c-365-369, 371-373, 375-379, 381-383.* **Aparo** *a-431-433, 434i, 435, 436, 437i, 438i, 439-452, 503r; c-431-452.* **Austin** *a-449i 451i.* **Bernard Baily** *c-48, 50, 52-59.* **Bolland** *c-475.* **Burnley** *c-61-72, 116-120p.* **Chaykin** *a-438.* **Ditko** *a-467-478p; c-467p.* **Creig Flessel** *c-32, 33, 40, 42, 44, 46, 47, 51, 60.* **Giffen** *c-491p-494p, 500p.* **Grell** *a-435-437, 440.* **Guardineer** *c-34, 35, 45.* **Infantino** *a-416r.* **Kaluta** *c-425.* **Bob Kane** *a-38.* **G. Kane** *a-414r, 425; c-496-499,*

Adventures #1 © STJ

Adventures in the DC Universe #13 © DC

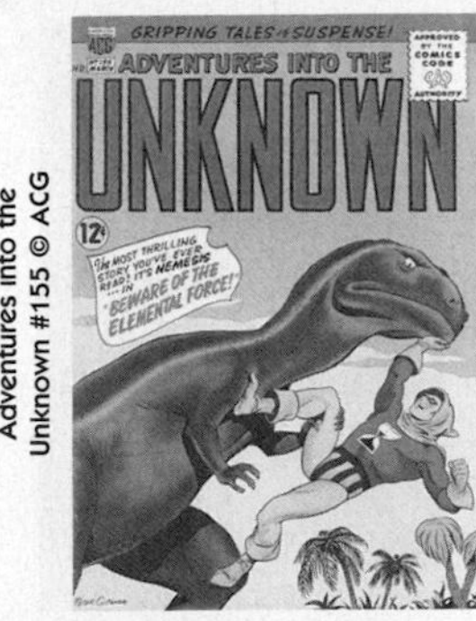

Adventures into the Unknown #155 © ACG

GD VG FN VF VF/NM NM-
2.0 4.0 6.0 8.0 9.0 9.2

537. ***Kirby*** *a-250-256.* ***Kubert*** *a-413.* ***Meskin*** *a-81,127.* ***Moldoff*** *a-494i; c-49.* ***Morrow*** *a-413-415, 417, 422, 502r, 503r.* ***Netzer/Nasser*** *a-449-451.* ***Newton*** *a-459-461, 464-466, 491p, 492p.* ***Paul Norris*** *a-69.* ***Orlando*** *a-457p, 458p.* ***Perez*** *c-484-486, 490p.* ***Simon/Kirby*** *a-503r; c-73-97, 100-102.* ***Starlin*** *c-471.* ***Staton*** *a-445-447i, 456-458p, 459, 460, 461p-465p, 466,467p-478p, 502p(r); c-458, 461(back).* ***Toth*** *a-418, 419, 425, 431, 495p-497p.* ***Tuska*** *a-494p.*

ADVENTURE COMICS (Also see All Star Comics 1999 crossover titles)
DC Comics: May, 1999 ($1.99, one-shot)

1-Golden Age Starman and the Atom; Snejbjerg-a 2.50

ADVENTURE INTO MYSTERY
Atlas Comics (BFP No. 1/OPI No. 2-8): May, 1956 - No. 8, July, 1957

1-Powell s/f-a; Forte-a; Everett-c 40 80 120 235 380 525
2-Flying Saucer story 22 44 66 129 207 285
3,6-Everett-c 20 40 60 115 183 250
4,5,7: 4-Williamson-a, 4 pgs; Powell-a. 5-Everett-c/a, Orlando-a. 7-Torres-a; Everett-c 21 42 63 123 197 270
8-Moreira, Sale, Torres, Woodbridge-a, Severin-c 20 40 60 115 183 250

ADVENTURE IS MY CAREER
U.S. Coast Guard Academy/Street & Smith: 1945 (44 pgs.)

nn-Simon, Milt Gross-a 21 42 63 123 197 270

ADVENTURERS, THE
Aircel Comics/Adventure Publ.: Aug, 1986 - No. 10, 1987? ($1.50, B&W)
V2#1, 1987 - V2#0, 1988; V3#1, Oct, 1989 - V3#6, 1990

1-Peter Hsu-a 1 2 3 5 6 8
1-Cover variant, limited ed. 2 4 6 9 12 15
1-2nd print (1986); 1st app. Elf Warrior 3.00
2,3, 0 (#4, 12/86)-Origin, 5-10, Book II, reg. & Limited Ed. #1 3.50
Book II, #2,3,0,4-9 2.50
Book III, #1 (10/89, $2.25)-Reg. & limited-c, Book III, #2-6 2.50

ADVENTURES (No. 2 Spectacular... on cover)
St. John Publishing Co.: Nov, 1949 - No. 2, Feb, 1950 (No. 1 ...in Romance on cover) (Slightly larger size)

1(Scarce); Bolle, Starr-a(2) 26 52 78 154 247 340
2(Scarce)-Slave Girl; China Bombshell app.; Bolle, L. Starr-a 40 80 120 235 380 525

ADVENTURES FOR BOYS
Bailey Enterprises: Dec, 1954

nn-Comics, text, & photos 8 16 24 40 50 60

ADVENTURES IN PARADISE (TV)
Dell Publishing Co.: Feb-Apr, 1962

Four Color#1301 6 12 18 39 62 85

ADVENTURES IN ROMANCE (See Adventures)

ADVENTURES IN SCIENCE (See Classics Illustrated Special Issue)

ADVENTURES IN THE DC UNIVERSE
DC Comics: Apr, 1997 - No. 19, Oct, 1998 ($1.75/$1.95/$1.99)

1-Animated style in all; JLA-c/app 5.00
2-11,13-17,19: 2-Flash app. 3-Wonder Woman. 4-Green Lantern. 6-Aquaman. 7-Shazam Family. 8-Blue Beetle & Booster Gold. 9-Flash. 10-Legion. 11-Green Lantern & Wonder Woman. 13-Impulse & Martian Manhunter. 14-Superboy/Flash race 3.50
12,18-JLA-c/app 3.50
Annual 1(1997, $3.95)-Dr. Fate, Impulse, Rose & Thorn, Superboy, Mister Miracle app. 4.50

ADVENTURES IN THE RIFLE BRIGADE
DC Comics (Vertigo): Oct, 2000 - No. 3, Dec, 2000 ($2.50, limited series)

1-3-Ennis-s/Ezquerra-a/Bolland-c 2.50
TPB (2004, $14.95) r/series and Operation Bollock series 15.00

ADVENTURES IN THE RIFLE BRIGADE: OPERATION BOLLOCK
DC Comics (Vertigo): Oct, 2001 - No. 3, Jan, 2002 ($2.50, limited series)

1-3-Ennis-s/Ezquerra-a/Fabry-c 2.50

ADVENTURES IN 3-D (With glasses)
Harvey Publications: Nov, 1953 - No. 2, Jan, 1954 (25¢)

1-Nostrand, Powell-a, 2-Powell-a 17 34 51 98 154 210

ADVENTURES INTO DARKNESS (See Seduction of the Innocent 3-D)
Better-Standard Publications/Visual Editions: No. 5, Aug, 1952- No. 14, 1954

5-Katz-c/a; Toth-a(p) 41 82 123 256 428 600
6-Tuska, Katz-a 29 58 87 172 276 380
7-9: 7-Katz-c/a. 8,9-Toth-a(p) 29 58 87 172 276 380
10-12: 10,11-Jack Katz-a. 12-Toth-a; lingerie panel 26 52 78 154 247 340
13-Toth-a(p); Cannibalism story cited by T. E. Murphy articles 33 66 99 192 309 425
14 20 40 60 115 183 250

NOTE: ***Fawcette*** *a-13.* ***Moreira*** *a-5.* ***Sekowsky*** *a-10, 11, 13(2).*

ADVENTURES INTO TERROR (Formerly Joker Comics)
Marvel/Atlas Comics (CDS): No. 43, Nov, 1950 - No. 31, May, 1954

43(#1) 68 136 204 428 727 1025
44(#2, 2/51)-Sol Brodsky-c 43 86 129 267 446 625
3(4/51), 4 31 62 93 184 295 405
5-Wolverton-c panel/Mystic #6; Rico-c panel also; Atom Bomb story 35 70 105 203 327 450
6,8: 8-Wolverton text illo r-/Marvel Tales #104; prototype of Spider-Man villain The Lizard 29 58 87 172 276 380
7-Wolverton-a "Where Monsters Dwell", 6 pgs.; Tuska-c; Maneely-c panels 59 118 177 372 629 885
9,10,12-Krigstein-a. 9-Decapitation panels 25 50 75 147 236 325
11,13-20 22 44 66 129 207 285
21-24,26-31 20 40 60 118 189 260
25-Matt Fox-a 25 50 75 147 236 325

NOTE: ***Ayers*** *a-21.* ***Colan*** *a-3, 5, 14, 21, 24, 25, 28, 29; c-27.* ***Colletta*** *a-30.* ***Everett*** *c-13, 21, 25.* ***Fass*** *a-28, 29.* ***Forte*** *a-28.* ***Heath*** *a-43, 44, 4-6, 22, 24, 26; c-43, 9, 11.* ***Lazarus*** *a-7.* ***Maneely*** *a-7(3 pg.), 10, 11, 21., 22 c-15, 29.* ***Don Rico*** *a-4, 5(3 pg.).* ***Sekowsky*** *a-43, 3, 4.* ***Sinnott*** *a-8, 9, 11, 28.* ***Tuska*** *a-14; c-7.*

ADVENTURES INTO THE UNKNOWN
American Comics Group: Fall, 1948 - No. 174, Aug, 1967 (No. 1-33: 52 pgs.)
(1st continuous series Supernatural comic; see Eerie #1)

1-Guardineer-a; adapt. of 'Castle of Otranto' by Horace Walpole 223 446 669 1405 2378 3350
2,3: 3-Feldstein-a (9 pgs) 78 156 234 491 833 1175
4,5: 5- 'Spirit Of Frankenstein' series begins, ends #12 (except #11) 41 82 123 253 419 585
6-10 35 70 105 203 327 450
11-16,18-20: 13-Starr-a 29 58 87 169 272 375
17-Story similar to movie 'The Thing' 34 68 102 198 319 440
21-26,28-30 25 50 75 147 236 325
27-Williamson/Krenkel-a (8 pgs.) 31 62 93 181 291 400
31-50: 38-Atom bomb panels 20 40 60 115 183 250
51-(1/54)-(3-D effect-c/story)-Only white cover 40 80 120 235 380 525
52-58: (3-D effect-c/stories with black covers). 52-E.C. swipe/Haunt Of Fear #14 37 74 111 219 352 485
59-3-D effect story only; new logo 29 58 87 169 272 375
60-Wood*esque*-a by Landau 15 30 45 86 133 180
61-Last pre-code issue (1-2/55) 15 30 45 86 133 180
62-70 8 16 24 54 90 125
71-90 6 12 18 43 69 95
91,96(#95 on inside),107,116-All have Williamson-a 7 14 21 47 76 105
92-95,97-99,101-106,108-115,117-128: 109-113,118-Whitney painted-c. 128-Williamson/Krenkel/Torres-a(r)/Forbidden Worlds #63; last 10¢ issue 5 10 15 34 55 75
100 6 12 18 39 62 85
129-153,157: 153,157-Magic Agent app. 4 8 12 24 37 50
154 Nemesis series begins (origin), ends #170 5 10 15 30 48 65
155,156,158-167,170-174 4 8 12 23 36 48
168-Ditko-a(p) 4 8 12 28 44 60
169-Nemesis battles Hitler 4 8 12 28 44 60
Nemesis Archives: Vol. One (Dark Horse Books, 9/08, $59.95) r/#154-170; creator bios 60.00

NOTE: *"Spirit of Frankenstein" series in 5, 6, 8-10, 12, 16.* ***Buscema*** *a-100, 106, 108-110, 158r, 165r.* ***Cameron*** *a-34.* ***Craig*** *a-152, 160.* ***Goode*** *a-45, 47, 60.* ***Landau*** *a-51, 59-63.* ***Lazarus*** *a-34, 48, 51, 52, 56, 58, 79, 87; c-31-56, 58.* ***Reinman*** *a-102, 111, 112, 115-118, 124, 130, 137, 141, 145, 164.* ***Whitney*** *c-12-30, 57, 59-on (most.)* ***Torres/Williamson*** *a-116.*

ADVENTURES INTO WEIRD WORLDS
Marvel/Atlas Comics (ACI): Jan, 1952 - No. 30, June, 1954

1-Atom bomb panels 73 146 219 460 780 1100
2-Sci/fic stories (2); one by Maneely 40 80 120 235 380 525
3-10: 7-Tongue ripped out. 10-Krigstein, Everett-a 28 56 84 164 265 365
11-20 22 44 66 129 207 285
21-Hitler in Hell story 27 54 81 158 254 350
22-26: 24-Man holds hypo & splits in two 20 40 60 118 189 260
27-Matt Fox end of world story-a; severed head-c 40 80 120 235 380 525
28-Atom bomb story; decapitation panels 22 44 66 129 207 285
29,30 18 36 54 103 162 220

NOTE: ***Ayers*** *a-8, 26.* ***Everett*** *a-4, 5; c-6, 8, 10-13, 18, 19, 22, 24, 25; a-4, 25.* ***Fass*** *a-7.* ***Forte*** *a-21, 24.* ***Al Hartley*** *a-2.* ***Heath*** *a-1, 4, 17, 22; c-7, 9, 20.* ***Maneely*** *a-2, 3, 11, 20, 22, 23, 25; c-1, 3, 22, 25-27, 29.* ***Reinman*** *a-24, 28.* ***Rico*** *a-13.* ***Robinson*** *a-13.* ***Sinnott*** *a-25, 30.* ***Tuska*** *a-1, 2, 12, 15.* ***Whitney*** *a-7.* ***Wildey*** *a-28. Bondage c-22.*

ADVENTURES IN WONDERLAND

Adventures of Alan Ladd #8 © DC

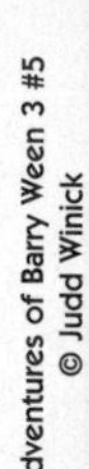

Adventures of Barry Ween 3 #5 © Judd Winick

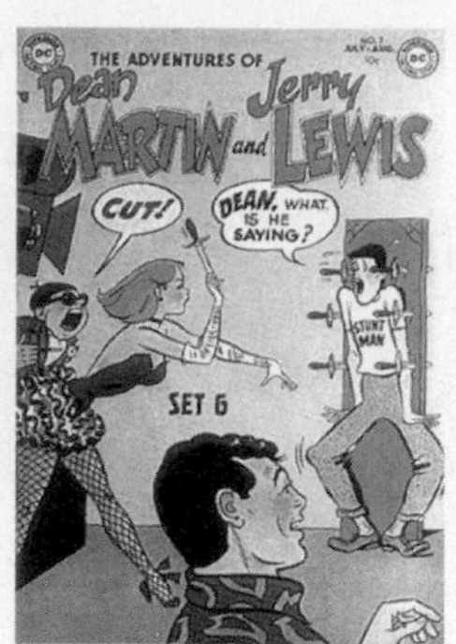

Adventures of Dean Martin and Jerry Lewis #7 © DC

	GD 2.0	VG 4.0	FN 6.0	VF 8.0	VF/NM 9.0	NM- 9.2
Lev Gleason Publications: April, 1955 - No. 5, Feb, 1956 (Jr. Readers Guild)						
1-Maurer-a	11	22	33	62	86	110
2-4	7	14	21	37	46	55
5-Christmas issue	8	16	24	40	50	60
ADVENTURES OF ALAN LADD, THE						
National Periodical Publ.: Oct-Nov, 1949 - No. 9, Feb-Mar, 1951 (All 52 pgs.)						
1-Photo-c	81	162	243	506	841	1175
2-Photo-c	42	84	126	256	421	585
3-6: Last photo-c	34	68	102	195	308	420
7-9	27	54	81	158	249	340
NOTE: *Dan Barry a-1. Moreira a-3-7.*						
ADVENTURES OF ALICE (Also see Alice in Wonderland & ...at Monkey Island)						
Civil Service Publ./Pentagon Publishing Co.: 1945						
1	15	30	45	83	124	165
2-Through the Magic Looking Glass	11	22	33	62	86	110
ADVENTURES OF BARON MUNCHAUSEN, THE						
Now Comics: July, 1989 - No. 4, Oct, 1989 ($1.75, limited series)						
1-4: Movie adaptation						2.50
ADVENTURES OF BARRY WEEN, BOY GENIUS, THE (Also see Free Comic Book Day Edition in the Promotional Comics section)						
Image Comics: Mar, 1999 - No. 3, May, 1999 ($2.95, B&W, limited series)						
1-3-Judd Winick-s/a						3.00
TPB (Oni Press, 11/99, $8.95)						9.00
ADVENTURES OF BARRY WEEN, BOY GENIUS 2.0, THE						
Oni Press: Feb, 2000 - No. 3, Apr, 2000 ($2.95, B&W, limited series)						
1-3-Judd Winick-s/a						3.00
TPB (2000, $8.95)						9.00
ADVENTURES OF BARRY WEEN, BOY GENIUS 3, THE : MONKEY TALES						
Oni Press: Feb, 2001 - No. 6, Feb, 2002 ($2.95, B&W, limited series)						
1-6-Judd Winick-s/a						3.00
TPB (2001, $8.95) r/#1-3; intro. by Peter David						9.00
...4 TPB (5/02, $8.95) r/#4-6						9.00
ADVENTURES OF BAYOU BILLY, THE (Based on video game)						
Archie Comics: Sept, 1989 - No. 5, June, 1990 ($1.00)						
1-5: Esposito-c/a(i). 5-Kelley Jones-c						3.00
ADVENTURES OF BOB HOPE, THE (Also see True Comics #59)						
National Per. Publ.: Feb-Mar, 1950 - No. 109, Feb-Mar, 1968 (#1-10: 52pgs.)						
1-Photo-c	190	380	570	1197	2024	2850
2-Photo-c	83	166	249	523	887	1250
3,4-Photo-c	52	104	156	322	536	750
5-10	40	80	120	240	390	540
11-20	28	56	84	162	261	360
21-31 (2-3/55; last precode)	19	38	57	112	176	240
32-40	10	20	30	68	119	170
41-50	9	18	27	60	100	140
51-70	7	14	21	49	80	110
71-93	5	10	15	34	55	75
94-Aquaman cameo	5	10	15	34	55	75
95-1st app. Super-Hip & 1st monster issue (11/65)	7	14	21	49	80	110
96-105: Super-Hip and monster stories in all. 103-Batman, Robin, Ringo Starr cameos	5	10	15	34	55	75
106-109-All monster-c/stories by N. Adams-c/a	7	14	21	49	80	110
NOTE: *Buzzy in #34. Kitty Karr of Hollywood in #15, 17-20, 23, 28. Liz in #26, 109. Miss Beverly Hills of Hollywood in #7, 8, 10, 13, 14. Miss Melody Lane of Broadway in #15. Rusty in #23, 25. Tommy in #24. No 2nd feature in #2-4, 6, 8, 11, 12, 28-108.*						
ADVENTURES OF CAPTAIN AMERICA						
Marvel Comics: Sept, 1991 - No. 4, Jan, 1992 ($4.95, 52 pgs., squarebound, limited series)						
1-4: 1-Origin in WW2; embossed-c; Nicieza scripts; Maguire-c/a(p) begins, ends #3. 2-4-Austin-c/a(i). 3,4-Red Skull app.						5.00
ADVENTURES OF CYCLOPS AND PHOENIX (Also See Askani'son & The Further Adventures of Cyclops And Phoenix)						
Marvel Comics: May, 1994 - No. 4, Aug, 1994 ($2.95, limited series)						
1-4-Characters from X-Men; origin of Cable						4.00
Trade paperback ($14.95)-reprints #1-4						15.00
ADVENTURES OF DEAN MARTIN AND JERRY LEWIS, THE (The Adventures of Jerry Lewis #41 on) (See Movie Love #12)						
National Periodical Publications: July-Aug, 1952 - No. 40, Oct, 1957						
1	110	220	330	693	1172	1650
2-3 pg origin on how they became a team	52	104	156	322	536	750
3-10: 3- I Love Lucy text featurette	31	62	93	181	291	400
11-19: Last precode (2/55)	20	40	60	115	183	250
20-30	15	30	45	86	133	180
31-40	14	28	42	76	108	140
ADVENTURES OF DETECTIVE ACE KING, THE (Also see Bob Scully-- & Detective Dan)						
Humor Publ. Corp.: No date (1933) (36 pgs., 9-1/2x12") (10¢, B&W, one-shot) (paper-c)						
Book 1-Along with Bob Scully & Detective Dan, the first comic w/original art & the first of a single theme.; Not reprints; Ace King by Martin Nadle (The American Sherlock Holmes). A Dick Tracy look-alike	375	750	1125	3000	-	-
ADVENTURES OF EVIL AND MALICE, THE						
Image Comics: June, 1999 - No. 3, Nov, 1999 ($3.50/$3.95, limited series)						
1,2-Jimmie Robinson-s/a						3.50
3-(3.95)						4.00
ADVENTURES OF FELIX THE CAT, THE						
Harvey Comics: May, 1992 ($1.25)						
1-Messmer-r						4.00
ADVENTURES OF FORD FAIRLANE, THE						
DC Comics: May, 1990 - No. 4, Aug, 1990 ($1.50, limited series, mature)						
1-4: Andrew Dice Clay movie tie-in; Don Heck inks						3.00
ADVENTURES OF HOMER COBB, THE						
Say/Bart Prod. : Sept, 1947 (Oversized) (Published in the U.S., but printed in Canada)						
1-(Scarce)-Feldstein-c/a	32	64	96	186	298	410
ADVENTURES OF HOMER GHOST (See Homer The Happy Ghost)						
Atlas Comics: June, 1957 - No. 2, Aug, 1957						
V1#1,2: 2-Robot-c	11	22	33	62	86	110
ADVENTURES OF JERRY LEWIS, THE (Adventures of Dean Martin & Jerry Lewis No. 1-40) (See Super DC Giant)						
National Periodical Publ.: No. 41, Nov, 1957 - No. 124, May-June, 1971						
41	9	18	27	63	107	150
42-60	7	14	21	49	80	110
61-67,69-73,75-80	6	12	18	41	66	90
68,74-Photo-c (movie)	9	18	27	60	100	140
81,82,85-87,90,91,94,96,98,99	5	10	15	34	55	75
83,84,88: 83-1st Monsters-c/s. 84-Jerry as a Super-hero-c/s. 88-1st Witch, Miss Kraft	6	12	18	41	66	90
89-Bob Hope app.; Wizard of Oz & Alfred E. Neuman in MAD parody	7	14	21	45	73	100
92-Superman cameo	7	14	21	45	73	100
93-Beatles parody as babies	6	12	18	41	66	90
95-1st Uncle Hal Wack-A-Boy Camp-c/s	6	12	18	41	66	90
97-Batman/Robin/Joker-c/story; Riddler & Penguin app; Dick Sprang-c.	9	18	27	63	107	150
100	6	12	18	43	69	95
101,103,104-Neal Adams-c/a	7	14	21	49	80	110
102-Beatles app.; Neal Adams c/a	9	18	27	63	107	150
105-Superman x-over	7	14	21	45	73	100
106-111,113-116	4	8	12	26	41	55
112,117: 112-Flash x-over. 117-W. Woman x-over	6	12	18	43	69	95
118-124	4	8	12	24	37	50
NOTE: *Monster-c/s-90,93,96,98,101. Wack-A-Buy Camp-c/s-96,99,102,107,108.*						
ADVENTURES OF JO-JOY, THE (See Jo-Joy)						
ADVENTURES OF LASSIE, THE (See Lassie)						
ADVENTURES OF LUTHER ARKWRIGHT, THE						
Valkyrie Press/Dark Horse Comics: Oct, 1987 - No. 9, Jan, 1989 ($2.00, B&W) V2, #1, Mar, 1990 - V2#9, 1990 ($1.95, B&W)						
1-9: 1-Alan Moore intro., V2#1-9 (Dark Horse): r-1st series; new-c						4.00
TPB (1997, $14.95) r/#1-9 w/Michael Moorcock intro.						15.00
ADVENTURES OF MIGHTY MOUSE (Mighty Mouse Adventures No. 1)						
St. John Publishing Co.: No. 2, Jan, 1952 - No. 18, May, 1955						
2	25	50	75	147	236	325
3-5	15	30	45	83	124	165
6-18	11	22	33	62	86	110
ADVENTURES OF MIGHTY MOUSE (2nd Series) (Becomes Mighty Mouse #161 on) (Two No. 144's; formerly Paul Terry's Comics; No. 129-137 have nn's)						
St. John/Pines/Dell/Gold Key: No. 126, Aug, 1955 - No. 160, Oct, 1963						

Adventures of Rex the Wonder Dog #1 © DC

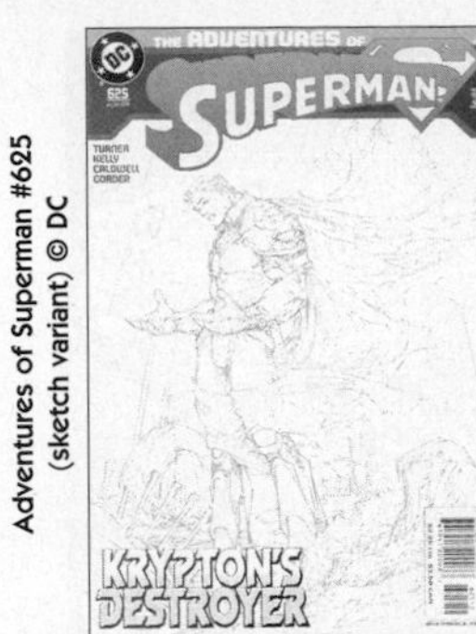

Adventures of Superman #625 (sketch variant) © DC

Adventures of the Jaguar #3 © AP

	GD 2.0	VG 4.0	FN 6.0	VF 8.0	VF/NM 9.0	NM- 9.2
126(8/55), 127(10/55), 128(11/55)-St. John	10	20	30	54	72	90
nn(129, 4/56)-144(8/59)-Pines	5	10	15	30	48	65
144(10-12/59)-155(7-9/62) Dell	4	8	12	28	44	60
156(10/62)-160(10/63) Gold Key	4	8	12	28	44	60

NOTE: *Early issues titled "Paul Terry's Adventures of ...."*

ADVENTURES OF MIGHTY MOUSE (Formerly Mighty Mouse)
Gold Key: No. 166, Mar, 1979 - No. 172, Jan, 1980

	GD 2.0	VG 4.0	FN 6.0	VF 8.0	VF/NM 9.0	NM- 9.2
166-172	1	2	3	5	6	8

ADVS. OF MR. FROG & MISS MOUSE (See Dell Junior Treasury No. 4)

ADVENTURES OF OZZIE & HARRIET, THE (See Ozzie & Harriet)

ADVENTURES OF PATORUZU
Green Publishing Co.: Aug, 1946 - Winter, 1946

	GD 2.0	VG 4.0	FN 6.0	VF 8.0	VF/NM 9.0	NM- 9.2
nn's-Contains Animal Crackers reprints	6	12	18	28	34	40

ADVENTURES OF PINKY LEE, THE (TV)
Atlas Comics: July, 1955 - No. 5, Dec, 1955

	GD 2.0	VG 4.0	FN 6.0	VF 8.0	VF/NM 9.0	NM- 9.2
1	24	48	72	140	225	310
2-5	15	30	45	85	130	175

ADVENTURES OF PIPSQUEAK, THE (Formerly Pat the Brat)
Archie Publications (Radio Comics): No. 34, Sept, 1959 - No. 39, July, 1960

	GD 2.0	VG 4.0	FN 6.0	VF 8.0	VF/NM 9.0	NM- 9.2
34	3	6	9	21	32	42
35-39	3	6	9	17	25	32

ADVENTURES OF QUAKE & QUISP, THE (See Quaker Oats "Plenty of Glutton")

ADVENTURES OF REX THE WONDER DOG, THE (Rex...No. 1)
National Periodical Publ.: Jan-Feb, 1952 - No. 45, May-June, 1959; No. 46, Nov-Dec, 1959

	GD 2.0	VG 4.0	FN 6.0	VF 8.0	VF/NM 9.0	NM- 9.2
1-(Scarce)-Toth-c/a	130	260	390	819	1385	1950
2-(Scarce)-Toth-c/a	59	110	177	372	629	885
3-(Scarce)-Toth-a	47	94	141	291	483	675
4,5	40	80	120	235	380	525
6-10	31	62	93	181	291	400
11-Atom bomb-c/story; dinosaur-c/sty	37	74	111	215	345	475
12-19: 19-Last precode (1-2/55)	20	40	60	115	183	250
20-46	15	30	45	84	127	170

NOTE: ***Infantino, Gil Kane** art in 5-19 (most)*

ADVENTURES OF ROBIN HOOD, THE (Formerly Robin Hood)
Magazine Enterprises (Sussex Publ. Co.): No. 7, 9/57 - No. 8, 11/57
(Based on Richard Greene TV Show)

	GD 2.0	VG 4.0	FN 6.0	VF 8.0	VF/NM 9.0	NM- 9.2
7,8-Richard Greene photo-c. 7-Powell-a	15	30	45	83	124	165

ADVENTURES OF ROBIN HOOD, THE
Gold Key: Mar, 1974 - No. 7, Jan, 1975 (Disney cartoon) (36 pgs.)

	GD 2.0	VG 4.0	FN 6.0	VF 8.0	VF/NM 9.0	NM- 9.2
1(90291-403)-Part-r of $1.50 editions	2	4	6	11	16	20
2-7: 1-7 are part-r	2	4	6	8	10	12

ADVENTURES OF SNAKE PLISSKEN
Marvel Comics: Jan, 1997 ($2.50, one-shot)

1-Based on Escape From L.A. movie; Brereton-c 3.50

ADVENTURES OF SPAWN, THE
Image Comics (Todd McFarlane Prods.): Jan, 2007 ($5.99, one-shot)

1-Printed adaptation of the Spawn.com web comic; Khary Randolph-a 6.00

ADVENTURES OF SPIDER-MAN, THE (Based on animated TV series)
Marvel Comics: Apr, 1996 - No. 12, Mar, 1997 (99¢)

1-12: 1-Punisher app. 2-Venom cameo. 3-X-Men. 6-Fantastic Four 3.00

ADVENTURES OF SUPERBOY, THE (See Superboy, 2nd Series)

ADVENTURES OF SUPERMAN (Formerly Superman)
DC Comics: No. 424, Jan, 1987 - No. 499, Feb, 1993; No. 500, Early June, 1993 - No. 649, Apr, 2006 (This title's numbering continues with Superman #650, May, 2006)

424-Ordway-c/a/Wolfman-s begin following Byrne's Superman revamp 3.00
425-435,437-462: 426-Legends x-over. 432-1st app. Jose Delgado who becomes Gangbuster in #434. 437-Millennium x-over. 438-New Brainiac app. 440-Batman app. 449-Invasion 3.00
436-Byrne scripts begin; Millennium x-over 3.50
463-Superman/Flash race; cover swipe/Superman #199 5.00
464-Lobo-c & app. (pre-dates Lobo #1) 4.00
465-495: 467-Part 2 of Batman story. 473-Hal Jordan, Guy Gardner x-over. 477-Legion app. 491-Last $1.00-c. 480-($1.75, 52 pgs.). 495-Forever People-c/story; Darkseid app. 2.50
496,497: 496-Doomsday cameo. 497-Doomsday battle issue 3.00
496,497-2nd printings 2.50
498,499-Funeral for a Friend; Supergirl app. 2.50
498-2nd & 3rd printings 2.50
500-($2.95, 68 pgs.)-Collector's edition w/card 3.50
500-($2.50, 68 pgs.)-Regular edition w/different-c 2.50
500-Platinum edition 30.00
501-($1.95)-Collector's edition with die-cut-c 2.50
501-($1.50)-Regular edition w/mini-poster & diff.-c 2.50
502-516: 502-Supergirl-c/story. 508-Challengers of the Unknown app. 510-Bizarro-c/story. 516-(9/94)-Zero Hour 2.50
505-($2.50)-Holo-grafx foil-c edition 2.50
0,517-523: 0-(10/94). 517-(11/94) 2.50
524-549,551-580: 524-Begin $1.95-c. 527-Return of Alpha Centurion (Zero Hour). 533-Impulse-c/app. 535-Luthor-c/app. 536-Brainiac app. 537-Parasite app. 540-Final Night x-over. 541-Superboy-c/app.; Lois & Clark honeymoon. 545-New powers. 546-New costume. 555-Red & Blue Supermen battle. 557-Millennium Giants x-over. 558-560: Superman Silver Age-style story; Krypto app. 561-Begin $1.99-c. 565-JLA app. 2.50
550-($3.50)-Double sized 3.50
581-588: 581-Begin $2.25-c. 583-Emperor Joker. 588-Casey-s 2.50
589-595: 589-Return to Krypton; Rivoche-c. 591-Wolfman-s. 593-595-Our Worlds at War x-over. 593-New Suicide Squad formed. 594-Doomsday-c/app. 2.50
596-Aftermath of "War" x-over has panel showing damaged World Trade Center buildings; issue went on sale the day after the Sept. 11 attack 5.00
597-599,601-624: 597-Joker: Last Laugh. 604,605-Ultraman, Owlman, Superwoman app. 606-Return to Krypton. 612-616,619-623-Nowlan-c. 624-Mr. Majestic app. 2.50
600-($3.95) Wieringo-a; painted-c by Adel; pin-ups by various 4.00
625,626-Godfall parts 2,5; Turner-c; Caldwell-a(p) 3.00
627-641,643-648: 627-Begin $2.50-c, Rucka-s/Clark-a/Ha-c begin. 628-Wagner-c. 631-Bagged with Sky Captain CD; Lois shot. 634-Mxyzptlk visits DC offices. 639-Capt. Marvel & Eclipso app. 641-OMAC app. 643-Sacrifice aftermath; Batman & Wonder Woman app. 2.50
642-OMAC Project x-over Sacrifice pt. 3; JLA app. 5.00
642-(2nd printing) red tone cover 2.50
649-Last issue; Infinite Crisis x-over, Superman vs. Earth-2 Superman 3.00
#1,000,000 (11/98) Gene Ha-c; 853rd Century x-over 3.00
Annual 1 (1987, $1.25, 52 pgs.)-Starlin-c & scripts 4.00
Annual 2,3 (1990, 1991, $2.00, 68 pgs.): 2-Byrne-c/a(i); Legion '90 (Lobo) app. 3-Armageddon 2001 x-over 3.00
Annual 4-6 ('92-'94, $2.50, 68 pgs.): 4-Guy Gardner/Lobo-c/story; Eclipso storyline; Quesada-c(p). 5-Bloodlines storyline. 6-Elseworlds sty. 3.00
Annual 7,9('95, '97, $3.95)-7-Year One story. 9-Pulp Heroes sty 4.00
Annual 8 (1996, $2.95)-Legends of the Dead Earth story 3.00

NOTE: ***Erik Larsen** a-431.*

ADVENTURES OF THE DOVER BOYS
Archie Comics (Close-up): September, 1950 - No. 2, 1950 (No month given)

	GD 2.0	VG 4.0	FN 6.0	VF 8.0	VF/NM 9.0	NM- 9.2
1,2	9	18	27	52	69	85

ADVENTURES OF THE FLY (The Fly #1-6; Fly Man No. 32-39; See The Double Life of Private Strong, The Fly, Laugh Comics & Mighty Crusaders)
Archie Publications/Radio Comics: Aug, 1959 - No. 30, Oct, 1964; No. 31, May, 1965

	GD 2.0	VG 4.0	FN 6.0	VF 8.0	VF/NM 9.0	NM- 9.2
1-Shield app.; origin The Fly; S&K-c/a	50	100	150	400	750	1100
2-Williamson, S&K-a	28	56	84	227	384	540
3-Origin retold; Davis, Powell-a	22	44	66	163	302	440
4-Neal Adams-a(p)(1 panel); S&K-c; Powell-a; 2 pg. Shield story	15	30	45	105	190	275
5,6,9,10: 9-Shield app. 9-1st app. Cat Girl. 10-Black Hood app.	10	20	30	73	129	185
7,8: 7-1st S.A. app. Black Hood (7/60). 8-1st S.A. app. Shield (9/60)	12	24	36	84	150	215
11-13,15-20: 13-1st app. Fly Girl w/o costume. 16-Last 10¢ issue. 20-Origin Fly Girl retold	7	14	21	49	80	110
14-Origin & 1st app. Fly Girl in costume	8	16	24	56	93	130
21-30: 23-Jaguar cameo. 27-29-Black Hood 1 pg. strips. 30-Comet x-over (1st S.A. app.) in Fly Girl	6	12	18	39	62	85
31-Black Hood, Shield, Comet app.	6	12	18	41	66	90

Vol. 1 TPB ('04, $12.95) r/#1-4 & Double Life of Private Strong #1,2; foreward by Joe Simon 13.00

NOTE: ***Simon** c-2-4. **Tuska** a-1. Cover title to #31 is Flyman; Advs. of the Fly inside.*

ADVENTURES OF THE JAGUAR, THE (See Blue Ribbon Comics, Laugh Comics & Mighty Crusaders)
Archie Publications (Radio Comics): Sept, 1961 - No. 15, Nov, 1963

	GD 2.0	VG 4.0	FN 6.0	VF 8.0	VF/NM 9.0	NM- 9.2
1-Origin Jaguar (1st app?) by J. Rosenberger	20	40	60	148	274	400
2,3: 3-Last 10¢ issue	11	22	33	75	133	190
4-6-Catgirl app. (#4's-c is same as splash pg.)	8	16	24	58	97	135
7-10	7	14	21	49	80	110
11-15:13,14-Catgirl, Black Hood app. in both	6	12	18	43	69	95

ADVENTURES OF THE MASK (TV cartoon)
Dark Horse Comics: Jan, 1996 - No. 12, Dec, 1996 ($2.50)

Adventures of the X-Men #6 © MAR

Agents of Law #2 © DH

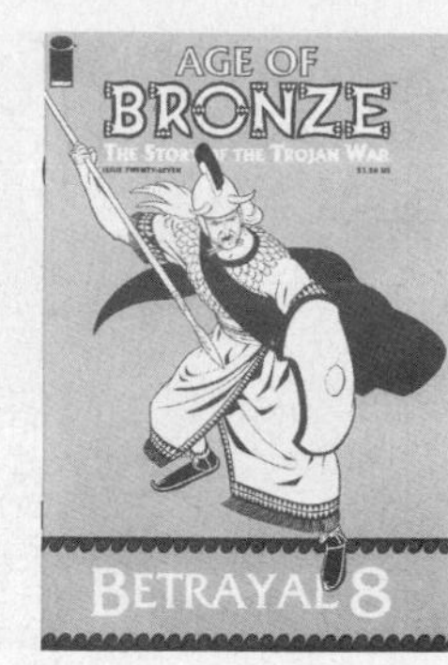

Age of Bronze #27 © Eric Shanower

1-12: Based on animated series 2.50

ADVENTURES OF THE NEW MEN (Formerly Newmen #1-21)
Maximum Press: No. 22, Nov, 1996; No. 23, March, 1997 ($2.50)
22,23-Sprouse-c/a 2.50

ADVENTURES OF THE OUTSIDERS, THE (Formerly Batman & The Outsiders; also see The Outsiders)
DC Comics: No. 33, May, 1986 - No. 46, June, 1987
33-46: 39-45-r/Outsiders #1-7 by Aparo 2.50

ADVENTURES OF THE SUPER MARIO BROTHERS (See Super Mario Bros.)
Valiant: 1990 - No. 9, Oct, 1991 ($1.50)
V2#1-9 5.00

ADVENTURES OF THE THING, THE (Also see The Thing)
Marvel Comics: Apr, 1992 - No. 4, July, 1992, ($1.25, limited series)
1-4: 1-r/Marvel Two-In-One #50 by Byrne; Kieth-c. 2-4-r/Marvel Two-In-One #80,51 & 77; 2-Ghost Rider-c/story; Quesada-c. 3-Miller-r/Quesada-c; new Perez-a (4 pgs.) 2.50

ADVENTURES OF THE X-MEN, THE (Based on animated TV series)
Marvel Comics: Apr, 1996 - No. 12, Mar, 1997 (99¢)
1-12: 1-Wolverine/Hulk battle. 3-Spider-Man-c. 5,6-Magneto-c/app. 3.00

ADVENTURES OF TINKER BELL (See Tinker Bell, 4-Color No. 896 & 982)

ADVENTURES OF TOM SAWYER (See Dell Junior Treasury No. 10)

ADVENTURES OF YOUNG DR. MASTERS, THE
Archie Comics (Radio Comics): Aug, 1964 - No. 2, Nov, 1964
1 3 6 9 18 27 35
2 3 6 9 14 19 24

ADVENTURES ON OTHER WORLDS (See Showcase #17 & 18)

ADVENTURES ON THE PLANET OF THE APES (Also see Planet of the Apes)
Marvel Comics Group: Oct, 1975 - No. 11, Dec, 1976
1-Planet of the Apes magazine-r in color; Starlin-c; adapts movie thru #6
3 6 9 17 25 32
2-5: 5-(25¢-c edition) 2 4 6 10 14 18
5-7-(30¢-c variants, limited distribution) 4 8 12 24 37 50
6-10: 6,7-(25¢-c edition). 7-Adapts 2nd movie (thru #11)
2 4 6 11 16 20
11-Last issue; concludes 2nd movie adaptation 3 6 9 14 19 24
NOTE: *Alcala a-6-11r. Buckler c-2p. Nasser c-7. Ploog a-1-9. Starlin c-6. Tuska a-1-5r.*

AEON FLUX (Based on the 2005 movie which was based on the MTV animated series)
Dark Horse Comics: Oct, 2005 - No. 4, Jan, 2006 ($2.99, limited series)
1-4-Timothy Green II-a/Mike Kennedy-s 3.00
TPB (5/06, $12.95) r/series; cover gallery 13.00

AFRICA
Magazine Enterprises: 1955
1(A-1#137)-Cave Girl, Thun'da;Powell-c/a(4) 27 54 81 158 254 350

AFRICAN LION (Disney movie)
Dell Publishing Co.: Nov, 1955
Four Color #665 6 12 18 37 59 80

AFTER DARK
Sterling Comics: No. 6, May, 1955 - No. 8, Sept, 1955
6-8-Sekowsky-a in all 9 18 27 52 69 85

AFTER THE CAPE
Image Comics (Shadowline): Mar, 2007 - No. 3, May, 2007 ($2.99, B&W, limited series)
1-3-Jim Valentino-s/Marco Rudy-a 3.00
... Volume One TPB (9/07, $12.99) r/series; scripts, sketch pages, character profiles 13.00
...II (11/07 - No. 3, 1/08, $2.99) 1-3-Jim Valentino-s/Sergio Carrera-a 3.00

AGAINST BLACKSHARD 3-D (Also see SoulQuest)
Sirius Comics: August, 1986 ($2.25)
1 3.50

AGENCY, THE
Image Comics (Top Cow): August, 2001 - No. 6, Mar, 2002 ($2.50/$2.95/$4.95)
1,2: 1-Jenkins-s/Hotz-a; three covers by Hotz, Turner, Silvestri 2.50
3-5 ($2.95) 3.00
6-($4.95) Flip-c preview of Jeremiah TV series 5.00
Preview (2001, 16 pgs.) B&W pages, cover previews, sketch pages 2.25

AGENT LIBERTY SPECIAL (See Superman, 2nd Series)
DC Comics: 1992 ($2.00, 52 pgs, one-shot)

GD VG FN VF VF/NM NM-
2.0 4.0 6.0 8.0 9.0 9.2

1-1st solo adventure; Guice-c/a(i) 2.50

AGENTS, THE
Image Comics: Apr, 2003 - No. 6, Sept, 2003 ($2.95, B&W)
1-6-Ben Dunn-c/a 3.00

AGENTS OF ATLAS
Marvel Comics: Oct, 2006 - No. 6, Mar, 2007 ($2.99, limited series)
1-6: 1-Golden Age heroes Marvel Boy & Venus app.; Kirk-a 3.00
HC (2007, $24.99, dustjacket) r/#1-6, What If? #9, agents' debuts in '40s-'50s Atlas comics, creator interviews, character design art 25.00

AGENTS OF LAW (Also see Comic's Greatest World)
Dark Horse Comics: Mar, 1995 - No. 6, Sept, 1995 ($2.50)
1-6: 5-Predator app. 6-Predator app.; death of Law 2.50

AGENT X (Continued from Deadpool)
Marvel Comics: Sept. 2002 - No. 15, Dec, 2003 ($2.99/$2.25)
1-($2.99) Simone-s/Udon Studios-a; Taskmaster app. 3.00
2-9-($2.25) 2-Punisher app. 2.50
10-15-($2.99) 10,11-Evan Dorkin-s. 12-Hotz-a 3.00

AGE OF APOCALYPSE: THE CHOSEN
Marvel Comics: Apr, 1995 ($2.50, one-shot)
1-Wraparound-c 3.00

AGE OF BRONZE
Image Comics: Nov, 1998 - Present ($2.95/$3.50, B&W, limited series)
1-6-Eric Shanower-c/s/a 3.00
7-27-($3.50) 3.50
...Behind the Scenes (5/02, $3.50) background info and creative process 3.50
...Special (6/99, $2.95) Story of Agamemnon and Menelaus 3.00
A Thousand Ships (7/01, $19.95, TPB) r/#1-9 20.00
Sacrifice (9/04, $19.95, TPB) r/#10-19 20.00

AGE OF HEROES, THE
Halloween Comics/Image Comics #3 on: 1996 - No. 5, 1999 ($2.95, B&W)
1-5: James Hudnall scripts; John Ridgway-c/a 3.00
...Special ($4.95) r/#1,2 5.00
...Special 2 ($6.95) r/#3,4 7.00
...Wex 1 ('98, $2.95) Hudnall-s/Angel Fernandez-a 3.00

AGE OF INNOCENCE: THE REBIRTH OF IRON MAN
Marvel Comics: Feb, 1996 ($2.50, one-shot)
1-New origin of Tony Stark 3.00

AGE OF REPTILES
Dark Horse Comics: Nov, 1993 - No. 4, Feb, 1994 ($2.50, limited series)
1-4: Delgado-c/a/scripts in all 3.00

AGE OF REPTILES: THE HUNT
Dark Horse Comics: May, 1996 - No. 5, Sept, 1996 ($2.95, limited series)
1-5: Delgado-c/a/scripts in all; wraparound-c 3.00

AGE OF THE SENTRY, THE
Marvel Comics: Nov, 2008 - No. 6 ($2.99, limited series)
1-Silver Age style stories. 1-Origin retold; Bullock-c 3.00

AGGIE MACK
Four Star Comics Corp./Superior Comics Ltd.: Jan, 1948 - No. 8, Aug, 1949
1-Feldstein-a, "Johnny Prep" 40 80 120 240 390 540
2,3-Kamen-c 21 42 63 123 197 270
4-Feldstein "Johnny Prep"; Kamen-c 28 56 84 162 261 360
5-8-Kamen-c/a 22 44 66 131 211 290

AGGIE MACK
Dell Publishing Co.: Apr - Jun, 1962
Four Color #1335 4 8 12 28 44 60

AIR ACE (Formerly Bill Barnes No. 1-12)
Street & Smith Publications: V2#1, Jan, 1944 - V3#8(No. 20), Feb-Mar, 1947
V2#1-Nazi concentration camp-c 41 82 123 256 428 600
V2#2-Classic-c 48 96 144 298 499 700
V2#3-12: 7-Powell-a 16 32 48 94 147 200
V3#1-6: 2-Atomic explosion on-c 14 28 42 80 115 150
V3#7-Powell bondage-c/a; all atomic issue 23 46 69 135 218 300
V3#8 (V5#8 on-c)-Powell-c/a 15 30 45 84 127 170

AIRBOY (Also see Airmaidens, Skywolf, Target: Airboy & Valkyrie)
Eclipse Comics: July, 1986 - No. 50, Oct, 1989 (#1-8, 50¢, 20 pgs., bi-weekly; #9-on, 36 pgs.;

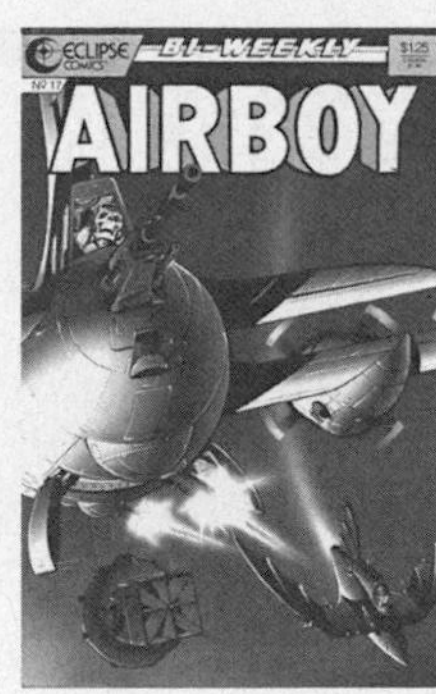

Airboy #17 © ECL

Air Fighters Comics #7 © HILL

Akiko #1 © Mark Crilley

	GD 2.0	VG 4.0	FN 6.0	VF 8.0	VF/NM 9.0	NM- 9.2
#34-on monthly)						
1-4: 2-1st Marisa; Skywolf gets new costume. 3-The Heap begins						4.00
5 Valkyrie returns; Dave Stevens-c						6.00
6-49: 9-Begin $1.25-c; Skywolf begins. 11-Origin of G.A. Airboy & his plane Birdie. 28-Mr. Monster vs. The Heap. 33-Begin $1.75-c. 38-40-The Heap by Infantino. 41-r/1st app. Valkyrie from Air Fighters. 42-Begin $1.95-c. 46,47-part-r/Air Fighters. 48-Black Angel-r/A.F						3.00
50 ($4.95, 52 pgs.)-Kubert-c						5.00

NOTE: *Evans* c-21. *Gulacy* c-7, 20. *Spiegle* a-34, 35, 37. *Ken Steacy* painted c-17, 33.

AIRBOY COMICS (Air Fighters Comics No. 1-22)
Hillman Periodicals: V2#11, Dec, 1945 - V10#4, May, 1953 (No V3#3)

	GD	VG	FN	VF	VF/NM	NM-
V2#11	73	146	219	460	780	1100
12-Valkyrie-c/app.	52	104	156	322	536	750
V3#1,2(no #3)	40	80	120	244	397	550
4-The Heap app. in Skywolf	37	74	111	218	349	480
5,7,8,10,11	33	66	99	192	309	425
6-Valkyrie-c/app.	36	72	108	210	338	465
9-Origin The Heap	37	74	111	219	352	485
12-Skywolf & Airboy x-over; Valkyrie-c/app.	40	80	120	235	380	525
V4#1-Iron Lady app.	33	66	99	192	309	425
2,3,12: 2-Rackman begins	25	50	75	147	236	325
4-Simon & Kirby-c	29	58	87	172	276	380
5-9,11 All S&K-a	28	56	84	164	265	365
10-Valkyrie-c/app.	30	60	90	176	283	390
V5#1-4,6-11: 4-Infantino Heap. 10-Origin The Heap	19	38	57	112	176	240
5-Skull-c.	22	44	66	127	204	280
12-Krigstein-a(p)	20	40	60	115	183	250
V6#1-3,5-12: 6,8-Origin The Heap	18	36	54	105	165	225
4-Origin retold	22	44	66	127	204	280
V7#1-12: 7,8,10-Origin The Heap	18	36	54	105	165	225
V8#1-3,5-12	16	32	48	96	151	205
4-Krigstein-a	17	34	51	100	158	215
V9#1,3,4,6-12: 7-One pg. Frazetta ad	15	30	45	83	124	165
2-Valkyrie app.	15	30	45	86	133	180
5(#100)	15	30	45	86	133	180
V10#1-4	14	28	42	80	115	150

NOTE: *Barry* a-V2#3, 7. *Bolle* a-V4#12. *McWilliams* a-V3#7, 9. *Powell* a-V7#2, 3, V8#1, 6. *Starr* a-V5#1, 12. *Dick Wood* a-V4#12. Bondage-c V5#8.

AIRBOY MEETS THE PROWLER
Eclipse Comics: Aug, 1987 ($1.95, one-shot)

1-John Snyder, III-c/a — 3.00

AIRBOY-MR. MONSTER SPECIAL
Eclipse Comics: Aug, 1987 ($1.75, one-shot)

1 — 3.00

AIRBOY VERSUS THE AIR MAIDENS
Eclipse Comics: July, 1988 ($1.95)

1 — 3.00

AIR FIGHTERS CLASSICS
Eclipse Comics: Nov, 1987 - No. 6, May, 1989 ($3.95, 68 pgs., B&W)

1-6: Reprints G.A. Air Fighters #2-7. 1-Origin Airboy — 4.00

AIR FIGHTERS COMICS (Airboy Comics #23 (V2#11) on)
Hillman Periodicals: Nov, 1941; No. 2, Nov, 1942 - V2#10, Fall, 1945

	GD	VG	FN	VF	VF/NM	NM-
V1#1-(Produced by Funnies, Inc.); Black Commander only app.	280	560	840	1764	2982	4200
2(11/42)-(Produced by Quality artists & Biro for Hillman); Origin & 1st app. Airboy & Iron Ace; Black Angel (1st app.), Flying Dutchman & Skywolf (1st app.) begin; Fuje-a; Biro-c/a	429	858	1287	2917	5109	7300
3-Origin/1st app. The Heap; origin Skywolf; 2nd Airboy app./c	187	374	561	1178	1989	2800
4-Japan war-c	137	274	411	863	1457	2050
5-Japanese octopus War-c	117	234	351	737	1244	1750
6-Japanese soldiers as rats-c	157	314	471	989	1670	2350
7-Classic Nazi swastika-c	153	306	459	964	1632	2300
8-12: 8,10,11-War covers	83	166	249	523	887	1250
V2#1-Classic Nazi War-c	87	174	261	548	924	1300
2-Skywolf by Giunta; Flying Dutchman by Fuje; 1st meeting Valkyrie & Airboy (she worked for the Nazis in beginning); 1st app. Valkyrie (11/43); Valkyrie-c	117	234	351	737	1244	1750
3,4,6,8,9	62	124	186	391	658	925
5,7: 5-Flag-c; Fuje-a. 7-Valkyrie app.	66	132	198	416	701	985
10-Origin The Heap & Skywolf	71	142	213	447	754	1060

NOTE: *Fuje* a-V1#2, 5, 7, V2#2, 3, 5, 7-9. *Giunta* a-V2#2, 3, 7, 9.

AIRFIGHTERS MEET SGT. STRIKE SPECIAL, THE
Eclipse Comics: Jan, 1988 ($1.95, one-shot, stiff-c)

1-Airboy, Valkyrie, Skywolf app. — 3.00

AIR FORCES (See American Air Forces)

AIRMAIDENS SPECIAL
Eclipse Comics: August, 1987 ($1.75, one-shot, Baxter paper)

1-Marisa becomes La Lupina (origin) — 3.00

AIR RAIDERS
Marvel Comics (Star Comics)/Marvel #3 on: Nov, 1987- No. 5, Mar, 1988 ($1.00)

1,5: Kelley Jones-a in all — 3.50
2-4: 2-Thunderhammer app. — 2.50

AIRTIGHT GARAGE, THE (Also see Elsewhere Prince)
Marvel Comics (Epic Comics): July, 1993 - No. 4, Oct, 1993 ($2.50, lim. series, Baxter paper)

1-4: Moebius-c/a/scripts — 4.00

AIR WAR STORIES
Dell Publishing Co.: Sept-Nov, 1964 - No. 8, Aug, 1966

	GD	VG	FN	VF	VF/NM	NM-
1-Painted-c; Glanzman-c/a begins	4	8	12	28	44	60
2-8: 2,3-Painted-c	3	6	9	18	27	35

A.K.A. GOLDFISH
Caliber Comics: 1994 - 1995 (B&W, $3.50/$3.95)

...:Ace; ...:Jack; ...:Queen; ...:Joker; ...:King -Brian Michael Bendis c/a — 4.00
TPB (1996, $17.95) — 20.00
Goldfish: The Definitive Collection (Image, 2001, $19.95) r/series plus promo art and new prose story; intro. by Matt Wagner — 20.00
10th Anniversary HC (Image, 2002, $49.95) — 50.00

AKIKO
Sirius: Mar, 1996 - Present ($2.50/$2.95, B&W)

1-Crilley-c/a/scripts in all — 5.00
2 — 4.00
3-39. 25-($2.95, 32 pgs.)-w/Asala back-up pages — 3.00
40-49,51,52: 40-Begin $2.95-c — 3.00
50-($3.50) — 3.50
Flights of Fancy TPB (5/02, $12.95) r/various features, pin-ups and gags — 13.00
TPB Volume 1,4 ('97, 2/00, $14.95) 1-r/#1-7. 4-r/#19-25 — 15.00
TPB Volume 2,3 ('98, '99, $11.95) 2-r/#8-13. 3- r/#14-18 — 12.00
TPB Volume 5 (12/01, $12.95) r/#26-31 — 13.00
TPB Volume 6,7 (6/03, 4/04, $14.95) 6-r/#32-38. 7-r/#40-47 — 15.00

AKIKO ON THE PLANET SMOO
Sirius: Dec, 1995 ($3.95, B&W)

V1#1-($3.95)-Crilley-c/a/scripts; gatefold-c — 5.00
Ashcan ('95, mail offer) — 3.00
Hardcover V1#1 (12/95, $19.95, B&W, 40 pgs.) — 20.00
The Color Edition(2/00,$4.95) — 5.00

AKIRA
Marvel Comics (Epic): Sept, 1988 - No. 38, Dec, 1995 ($3.50/$3.95/$6.95, deluxe, 68 pgs.)

	GD	VG	FN	VF	VF/NM	NM-
1-Manga by Katsuhiro Otomo	3	6	9	16	23	30
1,2-2nd printings (1989, $3.95)						5.00
2	2	4	6	9	12	15
3-5	2	4	6	8	10	12
6-16	1	2	3	5	7	9
17-33: 17-$3.95-c begins						6.00
34-37: 34-(1994)-$6.95-c begins. 35-37: 35-(1995). 37-Texeira back-up, Gibbons, Williams pin-ups	2	4	6	8	10	12
38-Moebius, Allred, Pratt, Toth, Romita, Van Fleet, O'Neill, Madureira pin-ups	2	4	6	8	11	14

ALADDIN & HIS WONDERFUL LAMP (See Dell Jr Treasury #2)

ALAN LADD (See The Adventures of...)

ALAN MOORE'S AWESOME UNIVERSE HANDBOOK (Also see Across the Universe:...)
Awesome Entertainment: Apr, 1999 ($2.95, B&W)

1-Alan Moore-text/ Alex Ross-sketch pages and 2 covers — 5.00

ALAN MOORE...
DC Comics (WildStorm): TPB

...'s Complete WildC.A.T.S. (2007, $29.99) r/#21-34,50; ...Homecoming & ...Gang War — 30.00
...: Wild Worlds (2007, $24.99) r/various WildStorm one-shots and limited series — 25.00

ALARMING ADVENTURES

Albion #5 © DC & IPC Media

Alias #12 © MAR

Alien Legion #16 © Carl Potts

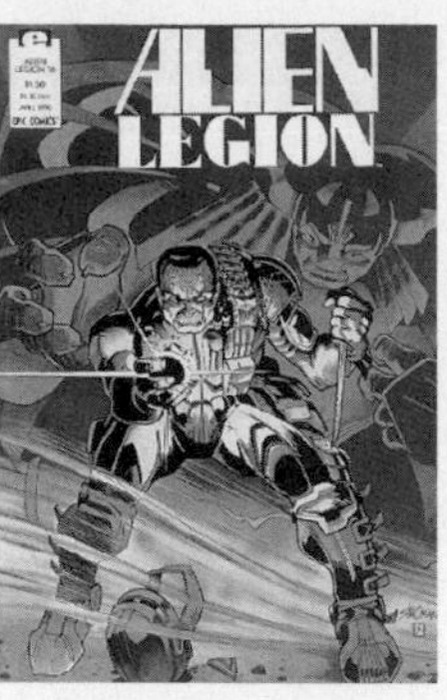

Harvey Publications: Oct, 1962 - No. 3, Feb, 1963

	GD 2.0	VG 4.0	FN 6.0	VF 8.0	VF/NM 9.0	NM- 9.2
1-Crandall/Williamson-a	8	16	24	54	90	125
2-Williamson/Crandall-a	5	10	15	35	55	75
3	5	10	15	30	48	65

NOTE: *Bailey a-1, 3. Crandall a-1p, 2i. Powell a-2(2). Severin c-1-3. Torres a-2? Tuska a-1. Williamson a-1i, 2p.*

ALARMING TALES
Harvey Publications (Western Tales): Sept, 1957 - No. 6, Nov, 1958

	GD 2.0	VG 4.0	FN 6.0	VF 8.0	VF/NM 9.0	NM- 9.2
1-Kirby-c/a(4); Kamandi prototype story by Kirby	29	58	87	169	272	375
2-Kirby-a(4)	20	40	60	117	186	255
3,4-Kirby-a. 4-Powell, Wildey-a	15	30	45	90	140	190
5-Kirby/Williamson-a; Wildey-a; Severin-c	16	32	48	96	151	205
6-Williamson-a?; Severin-c	14	28	42	78	112	145

ALBEDO
Thoughts And Images: Apr, 1985 - No. 14, Spring, 1989 (B&W)
Antarctic Press: (Vol. 2) Jun, 1991 - No. 10 ($2.50)

	GD 2.0	VG 4.0	FN 6.0	VF 8.0	VF/NM 9.0	NM- 9.2
0-Yellow cover; 50 copies	14	28	42	102	181	260
0-White cover, 450 copies	7	14	21	49	80	110
0-Blue, 1st printing, 500 copies	7	14	21	45	73	100
0-Blue, 2nd printing, 1000 copies	4	8	12	24	37	50
0-3rd & 4th printing	2	4	6	13	18	22
1-Dark red - low print run	7	14	21	50	83	115
1-Bright red - low print run	5	10	15	34	55	75
2 -1st app. Usagi Yojimbo by Stan Sakai; 2000 copies - no 2nd printing	31	62	93	239	445	650
3	3	6	9	18	27	35
4-Usagi Yojimbo-c	3	6	9	20	30	40
5-14	1	2	3	5	6	8
(Vol. 2) 1-10, Color Special						4.00

ALBEDO ANTHROPOMORPHICS
Antarctic Press: (Vol. 3) Spring, 1994 - No. 4, Jan, 1996 ($2.95, color); (Vol. 4) Dec, 1999 - No. 2, Jan, 1999 ($2.95/$2.99, B&W)

	NM- 9.2
V3#1-4-Steve Gallacci-c/a. V4#1,2	3.00

ALBERTO (See The Crusaders)

ALBERT THE ALLIGATOR & POGO POSSUM (See Pogo Possum)

ALBION (Inspired by 1960s IPC British comics characters)
DC Comics (WildStorm): Aug, 2005 - No. 6, Nov, 2006 ($2.99, limited series)

	NM- 9.2
1-6-Alan Moore, Leah Moore & John Reppion-s/Shane Oakley-a; Dave Gibbons-c	3.00
TPB (2007, $19.99) r/series; intro by Neil Gaiman; reprints from 1960s British comics	20.00

ALBUM OF CRIME (See Fox Giants)

ALBUM OF LOVE (See Fox Giants)

AL CAPP'S DOGPATCH (Also see Mammy Yokum)
Toby Press: No. 71, June, 1949 - No. 4, Dec, 1949

	GD 2.0	VG 4.0	FN 6.0	VF 8.0	VF/NM 9.0	NM- 9.2
71(#1)-Reprints from Tip Top #112-114	17	34	51	98	154	210
2-4: 4-Reprints from Li'l Abner #73	14	28	42	76	108	140

AL CAPP'S SHMOO (Also see Oxydol-Dreft & Washable Jones & Shmoo)
Toby Press: July, 1949 - No. 5, Apr, 1950 (None by Al Capp)

	GD 2.0	VG 4.0	FN 6.0	VF 8.0	VF/NM 9.0	NM- 9.2
1-1st app. Super-Shmoo	31	62	93	181	291	400
2-5: 3-Sci-fi trip to moon. 4-X-Mas-c	21	42	63	123	197	270

AL CAPP'S WOLF GAL
Toby Press: 1951 - No. 2, 1952

	GD 2.0	VG 4.0	FN 6.0	VF 8.0	VF/NM 9.0	NM- 9.2
1,2-Edited-r from Li'l Abner #63,64	24	48	72	140	225	310

ALEISTER ARCANE
IDW Publishing: Apr, 2004 - No. 3, June, 2004 ($3.99, limited series)

	NM- 9.2
1-3-Steve Niles-s/Breehn Burns-a	4.00
TPB (10/04, $17.99) r/series; sketch pages	18.00

ALEXANDER THE GREAT (Movie)
Dell Publishing Co.: No. 688, May, 1956

	GD 2.0	VG 4.0	FN 6.0	VF 8.0	VF/NM 9.0	NM- 9.2
Four Color 688-Buscema-a; photo-c	7	14	21	49	80	110

ALF (TV) (See Star Comics Digest)
Marvel Comics: Mar, 1988 - No. 50, Feb, 1992 ($1.00)

	GD 2.0	VG 4.0	FN 6.0	VF 8.0	VF/NM 9.0	NM- 9.2
1-Photo-c						4.00
1-2nd printing						2.50
2-19: 6-Photo-c						2.50
20-22: 20-Conan parody. 21-Marx Brothers. 22-X-Men parody						3.00
23-30: 24-Rhonda-c/app. 29-3-D cover						2.50
31-43,46-49						3.00
44,45: 44-X-Men parody. 45-Wolverine, Punisher, Capt. America-c						4.00
50-($1.75, 52 pgs.)-Final issue; photo-c						4.00
Annual 1-3: 1-Rocky & Bullwinkle app. 2-Sienkiewicz-c. 3-TMNT parody						3.00
...Comics Digest 1,2: 1-(1988)-Reprints Alf #1,2	1	3	4	6	8	10
Holiday Special 1,2 ('88, Wint. '89, 68 pgs.): 2-X-Men parody-c						3.00
Spring Special 1 (Spr/89, $1.75, 68 pgs.) Invisible Man parody						3.00
TPB (68 pgs.) r/#1-3; photo-c						5.00

ALFRED HARVEY'S BLACK CAT
Lorne-Harvey Productions: 1995 ($3.50, B&W/color)

	NM- 9.2
1-Origin by Mark Evanier & Murphy Anderson; contains history of Alfred Harvey & Harvey Publications; 5 pg. B&W Sad Sack story; Hildebrandts-c	5.00

ALGIE (LITTLE...)
Timor Publ. Co.: Dec, 1953 - No. 3, 1954

	GD 2.0	VG 4.0	FN 6.0	VF 8.0	VF/NM 9.0	NM- 9.2
1-Teenage	8	16	24	40	50	60
1-Misprint exists w/Secret Mysteries #19 inside	9	18	27	50	65	80
2,3	5	10	15	24	30	35
Accepted Reprint #2(nd)	3	6	8	12	14	16
Super Reprint #15	2	4	6	8	11	14

ALIAS:
Now Comics: July, 1990 - No. 5, Nov, 1990 ($1.75)

	NM- 9.2
1-5: 1-Sienkiewicz-c	2.50

ALIAS (Also see The Pulse)
Marvel Comics (MAX Comics): Nov, 2001 - No. 28, Jan, 2004 ($2.99)

	GD 2.0	VG 4.0	FN 6.0	VF 8.0	VF/NM 9.0	NM- 9.2
1-Bendis-s/Gaydos-a/Mack-c; intro Jessica Jones; Luke Cage app.	1	2	3	5	6	8
2-4						5.00
5-28: 7,8-Sienkiewicz-a (2 pgs.) 16-21-Spider-Woman app. 22,23-Jessica's origin. 24-28-Purple; Avengers app.; flashback-a by Bagley						3.00
HC (2002, $29.99) r/#1-9; intro. by Jeph Loeb						30.00
Omnibus (2006, $69.99, hardcover with dustjacket) r/#1-28 and What If Jessica Jones Had Joined the Avengers?; original pitch, script and sketch pages						70.00
Vol. 1: TPB (2003, $19.99) r/#1-9						20.00
Vol. 2: Come Home TPB (2003, $13.99) r/#11-15						14.00
Vol. 3: The Underneath TPB (2003, $16.99) r/#10,16-21						17.00

ALICE (New Adventures in Wonderland)
Ziff-Davis Publ. Co.: No. 10, 7-8/51 - No. 11(#2), 11-12/51

	GD 2.0	VG 4.0	FN 6.0	VF 8.0	VF/NM 9.0	NM- 9.2
10-Painted-c; Berg-a	26	52	78	152	244	335
11-(#2 on inside) Dave Berg-a	15	30	45	90	140	190

ALICE AT MONKEY ISLAND (See The Adventures of Alice)
Pentagon Publ. Co. (Civil Service): No. 3, 1946

	GD 2.0	VG 4.0	FN 6.0	VF 8.0	VF/NM 9.0	NM- 9.2
3	10	20	30	54	72	90

ALICE IN WONDERLAND (Disney; see Advs. of Alice, Dell Jr. Treasury #1, The Dreamery, Movie Comics,Walt Disney Showcase #22, and World's Greatest Stories)
Dell Publishing Co.: No. 24, 1940; No. 331, 1951; No. 341, July, 1951

	GD 2.0	VG 4.0	FN 6.0	VF 8.0	VF/NM 9.0	NM- 9.2
Single Series 24 (#1)(1940)	48	96	144	298	499	700
Four Color 331, 341-"Unbirthday Party w/..."	15	30	45	105	190	275
1-(Whitman, 3/84, pre-pack only)-r/4-Color #331	2	4	6	10	14	18

ALIEN ENCOUNTERS (Replaces Alien Worlds)
Eclipse Comics: June, 1985 - No. 14, Aug, 1987 ($1.75, Baxter paper, mature)

	NM- 9.2
1-10: Nudity, strong language in all. 9-Snyder-a	4.00
11-14-Low print run	5.00

ALIEN LEGION (See Epic & Marvel Graphic Novel #25)
Marvel Comics (Epic Comics): Apr, 1984 - No. 20, Sept, 1987

	NM- 9.2
nn-With bound-in trading card; Austin-i	4.00
2-20: 2-$1.50-c. 7,8-Portacio-i	3.00

ALIEN LEGION (2nd Series)
Marvel Comics (Epic): Aug, 1987(indicia)(10/87 on-c) - No. 18, Aug, 1990

	NM- 9.2
V2#1-18-Stroman-a in all. 7-18-Farmer-i	2.50
...: Force Nomad TPB (Checker Book Pub. Group, 2001, $24.95) r/#1-11	25.00
...: Piecemaker TPB (Checker Book Pub. Group, 2002, $19.95) r/#12-18	20.00

ALIEN LEGION: (Series of titles; all Marvel/Epic Comics)

	NM- 9.2
--BINARY DEEP, 1993 ($3.50, one-shot, 52 pgs.), nn-With bound-in trading card	3.50
--JUGGER GRIMROD, 8/92 ($5.95, one-shot, 52 pgs.) Book 1	6.00
--ONE PLANET AT A TIME, 5/93 - Book 3, 7/93 ($4.95, squarebound, 52 pgs.) Book 1-3: Hoang Nguyen-a	5.00

--ON THE EDGE (The... #2 & 3), 11/90 - No. 3, 1/91 ($4.50, 52 pgs.)

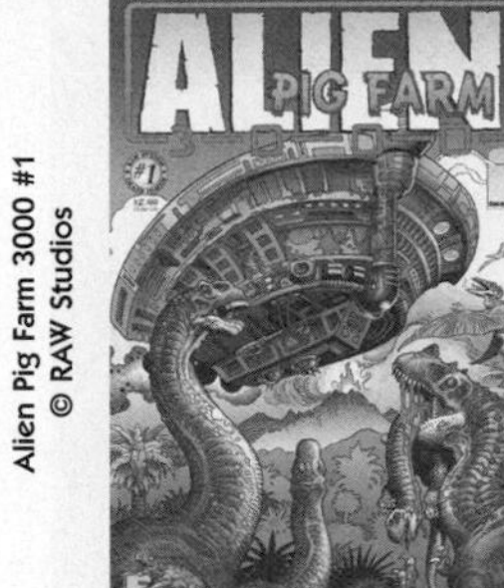

Alien Pig Farm 3000 #1
© RAW Studios

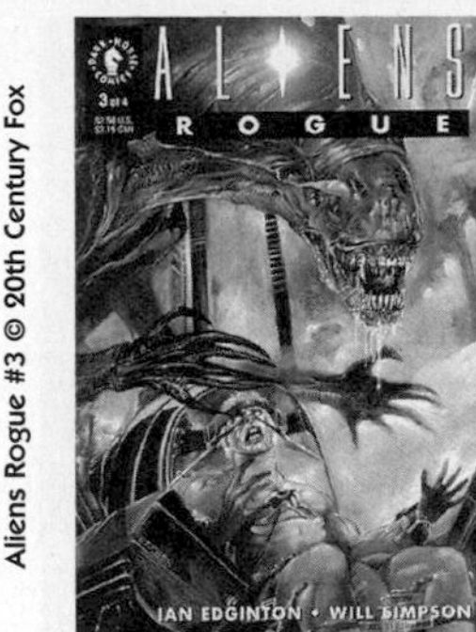

Aliens Rogue #3 © 20th Century Fox

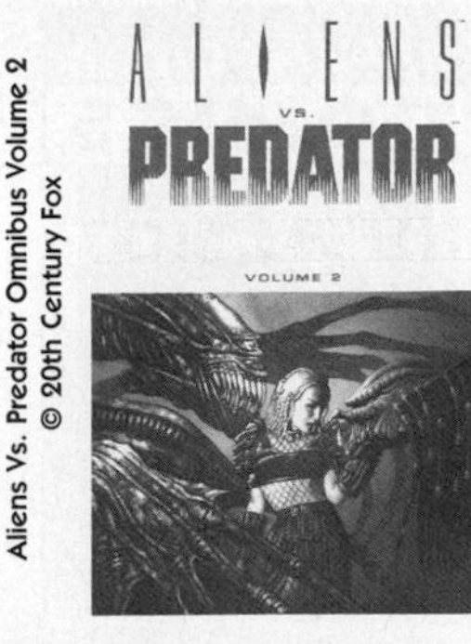

Aliens Vs. Predator Omnibus Volume 2
© 20th Century Fox

	GD 2.0	VG 4.0	FN 6.0	VF 8.0	VF/NM 9.0	NM- 9.2

1-3-Stroman & Farmer-a 4.50

--TENANTS OF HELL, '91 - No. 2, '1 ($4.50, squarebound, 52 pgs.)
Book 1,2-Stroman-c/a(p) 4.50

ALIEN NATION (Movie)
DC Comics: Dec, 1988 ($2.50; 68 pgs.)
1-Adaptation of film; painted-c 4.00

ALIEN PIG FARM 3000
Image Comics (RAW Studios): Apr, 2007 - No. 4, July, 2007 ($2.99, limited series)
1-4-Steve Niles, Thomas Jane & Todd Farmer-s/Don Marquez-a 3.00

ALIEN RESURRECTION (Movie)
Dark Horse Comics: Oct, 1997 - No. 2, Nov, 1997 ($2.50; limited series)
1,2-Adaptation of film; Dave McKean-c 3.00

ALIENS, THE (Captain Johner and...)(Also see Magnus Robot Fighter...)
Gold Key: Sept-Dec, 1967; No. 2, May, 1982
1-Reprints from Magnus #1,3,4,6-10; Russ Manning-a in all
3 6 9 20 30 40
2-(Whitman) Same contents as #1 1 2 3 5 6 8

ALIENS (Movie) (See Alien: The Illustrated..., Dark Horse Comics & Dark Horse Presents #24)
Dark Horse Comics: May, 1988 - No. 6, July, 1989 ($1.95, B&W, limited series)
1-Based on movie sequel;1st app. Aliens in comics 3 6 9 14 19 24
1-2nd - 6th printings; 4th w/new inside front-c 3.00
2 1 3 4 6 8 10
2-2nd & 3rd printing, 3-6-2nd printings 3.00
3 1 2 3 5 6 8
4-6 5.00
Mini Comic #1 (2/89, 4x6")-Was included with Aliens Portfolio 4.00
Collection 1 ($10.95,)-r/#1-6 plus Dark Horse Presents #24 plus new-a 12.00
Collection 1-2nd printing (1991, $11.95)-On higher quality paper than 1st print; Dorman painted-c 12.00
Hardcover ('90, $24.95, B&W)-r/1-6, DHP #24 30.00
... Omnibus Vol. 1 (7/07, $24.95, 9x6") r/1st & 2nd series and Aliens: Earth War 25.00
... Omnibus Vol. 2 (12/07, $24.95, 9x6") r/Genocide, Harvest and Colonial Marines series 25.00
... Omnibus Vol. 3 (3/08, $24.95, 9x6") r/Rogue, Salvation and Sacrifice, Labyrinth series 25.00
... Omnibus Vol. 4 (6/08, $24.95, 9x6") r/Music of the Spears, Stronghold, Berserker, Mondo Pest and Mondo Heat series and one-shots 25.00
... Outbreak (3rd printing, 8/96, $17.95)-Bolton-c 18.00
Platinum Edition - (See Dark Horse Presents: Aliens Platinum Edition) -

ALIENS
Dark Horse Comics: V2#1, Aug, 1989 - No. 4, 1990 ($2.25, limited series)
V2#1-Painted art by Denis Beauvais 5.00
1-2nd printing (1990), 2-4 3.00
...: Nightmare Asylum TPB (12/96, $16.95) r/series; Bolton-c 17.00

ALIENS: (Series of titles, all Dark Horse)
--ALCHEMY, 10/97 - No. 3, 11/97 ($2.95),1-3-Corben-c/a, Arcudi-s 3.00
--APOCALYPSE - THE DESTROYING ANGELS, 1/99 - No. 4, 4/99 ($2.95)
1-4-Doug Wheatly-a/Schultz-s 3.00
--BERSERKERS, 1/95 - No. 4, 4/95 ($2.50) 1-4 3.00
--COLONIAL MARINES, 1/93 - No. 10, 7/94 ($2.50) 1-10 3.00
--EARTH ANGEL, 8/94 ($2.95) 1-Byrne-a/story; wraparound-c 3.00
--EARTH WAR, 6/90 - No. 4, 10/90 ($2.50) 1-All have Sam Kieth-a & Bolton painted-c 5.00
1-2nd printing, 3,4 3.00
2 4.00
--GENOCIDE, 11/91 - No. 4, 2/92 ($2.50) 1-4-Suydam painted-c. 4-Wraparound-c, poster 3.00
--GLASS CORRIDOR, 6/98 ($2.95) 1-David Lloyd-s/a 3.00
--HARVEST (See Aliens: Hive)
--HAVOC, 6/97 - No. 2, 7/97 ($2.95) 1,2: Schultz-s, Kent Williams-c, 40 artists including Art Adams, Kelley Jones, Duncan Fegredo, Kevin Nowlan 3.00
--HIVE, 2/92 - No. 4,5/92 ($2.50) 1-4: Kelley Jones-c/a in all 3.00
...Harvest TPB ('98, $16.95) r/series; Bolton-c 17.00
--KIDNAPPED, 12/97 - No. 3, 2/98 ($2.50) 1-3 3.00
--LABYRINTH, 9/93 - No. 4, 1/94 ($2.50)1-4: 1-Painted-c 3.00
--LOVESICK, 12/96 ($2.95) 1 3.00
--MONDO HEAT, 2/96 ($2.50) nn-Sequel to Mondo Pest 3.00
--MONDO PEST, 4/95 ($2.95, 44 pgs.)nn-r/Dark Horse Comics #22-24 3.00
--MUSIC OF THE SPEARS, 1/94 - No. 4, 4/94 ($2.50) 1-4 3.00
--NEWT'S TALE, 6/92 - No. 2, 7/92 ($4.95) 1,2-Bolton-c 5.00
--PIG, 3/97 ($2.95)1 3.00
--PREDATOR: THE DEADLIEST OF THE SPECIES, 7/93 - No. 12,8/95 ($2.50)
1-Bolton painted-c; Guice-a(p) 5.00
1-Embossed foil platinum edition 10.00
2-12: Bolton painted-c. 2,3-Guice-a(p) 3.00
--PURGE, 8/97 ($2.95) nn-Hester-a 3.00
--ROGUE, 4/993 - No. 4, 7/93 ($2.50)1-4: Painted-c 3.00
--SACRIFICE, 5/93 ($4.95, 52 pgs.) nn-P. Milligan scripts; painted-c/a 5.00
--SALVATION, 11/93 ($4.95, 52 pgs.) nn-Mignola-c/a(p); Gibbons script 5.00
--SPECIAL, 6/97 ($2.50) 1 3.00
--STALKER, 6/98 ($2.50)1-David Wenzel-s/a 3.00
--STRONGHOLD, 5/94 - No. 4, 9/94 ($2.50) 1-4 3.00
--SURVIVAL, 2/98 - No. 3, 4/98 ($2.95) 1-3-Tony Harris-c 3.00
--TRIBES, 1992 ($24.95, hardcover graphic novel) Bissette text-s with Dorman painted-a 25.00
...softcover ($9.95) 10.00

ALIENS VS. PREDATOR (See Dark Horse Presents #36)
Dark Horse Comics: June, 1990 - No. 4, Dec, 1990 ($2.50, limited series)
1-Painted-c 1 2 3 5 6 8
1-2nd printing 3.00
0-(7/90, $1.95, B&W)-r/Dark Horse Pres. #34-36 1 2 3 5 7 9
2,3 5.00
4-Dave Dorman painted-c 4.00
Annual (7/99, $4.95) Jae Lee-c 5.00
... : Booty (1/96, $2.50) painted-c 3.00
... Omnibus Vol. 1 (5/07, $24.95, 9x6") r/#1-4 & Annual; ...: War; ...: Eternal 25.00
... Omnibus Vol. 2 (10/07, $24.95, 9x6") r/...: Xenogenesis #1-4; ...: Deadliest of the Species; ...: Booty and stories from ... Annual 25.00
... : Thrill of the Hunt (9/04, $6.95, digest-size TPB) Based on 2004 movie 7.00
... Wraith 1 (7/98, $2.95) Jay Stephens-s 3.00
--VS. PREDATOR: DUEL, 3/95 - No. 2, 4/95 ($2.50) 1,2 3.00
--VS. PREDATOR: ETERNAL, 6/98 - No. 4, 9/98 ($2.50)1-4: Edginton-s/Maleev-a; Fabry-c 3.00
--VS. PREDATOR VS. THE TERMINATOR, 4/00 - No. 4, 7/00 ($2.95) 1-4: Ripley app. 3.00
--VS. PREDATOR: WAR, No. 0, 5/95 - No. 4, 8/95 ($2.50) 0-4: Corben painted-c 3.00
--VS. PREDATOR: XENOGENESIS, 12/99 - No. 4, 3/00 ($2.95) 1-4: Watson-s/Mel Rubi-a 3.00
--XENOGENESIS, 8/99 - No. 4, 11/99 ($2.95) 1-4: T&M Bierbaum-s 3.00

ALIEN TERROR (See 3-D Alien Terror)

ALIEN: THE ILLUSTRATED STORY (Also see Aliens)
Heavy Metal Books: 1980 ($3.95, soft-c, 8x11")
nn-Movie adaptation; Simonson-a 3 6 9 14 19 24

ALIEN 3 (Movie)
Dark Horse Comics: June, 1992 - No. 3, July, 1992 ($2.50, limited series)
1-3: Adapts 3rd movie; Suydam painted-c 3.00

ALIEN WORLDS (Also see Eclipse Graphic Album #22)
Pacific Comics/Eclipse: Dec, 1982 - No. 9, Jan, 1985
1,2,4: 2,4-Dave Stevens-c/a 6.00
3,5-7 4.00
8,9 1 2 3 4 5 7
3-D No. 1-Art Adams 1st published art 1 2 3 4 5 7

ALISON DARE, LITTLE MISS ADVENTURES (Also see Return of ...)
Oni Press: Sept, 2000 ($4.50, B&W, one-shot)
1-J. Torres-s/J.Bone-c/a 4.50

ALISON DARE & THE HEART OF THE MAIDEN
Oni Press: Jan, 2002 - No. 2, Feb, 2002 ($2.95, B&W, limited series)
1,2-J. Torres-s/J.Bone-c/a 3.00

ALISTER THE SLAYER
Midnight Press: Oct, 1995 ($2.50)
1-Boris-c 2.50

ALL-AMERICAN COMICS (...Western #103-126, ...Men of War #127 on; also see The Big All-American Comic Book)
All-American/National Periodical Publ.: April, 1939 - No. 102, Oct, 1948
1-Hop Harrigan (1st app.), Scribbly by Mayer (1st DC app.), Toonerville Folks, Ben Webster,

All-American Comics #3 © DC

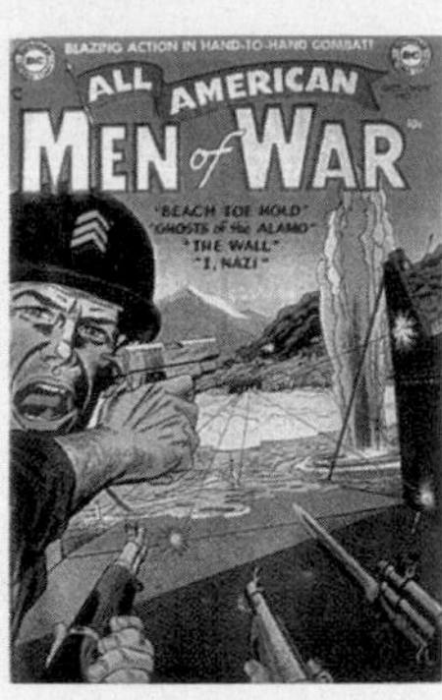

All American Men of War #7 © DC

All-American Western #112 © DC

	GD 2.0	VG 4.0	FN 6.0	VF 8.0	VF/NM 9.0	NM- 9.2

Spot Savage, Mutt & Jeff, Red White & Blue (1st app.), Adventures in the Unknown, Tippie, Reg'lar Fellers, Skippy, Bobby Thatcher, Mystery Men of Mars, Daiseybelle, Wiley of West Point begin 706 1412 2118 4236 6268 8300
2-Ripley's Believe It or Not begins, ends #24 204 408 612 1224 1812 2400
3-5: 5-The American Way begins, ends #10 155 310 465 930 1378 1825
6,7: 6-Last Spot Savage; Popsicle Pete begins, ends #26, 28. 7-Last Bobby Thatcher 110 220 330 693 1172 1650
8-The Ultra Man begins & 1st-c app. 280 560 840 1764 2982 4200
9,10: 10-X-Mas-c 95 190 285 599 1012 1425
11,15: 11-Ultra Man-c. 15-Last Tippie & Reg'lar Fellars; Ultra Man-c 113 226 339 712 1206 1700
12-14: 12-Last Toonerville Folks 90 180 270 567 959 1350
16-(Rare)-Origin/1st app. Green Lantern by Sheldon Moldoff (c/a)(7/40) & begin series; appears in costume on-c & only one panel inside; created by Martin Nodell. Inspired in 1940 by a switchman's green lantern that would give trains the go ahead to proceed 12,000 24,000 36,000 96,000 188,000 280,000
17-2nd Green Lantern 1450 2900 4350 10,750 19,125 27,500
18-N.Y. World's Fair-c/story (scarce) 1025 2050 3075 7700 13,850 20,000
19-Origin/1st app. The Atom (10/40); last Ultra Man 1750 3500 5250 13,200 23,600 34,000
20-Atom dons costume; Ma Hunkle becomes Red Tornado (1st app.)(1st DC costumed heroine, before Wonder Woman, 11/40); Rescue on Mars begins, ends #25; 1 pg. origin Green Lantern 500 1000 1500 3600 6300 9000
21-Last Wiley of West Point & Skippy; classic Moldoff-c 353 706 1059 2400 4200 6000
22,23: 23-Last Daiseybelle; 3 Idiots begin, end #82 317 634 951 1981 3541 5100
24-Sisty & Dinky become the Cyclone Kids; Ben Webster ends; origin Dr. Mid-Nite & Sargon, The Sorcerer in text with app. 324 648 972 2203 3852 5500
25-Origin & 1st story app. Dr. Mid-Nite by Stan Asch; Hop Harrigan becomes Guardian Angel; last Adventure in the Unknown (scarce) 1000 2000 3000 7400 13,200 19,000
26-Origin/1st story app. Sargon, the Sorcerer 371 742 1113 2523 4412 6300
27: #27-32 are misnumbered in indicia with correct No. appearing on-c. Intro. Doiby Dickles, Green Lantern's sidekick 388 776 1164 2638 4619 6600
28-Hop Harrigan gives up costumed i.d. 193 386 579 1216 2058 2900
29,30 193 386 579 1216 2058 2900
31-40: 35-Doiby learns Green Lantern's i.d. 140 280 420 882 1491 2100
41-50: 50-Sargon ends 115 230 345 725 1225 1725
51-60: 59-Scribbly & the Red Tornado ends 100 200 300 630 1065 1500
61-Origin/1st app. Solomon Grundy (11/44) 611 1222 1833 4399 7700 11,000
62-70: 70-Kubert Sargon; intro Sargon's helper, Maximillian O'Leary 88 176 264 554 940 1325
71-88: 71-Last Red White & Blue. 72-Black Pirate begins (not in #74-82); last Atom. 73-Winky, Blinky & Noddy begins, ends #82. 79,83-Mutt & Jeff-c. 70 140 210 441 746 1050
89-Origin & 1st app. Harlequin 117 234 351 737 1244 1750
90-99: 90-Origin/1st app. Icicle. 99-Last Hop Harrigan 113 226 339 712 1206 1700
100-1st app. Johnny Thunder by Alex Toth (8/48); western theme begins (Scarce) 197 394 591 1241 2096 2950
101-Last Mutt & Jeff (Scarce) 133 266 399 838 1419 2000
102-Last Green Lantern, Black Pirate & Dr. Mid-Nite (Scarce) 253 506 759 1594 2697 3800

NOTE: *No Atom in 47, 62-69.* **Kinstler** *Black Pirate-89.* **Stan Aschmeier** *a (Dr. Mid-Nite) 25-84; c-7.* **Mayer** *c-1, 2(part), 6, 10.* **Moldoff** *c-16-23.* **Nodell** *c-31.* **Paul Reinman** *a (Green Lantern)-53-55p, 56-84, 87; (Black Pirate)-83-88, 90; c-52, 55-76, 78, 80, 81, 87.* **Toth** *a-88, 92, 96, 98-102; c(p)-92, 96-102. Scribbly by* **Mayer** *in #1-59. Ultra Man by* **Mayer** *in #8-19.*

ALL AMERICAN COMICS
DC Comics: April 1939

nn - Ashcan comic, not distributed to newsstands, only for in house use. Cover art is Advenure Comics #33 and interior from Detective Comics #23 (no known sales)

ALL-AMERICAN COMICS (Also see All Star Comics 1999 crossover titles)
DC Comics: May, 1999 ($1.99, one-shot)

1-Golden Age Green Lantern and Johnny Thunder; Barreto-a 2.50

ALL-AMERICAN MEN OF WAR (Previously All-American Western)
National Periodical Publ.: No. 127, Aug-Sept, 1952 - No. 117, Sept-Oct, 1966

127 (#1, 1952) 96 192 288 816 1558 2300
128 (1952) 50 100 150 412 781 1150
2(12-1/'52-53)-5 45 90 135 360 673 985
6-Devil Dog story; Ghost Squadron story 34 68 102 269 495 720
7-10: 8-Sgt. Storm Cloud-s 34 68 102 269 495 720
11-16,18: 18-Last precode; 1st Kubert-c (2/55) 30 60 90 229 427 625
17-1st Frogman-s in this title 31 62 93 239 445 650
19,20,22-27 23 46 69 170 315 460
21-Easy Co. prototype 28 56 84 208 387 565
28 (12/55)-1st Sgt. Rock prototype; Kubert-a 38 76 114 293 547 800
29,30,32-Wood-a 23 46 69 170 315 460
31,33-38,40: 34-Gunner prototype-s. 35-Greytone-c. 36-Little Sure Shot prototype-s. 38-1st S.A. issue 20 40 60 143 264 385
39 (11/56)-2nd Sgt. Rock prototype; 1st Easy Co.? 30 60 90 225 420 615
41,43-47,49,50: 46-Tankbusters-c/s 16 32 48 118 219 320
42-Pre-Sgt. Rock Easy Co.-c/s 21 42 63 152 281 410
48-Easy Co.-c/s; Nick app.; Kubert-a 21 42 63 152 281 410
51-56,58-62,65,66: 61-Gunner-c/s 13 26 39 95 168 240
57(5/58),63,64 -Pre-Sgt. Rock Easy Co.-c/s 17 34 51 126 233 340
67-1st Gunner & Sarge by Andru & Esposito 36 72 108 277 514 750
68,69: 68-2nd app. Gunner & Sarge. 69-1st Tank Killer-c/s 15 30 45 111 206 300
70 12 24 36 86 153 220
71-80: 71,72,76-Tank Killer-c/s. 74-Minute Commandos-c/s 10 20 30 70 123 175
81,84-88: 88-Last 10¢ issue 9 18 27 60 100 140
82-Johnny Cloud begins(1st app.), ends #117 15 30 45 111 206 300
83-2nd Johnny Cloud 10 20 30 71 126 180
89-100: 89-Battle Aces of 3 Wars begins, ends #98 7 14 21 45 73 100
101-111,113-116: 111,114,115-Johnny Cloud 5 10 15 32 51 70
112-Balloon Buster series begins, ends #114,116 5 10 15 34 55 75
117-Johnny Cloud-c & 3-part story 5 10 15 34 55 75

NOTE: *Frogman stories in 17, 38, 44, 45, 50, 51, 53, 55-58, 63, 65, 66, 72, 76, 77.* **Colan** *a-112.* **Drucker** *a-47, 58, 61, 63, 65, 69, 71, 74, 77.* **Grandenetti** *c(p)-127, 128, 2-17(most).* **Heath** *a-14, 27, 32, 38, 41, 45, 47, 50, 51, 55-58, 62, 64, 71, 75, 76, 78, 95, 111-117; c-85, 91, 94-96, 100, 101, 110-112, others?* **Infantino** *a-8.* **Kirby** *a-29.* **Krigstein** *a-128('52), 2, 3, 5.* **Kubert** *a-22, 24, 28, 29, 33, 34, 36, 38, 39, 41-43, 47-50, 52, 53, 55, 56, 59, 60, 63-65, 69, 71-73, 76, 102, 103, 105, 106, 108, 114; c-41, 44, 52, 54, 55, 58, 64, 69, 76, 77, 79, 102-106, 108, 113-117, others? Tank Killer in 69, 71, 76 by* **Kubert**. **P. Reinman** *c-55, 57, 61, 62, 71, 72, 74-76, 80.* **J. Severin** *a-58.*

ALL AMERICAN MEN OF WAR
DC Comics: Aug/Sept. 1952

nn - Ashcan comic, not distributed to newsstands, only for in-house use. Cover art is All Star Western #58 and interior from Mr. District Attorney #21 (no known sales)

ALL-AMERICAN SPORTS
Charlton Comics: Oct, 1967

1 3 6 9 19 29 38

ALL-AMERICAN WESTERN (Formerly All-American Comics; Becomes All-American Men of War)
National Periodical Publ.: No. 103, Nov, 1948 - No. 126, June-July, 1952 (103-121: 52 pgs.)

103-Johnny Thunder & his horse Black Lightning continues by Toth, ends #126; Foley of The Fighting 5th, Minstrel Maverick, & Overland Coach begin; Captain Tootsie by Beck; mentioned in Love and Death 50 100 150 310 518 725
104-Kubert-a 37 74 111 215 345 475
105,107-Kubert-a 31 62 93 181 291 400
106,108-110,112: 112-Kurtzman's "Pot-Shot Pete" (1 pg.) 26 52 78 152 244 335
111,114-116-Kubert-a 27 54 81 158 254 350
113-Intro. Swift Deer, J. Thunder's new sidekick (4-5/50); classic Toth-c; Kubert-a 28 56 84 166 268 370
117-126: 121-Kubert-a; bondage-c 19 38 57 112 176 240

NOTE: **G. Kane** *c(p)-112, 119, 120, 123.* **Kubert** *a-103-105, 107, 111, 112(1 pg.), 113-116, 121.* **Toth** *a 103-125; c(p)-103-111,113-116, 121, 122, 124-126. Some copies of #125 have #12 on-c.*

ALL COMICS
Chicago Nite Life News: 1945

1 15 30 45 83 124 165

ALLEGRA
Image Comics (WildStorm): Aug, 1996 - No. 4, Dec, 1996 ($2.50)

1-4 2.50

ALLEY CAT (Alley Baggett)
Image Comics: July, 1999 - No. 6, Mar, 2000 ($2.50/$2.95)

Preview Edition 6.00
Prelude 5.00
Prelude w/variant-c 6.00
1-Photo-c 2.50
1-Painted-c by Dorian 3.50
1-Another Universe Edition, 1-Wizard World Edition 7.00
2-4: 4-Twin towers on-c 2.50
5,6-($2.95) 3.00
Lingerie Edition (10/99, $4.95) Photos, pin-ups, cover gallery 5.00
...Vs. Lady Pendragon ('99, $3.00) Stinsman-c 3.00

ALLEY OOP (See The Comics, The Funnies, Red Ryder and Super Book #9)

All-Flash Quarterly #2 © DC

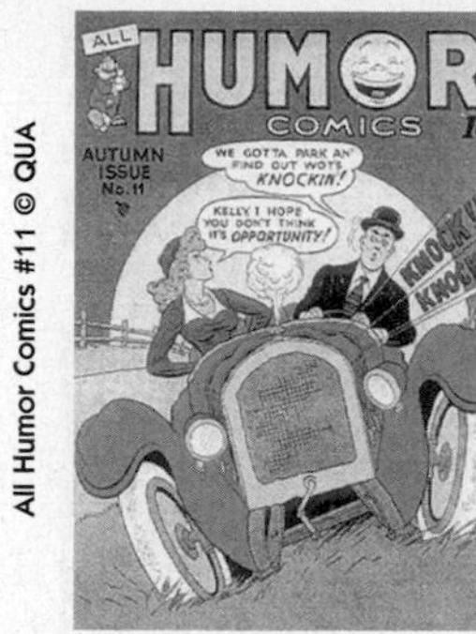

All Humor Comics #11 © QUA

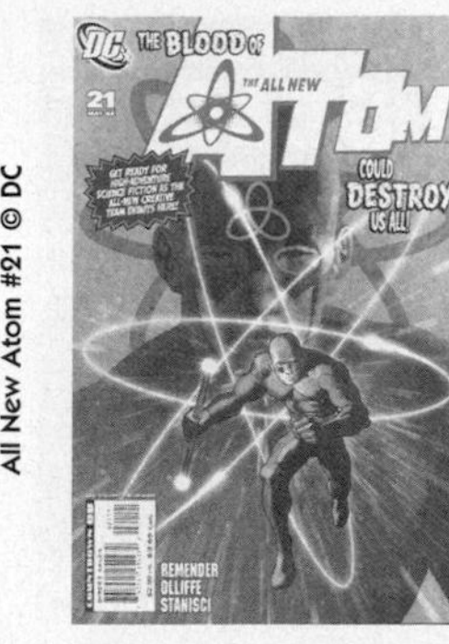

All New Atom #21 © DC

GD VG FN VF VF/NM NM-
2.0 4.0 6.0 8.0 9.0 9.2

Dell Publishing Co.: No. 3, 1942
Four Color 3 (#1) 43 86 129 344 647 950

ALLEY OOP
Argo Publ.: Nov, 1955 - No. 3, Mar, 1956 (Newspaper reprints)
1 16 32 48 92 144 195
2,3 12 24 36 67 94 120

ALLEY OOP
Dell Publishing Co.: 12-2/62-63 - No. 2, 9-11/63
1 6 12 18 41 66 90
2 5 10 15 34 55 75

ALLEY OOP
Standard Comics: No. 10, Sept, 1947 - No. 18, Oct, 1949
10 25 50 75 145 233 320
11-18: 17,18-Schomburg-c 20 40 60 115 183 250

ALLEY OOP ADVENTURES
Antarctic Press: Aug, 1998 - No. 3, Dec, 1998 ($2.95)
1-3-Jack Bender-s/a 3.00

ALLEY OOP ADVENTURES (Alley Oop Quarterly in indicia)
Antarctic Press: Sept, 1999 - No. 3, Mar, 2000 ($2.50/$2.99, B&W)
1-3-Jack Bender-s/a 3.00

ALL-FAMOUS CRIME (2nd series - Formerly Law Against Crime #1-3; becomes All-Famous Police Cases #6 on)
Star Publications: No. 8, 5/51 - No. 10, 11/51; No. 4, 2/52 - No. 5, 5/52;
8 (#1-1st series) 22 44 66 127 204 280
9 (#2)-Used in **SOTI**, illo- "The wish to hurt or kill couples in lovers' lanes is a not uncommon perversion;" L.B. Cole-c/a(r)/Law-Crime #3 37 74 111 215 345 475
10 (#3) 20 40 60 115 183 250
4 (#4-2nd series)-Formerly Law-Crime 19 38 57 109 172 235
5 (#5) Becomes All-Famous Police Cases #6 19 38 57 109 172 235
NOTE: *All have **L.B. Cole** covers.*

ALL FAMOUS CRIME STORIES (See Fox Giants)

ALL-FAMOUS POLICE CASES (Formerly All Famous Crime #5)
Star Publications: No. 6, Feb, 1952 - No. 16, Sept, 1954
6 19 38 57 112 176 240
7,8: 7-Baker story. 8-Marijuana story 18 36 54 105 165 225
9-16 16 32 48 94 147 200
NOTE: ***L. B. Cole** c-all; a-15, 1pg. **Hollingsworth** a-15.*

ALL-FLASH (...Quarterly No. 1-5)
National Per. Publ./All-American: Summer, 1941 - No. 32, Dec-Jan, 1947-48
1-Origin The Flash retold by E. E. Hibbard; Hibbard c-1-10,12-14,16,31p. 1425 2850 4275 10,700 18,850 27,000
2-Origin recap 353 706 1059 2400 4200 6000
3,4 177 354 531 1115 1883 2650
5-Winky, Blinky & Noddy begins (1st app.), ends #32 130 260 390 819 1385 1950
6-10 105 210 315 662 1119 1575
11-13: 12-Origin/1st The Thinker. 13-The King app. 90 180 270 567 959 1350
14-Green Lantern cameo 105 210 315 662 1119 1575
15-20: 18-Mutt & Jeff begins, ends #22 75 150 225 473 799 1125
21-31 64 128 192 403 682 960
32-Origin/1st app. The Fiddler; 1st Star Sapphire 120 240 360 756 1278 1800
NOTE: *Book length stories in 2-13, 16. Bondage c-31, 32. **Martin Nodell** c-15, 17-28.*

ALL FLASH (Leads into Flash [2nd series] #231)
DC Comics: Sept, 2007 ($2.99, one-shot)
1-Wally West hunts down Bart's killers; Waid-s; two covers by Middleton & Sienkiewicz 3.00

ALL FOR LOVE (Young Love V3#5-on)
Prize Publications: Apr-May, 1957 - V3#4, Dec-Jan, 1959-60
V1#1 8 16 24 52 86 120
2-6: 5-Orlando-c 5 10 15 30 48 65
V2#1-5(1/59), 5(3/59) 4 8 12 24 37 50
V3#1(5/59), 1(7/59)-4: 2-Powell-a 3 6 9 20 30 40

ALL FUNNY COMICS
Tilsam Publ./National Periodical Publications (Detective): Winter, 1943-44 - No. 23, May-June, 1948
1-Genius Jones (1st app.), Buzzy (1st app., ends #4), Dover & Clover (see More Fun #93) begin; Bailey-a 47 94 141 291 483 675
2 23 46 69 133 214 295
3-10 15 30 45 83 124 165
11-13,15,18,19-Genius Jones app. 14 28 42 80 115 150
14,17,20-23 10 20 30 56 76 95
16-DC Super Heroes app. 32 64 96 186 298 410

ALL GOOD
St. John Publishing Co.: Oct, 1949 (50¢, 260 pgs.)
nn-(8 St. John comics bound together) 68 136 204 428 727 1025
NOTE: *Also see Li'l Audrey Yearbook & Treasury of Comics.*

ALL GOOD COMICS (See Fox Giants)
Fox Features Syndicate: No.1, Spring, 1946 (36 pgs.)
1-Joy Family, Dick Transom, Rick Evans, One Round Hogan 27 54 81 158 254 350

ALL GREAT
William H. Wise & Co.: nd (1945?) (132 pgs.)
nn-Capt. Jack Terry, Joan Mason, Girl Reporter, Baron Doomsday; Torture scenes 41 82 123 253 419 585

ALL GREAT COMICS (See Fox Giants)
Fox Feature Syndicate: 1946 (36 pgs.)
1-Crazy House, Bertie Benson Boy Detective, Gussie the Gob 27 54 81 158 254 350

ALL GREAT COMICS (Formerly Phantom Lady #13? Dagar, Desert Hawk No. 14 on)
Fox Features Syndicate: No. 14, Oct, 1947 - No. 13, Dec, 1947 (Newspaper strip reprints)
14(#12)-Brenda Starr & Texas Slim-r (Scarce) 57 114 171 359 605 850
13-Origin Dagar, Desert Hawk; Brenda Starr (all-r); Kamen-c; Dagar covers begin 64 128 192 403 682 960

ALL-GREAT CONFESSIONS (See Fox Giants)

ALL GREAT CRIME STORIES (See Fox Giants)

ALL GREAT JUNGLE ADVENTURES (See Fox Giants)

ALL HALLOW'S EVE
Innovation Publishing: 1991 ($4.95, 52 pgs.)
1-Painted-c/a 1 2 3 4 5 7

ALL HERO COMICS
Fawcett Publications: Mar, 1943 (100 pgs., cardboard-c)
1-Capt. Marvel Jr., Capt. Midnight, Golden Arrow, Ibis the Invincible, Spy Smasher, Lance O'Casey; 1st Banshee O'Brien; Raboy-c 173 346 519 1090 1845 2600

ALL HUMOR COMICS
Quality Comics Group: Spring, 1946 - No. 17, December, 1949
1 21 42 63 123 197 270
2-Atomic Tot story; Gustavson-a 13 26 39 74 105 135
3-9: 3-Intro Kelly Poole who is cover feature #3 on. 5-1st app. Hickory? 8-Gustavson-a 9 18 27 47 61 75
10-17 8 16 24 42 54 65

ALLIANCE, THE
Image Comics (Shadowline Ink): Aug, 1995 - No. 3, Nov, 1995 ($2.50)
1-3: 2-(9/95) 2.50

ALL LOVE (...Romances No. 26)(Formerly Ernie Comics)
Ace Periodicals (Current Books): No. 26, May, 1949 - No. 32, May, 1950
26 (No. 1)-Ernie, Lily Belle app. 10 20 30 56 76 95
27-L. B. Cole-a 14 28 42 76 108 140
28-32 8 16 24 40 50 60

ALL-NEGRO COMICS
All-Negro Comics: June, 1947 (15¢)
1 (Rare) 1100 2200 3300 6000 8000 10,000
NOTE: *Seldom found in fine or mint condition; many copies have brown pages.*

ALL-NEW ATOM, THE (See The Atom and DCU Brave New World)
DC Comics: Sept, 2006 - Present ($2.99)
1-25: 1-18-Simone-s. 1-Intro Ryan Choi; Byrne-a thru #3. 4-11-Barrows-a. 12,13-Chronos app. 14,15-Countdown x-over. 17,18-Wonder Woman app. 3.00
...: Future/Past TPB (2007, $14.99) r/#7-11 15.00
...: My Life in Miniature TPB (2007, $14.99) r/#1-6 and app. in DCU Brave New World #1 15.00
...: The Hunt For Ray Palmer TPB (2008, $14.99) r/#12-16 15.00

ALL-NEW COLLECTORS' EDITION (Formerly Limited Collectors' Edition: see for C-57, C-59)
DC Comics, Inc.: Jan, 1978 - Vol. 8, No. C-62, 1979 (No. 54-58: 76 pgs.)
C-53-Rudolph the Red-Nosed Reindeer 4 8 12 28 44 60

All Select Comics #9 © MAR

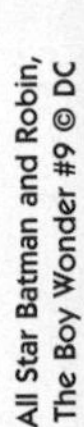
All Star Batman and Robin, The Boy Wonder #9 © DC

All Star Comics #3 © DC

GD VG FN VF VF/NM NM-
2.0 4.0 6.0 8.0 9.0 9.2

C-54-Superman Vs. Wonder Woman 4 8 12 24 37 50
C-55-Superboy & the Legion of Super-Heroes; Wedding of Lightning Lad & Saturn Girl; Grell-c/a 4 8 12 24 37 50
C-56-Superman Vs. Muhammad Ali: story & wraparound N. Adams-c/a 6 12 18 43 69 95
C-56-Superman Vs. Muhammad Ali (Whitman variant)-low print 7 14 21 49 80 110
C-57,C-59-(See Limited Collectors' Edition)
C-58-Superman Vs. Shazam; Buckler-c/a 4 8 12 25 39 52
C-60-Rudolph's Summer Fun(8/78) 4 8 12 25 39 52
C-61-(See Famous First Edition-Superman #1)
C-62-Superman the Movie (68 pgs.; 1979)-Photo-c from movie plus photos inside (also see DC Special Series #25) 3 6 9 15 21 27

ALL-NEW COMICS (...Short Story Comics No. 1-3)
Family Comics (Harvey Publications): Jan, 1943 - No. 14, Nov, 1946; No. 15, Mar-Apr, 1947 (10 x 13-1/2")

1-Steve Case, Crime Rover, Johnny Rebel, Kayo Kane, The Echo, Night Hawk, Ray O'Light, Detective Shane begin (all 1st app.?); Red Blazer on cover only; Sultan-a 300 600 900 1890 3195 4500
2-Origin Scarlet Phantom by Kubert 110 220 330 693 1172 1650
3-Nazi war-c 87 174 261 548 924 1300
4 71 142 213 447 754 1060
5-11: 5-Schomburg-c thru #11. 6-The Boy Heroes & Red Blazer (text story) begin, end #12; Black Cat app.; intro. Sparky in Red Blazer. 7-Kubert, Powell-a; Black Cat & Zebra app. 8,9: 8-Shock Gibson app.; Kubert, Powell-a; Schomburg-c. 9-Black Cat app.; Kubert-a. 10-The Zebra app. (from Green Hornet Comics); Kubert-a(3). 11-Girl Commandos, Man In Black app. 86 172 258 542 914 1285
12,13: 12-Kubert-a. 13-Stuntman by Simon & Kirby; Green Hornet, Joe Palooka, Flying Fool app.; Green Hornet-c 59 118 177 372 629 885
14-The Green Hornet & The Man in Black Called Fate by Powell, Joe Flying Fool app.; Flying Fool app.; J. Palooka-c by Ham Fisher 53 106 159 330 553 775
15-(Rare)-Small size (5-1/2x8-1/2"; B&W; 32 pgs.). Distributed to mail subscribers only. Black Cat and Joe Palooka app. 120 240 360 456 1278 1800

NOTE: *Also see Boy Explorers No. 2, Flash Gordon No. 5, and Stuntman No. 3.* ***Powell*** *a-11.* ***Schomburg*** *c-5-11. Captain Red Blazer & Spark on c-5-11 (w/Boy Heroes #12).*

ALL-NEW OFFICIAL HANDBOOK OF THE MARVEL UNIVERSE A TO Z
Marvel Comics: 2006 - No. 12, 2006 ($3.99, limited series)

1-12-Profile pages of Marvel characters not covered in 2004-2005 Official Handbooks 4.00
...: Update 1-4 (2007, $3.99) Profile pages 4.00

ALL-OUT WAR
DC Comics: Sept-Oct, 1979 - No. 6, Aug, 1980 ($1.00, 68 pgs.)

1-The Viking Commando(origin), Force Three(origin), & Black Eagle Squadron begin 2 4 6 9 12 15
2-6 1 2 3 5 7 9

NOTE: ***Ayers*** *a(p)-1-6.* ***Elias*** *r-2.* ***Evans*** *a-1-6.* ***Kubert*** *c-16.*

ALL PICTURE ADVENTURE MAGAZINE
St. John Publishing Co.: Oct, 1952 - No. 2, Nov, 1952 (100 pg. Giants, 25¢, squarebound)

1-War comics 32 64 96 190 305 420
2-Horror-crime comics 47 94 141 291 483 675

NOTE: *Above books contain three St. John comics rebound; variations possible.* ***Baker*** *art known in both.*

ALL PICTURE ALL TRUE LOVE STORY
St. John Publishing Co.: Oct., 1952 - No. 2, Nov., 1952 (100 pgs., 25¢)

1-Canteen Kate by Matt Baker 52 104 156 322 536 750
2-Baker-c/a 37 74 111 215 345 475

ALL-PICTURE COMEDY CARNIVAL
St. John Publishing Co.: October, 1952 (100 pgs., 25¢)(Contains 4 rebound comics)

1-Contents can vary; Baker-a 43 86 129 267 446 625

ALL REAL CONFESSION MAGAZINE (See Fox Giants)

ALL ROMANCES (Mr. Risk No. 7 on)
A. A. Wyn (Ace Periodicals): Aug, 1949 - No. 6, June, 1950

1 12 24 36 69 97 125
2 8 16 24 42 54 65
3-6 7 14 21 337 46 55

ALL-SELECT COMICS (Blonde Phantom No. 12 on)
Timely Comics (Daring Comics): Fall, 1943 - No. 11, Fall, 1946

1-Capt. America (by Rico #1), Human Torch, Sub-Mariner begin; Black Widow story (4 pgs.); Classic Schomburg-c 1333 2666 4000 10,000 18,000 26,000
2-Red Skull app. 423 846 1269 3000 5250 7500
3-The Whizzer begins 300 600 900 1910 3255 4600
4,5-Last Sub-Mariner 227 454 681 1430 2415 3400
6-9: 6-The Destroyer app. 8-No Whizzer 180 360 540 1134 1917 2700
10-The Destroyer & Sub-Mariner app.; last Capt. America & Human Torch issue 180 360 540 1134 1917 2700
11-1st app. Blonde Phantom; Miss America app.; all Blonde Phantom-c by Shores 273 546 819 1720 2910 4100

NOTE: ***Schomburg*** *c-1-10.* ***Sekowsky*** *a-7. #7 & 8 show 1944 in indicia, but should be 1945.*

ALL SPORTS COMICS (Formerly Real Sports Comics; becomes All Time Sports Comics No. 4 on)
Hillman Periodicals: No. 2, Dec-Jan, 1948-49; No. 3, Feb-Mar, 1949

2-Krigstein-a(p), Powell, Starr-a 34 68 102 198 319 440
3-Mort Lawrence-a 22 44 66 131 211 290

ALL STAR BATMAN & ROBIN, THE BOY WONDER
DC Comics: Sept, 2005 - Present ($2.99)

1-Two covers; retelling of Robin's origin; Frank Miller-s/Jim Lee-a/c 3.00
1-Diamond Retailer Summit Edition (9/05) sketch-c 100.00
2-9: 2-7-Two covers by Lee and Miller. 3-Black Canary app. 4-Six pg. Batcave gatefold 3.00
8,9-Variant cover by Neal Adams 5.00
... Special Edition (2/06, $3.99) r/#1 with Lee pencil pages and Miller script; new Miller-c 4.00
Vol. 1 HC (2008, $24.99, dustjacket) r/#1-9; cover gallery, sketch pages; Schreck intro. 25.00

ALL STAR COMICS
DC Comics: Spring 1940

1-Ashcan comic, not distributed to newsstands, only for in-house use. Cover art is Flash Comics #1 and interior from Detective Comics #37. A CGC certified 7.0 copy sold for $15,600 in 2002.

ALL STAR COMICS (All Star Western No. 58 on)
National Periodical Publ./All-American/DC Comics: Sum, '40 - No. 57, Feb-Mar, '51; No. 58, Jan-Feb, '76 -No. 74, Sept-Oct, '78

1-The Flash (#1 by E.E. Hibbard), Hawkman (by Shelly), Hourman (by Bernard Baily), The Sandman (by Creig Flessel), The Spectre (by Baily), Biff Bronson, Red White & Blue (ends #2) begin; Ultra Man's only app. (#1-3 are quarterly; #4 begins bi-monthly issues) 1155 2310 3456 8700 15,600 22,500
2-Green Lantern (by Martin Nodell), Johnny Thunder begin; Green Lantern figure swipe from the cover of All-American Comics #16; Flash figure swipe from cover of Flash Comics #8; Moldoff/Bailey-c (cut & paste-c.) 500 1000 1500 3600 6300 9000
3-Origin & 1st app. The Justice Society of America (Win/40); Dr. Fate & The Atom begin, Red Tornado cameo 4100 8200 12,300 30,800 55,400 80,000
3-Reprint, Oversize 13-1/2x10". **WARNING:** This comic is an exact reprint of the original except for its size. DC published it in 1974 with a second cover titling it as a Famous First Edition. There have been many reported cases of the outer cover being removed and the interior sold as the original edition. The reprint with the new outer cover removed is practically worthless. See Famous First Edition for value.
4-1st adventure for J.S.A. 500 1000 1500 3600 6300 9500
5-1st app. Shiera Sanders as Hawkgirl (1st costumed super-heroine, 6-7/41) 456 912 1368 3283 5742 8200
6-Johnny Thunder joins JSA 300 600 900 1910 3255 4600
7-Batman, Superman, Flash cameo; last Hourman; Doiby Dickles app. 329 658 987 2237 3919 5600
8-Origin & 1st app. Wonder Woman (12-1/41-42)(added as 9 pgs. making book 76 pgs.; origin cont'd in Sensation #1; see W.W. #1 for more detailed origin); Dr. Fate dons new helmet; Hop Harrigan text stories & Starman begin; Shiera app.; Hop Harrigan JSA guest; Starman & Dr. Mid-Nite become members 3333 6666 10,000 25,000 45,000 65,000
9-11: 9-JSA's girlfriends cameo; Shiera app.; J. Edgar Hoover of FBI made associate member of JSA. 10-Flash, Green Lantern cameo; Sandman new costume. 11-Wonder Woman begins; Spectre cameo; Shiera app.; Moldoff Hawkman-c 300 600 900 1890 3195 4500
12-Wonder Woman becomes JSA Secretary 273 546 819 1720 2910 4100
13,15: Sandman w/Sandy in #14 & 15. 15-Origin & 1st app. Brain Wave; Shiera app. 250 500 750 1575 2663 3750
14-(12/42) Junior JSA Club begins; w/membership offer & premiums 257 514 771 1619 2735 3850
16-20: 19-Sandman w/Sandy. 20-Dr. Fate & Sandman cameo 200 400 600 1260 2130 3000
21-23: 21-Spectre & Atom cameo; Dr. Fate by Kubert; Dr. Fate, Sandman end. 22-Last Hop Harrigan; Flag-c. 23-Origin/1st app. Psycho Pirate; last Spectre & Starman 163 326 489 1027 1739 2450
24-Flash & Green Lantern cameo; Mr. Terrific only app.; Wildcat, JSA guest; Kubert Hawkman begins; Hitler-c 163 326 489 1027 1739 2450
25-27: 25-Flash & Green Lantern start again. 26-Robot-c. 27-Wildcat, JSA guest (#24-26: only All-American imprint) 138 276 414 869 1472 2075
28-32 122 244 366 769 1297 1825
33-Solomon Grundy & Doiby Dickles app; classic Solomon Grundy cover & last G.A. app. 347 694 1041 2186 4043 5900

All-Star Comics #74 © DC

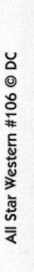

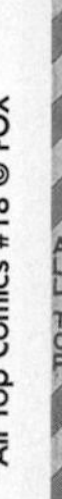

	GD 2.0	VG 4.0	FN 6.0	VF 8.0	VF/NM 9.0	NM- 9.2
34,35-Johnny Thunder cameo in both	117	234	351	737	1249	1760
36-Batman & Superman JSA guests	280	560	840	1764	2982	4200
37-Johnny Thunder cameo; origin & 1st app. Injustice Society; last Kubert Hawkman	157	314	471	989	1670	2350
38-Black Canary begins; JSA Death issue	213	426	639	1342	2271	3200
39,40: 39-Last Johnny Thunder	115	230	345	725	1225	1725
41-Black Canary joins JSA; Injustice Society app. (2nd app.?)	115	230	345	725	1225	1725
42-Atom & the Hawkman don new costumes	115	230	345	725	1225	1725
43-49,51-56: 43-New logo; Robot-c. 55-Sci/Fi story. 56-Robot-c	115	230	345	725	1225	1725
50-Frazetta art, 3 pgs.	123	246	369	775	1313	1850
57-Kubert-a, 6 pgs. (Scarce); last app. G.A. Green Lantern, Flash & Dr. Mid-Nite	167	334	501	1052	1776	2500
V12 #58-(1976) JSA (Flash, Hawkman, Dr. Mid-Nite, Wildcat, Dr. Fate, Green Lantern, Robin & Star Spangled Kid) app.; intro. Power Girl	6	12	18	37	59	80
V12 #59,60: 59-Estrada & Wood-a	3	6	9	16	23	30
V12 #61-68: 62-65-Superman app. 64,65-Wood-c/a; Vandal Savage app. 66-Injustice Society app. 68-Psycho Pirate app.	3	6	9	16	23	30
V12 #69-1st Earth-2 Huntress (Helena Wayne)	4	8	12	24	37	50
V12 #70-73: 70-Full intro. of Huntress	3	6	9	16	23	30
V12 #74-(44 pgs.) Last issue, story continues in Adventure Comics #461 & 462 (death of Earth-2 Batman; Staton-c/a	4	8	12	24	37	50

(See Justice Society Vol. 1 TPB for reprints of V12 revival)

NOTE: *No Atom-27, 36; no Dr. Fate-13; no Flash-8, 9, 11-23; no Green Lantern-8, 9,11-23; Hawkman in 1-57 (only one to app. in all 57 issues); no Johnny Thunder-5, 36; no Wonder Woman-9, 10, 23. Book length stories in 4-9, 11-14, 18-22, 25, 26, 29, 30, 32-36, 40, 42, 43. Johnny Peril in #42-46, 48, 49, 51, 52,54-57.* **Baily** *a-1-10, 12, 13, 14i, 15-20.* **Burnley** *Starman-8-13; c-12, 13.* **Grell** *c-58.* **E.E. Hibbard** *c-3, 4, 6-10.* **Infantino** *c-40.* **Kubert** *Hawkman-24-30, 33-37.* **Lampert/Baily/Flessel** *c-1, 2.* **Moldoff** *Hawkman-3-23; c-11.* **Mart Nodell** *c-25i, 26i, 27-32.* **Purcell** *c-5.* **Simon & Kirby** *Sandman 14-17, 19.* **Staton** *a-66-74p. c-74p.* **Toth** *a-37(2), 38(2), 40, 41; c-38, 41.* **Wood** *a-58i-63i, 64, 65; c-63i, 64, 65. Issues 1-7, 9-16 are 68 pgs.; #8 is 76 pgs., #17-19 are 60 pgs.; #20-57 are 52 pgs.*

ALL STAR COMICS (Also see crossover 1999 editions of Adventure, All-American, National, Sensation, Smash, Star Spangled and Thrilling Comics)
DC Comics: May, 1999 - No. 2, May, 1999 ($2.95, bookends for JSA x-over)

	GD 2.0	VG 4.0	FN 6.0	VF 8.0	VF/NM 9.0	NM- 9.2
1,2-Justice Society in World War 2; Robinson-s/Johnson-c						3.00
1-RRP Edition	(price will be based on future sales)					
...80-Page Giant (9/99, $4.95) Phantom Lady app.						5.00

ALL STAR INDEX, THE
Independent Comics Group (Eclipse): Feb, 1987 ($2.00, Baxter paper)

	GD 2.0	VG 4.0	FN 6.0	VF 8.0	VF/NM 9.0	NM- 9.2
1	1	2	3	5	6	8

ALL-STAR SQUADRON (See Justice League of America #193)
DC Comics: Sept, 1981 - No. 67, Mar, 1987

	GD 2.0	VG 4.0	FN 6.0	VF 8.0	VF/NM 9.0	NM- 9.2
1-Original Atom, Hawkman, Dr. Mid-Nite, Robotman (origin), Plastic Man, Johnny Quick, Liberty Belle, Shining Knight begin	1	2	3	4	5	7
2-10: 3-Solomon Grundy app. 4,7-Spectre app. 8-Re-intro Steel, the Indestructable Man						5.00
11-46,48,49: 12-Origin G.A. Hawkman retold. 23-Origin/1st app. The Amazing Man. 24-Batman app. 25-1st app. Infinity, Inc. (9/83), 26-Origin Infinity, Inc.(2nd app.); Robin app. 27-Dr. Fate vs. The Spectre. 30-35-Spectre app. 33-Origin Freedom Fighters of Earth-X. 36,37-Superman vs. Capt. Marvel; Ordway-c. 41-Origin Starman						4.00
47-Origin Dr. Fate; McFarlane-a (1st full story)/part-c (7/85)	1	3	4	6	8	10
50-Double size; Crisis x-over						6.00
51-66: 51-56-Crisis x-over. 61-Origin Liberty Belle. 62-Origin The Shining Knight. 63-Origin Robotman. 65-Origin Johnny Quick. 66-Origin Tarantula						4.50
67-Last issue; retells first case of the Justice Society						6.00
Annual 1-3: 1(11/82)-Retells origin of G.A. Atom, Guardian & Wildcat; Jerry Ordway's 1st pencils for DC.(1st work was inking Carmine Infantino in Mystery in Space #94). 2(11/83)-Infinity, Inc. app. 3(9/84)						4.50

NOTE: **Buckler** *a-1-5; c-1, 3-5, 51.* **Kubert** *c-2, 7-18. JLA app. in 14, 15. JSA app. in 4, 14, 15, 19, 27, 28.*

ALL-STAR STORY OF THE DODGERS, THE
Stadium Communications: Apr, 1979 ($1.00)

	GD 2.0	VG 4.0	FN 6.0	VF 8.0	VF/NM 9.0	NM- 9.2
1	2	4	6	9	13	16

ALL-STAR SUPERMAN
DC Comics: Jan, 2006 - No. 12, Oct, 2008 ($2.99)

	GD 2.0	VG 4.0	FN 6.0	VF 8.0	VF/NM 9.0	NM- 9.2
1-Grant Morrison-s/Frank Quitely-a/c						5.00
1-Variant-c by Neal Adams						20.00
2-12: 3-Lois gets super powers. 7,8-Bizarro app.						3.00
Vol. 1 HC (2007, $19.99, dustjacket) r/#1-6; Schreck intro.						20.00

ALL STAR WESTERN (Formerly All Star Comics No. 1-57)
National Periodical Publ.: No. 58, Apr-May, 1951 - No. 119, June-July, 1961

	GD 2.0	VG 4.0	FN 6.0	VF 8.0	VF/NM 9.0	NM- 9.2
58-Trigger Twins (ends #116), Strong Bow, The Roving Ranger & Don Caballero begin	45	90	135	279	465	650
59,60: Last 52 pgs.	27	54	81	156	251	345
61-66: 61-64-Toth-a	22	44	66	127	204	280
67-Johnny Thunder begins; Gil Kane-a	28	56	84	162	261	360
68-81: Last precode (2-3/55)	15	30	45	83	124	165
82-98: 97-1st S.A. issue	13	26	39	74	105	135
99-Frazetta-r/Jimmy Wakely #4	14	28	42	76	108	140
100	14	28	42	76	108	140
101-107,109-116,118,119	11	22	33	64	90	115
108-Origin J. Thunder; J. Thunder logo begins	22	44	66	127	204	280
117-Origin Super Chief	14	28	42	81	118	155

NOTE: **Gil Kane** *c(p) 58, 59, 61, 63, 64, 68, 69, 70-95(most), 97-199(most).* **Infantino** *art in most issues. Madame .44 app.- #117-119.*

ALL-STAR WESTERN (Weird Western Tales No. 12 on)
National Periodical Publications: Aug-Sept, 1970 - No. 11, Apr-May, 1972

	GD 2.0	VG 4.0	FN 6.0	VF 8.0	VF/NM 9.0	NM- 9.2
1-Pow-Wow Smith-r; Infantino-a	5	10	15	32	51	70
2-Outlaw begins; El Diablo by Morrow begins; has cameos by Williamson, Torres, Kane, Giordano & Phil Seuling	5	10	15	30	48	65
3-Origin El Diablo	4	8	12	28	44	60
4-6: 5-Last Outlaw issue. 6-Billy the Kid begins, ends #8	3	6	9	20	30	40
7-9-(52 pgs.) 9-Frazetta-a, 3pgs.(r)	4	8	12	23	36	48
10-(52 pgs.) Jonah Hex begins (1st app., 2-3/72)	35	70	105	270	498	725
11-(52 pgs.) 2nd app. Jonah Hex; 1st cover	15	30	45	107	196	285

NOTE: **Neal Adams** *c-2-5;* **Aparo** *a-5.* **G. Kane** *a-3, 4, 6, 8.* **Kubert** *a-4r, 7-9r.* **Morrow** *a-2-4, 10, 11. No. 7-11 have 52 pgs.*

ALL SURPRISE (Becomes Jeanie #13 on) (Funny animal)
Timely/Marvel (CPC): Fall, 1943 - No. 12, Winter, 1946-47

	GD 2.0	VG 4.0	FN 6.0	VF 8.0	VF/NM 9.0	NM- 9.2
1-Super Rabbit, Gandy & Sourpuss begin	38	76	114	226	363	500
2	18	36	54	105	165	225
3-10,12	15	30	45	84	127	170
11-Kurtzman "Pigtales" art	15	30	45	86	133	180

ALL TEEN (Formerly All Winners; All Winners & Teen Comics No. 21 on)
Marvel Comics (WFP): No. 20, January, 1947

	GD 2.0	VG 4.0	FN 6.0	VF 8.0	VF/NM 9.0	NM- 9.2
20-Georgie, Mitzi, Patsy Walker, Willie app.; Syd Shores-c	15	30	45	90	140	190

ALL-TIME SPORTS COMICS (Formerly All Sports Comics)
Hillman Per.: V2, No. 4, Apr-May, 1949 - V2, No. 7, Oct-Nov, 1949 (All 52 pgs.)

	GD 2.0	VG 4.0	FN 6.0	VF 8.0	VF/NM 9.0	NM- 9.2
V2#4	23	46	69	135	218	300
5-7: 5-(V1#5 inside)-Powell-a; Ty Cobb sty. 7-Krigstein-p; Walter Johnson & Knute Rockne sty	18	36	54	105	165	225

ALL TOP
William H. Wise Co.: 1944 (132 pgs.)

	GD 2.0	VG 4.0	FN 6.0	VF 8.0	VF/NM 9.0	NM- 9.2
nn-Capt. V, Merciless the Sorceress, Red Robbins, One Round Hogan, Mike the M.P., Snooky, Pussy Katnip app.	33	66	99	192	309	425

ALL TOP COMICS (My Experience No. 19 on)
Fox Features Synd./Green Publ./Norlen Mag.: 1945; No. 2, Sum, 1946 - No. 18, Mar, 1949; 1957 - 1959

	GD 2.0	VG 4.0	FN 6.0	VF 8.0	VF/NM 9.0	NM- 9.2
1-Cosmo Cat & Flash Rabbit begin (1st app.)	24	48	72	140	225	310
2 (#1-7 are funny animal)	14	28	42	76	108	140
3-7: 7-Two diff. issues (7/47 & 9/47)	10	20	30	56	76	95
8-Blue Beetle, Phantom Lady, & Rulah, Jungle Goddess begin (11/47); Kamen-c	273	546	819	1720	2910	4100
9-Kamen-c	142	284	426	895	1510	2125
10-Kamen bondage-c	147	294	441	926	1563	2200
11-13,15-17: 11,12-Rulah-c. 15-No Blue Beetle	117	234	351	737	1244	1750
14-No Blue Beetle; used in **SOTI**, illo- "Corpses of colored people strung up by their wrists"	160	320	480	1008	1704	2400
18-Dagar, Jo-Jo app; no Phantom Lady or Blue Beetle	75	150	225	473	799	1125
6(1957-Green Publ.)-Patoruzu the Indian; Cosmo Cat on cover only. 6(1958-Literary Ent.)-Muggy Doo; Cosmo Cat on cover only. 6(1959-Norlen)-Atomic Mouse; Cosmo Cat on-c only. 6(1959)-Little Eva. 6(Cornell)-Supermouse on-c	5	10	15	24	30	35

NOTE: *Jo-Jo by* **Kamen**-*12,18.*

ALL TRUE ALL PICTURE POLICE CASES
St. John Publishing Co.: Oct, 1952 - No. 2, Nov, 1952 (100 pgs.)

	GD 2.0	VG 4.0	FN 6.0	VF 8.0	VF/NM 9.0	NM- 9.2
1-Three rebound St. John crime comics	44	88	132	273	454	635
2-Three comics rebound	33	66	99	192	309	425

NOTE: *Contents may vary.*

ALL-TRUE CRIME (...Cases No. 26-35; formerly Official True Crime Cases)
Marvel/Atlas Comics: No. 26, Feb, 1948 - No. 52, Sept, 1952

All True Romance #1 © Artful Pub.

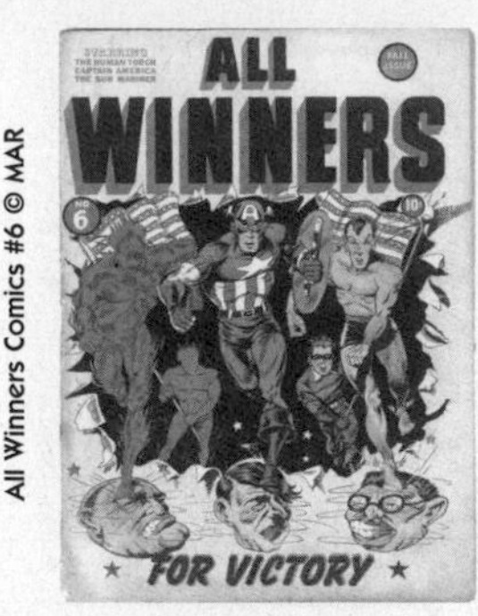

All Winners Comics #6 © MAR

Alpha Flight (2nd series) #12 © MAR

	GD 2.0	VG 4.0	FN 6.0	VF 8.0	VF/NM 9.0	NM- 9.2

(OFI #26,27/CFI #28,29/LCC #30-46/LMC #47-52)
26(#1)-Syd Shores-c 34 68 102 198 319 440
27(4/48)-Electric chair-c 27 54 81 160 258 355
28-41,43-48,50-52: 35-37-Photo-c 14 28 42 76 108 140
42,49-Krigstein-a. 49-Used in **POP**, Pg 79 14 28 42 80 115 150
NOTE: ***Robinson** a-47, 50. **Shores** c-26. **Tuska** a-48(3).*

ALL-TRUE DETECTIVE CASES (Kit Carson No. 5 on)
Avon Periodicals: #2, Apr-May, 1954 - No. 4, Aug-Sept, 1954
2(#1)-Wood-a 23 46 69 135 218 300
3-Kinstler-c 14 28 42 80 115 150
4-r/Gangsters And Gun Molls #2; Kamen-a 18 36 54 105 165 225
nn(100 pgs.)-7 pg. Kubert-a, Kinstler back-c 40 80 120 235 380 525

ALL TRUE ROMANCE (...Illustrated No. 3)
Artful Publ. #1-3/Harwell(Comic Media) #4-20?/Ajax-Farrell(Excellent Publ.) No. 22 on/Four Star Comic Corp.: 3/51 - No. 20, 12/54; No. 22, 3/55 - No. 30?, 7/57; No. 3(#31), 9/57;No. 4(#32), 11/57; No. 33, 2/58 - No. 34, 6/58
1 (3/51) 18 36 54 105 165 220
2 (10/51; 11/51 on-c) 11 22 33 62 86 110
3(12/51) - #5(5/52) 9 18 27 52 69 85
6-Wood-a, 9 pgs. (exceptional) 18 36 54 103 162 220
7-10 [two #7s: #7(11/52, 9/52 inside), #7(11/52, 11/52 inside)]. 10-Hollingsworth-c
9 18 27 47 61 75
11-13,16-19(9/54),20(12/54) (no #21): 11,13-Heck-a 7 14 21 37 46 55
14-Marijuana story 8 16 24 40 50 60
22: Last precode issue (1st Ajax, 3/55) 7 14 21 37 46 55
23-27,29,30(7/57): 29-Disbrow-a 6 12 18 31 38 45
28 (9/56)-L. B. Cole, Disbrow-a 11 22 33 62 86 110
3(#31, 9/57),4(#32, 11/57),33,34 (Farrell, '57- '58) 6 12 18 28 34 40

ALL WESTERN WINNERS (Formerly All Winners; becomes Western Winners with No. 5; see Two-Gun Kid No. 5)
Marvel Comics(CDS): No. 2, Winter, 1948-49 - No. 4, April, 1949
2-Black Rider (origin/1st app.) & his horse Satan, Kid Colt & his horse Steel, & Two-Gun Kid & his horse Cyclone begin; Shores c-2-4 76 152 228 479 810 1140
3-Anti-Wertham editorial 38 76 114 222 356 490
4-Black Rider i.d. revealed; Heath, Shores-a 38 76 114 222 356 490

ALL WINNERS COMICS (All Teen #20) (Also see Timely Presents: ...)
USA No. 1-7/WFP No. 10-19/YAI No. 21: Summer, 1941 - No. 19, Fall, 1946; No. 21, Winter, 1946-47; (No #20) (No. 21 continued from Young Allies No. 20)
1-The Angel & Black Marvel only app.; Capt. America by Simon & Kirby, Human Torch & Sub-Mariner begin (#1 was advertised as All Aces); 1st app. All-Winners Squad in text story by Stan Lee 2050 4100 6150 15,375 27,688 40,000
2-The Destroyer & The Whizzer begin; Simon & Kirby Captain America
500 1000 1500 3600 6300 9000
3 371 742 1113 2523 4412 6300
4-Classic War-c by Al Avison 400 800 1200 2720 4760 6800
5 267 534 801 1682 2841 4000
6-The Black Avenger only app.; no Whizzer story; Hitler, Hirohito & Mussolini-c
300 600 900 1950 3375 4800
7-10 233 466 699 1468 2484 3500
11,13-18: 11-1st Atlas globe on-c (Winter, 1943-44; also see Human Torch #14). 14-16-No Human Torch 163 326 489 1027 1739 2450
12-Red Skull story; last Destroyer; no Whizzer story
210 420 630 1323 2237 3150
19-(Scarce)-1st story app. & origin All Winners Squad (Capt. America & Bucky, Human Torch & Toro, Sub-Mariner, Whizzer, & Miss America; r-in Fantasy Masterpieces #10
556 1112 1668 4003 7002 10,000
21-(Scarce)-All Winners Squad; bondage-c 456 912 1368 3283 5742 8200
NOTE: ***Everett** Sub-Mariner-1, 3, 4; **Burgos** Torch-1, 3, 4. **Schomburg** c-1, 7-18. **Shores** c-19p, 21.*
(2nd Series - August, 1948, Marvel Comics (CDS))
(Becomes All Western Winners with No. 2)
1-The Blonde Phantom, Capt. America, Human Torch, & Sub-Mariner app.
300 600 900 1890 3195 4500

ALL YOUR COMICS (See Fox Giants)
Fox Feature Syndicate (R. W. Voight): Spring, 1946 (36 pgs.)
1-Red Robbins, Merciless the Sorceress app. 22 44 66 127 204 280

ALMANAC OF CRIME (See Fox Giants)

AL OF FBI (See Little Al of the FBI)

ALONE IN THE DARK (Based on video game)
Image Comics: Feb, 2003 ($4.95)
1-Matt Haley-c/a; Jean-Marc & Randy Lofficier-s 5.00

ALPHA AND OMEGA
Spire Christian Comics (Fleming H. Revell): 1978 (49¢)
nn 2 4 6 8 11 14

ALPHA CENTURION (See Superman, 2nd Series & Zero Hour)
DC Comics: 1996 ($2.95, one-shot)
1 3.00

ALPHA FLIGHT (See X-Men #120,121 & X-Men/Alpha Flight)
Marvel Comics: Aug, 1983 - No. 130, Mar, 1994 (#52-on are direct sales only)
1-(52 pgs.) Byrne-a begins (thru #28) -Wolverine & Nightcrawler cameo 4.00
2-28: 2-Vindicator becomes Guardian; origin Marrina & Alpha Flight. 3-Concludes origin Alpha Flight. 6-Origin Shaman. 7-Origin Snowbird. 10,11-Origin Sasquatch. 12-(52 pgs.)-Death of Guardian. 13-Wolverine app. 16,17-Wolverine cameo. 17-X-Men x-over (mostly r-/X-Men #109); 20-New headquarters. 25-Return of Guardian. 28-Last Byrne issue 3.00
29-32,35-50: 39-47,49-Portacio-a(i). 50-Double size; Portacio-a(i) 2.50
33,34-1st & 2nd app. Lady Deathstrike; Wolverine app. 34-Origin Wolverine 3.00
51-Jim Lee's 1st work at Marvel (10/87); Wolverine cameo; 1st Lee Wolverine; Portacio-a(i) 5.00
52,53-Wolverine app.; Lee-a on Wolverine; Portacio-a(i); 53-Lee/Portacio-a 3.00
54-73,76-86,91-99,101-105: 54,63,64-No Jim Lee-a. 54-Portacio-a(i). 55-62-Jim Lee-a(p). 71-Intro The Sorcerer (villain). 91-Dr. Doom app. 94-F.F. x-over. 99-Galactus, Avengers app. 102-Intro Weapon Omega 2.50
74,75,87-90,100: 74-Wolverine, Spider-Man & The Avengers app. 75-Double size ($1.95, 52 pgs.). 87-90-Wolverine. 4 part story w/Jim Lee-c. 89-Original Guardian returns. 100-($2.00, 52 pgs.)-Avengers & Galactus app. 3.00
106-Northstar revelation issue 2.50
106-2nd printing (direct sale only) 2.25
107-109,112-119,121-129: 107-X-Factor x-over. 112-Infinity War x-overs 2.50
110,111: Infinity War x-overs, Wolverine app. (brief). 111-Thanos cameo 3.00
120-($2.25)-Polybagged w/Paranormal Registration Act poster 2.50
130-($2.25, 52 pgs.) 3.00
Annual 1,2 (9/86, 12/87) 3.00
...Classics Vol. 1 TPB (2007, $24.99) r/#1-8; character profile pages; Byrne interview 25.00
Special V2#1(6/92, $2.50, 52 pgs.)-Wolverine-c/story 2.50
NOTE: ***Austin** c-1i, 2i, 53i. **Byrne** c-81, 82. **Guice** c-85, 91-99. **Jim Lee** a(p)-51, 53, 55-62, 64; c-53, 87-90. **Mignola** a-29-31p. **Whilce Portacio** a(i)-39-47, 49-54.*

ALPHA FLIGHT (2nd Series)
Marvel Comics: Aug, 1997 - No. 20, Mar, 1999 ($2.99/$1.99)
1-($2.99)-Wraparound cover 6.00
2,3: 2-Variant-c 4.00
4-11: 8,9-Wolverine-c/app. 3.00
12-($2.99) Death of Sasquatch; wraparound-c 4.00
13-20 3.00
.../Inhumans '98 Annual ($3.50) Raney-a 3.50

ALPHA FLIGHT (3rd Series)
Marvel Comics: May, 2004 - No. 12, April, 2005 ($2.99)
1-12: 1-6-Lobdell-s/Henry-c/a 3.00
... Vol. 1: You Gotta Be Kiddin' Me (2004, $14.99) r/#1-6 15.00

ALPHA FLIGHT: IN THE BEGINNING
Marvel Comics: July, 1997 ($1.95, one-shot)
(-1)-Flashback w/Wolverine 2.50

ALPHA FLIGHT SPECIAL
Marvel Comics: July, 1991 - No. 4, Oct, 1991 ($1.50, limited series)
1-4: 1-3-r-A. Flight #97-99 w/covers. 4-r-A.Flight #100 2.50

ALPHA KORPS
Diversity Comics: Sept, 1996 ($2.50)
1-Origin/1st app. Alpha Korps 2.50

ALTERED IMAGE
Image Comics: Apr, 1998 - No. 3, Sept, 1998 ($2.50, limited series)
1-3-Spawn, Witchblade, Savage Dragon; Valentino-s/a 3.00

ALTER EGO
First Comics: May, 1986 - No. 4, Nov, 1986 (Mini-series)
1-4 2.50

ALTER NATION
Image Comics: Feb, 2004 - No. 4, Jun, 2004 ($2.95, limited series)
1-4: 1-Two covers by Art Adams and Barberi; Barberi-a 3.00

ALVIN (TV) (See Four Color Comics No. 1042 or Three Chipmunks #1)
Dell Publishing Co.: Oct-Dec, 1962 - No. 28, Oct, 1973
12-021-212 (#1) 9 18 27 60 100 140

Amazing Adult Fantasy #12 © MAR

Amazing Adventures #2 © MAR

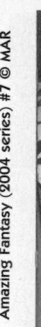

Amazing Fantasy (2004 series) #7 © MAR

	GD 2.0	VG 4.0	FN 6.0	VF 8.0	VF/NM 9.0	NM- 9.2
2	5	10	15	35	55	75
3-10	5	10	15	30	48	65
11-"Chipmunks sing the Beatles' Hits"	5	10	15	34	55	75
12-28	4	8	12	24	37	50
Alvin For President (10/64)	5	10	15	30	48	65
...& His Pals in Merry Christmas with Clyde Crashcup & Leonardo 1 (02-120-402)-(12-2/64)	7	14	21	50	83	115
Reprinted in 1966 (12-023-604)	4	8	12	24	37	50

ALVIN & THE CHIPMUNKS
Harvey Comics: July, 1992 - No. 5, May, 1994

1-5: 1-Richie Rich app. 4.00

AMALGAM AGE OF COMICS, THE: THE DC COMICS COLLECTION
DC Comics: 1996 ($12.95, trade paperback)

nn-r/Amazon, Assassins, Doctor Strangefate, JLX, Legends of the Dark Claw, & Super Soldier 13.00

AMANDA AND GUNN
Image Comics: Apr, 1997 - No. 4, Oct, 1997 ($2.95, B&W, limited series)

1-4 3.00

AMAZING ADULT FANTASY (Formerly Amazing Adventures #1-6; becomes Amazing Fantasy #15) (See Amazing Fantasy for Omnibus HC reprint of #1-15)
Marvel Comics Group (AMI): No. 7, Dec, 1961 - No. 14, July, 1962

	GD	VG	FN	VF	VF/NM	NM-
7-Ditko-c/a begins, ends #14	46	92	138	368	672	975
8-Last 10¢ issue	38	76	114	285	518	750
9-13: 12-1st app. Mailbag. 13-Anti-communist sty	36	72	108	270	498	725
13-2nd printing (1994)	2	4	6	8	10	12
14-Prototype issue (Professor X)	39	78	117	293	534	775

AMAZING ADVENTURE FUNNIES (Fantoman No. 2 on)
Centaur Publications: June, 1940 - No. 2, Sept. 1940

	GD	VG	FN	VF	VF/NM	NM-
1-The Fantom of the Fair by Gustavson (r/Amaz. Mystery Funnies V2#7,V2#8), The Arrow, Skyrocket Steele From the Year X by Everett (r/AMF #2); Burgos-a	173	346	519	1090	1845	2600
2-Reprints; Published after Fantoman #2	113	226	339	712	1206	1700

NOTE: ***Burgos*** *a-1(2).* ***Everett*** *a-1(3).* ***Gustavson*** *a-1(5), 2(3).* ***Pinajian*** *a-2.*

AMAZING ADVENTURES (Also see Boy Cowboy & Science Comics)
Ziff-Davis Publ. Co.: 1950; No. 1, Nov, 1950 - No. 6, Fall, 1952 (Painted covers)

	GD	VG	FN	VF	VF/NM	NM-
1950 (no month given) (8-1/2x11) (8 pgs.) Has the front & back cover plus Schomburg story used in Amazing Advs. #1 (Sent to subscribers of Z-D s/f magazines & ordered through mail for 10¢. Used to test market)	57	114	171	359	605	850
1-Wood, Schomburg, Anderson, Whitney-a	80	160	240	504	852	1200
2-5: 2-Schomburg-a. 2,4,5-Anderson-a. 3,5-Starr-a	40	80	120	244	397	550
6-Krigstein-a	40	80	120	246	403	560

AMAZING ADVENTURES (Becomes Amazing Adult Fantasy #7 on) (See Amazing Fantasy for Omnibus HC reprint of #1-15)
Atlas Comics (AMI)/Marvel Comics No. 3 on: June, 1961 - No. 6, Nov, 1961

	GD	VG	FN	VF	VF/NM	NM-
1-Origin Dr. Droom (1st Marvel-Age Superhero) by Kirby; Kirby/Ditko-a (5 pgs.) Ditko & Kirby-a in all; Kirby monster c-1-6	113	226	339	961	1781	2600
2	46	92	138	368	672	975
3-6: 6-Last Dr. Droom	40	80	120	310	568	825

AMAZING ADVENTURES
Marvel Comics Group: Aug, 1970 - No. 39, Nov, 1976

	GD	VG	FN	VF	VF/NM	NM-
1-Inhumans by Kirby(p) & Black Widow (1st app. in Tales of Suspense #52) double feature begins	6	12	18	43	69	95
2-4: 2-F.F. brief app. 4-Last Inhumans by Kirby	3	6	9	21	32	42
5-8: Adams-a(p); 8-Last Black Widow; last 15¢-c	5	10	15	30	48	65
9,10: Magneto app. 10-Last Inhumans (origin-r by Kirby)	3	6	9	19	29	38
11-New Beast begins(1st app. in mutated form; origin in flashback); X-Men cameo in flashback (#11-17 are X-Men tie-ins)	14	28	42	110	175	300
12-17: 12-Beast battles Iron Man. 13-Brotherhood of Evil Mutants x-over from X-Men. 15-X-Men app. 16-Rutland Vermont - Bald Mountain Halloween x-over; Juggernaut app. 17-Last Beast (origin); X-Men app.	6	12	18	39	62	100
18-War of the Worlds begins (5/73); 1st app. Killraven; Neal Adams-a(p)	3	6	9	18	27	35
19-35,38,39: 19-Chaykin-a. 25-Buckler-a. 35-Giffen's first published story (art), along with Deadly Hands of Kung-Fu #22 (3/76)	1	3	4	6	8	10
36,37-(Regular 25¢ edition)(7-8/76)	1	3	4	6	8	10
36,37-(30¢-c variants, limited distribution)	6	12	18	37	59	80

NOTE: ***N. Adams*** *c-6-8.* ***Buscema*** *a-1p, 2p.* ***Colan*** *a-3-5p, 26p.* ***Ditko*** *a-24r.* ***Everett*** *a(i)3-5, 7-9.* ***Giffen*** *a-35i, 38p.* ***G. Kane*** *c-11, 25p, 29p.* ***Ploog*** *a-12i.* ***Russell*** *a-27-32, 34-37, 39; c-28, 30-32, 33i, 34, 35, 37, 39i.* ***Starlin*** *a-17.* ***Starlin*** *c-15p, 16, 17, 27.* ***Sutton*** *a-11-15p.*

AMAZING ADVENTURES
Marvel Comics Group: Dec, 1979 - No. 14, Jan, 1981

	GD	VG	FN	VF	VF/NM	NM-
V2#1-Reprints story/X-Men #1 & 38 (origins)	1	2	3	5	6	8
2-14: 2-6-Early X-Men-r. 7,8-Origin Iceman						6.00

NOTE: ***Byrne*** *c-6p, 9p.* ***Kirby*** *a-1-14r; c-7, 9.* ***Steranko*** *a-12r.* ***Tuska*** *a-7-9.*

AMAZING ADVENTURES
Marvel Comics: July, 1988 ($4.95, squarebound, one-shot, 80 pgs.)

1-Anthology; Austin, Golden-a 5.00

AMAZING ADVENTURES OF CAPTAIN CARVEL AND HIS CARVEL CRUSADERS, THE
(See Carvel Comics in the Promotional Comics section)

AMAZING CHAN & THE CHAN CLAN, THE (TV)
Gold Key: May, 1973 - No. 4, Feb, 1974 (Hanna-Barbera)

	GD	VG	FN	VF	VF/NM	NM-
1-Warren Tufts-a in all	4	8	12	22	34	45
2-4	3	6	9	16	23	30

AMAZING COMICS (Complete Comics No. 2)
Timely Comics (EPC): Fall, 1944

	GD	VG	FN	VF	VF/NM	NM-
1-The Destroyer, The Whizzer, The Young Allies (by Sekowsky), Sergeant Dix; Schomburg-c	253	506	759	1594	2697	3800

AMAZING DETECTIVE CASES (Formerly Suspense No. 2?)
Marvel/Atlas Comics (CCC): No. 3, Nov, 1950 - No. 14, Sept, 1952

	GD	VG	FN	VF	VF/NM	NM-
3	30	60	90	176	283	390
4-6	17	34	51	100	158	215
7-10	15	30	45	90	140	190
11,12: 11-(3/52)-Horror format begins. 12-Krigstein-a	37	74	111	219	352	485
13-(Scarce)-Everett-a; electrocution-c/story	40	80	120	235	380	525
14	33	66	99	192	309	425

NOTE: ***Colan*** *a-9.* ***Maneely*** *c-13.* ***Sekowsky*** *a-12.* ***Sinnott*** *a-13.* ***Tuska*** *a-10.*

AMAZING FANTASY (Formerly Amazing Adult Fantasy #7-14)
Atlas Magazines/Marvel: #15, Aug, 1962 (Sept, 1962 shown in indicia); #16, Dec, 1995 - #18, Feb, 1996

	GD	VG	FN	VF	VF/NM	NM-
15-Origin/1st app. of Spider-Man by Steve Ditko (11 pgs.); 1st app. Aunt May & Uncle Ben; Kirby/Ditko-c	2400	4800	7200	21,000	43,000	65,000
16-18 ('95-'96, $3.95): Kurt Busiek scripts; painted-c/a by Paul Lee						4.00
Amazing Fantasy Omnibus HC ("Amazing Adult Fantasy" on-c) (2007, $75.00, dustjacket) r/Amazing Adventures #1-6, Amazing Adult Fantasy #7-14 and Amazing Fantasy #15 with letter pages; foreword by Bissette; cover gallery from '70s reprint titles						75.00

AMAZING FANTASY (Continues from #6 in Araña: The Heart of the Spider)
Marvel Comics: Aug, 2004 - No. 20, June, 2006 ($2.99)

1-Intro. Anya Corazon; Fiona Avery-s/Mark Brooks-c/a 4.00
2-14,16-20: 3,4-Roger Cruz-a. 7-Intro. new Scorpion; Kirk-a. 10-Intro. Vampire By Night 13,14-Back-up Captain Universe stories. 16-20-Death's Head 3.00
15-($3.99) Spider-Man app.; intro 6 new characters incl. Mastermind Excello seen in World War Hulk series; s/a by various 4.00
Death's Head 3.0: Unnatural Selection TPB (2006, $13.99) r/#16-20 14.00
Scorpion: Poison Tomorrow (2005, $7.99, digest) r/#7-13 8.00

AMAZING GHOST STORIES (Formerly Nightmare)
St. John Publishing Co.: No. 14, Oct, 1954 - No. 16, Feb, 1955

	GD	VG	FN	VF	VF/NM	NM-
14-Pit & the Pendulum story by Kinstler; Baker-c	34	68	102	198	319	440
15-r/Weird Thrillers #5; Baker-c, Powell-a	25	50	75	145	233	320
16-Kubert reprints of Weird Thrillers #4; Baker-c; Roussos, Tuska-a; Kinstler-a (1 pg.)	25	50	75	147	236	325

AMAZING HIGH ADVENTURE
Marvel Comics: 8/84; No. 2, 10/85; No. 3, 10/86 - No. 5, 1986 ($2.00)

1-5: Painted-c on all. 3,4-Baxter paper. 4-Bolton-c/a. 5-Bolton-a 3.50

NOTE: ***Bissette*** *a-4.* ***Severin*** *a-1, 3.* ***Sienkiewicz*** *a-1,2.* ***Paul Smith*** *a-2.* ***Williamson*** *a-2i.*

AMAZING JOY BUZZARDS
Image Comics: 2005 - No. 4, 2005 ($2.95, B&W with pink spot color in #1)

1-4-Mark Andrew Smith-s/Dan Hipp-a. 1-Mahfood back-c. 2-Morse back-c 3.00
Vol. 1 TPB (2005, $11.95) r/#1-4; bonus art and character design sketches 12.00
TPB (2008, $19.99) r/#1-4 and Vol. 2 #1-5 20.00

AMAZING JOY BUZZARDS (Volume 2)
Image Comics: Oct, 2005 - No. 5, Aug, 2006 ($2.99, B&W)

1-5: 1-Mark Andrew Smith-s/Dan Hipp-a. 4-Mahfood-a; Crosland-a. 5-Holgate-a 3.00
Vol. 2 TPB (2006, $12.99) r/#1-4; bonus art, pin-ups and character sketches 13.00

AMAZING-MAN COMICS (Formerly Motion Picture Funnies Weekly?)
(Also see Stars And Stripes Comics)
Centaur Publications: No. 5, Sept, 1939 - No. 26, Jan, 1942

Amazing Mystery Funnies V2 #6 © CEN

Amazing Spider-Girl #14 © MAR

Amazing Spider-Man #2 © MAR

GD VG FN VF VF/NM NM-
2.0 4.0 6.0 8.0 9.0 9.2

5(#1)(Rare)-Origin/1st app. A-Man the Amazing Man by Bill Everett; The Cat-Man by Tarpe Mills (also #8), Mighty Man by Filchock, Minimidget & sidekick Ritty, & The Iron Skull by Burgos begins 1440 2880 4320 10,800 19,400 28,000
6-Origin The Amazing Man retold; The Shark begins; Ivy Menace by Tarpe Mills app. 335 670 1005 2278 3989 5700
7-Magician From Mars begins; ends #11 243 486 729 1531 2591 3650
8-Cat-Man dresses as woman 183 366 549 1153 1952 2750
9-Magician From Mars battles the 'Elemental Monster,' swiped into The Spectre in More Fun #54 & 55. Ties w/Marvel Mystery #4 for 1st Nazi War-c on a comic (2/40) 190 380 570 1197 2024 2850
10,11: 11-Zardi, the Eternal Man begins; ends #16; Amazing Man dons costume; last Everett issue 135 270 405 851 1438 2025
12,13 125 250 375 788 1332 1875
14-Reef Kinkaid, Rocke Wayburn (ends #20), & Dr. Hypno (ends #21) begin; no Zardi or Chuck Hardy 100 200 300 630 1065 1500
15,17-20: 15-Zardi returns; no Rocke Wayburn. 17-Dr. Hypno returns; no Zardi 90 180 270 567 959 1350
16-Mighty Man's powers of super strength & ability to shrink & grow explained; Rocke Wayburn returns; no Dr. Hypno; Al Avison (a character) begins, ends #18 (a tribute to the famed artist) 93 186 279 586 993 1400
21-Origin Dash Dartwell (drug-use story); origin & only app. T.N.T. 100 200 300 630 1065 1500
22-Dash Dartwell, the Human Meteor & The Voice app; last Iron Skull & The Shark; Silver Streak app. (classic-c) 173 346 519 1090 1845 2600
23-Two Amazing Man stories; intro/origin Tommy the Amazing Kid; The Marksman only app. 80 160 240 504 852 1200
24-King of Darkness, Nightshade, & Blue Lady begin; end #26; 1st app. Super-Ann 80 160 240 504 852 1200
25,26 (Scarce): Meteor Martin by Wolverton in both; 26-Electric Ray app. 125 250 375 788 1332 1875

NOTE: ***Everett*** *a-5-11; c-5-11.* ***Gilman*** *a-14-20.* ***Giunta/Mirando*** *a-7-10.* ***Sam Glanzman*** *a-14-16, 18-21, 23.* ***Louis Glanzman*** *a-6, 9-11, 14-21; c-13-19, 21.* ***Robert Golden*** *a-9.* ***Gustavson*** *a-6; c-22, 23.* ***Lubbers*** *a-14-21.* ***Simon*** *a-10.* ***Frank Thomas*** *a-6, 9-11, 14, 15, 17-21.*

AMAZING MYSTERIES (Formerly Sub-Mariner Comics No. 31)
Marvel Comics (CCC): No. 32, May, 1949 - No. 35, Jan, 1950 (1st Marvel Horror Comic)

32-The Witness app. 85 170 255 536 906 1275
33-Horror format 40 80 120 244 397 550
34,35: Changes to Crime. 34,35-Photo-c 21 42 63 123 197 270

AMAZING MYSTERY FUNNIES
Centaur Publications: Aug, 1938 - No. 24, Sept, 1940 (All 52 pgs.)

V1#1-Everett-c(1st); Dick Kent Adv. story; Skyrocket Steele in the Year X on cover only 371 742 1113 2523 4412 6300
2-Everett 1st-a (Skyrocket Steele) 190 380 570 1197 2024 2850
3 98 196 294 617 1046 1475
3(#4, 12/38)-nn on cover, #3 on inside; bondage-c 90 180 270 567 959 1350
V2#1-4,6: 2-Drug use story. 3-Air-Sub DX begins by Burgos. 4-Dan Hastings, Sand Hog begins (ends #5). 6-Last Skyrocket Steele 80 160 240 504 852 1200
5-Classic Everett-c 160 320 480 108 1704 2400
7 (Scarce)-Intro. The Fantom of the Fair & begins; Everett, Gustavson, Burgos-a 353 706 1059 2400 4200 6000
8-Origin & 1st app. Speed Centaur 147 294 441 926 1563 2200
9-11: 11-Self portrait and biog. of Everett; Jon Linton begins; early Robot cover (11/39) 80 160 240 504 852 1200
12 (Scarce)-1st Space Patrol; Wolverton-a (12/39); new costume Phantom of the Fair 193 386 579 1216 2058 2900
V3#1(#17, 1/40)-Intro. Bullet; Tippy Taylor serial begins, ends #24 (continued in The Arrow #2) 80 160 240 504 852 1200
18,20: 18-Fantom of the Fair by Gustavson 77 154 231 481 816 1150
19,21-24: Space Patrol by Wolverton in all 93 186 279 586 993 1400

NOTE: ***Burgos*** *a-V2#3-9.* ***Eisner*** *a-V1#2, 3(2).* ***Everett*** *a-V1#2-4, V2#1, 3-6; c-V1#1-4,V2#3, 5, 18.* ***Filchock*** *a-V2#9.* ***Flessel*** *a-V2#6.* ***Guardineer*** *a-V1#4, V2#4-6;* ***Gustavson*** *a-V2#4, 5, 9-12, V3#1, 18, 19; c-V2#7, 9, 12, V3#1, 21, 22;* ***McWilliams*** *a-V2#9, 10.* ***TarpeMills*** *a-V2#2, 4-6, 9-12, V3#1.* ***Leo Morey****(Pulp artist) c-V2#10; text illo-V2#11.* ***FrankThomas*** *a-6-V2#11.* ***Webster*** *a-V2#4.*

AMAZING SAINTS
Logos International: 1974 (39¢)

nn-True story of Phil Saint 2 4 6 8 11 14

AMAZING SCARLET SPIDER
Marvel Comics: Nov, 1995 - No. 2, Dec, 1995 ($1.95, limited series)

1,2: Replaces "Amazing Spider-Man" for two issues. 1-Venom/Carnage cameos. 2-Green Goblin & Joystick-c/app. 2.50

AMAZING SCREW-ON HEAD, THE
Dark Horse Comics (Maverick): May, 2002 ($2.99, one-shot)

1-Mike Mignola-s/a/c 3.00

AMAZING SPIDER-GIRL (Also see Spider-Girl and What If...? (2nd series) #105)
Marvel Comics: No. 0, 2006; No. 1, Dec, 2006 - Present ($2.99)

0-($1.99) Recap of the Spider-Girl series and character profiles; A.F. #15 cover swipe 2.50
1-14,16-24-($2.99) Frenz & Buscema-a. 9-Carnage returns. 19-Has #17 on cover 3.00
15-($3.99) 10th Anniversary issue 4.00
... Vol. 1: What Ever Happened to the Daughter of Spider-Man? TPB (2007, $14.99) r/#0-6 15.00
... Vol. 2: Comes the Carnage! TPB (2007, $13.99) r/#7-12 14.00

AMAZING SPIDER-MAN, THE (See All Detergent Comics, Amazing Fantasy, America's Best TV Comics, Aurora, Deadly Foes of..., Fireside Book Series, Friendly Neighborhood..., Giant-Size..., Giant Size Super-Heroes Featuring..., Marvel Age..., Marvel Collectors Item Classics, Marvel Fanfare, Marvel Graphic Novel, Marvel Knoghts..., Marvel Spec. Ed., Marvel Tales, Marvel Team-Up, Marvel Treasury Ed., New Avengers, Nothing Can Stop the Juggernaut, Official Marvel Index To..., Peter Parker..., Power Record Comics, Spectacular..., Spider-Man, Spider-Man Digest, Spider-Man Saga, Spider-Man 2099, Spider-Man Vs. Wolverine, Spidey Super Stories, Strange Tales Annual #2, Superman Vs. ..., Try-Out Winner Book, Ultimate Marvel Team-Up, Ultimate Spider-Man, Web of Spider- Man & Within Our Reach)

AMAZING SPIDER-MAN, THE
Marvel Comics Group: March, 1963 - No. 441, Nov, 1998

1-Retells origin by Steve Ditko; 1st Fantastic Four x-over (ties with F.F. #12 as first Marvel x-over); intro. John Jameson & The Chameleon; Spider-Man's 2nd app.; Kirby/Ditko-c; Ditko-c/a #1-38 1375 2750 4125 12,400 28,200 44,000
1-Reprint from the Golden Record Comic set 15 30 45 111 206 300
With record (1966) 20 40 60 148 274 400
2-1st app. the Vulture & the Terrible Tinkerer 346 692 1038 3114 6057 9000
3-1st app. Doc Octopus; 1st full-length story; Human Torch cameo; Spider-Man pin-up by Ditko 288 576 864 2520 4860 7200
4-Origin & 1st app. The Sandman (see Strange Tales #115 for 2nd app.); 1st monthly issue; intro. Betty Brant & Liz Allen 240 480 720 2100 4050 6000
5-Dr. Doom app. 200 400 600 1750 3375 5000
6-1st app. Lizard 170 340 510 1488 2869 4250
7-Vs. The Vulture 115 230 345 978 1864 2750
8-Fantastic Four app. in back-up story by Kirby & Ditko 102 204 306 867 1509 2150
9-Origin & 1st app. Electro (2/64) 118 236 354 1003 1789 2575
10-1st app. Big Man & The Enforcers 100 200 300 850 1625 2400
11-1st app. Bennett Brant 88 176 264 748 1424 2100
12-Doc Octopus unmasks Spider-Man-c/story 79 158 237 672 1286 1900
13-1st app. Mysterio 102 204 306 867 1659 2450
14-(7/64)-1st app. The Green Goblin (c/story)(Norman Osborn); Hulk x-over 168 336 504 1470 2835 4200
15-1st app. Kraven the Hunter; 1st mention of Mary Jane Watson (not shown) 81 162 243 1377 1664 1950
16-Spider-Man battles Daredevil (1st x-over 9/64); still in old yellow costume 67 134 201 570 1085 1600
17-2nd app. Green Goblin (c/story); Human Torch x-over (also in #18 & #21) 72 144 216 612 1169 1725
18-1st app. Ned Leeds who later becomes Hobgoblin; Fantastic Four cameo; 3rd app. Sandman 51 102 153 408 767 1125
19-Sandman app. 40 80 120 308 574 840
20-Origin & 1st app. The Scorpion 57 114 171 485 930 1375
21-2nd app. The Beetle (see Strange Tales #123) 39 78 117 300 563 825
22-1st app. Princess Python 37 74 111 284 530 775
23-3rd app. The Green Goblin-c/story; Norman Osborn app. 47 94 141 376 701 1025
24 31 62 93 239 445 650
25-(6/65)-1st brief app. Mary Jane Watson (face not shown); 1st app. Spencer Smythe; Norman Osborn app. 38 76 114 293 547 800
26-4th app. The Green Goblin-c/story; 1st app. Crime Master; dies in #27 40 80 120 319 597 875
27-5th app. The Green Goblin-c/story; Norman Osborn app. 38 76 114 293 547 800
28-Origin & 1st app. Molten Man (9/65, scarcer in high grade) 71 142 213 604 1152 1700
29,30 26 52 78 192 359 525
31-1st app. Harry Osborn who later becomes 2nd Green Goblin, Gwen Stacy & Prof. Warren. 32 64 96 242 451 660
32-38: 34-4th app. Kraven the Hunter. 36-1st app. Looter. 37-Intro. Norman Osborn. 38-(7/66)-2nd brief app. Mary Jane Watson (face not shown); last Ditko issue 23 46 69 167 309 450
39-The Green Goblin-c/story; Green Goblin's i.d. revealed as Norman Osborn; Romita-a begins (8/66; see Daredevil #16 for 1st Romita-a on Spider-Man) 33 66 99 254 477 700

Amazing Spider-Man #47 © MAR

Amazing Spider-Man #250 © MAR

Amazing Spider-Man #291 © MAR

	GD 2.0	VG 4.0	FN 6.0	VF 8.0	VF/NM 9.0	NM- 9.2
40-1st told origin The Green Goblin-c/story	39	78	117	300	563	825
41-1st app. Rhino	31	62	93	239	445	650
42-(11/66)-3rd app. Mary Jane Watson (cameo in last 2 panels); 1st time face is shown	20	40	60	148	274	400
43-49: 44,45-2nd & 3rd app. The Lizard. 46-Intro. Shocker. 47-M. J. Watson & Peter Parker 1st date. 47-Green Goblin cameo; Harry & Norman Osborn app. 47,49-5th & 6th app. Kraven the Hunter	15	30	45	111	206	300
50-1st app. Kingpin (7/67)	56	112	168	476	913	1350
51-2nd app. Kingpin; Joe Robertson 1-panel cameo	21	42	63	155	288	420
52-58,60: 52-1st app. Joe Robertson & 3rd app. Kingpin. 56-1st app. Capt. George Stacy. 57,58-Ka-Zar app.	12	24	36	84	150	215
59-1st app. Brainwasher (alias Kingpin); 1st-c app. M. J. Watson	12	24	36	87	156	225
61-74: 61-1st Gwen Stacy cover app. 67-1st app. Randy Robertson. 69-Kingpin-c. 69,70-Kingpin app. 73-1st app. Silvermane. 74-Last 12¢ issue	9	18	27	65	113	160
75-83,87-89,91,92,95,99: 78,79-1st app. The Prowler. 83-1st app. Schemer & Vanessa (Kingpin's wife)	8	16	24	58	97	135
84-86,93: 84,85-Kingpin-c/story. 86-Re-intro & origin Black Widow in new costume. 93-1st app. Arthur Stacy	9	18	27	60	100	140
90-Death of Capt. Stacy	10	20	30	68	119	170
94-Origin retold	10	20	30	71	126	180
96-98-Green Goblin app. (97,98-Green Goblin-c); drug books not approved by CCA	10	20	30	73	129	185
100-Anniversary issue (9/71); Green Goblin cameo (2 pgs.)	15	30	45	108	199	290
101-1st app. Morbius the Living Vampire; Wizard cameo; last 15¢ issue (10/71)	17	34	51	120	223	325
101-Silver ink 2nd printing (9/92, $1.75)						2.50
102-Origin & 2nd app. Morbius (25¢, 52 pgs.)	12	24	36	82	146	210
103-118: 104,111-Kraven the Hunter-c/stories. 108-1st app. Sha-Shan. 109-Dr. Strange-c/story (6/72). 110-1st app. Gibbon. 113-1st app. Hammerhead. 116-118-reprints story from Spectacular Spider-Man Mag. in color with some changes	6	12	18	43	69	95
119,120-Spider-Man vs. Hulk (4 & 5/73)	9	18	27	60	100	140
121-Death of Gwen Stacy (6/73) (killed by Green Goblin) (reprinted in Marvel Tales #98 & 192)	19	38	57	139	257	375
122-Death of The Green Goblin-c/story (7/73) (reprinted in Marvel Tales #99 & 192)	20	40	60	143	264	385
123,126-128: 123-Cage app. 126-1st mention of Harry Osborn becoming Green Goblin	6	12	18	39	62	85
124-1st app. Man-Wolf (9/73)	7	14	21	45	73	100
125-Man-Wolf origin	6	12	18	41	66	90
129-1st app. The Punisher (2/74); 1st app. Jackal	38	76	114	293	547	800
130-133: 131-Last 20¢ issue	5	10	15	32	51	70
134-(7/74); 1st app. Tarantula; Harry Osborn discovers Spider-Man's ID; Punisher cameo	6	12	18	37	59	80
135-2nd full Punisher app. (8/74)	8	16	24	56	93	130
136-1st app. Harry Osborn Green Goblin in costume	8	16	24	52	86	120
137-Green Goblin-c/story (2nd Harry Osborn Goblin)	6	12	18	39	62	85
138-141: 139-1st Grizzly. 140-1st app. Glory Grant	4	8	12	22	34	45
142,143-Gwen Stacy clone cameos: 143-1st app. Cyclone	4	8	12	23	36	48
144-147: 144-Full app. of Gwen Stacy clone. 145,146-Gwen Stacy clone storyline continues. 147-Spider-Man learns Gwen Stacy is clone	4	8	12	23	36	48
148-Jackal revealed	4	8	12	26	41	55
149-Spider-Man clone story begins, clone dies (?); origin of Jackal	6	12	18	43	69	95
150-Spider-Man decides he is not the clone	4	8	12	24	37	50
151-Spider-Man disposes of clone body	4	8	12	24	37	50
152-160-(Regular 25¢ editions). 159-Last 25¢ issue(8/76)	3	6	9	18	27	35
155-159-(30¢-c variants, limited distribution)	7	14	21	49	80	110
161-Nightcrawler app. from X-Men; Punisher cameo; Wolverine & Colossus app.	4	8	12	22	34	45
162-Punisher, Nightcrawler app.; 1st Jigsaw	4	8	12	22	34	45
163-168,181-188: 167-1st app. Will O' The Wisp. 181-Origin retold; gives life history of Spidey; Punisher cameo in flashback (1 panel). 182-(7/78)-Peter's first proposal to Mary Jane, but she declines (in #183)	3	6	9	14	20	25
169-173-(Regular 30¢ edition). 169-Clone story recapped. 171-Nova app.	3	6	9	14	20	25
169-173-(35¢-c variants, limited dist.)(6-10/77)	15	30	45	106	193	280
174,175-Punisher app.	3	6	9	16	23	30
176-180-Green Goblin app.	3	6	9	17	25	32

	GD 2.0	VG 4.0	FN 6.0	VF 8.0	VF/NM 9.0	NM- 9.2
189,190-Byrne-a	3	6	9	16	22	28
191-193,196-199: 193-Peter & Mary Jane break up. 196-Faked death of Aunt May	2	4	6	11	16	20
NOTE: *Whitman 3-packs containing #192-194,196 exist.*						
194-1st app. Black Cat	4	8	12	28	44	60
195-2nd app. Black Cat	3	6	9	14	20	26
200-Giant origin issue (1/80)	3	6	9	21	32	42
201,202-Punisher app.	2	4	6	13	18	22
203-205,207,208,210-219: 203-3rd app. Dazzler (4/80). 210-1st app. Madame Web. 212-1st app. Hydro Man; origin Sandman	2	4	6	8	10	12
206-Byrne-a	2	4	6	9	12	15
209-Origin & 1st app. Calypso (10/80)	2	4	6	11	16	20
220-237: 225-(2/82)-Foolkiller-c/story. 226,227-Black Cat returns. 234-Free 16 pg. insert "Marvel Guide to Collecting Comics". 235-Origin Will-'O-The-Wisp. 236-Tarantula dies	1	3	4	6	8	10
238-(3/83)-1st app. Hobgoblin (Ned Leeds); came with skin "Tattooz" decal. NOTE: The same decal appears in the more common Fantastic Four #252 which is being removed & placed in this issue as incentive to increase value (Value listed is with or without tattooz)	7	14	21	49	80	110
239-2nd app. Hobgoblin & 1st battle w/Spidey	4	8	12	26	41	55
240-243,246-248: 241-Origin The Vulture. 242-Mary Jane Watson cameo (last panel). 243-Reintro Mary Jane after 4 year absence	1	2	3	5	7	9
244-3rd app. Hobgoblin (cameo)	2	4	6	9	12	15
245-(10/83)-4th app. Hobgoblin (cameo); Lefty Donovan gains powers of Hobgoblin & battles Spider-Man	2	4	6	9	12	15
249-251: 3 part Hobgoblin/Spider-Man battle. 249-Retells origin & death of 1st Green Goblin. 251-Last old costume	2	4	6	9	13	16
252-Spider-Man dons new black costume (5/84); ties with Marvel Team-Up #141 & Spectacular Spider-Man #90 for 1st new costume in regular title (See Marvel Super-Heroes Secret Wars #8 (12/84) for acquisition of costume)	4	8	12	26	41	55
253-1st app. The Rose	2	4	6	8	10	12
254-258: 256-1st app. Puma. 257-Hobgoblin cameo; 2nd app. Puma; M.J. Watson reveals she knows Spidey's i.d. 258-Hobgoblin app.	1	2	3	5	7	9
259-Full Hobgoblin app.; Spidey back to old costume; origin Mary Jane Watson	2	4	6	8	11	14
260-Hobgoblin app.	1	3	4	6	8	11
261-Hobgoblin-c/story; painted-c by Vess	2	4	6	8	10	12
262-Spider-Man unmasked; photo-c	1	2	3	5	7	9
263,264,266-274,277-280,282,283: 274-Zarathos (The Spirit of Vengeance) app. 277-Vess back-up art. 279-Jack O'Lantern-c/story. 282-X-Factor x-over	1	2	3	4	5	7
265-1st app. Silver Sable (6/85)	2	4	6	9	13	16
265-Silver ink 2nd printing ($1.25)						2.50
275-($1.25, 52 pgs.)-Hobgoblin-c/story; origin-r by Ditko	2	4	6	13	18	22
276-Hobgoblin app.	1	3	4	6	8	10
281-Hobgoblin battles Jack O'Lantern	1	3	4	6	8	10
284,285: 284-Punisher cameo; Gang War story begins; Hobgoblin-c/story. 285-Punisher app.; minor Hobgoblin app.	1	3	4	6	8	10
286-288: 286-Hobgoblin-c & app. (minor). 287-Hobgoblin app. (minor). 288-Full Hobgoblin app.; last Gang War	1	3	4	6	8	10
289-(6/87, $1.25, 52 pgs.)-Hobgoblin's i.d. revealed as Ned Leeds; death of Ned Leeds; Macendale (Jack O'Lantern) becomes new Hobgoblin (1st app.)	3	6	9	14	19	24
290-292,295-297: 290-Peter proposes to Mary Jane. 292-She accepts; leads into wedding in Amazing Spider-Man Annual #21	1	2	3	4	5	7
293,294-Part 2 & 5 of Kraven story from Web of Spider-Man. 294-Death of Kraven	2	4	6	8	10	12
298-Todd McFarlane-c/a begins (3/88); 1st brief app. Eddie Brock who becomes Venom; (last pg.)	5	10	15	30	48	65
299-1st brief app. Venom with costume	3	6	9	19	29	38
300 ($1.50, 52 pgs.; 25th Anniversary)-1st full Venom app.; last black costume (5/88)	8	16	24	58	97	135
301-305: 301 ($1.00 issues begin). 304-1st bi-weekly issue	2	4	6	9	13	16
306-311,313,314: 306-Swipes-c from Action #1	2	4	6	8	11	14
312-Hobgoblin battles Green Goblin	2	4	6	11	16	20
315-317-Venom app.	3	6	9	14	19	24
318-323,325: 319-Bi-weekly begins again	1	2	3	5	7	9
324-Sabretooth app.; McFarlane cover only	1	2	3	5	7	9
326,327,329: 327-Cosmic Spidey continues from Spectacular Spider-Man (no McFarlane-c/a)						5.00
328-Hulk x-over; last McFarlane issue	1	3	4	6	8	10
330,331-Punisher app. 331-Minor Venom app.						5.00

Amazing Spider-Man #432 © MAR

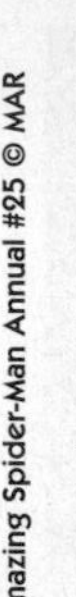
Amazing Spider-Man Annual #25 © MAR

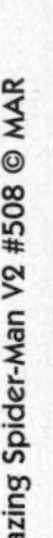
Amazing Spider-Man V2 #508 © MAR

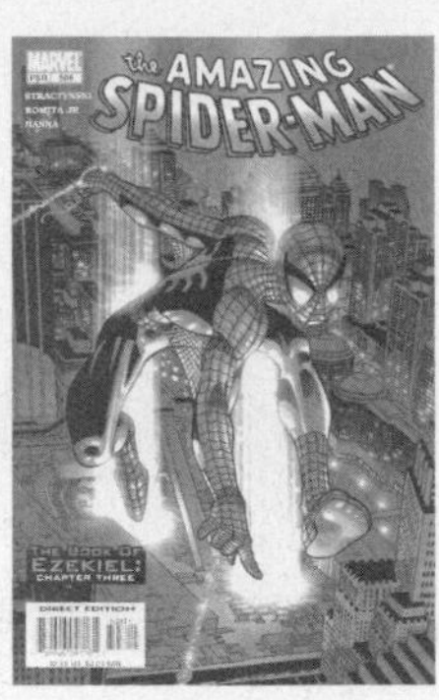

GD VG FN VF VF/NM NM-
2.0 4.0 6.0 8.0 9.0 9.2

332,333-Venom-c/story 1 3 4 6 8 10
334-336,338-343: 341-Tarantula app. 4.00
337-Hobgoblin app. 5.00
344-(2/91) 1st app. Cletus Kasady (Carnage) 2 4 6 9 12 15
345-1st full app. Cletus Kasady; Venom cameo on last pg.
2 4 6 9 12 15
346,347-Venom app. 1 3 4 6 8 10
348,349,351-359: 348-Avengers x-over. 351,352-Nova of New Warriors app. 353-Darkhawk app.; brief Punisher app. 354-Punisher cameo & Nova, Night Thrasher (New Warriors), Darkhawk & Moon Knight app. 357,358-Punisher, Darkhawk, Moon Knight, Night Thrasher, Nova x-over. 358-3 part gatefold-c; last $1.00-c. 360-Carnage cameo 3.00
350-($1.50, 52pgs.)-Origin retold; Spidey vs. Dr. Doom; pin-ups; Uncle Ben app. 5.00
360-Carnage cameo 4.00
361-(4/92) Intro Carnage (the Spawn of Venom); begin 3 part story; recap of how Spidey's alien costume became Venom 2 4 6 9 12 15
361-($1.25)-2nd printing; silver-c 2.50
362,363-Carnage & Venom-c/story 1 2 3 5 7 9
362-2nd printing 2.50
364,366-374,376-387: 364-The Shocker app. (old villain). 366-Peter's parents-c/story. 369-Harry Osborn back-up (Gr. Goblin II). 373-Venom back-up. 374-Venom-c/story. 376-Cardiac app. 378-Maximum Carnage part 3. 381,382-Hulk app. 383-The Jury app. 384-Venom/carnage app. 387-New costume Vulture 2.50
365-($3.95, 84 pgs.)-30th anniversary issue w/silver hologram on-c; Spidey/Venom/Carnage pull-out poster; contains 5 pg. preview of Spider-Man 2099 (1st app.); Spidey's origin retold; Lizard app.; reintro Peter's parents in Stan Lee 3 pg. text w/illo (story continues thru #370)
5.00
375-($3.95, 68 pgs.)-Holo-grafx foil-c; vs. Venom story; ties into Venom: Lethal Protector #1; Pat Olliffe-a. 5.00
388-($2.25, 68 pgs.)-Newsstand edition; Venom back-up & Cardiac & chance back-up 2.50
388-($2.95, 68 pgs.)-Collector's edition w/foil-c 3.00
389-396,398,399,401-420: 389-$1.50-c begins; bound-in trading card sheet; Green Goblin app. 394-Power & Responsibility Pt. 2. 396-Daredevil-c & app. 403-Carnage app. 406-1st New Doc Octopus. 407-Human Torch, Silver Sable, Sandman app. 409-Kaine, Rhino app. 410-Carnage app. 414-The Rose app. 415-Onslaught story; Spidey vs. Sentinels. 416-Epilogue to Onslaught; Garney-a(p); Williamson-a(i) 2.50
390-($2.95)-Collector's edition polybagged w/16 pg. insert of new animated Spidey TV show plus animation cel 3.00
394-($2.95, 48 pgs.)-Deluxe edition; flip book w/Birth of a Spider-Man Pt. 2; silver foil both-c; Power & Responsibility Pt. 2 3.00
397-($2.25)-Flip book w/Ultimate Spider-Man 2.50
400-($2.95)-Death of Aunt May 3.00
400-($3.95)-Death of Aunt May; embossed double-c 5.00
400-Collector's Edition; white-c 1 2 3 5 7 9
408-($2.95) Polybagged version with TV theme song cassette 8.00
421-424,426,428-433: 426-Begin $1.99-c. 432-Spiderhunt pt. 2 2.50
425-($2.99)-48 pgs., wraparound-c 3.00
427-($2.25) Return of Dr. Octopus; double gatefold-c 2.50
434-440: 434-Double-c with "Amazing Ricochet #1". 438-Daredevil app. 439-Avengers-c/app. 440-Byrne-s 2.50
441-Final issue; Byrne-s 4.00
#500-up (See Amazing Spider-Man Vol. 2; series resumed original numbering after Vol. 2 #58)
#(-1) Flashback issue (7/97, $1.95-c) 2.50
Annual 1 (1964, 72 pgs.)-Origin Spider-Man; 1st app. Sinister Six (Dr. Octopus, Electro, Kraven the Hunter, Mysterio, Sandman, Vulture) (new 41 pg. story); plus gallery of Spidey foes; early X-Men app. 85 170 255 723 1387 2050
Annual 2 (1965, 25¢, 72 pgs.)-Reprints from #1,2,5 plus new Doctor Strange story
35 70 105 270 498 725
Special 3 (11/66, 25¢, 72 pgs.)-New Avengers story & Hulk x-over; Doctor Octopus-r from #11,12; Romita-a 16 32 48 114 212 310
Special 4 (11/67, 25¢, 68 pgs.)-Spidey battles Human Torch (new 41 pg. story)
14 28 42 99 175 250
Special 5 (11/68, 25¢, 68 pgs.)-New 40 pg. Red Skull story; 1st app. Peter Parker's parents; last annual with new-a 12 24 36 82 146 210
Special 5-2nd printing (1994) 2 4 6 8 10 12
Special 6 (11/69, 25¢, 68 pgs.)-Reprints 41 pg. Sinister Six story from annual #1 plus 2 Kirby/Ditko stories (r) 5 10 15 32 51 70
Special 7 (12/70, 25¢, 68 pgs.)-All-r(#1,2) new Vulture-c
5 10 15 32 51 70
Special 8 (12/71)-All-r 5 10 15 32 51 70
King Size 9 ('73)-Reprints Spectacular Spider-Man (mag.) #2; 40 pg. Green Goblin-c/story (re-edited from 58 pgs.) 5 10 15 32 51 70
Annual 10 (1976)-Origin Human Fly (vs. Spidey); new-a begins
3 6 9 14 20 25
Annual 11-13 ('77-'79):12-Spidey vs. Hulk-r/#119,120. 13-New Byrne/Austin-a; Dr. Octopus x-over w/Spectacular S-M Ann. #1 2 4 6 9 13 16
Annual 14 (1980)-Miller-c/a(p); Dr. Strange app. 2 4 6 13 18 22
Annual 15 (1981)-Miller-c/a(p); Punisher app. 3 6 9 16 23 30
Annual 16-20:16 ('82)-Origin/1st app. new Capt. Marvel (female heroine). 17 ('83)-Kingpin app. 18 ('84)-Scorpion app.; JJJ weds. 19 ('85). 20 ('86)-Origin Iron Man of 2020
1 2 3 4 5 7
Annual 21 (1987)-Special wedding issue; newsstand & direct sale versions exist & are worth same 2 4 6 8 10 12
Annual 22 (1988, $1.75, 68 pgs.)-1st app. Speedball; Evolutionary War x-over; Daredevil app. 6.00
Annual 23 (1989, $2.00, 68 pgs.)-Atlantis Attacks; origin Spider-Man retold; She-Hulk app.; Byrne-c; Liefeld-a(p), 23 pgs. 4.00
Annual 24 (1990, $2.00, 68 pgs.)-Ant-Man app. 3.00
Annual 25 (1991, $2.00, 68 pgs.)-3 pg. origin recap; Iron Man app.; 1st Venom solo story; Ditko-a (6 pgs.) 5.00
Annual 26 (1992, $2.25, 68 pgs.)-New Warriors-c/story; Venom solo story cont'd in Spectacular Spider-Man Annual #12 4.00
Annual 27,28 ('93, '94, $2.95, 68 pgs.)-27-Bagged w/card; 1st app. Annex. 28-Carnage-c/story; Rhino & Cloak and Dagger back-ups 3.00
'96 Special-($2.95, 64 pgs.)-"Blast From The Past" 3.00
'97 Special-($2.99)-Wraparound-c,Sundown app. 3.00
Marvel Graphic Novel - Parallel Lives (3/89, $8.95) 2 4 6 8 10 12
Marvel Graphic Novel - Spirits of the Earth (1990, $18.95, HC)
3 6 9 16 22 28
Super Special 1 (4/95, $3.95)-Flip Book 4.00
...: Skating on Thin Ice 1(1990, $1.25, Canadian)-McFarlane-c; anti-drug issue; Electro app.
1 2 3 5 7 9
...: Skating on Thin Ice 1 (2/93, $1.50, American) 4.00
...: Double Trouble 2 (1990, $1.25, Canadian) 6.00
...: Double Trouble 2 (2/93, $1.50, American) 3.00
...: Hit and Run 3 (1990, $1.25, Canadian)-Ghost Rider-c/story
1 2 3 5 7 9
...: Hit and Run 3 (2/93. $1.50, American) 3.00
... : Carnage (6/93, $6.95)-r/ASM #344,345,359-363 1 2 3 4 5 7
...: Chaos in Calgary 4 (Canadian; part of 5 part series)-Turbine,Night Rider, Frightful app. 2 4 6 8 11 14
...: Chaos in Calgary 4 (2/93, $1.50, American) 3.00
...: Deadball 5 (1993, $1.60, Canadian)-Green Goblin-c/story; features Montreal Expos 2 4 6 10 14 18
Note: Prices listed above are for English Canadian editions. French editions are worth double.
...: Soul of the Hunter nn (8/92, $5.95, 52 pgs.)-Zeck-c/a(p) 6.00
Wizard #1 Ace Edition ($13.99) r/#1 w/ new Ramos acetate-c 14.00
Wizard #129 Ace Edition ($13.99) r/#129 w/ new Ramos acetate-c 14.00
NOTE: ***Austin*** *a(i)-248, 335, 337, Annual 13; c(i)-188, 241, 242, 248, 331, 334, 343, Annual 25.* ***J. Buscema*** *a(p)-72, 73, 76-81, 84, 85.* ***Byrne*** *a-189p, 190p, 206p, Annual 3r, 6r, 7r, 13p; c-189p, 268, 296, Annual 12.* ***Ditko*** *a-1-38, Annual 1, Special 3(r), 2, 24(2); c-1i, 2-38.* ***Guice*** *c/a-Annual 18i.* ***Gil Kane*** *a(p)-89-105, 120-124, 150, Annual 10, 12i, 24p; c-90p, 96, 98, 99, 101-105p, 129p, 131p, 132p, 137-140p, 143p, 148p, 149p, 151p, 153p, 160p, 161p, Annual 10p, 24.* ***Kirby*** *a-8.* ***Erik Larsen*** *a-324, 327, 329-350; c-327, 329-350, 354i, Annual 25.* ***McFarlane*** *a-298p, 299p, 300-303, 304-323p, 325p, 328; c-298-325, 328.* ***Miller*** *c-218, 219.* ***Mooney*** *a-65i, 67-82i, 84-88i, 173i, 178i, 189i, 190i, 192i, 193i, 196-202i, 207i, 211-219i, 221i, 222i, 226i, 227i, 229-233i, Annual 11i, 17i.* ***Nasser*** *c-228p.* ***Nebres*** *a-Annual 24i.* ***Russell*** *c-357i.* ***Simonson*** *c-222, 337i.* ***Starlin*** *a-113i, 114i, 187p.* ***Williamson*** *a-365i.*

AMAZING SPIDER-MAN (Volume 2) (Some issues reprinted in "Spider-Man, Best Of" hardcovers)
Marvel Comics: Jan, 1999 - Present ($2.99/$1.99/$2.25)

1-($2.99)-Byrne-a 6.00
1-Sunburst variant-c 1 2 3 5 6 8
1-($6.95) Dynamic Forces variant-c by the Romitas 1 3 4 6 8 10
1-Marvel Matrix sketch variant-c 1 3 4 6 8 10
2-($1.99) Two covers -by John Byrne and Andy Kubert 4.00
3-11: 4-Fantastic Four app. 5-Spider-Woman-c 2.50
12-($2.99) Sinister Six return (cont. in Peter Parker #12) 3.00
13-17: 13-Mary Jane's plane explodes 2.50
18,19,21-24,26-28: 18-Begin $2.25-c. 19-Venom-c. 24-Maximum Security 2.50
20-($2.99, 100 pgs.) Spider-Slayer issue; new story and reprints 3.00
25-($2.99) Regular cover; Peter Parker becomes the Green Goblin 3.00
25-($3.99) Holo-foil enhanced cover 4.00
29-Peter is reunited with Mary Jane 2.50
30-Straczynski-s/Campbell-c begin; intro. Ezekiel 6.00
31-35: Battles Morlun 4.00
36-Black cover; aftermath of the Sept. 11 tragedy in New York 10.00
37-49: 39-'Nuff Said issue 42-Dr. Strange app. 43-45-Doctor Octopus app. 46-48-Cho-c 2.50
50-Peter and MJ reunite; Captain America & Dr. Doom app.; Campbell-c 3.00
51-58: 51,52-Campbell-c. 55,56-Avery scripts. 57,58-Avengers, FF, Cyclops app. 2.50
(After #58 [Nov, 2003] numbering reverted back to original Vol. 1 with #500, Dec, 2003)
500-($3.50) J. Scott Campbell-c; Romita Jr. & Sr.-a; Uncle Ben app. 3.50
501-524: 501-Harris-c. 503-504-Loki app. 506-508-Ezekiel app. 509-514-Sins Past; intro.

Amazing Spider-Man V2 #545 © MAR

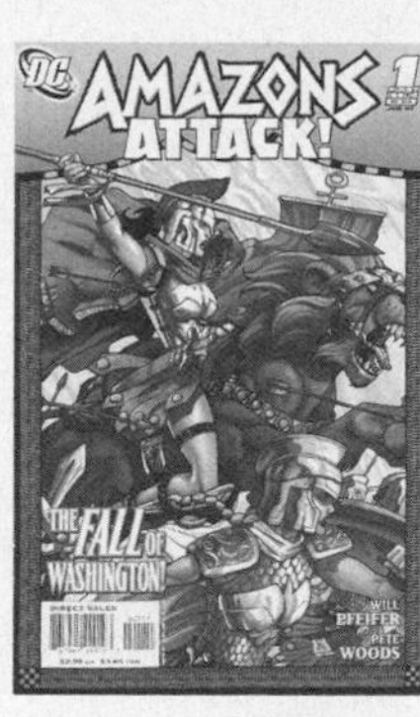

Amazons Attack #1 © DC

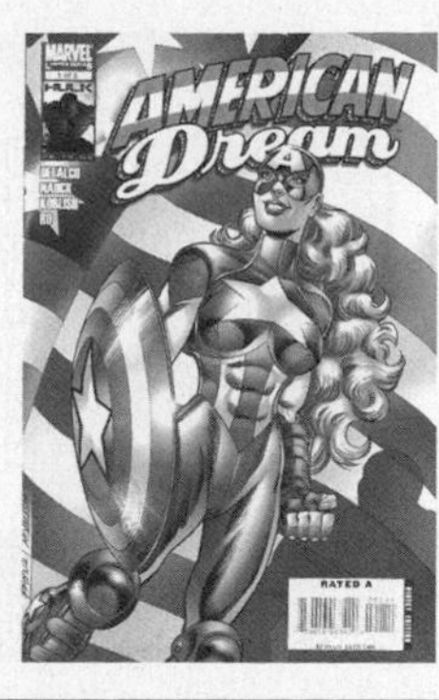

American Dream #1 © MAR

GD 2.0 | VG 4.0 | FN 6.0 | VF 8.0 | VF/NM 9.0 | NM- 9.2

Gabriel and Sarah Osborn; Deodato-a. 519-Moves into Avengers HQ. 521-Begin $2.50-c
524-Harris-c 2.50
525,526-Evolve or Die x-over. 525-David-s. 526-Hudlin-s; Spider-Man loses eye 4.00
525-528-2nd printings with variant-c. 525 Ben Reilly costume. 526-Six-Armed Spidey.
527-Spider-Man 2099. 528-Spider-Ham 5.00
527,528: Evolve or Die pt.9, 12 2.50
529-Debut of red and gold costume; Garney-a 10.00
529-2nd printing 5.00
529-3rd printing with Wieringo-c 3.00
530,531-Titanium Man app.; Kirkham-a. 531-Begin $2.99-c 6.00
532-538-Civil War tie-in. 538-Aunt May shot 5.00
539-543-Back in Black. 539-Peter wears the black costume 3.00
544-($3.99) "One More Day" pt. 1; Quesada-a/Straczynski-s 4.00
545-(12/08, $3.99) "One More Day" pt. 4; Quesada-a/Straczynski-s, Peter & MJ's marriage un-done; r/wedding from ASM Annual #21; 2 covers by Quesada and Djurdjevic 4.00
546-($3.99) Brand New Day begins; McNiven-a; Deodato, Winslade, Land, Romita Jr.-a 5.00
546-Variant-c by Bryan Hitch 8.00
546-Second printing with new McNiven-c of Peter Parker 4.00
547-567: 547,548-McNiven-a. 549-551-Larroca-a. 555-557-Bachalo-a. 559-Intro. Screwball. 560,561-MJ app. 565-New Kraven intro. 566,567-Spidey in Daredevil costume 3.00
568-($3.99) Romita Jr.-a begins; two covers by Romita Jr. and Alex Ross 6.00
568-Variant-c by John Romita Sr. 20.00
568-2nd printing with Romita Jr. Anti-Venom costume cover 4.00
569-Debut of Anti-Venom; Norman Osborn and Thunderbolts app.;Romita Jr.-c 3.00
569-Variant Venom-c by Granov 6.00
570-572-Two covers on each
1999, 2000 Annual (6/99, '00, $3.50) 1999-Buscema-a 3.50
2001 Annual ($2.99) Follows Peter Parker: S-M #29; last Mackie-s 3.00
Collected Edition #30-32 ($3.95) reprints #30-32 w/cover #30 4.00
... 500 Covers HC (2004, $49.99) reprints covers for #1-500 & Annuals, yearly re-caps 50.00
... Omnibus HC (2007, $99.99, dustjacket) r/Amazing Fantasy #15, Amazing Spider-Man #1-38, Annual #1,2, Strange Tales Annual #2 & Fantastic Four Annual #1; letter pages, bonus art, intro. by Stan Lee, bios, essays, Marvel Tales cover gallery 100.00
Spider-Man: Brand New Day - Extra!! #1 (9/08, $3.99) short stories; Bachalo,Ollifte-a 4.00
...: Swing Shift Director's Cut (2008, $3.99) story from 2007 FCBD; Brand New Day info 4.00
...Vol. 1: Coming Home (2001, $15.95) r/#30-35; J. Scott Campbell-c 16.00
...Vol. 2: Revelations (2002, $8.99) r/#36-39; Kaare Andrews-c 9.00
...Vol. 3: Until the Stars Turn Cold (2002, $12.99) r/#40-45; Romita Jr.-c 13.00
...Vol. 4: The Life and Death of Spiders (2003, $11.99) r/#46-50; Campbell-c 12.00
...Vol. 5: Unintended Consequences (2003, $12.99) r/#51-56; Dodson-c 13.00
...Vol. 6: Happy Birthday (2003, $12.99) r/#57,58,500-502 13.00
...Vol. 7: The Book of Ezekiel (2004, $12.99) r/#503-508; Romita Jr.-c 13.00
...Vol. 8: Sins Past (2005, $12.99) r/#509-514; cover sketch gallery 13.00
...Vol. 9: Skin Deep (2005, $9.99) r/#515-518 10.00
...Vol. 10: New Avengers (2005, $14.99) r/#519-524 15.00
Civil War: Amazing Spider-Man TPB (2007, $17.99) r/#532-538; variant covers 18.00

AMAAZING SPIDER-MAN FAMILY (Also see Spider-Man Family)
Marvel Comics: Oct, 2008 - Present ($4.99, anthology)
1-New tales and reprints. 1-Includes r/ASM #300; Granov-c 5.00

AMAZING WILLIE MAYS, THE
Famous Funnies Publ.: No date (Sept, 1954)

	GD	VG	FN	VF	VF/NM	NM-
nn	80	160	240	504	852	1200

AMAZING WORLD OF DC COMICS
DC Comics: Jul, 1974 - No. 17, 1978 ($1.50, B&W, mail-order DC Pro-zine)

	GD	VG	FN	VF	VF/NM	NM-
1-Kubert interview; unpublished Kirby-a; Infantino-c	7	14	21	45	73	100
2-4: 3-Julie Schwartz profile. 4-Batman; Robinson-c	5	10	15	30	48	65
5-Sheldon Mayer	4	8	12	26	41	55
6,8,13: 6-Joe Orlando; EC-r; Wrightson pin-up. 8-Infantino; Batman-r from Pop Tart giveaway. 13-Humor; Aragonés-c; Wood/Ditko-a; photos from serials of Superman, Batman, Captain Marvel	3	6	9	20	30	40
7,10-12: 7-Superman; r/1955 Pep comic giveaway. 10-Behind the scenes at DC; Showcase article. 11-Super-Villains; unpubl. Secret Society of S.V. story. 12-Legion; Grell-c/interview;	3	6	9	21	32	42
9-Legion of Super-Heroes; lengthy bios and history; Cockrum-c	7	14	21	47	76	105
14-Justice League	4	8	12	22	34	45
15-Wonder Woman; Nasser-c	4	8	12	28	44	60
16-Golden Age heroes	4	8	12	26	41	55
17-Shazam; G.A., 70s, TV and Fawcett heroes	4	8	12	22	34	45
Special 1 (Digest size)	3	6	9	18	27	35

AMAZING WORLD OF SUPERMAN (See Superman)

AMAZING X-MEN
Marvel Comics: Mar, 1995 - No. 4, July, 1995 ($1.95, limited series)
1-Age of Apocalypse; Andy Kubert-c/a 3.50
2-4 2.50

AMAZON
Comico: Mar, 1989 - No. 3, May, 1989 ($1.95, limited series)
1-3: Ecological theme 2.50

AMAZON (Also see Marvel Versus DC #3 & DC Versus Marvel #4)
DC Comics (Amalgam): Apr, 1996 ($1.95, one-shot)
1-John Byrne-c/a/scripts 2.50

AMAZON ATTACK 3-D
The 3-D Zone: Sept, 1990 ($3.95, 28 pgs.)
1-Chaykin-a 6.00

AMAZONS ATTACK (See Wonder Woman #8 - 2006 series)
DC Comics: Jun, 2007 - No. 6, Late Oct, 2007 ($2.99, limited series)
1-6-Queen Hippolyta and Amazons attacks Wash., DC; Pfeifer-s/Woods-a 3.00

AMAZON WOMAN (1st Series)
FantaCo: Summer, 1994 - No. 2, Fall, 1994 ($2.95, B&W, limited series, mature)
1,2: Tom Simonton-c/a/scripts 3.00

AMAZON WOMAN (2nd Series)
FantaCo: Feb, 1996 - No. 4, May, 1996 ($2.95, B&W, limited series, mature)
1-4: Tom Simonton-a/scripts 3.00
...: Invaders of Terror ('96, $5.95) Simonton-a/s 6.00

AMBUSH (See Zane Grey, Four Color 314)

AMBUSH BUG (Also see Son of...)
DC Comics: June, 1985 - No. 4, Sept, 1985 (75¢, limited series)
1-4: Giffen-c/a in all 3.00
Nothing Special 1 (9/92, $2.50, 68pg.)-Giffen-c/a 3.00
Stocking Stuffer (2/86, $1.25)-Giffen-c/a 3.00

AMBUSH BUG: YEAR NONE
DC Comics: Sept, 2008 - No. 6 ($2.99, limited series)
1-Giffen-s/a; Jonni DC app. 3.00

AMERICA AT WAR - THE BEST OF DC WAR COMICS (See Fireside Book Series)

AMERICA IN ACTION
Dell (Imp. Publ. Co.)/ Mayflower House Publ.: 1942; Winter, 1945 (36 pgs.)

	GD	VG	FN	VF	VF/NM	NM-
1942-Dell-(68 pgs.)	17	34	51	98	154	210
1-(1945)-Has 3 adaptations from American history; Kiefer, Schrotter & Webb-a	14	28	42	76	108	140

AMERICAN, THE
Dark Horse Comics: July, 1987 - No. 8, 1989 ($1.50/$1.75, B&W)
1-8: ($1.50) 2.50
Collection ($5.95, B&W)-Reprints 6.00
Special 1 (1990, $2.25, B&W) 2.50

AMERICAN AIR FORCES, THE (See A-1 Comics)
William H. Wise(Flying Cadet Publ. Co./Hasan(No.1)/Life's Romances/ Magazine Ent. No. 5 on): Sept-Oct, 1944-No. 4, 1945; No. 5, 1951-No. 12, 1954

	GD	VG	FN	VF	VF/NM	NM-
1-Article by Zack Mosley, creator of Smilin' Jack; German war-c	20	40	60	118	189	260
2-Classic-Japan war-c	34	68	102	198	319	440
3,4-Japan war-c	14	28	42	80	115	150

NOTE: *All part comic, part magazine. Art by* **Whitney, Chas. Quinlan, H. C. Kiefer,** *and* **Tony Dipreta.**

	GD	VG	FN	VF	VF/NM	NM-
5(A-1 45)(Formerly Jet Powers), 6(A-1 54), 7(A-1 58), 8(A-1 65), 9(A-1 67), 10(A-1 74), 11(A-1 79), 12(A-1 91)	9	18	27	47	61	75

NOTE: **Powell** *c/a-5-12.*

AMERICAN CENTURY
DC Comics (Vertigo): May, 2001 - No. 27, Oct, 2003 ($2.50/$2.75)
1-Chaykin-s/painted-c; Tischman-a 4.00
2-27: 5-New story arc begins. 10-16,22-27-Orbik-c. 17-21-Silke-c. 18-$2.75-c begins 2.75
Hollywood Babylon (2002, $12.95, TPB) r/#5-9; w/sketch-to-art pages 13.00
Scars & Stripes (2001, $8.95, TPB) r/#1-4; Tischman intro. 9.00

AMERICAN DREAM (From the M2 Avengers)
Marvel Comics: Jul, 2008 - No. 5, Sept, 2008 ($2.99, limited series)
1-5-DeFalco-s/Nauck-a 3.00

AMERICAN FLAGG! (See First Comics Graphic Novel 3,9,12,21 & Howard Chaykin's..)
First Comics: Oct, 1983 - No. 50, Mar, 1988

American Virgin #23 © Seagle & Cloonan

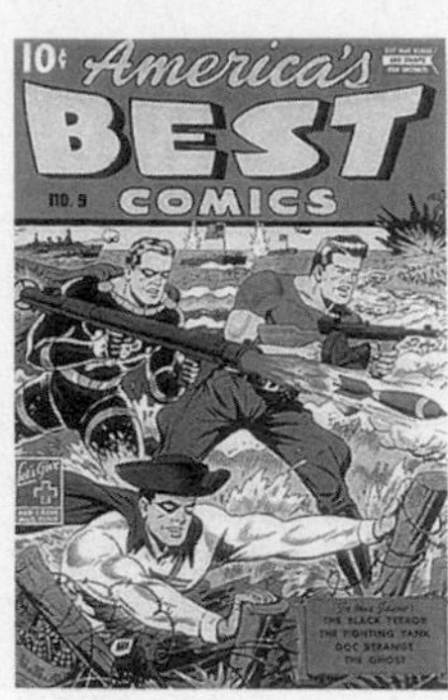

America's Best Comics #9 © STD

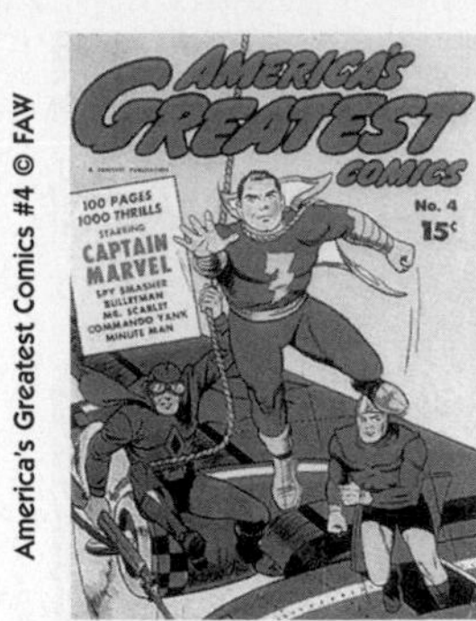

America's Greatest Comics #4 © FAW

GD VG FN VF VF/NM NM-
2.0 4.0 6.0 8.0 9.0 9.2

1,21-27: 1-Chaykin-c/a begins. 21-27-Alan Moore scripts 4.00
2-20,28-49: 31-Origin Bob Violence 3.00
50-Last issue 4.00
Special 1 (11/86)-Introduces Chaykin's Time[2] 4.00
...: Hard Times TPB (6/85, $11.95) r/#1-7; intro. by Michael Moorcock; bonus materials 12.00
...: Definitive Collection Volume 1 HC (2008, $49.99) r/#1-14 and material from the...: Hard Times TPB; intro by Michael Chabon; afterword by Jim Lee 50.00

AMERICAN FREAK: A TALE OF THE UN-MEN
DC Comics (Vertigo): Feb, 1994 - No. 5, Jun, 1994 ($1.95, mini-series, mature)
1-5 2.50

AMERICAN GRAPHICS
Henry Stewart: No. 1, 1954; No. 2, 1957 (25¢)
1-The Maid of the Mist, The Last of the Eries (Indian Legends of Niagara) (sold at Niagara Falls) 11 22 33 60 83 105
2-Victory at Niagara & Laura Secord (Heroine of the War of 1812) 8 16 24 40 50 60

AMERICAN INDIAN, THE (See Picture Progress)

AMERICAN LIBRARY
David McKay Publ.: 1943 - No. 6, 1944 (15¢, 68 pgs., B&W, text & pictures)
nn (#1)-Thirty Seconds Over Tokyo (movie) 38 76 114 226 363 500
nn (#2)-Guadalcanal Diary; painted-c (only 10¢) 28 56 84 162 261 360
3-6: 3-Look to the Mountain. 4-Case of the Crooked Candle (Perry Mason). 5-Duel in the Sun. 6-Wingate's Raiders 15 30 45 86 133 180

AMERICAN: LOST IN AMERICA, THE
Dark Horse Comics: July, 1992 - No. 4, Oct, 1992 ($2.50, limited series)
1-4: 1-Dorman painted-c. 2-Phillips painted-c. 3-Mignola-c. 4-Jim Lee-c 2.50

AMERICAN SPLENDOR: (Series of titles)
Dark Horse Comics: Aug, 1996 - Present (B&W, all one-shots)
--**COMIC-CON COMICS** (8/96) 1-H. Pekar script. --**MUSIC COMICS** (11/97) nn-H. Pekar-s/Sacco-a; r/Village Voice jazz strips. --**ODDS AND ENDS** (12/97) 1-Pekar-s. --**ON THE JOB** (5/97) 1-Pekar-s. --**A STEP OUT OF THE NEST** (8/94) 1-Pekar-s. --**TERMINAL** (9/99) 1-Pekar-s. --**TRANSATLANTIC** (7/98) 1-"American Splendour" on cover; Pekar-s 3.00
--**A PORTRAIT OF THE AUTHOR IN HIS DECLINING YEARS** (4/01, $3.99) 1-Photo-c. --**BEDTIME STORIES** (6/00, $3.95) 4.00

AMERICAN SPLENDOR
DC Comics: Nov, 2006 - No. 4, Feb, 2007 ($2.99, B&W)
1-4-Pekar-s/art by Haspiel and various. 1-Fabry-c 3.00
...: Another Day TPB (2007, $14.99) r/#1-4 15.00

AMERICAN SPLENDOR (Volume 2)
DC Comics (Vertigo): Jun, 2008 - No. 4, Sept, 2008 ($2.99, B&W)
1-4-Pekar-s/art by Haspiel and various. 1-Bond-c. 3-Cooke-c 3.00

AMERICAN SPLENDOR: UNSUNG HERO
Dark Horse Comics: Aug, 2002 - No. 3, Oct, 2002 ($3.99, B&W, limited series)
1-3-Pekar script/Collier-a; biography of Robert McNeill 4.00
TPB (8/03, $11.95) r/#1-3 12.00

AMERICAN SPLENDOR: WINDFALL
Dark Horse Comics: Sept, 1995 - No. 2, Oct,1995 ($3.95, B&W, limited series)
1,2-Pekar script 4.00

AMERICAN TAIL: FIEVEL GOES WEST, AN
Marvel Comics: Early Jan, 1992 - No. 3, Early Feb, 1992 ($1.00, limited series)
1-3-Adapts Universal animated movie; Wildman-a 3.00
1-($2.95-c, 69 pgs.) Deluxe squarebound edition 5.00

AMERICAN VIRGIN
DC Comics (Vertigo): May, 2006 - No. 23, Mar, 2008 ($2.99)
1-23-Steven Seagle-s/Becky Cloonan-a in most. 1-3-Quitely-c. 4-14-Middleton-c 3.00
...: Head (2006, $9.99, TPB) r/#1-4; interviews with the creators and page development 10.00
...: Going Down (2007, $14.99, TPB) r/#5-9 15.00
...: Wet (2007, $12.99, TPB) r/#10-14 13.00
...: Around the World (Vol. 4) (2008, $17.99, TPB) r/#15-23 18.00

AMERICAN WAY, THE
DC Comics (WildStorm): Apr, 2006 - No. 8, Nov, 2006 ($2.99, limited series)
1-8-John Ridley-s/Georges Jeanty-a/c 3.00
TPB (2007, $19.99) r/series; covers; Jeanty sketch pages 20.00

AMERICA'S BEST COMICS
Nedor/Better/Standard Publications: Feb, 1942; No. 2, Sept, 1942 - No. 31, July, 1949 (New logo with #9)

GD VG FN VF VF/NM NM-
2.0 4.0 6.0 8.0 9.0 9.2

1-The Woman in Red, Black Terror, Captain Future, Doc Strange, The Liberator, & Don Davis, Secret Ace begin 300 600 900 1930 3315 4700
2-Origin The American Eagle; The Woman in Red ends 108 216 324 680 1153 1625
3-Pyroman begins (11/42, 1st app.; also see Startling Comics #18, 12/42) 83 166 249 523 887 1250
4-6: 5-Last Capt. Future (not in #4); Lone Eagle app. 6-American Crusader app. 63 126 189 397 669 940
7-Hitler, Mussolini & Hirohito-c 123 246 369 775 1313 1850
8-Last Liberator 61 122 183 384 647 910
9-The Fighting Yank begins; The Ghost app. 67 134 201 422 711 1000
10-Flag-c 56 112 168 353 594 835
11-Hirohito & Tojo-c. (10/44) 77 154 231 481 816 1150
12-17,19-21: 14-American Eagle ends; Doc Strange vs. Hitler story. 21-Infinity-c 54 108 162 340 575 810
18-Classic-c 70 140 210 441 746 1050
22-Capt. Future app. 47 94 141 291 483 675
23-Miss Masque begins; last Doc Strange 54 108 162 340 575 810
24-Miss Masque bondage-c 53 106 159 331 558 785
25-Last Fighting Yank; Sea Eagle app. 42 84 126 252 409 565
26-31: 26-The Phantom Detective & The Silver Knight app.; Frazetta text illo & some panels in Miss Masque. 27,28-Commando Cubs. 27-Doc Strange. 28-Tuska Black Terror. 29-Last Pyroman 40 80 120 244 397 550
NOTE: *American Eagle not in 3, 8, 9, 13. Fighting Yank not in 10, 12. Liberator not in 2, 6, 7. Pyroman not in 9, 11, 14-16, 23, 25-27.* ***Schomburg (Xela)*** *c-5, 7-31. Bondage c-18, 24.*

AMERICA'S BEST COMICS
America's Best Comics: 1999 - Present
Preview (1999, Wizard magazine supplement) - Previews Tom Strong, Top Ten, Promethea, Tomorrow Stories 2.25
Sketchbook (2002, $5.95, square-bound)-Design sketches by Sprouse, Ross, Adams, Nowlan, Ha and others 6.00
Special 1 (2/01, $6.95)-Short stories of Alan Moore's characters; art by various; Ross-c 7.00
TPB (2004, $17.95) Reprints short stories and sketch pages from ABC titles 18.00

AMERICA'S BEST TV COMICS (TV)
American Broadcasting Co. (Prod. by Marvel Comics): 1967 (25¢, 68 pgs.)
1-Spider-Man, Fantastic Four (by Kirby/Ayers), Casper, King Kong, George of the Jungle, Journey to the Center of the Earth stories (promotes new TV cartoon show) 13 26 39 97 171 245

AMERICA'S BIGGEST COMICS BOOK
William H. Wise: 1944 (196 pgs., one-shot)
1-The Grim Reaper, The Silver Knight, Zudo, the Jungle Boy, Commando Cubs, Thunderhoof app. 40 80 120 235 380 525

AMERICA'S FUNNIEST COMICS
William H. Wise: 1944 - No. 2, 1944 (15¢, 80 pgs.)
nn(#1), 2 30 60 90 174 280 385

AMERICA'S GREATEST COMICS
Fawcett Publications: May?, 1941 - No. 8, Summer, 1943 (15¢, 100 pgs., soft cardboard-c)
1-Bulletman, Spy Smasher, Capt. Marvel, Minute Man & Mr. Scarlet begin; Classic Mac Raboy-c. 1st time that Fawcett's major super-heroes appear together as a group on a cover. Fawcett's 1st squarebound comic 335 670 1005 2278 3989 5700
2 145 290 435 914 1545 2175
3 103 206 309 649 1100 1550
4,5: 4-Commando Yank begins; Golden Arrow, Ibis the Invincible & Spy Smasher cameo in Captain Marvel 76 152 228 479 810 1140
6,7: 7-Balbo the Boy Magician app.; Captain Marvel, Bulletman cameo in Mr. Scarlet 67 134 201 422 711 1000
8-Capt. Marvel Jr. & Golden Arrow app.; Spy Smasher x-over in Capt. Midnight; no Minute Man or Commando Yank 67 134 201 422 711 1000

AMERICA'S SWEETHEART SUNNY (See Sunny, ...)

AMERICA VS. THE JUSTICE SOCIETY
DC Comics: Jan, 1985 - No. 4, Apr, 1985 ($1.00, limited series)
1-Double size; Alcala-a(i) in all 1 2 3 5 7 9
2-4: 3,4-Spectre cameo 1 2 3 4 5 7

AMERICOMICS
Americomics: April, 1983 - No. 6, Mar, 1984 ($2.00, Baxter paper/slick paper)
1-Intro/origin The Shade; Intro. The Slayer, Captain Freedom and The Liberty Corps; Perez-c 5.00
1,2-2nd printings ($2.00) 2.25
2-6: 2-Messenger app. & 1st app. Tara on Jungle Island. 3-New & old Blue Beetle battle. 4-Origin Dragonfly & Shade. 5-Origin Commando D. 6-Origin the Scarlet Scorpion 3.00

Amory Wars #5 © Evil Ink Comics

Anarky #2 © DC

Angel: After the Fall #10 © 20th Century Fox

	GD 2.0	VG 4.0	FN 6.0	VF 8.0	VF/NM 9.0	NM- 9.2
Special 1 (8/83, $2.00)-Sentinels of Justice (Blue Beetle, Captain Atom, Nightshade & The Question)						4.50

AMETHYST
DC Comics: Jan, 1985 - No. 16, Aug, 1986 (75¢)

	GD 2.0	VG 4.0	FN 6.0	VF 8.0	VF/NM 9.0	NM- 9.2
1-16: 8-Fire Jade's i.d. revealed						2.50
Special 1 (10/86, $1.25), 1-4 (11/87 - 2/88)(Limited series)						2.50

AMETHYST, PRINCESS OF GEMWORLD (See Legion of Super-Heroes #298)
DC Comics: May, 1983 - No. 12, Apr, 1984 (Maxi-series)

	GD 2.0	VG 4.0	FN 6.0	VF 8.0	VF/NM 9.0	NM- 9.2
1-(60¢)						2.50
1,2-(75¢): tested in Austin & Kansas City	3	6	9	17	25	32
2-12, Annual 1(9/84): 5-11-Pérez-c(p)						2.50

AMORY WARS (Based on the Coheed and Cambria album The Second Stage Turbine Blade)
Image Comics: Jun, 2007 - No. 5, Jan, 2008 ($2.99, limited series)

	GD 2.0	VG 4.0	FN 6.0	VF 8.0	VF/NM 9.0	NM- 9.2
1-5: 1-Claudio Sanchez-s/Gus Vasquez-a						3.00

AMORY WARS II
Image Comics: Jun, 2008 - No. 5 ($2.99, limited series)

	GD 2.0	VG 4.0	FN 6.0	VF 8.0	VF/NM 9.0	NM- 9.2
1-4-Claudio Sanchez-s/Gabriel Guzman-a						3.00

AMY RACECAR COLOR SPECIAL (See Stray Bullets)
El Capitán Books: July, 1997; Oct, 1999 ($2.95/$3.50)

	GD 2.0	VG 4.0	FN 6.0	VF 8.0	VF/NM 9.0	NM- 9.2
1,2-David Lapham-a/scripts. 2-($3.50)						3.50

ANARCHO DICTATOR OF DEATH (See Comics Novel)

ANARKY (See Batman titles)
DC Comics: May, 1997 - No. 4, Aug, 1997 ($2.50, limited series)

	GD 2.0	VG 4.0	FN 6.0	VF 8.0	VF/NM 9.0	NM- 9.2
1						3.50
2-4						2.50

ANARKY (See Batman titles)
DC Comics: May, 1999 - No. 8, Dec, 1999 ($2.50)

	GD 2.0	VG 4.0	FN 6.0	VF 8.0	VF/NM 9.0	NM- 9.2
1-8: 1-JLA app.; Grant-s/Breyfogle-a. 3-Green Lantern app. 7-Day of Judgment; Haunted Tank app. 8-Joker-c/app.						2.50

ANCHORS ANDREWS (The Saltwater Daffy)
St. John Publishing Co.: Jan, 1953 - No. 4, July, 1953 (Anchors the Saltwater... No. 4)

	GD 2.0	VG 4.0	FN 6.0	VF 8.0	VF/NM 9.0	NM- 9.2
1-Canteen Kate by Matt Baker (9 pgs.)	20	40	60	118	189	260
2-4	9	18	27	50	65	80

ANDY & WOODY (See March of Comics No. 40, 55, 76)

ANDY BURNETT (TV, Disney)
Dell Publishing Co.: Dec, 1957

	GD 2.0	VG 4.0	FN 6.0	VF 8.0	VF/NM 9.0	NM- 9.2
Four Color 865-Photo-c	8	16	24	58	97	135

ANDY COMICS (Formerly Scream Comics; becomes Ernie Comics)
Current Publications (Ace Magazines): No. 20, June, 1948-No. 21, Aug, 1948

	GD 2.0	VG 4.0	FN 6.0	VF 8.0	VF/NM 9.0	NM- 9.2
20,21: Archie-type comic	8	16	24	42	54	65

ANDY DEVINE WESTERN
Fawcett Publications: Dec, 1950 - No. 2, 1951

	GD 2.0	VG 4.0	FN 6.0	VF 8.0	VF/NM 9.0	NM- 9.2
1	50	100	150	305	503	700
2	40	80	120	235	368	500

ANDY GRIFFITH SHOW, THE (TV)(1st show aired 10/3/60)
Dell Publishing Co.: #1252, Jan-Mar, 1962; #1341, Apr-Jun, 1962

	GD 2.0	VG 4.0	FN 6.0	VF 8.0	VF/NM 9.0	NM- 9.2
Four Color 1252(#1)	35	70	105	270	498	725
Four Color 1341-Photo-c	32	64	96	246	461	675

ANDY HARDY COMICS (See Movie Comics #3 by Fiction House)
Dell Publishing Co.: April, 1952 - No. 6, Sept-Nov, 1954

	GD 2.0	VG 4.0	FN 6.0	VF 8.0	VF/NM 9.0	NM- 9.2
Four Color 389(#1)	5	10	15	34	55	75
Four Color 447,480,515, #5,#6	4	8	12	26	41	55

ANDY PANDA (Also see Crackajack Funnies #39, The Funnies, New Funnies & Walter Lantz...)
Dell Publishing Co.: 1943 - No. 56, Nov-Jan, 1961-62 (Walter Lantz)

	GD 2.0	VG 4.0	FN 6.0	VF 8.0	VF/NM 9.0	NM- 9.2
Four Color 25(#1, 1943)	52	104	156	416	783	1150
Four Color 54(1944)	29	58	87	213	394	575
Four Color 85(1945)	16	32	48	114	212	310
Four Color 130(1946),154,198	12	24	36	82	146	210
Four Color 216,240,258,280,297	8	16	24	58	97	135
Four Color 326,345,358	6	12	18	43	69	95
Four Color 383,409	5	10	15	34	55	75
16(11-1/52-53) - 30	4	8	12	26	41	55
31-56	3	6	9	20	30	40

(See March of Comics #5, 22, 79, & Super Book #4, 15, 27.)

A-NEXT (See Avengers)
Marvel Comics: Oct, 1998 - No. 12, Sept, 1999 ($1.99)

	GD 2.0	VG 4.0	FN 6.0	VF 8.0	VF/NM 9.0	NM- 9.2
1-Next generation of Avengers; Frenz-a						3.00
2-12: 2-Two covers. 3-Defenders app.						2.50
Spider-Girl Presents Avengers Next Vol. 1: Second Coming (2006, $7.99, digest) r/#1-6						8.00

ANGEL
Dell Publishing Co.: Aug, 1954 - No. 16, Nov-Jan, 1958-59

	GD 2.0	VG 4.0	FN 6.0	VF 8.0	VF/NM 9.0	NM- 9.2
Four Color 576(#1, 8/54)	4	8	12	26	41	55
2(5-7/55) - 16	3	6	9	18	27	35

ANGEL (TV) (Also see Buffy the Vampire Slayer)
Dark Horse Comics: Nov, 1999 - No. 17, Apr, 2001 ($2.95/$2.99)

	GD 2.0	VG 4.0	FN 6.0	VF 8.0	VF/NM 9.0	NM- 9.2
1-17: 1-3,5-7,10-14-Zanier-a. 1-4,7,10-Matsuda & photo-c. 16-Buffy-c/app.						3.00
...: Earthly Possessions TPB (4/01, $9.95) r/#5-7, photo-c						10.00
...: Surrogates TPB (12/00, $9.95) r/#1-3; photo-c						10.00

ANGEL (Buffy the Vampire Slayer)
Dark Horse Comics: Sept, 2001 - No. 4, May, 2002 ($2.99, limited series)

	GD 2.0	VG 4.0	FN 6.0	VF 8.0	VF/NM 9.0	NM- 9.2
1-4-Joss Whedon & Matthews-s/Rubi-a; photo-c and Rubi-c on each						3.00

ANGEL (one-shots) (Buffy the Vampire Slayer)
IDW Publishing: ($3.99/$7.49)

	GD 2.0	VG 4.0	FN 6.0	VF 8.0	VF/NM 9.0	NM- 9.2
...: Connor (8/06, $3.99) Jay Faerber-s/Bob Gill-a; 4 covers + 1 retailer cover						4.00
...: Doyle (7/06, $3.99) Jeff Mariotte-s/David Messina-a; 4 covers + 1 retailer cover						4.00
...: Gunn (5/06, $3.99) Dan Jolley-s/Mark Pennington-a; 4 covers + 2 retailer covers						4.00
...: Illyria (4/06, $3.99) Peter David-s/Nicola Scott-a; 4 covers + 2 retailer covers						4.00
...: Masks (10/06, $7.49) short stories of Angel, Illyria, Cordilia & Lindsay; puppet Angel app.						8.00
...: Wesley (6/06, $3.99) Scott Tipton-s/Mike Norton-a; 4 covers + 1 retailer cover						4.00
Spotlight TPB (12/06, $19.99) r/Connor, Doyle, Gunn, Illyria & Wesley one-shots						20.00

ANGELA
Image Comics (Todd McFarlane Prod.): Dec, 1994 - No. 3, Feb, 1995 ($2.95, lim. series)

	GD 2.0	VG 4.0	FN 6.0	VF 8.0	VF/NM 9.0	NM- 9.2
1-Gaiman scripts & Capullo-c/a in all; Spawn app.	1	2	3	5	6	8
2						6.00
3						5.00
Special Edition (1995)-Pirate Spawn-c	3	6	9	14	20	25
Special Edition (1995)-Angela-c	3	6	9	14	20	25
TPB ($9.95, 1995) reprints #1-3 & Special Ed. w/additional pin-ups						10.00

ANGEL: AFTER THE FALL (Buffy the Vampire Slayer) (Follows the last TV episode)
IDW Publishing: Nov, 2007 - Present ($3.99)

	GD 2.0	VG 4.0	FN 6.0	VF 8.0	VF/NM 9.0	NM- 9.2
1-Whedon & Lynch-s; multiple covers						5.00
2-12: Multiple covers on all						4.00

ANGELA/GLORY: RAGE OF ANGELS (See Glory/Angela: Rage of Angels)
Image Comics (Todd McFarlane Productions): Mar, 1996 ($2.50, one-shot)

	GD 2.0	VG 4.0	FN 6.0	VF 8.0	VF/NM 9.0	NM- 9.2
1-Liefeld-c/Cruz-a(p); Darkchylde preview flip book						4.00
1-Variant-c						4.00

ANGEL AND THE APE (Meet Angel No. 7) (See Limited Collector's Edition C-34 & Showcase No. 77)
National Periodical Publications: Nov-Dec, 1968 - No. 6, Sept-Oct, 1969

	GD 2.0	VG 4.0	FN 6.0	VF 8.0	VF/NM 9.0	NM- 9.2
1-(11-12/68)-Not Wood-a	5	10	15	30	48	65
2-5-Wood inks in all. 4-Last 12¢ issue	3	6	9	20	30	40
6-Wood inks	4	8	12	22	34	45

ANGEL AND THE APE (2nd Series)
DC Comics: Mar, 1991 - No. 4, June, 1991 ($1.00, limited series)

	GD 2.0	VG 4.0	FN 6.0	VF 8.0	VF/NM 9.0	NM- 9.2
1-4						3.00

ANGEL AND THE APE (3rd Series)
DC Comics (Vertigo): Oct, 2001 - No. 4, Jan 2002 ($2.95, limited series)

	GD 2.0	VG 4.0	FN 6.0	VF 8.0	VF/NM 9.0	NM- 9.2
1-4-Chaykin & Tischman-s/Bond-a/Art Adams-c						3.00

ANGEL: AULD LANG SYNE (Buffy the Vampire Slayer)
IDW Publishing: Nov, 2006 - No. 5, Mar, 2007 ($3.99, limited series)

	GD 2.0	VG 4.0	FN 6.0	VF 8.0	VF/NM 9.0	NM- 9.2
1-5: 1-Three covers plus photo-c; Tipton-s/Messina-a						4.00

ANGEL LOVE
DC Comics: Aug, 1986 - No. 8, Mar, 1987 (75¢, limited series)

	GD 2.0	VG 4.0	FN 6.0	VF 8.0	VF/NM 9.0	NM- 9.2
1-8, Special 1 (1987, $1.25, 52 pgs.)						2.50

ANGEL OF LIGHT, THE (See The Crusaders)

ANGEL: OLD FRIENDS (Buffy the Vampire Slayer)
IDW Publishing: Nov, 2005 - No. 5, Mar, 2006 ($3.99, limited series)

	GD 2.0	VG 4.0	FN 6.0	VF 8.0	VF/NM 9.0	NM- 9.2
1-5: Four covers plus photo-c on each; Mariotte-s/Messina-a; Gunn, Spike and Illyria app.						4.00
... Cover Gallery (6/06, $3.99) gallery of variant covers for the series						4.00

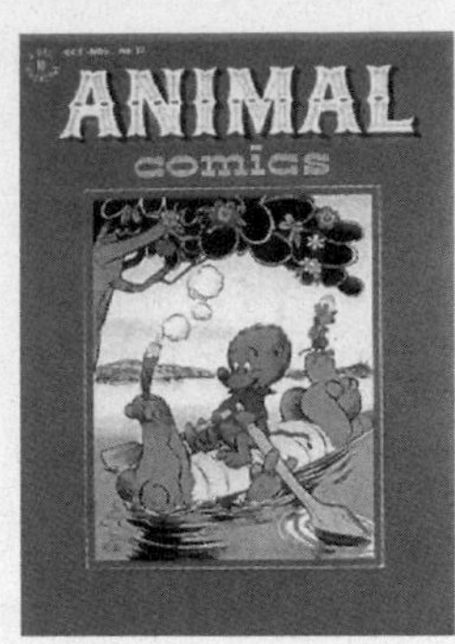

Animal Comics #17 © Bobs-Merrill

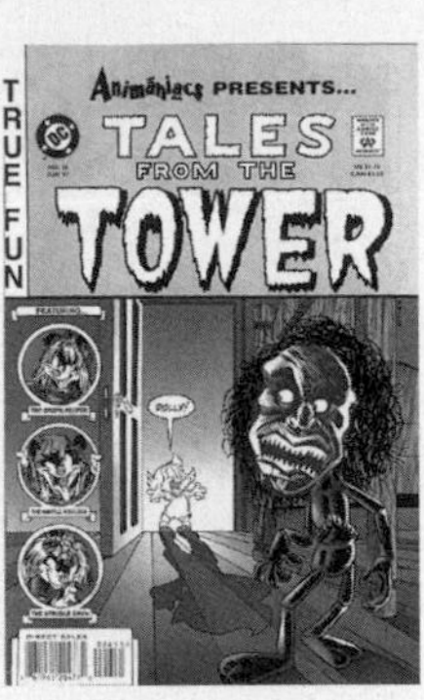

Animaniacs #26 © WB

Anita Blake - Vampire Hunter: Guilty Pleasures #9 © Laurell K. Hamilton

	GD 2.0	VG 4.0	FN 6.0	VF 8.0	VF/NM 9.0	NM- 9.2

... Cover Gallery (12/06, $3.99) gallery of variant covers; preview of Angel: Auld Lang Syne 4.00
TPB (2006, $19.99) r/series; gallery of Messina covers 20.00

ANGEL: REVELATIONS (X-Men character)
Marvel Comics: July, 2008 - No. 5, Nov, 2008 ($3.99, limited series)
1-5-Origin from childhood re-told; Adam Pollina-a/Aquirre-Sacasa-s 4.00

ANGEL: THE CURSE (Buffy the Vampire Slayer)
IDW Publishing: June, 2005 - No. 5, Oct, 2005 ($3.99, limited series)
1-5-Four covers on each; Mariotte-s/Messina-a 4.00
TPB (1/06, $19.99) r/#1-5; cover gallery of Messina covers 20.00

ANGELTOWN
DC Comics (Vertigo): Jan, 2005 - No. 5, May, 2005 ($2.95, limited series)
1-5-Gary Phillips-s/Shawn Martinbrough-a 3.00

ANGELUS
Image Comics (Top Cow): Dec, 2007 ($2.99)
... Pilot Season 1-Sejic-a/c; Edington-s; origin re-told 3.00

ANGRY CHRIST COMIX (See Cry For Dawn)

ANIMA
DC Comics: Mar, 1994 - No. 15, July, 1995 ($1.75/$1.95/$2.25)
1-7,0,8-15: 7-(9/94)-Begin $1.95-c; Zero Hour x-over 2.50

ANIMAL ADVENTURES
Timor Publications/Accepted Publ. (reprints): Dec, 1953 - No. 3, May?, 1954

	GD	VG	FN	VF	VF/NM	NM-
1-Funny animal	8	16	24	40	50	60
2,3: 2-Featuring Soopermutt (2/54)	6	12	18	28	34	40
1-3 (reprints, nd)	3	6	8	11	13	15

ANIMAL ANTICS
DC Comics: Feb, 1946
nn - Ashcan comic, not distributed to newsstands, only for in-house use. Cover art is Star Spangled Comics #49 and interior is Boy Commandos #12 ; a cover sold for $600 in 2006.

ANIMAL ANTICS (Movietown... No. 24 on)
National Periodical Publ: Mar-Apr, 1946 - No. 23, Nov-Dec, 1949 (All 52 pgs.?)

	GD	VG	FN	VF	VF/NM	NM-
1-Raccoon Kids begins by Otto Feuer, many-c by Grossman; Seaman Sy Wheeler by Kelly in some issues; Grossman-a in most issues	45	90	135	279	465	650
2	25	50	75	145	233	320
3-10: 10-Post-c/a	16	32	48	92	144	195
11-23: 14,15,18,19-Post-a	12	24	36	67	94	120

ANIMAL COMICS
Dell Publishing Co.: Dec-Jan, 1941-42 - No. 30, Dec-Jan, 1947-48

	GD	VG	FN	VF	VF/NM	NM-
1-1st Pogo app. by Walt Kelly (Dan Noonan art in most issues)	97	194	291	611	1031	1450
2-Uncle Wiggily begins	50	100	150	310	518	725
3,5	28	56	84	207	384	560
4,6,7-No Pogo	16	32	48	114	212	310
8-10	19	38	57	137	254	370
11-15	13	26	39	95	168	240
16-20	9	18	27	63	107	150
21-30: 24-30- "Jigger" by John Stanley	8	16	24	52	86	120

NOTE: ***Dan Noonan** a-18-30. **Gollub** art in most later issues; c-29, 30. **Kelly** c-7-26, part #27-30.*

ANIMAL CRACKERS (Also see Adventures of Patoruzu)
Green Publ. Co./Norlen/Fox Feat.(Hero Books): 1946; No. 31, July, 1950; No. 9, 1959

	GD	VG	FN	VF	VF/NM	NM-
1-Super Cat begins (1st app.)	19	38	57	112	176	240
2	10	20	30	58	79	100
31(Fox)-Formerly My Love Secret	8	16	24	42	54	65
9(1959-Norlen)-Infinity-c	5	10	14	20	24	28
nn, nd ('50s), no publ.; infinity-c	5	10	14	20	24	28

ANIMAL FABLES
E. C. Comics (Fables Publ. Co.): July-Aug, 1946 - No. 7, Nov-Dec, 1947

	GD	VG	FN	VF	VF/NM	NM-
1-Freddy Firefly (clone of Human Torch), Korky Kangaroo, Petey Pig, Danny Demon begin	52	104	156	322	536	750
2-Aesop Fables begin	32	64	96	190	305	420
3-6	27	54	81	158	254	350
7-Origin Moon Girl	67	134	201	422	711	1000

ANIMAL FAIR (Fawcett's...)
Fawcett Publications: Mar, 1946 - No. 11, Feb, 1947

	GD	VG	FN	VF	VF/NM	NM-
1	28	56	84	162	261	360
2	14	28	42	82	121	160
3-6	12	24	36	67	94	120
7-11	10	20	30	54	72	90

ANIMAL FUN
Premier Magazines: 1953 (25¢, came w/glasses)

	GD	VG	FN	VF	VF/NM	NM-
1-(3-D)-Ziggy Pig, Silly Seal, Billy & Buggy Bear	35	70	105	203	327	450

ANIMAL MAN (See Action Comics #552, 553, DC Comics Presents #77, 78, Secret Origins #39, Strange Adventures #180 & Wonder Woman #267, 268)
DC Comics (Vertigo imprint #57 on): Sept, 1988 - No. 89, Nov, 1995 ($1.25/$1.50/$1.75/$1.95/$2.25, mature)

	GD	VG	FN	VF	VF/NM	NM-
1-Grant Morrison scripts begin, ends #26	1	3	4	6	8	10

2-10: 2-Superman cameo. 6-Invasion tie-in. 9-Manhunter-c/story. 10-Psycho Pirate app. 6.00
11-49,51-55,57-89: 23,24-Psycho Pirate app. 24-Arkham Asylum story; Bizarro Superman app. 25-Inferior Five app. 26-Morrison apps. in story; part photo-c (of Morrison?) 3.00
50-($2.95, 52 pgs.)-Last issue w/Veitch scripts 5.00
56-($3.50, 68 pgs.) 5.00
Annual 1 (1993, $3.95, 68 pgs.)-Bolland-c; Children's Crusade Pt. 3 6.00
...: Deus Ex Machina TPB (2003, $19.95) r/#18-26; Morrison-a; new Bolland-c 20.00
...: Origin of the Species TPB (2002, $19.95) r/#10-17 & Secret Origins #39 20.00
NOTE: ***Bolland** c-1-63. 71-**Sutton**-a(i)*

ANIMAL MYSTIC (See Dark One...)
Cry For Dawn/Sirius: 1993 - No. 4, 1995 ($2.95?/$3.50, B&W)

	GD	VG	FN	VF	VF/NM	NM-
1	3	6	9	14	19	24
1-Alternate	4	8	12	22	34	45
1-2nd printing						5.00
2	2	4	6	10	14	18
2,3-2nd prints (Sirius)						3.50
3 ,4: 4-Color poster insert, Linsner-s	1	2	3	5	7	9
TPB ($14.95) r/series						18.00

ANIMAL MYSTIC WATER WARS
Sirius: 1996 - No. 6 ($2.95, limited series)
1-6-Dark One-c/a/scripts 5.00

ANIMAL WORLD, THE (Movie)
Dell Publishing Co.: No. 713, Aug, 1956

	GD	VG	FN	VF	VF/NM	NM-
Four Color 713	4	8	12	26	41	55

ANIMANIACS (TV)
DC Comics: May, 1995 - No. 59, Apr, 2000 ($1.50/$1.75/$1.95/$1.99)

	GD	VG	FN	VF	VF/NM	NM-
1	1	2	3	4	5	7

2-20: 13-Manga issue. 19-X-Files parody; Miran Kim-c; Adlard-a (4 pgs.) 4.00
21-59: 26-E.C. parody-c. 34-Xena parody. 43-Pinky & the Brain take over 3.00
A Christmas Special (12/94, $1.50, "1" on-c) 3.00

ANIMATED COMICS
E. C. Comics: No date given (Summer, 1947?)

	GD	VG	FN	VF	VF/NM	NM-
1 (Rare)	80	160	240	504	852	1200

ANIMATED FUNNY COMIC TUNES (See Funny Tunes)

ANIMATED MOVIE-TUNES (Movie Tunes No. 3)
Margood Publishing Corp. (Timely): Fall, 1945 - No. 2, Sum, 1946

	GD	VG	FN	VF	VF/NM	NM-
1,2-Super Rabbit, Ziggy Pig & Silly Seal	31	62	93	181	291	400

ANIMAX
Marvel Comics (Star Comics): Dec, 1986 - No. 4, June, 1987
1-4: Based on toys; Simonson-a 3.00

ANITA BLAKE: VAMPIRE HUNTER GUILTY PLEASURES
Marvel Comics (Dabel Brothers): Dec, 2006 - No. 12, Aug, 2008 ($2.99)
1-Laurell K. Hamilton-s/Brett Booth-a; blue cover 6.00
1-Variant-c by Greg Horn 20.00
1-Sketch cover 25.00
1-2nd printing with red cover 3.00
2-Two covers 5.00
3-12 3.00
...: Handbook (2007, $3.99) profile pages of characters; glossary 4.00
... Volume One HC (6/07, $19.99, dust jacket) r/#1-6; cover gallery 20.00

ANITA BLAKE: VAMPIRE HUNTER THE FIRST DEATH, (LAURELL K. HAMILTONS...)
Marvel Comics (Dabel Brothers): July, 2007 - No. 2, Dec, 2007 ($3.99)
1,2-Laurell K. Hamilton & Jonathon Green-s/Wellington Alves-a. 2-Marvel Zombie var-c 4.00
... HC (2008, $19.99, dust jacket) r/#1,2 & Guilty Pleasures Handbook 20.00

ANNE RICE'S INTERVIEW WITH THE VAMPIRE
Innovation Books: 1991 - No. 12, Jan, 1994 ($2.50, limited series)

Annie Oakley #9 © MAR

Annihilation: Conquest #1 © MAR

A-1 Comics #49 © ME

GD 2.0 | VG 4.0 | FN 6.0 | VF 8.0 | VF/NM 9.0 | NM- 9.2

1-12: Adapts novel; Moeller-a 3.00

ANNE RICE'S THE MASTER OF RAMPLING GATE
Innovation Books: 1991 ($6.95, one-shot)
1-Bolton painted-c; Colleen Doran painted-a 7.00

ANNE RICE'S THE MUMMY OR RAMSES THE DAMNED
Millennium Publications: Oct, 1990 - No. 12, Feb, 1992 ($2.50, limited series)
1-12: Adapts novel; Mooney-p in all 3.00

ANNE RICE'S THE WITCHING HOUR
Millennium Publ./Comico: 1992 - No. 13, Jan, 1993 ($2.50, limited series)
1-13 3.00

ANNETTE (Disney, TV)
Dell Publishing Co.: No. 905, May, 1958; No. 1100, May, 1960 (Mickey Mouse Club)

	GD	VG	FN	VF	VF/NM	NM-
Four Color 905-Annette Funicello photo-c	26	52	78	182	359	525
Four Color 1100-...'s Life Story (Movie); A. Funicello photo-c	22	44	66	157	291	425

ANNEX (See Amazing Spider-Man Annual #27 for 1st app.)
Marvel Comics: Aug, 1994 - No. 4, Nov, 1994 ($1.75)
1-4: 1,4-Spider-Man app. 2.50

ANNIE
Marvel Comics Group: Oct, 1982 - No. 2, Nov, 1982 (60¢)

	GD	VG	FN	VF	VF/NM	NM-
1,2-Movie adaptation						4.00
Treasury Edition ($2.00, tabloid size)	3	6	9	17	25	32

ANNIE OAKLEY (See Tessie The Typist #19, Two-Gun Kid & Wild Western)
Marvel/Atlas Comics(MPI No. 1-4/CDS No. 5 on): Spring, 1948 - No. 4, 11/48; No. 5, 6/55 - No. 11, 6/56

	GD	VG	FN	VF	VF/NM	NM-
1 (1st Series, 1948)-Hedy Devine app.	45	90	135	279	465	650
2 (7/48, 52 pgs.)-Kurtzman-a, "Hey Look", 1 pg; Intro. Lana; Hedy Devine app; Captain Tootsie by Beck	26	52	78	152	244	335
3,4	22	44	66	129	207	285
5 (2nd Series, 1955)-Reinman-a ; Maneely-c	16	32	48	96	151	205
6-9: 6,8-Woodbridge-a. 9-Williamson-a (4 pgs.)	14	28	42	80	115	150
10,11: 11-Severin-c	13	26	39	74	105	135

ANNIE OAKLEY AND TAGG (TV)
Dell Publishing Co./Gold Key: 1953 - No. 18, Jan-Mar, 1959; July, 1965 (Gail Davis photo-c #3 on)

	GD	VG	FN	VF	VF/NM	NM-
Four Color 438 (#1)	14	28	42	103	184	265
Four Color 481,575 (#2,3)	9	18	27	64	110	155
4(7-9/55)-10	8	16	24	56	93	130
11-18(1-3/59)	7	14	21	47	76	105
1(7/65-Gold Key)-Photo-c (c-r/#6)	5	10	15	30	48	65

NOTE: *Manning a-13. Photo back c-4, 9, 11.*

ANNIHILATION
Marvel Comics: May, 2006 - No. 6, Mar, 2007 ($3.99/$2.99, limited x-over series)

Prologue (5/06, $3.99, one-shot) Nova, Thanos and Silver Surfer app. 4.00
1-6: 1-(10/06) Giffen-s/DiVito-a; Annihilus app. 3.00
...: Heralds of Galactus 1,2 (4/07-5/07, $3.99) 2-Silver Surfer app. 4.00
...: Nova 1-4 (6/06-9/06, $2.99) Abnett & Lanning-s/Walker-a/Dell'Otto-c. 2,3-Quasar app. 3.00
...: Ronan 1-4 (6/06-9/06, $2.99) Furman-s/Lucas-a/Dell'Otto-c 3.00
... Saga (2007, $1.99) re-cap of the series; DiVito-c 2.50
...: Silver Surfer 1-4 (6/06-9/06, $2.99) Giffen-s/Arlem-a/Dell'Otto-c 3.00
...: Super-Skrull 1-4 (6/06-9/06, $2.99) Grillo-Marxuach-s/Titus-a/Dell'Otto-c 3.00
...: The Nova Corps Files (2006, $3.99) profile pages of characters and alien races 4.00
Annihilation Book 1 HC (2007, $29.99, dustjacket) r/Drax the Destroyer #1-4, Annihilation Prologue and Annihilation: Nova #1-4; sketch and layout pages 30.00
Annihilation Book 1 SC (2007, $24.99) same content as HC 25.00
Annihilation Book 2 HC (2007, $29.99, dustjacket) r/Annihilation: Silver Surfer #1-4, ...: Super Skrull #1-4 and ...: Ronan #1-4; sketch and layout pages 30.00
Annihilation Book 2 SC (2007, $24.99) same content as HC 25.00
Annihilation Book 3 HC (2007, $29.99, dustjacket) r/Annihilation #1-6, Annihilation: Heralds of Galactus #1,2 and Annihilation: Nova Corps Files; sketch pages 30.00
Annihilation Book 3 SC (2007, $24.99) same content as HC 25.00

ANNIHILATION: CONQUEST (Also see Nova 2007 series)
Marvel Comics: Jan, 2008 - No. 6, Jun, 2008 ($3.99/$2.99, limited x-over series)

Prologue (8/07, $3.99, one-shot) the new Quasar, Moondragon app.; Perkins-a 4.00
1-5-Raney-a; Ultron app. 3-Moondragon dies 3.00
6-($3.99) 4.00
... - Quasar 1-4 (9/07-No. 4, 12/07, $2.99) Gage-s/Lilly-a. 1-Super-Adaptoid app. 3.00
... - Starlord 1-4 (9/07-No. 4, 12/07, $2.99) Giffen-s/Green-a 3.00
... - Wraith 1-4 (9/07-No. 4, 12/07, $2.99) Hotz-a/Grillo-Marxuach-s 3.00
Annihilation: Conquest Book 1 HC (2008, $29.99, dustjacket) r/Prologue; ...Quasar #1-4, ...Star-Lord #1-4; Annihilation Saga; design pages 30.00

ANOTHER WORLD (See Strange Stories From...)

ANT
Image Comics: Aug, 2005 - Present ($2.99)
1-11: 1-Mario Gulley-s/a. 2-Savage Dragon & Spawn app. 3-Spawn-c/app. 3.00
Vol. 1: Reality Bites TPB (2006, $12.99) r/#1-4; sketch and concept art 13.00

ANTHRO (See Showcase #74)
National Periodical Publications: July-Aug, 1968 - No. 6, July-Aug, 1969

	GD	VG	FN	VF	VF/NM	NM-
1-(7-8/68)-Howie Post-a in all	6	12	18	37	59	80
2-5: 5-Last 12¢ issue	4	8	12	22	34	45
6-Wood-c/a (inks)	4	8	12	24	37	50

ANTI-HITLER COMICS
New England Comics Press: Summer, 1992 ($2.75, B&W, one-shot)
1-Reprints Hitler as Devil stories from wartime comics 5.00

ANT-MAN (See Irredeemable Ant-Man, The)

ANT-MAN'S BIG CHRISTMAS
Marvel Comics: Feb, 2000 ($5.95, square-bound, one-shot)
1-Bob Gale-s/Phil Winslade-a; Avengers app. 6.00

ANTONY AND CLEOPATRA (See Ideal, a Classical Comic)

ANYTHING GOES
Fantagraphics Books: Oct, 1986 - No. 6, 1987 ($2.00, #1-5 color & B&W/#6 B&W, lim. series)
1-6: 1-Flaming Carrot app. (1st in color?); G. Kane-c. 2-6: 2-Miller-c(p); Alan Moore scripts; Kirby a; early Sam Kieth-a (2 pgs.). 3-Capt. Jack, Cerebus app.; Cerebus-c by N. Adams. 4-Perez-c. 5-3rd color Teenage Mutant Ninja Turtles app. 3.50

A-1
Marvel Comics (Epic Comics): 1992 - No. 4, 1993 ($5.95, limited series, mature)

	GD	VG	FN	VF	VF/NM	NM-
1-4: 1-Fabry-c/a, Russell-a, S. Hampton-a. 3-Bisley-c; Kent Williams-a. 4-McKean-a; Dorman-s/a	1	2	3	4	5	7

A-1 COMICS (A-1 appears on covers No. 1-17 only)(See individual title listings for #11-139) (1st two issues not numbered.)
Life's Romances Publ.-No. 1/Compix/Magazine Ent.: 1944 - No. 139, Sept-Oct, 1955 (No #2)

nn-(1944) (See Kerry Drake Detective Cases)

	GD	VG	FN	VF	VF/NM	NM-
1-Dotty Dripple (1 pg.), Mr. Ex, Bush Berry, Rocky, Lew Loyal (20 pgs.)	15	30	45	84	127	170
3-8,10: Texas Slim & Dirty Dalton, The Corsair, Teddy Rich, Dotty Dripple, Inca Dinca, Tommy Tinker, Little Mexico & Tugboat Tim, The Masquerader & others. 7-Corsair-c/s. 8-Intro Rodeo Ryan	10	20	30	54	72	90
9-All Texas Slim	10	20	30	56	76	95

(See Individual Alphabetical listings for prices)

11-Teena; Ogden Whitney-c
12,15-Teena
13-Guns of Fact & Fiction (1948). Used in **SOTI**, pg. 19; Ingels & Johnny Craig-a
14-Tim Holt Western Adventures #1
16-Vacation Comics; The Pixies, Tom Tom, Flying Fredd, & Koko & Kola
17-Tim Holt #2; photo-c; last issue to carry A-1 on cover (9-10/48)
18,20-Jimmy Durante; photo covers on both
19-Tim Holt #3; photo-c
21-Joan of Arc (1949)-Movie adaptation; Ingrid Bergman photo-covers & interior photos; Whitney-a
22-Dick Powell (1949)-Photo-c
23-Cowboys and Indians #6; Doc Holiday-c/story
24-Trail Colt #1-Frazetta-r in-Manhunt #13; Ingels-c; L. B. Cole-a
25-Fibber McGee & Molly (1949) (Radio)
26-Trail Colt #2-Ingels-c
27-Ghost Rider #1(1950)-Origin
28-Christmas-(Koko & Kola #6) ('50)
29-Ghost Rider #2-Frazetta-c (1950)
30-Jet Powers #1-Powell-a
31-Ghost Rider #3-Frazetta-c & origin ('51)
32-Jet Powers #2
33-Muggsy Mouse #1('51)
34-Ghost Rider #4-Frazetta-c (1951)
35-Jet Powers #3-Williamson/Evans-a
36-Muggsy Mouse #2; Racist-c
37-Ghost Rider #5-Frazetta-c (1951)
38-Jet Powers #4-Williamson/Wood-a
39-Muggsy Mouse #3
40-Dogface Dooley #1('51)
41-Cowboys 'N' Indians #7 (1951)
42-Best of the West #1-Powell-a
43-Dogface Dooley #2
44-Ghost Rider #6
45-American Air Forces #5-Powell-c/a
46-Best of the West #2
47-Thun'da, King of the Congo #1-Frazetta-c/a('52)
48-Cowboys 'N' Indians #8
49-Dogface Dooley #3
50-Danger Is Their Business #11 ('52)-Powell-a
51-Ghost Rider #7 ('52)
52-Best of the West #3

A-1 Comics #82 © ME

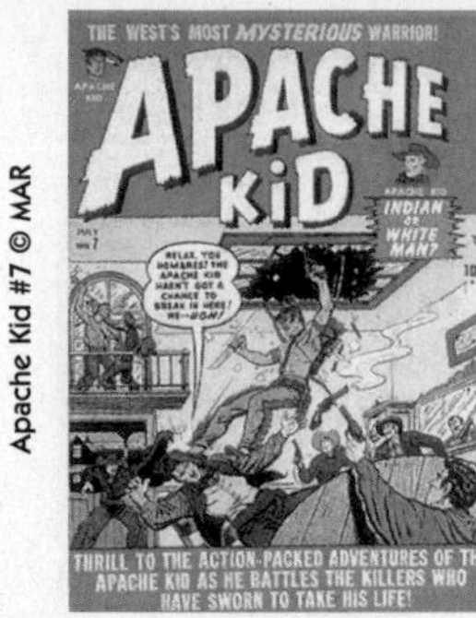

Apache Kid #7 © MAR

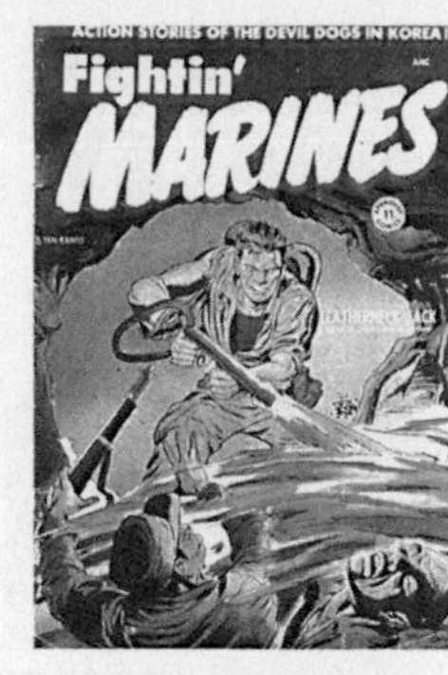

Approved Comics #11 © STJ

	GD 2.0	VG 4.0	FN 6.0	VF 8.0	VF/NM 9.0	NM- 9.2

53-Dogface Dooley #4
55-U.S. Marines #5-Powell-a
56-Thun'da #2-Powell-c/a
58-American Air Forces #7-Powell-a
60-The U.S. Marines #6-Powell-a
62-Starr Flagg, Undercover Girl #5 (#1) reprinted from A-1 #24
65-American Air Forces #8-Powell-a
67-American Air Forces #9-Powell-a
69-Ghost Rider #9(10/52)
71-Ghost Rider #10(12/52)- Vs. Frankenstein
74-American Air Forces #10-Powell-a
76-Best of the West #7
78-Thun'da #4-Powell-c/a
80-Ghost Rider #12(6/52)- One-eyed Devil-c
83-Thun'da #5-Powell-c/a
84-Ghost Rider #13(7-8/53)
86-Thun'da #6-Powell-c/a
88-Bobby Benson's B-Bar-B Riders #20
90-Red Hawk #11(1953)-Powell-c/a
91-American Air Forces #12-Powell-a
93-Great Western #8('54)-Origin The Ghost Rider; Powell-a
95-Muggsy Mouse #4
96-Cave Girl #12, with Thun'da; Powell-c/a
99-Muggsy Mouse #5
101-White Indian #12-Frazetta-a(r)
101-Dream Book of Romance #6 (4-6/54); Marlon Brando photo-c; Powell, Bolle, Guardineer-a
105-Great Western #9-Ghost Rider app.; Powell-a, 6 pgs.; Bolle-c
107-Hot Dog #1
108-Red Fox #15 (1954)-L.B. Cole-c/a; Powell-a
110-Dream Book of Romance #8 (10/54)-Movie photo-c
112-Ghost Rider #14 ('54)
114-Dream Book of Love #2- Guardineer, Bolle-a; Piper Laurie, Victor Mature photo-c
118-Undercover Girl #7-Powell-c
120-Badmen of the West #2
121-Mysteries of Scotland Yard #1; reprinted from Manhunt (5 stories)
124-Dream Book of Romance #8 (10-11/54)
126-I'm a Cop #2-Powell-a
128-I'm a Cop #3-Powell-a
130-Strongman #1-Powell-a (2-3/55)
132-Strongman #2
134-Strongman #3
136-Hot Dog #4
138-The Avenger #4-Powell-c/a

54-American Air Forces #6(8/52)- Powell-a
57-Ghost Rider #8
59-Best of the West #4
61-Space Ace #5('53)-Guardineer-a
63-Manhunt #13-Frazetta
64-Dogface Dooley #5
66-Best of the West #5
68-U.S. Marines #7-Powell-a
70-Best of the West #6
72-U.S. Marines #8-Powell-a(3)
73-Thun'da #3-Powell-c/a
75-Ghost Rider #11(3/52)
77-Manhunt #14
79-American Air Forces #11-Powell-a
81-Best of the West #8
82-Cave Girl #11(1953)-Powell-c/a; origin (#1)
85-Best of the West #9
87-Best of the West #10(9-10/53)
89-Home Run #3-Powell-a; Stan Musial photo-c
92-Dream Book of Romance #5- Photo-c; Guardineer-a
94-White Indian #11-Frazetta-a(r); Powell-c
97-Best of the West #11
98-Undercover Girl #6-Powell-c
100-Badmen of the West #1- Meskin-a(?)
103-Best of the West #12-Powell-a
104-White Indian #13-Frazetta-a(r) ('54)
106-Dream Book of Love #1 (6-7/54) -Powell, Bolle-a; Montgomery Clift, Donna Reed photo-c
109-Dream Book of Romance #7 (7-8/54). Powell-a; movie photo-c
111-I'm a Cop #1 ('54); drug mention story; Powell-a
113-Great Western #10; Powell-a
115-Hot Dog #3
116-Cave Girl #13 Powell-c/a
117-White Indian #14
119-Straight Arrow's Fury #1 (origin); Fred Meagher-c/a
122-Black Phantom #1 (11/54)
123-Dream Book of Love #3 (10-11/54)-Movie photo-c
125-Cave Girl #14-Powell-c/a
127-Great Western #11('54)-Powell-a
129-The Avenger #1('55)-Powell-c
131-The Avenger #2('55)-Powell-c/a
133-The Avenger #3-Powell-c/a
135-White Indian #15
137-Africa #1-Powell-c/a(4)
139-Strongman #4-Powell-a

NOTE: *Bolle a-110. Photo-c-17-22, 89, 92, 101, 106, 109, 110, 114, 123, 124.*

APACHE
Fiction House Magazines: 1951

	GD 2.0	VG 4.0	FN 6.0	VF 8.0	VF/NM 9.0	NM- 9.2
1	22	44	66	131	211	290
I.W. Reprint No. 1-r/#1 above	3	6	9	18	27	35

APACHE KID (Formerly Reno Browne; Western Gunfighters #20 on) (Also see Two-Gun Western & Wild Western)
Marvel/Atlas Comics(MPC No. 53-10/CPS No. 11 on): No. 53, 12/50 - No. 10, 1/52; No. 11, 12/54 - No. 19, 4/56

	GD 2.0	VG 4.0	FN 6.0	VF 8.0	VF/NM 9.0	NM- 9.2
53(#1)-Apache Kid & his horse Nightwind (origin), Red Hawkins by Syd Shores begins	35	70	105	203	327	450
2(2/51)	17	34	51	98	154	210
3-5	13	26	39	72	101	130
6-10 (1951-52): 7-Russ Heath-a	11	22	33	60	83	105
11-19 (1954-56)	9	18	27	50	65	80

NOTE: ***Heath** a-7. c-11, 13. **Maneely** a-53; c-53(#1), 12, 14-16. **Powell** a-14. **Severin** c-17.*

APACHE MASSACRE (See Chief Victorio's...)

APACHE SKIES
Marvel Comics: Sept, 2002 - No. 4, Dec, 2002 ($2.99, limited series)

	GD 2.0	VG 4.0	FN 6.0	VF 8.0	VF/NM 9.0	NM- 9.2
1-4-Apache Kid app.; Ostrander-s/Manco-c/a						3.00
TPB (2003, $12.99) r/#1-4						13.00

APACHE TRAIL
Steinway/America's Best: Sept, 1957 - No. 4, June, 1958

	GD 2.0	VG 4.0	FN 6.0	VF 8.0	VF/NM 9.0	NM- 9.2
1	11	22	33	62	86	110
2-4: 2-Tuska-a	8	16	24	40	50	60

APE (Magazine)
Dell Publishing Co.: 1961 (52 pgs., B&W)

	GD 2.0	VG 4.0	FN 6.0	VF 8.0	VF/NM 9.0	NM- 9.2
1-Comics and humor	4	8	12	24	37	50

APHRODITE IX
Image Comics (Top Cow): Sept, 2000 - No. 4, Mar, 2002 ($2.50)

	GD 2.0	VG 4.0	FN 6.0	VF 8.0	VF/NM 9.0	NM- 9.2
1-3: 1-Four covers by Finch, Turner, Silvestri, Benitez						4.00
1-Tower Record Ed.; Finch-c						3.00
1-DF Chrome ($14.99)						15.00
4-($4.95) Double-sized issue; Finch-c						5.00
Convention Preview						10.00
...: Time Out of Mind TPB (6/04, $14.99) r/#1-4, & #0; cover gallery						15.00
Wizard #0 (4/00, bagged w/Tomb Raider magazine) Preview & sketchbook						5.00
#0-(6/01, $2.95) r/Wizard #0 with cover gallery						3.00

APOCALYPSE NERD
Dark Horse Comics: January, 2005 - No. 6, Oct, 2007 ($2.99, B&W)

	GD 2.0	VG 4.0	FN 6.0	VF 8.0	VF/NM 9.0	NM- 9.2
1-6-Peter Bagge-s/a						3.00

APPARITION
Caliber Comics: 1995 ($3.95, 52 pgs., B&W)

	GD 2.0	VG 4.0	FN 6.0	VF 8.0	VF/NM 9.0	NM- 9.2
1 ($3.95)						4.00
V2#1-6 ($2.95)						3.00
Visitations						4.00

APPLESEED
Eclipse Comics: Sept, 1988 - Book 4, Vol. 4, Aug, 1991 ($2.50/$2.75/$3.50, 52/68 pgs, B&W)

	GD 2.0	VG 4.0	FN 6.0	VF 8.0	VF/NM 9.0	NM- 9.2
Book One, Vol. 1-5: 5-(1/89), Book Two, Vol. 1(2/89) -5(7/89): Art Adams-c, Book Three, Vol. 1(8/89) -4 ($2.75), Book Three, Vol. 5 ($3.50), Book Four, Vol. 1 (1/91) - 4 (8/91) ($3.50, 68 pgs.)						6.00

APPLESEED DATABOOK
Dark Horse Comics: Apr, 1994 - No. 2, May, 1994 ($3.50, B&W, limited series)

	GD 2.0	VG 4.0	FN 6.0	VF 8.0	VF/NM 9.0	NM- 9.2
1,2: 1-Flip book format						3.50

APPROVED COMICS (Also see Blue Ribbon Comics)
St. John Publishing Co. (Most have no c-price): March, 1954 - No. 12, Aug, 1954 (Painted-c on #1-5,7,8,10)

	GD 2.0	VG 4.0	FN 6.0	VF 8.0	VF/NM 9.0	NM- 9.2
1-The Hawk #5-r	10	20	30	56	76	95
2-Invisible Boy (3/54)-Origin; Saunders-c	16	32	48	92	144	195
3-Wild Boy of the Congo #11-r (4/54)	10	20	30	56	76	95
4,5: 4-Kid Cowboy-r. 5-Fly Boy-r	10	20	30	56	76	95
6-Daring Adv.-r (5/54); Krigstein-a(2); Baker-c	13	26	39	72	101	130
7-The Hawk #6-r	10	20	30	56	76	95
8-Crime on the Run (6/54); Powell-a; Saunders-c	10	20	30	56	76	95
9-Western Bandit Trails #3-r, with new-c; Baker-c/a	13	26	39	72	101	130
10-Dinky Duck (Terrytoons)	6	12	18	31	38	45
11-Fightin' Marines #3-r (8/54); Canteen Kate app; Baker-c/a	14	28	42	76	108	140
12-Northwest Mounties #4-r(8/54); new Baker-c	14	28	42	76	108	140

AQUAMAN (See Adventure Comics #260, Brave & the Bold, DC Comics Presents #5, DC Special #28, DC Special Series #1, DC Super Stars #7, Detective Comics, JLA, Justice League of America, More Fun #73, Showcase #30-33, Super DC Giant, Super Friends, and World's Finest Comics)

AQUAMAN (1st Series)
National Periodical Publications/DC Comics: Jan-Feb, 1962 - #56, Mar-Apr, 1971; #57, Aug-Sept,1977 - #63, Aug-Sept, 1978

	GD 2.0	VG 4.0	FN 6.0	VF 8.0	VF/NM 9.0	NM- 9.2
1-(1-2/62)-Intro. Quisp	83	166	249	706	1353	2000
2	31	62	93	242	451	660
3-5	19	38	57	139	257	375
6-10	13	26	39	95	168	240
11,18: 11-1st app. Mera. 18-Aquaman weds Mera; JLA cameo	10	20	30	73	129	185
12-17,19,20	10	20	30	70	123	175
21-32: 23-Birth of Aquababy. 26-Huntress app.(3-4/66). 29-1st app. Ocean Master, Aquaman's step-brother. 30-Batman & Superman-c & cameo	7	14	21	47	76	105

Aquaman #29 © DC

Aquaman (4th series) #54 © DC

Archer & Armstrong #3 © VAL

	GD 2.0	VG 4.0	FN 6.0	VF 8.0	VF/NM 9.0	NM- 9.2
33-1st app. Aqua-Girl (see Adventure #266)	7	14	21	50	83	115
34-40: 35-1st app. Black Manta. 40-Jim Aparo's 1st DC work (8/68)	6	12	18	37	59	80
41-46,47,49: 45-Last 12¢-c	5	10	15	32	51	70
48-Origin reprinted	5	10	15	34	55	75
50-52-Deadman by Neal Adams	8	16	24	52	86	120
53-56('71): 56-1st app. Crusader; last 15¢-c	2	4	6	9	13	16
57('77)-63: 58-Origin retold	1	2	3	5	7	9

NOTE: *Aparo a-40-45, 46p, 47-59; c-58-63.* ***Nick Cardy*** *c-1-40.* ***Newton*** *a-60-63.*

AQUAMAN (1st limited series)
DC Comics: Feb, 1986 - No. 4, May, 1986 (75¢, limited series)

1-New costume; 1st app. Nuada of Thierna Na Oge. 5.50
2-4: 3-Retelling of Aquaman & Ocean Master's origins. 4.00
Special 1 (1988, $1.50, 52 pgs.) 3.75
NOTE: ***Craig Hamilton*** *c/a-1-4p.* ***Russell*** *c-2-4i.*

AQUAMAN (2nd limited series)
DC Comics: June, 1989 - No. 5, Oct, 1989 ($1.00, limited series)

1-5: Giffen plots/breakdowns; Swan-a(p). 3.00
Special 1 (Legend of..., $2.00, 1989, 52 pgs.)-Giffen plots/breakdowns; Swan-a(p) 3.00

AQUAMAN (2nd Series)
DC Comics: Dec, 1991 - No. 13, Dec, 1992 ($1.00/$1.25)

1-5 2.50
6-13: 6-Begin $1.25-c. 9-Sea Devils app. 2.50

AQUAMAN (3rd Series)(Also see Atlantis Chronicles)
DC Comics: Aug, 1994 - No. 75, Jan, 2001 ($1.50/$1.75/$1.95/$1.99/$2.50)

1-(8/94)-Peter David scripts begin; reintro Dolphin 6.00
2 (9/94)-Aquaman loses hand 6.50
0-(10/94)-Aquaman replaces lost hand with hook. 6.50
3-8: 3-(11/94)-Superboy-c/app. 4-Lobo app. 6-Deep Six app. 3.50
9-69: 9-Begin $1.75-c. 10-Green Lantern app. 11-Reintro Mera. 15-Re-intro Kordax. 16-vs. JLA. 18-Reintro Ocean Master & Atlan (Aquaman's father). 19-Reintro Garth (Aqualad). 23-1st app. Deep Blue (Neptune Perkins & Tsunami's daughter). 23,24-Neptune Perkins, Nuada, Tsunami, Arion, Power Girl, & The Sea Devils app. 26-Final Night. 28-Martian Manhunter-c/app. 29-Black Manta-c/app. 32-Swamp Thing-c/app. 37-Genesis x-over. 41-Maxima-c/app. 43-Millennium Giants x-over; Superman-c/app. 44-G.A. Flash & Sentinel app. 50-Larsen-s begins. 53-Superman app. 60-Tempest marries Dolphin; Teen Titans app. 63-Kaluta covers begin. 66-JLA app. 2.50
70-75: 70-Begin $2.50-c. 71-73-Warlord-c/app. 75-Final issue 2.50
#1,000,000 (11/98) 853rd Century x-over 3.00
Annual 1 (1995, $3.50)-Year One story 3.50
Annual 2 (1996, $2.95)-Legends of the Dead Earth story 3.00
Annual 3 (1997, $3.95)-Pulp Heroes story 4.00
Annual 4,5 ('98, '99, $2.95)-4-Ghosts; Wrightson-c. 5-JLApe 3.00
...Secret Files 1 (12/98, $4.95) Origin-s and pin-ups 5.00
NOTE: ***Art Adams****-c, Annual 5.* ***Mignola*** *c-6.* ***Simonson*** *c-15.*

AQUAMAN (4th Series)(Titled Aquaman: Sword of Atlantis #40-on) (Also see JLA #69-75)
DC Comics: Feb, 2003 - No. 57, Dec, 2007 ($2.50/$2.99)

1-Veitch-s/Guichet-a/Maleev-c 3.00
2-14: 2-Martian Manhunter app. 8-11-Black Manta app. 2.50
15-39: 15-San Diego flooded; Pfeifer-s/Davis-c begin. 23,24-Sea Devils app. 33-Mera returns. 39-Black Manta app. 2.50
40-Sword of Atlantis; One Year Later begins ($2.99-c) Guice-a ; two covers 4.00
41-49,51-57: 41-Two covers. 42-Sea Devils app. 44-Ocean Master app. 3.00
50-($3.99) Tempest app.; McManus-a 4.00
...Secret Files 2003 (5/03, $4.95) background on Aquaman's new powers; pin-ups 5.00
...: Once and Future TPB (2006, $12.99) r/#40-45 13.00
...: The Waterbearer TPB (2003, $12.95) r/#1-4, stories from Aquaman Secret Files and JLA/JSA Secret Files #1; JG Jones-c 13.00

AQUAMAN: TIME & TIDE (3rd limited series) (Also see Atlantis Chronicles)
DC Comics: Dec, 1993 - No. 4, Mar, 1994 ($1.50, limited series)

1-4: Peter David scripts; origin retold. 3.00
Trade paperback ($9.95) 10.00

AQUANAUTS (TV)
Dell Publishing Co.: May - July, 1961

	GD 2.0	VG 4.0	FN 6.0	VF 8.0	VF/NM 9.0	NM- 9.2
Four Color 1197-Photo-c	7	14	21	47	76	105

ARABIAN NIGHTS (See Cinema Comics Herald)

ARACHNOPHOBIA (Movie)
Hollywood Comics (Disney Comics): 1990 ($5.95, 68 pg. graphic novel)

nn-Adaptation of film; Spiegle-a 6.00

Comic edition ($2.95, 68 pgs.) 3.00

ARAK/SON OF THUNDER (See Warlord #48)
DC Comics: Sept, 1981 - No. 50, Nov, 1985

1,24,50: 1-1st app. Angelica, Princess of White Cathay. 24,50-(52 pgs.) 3.00
2-23,25-49: 3-Intro Valda. 12-Origin Valda. 20-Origin Angelica 2.50
Annual 1(10/84) 3.00

ARAÑA THE HEART OF THE SPIDER (See Amazing Fantasy (2004) #1-6)
Marvel Comics: March, 2005 - No. 12, Feb, 2006 ($2.99)

1-12: 1-Avery-s/Cruz-a. 4-Spider-Man-c/app. 3.00
Vol. 1: Heart of the Spider (2005, $7.99, digest) r/Amazing Fantasy (2004) #1-6 8.00
Vol. 2: In the Beginning (2005, $7.99, digest) r/#1-6 8.00
Vol. 3: Night of the Hunter (2006, $7.99, digest) r/#7-12 8.00

ARCANA (Also see Books of Magic limited & ongoing series and Mister E)
DC Comics (Vertigo): 1994 ($3.95, 68 pgs., annual)

1-Bolton painted-c; Children's Crusade/Tim Hunter story 4.00

ARCANUM
Image Comics (Top Cow Productions): Apr, 1997 - No. 8, Feb, 1998 ($2.50)

1/2 Gold Edition 12.00
1-Brandon Peterson-s/a(p), 1-Variant-c, 4-American Ent. Ed. 3.00
2-8 2.50
3-Variant-c 4.00
...: Millennium's End TPB (2005, $16.99) r/#1-8 & #1/2; cover gallery and sketch pages 17.00

ARCHANGEL (See Uncanny X-Men, X-Factor & X-Men)
Marvel Comics: Feb, 1996 ($2.50, B&W, one-shot)

1-Milligan story 2.50

ARCHARD'S AGENTS (See Ruse)
CrossGeneration Comics: Jan, 2003; Nov, 2003; Apr, 2004 ($2.95)

1-Dixon-s/Perkins-a 3.00
...: The Case of the Puzzled Pugilist (11/03) Dixon-s/Perkins-a 3.00
Vol. 3 - Deadly Dare (4/04) Dixon-s/McNiven-a; preview of Lady Death: The Wild Hunt 3.00

ARCHENEMIES
Dark Horse Comics: Apr, 2006 - No. 4, July, 2006 ($2.99, limited series)

1-4-Melbourne-s/Guichet-a 3.00

ARCHER & ARMSTRONG
Valiant: July (June inside), 1992 - No. 26, Oct, 1994 ($2.50)

0-(7/92)-B. Smith-c/a; Reese-i assists 4.00

	GD 2.0	VG 4.0	FN 6.0	VF 8.0	VF/NM 9.0	NM- 9.2
0-(with Gold Valiant Logo)	2	4	6	8	10	12

1-7,9-26: 1-(8/92)-Origin & 1st app. Archer; Miller-c; B. Smith/Layton-a. 2-2nd app. Turok (c/story); Smith/Layton-a; Simonson-c. 3,4-Smith-c&a(p) & scripts. 10-2nd app. Ivar. 10,11-B. Smith-c. 21,22-Shadowman app. 22-w/bound-in trading card. 25-Eternal Warrior app. 26-Flip book w/Eternal Warrior #26 2.50
8-($4.50, 52 pgs.)-Combined with Eternal Warrior #8; B. Smith-c/a & scripts; 1st app. Ivar the Time Walker 4.50

ARCHIE (See Archie Comics) (Also see Christmas & Archie, Everything's..., Explorers of the Unknown, Jackpot, Little..., Oxydol-Dreft, Pep, Riverdale High, Teenage Mutant Ninja Turtles Adventures & To Riverdale and Back Again)

ARCHIE ALL CANADIAN DIGEST
Archie Publications: Aug, 1996 ($1.75, 96 pgs.)

1 6.00

ARCHIE AMERICANA SERIES, BEST OF THE FORTIES
Archie Publications: 1991,2002 ($10.95, trade paperback)

Vol. 1,2-r/early strips from 1940s 1-Intro. by Steven King. 2-Intro. by Paul Castiglia 11.00

ARCHIE AMERICANA SERIES, BEST OF THE FIFTIES
Archie Publications: 1991 ($8.95, trade paperback)

Vol. 2-r/strips from 1950's; 9.00
2nd printing (1998, $9.95) 10.00
Book 2 (2003, $10.95) 11.00

ARCHIE AMERICANA SERIES, BEST OF THE SIXTIES
Archie Publications: 1995 ($9.95, trade paperback)

Vol. 3-r/strips from 1960s; intro. by Frankie Avalon. 10.00

ARCHIE AMERICANA SERIES, BEST OF THE SEVENTIES
Archie Publications: 1997, 2008 ($9.95/$10.95, trade paperback)

Vol. 4 (1997, $9.95)-r/strips from 1970s 10.00
Vol. 8 Book 2 (2008, $10.95)-r/other strips from 1970s 11.00

ARCHIE AMERICANA SERIES, BEST OF THE EIGHTIES

Archie & Friends #100 © AP

Archie at Riverdale High #3 © AP

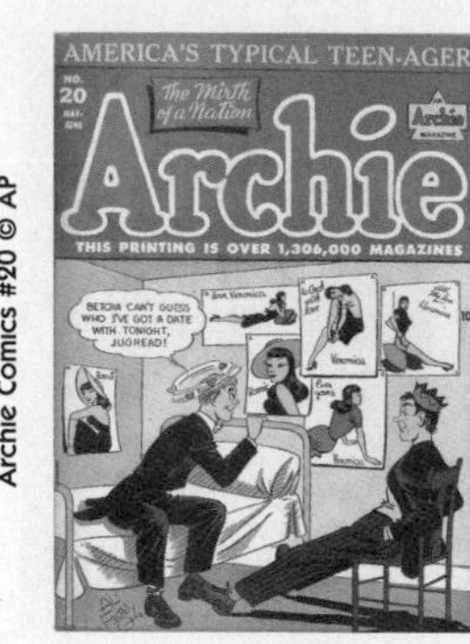

Archie Comics #20 © AP

	GD	VG	FN	VF	VF/NM	NM-
	2.0	4.0	6.0	8.0	9.0	9.2

Archie Publications: 2001 ($10.95, trade paperback)
Vol. 5-r/strips from 1980s; foreward by Steve Geppi 11.00

ARCHIE AMERICANA SERIES, BEST OF THE '90S
Archie Publications: 2008 ($11.95, trade paperback)
Vol. 9-r/strips from 1990s; new Lindsey cover 12.00

ARCHIE AND BIG ETHEL
Spire Christian Comics (Fleming H. Revell Co.): 1982 (69¢)
nn-(Low print run) 2 4 6 10 14 18

ARCHIE & FRIENDS
Archie Comics: Dec, 1992 - Present ($1.25/$1.50/$1.75/$1.79/$1.99/$2.19/$2.25, bi-monthly)
1 5.00
2,4,10-14,17,18,20-Sabrina app. 20-Archie's Band-c 4.00
3,5-9,16 2.50
15-Babewatch-s with Sabrina app. 6.00
19-Josie and the Pussycats app.; E.T. parody-c/s 5.00
21-46 2.50
47-All Josie and the Pussycats issue; movie and actress profiles/photos 3.00
48-126: 48-56,58,60,96-Josie and the Pussycats-c/s. 79-Cheryl Blossom returns. 100-The Veronicas-c/app. 101-Katy Keene begins 2.50

ARCHIE AND ME (See Archie Giant Series Mag. #578, 591, 603, 616, 626)
Archie Publications: Oct, 1964 - No. 161, Feb, 1987
1 15 30 45 106 193 280
2 9 18 27 60 100 140
3-5 6 12 18 39 62 85
6-10 4 8 12 24 37 50
11-20 3 6 9 17 25 32
21(6/68)-26,28-30: 21-UFO story. 26-X-Mas-c 3 6 9 15 21 26
27-Groovyman & Knowman superhero-s; UFO-sty 3 6 9 17 25 32
31-42: 37-Japan Expo '70-c/s 2 4 6 10 14 18
43-48,50-63-(All Giants): 43-(8/71) Mummy-s. 44-Mermaid-s. 62-Elvis cameo-c. 63-(2/74) 3 6 9 15 21 26
49-(Giant) Josie & the Pussycats-c/app. 3 6 9 18 27 35
64-66,68-99-(Regular size): 85-Bicentennial-s. 98-Collectors Comics 1 3 4 6 8 10
67-Sabrina app.(8/74) 2 4 6 9 13 16
100-(4/78) 2 4 6 8 10 12
101-120: 107-UFO-s 6.00
121(8/80)-159: 134-Riverdale 2001 5.00
160,161: 160-Origin Mr. Weatherbee. 161-Last issue 6.00

ARCHIE AND MR. WEATHERBEE
Spire Christian Comics (Fleming H. Revell Co.): 1980 (59¢)
nn - (Low print run) 2 4 6 9 13 16

ARCHIE...ARCHIE ANDREWS, WHERE ARE YOU? (...Comics Digest #9, 10; ...Comics Digest Mag. No. 11 on)
Archie Publications: Feb, 1977 - No. 114, May, 1998 (Digest size, 160-128 pgs., quarterly)
1 3 6 9 16 23 30
2,3,5,7-9-N. Adams-a; 8-r-/origin The Fly by S&K. 9-Steel Sterling-r 2 4 6 9 13 16
4,6,10 ($1.00/$1.50) 2 4 6 8 10 12
11-20: 17-Katy Keene story 1 2 3 5 7 9
21-50,100 1 2 3 4 5 7
51-70 4.00
71-99,101-114: 113-Begin $1.95-c 3.00

ARCHIE AS PUREHEART THE POWERFUL (Also see Archie Giant Series #142, Jughead as Captain Hero, Life With Archie & Little Archie)
Archie Publications (Radio Comics): Sept, 1966 - No. 6, Nov, 1967
1-Super hero parody 10 20 30 70 123 175
2 6 12 18 41 66 90
3-6 5 10 15 34 55 75
NOTE: *Evilheart cameos in all. Title: Archie As Pureheart the Powerful #1-3; ...As Capt. Pureheart-#4-6.*

ARCHIE AT RIVERDALE HIGH (See Archie Giant Series Magazine #573, 586, 604 & Riverdale High)
Archie Publications: Aug, 1972 - No. 113, Feb, 1987
1 6 12 18 39 62 85
2 3 6 9 20 30 40
3-5 3 6 9 16 23 30
6-10 2 4 6 11 16 20
11-30 2 4 6 8 10 12
31(12/75)-46,48-50(12/77) 1 2 3 5 7 9
47-Archie in drag-s; Betty mud wrestling-s 2 4 6 9 12 15
51-80,100 (12/84) 6.00
81(8/81)-88, 91,93-95,98 5.00
89,90-Early Cheryl Blossom app. 90-Archies Band app. 2 4 6 10 14 18
92,96,97,99-Cheryl Blossom app. 96-Anti-smoking issue 2 4 6 8 11 14
101,102,104-109,111,112: 102-Ghost-c 4.00
103-Archie dates Cheryl Blossom-s 2 4 6 8 11 14
110,113: 110-Godzilla-s. 113-Last issue 6.00

ARCHIE COMICS (Archie #114 on; 1st Teen-age comic; Radio show aired 6/2/45 by NBC)
MLJ Magazines No. 1-19/Archie Publ. No. 20 on: Winter, 1942-43 - No. 19, 3-4/46; No. 20, 5-6/46 - Present
1 (Scarce)-Jughead, Veronica app.; 1st app. Mrs. Andrews 2100 4200 6300 16,000 27,000 38,000
2 444 888 1332 3197 5599 8000
3 (60 pgs.)(scarce) 324 648 972 2203 3852 5500
4,5: 4-Article about Archie radio series. 5-Halloween-c 207 414 621 1304 2202 3100
6,8-10: 6-X-Mas-c. 9-1st Miss Grundy cover 147 294 441 926 1563 2200
7-1st definitive love triangle story 157 314 471 989 1670 2350
11-20: 15,17,18-Dotty & Ditto by Woggon. 16,19-Woggon-a. 18-Halloween pumpkin-c. 93 186 279 586 993 1400
21-30: 23-Betty & Veronica by Woggon. 25-Woggon-a. 30-Coach Piffle app., a Coach Kleets prototype. 34-Pre-Dilton try-out (named Dilbert) 58 116 174 365 620 875
31-40 40 80 120 235 380 525
41-50 29 58 87 169 272 375
51-60 13 26 39 93 164 235
61-70 (1954): 65-70, Katy Keene app. 10 20 30 70 123 175
71-80: 72-74-Katy Keene app. 8 16 24 56 93 130
81-93,95-99 7 14 21 47 76 105
94-1st Coach Kleets 8 16 24 52 86 120
100 8 16 24 58 97 135
101-122,126,128-130 (1962) 5 10 15 32 51 70
123-125,127-Horror/SF covers. 123-UFO-c/s 6 12 18 41 66 90
131,132,134-157,159,160: 137-1st Caveman Archie gang story 3 6 9 19 29 38
133 (12/62)-1st app. Cricket O'Dell 4 8 12 23 36 48
158-Archie in drag story 3 6 9 20 30 40
161(2/66)-184,186-188,190-195,197-199: 168-Superhero gag-c. 176,178-Twiggy-c 183-Caveman Archie gang story 3 6 9 14 20 25
185-1st "The Archies" Band story 4 8 12 22 34 45
189 (3/69)-Archie's band meets Don Kirshner who developed the Monkees 3 6 9 17 25 32
196 (12/69)-Early Cricket O'Dell app. 3 6 9 17 25 32
200 (6/70) 3 6 9 16 22 28
201-230(11/73): 213-Sabrina/Josie-c cameos. 229-Lost Child issue 2 4 6 9 12 15
231-260(3/77): 253-Tarzan parody 1 3 4 6 8 10
261-282, 284-299 1 2 3 5 6 8
283(8/79)-Cover/story plugs "International Children's Appeal" which was a fraudulent charity, according to TV's 20/20 news program broadcast July 20, 1979 1 2 3 5 7 9
300(1/81)-Anniversary issue 1 3 4 6 8 10
301-321,323-325,327-335,337-350: 323-Cheryl Blossom pin-up. 325-Cheryl Blossom app. 5.00
322-E.T. story 6.00
326-Early Cheryl Blossom story 2 4 6 9 13 16
336-Michael Jackson/Boy George parody 6.00
351-399: 356-Calgary Olympics Special. 393-Infinity-c; 1st comic book printed on recycled paper 4.00
400 (6/92)-Shows 1st meeting of Little Archie and Veronica 6.00
401-428 3.00
429-Love Showdown part 1 5.00
430-592: 467- "A Storm Over Uniforms" x-over parts 3,4. 538-Comic-Con issue 2.50
Annual 1 ('50)-116 pgs. (Scarce) 213 426 639 1342 2271 3200
Annual 2 ('51) 100 200 300 630 1065 1500
Annual 3 ('52) 58 116 174 365 620 875
Annual 4,5 (1953-54) 41 82 123 256 428 600
Annual 6-10 (1955-59): 8,9-(100 pgs.). 10-(84 pgs.) Elvis record on-c 15 30 45 111 206 300
Annual 11-15 (1960-65): 12,13-(84 pgs.) 14,15-(68 pgs.) 9 18 27 63 107 150
Annual 16-20 (1966-70)(all 68 pgs.): 20-Archie's band-c 6 12 18 37 59 80

Archie Digest Magazine #158 © AP

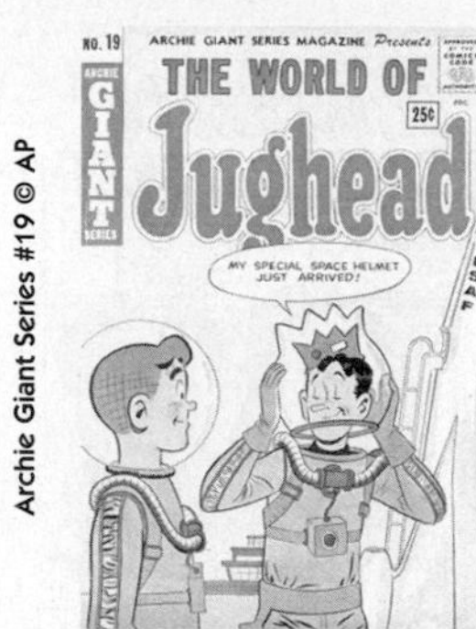

Archie Giant Series #19 © AP

Archie Giant Series #141 © AP

GD VG FN VF VF/NM NM-
2.0 4.0 6.0 8.0 9.0 9.2

Annual 21,22,24-26 (1971-75): 21,22-(68 pgs.). 22-Archie's band-s. 24-26-(52 pgs.). 25-Cavemen-s 3 6 9 20 30 40
Annual 23-Archie's band-c/s; Josie/Sabrina-c 4 8 12 26 41 55
Annual Digest 27 ('75) 4 8 12 22 34 45
...28-30 3 6 9 14 19 24
...31-34 2 4 6 9 13 16
...35-40 (...Magazine #35 on) 1 3 4 6 8 10
...41-65 ('94) 5.00
...66-69 3.00
...All-Star Specials (Winter '75, $1.25)-6 remaindered Archie comics rebound in each; titles: "The World of Giant Comics", "Giant Grab Bag of Comics", "Triple Giant Comics" & "Giant Spec. Comics 4 8 12 28 44 60
NOTE: *Archies Band-s-185, 188-192, 197, 198, 201, 204, 205, 208, 209, 215, 329, 330; Band-c-191, 330. Cavemen Archie Gang-s-183, 192, 197, 208, 210, 220, 223, 282, 333, 335, 338, 340.* ***Al Fagly*** *c-17-35.* ***Bob Montana*** *c-38, 41-50, 58, Annual 1-4.* ***Bill Woggon*** *c-53, 54.*

ARCHIE COMICS DIGEST (...Magazine No. 37-95)
Archie Publications: Aug, 1973 - Present (Small size, 160-128 pgs.)

1-1st Archie digest 9 18 27 63 107 150
2 5 10 15 32 51 70
3-5 4 8 12 24 37 50
6-10 3 6 9 16 23 30
11-33: 32,33-The Fly-r by S&K 2 4 6 10 14 18
34-60 1 3 4 6 8 10
61-80,100 1 2 3 5 6 8
81-99 5.00
101-140: 36-Katy Keene story 4.00
141-165 3.00
166-250: 194-Begin $2.39-c. 225-Begin $2.49-c. 236-65th Anniversary issue, r/1st app. in Pep #22 and entire Archie Comics #1 (1942) 2.50
NOTE: ***Neal Adams*** *a-1, 2, 4, 5, 19-21, 24, 25, 27, 29, 31, 33. X-mas c-88, 94, 100, 106.*

ARCHIE COMICS PRESENTS: THE LOVE SHOWDOWN COLLECTION
Archie Publications: 1994 ($4.95, squarebound)

nn-r/Archie #429, Betty #19, Betty & Veronica #82, & Veronica #39 1 2 3 4 5 7

ARCHIE GETS A JOB
Spire Christian Comics (Fleming H. Revell Co.): 1977

nn 2 4 6 10 14 18

ARCHIE GIANT SERIES MAGAZINE
Archie Publications: 1954 - No. 632, July, 1992 (No #36-135, no #252-451)
(#1 not code approved) (#1-233 are Giants; #12-184 are 68 pgs.,#185-194,197-233 are 52 pgs.; #195,196 are 84 pgs.; #234-up are 36 pgs.)

1-Archie's Christmas Stocking 140 280 420 882 1491 2100
2-Archie's Christmas Stocking('55) 75 150 225 473 799 1125
3-6-Archie's Christmas Stocking('56- '59) 52 104 156 322 536 750
7-10: 7-Katy Keene Holiday Fun(9/60); Bill Woggon-c. 8-Betty & Veronica Summer Fun (10/60); baseball story w/Babe Ruth & Lou Gehrig. 9-The World of Jughead (12/60); Neal Adams-a. 10-Archie's Christmas Stocking(1/61) 40 80 120 235 380 525
11,13,16,18: 11-Betty & Veronica Spectacular (6/61). 13-Betty & Veronica Summer Fun (10/61). 16-Betty & Veronica Spectacular (6/62). 18-Betty & Veronica Summer Fun (10/62) 25 50 75 147 236 325
12,14,15,17,19,20: 12-Katy Keene Holiday Fun (9/61). 14-The World of Jughead (12/61); Vampire-s. 15-Archie's Christmas Stocking (1/62). 17-Archie's Jokes (9/62); Katy Keene app. 19-The World of Jughead (12/62). 20-Archie's Christmas Stocking (1/63) 18 36 54 107 169 230
21,23,28: 21-Betty & Veronica Spectacular (6/63). 23-Betty & Veronica Summer Fun (10/63). 28-Betty & Veronica Summer Fun (9/64) 10 20 30 67 116 165
22,24,25,27,29,30: 22-Archie's Jokes (9/63). 24-The World of Jughead (12/63). 25-Archie's Christmas Stocking (1/64). 27-Archie's Jokes (8/64). 29-Around the World with Archie (10/64); Doris Day-s. 30-The World of Jughead (12/64) 9 18 27 60 100 140
26-Betty & Veronica Spectacular (6/64); all pin-ups; DeCarlo-c/a 10 20 30 68 119 170
31,33-35: 31-Archie's Christmas Stocking (1/65). 33-Archie's Jokes (8/65). 34-Betty & Veronica Summer Fun (9/65). 35-Around the World with Archie (10/65). 6 12 18 43 69 95
32-Betty & Veronica Spectacular (6/65); all pin-ups; DeCarlo-c/a 8 16 24 52 86 120
36-135-**Do not exist**
136-141: 136-The World of Jughead (12/65). 137-Archie's Christmas Stocking (1/66). 138-Betty & Veronica Spect. (6/66). 139-Archie's Jokes (6/66). 140-Betty & Veronica Summer Fun (8/66). 141-Around the World with Archie (9/66) 6 12 18 43 69 95
142-Archie's Super-Hero Special (10/66)-Origin Capt. Pureheart, Capt. Hero, and Evilheart 8 16 24 52 86 120

GD VG FN VF VF/NM NM-
2.0 4.0 6.0 8.0 9.0 9.2

143-The World of Jughead (12/66); Capt. Hero-c/s; Man From R.I.V.E.R.D.A.L.E., Pureheart, Superteen app. 6 12 18 41 66 90
144-160: 144-Archie's Christmas Stocking (1/67). 145-Betty & Veronica Spectacular (6/67). 146-Archie's Jokes (6/67). 147-Betty & Veronica Summer Fun (8/67) 148-World of Archie (9/67). 149-World of Jughead (10/67). 150-Archie's Christmas Stocking (1/68). 151-World of Archie (2/68). 152-World of Jughead (2/68). 153-Betty & Veronica Spectacular (6/68). 154-Archie Jokes (6/68). 155-Betty & Veronica Summer Fun (8/68). 156-World of Archie (10/68). 157-World of Jughead (12/68). 158-Archie's Christmas Stocking (1/69). 159-Betty & Veronica Christmas Spectacular (1/69). 160-World of Archie (2/69); Frankenstein-s each... 4 8 12 22 34 45
161-World of Jughead (2/69); Super-Jughead-s; 11 pg.early Cricket O'Dell-s 4 8 12 24 37 50
162-183: 162-Betty & Veronica Spectacular (6/69). 163-Archie's Jokes(8/69). 164-Betty & Veronica Summer Fun (9/69). 165-World of Archie (9/69). 166-World of Jughead (9/69). 167-Archie's Christmas Stocking (1/70). 168-Betty & Veronica Christmas Spect. (1/70). 169-Archie's Christmas Love-In (1/70). 170-Jughead's Eat-Out Comic Book Mag. (12/69). 171-World of Archie (2/70). 172-World of Jughead (2/70). 173-Betty & Veronica Spectacular (6/70). 174-Archie's Jokes (8/70). 175-Betty & Veronica Summer Fun (9/70). 176-Li'l Jinx Giant Laugh-Out (8/70). 177-World of Archie (9/70). 178-World of Jughead (9/70). 179-Archie's Christmas Stocking(1/71). 180-Betty & Veronica Christmas Spect. (1/71). 181-Archie's Christmas Love-In (1/71). 182-World of Archie (2/71). 183-World of Jughead (2/71)-Last squarebound each... 3 6 9 17 25 32
184-189,193,194,197-199 (52 pgs.): 184-Betty & Veronica Spectacular (6/71). 185-Li'l Jinx Giant Laugh-Out (6/71). 186-Archie's Jokes (8/71). 187-Betty & Veronica Summer Fun (9/71). 188-World of Archie (9/71). 189-World of Jughead (9/71). 193-World of Archie (3/72).194-World of Jughead (4/72). 197-Betty & Veronica Spectacular (6/72). 198-Archie's Jokes (8/72). 199-Betty & Veronica Summer Fun (9/72) each... 3 6 9 14 20 25
190-Archie's Christmas Stocking (12/71); Sabrina-c 4 8 12 26 41 55
191-Betty & Veronica Christmas Spect.(2/72); Sabrina app. 4 8 12 24 37 50
192-Archie's Christmas Love-In (1/72); Archie Band-c/s 3 6 9 21 32 42
195-(84 pgs.)-Li'l Jinx Christmas Bag (1/72). 4 8 12 22 34 45
196-(84 pgs.)-Sabrina's Christmas Magic (1/72) 6 12 18 37 59 80
200-(52 pgs.)-World of Archie (10/72) 3 6 9 21 32 42
201-206,208-219,221-230,232,233 (All 52 pgs.): 201-Betty & Veronica Spectacular (10/72). 202-World of Jughead (11/72). 203-Archie's Christmas Stocking (12/72). 204-Betty & Veronica Christmas Spectacular (2/73). 205-Archie's Christmas Love-In (1/73). 206-Li'l Jinx Christmas Bag (12/72). 208-World of Archie (3/73). 209-World of Jughead (4/73). 210-Betty & Veronica Spectacular (6/73). 211-Archie's Jokes (8/73). 212-Betty & Veronica Summer Fun (9/73). 213-World of Archie (10/73). 214-Betty & Veronica Spectacular (10/73). 215-World of Jughead (11/73). 216-Archie's Christmas Stocking (12/73). 217-Betty & Veronica Christmas Spectacular (2/74). 218-Archie's Christmas Love-In (1/74). 219-Li'l Jinx Christmas Bag (12/73). 221-Betty & Veronica Spectacular (Advertised as World of Archie) (6/74). 222-Archie's Jokes (advertised as World of Jughead) (8/74). 223-Li'l Jinx (8/74). 224-Betty & Veronica Summer Fun (9/74). 225-World of Archie (9/74). 226-Betty & Veronica Spectacular (10/74). 227-World of Jughead (10/74). 228-Archie's Christmas Stocking (12/74). 229-Betty & Veronica Christmas Spectacular (12/74). 230-Archie's Christmas Love-In (1/75). 232-World of Archie (3/75). 233-World of Jughead (4/75) each... 2 4 6 10 14 18
207,220,231,243: Sabrina's Christmas Magic. 207-(12/72). 220-(12/73). 231-(1/75). 243-(1/76) each... 3 6 9 17 25 32
234-242,244-251 (36 pgs.): 234-Betty & Veronica Spectacular (6/75). 235-Archie's Jokes (8/75). 236-Betty & Veronica Summer Fun (9/75). 237-World of Archie (9/75) 238-Betty & Veronica Spectacular (10/75). 239-World of Jughead (10/75). 240-Archie's Christmas Stocking (12/75). 241-Betty & Veronica Christmas Spectacular (12/75). 242-Archie's Christmas Love-In (1/76). 244-World of Archie (3/76). 245-World of Jughead (4/76). 246-Betty & Veronica Spectacular (6/76). 247-Archie's Jokes (8/76). 248-Betty & Veronica Summer Fun (9/76). 249-World of Archie (9/76). 250-Betty & Veronica Spectacular (10/76). 251-World of Jughead each.... 2 4 6 9 12 15
252-451-**Do not exist**
452-454,456-466,468-478, 480-490,492-499: 452-Archie's Christmas Stocking (12/76). 453-Betty & Veronica Christmas Spectacular (12/76). 454-Archie's Christmas Love-In (1/77). 456-World of Archie (3/77). 457-World of Jughead (4/77). 458-Betty & Veronica Spectacular (6/77). 459-Archie's Jokes (8/77)-Shows 8/76 in error. 460-Betty & Veronica Summer Fun (9/77). 461-World of Archie (9/77). 462-Betty & Veronica Spectacular (10/77). 463-World of Jughead (10/77). 464-Archie's Christmas Stocking (12/77). 465-Betty & Veronica Christmas Spectacular (12/77). 466-Archie's Christmas Love-In (1/78). 468-World of Archie (2/78). 469-World of Jughead (2/78). 470-Betty & Veronica Spectacular(6/78). 471-Archie's Jokes (8/78). 472-Betty & Veronica Summer Fun (9/78). 473-World of Archie (9/78). 474-Betty & Veronica Spectacular (10/78). 475-World of Jughead (10/78). 476-Archie's Christmas Stocking (12/78). 477-Betty & Veronica Christmas Spectacular (12/78). 478-Archie's Christmas Love-In (1/79). 480-The World of Archie (3/79). 481-World of Jughead (4/79).

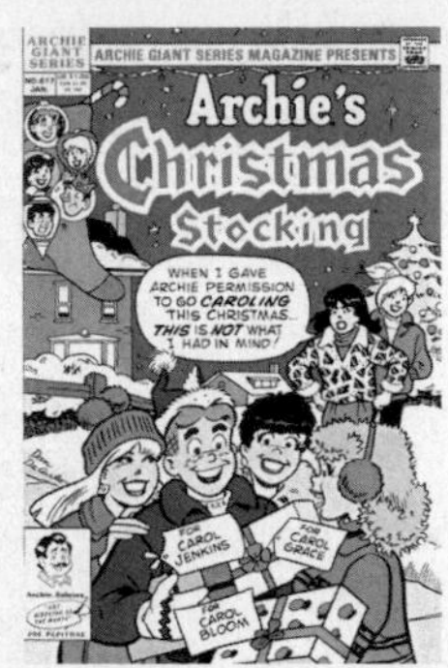

Archie Giant Series #617 © AP

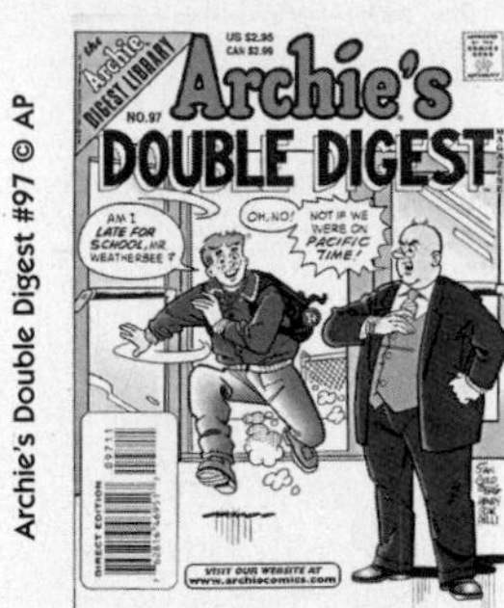

Archie's Double Digest #97 © AP

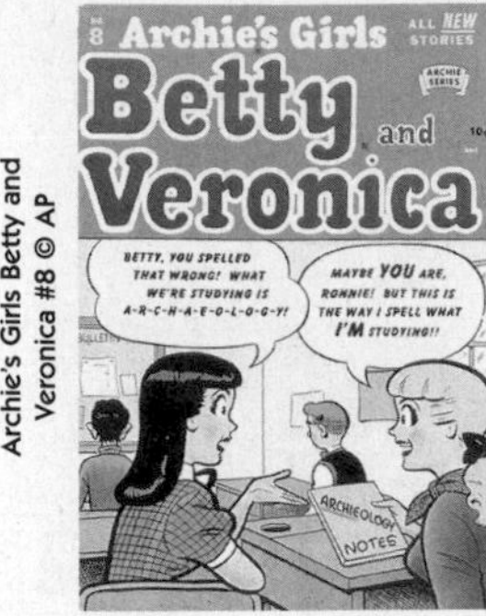

Archie's Girls Betty and Veronica #8 © AP

GD 2.0 | VG 4.0 | FN 6.0 | VF 8.0 | VF/NM 9.0 | NM- 9.2

482-Betty & Veronica Spectacular (6/79). 483-Archie's Jokes (8/79). 484-Betty & Veronica Summer Fun(9/79). 485-The World of Archie (9/79). 486-Betty & Veronica Spectacular (10/79). 487-The World of Jughead (10/79). 488-Archie's Christmas Stocking (12/79). 489-Betty & Veronica Christmas Spectacular (1/80). 490-Archie's Christmas Love-in (1/80). 492-The World of Archie (2/80). 493-The World of Jughead (4/80). 494-Betty & Veronica Spectacular (6/80). 495-Archie's Jokes (8/80). 496-Betty & Veronica Summer Fun (9/80). 497-The World of Archie (9/80). 498-Betty & Veronica Spectacular (10/80). 499-The World of Jughead (10/80) each... 2 4 6 8 10 12

455,467,479,491,503-Sabrina's Christmas Magic: 455-(1/77). 467-(1/78). 479-(1/79) Dracula/ Werewolf-s. 491-(1/80), 503(1/81) 2 4 6 11 16 20

500-Archie's Christmas Stocking (12/80) 2 4 6 8 11 14

501-514,516-527,529-532,534-539,541-543,545-550: 501-Betty & Veronica Christmas Spectacular (12/80). 502-Archie's Christmas Love-in (1/81). 504-The World of Archie (3/81). 505-The World of Jughead (4/81). 506-Betty & Veronica Spectacular (6/81). 507-Archie's Jokes (8/81). 508-Betty & Veronica Summer Fun (9/81). 509-The World of Archie (9/81). 510-Betty & Vernonica Spectacular (9/81). 511-The World of Jughead (10/81). 512-Archie's Christmas Stocking (12/81). 513-Betty & Veronica Christmas Spectacular (12/81). 514-Archie's Christmas Love-in (1/82). 516-The World of Archie(3/82). 517-The World of Jughead (4/82). 518-Betty & Veronica Spectacular (6/82). 519-Archie's Jokes (8/82). 520-Betty & Veronica Summer Fun (9/82). 521-The World of Archie (9/82). 522-Betty & Veronica Spectacular (10/82). 523-The World of Jughead (10/82).524-Archie's Christmas Stocking (1/83). 525-Betty and Veronica Christmas Spectacular (1/83). 526-Betty and Veronica Spectacular (5/83). 527-Little Archie (8/83). 529-Betty and Veronica Summer Fun (8/83). 530-Betty and Veronica Spectacular (9/83). 531-The World of Jughead (9/83). 532-The World of Archie (10/83). 534-Little Archie (1/84). 535-Archie's Christmas Stocking (1/84). 536-Betty and Veronica Christmas Spectacular (1/84). 537-Betty and Veronica Spectacular (6/84). 538-Little Archie (8/84). 539-Betty and Veronica Summer Fun (8/84). 541-Betty and Veronica Spectacular (9/84). 542-The World of Jughead (9/84). 543-The World of Archie (10/84). 545-Little Archie (12/84). 546-Archie's Christmas Stocking (12/84). 547-Betty and Veronica Christmas Spectacular (12/84). 548-?. 549-Little Archie. 550-Betty and Veronica Summer Fun each... 1 2 3 5 7 9

515,528,533,540,544: 515-Sabrina's Christmas Magic (1/82). 528-Josie and the Pussycats (8/83). 533-Sabrina; Space Pirates by Frank Bolling (10/83). 540-Josie and the Pussycats (8/84). 544-Sabrina the Teen-Age Witch (10/84). each... 2 4 6 10 14 18

551,562,571,584,597-Josie and the Pussycats 2 4 6 8 10 12

552-561,563-570,572-583,585-596,598-600: 552-Betty & Veronica Spectacular. 553-The World of Jughead. 554-The World of Archie. 555-Betty's Diary. 556-Little Archie (1/86). 557-Archie's Christmas Stocking (1/86). 558-Betty & Veronica Christmas Spectacular (1/86). 559-Betty & Veronica Spectacular. 560-Little Archie. 561-Betty & Veronica Summer Fun. 563-Betty & Veronica Spectacular. 564-World of Jughead. 565-World of Archie. 566-Little Archie. 567-Archie's Christmas Stocking. 568-Betty & Veronica Christmas Spectacular. 569-Betty & Veronica Spring Spectacular. 570-Little Archie. 571-Dracula-c/s. 572-Betty & Veronica Summer Fun. 573-Archie At Riverdale High. 574-World of Archie. 575-Betty & Veronica Spectacular. 576-Pep. 577-World of Jughead. 578-Archie And Me. 579-Archie's Christmas Stocking. 580-Betty and Veronica Christmas Spectacular. 581-Little Archie Christmas Special. 582-Betty & Veronica Spring Spectacular. 583-Little Archie. 585-Betty & Veronica Summer Fun. 586-Archie At Riverdale High. 587-The World of Archie (10/88); 1st app. Explorers of the Unknown. 588-Betty & Veronica Spectacular. 589-Pep (10/88). 590-The World of Jughead. 591-Archie & Me. 592-Archie's Christmas Stocking. 593-Betty & Veronica Christmas Spectacular. 594-Little Archie. 595-Betty & Veronica Spring Spectacular. 596-Little Archie. 598-Betty & Veronica Summer Fun. 599-The World of Archie (10/89); 2nd app. Explorers of the Unknown. 600-Betty and Veronica Spectacular each.... 6.00

601,602,604-609,611-629: 601-Pep. 602-The World of Jughead. 604-Archie at Riverdale High. 605-Archie's Christmas Stocking. 606-Betty and Veronica Christmas Spectacular. 607-Little Archie. 608-Betty and Veronica Spectacular. 609-Little Archie. 611-Betty and Veronica Summer Fun. 612-The World of Archie. 613-Betty and Veronica Spectacular. 614-Pep (10/90). 615-Veronica's Summer Special. 616-Archie and Me. 617-Archie's Christmas Stocking. 618-Betty & Veronica Christmas Spectacular. 619-Little Archie. 620-Betty and Veronica Spectacular. 621-Betty and Veronica Summer Fun. 622-Josie & the Pussycats; not published. 623-Betty and Veronica Spectacular. 624-Pep Comics. 625-Veronica's Summer Special. 626-Archie and Me. 627-World of Archie. 628-Archie's Pals 'n' Gals Holiday Special. 629-Betty & Veronica Christmas Spectacular. each.... 4.00

603-Archie and Me; Titanic app. 5.00

610-Josie and the Pussycats 1 2 3 4 5 7

630-631: 630-Archie's Christmas Stocking. 631-Archie's Pals 'n' Gals 4.00

632-Last issue; Betty & Veronica Spectacular 1 2 3 4 5 7

NOTE: *Archies Band-c-173,180,192; s-189,192. Archie Cavemen-165,225,232,244,249. Little Sabrina-527,534, 538,545,556,566. UFO-s-178,487,594.*

ARCHIE MEETS THE PUNISHER (Same contents as The Punisher Meets Archie)
Marvel Comics & Archie Comics Publ.: Aug, 1994 ($2.95, 52 pgs., one-shot)

1-Batton Lash story, J. Buscema-a on Punisher, S. Goldberg-a on Archie 6.00

ARCHIE'S ACTIVITY COMICS DIGEST MAGAZINE
Archie Enterprises: 1985 - No. 4 (Annual, 128 pgs., digest size)

1 (Most copies are marked) 2 4 6 9 13 16
2-4 1 2 3 5 7 9

ARCHIE'S CAR
Spire Christian Comics (Fleming H. Revell co.): 1979 (49¢)

nn 2 4 6 8 11 14

ARCHIE'S CHRISTMAS LOVE-IN (See Archie Giant Series Mag. No. 169, 181,192, 205, 218, 230, 242, 454, 466, 478, 490, 502, 514)

ARCHIE'S CHRISTMAS STOCKING (See Archie Giant Series Mag. No. 1-6,10, 15, 20, 25, 31, 137, 144, 150, 158, 167, 179, 190, 203, 216, 228, 240, 452, 464, 476, 488, 500, 512, 524, 535, 546, 557, 567, 579, 592, 605, 617, 630)

ARCHIE'S CHRISTMAS STOCKING
Archie Comics: 1993 - No. 7, 1999 ($2.00-$2.29, 52 pgs.)(Bound-in calendar poster in all)

1-Dan DeCarlo-c/a 5.00
2-5 4.00
6,7: 6-(1998, $2.25). 7-(1999, $2.29) 3.00

ARCHIE'S CIRCUS
Barbour Christian Comics: 1990 (69¢)

nn 2 4 6 8 11 14

ARCHIE'S CLASSIC CHRISTMAS STORIES
Archie Comics: 2002 ($10.95, TPB)

Volume 1 - Reprints stories from 1955-1964 Archie's Christmas Stocking issues 11.00

ARCHIE'S CLEAN SLATE
Spire Christian Comics (Fleming H. Revell Co.): 1973 (35/49¢)

1-(35¢-c edition)(Some issues have nn) 2 4 6 10 14 18
1-(49¢-c edition) 2 4 6 9 12 15

ARCHIE'S DATE BOOK
Spire Christian comics (Fleming H. Revell Co.): 1981

nn-(Low print) 2 4 6 10 14 18

ARCHIE'S DOUBLE DIGEST QUARTERLY MAGAZINE
Archie Comics: 1981 - Present ($1.95-$3.69, 256 pgs.) (Archie's Double Digest Magazine No. 10 on)

1 3 6 9 16 23 30
2-10; 6-Katy Keene story. 2 4 6 10 14 18
11-30: 29-Pureheart story 2 4 6 8 10 12
31-50 1 2 3 4 5 7
51-70,100 5.00
71-99 4.00
101-194: 115-Begin $3.19-c. 123-Begin $3.29-c. 139-Begin $3.59-c. 170-Begin $3.69 3.75

ARCHIE'S FAMILY ALBUM
Spire Christian Comics (Fleming H. Revell Co.): 1978 (39¢/49¢, 36 pgs.)

nn 2 4 6 9 12 15
nn (49¢-c edition) 1 3 4 6 8 10

ARCHIE'S FESTIVAL
Spire Christian Comics (Fleming H. Revell Co.): 1980 (49¢)

nn 2 4 6 9 12 15

ARCHIE'S GIRLS, BETTY AND VERONICA (Becomes Betty & Veronica)(Also see Veronica)
Archie Publications (Close-Up): 1950 - No. 347, Apr, 1987

1 247 494 741 1556 2628 3700
2 100 200 300 630 1065 1500
3-5: 3-Betty's 1st ponytail. 4-Dan DeCarlo's 1st Archie work 57 114 171 359 605 850
6-10: 10-Katy Keene app. (2 pgs.) 46 92 138 285 473 660
11-20: 11,13,14,17-19-Katy Keene app. 17-Last pre-code issue (3/55). 20-Debbie's Diary (2 pgs.) 37 74 111 215 345 475
21-30: 27,30-Katy Keene app. 29-Tarzan 25 50 75 147 236 325
31-43,45-50: 41-Marilyn Monroe and Brigitte Bardot mentioned. 45-Fabian 1 pg. photo & bio. 46-Bobby Darin 1 pg. photo & bio 18 36 54 103 162 220
44-Elvis Presley 1 pg. photo & bio 20 40 60 115 183 250
51-55,57-74: 67-Jackie Kennedy homage. 73-Sci-fi-c 8 16 24 56 93 130
56-Elvis and Bobby Darin records parody 9 18 27 65 113 160
75-Betty & Veronica sell souls to Devil 15 30 45 107 196 285
76-99: 82-Bobby Rydell 1 pg. illustrated bio; Elvis mentioned on-c. 84-Connie Francis 1 pg. illustrated bio 6 12 18 37 59 80
100 6 12 18 43 69 95
101-104, 106-117,120 (12/65): 113-Monsters-s 4 8 12 28 44 60

Archie's Joke Book #42 © AP

Archie's Madhouse #64 © AP

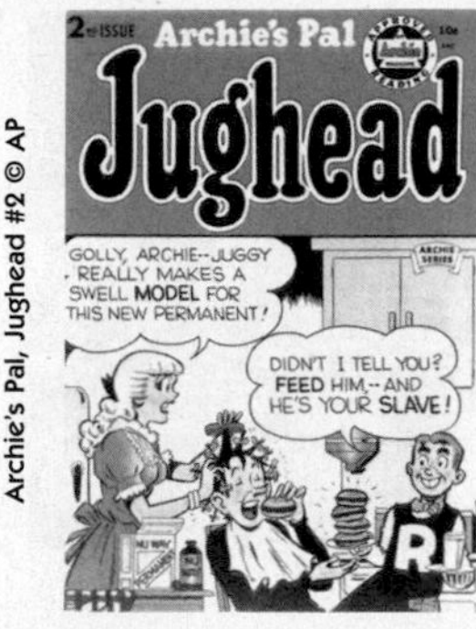

Archie's Pal, Jughead #2 © AP

	GD 2.0	VG 4.0	FN 6.0	VF 8.0	VF/NM 9.0	NM- 9.2
105-Beatles wig parody (5 pg. story)(9/64)	5	10	15	30	48	65
118-(10/65) 1st app./origin Superteen (also see Betty & Me #3)	6	12	18	43	69	95
119-2nd app./last Superteen story	5	10	15	32	51	70
121,122,124-126,128-140 (8/67): 135,140-Mod-c. 136-Slave Girl-s	3	6	9	19	29	38
123-"Jingo"-Ringo parody-c	4	8	12	22	34	45
127-Beatles Fan Club-s	5	10	15	30	48	65
141-156,158-163,165-180 (12/70)	3	6	9	14	20	26
157,164-Archies Band	3	6	9	18	27	35
181-193,195-199	2	4	6	10	14	18
194-Sabrina-c/s	3	6	9	18	27	35
200-(8/72)	2	4	6	13	18	22
201-205,207,209,211-215,217-240	2	4	6	8	10	12
206,208,210, 216: 206,208,216-Sabrina c/app. 206-Josie-c. 210-Sabrina app.	3	6	9	14	19	24
241 (1/76)-270 (6/78)	1	3	4	6	8	10
271-299: 281-UFO-s	1	2	3	5	7	9
300 (12/80)-Anniversary issue	2	4	6	8	10	12
301-309	1	2	3	4	5	7
310-John Travolta parody story	1	3	4	6	8	10
311-319						6.00
320 (10/82)-Intro. of Cheryl Blossom on cover and inside story (she also appears, but not on the cover, in Jughead #325 with same 10/82 publication date)	8	16	24	52	86	120
321,322-Cheryl Blossom app.	3	6	9	18	27	35
323,326,329,330,331,333-338: 333-Monsters-s	1	2	3	5	7	9
324,325-Crickett O'Dell app.	2	4	6	8	10	12
327,328-Cheryl Blossom app.	3	6	9	16	23	30
332,339: 332-Superhero costume party. 339-(12/85) Betty dressed as Madonna.	2	4	6	8	10	12
340-346 Low print	1	2	3	5	6	8
347 (4/87) Last issue; low print	1	2	3	5	7	9
Annual 1 (1953)	113	226	339	712	1206	1700
Annual 2 (1954)	46	92	138	285	473	660
Annual 3-5 (1955-1957)	37	74	111	219	352	485
Annual 6-8 (1958-1960)	26	52	78	152	244	335

ARCHIE'S HOLIDAY FUN DIGEST
Archie Comics: 1997 - Present ($1.75/$1.95/$1.99/$2.19/$2.39/$2.49, annual)

	GD	VG	FN	VF	VF/NM	NM-
1-12-Christmas stories						2.50

ARCHIE'S JOKEBOOK COMICS DIGEST ANNUAL (See Jokebook...)

ARCHIE'S JOKE BOOK MAGAZINE (See Joke Book ...)
Archie Publ: 1953 - No. 3, Sum, 1954; No. 15, Fall, 1954 - No. 288, 11/82 (subtitled...Laugh-In #127-140; ...Laugh-Out #141-194)

	GD	VG	FN	VF	VF/NM	NM-
1953-One Shot (#1)	103	206	309	649	1100	1550
2	48	96	144	298	499	700
3 (no #4-14)	40	80	120	235	380	525
15-20: 15-Formerly Archie's Rival Reggie #14; last pre-code issue (Fall/54). 15-17-Katy Keene app.	24	48	72	140	225	310
21-30	15	30	45	86	133	180
31-43: 42-Bio of Ed "Kookie" Byrnes. 43-story about guitarist Duane Eddy	12	24	36	69	97	125
44-1st professional comic work by Neal Adams, 4 pgs.	28	56	84	166	268	370
45-47-N. Adams-a in all, 2-6 pgs.	15	30	45	94	147	200
48-Four pgs. N. Adams-a	15	30	45	94	147	200
49,50	5	10	15	34	55	75
51-56,60 (1962)	4	8	12	26	41	55
57-Elvis mentioned; Marilyn Monroe cameo	5	10	15	34	55	75
58,59-Horror/Sci-Fi-c	5	10	15	32	51	70
61-80 (8/64): 66-(12¢ cover)	3	6	9	17	25	32
66-(15¢ cover variant)	3	6	9	20	30	40
81-89,91,92,94-99	2	4	6	13	18	22
90,93: 90-Beatles gag. 93-Beatles cameo	3	6	9	16	23	30
100 (5/66)	3	6	9	16	22	28
101,103-117,119-123,127,129,131-140 (9/69): 105-Superhero gag-c. 108-110-Archies Archers Band-s. 116-Beatles/Monkees/Bob Dylan cameos (posters)	2	4	6	10	14	18
102 (7/66) Archie Band prototype-c; Elvis parody panel, Rolling Stones mention	3	6	9	17	25	32
118,124,125,126,128,130: 118-Archie Band-c; Veronica & Groovers band-s. 124-Archies Band-c/app. 125-Beatles cameo (poster). 126,130-Monkees cameo. 128-Veronica/Archies Band app.	3	6	9	16	22	28
141-173,175-181,183-199	2	4	6	8	10	12
174-Sabrina-c. 182-Sabrina cameo	2	4	6	9	12	15
200 (9/74)	2	4	6	9	12	15
201-230 (3/77)	1	2	3	5	6	8
231-239,241-287						6.00
240-Elvis record-c	1	2	3	5	7	9
288-Last issue	1	2	3	4	5	7

NOTE: *Archies Band-c-118,124,147,172; 1 pg.-s-127,128,138,140,143,147,167; 2 pg.-s-124,131, 155. Sabrina app.-247,248,252-259,261,262,264,266-270,274,277,284-286.*

ARCHIE'S JOKES (See Archie Giant Series Mag. No. 17, 22, 27, 33, 139, 146, 154, 163, 174, 186, 198, 211, 222, 235, 247, 459, 471, 483, 495, 519)

ARCHIE'S LOVE SCENE
Spire Christian Comics (Fleming H. Revell Co.): 1973 (35¢/39¢/49¢/no price)

	GD	VG	FN	VF	VF/NM	NM-
1-(35¢ Edition)	2	4	6	10	14	18
1-(39¢/49¢ Edition/no price) (Some copies have nn)	2	4	6	8	10	12

ARCHIE'S LOVE SHOWDOWN SPECIAL
Archie Publications: 1994 ($2.00, one-shot)

	GD	VG	FN	VF	VF/NM	NM-
1-Concludes x-over from Archie #429, Betty #19, B&V #82, Veronica #39						4.00

ARCHIE'S MADHOUSE (Madhouse Ma-ad No. 67 on)
Archie Publications: Sept, 1959 - No. 66, Feb, 1969

	GD	VG	FN	VF	VF/NM	NM-
1-Archie begins	21	42	63	155	288	420
2	12	24	36	82	146	210
3-5	8	16	24	58	97	135
6-10	6	12	18	41	66	90
11-17 (Last w/regular characters)	5	10	15	32	51	70
18-21,23,29: 18-New format begins. 23-No Sabrina	4	8	12	26	41	55
22-1st app. Sabrina, the Teen-age Witch (10/62)	23	46	69	170	315	460
24-2nd app.Sabrina a	10	20	30	70	123	175
25,26,28-Sabrina app. 25-1st app. Captain Sprocket (4/63)	8	16	24	52	86	120
27-Sabrina-c; no story	6	12	18	41	66	90
30,34,38-40: No Sabrina. 34-Bordered-c begin.	3	6	9	17	25	32
31,33,37-Sabrina app.	6	12	18	39	62	85
32-Sabrina app.?	3	6	9	17	25	32
35-Beatles cameo. No Sabrina	3	6	9	19	29	38
36-1st Salem the Cat w/Sabrina story	8	16	24	56	93	130
41-48,51-57,60-62,64-66: No Sabrina 43-Mighty Crusaders cameo. 44-Swipes Mad #4 (Super-Duperman) in "Bird Monsters From Outer Space"	3	6	9	14	20	26
49,50,58,59,63-Sabrina stories	5	10	15	30	48	65
Annual 1 (1962-63) no Sabrina	7	14	21	47	76	105
Annual 2 (1964) no Sabrina	5	10	15	30	48	65
Annual 3 (1965)-Origin Sabrina the Teen-Age Witch	9	18	27	65	113	160
Annual 4,5('66-68)(Becomes Madhouse Ma-ad Annual #7 on); no Sabrina	3	6	9	18	27	35
Annual 6 (1969)-Sabrina the Teen-Age Witch-sty	6	12	18	41	66	90

NOTE: *Cover title to #61-65 is "Madhouse" and to #66 is "Madhouse Ma-ad Jokes". Sci-Fi/Horror covers 6, 8, 11, 13, 15-26, 29, 35, 36, 38, 42, 43, 48, 51, 58, 60.*

ARCHIE'S MECHANICS
Archie Publications: Sept, 1954 - No. 3, 1955

	GD	VG	FN	VF	VF/NM	NM-
1-(15¢; 52 pgs.)	85	170	255	536	906	1275
2-(10¢)-Last pre-code issue	48	96	144	298	499	700
3-(10¢)	40	80	120	247	404	560

ARCHIE'S MYSTERIES (Continued from Archie's Weird Mysteries)
Archie Comics: No. 25, Feb, 2003 - No. 34, June, 2004 ($2.19)

	GD	VG	FN	VF	VF/NM	NM-
25-34- Archie and gang as "Teen Scene Investigators"						2.50

ARCHIE'S ONE WAY
Spire Christian Comics (Fleming H. Revell Co.): 1972 (35¢/39¢/49¢, 36 pgs.)

	GD	VG	FN	VF	VF/NM	NM-
nn-(35¢ Edition)	2	4	6	10	14	18
nn-(39¢, 49¢, no price editions)	2	4	6	8	10	12

ARCHIE'S PAL, JUGHEAD (Jughead No. 127 on)
Archie Publications: 1949 - No. 126, Nov, 1965

	GD	VG	FN	VF	VF/NM	NM-
1 (1949)-1st app. Moose (see Pep #33)	207	414	621	1304	2202	3100
2 (1950)	80	160	240	504	852	1200
3-5	47	94	141	291	483	675
6-10: 7-Suzie app.	33	66	99	196	316	435
11-20: 20-Jughead as Sherlock Holmes parody	22	44	66	129	207	285
21-30: 23-25,28-30-Katy Keene app. 23-Early Dilton-s. 28-Debbie's Diary app.	15	30	45	90	140	190
31-50: 49-Archies Rock 'N' Rollers band-c	7	14	21	47	76	105

Archie's Pals 'N' Gals #2 © AP

Archie's Rival Reggie #9 © AP

Archie's TV Laugh-Out #2 © AP

	GD 2.0	VG 4.0	FN 6.0	VF 8.0	VF/NM 9.0	NM- 9.2
51-57,59-70: 59- Bio of Will Hutchins of TV's Sugarfoot. 67-Betty seducing Jughead-c. 68-Early Archie Gang Cavemen-s	5	10	15	32	51	70
58-Neal Adams-a	6	12	18	39	62	85
71-76,83,84,89-99: 72-Jughead dates Betty & Veronica. 84-1st app. Big Ethel (5/62). 95-2nd app. Cricket O'Dell	4	8	12	22	34	45
77,78,80-82,85,86,88-Horror/Sci-Fi-c	5	10	15	34	55	75
79-Creature From the Black Lagoon-c	6	12	18	43	69	95
87-Early Big Ethel app.; UGAJ (United Girls Against Jughead)-s	4	8	12	28	44	60
100	4	8	12	26	41	55
101-Return of Big Ethyl	4	8	12	23	36	48
102-126	3	6	9	17	25	32
Annual 1 (1953, 25¢)	70	140	210	441	746	1050
Annual 2 (1954, 25¢)-Last pre-code issue	40	80	120	244	397	550
Annual 3-5 (1955-57, 25¢)	29	58	87	169	272	375
Annual 6-8 (1958-60, 25¢)	19	38	57	109	172	235

ARCHIE'S PAL JUGHEAD COMICS (Formerly Jughead #1-45)
Archie Comic Publ.: No. 46, June, 1993 - Present ($1.25-$2.25)

	GD	VG	FN	VF	VF/NM	NM-
46-60						3.00
61-192: 100-"A Storm Over Uniforms" x-over part 1,2. 166-Three Geeks cameo						2.25

ARCHIE'S PALS 'N' GALS (Also see Archie Giant Series Magazine #628)
Archie Publ: 1952-53 - No. 6, 1957-58; No. 7, 1958 - No. 224, Sept, 1991
(...All News Stories on-c #49-59)

	GD	VG	FN	VF	VF/NM	NM-
1-(116 pgs., 25¢)	87	174	261	548	924	1300
2(Annual)('54, 25¢)	41	82	123	256	428	600
3-5(Annual, '55-57, 25¢): 3-Last pre-code issue	31	62	93	181	291	400
6-10('58-'60)	19	38	57	112	176	240
11,13,14,16,17,20-(84 pgs.): 17-B&V paper dolls	12	24	36	67	94	120
12,15-(84 pgs.) Neal Adams-a. 12-Harry Belafonte 2 pg. photos & bio.	14	28	42	76	108	140
18-(84 pgs.) Horror/Sci-Fi-c	13	26	39	74	105	135
19-Marilyn Monroe app.	15	30	45	94	147	200
21,22,24-28,30 (68 pgs.)	6	12	18	39	62	85
23-(Wint./62) 6 pg. Josie-s with Pepper and Melody (1st app.) by DeCarlo; Betty in towel pin-up	15	30	45	108	199	290
29-Beatles satire (68 pgs.)	9	18	27	60	100	140
31(Wint. 64/65)-39 -(68 pgs.)	5	10	15	34	55	75
40-Early Superteen-s; with Pureheart	7	14	21	45	73	100
41(8/67)-43,45-50(2/69) (68 pgs.)	4	8	12	24	37	50
44-Archies Band-s; WEB cameo	4	8	12	28	44	60
51(4/69),52,55-64(6/71): 62-Last squarebound	3	6	9	18	27	35
53-Archies Band-c/s	3	6	9	21	32	42
54-Satan meets Veronica-s	5	10	15	30	48	65
65(8/70),67-70,73,74,76-81,83(6/74) (52 pgs.)	3	6	9	14	19	24
66,82-Sabrina-c	3	6	9	20	30	40
71,72-Two part drug story (8/72,9/72)	3	6	9	20	30	40
75-Archies Band-s	3	6	9	16	23	30
84-99	1	3	4	6	8	10
100 (12/75)	2	4	6	9	12	15
101-130(3/79): 125,126-Riverdale 2001-s	1	2	3	5	6	8
131-160,162-170 (7/84)						6.00
161 (11/82) 3rd app./1st solo Cheryl Blossom-s and pin-up; 2nd Jason Blossom	3	6	9	19	29	38
171-173,175,177-197,199: 197-G. Colan-a						4.00
174,176,198: 174-New Archies Band-s. 176-Cyndi Lauper-c. 198-Archie gang on strike at Archie Ent. offices						6.00
200(9/88)-Illiteracy-s						6.00
201,203-223: Later issues $1.00 cover						3.00
202-Explains end of Archie's jalopy; Dezerland-c/s; James Dean cameo						6.00
224-Last issue						5.00

NOTE: *Archies Band-c-45,47,49,53,56; s-44,53,75,174. UFO-s-50,63,209,220.*

ARCHIE'S PALS 'N' GALS DOUBLE DIGEST MAGAZINE
Archie Comic Publications: Nov, 1992 - Present ($2.50-$3.69)

	GD	VG	FN	VF	VF/NM	NM-
1-Capt. Hero story; Pureheart app.	2	4	6	8	10	12
2-10: 2-Superduck story; Little Jinx in all. 4-Begin $2.75-c	1	2	3	4	5	7
11-29						4.00
30-128: 40-Begin $2.99-c. 48-Begin $3.19-c. 56-Begin $3.29-c. 72-Begin $3.59-c. 100-Story uses screen captures from classic animated series. 102-Begin $3.69-c 125-128-"New Look" art						3.75

ARCHIE'S PARABLES
Spire Christian Comics (Fleming H. Revell Co.): 1973,1975 (39/49¢, 36 pgs.)

	GD	VG	FN	VF	VF/NM	NM-
nn-By Al Hartley; 39¢ Edition	2	4	6	10	14	18
49¢, no price editions	2	4	6	8	10	12

ARCHIE'S R/C RACERS (Radio controlled cars)
Archie Comics: Sept, 1989 - No. 10, Mar, 1991 (95¢/$1)

	GD	VG	FN	VF	VF/NM	NM-
1						6.00
2,5-7,10: 5-Elvis parody. 7-Supervillain-c/s. 10-UFO-c/s						4.00
3,4,8,9						3.00

ARCHIE'S RIVAL REGGIE (Reggie & Archie's Joke Book #15 on)
Archie Publications: 1949 - No. 14, Aug, 1954

	GD	VG	FN	VF	VF/NM	NM-
1-Reggie 1st app. in Jackpot Comics #5	85	170	255	536	906	1275
2	41	82	123	250	413	575
3-5	31	62	93	184	295	405
6-10	22	44	66	127	204	280
11-14: Katy Keene in No. 10-14, 1-2 pgs.	16	32	48	96	151	205

ARCHIE'S RIVERDALE HIGH (See Riverdale High)

ARCHIE'S ROLLER COASTER
Spire Christian Comics (Fleming H. Revell Co.): 1981 (69¢)

	GD	VG	FN	VF	VF/NM	NM-
nn-(Low print)	2	4	6	10	14	18

ARCHIE'S SOMETHING ELSE
Spire Christian Comics (Fleming H. Revell Co.): 1975 (39/49¢, 36 pgs.)

	GD	VG	FN	VF	VF/NM	NM-
nn-(39¢-c) Hell's Angels Biker on motorcycle-c	2	4	6	10	14	18
nn-(49¢-c)	2	4	6	8	10	12
Barbour Christian Comics Edition ('86, no price listed)	1	2	3	5	7	9

ARCHIE'S SONSHINE
Spire Christian Comics (Fleming H. Revell Co.): 1973, 1974 (39/49¢, 36 pgs.)

	GD	VG	FN	VF	VF/NM	NM-
39¢ Edition	2	4	6	10	14	18
49¢, no price editions	2	4	6	8	10	12

ARCHIE'S SPORTS SCENE
Spire Christian Comics (Fleming H. Revell Co.): 1983 (no cover price)

	GD	VG	FN	VF	VF/NM	NM-
nn-(Low print)	2	4	6	10	14	18

ARCHIE'S SPRING BREAK
Archie Comics: 1996 - Present ($2.00, 48 pgs., annual)

	GD	VG	FN	VF	VF/NM	NM-
1-Dan DeCarlo-c						4.00
2-4: 2-Dan DeCarlo-c						3.00

ARCHIE'S STORY & GAME COMICS DIGEST MAGAZINE
Archie Enterprises: Nov, 1986 - No. 39, Jan, 1998 ($1.25-$1.95, 128 pgs., digest-size)

	GD	VG	FN	VF	VF/NM	NM-
1: Marked-up copies are common	2	4	6	10	14	18
2-10	1	3	4	6	8	10
11-20						6.00
21-38						3.00
39-($1.95)						2.50

ARCHIE'S SUPER HERO SPECIAL (See Archie Giant Series Mag. No. 142)

ARCHIE'S SUPER HERO SPECIAL (...Comics Digest Mag. 2)
Archie Publications (Red Circle): Jan, 1979 - No. 2, Aug, 1979 (95¢, 148 pgs.)

	GD	VG	FN	VF	VF/NM	NM-
1-Simon & Kirby r-/Double Life of Pvt. Strong #1,2; Black Hood, The Fly, Jaguar, The Web app.	2	4	6	11	16	20
2-Contains contents to the never published Black Hood #1; origin Black Hood; N. Adams, Wood, McWilliams, Morrow, S&K-a(r); N. Adams-c. The Shield, The Fly, Jaguar, Hangman, Steel Sterling, The Web, The Fox-r	2	4	6	11	16	20

ARCHIE'S SUPER TEENS
Archie Comic Publications, Inc.: 1994 - No. 4, 1996 ($2.00, 52 pgs.)

	GD	VG	FN	VF	VF/NM	NM-
1-Staton/Esposito-c/a; pull-out poster						4.00
2-4: 2-Fred Hembeck script; Bret Blevins/Terry Austin-a						3.00

ARCHIE'S TV LAUGH-OUT ("...Starring Sabrina" on-c #1-50)
Archie Publications: Dec, 1969 - No. 105, Feb, 1986 (#1-7: 68 pgs.)

	GD	VG	FN	VF	VF/NM	NM-
1-Sabrina begins, thru #106	10	20	30	68	119	170
2 (68 pgs.)	6	12	18	39	62	85
3-6 (68 pgs.)	5	10	15	30	48	65
7-Josie begins, thru #105; Archie's & Josie's Bands cover logos begin	7	14	21	47	76	105
8-23 (52 pgs.): 10-1st Josie on-c. 12-1st Josie and Pussycats on-c. 14-Beatles cameo on poster	4	8	12	24	37	50
24-40: 37,39,40-Bicentennial-c	3	6	9	14	20	25
41,47,56: 41-Alexandra rejoins J&P band. 47-Fonz cameo; voodoo-s. 56-Fonz parody; B&V with Farrah hair-c	3	6	9	16	22	28

Area 52 #1 © Brian Haberlin

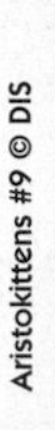
Aristokittens #9 © DIS

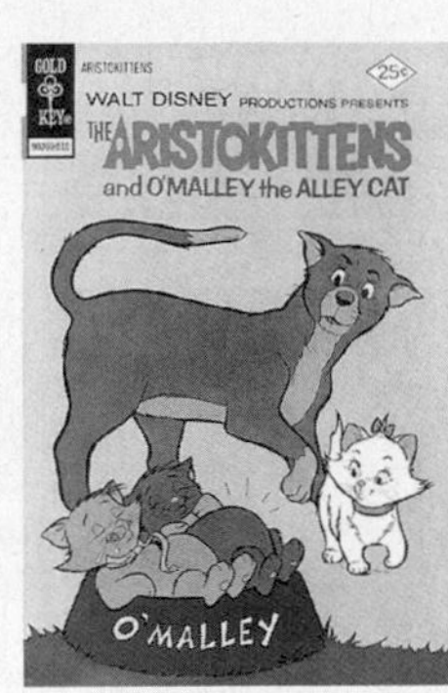

Armageddon 2001 #2 © DC

GD VG FN VF VF/NM NM-
2.0 4.0 6.0 8.0 9.0 9.2

42-46,48-55,57-60 2 4 6 9 12 15
61-68,70-80: 63-UFO-s. 79-Mummy-s 1 3 4 6 8 10
69-Sherlock Holmes parody 1 3 4 6 8 10
81-90,94,95,97-99: 84 Voodoo-s 1 2 3 5 6 8
91-Early Cheryl Blossom-s; Sabrina/Archies Band-c 2 4 6 13 18 22
92-A-Team parody 1 3 4 6 8 10
93-(2/84) Archie in drag-s; Hill Street Blues-s; Groucho Marx parody; cameo parody app. of Batman, Spider-Man, Wonder Woman and others 2 4 6 9 12 15
96-MASH parody-s; Jughead in drag; Archies Band-c 1 3 4 6 8 10
100-(4/85) Michael Jackson parody-c/s; J&P band and Archie band on-c 2 4 6 9 12 15
101-104-Lower print run. 104-Miami Vice parody-c 1 2 3 5 7 9
105-Wrestling/Hulk Hogan parody-c; J&P band-s 2 4 6 9 12 15

NOTE: ***Dan DeCarlo-a*** *78-up(most),* ***c****-89-up(most).* ***Archies Band-s*** *2,7,9-11,15,20,25,37,64,65,67,68,70,73, 76,78,79,83,84,86,90,96,100,101;* ***Archies Band-c*** *2,17,20,91,94,96,99-103.* ***Josie-s*** *12,21,26,35,52,78,80,90.* ***Josie-c*** *10,91,94.* ***Josie and the Pussycats (as a band in costume)-s*** *7,9,10,37,38,41,42,66,84,99-101,105.* ***Josie w/Pussycats member Valerie &/or Melody-s*** *17,20,22,25,27-29,31,33,36,39,40,43-51,53-65,67-77,79,81-83,85-89,92-94,102-104.* ***Josie w/Pussycats band-c*** *12,14,17,18,22,24.* ***Sabrina-s*** *1-9,11-86,88-106.* ***Sabrina-c*** *1-18,21,23,27,49,91,94.*

ARCHIE'S VACATION SPECIAL
Archie Publications: Winter, 1994 - Present ($2.00/$2.25/$2.29/$2.49, annual)

1 4.00
2-8: 8-(2000, $2.49) 3.00

ARCHIE'S WEIRD MYSTERIES (Continues as Archie's Mysteries)
Archie Comics: Feb, 2000 - No. 24, Dec, 2002 ($1.79/$1.99)

1 3.50
2-10: 3-Mighty Crusaders app. 3.00
11-24: 14-Super Teens-c/app.; Mighty Crusaders app. 2.50

ARCHIE'S WORLD
Spire Christian Comics (Fleming H. Revell Co.): 1973, 1976 (39/49¢)

39¢ Edition 2 4 6 10 14 18
49¢ Edition, no price editions 2 4 6 8 10 12

ARCHIE 3000
Archie Comics: May, 1989 - No. 16, July, 1991 (75¢/95¢/$1.00)

1,16: 16-Aliens-c/s 4.00
2-15: 6-Begin $1.00-c; X-Mas-c 3.00

ARCOMICS PREMIERE
Arcomics: July, 1993 ($2.95)

1-1st lenticular-c on a comic (flicker-c) 3.00

AREA 52
Image Comics: Jan, 2001 - No. 4, June, 2001 ($2.95)

1-4-Haberlin-s/Henry-a 3.00

ARES
Marvel Comics: Mar, 2006 - No. 5, July, 2006 ($2.99, limited series)

1-5-Oeming-s/Foreman-a 3.00
...: God of War TPB (2006, $13.99) r/series 14.00

ARGUS (See Flash, 2nd Series) (Also see Showcase '95 #1,2)
DC Comics: Apr, 1995 - No. 6, Oct, 1995 ($1.50, limited series)

1-6: 4-Begin $1.75-c 2.50

ARIA
Image Comics (Avalon Studios): Jan, 1999 - Present ($2.50)

Preview (11/98, $2.95) 5.00
1-Anacleto-c/a 1 2 3 5 6 8
1-Variant-c by Michael Turner 1 2 3 5 6 8
1-($10.00) Alternate-c by Turner 1 3 4 6 8 10
1,2-(Blanc & Noir) Black and white printing of pencil art 3.00
1-(Blanc & Noir) DF Edition 5.00
2-4: 2,4-Anacleto-c/a. 3-Martinez-a 3.00
4-($6.95) Glow in the Dark-c 1 3 4 6 8 10
Aria Angela 1 (2/00, $2.95) Anacleto-a; 4 covers by Anacleto, JG Jones, Portacio and Quesada 3.00
Aria Angela Blanc & Noir 1 (4/00, $2.95) Anacleto-c 3.00
Aria Angela European Ashcan 10.00
Aria Angela 2 (10/00, $2.95) Anacleto-a/c 3.00
...: A Midwinter's Dream 1 (1/02, $4.95, 7"x7") text-s w/Anacleto panels 5.00
...: The Enchanted Collection (5/04, $16.95) r/Summer's Spell & The Uses of Enchantment 17.00

ARIA: SUMMER'S SPELL
Image Comics (Avalon Studios): Mar, 2002 - No. 2, Jun, 2002 ($2.95)

1,2-Anacleto-c/Holguin-s/Pajarillo & Medina-a 3.00

ARIA: THE SOUL MARKET
Image Comics (Avalon Studios): Mar, 2001 - No. 6, Dec, 2001 ($2.95)

1-6-Anacleto-c/Holguin-s 3.00
HC (2002, $26.95, 8.25" x 12.25") oversized r/#1-6 27.00
SC (2004, $16.95, 8.25" x 12.25") oversized r/#1-6 17.00

ARIA: THE USES OF ENCHANTMENT
Image Comics (Avalon Studios): Feb, 2003 - No. 4, Sept, 2003 ($2.95)

1-4-Anacleto-c/Holguin-s/Medina-a 3.00

ARIANE AND BLUEBEARD (See Night Music #8)

ARIEL & SEBASTIAN (See Cartoon Tales & The Little Mermaid)

ARION, LORD OF ATLANTIS (Also see Warlord #55)
DC Comics: Nov, 1982 - No. 35, Sept, 1985

1-Story cont'd from Warlord #62 3.00
2-35, Special #1 (11/85) 2.50

ARION THE IMMORTAL (Also see Showcase '95 #7)
DC Comics: July, 1992 - No. 6, Dec, 1992 ($1.50, limited series)

1 3.00
2-6: 4-Gustovich-a(i) 2.50

ARISTOCATS (See Movie Comics & Walt Disney Showcase No. 16)

ARISTOKITTENS, THE (...Meet Jiminy Cricket No. 1)(Disney)
Gold Key: Oct, 1971 - No. 9, Oct, 1975

1 3 6 9 20 30 40
2-5,7-9 3 6 9 14 19 24
6-(52 pgs.) 3 6 9 16 22 28

ARIZONA KID, THE (Also see The Comics & Wild Western)
Marvel/Atlas Comics(CSI): Mar, 1951 - No. 6, Jan, 1952

1 22 44 66 127 204 280
2-4: 2-Heath-a(3) 12 24 36 69 97 125
5,6 10 20 30 56 76 95

NOTE: ***Heath*** *a-1-3; c-1-3.* ***Maneely*** *c-4-6.* ***Morisi*** *a-4-6.* ***Sinnott*** *a-6.*

ARK, THE (See The Crusaders)

ARKAGA
Image Comics: Sept, 1997 ($2.95, one-shot)

1-Jorgensen-s/a 3.00

ARKANIUM
Dreamwave Productions: Sept, 2002 - No. 5 ($2.95)

1-5: 1-Gatefold wraparound-c 3.00

ARKHAM ASYLUM: LIVING HELL
DC Comics: July, 2003 - No. 6, Dec, 2003 ($2.50, limited series)

1-6-Ryan Sook-a; Batman app. 3-Batgirl-c/app. 2.50

ARMAGEDDON
Chaos! Comics: Oct, 1999 - No. 4, Jan, 2000 ($2.95, limited series)

Preview 5.00
1-4-Lady Death, Evil Ernie, Purgatori app. 3.00

ARMAGEDDON: ALIEN AGENDA
DC Comics: Nov, 1991 - No. 4, Feb, 1992 ($1.00, limited series)

1-4 2.50

ARMAGEDDON FACTOR, THE
AC Comics: 1987 - No. 2, 1987; No. 3, 1990 ($1.95)

1,2: Sentinels of Justice, Dragonfly, Femforce 2.50
3-($3.95, color)-Almost all AC characters app. 4.00

ARMAGEDDON: INFERNO
DC Comics: Apr, 1992 - No. 4, July, 1992 ($1.00, limited series)

1-4: Many DC heroes app. 3-A. Adams/Austin-a 2.50

ARMAGEDDON 2001
DC Comics: May, 1991 - No. 2, Oct, 1991 ($2.00, squarebound, 68 pgs.)

1-Features many DC heroes; intro Waverider 4.00
1-2nd & 3rd printings; 3rd has silver ink-c 2.50
2 3.00

ARMED & DANGEROUS
Acclaim Comics (Armada): Apr, 1996 - No.4, July, 1996 ($2.95, B&W)

1-4-Bob Hall-c/a & scripts 3.00
Special 1 (8/96, $2.95, B&W)-Hall-c/a & scripts. 3.00

Army and Navy Comics #4 © CN

Army@Love #12 © Rick Veitch

Arsenal #2 © DC

	GD	VG	FN	VF	VF/NM	NM-
	2.0	4.0	6.0	8.0	9.0	9.2

ARMED & DANGEROUS HELL'S SLAUGHTERHOUSE
Acclaim Comics (Armada): Oct, 1996 - No. 4, Jan, 1997 ($2.95, B&W)
1-4: Hall-c/a/scripts. 3.00

ARMOR (AND THE SILVER STREAK) (Revengers Featuring... in indicia for #1-3)
Continuity Comics: Sept, 1985 - No.13, Apr, 1992 ($2.00)
1-13: 1-Intro/origin Armor & the Silver Streak; Neal Adams-c/a. 7-Origin Armor; Nebres-i 3.50

ARMOR (DEATHWATCH 2000)
Continuity Comics: Apr, 1993 - No. 6, Nov, 1993 ($2.50)
1-6: 1-3-Deathwatch 2000 x-over 3.00

ARMORINES (See X-O Manowar #25 for 16 pg. bound-in Armorines #0)
Valiant: June, 1994 - No. 12, June, 1995 ($2.25)
0-Stand-alone edition with cardstock-c 25.00
0-Gold 15.00
1-12: 7-Wraparound-c. 12-Byrne-c/swipe (X-Men, 1st Series #138) 2.50

ARMORINES (Volume 2)
Acclaim Comics: Oct, 1999 - No. 4 ($3.95/$2.50, limited series)
1-($3.95) Calafiore & P. Palmiotti-a 4.00
2,3-($2.50) 2.50

ARMOR X
Image Comics: March, 2005 - No. 4, June, 2005 ($2.95, limited series)
1-Keith Champagne-s/Andy Smith-a; flip covers on #2-4 3.00

ARMY AND NAVY COMICS (Supersnipe No. 6 on)
Street & Smith Publications: May, 1941 - No. 5, July, 1942
1-Cap Fury & Nick Carter 53 106 159 329 550 770
2-Cap Fury & Nick Carter 31 62 93 181 291 400
3,4: 4-Jack Farr-c/a 23 46 69 133 214 295
5-Supersnipe app.; see Shadow V2#3 for 1st app.; Story of Douglas MacArthur; George Marcoux-c/a 53 106 159 332 556 780

ARMY @ LOVE
DC Comics (Vertigo): May, 2007 - No. 12, Apr, 2008; V2 #1, Oct, 2008 - Present ($2.99)
1-12-Rick Veitch-s/a(p); Gary Erskine-a(i) 3.00
(Vol. 2) 1-Veitch-s/a(p); Erskine-a(i) 3.00
...: The Hot Zone Club TPB (2007, $9.99) r/#1-5; intro. by Peter Kuper 10.00

ARMY ATTACK
Charlton Comics: July, 1964 - No. 4, Feb, 1965; V2#38, July, 1965 - No. 47, Feb, 1967
V1#1 4 8 12 28 44 60
2-4(2/65) 3 6 9 18 27 35
V2#38(7/65)-47 (formerly U.S. Air Force #1-37) 3 6 9 15 21 26
NOTE: *Glanzman a-1-3. Montes/Bache a-44.*

ARMY AT WAR (Also see Our Army at War & Cancelled Comic Cavalcade)
DC Comics: Oct-Nov, 1978
1-Kubert-c; all new story and art 2 4 6 9 13 16

ARMY OF DARKNESS (Movie)
Dark Horse Comics: Nov, 1992 - No. 2, Dec, 1992; No. 3, Oct, 1993 ($2.50, limited series)
1-3-Bolton painted-c/a 2 4 6 9 12 15
... Movie Adaptation TPB (2006, $14.99) r/#1-3; intro. by Busiek; Bruce Campbell interview 15.00

ARMY OF DARKNESS (Also see Marvel Zombies vs. Army of Darkness)
Dynamite Entertainment: 2005 - No. 13, 2007 ($2.99)
1-4 (Vs. Re-Animator):1,2-Four covers; Greene-a/Kuhoric-s. 3,4-Three covers 3.00
5-13: 5-7-Kuhoric-s/Sharpe-a; four covers. 8-11-Ash Vs. Dracula. 12,13-Death of Ash 3.00

ARMY OF DARKNESS: ...
Dynamite Entertainment: 2007 - Present ($3.50)
... From the Ashes 1-4-Kuhoric-s/Blanco-a; covers by Blanco & Suydam 3.50
... The Long Road Home 5-8-Two covers on each 3.50
... Home Sweet Hell 9-12 3.50

ARMY OF DARKNESS: ASHES 2 ASHES (Movie)
Devil's Due Publ.: July, 2004 - No. 4, 2004 ($2.99, limited series)
1-4-Four covers for each; Nick Bradshaw-a 3.00
1-Director's Cut (12/04, $4.99) r/#1, cover gallery, script and sketch pages 5.00
TPB (2005, $14.99) r/series; cover gallery; Bradshaw interview and sketch pages 15.00

ARMY OF DARKNESS: SHOP TILL YOU DROP DEAD (Movie)
Devil's Due Publ.: Jan, 2005 - No. 4, July, 2005 ($2.99, limited series)
1-4:1-Five covers; Bradshaw-a/Kuhoric-s. 2-4: Two covers. 3-Greene-a 3.00

ARMY OF DARKNESS / XENA
Dynamite Entertainment: 2008 - No. 4, 2008 ($3.50)
1-4-Layman-s/Montenegro-a; two covers on each 3.50

ARMY SURPLUS KOMIKZ FEATURING CUTEY BUNNY
Army Surplus Komikz/Eclipse Comics: 1982 - No. 5, 1985 ($1.50, B&W)
1-Cutey Bunny begins 2 4 6 8 10 12
2-5: 5-(Eclipse)-JLA/X-Men/Batman parody 4.50

ARMY WAR HEROES (Also see Iron Corporal)
Charlton Comics: Dec, 1963 - No. 38, June, 1970
1 5 10 15 32 51 70
2-10 3 6 9 18 27 35
11-21,23-30: 24-Intro. Archer & Corp. Jack series 3 6 9 14 20 25
22-Origin/1st app. Iron Corporal series by Glanzman 4 8 12 22 34 45
31-38 2 4 6 9 13 16
Modern Comics Reprint 36 ('78) 4.00
NOTE: *Montes/Bache a-1, 16, 17, 21, 23-25, 27-30.*

AROUND THE BLOCK WITH DUNC & LOO (See Dunc and Loo)

AROUND THE WORLD IN 80 DAYS (Movie) (See A Golden Picture Classic)
Dell Publishing Co.: Feb, 1957
Four Color 784-Photo-c 7 14 21 50 83 115

AROUND THE WORLD UNDER THE SEA (See Movie Classics)

AROUND THE WORLD WITH ARCHIE (See Archie Giant Series Mag. #29, 35, 141)

AROUND THE WORLD WITH HUCKLEBERRY & HIS FRIENDS (See Dell Giant No. 44)

ARRGH! (Satire)
Marvel Comics Group: Dec, 1974 - No. 5, Sept, 1975 (25¢)
1-Dracula story; Sekowsky-a(p) 3 6 9 16 23 30
2-5: 2-Frankenstein. 3-Mummy. 4-Nightstalker(TV); Dracula-c/app., Hunchback. 5-Invisible Man, Dracula 2 4 6 12 16 20
NOTE *Alcala a-2; c-3. Everett a-1r, 2r. Grandenetti a-4. Maneely a-4r. Sutton a-1-3.*

ARROW (See Protectors)
Malibu Comics: Oct, 1992 ($1.95, one-shot)
1-Moder-a(p) 2.50

ARROW, THE (See Funny Pages)
Centaur Publications: Oct, 1940 - No. 2, Nov, 1940; No. 3, Oct, 1941
1-The Arrow begins(r/Funny Pages) 300 600 900 2040 3570 5100
2,3: 2-Tippy Taylor serial continues from Amazing Mystery Funnies #24. 3-Origin Dash Dartwell, the Human Meteor; origin The Rainbow-r; bondage-c 135 270 405 851 1438 2025
NOTE: *Gustavson a-1, 2; c-3.*

ARROWHEAD (See Black Rider and Wild Western)
Atlas Comics (CPS): April, 1954 - No. 4, Nov, 1954
1-Arrowhead & his horse Eagle begin 15 30 45 88 137 185
2-4: 4-Forte-a 10 20 30 54 72 90
NOTE: *Heath c-3. Jack Katz a-3. Maneely c-2. Pakula a-2. Sinnott a-1-4; c-1.*

ARROWSMITH (Also see Astro City/Arrowsmith flip book)
DC Comics (Cliffhanger): Sept, 2003 - No. 6, May, 2004 ($2.95)
1-6-Pacheco-a/Busiek-s 3.00
...: So Smart in Their Fine Uniforms TPB (2004, $14.95) r/#1-6 15.00

ARSENAL (Teen Titans' Speedy)
DC Comics: Oct, 1998 - No. 4, Jan, 1999 ($2.50, limited series)
1-4: Grayson-s. 1-Black Canary app. 2-Green Arrow app. 2.50

ARSENAL SPECIAL (See New Titans, Showcase '94 #7 & Showcase '95 #8)
DC Comics: 1996 ($2.95, one-shot)
1 3.00

ARTBABE
Fantagraphics Books: May, 1996 - Apr, 1999 ($2.50/$2.95/$3.50, B&W)
V1 #5, V2 #1-3 3.00
#4-($3.50) 3.50

ARTEMIS: REQUIEM (Also see Wonder Woman, 2nd Series #90)
DC Comics: June, 1996 - No. 6, Nov, 1996 ($1.75, limited series)
1-6: Messner-Loebs scripts & Benes-c/a in all. 1,2-Wonder Woman app. 3.00

ART OF HOMAGE STUDIOS, THE
Image Comics: Dec, 1993 ($4.95, one-shot)
1-Short stories and pin-ups by Jim Lee, Silvestri, Williams, Portacio & Chiodo 5.00

ART OF ZEN INTERGALACTIC NINJA, THE

Ash: Cinder & Smoke #2 © Q&P

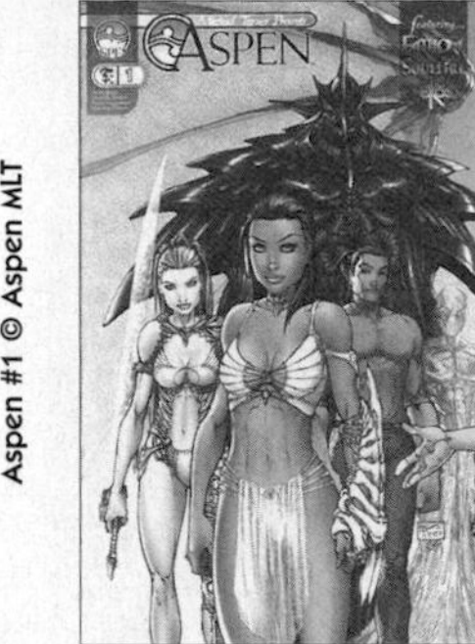

Aspen #1 © Aspen MLT

Astonishing #36 © MAR

GD VG FN VF VF/NM NM-
2.0 4.0 6.0 8.0 9.0 9.2

Entity Comics: 1994 - No. 2, 1994 ($2.95)
1,2 3.00

ARZACH (See Moebius...)
Dark Horse Comics: 1996 ($6.95, one-shot)
nn-Moebius-c/a/scripts 1 2 3 4 5 7

ASCENSION
Image Comics (Top Cow Productions): Oct, 1997 - No. 22, Mar, 2000 ($2.50)
Preview 5.00
Preview Gold Edition 8.00
Preview San Diego Edition 2 4 6 8 10 12
0 4.00
1/2 6.00
1-David Finch-s/a(p)/Batt-s/a(i) 4.00
1-Variant-c w/Image logo at lower right 6.00
2-6 3.00
7-22 2.50
Fan Club Edition 5.00

...COLLECTED EDITION
1998 - No. 2 ($4.95, squarebound) 1,2: 1-r/#1,2. 2-r/#3,4 5.00

ASH
Event Comics: Nov, 1994 - No. 6, Dec, 1995; No. 0, May, 1996 ($2.50/$3.00)
0-Present & Future (Both 5/96, $3.00, foil logo-c)-w/pin-ups 3.00
0-Blue Foil logo-c (Present and Future) (1000 each) 4.00
0-Silver Prism logo-c (Present and Future) (500 each) 10.00
0-Red Prism logo-c (Present and Future) (250 each) 20.00
0-Gold Hologram logo-c (Present and Future) (1000 each) 8.00
1-Quesada p/story; Palmiotti-i/story; Barry Windsor-Smith pin-up 2 4 6 8 10 12
2-Mignola Hellboy pin-up 1 2 3 4 5 7
3,4: 3-Big Guy pin-up by Geoff Darrow. 4-Jim Lee pin-up 4.00
4-Fahrenheit Gold 7.00
4-6-Fahrenheit Red (5,6-1000) 8.00
4-6-Fahrenheit White 12.00
5, 6-Double-c w/Hildebrandt Bros.-a, Quesada & Palmiotti. 6-Texeira-c 3.00
5,6-Fahrenheit Gold (2000) 4.00
6-Fahrenheit White (500)-Texeira-c 12.00
Volume 1 (1996, $14.95, TPB)-r/#1-5, intro by James Robinson 15.00
Wizard Mini-Comic (1996, magazine supplement) 2.25
Wizard #1/2 (1997, mail order) 4.00

ASH: CINDER & SMOKE
Event Comics: May, 1997 - No. 6, Oct, 1997 ($2.95, limited series)
1-6: Ramos-a/Waid, Augustyn-s in all. 2-6-variant covers by Ramos and Quesada 3.00

ASH: FILES
Event Comics: Mar, 1997 ($2.95, one-shot)
1-Comics w/text 3.00

ASH: FIRE AND CROSSFIRE
Event Comics: Jan, 1999 - No. 5 ($2.95, limited series)
1,2-Robinson-s/Quesada & Palmiotti-c/a 3.00

ASH: FIRE WITHIN, THE
Event Comics: Sept, 1996 - No. 2, Jan, 1997 ($2.95, unfinished limited series)
1,2: Quesada & Palmiotti-c/s/a 3.00

ASH/ 22 BRIDES
Event Comics: Dec, 1996 - No. 2, Apr, 1997 ($2.95, limited series)
1,2: Nicieza-s/Ramos-c/a 3.00

ASKANI'SON (See Adventures of Cyclops & Phoenix limited series)
Marvel Comics: Jan, 1996 - No. 4, May, 1996 ($2.95, limited series)
1-4: Story cont'd from Advs. of Cyclops & Phoenix; Lobdell/Loeb story; Gene Ha-c/a(p) 3.00
TPB (1997, $12.99) r/#1-4; Gene Ha painted-c 13.00

ASPEN (MICHAEL TURNER PRESENTS:...) (Also see Fathom)
Aspen MLT, Inc.: July, 2003 - No. 3, Aug, 2003 ($2.99)
1-Fathom story; Turner-a/Johns-s; interviews w/Turner & Johns; two covers by Turner 3.00
2,3:2-Fathom story; Turner-a/Johns-s; two covers by Turner; pin-ups and interviews 3.00
... Seasons: Fall 2005 (12/05, $2.99) short stories by various; Turner-c 3.00
... Seasons: Spring 2005 (4/05, $2.99) short stories by various; Turner-c 3.00
... Seasons: Summer 2006 (10/06, $2.99) short stories by various; Turner-c 3.00
... Showcase: Aspen Matthews 1 (7/08, $2.99) Caldwell-a 3.00
... Sketchbook 1 (2003, $2.99) sketch pages by Michael Turner and Talent Caldwell 3.00
... Splash: 2006 Swimsuit Spectacular 1 (3/06, $2.99) pin-up pages by various; Turner-c 3.00
... Splash: 2007 Swimsuit Spectacular 1 (8/07, $2.99) pin-up pages by various; Turner-c 3.00
... Splash: 2008 Swimsuit Spectacular 1 (7/08, $2.99) pin-up pages by various; Turner-c 3.00

ASPEN SHOWCASE
Aspen MLT: Oct, 2008 ($2.99)
...: Benoist 1 - Krul-s/Gunnell-a; two covers by Gunnell & Manapul 3.00

ASSASSINS
DC Comics (Amalgam): Apr, 1996 ($1.95)
1 2.50

ASTONISHING (Formerly Marvel Boy No. 1, 2)
Marvel/Atlas Comics(20CC): No. 3, Apr, 1951 - No. 63, Aug, 1957
3-Marvel Boy continues; 3-5-Marvel Boy-c 93 186 279 586 993 1400
4-6-Last Marvel Boy; 4-Stan Lee app. 66 132 198 416 701 985
7-10: 7-Maneely s/f story. 10-Sinnott s/f story 35 70 105 203 327 450
11,12,15,17,20 30 60 90 176 283 390
13,14,16,18,19-Krigstein-a. 18-Jack The Ripper sty 31 62 93 181 291 400
21,22,24 26 52 78 152 244 335
23-E.C. swipe "The Hole In The Wall" from Vault Of Horror #16 27 54 81 156 251 345
25,29: 25-Crandall-a. 29-Decapitation-c 24 48 72 140 225 310
26-28 22 44 66 129 207 285
30-Tentacled eyeball-c/story; classic-c 45 90 135 279 465 650
31-37-Last pre-code issue 20 40 60 115 183 250
38-43,46,48-52,56,58,59,61 15 30 45 90 140 190
44,45,47,53-55,57,60: 44-Crandall swipe/Weird Fantasy #22. 45,47-Krigstein-a. 53-Ditko-a. 54-Torres-a, 55-Crandall, Torres-a. 57-Williamson/Krenkel-a (4 pgs.). 60-Williamson/Mayo-a (4 pgs.) 16 32 48 96 151 205
62,63: 62-Torres, Powell-a. 63-Woodbridge-a 15 30 45 94 147 200
NOTE: ***Ayers** a-16. **Berg** a-36, 53, 56. **Cameron** a-50. **Gene Colan** a-12, 20, 29, 56. **Ditko** a-53. **Drucker** a-41, 62. **Everett** a-3-6(3), 6, 10, 12, 37, 47, 48, 58; c-3-5, 13,15, 16, 18, 29, 47, 49, 51, 53-55, 57, 59-63. **Fass** a-11, 34. **Forte** a-53, 58, 60. **Fuje** a-11. **Heath** a-8, 29; c-8, 9, 19, 22, 25, 26. **Kirby** a-56. **Lawrence** a-28, 37, 38, 42. **Maneely** a-7(2); c-7, 31, 33, 34, 56. **Moldoff** a-33. **Morisi** a-10, 60. **Morrow** a-52, 61. **Orlando** a-47, 58, 61. **Pakula** a-10. **Powell** a-43, 44, 48. **Ravielli** a-28. **Reinman** a-32, 34, 38. **Robinson** a-20. **J. Romita** a-7, 18, 24, 43, 57,61. **Roussos** a-55. **Sale** a-28, 38, 59; c-32. **Sekowsky** a-13. **Severin** c-46. **Shores** a-16, 60. **Sinnott** a-11, 30. **Whitney** a-13. **Ed Win** a-20. Canadian reprints exist.*

ASTONISHING TALES (See Ka-Zar)
Marvel Comics Group: Aug, 1970 - No. 36, July, 1976 (#1-7: 15¢; #8: 25¢)
1-Ka-Zar (by Kirby(p) #1,2; by B. Smith #3-6) & Dr. Doom (by Wood #1-4; by Tuska #5,6; by Colan #7,8; 1st Marvel villain solo series) double feature begins; Kraven the Hunter-c/story; Nixon cameo 6 12 18 41 66 90
2-Kraven the Hunter-c/story; Kirby, Wood-a 3 6 9 20 30 40
3-6: B. Smith-p; Wood-a-#3,4. 5,6-Red Skull 2-part story 4 8 12 22 34 45
7-Last 15¢ issue; Black Panther app. 3 6 9 15 21 26
8-(25¢, 52 pgs.)-Last Dr. Doom of series 3 6 9 20 30 40
9-All Ka-Zar issues begin; Lorna-r/Lorna #14 2 4 6 10 14 18
10-B. Smith/Sal Buscema-a. 3 6 9 14 19 24
11-Origin Ka-Zar & Zabu; death of Ka-Zar's father 2 4 6 11 16 20
12-2nd app.Man-Thing; by Neal Adams (see Savage Tales #1 for 1st app.) 4 8 12 24 37 50
13-3rd app.Man-Thing 3 6 9 18 27 35
14-20: 14-Jann of the Jungle-r (1950s); reprints censored Ka-Zar-s from Savage Tales #1. 17-S.H.I.E.L.D. begins. 19-Starlin-a(p). 20-Last Ka-Zar (continues into 1974 Ka-Zar series) 1 3 4 6 8 10
21-(12/73)-It! the Living Colossus begins, ends #24 (see Supernatural Thrillers #1) 3 6 9 20 30 40
22-24: 23,24-IT vs. Fin Fang Foom 3 6 9 16 23 30
25-1st app. Deathlok the Demolisher; full length stories begin, end #36; Perez's 1st work, 2 pgs. (8/74) 5 10 15 32 51 70
26-28,30 2 4 6 10 14 18
29-r/origin/1st app. Guardians of the Galaxy from Marvel Super-Heroes #18 plus-c w/4 pgs. omitted; no Deathlok story 1 3 4 6 8 10
31-34: 31-Watcher-r/Silver Surfer #3 2 4 6 8 11 14
35,36-(Regular 25¢ edition)(5,7/76) 2 4 6 8 11 14
35,36-(30¢-c, low distribution) 5 10 15 32 51 70
NOTE: ***Buckler** a-13i, 16p, 25, 26p, 27p, 28, 29p-36p; c-13, 25p, 26-30, 32-35p, 36. **John Buscema** a-9, 12p-14p, 16p; c-4-6p, 12p. **Colan** a-7p, 8p. **Ditko** a-21r. **Everett** a-6i. **G. Kane** a-11p, 15p; c-9, 10p, 11p, 14, 15p, 21p. **McWilliams** a-30i. **Starlin** a-19p; c-16p. **Sutton & Trimpe** a-8. **Tuska** a-5p, 6p, 8p. **Wood** a-1-4. **Wrightson** c-31i.*

ASTONISHING X-MEN
Marvel Comics: Mar, 1995 - No. 4, July, 1995 ($1.95, limited series)
1-Age of Apocalypse; Magneto-c 4.00
2-4 3.00

Astonishing X-Men #25 © MAR

Atari Force #4 © Atari

Atom and Hawkman #40 © DC

GD VG FN VF VF/NM NM-
2.0 4.0 6.0 8.0 9.0 9.2

ASTONISHING X-MEN
Marvel Comics: Sept, 1999 - No.3, Nov, 1999 ($2.50, limited series)
1-3-New team, Cable & X-Man app.; Peterson-a 2.50
TPB (11/00, $15.95) r/#1-3, X-Men #92 & #95, Uncanny X-Men #375 16.00

ASTONISHING X-MEN (See Giant-Size Astonishing X-Men for story folllowing #24)
Marvel Comics: July, 2004 - Present ($2.99)
1-Whedon-s/Cassaday-c/a; team of Cyclops, Beast, Wolverine, Emma Frost & Kitty Pryde 3.00
1-Director's Cut (2004, $3.99) different Cassaday partial sketch-c; cover gallery, sketch pages and script excerpt 4.00
1-Variant-c by Cassaday 10.00
1-Variant-c by Dell'Otto 5.00
2,3,5,6-X-Men battle Ord 3.00
4-Colossus returns 4.00
4-Variant Colossus cover by Cassaday 5.00
7-24: 7-Fantastic Four app. 9,10-X-Men vs. the Danger Room 3.00
7,9,10-12,19-24-Second printing variant covers 3.00
25,26: 25-Ellis-s/Bianchi-a begins; Bianchi wraparound-c 3.00
... Saga (2006, $3.99) reprints highlights from #1-12; sketch pages and cover gallery 4.00
... Sketchbook Special ('08, $2.99) Costume sketches & blueprints by Bianchi & Larroca 3.00
...Vol. 1 HC (2006, $29.99, dust jacket) r/#1-12; interviews, sketch pages and covers 30.00
...Vol. 1: Gifted (2004, $14.99) r/#1-6; variant cover gallery 15.00
...Vol. 2: Dangerous (2005, $14.99) r/#7-12; variant cover gallery 15.00
...Vol. 3: Torn (2007, $14.99) r/#13-18; variant & sketch cover gallery 15.00

ASTOUNDING SPACE THRILLS: THE COMIC BOOK
Image Comics: Apr, 2000 - No. 4, Dec, 2000 ($2.95, limited series)
1-4-Steve Conley-s/a. 2,3-Flip book w/Crater Kid 3.00
Galaxy-Sized Astounding Space Thrills 1 (10/01, $4.95) 5.00

ASTOUNDING WOLF-MAN
Image Comics: Jun, 2007 - Present ($2.99)
1-Free Comic Boy Day issue; Kirkman-s/Howard-a; origin story 3.00
2-8 3.00
Vol. 1 TPB (2008, $14.99) r/#1-7; sketch pages; Kirkman intro. 15.00

ASTRA
CPM Manga: 2001 - No. 8 ($2.95, B&W, limited series)
1-8: Created by Jerry Robinson; Tanaka-a. 1-Balent variant-c 3.00
TPB (2002, $15.95) r/#1-8; JH Williams III-c from #3 16.00

ASTRO BOY (TV) (See March of Comics #285 & The Original...)
Gold Key: August, 1965 (12¢)
1(10151-508)-Scarce;1st app. Astro Boy in comics 30 60 90 222 411 600

ASTRO CITY / ARROWSMITH (Flip book)
DC Comics (WildStorm Productions): Jun, 2004 ($2.95, one-shot flip book)
1-Intro. Black Badge; Ross-c; Arrowsmith a/c by Pacheco 3.00

ASTRO CITY (Also see Kurt Busiek's Astro City)
DC Comics (WildStorm Productions): Dec, 2004; Sept, 2006 (one-shots)
... A Visitor's Guide (12/04, $5.95) short story, city guide and pin-ups by various; Ross-c 6.00
...: Beautie (4/08, $3.99) Busiek-s/Anderson-a/Ross-c; origin 4.00
...: Samaritan (9/06, $3.99) Busiek-s/Anderson-a/Ross-c; origin of Infidel 4.00

ASTRO CITY: DARK AGE
DC Comics (WildStorm Productions): Aug, 2005 - No. 4, Dec, 2005 ($2.95, limited series)
1-4-Busiek-s/Anderson-a/Ross-c; Silver Agent and The Blue Knight app. 3.00
Book Two #1-4 (1/07-11/07, $2.99) Busiek-s/Anderson-a/Ross-c 3.00

ASTRO CITY: LOCAL HEROES
DC Comics (WildStorm Productions): Apr, 2003 - No. 5, Feb, 2004 ($2.95, limited series)
1-5-Busiek-s/Anderson-a/Ross-c 3.00
HC (2005, $24.95) r/series; Kurt Busiek's Astro City V2 #21,22; stories from Astro City/ Arrowsmith #1; and 9-11, The World's Finest... Vol. 2; Alex Ross sketch pages 25.00
SC (2005, $17.99) same contents as HC 18.00

ASYLUM
Millennium Publications: 1993 ($2.50)
1-3: 1-Bolton-c/a; Russell 2-pg. illos 2.50

ASYLUM
Maximum Press: Dec, 1995 - No. 11, Jan, 1997 ($2.95/$2.99, anthology)
(#1-6 are flip books)
1-11: 1-Warchild by Art Adams, Beanworld, Avengelyne, Battlestar Galactica. 2-Intro Mike Deodato's Deathkiss. 4-1st app.Christian; painted Battlestar Galactica story begins. 6-Intro Bionix (Six Million Dollar Man & the Bionic Woman). 7-Begin $2.99-c. 8-B&W-a. 9- Foot Soldiers & Kid Supreme. 10-Lady Supreme by Terry Moore-c/app. 4.00

GD VG FN VF VF/NM NM-
2.0 4.0 6.0 8.0 9.0 9.2

ATARI FORCE (Also see Promotional comics section)
DC Comics: Jan, 1984 - No. 20, Aug, 1985 (Mando paper)
1-(1/84)-Intro Tempest, Packrat, Babe, Morphea, & Dart 4.00
2-20 3.00
Special 1 (4/86) 3.00
NOTE: ***Byrne*** *c-Special 1i.* ***Giffen*** *a-12p, 13i.* ***Rogers*** *a-18p, Special 1p.*

A-TEAM, THE (TV) (Also see Marvel Graphic Novel)
Marvel Comics Group: Mar, 1984 - No. 3, May, 1984 (limited series)
1-3 5.00
1,2-(Whitman bagged set) w/75¢-c 2 4 6 8 10 12
3-(Whitman, no bag) w/75¢-c 1 2 3 5 6 8

ATHENA INC. THE MANHUNTER PROJECT
Image Comics: Dec, 2001; Apr, 2002 - No. 6 ($2.95/$4.95/$5.95)
...The Beginning (12/01, $5.95) Anacleto-c/a; Haberlin-s 6.00
1-5: 1-(4/02, $2.95) two covers by Anacleto 3.00
6-($4.95) 5.00
...: Agents Roster #1 (11/02, $5.95, 8 1/2 x 11") bios and sketch pages by Anacleto 6.00
Vol. 1 TPB (4/03, $19.95) r/#1-6 & Agents Roster; cover gallery 20.00

ATLANTIS CHRONICLES, THE (Also see Aquaman, 3rd Series & Aquaman: Time & Tide)
DC Comics: Mar, 1990 - No. 7, Sept, 1990 ($2.95, limited series, 52 pgs.)
1-7: 1-Peter David scripts. 7-True origin of Aquaman; nudity panels 3.25

ATLANTIS, THE LOST CONTINENT
Dell Publishing Co.: May, 1961
Four Color #1188-Movie, photo-c 10 20 30 68 119 170

ATLAS (See 1st Issue Special)

ATLAS
Dark Horse Comics: Feb, 1994 - No. 4, 1994 ($2.50, limited series)
1-4 2.50

ATMOSPHERICS
Avatar Press: June, 2002 ($5.95, B&W, one-shot graphic novel)
1-Warren Ellis-s/Ken Meyer Jr.-painted-a/c 6.00

ATOM, THE (See Action #425, All-American #19, Brave & the Bold, D.C. Special Series #1, Detective Comics, Flash Comics #80, Hawkman, Identity Crisis, JLA, Power Of The Atom, Showcase #34 -36, Super Friends, Sword of The Atom, Teen Titans & World's Finest)

ATOM, THE (...& the Hawkman No. 39 on)
National Periodical Publ.: June-July, 1962 - No. 38, Aug-Sept, 1968
1-(6-7/62)-Intro Plant-Master; 1st app. Maya 83 166 249 706 1353 2000
2 31 62 93 242 451 660
3-1st Time Pool story; 1st app. Chronos (origin) 21 42 63 155 288 420
4,5: 4-Snapper Carr x-over 16 32 48 116 216 315
6,9,10 13 26 39 90 160 230
7-Hawkman x-over (6-7/63; 1st Atom & Hawkman team-up); 1st app. Hawkman since Brave & the Bold tryouts 28 56 84 207 384 560
8-Justice League, Dr. Light app. 13 26 39 95 168 240
11-15: 13-Chronos-c/story 10 20 30 68 119 170
16-20: 19-Zatanna x-over 8 16 24 52 86 120
21-28,30: 26-Two-page pin-up. 28-Chronos-c/story 7 14 21 47 76 105
29-1st solo Golden Age Atom x-over in S.A. 14 28 42 100 178 255
31-35,37,38: 31-Hawkman x-over. 37-Intro. Major Mynah; Hawkman cameo 6 12 18 39 62 85
36-G.A. Atom x-over 7 14 21 47 76 105
NOTE: ***Anderson*** *a-1-11i, 13i; c-inks-1-25, 31-35, 37.* ***Sid Greene*** *a-8i-37i.* ***Gil Kane*** *a-1p-37p; c-1p-28p, 29, 33p, 34; c-26i.* ***George Roussos*** *a-38i.* ***Mike Sekowsky*** *a-38p. Time Pool stories also in 6, 9,12, 17, 21, 27, 35.*

ATOM, THE (See All New Atom and Tangent Comics/ The Atom)

ATOM AGE (See Classics Illustrated Special Issue)

ATOM-AGE COMBAT
St. John Publishing Co.: June, 1952 - No. 5, Apr, 1953; Feb, 1958
1-Buck Vinson in all 47 94 141 291 488 685
2-Flying saucer story 30 60 90 174 280 385
3,5: 3-Mayo-a (6 pgs.). 5-Flying saucer-c/story 26 52 78 152 244 335
4 (Scarce) 30 60 90 174 280 385
1(2/58-St. John) 22 44 66 127 204 280

ATOM-AGE COMBAT
Fago Magazines: No. 2, Jan, 1959 - No. 3, Mar, 1959
2-A-Bomb explosion-c; 27 54 81 158 254 350
3 21 42 63 123 197 270

ATOMAN

Atomic Comics #2 © Green Pub.

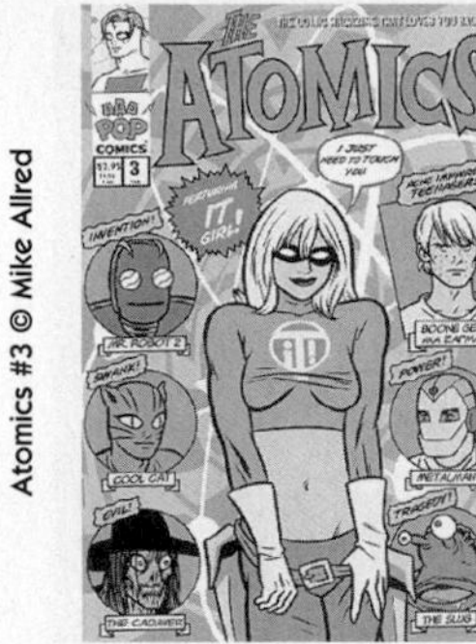

Atomics #3 © Mike Allred

Attack #4 © YM

GD VG FN VF VF/NM NM-
2.0 4.0 6.0 8.0 9.0 9.2

Spark Publications: Feb, 1946 - No. 2, April, 1946
1-Origin & 1st app. Atoman; Robinson/Meskin-a; Kidcrusaders, Wild Bill Hickok, Marvin the Great app. 66 132 198 416 701 985
2-Robinson/Meskin-a; Robinson c-1,2 41 82 123 250 413 575

ATOM & HAWKMAN, THE (Formerly The Atom)
National Periodical Publ: No. 39, Oct-Nov, 1968 - No. 45, Oct-Nov, 1969
39-43: 40-41-Kubert/Anderson-a. 43-(7/69)-Last 12¢ issue; 1st S.A. app. Gentleman Ghost 6 12 18 37 59 80
44,45: 44-(9/69)-1st 15¢-c; origin Gentleman Ghost 6 12 18 37 59 80
NOTE: M. Anderson a-39, 40i, 41i, 43, 44. Sid Greene a-40i-45i. Kubert a-40p; 41p; c-39-45.

ATOM ANT (TV) (See Golden Comics Digest #2) (Hanna-Barbera)
Gold Key: January, 1966 (12¢)
1(10170-601)-1st app. Atom Ant, Precious Pup, and Hillbilly Bears 19 38 57 139 257 375

ATOM ANT & SECRET SQUIRREL (See Hanna-Barbera Presents)

ATOMIC AGE
Marvel Comics (Epic Comics): Nov, 1990 - No. 4, Feb, 1991 ($4.50, limited series, squarebound, 52 pgs.)
1-4: Williamson-a(i); sci-fi story set in 1957 4.50

ATOMIC ATTACK (True War Stories; formerly Attack, first series)
Youthful Magazines: No. 5, Jan, 1953 - No. 8, Oct, 1953 (1st story is sci/fi in all issues)
5-Atomic bomb-c; science fiction stories in all 40 80 120 235 380 525
6-8 25 50 75 147 236 325

ATOMIC BOMB
Jay Burtis Publications: 1945 (36 pgs.)
1-Airmale & Stampy (scarce) 69 138 207 435 738 1040

ATOMIC BUNNY (Formerly Atomic Rabbit)
Charlton Comics: No. 12, Aug, 1958 - No. 19, Dec, 1959
12 12 24 36 69 97 125
13-19 8 16 24 42 54 65

ATOMIC COMICS
Daniels Publications (Canadian): Jan, 1946 (Reprints, one-shot)
1-Rocketman, Yankee Boy, Master Key app. 40 80 120 235 380 525

ATOMIC COMICS
Green Publishing Co.: Jan, 1946 - No. 4, July-Aug, 1946 (#1-4 were printed w/o cover gloss)
1-Radio Squad by Siegel & Shuster; Barry O'Neal app.; Fang Gow cover-r/ Detective Comics (Classic-c) 103 206 309 644 1072 1500
2-Inspector Dayton; Kid Kane by Matt Baker; Lucky Wings, Congo King, Prop Powers (only app.) begin 59 118 177 369 610 850
3,4: 3-Zero Ghost Detective app.; Baker-a(2) each; 4-Baker-c 41 82 123 252 406 560

ATOMIC KNIGHTS (See Strange Adventures #117)

ATOMIC MOUSE (TV, Movies) (See Blue Bird, Funny Animals, Giant Comics Edition & Wotalife Comics)
Capitol Stories/Charlton Comics: 3/53 - No. 54, 6/63; No. 1, 12/84; V2#10, 19/85 - No. 12, 1/86
1-Origin & 1st app.; Al Fago-c/a in most 33 66 99 192 309 425
2 15 30 45 84 127 170
3-10: 5-Timmy The Timid Ghost app.; see Zoo Funnies 10 20 30 58 79 100
11-13,16-25 8 16 24 40 50 60
14,15-Hoppy The Marvel Bunny app. 9 18 27 50 65 80
26-(68 pgs.) 12 24 36 67 94 120
27-40: 36,37-Atom The Cat app. 6 12 18 29 36 42
41-54 5 10 15 22 26 30
1 (1984)-Low print run; rep/#7-c w/diff. stories 2 4 6 8 10 12
V2#10 (9/85) -12(1/86)-Low print run 1 3 4 6 8 10

ATOMIC RABBIT (Atomic Bunny #12 on; see Giant Comics #3 & Wotalife)
Charlton Comics: Aug, 1955 - No. 11, Mar, 1958
1-Origin & 1st app.; Al Fago-c/a in all? 30 60 90 174 280 385
2 14 28 42 80 115 150
3-10 10 20 30 56 76 95
11-(68 pgs.) 14 28 42 80 115 150

ATOMICS, THE
AAA Pop Comics: Jan, 2000 - No. 15, Nov, 2001 ($2.95)
1-11-Mike Allred-s/a; 1-Madman-c/app. 3.00
12-15-($3.50): 13-15-Savage Dragon-c/app. 15-Afterword by Alex Ross; colored reprint of 1st Frank Einstein story 3.50
...King-Size Giant Spectacular: Jigsaw (2000, $10.00) r/#1-4 10.00
...King-Size Giant Spectacular: Lessons in Light, Lava, & Lasers (2000, $8.95) r/#5-8 9.00
...King-Size Giant Spectacular: Running With the Dragon ('02, $8.95) r/#13-15 and r/1st Frank Einstein app. in color 9.00
...King-Size Giant Spectacular: Worlds Within Worlds ('01, $8.95) r/#9-12 9.00
Madman and the Atomics, Vol. 1 TPB (2007, $24.99) r/#1-15, cover gallery, pin-ups, afterword by Alex Ross 25.00
...: Spaced Out & Grounded in Snap City TPB (10/03, $12.95) r/one-shots - It Girl, Mr. Gum, Spaceman and Crash Metro & the Star Squad; sketch pages 13.00

ATOMIC SPY CASES
Avon Periodicals: Mar-Apr, 1950 (Painted-c)
1-No Wood-a; A-bomb blast panels; Fass-a 35 70 105 203 327 450

ATOMIC THUNDERBOLT, THE
Regor Company: Feb, 1946 (one-shot) (scarce)
1-Intro. Atomic Thunderbolt & Mr. Murdo 63 126 189 397 669 940

ATOMIC TOYBOX
Image Comics: Dec, 1999 ($2.95)
1- Aaron Lopresti-c/s/a 3.00

ATOMIC WAR!
Ace Periodicals (Junior Books): Nov, 1952 - No. 4, Apr, 1953
1-Atomic bomb-c 103 206 309 649 1100 1550
2,3: 3-Atomic bomb-c 60 120 180 378 639 900
4-Used in **POP**, pg. 96 & illo. 60 120 180 378 639 900

ATOMIKA
Speakeasy Comics/Mercury Comics: Mar, 2005 - No. 6 ($2.99)
1-6: 1-Alex Ross-c/Sal Abbinanti-a/Dabb-s. 3-Fabry-c. 4-Four covers; Romita back-c 3.00
... God is Red TPB (5/06, $19.99) r/#1-6; cover gallery; Dabb foreword 20.00

ATOMIK ANGELS
Crusade Comics: May, 1996 - No. 4, Nov. 1996 ($2.50)
1-4: 1-Freefall from Gen 13 app. 3.00
1-Variant-c 4.00
Intrep-Edition (2/96, B&W, giveaway at launch party)-Previews Atomik Angels #1; includes Billy Tucci interview. 4.00

ATOM SPECIAL (See Atom & Justice League of America)
DC Comics: 1993/1995 ($2.50/$2.95)(68pgs.)
1,2: 1-Dillon-c/a. 2-McDonnell-a/Bolland-c/Peyer-s 3.00

ATOM THE CAT (Formerly Tom Cat; see Giant Comics #3)
Charlton Comics: No. 9, Oct, 1957 - No. 17, Aug, 1959
9 10 20 30 54 72 90
10,13-17 7 14 21 35 43 50
11,12: 11(64 pgs)-Atomic Mouse app. 12(100 pgs.) 11 22 33 62 86 110

ATTACK
Youthful Mag./Trojan No. 5 on: May, 1952 - No. 4, Nov, 1952; No. 5, Jan, 1953 - No. 5, Sept, 1953
1-(1st series)-Extreme violence 32 64 96 190 305 420
2,3-Both Harrison-c/a; bondage, whipping 18 36 54 103 162 220
4-Krenkel-a (7 pgs.); Harrison-a (becomes Atomic Attack #5 on) 18 36 54 103 162 220
5-(#1, Trojan, 2nd series) 14 28 42 81 118 155
6-8 (#2-4), 5 11 22 33 60 83 105

ATTACK
Charlton Comics: No. 54, 1958 - No. 60, Nov, 1959
54 (25¢, 100 pgs.) 12 24 36 69 97 125
55-60 7 14 21 35 43 50

ATTACK!
Charlton Comics: 1962 - No. 15, 3/75; No. 16, 8/79 - No. 48, 10/84
nn(#1)-('62) Special Edition 5 10 15 32 51 70
2('63), 3(Fall, '64) 3 6 9 20 30 40
V4#3(10/66), 4(10/67)-(Formerly Special War Series #2; becomes Attack At Sea V4#5) 3 6 9 16 23 30
1(9/71) 3 6 9 16 22 28
2-5: 4-American Eagle app. 2 4 6 9 12 15
6-15(3/75): 1 3 4 6 8 10
16(8/79) - 40 5.00
41-47 Low print run 7.00
48(10/84)-Wood-r; S&K-c (low print) 1 3 4 6 8 10

Authentic Police Cases #2 © STJ

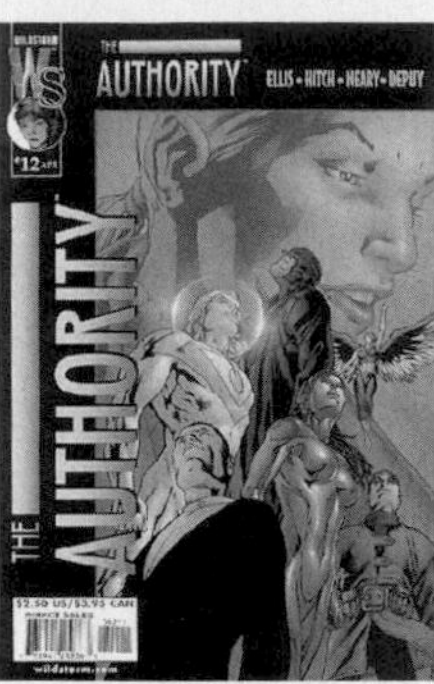

The Authority #12 © WSP

Avengelyne V2 #3 © Rob Liefeld

GD VG FN VF VF/NM NM-
2.0 4.0 6.0 8.0 9.0 9.2

Modern Comics 13('78)-r 4.00
NOTE: *Sutton a-9,10,13.*

ATTACK!
Spire Christian Comics (Fleming H. Revell Co.): 1975 (39¢/49¢, 36 pgs.)
nn 2 4 6 8 11 14

ATTACK AT SEA (Formerly Attack!, 1967)
Charlton Comics: V4#5, Oct, 1968 (one-shot)
V4#5 3 6 9 16 23 30

ATTACK ON PLANET MARS (See Strange Worlds #18)
Avon Periodicals: 1951
nn-Infantino, Fawcette, Kubert & Wood-a; adaptation of Tarrano the Conqueror by Ray Cummings 80 160 240 504 852 1200

ATTITUDE LAD
Slave Labor Graphics: Apr, 1994 - No. 3, Nov, 1994 ($2.95, B&W)
1-3 3.00

AUDREY & MELVIN (Formerly Little...)(See Little Audrey & Melvin)
Harvey Publications: No. 62, Sept, 1974
62 2 4 6 8 11 14

AUGIE DOGGIE (TV) (See Hanna-Barbera Band Wagon, Quick-Draw McGraw, Spotlight #2, Top Cat & Whitman Comic Books)
Gold Key: October, 1963 (12¢)
1-Hanna-Barbera character 17 34 51 120 223 325

AUTHENTIC POLICE CASES
St. John Publishing Co.: 2/48 - No. 6, 11/48; No. 7, 5/50 - No. 38, 3/55
1-Hale the Magician by Tuska begins 44 88 132 273 457 640
2-Lady Satan, Johnny Rebel app. 28 56 84 162 261 360
3-Veiled Avenger app.; blood drainage story plus 2 Lucky Coyne stories; used in **SOTI**, illo. from Red Seal #16 47 94 141 291 486 680
4,5: 4-Masked Black Jack app. 5-Late 1930s Jack Cole-a(r); transvestism story 28 56 84 162 261 360
6-Matt Baker-c; used in **SOTI**, illo- "An invitation to learning", r-in Fugitives From Justice #3; Jack Cole-a; also used by the N.Y. Legis. Comm. 50 100 150 310 518 725
7,8,10-14: 7-Jack Cole-a; Matt Baker-a begins #8, ends #?; Vic Flint in #10-14. 10-12-Baker-a(2 each) 27 54 81 158 254 350
9-No Vic Flint 22 44 66 127 204 280
15-Drug-c/story; Vic Flint app.; Baker-c 28 56 84 162 261 360
16,18,20,21,23: Baker-a(i) 17 34 51 100 158 215
17,19,22-Baker-c 20 40 60 120 193 265
24-28 (All 100 pgs.): 26-Transvestism 37 74 111 215 345 475
29,31,32-Baker-c 15 30 45 85 130 175
30 14 28 42 80 115 150
33-38: 33-Baker-c. 34-Baker-c; r/#9. 35-Baker-c/a(2); r/#10. 36-r/#11; Vic Flint strip-r; Baker-c/a(2) unsigned. 37-Baker-c; r/#17. 38- Baker-c/a; r/#18 16 32 48 96 151 205
NOTE: *Matt Baker c-6-16, 17, 19, 22, 27, 29, 31-38; a-13, 16. Bondage c-1, 3.*

AUTHORITY, THE (See Stormwatch and Jenny Sparks: The Secret History of...)
DC Comics (WildStorm): May, 1999 - No. 29, Jul, 2002 ($2.50)
1-Wraparound-c; Warren Ellis-s/Bryan Hitch and Paul Neary-a 2 4 6 8 11 14
2-4 1 3 4 6 8 10
5-12: 12-Death of Jenny Sparks; last Ellis-s 1 2 3 5 6 8
13-Mark Millar-s/Frank Quitely-c/a begins 2 4 6 8 10 12
14-16-Authority vs. Marvel-esque villains 1 2 3 4 5 7
17-22: 17,18-Weston-a. 19,20,22-Quitely-a. 21-McCrea-a 5.00
23-29: 23-26-Peyer-s/Nguyen-a; new Authority. 24-Preview of "The Establishment." 25,26-Jenny Sparks app. 27,28-Millar-s/Adams-a/c 4.00
Annual 2000 ($3.50) Devil's Night x-over; Hamner-a/Bermejo-c 1 2 3 4 5 7
Absolute Authority Slipcased Hardcover (2002, $49.95) oversized r/#1-12 plus script pages by Ellis and sketch pages by Hitch 50.00
...: Earth Inferno and Other Stories TPB (2002, $14.95) r/#17-20, Annual 2000, and Wildstorm Summer Special; new Quitely-c 15.00
...: Human on the Inside HC (2004, $24.95, dust jacket) Ridley-s/Oliver-a/c 25.00
...: Human on the Inside SC (2004, $17.99) Ridley-s/Oliver-a/c 18.00
...: Kev (10/02, $4.95) Ennis-s/Fabry-c/a 5.00
...: Relentless TPB (2000, $17.95) r/#1-8 18.00
...: Scorched Earth (2/03, $4.95) Robbie Morrison-s/Frazer Irving-a/Ashley Wood-c 5.00
...: Transfer of Power TPB (2002, $17.95) r/#22-29 18.00
...: Under New Management TPB (2000, $17.95) r/#9-16; new Quitely-c 18.00

AUTHORITY, THE (See previews in Sleeper, Stormwatch: Team Achilles and Wildcats Version 3.0)
DC Comics (WildStorm): Jul, 2003 - No. 14, Oct, 2004 ($2.95)
1-14: 1-Robbie Morrison-s/Dwayne Turner-a. 5-Huat-a. 14-Portacio-a 3.00
#0 (10/03, $2.95) r/preview back-up-s listed above; Turner sketch pages 3.00
...: Fractured Worlds TPB (2005, $17.95) r/#6-14; cover gallery 18.00
...: Harsh Realities TPB (2004, $14.95) r/#0-5; cover gallery 15.00
.../Lobo: Jingle Hell (2/04, $4.95) Bisley-c/a; Giffen & Grant-s 5.00
.../Lobo: Spring Break Massacre (8/05, $4.99) Bisley-c/a; Giffen & Grant-s 5.00

AUTHORITY, THE
DC Comics (WildStorm): Dec, 2006 - No. 2, May 2007 ($2.99, unfinished series)
1,2-Grant Morrison-s/Gene Ha-a/c 3.00
1-Variant cover by Art Adams 5.00

AUTHORITY, THE (Volume 5) (World's End on cover)
DC Comics (WildStorm): Oct, 2008 - Present ($2.99)
1-Simon Coleby-a/c; Lynch back-up story w/Hairsine-a/Gage-s 3.00

AUTHORITY, THE: MORE KEV
DC Comics (WildStorm): Jul, 2004 - No. 4, Dec, 2004 ($2.95, limited series)
1-4-Garth Ennis-s/Glenn Fabry-c/a 3.00
...: Kev TPB (2005, $14.99) r/Authority: Kev one-shot and Authority: More Kev series 15.00

AUTHORITY, THE: PRIME
DC Comics (WildStorm): Dec, 2007 - No. 6, May, 2008 ($2.99, limited series)
1-6-Gage-s/Robertson-c/a; Bendix app. 3.00

AUTHORITY, THE: REVOLUTION
DC Comics (WildStorm): Dec, 2004 - No. 12, Dec, 2005 ($2.95/$2.99)
1-12-Brubaker-s/Nguyen-a. 5-Henry Bendix returns. 7-Jenny Sparks app. 3.00
...: Book One TPB (2005, $14.99) r/#1-6; cover gallery and Nguyen sketch pages 15.00
...: Book Two TPB (2006, $14.99) r/#7-12; cover gallery and Nguyen sketch pages 15.00

AUTHORITY, THE: THE MAGNIFICENT KEV
DC Comics (WildStorm): Nov, 2005 - No. 5, Feb, 2006 ($2.99, limited series)
1-5-Garth Ennis-s/Carlos Ezquerra-a/Glenn Fabry-c 3.00
TPB (2006, $14.99) r/#1-5 15.00

AUTOMATIC KAFKA
DC Comics (WildStorm): Sept, 2002 - No. 9, Jul, 2003 ($2.95)
1-9-Ashley Wood-c/a; Joe Casey-s 3.00

AUTOMATON
Image Comics (Flypaper Press): Sept, 1998 - No. 3, 1998 ($2.95, lim. series)
1-3-R.A. Jones-s/Peter Vale-a 3.00

AUTUMN
Caliber Comics: 1995 - No. 3, 1995 ($2.95, B&W)
1-3 3.00

AUTUMN ADVENTURES (Walt Disney's...)
Disney Comics: Autumn, 1990; No. 2, Autumn, 1991 ($2.95, 68 pgs.)
1-Donald Duck-r(2) by Barks, Pluto-r, & new-a 4.00
2-D. Duck-r by Barks; new Super Goof story 4.00

AVATAARS: COVENANT OF THE SHIELD
Marvel Comics: Sept, 2000 - No. 3, Nov, 2000 ($2.99, limited series)
1-3-Kaminski-s/Oscar Jimenez-a 3.00

AVATAR
DC Comics: Feb, 1991 - No. 3, Apr, 1991 ($5.95, limited series, 100 pgs.)
1-3: Based on TSR's Forgotten Realms 6.00

AVENGELYNE
Maximum Press: May, 1995 - No. 3, July, 1995 ($2.50/$3.50, limited series)
1/2 2 4 6 8 10 12
1/2 Platinum 15.00
1-Newstand ($2.50)-Photo-c; poster insert 6.00
1-Direct Market ($3.50)-Chromium-c; poster 1 2 3 4 5 7
1-Glossy edition 2 4 6 12 16 20
1-Gold 12.00
2-3: 2-Polybagged w/card 3.00
3-Variant-c; Deodato pin-up 5.00
...Bible (10/96, $3.50) 4.00
.../Glory (9/95, $3.95) 2 covers 4.00
.../Glory Swimsuit Special (6/96, $2.95) photo and illos. covers 3.00
.../Glory: The Godyssey (9/96, $2.99) 2 covers (1 photo) 3.00
...Revelation One (Avatar, 1/01, $3.50) 3 covers by Haley, Rio, Shaw; Shaw-a 3.50

The Avengers #1 © GK

The Avengers #7 © MAR

The Avengers #183 © MAR

	GD 2.0	VG 4.0	FN 6.0	VF 8.0	VF/NM 9.0	NM- 9.2
.../Shi (Avatar, 11/01, $3.50) Eight covers; Waller-a						3.50
...Swimsuit (8/95, $2.95)-Pin-ups/photos. 3-Variant-c exist (2 photo, 1 Liefeld-a)						4.00
...Swimsuit (1/96, $3.50, 2nd printing)-photo-c						4.00
Trade paperback (12/95, $9.95)						10.00
.../Warrior Nun Areala 1 (11/96, $2.99) also see Warrior Nun/Avengelyne						3.00

AVENGELYNE
Maximum Press: V2#1, Apr, 1996 - No. 14, Apr, 1997 ($2.95/$2.50)

	GD	VG	FN	VF	VF/NM	NM-
V2#1-Four covers exist (2 photo-c).						4.00
V2#2-Three covers exist (1 photo-c); flip book w/Darkchylde						5.00
V2#0, 3-14: 0-(10/96).3-Flip book w/Priest preview. 5-Flip book w/Blindside						3.00

AVENGELYNE (Volume 3)
Awesome Comics: Mar, 1999 ($2.50)

	GD	VG	FN	VF	VF/NM	NM-
1-Fraga & Liefeld-a						3.00

AVENGELYNE: ARMAGEDDON
Maximum Press: Dec, 1996 - No. 3, Feb, 1997 ($2.99, limited series)

	GD	VG	FN	VF	VF/NM	NM-
1-3-Scott Clark-a(p)						3.00

AVENGELYNE: DEADLY SINS
Maximum Press: Feb, 1996 - No. 2, Mar, 1996 ($2.95, limited series)

	GD	VG	FN	VF	VF/NM	NM-
1,2: 1-Two-c exist (1 photo, 1 Liefeld-a). 2-Liefeld-c; Pop Mhan-a(p)						3.00

AVENGELYNE/POWER
Maximum Press: Nov, 1995 - No.3, Jan, 1996 ($2.95, limited series)

	GD	VG	FN	VF	VF/NM	NM-
1-3: 1,2-Liefeld-c. 3-Three variant-c. exist (1 photo-c)						3.00

AVENGELYNE • PROPHET
Maximum Press: May, 1996; No. 2, Feb. 1997 ($2.95, unfinished lim. series)

	GD	VG	FN	VF	VF/NM	NM-
1,2-Liefeld-c/a(p)						3.00

AVENGER, THE (See A-1 Comics)
Magazine Enterprises: Feb-Mar, 1955 - No. 4, Aug-Sept, 1955

	GD	VG	FN	VF	VF/NM	NM-
1(A-1 #129)-Origin	40	80	120	235	380	525
2(A-1 #131), 3(A-1 #133) Robot-c, 4(A-1 #130)	27	54	81	156	251	345
IW Reprint #9('64)-Reprints #1 (new cover)	4	8	12	20	29	38

NOTE: *Powell a-2-4; c-1-4.*

AVENGERS, THE (TV)(Also see Steed and Mrs. Peel)
Gold Key: Nov, 1968 ("John Steed & Emma Peel" cover title) (15¢)

	GD	VG	FN	VF	VF/NM	NM-
1-Photo-c	15	30	45	111	206	300
1-(Variant with photo back-c)	20	40	60	148	274	400

AVENGERS, THE (See Essential..., Giant-Size..., JLA/..., Kree/Skrull War Starring..., Marvel Graphic Novel #27, Marvel Super Action, Marvel Super Heroes('66), Marvel Treasury Ed., Marvel Triple Action, New Avengers, Solo Avengers, Tales Of Suspense #49, West Coast Avengers & X-Men Vs....)

AVENGERS, THE (The Mighty Avengers on cover only #63-69)
Marvel Comics Group: Sept, 1963 - No. 402, Sept, 1996

	GD	VG	FN	VF	VF/NM	NM-
1-Origin & 1st app. The Avengers (Thor, Iron Man, Hulk, Ant-Man, Wasp); Loki app.	354	708	1062	3186	6193	9200
2-Hulk leaves Avengers	75	150	225	638	1219	1800
3-2nd Sub-Mariner x-over outside the F.F. (see Strange Tales #107 for 1st); Sub-Mariner & Hulk team-up & battle Avengers; Spider-Man cameo (1/64)	50	100	150	425	813	1200
4-Revival of Captain America who joins the Avengers; 1st Silver Age app. of Captain America & Bucky (3/64)	131	262	393	1114	2132	3150
4-Reprint from the Golden Record Comic set	11	22	33	79	140	200
With Record (1966)	15	30	45	111	206	300
5-Hulk app.	39	78	117	300	563	825
6,8: 6-Intro/1st app. original Zemo & his Masters of Evil. 8-Intro Kang	29	58	87	213	394	575
7-Rick Jones app. in Bucky costume	32	64	96	246	461	675
9-Intro Wonder Man who dies in same story	38	76	114	293	547	800
10-Intro/1st app. Immortus; early Hercules app. (11/64)	25	50	75	185	343	500
11-Spider-Man-c & x-over (12/64)	31	62	93	239	445	650
12-15: 15-Death of original Zemo	17	34	51	120	223	325
16-New Avengers line-up (Hawkeye, Quicksilver, Scarlet Witch join; Thor, Iron Man, Giant-Man, Wasp leave)	20	40	60	148	274	400
17,18	12	24	36	87	156	225
19-1st app. Swordsman; origin Hawkeye (8/65)	14	28	42	99	175	250
20-22: Wood inks	9	18	27	63	107	150
23-30: 23-Romita Sr. inks (1st Silver Age Marvel work). 25-Dr. Doom-c/story. 28-Giant-Man becomes Goliath (5/66)	8	16	24	54	90	125
31-40	7	14	21	45	73	100
41-46,49-52,54-56: 43-1st app. Red Guardian (dies in #44) . 46-Ant-Man returns (re-intro, 11/67). 52-Black Panther joins; 1st app. The Grim Reaper. 54-1st app. new Masters of Evil. 56-Zemo app; story explains how Capt. America became imprisoned in ice during WWII, only to be rescued in Avengers #4	6	12	18	39	62	85
47-Magneto-c/story	6	12	18	41	66	90
48-Origin/1st app. new Black Knight (1/68)	6	12	18	41	66	90
53-X-Men app.	8	16	24	56	93	130
57-1st app. S.A. Vision (10/68)	14	28	42	104	187	270
58-Origin The Vision	8	16	24	58	97	135
59-65: 59-Intro. Yellowjacket. 60-Wasp & Yellowjacket wed. 63-Goliath becomes Yellowjacket; Hawkeye becomes the new Goliath. 65-Last 12¢ issue	5	10	15	32	51	70
66,67-B. Smith-a	5	10	15	34	55	75
68-70: 69-Nighthawk cameo. 70-1st full app. Nighthawk	5	10	15	30	48	65
71-1st app. The Invaders (12/69); Black Knight joins	7	14	21	49	80	110
72-79,81,82,84-86,89-91: 82-Daredevil app	4	8	12	26	44	60
80-Intro. Red Wolf (9/70)	5	10	15	30	48	65
83-Intro. The Liberators (Wasp, Valkyrie, Scarlet Witch, Medusa & the Black Widow)	5	10	15	32	51	70
87-Origin The Black Panther	5	10	15	32	51	70
88-Written by Harlan Ellison	5	10	15	30	48	65
88-2nd printing (1994)	2	4	6	8	10	12
92-Last 15¢ issue; Neal Adams-c	5	10	15	34	55	75
93-(52 pgs.)-Neal Adams-c/a	12	24	36	87	156	225
94-96-Neal Adams-c/a	7	14	21	47	76	105
97-G.A. Capt. America, Sub-Mariner, Human Torch, Patriot, Vision, Blazing Skull, Fin, Angel, & new Capt. Marvel x-over	5	10	15	32	51	70
98,99: 98-Goliath becomes Hawkeye; Smith c/a(i). 99-Smith-c, Smith/Sutton-a	4	8	12	26	41	55
100-(6/72)-Smith-c/a; featuring everyone who was an Avenger	9	18	27	60	100	140
101-Harlan Ellison scripts	3	6	9	21	32	42
102-106,108,109	3	6	9	19	29	38
107-Starlin-a(p)	3	6	9	21	32	42
110,111-X-Men app.	5	10	15	32	51	70
112-1st app. Mantis	4	8	12	26	41	55
113-115,119-124,126-130: 123-Origin Mantis	3	6	9	16	23	30
116-118-Defenders/Silver Surfer app.	4	8	12	28	44	60
125-Thanos-c & brief app.	3	6	9	19	29	38
131-133,136-140: 136-Ploog-r/Amazing Advs. #12	2	4	6	11	16	20
134,135-Origin of the Vision revised (also see Avengers Forever mini-series)	3	6	9	18	27	35
141-143,145,152-163	2	4	6	8	10	12
144-Origin & 1st app. Hellcat	2	4	6	13	18	22
146-149-(Reg.25¢ editions)(4-7/76)	2	4	6	8	10	12
146-149-(30¢-c variants, limited distribution)	4	8	12	26	41	45
150-Kirby-a(r); new line-up: Capt. America, Scarlet Witch, Iron Man, Wasp, Yellowjacket, Vision & The Beast	2	4	6	9	12	15
150-(30¢-c variant, limited distribution)	4	8	12	26	41	55
151-Wonder Man returns w/new costume	2	4	6	8	11	14
160-164-(35¢-c variants, limited dist.)(6-10/77)	7	14	21	47	76	105
164-166: Byrne-a	2	4	6	8	11	14
167-180: 168-Guardians of the Galaxy app. 174-Thanos cameo. 176-Starhawk app.	1	2	3	4	5	7
181-191-Byrne-a: 181-New line-up: Capt. America, Scarlet Witch, Iron Man, Wasp, Vision, Beast & The Falcon. 183-Ms. Marvel joins. 185-Origin Quicksilver & Scarlet Witch	1	3	4	6	8	10
192-194,197-199						6.00
195,196: 195-1st Taskmaster cameo. 196-1st Taskmaster full app.	1	3	4	6	8	10
200-(10/80, 52 pgs.)-Ms. Marvel leaves.	1	3	4	6	8	10
201-213,217-238: 211-New line-up: Capt. America, Iron Man, Tigra, Thor, Wasp & Yellowjacket. 213-Yellowjacket leaves. 217-Yellowjacket & Wasp return. 221-Hawkeye & She-Hulk join. 227-Capt. Marvel (female) joins; origins of Ant-Man, Wasp, Giant-Man, Goliath, Yellowjacket, & Avengers. 230-Yellowjacket quits. 231-Iron Man leaves. 232-Starfox (Eros) joins. 234-Origin Quicksilver, Scarlet Witch. 238-Origin Blackout						4.50
214-Ghost Rider-c/story						6.00
215,216,239,240,250: 215,216-Silver Surfer app. 216-Tigra leaves. 239-(1/84) Avengers app. on David Letterman show. 240-Spider-Woman revived. 250-($1.00, 52 pgs.)						4.00
241-249, 251-262						3.50
263-1st app. X-Factor (1/86)(story continues in Fant. Four #286)						6.00
264-299: 272-Alpha Flight app. 291-$1.00 issues begin. 297-Black Knight, She-Hulk & Thor resign. 298-Inferno tie-in						3.00
300 (2/89, $1.75, 68 pgs.)-Thor joins; Simonson-a						4.00

The Avengers #374 © MAR

The Avengers V3 #39 © MAR

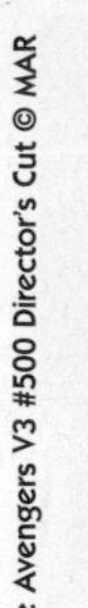
The Avengers V3 #500 Director's Cut © MAR

GD 2.0 | VG 4.0 | FN 6.0 | VF 8.0 | VF/NM 9.0 | NM- 9.2

301-304,306-313,319-325,327,329-343: 302-Re-intro Quasar. 320-324-Alpha Flight app. (320-cameo). 327-2nd app. Rage. 341,342-New Warriors app. 343-Last $1.00-c 3.00
305,314-318: 305-Byrne scripts begin. 314-318-Spider-Man x-over 3.50
326-1st app. Rage (11/90) 4.00
328,344-349,351-359,361,362,364,365,367: 328-Origin Rage. 365-Contains coupon for Hunt for Magneto contest 3.00
350-($2.50, 68 pgs.)-Double gatefold-c showing-c to #1; r/#53 w/cover in flip book format; vs. The Starjammers 3.50
360-($2.95, 52 pgs.)-Embossed all-foil-c; 30th ann. 4.00
363-($2.95, 52 pgs.)-All silver foil-c 4.00
366-($3.95, 68 pgs.)-Embossed all gold foil-c 4.00
368,370-374,376-399: 368-Bloodties part 1; Avengers/X-Men x-over. 374-bound-in trading card sheet. 380-Deodato-a. 390,391-"The Crossing." 395-Death of "old" Tony Stark; wraparound-c. 3.00
369-($2.95)-Foil embossed-c; Bloodties part 5 4.00
375-($2.00, 52 pgs.)-Regular ed.; Thunderstrike returns; leads into Malibu Comics' Black September. 3.00
375-($2.50, 52 pgs.)-Collector's ed. w/bound-in poster; leads into Malibu Comics' Black September. 3.50
400-402: Waid-s; 402-Deodato breakdowns; cont'd in X-Men #56 & Onslaught: Marvel Universe. 4.00
#500-503 (See Avengers Vol. 3; series resumed original numbering after Vol. 3 #84)
Special 1 (9/67, 25¢, 68 pgs.)-New-a; original & new Avengers team-up 10 20 30 71 126 180
Special 2 (9/68, 25¢, 68 pgs.)-New-a; original vs. new Avengers 6 12 18 43 69 95
Special 3 (9/69, 25¢, 68 pgs.)-r/Avengers #4 plus 3 Capt. America stories by Kirby (art); origin Red Skull 4 8 12 26 41 55
Special 4 (1/71, 25¢, 68 pgs.)-Kirby-r/Avengers #5,6 3 6 9 16 23 30
Special 5 (1/72, 52 pgs.)-Spider-Man x-over 3 6 9 16 23 30
Annual 6 (11/76) Perez-a; Kirby-c 2 4 6 10 14 18
Annual 7 (11/77)-Starlin-c/a; Warlock dies; Thanos app. 5 10 15 30 48 65
Annual 8 (1978)-Dr. Strange, Ms. Marvel app. 2 4 6 8 10 12
Annual 9 (1979)-Newton-a(p) 1 2 3 5 7 9
Annual 10 (1981)-Golden-p; X-Men cameo; 1st app. Rogue & Madelyne Pryor 5 10 15 30 48 65
Annual 11-13: 11(1982)-Vs. The Defenders. 12('83), 13('84) 4.00
Annual 14-18: 14('85),15('86),16('87),17('88)-Evolutionary War x-over, 18('89)-Atlantis Attacks 4.00
Annual 19-23 (90-'94, 68 pgs.). 22-Bagged/card 3.00
...: Galactic Storm Vol. 1 ('06, $29.99, TPB) r/Kree-Shi'ar war from Avengers #345-346, Capt. America #398-399, Avengers West Coast #80-81, Quasar #32-33, Wonder Man #7-8, Iron Man #270 and Thor #445; new Epting-c 30.00
...: Galactic Storm Vol. 2 ('06, $29.99, TPB) r/Kree-Shi'ar war from Avengers #347, Capt. America #400-401, Avengers West Coast #82, Quasar #34-36, Wonder Man #9, Iron Man #279, Thor #446 and What If #55-56 30.00
...: Kang - Time and Time Again ('05, $19.99, TPB) r/Avengers #69-71 & 267-269, Thor #140 and Incredible Hulk #135 20.00
...Kree-Skrull War ('00, $24.95, TPB) new Neal Adams-c 25.00
...: Legends Vol. 3: George Perez ('03, $16.99)-r/#161,162,194-196,201, Ann. #6 & 8 17.00
Marvel Double Feature...Avengers/Giant-Man #379 ($2.50, 52 pgs.)-Same as Avengers #379 w/Giant-Man flip book 2.50
Marvel Graphic Novel - Deathtrap: The Vault (1991, $9.95) Venom-c/app. 2 4 6 8 10 12
The Korvac Saga TPB (2003, $19.95)-r/#167,168,170-177; Perez-c 20.00
The Serpent Crown TPB (2005, $15.99)-r/#141-144,147-149; Hellcat app. 16.00
The Yesterday Quest ($6.95)-r/#181,182,185-187 1 2 3 4 5 7
Under Siege ('98, $16.95, TPB) r/#270,271,273-277 17.00
...: Vision and the Scarlet Witch TPB (2005, $15.99) r/wedding from Giant-Size Avengers #4 and "Vision and the Scarlet Witch" mini-series #1-4 16.00
...: Visionaries ('99, $16.95)-r/early George Perez art 17.00

NOTE: **Austin** *c(i)-157, 167, 168, 170-177, 181, 183-188, 198-201, Annual 8.* **John Buscema** *a-41-44p, 46p, 47p, 49, 50, 51-62p, 74-77, 79-85, 87-91, 97, 105p, 121p, 124p,125p, 152, 153p, 255-279p, 281-302p; c-41-66, 68-71, 73-91, 97-99, 178, 256-259p, 261-279p, 281-302p.* **Byrne** *a-164-166p, 181-191p, 233p, Annual 13i, 14p; c-186-190p, 233p, 260, 305p; scripts-305-312.* **Colan** *a(p)-63-65, 111, 206-208, 210, 211; c(p)-65, 206-208, 210, 211.* **Ditko** *a-Annual 13.* **Guice** *a-Annual 12p.* **Don Heck** *a-9-15, 17-40, 157.* **Kane** *c-37p, 159p.* **Kane/Everett** *c-97.* **Kirby** *a-1-8p, Special 3r, 4r(p); c-1-30, 148, 151-158; layouts-14-16.* **Ron Lim** *c(p)-335-341.* **Miller** *c-193p.* **Mooney** *a-86i, 179p, 180p.* **Nebres** *a-178i; c-179i.* **Newton** *a-204p, Annual 9p.* **Perez** *a(p)-141, 143, 144, 148, 150, 154, 155, 160, 161, 162, 167,168, 170, 171, 194-196, 198-202, Annual 6, 8; c(p)-160-162, 164-166, 170-174, 181,183-185, 191, 192, 194-201, 379-382, Annual 8.* **Starlin** *c-121, 135.* **Staton** *a-127-134i.* **Tuska** *a-47i,48i, 51i, 53i, 54i, 106p, 107p, 135p, 137-140p, 163p. Guardians of the Galaxy app. in #167, 168, 170, 173, 175, 181.*

AVENGERS, THE (Volume Two)
Marvel Comics: V2#1, Nov, 1996 - No. 13, Nov, 1997 ($2.95/$1.95/$1.99) (Produced by Extreme Studios)

GD 2.0 | VG 4.0 | FN 6.0 | VF 8.0 | VF/NM 9.0 | NM- 9.2

1-($2.95)-Heroes Reborn begins; intro new team (Captain America, Swordsman, Scarlet Witch, Vision, Thor, Hellcat & Hawkeye); 1st app. Avengers Island; Loki & Enchantress app.; Rob Liefeld-p & plot; Chap Yaep-p; Jim Valentino scripts; variant-c exists 5.00
1-($1.95)-Variant-c 6.00
2-13: 2,3-Jeph Loeb scripts begin, Kang app. 4-Hulk-c/app. 5-Thor/Hulk battle; 2 covers. 10,11,13-"World War 3"-pt. 2, x-over w/Image characters. 12-($2.99) "Heroes Reunited"-pt. 2 4.00
Heroes Reborn: Avengers (2006, $29.99, TPB) r/#1-12; pin-up and cover gallery 30.00

AVENGERS, THE (Volume Three)(See New Avengers for next series)
Marvel Comics: Feb, 1998 - No. 84, Aug, 2004; No. 500, Sept, 2004 - No. 503, Dec, 2004 ($2.99/$1.99/$2.25)

1-($2.99, 48 pgs.) Busiek-s/Perez-a/wraparound-c; Avengers reassemble after Heroes Return 5.00
1-Variant Heroes Return cover 1 2 3 4 5 7
1-Rough Cut-Features original script and pencil pages 3.00
2-($1.99)Perez-c, 2-Lago painted-c 4.00
3,4: 3-Wonder Man-c/app. 4-Final roster chosen; Perez poster 3.00
5-11: 5,6-Squadron Supreme-c/app. 8-Triathlon-c/app. 2.50
12-($2.99) Thunderbolts app. 3.00
12-Alternate-c of Avengers w/white background; no logo 15.00
13-24,26,28: 13-New Warriors app. 16-18-Ordway-s/a. 19-Ultron returns. 26-Immonen-a 2.50
16-Variant-c with purple background 5.00
25,27-($2.99) 25-vs. the Exemplars; Spider-Man app. 27-100 pgs. 3.00
29-33,35-47: 29-Begin $2.25-c. 35-Maximum Security x-over; Romita Jr.-a. 36-Epting-a; poster by Alan Davis. 38-Davis-a begins ($1.99-c) 2.50
34-($2.99) Last Pérez-a; Thunderbirds app. 3.00
48-($3.50, 100 pgs.) new story w/Dwyer-a & r/#98-100 3.50
49,51-59: 49-'Nuff Said story. 51-Anderson-a. 52-Reis-a. 57-Johns-s begin 2.50
50,60-($3.50): 50 Dwyer-a; Quasar app. 3.50
61-84: 61,62-Frank-a; new line-up. 63-Davis-a. 64-Reis-a. 65-70-Coipel-a. 75-Hulk app. 76-Jack of Hearts dies; Jae Lee-c. 77-(50¢-c) Coipel-a/Cassaday-c. 78,80,81Coipel-a. 83,84-New Invaders app. 2.50
(After #84 [Aug, 2004], numbering reverted back to original Vol. 1 with #500, Sept, 2004)
500-($3.50) "Avengers Disassembled" begins; Bendis-s/Finch-a; Ant-Man (Scott Lang) killed, Vision destroyed 3.50
500-Director's Cut ($4.99) Cassaday foil variant-c plus interviews and galleries 5.00
501, 502-($2.25): 502-Hawkeye killed 2.50
503-($3.50) "Avengers Disassembled" ends; reprint pages from Avengers V1#16 3.50
#1 1/2 (12/99, $2.50) Timm-c/a/Stern-s; 1963-style issue 2.50
.../ Squadron Supreme '98 Annual ($2.99) 3.00
1999, 2000 Annual (7/99, '00, $3.50) 1999-Manco-a. 2000-Breyfogle-a 3.50
2001 Annual ($2.99) Reis-a; back-up-s art by Churchill 3.00
...: Above and Beyond TPB ('05, $24.99) r/#36-40,56, Annual 2001, & Avengers: The Ultron Imperative; Alan Davis-c 25.00
... Assemble HC ('04, $29.95, oversized) r/#1-11 & '98 Annual; Busiek intro.; Pérez pencil art and Busiek script from Avengers #1 30.00
... Assemble Vol. 2 HC ('05, $29.95, oversized) r/#12-22, #0 & Ann. 1999; Ordway intro. 30.00
... Assemble Vol. 3 HC ('06, $34.99, oversized) r/#23-34, #1 1/2 & Thunderbolts #42-44 35.00
... Assemble Vol. 4 HC ('07, $34.99, oversized) r/#35-40, Avengers 2000, Avengers 2001, Avengers: The Ultron Imperative, Maximum Security #1-3 & ...Dangerous Planet 35.00
... Assemble Vol. 5 HC ('07, $39.99, oversized) r/#41-56 and Avengers 2001 40.00
...: Clear and Present Dangers TPB ('01, $19.95) r/#8-15 20.00
...: Defenders War HC ('07, $19.99) r/#115-118 & Defenders #8-11; Englehart intro. 20.00
...: Disassembled HC ('06, $24.99) r/#500-503 & Avengers Finale; Director's Cut extras 25.00
...: Disassembled TPB ('05, $15.99) r/#500-503 & Avengers Finale; Director's Cut extras 16.00
...Finale 1 (1/05, $3.50) Epilogue to Avengers Disassembled; Neal Adams-c; art by various incl. Peréz, Maleev, Oeming, Powell, Mayhew, Mack, McNiven, Cheung, Frank 3.50
...: Living Legends TPB ('04, $19.99) r/#23-30; last Busiek/Pérez arc 20.00
...Supreme Justice TPB (4/01, $17.95) r/Squadron Supreme appearances in Avengers #5-7, '98 Annual, Iron Man #7, Capt. America #8, Quicksilver #10; Pérez-c 18.00
The Kang Dynasty TPB ('02, $29.99) r/#41-55 & 2001 Annual 30.00
The Morgan Conquest TPB ('00, $14.95) r/#1-4 15.00
.../Thunderbolts Vol. 1: The Nefaria Protocols (2004, $19.99) r/#31-34, 42-44 20.00
Ultron Unleashed TPB (8/99, $3.50) reprints early app. 3.50
Ultron Unlimited TPB (4/01, $14.95) r/#19-22 & #0 prelude 15.00
Wizard #0-Ultron Unlimited prelude 2.50
Vol. 1: World Trust TPB ('03, $14.99) r/#57-62 & Marvel Double-Shot #2 15.00
Vol. 2: Red Zone TPB ('04, $14.99) r/#64-70 15.00
Vol. 3: The Search For She-Hulk TPB ('04, $12.99) r/#71-76 13.00
Vol. 4: The Lionheart of Avalon TPB ('04, $11.99) r/#77-81 12.00
Vol. 5: Once an Invader TPB ('04, $14.99) r/#82-84, V1 #71; Invaders #0 & Ann #1 ('77) 15.00

AVENGERS AND POWER PACK ASSEMBLE!
Marvel Comics: June, 2006 - No. 4 ($2.99, limited series)

Avengers Classic #4 © MAR

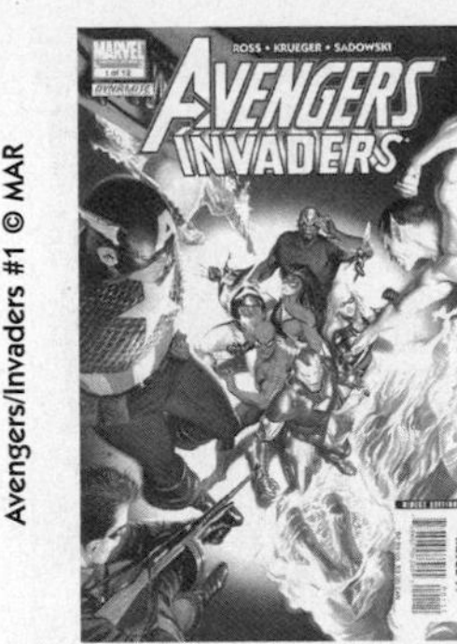

Avengers/Invaders #1 © MAR

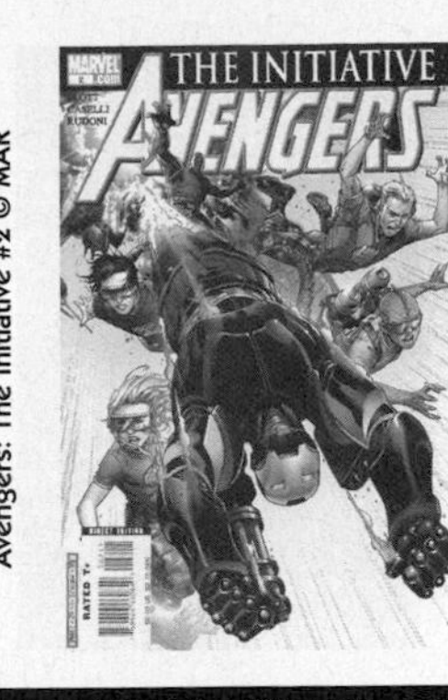

Avengers: The Initiative #2 © MAR

GD 2.0 VG 4.0 FN 6.0 VF 8.0 VF/NM 9.0 NM- 9.2

1-4-GuriHiru-a/Sumerak-s. 1-Capt. America app. 2-Iron Man. 3-Spider-Man, Kang app. 3.00
TPB (2006, $6.99, digest-size) r/#1-4 7.00

AVENGERS: CELESTIAL QUEST
Marvel Comics: Nov, 2001 - No. 8, June, 2002 ($2.50/$3.50, limited series)
1-7-Englehart-s/Santamaria-a; Thanos app. 2.50
8-($3.50) 3.50

AVENGERS: CLASSIC
Marvel Comics: Aug, 2007 - Present ($3.99/$2.99)
1,12-($3.99) 1-Reprints Avengers #1 ('63) with new stories about that era; Art Adams-c 4.00
2-11-($2.99) R/#2-11 with back-up w/art by Oeming and others 3.00

AVENGERS COLLECTOR'S EDITION, THE
Marvel Comics: 1993 (Ordered through mail w/candy wrapper, 20 pgs.)
1-Contains 4 bound-in trading cards 5.00

AVENGERS: EARTH'S MIGHTIEST HEROES
Marvel Comics: Jan, 2005 - No. 8, Apr, 2005 ($3.50, limited series)
1-8-Retells origin; Casey-s/Kolins-a 3.50
HC (2005, $24.99, 7 1/2" x 11" with dustjacket) r/#1-8 25.00

AVENGERS: EARTH'S MIGHTIEST HEROES II
Marvel Comics: Jan, 2007 - No. 8, May, 2007 ($3.99, limited series)
1-8-Retells time when the Vision joined; Casey-s/Rosado-a. 6-Hank & Janet's wedding 4.00
HC (2007, $24.99, 7 1/2" x 11" with dustjacket) r/#1-8; cover sketches 25.00

AVENGERS FAIRY TALES
Marvel Comics: May, 2008 - No. 4 ($2.99, limited series)
1-2: 1-Peter Pan-style tale; Cebulski-a/Lemos-a. 2-The Vision. 3-Miyazawa-a 3.00

AVENGERS FOREVER
Marvel Comics: Dec, 1998 - No. 12, Feb, 2000 ($2.99)
1-Busiek-s/Pacheco-a in all 4.00
2-12: 4-Four covers. 6-Two covers. 8-Vision origin revised. 12-Rick Jones becomes Capt. Marvel 3.00
TPB (1/01, $24.95) r/#1-12; Busiek intro.; new Pacheco-c 25.00

AVENGERS INFINITY
Marvel Comics: Sept, 2000 - No. 4, Dec, 2000 ($2.99, limited series)
1-4-Stern-s/Chen-a 3.00

AVENGERS/ INVADERS
Marvel Comics: Jul, 2008 - No. 12 ($2.99, limited series)
1-Invaders journey to the present; Alex Ross-c/Sadowski-a; Thunderbolts app. 3.00
2-4: 2-New Avengers app.; Perkins variant-c. 3-Granov variant-c. 4-Davis var-c 3.00
... Sketchbook (2008, giveaway) Ross and Sadowski sketch art; Krueger commentary 2.50

AVENGERS/ JLA (See JLA/Avengers for #1 & #3)
DC Comics: No, 2, 2003; No. 4, 2003 ($5.95, limited series)
2-Busiek-s/Pérez-a; wraparound-c; Krona, Galactus app. 6.00
4-Busiek-s/Pérez-a; wraparound-c 6.00

AVENGERS LOG, THE
Marvel Comics: Feb, 1994 ($1.95)
1-Gives history of all members; Perez-c 2.50

AVENGERS NEXT (See A-Next and Spider-Girl)
Marvel Comics: Jan, 2007 - No. 5 ($2.99, limited series)
1-5-Lim-a/Wieringo-c; Spider-Girl app. 1-Avengers vs. zombies. 2-Thena app. 3.00
...: Rebirth TPB (2007, $13.99) r/#1-5 14.00

AVENGERS SPOTLIGHT (Formerly Solo Avengers #1-20)
Marvel Comics: No. 21, Aug, 1989 - No. 40, Jan, 1991 (75¢/$1.00)
21-Byrne-c/a 3.00
22-40: 26-Acts of Vengeance story. 31-34-U.S. Agent series. 36-Heck-i. 37-Mortimer-i. 40-The Black Knight app. 2.50

AVENGERS STRIKEFILE
Marvel Comics: Jan, 1994 ($1.75, one-shot)
1 2.50

AVENGERS: THE CROSSING
Marvel Comics: July, 1995 ($4.95, one-shot)
1-Deodato-c/a; 1st app. Thor's new costume 5.00

AVENGERS: THE INITIATIVE (See Civil War and related titles)
Marvel Comics: Jun, 2007 - Present ($2.99)
1-Caselli-a/Slott-s/Cheung-c; War Machine app. 4.00
2-17: 4,5-World War Hulk. 6-Uy-a. 14-16-Secret Invasion; 3-D Man app. 16-Skrull Kill Krew returns 3.00
Annual 1 (1/08, $3.99) Secret Invasion tie-in; Cheung-c 4.00
...: Vol. 1 - Basic Training HC (2007, $19.99, d.j.) r/#1-6 20.00
...: Vol. 1 - Basic Training SC (2008, $14.99) r/#1-6 15.00

AVENGERS: THE TERMINATRIX OBJECTIVE
Marvel Comics: Sept, 1993 - No. 4, Dec, 1993 ($1.25, limited series)
1 ($2.50)-Holo-grafx foil-c 3.00
2-4-Old vs. current Avengers 2.50

AVENGERS: THE ULTRON IMPERATIVE
Marvel Comics: Nov, 2001 ($5.99, one-shot)
1-Follow-up to the Ultron Unlimited ending in Avengers #42; BWS-c 6.00

AVENGERS/THUNDERBOLTS
Marvel Comics: May, 2004 - No. 6, Sept, 2004 ($2.99, limited series)
1-6: Busiek & Nicieza-s/Kitson-c. 1,2-Kitson-a. 3-6-Grummett-a 3.00
Vol. 2: Best Intentions (2004, $14.99) r/#1-6 15.00

AVENGERS: TIMESLIDE
Marvel Comics: Feb, 1996 ($4.95, one-shot)
1-Foil-c 5.00

AVENGERS TWO: WONDER MAN & BEAST
Marvel Comics: May, 2000 - No. 3, July, 2000 ($2.99, limited series)
1-3: Stern-s/Bagley-c/a 3.00

AVENGERS/ULTRAFORCE (See Ultraforce/Avengers)
Marvel Comics: Oct, 1995 ($3.95, one-shot)
1-Wraparound foil-c by Perez 4.00

AVENGERS UNITED THEY STAND
Marvel Comics: Nov, 1999 - No. 7, June, 2000 ($2.99/$1.99)
1-Based on the animated series 3.00
2-6-($1.99) 2-Avengers battle Hydra 2.50
7-($2.99) Devil Dinosaur-c/app.; reprints Avengers Action Figure Comic 3.00

AVENGERS UNIVERSE
Marvel Comics: Jun, 2000 - No. 3, Oct, 2000 ($3.99)
1-3-Reprints recent stories 4.00

AVENGERS UNPLUGGED
Marvel Comics: Oct, 1995 - No. 6, Aug, 1996 (99¢, bi-monthly)
1-6 2.50

AVENGERS WEST COAST (Formerly West Coast Avengers)
Marvel Comics: No. 48, Sept, 1989 - No. 102, Jan, 1994 ($1.00/$1.25)
48,49: 48-Byrne-c/a & scripts continue thru #57 3.00
50-Re-intro original Human Torch 4.00
51-69,71-74,76-83,85,86,89-99: 54-Cover swipe/F.F. #1. 78-Last $1.00-c. 79-Dr. Strange x-over. 93-95-Darkhawk app. 2.50
70,75,84,87,88: 70-Spider-Woman app. 75 (52 pgs.)-Fantastic Four x-over. 84-Origin Spider-Woman retold; Spider-Man app. (also in #85,86). 87,88-Wolverine-c/story 3.00
100-($3.95, 68 pgs.)-Embossed all red foil-c 4.00
101,102: 101-X-Men x-over 4.00
Annual 5-8 ('90- '93, 68 pgs.)-5,6-West Coast Avengers in indicia. 7-Darkhawk app. 8-Polybagged w/card 3.00
...: Darker Than Scarlet TPB (2008, $24.99) r/#51-57,60-62; Byrne-s/a 25.00
...: Vision Quest TPB (2005, $24.99) r/#42-50; Byrne-s/a 25.00

AVIATION ADVENTURES AND MODEL BUILDING (True Aviation Advs. ...No. 15)
Parents' Magazine Institute: No. 16, Dec, 1946 - No. 17, Feb, 1947
16,17-Half comics and half pictures 8 16 24 42 54 65

AVIATION CADETS
Street & Smith Publications: 1943
nn 19 37 57 109 172 235

A-V IN 3-D
Aardvark-Vanaheim: Dec, 1984 ($2.00, 28 pgs. w/glasses)
1-Cerebus, Flaming Carrot, Normalman & Ms. Tree 4.00

AWAKENING, THE
Image Comics: Oct, 1997 - No. 4, Apr, 1998 ($2.95, B&W, limited series)
1-4-Stephen Blue-s/c/a 3.00

AWESOME ADVENTURES
Awesome Entertainment: Aug, 1999 ($2.50)
1-Alan Moore-s/ Steve Skroce-a; Youngblood story 3.00

Azrael #73 © DC

Baby Huey Duckland #12 © HARV

Babylon 5 #7 © WB

AWESOME HOLIDAY SPECIAL
Awesome Entertainment: Dec, 1997 ($2.50, one-shot)

	GD 2.0	VG 4.0	FN 6.0	VF 8.0	VF/NM 9.0	NM- 9.2
1-Flip book w/covers of Fighting American & Coven. Holiday stories also featuring Kaboom and Shaft by regular creators.						3.00
1-Gold Edition						5.00

AWFUL OSCAR (Formerly & becomes Oscar Comics with No. 13)
Marvel Comics: No. 11, June, 1949 - No. 12, Aug, 1949

	GD 2.0	VG 4.0	FN 6.0	VF 8.0	VF/NM 9.0	NM- 9.2
11,12	14	28	42	80	115	150

AWKWARD UNIVERSE
Slave Labor Graphics: 12/95 ($9.95, graphic novel)

	GD 2.0	VG 4.0	FN 6.0	VF 8.0	VF/NM 9.0	NM- 9.2
nn						10.00

AXA
Eclipse Comics: Apr, 1987 - No. 2, Aug, 1987 ($1.75)

	GD 2.0	VG 4.0	FN 6.0	VF 8.0	VF/NM 9.0	NM- 9.2
1,2						2.50

AXEL PRESSBUTTON (Pressbutton No. 5; see Laser Eraser &...)
Eclipse Comics: Nov, 1984 - No. 6, July, 1985 ($1.50/$1.75, Baxter paper)

	GD 2.0	VG 4.0	FN 6.0	VF 8.0	VF/NM 9.0	NM- 9.2
1-6: Reprints Warrior (British mag.). 1-Bolland-c; origin Laser Eraser & Pressbutton						3.00

AXIS ALPHA
Axis Comics: Feb, 1994 ($2.50, one-shot)

	GD 2.0	VG 4.0	FN 6.0	VF 8.0	VF/NM 9.0	NM- 9.2
V1-Previews Axis titles including, Tribe, Dethgrip, B.E.A.S.T.I.E.S. & more; Pitt app. in Tribe story.						3.00

AZRAEL (...Agent of the Bat #47 on)(Also see Batman: Sword of Azrael)
DC Comics: Feb, 1995 - No. 100, May, 2003 ($1.95/$2.25/$2.50/$2.95)

	GD 2.0	VG 4.0	FN 6.0	VF 8.0	VF/NM 9.0	NM- 9.2
1-Dennis O'Neil scripts begin						5.00
2,3						3.00
4-46,48-62: 5,6-Ras Al Ghul app. 13-Nightwing-c/app. 15-Contagion Pt. 5 (Pt. 4 on-c). 16-Contagion Pt. 10. 22-Batman-c/app. 23,27-Batman app. 27,28-Joker app. 35-Hitman app. 36-39-Batman, Bane app. 50-New costume. 53-Joker-c/app. 56,57,60-New Batgirl app.						2.50
47-($3.95) Flip book with Batman: Shadow of the Bat #80						4.00
63-74,76-92: 63-Huntress-c/app.; Azrael returns to old costume. 67-Begin $2.50-c. 70-79-Harris-c. 83-Joker x-over. 91-Bruce Wayne: Fugitive pt. 15						2.50
75-($3.95) New costume; Harris-c						4.00
93-100: 93-Begin $2.95-c. 95,96-Two-Face app. 100-Last issue; Zeck-c						3.00
#1,000,000 (11/98) Giarrano-a						2.50
Annual 1 (1995, $3.95)-Year One story						4.00
Annual 2 (1996, $2.95)-Legends of the Dead Earth story						3.00
Annual 3 (1997, $3.95)-Pulp Heroes story; Orbik-c						4.00
Plus (12/96, $2.95)-Question-c/app.						3.00

AZRAEL/ ASH
DC Comics: 1997 ($4.95, one-shot)

	GD 2.0	VG 4.0	FN 6.0	VF 8.0	VF/NM 9.0	NM- 9.2
1-O'Neil-s/Quesada, Palmiotti-a						5.00

AZTEC ACE
Eclipse Comics: Mar, 1984 - No. 15, Sept, 1985 ($2.25/$1.50/$1.75, Baxter paper)

	GD 2.0	VG 4.0	FN 6.0	VF 8.0	VF/NM 9.0	NM- 9.2
1-$2.25-c (52 pgs.)						3.00
2-15: 2-Begin 36 pgs.						2.50

NOTE: *N. Redondo a-1i-8i, 10i. c-6-8i.*

AZTEK: THE ULTIMATE MAN
DC Comics: Aug, 1996 - No. 10, May 1997 ($1.75)

	GD 2.0	VG 4.0	FN 6.0	VF 8.0	VF/NM 9.0	NM- 9.2
1-1st app. Aztek & Synth; Grant Morrison & Mark Millar scripts in all						6.00
2-9: 2-Green Lantern app. 3-1st app. Death-Doll. 4-Intro The Lizard King. 5-Origin. 6-Joker app.; Batman cameo. 7-Batman app. 8-Luthor app. 9-vs. Parasite-c/app.						4.00
10-JLA-c/app.	1	2	4	6	8	10
JLA Presents: Aztek the Ultimate Man TPB (2008, $19.99) r/#1-10						20.00

NOTE: ***Breyfogle** c-5p. **N. Steven Harris** a-1-5p. **Porter** c-1p. **Wieringo** c-2p.*

BABE (...Darling of the Hills, later issues)(See Big Shot and Sparky Watts)
Prize/Headline/Feature: June-July, 1948 - No. 11, Apr-May, 1950

	GD 2.0	VG 4.0	FN 6.0	VF 8.0	VF/NM 9.0	NM- 9.2
1-Boody Rogers-a	26	52	78	154	247	340
2-Boody Rogers-a	15	30	45	88	137	185
3-11-All by Boody Rogers	14	28	42	82	121	160

BABE
Dark Horse Comics (Legend): July, 1994 - No. 4, Jan, 1994 ($2.50, lim. series)

	GD 2.0	VG 4.0	FN 6.0	VF 8.0	VF/NM 9.0	NM- 9.2
1-4: John Byrne-c/a/scripts; ProtoTykes back-up story						2.50

BABE RUTH SPORTS COMICS (Becomes Rags Rabbit #11 on?)
Harvey Publications: April, 1949 - No. 11, Feb, 1951

	GD 2.0	VG 4.0	FN 6.0	VF 8.0	VF/NM 9.0	NM- 9.2
1-Powell-a	41	82	123	250	413	575
2-Powell-a	28	56	84	162	261	360
3-11: Powell-a in most	23	46	69	133	214	295

NOTE: *Baseball c-2-4, 9. Basketball c-1, 6. Football c-5. Yogi Berra c/story-8. Joe DiMaggio c/story-3. Bob Feller c/story-4. Stan Musial c-9.*

BABES IN TOYLAND (Disney, Movie) (See Golden Pix Story Book ST-3)
Dell Publishing Co.: No. 1282, Feb-Apr, 1962

	GD 2.0	VG 4.0	FN 6.0	VF 8.0	VF/NM 9.0	NM- 9.2
Four Color 1282-Annette Funicello photo-c	14	28	42	99	175	250

BABES OF BROADWAY
Broadway Comics: May, 1996 ($2.95, one-shot)

	GD 2.0	VG 4.0	FN 6.0	VF 8.0	VF/NM 9.0	NM- 9.2
1-Pin-ups of Broadway Comics' female characters; Alan Davis, Michael Kaluta, J. G. Jones, Alan Weiss, Guy Davis & others-a; Giordano-c.						3.00

BABE 2
Dark Horse Comics (Legend): Mar, 1995 - No. 2, May, 1995 ($2.50, lim. series)

	GD 2.0	VG 4.0	FN 6.0	VF 8.0	VF/NM 9.0	NM- 9.2
1,2: John Byrne-c/a/scripts						2.50

BABY HUEY
Harvey Comics: No. 1, Oct, 1991 - No. 9, June, 1994 ($1.00/$1.25/$1.50, quarterly)

	GD 2.0	VG 4.0	FN 6.0	VF 8.0	VF/NM 9.0	NM- 9.2
1 ($1.00): 1-Cover says "Big Baby Huey"						5.00
2-9 ($1.25-$1.50)						3.00

BABY HUEY AND PAPA (See Paramount Animated...)
Harvey Publications: May, 1962 - No. 33, Jan, 1968 (Also see Casper The Friendly Ghost)

	GD 2.0	VG 4.0	FN 6.0	VF 8.0	VF/NM 9.0	NM- 9.2
1	15	30	45	107	196	285
2	8	16	24	58	97	135
3-5	6	12	18	37	59	80
6-10	3	6	9	21	32	42
11-20	3	6	9	16	22	28
21-33	2	4	6	13	18	22

BABY HUEY DIGEST
Harvey Publications: June, 1992 (Digest-size, one-shot)

	GD 2.0	VG 4.0	FN 6.0	VF 8.0	VF/NM 9.0	NM- 9.2
1-Reprints	1	3	4	6	8	10

BABY HUEY DUCKLAND
Harvey Publications: Nov, 1962 - No. 15, Nov, 1966 (25¢ Giants, 68 pgs.)

	GD 2.0	VG 4.0	FN 6.0	VF 8.0	VF/NM 9.0	NM- 9.2
1	12	24	36	82	146	210
2-5	6	12	18	39	62	85
6-15	4	8	12	22	34	45

BABY HUEY, THE BABY GIANT (Also see Big Baby Huey, Casper, Harvey Hits #22, Harvey Comics Hits #60, & Paramount Animated Comics)
Harvey Publ: 9/56 - #97, 10/71; #98, 10/72; #99, 10/80; #100, 10/90; #101, 11/90

	GD 2.0	VG 4.0	FN 6.0	VF 8.0	VF/NM 9.0	NM- 9.2
1-Infinity-c	48	96	144	384	717	1050
2	23	46	69	167	309	450
3-Baby Huey takes anti-pep pills	15	30	45	105	190	275
4,5	10	20	30	71	126	180
6-10	7	14	21	47	76	105
11-20	5	10	15	35	55	75
21-40	4	8	12	24	37	50
41-60	3	6	9	16	23	30
61-79 (12/67)	2	4	6	13	18	22
80(12/68) - 95-All 68 pg. Giants	3	6	9	17	25	32
96,97-Both 52 pg. Giants	3	6	9	14	19	24
98-Regular size	2	4	6	9	12	15
99-Regular size	1	2	3	5	6	8
100,101 ($1.00)						4.00

BABYLON 5 (TV)
DC Comics: Jan, 1995 - No. 11, Dec, 1995 ($1.95/$2.50)

	GD 2.0	VG 4.0	FN 6.0	VF 8.0	VF/NM 9.0	NM- 9.2
1	2	4	6	8	11	14
2-5	1	2	3	5	7	9
6-11: 7-Begin $2.50-c	1	2	3	4	5	7
... The Price of Peace (1998, $9.95, TPB) r/#1-4,11						10.00

BABYLON 5: IN VALEN'S NAME
DC Comics: Mar, 1998 - No. 3, May, 1998 ($2.50, limited series)

	GD 2.0	VG 4.0	FN 6.0	VF 8.0	VF/NM 9.0	NM- 9.2
1-3						4.00

BABY SNOOTS (Also see March of Comics #359,371,396,401,419,431,443,450,462,474,485)
Gold Key: Aug, 1970 - No. 22, Nov, 1975

	GD 2.0	VG 4.0	FN 6.0	VF 8.0	VF/NM 9.0	NM- 9.2
1	3	6	9	20	30	40
2-11	2	4	6	11	16	20
12-22: 22-Titled Snoots, the Forgetful Elefink	2	4	6	8	10	12

BACCHUS (Also see Eddie Campbell's ...)
Harrier Comics (New Wave): 1988 - No. 2, Aug, 1988 ($1.95, B&W)

Bad Company #6 © IFC

Baffling Mysteries #8 © ACE

Ball and Chain #1 © Stray Thoughts Inc.

GD 2.0 | VG 4.0 | FN 6.0 | VF 8.0 | VF/NM 9.0 | NM- 9.2

1,2: Eddie Campbell-c/a/scripts. 2.50

BACHELOR FATHER (TV)
Dell Publishing Co.: No. 1332, 4-6/62 - No. 2, Sept.-Nov., 1962

Four Color 1332 (#1), 2-Written by Stanley 7 14 21 50 83 115

BACHELOR'S DIARY
Avon Periodicals: 1949 (15¢)

1(Scarce)-King Features panel cartoons & text-r; pin-up, girl wrestling photos; similar to Sideshow 63 126 189 397 674 950

BACKPACK MARVELS (B&W backpack-sized reprint collections)
Marvel Comics: Nov, 2000 ($6.95, B&W, digest-size)

Avengers 1 -r/Avengers #181-189; profile pages 7.00
Spider-Man 1-r/ASM #234-240 7.00
X-Men 1-r/Uncanny X-Men #167-173 7.00
X-Men 2-r/Uncanny X-Men #174-179, new painted-c by Greg Horn 7.00

BACK DOWN THE LINE
Eclipse Books: 1991 (Mature adults, 8-1/2 x 11", 52 pgs.)

nn (Soft-c, $8.95)-Bolton-c/a 9.00
nn (Limited Hard-c, $29.95) 30.00

BACKLASH (Also see The Kindred)
Image Comics (WildStorm Prod.): Nov,1994 - No. 32, May, 1997 ($1.95/$2.50)

1-Double-c; variant-double-c 3.00
2-7,9-32: 5-Intro Mindscape; 2 pinups. 19-Fire From Heaven Pt 2. 20-Fire From Heaven Pt 10. 31-WildC.A.T.S app. 2.50
8-($1.95, newsstand)-Wildstorm Rising Pt. 8 2.50
8-($2.50, direct market)-Wildstorm Rising Pt. 8 2.50
25-($3.95)-Double-size 4.00
...& Taboo's African Holiday (9/99, $5.95) Booth-s/a(p) 6.00

BACKLASH/SPIDER-MAN
Image Comics (WildStorm Productions): Aug, 1996 - No. 2, Sept, 1996 ($2.50, lim. series)

1,2: Pike (villain from WildC.A.T.S) & Venom app. 3.00

BACK TO THE FUTURE (Movie, TV cartoon)
Harvey Comics: Nov, 1991 - No. 4, June, 1992 ($1.25)

1-4: 1,2-Gil Kane-c; based on animated cartoon 3.00

BACK TO THE FUTURE: FORWARD TO THE FUTURE
Harvey Comics: Oct, 1992 - No. 3, Feb, 1993 ($1.50, limited series)

1-3 3.00

BAD BOY
Oni Press: Dec, 1997 ($4.95, one-shot)

1-Frank Miller-s/Simon Bisley-a/painted-c 5.00

BAD COMPANY
Quality Comics/Fleetway Quality #15 on: Aug, 1988 - No. 19?, 1990 ($1.50/$1.75, high quality paper)

1-19: 5,6-Guice-c 2.50

BADGE OF JUSTICE (Formerly Crime And Justice #21)
Charlton Comics: No. 22, 1/55 - No. 2, 4/55 - No. 4, 10/55

22(#1)(1/55) 10 20 30 58 79 100
2-4 7 14 21 35 43 50

BADGER, THE
Capital Comics(#1-4)/First Comics: Dec, 1983 - No. 70, Apr, 1991; V2#1, Spring, 1991

1 5.00
2-70: 52-54-Tim Vigil-c/a 3.00
50-($3.95, 52 pgs.) 4.00
V2#1 (Spring, 1991, $4.95) 5.00

BADGER, THE
Image Comics: V3#78, May, 1997 - V3#88 ($2.95, B&W)

78-Cover lists #1, Baron-s 3.00
79/#2, 80/#3, 81(indicia lists #80)/#4,82-88/#5-11 3.00

BADGER GOES BERSERK
First Comics: Sept, 1989 - No. 4, Dec, 1989 ($1.95, lim. series, Baxter paper)

1-4: 2-Paul Chadwick-c/a(2pgs.) 3.00

BADGER: SHATTERED MIRROR
Dark Horse Comics: July, 1994 - No. Oct, 1994 ($2.50, limited series)

1-4 3.00

BADGER: ZEN POP FUNNY-ANIMAL VERSION
Dark Horse Comics: July, 1994 - No. 2, Aug, 1994 ($2.50, limited series)

1,2 3.00

BAD GIRLS
DC Comics: Oct, 2003 - No. 5, Feb, 2004 ($2.50, limited series)

1-5-Vance-s/Graves-a/Cook-c 2.50

BAD IDEAS
Image Comics: Apr, 2004 - No. 2, July, 2004 ($5.95, B&W, limited series)

1,2-Chinsang-s/Mahfood & Crosland-a 6.00
, Vol. 1: Collected! (2005, $12.99) r/#1,2 13.00

BADLANDS
Vortex Comics: May, 1990 ($3.00, glossy stock, mature)

1-Chaykin-c 3.00

BADLANDS
Dark Horse Comics: July, 1991 - No. 6, Dec, 1991 ($2.25, B&W, limited series)

1-6: 1-John F. Kennedy-c; reprints Vortex Comics issue 2.50

BADMEN OF THE WEST
Avon Periodicals: 1951 (Giant) (132 pgs., painted-c)

1-Contains rebound copies of Jesse James, King of the Bad Men of Deadwood, Badmen of Tombstone; other combinations possible.
Issues with Kubert-a... 40 80 120 235 380 525

BADMEN OF THE WEST! (See A-1 Comics)
Magazine Enterprises: 1953 - No. 3, 1954

1(A-1 100)-Meskin-a? 23 46 69 133 214 295
2(A-1 120), 3: 2-Larsen-a 15 30 45 85 130 175

BADMEN OF TOMBSTONE
Avon Periodicals: 1950

nn 15 30 45 94 147 200

BAD PLANET
Image Comics (Raw Studios): Dec, 2005 - Present ($2.99)

1-5: 1-Thomas Jane & Steve Niles-s/Larosa & Bradstreet-a/c. 2-Wrightson-c. 3-3-D pages 3.00

BADROCK (Also see Youngblood)
Image Comics (Extreme Studios): Mar, 1995 - No. 2, Jan, 1996 ($1.75/$2.50)

1-Variant-c (3) 3.00
2-Liefeld-c/a & story; Savage Dragon app, flipbook w/Grifter/Badrock #2; variant-c exist 2.50
Annual 1(1995,$2.95)-Arthur Adams-c 3.00
Annual 1 Commemorative ($9.95)-3,000 printed 10.00
.../Wolverine (6/96, $4.95, squarebound)-Sauron app; pin-ups; variant-c exists 5.00
.../Wolverine (6/96)-Special Comicon Edition 5.00

BADROCK AND COMPANY (Also see Youngblood)
Image Comics (Extreme Studios): Sept, 1994 - No.6, Feb, 1995 ($2.50)

1-6 : 6-Indicia reads "October 1994"; story cont'd in Shadowhawk #17 2.50

BAFFLING MYSTERIES (Formerly Indian Braves No. 1-4; Heroes of the Wild Frontier No. 26-on)
Periodical House (Ace Magazines): No. 5, Nov, 1951 - No. 26, Oct, 1955

5 40 80 120 244 397 550
6-19,21-24: 8-Woodish-a by Cameron. 10-E.C. Crypt Keeper swipe on-c. 24-Last pre-code issue 25 50 75 147 236 325
20-Classic-c 33 66 99 192 309 425
25-Reprints; surrealistic-c 19 38 57 112 176 240
26-Reprints 17 34 51 100 158 215

NOTE: *Cameron a-8, 10, 16-18, 20-22. Colan a-5, 11, 25r/5. Sekowsky a-5, 6, 22. Bondage c-20, 23. Reprints in 18(1), 19(1), 24(3).*

BALBO (See Master Comics #33 & Mighty Midget Comics)

BALDER THE BRAVE
Marvel Comics Group: Nov, 1985 - No. 4, 1986 (Limited series)

1-4: Simonson-c/a; character from Thor 3.00

BALLAD OF HALO JONES, THE
Quality Comics: Sept, 1987 - No. 12, Aug, 1988 ($1.25/$1.50)

1-12: Alan Moore scripts in all 2.50

BALL AND CHAIN
DC Comics (Homage): Nov, 1999 - No. 4, Feb, 2000 ($2.50, limited series)

1-4-Lobdell-s/Garza-a 2.50

BALLISTIC (Also See Cyberforce)
Image Comics (Top Cow Productions): Sept, 1995 - No. 3, Dec, 1995 ($2.50, limited series)

1-3: Wetworks app, Turner-c/a 3.00

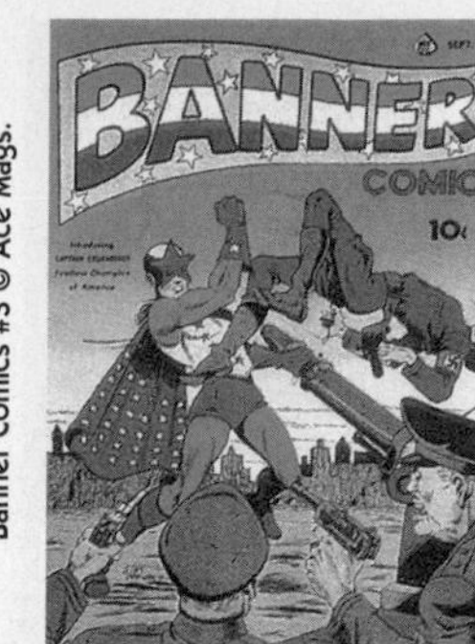

Banner Comics #3 © Ace Mags.

Barb Wire: Ace of Spades #1 © DH

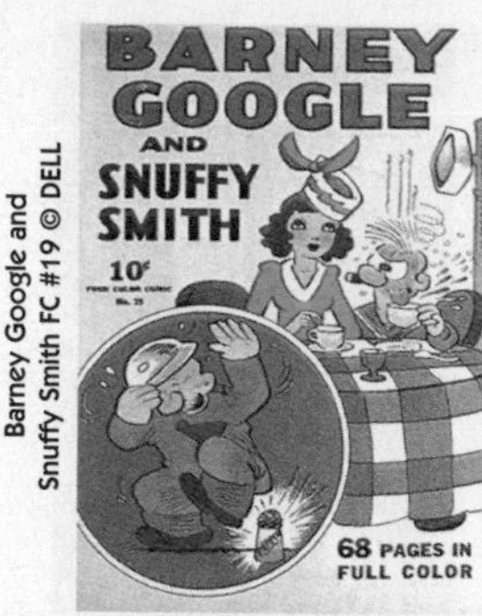

Barney Google and Snuffy Smith FC #19 © DELL

	GD 2.0	VG 4.0	FN 6.0	VF 8.0	VF/NM 9.0	NM- 9.2
... Action (5/96, $2.95) Pin-ups of Top Cow characters participating in outdoor sports						3.00
... Imagery (1/96, $2.50, anthology) Cyberforce app.						2.50
.../ Wolverine (2/97, $2.95) Devil's Reign pt. 4; Witchblade cameo (1 page)						4.00

BALOO & LITTLE BRITCHES (Disney)
Gold Key: Apr, 1968

	GD	VG	FN	VF	VF/NM	NM-
1-From the Jungle Book	4	8	12	22	34	45

BAMBI (Disney) (See Movie Classics, Movie Comics, and Walt Disney Showcase No. 31)
Dell Publishing Co.: No. 12, 1942; No. 30, 1943; No. 186, Apr, 1948; 1984

	GD	VG	FN	VF	VF/NM	NM-
Four Color 12-Walt Disney's...	50	100	150	400	750	1100
Four Color 30-Bambi's Children (1943)	44	88	132	352	664	975
Four Color 186-Walt Disney's...; reprinted as Movie Classic Bambi #3 (1956)	16	32	48	114	212	310
1-(Whitman, 1984; 60¢)-r/Four Color #186 (3-pack)	2	4	6	9	13	16

BAMBI (Disney)
Grosset & Dunlap: 1942 (50¢, 7"x8-1/2", 32pg, hard-c w/dust jacket)

	GD	VG	FN	VF	VF/NM	NM-
nn-Given away w/a copy of Thumper for a $2.00, 2-yr. subscription to WDC&S in 1942 (Xmas offer). Book only	22	44	66	131	211	290
w/dust jacket	40	80	120	235	380	525

BAMM BAMM & PEBBLES FLINTSTONE (TV)
Gold Key: Oct, 1964 (Hanna-Barbera)

	GD	VG	FN	VF	VF/NM	NM-
1	9	18	27	60	100	140

BANANA SPLITS, THE (TV) (See Golden Comics Digest & March of Comics No. 364)
Gold Key: June, 1969 - No. 8, Oct, 1971 (Hanna-Barbera)

	GD	VG	FN	VF	VF/NM	NM-
1-Photo-c on all	10	20	30	68	119	170
2-8	6	12	18	41	66	90

BANANA SUNDAY
Oni Press: July, 2005 - No. 4, Oct, 2005 ($2.99, B&W, limited series)

	GD	VG	FN	VF	VF/NM	NM-
1-4-Root Nibot-s/Colleen Coover-a						3.00
TPB (3/06, $11.95) r/#1-4; sketch gallery						12.00

BAND WAGON (See Hanna-Barbera Band Wagon)

BANG-UP COMICS
Progressive Publishers: Dec, 1941 - No. 3, June, 1942

	GD	VG	FN	VF	VF/NM	NM-
1-Cosmo Mann & Lady Fairplay begin; Buzz Balmer by Rick Yager in all (origin #1)	93	186	279	586	993	1400
2,3	45	90	135	279	465	650

BANISHED KNIGHTS (See Warlands)
Image Comics: Dec, 2001 - No. 4, June, 2002 ($2.95)

	GD	VG	FN	VF	VF/NM	NM-
1-4-Two covers (Alvin Lee, Pat Lee)						3.00

BANNER COMICS (Becomes Captain Courageous No. 6)
Ace Magazines: No. 3, Sept, 1941 - No. 5, Jan, 1942

	GD	VG	FN	VF	VF/NM	NM-
3-Captain Courageous (1st app.) & Lone Warrior & Sidekick Dicky begin; Jim Mooney-c	107	214	321	674	1137	1600
4,5: 4-Flag-c	66	132	198	416	701	985

BARACK OBAMA (See Presidential Material: Barack Obama)

BARBARIANS, THE
Atlas Comics/Seaboard Periodicals: June, 1975

	GD	VG	FN	VF	VF/NM	NM-
1-Origin, only app. Andrax; Iron Jaw app.; Marcos-a	2	4	6	8	10	12

BARBIE
Marvel Comics: Jan, 1991 - No. 63, Mar, 1996 ($1.00/$1.25/$1.50)

	GD	VG	FN	VF	VF/NM	NM-
1-Polybagged w/doorknob hanger; Romita-c	2	4	6	9	12	15
2-49,51-62	1	2	3	5	7	9
50,63: 50-(Giant). 63-Last issue	2	4	6	8	10	12
... And Baby Sister Kelly (1995, 99¢-c, part of a Marvel 4-pack) scarce	3	6	9	14	20	25

BARBIE & KEN
Dell Publishing Co.: May-July, 1962 - No. 5, Nov-Jan, 1963-64

	GD	VG	FN	VF	VF/NM	NM-
01-053-207(#1)-Based on Mattel toy dolls	36	72	108	277	514	750
2-4	29	58	87	216	398	580
5 (Rare)	30	60	90	222	411	600

BARBIE FASHION
Marvel Comics: Jan, 1991 - No. 53, May, 1995 ($1.00/$1.25/$1.50)

	GD	VG	FN	VF	VF/NM	NM-
1-Polybagged w/Barbie Pink Card	2	4	6	9	12	15
2-49,51,52: 4-Contains preview to Sweet XVI	1	2	3	5	7	9
50,53: 50-(Giant). 53-Last issue	2	4	6	8	10	12

BARB WIRE (See Comics' Greatest World)
Dark Horse Comics: Apr, 1994 - No. 9, Feb, 1995 ($2.00/$2.50)

	GD	VG	FN	VF	VF/NM	NM-
1-9: 1-Foil logo						3.00
Trade paperback (1996, $8.95)-r/#2,3,5,6 w/Pamela Anderson bio						9.00

BARB WIRE: ACE OF SPADES
Dark Horse Comics: May, 1996 - No. 4, Sept, 1996 ($2.95, limited series)

	GD	VG	FN	VF	VF/NM	NM-
1-4: Chris Warner-c/a(p)/scripts; Tim Bradstreet-c/a(i) in all						3.00

BARB WIRE COMICS MAGAZINE SPECIAL
Dark Horse Comics: May, 1996 ($3.50, B&W, magazine, one-shot)

	GD	VG	FN	VF	VF/NM	NM-
nn-Adaptation of film; photo-c; poster insert.						3.50

BARB WIRE MOVIE SPECIAL
Dark Horse Comics: May, 1996 ($3.95, one-shot)

	GD	VG	FN	VF	VF/NM	NM-
nn-Adaptation of film; photo-c; 1st app. new look						4.00

BARKER, THE (Also see National Comics #42)
Quality Comics Group/Comic Magazine: Autumn, 1946 - No. 15, Dec, 1949

	GD	VG	FN	VF	VF/NM	NM-
1	23	46	69	135	218	300
2	14	28	42	80	115	150
3-10	11	22	33	62	86	110
11-14	9	18	27	50	65	80
15-Jack Cole-a(p)	9	18	27	52	69	85

NOTE: ***Jack Cole** art in some issues.*

BARNABY
Civil Service Publications Inc.: 1945 (25¢,102 pgs., digest size)

	GD	VG	FN	VF	VF/NM	NM-
V1#1-r/Crocket Johnson strips from 1942	5	10	14	20	24	28

BARNEY AND BETTY RUBBLE (TV) (Flintstones' Neighbors)
Charlton Comics: Jan, 1973 - No. 23, Dec, 1976 (Hanna-Barbera)

	GD	VG	FN	VF	VF/NM	NM-
1	4	8	12	24	37	50
2-11: 11(2/75)-1st Mike Zeck-a (illos)	3	6	9	14	20	25
12-23	2	4	6	10	14	18
Digest Annual (1972, B&W, 100 pgs.) (scarce)	4	8	12	22	34	45

BARNEY BAXTER (Also see Magic Comics)
David McKay/Dell Publishing Co./Argo: 1938 - No. 2, 1956

	GD	VG	FN	VF	VF/NM	NM-
Feature Books 15(McKay-1938)	40	80	120	244	397	550
Four Color 20(1942)	25	50	75	185	343	500
1,2 (1956-Argo)	9	18	27	50	65	80

BARNEY BEAR ...
Spire Christian Comics (Fleming H. Revell Co.): 1977-1981

	GD	VG	FN	VF	VF/NM	NM-
...Home Plate nn-(1979, 49¢), ...Lost and Found nn-(1979, 49¢), Out of The Woods nn-(1980, 49¢), Sunday School Picnic nn-(1981, 69¢, The Swamp Gang!-(1977, 39¢)	2	4	6	8	10	12

BARNEY GOOGLE & SNUFFY SMITH
Dell Publishing Co./Gold Key: 1942 - 1943; April, 1964

	GD	VG	FN	VF	VF/NM	NM-
Four Color 19(1942)	47	94	141	291	483	675
Four Color 40(1944)	21	42	63	152	281	410
Large Feature Comic 11(1943)	38	76	114	222	356	490
1(10113-404)-Gold Key (4/64)	4	8	12	26	41	55

BARNEY GOOGLE & SNUFFY SMITH
Toby Press: June, 1951 - No. 4, Feb, 1952 (Reprints)

	GD	VG	FN	VF	VF/NM	NM-
1	14	28	42	76	108	140
2,3	8	16	24	44	57	70
4-Kurtzman-a "Pot Shot Pete", 5 pgs.; reprints John Wayne #5	12	24	36	69	97	125

BARNEY GOOGLE AND SNUFFY SMITH
Charlton Comics: Mar, 1970 - No. 6, Jan, 1971

	GD	VG	FN	VF	VF/NM	NM-
1	3	6	9	16	23	30
2-6	2	4	6	10	14	18

BARNUM!
DC Comics (Vertigo): 2003; 2005 ($29.95, $19.95)

	GD	VG	FN	VF	VF/NM	NM-
Hardcover (2003, $29.95, with dust jacket)-Chaykin & Tischman-s/Henrichon-a						30.00
Softcover (2005, $19.95)-Chaykin & Tischman-s/Henrichon-a						20.00

BARNYARD COMICS (Dizzy Duck No. 32 on)
Nedor/Polo Mag./Standard(Animated Cartoons): June, 1944 - No. 31, Sept, 1950; No. 10, 1957

	GD	VG	FN	VF	VF/NM	NM-
1 (nn, 52 pgs.)-Funny animal	20	40	60	115	183	250
2 (52 pgs.)	12	24	36	69	97	125
3-5	9	18	27	52	69	85

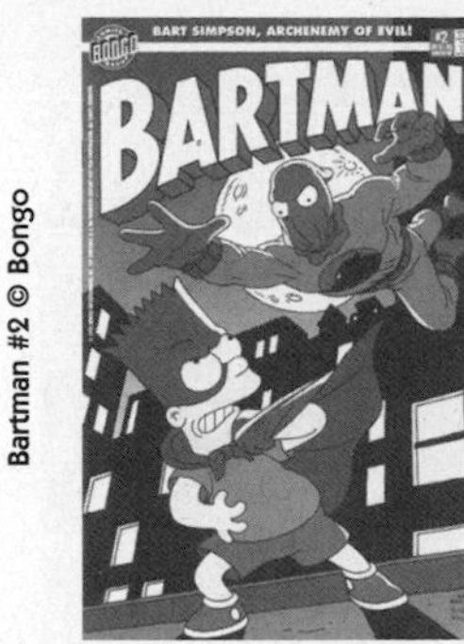

Bartman #2 © Bongo

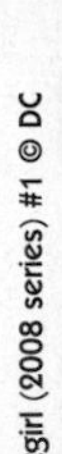
Batgirl (2008 series) #1 © DC

Bat Lash (2008 series) #1 © DC

GD VG FN VF VF/NM NM-
2.0 4.0 6.0 8.0 9.0 9.2

6-12,16 8 16 24 44 57 70
13-15,17,21,23,26,27,29-All contain Frazetta text illos
10 20 30 54 72 90
18-20,22,24,25-All contain Frazetta-a & text illos 12 24 36 69 97 125
28,30,31 7 14 21 37 46 50
10 (1957)(Exist?) 4 7 10 14 17 20

BARRY M. GOLDWATER
Dell Publishing Co.: Mar, 1965 (Complete life story)
12-055-503-Photo-c 4 8 12 23 36 48

BARRY WINDSOR-SMITH: STORYTELLER
Dark Horse Comics: Oct, 1996 - No. 9, July, 1997 ($4.95, oversize)
1-9: 1-Intro Young Gods, Paradox Man & the Freebooters; Barry Smith-c/a/scripts 5.00
Preview 4.00

BAR SINISTER (Also see Shaman's Tears)
Acclaim Comics (Windjammer): Jun, 1995 - No. 4, Sept, 1995 ($2.50, lim. series)
1-4: Mike Grell-c/a/scripts 2.50

BARTMAN (Also see Simpson's Comics & Radioactive Man)
Bongo Comics: 1993 - No. 6, 1994 ($1.95/$2.25)
1-($2.95)-Foil-c; bound-in jumbo Bartman poster 6.00
2-6: 3-w/trading card 4.00

BART SIMPSON (See Simpsons Comics Presents Bart Simpson)

BASEBALL COMICS
Will Eisner Productions: Spring, 1949 (Reprinted later as a Spirit section)
1-Will Eisner-c/a 67 134 201 422 711 1000

BASEBALL COMICS
Kitchen Sink Press: 1991 ($3.95, coated stock)
1-r/1949 ish. by Eisner; contains trading cards 6.00

BASEBALL HEROES
Fawcett Publications: 1952 (one-shot)
nn (Scarce)-Babe Ruth photo-c; baseball's Hall of Fame biographies
80 160 240 504 852 1200

BASEBALL'S GREATEST HEROES
Magnum Comics: Dec, 1991 - No. 2, May, 1992 ($1.75)
1-Mickey Mantle #1; photo-c; Sinnott-a(p) 5.00
2-Brooks Robinson #1; photo-c; Sinnott-a(i) 4.00

BASEBALL THRILLS
Ziff-Davis Publ. Co.: No. 10, Sum, 1951 - No. 3, Sum, 1952 (Saunders painted-c No.1,2)
10(#1)-Bob Feller, Musial, Newcombe & Boudreau stories
43 86 129 267 446 625
2-Powell-a(2)(Late Sum, '51); Feller, Berra & Mathewson stories
31 62 93 184 295 405
3-Kinstler-c/a; Joe DiMaggio story 31 62 93 184 295 405

BASEBALL THRILLS 3-D
The 3-D Zone: May, 1990 ($2.95, w/glasses)
1-New L.B. Cole-c; life stories of Ty Cobb & Ted Williams 6.00

BASICALLY STRANGE (Magazine)
John C. Comics (Archie Comics Group): Dec, 1982 ($1.95, B&W)
1-(21,000 printed; all but 1,000 destroyed; pgs. out of sequence)
3 6 9 16 23 30
1-Wood, Toth-a; Corben-c; reprints & new art 2 4 6 13 18 22

BASIC HISTORY OF AMERICA ILLUSTRATED
Pendulum Press: 1976 (B&W) (Soft-c $1.50; Hard-c $4.50)
07-1999-America Becomes a World Power 1890-1920. 07-2251-The Industrial Era 1865-1915. 07-226x-Before the Civil War 1830-1860. 07-2278-Americans Move Westward 1800-1850. 07-2286-The Civil War 1850-1876; Redondo-a. 07-2294-The Fight for Freedom 1750-1783. 07-2308-The New World 1500-1750. 07-2316-Problems of the New Nation 1800-1830. 07-2324-Roaring Twenties and the Great Depression 1920-1940. 07-2332-The United States Emerges 1783-1800. 07-2340-America Today 1945-1976. 07-2359-World War II 1940-1945
Softcover editions each 1 2 3 4 5 7
Hardcover editions each 14.00

BASIL (...the Royal Cat)
St. John Publishing Co.: Jan, 1953 - No. 4, Sept, 1953
1-Funny animal 7 14 21 37 46 55
2-4 5 10 15 22 26 30
I.W. Reprint 1 2 4 6 9 12 15

BASIL WOLVERTON'S FANTASTIC FABLES
Dark Horse Comics: Oct, 1993 - No. 2, Dec, 1993 ($2.50, B&W, limited series)
1,2-Wolverton-c/a(r) 6.00

BASIL WOLVERTON'S GATEWAY TO HORROR
Dark Horse Comics: June, 1988 ($1.75, B&W, one-shot)
1-Wolverton-r 6.00

BASIL WOLVERTON'S PLANET OF TERROR
Dark Horse Comics: Oct, 1987 ($1.75, B&W, one-shot)
1-Wolverton-r; Alan Moore-c 6.00

BASTARD SAMURAI
Image Comics: Apr, 2002 - No. 3, Aug, 2002 ($2.95)
1-3-Oeming & Gunter-s; Shannon-a/Oeming-i 3.00
TPB (2003, $12.95) r/#1-3; plus sketch pages and pin-ups 13.00

BATGIRL (See Batman: No Man's Land stories)
DC Comics: Apr, 2000 - No. 73, Apr, 2006 ($2.50)
1-Scott & Campanella-a 6.00
1-(2nd printing) 2.50
2-10: 8-Lady Shiva app. 4.50
11-24: 12-"Officer Down" x-over. 15-Joker-c/app. 24-Bruce Wayne: Murderer pt. 2. 4.00
25-($3.25) Batgirl vs Lady Shiva 3.50
26-29: 27- Bruce Wayne: Fugitive pt. 5; Noto-a. 29-B.W.:F. pt. 13 3.50
30-49,51-73: 30-32-Connor Hawke app. 39-Intro. Black Wind. 41-Superboy-c/app. 53-Robin (Spoiler) app. 54-Bagged with Sky Captain CD. 55-57-War Games. 63,64-Deathstroke app. 67 Birds of Prey app. 73-Lady Shiva origin; Salo-c 2.50
50-($3.25) Batgirl vs Batman 3.25
Annual 1 ('00, $3.50) Planet DC; intro. Aruna 5.00
...: A Knight Alone (2001, $12.95, TPB) r/#7-11,13,14 13.00
...: Death Wish (2003, $14.95, TPB) r/#17-20,22,23,25 & Secret Files and Origins #1 15.00
.... Destruction's Daughter (2006, $19.99, TPB) r/#65-73 20.00
...: Fists of Fury (2004, $14.95, TPB) r/#15,16,21,26-28 15.00
...: Kicking Assassins (2005, $14.99, TPB) r/#60-64 15.00
... Secret Files and Origins (8/02, $4.95) origin-s Noto-a; profile pages and pin-ups 5.00
...: Silent Running (2001, $12.95, TPB) r/#1-6 13.00

BATGIRL (Cassandra Cain)
DC Comics: Sept, 2008 - Present ($2.99)
1-Beechen-s/Calafiore-a 3.00

BATGIRL ADVENTURES (See Batman Adventures, The)
DC Comics: Feb, 1998 ($2.95, one-shot) (Based on animated series)
1-Harley Quinn and Poison Ivy app.; Timm-c 5.00

BATGIRL SPECIAL
DC Comics: 1988 ($1.50, one-shot, 52 pgs)
1-Kitson-a/Mignola-c 1 2 3 5 7 9

BATGIRL: YEAR ONE
DC Comics: Feb, 2003 - No. 9, Oct, 2003 ($2.95, limited series)
1-9-Barbara Gordon becomes Batgirl; Killer Moth app.; Beatty & Dixon-s 3.00
TPB (2003, $17.95) r/#1-9 18.00

BAT LASH (See DC Special Series #16, Showcase #76, Weird Western Tales)
National Periodical Publications: Oct-Nov, 1968 - No. 7, Oct-Nov, 1969
(All 12¢ issues)
1-(10-11/68)-2nd app. Bat Lash 6 12 18 37 59 80
2-7 4 8 12 24 37 50

BAT LASH
DC Comics: Feb, 2008 - No. 6, Jul, 2008 ($2.99, limited series)
1-6-Aragonés & Brandvold-s/John Severin-a. 1-Two covers by Severin and Simonson 3.00

BATMAN (See All Star Batman & Robin, Anarky, Aurora [in Promo. Comics section], Azrael, The Best of DC #2, Blind Justice, The Brave & the Bold, Cosmic Odyssey, DC 100-Page Super Spec. #14,20, DC Special, DC Special Series, Detective, Dynamic Classics, 80-Page Giants, Gotham By Gaslight, Gotham Nights, Greatest Batman Stories Ever Told, Greatest Joker Stories Ever Told, Heroes Against Hunger, JLA,The Joker, Justice League of America, Justice League Int., Legends of the Dark Knight, Limited Coll. Ed., Man-Bat, Nightwing, Power Record Comics, Real Fact #5, Robin, Saga of Ra's Al Ghul, Shadow of the..., Star Spangled, Super Friends, 3-D Batman, Untold Legend of..., Wanted... & World's Finest Comics)

BATMAN
National Per. Publ./Detective Comics/DC Comics: Spring, 1940 - Present
(#1-5 were quarterly)
1-Origin The Batman reprinted (2 pgs.) from Det. #33 w/splash from #34 by Bob Kane; see Detective #33 for 1st origin; 1st app. Joker (2 stories intended for 2 separate issues of Det. Comics which would have been 1st & 2nd app.); splash pg. to 2nd Joker story is similar to cover of Det. #40 (story intended for #40); 1st app. The Cat (Catwoman)

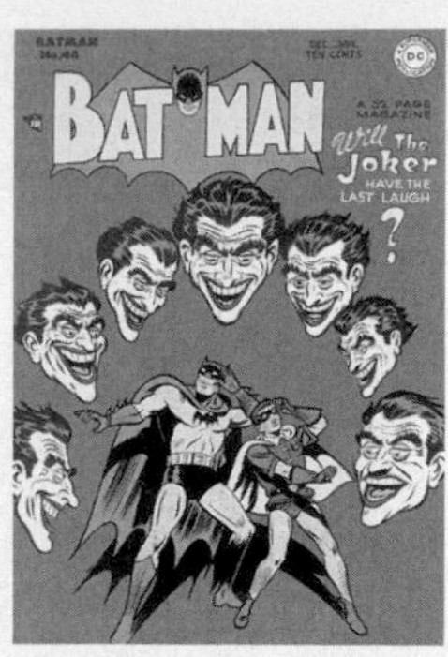

Batman #44 © DC

Batman #139 © DC

Batman #255 © DC

GD VG FN VF VF/NM NM-
2.0 4.0 6.0 8.0 9.0 9.2

(1st villainess in comics); has Batman story (w/Hugo Strange) without Robin originally planned for Det. #38; mentions location (Manhattan) where Batman lives (see Det. #31). This book was created entirely from the inventory of Det. Comics; 1st Batman/Robin pin-up on back-c; has text piece & photo of Bob Kane 9500 19,000 28,500 67,000 141,000 215,000

1-Reprint, oversize 13-1/2x10". **WARNING**: This comic is an exact duplicate reprint of the original except for its size. DC published it in 1974 with a second cover titling it as a Famous First Edition. There have been many reported cases of the outer cover being removed and the interior sold as the original edition. The reprint with the new outer cover removed is practically worthless. See Famous First Edition for value.

2-2nd app. The Joker; 2nd app. Catwoman (out of costume) in Joker story; 1st time called Catwoman (NOTE: A 15¢-c for Canadian distr. exists.) 1500 3000 4500 11,250 20,625 30,000
3-3rd app Catwoman (1st in costume & 1st costumed villainess); 1st Puppet Master app.; classic Kane & Robinson-c 944 1888 2832 6797 11,899 17,000
4-4th app. The Joker (see Det. #45 for 3rd); 1st mention of Gotham City in a Batman comic (on newspaper)(Win/40) 722 1444 2166 5198 9099 13,000
5-1st app. the Batmobile with its bat-head front 528 1056 1584 3802 6651 9500
6,7: 7-Bullseye-c; Joker app. 456 912 1368 3283 5742 8200
8-Infinity-c by Fred Ray; Joker app. 382 764 1146 2598 4549 6500
9-10:9-1st Batman x-mas story; Burnley-c. 10-Catwoman story (gets new costume) 371 742 1113 2523 4412 6300
11-Classic Joker-c by Ray/Robinson (3rd Joker-c, 6-7/42); Joker & Penguin app. 750 1500 2250 5400 9450 13,500
12,15: 12-Joker app. 15-New costume Catwoman 306 612 918 1989 3445 4900
13-Jerry Siegel (Superman's co-creator) appears in a Batman story. 300 600 900 2010 3505 5000
14-2nd Penguin-c; Penguin app. (12-1/42-43) 300 600 900 2040 3570 5100
16-Intro/origin Alfred (4-5/43); cover is a reverse of #9 cover by Burnley; 1st small logo 528 1056 1584 3802 6651 9500
17,20: 17-Classic war-c; Penguin app. 20-1st Batmobile-c (12-1/43-44); Joker app. 260 520 780 1638 2769 3900
18-Hitler, Hirohito, Mussolini-c. 300 600 900 2040 3570 5100
19-Joker app. 207 414 621 1304 2202 3100
21,22,24,26,28-30: 21-1st skinny Alfred in Batman (2-3/44). 21,30-Penguin app. 22-1st Alfred solo-c/story (Alfred solo stories in 22-32,36); Catwoman & The Cavalier app. 28-Joker story 157 314 471 989 1670 2350
23-Joker-c/story; classic black-c 267 534 801 1682 2841 4000
25-Only Joker/Penguin team-up; 1st team-up between two major villains 243 486 729 1531 2591 3650
27-Classic Burnley Christmas-c; Penguin app. 210 420 630 1323 2237 3150
31,32,34-36,39: 32-Origin Robin retold; Joker app. 35-Catwoman story (in new costume w/o cat head mask). 36-Penguin app. 118 236 354 743 1259 1775
33-Christmas-c 140 280 420 882 1491 2100
37,40,44-Joker-c/stories 167 334 501 1052 1776 2500
38-Penguin-c/story 140 280 420 882 1491 2100
41,45,46: 41-1st Sci-fi cover/story in Batman; Penguin app.(6-7/47). 45-Christmas-c/story; Catwoman story. 46-Joker app. 87 174 261 548 924 1300
42-2nd Catwoman-c (1st in Batman)(8-9/47); Catwoman story also. 153 306 459 964 1632 2300
43-Penguin-c/story 122 244 366 769 1297 1825
47-1st detailed origin The Batman (6-7/48); 1st Bat-signal-c this title (see Detective #108); Batman tracks down his parent's killer and reveals i.d. to him 353 706 1059 2400 4200 6000
48-1000 Secrets of the Batcave; r-in #203; Penguin story 118 236 354 743 1259 1775
49-Joker-c/story; 1st app. Mad Hatter; 1st app. Vicki Vale 190 380 570 1292 2071 2850
50-Two-Face impostor app. 100 200 300 630 1065 1500
51,54,56,57,59,60: 57-Centerfold is a 1950 calendar; Joker app. 59-1st app. Deadshot; Batman in the future-c/story 85 170 255 536 906 1275
52,55-Joker-c/stories 120 240 360 756 1278 1800
53-Joker story 88 176 264 554 940 1325
58,61: 58-Penguin-c. 61-Origin Batman Plane II 95 190 285 599 1012 1425
62-Origin Catwoman; Catwoman-c 143 286 429 901 1526 2150
63,80-Joker stories. 63-1st app. Killer Moth; flying saucer story(2-3/51) 80 160 240 504 852 1200
64,70-72,74-77,79: 70-Robot-c. 72-Last 52 pg. issue. 74-Used in **POP**, Pg. 90. 76-Penguin story. 79-Vicki Vale in "The Bride of Batman" 67 134 201 422 711 1000
65,69-Catwoman-c/stories 100 200 300 630 1065 1500
66,73-Joker-c/stories. 66-Pre-2nd Batman & Robin team try-out. 73-Vicki Vale story 103 206 309 649 1100 1550
67-Joker story 80 160 240 504 852 1200
68,81-Two-Face-c/stories 83 166 249 523 887 1250

GD VG FN VF VF/NM NM-
2.0 4.0 6.0 8.0 9.0 9.2

78-(8-9/53)-Roh Kar, The Man Hunter from Mars story-the 1st lawman of Mars to come to Earth (green skinned) 82 164 246 517 871 1225
82,83,87-89: 89-Last pre-code issue 63 126 189 397 674 950
84-Catwoman-c/story; Two-Face app. 93 186 279 586 993 1400
85,86-Joker story. 86-Intro Batmarine (Batman's submarine) 65 130 195 410 693 975
90,91,93-96,98,99: 99-(4/56)-Last G.A. Penguin app. 55 110 165 347 586 825
92-1st app. Bat-Hound-c/story 90 180 270 567 959 1350
97-2nd app. Bat-Hound-c/story; Joker story 60 120 180 378 639 900
100-(6/56) 277 554 831 1745 2948 4150
101-(8/56)-Clark Kent x-over who protects Batman's i.d. (3rd story) 56 112 168 353 597 840
102-104,106-109: 103-1st S.A. issue; 3rd Bat-Hound-c/story 52 104 156 322 536 750
105-1st Batwoman in Batman (2nd anywhere) 73 146 219 460 780 1100
110-Joker story 53 106 159 330 553 775
111-120: 112-1st app. Signalman (super villain). 113-1st app. Fatman; Batman meets his counterpart on Planet X w/a chest plate similar to S.A. Batman's design (yellow oval w/black design inside). 43 86 129 267 446 625
121- Origin/1st app. of Mr. Zero (Mr. Freeze). 60 120 180 378 639 900
122,124-126,128,130: 122,126-Batwoman-c/story. 124-2nd app. Signal Man. 128-Batwoman cameo. 130-Lex Luthor app. 37 74 111 215 345 475
123,127: 123-Joker story; Bat-Hound app. 127-(10/59)-Batman vs. Thor the Thunder God c/story; Joker story; Superman cameo 38 76 114 226 363 500
129-Origin Robin retold; bondage-c; Batwoman-c/story (reprinted in Batman Family #8) 41 82 123 256 428 600
131-135,137-139,141-143: 131-Intro 2nd Batman & Robin series (see #66; also in #135,145, 154,159,163). 133-1st Bat-Mite in Batman (3rd app. anywhere). 134-Origin The Dummy (not Vigilante's villain). 139-Intro 1st original Bat-Girl; only app. Signalman as the Blue Bowman. 141-2nd app. original Bat-Girl. 143-(10/61)-Last 10¢ issue 29 58 87 169 272 375
136-Joker-c/story 35 70 105 203 327 450
140-Joker story, Batwoman-c/s; Superman cameo 30 60 90 176 283 390
144-(12/61)-1st 12¢ issue; Joker story 20 40 60 143 264 385
145,148-Joker-c/stories 22 44 66 157 291 425
146,147,149,150 17 34 51 120 223 325
151-154,156-158,160-162,164-168,170: 152-Joker story. 156-Ant-Man/Robin team-up(6/63). 164-New Batmobile(6/64) new look & Mystery Analysts series begins 14 28 42 99 175 250
155-1st S.A. app. The Penguin (5/63) 31 62 93 239 445 650
159,163-Joker-c/stories. 159-Bat-Girl app. 163-Last Bat-Girl app. until Teen Titans #50 15 30 45 111 206 300
169-2nd SA Penguin app. 15 30 45 111 206 300
171-1st Riddler app.(5/65) since Dec. 1948 40 80 120 312 581 850
172-175,177,178,180,184 10 20 30 71 126 180
176-(80-Pg. Giant G-17); Joker-c/story; Penguin app. in strip-r; Catwoman reprint 12 24 36 87 156 225
179-2nd app. Silver Age Riddler 16 32 48 118 219 320
181-Batman & Robin poster insert; intro. Poison Ivy 20 40 60 148 274 400
182,187-(80 Pg. Giants G-24, G-30); Joker-c/stories 11 22 33 77 136 195
183-2nd app. Poison Ivy 13 26 39 95 168 240
185-(80 Pg. Giant G-27) 11 22 33 75 133 190
186-Joker-c/story 11 22 33 77 136 195
188,191,192,194-196,199 8 16 24 54 90 125
189-1st S.A. app. Scarecrow; retells origin of G.A. Scarecrow from World's Finest #3(1st app.) 14 28 42 99 175 250
190-Penguin-c/app. 10 20 30 70 123 175
193-(80-Pg. Giant G-37) 10 20 30 68 119 170
197-4th S.A. Catwoman app. cont'd from Det. #369; 1st new Batgirl app. in Batman (5th anywhere) 11 22 33 75 133 190
198-(80-Pg. Giant G-43); Joker-c/story-r/World's Finest #61; Catwoman-r/Det. #211; Penguin-r; origin-r/#47 10 20 30 71 126 180
200-(3/68)-Joker cameo; retells origin of Batman & Robin; 1st Neal Adams work this title (cover only) 12 24 36 87 156 225
201-Joker story 6 12 18 43 69 95
202,204-207,209-212: 210-Catwoman-c/app. 212-Last 12¢ issue 6 12 18 39 62 85
203-(80 Pg. Giant G-49); r/#48, 61, & Det. 185; Batcave Blueprints 8 16 24 54 90 125
208-(80 Pg. Giant G-55); New origin Batman by Gil Kane plus 3 G.A. Batman reprints w/Catwoman, Vicki Vale & Batwoman 8 16 24 54 90 125
213-(80-Pg. Giant G-61); 30th anniversary issue (7-8/69); origin Alfred (r/Batman #16), Joker(r/Det. #168), Clayface; new origin Robin with new facts

Batman #348 © DC

Batman #454 © DC

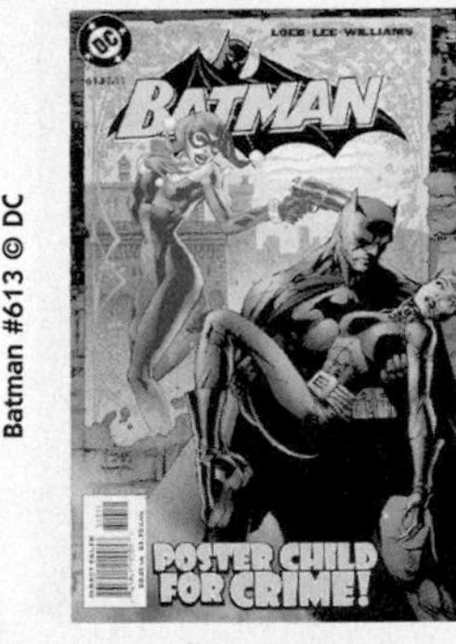

Batman #613 © DC

GD VG FN VF VF/NM NM-
2.0 4.0 6.0 8.0 9.0 9.2

9 18 27 63 107 150
214-217: 214-Alfred given a new last name- "Pennyworth" (see Detective #96) 5 10 15 32 51 70
218-(80-Pg. Giant G-67) 7 14 21 45 73 100
219-Neal Adams-a 7 14 21 45 73 100
220,221,224-226,229-231 4 8 12 28 44 60
222-Beatles take-off; art lesson by Joe Kubert 6 12 18 39 62 85
223,228,233: 223,228-(80-Pg. Giants G-73,G-79). 233-G-85-(68 pgs., "64 pgs." on-c) 6 12 18 43 69 95
227-Neal Adams cover swipe of Detective #31 7 14 21 49 80 110
232-(6/71) Adams-a. Intro/1st app. Ra's al Ghul; origin Batman & Robin retold; last 15¢ issue (see Detective #411 (5/71) for Talia's debut) 15 30 45 105 190 275
234-(9/71)-1st modern app. of Harvey Dent/Two-Face; (see World's Finest #173 for Batman as Two-Face; only S.A. mention of character); N. Adams-a; 52 pg. issues begin, end #242 15 30 45 111 206 300
235,236,239-242: 239-XMas-c. 241-Reprint/#5 5 10 15 30 48 65
237-N. Adams-a. 1st Rutland Vermont - Bald Mountain Halloween x-over. G.A. Batman-r/Det. #37; 1st app. The Reaper; Wrightson/Ellison plots 12 24 36 82 146 210
238-Also listed as DC 100 Page Super Spectacular #8; Batman, Legion, Aquaman-r; G.A. Atom, Sargon (r/Sensation #57), Plastic Man (r/Police #14) stories; Doom Patrol origin-r; N. Adams wraparound-c
(see DC 100 Pg. Super Spectacular #8 for price)
243-245-Neal Adams-a 7 14 21 45 73 100
246-250,252,253: 246-Scarecrow app. 253-Shadow-c & app. 4 8 12 28 44 60
251-(9/73)-N. Adams-c/a; Joker-c/story 8 16 24 58 97 135
254,256-259,261-All 100 pg. editions; part-r: 254-(2/74)-Man-Bat-c & app. 256-Catwoman app. 257-Joker & Penguin app. 258-The Cavalier-r. 259-Shadow-c/app. 6 12 18 41 66 90
255-(100 pgs.)-N. Adams-c/a; tells of Bruce Wayne's father who wore bat costume & fought crime (r/Det. #235); r/story Batman #22 7 14 21 49 80 110
260-Joker-c/story (100 pgs.) 7 14 21 49 80 110
262 (68pgs.) 4 8 12 28 44 60
263,264,266-285,287-290,292,293,295-299: 266-Catwoman back to old costume 2 4 6 11 16 20
265-Wrightson-a(i) 2 4 6 13 18 22
286,291,294: 294-Joker-c/stories 3 6 9 16 23 30
300-Double-size 3 6 9 17 25 32
301-(7/78)-310,312-315,317-320,325-331,333-352: 304-(44 pgs.). 306-3rd app. Black Spider. 308-Mr. Freeze app. 310-1st modern app. The Gentleman Ghost in Batman; Kubert-c. 312,314,346-Two-Face-c/stories. 313-2nd app. Calendar Man. 318-Intro Firebug. 319-2nd modern age app. The Gentleman Ghost; Kubert-c. 344-Poison Ivy app. 345-1st app. new Dr. Death. 345,346,351-Catwoman back-ups 2 4 6 8 10 12
306-308,311-320,323,324,326-(Whitman variants; low print run; none show issue # on cover) 2 4 6 10 14 18
311,316,322-324: 311-Batgirl-c/story; Batgirl reteams w/Batman. 316-Robin returns. 322-324-Catwoman (Selina Kyle) app. 322,323-Cat-Man cameos (1st in Batman, 1 panel each). 323-1st meeting Catwoman & Cat-Man. 324-1st full app. Cat-Man this title 2 4 6 9 12 15
321,353,359-Joker-c/stories 2 4 6 13 18 22
332-Catwoman's 1st solo 2 4 6 10 14 18
354-356,358,360-365,369,370: 361-1st app Harvey Bullock 1 2 3 5 7 9
357-1st app. Jason Todd (3/83); see Det. #524; 1st brief app. Croc 2 4 6 9 13 16
366-Jason Todd 1st in Robin costume; Joker-c/story 2 4 6 11 16 20
367-Jason in red & green costume (not as Robin) 2 4 6 8 10 12
368-1st new Robin in costume (Jason Todd) 2 4 6 9 13 16
371-399,401-403: 371-Cat-Man-c/story; brief origin Cat-Man (cont'd in Det. #538). 386,387-Intro Black Mask (villain). 380-391-Catwoman app. 398-Catwoman & Two-Face app. 401-2nd app. Magpie (see Man of Steel #3 for 1st). 403-Joker cameo 6.00

NOTE: *Issues 397-399, 401-403, 408-416, 421-425, 430-432 all have 2nd printings in 1989; some with up to 8 printings. Some are not identified as reprints but have newer ads copyrighted after cover dates. All reprints have different back-c ads. All reprints are scarcer than 1st prints and have same value to variant collectors.*

400 ($1.50, 68pgs.)-Dark Knight special; intro by Stephen King; Art Adams/Austin-a 3 6 9 16 23 30
404-Miller scripts begin (end 407); Year 1; 1st modern app. Catwoman (2/87) 3 6 9 16 22 28
405-407: 407-Year 1 ends (See Detective Comics #575-578 for Year 2) 2 4 6 13 18 22
408-410: New Origin Jason Todd (Robin) 2 4 6 13 18 22
411-416,421-425: 411-Two-face app. 412-Origin/1st app. Mime. 414-Starlin scripts begin, end #429. 416-Nightwing-c/story. 423-McFarlane-c 5.00
417-420: "Ten Nights of the Beast" storyline 2 4 6 8 10 12
426-($1.50, 52 pgs.)- "A Death In The Family" storyline begins, ends #429 2 4 6 11 16 20
427- "A Death In The Family" part 2. 2 4 6 9 12 15
428-Death of Robin (Jason Todd) 2 4 6 11 16 20
429-Joker-c/story; Superman app. 2 4 6 8 10 12
430-432 3.00
433-435-Many Deaths of the Batman story by John Byrne-c/scripts 3.00
436-Year 3 begins (ends #439); origin original Robin retold by Nightwing (Dick Grayson); 1st app. Timothy Drake (8/89) 4.00
436-441: 436-2nd printing. 437-Origin Robin cont. 440,441: "A Lonely Place of Dying" Parts 1 & 3 3.00
442-1st app. Timothy Drake in Robin costume 4.00
443-456,458,459,462-464: 445-447-Batman goes to Russia. 448,449-The Penguin Affair Pts 1 & 3. 450-Origin Joker. 450,451-Joker-c/stories. 452-454-Dark Knight Dark City storyline; Riddler app. 455-Alan Grant scripts begin, ends #466, 470. 464-Last solo Batman story; free 16 pg. preview of Impact Comics line 3.00
457-Timothy Drake officially becomes Robin & dons new costume 5.00
457-Direct sale edition (has #000 in indicia) 5.00
460,461,465-487: 460,461-Two part Catwoman story. 465-Robin returns to action with Batman. 470-War of the Gods x-over. 475-1st app. Renee Montoya. 475,476-Return of Scarface. 476-Last $1.00-c. 477,478-Photo-c 3.00
488-Cont'd from Batman: Sword of Azrael #4; Azrael-c & app. 1 2 3 5 6 8
489-Bane-c/story; 1st app. Azrael in Bat-costume 5.00
490-Riddler-c/story; Azrael & Bane app. 6.00
491,492: 491-Knightfall lead-in; Joker-c/story; Azrael & Bane app.; Kelley Jones-c begin. 492-Knightfall part 1; Bane app. 4.00
492-Platinum edition (promo copy) 10.00
493-496: 493-Knightfall Pt. 3. 494-Knightfall Pt. 5; Joker-c & app. 495-Knightfall Pt. 7; brief Bane & Joker apps. 496-Knightfall Pt. 9, Joker-c/story; Bane cameo 3.00
497-(Late 7/93)-Knightfall Pt. 11; Bane breaks Batman's back; B&W outer c; Aparo-a(p); Giordano-a(i) 5.00
497-499: 497-2nd printing. 497-Newsstand edition w/o outer cover. 498-Knightfall part 15; Bane & Catwoman-c & app. (see Showcase 93 #7 & 8) 499-Knightfall Pt. 17; Bane app. 3.00
500-($2.50, 68 pgs.)-Knightfall Pt. 19; Azrael in new Bat-costume; Bane-c/story 3.00
500-($3.95, 68 pgs.)-Collector's Edition w/die-cut double-c w/foil by Joe Quesada & 2 bound-in post cards 5.00
501-508,510,511: 501-Begin $1.50-c. 501-508-Knightquest. 503,504-Catwoman app. 507-Ballistic app.; Jim Balent-a(p). 510-KnightsEnd Pt. 7. 511-(9/94)-Zero Hour; Batgirl-c/story 2.50
509-($2.50, 52 pgs.)-KnightsEnd Pt. 1 3.00
512-514,516-518: 512-(11/94)-Dick Grayson assumes Batman role 2.50
515-Special Ed.($2.50)-Kelley Jones-a begins; all black embossed-c; Troika Pt. 1 3.00
515-Regular Edition 2.50
519-534,536-549: 519-Begin $1.95-c. 521-Return of Alfred, 522-Swamp Thing app. 525-Mr. Freeze app. 527,528-Two Face app. 529-Contagion Pt. 6. 530-532-Deadman app. 533-Legacy prelude. 534-Legacy Pt. 5. 536-Final Night x-over; Man-Bat-c/app. 540,541-Spectre-c-app. 544-546-Joker & The Demon. 548,549-Penguin-c/app. 2.50
530-532 ($2.50)-Enhanced edition; glow-in-the-dark-c. 3.00
535-(10/96, $2.95)-1st app. The Ogre 3.00
535-(10/96, $3.95)-1st app. The Ogre; variant, cardboard, foldout-c 4.00
550-($3.50)-Collector's Ed., includes 4 collector cards; intro. Chase, return of Clayface; Kelley Jones-c 3.50
550-($2.95)-Standard Ed.; Williams & Gray-c 3.00
551,552,554-562: 551,552-Ragman c/app. 554-Cataclysm pt. 12. 2.50
553-Cataclysm pt.3 4.00
563-No Man's Land; Joker-c by Campbell; Bob Gale-s 5.00
564-574: 569-New Batgirl-c/app. 572-Joker and Harley app. 2.50
575-579: 575-New look Batman begins; McDaniel-a 2.50
580-598: 580-Begin $2.25-c. 587-Gordon shot. 591,592-Deadshot-c/app. 2.50
599-Bruce Wayne: Murderer pt. 7 2.50
600-($3.95) Bruce Wayne: Fugitive pt. 1; back-up homage stories in '50s, 60's, & 70s styles; by Aragonés, Gaudiano, Shanower and others 5.00
600-(2nd printing) 4.00
601-604, 606,607: 601,603-Bruce Wayne: Fugitive pt.3,13. 606,607-Deadshot-c/app. 2.50
605-($2.95) Conclusion to Bruce Wayne: Fugitive x-over; Noto-c 3.00
608-(12/02) Jim Lee-a/c & Jeph Loeb-s begin; Poison Ivy & Catwoman app. 8.00
608-2nd printing; has different cover with Batman standing on gargoyle 12.00
608-Special Edition; has different cover; 200 printed; used for promotional purposes (a CGC certified 9.2 copy sold for $700, and a CGC certified 9.8 copy sold for $2,100)
609-Huntress app. 9.00
610,611: 610-Killer Croc-c/app.; Batman & Catwoman kiss 8.00
612-Batman vs. Superman; 1st printing with full color cover 9.00

Batman #627 © DC

Batman #677 © DC

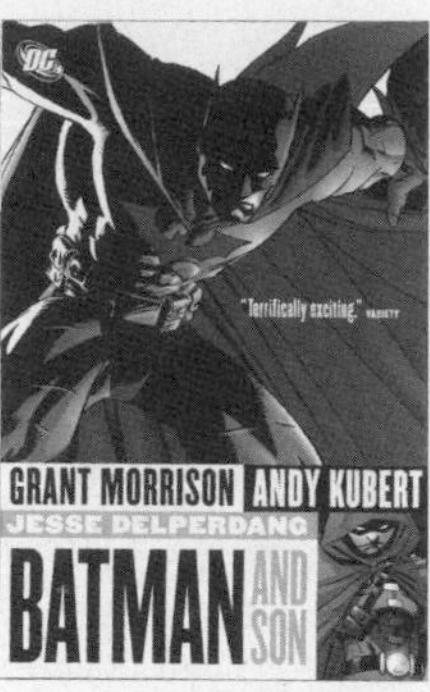

Batman and Son HC © DC

GD VG FN VF VF/NM NM-
2.0 4.0 6.0 8.0 9.0 9.2

612-2nd printing with B&W sketch cover 15.00
613,614: 614-Joker-c/app. 7.00
615-617: 615-Reveals ID to Catwoman. 616-Ra's al Ghul app. 617-Scarecrow app. 5.00
618- Batman vs. "Jason Todd" 4.00
619-Newsstand cover; Hush story concludes; Riddler app. 5.00
619-Two variant tri-fold covers; one Heroes group, one Villains group 5.00
619-2nd printing with Riddler chess cover 5.00
620-Broken City pt. 1; Azzarello-s/Risso-a/c begin; Killer Croc app. 3.00
621-633: 621-625-Azzarello-s/Risso-a/c. 626-630-Winick-s/Nguyen-a/Wagner-c; Penguin & Scarecrow app. 631-633-War Games. 633-Conclusion to War Games x-over 3.00
634-637-Winick-s/Nguyen-a/Wagner-c; Red Hood app. 637-Amazo app. 638-Red Hood unmasked as Jason Todd 2.50
639-650: 640-Superman app. 641-Begin $2.50-c. 643,644-War Crimes; Joker app. 650-Infinite Crisis; Joker and Jason Todd app. 2.50
651-654-One Year Later; Bianchi-c 3.00
655-Begin Grant Morrison-s/Andy Kubert-a; Kubert-c w/red background 5.00
655-Variant cover by Adam Kubert, brown-toned image 15.00
656-665: 656-Intro. Damien, son of Talia and Batman (see Batman: Son of the Demon). 657-Damien in Robin costume. 659-662-Mandrake-a. 663-Van Fleet-a. 664-Bane app. 3.00
666-675: 666-Future story of adult Damien; Andy Kubert-a. 667-669-Williams III-a. 670,671-Resurrection of Ra's al Ghul; Daniel-a. 671-2nd printing 3.00
676-Batman R.I.P. begins; Morrison-s/Daniel-a/Alex Ross-c 4.00
676-Variant-c by Tony Daniel 12.00
676-Second (red-tinted Daniel-c) & third (B&W Daniel-c) printings 3.00
677-Batman R.I.P.; Alex Ross-c 3.00
677-Variant-c by Tony Daniel 10.00
677-Second printing with B&W&red-tinted Daniel-c 3.00
678-Bat-Mite app. 3.00
#0 (10/94)-Zero Hour issue released between #511 & #512; Origin retold 2.50
#1,000,000 (11/98) 853rd Century x-over 2.50
Annual 1 (8-10/61)-Swan-c 55 110 165 468 897 1325
Annual 2 28 56 84 198 369 540
Annual 3 (Summer, '62)-Joker-c/story 28 56 84 203 377 550
Annual 4,5 14 28 42 103 184 265
Annual 6,7 (7/64, 25¢, 80 pgs.) 12 24 36 82 146 210
Annual V5#8 (1982)-Painted-c 1 2 3 5 6 8
Annual 9,10,12: 9(7/85). 10(1986). 12(1988, $1.50) 6.00
Annual 11 (1987, $1.25)-Penguin-c/story; Moore-s 1 2 3 5 6 8
Annual 13 (1989, $1.75, 68 pgs.)-Gives history of Bruce Wayne, Dick Grayson, Jason Todd, Alfred, Comm. Gordon, Barbara Gordon (Batgirl) & Vicki Vale; Morrow-i 5.00
Annual 14-17 ('90-'93, 68 pgs.)-14-Origin Two-Face. 15-Armageddon 2001 x-over; Joker app. 15 (2nd printing). 16-Joker-c/s; Kieth-c. 17 (1993, $2.50, 68 pgs.)-Azrael in Bat-costume; intro Ballistic 4.00
Annual 18 (1994, $2.95) 3.00
Annual 19 (1995, $3.95)-Year One story; retells Scarecrow's origin 4.00
Annual 20 (1996, $2.95)-Legends of the Dead Earth story; Giarrano-a 3.00
Annual 21 (1997, $3.95)-Pulp Heroes story 4.00
Annual 22,23 ('98, '99, $2.95)-22-Ghosts; Wrightson-c. 23-JLApe; Art Adams-c 3.00
Annual 24 ('00, $3.50) Planet DC; intro. The Boggart; Aparo-a 3.50
Annual 25 ('06, $4.99) Infinite Crisis-revised story of Jason Todd; unused Aparo page 6.00
Annual 26 ('07, $3.99) Origin of Ra's al Ghul; Damien app. 4.00

NOTE: ***Art Adams*** *a-400p.* ***Neal Adams*** *c-200, 203, 210, 217, 219-222, 224-227, 229, 230, 232, 234, 236-241, 243-246, 251, 255, Annual 14.* ***Aparo*** *a-414-420, 426-435, 440-448, 450, 451, 480-483, 486-491, 494-500; c-414-416, 481, 482, 463i, 486, 487i.* ***Bolland*** *a-400; c-445-447.* ***Burnley*** *a-10, 12-18, 20, 22, 25, 27; c-9, 15, 16, 27, 28p, 40p, 42p.* ***Byrne*** *c-401, 433-435, 533-535, Annual 11.* ***Travis Charest*** *c-488-490p.* ***Colan*** *a-340p, 343-345p, 348-351p, 373p, 383p; c-343p, 345p, 350p.* ***J. Cole*** *a-238r.* ***Cowan*** *a-Annual 10p.* ***Golden*** *a-295p, 303p, 484, 485.* ***Alan Grant*** *scripts-455-466, 470, 474-476, 479, 480, Annual 16(part).* ***Grell*** *a-287, 288p, 289p, 290; c-287-290.* ***Infantino/Anderson*** *c-167, 173, 175, 181, 186, 191, 192, 194, 195, 198, 199.* ***Infantino/Giella*** *c-190.* ***Kelley Jones*** *a-513-519, 521-525, 527; c-491-499, 500(newsstand), 501-510, 513.* ***Kaluta*** *c-242, 248, 253, Annual 12.* ***G. Kane/Anderson*** *c-178-180.* ***Bob Kane*** *a-1, 2, 5; c-1-5, 7, 17.* ***G. Kane*** *a-(r)-254, 255, 259, 261, 353i.* ***Kubert*** *a-238r, 400; c-310, 319p, 327, 328, 344.* ***McFarlane*** *c-423.* ***Mignola*** *c-426-429, 452-454, Annual 18.* ***Moldoff*** *c-101-140.* ***Moldoff/Giella*** *a-164-175, 177-181, 183, 184, 186.* ***Moldoff/Greene*** *a-169, 172-174, 177-179, 181, 184.* ***Mooney*** *a-255r.* ***Morrow*** *a-Annual 13i.* ***Newton*** *a-305, 306, 328p, 331p, 332p, 337p, 338p, 346p, 352-357p, 360-372p, 374-378p; c-374p, 378p.* ***Nino*** *a-Annual 9.* ***Irv Novick*** *c-201, 202.* ***Perez*** *a-400; c-436-442.* ***Fred Ray*** *c-8, 10; w/Robinson-11.* ***Robinson/Roussos*** *a-12-17, 20, 22, 24, 25, 27, 28, 31, 33, 37.* ***Robinson*** *a-12, 14, 18, 22-32,34, 36, 37, 255r, 260r, 261r; c-6, 10, 12-14, 18, 21, 24, 26, 30, 37, 39.* ***Simonson*** *a-300p, 312p, 321p; c-300p, 312p, 366, 413i.* ***P. Smith*** *a-Annual 9.* ***Dick Sprang*** *c-19, 20, 22, 23, 25, 29, 31-36, 38, 51, 55, 66, 73, 76.* ***Starlin*** *c/a-402.* ***Staton*** *a-334.* ***Sutton*** *a-400.* ***Wrightson*** *a-265i, 400; c-320r. Bat-Hound app. in 92, 97, 103, 123, 125, 133, 156, 158. Bat-Mite app. in 133, 136, 144, 146, 158, 161. Batwoman app. in 105, 116, 122, 125, 128, 129, 131, 133, 139, 140, 141, 144, 145, 150, 151, 153, 154, 157, 159, 162, 163.* ***Zeck*** *c-417-420. Catwoman back-ups in 332, 345, 346, 348-351. Joker app. in 1, 2, 4, 5, 7-9, 11-13, 19, 20, 23, 25, 28, 32 & many more. Robin solo back-up stories in 337-339, 341-343.*

BATMAN (Hardcover books and trade paperbacks)
...: ABSOLUTION (2002, $24.95)-Hard-c.; DeMatteis-s/Ashmore painted-a 25.00
...: ABSOLUTION (2003, $17.95)-Soft-c.; DeMatteis-s/Ashmore painted-a 18.00
...: A LONELY PLACE OF DYING (1990, $3.95, 132 pgs.)-r/Batman #440-442 & New Titans #60,61; Perez-c 4.00

GD VG FN VF VF/NM NM-
2.0 4.0 6.0 8.0 9.0 9.2

...: ANARKY TPB (1999, $12.95) r/early appearances 13.00
...AND DRACULA: RED RAIN nn (1991, $24.95)-Hard-c.; Elseworlds storyline 32.00
...AND DRACULA: RED RAIN nn (1992, $9.95)-SC 12.00
...AND SON HC (2007, $24.99, dustjacket) r/Batman #655-658,663-666 25.00
...AND SON SC (2008, $14.99) r/Batman #655-658,663-666 15.00
ARKHAM ASYLUM Hard-c; Morrison-s/McKean-a (1989, $24.95) 30.00
ARKHAM ASYLUM Soft-c ($14.95) 15.00
ARKHAM ASYLUM 15TH ANNIVERSARY EDITION Hard-c (2004, $29.95) reprint with Morrison's script and annotations, original page layouts; Karen Berger afterword 30.00
ARKHAM ASYLUM 15TH ANNIVERSARY EDITION Soft-c (2005, $17.99) 18.00
...: AS THE CROW FLIES-(2004, $12.95) r/#626-630; Nguyen sketch pages 13.00
BIRTH OF THE DEMON Hard-c (1992, $24.95)-Origin of Ra's al Ghul 25.00
BIRTH OF THE DEMON Soft-c (1993, $12.95) 13.00
BLIND JUSTICE nn (1992, $7.50)-r/Det. #598-600 7.50
BLOODSTORM (1994, $24.95,HC) Kelley Jones-c/a 28.00
BRIDE OF THE DEMON Hard-c (1990, $19.95) 20.00
BRIDE OF THE DEMON Soft-c ($12.95) 13.00
...: BROKEN CITY HC-(2004, $24.95) r/#620-625; new Johnson-c; intro by Schreck 25.00
...: BROKEN CITY SC-(2004, $14.99) r/#620-625; new Johnson-c; intro by Schreck 15.00
...: BRUCE WAYNE: FUGITIVE Vol. 1 ('02, $12.95)-r/ story arc 13.00
...: BRUCE WAYNE: FUGITIVE Vol. 2 ('03, $12.95)-r/ story arc 13.00
...: BRUCE WAYNE: FUGITIVE Vol. 3 ('03, $12.95)-r/ story arc 13.00
...: BRUCE WAYNE-MURDERER? ('02, $19.95)-r/ story arc 20.00
...: CASTLE OF THE BAT ($5.95)-Elseworlds story 6.00
...: CATACLYSM ('99, $17.95)-r/ story arc 18.00
...: CHILD OF DREAMS (2003, $24.95, B&W, HC) Reprint of Japanese manga with Kia Asamiya-s/a/c; English adaptation by Max Allan Collins; Asamiya interview 25.00
...: CHILD OF DREAMS (2003, $19.95, B&W, SC) 20.00
...CHRONICLES VOL. 1 (2005, $14.99)-r/apps. in Detective Comics #27-38; Batman #1 15.00
...CHRONICLES VOL. 2 (2006, $14.99)-r/apps. in Detective Comics #39-45 and NY World's Fair 1940; Batman #2,3 15.00
...CHRONICLES VOL. 3 (2007, $14.99)-r/apps. in Detective Comics #46-50 and World's Best Comics #1; Batman #4,5 15.00
...CHRONICLES VOL. 4 (2007, $14.99)-r/apps. in Detective Comics #51-56 and World's Finest Comics #2,3; Batman #6,7 15.00
...CHRONICLES VOL. 5 (2008, $14.99)-r/apps. in Detective Comics #57-61 and World's Finest Comics #4; Batman #8,9 15.00
...: CITY OF CRIME (2006, $19.99) r/Detective Comics #800-808,811-814; Lapham-s 20.00
...: COLLECTED LEGENDS OF THE DARK KNIGHT nn (1994, $12.95)-r/Legends of the Dark Knight #32-34,38,42,43 13.00
...: CRIMSON MIST (1999, $24.95,HC)-Vampire Batman Elseworlds story Doug Moench-s/Kelley Jones-c/a 25.00
...: CRIMSON MIST (2001, $14.95,SC) 25.00
...: DARK JOKER-THE WILD (1993, $24.95,HC)-Elseworlds story; Moench-s/Jones-c/a 25.00
...: DARK JOKER-THE WILD (1993, $9.95,SC) 10.00
...DARK KNIGHT DYNASTY nn (1997, $24.95)-Hard-c.; 3 Elseworlds stories; Barr-s/ S. Hampton painted-a, Gary Frank, McDaniel-a(p) 25.00
...DARK KNIGHT DYNASTY Softcover (2000, $14.95) Hampton-c 15.00
...DEADMAN: DEATH AND GLORY nn (1996, $24.95)-Hard-c.; Robinson-s/ Estes-c/a 25.00
...DEADMAN: DEATH AND GLORY ($12.95)-SC 13.00
DEATH AND THE CITY (2007, $14.99, TPB)-r/Detective #827-834 15.00
DEATH IN THE FAMILY (1988, $3.95, trade paperback)-r/Batman #426-429 by Aparo 5.00
DEATH IN THE FAMILY: (2nd - 5th printings) 4.00
...: DETECTIVE (2007, $14.99, SC)-r/Detective Comics #821-826 15.00
...: DETECTIVE #27 HC (2003, $19.95)-Elseworlds; Uslan-s/Snejbjerg-a 20.00
...: DETECTIVE #27 SC (2004, $12.95)-Elseworlds; Uslan-s/Snejbjerg-a 13.00
DIGITAL JUSTICE nn (1990, $24.95, Hard-c.)-Computer generated art 25.00
... :EVOLUTION (2001, $12.95, SC)-r/Detective Comics #743-750 13.00
... FACES (1995, $9.95, TPB) 10.00
...: FACE THE FACE (2006, $14.99, TPB)-r/Batman #651-654, Detective #817-820 15.00
...: FALSE FACES HC (2008, $19.99)-r/Batman #588-590, Wonder Woman #160,161; Batman: Gotham City Secret Files #1 and Detective #787; Brian K. Vaughn intro. 20.00
...: FORTUNATE SON HC (1999, $24.95) Gene Ha-a 25.00
...: FORTUNATE SON SC (2000, $14.95) Gene Ha-a 15.00
FOUR OF A KIND TPB (1998, $14.95)-r/1995 Year One Annuals featuring Poison Ivy, Riddler, Scarecrow, & Man-Bat 15.00
...: GOTHAM BY GASLIGHT (2006, $12.99, TPB) r/Gotham By Gaslight & Master of the Future one-shots; Elseworlds Batman vs. Jack the Ripper 13.00
...GOTHIC (1992, $12.95, TPB)-r/Legends of the Dark Knight #6-10 13.00
...GOTHIC (2007, $14.99, TPB)-r/Legends of the Dark Knight #6-10 15.00
...: HARVEST BREED-(2000, $24.95) George Pratt-s/painted-a 25.00
...: HARVEST BREED-(2003, $17.95) George Pratt-s/painted-a 18.00
...: HAUNTED KNIGHT-(1997, $12.95) r/ Halloween specials 13.00
...: HONG KONG HC (2003, $24.95, with dustjacket) Doug Moench-s/Tony Wong-a 25.00

Batman: Prey TPB © DC

Batman: Secrets of the Batcave HC © DC

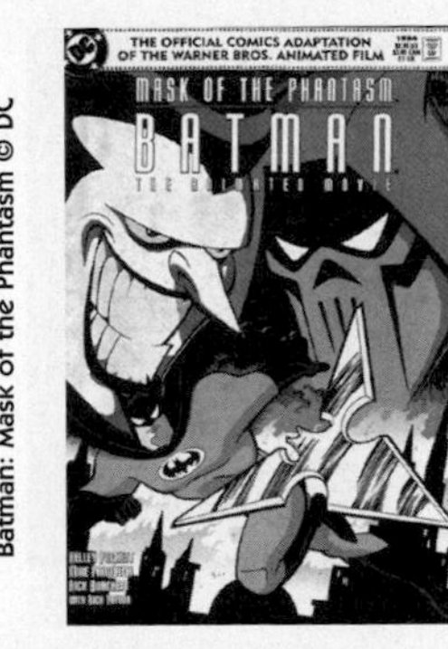

Batman: Mask of the Phantasm © DC

GD VG FN VF VF/NM NM-
2.0 4.0 6.0 8.0 9.0 9.2

...: HONG KONG SC (2004, $17.95) Doug Moench-s/Tony Wong-a 18.00
...: HUSH DOUBLE FEATURE-(2003, $3.95) r/#608,609(1st 2 Jim Lee-a issues) 4.00
...: HUSH VOLUME 1 HC-(2003, $19.95) r/#608-612; & new 2 pg. origin w/Lee-a 20.00
...: HUSH VOLUME 1 SC-(2004, $12.95) r/#608-612; includes CD of DC GN art 13.00
...: HUSH VOLUME 2 HC-(2003, $19.95) r/#613-619; Lee intro & sketchpages 20.00
...: HUSH VOLUME 2 SC-(2004, $12.95) r/#613-619; Lee intro & sketchpages 13.00
...: ILLUSTRATED BY NEAL ADAMS VOLUME 1 HC-(2003, $49.95) r/Batman, Brave and the Bold, and Detective Comics stories and covers 50.00
...: ILLUSTRATED BY NEAL ADAMS VOLUME 2 HC-(2004, $49.95) r/Adams' Batman art from 1969-71, intro. by Dick Giordano 50.00
... IN THE FORTIES TPB ($19.95) Intro. by Bill Schelly 20.00
... IN THE FIFTIES TPB ($19.95) Intro. by Michael Uslan 20.00
... IN THE SIXTIES TPB ($19.95) Intro. by Adam West 20.00
... IN THE SEVENTIES TPB ($19.95) Intro. by Dennis O'Neil 20.00
... IN THE EIGHTIES TPB ($19.95) Intro. by John Wells 20.00
.../ JUDGE DREDD FILES (2004, $14.95) reprints cross-overs 15.00
... LEGACY-(1996,17.95) reprints Legacy 10.00
...: THE MANY DEATHS OF THE BATMAN (1992, $3.95, 84 pgs.)-r/Batman #433-435 w/new Byrne-c 4.00
...: THE MOVIES (1997, $19.95)-r/movie adaptations of Batman, Batman Returns, Batman Forever, Batman and Robin 20.00
...: NINE LIVES HC (2002, $24.95, sideways format) Motter-s/Lark-a 25.00
...: NINE LIVES SC (2003, $17.95, sideways format) Motter-s/Lark-a 18.00
...: OFFICER DOWN (2001, $12.95)-r/Commissioner shot x-over; Talon-c 13.00
...: PREY (1992, $12.95)-Gulacy/Austin-a 13.00
...: PRODIGAL (1997, $14.95)-Gulacy/Austin-a 15.00
... SCARECROW TALES (2005, $19.99, TPB) r/Scarecrow stories & pin-ups from World's Finest #3 to present 20.00
...: SECRETS OF THE BATCAVE (2007, $17.99, TPB) r/Batcave stories 18.00
SHAMAN (1993, $12.95)-r/Legends/D.K. #1-5 13.00
...: SNOW (2007, $14.99, TPB)-r/Legends of the Dark Knight #192-196; Fisher-a 15.00
...: SON OF THE DEMON Hard-c (9/87, $14.95) (see Batman #655-658) 30.00
...: SON OF THE DEMON limited signed & numbered Hard-c (1,700) 45.00
...: SON OF THE DEMON Soft-c w/new-c ($8.95) 10.00
...: SON OF THE DEMON Soft-c (1989, $9.95, 2nd printing - 5th printing) 10.00
... : STRANGE APPARITIONS ($12.95) r/'77-'78 Englehart/Rogers stories from Detective #469-479; also Simonson-a 13.00
...: TALES OF THE DEMON (1991, $17.95, 212 pgs.)-Intro by Sam Hamm; reprints by Neal Adams(3) & Golden; contains Saga of Ra's al Ghul #1 18.00
TALES OF THE MULTIVERSE: BATMAN - VAMPIRE (2007, $19.99) r/Batman & Dracula: Red Rain, Batman: Bloodstorm and Batman: Crimson Mist; Van Lustbader foreword 20.00
...: TEN NIGHTS OF THE BEAST (1994, $5.95)-r/Batman #417-420 6.00
...: TERROR (2003, $12.95, TPB)-r/Legends of the Dark Knight #137-141; Gulacy-c 13.00
...: THE CHALICE (HC, '99, $24.95) Van Fleet painted-a 25.00
...: THE CHALICE (SC, '00, $14.95) Van Fleet painted-a 15.00
...: THE GREATEST STORIES EVER TOLD (2005, $19.99, TPB) Les Daniels intro. 20.00
...: THE GREATEST STORIES EVER TOLD VOLUME TWO (2007, $19.99, TPB) 20.00
...: THE JOKER'S LAST LAUGH ('08, $17.99) r/Joker's Last Laugh series #1-6 18.00
...: THE LAST ANGEL (1994, $12.95, TPB) Lustbader-s 13.00
...: THE RESURRECTION OF RA'S AL GHUL (2008, $29.99, HC w/DJ) r/x-over 30.00
...: THE RING, THE ARROW AND THE BAT (2003, $19.95, TPB) r/Legends of the DCU #7-9 & Batman: Legends of the Dark Knight #127-131; Green Lantern & Green Arrow app. 20.00
...: THRILLKILLER (1998, $12.95, TPB)-r/series & Thrillkiller '62 13.00
...: UNDER THE HOOD (2005, $9.99, TPB)-r/Batman #635-641 10.00
...: UNDER THE HOOD Vol. 2 (2006, $9.99, TPB)-r/Batman #645-650 & Annual #25 10.00
...: VENOM (1993, $9.95, TPB)-r/Legends of the Dark Knight #16-20; embossed-c 10.00
... VS. TWO-FACE (2008, $19.99, TPB) r/initial (Det. #80) & classic battles; Bianchi-c 20.00
...: WAR CRIMES (2006, $12.99, TPB) r/x-over; James Jean-c 13.00
... WAR DRUMS (2004, $17.95) r/Detective #790-796 & Robin #126-128 18.00
...: WAR GAMES ACT 1,2,3 (2005, $14.95/$14.99, TPB) r/x-over; James Jean-c; each.. 15.00
YEAR ONE Hard-c (1988, $12.95) r/Batman #404-407 18.00
YEAR ONE (1988, $9.95, TPB)-r/Batman #404-407 by Miller; intro by Miller 10.00
YEAR ONE (TPB, 2nd & 3rd printings) 10.00
YEAR ONE Deluxe HC (2005, $19.99, die-cut d.j.) new intro. by Miller and developmental material from Mazzucchelli; script pages and sketches 20.00
YEAR ONE (Deluxe) SC (2007, $14.99) r/story plus bonus material from 2005 HC 15.00
YEAR TWO (1990, $9.95, TPB)-r/Det. 575-578 by McFarlane; wraparound-c 10.00

BATMAN (one-shots)
... ABDUCTION, THE (1998, $5.95) 6.00
... ALLIES SECRET FILES AND ORIGINS 2005 (8/05, $4.99) stories/pin-ups by various 5.00
... & ROBIN (1997, $5.95)-Movie adaptation 6.00
...: ARKHAM ASYLUM - TALES OF MADNESS (5/98, $2.95) Cataclysm x-over pt. 16 3.00
... : BANE (1997, $4.95)-Dixon-s/Burchett-a; Stelfreeze-c; cover art interlocks w/Batman:(Batgirl, Mr. Freeze, Poison Ivy) 5.00

GD VG FN VF VF/NM NM-
2.0 4.0 6.0 8.0 9.0 9.2

... : BATGIRL (1997, $4.95)-Puckett-s/Haley,Kesel-a; Stelfreeze-c; cover art interlocks w/Batman:(Bane, Mr. Freeze, Poison Ivy) 5.00
... : BATGIRL (6/98, $1.95)-Girlfrenzy; Balent-a 2.50
... : BLACKGATE (1/97, $3.95) Dixon-s 4.00
... : BLACKGATE - ISLE OF MEN (4/98, $2.95) Cataclysm x-over pt. 8; Moench-s/Aparo-a 3.00
... BOOK OF SHADOWS, THE (1999, $5.95) 6.00
BROTHERHOOD OF THE BAT (1995, $5.95)-Elseworlds-s 6.00
... BULLOCK'S LAW (8/99, $4.95) Dixon-s 5.00
.../CAPTAIN AMERICA (1996, $5.95, DC/Marvel) Elseworlds story; Byrne-c/s/a 6.00
... : CATWOMAN DEFIANT nn (1992, $4.95, prestige format)-Milligan scripts; cover art interlocks w/Batman: Penguin Triumphant; special foil logo 5.00
... /DANGER GIRL (2/05, $4.95)-Leinil Yu-a/c; Joker, Harley Quinn & Catwoman app 5.00
... /DAREDEVIL (2000, $5.95)-Barreto-a 6.00
...: DARK ALLEGIANCES (1996, $5.95)-Elseworlds story, Chaykin-c/a 6.00
...: DARK KNIGHT GALLERY (1/96, $3.50)-Pin-ups by Pratt, Balent, & others 3.50
...:DAY OF JUDGMENT (11/99, $3.95) 4.00
...:DEATH OF INNOCENTS (12/96, $3.95)-O'Neil-s/ Staton-a(p) 4.00
.../DEMON (1996, $4.95)-Alan Grant scripts 5.00
.../DEMON: A TRAGEDY (2000, $5.95)-Grant-s/Murray painted-a 6.00
...:D.O.A. (1999, $6.95)-Bob Hall-s/a 7.00
...:DREAMLAND (2000, $5.95)-Grant-s/Breyfogle-a 6.00
... : EGO (2000, $6.95)-Darwyn Cooke-s/a 7.00
... 80-PAGE GIANT (8/98, $4.95) Stelfreeze-c 6.00
... 80-PAGE GIANT 2 (10/99, $4.95) Luck of the Draw 6.00
... 80-PAGE GIANT 3 (7/00, $5.95) Calendar Man 6.00
... FOREVER (1995, $5.95, direct market) 6.00
... FOREVER (1995, $3.95, newsstand) 4.00
FULL CIRCLE nn (1991, $5.95, 68 pgs.)-Sequel to Batman: Year Two 6.00
...GALLERY, The 1 (1992, $2.95)-Pin-ups by Miller, N. Adams & others 3.00
...GOLDEN STREETS OF GOTHAM (2003, $6.95) Elseworlds in early 1900s 7.00
...GOTHAM BY GASLIGHT (1989, $3.95) Elseworlds; Mignola-a/Augustyn-s 4.00
...GOTHAM CITY SECRET FILES 1 (4/00, $4.95) Batgirl app. 5.00
...: GOTHAM NOIR (2001, $6.95)-Elseworlds; Brubaker-s/Phillips-c/a 7.00
.../GREEN ARROW: THE POISON TOMORROW nn (1992, $5.95, square-bound, 68 pgs.) Netzer-c/a 6.00
HOLY TERROR nn (1991, $4.95, 52 pgs.)-Elseworlds story 5.00
.../HOUDINI: THE DEVIL'S WORKSHOP (1993, $5.95) 6.00
... :HUNTRESS/SPOILER - BLUNT TRAUMA (5/98, $2.95) Cataclysm pt. 13; Dixon-s/Barreto & Sienkiewicz-a 3.00
...: I, JOKER nn (1998, $4.95)-Elseworlds story; Bob Hall-s/a 5.00
...: IN DARKEST KNIGHT nn (1994, $4.95, 52 pgs.)-Elseworlds story; Batman w/Green Lantern's ring. 5.00
...:JOKER'S APPRENTICE (5/99, $3.95) Von Eeden-a 4.00
.../ JOKER: SWITCH (2003, $6.95)-Bolton-a/Grayson-s 7.00
...:JUDGE DREDD: JUDGEMENT ON GOTHAM nn (1991, $5.95, 68 pgs.) Simon Bisley-c/a; Grant/Wagner scripts 6.00
...:JUDGE DREDD: JUDGEMENT ON GOTHAM nn (2nd printing) 6.00
...:JUDGE DREDD: THE ULTIMATE RIDDLE (1995, $4.95) 5.00
...:JUDGE DREDD: VENDETTA IN GOTHAM (1993, $5.95) 6.00
...: KNIGHTGALLERY (1995, $3.50)-Elseworlds sketchbook. 3.50
.../ LOBO (2000, $5.95)-Elseworlds; Joker app.; Bisley-a 6.00
...: MASK OF THE PHANTASM (1994, $2.95)-Movie adapt. 3.00
...: MASK OF THE PHANTASM (1994, $4.95)-Movie adapt. 5.00
...: MASQUE (1997, $6.95)-Elseworlds; Grell-c/s/a 7.00
...: MASTER OF THE FUTURE nn (1991, $5.95, 68 pgs.)-Elseworlds; sequel to Gotham By Gaslight; Barreto-a; embossed-c 6.00
...: MITEFALL (1995, $4.95)-Alan Grant script, Kevin O'Neill-a 5.00
... : MR. FREEZE (1997, $4.95)-Dini-s/Buckingham-a; Stelfreeze-c; cover art interlocks w/Batman:(Bane, Batgirl, Poison Ivy) 5.00
... /NIGHTWING: BLOODBORNE (2002, $5.95) Cypress-a; McKeever-c 6.00
...: NOSFERATU (1999, $5.95) McKeever-a 6.00
...: OF ARKHAM (2000, $5.95)-Elseworlds; Grant-s/Alcatena-a 6.00
...: OUR WORLDS AT WAR (8/01, $2.95)-Jae Lee-c 3.00
...: PENGUIN TRIUMPHANT nn (1992, $4.95)-Staton-a(p); foil logo 5.00
...PHANTOM STRANGER nn (1997, $4.95) nn-Grant-s/Ransom-a 5.00
... : PLUS (2/97, $2.95) Arsenal-c/app. 3.00
... : POISON IVY (1997, $4.95)-J.F. Moore-s/Apthorp-a; Stelfreeze-c; cover art interlocks w/Batman:(Bane, Batgirl, Mr. Freeze) 5.00
.../POISON IVY: CAST SHADOWS (2004, $6.95) Van Fleet-c/a; Nocenti-s 7.00
.../PUNISHER: LAKE OF FIRE (1994, $4.95, DC/Marvel) 5.00
... :REIGN OF TERROR ('99, $4.95) Elseworlds 5.00
...RETURNS MOVIE SPECIAL (1992, $3.95) 4.00
...RETURNS MOVIE PRESTIGE (1992, $5.95, squarebound)-Dorman painted-c 6.00
...:RIDDLER-THE RIDDLE FACTORY (1995, $4.95)-Wagner script 5.00

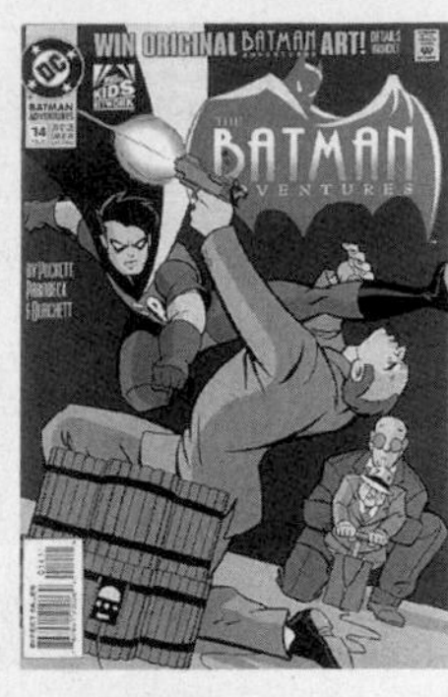

Batman Adventures #14 © DC

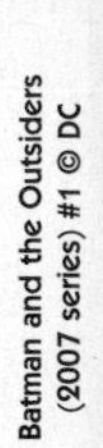

Batman and the Outsiders (2007 series) #1 © DC

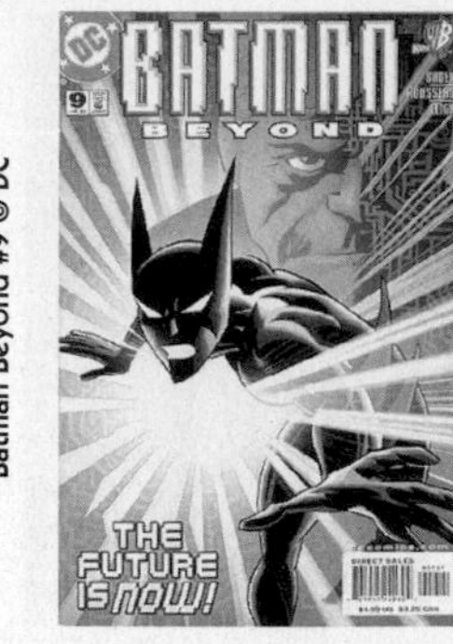

Batman Beyond #9 © DC

GD VG FN VF VF/NM NM-
2.0 4.0 6.0 8.0 9.0 9.2

GD VG FN VF VF/NM NM-
2.0 4.0 6.0 8.0 9.0 9.2

...: ROOM FULL OF STRANGERS (2004, $5.95) Scott Morse-s/c/a 6.00
...: SCARECROW 3-D (12/98, $3.95) w/glasses 4.00
.../ SCARFACE: A PSYCHODRAMA (2001, $5.95)-Adlard-a/Sienkiewicz-c 6.00
...: SCAR OF THE BAT nn (1996, $4.95)-Elseworlds; Max Allan Collins script; Barreto-a 5.00
... :SCOTTISH CONNECTION (1998, $5.95) Quitely-a 6.00
... :SEDUCTION OF THE GUN nn (1992, $2.50, 68 pgs.) 3.00
.../SPAWN: WAR DEVIL nn (1994, $4.95, 52 pgs.) 5.00
... SPECIAL 1 (4/84)-Mike W. Barr story; Golden-c/a 1 2 3 5 6 8
.../SPIDER-MAN (1997, $4.95) Dematteis-s/Nolan & Kesel-a 5.00
... : THE ABDUCTION ('98, $5.95) 6.00
...: THE BLUE, THE GREY, & THE BAT (1992, $5.95)-Weiss/Lopez-a 6.00
... :THE HILL (5/00, $2.95)-Priest-s/Martinbrough-a 3.00
... :THE KILLING JOKE (1988, deluxe 52 pgs., mature readers)-Bolland-c/a; Alan Moore scripts; Joker cripples Barbara Gordon 2 4 6 11 16 20
...: THE KILLING JOKE (2nd thru 11th printings) 2 4 6 8 10 12
...: THE KILLING JOKE : THE DELUXE EDITION (2008, $17.99, HC) re-colored version along with Bolland-s/a from Batman Black and White #4; sketch pages; Tim Sale intro. 18.00
...: THE MAN WHO LAUGHS (2005, $6.95)-Retells 1st meeting with the Joker; Mahnke-a 7.00
...: THE OFFICIAL COMIC ADAPTATION OF THE WARNER BROS. MOTION PICTURE (1989, $2.50, regular format, 68 pgs.)-Ordway-c 3.00
...: THE OFFICIAL COMIC ADAPTATION OF THE WARNER BROS. MOTION PICTURE (1989, $4.95, prestige format, 68 pgs.)-same interiors but different-c 5.00
...: THE ORDER OF BEASTS (2004, $5.95)-Elseworlds; Eddie Campbell-a 6.00
...: THE SPIRIT (1/07, $4.99)-Loeb-s/Cooke-a; P'Gell & Commissioner Dolan app. 5.00
...: THE 10-CENT ADVENTURE (3/02, 10¢) intro. to the "Bruce Wayne: Murderer" x-over; Rucka-s/Burchett & Janson-a/Dave Johnson-c 2.00
NOTE: (Also see Promotional Comics section for alternate copies with special outer half-covers promoting local comic shops)
...: THE 12-CENT ADVENTURE (10/04, 12¢) intro. to the "War Games" x-over; Grayson-s/Bachs-a; Catwoman & Spoiler app. 2.00
...: TWO-FACE-CRIME AND PUNISHMENT-(1995, $4.95)-McDaniel-a 5.00
... : TWO FACES (11/98, $4.95) Elseworlds 5.00
...: VENGEANCE OF BANE SPECIAL 1 (1992, $2.50, 68 pgs.)-Origin & 1st app. Bane (see Batman #491) 2 4 6 8 10 12
...: VENGEANCE OF BANE SPECIAL 1 (2nd printing) 3.00
...:VENGEANCE OF BANE II nn (1995, $3.95)-sequel 4.00
Vs. THE INCREDIBLE HULK (1995, $3.95)-r/DC Special Series #27 4.00
...: VILLAINS SECRET FILES (10/98, $4.95) Origin-s 5.00
... VILLAINS SECRET FILES AND ORIGINS 2005 (7/05, $4.99) Clayface origin w/ Mignola-a; Black Mask story, pin-up of villains by various; Barrionuevo-c 5.00

BATMAN ADVENTURES, THE (Based on animated series)
DC Comics: Oct, 1992 - No. 36, Oct, 1995 ($1.25/$1.50)

1-Penguin-c/story 4.00
1 ($1.95, Silver Edition)-2nd printing 2.50
2-6,8-19: 2,12-Catwoman-c/story. 3-Joker-c/story. 5-Scarecrow-c/story. 10-Riddler-c/story. 11-Man-Bat-c/story. 12-Batgirl & Catwoman-c/story. 16-Joker-c/story; begin $1.50-c. 18-Batgirl-c/story. 19-Scarecrow-c/story. 3.00
7-Special edition polybagged with Man-Bat trading card 5.00
20-24,26-32: 26-Batgirl app. 2.50
25-($2.50, 52 pgs.)-Superman app. 3.00
33-36: 33-Begin $1.75-c 2.50
Annual 1,2 ('94, '95): 2-Demon-c/story; Ra's al Ghul app. 3.50
...: Dangerous Dames & Demons (2003, $14.95, TPB) r/Annual 1,2, Mad Love & Adventures in the DC Universe #3; Bruce Timm painted-c 15.00
Holiday Special 1 (1995, $2.95) 4.00
The Collected Adventures Vol. 1,2 ('93, '95, $5.95) 6.00
TPB ('98, $7.95) r/#1-6; painted wraparound-c 8.00

BATMAN ADVENTURES (Based on animated series)
DC Comics: Jun, 2003 - No. 17, Oct, 2004 ($2.25)

1-Timm-c (2003 Free Comic Book Day edition is listed in Promotional Comics section) 2.25
2-17: 3,16-Joker-c/app. 4-Ra's al Ghul app. 6-8-Phantasm app. 14-Grey Ghost app. 2.50
Vol. 1: Rogues Gallery (2004, $6.95, digest size) r/#1-4 & Batman: Gotham Advs. #50 7.00
Vol. 2: Shadows & Masks (2004, $6.95, digest size) r/#5-9 7.00

BATMAN ADVENTURES, THE: MAD LOVE
DC Comics: Feb, 1994 ($3.95/$4.95)

1-Origin of Harley Quinn; Dini-s/Timm-c/a 2 4 6 8 10 12
1-($4.95, Prestige format) new Timm painted-c 1 2 3 5 6 8

BATMAN ADVENTURES, THE: THE LOST YEARS (TV)
DC Comics: Jan, 1998 - No. 5, May, 1998 ($1.95) (Based on animated series)

1-5-Leads into Fall '97's new animated episodes. 4-Tim Drake becomes Robin. 5-Dick becomes Nightwing 2.50
TPB-(1999, $9.95) r/series 10.00

BATMAN/ALIENS
DC Comics/Dark Horse: Mar, 1997 - No. 2, Apr, 1997 ($4.95, limited series)

1,2: Wrightson-c/a. 5.00
TPB-(1997, $14.95) w/prequel from DHP #101,102 15.00

BATMAN/ALIENS II
DC Comics/Dark Horse: 2003 - No. 3, 2003 ($5.95, limited series)

1-3-Edginton-s/Staz Johnson-a 6.00
TPB-(2003, $14.95) r/#1-3 15.00

BATMAN AND ROBIN ADVENTURES (TV)
DC Comics: Nov, 1995 - No. 25, Dec, 1997 ($1.75) (Based on animated series)

1-Dini-s. 3.00
2-24: 2-4-Dini script. 4-Penguin-c/story. 5-Joker-c/story; Poison Ivy, Harley Quinn-c/app. 9-Batgirl & Talia-c/story. 10-Ra's al Ghul-c/story. 11-Man-Bat app. 12-Bane-c/app. 13-Scarecrow-c/app. 15 Deadman-c/app. 16-Catwoman-c/app. 18-Joker-c/app. 24-Poison Ivy app. 2.50
25-($2.95, 48 pgs.) 3.00
Annual 1,2 (11/96, 11/97): 1-Phantasm-c/app. 2-Zatara & Zatanna-c/app. 4.00
...: Sub-Zero(1998, $3.95) Adaptation of animated video 4.00

BATMAN AND SUPERMAN ADVENTURES: WORLD'S FINEST
DC Comics: 1997 ($6.95, square-bound, one-shot) (Based on animated series)

1-Adaptation of animated crossover episode; Dini-s/Timm-c. 7.00

BATMAN AND SUPERMAN: WORLD'S FINEST
DC Comics: Apr, 1999 - No. 10, Jan, 2000 ($4.95/$1.99, limited series)

1,10-($4.95, squarebound) Taylor-a 5.00
2-9-($1.99) 5-Batgirl app. 8-Catwoman-c/app. 2.50
TPB (2003, $19.95) r/#1-10 20.00

BATMAN AND THE OUTSIDERS (The Adventures of the Outsiders #33 on)
(Also see Brave & The Bold #200 & The Outsiders) (Replaces The Brave and the Bold)
DC Comics: Aug, 1983 - No. 32, Apr, 1986 (Mando paper #5 on)

1-Batman, Halo, Geo-Force, Katana, Metamorpho & Black Lightning begin 4.00
2-32: 5-New Teen Titans x-over. 9-Halo begins. 11,12-Origin Katana. 18-Moro info on Motamorpho's origin. 28-31-Lookers origin. 32-Team disbands 2.50
Annual 1,2 (9/84, 9/85): 2-Metamorpho & Sapphire Stagg wed 3.00
NOTE: *Aparo a-1-9, 11-13p, 16-20; c-1-4, 5i, 6-21, Annual 1, 2.* ***B. Kane*** *a-3r.* ***Layton*** *a-19i, 20i.* ***Lopez*** *a-3p.* ***Miller*** *c-Annual 1.* ***Perez*** *c-5p.* ***B. Willingham*** *a-14p.*

BATMAN AND THE OUTSIDERS (Continued from The Outsiders)
DC Comics: Dec, 2007 - Present ($2.99)

1-9: 1-Batman, Catwoman, Martian Manhunter, Katana, Metamorpho, Thunder & Grace begin. 4-Batgirl app. 3.00

BATMAN: BANE OF THE DEMON
DC Comics: Mar, 1998 - No. 4, June, 1998 ($1.95, limited series)

1-4-Dixon-s/Nolan-a; prelude to Legacy x-over 2.50

BATMAN BEYOND (Based on animated series)(Mini-series)
DC Comics: Mar, 1999 - No. 6, Aug, 1999 ($1.99)

1-6: 1,2-Adaptation of pilot episode, Timm-c 2.50
TPB (1999, $9.95) r/#1-6 10.00

BATMAN BEYOND (Based on animated series)(Continuing series)
DC Comics: Nov, 1999 - No. 24, Oct, 2001 ($1.99)

1-24: 1-Rousseau-a; Batman vs. Batman. 14-Demon-c/app. 21,22-Justice League Unlimited-c/app. 2.50
...: Return of the Joker (2/01, $2.95) adaptation of video release 3.00

BATMAN: BLACK & WHITE
DC Comics: June, 1996 - No. 4, Sept, 1996 ($2.95, B&W, limited series)

1-Stories by McKeever, Timm, Kubert, Chaykin, Goodwin; Jim Lee-c; Allred inside front-c; Moebius inside back-c 4.00
2-4: 2-Stories by Simonson, Corben, Bisley & Gaiman; Miller-c. 3-Stories by M. Wagner, Janson, Sienkiewicz, O'Neil & Kristiansen; B. Smith-c; Russell inside front-c; Silvestri inside back-c. 4-Stories by Bolland, Goodwin & Gianni, Strnad & Nowlan, O'Neil & Stelfreeze; Toth-c; pin-ups by Neal Adams & Alex Ross 3.00
Hardcover ('97, $39.95) r/series w/new art & cover plate 40.00
Softcover ('00, $19.95) r/series 20.00
Volume 2 HC ('02, $39.95, 7 3/4"x12") r/B&W back-up-s from Batman: Gotham Knights #1-16; stories and art by various incl. Ross, Buscema, Byrne, Ellison, Sale; Mignola-c 40.00
Volume 2 SC ('03, $19.95, 7 3/4"x12") same contents as HC 20.00
Volume 3 HC ('07, $24.99, reg. size) r/B&W back-up-s from Batman: Gotham Knights #17-49; stories and art by various incl. Davis, DeCarlo, Morse, Schwartz, Thompson; Miller-c 25.00

BATMAN: BOOK OF THE DEAD

Batman Confidential #12 © DC

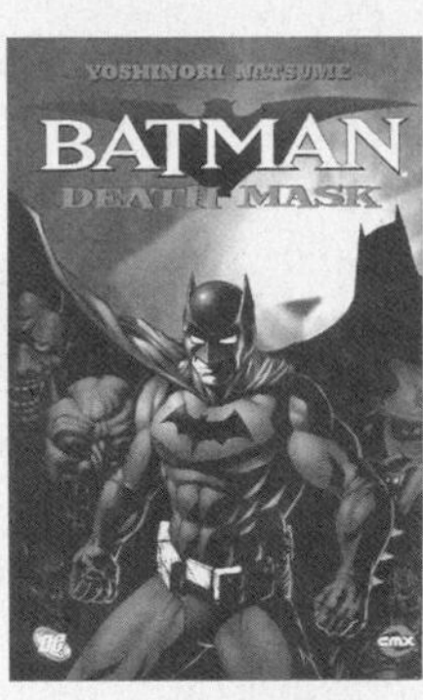

Batman: Death Mask #1 © DC

Batman: Gotham Adventures #60 © DC

GD VG FN VF VF/NM NM-
2.0 4.0 6.0 8.0 9.0 9.2

DC Comics: Jun, 1999 - No. 2, July, 1999 ($4.95, limited series, prestige format)

1,2-Elseworlds; Kitson-a 5.00

BATMAN: CATWOMAN DEFIANT (See Batman one-shots)

BATMAN/ CATWOMAN: TRAIL OF THE GUN
DC Comics: 2004 - No. 2, 2004 ($5.95, limited series, prestige format)

1,2-Elseworlds; Van Sciver-a/Nocenti-s 6.00

BATMAN CHRONICLES, THE
DC Comics: Summer, 1995 - No. 23, Winter, 2001 ($2.95, quarterly)

1-3,5-19: 1-Dixon/Grant/Moench script. 3-Bolland-c. 5-Oracle Year One story, Richard Dragon app.,Chaykin-c. 6-Kaluta-c; Ra's al Ghul story. 7-Superman-c/app.11-Paul Pope-s/a. 12-Cataclysm pt. 10. 18-No Man's Land 3.50
4-Hitman story by Ennis, Contagion tie-in; Balent-c 2 4 6 8 10 12
20-23: 20-Catwoman and Relative Heroes-c/app. 21-Pander Bros.-a 3.00
...Gallery (3/97, $3.50) Pin ups 3.50
...Gauntlet, The (1997, $4.95, one-shot) 5.00

BATMAN: CITY OF LIGHT
DC Comics: Dec, 2003 - No. 8, July, 2004 ($2.95, limited series)

1-8-Pander Brothers-a/s; Paniccia-s 3.00

BATMAN CONFIDENTIAL
DC Comics: Feb, 2007 - Present ($2.99)

1-19: 1-6-Diggle-s/Portacio a/c. 7-12-Cowan-a; Joker's origin. 13-16-Morales-a 3.00
...: Lovers and Madmen HC (2008, $24.99, dustjacket) r/#7-12; Brad Meltzer Intro. 25.00
...: Rules of Engagement HC (2007, $24.99, dustjacket) r/#1-6 25.00

BATMAN: DARK DETECTIVE
DC Comics: Early July, 2005 - No. 6, Late September, 2005 ($2.99, limited series)

1-6-Englehart-s/Rogers & Austin-a; Silver St. Cloud and The Joker app. 3.00

BATMAN: DARK KNIGHT OF THE ROUND TABLE
DC Comics: 1999 - No. 2, 1999 ($4.95, limited series, prestige format)

1,2-Elseworlds; Giordano-a 5.00

BATMAN: DARK VICTORY
DC Comics: 1999 - No. 13, 2000 ($4.95/$2.95, limited series)

Wizard #0 Preview 2.25
1-($4.95) Loeb-s/Sale-c/a 5.00
2-12-($2.95) 3.00
13-($4.95) 5.00
Hardcover (2001, $29.95) with dust jacket; r/#0,1-13 30.00
Softcover (2002, $19.95) r/#0,1-13 20.00

BATMAN: DEATH AND THE MAIDENS
DC Comics: Oct, 2003 - No. 9, Aug, 2004 ($2.95, limited series)

1-Ra's al Ghul app.; Rucka-s/Janson-a 4.00
2-9: 9-Ra's al Ghul dies 3.00
TPB (2004, $19.95) r/#1-9 & Detective #783 20.00

BATMAN/ DEATHBLOW: AFTER THE FIRE
DC Comics/WildStorm: 2002 - No. 3, 2002 ($5.95, limited series)

1-3-Azzarello-s/Bermejo & Bradstreet-a 6.00
TPB (2003, $12.95) r/#1-3; plus concept art 13.00

BATMAN: DEATH MASK
DC Comics/CMX: Jun, 2008 - No. 4, Sept, 2008 ($2.99, B&W, limited series, right-to-left manga style)

1-4-Yoshinori Natsume-s/a 3.00

BATMAN FAMILY, THE
National Periodical Pub./DC Comics: Sept-Oct, 1975 - No. 20, Oct-Nov, 1978
(#1-4, 17-on: 68 pgs.) (Combined with Detective Comics with No. 481)

1-Origin/2nd app. Batgirl-Robin team-up (The Dynamite Duo); reprints plus one new story begins; N. Adams-a(r); r/1st app. Man-Bat from Det. #400
4 8 12 22 34 45
2-5: 2-r/Det. #369. 3-Batgirl & Robin learn each's i.d.; r/Batwoman app. from Batman #105. 4-r/1st Fatman app. from Batman #113. 5-r/1st Bat-Hound app. from Batman #92
3 6 9 14 20 25
6,9-Joker's daughter on cover (1st app?) 3 6 9 16 22 28
7,8,14-16: 8-r/Batwoman app.14-Batwoman app. 15-3rd app. Killer Moth. 16-Bat-Girl cameo (last app. in costume until New Teen Titans #47) 2 4 6 10 14 18
10-1st revival Batwoman; Cavalier app.; Killer Moth app.
3 6 9 17 25 32
11-13,17-20: 11-13-Rogers-a(p): 11-New stories begin; Man-Bat begins. 13-Batwoman cameo. 17-($1.00 size)-Batman, Huntress begin; Batwoman & Catwoman 1st meet.

GD VG FN VF VF/NM NM-
2.0 4.0 6.0 8.0 9.0 9.2

18-20: Huntress by Staton in all. 20-Origin Ragman retold
3 6 9 16 23 30

NOTE: *Aparo a-17; c-11-16.* ***Austin*** *a-12i.* ***Chaykin*** *a-14p.* ***Michael Golden*** *a-15-17,18-20p.* ***Grell*** *a-1; c-1.* ***Gil Kane*** *a-2r.* ***Kaluta*** *c-17, 19.* ***Newton*** *a-13.* ***Robinson*** *a-1r, 3i(r), 9r.* ***Russell*** *a-18i, 19i.* ***Starlin*** *a-17; c-18, 20.*

BATMAN: FAMILY
DC Comics: Dec, 2002 - No. 8, Feb, 2003 ($2.95/$2.25, weekly limited series)

1,8-($2.95). John Francis Moore-s/Hoberg & Gaudiano-a 3.00
2-7-($2.25). 3-Orpheus & Black Canary app. 2.50

BATMAN: GCPD
DC Comics: Aug, 1996 - No. 4, Nov, 1996 ($2.25, limited series)

1-4: Features Jim Gordon; Aparo/Sienkiewicz-a 2.50

BATMAN: GORDON OF GOTHAM
DC Comics: June, 1998 - No. 4, Sept, 1998 ($1.95, limited series)

1-4: Gordon's early days in Chicago 2.50

BATMAN: GORDON'S LAW
DC Comics: Dec, 1996 - No. 4, Mar, 1997 ($1.95, limited series)

1-4: Dixon-s/Janson-c/a 2.50

BATMAN: GOTHAM ADVENTURES (TV)
DC Comics: June, 1998 - No. 60, May, 2003 ($2.95/$1.95/$1.99/$2.25)

1-($2.95) Based on Kids WB Batman animated series 3.00
2-3-($1.95): 2-Two-Face-c/app. 2.50
4-22: 4-Begin $1.99-c. 5-Deadman-c. 13-MAD #1 cover swipe 2.50
23-60: 31,60-Joker-c/app. 50-Catwoman c/app. 53-Begin $2.25-c. 58-Creeper-c/app. 2.50
TPB (2000, $9.95) r/#1-6 10.00

BATMAN: GOTHAM AFTER MIDNIGHT
DC Comics: July, 2008 - No. 12 ($2.99, limited series)

1-3-Steve Niles-s/Kelley Jones-a/c. 1-Scarecrow app. 2-Man-Bat app. 3.00

BATMAN: GOTHAM COUNTY LINE
DC Comics: 2005 - No. 3, 2005 ($5.99, square-bound, limited series)

1-3-Steve Niles-s/Scott Hampton-a. 2,3-Deadman app. 6.00
TPB (2006, $17.99) r/#1-3 18.00

BATMAN: GOTHAM KNIGHTS
DC Comics: Mar, 2000 - No. 74, Apr, 2006 ($2.50/$2.75)

1-Grayson-s; B&W back-up by Warren Ellis & Jim Lee 4.00
2-10-Grayson-s; B&W back-ups by various 2.75
11-($3.25) Bolland-c; Kyle Baker back-up story 3.25
12-24: 13-Officer Down x-over; Ellison back-up-s. 15-Colan back-up. 20-Superman-c/app. 2.75
25,26-Bruce Wayne: Murderer pt. 4,10 3.00
27-31: 28,30,31-Bruce Wayne: Fugitive pt. 7,14,17 2.75
32-49: 32-Begin $2.75-c; Kaluta-a back-up. 33,34-Bane-c/app. 35-Mahfood-a back-up. 38-Bolton-a back-up. 43-Jason Todd & Batgirl app. 44-Jason Todd flashback 2.75
50-54-Hush returns-Barrionuevo-a/Bermejo-c. 53,54-Green Arrow app. 3.00
55-($3.75) Batman vs. Hush; Joker & Riddler app. 4.00
56-74: 56-58-War Games; Jae Lee-c. 60-65-Hush app. 66-Villains United tie-in; Talia app. 2.50
Batman: Hush Returns TPB (2006, $12.99) r/#50-55,66; cover gallery 13.00

BATMAN: GOTHAM NIGHTS II (First series listed under Gotham Nights)
DC Comics: Mar, 1995 - No. 4, June, 1995 ($1.95, limited series)

1-4 2.50

BATMAN/GRENDEL (1st limited series)
DC Comics: 1993 - No. 2, 1993 ($4.95, limited series, squarebound; 52 pgs.)

1,2: Batman vs. Hunter Rose. 1-Devil's Riddle; Matt Wagner-c/a/scripts. 2-Devil's Masque; Matt Wagner-c/a/scripts 6.00

BATMAN/GRENDEL (2nd limited series)
DC Comics: June, 1996 - No. 2, July, 1996 ($4.95, limited series, squarebound)

1,2: Batman vs. Grendel Prime. 1-Devil's Bones. 2-Devil's Dance; Wagner-c/a/s 5.00

BATMAN: HARLEY & IVY
DC Comics: Jun, 2004 - No. 3, Aug, 2004 ($2.50, limited series)

1-3-Paul Dini-s/Bruce Timm-c/a 2.50
TPB (2007, $14.99) r/series; newly colored story from Batman: Gotham Knights #14 and Harley and Ivy: Love on the Lam series 15.00

BATMAN: HARLEY QUINN
DC Comics: 1999 ($5.95, prestige format)

1-Intro. of Harley Quinn into regular DC continuity; Dini-s/Alex Ross-c 9.00
1-(2nd printing) 6.00

BATMAN: HAUNTED GOTHAM
DC Comics: 2000 - No. 4, 2000 ($4.95, limited series, squarebound)

Batman: Journey Into Knight #1 © DC

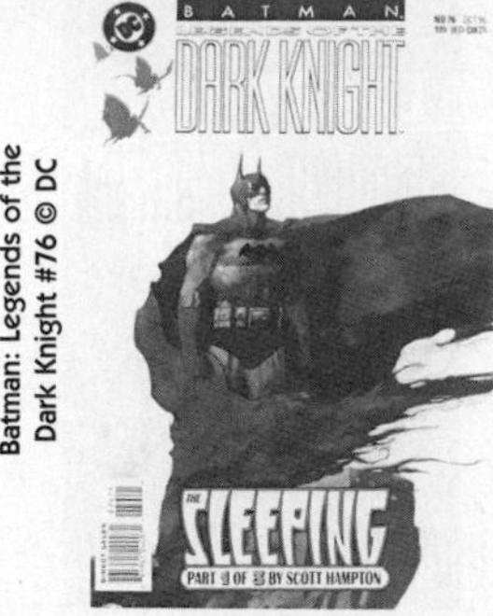

Batman: Legends of the Dark Knight #76 © DC

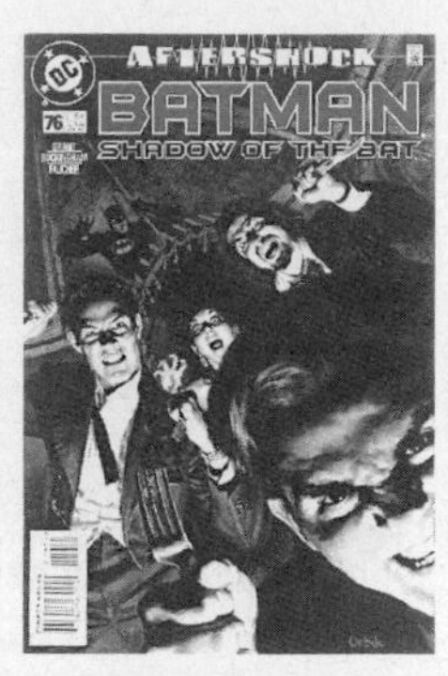

Batman: Shadow of the Bat #76 © DC

GD VG FN VF VF/NM NM-
2.0 4.0 6.0 8.0 9.0 9.2

1-4-Moench-s/Kelley Jones-c/a 5.00

BATMAN/ HELLBOY/STARMAN
DC Comics/Dark Horse: Jan, 1999 - No. 2, Feb, 1999 ($2.50, limited series)

1,2: Robinson-s/Mignola-a. 2-Harris-c 2.50

BATMAN: HOLLYWOOD KNIGHT
DC Comics: Apr, 2001 - No. 3, Jun, 2001 ($2.50, limited series)

1-3-Elseworlds Batman as a 1940's movie star; Giordano-a/Layton-s 2.50

BATMAN/ HUNTRESS: CRY FOR BLOOD
DC Comics: Jun, 2000 - No. 6, Nov, 2000 ($2.50, limited series)

1-6: Rucka-s/Burchett-a; The Question app. 2.50
TPB (2002, $12.95) r/#1-6 13.00

BATMAN: JEKYLL & HYDE
DC Comics: June, 2005 - No. 6, Nov, 2005 ($2.99, limited series)

1-6-Paul Jenkins-s; Two-Face app. 1-3-Jae Lee-a. 4-6-Sean Phillips-a 3.00
TPB (2008, $14.99) r/#1-6 15.00

BATMAN: JOKER TIME (...: It's Joker Time! on cover)
DC Comics: 2000 - No. 3 ($4.95, limited series, squarebound)

1-3-Bob Hall-s/a 5.00

BATMAN: JOURNEY INTO KNGHT
DC Comics: Oct, 2005 - No. 12, Nov, 2006 ($2.50/$2.99, limited series)

1-9-Andrew Helfer-s/Tan Eng Huat-a/Pat Lee-c 2.50
10-12-($2.99) Joker app. 3.00

BATMAN/ JUDGE DREDD "DIE LAUGHING"
DC Comics: 1998 - No. 2, 1999 ($4.95, limited series, squarebound)

1,2: 1-Fabry-c/a. 2-Jim Murray-c/a 5.00

BATMAN: KNIGHTGALLERY (See Batman one-shots)

BATMAN: LEAGUE OF BATMEN
DC Comics: 2001 - No. 2, 2001 ($5.95, limited series, squarebound)

1,2-Elseworlds; Moench-s/Bright & Tanghal-a/Van Fleet-c 6.00

BATMAN: LEGENDS OF THE DARK KNIGHT (Legends of the Dark...#1-36)
DC Comics: Nov, 1989 - No. 214, Mar, 2007 ($1.50/$1.75/$1.95/$1.99/$2.25/$2.50/$2.99)

1- "Shaman" begins, ends #5; outer cover has four different color variations, all worth same 4.00
2-10: 6-10- "Gothic" by Grant Morrison (scripts) 3.00
11-15: 11-15-Gulacy/Austin-a. 13-Catwoman app. 3.00
16-Intro drug Bane uses; begin Venom story 5.00
17-20 4.00
21-49,51-63: 38-Bat-Mite-c/story. 46-49-Catwoman app. w/Heath-c/a. 51-Ragman app.; Joe Kubert-c. 59,60,61-Knightquest x-over. 62,63-KnightsEnd Pt. 4 & 10 3.00
50-($3.95, 68 pgs.)-Bolland embossed gold foil-c; Joker-c/story; pin-ups by Chaykin, Simonson, Williamson, Kaluta, Russell, others 5.00
64-99: 64-(9/94)-Begin $1.95-c. 71-73-James Robinson-s,Watkiss-c/a. 74,75-McKeever-c/a/s. 76-78-Scott Hampton-c/a/s. 81-Card insert. 83,84-Ellis-s. 85-Robinson-s. 91-93-Ennis-s. 94-Michael T. Gilbert-s/a. 3.00
100-($3.95) Alex Ross painted-c; gallery by various 5.00
101-115: 101-Ezquerra-a. 102-104-Robinson-s 2.50
116-No Man's Land stories begin; Huntress-c 4.00
117-119,121-126: 122-Harris-c 2.50
120-ID of new Batgirl revealed 4.00
127-131: Return to Legends stories; Green Arrow app. 2.50
132-199, 201-204: 132-136 ($2.25-c) Archie Goodwin-s/Rogers-a. 137-141-Gulacy-a. 142-145-Joker and Ra's al Ghul app. 146-148-Kitson-a. 158-Begin $2.50-c 169-171-Tony Harris-c/a. 182-184-War Games. 182-Bagged with Sky Captain CD 2.50
200-($4.99) Joker-c/app. 5.00
205-214: 205-Begin $2.99-c. 207,208-Olivetti-a. 214-Deadshot app. 3.00
#0-(10/94)-Zero Hour; Quesada/Palmiotti-c; released between #64&65 3.00
Annual 1-7 ('91-'97, $3.50-$3.95, 68 pgs.): 1-Joker app. 2-Netzer-c/a. 3-New Batman (Azrael) app. 4-Elseworlds story. 5-Year One; Man-Bat app. 6-Legend of the Dead Earth story. 7-Pulp Heroes story 4.00
Halloween Special 1 (12/93, $6.95, 84 pgs.)-Embossed & foil stamped-c 1 2 3 4 5 7
Batman Madness-...Halloween Special (1994, $4.95) 5.00
Batman Ghosts-...Halloween Special (1995, $4.95) 5.00

NOTE: *Aparo a-Annual 1.* ***Chaykin*** *scripts-24-26.* ***Giffen*** *a-Annual 1.* ***Golden*** *a-Annual 1.* ***Alan Grant*** *scripts-38, 52, 53.* ***Gil Kane*** *c/a-24-26.* ***Mignola*** *a-54; c-54, 62.* ***Morrow*** *a-Annual 3i.* ***Quesada*** *a-Annual 1.* ***James Robinson*** *scripts- 71-73.* ***Russell*** *c/a-42, 43.* ***Sears*** *a-21, 23; c-21, 23.* ***Zeck*** *a-69, 70; c-69, 70.*

BATMAN-LEGENDS OF THE DARK KNIGHT: JAZZ
DC Comics: Apr, 1995 - No. 3, June, 1995 ($2.50, limited series)

GD VG FN VF VF/NM NM-
2.0 4.0 6.0 8.0 9.0 9.2

1-3 2.50

BATMAN/LOBO
DC Comics: Oct, 2007 - No. 2, Nov, 2007 ($5.99, squarebound, limited series)

1,2-Sam Kieth-s/a 6.00

BATMAN: MANBAT
DC Comics: Oct, 1995 - No. 3, Dec, 1995 ($4.95, limited series)

1-3-Elseworlds-Delano-script; Bolton-a. 5.00
TPB-(1997, $14.95) r/#1-3 15.00

BATMAN: MITEFALL (See Batman one-shots)

BATMAN MINIATURE (See Batman Kellogg's)

BATMAN: NEVERMORE
DC Comics: June, 2003 - No. 5, Oct, 2003 ($2.50, limited series)

1-5-Elseworlds Batman & Edgar Allan Poe; Wrightson-c/Guy Davis-a/Len Wein-s 2.50

BATMAN: NO MAN'S LAND (Also see 1999 Batman titles)
DC Comics: (one shots)

nn (3/99, $2.95) Alex Ross-c; Bob Gale-s; begins year-long story arc 3.00
Collector's Ed. (3/99, $3.95) Ross lenticular-c 5.00
#0 (: Ground Zero on cover) (12/99, $4.95) Orbik-c 5.00
...: Gallery (7/99, $3.95) Jim Lee-c 4.00
...: Secret Files (12/99, $4.95) Maleev-c 5.00
TPB ('99, $12.95) r/early No Man's Land stories; new Batgirl early app. 13.00
No Law and a New Order TPB(1999, $5.95) Ross-c 6.00
Volume 2 ('00, $12.95) r/later No Man's Land stories; Batgirl(Huntress) app.; Deodato-c 13.00
Volume 3-5 ('00,'01 $12.95) 3-Intro. new Batgirl. 4-('00). 5-('01) Land-c 13.00

BATMAN: ORPHEUS RISING
DC Comics: Oct, 2001 - No. 5, Feb, 2002 ($2.50, limited series)

1-5-Intro. Orpheus; Simmons-s/Turner & Miki-a 2.50

BATMAN: OUTLAWS
DC Comics: 2000 - No. 3, 2000 ($4.95, limited series)

1-3-Moench-s/Gulacy-a 5.00

BATMAN: PENGUIN TRIUMPHANT (See Batman one-shots)

BATMAN/PREDATOR III: BLOOD TIES
DC Comics/Dark Horse Comics: Nov, 1997 - No. 4, Feb, 1998 ($1.95, lim. series)

1-4: Dixon-s/Damaggio-c/a 2.50
TPB-(1998, $7.95) r/#1-4 8.00

BATMAN/RA'S AL GHUL (See Year One:...)

BATMAN RETURNS MOVIE SPECIAL (See Batman one-shots)

BATMAN: RIDDLER-THE RIDDLE FACTORY (See Batman one-shots)

BATMAN: RUN, RIDDLER, RUN
DC Comics: 1992 - Book 3, 1992 ($4.95, limited series)

Book 1-3: Mark Badger-a & plot 5.00

BATMAN SCARECROW (See Year One:...)

BATMAN: SECRET FILES
DC Comics: Oct, 1997 ($4.95)

1-New origin-s and profiles 5.00

BATMAN: SECRETS
DC Comics: May, 2006 - No. 5, Sept, 2006 ($2.99, limited series)

1-5-Sam Kieth-s/a/c; Joker app. 3.00
TPB (2007, $12.99) r/series 13.00

BATMAN: SHADOW OF THE BAT
DC Comics: June, 1992 - No. 94, Feb, 2000 ($1.50/$1.75/$1.95/$1.99)

1-The Last Arkham-c/story begins; Alan Grant scripts in all 4.00
1-($2.50)-Deluxe edition polybagged w/poster, pop-up & book mark 5.00
2-7: 4-The Last Arkham ends. 7-Last $1.50-c 3.00
8-28: 14,15-Staton-a(p). 16-18-Knightfall tie-ins. 19-28-Knightquest tie-ins w/Azrael as Batman. 25-Silver ink-c; anniversary issue 2.50
29-($2.95, 52 pgs.)-KnightsEnd Pt. 2 3.00
30-72: 30-KnightsEnd Pt. 8. 31-(9.94)-Begin $1.95-c; Zero Hour. 32-(11/94). 33-Robin-c. 35-Troika-Pt.2. 43,44-Cat-Man & Catwoman-c. 48-Contagion Pt. 1; card insert. 49-Contagion Pt.7. 56,57,58-Poison Ivy-c/app. 62-Two-Face app. 69,70-Fate app. 2.50
35-($2.95)-Variant embossed-c 3.00
73,74,76-78: Cataclysm x-over pts. 1,9. 76-78-Orbik-c 2.50
75-($2.95) Mr. Freeze & Clayface app.; Orbik-c 3.00
79,81,82: 79-Begin $1.99-c; Orbik-c 2.50
80-($3.95) Flip book with Azrael #47 4.00

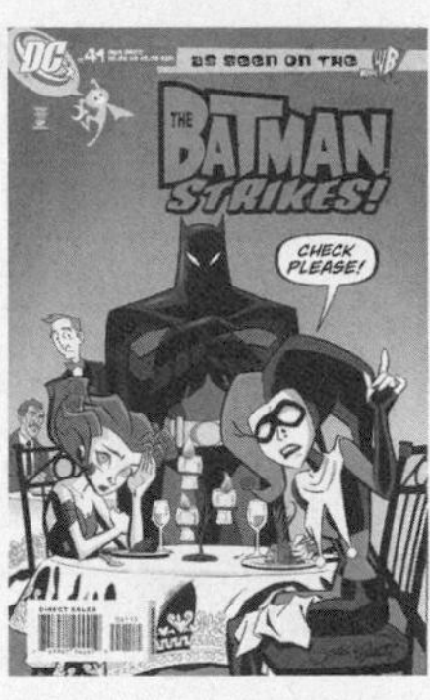

The Batman Strikes! #41 © DC

Batman: The Long Halloween #8 © DC

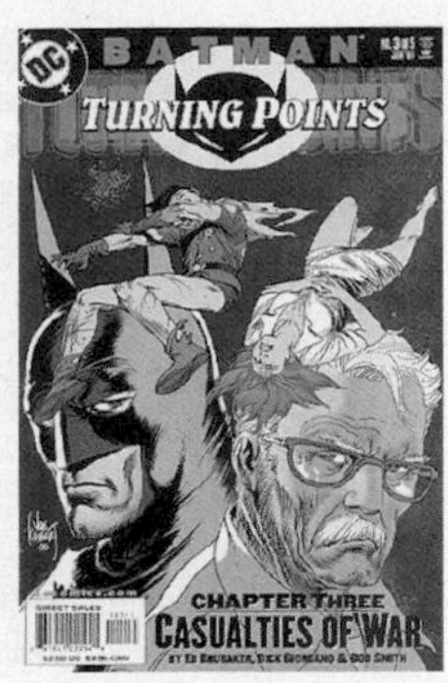

Batman: Turning Points #3 © DC

GD VG FN VF VF/NM NM-
2.0 4.0 6.0 8.0 9.0 9.2

GD VG FN VF VF/NM NM-
2.0 4.0 6.0 8.0 9.0 9.2

83-No Man's Land; intro. new Batgirl (Huntress) 12.00
84,85-No Man's Land 4.00
86-94: 87-Deodato-a. 90-Harris-c. 92-Superman app. 93-Joker and Harley app.
94-No Man's Land ends 3.00
#0 (10/94) Zero Hour; released between #31&32 3.00
#1,000,000 (11/98) 853rd Century x-over; Orbik-c 2.50
Annual 1-5 ('93-'97 $2.95-$3.95, 68 pgs.): 3-Year One story; Poison Ivy app. 4-Legends of the Dead Earth story; Starman cameo. 5-Pulp Heroes story; Poison Ivy app. 4.00

BATMAN: SON OF THE DEMON (Also see Batman #655-658 and Batman Hardcovers)
DC Comics: 2006 ($5.99, reprints the 1987 HC in comic book format)
nn-Talia has Batman's son; Mike W. Barr-s/Jerry Bingham-a; new Andy Kubert-c 6.00

BATMAN-SPAWN: WAR DEVIL (See Batman one-shots)

BATMAN SPECTACULAR (See DC Special Series No. 15)

BATMAN STRIKES!, THE (Based on the 2004 animated series) (2005 Free Comic Book Day edition is listed in Promotional Comics section)
DC Comics: Nov, 2004 - Present ($2.25)
1,2,4-47: 1,11-Penguin app. 2-Man-Bat app. 4-Bane app. 9-Joker app. 18-Batgirl debut. 29-Robin debuts. 32,33-Cal Ripken 8-pg. insert. 44-Superman app. 2.50
3-($2.95) Joker-c/app.; Catwoman & Wonder Woman-r from Advs. in the DCU 3.00
Jam Packed Action (2005, $7.99, digest) adaptations of two TV episodes 8.00
... Vol. 1: Crime Time (2005, $6.99, digest) r/#1-5 7.00
... Vol. 2: In Darkest Knight (2005, $6.99, digest) r/#6-10 7.00

BATMAN/ SUPERMAN/WONDER WOMAN: TRINITY
DC Comics: 2003 - No. 3, 2003 ($6.95, limited series, squarebound)
1-3-Matt Wagner-s/a/c. 1-Ra's al Ghul & Bizarro app. 7.00
HC (2004, $24.95, with dust-jacket) r/series; intro. by Brad Meltzer 30.00
SC (2004, $17.99) r/series; intro. by Brad Meltzer 18.00

BATMAN: SWORD OF AZRAEL (Also see Azrael & Batman #488,489)
DC Comics: Oct, 1992 - No. 4, Jan, 1993 ($1.75, limited series)
1-Wraparound gatefold-c; Quesada-c/a(p) in all; 1st app. Azrael 2 4 6 8 10 12
2-4: 4-Cont'd in Batman #488 1 2 3 5 6 8
Silver Edition 1-4 (1993, $1.95)-Reprints #1-4 2.50
Trade Paperback (1993, $9.95)-Reprints #1-4 10.00
Trade Paperback Gold Edition 15.00

BATMAN/ TARZAN: CLAWS OF THE CAT-WOMAN
Dark Horse Comics/DC Comics: Sept, 1999 - No. 4, Dec, 1999 ($2.95, limited series)
1-4: Marz-s/Kordey-a 3.00

BATMAN: TENSES
DC Comics: 2003 - No. 2, 2003 ($6.95, limited series)
1,2-Joe Casey-s/Cully Hamner-a; Bruce Wayne's first year back in Gotham 7.00

BATMAN: THE ANKH
DC Comics: 2002 - No. 2, 2002 ($5.95, limited series)
1,2-Dixon-s/Van Fleet-a 6.00

BATMAN: THE CULT
DC Comics: 1988 - No. 4, Nov, 1988 ($3.50, deluxe limited series)
1-Wrightson-a/painted-c in all 6.00
2-4 5.00
Trade Paperback ('91, $14.95)-New Wrightson-c 15.00

BATMAN: THE DARK KNIGHT RETURNS (Also see Dark Knight Strikes Again)
DC Comics: Mar, 1986 - No. 4, 1986 ($2.95, squarebound, limited series)
1-Miller story & c/a(p); set in the future 5 10 15 30 48 65
1,2-2nd & 3rd printings, 3-2nd printing 6.00
2-Carrie Kelly becomes 1st female Robin 3 6 9 16 23 30
3-Death of Joker; Superman app. 3 6 9 14 20 25
4-Death of Alfred; Superman app. 2 4 6 11 16 20
Hardcover, signed & numbered edition ($40.00)(4000 copies) 250.00
Hardcover, trade edition 50.00
Softcover, trade edition (1st printing only) 2 4 6 9 12 15
Softcover, trade edition (2nd thru 8th printings) 1 2 3 4 5 7
10th Anniv. Slipcase set ('96, $100.00): Signed & numbered hard-c edition (10,000 copies), sketchbook, copy of script for #1, 2 color prints 100.00
10th Anniv. Hardcover ('96, $45.00) 45.00
10th Anniv. Softcover ('97, $14.95) 15.00
Hardcover 2nd printing ('02, $24.95) with 3 1/4" tall partial dustjacket 25.00
NOTE: The #2 second printings can be identified by matching the grey background colors on the inside front cover and facing page. The inside front cover of the second printing has a dark grey background which does not match the lighter grey of the facing page. On the true 1st printings, the backgrounds are both light grey. All other issues are clearly marked.

BATMAN: THE DOOM THAT CAME TO GOTHAM
DC Comics: 2000 - No. 3, 2001 ($4.95, limited series)
1-3-Elseworlds; Mignola-c/s; Nixey-a; Etrigan app. 5.00

BATMAN: THE KILLING JOKE (See Batman one-shots)

BATMAN: THE LONG HALLOWEEN
DC Comics: Oct, 1996 - No. 13, Oct, 1997 ($2.95/$4.95, limited series)
1-($4.95)-Loeb-s/Sale-c/a in all 1 2 3 5 6 8
2-5($2.95): 2-Solomon Grundy-c/app. 3-Joker-c/app., Catwoman, Poison Ivy app. 6.00
6-10: 6-Poison Ivy-c. 7-Riddler-c/app. 5.00
11,12 4.00
13-($4.95, 48 pgs.)-Killer revelations 5.00
Absolute Batman: The Long Halloween (2007, $75.00, oversized HC) r/series; interviews with the creators; Sale sketch pages; action figure line; unpubbed 4-page sequence 75.00
HC-($29.95) r/series 30.00
SC-($19.95) 20.00

BATMAN: THE MAD MONK ("Batman & the Mad Monk" on cover)
DC Comics: Oct, 2006 - No. 6, ($3.50, limited series)
1-5-Matt Wagner-s/a/c. 1-Catwoman app. 3.50
TPB (2007, $14.99) r/#1-6 15.00

BATMAN: THE MONSTER MEN ("Batman & the Monster Men" on cover)
DC Comics: Jan, 2006 - No. 6, June, 2006 ($2.99, limited series)
1-6-Matt Wagner-s/a/c 3.00
TPB (2006, $14.99) r/#1-6 15.00

BATMAN: THE OFFICIAL COMIC ADAPTATION OF THE WARNER BROS. MOTION PICTURE (See Batman one-shots)

BATMAN: THE ULTIMATE EVIL
DC Comics: 1995 ($5.95, limited series, prestige format)
1,2-Barrett, Jr. adaptation of Vachss novel. 6.00

BATMAN 3-D (Also see 3-D Batman)
DC Comics: 1990 ($9.95, w/glasses, 8-1/8x10-3/4")
nn-Byrne-a/scripts; Riddler, Joker, Penguin & Two-Face app. plus r/1953 3-D Batman; pin-ups by many artists 2 4 6 8 10 12

BATMAN: TOYMAN
DC Comics: Nov, 1998 - No. 4, Feb, 1999 ($2.25, limited series)
1-4-Hama-s 2.50

BATMAN: TURNING POINTS
DC Comics: Jan, 2001 - No. 5, Jan, 2001 ($2.50, weekly limited series)
1-5: 2-Giella-a. 3-Kubert-c/Giordano-a. 4-Chaykin-c/Brent Anderson-a. 5-Pope-c/a 2.50
TPB (2007, $14.99) r/#1-5 15.00

BATMAN: TWO-FACE-CRIME AND PUNISHMENT (See Batman one-shots)

BATMAN: TWO-FACE STRIKES TWICE
DC Comics: 1993 - No. 2, 1993 ($4.95, 52 pgs.)
1,2-Flip book format w/Staton-a (G.A. side) 5.00

BATMAN VERSUS PREDATOR
DC Comics/Dark Horse Comics: 1991 - No. 3, 1992 ($4.95/$1.95, limited series) (1st DC/Dark Horse x-over)
1 (Prestige format, $4.95)-1 & 3 contain 8 Batman/Predator trading cards; Andy & Adam Kubert-a; Suydam painted-c 6.00
1-3 (Regular format, $1.95)-No trading cards 3.00
2,3-(Prestige)-2-Extra pin-ups inside; Suydam-c 5.00
TPB (1993, $5.95, 132 pgs.)-r/#1-3 w/new introductions & forward plus new wraparound-c by Dave Gibbons 6.00

BATMAN VERSUS PREDATOR II: BLOODMATCH
DC Comics: Late 1994 - No. 4, 1995 ($2.50, limited series)
1-4-Huntress app.; Moench scripts; Gulacy-a 3.00
TPB (1995, $6.95)-r/#1-4 7.00

BATMAN VS. THE INCREDIBLE HULK (See DC Special Series No. 27)

BATMAN: WAR ON CRIME
DC Comics: Nov, 1999 ($9.95, treasury size, one-shot)
nn-Painted art by Alex Ross; story by Alex Ross and Paul Dini 10.00

BATMAN/ WILDCAT
DC Comics: Apr, 1997 - No.3, June, 1997 ($2.25, mini-series)

Battle #3 © MAR

Battle Chasers #3 © Joe Madureira

Battle Classics #1 © DC

	GD 2.0	VG 4.0	FN 6.0	VF 8.0	VF/NM 9.0	NM- 9.2
1-3: Dixon/Smith-s: 1-Killer Croc app.						2.50

BATMAN: YEAR 100
DC Comics: 2006 - No. 4, 2006 ($5.99, squarebound, limited series)

	GD 2.0	VG 4.0	FN 6.0	VF 8.0	VF/NM 9.0	NM- 9.2
1-4-Paul Pope-s/a/c						6.00
TPB (2007, $19.99) r/series						20.00

BAT MASTERSON (TV) (Also see Tim Holt #28)
Dell Publishing Co.: Aug-Oct, 1959; Feb-Apr, 1960 - No. 9, Nov-Jan, 1961-62

	GD 2.0	VG 4.0	FN 6.0	VF 8.0	VF/NM 9.0	NM- 9.2
Four Color 1013 (#1) (8-10/59)	11	22	33	79	140	200
2-9: Gene Barry photo-c on all. 2-Two different back-c exist	7	14	21	45	73	100

BATS (See Tales Calculated to Drive You Bats)

BATS, CATS & CADILLACS
Now Comics: Oct, 1990 - No. 2, Nov, 1990 ($1.75)

	GD 2.0	VG 4.0	FN 6.0	VF 8.0	VF/NM 9.0	NM- 9.2
1,2: 1-Gustovich-a(i); Snyder-c						2.50

BAT-THING
DC Comics (Amalgam): June, 1997 ($1.95, one-shot)

	GD 2.0	VG 4.0	FN 6.0	VF 8.0	VF/NM 9.0	NM- 9.2
1-Hama-s/Damaggio & Sienkiewicz-a						2.50

BATTLE
Marvel/Atlas Comics(FPI #1-62/ Male #63 on): Mar, 1951 - No. 70, Jun, 1960

	GD 2.0	VG 4.0	FN 6.0	VF 8.0	VF/NM 9.0	NM- 9.2
1	32	64	96	190	305	420
2	17	34	51	98	154	210
3-10: 4-1st Buck Pvt. O'Toole. 10-Pakula-a	14	28	42	80	115	150
11-20: 11-Check-a	11	22	33	62	86	110
21,23-Krigstein-a	12	24	36	67	94	120
22,24-36: 32-Tuska-a. 36-Everett-a	10	20	30	54	72	90
37-Kubert-a (Last precode, 2/55)	10	20	30	58	79	100
38-40,42-48	9	18	27	52	69	85
41,49: 41-Kubert/Moskowitz-a. 49-Davis-a	10	20	30	56	76	95
50-54,56-58: 56-Colan-a; Ayers-a	9	18	27	50	65	80
55-Williamson-a (5 pgs.)	10	20	30	56	76	95
59-Torres-a	9	18	27	52	69	85
60-62: 60,62-Combat Kelly app. 61-Combat Casey app.	9	18	27	50	65	80
63-Ditko-a	14	28	42	80	115	150
64-66-Kirby-a. 66-Davis-a; has story of Fidel Castro in pre-Communism days (an admiring profile)	15	30	45	86	133	180
67,68: 67-Williamson/Crandall-a (4 pgs.); Kirby, Davis-a. 68-Kirby/Williamson-a (4 pgs.); Kirby/Ditko-a	15	30	45	88	137	185
69,70: 69-Kirby-a. 70-Kirby/Ditko-a	15	30	45	86	133	180

NOTE: ***Andru** a-37. **Berg** a 38, 14, 60 62. **Colan** a-19, 33, 55. **Everett** a-36, 50, 70; c-56, 57. **Heath** a-6, 9, 13, 31, 69; c-6, 9, 12, 26, 35, 37. **Kirby** c-64-69. **Maneely** a-4, 6, 31, 61; c-4, 22, 33, 48, 59, 61. **Orlando** a-47. **Powell** a-53, 55. **Reinman** a-8-10, 14, 26, 32, 48. **Robinson** a-9, 39. **Romita** a-14, 26. **Severin** a-28, 32-34, 66-69; c-36, 55. **Sinnott** a-33, 37, 63, 66. **Whitney** s-10.**Woodbridge** a-52, 55.*

BATTLE ACTION
Atlas Comics (NPI): Feb, 1952 - No. 12, 5/53; No. 13, 10/54 - No. 30, 8/57

	GD 2.0	VG 4.0	FN 6.0	VF 8.0	VF/NM 9.0	NM- 9.2
1-Pakula-a	26	52	78	154	247	340
2	15	30	45	84	127	170
3,4,6,7,9,10: 6-Robinson-c/a. 7-Partial nudity	10	20	30	58	79	100
5-Used in **POP**, pg. 93,94	11	22	33	60	83	105
8-Krigstein-a	11	22	33	62	86	110
11-15 (Last precode, 2/55)	10	20	30	56	76	95
16-30: 22-Pakula-a. 27,30-Torres-a	10	20	30	54	72	90

NOTE: *Battle Brady app. 5-7, 10-12. **Berg** a-3. **Check** a-11. **Everett** a-7; c-13, 25. **Heath** a-3, 8, 18; c-3,15, 18, 21. **Maneely** a-1; c-5. **Reinman** a-1, 2. **Robinson** a-6, 7; c-6. **Shores** a-7(2), 12; c-11. **Sinnott** a-3, 27. **Woodbridge** a-28, 30.*

BATTLE ATTACK
Stanmor Publications: Oct, 1952 - No. 8, Dec, 1955

	GD 2.0	VG 4.0	FN 6.0	VF 8.0	VF/NM 9.0	NM- 9.2
1	13	26	39	72	101	130
2	8	16	24	42	54	65
3-8: 3-Hollingsworth-a	7	14	21	37	46	55

BATTLEAXES
DC Comics (Vertigo): May, 2000 - No. 4, Aug, 2000 ($2.50, limited series)

	GD 2.0	VG 4.0	FN 6.0	VF 8.0	VF/NM 9.0	NM- 9.2
1-4: Terry LaBan-s/Alex Horley-a						2.50

BATTLE BEASTS
Blackthorne Publishing: Feb, 1988 - No. 4, 1988 ($1.50/$1.75, B&W/color)

	GD 2.0	VG 4.0	FN 6.0	VF 8.0	VF/NM 9.0	NM- 9.2
1-4: 1-3- (B&W)-Based on Hasbro toys. 4-Color						2.50

BATTLE BRADY (Formerly Men in Action No. 1-9; see 3-D Action)
Atlas Comics (IPC): No. 10, Jan, 1953 - No. 14, June, 1953

	GD 2.0	VG 4.0	FN 6.0	VF 8.0	VF/NM 9.0	NM- 9.2
10: 10-12-Syd Shores-c	16	32	48	96	147	205
11-Used in **POP**, pg. 95 plus B&W & color illos	11	22	33	60	83	105
12-14	10	20	30	54	72	90

BATTLE CHASERS
Image Comics (Cliffhanger): Apr, 1998 - No. 4, Dec, 1998;
DC Comics (Cliffhanger): No. 5, May, 1999 - No. 8, May, 2001 ($2.50)
Image Comics: No. 9, Sept, 2001 ($3.50)

	GD 2.0	VG 4.0	FN 6.0	VF 8.0	VF/NM 9.0	NM- 9.2
Prelude (2/98)	1	3	4	6	8	10
Prelude Gold Ed.	1	3	4	6	8	10
1-Madureira & Sharrieff-s/Madureira-a(p)/Charest-c	1	2	3	5	7	9
1-American Ent. Ed. w/"racy" cover	1	3	4	6	8	10
1-Gold Edition						9.00
1-Chromium cover						40.00
1-2nd printing						3.00
2						5.00
2-Dynamic Forces BattleChrome cover	2	4	6	8	10	12
3-Red Monika cover by Madureira						4.00
4-8: 4-Four covers. 6-Back-up by Adam Warren-s/a. 7-Three covers (Madureira, Ramos, Campbell)						3.00
9-($3.50, Image) Flip cover/story by Adam Warren						3.50
...: A Gathering of Heroes HC ('99, $24.95) r/#1-5, Prelude, Frank Frazetta Fantasy Ill.; cover gallery						25.00
...: A Gathering of Heroes SC ('99, $14.95)						15.00
...Collected Edition 1,2 (11/98, 5/99, $5.95) 1-r/#1,2. 2-r/#3,4						6.00

BATTLE CLASSICS (See Cancelled Comic Cavalcade)
DC Comics: Sept-Oct, 1978 (44 pgs.)

	GD 2.0	VG 4.0	FN 6.0	VF 8.0	VF/NM 9.0	NM- 9.2
1-Kubert-r; new Kubert-c	1	3	4	6	8	10

BATTLE CRY
Stanmor Publications: 1952 (May) - No. 20, Sept, 1955

	GD 2.0	VG 4.0	FN 6.0	VF 8.0	VF/NM 9.0	NM- 9.2
1	15	30	45	86	133	180
2	10	20	30	54	72	90
3,5-10: 8-Pvt. Ike begins, ends #13,17	8	16	24	42	54	65
4-Classic E.C. swipe	9	18	27	50	65	80
11-20	7	14	21	37	46	55

NOTE: ***Hollingsworth** a-9; c-20.*

BATTLEFIELD (War Adventures on the...)
Atlas Comics (ACI): April, 1952 - No. 11, May, 1953

	GD 2.0	VG 4.0	FN 6.0	VF 8.0	VF/NM 9.0	NM- 9.2
1-Pakula, Reinman-a	22	44	66	127	204	280
2-5: 2-Heath, Maneely, Pakula, Reinman-a	14	28	42	76	108	140
6-11	10	20	30	58	79	100

NOTE: ***Colan** a-11. **Everett** a-8. **Heath** a-1, 2, 5p,7; c-2, 8, 9, 11. **Ravielli** a-11.*

BATTLEFIELD ACTION (Formerly Foreign Intrigues)
Charlton Comics: No. 16, Nov, 1957 - No. 62, 2-3/66; No. 63, 7/80 - No. 89, 11/84

	GD 2.0	VG 4.0	FN 6.0	VF 8.0	VF/NM 9.0	NM- 9.2
V2#16	8	16	24	42	54	65
17,20-30	5	10	15	24	30	35
18,19-Check-a (2 stories in #18)	3	6	9	20	30	40
31-62(1966)	3	6	9	14	20	26
63-80(1983-84)						5.00
81-83,85-89 (Low print run)	1	2	3	4	5	7
84-Kirby reprints; 3 stories	1	3	4	6	8	10

NOTE: ***Montes/Bache** a-43, 55, 62. **Glanzman** a-87r.*

BATTLE FIRE
Aragon Magazine/Stanmor Publications: Apr, 1955 - No. 7, 1955

	GD 2.0	VG 4.0	FN 6.0	VF 8.0	VF/NM 9.0	NM- 9.2
1	12	24	36	69	97	125
2	8	16	24	42	54	65
3-7	7	14	21	35	43	50

BATTLE FOR A THREE DIMENSIONAL WORLD
3D Cosmic Publications: May, 1983 (20 pgs., slick paper w/stiff-c, $3.00)

	GD 2.0	VG 4.0	FN 6.0	VF 8.0	VF/NM 9.0	NM- 9.2
nn-Kirby c/a in 3-D; shows history of 3-D	2	4	6	8	10	12

BATTLEFORCE
Blackthorne Publishing: Nov, 1987 - No. 2, 1988 ($1.75, color/B&W)

	GD 2.0	VG 4.0	FN 6.0	VF 8.0	VF/NM 9.0	NM- 9.2
1,2: Based on game. 1-In color. 2-B&W						2.50

BATTLE FOR INDEPENDENTS, THE (Also See Cyblade/Shi & Shi/Cyblade: The Battle For Independents)
Image Comics (Top Cow Productions)/Crusade Comics: 1995 ($29.95)

	GD 2.0	VG 4.0	FN 6.0	VF 8.0	VF/NM 9.0	NM- 9.2
nn-boxed set of all editions of Shi/Cyblade & Cyblade/Shi plus new variant.	3	6	9	20	30	40

BATTLE FOR THE PLANET OF THE APES (See Power Record Comics)

Battlefront #4 © MAR

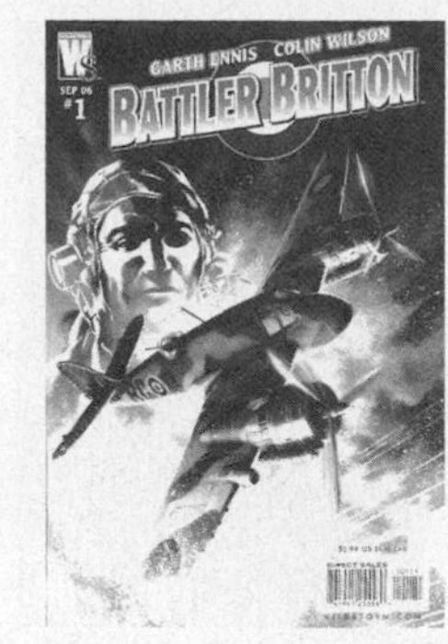

Battler Britton #1 © DC & IPC Media

Battlestar Galactica Season Zero #8 © USA Cable

	GD 2.0	VG 4.0	FN 6.0	VF 8.0	VF/NM 9.0	NM- 9.2

BATTLEFRONT
Atlas Comics (PPI): June, 1952 - No. 48, Aug, 1957

1-Heath-c	30	60	90	176	283	390
2-Robinson-a(4)	15	30	45	88	137	185
3-5-Robinson-a	14	28	42	78	112	145
6-10: Combat Kelly in No. 6-10. 6-Romita-a	11	22	33	64	90	115
11-22,24-28: 14,16-Battle Brady app. 22-Teddy Roosevelt & His Rough Riders story. 28-Last pre-code (2/55)	10	20	30	56	76	95
23,43-Check-a	10	20	30	58	79	100
29-39,41,44-47	9	18	27	52	69	85
40,42-Williamson-a	11	22	33	60	83	105
48-Crandall-a	10	20	30	56	76	95

NOTE: ***Ayers** a-19, 32. **Berg** a-44. **Colan** a-21, 22, 32, 33, 40. **Drucker** a-28, 29. **Everett** a-44. **Heath** c-23, 26, 27, 29, 32. **Maneely** a-22, 23, 26; c-2, 7, 13, 22, 34, 35. **Morisi** a-42. **Morrow** a-41.**Orlando** a-47. **Powell** a-19, 21, 25, 29, 32, 40, 47. **Robinson** a-1-3, 4&5(4); c-4, 5. **Robert Sale** a-19. **Severin** a-32; c-40, 45. **Sinnott** a-26; 48. **Woodbridge** a-45, 46.*

BATTLEFRONT
Standard Comics: No. 5, June, 1952

5-Toth-a	15	30	45	83	124	165

BATTLE GODS: WARRIORS OF THE CHAAK
Dark Horse Comics: Apr, 2000 - No. 4, July, 2000 ($2.95)

1-4-Francisco Ruiz Velasco-s/a 3.00

BATTLE GROUND
Atlas Comics (OMC): Sept, 1954 - No. 20, Aug, 1957

1	22	44	66	127	204	280
2-Jack Katz-a	14	28	42	76	108	140
3,4: 3-Jack Katz-a. 4-Last precode (3/55)	11	22	33	60	83	105
5-8,10	10	20	30	56	76	95
9,11,13,18: 9-Krigstein-a. 11,13,18-Williamson-a in each	11	22	33	64	90	115
12,15-17,19,20	10	20	30	54	72	90
14-Kirby-a	13	26	39	72	101	130

NOTE: ***Ayers** a-4, 13, 16. **Colan** a-3, 11, 13. **Drucker** a-7, 12, 13, 20. **Heath** c-2, 3, 5, 7, 13. **Maneely** a-3, 14, 19; c-1, 18, 19. **Orlando** a-17. **Pakula** a-11. **Reinman** a-2. **Severin** a-4, 5, 12, 19. c-20. **Sinnott** a-7, 16. **Tuska** a-11.*

BATTLE HEROES
Stanley Publications: Sept, 1966 - No. 2, Nov, 1966 (25¢, squarebound giants)

1	3	6	9	21	32	42
2	3	6	9	16	22	28

BATTLE HYMN
Image Comics: Jan, 2005 - No. 5, Oct, 2005 ($2.95/$2.99, limited series)

1-5-WW2 super team; B. Clay Moore-s/Jeremy Haun-a; flip cover on #1-4 3.00

BATTLE OF THE BULGE (See Movie Classics)

BATTLE OF THE PLANETS (Based on syndicated cartoon by Sandy Frank)
Gold Key/Whitman No. 6 on: 6/79 - No. 10, 12/80

1: Mortimer a-1-4,7-10	4	8	12	24	37	50
2-6,10	3	6	9	16	23	30
7-Low print run	5	10	15	30	48	65
8,9-Low print run: 8(11/80). 9-(3-pack only?)	4	8	12	26	41	55

BATTLE OF THE PLANETS (Also see Thundercats/...)
Image Comics (Top Cow): Aug, 2002 - No. 12, Sept, 2003 ($2.95/$2.99)

1-($2.95) Alex Ross-c & art director; Tortosa-a(p); re-intro. G-Force 3.00
1-($5.95) Holofoil-c by Ross 6.00
2-11-($2.99) Ross-c on all 3.00
12-($4.99) 5.00
#1/2 (7/03, $2.99) Benitez-c; Alex Ross sketch pages 3.00
... Battle Book 1 (5/03, $4.99) background info on characters, equipment, stories 5.00
... : Jason 1 (7/03, $4.99) Ross-c; Erwin David-a; preview of Tomb Raider: Epiphany 5.00
... : Mark 1 (5/03, $4.99) Ross-c; Erwin David-a; preview of BotP: Jason 5.00
.../Thundercats 1 (Image/WildStorm, 5/03, $4.99) 2 covers by Ross & Campbell 5.00
.../Witchblade 1 (2/03, $5.95) Ross-c; Christina and Jo Chen-a 6.00
Vol. 1: Trial By Fire (2003, $7.99) r/#1-3 8.00
Vol. 2: Blood Red Sky (9/03, $16.95) r/#4-9 17.00
Vol. 3: Destroy All Monsters (11/03, $19.95) r/#10-12, ...: Jason, ...: Mark, .../Witchblade 20.00
Vol. 1: Digest (1/04, $9.99, 7-3/8x5", B&W) r/#1-9 & ...: Mark 10.00
Vol. 2: Digest (8/04, $9.99, B&W) r/#10-12, ...: Jason, ...: Manga #1-3, .../Witchblade 10.00

BATTLE OF THE PLANETS: MANGA
Image Comics (Top Cow): Nov, 2003 - No. 3, Jan, 2004 ($2.99, B&W)

1-3-Edwin David-a/David Wohl-s; previews for Wanted & Tomb Raider #35 3.00

BATTLE OF THE PLANETS: PRINCESS
Image Comics (Top Cow): Nov, 2004 - No. 6, May, 2005 ($2.99, B&W, limited series)

1-6-Tortosa-a/Wohl-s. 1-Ross-c. 2-Tortosa-c 3.00

BATTLE POPE
Image Comics: June, 2005 - No. 14, Apr, 2007 ($2.99/$3.50, reprints 2000 B&W series in color)

1-5-Kirkman-s/Moore-a 3.00
6-10,12-14-($3.50) 14-Wedding 3.50
11-($4.99) Christmas issue 5.00
... Vol. 1: Genesis TPB (2006, $12.95) r/#1-4; sketch pages 13.00
... Vol. 2: Mayhem TPB (2006, $12.99) r/#5-8; sketch pages 13.00
... Vol. 3: Pillow Talk TPB (2007, $12.99) r/#9-11; sketch pages 13.00

BATTLER BRITTON (British comics character who debuted in 1956)
DC Comics (WildStorm): Sept, 2006 - No. 5, Jan, 2007 ($2.99, limited series)

1-5-WWII fighter pilots; Garth Ennis-s/Colin Wilson-a 3.00
TPB (2007, $19.99) r/#1-5; background of the character's British origins in the 1950s 20.00

BATTLE REPORT
Ajax/Farrell Publications: Aug, 1952 - No. 6, June, 1953

1	11	22	33	62	86	110
2-6	7	14	21	37	46	55

BATTLE SQUADRON
Stanmor Publications: April, 1955 - No. 5, Dec, 1955

1	10	20	30	54	72	90
2-5: 3-Iwo Jima & flag-c	6	12	18	31	38	45

BATTLESTAR GALACTICA (TV) (Also see Marvel Comics Super Special #8)
Marvel Comics Group: Mar, 1979 - No. 23, Jan, 1981

1: 1-5 adapt TV episodes	2	4	6	8	10	12
2-23: 1-3-Partial-r	1	2	3	5	6	8

NOTE: ***Austin** c-9i, 10i. **Golden** c-18. **Simonson** a(p)-4, 5, 11-13, 15-20, 22, 23; c(p)-4, 5,11-17, 19, 20, 22, 23.*

BATTLESTAR GALACTICA (TV) (Also see Asylum)
Maximum Press: July, 1995 - No. 4, Nov, 1995 ($2.50, limited series)

1-4: Continuation of 1978 TV series 4.00
Trade paperback (12/95, $12.95)-reprints series 13.00

BATTLESTAR GALACTICA (1978 TV series)
Realm Press: Dec, 1997 - No. 5, July, 1998 ($2.99)

1-5-Chris Scalf-s/painted-a/c 3.00
...Search For Sanctuary (9/98, $2.99) Scalf & Kuhoric-s 3.00
...Search For Sanctuary Special (4/00, $3.99) Kuhoric-s/Scalf & Scott-a 4.00

BATTLESTAR GALACTICA (2003-Present TV series)
Dynamite Entertainment: No. 0, 2006 - No. 12, 2007 (25¢/$2.99)

0-(25¢-c) Two covers; Pak-s/Raynor-a 2.25
1-($2.99) Covers by Turner, Tan, Raynor & photo-c; Pak-s/Raynor-a 3.00
2-12-Four covers on each 3.00
... Pegasus (2007, $4.99) story of Battlestar Pegasus & Admiral Cain; 2 covers 5.00
... Volume 1 HC (2007, $19.99) r/#0-4; cover gallery; Raynor sketch pages; commentary 20.00
... Volume 1 TPB (2007, $14.99) r/#0-4; cover gallery; Raynor sketch pages; commentary 15.00
... Volume 2 HC (2007, $19.99) r/#5-8; cover gallery; Raynor sketch pages 20.00
... Volume 2 TPB (2007, $14.99) r/#5-8; cover gallery; Raynor sketch pages 15.00

BATTLESTAR GALACTICA, (Classic...) (1978 TV series characters)
Dynamite Entertainment: 2006 - Present ($2.99)

1-5: 1-Two covers by Dorman & Caldwell; Rafael-a. 2-Two covers 3.00

BATTLESTAR GALACTICA: APOLLO'S JOURNEY (1978 TV series)
Maximum Press: Apr, 1996 - No. 3, June, 1996 ($2.95, limited series)

1-3: Richard Hatch scripts 4.00

BATTLESTAR GALACTICA: CYLON APOCALYPSE (1978 TV series characters)
Dynamite Entertainment: 2007 - No. 4, 2007 ($2.99, limited series)

1-4-Carlos Rafael-a; 4 covers on each 3.00
TPB (2007, $14.99) r/series with cover gallery 15.00

BATTLESTAR GALACTICA: JOURNEY'S END (1978 TV series)
Maximum Press: Aug, 1996 - No. 4, Nov, 1996 ($2.99, limited series)

1-4-Continuation of the T.V. series 4.00

BATTLESTAR GALACTICA: ORIGINS (2003-Present TV series)
Dynamite Entertainment: 2007 - Present ($3.50)

1-9: 1-4-Baltar's origin; multiple covers. 5-8-Adama's origin. 9-Starbuck & Helo 3.50

BATTLESTAR GALACTICA: SEASON III
Realm Press: June/July, 1999 - No. 3, Sept, 1999 ($2.99)

1-3: 1-Kuhoric-s/Scalf & Scott-a; two covers by Scalf & Jae Lee. 2,3-Two covers 3.00

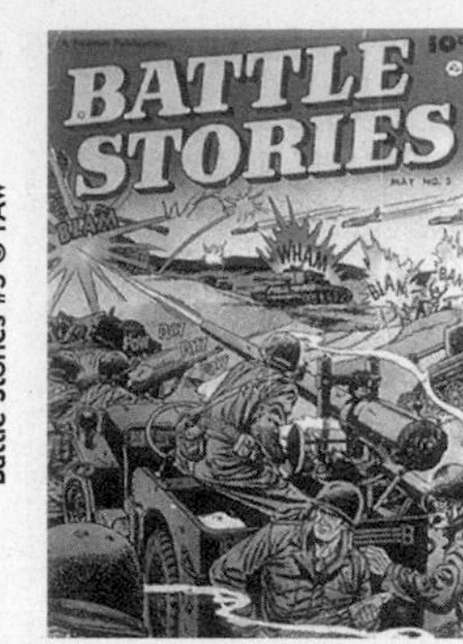

Battle Stories #3 © FAW

Beagle Boys #9 © DIS

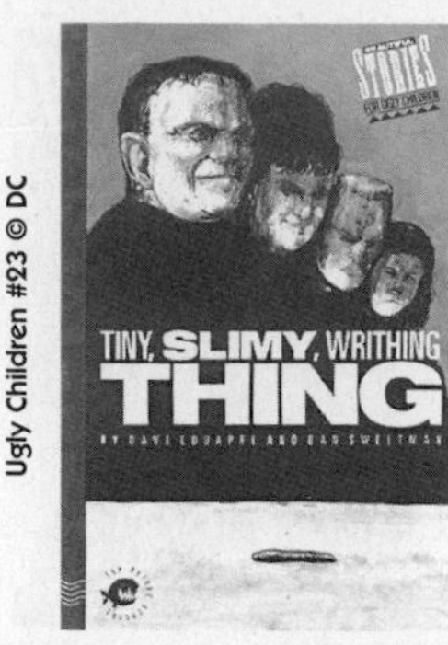

Beautiful Stories For Ugly Children #23 © DC

	GD 2.0	VG 4.0	FN 6.0	VF 8.0	VF/NM 9.0	NM- 9.2

Gallery (4/00, $3.99) short story and pin-ups 4.00
1999 Tour Book (5/99, $2.99) 3.00
1999 Tour Book Convention Edition (6.99) 7.00
...Special: Centurion Prime (12/99, $3.99) Kuhoric-s 4.00

BATTLESTAR GALACTICA: SEASON ZERO (2003-Present TV series)
Dynamite Entertainment: 2007 - No. 12, 2008 ($2.99)
1-12-Set 2 years before the Cylon attack; multiple covers 3.00

BATTLESTAR GALACTICA: SPECIAL EDITION (TV)
Maximum Press: Jan, 1997 ($2.99, one-shot)
1-Fully painted; Scalf-c/s/a; r/Asylum 3.00

BATTLESTAR GALACTICA: STARBUCK (TV)
Maximum Press: Dec, 1995 - No. 3, Mar, 1996 ($2.50, limited series)
1-3 4.00

BATTLESTAR GALACTICA: THE COMPENDIUM (TV)
Maximum Press: Feb, 1997 ($2.99, one-shot)
1 3.00

BATTLESTAR GALACTICA: THE ENEMY WITHIN (TV)
Maximum Press: Nov, 1995 - No. 3, Feb, 1996 ($2.50, limited series)
1-3: 3-Indicia reads Feb, 1995 in error. 4.00

BATTLESTAR GALACTICA ZAREK (2003 series)
Dynamite Entertainment: 2007 - No. 4, 2007 ($3.50, limited series)
1-4-Origin story of political activist Tom Zarek; 2 covers on each 3.50

BATTLE STORIES (See XMas Comics)
Fawcett Publications: Jan, 1952 - No. 11, Sept, 1953
1-Evans-a 16 32 48 92 144 195
2 10 20 30 56 76 95
3-11 9 18 27 47 61 75

BATTLE STORIES
Super Comics: 1963 - 1964
Reprints #10-13,15-18: 10-r/U.S Tank Commandos #? 11-r/? 11, 12,17-r/Monty Hall #?; 13-Kintsler-a (1pg).15-r/American Air Forces #7 by Powell; Bolle-r. 18-U.S. Fighting Air Force #? 2 4 6 9 13 16

BATTLETECH (See Blackthorne 3-D Series #41 for 3-D issue)
Blackthorne Publishing: Oct, 1987 - No. 6, 1988 ($1.75/$2.00)
1-6: Based on game. 1-Color. 2-Begin B&W 3.00
Annual 1 ($4.50, B&W) 5.00

BATTLETECH
Malibu Comics: Feb, 1995 ($2.95)
0 3.00

BATTLETECH FALLOUT
Malibu Comics: Dec, 1994 - No. 4, Mar, 1995 ($2.95)
1-4-Two edi. exist #1; normal logo 3.00
1-Gold version w/foil logo stamped "Gold Limited Edition 8.00
1-Full-c holographic limited edition 6.00

BATTLETIDE (Death's Head II & Killpower...)
Marvel Comics UK, Ltd.: Dec, 1992 - No. 4, Mar, 1993 ($1.75, mini-series)
1-4: Wolverine, Psylocke, Dark Angel app. 2.50

BATTLETIDE II (Death's Head II & Killpower...)
Marvel Comics UK, Ltd.: Aug, 1993 - No. 4, Nov, 1993 ($1.75, mini-series)
1-($2.95)-Foil embossed logo 3.00
2-4: 2-Hulk-c/story 2.50

BAY CITY JIVE
DC Comics (WildStorm): Jul, 2001 - No. 3, Sept, 2001 ($2.95, limited series)
1-3: Intro Sugah Rollins in 1970s San Francisco; Layman-s/Johnson-a 3.00

BAYWATCH COMIC STORIES (TV) (Magazine)
Acclaim Comics (Armada): May, 1996 - No. 4, 1997 ($4.95) (Photo-c on all)
1-4: Photo comics based on TV show 5.00

BEACH BLANKET BINGO (See Movie Classics)

BEAGLE BOYS, THE (Walt Disney)(See The Phantom Blot)
Gold Key: 11/64; No. 2, 11/65; No. 3, 8/66 - No. 47, 2/79 (See WDC&S #134)
1 5 10 15 32 51 70
2-5 3 6 9 18 27 35
6-10 3 6 9 16 22 28
11-20: 11,14,19-r 2 4 6 11 16 20
21-30: 27-r 2 4 6 8 11 14
31-47 1 3 4 6 8 10

BEAGLE BOYS VERSUS UNCLE SCROOGE
Gold Key: Mar, 1979 - No. 12, Feb, 1980
1 2 4 6 9 13 16
2-12: 9-r 1 2 3 5 6 8

BEANBAGS
Ziff-Davis Publ. Co. (Approved Comics): Winter, 1951 - No. 2, Spring, 1952
1,2 12 24 36 69 97 125

BEANIE THE MEANIE
Fago Publications: No. 3, May, 1959
3 5 10 15 24 30 35

BEANY AND CECIL (TV) (Bob Clampett's...)
Dell Publishing Co.: Jan, 1952 - 1955; July-Sept, 1962 - No. 5, July-Sept, 1963
Four Color 368 24 48 72 172 319 465
Four Color 414,448,477,530,570,635(1/55) 15 30 45 105 190 275
01-057-209 (#1) 14 28 42 100 178 255
2-5 10 20 30 68 119 170

BEAR COUNTRY (Disney)
Dell Publishing Co.: No. 758, Dec, 1956
Four Color 758-Movie 5 10 15 34 55 75

BEAST (See X-Men)
Marvel Comics: May, 1997 - No. 3, 1997 ($2.50, mini-series)
1-3-Giffen-s/Nocon-a 3.00

BEAST BOY (See Titans)
DC Comics: Jan, 2000 - No. 4, Apr, 2000 ($2.95, mini-series)
1-4-Justiano-c/a; Raab & Johns-s 3.00

B.E.A.S.T.I.E.S. (Also see Axis Alpha)
Axis Comics: Apr, 1994 ($1.95)
1-Javier Saltares-c/a/scripts 2.50

BEATLES, THE (See Girls' Romances #109, Go-Go, Heart Throbs #101, Herbie #5, Howard the Duck Mag. #4, Laugh #166, Marvel Comics Super Special #4, My Little Margie #54, Not Brand Echh, Strange Tales #130, Summer Love, Superman's Pal Jimmy Olsen #79, Teen Confessions #37, Tippy's Friends & Tippy Teen)

BEATLES, THE (Life Story)
Dell Publishing Co.: Sept-Nov, 1964 (35¢)
1-(Scarce)-Stories with color photo pin-ups; Paul S. Newman-s
40 80 120 312 581 850

BEATLES EXPERIENCE, THE
Revolutionary Comics: Mar, 1991 - No. 8, 1991 ($2.50, B&W, limited series)
1-8: 1-Gold logo 5.00

BEATLES YELLOW SUBMARINE (See Movie Comics under Yellow...)

BEAUTIFUL KILLER
Black Bull Comics: Sept., 2002 - No. 3, Jan, 2003 ($2.99, limited series)
...Limited Preview Edition (5/02, $5.00) preview pgs. & creator interviews 5.00
1-Noto-a/Palmiotti-s; Hughes-c; intro Brigit Cole 3.00
2,3: 2-Jusko-c. 3-Noto-c 3.00
TPB (5/03, $9.99) r/#1-3; cover gallery and Adam Hughes sketch pages 10.00

BEAUTIFUL PEOPLE
Slave Labor Graphics: Apr, 1994 ($4.95, 8-1/2x11", one-shot)
nn 5.00

BEAUTIFUL STORIES FOR UGLY CHILDREN
DC Comics (Piranha Press): 1989 - No. 30, 1991 ($2.00/$2.50, B&W, mature)
Vol. 1-20: 12-$2.50-c begins 3.50
21-25 4.50
26-30-(Lower print run) 6.00
A Cotton Candy Autopsy ($12.95, B&W)-Reprints 1st two volumes 13.00

BEAUTY AND THE BEAST, THE
Marvel Comics Group: Jan, 1985 - No. 4, Apr, 1985 (limited series)
1-4: Dazzler & the Beast from X-Men; Sienkiewicz-c on all 3.00

BEAUTY AND THE BEAST (Graphic novel)(Also see Cartoon Tales & Disney's New Adventures of...)
Disney Comics: 1992
nn-($4.95, prestige edition)-Adapts animated film 7.00

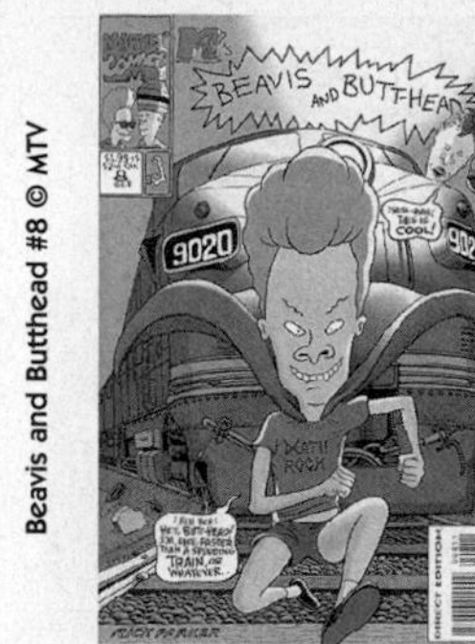

Beavis and Butthead #8 © MTV

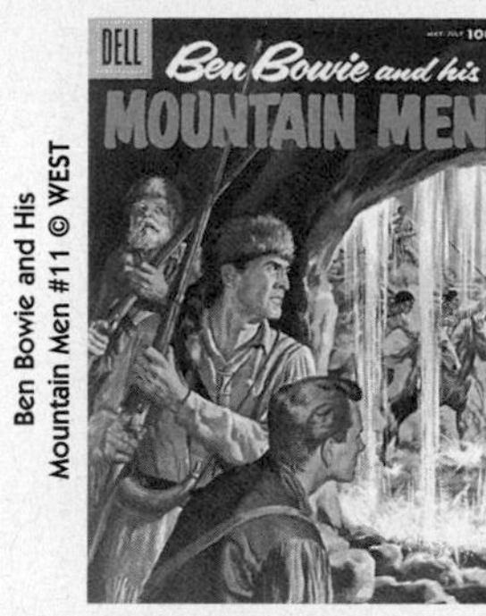

Ben Bowie and His Mountain Men #11 © WEST

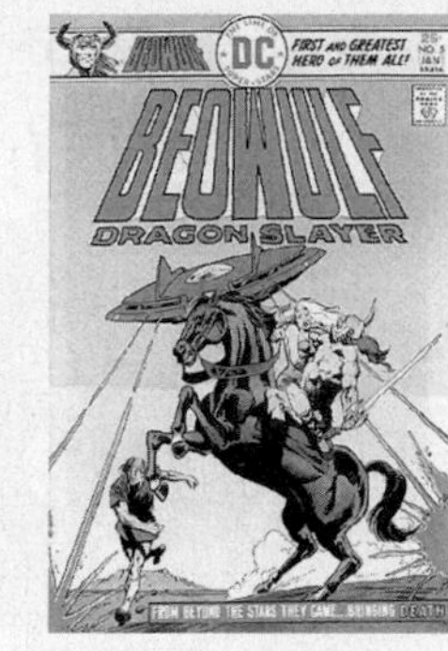

Beowulf #5 © DC

	GD 2.0	VG 4.0	FN 6.0	VF 8.0	VF/NM 9.0	NM- 9.2
nn-($2.50, newsstand edition)						3.00

BEAUTY AND THE BEAST
Disney Comics: Sept., 1992 - No. 2, 1992 ($1.50, limited series)

	GD	VG	FN	VF	VF/NM	NM-
1,2						3.00

BEAUTY AND THE BEAST: PORTRAIT OF LOVE (TV)
First Comics: May, 1989 - No. 2, Mar, 1990 ($5.95, 60 pgs., squarebound)

	GD	VG	FN	VF	VF/NM	NM-
1,2: 1-Based on TV show, Wendy Pini-a/scripts. 2-...: Night of Beauty; by Wendy Pini						6.00

BEAVER VALLEY (Movie)(Disney)
Dell Publishing Co.: No. 625, Apr, 1955

	GD	VG	FN	VF	VF/NM	NM-
Four Color 625	6	12	18	41	66	90

BEAVIS AND BUTTHEAD (MTV's...)(TV cartoon)
Marvel Comics: Mar, 1994 - No. 28, June, 1996 ($1.95)

	GD	VG	FN	VF	VF/NM	NM-
1-Silver ink-c. 1, 2-Punisher & Devil Dinosaur app.						4.00
1-2nd printing						2.50
2,3: 2-Wolverine app. 3-Man-Thing, Spider-Man, Venom, Carnage, Mary Jane & Stan Lee cameos; John Romita, Sr. art (2 pgs.)						2.50
4-28: 5-War Machine, Thor, Loki, Hulk, Captain America & Rhino cameos. 6-Psylocke, Polaris, Daredevil & Bullseye app. 7-Ghost Rider & Sub-Mariner app. 8-Quasar & Eon app. 9-Prowler & Nightwatch app. 11-Black Widow app. 12-Thunderstrike & Bloodaxe app. 13-Night Thrasher app. 14-Spider-Man 2099 app. 15-Warlock app. 16-X-Factor app. 25-Juggernaut app.						2.50

BECK & CAUL INVESTIGATIONS
Gauntlet Comics (Caliber): Jan, 1994 - No. 5, 1995? ($2.95, B&W)

	GD	VG	FN	VF	VF/NM	NM-
1-5						3.00
Special 1 ($4.95)						5.00

BEDKNOBS AND BROOMSTICKS (See Walt Disney Showcase No. 6 & 50)

BEDLAM!
Eclipse Comics: Sept, 1985 - No. 2, Sept, 1985 (B&W-r in color)

	GD	VG	FN	VF	VF/NM	NM-
1,2: Bissette-a						3.00

BEDTIME STORY (See Cinema Comics Herald)

BEELZELVIS
Slave Labor Graphics: Feb, 1994 ($2.95, B&W, one-shot)

	GD	VG	FN	VF	VF/NM	NM-
1						3.00

BEEP BEEP, THE ROAD RUNNER (TV) (See Dell Giant Comics Bugs Bunny Vacation Funnies #8 for 1st app.) (Also see Daffy & Kite Fun Book)
Dell Publishing Co./Gold Key No. 1-88/Whitman No. 89 on: July, 1958 - No. 14, Aug-Oct, 1962; Oct, 1966 - No. 105, 1984

	GD	VG	FN	VF	VF/NM	NM-
Four Color 918 (#1, 7/58)	11	22	33	75	133	190
Four Color 1008,1046 (11-1/59-60)	6	12	18	43	69	95
4(2-4/60)-14(Dell)	6	12	18	39	62	85
1(10/66, Gold Key)	6	12	18	39	62	85
2-5	4	8	12	24	37	50
6-14	3	6	9	18	27	35
15-18,20-40	3	6	9	14	20	26
19-With pull-out poster	4	8	12	22	34	45
41-50	2	4	6	11	16	20
51-70	2	4	6	8	11	14
71-88	1	2	3	5	7	9
89,90,94-101: 100(3/82), 101(4/82)	1	3	4	6	8	10
91(8/80), 92(9/80), 93 (3-pack?) (low printing)	3	6	9	21	32	42
102-105 (All #90189 on-c; nd or date code; pre-pack) 102(6/83), 103(7/83), 104(5/84), 105(6/84)	3	6	9	14	20	26
#63-2970 (Now Age Books/Pendulum Pub. Comic Digest, 1971, 75¢, 100 pages, B&W) collection of one-page gags	4	8	12	24	37	50

NOTE: *See March of Comics #351, 353, 375, 387, 397, 416, 430, 442, 455. #5, 8-10, 35, 53, 59-62, 68-r; 96-102, 104 are 1/3-r.*

BEETLE BAILEY (See Giant Comic Album, Sarge Snorkel; also Comics Reading Libraries in the Promotional Comics section)
Dell Publishing Co./Gold Key #39-53/King #54-66/Charlton #67-119/Gold Key #120-131/ Whitman #132: #459, 5/53 - #38, 5-7/62; #39, 11/62 - #53, 5/66; #54, 8/66 - #65, 12/67;#67, 2/69 - #119, 11/76; #120, 4/78 - #132, 4/80

	GD	VG	FN	VF	VF/NM	NM-
Four Color 469 (#1)-By Mort Walker	11	22	33	75	133	190
Four Color 521,552,622	6	12	18	43	69	95
5(2-4/56)-10(5-7/57)	6	12	18	37	59	80
11-20(4-5/59)	4	8	12	26	41	55
21-38(5-7/62)	3	6	9	19	29	38
39-53(5/66)	3	6	9	16	23	30
54-65 (No. 66 publ. overseas only?)	3	6	9	14	20	25
67-69: 69-Last 12¢ issue	2	4	6	13	18	22
70-99	2	4	6	9	13	16
100	2	4	6	11	16	20
101-111,114-119	1	3	4	6	8	10
112,113-Byrne illos. (4 each)	2	4	6	9	12	15
120-132						6.00

BEETLE BAILEY
Harvey Comics: V2#1, Sept, 1992 - V2#9, Aug, 1994 ($1.25/$1.50)

	GD	VG	FN	VF	VF/NM	NM-
V2#1						4.00
2-9-($1.50)						3.00
Big Book 1(11/92),2(5/93)(Both $1.95, 52 pgs.)						3.50
Giant Size V2#1(10/92),2(3/93)(Both $2.25,68 pgs.)						3.50

BEETLEJUICE (TV)
Harvey Comics: Oct, 1991 ($1.25)

	GD	VG	FN	VF	VF/NM	NM-
1						3.00

BEETLEJUICE CRIMEBUSTERS ON THE HAUNT
Harvey Comics: Sept, 1992 - No. 3, Jan, 1993 ($1.50, limited series)

	GD	VG	FN	VF	VF/NM	NM-
1-3						3.00

BEE 29, THE BOMBARDIER
Neal Publications: Feb, 1945

	GD	VG	FN	VF	VF/NM	NM-
1-(Funny animal)	33	66	99	192	309	425

BEFORE THE FANTASTIC FOUR: BEN GRIMM AND LOGAN
Marvel Comics: July, 2000 - No. 3, Sept, 2000 ($2.99, limited series)

	GD	VG	FN	VF	VF/NM	NM-
1-3-The Thing and Wolverine app.; Hama-s						3.00

BEFORE THE FANTASTIC FOUR: REED RICHARDS
Marvel Comics: Sept, 2000 - No. 3, Dec, 2000 ($2.99, limited series)

	GD	VG	FN	VF	VF/NM	NM-
1-3-Peter David-s/Duncan Fegredo-c/a						3.00

BEFORE THE FANTASTIC FOUR: THE STORMS
Marvel Comics: Dec, 2000 - No. 3, Feb, 2001 ($2.99, limited series)

	GD	VG	FN	VF	VF/NM	NM-
1-3-Adlard-a						3.00

BEHIND PRISON BARS
Realistic Comics (Avon): 1952

	GD	VG	FN	VF	VF/NM	NM-
1-Kinstler-c	32	64	96	186	298	410

BEHOLD THE HANDMAID
George Pflaum: 1954 (Religious) (25¢ with a 20¢ sticker price)

	GD	VG	FN	VF	VF/NM	NM-
nn	6	12	18	29	36	42

BELIEVE IT OR NOT (See Ripley's...)

BELLE STARR: QUEEN OF BANDITS
Moonstone: 2005 - Present ($2.95, B&W)

	GD	VG	FN	VF	VF/NM	NM-
1,2-Ricketts-s/Buccallato-a/Beck-c						3.00

BEN AND ME (Disney)
Dell Publishing Co.: No. 539, Mar, 1954

	GD	VG	FN	VF	VF/NM	NM-
Four Color 539	4	8	12	26	41	55

BEN BOWIE AND HIS MOUNTAIN MEN
Dell Publishing Co.: 1952 - No. 17, Nov-Jan, 1958-59

	GD	VG	FN	VF	VF/NM	NM-
Four Color 443 (#1)	8	16	24	56	93	130
Four Color 513,557,599,626,657	5	10	15	30	48	65
7(5-7/56)-11: 11-Intro/origin Yellow Hair	4	8	12	24	37	50
12-17	4	8	12	22	34	45

BEN CASEY (TV)
Dell Publishing Co.: June-July, 1962 - No. 10, June-Aug, 1965 (Photo-c)

	GD	VG	FN	VF	VF/NM	NM-
12-063-207 (#1)	6	12	18	41	66	90
2(10/62),3,5-10	4	8	12	24	37	50
4-Marijuana & heroin use story	4	8	12	28	44	60

BEN CASEY FILM STORY (TV)
Gold Key: Nov, 1962 (25¢) (Photo-c)

	GD	VG	FN	VF	VF/NM	NM-
30009-211-All photos	8	16	24	52	86	120

BENEATH THE PLANET OF THE APES (See Movie Comics & Power Record Comics)

BEN FRANKLIN (See Kite Fun Book)

BEN HUR
Dell Publishing Co.: No. 1052, Nov, 1959

	GD	VG	FN	VF	VF/NM	NM-
Four Color 1052-Movie, Manning-a	10	20	30	67	116	165

BEN ISRAEL

Best of Bugs Bunny #1 © WB

Best of DC Comics #13 © DC

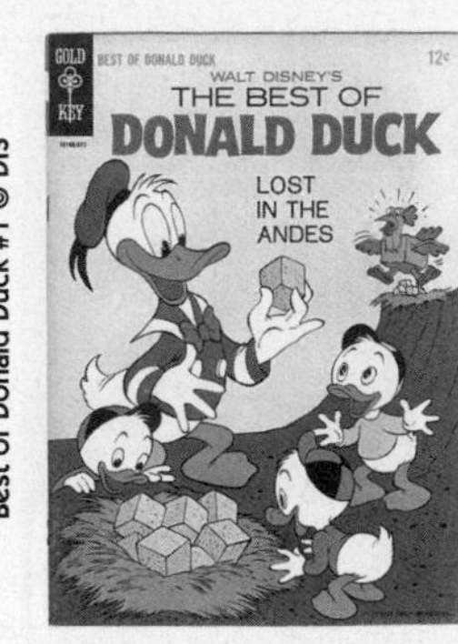

Best of Donald Duck #1 © DIS

GD VG FN VF VF/NM NM-
2.0 4.0 6.0 8.0 9.0 9.2

Logos International: 1974 (39¢)
nn-Christian religious 2 4 6 9 13 16

BEOWULF (Also see First Comics Graphic Novel #1)
National Periodical Publications: Apr-May, 1975 - No. 6, Feb-Mar, 1976
1 2 4 6 8 11 14
2,3,5,6: 5-Flying saucer-c/story 1 2 3 5 6 8
4-Dracula-c/s 1 2 3 5 7 9

BERNI WRIGHTSON, MASTER OF THE MACABRE
Pacific Comics/Eclipse Comics No. 5: July, 1983 - No. 5, Nov, 1984 ($1.50, Baxter paper)
1-5: Wrightson-c/a(r). 4-Jeff Jones-r (11 pgs.) 5.00

BERRYS, THE (Also see Funny World)
Argo Publ.: May, 1956
1-Reprints daily & Sunday strips & daily Animal Antics by Ed Nofziger 6 12 18 29 36 42

BERZERKERS (See Youngblood V1#2)
Image Comics (Extreme Studios): Aug, 1995 - No. 3, Oct, 1995 ($2.50, limited series)
1-3: Beau Smith scripts, Fraga-a 2.50

BEST COMICS
Better Publications: Nov, 1939 - No. 4, Feb, 1940(10-11/16" wide x 8" tall, reads sideways)
1-(Scarce)-Red Mask begins(1st app.) & c/s-all 87 174 261 548 924 1300
2-4: 4-Cannibalism story 48 96 144 298 499 700

BEST FROM BOY'S LIFE, THE
Gilberton Company: Oct, 1957 - No. 5, Oct, 1958 (35¢)
1-Space Conquerors & Kam of the Ancient Ones begin, end #5; Bob Cousy photo/story 13 26 39 72 101 130
2,3,5 8 16 24 42 54 65
4-L.B. Cole-a 8 16 24 44 57 70

BEST LOVE (Formerly Sub-Mariner Comics No. 32)
Marvel Comics (MPI): No. 33, Aug, 1949 - No. 36, April, 1950 (Photo-c 33-36)
33-Kubert-a 14 28 42 80 115 150
34 9 18 27 52 69 85
35,36-Everett-a 10 20 30 58 79 100

BEST OF ARCHIE, THE
Perigee Books: 1980 ($7.95, softcover TPB)
nn-Intro by Michael Uslan & Jeffrey Mendel 5 10 15 35 55 75

BEST OF BUGS BUNNY, THE
Gold Key: Oct, 1966 - No. 2, Oct, 1968
1,2-Giants 4 8 12 28 44 60

BEST OF DC, THE (Blue Ribbon Digest) (See Limited Coll. Ed. C-52)
DC Comics: Sept-Oct, 1979 - No. 71, Apr, 1986 (100-148 pgs; mostly reprints)
1-Superman, w/"Death of Superman"-r 2 4 6 11 16 20
2,5-9: 2-Batman 40th Ann. Special. 5-Best of 1979. 6,8-Superman. 7-Superboy. 9-Batman, Creeper app. 2 4 6 8 10 12
3-Superfriends 2 4 6 9 12 15
4-Rudolph the Red Nosed Reindeer 2 4 6 9 13 16
10-Secret Origins of Super Villains; 1st ever Penguin origin-s 3 6 9 16 22 28
11-16,18-20: 11-The Year's Best Stories. 12-Superman Time and Space Stories.13-Best of DC Comics Presents. 14-New origin stories of Batman villains. 15-Superboy. 16-Superman Anniv. 18-Teen Titans new-s., Adams, Kane-a; Perez-c. 19-Superman. 20-World's Finest 1 2 3 5 7 9
17-Supergirl 2 4 6 8 10 12
21,22: 21-Justice Society. 22-Christmas; unpublished Sandman story w/Kirby-a 2 4 6 10 14 18
23-27: 23-(148 pgs.)-Best of 1981. 24 Legion, new story and 16 pgs. new costumes. 25-Superman. 26-Brave & Bold. 27-Superman vs. Luthor 2 4 6 9 12 15
28,29: 28-Binky, Sugar & Spike app. 29-Sugar & Spike, 3 new stories; new Stanley & his Monster story 2 4 6 9 13 16
30,32-36,38,40: 30-Detective Comics. 32-Superman. 33-Secret origins of Legion Heroes and Villains. 34-Metal Men; has #497 on-c from Adv. Comics. 35-The Year's Best Comics Stories (148 pgs.). 36-Superman vs. Kryptonite. 38-Superman. 40-World of Krypton 2 4 6 9 12 15
31-JLA 2 4 6 10 14 18
37,39: 37-"Funny Stuff", Mayer-a. 39-Binky 2 4 6 10 14 18
41,43,45,47,49,53,55,58,60,63,65,68,70: 41-Sugar & Spike new stories with Mayer-a. 43,49,55-Funny Stuff. 45,53,70-Binky. 47,65,68-Sugar & Spike. 58-Super Jrs. Holiday Special; Sugar & Spike. 60-Plop!; Wood-c(r) & Aragonés-r (5/85). 63-Plop!; Wrightson-a(r) 3 6 9 14 19 24
42,44,46,48,50-52,54,56,57,59,61,62,64,66,67,69,71: 42,56-Superman vs. Aliens. 44,57,67-Superboy & LSH. 46-Jimmy Olsen. 48-Superman Team-ups. 50-Year's best Superman. 51-Batman Family. 52 Best of 1984. 54,56,59-Superman. 61-(148 pgs.)Year's best. 62-Best of Batman 1985. 69-Year's best Team stories. 71-Year's best 2 4 6 10 14 18

NOTE: ***N. Adams** a-2r, 14r, 18r, 26, 51. **Aparo** a-9, 14, 26, 30; c-9, 14, 26. **Austin** a-51i. **Buckler** a-40p; c-16, 22. **Giffen** a-50, 52; c-33p. **Grell** a-33p. **Grossman** a-37. **Heath** a-26. **Infantino** a-10r, 18. **Kaluta** a-40. **G. Kane** a-10r, 18r; c-40, 44. **Kubert** a-10r, 21, 26. **Layton** a-21. **S. Mayer** c-29, 37, 41, 43, 47; a-28, 29, 37, 41, 43, 47, 58, 65, 68. **Moldoff** c-64p. **Morrow** a-40; c-40. **W. Mortimer** a-39p. **Newton** a-5, 51. **Perez** a-24, 50p; c-18, 21, 23. **Rogers** a-14, 51p. **Simonson** a-11r. **Spiegle** a-52. **Starlin** a-51. **Staton** a-5, 21. **Tuska** a-24. **Wolverton** a-60. **Wood** a-60, 63; c-60, 63. **Wrightson** a-60. New art in #14, 18, 24.*

BEST OF DENNIS THE MENACE, THE
Hallden/Fawcett Publications: Summer, 1959 - No. 5, Spring, 1961 (100 pgs.)
1-All reprints; Wiseman-a 7 14 21 45 73 100
2-5 4 8 12 28 44 60

BEST OF DONALD DUCK, THE
Gold Key: Nov, 1965 (12¢, 36 pgs.)(Lists 2nd printing in indicia)
1-Reprints Four Color #223 by Barks 8 16 24 54 90 125

BEST OF DONALD DUCK & UNCLE SCROOGE, THE
Gold Key: Nov, 1964 - No. 2, Sept, 1967 (25¢ Giants)
1(30022-411)('64)-Reprints 4-Color #189 & 408 by Carl Barks; cover of F.C. #189 redrawn by Barks 9 18 27 63 107 150
2(30022-709)('67)-Reprints 4-Color #256 & "Seven Cities of Cibola" & U.S. #8 by Barks 8 16 24 52 86 120

BEST OF HORROR AND SCIENCE FICTION COMICS
Bruce Webster: 1987 ($2.00)
1-Wolverton, Frazetta, Powell, Ditko-r 5.00

BEST OF JOSIE AND THE PUSSYCATS
Archie Comics: 2001 ($10.95, TPB)
1-Reprints 1st app. and noteworthy stories 11.00

BEST OF MARMADUKE, THE
Charlton Comics: 1960
1-Brad Anderson's strip reprints 3 6 9 19 29 38

BEST OF MS. TREE, THE
Pyramid Comics: 1987 - No. 4, 1988 ($2.00, B&W, limited series)
1-4 2.50

BEST OF RAY BRADBURY, THE
ibooks: 2003 ($18.95, TPB)
The Graphic Novel - Reprints from Ray Bradbury Comics; adaptations by various 19.00

BEST OF THE BRAVE AND THE BOLD, THE (See Super DC Giant)
DC Comics: Oct, 1988 - No. 6, Jan, 1989 ($2.50, limited series)
1-6: Neal Adams-r, Kubert-r & Heath-r in all 4.00

BEST OF THE SPIRIT, THE
DC Comics: 2005 ($14.99, TPB)
nn-Reprints 1st app. and noteworthy stories; intro by Neil Gaiman; Eisner bio. 15.00

BEST OF THE WEST (See A-1 Comics)
Magazine Enterprises: 1951 - No. 12, April-June, 1954
1(A-1 42)-Ghost Rider, Durango Kid, Straight Arrow, Bobby Benson begin 41 82 123 250 413 575
2(A-1 46) 22 44 66 127 204 280
3(A-1 52), 4(A-1 59), 5(A-1 66) 18 36 54 105 165 225
6(A-1 70), 7(A-1 76), 8(A-1 81), 9(A-1 85), 10(A-1 87), 11(A-1 97), 12(A-1 103) 15 30 45 84 127 170

NOTE: ***Bolle** a-9. **Borth** a-12. **Guardineer** a-5, 12. **Powell** a-1, 12.*

BEST OF UNCLE SCROOGE & DONALD DUCK, THE
Gold Key: Nov, 1966 (25¢)
1(30030-611)-Reprints part 4-Color #159 & 456 & Uncle Scrooge #6,7 by Carl Barks 8 16 24 52 86 120

BEST OF WALT DISNEY COMICS, THE
Western Publishing Co.: 1974 ($1.50, 52 pgs.) (Walt Disney)
(8-1/2x11" cardboard covers; 32,000 printed of each)
96170-Reprints 1st two stories less 1 pg. each from 4-Color #62 6 12 18 37 59 80
96171-Reprints Mickey Mouse and the Bat Bandit of Inferno Gulch from 1934 (strips) by Gottfredson 6 12 18 37 59 80

Betty #4 © AP

Betty and Veronica #40 © AP

Beverly Hillbillies #5 © CBS

	GD 2.0	VG 4.0	FN 6.0	VF 8.0	VF/NM 9.0	NM- 9.2

96172-r/Uncle Scrooge #386 & two other stories 6 12 18 37 59 80
96173-Reprints "Ghost of the Grotto" (from 4-Color #159) & "Christmas on Bear Mountain" (from 4-Color #178) 6 12 18 37 59 80

BEST ROMANCE
Standard Comics (Visual Editions): No. 5, Feb-Mar, 1952 - No. 7, Aug, 1952
5-Toth-a; photo-c 14 28 42 78 112 145
6,7-Photo-c 8 16 24 44 57 70

BEST SELLER COMICS (See Tailspin Tommy)

BEST WESTERN (Formerly Terry Toons? or Miss America Magazine
Marvel Comics (IPC): V7#24(#57)?; Western Outlaws & Sheriffs No. 60 on)
No. 58, June, 1949 - No. 59, Aug, 1949
58,59-Black Rider, Kid Colt, Two-Gun Kid app.; both have Syd Shores-c
20 40 60 117 186 255

BETTIE PAGE COMICS
Dark Horse Comics: Mar, 1996 ($3.95)
1-Dave Stevens-c; Blevins & Heath-a; Jaime Hernandez pin-up
1 2 3 4 5 7

BETTIE PAGE COMICS: QUEEN OF THE NILE
Dark Horse Comics: Dec, 1999 - No. 3, Apr, 2000 ($2.95, limited series)
1-3-Silke-s/a; Stevens-c 3.00

BETTIE PAGE COMICS: SPICY ADVENTURE
Dark Horse Comics: Jan, 1997 ($2.95, one-shot, mature)
nn-Silke-c/s/a 4.00

BETTY (See Pep Comics #22 for 1st app.)
Archie Comics: Sept, 1992 - Present ($1.25/$1.50/$1.75/$1.79/$1.99/$2.19/$2.25)
1 5.00
2-18,20-24: 20-1st Super Sleuther-s 3.00
19-Love Showdown part 2 5.00
25-Pin-up page of Betty as Marilyn Monroe, Madonna, Lady Di 5.00
26-50 3.00
51-177: 57- "A Storm Over Uniforms" x-over part 5,6 2.50

BETTY AND HER STEADY (Going Steady with Betty No. 1)
Avon Periodicals: No. 2, Mar-Apr, 1950
2 10 20 30 56 76 95

BETTY AND ME
Archie Publications: Aug, 1965 - No. 200, Aug, 1992
1 9 18 27 65 113 160
2,3: 3-Origin Superteen 6 12 18 37 59 80
4-8: Superteen in new costume #4-7; dons new helmet in #5, ends #8. 4 8 12 26 41 55
9,10: Girl from R.I.V.E.R.D.A.L.E. 9-UFO-s 3 6 9 20 30 40
11-15,17-20(4/69) 3 6 9 16 23 30
16-Classic cover; w/risqué cover dialogue 4 8 12 26 41 55
21,24-35: 33-Paper doll page 3 6 9 14 19 24
22-Archies Band-s 3 6 9 14 20 26
23-I Dream of Jeannie parody 3 6 9 16 23 30
36(8/71),37,41-55 (52 pgs.): 42-Betty as vamp-s 3 6 9 14 19 24
38-Sabrina app. 3 6 9 21 32 42
39-Josie and Sabrina cover cameos 3 6 9 17 25 32
40-Archie & Betty share a cabin 3 6 9 14 20 25
56(4/71)-80(12/76): 79 Betty Cooper mysteries thru #86. 79-81-Drago the Vampire-s
2 4 6 8 11 14
81-99: 83-Harem-c. 84-Jekyll & Hyde-c/s 1 3 4 6 8 10
100(3/79) 2 4 6 8 11 14
101,118: 101-Elvis mentioned. 118-Tarzan mentioned 1 2 3 5 6 8
102-117,119-130(9/82): 103,104-Space-s. 124-DeCarlo-c begins 6.00
131-138,140,142-147,149-154,156-158: 135,136-Jason Blossom app. 136-Cheryl Blossom cameo. 137-Space-s. 138-Tarzan parody 4.00
139,141,148: 139-Katy Keene collecting-s; Archie in drag-s. 141-Tarzan parody-s. 148-Cyndi Lauper parody-s 5.00
155,159,160(8/87): 155-Archie in drag-s. 159-Superhero gag-c. 160-Wheel of Fortune parody 5.00
161-169,171-199 3.00
170,200: 170-New Archie Superhero-s 5.00

BETTY AND VERONICA (Also see Archie's Girls...)
Archie Enterprises: June, 1987 - Present (75¢ /$1.25/$1.50/$1.75/$1.79/$1.99/$2.19/$2.25)
1 1 2 3 5 7 9
2-10 5.50
11-30 4.00
31-50 3.00
51-81 2.50
82-Love Showdown part 3 5.00
83-158 2.50
159-239 2.25
NOTE: *2005 Free Comic Book Day edition is listed in Promotional Comics section.*

BETTY & VERONICA ANNUAL DIGEST (...Digest Magazine #1-4, 44 on; ...Comics Digest Mag. #5-43)
Archie Publications: Nov, 1980 - Present ($1.00/-$2.49, digest size)
1 3 6 9 16 22 28
2-10: 2(11/81-Katy Keene story), 3(8/82) 2 4 6 9 13 16
11-30 1 3 4 6 8 10
31-50 1 2 3 4 5 7
51-70 4.00
71-190: 110-Begin $2.19-c. 135-Begin $2.39-c. 165-Begin $2.49. 185-Includes reprint of Archie's Girls B&V #1 (1950) and new story where 1950 & 2008 B&V meet 2.50

BETTY & VERONICA ANNUAL DIGEST MAGAZINE
Archie Comics: Sept, 1989 - No. 16, Aug, 1997 ($1.50/$1.75/$1.79, 128 pgs.)
1 1 2 3 5 7 9
2-10: 9-Neon ink logo 5.00
11-16: 16-Begin $1.79-c 3.00

BETTY & VERONICA CHRISTMAS SPECTACULAR (See Archie Giant Series Magazine #159, 168, 180, 191, 204, 217, 229, 241, 453, 465, 477, 489, 501, 513, 525, 536, 547, 558, 568, 580, 593, 606, 618)

BETTY & VERONICA DOUBLE DIGEST MAGAZINE
Archie Enterprises: 1987 - Present ($2.25-$3.69, digest size, 256 pgs.)(...Digest #12 on)
1 2 4 6 8 10 12
2-10 1 2 3 4 5 7
11-25: 5,17-Xmas-c. 16-Capt. Hero story 5.00
26-50 4.00
51-150: 87-Begin $3.19-c. 95-Begin $3.29-c. 114-Begin $3.59-c. 142-Begin $3.69-c 3.75
151-167: 151 (7/07)-Realistic style Betty & Veronica debuts (thru #154). 160 Cheryl Blossom spotlight 4.00
Betty & Veronica: in Bad Boy Trouble Vol.1 TPB (2007, $7.49) r/new style from #151-154 8.00

BETTY & VERONICA SPECTACULAR (See Archie Giant Series Mag. #11, 16, 21, 26, 32, 138, 145, 153, 162, 173, 184, 197, 201, 210, 214, 221, 226, 234, 238, 246, 250, 458, 462, 470, 482, 486, 494, 498, 506, 510, 518, 522, 526, 530, 537, 552, 559, 563, 569, 575, 582, 588, 600, 608, 613, 620, 623, and Betty & Veronica)

BETTY AND VERONICA SPECTACULAR
Archie Comics: Oct, 1992 - Present ($1.25/$1.50/$1.75/$1.99/$2.19/$2.25)
1-Dan DeCarlo-c/a 5.00
2-20 3.00
21-86: 48-Cheryl Blossom leaves Riverdale. 64-Cheryl Blossom returns 2.50

BETTY & VERONICA SPRING SPECTACULAR (See Archie Giant Series Magazine #569, 582, 595)

BETTY & VERONICA SUMMER FUN (See Archie Giant Series Mag. #8, 13, 18, 23, 28, 34, 140, 147, 155, 164, 175, 187, 199, 212, 224, 236, 248, 460, 484, 496, 508, 520, 529, 539, 550, 561, 572, 585, 598, 611, 621)
Archie Comics: 1994 - Present ($2.00/$2.25/$2.29)
1-6: 1-($2.00, 52 pgs. plus poster). 5-($2.25-c). 6-($2.29-c) 2.50
Vol. 1 (2003, $10.95) reprints stories from Archie Giant Series editions 11.00

BETTY BOOP'S BIG BREAK
First Publishing: 1990 ($5.95, 52 pgs.)
nn-By Joshua Quagmire; 60th anniversary ish. 6.00

BETTY PAGE 3-D COMICS
The 3-D Zone: 1991 ($3.95, "7-1/2x10-1/4," 28 pgs., no glasses)
1-Photo inside covers; back-c nudity 1 2 3 5 7 9

BETTY'S DIARY (See Archie Giant Series Magazine No. 555)
Archie Enterprises: April, 1986 - No. 40, Apr, 1991 (#1:65¢; 75¢/95¢)
1 6.00
2-10 4.00
11-40 2.50

BETTY'S DIGEST
Archie Enterprises: Nov, 1996 - No. 2 ($1.75/$1.79)
1,2 3.00

BEVERLY HILLBILLIES (TV)
Dell Publishing Co.: 4-6/63 - No. 18, 8/67; No. 19, 10/69; No. 20, 10/70; No. 21, Oct, 1971
1-Photo-c 15 30 45 106 193 280
2-Photo-c 9 18 27 60 100 140
3-9: All have photo covers 7 14 21 47 76 105

Beware #2 © MAR

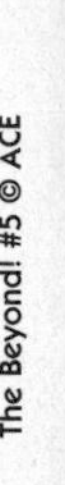
The Beyond! #5 © ACE

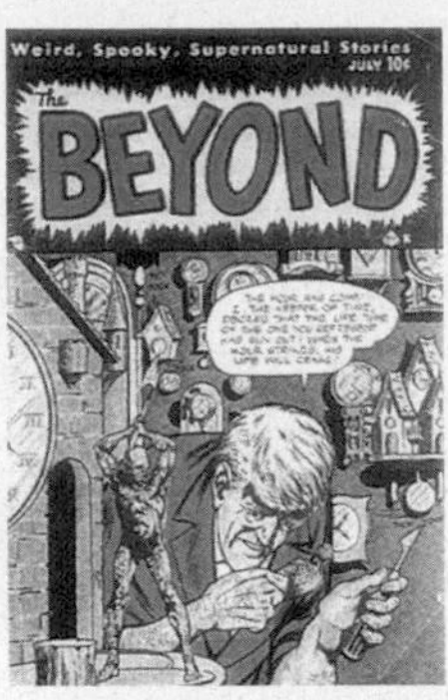

Big Bang Comics #27 © Carlson

GD 2.0 | VG 4.0 | FN 6.0 | VF 8.0 | VF/NM 9.0 | NM- 9.2

10: No photo cover 5 10 15 32 51 70
11-21: All have photo covers. 18-Last 12¢ issue. 19-21-Reprint #1-3 (covers and insides)
6 12 18 37 59 80
NOTE: *#1-9, 11-21 are photo covers.*

BEWARE (Formerly Fantastic; Chilling Tales No. 13 on)
Youthful Magazines: No. 10, June, 1952 - No. 12, Oct, 1952
10-E.A. Poe's Pit & the Pendulum adaptation by Wildey; Harrison/Bache-a; atom bomb and shrunken head-c 57 114 171 359 610 860
11-Harrison-a; Ambrose Bierce adapt. 38 76 114 226 363 500
12-Used in **SOTI**, pg. 388; Harrison-a 38 76 114 226 363 500

BEWARE
Trojan Magazines/Merit Publ. No. ?: No. 13, 1/53 - No. 16, 7/53; No. 5, 9/53 - No. 15, 5/55
13(#1)-Harrison-a 56 112 168 353 597 840
14(#2, 3/53)-Krenkel/Harrison-c; dismemberment, severed head panels
38 76 114 226 363 500
15,16(#3, 5/53; #4, 7/53)-Harrison-a 33 66 99 196 316 435
5,9,12,13 33 66 99 192 309 425
6-Ill. in **SOTI**- "Children are first shocked and then desensitized by all this brutality." Corpse on cover swipe/V.O.H. #26; girl on cover swipe/Advs. Into Darkness #10
62 124 186 391 658 925
7,8-Check-a 33 66 99 196 316 435
10-Frazetta/Check-c; Disbrow, Check-a 70 140 210 441 746 1050
11-Disbrow-a; heart torn out, blood drainage 38 76 114 226 363 500
14,15: 14-Myron Fass-c. 15-Harrison-a 28 56 84 162 261 360
NOTE: ***Fass** a-5, 6, 8; c-6, 11, 14. **Forte** a-8. **Hollingsworth** a-15(#3), 16(#4), 9; c-16(#4), 8, 9. **Kiefer** a-16(#4), 5, 6, 10.*

BEWARE (Becomes Tomb of Darkness No. 9 on)
Marvel Comics Group: Mar, 1973 - No. 8, May, 1974 (All reprints)
1-Everett-c; Kirby & Sinnott-r ('54) 3 6 9 16 22 28
2-8: 2-Forte, Colan-r. 6-Tuska-a. 7-Torres-r/Mystical Tales #7
2 4 6 10 14 18
NOTE: ***Infantino** a-4r. **Gil Kane** c-4. **Wildey** a-7r.*

BEWARE TERROR TALES
Fawcett Publications: May, 1952 - No. 8, July, 1953
1-E.C. art swipe/Haunt of Fear #5 & Vault of Horror #26
47 94 141 291 488 685
2 32 64 96 186 298 410
3-5,7 26 52 78 154 247 340
6-Classic skeleton-c 28 56 84 162 261 360
8-Tothish-a; people being cooked-c 31 62 93 181 291 400
NOTE: ***Andru** a-2. **Bernard Bailey** a-1; c-1-5. **Powell** a-1, 2, 8. **Sekowsky** a-2.*

BEWARE THE CREEPER (See Adventure, Best of the Brave & the Bold, Brave & the Bold, 1st Issue Special, Flash #318-323, Showcase #73, World's Finest Comics #249)
National Periodical Publications: May-June, 1968 - No. 6, Mar-Apr, 1969 (All 12¢ issues)
1-(5-6/68)-Classic Ditko-c; Ditko-a in all 9 18 27 63 107 150
2-6: 2-5-Ditko-c. 2-Intro. Proteus. 6-Gil Kane-c 5 10 15 34 55 75

BEWARE THE CREEPER
DC Comics (Vertigo): June, 2003 - No. 5, Oct, 2003 ($2.95, limited series)
1-5-Female vigilante in 1920s Paris; Jason Hall-s/Cliff Chiang-a 3.00

BEWITCHED (TV)
Dell Publishing Co.: 4-6/65 - No. 11, 10/67; No. 12, 10/68 - No. 13, 1/69; No. 14, 10/69
1-Photo-c 15 30 45 105 190 275
2-No photo-c 8 16 24 54 90 125
3-13-All have photo-c. 12-Rep. #1. 13-Last 12¢-c 7 14 21 47 76 105
14-No photo-c; reprints #2 5 10 15 34 55 75

BEYOND!
Marvel Comics: Sept, 2006 - No. 6, Feb, 2007 ($2.99, limited series)
1-6-McDuffie-s/Kolins-a; Spider-Man, Venom, Gravity, Wasp app. 6-Gravity dies 3.00
HC (2007, $19.99, dustjacket) r/series; cover sketches and sketch design pages 20.00
SC (2008, $14.99) r/series; cover sketches and sketch design pages 15.00

BEYOND, THE
Ace Magazines: Nov, 1950 - No. 30, Jan, 1955
1-Bakerish-a(p) 43 86 129 267 446 625
2-Bakerish-a(p) 28 56 84 162 261 360
3-10: 10-Woodish-a by Cameron 20 40 60 117 186 255
11-20: 18-Used in **POP**, pgs. 81,82 15 30 45 94 147 200
21-26,28-30 15 30 45 92 144 195
27-Used in **SOTI**, pg. 111 15 30 45 94 147 200
NOTE: ***Cameron** a-10, 11p, 12p, 15, 16, 21-27, 30; c-20. **Colan** a-6, 13, 17. **Sekowsky** a-2, 3, 5, 7, 11, 14, 27r. No. 1 was to appear as Challenge of the Unknown No. 7.*

BEYOND THE GRAVE
Charlton Comics: July, 1975 - No. 6, June, 1976; No. 7, Jan, 1983 - No. 17, Oct, 1984
1-Ditko-a (6 pgs.); Sutton painted-c 3 6 9 18 27 35
2-6: 2-5-Ditko-a; Ditko c-2,3,6 2 4 6 10 14 18
7-17: ('83-'84) Reprints. 13-Aparo-c(r). 15-Sutton-c (low print run) 6.00
Modern Comics Reprint 2('78) 4.00
NOTE: ***Howard** a-4. **Kim** a-1. **Larson** a-4, 6.*

BIBLE, THE: EDEN
IDW Publishing: 2003 ($21.99, hardcover graphic novel)
HC-Scott Hampton painted-a; adaptation of Genesis by Dave Elliot and Keith Giffen 22.00

BIBLE TALES FOR YOUNG FOLK (...Young People No. 3-5)
Atlas Comics (OMC): Aug, 1953 - No. 5, Mar, 1954
1 26 52 78 152 244 355
2-Everett, Krigstein-a; Robinson-c 18 36 54 105 165 225
3-5: 4,5-Robinson-c 15 30 45 88 137 185

BIG (Movie)
Hit Comics (Dark Horse Comics): Mar, 1989 ($2.00)
1-Adaptation of film; Paul Chadwick-c 2.50

BIG ALL-AMERICAN COMIC BOOK, THE (See All-American Comics)
All-American/National Per. Publ.: 1944 (132 pgs., one-shot) (Early DC Annual)
1-Wonder Woman, Green Lantern, Flash, The Atom, Wildcat, Scribbly, The Whip, Ghost Patrol, Hawkman by Kubert (1st on Hawkman), Hop Harrigan, Johnny Thunder, Little Boy Blue, Mr. Terrific, Mutt & Jeff app.; Sargon on cover only; cover by Kubert/Hibbard/Mayer and others 800 1600 2400 5600 9,800 14,000

BIG BABY HUEY (See Baby Huey)

BIG BANG COMICS (Becomes Big Bang #4)
Caliber Press: Spring, 1994 - No. 4, Feb, 1995; No. 0, May, 1995 ($1.95, lim. series)
1-4-($1.95-c) 2.50
0-(5/95, $2.95) Alex Ross-c; color and B&W pages 3.00
Your Big Book of Big Bang Comics TPB ('98, $11.00) r/#0-2 11.00

BIG BANG COMICS (Volume 2)
Image Comics (Highbrow Ent.): V2#1, May, 1996 - No. 35, Jan, 2001 ($1.95-$3.95)
1-23,26: 1-Mighty Man app. 2-4-S.A. Shadowhawk app. 5-Begin $2.95-c. 6-Curt Swan/Murphy Anderson-c. 7-Begin B&W. 12-Savage Dragon-c/app. 16,17,21-Shadow Lady 3.00
24,25,27-35-($3.95): 35-Big Bang vs. Alan Moore's "1963" characters 4.00
...Presents the Ultiman Family (2/05, $3.50) 3.50
...Round Table of America (2/04, $3.95) Don Thomas-a 4.00
...Summer Special (8/03, $4.95) World's Nastiest Nazis app. 5.00

BIG BANG PRESENTS (Volume 3)
Big Bang Comics: July, 2006 - Present ($2.95/$3.95, B&W)
1,2: 1-Protoplasman (Plastic Man homage) 3.00
3-5-($3.95) 3-Origin of Protoplasman. 4-Flip book 4.00

BIG BLACK KISS
Vortex Comics: Sep, 1989 - No, 3, Nov, 1989 ($3.75, B&W, lim. series, mature)
1-3-Chaykin-s/a 4.00

BIG BLOWN BABY (Also see Dark Horse Presents)
Dark Horse Comics: Aug, 1996 - No. 4, Nov, 1996 ($2.95, lim. series, mature)
1-4: Bill Wray-c/a/scripts 3.00

BIG BOOK OF ..., THE
DC Comics (Paradox Press): 1994 - Present (B&W)($12.95 - $14.95)
nn-...**BAD**,1998 ($14.95), ...**CONSPIRACIES**, 1995 ($12.95), ...**DEATH**,1994 ($12.95), ...**FREAKS**, 1996 ($14.95), ...**GRIMM**, 1999 ($14.95), ...**HOAXES**, 1996 ($14.95), ...**LITTLE CRIMINALS**, 1996 ($14.95), ...**LOSERS**,1997 ($14.95), **MARTYRS**, 1997 ($14.95), ...**SCANDAL**,1997 ($14.95), ...**THE WEIRD WILD WEST**,1998 ($14.95), ...**THUGS**, 1997 ($14.95), ...**UNEXPLAINED**, 1997 ($14.95), ...**URBAN LEGENDS**, 1994 ($12.95), ...**VICE**, 1999 ($14.95), ...**WEIRDOS**, 1995 ($12.95) cover price

BIG BOOK OF FUN COMICS (See New Book of Comics)
National Periodical Publications: Spring, 1936 (Large size, 52 pgs.)
(1st comic book annual & DC annual)
1 (Very rare)-r/New Fun #1-5 2300 4600 6900 15,000 - -

BIG BOOK ROMANCES
Fawcett Publications: Feb, 1950 (no date given) (148 pgs.)
1-Contains remaindered Fawcett romance comics - several combinations possible
41 82 123 250 413 575

Big Chief Wahoo #1 © EAS

Big Hero 6 #1 © MAR

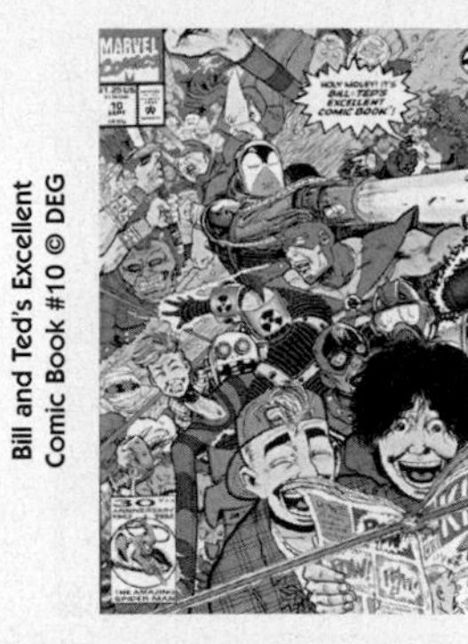

Bill and Ted's Excellent Comic Book #10 © DEG

	GD	VG	FN	VF	VF/NM	NM-
	2.0	4.0	6.0	8.0	9.0	9.2

BIG CHIEF WAHOO
Eastern Color Printing/George Dougherty (distr. by Fawcett): July, 1942 - No. 7, Wint., 1943/44?(no year given)(Quarterly)

1-Newspaper-r (on sale 6/15/42) 41 82 123 256 428 600
2-Steve Roper app. 23 46 69 133 214 295
3-5: 4-Chief is holding a Katy Keene comic 18 36 54 105 165 225
6-7 14 28 42 82 121 160
NOTE: *Kerry Drake in some issues.*

BIG CIRCUS, THE (Movie)
Dell Publishing Co.: No. 1036, Sept-Nov, 1959

Four Color 1036-Photo-c 6 12 18 43 69 95

BIG COUNTRY, THE (Movie)
Dell Publishing Co.: No. 946, Oct, 1958

Four Color 946-Photo-c 7 14 21 47 76 105

BIG DADDY DANGER
DC Comics: Oct, 2002 - No. 9, June, 2003 ($2.95, limited series)

1-9-Adam Pollina-s/a/c 3.00

BIG DADDY ROTH (Magazine)
Millar Publications: Oct-Nov, 1964 - No. 4, Apr-May, 1965 (35¢)

1-Toth-a 17 34 51 120 223 325
2-4-Toth-a 11 22 33 79 140 200

BIGFOOT
IDW Publishing: Feb, 2005 - No. 4, May, 2005 ($3.99, limited series)

1-4-Steve Niles & Rob Zombie-s/Richard Corben-a/c 4.00

BIGG TIME
DC Comics (Vertigo): 2002 ($14.95, B&W, graphic novel)

nn-Ty Templeton-s/c/a 15.00

BIG GUY AND RUSTY THE BOY ROBOT, THE (Also See Madman Comics #6,7 & Martha Washington Stranded In Space)
Dark Horse (Legend): July, 1995 - No. 2, Aug, 1995 ($4.95, oversize, limited series)

1,2-Frank Miller scripts & Geoff Darrow-c/a 1 2 3 4 5 7
Trade paperback (10/96, $14.95)-r/1,2 w/cover gallery 15.00

BIG HAIR PRODUCTIONS
Image Comics: Feb, 2000 - No. 2, Mar, 2000 ($3.50, B&W)

1,2 3.50

BIG HERO ADVENTURES (See Jigsaw)

BIG HERO 6 (Also see Sunfire & Big Hero Six)
Marvel Comics: Nov, 2008 - No. 5 ($3.99, limited series)

1-Claremont-s/Nakayama-a; character design pages & Handbook entries 4.00

BIG JON & SPARKIE (Radio)(Formerly Sparkie, Radio Pixie)
Ziff-Davis Publ. Co.: No. 4, Sept-Oct, 1952 (Painted-c)

4-Based on children's radio program 18 36 54 107 169 230

BIG LAND, THE (Movie)
Dell Publishing Co.: No. 812, July, 1957

Four Color 812-Alan Ladd photo-c 9 18 27 60 100 140

BIG RED (See Movie Comics)

BIG SHOT COMICS
Columbia Comics Group: May, 1940 - No. 104, Aug, 1949

1-Intro. Skyman; The Face (1st app.; Tony Trent), The Cloak (Spy Master), Marvelo, Monarch of Magicians, Joe Palooka, Charlie Chan, Tom Kerry, Dixie Dugan, Rocky Ryan begin; Charlie Chan moves over from Feature Comics #31 (4/40)
253 506 759 1594 2697 3800
2 88 176 264 554 940 1325
3-The Cloak called Spy Chief; Skyman-c 78 156 234 491 833 1175
4,5 57 114 171 359 605 850
6-10: 8-Christmas-c 46 92 138 285 473 660
11-13 41 82 123 256 428 600
14-Origin & 1st app. Sparky Watts (6/41) 45 90 135 279 465 650
15-Origin The Cloak 46 92 138 285 473 660
16-20 35 70 105 203 327 450
21-23,26,27,29,30: 29-Intro. Capt. Yank; Bo (a dog) newspaper strip-r by Frank Beck begin, ends #104. 30-X-Mas-c 30 60 90 174 280 385
24-Classic Tojo-c. 50 100 150 310 518 725
25-Hitler-c 41 82 123 250 413 575
28-Hitler, Tojo & Mussolini-c 53 106 159 334 567 800
31,33-40 22 44 66 127 204 280
32-Vic Jordan newspaper strip reprints begin, ends #52; Hitler, Tojo & Mussolini-c
43 86 129 267 446 625
41,42,44,45,47-50: 42-No Skyman. 50-Origin The Face retold
19 38 57 112 176 240
43-Hitler-c 38 76 114 220 363 500
46-Hitler, Tojo-c (6/44) 37 74 111 215 345 475
51-56,58-60: 51-Tojo Japanese war-c 15 30 45 94 147 200
57-Hitler, Tojo Halloween mask-c 27 54 81 158 254 350
61-70: 63 on-Tony Trent, the Face 14 28 42 80 115 150
71-80: 73-The Face cameo. 74-(2/47)-Mickey Finn begins. 74,80-The Face app. in Tony Trent. 78-Last Charlie Chan strip-r 14 28 42 76 108 140
81-90: 85-Tony Trent marries Babs Walsh. 86-Valentines-c
11 22 33 62 86 110
91-99,101-104: 69-94-Skyman in Outer Space. 96-Xmas-c
10 20 30 56 76 95
100 11 22 33 64 90 115
NOTE: ***Mart Bailey** art on "The Face" No. 1-104. **Guardineer** a-5. Sparky Watts by **Boody Rogers**-No. 14-42, 77-104, (by others No. 43-76). Others than Tony Trent wear "The Face" mask in No. 46-63, 93. Skyman by **Ogden Whitney**-No. 1, 2, 4, 12-37, 49, 70-101. Skyman covers-No. 1, 3, 7-12, 14, 16, 20, 27, 89, 95, 100.*

BIG SMASH BARGAIN COMICS
No publisher listed: Early 1950s (25¢, 160pgs., Canadian reprints)

1-4: Contains 4 comics from various companies bundled with new cover (scarce)
28 56 84 164 265 365

BIG TEX
Toby Press: June, 1953

1-Contains (3) John Wayne stories-r with name changed to Big Tex
10 20 30 58 79 100

BIG-3
Fox Features Syndicate: Fall, 1940 - No. 7, Jan, 1942

1-Blue Beetle, The Flame, & Samson begin 223 446 669 1405 2378 3350
2 83 166 249 523 887 1250
3-5 59 118 177 372 629 885
6,7: 6-Last Samson. 7-V-Man app. 45 90 135 279 465 650

BIG TOP COMICS, THE (TV's Great Circus Show)
Toby Press: 1951 - No. 2, 1951 (No month)

1 10 20 30 58 79 100
2 9 18 27 47 61 75

BIG TOWN (Radio/TV) (Also see Movie Comics, 1946)
National Periodical Publ: Jan, 1951 - No. 50, Mar-Apr, 1958 (No. 1-9: 52pgs.)

1-Dan Barry-a begins 66 132 198 416 701 985
2 35 70 105 203 327 450
3-10 21 42 63 123 197 270
11-20 15 30 45 90 140 190
21-31: Last pre-code (1-2/55) 13 26 39 72 101 130
32-50: 46-Grey tone cover 10 20 30 56 76 95

BIG VALLEY, THE (TV)
Dell Publishing Co.: June, 1966 - No. 5, Oct, 1967; No. 6, Oct, 1969

1: Photo-c #1-5 5 10 15 34 55 75
2-6: 6-Reprints #1 4 8 12 22 34 45

BIKER MICE FROM MARS (TV)
Marvel Comics: Nov, 1993 - No. 3, Jan, 1994 ($1.50, limited series)

1-3: 1-Intro Vinnie, Modo & Throttle. 2-Origin 3.50

BILL & TED'S BOGUS JOURNEY
Marvel Comics: Sept, 1991 ($2.95, squarebound, 84 pgs.)

1-Adapts movie sequel 3.00

BILL & TED'S EXCELLENT COMIC BOOK (Movie)
Marvel Comics: Dec, 1991 - No. 12, 1992 ($1.00/$1.25)

1-12: 3-Begin $1.25-c 2.50

BILL BARNES COMICS (...America's Air Ace Comics No. 2 on) (Becomes Air Ace V2#1 on; also see Shadow Comics)
Street & Smith Publications: Oct, 1940(No. month given) - No. 12, Oct, 1943

1-23 pgs.-comics; Rocket Rooney begins 87 174 261 548 924 1300
2-Barnes as The Phantom Flyer app.; Tuska-a 43 86 129 267 446 625
3-5 40 80 120 235 380 525
6-12 34 68 102 198 319 440

BILL BATTLE, THE ONE MAN ARMY (Also see Master Comics No. 133)
Fawcett Publications: Oct, 1952 - No. 4, Apr, 1953 (All photo-c)

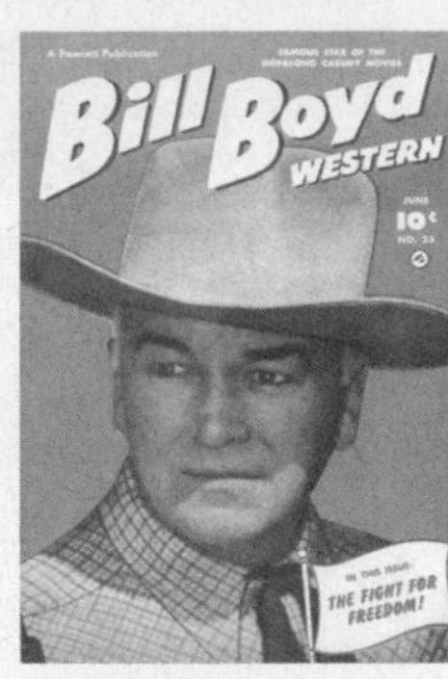

Bill Boyd Western #23 © FAW

Billy Batson and the Magic of Shazam! #1 © DC

Billy West #6 © STD

	GD 2.0	VG 4.0	FN 6.0	VF 8.0	VF/NM 9.0	NM- 9.2
1	14	28	42	76	108	140
2	8	16	24	44	57	70
3,4	8	16	24	40	50	60

BILL BLACK'S FUN COMICS
Paragon #1-3/Americomics #4: Dec, 1982 - No. 4, Mar, 1983 ($1.75/$2.00, Baxter paper) (1st AC comic)

	GD 2.0	VG 4.0	FN 6.0	VF 8.0	VF/NM 9.0	NM- 9.2
1-(B&W fanzine; 7x8-1/2"; low print) Intro. Capt. Paragon, Phantom Lady & Commando D	2	4	6	13	18	22
2-4: 2,3-(B&W fanzines; 8-1/2x11"). 3-Kirby-c. 4-($2.00, color)-Origin Nightfall (formerly Phantom Lady); Nightveil app.; Kirby-a	1	3	4	6	8	10

BILL BOYD WESTERN (Movie star; see Hopalong Cassidy & Western Hero)
Fawcett Publ: Feb, 1950 - No. 23, June, 1952 (1-3,7,11,14-on: 36 pgs.)

	GD 2.0	VG 4.0	FN 6.0	VF 8.0	VF/NM 9.0	NM- 9.2
1-Bill Boyd & his horse Midnite begin; photo front/back-c	41	82	123	257	419	580
2-Painted-c	23	46	69	135	213	290
3-Photo-c begin, end #23; last photo back-c	18	36	54	105	165	225
4-6(52 pgs.)	15	30	45	88	137	185
7,11(36 pgs.)	14	28	42	76	108	140
8-10,12,13(52 pgs.)	14	28	42	78	112	145
14-22	13	26	39	72	101	130
23-Last issue	14	28	42	76	108	140

BILL BUMLIN (See Treasury of Comics No. 3)

BILL ELLIOTT (See Wild Bill Elliott)

BILLI 99
Dark Horse Comics: Sept, 1991 - No. 4, 1991 ($3.50, B&W, lim. series, 52 pgs.)

	GD 2.0	VG 4.0	FN 6.0	VF 8.0	VF/NM 9.0	NM- 9.2
1-4: Tim Sale-c/a						3.50

BILL STERN'S SPORTS BOOK
Ziff-Davis Publ. Co.(Approved Comics): Spring-Sum, 1951 - V2#2, Win, 1952

	GD 2.0	VG 4.0	FN 6.0	VF 8.0	VF/NM 9.0	NM- 9.2
V1#10-(1951) Whitney painted-c	22	44	66	126	198	270
2-(Sum/52; reg. size)	16	32	48	94	147	200
V2#2-(1952, 96 pgs.)-Krigstein, Kinstler-a	23	46	69	130	205	280

BILL THE BULL: ONE SHOT, ONE BOURBON, ONE BEER
Boneyard Press: Dec, 1994 ($2.95, B&W, mature)

	GD 2.0	VG 4.0	FN 6.0	VF 8.0	VF/NM 9.0	NM- 9.2
1						3.00

BILLY AND BUGGY BEAR (See Animal Fun)
I.W. Enterprises/Super: 1958; 1964

	GD 2.0	VG 4.0	FN 6.0	VF 8.0	VF/NM 9.0	NM- 9.2
I.W. Reprint #1, #7('58)-All Surprise Comics #?(Same issue-r for both)	2	4	6	10	14	18
Super Reprint #10(1964)	2	4	6	8	11	14

BILLY BATSON AND THE MAGIC OF SHAZAM! (Follows Shazam: The Monster Society of Evil mini-series)
DC Comics: Sept, 2008 - Present ($2.25, all ages title)

	GD 2.0	VG 4.0	FN 6.0	VF 8.0	VF/NM 9.0	NM- 9.2
1-Mike Kunkel-s/a/c; Theo (Black) Adam app.						3.00

BILLY BUCKSKIN WESTERN (2-Gun Western No. 4)
Atlas Comics (IMC No. 1/MgPC No. 2,3): Nov, 1955 - No. 3, Mar, 1956

	GD 2.0	VG 4.0	FN 6.0	VF 8.0	VF/NM 9.0	NM- 9.2
1-Mort Drucker-a; Maneely-c/a	16	32	48	88	137	185
2-Mort Drucker-a	10	20	30	56	76	95
3-Williamson, Drucker-a	12	24	36	67	94	120

BILLY BUNNY (Black Cobra No. 6 on)
Excellent Publications: Feb-Mar, 1954 - No. 5, Oct-Nov, 1954

	GD 2.0	VG 4.0	FN 6.0	VF 8.0	VF/NM 9.0	NM- 9.2
1	9	18	27	50	65	80
2	6	12	18	28	34	40
3-5	5	10	15	24	30	35

BILLY BUNNY'S CHRISTMAS FROLICS
Farrell Publications: 1952 (25¢ Giant, 100 pgs.)

	GD 2.0	VG 4.0	FN 6.0	VF 8.0	VF/NM 9.0	NM- 9.2
1	21	42	63	122	191	260

BILLY COLE
Cult Press: May, 1994 - No. 4, Aug, 1994 ($2.75, B&W, limited series)

	GD 2.0	VG 4.0	FN 6.0	VF 8.0	VF/NM 9.0	NM- 9.2
1-4						2.75

BILLY MAKE BELIEVE
United Features Syndicate: No. 14, 1939

	GD 2.0	VG 4.0	FN 6.0	VF 8.0	VF/NM 9.0	NM- 9.2
Single Series 14	32	64	96	186	293	400

BILLY NGUYEN, PRIVATE EYE
Caliber Press: V2#1, 1990 ($2.50)

	GD 2.0	VG 4.0	FN 6.0	VF 8.0	VF/NM 9.0	NM- 9.2
V2#1						2.50

BILLY THE KID (Formerly The Masked Raider; also see Doc Savage Comics & Return of the Outlaw)
Charlton Publ. Co.: No. 9, Nov, 1957 - No. 121, Dec, 1976; No. 122, Sept, 1977 - No. 123, Oct, 1977; No. 124, Feb, 1978 - No. 153, Mar, 1983

	GD 2.0	VG 4.0	FN 6.0	VF 8.0	VF/NM 9.0	NM- 9.2
9	10	20	30	58	79	100
10,12,14,17-19: 12-2 pg Check-sty	8	16	24	40	50	60
11-(68 pgs.)-Origin & 1st app. The Ghost Train	9	18	27	50	65	80
13-Williamson/Torres-a	8	16	24	44	57	70
15-Origin; 2 pgs. Williamson-a	8	16	24	44	57	70
16-Williamson-a, 2 pgs.	8	16	24	42	54	65
20-26-Severin-a(3-4 each)	8	16	24	44	57	70
27-30: 30-Masked Rider app.	3	6	9	19	29	38
31-40	3	6	9	16	22	28
41-60	2	4	6	13	18	22
61-65	2	4	6	10	14	18
66-Bounty Hunter series begins.	2	4	6	11	16	20
67-80: Bounty Hunter series; not in #79,82,84-86	2	4	6	9	13	16
81-84,86-90: 87-Last Bounty Hunter	1	3	4	6	8	10
85-Early Kaluta-a (4 pgs.)	2	4	6	8	11	14
91-123: 110-Dr. Young of Boothill app. 111-Origin The Ghost Train. 117-Gunsmith & Co., The Cheyenne Kid app.	1	2	3	4	5	7
124(2/78)-153						5.00
Modern Comics 109 (1977 reprint)						4.00

NOTE: ***Boyette** a-91-110. **Kim** a-73. **Morsi** a-12,14. **Sattler** a-118-123. **Severin** a(r)-121-129, 134; c-23, 25. **Sutton** a-111.*

BILLY THE KID ADVENTURE MAGAZINE
Toby Press: Oct, 1950 - No. 29, 1955

	GD 2.0	VG 4.0	FN 6.0	VF 8.0	VF/NM 9.0	NM- 9.2
1-Williamson/Frazetta-a (2 pgs) r/from John Wayne Adventure Comics #2; photo-c	31	62	93	181	291	400
2-Photo-c	12	24	36	69	97	125
3-Williamson/Frazetta "The Claws of Death", 4 pgs. plus Williamson art	34	68	102	198	319	440
4,5,7,8,10: 4,7-Photo-c	9	18	27	52	69	85
6-Frazetta assist on "Nightmare"; photo-c	15	30	45	83	124	165
9-Kurtzman Pot-Shot Peto; photo-c	11	22	33	64	90	115
11,12,15-20: 11-Photo-c	8	16	24	42	54	65
13-Kurtzman-r/John Wayne #12 (Genius)	9	18	27	47	61	75
14-Williamson/Frazetta; r-of #1 (2 pgs.)	10	20	30	56	76	95
21,23-29	7	14	21	37	46	55
22-Williamson/Frazetta-r(1pg.)/#1; photo-c	8	16	24	42	54	65

BILLY THE KID AND OSCAR (Also see Fawcett's Funny Animals)
Fawcett Publications: Winter, 1945 - No. 3, Fall, 1946 (Funny animal)

	GD 2.0	VG 4.0	FN 6.0	VF 8.0	VF/NM 9.0	NM- 9.2
1	15	30	45	84	127	170
2,3	10	20	30	56	76	95

BILLY THE KID'S OLD TIMEY ODDITIES
Dark Horse Comics: Apr, 2005 - No. 4, July, 2005 ($2.99, limited series)

	GD 2.0	VG 4.0	FN 6.0	VF 8.0	VF/NM 9.0	NM- 9.2
1-4-Eric Powell-s/c; Kyle Hotz-a						3.00
TPB (2005, $13.95) r/series						14.00

BILLY WEST (Bill West No. 9,10)
Standard Comics (Visual Editions): 1949-No. 9, Feb, 1951; No. 10, Feb, 1952

	GD 2.0	VG 4.0	FN 6.0	VF 8.0	VF/NM 9.0	NM- 9.2
1	14	28	42	82	121	160
2	9	18	27	50	65	80
3-6,9,10	8	16	24	42	54	65
7,8-Schomburg-c	9	18	27	47	61	75

NOTE: ***Celardo** a-1-6, 9; c-1-3. **Moreira** a-3. **Roussos** a-2.*

BING CROSBY (See Feature Films)

BINGO (...Comics) (H. C. Blackerby)
Howard Publ.: 1945 (Reprints National material)

	GD 2.0	VG 4.0	FN 6.0	VF 8.0	VF/NM 9.0	NM- 9.2
1-L. B. Cole opium-c; blank back-c	36	72	108	212	341	470

BINGO, THE MONKEY DOODLE BOY
St. John Publishing Co.: Aug, 1951; Oct, 1953

	GD 2.0	VG 4.0	FN 6.0	VF 8.0	VF/NM 9.0	NM- 9.2
1(8/51)-By Eric Peters	8	16	24	40	50	60
1(10/53)	6	12	18	28	34	40

BINKY (Formerly Leave It to...)
National Periodical Publ./DC Comics: No. 72, 4-5/70 - No. 81, 10-11/71; No. 82, Summer/77

	GD 2.0	VG 4.0	FN 6.0	VF 8.0	VF/NM 9.0	NM- 9.2
72-76	3	6	9	20	30	40
77-79: (68 pgs.). 77-Bobby Sherman 1pg. story w/photo. 78-1 pg. sty on Barry Williams of Brady Bunch. 79-Osmonds 1pg. story	5	10	15	34	55	75

Birds of Prey #66 © DC

Bishop The Last X-Man #2 © MAR

Black Adam #1 © DC

	GD 2.0	VG 4.0	FN 6.0	VF 8.0	VF/NM 9.0	NM- 9.2

80,81 (52 pgs.)-Sweat Pain story 4 8 12 28 44 60
82 (1977, one-shot) 3 6 9 21 32 42

BINKY'S BUDDIES
National Periodical Publications: Jan-Feb, 1969 - No. 12, Nov-Dec, 1970

1 6 12 18 41 66 90
2-12: 3-Last 12¢ issue 4 8 12 22 34 45

BIONIC WOMAN, THE (TV)
Charlton Publications: Oct, 1977 - No. 5, June, 1978

1 3 6 9 18 27 35
2-5 2 4 6 11 16 20

BIRDS OF PREY (Also see Black Canary/Oracle: Birds of Prey)
DC Comics: Jan, 1999 - Present ($1.99/$2.50)

1-Dixon-s/Land-c/a 1 3 4 6 8 10
2-4 6.00
5-7,9-15: 15-Guice-a begins. 4.00
8-Nightwing-c/app.; Barbara & Dick's circus date 2 4 6 9 12 15
16-38: 23-Grodd-c/app. 26-Bane app. 32-Noto-c begin 2.50
39,40-Bruce Wayne: Murderer pt. 5,12 3.00
41-Bruce Wayne: Fugitive pt. 2 4.00
42-46: 42-Fabry-a. 45-Deathstroke-c/app. 2.50
47-74,76-91: 47-49-Terry Moore-s/Conner & Palmiotti-a; Noto-c. 50-Gilbert Hernandez-s begin. 52,54-Metamorpho app. 56-Simone-s/Benes-a begin. 65,67,68,70-Land-c. 76-Debut of Black Alice (from Day of Vengeance). 86-Timm-a (7 pgs.) 2.50
75-($2.95) Pearson-c; back-up story of Lady Blackhawk 3.00
92-99,101-120: 92-One Year Later. 94-Begin $2.99-c; Prometheus app. 96,97-Black Alice app. 98,99-New Batgirl app. 99-Black Canary leaves the team. 104-107-Secret Six app. 3.00
100-($3.99) new team recruited; Black Canary origin re-told 4.00
TPB (1999, $17.95) r/ previous series and one-shots 18.00
...: Batgirl 1 (2/98, $2.95) Dixon-s/Frank-c 5.00
...: Batgirl/Catwoman 1 ('03, $5.95) Robertson-a; cont'd in BOP: Catwoman/Oracle 1 6.00
...: Between Dark & Dawn TPB (2006, $14.99) r/#69-75 15.00
...: Blood and Circuits TPB (2007, $17.99) r/#96-103 18.00
...: Catwoman/Oracle 1 ('03, $5.95) Cont'd from BOP: Batgirl/Catwoman 1; David Ross-a 6.00
...: Dead of Winter TPB (2008, $17.99) r/#104-108 18.00
...: Of Like Minds TPB (2004, $14.95) r/#55-61 15.00
...: Old Friends, New Enemies TPB (2003, $17.95) r/#1-6, ...: Batgirl, ...: Wolves 18.00
...: Perfect Pitch TPB (2007, $17.99) r/#86-90,92-95 18.00
...: Revolution 1 (1997, $2.95) Frank-c/Dixon-s 5.00
... Secret Files 2003 (8/03, $4.95) Short stories, pin-ups and profile pages; Noto-c 5.00
...: Sensei and Student TPB (2005, $17.95) r/#62-68 18.00
...: The Battle Within TPB (2006, $17.99) r/#76-85 18.00
...: The Ravens 1 (6/98, $1.95)-Dixon-s; Girlfrenzy issue 4.00
...: Wolves 1 (10/97, $2.95) Dixon-s/Giordano & Faucher-a 5.00

BIRDS OF PREY: MANHUNT
DC Comics: Sept, 1996 - No. 4, Dec, 1996 ($1.95, limited series)

1-Features Black Canary, Oracle, Huntress, & Catwoman; Chuck Dixon scripts; Gary Frank-c on all. 1-Catwoman cameo only 1 2 3 5 6 8
2-4 6.00
NOTE: *Gary Frank c-1-4. Matt Haley a-1-4p. Wade Von Grawbadger a-1i.*

BIRTH CAUL, THE
Eddie Campbell Comics: 1999 ($5.95, B&W, one-shot)

1-Alan Moore-s/Eddie Campbell-a 6.00

BIRTH OF THE DEFIANT UNIVERSE, THE
Defiant Comics: May, 1993

nn-Contains promotional artwork & text; limited print run of 1000 copies. 2 4 6 8 10 12

BISHOP (See Uncanny X-Men & X-Men)
Marvel Comics: Dec, 1994 - No.4, Mar, 1995 ($2.95, limited series)

1-4: Foil-c; Shard & Mountjoy in all. 1-Storm app. 3.00

BISHOP THE LAST X-MAN
Marvel Comics: Oct, 1999 - No. 16, Jan, 2001 ($2.99/$1.99/$2.25)

1-($2.99)-Jeanty-a 3.50
2-8-($1.99): 2-Two covers 2.50
9-11,13-16: 9-Begin $2.25-c. 15-Maximum Security x-over; Xavier app. 2.50
12-($2.99) 3.00

BISHOP: XAVIER SECURITY ENFORCER
Marvel Comics: Jan, 1998 - No.3, Mar, 1998 ($2.50, limited series)

1-3: Ostrander-s 3.00

BITE CLUB
DC Comics (Vertigo): Jun, 2004 - No. 6, Nov, 2004 ($2.95, limited series)

1-6-Chaykin-s/Tischman-a/Quitely-c 3.00
TPB Digest (2005, $9.99) r/#1-6; cover gallery 10.00
The Complete Bite Club TPB (2007, $19.99) r/#1-6 and ...: Vampire Crime Unit #1-5 20.00

BITE CLUB: VAMPIRE CRIME UNIT
DC Comics (Vertigo): Jun, 2006 - No. 5 ($2.99, limited series)

1-5:1-Chaykin & Tischman-s/Hahn-a/Quitely-c. 4-Chaykin-c 3.00

BIZARRE ADVENTURES (Formerly Marvel Preview)
Marvel Comics Group: No. 25, 3/81 - No. 34, 2/83 (#25-33: Magazine-$1.50)

25,26: 25-Lethal Ladies. 26-King Kull; Bolton-c/a 1 3 4 6 8 10
27,28: 27-Phoenix, Iceman & Nightcrawler app. 28-The Unlikely Heroes; Elektra by Miller; Neal Adams-a 2 4 6 9 13 16
29,30,32,33: 29-Stephen King's Lawnmower Man. 30-Tomorrow; 1st app. Silhouette. 32-Gods; Thor-c/s. 33-Horror; Dracula app.; photo-c 1 2 3 5 7 9
31-After The Violence Stops; new Hangman story; Miller-a 1 3 4 6 8 10
34 ($2.00, Baxter paper, comic size)-Son of Santa; Christmas special; Howard the Duck by Paul Smith 1 2 3 5 6 8
NOTE: *Alcala a-27i. Austin a-25i, 28i. Bolton a-26, 32. J. Buscema a-27p, 29, 30p; c-26. Byrne a-31 (2 pg.). Golden a-25p, 28p. Perez a-27p. Rogers a-25p. Simonson a-29; c-29. Paul Smith a-34.*

BIZARRO COMICS!
DC Comics: 2001 ($29.95, hardcover, one-shot)

HC-Short stories of DC heroes by various alternative cartoonists including Dorkin, Pope, Haspiel, Kidd, Kochalka, Millionaire, Stephens, Wray; includes "Superman's Babysitter" by Kyle Baker from Elseworlds 80-Page Giant recalled by DC; Groening-c 30.00
Softcover (2003, $19.95) 20.00

BIZARRO WORLD
DC Comics: 2005 ($29.95, hardcover, one-shot)

HC-Short stories by various alternative cartoonists including Bagge, Baker, Dorkin, Dunn, Kupperman, Morse, Oswalt, Pekar, Simpson, Stewart; Jaime Hernandez-c 30.00
Softcover (2006, $19.99) 20.00

BLACK ADAM (See 52 and Countdown)
DC Comics: Oct, 2007 - No. 6, Mar, 2008 ($2.99, limited series)

1-6: 1-Mahnke-a/c; Isis returns; Felix Faust app. 3.00
...: The Dark Age TPB (2008, $17.99) r/#1-6; Alex Ross-c 18.00

BLACK AND WHITE (See Large Feature Comic, Series I)

BLACK & WHITE (Also see Codename: Black & White)
Image Comics (Extreme): Oct, 1994 - No. 3, Jan, 1995 ($1.95, limited series)

1-3: Thibert-c/story 2.50

BLACK & WHITE MAGIC
Innovation Publishing: 1991 ($2.95, 98 pgs., B&W w/30 pgs. color, squarebound)

1-Contains rebound comics w/covers removed; contents may vary 3.00

BLACK AXE
Marvel Comics (UK): Apr, 1993 - No. 7, Oct, 1993 ($1.75)

1-4: 1-Romita Jr.-c. 2-Sunfire-c/s 3.00
5-7: 5-Janson-c; Black Panther app. 6,7-Black Panther-c/s 3.00

BLACKBALL COMICS
Blackball Comics: Mar, 1994 ($3.00)

1-Trencher-c/story by Giffen; John Pain by O'Neill 3.00

BLACKBEARD'S GHOST (See Movie Comics)

BLACK BEAUTY (See Son of Black Beauty)
Dell Publishing Co.: No. 440, Dec, 1952

Four Color 440 5 10 15 30 48 65

BLACKBURNE COVENANT, THE
Dark Horse Comics: Apr, 2003 - No. 4, July, 2003 ($2.99, limited series)

1-4-Nicieza-s/Raffaele-a 3.00
TPB (2003, $12.95) r/#1-4 13.00

BLACK CANARY (See All Star Comics #38, Flash Comics #86, Justice League of America #75 & World's Finest #244)
DC Comics: Nov, 1991 - No. 4, Feb, 1992 ($1.75, limited series)

1-4 2.50

BLACK CANARY
DC Comics: Jan, 1993 - No. 12, Dec, 1993 ($1.75)

1-7 2.50

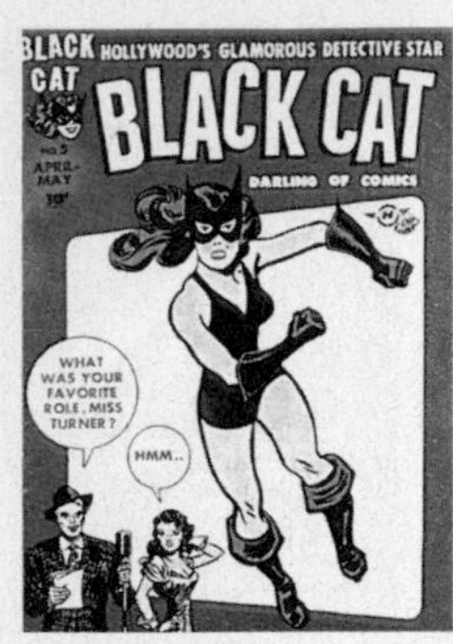

Black Cat Comics #5 © HARV

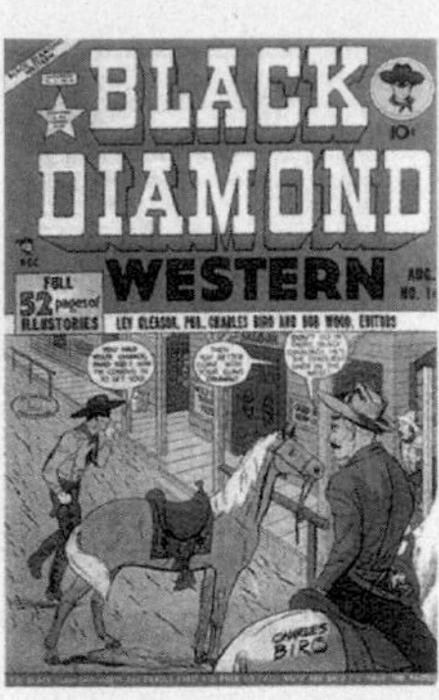

Black Diamond Western #14 © LEV

Blackhawk #30 © QUA

GD VG FN VF VF/NM NM-
2.0 4.0 6.0 8.0 9.0 9.2

GD VG FN VF VF/NM NM-
2.0 4.0 6.0 8.0 9.0 9.2

8-12: 8-The Ray-c/story. 9,10-Huntress-c/story 3.00

BLACK CANARY (Follows Oliver Queen's marriage proposal in Green Arrow #75)
DC Comics: Early Sept, 2007 - No. 4, Late Oct, 2007 ($2.99, bi-weekly limited series)
1-4-Bedard-s/Siqueira-a 3.00
... Wedding Planner 1 (11/07, $2.99) Roux-c/Ferguson & Norrie-a 3.00

BLACK CANARY/ORACLE: BIRDS OF PREY (Also see Showcase '96 #3)
DC Comics: 1996 ($3.95, one-shot)
1-Chuck Dixon scripts & Gary Frank-c/a. 1 2 3 5 7 9

BLACK CAT COMICS (...Western #16-19; ...Mystery #30 on)
(See All-New #7,9, The Original Black Cat, Pocket & Speed Comics)
Harvey Publications (Home Comics): June-July, 1946 - No. 29, June, 1951
1-Kubert-a; Joe Simon c-1,2 73 146 219 460 780 1100
2-Kubert-a 40 80 120 235 380 525
3,4: 4-The Red Demons begin (The Demon #4 & 5)
32 64 96 190 305 420
5,6,7: 5,6-The Scarlet Arrow app. in ea. by Powell; S&K-a in both. 6-Origin Red Demon.
7-Vagabond Prince by S&K plus 1 more story 40 80 120 235 380 525
8-S&K-a; Kerry Drake begins, ends #13 35 70 105 203 327 450
9-Origin Stuntman (r/Stuntman #1) 38 76 114 222 356 490
10-20: 14,15,17-Mary Worth app. plus Invisible Scarlet O'Neil-#15,20,24
26 52 78 152 244 335
21-26 21 42 63 123 197 270
27,28: 27-Used in **SOTI**, pg. 193; X-Mas-c; 2 pg. John Wayne story. 28-Intro.
Kit, Black Cat's new sidekick 23 46 69 133 214 295
29-Black Cat bondage-c; Black Cat stories 22 44 66 127 204 280

BLACK CAT MYSTERY (Formerly Black Cat; ...Western Mystery #54; ...Western #55,56; ...Mystery #57; ...Mystic #58-62; Black Cat #63-65)
Harvey Publications: No. 30, Aug, 1951 - No. 65, Apr, 1963
30-Black Cat on cover and splash page only 31 62 93 181 291 400
31,32,34,37,38,40 25 50 75 147 236 325
33-Used in **POP**, pg. 89; electrocution-c 27 54 81 158 254 350
35-Atomic disaster cover/story 30 60 90 176 283 390
36,39-Used in **SOTI**: #36-Pgs. 270,271; #39-Pgs. 386-388
29 58 87 169 272 375
41-43 24 48 72 143 229 315
44-Eyes, ears, tongue cut out; Nostrand-a 26 52 78 154 247 340
45-Classic "Colorama" by Powell; Nostrand-a 41 82 123 256 428 600
46-49,51-Nostrand-a in all 25 50 75 147 236 325
50-Check-a; classic Warren Kremer-c showing a man's face & hands burning away
93 186 279 586 993 1400
52,53 (r/#34 & 35) 15 30 45 92 144 195
54-Two Black Cat stories (2/55, last pre-code) 18 36 54 107 169 230
55,56-Black Cat app. 15 30 45 92 144 195
57(7/56)-Kirby-c 17 34 51 98 154 210
58-60-Kirby-a(4). 58,59-Kirby-c. 60,61-Simon-c 21 42 63 123 197 270
61-Nostrand-a; "Colorama" r/#45 18 36 54 107 169 230
62 (3/58)-E.C. story swipe 15 30 45 92 144 195
63-65: Giants(10/62,1/63, 4/63); Reprints; Black Cat app. 63-origin Black Kitten.
65-1 pg. Powell-a 19 38 57 112 176 240
NOTE: ***Kremer*** *a-37, 39, 43; c-36, 37, 47.* ***Meskin*** *a-51.* ***Palais*** *a-30, 31(2), 32(2), 33-35, 37-40.* ***Powell*** *a-32-35, 36(2), 40, 41, 43-53, 57.* ***Simon*** *c-63-65.* ***Sparling*** *a-44. Bondage c-32, 34, 43.*

BLACK COBRA (Bride's Diary No. 4 on) (See Captain Flight #8)
Ajax/Farrell Publications(Excellent Publ.): No. 1, 10-11/54; No. 6(No. 2), 12-1/54-55; No. 3, 2-3/55
1-Re-intro Black Cobra & The Cobra Kid (costumed heroes)
35 70 105 203 327 450
6(#2)-Formerly Billy Bunny 19 38 57 109 172 235
3-(Pre-code)-Torpedoman app. 18 36 54 103 162 220

BLACK CONDOR (Also see Crack Comics, Freedom Fighters & Showcase '94 #10,11)
DC Comics: June, 1992 - No. 12, May, 1993 ($1.25)
1-8-Heath-c 2.50
9-12: 9,10,12-Heath-c. 9,10-The Ray app. 12-Batman-c/app. 3.00

BLACK CROSS SPECIAL (See Dark Horse Presents)
Dark Horse Comics: Jan, 1988 ($1.75, B&W, one-shot)(Reprints & new-a)
1-1st printing 3.00
1-(2nd printing) has 2 pgs. new-a 2.50

BLACK CROSS: DIRTY WORK (See Dark Horse Presents)
Dark Horse Comics: Apr, 1997 ($2.95, one-shot)
1-Chris Warner-c/s/a 3.00

BLACK DIAMOND
Americomics: May, 1983 - No. 5, 1984 (no month)($2.00-$1.75, Baxter paper)
1-3-Movie adapt.; 1-Colt back-up begins 4.00
4,5 3.00
NOTE: ***Bill Black*** *a-1i; c-1.* ***Gulacy*** *c-2-5. Sybil Danning photo back-c-1.*

BLACK DIAMOND WESTERN (Formerly Desperado No. 1-8)
Lev Gleason Publ: No. 9, Mar, 1949 - No. 60, Feb, 1956 (No. 9-28: 52 pgs.)
9-Black Diamond & his horse Reliapon begin; origin & 1st app. Black Diamond
21 42 63 123 197 270
10 12 24 36 69 97 125
11-15 10 20 30 54 72 90
16-28(11/49-11/51)-Wolverton's Bingbang Buster 14 28 42 76 108 140
29-40: 31-One pg. Frazetta anti-drug ad 9 18 27 47 61 75
41-50,53-59 8 16 24 40 50 60
51-3-D effect-c/story 15 30 45 85 130 175
52-3-D effect story 14 28 42 81 118 155
60-Last issue 8 16 24 44 57 70
NOTE: ***Biro*** *c-9-35?.* ***Fass*** *a-58, c-54-56, 58.* ***Guardineer*** *a-9, 15, 18.* ***Kida*** *a-9.* ***Maurer*** *a-10.* ***Ed Moore*** *a-16.* ***Morisi*** *a-55.* ***Tuska*** *a-10, 48.*

BLACK DRAGON, THE
Marvel Comics (Epic Comics): 5/85 - No. 6, 10/85 (Baxter paper, mature)
1-6: 1-Chris Claremont story & John Bolton painted-c/a in all 3.00

BLACK DRAGON, THE
Dark Horse Comics: Apr, 1996 ($17.95, B&W, trade paperback)
nn-Reprints Epic Comics limited series; intro by Anne McCaffrey 18.00

BLACK FLAG (See Asylum #5)
Maximum Press: Jan, 1995 - No.4, 1995; No. 0, July, 1995 ($2.50, B&W) (No. 0 in color)
Preview Edition (6/94, $1.95, B&W)-Fraga/McFarlane-c. 3.00
0-4: 0-(7/95)-Liefeld/Fraga-c. 1-(1/95). 3.00
1-Variant cover 5.00
2,4-Variant covers 3.00
NOTE: ***Fraga*** *a-0 1, Preview Edition; c-1-4.* ***Liefeld/Fraga*** *c-0.* ***McFarlane/Fraga*** *c-Preview Edition.*

BLACK FOREST, THE
Image Comics: Mar, 2004; 2005 ($9.95/$6.99, B&W, graphic novels)
nn-Livingston & Tinnell-s/Vokes-a/Oeming-c 10.00
... 2:Castle of Shadows (2005, $6.99) Livingston & Tinnell-s/Vokes-a/c 7.00

BLACK FURY (Becomes Wild West No. 58) (See Blue Bird)
Charlton Comics Group: May, 1955 - No. 57, Mar-Apr, 1966 (Horse stories)
1 10 20 30 58 79 100
2 7 14 21 35 43 50
3-10 5 10 15 24 30 35
11-15,19,20 4 8 10 16 19 22
16-18-Ditko-a 10 20 30 58 79 100
21-30 4 7 9 14 16 18
31-57 3 5 7 10 12 14

BLACK GOLIATH (See Avengers #32-35,41,54 and Civil War #4)
Marvel Comics Group: Feb, 1976 - No. 5, Nov, 1976
1-Tuska-a(p) thru #3 2 4 6 10 14 18
2-5: 2-4-(Regular 25¢ editions). 4-Kirby-c/Buckler-a 2 4 6 8 10 12
2-4-(30¢-c variants, limited distribution)(4,6,8/76) 4 8 12 24 37 50

BLACKHAWK (Formerly Uncle Sam #1-8; see Military & Modern Comics)
Comic Magazines(Quality)No. 9-107(12/56); National Periodical Publications No. 108 (1/57) -250; DC Comics No. 251 on: No. 9, Winter, 1944 - No. 243, 10-11/68; No. 244, 1-2/76 - No. 250, 1-2/77; No. 251, 10/82 - No. 273, 11/84
9 (1944) 341 682 1023 2319 4060 5800
10 (1946) 103 206 309 649 1100 1550
11-15: 14-Ward-a; 13,14-Fear app. 70 140 210 441 746 1050
16-19 60 120 180 378 639 900
20-Classic Crandall bondage-c; Ward Blackhawk 48 96 144 384 717 1050
21-30 (1950) 45 90 135 279 465 650
31-40: 31-Chop Chop by Jack Cole 38 76 114 222 356 490
41-49,51-60: 42-Robot-c 31 62 93 181 291 400
50-1st Killer Shark; origin in text 34 68 102 198 319 440
61,62: 61-Used in **POP**, pg. 91. 62-Used in **POP**, pg. 92 & color illo
27 54 81 160 258 355
63-70,72-80: 65-H-Bomb explosion panel. 66-B&W & color illos **POP**. 67-Hitler-s. 70-Return of Killer Shark; atomic explosion panel. 75-Intro. Blackie the Hawk
26 52 78 152 244 335
71-Origin retold; flying saucer-c; A-Bomb panels 29 58 87 172 276 380

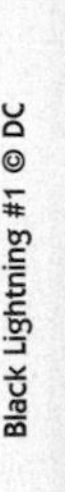
Black Hood #1 © AP

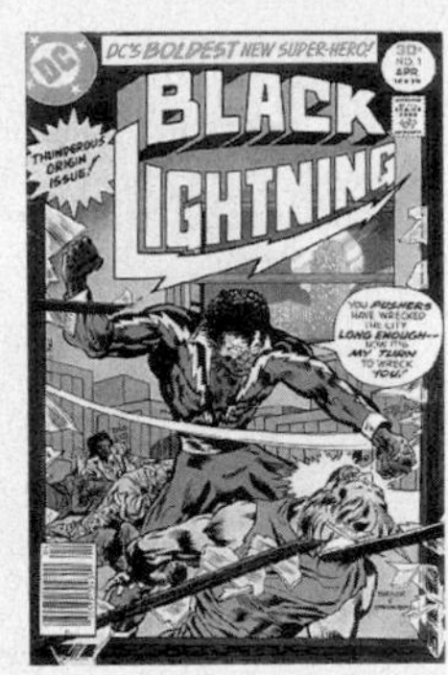

Black Lightning #1 © DC

Black Magic #4 © Headline

GD 2.0 | VG 4.0 | FN 6.0 | VF 8.0 | VF/NM 9.0 | NM- 9.2

81-86: Last precode (3/55) 23 46 69 133 214 295
87-92,94-99,101-107: 91-Robot-c. 105-1st S.A. 19 38 57 109 172 235
93-Origin in text 19 38 57 112 176 240
100 23 46 69 133 214 295
108-1st DC issue (1/57); re-intro. Blackie, the Hawk, their mascot; not in #115
38 76 114 293 547 800
109-117: 117-(10/57)-Mr. Freeze app. 15 30 45 105 190 275
118-(11/57)-Frazetta-r/Jimmy Wakely #4 (3 pgs.) 15 30 45 108 199 290
119-130 (11/58); 120-Robot-c 11 22 33 77 136 195
131-140 (9/59): 133-Intro. Lady Blackhawk 9 10 27 65 113 160
141-150,152-163,165,166: 141-Cat-Man returns-c/s. 143-Kurtzman-r/Jimmy Wakely #4. 150-(7/60)-King Condor returns. 166-Last 10¢ issue
7 14 21 50 83 115
151-Lady Blackhawk receives & loses super powers 8 16 24 54 90 125
164-Origin retold 8 16 24 54 90 125
167-180 6 12 18 37 59 80
181-190 5 10 15 30 48 65
191-196,199: 196-Combat Diary series begins 4 8 12 24 37 50
197,198,200: 197-New look for Blackhawks. 198-Origin retold
4 8 12 26 41 55
201,202,204-210 4 8 12 22 34 45
203-Origin Chop Chop (12/64) 4 8 12 26 41 55
211-227,229-243(1968): 230-Blackhawks become superheroes; JLA cameo
242-Return to old costumes 3 6 9 18 27 35
228-Batman, Green Lantern, Superman, The Flash cameos.
3 6 9 20 30 40
244 ('76) -250: 250-Chuck dies 1 2 3 4 5 7
251-273; 251-Origin retold; Black Knights return. 252-Intro Domino. 253-Part origin Hendrickson. 258-Blackhawk's Island destroyed. 259-Part origin Chop-Chop.
265-273 (75¢ cover price) 3.00

NOTE: ***Chaykin** a-260; c-257-260, 262. **Crandall** a-10, 11, 13, 16?, 18-20, 22-26, 30-33, 35p, 36(2), 37, 38?, 39-44, 46-50, 52-58, 60, 63, 64, 66, 67; c-14-20, 22-63(most except #28-33, 36, 37, 39). **Evans** a-244, 245,246i, 248-250i. **G. Kane** c-263, 264. **Kubert** c-244, 245. **Newton** a-266p. **Severin** a-257.**Spiegle** a-261-267, 269-273; c-265-272. **Toth** a-260p. **Ward** a-16-27(Chop Chop, 8pgs. ea.); pencilled stories-No. 17-63(approx.). **Wildey** a-268. Chop Chop solo stories in #10-95?*

BLACKHAWK
DC Comics: Mar, 1988 - No. 3, May, 1988 ($2.95, limited series, mature)

1-3: Chaykin painted-c/a/scripts 4.00

BLACKHAWK (Also see Action Comics #601)
DC Comics: Mar, 1989 - No. 16, Aug, 1990 ($1.50, mature)

1 3.50
2-6,8-16: 16-Crandall-c swipe 2.50
7-($2.50, 52 pgs.)-Story-r/Military #1 3.00
Annual 1 (1989, $2.95, 68 pgs.)-Recaps origin of Blackhawk, Lady Blackhawk, and others 3.50
Special 1 (1992, $3.50, 68 pgs.)-Mature readers 3.50

BLACKHAWK INDIAN TOMAHAWK WAR, THE
Avon Periodicals: 1951 (Also see Fighting Indians of the Wild West)

nn-Kinstler-c; Kit West story 20 40 60 115 183 250

BLACK HEART ASSASSIN
Iguana Comics: Jan, 1994 ($2.95)

1 3.00

BLACK HOLE (See Walt Disney Showcase #54) (Disney, movie)
Whitman Publishing Co.: Mar, 1980 - No. 4, Sept, 1980

11295(#1) (1979, Golden, $1.50-c, 52 pgs., graphic novel; 8 1/2x11") Photo-c; Spiegle-a. 2 4 6 13 18 22
1-3: 1,2-Movie adaptation. 2,3-Spiegle-a. 3-McWilliams-a; photo-c.
3-New stories 2 4 6 8 10 12
4-Sold only in pre-packs; new story; Spiegle-a 6 12 18 41 66 90

BLACK HOOD, THE (See Blue Ribbon, Flyman & Mighty Comics)
Red Circle Comics (Archie): June, 1983 - No. 3, Oct, 1983 (Mandell paper)

1-Morrow, McWilliams, Wildey-a; Toth-c 6.00
2,3: The Fox by Toth-c/a; Boyette-a. 3-Morrow-a; Toth wraparound-c 4.00
(Also see Archie's Super-Hero Special Digest #2)

BLACK HOOD
DC Comics (Impact Comics): Dec, 1991 - No. 12, Dec, 1992 ($1.00)

1 3.50
2-12: 11-Intro The Fox. 12-Origin Black Hood 2.50
Annual 1 (1992, $2.50, 68 pgs.)-w/Trading card 3.00

BLACK HOOD COMICS (Formerly Hangman #2-8; Laugh Comics #20 on; also see Black Swan, Jackpot, Roly Poly & Top-Notch #9)
MLJ Magazines: No. 9, Wint., 1943-44 - No. 19, Sum., 1946 (on radio in 1943)

9-The Hangman & The Boy Buddies cont'd 110 220 330 693 1172 1650
10-Hangman & Dusty, the Boy Detective app. 62 124 186 391 663 935
11-Dusty app.; no Hangman 48 96 144 298 499 700
12-18: 14-Kinstler blood-c. 17-Hal Foster swipo from Prince Valiant; 1st issue with "An Archie Magazine" on-c 42 84 126 260 438 615
19-I.D. exposed; last issue 52 104 156 322 536 750

NOTE: *Hangman by **Fuje** in 9, 10. **Kinstler** a-15, c-14-16.*

BLACK JACK (Rocky Lane's...; formerly Jim Bowie)
Charlton Comics: No. 20, Nov, 1957 - No. 30, Nov, 1959

20 9 10 27 52 69 85
21,27,29,30 6 12 18 31 38 45
22,23: 22-(68 pgs.). 23-Williamson/Torres-a 8 16 24 42 54 65
24-26,28-Ditko-a 10 20 30 56 76 95

BLACK KNIGHT, THE
Toby Press: May, 1953; 1963

1-Bondage-c 27 54 81 158 254 350
Super Reprint No. 11 (1963)-Reprints 1953 issue 3 6 9 19 25 32

BLACK KNIGHT, THE
Atlas Comics (MgPC): May, 1955 - No. 5, April, 1956

1-Origin Crusader; Maneely-c/a 88 176 264 554 940 1325
2-Maneely-c/a(4) 60 120 180 378 639 900
3-5: 4-Maneely-c/a. 5-Maneely-c, Shores-a 46 92 138 285 478 670

BLACK KNIGHT (See The Avengers #48, Marvel Super Heroes & Tales To Astonish #52)
Marvel Comics: June, 1990 - No. 4, Sept, 1990 ($1.50, limited series)

1-4: 1-Original Black Knight returns. 3,4-Dr. Strange app. 2.50

NOTE: ***Buckler** c-1-4p*

BLACK KNIGHT: EXODUS
Marvel Comics: Dec, 1996 ($2.50, one-shot)

1-Raab-s; Apocalypse-c/app. 2.50

BLACK LAMB, THE
DC Comics (Helix): Nov, 1996 - No, 6, Apr, 1997 ($2.50, limited series)

1-6: Tim Truman-c/a/scripts 2.50

BLACKLIGHT (From ShadowHawk)
Image Comics: June, 2005 - Present ($2.99)

1,2-Toledo & Deering-a/Wherle-s 3.00

BLACK LIGHTNING (See The Brave & The Bold, Cancelled Comic Cavalcade, DC Comics Presents #16, Detective #490 and World's Finest #257)
National Periodical Publ./DC Comics: Apr, 1977 - No. 11, Sept-Oct, 1978

1-Origin Black Lightning 2 4 6 8 10 12
2,3,6-10 6.00
4,5-Superman-c/s. 4-Intro Cyclotronic Man 1 2 3 4 5 7
11-The Ray new solo story 1 2 3 5 7 9

NOTE: ***Buckler** c-1-3p, 6-11p. #11 is 44 pgs.*

BLACK LIGHTNING (2nd Series)
DC Comics: Feb, 1995 - No. 13, Feb, 1996 ($1.95/$2.25)

1-5-Tony Isabella scripts begin, ends #8 3.00
6-13: 6-Begin $2.25-c. 13-Batman-c/app. 3.00

BLACK MAGIC (...Magazine) (Becomes Cool Cat V8#6 on)
Crestwood Publ. V1#1-4,V6#1-V7#5/Headline V1#5-V5#3,V7#6-V8#5: 10-11/50 - V4#1, 6-7/53: V4#2, 9-10/53 - V5#3, 11-12/54; V6#1, 9-10/57 - V7#2, 11-12/58: V7#3, 7-8/60 - V8#5, 11-12/61 (V1#1-5, 52pgs.; V1#6-V3#3, 44pgs.)

V1#1-S&K-a, 10 pgs.; Meskin-a(2) 140 280 420 882 1491 2100
2-S&K-a, 17 pgs.; Meskin-a 62 124 186 391 658 925
3-6(8-9/51)-S&K, Roussos, Meskin-a 53 106 159 331 558 785
V2#1(10-11/51),4,5,7(#13),9(#15),12(#18)-S&K-a 38 76 114 222 356 490
2,3,6,8,10,11(#17) 29 58 87 169 272 375
V3#1(#19, 12/52) - 6(#24, 5/53)-S&K-a 30 60 90 176 283 390
V4#1(#25, 6-7/53), 2(#26, 9-10/53)-S&K-a(3-4) 31 62 93 181 291 400
3(#27, 11-12/53)-S&K-a; Ditko-a (2nd published-a); also see Captain 3-D, Daring Love #1, Strange Fantasy #9, & Fantastic Fears #5 (Fant. Fears was 1st drawn, but not 1st publ.)
48 96 144 298 499 700
4(#28)-Eyes ripped out/story-S&K, Ditko-a 40 80 120 245 403 560
5(#29, 3-4/54)-S&K, Ditko-a 32 64 96 188 302 415
6(#30, 5-6/54)-S&K, Powell?-a 25 50 75 149 240 330
V5#1(#31, 7-8/54 - 3(#33, 11-12/54)-S&K-a 19 38 57 109 172 235
V6#1(#34, 9-10/57), 2(#35, 11-12/57) 12 24 36 67 94 120
3(1-2/58) - 6(7-8/58) 12 24 36 67 94 120

Black Panther #1 © MAR

Black Panther (2005 series) #14 © MAR

Blackstone, The Magician #2 © MAR

GD 2.0 | VG 4.0 | FN 6.0 | VF 8.0 | VF/NM 9.0 | NM- 9.2

V7#1(9-10/58) - 3(7-8/60), 4(9-10/60) 10 20 30 56 76 95
5(11-12/60)-Hitler-c; Torres-a 14 28 42 82 121 160
6(1-2/61)-Powell-a(2) 10 20 30 56 76 95
V8#1(3-4/61)-Powell-c/a 10 20 30 56 76 95
2(5-6/61)-E.C. story swipe/W.F. #22; Ditko, Powell-a
11 22 33 60 83 105
3(7-8/61)-E.C. story swipe/W.F. #22; Powell-a(2) 11 22 33 60 83 105
4(9-10/61)-Powell-a(5) 10 20 30 56 76 95
5-E.C. story swipe/W.S.F. #28; Powell-a(3) 11 22 33 60 83 105

NOTE: ***Bernard Baily*** *a-V4#6?, V5#3(2).* ***Grandenetti*** *a-V2#3, 11.* ***Kirby*** *c-V1#1-6, V2#1-12, V3#1-6, V4#1, 2, 4-6, V5#1-3.* ***McWilliams*** *a-V3#2i.* ***Meskin*** *a-V1#1(2), 2, 3, 4(2), 5(2), 6, V2/1, 2, 3(2), 4(3), 5, 6(2), 7-9, 11, 12i, V3#1(2), 5, 6, V5#1(2), 2.* ***Orlando*** *a-V6#1, 4, V7#2; c-V6/1-6.* ***Powell*** *a-V5#1?.* ***Roussos*** *a-V1#3-5, 6(2), V2#3(2), 4, 5(2), 6, 8, 9, 10(2), 11, 12p, V3#1(2), 2i, 5, V5#2.* ***Simon*** *a-V2#12, V3#2, V7#5? c-V4#3?, V7#3?, 4, 5?, 6?, V8#1-5.* ***Simon & Kirby*** *a-V1#1, 2(2), 3-6, V2#1, 4, 5, 7, 9, 12, V3#1-6, V4#1(3), 2(4), 3(2), 4(2), 5, 6, V5#1-3; c-V2#1.* ***Leonard Starr*** *a-V1#1.* ***Tuska*** *a-V6#3, 4.* ***Woodbridge*** *a-V7#4.*

BLACK MAGIC
National Periodical Publications: Oct-Nov, 1973 - No. 9, Apr-May, 1975
1-S&K reprints 3 6 9 18 23 30
2-8-S&K reprints 2 4 6 9 13 16
9-S&K reprints 2 4 6 10 14 18

BLACKMAIL TERROR (See Harvey Comics Library)

BLACK MASK
DC Comics: 1993 - No. 3, 1994 ($4.95, limited series, 52 pgs.)
1-3 5.00

BLACK OPS
Image Comics (WildStorm): Jan, 1996 - No. 5, May, 1996 ($2.50, lim. series)
1-5 2.50

BLACK ORCHID (See Adventure Comics #428 & Phantom Stranger)
DC Comics: Holiday, 1988-89 - No. 3, 1989 ($3.50, lim. series, prestige format)
Book 1,3: Gaiman scripts & McKean painted-a in all 6.00
Book 2-Arkham Asylum story; Batman app. 1 2 3 5 6 8
TPB (1991, $19.95) r/#1-3; new McKean-c 20.00

BLACK ORCHID
DC Comics: Sept, 1993 - No. 22, June, 1995 ($1.95/$2.25)
1-22: Dave McKean-c all issues 2.50
1-Platinum Edition 12.00
Annual 1 (1993, $3.95, 68 pgs.)-Children's Crusade 4.00

BLACKOUTS (See Broadway Hollywood...)

BLACK PANTHER, THE (Also see Avengers #52, Fantastic Four #52, Jungle Action & Marvel Premiere #51-53)
Marvel Comics Group: Jan, 1977 - No. 15, May, 1979
1-Jack Kirby-s/a thru #12 3 6 9 18 27 35
2-13: 4,5-(Regular 30¢ editions). 8-Origin 2 4 6 8 10 12
4,5-(35¢-c variants, limited dist.)(7,9/77) 6 12 18 39 62 85
14,15-Avengers x-over. 14-Origin 2 4 6 11 16 20
...By Jack Kirby Vol. 1 TPB (2005, $19.99) r/#1-7; unused covers and sketch pages 20.00
...By Jack Kirby Vol. 2 TPB (2006, $19.99) r/#8-12 by Kirby and #13 non-Kirby 20.00
NOTE: ***J. Buscema*** *c-15p.* ***Layton*** *c-13i.*

BLACK PANTHER
Marvel Comics Group: July, 1988 - No. 4, Oct, 1988 ($1.25)
1-4-Gillis-s/Cowan & Delarosa-a 2.50

BLACK PANTHER (Marvel Knights)
Marvel Comics: Nov, 1998 - No. 62, Sept, 2003 ($2.50)
1-Texeira-a/c; Priest-s 6.00
1-($6.95) DF edition w/Quesada & Palmiotti-c 1 2 3 5 6 8
2-4: 2-Two covers by Texeira and Timm. 3-Fantastic Four app. 3.50
5-35,37-40: 5-Evans-a. 6-8-Jusko-a. 8-Avengers-c/app. 15-Hulk app. 22-Moon Knight app. 23-Avengers app. 25-Maximum Security x-over. 26-Storm-c/app. 28-Magneto & Sub-Mariner-c/app. 29-WWII flashback meeting w/Captain America. 35-Defenders-c/app. 37-Luke Cage and Falcon-c/app. 2.50
36-($3.50, 100 pgs.) 35th Anniversary issue incl. r/1st app. in FF #52 3.50
41-56: 41-44-Wolverine app. 47-Thor app. 48,49-Magneto app. 2.50
57-62: 57-Begin $2.99-c. 59-Falcon app. 3.00
...: The Client (6/01, $14.95, TPB) r/#1-5 15.00
... 2099 #1 (11/04, $2.99) Kirkman-s/Hotz-a/Pat Lee-c 3.00

BLACK PANTHER (Marvel Knights)
Marvel Comics: Apr, 2005 - Present ($2.99)
1-Reginald Hudlin-s/John Romita Jr. & Klaus Janson-a; covers by Romita & Ribic 5.00
1-2nd printing; variant-c by Ribic 3.00

GD 2.0 | VG 4.0 | FN 6.0 | VF 8.0 | VF/NM 9.0 | NM- 9.2

2-7,9-15,17-20: 7-House of M; Hairsine-a. 10-14-Luke Cage app. 12,13-Blade app. 17-Linsner-c. 19-Doctor Doom app. 3.00
8-Cho-c; X-Men app. 4.00
8-2nd printing variant-c 3.00
16-($3.99) Wedding of T'Challa and Storm; wraparound Cho-c; Hudlin-s/Eaton-a 4.00
21-Civil War x-over; Namor app. 8.00
21-2nd printing with new cover and Civil War logo 3.00
22-25-Civil War: 23-25-Turner-c 4.00
26-41: 26-30-T'Challa and Storm join the Fantastic Four. 27-30-Marvel Zombies app. 28-30-Suydam-c. 39-41-Secret Invasion 3.00
Annual 1 (4/08, $3.99) Hudlin-s/Stroman & Lashley-a; alternate future; Uatu app. 4.00
...: Bad Mutha TPB (2006, $10.99) r/#10-13 11.00
...: Civil War TPB (2007, $17.99) r/#19-25 18.00
...: Four the Hard Way TPB (2007, $13.99) r/#26-30; page layouts and character designs 14.00
...: Little Green Men TPB (2008, $10.99) r/#31-34 11.00
...: The Bride TPB (2006, $14.99) r/#14-18; interview with the dress designer 15.00
...: Who Is The Black Panther HC (2005, $21.99) r/#1-6; Hudlin afterword; cover gallery 22.00
...: Who Is The Black Panther SC (2006, $14.99) r/#1-6; Hudlin afterword; cover gallery 15.00

BLACK PANTHER: PANTHER'S PREY
Marvel Comics: May, 1991 - No. 4, Oct, 1991 ($4.95, squarebound, lim. series, 52 pgs.)
1-4: McGregor-s/Turner-a 5.00

BLACK PEARL, THE
Dark Horse Comics: Sept, 1996 - No. 5, Jan, 1997 ($2.95, limited series)
1-5: Mark Hamill scripts 3.00

BLACK PHANTOM (See Tim Holt #25, 38)
Magazine Enterprises: Nov, 1954 (one-shot) (Female outlaw)
1 (A-1 #122)-The Ghost Rider story plus 3 Black Phantom stories; Headlight-c/a
36 72 108 212 341 470

BLACK PHANTOM
AC Comics: 1989 - No. 3, 1990 ($2.50, B&W; #2 color)(Reprints & new-a)
1-3: 1-Ayers-r, Bolle-r/B.P. #1-3-Redmask-r 2.75

BLACK PHANTOM, RETURN OF THE (See Wisco)

BLACK RIDER (Western Winners #1-7; Western Tales of Black Rider #28-31; Gunsmoke Western #32 on)(See All Western Winners, Best Western, Kid Colt, Outlaw Kid, Rex Hart, Two-Gun Kid, Two-Gun Western, Western Gunfighters, Western Winners, & Wild Western)
Marvel/Atlas Comics(CDS No. 8-17/CPS No. 19 on): No. 8, 3/50 - No. 18, 1/52; No. 19, 11/53 - No. 27, 3/55
8 (#1)-Black Rider & his horse Satan begin; 36 pgs; Stan Lee photo-c as Black Rider) 42 84 126 260 435 610
9-52 pgs. begin, end #14 23 46 69 133 214 295
10-Origin Black Rider 27 54 81 158 254 350
11-14: 14-Last 52pgs. 17 34 51 98 154 210
15-19: 19-Two-Gun Kid app. 15 30 45 85 130 175
20-Classic-c; Two-Gun Kid app. 16 32 48 92 144 195
21-27: 21-23-Two-Gun Kid app. 24,25-Arrowhead app. 26-Kid Colt app. 27-Last issue; last precode. Kid Colt app. The Spider (a villain) burns to death
14 28 42 81 118 155
NOTE: ***Ayers*** *c-22.* ***Jack Keller*** *a-15, 26, 27.* ***Maneely*** *a-14; c-16, 17, 25, 27.* ***Syd Shores*** *a-19, 21, 22, 23(3), 24(3), 25-27; c-19, 21, 23.* ***Sinnott*** *a-24, 25.* ***Tuska*** *a-12, 19-21.*

BLACK RIDER RIDES AGAIN!, THE
Atlas Comics (CPS): Sept, 1957
1-Kirby-a(3); Powell-a; Severin-c 25 50 75 145 233 320

BLACK SEPTEMBER (Also see Avengers/Ultraforce, Ultraforce (1st series) #10 & Ultraforce/Avengers)
Malibu Comics (Ultraverse): 1995 ($1.50, one-shot)
Infinity-Intro to the new Ultraverse; variant-c exists. 2.50

BLACKSTONE (See Super Magician Comics & Wisco Giveaways)

BLACKSTONE, MASTER MAGICIAN COMICS
Vital Publ./Street & Smith Publ.: Mar-Apr, 1946 - No. 3, July-Aug, 1946
1 32 64 96 186 298 410
2,3 19 38 57 112 176 240

BLACKSTONE, THE MAGICIAN (...Detective on cover only #3 & 4)
Marvel Comics (CnPC): No. 2, May, 1948 - No. 4, Sept, 1948 (No #1) (Cont'd from E.C. #1?)
2-The Blonde Phantom begins, ends #4 65 130 195 410 693 975
3,4: 3-Blonde Phantom by Sekowsky 40 80 120 244 397 550

BLACKSTONE, THE MAGICIAN DETECTIVE FIGHTS CRIME
E. C. Comics: Fall, 1947

Blackwulf #3 © MAR

Blade V2 #3 © MAR

Blade of the Immortal #107 © Hiroaki Samura

	GD	VG	FN	VF	VF/NM	NM-
	2.0	4.0	6.0	8.0	9.0	9.2
1-1st app. Happy Houlihans	50	100	150	310	518	725

BLACK SUN (X-Men Black Sun on cover)
Marvel Comics: Nov, 2000 - No. 5, Nov, 2000 ($2.99, weekly limited series)

1-(...: X-Men), 2-(...: Storm), 3-(...: Banshee and Sunfire), 4-(...: Colossus and Nightcrawler), 5-(...: Wolverine and Thunderbird); Claremont-s in all; Evans interlocking painted covers; Magik returns 3.00

BLACK SUN
DC Comics (WildStorm): Nov, 2002 - No. 6, Jun, 2003 ($2.95, limited series)

1-6-Andreyko-s/Scott-a 3.00

BLACK SWAN COMICS
MLJ Magazines (Pershing Square Publ. Co.): 1945

	GD	VG	FN	VF	VF/NM	NM-
1-The Black Hood reprints from Black Hood No. 14; Bill Woggon-a; Suzie app.	21	42	63	123	197	270

BLACK TARANTULA (See Feature Presentations No. 5)

BLACK TERROR (See America's Best Comics & Exciting Comics)
Better Publications/Standard: Winter, 1942-43 - No. 27, June, 1949

	GD	VG	FN	VF	VF/NM	NM-
1-Black Terror, Crime Crusader begin	300	600	900	2010	3505	5000
2	118	236	354	743	1259	1775
3	82	164	246	517	871	1225
4,5	68	136	204	428	724	1020
6-10: 7-The Ghost app.	58	116	174	365	618	870
11-20: 20-The Scarab app.	50	100	150	310	518	725
21-Miss Masque app.	53	106	159	330	553	775
22-Part Frazetta-a on one Black Terror story	50	100	150	310	518	725
23,25-27	45	90	135	279	465	650
24 Frazetta-a (1/4 pg.)	46	92	138	285	473	660

NOTE: ***Schomburg (Xela)** c-2-27; bondage c-2, 17, 24. **Meskin** a-27. **Moreira** a-27. **Robinson/Meskin** a-23, 24(3), 25, 26. **Roussos/Mayo** a-24. **Tuska** a-26, 27.*

BLACK TERROR, THE (Also see Total Eclipse)
Eclipse Comics: Oct, 1989 - No. 3, June, 1990 ($4.95, 52 pgs., squarebound, limited series)

1-3: Beau Smith & Chuck Dixon scripts; Dan Brereton painted-c/a 5.00

BLACKTHORNE 3-D SERIES
Blackthorne Publishing Co.: May, 1985 - No. 80, 1989 ($2.25/$2.50)

	GD	VG	FN	VF	VF/NM	NM-
1-Sheena in 3-D #1. D. Stevens-c/retouched-a	1	2	3	5	6	8
2-10: 2-MerlinRealm in 3-D #1. 3-3-D Heroes #1. Goldyn in 3-D #1. 5-Bizarre 3-D Zone #1. 6-Salimba in 3-D #1. 7-Twisted Tales in 3-D #1. 8-Dick Tracy in 3-D #1. 9-Salimba in 3-D #2. 10-Gumby in 3-D #1						6.00
11-19: 11-Betty Boop in 3-D #1. 12-Hamster Vice in 3-D #1. 13-Little Nemo in 3-D #1. 14-Gumby in 3-D #2. 15-Hamster Vice #6 in 3-D. 16-Laffin' Gas #6 in 3-D. 17-Gumby in 3-D #3. 18-Bullwinkle and Rocky in 3-D #1. 19-The Flintstones in 3-D #1						6.00
20(#1),26(#2),35(#3),39(#4),52(#5),62,71(#6)-G.I. Joe in 3-D. 62-G.I. Joe Annual	2	4	6	8	11	14
21-24,27-28: 21-Gumby in 3-D #4. 22-The Flintstones in 3-D #2. 23-Laurel & Hardy in 3-D #1. 24-Bozo the Clown in 3-D #1. 27-Bravestarr in 3-D #1. 28- Gumby in 3-D #5						6.00
25,29,37-The Transformers in 3-D	2	4	6	10	14	18
30-Star Wars in 3-D #1	3	6	9	14	19	24
31-34,36,38,40: 31-The California Raisins in 3-D #1. 32-Richie Rich & Casper in 3-D #1. 33-Gumby in 3-D #6. 34-Laurel & Hardy in 3-D #2. 36-The Flintstones in 3-D #3. 38-Gumby in 3-D #7. 40-Bravestarr in 3-D #2						6.00
41-46,49,50: 41-Battletech in 3-D #1. 42-The Flintstones in 3-D #4. 43-Underdog in 3-D #1 44-The California Raisins in 3-D #2. 45-Red Heat in 3-D #1 (movie adapt.). 46-The California Raisins in 3-D #3. 49-Rambo in 3-D #1. 49-Sad Sack in 3-D #1. 50-Bullwinkle For President in 3-D #1						6.00
47,48-Star Wars in 3-D #2,3	2	4	6	9	13	16
51,53-60: 51-Kull in 3-D #1. 53-Red Sonja in 3-D #1. 54-Bozo in 3-D #2. 55-Waxwork in 3-D #1 (movie adapt.). 57-Casper in 3-D #1. 58-Baby Huey in 3-D #1. 59-Little Dot in 3-D #1. 60-Solomon Kane in 3-D #1						6.00
61,63-70,72-80: 61-Werewolf in 3-D #1. 63-The California Raisins in 3-D #4. 64-To Die For in 3-D #1. 65-Capt. Holo in 3-D #1. 66-Playful Little Audrey in 3-D #1. 67-Kull in 3-D #2. 69-The California Raisins in 3-D #5. 70-Wendy in 3-D #1. 72-Sports Hall of Shame #1. 74-The Noid in 3-D #1. 75-Moonwalker in 3-D #1 (Michael Jackson movie adapt.). 76-79. 80-The Noid in 3-D #2	1	2	3	4	5	7

BLACK WIDOW (Marvel Knights) (Also see Marvel Graphic Novel)
Marvel Comics: May, 1999 - No. 3, Aug, 1999 ($2.99, limited series)

1-(June on-c) Devin Grayson-s/J.G. Jones-c/a; Daredevil app. 5.00
1-Variant-c by J.G. Jones 6.00
2,3 4.00
...Web of Intrigue (6/99, $3.50) r/origin & early appearances 3.50
TPB (7/01, $15.95) r/Vol. 1 & 2; Jones-c 16.00

GD VG FN VF VF/NM NM-
2.0 4.0 6.0 8.0 9.0 9.2

BLACK WIDOW (Marvel Knights) (Volume 2)
Marvel Comics: Jan, 2001 - No. 3, May, 2001 ($2.99, limited series)

1-3-Grayson & Rucka-s/Scott Hampton-c/a; Daredevil app. 3.00

BLACK WIDOW (Marvel Knights)
Marvel Comics: Nov, 2004 - No. 6, Apr, 2005 ($2.99, limited series)

1-6-Sienkiewicz-a/Land-c 3.00

BLACK WIDOW: PALE LITTLE SPIDER (Marvel Knights) (Volume 3)
Marvel Comics: Jun, 2002 - No. 3, Aug, 2002 ($2.99, limited series)

1-3-Rucka-s/Kordey-a/Horn-c 3.00

BLACK WIDOW 2 (THE THINGS THEY SAY ABOUT HER) (Marvel Knights)
Marvel Comics: Nov, 2005 - No. 6, Apr, 2006 ($2.99, limited series)

1-6-Phillips & Sienkiewicz-a/Morgan-s; Daredevil app. 3.00
TPB (2006, $15.99) r/#1-6 16.00

BLACKWULF
Marvel Comics: June, 1994 - No. 10, Mar, 1995 ($1.50)

1-($2.50)-Embossed-c; Angel Medina-a 3.00
2-10 2.50

BLADE (The Vampire Hunter)
Marvel Comics

1-(3/98, $3.50) Colan-a(p)/Christopher Golden-s 3.50
... Black & White TPB (2004, $15.99, B&W) reprints from magazines Vampire Tales #8,9; Marvel Preview #3,6; Crescent City Blues #1 and Marvel Shadow and Light #1 16.00
San Diego Con Promo (6/97) Wesley Snipes photo-c 3.00
...Sins of the Father (10/98, $5.99) Sears-a; movie adaption 6.00
Blade 2: Movie Adaptation (5/02, $5.95) Ponticelli-a/Bradstreet-c 6.00

BLADE (The Vampire Hunter)
Marvel Comics: Nov, 1998 - No. 3, Jan, 1999 ($3.50/$2.99)

1-($3.50) Contains Movie insider pages; McKean-a 3.50
2,3-($2.99): 2-Two covers 3.00

BLADE (Volume 2)
Marvel Comics (MAX): May, 2002 -No. 6, Oct, 2002 ($2.99)

1-6-Bradstreet-c/Hinz-s. 1-5-Pugh-a. 6-Homs-a 3.00

BLADE
Marvel Comics: Nov, 2006 - No. 12, Oct, 2007 ($2.99)

1-12: 1-Chaykin-a/Guggenheim-s; origin retold; Spider-Man app. 2-Dr. Doom-c/app. 5-Civil War tie-in; Wolverine app. 6-Blade loses a hand. 10-Spider-Man app. 3.00
...: Sins of the Father TPB (2007, $14.99) r/#7-12; afterword by Guggenheim 15.00
...: Undead Again TPB (2007, $14.99) r/#1-6; letters pages from #1&2 15.00

BLADE OF THE IMMORTAL (Manga)
Dark Horse Comics: June, 1996 - No. 131, Nov, 2007 ($2.95/$2.99/$3.95, B&W)

	GD	VG	FN	VF	VF/NM	NM-
1-Hiroaki Samura-s/a in all	1	3	4	6	8	10
2-5: 2-#1 on cover in error						6.00
6-10						5.00
11,19,20,34-($3.95, 48 pgs.): 34-Food one-shot						4.00
12-18,21-33,35-41,43-105,107-131: 12-20-Dreamsong. 21-28-On Silent Wings. 29-33-Dark Shadow. 35-42-Heart of Darkness. 43-57-The Gathering						3.00
42-($3.50) Ends Heart of Darkness						3.50
106-($3.99)						4.00

BLADE RUNNER (Movie)
Marvel Comics Group: Oct, 1982 - No. 2, Nov, 1982

1,2-r/Marvel Super Special #22; 1-Williamson-c/a. 2-Williamson-a 3.50

BLADE: THE VAMPIRE-HUNTER
Marvel Comics: July, 1994 - No. 10, Apr, 1995 ($1.95)

1-($2.95)-Foil-c; Dracula returns; Wheatley-c/a 3.50
2-10: 2,3,10-Dracula-c/app. 8-Morbius app. 2.50

BLADE: VAMPIRE-HUNTER
Marvel Comics: Dec, 1999 - No. 6, May, 2000 ($3.50/$2.50)

1-($3.50)-Bart Sears-s; Sears and Smith-a 3.50
2-6-($2.50): 2-Regular & Wesley Snipes photo-c 2.50

BLAIR WITCH CHRONICLES, THE
Oni Press: Mar, 2000 - No. 4, July, 2000 ($2.95, B&W, limited series)

1-4-Van Meter-s.1-Guy Davis-a. 2-Mireault-a 3.00
1-DF Alternate-c by John Estes 7.00
TPB (9/00, $15.95) r/#1-4 & Blair Witch Project one-shot 16.00

BLAIR WITCH: DARK TESTAMENTS

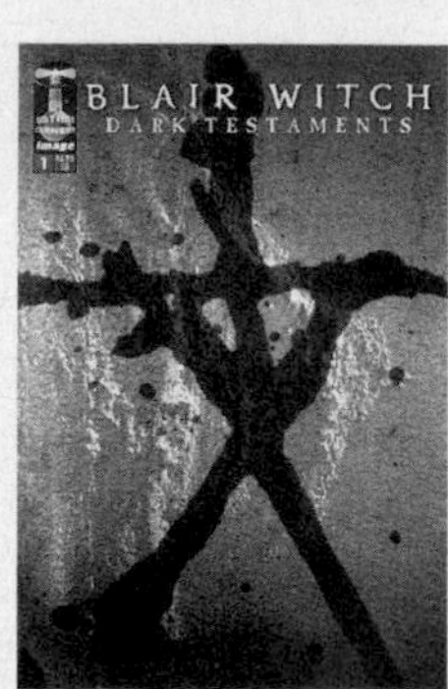

Blair Witch: Dark Testaments #1 © Oni

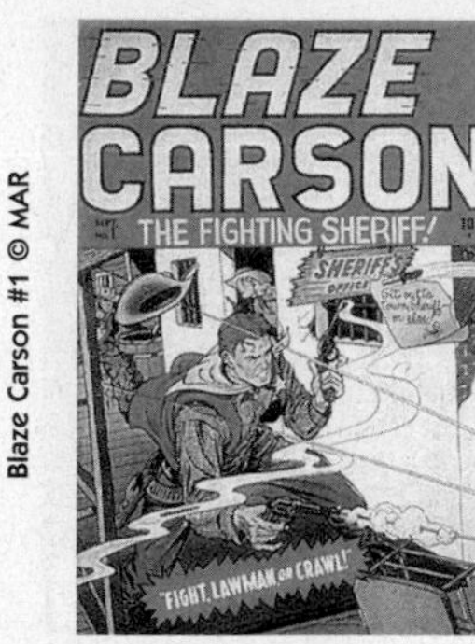

Blaze Carson #1 © MAR

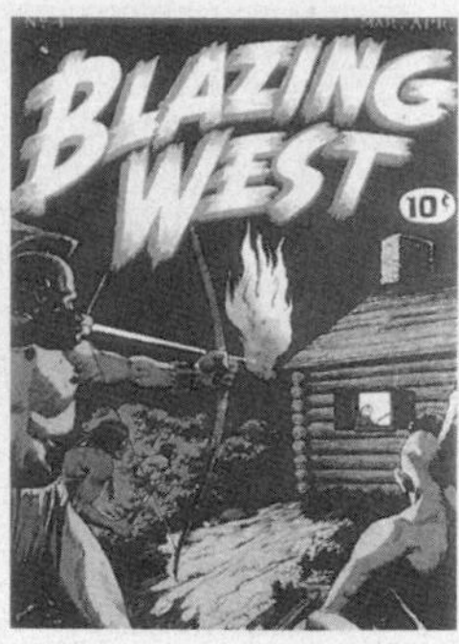

Blazing West #4 © ACG

	GD 2.0	VG 4.0	FN 6.0	VF 8.0	VF/NM 9.0	NM- 9.2

Image Comics: Oct, 2000 ($2.95, one-shot)
1-Edington-s/Adlard-a; story of murderer Rustin Parr 3.00

BLAIR WITCH PROJECT, THE (Movie companion, not adaptation)
Oni Press: July, 1999 ($2.95, B&W, one-shot)
1-(1st printing) History of the Blair Witch, art by Edwards, Mireault, and Davis; Van Meter-s; only the stick figure is red on the cover 12.00
1-(2nd printing) Stick figure and title lettering are red on cover 4.00
1-(3rd printing) Stick figure, title, and creator credits are red on cover 3.00
DF Glow in the Dark variant-c ($10.00) 10.00

BLAST (Satire Magazine)
G & D Publications: Feb, 1971 - No. 2, May, 1971
1-Wrightson & Kaluta-a/Everette-c 7 14 21 47 76 105
2-Kaluta-c/a 5 10 15 35 55 75

BLAST CORPS
Dark Horse Comics: Oct, 1998 ($2.50, one-shot, based on Nintendo game)
1-Reprints from Nintendo Power magazine; Mahn-a 2.50

BLASTERS SPECIAL
DC Comics: 1989 ($2.00, one-shot)
1-Peter David scripts; Invasion spin-off 2.50

BLAST-OFF (Three Rocketeers)
Harvey Publications (Fun Day Funnies): Oct, 1965 (12¢)
1-Kirby/Williamson-a(2); Williamson/Crandall-a; Williamson/Torres/Krenkel-a; Kirby/Simon-c 6 12 18 41 66 90

BLAZE
Marvel Comics: Aug, 1994 - No. 12, July, 1995 ($1.95)
1-($2.95)-Foil embossed-c 3.50
2-12: 2-Man-Thing-c/story. 11,12-Punisher app. 2.50

BLAZE CARSON (Rex Hart #6 on)(See Kid Colt, Tex Taylor, Wild Western, Wisco)
Marvel Comics (USA): Sept, 1948 - No. 5, June, 1949
1: 1,2-Shores-c 27 54 81 156 251 345
2,4,5: 4-Two-Gun Kid app. 5-Tex Taylor app. 18 36 54 105 165 225
3-Used by N.Y. State Legis. Comm. (injury to eye splash); Tex Morgan app. 19 38 57 112 176 240

BLAZE: LEGACY OF BLOOD (See Ghost Rider & Ghost Rider/Blaze)
Marvel Comics (Midnight Sons imprint): Dec, 1993 - No. 4, Mar, 1994 ($1.75, limited series)
1-4 2.50

BLAZE OF GLORY
Marvel Comics: Feb, 2000 - No. 4, Mar, 2000 ($2.99, limited series)
1-4-Ostrander-s/Manco-a; Two-Gun Kid, Rawhide Kid, Red Wolf and Ghost Rider app. 3.00
TPB (7/02, $9.99) r/#1-4 10.00

BLAZE THE WONDER COLLIE (Formerly Molly Manton's Romances #1?)
Marvel Comics(SePI): No. 2, Oct, 1949 - No. 3, Feb, 1950 (Both have photo-c)
2(#1), 3-(Scarce) 23 46 69 133 214 295

BLAZING BATTLE TALES
Seaboard Periodicals (Atlas): July, 1975
1-Intro. Sgt. Hawk & the Sky Demon; Severin, McWilliams, Sparling-a; Nazi-c by Thorne 2 4 6 8 11 14

BLAZING COMBAT (Magazine)
Warren Publishing Co.: Oct, 1965 - No. 4, July, 1966 (35¢, B&W)
1-Frazetta painted-c on all 25 50 75 185 343 500
2 8 16 24 52 86 120
3,4: 4-Frazetta half pg. ad 7 14 21 47 76 105
nn-Anthology (reprints from No. 1-4) (low print) 7 14 21 50 83 115
NOTE: ***Adkins** a-4. **Colan** a-3,4,nn. **Crandall** a-all. **Evans** a-1,4. **Heath** a-4,nn. **Morrow** a-1-3,nn. **Orlando** a-1-3,nn. **J. Severin** a-all. **Torres** a-1-4. **Toth** a-all. **Williamson** a-2. and **Wood** a-3,4,nn.*

BLAZING COMBAT: WORLD WAR I AND WORLD WAR II
Apple Press: Mar, 1994 ($3.75, B&W)
1,2: 1-r/Colan, Toth, Goodwin, Severin, Wood-a. 2-r/Crandall, Evans, Severin, Torres, Williamson-a 4.00

BLAZING COMICS (Also see Blue Circle Comics and Red Circle Comics)
Enwil Associates/Rural Home: 6/44 - #3, 9/44; #4, 2/45; #5, 3/45; #5(V2#2), 3/55 - #6(V2#3), 1955?
1-The Green Turtle, Red Hawk, Black Buccaneer begin; origin Jun-Gal 51 102 153 316 526 735
2-5: 3-Briefer-a. 5-(V2#2 inside) 34 68 102 198 319 440
5(3/55, V2#2-inside)-Black Buccaneer-c, 6(V2#3-inside, 1955)-Indian/Japanese-c; cover is from Apr. 1945 18 36 54 105 165 225
NOTE: *No. 5 & 6 contain remaindered comics rebound and the contents can vary. Cloak & Daggar, Will Rogers, Superman 64, Star Spangled 130, Kaanga known. Value would be half of contents.*

BLAZING SIXGUNS
Avon Periodicals: Dec, 1952
1-Kinstler-c/a; Larsen/Alascia-a(2), Tuska?-a; Jesse James, Kit Carson, Wild Bill Hickok app. 17 34 51 100 158 215

BLAZING SIXGUNS
I.W./Super Comics: 1964
I.W. Reprint #1,8,9: 1-r/Wild Bill Hickok #26, Western True Crime #? & Blazing Sixguns #1 by Avon; Kinstler-c. 8-r/Blazing Western #?; Kinstler-c. 9-r/Blazing Western #1; Ditko-r; Kintsler-c reprinted from Dalton Boys #1 2 4 6 10 14 18
Super Reprint #10,11,15-17: 10,11-r/The Rider #2,1. 15-r/Silver Kid Western #?. 16-r/Buffalo Bill #?; Wildey-r; Severin-c. 17(1964)-r/Western True Crime #? 2 4 6 10 14 18
12-Reprints Bullseye #3; S&K-a 4 8 12 19 29 38
18-r/Straight Arrow #? by Powell; Severin-c 2 4 6 10 14 18

BLAZING SIX-GUNS (Also see Sundance Kid)
Skywald Comics: Feb, 1971 - No. 2, Apr, 1971 (52 pgs.)
1-The Red Mask (3-D effect, not true 3-D), Sundance Kid begin (new-s), Avon's Geronimo reprint by Kinstler; Wyatt Earp app. 3 6 9 14 20 25
2-Wild Bill Hickok, Jesse James, Kit Carson-r plus M.E. Red Mask-r (3-D effect) 2 4 6 10 14 18

BLAZING WEST (The Hooded Horseman #21 on)
American Comics Group (B&I Publ./Michel Publ.): Fall, 1948 - No. 20, Nov-Dec, 1951
1-Origin & 1st app. Injun Jones, Tenderfoot & Buffalo Belle; Texas Tim & Ranger begins, ends #13 20 40 60 115 183 250
2,3 (1-2/49) 11 22 33 62 86 110
4-Origin & 1st app. Little Lobo; Starr-a (3-4/49) 10 20 30 56 76 95
5-10: 5-Starr-a 9 18 27 50 65 80
11-13 8 16 24 42 54 65
14(11-12/50)-Origin/1st app. The Hooded Horseman 13 26 39 74 105 135
15-20: 15,16,18,19-Starr-a 9 18 27 50 65 80

BLAZING WESTERN
Timor Publications: Jan, 1954 - No. 5, Sept, 1954
1-Ditko-a (1st Western-a?); text story by Bruce Hamilton 16 32 48 94 147 200
2-4 9 18 27 50 65 80
5-Disbrow-a 9 18 27 52 69 85

BLINDSIDE
Image Comics (Extreme Studios): Aug, 1996 ($2.50)
1-Variant-c exists 2.50

BLINK (See X-Men Age of Apocalypse storyline)
Marvel Comics: March, 2001 - No. 4, June, 2001 ($2.99, limited series)
1-4-Adam Kubert-c/Lobdell-s/Winick-script; leads into Exiles #1 3.00

BLIP
Marvel Comics Group: 2/1983 - 1983 (Video game mag. in comic format)
1-1st app. Donkey Kong & Mario Bros. in comics, 6pgs. comics; photo-c 1 2 3 5 6 8
2-Spider-Man photo-c; 6pgs. Spider-Man comics w/Green Goblin 1 3 4 6 8 10
3,4,6 5.00
5-E.T., Indiana Jones; Rocky-c 6.00
7-6pgs. Hulk comics; Pac-Man & Donkey Kong Jr. Hints 1 2 3 4 5 7

BLISS ALLEY
Image Comics: July, 1997 - No. 2, Sept, 1997 ($2.95, B&W)
1,2-Messner-Loebs-s/a 3.00

BLITZKRIEG
National Periodical Publications: Jan-Feb, 1976 - No. 5, Sept-Oct, 1976
1-Kubert-c on all 4 8 12 22 34 45
2-5 3 6 9 14 20 25

BLONDE PHANTOM (Formerly All-Select #1-11; Lovers #23 on)(Also see Blackstone, Marvel Mystery, Millie The Model #2, Sub-Mariner Comics #25 & Sun Girl)
Marvel Comics (MPC): No. 12, Winter, 1946-47 - No. 22, Mar, 1949
12-Miss America begins, ends #14 170 340 510 1071 1811 2550
13-Sub-Mariner begins (not in #16) 100 200 300 630 1065 1500

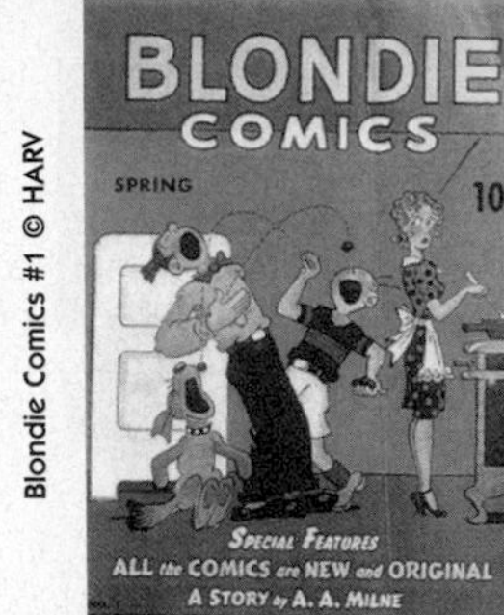

Blondie Comics #1 © HARV

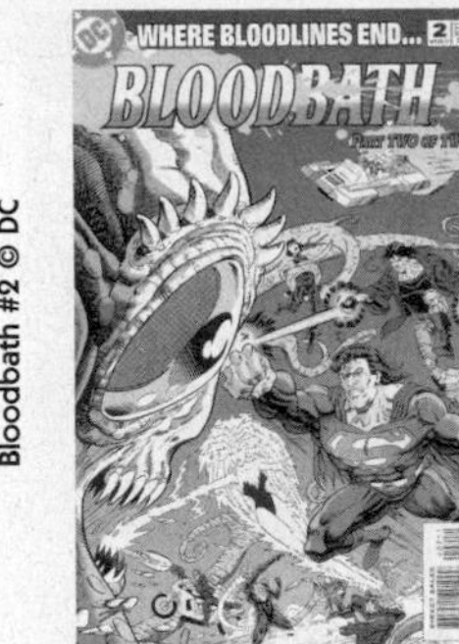

Bloodbath #2 © DC

Bloodstone #1 © MAR

	GD 2.0	VG 4.0	FN 6.0	VF 8.0	VF/NM 9.0	NM- 9.2
14,15: 15-Kurtzman's "Hey Look"	93	186	279	586	993	1400
16-Captain America with Bucky story by Rico(p), 6 pgs.; Kurtzman's "Hey Look" (1 pg.)	125	250	375	788	1332	1875
17-22: 22-Anti Wertham editorial	78	156	234	491	833	1175

NOTE: ***Shores** c-12-18.*

BLONDIE (See Ace Comics, Comics Reading Libraries (Promotional Comics section), Dagwood, Daisy & Her Pups, Eat Right to Work..., King & Magic Comics)
David McKay Publications: 1942 - 1946

	GD	VG	FN	VF	VF/NM	NM-
Feature Books 12 (Rare)	82	164	246	517	871	1225
Feature Books 27-29,31,34(1940)	21	42	63	123	197	270
Feature Books 36,38,40,42,43,45,47	20	40	60	115	183	250
...1944 (Hard-c, 1938, B&W, 128 pgs.)-1944 daily strip-r	16	32	48	94	147	200

BLONDIE & DAGWOOD FAMILY
Harvey Publ. (King Features Synd.): Oct, 1963 - No. 4, Dec, 1965 (68 pgs.)

	GD	VG	FN	VF	VF/NM	NM-
1	5	10	15	32	51	70
2-4	3	6	9	20	30	40

BLONDIE COMICS (...Monthly No. 16-141)
David McKay #1-15/Harvey #16-163/King #164-175/Charlton #177 on:
Spring, 1947 - No. 163, Nov, 1965; No. 164, Aug, 1966 - No. 175, Dec, 1967; No. 177, Feb, 1969 - No. 222, Nov, 1976

	GD	VG	FN	VF	VF/NM	NM-
1	33	66	99	192	309	425
2	17	34	51	98	154	210
3-5	14	28	42	82	121	160
6-10	13	26	39	72	101	130
11-15	9	18	27	52	69	85
16-(3/50; 1st Harvey issue)	11	22	33	60	83	105
17-20: 20-(3/51)-Becomes Daisy & Her Pups #21 & Chamber of Chills #21	6	12	18	37	59	80
21-30	5	10	15	32	51	70
31-50	4	8	12	24	37	50
51-80	4	8	12	22	34	45
81-99	3	6	9	20	30	40
100	4	8	12	24	37	50
101-124,126-130	3	6	9	16	23	30
125 (80 pgs.)	4	8	12	26	41	55
131-136,138,139	3	6	9	16	22	28
137,140-(80 pgs.)	4	8	12	25	39	52
141-147,149-154,156,160,164-167	3	6	9	16	22	28
148,155,157-159,161-163 are 68 pgs.	3	6	9	21	32	42
168-175	2	4	6	11	16	20
177-199 (no #176)	2	4	6	9	13	16
200	2	4	6	10	14	18
201-210,213-222	2	4	6	8	10	12
211,212-1st & 2nd app. Super Dagwood	2	4	6	9	13	16
Blondie, Dagwood & Daisy by Chic Young #1(Harvey, 1953, 100 pg. squarebound giant) new stories; Popeye (1 pg.) and Felix (1pg.) app.	29	58	87	169	272	375

BLOOD
Marvel Comics (Epic Comics): Feb, 1988 - No. 4, Apr, 1988 ($3.25, mature)

1-4: DeMatteis scripts & Kent Williams-c/a — 3.50

BLOOD AND GLORY (Punisher & Captain America)
Marvel Comics: Oct, 1992 - No. 3, Dec, 1992 ($5.95, limited series)

1-3: 1-Embossed wraparound-c by Janson; Chichester & Clarke-s — 6.00

BLOOD & ROSES: FUTURE PAST TENSE (Bob Hickey's...)
Sky Comics: Dec, 1993 ($2.25)

1-Silver ink logo — 2.50

BLOOD & ROSES: SEARCH FOR THE TIME-STONE (Bob Hickey's...)
Sky Comics: Apr, 1994 ($2.50)

1 — 2.50

BLOOD AND SHADOWS
DC Comics (Vertigo): 1996 - Book 4, 1996 ($5.95, squarebound, mature)

Books 1-4: Joe R. Lansdale scripts; Mark A. Nelson-c/a. — 6.00

BLOOD AND WATER
DC Comics (Vertigo): May, 2003 - No. 5, Sept, 2003 ($2.95, limited series)

1-5-Judd Winick-s/Tomm Coker-a/Brian Bolland-c — 3.00

BLOOD: A TALE
DC Comics (Vertigo): Nov, 1996 - No. 4, Feb, 1997 ($2.95, limited series)

1-4: Reprints Epic series w/new-c; DeMatteis scripts; Kent Williams-c/a — 3.00

TPB (2004, $19.95) r/#1-4 — 20.00

BLOODBATH
DC Comics: Early Dec, 1993 - No. 2, Late Dec, 1993 ($3.50, 68 pgs.)

	GD	VG	FN	VF	VF/NM	NM-
1-Neon ink-c; Superman app.; new Batman-c /app.						3.50
2-Hitman 2nd app.	1	2	3	4	5	7

BLOODHOUND
DC Comics: Sept, 2004 - No. 10, June, 2005 ($2.95)

1-10: 1-Jolley-s/Kirk-a/Johnson-c. 5-Firestorm app. (cont. from Firestorm #7) — 3.00

BLOOD LEGACY
Image Comics (Top Cow): May, 2000 - No. 4, Nov, 2000, Apr, 2003 ($2.50/$4.99)

...: The Story of Ryan 1-4-Kerri Hawkins-s. 1-Andy Park-a(p); 3 covers — 2.50
...: The Young Ones 1 (4/03, $4.99, one-shot) Basaldua-c/a — 5.00
Preview Special ('00, $4.95) B&W flip-book w/The Magdalena Preview — 5.00

BLOODLINES: A TALE FROM THE HEART OF AFRICA (See Tales From the Heart of Africa)
Marvel Comics (Epic Comics): 1992 ($5.95, 52 pgs.)

1-Story cont'd from Tales From... — 6.00

BLOOD OF DRACULA
Apple Comics: Nov, 1987 - No. 20?, 1990 ($1.75/$1.95, B&W)($2.25 #14,16 on)

	GD	VG	FN	VF	VF/NM	NM-
1-3,5-14,20: 1-10-Chadwick-c						4.00
4,16-19-Lost Frankenstein pgs. by Wrightson	1	2	3	4	5	7
15-Contains stereo flexidisc ($3.75)						5.00

BLOOD OF THE DEMON (Etrigan the Demon)
DC Comics: May, 2005 - No. 17, Sept, 2006 ($2.50/$2.99)

1-14-Byrne-a(p) & plot/Pfeifer-script. 3,4-Batman app. 13-One Year Later — 2.50
15-17-($2.99) — 3.00

BLOOD OF THE INNOCENT (See Warp Graphics Annual)
WaRP Graphics: 1/7/86 - No. 4, 1/28/86 (Weekly mini-series, mature)

1-4 — 2.50

BLOODPACK
DC Comics: Mar, 1995 - No. 4, June,1995 ($1.50, limited series)

1-4 — 2.50

BLOODPOOL
Image Comics (Extreme): Aug, 1995 - No. 4, Nov, 1995 ($2.50, limited series)

1-4: Jo Duffy scripts in all — 2.50
Special (3/96, $2.50)-Jo Duffy scripts — 2.50
Trade Paperback (1996, $12.95)-r/#1-4 — 13.00

BLOODSCENT
Comico: Oct, 1988 ($2.00, one-shot, Baxter paper)

1-Colan-p — 2.50

BLOODSEED
Marvel Comics (Frontier Comics): Oct, 1993 - No. 2, Nov, 1993 ($1.95)

1,2: Sharp/Cam Smith-a — 3.00

BLOODSHOT (See Eternal Warrior #4 & Rai #0)
Valiant/Acclaim Comics (Valiant): Feb, 1993 - No. 51, Aug, 1996 ($2.25/$2.50)

0-(3/94, $3.50)-Wraparound chromium-c by Quesada(p); origin — 4.00
0-Gold variant; no cover price — 10.00
Note: There is a "Platinum variant"; press run error of Gold ed. (25 copies exist) (A CGC certified 9.8 copy sold for $2,067 in 2004)
1-($3.50)-Chromium embossed-c by B. Smith w/poster — 4.00
2-5,8-14: 3-$2.25-c begins; cont'd in Hard Corps #5. 4-Eternal Warrior-c/story. 5-Rai & Eternal Warrior app. 14-(3/94)-Reese-c(i) — 2.50
6,7: 6-1st app. Ninjak (out of costume). 7-In costume — 2.50
15(4/94)-51: 16-w/bound-in trading card. 51-Bloodshot dies? — 2.50
Yearbook 1 (1994, $3.95) — 4.00
Special 1 (3/94, $5.95)-Zeck-c/a(p); Last Stand — 6.00

BLOODSHOT (Volume Two)
Acclaim Comics (Valiant): July, 1997 - No. 16, Oct, 1998 ($2.50)

1-16: 1-Two covers. 5-Copycat-c. X-O Manowar-c/app — 2.50

BLOODSTONE
Marvel Comics: Dec, 2001 - No. 4, Mar, 2002 ($2.99)

1-4-Intro. Elsa Bloodstone; Abnett & Lanning-s/Lopez-a — 3.00

BLOODSTREAM
Image Comics: Jan, 2004 - No. 4, Dec, 2004 ($2.95)

1-4-Adam Shaw painted-a — 3.00

Blood Syndicate #9 © Milestone Media

Blue Beetle #51 © FOX

Blue Beetle (2006 series) #20 © DC

GD VG FN VF VF/NM NM-
2.0 4.0 6.0 8.0 9.0 9.2

BLOODSTRIKE (See Supreme V2#3)
Image Comics (Extreme Studios): 1993 - No. 22, May, 1995; No. 25, May, 1994 ($1.95/$2.50)
1-22, 25: Liefeld layouts in early issues. 1-Blood Brothers prelude. 2-1st app. Lethal. 5-1st app. Noble. 9-Black and White part 6 by Art Thibert; Liefeld pin-up. 9,10-Have coupon #3 & 7 for Extreme Prejudice #0. 10-(4/94). 11-(7/94). 16:Platt-c; Prophet app. 17-19-polybagged w/card . 25-(5/94)-Liefeld/Fraga-c 3.00
NOTE: *Giffen story/layouts-4-6.* ***Jae Lee*** *c-7, 8.* ***Rob Liefeld*** *layouts-1-3.* ***Art Thibert*** *c-6i.*

BLOODSTRIKE ASSASSIN
Image Comics (Extreme Studios): June, 1995 - No. 3, Aug, 1995; No. 0, Oct, 1995 ($2.50, limited series)
0-3: 3-(8/95)-Quesada-c. 0-(10/95)-Battlestone app. 3.00

BLOOD SWORD, THE
Jademan Comics: Aug, 1988 - No. 53, Dec, 1992 ($1.50/$1.95, 68 pgs.)
1-53-Kung Fu stories in all 3.00

BLOOD SWORD DYNASTY
Jademan Comics: 1989 -No. 41, Jan, 1993 ($1.25, 36 pgs.)
1-Ties into Blood Sword 2.50
2-41: Ties into Blood Sword 2.50

BLOOD SYNDICATE
DC Comics (Milestone): Apr, 1993 - No. 35, Feb, 1996 ($1.50/-$3.50)
1-($2.95)-Collector's Edition; polybagged with poster, trading card, & acid-free backing board (direct sale only) 3.50
1-9,11-24,26,27,29,33-34: 8-Intro Kwai. 15-Byrne-c. 16-Worlds Collide Pt. 6; Superman-c/app. 17-Worlds Collide Pt. 13. 29-(99¢); Long Hot Summer x-over 2.50
10,28,30-32: 10-Simonson-c. 30-Long Hot Summer x-over 2.50
25-($2.95, 52 pgs.) 3.00
35-Kwai disappears; last issue 3.50

BLOODWULF
Image Comics (Extreme): Feb, 1995 - No. 4, May, 1995 ($2.50, limited series)
1-4: 1-Liefeld-c w/4 diferent captions & alternate-c. 2.50
Summer Special (8/95, $2.50)-Jeff Johnson-c/a; Supreme app; story takes place between Legend of Supreme #3 & Supreme #23. 2.50

BLOODY MARY
DC Comics (Helix): Oct, 1996 - No. 4, Jan, 1997 ($2.25, limited series)
1-4: Garth Ennis scripts; Ezquerra-c/a in all 3.50
TPB (2005, $19.99) r/#1-4 and Bloody Mary: Lady Liberty #1-4 20.00

BLOODY MARY: LADY LIBERTY
DC Comics (Helix): Sept, 1997 - No. 4, Dec, 1997 ($2.50, limited series)
1-4: Garth Ennis scripts; Ezquerra-c/a in all 3.00

BLUE
Image Comics (Action Toys): Aug, 1999 - No. 2, Apr, 2000 ($2.50)
1,2-Aronowitz-s/Struzan-c 2.50

BLUEBEARD
Slave Labor Graphics: Nov, 1993 - No. 3, Mar, 1994 ($2.95, B&W, lim. series)
1-3: James Robinson scripts. 2-(12/93) 3.00
Trade paperback (6/94, $9.95) 13.00
Trade paperback (2nd printing, 7/96, $12.95)-New-c 13.00

BLUE BEETLE, THE (Also see All Top, Big-3, Mystery Men & Weekly Comic Magazine)
Fox Publ. No. 1-11, 31-60; Holyoke No. 12-30: Winter, 1939-40 - No. 57, 7/48; No. 58, 4/50 - No. 60, 8/50

	GD	VG	FN	VF	VF/NM	NM-
1-Reprints from Mystery Men #1-5; Blue Beetle origin; Yarko the Great-r/from Wonder Comics /Wonderworld #2-5 all by Eisner; Master Magician app.; (Blue Beetle in 4 different costumes)	458	916	1374	3298	5774	8250
2-K-51-r by Powell/Wonderworld #8,9	160	320	480	1008	1704	2400
3-Simon-c	117	234	351	737	1244	1750
4-Marijuana drug mention story	78	156	234	491	833	1175
5-Zanzibar The Magician by Tuska	68	136	204	428	727	1025
6-Dynamite Thor begins (1st); origin Blue Beetle	64	128	192	403	682	960
7,8-Dynamo app. in both. 8-Last Thor	58	116	174	365	615	865
9-12: 9,10-The Blackbird & The Gorilla app. in both. 10-Bondage/hypo-c. 11(2/42)-The Gladiator app. 12(6/42)-The Black Fury app.	52	104	156	322	541	760
13-V-Man begins (1st app.), ends #18; Kubert-a; centerfold spread	60	120	180	378	639	900
14,15-Kubert-a in both. 14-Intro. side-kick (c/text only), Sparky (called Spunky #17-19)	53	106	159	330	553	775
16-18: 17-Brodsky-c	43	86	129	267	446	625
19-Kubert-a	45	90	135	279	465	650
20-Origin/1st app. Tiger Squadron; Arabian Nights begin	47	94	141	291	488	685
21-26: 24-Intro. & only app. The Halo. 26-General Patton story & photo	37	74	111	215	345	475
27-Tamaa, Jungle Prince app.	34	68	102	198	319	440
28-30(2/44)	30	60	90	174	280	385
31(6/44), 33,34,36-40: 34-38-"The Threat from Saturn" serial.	28	56	84	162	261	360
32-Hitler-c	50	100	150	310	518	725
35-Extreme violence	34	68	102	198	319	440
41-45 (#43 exist?)	26	52	78	152	244	335
46-The Puppeteer app.	29	58	87	169	272	375
47-Kamen & Baker-a begin	132	264	396	832	1404	1975
48-50	100	200	300	630	1065	1500
51,53	86	172	258	542	914	1285
52-Kamen bondage-c; true crime stories begin	127	254	381	800	1350	1900
54-Used in **SOTI**. Illo, "Children call these 'headlights' comics"	177	354	531	1115	1883	2650
55-57: 56-Used in **SOTI**, pg. 145. 57(7/48)-Last Kamen issue; becomes Western Killers?	83	166	249	523	887	1250
58(4/50)-60-No Kamen-a	18	36	54	105	165	225

NOTE: ***Kamen*** *a-47-51, 53, 55-57; c-47, 49-52.* ***Powell*** *a-4(2). Bondage-c 9-12, 46, 52.*

BLUE BEETLE (Formerly The Thing; becomes Mr. Muscles No. 22 on) (See Charlton Bullseye & Space Adventures)
Charlton Comics: No. 18, Feb, 1955 - No. 21, Aug, 1955

	GD	VG	FN	VF	VF/NM	NM-
18,19-(Pre-1944-r). 18-Last pre-code issue. 19-Bouncer, Rocket Kelly-r	20	40	60	118	189	260
20-Joan Mason by Kamen	25	50	75	145	233	320
21-New material	20	40	60	115	183	250

BLUE BEETLE (Unusual Tales #1-49; Ghostly Tales #55 on)(See Captain Atom #83 & Charlton Bullseye)
Charlton Comics: V2#1, June, 1964 - V2#5, Mar-Apr, 1965; V3#50, July, 1965 - V3#54, Feb-Mar, 1966; #1, June, 1967 - #5, Nov, 1968

	GD	VG	FN	VF	VF/NM	NM-
V2#1-Origin/1st S.A. app. Dan Garrett-Blue Beetle	8	16	24	58	97	135
2-5: 5-Weiss illo; 1st published-a?	5	10	15	34	55	75
V3#50-54-Formerly Unusual Tales	5	10	15	32	51	70
1(1967)-Question series begins by Ditko	10	20	30	70	123	175
2-Origin Ted Kord-Blue Beetle (see Capt. Atom #83 for 1st Ted Kord Blue Beetle); Dan Garrett x-over	6	12	18	39	62	85
3-5 (All Ditko-c/a in #1-5)	5	10	15	34	55	75
1,3(Modern Comics-1977)-Reprints	1	2	3	5	6	8

NOTE: *#6 only appeared in the fanzine 'The Charlton Portfolio.'*

BLUE BEETLE (Also see Americomics, Crisis On Infinite Earths, Justice League & Showcase '94 #2-4)
DC Comics: June, 1986 - No. 24, May, 1988
1-Origin retold; intro. Firefist 4.00
2-10,15-19,21-24: 2-Origin Firefist. 5-7-The Question app. 21-Millennium tie-in 2.50
11-14-New Teen Titans x-over 3.00
20-Justice League app.; Millennium tie-in 3.00

BLUE BEETLE (See Infinite Crisis)
DC Comics: May, 2006 - Present ($2.99)
1-Hamner-a/Giffen & Rogers-s; Guy Gardner app. 4.00
1-2nd & 3rd printings 3.00
2-29: 2-2nd printing exists. 2-4-Oracle app. 5-Phantom Stranger app. 14-Guy Gardner 16-Eclipso app. 18-Teen Titans app. 20-Sinestro Corps. 21-Spectre app. 3.00
...: Reach For the Stars TPB (2008, $14.99) r/#13-19 15.00
...: Road Trip TPB (2007, $12.99) r/#7-12 13.00
...: Shellshocked TPB (2006, $12.99) r/#1-6 13.00

BLUEBERRY (See Lt. Blueberry & Marshal Blueberry)
Marvel Comics (Epic Comics): 1989 - No. 5, 1990 ($12.95/$14.95, graphic novel)

	GD	VG	FN	VF	VF/NM	NM-
1,3,4,5-($12.95)-Moebius-a in all	2	4	6	11	16	20
2-($14.95)	2	4	6	13	18	22

BLUE BOLT
Funnies, Inc. No. 1/Novelty Press/Premium Group of Comics: June, 1940 - No. 101 (V10#2), Sept-Oct, 1949

	GD	VG	FN	VF	VF/NM	NM-
V1#1-Origin Blue Bolt by Joe Simon, Sub-Zero Man, White Rider & Super Horse, Dick Cole, Wonder Boy & Sgt. Spook (1st app. of each)	318	636	954	2162	3781	5400
2-Simon & Kirby's 1st art & 1st super-hero (Blue Bolt)	180	360	540	1134	1917	2700

3-1 pg. Space Hawk by Wolverton; 2nd S&K-a on Blue Bolt (same cover date as Red Raven #1); 1st time S&K names app. in a comic; Simon-c

Blue Bolt V3 #4 © NOVP

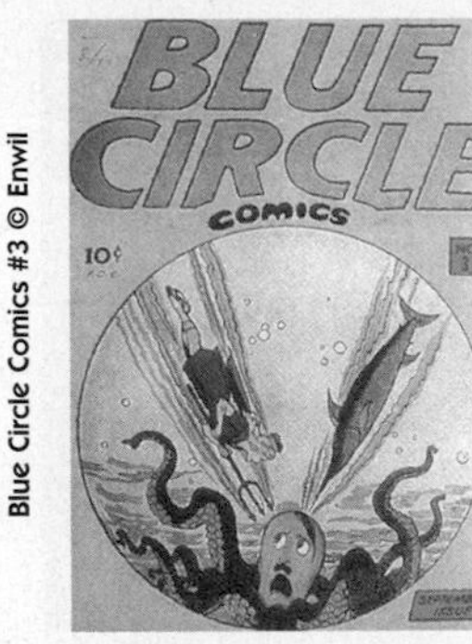

Blue Circle Comics #3 © Enwil

Blue Monday: Lovecats © Chynna Clugston

	GD 2.0	VG 4.0	FN 6.0	VF 8.0	VF/NM 9.0	NM- 9.2
	157	314	471	989	1670	2350
4-S&K-a; classic Everett shark-c	153	306	459	964	1632	2300
5-S&K-a; Everett-a begins on Sub-Zero	133	266	399	838	1419	2000
6,8-10-S&K-a	122	244	366	769	1297	1825
7-S&K-c/a	142	284	426	895	1510	2125
11,12: 11-Robot-c	115	230	345	725	1225	1725
V2#1-Origin Dick Cole & The Twister; Twister x-over in Dick Cole, Sub-Zero, & Blue Bolt; origin Simba Karno who battles Dick Cole thru V2#5 & becomes main supporting character V2#6 on; battle-c	40	80	120	247	404	560
2-Origin The Twister retold in text	34	68	102	198	319	440
3-5: 5-Intro. Freezum	30	60	90	174	280	385
6-Origin Sgt. Spook retold	26	52	78	152	244	335
7-12: 7-Lois Blake becomes Blue Bolt's costume aide; last Twister. 12-Text-sty by Mickey Spillaine	22	44	66	127	204	280
V3#1-3	18	36	54	105	165	225
4-12: 4-Blue Bolt abandons costume	15	30	45	85	130	175
V4#1-Hitler, Tojo, Mussolini-c	40	80	120	235	380	525
V4#2-12: 3-Shows V4#3 on-c, V4#4 inside (9-10/43). 5-Infinity-c. 8-Last Sub-Zero	12	24	36	69	97	125
V5#1-8, V6#1-3,5-10, V7#1-12	11	22	33	62	86	110
V6#4-Racist cover	18	36	54	105	165	225
V8#1-6,8-12, V9#1-4,7,8, V10#1(#100),V10#2(#101)-Last Dick Cole, Blue Bolt	10	20	30	56	76	95
V9#7,V9#6,9-L. B. Cole-c	22	44	66	127	204	280
V9#5-Classic fish in the face-c	21	42	63	123	197	270

NOTE: ***Everett** c-V1#4, 11, V2#1, 2. **Gustavson** a-V1#1-12, V2#1-7. **Kiefer** c-V3#1. **Rico** a-V6#10, V7#4. Blue Bolt not in V9#8.*

BLUE BOLT (Becomes Ghostly Weird Stories #120 on; continuation of Novelty Blue Bolt) (...Weird Tales of Terror #111,112,...Weird Tales #113-119)
Star Publications: No. 102, Nov-Dec, 1949 - No. 119, May-June, 1953

	GD 2.0	VG 4.0	FN 6.0	VF 8.0	VF/NM 9.0	NM- 9.2
102-The Chameleon, & Target app.	39	78	117	230	370	510
103,104-The Chameleon app. 104-Last Target	38	76	114	222	356	490
105-Origin Blue Bolt (from #1) retold by Simon; Chameleon & Target app.; opium den story	55	110	165	347	586	825
106-Blue Bolt by S&K begins; Spacehawk reprints from Target by Wolverton begin, ends #110; Sub-Zero begins; ends #109	53	106	159	330	553	775
107-110: 108-Last S&K Blue Bolt reprint. 109-Wolverton-c(r)/inside Spacehawk splash. 110-Target app.	52	104	156	322	536	750
111,112: 111-Red Rocket & The Mask-r; last Blue Bolt; 1pg. L. B. Cole-a. 112-Last Torpedo Man app.	46	92	138	285	485	685
113-Wolverton's Spacehawk-r/Target V3#7	49	98	147	304	507	710
114,116: 116-Jungle Jo-r	46	92	138	285	485	685
115-Sgt. Spook app.	49	98	147	304	507	710
117-Jo-Jo & Blue Bolt-r	48	96	144	298	499	700
118-"White Spirit" by Wood	49	98	147	304	507	710
119-Disbrow/Cole-c; Jungle Jo-r	48	96	144	298	499	700
Accepted Reprint #103(1957?, nd)	14	28	42	80	115	150

NOTE: ***L. B. Cole** c-102-108, 110 on. **Disbrow** a-112(2), 113(3), 114(2), 115(2), 116-118. **Hollingsworth** a-117. **Palais** a-112r. Sci/Fi c-105-110. Horror c-111.*

BLUE BULLETEER, THE (Also see Femforce Special)
AC Comics: 1989 ($2.25, B&W, one-shot)

	NM- 9.2
1-Origin by Bill Black; Bill Ward-a	4.00

BLUE BULLETEER (Also see Femforce Special)
AC Comics: 1996 ($5.95, B&W, one-shot)

	NM- 9.2
1-Photo-c	6.00

BLUE CIRCLE COMICS (Also see Red Circle Comics, Blazing Comics & Roly Poly Comic Book)
Enwil Associates/Rural Home: June, 1944 - No. 6, Apr, 1945

	GD 2.0	VG 4.0	FN 6.0	VF 8.0	VF/NM 9.0	NM- 9.2
1-The Blue Circle begins (1st app.); origin & 1st app. Steel Fist	32	64	96	186	298	410
2	20	40	60	115	183	250
3-Hitler parody-c	30	60	90	174	280	385
4-6: 5-Last Steel Fist.	17	34	51	100	158	215
6-(Dated 4/45, Vol. 2#3 inside)-Leftover covers to #6 were later restapled over early 1950's coverless comics; variations of the coverless comics exist. Colossal Features known.	17	34	51	100	158	215

BLUE DEVIL (See Fury of Firestorm #24, Underworld Unleashed, Starman (2nd) #38, Infinite Crisis and Shadowpact)
DC Comics: June, 1984 - No. 31, Dec, 1986 (75¢/$1.25)

	NM- 9.2
1	4.00
2-16,19-31: 4-Origin Nebiros. 7-Gil Kane-a. 8-Giffen-a	2.50
17,18-Crisis x-over	3.00

	NM- 9.2
Annual 1 (11/85)-Team-ups w/Black Orchid, Creeper, Demon, Madame Xanadu, Man-Bat & Phantom Stranger	3.00

BLUE MONDAY: ... (one-shots)
Oni Press: Feb, 2002 - Present (B&W, Chynna Clugston-Major-s/a/c in all)

	NM- 9.2
Dead Man's Party (10/02, $2.95) Dan Brereton painted back-c	3.00
Inbetween Days (9/03, $9.95, 8" x 5-1/2") r/Dead Man's Party, Lovecats, & Nobody's Fool	10.00
Lovecats (2/02, $2.95) Valentine's Day themed	3.00
Nobody's Fool (2/03, $2.95) April Fool's Day themed	3.00

BLUE MONDAY: ABSOLUTE BEGINNERS
Oni Press: Feb, 2001 - No. 4, Sept, 2001 ($2.95, B&W, limited series)

	NM- 9.2
1-4-Chynna Clugston-Major-s/a/c	3.00
TPB (12/01, $11.95, 8" x 6") r/series	12.00

BLUE MONDAY: PAINTED MOON
Oni Press: Feb, 2004 - No. 4, Mar, 2005 ($2.99, B&W, limited series)

	NM- 9.2
1-4-Chynna Clugston-Major-s/a/c	3.00
TPB (4/05, $11.95, digest-sized) r/series; sketch pages	12.00

BLUE MONDAY: THE KIDS ARE ALRIGHT
Oni Press: Feb, 2000 - No. 3, May, 2000 ($2.95, B&W, limited series)

	NM- 9.2
1-3-Chynna Clugston-Major-s/a/c. 1-Variant-c by Warren. 2-Dorkin-c	3.00
3-Variant cover by J. Scott Campbell	4.00
TPB (12/00, $10.95, digest-sized) r/#1-3 & earlier short stories	11.00

BLUE PHANTOM, THE
Dell Publishing Co.: June-Aug, 1962

	GD 2.0	VG 4.0	FN 6.0	VF 8.0	VF/NM 9.0	NM- 9.2
1(01-066-208)-by Fred Fredericks	3	6	9	21	32	42

BLUE RIBBON COMICS (...Mystery Comics No. 9-18)
MLJ Magazines: Nov, 1939 - No. 22, Mar, 1942 (1st MLJ series)

	GD 2.0	VG 4.0	FN 6.0	VF 8.0	VF/NM 9.0	NM- 9.2
1-Dan Hastings, Richy the Amazing Boy, Rang-A-Tang the Wonder Dog begin (1st app. of each); Little Nemo app. (not by W. McCay), Jack Cole a(3) (1st MLJ comic)	300	600	900	2010	3505	5000
2-Bob Phantom, Silver Fox (both in #3), Rang-A-Tang Club & Cpl. Collins begin (1st app. of each); Jack Cole-a	117	234	351	737	1244	1750
3-J. Cole-a	77	154	231	481	816	1150
4-Doc Strong, The Green Falcon, & Hercules begin (1st app. each); origin & 1st app. The Fox & Ty-Gor, Son of the Tiger	85	170	255	536	906	1275
5-8: 8-Last Hercules; 6,7-Biro, Meskin-a. 7-Fox app. on-c	63	126	189	397	669	940
9-(Scarce)-Origin & 1st app. Mr. Justice (2/41)	300	600	900	1930	3315	4700
10-13: 12-Last Doc Strong. 13-Inferno, the Flame Breather begins, ends #19; Devil-c	103	206	309	649	1100	1550
14,15,17,18: 15-Last Green Falcon	87	174	261	548	924	1300
16-Origin & 1st app. Captain Flag (9/41)	160	320	480	1008	1704	2400
19-22: 20-Last Ty-Gor. 22-Origin Mr. Justice retold	87	174	261	548	924	1300

NOTE: ***Biro** c-3-5; a-2 (Cpl. Collins & Scoop Cody). **S. Cooper** c-9-17. 20-22 contain "Tales From the Witch's Cauldron" (same strip as "Stories of the Black Witch" in Zip Comics). Mr. Justice c-9-18. Captain Flag c-16-18 (w/Mr. Justice), 19-22.*

BLUE RIBBON COMICS (Becomes Teen-Age Diary Secrets #4)
(Also see Approved Comics, Blue Ribbon Comics and Heckle &Jeckle)
Blue Ribbon (St. John): Feb, 1949 - No. 6, Aug, 1949

	GD 2.0	VG 4.0	FN 6.0	VF 8.0	VF/NM 9.0	NM- 9.2
1-Heckle & Jeckle (Terrytoons)	14	28	42	78	112	145
2(4/49)-Diary Secrets; Baker-c	29	58	87	169	272	375
3-Heckle & Jeckle (Terrytoons)	11	22	33	60	83	105
4(6/49)-Teen-Age Diary Secrets; Baker c/a(2)	29	58	87	169	272	375
5(8/49)-Teen-Age Diary Secrets; Oversize; photo-c; Baker-a(2)- Continues as Teen-Age Diary Secrets	35	70	105	203	327	450
6-Dinky Duck(8/49)(Terrytoons)	8	16	24	42	54	65

BLUE RIBBON COMICS
Red Circle Prod./Archie Ent. No. 5 on: Nov, 1983 - No. 14, Dec, 1984

	NM- 9.2
1-S&K-r/Advs. of the Fly #1,2; Williamson/Torres-r/Fly #2; Ditko-c	6.00
2-7,9,10: 3-Origin Steel Sterling. 5-S&K Shield-r; new Kirby-c. 6,7-The Fox app.	5.00
8-Toth centerspread; Black Hood app.; Neal Adams-a(r)	6.00
11,13,14: 11-Black Hood. 13-Thunder Bunny. 14-Web & Jaguar	5.00
12-Thunder Agents; Noman new Ditko-a	6.00

NOTE: ***N. Adams** a(r)-8. **Buckler** a-4i. **Nino** a-2i. **McWilliams** a-8. **Morrow** a-8.*

BLUE STREAK (See Holyoke One-Shot No. 8)

BLUNTMAN AND CHRONIC TPB(Also see Jay and Silent Bob, Clerks, and Oni Double Feature)
Image Comics: Dec, 2001 ($14.95, TPB)

	NM- 9.2
nn-Tie-in for "Jay & Silent Bob Strike Back" movie; new Kevin Smith-s/Michael Oeming-a; r/app. from Oni Double Feature #12 in color; Ben Affleck & Jason Lee afterwords	15.00

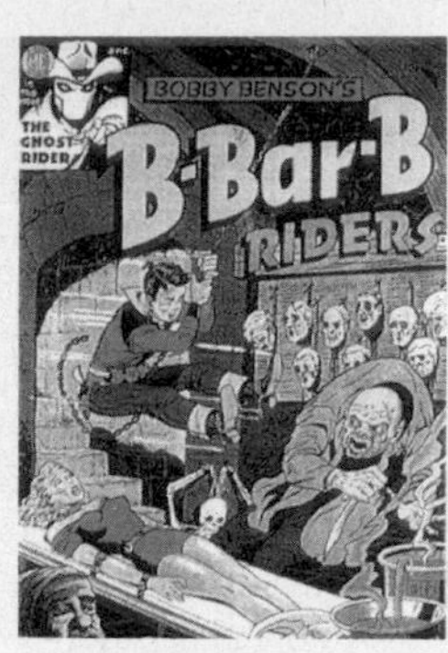

Bobby Benson's B-Bar-B Riders #14 © ME

Bob Steele Western #7 © FAW

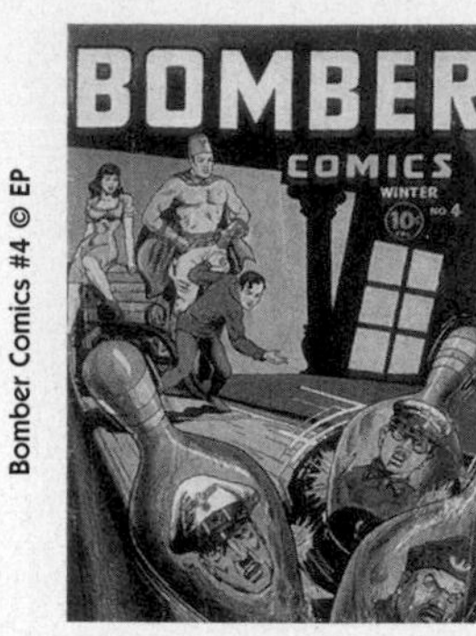

Bomber Comics #4 © EP

GD VG FN VF VF/NM NM-
2.0 4.0 6.0 8.0 9.0 9.2

BLYTHE (Marge's)
Dell Publishing Co.: No. 1072, Jan-Mar, 1960
Four Color 1072 — 5 10 15 34 55 75

B-MAN (See Double-Dare Adventures)

BO (Tom Cat #4 on) (Also see Big Shot #29 & Dixie Dugan)
Charlton Comics Group: June, 1955 - No. 3, Oct, 1955 (A dog)
1-3: Newspaper reprints by Frank Beck — 8 16 24 40 50 60

BOATNIKS, THE (See Walt Disney Showcase No. 1)

BOB BURDEN'S ORIGINAL MYSTERYMEN PRESENTS
Dark Horse Comics: 1999 - No. 4 ($2.95/$3.50)
1-3-Bob Burden-s/Sadowski-a(p) — 3.50
4-($3.50) All Villain issue — 3.50

BOBBY BENSON'S B-BAR-B RIDERS (Radio) (See Best of The West, The Lemonade Kid & Model Fun)
Magazine Enterprises/AC Comics: May-June, 1950 - No. 20, May-June, 1953
1-The Lemonade Kid begins; Powell-a (Scarce) — 41 82 123 250 413 575
2 — 17 34 51 98 154 210
3-5: 4,5-Lemonade Kid-c (#4-Spider-c) — 14 28 42 76 108 140
6-8,10 — 13 26 39 72 101 130
9,11,13-Frazetta-c; Ghost Rider in #13-15 by Ayers-a. 13-Ghost Rider-c — 37 74 111 215 345 475
12,17-20: 20-(A-1 #88) — 11 22 33 64 90 115
14-Decapitation/Bondage-c & story; classic horror-c — 28 56 84 162 261 360
15-Ghost Rider-c — 22 44 66 127 204 280
16-Photo-c — 14 28 42 80 115 150
1 (1990, $2.75, B&W)-Reprints; photo-c & inside covers — 3.00
NOTE: *Ayers a-13-15, 20. Powell a-1-12(4 ea.), 13(3), 14-16(Red Hawk only); c-1-8,1 0, 12. Lemonade Kid in most 1-13.*

BOBBY COMICS
Universal Phoenix Features: May, 1946
1-By S. M. Iger — 9 18 27 47 61 75

BOBBY SHERMAN (TV)
Charlton Comics: Feb, 1072 - No. 7, Oct, 1972
1-Based on TV show "Getting Together" — 5 10 15 35 55 75
2-7: 2,4-Photo-c — 4 8 12 22 34 45

BOB COLT (Movie star)(See XMas Comics)
Fawcett Publications: Nov, 1950 - No. 10, May, 1952
1-Bob Colt, his horse Buckskin & sidekick Pablo begin; photo front/back-c begin — 36 72 108 208 329 450
2 — 18 36 54 105 165 225
3-5 — 15 30 45 85 130 175
6-Flying Saucer story — 14 28 42 80 115 150
7-10: 9-Last photo back-c — 13 26 39 74 105 135

BOB HOPE (See Adventures of... & Calling All Boys #12)

BOB MARLEY, TALE OF THE TUFF GONG (Music star)
Marvel Comics: Aug, 1994 - No, 3, Nov, 1994 ($5.95, limited series)
1-3 — 6.00

BOB POWELL'S TIMELESS TALES
Eclipse Comics: March, 1989 ($2.00, B&W)
1-Powell-r/Black Cat #5 (Scarlet Arrow), 9 & Race for the Moon #1 — 3.00

BOB SCULLY, THE TWO-FISTED HICK DETECTIVE (Also see Advs. of Detective Ace King and Detective Dan)
Humor Publ. Co.: No date (1933) (36 pgs., 9-1/2x11", B&W, paper-c; 10¢-c)
nn-By Howard Dell; not reprints; along with Advs. of Det. Ace King and Detective Dan, the first comic w/original art & the first of a single theme; has a blue 2-tone cover — 375 750 1125 3000 - -

BOB SON OF BATTLE
Dell Publishing Co.: No. 729, Nov, 1956
Four Color 729 — 4 8 12 24 37 50

BOB STEELE WESTERN (Movie star)
Fawcett Publications/AC Comics: Dec, 1950 - No. 10, June, 1952; 1990
1-Bob Steele & his horse Bullet begin; photo front/back-c begin — 43 86 129 262 431 600
2 — 22 44 66 128 202 275
3-5: 4-Last photo back-c — 15 30 45 90 140 190
6-10: 10-Last photo-c — 14 28 42 80 115 150
1 (1990, $2.75, B&W)-Bob Steele & Rocky Lane reprints; photo-c & inside covers — 3.00

BOB SWIFT (Boy Sportsman)
Fawcett Publications: May, 1951 - No. 5, Jan, 1952
1 — 10 20 30 58 79 100
2-5: Saunders painted-c #1-5 — 7 14 21 35 43 50

BOB, THE GALACTIC BUM
DC Comics: Feb, 1995 - No. 4, June, 1995 ($1.95, limited series)
1-4: 1-Lobo app. — 2.50

BODY BAGS
Dark Horse Comics (Blanc Noir): Sept, 1996 - No. 4, Jan, 1997 ($2.95, mini-series, mature) (1st Blanc Noir series)
1-Jason Pearson-c/a/scripts in all. 1-Intro Clownface & Panda. — 1 2 3 5 6 8
2 — 1 3 4 6 8 10
3,4 — 6.00
Body Bags 1 (Image Comics, 7/05, $5.99) r/#1&2 — 6.00
Body Bags 2 (Image Comics, 8/05, $5.99) r/#3&4 — 6.00
...: 3 The Hard Way (Image, 2/06, $5.99) new story & r/Dark Horse Presents Annual 1997 and Dark Horse Maverick 2000; Pearson-c — 6.00

BODYCOUNT (Also see Casey Jones & Raphael)
Image Comics (Highbrow Entertainment): Mar, 1996 - No. 4, July, 1996 ($2.50, lim. series)
1-4: Kevin Eastman-a(p)/scripts; Simon Bisley-c/a(i); Turtles app. — 2.50

BODY DOUBLES (See Resurrection Man)
DC Comics: Oct, 1999 - No. 4, Jan, 2000 ($2.50, limited series)
1-4-Lanning & Abnett-s. 2-Black Canary app. 4-Wonder Woman app. — 2.50
...(Villains) (2/98, $1.95, one-shot) 1-Pearson-c; Deadshot app. — 2.50

BOFFO LAFFS
Paragraphics: 1986 - No. 5 ($2.50/$1.95)
1-($2.50) First comic cover with hologram — 3.00
2-5 — 2.50

BOLD ADVENTURES
Pacific Comics: Oct, 1983 - No. 3, June, 1984 ($1.50)
1-Time Force, Anaconda, & The Weirdling begin — 3.00
2,3: 2-Soldiers of Fortune begins. 3-Spitfire — 3.00
NOTE: *Kaluta c-3. Nebres a-1-3. Nino a-2, 3. Severin a-3.*

BOLD STORIES (Also see Candid Tales & It Rhymes With Lust)
Kirby Publishing Co.: Mar, 1950 - July, 1950 (Digest size, 144 pgs.)
March issue (Very Rare) - Contains "The Ogre of Paris" by Wood — 143 286 429 901 1526 2150
May issue (Very Rare) - Contains "The Cobra's Kiss" by Graham Ingels (21 pgs.) — 127 254 381 800 1350 1900
July issue (Very Rare) - Contains "The Ogre of Paris" by Wood — 115 230 345 725 1225 1725

BOLT AND STAR FORCE SIX
Americomics: 1984 ($1.75)
1-Origin Bolt & Star Force Six — 3.00
Special 1 (1984, $2.00, 52pgs., B&W) — 3.00

BOMBARDIER (See Bee 29, the Bombardier & Cinema Comics Herald)

BOMBAST
Topps Comics: 1993 ($2.95, one-shot) (Created by Jack Kirby)
1-Polybagged w/Kirbychrome trading card; Savage Dragon app.; Kirby-c; has coupon for Amberchrome Secret City Saga #0 — 3.00

BOMBA THE JUNGLE BOY (TV)
National Periodical Publ.: Sept-Oct, 1967 - No. 7, Sept-Oct, 1968 (12¢)
1-Intro. Bomba; Infantino/Anderson-c — 4 8 12 24 37 50
2-7 — 3 6 9 16 23 30

BOMBER COMICS
Elliot Publ. Co./Melverne Herald/Farrell/Sunrise Times: Mar, 1944 - No. 4, Winter, 1944-45
1-Wonder Boy, & Kismet, Man of Fate begin — 80 160 240 504 852 1200
2-Hitler-c and 8 pg. story — 73 146 219 460 780 1100
3: 2-4-Have Classics Comics ad to HRN 20 — 45 90 135 279 465 650
4-Hitler, Tojo & Mussolini-c; Sensation Comics #13-c/swipe; has Classics Comics ad to HRN 20. — 72 144 216 454 765 1075

BOMB QUEEN
Image Comics (Shadowline): Feb, 2006 - No. 4, May, 2006 ($3.50, mature)

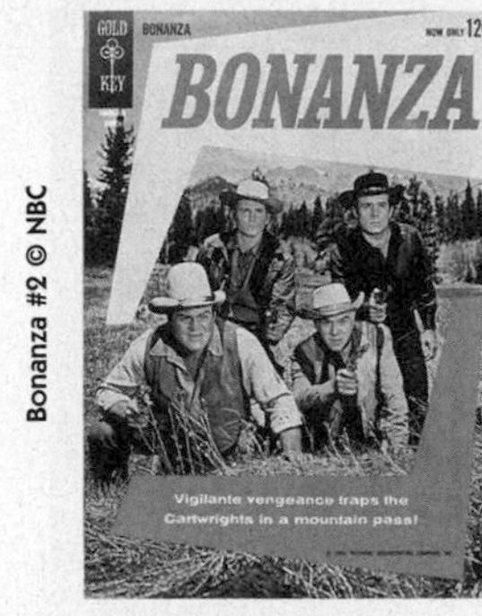

Bonanza #2 © NBC

Bone #12 © Jeff Smith

Books of Magic #50 © DC

	GD	VG	FN	VF	VF/NM	NM-
	2.0	4.0	6.0	8.0	9.0	9.2

1-4-Jimmie Robinson-s/a 3.50
... Vs. Blacklight One Shot #1 (8/06, $3.50) Robinson-a; Shadowhawk app. 3.50
..., Vol. 1: WMD: Woman of Mass Destruction TPB (7/06, $12.99) r/#1-4; bonus art 13.00

BOMB QUEEN II
Image Comics (Shadowline): Oct, 2006 - No. 3, Dec, 2006 ($3.50, mature)

1-3-Jimmie Robinson-s/a; intro. The Four Queens 3.50
..., Vol. 2: Dirty Bomb - Queen of Hearts TPB (7/07, $14.99) r/#1-3 & Blacklight One Shot; bonus art; Robinson interview 15.00

BOMB QUEEN III THE GOOD, THE BAD & THE LOVELY
Image Comics (Shadowline): Mar, 2007 - No. 4, Jun, 2007 ($3.50, mature)

1-4-Jimmie Robinson-a/Jim Valentino-s; Blacklight & Rebound app. 1-Linsner-c 3.50

BOMB QUEEN IV SUICIDE BOMBER
Image Comics (Shadowline): Aug, 2007 - No. 4, Dec, 2007 ($3.50, mature)

1-4-Jim Robinson-s/a. 3-She-Spawn app. 3.50

BOMB QUEEN (Volume 5)
Image Comics (Shadowline): May, 2008 - No. 6 ($3.50, mature)

1-3-Jim Robinson-s/a 3.50

BONANZA (TV)
Dell/Gold Key: June-Aug, 1960 - No. 37, Aug, 1970 (All Photo-c)

	GD	VG	FN	VF	VF/NM	NM-
Four Color 1110 (6-8/60)	31	62	93	239	445	650
Four Color 1221,1283, & #01070-207, 01070-210	17	34	51	120	223	325
1(12/62-Gold Key)	18	36	54	128	237	345
2	10	20	30	68	119	170
3-10	8	16	24	52	86	120
11-20	6	12	18	39	62	85
21-37: 29-Reprints	5	10	15	32	51	70

BONE
Cartoon Books #1-20, 28 on/Image Comics #21-27: Jul, 1991 - No. 55, Jun, 2004 ($2.95, B&W)

	GD	VG	FN	VF	VF/NM	NM-
1-Jeff Smith-c/a in all	7	14	21	50	83	115
1-2nd printing	2	4	6	8	10	12
1-3rd thru 5th printings						4.00
2-1st printing	4	8	12	26	41	55
2-2nd & 3rd printings						4.00
3-1st printing	3	6	9	20	30	40
3-2nd thru 4th printings						4.00
4,5	2	4	6	13	18	22
6-10	1	3	4	6	8	11
11-37: 21-1st Image issue						4.00
13 1/2 (1/95, Wizard)	1	3	4	6	8	10
13 1/2 (Gold)	2	4	6	8	10	12
38-($4.95) Three covers by Miller, Ross, Smith						5.00
39-55-($2.95)						3.00
1-27-($2.95): 1-Image reprints begin w/new-c. 2-Allred pin-up.						3.00
... Holiday Special (1993, giveaway)						3.00
... Reader -($9.95) Behind the scenes info						10.00
... Sourcebook-San Diego Edition						3.00
...10th Anniversary Edition (8/01, $5.95) r/#1 in color; came with figure						6.00
Complete Bone Adventures Vol 1,2 ('93, '94, $12.95, r/#1-6 & #7-12)						13.00
...: One Volume Edition (2004, $39.95, 1300 pgs.) r/#1-54; extra material						40.00
Volume 1-($19.95, hard-c)-"Out From Boneville"						20.00
Volume 1-($12.95, soft-c)						13.00
Volume 2,5-($22.95, hard-c)-"The Great Cow Race" & "Rock Jaw"						23.00
Volume 2,5-($14.95, soft-c)						15.00
Volume 3,4-($24.95, hard-c)-"Eyes of the Storm" & "The Dragonslayer"						25.00
Volume 3,4,7-($16.95, soft-c)						17.00
Volume 6-($15.95, soft-c)-"Old Man's Cave"						16.00
Volume 7-($24.95, hard-c)-"Ghost Circles"						25.00
Volume 8-($23.95, hard-c)-"Treasure Hunters"						24.00

NOTE: *Printings not listed sell for cover price.*

BONGO (See Story Hour Series)

BONGO & LUMPJAW (Disney, see Walt Disney Showcase #3)
Dell Publishing Co.: No. 706, June, 1956; No. 886, Mar, 1958

	GD	VG	FN	VF	VF/NM	NM-
Four Color 706 (#1)	6	12	18	37	59	80
Four Color 886	5	10	15	30	48	65

BONGO COMICS PRESENTS RADIOACTIVE MAN (See Radioactive Man)

BON VOYAGE (See Movie Classics)

BOOF
Image Comics (Todd McFarlane Prod.): July, 1994 - No. 6, Dec, 1994 ($1.95)

1-6 2.50

BOOF AND THE BRUISE CREW
Image Comics (Todd McFarlane Prod.): July, 1994 - No. 6, Dec, 1994 ($1.95)

1-6 2.50

BOOK AND RECORD SET (See Power Record Comics)

BOOK OF ALL COMICS
William H. Wise: 1945 (196 pgs.)(Inside f/c has Green Publ. blacked out)

	GD	VG	FN	VF	VF/NM	NM-
nn-Green Mask, Puppeteer & The Bouncer	43	86	129	267	446	625

BOOK OF ANTS, THE
Artisan Entertainment: 1998 ($2.95, B&W)

1-Based on the movie Pi; Aronofsky-s 3.00

BOOK OF BALLADS AND SAGAS, THE
Green Man Press: Oct, 1995 - No. 4 ($2.95/$3.50/$3.25, B&W)

1-4: 1-Vess-c/a; Gaiman story. 3.50

BOOK OF COMICS, THE
William H. Wise: No date (1944) (25¢, 132 pgs.)

	GD	VG	FN	VF	VF/NM	NM-
nn-Captain V app.	41	82	123	247	406	565

BOOK OF FATE, THE (See Fate)
DC Comics: Feb, 1997 - No. 12, Jan, 1998 ($2.25/$2.50)

1-12: 4-Two-Face-c/app. 6-Convergence. 11-Sentinel app. 3.00

BOOK OF LOST SOULS, THE
Marvel Comics (Icon): Dec, 2005 - No. 6, June, 2006 ($2.99)

1-6-Colleen Doran-a/c; J. Michael Straczynski-s 3.00
... Vol. 1: Introductions All Around TPB (2006, $16.99) r/series 17.00

BOOK OF LOVE (See Fox Giants)

BOOK OF NIGHT, THE
Dark Horse Comics: July, 1987 - No. 3, 1987 ($1.75, B&W)

1-3: Reprints from Epic Illustrated; Vess-a 2.50
TPB-r/#1-3 15.00
Hardcover-Black-c with red crest 100.00
Hardcover w/slipcase (1991) signed and numbered 50.00

BOOK OF THE DEAD
Marvel Comics: Dec, 1993 - No. 4, Mar, 1994 ($1.75, limited series, 52 pgs.)

	GD	VG	FN	VF	VF/NM	NM-
1-4: 1-Ploog Frankenstein & Morrow Man-Thing-r begin; Wrightson-r/Chamber of Darkness #7. 2-Morrow new painted-c; Chaykin/Morrow Man-Thing; Krigstein-r/Uncanny Tales #54; r/Fear #10. 3-r/Astonishing Tales #10 & Starlin Man-Thing. 3,4-Painted-c	1	2	3	4	5	7

BOOKS OF DOOM (Dr. Doom from Fantastic Four)
Marvel Comics: Jan, 2006 - No. 6, June, 2006 ($2.99, limited series)

1-6-Life story/origin of Dr. Doom; Brubaker-s/Raimondi-a/Rivera-c 3.00
Fantastic Four: Books of Doom HC (2006, $19.99) r/#1-6 20.00
Fantastic Four: Books of Doom SC (2007, $14.99) r/#1-6 15.00

BOOKS OF FAERIE, THE
DC Comics (Vertigo): Mar, 1997 - No. 3, May, 1997 ($2.50, limited series)

1-3-Gross-a 3.00
TPB (1998, $14.95) r/#1-3 & Arcana Annual #1 15.00

BOOKS OF FAERIE, THE : AUBERON'S TALE
DC Comics (Vertigo): Aug, 1998 - No. 3, Oct, 1998 ($2.50, limited series)

1-3-Gross-a 3.00

BOOKS OF FAERIE, THE : MOLLY'S STORY
DC Comics (Vertigo): Sept, 1999 - No. 4, Dec, 1999 ($2.50, limited series)

1-4-Ney Rieber-s/Mejia-a 3.00

BOOKS OF MAGIC
DC Comics: 1990 - No. 4, 1991 ($3.95, 52 pgs., limited series, mature)

	GD	VG	FN	VF	VF/NM	NM-
1-Bolton painted-c/a; Phantom Stranger app.; Gaiman scripts in all	1	3	4	6	8	10
2,3: 2-John Constantine, Dr. Fate, Spectre, Deadman app. 3-Dr. Occult app.; minor Sandman app.	1	2	3	4	5	7
4-Early Death-c/app. (early 1991)	1	2	3	5	6	8
Trade paperback-($19.95)-Reprints limited series						20.00

BOOKS OF MAGIC (Also see Hunter: The Age of Magic and Names of Magic)
DC Comics (Vertigo): May, 1994 - No. 75, Aug, 2000 ($1.95/$2.50, mature)

Booster Gold (2007 series) #4 © DC

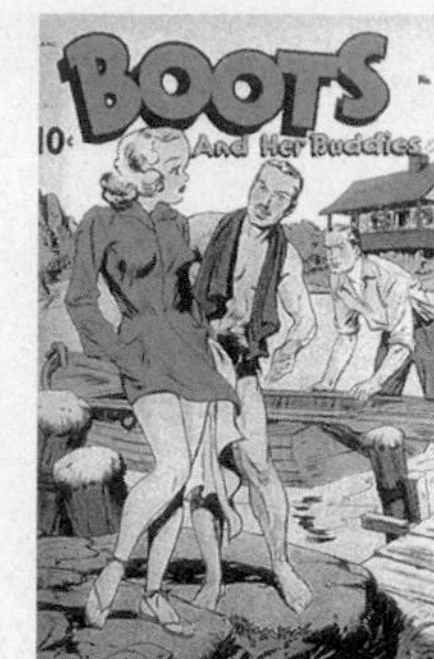

Boots and Her Buddies #5 © STD

Boy Comics #30 © LEV

	GD 2.0	VG 4.0	FN 6.0	VF 8.0	VF/NM 9.0	NM- 9.2
1-Charles Vess-c	2	4	6	8	10	12
1-Platinum	2	4	6	13	18	22
2-4: 4-Death app.	1	2	3	4	5	7
5-14; Charles Vess-c						4.00
15-50: 15-$2.50-c begins. 22-Kaluta-c. 25-Death-c/app; Bachalo-c						3.00
51-75: 51-Peter Gross-s/a begins. 55-Medley-a						2.50
Annual 1-3 (2/97, 2/98, '99, $3.95)						4.00
Bindings (1995, $12.95, TPB)-r/#1-4						13.00
Death After Death (2001, $19.95, TPB)-r/#42-50						20.00
Girl in the Box (1999, $14.95, TPB)-r/#26-32						15.00
Reckonings (1997, $12.95, TPB)-r/#14-20						13.00
Summonings (1996, $17.50, TPB)-r/#5-13, Vertigo Rave #1						17.50
The Burning Girl (2000, $17.95, TPB)-r/#33-41						18.00
Transformations (1998, $12.95, TPB)-r/#21-25						13.00

BOOKS OF MAGICK, THE : LIFE DURING WARTIME (See Books of Magic)
DC Comics (Vertigo): Sept, 2004 - No. 15, Dec, 2005 ($2.50/$2.75)

	GD 2.0	VG 4.0	FN 6.0	VF 8.0	VF/NM 9.0	NM- 9.2
1-15: 1-Spencer-s/Ormston-a/Quitely-c; Constantine app. 2-Bagged with Sky Captain CD 6-Fegredo-a. 7-Constantine & Zatanna-c						2.75
... Book One TPB (2005, $9.95) r/#1-5						10.00

BOOSTER GOLD (See Justice League #4)
DC Comics: Feb, 1986 - No. 25, Feb, 1988 (75¢)

	GD 2.0	VG 4.0	FN 6.0	VF 8.0	VF/NM 9.0	NM- 9.2
1-Dan Jurgens-s/a(p)						3.00
2-25: 4-Rose & Thorn app. 6-Origin. 6,7,23-Superman app. 8,9-LSH app. 22-JLI app. 24,25-Millennium tie-ins						2.50

NOTE: *Austin c-22i. Byrne c-23i.*

BOOSTER GOLD (See DC's weekly series 52)
DC Comics: Oct, 2007 - Present ($3.50/$2.99)

	GD 2.0	VG 4.0	FN 6.0	VF 8.0	VF/NM 9.0	NM- 9.2
1-Geoff Johns-s/Dan Jurgens-a(p); covers by Jurgens and Art Adams; Rip Hunter app.						5.00
2-10: 3-Jonah Hex app. 4-Barry Allen app. 5-Joker and Batgirl app. 8-Superman app.						3.00
#0-(4/08) Blue Beetle (Ted Cord) returns; takes place between #6&7						3.00
#1,000,000-(9/08) Michelle Carter returns; takes place between #10&11						3.00
...: 52 Pick-Up (2008, $24.99, HC w/d.j.) r/#1-6, original design sketches from Jurgens						25.00

BOOTS AND HER BUDDIES
Standard Comics/Visual Editions/Argo (NEA Service):
No. 5, 9/48 - No. 9, 9/49; 12/55 - No. 3, 1956

	GD 2.0	VG 4.0	FN 6.0	VF 8.0	VF/NM 9.0	NM- 9.2
5-Strip-r	16	32	48	94	147	200
6,8	11	22	33	64	90	115
7-(Scarce)	14	28	42	80	115	150
9-(Scarce)-Frazetta-a (2 pgs.)	26	52	78	152	244	335
1-3(Argo-1955-56)-Reprints	6	12	18	31	38	45

BOOTS & SADDLES (TV)
Dell Publ. Co.: No. 919, July, 1958; No. 1029, Sept, 1959; No. 1116, Aug, 1960

	GD 2.0	VG 4.0	FN 6.0	VF 8.0	VF/NM 9.0	NM- 9.2
Four Color 919 (#1)-Photo-c	7	14	21	50	83	115
Four Color 1029, 1116-Photo-c	5	10	15	34	55	75

BORDERLINE
Friction Press: June, 1992 ($2.25, B&W)

	GD 2.0	VG 4.0	FN 6.0	VF 8.0	VF/NM 9.0	NM- 9.2
0-Ashcan edition; 1st app. of Cliff Broadway						2.25
1-Painted-c						3.00
1-Special Edition (bagged w/ photo, S&N)						4.00

BORDER PATROL
P. L. Publishing Co.: May-June, 1951 - No. 3, Sept-Oct, 1951

	GD 2.0	VG 4.0	FN 6.0	VF 8.0	VF/NM 9.0	NM- 9.2
1	14	28	42	80	115	150
2,3	10	20	30	54	72	90

BORDER WORLDS (Also see Megaton Man)
Kitchen Sink Press: 7/86 - No. 7, 1987; V2#1, 1990 - No. 4, 1990 ($1.95-$2.00, B&W, mature)

	GD 2.0	VG 4.0	FN 6.0	VF 8.0	VF/NM 9.0	NM- 9.2
1-7, V2#1-4: Donald Simpson-c/a/scripts						3.00

BORIS KARLOFF TALES OF MYSTERY (TV) (...Thriller No. 1,2)
Gold Key: No. 3, April, 1963 - No. 97, Feb, 1980

	GD 2.0	VG 4.0	FN 6.0	VF 8.0	VF/NM 9.0	NM- 9.2
3-5-(Two #5's, 10/63,11/63): 5-(10/63)-11 pgs. Toth-a.	5	10	15	30	48	65
6-8,10: 10-Orlando-a	4	8	12	22	34	45
9-Wood-a	4	8	12	23	36	48
11-Williamson-a, 8 pgs.; Orlando-a, 5 pgs.	4	8	12	23	36	48
12-Torres, McWilliams-a; Orlando-a(2)	3	6	9	19	29	38
13,14,16-20	3	6	9	17	25	32
15-Crandall	3	6	9	18	27	35
21-Jeff Jones-a(3 pgs.) "The Screaming Skull"	3	6	9	18	27	35
22-Last 12¢ issue	3	6	9	14	20	26
23-30: 23-Reprint; photo-c	3	6	9	14	19	24
31-50: 36-Weiss-a	2	4	6	11	16	20
51-74: 74-Origin & 1st app. Taurus	2	4	6	9	12	15
75-79,87-97: 90-r/Torres, McWilliams-a/#12; Morrow-c	2	4	6	8	10	12
80-86-(52 pgs.)	2	4	6	9	12	15
Story Digest 1(7/70-Gold Key)-All text/illos.; 148 pp.	5	10	15	34	55	75

(See Mystery Comics Digest No. 2, 5, 8, 11, 14, 17, 20, 23, 26)
NOTE: *Bolle a-51-54, 56, 58, 59. McWilliams a-12, 14, 18, 19, 72, 80, 81, 93. Orlando a-11-15, 21. Reprints: 78, 81-86, 88, 90, 92, 95, 97.*

BORIS KARLOFF THRILLER (TV) (Becomes Boris Karloff Tales...)
Gold Key: Oct, 1962 - No. 2, Jan, 1963 (84 pgs.)

	GD 2.0	VG 4.0	FN 6.0	VF 8.0	VF/NM 9.0	NM- 9.2
1-Photo-c	10	20	30	67	116	165
2	6	12	18	43	69	95

BORIS THE BEAR
Dark Horse Comics/Nicotat Comics #13 on: Aug, 1986 - No. 34, 1990 ($1.50/$1.75/$1.95, B&W)

	GD 2.0	VG 4.0	FN 6.0	VF 8.0	VF/NM 9.0	NM- 9.2
1 , Annual 1 (1988, $2.50)						3.00
1 (2nd printing),2,3,4A,4B,5-12, 14-34: 8-(44 pgs.)						2.50
13-1st Nicotat Comics issue						3.00

BORIS THE BEAR INSTANT COLOR CLASSICS
Dark Horse Comics: July, 1987 - No. 3, 1987 ($1.75/$1.95)

	GD 2.0	VG 4.0	FN 6.0	VF 8.0	VF/NM 9.0	NM- 9.2
1-3						2.50

BORN
Marvel Comics: 2003 - No. 4, 2003 ($3.50, limited series)

	GD 2.0	VG 4.0	FN 6.0	VF 8.0	VF/NM 9.0	NM- 9.2
1-4-Frank Castle (the Punisher) in 1971 Vietnam; Ennis-s/Robertson-a						3.50
HC (2004, $17.99) oversized reprint of series; proposal, layout pages						18.00
Punisher: Born SC (2004, $13.99) r/series; proposal, layout pages						14.00

BORN AGAIN
Spire Christian Comics (Fleming H. Revell Co.): 1978 (39¢)

	GD 2.0	VG 4.0	FN 6.0	VF 8.0	VF/NM 9.0	NM- 9.2
nn-Watergate, Nixon, etc.	2	4	6	8	11	14

BOUNCER, THE (Formerly Green Mask #9)
Fox Features Syndicate: 1944 - No. 14, Jan, 1945

	GD 2.0	VG 4.0	FN 6.0	VF 8.0	VF/NM 9.0	NM- 9.2
nn(1944, #10?)	31	62	93	181	291	400
11 (9/44)-Origin; Rocket Kelly, One Round Hogan app.	23	46	69	135	218	300
12-14: 14-Reprints no # issue	19	38	57	112	176	240

BOUNTY GUNS (See Luke Short's..., Four Color 739)

BOX OFFICE POISON
Antarctic Press: 1996 - No. 21, Sept, 2000 ($2.95, B&W)

	GD 2.0	VG 4.0	FN 6.0	VF 8.0	VF/NM 9.0	NM- 9.2
1-Alex Robinson-s/a in all	1	2	3	4	5	7
2-5						4.00
6-21, ...Kolor Karnival 1 (5/99, $2.99)						3.00
...Super Special 0 (5/97, $4.95)						5.00
Sherman's March: Collected BOP Vol. 1 (9/98, $14.95) r/#0-4						15.00
TPB (2002, $29.95, 608 pgs.) r/entire series						30.00

BOY AND HIS 'BOT, A
Now Comics: Jan, 1987 ($1.95)

	GD 2.0	VG 4.0	FN 6.0	VF 8.0	VF/NM 9.0	NM- 9.2
1-A Holiday Special						3.00

BOY AND THE PIRATES, THE (Movie)
Dell Publishing Co.: No. 1117, Aug, 1960

	GD 2.0	VG 4.0	FN 6.0	VF 8.0	VF/NM 9.0	NM- 9.2
Four Color 1117-Photo-c	6	12	18	43	69	95

BOY COMICS (Captain Battle No. 1 & 2; Boy Illustories No. 43-108) (Stories by Charles Biro) (Also see Squeeks)
Lev Gleason Publ. (Comic House): No. 3, Apr, 1942 - No. 119, Mar, 1956

	GD 2.0	VG 4.0	FN 6.0	VF 8.0	VF/NM 9.0	NM- 9.2
3(No.1)-1st app. & origin Crimebuster, Bombshell & Young Robin Hood; Yankee Longago, Case 1001-1008, Swoop Storm, & Boy Movies begin; 1st app. Iron Jaw; Crimebuster's pet monkey Squeeks begins	306	612	918	2081	3641	5200
4-Hitler, Tojo, Mussolini-c	133	266	399	838	1419	2000
5	90	180	270	567	959	1350
6-Origin Iron Jaw; origin & death of Iron Jaw's son; Little Dynamite begins, ends #39; 1st Iron Jaw-c	300	600	900	2040	3570	5100
7-Flag & Hitler, Tojo, Mussolini-c	100	200	300	630	1065	1500
8-Death of Iron Jaw; Iron Jaw-c	97	194	291	611	1031	1450
9-Iron Jaw-c	87	174	261	548	924	1300
10-Return of Iron Jaw; classic Biro-c; Iron Jaw-c	130	260	390	819	1385	1950
11-Classic Iron Jaw-c	92	184	276	580	978	1375
12,13: 12-Torture-c	56	112	168	353	597	840

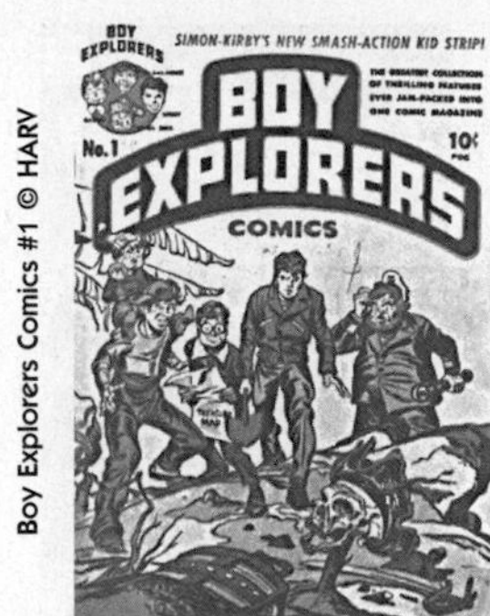

Boy Explorers Comics #1 © HARV

The Boys #14 © Spitfire & Darick Robertson

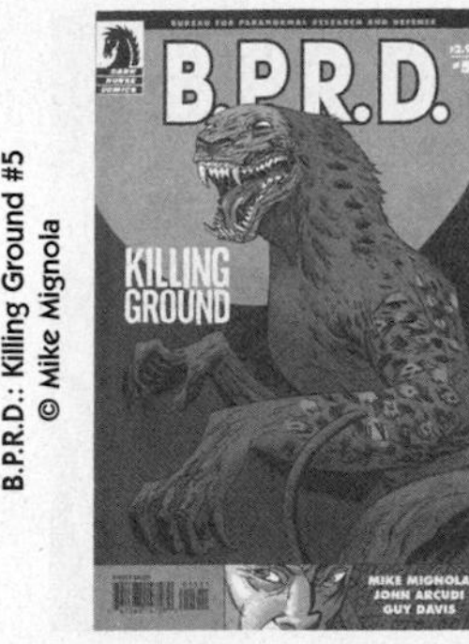

B.P.R.D.: Killing Ground #5 © Mike Mignola

	GD 2.0	VG 4.0	FN 6.0	VF 8.0	VF/NM 9.0	NM- 9.2
14-Iron Jaw-c	65	130	195	410	693	975
15-Death of Iron Jaw	75	150	225	473	799	1125
16,18-20	40	80	120	247	404	560
17-Flag-c	41	82	123	250	413	575
21-29,31,32-(All 68 pgs.). 28-Yankee Longago ends. 32-Swoop Storm & Young Robin Hood end	28	56	84	162	261	360
30-(68 pgs.)-Origin Crimebuster retold	37	74	111	215	345	475
33-40: 34-Crimebuster story(2); suicide-c/story	21	42	63	125	200	275
41-50	18	36	54	103	162	220
51-59: 57-Dilly Duncan begins, ends #71	15	30	45	88	137	105
60-Iron Jaw returns	15	30	45	94	147	200
61-Origin Crimebuster & Iron Jaw retold	18	36	54	105	165	225
62-Death of Iron Jaw explained	17	34	51	100	158	215
63-73: 63-McWilliams-a. 73-Frazetta 1-pg. ad	13	26	39	72	101	130
74-88: 80-1st app. Rocky X of the Rocketeers; becomes "Rocky X" #101; Iron Jaw, Sniffer & the Deadly Dozen in 80-118	10	20	30	58	79	100
89-92-The Claw serial app. in all	11	22	33	60	83	105
93-Claw cameo; Rocky X by Sid Check	10	20	30	58	79	100
94-97,99	10	20	30	56	76	95
98,100: 98-Rocky X by Sid Check	10	20	30	58	79	100
101-107,109,111,119: 101-Rocky X becomes spy strip. 106-Robin Hood app. 119-Last Crimebuster. 111-Crimebuster becomes Chuck Chandler.	9	18	27	52	69	85
108,110,112-118-Kubert-a; 108-Ditko-a	10	20	30	56	76	95

(See Giant Boy Book of Comics)

NOTE: *Boy Movies in 3-5,40,41. Iron Jaw app.-3, 4, 6, 8, 10, 11, 13-15; returns-60-62, 68, 69, 72-79, 81-118.* ***Biro*** *c-all.* ***Briefer*** *a-5, 13, 14, 16-20 among others.* ***Fuje*** *a-55, 18 pgs.* ***Palais*** *a-14, 16, 17, 19, 20 among others.*

BOY COMMANDOS (See Detective #64 & World's Finest Comics #8)
National Periodical Publications: Winter, 1942-43 - No. 36, Nov-Dec, 1949

	GD 2.0	VG 4.0	FN 6.0	VF 8.0	VF/NM 9.0	NM- 9.2
1-Origin Liberty Belle; The Sandman & The Newsboy Legion x-over in Boy Commandos, S&K-a, 48 pgs.; S&K cameo? (classic WWII-c)	506	1012	1518	3643	6372	9100
2-Last Liberty Belle; Hitler-c; S&K-a, 46 pgs.; WWII-c	233	466	699	1468	2484	3500
3-S&K-a, 45 pgs.; WWII-c	133	266	399	838	1419	2000
4-6: All WWII-c. 6-S&K-a	83	166	249	523	887	1250
7-10: All WWII-c	53	106	159	330	553	775
11-13: All WWII-c. 11-Infinity-c	40	80	120	235	380	525
14,16,18-19-All have S&K-a. 18-2nd Crazy Quilt-c	31	62	93	181	291	400
15-1st app. Crazy Quilt, their arch nemesis	40	80	120	244	397	550
17,20-Sci/fi-c/stories	38	76	114	226	363	500
21,22,25: 22-3rd Crazy Quilt-c; Judy Canova x-over	25	50	75	147	236	325
23-S&K-c/a(all)	34	68	102	198	319	440
24-1st costumed superhero satire-c (11-12/47).	30	60	90	174	280	385
26-Flying Saucer story (3-4/48)-4th of this theme; see The Spirit 9/28/47(1st), Shadow Comics V7#10 (2nd, 1/48) & Captain Midnight #60 (3rd, 2/48)	30	60	90	176	283	390
27,28,30: 30-Cleveland Indians story	24	48	72	143	229	315
29-S&K story (1)	26	52	78	152	244	335
31-35: 32-Dale Evans app. on-c & in story. 33-Last Crazy Quilt-c. 34-Intro. Wolf, their mascot	22	44	66	127	204	280
36-Intro The Atomobile c/sci-fi story (Scarce)	40	80	120	244	397	550

NOTE: *Most issues signed by* ***Simon & Kirby*** *are not by them.* ***S&K*** *c-1-9, 13, 14, 17, 21, 23, 24, 30-32.* ***Feller*** *c-30.*

BOY COMMANDOS
National Per. Publ.: Sept-Oct, 1973 - No. 2, Nov-Dec, 1973 (G.A. S&K reprints)

	GD 2.0	VG 4.0	FN 6.0	VF 8.0	VF/NM 9.0	NM- 9.2
1,2: 1-Reprints story from Boy Commandos #1 plus-c & Detective #66 by S&K. 2-Infantino/Orlando-c	2	4	6	9	13	16

BOY COMMANDOS COMICS
DC Comics: Sept/Oct. 1942

1-Ashcan comic, not distributed to newsstands, only for in-house use. Cover art is the splash page from the Boy Commandos story in Detective Comics #68 interior is from an unidentified issue of Detective Comics (no known sales)

nn - (9-10/42) Ashcan comic, not distributed to newsstands, only for in-house use. Cover art is the splash page from the Boy Commandos story in Detective Comics #68 interior is from Detective Comics #68 (no known sales)

BOY COWBOY (Also see Amazing Adventures & Science Comics)
Ziff-Davis Publ. Co.: 1950 (8 pgs. in color)

	GD 2.0	VG 4.0	FN 6.0	VF 8.0	VF/NM 9.0	NM- 9.2
nn-Sent to subscribers of Ziff-Davis mags. & ordered through mail for 10¢; used to test market for Kid Cowboy	27	54	81	158	254	350

BOY DETECTIVE
Avon Periodicals: May-June, 1951 - No. 4, May, 1952

	GD 2.0	VG 4.0	FN 6.0	VF 8.0	VF/NM 9.0	NM- 9.2
1	20	40	60	115	183	250
2-4: 3,4-Kinstler-c	14	28	42	80	115	150

BOY EXPLORERS COMICS (Terry and The Pirates No. 3 on)
Family Comics (Harvey Publ.): May-June, 1946 - No. 2, Sept-Oct, 1946

	GD 2.0	VG 4.0	FN 6.0	VF 8.0	VF/NM 9.0	NM- 9.2
1-Intro The Explorers, Duke of Broadway, Calamity Jane & Danny Dixon...Cadet; S&K-c/a, 24 pgs.	65	130	195	410	693	975
2-(Scarce)-Small size (5-1/2x8-1/2"; B&W; 32 pgs.) Distributed to mail subscribers only; S&K-a	120	240	360	756	1278	1800

(Also see All New No. 15, Flash Gordon No. 5, and Stuntman No. 3)

BOY ILLUSTORIES (See Boy Comics)

BOY LOVES GIRL (Boy Meets Girl No. 1-24)
Lev Gleason Publications: No. 25, July, 1952 - No. 57, June, 1956

	GD 2.0	VG 4.0	FN 6.0	VF 8.0	VF/NM 9.0	NM- 9.2
25(#1)	10	20	30	56	70	85
26,27,29-33: 30-33-Serial, 'Loves of My Life	8	16	24	40	50	60
34-42: 39-Lingerie panels	7	14	21	37	46	55
28-Drug propaganda story	8	16	24	40	50	60
43 Toth-a	8	16	24	42	54	65
44-50: 47-Toth-a? 50-Last pre-code (2/55)	7	14	21	35	43	50
51-57: 57-Ann Brewster-a	6	12	18	28	34	40

BOY MEETS GIRL (Boy Loves Girl No. 25 on)
Lev Gleason Publications: Feb, 1950 - No. 24, June, 1952 (No. 1-17: 52 pgs.)

	GD 2.0	VG 4.0	FN 6.0	VF 8.0	VF/NM 9.0	NM- 9.2
1-Guardineer-a	15	30	45	84	127	170
2	9	18	27	52	69	85
3-10	9	18	27	47	61	75
11-24	8	16	24	44	57	70

NOTE: ***Briefer*** *a-24.* ***Fuje*** *c-3,7. Painted-c 1-17. Photo-c 19-21, 23.*

BOYS, THE
DC Comics (WildStorm)/Dynamite Ent. #7 on: Oct, 2006 - Present ($2.99, mature)

	GD 2.0	VG 4.0	FN 6.0	VF 8.0	VF/NM 9.0	NM- 9.2
1-Garth Ennis-s/Darick Robertson-a						6.00
2-6						4.00
7-22-(Dynamite Ent.,). 19-Origin of the Homelander						3.00
... Volume 1: The Name of the Game TPB (2007, $14.99) r/#1-6; intro. by Simon Pegg						15.00
... Volume 2: Get Some TPB (2008, $19.99) r/#7-14						20.00

BOYS' AND GIRLS' MARCH OF COMICS (See March of Comics)

BOYS' RANCH (Also see Western Tales & Witches' Western Tales)
Harvey Publ.: Oct, 1950 - No. 6, Aug, 1951 (No.1-3, 52 pgs.; No. 4-6, 36 pgs.)

	GD 2.0	VG 4.0	FN 6.0	VF 8.0	VF/NM 9.0	NM- 9.2
1-S&K-c/a(3)	60	120	180	378	639	900
2-S&K-c/a(3)	41	82	123	250	413	575
3-S&K-c/a(2); Meskin-a	40	80	120	235	380	525
4-S&K-c/a, 5 pgs.	35	70	105	203	327	450
5,6-S&K-c, splashes & centerspread only; Meskin-a	20	40	60	115	183	250

BOZO (Larry Harmon's Bozo, the World's Most Famous Clown)
Innovation Publishing: 1992 ($6.95, 68 pgs.)

	GD 2.0	VG 4.0	FN 6.0	VF 8.0	VF/NM 9.0	NM- 9.2
1-Reprints Four Color #285(#1)	1	2	3	4	5	7

BOZO THE CLOWN (TV) (Bozo No. 7 on)
Dell Publishing Co.: July, 1950 - No. 4, Oct-Dec, 1963

	GD 2.0	VG 4.0	FN 6.0	VF 8.0	VF/NM 9.0	NM- 9.2
Four Color 285(#1)	18	36	54	130	240	350
2(7-9/51)-7(10-12/52)	11	22	33	75	133	190
Four Color 464,508,551,594(10/54)	9	18	27	65	113	160
1(nn, 5-7/62)	7	14	21	50	83	115
2 - 4(1963)	6	12	18	39	62	85

BOZZ CHRONICLES, THE
Marvel Comics (Epic Comics): Dec, 1985 - No. 6, 1986 (Lim. series, mature)

	GD 2.0	VG 4.0	FN 6.0	VF 8.0	VF/NM 9.0	NM- 9.2
1-6-Logan/Wolverine look alike in 19th century. 1,3,5-Blevins-a						3.00

B.P.R.D. (Bureau of Paranormal Research and Defense) (Also see Hellboy titles)
Dark Horse Comics: (one-shots)

	GD 2.0	VG 4.0	FN 6.0	VF 8.0	VF/NM 9.0	NM- 9.2
... Dark Waters (7/03, $2.99) Guy Davis-c/a; Augustyn-s						3.00
... Night Train (9/03, $2.99) Johns & Kolins-s; Kolins & Stewart-a						3.00
... The Ectoplasmic Man (6/08, $2.99) Stenbeck-a/Mignola-c; origin of Johann Kraus						3.00
... There's Something Under My Bed (11/03, $2.99) Pollina-a/c						3.00
... The Soul of Venice (5/03, $2.99) Oeming-a/c; Gunter & Oeming-s						3.00
... The Soul of Venice and Other Stories TPB (8/04, $17.95) r/one-shots & new story by Mignola and Cam Stewart; sketch pages by various						18.00
... War on Frogs (6/08, $2.99) Trimpe-a/Mignola-c; Abe Sapien app.						3.00

B.P.R.D.: GARDEN OF SOULS
Dark Horse Comics: Mar, 2007 - No. 5, July, 2007 ($2.99, limited series)

	GD 2.0	VG 4.0	FN 6.0	VF 8.0	VF/NM 9.0	NM- 9.2
1-5-Mignola & Arcudi-s/Guy Davis-a/Mignola-c						3.00

B.P.R.D.: HOLLOW EARTH (Mike Mignola's...)

Brats Bizarre #1 © MAR

Brave and the Bold #14 © DC

Brave and the Bold #25 © DC

	GD	VG	FN	VF	VF/NM	NM-
	2.0	4.0	6.0	8.0	9.0	9.2

Dark Horse Comics: Jan, 2002 - No. 3, June, 2002 ($2.99, limited series)
1-3-Mignola, Golden & Sniegoski-s/Sook-a/Mignola-c; Hellboy and Abe Sapien app. 3.00
... and Other Stories TPB (1/03; 7/04, $17.95) r/#1-3, Hellboy: Box Full of Evil, Abe Sapien: Drums of the Dead, and Dark Horse Extra; plus sketch pages 18.00

B.P.R.D.: KILLING GROUND
Dark Horse Comics: Aug, 2007 - No. 5, Dec, 2007 ($2.99, limited series)
1-5-Mignola & Arcudi-s/Guy Davis-a/c 3.00

B.P.R.D.: 1946
Dark Horse Comics: Jan, 2008 - No. 5, May, 2008 ($2.99, limited series)
1-5-Mignola & Dysart-s/Azaceta-a; Mignola/c 3.00

B.P.R.D.: PLAGUE OF FROGS
Dark Horse Comics: Mar, 2004 - No. 5, July, 2004 ($2.99, limited series)
1-5-Mignola-s/Guy Davis-c/a 3.00
TPB (1/05, $17.95) r/series; sketchbook pages & afterword by Davis & Mignola 18.00

B.P.R.D.: THE BLACK FLAME
Dark Horse Comics: Sept, 2005 - No. 6, Jan, 2006 ($2.99, limited series)
1-6-Mignola & Arcudi-s/Guy Davis-a/ Mignola-c 3.00
TPB (7/06, $17.95) r/series; sketchbook pages & afterword by Davis & Mignola 18.00

B.P.R.D.: THE DEAD
Dark Horse Comics: Nov, 2004 - No. 5, Mar, 2005 ($2.99, limited series)
1-5-Mignola-s/Guy Davis-c/a 3.00

B.P.R.D.: THE UNIVERSAL MACHINE
Dark Horse Comics: Apr, 2006 - No. 5, Aug, 2006 ($2.99, limited series)
1-5-Mignola & Arcudi-s/Guy Davis-a/Mignola-c. 5-Mignola-a (5 pgs.) 3.00
TPB (1/07, $17.95) r/series; sketchbook pages by Davis; Mignola afterword 18.00

B.P.R.D.: THE WARNING
Dark Horse Comics: July, 2008 - No. 5, ($2.99, limited series)
1-3-Mignola & Arcudi-s/Guy Davis-c/a 3.00

BRADLEYS, THE (Also see Hate)
Fantagraphics Books: Apr, 1999 - No. 6, Jan, 2000 ($2.95, B&W, limited series)
1-6-Reprints Peter Bagge's-s/a 3.00

BRADY BUNCH, THE (TV)(See Kite Fun Book and Binky #78)
Dell Publishing Co.: Feb, 1970 - No. 2, May, 1970
1 11 22 33 75 133 190
2 8 16 24 54 90 125

BRAIN, THE
Sussex Publ. Co./Magazine Enterprises: Sept, 1956 - No. 7, 1958
1-Dan DeCarlo-a in all including reprints 12 24 36 67 94 120
2,3 8 16 24 40 50 60
4-7 4 8 12 24 37 50
I.W. Reprints #1-4,8-10('63),14: 2-Reprints Sussex #2 with new cover added 2 4 6 9 13 16
Super Reprint #17,18(nd) 2 4 6 9 13 16

BRAINBANX
DC Comics (Helix): Mar, 1997 - No. 6, Aug, 1997 ($2.50, limited series)
1-6: Elaine Lee-s/Temujin-a 2.50

BRAIN BOY
Dell Publishing Co.: Apr-June, 1962 - No. 6, Sept-Nov, 1963 (Painted c-#1-6)
Four Color 1330(#1)-Gil Kane-a; origin 11 22 33 79 140 200
2(7-9/62),3-6: 4-Origin retold 7 14 21 49 80 110

BRAM STOKER'S BURIAL OF THE RATS (Movie)
Roger Corman's Cosmic Comics: Apr, 1995 - No.3, June, 1995 ($2.50)
1-3: Adaptation of film; Jerry Prosser scripts 2.50

BRAM STOKER'S DRACULA (Movie)(Also see Dracula: Vlad the Impaler)
Topps Comics: Oct, 1992 - No. 4, Jan, 1993 ($2.95, limited series, polybagged)
1-(1st & 2nd printing)-Adaptation of film begins; Mignola-c/a in all; 4 trading cards & poster; photo scenes of movie 3.00
1-Crimson foil edition (limited to 500) 8.00
2-4: 2-Bound-in poster & cards. 4 trading cards in both. 3-Contains coupon to win 1 of 500 crimson foil-c edition of #1. 4-Contains coupon to win 1 of 500 uncut sheets of all 16 trading cards 3.00

BRAND ECHH (See Not Brand Echh)

BRAND OF EMPIRE (See Luke Short's...Four Color 771)

BRASS
Image Comics (WildStorm Productions): Aug, 1996 - No. 3, May, 1997 ($2.50, lim. series)
1-($4.50) Folio Ed.; oversized 4.50
1-3: Wiesenfeld-s/Bennett-a. 3-Grunge & Roxy(Gen 13) cameo 2.50

BRASS
DC Comics (WildStorm): Aug, 2000 - No. 6, Jan, 2001 ($2.50, limited series)
1-6-Arcudi-s 2.50

BRATH
CrossGeneration Comics: Feb, 2003 - No. 14, June, 2004 ($2.95)
Prequel-Dixon-s/Di Vito-a 3.00
1-14: 1-(3/03)-Dixon-s/Di Vito-a 3.00
Vol. 1: Hammer of Vengeance (2003, $9.95) Digest-sized reprint of Prequel & #1-6 10.00

BRATPACK/MAXIMORTAL SUPER SPECIAL
King Hell Press: 1996 ($2.95, B&W, limited series)
1,2: Veitch-s/a 3.00

BRATS BIZARRE
Marvel Comics (Epic/Heavy Hitters): 1994 - No. 4, 1994 ($2.50, limited series)
1-4: All w/bound-in trading cards 2.50

BRAVADOS, THE (See Wild Western Action)
Skywald Publ. Corp.: Aug, 1971 (52 pgs., one-shot)
1-Red Mask, The Durango Kid, Billy Nevada-r; Bolle-a; 3-D effect story 3 6 9 14 19 24

BRAVE AND THE BOLD, THE (See Best Of... & Super DC Giant) (Replaced by Batman & The Outsiders)
National Periodical Publ./DC Comics: Aug-Sept, 1955 - No. 200, July, 1983
1-Viking Prince by Kubert, Silent Knight, Golden Gladiator begin; part Kubert-c 272 544 816 2380 4590 6800
2 113 226 339 961 1831 2700
3,4 59 118 177 502 964 1425
5-Robin Hood begins (4-5/56, 1st DC app.), ends #15; see Robin Hood Tales #7 61 122 183 519 997 1475
6-10: 6-Robin Hood by Kubert; last Golden Gladiator app.; Silent Knight; no Viking Prince. 8-1st S.A. issue 44 88 132 352 664 975
11-22,24: 12,14-Robin Hood-c. 18,21-23-Grey tone-c. 22-Last Silent Knight. 24-Last Viking Prince by Kubert (2nd solo book) 36 72 108 277 514 750
23-Viking Prince origin by Kubert; 1st B&B single theme issue & 1st Viking Prince solo book 44 88 132 352 664 975
25-1st app. Suicide Squad (8-9/59) 42 84 126 336 631 925
26,27-Suicide Squad 30 60 90 217 401 585
28-(2-3/60)-Justice League intro./1st app.; origin/1st app. Snapper Carr 500 1000 1500 4600 8800 13,000
29-Justice League (4-5/60)-2nd app. battle the Weapons Master; robot-c 184 368 552 1610 3105 4600
30-Justice League (6-7/60)-3rd app.; vs. Amazo 150 300 450 1275 2438 3600
31-1st app. Cave Carson (8-9/60); scarce in high grade; 1st try-out series 39 78 117 300 563 825
32,33-Cave Carson 23 46 69 167 309 450
34-Origin/1st app. Silver-Age Hawkman, Hawkgirl & Byth (2-3/61); Gardner Fox story, Kubert-c/a ; 1st S.A. Hawkman tryout series; 2nd in #42-44; both series predate Hawkman #1 (4-5/64) 176 352 528 1540 2970 4400
35-Hawkman by Kubert (4-5/61)-2nd app. 43 86 129 344 647 950
36-Hawkman by Kubert; origin & 1st app. Shadow Thief (6-7/61)-3rd app. 39 78 117 300 563 825
37-Suicide Squad (2nd tryout series) 21 42 63 152 281 410
38,39-Suicide Squad. 38-Last 10¢ issue 18 36 54 130 240 350
40,41-Cave Carson Inside Earth (2nd try-out series). 40-Kubert-a. 41-Meskin-a 14 28 42 104 187 270
42-Hawkman by Kubert (2nd tryout series); Hawkman earns helmet wings; Byth app. 26 52 78 192 359 525
43-Hawkman by Kubert; more detailed origin 31 62 93 239 445 650
44-Hawkman by Kubert; grey-tone-c 25 50 75 185 343 500
45-49-Strange Sports Stories by Infantino 9 18 27 65 113 160
50-The Green Arrow & Manhunter From Mars (10-11/63); 1st Manhunter x-over outside of Detective Comics (pre-dates House of Mystery #143); team-ups begin 18 36 54 128 237 345
51-Aquaman & Hawkman (12-1/63-64); pre-dates Hawkman #1 21 42 63 152 281 410
52-(2-3/64)-3 Battle Stars; Sgt. Rock, Haunted Tank, Johnny Cloud, & Mlle. Marie team-up for 1st time by Kubert (c/a) 20 40 60 148 274 400
53-Atom & The Flash by Toth 9 18 27 65 113 160
54-Kid Flash, Robin & Aqualad; 1st app./origin Teen Titans (6-7/64)

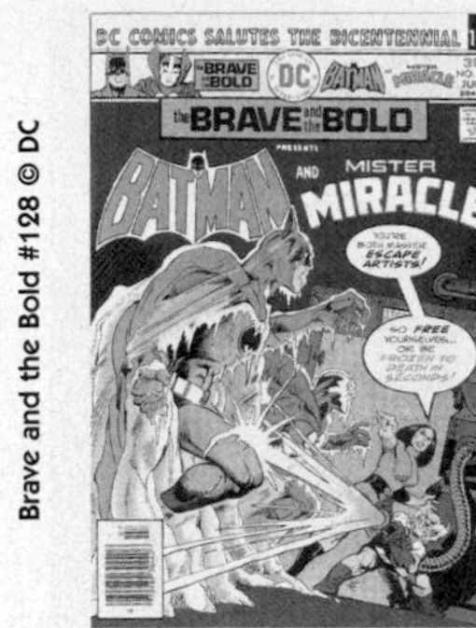

Brave and the Bold #128 © DC

Brave and the Bold #184 © DC

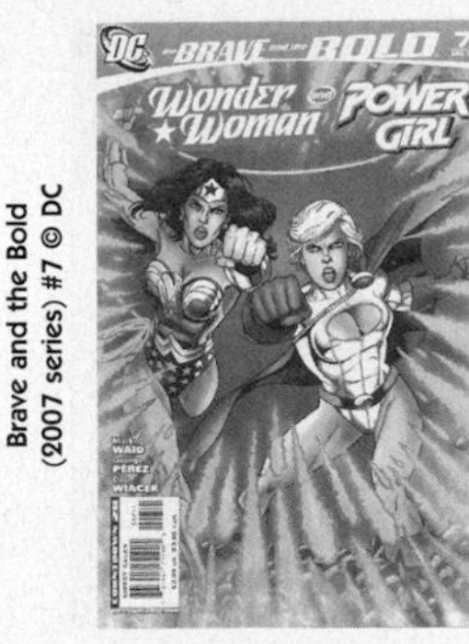

Brave and the Bold (2007 series) #7 © DC

GD VG FN VF VF/NM NM-
2.0 4.0 6.0 8.0 9.0 9.2

30 60 90 229 427 625
55-Metal Men & The Atom 8 16 24 58 97 135
56-The Flash & Manhunter From Mars 8 16 24 58 97 135
57-Origin & 1st app. Metamorpho (12-1/64-65) 17 34 51 120 223 325
58-2nd app. Metamorpho by Fradon 10 20 30 67 116 165
59-Batman & Green Lantern; 1st Batman team-up in Brave and the Bold
12 24 36 86 153 220
60-Teen Titans (2nd app.)-1st app. new Wonder Girl (Donna Troy), who joins Titans (6-7/65) 14 28 42 102 181 260
61-Origin Starman & Black Canary by Anderson 13 26 39 90 160 230
62-Origin Starman & Black Canary cont'd. 62-1st S.A. app. Wildcat (10-11/65); 1st S.A. app. of G.A. Huntress (W.W. villain) 11 22 33 79 140 200
63-Supergirl & Wonder Woman 8 16 24 56 93 130
64-Batman Versus Eclipso (see H.O.S. #61) 8 16 24 58 97 135
65-Flash & Doom Patrol (4-5/66) 6 12 18 39 62 85
66-Metamorpho & Metal Men (6-7/66) 6 12 18 39 62 85
67-Batman & The Flash by Infantino; Batman team-ups begin, end #200 (8-9/66)
7 14 21 47 76 105
68-Batman/Metamorpho/Joker/Riddler/Penguin-c/story; Batman as Bat-Hulk (Hulk parody)
9 18 27 60 100 140
69-Batman & Green Lantern 6 12 18 41 66 90
70-Batman & Hawkman; Craig-a(p) 6 12 18 41 66 90
71-Batman & Green Arrow 6 12 18 41 66 90
72-Spectre & Flash (6-7/67); 4th app. The Spectre; predates Spectre #1
6 12 18 43 69 95
73-Aquaman & The Atom 6 12 18 39 62 85
74-Batman & Metal Men 6 12 18 39 62 85
75-Batman & The Spectre (12-1/67-68); 6th app. Spectre; came out between Spectre #1 & #2 6 12 18 41 66 90
76-Batman & Plastic Man (2-3/68); came out between Plastic Man #8 & #9
6 12 18 39 62 85
77-Batman & The Atom 6 12 18 39 62 85
78-Batman, Wonder Woman & Batgirl 6 12 18 39 62 85
79-Batman & Deadman by Neal Adams (8-9/68); early Deadman app.
9 18 27 60 100 140
80-Batman & Creeper (10-11/68); N. Adams-a; early app. The Creeper; came out between Creeper #3 & #4 7 14 21 50 83 115
81-Batman & Flash; N. Adams-a 7 14 21 50 83 115
82-Batman & Aquaman; N. Adams-a; origin Ocean Master retold (2-3/69)
7 14 21 50 83 115
83-Batman & Teen Titans; N. Adams-a (4-5/69) 7 14 21 50 83 115
84-Batman (G.A., 1st S.A. app.) & Sgt. Rock; N. Adams-a; last 12¢ issue (6-7/69)
7 14 21 50 83 115
85-Batman & Green Arrow; 1st new costume for Green Arrow by Neal Adams (8-9/69)
8 16 24 52 86 120
86-Batman & Deadman (10-11/69); N. Adams-a; story concludes from Strange Adventures #216 (1-2/69) 7 14 21 50 83 115
87-Batman & Wonder Woman 4 8 12 26 41 55
88-Batman & Wildcat 4 8 12 26 41 55
89-Batman & Phantom Stranger (4-5/70); early Phantom Stranger app. (came out between Phantom Stranger #6 & 7 4 8 12 24 37 50
90-Batman & Adam Strange 4 8 12 24 37 50
91-Batman & Black Canary (8-9/70) 4 8 12 24 37 50
92-Batman; intro the Bat Squad 4 8 12 24 37 50
93-Batman-House of Mystery; N. Adams-a 6 12 18 43 69 95
94-Batman-Teen Titans 4 8 12 22 34 45
95-Batman & Plastic Man 3 6 9 20 30 40
96-Batman & Sgt. Rock; last 15¢ issue 3 6 9 21 32 42
97-Batman & Wildcat; 52 pg. issues begin, end #102; reprints origin & 1st app. Deadman from Strange Advs. #205 3 6 9 21 32 42
98-Batman & Phantom Stranger; 1st Jim Aparo Batman-a?
3 6 9 21 32 42
99-Batman & Flash 3 6 9 21 32 42
100-(2-3/72, 25¢, 52 pgs.)-Batman-Green Lantern-Green Arrow-Black Canary-Robin; Deadman-r by Adams/Str. Advs. #210 6 12 18 39 62 85
101-Batman & Metamorpho; Kubert Viking Prince 3 6 9 20 30 40
102-Batman-Teen Titans; N. Adams-a(p) 5 10 15 30 48 65
103-107,109,110: Batman team-ups: 103-Metal Men. 104-Deadman. 105-Wonder Woman. 106-Green Arrow. 107-Black Canary. 109-Demon. 110-Wildcat
3 6 9 14 19 24
108-Sgt. Rock 3 6 9 14 20 26
111-Batman/Joker-c/story 3 6 9 18 27 35
112-117: All 100 pgs.; Batman team-ups: 112-Mr. Miracle. 113-Metal Men; reprints origin/1st Hawkman from Brave and the Bold #34; r/origin Multi-Man/Challengers #14. 114-Aquaman. 115-Atom; r/origin Viking Prince from #23; r/Dr. Fate/Hourman/Solomon Grundy/Green Lantern from Showcase #55. 116-Spectre. 117-Sgt. Rock; last 100 pg. issue
5 10 15 30 48 65
118-Batman/Wildcat/Joker-c/story 3 6 9 17 25 32
119,121-123,125-128,132-140: Batman team-ups: 119-Man-Bat. 121-Metal Men. 122-Swamp Thing. 123-Plastic Man/Metamorpho. 125-Flash. 126-Aquaman. 127-Wildcat. 128-Mr. Miracle. 132-Kung-Fu Fighter. 133-Deadman. 134-Green Lantern. 135-Metal Men. 136-Metal Men/Green Arrow. 137-Demon. 138-Mr. Miracle. 139-Hawkman. 140-Wonder Woman 2 4 6 8 10 12
120-Kamandi (68 pgs.) 3 6 9 14 19 24
124-Sgt. Rock 2 4 6 9 12 15
129,130-Batman/Green Arrow/Atom parts 1 & 2; Joker & Two Face-c/stories
2 4 6 13 18 22
131-Batman & Wonder Woman vs. Catwoman-c/sty 2 4 6 10 14 18
141-Batman/Black Canary vs. Joker-c/story 2 4 6 13 18 22
142-160: Batman team-ups: 142-Aquaman. 143-Creeper; origin Human Target (44 pgs.). 144-Green Arrow; origin Human Target part 2 (44 pgs.). 145-Phantom Stranger. 146-G.A. Batman/Unknown Soldier. 147-Supergirl. 148-Plastic Man; X-Mas-c. 149-Teen Titans. 150-Anniversary issue; Superman. 151-Flash. 152-Atom. 153-Red Tornado. 154-Metamorpho. 155-Green Lantern. 156-Dr. Fate. 157-Batman vs. Kamandi (ties into Kamandi #59). 158-Wonder Woman. 159-Ra's Al Ghul. 160-Supergirl.
1 3 4 6 8 10
145(11/79)-147,150-159,165(8/80)-(Whitman variants; low print run, none show issue # on cover) 2 4 6 9 13 16
161-181,183-190,192-195,198,199: Batman team-ups: 161-Adam Strange. 162-G.A. Batman/Sgt. Rock. 163-Black Lightning. 164-Hawkman. 165-Man-Bat. 166-Black Canary; Nemesis (intro) back-up story begins, ends #192; Penguin-c/story. 167-G.A. Batman/Blackhawk; origin Nemesis. 168-Green Arrow. 169-Zatanna. 170-Nemesis. 171-Scalphunter. 172-Firestorm. 173-Guardians of the Universe. 174-Green Lantern. 175-Lois Lane. 176-Swamp Thing. 177-Elongated Man. 178-Creeper. 179-Legion. 180-Spectre. 181-Hawk & Dove. 183-Riddler. 184-Huntress & Earth II Batman. 185-Green Arrow. 186-Hawkman. 187-Metal Men. 188,189-Rose & the Thorn. 190-Adam Strange. 192-Superboy vs. Mr. I.Q. 194-Flash. 195-I...Vampire. 198-Karate Kid. 199-Batman vs. The Spectre 6.00
182-G.A. Robin; G.A. Starman app.; 1st modern app. G.A. Batwoman
2 4 6 8 10 12
191-Batman/Joker-c/story; Nemesis app. 2 4 6 8 11 14
196-Ragman; origin Ragman retold. 1 2 3 5 6 8
197-Catwoman; Earth II Batman & Catwoman marry; 2nd modern app. of G.A. Batwoman; Scarecrow story in Golden Age style 2 4 6 9 12 15
200-Double-sized (64 pgs.); printed on Mando paper; Earth One & Earth Two Batman app. in separate stories; intro/1st app. Batman & The Outsiders
2 4 6 8 10 12

NOTE: ***Neal Adams*** *a-79-86, 93, 100r, 102; c-75, 76, 79-86, 88-90, 93, 95, 99, 100r.* ***M. Anderson*** *a-115r; c-72i, 96i.* ***Andru/Esposito*** *c-25-27.* ***Aparo*** *a-98, 100-102, 104-125, 126i, 127-136, 138-145, 147, 148i, 149-152, 154, 155, 157-162, 168-170, 173-178, 180-182, 184, 186i-189i, 191i-193i, 195, 196, 200; c-105-109, 111-136, 137i, 138-175, 177, 180-184, 186-200.* ***Austin*** *a-166i.* ***Bernard Baily*** *c-32, 33, 58.* ***Buckler*** *a-185, 186p; c-137, 178p, 185p, 186p.* ***Giordano*** *a-143, 144.* ***Infantino*** *a-67p, 72p, 97r, 98r, 115r, 172p, 183p, 190p, 194p; c-45-49, 67p, 69p, 70p, 72p, 96p, 98r.* ***Kaluta*** *c-176.* ***Kane*** *a-115r; c-59, 64.* ***Kubert*** *&/or* ***Heath*** *a-1-24; reprints-101, 113, 115, 117.* ***Kubert*** *a-99r; c-22-24, 34-36, 40, 42-44, 52.* ***Mooney*** *a-114r.* ***Mortimer*** *a-64, 69.* ***Newton*** *a-153p, 156p, 165p.* ***Irv Novick*** *c-1(part), 2-21.* ***Fred Ray*** *a-78r.* ***Roussos*** *a-50, 76i, 114r.* ***Staton*** *148p. 52 pgs.-97, 100; 68 pgs.-120; 100 pgs.-112-117.*

BRAVE AND THE BOLD, THE
DC Comics: Dec, 1991 - No. 6, June, 1992 ($1.75, limited series)

1-6: Green Arrow, The Butcher, The Question in all; Grell scripts in all 2.50
NOTE: ***Grell*** *c-3, 4-6.*

BRAVE AND THE BOLD, THE
DC Comics: Apr, 2007 - Present ($2.99)

1-Batman & Green Lantern team-up; Roulette app.; Waid-c/Peréz-c/a; 2 covers 4.00
2-15: 2-GL & Supergirl. 3-Batman & Blue Beetle vs. Fatal Five; Lobo app. 4-6-LSH app. 12-Megistus conclusion; Ordway-a. 14-Kolins-a 3.00
...: The Lords of Luck HC (2007, $24.99, dustjacket) r/#1-6 with Waid intro & annotations 25.00

BRAVE AND THE BOLD ANNUAL NO. 1 1969 ISSUE, THE
DC Comics: 2001 ($5.95, one-shot)

1-Reprints silver age team-ups in 1960s-style 80 pg. Giant format 6.00

BRAVE AND THE BOLD SPECIAL, THE (See DC Special Series No. 8)

BRAVE EAGLE (TV)
Dell Publishing Co.: No. 705, June, 1956 - No. 929, July, 1958

Four Color 705 (#1)-Photo-c 6 12 18 43 69 95
Four Color 770, 816, 879 (2/58), 929-All photo-c 4 8 12 26 41 55

BRAVE NEW WORLD (See DCU Brave New World)

BRAVE OLD WORLD (V2K)
DC Comics (Vertigo): Feb, 2000 - No. 4, May, 2000 ($2.50, mini-series)

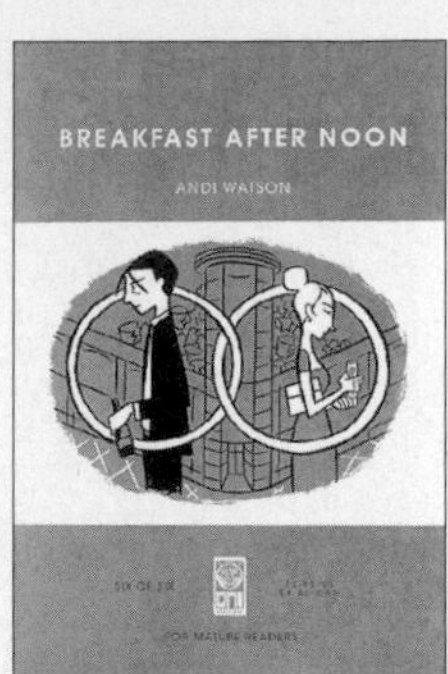

Breakfast After Noon #6 © Andi Watson

Brenda Starr #13 (#1) © SUPR

Brigade #2 © Rob Liefeld

	GD 2.0	VG 4.0	FN 6.0	VF 8.0	VF/NM 9.0	NM- 9.2

1-4-Messner-Loeb-s/Guy Davis & Phil Hester-a 2.50

BRAVE ONE, THE (Movie)
Dell Publishing Co.: No. 773, Mar, 1957

	GD	VG	FN	VF	VF/NM	NM-
Four Color 773-Photo-c	5	10	15	34	55	75

BRAVURA
Malibu Comics (Bravura): 1995 (mail-in offer)

0-wraparound holographic-c; short stories and promo pin-ups of Chaykin's Power & Glory, Gil Kane's & Steven Grant's Edge, Starlin's Breed, & Simonson's Star Slammers 5.00
1 1/2 7.00

BREACH
DC Comics: Mar, 2005 - No. 11, Jan, 2006 ($2.95/$2.50)

1-11: 1-Marcos Martin-a/Bob Harras-s; origin. 4-JLA-c/app. 3.00

BREAKDOWN
Devil's Due Publ.: Oct, 2004 - No. 6, Apr, 2005 ($2.95)

1-6: 1-Two covers by Dave Ross and Leinil Yu; Dixon-s/Ross-a 3.00

BREAKFAST AFTER NOON
Oni Press: May, 2000 - No. 6, Jan, 2001($2.95, B&W, limited series)

1-6-Andi Watson-s/a 3.00
TPB (2001, $19.95) r/series 20.00

BREAKNECK BLVD.
MotioN Comics/Slave Labor Graphics Vol. 2: No. 0, Feb, 1994 - No. 2, Nov, 1994; Vol. 2#1, Jul, 1995 - #6, Dec., 1996 ($2.50/$2.95, B&W)

0-2, V2#1-6: 0-Perez/Giordano-c 3.00

BREAK-THRU (Also see Exiles V1#4)
Malibu Comics (Ultraverse): Dec, 1993 - No. 2, Jan, 1994 ($2.50, 44 pgs.)

1,2-Perez-c/a(p); has x-overs in Ultraverse titles 2.50

BREATHTAKER
DC Comics: 1990 - No. 4, 1990 ($4.95, 52 pgs., prestige format, mature)

Book 1-4: Mark Wheatley-painted-c/a & scripts; Marc Hempel-a 5.00
TPB (1994, $14.95) r/#1-4; intro by Neil Gaiman 15.00

'BREED
Malibu Comics (Bravura): Jan, 1994 - No. 6, 1994 ($2.50, limited series)

1-6: 1-(48 pgs.)-Origin/1st app. of 'Breed by Starlin; contains Bravura stamps; spot varnish-c. 2-5-contains Bravura stamps. 6-Death of Rachel 3.00
...:Book of Genesis (1994, $12.95)-reprints #1-6 13.00

'BREED II
Malibu Comics (Bravura): Nov, 1994 - No. 6, Apr, 1995 ($2.95, limited series)

1-6: Starlin-c/a/scripts in all. 1-Gold edition 3.00

BREEZE LAWSON, SKY SHERIFF (See Sky Sheriff)

BRENDA LEE'S LIFE STORY
Dell Publishing Co.: July-Sept., 1962

	GD	VG	FN	VF	VF/NM	NM-
01-078-209	8	16	24	52	86	120

BRENDA STARR (Also see All Great)
Four Star Comics Corp./Superior Comics Ltd.: No. 13, 9/47; No. 14, 3/48; V2#3, 6/48 - V2#12, 12/49

	GD	VG	FN	VF	VF/NM	NM-
V1#13-By Dale Messick	83	166	249	523	887	1250
14-Classic Kamen bondage-c	133	266	399	838	1419	2000
V2#3-Baker-a?	67	134	201	422	711	1000
4-Used in **SOTI**, pg. 21; Kamen-c	82	164	246	517	871	1225
5-10	66	132	198	416	701	985
11,12 (Scarce)	68	136	204	428	727	1025

NOTE: *Newspaper reprints plus original material through #6. All original #7 on.*

BRENDA STARR (...Reporter)(Young Lovers No. 16 on?)
Charlton Comics: No. 13, June, 1955 - No. 15, Oct, 1955

	GD	VG	FN	VF	VF/NM	NM-
13-15-Newspaper-r	32	64	96	186	298	410

BRENDA STARR REPORTER
Dell Publishing Co.: Oct, 1963

	GD	VG	FN	VF	VF/NM	NM-
1	12	24	36	86	153	220

BRER RABBIT (See Kite Fun Book, Walt Disney Showcase #28 and Wheaties)
Dell Publishing Co.: No. 129, 1946; No. 208, Jan, 1949; No. 693, 1956 (Disney)

	GD	VG	FN	VF	VF/NM	NM-
Four Color 129 (#1)-Adapted from Disney movie "Song of the South"	26	52	78	191	356	520
Four Color 208 (1/49)	11	22	33	79	140	200
Four Color 693-Part-r #129	8	16	24	56	93	130

BRIAN BOLLAND'S BLACK BOOK
Eclipse Comics: July, 1985 (one-shot)

1-British B&W-r in color 3.00

BRIAN PULIDO'S LADY DEATH... (See Lady Death)

BRICK BRADFORD (Also see Ace Comics & King Comics)
King Features Syndicate/Standard: No. 5, July, 1948 - No. 8, July, 1949 (Ritt & Grey reprints)

	GD	VG	FN	VF	VF/NM	NM-
5	19	38	57	112	176	240
6-Robot-c (by Schomburg?).	35	70	105	203	327	450
7-Schomburg-c. 8-Says #7 inside, #8 on-c	15	30	45	94	147	200

BRIDE'S DIARY (Formerly Black Cobra No. 3)
Ajax/Farrell Publ.: No. 4, May, 1955 - No. 10, Aug, 1956

	GD	VG	FN	VF	VF/NM	NM-
4 (#1)	9	18	27	50	65	80
5-8	6	12	18	31	38	45
9,10-Disbrow-a	8	16	24	42	54	65

BRIDES IN LOVE (Hollywood Romances & Summer Love No. 46 on)
Charlton Comics: Aug, 1956 - No. 45, Feb, 1965

	GD	VG	FN	VF	VF/NM	NM-
1	11	22	33	62	86	110
2	7	14	21	37	46	55
3-6,8-10	3	6	9	20	30	40
7-(68 pgs.)	4	8	12	26	41	55
11-20	3	6	9	16	22	28
21-45	2	4	6	10	14	18

BRIDES ROMANCES
Quality Comics Group: Nov, 1953 - No. 23, Dec, 1956

	GD	VG	FN	VF	VF/NM	NM-
1	15	30	45	84	127	170
2	9	18	27	47	61	75
3-10: Last precode (3/55)	8	16	24	44	57	70
11-17,19-22: 15-Baker-a(p)?; Colan-a	8	16	24	40	50	60
18-Baker-a	8	16	24	44	57	70
23-Baker-c/a	12	24	36	67	94	120

BRIDE'S SECRETS
Ajax/Farrell(Excellent Publ.)/Four-Star: Apr-May, 1954 - No. 19, May, 1958

	GD	VG	FN	VF	VF/NM	NM-
1	12	24	36	69	97	125
2	8	16	24	40	50	60
3-6: Last precode (3/55)	6	12	18	31	38	45
7-11,13-19: 18-Hollingsworth-a	6	12	18	28	34	40
12-Disbrow-a	6	12	18	33	41	48

BRIDE-TO-BE ROMANCES (See True...)

BRIGADE
Image Comics (Extreme Studios): Aug, 1992 - No. 4, 1993 ($1.95, lim. series)

1-Liefeld part plots/scripts in all, Liefeld-c(p); contains 2 Brigade trading cards 3.00
1-Gold foil stamped logo edition 8.00
2-Contains coupon for Image Comics #0 & 2 trading cards 3.00
2-With coupon missing 2.25
3,4: 3-Contains 2 trading cards; 1st Birds of Prey. 4-Flip book featuring Youngblood #5 2.50

BRIGADE
Image Comics (Extreme): V2#1, May, 1993 - V2#22, July, 1995, V2#25, May, 1996 ($1.95/$2.50)

V2#1-22,25: 1-Gatefold-c; Liefeld co-plots; Blood Brothers part 1; Bloodstrike app. 2-(6/93, V2#1 on inside)-Foil merricote-c (newsstand ed. w/out foil-c exists). 3-Perez-c(i); Liefeld scripts. 8,9-Coupons #2 & 6 for Extreme Prejudice #0 bound-in. 11-(8/94, $2.50) WildC.A.T.S app. 16-Polybagged w/ trading card. 22-"Supreme Apocalypse" Pt. 4; w/ trading card 2.50
0-(9/93)-Liefeld scripts; 1st app. Warcry; Youngblood & Wildcats app.; 2.50
20-Variant-c. by Quesada & Palmiotti 2.50
Sourcebook 1 (8/94, $2.95) 3.00

BRIGADE
Awesome Entertainment: July, 2000 ($2.99)

1-Flip book w/Century preview 3.00

BRIGAND, THE (See Fawcett Movie Comics No. 18)

BRINGING UP FATHER
Dell Publishing Co.: No. 9, 1942 - No. 37, 1944

	GD	VG	FN	VF	VF/NM	NM-
Large Feature Comic 9	30	60	90	174	280	385
Four Color 37	19	38	57	135	250	365

BRING BACK THE BAD GUYS (Also see Fireside Book Series)
Marvel Comics: 1998 ($24.95, TPB)

1-Reprints stories of Marvel villains' secrets 25.00

The Brotherhood #4 © MAR

Bruce Gentry #4 © SUPR

Buccaneers #23 © QUA

GD 2.0 | VG 4.0 | FN 6.0 | VF 8.0 | VF/NM 9.0 | NM- 9.2

BRING ON THE BAD GUYS (See Fireside Book Series)

BROADWAY HOLLYWOOD BLACKOUTS
Stanhall: Mar-Apr, 1954 - No. 3, July-Aug, 1954
1 13 26 39 74 105 135
2,3 9 18 27 50 65 80

BROADWAY ROMANCES
Quality Comics Group: January, 1950 - No. 5, Sept, 1950
1-Ward-c/a (9 pgs.), Gustavson-a 38 76 114 222 356 490
2-Ward-a (9 pgs.); photo-c 26 52 78 152 244 335
3-5: All-Photo-c 15 30 45 83 124 165

BROKEN ARROW (TV)
Dell Publishing Co.: No. 855, Oct, 1957 - No. 947, Nov, 1958
Four Color 855 (#1)-Photo-c 6 12 18 37 59 80
Four Color 947-Photo-c 5 10 15 32 51 70

BROKEN CROSS, THE (See The Crusaders)

BROKEN TRILOGY
Image Comics (Top Cow): July, 2008 - No. 3 ($2.99, limited series)
1,2-Witchblade, Darkness & Angelus app.; Marz-s/Sojic & Hester-a; two covers 3.00
...: The Darkness 1 (8/08, $2.99) Hester-s/Lucas-a; two covers 3.00

BRONCHO BILL (See Comics On Parade, Sparkler & Tip Top Comics)
United Features Syndicate/Standard(Visual Editions) No. 5-on: 1939 - 1940; No. 5, 12/48 - No. 16, 8?/50
Single Series 2 ('39) 52 104 156 322 536 750
Single Series 19 ('40)(#2 on cvr) 41 82 123 256 428 600
5 15 30 45 83 124 165
6(4/48)-10(4/49) 9 18 27 52 69 85
11(6/49)-16 8 16 24 44 57 70
NOTE: *Schomburg c-6, 7, 9-13, 15, 16.*

BROOKS ROBINSON (See Baseball's Greatest Heroes #2)

BROTHER BILLY THE PAIN FROM PLAINS
Marvel Comics Group: 1979 (68pgs.)
1-B&W comics, satire, Jimmy Carter-c & x-over w/Brother Billy peanut jokes. Joey Adams-a (scarce) 3 6 9 20 30 40

BROTHERHOOD, THE (Also see X-Men titles)
Marvel Comics: July, 2001 - No. 9, Mar, 2002 ($2.25)
1-Intro. Orwell & the Brotherhood; Ribic-a/X-s/Sienkiewicz-c 2.50
2-9: 2-Two covers (JG Jones & Sienkiewicz). 4-6-Fabry-c. 7-9-Phillips-c/a 2.50

BROTHER POWER, THE GEEK (See Saga of Swamp Thing Annual & Vertigo Visions)
National Periodical Publications: Sept-Oct, 1968 - No. 2, Nov-Dec, 1968
1-Origin; Simon-c(i?) 5 10 15 34 55 75
2 3 6 9 20 30 40

BROTHERS, HANG IN THERE, THE
Spire Christian Comics (Fleming H. Revell Co.): 1979 (49¢)
nn 2 4 6 8 11 14

BROTHERS IN ARMS (Based on the World War II military video game)
Dynamite Entertainment: 2008 - Present ($3.99/$3.50)
1-($3.99) Fabbri-a; two covers by Fabbri & Sejic 4.00
2,3-($3.50) Two covers by Fabbri & Sejic on each 3.50

BROTHERS OF THE SPEAR (Also see Tarzan)
Gold Key/Whitman No. 18: June, 1972 - No. 17, Feb, 1976; No. 18, May, 1982
1 5 10 15 30 48 65
2-Painted-c begin, end #17 3 6 9 17 25 32
3-10 3 6 9 14 19 24
11-18: 12-Line drawn-c. 13-17-Spiegle-a. 18(5/82)-r/#2; Leopard Girl-r 2 4 6 9 12 15

BROTHERS, THE CULT ESCAPE, THE
Spire Christian Comics (Fleming H. Revell Co.): 1980 (49¢)
nn 2 4 6 8 13 16

BROWNIES (See New Funnies)
Dell Publishing Co.: No. 192, July, 1948 - No. 605, Dec, 1954
Four Color 192(#1)-Kelly-a 14 28 42 99 175 250
Four Color 244(9/49), 293 (9/50)-Last Kelly c/a 10 20 30 68 119 170
Four Color 337(7-8/51), 365(12-1/51-52), 398(5/52) 6 12 18 37 59 80
Four Color 436(11/52), 482(7/53), 522(12/53), 605 5 10 15 34 55 75

BRUCE GENTRY
Better/Standard/Four Star Publ./Superior No. 3: Jan, 1948 - No. 8, Jul, 1949
1-Ray Bailey strip reprints begin, end #3; E. C. emblem appears as a monogram on stationery in story; negligee panels 58 116 174 365 620 875
2,3 37 74 111 220 353 485
4-8 25 50 75 147 236 325
NOTE: *Kamenish a-2-7; c-1-8.*

BRUCE LEE (Also see Deadly Hands of Kung Fu)
Malibu Comics: July, 1994 - No. 6, Dec, 1994 ($2.95, 36 pgs.)
1-6: 1-(44 pgs.)-Mortal Kombat prev., 1st app. in comics. 2,6-(36 pgs.) 5.00

BRUCE JONES' OUTER EDGE
Innovation: 1993 ($2.50, B&W, one-shot)
1-Bruce Jones-c/a/script 2.50

BRUCE WAYNE: AGENT OF S.H.I.E.L.D. (Also see Marvel Vs. DC #3 & DC Vs. Marvel #4)
Marvel Comics (Amalgam): Apr, 1996 ($1.95, one-shot)
1-Chuck Dixon scripts & Cary Nord-c/a. 2.50

BRUISER
Anthem Publications: Feb, 1994 ($2.45)
1 2.50

BRUTE, THE
Seaboard Publ. (Atlas): Feb, 1975 - No. 3, July, 1975
1-Origin & 1st app; Sekowsky-a(p) 2 4 6 8 10 12
2-Sekowsky-a(p); Fleisher-s 1 2 3 5 6 8
3-Brunner/Starlin/Weiss-a(p) 1 2 3 5 7 9

BRUTE & BABE
Ominous Press: July, 1994 - No. 2, Aug, 1994
1-($3.95, 8 tablets plus c)-"...It Begins..."; tablet format 4.00
2-($2.50, 36 pgs.)-"Mael's Rage", 2-(40 pgs.)-Stiff additional variant-c 2.50

BRUTE FORCE
Marvel Comics: Aug, 1990 - No. 4, Nov, 1990 ($1.00, limited series)
1-4: Animal super-heroes; Delbo & DeCarlo-a 2.50

B-SIDES (The Craptacular...)
Marvel Comics: Nov, 2002 - No. 3, Jan, 2003 ($2.99, limited series)
1-3-Kieth-c/Weldele-a. 2-Dorkin-a (1 pg.) 2-FF cameo. 3-FF app. 3.00

BUBBLEGUM CRISIS: GRAND MAL
Dark Horse Comics: Mar, 1994 - No. 4, June, 1994 ($2.50, limited series)
1-4-Japanese manga 2.50

BUCCANEER
I. W. Enterprises: No date (1963)
I.W. Reprint #1(r-/Quality #20), #8(r-/#23): Crandall-a in each 3 6 9 16 23 30

BUCCANEERS (Formerly Kid Eternity)
Quality Comics: No. 19, Jan, 1950 - No. 27, May, 1951 (No. 24-27: 52 pgs.)
19-Captain Daring, Black Roger, Eric Falcon & Spanish Main begin; Crandall-a 48 96 144 298 499 700
20,23-Crandall-a 36 72 108 212 341 470
21-Crandall-c/a 40 80 120 235 380 525
22-Bondage-c 28 56 84 162 261 360
24-26: 24-Adam Peril, U.S.N. begins. 25-Origin & 1st app. Corsair Queen. 26-last Spanish Main 24 48 72 140 225 310
27-Crandall-c/a 35 70 105 203 327 450
Super Reprint #12 (1964)-Crandall-r/#21 3 6 9 16 23 30

BUCCANEERS, THE (TV)
Dell Publishing Co.: No. 800, 1957
Four Color 800-Photo-c 7 14 21 47 76 105

BUCKAROO BANZAI (Movie)
Marvel Comics Group: Dec, 1984 - No. 2, Feb, 1985
1,2-Movie adaptation; r/Marvel Super Special #33; Texiera-c/a 3.00

BUCKAROO BANZAI: RETURN OF THE SCREW
Moonstone: 2006 - No. 3, 2006 ($3.50, limited series)
1-3: 1-Three covers by Haley, Stribling, Beck; Thompson-a 3.50
Preview (2006, 50¢) B&W preview; history of movie and spin-off projects 2.25

BUCK DUCK
Atlas Comics (ANC): June, 1953 - No. 4, Dec, 1953
1-Funny animal stories in all 15 30 45 85 130 175

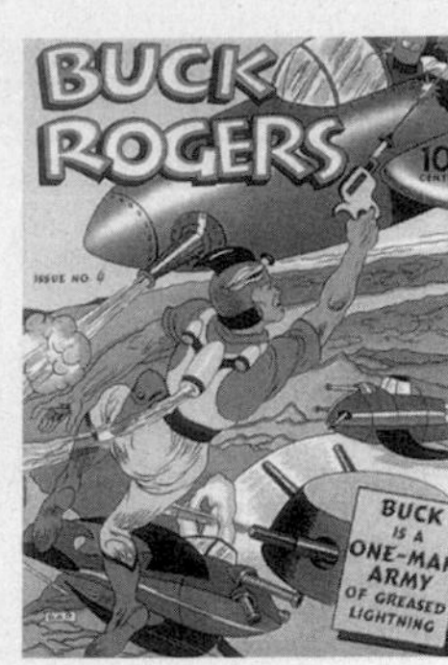

Buck Rogers #4 © KING

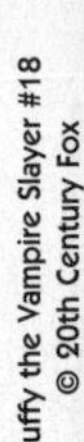
Buffy the Vampire Slayer #18 © 20th Century Fox

Buffy the Vampire Slayer: Giles #1 © 20th Century Fox

	GD 2.0	VG 4.0	FN 6.0	VF 8.0	VF/NM 9.0	NM- 9.2
2-4: 2-Ed Win-a(5)	9	18	27	52	69	85

BUCK JONES (Also see Crackajack Funnies, Famous Feature Stories, Master Comics #7 & Wow Comics #1, 1936)
Dell Publishing Co.: No. 299, Oct, 1950 - No. 850, Oct, 1957 (All Painted-c)

	GD	VG	FN	VF	VF/NM	NM-
Four Color 299(#1)-Buck Jones & his horse Silver-B begin; painted back-c begins, ends #5	13	26	39	93	164	235
2(4-6/51)	7	14	21	50	83	115
3-8(10-12/52)	6	12	18	43	69	95
Four Color 460,500,546,589	6	12	18	41	66	90
Four Color 652,733,850	5	10	15	32	51	70

BUCK ROGERS (Also see Famous Funnies, Pure Oil Comics, Salerno Carnival of Comics, 24 Pages of Comics, & Vicks Comics)
Famous Funnies: Winter, 1940-41 - No. 6, Sept, 1943
NOTE: Buck Rogers first appeared in the pulp magazine Amazing Stories Vol. 3 #5 in Aug, 1928.

	GD	VG	FN	VF	VF/NM	NM-
1-Sunday strip reprints by Rick Yager; begins with strip #190; Calkins-c	306	612	918	2081	3641	5200
2 (7/41)-Calkins-c	130	260	390	819	1385	1950
3 (12/41), 4 (7/42)	112	224	336	706	1196	1685
5,6: 5-Story continues with Famous Funnies No. 80; Buck Rogers, Sky Roads. 6-Reprints of 1939 dailies; contains B.R. story "Crater of Doom" (2 pgs.) by Calkins not-r from Famous Funnies	95	190	285	599	1012	1425

BUCK ROGERS
Toby Press: No. 100, Jan, 1951 - No. 9, May-June, 1951

	GD	VG	FN	VF	VF/NM	NM-
100(#7)-All strip-r begin	30	60	90	174	280	385
101(#8), 9-All Anderson-a(1947-49-r/dailies)	23	46	69	133	214	295

BUCK ROGERS (...in the 25th Century No. 5 on) (TV)
Gold Key/Whitman No. 7 on: Oct, 1964; No. 2, July, 1979 - No. 16, May, 1982 (No #10; story was written but never released. #17 exists only as a press proof without covers and was never published)

	GD	VG	FN	VF	VF/NM	NM-
1(10128-410, 12¢)-1st S.A. app. Buck Rogers & 1st new B. R. in comics since 1933 giveaway; painted-c; back-c pin-up	10	20	30	68	119	170
2(7/79)-6: 3,4,6-Movie adaptation; painted-c	2	4	6	9	12	15
7,11 (Whitman)	2	4	6	11	16	20
8,9 (prepack)(scarce)	3	6	9	18	27	35
12-16: 14(2/82), 15(3/82), 16(5/82)	2	4	6	8	10	12
Giant Movie Edition 11296(64pp, Whitman, $1.50), reprints GK #2-4 minus cover; tabloid size; photo-c (See Marvel Treasury)	3	6	9	19	26	34
Giant Movie Edition 02489(Western/Marvel, $1.50), reprints GK #2-4 minus cover	3	6	9	17	25	32

NOTE: *Bolle a-2p,3p, Movie Ed.(p). McWilliams a-2i,3i, 5-11, Movie Ed.(i). Painted c-1-9,11-13.*

BUCK ROGERS (Comics Module)
TSR, Inc.: 1990 - No. 10, 1991 ($2.95, 44 pgs.)

1-10 (1990): 1-Begin origin in 3 parts. 2-Indicia says #1. 2,3-Black Barney back-up story. 4-All Black Barney issue; B. B.-c. 5-Indicia says #6; Black Barney-c & lead story; Buck Rogers back-up story. 10-Flip book (72pgs.) 3.00

BUCKSKIN (TV)
Dell Publishing Co.: No. 1011, July, 1959 - No. 1107, June-Aug, 1960

	GD	VG	FN	VF	VF/NM	NM-
Four Color 1011 (#1)-Photo-c	7	14	21	47	76	105
Four Color 1107-Photo-c	6	12	18	43	69	95

BUCKY O'HARE (Funny Animal)
Continuity Comics: 1988 ($5.95, graphic novel)

	GD	VG	FN	VF	VF/NM	NM-
1-Golden-c/a(r); r/serial-Echo of Futurepast #1-6	1	2	3	4	5	7
Deluxe Hardcover ($40.00, 52 pg., 8 x 11")						40.00

BUCKY O'HARE
Continuity Comics: Jan, 1991 - No. 5, 1991 ($2.00)

1-6: 1-Michael Golden-c/a 2.50

BUDDIES IN THE U.S. ARMY
Avon Periodicals: Nov, 1952 - No. 2, 1953

	GD	VG	FN	VF	VF/NM	NM-
1-Lawrence-c	14	28	42	80	115	150
2-Mort Lawrence-c/a	10	20	30	54	72	90

BUFFALO BEE (TV)
Dell Publishing Co.: No. 957, Nov, 1958 - No. 1061, Dec-Feb, 1959-60

	GD	VG	FN	VF	VF/NM	NM-
Four Color 957 (#1)	8	16	24	58	97	135
Four Color 1002 (8-10/59), 1061	7	14	21	45	73	100

BUFFALO BILL (See Frontier Fighters, Super Western Comics & Western Action Thrillers)
Youthful Magazines: No. 2, Oct, 1950 - No. 9, Dec, 1951

	GD	VG	FN	VF	VF/NM	NM-
2-Annie Oakley story	14	28	42	78	112	145
3-9: 2-4-Walter Johnson-c/a. 9-Wildey-a	10	20	30	54	72	90

BUFFALO BILL CODY (See Cody of the Pony Express)

BUFFALO BILL, JR. (TV) (See Western Roundup)
Dell/Gold Key: Jan, 1956 - No. 13, Aug-Oct, 1959; 1965 (All photo-c)

	GD	VG	FN	VF	VF/NM	NM-
Four Color 673 (#1)	9	18	27	60	100	140
Four Color 742,766,798,828,856(11/57)	6	12	18	39	62	85
7(2-4/58)-13	5	10	15	34	55	75
1(6/65, Gold Key)-Photo-c(r/F.C. #798); photo-b/c	4	8	12	24	37	50

BUFFALO BILL PICTURE STORIES
Street & Smith Publications: June-July, 1949 - No. 2, Aug-Sept, 1949

	GD	VG	FN	VF	VF/NM	NM-
1,2-Wildey, Powell-a in each	14	28	42	78	112	145

BUFFY THE VAMPIRE SLAYER (Based on the TV series)(Also see Tales of the Vampires)
Dark Horse Comics: 1998 - No. 63, Nov, 2003 ($2.95/$2.99)

	GD	VG	FN	VF	VF/NM	NM-
1-Bennett-a/Watson-s; Art Adams-c	1	2	3	5	7	9
1-Variant photo-c	1	2	3	5	7	9
1-Gold foil logo Art Adams-c						15.00
1-Gold foil logo photo-c						20.00
2-15-Regular and photo-c. 4-7-Gomez-a. 5,8-Green-c						5.00
16-48: 29,30-Angel x-over. 43-45-Death of Buffy. 47-Lobdell-s begin. 48-Pike returns						3.00
50-($3.50) Scooby gang battles Adam; back-up story by Watson						3.50
51-63: 51-54-Viva Las Buffy; pre-Sunnydale Buffy & Pike in Vegas						3.00
Annual '99 ($4.95)-Two stories and pin-ups	1	2	3	4	5	7
...: A Stake to the Heart TPB (3/04, $12.95) r/#60-63						13.00
...: Chaos Bleeds (6/03, $2.99) Based on the video game; photo & Campbell-c						3.00
...: Creatures of Habit (3/02, $17.95) text with Horton & Paul Lee-a						18.00
...: Jonathan 1 (1/01, $2.99) two covers; Richards-a						3.00
...: Lost and Found 1 (3/02, $2.99) aftermath of Buffy's death; Richards-a						3.00
... Lovers Walk (2/01, $2.99) short stories by various; Richards & photo-c						3.00
...: Note From the Underground (3/03, $12.95) r/#47-50						13.00
...: Omnibus Vol. 1 (7/07, $24.95, 9x6") r/Spike & Dru #3, Origin #1-3 and Buffy #51-59						25.00
...: Omnibus Vol. 2 (9/07, $24.95, 9x6") r/Buffy #60-63 and various one-shots & specials						25.00
...: Omnibus Vol. 3 (1/08, $24.95, 9x6") r/Buffy #1 8,12,16, Annual '99						25.00
...: Omnibus Vol. 4 (5/08, $24.95, 9x6") r/Buffy #9-11,13-15,17-20,50 and various						25.00
...: Omnibus Vol. 5 (9/08, $24.95, 9x6") r/Buffy #21-28 and various one-shots & specials						25.00
...: Reunion (6/02, $3.50) Buffy & Angel's; Espenson-s; art by various						3.50
...: Slayer Interrupted TPB (2003, $14.95) r/#56-59						15.00
...: Tales of the Slayers (10/02, $3.50) art by Matsuda and Colan; art & photo-c						3.50
...: The Death of Buffy TPB (8/02, $15.95) r/#43-46						16.00
...: Viva Las Buffy TPB (7/03, $12.95) r/#51-54						13.00
Wizard #1/2	1	2	3	6	8	9

BUFFY THE VAMPIRE SLAYER ("Season Eight" of the TV series)
Dark Horse Comics: Mar, 2007 - Present ($2.99)

	NM-
1-Joss Whedon-s/Georges Jeanty-a/Jo Chen-c	7.00
1-Variant cover by Jeanty	10.00
1-RRP with B&W Jeanty cover (edition of 1000)	70.00
1-4: 1-2nd thru 5th printings. 2-2nd-4th printings. 3,4-2nd & 3rd printings	3.00
2-5-Chen-c/Jeanty-a	4.00
2-5-Variant-c by Jeanty	6.00
6-18: 6-9-Faith app.; Vaughan-s. 10,11-Whedon-s. 12-15-Goddard-s; Dracula app. 16-18-Fray app.; Whedon-s/Moline-a	3.00
6-18-Variant-c by Jeanty	4.00
...: Volume One: The Long Way Home TPB (11/07, $15.95) r/#1-5 and variant covers	16.00

NOTE: *Later printings have Jo Chen art with different credit graphics.*

BUFFY THE VAMPIRE SLAYER: ANGEL
Dark Horse Comics: May, 1999 - No. 3, July, 1999 ($2.95, limited series)

1-3-Gomez-a; Matsuda-c & photo-c for each 3.00

BUFFY THE VAMPIRE SLAYER: GILES
Dark Horse Comics: Oct, 2000 ($2.95, one-shot)

1-Eric Powell-a; Powell & photo-c 3.00

BUFFY THE VAMPIRE SLAYER: HAUNTED
Dark Horse Comics: Dec, 2001 - No. 4, Mar, 2002 ($2.99, limited series)

1-4-Faith and the Mayor app.; Espenson-s/Richards-a 3.00
TPB (9/02, $12.95) r/series; photo-c 13.00

BUFFY THE VAMPIRE SLAYER: OZ
Dark Horse Comics: July, 2001 - No. 3, Sept, 2001 ($2.99, limited series)

1-3-Totleben & photo-c; Golden-s 3.00

BUFFY THE VAMPIRE SLAYER: SPIKE AND DRU
Dark Horse Comics: Apr, 1999; No. 2, Oct, 1999; No. 3, Dec, 2000 ($2.95)

Bugs Bunny #105 © WB

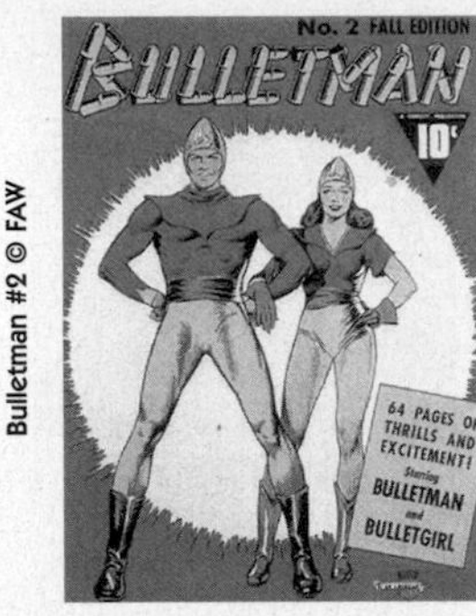

Bulletman #2 © FAW

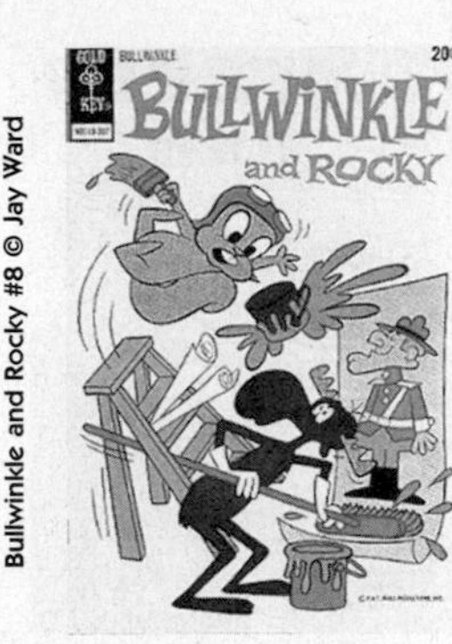

Bullwinkle and Rocky #8 © Jay Ward

GD VG FN VF VF/NM NM-
2.0 4.0 6.0 8.0 9.0 9.2

1-3: 1,2-Photo-c. 3-Two covers (photo & Sook) 3.00

BUFFY THE VAMPIRE SLAYER: THE ORIGIN (Adapts movie screenplay)
Dark Horse Comics: Jan, 1999 - No. 3, Mar, 1999 ($2.95, limited series)

1-3-Brereton-s/Bennett-a; reg & photo-c for each 3.00

BUFFY THE VAMPIRE SLAYER: WILLOW & TARA
Dark Horse Comics: Apr, 2001 ($2.99, one-shot)

1-Terry Moore-a/Chris Golden & Amber Benson-s; Moore-c & photo-c 3.00
TPB (4/03, $9.95) r/#1 & W&T - Wilderness; photo-c 10.00

BUFFY THE VAMPIRE SLAYER: WILLOW & TARA - WILDERNESS
Dark Horse Comics: Jul, 2002 - No. 2, Sept, 2002 ($2.99, limited series)

1,2-Chris Golden & Amber Benson-s; Jothikaumar-c & photo-c 3.00

BUG
Marvel Comics: Mar, 1997 ($2.99, one-shot)

1-Micronauts character 3.00

BUGALOOS (TV)
Charlton Comics: Sept, 1971 - No. 4, Feb, 1972

	GD 2.0	VG 4.0	FN 6.0	VF 8.0	VF/NM 9.0	NM- 9.2
1	5	10	15	30	48	65
2-4	3	6	9	19	29	38

NOTE: *No. 3(1/72) went on sale late in 1972 (after No. 4) with the 1/73 issues.*

BUGHOUSE (Satire)
Ajax/Farrell (Excellent Publ.): Mar-Apr, 1954 - No. 4, Sept-Oct, 1954

	GD 2.0	VG 4.0	FN 6.0	VF 8.0	VF/NM 9.0	NM- 9.2
V1#1	21	42	63	123	197	270
2-4	14	28	42	78	112	145

BUGS BUNNY (See The Best of..., Camp Comics, Comic Album #2, 6, 10, 14, Dell Giant #28, 32, 46, Dynabrite, Golden Comics Digest #1, 3, 5, 6, 8, 10, 14, 15, 17, 21, 26, 30, 34, 39, 42, 47, Kite Fun Book, Large Feature Comic #8, Looney Tunes and Merry Melodies, March of Comics #44, 59, 75, 83, 97, 115, 132, 149, 160, 179, 188, 201, 220, 231, 245, 259, 273, 287, 301, 315, 329, 343, 363, 367, 380, 392, 403, 415, 428, 440, 452, 464, 476, 487, Porky Pig, Puffed Wheat, Story Hour Series #802, Super Book #14, 26 and Whitman Comic Books)

BUGS BUNNY (See Dell Giants for annuals)
Dell Publishing Co./Gold Key No. 86-218/Whitman No. 219 on: 1942 - No. 245, April, 1984

	GD 2.0	VG 4.0	FN 6.0	VF 8.0	VF/NM 9.0	NM- 9.2
Large Feature Comic 8(1942)-(Rarely found in fine-mint condition)	187	374	561	1178	1989	2800
Four Color 33 ('43)	96	192	288	816	1558	2300
Four Color 51	32	64	96	246	461	675
Four Color 88	22	44	66	163	302	440
Four Color 123('46),142,164	15	30	45	110	203	295
Four Color 187,200,217,233	12	24	36	82	146	210
Four Color 250-Used in **SOTI**, pg. 309	12	24	36	86	153	220
Four Color 266,274,281,289,298('50)	9	18	27	65	113	160
Four Color 307,317(#1),327(#2),338,347,355,366,376,393	9	18	27	60	100	140
Four Color 407,420,432(10/52)	7	14	21	50	83	115
Four Color 498(9/53),585(9/54), 647(9/55)	6	12	18	39	62	85
Four Color 724(9/56),838(9/57),1064(12/59)	5	10	15	34	55	75
28(12-1/52-53)-30	6	12	18	39	62	85
31-50	5	10	15	30	48	65
51-85(7-9/62)	4	8	12	24	37	50
86(10/62)-88-Bugs Bunny's Showtime-(25¢, 80pgs.)	6	12	18	41	66	90
89-99	3	6	9	17	25	32
100	3	6	9	18	27	35
101-118: 108-1st Honey Bunny. 118-Last 12¢ issue	3	6	9	14	19	24
119-140	2	4	6	11	16	20
141-170	2	4	6	9	12	15
171-218	2	4	6	8	10	12
219,220,225-237(5/82): 229-Swipe of Barks story/WDC&S #223. 233(2/82)	2	4	6	8	10	12
221(9/80),222(11/80)-Pre-pack? (Scarce)	3	6	9	19	29	38
223 (1/81, 50¢-c), 224 (3/81)-Low distr.	2	4	6	11	16	20
223 (1/81, 40¢-c) Cover price error variant	3	6	9	14	20	25
238-245 (#90070 on-c, nd, nd code; pre-pack): 238(5/83), 239(6/83), 240(7/83), 241(7/83), 242(8/83), 243(8/83), 244(3/84), 245(4/84)	2	4	6	13	18	22

NOTE: *Reprints-100,102-104,110,115,123,143,144,147,167,173,175-177,179-185,187,190.*

	GD 2.0	VG 4.0	FN 6.0	VF 8.0	VF/NM 9.0	NM- 9.2
nn (Xerox Pub. Comic Digest, 1971, 100 pages, B&W) collection of one-page gags	4	8	12	22	34	45
...Comic-Go-Round 11196-(224 pgs.)($1.95)(Golden Press, 1979)	4	8	12	23	36	48
...Winter Fun 1(12/67-Gold Key)-Giant	5	10	15	32	51	70

BUGS BUNNY
DC Comics: June, 1990 - No. 3, Aug, 1990 ($1.00, limited series)

GD VG FN VF VF/NM NM-
2.0 4.0 6.0 8.0 9.0 9.2

1-3: Daffy Duck, Elmer Fudd, others app. 4.00

BUGS BUNNY (...Monthly on-c)
DC Comics: 1993 - No. 3, 1994? ($1.95)

1-3-Bugs, Porky Pig, Daffy, Road Runner 3.50

BUGS BUNNY (Digest-size reprints from Looney Tunes)
DC Comics: 2005 - Present ($6.99, digest)

Vol. 1: What's Up Doc? - Reprints from Looney Tunes #37,41,43-45,48,52,55,57-59,63 7.00

BUGS BUNNY & PORKY PIG
Gold Key: Sept, 1965 (Paper-c, giant, 100 pgs.)

	GD 2.0	VG 4.0	FN 6.0	VF 8.0	VF/NM 9.0	NM- 9.2
1(30025-509)	7	14	21	40	80	110

BUGS BUNNY'S ALBUM (See Bugs Bunny, Four Color No. 498,585,647,724)

BUGS BUNNY LIFE STORY ALBUM (See Bugs Bunny, Four Color No. 838)

BUGS BUNNY MERRY CHRISTMAS (See Bugs Bunny, Four Color No. 1064)

BUILDING, THE
Kitchen Sink Press: 1987; 2000 (8 1/2" x 11" sepia toned graphic novel)

nn-Will Eisner-s/c/a 10.00
nn-(DC Comics, 9/00, $9.95) reprints 1987 edition 10.00

BULLET CROW, FOWL OF FORTUNE
Eclipse Comics: Mar, 1987 - No. 2, Apr, 1987 ($2.00, B&W, limited series)

1,2-The Comic Reader-r & new-a 2.50

BULLETMAN (See Fawcett Miniatures, Master Comics, Mighty Midget Comics, Nickel Comics & XMas Comics)
Fawcett Publications: Sum, 1941 - #12, 2/12/43; #14, Spr, 1946 - #16, Fall, 1946 (No #13)

	GD 2.0	VG 4.0	FN 6.0	VF 8.0	VF/NM 9.0	NM- 9.2
1-Silver metallic-c	376	752	1128	2557	4479	6400
2-Raboy-c	163	326	489	1027	1739	2450
3,5-Raboy-c each	120	240	360	756	1278	1800
4	97	194	291	611	1031	1450
6,8-10: 10-Intro. Bulletdog	80	160	240	504	852	1200
7-Ghost Stories told by night watchman of cemetery begins; Eisnerish-a; hidden message "Chic Stone is a jerk".	83	166	249	523	887	1250
11,12,14-16 (nn 13): 12-Robot-c	60	120	180	378	639	900

NOTE: ***Mac Raboy** c-1-3, 5, 6, 10. "Bulletman the Flying Detective" on cover #8 on.*

BULLET POINTS
Marvel Comics: Jan, 2007 - No. 5 ($2.99, limited series)

1-5: 1-Steve Rogers becomes Iron Man; Straczynski-s/Edwards-a. 4,5-Galactus app. 3.00
TPB (2007, $13.99) r/#1-5, layout pages by Edwards 14.00

BULLETPROOF MONK (Inspired the 2003 film)
Image Comics (Flypaper Press): 1998 - No. 3, 1999 ($2.95, limited series)

1-3-Oeming-a 3.00
...: Tales of the BPM (3/03, $2.95) Flip book; 2 covers by Sale; art by Sale, Oeming, Dave Johnson; Seann William Scott afterword 3.00
TPB (2002, $9.95) r/#1-3; foreword by John Woo 10.00

BULLETS AND BRACELETS (Also see Marvel Versus DC #3 & DC Versus Marvel #4)
Marvel Comics (Amalgam): Apr, 1996 ($1.95)

1-John Ostrander script & Gary Frank-c/a 2.50

BULLSEYE: GREATEST HITS (Daredevil villain)
Marvel Comics: Nov, 2004 - No. 5, Mar, 2005 ($2.99, limted series)

1-5-Origin of Bullseye; Steve Dillon-a/Deodato-c. 3-Punisher app. 3.00
TPB (2005, $13.99) r/#1-5 14.00

BULLS-EYE (Cody of The Pony Express No. 8 on)
Mainline No. 1-5/Charlton No. 6,7: 7-8/54-No. 5, 3-4/55; No. 6, 6/55; No. 7, 8/55

	GD 2.0	VG 4.0	FN 6.0	VF 8.0	VF/NM 9.0	NM- 9.2
1-S&K-c, 2 pgs.-a	56	112	168	353	597	840
2-S&K-c/a	47	94	141	291	486	680
3-5-S&K-c/a(2 each). 4-Last pre-code issue (1-2/55). 5-Censored issue with tomahawks removed in battle scene	40	80	120	244	397	550
6-S&K-c/a	35	70	105	208	334	460
7-S&K-c/a(3)	40	80	120	244	397	550

BULLS-EYE COMICS (Formerly Komik Pages #10; becomes Kayo #12)
Harry 'A' Chesler: No. 11, 1944

	GD 2.0	VG 4.0	FN 6.0	VF 8.0	VF/NM 9.0	NM- 9.2
11-Origin K-9, Green Knight's sidekick, Lance; The Green Knight, Lady Satan, Yankee Doodle Jones app.	43	86	129	267	446	625

BULLWHIP GRIFFIN (See Movie Comics)

BULLWINKLE (...and Rocky No. 22 on; See March of Comics #233 and Rocky & Bullwinkle) (TV) (Jay Ward)
Dell/Gold Key: 3-5/62 - #11, 4/74; #12, 6/76 - #19, 3/78; #20, 4/79 - #25, 2/80

Burke's Law #1 © DELL

Buzzy #12 © DC

Cable #100 © MAR

GD 2.0 | VG 4.0 | FN 6.0 | VF 8.0 | VF/NM 9.0 | NM- 9.2

Four Color 1270 (3-5/62) 18 36 54 133 247 360
01-090-209 (Dell, 7-9/62) 15 30 45 106 193 280
1(11/62, Gold Key) 14 28 42 99 175 250
2(2/63) 9 18 27 63 107 150
3(4/72)-11(4/74-Gold Key) 5 10 15 34 55 75
12-14: 12(6/76)-Reprints. 13(9/76), 14-New stories 3 6 9 18 27 35
15-25 2 4 6 11 16 20
Mother Moose Nursery Pomes 01-530-207 (5-7/62, Dell) 17 34 51 122 226 330
NOTE: *Reprints: 6, 7, 20-24.*

BULLWINKLE (...& Rocky No. 2 on)(TV)
Charlton Comics: July, 1970 - No. 7, July, 1971
1 7 14 21 47 76 105
2-7 5 10 15 32 51 70

BULLWINKLE AND ROCKY
Star Comics/Marvel Comics No. 3 on: Nov, 1987 - No. 9, Mar, 1989
1-9: Boris & Natasha in all. 3,5,8-Dudley Do-Right app. 4-Reagan-c 4.00
Marvel Moosterworks (1/92, $4.95) 1 3 4 6 8 10

BUMMER
Fantagraphics Books: June, 1995 ($3.50, B&W, mature)
1 3.50

BUNNY (Also see Harvey Pop Comics)
Harvey Publications: Dec, 1966 - No. 20, Dec, 1971; No. 21, Nov, 1976
1-68 pg. Giants begin 8 16 24 52 86 120
2-10 4 8 12 28 44 60
11-18: 18-Last 68 pg. Giant 4 8 12 26 41 55
19-21-52 pg. Giants: 21-Fruitman app. 4 8 12 24 37 50

BURKE'S LAW (TV)
Dell Publ.: 1-3/64; No. 2, 5-7/64; No. 3, 3-5/65 (All have Gene Barry photo-c)
1-Photo-c 5 10 15 34 55 75
2,3-Photo-c 4 8 12 24 37 50

BURNING ROMANCES (See Fox Giants)

BUSTER BEAR
Quality Comics Group (Arnold Publ.): Dec, 1953 - No. 10, June, 1955
1-Funny animal 11 22 33 60 83 105
2 7 14 21 35 43 50
3-10 6 12 18 28 34 40
I.W. Reprint #9,10 (Super on inside) 2 4 6 9 13 16

BUSTER BROWN COMICS (See Promotional Comics section)

BUSTER BUNNY
Standard Comics(Animated Cartoons)/Pines: Nov, 1949 - No. 16, Oct, 1953
1-Frazetta 1 pg. text illo. 11 22 33 60 83 105
2 7 14 21 35 43 50
3-14,16 6 12 18 28 34 40
15-Racist-c 8 16 24 40 50 60

BUSTER CRABBE (TV)
Famous Funnies Publ.: Nov, 1951 - No. 12, 1953
1-1st app.(?) Frazetta anti-drug ad; text story about Buster Crabbe & Billy the Kid 40 80 120 235 380 525
2-Williamson/Evans-c; text story about Wild Bill Hickok & Pecos Bill 38 76 114 222 356 490
3-Williamson/Evans-c/a 40 80 120 235 380 525
4-Frazetta-c/a, 1pg.; bondage-c 48 96 144 298 499 700
5-Frazetta-c; Williamson/Krenkel/Orlando-a, 11pgs. (per Mr. Williamson) 123 246 369 775 1313 1850
6,8 19 38 57 109 172 235
7-Frazetta one pg. ad 19 38 57 112 176 240
9-One pg. Frazetta Boy Scouts ad (1st?) 16 32 48 92 144 195
10-12 12 24 36 69 97 125
NOTE: Eastern Color sold 3 dozen each NM file copies of #s 9-12 a few years ago.

BUSTER CRABBE (The Amazing Adventures of...)(Movie star)
Lev Gleason Publications: Dec, 1953 - No. 4, June, 1954
1,4: 1-Photo-c. 4-Flash Gordon-c 21 42 63 123 197 270
2,3-Toth-a 19 38 57 112 176 240

BUTCH CASSIDY
Skywald Comics: June, 1971 - No. 3, Oct, 1971 (52 pgs.)
1-Pre-code reprints and new material; Red Mask reprint, retitled Maverick; Bolle-a; Sutton-a 3 6 9 14 20 26
2,3: 2-Whip Wilson-r. 3-Dead Canyon Days reprint/Crack Western No. 63; Sundance Kid app.; Crandall-a 2 4 6 9 13 16

BUTCH CASSIDY (...& the Wild Bunch)
Avon Periodicals: 1951
1-Kinstler-c/a 19 38 57 112 176 240
NOTE: *Reinman story; Issue number on inside spine.*

BUTCH CASSIDY (See Fun-In No. 11 & Western Adventure Comics)

BUTCHER, THE (Also see Brave and the Bold, 2nd Series)
DC Comics: May, 1990 - No. 5, Sept, 1990 ($1.50, mature)
1-5: 1-No indicia inside 2.50

BUTCHER KNIGHT
Image Comics (Top Cow): Jan, 2001 - No. 4, June, 2001 ($2.95, limited series)
Preview (B&W, 16 pgs.) Dwayne Turner-c/a 2.25
1-4-Dwayne Turner-c/a 3.00

BUZ SAWYER (Sweeney No. 4 on)
Standard Comics: June, 1948 - No. 3, 1949
1-Roy Crane-a 25 50 75 145 233 320
2-Intro his pal Sweeney 15 30 45 86 133 180
3 12 24 36 69 97 125

BUZ SAWYER'S PAL, ROSCOE SWEENEY (See Sweeney)

BUZZ, THE (Also see Spider-Girl)
Marvel Comics: July, 2000 - No. 3, Sept, 2000 ($2.99, limited series)
1-3-Buscema-a/DeFalco & Frenz-s 3.00

BUZZ BUZZ COMICS MAGAZINE
Horse Press: May, 1996 ($4.95, B&W, over-sized magazine)
1-Paul Pope-c/a/scripts; Moebius-a 5.00

BUZZY (See All Funny Comics)
National Periodical Publications/Detective Comics: Winter, 1944-45 - No. 75, 1-2/57; No. 76, 10/57; No. 77, 10/58
1 (52 pgs. begin); "America's favorite teenster" 31 62 93 181 291 400
2 (Spr, 1945) 15 30 45 92 144 195
3-5 12 24 36 69 97 125
6-10 10 20 30 56 76 95
11-20 9 18 27 50 65 80
21-30 8 16 24 42 54 65
31,35-38 8 16 24 40 50 60
32-34,39-Last 52 pgs. Scribbly story by Mayer in each (these four stories were done for Scribbly #14 which was delayed for a year) 8 16 24 44 57 70
40-77: 62-Last precode (2/55) 7 14 21 37 46 55

BUZZY THE CROW (See Harvey Comics Hits #60 & 62, Harvey Hits #18 & Paramount Animated Comics #1)

BY BIZARRE HANDS
Dark Horse Comics: Apr, 1994 - No. 3, June, 1994 ($2.50, B&W, mature)
1-3: Lansdale stories 2.50

CABBOT: BLOODHUNTER (Also see Bloodstrike & Bloodstrike: Assassin)
Maximum Press: Jan, 1997 ($2.50, one-shot)
1-Rick Veitch-a/script; Platt-c; Thor, Chapel & Prophet cameos 2.50

CABLE (See Ghost Rider &..., & New Mutants #87) (Title becomes Soldier X)
Marvel Comics: May, 1993 - No. 107, Sept, 2002 ($3.50/$1.95/$1.50-$2.25)
1-($3.50, 52 pgs.)-Gold foil & embossed-c; Thibert a-1-4p; c-1-3 5.00
2-15: 3-Extra 16 pg. X-Men/Avengers ann. preview. 4-Liefeld-a assist; last Thibert-a(p). 6-8-Reveals that Baby Nathan is Cable; gives background on Stryfe. 9-Omega Red-c/story. 11-Bound-in trading card sheet 3.50
16-Newsstand edition 2.50
16-Enhanced edition 5.00
17-20-($1.95)-Deluxe edition, 20-w/bound in '95 Fleer Ultra cards 3.00
17-20-($1.50)-Standard edition 2.50
21-24, 26-44, -1(7/97): 21-Begin $1.95-c; return from Age of Apocalyse. 24-Grizzly dies. 28-vs. Sugarman; Mr. Sinister app. 30-X-Man-c/app.; Exodus app. 31-vs. X-Man. 32-Post app. 33-Post-c/app; Mandarin app (flashback); includes "Onslaught Update". 34-Onslaught x-over; Hulk-c/app; Apocalypse app. (cont'd in Hulk #444). 35-Onslaught x-over; Apocalypse vs. Cable. 36-w/card insert. 38-Weapon X-c/app; Psycho Man & Micronauts app. 40-Scott Clark-a(p). 41-Bishop-c/app. 3.00
25 ($3.95)-Foil gatefold-c 4.00
45-49,51-74: 45-Operation Zero Tolerance. 51-1st Casey-s. 54-Black Panther. 55-Domino-c/app. 62-Nick Fury-c/app.63-Stryfe-c/app. 67,68-Avengers-c/app. 71,73-Liefeld-a 2.50
50-($2.99) Double sized w/wraparound-c 3.00

Cable (2008 series) #1 © MAR

Cage #9 © MAR

Calling All Boys #3 © PMI

	GD 2.0	VG 4.0	FN 6.0	VF 8.0	VF/NM 9.0	NM- 9.2
75 -($2.99) Liefeld-c/a; Apocalypse: The Twelve x-over						3.00
76-79: 76-Apocalypse: The Twelve x-over						2.50
80-96: 80-Begin $2.25-c. 87-Mystique-c/app.						2.50
97-99,101-107: 97-Tischman-s/Kordey-a/c begin						2.50
100-($3.99) Dialogue-free 'Nuff Said back-up story						4.00
... Classic Vol. 1 TPB (2008, $29.99) r/#1-4, New Mutants #87, Cable: Blood & Metal #1,2						30.00
.../Machine Man '98 Annual ($2.99) Wraparound-c						3.00
.../X-Force '96 Annual ($2.95) Wraparound-c						3.00
...'99 Annual ($3.50) vs. Sinister; computer photo-c						3.50
...Second Genesis 1 (9/99, $3.99) r/New Mutants #99, 100 and X-Force #1; Liefeld-c						4.00
...: The End (2002, $14.99, TPB) r/#101-107						15.00

CABLE
Marvel Comics: May, 2008 - Present ($2.99)

1-6-Olivetti-c/a. 1-Liefeld var-c. 2-Finch var-c. 3-Romita Jr. var-c. 4-Bishop app.; Djurdjevic var-c. 5-Silvestri var-c. 6-Liefeld var-c						3.00

CABLE - BLOOD AND METAL (Also see New Mutants #87 & X-Force #8)
Marvel Comics: Oct, 1992 - No. 2, Nov, 1992 ($2.50, limited series, 52 pgs.)

1-Fabian Nicieza scripts; John Romita, Jr.-c/a in both; Cable vs. Stryfe; 2nd app. of The Wild Pack (becomes The Six Pack); wraparound-c						4.00
2-Prelude to X-Cutioner's Song						3.00

CABLE/DEADPOOL ("Cable & Deadpool" on cover)
Marvel Comics: May, 2004 - No. 50, Apr, 2008 ($2.99)

1-49: 1-Nicieza-s/Liefeld-c. 7-9-X-Men app. 17-House of M. 21-Heroes For Hire app. 30,31-Civil War. 30-Great Lakes Avengers app. 33-Liefeld-c. 43,44-Wolverine app.						3.00
50-($3.99) Final issue; Spider-Man and the Avengers app.						4.00
... Vol. 1: If Looks Could Kill TPB (2004, $14.99) r/#1-6						15.00
... Vol. 2: The Burnt Offering TPB (2005, $14.99) r/#7-12						15.00
... Vol. 3: The Human Race TPB (2005, $14.99) r/#13-18						15.00
... Vol. 4: Bosom Buddies TPB (2006, $14.99) r/#19-24						15.00
... Vol. 5: Living Legends TPB (2006, $13.99) r/#25-29						14.00
... Vol. 6: Paved With Good Intentions TPB (2007, $14.99) r/#30-35						15.00
... Vol. 7: Separation Anxiety TPB (2007, $17.99) r/#36-42; sketch pages						18.00
Deadpool Vs. The Marvel Universe TPB (2008, $24.99) r/#43-50						25.00

CADET GRAY OF WEST POINT (See Dell Giants)

CADILLACS & DINOSAURS (TV)
Marvel Comics (Epic Comics): Nov, 1990 - No. 6, Apr, 1991 ($2.50, limited series)

1-6: r/Xenozoic Tales in color w/new-c						3.00
...In 3-D #1 (7/92, $3.95, Kitchen Sink)-With glasses						6.00

CADILLACS AND DINOSAURS (TV)
Topps Comics: V2#1, Feb, 1994 - V2#9, 1995 ($2.50, limited series)

V2#1-($2.95)-Collector's edition w/Stout-c & bound-in poster; Buckler-a; foil stamped logo; Giordano-a in all						6.00
V2#1-9: 1-Newsstand edition w/Giordano-c. 2,3-Collector's editions w/Stout-c & posters. 2,3-Newsstand ed. w/Giordano-c; w/o posters. 4-6-Collectors & Newsstand editions; Kieth-c. 7-9-Linsner-c						3.00

CAGE (Also see Hero for Hire, Power Man & Punisher)
Marvel Comics: Apr, 1992 - No. 20, Nov, 1993 ($1.25)

1,3,10,12: 3-Punisher-c & minor app. 10-Rhino & Hulk-c/app. 12-(52 pgs.)-Iron Fist app.						3.00
2,4-9,11,13-20: 9-Rhino-c/story; Hulk cameo						2.50

CAGE (Volume 3)
Marvel Comics (MAX): Mar, 2002 - No. 5, Sept, 2002 ($2.99, mature)

1-5-Corben-c/a; Azzarello-s						3.00
HC (2002, $19.99, with dustjacket) r/#1-5; intro. by Darius James; sketch pages						20.00
SC (2003, $13.99) r/#1-5; intro. by Darius James						14.00

CAGED HEAT 3000 (Movie)
Roger Corman's Cosmic Comics: Nov, 1995 - No. 3, Jan, 1996 ($2.50)

1-3: Adaptation of film						2.50

CAGES
Tundra Publ.: 1991 - No. 10, May, 1996 ($3.50/$3.95/$4.95, limited series)

1-Dave McKean-c/a in all	2	4	6	8	10	12
2-Misprint exists	1	2	3	5	6	8
3-9: 5-$3.95-c begins						4.00
10-($4.95)						5.00

CAIN'S HUNDRED (TV)
Dell Publishing Co.: May-July, 1962 - No. 2, Sept-Nov, 1962

nn(01-094-207)	3	6	9	20	30	40
2	3	6	9	16	22	28

CAIN/VAMPIRELLA FLIP BOOK
Harris Comics: Oct, 1994 ($6.95, one-shot, squarebound)

nn-contains Cain #3 & #4; flip book is r/Vampirella story from 1993 Creepy Fearbook	1	2	3	5	7	9

CALIBER PRESENTS
Caliber Press: Jan, 1989 - No. 24, 1991 ($1.95/$2.50, B&W, 52 pgs.)

1-Anthology; 1st app. The Crow; Tim Vigil-c/a	6	12	18	39	62	85
2-Deadworld story; Tim Vigil-a	2	4	6	9	13	16
3-24: 15-24 ($3.50, 68 pgs.)						3.50

CALIBER PRESENTS: CINDERELLA ON FIRE
Caliber Press: 1994 ($2.95, B&W, mature)

1						3.00

CALIBER SPOTLIGHT
Caliber Press: May, 1995 ($2.95, B&W)

1-Kabuki app						3.50

CALIFORNIA GIRLS
Eclipse Comics: June, 1987 - No. 8, May, 1988 ($2.00, 40 pgs, B&W)

1-8: All contain color paper dolls						3.00

CALL, THE
Marvel Comics: June, 2003 - No. 4, Sept, 2003 ($2.25)

1-4-Austen-s/Olliffe-a						2.50

CALLING ALL BOYS (Tex Granger No. 18 on)
Parents' Magazine Institute: Jan, 1946 - No. 17, May, 1948 (Photo c-1-5,7,8)

1	14	28	42	81	118	155
2-Contains Roy Rogers article	9	18	27	47	61	75
3-7,9,11,14-17: 6-Painted-c. 11-Rin Tin Tin photo on-c; Tex Granger begins. 14-J. Edgar Hoover photo on-c. 15-Tex Granger-c begin	7	14	21	35	43	50
8-Milton Caniff story	9	18	27	50	65	80
10-Gary Cooper photo on-c	9	18	27	50	65	80
12-Bob Hope photo on-c	14	28	42	76	108	140
13-Bing Crosby photo on-c	12	24	36	67	94	120

CALLING ALL GIRLS
Parents' Magazine Institute: Sept, 1941 - No. 89, Sept, 1949 (Part magazine, part comic)

1	18	36	54	103	162	220
2-Photo-c	10	20	30	58	79	100
3-Shirley Temple photo-c	14	28	42	80	115	150
4-10: 4,5,7,9-Photo-c. 9-Flag-c	9	18	27	50	65	80
11-Tina Thayer photo-c; Mickey Rooney photo-b/c; B&W photo inside of Gary Cooper as Lou Gehrig in "Pride of Yankees"	10	20	30	58	79	100
12-20	8	16	24	42	54	65
21-39,41-43(10-11/45)-Last issue with comics	8	16	24	40	50	60
40-Liz Taylor photo-c	20	40	60	118	189	260
44-51(7/46)-Last comic book size issue	6	12	18	33	41	48
52-89	6	12	18	27	33	38

NOTE: ***Jack Sparling*** *art in many issues; becomes a girls' magazine "Senior Prom" with #90.*

CALLING ALL KIDS (Also see True Comics)
Parents' Magazine Institute: Dec-Jan, 1945-46 - No. 26, Aug, 1949

1-Funny animal	14	28	42	80	115	150
2	8	16	24	44	57	70
3-10	7	14	21	35	43	50
11-26	6	12	18	31	38	45

CALL OF DUTY, THE : THE BROTHERHOOD
Marvel Comics: Aug, 2002 - No. 6, Jan, 2003 ($2.25)

1-Exploits of NYC Fire Dept.; Finch-c/a; Austen & Bruce Jones-s						4.00
2-6-Austen-s						2.50
...Vol 1: The Brotherhood & The Wagon TPB (2002, $14.99) r/#1-6 & ...The Wagon #1-4						15.00

CALL OF DUTY, THE : THE PRECINCT
Marvel Comics: Sept, 2002 - No. 5, Jan, 2003 ($2.25, limited series)

1-Exploits of NYC Police Dept.; Finch-c; Bruce Jones-s/Mandrake-a						3.00
2-4						2.50
...Vol 2: The Precinct TPB (2003, $9.99) r/#1-4						10.00

CALL OF DUTY, THE : THE WAGON
Marvel Comics: Oct, 2002 - No. 4, Jan, 2003 ($2.25, limited series)

1-4-Exploits of NYC EMS Dept.; Finch-c; Austen-s/Zelzej-a						2.50

CALVIN (See Li'l Kids)

CALVIN & THE COLONEL (TV)

Camelot 3000 #9 © DC

Canteen Kate #2 © STJ

Captain Action #0 © Capt. Action Ents.

	GD 2.0	VG 4.0	FN 6.0	VF 8.0	VF/NM 9.0	NM- 9.2

Dell Publishing Co.: No. 1354, Apr-June, 1962 - No. 2, July-Sept, 1962

Issue	GD 2.0	VG 4.0	FN 6.0	VF 8.0	VF/NM 9.0	NM- 9.2
Four Color 1354(#1)	8	16	24	56	93	130
2	6	12	18	39	62	85

CAMELOT 3000
DC Comics: Dec, 1982 - No. 11, July, 1984; No. 12, Apr, 1985 (Direct sales, maxi series, Mando paper)

Issue	GD 2.0	VG 4.0	FN 6.0	VF 8.0	VF/NM 9.0	NM- 9.2
1-12: 1-Mike Barr scripts & Brian Bolland-c/a begin. 5-Intro Knights of New Camelot						4.00
TPB (1988, $12.95) r/#1-12						15.00

NOTE: ***Austin** a-7i-12i. **Bolland** a-1-12p; c-1-12.*

CAMERA COMICS
U.S. Camera Publishing Corp./ME: July, 1944 - No. 9, Summer, 1946

Issue	GD 2.0	VG 4.0	FN 6.0	VF 8.0	VF/NM 9.0	NM- 9.2
nn (7/44)	25	50	75	145	233	320
nn (9/44)	18	36	54	107	169	230
1(10/44)-The Grey Comet (slightly smaller page size than subsequent issues)	18	36	54	107	169	230
2-16 pgs. of photos with 32 pgs. of comics	14	28	42	82	121	160
3-Nazi WW II-c; photos	14	28	42	82	121	160
4-9: All 1/3 photos	13	26	39	74	105	135

CAMP CANDY (TV)
Marvel Comics: May, 1990 - No. 6, Oct, 1990 ($1.00, limited series)

Issue	GD 2.0	VG 4.0	FN 6.0	VF 8.0	VF/NM 9.0	NM- 9.2
1-6: Post-c/a(p); featuring John Candy						4.00

CAMP COMICS
Dell Publishing Co.: Feb, 1942 - No. 3, April, 1942 (All have photo-c)

Issue	GD 2.0	VG 4.0	FN 6.0	VF 8.0	VF/NM 9.0	NM- 9.2
1- "Seaman Sy Wheeler" by Kelly, 7 pgs.; Bugs Bunny app.; Mark Twain adaptation (scarce)	82	164	246	517	871	1225
2-Kelly-a, 12 pgs.; Bugs Bunny app.; classic-c	82	164	246	517	871	1225
3-(Scarce)-Dave Berg & Walt Kelly-a	62	124	186	391	663	935

CAMP RUNAMUCK (TV)
Dell Publishing Co.: Apr, 1966

Issue	GD 2.0	VG 4.0	FN 6.0	VF 8.0	VF/NM 9.0	NM- 9.2
1-Photo-c	4	8	12	21	32	42

CAMPUS LOVES
Quality Comics Group (Comic Magazines): Dec, 1949 - No. 5, Aug, 1950

Issue	GD 2.0	VG 4.0	FN 6.0	VF 8.0	VF/NM 9.0	NM- 9.2
1-Ward-c/a (9 pgs.)	35	70	105	203	327	450
2-Ward-c/a	26	52	78	152	244	335
3-5	14	28	42	82	121	160

NOTE: ***Gustavson** a-1-5. Photo c-3-5.*

CAMPUS ROMANCE (...Romances on cover)
Avon Periodicals/Realistic: Sept-Oct, 1949 - No. 3, Feb-Mar, 1950

Issue	GD 2.0	VG 4.0	FN 6.0	VF 8.0	VF/NM 9.0	NM- 9.2
1-Walter Johnson-a; c-/Avon paperback #348	26	52	78	154	247	340
2-Grandenetti-a; c-/Avon paperback #151	19	38	57	109	172	235
3-c-/Avon paperback #201	19	38	57	109	172	235
Realistic reprint	10	20	30	54	72	90

CANADA DRY PREMIUMS (See Swamp Fox, The & Terry & The Pirates in the Promotional Comics section)

CANCELLED COMIC CAVALCADE (See the Promotional Comics section)

CANDID TALES (Also see Bold Stories & It Rhymes With Lust)
Kirby Publ. Co.: April, 1950; June, 1950 (Digest size) (144 pgs.) (Full color)

Issue	GD 2.0	VG 4.0	FN 6.0	VF 8.0	VF/NM 9.0	NM- 9.2
nn-(Scarce) Contains Wood female pirate story, 15 pgs., and 14 pgs. in June issue; Powell-a	107	214	321	674	1137	1600

NOTE: *Another version exists with Dr. Kilmore by Wood; no female pirate story.*

CANDY
William H. Wise & Co.: Fall, 1944 - No. 3, Spring, 1945

Issue	GD 2.0	VG 4.0	FN 6.0	VF 8.0	VF/NM 9.0	NM- 9.2
1-Two Scoop Scuttle stories by Wolverton	40	80	120	235	380	525
2,3-Scoop Scuttle by Wolverton, 2-4 pgs.	26	52	78	152	244	335

CANDY (Teen-age)(Also see Police Comics #37)
Quality Comics Group (Comic Magazines): Autumn, 1947 - No. 64, Jul, 1956

Issue	GD 2.0	VG 4.0	FN 6.0	VF 8.0	VF/NM 9.0	NM- 9.2
1-Gustavson-a	23	46	69	135	218	300
2-Gustavson-a	14	28	42	78	112	145
3-10	10	20	30	54	72	90
11-30	8	16	24	40	50	60
31-64: 64-Ward-c(p)?	7	14	21	35	43	50
Super Reprint No. 2,10,12,16,17,18('63- '64):17-Candy #12	2	4	6	10	14	18

NOTE: ***Jack Cole** 1-2 pg. art in many issues.*

CANNON (See Heroes, Inc. Presents Cannon)

CANNON: DAWN OF WAR (Michael Turner's...)
Aspen MLT, Inc.: Nov, 2004 ($2.99)

Issue	GD 2.0	VG 4.0	FN 6.0	VF 8.0	VF/NM 9.0	NM- 9.2
1-Turnbull-a; two covers by Turnbull and Turner						3.00

CANNONBALL COMICS
Rural Home Publishing Co.: Feb, 1945 - No. 2, Mar, 1945

Issue	GD 2.0	VG 4.0	FN 6.0	VF 8.0	VF/NM 9.0	NM- 9.2
1-The Crash Kid, Thunderbrand, The Captive Prince & Crime Crusader begin; skull-c	93	186	279	586	993	1400
2-Devil-c	67	134	201	422	711	1000

CANTEEN KATE (See All Picture All True Love Story & Fightin' Marines)
St. John Publishing Co.: June, 1952 - No. 3, Nov, 1952

Issue	GD 2.0	VG 4.0	FN 6.0	VF 8.0	VF/NM 9.0	NM- 9.2
1-Matt Baker-c/a	70	140	210	441	746	1050
2-Matt Baker-c/a	45	90	135	279	465	650
3-(Rare)-Used in **POP**, pg. 75; Baker-c/a	52	104	156	325	543	760

CAPER
DC Comics: Dec, 2003 - No. 12, Nov, 2004 ($2.95, limited series)

Issue	GD 2.0	VG 4.0	FN 6.0	VF 8.0	VF/NM 9.0	NM- 9.2
1-12: 1-4-Judd Winick-s/Farel Dalrymple-a. 5-8-John Severin-a. 9-12-Fowler-a						3.00

CAPES
Image Comics: Sept, 2003 - No. 3, Nov, 2003 ($3.50)

Issue	GD 2.0	VG 4.0	FN 6.0	VF 8.0	VF/NM 9.0	NM- 9.2
1-3-Robert Kirkman-s/Mark Englert-a/c						3.50

CAP'N QUICK & A FOOZLE (Also see Eclipse Mag. & Monthly)
Eclipse Comics: July, 1984 - No. 3, Nov, 1985 ($1.50, color, Baxter paper)

Issue	GD 2.0	VG 4.0	FN 6.0	VF 8.0	VF/NM 9.0	NM- 9.2
1-3-Rogers-c/a						3.00

CAPTAIN ACTION (Toy)
National Periodical Publications: Oct-Nov, 1968 - No. 5, June-July, 1969 (Based on Ideal toy)

Issue	GD 2.0	VG 4.0	FN 6.0	VF 8.0	VF/NM 9.0	NM- 9.2
1-Origin; Wood-a; Superman-c app.	7	14	21	49	80	110
2,3,5-Kane/Wood-a	6	12	18	39	62	85
4	5	10	15	32	51	70

CAPTAIN ACTION COMICS (Toy)
Moonstone: No. 0, 2008 - Present (Based on the Ideal toy)

Issue	GD 2.0	VG 4.0	FN 6.0	VF 8.0	VF/NM 9.0	NM- 9.2
0-($1.99) Origin re-told; Sparacio-a; three covers; character history by Michael Eury						2.50
...: First Mission, Last Day (2008, $3.99) origin story re-told; Nicieza-s/Procopio-a						4.00

CAPTAIN AERO COMICS (Samson No. 1-6; also see Veri Best Sure Fire & Veri Best Sure Shot Comics)
Holyoke Publishing Co.: V1#7(#1), Dec, 1941 - V2#4(#10), Jan, 1943; V3#9(#11), Sept, 1943 -V4#3(#17), Oct, 1944; #21, Dec, 1944 - #26, Aug, 1946 (No #18-20)

Issue	GD 2.0	VG 4.0	FN 6.0	VF 8.0	VF/NM 9.0	NM- 9.2
V1#7(#1)-Flag-Man & Solar, Master of Magic, Captain Aero, Cap Stone, Adventurer begin; Nazi WWII-c	177	354	531	1115	1883	2650
8,10: 8(#2)-Pals of Freedom app. 10(#4)-Origin The Gargoyle; Kubert-a	90	180	270	567	959	1350
9(#3)-Hitler-sty; Catman back-c; Alias X begins; Pals of Freedom app.	100	200	300	630	1065	1500
11,12(#5,6)-Kubert-a; Miss Victory in #6	72	144	216	454	770	1085
V2#1,2(#7,8): 8-Origin The Red Cross; Miss Victory app.; Brodsky-c(i)	43	86	129	267	446	625
3(#9)-Miss Victory app.	42	84	126	252	409	565
4(#10)-Miss Victory app.; Japanese WWII-c	35	70	105	203	327	450
V3#9 - V3#12(#11-14): 9-Quinlan Japanese WWII-c; Miss Victory app.	28	56	84	164	265	365
V3#13(#15),V4#2(#16): Schomburg Japanese WWII-c. 13-Miss Victory app.	30	60	90	176	283	390
V4#3(#17), 21-24-L. B. Cole Japanese WWII covers. 22-Intro/origin Mighty Mite.	50	100	150	310	518	725
25-L. B. Cole SciFi-c	50	100	150	310	518	725
26-L. B. Cole SciFi-c; Palais-a(2) (scarce)	107	214	321	674	1137	1600

NOTE: ***L.B. Cole** c-17. **Hollingsworth** a-23. **Infantino** a-23, 26. **Schomburg** c-15, 16.*

CAPTAIN AMERICA (See Adventures of..., All-Select, All Winners, Aurora, Avengers #4, Blood and Glory, Captain Britain 16-20, Giant-Size..., The Invaders, Marvel Double Feature, Marvel Fanfare, Marvel Mystery, Marvel Super-Action, Marvel Super Heroes V2#3, Marvel Team-Up, Marvel Treasury Special, Power Record Comics, Ultimates, USA Comics, Young Allies & Young Men)

CAPTAIN AMERICA (Formerly Tales of Suspense #1-99) (Captain America and the Falcon #134-223 & Steve Rogers: Captain America #444-454 appears on cover only)
Marvel Comics Group: No. 100, Apr, 1968 - No. 454, Aug, 1996

Issue	GD 2.0	VG 4.0	FN 6.0	VF 8.0	VF/NM 9.0	NM- 9.2
100-Flashback on Cap's revival with Avengers & Sub-Mariner; story continued from Tales of Suspense #99; Kirby-c/a begins	24	48	72	176	326	475
101-The Sleeper-c/story; Red Skull app.	8	16	24	54	90	125
102-104: 102-Sleeper-c/s. 103,104-Red Skull-c/sty	6	12	18	41	66	90
105-108	5	10	15	34	55	75
109-Origin Capt. America retold in detail	7	14	21	50	83	115
109-2nd printing (1994)	2	4	6	8	10	12
110-Rick Jones dons Bucky's costume & becomes Cap's partner; Hulk x-over; Steranko-c/a	9	18	27	65	113	160

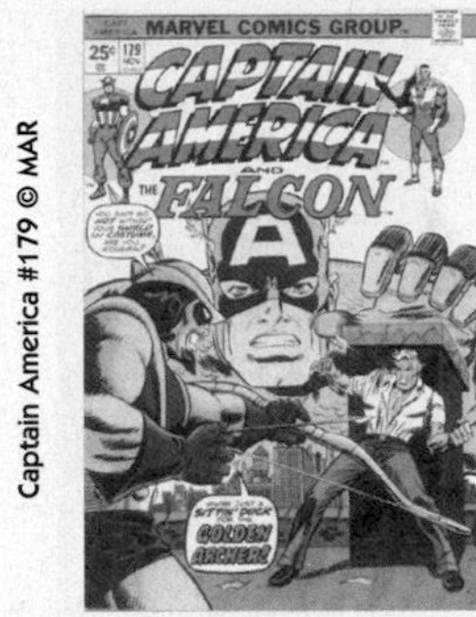

Captain America #179 © MAR

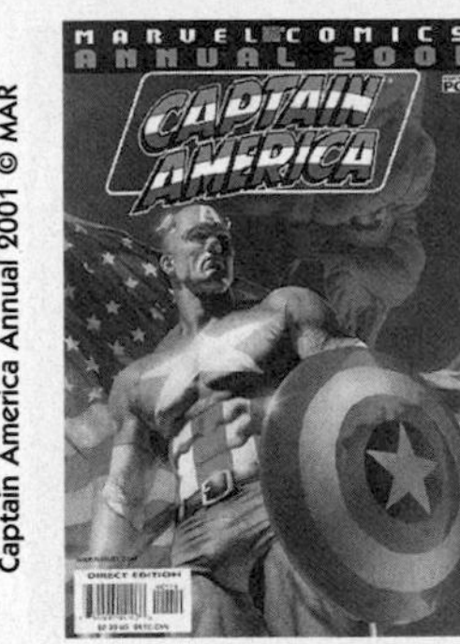

Captain America Annual 2001 © MAR

Captain America (2005 series) #34 © MAR

	GD 2.0	VG 4.0	FN 6.0	VF 8.0	VF/NM 9.0	NM- 9.2
111,113-Classic Steranko-c/a: 111-Death of Steve Rogers. 113-Cap's funeral; Avengers app.	8	16	24	58	97	135
112-S.A. recovery retold; last Kirby-c/a	5	10	15	30	48	65
114-116,118-120: 115-Last 12¢ issue	4	8	12	22	34	45
117-1st app. The Falcon (9/69)	9	18	27	63	107	150
121-136,139,140: 121-Retells origin. 133-The Falcon becomes Cap's partner; origin Modok. 140-Origin Grey Gargoyle retold	3	6	9	16	23	30
137,138-Spider-Man x-over	3	6	9	19	29	38
141,142: 142-Last 15¢ issue	3	6	9	14	19	24
143 (52 pgs).	3	6	9	17	25	32
144-153: 144-New costume Falcon. 153-1st brief app. Jack Monroe	2	4	6	11	16	20
154-1st full app. Jack Monroe (Nomad)(10/72)	2	4	6	13	18	22
155-Origin re-told; origin Jack Monroe	2	4	6	13	18	22
156-171,176-179: 155-158-Cap's strength increased. 160-1st app. Solarr. 164-1st app. Nightshade. 176-End of Capt. America.	2	4	6	8	10	12
172-175: X-Men x-over	2	4	6	11	16	20
180-Intro/origin of Nomad (Steve Rogers)	2	4	6	13	18	22
181-Intro/origin new Cap.	2	4	6	10	14	18
182,184-192: 186-True origin The Falcon	1	2	3	5	7	9
183-Death of new Cap; Nomad becomes Cap	2	4	6	8	11	14
193-Kirby-c/a begins	2	4	6	13	18	22
194-199-(Regular 25¢ edition)(4-7/76)	2	4	6	10	14	18
196-199-(30¢-c variants, limited distribution)	5	10	15	32	51	70
200-(Regular 25¢ edition)(8/76)	2	4	6	11	16	20
200-(30¢-c variant, limited distribution)	6	12	18	37	59	80
201-214-Kirby-c/a	2	4	6	8	11	14
210-214-(35¢-c variants, limited dist.)(6-10/77)	7	14	21	45	73	100
215,216,218-229,231-234,236-240,242-246: 215-Retells Cap's origin. 216-r/story from Strange Tales #114. 229-Marvel Man app. 233-Death of Sharon Carter. 234-Daredevil x-over. 244,245-Miller-c						6.00
217,230,235: 217-1st app. Marvel Man (later Quasar). 230-Battles Hulk-c/story cont'd in Hulk #232. 235-(7/79) Daredevil x-over; Miller-a(p)	1	2	3	4	5	7
241-Punisher app.; Miller-c.	3	6	9	17	25	32
241-2nd print						3.00
247-255-Byrne-a. 255-Origin; Miller-c.	1	2	3	5	7	9
256-281,284,285,289-322,324-326,328-331: 264-Old X-Men cameo in flashback. 265,266-Nick Fury & Spider-Man app. 267-1st app. Everyman. 269-1st Team America. 279-(3/83)-Contains Tattooz skin decals. 281-1950s Bucky returns. 284-Patriot (Jack Mace) app. 285-Death of Patriot. 298-Origin Red Skull. 328-Origin & 1st app. D-Man						3.00
282-Bucky becomes new Nomad (Jack Monroe)						5.00
282-Silver ink 2nd print ($1.75) w/original date (6/83)						2.50
283,327,333-340: 283-2nd app. Nomad. 327-Capt. Amer. battles Super Patriot. 333-Intro & origin new Captain (Super Patriot). 339-Fall of the Mutants tie-in						4.00
286-288-Deathlok app.						4.00
323-1st app. new Super Patriot (see Nick Fury)						4.00
332-Old Cap resigns	1	2	3	5	6	8
341-343,345-349						3.00
344-($1.50, 52 pgs.)-Ronald Reagan cameo						4.00
350-($1.75, 68 pgs.)-Return of Steve Rogers (original Cap) to original costume						4.00
351-382,384-396: 351-Nick Fury app. 354-1st app. U.S. Agent (6/89, see Avengers West Coast). 360-1st app. Crossbones. 375-Daredevil app. 386-U.S. Agent app. 387-389-Red Skull back-up stories. 396-Last $1.00-c. 396,397-1st app. all new Jack O'Lantern						2.50
383-($2.00, 68 pgs.)-50th anniversary issue; Red Skull story; Jim Lee-c(i)						4.00
397-399,401-424,425: 402-Begin 6 part Man-Wolf story w/Wolverine in #403-407. 405-410-New Jack O'Lantern app. in back-up story. 406-Cable & Shatterstar cameo. 407-Capwolf vs. Cable-c/story. 408-Infinity War x-over; Falcon solo back-up. 423-Vs. Namor-c/story						2.50
400-($2.25, 84 pgs.)-Flip book format w/double gatefold-c; r/Avengers #4 plus-c; contains cover pin-ups.						3.00
425-($2.95, 52 pgs.)-Embossed Foil-c ed.n; Fighting Chance Pt. 1						3.00
426-443,445,446,447,449-453: 427-Begin $1.50-c; bound-in trading card sheet. 449-Thor app. 450-"Man Without A Country" storyline begins, ends #453; Bill Clinton app; variant-c exists. 451-1st app.Cap's new costume. 453-Cap gets old costume back; Bill Clinton app.						2.50
444-Mark Waid scripts & Ron Garney-c/a(p) begins, ends #454; Avengers app.						5.00
445,454: 445-Sharon Carter & Red Skull return.						3.00
448-($2.95, double-sized issue)-Waid script & Garney-c/a; Red Skull "dies"						4.00
Special 1(1/71)-Origin retold	5	10	15	32	51	70
Special 2(1/72, 52 pgs.)-Colan-r/Not Brand Echh; all-r	3	6	9	20	30	40
Annual 3('76, 52 pgs.)-Kirby-c/a(new)	3	6	9	14	20	26
Annual 4('77, 34 pgs.)-Magneto-c/story	3	6	9	14	20	26
Annual 5-7: (52 pgs.)('81-'83)						5.00
Annual 8(9/86)-Wolverine-c/story	3	6	9	19	29	38
Annual 9-13('90-'94, 68 pgs.)-9-Nomad back-up. 10-Origin retold (2 pgs.). 11-Falcon solo story. 12-Bagged w/card. 13-Red Skull-c/story						3.00
...Ashcan Edition ('95, 75¢)						3.00
... and the Falcon: Madbomb TPB (2004, $16.99) r/#193-200; Kirby-s/a						17.00
... and the Falcon: Nomad TPB (2006, $24.99) r/#177-186; Cap becomes Nomad						25.00
... and the Falcon: Secret Empire TPB (2005, $19.99) r/#169-176						20.00
... and the Falcon: The Swine TPB (2006, $29.99) r/#206-214 & Annual #3,4						30.00
... By Jack Kirby: Bicentennial Battles TPB (2005, $19.99) r/#201-205 & Marvel Treasury Special Featuring Captain America's Bicentennial Battles; Kirby-s/a						20.00
...: Deathlok Lives! nn(10/93, $4.95)-r/#286-288						5.00
...Drug War 1-(1994, $2.00, 52 pgs.)-New Warriors app.						3.00
...Man Without a Country(1998, $12.99, TPB)-r/#450-453						13.00
...Medusa Effect 1 (1994, $2.95, 68 pgs.) Origin Baron Zemo						3.00
...Operation Rebirth (1996, $9.95)-r/#445-448						10.00
... 65th Anniversary Special (5/06, $3.99) WWII flashback with Bucky; Brubaker-s						4.00
...Streets of Poison ($15.95)-r/#372-378						16.00
...: The Movie Special nn (5/92, $3.50, 52 pgs.)-Adapts movie; printed on coated stock; The Red Skull app.						3.50

NOTE: ***Austin*** *c-225i, 239i, 240i.* ***Buscema*** *a-115p, 217p; c-136p, 217, 297.* ***Byrne*** *c-223(part), 238, 239, 247p-254p, 290, 291, 313p; a-247-254p, 255, 313p, 350.* ***Colan*** *a(p)-116-137, 256, Annual 5; c(p)-116-123, 126, 129.* ***Everett*** *a-136i, 137i; c-126i.* ***Garney*** *a(p)-444-454.* ***Gil Kane*** *a-145p; c-147p, 149p, 150p, 170p, 172-174, 180, 181p, 183-190p, 215, 216, 220, 221.* ***Kirby*** *a(p)-100-109, 112, 193-214, 216, Special 1, 2(layouts), Annual 3, 4; c-100-109, 112, 126p, 193-214.* ***Ron Lim*** *a(p)-366, 368-378, 380-386; c-366p, 368-378p, 379, 380-393p.* ***Miller*** *c-241p, 244p, 245p, 255p, Annual 5.* ***Mooney*** *a-149i.* ***Morrow*** *a-144.* ***Perez*** *c-243p, 246p.* ***Robbins*** *c(p)-183-187, 189-192, 225.* ***Roussos*** *a-140i, 168i.* ***Shores*** *a-102i, 107i, 109i.* ***Starlin/Sinnott*** *c-162.* ***Sutton*** *a-244i.* ***Tuska*** *a-112i, 215p, Special 2.* ***Waid*** *scripts-444-454.* ***Williamson*** *a-313i.* ***Wood*** *a-127i.* ***Zeck*** *a-263-289; c-300.*

CAPTAIN AMERICA (Volume Two)
Marvel Comics: V2#1, Nov, 1996 - No. 13, Nov, 1997($2.95/$1.95/$1.99)
(Produced by Extreme Studios)

	GD 2.0	VG 4.0	FN 6.0	VF 8.0	VF/NM 9.0	NM- 9.2
1-($2.95)-Heroes Reborn begins; Liefeld-c/a; Loeb scripts; reintro Nick Fury						6.00
1-($2.95)-(Variant-c)-Liefeld-c/a						6.00
1-(7/96, $2.95)-(Exclusive Comicon Ed.)-Liefeld-c/a.	1	2	3	5	6	8
2-11,13: 5-Two-c. 6-Cable-c/app. 13-"World War 3"-pt. 4, x-over w/Image						3.00
12-($2.99) "Heroes Reunited"-pt. 4						4.00
Heroes Reborn: Captain America (2006, $29.99, TPB) r/#1-12 & Heroes Reborn #1/2						30.00

CAPTAIN AMERICA (Vol. Three) (Also see Capt. America: Sentinel of Liberty)
Marvel Comics: Jan, 1998 - No. 50, Feb, 2002 ($2.99/$1.99/$2.25)

	NM- 9.2
1-($2.99) Mark Waid-s/Ron Garney-a	4.00
1-Variant cover	6.00
2-($1.99): 2-Two covers	3.00
3-11: 3-Returns to old shield. 4-Hawkeye app. 5-Thor-c/app. 7-Andy Kubert-c/a begin. 9-New shield	2.50
12-($2.99) Battles Nightmare; Red Skull back-up story	3.50
13-17,19-Red Skull returns	2.50
18-($2.99) Cap vs. Korvac in the Future	3.00
20-24,26-29: 20,21-Sgt. Fury back-up story painted by Evans	2.50
25-($2.99) Cap & Falcon vs. Hatemonger	3.00
30-49: 30-Begin $2.25-c. 32-Ordway-a. 33-Jurgens-s/a begins; U.S. Agent app. 36-Maximum Security x-over. 41,46-Red Skull app.	2.50
.../Citizen V '98 Annual ($3.50) Busiek & Kesel-s	3.50
50-($5.95) Stories by various incl. Jurgens, Quitely, Immonen; Ha-c	6.00
1999 Annual ($3.50) Flag Smasher app.	3.50
2000 Annual ($3.50) Continued from #35 vs. Protocide; Jurgens-s	3.50
2001 Annual ($2.99) Golden Age flashback; Invaders app.	3.00
...: To Serve and Protect TPB (2/02, $17.95) r/Vol. 3 #1-7	18.00

CAPTAIN AMERICA (Volume 4)
Marvel Comics: Jun, 2002 - No. 32, Dec, 2004 ($3.99/$2.99)

	NM- 9.2
1-Ney Rieber-s/Cassaday-c/a	4.00
2-9-($2.99) 3-Cap reveals Steve Rogers ID. 7-9-Hairsine-a	3.00
10-32: 10-16-Jae Lee-a. 17-20-Gibbons-s/Weeks-a. 21-26-Bachalo-a. 26-Bucky flashback. 27,28-Eddie Campbell-a. 29-32-Red Skull app.	3.00
...Vol. 1: The New Deal HC (2003, $22.99) r/#1-6; foreward by Max Allan Collins	23.00
...Vol. 2: The Extremists TPB (2003, $13.99) r/#7-11; Cassaday-c	14.00
...Vol. 3: Ice TPB (2003, $12.99) r/#12-16; Jae Lee-a; Cassaday-c	13.00
...Vol. 4: Cap Lives TPB (2004, $12.99) r/#17-22 & Tales of Suspense #66	13.00
Avengers Disassembled: Captain America TPB (2004, $17.99) r/#29-32 and Captain America and the Falcon #5-7	18.00

CAPTAIN AMERICA
Marvel Comics: Jan, 2005 - Present ($2.99)

	NM- 9.2
1-Brubaker-s/Epting-c/a; Red Skull app.	4.00
2-24: 10-House of M. 11-Origin of the Winter Soldier. 13-Iron Man app. 24-Civil War	3.00
6,8-Retailer variant covers	6.00
25-($3.99) Captain America shot dead; handcuffed red glove cover by Epting	8.00
25-($3.99) Variant edition with running Cap cover by McGuinness	12.00

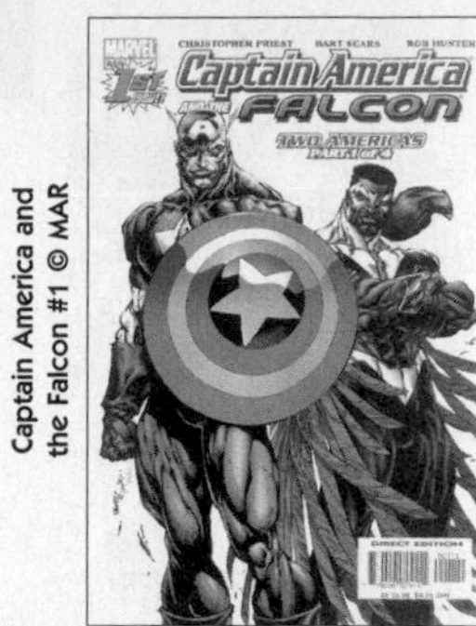

Captain America and the Falcon #1 © MAR

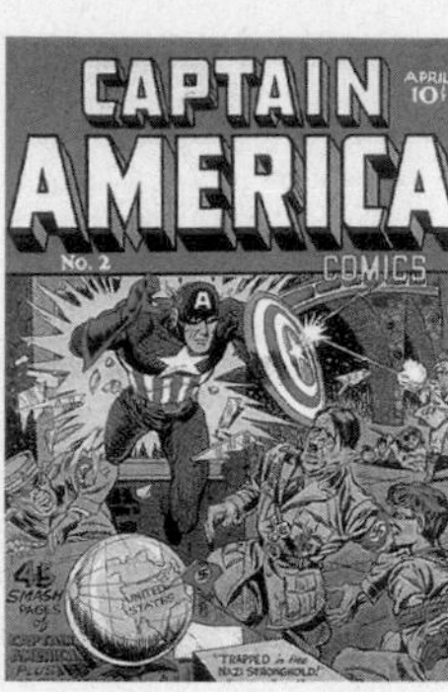

Captain America Comics #2 © MAR

Captain America: The Chosen #4 © MAR

GD VG FN VF VF/NM NM-
2.0 4.0 6.0 8.0 9.0 9.2

GD VG FN VF VF/NM NM-
2.0 4.0 6.0 8.0 9.0 9.2

25-($3.99) 2nd printing with "The Death of The Dream" cover by Epting 4.00
25 Director's Cut-($4.99) w/script with Brubaker commentary; pencil pages, variant and un-used covers gallery; article on media hype 5.00
26-33-Falcon & Winter Soldier app. 3.00
34-(3/08) Bucky becomes the new Captain America; Alex Ross-c 3.00
34-Variant-c by Steve Epting 3.00
34-($3.99) Director's Cut; includes script; pencil art, costume designs, cover gallery 4.00
34-DF Edition with Alex Ross portrait cover; signed by Ross 25.00
35-42-Bucky as Captain America 3.00
... By Ed Brubaker Omnibus Vol. 1 HC (2007, $74.99, dustjacket) r/#1-25; Capt. America 65th Anniv. Spec. and Winter Soldier: Winter Kills; Brubaker intro.; bonus material 75.00
Civil War: Captain America TPB (2007, $11.99) r/#22-24 & Winter Soldier: Winter Kills 12.00
...: Red Menace Vol. 1 SC (2006, $11.99) r/#15-17 and 65th Anniversary Special 12.00
...: Red Menace Vol. 2 SC (2006, $10.99) r/#18-21; Brubaker interview 11.00
...: The Death of Captan America Vol. 1 HC (2007, $19.99) r/#25-30; variant covers 20.00
...: The Death of Captan America Vol. 2 HC (2008, $19.99) r/#31-36; variant covers 20.00
...Vol. 1: Winter Soldier HC (2005, $21.99) r/#1-7; concept sketches 22.00
...Vol. 1: Winter Soldier SC (2006, $16.99) r/#1-7; concept sketches 17.00
...: Winter Soldier Vol. 2 HC (2006, $19.99) r/#8,9,11-14 20.00
...: Winter Soldier Vol. 2 SC (2006, $14.99) r/#8,9,11-14 15.00

CAPTAIN AMERICA AND THE FALCON
Marvel Comics: May, 2004 - No. 14, June, 2005 ($2.99, limited series)

1-4-Priest-s/Sears-a 3.00
5-14: 5-8-Avengers Disassembled x-over. 6,7-Scarlet Witch app. 8-12-Modok app. 3.00
... Vol. 1: Two Americas (2005, $9.99) r/#1-4 10.00
... Vol. 2: Brothers and Keepers (2005, $17.99) r/#8-14 18.00

CAPTAIN AMERICA COMICS
Timely/Marvel Comics (TCI 1-20/CmPS 21-68/MjMC 69-75/Atlas Comics (PrPI 76-78): Mar, 1941 - No. 75, Feb, 1950; No. 76, 5/54 - No. 78, 9/54
(No. 74 & 75 titled Capt. America's Weird Tales)

1-Origin & 1st app. Captain America & Bucky by S&K; Hurricane, Tuk the Caveboy begin by S&K; 1st app. Red Skull; Hitler-c (by Simon?); intro of the "Capt. America Sentinels of Liberty Club" (advertised on inside front-c.); indicia reads Vol. 2, Number 1
8200 16,400 24,600 58,500 124,250 190,000
2-S&K Hurricane; Tuk by Avison (Kirby splash); classic Hitler-c
1475 2950 4425 11,000 20,000 29,000
3-Classic Red Skull-c & app; Stan Lee's 1st text (1st work for Marvel)
1200 2400 3600 9000 16,500 24,000
4-Early use of full pg. panel in comic 806 1612 2418 5803 10,152 14,500
5 750 1500 2250 5400 9450 13,500
6-Origin Father Time; Tuk the Caveboy ends 639 1278 1917 4601 8051 11,500
7-Red Skull app.; classic-c 711 1422 2133 5119 8960 12,800
8-10-Last S&K issue, (S&K centerfold #6-10) 511 1022 1533 3679 6440 9200
11-Last Hurricane, Headline Hunter; Al Avison Captain America begins, ends #20; Avison-c(p) 423 846 1269 2770 5085 7400
12-The Imp begins, ends #16; last Father Time 411 822 1233 2795 4898 7000
13-Origin The Secret Stamp; classic-c 444 888 1332 3197 5599 8000
14,15 411 822 1233 2795 4898 7000
16-Red Skull unmasks Cap; Red Skull-c 500 1000 1500 3600 6300 9000
17-The Fighting Fool only app. 359 718 1077 2441 4271 6100
18-Classic-c 359 718 1077 2441 4271 6100
19-Human Torch begins #19 303 606 909 2060 3605 5150
20-Sub-Mariner app.; no H. Torch 300 600 900 2040 3570 5100
21-25: 25-Cap drinks liquid opium 300 600 900 1950 3375 4800
26-30: 27-Last Secret Stamp; last 68 pg. issue. 28-60 pg. issues begin.
300 600 900 1911 3256 4600
31-35,38-40: 34-Centerfold poster of Cap 267 534 801 1682 2841 4000
36-Classic Hitler-c 329 658 987 2237 3919 5600
37-Red Skull app. 300 600 900 1980 3440 4900
41-45,47: 41-Last Japan War-c. 47-Last German War-c
223 446 669 1405 2378 3350
46-German Holocaust-c; classic 300 600 900 1930 3315 4700
48-58,60 160 320 480 1008 1704 2400
59-Origin retold 312 624 936 2122 3711 5300
61-Red Skull-c/story 300 600 900 2010 3505 5000
62,64,65: 65-Kurtzman's "Hey Look" 207 414 621 1304 2202 3100
63-Intro/origin Asbestos Lady 210 420 630 1323 2237 3150
66-Bucky is shot; Golden Girl teams up with Captain America & learns his i.d; origin Golden Girl 257 514 771 1619 2735 3850
67-73: 67-Captain America/Golden Girl team-up; Mxyztplk swipe; last Toro in Human Torch. 68,70-Sub-Mariner/Namora, and Captain America/Golden Girl team-up in each. 69-Human Torch/Sun Girl team-up. 70-Science fiction-c/story. 71-Anti Wertham editorial; The Witness, Bucky app. 253 506 759 1594 2697 3800
74-(Scarce)(10/49)-Titled "Captain America's Weird Tales"; Red Skull-c & app.; classic-c 694 1388 2082 4997 8749 12,500
75(2/50)-Titled "C.A.'s Weird Tales"; no C.A. app.; horror cover/stories
250 500 750 1575 2663 3750
76-78(1954): Human Torch/Toro stories; all have communist-c/stories
143 286 429 901 1526 2150
132-Pg. Issue (B&W-1942)(Canadian)-Very rare. Has blank inside-c and back-c; contains Marvel Mystery #33 & Captain America #18 w/cover from Captain America #22; same contents as one version of the Marvel Mystery annuals
5000 10,000 15,000 30,000 - -

NOTE: ***Crandall*** *a-2i, 3i, 9i, 10i.* ***Kirby*** *c-1, 2, 5-8p.* ***Rico*** *c-69-71.* ***Romita*** *c-77, 78.* ***Schomburg*** *c-3, 4, 26-29, 31, 33, 37-39, 41, 42, 45-54, 58.* ***Sekowsky*** *c-55, 56.* ***Shores*** *c-1i, 2i, 5-7i, 11i, 20-25, 30, 32, 34, 35, 40, 57, 59-67.* ***S&K*** *c-9, 10. Bondage c-3, 7, 15, 16, 34, 38.*

CAPTAIN AMERICA: DEAD MEN RUNNING
Marvel Comics: Mar, 2002 - No. 3, May, 2002 ($2.99, limited series)

1-3-Macan-s/Zezelj-a 3.00

CAPTAIN AMERICA/NICK FURY: BLOOD TRUCE
Marvel Comics: Feb, 1995 ($5.95, one-shot, squarebound)

nn-Chaykin story 6.00

CAPTAIN AMERICA/NICK FURY: THE OTHERWORLD WAR
Marvel Comics: Oct, 2001 ($6.95, one-shot, squarebound)

nn-Manco-a; Bucky and Red Skull app. 7.00

CAPTAIN AMERICA: RED, WHITE & BLUE
Marvel Comics: Sept, 2002 ($29.99, one-shot, hardcover with dustjacket)

nn-Reprints from Lee & Kirby, Steranko, Miller and others; and new short stories and pin-ups by various incl. Ross, Dini, Timm, Waid, Dorkin, Sienkiewicz, Miller, Bruce Jones, Collins, Piers-Rayner, Pope, Deodato, Quitely, Nino; Stelfreeze-c 30.00
TPB (2007, $19.99) 20.00

CAPTAIN AMERICA, SENTINEL OF LIBERTY (See Fireside Book Series)

CAPTAIN AMERICA: SENTINEL OF LIBERTY
Marvel Comics: Sept, 1998 - No. 12, Aug, 1999 ($1.99)

1-Waid-s/Garney-a 3.00
1-Rough Cut ($2.99) Features original script and pencil pages 3.00
2-5: 2-Two-c; Invaders WW2 story 2.50
6-($2.99) Iron Man-c/app. 3.00
7-11: 8-Falcon-c/app. 9-Falcon poses as Cap 2.50
12-($2.99) Final issue; Bucky-c/app. 3.00

CAPTAIN AMERICA SPECIAL EDITION
Marvel Comics Group: Feb, 1984 - No. 2, Mar, 1984 ($2.00, Baxter paper)

1-Steranko-c/a(r) in both; r/ Captain America #110,111 6.00
2-Reprints the scarce Our Love Story #5, and C.A. #113
1 2 3 5 6 8

CAPTAIN AMERICA: THE CHOSEN
Marvel Comics: Nov, 2007 - No. 6 ($3.99, limited series)

1-6-Breitweiser-a/Morrell-s 4.00

CAPTAIN AMERICA: THE CLASSIC YEARS
Marvel Comics: Jun, 1998 -No. 2 (trade paperbacks)

1-($19.95) Reprints Captain America Comics #1-5 25.00
2-($24.95) Reprints Captain America Comics #6-10 25.00

CAPTAIN AMERICA: THE LEGEND
Marvel Comics: Sept, 1996 ($3.95, one-shot)

1-Tribute issue; wraparound-c 4.00

CAPTAIN AMERICA: WHAT PRICE GLORY
Marvel Comics: May, 2003 - No. 4, May, 2003 ($2.99, weekly limited series)

1-4-Bruce Jones-s/Steve Rude & Mike Royer-a 3.00

CAPTAIN AMERICA: WHITE
Marvel Comics: No. 0, Sept, 2008 - No. 6 ($2.99, limited series)

0-Bucky's origin retold; Loeb-s/Sale-a; interviews with creators; Sale sketch art 3.00

CAPTAIN AND THE KIDS, THE (See Famous Comics Cartoon Books)

CAPTAIN AND THE KIDS, THE (See Comics on Parade, Katzenjammer Kids, Okay Comics & Sparkler Comics)
United Features Syndicate/Dell Publ. Co.: 1938 -12/39; Sum, 1947 - No. 32, 1955; Four Color No. 881, Feb, 1958

Single Series 1(1938) 97 194 291 611 1031 1450
Single Series 1(Reprint)(12/39- "Reprint" on-c) 48 96 144 298 499 700
1(Summer, 1947-UFS)-Katzenjammer Kids 17 34 51 98 154 210

Captain Battle Comics #1 © LEV

Captain Britain and MI:13 #1 © MAR

Captain Easy #14 © NEA

GD 2.0 | VG 4.0 | FN 6.0 | VF 8.0 | VF/NM 9.0 | NM- 9.2

2 11 22 33 60 83 105
3-10 9 18 27 52 69 85
11-20 8 16 24 42 54 65
21-32 (1955) 8 16 24 40 50 60
50th Anniversary issue-(1948)-Contains a 2 pg. history of the strip, including an account of the famous Supreme Court decision allowing both Pulitzer & Hearst to run the same strip under different names 15 30 45 94 147 200
Special Summer issue, Fall issue (1948) 11 22 33 60 83 105
Four Color 881 (Dell) 4 8 12 28 44 60

CAPTAIN ATOM
Nationwide Publishers: 1950 - No. 7, 1951 (5¢, 5x7-1/4", 52 pgs.)
1-Science fiction 41 82 123 250 413 575
2-7 22 44 66 129 207 285

CAPTAIN ATOM (Formerly Strange Suspense Stories #77)(Also see Space Adventures)
Charlton Comics: V2#78, Dec, 1965 - V2#89, Dec, 1967
V2#78-Origin retold; Bache-a (3 pgs.) 8 16 24 56 93 130
79-82: 79-1st app. Dr. Spectro; 3 pg. Ditko cut & paste /Space Adventures #24. 82-Intro. Nightshade (9/66) 6 12 18 37 59 80
83-86: Ted Kord Blue Beetle in all. 83-(11/66)-1st app. Ted Kord. 84-1st app. new Captain Atom 5 10 15 32 51 70
87-89: Nightshade by Aparo in all 5 10 15 32 51 70
83-85(Modern Comics-1977)-reprints 1 2 3 4 5 7
NOTE: *Aparo a-87-89. Ditko c/a(p) 78-89. #90 only published in fanzine 'The Charlton Bullseye' #1, 2.*

CAPTAIN ATOM (Also see Americomics & Crisis On Infinite Earths)
DC Comics: Mar, 1987 - No. 57, Sept, 1991 (Direct sales only #35 on)
1-(44 pgs.)-Origin/1st app. with new costume 4.00
2-40: 5-Firestorm x-over. 6-Intro. new Dr. Spectro. 11-Millennium tie-in. 14-Nightshade app. 16-Justice League app. 17-$1.00-c begins; Swamp Thing app. 20-Blue Beetle x-over. 24,25-Invasion tie-in 2.50
51-57: 50-($2.00, 52 pgs.). 57-War of the Gods x-over 2.50
Annual 1,2 ('88, '89)-1-Intro Major Force 3.00

CAPTAIN ATOM: ARMAGEDDON (Restarts the WildStorm Universe)
DC Comics (WildStorm): Dec, 2005 - No. 9, Aug, 2006 ($2.99, limited series)
1-9-Captain Atom appears in WildStorm Universe; Pfeifer-s/Camuncoli-a. 1-Lee-c 3.00
TPB (2007, $19.99) r/series 20.00

CAPTAIN BATTLE (Boy Comics #3 on) (See Silver Streak Comics)
New Friday Publ./Comic House: Summer, 1941 - No. 2, Fall, 1941
1-Origin Blackout by Rico; Captain Battle begins (1st appeared in Silver Streak #10, 5/41) 145 290 435 914 1545 2175
2 80 160 240 504 852 1200

CAPTAIN BATTLE (2nd Series)
Magazine Press/Picture Scoop No. 5: No. 3, Wint, 1942-43; No. 5, Sum, 1943 (No #4)
3-Origin Silver Streak-r/SS#3; origin Lance Hale-r/Silver Streak; Simon-a(r) (52 pgs., nd) 71 142 213 447 754 1060
5-Origin Blackout retold (68 pgs.) 50 100 150 310 518 725

CAPTAIN BATTLE, JR.
Comic House (Lev Gleason): Fall, 1943 - No. 2, Winter, 1943-44
1-The Claw vs. The Ghost 135 270 405 851 1438 2025
2-Wolverton's Scoop Scuttle; Don Rico-c/a; The Green Claw story is reprinted from Silver Streak #6; bondage/torture-c 80 160 240 504 852 1200

CAPTAIN BEN DIX (See Promotional Comics section)

CAPTAIN BRITAIN (Also see Marvel Team-Up No. 65, 66)
Marvel Comics International: Oct. 13, 1976 - No. 39, July 6, 1977 (Weekly)
1-Origin; with Capt. Britain's face mask inside 2 4 6 10 14 18
2-Origin, part II; Capt. Britain's Boomerang inside 2 4 6 8 10 12
3-11: 3,8-Vs. Bank Robbers. 4-7-Vs. Hurricane. 9-11: Vs. Dr. Synne 6.00
12-23,25-27: (scarce)-12,13-Vs. Dr. Synne. 14,15-Vs. Mastermind. 16-23,25,26-With Captain America. 17 misprinted & color section reprinted in #18. 27-Origin retold 2 4 6 8 11 14
24-With C.B.'s Jet Plane inside 2 4 6 10 14 18
28-32,36-39: 28-32-Vs. Lord Hawk. 37-39-Vs. Highwayman & Munipulator 3.50
33-35-More on origin 4.00
Annual (1978, Hardback, 64 pgs.)-Reprints #1-7 with pin-ups of Marvel characters 2 4 6 9 13 16
Summer Special (1980, 52 pgs.)-Reprints 5.00
NOTE: *No. 1, 2, & 24 are rarer in mint due to inserts. Distributed in Great Britain only. Nick Fury-r by* ***Steranko*** *in 1-20, 24-31, 35-37. Fantastic Four-r by* ***J. Buscema*** *in all. New* ***Buscema****-a in 24-30. Story from No. 39 continues in Super Spider-Man (British weekly) No. 231-247. Following cancellation of his series, new Captain Britain stories appeared in "Super Spider-Man" (British weekly) No. 231-247. Captain Britain stories which appear in Super-Spider-Man No 248-253 are reprints of Marvel Team-Up No. 65&66. Capt. Britain strips also appeared in Hulk Comic (weekly) 1, 3-30, 42-55, 57-60, in Marvel Superheroes (monthly) 377-388, in Daredevils (monthly) 1-11, Mighty World of Marvel (monthly) 7-16 & Captain Britain (monthly) 1-14. Issues 1-23 have B&W & color, paper-c, & are 32 pgs. Issues 24 on are all B&W w/glossy-c & are 36 pgs.*

CAPTAIN BRITAIN AND MI: 13 (Also see Secret Invasion x-over titles)
Marvel Comics: Jul, 2008 - Present ($2.99)
1-Skrull invasion; Black Knight app.; Kirk-a 4.00
1-2nd printing with Kirk variant-c; 3rd printing with B&W cover 3.00
2-5: 5-Blade app. 3.00

CAPTAIN CANUCK
Comely Comix (Canada)(All distr. in U. S.): 7/75 - No. 4, 7/77; No. 4, 7-8/79 - No. 14, 3-4/81
1-1st app. Bluefox 5.00
2,3(5-7/76)-2-1st app. Dr. Walker, Redcoat & Kebec. 3-1st app. Heather 4.00
4(1st printing-2/77)-10x14-1/2"; (5.00); B&W; 300 copies serially numbered and signed with one certificate of authenticity 7 14 21 49 80 110
4(2nd printing-7/77)-11x17", B&W; only 15 copies printed; signed by creator Richard Comely, serially #'d and two certificates of authenticity inserted; orange cardboard covers (Very Rare) 9 18 27 65 113 160
4-14: 4(7-8/79)-1st app. Tom Evans & Mr. Gold; origin The Catman. 5-Origin Capt. Canuck's powers; 1st app. Earth Patrol & Chaos Corps. 8-Jonn 'The Final Chapter'. 9-1st World Beyond. 11-1st 'Chariots of Fire' story 4.00
15-(8/04, $15.00) Limited edition of unpublished issue from 1981; serially #'d edition of 150; signed by creator Richard Comely 3 6 9 16 23 30
... Legacy 1 (9-10/06) Comely-s/a 3.00
... Legacy Special Edition ($7.95, 52 pgs., limited ed. of 1000) Comely-s/a 1 2 3 5 6 8
Special Collectors Pack (polybagged) 1 3 4 6 8 10
Summer Special 1(7-9/80, 95¢, 64 pgs.) 4.00
NOTE: *30,000 copies of No. 2 were destroyed in Winnipeg.*

CAPTAIN CANUCK: UNHOLY WAR
Comely Comix: Oct, 2004 - No. 0 ($2.50, limited series)
1-Riel Langlois-s/Drue Langlois-a 2.50

CAPTAIN CARROT AND HIS AMAZING ZOO CREW (Also see New Teen Titans & Oz-Wonderland War)
DC Comics: Mar, 1982 - No. 20, Nov, 1983
1-20: 1-Superman app. 3-Re-intro Dodo & The Frog. 9-Re-intro Three Mouseketeers, the Terrific Whatzit. 10,11-Pig Iron reverts back to Peter Porkchops. 20-Changeling app. 3.00

CAPTAIN CARROT AND THE FINAL ARK (DC Countdown tie-in)
DC Comics: Dec, 2007 - No. 3, Feb, 2008 ($2.99, limited series)
1-3-Bill Morrison-s/Scott Shaw!-a. 3-Batman, Red Arrow, Hawkgirl & Zatanna app. 3.00
TPB (2008, $19.99) r/#1-3; Captain Carrot and His Amazing Zoo Crew #1,14,15; New Teen Titans #16 and stories from Teen Titans (2003 series) #30,31; cover gallery 20.00

CAPTAIN CARVEL AND HIS CARVEL CRUSADERS (See Carvel Comics)

CAPTAIN CONFEDERACY
Marvel Comics (Epic Comics): Nov, 1991 - No. 4, Feb, 1992 ($1.95)
1-4: All new stories 2.25

CAPTAIN COURAGEOUS COMICS (Banner #3-5; see Four Favorites #5)
Periodical House (Ace Magazines): No. 6, March, 1942
6-Origin & 1st app. The Sword; Lone Warrior, Capt. Courageous app.; Capt. moves to Four Favorites #5 in May 77 154 231 481 816 1150

CAPT'N CRUNCH COMICS (See Cap'n...)

CAPTAIN DAVY JONES
Dell Publishing Co.: No. 598, Nov, 1954
Four Color 598 5 10 15 30 48 65

CAPTAIN EASY (See The Funnies & Red Ryder #3-32)
Hawley/Dell Publ./Standard(Visual Editions)/Argo: 1939 - No. 17, Sept, 1949; April, 1956
nn-Hawley(1939)-Contains reprints from The Funnies & 1938 Sunday strips by Roy Crane 88 176 264 554 940 1325
Four Color 24 (1943) 50 100 150 310 518 725
Four Color 111(6/46) 14 28 42 99 175 250
10(Standard-10/47) 13 26 39 72 101 130
11,12,14,15,17: 11-17 all contain 1930s & '40s strip-r 10 20 30 54 72 90
13,16: Schomburg-c 11 22 33 62 86 110
Argo 1(4/56)-Reprints 7 14 21 37 46 55

CAPTAIN EASY & WASH TUBBS (See Famous Comics Cartoon Books)

CAPTAIN ELECTRON
Brick Computer Science Institute: Aug, 1986 ($2.25)
1-Disbrow-a 2.50

Captain Fearless Comics #1 © HOKE

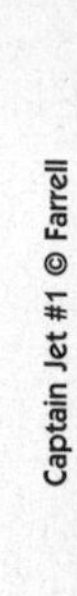
Captain Jet #1 © Farrell

Captain Marvel #1 © MAR

	GD	VG	FN	VF	VF/NM	NM-
	2.0	4.0	6.0	8.0	9.0	9.2

CAPTAIN EO 3-D (Disney)
Eclipse Comics: July, 1987 (Eclipse 3-D Special #18, $3.50, Baxter)

	GD	VG	FN	VF	VF/NM	NM-
1-Adapts 3-D movie						4.00
1-2-D limited edition	1	2	3	4	5	7
1-Large size (11x17", 8/87)-Sold only at Disney Theme parks ($6.95)	2	4	6	10	14	18

CAPTAIN FEARLESS COMICS (Also see Holyoke One-Shot #6, Old Glory Comics & Silver Streak #1)
Helnit Publishing Co. (Holyoke Publ. Co.): Aug, 1941 - No. 2, Sept, 1941

	GD	VG	FN	VF	VF/NM	NM-
1-Origin Mr. Miracle, Alias X, Captain Fearless, Citizen Smith Son of the Unknown Soldier; Miss Victory (1st app.) begins (1st patriotic heroine? before Wonder Woman)	83	166	249	523	887	1250
2-Grit Grady, Captain Stone app.	50	100	150	310	518	725

CAPTAIN FLAG (See Blue Ribbon Comics #16)

CAPTAIN FLASH
Sterling Comics: Nov, 1954 - No. 4, July, 1955

	GD	VG	FN	VF	VF/NM	NM-
1-Origin; Sekowsky-a; Tomboy (female super hero) begins; only pre-code issue; atomic rocket-c	40	80	120	235	380	525
2-4: 4-Flying saucer invasion-c	22	44	66	127	204	280

CAPTAIN FLEET (Action Packed Tales of the Sea)
Ziff-Davis Publishing Co.: Fall, 1952

	GD	VG	FN	VF	VF/NM	NM-
1-Painted-c	15	30	45	88	137	185

CAPTAIN FLIGHT COMICS
Four Star Publications: Mar, 1944 - No. 10, Dec, 1945; No. 11, Feb-Mar, 1947

	GD	VG	FN	VF	VF/NM	NM-
nn	43	86	129	267	446	625
2-4: 4-Rock Raymond begins, ends #7	25	50	75	145	233	320
5-Bondage, classic torture-c; Red Rocket begins; the Grenade app. (scarce)	113	226	339	712	1206	1700
6	23	46	69	135	218	300
7-10: 7-L. B. Cole covers begin, end #11. 8-Yankee Girl begins; intro. Black Cobra & Cobra Kid & begins. 9-Torpedoman app.; last Yankee Girl; Kinstler-a. 10-Deep Sea Dawson, Zoom of the Jungle, Rock Raymond, Red Rocket, & Black Cobra app; bondage-c	52	104	156	322	536	750
11-Torpedoman, Blue Flame (Human Torch clone) app.; last Black Cobra, Red Rocket; classic L. B. Cole robot-c (scarce)	150	300	450	945	1598	2250

CAPTAIN GALLANT (...of the Foreign Legion) (TV) (Texas Rangers in Action No. 5 on?)
Charlton Comics: 1955; No. 2, Jan, 1956 - No. 4, Sept, 1956

	GD	VG	FN	VF	VF/NM	NM-
Non-Heinz version (#1)-Buster Crabbe photo on-c; full page Buster Crabbe photo inside front-c	9	18	27	47	61	75
(Heinz version is listed in the Promotional Comics section)						
2-4: Buster Crabbe in all	8	16	24	42	54	65

CAPTAIN GLORY
Topps Comics: Apr, 1993 ($2.95) (Created by Jack Kirby)

	GD	VG	FN	VF	VF/NM	NM-
1-Polybagged w/Kirbychrome trading card; Ditko-a & Kirby-c; has coupon for Amberchrome Secret City Saga #0						3.00

CAPTAIN HERO (See Jughead as...)

CAPTAIN HERO COMICS DIGEST MAGAZINE
Archie Publications: Sept, 1981

	GD	VG	FN	VF	VF/NM	NM-
1-Reprints of Jughead as Super-Guy	2	4	6	10	14	18

CAPTAIN HOBBY COMICS
Export Publication Ent. Ltd. (Dist. in U.S. by Kable News Co.): Feb, 1948 (Canadian)

	GD	VG	FN	VF	VF/NM	NM-
1	8	16	24	40	50	60

CAPT. HOLO IN 3-D (See Blackthorne 3-D Series #65)

CAPTAIN HOOK & PETER PAN (Movie)(Disney)
Dell Publishing Co.: No. 446, Jan, 1953

	GD	VG	FN	VF	VF/NM	NM-
Four Color 446	9	18	27	60	100	140

CAPTAIN JET (Fantastic Fears No. 7 on)
Four Star Publ./Farrell/Comic Media: May, 1952 - No. 5, Jan, 1953

	GD	VG	FN	VF	VF/NM	NM-
1-Bakerish-a	22	44	66	131	211	290
2	14	28	42	78	112	145
3-5,6(?)	12	24	36	67	94	120

CAPTAIN JOHNER & THE ALIENS
Valiant: May, 1995 - No. 2, May, 1995 ($2.95, shipped in same month)

	GD	VG	FN	VF	VF/NM	NM-
1,2: Reprints Magnus Robot Fighter 4000 A.D. back-up stories; new Paul Smith-c						3.00

CAPTAIN JUSTICE (TV)
Marvel Comics: Mar, 1988 - No. 2, Apr, 1988 (limited series)

	GD	VG	FN	VF	VF/NM	NM-
1,2-Based on the 1987 "Once a Hero" television series						2.50

CAPTAIN KANGAROO (TV)
Dell Publishing Co.: No. 721, Aug, 1956 - No. 872, Jan, 1958

	GD	VG	FN	VF	VF/NM	NM-
Four Color 721 (#1)-Photo-c	15	30	45	108	199	290
Four Color 780, 872-Photo-c	13	26	39	93	164	235

CAPTAIN KIDD (Formerly Dagar; My Secret Story #26 on)(Also see Comic Comics & Fantastic Comics)
Fox Feature Syndicate: No. 24, June, 1949 - No. 25, Aug, 1949

	GD	VG	FN	VF	VF/NM	NM-
24,25: 24-Features Blackbeard the Pirate	15	30	45	83	124	165

CAPTAIN MARVEL (See All Hero, All-New Collectors' Ed., America's Greatest, Fawcett Miniature, Gift, JSA, Kingdom Come, Legends, Limited Collectors' Ed., Marvel Family, Master No. 21, Mighty Midget Comics, Power of Shazam!, Shazam, Special Edition Comics, Whiz, Wisco (in Promotional Comics section), World's Finest #253 and XMas Comics)

CAPTAIN MARVEL (Becomes ...Presents the Terrible 5 No. 5)
M. F. Enterprises: April, 1966 - No. 4, Nov, 1966 (25¢ Giants)

	GD	VG	FN	VF	VF/NM	NM-
nn-(#1 on pg. 5)-Origin; created by Carl Burgos	4	8	12	28	44	60
2-4: 3-(#3 on pg. 4)-Fights the Bat	3	6	9	18	27	35

CAPTAIN MARVEL (Marvel's Space-Born Super-Hero! Captain Marvel #1-6; see Giant-Size..., Life Of..., Marvel Graphic Novel #1, Marvel Spotlight V2#1 & Marvel Super-Heroes #12)
Marvel Comics Group: May, 1968 - No. 19, Dec, 1969; No. 20, June, 1970 - No. 21, Aug, 1970; No. 22, Sept, 1972 - No. 62, May, 1979

	GD	VG	FN	VF	VF/NM	NM-
1	12	24	36	87	156	225
2-Super Skrull-c/story	6	12	18	39	62	85
3-5: 4-Captain Marvel battles Sub-Mariner	5	10	15	30	48	65
6-11: 11-Capt. Marvel given great power by Zo the Ruler; Smith/Trimpe-c; Death of Una	3	6	9	20	30	40
12,13,15-20: 16,17-New costume	3	6	9	14	19	24
14,21: 14-Capt. Marvel vs. Iron Man; last 12¢ issue. 21-Capt. Marvel battles Hulk; last 15¢ issue	3	6	9	20	30	40
22-24	2	4	6	11	16	20
25,26: 25-Starlin-c/a begins; Starlin's 1st Thanos saga begins (3/73), ends #34; Thanos cameo (5 panels). 26-Minor Thanos app. (see Iron Man #55); 1st Thanos-c	4	8	12	26	41	55
27,28-2nd & 3rd app. Thanos. 28-Thanos-c/s	4	8	12	22	34	45
29,30-Thanos cameos. 29-C.M. gains more powers	3	6	9	16	22	28
31,32: Thanos app. 31-Last 20¢ issue. 32-Thanos-c	3	6	9	16	23	30
33-Thanos-c & app.; Capt. Marvel battles Thanos; Thanos origin re-told	4	8	12	22	34	45
34-1st app. Nitro; C.M. contracts cancer which eventually kills him; last Starlin-c/a	3	6	9	16	22	28
35,37-40,42,46-48,50,53-56,58-62: 39-Origin Watcher. 58-Thanos cameo	1	3	4	6	8	10
36,41,43,49: 36-R-origin/1st app. Capt. Marvel from Marvel Super-Heroes #12. 41,43-Wrightson part inks; #43-c(i). 49-Starlin & Weiss-p assists	1	3	4	6	8	11
44,45-(Regular 25¢ editions)(5,7/76)	1	3	4	6	8	10
44,45-(30¢-c variants, limited distribution)	4	8	12	28	44	60
51,52-(Regular 30¢ editions)(7,9/77)	1	3	4	6	8	10
51,52-(35¢-c variants, limited distribution)	5	10	15	32	51	70
57-Thanos appears in flashback	2	4	6	8	11	14

NOTE: ***Alcala** a-35. **Austin** a-46i, 49-53i; c-52i. **Buscema** a-18p-21p. **Colan** a(p)-1-4; c(p)-1-4, 8, 9. **Heck** a-5-10p, 16p. **Gil Kane** a-17-21p; c-17-24p, 37p, 53. **Starlin** a-36. **McWilliams** a-40i. #25-34 were reprinted in The Life of Captain Marvel.*

CAPTAIN MARVEL
Marvel Comics: Nov, 1989 ($1.50, one-shot, 52 pgs.)

	GD	VG	FN	VF	VF/NM	NM-
1-Super-hero from Avengers; new powers						3.00

CAPTAIN MARVEL
Marvel Comics: Feb, 1994 ($1.75, 52 pgs.)

	GD	VG	FN	VF	VF/NM	NM-
1-(Indicia reads Vol 2 #2)-Minor Captain America app.						2.50

CAPTAIN MARVEL
Marvel Comics: Dec, 1995 - No. 6, May, 1996 ($2.95/$1.95)

	GD	VG	FN	VF	VF/NM	NM-
1 ($2.95)-Advs. of Mar-Vell's son begins; Fabian Nicieza scripts; foil-c						3.50
2-6: 2-Begin $1.95-c						2.50

CAPTAIN MARVEL (Vol. 3) (See Avengers Forever)
Marvel Comics: Jan, 2000 - No. 35, Oct, 2002 ($2.50)

	GD	VG	FN	VF	VF/NM	NM-
1-Peter David-s in all; two covers						4.00
2-10: 2-Two covers; Hulk app. 9-Silver Surfer app.						3.00
11-35: 12-Maximum Security x-over. 17,18-Starlin-a. 27-30-Spider-Man 2099 app.						2.50
Wizard #0-Preview and history of Rick Jones						4.00
...: First Contact (8/01, $16.95, TPB) r/#0,1-6						17.00

Captain Marvel V5 #1 © MAR

Captain Marvel Adventures #27 © FAW

Captain Marvel, Jr. #4 © FAW

	GD 2.0	VG 4.0	FN 6.0	VF 8.0	VF/NM 9.0	NM- 9.2

CAPTAIN MARVEL (Vol. 4) (See Avengers Forever)
Marvel Comics: Nov, 2002 - No. 25, Sept, 2004 ($2.25/$2.99)

1-Peter David-s/Chriscross-a ; 3 covers by Ross, Jusko & Chriscross 3.00
2-7: 2,3-Punisher app. 3-Alex Ross-c; new costume debuts. 4-Noto-c. 7-Thor app. 2.50
3-Sketchbook Edition-($3.50) includes Ross' concept design pages for new costume 3.50
8-25: 8-Begin $2.99-c; Thor app.; Manco-c. 10-Spider-Man-c/app. 15-Neal Adams-c 3.00
Vol. 1: Nothing To Lose (2003, $14.99, TPB) r/#1-6 15.00
Vol. 2: Coven (2003, $14.99, TPB) r/#7-12 15.00
Vol. 3: Crazy Like a Fox (2004, $14.99, TPB) r/#13-18 15.00
Vol. 4: Odyssey (2004, $16.99, TPB) r/#19-25 17.00

CAPTAIN MARVEL (Vol. 5) (See Secret Invasion x-over titles)
Marvel Comics: Jan, 2008 - No. 5, Jun, 2008 ($2.99)

1-5-Mar-Vell "from the past in the present"; McGuinness-c/Weeks-a 3.00
3,4-Skrull variant-c 4.00

CAPTAIN MARVEL ADVENTURES (See Special Edition Comics for pre #1)
Fawcett Publications: 1941 (March) - No. 150, Nov, 1953 (#1 on stands 1/16/41)

	GD	VG	FN	VF	VF/NM	NM-
nn(#1)-Captain Marvel & Sivana by Jack Kirby. The cover was printed on unstable paper stock and is rarely found in Fine or Mint condition; blank back inside-c	2750	5500	8250	21,000	36,000	51,000
2-(Advertised as #3, which was counting Special Edition Comics as the real #1); Tuska-a	423	846	1269	2876	5038	7200
3-Metallic silver-c	307	614	921	1934	3267	4600
4-Three Lt. Marvels app.	207	414	621	1304	2202	3100
5	160	320	480	1008	1704	2400
6-10: 9-1st Otto Binder scripts on Capt. Marvel	122	244	366	769	1297	1825
11-15: 12-Capt. Marvel joins the Army. 13-Two pg. Capt. Marvel pin-up. 15-Comic cards on back-c begin, end #26	93	186	279	586	993	1400
16,17: 17-Painted-c	88	176	264	554	940	1325
18-Origin & 1st app. Mary Marvel & Marvel Family (12/11/42); painted-c; Mary Marvel by Marcus Swayze	247	494	741	1556	2628	3700
19-Mary Marvel x-over; Christmas-c	75	150	225	473	799	1125
20,21,23-Attached to the cover, each has a miniature comic just like the Mighty Midget Comics #11, except that each has a full color promo ad on the back cover. Most copies were circulated without the miniature comic. These issues with miniatures attached are very rare, and should not be mistaken for copies with the similar Mighty Midget glued in its place. The Mighty Midgets had blank back covers except for a small victory stamp seal. Only the Capt. Marvel, Captain Marvel Jr. and Golden Arrow No. 11 miniatures have been positively documented as having been affixed to these covers. Each miniature was only partially glued by its back cover to the Captain Marvel comic making it easy to see if it's the genuine miniature rather than a Mighty Midget. with comic attached....	359	718	1077	2441	4271	6100
20,23-Without miniature	68	136	204	428	727	1025
21-Without miniature; Hitler-c	112	224	336	706	1191	1675
22-Mr. Mind serial begins; Mr. Mind first heard	95	190	285	599	1012	1425
24,25	67	134	201	422	711	1000
26-28,30: 26-Flag-c; subtle Mr. Mind 2-panel cameo. 27-1st full Mr. Mind app. (his voice was only heard over the radio before now) (9/43)	55	110	165	347	586	825
29-1st Mr. Mind-c (11/43)	58	116	174	365	615	865
31-35: 35-Origin Radar (5/44, see Master #50)	49	98	147	304	507	710
36-40: 37-Mary Marvel x-over	46	92	138	285	473	660
41-46: 42-Christmas-c. 43-Capt. Marvel 1st meets Uncle Marvel; Mary Batson cameo. 46-Mr. Mind serial ends	40	80	120	235	380	525
47-50	38	76	114	222	356	490
51-53,55-60: 51-63-Bi-weekly issues. 52-Origin & 1st app. Sivana Jr.; Capt. Marvel Jr. x-over	32	64	96	188	302	415
54-Special oversize 68 pg. issue	33	66	99	192	309	425
61-The Cult of the Curse serial begins	35	70	105	203	327	450
62-65-Serial cont.; Mary Marvel x-over in #65	32	64	96	188	302	415
66-Serial ends; Atomic War-c	36	72	108	212	341	470
67-77,79: 69-Billy Batson's Christmas; Uncle Marvel, Mary Marvel, Capt. Marvel Jr. x-over. 71-Three Lt. Marvels app. 79-Origin Mr. Tawny	29	58	87	169	272	375
78-Origin Mr. Atom	33	66	99	192	309	425
80-Origin Capt. Marvel retold	64	128	192	403	682	960
81-84,86-90: 81,90-Mr. Atom app. 82-Infinity-c. 82,86,88,90-Mr. Tawny app.	27	54	81	158	254	350
85-Freedom Train issue	32	64	96	186	298	410
91-99: 92-Mr. Tawny app. 96-Gets 1st name "Tawky"	26	52	78	154	247	340
100-Origin retold; silver metallic-c	47	94	141	291	483	675
101-115,117-120	26	52	78	152	244	335
116-Flying Saucer issue (1/51)	29	58	87	172	276	380
121-Origin retold	34	68	102	198	319	440
122-137,139,140	25	50	75	147	236	325
138-Flying Saucer issue (11/52)	29	58	87	172	276	380
141-Pre-code horror story "The Hideous Head-Hunter"	27	54	81	156	251	345
142-149: 142-used in **POP**, pgs. 92,96	26	52	78	152	244	335
150-(Low distribution)	47	94	141	291	483	675

NOTE: ***Swayze** a-12, 14, 15, 18, 19, 40; c-12, 15, 19.*

CAPTAIN MARVEL AND THE GOOD HUMOR MAN (Movie)
Fawcett Publications: 1950

	GD	VG	FN	VF	VF/NM	NM-
nn-Partial photo-c w/Jack Carson & the Captain Marvel Club Boys	47	94	141	291	483	675

CAPTAIN MARVEL COMIC STORY PAINT BOOK (See Comic Story...)

CAPTAIN MARVEL, JR. (See Fawcett Miniatures, Marvel Family, Master Comics, Mighty Midget Comics, Shazam & Whiz Comics)

CAPTAIN MARVEL, JR.
Fawcett Publications: Nov, 1942 - No. 119, June, 1953 (No #34)

	GD	VG	FN	VF	VF/NM	NM-
1-Origin Capt. Marvel Jr. retold (Whiz #25); Capt. Nazi app. Classic Raboy-c	544	1088	1632	3917	6859	9800
2-Vs. Capt. Nazi; origin Capt. Nippon	200	400	600	1260	2130	3000
3	112	224	336	706	1191	1675
4-Classic Raboy-c	118	236	354	743	1259	1775
5-Vs. Capt. Nazi	95	190	285	599	1012	1425
6-8: 8-Vs. Capt. Nazi	78	156	234	491	833	1175
9-Classic flag-c	85	170	255	536	906	1275
10-Hitler-c	112	224	336	706	1191	1675
11,12,15-Capt. Nazi app.	67	134	201	422	711	1000
13-Classic Hitler, Tojo and Mussolini football-c	112	224	336	706	1191	1675
14,16-20: 14-X-Mas-c. 16-Capt. Marvel & Sivana x-over. 19-Capt. Nazi & Capt. Nippon app.	55	110	165	347	586	825
21-30: 25-Flag-c	45	90	135	279	465	650
31-33,36-40: 37-Infinity-c	32	64	96	186	298	410
35-#34 on inside; cover shows origin of Sivana Jr. which is not on inside. Evidently the cover to #35 was printed out of sequence and bound with contents to #34	32	64	96	186	298	410
41-70: 42-Robot-c. 53-Atomic Bomb-c/story	26	52	78	152	244	335
71-99,101-104: 87-Robot-c. 104-Used in **POP**, pg. 89	20	40	60	118	189	260
100	21	48	72	140	225	310
105-114,116-118: 116-Vampira, Queen of Terror app.	20	40	60	114	180	245
115-Injury to eye-c; Eyeball story w/injury-to-eye panels	46	92	138	285	473	660
119-Electric chair-c (scarce)	51	102	153	316	526	735

NOTE: ***Mac Raboy** c-1-28, 30-32, 57, 59 among others.*

CAPTAIN MARVEL PRESENTS THE TERRIBLE FIVE
M. F. Enterprises: Aug, 1966; V2#5, Sept, 1967 (No #2-4) (25¢)

	GD	VG	FN	VF	VF/NM	NM-
1	4	8	12	26	41	55
V2#5-(Formerly Captain Marvel)	3	6	9	17	25	32

CAPTAIN MARVEL'S FUN BOOK
Samuel Lowe Co.: 1944 (1/2" thick) (cardboard covers)(25¢)

	GD	VG	FN	VF	VF/NM	NM-
nn-Puzzles, games, magic, etc.; infinity-c	36	72	108	212	341	470

CAPTAIN MARVEL SPECIAL EDITION (See Special Edition)

CAPTAIN MARVEL STORY BOOK
Fawcett Publications: Summer, 1946 - No. 4, Summer?, 1948

	GD	VG	FN	VF	VF/NM	NM-
1-Half text	52	104	156	322	536	750
2-4	37	74	111	218	349	480

CAPTAIN MARVEL THRILL BOOK (Large-Size)
Fawcett Publications: 1941 (B&W w/color-c)

	GD	VG	FN	VF	VF/NM	NM-
1-Reprints from Whiz #8,10, & Special Edition #1 (Rare)	300	600	900	3000	-	-

NOTE: *Rarely found in Fine or Mint condition.*

CAPTAIN MIDNIGHT (TV, radio, films) (See The Funnies, Popular Comics & Super Book of Comics)(Becomes Sweethearts No. 68 on)
Fawcett Publications: Sept, 1942 - No. 67, Fall, 1948 (#1-14: 68 pgs.)

	GD	VG	FN	VF	VF/NM	NM-
1-Origin Captain Midnight, star of radio and movies; Captain Marvel cameo on cover	300	600	900	2040	3570	5100
2-Smashes the Jap Juggarnaut	138	276	414	869	1472	2075
3-Classic Nazi war-c	124	248	372	781	1321	1860
4,5: 4-Grapples the Gremlins	108	216	324	680	1153	1625
6-8	67	134	201	422	711	1000
9-Raboy-c	69	138	207	435	735	1035
10-Raboy Flag-c	71	142	213	447	754	1060
11-20: 11,17,18-Raboy-c. 16 (1/44)	50	100	150	310	518	725
21-Classic-c	45	90	135	279	465	650

Capt. Storm #6 © DC

Captain 3-D #1 © HARY

Captain Universe: Power Unimaginable TPB © MAR

	GD 2.0	VG 4.0	FN 6.0	VF 8.0	VF/NM 9.0	NM- 9.2
22,23,25-30: 22-War savings stamp-c	41	82	123	250	413	575
24-Japan flag sunburst-c	48	96	144	298	499	700
31-40	32	64	96	186	298	410
41-59,61-67: 50-Sci/fi theme begins?	24	48	72	140	225	310
60-Flying Saucer issue (2/48)-3rd of this theme; see The Spirit 9/28/47(1st), Shadow Comics V7#10 (2nd, 1/48) & Boy Commandos #26 (4th, 3-4/48)	35	70	105	203	327	450

CAPTAIN NICE (TV)
Gold Key: Nov, 1967 (one-shot)

1(10211-711)-Photo-c 7 14 21 47 76 105

CAPTAIN N: THE GAME MASTER (TV)
Valiant Comics: 1990 - No. 6? ($1.95, thick stock, coated-c)

1-6: 4-6-Layton-c 3.00

CAPTAIN PARAGON (See Bill Black's Fun Comics)
Americomics: Dec, 1983 - No. 4, 1985

1-Intro/1st app. Ms. Victory 4.00
2-4 3.00

CAPTAIN PARAGON AND THE SENTINELS OF JUSTICE
AC Comics: April, 1985 - No. 6, 1986 ($1.75)

1-6: 1-Capt. Paragon, Commando D., Nightveil, Scarlet Scorpion, Stardust & Atoman 3.00

CAPTAIN PLANET AND THE PLANETEERS (TV cartoon)
Marvel Comics: Oct, 1991 - No. 12, Oct, 1992 ($1.00/$1.25)

1-N. Adams painted-c 4.00
2-12: 3-Romita-c 3.00

CAPTAIN POWER AND THE SOLDIERS OF THE FUTURE (TV)
Continuity Comics: Aug, 1988 - No. 2, 1988 ($2.00)

1,2: 1-Neal Adams-c/layouts/inks; variant-c exists. 3.00

CAPTAIN PUREHEART (See Archie as...)

CAPTAIN ROCKET
P. L. Publ. (Canada): Nov, 1951

1 43 86 129 267 446 625

CAPT. SAVAGE AND HIS LEATHERNECK RAIDERS (...And His Battlefield Raiders #9 on)
Marvel Comics Group (Animated Timely Features): Jan, 1968 - No. 19, Mar, 1970
(See Sgt. Fury No. 10)

	GD	VG	FN	VF	VF/NM	NM-
1-Sgt. Fury & Howlers cameo	5	10	15	30	48	65
2,7,11: 2,4-Origin Hydra. 7-Pre-"Thing" Ben Grimm story. 11-Sgt. Fury app.	3	6	9	17	25	32
3-6,8-10,12-14: 14-Last 12¢ issue	3	6	9	16	22	28
15-19	2	4	6	13	18	22

NOTE: *Ayres/Shores a-1-8,11. Ayres/Severin a-9,10,17-19. Heck/Shores a-12-15.*

CAPTAIN SCIENCE (Fantastic No. 8 on)
Youthful Magazines: Nov, 1950 - No. 7, Dec, 1951

	GD	VG	FN	VF	VF/NM	NM-
1-Wood-a; origin; 2 pg. text w/ photos of George Pal's "Destination Moon."	88	176	264	554	940	1325
2-Flying saucer-c swipes Weird Science #13(#2)	48	96	144	298	499	700
3,6,7; 3,6-Bondage c-swipes/Wings #94,91	41	82	123	250	413	575
4,5-Wood/Orlando-c/a(2) each	80	160	240	504	852	1200

NOTE: *Fass a-4. Bondage c-3, 6, 7.*

CAPTAIN SILVER'S LOG OF SEA HOUND (See Sea Hound)

CAPTAIN SINBAD (Movie Adaptation) (See Fantastic Voyages of... & Movie Comics)

CAPTAIN STERNN: RUNNING OUT OF TIME
Kitchen Sink Press: Sept, 1993 - No. 5, 1994 ($4.95, limited series, coated stock, 52 pgs.)

1-5: Berni Wrightson-c/a/scripts 6.00
1-Gold ink variant 10.00

CAPTAIN STEVE SAVAGE (...& His Jet Fighters, No. 2-13)
Avon Periodicals: 1950 - No. 8, 1/53; No. 5, 9-10/54 - No. 13, 5-6/56

	GD	VG	FN	VF	VF/NM	NM-
nn(1st series)-Wood art, 22 pgs. (titled "...Over Korea")	40	80	120	235	380	525
1(4/51)-Reprints nn issue (Canadian)	17	34	51	100	158	215
2-Kamen-a	14	28	42	78	112	145
3-11 (#6, 9-10/54, last precode)	10	20	30	56	76	95
12-Wood-a (6 pgs.)	14	28	42	80	115	150
13-Check, Lawrence-a	10	20	30	58	79	100

NOTE: *Kinstler c-2-5, 7-9, 11. Lawrence a-8. Ravielli a-5, 9.*

	GD	VG	FN	VF	VF/NM	NM-
5(9-10/54-2nd series)(Formerly Sensational Police Cases)	9	18	27	52	69	85
6-Reprints nn issue; Wood-a	10	20	30	56	76	95
7-13: 9,10-Kinstler-c. 10-r/cover #2 (1st series). 13-r/cover #8 (1st series)	8	16	24	42	54	65

CAPTAIN STONE (See Holyoke One-Shot No. 10)

CAPT. STORM (Also see G. I. Combat #138)
National Periodical Publications: May-June, 1964 - No. 18, Mar-Apr, 1967

	GD	VG	FN	VF	VF/NM	NM-
1-Origin	8	16	24	58	97	135
2-7,9-18: 3,6,13-Kubert-a. 4-Colan-a. 12-Kubert-c	5	10	15	34	55	75
8-Grey-tone-c	6	12	18	41	66	90

CAPTAIN 3-D (Super hero)
Harvey Publications: December, 1953 (25¢, came with 2 pairs of glasses)

1-Kirby/Ditko-a (Ditko's 3rd published work tied with Strange Fantasy #9, see also Daring Love #1 & Black Magic V4 #3); shows cover in 3-D on inside; Kirby/Meskin-c 12 24 36 69 97 125

NOTE: *Half price without glasses*

CAPTAIN THUNDER AND BLUE BOLT
Hero Comics: Sept, 1987 - No. 10, 1988 ($1.95)

1-10: 1-Origin Blue Bolt. 3-Origin Capt. Thunder. 6-1st app. Wicket. 8-Champions x-over 2.50

CAPTAIN TOOTSIE & THE SECRET LEGION (Advs. of...)(Also see Monte Hale #30,39 & Real Western Hero)
Toby Press: Oct, 1950 - No. 2, Dec, 1950

	GD	VG	FN	VF	VF/NM	NM-
1-Not Beck-a; both have sci/fi covers	32	64	96	186	298	410
2-The Rocketeer Patrol app.; not Beck-a	20	40	60	115	183	250

CAPTAIN TRIUMPH (See Crack Comics #27)

CAPTAIN UNIVERSE... (5-part x-over)
Marvel Comics: 2005; Jan, 2006

.../ Daredevil 1 (1/06, $2.99) Part 2; Faerber-s/Santacruz-a 3.00
.../ Hulk 1 (1/06, $2.99) Part 1; Faerber-s/Magno-a 3.00
.../ Invisible Woman 1 (1/06, $2.99) Part 4; Faerber-s/Raiz-a; Gladiator app. 3.00
.../ Silver Surfer 1 (1/06, $2.99) Part 5; Faerber-s/Magno-a 3.00
.../ X-23 1 (1/06, $2.99) Part 3; Faerber-s/Portella-a; Scorpion app. 3.00
...: Power Unimaginable TPB (2005, $19.99)-Reprints from Marvel Spotlight #9-11, Incredible Hulk Ann. #10, Marvel Fanfare #25, Web of Spider-Man Ann. #5&6, Marvel Comics Presents #148, Cosmic Power Unlimited #5 20.00
...: Universal Heroes TPB (2005, $13.99) reprints .../Hulk, .../Daredevil, ...X-23 and back-up stories from Amazing Fantasy (2005) #13,14 14.00

CAPTAIN VENTURE & THE LAND BENEATH THE SEA (See Space Family Robinson)
Gold Key: Oct, 1968 - No. 2, Oct, 1969

	GD	VG	FN	VF	VF/NM	NM-
1-r/Space Family Robinson serial; Spiegle-a	4	8	12	28	44	60
2-Spiegle-a	4	8	12	24	37	50

CAPTAIN VICTORY AND THE GALACTIC RANGERS
Pacific Comics: Nov, 1981 - No. 13, Jan, 1984 ($1.00, direct sales, 36-48 pgs.)
(Created by Jack Kirby)

1-1st app. Mr. Mind 4.00
2-13: 3-N. Adams-a 3.00
Special 1-(10/83)-Kirby c/a(p) 4.00

NOTE: *Conrad a-10, 11. Ditko a-6. Kirby a-1-3p; c-1-13.*

CAPTAIN VICTORY AND THE GALACTIC RANGERS
Jack Kirby Comics: July, 2000 - No. 2, Sept, 2000 ($2.95, B&W)

1,2-New Jeremy Kirby-s with reprinted Jack Kirby-a; Liefeld pin-up art 3.00

CAPTAIN VIDEO (TV) (See XMas Comics)
Fawcett Publications: Feb, 1951 - No. 6, Dec, 1951 (No. 1,5,6-36pgs.; 2-4, 52 pgs.)

	GD	VG	FN	VF	VF/NM	NM-
1-George Evans-a(2); 1st TV hero comic	103	206	309	644	1072	1500
2-Used in **SOTI**, pg. 382	67	134	201	419	697	975
3-6-All Evans-a except #5 mostly Evans	55	110	165	344	572	800

NOTE: *Minor Williamson assists on most issues. Photo c-1, 5, 6; painted c-2-4.*

CAPTAIN WILLIE SCHULTZ (Also see Fightin' Army)
Charlton Comics: No. 76, Oct, 1985 - No. 77, Jan, 1986

76,77-Low print run 1 2 3 5 6 8

CAPTAIN WIZARD COMICS (See Meteor, Red Band & Three Ring Comics)
Rural Home: 1946

1-Capt. Wizard dons new costume; Impossible Man, Race Wilkins app. 34 68 102 198 319 440

CARE BEARS (TV, Movie)(See Star Comics Magazine)
Star Comics/Marvel Comics No. 15 on: Nov, 1985 - No. 20, Jan, 1989

1-20: Post-a begins. 11-$1.00-c begins. 13-Madballs app. 4.00

Career Girl Romances #46 © CC

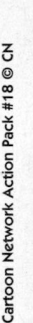

Cartoon Network Action Pack #18 © CN

Casanova #10 © Fraction & Bá

	GD 2.0	VG 4.0	FN 6.0	VF 8.0	VF/NM 9.0	NM- 9.2

CAREER GIRL ROMANCES (Formerly Three Nurses)
Charlton Comics: June, 1964 - No. 78, Dec, 1973

V4#24-31 3 6 9 14 20 25
32-Elvis Presley, Herman's Hermits, Johnny Rivers line drawn-c
10 20 30 68 119 170
33-38,40-50 2 4 6 13 18 22
39-(4/67) 1st app. Tiffany Sinn, C.I.A. Sweetheart, Undercover Agent (also see Secret Agent #10; Dominguel-a 3 6 9 16 23 30
51-78: 70-David Cassidy poster 2 4 6 9 13 16

CAR 54, WHERE ARE YOU? (TV)
Dell Publishing Co.: Mar-May, 1962 - No. 7, Sept-Nov, 1963; 1964 - 1965 (All photo-c)

Four Color 1257(#1, 3-5/62) 8 16 24 56 93 130
2(6-8/62)-7 5 10 15 32 51 70
2,3(10-12/64), 4(1-3/65)-Reprints #2,3,&4 of 1st series
3 6 9 20 30 40

CARL BARKS LIBRARY OF WALT DISNEY'S GYRO GEARLOOSE COMICS AND FILLERS IN COLOR, THE
Gladstone: 1993 ($7.95, 8-1/2x11", limited series, 52 pgs.)

1-6: Carl Barks reprints 1 3 4 6 8 10

CARL BARKS LIBRARY OF WALT DISNEY'S COMICS AND STORIES IN COLOR, THE
Gladstone: Jan, 1992 - No. 51, Mar, 1996 ($8.95, 8-1/2x11", 60 pgs.)

1,2,6,8-51: 1-Barks Donald Duck-r/WDC&S #31-35; 2-r/#36,38-41; 6-r/#57-61; 8-r/#67-71; 9-r/#72-76; 10-r/#77-81; 11-r/#82-86; 12-r/#87-91; 13-r/#92-96; 14-r/#97-101; 15-r/#102-106; 16-r/#107-111; 17-r/#112,114,117,124,125; 18-r/#126-130; 19-r/#131,132(2),133,134; 20-r/#135-139; 21-r/#140-144; 22-r/#145-149; 23-r/#150-154; 24-r/#155-159; 25-r/#160-164; 26-r/#165-169; 27-r/#170-174;28-r/#175-179; 29-r/#180-184; 30-r/#185-189; 31-r/#190-194; 32-r/#195-199;33-r/#200-204; 34-r/#205-209; 35-r/#210-214; 36-r/#215-219; 37-r/#220-224; 38-r/#225-229; 39-r/#230-234; 40-r/#235-239; 41-r/#240-244; 42r/#245-249; 43-r/#250-254; 44-50; All contain one Heroes & Villains trading card each
1 3 4 6 8 10
3,4,7: 3-r/#42-46. 4-r/#47-51. 7-r/#62-66. 2 4 6 9 12 15
5-r/#52-56 2 4 6 11 16 20

CARL BARKS LIBRARY OF WALT DISNEY'S DONALD DUCK ADVENTURES IN COLOR, THE
Gladstone: Jan, 1994 - No. 25, Jan, 1996 ($7.95-$9.95, 44-68 pgs., 8-1/2"x11")
(all contain one Donald Duck trading card each)

1-5,7-25-Carl Barks-r: 1-r/FC #9; 2-r/FC #29; 3-r/FC #62; 4-r/FC #108; 5-r/FC #147 & #79(Mickey Mouse); 7-r/FC #159. 8-r/FC #178 & 189. 9-r/FC #199 & 203; 10-r/FC 223 & 238; 11-r/Christmas Parade #1 & 2; 12-r/FC #296; 13-r/FC #263; 14-r/MOC #20 & 41; 15-r/FC 275 & 282; 16-r/FC #291&300; 17-r/FC #308 & 318; 18-r/Vac. Parade #1 & Summer Fun #2; 19-r/FC #328 & 367 2 4 6 8 10 12
6-r/MOC #4, Cheerios "Atom Bomb," D.D. Tells About Kites
2 4 6 11 16 20

CARL BARKS LIBRARY OF WALT DISNEY'S DONALD DUCK CHRISTMAS STORIES IN COLOR, THE
Gladstone: 1992 ($7.95, 44pgs., one-shot)

nn-Reprints Firestone giveaways 1945-1949 2 4 6 9 12 15

CARL BARKS LIBRARY OF WALT DISNEY'S UNCLE SCROOGE COMICS ONE PAGERS IN COLOR, THE
Gladstone: 1992 - No. 2, 1993 ($8.95, limited series, 60 pgs., 8-1/2x11")

1-Carl Barks one pg. reprints 3 6 9 14 20 25
2-Carl Barks one pg. reprints 2 4 6 9 12 15

CARNAGE: IT'S A WONDERFUL LIFE
Marvel Comics: Oct, 1996 ($1.95, one-shot)

1-David Quinn scripts 3.00

CARNAGE: MIND BOMB
Marvel Comics: Feb, 1996 ($2.95, one-shot)

1-Warren Ellis script; Kyle Hotz-a 3.00

CARNATION MALTED MILK GIVEAWAYS (See Wisco)

CARNEYS, THE
Archie Comics: Summer, 1994 ($2.00, 52 pgs)

1-Bound-in pull-out poster 2.50

CARNIVAL COMICS (Formerly Kayo #12; becomes Red Seal Comics #14)
Harry 'A' Chesler/Pershing Square Publ. Co.: 1945

nn (#13)-Guardineer-a 18 36 54 105 165 225

CAROLINE KENNEDY
Charlton Comics: 1961 (one-shot)

nn-Interior photo covers of Kennedy family 9 18 27 60 100 140

CAROUSEL COMICS
F. E. Howard, Toronto: V1#8, April, 1948

V1#8 8 16 24 42 54 65

CARTOON CARTOONS (Anthology)
DC Comics: Mar, 2001 - No. 33, Oct, 2004 ($1.99/$2.25)

1-33-Short stories of Cartoon Network characters. 3,6,10,13,15-Space Ghost. 13-Begin $2.25-c. 17-Dexter's Laboratory begins 2.50

CARTOON KIDS
Atlas Comics (CPS): 1957 (no month)

1-Maneely-c/a; Dexter The Demon, Willie The Wise-Guy, Little Zelda app.
11 22 33 62 86 110

CARTOON NETWORK ACTION PACK (Anthology)
DC Comics: July, 2006 - Present ($2.25)

1-27-Short stories of Cartoon Network characters. 1,4,6-Rowdyruff Boys app. 2.25

CARTOON NETWORK BLOCK PARTY (Anthology)
DC Comics: Nov, 2004 - Present ($2.25)

1,2,4-47-Short stories of Cartoon Network characters 2.25
3-($2.95) Bonus pages 3.00
... Vol. 1: Get Down! (2005, $6.99, digest) reprints from Dexter's Lab and Cartoon Cartoons 7.00
... Vol. 2: Read All About It! (2005, $6.99, digest) reprints 7.00
... Vol. 3: Can You Dig It?; ... Vol. 4: Blast Off! (2006, $6.99, digest) reprints 7.00

CARTOON NETWORK PRESENTS
DC Comics: Aug, 1997 - No. 24, Aug, 1999 ($1.75-$1.99, anthology)

1-Dexter's Lab 5.00
1-Platinum Edition 1 2 3 5 7 9
2-10: 2-Space Ghost 3.50
11-24: 12-Bizarro World 2.50

CARTOON NETWORK PRESENTS SPACE GHOST
Archie Comics: Mar, 1997 ($1.50)

1-Scott Rosema-p 6.00

CARTOON NETWORK STARRING... (Anthology)
DC Comics: Sept, 1999 - No. 18, Feb, 2001 ($1.99)

1-Powerpuff Girls 5.00
2-18: 2,8,11,14,17-Johnny Bravo. 12,15,18-Space Ghost 3.00

CARTOON TALES (Disney's...)
W.D. Publications (Disney): nd, nn (1992) ($2.95, 6-5/8x9-1/2", 52 pgs.)

nn-Ariel & Sebastian-Serpent Teen; Beauty and the Beast; A Tale of Enchantment; Darkwing Duck - Just Us Justice Ducks; 101 Dalmatians - Canine Classics; Tale Spin - Surprise in the Skies; Uncle Scrooge - Blast to the Past 4.00

CARVERS
Image Comics (Flypaper Press): 1998 - No. 3, 1999 ($2.95)

1-3-Pander Bros.-a/Fleming-s 3.00

CAR WARRIORS
Marvel Comics (Epic): June, 1991 - No. 4, Sept, 1991 ($2.25, lim. series)

1-4: 1-Says April in indicia 2.50

CASANOVA
Image Comics: June, 2006 - Present ($1.99, B&W& olive green or blue)

1-14: 1-7-Matt Fraction-s/Gabriel Bá-a/c. 8-14-Fabio Moon-a 2.50
...: Luxuria TPB (2008, $12.99) r/#1-7; sketch pages and cover gallery 13.00

CASE FILES: SAM & TWITCH (Also see the Spawn titles)
Image Comics: May, 2003 - No. 25, July, 2006 ($2.50/$2.95, color #1-6/B&W #7-on)

1-25: 1-5-Scott Morse-a/Marc Andreyko-s. 7-13-Paul Lee-a. 13-Niles-s 3.00

CASE OF THE SHOPLIFTER'S SHOE (See Perry Mason, Feature Book No.50)

CASE OF THE WINKING BUDDHA, THE
St. John Publ. Co.: 1950 (132 pgs.; 25¢; B&W; 5-1/2x7-5-1/2x8")

nn-Charles Raab-a; reprinted in Authentic Police Cases No. 25
29 58 87 169 272 375

CASEY BLUE
DC Comics (WildStorm): Jul, 2008 - No. 6 ($2.99, limited series)

1-3-B. Clay Moore-s/Carlos Barberi-a 3.00

CASEY-CRIME PHOTOGRAPHER (Two-Gun Western No. 5 on)(Radio)
Marvel Comics (BFP): Aug, 1949 - No. 4, Feb, 1950

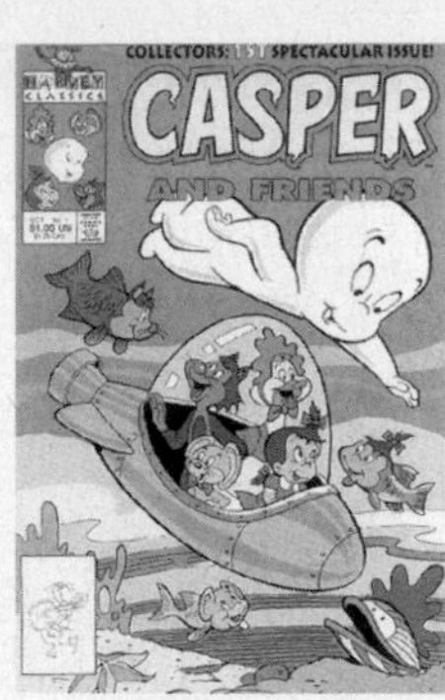

Casper and Friends #1 © HARV

Casper and Nightmare #14 © HARV

Casper, The Friendly Ghost #9 © Paramount

	GD 2.0	VG 4.0	FN 6.0	VF 8.0	VF/NM 9.0	NM- 9.2
1-Photo-c; 52 pgs.	25	50	75	147	236	325
2-4: Photo-c	18	36	54	105	165	225

CASEY JONES (TV)
Dell Publishing Co.: No. 915, July, 1958

	GD	VG	FN	VF	VF/NM	NM-
Four Color 915-Alan Hale photo-c	5	10	15	34	55	75

CASEY JONES & RAPHAEL (See Bodycount)
Mirage Studios: Oct, 1994 ($2.75, unfinished limited series)

1-Bisley-c; Eastman story & pencils — 2.75

CASEY JONES: NORTH BY DOWNEAST
Mirage Studios: May, 1994 - No. 2, July, 1994 ($2.75, limited series)

1,2-Rick Veitch script & pencils; Kevin Eastman story & inks — 2.75

CASPER ADVENTURE DIGEST
Harvey Comics: V2#1, Oct, 1992 - V2#8, Apr, 1994 ($1.75/$1.95, digest-size)

V2#1: Casper, Richie Rich, Spooky, Wendy — 5.00
2-8 — 3.50

CASPER AND...
Harvey Comics: Nov, 1987 - No. 12, June, 1990 (.75/$1.00, all reprints)

1-Ghostly Trio — 5.00
2-12: 2-Spooky; begin $1.00-c. 3-Wendy. 4-Nightmare. 5-Ghostly Trio. 6-Spooky. 7-Wendy. 8-Hot Stuff. 9-Baby Huey. 10-Wendy.11-Ghostly Trio. 12-Spooky — 3.00

CASPER AND FRIENDS
Harvey Comics: Oct, 1991 - No. 5, July, 1992 ($1.00/$1.25)

1-Nightmare, Ghostly Trio, Wendy, Spooky — 4.00
2-5 — 3.00

CASPER AND FRIENDS MAGAZINE: Mar, 1997 - No. 3, July, 1997 ($3.99)

1-3 — 4.00

CASPER AND NIGHTMARE (See Harvey Hits# 37, 45, 52, 56, 59, 62, 65, 68,71, 75)

CASPER AND NIGHTMARE (Nightmare & Casper No. 1-5)
Harvey Publications: No. 6, 11/64 - No. 44, 10/73; No. 45, 6/74 - No. 46, 8/74 (25¢)

	GD	VG	FN	VF	VF/NM	NM-
6: 68 pg. Giants begin, ends #32	5	10	15	34	55	76
7-10	4	8	12	22	34	45
11-20	3	6	9	18	27	35
21-37: 33-37-(52 pg. Giants)	3	6	9	14	20	26
38-46	2	4	6	10	14	18

NOTE: *Many issues contain reprints.*

CASPER AND SPOOKY (See Harvey Hits No. 20)
Harvey Publications: Oct, 1972 - No. 7, Oct, 1973

	GD	VG	FN	VF	VF/NM	NM-
1	3	6	9	18	27	35
2-7	2	4	6	10	14	18

CASPER AND THE GHOSTLY TRIO
Harvey Pub.: Nov, 1972 - No. 7, Nov, 1973; No. 8, Aug, 1990 - No. 10, Dec, 1990

	GD	VG	FN	VF	VF/NM	NM-
1	3	6	9	18	27	35
2-7	2	4	6	10	14	18
8-10						6.00

CASPER AND WENDY
Harvey Publications: Sept, 1972 - No. 8, Nov, 1973

	GD	VG	FN	VF	VF/NM	NM-
1: 52 pg. Giant	3	6	9	18	27	35
2-8	2	4	6	10	14	18

CASPER BIG BOOK
Harvey Comics: V2#1, Aug, 1992 - No. 3, May, 1993 ($1.95, 52 pgs.)

V2#1-Spooky app. — 4.00
2,3 — 3.00

CASPER CAT (See Dopey Duck)
I. W. Enterprises/Super: 1958; 1963

	GD	VG	FN	VF	VF/NM	NM-
1,7:1-Wacky Duck #?.7-Reprint, Super No. 14('63)	2	4	6	9	13	16

CASPER DIGEST (...Magazine #?; ...Halloween Digest #8, 10)
Harvey Publications: Oct, 1986 - No. 18, Jan, 1991 ($1.25/$1.75, digest-size)

	GD	VG	FN	VF	VF/NM	NM-
1	1	3	4	6	8	10
2-18: 11-Valentine-c. 18-Halloween-c						6.00

CASPER DIGEST (...Magazine #? on)
Harvey Comics: V2#1, Sept, 1991 - V2#14, Nov, 1994 ($1.75/$1.95, digest-size)

V2#1 — 5.00
2-14 — 3.50

CASPER DIGEST STORIES
Harvey Publications: Feb, 1980 - No. 4, Nov, 1980 (95¢, 132 pgs., digest size)

	GD	VG	FN	VF	VF/NM	NM-
1	2	4	6	9	13	16
2-4	1	2	3	5	7	9

CASPER DIGEST WINNERS
Harvey Publications: Apr, 1980 - No. 3, Sept, 1980 (95¢, 132 pgs., digest size)

	GD	VG	FN	VF	VF/NM	NM-
1	2	4	6	9	13	16
2,3	1	2	3	5	7	9

CASPER ENCHANTED TALES DIGEST
Harvey Comics: May, 1992 - No. 10, Oct, 1994 ($1.75, digest-size, 98 pgs.)

1-Casper, Spooky, Wendy stories — 5.00
2-10 — 3.50

CASPER GHOSTLAND
Harvey Comics: May, 1992 ($1.25)

1 — 3.00

CASPER GIANT SIZE
Harvey Comics: Oct, 1992 - No. 4, Nov, 1993 ($2.25, 68 pgs.)

V2#1-Casper, Wendy, Spooky stories — 5.00
2-4 — 4.00

CASPER HALLOWEEN TRICK OR TREAT
Harvey Publications: Jan, 1976 (52 pgs.)

	GD	VG	FN	VF	VF/NM	NM-
1	3	6	9	18	27	35

CASPER IN SPACE (Formerly Casper Spaceship)
Harvey Publications: No. 6, June, 1973 - No. 8, Oct, 1973

	GD	VG	FN	VF	VF/NM	NM-
6-8	2	4	6	10	14	18

CASPER'S GHOSTLAND
Harvey Publications: Winter, 1958-59 - No. 97, 12/77; No. 98, 12/79 (25¢)

	GD	VG	FN	VF	VF/NM	NM-
1-84 pgs. begin, ends #10	18	36	54	133	247	360
2	10	20	30	68	119	170
3-10	7	14	21	50	83	115
11-20: 11-68 pgs. begin, ends #61. 13-X-Mas-c	6	12	18	41	66	90
21-40	5	10	15	30	48	65
41-61	3	6	9	17	25	32
62-77: 62-52 pgs. begin	2	4	6	9	13	16
78-98: 94-X-Mas-c	2	4	6	8	10	12

NOTE: *Most issues contain reprints w/new stories.*

CASPER SPACESHIP (Casper in Space No. 6 on)
Harvey Publications: Aug, 1972 - No. 5, April, 1973

	GD	VG	FN	VF	VF/NM	NM-
1: 52 pg. Giant	3	6	9	19	27	38
2-5	2	4	6	11	16	20

CASPER STRANGE GHOST STORIES
Harvey Publications: October, 1974 - No. 14, Jan, 1977 (All 52 pgs.)

	GD	VG	FN	VF	VF/NM	NM-
1	3	6	9	19	29	38
2-14	2	4	6	11	16	20

CASPER, THE FRIENDLY GHOST (See America's Best TV Comics, Famous TV Funday Funnies, The Friendly Ghost..., Nightmare &..., Richie Rich and..., Tastee-Freez, Treasury of Comics, Wendy the Good Little Witch & Wendy Witch World)

CASPER, THE FRIENDLY GHOST (Becomes Harvey Comics Hits No. 61 (No. 6), and then continued with Harvey issue No. 7)(1st Series)
St. John Publishing Co.: Sept, 1949 - No. 5, Aug, 1951

	GD	VG	FN	VF	VF/NM	NM-
1(1949)-Origin & 1st app. Baby Huey & Herman the Mouse (1st comic app. of Casper and the 1st time the name Casper app. in any media, even films)	253	506	759	1594	2697	3800
2,3 (2/50 & 8/50)	92	184	276	580	978	1375
4,5 (3/51 & 8/51)	70	140	210	441	746	1050

CASPER, THE FRIENDLY GHOST (Paramount Picture Star...)(2nd Series)
Harvey Publications (Family Comics): No. 7, Dec, 1952 - No. 70, July, 1958
Note: No. 6 is Harvey Comics Hits No. 61 (10/52)

	GD	VG	FN	VF	VF/NM	NM-
7-Baby Huey begins, ends #9	32	64	96	250	468	685
8,9	20	40	60	148	274	400
10-Spooky begins (1st app., 6/53), ends #70?	25	50	75	185	343	500
11,12: 2nd & 3rd app. Spooky	14	28	42	103	184	265
13-18: Alfred Harvey app. in story	13	26	39	95	168	240
19-1st app. Nightmare (4/54)	20	40	60	148	274	400
20-Wendy the Witch begins (1st app., 5/54)	24	48	72	179	332	485
21-30: 24-Infinity-c	10	20	30	67	116	165
31-40: 38-Early Wendy app. 39-1st app. Samson Honeybun. 40-1st app. Dr. Brainstorm	8	16	24	54	90	125

The Cat #2 © MAR

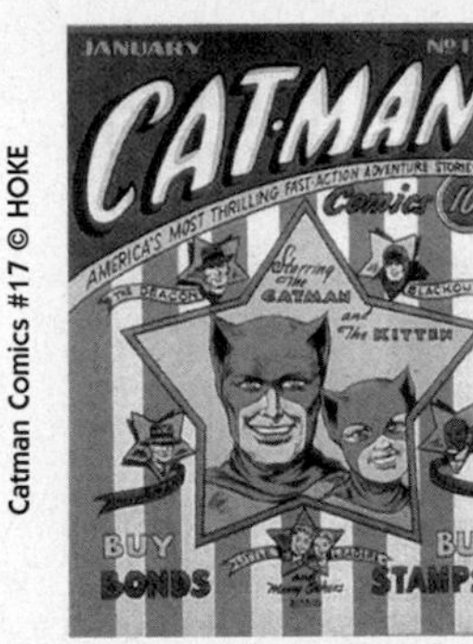

Catman Comics #17 © HOKE

Catwoman #65 © DC

GD VG FN VF VF/NM NM-
2.0 4.0 6.0 8.0 9.0 9.2

41-1st Wendy app. on-c 8 16 24 58 97 135
42-50: 43-2nd Wendy-c. 46-1st app. Spooky's girl Pearl.
6 12 18 43 69 95
51-70 (Continues as Friendly Ghost... 8/58) 58-Early app. Bat Balfrey. 63-2nd app. Something the Baby Ghost. 66-1st app. Wildcat Witch 5 10 15 34 55 75
Harvey Comics Classics Vol. 1 TPB (Dark Horse Books, 6/07, $19.95) Reprints Casper's earliest appearances in this title, Little Audrey, and The Friendly Ghost Casper, mostly B&W with some color stories; history, early concept drawings and animation art 20.00
NOTE: *Baby Huey app. 7 0, 11, 121, 14, 16, 20. Buzzy app. 14, 16, 20. Nightmare app. 19, 27, 36, 37, 42, 46, 51, 53, 56, 70. Spooky app. 10-70. Wendy app. 20, 29-31, 35, 37, 00, 41 40, 51, 52, 54-58, 61, 64, 68.*

CASPER THE FRIENDLY GHOST (Formerly The Friendly Ghost...)(3rd Series)
Harvey Comics: No. 254, July, 1990 - No. 260, Jan, 1991 ($1.00)
254-260 3.00

CASPER THE FRIENDLY GHOST (4th Series)
Harvey Comics: Mar, 1991 - No. 28, Nov, 1994 ($1.00/$1.25/$1.50)
1-Casper becomes Mighty Ghost; Spooky & Wendy app. 5.00
2-10: 7,8-Post-a 3.00
11-28-($1.50) 2.50

CASPER T.V. SHOWTIME
Harvey Comics: Jan, 1980 - No. 5, Oct, 1980
1 2 4 6 9 13 16
2-5 1 2 3 5 7 9

CASSETTE BOOKS (Classics Illustrated)
Cassette Book Co./I.P.S. Publ.: 1984 (48 pgs, b&w comic with cassette tape)
NOTE: *This series was illegal. The artwork was illegally obtained, and the Classics Illustrated copyright owner, Twin Circle Publ. sued to get an injunction to prevent the continued sale of this series. Many C.I. collectors obtained copies before the 1987 injunction, but now they are already scarce. Here again the market is just developing, but sealed mint copies of com ic and tapo should he worth at least $25.*
1001 (CI#1-A2)New-PC 1002(CI#3-A2)CI-PC 1003(CI#13-A2)CI-PC
1004(CI#25)CI-LDC 1005(CI#10-A2)New-PC 1006(CI#64)CI-LDC

CASTILIAN (See Movie Classics)

CASTLEVANIA: THE BELMONT LEGACY
IDW Publishing: March 2005 - No. 5, July, 2005 ($3.99, limited series)
1-5-Marc Andreyko-s/E.J. Su-a 4.00

CASTLE WAITING
Olio: 1997 - No. 7, 1999 ($2.95, B&W)
Cartoon Books: Vol. 2, Aug, 2000 - No. 16 ($2.95/$3.95, B&W)
Fantagraphics Books: Vol. 3, 2006 - Present ($5.95/$3.95, B&W)
1-Linda Medley-s/a in all 1 2 3 5 6 8
2 4.00
3-7 3.00
The Lucky Road TPB r/#1-7 17.00
Hiatus Issue (1999) Crilley-c; short stories and previews 3.00
Vol. 2 #1-6,14-16 (#5&6 also have #12&13 on cover, for series numbering) 3.00
Vol. 3 #1 ($5.95) r/#15,16 and new story 6.00
Vol. 3 #2-12 ($3.95) 4.00

CASUAL HEROES
Image Comics (Motown Machineworks): Apr, 1996 ($2.25, unfinished lim. series)
1-Steve Rude-c 2.50

CAT, T.H.E. (TV) (See T.H.E. Cat)

CAT, THE (See Movie Classics)

CAT, THE (Female hero)
Marvel Comics Group: Nov, 1972 - No. 4, June, 1973
1-Origin & 1st app. The Cat (who later becomes Tigra); Mooney-a(i); Wood-c(i)/a(i)
4 8 12 23 36 48
2,3: 2-Marie Severin/Mooney-a. 3-Everett inks 3 6 9 14 19 24
4-Starlin/Weiss-a(p) 3 6 9 15 21 26

CATALYST: AGENTS OF CHANGE (Also see Comics' Greatest World)
Dark Horse Comics: Feb, 1994 - No.7, Nov, 1994 ($2.00, limited series)
1-7: 1-Foil stamped logo 2.50

CAT & MOUSE
EF Graphics (Silverline): Dec, 1988 ($1.75, color w/part B&W)
1-1st printing (12/88, 32 pgs.), 1-2nd printing (5/89, 36 pgs.) 2.50

CAT FROM OUTER SPACE (See Walt Disney Showcase #46)

CATHOLIC COMICS (See Heroes All Catholic...)
Catholic Publications: June, 1946 - V3#10, July, 1949
1 30 60 90 176 283 390
2 15 30 45 92 144 195
3-13(7/47): 11-Hollingsworth-a 14 28 42 81 118 155
V2#1-10 11 22 33 60 83 105
V3#1-10: Reprints 10-part Treasure Island serial from Target V2#2-11 (see Key Comics #5)
11 22 33 62 86 110
NOTE: ***Orlando** c-V2#10, V3#5, 6, 8.*

CATHOLIC PICTORIAL
Catholic Guild: 1947
1-Toth-a(2) (Rare) 40 80 120 235 380 525

CATMAN COMICS (Formerly Crash Comics No. 1-5)
Holyoke Publishing Co./Continental Magazines V2#12, 7/44 on:
5/41 - No. 17, 1/43; No. 18, 7/43 - No. 22, 12/43; No. 23, 3/44 - No. 26, 11/44; No. 27, 4/45 - No. 30, 12/45; No. 31, 6/46 - No. 32, 8/46
1(V1#6)-Origin The Deacon & Sidekick Mickey, Dr. Diamond & Rag-Man; The Black Widow app.; The Catman by Chas. Quinlan & Blaze Baylor begin
400 800 1200 2720 4760 6800
2(V1#7) 167 334 501 1052 1776 2500
3(V1#8)-The Pied Piper begins; classic Hitler, Stalin & Mussolini-c
153 306 459 964 1632 2300
4(V1#9) 110 220 330 693 1172 1650
5(V2#10)-1st app. Kitten; The Hood begins (c-redated), 6,7(V2#11,12)
92 184 276 580 978 1375
8(V2#13,3/42)-Origin Little Leaders; Volton by Kubert begins (his 1st comic book work)
113 226 339 712 1206 1700
9,10(V2#14,15): 10-Origin Blackout; Phantom Falcon begins
77 154 231 481 816 1150
11 (V3#1)-Kubert-a 77 154 231 481 816 1150
12 (V3#2), 14, 15, 17. 12-Volton by Brodsky, not Kubert. 14-Brodsky-a
62 124 186 391 658 925
13-(scarce) 107 214 321 674 1137 1600
16 (V3#5)-Hitler, Tojo, Mussolini, Goehring-c 100 200 300 630 1065 1500
18(V3#8, 7/43)-(scarce) 72 144 216 454 765 1075
19,20: 19 (V2#6)-Hitler, Tojo, Mussolini-c. 20 (V2#7): Classic Hitler-c
103 06 309 649 1100 1550
21-23 (V2#10, 3/44) 60 120 180 378 639 900
nn(V3#13, 5/44)-Rico-a; Schomburg bondage-c 58 116 174 365 620 875
nn(V2#12, 7/44, nn(V3#1, 9/44)-Origin The Golden Archer; Leatherface app.
53 106 159 334 567 800
nn(V3#2, 11/44)-L. B. Cole-c 92 184 276 580 978 1375
27-Origins Catman & Kitten retold; L. B. Cole Flag-c; Infantino-a
110 220 330 693 1172 1650
28-Dr. Macabre app.; L. B. Cole-c/a 120 240 360 756 1278 1800
29-32-L. B. Cole-c; bondage-#30 107 214 321 674 1137 1600
NOTE: ***Fuje** a-11, 27, 28(2), 29(3), 30. **Palais** a-11, 16, 27, 28, 29(2), 30(2), 32; c-25(7/44). **Rico** a-11(2), 23, 27, 28.*

CAT TALES (3-D)
Eternity Comics: Apr, 1989 ($2.95)
1-Felix the Cat-r in 3-D 5.00

CATWOMAN (Also see Action Comics Weekly #611, Batman #404-407, Detective Comics, & Superman's Girlfriend Lois Lane #70, 71)
DC Comics: Feb, 1989 - No. 4, May, 1989 ($1.50, limited series, mature)
1 1 3 4 6 8 10
2-4: 3-Batman cameo. 4-Batman app. 1 2 3 5 7 9
Her Sister's Keeper (1991, $9.95, trade paperback)-r/#1-4 10.00

CATWOMAN (Also see Showcase '93, Showcase '95 #4, & Batman #404-407)
DC Comics: Aug, 1993 - No. 94, Jul, 2001 ($1.50-$2.25)
0-(10/94)-Zero Hour; origin retold. Released between #14&15 3.00
1-($1.95)-Embossed-c; Bane app.; Balent c-1-10; a-1-10p 4.00
2-20: 3-Bane flashback cameo. 4-Brief Bane app. 6,7-Knightquest tie-ins; Batman (Azrael) app. 8-1st app. Zephyr. 12-KnightsEnd pt. 6. 13-new Knights End Aftermath. 14-(9/94)-Zero Hour 3.00
21-24, 26-30, 33-49: 21-$1.95-c begins. 28,29-Penguin cameo app. 36-Legacy pt. 2. 38-40-Year Two; Batman, Joker, Penguin & Two-Face app. 46-Two-Face app. 2.50
25,31,32: 25-($2.95)-Robin app. 31,32-Contagion pt. 4 (Reads pt. 5 on-c) & pt. 9. 3.00
50-($2.95, 48 pgs.)-New armored costume 3.00
50-($2.95, 48 pgs.)-Collector's Ed.w/metallic ink-c 3.00
51-77: 51-Huntress-c/app. 54-Grayson-s begins. 56-Cataclysm pt.6. 57-Poison Ivy-c/app. 63-65-Joker-c/app. 72-No Man's Land; Ostrander-s begins 2.50
78-82: 80-Catwoman goes to jail 2.50
83-94: 83-Begin $2.25-c. 83,84,89-Harley Quinn-c/app. 2.50
#1,000,000 (11/98) 853rd Century x-over 2.50

Catwoman (2002 series) #58 © DC

Cave Girl #1 © AC

Cerebus the Aardvark #3 © Dave Sim

	GD 2.0	VG 4.0	FN 6.0	VF 8.0	VF/NM 9.0	NM- 9.2
Annual 1 (1994, $2.95, 68 pgs.)-Elseworlds story; Batman app.; no Balent-a						3.00
Annual 2,4 ('95, '97, $3.95) 2-Year One story. 4-Pulp Heroes						4.00
Annual 3 (1996, $2.95)-Legends of the Dead Earth story						3.00
...Plus 1 (11/97, $2.95) Screamqueen (Scare Tactics) app.						3.00
TPB ($9.95) r/#15-19, Balent-c						10.00

CATWOMAN (Also see Detective Comics #759-762)
DC Comics: Jan, 2002 - No. 82, Oct, 2008 ($2.50/$2.99)

1-Darwyn Cooke & Mike Allred-a; Ed Brubaker-s						6.00
2-4						3.00
5-54: 5-9-Rader-a/Paul Pope-c. 10-Morse-c. 16-JG Jones-c. 22-Batman-c/app. 34-36-War Games. 43-Killer Croc app. 44-Hughes-c begin. 50-Zatanna app. 52-Catwoman kills Black Mask. 53-One Year Later; Helena born						2.50
55-81: 55-Begin $2.99-c. 56-58-Wildcat app. 74-Zatanna app. 75-78-Salvation Run						3.00
...: Catwoman Dies TPB (2008, $14.99) r/#66-72; Hughes cover gallery						15.00
...: Crooked Little Town TPB (2003, $14.95) r/#5-10 & Secret Files; Oeming-c						15.00
...: It's Only a Movie TPB (2007, $19.99) r/#59-65						20.00
...: Relentless TPB (2005, $19.95) r/#12-19 & Secret Files						20.00
... Secret Files and Origins (10/02, $4.95) origin-s Oeming-a; profiles and pin-ups						5.00
...Selina's Big Score HC (2002, $24.95) Cooke-s/a; pin-ups by various						25.00
...Selina's Big Score SC (2003, $17.95) Cooke-s/a; pin-ups by various						18.00
...: The Dark End of the Street TPB (2002, $12.95) r/#1-4 & Slam Bradley back-up stories from Detective Comics #759-762						13.00
...: The Replacements TPB (2007, $14.99) r/#53-58						15.00
...: Wild Ride TPB (2005, $14.99) r/#20-24 & Secret Files #1						15.00

CATWOMAN/ GUARDIAN OF GOTHAM
DC Comics: 1999 - No. 2, 1999 ($5.95, limited series)

1,2-Elseworlds; Moench-s/Balent-a 6.00

CATWOMAN: NINE LIVES OF A FELINE FATALE
DC Comics: 2004 ($14.95, TPB)

nn-Reprints notable stories from Batman #1 to the present; pin-ups by various; Bolland-c 15.00

CATWOMAN: THE MOVIE (2004 Halle Berry movie)
DC Comics: 2004 ($4.95/$9.95)

1-($4.95) Movie adaptation; Jim Lee-c and sketch pages; Derenick-a 5.00
... & Other Cat Tales TPB (2004, $9.95)-r/Movie adaptation; Jim Lee sketch pages, r/Catwoman #0, Catwoman (2nd series) #11 & 25; photo-c 10.00

CATWOMAN/VAMPIRELLA: THE FURIES
DC Comics/Harris Publ.: Feb, 1997 ($4.95, squarebound, 46 pgs.) (1st DC/Harris x-over)

nn-Reintro Pantha; Chuck Dixon scripts; Jim Balent-c/a 5.00

CATWOMAN: WHEN IN ROME
DC Comics: Nov, 2004 - No. 6, Aug, 2005 ($3.50, limited series)

1-6-Jeph Loeb-s/Tim Sale-a/c; Riddler app. 3.50
HC (2005, $19.99, dustjacket) r/series; intro by Mark Chiarello; sketch pages 20.00
SC (2007, $12.99) r/series; intro by Mark Chiarello; sketch pages 13.00

CATWOMAN/WILDCAT
DC Comics: Aug, 1998 - No. 4, Nov, 1998 ($2.50, limited series)

1-4-Chuck Dixon & Beau Smith-s; Stelfreeze-c 3.00

CAUGHT
Atlas Comics (VPI): Aug, 1956 - No. 5, Apr, 1957

	GD	VG	FN	VF	VF/NM	NM-
1	22	44	66	127	204	280
2-4: 3-Maneely, Pakula, Torres-a. 4-Maneely-a	13	26	39	74	105	135
5-Crandall, Krigstein-a	14	28	42	78	112	145

NOTE: ***Drucker** a-2. **Heck** a-4. **Severin** c-1, 2, 4, 5. **Shores** a-4.*

CAVALIER COMICS
A. W. Nugent Publ. Co.: 1945; 1952 (Early DC reprints)

	GD	VG	FN	VF	VF/NM	NM-
2(1945)-Speed Saunders, Fang Gow	20	40	60	117	186	255
2(1952)	11	22	33	64	90	115

CAVE GIRL (Also see Africa)
Magazine Enterprises: No. 11, 1953 - No. 14, 1954

	GD	VG	FN	VF	VF/NM	NM-
11(A-1 82)-Origin; all Cave Girl stories	47	94	141	291	483	675
12(A-1 96), 13(A-1 116), 14(A-1 125)-Thunda by Powell in each	37	74	111	215	345	475

NOTE: ***Powell** c/a in all.*

CAVE GIRL
AC Comics: 1988 ($2.95, 44 pgs.) (16 pgs. of color, rest B&W)

1-Powell-r/Cave Girl #11; Nyoka photo back-c from movie; Powell/Bill Black-c; Special Limited Edition on-c 4.00

CAVE KIDS (TV) (See Comic Album #16)
Gold Key: Feb, 1963 - No. 16, Mar, 1967 (Hanna-Barbera)

	GD	VG	FN	VF	VF/NM	NM-
1	7	14	21	45	73	100
2-5	4	8	12	24	37	50
6-16: 7,12-Pebbles & Bamm Bamm app. 16-1st Space Kidettes	3	6	9	20	30	40

CAVEWOMAN
Basement Comics: Jan, 1994 - No. 6, 1995 ($2.95)

	GD	VG	FN	VF	VF/NM	NM-
1	3	6	9	16	23	30
2	2	4	6	9	12	15
3-6	1	2	3	5	6	8
...: Meets Explorers ('97, $2.95)						3.00
...: One-Shot Special (7/00, $2.95) Massey-s/a						3.00

CELESTINE (See Violator Vs. Badrock #1)
Image Comics (Extreme): May, 1996 - No. 2, June, 1996 ($2.50, limited series)

1,2: Warren Ellis scripts 2.50

CENTURION OF ANCIENT ROME, THE
Zondervan Publishing House: 1958 (no month listed) (B&W, 36 pgs.)

	GD	VG	FN	VF	VF/NM	NM-
(Rare) All by Jay Disbrow	55	110	165	347	586	825

CENTURIONS (TV)
DC Comics: June, 1987 - No. 4, Sept, 1987 (75¢, limited series)

1-4 2.50

CENTURY: DISTANT SONS
Marvel Comics: Feb, 1996 ($2.95, one-shot)

1-Wraparound-c 3.00

CENTURY OF COMICS (See Promotional Comics section)

CEREBUS BI-WEEKLY
Aardvark-Vanaheim: Dec. 2, 1988 - No. 26, Nov. 11, 1989 ($1.25, B&W)

	GD	VG	FN	VF	VF/NM	NM-
Reprints Cerebus The Aardvark#1-26						
1-16, 18, 19, 21-26:						3.00
17-Hepcats app.	2	4	6	8	10	12
20-Milk & Cheese app.	2	4	6	10	12	15

CEREBUS: CHURCH & STATE
Aardvark-Vanaheim: Feb, 1991 - No. 30, Apr, 1992 ($2.00, B&W, bi-weekly)

1-30: r/Cerebus #51-80 3.00

CEREBUS: HIGH SOCIETY
Aardvark-Vanaheim: Feb, 1990 - No. 25, 1991 ($1.70, B&W)

1-25: r/Cerebus #26-50 3.00

CEREBUS JAM
Aardvark-Vanaheim: Apr, 1985

1-Eisner, Austin, Dave Sim-a (Cerebus vs. Spirit) 6.00

CEREBUS THE AARDVARK (See A-V in 3-D, Nucleus, Power Comics)
Aardvark-Vanaheim: Dec, 1977 - No. 300, March, 2004 ($1.70/$2.00/$2.25, B&W)

	GD	VG	FN	VF	VF/NM	NM-
0						3.00
0-Gold						20.00
1-1st app. Cerebus; 2000 print run; most copies poorly printed	45	90	135	360	680	1000

Note: *There is a counterfeit version known to exist. It can be distinguished from the original in the following ways: inside cover is glossy instead of flat, black background on the front cover is blotted or spotty. Reports show that a counterfeit #2 also exists.*

	GD	VG	FN	VF	VF/NM	NM-
2-Dave Sim art in all	13	26	39	93	167	235
3-Origin Red Sophia	10	20	30	73	129	185
4-Origin Elrod the Albino	8	16	24	58	97	135
5,6	7	14	21	49	80	110
7-10	6	12	18	39	62	85
11,12: 11-Origin The Cockroach	5	10	15	30	48	65
13-15: 14-Origin Lord Julius	4	8	12	26	41	55
16-20	3	6	9	18	27	35
21-B. Smith letter in letter column	6	12	18	39	62	85
22-Low distribution; no cover price	4	8	12	22	34	45
23-30: 23-Preview of Wandering Star by Teri S. Wood. 26-High Society begins, ends #50	3	6	9	14	20	25
31-Origin Moonroach	3	6	9	16	22	28
32-40, 53-Intro. Wolveroach (brief app.)	2	4	6	8	10	12
41-50,52: 52-Church & State begins, ends #111; Cutey Bunny app.	1	2	3	5	7	9
51,54: 51-Cutey Bunny app. 54-1st full Wolveroach story	2	4	6	8	11	14

The Challenger #2 © T.C. Comics

Challengers of the Unknown (1991 series) #1 © DC

Chamber of Chills #14 © HARV

GD VG FN VF VF/NM NM-
2.0 4.0 6.0 8.0 9.0 9.2

55,56-Wolveroach app.; Normalman back-ups by Valentino
1 3 4 6 8 10
57-100: 61,62: Flaming Carrot app. 65-Gerhard begins 4.00
101-160: 104-Flaming Carrot app. 112/113-Doublo issue. 114-Jaka's Story begins, ends #136. 139-Melmoth begins, ends #150. 151-Mothers & Daughters begins, ends #200 3.00
161-Bone app. 1 3 4 6 8 10
162-231: 175-($2.25, 44 pgs). 186-Strangers in Paradise cameo. 201-Guys storyline begins; Eddie Campbell's Bacchus app. 220-231-Rick's Story 2.50
232-265-Going Home 2.50
266-288,291-299-Latter Days. 267-Five Bar Gate. 270-Sporn (Spawn spoof) 2.50
289&290 ($4.50) Two issues combined 5.00
300-Final issue 2.50
Free Cerebus (Giveaway, 1991-92?, 36 pgs.)-All-r 4.00

CHAIN GANG WAR
DC Comics: July, 1993 - No. 12, June, 1994 ($1.75)

1-($2.50)-Embossed silver foil-c, Dave Johnson-c/a 3.00
2-4,6-12: 3-Deathstroke app. 4-Brief Deathstroke app. 6-New Batman (Azrael) cameo. 11-New Batman-c/story. 12-New Batman app. 2.50
5-($2.50)-Foil-c; Deathstroke app; new Batman cameo (1 panel) 3.00

CHAINS OF CHAOS
Harris Comics: Nov, 1994 - No. 3, Jan, 1995 ($2.95, limited series)

1-3-Re-Intro of The Rook w/ Vampirella 3.00

CHALLENGE OF THE UNKNOWN (Formerly Love Experiences)
Ace Magazines: No. 6, Sept, 1950 (See Web Of Mystery No. 19)

6- "Villa of the Vampire" used in N.Y. Joint Legislative Comm. Publ; Sekowsky-a
35 70 105 208 334 460

CHALLENGER, THE
Interfaith Publications/T.C. Comics: 1945 - No. 4, Oct-Dec, 1946

nn; nd; 32 pgs.; Origin the Challenger Club; Anti-Fascist with funny animal filler
50 100 150 310 518 725
2-4: Kubert-a; 4-Fuje-a 40 80 120 235 380 525

CHALLENGERS OF THE FANTASTIC
Marvel Comics (Amalgam): June 1997 ($1.95, one-shot)

1-Karl Kesel-s/Tom Grummett-a 2.50

CHALLENGERS OF THE UNKNOWN (See Showcase #6, 7, 11, 12, Super DC Giant, and Super Team Family) (See Showcase Presents for B&W reprints)
National Per. Publ./DC Comics: 4-5/58 - No. 77, 12-1/70-71; No. 78, 2/73 - No. 80, 6-7/73; No. 81, 6-7/77 - No. 87, 6-7/78

1-(4-5/58)-Kirby/Stein-a(2); Kirby-c 200 400 600 1750 3375 5000
2-Kirby/Stein-a(2) 65 130 195 553 1052 1550
3-Kirby/Stein-a(2); Rocky returns from space with powers similar to the Fantastic Four (9/58)
56 112 168 476 908 1340
4-8-Kirby/Wood-a plus cover to #8 43 86 129 344 647 950
9,10 25 50 75 188 349 510
11-Grey tone-c 23 46 69 167 309 450
12-15: 14-Origin/1st app. Multi-Man (villain) 18 36 54 130 240 350
16-22: 18-Intro. Cosmo, the Challengers Spacepet. 22-Last 10¢ issue
13 26 39 95 168 240
23-30 8 16 24 58 97 135
31-Retells origin of the Challengers 9 18 27 60 100 140
32-40 6 12 18 41 66 90
41-47,49,50,52-60: 43-New look begins. 49-Intro. Challenger Corps. 55-Death of Red Ryan. 60-Red Ryan returns 4 8 12 28 44 60
48,51: 48-Doom Patrol app. 51-Sea Devils app. 5 10 15 30 48 65
61-68: 64,65-Kirby origin-r, parts 1 & 2. 66-New logo. 68-Last 12¢ issue.
3 6 9 20 30 40
69-73,75-80: 69-1st app. Corinna. 77-Last 15¢ issue 2 4 6 13 18 22
74-Deadman by Tuska/Adams; 1 pg. Wrightson-a 5 10 15 34 55 75
81,83-87: 81-(6-7/77). 83-87-Swamp Thing app. 84-87-Deadman app.
1 3 4 6 8 10
82-Swamp Thing begins (thru #87, c/s 2 4 6 8 11 14

NOTE: ***N. Adams*** *c-67, 68, 70, 72, 74i, 81i.* ***Buckler*** *c-83-86p.* ***Giffen*** *a-83-87p.* ***Kirby*** *a-75-80r; c-75, 77, 78.* ***Kubert*** *c-64, 66, 69, 76, 79.* ***Nasser*** *c/a-81p, 82p.* ***Tuska*** *a-73.* ***Wood*** *r-76.*

CHALLENGERS OF THE UNKNOWN
DC Comics: Mar, 1991 - No. 8, Oct, 1991 ($1.75, limited series)

1-Jeph Loeb scripts & Tim Sale-a in all (1st work together); Bolland-c 3.00
2-8: 2-Superman app. 3-Dr. Fate app. 6-G. Kane-c(p). 7-Steranko-c/swipe by Art Adams 2.50
... Must Die! (2004, $19.95, TPB) r/series; intro by Bendis; Sale sketch pages 20.00

NOTE: ***Art Adams*** *c-7.* ***Hempel*** *c-5.* ***Gil Kane*** *c-6p.* ***Sale*** *a-1-8; c-3, 8.* ***Wagner*** *c-4.*

CHALLENGERS OF THE UNKNOWN
DC Comics: Feb, 1997 - No. 18, July, 1998 ($2.25)

1-18: 1-Intro new team; Leon-c/a(p) begins. 4-Origin of new team. 11,12-Batman app. 15-Millennium Giants x-over; Superman-c/app. 2.50

CHALLENGERS OF THE UNKNOWN
DC Comics: Aug, 2004 - No. 6, Jan, 2005 ($2.95, limited series)

1-6-Intro. new team; Howard Chaykin-s/a 3.00

CHALLENGE TO THE WORLD
Catechetical Guild: 1951 (10¢, 36 pgs.)

nn 6 12 18 28 34 40

CHAMBER (See Generation X and Uncanny X-Men)
Marvel Comics: Oct, 2002 - No. 4, Jan, 2003 ($2.99, limited series)

1-4-Bachalo-c/Vaughan-s/Ferguson-a. 1-Cyclops app. 3.00

CHAMBER OF CHILLS (Formerly Blondie Comics #20; ...of Clues No. 27 on)
Harvey Publications/Witches Tales: No. 21, June, 1951 - No. 26, Dec, 1954

21 (#1) 48 96 144 298 499 700
22,24 (#2,4) 35 70 105 203 327 450
23 (#3)-Excessive violence; eyes torn out 37 74 111 215 345 475
5(2/52)-Decapitation, acid in face scene 37 74 111 215 345 475
6-Woman melted alive 35 70 105 208 334 460
7-Used in **SOTI**, pg. 389; decapitation/severed head panels
33 66 99 196 316 435
8-10: 8-Decapitation panels 27 54 81 160 258 355
11,12,14 22 44 66 129 207 285
13,15-24-Nostrand-a in all. 13,21-Decapitation panels. 18-Atom bomb panels. 20-Nostrand-c
27 54 81 158 254 350
25,26 18 36 54 105 165 225

NOTE: *About half the issues contain bondage, torture, sadism, perversion, gore, cannabalism, eyes ripped out, acid in face, etc.* ***Elias*** *c-4-11, 14-19, 21-26.* ***Kremer*** *a-12, 17.* ***Palais*** *a-21(1), 23.* ***Nostrand/Powell*** *a-13, 15, 16.* ***Powell*** *a-21, 23, 24('51), 5-8, 11, 13, 18-21, 23-25. Bondage-c-21, 24('51), 7. 25-r/#5; 26-r/#9.*

CHAMBER OF CHILLS
Marvel Comics Group: Nov, 1972 - No. 25, Nov, 1976

1-Harlan Ellison adaptation 3 6 9 20 30 40
2-5: 2-1st app. John Jakes' Brak the Barbarian 2 4 6 10 14 18
6-25: 22,23-(Regular 25¢ editions) 2 4 6 8 11 14
22,23-(30¢-c variants, limited distribution)(5,7/76) 4 8 12 24 37 50

NOTE: ***Adkins*** *a-1i, 2i.* ***Brunner*** *a-2-4; c-4.* ***Chaykin*** *a-4.* ***Ditko*** *r-14, 16, 19, 23, 24.* ***Everett*** *a-3i, 11r,21r.* ***Heath*** *a-1r.* ***Gil Kane*** *c-2p.* ***Kirby*** *r-11, 18, 19, 22.* ***Powell*** *a-13r.* ***Russell*** *a-1p, 2p.* ***Shores*** *a-5 .* ***Williamson/Mayo*** *a-13r.* ***Robert E. Howard*** *horror story adaptation-2, 3.*

CHAMBER OF CLUES (Formerly Chamber of Chills)
Harvey Publications: No. 27, Feb, 1955 - No. 28, April, 1955

27-Kerry Drake-r/#19; Powell-a; last pre-code 7 14 21 35 43 50
28-Kerry Drake 6 12 18 28 34 40

CHAMBER OF DARKNESS (Monsters on the Prowl #9 on)
Marvel Comics Group: Oct, 1969 - No. 8, Dec, 1970

1-Buscema-a(p) 7 14 21 45 73 100
2,3: 2-Neal Adams scripts. 3-Smith, Buscema-a 4 8 12 24 37 50
4-A Conan-esque tryout by Smith (4/70); reprinted in Conan #16; Marie Severin/Everett-c 8 16 24 54 90 125
5,8: 5-H.P. Lovecraft adaptation. 8-Wrightson-c 3 6 9 21 31 42
6 3 6 9 18 27 35
7-Wrightson-c/a, 7pgs. (his 1st work at Marvel); Wrightson draws himself in 1st & last panels; Kirby/Ditko-r; last 15¢-c 5 10 15 32 51 70
1-(1/72; 25¢ Special, 52 pgs.) 4 8 12 22 34 45

NOTE: ***Adkins/Everett*** *a-8.* ***Buscema*** *a-Special 1r.* ***Craig*** *a-5.* ***Ditko*** *a-6-8r.* ***Heck*** *a-1, 2, 8, Special 1r.* ***Kirby*** *a(p)-4, 5, 7r.* ***Kirby/Everett*** *c-5.* ***Severin/Everett*** *c-6.* ***Shores*** *a-2, 3i, Special 1r.* ***Sutton*** *a-1, 2i, 4, 7, Special 1r.* ***Wrightson*** *c-7, 8.*

CHAMP COMICS (Formerly Champion No. 1-10)
Worth Publ. Co./Champ Publ./Family Comics(Harvey Publ.): No. 11, Oct, 1940 - No. 24, Dec, 1942; No. 25, April, 1943

11-Human Meteor cont'd. from Champion 92 184 276 580 978 1375
12-17,20: 14,15-Crandall-c. 20-The Green Ghost app.
71 142 213 447 756 1065
18,19-Simon-c. 19-The Wasp app. 88 176 264 554 940 1325
21-23,25: 22-The White Mask app. 23-Flag-c 52 104 156 322 536 750
24-Hitler, Tojo & Mussolini-c 65 130 195 410 693 975

CHAMPION (See Gene Autry's...)

CHAMPION COMICS
Worth Publ. Co.: Oct, 1939 (ashcan)

nn-Ashcan comic, not distributed to newsstands, only for in house use (no known sales)

The Champions #13 © MAR

Charlie Chan #9 © CC

Chase #1 © DC

	GD 2.0	VG 4.0	FN 6.0	VF 8.0	VF/NM 9.0	NM- 9.2

CHAMPION COMICS (Formerly Speed Comics #1?; Champ Comics No. 11 on)
Worth Publ. Co.(Harvey Publications): No. 2, Dec, 1939 - No. 10, Aug, 1940 (no No.1)

2-The Champ, The Blazing Scarab, Neptina, Liberty Lads, Jungleman, Bill Handy, Swingtime Sweetie begin	173	346	519	1090	1845	2600
3-7: 7-The Human Meteor begins?	79	158	237	498	842	1185
8-10: 8-Simon-c. 9-1st S&K-c (1st collaboration together). 10-Bondage-c by Kirby	163	326	489	1027	1739	2450

CHAMPIONS, THE
Marvel Comics Group: Oct, 1975 - No. 17, Jan, 1978

1-Origin & 1st app. The Champions (The Angel, Black Widow, Ghost Rider, Hercules, Iceman); Venus x-over	4	8	12	22	34	45
2-4,8-10,16: 2,3-Venus x-over	2	4	6	10	14	18
5-7-(Regular 25¢ edition)(4-8/76) 6-Kirby-c	2	4	6	10	14	18
5-7-(30¢-c variants, limited distribution)	5	10	15	30	48	65
11-14,17-Byrne-a. 14-(Regular 30¢ edition)	2	4	6	10	14	18
14,15-(35¢-c variant, limited distribution)	6	12	18	37	59	80
15-(Regular 30¢ edition)(9/77)-Byrne-a	2	4	6	10	14	18
... Classic Vol. 1 TPB (2006, $19.99) r/#1-11; unused cover to #7						20.00
... Classic Vol. 2 TPB (2007, $19.99) r/#12-17, Iron Man Ann. #4, Avengers #163, Super-Villain Team-Up #14 and Peter Parker, The Spectacular Spider-Man #17-18						20.00

NOTE: ***Buckler/Adkins** c-3. **Byrne** a-11-15, 17. **Kane/Adkins** c-1. **Kane/Layton** c-11. **Tuska** a-3p, 4p, 6p, 7p. Ghost Rider c-1-4, 7, 8, 10, 14, 16, 17 (4, 10, 14 are more prominent).*

CHAMPIONS (Game)
Eclipse Comics: June, 1986 - No. 6, Feb, 1987 (limited series)

1-6: 1-Intro Flare; based on game. 5-Origin Flare — 2.50

CHAMPIONS (Also see The League of Champions)
Hero Comics: Sept, 1987 - No. 12, 1989 ($1.95)

1-12: 1-Intro The Marksman & The Rose. 14-Origin Malice — 2.50
Annual 1(1988, $2.75, 52pgs.)-Origin of Giant — 2.75

CHAMPION SPORTS
National Periodical Publications: Oct-Nov, 1973 - No. 3, Feb-Mar, 1974

1	3	6	9	16	23	30
2,3	2	4	6	9	12	15

CHANNEL ZERO
Image Comics: Feb, 1998 - No. 5 ($2.95, B&W, limited series)

1-5, ...Dupe (1/99) -Brian Wood-s/a — 3.00

CHAOS (See The Crusaders)

CHAOS! BIBLE
Chaos! Comics: Nov, 1995 ($3.30, one-shot)

1-Profiles of characters & creators — 3.50

CHAOS! CHRONICLES
Chaos! Comics: Feb, 2000 ($3.50, one-shot)

1-Profiles of characters, checklist of Chaos! comics and products — 3.50

CHAOS EFFECT, THE
Valiant: 1994

Alpha (Giveaway w/trading card checklist) — 2.25
Alpha-Gold variant, Alpha-Red variant, Omega-Gold variant — 5.00
Omega (11/94, $2.25); Epilogue Pt. 1, 2 (12/94, 1/95; $2.95) — 3.00

CHAOS! GALLERY
Chaos! Comics: Aug, 1997 ($2.95, one-shot)

1-Pin-ups of characters — 3.00

CHAOS! QUARTERLY
Chaos! Comics: Oct, 1995 -No. 3, May, 1996 ($4.95, quarterly)

1-3: 1-anthology; Lady Death-c by Julie Bell. 2-Boris "Lady Demon"-c — 5.00
1-Premium Edition (7,500) — 25.00

CHAPEL (Also see Youngblood & Youngblood Strikefile #1-3)
Image Comics (Extreme Studios): No. 1 Feb, 1995 - No. 2, Mar, 1995 ($2.50, limited series)

1,2 — 2.50

CHAPEL (Also see Youngblood & Youngblood Strikefile #1-3)
Image Comics (Extreme Studios): V2 #1, Aug, 1995 - No. 7, Apr, 1996 ($2.50)

V2#1-7: 4-Babewatch x-over. 5-vs. Spawn. 7-Shadowhawk-c/app; Shadowhunt x-over — 2.50
#1-Quesada & Palmiotti variant-c — 2.50

CHAPEL (Also see Youngblood & Youngblood Strikefile #1-3)
Awesome Entertainment: Sept, 1997 ($2.99, one-shot)

1 (Reg. & alternate covers) — 3.00

CHARLEMAGNE (Also see War Dancer)
Defiant Comics: Mar, 1994 - No. 5, July, 1994 ($2.50)

1/2 (Hero Illustrated giveaway)-Adam Pollina-c/a.
1-(3/94, $3.50, 52 pgs.)-Adam Pollina-c/a. — 3.50
2,3,5: Adam Pollina-c/a. 2-War Dancer app. 5-Pre-Schism issue. — 2.50
4-($3.25, 52 pgs.) — 3.25

CHARLIE CHAN (See Big Shot Comics, Columbia Comics, Feature Comics & The New Advs. of...)

CHARLIE CHAN (The Adventures of...) (Zaza The Mystic No. 10 on) (TV)
Crestwood(Prize) No. 1-5; Charlton No. 6(6/55) on: 6-7/48 - No. 5, 2-3/49; No.6, 6/55 - No. 9, 3/56

1-S&K-c, 2 pgs.; Infantino-a	83	166	249	523	887	1250
2-5-S&K-c: 3-S&K-c/a	50	100	150	310	518	725
6 (6/55-Charlton)-S&K-c	37	74	111	215	345	475
7-9	20	40	60	117	186	255

CHARLIE CHAN
Dell Publishing Co.: Oct-Dec, 1965 - No. 2, Mar, 1966

1-Springer-a/c	5	10	15	35	55	75
2	4	8	12	22	34	45

CHARLIE McCARTHY (See Edgar Bergen Presents...)
Dell Publishing Co.: No. 171, Nov, 1947 - No. 571, July, 1954 (See True Comics #14)

Four Color 171	24	48	72	176	326	475
Four Color 196-Part photo-c; photo back-c	15	30	45	108	199	290
1(3-5/49)-Part photo-c; photo back-c	14	28	42	102	181	260
2-9(7/52; #5,6-52 pgs.)	8	16	24	56	93	130
Four Color 445,478,527,571	6	12	18	39	62	85

CHARLTON BULLSEYE
CPL/Gang Publications: 1975 - No. 5, 1976 ($1.50, B&W, bi-monthly, magazine format)

1: 1 & 2 are last Capt. Atom by Ditko/Byrne intended for the never published Capt. Atom #90; Nightshade app.; Jeff Jones-a	5	10	15	30	48	65
2-Part 2 Capt. Atom story by Ditko/Byrne	3	6	9	21	32	42
3-Wrong Country by Sanho Kim	2	4	6	13	18	22
4-Doomsday + 1 by John Byrne	3	6	9	17	25	32
5-Doomsday + 1 by Byrne, The Question by Toth; Neal Adams back-c; Toth-c	4	8	12	24	37	50

CHARLTON BULLSEYE
Charlton Publications: June, 1981 - No. 10, Dec, 1982; Nov, 1986

1-Blue Beetle, The Question app.; 1st app. Rocket Rabbit	1	2	3	5	7	9
2-5: 2-1st app. Neil The Horse; Rocket Rabbit app. 4-Vanguards						6.00
6-10: Low print run. 6-Origin & 1st app. Thunderbunny	1	2	3	5	7	9

NOTE: *Material intended for issue #11-up was published in **Scary Tales** #37-up.*

CHARLTON CLASSICS
Charlton Comics: Apr, 1980 - No. 9, Aug, 1981

1-Hercules-r by Glanzman in all — 6.00
2-9 — 5.00

CHARLTON CLASSICS LIBRARY (1776)
Charlton Comics: V10 No.1, Mar, 1973 (one-shot)

1776 (title) - Adaptation of the film musical "1776"; given away at movie theatres; also a newsstand version	3	6	9	14	19	24

CHARLTON PREMIERE (Formerly Marine War Heroes)
Charlton Comics: V1#19, July, 1967; V2#1, Sept, 1967 - No. 4, May, 1968

V1#19, V2#1,2,4: V1#19-Marine War Heroes. V2#1-Trio; intro. Shape, Tyro Team & Spookman. 2-Children of Doom; Boyette classic-a. 4-Unlikely Tales; Aparo, Ditko-a	3	6	9	16	22	28
V2#3-Sinistro Boy Fiend; Blue Beetle & Peacemaker x-over	3	6	9	18	27	35

CHARLTON SPORT LIBRARY - PROFESSIONAL FOOTBALL
Charlton Comics: Winter, 1969-70 (Jan. on cover) (68 pgs.)

1	3	6	9	20	30	40

CHASE (See Batman #550 for 1st app.)
DC Comics: Feb, 1998 - No. 9, Oct, 1998; #1,000,000 Nov, 1998 ($2.50)

1-9: Williams III & Gray-a. 1-Includes 4 Chase cards. 4-Teen Titans app. 7,8-Batman app. 9-GL Hal Jordan-c/app. — 2.50
#1,000,000 (11/98) Final issue; 853rd Century x-over — 2.50

CHASING DOGMA (See Jay and Silent Bob)

Checkmate #22 © DC

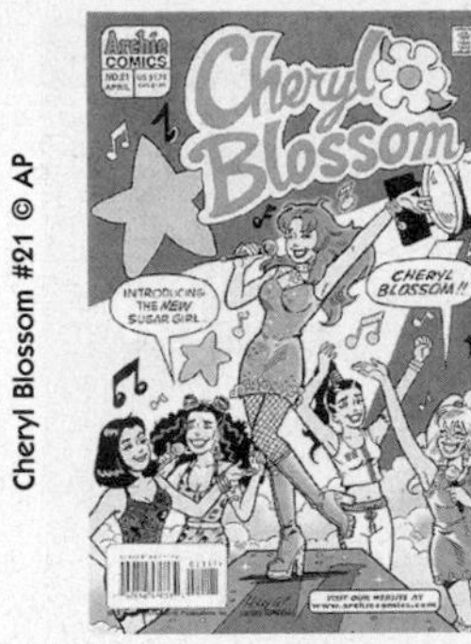

Cheryl Blossom #21 © AP

Cheyenne #17 © DELL

GD VG FN VF VF/NM NM-
2.0 4.0 6.0 8.0 9.0 9.2

CHASSIS
Millenium Publications: 1996 - No. 3 ($2.95)
1-3: 1-Adam Hughes-c. 2-Conner var-c. 3.00

CHASSIS
Hurricane Entertainment: 1998 - No. 3 ($2.95)
0,1-3: 1-Adam Hughes-c. 0-Green var-c. 3.00

CHASSIS (Vol. 3)
Image Comics: Nov, 1999 - No. 4 ($2.95, limited series)
1-4: 1-Two covers by O'Neil and Green. 2-Busch var-c. 3.00
1-($6.95) DF Edition alternate-c by Wieringo 7.00

CHASTITY
Chaos! Comics: (one-shots)
#1/2 (1/01, $2.95) Batista-a 3.00
Heartbreaker (3/02, $2.99) Adrian-a/Molenaar-c 3.00
Love Bites (3/01, $2.99) Vale-a/Romano-c 3.00
Reign of Terror 1 (10/00, $2.95) Grant-s/Ross-a/Rio-c 3.00
Re-Imagined 1 (7/02, $2.99) Conner-c; Toledo-a 3.00

CHASTITY: CRAZYTOWN
Chaos! Comics: Apr, 2002 - No. 3, June, 2002 ($2.99, limited series)
1-3-Nicieza-s/Batista-c/a 3.00

CHASTITY: LUST FOR LIFE
Chaos! Comics: May, 1999 - No. 3, July, 1999 ($2.95, limited series)
1-3-Nutman-s/Benes-c/a 3.00

CHASTITY: ROCKED
Chaos! Comics: Nov, 1998 - No. 4, Feb, 1999 ($2.95, limited series)
1-4-Nutman-s/Justiniano-c/a 3.00

CHASTITY: SHATTERED
Chaos! Comics: Jun, 2001 - No. 3, Sept, 2001 ($2.99, limited series)
1-3-Kaminski & Pulido-s/Batista-c/a 3.00

CHASTITY: THEATER OF PAIN
Chaos! Comics: Feb, 1997 - No. 3, June, 1997 ($2.95, limited series)
1-3-Pulido-s/Justiniano-c/a 3.00
TPB (1997, $9.95) r/#1-3 10.00

CHECKMATE (TV)
Gold Key: Oct, 1962 - No. 2, Dec, 1962
1-Photo-c on both 6 12 18 37 59 80
2 5 10 15 32 51 70

CHECKMATE! (See Action Comics #598 and The OMAC Project)
DC Comics: Apr, 1988 - No. 33, Jan, 1991 ($1.25)
1-33: 13: New format begins 2.50
NOTE: ***Gil Kane*** *c-2, 4, 7, 8, 10, 11, 15-19.*

CHECKMATE (See Infinite Crisis and The OMAC Project)
DC Comics: Jun, 2006 - Present ($2.99)
1-Rucka-s/Saiz-a/Bermejo-c; Alan Scott, Mr. Terrific, Sasha Bordeaux app. 4.00
1-2nd printing with B&W cover 3.00
2-28: 2,3-Kobra, King Faraday, Amanda Waller, Fire app. 13-15-Outsiders app. 26-Chimera origin 3.00
...: A King's GameTPB (2007, $14.99) r/#1-7 15.00
...: Fall of the Wall TPB (2008, $14.99) r/#16-22 15.00
...: Pawn Breaks TPB (2007, $14.99) r/#8-12 15.00

CHERYL BLOSSOM (See Archie's Girls, Betty and Veronica #320 for 1st app.)
Archie Publications: Sept, 1995 - No. 3, Nov, 1995 ($1.50, limited series)
1-3 6.00
Special 1-4 ('95, '96, $2.00) 6.00

CHERYL BLOSSOM (Cheryl's Summer Job)
Archie Publications: July, 1996 - No. 3, Sept, 1996 ($1.50, limited series)
1-3 4.50

CHERYL BLOSSOM (...Goes Hollywood)
Archie Publications: Dec, 1996 - No. 3, Feb, 1997 ($1.50, limited series)
1-3 4.00

CHERYL BLOSSOM
Archie Publications: Apr, 1997 - No. 37, Mar, 2001 ($1.50/$1.75/$1.79/$1.99)
1-Dan DeCarlo-c/a 1 2 3 5 6 8
2-10: 2-7-Dan DeCarlo-c/a 4.50
11-37: 32-Begin $1.99-c. 34-Sabrina app. 2.50

GD VG FN VF VF/NM NM-
2.0 4.0 6.0 8.0 9.0 9.2

CHESTY SANCHEZ
Antarctic Press: Nov, 1995 - No. 2, Mar, 1996 ($2.95, B&W)
1,2 3.00
...Super Special (2/99, $5.99) 6.00

CHEVAL NOIR
Dark Horse Comics: 1989 - No. 48, Nov, 1993 ($3.50, B&W, 68 pgs.)
1-8,10 ($3.50): 6-Moebius poster insert 3.50
9,11,13,15,17,20,22 ($4.50, 84 pgs.) 4.50
12,18,19,21,23 ($3.95): 12-Geary a; Mignola c 4.00
14 ($4.95, 76 pgs.)(7 pgs. color) 5.00
16,24 ($3.75): 16-19-Contain trading cards 3.75
25,26 ($3.95): 26-Moebius-a begins 4.00
27-48 ($2.95): 33-Snyder III-c 3.00
NOTE: ***Bolland*** *a-2, 6, 7, 13, 14.* ***Bolton*** *a-2, 4, 45; c-4, 20.* ***Chadwick*** *c-13.* ***Dorman*** *painted c-16.* ***Geary*** *a-13, 14.* ***Kelley Jones*** *c-27.* ***Kaluta*** *a-6; c-6, 18.* ***Moebius*** *c-5, 9, 26.* ***Dave Stevens*** *c-1, 7.* ***Sutton*** *painted c-36.*

CHEYENNE (TV)
Dell Publishing Co.: No. 734, Oct, 1956 - No. 25, Dec-Jan, 1961-62
Four Color 734(#1)-Clint Walker photo-c 15 30 45 107 196 285
Four Color 772,803: Clint Walker photo-c 9 18 27 60 100 140
4(8-10/57) - 20: 4-9,13-20-Clint Walker photo-c. 10-12-Ty Hardin photo-c 6 12 18 43 69 95
21-25-Clint Walker photo-c on all 7 14 21 45 73 100

CHEYENNE AUTUMN (See Movie Classics)

CHEYENNE KID (Formerly Wild Frontier No. 1-7)
Charlton Comics: No. 8, July, 1957 - No. 99, Nov, 1973
8 (#1) 8 16 24 40 50 65
9,15-19 6 12 18 29 36 42
10-Williamson/Torres-a(3); Ditko-c 11 22 33 60 83 105
11-(68 pgs.)-Cheyenne Kid meets Geronimo 10 20 30 58 79 100
12 Williamson/Torres-a(2) 10 20 30 58 79 100
13-Williamson/Torres-a (5 pgs.) 8 16 24 44 57 70
14-Williamson-a (5 pgs.?) 8 16 24 42 54 65
20-22,24,25-Severin c/a(3) each 4 8 12 22 34 45
23,27-29 3 6 9 16 22 28
26,30-Severin-a 3 6 9 18 27 35
31-59 2 4 6 10 14 18
60-65,67-80 2 4 6 8 11 14
66-Wander by Aparo begins, ends #87 2 4 6 10 14 18
81-99: Apache Red begins #88, origin in #89 2 4 6 8 11 14
Modern Comics Reprint 87,89(1978) 4.00

CHIAROSCURO (THE PRIVATE LIVES OF LEONARDO DA VINCI)
DC Comics (Vertigo): July, 1995 - No. 10, Apr, 1996 ($2.50/$2.95, limited series, mature)
1-9: McGreal and Rawson-s/Truog & Kayanan-a 2.50
10-($2.95) 3.00
TPB (2005, $24.99) r/series; intro. by Alisa Kwitney, afterword by Pat McGreal 25.00

CHICAGO MAIL ORDER (See C-M-O Comics)

CHIEF, THE (Indian Chief No. 3 on)
Dell Publishing Co.: No. 290, Aug, 1950 - No. 2, Apr-June, 1951
Four Color 290(#1) 7 14 21 49 80 110
2 6 12 18 39 62 85

CHIEF CRAZY HORSE (See Wild Bill Hickok #21)
Avon Periodicals: 1950 (Also see Fighting Indians of the Wild West!)
nn-Fawcette-c 21 42 63 123 197 270

CHIEF VICTORIO'S APACHE MASSACRE (See Fight Indians of/Wild West!)
Avon Periodicals: 1951
nn-Williamson/Frazetta-a (7 pgs.); Larsen-a; Kinstler-c 45 90 135 279 465 650

CHILDREN OF FIRE
Fantagor Press: Nov, 1987 - No. 3, 1988 ($2.00, limited series)
1-3: by Richard Corben 4.00

CHILDREN OF THE VOYAGER (See Marvel Frontier Comics Unlimited)
Marvel Frontier Comics: Sept, 1993 - No. 4, Dec, 1993 ($1.95, limited series)
1-($2.95)-Embossed glow-in-the-dark-c; Paul Johnson-c/a 3.00
2-4 2.50

CHILDREN'S BIG BOOK
Dorene Publ. Co.: 1945 (25¢, stiff-c, 68 pgs.)

Chiller #2 © MAR

Chip 'n' Dale #17 © DIS

Christmas Carnival © Z-D

	GD 2.0	VG 4.0	FN 6.0	VF 8.0	VF/NM 9.0	NM- 9.2
nn-Comics & fairy tales; David Icove-a	14	28	42	78	112	145

CHILDREN'S CRUSADE, THE
DC Comics (Vertigo): Dec, 1993 - No. 2, Jan, 1994 ($3.95, limited series)

	GD	VG	FN	VF	VF/NM	NM-
1,2-Neil Gaiman scripts & Chris Bachalo-a; framing issues for Children's Crusade x-over						4.00

CHILD'S PLAY: THE SERIES (Movie)
Innovation Publishing: May, 1991 - #3, 1991 ($2.50, 28pgs.)

	GD	VG	FN	VF	VF/NM	NM-
1-3						2.50

CHILD'S PLAY 2 THE OFFICIAL MOVIE ADAPTATION (Movie)
Innovation Publishing: 1990 - No. 3, 1990 ($2.50, bi-weekly limited series)

	GD	VG	FN	VF	VF/NM	NM-
1-3: Adapts movie sequel						2.50

CHILI (Millie's Rival)
Marvel Comics Group: 5/69 - No. 17, 9/70; No. 18, 8/72 - No. 26, 12/73

	GD	VG	FN	VF	VF/NM	NM-
1	8	16	24	56	93	130
2,4,5	5	10	15	30	48	65
3-Millie & Chili visit Marvel and meet Stan Lee & Stan Goldberg (6 pgs.)	5	10	15	32	51	70
6-17	4	8	12	24	37	50
18-26	3	6	9	20	30	40
Special 1(12/71, 52 pgs.)	5	10	15	32	51	70

CHILLER
Marvel Comics (Epic): Nov, 1993 - No. 2, Dec, 1993 ($7.95, lim. series)

	GD	VG	FN	VF	VF/NM	NM-
1,2-(68 pgs.)	1	2	3	5	6	8

CHILLING ADVENTURES IN SORCERY (...as Told by Sabrina #1, 2)
(Red Circle Sorcery No. 6 on)
Archie Publications (Red Circle Prods.): 9/72 - No. 2, 10/72; No. 3, 10/73 - No. 5, 2/74

	GD	VG	FN	VF	VF/NM	NM-
1-Sabrina cameo as narrator	5	10	15	30	48	65
2-Sabrina cameo as narrator	3	6	9	17	25	32
3-5: Morrow-c/a, all. 4,5-Alcazar-a	2	4	6	10	14	18

CHILLING TALES (Formerly Beware)
Youthful Magazines: No. 13, Dec, 1952 - No. 17, Oct, 1953

	GD	VG	FN	VF	VF/NM	NM-
13(No.1)-Harrison-a; Matt Fox-c/a	67	134	201	422	711	1000
14-Harrison-a	44	88	132	273	454	635
15-Has #14 on-c; Matt Fox-c; Harrison-a	52	104	156	322	541	760
16-Poe adapt.-'Metzengerstein'; Rudyard Kipling adapt.- 'Mark of the Beast,' by Kiefer; bondage-c	40	80	120	239	387	535
17-Matt Fox-c; Sir Walter Scott & Poe adapt.	44	88	132	273	454	635

CHILLING TALES OF HORROR (Magazine)
Stanley Publications: V1#1, 6/69 - V1#7, 12/70; V2#2, 2/71 - V2#6, 10/71(50¢, B&W, 52 pgs.)

	GD	VG	FN	VF	VF/NM	NM-
V1#1	7	14	21	45	73	100
2-4,(no #5),6,7: 7-Cameron-a	5	10	15	30	48	65
V2#2-6: 2-Two different #2 issues exist (2/71 & 4/71). 2-(2/71) Spirit of Frankenstein -r/Adventures into the Unknown #16. 4-(8/71) different from other V2#4(6/71)	4	8	12	28	44	60
V2#4-(6/71) r/9 pg. Feldstein-a from Adventures into the Unknown #3	5	10	15	30	48	65

NOTE: *Two issues of V2#2 exist, Feb, 1971 and April, 1971. Two issues of V2#4 exist, Jun, 1971 and Aug, 1971.*

CHILLY WILLY (Also see New Funnies #211)
Dell Publ. Co.: No. 740, Oct, 1956 - No. 1281, Apr-June, 1962 (Walter Lantz)

	GD	VG	FN	VF	VF/NM	NM-
Four Color 740 (#1)	7	14	21	45	73	100
Four Color 852 (2/58),967 (2/59),1017 (9/59),1074 (2-4/60),1122 (8/60), 1177 (4-6/61), 1212 (7-9/61), 1281	5	10	15	30	48	65

CHIMERA
CrossGeneration Comics: Mar, 2003 - No. 4, July, 2003 ($2.95, limited series)

	GD	VG	FN	VF	VF/NM	NM-
1-4-Marz-s/Peterson-c/a						3.00
Vol. 1 TPB (2003, $15.95) r/#1-4 plus sketch pages, 3-D models, how-to guides						16.00

CHINA BOY (See Wisco in the Promotional Comics section)

CHIP 'N' DALE (Walt Disney)(See Walt Disney's C&S #204)
Dell Publishing Co./Gold Key/Whitman No. 65 on: Nov, 1953 - No. 30, June-Aug, 1962; Sept, 1967 - No. 83, July, 1984

	GD	VG	FN	VF	VF/NM	NM-
Four Color 517(#1)	10	20	30	73	129	185
Four Color 581	6	12	18	43	69	95
Four Color 636	6	12	18	43	69	95
4(12/55-2/56)-10	6	12	18	37	59	80
11-30	5	10	15	30	48	65
1(Gold Key, 1967)-Reprints	3	6	9	19	29	38
2-10	2	4	6	11	16	20
11-20	2	4	6	8	11	14
21-40	1	3	4	6	8	10
41-64,70-77: 75(2/82), 76(2-3/82), 77(3/82)	1	2	3	5	6	8
65,66 (Whitman)	2	4	6	8	10	12
67-69 (3-pack? 1980): 67(8/80), 68(10/80) (scarce)	4	8	12	22	34	45
78-83 (All #90214; 3-pack, nd, nd code): 78(4/83), 79(5/83), 80(7/83), 81(8/83), 82(5/84), 83(7/84)	3	6	9	14	20	26

NOTE: *All Gold Key/Whitman issues have reprints except No. 32-35, 38-41, 45-47. No. 23-28, 30-42, 45-47, 49 have new covers.*

CHIP 'N DALE RESCUE RANGERS
Disney Comics: June, 1990 - No. 19, Dec, 1991 ($1.50)

	GD	VG	FN	VF	VF/NM	NM-
1-New stories; origin begins						3.00
2-19: 2-Origin continued						2.50

CHITTY CHITTY BANG BANG (See Movie Comics)

C.H.I.X.
Image Comics (Studiosaurus): Jan, 1998 ($2.50)

	GD	VG	FN	VF	VF/NM	NM-
1-Dodson, Haley, Lopresti, Randall, and Warren-s/c/a						3.00
1-($5.00) "X-Ray Variant" cover						5.00
C.H.I.X. That Time Forgot 1 (8/98, $2.95)						3.00

CHOICE COMICS
Great Publications: Dec, 1941 - No. 3, Feb, 1942

	GD	VG	FN	VF	VF/NM	NM-
1-Origin Secret Circle; Atlas the Mighty app.; Zomba, Jungle Fight, Kangaroo Man, & Fire Eater begin	152	304	456	958	1617	2275
2	76	152	228	479	810	1140
3-Double feature; Features movie "The Lost City" (classic cover); continued from Great Comics #3	137	274	411	863	1457	2050

CHOLLY AND FLYTRAP (Arthur Suydam's...)
Image Comics: Nov, 2004 - No. 4, June, 2005 ($4.95/$5.95, limited series)

	GD	VG	FN	VF	VF/NM	NM-
1-($4.95) Arthur Suydam-s/a/c						5.00
2-4-($5.95)						6.00

CHOO CHOO CHARLIE
Gold Key: Dec, 1969

	GD	VG	FN	VF	VF/NM	NM-
1-John Stanley-a	9	18	27	63	107	150

CHOSEN
Dark Horse Comics: Jan, 2004 - No. 3, Aug, 2004 ($2.99, limited series)

	GD	VG	FN	VF	VF/NM	NM-
1-Story of the second coming; Mark Millar-s/Peter Gross-a						4.00
2,3						3.00

CHRISTIAN (See Asylum)
Maximum Press: Jan, 1996 ($2.99, one-shot)

	GD	VG	FN	VF	VF/NM	NM-
1-Pop Mhan-a						3.00

CHRISTIAN HEROES OF TODAY
David C. Cook: 1964 (36 pgs.)

	GD	VG	FN	VF	VF/NM	NM-
nn	3	6	9	17	25	32

CHRISTMAS (Also see A-1 Comics)
Magazine Enterprises: No. 28, 1950

	GD	VG	FN	VF	VF/NM	NM-
A-1 28	8	16	24	40	50	60

CHRISTMAS ADVENTURE, A (See Classics Comics Giveaways, 12/69)

CHRISTMAS ALBUM (See March of Comics No. 312)

CHRISTMAS ANNUAL
Golden Special: 1975 ($1.95, 100 pgs., stiff-c)

	GD	VG	FN	VF	VF/NM	NM-
nn-Reprints Mother Goose stories with Walt Kelly-a	4	8	12	22	34	45

CHRISTMAS & ARCHIE
Archie Comics: Jan, 1975 ($1.00, 68 pgs., 10-1/4x13-1/4" treasury-sized)

	GD	VG	FN	VF	VF/NM	NM-
1-(scarce)	6	12	18	39	62	85

CHRISTMAS BELLS (See March of Comics No. 297)

CHRISTMAS CARNIVAL
Ziff-Davis Publ. Co./St. John Publ. Co. No. 2: 1952 (25¢, one-shot, 100 pgs.)

	GD	VG	FN	VF	VF/NM	NM-
nn	35	70	105	203	327	450
2-Reprints Ziff-Davis issue plus-c	17	34	51	98	154	210

CHRISTMAS CAROL, A (See March of Comics No. 33)

CHRISTMAS EVE, A (See March of Comics No. 212)

CHRISTMAS IN DISNEYLAND (See Dell Giants)

CHRISTMAS PARADE (See Dell Giant No. 26, Dell Giants, March of Comics No. 284, Walt Disney Christmas Parade & Walt Disney's...)

Chromium Man #7 © CKH

Chuck #1 © WB

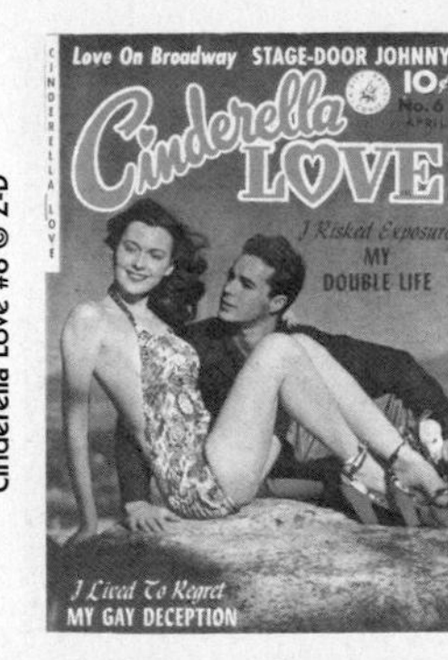

Cinderella Love #6 © Z-D

	GD 2.0	VG 4.0	FN 6.0	VF 8.0	VF/NM 9.0	NM- 9.2

CHRISTMAS PARADE (Walt Disney's)
Gold Key: 1962 (no month listed) - No. 9, Jan, 1972 (#1,5: 80 pgs.; #2-4,7-9: 36 pgs.)

	GD	VG	FN	VF	VF/NM	NM-
1 (30018-301)-Giant	9	18	27	60	100	140
2-6: 2-r/F.C. #367 by Barks. 3-r/F.C. #178 by Barks. 4-r/F.C. #203 by Barks. 5-r/Christmas Parade #1 (Dell) by Barks; giant. 6-r/Christmas Parade #2 (Dell) by Barks (64 pgs.); giant	6	12	18	41	66	90
7-Pull-out poster (half price w/o poster)	5	10	15	32	51	70
8-r/F.C. #367 by Barks; pull-out poster	6	12	18	41	66	90
9	4	8	12	26	41	55

CHRISTMAS PARTY (See March of Comics No. 256)

CHRISTMAS STORIES (See Little People No. 959, 1062)

CHRISTMAS STORY (See March of Comics No. 326 in the Promotional Comics section)

CHRISTMAS STORY BOOK (See Woolworth's Christmas Story Book)

CHRISTMAS TREASURY, A (See Dell Giants & March of Comics No. 227)

CHRISTMAS WITH ARCHIE
Spire Christian Comics (Fleming H. Revell Co.): 1973, 1974 (49¢, 52 pgs.)

	GD	VG	FN	VF	VF/NM	NM-
nn-Low print run	2	4	6	11	16	20

CHRISTMAS WITH MOTHER GOOSE
Dell Publishing Co.: No. 90, Nov, 1945 - No. 253, Nov, 1949

	GD	VG	FN	VF	VF/NM	NM-
Four Color 90 (#1)-Kelly-a	17	34	51	122	226	330
Four Color 126 ('46), 172 (11/47)-By Walt Kelly	13	26	39	95	168	240
Four Color 201 (10/48), 253-By Walt Kelly	11	22	33	79	140	200

CHRISTMAS WITH SANTA (See March of Comics No. 92)

CHRISTMAS WITH THE SUPER-HEROES (See Limited Collectors' Edition)
DC Comics: 1988; No. 2, 1989 ($2.95)

	GD	VG	FN	VF	VF/NM	NM-
1,2: 1-(100 pgs.)-All reprints; N. Adams-r, Byrne-c; Batman, Superman, JLA, LSH Christmas stories; r-Miller's 1st Batman/DC Special Series #21. 2-(68 pgs.)-Superman by Chadwick; Batman, Wonder Woman, Deadman, Green Lantern, Flash app.; Morrow-a; Enemy Ace by Byrne; all new-a						5.00

CHROMA-TICK, THE (...Special Edition, #1,2) (Also see The Tick)
New England Comics Press: Feb, 1992 - No. 8, Nov, 1993 ($3.95/$3.50, 44 pgs.)

	GD	VG	FN	VF	VF/NM	NM-
1,2-Includes serially numbered trading card set						5.00
3-8 ($3.50, 36 pgs.): 6-Bound-in card						4.00

CHROME
Hot Comics: 1986 - No. 3, 1986 ($1.50, limited series)

	GD	VG	FN	VF	VF/NM	NM-
1-3						2.50

CHROMIUM MAN, THE
Triumphant Comics: Aug, 1993 - No.10, May, 1994 ($2.50)

	GD	VG	FN	VF	VF/NM	NM-
1-1st app. Mr. Death; all serially numbered						2.50
2-10: 2-1st app. Prince Vandal. 3-1st app. Candi, Breaker & Coil. 4,5-Triumphant Unleashed x-over. 8,9-(3/94). 10-(5/94)						2.50
0-(4/94)-Four color-c, 0-All pink-c & all blue-c; no cover price						2.50

CHROMIUM MAN: VIOLENT PAST, THE
Triumphant Comics: Jan, 1994 - No. 2, Jan, 1994 ($2.50, limited series)

	GD	VG	FN	VF	VF/NM	NM-
1,2-Serially numbered to 22,000 each						2.50

CHRONICLES OF CONAN, THE (See Conan the Barbarian)

CHRONICLES OF CORUM, THE (Also see Corum...)
First Comics: Jan, 1987 - No. 12, Nov, 1988 ($1.75/$1.95, deluxe series)

	GD	VG	FN	VF	VF/NM	NM-
1-12: Adapts Michael Moorcock's novel						2.50

CHRONOS
DC Comics: Mar, 1998 - No. 11, Feb. 1999 ($2.50)

	GD	VG	FN	VF	VF/NM	NM-
1-11-J.F. Moore-s/Guinan-a						2.50
#1,000,000 (11/98) 853rd Century x-over						2.50

CHUCK (Based on the NBC TV series)
DC Comics (WildStorm): Aug, 2008 - No. 6 ($2.99, limited series)

	GD	VG	FN	VF	VF/NM	NM-
1,2-Jeremy Haun-a/Kristian Donaldson-c; Noto back-up-a						3.00

CHUCKLE, THE GIGGLY BOOK OF COMIC ANIMALS
R. B. Leffingwell Co.: 1945 (132 pgs., one-shot)

	GD	VG	FN	VF	VF/NM	NM-
1-Funny animal	22	44	66	127	204	280

CHUCK NORRIS (TV)
Marvel Comics (Star Comics): Jan, 1987 - No. 4, July, 1987

	GD	VG	FN	VF	VF/NM	NM-
1-3: Ditko-a						3.50
4-No Ditko-a (low print run)						5.00

	GD 2.0	VG 4.0	FN 6.0	VF 8.0	VF/NM 9.0	NM- 9.2

CHUCK WAGON (See Sheriff Bob Dixon's...)

CHUCKY (Based on the 1988 killer doll movie Child's Play)
Devil's Due Publishing: Apr, 2007 - No. 4, Nov, 2007 ($3.50/$5.50)

	GD	VG	FN	VF	VF/NM	NM-
1-3-Pulido-s/Medors-a; art & photo covers						3.50
4-($5.50)						5.50
TPB (2007, $18.99) r/series; gallery of variant covers; 4 pages of script and sketch art						19.00

CHYNA (WWF Wrestling)
Chaos! Comics: Sept, 2000; July, 2001 ($2.95/$2.99, one-shots)

	GD	VG	FN	VF	VF/NM	NM-
1-Grant-s/Barrows-a; photo-c						3.00
1-($9.95) Premium Edition; Cleavenger-c						10.00
II -(7/01, $2.99) Deodato-a; photo-c						0.00

CICERO'S CAT
Dell Publishing Co.: July-Aug, 1959 - No. 2, Sept-Oct, 1959

	GD	VG	FN	VF	VF/NM	NM-
1-Cat from Mutt & Jeff	5	10	15	30	48	65
2	4	8	12	26	41	55

CIMARRON STRIP (TV)
Dell Publishing Co.: Jan, 1968

	GD	VG	FN	VF	VF/NM	NM-
1-Stuart Whitman photo-c	4	8	12	24	37	50

CINDER AND ASHE
DC Comics: May, 1988 - No. 4, Aug, 1988 ($1.75, limited series)

	GD	VG	FN	VF	VF/NM	NM-
1-4: Mature readers						2.50

CINDERELLA (Disney) (See Movie Comics)
Dell Publishing Co.: No. 272, Apr, 1950 - No. 786, Apr, 1957

	GD	VG	FN	VF	VF/NM	NM-
Four Color 272	12	24	36	87	156	225
Four Color 786-Partial-r #272	7	14	21	45	73	100

CINDERELLA
Whitman Publishing Co.: Apr, 1982

	GD	VG	FN	VF	VF/NM	NM-
nn-Reprints 4-Color #272	1	2	3	4	5	7

CINDERELLA LOVE
Ziff-Davis/St. John Publ. Co. No. 12 on: No. 10, 1950, No. 11, 4 5/51; No. 12, 9/51; No. 4, 10-11/51 - No. 11, Fall, 1952; No. 12, 10/53 - No. 15, 8/54; No. 25, 12/54 - No. 29, 10/55 (No #16-24)

	GD	VG	FN	VF	VF/NM	NM-
10(#1)(1st Series, 1950)-Painted-c	15	30	45	90	140	190
11(#2, 4-5/51)-Crandall-a; Saunders painted-c	11	22	33	62	86	110
12(#3, 9/51)-Photo-c	10	20	30	54	72	90
4-8: 4,6,7-Photo-c	9	18	27	50	65	80
9-Kinstler-a; photo-c	10	20	30	56	76	95
10,11(Fall/'52), 14: 10,11-Photo-c. 14-Baker-a	10	20	30	54	72	90
12(St. John-10/53)-#13:13-Painted-c.	9	18	27	47	61	75
15(8/54)-Matt Baker-c	11	22	33	62	86	110
25(2nd Series)(Formerly Romantic Marriage) Baker-c	11	22	33	62	86	110
26-Baker-c; last precode (2/55)	11	22	33	62	86	110
27,29: Both Matt Baker-c	11	22	33	62	86	110
28	8	16	24	42	54	65

CINDY COMICS (...Smith No. 39, 40; Crime Can't Win No. 41 on)(Formerly Krazy Komics)
(See Junior Miss & Teen Comics)
Timely Comics: No. 27, Fall, 1947 - No. 40, July, 1950

	GD	VG	FN	VF	VF/NM	NM-
27-Kurtzman-a, 3 pgs: Margie, Oscar begin	22	44	66	129	207	285
28-31-Kurtzman-a	14	28	42	82	121	160
32-40: 33-Georgie story; anti-Wertham editorial	11	22	33	62	86	110

NOTE: *Kurtzman's "Hey Look"-#27(3), 29(2), 30(2), 31; "Giggles 'n' Grins"-28.*

CINNAMON: EL CICLO
DC Comics: Oct, 2003 - No. 5, Feb, 2004 ($2.50, limited series)

	GD	VG	FN	VF	VF/NM	NM-
1-5-Van Meter-s/Chaykin-c/Paronzini-a						2.50

CIRCLE, THE
Image Comics: Nov, 2007 - Present ($2.99)

	GD	VG	FN	VF	VF/NM	NM-
1-5-Reed-s/Hosfeld-a						3.00

CIRCUS (...the Comic Riot)
Globe Syndicate: June, 1938 - No. 3, Aug, 1938

	GD	VG	FN	VF	VF/NM	NM-
1-(Scarce)-Spacehawks (2 pgs.), & Disk Eyes by Wolverton (2 pgs.), Pewee Throttle by Cole (2nd comic book work; see Star Comics V1#11), Beau Gus, Ken Craig & The Lords of Crillon, Jack Hinton by Eisner, Van Bragger by Kane	517	1034	1551	3722	6511	9300
2,3-(Scarce)-Eisner, Cole, Wolverton, Bob Kane-a in each	300	600	900	1890	3195	4500

CIRCUS BOY (TV) (See Movie Classics)
Dell Publishing Co.: No. 759, Dec, 1956 - No. 813, July, 1957

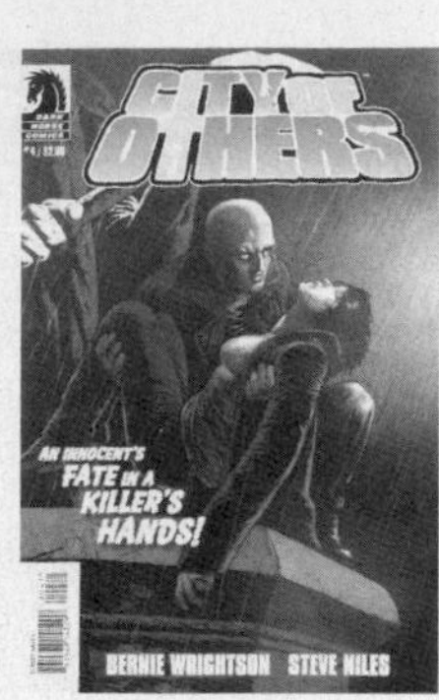

City of Others #4 © Niles & Wrightson

Civil War #4 © MAR

Clandestine (2008 series) #1 © MAR

GD 2.0 | VG 4.0 | FN 6.0 | VF 8.0 | VF/NM 9.0 | NM- 9.2

Four Color 759 (#1)-The Monkees' Mickey Dolenz photo-c 12 24 36 87 156 225
Four Color 785 (4/57),813-Mickey Dolenz photo-c 10 20 30 70 123 175

CIRCUS COMICS
Farm Women's Pub. Co./D. S. Publ.: 1945 - No. 2, Jun, 1945; Wint., 1948-49
1-Funny animal 14 28 42 80 115 150
2 9 18 27 50 65 80
1(1948)-D.S. Publ.; 2 pgs. Frazetta 24 48 72 140 225 310

CIRCUS OF FUN COMICS
A. W. Nugent Publ. Co.: 1945 - No. 3, Dec, 1947 (A book of games & puzzles)
1 15 30 45 83 124 165
2,3 10 20 30 54 72 90

CISCO KID, THE (TV)
Dell Publishing Co.: July, 1950 - No. 41, Oct-Dec, 1958
Four Color 292(#1)-Cisco Kid, his horse Diablo, & sidekick Pancho & his horse Loco begin; painted-c begin 22 44 66 157 291 425
2(1/51) 11 22 33 79 140 200
3-5 10 20 30 70 123 175
6-10 9 18 27 60 100 140
11-20 8 16 24 52 86 120
21-36-Last painted-c 6 12 18 43 69 95
37-41: All photo-c 8 16 24 54 90 125
NOTE: ***Buscema** a-40. **Ernest Nordli** painted c-5-16, 20, 35.*

CISCO KID COMICS
Bernard Bailey/Swappers Quarterly: Winter, 1944 (one-shot)
1-Illustrated Stories of the Operas: Faust; Funnyman by Giunta; Cisco Kid (1st app.) & Superbaby begin; Giunta-c 43 86 129 267 446 625

CITIZEN SMITH (See Holyoke One-Shot No. 9)

CITIZEN V AND THE V-BATTALION (See Thunderbolts)
Marvel Comics: June, 2001 - No. 3, Aug, 2001 ($2.99, limited series)
1-3-Nicieza-a; Michael Ryan-c/a 3.00
...: The Everlasting 1-4 (3/02 - No. 4, 7/02) Nicieza-s/LaRosa-a(p) 3.00

CITY OF HEROES (Online game)
Dark Horse Comics/Blue King Studios: Sept, 2002; May, 2004 - No. 7 ($2.95)
1-(no cover price) Dakan-s/Zombo-a 2.50
1-7-($2.95) 3.00

CITY OF HEROES (Online game)
Image Comics: June, 2005 - No. 20, Aug, 2007 ($2.99)
1-20: 1-Waid-s; Pérez-c. 6-Flp-c with City of Villains. 7-9-Jurgens-s 3.00

CITY OF OTHERS
Dark Horse Comics: Apr, 2007 - No. 4, Aug, 2007 ($2.99, limited series)
1-4-Bernie Wrightson-a/c; Steve Niles & Wrightson-s 3.00
TPB (2/08, $14.95) r/#1-4; Wrightson sketch pages 15.00

CITY OF SILENCE
Image Comics: May, 2000 - No. 3, July, 2000 ($2.50)
1-3-Ellis-s/Erskine-a 2.50
TPB (6/04, $9.95) r/#1-3; pin-up gallery 10.00

CITY OF THE LIVING DEAD (See Fantastic Tales No. 1)
Avon Periodicals: 1952
nn-Hollingsworth-c/a 48 96 144 298 499 700

CITY OF TOMORROW
DC Comics (WildStorm): June, 2005 - No. 6, Nov, 2005 ($2.99, limited series)
1-6-Howard Chaykin-s/a 3.00
TPB (2006, $19.99) r/#1-6 20.00

CITY PEOPLE NOTEBOOK
Kitchen Sink Press: 1989 ($9.95, B&W, magazine sized)
nn-Will Eisner-s/a 10.00
nn-(DC Comics, 2000) Reprint 10.00

CITY SURGEON (Blake Harper...)
Gold Key: August, 1963
1(10075-308)-Painted-c 4 8 12 24 37 50

CIVIL WAR (Also see Amazing Spider-Man for TPB)
Marvel Comics: July, 2006 - No. 7, Jan, 2007 ($3.99/$2.99, limited series)
1-($3.99) Millar-s/McNiven-a & wraparound-c 1 2 3 5 6 8
1-Variant cover by Michael Turner 2 4 6 9 12 15
1-Aspen Comics Variant cover by Turner 2 4 6 9 12 15
1-Director's Cut (2006, $4.99) r/#1 plus promo art, variant covers, sketches and script 5.00
2-($2.99) Spider-Man unmasks 1 2 3 4 5 7
2-Turner variant cover 5.00
2-B&W sketch variant cover 20.00
2-2nd printing 4.00
3-7: 3-Thor returns. 4-Goliath killed 4.00
3-7-Turner variant covers 5.00
3-7-B&W sketch variant covers 15.00
TPB (2007, $24.99) r/#1-7; gallery of variant covers 25.00
...: Battle Damage Report (2007, $3.99) Post-Civil War character profiles; McGuiness-c 4.00
...: Choosing Sides (2/07, $3.99) Colan-c; Howard the Duck app.; 2 covers by Yu & Colan 4.00
... Companion TPB (2007, $13.99) r/Civil War Files, ...:Battle Damage Report, Marvel Spotlight: Millar/McNiven, Marvel Spotlight: Civil War Aftermath and Daily Bugle CW 14.00
Daily Bugle Civil War Newspaper Special #1 (9/06, 50¢, newsprint) Daily Bugle "newspaper" overview of the crossover; Mayhew-a 2.50
...Files (2006, $3.99) profile pages of major Civil War characters; McNiven-c 4.00
...: Marvel Universe TPB (2007, $11.99) r/Civil War: Choosing Sides, CW: The Return, She-Hulk #8, CW: The Initiative; She-Hulk sketch page; variant cover gallery 12.00
...: The Initiative (4/07, $4.99) Silvestri-c/a; previews of post-Civil War series 5.00
...: The Return (3/07, $2.99) Captain Marvel returns; The Sentry app.; Raney-a 3.00
...: The Road to Civil War TPB (2007, $14.99) r/New Avengers: Illuminati, Fantastic Four #536 & 537, Amazing Spider-Man #529-531; Spider-Man costume sketches by Bachalo 15.00
... War Crimes (2/07, $3.99) Kingpin in prison; Tieri-s/Staz Johnson-a 4.00
... War Crimes TPB (2007, $17.99) r/Civil War: War Crimes one-shot and Underworld #1-5 18.00
... X-Men Universe TPB (2007, $13.99) r/Cable & Deadpool #30-32; X-Factor #8,9 14.00

CIVIL WAR CHRONICLES (Reprints of Civil War and related Marvel issues)
Marvel Comics: Oct, 2007 - No. 12, Sept, 2008 ($4.99, limited series)
1-12: Reprints Civil War, Civil War: Frontline and x-over issues 5.00

CIVIL WAR: FRONTLINE (Tie-in to Civil War and related Marvel issues)
Marvel Comics: Aug, 2006 - No. 11, Apr, 2007 ($2.99, limited series)
1-Jenkins-s/Bachs-a/Watson-c; back-up stories by various 4.00
2-11: 3-Green Goblin app. 11-Aftermath of Civil War #7 3.00
... Book 1 TPB (2007, $14.99) r/#1 6 15.00
... Book 2 TPB (2007, $14.99) r/#7-11 15.00

CIVIL WAR: HOUSE OF M
Marvel Comics: Nov, 2008 - No. 5 ($2.99, limited series)
1-Gage-s/DiVito-a 3.00

CIVIL WAR MUSKET, THE (Kadets of America Handbook)
Custom Comics, Inc.: 1960 (25¢, half-size, 36 pgs.)
nn 3 6 9 16 22 28

CIVIL WAR: X-MEN (Tie-in to Civil War)
Marvel Comics: Sept, 2006 - No. 4, Dec, 2006 ($2.99, limited series)
1-4-Paquette-a/Hine-s; Bishop app. 3.00
1-Variant cover by Michael Turner 10.00
TPB (2007, $11.99) r/#1-4, profile pages of minor characters 12.00

CIVIL WAR: YOUNG AVENGERS & RUNAWAYS (Tie-in to Civil War)
Marvel Comics: Sept, 2006 - No. 4, Dec, 2006 ($2.99, limited series)
1-4-Caselli-a/Wells-s/Cheung-c 3.00
TPB (2007, $11.99) r/#1-4, profile pages of characters 12.00

CLAIRE VOYANT (Also see Keen Teens)
Leader Publ./Standard/Pentagon Publ.: 1946 - No. 4, 1947 (Sparling strip reprints)
nn 66 132 198 416 701 985
2,4: 2-Kamen-c. 4-Kamen bondage-c 49 98 147 304 507 710
3-Kamen bridal-c; contents mentioned in Love and Death, a book by Gershom Legman(1949) referenced by Dr. Wertham in **SOTI** 57 114 171 359 605 850

CLANDESTINE (Also see Marvel Comics Presents & X-Men: ClanDestine)
Marvel Comics: Oct, 1994 - No.12, Sept, 1995 ($2.95/$2.50)
1-($2.95)-Alan Davis-c/a(p)/scripts & Mark Farmer-c/a(i) begin, ends #8; Modok app.; Silver Surfer cameo; gold foil-c 3.00
2-12: 2-Wraparound-c. 2,3-Silver Surfer app. 5-Origin of ClanDestine. 6-Capt. America, Hulk, Spider-Man, Thing & Thor-c; Spider-Man cameo. 7-Spider-Man-c/app; Punisher cameo. 8-Invaders & Dr. Strange app. 10-Captain Britain-c/app. 11-Sub-Mariner app. 2.50
Preview (10/94, $1.50) 2.50
... Classic HC (2008, $29.99, DJ) r/#1-8, Marvel Comics Presents #158, X-Men and Clandestine #1&2, sketch pages and cover gallery; Alan Davis afterword 30.00

CLANDESTINE
Marvel Comics: Apr, 2008 - No. 5, Aug, 2008 ($2.99, limited series)

Classic Comics #1 © GIL

Classic Comics #2 © GIL

Classic Comics #3 © GIL

1-5: 1-Alan Davis-c/a(p)/scripts & Mark Farmer-c/a(i). 2-5-Excalibur app. 3.00

CLASH
DC Comics: 1991 - No. 3, 1991 ($4.95, limited series, 52 pgs.)

Book One - Three: Adam Kubert-c/a 5.00

CLASSIC BATTLESTAR GALACTICA (See Battlestar Galactica, Classic...)

CLASSIC COMICS/ILLUSTRATED - INTRODUCTION
by Dan Malan

Since the first publication of this special introduction to the **Classics** section, a number of revisions have been made to further clarify the listings. **Classics** reprint editions prior to 1963 had either incorrect dates or no dates listed. Those reprint editions should be identified only by the highest number on the reorder list (HRN). Past *Guides* listed what were calculated to be approximately correct dates, but many people found it confusing for the *Guide* to list a date not listed in the comic itself.

We have also attempted to clear up confusion about edition variations, such as color, printer, etc. Such variations are identified by letters. Editions are determined by three categories. Original edition variations are designated as Edition 1A, 1B, etc. All reprint editions prior to 1963 are identified by HRN only. All reprint editions from 9/63 on are identified by the correct date listed in the comic.

Information is also included on four reprintings of **Classics**. From 1968-1976, Twin Circle, the Catholic newspaper, serialized over 100 **Classics** titles. That list can be found under non-series items at the end of this section. In 1972, twelve **Classics** were reissued as **Now Age Books Illustrated**. They are listed under **Pendulum Illustrated Classics**. In 1982, 20 **Classics** were reissued, adapted for teaching English as a second language. They are listed under **Regents Illustrated Classics**. Then in 1984, six **Classics** were reissued with cassette tapes. See the listing under **Cassette Books**.

UNDERSTANDING CLASSICS ILLUSTRATED
by Dan Malan

Since **Classics Illustrated** is the most complicated comic book series, with all its reprint editions and variations, changes in covers and artwork, a variety of means of identifying editions, and the most extensive worldwide distribution of any comic-book series, this introductory section is provided to assist you in gaining expertise about this series.

THE HISTORY OF CLASSICS

The **Classics** series was the brain child of Albert L. Kantor, who saw in the new comic-book medium a means of introducing children to the great classics of literature. In October of 1941 his Gilberton Co. began the **Classic Comics** series with **The Three Musketeers**, with 64 pages of storyline. In those early years, the struggling series saw irregular schedules and numerous printers, not to mention variable art quality and liberal story adaptations. With No.13 the page total was reduced to 56 (except for No. 33, originally scheduled to be No. 9), and with No. 15 the coming-next ad on the outside back cover moved inside. In 1945 the Jerry Iger Shop began producing all new CC titles, beginning with No. 23. In 1947 the search for a classier logo resulted in **Classics Illustrated**, beginning with No. 35, **Last Days of Pompeii**. With No. 45 the page total dropped again to 48, which was to become the standard.

Two new developments in 1951 had a profound effect upon the success of the series. One was the introduction of painted covers, instead of the old line drawn covers, beginning with No. 81, **The Odyssey**. The second was the switch to the major national distributor Curtis. They raised the cover price from 10 to 15 cents, making it the highest priced comic-book, but it did not slow the growth of the series, because they were marketed as books, not comics. Because of this higher quality image, **Classics** flourished during the fifties while other comic series were reeling from outside attacks. They diversified with their new **Juniors**, **Specials**, and **World Around Us** series.

Classics artwork can be divided into three distinct periods. The pre-Iger era (1941-44) was mentioned above for its variable art quality. The Iger era (1945-53) was a major improvement in art quality and adaptations. It came to be dominated by artists Henry Kiefer and Alex Blum, together accounting for some 50 titles. Their styles gave the first real personality to the series. The EC era (1954-62) resulted from the demise of the EC horror series, when many of their artists made the major switch to classical art.

But several factors brought the production of new CI titles to a complete halt in 1962. Gilberton lost its 2nd class mailing permit. External factors like television, cheap paperback books, and Cliff Notes were all eating away at their market. Production halted with No.167, **Faust**, even though many more titles were already in the works. Many of those found their way into foreign series, and are very desirable to collectors. In 1967, **Classics Illustrated** was sold to Patrick Frawley and his Catholic publication, Twin Circle. They issued two new titles in 1969 as part of an attempted revival, but succumbed to major distribution problems in 1971. In 1988, First Publishing acquired the rights to use the old CI series art, logo, and name from the Frawley Group, and released a short-lived series featuring contributions of modern creators. Acclaim Books and Twin Circles issued a series of **Classics** reprints from 1997-1998.

One of the unique aspects of the **Classics Illustrated** (CI) series was the proliferation of reprint variations. Some titles had as many as 25 editions. Reprinting began in 1943. Some **Classic Comics** (CC) reprints (r) had the logo format revised to a banner logo, and added a motto under the banner. In 1947 CC titles changed to the CI logo, but kept their line drawn covers (LDC). In 1948, Nos. 13, 18, 29 and 41 received second covers (LDC2), replacing covers considered too violent, and reprints of Nos. 13-44 had pages reduced to 48, except for No. 26, which had 48 pages to begin with.

Starting in the mid-1950s, 70 of the 80 LDC titles were reissued with new painted covers (PC). Thirty of them also received new interior artwork (A2). The new artwork was generally higher quality with larger art panels and more faithful but abbreviated storylines. Later on, there were 29 second painted covers (PC2), mostly by Twin Circle. Altogether there were 199 interior art variations (169 (O)s and 30 A2 editions) and 272 different covers (169 (O)s, four LDC2s, 70 new PCs of LDC (O)s, and 29 PC2s). It is mildly astounding to realize that there are nearly 1400 different editions in the U.S. CI series.

FOREIGN CLASSICS ILLUSTRATED

If U.S. Classics variations are mildly astounding, the veritable plethora of foreign CI variations will boggle your imagination. While we still anticipate additional discoveries, we presently know about series in 25 languages and 27 countries. There were 250 new CI titles in foreign series, and nearly 400 new foreign covers of U.S. titles. The 1400 U.S. CI editions pale in comparison to the 4000 plus foreign editions. The very nature of CI lent itself to flourishing as an international series. Worldwide, they published over one billion copies! The first foreign CI series consisted of six Canadian Classic Comic reprints in 1946.

The following chart shows when CI series first began in each country:
1946: Canada. 1947: Australia. 1948: Brazil/The Netherlands. 1950: Italy. 1951: Greece/Japan/Hong Kong(?)/England/Argentina/Mexico. 1952: West Germany. 1954: Norway. 1955: New Zealand/South Africa. 1956: Denmark/Sweden/Iceland. 1957: Finland/France. 1962: Singapore(?). 1964: India (8 languages). 1971: Ireland (Gaelic). 1973: Belgium(?) /Philippines(?) & Malaysia(?).

Significant among the early series were Brazil and Greece. In 1950, Brazil was the first country to begin doing its own new titles. They issued nearly 80 new CI titles by Brazilian authors. In Greece in 1951 they actually had debates in parliament about the effects of Classics Illustrated on Greek culture, leading to the inclusion of 88 new Greek History & Mythology titles in the CI series.

But by far the most important foreign CI development was the joint European series which began in 1956 in 10 countries simultaneously. By 1960, CI had the largest European distribution of any American publication, not just comics! So when all the problems came up with U.S. distribution, they literally moved the CI operation to Europe in 1962, and continued producing new titles in all four CI series. Many of them were adapted and drawn in the U.S., the most famous of which was the British CI #158A. Dr. No, drawn by Norman Nodel. Unfortunately, the British CI series ended in late 1963, which limited the European CI titles available in English to 15. Altogether there were 82 new CI art titles in the joint European series, which ran until 1976.

IDENTIFYING CLASSICS EDITIONS

HRN: This is the highest number on the reorder list. It should be listed in ( ) after the title number. It is crucial to understanding various CI editions.

ORIGINALS (O): This is the all-important First Edition. To determine (O)s,there is one primary rule and two secondary rules (with exceptions):

Rule No. 1: All (O)s and only (O)s have coming-next ads for the next number. **Exceptions**: No. 14(15) (reprint) has an ad on the last inside text page only. No. 14(0) also has a full-page outside back cover ad (also rule 2). Nos.55(75) and 57(75) have coming-next ads. (Rules 2 and 3 apply here). Nos. 168(0) and 169(0) do not have coming-next ads. No.168 was never reprinted; No. 169(0) has HRN (166). No. 169(169) is the only reprint.

Rule No. 2: On nos.1-80, all (O)s and only (O)s list 10c on the front cover. **Exceptions**: Reprint variations of Nos. 37(62), 39(71), and 46(62) list 10c on the front cover. (Rules 1 and 3 apply here.)

Rule No. 3: All (O)s have HRN close to that title No. **Exceptions**: Some reprints also have HRNs close to that title number: a few CC(r)s, 58(62), 60(62), 149(149), 152(149) 153(149), and title nos. in the 160's. (Rules 1 and 2 apply here.)

DATES: Many reprint editions list either an incorrect date or no date. Since Gilberton apparently kept track of CI editions by HRN, they often left the (O) date on reprints. Often, someone with a CI collection for sale will swear that all their copies are originals. That is why we are so detailed in pointing out how to identify original editions. Except for original editions, which should have a coming-next ad, etc., all CI dates prior to 1963 are incorrect! So you want to go by HRN only if it is (165) or below, and go by listed date if it is 1963 or later. There are a few (167) editions with incorrect dates. They could be listed either as (167) or (62/3), which is meant to indicate that they were issued sometime between late 1962 and early 1963.

COVERS: A change from CC to LDC indicates a logo change, not a cover change; while a change from LDC to LDC2, LDC to PC, or from PC to PC2 does indicate a new cover. New PCs can be identified by HRN, and PC2s can be identified by HRN and date. Several covers had color changes, particularly from purple to blue.

Notes: If you see 15 cents in Canada on a front cover, it does not necessarily indicate a Canadian edition. Editions with an HRN between 44 and 75, with 15 cents on the cover are Canadian. Check the publisher's address. An HRN listing two numbers with a / between them indicates that there are two different reorder lists in the front and back covers. Official Twin Circle editions have a full-page back cover ad for their TC magazine, with no CI reorder list.

Classic Comics #4 © GIL

Classic Comics #5 © GIL

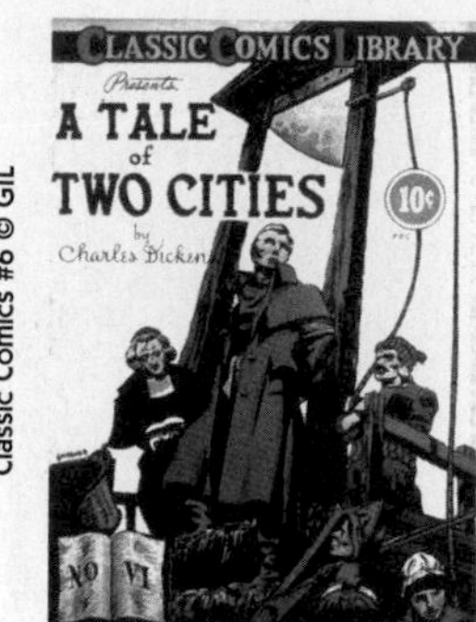

Classic Comics #6 © GIL

Any CI with just a Twin Circle sticker on the front is not an official TC edition.

TIPS ON LISTING CLASSICS FOR SALE

It may be easy to just list Edition 17, but Classics collectors keep track of CI editions in terms of HRN and/or date, (O) or (r), CC or LDC, PC or PC2, A1 or A2, soft or stiff cover, etc. Try to help them out. For originals, just list (0), unless there are variations such as color (Nos. 10 and 61), printer (Nos. 18-22), HRN (Nos. 95, 108, 160), etc. For reprints, just list HRN if it's (165) or below. Above that, list HRN and date. Also, please list type of logo/cover/art for the convenience of buyers. They will appreciate it.

CLASSIC COMICS (Also see Best from Boys Life, Cassette Books, Famous Stories, Fast Fiction, Golden Picture Classics, King Classics, Marvel Classics Comics, Pendulum Illustrated Classics, Picture Parade, Picture Progress, Regents Ill. Classics, Spitfire, Stories by Famous Authors, Superior Stories, and World Around Us.)

CLASSIC COMICS (Classics Illustrated No. 35 on)
Elliot Publishing #1-3 (1941-1942)/Gilberton Publications #4-167 (1942-1967) /Twin Circle Pub. (Frawley) #168-169 (1968-1971):
10/41 - No. 34, 2/47; No. 35, 3/47 - No. 169, Spring 1969
(Reprint Editions of almost all titles 5/43 - Spring 1971)
(Painted Covers (0)s No. 81 on, and (r)s of most Nos. 1-80)

Abbreviations:
A–Art; C or c–Cover; CC–Classic Comics; CI–Classics Ill.; Ed–Edition; LDC–Line Drawn Cover; PC–Painted Cover; r–Reprint

1. The Three Musketeers

Ed	HRN	Date	Details	A	C	GD 2.0	VG 4.0	FN 6.0	VF 8.0	VF/NM 9.0	NM- 9.2
1	–	10/41	Date listed-1941; Elliot Pub; 68 pgs.	1	1	444	888	1332	3197	5599	8000
2	10	–	10¢ price removed on all (r)s; Elliot Pub; CC-r	1	1	34	68	102	198	319	440
3	15	–	Long Isl. Ind. Ed.; CC-r	1	1	24	48	72	143	229	315
4	18/20	–	Sunrise Times Ed.; CC-r	1	1	18	36	54	103	162	220
5	21	–	Richmond Courier Ed.; CC-r	1	1	15	30	45	92	144	195
6	28	1946	CC-r	1	1	14	28	42	78	112	145
7	36	–	LDC-r	1	1	8	16	24	42	54	65
8	60	–	LDC-r	1	1	6	12	18	27	33	38
9	64	–	LDC-r	1	1	5	10	15	22	26	30
10	78	–	C-price 15¢;LDC-r	1	1	4	9	13	18	22	26
11	93	–	LDC-r	1	1	4	9	13	18	22	26
12	114	–	Last LDC-r	1	1	4	8	11	16	19	22
13	134	–	New-c; old-a; 64 pg. PC-r	1	2	3	6	9	19	29	38
14	143	–	Old-a; PC-r; 64 pg.	1	2	2	4	6	11	16	20
15	150	–	New-a; PC-r; Evans/Crandall-a	2	2	3	6	9	17	25	32
16	149	–	PC-r	2	2	2	4	6	8	10	12
17	167	–	PC-r	2	2	2	4	6	8	10	12
18	167	4/64	PC-r	2	2	2	4	6	8	10	12
19	167	1/65	PC-r	2	2	2	4	6	8	10	12
20	167	3/66	PC-r	2	2	2	4	6	8	10	12
21	166	11/67	PC-r	2	2	2	4	6	8	10	12
22	166	Spr/69	C-price 25¢ ; stiff-c; PC-r	2	2	2	4	6	8	10	12
23	169	Spr/71	PC-r; stiff-c	2	2	2	4	6	8	10	12

2. Ivanhoe

Ed	HRN	Date	Details	A	C	GD 2.0	VG 4.0	FN 6.0	VF 8.0	VF/NM 9.0	NM- 9.2
1	(O)	12/41?	Date listed-1941; Elliot Pub; 68 pgs.	1	1	230	460	690	1449	2450	3450
2	10	–	Price & 'Presents' removed; Elliot Pub; CC-r	1	1	31	62	93	181	291	400
3	15	–	Long Isl. Ind. ed.; CC-r	1	1	20	40	60	115	183	250
4	18/20	–	Sunrise Times ed.; CC-r	1	1	18	36	54	103	162	220
5	21	–	Richmond Courier ed.; CC-r	1	1	15	30	45	92	144	195
6	28	1946	Last 'Comics'-r	1	1	14	28	42	78	112	145
7	36	–	1st LDC-r	1	1	9	18	27	47	61	75
8	60	–	LDC-r	1	1	6	12	18	27	33	38
9	64	–	LDC-r	1	1	5	10	15	22	26	30
10	78	–	C-price 15¢; LDC-r	1	1	4	9	13	18	22	26
11	89	–	LDC-r	1	1	4	8	12	17	21	24
12	106	–	LDC-r	1	1	4	7	10	14	17	20
13	121	–	Last LDC-r	1	1	4	7	10	14	17	20
14	136	–	New-c&a; PC-r	2	2	5	10	15	25	31	36
15	142	–	PC-r	2	2	2	4	6	8	11	14
16	153	–	PC-r	2	2	2	4	6	8	11	14
17	149	–	PC-r	2	2	2	4	6	8	11	14
18	167	–	PC-r	2	2	2	4	6	8	10	12
19	167	5/64	PC-r	2	2	2	4	6	8	10	12
20	167	1/65	PC-r	2	2	2	4	6	8	10	12
21	167	3/66	PC-r	2	2	2	4	6	8	10	12
22A	166	9/67	PC-r	2	2	2	4	6	8	10	12
22B	166	–	Center ad for Children's Digest & Young Miss; rare; PC-r	2	2	7	14	21	47	76	105
23	166	R/68	C-Price 25¢; PC-r	2	2	2	4	6	8	10	12
24	169	Win/69	Stiff-c	2	2	2	4	6	8	10	12
25	169	Win/71	PC-r; stiff-c	2	2	2	4	6	8	10	12

3. The Count of Monte Cristo

Ed	HRN	Date	Details	A	C	GD 2.0	VG 4.0	FN 6.0	VF 8.0	VF/NM 9.0	NM- 9.2
1	(O)	3/42	Elliot Pub; 68 pgs.	1	1	147	294	441	926	1563	2200
2	10	–	Conray Prods; CC-r	1	1	26	52	78	152	244	335
3	15	–	Long Isl. Ind. ed.; CC-r	1	1	20	40	60	117	186	255
4	18/20	–	Sunrise Times ed.; CC-r	1	1	18	36	54	107	169	230
5	20	–	Sunrise Times ed.; CC-r	1	1	16	32	48	96	151	205
6	21	–	Richmond Courier ed.; CC-r	1	1	15	30	45	92	144	195
7	28	1946	CC-r; new Banner logo	1	1	14	28	42	78	112	145
8	36	–	1st LDC-r	1	1	9	18	27	47	61	75
9	60	–	LDC-r	1	1	6	12	18	27	33	38
10	62	–	LDC-r	1	1	6	12	18	29	36	42
11	71	–	LDC-r	1	1	5	10	14	20	24	28
12	87	–	C-price 15¢; LDC-r	1	1	4	9	13	18	22	26
13	113	–	LDC-r	1	1	4	7	10	14	17	20
14	135	–	New-c&a; PC-r; Cameron-a	2	2	3	6	9	18	27	35
15	143	–	PC-r	2	2	2	4	6	8	11	14
16	153	–	PC-r	2	2	2	4	6	8	11	14
17	161	–	PC-r	2	2	2	4	6	8	11	14
18	167	–	PC-r	2	2	2	4	6	8	10	12
19	167	7/64	PC-r	2	2	2	4	6	8	10	12
20	167	7/65	PC-r	2	2	2	4	6	8	10	12
21	167	7/66	PC-r	2	2	2	4	6	8	10	12
22	166	R/68	C-price 25¢; PC-r	2	2	2	4	6	8	10	12
23	169	–	Win/69 Stiff-c; PC-r	2	2	2	4	6	8	10	12

4. The Last of the Mohicans

Ed	HRN	Date	Details	A	C	GD 2.0	VG 4.0	FN 6.0	VF 8.0	VF/NM 9.0	NM- 9.2
1	(O)	8/42	Date listed-1942; Gilberton #4(0) on; 68 pgs.	1	1	125	250	375	788	1332	1875
2	12	–	Elliot Pub; CC-r	1	1	26	52	78	154	247	340
3	15	–	Long Isl. Ind. ed.; CC-r	1	1	20	40	60	117	186	255
4	20	–	Long Isl. Ind. ed.; CC-r; banner logo	1	1	18	36	54	103	162	220
5	21	–	Queens Home News ed.; CC-r	1	1	15	30	45	92	144	195
6	28	1946	Last CC-r; new	1	1	14	28	42	78	112	145
7	36	–	1st LDC-r	1	1	9	18	27	47	61	75
8	60	–	LDC-r	1	1	6	12	18	27	33	38
9	64	–	LDC-r	1	1	5	10	14	20	24	28
10	78	–	C-price 15¢; LDC-r	1	1	4	9	13	18	22	26
11	89	–	LDC-r	1	1	4	8	12	17	21	24
12	117	–	Last LDC-r	1	1	4	7	10	14	17	20
13	135	–	New-c; PC-r	1	2	5	10	15	24	30	35
14	141	–	PC-r	1	2	3	6	8	12	14	16
15	150	–	New-a; PC-r;	2	2	6	12	18	27	33	38

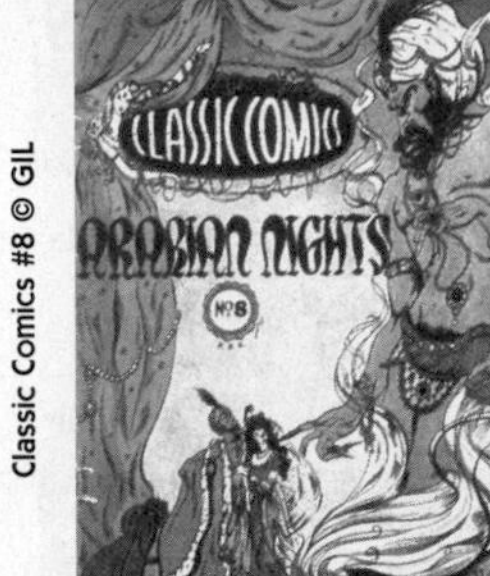

Classic Comics #8 © GIL

Classic Comics #9 © GIL

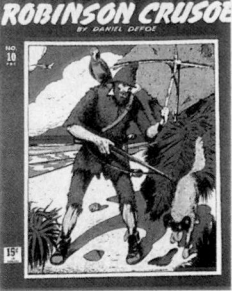

Classic Comics #10 © GIL

Ed	HRN	Date	Details	A	C	GD 2.0	VG 4.0	FN 6.0	VF 8.0	VF/NM 9.0	NM- 9.2
			Severin, L.B. Cole-a								
16	161	–	PC-r	2	2	2	4	6	8	10	12
17	167	–	PC-r	2	2	2	4	6	8	10	12
18	167	6/64	PC-r	2	2	2	4	6	8	10	12
19	167	8/65	PC-r	2	2	2	4	6	8	10	12
20	167	8/66	PC-r	2	2	2	4	6	8	10	12
21	166	R/67	C-price 25¢; PC-r	2	2	2	4	6	8	10	12
22	169	Spr/69	Stiff-c; PC-r	2	2	2	4	6	8	10	12

5. Moby Dick

Ed	HRN	Date	Details	A	C	GD 2.0	VG 4.0	FN 6.0	VF 8.0	VF/NM 9.0	NM- 9.2
1A	(O)	9/42	Date listed-1942; Gilberton; 68 pgs.	1	1	152	304	456	958	1617	2275
1B			inside-c, rare free promo			230	460	690	1449	2450	3450
2	10	–	Conray Prods; Pg. 64 changed from 105 title list to letter from Editor; CC-r	1	1	27	54	81	160	258	355
3	15	–	Long Isl. Ind. ed.; Pg. 64 changed from Letter to the Editor to Ill. poem-Concord Hymn; CC-r	1	1	23	46	69	133	214	295
4	18/20	–	Sunrise Times ed.; CC-r	1	1	18	36	54	107	169	230
5	20	–	Sunrise Times ed.; CC-r	1	1	18	36	54	103	162	220
6	21		Sunrise Times ed.; CC-r	1	1	15	30	45	92	144	195
7	28	1946	CC-r; new banner logo	1	1	14	28	42	81	118	155
8	36	–	1st LDC-r	1	1	9	18	27	47	61	75
9	60	–	LDC-r	1	1	6	12	18	27	33	38
10	62	–	LDC-r	1	1	6	12	18	29	36	42
11	71	–	LDC-r	1	1	5	10	15	22	26	30
12	87	–	C-price 15¢; LDC-r	1	1	5	10	14	20	24	28
13	118	–	LDC-r	1	1	4	8	12	17	21	24
14	131	–	New c&a; PC-r	2	2	5	10	15	25	31	36
15	138	–	PC-r	2	2	2	4	6	8	11	14
16	148	–	PC-r	2	2	2	4	6	8	11	14
17	158	–	PC-r	2	2	2	4	6	8	11	14
18	167	–	PC-r	2	2	2	4	6	8	10	12
19	167	6/64	PC-r	2	2	2	4	6	8	10	12
20	167	7/65	PC-r	2	2	2	4	6	8	10	12
21	167	3/66	PC-r	2	2	2	4	6	8	10	12
22	166	9/67	PC-r	2	2	2	4	6	8	10	12
23	166	Win/69	New-c & c-price 25¢; Stiff-c; PC-r	2	3	3	6	9	16	22	28
24	169	Win/71	PC-r	2	3	2	4	6	13	18	22

6. A Tale of Two Cities

Ed	HRN	Date	Details	A	C	GD 2.0	VG 4.0	FN 6.0	VF 8.0	VF/NM 9.0	NM- 9.2
1	(O)	10/42	Date listed-1942; 68 pgs. Zeckerberg c/a	1	1	125	250	375	788	1332	1875
2	14	–	Elliot Pub; CC-r	1	1	24	48	72	143	229	315
3	18	–	Long Isl. Ind. ed.; CC-r	1	1	20	40	60	114	180	245
4	20	–	Sunrise Times ed.; CC-r	1	1	18	36	54	103	162	220
5	28	1946	Last CC-r; new banner logo	1	1	14	28	42	78	112	145
6	51	–	1st LDC-r	1	1	8	16	24	42	54	65
7	64	–	LDC-r	1	1	5	10	15	23	28	32
8	78	–	C-price 15¢; LDC-r	1	1	5	10	14	20	24	28
9	89	–	LDC-r	1	1	4	7	10	14	17	20
10	117	–	LDC-r	1	1	4	7	10	14	17	20
11	132	–	New-c&a; PC-r; Joe Orlando-a	2	2	5	10	15	25	31	36
12	140	–	PC-r	2	2	2	4	6	8	10	12
13	147	–	PC-r	2	2	2	4	6	8	10	12
14	152	–	PC-r; very rare	2	2	17	34	51	98	154	210
15	153	–	PC-r	2	2	2	4	6	8	11	14
16	149	–	PC-r	2	2	2	4	6	8	11	14
17	167	–	PC-r	2	2	2	4	6	8	10	12
18	167	6/64	PC-r	2	2	2	4	6	8	10	12
19	167	8/65	PC-r	2	2	2	4	6	8	10	12
20	166	5/67	PC-r	2	2	2	4	6	8	10	12
21	166	Fall/68	New-c & 25¢; PC-r	2	3	3	6	9	16	23	30
22	169	Sum/70	Stiff-c; PC-r	2	3	2	4	6	11	16	20

7. Robin Hood

Ed	HRN	Date	Details	A	C	GD 2.0	VG 4.0	FN 6.0	VF 8.0	VF/NM 9.0	NM- 9.2
1	(O)	12/42	Date listed-1942; first Gift Box ad-bc; 68 pgs.	1	1	93	186	279	586	993	1400
2	12	–	Elliot Pub; CC-r	1	1	23	46	69	135	218	300
3	18	–	Long Isl. Ind. ed.; CC-r	1	1	19	38	57	109	172	235
4	20	–	Nassau Bulletin ed.; CC-r	1	1	18	36	54	103	162	220
5	22	–	Queens Cty. Times ed.; CC-r	1	1	15	30	45	92	144	195
6	28	–	CC-r	1	1	14	28	42	81	118	155
7	51	–	LDC-r	1	1	8	16	24	42	54	65
8	64	–	LDC-r	1	1	5	10	15	24	30	35
9	78	–	LDC-r	1	1	4	9	13	18	22	26
10	97	–	LDC-r	1	1	4	8	12	17	21	24
11	106	–	LDC-r	1	1	4	7	10	14	17	20
12	121	–	LDC-r	1	1	4	7	10	14	17	20
13	129	–	New-c; PC-r	1	2	5	10	15	25	31	36
14	136	–	New-a; PC-r	2	2	5	10	15	24	29	34
15	143	–	PC-r	2	2	2	4	6	8	11	14
16	153	–	PC-r	2	2	2	4	6	8	11	14
17	164	–	PC-r	2	2	2	4	6	8	10	12
18	167	–	PC-r	2	2	2	4	6	8	10	12
19	167	6/64	PC-r	2	2	2	4	6	8	10	12
20	167	5/65	PC-r	2	2	2	4	6	8	10	12
21	167	7/66	PC-r	2	2	2	4	6	8	10	12
22	166	12/67	PC-r	2	2	2	4	6	8	10	12
23	169	Sum/69	Stiff-c; c-price 25¢; PC-r	2	2	2	4	6	8	10	12

8. Arabian Nights

Ed	HRN	Date	Details	A	C	GD 2.0	VG 4.0	FN 6.0	VF 8.0	VF/NM 9.0	NM- 9.2
1	(O)	2/43	Original; 68 pgs. Lilian Chestney-c/a	1	1	150	300	450	945	1598	2250
2	17	–	Long Isl. ed.; pg. 64 changed from Gift Box ad to Letter from British Medical Worker; CC-r	1	1	52	104	156	322	536	750
3	20	–	Nassau Bulletin; Pg. 64 changed from letter to article-Three Men Named Smith; CC-r	1	1	42	84	126	260	435	610
4A	28	1946	CC-r; new banner logo, slick-c	1	1	31	62	93	181	291	400
4B	28	1946	Same, but w/stiff-c	1	1	31	62	93	181	291	400
5	51	–	LDC-r	1	1	22	44	66	127	204	280
6	64	–	LDC-r	1	1	19	38	57	109	172	235
7	78	–	LDC-r	1	1	18	36	54	103	162	220
8	164	–	New-c&a; PC-r	2	2	15	30	45	88	137	185

9. Les Miserables

Ed	HRN	Date	Details	A	C	GD 2.0	VG 4.0	FN 6.0	VF 8.0	VF/NM 9.0	NM- 9.2
1A	(O)	3/43	Original; slick paper cover; 68 pgs.	1	1	93	186	279	586	993	1400
1B	(O)	3/43	Original; rough, pulp type-c; 68 pgs.	1	1	110	220	330	693	1172	1650
2	14	–	Elliot Pub; CC-r	1	1	26	52	78	152	244	335
3	18	3/44	Nassau Bul. Pg. 64 changed from Gift Box ad to Bill of Rights article; CC-r	1	1	22	44	66	127	204	280
4	20	–	Richmond Courier ed.; CC-r	1	1	18	36	54	107	162	230
5	28	1946	Gilberton; pgs. 60-64 rearranged/ illos added; CC-r	1	1	14	28	42	81	118	155

Classic Comics #11 © GIL

Classic Comics #13 © GIL

Classic Comics #14 © GIL

Ed	HRN	Date	Details	A	C	GD 2.0	VG 4.0	FN 6.0	VF 8.0	VF/NM 9.0	NM- 9.2
6	51	–	LDC-r	1	1	9	18	27	47	61	75
7	71	–	LDC-r	1	1	6	12	18	29	36	42
8	87	–	C-price 15¢; LDC-r	1	1	6	12	18	27	33	38
9	161	–	New-c&a; PC-r	2	2	7	14	21	37	46	55
10	167	9/63	PC-r	2	2	2	4	6	11	16	20
11	167	12/65	PC-r	2	2	2	4	6	11	16	20
12	166	R/1968	New-c & price 25¢; PC-r	2	3	3	6	9	18	27	35

10. Robinson Crusoe (Used in **SOTI**, pg. 142)

Ed	HRN	Date	Details	A	C	GD 2.0	VG 4.0	FN 6.0	VF 8.0	VF/NM 9.0	NM- 9.2
1A	(O)	4/43	Original; Violet-c; 68 pgs; Zuckerberg c/a	1	1	83	166	249	523	887	1250
1B	(O)	4/43	Original; blue-grey-c, 68 pgs.	1	1	92	184	276	580	978	1375
2A	14	–	Elliot Pub; violet-c; 68 pgs; CC-r	1	1	28	56	84	166	268	370
2B	14	–	Elliot Pub; blue-grey-c; CC-r	1	1	25	50	75	145	233	320
3	18	–	Nassau Bul. Pg. 64 changed from Gift Box ad to Bill of Rights article; CC-r	1	1	19	38	57	109	172	235
4	20	–	Queens Home News ed.; CC-r	1	1	15	30	45	90	140	190
5	28	1946	Gilberton; pg. 64 changes from Bill of Rights to WWII article-One Leg Shot Away; last CC-r	1	1	14	28	42	78	112	145
6	51	–	LDC-r	1	1	8	16	24	42	54	65
7	64	–	LDC-r	1	1	6	12	18	27	33	38
8	78	–	C-price 15¢; LDC-r	1	1	5	10	14	20	24	28
9	97	–	LDC-r	1	1	4	9	13	18	22	26
10	114	–	LDC-r	1	1	4	7	10	14	17	20
11	130	–	New-c; PC-r	1	2	5	10	15	25	31	36
12	140	–	New-a; PC-r	2	2	5	10	15	24	29	34
13	153	–	PC-r	2	2	2	4	6	8	10	12
14	164	–	PC-r	2	2	2	4	6	8	10	12
15	167	–	PC-r	2	2	2	4	6	8	10	12
16	167	7/64	PC-r	2	2	2	4	6	10	13	16
17	167	5/65	PC-r	2	2	2	4	6	10	13	16
18	167	6/66	PC-r	2	2	2	4	6	8	10	12
19	166	Fall/68	C-price 25¢; PC-r	2	2	2	4	6	8	10	12
20	166	R/68	(No Twin Circle ad)	2	2	2	4	6	8	11	14
21	169	Sm/70	Stiff-c; PC-r	2	2	2	4	6	8	11	14

11. Don Quixote

Ed	HRN	Date	Details	A	C	GD 2.0	VG 4.0	FN 6.0	VF 8.0	VF/NM 9.0	NM- 9.2
1	10	5/43	First (O) with HRN list; 68 pgs.	1	1	87	174	261	548	924	1300
2	18	–	Nassau Bulletin ed.; CC-r	1	1	23	46	69	133	214	295
3	21	–	Queens Home News ed.; CC-r	1	1	19	38	57	109	172	235
4	28	–	CC-r	1	1	14	28	42	81	118	155
5	110	–	New-PC; PC-r	1	2	7	14	21	35	43	50
6	156	–	Pgs. reduced 68 to 52; PC-r	1	2	4	7	10	14	17	20
7	165	–	PC-r	1	2	2	4	6	9	11	14
8	167	1/64	PC-r	1	2	2	4	6	9	11	14
9	167	11/65	PC-r	1	2	2	4	6	9	11	14
10	166	R/1968	New-c & price 25¢; PC-r	1	3	3	6	9	18	27	36

12. Rip Van Winkle and the Headless Horseman

Ed	HRN	Date	Details	A	C	GD 2.0	VG 4.0	FN 6.0	VF 8.0	VF/NM 9.0	NM- 9.2
1	11	6/43	Original; 68 pgs.	1	1	87	174	261	548	924	1300
2	15	–	Long Isl. Ind. ed.; CC-r	1	1	23	46	69	133	214	295
3	20	–	Long Isl. Ind. ed.;	1	1	19	38	57	109	172	235
4	22	–	Queens Cty. Times ed.; CC-r	1	1	15	30	45	92	144	195
5	28	–	CC-r	1	1	14	28	42	78	112	145
6	60	–	1st LDC-r	1	1	8	16	24	40	50	60
7	62	–	LDC-r	1	1	5	10	15	23	28	32
8	71	–	LDC-r	1	1	4	9	13	18	22	26
9	89	–	C-price 15¢; LDC-r	1	1	4	8	12	17	21	24
10	118	–	LDC-r	1	1	4	7	10	14	17	20
11	132	–	New-c; PC-r	1	2	5	10	15	25	31	36
12	150	–	New-a; PC-r	2	2	5	10	15	24	29	34
13	158	–	PC-r	2	2	2	4	6	8	11	14
14	167	–	PC-r	2	2	2	4	6	8	11	14
15	167	12/63	PC-r	2	2	2	4	6	8	10	12
16	167	4/65	PC-r	2	2	2	4	6	8	10	12
17	167	4/66	PC-r	2	2	2	4	6	8	10	12
18	166	R/1968	New-c&price 25¢; PC-r; stiff-c	2	3	3	6	9	14	19	24
19	169	Sm/70	PC-r; stiff-c	2	3	2	4	6	9	13	16

13. Dr. Jekyll and Mr. Hyde (Used in **SOTI**, pg. 143)(1st horror comic?)

Ed	HRN	Date	Details	A	C	GD 2.0	VG 4.0	FN 6.0	VF 8.0	VF/NM 9.0	NM- 9.2
1	12	8/43	Original 60 pgs.	1	1	128	256	384	806	1366	1925
2	15	–	Long Isl. Ind. ed.; CC-r	1	1	33	66	99	192	309	425
3	20	–	Long Isl. Ind. ed.; CC-r	1	1	23	46	69	133	214	295
4	28	–	No c-price; CC-r	1	1	18	36	54	103	162	220
5	60	–	New-c; Pgs. reduced from 60 to 52; H.C. Kiefer-c; LDC-r	1	2	9	18	27	47	61	75
6	62	–	LDC-r	1	2	6	12	18	28	34	40
7	71	–	LDC-r	1	2	5	10	15	23	28	32
8	87	–	Date returns (erroneous); LDC-r	1	2	5	10	15	22	26	30
9	112	–	New-c&a; PC-r; Cameron-a	2	3	7	14	21	35	43	50
10	153	–	PC-r	2	3	2	4	6	9	12	15
11	161	–	PC-r	2	3	2	4	6	9	12	15
12	167	–	PC-r	2	3	2	4	6	8	10	12
13	167	8/64	PC-r	2	3	2	4	6	8	10	12
14	167	11/65	PC-r	2	3	2	4	6	8	10	12
15	166	R/68	C-price 25¢; PC-r	2	3	2	4	6	8	10	12
16	169	Wn/69	PC-r; stiff-c	2	3	2	4	6	8	10	12

14. Westward Ho!

Ed	HRN	Date	Details	A	C	GD 2.0	VG 4.0	FN 6.0	VF 8.0	VF/NM 9.0	NM- 9.2
1	13	9/43	Original; last outside bc coming-next ad; 60 pgs.	1	1	193	386	579	1216	2058	2900
2	15	–	Long Isl. Ind. ed.; CC-r	1	1	57	114	171	359	605	850
3	21	–	Queens Home News; Pg. 56 changed from coming-next ad to Three Men Named Smith; CC-r	1	1	45	90	135	279	465	650
4	28	1946	Gilberton; Pg. 56 changed again to WWII article-Speaking for America; last CC-r	1	1	40	80	120	235	380	525
5	53	–	Pgs. reduced from 60 to 52; LDC-r	1	1	35	70	105	208	334	460

15. Uncle Tom's Cabin (Used in **SOTI**, pgs. 102, 103)

Ed	HRN	Date	Details	A	C	GD 2.0	VG 4.0	FN 6.0	VF 8.0	VF/NM 9.0	NM- 9.2
1	14	11/43	Original; Outside-bc ad: 2 Gift Boxes; 60 pgs.; color var. on-c; green trunk,root on left & brown trunk, root on left	1	1	73	146	219	460	780	1100
2	15	–	Long Isl. Ind. listed- bottom inside-fc; also Gilberton listed bottom-pg. 1; CC-r; green root vs. brown root var. occurs again	1	1	25	50	75	145	233	320
3	21	–	Nassau Bulletin ed.; CC-r	1	1	20	40	60	114	180	245
4	28	–	No c-price; CC-r	1	1	14	28	42	81	118	155

NO. 16 CLASSIC COMICS GULLIVER'S TRAVELS

Classic Comics #16 © GIL

NO. 18 CLASSIC COMICS The HUNCHBACK of NOTRE DAME

Classic Comics #18 © GIL

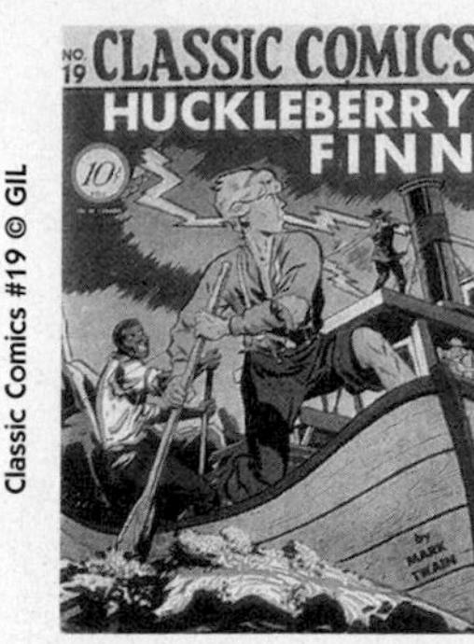

Classic Comics #19 © GIL

Ed	HRN	Date	Details	A	C	GD 2.0	VG 4.0	FN 6.0	VF 8.0	VF/NM 9.0	NM- 9.2
5	53	–	Pgs. reduced 60 to 52; LDC-r	1	1	8	16	24	42	54	65
6	71	–	LDC-r	1	1	6	12	18	27	33	38
7	89	–	C-price 15¢; LDC-r	1	1	5	10	15	24	30	35
8	117	–	New-c/lettering changes; PC-r	1	2	5	10	15	25	31	36
9	128	–	'Picture Progress' promo; PC-r	1	2	2	4	6	9	13	16
10	137	–	PC-r	1	2	2	4	6	8	11	14
11	146	–	PC-r	1	2	2	4	6	8	11	14
12	154	–	PC-r	1	2	2	4	6	8	11	14
13	161	–	PC-r	1	2	2	4	6	8	10	12
14	167	–	PC-r	1	2	2	4	6	8	10	12
15	167	6/64	PC-r	1	2	2	4	6	8	10	12
16	167	5/65	PC-r	1	2	2	4	6	8	10	12
17	166	5/67	PC-r	1	2	2	4	6	8	10	12
18	166	Wn/69	New-stiff-c; PC-r	1	3	3	6	9	16	22	28
19	169	Sm/70	PC-r; stiff-c	1	3	2	4	6	10	13	16

16. Gullivers Travels

Ed	HRN	Date	Details	A	C	GD 2.0	VG 4.0	FN 6.0	VF 8.0	VF/NM 9.0	NM- 9.2
1	15	12/43	Original-Lilian Chestney c/a; 60 pgs.	1	1	75	150	225	473	799	1125
2	18/20	–	Price deleted; Queens Home News ed; CC-r	1	1	22	44	66	127	204	280
3	22	–	Queens Cty. Times ed.; CC-r	1	1	18	36	54	103	162	220
4	28	–	CC-r	1	1	14	28	42	78	112	145
5	60	–	Pgs. reduced to 48; LDC-r	1	1	6	12	18	31	38	45
6	62	–	LDC-r	1	1	5	10	15	23	28	32
7	78	–	C-price 15¢; LDC-r	1	1	5	10	14	20	24	28
8	89	–	LDC-r	1	1	4	8	12	17	21	24
9	155	–	New-c; PC-r	1	2	5	10	15	25	31	36
10	165	–	PC-r	1	2	2	4	6	8	10	12
11	167	5/64	PC-r	1	2	2	4	6	8	10	12
12	167	11/65	PC-r	1	2	2	4	6	8	10	12
13	166	R/1968	C-price 25¢; PC-r	1	2	2	4	6	8	10	12
14	169	Wn/69	PC-r; stiff-c	1	2	2	4	6	8	10	12

17. The Deerslayer

Ed	HRN	Date	Details	A	C	GD 2.0	VG 4.0	FN 6.0	VF 8.0	VF/NM 9.0	NM- 9.2
1	16	1/44	Original; Outside-bc ad: 3 Gift Boxes; 60 pgs.	1	1	64	128	192	403	682	960
2A	18	–	Queens Cty Times (inside-fc); CC-r	1	1	23	46	69	135	218	300
2B	18	–	Gilberton (bottom-pg. 1); CC-r; Scarce	1	1	33	66	99	192	309	425
3	22	–	Queens Cty. Times ed.; CC-r	1	1	19	38	57	109	172	235
4	28	–	CC-r	1	1	14	28	42	81	118	155
5	60	–	Pgs.reduced to 52; LDC-r	1	1	7	14	21	37	46	55
6	64	–	LDC-r	1	1	5	10	15	22	26	30
7	85	–	C-price 15¢; LDC-r	1	1	4	8	12	17	21	24
8	118	–	LDC-r	1	1	4	7	10	14	17	20
9	132	–	LDC-r	1	1	4	7	10	14	17	20
10	167	11/66	Last LDC-r	1	1	2	4	6	11	16	20
11	166	R/1968	New-c & price 25¢; PC-r	1	2	3	6	9	18	27	35
12	169	Spr/71	Stiff-c; letters from parents & educators; PC-r	1	2	2	4	6	10	14	18

18. The Hunchback of Notre Dame

Ed	HRN	Date	Details	A	C	GD 2.0	VG 4.0	FN 6.0	VF 8.0	VF/NM 9.0	NM- 9.2
1A	17	3/44	Orig.; Gilberton ed; 60 pgs.	1	1	87	174	261	548	924	1300
1B	17	3/44	Orig.; Island Pub. Ed.; 60 pgs.	1	1	77	154	231	481	816	1150
2	18/20	–	Queens Home News ed.; CC-r	1	1	24	48	72	140	225	310
3	22	–	Queens Cty. Times ed.; CC-r	1	1	19	38	57	109	172	235
4	28	–	CC-r	1	1	15	30	45	92	144	195
5	60	–	New-c; 8pgs. deleted; Kiefer-c; LDC-r	1	2	9	18	27	47	61	75
6	62	–	LDC-r	1	2	5	10	15	22	26	30
7	78	–	C-price 15¢; LDC-r	1	2	5	10	14	20	24	28
8A	89	–	H.C.Kiefer on bottom right-fc; LDC-r	1	2	4	9	13	18	22	26
8B	89	–	Name omitted; LDC-r	1	2	5	10	15	24	30	35
9	118	–	LDC-r	1	2	4	8	12	17	21	24
10	140	–	New-c; PC-r	1	3	7	14	21	35	43	50
11	146	–	PC-r	1	3	4	9	13	18	22	26
12	158	–	New-c&a; PC-r; Evans/Crandall-a	2	4	5	10	15	25	31	36
13	165	–	PC-r	2	4	2	4	6	8	11	14
14	167	9/63	PC-r	2	4	2	4	6	8	11	14
15	167	10/64	PC-r	2	4	2	4	6	8	11	14
16	167	4/66	PC-r	2	4	2	4	6	8	10	12
17	166	R/1968	New price 25¢; PC-r	2	4	2	4	6	8	10	12
18	169	Sp/70	Stiff-c; PC-r	2	4	2	4	6	8	10	12

19. Huckleberry Finn

Ed	HRN	Date	Details	A	C	GD 2.0	VG 4.0	FN 6.0	VF 8.0	VF/NM 9.0	NM- 9.2
1A	18	4/44	Orig.; Gilberton ed., 60 pgs.	1	1	53	106	159	330	553	775
1B	18	4/44	Orig.; Island Pub.; 60 pgs.	1	1	55	110	165	347	586	825
2	18	–	Nassau Bulletin ed.; fc-price 15¢-Canada; no coming-next ad; CC-r	1	1	23	46	69	133	214	295
3	22	–	Queens City Times ed.; CC-r	1	1	19	38	57	109	172	235
4	28	–	CC-r	1	1	14	28	42	78	112	145
5	60	–	Pgs. reduced to 48; LDC-r	1	1	6	12	18	31	38	45
6	62	–	LDC-r	1	1	5	10	15	23	28	32
7	78	–	LDC-r	1	1	4	9	13	18	22	26
8	89	–	LDC-r	1	1	4	8	12	17	21	24
9	117	–	LDC-r	1	1	4	7	10	14	17	20
10	131	–	New-c&a; PC-r	2	2	5	10	15	24	30	35
11	140	–	PC-r	2	2	2	4	6	8	11	14
12	150	–	PC-r	2	2	2	4	6	8	11	14
13	158	–	PC-r	2	2	2	4	6	8	11	14
14	165	–	PC-r (scarce)	2	2	3	6	9	14	19	24
15	167	–	PC-r	2	2	2	4	6	8	10	12
16	167	6/64	PC-r	2	2	2	4	6	8	10	12
17	167	6/65	PC-r	2	2	2	4	6	8	10	12
18	167	10/65	PC-r	2	2	2	4	6	8	10	12
19	166	9/67	PC-r	2	2	2	4	6	8	10	12
20	166	Win/69	C-price 25¢; PC-r; stiff-c	2	2	2	4	6	8	10	12
21	169	Sm/70	PC-r; stiff-c	2	2	2	4	6	9	11	12

20. The Corsican Brothers

Ed	HRN	Date	Details	A	C	GD 2.0	VG 4.0	FN 6.0	VF 8.0	VF/NM 9.0	NM- 9.2
1A	20	6/44	Orig.; Gilberton ed.; bc-ad: 4 Gift Boxes; 60 pgs.	1	1	47	94	141	291	483	675
1B	20	6/44	Orig.; Courier ed.; 60 pgs.	1	1	40	80	120	244	397	550
1C	20	6/44	Orig.; Long Island Ind. ed.; 60 pgs.	1	1	40	80	120	244	397	550
2	22	–	Queens Cty. Times ed.; white logo banner; CC-r	1	1	20	40	60	114	180	245
3	28	–	CC-r	1	1	19	38	57	109	172	235
4	60	–	CI logo; no price; 48 pgs.; LDC-r	1	1	15	30	45	90	140	190
5A	62	–	LDC-r; Classics Ill. logo at top of pgs.	1	1	15	30	45	83	124	165
5B	62	–	w/o logo at top of pg. (scarcer)	1	1	15	30	45	86	133	180
6	78	–	C-price 15¢; LDC-r	1	1	14	28	42	81	118	155
7	97	–	LDC-r	1	1	14	28	42	78	112	145

Classic Comics #23 © GIL

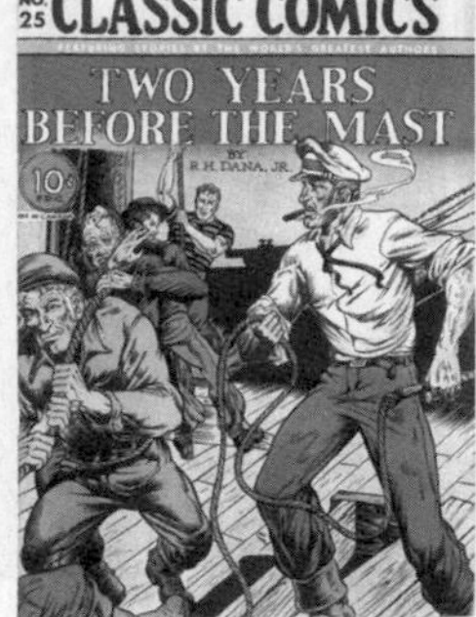

Classic Comics #25 © GIL

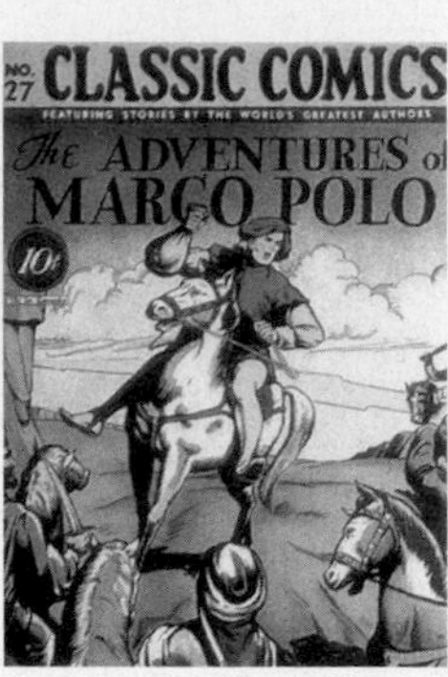

Classic Comics #27 © GIL

21. 3 Famous Mysteries ("The Sign of the 4", "The Murders in the Rue Morgue", "The Flayed Hand")

Ed	HRN	Date	Details	A	C	GD 2.0	VG 4.0	FN 6.0	VF 8.0	VF/NM 9.0	NM- 9.2
1A	21	7/44	Orig.; Gilberton ed.; 60 pgs.	1	1	93	186	279	586	993	1400
1B	21	7/44	Orig. Island Pub. Co.; 60 pgs.	1	1	97	194	291	611	1031	1450
1C	21	7/44	Original; Courier Ed.; 60 pgs.	1	1	83	166	249	523	887	1250
2	22	–	Nassau Bulletin ed.; CC-r	1	1	38	76	114	226	363	500
3	30	–	CC-r	1	1	28	56	84	162	261	360
4	62	–	LDC-r; 8 pgs. deleted; LDC-r	1	1	22	44	66	127	204	280
5	70	–	LDC-r	1	1	20	40	60	115	183	250
6	85	–	C-price 15¢; LDC-r	1	1	18	36	54	103	162	220
7	114	–	New-c; PC-r	1	2	18	36	54	103	162	220

22. The Pathfinder

Ed	HRN	Date	Details	A	C	GD 2.0	VG 4.0	FN 6.0	VF 8.0	VF/NM 9.0	NM- 9.2
1A	22	10/44	Orig.; No printer listed; ownership statement inside fc lists Gilberton & date; 60 pgs.	1	1	45	90	135	279	465	650
1B	22	10/44	Orig.; Island Pub. ed.; 60 pgs.	1	1	40	80	120	244	397	550
1C	22	10/44	Orig.; Queens Cty Times ed. 60 pgs.	1	1	40	80	120	244	397	550
2	30	–	C-price removed; CC-r	1	1	15	30	45	84	127	170
3	60	–	Pgs. reduced to 52; LDC-r	1	1	6	12	18	27	33	38
4	70	–	LDC-r	1	1	5	10	15	22	26	30
5	85	–	C-price 15¢; LDC-r	1	1	4	9	13	18	22	26
6	118	–	LDC-r	1	1	4	8	12	17	21	24
7	132	–	LDC-r	1	1	4	7	10	14	17	20
8	146	–	LDC-r	1	1	4	7	10	14	17	20
9	167	11/63	New-c; PC-r	1	2	4	8	12	24	37	50
10	167	12/65	PC-r	1	2	2	4	6	11	16	20
11	166	8/67	PC-r	1	2	2	4	6	11	16	20

23. Oliver Twist (1st Classic produced by the Iger Shop)

Ed	HRN	Date	Details	A	C	GD 2.0	VG 4.0	FN 6.0	VF 8.0	VF/NM 9.0	NM- 9.2
1	23	7/45	Original; 60 pgs.	1	1	45	90	135	279	465	650
2A	30	–	Printers Union logo on bottom left-fc same as 23(Orig.) (very rare); CC-r	1	1	30	60	90	176	283	390
2B	30	–	Union logo omitted; CC-r	1	1	14	28	42	82	121	160
3	60	–	Pgs. reduced to 48; LDC-r	1	1	6	12	18	29	36	42
4	62	–	LDC-r	1	1	5	10	15	23	28	32
5	71	–	LDC-r	1	1	5	10	14	20	24	28
6	85	–	C-price 15¢; LDC-r	1	1	4	9	13	18	22	26
7	94	–	LDC-r	1	1	4	7	10	14	17	20
8	118	–	LDC-r	1	1	4	7	10	14	17	20
9	136	–	New-PC, old-a; PC-r	1	2	5	10	15	24	30	35
10	150	–	Old-a; PC-r	1	2	4	7	10	14	17	20
11	164	–	Old-a; PC-r	1	2	4	8	11	16	19	22
12	164	–	New-a; PC-r; Evans/Crandall-a	2	2	4	8	12	24	37	50
13	167	–	PC-r	2	2	2	4	6	11	16	20
14	167	8/64	PC-r	2	2	2	4	6	8	10	12
15	167	12/65	PC-r	2	2	2	4	6	8	10	12
16	166	R/1968	New 25¢; PC-r	2	2	2	4	6	8	10	12
17	169	Win/69	Stiff-c; PC-r	2	2	2	4	6	8	10	12

24. A Connecticut Yankee in King Arthur's Court

Ed	HRN	Date	Details	A	C	GD 2.0	VG 4.0	FN 6.0	VF 8.0	VF/NM 9.0	NM- 9.2
1	–	9/45	Original	1	1	40	80	120	244	397	550
2	30	–	No price circle; CC-r	1	1	14	28	42	82	121	160
3	60	–	8 pgs. deleted; LDC-r	1	1	6	12	18	27	33	38
4	62	–	LDC-r	1	1	5	10	15	23	28	32
5	71	–	LDC-r	1	1	5	10	15	22	26	30
6	87	–	C-price 15¢; LDC-r	1	1	4	9	13	18	22	26
7	121	–	LDC-r	1	1	4	8	12	17	21	24
8	140	–	New-c&a; PC-r	2	2	5	10	15	25	31	36
9	153	–	PC-r	2	2	2	4	6	8	11	14
10	164	–	PC-r	2	2	2	4	6	8	10	12
11	167	–	PC-r	2	2	2	4	6	8	10	12
12	167	7/64	PC-r	2	2	2	4	6	8	10	12
13	167	6/66	PC-r	2	2	2	4	6	8	10	12
14	166	R/1968	C-price 25¢; PC-r	2	2	2	4	6	8	10	12
15	169	Spr/71	PC-r; stiff-c	2	2	2	4	6	8	10	12

25. Two Years Before the Mast

Ed	HRN	Date	Details	A	C	GD 2.0	VG 4.0	FN 6.0	VF 8.0	VF/NM 9.0	NM- 9.2
1	–	10/45	Original; Webb/Heames-a&c	1	1	40	80	120	244	397	550
2	30	–	Price circle blank; CC-r	1	1	14	28	42	82	121	160
3	60	–	8 pgs. deleted; LDC-r	1	1	6	12	18	27	33	38
4	62	–	LDC-r	1	1	5	10	15	23	28	32
5	71	–	LDC-r	1	1	4	9	13	18	22	26
6	85	–	C-price 15¢; LDC-r	1	1	4	8	12	17	21	24
7	114	–	LDC-r	1	1	4	7	10	14	17	20
8	156	–	3 pgs. replaced by fillers; new-c; PC-r	1	2	5	10	15	25	31	36
9	167	12/63	PC-r	1	2	2	4	6	8	10	12
10	167	12/65	PC-r	1	2	2	4	6	8	10	12
11	166	9/67	PC-r	1	2	2	4	6	8	10	12
12	169	Win/69	C-price 25¢; stiff-c PC-r	1	2	2	4	6	8	10	12

26. Frankenstein (2nd horror comic?)

Ed	HRN	Dato	Details	A	C	GD 2.0	VG 4.0	FN 6.0	VF 8.0	VF/NM 9.0	NM- 9.2
1	26	12/45	Orig.; Webb/Brewster a&c; 52 pgs.	1	1	103	206	309	649	1100	1550
2A	30	–	Price circle blank; no indicia; CC-r	1	1	29	58	87	172	276	380
2B	30	–	With indicia; scarce; CC-r	1	1	34	68	102	198	319	440
3	60	–	LDC-r	1	1	15	30	45	92	144	195
4	62	–	LDC-r	1	1	15	30	45	84	127	170
5	71	–	LDC-r	1	1	8	16	24	40	50	60
6A	82	–	C-price 15¢; soft-c LDC-r	1	1	7	14	21	35	43	50
6B	82	–	Stiff-c; LDC-r	1	1	8	16	24	40	50	60
7	117	–	LDC-r	1	1	4	8	12	18	22	25
8	146	–	New Saunders-c; PC-r	1	2	6	12	18	29	36	42
9	152	–	Scarce; PC-r	1	2	8	16	24	40	50	60
10	153	–	PC-r	1	2	2	4	6	8	11	14
11	160	–	PC-r	1	2	2	4	6	8	11	14
12	165	–	PC-r	1	2	2	4	6	8	10	12
13	167	–	PC-r	1	2	2	4	6	8	10	12
14	167	6/64	PC-r	1	2	2	4	6	8	10	12
15	167	6/65	PC-r	1	2	2	4	6	8	10	12
16	167	10/65	PC-r	1	2	2	4	6	8	10	12
17	166	9/67	PC-r	1	2	2	4	6	8	10	12
18	169	Fall/69	C-price 25¢; stiff-c PC-r	1	2	2	4	6	8	10	12
19	169	Spr/71	PC-r; stiff-c	1	2	2	4	6	8	10	12

27. The Adventures of Marco Polo

Ed	HRN	Date	Details	A	C	GD 2.0	VG 4.0	FN 6.0	VF 8.0	VF/NM 9.0	NM- 9.2
1	–	4/46	Original	1	1	40	80	120	244	397	550
2	30	–	Last 'Comics' reprint; CC-r	1	1	14	28	42	82	121	160
3	70	–	8 pgs. deleted; no c-price; LDC-r	1	1	5	10	15	24	30	35
4	87	–	C-price 15¢; LDC-r	1	1	4	9	13	18	22	26
5	117	–	LDC-r	1	1	4	7	10	14	17	20
6	154	–	New-c; PC-r	1	2	5	10	15	24	30	35
7	165	–	PC-r	1	2	2	4	6	8	10	12
8	167	4/64	PC-r	1	2	2	4	6	8	10	12

Classic Comics #29 © GIL

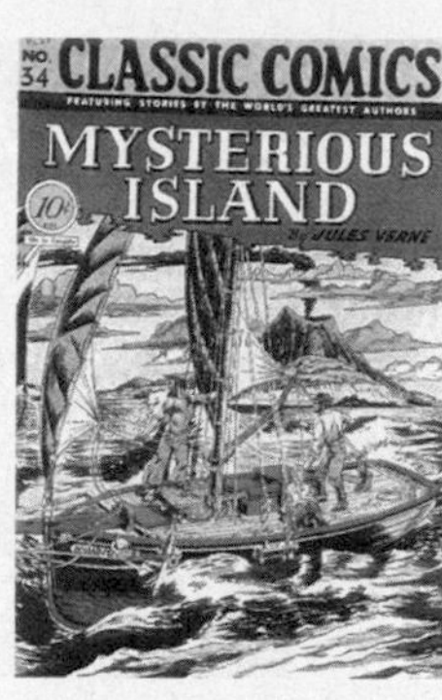

Classic Comics #34 © GIL

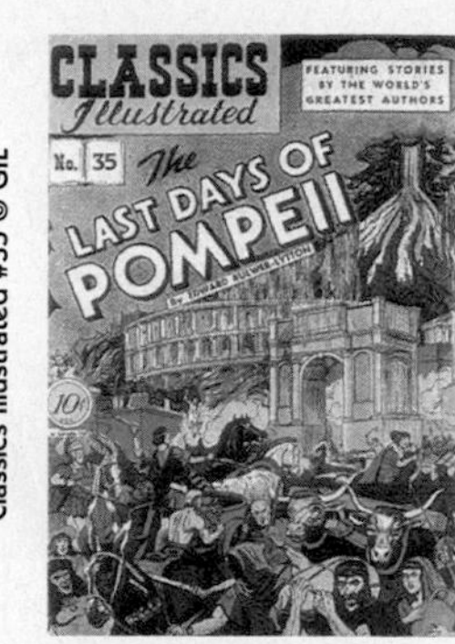

Classics Illustrated #35 © GIL

Ed	HRN	Date	Details	A	C	GD 2.0	VG 4.0	FN 6.0	VF 8.0	VF/NM 9.0	NM- 9.2
9	167	6/66	PC-r	1	2	2	4	6	8	10	12
10	169	Spr/69	New price 25¢; stiff-c; PC-r	1	2	2	4	6	8	10	12

28. Michael Strogoff

Ed	HRN	Date	Details	A	C	GD 2.0	VG 4.0	FN 6.0	VF 8.0	VF/NM 9.0	NM- 9.2
1	–	6/46	Original	1	1	40	80	120	244	397	550
2	51	–	8 pgs. cut; LDC-r	1	1	14	28	42	82	121	160
3	115	–	New-c; PC-r	1	2	6	12	18	31	38	45
4	155	–	PC-r	1	2	4	7	10	14	17	20
5	167	11/63	PC-r	1	2	2	4	6	9	13	16
6	167	7/66	PC-r	1	2	2	4	6	9	13	16
7	169	Sm/69	C-price 25¢; stiff-c PC-r	1	3	3	6	9	15	21	26

29. The Prince and the Pauper

Ed	HRN	Date	Details	A	C	GD 2.0	VG 4.0	FN 6.0	VF 8.0	VF/NM 9.0	NM- 9.2
1	–	7/46	Orig.; "Horror"-c	1	1	57	114	171	359	605	850
2	60	–	8 pgs. cut; new-c by Kiefer; LDC-r	1	2	9	18	27	50	65	80
3	62	–	LDC-r	1	2	5	10	15	24	30	35
4	71	–	LDC-r	1	2	4	9	13	18	22	26
5	93	–	LDC-r	1	2	4	8	12	17	21	24
6	114	–	LDC-r	1	2	4	7	10	14	17	20
7	128	–	New-c; PC-r	1	3	5	10	15	24	30	35
8	138	–	PC-r	1	3	2	4	6	8	11	14
9	150	–	PC-r	1	3	2	4	6	8	11	14
10	164	–	PC-r	1	3	2	4	6	8	10	12
11	167	–	PC-r	1	3	2	4	6	8	10	12
12	167	7/64	PC-r	1	3	2	4	6	8	10	12
13	167	11/65	PC-r	1	3	2	4	6	8	10	12
14	166	R/68	C-price 25¢; PC-r	1	3	2	4	6	8	10	12
15	169	Sm/70	PC-r; stiff-c	1	3	2	4	6	8	10	12

30. The Moonstone

Ed	HRN	Date	Details	A	C	GD 2.0	VG 4.0	FN 6.0	VF 8.0	VF/NM 9.0	NM- 9.2
1	–	9/46	Original; Rico-c/a	1	1	40	80	120	244	397	550
2	60	–	LDC-r; 8pgs. cut	1	1	9	18	27	47	61	75
3	70	–	LDC-r	1	1	8	16	24	42	54	65
4	155	–	New L.B. Cole-c; PC-r	1	2	4	8	12	28	44	60
5	165	–	PC-r; L.B. Cole-c	1	2	3	6	9	16	23	30
6	167	1/64	PC-r; L.B. Cole-c	1	2	2	4	6	10	14	18
7	167	9/65	PC-r; L.B. Cole-c	1	2	2	4	6	9	13	16
8	166	R/1968	C-price 25¢; PC-r	1	2	2	4	6	8	11	14

31. The Black Arrow

Ed	HRN	Date	Details	A	C	GD 2.0	VG 4.0	FN 6.0	VF 8.0	VF/NM 9.0	NM- 9.2
1	30	10/46	Original	1	1	38	76	114	226	363	500
2	51	–	CI logo; LDC-r 8pgs. deleted	1	1	6	12	18	33	41	48
3	64	–	LDC-r	1	1	4	9	13	18	22	26
4	87	–	C-price 15¢; LDC-r	1	1	4	8	12	17	21	24
5	108	–	LDC-r	1	1	4	7	10	14	17	20
6	125	–	LDC-r	1	1	4	7	10	14	17	20
7	131	–	New-c; PC-r	1	2	5	10	15	24	30	35
8	140	–	PC-r	1	2	2	4	6	8	11	14
9	148	–	PC-r	1	2	2	4	6	8	11	14
10	161	–	PC-r	1	2	2	4	6	8	10	12
11	167	–	PC-r	1	2	2	4	6	8	10	12
12	167	7/64	PC-r	1	2	2	4	6	8	10	12
13	167	11/65	PC-r	1	2	2	4	6	8	10	12
14	166	R/1968	C-price 25¢; PC-r	1	2	2	4	6	8	10	12

32. Lorna Doone

Ed	HRN	Date	Details	A	C	GD 2.0	VG 4.0	FN 6.0	VF 8.0	VF/NM 9.0	NM- 9.2
1	–	12/46	Original; Matt Baker c&a	1	1	40	80	120	244	397	550
2	53/64	–	8 pgs. deleted; LDC-r	1	1	9	18	27	47	61	75
3	85	1951	C-price 15¢; LDC-r; Baker c&a	1	1	7	14	21	37	46	55
4	118	–	LDC-r	1	1	4	9	13	18	22	26
5	138	–	New-c; old-c becomes new title pg.; PC-r	1	2	6	12	18	28	34	40
6	150	–	PC-r	1	2	2	4	6	8	10	12
7	165	–	PC-r	1	2	2	4	6	8	10	12
8	167	1/64	PC-r	1	2	2	4	6	8	11	14
9	167	11/65	PC-r	1	2	2	4	6	8	11	14
10	166	R/1968	New-c; PC-r	1	3	3	6	9	17	25	32

33. The Adventures of Sherlock Holmes

Ed	HRN	Date	Details	A	C	GD 2.0	VG 4.0	FN 6.0	VF 8.0	VF/NM 9.0	NM- 9.2
1	33	1/47	Original; Kiefer-c; contains Study in Scarlet & Hound of the Baskervilles; 68 pgs.	1	1	122	244	366	769	1297	1825
2	53	–	"A Study in Scarlet" (17 pgs.) deleted; LDC-r	1	1	45	90	135	279	465	650
3	71	–	LDC-r	1	1	37	74	111	215	345	475
4A	89	–	C-price 15¢; LDC-r	1	1	29	58	87	169	272	375
4B	89	–	Kiefer's name omitted from-c	1	1	30	60	90	176	283	390

34. Mysterious Island (Last "Classic Comic")

Ed	HRN	Date	Details	A	C	GD 2.0	VG 4.0	FN 6.0	VF 8.0	VF/NM 9.0	NM- 9.2
1	35	2/47	Original; Webb/Heames-c/a	1	1	40	80	120	244	397	550
2	60	–	8 pgs. deleted; LDC-r	1	1	7	14	21	37	46	55
3	62	–	LDC-r	1	1	5	10	15	23	28	32
4	71	–	LDC-r	1	1	6	12	18	31	38	45
5	78	–	C-price 15¢ in circle; LDC-r	1	1	5	10	14	20	24	28
6	92	–	LDC-r	1	1	4	9	13	18	22	26
7	117	–	LDC-r	1	1	4	7	10	14	17	20
8	140	–	New-c; PC-r	1	2	5	10	15	24	30	35
9	156	–	PC-r	1	2	2	4	6	8	11	14
10	167	10/63	PC-r	1	2	2	4	6	8	10	12
11	167	5/64	PC-r	1	2	2	4	6	8	10	12
12	167	6/66	PC-r	1	2	2	4	6	8	10	12
13	166	R/1968	C-price 25¢; PC-r	1	2	2	4	6	8	10	12

35. Last Days of Pompeii (First "Classics Illustrated")

Ed	HRN	Date	Details	A	C	GD 2.0	VG 4.0	FN 6.0	VF 8.0	VF/NM 9.0	NM- 9.2
1	35	3/47	Original; LDC; Kiefer-c/a	1	1	40	80	120	244	397	550
2	161	–	New c&a; 15¢; PC-r; Kirby/Ayers-a	2	2	5	10	15	30	48	65
3	167	1/64	PC-r	2	2	3	6	9	15	21	26
4	167	7/66	PC-r	2	2	3	6	9	15	21	26
5	169	Spr/70	New price 25¢; stiff-c; PC-r	2	2	3	6	9	15	21	26

36. Typee

Ed	HRN	Date	Details	A	C	GD 2.0	VG 4.0	FN 6.0	VF 8.0	VF/NM 9.0	NM- 9.2
1	36	4/47	Original	1	1	26	52	78	154	247	340
2	64	–	No c-price; 8 pg. ed.; LDC-r	1	1	7	14	21	37	46	55
3	155	–	New-c; PC-r	1	2	5	10	15	24	30	35
4	167	9/63	PC-r	1	2	2	4	6	9	12	15
5	167	7/65	PC-r	1	2	2	4	6	9	12	15
6	169	Sm/69	C-price 25¢; stiff-c PC-r	1	2	2	4	6	9	12	15

37. The Pioneers

Ed	HRN	Date	Details	A	C	GD 2.0	VG 4.0	FN 6.0	VF 8.0	VF/NM 9.0	NM- 9.2
1	37	5/47	Original; Palais-c/a	1	1	24	48	72	143	229	315
2A	62	–	8 pgs. cut; LDC-r; price circle blank	1	1	6	12	18	28	34	40
2B	62	–	10¢; LDC-r;	1	1	26	52	78	154	247	340
3	70	–	LDC-r	1	1	4	8	12	17	21	24
4	92	–	15¢; LDC-r	1	1	4	8	11	16	19	22
5	118	–	LDC-r	1	1	4	7	10	14	17	20
6	131	–	LDC-r	1	1	4	7	10	14	17	20
7	132	–	LDC-r	1	1	4	7	10	14	17	20
8	153	–	LDC-r	1	1	4	7	10	14	17	20
9	167	5/64	LDC-r	1	1	2	4	6	8	11	14
10	167	6/66	LDC-r	1	1	2	4	6	8	11	14
11	166	R/1968	New-c; 25¢; PC-r	1	2	3	6	9	18	27	36

38. Adventures of Cellini

Ed	HRN	Date	Details	A	C

Classics Illustrated #40 © GIL

Classics Illustrated #42 © GIL

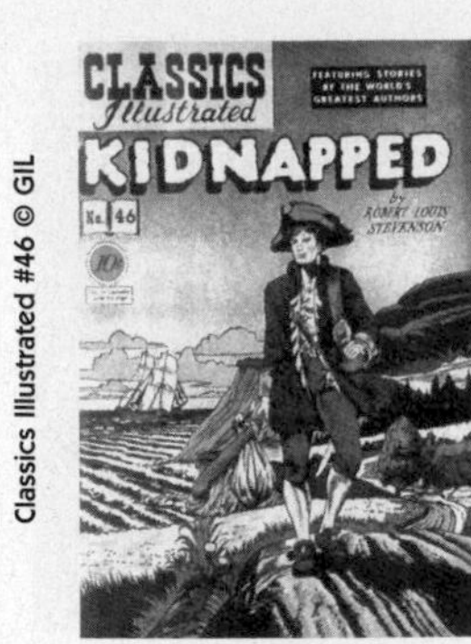

Classics Illustrated #46 © GIL

Ed	HRN	Date	Details	A	C	GD 2.0	VG 4.0	FN 6.0	VF 8.0	VF/NM 9.0	NM- 9.2
1	–	6/47	Original; Froehlich c/a	1	1	32	64	96	188	302	415
2	164	–	New-c&a; PC-r	2	2	3	6	9	18	27	36
3	167	12/63	PC-r	2	2	2	4	6	10	14	18
4	167	7/66	PC-r	2	2	2	4	6	10	14	18
5	169	Spr/70	Stiff-c; new price 25¢; PC-r	2	2	2	4	6	11	16	20

39. Jane Eyre

Ed	HRN	Date	Details	A	C	GD 2.0	VG 4.0	FN 6.0	VF 8.0	VF/NM 9.0	NM- 9.2
1	–	7/47	Original	1	1	31	62	93	181	291	400
2	60	–	No c-price; 8 pgs. cut; LDC-r	1	1	6	12	18	31	38	45
3	62	–	LDC-r	1	1	5	10	15	24	30	35
4	71	–	LDC-r; c-price 10¢	1	1	5	10	15	22	26	30
5	92	–	C-price 15¢; LDC-r	1	1	4	9	13	18	22	26
6	118	–	LDC-r	1	1	4	8	12	17	21	24
7	142	–	New-c; old-a; PC-r	1	2	6	12	18	28	34	40
8	154	–	Old-a; PC-r	1	2	4	8	12	17	21	24
9	165	–	New-a; PC-r	2	2	3	6	9	18	27	35
10	167	12/63	PC-r	2	2	3	6	9	14	19	24
11	167	4/65	PC-r	2	2	2	4	6	13	18	22
12	167	8/66	PC-r	2	2	2	4	6	13	18	22
13	166	R/1968	New-c; PC-r	2	3	5	10	15	34	55	75

40. Mysteries ("The Pit and the Pendulum", "The Advs. of Hans Pfall" & "The Fall of the House of Usher")

Ed	HRN	Date	Details	A	C	GD 2.0	VG 4.0	FN 6.0	VF 8.0	VF/NM 9.0	NM- 9.2
1	40	8/47	Original; Kiefer-c/a, Froehlich, Griffiths-a	1	1	59	118	177	372	629	885
2	62	–	LDC-r; 8pgs. cut	1	1	23	46	69	133	214	295
3	75	–	LDC-r	1	1	19	38	57	109	172	235
4	92	–	C-price 15¢; LDC-r	1	1	15	30	45	94	147	200

41. Twenty Years After

Ed	HRN	Date	Details	A	C	GD 2.0	VG 4.0	FN 6.0	VF 8.0	VF/NM 9.0	NM- 9.2
1	–	9/47	Original; 'horror' c	1	1	39	78	117	230	370	510
2	62	–	New-c; no c-price 8 pgs. cut; LDC-r; Kiefer-c	1	2	7	14	21	37	46	55
3	78	–	C-price 15¢; LDC-r	1	2	5	10	15	23	28	32
4	156	–	New-c; PC-r	1	3	5	10	15	24	30	35
5	167	12/63	PC-r	1	3	2	4	6	8	10	12
6	167	11/66	PC-r	1	3	2	4	6	8	10	12
7	169	Spr/70	New price 25¢; stiff-c; PC-r	1	3	2	4	6	8	10	12

42. Swiss Family Robinson

Ed	HRN	Date	Details	A	C	GD 2.0	VG 4.0	FN 6.0	VF 8.0	VF/NM 9.0	NM- 9.2
1	42	10/47	Orig.; Kiefer-c&a;	1	1	23	46	69	135	218	300
2A	62	–	8 pgs. cut; outside bc: Gift Box ad; LDC-r	1	1	6	12	18	31	38	45
2B	62	–	8 pgs. cut; outside-bc: Reorder list; scarce; LDC-r	1	1	10	20	30	58	79	100
3	75	–	LDC-r	1	1	5	10	14	20	24	28
4	93	–	LDC-r	1	1	5	10	14	20	24	28
5	117	–	LDC-r	1	1	3	6	9	14	19	24
6	131	–	New-c; old-a; PC-r	1	2	3	6	9	15	21	26
7	137	–	Old-a; PC-r	1	2	2	4	6	10	14	18
8	141	–	Old-a; PC-r	1	2	2	4	6	10	14	18
9	152	–	New-a; PC-r	2	2	3	6	9	16	23	30
10	158	–	PC-r	2	2	2	4	6	8	10	12
11	165	–	PC-r	2	2	3	6	9	17	25	32
12	167	12/63	PC-r	2	2	2	4	6	8	11	14
13	167	4/65	PC-r	2	2	2	4	6	8	10	12
14	167	5/66	PC-r	2	2	2	4	6	8	10	12
15	166	11/67	PC-r	2	2	2	4	6	8	10	12
16	169	Spr/69	PC-r; stiff-c	2	2	2	4	6	8	10	12

43. Great Expectations (Used in **SOTI**, pg. 311)

Ed	HRN	Date	Details	A	C	GD 2.0	VG 4.0	FN 6.0	VF 8.0	VF/NM 9.0	NM- 9.2
1	43	11/47	Original; Kiefer-a/c	1	1	88	176	264	554	940	1325
2	62	–	No c-price; 8 pgs. cut; LDC-r	1	1	57	114	171	359	610	860

44. Mysteries of Paris (Used in **SOTI**, pg. 323)

Ed	HRN	Date	Details	A	C	GD 2.0	VG 4.0	FN 6.0	VF 8.0	VF/NM 9.0	NM- 9.2
1A	44	12/47	Original; 56 pgs.; Kiefer-c/a	1	1	64	128	192	403	682	960
1B	44	12/47	Orig.; printed on white/heavier paper; (rare)	1	1	75	150	225	473	799	1125
2A	62	–	8 pgs. cut; outside-bc: Gift Box ad; LDC-r	1	1	29	58	87	172	276	380
2B	62	–	8 pgs. cut; outside-bc: reorder list; LDC-r	1	1	29	58	87	172	276	380
3	78	–	C-price 15¢; LDC-r	1	1	25	50	75	145	233	320

45. Tom Brown's School Days

Ed	HRN	Date	Details	A	C	GD 2.0	VG 4.0	FN 6.0	VF 8.0	VF/NM 9.0	NM- 9.2
1	44	1/48	Original; 1st 48pg. issue	1	1	18	36	54	103	162	220
2	64	–	No c-price; LDC-r	1	1	7	14	21	35	43	50
3	161	–	New-c&a; PC-r	2	2	3	6	9	17	25	32
4	167	2/64	PC-r	2	2	2	4	6	8	11	14
5	167	8/66	PC-r	2	2	2	4	6	8	11	14
6	166	R/1968	C-price 25¢; PC-r	2	2	2	4	6	8	11	14

46. Kidnapped

Ed	HRN	Date	Details	A	C	GD 2.0	VG 4.0	FN 6.0	VF 8.0	VF/NM 9.0	NM- 9.2
1	47	4/48	Original; Webb-c/a	1	1	18	36	54	103	162	220
2A	62	–	Price circle blank; LDC-r	1	1	7	14	21	35	43	50
2B	62	–	C-price 10¢; rare; LDC-r	1	1	30	60	90	176	283	390
3	78	–	C-price 15¢; LDC-r	1	1	5	10	14	20	24	28
4	87	–	LDC-r	1	1	4	9	13	18	22	26
5	118	–	LDC-r	1	1	4	7	10	14	17	20
6	131	–	New-c; PC-r	1	2	5	10	16	20	28	32
7	140	–	PC-r	1	2	2	4	6	8	11	14
8	150	–	PC-r	1	2	2	4	6	8	11	14
9	164	–	Reduced pg.width; PC-r	1	2	2	4	6	8	10	12
10	167	–	PC-r	1	2	2	4	6	8	10	12
11	167	3/64	PC-r	1	2	2	4	6	8	10	12
12	167	6/65	PC-r	1	2	2	4	6	8	10	12
13	167	12/65	PC-r	1	2	2	4	6	8	10	12
14	166	9/67	PC-r	1	2	2	4	6	8	10	12
15	166	Win/69	New price 25¢; PC-r; stiff-c	1	2	2	4	6	8	10	12
16	169	Sm/70	PC-r; stiff-c	1	2	2	4	6	8	10	12

47. Twenty Thousand Leagues Under the Sea

Ed	HRN	Date	Details	A	C	GD 2.0	VG 4.0	FN 6.0	VF 8.0	VF/NM 9.0	NM- 9.2
1	47	5/48	Orig.; Kiefer-a&c;	1	1	19	38	57	109	172	235
2	64	–	No c-price; LDC-r	1	1	6	12	18	27	33	38
3	78	–	C-price 15¢; LDC-r	1	1	4	9	13	18	22	26
4	94	–	LDC-r	1	1	4	8	12	17	21	24
5	118	–	LDC-r	1	1	4	7	10	14	17	20
6	128	–	New-c; PC-r	1	2	5	10	15	24	30	35
7	133	–	PC-r	1	2	2	4	6	9	13	16
8	140	–	PC-r	1	2	2	4	6	8	11	14
9	148	–	PC-r	1	2	2	4	6	8	11	14
10	156	–	PC-r	1	2	2	4	6	8	11	14
11	165	–	PC-r	1	2	2	4	6	8	11	14
12	167	–	PC-r	1	2	2	4	6	8	11	14
13	167	3/64	PC-r	1	2	2	4	6	8	11	14
14	167	8/65	PC-r	1	2	2	4	6	8	11	14
15	167	10/66	PC-r	1	2	2	4	6	8	11	14
16	166	R/1968	C-price 25¢; new-c PC-r	1	3	3	6	9	14	20	25
17	169	Spr/70	Stiff-c; PC-r	1	3	2	4	6	11	16	20

48. David Copperfield

Ed	HRN	Date	Details	A	C	GD 2.0	VG 4.0	FN 6.0	VF 8.0	VF/NM 9.0	NM- 9.2
1	47	6/48	Original; Kiefer-c/a	1	1	18	36	54	103	162	220
2	64	–	Price circle replaced by motif of boy reading; LDC-r	1	1	6	12	18	27	33	38
3	87	–	C-price 15¢; LDC-r	1	1	4	8	12	17	21	24

Classics Illustrated #51 © GIL

Classics Illustrated #55 © GIL

Classics Illustrated #59 © GIL

Ed	HRN	Date	Details	A	C	GD 2.0	VG 4.0	FN 6.0	VF 8.0	VF/NM 9.0	NM- 9.2
4	121	–	New-c; PC-r	1	2	5	10	15	22	26	30
5	130	–	PC-r	1	2	2	4	6	8	11	14
6	140	–	PC-r	1	2	2	4	6	8	11	14
7	148	–	PC-r	1	2	2	4	6	8	11	14
8	156	–	PC-r	1	2	2	4	6	8	11	14
9	167	–	PC-r	1	2	2	4	6	8	10	12
10	167	4/64	PC-r	1	2	2	4	6	8	10	12
11	167	6/65	PC-r	1	2	2	4	6	8	10	12
12	166	5/67	PC-r	1	2	2	4	6	8	10	12
13	166	R/67	PC-r; C-price 25¢	1	2	2	4	6	9	13	16
14	166	Spr/69	C-price 25¢; stiff-c PC-r	1	2	2	4	6	8	10	12
15	169	Win/69	Stiff-c; PC-r	1	2	2	4	6	8	10	12

49. Alice in Wonderland

Ed	HRN	Date	Details	A	C	GD 2.0	VG 4.0	FN 6.0	VF 8.0	VF/NM 9.0	NM- 9.2
1	47	7/48	Original; 1st Blum a & c	1	1	21	42	63	123	197	270
2	64	–	No c-price; LDC-r	1	1	8	16	24	40	50	60
3A	85	–	C-price 15¢; soft-c LDC-r	1	1	7	14	21	35	43	50
3B	85	–	Stiff-c; LDC-r	1	1	7	14	21	37	46	55
4	155	–	New PC, similar to orig.; PC-r	1	2	4	8	12	24	37	50
5	165	–	PC-r	1	2	3	6	9	16	23	30
6	167	3/64	PC-r	1	2	3	6	9	15	21	26
7	167	6/66	PC-r	1	2	3	6	9	15	21	26
8A	166	Fall/68	New-c; soft-c; 25¢ c-price; PC-r	1	3	4	8	12	24	37	50
8B	166	Fall/68	New-c; stiff-c; 25¢ c-price; PC-r	1	3	6	12	18	43	69	95

50. Adventures of Tom Sawyer (Used in **SOTI**, pg. 37)

Ed	HRN	Date	Details	A	C	GD 2.0	VG 4.0	FN 6.0	VF 8.0	VF/NM 9.0	NM- 9.2
1A	51	8/48	Orig.; Aldo Rubano a&c	1	1	18	36	54	103	162	220
1B	51	9/48	Orig.; Rubano c&a	1	1	18	36	54	103	162	220
1C	51	9/48	Orig.; outside-bc: blue & yellow only; rare	1	1	23	46	69	135	218	300
2	64	–	No c-price; LDC-r	1	1	5	10	15	23	28	32
3	78	–	C-price 15¢; LDC-r	1	1	4	8	12	17	21	24
4	94	–	LDC-r	1	1	4	7	10	14	17	20
5	117	–	LDC-r	1	1	2	4	6	10	14	18
6	132	–	LDC-r	1	1	2	4	6	10	14	18
7	140	–	New-c; PC-r	1	2	3	6	9	18	27	35
8	150	–	PC-r	1	2	2	4	6	8	11	14
9	164	–	New-a; PC-r	2	2	3	6	9	18	27	35
10	167	–	PC-r	2	2	2	4	6	8	11	14
11	167	1/65	PC-r	2	2	2	4	6	8	10	12
12	167	5/66	PC-r	2	2	2	4	6	8	10	12
13	166	12/67	PC-r	2	2	2	4	6	8	10	12
14	169	Fall/69	C-price 25¢; stiff-c; PC-r	2	2	2	4	6	8	10	12
15	169	Win/71	PC-r	2	2	2	4	6	8	10	12

51. The Spy

Ed	HRN	Date	Details	A	C	GD 2.0	VG 4.0	FN 6.0	VF 8.0	VF/NM 9.0	NM- 9.2
1A	51	9/48	Original; inside-bc illo: Christmas Carol	1	1	17	34	51	98	154	210
1B	51	9/48	Original; inside-bc illo: Man in Iron Mask	1	1	17	34	51	98	154	210
1C	51	8/48	Original; outside-bc: full color	1	1	17	34	51	98	154	210
1D	51	8/48	Original; outside-bc: blue & yellow only; scarce	1	1	18	36	54	107	169	230
2	89	–	C-price 15¢; LDC-r	1	1	5	10	14	20	24	28
3	121	–	LDC-r	1	1	4	8	12	17	21	24
4	139	–	New-c; PC-r	1	2	3	6	9	18	27	35
5	156	–	PC-r	1	2	2	4	6	8	11	14
6	167	11/63	PC-r	1	2	2	4	6	8	10	12
7	167	7/66	PC-r	1	2	2	4	6	8	10	12
8A	166	Win/69	C-price 25¢; soft-c; scarce; PC-r	1	2	3	6	9	15	21	26
8B	166	Win/69	C-price 25¢; stiff-c; PC-r	1	2	2	4	6	8	10	12

52. The House of the Seven Gables

Ed	HRN	Date	Details	A	C	GD 2.0	VG 4.0	FN 6.0	VF 8.0	VF/NM 9.0	NM- 9.2
1	53	10/48	Orig.; Griffiths a&c	1	1	17	34	51	98	154	210
2	89	–	C-price 15¢; LDC-r	1	1	5	10	14	20	24	28
3	121	–	LDC-r	1	1	4	8	12	17	21	24
4	142	–	New-c&a; PC-r; Woodbridge-a	2	2	5	10	15	25	31	36
5	156	–	PC-r	2	2	2	4	6	8	11	14
6	165	–	PC-r	2	2	2	4	6	8	10	12
7	167	5/64	PC-r	2	2	2	4	6	8	11	14
8	167	3/66	PC-r	2	2	2	4	6	8	10	12
9	166	R/1968	C-price 25¢; PC-r	2	2	2	4	6	8	10	12
10	169	Spr/70	Stiff-c; PC-r	2	2	2	4	6	8	10	12

53. A Christmas Carol

Ed	HRN	Date	Details	A	C	GD 2.0	VG 4.0	FN 6.0	VF 8.0	VF/NM 9.0	NM- 9.2
1	53	11/48	Original & only ed; Kiefer-c/a	1	1	23	46	69	135	218	300

54. Man in the Iron Mask

Ed	HRN	Date	Details	A	C	GD 2.0	VG 4.0	FN 6.0	VF 8.0	VF/NM 9.0	NM- 9.2
1	55	12/48	Original; Froehlich-a, Kiefer-c	1	1	17	34	51	98	154	210
2	93	–	C-price 15¢; LDC-r	1	1	5	10	15	23	28	32
3A	111	–	(O) logo lettering; scarce; LDC-r	1	1	6	12	18	31	38	45
3B	111	–	New logo as PC; LDC-r	1	1	5	10	15	23	28	32
4	142	–	New-c&a; PC-r	2	2	5	10	15	24	30	35
5	154	–	PC-r	2	2	2	4	6	8	11	14
6	165	–	PC-r	2	2	2	4	6	8	10	12
7	167	5/64	PC-r	2	2	2	4	6	8	10	12
8	167	4/66	PC-r	2	2	2	4	6	8	10	12
9A	166	Win/69	C-price 25¢; soft-c PC-r	2	2	3	6	9	15	21	26
9B	166	Win/69	Stiff-c	2	2	2	4	6	8	10	12

55. Silas Marner (Used in **SOTI**, pgs. 311, 312)

Ed	HRN	Date	Details	A	C	GD 2.0	VG 4.0	FN 6.0	VF 8.0	VF/NM 9.0	NM- 9.2
1	55	1/49	Original-Kiefer-c	1	1	17	34	51	98	154	210
2	75	–	Price circle blank; 'Coming Next' ad; LDC-r	1	1	5	10	15	24	30	35
3	97	–	LDC-r	1	1	3	6	9	14	19	24
4	121	–	New-c; PC-r	1	2	3	6	9	18	27	35
5	130	–	PC-r	1	2	2	4	6	8	11	14
6	140	–	PC-r	1	2	2	4	6	8	11	14
7	154	–	PC-r	1	2	2	4	6	8	11	14
8	165	–	PC-r	1	2	2	4	6	8	10	12
9	167	2/64	PC-r	1	2	2	4	6	8	10	12
10	167	6/65	PC-r	1	2	2	4	6	8	10	12
11	166	5/67	PC-r	1	2	2	4	6	8	10	12
12A	166	Win/69	C-price 25¢; soft-c PC-r	1	2	3	6	9	15	21	26
12B	166	Win/69	C-price 25¢; stiff-c PC-r	1	2	2	4	6	8	10	12

56. The Toilers of the Sea

Ed	HRN	Date	Details	A	C	GD 2.0	VG 4.0	FN 6.0	VF 8.0	VF/NM 9.0	NM- 9.2
1	55	2/49	Original; A.M. Froehlich-c/a	1	1	24	48	72	140	225	310
2	165	–	New-c&a; PC-r; Angelo Torres-a	2	2	7	14	21	37	46	55
3	167	3/64	PC-r	2	2	3	6	9	16	22	28
4	167	10/66	PC-r	2	2	3	6	9	16	22	28

57. The Song of Hiawatha

Ed	HRN	Date	Details	A	C	GD 2.0	VG 4.0	FN 6.0	VF 8.0	VF/NM 9.0	NM- 9.2
1	55	3/49	Original; Alex Blum-c/a	1	1	15	30	45	92	144	195
2	75	–	No c-price w/15¢ sticker; 'Coming Next' ad; LDC-r	1	1	5	10	15	24	30	35
3	94	–	C-price 15¢; LDC-r	1	1	5	10	14	20	24	28
4	118	–	LDC-r	1	1	3	6	9	14	19	24

Classics Illustrated #60 © GIL

Classics Illustrated #62 © GIL

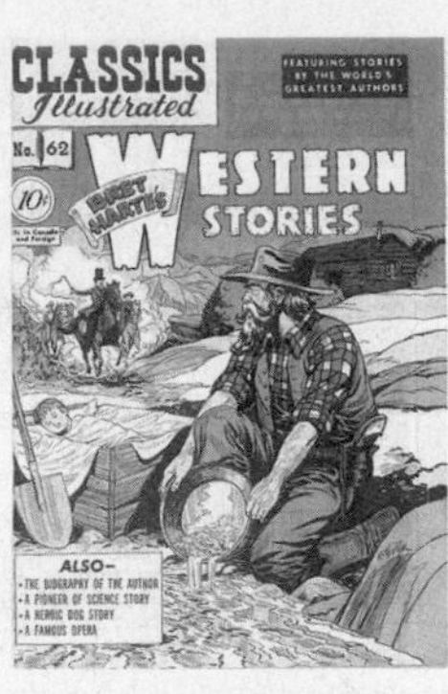

Classics Illustrated #68 © GIL

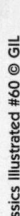

Ed	HRN	Date	Details	A	C	GD 2.0	VG 4.0	FN 6.0	VF 8.0	VF/NM 9.0	NM- 9.2
5	134	–	New-c; PC-r	1	2	3	6	9	18	27	35
6	139	–	PC-r	1	2	2	4	6	8	11	14
7	154	–	PC-r	1	2	2	4	6	8	11	14
8	167	–	Has orig.date; PC-r	1	2	2	4	6	8	10	12
9	167	9/64	PC-r	1	2	2	4	6	8	10	12
10	167	10/65	PC-r	1	2	2	4	6	8	10	12
11	166	F/1968	C-price 25¢; PC-r	1	2	2	4	6	8	10	12

58. The Prairie

Ed	HRN	Date	Details	A	C	GD 2.0	VG 4.0	FN 6.0	VF 8.0	VF/NM 9.0	NM- 9.2
1	60	4/49	Original; Palais c/a	1	1	15	30	45	92	144	195
2A	62	–	No c-price; no coming-next ad; LDC-r	1	1	9	18	27	47	61	75
2B	62		10¢ (rare)	1	1	18	36	54	105	165	225
3	78	–	C-price 15¢ in dbl. circle; LDC-r	1	1	5	10	15	22	26	30
4	114	–	LDC-r	1	1	4	8	12	17	21	24
5	131	–	LDC-r	1	1	4	7	10	14	17	20
6	132	–	LDC-r	1	1	4	7	10	14	17	20
7	146	–	New-c; PC-r	1	2	5	10	15	23	28	32
8	155	–	PC-r	1	2	2	4	6	8	11	14
9	167	5/64	PC-r	1	2	2	4	6	8	10	12
10	167	4/66	PC-r	1	2	2	4	6	8	10	12
11	169	Sm/69	New price 25¢; stiff-c; PC-r	1	2	2	4	6	8	10	12

59. Wuthering Heights

Ed	HRN	Date	Details	A	C	GD 2.0	VG 4.0	FN 6.0	VF 8.0	VF/NM 9.0	NM- 9.2
1	60	5/49	Original; Kiefer-c/a	1	1	17	34	51	98	154	210
2	85	–	C-price 15¢; LDC-r	1	1	6	12	18	28	34	40
3	156	–	New-c; PC-r	1	2	5	10	15	25	31	36
4	167	1/64	PC-r	1	2	2	4	6	8	11	14
5	167	10/66	PC-r	1	2	2	4	6	8	11	14
6	169	Sm/69	C-price 25¢; stiff-c; PC-r	1	2	2	4	6	8	11	14

60. Black Beauty

Ed	HRN	Date	Details	A	C	GD 2.0	VG 4.0	FN 6.0	VF 8.0	VF/NM 9.0	NM- 9.2
1	62	6/49	Original; Froehlich-c/a	1	1	15	30	45	92	144	195
2	62	–	No c-price; no coming-next ad; LDC-r (rare)	1	1	18	36	54	105	165	225
3	85	–	C-price 15¢; LDC-r	1	1	5	10	15	23	28	32
4	158	–	New L.B. Cole-c/a; PC-r	2	2	7	14	21	35	43	50
5	167	2/64	PC-r	2	2	2	4	6	11	16	20
6	167	3/66	PC-r	2	2	2	4	6	11	16	20
7	166	R/1968	New-c&price, 25¢; PC-r	2	3	5	10	15	32	51	70

61. The Woman in White

Ed	HRN	Date	Details	A	C	GD 2.0	VG 4.0	FN 6.0	VF 8.0	VF/NM 9.0	NM- 9.2
1A	62	7/49	Original; Blum-c/a fc-purple; bc: top illos light blue	1	1	17	34	51	98	154	210
1B	62	7/49	Original; Blum-c/a fc-pink; bc: top illos light violet	1	1	17	34	51	98	154	210
2	156	–	New-c; PC-r	1	2	6	12	18	28	34	40
3	167	1/64	PC-r	1	2	2	4	6	11	16	20
4	166	R/1968	C-price 25¢; PC-r	1	2	2	4	6	11	16	20

62. Western Stories ("The Luck of Roaring Camp" and "The Outcasts of Poker Flat")

Ed	HRN	Date	Details	A	C	GD 2.0	VG 4.0	FN 6.0	VF 8.0	VF/NM 9.0	NM- 9.2
1	62	8/49	Original; Kiefer-c/a	1	1	15	30	45	88	137	185
2	89	–	C-price 15¢; LDC-r	1	1	5	10	15	23	28	32
3	121	–	LDC-r	1	1	3	6	9	15	21	26
4	137	–	New-c; PC-r	1	2	3	6	9	18	27	35
5	152	–	PC-r	1	2	2	4	6	8	10	12
6	167	10/63	PC-r	1	2	2	4	6	8	10	12
7	167	6/64	PC-r	1	2	2	4	6	8	10	12
8	167	11/66	PC-r	1	2	2	4	6	8	10	12
9	166	R/1968	New-c&price 25¢; PC-r	1	3	3	6	9	17	25	32

63. The Man Without a Country

Ed	HRN	Date	Details	A	C	GD 2.0	VG 4.0	FN 6.0	VF 8.0	VF/NM 9.0	NM- 9.2
1	62	9/49	Original; Kiefer-c/a	1	1	15	30	45	92	144	195
2	78	–	C-price 15¢ in double circle; LDC-r	1	1	5	10	15	23	28	32
3	156	–	New-c, old-a; PC-r	1	2	6	12	18	28	34	40
4	165	–	New-a & text pgs.; PC-r; A. Torres-a	2	2	5	10	15	23	28	32
5	167	3/64	PC-r	2	2	2	4	6	8	10	12
6	167	8/66	PC-r	2	2	2	4	6	8	10	12
7	169	Sm/69	New price 25¢; stiff-c; PC-r	2	2	2	4	6	8	10	12

64. Treasure Island

Ed	HRN	Date	Details	A	C	GD 2.0	VG 4.0	FN 6.0	VF 8.0	VF/NM 9.0	NM- 9.2
1	62	10/49	Original; Blum-c/a	1	1	17	34	51	98	154	210
2A	82	–	C-price 15¢; soft-c LDC-r	1	1	5	10	15	22	26	30
2B	82	–	Stiff-c; LDC-r	1	1	5	10	15	23	28	32
3	117	–	LDC-r	1	1	3	6	9	15	21	26
4	131	–	New-c; PC-r	1	2	3	6	9	18	27	35
5	138	–	PC-r	1	2	2	4	6	8	11	14
6	146	–	PC-r	1	2	2	4	6	8	11	14
7	158	–	PC-r	1	2	2	4	6	8	11	14
8	165	–	PC-r	1	2	2	4	6	8	10	12
9	167	–	PC-r	1	2	2	4	6	8	10	12
10	167	6/64	PC-r	1	2	2	4	6	8	10	12
11	167	12/65	PC-r	1	2	2	4	6	8	10	12
12A	166	10/67	PC-r	1	2	2	4	6	8	10	12
12B	166	10/67	w/Grit ad stapled in book	1	2	9	18	27	65	113	160
13	169	Spr/69	New price 25¢; stiff-c; PC-r	1	2	2	4	6	8	11	14
14	–	1989	Long John Silver's Seafood Shoppes; $1.95, First/Berkley Publ.; Blum-r	1	2						5.00

65. Benjamin Franklin

Ed	HRN	Date	Details	A	C	GD 2.0	VG 4.0	FN 6.0	VF 8.0	VF/NM 9.0	NM- 9.2
1	64	11/49	Original; Kiefer-c; Iger Shop-a	1	1	15	30	45	92	144	195
2	131	–	New-c; PC-r	1	2	5	10	15	24	30	35
3	154	–	PC-r	1	2	2	4	6	9	12	15
4	167	2/64	PC-r	1	2	2	4	6	8	11	14
5	167	4/66	PC-r	1	2	2	4	6	8	11	14
6	169	Fall/69	New price 25¢; stiff-c; PC-r	1	2	2	4	6	8	11	14

66. The Cloister and the Hearth

Ed	HRN	Date	Details	A	C	GD 2.0	VG 4.0	FN 6.0	VF 8.0	VF/NM 9.0	NM- 9.2
1	67	12/49	Original & only ed; Kiefer-a & c	1	1	30	60	90	176	283	390

67. The Scottish Chiefs

Ed	HRN	Date	Details	A	C	GD 2.0	VG 4.0	FN 6.0	VF 8.0	VF/NM 9.0	NM- 9.2
1	67	1/50	Original; Blum-a&c	1	1	15	30	45	84	127	170
2	85	–	C-price 15¢; LDC-r	1	1	5	10	15	23	28	32
3	118	–	LDC-r	1	1	3	6	9	15	21	26
4	136	–	New-c; PC-r	1	2	3	6	9	18	27	36
5	154	–	PC-r	1	2	2	4	6	8	11	14
6	167	11/63	PC-r	1	2	2	4	6	9	13	16
7	167	8/65	PC-r	1	2	2	4	6	8	11	14

68. Julius Caesar (Used in SOTI, pgs. 36, 37)

Ed	HRN	Date	Details	A	C	GD 2.0	VG 4.0	FN 6.0	VF 8.0	VF/NM 9.0	NM- 9.2
1	70	2/50	Original; Kiefer-c/a	1	1	15	30	45	84	127	170
2	85	–	C-price 15¢; LDC-r	1	1	5	10	15	22	26	30
3	108	–	LDC-r	1	1	4	9	13	18	22	26
4	156	–	New L.B. Cole-c; PC-r	1	2	6	12	18	28	34	40
5	165	–	New-a by Evans, Crandall; PC-r	2	2	5	10	15	24	30	35
6	167	2/64	PC-r	2	2	2	4	6	8	10	12
7	167	10/65	Tarzan books inside cover; PC-r	2	2	2	4	6	8	10	12
8	166	R/1967	PC-r	2	2	2	4	6	8	10	12
9	169	Win/69	PC-r; stiff-c	2	2	2	4	6	8	10	12

Classics Illustrated #72 © GIL

Classics Illustrated #78 © GIL

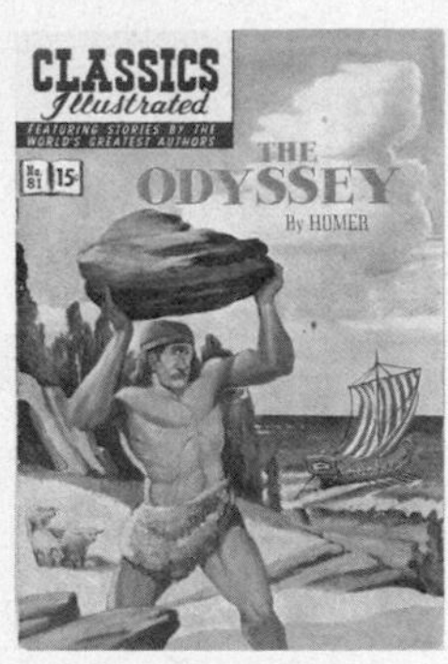

Classics Illustrated #81 © GIL

69. Around the World in 80 Days

Ed	HRN	Date	Details	A	C	GD 2.0	VG 4.0	FN 6.0	VF 8.0	VF/NM 9.0	NM- 9.2
1	70	3/50	Original; Kiefer-c/a	1	1	15	30	45	84	127	170
2	07		C-price 15¢; LDC-r	1	1	5	10	15	22	26	30
3	125	–	LDC-r	1	1	4	9	13	18	22	26
4	136	–	New-c; PC-r	1	2	5	10	15	25	31	36
5	146	–	PC-r	1	2	2	4	6	8	11	14
6	152	–	PC-r	1	2	2	4	6	8	11	14
7	164	–	PC-r	1	2	2	4	6	8	10	12
8	167	–	PC-r	1	2	2	4	6	8	10	12
9	167	7/64	PC-r	1	2	2	4	6	8	10	12
10	167	11/65	PC-r	1	2	2	4	6	8	10	12
11	166	7/67	PC-r	1	2	2	4	6	8	10	12
12	169	Spr/69	C-price 25¢; stiff-c; PC-r	1	2	2	4	6	8	10	12

70. The Pilot

Ed	HRN	Date	Details	A	C	GD 2.0	VG 4.0	FN 6.0	VF 8.0	VF/NM 9.0	NM- 9.2
1	71	4/50	Original; Blum-c/a	1	1	13	26	39	74	105	135
2	92	–	C-price 15¢; LDC-r	1	1	5	10	15	23	28	32
3	125	–	LDC-r	1	1	4	9	13	18	22	26
4	156	–	New-c; PC-r	1	2	6	12	18	28	34	40
5	167	2/64	PC-r	1	2	2	4	6	11	16	20
6	167	5/66	PC-r	1	2	2	4	6	9	13	16

71. The Man Who Laughs

Ed	HRN	Date	Details	A	C	GD 2.0	VG 4.0	FN 6.0	VF 8.0	VF/NM 9.0	NM- 9.2
1	71	5/50	Original; Blum-c/a	1	1	18	36	54	107	169	230
2	165	–	New-c&a; PC-r	2	2	14	28	42	80	115	150
3	167	4/64	PC-r	2	2	11	22	33	62	86	110

72. The Oregon Trail

Ed	HRN	Date	Details	A	C	GD 2.0	VG 4.0	FN 6.0	VF 8.0	VF/NM 9.0	NM- 9.2
1	73	6/50	Original; Kiefer-c/a	1	1	13	26	39	74	105	135
2	80	–	C-price 15¢; LDC-r	1	1	5	10	15	23	28	32
3	121	–	LDC-r	1	1	4	9	13	18	22	28
4	131	–	New-c; PC-r	1	2	5	10	15	25	31	36
5	140	–	PC-r	1	2	2	4	6	8	11	14
6	150	–	PC-r	1	2	2	4	6	8	11	14
7	164	–	PC-r	1	2	2	4	6	8	10	12
8	167	–	PC-r	1	2	2	4	6	8	10	12
9	167	8/64	PC-r	1	2	2	4	6	8	10	12
10	167	10/65	PC-r	1	2	2	4	6	8	10	12
11	166	R/1968	C-price 25¢; PC-r	1	2	2	4	6	8	10	12

73. The Black Tulip

Ed	HRN	Date	Details	A	C	GD 2.0	VG 4.0	FN 6.0	VF 8.0	VF/NM 9.0	NM- 9.2
1	75	7/50	1st & only ed.; Alex Blum-c/a	1	1	35	70	105	203	327	450

74. Mr. Midshipman Easy

Ed	HRN	Date	Details	A	C	GD 2.0	VG 4.0	FN 6.0	VF 8.0	VF/NM 9.0	NM- 9.2
1	75	8/50	1st & only edition	1	1	35	70	105	203	327	450

75. The Lady of the Lake

Ed	HRN	Date	Details	A	C	GD 2.0	VG 4.0	FN 6.0	VF 8.0	VF/NM 9.0	NM- 9.2
1	75	9/50	Original; Kiefer-c/a	1	1	13	26	39	74	105	135
2	85	–	C-price 15¢; LDC-r	1	1	5	10	15	24	30	35
3	118	–	LDC-r	1	1	5	10	14	20	24	28
4	139	–	New-c; PC-r	1	2	5	10	15	25	31	36
5	154	–	PC-r	1	2	2	4	6	8	11	14
6	165	–	PC-r	1	2	2	4	6	8	10	12
7	167	4/64	PC-r	1	2	2	4	6	8	10	12
8	167	5/66	PC-r	1	2	2	4	6	8	10	12
9	169	Spr/69	New price 25¢; stiff-c; PC-r	1	2	2	4	6	8	10	12

76. The Prisoner of Zenda

Ed	HRN	Date	Details	A	C	GD 2.0	VG 4.0	FN 6.0	VF 8.0	VF/NM 9.0	NM- 9.2
1	75	10/50	Original; Kiefer-c/a	1	1	13	26	39	74	105	135
2	85	–	C-price 15¢; LDC-r	1	1	5	10	15	23	28	32
3	111	–	LDC-r	1	1	3	6	9	16	21	26
4	128	–	New-c; PC-r	1	2	3	6	9	18	27	35
5	152	–	PC-r	1	2	2	4	6	8	11	14
6	165	–	PC-r	1	2	2	4	6	8	10	12
7	167	4/64	PC-r	1	2	2	4	6	8	10	12
8	167	9/66	PC-r	1	2	2	4	6	8	10	12
9	169	Fall/69	New price 25¢; stiff-c; PC-r	1	2	2	4	6	8	10	12

77. The Iliad

Ed	HRN	Date	Details	A	C	GD 2.0	VG 4.0	FN 6.0	VF 8.0	VF/NM 9.0	NM- 9.2
1	78	11/50	Original; Blum-c/a	1	1	13	26	39	74	105	135
2	87	–	C-price 15¢; LDC-r	1	1	5	10	15	24	30	35
3	121	–	LDC-r	1	1	3	6	9	15	21	26
4	139	–	New-c; PC-r	1	2	3	6	9	17	25	32
5	150	–	PC-r	1	2	2	4	6	8	11	14
6	165	–	PC-r	1	2	2	4	6	8	10	12
7	167	10/63	PC-r	1	2	2	4	6	8	10	12
8	167	7/64	PC-r	1	2	2	4	6	8	10	12
9	167	5/66	PC-r	1	2	2	4	6	8	10	12
10	166	R/1968	C-price 25¢; PC-r	1	2	2	4	6	8	10	12

78. Joan of Arc

Ed	HRN	Date	Details	A	C	GD 2.0	VG 4.0	FN 6.0	VF 8.0	VF/NM 9.0	NM- 9.2
1	78	12/50	Original; Kiefer-c/a	1	1	13	26	39	74	105	135
2	87	–	C-price 15¢; LDC-r	1	1	5	10	15	23	28	32
3	113	–	LDC-r	1	1	3	6	9	15	21	26
4	128	–	New-c; PC-r	1	2	3	6	9	18	27	35
5	140	–	PC-r	1	2	2	4	6	8	11	14
6	150	–	PC-r	1	2	2	4	6	8	11	14
7	159	–	PC-r	1	2	2	4	6	8	11	14
8	167	–	PC-r	1	2	2	4	6	8	10	12
9	167	12/63	PC-r	1	2	2	4	6	8	10	12
10	167	6/65	PC-r	1	2	2	4	6	8	10	12
11	166	6/67	PC-r	1	2	2	4	6	8	10	12
12	166	Win/69	New-c&price, 25¢; PC-r; stiff-c	1	3	3	6	9	16	23	30

79. Cyrano de Bergerac

Ed	HRN	Date	Details	A	C	GD 2.0	VG 4.0	FN 6.0	VF 8.0	VF/NM 9.0	NM- 9.2
1	78	1/51	Orig., movie promo inside front-c; Blum-c/a	1	1	13	26	39	74	105	135
2	85	–	C-price 15¢; LDC-r	1	1	5	10	15	23	28	32
3	118	–	LDC-r	1	1	3	6	9	17	23	28
4	133	–	New-c; PC-r	1	2	3	6	9	17	25	32
5	156	–	PC-r	1	2	2	4	6	11	16	20
6	167	8/64	PC-r	1	2	2	4	6	11	16	20

80. White Fang (Last line drawn cover)

Ed	HRN	Date	Details	A	C	GD 2.0	VG 4.0	FN 6.0	VF 8.0	VF/NM 9.0	NM- 9.2
1	79	2/51	Orig.; Blum-c/a	1	1	13	26	39	74	105	135
2	87	–	C-price 15¢; LDC-r	1	1	5	10	15	24	30	35
3	125	–	LDC-r	1	1	3	6	9	15	21	26
4	132	–	New-c; PC-r	1	2	3	6	9	17	25	32
5	140	–	PC-r	1	2	2	4	6	8	11	14
6	153	–	PC-r	1	2	2	4	6	8	11	14
7	167	–	PC-r	1	2	2	4	6	8	10	12
8	167	9/64	PC-r	1	2	2	4	6	8	10	12
9	167	7/65	PC-r	1	2	2	4	6	8	10	12
10	166	6/67	PC-r	1	2	2	4	6	8	10	12
11	169	Fall/69	New price 25¢; PC-r; stiff-c	1	2	2	4	6	8	10	12

81. The Odyssey (1st painted cover)

Ed	HRN	Date	Details	A	C	GD 2.0	VG 4.0	FN 6.0	VF 8.0	VF/NM 9.0	NM- 9.2
1	82	3/51	First 15¢ Original; Blum-c	1	1	13	26	39	74	105	135
2	167	8/64	PC-r	1	1	2	4	6	11	16	20
3	167	10/66	PC-r	1	1	2	4	6	11	16	20
4	169	Spr/69	New, stiff-c; PC-r	1	2	3	6	9	18	27	36

82. The Master of Ballantrae

Ed	HRN	Date	Details	A	C	GD 2.0	VG 4.0	FN 6.0	VF 8.0	VF/NM 9.0	NM- 9.2
1	82	4/51	Original; Blum-c	1	1	11	22	33	62	86	110
2	167	8/64	PC-r	1	1	3	6	9	14	19	24
3	166	Fall/68	New, stiff-c; PC-r	1	2	3	6	9	18	27	36

83. The Jungle Book

Ed	HRN	Date	Details	A	C	GD 2.0	VG 4.0	FN 6.0	VF 8.0	VF/NM 9.0	NM- 9.2
1	85	5/51	Original; Blum-c Bossert/Blum-a	1	1	11	22	33	62	86	110
2	110	–	PC-r	1	1	2	4	6	9	13	16
3	125	–	PC-r	1	1	2	4	6	8	11	14
4	134	–	PC-r	1	1	2	4	6	8	11	14
5	142	–	PC-r	1	1	2	4	6	8	11	14
6	150	–	PC-r	1	1	2	4	6	8	11	14

Classics Illustrated #88 © GIL

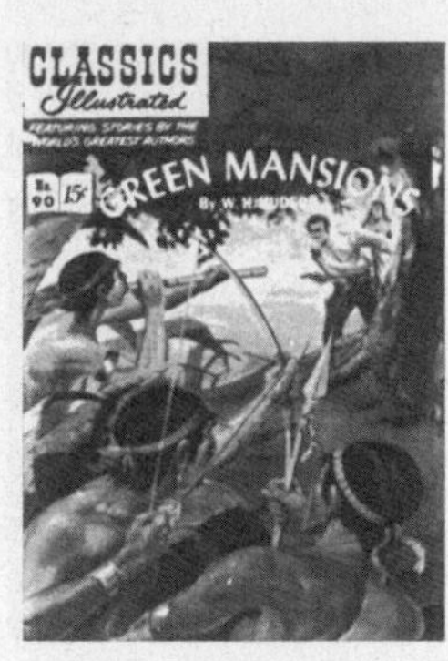

Classics Illustrated #90 © GIL

Classics Illustrated #97 © GIL

Ed	HRN	Date	Details	A	C	GD 2.0	VG 4.0	FN 6.0	VF 8.0	VF/NM 9.0	NM- 9.2
7	159	–	PC-r	1	1	2	4	6	8	11	14
8	167	–	PC-r	1	1	2	4	6	8	10	12
9	167	3/65	PC-r	1	1	2	4	6	8	10	12
10	167	11/65	PC-r	1	1	2	4	6	8	10	12
11	167	5/66	PC-r	1	1	2	4	6	8	10	12
12	166	R/1968	New c&a; stiff-c; PC-r	2	2	3	6	9	18	27	36

84. The Gold Bug and Other Stories ("The Gold Bug", "The Tell-Tale Heart", "The Cask of Amontillado")

Ed	HRN	Date	Details	A	C	GD	VG	FN	VF	VF/NM	NM-
1	85	6/51	Original; Blum-c/a; Palais, Laverly-a	1	1	14	28	42	82	121	160
2	167	7/64	PC-r	1	1	11	22	33	60	83	105

85. The Sea Wolf

Ed	HRN	Date	Details	A	C	GD	VG	FN	VF	VF/NM	NM-
1	85	7/51	Original; Blum-c/a	1	1	10	20	30	58	79	100
2	121	–	PC-r	1	1	2	4	6	8	11	14
3	132	–	PC-r	1	1	2	4	6	8	11	14
4	141	–	PC-r	1	1	2	4	6	8	11	14
5	161	–	PC-r	1	1	2	4	6	8	10	12
6	167	2/64	PC-r	1	1	2	4	6	8	10	12
7	167	11/65	PC-r	1	1	2	4	6	8	10	12
8	169	Fall/69	New price 25¢; stiff-c; PC-r	1	1	2	4	6	8	10	12

86. Under Two Flags

Ed	HRN	Date	Details	A	C	GD	VG	FN	VF	VF/NM	NM-
1	87	8/51	Original; first delBourgo-a	1	1	10	20	30	58	79	100
2	117	–	PC-r	1	1	2	4	6	9	13	16
3	139	–	PC-r	1	1	2	4	6	8	11	14
4	158	–	PC-r	1	1	2	4	6	8	11	14
5	167	2/64	PC-r	1	1	2	4	6	8	10	12
6	167	8/66	PC-r	1	1	2	4	6	8	10	12
7	169	Sm/69	New price 25¢; stiff-c; PC-r	1	1	2	4	6	8	10	12

87. A Midsummer Nights Dream

Ed	HRN	Date	Details	A	C	GD	VG	FN	VF	VF/NM	NM-
1	87	9/51	Original; Blum c/a	1	1	10	20	30	58	79	100
2	161	–	PC-r	1	1	2	4	6	8	11	14
3	167	4/64	PC-r	1	1	2	4	6	8	10	12
4	167	5/66	PC-r	1	1	2	4	6	8	10	12
5	169	Sm/69	New price 25¢; stiff-c; PC-r	1	1	2	4	6	8	10	12

88. Men of Iron

Ed	HRN	Date	Details	A	C	GD	VG	FN	VF	VF/NM	NM-
1	89	10/51	Original	1	1	10	20	30	58	79	100
2	154	–	PC-r	1	1	2	4	6	8	11	14
3	167	1/64	PC-r	1	1	2	4	6	8	10	12
4	166	R/1968	C-price 25¢; PC-r	1	1	2	4	6	8	10	12

89. Crime and Punishment (Cover illo. in **POP**)

Ed	HRN	Date	Details	A	C	GD	VG	FN	VF	VF/NM	NM-
1	89	11/51	Original; Palais-a	1	1	10	20	30	58	79	100
2	152	–	PC-r	1	1	2	4	6	8	11	14
3	167	4/64	PC-r	1	1	2	4	6	8	10	12
4	167	5/66	PC-r	1	1	2	4	6	8	10	12
5	169	Fall/69	New price 25¢ stiff-c; PC-r	1	1	2	4	6	8	10	12

90. Green Mansions

Ed	HRN	Date	Details	A	C	GD	VG	FN	VF	VF/NM	NM-
1	89	12/51	Original; Blum-c/a	1	1	10	20	30	58	79	100
2	148	–	New L.B. Cole-c; PC-r	1	2	5	10	15	22	26	30
3	165	–	PC-r	1	2	2	4	6	8	10	12
4	167	4/64	PC-r	1	2	2	4	6	8	10	12
5	167	9/66	PC-r	1	2	2	4	6	8	10	12
6	169	Sm/69	New price 25¢; stiff-c; PC-r	1	2	2	4	6	8	10	12

91. The Call of the Wild

Ed	HRN	Date	Details	A	C	GD	VG	FN	VF	VF/NM	NM-
1	92	1/52	Orig.; delBourgo-a	1	1	10	20	30	58	79	100
2	112	–	PC-r	1	1	2	4	6	8	11	14
3	125	–	'Picture Progress' on back-c; PC-r	1	1	2	4	6	8	11	14
4	134	–	PC-r	1	1	2	4	6	8	11	14
5	143	–	PC-r	1	1	2	4	6	8	11	14
6	165	–	PC-r	1	1	2	4	6	8	11	14
7	167	–	PC-r	1	1	2	4	6	8	10	12
8	167	4/65	PC-r	1	1	2	4	6	8	10	12
9	167	3/66	PC-r	1	1	2	4	6	8	10	12
10	166	11/67	PC-r	1	1	2	4	6	8	10	12
11	169	Spr/70	New price 25¢; stiff-c; PC-r	1	1	2	4	6	8	10	12

92. The Courtship of Miles Standish

Ed	HRN	Date	Details	A	C	GD	VG	FN	VF	VF/NM	NM-
1	92	2/52	Original; Blum-c/a	1	1	10	20	30	58	79	100
2	165	–	PC-r	1	1	2	4	6	8	11	14
3	167	3/64	PC-r	1	1	2	4	6	8	11	14
4	166	5/67	PC-r	1	1	2	4	6	8	11	14
5	169	Win/69	New price 25¢ stiff-c; PC-r	1	1	2	4	6	8	11	14

93. Pudd'nhead Wilson

Ed	HRN	Date	Details	A	C	GD	VG	FN	VF	VF/NM	NM-
1	94	3/52	Orig.; Kiefer-c/a;	1	1	10	20	30	58	79	100
2	165	–	New-c; PC-r	1	2	2	4	6	11	16	25
3	167	3/64	PC-r	1	2	2	4	6	8	11	14
4	166	R/1968	New price 25¢; soft-c; PC-r	1	2	2	4	6	9	12	15

94. David Balfour

Ed	HRN	Date	Details	A	C	GD	VG	FN	VF	VF/NM	NM-
1	94	4/52	Original; Palais-a	1	1	10	20	30	58	79	100
2	167	5/64	PC-r	1	1	2	4	6	11	16	20
3	166	R/1968	C-price 25¢; PC-r	1	1	2	4	6	13	18	22

95. All Quiet on the Western Front

Ed	HRN	Date	Details	A	C	GD	VG	FN	VF	VF/NM	NM-
1A	96	5/52	Orig.; del Bourgo-a	1	1	14	28	42	78	112	145
1B	99	5/52	Orig.; del Bourgo-a	1	1	12	24	36	67	94	120
2	167	10/64	PC-r	1	1	3	6	9	15	21	26
3	167	11/66	PC-r	1	1	3	6	9	15	21	26

96. Daniel Boone

Ed	HRN	Date	Details	A	C	GD	VG	FN	VF	VF/NM	NM-
1	97	6/52	Original; Blum-a	1	1	10	20	30	56	76	95
2	117	–	PC-r	1	1	2	4	6	8	11	14
3	128	–	PC-r	1	1	2	4	6	8	11	14
4	132	–	PC-r	1	1	2	4	6	8	11	14
5	134	–	"Story of Jesus" on back-c; PC-r	1	1	2	4	6	8	11	14
6	158	–	PC-r	1	1	2	4	6	8	11	14
7	167	1/64	PC-r	1	1	2	4	6	8	10	12
8	167	5/65	PC-r	1	1	2	4	6	8	10	12
9	167	11/66	PC-r	1	1	2	4	6	8	10	12
10	166	Win/69	New-c; price 25¢; PC-r; stiff-c	1	2	3	6	9	16	22	28

97. King Solomon's Mines

Ed	HRN	Date	Details	A	C	GD	VG	FN	VF	VF/NM	NM-
1	96	7/52	Orig.; Kiefer-a	1	1	10	20	30	56	76	95
2	118	–	PC-r	1	1	2	4	6	8	11	14
3	131	–	PC-r	1	1	2	4	6	8	11	14
4	141	–	PC-r	1	1	2	4	6	8	11	14
5	158	–	PC-r	1	1	2	4	6	8	11	14
6	167	2/64	PC-r	1	1	2	4	6	8	10	12
7	167	9/65	PC-r	1	1	2	4	6	8	10	12
8	169	Sm/69	New price 25¢; stiff-c; PC-r	1	1	2	4	6	8	10	12

98. The Red Badge of Courage

Ed	HRN	Date	Details	A	C	GD	VG	FN	VF	VF/NM	NM-
1	98	8/52	Original	1	1	10	20	30	56	76	95
2	118	–	PC-r	1	1	2	4	6	8	11	14
3	132	–	PC-r	1	1	2	4	6	8	11	14
4	142	–	PC-r	1	1	2	4	6	8	11	14
5	152	–	PC-r	1	1	2	4	6	8	11	14
6	161	–	PC-r	1	1	2	4	6	8	11	14
7	167	–	Has orig.date; PC-r	1	1	2	4	6	8	11	14
8	167	9/64	PC-r	1	1	2	4	6	8	11	14
9	167	10/65	PC-r	1	1	2	4	6	8	11	14

Classics Illustrated #106 © GIL

Classics Illustrated #107 © GIL

Classics Illustrated #114 © GIL

Ed	HRN	Date	Details	A	C	GD 2.0	VG 4.0	FN 6.0	VF 8.0	VF/NM 9.0	NM- 9.2
10	166	R/1968	New-c&price 25¢; PC-r; stiff-c	1	2	3	6	9	16	23	30

99. Hamlet (Used in **POP**, pg. 102)

Ed	HRN	Date	Details	A	C	GD 2.0	VG 4.0	FN 6.0	VF 8.0	VF/NM 9.0	NM- 9.2
1	98	9/52	Original; Blum-a	1	1	10	20	30	58	79	100
2	121	–	PC-r	1	1	2	4	6	8	11	14
3	141	–	PC-r	1	1	2	4	6	8	11	14
4	158	–	PC-r	1	1	2	4	6	8	11	14
5	167	–	Has orig.date; PC-r	1	1	2	4	6	8	10	12
6	167	7/65	PC-r	1	1	2	4	6	8	10	12
7	166	4/67	PC-r	1	1	2	4	6	8	10	12
8	169	Spr/69	New-c&price 25¢; PC-r; stiff-c	1	2	3	6	9	16	23	30

100. Mutiny on the Bounty

Ed	HRN	Date	Details	A	C	GD 2.0	VG 4.0	FN 6.0	VF 8.0	VF/NM 9.0	NM- 9.2
1	100	10/52	Original	1	1	10	20	30	56	76	95
2	117	–	PC-r	1	1	2	4	6	8	11	14
3	132	–	PC-r	1	1	2	4	6	8	11	14
4	142	–	PC-r	1	1	2	4	6	8	11	14
5	155	–	PC-r	1	1	2	4	6	8	11	14
6	167	–	Has orig. date;PC-r	1	1	2	4	6	8	10	12
7	167	5/64	PC-r	1	1	2	4	6	8	10	12
8	167	3/66	PC-r	1	1	2	4	6	8	10	12
9	169	Spr/70	PC-r; stiff-c	1	1	2	4	6	8	10	12

101. William Tell

Ed	HRN	Date	Details	A	C	GD 2.0	VG 4.0	FN 6.0	VF 8.0	VF/NM 9.0	NM- 9.2
1	101	11/52	Original; Kiefer-c delBourgo-a	1	1	10	20	30	56	76	95
2	118	–	PC-r	1	1	2	4	6	8	11	14
3	141	–	PC-r	1	1	2	4	6	8	11	14
4	158	–	PC-r	1	1	2	4	6	8	11	14
5	167	–	Has orig.date; PC-r	1	1	2	4	6	8	10	12
6	167	11/64	PC-r	1	1	2	4	6	8	10	12
7	166	4/67	PC-r	1	1	2	4	6	8	10	12
8	169	Win/69	New price 25¢; stiff-c; PC-r	1	1	2	4	6	8	10	12

102. The White Company

Ed	HRN	Date	Details	A	C	GD 2.0	VG 4.0	FN 6.0	VF 8.0	VF/NM 9.0	NM- 9.2
1	101	12/52	Original; Blum-a	1	1	13	26	39	72	101	130
2	165	–	PC-r	1	1	3	6	9	16	22	28
3	167	4/64	PC-r	1	1	3	6	9	16	22	28

103. Men Against the Sea

Ed	HRN	Date	Details	A	C	GD 2.0	VG 4.0	FN 6.0	VF 8.0	VF/NM 9.0	NM- 9.2
1	104	1/53	Original; Kiefer-c; Palais-a	1	1	10	20	30	58	79	100
2	114	–	PC-r	1	1	4	8	11	16	19	22
3	131	–	New-c; PC-r	1	2	5	10	15	24	30	35
4	158	–	PC-r	1	2	4	7	10	14	17	20
5	149	–	White reorder list; came after HRN-158; PC-r	1	2	5	10	15	22	26	30
6	167	3/64	PC-r	1	2	2	4	6	8	11	14

104. Bring 'Em Back Alive

Ed	HRN	Date	Details	A	C	GD 2.0	VG 4.0	FN 6.0	VF 8.0	VF/NM 9.0	NM- 9.2
1	105	2/53	Original; Kiefer-c/a	1	1	10	20	30	56	76	95
2	118	–	PC-r	1	1	2	4	6	8	11	14
3	133	–	PC-r	1	1	2	4	6	8	11	14
4	150	–	PC-r	1	1	2	4	6	8	11	14
5	158	–	PC-r	1	1	2	4	6	8	11	14
6	167	10/63	PC-r	1	1	2	4	6	8	10	12
7	167	9/65	PC-r	1	1	2	4	6	8	10	12
8	169	Win/69	New price 25¢; stiff-c; PC-r	1	1	2	4	6	8	10	12

105. From the Earth to the Moon

Ed	HRN	Date	Details	A	C	GD 2.0	VG 4.0	FN 6.0	VF 8.0	VF/NM 9.0	NM- 9.2
1	106	3/53	Original; Blum-a	1	1	10	20	30	56	76	95
2	118	–	PC-r	1	1	2	4	6	8	11	14
3	132	–	PC-r	1	1	2	4	6	8	11	14
4	141	–	PC-r	1	1	2	4	6	8	11	14
5	146	–	PC-r	1	1	2	4	6	8	11	14
6	156	–	PC-r	1	1	2	4	6	8	11	14
7	167	–	Has orig. date; PC-r	1	1	2	4	6	8	10	12
8	167	5/64	PC-r	1	1	2	4	6	8	10	12
9	167	5/65	PC-r	1	1	2	4	6	8	10	12
10A	166	10/67	PC-r	1	1	2	4	6	8	10	12
10B	166	10/67	w/Grit ad stapled in book	1	1	8	16	24	54	90	125
11	169	Sm/69	New price 25¢; stiff-c; PC-r	1	1	2	4	6	8	10	12
12	169	Spr/71	PC-r	1	1	2	4	6	8	10	12

106. Buffalo Bill

Ed	HRN	Date	Details	A	C	GD 2.0	VG 4.0	FN 6.0	VF 8.0	VF/NM 9.0	NM- 9.2
1	107	4/53	Orig.; delBourgo-a	1	1	10	20	30	54	72	90
2	118	–	PC-r	1	1	2	4	6	8	11	14
3	132	–	PC-r	1	1	2	4	6	8	11	14
4	142	–	PC-r	1	1	2	4	6	8	11	14
5	161	–	PC-r	1	1	2	4	6	8	10	12
6	167	3/64	PC-r	1	1	2	4	6	8	10	12
7	166	7/67	PC-r	1	1	2	4	6	8	10	12
8	169	Fall/69	PC-r; stiff-c	1	1	2	4	6	8	10	12

107. King of the Khyber Rifles

Ed	HRN	Date	Details	A	C	GD 2.0	VG 4.0	FN 6.0	VF 8.0	VF/NM 9.0	NM- 9.2
1	108	5/53	Original	1	1	10	20	30	54	72	90
2	118	–	PC-r	1	1	2	4	6	8	11	14
3	146	–	PC-r	1	1	2	4	6	8	11	14
4	158	–	PC-r	1	1	2	4	6	8	11	14
5	167	–	Has orig.date; PC-r	1	1	2	4	6	8	10	12
6	167	–	PC-r	1	1	2	4	6	8	10	12
7	167	10/66	PC-r	1	1	2	4	6	8	10	12

108. Knights of the Round Table

Ed	HRN	Date	Details	A	C	GD 2.0	VG 4.0	FN 6.0	VF 8.0	VF/NM 9.0	NM- 9.2
1A	108	6/53	Original; Blum-a	1	1	10	20	30	58	79	100
1B	109	6/53	Original; scarce	1	1	11	22	33	60	83	105
2	117	–	PC-r	1	1	2	4	6	8	11	14
3	165	–	PC-r	1	1	2	4	6	8	10	12
4	167	4/64	PC-r	1	1	2	4	6	8	10	12
5	166	4/67	PC-r	1	1	2	4	6	8	10	12
6	169	Sm/69	New price 25¢, stiff-c; PC-r	1	1	2	4	6	8	10	12

109. Pitcairn's Island

Ed	HRN	Date	Details	A	C	GD 2.0	VG 4.0	FN 6.0	VF 8.0	VF/NM 9.0	NM- 9.2
1	110	7/53	Original; Palais-a	1	1	10	20	30	58	79	100
2	165	–	PC-r	1	1	2	4	6	8	11	14
3	167	3/64	PC-r	1	1	2	4	6	8	11	14
4	166	6/67	PC-r	1	1	2	4	6	8	11	14

110. A Study in Scarlet

Ed	HRN	Date	Details	A	C	GD 2.0	VG 4.0	FN 6.0	VF 8.0	VF/NM 9.0	NM- 9.2
1	111	8/53	Original	1	1	14	28	42	82	121	160
2	165	–	PC-r	1	1	11	22	33	60	83	105

111. The Talisman

Ed	HRN	Date	Details	A	C	GD 2.0	VG 4.0	FN 6.0	VF 8.0	VF/NM 9.0	NM- 9.2
1	112	9/53	Original; last H.C. Kiefer-a	1	1	10	20	30	58	79	100
2	165	–	PC-r	1	1	2	4	6	8	11	14
3	167	5/64	PC-r	1	1	2	4	6	8	11	14
4	166	Fall/68	C-price 25¢; PC-r	1	1	2	4	6	8	11	14

112. Adventures of Kit Carson

Ed	HRN	Date	Details	A	C	GD 2.0	VG 4.0	FN 6.0	VF 8.0	VF/NM 9.0	NM- 9.2
1	113	10/53	Original; Palais-a	1	1	10	20	30	56	76	95
2	129	–	PC-r	1	1	2	4	6	8	11	14
3	141	–	PC-r	1	1	2	4	6	8	11	14
4	152	–	PC-r	1	1	2	4	6	8	11	14
5	161	–	PC-r	1	1	2	4	6	8	10	12
6	167	–	PC-r	1	1	2	4	6	8	10	12
7	167	2/65	PC-r	1	1	2	4	6	8	10	12
8	167	5/66	PC-r	1	1	2	4	6	8	10	12
9	166	Win/69	New-c&price 25¢; PC-r; stiff-c	1	2	3	6	9	14	20	25

113. The Forty-Five Guardsmen

Ed	HRN	Date	Details	A	C	GD 2.0	VG 4.0	FN 6.0	VF 8.0	VF/NM 9.0	NM- 9.2
1	114	11/53	Orig.; delBourgo-a	1	1	12	24	36	67	94	120
2	166	7/67	PC-r	1	1	3	6	9	19	29	38

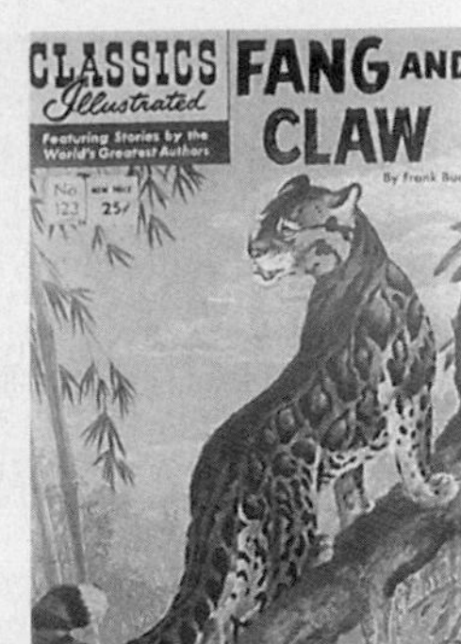

Classics Illustrated #123 © GIL

Classics Illustrated #125 © GIL

Classics Illustrated #131 © GIL

114. The Red Rover

Ed	HRN	Date	Details	A	C	GD 2.0	VG 4.0	FN 6.0	VF 8.0	VF/NM 9.0	NM- 9.2
1	115	12/53	Original	1	1	12	24	36	67	94	120
2	166	7/67	PC-r	1	1	3	6	9	19	29	38

115. How I Found Livingstone

Ed	HRN	Date	Details	A	C	GD 2.0	VG 4.0	FN 6.0	VF 8.0	VF/NM 9.0	NM- 9.2
1	116	1/54	Original	1	1	13	26	39	72	101	130
2	167	1/67	PC-r	1	1	4	8	12	24	37	50

116. The Bottle Imp

Ed	HRN	Date	Details	A	C	GD 2.0	VG 4.0	FN 6.0	VF 8.0	VF/NM 9.0	NM- 9.2
1	117	2/54	Orig.; Cameron-a	1	1	13	26	39	72	101	130
2	167	1/67	PC-r	1	1	4	8	12	24	37	50

117. Captains Courageous

Ed	HRN	Date	Details	A	C	GD 2.0	VG 4.0	FN 6.0	VF 8.0	VF/NM 9.0	NM- 9.2
1	118	3/54	Orig.; Costanza-a	1	1	12	24	36	67	94	120
2	167	2/67	PC-r	1	1	3	6	9	14	19	24
3	169	Fall/69	New price 25¢; stiff-c; PC-r	1	1	3	6	9	14	19	24

118. Rob Roy

Ed	HRN	Date	Details	A	C	GD 2.0	VG 4.0	FN 6.0	VF 8.0	VF/NM 9.0	NM- 9.2
1	119	4/54	Original; Rudy & Walter Palais-a	1	1	13	26	39	72	101	130
2	167	2/67	PC-r	1	1	4	8	12	24	37	50

119. Soldiers of Fortune

Ed	HRN	Date	Details	A	C	GD 2.0	VG 4.0	FN 6.0	VF 8.0	VF/NM 9.0	NM- 9.2
1	120	5/54	Schaffenberger-a	1	1	11	22	33	62	86	110
2	166	3/67	PC-r	1	1	3	6	9	14	19	24
3	169	Spr/70	New price 25¢; stiff-c; PC-r	1	1	3	6	9	14	19	24

120. The Hurricane

Ed	HRN	Date	Details	A	C	GD 2.0	VG 4.0	FN 6.0	VF 8.0	VF/NM 9.0	NM- 9.2
1	121	6/54	Orig.; Cameron-a	1	1	11	22	33	62	86	110
2	166	3/67	PC-r	1	1	3	6	9	20	30	40

121. Wild Bill Hickok

Ed	HRN	Date	Details	A	C	GD 2.0	VG 4.0	FN 6.0	VF 8.0	VF/NM 9.0	NM- 9.2
1	122	7/54	Original	1	1	10	20	30	54	72	90
2	132	–	PC-r	1	1	2	4	6	8	11	14
3	141	–	PC-r	1	1	2	4	6	8	11	14
4	154	–	PC-r	1	1	2	4	6	8	11	14
5	167	–	PC-r	1	1	2	4	6	8	10	12
6	167	8/64	PC-r	1	1	2	4	6	8	10	12
7	166	4/67	PC-r	1	1	2	4	6	8	10	12
8	169	Win/69	PC-r; stiff-c	1	1	2	4	6	8	10	12

122. The Mutineers

Ed	HRN	Date	Details	A	C	GD 2.0	VG 4.0	FN 6.0	VF 8.0	VF/NM 9.0	NM- 9.2
1	123	9/54	Original	1	1	10	20	30	58	79	100
2	136	–	PC-r	1	1	2	4	6	8	11	14
3	146	–	PC-r	1	1	2	4	6	8	11	14
4	158	–	PC-r	1	1	2	4	6	8	11	14
5	167	11/63	PC-r	1	1	2	4	6	8	10	12
6	167	3/65	PC-r	1	1	2	4	6	8	10	12
7	166	8/67	PC-r	1	1	2	4	6	8	10	12

123. Fang and Claw

Ed	HRN	Date	Details	A	C	GD 2.0	VG 4.0	FN 6.0	VF 8.0	VF/NM 9.0	NM- 9.2
1	124	11/54	Original	1	1	10	20	30	58	79	100
2	133	–	PC-r	1	1	2	4	6	8	11	14
3	143	–	PC-r	1	1	2	4	6	8	11	14
4	154	–	PC-r	1	1	2	4	6	8	11	14
5	167	–	Has orig.date; PC-r	1	1	2	4	6	8	10	12
6	167	9/65	PC-r	1	1	2	4	6	8	10	12

124. The War of the Worlds

Ed	HRN	Date	Details	A	C	GD 2.0	VG 4.0	FN 6.0	VF 8.0	VF/NM 9.0	NM- 9.2
1	125	1/55	Original; Cameron-c/a	1	1	13	26	39	72	101	130
2	131	–	PC-r	1	1	2	4	6	9	13	16
3	141	–	PC-r	1	1	2	4	6	9	13	16
4	148	–	PC-r	1	1	2	4	6	9	13	16
5	156	–	PC-r	1	1	2	4	6	9	13	16
6	165	–	PC-r	1	1	2	4	6	11	16	20
7	167	–	PC-r	1	1	2	4	6	8	11	14
8	167	11/64	PC-r	1	1	2	4	6	9	13	16
9	167	11/65	PC-r	1	1	2	4	6	8	11	14
10	166	R/1968	C-price 25¢; PC-r	1	1	2	4	6	8	11	14
11	169	Sm/70	PC-r; stiff-c	1	1	2	4	6	8	11	14

125. The Ox Bow Incident

Ed	HRN	Date	Details	A	C	GD 2.0	VG 4.0	FN 6.0	VF 8.0	VF/NM 9.0	NM- 9.2
1	–	3/55	Original; Picture Progress replaces reorder list	1	1	10	20	30	54	72	90
2	143	–	PC-r	1	1	2	4	6	8	11	14
3	152	–	PC-r	1	1	2	4	6	8	11	14
4	149	–	PC-r	1	1	2	4	6	8	11	14
5	167	–	PC-r	1	1	2	4	6	8	10	12
6	167	11/64	PC-r	1	1	2	4	6	8	10	12
7	166	4/67	PC-r	1	1	2	4	6	8	10	12
8	169	Win/69	New price 25¢; stiff-c; PC-r	1	1	2	4	6	8	10	12

126. The Downfall

Ed	HRN	Date	Details	A	C	GD 2.0	VG 4.0	FN 6.0	VF 8.0	VF/NM 9.0	NM- 9.2
1	5/55	–	Orig.; 'Picture Progress' replaces reorder list; Cameron-c/a	1	1	10	20	30	58	79	100
2	167	8/64	PC-r	1	1	2	4	6	11	16	20
3	166	R/1968	C-price 25¢; PC-r	1	1	2	4	6	11	16	20

127. The King of the Mountains

Ed	HRN	Date	Details	A	C	GD 2.0	VG 4.0	FN 6.0	VF 8.0	VF/NM 9.0	NM- 9.2
1	128	7/55	Original	1	1	10	20	30	58	79	100
2	167	6/64	PC-r	1	1	2	4	6	9	13	16
3	166	F/1968	C-price 25¢; PC-r	1	1	2	4	6	9	13	16

128. Macbeth (Used in **POP**, pg. 102)

Ed	HRN	Date	Details	A	C	GD 2.0	VG 4.0	FN 6.0	VF 8.0	VF/NM 9.0	NM- 9.2
1	128	9/55	Orig.; last Blum-a	1	1	10	20	30	58	79	100
2	143	–	PC-r	1	1	2	4	6	8	11	14
3	158	–	PC-r	1	1	2	4	6	8	11	14
4	167	–	PC-r	1	1	2	4	6	8	10	12
5	167	6/64	PC-r	1	1	2	4	6	8	10	12
6	166	4/67	PC-r	1	1	2	4	6	8	10	12
7	166	R/1968	C-Price 25¢; PC-r	1	1	2	4	6	8	10	12
8	169	Spr/70	Stiff-c; PC-r	1	1	2	4	6	8	10	12

129. Davy Crockett

Ed	HRN	Date	Details	AC		GD 2.0	VG 4.0	FN 6.0	VF 8.0	VF/NM 9.0	NM- 9.2
1	129	11/55	Orig.; Cameron-a	1	1	14	28	42	80	115	150
2	167	9/66	PC-r	1	1	11	22	33	60	83	105

130. Caesar's Conquests

Ed	HRN	Date	Details	A	C	GD 2.0	VG 4.0	FN 6.0	VF 8.0	VF/NM 9.0	NM- 9.2
1	130	1/56	Original; Orlando-a	1	1	10	20	30	58	79	100
2	142	–	PC-r	1	1	2	4	6	8	11	14
3	152	–	PC-r	1	1	2	4	6	8	11	14
4	149	–	PC-r	1	1	2	4	6	8	11	14
5	167	–	PC-r	1	1	2	4	6	8	10	12
6	167	10/64	PC-r	1	1	2	4	6	8	10	12
7	167	4/66	PC-r	1	1	2	4	6	8	10	12

131. The Covered Wagon

Ed	HRN	Date	Details	A	C	GD 2.0	VG 4.0	FN 6.0	VF 8.0	VF/NM 9.0	NM- 9.2
1	131	3/56	Original	1	1	6	12	18	41	66	90
2	143	–	PC-r	1	1	2	4	6	8	11	14
3	152	–	PC-r	1	1	2	4	6	8	11	14
4	158	–	PC-r	1	1	2	4	6	8	11	14
5	167	–	PC-r	1	1	2	4	6	8	10	12
6	167	11/64	PC-r	1	1	2	4	6	8	10	12
7	167	4/66	PC-r	1	1	2	4	6	8	10	12
8	169	Win/69	New price 25¢; stiff-c; PC-r	1	1	2	4	6	8	10	12

132. The Dark Frigate

Ed	HRN	Date	Details	A	C	GD 2.0	VG 4.0	FN 6.0	VF 8.0	VF/NM 9.0	NM- 9.2
1	132	5/56	Original	1	1	10	20	30	58	79	100
2	150	–	PC-r	1	1	2	4	6	9	12	15
3	167	1/64	PC-r	1	1	2	4	6	8	11	14
4	166	5/67	PC-r	1	1	2	4	6	8	11	14

133. The Time Machine

Ed	HRN	Date	Details	A	C

Classics Illustrated #138 © GIL

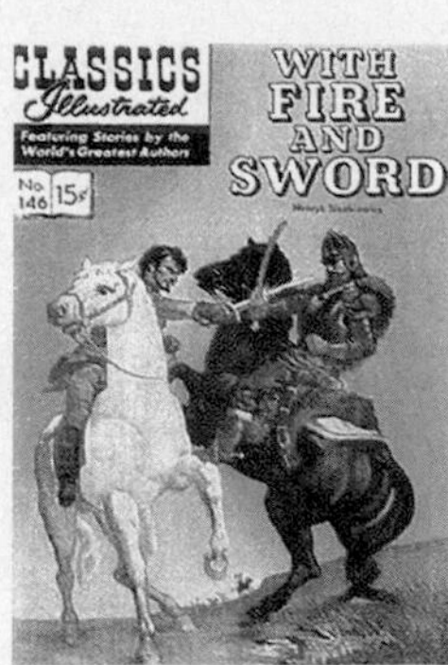

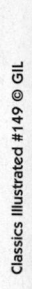

Classics Illustrated #146 © GIL

Classics Illustrated #149 © GIL

Ed	HRN	Date	Details	A	C	GD 2.0	VG 4.0	FN 6.0	VF 8.0	VF/NM 9.0	NM- 9.2
1	132	7/56	Orig.; Cameron-a	1	1	7	14	21	49	80	110
2	142	–	PC-r	1	1	2	4	6	9	13	16
3	152	–	PC-r	1	1	2	4	6	9	13	16
4	158	–	PC-r	1	1	2	4	6	9	13	16
5	167	–	PC-r	1	1	2	4	6	8	11	14
6	167	6/64	PC-r	1	1	2	4	6	9	13	16
7	167	3/66	PC-r	1	1	2	4	6	8	11	14
8	166	12/67	PC-r	1	1	2	4	6	8	11	14
9	169	Win/71	New price 25¢; stiff-c; PC-r	1	1	2	4	6	8	11	14

134. Romeo and Juliet

Ed	HRN	Date	Details	A	C	GD	VG	FN	VF	VF/NM	NM-
1	134	9/56	Original; Evans-a	1	1	7	14	21	45	73	100
2	161	–	PC-r	1	1	2	4	6	8	11	14
3	167	9/63	PC-r	1	1	2	4	6	8	10	12
4	167	5/65	PC-r	1	1	2	4	6	8	10	12
5	166	6/67	PC-r	1	1	2	4	6	8	10	12
6	166	Win/69	New c&price 25¢; stiff-c; PC-r	1	2	3	6	9	17	25	32

135. Waterloo

Ed	HRN	Date	Details	A	C	GD	VG	FN	VF	VF/NM	NM-
1	135	11/56	Orig.; G. Ingels-a	1	1	7	14	21	45	73	100
2	153	–	PC-r	1	1	2	4	6	8	11	14
3	167	–	PC-r	1	1	2	4	6	8	10	12
4	167	9/64	PC-r	1	1	2	4	6	8	10	12
5	166	R/1968	C-price 25¢; PC-r	1	1	2	4	6	8	10	12

136. Lord Jim

Ed	HRN	Date	Details	A	C	GD	VG	FN	VF	VF/NM	NM-
1	136	1/57	Original; Evans-a	1	1	7	14	21	45	73	100
2	165	–	PC-r	1	1	2	4	6	8	10	12
3	167	3/64	PC-r	1	1	2	4	6	8	10	12
4	167	9/66	PC-r	1	1	2	4	6	8	10	12
5	169	Sm/69	New price 25 ¢; stiff-c; PC-r	1	1	2	4	6	8	10	12

137. The Little Savage

Ed	HRN	Date	Details	A	C	GD	VG	FN	VF	VF/NM	NM-
1	136	3/57	Original; Evans-a	1	1	7	14	21	45	73	100
2	148	–	PC-r	1	1	2	4	6	8	11	14
3	156	–	PC-r	1	1	2	4	6	8	11	14
4	167	–	PC-r	1	1	2	4	6	8	10	12
5	167	10/64	PC-r	1	1	2	4	6	8	10	12
6	166	8/67	PC-r	1	1	2	4	6	8	10	12
7	169	Spr/70	New price 25¢; stiff-c; PC-r	1	1	2	4	6	8	10	12

138. A Journey to the Center of the Earth

Ed	HRN	Date	Details	A	C	GD	VG	FN	VF	VF/NM	NM-
1	136	5/57	Original	1	1	8	16	24	54	90	125
2	146	–	PC-r	1	1	2	4	6	10	14	18
3	156	–	PC-r	1	1	2	4	6	10	14	18
4	158	–	PC-r	1	1	2	4	6	10	14	18
5	167	–	PC-r	1	1	2	4	6	8	11	14
6	167	6/64	PC-r	1	1	2	4	6	11	16	20
7	167	4/66	PC-r	1	1	2	4	6	11	16	20
8	166	R/68	C-price 25¢; PC-r	1	1	2	4	6	9	13	16

139. In the Reign of Terror

Ed	HRN	Date	Details	A	C	GD	VG	FN	VF	VF/NM	NM-
1	139	7/57	Original; Evans-a	1	1	6	12	18	41	66	90
2	154	–	PC-r	1	1	2	4	6	8	11	14
3	167	–	Has orig.date; PC-r	1	1	2	4	6	8	10	12
4	167	7/64	PC-r	1	1	2	4	6	8	10	12
5	166	R/1968	C-price 25¢; PC-r	1	1	2	4	6	8	10	12

140. On Jungle Trails

Ed	HRN	Date	Details	A	C	GD	VG	FN	VF	VF/NM	NM-
1	140	9/57	Original	1	1	6	12	18	41	66	90
2	150	–	PC-r	1	1	2	4	6	8	11	14
3	160	–	PC-r	1	1	2	4	6	8	11	14
4	167	9/63	PC-r	1	1	2	4	6	8	10	12
5	167	9/65	PC-r	1	1	2	4	6	8	10	12

141. Castle Dangerous

Ed	HRN	Date	Details	A	C	GD	VG	FN	VF	VF/NM	NM-
1	141	11/57	Original	1	1	7	14	21	47	76	105
2	152	–	PC-r	1	1	2	4	6	8	11	14
3	167	–	PC-r	1	1	2	4	6	8	11	14
4	166	7/67	PC-r	1	1	2	4	6	8	11	14

142. Abraham Lincoln

Ed	HRN	Date	Details	A	C	GD	VG	FN	VF	VF/NM	NM-
1	142	1/58	Original	1	1	7	14	21	45	73	100
2	154	–	PC-r	1	1	2	4	6	8	11	14
3	158	–	PC-r	1	1	2	4	6	8	11	14
4	167	10/63	PC-r	1	1	2	4	6	8	10	12
5	167	7/65	PC-r	1	1	2	4	6	8	10	12
6	166	11/67	PC-r	1	1	2	4	6	8	10	12
7	169	Fall/69	New price 25¢, stiff-c; PC-r	1	1	2	4	6	8	10	12

143. Kim

Ed	HRN	Date	Details	A	C	GD	VG	FN	VF	VF/NM	NM-
1	143	3/58	Original; Orlando-a	1	1	6	12	18	41	66	90
2	165	–	PC-r	1	1	2	4	6	8	10	12
3	167	11/63	PC-r	1	1	2	4	6	8	10	12
4	167	8/65	PC-r	1	1	2	4	6	8	10	12
5	169	Win/69	New price 25¢; stiff-c; PC-r	1	1	2	4	6	8	10	12

144. The First Men in the Moon

Ed	HRN	Date	Details	A	C	GD	VG	FN	VF	VF/NM	NM-
1	143	5/58	Original; Woodbridge/Williamson/Torres-a	1	1	7	14	21	49	80	110
2	152	–	(Rare)-PC-r	1	1	8	16	24	54	90	125
3	153	–	PC-r	1	1	2	4	6	8	11	14
4	161	–	PC-r	1	1	2	4	6	8	10	12
5	167	–	PC-r	1	1	2	4	6	8	10	12
6	167	12/65	PC-r	1	1	2	4	6	8	10	12
7	166	Fall/68	New-c&price 25¢; PC-r; stiff-c	1	2	3	6	9	16	22	28
8	169	Win/69	Stiff-c; PC-r	1	2	2	4	6	10	14	18

145. The Crisis

Ed	HRN	Date	Details	A	C	GD	VG	FN	VF	VF/NM	NM-
1	143	7/58	Original; Evans-a	1	1	7	14	21	45	73	100
2	156	–	PC-r	1	1	2	4	6	8	11	14
3	167	10/63	PC-r	1	1	2	4	6	8	10	12
4	167	3/65	PC-r	1	1	2	4	6	8	10	12
5	166	R/68	C-price 25¢; PC-r	1	1	2	4	6	8	10	12

146. With Fire and Sword

Ed	HRN	Date	Details	A	C	GD	VG	FN	VF	VF/NM	NM-
1	143	9/58	Original; Woodbridge-a	1	1	7	14	21	45	73	100
2	156	–	PC-r	1	1	2	4	6	9	13	16
3	167	11/63	PC-r	1	1	2	4	6	8	11	14
4	167	3/65	PC-r	1	1	2	4	6	8	11	14

147. Ben-Hur

Ed	HRN	Date	Details	A	C	GD	VG	FN	VF	VF/NM	NM-
1	147	11/58	Original; Orlando-a	1	1	6	12	18	43	69	95
2	152	–	Scarce; PC-r	1	1	7	14	21	45	73	100
3	153	–	PC-r	1	1	2	4	6	8	11	14
4	158	–	PC-r	1	1	2	4	6	8	11	14
5	167	–	Orig.date; but PC-r	1	1	2	4	6	8	10	12
6	167	2/65	PC-r	1	1	2	4	6	8	10	12
7	167	9/66	PC-r	1	1	2	4	6	8	10	12
8A	166	Fall/68	New-c&price 25¢; PC-r; soft-c	1	2	3	6	9	17	25	32
8B	166	Fall/68	New-c&price 25¢; PC-r; stiff-c; scarce	1	2	4	8	12	22	34	45

148. The Buccaneer

Ed	HRN	Date	Details	A	C	GD	VG	FN	VF	VF/NM	NM-
1	148	1/59	Orig.; Evans/Jenny-a; Saunders-c	1	1	6	12	18	41	66	90
2	568	–	Juniors list only PC-r	1	1	2	4	6	8	11	14
3	167	–	PC-r	1	1	2	4	6	8	10	12
4	167	9/65	PC-r	1	1	2	4	6	8	10	12
5	169	Sm/69	New price 25¢; PC-r; stiff-c	1	1	2	4	6	8	10	12

149. Off on a Comet

Ed	HRN	Date	Details	A	C

Classics Illustrated #152 © GIL

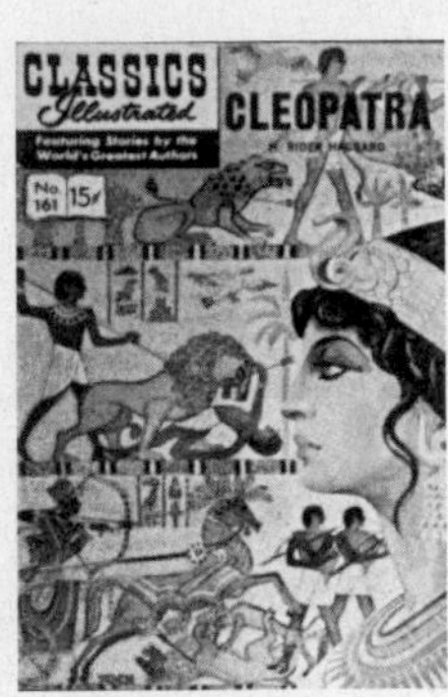

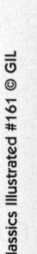

Classics Illustrated #161 © GIL

Classics Illustrated #168 © GIL

Ed	HRN	Date	Details	A	C	GD 2.0	VG 4.0	FN 6.0	VF 8.0	VF/NM 9.0	NM- 9.2
1	149	3/59	Orig.;G.McCann-a; blue reorder list	1	1	7	14	21	45	73	100
2	155	–	PC-r	1	1	2	4	6	8	11	14
3	149	–	PC-r; white reorder list; no coming-next ad	1	1	2	4	6	8	11	14
4	167	12/63	PC-r	1	1	2	4	6	8	10	12
5	167	2/65	PC-r	1	1	2	4	6	8	10	12
6	167	10/66	PC-r	1	1	2	4	6	8	10	12
7	166	Fall/68	New-c & price 25¢; PC-r	1	2	3	6	9	16	23	30

150. The Virginian

Ed	HRN	Date	Details	A	C	GD 2.0	VG 4.0	FN 6.0	VF 8.0	VF/NM 9.0	NM- 9.2
1	150	5/59	Original	1	1	7	14	21	47	76	105
2	164	–	PC-r	1	1	2	4	6	11	16	20
3	167	10/63	PC-r	1	1	3	6	9	15	21	26
4	167	12/65	PC-r	1	1	2	4	6	11	16	20

151. Won By the Sword

Ed	HRN	Date	Details	A	C	GD 2.0	VG 4.0	FN 6.0	VF 8.0	VF/NM 9.0	NM- 9.2
1	150	7/59	Original	1	1	7	14	21	45	73	100
2	164	–	PC-r	1	1	2	4	6	9	13	16
3	167	10/63	PC-r	1	1	2	4	6	9	13	16
4	166	7/67	PC-r	1	1	2	4	6	9	13	16

152. Wild Animals I Have Known

Ed	HRN	Date	Details	A	C	GD 2.0	VG 4.0	FN 6.0	VF 8.0	VF/NM 9.0	NM- 9.2
1	152	9/59	Orig.; L.B. Cole c/a	1	1	7	14	21	49	80	110
2A	149	–	PC-r; white reorder list; no coming-next ad; IBC: Jr. list #572	1	1	2	4	6	8	11	14
2B	149	–	PC-r; inside-bc: Jr. list to #555	1	1	2	4	6	9	12	15
2C	149	–	PC-r; inside-bc: has World Around Us ad; scarce	1	1	3	6	9	15	21	26
3	167	9/63	PC-r	1	1	2	4	6	8	10	12
4	167	8/65	PC-r	1	1	2	4	6	8	10	12
5	169	Fall/69	New price 25¢; stiff-c; PC-r	1	1	2	4	6	8	10	12

153. The Invisible Man

Ed	HRN	Date	Details	A	C	GD 2.0	VG 4.0	FN 6.0	VF 8.0	VF/NM 9.0	NM- 9.2
1	153	11/59	Original	1	1	8	16	24	52	86	120
2A	149	–	PC-r; white reorder list; no coming-next ad; inside-bc: Jr. list to #572	1	1	2	4	6	10	14	18
2B	149	–	PC-r; inside-bc: Jr. list to #555	1	1	2	4	6	11	16	20
3	167	–	PC-r	1	1	2	4	6	9	12	15
4	167	2/65	PC-r	1	1	2	4	6	9	12	15
5	167	9/66	PC-r	1	1	2	4	6	9	12	15
6	166	Win/69	New price 25¢; PC-r; stiff-c	1	1	2	4	6	9	12	15
7	169	Spr/71	Stiff-c; letters spelling 'Invisible Man' are 'solid' not 'invisible;' PC-r	1	1	2	4	6	9	12	15

154. The Conspiracy of Pontiac

Ed	HRN	Date	Details	A	C	GD 2.0	VG 4.0	FN 6.0	VF 8.0	VF/NM 9.0	NM- 9.2
1	154	1/60	Original	1	1	7	14	21	47	76	105
2	167	11/63	PC-r	1	1	2	4	6	11	16	20
3	167	7/64	PC-r	1	1	2	4	6	11	16	20
4	166	12/67	PC-r	1	1	2	4	6	11	16	20

155. The Lion of the North

Ed	HRN	Date	Details	A	C	GD 2.0	VG 4.0	FN 6.0	VF 8.0	VF/NM 9.0	NM- 9.2
1	154	3/60	Original	1	1	7	14	21	45	73	100
2	167	1/64	PC-r	1	1	2	4	6	10	14	18
3	166	R/1967	C-price 25¢; PC-r	1	1	2	4	6	9	12	15

156. The Conquest of Mexico

Ed	HRN	Date	Details	A	C	GD 2.0	VG 4.0	FN 6.0	VF 8.0	VF/NM 9.0	NM- 9.2
1	156	5/60	Orig.; Bruno Premiani-c/a	1	1	7	14	21	45	73	100
2	167	1/64	PC-r	1	1	2	4	6	9	12	15
3	166	8/67	PC-r	1	1	2	4	6	9	12	15
4	169	Spr/70	New price 25¢; stiff-c; PC-r	1	1	2	4	6	8	10	12

157. Lives of the Hunted

Ed	HRN	Date	Details	A	C	GD 2.0	VG 4.0	FN 6.0	VF 8.0	VF/NM 9.0	NM- 9.2
1	156	7/60	Orig.; L.B. Cole-c	1	1	7	14	21	47	76	105
2	167	2/64	PC-r	1	1	2	4	6	11	16	20
3	166	10/67	PC-r	1	1	2	4	6	11	16	20

158. The Conspirators

Ed	HRN	Date	Details	A	C	GD 2.0	VG 4.0	FN 6.0	VF 8.0	VF/NM 9.0	NM- 9.2
1	156	9/60	Original	1	1	7	14	21	47	76	105
2	167	7/64	PC-r	1	1	2	4	6	11	16	20
3	166	10/67	PC-r	1	1	2	4	6	11	16	20

159. The Octopus

Ed	HRN	Date	Details	A	C	GD 2.0	VG 4.0	FN 6.0	VF 8.0	VF/NM 9.0	NM- 9.2
1	159	11/60	Orig.; Gray Morrow-a; L.B. Cole-c	1	1	7	14	21	47	76	105
2	167	2/64	PC-r	1	1	2	4	6	11	16	20
3	166	R/1967	C-price 25¢; PC-r	1	1	2	4	6	11	16	20

160. The Food of the Gods

Ed	HRN	Date	Details	A	C	GD 2.0	VG 4.0	FN 6.0	VF 8.0	VF/NM 9.0	NM- 9.2
1A	159	1/61	Original	1	1	7	14	21	49	80	110
1B	160	1/61	Original; same, except for HRN	1	1	7	14	21	47	76	105
2	167	1/64	PC-r	1	1	2	4	6	11	16	20
3	166	6/67	PC-r	1	1	2	4	6	11	16	20

161. Cleopatra

Ed	HRN	Date	Details	A	C	GD 2.0	VG 4.0	FN 6.0	VF 8.0	VF/NM 9.0	NM- 9.2
1	161	3/61	Original	1	1	7	14	21	47	76	105
2	167	1/64	PC-r	1	1	2	4	6	13	18	22
3	166	8/67	PC-r	1	1	2	4	6	13	18	22

162. Robur the Conqueror

Ed	HRN	Date	Details	A	C	GD 2.0	VG 4.0	FN 6.0	VF 8.0	VF/NM 9.0	NM- 9.2
1	162	5/61	Original	1	1	7	14	21	47	76	105
2	167	7/64	PC-r	1	1	2	4	6	13	18	22
3	166	8/67	PC-r	1	1	2	4	6	13	18	22

163. Master of the World

Ed	HRN	Date	Details	A	C	GD 2.0	VG 4.0	FN 6.0	VF 8.0	VF/NM 9.0	NM- 9.2
1	163	7/61	Original; Gray Morrow-a	1	1	7	14	21	47	76	105
2	167	1/65	PC-r	1	1	2	4	6	12	16	20
3	166	R/1968	C-price 25¢; PC-r	1	1	2	4	6	12	16	20

164. The Cossack Chief

Ed	HRN	Date	Details	A	C	GD 2.0	VG 4.0	FN 6.0	VF 8.0	VF/NM 9.0	NM- 9.2
1	164	(1961)	Orig.; nd(10/61?)	1	1	6	12	18	41	66	90
2	167	4/65	PC-r	1	1	2	4	6	11	16	20
3	166	Fall/68	C-price 25¢; PC-r	1	1	2	4	6	11	16	20

165. The Queen's Necklace

Ed	HRN	Date	Details	A	C	GD 2.0	VG 4.0	FN 6.0	VF 8.0	VF/NM 9.0	NM- 9.2
1	164	1/62	Original; Morrow-a	1	1	7	14	21	47	76	105
2	167	4/65	PC-r	1	1	2	4	6	11	16	20
3	166	Fall/68	C-price 25¢; PC-r	1	1	2	4	6	11	16	20

166. Tigers and Traitors

Ed	HRN	Date	Details	A	C	GD 2.0	VG 4.0	FN 6.0	VF 8.0	VF/NM 9.0	NM- 9.2
1	165	5/62	Original	1	1	9	18	27	60	100	140
2	167	2/64	PC-r	1	1	3	6	9	19	29	40
3	167	11/66	PC-r	1	1	3	6	9	19	29	40

167. Faust

Ed	HRN	Date	Details	A	C	GD 2.0	VG 4.0	FN 6.0	VF 8.0	VF/NM 9.0	NM- 9.2
1	165	8/62	Original	1	1	12	24	36	87	156	225
2	167	2/64	PC-r	1	1	6	12	18	37	59	80
3	166	6/67	PC-r	1	1	6	12	18	37	59	80

168. In Freedom's Cause

Ed	HRN	Date	Details	A	C	GD 2.0	VG 4.0	FN 6.0	VF 8.0	VF/NM 9.0	NM- 9.2
1	169	Win/69	Original; Evans/Crandall-a; stiff-c; 25¢; no coming-next ad;	1	1	14	28	42	99	175	250

169. Negro Americans The Early Years

Classics Illustrated Junior #502 © GIL

Classics Illustrated Junior #513 © GIL

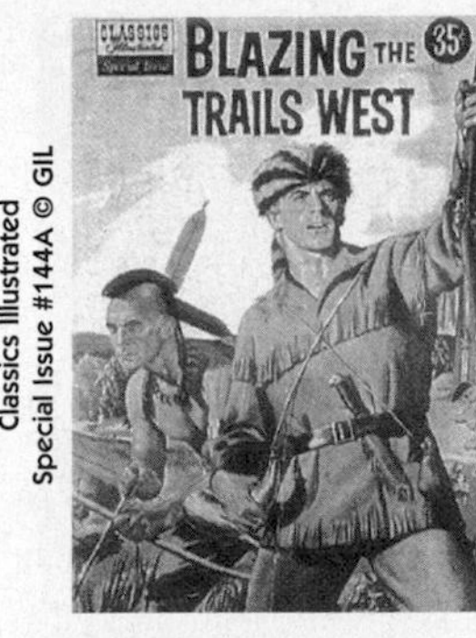

Classics Illustrated Special Issue #144A © GIL

	GD 2.0	VG 4.0	FN 6.0	VF 8.0	VF/NM 9.0	NM- 9.2

Ed	HRN	Date	Details	A	C						
1	166	Spr/69	Orig. & last issue; 25¢; Stiff-c; no coming-next ad; other sources indicate publication date of 5/69	1	1	12	24	36	87	156	225
2	169	Spr/69	Stiff-c	1	1	7	14	21	47	76	105

NOTE: *Many other titles were prepared or planned but were only issued in British/European series.*

CLASSIC PUNISHER (Also see Punisher)
Marvel Comics: Dec, 1989 ($4.95, B&W, deluxe format, 68 pgs.)

1-Reprints Marvel Super Action #1 & Marvel Preview #2 plus new story 5.00

CLASSICS ILLUSTRATED
First Publishing/Berkley Publishing: Feb, 1990 - No. 27, July, 1991 ($3.75/$3.95, 52 pgs.)

1-27: 1-Gahan Wilson-c/a. 4-Sienkiewicz painted-c/a. 6-Russell scripts/layouts. 7-Spiegle-a. 9-Ploog-c/a. 16-Staton-a. 18-Gahan Wilson-c/a; 20-Geary-a. 26-Aesop's Fables (6/91). 26,27-Direct sale only 5.00

CLASSICS ILLUSTRATED
Acclaim Books/Twin Circle PublishingCo.: Feb, 1997 - Present ($4.99, digest-size) (Each book contains study notes)

A Christmas Carol-(12/97), A Connecticut Yankee in King Arthur's Court-(5/97), All Quiet on the Western Front-(1/98), A Midsummer's Night Dream-(4/97) Around the World in 80 Days-(1/98), A Tale of Two Cities-(2/97)Joe Orlando-r, Captains Courageous-(11/97), Crime and Punishment-(3/97), Dr. Jekyll and Mr. Hyde-(10/97), Don Quixote-(12/97), Frankenstein-(10/97), Great Expectations-(4/97), Hamlet-(3/97), Huckleberry Finn-(3/97), Jane Eyre-(2/97), Kidnapped-(1/98), Les Miserables-(5/97), Lord Jim-(9/97),Macbeth-(5/97), Moby Dick-(4/97), Oliver Twist-(5/97), Robinson Crusoe-(9/97), Romeo & Juliet-(2/97), Silas Marner-(11/97), The Call of the Wild-(9/97), The Count of Monte Cristo-(1/98), The House of the Seven Gables-(9/97), The Iliad-(12/97), The Invisible Man-(10/97), The Last of the Mohicans-(12/97), The Master of Ballantrae-(11/97), The Odyssey-(3/97), The Prince and the Pauper-(4/97), The Red Badge Of Courage-(9/97), Tom Sawyer-(2/97) Wuthering Heights-(11/97) 5.00

NOTE: *Stories reprinted from the original Gilberton Classic Comics and Classics Illustrated.*

CLASSICS ILLUSTRATED GIANTS
Gilberton Publications: Oct, 1949 (One-Shots - "OS")

These Giant Editions, all with new front and back covers, were advertised from 10/49 to 2/52. They were 50¢ on the newsstand and 60¢ by mail. They are actually four Classics in one volume. All the stories are reprints of the Classics Illustrated Series.

NOTE: There were also British hardback Adventure & Indian Giants in 1952, with the same covers but different contents: Adventure - 2, 7, 10; Indian - 17, 22, 37, 58. They are also rare.

	GD	VG	FN	VF	VF/NM	NM-
"An Illustrated Library of Great Adventure Stories" - reprints of No. 6,7,8,10 (Rare); Kiefer-c	147	294	441	926	1563	2200
"An Illustrated Library of Exciting Mystery Stories" - reprints of No. 30,21,40, 13 (Rare); Blum-c	158	316	474	995	1685	2375
"An Illustrated Library of Great Indian Stories" - reprints of No. 4,17,22,37 (Rare); Blum-c	147	294	441	926	1563	2200

INTRODUCTION TO CLASSICS ILLUSTRATED JUNIOR

Collectors of Juniors can be put into one of two categories: those who want any copy of each title, and those who want all the originals. Those seeking every original and reprint edition are a limited group, primarily because Juniors have no changes in art or covers to spark interest, and because reprints are so low in value it is difficult to get dealers to look for specific reprint editions.

In recent years it has become apparent that most serious Classics collectors seek Junior originals. Those seeking reprints seek them for low cost. This has made the previous note about the comparative market value of reprints inadequate. Three particular reprint editions are worth even more. For the 535-Twin Circle edition, see Giveaways. There are also reprint editions of 501 and 503 which have a full-page bc ad for the very rare Junior record. Those may sell as high as $10-$15 in mint. Original editions of 557 and 558 also have that ad.

There are no reprint editions of 577. The only edition, from 1969, is a 25 cent stiff-cover edition with no ad for the next issue. All other original editions have coming-next ad. But 577, like C.I. #168, was prepared in 1962 but not issued. Copies of 577 can be found in 1963 British/European series, which then continued with dozens of additional new Junior titles.

PRICES LISTED BELOW ARE FOR ORIGINAL EDITIONS, WHICH HAVE AN AD FOR THE NEXT ISSUE.

NOTE: *Non HRN 576 copies- many are written on or colored . Reprints with 576 HRN are worth about 1/3 original prices. All other HRN #'s are 1/2 original price*

CLASSICS ILLUSTRATED JUNIOR
Famous Authors Ltd. (Gilberton Publications): Oct, 1953 - Spring, 1971

	GD	VG	FN	VF	VF/NM	NM-
501-Snow White & the Seven Dwarfs; Alex Blum-a	12	24	36	69	97	125
502-The Ugly Duckling	9	18	27	47	61	75
503-Cinderella	8	16	24	40	50	60
504-512: 504-The Pied Piper. 505-The Sleeping Beauty. 506-The Three Little Pigs. 507-Jack & the Beanstalk. 508-Goldilocks & the Three Bears. 509-Beauty and the Beast. 510-Little Red Riding Hood. 511-Puss-N Boots. 512-Rumpelstiltskin	6	12	18	27	33	38
513-Pinocchio	7	14	21	37	46	55
514 The Steadfast Tin Soldier	8	16	24	44	57	70
515-Johnny Appleseed	6	12	18	27	33	38
516-Aladdin and His Lamp	6	12	18	29	36	42
517-519: 517-The Emperor's New Clothes. 518-The Golden Goose. 519-Paul Bunyan	6	12	18	27	33	38
520-Thumbelina	6	12	18	29	36	42
521-King of the Golden River	6	12	18	27	33	38
522,523,530: 522-The Nightingale. 523-The Gallant Tailor. 530-The Golden Bird	5	10	15	24	30	35
524-The Wild Swans	6	12	18	29	36	42
525,526: 525-The Little Mermaid. 526-The Frog Prince	6	12	18	29	36	42
527-The Golden-Haired Giant	6	12	18	27	33	38
528-The Penny Prince	6	12	18	27	33	38
529-The Magic Servants	6	12	18	27	33	38
531-Rapunzel	6	12	18	27	33	38
532-534: 532-The Dancing Princesses. 533-The Magic Fountain. 534-The Golden Touch	5	10	15	23	28	32
535-The Wizard of Oz	8	16	24	44	57	70
536-The Chimney Sweep	6	12	18	27	33	38
537-The Three Fairies	6	12	18	28	34	40
538-Silly Hans	5	10	15	23	28	32
539-The Enchanted Fish	6	12	18	31	38	45
540-The Tinder-Box	6	12	18	31	38	45
541-Snow White & Rose Red	5	10	15	24	30	35
542-The Donkey's Tale	5	10	15	24	30	35
543-The House in the Woods	6	12	18	27	33	38
544-The Golden Fleece	6	12	18	31	38	45
545-The Glass Mountain	5	10	15	24	30	35
546-The Elves & the Shoemaker	5	10	15	24	30	35
547-The Wishing Table	6	12	18	27	33	38
548-551: 548-The Magic Pitcher. 549-Simple Kate. 550-The Singing Donkey. 551-The Queen Bee	5	10	15	23	28	32
552-The Three Little Dwarfs	6	12	18	27	33	38
553,556: 553-King Thrushbeard. 556-The Elf Mound	5	10	15	23	28	32
554-The Enchanted Deer	6	12	18	29	36	42
555-The Three Golden Apples	5	10	15	24	30	35
557-Silly Willy	6	12	18	28	34	40
558-The Magic Dish; L.B. Cole-c; soft and stiff-c exist on original	7	14	21	35	43	50
559-The Japanese Lantern; 1 pg. Ingels-a; L.B. Cole-c	7	14	21	35	43	50
560-The Doll Princess; L.B. Cole-c	7	14	21	35	43	50
561-Hans Humdrum; L.B. Cole-c	6	12	18	29	36	42
562-The Enchanted Pony; L.B. Cole-c	7	14	21	35	43	50
563,565-568,570: 563-The Wishing Well; L.B. Cole-c. 565-The Silly Princess; L.B. Cole-c. 566-Clumsy Hans; L.B. Cole-c. 567-The Bearskin Soldier; L.B. Cole-c. 570-The Pearl Princess	6	12	18	27	33	38
564-The Salt Mountain; L.B.Cole-c. 568-The Happy Hedgehog; L.B. Cole-c.	6	12	18	28	34	40
569,573: 569-The Three Giants.573-The Crystal Ball	5	10	15	23	28	32
571,572: 571-How Fire Came to the Indians. 572-The Drummer Boy	6	12	18	29	36	42
574-Brightboots	5	10	15	24	30	35
575-The Fearless Prince	6	12	18	28	34	40
576-The Princess Who Saw Everything	7	14	21	35	43	50
577-The Runaway Dumpling	8	16	24	44	57	70

NOTE: *Prices are for original editions. Last reprint - Spring, 1971.* ***Costanza & Schaffenberger*** *art in many issues.*

CLASSICS ILLUSTRATED SPECIAL ISSUE
Gilberton Co.: (Came out semi-annually) Dec, 1955 - Jul, 1962 (35¢, 100 pgs.)

	GD	VG	FN	VF	VF/NM	NM-
129-The Story of Jesus (titled ...Special Edition) "Jesus on Mountain" cover	13	26	39	74	105	135
"Three Camels" cover (12/58)	14	28	42	81	118	155
"Mountain" cover (no date)-Has checklist on inside b/c to HRN #161 & different testimonial on back-c	11	22	33	62	86	110
"Mountain" cover (1968 re-issue; has white 50¢ circle)	8	16	24	44	57	70
132A-The Story of America (6/56); Cameron-a	10	20	30	58	79	100
135A-The Ten Commandments(12/56)	10	20	30	54	72	90
138A-Adventures in Science(6/57); HRN to 137	9	18	27	52	69	85
138A-(6/57)-2nd version w/HRN to 149	7	14	21	35	43	50
138A-(12/61)-3rd version w/HRN to 149	7	14	21	35	43	50

Classics Illustrated Special Issue #167A © GIL

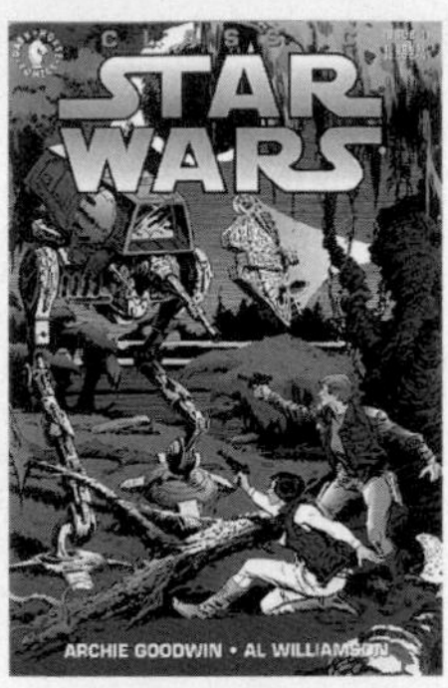

Classic Star Wars #1 © LucasFilm

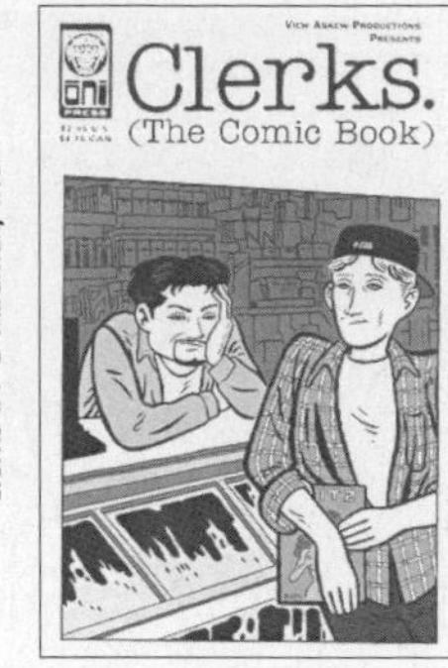

Clerks #1 © Miramax, Inc.

GD VG FN VF VF/NM NM-
2.0 4.0 6.0 8.0 9.0 9.2

141A-The Rough Rider (Teddy Roosevelt)(12/57); Evans-a
10 20 30 54 72 90
144A-Blazing the Trails West(6/58)- 73 pgs. of Crandall/Evans plus Severin-a 10 20 30 56 76 95
147A-Crossing the Rockies(12/58)-Crandall/Evans-a 10 20 30 54 72 90
150A-Royal Canadian Police(6/59)-Ingels, Sid Check-a
10 20 30 54 72 90
153A-Men, Guns & Cattle(12/59)-Evans-a (26 pgs.); Kinstler-a
10 20 30 54 72 90
156A-The Atomic Age(6/60)-Crandall/Evans, Torres-a
10 20 30 54 72 90
159A-Rockets, Jets and Missiles(12/60)-Evans, Morrow-a
10 20 30 54 72 90
162A-War Between the States(6/61)-Kirby & Crandall/Evans-a; Ingels-a
15 30 45 86 133 180
165A-To the Stars(12/61)-Torres, Crandall/Evans, Kirby-a
11 22 33 60 83 105
166A-World War II('62)-Torres, Crandall/Evans, Kirby-a
13 26 39 72 101 130
167A-Prehistoric World(7/62)-Torres & Crandall/Evans-a; two versions exist (HRN to 165 & HRN to 167) 12 24 36 67 94 120
nn Special Issue-The United Nations (1964; 50¢; scarce); this is actually part of the European Special Series, which cont'd on after the U.S. series stopped issuing new titles in 1962. This English edition was prepared specifically for sale at the U.N. It was printed in Norway
40 80 120 235 380 525

NOTE: *There was another U.S. Special Issue prepared in 1962 with artwork by* ***Torres*** *entitled World War I. Unfortunately, it was never issued in any English-language edition. It was issued in 1964 in West Germany, The Netherlands, and some Scandanavian countries, with another edition in 1974 with a new cover.*

CLASSICS LIBRARY (See King Classics)

CLASSIC STAR WARS (Also see Star Wars)
Dark Horse Comics: Aug, 1992 - No. 20, June, 1994 ($2.50)

1-Begin Star Wars strip-r by Williamson; Williamson redrew portions of the panels to fit comic book format 6.00
2-10: 8-Polybagged w/Star Wars Galaxy trading card. 8-M. Schultz-c 4.00
11-19: 13-Yeates-c. 17-M. Schultz-c. 19-Evans-c 3.00
20-($3.50, 52 pgs.)-Polybagged w/trading card 3.50
Escape To Hoth TPB ($16.95) r/#15-20 17.00
The Rebel Storm TPB - r/#8-14 17.00
Trade paperback ($29.95, slip-cased)-Reprints all movie adaptations 30.00
NOTE: *Williamson c-1-5,7,9,10,14,15,20.*

CLASSIC STAR WARS: (Title series). **Dark Horse Comics**

--A NEW HOPE, 6/94 - No. 2, 7/94 ($3.95)
1,2: 1 r/Star Wars #1-3, 7-9 publ; 2-r/Star Wars #4-6, 10-12 publ. by Marvel Comics 4.00

--DEVILWORLDS, 8/96 - No.2, 9/96 ($2.50s)1,2: r/Alan Moore-s 2.50

--HAN SOLO AT STARS' END, 3/97 - No. 3, 5/97 ($2.95)
1-3: r/strips by Alfredo Alcala 3.00

--RETURN OF THE JEDI, 10/94 - No.2, 11/94 ($3.50)
1,2: 1-r/1983-84 Marvel series; polybagged with w/trading card 3.50

--THE EARLY ADVENTURES, 8/94 - No. 9, 4/95 ($2.50)1-9 2.50

--THE EMPIRE STRIKES BACK, 8/94 - No. 2, 9/94 ($3.95)
1-r/Star Wars #39-44 published by Marvel Comics 4.00

CLASSIC X-MEN (Becomes X-Men Classic #46 on)
Marvel Comics Group: Sept, 1986 - No. 45, Mar, 1990

1-Begins-r of New X-Men 5.00
2-10: 10-Sabretooth app. 4.00
11-45: 11-1st origin of Magneto in back-up story. 17-Wolverine-c. 27-r/X-Men #121. 26-r/X-Men #120; Wolverine-c/app. 35-r/X-Men #129. 39-New Jim Lee back-up story (2nd-a on X-Men). 43-Byrne-c/a(r); $1.75, double-size 3.00
NOTE: ***Art Adams*** *c(p)-1-10, 12-16, 18-23.* ***Austin*** *c-10,15-21,24-28i.* ***Bolton*** *back up stories in 1-28,30-35.* ***Williamson*** *c-12-14i.*

CLAW (See Capt. Battle, Jr., Daredevil Comics & Silver Streak Comics)

CLAWS
Marvel Comics: Oct, 2006 - No. 3, Dec, 2006 ($3.99, limited series)

1-3-Wolverine and Black Cat team-up; Linsner-a/c 4.00
Wolverine & Black Cat: Claws HC (2007, $17.99, dustjacket) r/#1-3 & bonus Linsner art 18.00

CLAW THE UNCONQUERED (See Cancelled Comic Cavalcade)
National Periodical Publications/DC Comics: 5-6/75 - No. 9, 9-10/76; No. 10, 4-5/78 - No. 12, 8-9/78

1-1st app. Claw 2 4 6 8 10 12
2-12: 3-Nudity panel. 9-Origin 1 2 3 4 5 7
NOTE: ***Giffen*** *a-8-12p.* ***Kubert*** *c-10-12.* ***Layton*** *a-9i, 12i.*

CLAW THE UNCONQUERED (See Red Sonja/Claw: The Devil's Hands)
DC Comics: Aug, 2006 - No. 6, Jan, 2007 ($2.99)

1-6: 1,2-Chuck Dixon-s/Andy Smith; two covers by Smith & Van Sciver 3.00
TPB (2007, $17.99) r/#1-6; cover gallery 18.00

CLAY CODY, GUNSLINGER
Pines Comics: Fall, 1957

1-Painted-c 6 12 18 31 38 45

CLEAN FUN, STARRING "SHOOGAFOOTS JONES"
Specialty Book Co.: 1944 (10¢, B&W, oversized covers, 24 pgs.)

nn-Humorous situations involving Negroes in the Deep South
White cover issue... 15 30 45 86 133 180
Dark grey cover issue... 15 30 45 90 140 190

CLEMENTINA THE FLYING PIG (See Dell Jr. Treasury)

CLEOPATRA (See Ideal, a Classical Comic No. 1)

CLERKS: THE COMIC BOOK (Also see Tales From the Clerks and Oni Double Feature #1)
Oni Press: Feb, 1998 ($2.95, B&W, one-shot)

1-Kevin Smith-s 2 4 6 8 10 12
1-Second printing 4.00
...Holiday Special (12/98, $2.95) Smith-s 5.00
...The Lost Scene (12/99, $2.95) Smith-s/Hester-a 5.00

CLIFFHANGER (See Battle Chasers, Crimson, and Danger Girl)
WildStorm Prod./Wizard Press: 1997 (Wizard supplement)

0-Sketchbook preview of Cliffhanger titles 6.00

CLIMAX! (Mystery)
Gillmor Magazines: July, 1955 - No. 2, Sept, 1955

1 16 32 48 94 147 200
2 14 28 42 76 108 140

CLINT (Also see Adolescent Radioactive Black Belt Hamsters)
Eclipse Comics: Sept, 1986 - No. 2, Jan, 1987 ($1.50, B&W)

1,2 2.50

CLINT & MAC (TV, Disney)
Dell Publishing Co.: No. 889, Mar, 1958

Four Color 889-Alex Toth-a, photo-c 11 22 33 79 140 200

CLIVE BARKER'S BOOK OF THE DAMNED: A HELLRAISER COMPANION
Marvel Comics (Epic): Oct, 1991 - No. 3, Nov, 1992 ($4.95, semi-annual)

Volume 1-3-(52 pgs.): 1-Simon Bisley-c. 2-(4/92). 3-(11/92)-McKean-a (1 pg.) 5.00

CLIVE BARKER'S HELLRAISER (Also see Epic, Hellraiser Nightbreed –Jihad, Revelations, Son of Celluloid, Tapping the Vein & Weaveworld)
Marvel Comics (Epic Comics): 1989 - No. 20, 1993 ($4.50-6.95, mature, quarterly, 68 pgs.)

Book 1-4,10-16,18,19: Based on Hellraiser & Hellbound movies; Bolton-c/a; Spiegle & Wrightson-a (graphic album). 10-Foil-c. 12-Sam Kieth-a 6.00
Book 5-9 ($5.95): 7-Bolton-a. 8-Morrow-a 6.00
Book 17-Alex Ross-a, 34 pgs. 2 4 6 8 10 12
Book 20-By Gaiman/McKean 1 2 3 5 6 8
...Collected Best (Checker Books, '02, $21.95)-r/by various incl. Ross, Gaiman, Mignola 22.00
...Collected Best II ('03, $19.95)-r/by various incl. Bolton, L. Wachowski, Dorman 20.00
...Collected Best III ('04, $26.95)-r/by various incl. Bolton, L. Wachowski, Wrightson 27.00
...Dark Holiday Special ('92, $4.95)-Conrad-a 6.00
...Spring Slaughter 1 ('94, $6.95, 52 pgs.)-Painted-c 7.00
...Summer Special 1 ('92, $5.95, 68 pgs.) 6.00

CLIVE BARKER'S NIGHTBREED (Also see Epic)
Marvel Comics (Epic Comics): Apr, 1990 - No. 25, Mar, 1993 ($1.95/$2.25/$2.50, mature readers)

1-25: 1-4-Adapt horror movie. 5-New stories; Guice-a(p) 2.50

CLIVE BARKER'S THE HARROWERS
Marvel Comics (Epic Comics): Dec, 1993 - No. 6, May, 1994 ($2.50)

1-($2.95)-Glow-in-the-dark-c; Colan-c/a in all 3.00
2-6 2.50
NOTE: ***Colan*** *a(p)-1-6; c-1-3, 4p, 5p.* ***Williamson*** *a(i)-2, 4, 5(part).*

CLOAK AND DAGGER
Ziff-Davis Publishing Co.: Fall, 1952

1-Saunders painted-c 28 56 84 162 261 360

CLOAK AND DAGGER (Also see Marvel Fanfare)
Marvel Comics Group: Oct, 1983 - No. 4, Jan, 1984 (Mini-series)

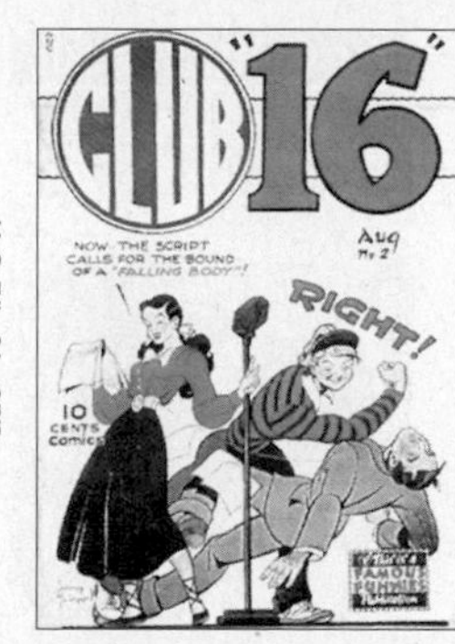

Club "16" #2 © FF

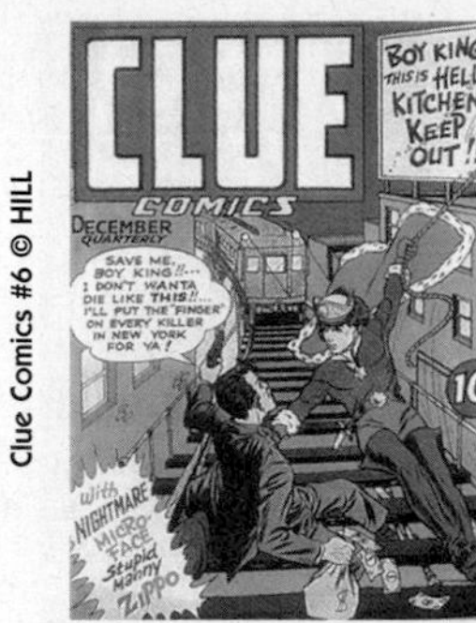

Clue Comics #6 © HILL

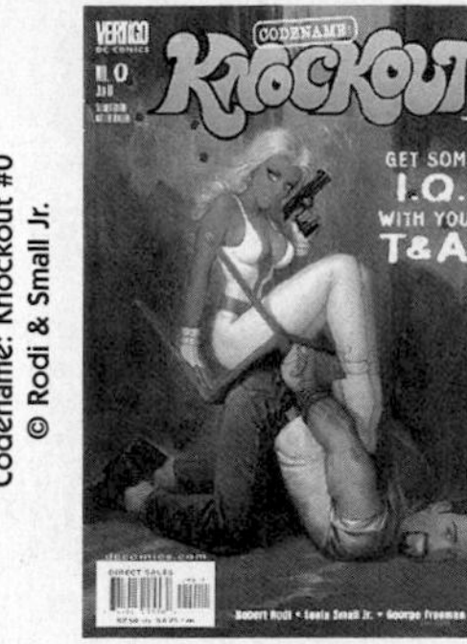

Codename: Knockout #0 © Rodi & Small Jr.

	GD 2.0	VG 4.0	FN 6.0	VF 8.0	VF/NM 9.0	NM- 9.2

(See Spectacular Spider-Man #64)
1-4-Austin-c/a(i) in all. 4-Origin 3.00

CLOAK AND DAGGER (2nd Series)(Also see Marvel Graphic Novel #34 & Strange Tales)
Marvel Comics Group: July, 1985 - No. 11, Jan, 1987
1-11: 9-Art Adams-p 2.50
...And Power Pack (1990, $7.95, 68 pgs.) 8.00
NOTE: *Mignola c-7, 8.*

CLOAK AND DAGGER (3rd Series listed as Mutant Misadventures Of...)

CLOBBERIN' TIME
Marvel Comics: Sept, 1995 ($1.95) (Based on card game)
nn-Overpower game guide; Ben Grimm story 2.50

CLOCK MAKER, THE
Image Comics: Jan, 2003 - No. 4, May, 2003 ($2.50, comic unfolds to 10"x13" pages)
1-4-Krueger-s 2.50
... Act Two (4/04, $4.95, standard format) Krueger-s/Matt Smith-c 5.00

CLONEZONE SPECIAL
Dark Horse Comics/First Comics: 1989 ($2.00, B&W)
1-Back-up series from Badger & Nexus 2.50

CLOSE ENCOUNTERS (See Marvel Comics Super Special & Marvel Special Edition)

CLOSE SHAVES OF PAULINE PERIL, THE (TV cartoon)
Gold Key: June, 1970 - No. 4, March, 1971
1 3 6 9 21 32 42
2-4 3 6 9 16 22 28

CLOWN COMICS (No. 1 titled Clown Comic Book)
Clown Comics/Home Comics/Harvey Publ.: 1945 - No. 3, Win, 1946
nn (#1) 13 26 39 74 105 135
2,3 9 18 27 47 61 75

CLOUDBURST
Image Comics: June, 2004 ($7.95, squarebound)
1-Gray & Palmiotti-s/Shy & Gouveia-a 8.00

CLOUDFALL
Image Comics: Nov, 2003 ($4.95, B&W, squarebound)
1-Kirkman-s/Su-a/c 5.00

CLOWNS, THE (I Pagliacci)
Dark Horse Comics: 1998 ($2.95, B&W, one-shot)
1-Adaption of the opera; P. Craig Russell-script 3.00

CLUBHOUSE RASCALS (#1 titled ...Presents?) (Also see Three Rascals)
Sussex Publ. Co. (Magazine Enterprises): June, 1956 - No. 2, Oct, 1956
1-The Brain app. in both; DeCarlo-a 8 16 24 44 57 70
2 7 14 21 35 43 50

CLUB "16"
Famous Funnies: June, 1948 - No. 4, Dec, 1948
1-Teen-age humor 14 28 42 76 108 140
2-4 8 16 24 44 57 70

CLUE COMICS (Real Clue Crime V2#4 on)
Hillman Periodicals: Jan, 1943 - No. 15(V2#3), May, 1947
1-Origin The Boy King, Nightmare, Micro-Face, Twilight, & Zippo
160 320 480 1008 1704 2400
2 (scarce) 82 164 246 517 871 1225
3-5 (9/43) 44 88 132 273 454 635
6,8,9: 8-Palais-c/a(2) 33 66 99 196 316 435
7-Classic concentration camp torture-c (3/44) 63 126 189 397 674 950
10-Origin/1st app. The Gun Master & begin series; content changes to crime (10/46) 35 70 105 208 334 460
11 (12/46) 25 50 75 145 233 320
12-Origin Rackman; McWilliams-a, Guardineer-a(2) 30 60 90 176 283 390
V2#1-Nightmare new origin; Iron Lady app.; Simon & Kirby-a (3/47)
53 106 159 330 553 775
V2#2-S&K-a(2)-Bondage/torture-c; man attacks & kills people with electric iron. Infantino-a 68 136 204 428 727 1025
V2#3-S&K-a(3) 53 106 159 334 567 800

CLUELESS SPRING SPECIAL (TV)
Marvel Comics: May, 1997 ($3.99, magazine sized, one-shot)
1-Photo-c from TV show 4.00

CLUTCHING HAND, THE
American Comics Group: July-Aug, 1954
1 40 80 120 235 380 525

CLYDE BEATTY COMICS (Also see Crackajack Funnies)
Commodore Productions & Artists, Inc.: October, 1953 (84 pgs.)
1-Photo front/back-c; movie scenes and comics 23 46 69 135 218 300

CLYDE CRASHCUP (TV)
Dell Publishing Co.: Aug-Oct, 1963 - No. 5, Sept-Nov, 1964
1-All written by John Stanley 10 20 30 70 123 175
2-5 9 18 27 60 100 140

COBALT BLUE (Also see Power Comics)
Innovation Publishing: Sept, 1989 - No. 2, Oct, 1989 ($1.95, 28 pgs.)
1,2-Gustovich-c/a/scripts 2.50
The Graphic Novel ($6.95, color, 52 pgs.)-r/1,2 7.00

COBB
IDW Publishing: May, 2006 - No. 3, July, 2007 ($3.99, B&W)
1-3-Beau Smith-s/Eduardo Barreto-a/c; regular and retailer incentive covers 4.00

CODE NAME: ASSASSIN (See 1st Issue Special)

CODENAME: DANGER
Lodestone Publishing: Aug, 1985 - No. 4, May, 1986 ($1.50)
1-4 2.50

CODENAME: FIREARM (Also see Firearm)
Malibu Comics (Ultraverse): June, 1995 - No. 5, Sept, 1995 ($2.95, bimonthly limited series)
0-5: 0-2-Alec Swan back-up story by James Robinson 3.00
NOTE: *Perez c-0.*

CODENAME: GENETIX
Marvel Comics UK: Jan, 1993 - No. 4, May, 1993 ($1.75, limited series)
1-4: Wolverine in all 3.00

CODENAME: KNOCKOUT
DC Comics (Vertigo): No. 0, Jun, 2001 - No. 23, June, 2003 ($2.50/$2.75)
0-15: Rodi-s in all. 0-6-Small Jr. -a. 1-Two covers by Chiodo & Cho. 7,8,10,11,12-Paquette-a. 9,13,14-Conner-a 2.50
16-23: 16-Begin $2.75-c. 23-Last issue; JG Jones-c 2.75

CODENAME SPITFIRE (Formerly Spitfire And The Troubleshooters)
Marvel Comics Group: No. 10, July, 1987 - No. 13, Oct, 1987
10-13: 10-Rogers-c/a (low printing) 3.50

CODENAME: STRYKE FORCE (Also See Cyberforce V1#4 & Cyberforce/Stryke Force: Opposing Forces
Image Comics (Top Cow Productions): Jan, 1994 - No. 14, Sept, 1995 ($1.95-$2.25)
0,1-14: 1-12-Silvestri stories, Peterson-a. 4-Stormwatch app. 14-Story continues in Cyberforce/Stryke Force: Opposing Forces; Turner-a 2.50
1-Gold, 1-Blue 4.00

CODE NAME: TOMAHAWK
Fantasy General Comics: Sept, 1986 ($1.75, high quality paper)
1-Sci/fi 2.50

CODE OF HONOR
Marvel Comics: Feb, 1997 - No. 4, May, 1997 ($5.95, limited series)
1-4-Fully painted by various; Dixon-s 6.00

CODY OF THE PONY EXPRESS (See Colossal Features Magazine)
Fox Features Syndicate: Sept, 1950 (See Women Outlaws)(One shot)
1-Painted-c 14 28 42 81 118 155

CODY OF THE PONY EXPRESS (Buffalo Bill...) (Outlaws of the West #11 on; Formerly Bullseye)
Charlton Comics: No. 8, Oct, 1955; No. 9, Jan, 1956; No. 10, June, 1956
8-Bullseye on splash pg; not S&K-a 8 16 24 44 57 70
9,10: Buffalo Bill app. in all 6 12 18 29 36 42

CODY STARBUCK (1st app. in Star Reach #1)
Star Reach Productions: July, 1978
nn-Howard Chaykin-c/a 2 4 6 12 16 20
2nd printing 1 2 3 5 6 8
NOTE: *Both printings say First Printing. True first printing is on lower-grade paper, somewhat off-register, and snow in snow sequence has green tint.*

CO-ED ROMANCES
P. L. Publishing Co.: November, 1951

Colossus Comics #1 © Sun Publ.

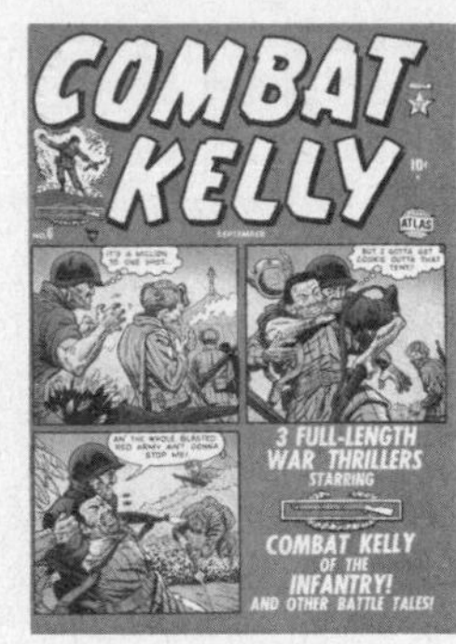

Combat Kelly #6 © MAR

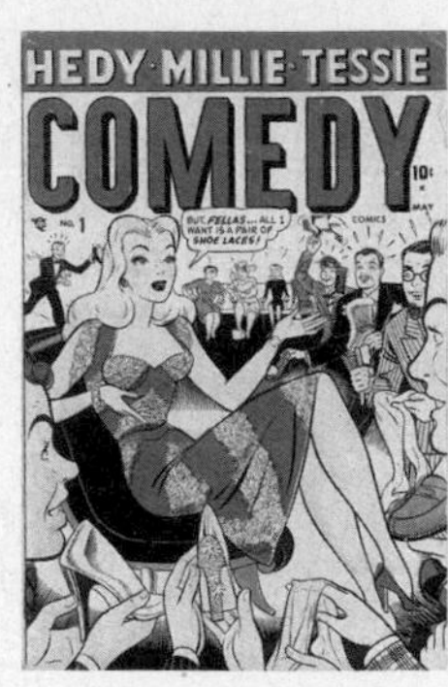

Comedy Comics #1 © MAR

	GD 2.0	VG 4.0	FN 6.0	VF 8.0	VF/NM 9.0	NM- 9.2
1	9	18	27	47	61	75

COFFEE WORLD
World Comics: Oct, 1995 ($1.50, B&W, anthology)

1-Shannon Wheeler's Too Much Coffee Man story						3.00

COFFIN, THE
Oni Press: Sept, 2000 - No. 4, May, 2001 ($2.95, B&W, limited series)

1-4-Hester-s/Huddleston-a						3.00
TPB (8/01, $11.95, TPB) r/#1-4						12.00

COLLECTORS DRACULA, THE
Millennium Publications: 1994 - No. 2, 1994 ($3.95, color/B&W, 52 pgs., limited series)

1,2-Bolton-a (7 pgs.)						4.00

COLLECTORS ITEM CLASSICS (See Marvel Collectors Item Classics)

COLORS IN BLACK
Dark Horse Comics: Mar, 1995 - No. 4, June, 1995 ($2.95, limited series)

1-4						3.00

COLOSSAL FEATURES MAGAZINE (Formerly I Loved) (See Cody of the Pony Express)
Fox Features Syndicate: No. 33, 5/50 - No. 34, 7/50; No. 3, 9/50 (Based on Columbia serial)

33,34: Cody of the Pony Express begins. 33-Painted-c. 34-Photo-c	14	28	42	80	115	150
3-Authentic criminal cases	14	28	42	80	115	150

COLOSSAL SHOW, THE (TV cartoon)
Gold Key: Oct, 1969

1	5	10	15	32	51	70

COLOSSUS (See X-Men)
Marvel Comics: Oct, 1997 ($2.99, 48 pgs., one-shot)

1-Raab-s/Hitch & Neary-a, wraparound-c						3.00

COLOSSUS COMICS (See Green Giant & Motion Picture Funnies Weekly)
Sun Publications (Funnies, Inc.?): March, 1940

1-(Scarce)-Tulpa of Tsang(hero); Colossus app.	639	1278	1917	4600	8050	11,500

NOTE: *Cover by artist that drew Colossus in Green Giant Comics.*

COLOUR OF MAGIC, THE (Terry Pratchett's...)
Innovation Publishing: 1991 - No. 4, 1991 ($2.50, limited series)

1-4: Adapts 1st novel of the Discworld series						3.00

COLT .45 (TV)
Dell Publishing Co.: No. 924, 8/58 - No. 1058, 11-1/59-60; No. 4, 2-4/60 - No. 9, 5-7/61

Four Color 924(#1)-Wayde Preston photo-c on all	10	20	30	70	123	175
Four Color 1004,1058, #4,5,7-9: 1004-Photo-b/c	8	16	24	56	93	130
6-Toth-a	9	18	27	60	100	140

COLUMBIA COMICS
William H. Wise Co.: 1943

1-Joe Palooka, Charlie Chan, Capt. Yank, Sparky Watts, Dixie Dugan app.	27	54	81	156	251	345

COMANCHE
Dell Publishing Co.: No. 1350, Apr-Jun, 1962

Four Color 1350-Disney movie; reprints FC #966 with title change from "Tonka" to "Comanche"; Sal Mineo photo-c	5	10	15	35	55	75

COMANCHEROS, THE
Dell Publishing Co.: No. 1300, Mar-May, 1962

Four Color 1300-Movie, John Wayne photo-c	15	30	45	105	188	270

COMBAT
Atlas Comics (ANC): June, 1952 - No. 11, April, 1953

1	26	52	78	154	247	340
2-Heath-c/a	15	30	45	84	127	170
3,5-9,11: 3-Romita-a. 6-Robinson-c; Romita-a	11	22	33	64	90	115
4-Krigstein-a	12	24	36	67	94	120
10-B&W and color illos. in **POP**; Sale-a, Forte-a	12	24	36	67	94	120

NOTE: *Combat Casey in 7-11.* ***Heath*** *a-2, 3; c-1, 2, 5, 9.* ***Maneely*** *a-1; c-3, 10.* ***Pakula*** *a-1.* ***Reinman*** *a-1.*

COMBAT
Dell Publishing Co.: Oct-Nov, 1961 - No. 40, Oct, 1973 (No #9)

1	6	12	18	43	69	95
2,3,5	4	8	12	26	41	55
4-John F. Kennedy c/story (P.T. 109)	5	10	15	34	55	75
6,7,8(4-6/63), 8(7-9/63)	4	8	12	24	37	50
10-26: 26-Last 12¢ issue	3	6	9	20	30	40
27-40(reprints #1-14). 30-r/#4	3	6	9	14	19	24

COMBAT CASEY (Formerly War Combat)
Atlas Comics (SAI): No. 6, Jan, 1953 - No. 34, July, 1957

6 (Indicia shows 1/52 in error)	17	34	51	98	154	210
7-R.Q. Sale-a	11	22	33	60	83	105
8-Used in **POP**, pg. 94	10	20	30	54	72	90
9-Violent art by R.Q. Sale	9	18	27	50	65	80
10,13-19-Violent art by R.Q. Sale; Battle Brady x-over #10	13	26	39	72	101	130
11,12,20-Last Precode (2/55)	9	18	27	50	65	80
21-34: 22,25-R.Q. Sale-a	9	18	27	47	61	75

NOTE: ***Everett*** *a-6.* ***Heath*** *c-10, 17, 19, 23, 30.* ***Maneely*** *c-6, 8, 15.* ***Powell*** *a-29(5), 30(5), 34.* ***Severin*** *c-26, 33.*

COMBAT KELLY
Atlas Comics (SPI): Nov, 1951 - No. 44, Aug, 1957

1-1st app. Combat Kelly; Heath-a	31	62	93	181	291	400
2	15	30	45	90	140	190
3-10	13	26	39	74	105	135
11-Used in **POP**, pgs. 94,95 plus color illo.	11	22	33	60	83	105
12-Color illo. in **POP**	11	22	33	60	83	105
13-16	10	20	30	56	76	95
17-Violent art by R. Q. Sale; Combat Casey app.	14	28	42	76	108	140
18-20,22-44: 18-Battle Brady app. 28-Last precode (1/55). 38-Green Berets story (8/56)	9	18	27	52	69	85
21-Transvestism-c	10	20	30	54	72	90

NOTE: ***Berg*** *a-8, 12-14, 15-17, 19-23, 25, 26, 28, 31-37, 39, 41-44; c-2.* ***Colan*** *a-42.* ***Heath*** *a-4, 18; c-31.* ***Lawrence*** *a-23.* ***Maneely*** *a-4(2), 6, 7(3), 8; c-4, 5, 7, 8, 10, 25, 29, 39.* ***R.Q. Sale*** *a-17, 25.* ***Severin*** *c-41, 42.* ***Whitney*** *a-5.*

COMBAT KELLY (...and the Deadly Dozen)
Marvel Comics Group: June, 1972 - No. 9, Oct, 1973

1-Intro & origin new Combat Kelly; Ayers/Mooney-a; Severin-c (20¢)	3	6	9	18	27	35
2,5-8	2	4	6	10	14	18
3,4: 3-Origin. 4-Sgt. Fury-c/s	2	4	6	13	18	22
9-Death of the Deadly Dozen	3	6	9	14	20	25

COMBAT ZONE: TRUE TALES OF GIS IN IRAQ
Marvel Comics: 2005 ($19.99, squarebound)

Vol. 1-Karl Zinsmeister scripts adapted from his non-fiction books; Dan Jurgens-a						20.00

COMBINED OPERATIONS (See The Story of the Commandos)

COMEBACK (See Zane Grey 4-Color 357)

COMEDY CARNIVAL
St. John Publishing Co.: no date (1950's) (100 pgs.)

nn-Contains rebound St. John comics	35	70	105	203	327	450

COMEDY COMICS (1st Series) (Daring Mystery #1-8) (Becomes Margie Comics #35 on)
Timely Comics (TCI 9,10): No. 9, April, 1942 - No. 34, Fall, 1946

9-(Scarce)-The Fin by Everett, Capt. Dash, Citizen V, & The Silver Scorpion app.; Wolverton-a; 1st app. Comedy Kid; satire on Hitler & Stalin; The Fin, Citizen V & Silver Scorpion cont. from Daring Mystery	300	600	900	1950	3375	4800
10-(Scarce)-Origin The Fourth Musketeer, Victory Boys; Monstro, the Mighty app.	233	466	699	1468	2484	3500
11-Vagabond, Stuporman app.	53	106	159	333	554	775
12,13	17	34	51	98	154	210
14-Origin/1st app. Super Rabbit (3/43) plus-c	53	106	159	334	567	800
15-20: 20-Hitler parody-c	15	30	45	92	144	195
21-32: 21-Tojo-c. 22-Hitler parody-c	14	28	42	76	108	140
33-Kurtzman-a (5 pgs.)	15	30	45	84	127	170
34-Intro Margie; Wolverton-a (5 pgs.)	22	44	66	131	211	290

COMEDY COMICS (2nd Series)
Marvel Comics (ACI): May, 1948 - No. 10, Jan, 1950

1-Hedy, Tessie, Millie begin; Kurtzman's "Hey Look" (he draws himself)	36	72	108	212	341	470
2	15	30	45	94	147	200
3,4-Kurtzman's "Hey Look" (?&3)	17	34	51	98	154	210
5-10	11	22	33	64	90	115

COMET, THE (See The Mighty Crusaders & Pep Comics #1)
Red Circle Comics (Archie): Oct, 1983 - No. 2, Dec, 1983

1-Re-intro & origin The Comet; The American Shield begins. Nino & Infantino art in both. Hangman in both						5.00
2-Origin continues.						4.00

The Comet #5 © AP

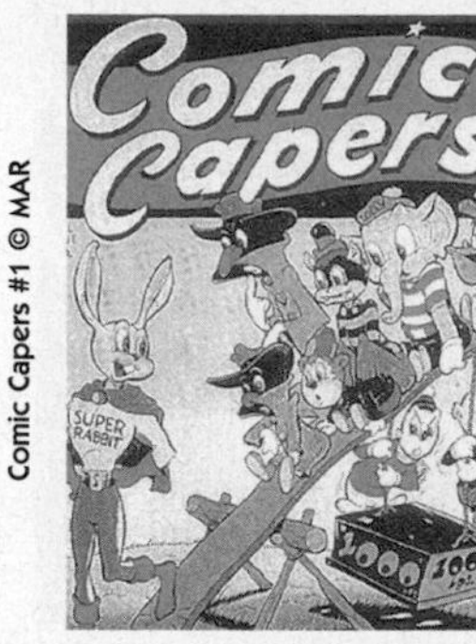

Comic Capers #1 © MAR

Comic Cavalcade #2 © DC

GD	VG	FN	VF	VF/NM	NM-
2.0	4.0	6.0	8.0	9.0	9.2

COMET, THE
DC Comics (Impact Comics): July, 1991 - No. 18, Dec, 1992 ($1.00/$1.25)

1 3.00
2-18: 4-Black Hood app. 6-Re-intro Hangman. 8-Web x-over. 10-Contains Crusaders trading card. 4-Origin. Netzer(Nasser) c(p)-11,14-17 2.50
Annual 1 (1992, $2.50, 68 pgs.)-Contains Impact trading card; Shield back-up story 2.50

COMET MAN, THE (Movie)
Marvel Comics Group: Feb, 1987 - No. 6, July, 1987 (limited series)

1-6: 3-Hulk app. 4-She-Hulk shower scene-c/s. Fantastic 4 app. 5-Fantastic 4 app. 2.50
NOTE: ***Kelley Jones** a-1-6p.*

COMIC ALBUM (Also see Disney Comic Album)
Dell Publishing Co.: Mar-May, 1958 - No. 18, June-Aug, 1962

1-Donald Duck 9 18 27 60 100 140
2-Bugs Bunny 5 10 15 32 51 70
3-Donald Duck 7 14 21 47 76 105
4-6,8-10: 4-Tom & Jerry. 5-Woody Woodpecker. 6,10-Bugs Bunny. 8-Tom & Jerry. 9-Woody Woodpecker 4 8 12 28 44 60
7,11,15: Popeye. 11-(9-11/60) 6 12 18 33 49 65
12-14: 12-Tom & Jerry. 13-Woody Woodpecker. 14-Bugs Bunny 5 10 15 30 48 60
16-Flintstones (12-2/61-62)-3rd app. Early Cave Kids app. 8 16 24 54 90 125
17-Space Mouse (3rd app.) 5 10 15 32 51 70
18-Three Stooges; photo-c 8 16 24 54 90 125

COMIC BOOK
Marvel Comics-#1/Dark Horse Comics-#2: 1995 ($5.95, oversize)

1-Spumco characters by John K. 1 2 3 4 5 7
2-(Dark Horse) 0.00

COMIC CAPERS
Red Circle Mag./Marvel Comics: Fall, 1944 - No. 6, Summer, 1946

1-Super Rabbit, The Creeper, Silly Seal, Ziggy Pig, Sharpy Fox begin 30 60 90 174 280 385
2 15 30 45 92 144 195
3-6 14 28 42 81 118 155

COMIC CAVALCADE
All-American/National Periodical Publications: Winter, 1942-43 - No. 63, June-July, 1954 (Contents change with No. 30, Dec-Jan, 1948-49 on)

1-The Flash, Green Lantern, Wonder Woman, Wildcat, The Black Pirate by Moldoff (also #2), Ghost Patrol, and Red White & Blue begin; Scribbly app.; Minute Movie 861 1722 2583 6199 10,850 15,500
2-Mutt & Jeff begin; last Ghost Patrol & Black Pirate; Minute Movies 243 486 729 1531 2591 3650
3-Hop Harrigan & Sargon, the Sorcerer begin; The King app. 160 320 480 1008 1704 2400
4,5: 4-The Gay Ghost, The King, Scribbly, & Red Tornado app. 5-Christmas-c. 5-Prints ad for Jr. JSA membership kit that includes "The Minute Man Answers The Call" 145 290 435 914 1545 2175
6-10: 7-Red Tornado & Black Pirate app.; last Scribbly. 9-Fat & Slat app.; X-Mas-c 116 232 348 731 1236 1740
11,12,14: 12-Last Red White & Blue 97 194 291 611 1031 1450
13-Solomon Grundy app.; X-Mas-c 162 324 486 1021 1723 2425
15-Just a Story begins 98 196 294 617 1046 1475
16-20: 19-Christmas-c 89 178 267 561 951 1340
21-23: 22-Johnny Peril begins. 23-Harry Lampert-c (Toth swipes) 85 170 255 536 906 1275
24-Solomon Grundy x-over in Green Lantern 113 226 339 712 1206 1700
25-28: 25-Black Canary app.; X-Mas-c. 26-28-Johnny Peril app. 28-Last Mutt & Jeff 76 152 228 479 810 1140
29-(10-11/48)-Last Flash, Wonder Woman, Green Lantern & Johnny Peril; Wonder Woman invents "Thinking Machine"; 2nd computer in comics (after Flash Comics #52); Leave It to Binky story (early app.) 87 174 261 548 924 1300
30-(12-1/48-49)-The Fox & the Crow, Dodo & the Frog & Nutsy Squirrel begin 41 82 123 250 413 575
31-35 24 48 72 140 225 310
36-49: 41-Last squarebound issue 17 34 51 100 158 215
50-62(Scarce) 21 42 63 123 197 270
63(Rare) 34 68 102 198 319 440
*NOTE: **Grossman** a-30-63. **E.E. Hibbard** c-(Flash only)-1-4, 7-14, 16-19, 21. **Sheldon Mayer** a(2-3)-40-63. **Moulson** c(G.L.)-7, 15. **Nodell** c(G.L.)-9. **H.G. Peter** c(W. Woman only)-1, 3-21, 24. **Post** a-31, 36. **Purcell** c(G.L.)-2-5, 10. **Reinman** a(Green Lantern)-4-6, 8, 9, 13, 15-21; c(Gr. Lantern)-6, 8, 19. **Toth** a(Green Lantern)-26-28; c-27. Atom app.-22, 23.*

COMIC COMICS
Fawcett Publications: Apr, 1946 - No. 10, Feb, 1947

1-Captain Kid; Nutty Comics #1 in indicia 15 30 45 83 124 165
2-10-Wolverton-a, 4 pgs. each. 5-Captain Kidd app. Mystic Moot by Wolverton in #2-10? 15 30 45 84 127 170

COMIC LAND
Fact and Fiction Publ.: March, 1946

1-Sandusky & the Senator, Sam Stupor, Sleuth, Marvin the Great, Sir Passer, Phineas Gruff app.; Irv Tirman & Perry Williams art 15 30 45 84 127 170

COMICO CHRISTMAS SPECIAL
Comico: Dec, 1988 ($2.50, 44pgs.)

1-Rude/Williamson-a; Dave Stevens-c 4.00

COMICO COLLECTION (Also see Grendel)
Comico: 1987 ($9.95, slipcased collection)

nn-Contains exclusive Grendel: Devil's Vagary, 9 random Comico comics, a poster and newsletter in black slipcase w/silver ink 25.00

COMICO PRIMER (See Primer)

COMIC PAGES (Formerly Funny Picture Stories)
Centaur Publications: V3#4, July, 1939 - V3#6, Dec, 1939

V3#4-Bob Wood-a 53 106 159 330 553 775
5,6: 6-Schwab-c 43 86 129 267 446 625

COMICS (See All Good)

COMICS, THE
Dell Publ. Co.: Mar, 1937 - No. 11, Nov, 1938 (Newspaper strip-r; bi-monthly)

1-1st app. Tom Mix in comics; Wash Tubbs, Tom Beatty, Myra North, Arizona Kid, Erik Noble & International Spy w/Doctor Doom begin 187 374 561 1178 1989 2800
2 82 164 246 517 871 1225
3-11: 3-Alley Oop begins 66 132 198 416 701 985

COMICS AND STORIES (See Walt Disney's Comics and Stories)

COMICS & STORIES (Also see Wolf & Red)
Dark Horse Comics: Apr, 1996 - No. 4, July, 1996 ($2.95, lim. series) (Created by Tex Avery)

1-4: Wolf & Red app; reads Comics and Stories on-c. 1-Terry Moore-a. 2-Reed Waller-a 3.00

COMICS CALENDAR, THE (The 1946...)
True Comics Press (ordered through the mail): 1946 (25¢, 116 pgs.) (Stapled at top)

nn-(Rare) Has a "strip" story for every day of the year in color 40 80 120 235 380 525

COMICS DIGEST (Pocket size)
Parents' Magazine Institute: Winter, 1942-43 (B&W, 100 pgs)

1-Reprints from True Comics (non-fiction World War II stories) 10 20 30 54 72 90

COMICS EXPRESS
Eclipse Comics: Nov, 1989 - No. 2, Jan, 1990 ($2.95, B&W, 68pgs.)

1,2: Collection of strip-r; 2(12/89-c, 1/90 inside) 3.00

COMICS FOR KIDS
London Publ. Co./Timely: 1945 (no month); No. 2, Sum, 1945 (Funny animal)

1,2-Puffy Pig, Sharpy Fox 16 32 48 94 147 200

COMICS' GREATEST WORLD
Dark Horse Comics: Jun, 1993 - V4#4, Sept, 1993 ($1.00, weekly, lim. series)

Arcadia (Wk 1): V1#1,2,4: 1-X: Frank Miller-c. 2-Pit Bulls. 4-Monster. 2.50
1-B&W Press Proof Edition (1500 copies) 1 3 4 6 8 10
1-Silver-c; distr. retailer bonus w/print & cards 1 2 3 5 6 8
3-Ghost, Dorman-c; Hughes-a 4.00
Retailer's Prem. Emb. Silver Foil Logo-r/V1#1-4 1 3 4 6 8 10
Golden City (Wk 2: V2#1-4: 1-Rebel; Ordway-c. 2-Mecha; Dave Johnson-c. 3-Titan; Walt Simonson-c. 4-Catalyst; Perez-c. 2.50
1-Gold-c; distr. retailer bonus w/print & cards. 6.00
Retailer's Prem. Embos. Gold Foil Logo-r/V2#1-4 1 2 3 5 6 8
Steel Harbor (Week 3): V3#1-Barb Wire; Dorman-c; Gulacy-a(p) 4.00
2-4: 2-The Machine. 3-Wolfgang. 4-Motorhead 2.50
1-Silver-c; distr. retailer bonus w/print & cards 1 2 3 5 6 8
Retailer's Prem. Emb. Red Foil Logo-r/V3#1-4. 1 3 4 6 8 10
Vortex (Week 4): V4#1-4: 1-Division 13; Dorman-c. 2-Hero Zero; Art Adams-c. 3-King Tiger; Chadwick-a(p); Darrow-c. 4-Vortex; Miller-c. 2.50
1-Gold-c; distr. retailer bonus w/print & cards. 6.00
Retailer's Prem. Emb. Blue Foil Logo-r/V4#1-4. 1 2 3 5 6 8

Comics on Parade #38 © UFS

Commander Battle and the Atomic Sub #7 © ACG

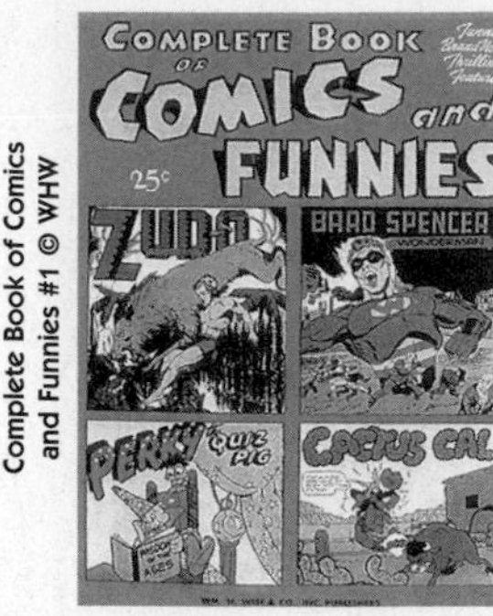

Complete Book of Comics and Funnies #1 © WHW

	GD 2.0	VG 4.0	FN 6.0	VF 8.0	VF/NM 9.0	NM- 9.2

COMICS' GREATEST WORLD: OUT OF THE VORTEX (See Out of The Vortex)

COMICS HITS (See Harvey Comics Hits)

COMICS MAGAZINE, THE (...Funny Pages #3)(Funny Pages #6 on)
Comics Magazine Co. (1st Comics Mag./Centaur Publ.): May, 1936 - No. 5, Sept, 1936 (Paper covers)

Issue	GD	VG	FN	VF	VF/NM	NM-
1-1st app. Dr. Mystic (a.k.a. Dr. Occult) by Siegel & Shuster (the 1st app. of a Superman prototype in comics). Dr. Mystic is not in costume but later appears in costume as a more pronounced prototype in More Fun #14-17. (1st episode of "The Koth and the Seven"; continues in More Fun #14; originally scheduled for publication at DC). 1 pg. Kelly-a; Sheldon Mayer-a	3000	6000	9000	18,000	-	-
2-Federal Agent (a.k.a. Federal Men) by Siegel & Shuster; 1 pg. Kelly-a	350	700	1050	2100	2800	3500
3-5	300	600	900	1800	2400	3000

COMICS NOVEL (Anarcho, Dictator of Death)
Fawcett Publications: 1947

Issue	GD	VG	FN	VF	VF/NM	NM-
1-All Radar; 51 pg anti-fascism story	32	64	96	186	298	410

COMICS ON PARADE (No. 30 on are a continuation of Single Series)
United Features Syndicate: Apr, 1938 - No. 104, Feb, 1955

Issue	GD	VG	FN	VF	VF/NM	NM-
1-Tarzan by Foster; Captain & the Kids, Little Mary Mixup, Abbie & Slats, Ella Cinders, Broncho Bill, Li'l Abner begin	359	718	1077	2441	4271	6100
2 (Tarzan & others app. on-c of #1-3,17)	127	254	381	800	1350	1900
3	97	194	291	611	1031	1450
4,5	76	152	228	479	810	1140
6-10	53	106	159	330	553	775
11-16,18-20	42	84	126	260	435	610
17-Tarzan-c	49	98	147	304	507	710
21-29: 22-Son of Tarzan begins. 22,24,28-Tailspin Tommy-c. 29-Last Tarzan issue	36	72	108	212	341	470
30-Li'l Abner	20	40	60	115	183	250
31-The Captain & the Kids	15	30	45	85	130	175
32-Nancy & Fritzi Ritz	14	28	42	78	112	145
33,36,39,42-Li'l Abner	16	32	48	94	147	200
34,37,40-The Captain & the Kids (10/41,6/42,3/43)	15	30	45	83	124	165
35,38-Nancy & Fritzi Ritz. 38-Infinity-c	14	28	42	76	108	140
41-Nancy & Fritzi Ritz	11	22	33	60	83	105
43-The Captain & the Kids	15	30	45	83	124	165
44 (3/44),47,50: Nancy & Fritzi Ritz	11	22	33	60	83	105
45-Li'l Abner	15	30	45	84	127	170
46,49-The Captain & the Kids	13	26	39	74	105	135
48-Li'l Abner (3/45)	15	30	45	84	127	170
51,54-Li'l Abner	14	28	42	76	108	140
52-The Captain & the Kids (3/46)	10	20	30	56	76	95
53,55,57-Nancy & Fritzi Ritz	10	20	30	56	76	95
56-The Captain & the Kids (r/Sparkler)	10	20	30	56	76	95
58-Li'l Abner; continues as Li'l Abner #61?	14	28	42	76	108	140
59-The Captain & the Kids	9	18	27	47	61	75
60-70-Nancy & Fritzi Ritz	8	16	24	44	57	70
71-99,101-104-Nancy & Sluggo: 71-76-Nancy only	8	16	24	42	54	65
100-Nancy & Sluggo	14	28	42	76	108	140
Special Issue, 7/46; Summer, 1948 - The Captain & the Kids app.	11	22	33	62	86	110
NOTE: Bound Volume (Very Rare) includes No. 1-12; bound by publisher in pictorial comic boards & distributed at the 1939 World's Fair and through mail order from ads in comic books (also see Tip Top)	280	560	840	1764	2982	4200

NOTE: *Li'l Abner reprinted from Tip Top.*

COMICS READING LIBRARIES (See the Promotional Comics section)

COMICS REVUE
St. John Publ. Co. (United Features Synd.): June, 1947 - No. 5, Jan, 1948

Issue	GD	VG	FN	VF	VF/NM	NM-
1-Ella Cinders & Blackie	11	22	33	64	90	115
2,4: 2-Hap Hopper (7/47). 4-Ella Cinders (9/47)	9	18	27	47	61	75
3,5: 3-Iron Vic (8/47). 5-Gordo No. 1 (1/48)	8	16	24	44	57	70

COMIC STORY PAINT BOOK
Samuel Lowe Co.: 1943 (Large size, 68 pgs.)

Issue	GD	VG	FN	VF	VF/NM	NM-
1055-Captain Marvel & a Captain Marvel Jr. story to read & color; 3 panels in color per pg. (reprints)	75	150	225	473	799	1125

COMIX BOOK
Marvel Comics Group/Krupp Comics Works No. 4,5: 1974 - No. 5, 1976 ($1.00, B&W, magazine) (#1-3 newsstand; #4,5 were direct distribution only)

Issue	GD	VG	FN	VF	VF/NM	NM-
1-Underground comic artists; 2 pgs. Wolverton-a	3	6	9	16	22	28
2,3: 2-Wolverton-a (1 pg.)	3	6	9	14	19	24
4(2/76), 4(5/76), 5 (Low distribution)	3	6	9	16	23	30

NOTE: *Print run No. 1-3: 200-250M; No. 4&5: 10M each.*

COMIX INTERNATIONAL
Warren Magazines: Jul, 1974 - No. 5, Spring, 1977 (Full color, stiff-c, mail only)

Issue	GD	VG	FN	VF	VF/NM	NM-
1-Low distribution; all Corben story remainders from Warren; Corben-c on all	9	18	27	60	100	140
2,4: 2-Two Dracula stories; Wood, Wrightson-r; Crandall-a; Maroto-a. 4-Printing w/ 3 Corben sty	5	10	15	32	51	70
3-5: 3-Dax story. 4-(printing without Corben story). 4-Crandall-a. 4,5-Vampirella stories. 5-Spirit story; Eisner-a	4	8	12	26	41	55

NOTE: *No. 4 had two printings with extra **Corben** story in one. No. 3 may also have a variation. No. 3 has two Jeff Jones reprints from Vampirella.*

COMMANDER BATTLE AND THE ATOMIC SUB
Amer. Comics Group (Titan Publ. Co.): Jul-Aug, 1954 - No. 7, Aug-Sep, 1955

Issue	GD	VG	FN	VF	VF/NM	NM-
1 (3-D effect)-Moldoff flying saucer-c	47	94	141	291	483	675
2,4-7: 2-Moldoff-c. 4-(1-2/55)-Last pre-code; Landau-a. 5-3-D effect story (2 pgs.). 6,7-Landau-a. 7-Flying saucer-c	31	62	93	181	291	400
3-H-Bomb-c; Atomic Sub becomes Atomic Spaceship	32	64	96	188	302	415

COMMANDO ADVENTURES
Atlas Comics (MMC): June, 1957 - No. 2, Aug, 1957

Issue	GD	VG	FN	VF	VF/NM	NM-
1-Severin-c	14	28	42	76	108	140
2-Severin-c; Drucker-a?	10	20	30	54	72	90

COMMANDOS
DC Comics: Oct. 1942

1-Ashcan comic, not distributed to newsstands, only for in-house use. Cover art is Boy Commandos #1 with interior being a Boy Commandos story from an unidentified issue of Detective Comics (no known sales)

COMMANDO YANK (See The Mighty Midget Comics & Wow Comics)

COMMON GROUNDS
Image Comics (Top Cow): Feb, 2004 - No. 6, July, 2004 ($2.99)

Issue	Price
1-6: 1-Two covers; art by Jurgens and Oeming. 3-Bachalo, Jurgens-a. 4-Peréz-a	3.00
...: Baker's Dozen TPB (12/04, $14.99) r/#1-6; cover gallery; Holey Crullers pages	15.00

COMPLETE BOOK OF COMICS AND FUNNIES
William H. Wise & Co.: 1944 (25¢, one-shot, 196 pgs.)

Issue	GD	VG	FN	VF	VF/NM	NM-
1-Origin Brad Spencer, Wonderman; The Magnet, The Silver Knight by Kinstler, & Zudo the Jungle Boy app.	43	86	129	267	446	625

COMPLETE BOOK OF TRUE CRIME COMICS
William H. Wise & Co.: No date (Mid 1940's) (25¢, 132 pgs.)

Issue	GD	VG	FN	VF	VF/NM	NM-
nn-Contains Crime Does Not Pay rebound (includes #22)	123	246	369	775	1313	1850

COMPLETE COMICS (Formerly Amazing Comics No. 1)
Timely Comics (EPC): No. 2, Winter, 1944-45

Issue	GD	VG	FN	VF	VF/NM	NM-
2-The Destroyer, The Whizzer, The Young Allies & Sergeant Dix; Schomburg-c	163	326	489	1027	1739	2450

COMPLETE FRANK MILLER BATMAN, THE
Longmeadow Press: 1989 ($29.95, hardcover, silver gilded pages)

Issue	Price
HC-Reprints Batman: Year One, Wanted: Santa Claus--Dead or Alive, and The Dark Knight Returns	30.00

COMPLETE GUIDE TO THE DEADLY ARTS OF KUNG FU AND KARATE
Marvel Comics: 1974 (68 pgs., B&W magazine)

Issue	GD	VG	FN	VF	VF/NM	NM-
V1#1-Bruce Lee-c and 5 pg. story (scarce)	6	12	18	37	59	80

COMPLETE LOVE MAGAZINE (Formerly a pulp with same title)
Ace Periodicals (Periodical House): V26#2, May-June, 1951 - V32#4(#191), Sept, 1956

Issue	GD	VG	FN	VF	VF/NM	NM-
V26#2-Painted-c (52 pgs.)	10	20	30	58	79	100
V26#3-6(2/52), V27#1(4/52)-6(1/53)	8	16	24	44	57	70
V28#1(3/53), V28#2(5/53), V29#3(7/53)-6(12/53)	8	16	24	42	54	65
V30#1(2/54), V30#1(#176, 4/54),2,4-6(#181, 1/55)	8	16	24	42	54	65
V30#3(#178)-Rock Hudson photo-c	8	16	24	44	57	70
V31#1(#182, 3/55)-Last precode	8	16	24	40	50	60
V31#2(5/55)-6(#187, 1/56)	7	14	21	37	46	55
V32#1(#188, 3/56)-4(#191, 9/56)	7	14	21	37	46	55

NOTE: *(34 total issues). Photo-c V27#5-on. Painted-c V26#3.*

COMPLETE MYSTERY (True Complete Mystery No. 5 on)
Marvel Comics (PrPl): Aug, 1948 - No. 4, Feb, 1949 (Full length stories)

Issue	GD	VG	FN	VF	VF/NM	NM-
1-Seven Dead Men	45	90	135	279	465	650

2-4: 2-Jigsaw of Doom! 3-Fear in the Night; Burgos-c/a (28 pgs.). 4-A Squealer Dies Fast

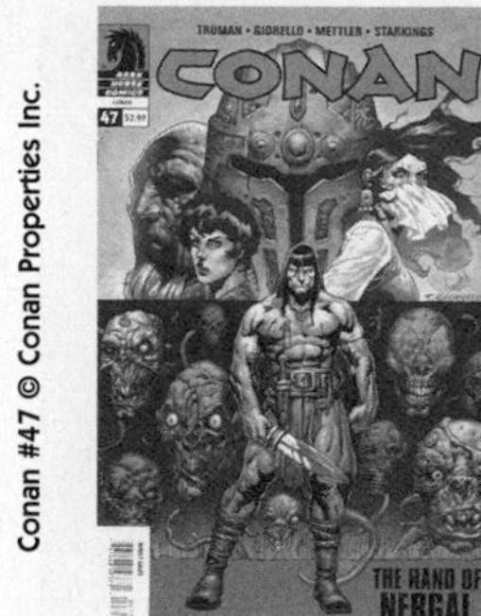
Conan #47 © Conan Properties Inc.

Conan Classic #5 © Conan Properties Inc.

Conan the Barbarian #57 © Conan Properties Inc.

GD VG FN VF VF/NM NM-
2.0 4.0 6.0 8.0 9.0 9.2

39 78 117 228 369 510

COMPLETE ROMANCE
Avon Periodicals: 1949
1-(Scarce)-Reprinted as Women to Love 40 00 120 244 397 550

CONAN (See Chamber of Darkness #4, Giant-Size..., Handbook of..., King Conan, Marvel Graphic Novel #19, 28, Marvel Treasury Ed., Power Record Comics, Robert E. Howard's.., Savage Sword of Conan, and Savage Tales)

CONAN
Dark Horse Comics: Feb, 2004 - No. 50, May, 2008 ($2.99)
0-(11/03, 25¢-c) Busiek-s/Nord-a 2.25
1-($2.99) Linsner-c/Busiek-s/Nord-a 5.00
1-(2nd printing) J. Scott Campell-c 3.00
1-(3rd printing) Nord-c 3.00
2-49: 18-Severin & Timm-a. 22-Kaluta-a (6 pgs.) 24-Harris-c. 29-31-Mignola-s 3.00
24-Variant c with nude woman (also see Conan and the Demons of Khitai #3 for ad) 20.00
50-($4.99) Harris-c; new story and reprint from Conan the Barbarian #30 5.00
... and the Daughters of Midora (10/04, $4.99) Texiera-a/c 5.00
...: Born on the Battlefield TPB (6/08, $17.95) r/#0,8,15,23,32,45,46; Ruth sketch pages 18.00
...: The Blood-Stained Crown and Other Stories TPB (1/08, $14.95) r/#18,26-28,39 15.00
...: The Frazetta Cover Series (12/07 - No. 8, $3.50) 1,2-Reprints with Frazetta covers 3.50
HC Vol. 1: The Frost Giant's Daughter and Other Stories (2005, $24.95) r/#1-6, partial #7; signed by Busiek; Nord sketch pages 25.00
Vol. 1: The Frost Giant's Daughter and Other Stories (2005, $15.95) r/#1-6, partial #7 16.00
Vol. 2: The God in the Bowl and Other Stories HC (2005, $24.95) r/#9-14 25.00
Vol. 2: The God in the Bowl and Other Stories SC (2006, $15.95) r/#9-14 16.00
Vol. 3: The Tower of the Elephant and Other Stories HC (5/06, $24.95) r/#0,16,17,19-22 25.00
Vol. 3: The Tower of the Elephant and Other Stories SC (6/06, $15.95) r/#0,16,17,19-22 16.00
Vol. 4: The Hall of the Dead and Other Stories HC (5/07, $24.95) r/#0,24,25,29-31,33,34 25.00
Vol. 4: The Hall of the Dead and Other Stories SC (6/07, $17.95) r/#0,24,25,29-31,33,34 18.00

CONAN AND THE DEMONS OF KHITAI
Dark Horse Comics: Oct, 2005 - No. 4, Jan, 2006 ($2.99, limited series)
1,2,4-Paul Lee-a/Akira Yoshida-s/Pat Lee-c 3.00
3-1st printing with red cover logo; letters page has image of Conan #24 nude variant-c 5.00
3-2nd printing with black cover logo; letters page has image of Conan #24 regular-c 3.00
TPB (7/06, $12.95) r/series 13.00

CONAN AND THE JEWELS OF GWAHLUR
Dark Horse Comics: Apr, 2005 - No. 3, June, 2005 ($2.99, limited series)
1-3-P. Craig Russell-s/a/c 3.00
HC (12/05, $13.95) r/series; P. Craig Russell interview and sketch pages 14.00

CONAN AND THE MIDNIGHT GOD
Dark Horse Comics: Dec, 2006 - No. 5, May, 2007 ($2.99, limited series)
1-5-Dysart-s/Conrad-a/Alexander-c 3.00
TPB (10/07, $14.95) r/#1-5 and Age of Conan: Hyborian Adventures one-shot 15.00

CONAN AND THE SONGS OF THE DEAD
Dark Horse Comics: July, 2006 - No. 5, Nov, 2006 ($2.99, limited series)
1-5-Timothy Truman-a/c; Joe Lansdale-s 3.00
TPB (4/07, $14.95) r/series; Truman sketch pages 15.00

CONAN: (Title Series): Marvel Comics
CONAN, 8/95 - No. 11, 6/96 ($2.95), 1-11: 4-Malibu Comic's Rune app. 3.00
...CLASSIC, 6/94 - No. 11, 4/95 ($1.50), 1-11: 1-r/Conan #1 by B. Smith, r/covers w/changes. 2-11-r/Conan #2-11 by Smith. 2-Bound w/cover to Conan The Adventurer #2 by mistake 2.50
...DEATH COVERED IN GOLD, 9/99 - No. 3, 11/99 ($2.99), 1-3-Roy Thomas-s/ John Buscema-a 3.00
...FLAME AND THE FIEND, 8/00 - No. 3, 10/00 ($2.99), 1-3-Thomas-s 3.00
...RETURN OF STYRM, 9/98 - No. 3, 11/98 ($2.99), 1-3-Parente & Soresina-a; painted-c 3.00
...RIVER OF BLOOD, 6/98 - No. 3, 8/98 ($2.50), 1-3 2.50
...SCARLET SWORD, 12/98 - No. 3, 2/99 ($2.99), 1-3-Thomas-s/Raffaele-a 3.00

CONAN SAGA, THE
Marvel Comics: June, 1987 - No. 97, Apr, 1995 ($2.00/$2.25, B&W, magazine)
1-Barry Smith-r; new Smith-c 1 2 3 5 6 8
2-27: 2-9,11-new Barry Smith-c. 13,15-Boris-c. 17-Adams-r.18,25-Chaykin-r. 22-r/Giant-Size Conan 1,2 4.00
28-90: 28-Begin $2.25-c. 31-Red Sonja-r by N. Adams/SSOC #1; 1 pg. Jeff Jones-r. 32-Newspaper strip-r begin by Buscema. 33-Smith/Conrad-a. 39-r/Kull #1('71) by Andru & Wood. 44-Swipes-c/Savage Tales #1. 57-Brunner-r/SSOC #30. 66-r/Conan Annual #2 by Buscema. 79-r/Conan #43-45 w/Red Sonja. 85-Based on Conan #57-63 3.00
91-96 4.50
97-Last issue 1 2 3 4 5 7
NOTE: ***J. Buscema*** *r-32-on; c-86.* ***Chaykin*** *r-34.* ***Chiodo*** *painted c-63, 65, 66, 82.* ***G. Colan*** *a-47p.* ***Jusko*** *painted c-64, 83.* ***Kaluta*** *c-84.* ***Nino*** *a-37.* ***Ploog*** *a-50.* ***N. Redondo*** *painted c-48, 50, 51, 53, 57, 62.* ***Simonson*** *r-50-54, 56.* ***B. Smith*** *r-51.* ***Starlin*** *c-34.* ***Williamson*** *r-50i.*

CONAN THE ADVENTURER
Marvel Comics: June, 1994 - No. 14, July, 1995 ($1.50)
1-($2.50)-Embossed foil-c; Kayaran-a 3.00
2-14 2.50
2-Contents are Conan Classics #2 by mistake 2.50

CONAN THE BARBARIAN
Marvel Comics: Oct, 1970 - No. 275, Dec, 1993
1-Origin/1st app. Conan (in comics) by Barry Smith; 1st brief app. Kull; #1-9 are 15¢ issues 20 40 60 148 274 400
2 9 18 27 60 100 140
3-(Low distribution in some areas) 14 28 42 99 175 250
4,5 7 14 21 50 83 115
6-9: 8-Hidden panel message, pg. 14. 9-Last 15¢-c 6 12 18 39 62 85
10,11 (25¢ 52 pg. giants): 10-Black Knight-r; Kull story by Severin 7 14 21 47 76 105
12,13: 12-Wrightson-c(i) 5 10 15 34 55 75
14,15-Elric app. 6 12 18 41 66 90
16,19,20: 16-Conan-r/Savage Tales #1 5 10 15 32 51 70
17,18-No Barry Smith-a 4 8 12 24 37 50
21,22: 22-Has reprint from #1 4 8 12 26 41 55
23-1st app. Red Sonja (2/73) 6 12 18 37 59 80
24-1st full Red Sonja story; last Smith-a 5 10 15 34 55 75
25-John Buscema-c/a begins 3 6 9 16 22 28
26-30 2 4 6 11 16 20
31-36,38-40 2 4 6 8 11 14
37-Neal Adams-c/a; last 20¢ issue; contains pull-out subscription form 3 6 9 16 23 30
41-43,46-50: 48-Origin retold 1 3 4 6 8 10
44,45-N. Adams-i(Crusty Bunkers). 45-Adams-c 2 4 6 8 11 14
51-57,59,60: 59-Origin Belit 1 2 3 4 5 7
58-2nd Belit app. (see Giant-Size Conan #1) 2 4 6 8 10 12
61-65-(Regular 25¢ editions)(4-8/76) 6.00
61-65-(30¢-c variants, limited distribution) 5 10 15 30 48 65
66-99: 68-Red Sonja story cont'd from Marvel Feature #7. 75-79-(Reg. 30¢-c). 84-Intro. Zula. 85-Origin Zula. 87-r/Savage Sword of Conan #3 in color 5.00
75-79-(35¢-c variants, limited distribution) 4 8 12 26 41 55
100-(52 pg. Giant)-Death of Belit 1 2 3 5 6 8
101-114 3.00
115-Double size 4.00
116-199,201-231,233-249: 116-r/Power Record Comic PR31. 244-Zula returns 3.00
200,232: 200-(52 pgs.). 232-Young Conan storyline begins; Conan is born 4.50
250-(60 pgs.) 5.00
251-270: 262-Adapted from R.E. Howard story 4.00
271-274 6.00
275-($2.50, 68 pgs.)-Final issue; painted-c (low print) 2 4 6 10 14 18
King Size 1(1973, 35¢)-Smith-r/#2,4; Smith-c 3 6 9 17 25 32
Annual 2(1976, 50¢)-New full length story 2 4 6 0 11 14
Annual 3,4: 3('78)-Chaykin/N. Adams-r/SSOC #2. 4('78)-New full length story 1 3 4 6 8 10
Annual 5,6: 5(1979)-New full length Buscema story & part-c, 6(1981)-Kane-c/a 6.00
Annual 7-12: 7('82)-Based on novel "Conan of the Isles" (new-a). 8(1984). 9(1984). 10(1986). 11(1986). 12(1987) 4.00
Special Edition 1 (Red Nails) 4.00
The Chronicles of Conan Vol. 1: Tower of the Elephant and Other Stories (Dark Horse, 2003, $15.95) r/#1-8; afterword by Roy Thomas 16.00
The Chronicles of Conan Vol. 2: Rogues in the House and Other Stories (Dark Horse, 2003, $15.95) r/#9-13,16; afterword by Roy Thomas 16.00
The Chronicles of Conan Vol. 3: The Monster of the Monoliths and Other Stories (Dark Horse, 2003, $15.95) r/#14,15,17-21; afterword by Roy Thomas 16.00
The Chronicles of Conan Vol. 4: The Song of Red Sonja and Other Stories (Dark Horse, 2004, $15.95) r/#23-26 & "Red Nails" from Savage Tales; afterword by Roy Thomas 16.00
The Chronicles of Conan Vol. 5: The Shadow in the Tomb and Other Stories (Dark Horse, 2004, $15.95) r/#27-34; afterword by Roy Thomas 16.00
The Chronicles of Conan Vol. 6: The Curse of the Skull and Other Stories (Dark Horse, 2004, $15.95) r/#35-42; afterword by Roy Thomas 16.00
The Chronicles of Conan Vol. 7: The Dweller in the Pool and Other Stories (Dark Horse, 2005, $15.95) r/#43-51; afterword by Roy Thomas 16.00
The Chronicles of Conan Vol. 8: Brothers of the Blade and Other Stories (Dark Horse,

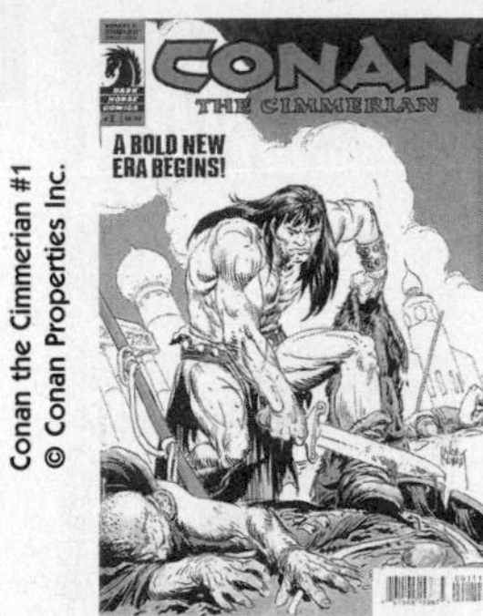

Conan the Cimmerian #1
© Conan Properties Inc.

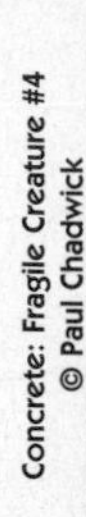
Concrete: Fragile Creature #4
© Paul Chadwick

Confessions of Love #14 © STAR

GD VG FN VF VF/NM NM-
2.0 4.0 6.0 8.0 9.0 9.2

2005, $16.95) r/#52-59; afterword by Roy Thomas 17.00
The Chronicles of Conan Vol. 9: Riders of the River-Dragons and Other Stories (Dark Horse, 11/05, $16.95) r/#60-63,65,69-71; afterword by Roy Thomas 17.00
The Chronicles of Conan Vol. 10: When Giants Walk the Earth and Other Stories (Dark Horse, 3/06, $16.95) r/#72-77,79-82; afterword by Roy Thomas 17.00
The Chronicles of Conan Vol. 11: The Dance of the Skull and Other Stories (Dark Horse, 2/07, $16.95) r/#82-86,88-90; afterword by Roy Thomas 17.00
The Chronicles of Conan Vol. 12: The King Beast of Abombi and Other Stories (Dark Horse, 7/07, $16.95) r/#91,93-100; afterword by Roy Thomas 17.00
The Chronicles of Conan Vol. 13: Whispering Shadows and Other Stories (Dark Horse, 12/07, $16.95) r/#92,100-107; afterword by Roy Thomas 17.00
The Chronicles of Conan Vol. 14: Shadow of the Beast and Other Stories (Dark Horse, 3/08, $16.95) r/#92,108-115; afterword by Roy Thomas 17.00
The Chronicles of Conan Vol. 15: The Corridor of Mullah-Kajar and Other Stories (Dark Horse, 7/08, $16.95) r/#116-121 & Annual #2; afterword by Roy Thomas 17.00

NOTE: ***Arthur Adams** c-248, 249. **Neal Adams** a-116r(i); c-49i. **Austin** a-125, 126; c-125i, 126i. **Brunner** c-17i. c-40. **Buscema** a-25-36p, 38, 39, 41-56p, 58-63p, 65-67p, 68, 70-78p, 84-86p, 88-91p, 93-126p, 136p, 140, 141-144p, 146-158p, 159, 161, 162, 163p, 165-185p, 187-190p, Annual 2(3pgs.). 3-5p, 7p; c(p)-26, 36, 44, 46, 52, 56, 58, 59, 64, 65, 72, 78-80, 83-91, 93-103, 105-126, 136-151, 155-159, 161, 162, 168, 169, 171, 172, 174, 175, 178-185, 188, 189, Annual 4, 5, 7. **Chaykin** a-79-83. **Golden** c-152. **Kaluta** c-167. **Gil Kane** a-12p, 17p, 18p, 127-130, 131-134p; c-12p, 17p, 18p, 23, 25, 27-32, 34, 35, 38, 39, 41-43, 45-51, 53-55, 57, 60-63, 65-71, 73p, 76p, 127-134. **Jim Lee** c-242. **McFarlane** c-241p. **Ploog** a-57. **Russell** a-21; c-251i. **Simonson** c-135. **B. Smith** a-1-11p, 12, 13-15p, 16, 19-21, 23, 24; c-1-11, 13-16, 19-24p. **Starlin** a-64. **Wood** a-47r. Issue Nos. 3-5, 7-9, 11, 16-18, 21, 23, 25, 27-30, 35, 37, 38, 42, 45, 52, 57, 58, 65, 69-71, 73, 79-83, 99, 100, 104, 114, Annual 2 have original Robert E. Howard stories adapted. Issues #32-34 adapted from Norvell Page's novel **Flame Winds**.*

CONAN THE BARBARIAN (Volume 2)
Marvel Comics: July, 1997 - No. 3, Oct, 1997 ($2.50, limited series)

1-3-Castellini-a 3.00

CONAN THE BARBARIAN MOVIE SPECIAL (Movie)
Marvel Comics Group: Oct, 1982 - No. 2, Nov, 1982

1,2-Movie adaptation; Buscema-a 3.50

CONAN THE BARBARIAN: THE USURPER
Marvel Comics: Dec, 1997 - No. 3, Feb, 1998 ($2.50, limited series)

1-3-Dixon-s 3.00

CONAN: THE BOOK OF THOTH
Dark Horse Comics: Mar, 2006 - No. 4, June, 2006 ($4.99, limited series)

1-4-Origin of Thoth-amon; Len Wein & Kurt Busiek-s/Kelley Jones-a/c 5.00
TPB (12/06, $17.95) r/#1-4 18.00

CONAN THE CIMMERIAN
Dark Horse Comics: No. 0, Jun, 2008 - Present (99¢/$2.99)

0-Follows Conan #50; Truman-s/Giorello-a/c 3.00
1-(7/08, $2.99) Two covers by Joe Kubert and Cho; Giorello & Corben-a 3.00
2-Cho-c; Giorello & Corben-a 3.00

CONAN THE DESTROYER (Movie)
Marvel Comics Group: Jan, 1985 - No. 2, Mar, 1985

1,2-r/Marvel Super Special 3.00

CONAN THE KING (Formerly King Conan)
Marvel Comics Group: No. 20, Jan, 1984 - No. 55, Nov, 1989

20-49 4.00
50-54 5.00
55-Last issue 1 2 3 5 6 8

NOTE: ***Kaluta** c-20-23, 24i, 26, 27, 30, 50, 52. **Williamson** a-37i; c-37i, 38i.*

CONAN: THE LEGEND (See Conan 2004 series)

CONAN: THE LORD OF THE SPIDERS
Marvel Comics: Mar, 1998 - No. 3, May, 1998 ($2.50, limited series)

1-3-Roy Thomas-s/Raffaele-a 3.00

CONAN THE SAVAGE
Marvel Comics: Aug, 1995 - No. 10, May, 1996 ($2.95, B&W, Magazine)

1-10: 1-Bisley-c. 4-vs. Malibu Comics' Rune. 5,10-Brereton-c 4.00

CONAN VS. RUNE (Also See Conan #4)
Marvel Comics: Nov, 1995 ($2.95, one-shot)

1-Barry Smith-c/a/scripts 4.00

CONCRETE (Also see Dark Horse Presents & Within Our Reach)
Dark Horse Comics: March, 1987 - No. 10, Nov, 1988 ($1.50, B&W)

1-Paul Chadwick-c/a in all 1 3 4 6 8 10
1-2nd print 3.00
2 6.00
3-Origin 5.00
4-10 4.00
A New Life 1 (1989, $2.95, B&W)-r/#3,4 plus new-a (11 pgs.) 3.00
Celebrates Earth Day 1990 ($3.50, 52 pgs.) 6.00
Color Special 1 (2/89, $2.95, 44 pgs.)-r/1st two Concrete apps. from Dark Horse Presents #1,2 plus new-a 6.00
Depths TPB (7/05, $12.95)-r/#1-5, stories from DHP #1,8,10,150; other short stories 13.00
Land And Sea 1 (2/89, $2.95, B&W)-r/#1,2 6.00
Odd Jobs 1 (7/90, $3.50)-r/5,6 plus new-a 3.50
...Vol. 1: Depths ('05, $12.95, 9"x6") r/#1-5 & short stories 13.00
...Vol. 2: Heights ('05, $12.95, 9"x6") r/#6-10 & short stories 13.00
...Vol. 3: Fragile Creatures (1/06, $12.95, 9"x6") r/mini-series & short stories from DHP 13.00
...Vol. 4: Killer Smile (3/06, $12.95, 9"x6") r/mini-series & short stories from various 13.00
...Vol. 5: Think Like a Mountain (5/06, $12.95, 9"x6") r/mini-series & short stories 13.00
...Vol. 6: Strange Armor (7/06, $12.95, 9"x6") r/mini-series & short stories 13.00
...Vol. 7: The Human Dilemma (4/06, $12.95, 9"x6") r/mini-series 13.00

CONCRETE: (Title series), **Dark Horse Comics**

--ECLECTICA, 4/93 - No. 2, 5/93 ($2.95) 1,2 3.00

--FRAGILE CREATURE, 6/91 - No. 4, 2/92 ($2.50) 1-4 3.00

--KILLER SMILE, (Legend), 7/94 - No. 4, 10/94 ($2.9) 1-4 3.00

--STRANGE ARMOR, 12/97 - No. 5, 5/98 ($2.95, color) 1-5-Chadwick-s/c/a; retells origin 3.00

--THE HUMAN DILEMMA, 12/04 - No. 6, 5/05 ($3.50)
1-6: Chadwick-a/c & scripts; Concrete has a child 3.50

--THINK LIKE A MOUNTAIN, (Legend), 3/96 - No. 6, 8/96 ($2.95)
1-6: Chadwick-a/scripts & Darrow-c in all 3.00

CONDORMAN (Walt Disney)
Whitman Publishing: Oct, 1981 - No. 3, Jan, 1982

1-3: 1,2-Movie adaptation; photo-c 1 3 4 6 8 10

CONEHEADS
Marvel Comics: June, 1994 - No. 4, 1994 ($1.75, limited series)

1-4 2.50

CONFESSIONS ILLUSTRATED (Magazine)
E. C. Comics: Jan-Feb, 1956 - No. 2, Spring, 1956

1-Craig, Kamen, Wood, Orlando-a 29 58 87 169 272 375
2-Craig, Crandall, Kamen, Orlando-a 21 42 63 125 200 275

CONFESSIONS OF LOVE
Artful Publ.: Apr, 1950 - No. 2, July, 1950 (25¢, 7-1/4x5-1/4", 132 pgs.)

1-Bakerish-a 29 58 87 169 272 375
2-Art & text; Bakerish-a 18 36 54 105 165 225

CONFESSIONS OF LOVE (Formerly Startling Terror Tales #10; becomes Confessions of Romance No. 7 on)
Star Publications: No. 11, 7/52 - No. 14, 1/53; No. 4, 3/53- No. 6, 8/53

11-13: 12,13-Disbrow-a 15 30 45 90 140 190
14,5,6 14 28 42 78 112 145
4-Disbrow-a 14 28 42 81 118 155

NOTE: *All have **L. B. Cole** covers.*

CONFESSIONS OF ROMANCE (Formerly Confessions of Love)
Star Publications: No. 7, Nov, 1953 - No. 11, Nov, 1954

7 15 30 45 90 140 190
8 14 28 42 78 112 145
9-Wood-a 15 30 45 84 127 170
10,11-Disbrow-a 14 28 42 81 118 155

NOTE: *All have **L. B. Cole** covers.*

CONFESSIONS OF THE LOVELORN (Formerly Lovelorn)
American Comics Group (Regis Publ./Best Synd. Features): No. 52, Aug, 1954 - No. 114, June-July, 1960

52 (3-D effect) 29 58 87 169 272 375
53,55 11 22 33 60 83 105
54 (3-D effect) 29 58 87 169 272 375
56-Anti-communist propaganda story, 10 pgs; last pre-code (2/55)
14 28 42 80 115 150
57-90,100 8 16 24 44 57 70
91-Williamson-a 10 20 30 54 72 90
92-99,101-114 7 14 21 37 46 55

NOTE: ***Whitney** a-most issues; c-52, 53. Painted c-106, 107.*

CONFIDENTIAL DIARY (Formerly High School Confidential Diary; Three Nurses #18 on)
Charlton Comics: No. 12, May, 1962 - No. 17, Mar, 1963

12-17 3 6 9 15 21 26

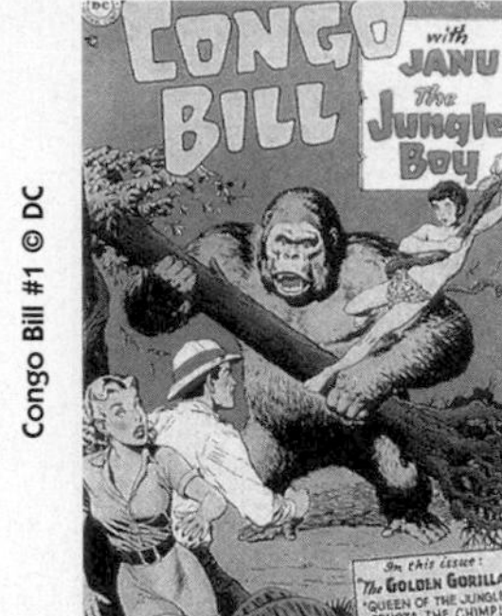

Congo Bill #1 © DC

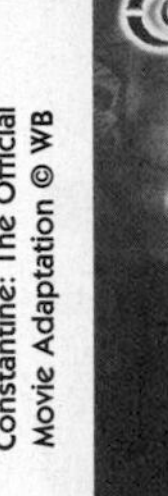

Constantine: The Official Movie Adaptation © WB

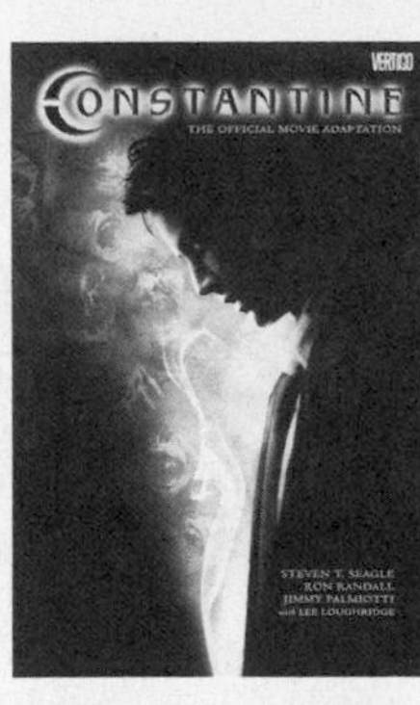

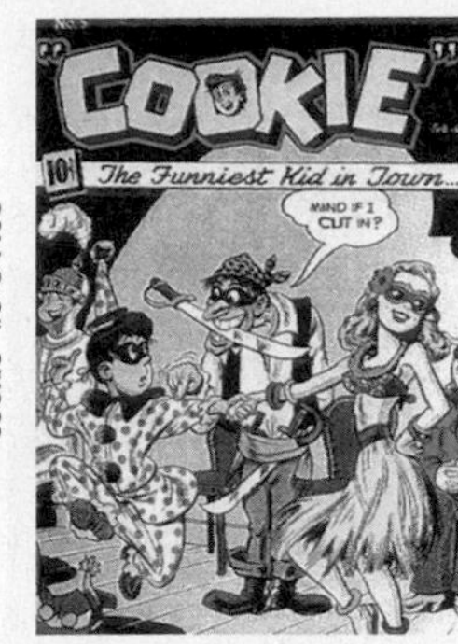

"Cookie" #5 © ACG

GD VG FN VF VF/NM NM-
2.0 4.0 6.0 8.0 9.0 9.2

GD VG FN VF VF/NM NM-
2.0 4.0 6.0 8.0 9.0 9.2

CONGO BILL (See Action Comics & More Fun Comics #56)
National Periodical Publication: Aug-Sept, 1954 - No. 7, Aug-Sept, 1955
1 (Scarce) 181 388 582 1550 - -
2,7 (Scarce) 122 244 366 975 - -
3-6 (Scarce). 4-Last pre-code issue 97 194 291 775 - -
NOTE: *(Rarely found in fine to mint condition.)* ***Nick Cardy** c-1-7.*

CONGO BILL
DC Comics (Vertigo): Oct, 1999 - No. 4, Jan, 2000 ($2.95, limited series)
1-4-Corben-c 3.00

CONGORILLA (Also see Actions Comics #224)
DC Comics: Nov, 1992 - No. 4, Feb, 1993 ($1.75, limited series)
1-4: 1,2-Brian Bolland-c 3.00

CONJURORS
DC Comics: Apr, 1999 - No. 3, Jun, 1999 ($2.95, limited series)
1-3-Elseworlds; Phantom Stranger app.; Barreto-c/a 3.00

CONNECTICUT YANKEE, A (See King Classics)

CONNOR HAWKE: DRAGON'S BLOOD (Also see Green Arrow titles)
DC Comics: Jan, 2007 - No. 6, Jun, 2007 ($2.99, limited series)
1-6-Chuck Dixon-s/Derec Donovan-a/c 3.00
SC (2008, $19.99) r/#1-6 20.00

CONQUEROR, THE
Dell Publishing Co.: No., 690, Mar, 1956
Four Color 690-Movie, John Wayne photo-c 15 30 45 108 199 290

CONQUEROR COMICS
Albrecht Publishing Co.: Winter, 1945
nn 21 42 63 123 197 270

CONQUEROR OF THE BARREN EARTH (See The Warlord #63)
DC Comics: Feb, 1985 - No. 4, May, 1985 (Limited series)
1-4: Back-up series from Warlord 2.50

CONQUEST
Store Comics: 1953 (6¢)
1-Richard the Lion Hearted, Beowulf, Swamp Fox 7 14 21 35 43 50

CONQUEST
Famous Funnies: Spring, 1955
1-Crandall-a, 1 pg.; contains contents of 1953 ish. 5 10 15 22 26 30

CONSPIRACY
Marvel Comics: Feb, 1998 - No. 2, Mar, 1998 ($2.99, limited series)
1,2-Painted art by Korday/Abnett-s 3.00

CONSTANTINE (Also see Hellblazer)
DC Comics (Vertigo): 2005 (Based on the 2005 Keanu Reeves movie)
...: The Hellblazer Collection (2005, $14.95) Movie adaptation and r/#1, 27, 41; photo-c 15.00
...: The Official Movie Adaptation (2005, $6.95) Seagle-s/Randall-a/photo-c 7.00

CONSTRUCT
Caliber (New Worlds): 1996 - No. 6, 1997 ($2.95, B&W, limited series)
1-6: Paul Jenkins scripts 3.00

CONSUMED
Platinum Studios: July, 2007 - No. 4, Oct, 2007 ($2.99, limited series)
1-4-Linsner-c/Budd-a/Shumskas-Tait-s 3.00

CONTACT COMICS
Aviation Press: July, 1944 - No. 12, May, 1946
nn-Black Venus, Flamingo, Golden Eagle, Tommy Tomahawk begin 53 106 159 331 558 785
2-5: 3-Last Flamingo. 3,4-Black Venus by L. B. Cole. 5-The Phantom Flyer app. 40 80 120 240 390 540
6,11-Kurtzman's Black Venus; 11-Last Golden Eagle, last Tommy Tomahawk; Feldstein-a 46 92 138 285 478 670
7-10 40 80 120 235 380 525
12-Sky Rangers, Air Kids, Ace Diamond app.; L.B. Cole sci-fi cover 110 220 330 693 1172 1650
NOTE: ***L. B. Cole** a-3, 9; c-1-12. **Giunta** a-3. **Hollingsworth** a-5, 7, 10. **Palais** a-11, 12.*

CONTEMPORARY MOTIVATORS
Pendelum Press: 1977 - 1978 ($1.45, 5-3/8x8", 31 pgs., B&W)
14-3002 The Caine Mutiny; 14-3010 Banner in the Sky; 14-3029 God Is My Co-Pilot; 14-3037 Guadalcanal Diary; 14-3045 Hiroshima; 14-3053 Hot Rod; 14-3061 Just Dial a Number; 14-3088 The Diary of Anne Frank; 14-3096 Lost Horizon 1 3 4 6 8 10
NOTE: *Also see Pendulum Illustrated Classics. Above may have been distributed the same.*

CONTEST OF CHAMPIONS (See Marvel Super-Hero...)

CONTEST OF CHAMPIONS II
Marvel Comics: Sept, 1999 - No. 5 ($2.50, limited series)
1-5-Claremont-s/Jimenez-a 2.50

CONTRACTORS
Eclipse Comics: June, 1987 ($2.00, B&W, one-shot)
1-Funny animal 2.50

CONTRACT WITH GOD, A
Baronet Publishing Co./Kitchen Sink Press: 1978 ($4.95/$7.95, B&W, graphic novel)
nn-Will Eisner-s/a 2 4 6 13 18 22
Reprint (DC Comics, 2000, $12.95) 13.00

CONVOCATIONS: A MAGIC THE GATHERING GALLERY
Acclaim Comics (Armada): Jan, 1996 ($2.50, one-shot)
1-pin-ups by various artists including Kaluta, Vess, and Dringenberg 2.50

COO COO COMICS (...the Bird Brain No. 57 on)
Nedor Publ. Co./Standard (Animated Cartoons): Oct, 1942 - No. 62, Apr, 1952
1-Origin/1st app. Super Mouse & begin series (cloned from Superman); the first funny animal super hero series (see Looney Tunes #5 for 1st funny animal super hero) 31 62 93 181 291 400
2 15 30 45 86 133 180
3-10: 10-(3/44) 11 22 33 60 83 105
11-33: 33-1 pg. Ingels-a 9 18 27 50 65 80
34-40,43-46,48-Text illos by Frazetta in all. 36-Super Mouse covers begin 11 22 33 64 90 115
41-Frazetta-a (6-pg. story & 3 text illos) 21 42 63 125 200 275
42,47-Frazetta-a & text illos. 15 30 45 86 133 180
49-(1/50) 3-D effect story; Frazetta text illo 14 28 42 76 108 140
50,51-3-D effect-c only. 50-Frazetta text illo 13 26 39 72 101 130
52-62: 56-58,61-Super Mouse app. 8 16 24 42 54 65

"COOKIE" (Also see Topsy-Turvy)
Michel Publ./American Comics Group(Regis Publ.): Apr, 1946 - No. 55, Aug-Sept, 1955
1-Teen-age humor 22 44 66 131 211 290
2 14 28 42 78 112 145
3-10 11 22 33 60 83 105
11-20 9 18 27 52 69 85
21-23,26,28-30 8 16 24 42 54 65
24,25,27-Starlett O'Hara stories 8 16 24 44 57 70
31-34,37-48,50,52-55 7 14 21 37 46 55
35,36-Starlett O'Hara stories 8 16 24 42 54 65
49,51: 49-(6-7/54)-3-D effect-c/s. 51-(10-11/54) 8pg. TrueVision 3-D effect story 12 24 36 67 94 120

COOL CAT (Formerly Black Magic)
Prize Publications: V8#6, Mar-Apr, 1962 - V9#2, July-Aug, 1962
V8#6, nn(V9#1, 5-6/62), V9#2 3 6 9 17 25 32

COOL WORLD (Movie by Ralph Bakshi)
DC Comics: Apr, 1992 - No. 4, Sept, 1992 ($1.75, limited series)
1-4: Prequel to animated/live action movie. 1-Bakshi-c. Bill Wray inks in all 2.50
Movie Adaptation nn ('92, $3.50, 68pg.)-Bakshi-c 3.50

COPPER CANYON (See Fawcett Movie Comics)

COPS (TV)
DC Comics: Aug, 1988 - No. 15, Aug, 1989 ($1.00)
1 ($1.50, 52 pgs.)-Based on Hasbro Toys 3.00
2-15: 14-Orlando-c(p) 2.50

COPS: THE JOB
Marvel Comics: June, 1992 - No. 4, Sept, 1992 ($1.25, limited series)
1-4: All have Jusko scripts & Golden-c 2.50

CORBEN SPECIAL, A
Pacific Comics: May, 1984 (one-shot)
1-Corben-c/a; E.A. Poe adaptation 5.00

CORE, THE
Image Comics: July, 2008 ($3.99)
Pilot Season - Hickman-s/Rocafort-a 4.00

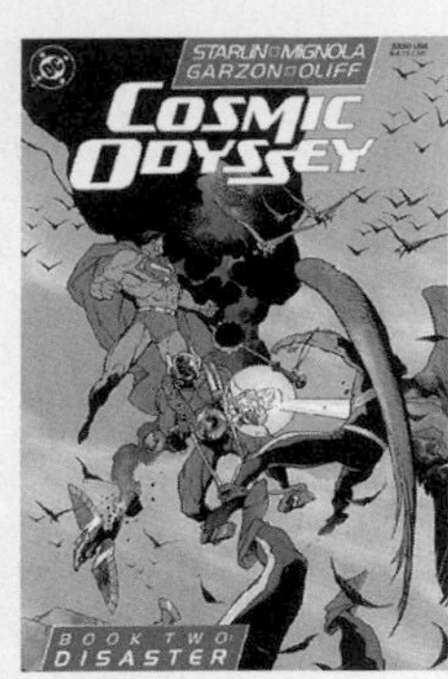

Cosmic Odyssey #2 © DC

Cosmo Cat #5 © FOX

Countdown #36 © DC

GD 2.0 | VG 4.0 | FN 6.0 | VF 8.0 | VF/NM 9.0 | NM- 9.2

CORKY & WHITE SHADOW (Disney, TV)
Dell Publishing Co.: No. 707, May, 1956 (Mickey Mouse Club)

	GD	VG	FN	VF	VF/NM	NM-
Four Color 707-Photo-c	7	14	21	47	76	105

CORLISS ARCHER (See Meet Corliss Archer)

CORMAC MAC ART (Robert E. Howard's...)
Dark Horse Comics: 1990 - No. 4, 1990 ($1.95, B&W, mini-series)

1-4: All have Bolton painted-c; Howard adapts. 3.00

CORNY'S FETISH
Dark Horse Comics: Apr, 1998 ($4.95, B&W, one-shot)

1-Renée French-s/a; Bolland-c 5.00

CORPORAL RUSTY DUGAN (See Holyoke One-Shot #2)

CORPSES OF DR. SACOTTI, THE (See Ideal a Classical Comic)

CORSAIR, THE (See A-1 Comics No. 5, 7, 10 under Texas Slim)

CORTEZ AND THE FALL OF THE AZTECS
Tome Press: 1993 ($2.95, B&W, limited series)

1,2 3.00

CORUM: THE BULL AND THE SPEAR (See Chronicles Of Corum)
First Comics: Jan, 1989 - No. 4, July, 1989 ($1.95)

1-4: Adapts Michael Moorcock's novel 2.50

COSMIC BOOK, THE
Ace Comics: Dec, 1986 - No. 1, 1987 ($1.95)

1,2: 1-(44pgs.)-Wood, Toth-a. 2-(B&W) 2.50

COSMIC BOY (Also see The Legion of Super-Heroes)
DC Comics: Dec, 1986 - No. 4, Mar, 1987 (limited series)

1-4: Legends tie-ins all issues 2.50

COSMIC GUARD
Devil's Due Publ.: Aug, 2004 - No. 6, Dec, 2005 ($2.99)

1-6-Jim Starlin-s/a 3.00

COSMIC HEROES
Eternity/Malibu Graphics: Oct, 1988 - No. 11, Dec, 1989 ($1.95, B&W)

1-11: Reprints 1934-1936's Buck Rogers newspaper strips #1-728 2.50

COSMIC ODYSSEY
DC Comics: 1988 - No. 4, 1988 ($3.50, limited series, squarebound)

1-4: Reintro. New Gods into DC continuity; Superman, Batman, Green Lantern (John Stewart) app; Starlin scripts, Mignola-c/a in all. 2-Darkseid merges Demon & Jason Blood (separated in Demon limited series #4) 5.00
Trade paperback-r/#1-4. 20.00

COSMIC POWERS
Marvel Comics: Mar, 1994 - No. 6, Aug, 1994 ($2.50, limited series)

1-6: 1-Ron Lim-c/a(p). 1,2-Thanos app. 2-Terrax. 3-Ganymede & Jack of Hearts app. 2.50

COSMIC POWERS UNLIMITED
Marvel Comics: May, 1995 - No. 5, May, 1996 ($3.95, quarterly)

1-5 4.00

COSMIC RAY
Image Comics: June, 1999 - No. 2 ($2.95, B&W)

1,2-Steven Blue-s/a 3.00

COSMIC SLAM
Ultimate Sports Entertainment: 1999 ($3.95, one-shot)

1-McGwire, Sosa, Bagwell, Justice battle aliens; Sienkiewicz-c 4.00

COSMO CAT (Becomes Sunny #11 on; also see All Top & Wotalife Comics)
Fox Publications/Green Publ. Co./Norlen Mag.: July-Aug, 1946 - No. 10, Oct, 1947; 1957; 1959

	GD	VG	FN	VF	VF/NM	NM-
1	26	52	78	154	247	340
2	15	30	45	84	127	170
3-Origin (11-12/46)	18	36	54	107	169	230
4-Robot-c	14	28	42	76	108	140
5-10	11	22	33	60	83	105
2-4(1957-Green Publ. Co.)	6	12	18	27	33	38
2-4(1959-Norlen Mag.)	5	10	15	23	28	32
I.W. Reprint #1	2	4	6	11	16	20

COSMO THE MERRY MARTIAN
Archie Publications (Radio Comics): Sept, 1958 - No. 6, Oct, 1959

	GD	VG	FN	VF	VF/NM	NM-
1-Bob White-a in all	15	30	45	84	127	170
2-6	11	22	33	60	83	105

COTTON WOODS
Dell Publishing Co.: No. 837, Sept, 1957

	GD	VG	FN	VF	VF/NM	NM-
Four Color 837	4	8	12	24	37	50

COUGAR, THE (Cougar No. 2)
Seaboard Periodicals (Atlas): April, 1975 - No. 2, July, 1975

	GD	VG	FN	VF	VF/NM	NM-
1,2: 1-Vampire; Adkins-a(p). 2-Cougar origin; werewolf-s; Buckler-c(p)	1	3	4	6	8	10

COUNTDOWN (See Movie Classics)

COUNTDOWN
DC Comics (WildStorm): June, 2000 - No. 8, Jan, 2001 ($2.95)

1-8-Mariotte-s/Lopresti-a 3.00

COUNTDOWN (Continued from 52 weekly series)
DC Comics: No. 51, July, 2007 - No. 1, June, 2008 ($2.99, weekly, limited series) (issue #s go in reverse)

51-Gatefold wraparound-c by Andy Kubert; Duela Dent killed; the Monitors app. 3.00
50-1: 50-Joker-c. 48-Lightray dies. 47-Mary Marvel gains Black Adam's powers. 46-Intro. Forerunner. 43-Funeral for Bart Allen. 39-Karate Kid-c 3.00
Countdown to Final Crisis Vol. 1 TPB (2008, $19.99) r/#51-39 20.00

COUNTDOWN: ARENA (Takes place during Countdown #21-18)
DC Comics: Feb, 2008 - No. 4, Feb, 2008 ($3.99, weekly, limited series)

1-4-Battles between alternate earth heroes; McDaniel-a; Andy Kubert variant-c on each 4.00

COUNTDOWN PRESENTS: LORD HAVOK & THE EXTREMISTS
DC Comics: Dec, 2007 - No. 8 ($2.99, limited series)

1-6: 1-Tieri-s/Sharp-a/c; Challengers From Beyond app. 3.00

COUNTDOWN PRESENTS THE SEARCH FOR RAY PALMER (Leads into Countdown #18)
DC Comics: Nov, 2007 - Feb, 2008 ($2.99, series of one-shots)

...: Wildstorm (11/07) Part 1; The Authority app.; Art Adams-c/Unzueta-a 3.00
...: Crime Society (12/07) Earth-3 Owlman & Jokester app.; Igle-a 3.00
...: Red Rain (1/08) Vampire Batman app.; Kelley Jones-c; Jones, Battle & Unzueta-a 3.00
...: Gotham By Gaslight (1/08) Victorian Batman app.; Tocchini-a/Nguyen-c 3.00
...: Red Son (2/08) Soviet Superman app.; Foreman-a 3.00
...: Superwoman/Batwoman (2/08) Conclusion; gender-reversed heroes; Sook-c 3.00
TPB (2008, $17.99) r/one-shots 18.00

COUNTDOWN SPECIAL
DC Comics: Dec, 2007 - Jun, 2008 ($4.99, collection of reprints related to Countdown)

...: Eclipso (5/08) r/Eclipso #10 & Spectre #17,18 (1994); Sook-c 5.00
...: Jimmy Olsen (1/08) r/Superman's Pal, Jimmy Olsen #136,147,148; Kirby-s/a; Sook-c 5.00
...: Kamandi (6/08) r/Kamandi: The Last Boy on Earth #1,10,29; Kirby-s/a; Sook-c 5.00
...: New Gods (3/08) r/Forever People #1, Mr. Miracle #1, New Gods #7; Kirby-s/a; Sook-c 5.00
...: Omac (4/08) r/Omac (1974) #1, Warlord #37-39, DC Comics Presents #61; Sook-c 5.00
...: The Atom 1,2 (2/08) r/stories from Super-Team Family #11-14; Sook-c on both 5.00
...: The Flash (12/07) r/Rogues Gallery in Flash (1st series) #106,113,155,174; Sook-c 5.00

COUNTDOWN TO ADVENTURE
DC Comics: Oct, 2007 - No. 8, May, 2008 ($3.99, limited series)

1-8: 1-Adam Strange, Animal Man and Starfire app.; origin of Forerunner 4.00

COUNTDOWN TO INFINITE CRISIS (See DC Countdown)

COUNTDOWN TO MYSTERY
DC Comics: Nov, 2007 - No. 8, Jun, 2008 ($3.99, limited series)

1-8: 1-Doctor Fate, Eclipso, The Spectre and Plastic Man app. 4.00

COUNT DUCKULA (TV)
Marvel Comics: Nov, 1988 - No. 15, Jan, 1991 ($1.00)

1,8: 1-Dangermouse back-up. 8-Geraldo Rivera photo-c/& app.; Sienkiewicz-a(i) 5.00
2-7,9-15: Dangermouse back-ups in all 4.00

COUNT OF MONTE CRISTO, THE
Dell Publishing Co.: No. 794, May, 1957

	GD	VG	FN	VF	VF/NM	NM-
Four Color 794-Movie, Buscema-a	8	16	24	56	93	130

COUP D'ETAT (Oneshots)
DC Comics (WildStorm): April, 2004 ($2.95, weekly limited series)

...: Sleeper 1 (part 1 of 4) Jim Lee-a; 2 covers by Lee and Bermejo 3.00
...: Stormwatch 1 (part 2 of 4) D'Anda-a; 2 covers by D'Anda and Bermejo 3.00
...: Wildcats Version 3.0 1 (part 3 of 4) Garza-a; 2 covers by Garza and Bermejo 3.00
...: The Authority 1 (part 4 of 4) Portacio-a; 2 covers by Portacio and Bermejo 3.00
...: Afterword 1 (5/04) Profile pages and prelude stories for Sleeper & Wetworks 3.00
TPB (2004, $12.95) r/series and profile pages from Afterword 13.00

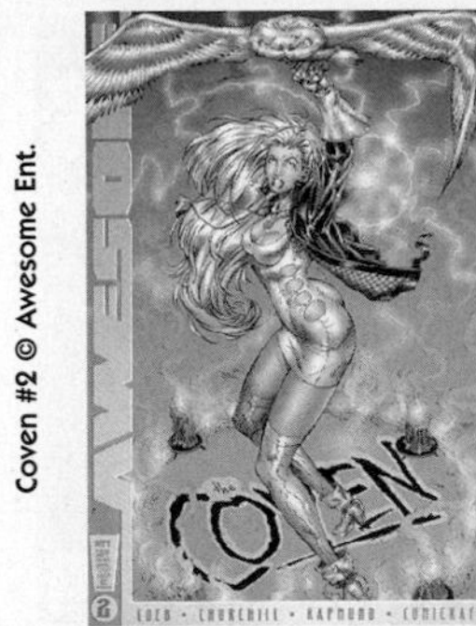

Coven #2 © Awesome Ent.

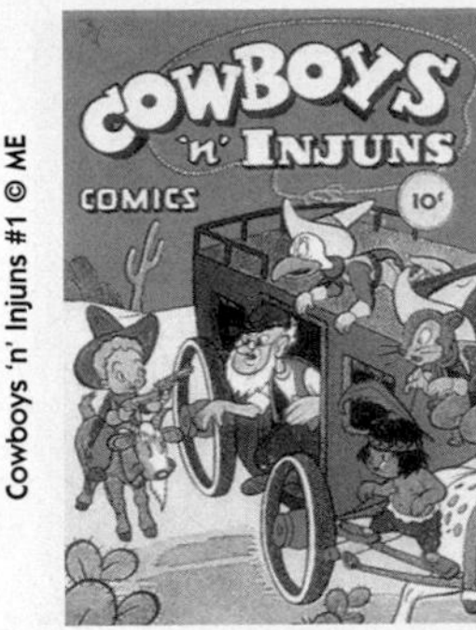

Cowboys 'n' Injuns #1 © ME

Cowboy Western Comics #27 © CC

	GD 2.0	VG 4.0	FN 6.0	VF 8.0	VF/NM 9.0	NM- 9.2

COURAGE COMICS
J. Edward Slavin: 1945

1,2,77	14	28	42	80	115	150

COURTNEY CRUMRIN...
Oni Press: July, 2005; July 2007 ($5.95, B&W, series of one-shots)

... And The Fire Thief's Tale (7/07) Naifeh-s/a						6.00
... Tales Portrait of the Warlock as a Young Man (7/05) origin Uncle Aloysius; Naifeh-s/a						6.00

COURTNEY CRUMRIN & THE COVEN OF MYSTICS
Oni Press: Dec, 2002 - No. 4, March, 2003 ($2.95, B&W, limited series)

1-4-Ted Naifeh-s/a						3.00
TPB (9/03, $11.95, 8" x 5-1/2") r/#1-4						12.00

COURTNEY CRUMRIN & THE NIGHT THINGS (Also see Promotional Section for FCBD Ed.)
Oni Press: Mar, 2002 - No. 4, June, 2002 ($2.95, B&W, limited series)

1-4-Ted Naifeh-s/a						3.00
TPB (12/02, $11.95) r/#1-4						12.00

COURTNEY CRUMRIN IN THE TWILIGHT KINGDOM
Oni Press: Dec, 2003 - No. 4, May, 2004 ($2.99, B&W, limited series)

1-4-Ted Naifeh-s/a						3.00
TPB (9/04, $11.95, digest-size) r/#1-4						12.00

COURTSHIP OF EDDIE'S FATHER (TV)
Dell Publishing Co.: Jan, 1970 - No. 2, May, 1970

1-Bill Bixby photo-c on both	6	12	18	37	59	80
2	4	8	12	24	37	50

COVEN
Awesome Entertainment: Aug, 1997 - No. 5, Mar, 1998 ($2.50)

Preview	1	2	3	5	6	8
1-Loeb-s/Churchill-a; three covers by Churchill, Liefeld, Pollina	1	2	3	5	6	8
1-Fan Appreciation Ed (3/98); new Churchill-c						3.00
1+ :Includes B&W art from Kaboom	1	3	4	6	8	10
2-Regular-c w/leaping Fantom						6.00
2-Variant-c w/circle of candles	1	2	3	5	6	8
3-6-Contains flip book preview of ReGex						3.00
3-White variant-c	1	2	3	4	5	7
3,4: 3-Halloween wraparound-c. 4-Purple variant-c						3.00
...Black & White (9/98) Short stories						3.00
...Fantom Special (2/98) w/sketch pages						5.00

COVEN
Awesome Entertainment: Jan, 1999 - No. 3, June, 1999 ($2.50)

1-3: 1-Loeb-s/Churchill-a; 6 covers by various. 2-Supreme-c/app. 3-Flip book w/Kaboom preview						2.50
... Dark Origins (7/99, 2.50) w/Lionheart gallery						2.50

COVENANT, THE
Image Comics (Top Cow): 2005 ($9.99, squarebound, one-shot)

nn-Tone Rodriguez-a/Aron Coleite-s						10.00

COVERED WAGONS, HO (Disney, TV)
Dell Publishing Co.: No. 814, June, 1957 (Donald Duck)

Four Color 814-Mickey Mouse app.	5	10	15	34	55	75

COWBOY ACTION (Formerly Western Thrillers No. 1-4; Becomes Quick-Trigger Western No. 12 on)
Atlas Comics (ACI): No. 5, March, 1955 - No. 11, March, 1956

5	14	28	42	76	108	140
6-10: 6-8-Heath-c	10	20	30	54	72	90
11-Williamson-a (4 pgs.); Baker-a	11	22	33	62	86	110

NOTE: *Ayers a-8. **Drucker** a-6. **Maneely** c/a-5, 6. **Severin** c-10. **Shores** a-7.*

COWBOY COMICS (Star Ranger #12, Stories #14)(Star Ranger Funnies #15)
Centaur Publishing Co.: No. 13, July, 1938 - No. 14, Aug, 1938

13-(Rare)-Ace and Deuce, Lyin Lou, Air Patrol, Aces High, Lee Trent, Trouble Hunters begin	127	254	381	800	1350	1900
14-Filchock-c	87	174	261	548	924	1300

NOTE: ***Guardineer** a-13, 14. **Gustavson** a-13, 14.*

COWBOY IN AFRICA (TV)
Gold Key: Mar, 1968

1(10219-803)-Chuck Connors photo-c	4	8	12	26	41	55

COWBOY LOVE (Becomes Range Busters?)
Fawcett Publications/Charlton Comics No. 28 on: 7/49 - V2#10, 6/50; No. 11, 1951; No. 28, 2/55 - No. 31, 8/55

V1#1-Rocky Lane photo back-c	15	30	45	88	137	185
2	8	16	24	44	57	70
V1#3,4,6 (12/49)	8	16	24	40	50	60
5-Bill Boyd photo back-c (11/49)	9	18	27	47	61	75
V2#7-Williamson/Evans-a	10	20	30	54	72	90
V2#8-11	7	14	21	35	43	50
V1#28 (Charlton)-Last precode (2/55) (Formerly Romantic Story?)	6	12	18	31	38	45
V1#29-31 (Charlton; becomes Sweetheart Diary #32 on)	6	12	18	28	34	40

NOTE: ***Powell** a-10. **Marcus Swayze** a-2, 3. Photo c-1-11. No. 1-3, 5-7, 9, 10 are 52 pgs.*

COWBOY ROMANCES (Young Men No. 4 on)
Marvel Comics (IPC): Oct, 1949 - No. 3, Mar, 1950 (All photo-c & 52 pgs.)

1-Photo-c	23	46	69	133	214	295
2-William Holden, Mona Freeman "Streets of Laredo" photo-c	16	32	48	94	147	200
3-Photo-c	15	30	45	84	127	170

COWBOYS 'N' INJUNS (...and Indians No. 6 on)
Compix No. 1-5/Magazine Enterprises No. 6 on: 1946 - No. 5, 1947; No. 6, 1949 - No. 8, 1952

1-Funny animal western	14	28	42	82	121	160
2-5-All funny animal western	10	20	30	54	72	90
6(A-1 23)-Half violent, half funny; Ayers-a	13	26	39	74	105	135
7(A-1 41, 1950), 8(A-1 48)-All funny	9	18	27	47	61	75
I.W. Reprint No. 1,7 (Reprinted in Canada by Superior, No. 7)	2	4	6	11	16	20
Super Reprint #10 (1963)	2	4	6	11	16	20

COWBOY WESTERN COMICS (TV)(Formerly Jack In The Box; Becomes Space Western No. 40-45 & Wild Bill Hickok & Jingles No. 68 on; title:Cowboy Western Heroes No. 47 & 48; Cowboy Western No. 49 on)
Charlton (Capitol Stories): No. 17, 7/48 - No. 39, 8/52; No. 46, 10/53; No. 47, 12/53; No. 48, Spr, '54; No. 49, 5-6/54 - No. 67, 3/58 (nn 40-45)

17-Jesse James, Annie Oakley, Wild Bill Hickok begin; Texas Rangers app.	16	32	48	94	147	200
18,19-Orlando-c/a. 18-Paul Bunyan begins. 19-Wyatt Earp story	10	20	30	58	79	100
20-25: 21-Buffalo Bill story. 22-Texas Rangers-c/story. 24-Joel McCrea photo-c & adaptation from movie "Three Faces West". 25-James Craig photo-c & adaptation from movie "Northwest Stampede"	9	18	27	52	69	85
26-George Montgomery photo-c and adaptation from movie "Indian Scout"; 1 pg. bio on Will Rogers	10	20	30	58	79	100
27-Sunset Carson photo-c & adapts movie "Sunset Carson Rides Again" plus 1 other Sunset Carson story	41	82	123	250	400	550
28-Sunset Carson line drawn-c; adapts movies "Battling Marshal" & "Fighting Mustangs" starring Sunset Carson	20	40	60	117	184	250
29-Sunset Carson line drawn-c; adapts movies "Rio Grande" with Sunset Carson & "Winchester '73" w/James Stewart plus 5 pg. life history of Sunset Carson featuring Tom Mix	20	40	60	117	184	250
30-Sunset Carson photo-c; adapts movie "Deadline" starring Sunset Carson plus 1 other Sunset Carson story	41	82	123	250	400	550
31-34,38,39,47-50 (no #40-45): 50-Golden Arrow, Rocky Lane & Blackjack (r?) stories	9	18	27	47	61	75
35,36-Sunset Carson-c/stories (2 in each). 35-Inside front-c photo of Sunset Carson plus photo on-c	22	44	66	126	198	270
37-Sunset Carson stories (2)	16	32	48	94	147	200
46-(Formerly Space Western)-Space western story	16	32	48	94	147	200
51-57,59-66: 51-Golden Arrow(r?) & Monte Hale-r renamed Rusty Hall. 53,54-Tom Mix-r. 55-Monte Hale story(r?). 66-Young Eagle story. 67-Wild Bill Hickok and Jingles-c/story	7	14	21	35	43	50
58-(1/56, 15¢, 68 pgs.)-Wild Bill Hickok, Annie Oakley & Jesse James stories; Forgione-a	8	16	24	44	57	70
67-(15¢, 68 pgs.)-Williamson/Torres-a, 5 pgs.	9	18	27	50	65	80

NOTE: *Many issues trimmed 1" shorter. **Maneely** a-67(5). Inside front/back photo c-29.*

COWGIRL ROMANCES
Marvel Comics (CCC): No. 28, Jan, 1950 (52 pgs.)

28(#1)-Photo-c	22	44	66	126	198	270

COWGIRL ROMANCES
Fiction House Magazines: 1950 - No. 12, Winter, 1952-53 (No. 1-3: 52 pgs.)

1-Kamen-a	40	80	120	244	397	550
2	20	40	60	120	193	265

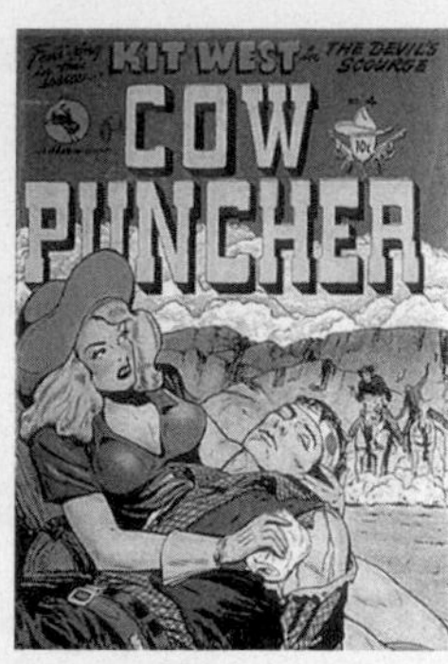

Cow Puncher #4 © AVON

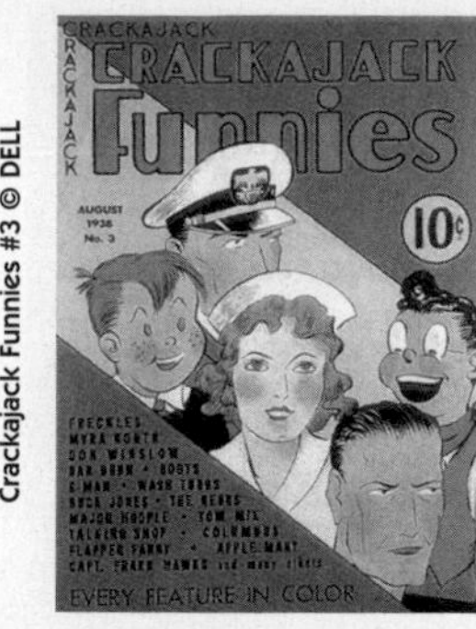

Crackajack Funnies #3 © DELL

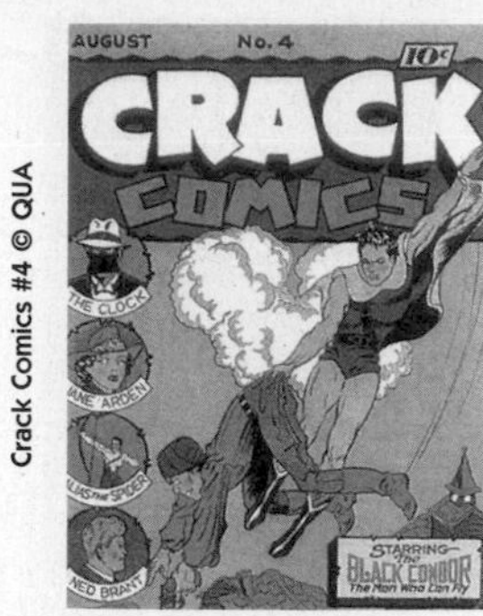

Crack Comics #4 © QUA

GD VG FN VF VF/NM NM-
2.0 4.0 6.0 8.0 9.0 9.2

3-5: 5-12-Whitman-c (most) 18 36 54 105 165 225
6-9,11,12 17 34 51 100 158 215
10-Frazetta?/Williamson?-a; Kamen?/Baker-a; r/Mitzi story from Movie Comics #4
w/all new dialogue 31 62 93 181 291 400

COW PUNCHER (...Comics)
Avon Periodicals: Jan, 1947; No. 2, Sept, 1947 - No. 7, 1949

1-Clint Cortland, Texas Ranger, Kit West, Pioneer Queen begin; Kubert-a; Alabam stories
begin 44 88 132 273 454 635
2-Kubert, Kamen/Feldstein-a; Kamen-c 38 76 114 222 356 490
3-5,7: 3-Kiefer story 27 54 81 158 254 350
6-Opium drug mention story; bondage, headlight-c; Reinman-a
35 70 105 208 334 460

COWPUNCHER
Realistic Publications: 1953 (nn) (Reprints Avon's No. 2)

nn-Kubert-a 11 22 33 64 90 115

COWSILLS, THE (See Harvey Pop Comics)

COW SPECIAL, THE
Image Comics (Top Cow): Spring-Summer 2000; 2001 ($2.95)

1-Previews upcoming Top Cow projects; Yancy Butler photo-c 3.00
Vol. 2 #1-Witchblade-c; previews and interviews 3.00

COYOTE
Marvel Comics (Epic Comics): June, 1983 - No. 16, Mar, 1986

1-10,15: 7-10-Ditko-a 2.50
11-1st McFarlane-a. 6.00
12-14,16: 12-14-McFarlane-a. 14-Badger x-over. 16-Reagan c/app. 4.00
Coyote Collection Vol. 1 (2005, $14.99) reprints from Coyote #1-7 & Scorpio Rose #1,2 plus
Rogers layout pages for unpublished #3; Englehart intro. 15.00
Coyote Collection Vol. 2 (2005, $12.99) reprints from Coyote #1-4 13.00
Coyote Collection Vol. 3 (2006, $12.99) reprints from Coyote #5-8 13.00
Coyote Collection Vol. 4 (2007, $14.99) reprints from Coyote #9-12 15.00
Coyote Collection Vol. 5 (2007, $12.99) reprints from Coyote #13-16 13.00

CRACKAJACK FUNNIES (Also see The Owl)
Dell Publishing Co.: June, 1938 - No. 43, Jan, 1942

1-Dan Dunn, Freckles, Myra North, Wash Tubbs, Apple Mary, The Nebbs, Don Winslow,
Tom Mix, Buck Jones, Major Hoople, Clyde Beatty, Boots begin
237 474 711 1493 2522 3550
2 90 180 270 567 959 1350
3 66 132 198 416 701 985
4 50 100 150 310 518 725
5-Nude woman on cover 52 104 156 322 536 750
6-8,10: 8-Speed Bolton begins (1st app.) 41 82 123 256 428 600
9-(3/39)-Red Ryder strip-r begin by Harman; 1st app. in comics & 1st cover app.
187 374 561 1178 1989 2800
11-14 40 80 120 235 380 525
15-Tarzan text feature begins by Burroughs (9/39); not in #26,35
41 82 123 253 419 585
16-24: 18-Stratosphere Jim begins (1st app., 12/39). 23-Ellery Queen begins plus-c
(1st comic book app., 5/40) 32 64 96 190 305 420
25-The Owl begins (1st app., 7/40); in new costume #26 by Frank Thomas
(also see Popular Comics #72) 80 160 240 504 852 1200
26-30: 28-Part Owl-c 53 106 159 328 547 765
31-Owl covers begin, end #42 53 106 159 331 558 785
32-Origin Owl Girl 58 116 174 365 615 865
33-38: 36-Last Tarzan issue. 37-Cyclone & Midge begin (1st app.)
52 104 156 327 544 760
39-Andy Panda begins (intro/1st app., 9/41) 62 124 186 391 658 925
40-42: 42-Last Owl-c. 40 80 120 235 380 525
43-Terry & the Pirates-r 30 60 90 174 280 385
NOTE: *McWilliams art in most issues.*

CRACK COMICS (Crack Western No. 63 on)
Quality Comics Group: May, 1940 - No. 62, Sept, 1949

1-Origin & 1st app. The Black Condor by Lou Fine, Madame Fatal, Red Torpedo, Rock
Bradden & The Space Legion; The Clock, Alias the Spider (by Gustavson), Wizard Wells,
& Ned Brant begin; Powell-a; Note: Madame Fatal is a man dressed as a woman
467 934 1401 3362 5881 8400
2 222 444 666 1399 2362 3325
3 152 304 456 958 1617 2275
4 122 244 366 769 1297 1825
5-10: 5-Molly The Model begins. 10-Tor, the Magic Master begins
92 184 276 580 978 1375

GD VG FN VF VF/NM NM-
2.0 4.0 6.0 8.0 9.0 9.2

11-20: 13-1 pg. J. Cole-a. 15-1st app. Spitfire 82 164 246 517 871 1225
21-24: 23-Pen Miller begins; continued from National Comics #22. 24-Last Fine Black Condor
64 128 192 403 682 960
25,26: 26-Flag-c 48 96 144 298 499 700
27-(1/43)-Intro & origin Captain Triumph by Alfred Andriola (Kerry Drake artist)
& begin series 90 180 270 567 959 1350
28-30 41 82 123 250 413 575
31-39: 31-Last Black Condor 24 48 72 140 225 310
40-46 17 34 51 98 154 210
47-57,59,60-Capt. Triumph by Crandall 18 36 54 105 165 225
58,61,62-Last Captain Triumph 15 30 45 84 127 170
NOTE: *Black Condor by* ***Fine****: No. 1, 2, 5, 6, 8, 10-24; by* ***Sultan****: No. 3, 7; by* ***Fugitani****: No. 9.* ***Cole*** *a-34.* ***Crandall*** *a-61(unsigned); c-48, 49, 51-61.* ***Guardineer*** *a-17.* ***Gustavson*** *a-1, 2, 4, 7, 13, 17, 23.* ***McWilliams*** *a-15-27. Black Condor c-2, 4, 6, 8, 10, 12, 14, 16, 18, 20-26. Capt. Triumph c-27-62. The Clock c-1, 3, 5, 7, 9, 11, 13, 15, 17, 19.*

CRACK COMICS
Quality Comics: May 1940

1-Ashcan comic, not distributed to newsstands, only for in-house use. Cover art is the same
as published version of Crack Comics #1with exception of text panel on bottom left of
cover. A CGC certified 4.0 copy sold for $1,495 in 2005.

CRACKED (Magazine) (Satire) (Also see The 3-D Zone #19)
Major Magazines(#1-212)/Globe Communications(#213-346/American Media #347 on):
Feb-Mar, 1958 - No. 365, Nov, 2004

1-One pg. Williamson-a; Everett-c; Gunsmoke-s 17 34 51 126 233 340
2-1st Shut-Ups & Bonus Cut-Outs; Superman parody-c by Severin (his 1st cover on the title)
Frankenstein-s 9 18 27 65 113 160
3-5 7 14 21 49 80 110
6-10: 7-Reprints 1st 6 covers on-c. 8-Frankenstein-c. 10-Wolverton-a
6 12 18 39 62 85
11-12, 13(nn,3/60), 5 10 15 34 55 75
14-Kirby-a 6 12 18 41 66 90
15-17, 18(nn,2/61), 19,20 5 10 15 32 51 70
21-27(11/62), 27(No.28, 2/63; mis-#d), 29(5/63) 4 8 12 28 44 60
30-40(11/64): 37-Beatles and Superman cameos 4 8 12 24 37 50
41-45,47-56,59,60: 47,49,52-Munsters. 51-Beatles inside-c. 59-Laurel and Hardy photos
3 6 9 20 30 40
46,57,58: 46,58-Man From U.N.C.L.E. 46-Beatles. 57-Rolling Stones
3 6 9 20 30 40
61-80: 62-Beatles cameo. 69-Batman, Superman app. 70-(8/68) Elvis cameo.
71-Garrison's Gorillas; W.C. Fields photos 3 6 9 16 22 28
81-99: 99-Alfred E. Neuman on-c 3 6 9 14 19 24
100 3 6 9 18 27 35
101-119: 104-Godfather-c/s. 108-Archie Bunker-s. 112,119-Kung Fu (TV). 113-Tarzan-s.
115-MASH. 117-Cannon. 118-The Sting-c/s 2 4 6 10 14 18
120(12/74) Six Million Dollar Man-c/s; Ward-a 2 4 6 13 18 22
121,122,124-126,128-133,136-140: 121-American Graffiti. 122-Korak-c/s.
124,131-Godfather-c/s. 128-Capone-c. 129,131-Jaws. 132-Baretta-c/s. 133-Space 1999.
136-Laverne and Shirley/Fonz-c. 137-Travolta/Kotter-c/s. 138-Travolta/Laverne and Shirley/
Fonz-c. 139-Barney Miller-c/s. 140-King Kong-c/s; Fonz-s
2 4 6 10 14 18
123-Planet of the Apes-c/s; Six Million Dollar Man 2 4 6 13 18 22
127,134,135: 127-Star Trek-c/s; Ward-a. 134-Fonz-c/s; Starsky and Hutch. 135-Bionic Woman-
c/s; Ward-a 2 4 6 11 16 20
141,151-Charlie's Angels-c/s. 151-Frankenstein 2 4 6 11 16 20
142,143,150,152-155,157: 142-MASH-c/s. 143-Rocky-c/s; King Kong-s. 150-(5/78) Close
Encounters-c/s. 152-Close Enc./Star Wars-c/s. 153-Close Enc./Fonz-c/s. 154-Jaws II-c/s;
Star Wars-s. 155-Star Wars/Fonz-c 2 4 6 9 13 16
144,149,156,158-160: 144-Fonz/Happy Days-c. 149-Star Wars/Six Mil.$ Man-c/s.
156-Grease/Travolta-c. 158-Mork & Mindy. 159-Battlestar Galactica-c/s; MASH-s.
160-Superman-c/s 2 4 6 11 16 20
145,147-Both have insert postcards: 145-Fonz/Rocky/L&S-c/s. 147-Star Wars-s;
Farrah photo page (missing postcards-1/2 price) 3 6 9 14 20 26
146,148: 46-Star Wars-c/s with stickers insert (missing stickers-1/2 price). 148-Star Wars-c/s
with inside-c color poster 3 6 9 16 23 30
161,170-Ward-a: 161-Mork & Mindy-c/s. 170-Dukes of Hazzard-c/s
2 4 6 8 11 14
162,165-168,171,172,175-178,180-Ward-a: 162-Sherlock Holmes-s. 165-Dracula-c/s.
167-Mork-c/s. 168,175-MASH-c/s. 168-Mork-s. 172-Dukes of Hazzard/CHiPs-c/s.
176-Barney Miller-c/s 2 4 6 8 10 12
163,179:163-Postcard insert; Mork & Mindy-c/s. 179-Insult cards insert; Popeye,
Dukes of Hazzard-c/s 3 6 9 14 19 24
164,169,173,174: 164-Alien movie-c/s; Mork & Mindy-s. 169-Star Trek. 173,174-Star Wars-
Empire Strikes Back. 173-SW poster 2 4 6 9 13 16
181,182,185-191,193,194,196-198-most Ward-a: 182-MASH-c/s. 185-Dukes of Hazzard-c/s;

Cracked #2 © Major Mags.

Cracked #250 © Major Mags.

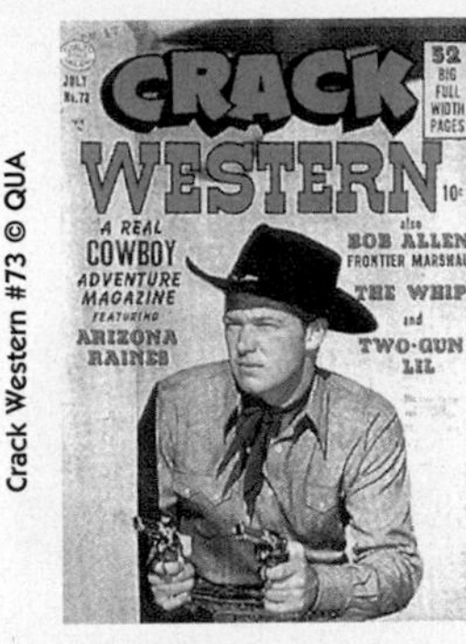

Crack Western #73 © QUA

	GD 2.0	VG 4.0	FN 6.0	VF 8.0	VF/NM 9.0	NM- 9.2
Jefferson-s. 187-Love Boat. 188-Fall Guy-s. 189-Fonz/Happy Days-c. 190,194-MASH-c/s. 191-Magnum P.I./Rocky-c; Magnum-s. 193-Knight Rider-s. 196-Dukes of Hazzard/Knight Rider-c/s. 198 Jaws III-c/s; Fall Guy-s	1	2	3	5	7	9
183,184,192,195,199,200-Ward-a in all: 183-Superman-c/s. 184-Star Trek-c/s. 192-E.T.-c/s; Rocky-s. 195-E.T.-c/s. 199-Jabba-c; Star Wars-s. 200-(12/83)	1	3	4	6	8	10
201,203,210-A-Team-c/s						6.00
202,204-206,211-224,226,227,230-233: 202-Knight Rider-s. 204-Magnum P.I.; A-Team-s. 206-Michael Jackson/Mr. T-c/s. 212-Prince-s; Cosby-s. 213-Monsters issue-c/s. 215-Hulk Hogan/Mr. T-c/s. 216-Miami Vice-s; James Bond-s. 217-Rambo-s; Cosby-s; A-Team-s. 218-Rocky-c/s. 219-Arnold/Commando-c/s; Rocky-s; Godzilla. 220-Rocky-c/s. 221-Stephen King app. 223-Miami Vice-s. 224-Cosby-s. 226-29th Anniv.; Tarzan-s; Aliens-s; Family Ties-s. 227-Cosby, Family Ties, Miami Vice-s. 230-Monkees-c/s; Elvis on-c; 232-Alf, Cheers, StarTrek-s. 233-Superman/James Bond-c/s; Robocop, Predator-s						5.00
207-209,225,234: 207-Michael Jackson-c/s. 208-Indiana Jones-c/s. 209-MichaelJackson/Gremlins-c/s; Star Trek III-s. 225-Schwarzenegger/Stallone/G.I. Joe-c/s. 234-Don Martin-a begins; Batman/Robocop/Clint Eastwood-c/s						6.00
228,229: 228-Star Trek-c/s; Alf, Pee Wee Herman-s. 229-Monsters issue-c/s; centerfold with many superheroes						6.00
235,239,243,249: 235-1st Martin-c; Star Trek:TNG-s; Alf-s. 239-Beetlejuice-c/s; Mike Tyson-s. 243-X-Men and other heroes app. 249-Batman/Indiana Jones/Ghostbusters-c/s						6.00
236,244,245,248: 236-Madonna/Stallone-c/s; Twilight Zone-s. 244-Elvis-c/s; Martin-c. 245-Roger Rabbit-c/s. 248-Batman issue						6.00
237,238,240-242,246,247,250: 237-Robocop-s. 238-Rambo-c/s; Star Trek-s. 242-Dirty Harry-s, Ward-a. 246-Alf-s; Star Trek-s., Ward-a. 247-Star Trek-s. 250-Batman/Ghostbusters-s						4.00
251-253,255,256,259,261-265,275-278,281,284,286-297,299: 252-Star Trek-s. 253-Back to the Future-c/s. 255-TMNT-c/s. 256-TMNT-c/s; Batman, Bart Simpson on-c. 259-Die Hard II, Robocop-s. 261-TMNT, Twin Peaks-s. 262-Rocky-c/s; Rocky Horror-s. 265-TMNT-s. 276-Aliens III, Batman-s. 277-Clinton-c. 284-Bart Simpson-c; 90210-s. 297-Van Damme-s/photo-c. 299-Dumb & Dumber-c/s						4.00
254,257,266,267,272,280,282,285,298,300: 254-Back to the Future, Punisher-s; Wolverton-a, Batman-c, Ward-a. 257-Batman, Simpsons-s; Spider-Man and other heroes app. 266-Terminator-c/s. 267-Toons-c/s. 272-Star Trek VI-s. 280-Swimsuit issue. 282-Cheers-c/s. 285-Jurassic Park-c/s. 298-Swimsuit issue; Martin-c. 300-(8/95) Brady Bunch-c/s						5.00
258,260,274,279,283: 258-Simpsons-c/s; Back to the Future-s. 260-Spider-Man-c/s; Simpsons-s. 274-Batman-c/s. 279-Madonna-c/s. 283-Jurassic Park-c/s; Wolverine app. inside back-c						5.00
301-305,307-365: 365-Freas-c						2.50
306-Toy Story-c/s						4.00
Biggest... (Winter, 1977)	2	4	6	13	18	22
Biggest, Greatest... nn('65)	5	10	15	30	48	65
Biggest, Greatest... 2('66/67) - #5('69/70)	3	6	9	20	30	40
Biggest, Greatest... 6('70) - #12(Wint. '77)	3	6	9	14	19	24
Biggest, Greatest...13(Fall '78) - #21(Fall/Wint. '86)	2	4	6	8	11	14
...Blockbuster 1(Sum '87), 2('88), 3(Sum. '89)	1	3	4	6	8	10
...Blockbuster 4 - 6(Sum. '92)						6.00
...Collectors' Edition 4 ('73; formerly ...Special)	2	4	6	13	18	22
5-9,10(10/75)	2	4	6	11	16	20
11-19,20(11/17)	2	4	6	8	11	14
21,22,23(5/78): 23-Ward-a	2	4	6	8	11	14
(#24-62,64 not numbered)						
1978 (nn; July, Sept, Nov, Dec) (#24-27)	2	4	6	8	11	14
1979 (nn; May, July, Sept, Nov, Dec) (#28-33)	2	4	6	8	11	14
1980 (nn; Feb, May, July, Sept, Nov, Dec) (#34-39)	1	3	4	6	8	10
1981 (nn; Feb, May, July, Sept, Nov, Dec) (#40-45)	1	3	4	6	8	10
1982 (nn; Feb, May, July, Sept, Nov, Dec) (#46-51)	1	3	4	6	8	10
1983 (nn; Feb, May, Sept, Nov, Dec) (#52-56)	1	3	4	6	8	10
1984 (nn; Feb, May, July, Nov) (#57-60)	1	2	3	4	5	7
1985 (nn; Feb) (#61)	1	2	3	4	5	7
62(9/85), nn(#63,11/85), 64(12/85), 65-69, 70(4/87)	1	2	3	4	5	7
71,72,73(100 pgs., 1/88), 74-79, 80(9/89)						5.00
81-96, 97(two diff. issues), 98-115: 83-Elvis, Batman parodies						5.00
116('98)-Last issue?						6.00
...Digest 1(Fall, '86, 148 pgs.), 2(1/87)	1	2	3	6	8	10
...Digest 3-5	1	2	3	4	5	7
...Party Pack 1,2('88) - 4('90)						4.00
...Shut-Ups 1(2/72)	3	6	9	18	27	35
...Shut-Ups 2('72) becomes Cracked Spec. #3	3	6	9	14	19	24
...Special 3('73; formerly Cracked Shut-Ups; ...Collectors' Edition#4 on)	2	4	6	13	18	22
... Summer Special 1(Sum. '91), 2(Sum. '92)-Don Martin-a						4.00
... Summer Special 3(Sum. '93) - 8(Sum. '98)						3.00
... Super (Vol. 2, formerly Super Cracked) 5(Wint. '91/92) - 14(Wint.'97/98)						3.00
Extra Special... 1(Spr. '76)	2	4	6	11	16	20
Extra Special... 2(Spr./Sum. '77)	2	4	6	10	14	18
Extra Special... 3(Wint. '79) - 9(Wint. '86)	1	2	3	4	5	7
Giant... nn('65)	6	12	18	37	59	80
Giant... 2('66) - 5('69)	4	8	12	22	34	45
Giant...6('70) - 12('76)	3	6	9	17	25	32
Giant...nn(9/77, #13), nn(1/78, #14), nn(3/78, #15), nn(5/78, #16), nn(7/78, #17), nn(11/78, #18), nn(3/79, #19), nn(7/79, #20), nn(10/79, #21), nn(12/79, #22), nn(3/80, #23), nn(7/80, #24)	2	4	6	11	16	20
Giant...nn(10/80, #25), nn(12/80, #26), nn(3/81, #27), nn(7/81, #28), nn(10/81, #29), nn(12/81, #30), nn(7/82, #31), nn(10/82, #32), nn(12/82, #33), nn(7/83, #34),	2	4	6	8	11	14
Giant...nn(10/83, #35), nn(12/83, #36), nn(3/84, #37), nn(7/84, #38), nn(10/84, #39), nn(3/85, #40), nn(7/85, #41), nn(10/85, #42)	1	2	3	5	7	9
Giant...43(3/86) - 46(1/87), 47(Wint. '88), 48(Wint. '89)	1	2	3	4	5	7
King Sized... 1('67)	4	8	12	26	41	55
King Sized... 2('68) - 5('71)	3	6	9	18	27	35
King Sized... 6('72) - 11('77)	3	6	9	14	20	26
King Sized... 12(Fall '78) - 17(Sum. '83)	2	4	6	8	11	14
King Sized... 18-20 (Sum/'86) (#21,22 exist?)	1	3	4	6	8	10
Spaced Out... 1-4 ('93 - '94)						5.00
Super... 1('68)	4	8	12	26	41	55
Super... 2('69) - 6('73)	3	6	9	20	30	40
Super... 7('74), 8(Spr. '75) - 10(Spr. '77)	3	6	9	16	22	28
Super... 11(Sum. '78) - 16(Fall '81)	2	4	6	11	16	20
Super... 17(Spr. '82) - 22(Fall '83)	2	4	6	8	11	14
Super... 23(Sum. '84, mis-numbered as #24)	2	4	6	8	11	14
Super... 24(Fall '84, correctly numbered)	2	4	6	8	11	14
Super... 25(Wint. '85) - 32(Fall '86)	2	4	6	8	10	12
Super... (Vol. 2) 1('87, 100 pgs.)-Severin & Elder-a	1	3	4	6	8	10
Super... (Vol. 2) 2(Sum. '88), 3(Wint. '89), 4(exist?)(Becomes Cracked Super)						6.00

NOTE: ***Burgos*** *a-1-10.* ***Colan*** *a-257.* ***Davis*** *a-5, 11-17, 24, 40, 80; c-12-14, 16.* ***Elder*** *a-5, 6, 10-13; c-10.* ***Everett*** *a-1-10, 23-25, 61; c-1.* ***Heath*** *a-1-3, 6, 13, 14, 17, 110; c-6.* ***Jaffee*** *a-5, 6.* ***Don Martin*** *c-235, 244, 247, 259, 261, 264.* ***Morrow*** *a-8-10.* ***Reinman*** *a-1-4.* ***Severin*** *c/a-in most all issues.* ***Shores*** *a-3-7.* ***Torres*** *a-7-10.* ***Ward*** *a-22-24, 27, 35, 40, 120-193, 195, 197-205, 242, 244, 246, 247, 250, 252-257.* ***Williamson*** *a-1 (1 pg.).* ***Wolverton*** *a-10 (2 pgs.), Giant nn('65).* ***Wood*** *a-27, 35, 40. Alfred E. Neuman c-177, 200, 202. Batman c-234, 248, 249, 256, 274. Captain America c-256. Christmas c-234, 243. Spider-Man c-260. Star Trek c-127, 189, 207, 228. Star Wars c-145, 146, 148, 149, 152, 155, 173, 174, 199. Superman c-183, 233. #144, 146 have free full-color pre-glued stickers. #145, 147, 155, 163 have free full-color postcards. #123, 137, 154, 157 have free iron-ons.*

CRACKED MONSTER PARTY
Globe Communications: July, 1988 - No. 27, Wint. 1999/2000

	GD 2.0	VG 4.0	FN 6.0	VF 8.0	VF/NM 9.0	NM- 9.2
1	2	4	6	10	14	18
2-10	2	4	6	8	10	12
11-26	1	2	3	4	5	7
27-Interview with a Vampire-c/s	2	4	6	8	10	12

CRACKED'S FOR MONSTERS ONLY
Major Magazines: Sept, 1969 - No. 9, Sept, 1969; June, 1972

	GD 2.0	VG 4.0	FN 6.0	VF 8.0	VF/NM 9.0	NM- 9.2
1	5	10	15	30	48	65
2-9, nn(6/72)	3	6	9	20	30	40

CRACK WESTERN (Formerly Crack Comics; Jonesy No. 85 on)
Quality Comics Group: No. 63, Nov, 1949 - No. 84, May, 1953 (36 pgs., 63-68,74-on)

	GD 2.0	VG 4.0	FN 6.0	VF 8.0	VF/NM 9.0	NM- 9.2
63(#1)-Ward-c; Two-Gun Lil (origin & 1st app.)(ends #84), Arizona Ames, his horse Thunder (with sidekick Spurs & his horse Calico), Frontier Marshal (ends #70), & Dead Canyon Days (ends #69) begin; Crandall-a	18	36	54	107	169	230
64,65: 64-Ward-c. Crandall-a in both.	15	30	45	83	124	165
66,68-Photo-c. 66-Arizona Ames becomes A. Raines (ends #84)	13	26	39	72	101	130
67-Randolph Scott photo-c; Crandall-a	14	28	42	80	115	150
69(52pgs.)-Crandall-a	13	26	39	72	101	130
70(52pgs.)-The Whip (origin & 1st app.) & his horse Diablo begin (ends #84); Crandall-a	13	26	39	72	101	130
71(52pgs.)-Frontier Marshal becomes Bob Allen F. Marshal (ends #84); Crandall-c/a	14	28	42	80	115	150
72(52pgs.)-Tim Holt photo-c	12	24	36	67	94	120
73(52pgs.)-Photo-c	10	20	30	58	79	100
74-76,78,79,81,83-Crandall-c. 83-Crandall-a(p)	11	22	33	62	86	110
77,80,82	8	16	24	44	57	70
84-Crandall-c/a	12	24	36	67	94	120

NOTE: ***Crandall*** *c-71p, 74-81, 83p(w/****Cuidera****-i).*

CRASH COMICS (Catman Comics No. 6 on)
Tem Publishing Co.: May, 1940 - No. 5, Nov, 1940

	GD 2.0	VG 4.0	FN 6.0	VF 8.0	VF/NM 9.0	NM- 9.2
1-The Blue Streak, Strongman (origin), The Perfect Human, Shangra begin (1st app. of each); Kirby-a	318	636	954	2162	3781	5400
2-Simon & Kirby-a	160	320	480	1008	1704	2400

Crazy Magazine #4 © MAR

Crazy Magazine #45 © MAR

Crazyman #2 © Continuity

	GD 2.0	VG 4.0	FN 6.0	VF 8.0	VF/NM 9.0	NM- 9.2

3,5-Simon & Kirby-a — 135 270 405 851 1438 2025
4-Origin & 1st app. The Catman; S&K-a — 324 648 972 2203 3852 5500

NOTE: *Solar Legion by* **Kirby** *No. 1-5 (5 pgs. each). Strongman c-1-4. Catman c-5.*

CRASH DIVE (See Cinema Comics Herald)

CRASH METRO AND THE STAR SQUAD
Oni Press: May, 1999 ($2.95, B&W, one-shot)

1-Allred-s/Ontiveros-a — 3.00

CRASH RYAN (Also see Dark Horse Presents #44)
Marvel Comics (Epic): Oct, 1984 - No. 4, Jan, 1985 (Baxter paper, lim. series)

1-4 — 2.50

CRAZY (Also see This Magazine is Crazy)
Atlas Comics (CSI): Dec, 1953 - No. 7, July, 1954

1-Everett-c/a — 30 60 90 176 283 390
2 — 20 40 60 118 189 260
3-7: 4-I Love Lucy satire. 5-Satire on censorship — 17 34 51 98 154 210

NOTE: ***Ayers** a-5. **Berg** a-1, 2. **Burgos** c-5, 6. **Drucker** a-6. **Everett** a-1-4. **Al Hartley** a-4. **Heath** a-3, 7; c-7. **Maneely** a-1-7, c-3, 4. **Post** a-3-6. Funny monster c-1-4.*

CRAZY (Satire)
Marvel Comics Group: Feb, 1973 - No. 3, June, 1973

1-Not Brand Echh-r; Beatles cameo (r) — 3 6 9 16 22 28
2,3-Not Brand Echh-r; Kirby-a — 2 4 6 10 14 18

CRAZY MAGAZINE (Satire)
Oct, 1973 - No. 94, Apr, 1983 (40-90¢, B&W magazine)
Marvel Comics: (#1, 44 pgs; #2-90, reg. issues, 52 pgs; #92-95, 68 pgs)'

1-Wolverton(1 pg.), Bode-a; 3 pg. photo story of Neal Adams & Dick Giordano; Harlan Ellison story; TV Kung Fu sty. — 5 10 15 30 48 65
2-"Live & Let Die" c/s; 8pgs; Adams/Buscema-a; McCloud w5 pgs. Adams-a; Kurtzman's "Hey Look" 2 pg.-r — 3 6 9 20 30 40
3-5: 3-"High Plains Drifter" w/Clint Eastwood c/s; Waltons app; Drucker, Reese-a. 4-Shaft-c/s; Ploog-a; Nixon 3 pg. app; Freas-a. 5-Michael Crichton's "Westworld" c/s; Nixon app. — 3 6 9 17 25 32
6,7,18: 6-Exorcist c/s; Nixon app. 7-TV's Kung Fu c/s; Nixon app.; Ploog & Freas-a. 18-Six Million Dollar Man/Bionic Woman c/s; Welcome Back Kotter story — 3 6 9 16 22 28
8-10: 8-Serpico c/s; Casper parody; TV's Police Story. 9-Joker cameo; Chinatown story; Eisner s/a begins; Has 1st 8 covers on-c. 10-Playboy Bunny-c; M. Severin-a; Lee Marrs-a begins; "Deathwish" story — 3 6 9 14 20 26
11-17,19: 11-Towering Inferno. 12-Rhoda. 13-"Tommy" the Who Rock Opera. 14-Mandingo. 15-Jaws story. 16-Santa/Xmas-c; "Good Times" TV story; Jaws. 17-Bicentennial issue; Baretta; Woody Allen. 19-King Kong c/s; Reagan, J. Carter, Howard the Duck cameos, "Laverne & Shirley" — 2 4 6 11 16 20
20,24,27: 20-Bicentennial-c; Space 1999 sty; Superheroes song sheet, 4pgs. 24-Charlie's Angels. 27-Charlie's Angels/Travolta/Fonz-c; Bionic Woman sty — 3 6 9 14 19 24
21-23,25,26,28-30: 21-Starsky & Hutch. 22-Mount Rushmore/J. Carter-c; TV's Barney Miller; Superheroes spoof. 23-Santa/Xmas-c; "Happy Days" sty; "Omen" sty. 25-J. Carter-c/s; Grandenetti-a begins; TV's Alice; Logan's Run. 26-TV Stars-c; Mary Hartman, King Kong. 28-Donny & Marie Osmond-c/s; Marathon Man. 29-Travolta/Kotter-c; "One Day at a Time", Gong Show. 30-1977, 84 pgs. w/bonus; Jaws, Baretta, King Kong, Happy Days — 2 4 6 9 12 15
31,33-35,38,40: 31-"Rocky"-c/s; TV game shows. 33-Peter Benchley's "Deep". 34-J. Carter-c; TV's "Fish". 35-Xmas-c with Fonz/Six Million Dollar Man/Wonder Woman/Darth Vader/Travolta, TV's "Mash" & "Family Matters". 38-Close Encounters of the Third Kind-c/s. 40-"Three's Company-c/s — 1 3 4 6 8 11
32-Star Wars/Darth Vader-c/s; "Black Sunday" — 3 6 9 14 19 24
36,42,47,49: 36-Farrah Fawcett/Six Million Dollar Man-c; TV's Nancy Drew & Hardy Boys; 1st app. Howard The Duck in Crazy, 2 pgs. 42-84 pgs. w/bonus; TV Hulk/Spider-Man-c; Mash, Gong Show, One Day at a Time, Disco, Alice. 47-Battlestar Galactica xmas-c; movie "Foul Play". 49-1979, 84 pgs. w/bonus; Mork & Mindy-c; Jaws, Saturday Night Fever, Three's Company — 2 4 6 9 12 15
37-1978, 84 pgs. w/bonus. Darth Vader-c; Barney Miller, Laverne & Shirley, Good Times, Rocky, Donny & Marie Osmond, Bionic Woman — 2 4 6 13 18 22
39,44: 39-Saturday Night Fever-c/s. 44-"Grease"-c w/Travolta/O. Newton-John — 2 4 6 11 16 20
41-Kiss-c & 1pg. photos; Disaster movies, TV's "Family", Annie Hall — 4 8 12 28 44 60
43,45,46,48,51: 43-Jaws-c; Saturday Night Fever. 43-E.C. swipe from Mad #131. 45-Travolta/O. Newton-John/J. Carter-c; Eight is Enough. 46-TV Hulk-c/s; Punk Rock. 48-"Wiz"-c, Battlestar Galactica-s. 51-Grease/Mork & Mindy/D&M Osmond-c, Mork & Mindy-sty. "Boys from Brazil" — 1 3 4 6 8 11
50,58: 50-Superman movie-c/sty, Playboy Mag., TV Hulk, Fonz; Howard the Duck, 1 pg. 58-1980, 84 pgs. w/32 pg. color comic bonus insert-Full reprint of Crazy Comic #1, Battlestar Galactica, Charlie's Angels, Starsky & Hutch — 2 4 6 11 16 20
52,59,60,64: 52-1979, 84 pgs. w/bonus. Marlon Brando-c; TV Hulk, Grease. Kiss, 1 pg. photos. 59-Santa Ptd-c by Larkin; "Alien", "Moonraker", Rocky-2, Howard the Duck, 1 pg. 60-Star Trek w/Muppets-c; Star Trek sty; 1st app/origin Teen Hulk; Severin-a. 64-84 pgs. w/bonus Monopoly game satire. "Empire Strikes Back", 8 pgs., One Day at a Time — 2 4 6 11 16 20
53,54,65,67-70: 53-"Animal House"-c/sty; TV's "Vegas", Howard the Duck, 1 pg. 54-Love at First Bite-c/sty, Fantasy Island sty, Howard the Duck 1 pg. 65-(Has #66 on-c, Aug/'80). "Black Hole" w/Janson-a; Kirby,Wood/Severin-a(r), 5 pgs. Howard the Duck, 3 pgs.; Broderick-a; Buck Rogers, Mr. Rogers. 67-84 pgs. w/bonus; TV's Kung Fu, Exorcist; Ploog-a(r). 68-American Gigolo, Dukes of Hazzard, Teen Hulk; Howard the Duck, 3 pgs. Broderick-a; Monster sty/5 pg. Ditko-a(r). 69-Obnoxio the Clown-c/sty; Stephen King's "Shining", Teen Hulk, Richie Rich, Howard the Duck, 3pgs; Broderick-a. 70-84 pgs. Towering Inferno, Daytime TV; Trina Robbins-a — 1 3 4 6 8 10
55-57,61,63: 55-84 pgs. w/bonus; Love Boat, Mork & Mindy, Fonz, TV Hulk. 56-Mork/Rocky/J. Carter-c; China Syndrome. 57-TV Hulk with Miss Piggy-c, Dracula, Taxi, Muppets. 61-1980, 84 pgs. Adams-a(r), McCloud, Pro wrestling, Casper, TV's Police Story. 63-Apocalypse Now-Coppola's cult movie; 3rd app. Teen Hulk, Howard the Duck, 3 pgs. — 2 4 6 8 11 14
62-Kiss-c & 2 pg. app; Quincy, 2nd app. Teen Hulk — 4 8 12 24 37 50
66-Sept/'80, Empire Strikes Back-c/sty; Teen Hulk by Severin, Howard the Duck, 3pgs. by Broderick — 2 4 6 10 14 18
71,72,75-77,79: 71-Blues Brothers parody, Teen Hulk, Superheroes parody, WKRP in Cincinnati, Howard the Duck, 3pgs. by Broderick. 72-Jackie Gleason/Smokey & the Bandit II-c/sty, Shogun, Teen Hulk. Howard the Duck, 3pgs. by Broderick. 75-Flash Gordon movie c/sty; Teen Hulk, Cat in the Hat, Howard the Duck 3pgs. by Broderick. 76-84 pgs. w/bonus; Monster-sty w/ Crandall-a(r), Monster-stys(2) w/Kirby-a(r), 5pgs. ea; Mash, TV Hulk, Chinatown. 77-Popeye movie/R. Williams-c/sty; Teen Hulk, Love Boat, Howard the Duck 3 pgs. 79-84 pgs. w/bonus color stickers; has new material; "9 to 5" w/Dolly Parton, Teen Hulk, Magnum P.I., Monster-sty w/5pgs, Ditko-a(r), "Rat" w/Sutton-a(r), Everett-a, 4 pgs.(r) — 1 3 4 6 8 10
73,74,78,80: 73-84 pgs. w/bonus Hulk/Spiderman Finger Puppets-c & bonus; "Live & Let Die, Jaws, Fantasy Island. 74-Dallas/"Who Shot J.R."-c/sty; Elephant Man, Howard the Duck 3pgs. by Broderick. 78-Clint Eastwood-c/sty; Teen Hulk, Superheroes parody, Lou Grant. 80-Star Wars, 2 pg. app; "Howling", TV's "Greatest American Hero" — 2 4 6 8 11 14
81,84,86,87,89: 81-.Superman Movie II-c/sty; Wolverine cameo, Mash, Teen Hulk. 84-American Werewolf in London, Johnny Carson app; Teen Hulk. 86-Time Bandits-c/sty; Private Benjamin. 87-Rubix Cube-c; Hill Street Blues, "Ragtime", Origin Obnoxio the Clown; Teen Hulk. 89-Burt Reynolds "Sharkey's Machine", Teen Hulk — 1 3 4 6 8 10
82-X-Men-c w/new Byrne-a, 84 pgs. w/new material; Fantasy Island, Teen Hulk, "For Your Eyes Only", Spiderman/Human Torch-r by Kirby/Ditko; Sutton-a(r); Rogers-a; Hunchback of Notre Dame, 5 pgs. — 2 4 6 11 16 20
83-Raiders of the Lost Ark-c/sty; Hart to Hart; Reese-a; Teen Hulk — 2 4 6 9 13 20
85,88: 85-84 pgs; Escape from New York, Teen Hulk; Kirby-a(r), 5 pgs, Poseidon Adventure, Flintstones, Sesame Street. 88-84 pgs. w/bonus Dr. Strange Game; some new material; Jeffersons, X-Men/Wolverine, 10 pgs.; Byrne-a; Apocalypse Now, Teen Hulk — 1 3 4 6 8 11
90-94: 90-Conan-c/sty; M. Severin-a; Teen Hulk. 91-84 pgs, some new material; Bladerunner-c/sty, "Deathwish-II, Teen Hulk, Black Knight, 10 pgs.-'50s-r w/Maneely-a. 92-Wrath of Khan Star Trek-c/sty; Joanie & Chachi, Teen Hulk. 93-"E.T."-c/sty, Teen Hulk, Archie Bunkers Place, Dr. Doom Game. 94-Poltergeist, Smurfs, Teen Hulk, Casper, Avengers parody-8pgs. Adams-a — 2 4 6 10 14 18
Crazy Summer Special #1 (Sum, '75, 100 pgs.)-Nixon, TV Kung Fu, Babe Ruth, Joe Namath, Waltons, McCloud, Chariots of the Gods — 3 6 9 14 19 24

NOTE: ***N. Adams** a-2, 61r, 94p. **Austin** a-82i. **Buscema** a-2, 82. **Byrne** c-82p. **Nick Cardy** c-7, 8, 10, 12-16, Super Special 1. **Crandall** a-76r. **Ditko** a-68r, 79r, 82r. **Drucker** a-3. **Eisner** a-9-16. **Kelly Freas** c-1-6, 9, 11; a-7. **Kirby/Wood** a-66r. **Ploog** a-1, 4, 7, 67r, 73r. **Rogers** a-82. **Sparling** a-92. **Wood** a-65r. Howard the Duck in 36, 50, 51, 53, 54, 59, 63, 65, 66, 68, 69, 71, 72, 74, 75, 77. Hulk in 46, c-42, 46, 57, 73. Star Wars in 32, 66; c-37.*

CRAZYMAN
Continuity Comics: Apr, 1992 - No. 3, 1992 ($2.50, high quality paper)

1-($3.95, 52 pgs.)-Embossed-c; N. Adams part-i — 4.00
2,3 ($2.50): 2-N. Adams/Bolland-c — 2.50

CRAZYMAN
Continuity Comics: V2#1, 5/93 - No. 4, 1/94 ($2.50, high quality paper)

V2#1-4: 1-Entire book is die-cut. 2-(12/93)-Adams-c(p) & part scripts. 3-(12/93). 4-Indicia says #3, Jan. 1993 — 2.50

CRAZY, MAN, CRAZY (Magazine) (Becomes This Magazine is...?)
(Formerly From Here to Insanity)

Creature Commandos #6 © DC

The Creeper #7 © DC

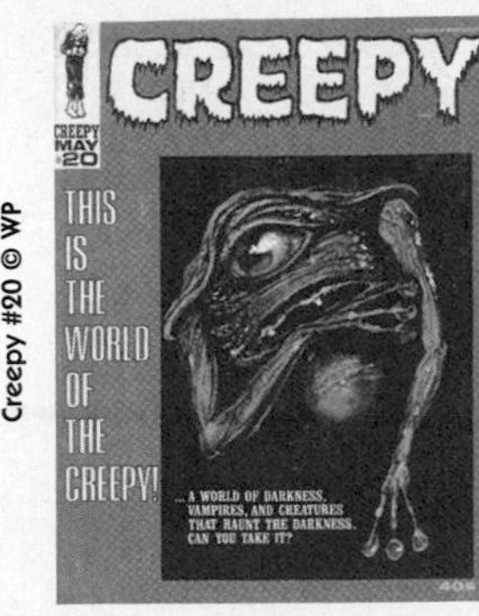

Creepy #20 © WP

GD 2.0 VG 4.0 FN 6.0 VF 8.0 VF/NM 9.0 NM- 9.2

Humor Magazines (Charlton): V2#1, Dec, 1955 - V2#2, June, 1956
V2#1,V2#2-Satire; Wolverton-a, 3 pgs. 15 30 45 85 130 175

CREATURE, THE (See Movie Classics)

CREATURE COMMANDOS (See Weird War Tales #93 for 1st app.)
DC Comics: May, 2000 - No. 8, Dec, 2000 ($2.50, limited series)
1-8: Truman-s/Eaton-a 2.50

CREATURES OF THE ID
Caliber Press: 1990 ($2.95, B&W)
1-Frank Einstein (Madman) app.; Allred-a 3 6 9 16 23 30

CREATURES OF THE NIGHT
Dark Horse Books: Nov, 2004 ($12.95, hardcover graphic novel)
HC-Neil Gaiman-s/Michael Zulli-a/c 13.00

CREATURES ON THE LOOSE (Formerly Tower of Shadows No. 1-9)(See Kull)
Marvel Comics: No. 10, March, 1971 - No. 37, Sept, 1975 (New-a & reprints)
10-(15¢)-1st full app. King Kull; see Kull the Conqueror; Wrightson-a
7 14 21 45 73 100
11-15: 13-Last 15¢ issue 3 6 9 16 22 28
16-Origin Warrior of Mars (begins, ends #21) 2 4 6 13 18 22
17-20 2 4 6 8 11 14
21-Steranko-c 3 6 9 14 19 24
22-Steranko-c; Thongor stories begin 3 6 9 14 20 26
23-29-Thongor-c/stories 1 2 3 5 7 9
30-Manwolf begins 3 6 9 16 23 30
31-33 2 4 6 9 12 15
34-37 2 4 6 8 10 12
NOTE: ***Crandall*** *a-13.* ***Ditko*** *r-15, 17, 18, 20, 22, 24, 27, 28.* ***Everett*** *a-16i(new).* ***Matt Fox*** *r-21i.* ***Howard*** *a-26i.* ***Gil Kane*** *a-16p, 17p, 19i; c-16, 17, 19, 20, 25, 29, 33p, 35p, 36p.* ***Kirby*** *a-10-15r, 16(2)r, 17r, 19r.* ***Morrow*** *a-20, 21.* ***Perez*** *a-33-37; c-34p.* ***Shores*** *a-11.* ***Sinnott*** *r-21.* ***Sutton*** *c-10.* ***Tuska*** *a-30-32p.*

CREECH, THE
Image Comics: Oct, 1997 - No. 3, Dec, 1997 ($1.95/$2.50, limited series)
1-3: 1-Capullo-s/c/a(p) 2.50
TPB (1999, $9.95) r/#1-3, McFarlane intro. 10.00
Out for Blood 1-3 (7/01 - No. 3, 11/01; $4.95) Capullo-s/c/a 5.00

CREED
Hall of Heroes Comics: Dec, 1994 - No. 2, Jan, 1995 ($2.50, B&W)
1 2 4 6 9 12 15
2 2 4 6 8 10 12

CREED
Lightning Comics: June, 1995 - No. 3 ($2.75/$3.00, B&W/color)
1-($2.75) 4.00
1-($3.00, color) 5.00
1-($9.95)-Commemorative Edition 10.00
1-TwinVariant Edition (1250? print run) 10.00
1-Special Edition; polybagged w/certificate 4.00
1 Gold Collectors Edition; polybagged w/certificate 3.00
2,3-($3.00, color)-Butt Naked Edition & regular-c 3.00
3-($9.95)-Commemorative Edition; polybagged w/certificate & card 10.00

CREED: CRANIAL DISORDER
Lightning Comics: Oct, 1996 ($3.00, limited series)
1-3-Two covers 3.00
1-($5.95)-Platinum Edition 6.00
2,3-($9.95)Ltd.I Edition 10.00

CREED/TEENAGE MUTANT NINJA TURTLES
Lightning Comics: May, 1996 ($3.00, one-shot)
1-Kaniuga-a(p)/scripts; Laird-c; variant-c exists 3.00
1-($9.95)-Platinum Edition 10.00
1-Special Edition; polybagged w/certificate 5.00

CREEPER, THE (See Beware... , Showcase #73 & 1st Issue Special #7)
DC Comics: Dec, 1997 - No. 11; #1,000,000 Nov, 1998 ($2.50)
1-11-Kaminski-s/Martinbrough-a(p). 7,8-Joker-c/app. 3.00
#1,000,000 (11/98) 853rd Century x-over 3.00

CREEPER, THE (See DCU Brave New World)
DC Comics: Oct, 2006 - No. 6, Mar, 2007 ($2.99, limited series)
1-6-Niles-s/Justiniano-a/c; Jack Ryder becomes the Creeper. 2-6-Batman app. 3.00
... - Welcome to Creepsville TPB ('07, $19.99) r/#1-6 & story from DCU Brave New World 20.00

CREEPS

GD 2.0 VG 4.0 FN 6.0 VF 8.0 VF/NM 9.0 NM- 9.2

Image Comics: Oct, 2001 - No. 4, May, 2002 ($2.95)
1-4-Mandrake-a/Mishkin-s 3.00

CREEPSHOW
Plume/New American Library Pub.: July, 1982 (softcover graphic novel)
1st edition-nn-(68 pgs.) Kamen-c/Wrightson-a; screenplay by Stephen King for the George Romero movie 4 8 12 22 34 45
2nd-7th printings 3 6 9 16 23 30

CREEPSVILLE
Laughing Reindeer Press: V2#1, Winter, 1995 ($4.95)
V2#1-Comics w/text 5.00

CREEPY (See Warren Presents)
Warren Publishing Co./Harris Publ. #146: 1964 - No. 145, Feb, 1983; No. 146, 1985 (B&W, magazine)
1-Frazetta-a (his last story in comics?); Jack Davis-c; 1st Warren all comics magazine; 1st app. Uncle Creepy 12 24 36 82 146 210
2-Frazetta-c & 1 pg. strip 7 14 21 49 80 110
3-8,11-13,15-17: 3-7,9-11,15-17-Frazetta-c. 7-Frazetta 1 pg. strip. 15,16-Adams-a. 16-Jeff Jones-a 5 10 15 30 48 65
9-Creepy fan club sketch by Wrightson (1st published-a); has 1/2 pg. anti-smoking strip by Frazetta; Frazetta-c; 1st Wood and Ditko art on this title; Toth-a (low print)
7 14 21 47 76 105
10-Brunner fan club sketch (1st published work) 5 10 15 32 51 70
14-Neal Adams 1st Warren work 5 10 15 32 51 70
18-28,30,31: 27-Frazetta-c 4 8 12 22 34 45
29,34: 29-Jones-a 4 8 12 24 37 50
32-(scarce) Frazetta-c; Harlan Ellison sty 6 12 18 39 62 85
33,35,37,39,40,42-47,49: 35-Hitler/Nazi-s. 39-1st Uncle Creepy solo-s, Cousin Eerie app.; early Brunner-a. 42-1st San Julian-c. 44-1st Ploog-a. 46-Corben-a
3 6 9 20 30 40
36-(11/70)1st Corben art at Warren 4 8 12 24 37 50
38,41-(scarce): 38-1st Kelly-c. 41-Corben-a 4 8 12 28 44 60
48,55,65-(1972, 1973, 1974 Annuals) #55 & 65 contain an 8 pg. slick comic insert. 48-(84 pgs.). 55-Color poster bonus (1/2 price if missing). 65-(100 pgs.) Summer Giant 4 8 12 24 37 50
50-Vampirella/Eerie/Creepy-c 4 8 12 28 44 60
51,54,56-61,64: All contain an 8 pg. slick comic insert in middle. 59-Xmas horror. 54,64-Chaykin-a 4 8 12 22 34 45
52,53,66,71,72,75,76,78-80: 71-All Bermejo-a; Space & Time issue. 72-Gual-a. 78-Fantasy issue. 79,80-Monsters issue 3 6 9 16 23 30
62,63-1st & 2nd full Wrightson story art; Corben-a; 8 pg. color comic insert
4 8 12 22 34 45
67,68,73 3 6 9 18 27 35
69,70-Edgar Allan Poe issues; Corben-a 3 6 9 17 25 32
74,77: 74-All Crandell-a. 77-Xmas Horror issue; Corben-a,Wrightson-a
3 6 9 20 30 40
81,84,85,88-90,92-94,96-99,102,104-112,114-118,120,122-130: 84,93-Sports issue. 85,97,102-Monster issue. 89-All war issue; Nino-a. 94-Weird Children issue. 96,109-Aliens issue. 99-Disasters. 103-Corben-a. 104-Robots issue. 106-Sword & Sorcery.107-Sci-fi. 116-End of Man. 125-Xmas Horror 2 4 6 9 12 15
82,100,101: 82-All Maroto issue. 100-(8/78) Anniversary. 101-Corben-a
2 4 6 13 18 22
83,95-Wrightson-a. 83-Corben-a. 95-Gorilla/Apes. 2 4 6 10 14 18
86,87,91,103-Wrightson-a. 86-Xmas Horror 2 4 6 10 14 18
113-All Wrightson-r issue 3 6 9 17 25 32
119,121: 119-All Nino issue.121-All Severin-r issue 2 4 6 10 14 18
131,133-136,138,140: 135-Xmas issue 2 4 6 10 14 18
132,137,139: 132-Corben. 137-All Williamson-r issue. 139-All Toth-r issue
2 4 6 13 18 22
141,143,144 (low dist.): 144-Giant, $2.25; Frazetta-c 3 6 9 15 21 26
142,145 (low dist.): 142-(10/82, 100 pgs.) All Torres issue. 145-(2/83) last Warren issue
3 6 9 16 23 30
146 ($2.95)-1st from Harris; resurrection issue 6 12 18 43 69 95
Year Book '68-'70: '70-Neal Adams, Ditko-a(r) 5 10 15 32 51 70
Annual 1971,1972 5 10 15 30 48 65
1993 Fearbook ($3.95)-Harris Publ.; Brereton-c; Vampirella by Busiek-s/Art Adams-a; David-s; Paquette-a 4 8 12 24 37 50
... Archives - Volume One HC (Dark Horse, 8/08, $49.95) r/#1-5; Jon B. Cooke intro. 50.00
...:The Classic Years TPB (Harris/Dark Horse, '91, $12.95) Kaluta-c; art by Frazetta,Torres, Crandall, Ditko, Morrow, Williamson, Wrightson 25.00
NOTE: *All issues contain many good artists works:* ***Neal Adams, Brunner, Corben, Craig (Taycee), Crandall, Ditko, Evans, Frazetta, Heath, Jeff Jones, Krenkel, McWilliams, Morrow, Nino, Orlando, Ploog, Severin, Torres, Toth, Williamson, Wood, & Wrightson****; covers by* ***Crandall, Davis, Frazetta, Morrow, San Julian, Todd/Bode****; Otto Binder's "Adam Link" stories in No. 2, 4, 6, 8, 9, 12, 13, 15 with* ***Orlando*** *art.* ***Frazetta*** *c-2-7, 9-*

Crime and Punishment #31 © LEV

Crime Bible: The Five Lessons #2 © DC

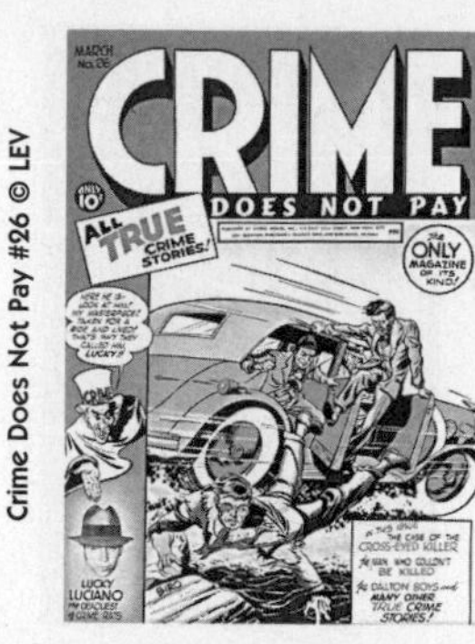

Crime Does Not Pay #26 © LEV

	GD 2.0	VG 4.0	FN 6.0	VF 8.0	VF/NM 9.0	NM- 9.2

GD VG FN VF VF/NM NM- 2.0 4.0 6.0 8.0 9.0 9.2

*11, 15-17, 27, 32, 83r, 89r, 91r. **E.A. Poe** adaptations in 66, 69, 70.*

CREEPY (Mini-series)
Harris Comics/Dark Horse: 1992 - Book 4, 1992 (48 pgs, B&W, squarebound)

	GD	VG	FN	VF	VF/NM	NM-
Book 1-4: Brereton painted-c on all. Stories and art by various incl. David (all), Busiek(2), Infantino(2), Guice(3), Colan(1)	2	4	6	8	10	12

CREEPY THINGS
Charlton Comics: July, 1975 - No. 6, June, 1976

	GD	VG	FN	VF	VF/NM	NM-
1-Sutton-c/a	2	4	6	12	16	20
2-6: Ditko-a in 3,5. Sutton c-3,4. 6-Zeck-c	1	3	4	6	8	10
Modern Comics Reprint 2-6(1977)						4.00

NOTE: *Larson a-2,6. **Sutton** a-1,2,4,6. **Zeck** a-2.*

CREW, THE
Marvel Comics: July, 2003 - No. 7, Jan, 2004 ($2.50)

	GD	VG	FN	VF	VF/NM	NM-
1-7-Priest-s/Bennett-a; James Rhodes (War Machine) app.						2.50

CRIME AND JUSTICE (Badge Of Justice #22 on; Rookie Cop? No. 27 on)
Capitol Stories/Charlton Comics: March, 1951 - No. 21; No. 23 - No. 26, Sept, 1955 (No #22)

	GD	VG	FN	VF	VF/NM	NM-
1	34	68	102	198	319	440
2	15	30	45	84	127	170
3-8,10-13: 6-Negligee panels	14	28	42	76	108	140
9-Classic story "Comics Vs. Crime"	25	50	75	145	233	320
14-Color illos in **POP**; gory story of man who beheads women	20	40	60	120	193	265
15-17,19-21,23,24: 15-Negligee panels. 23-Rookie Cop (1st app.)	10	20	30	56	76	95
18-Ditko-a	25	50	75	147	236	325
25,26: (scarce)	15	30	45	84	127	170

NOTE: ***Alascia** c-20. **Ayers** a-17. **Shuster** a-19-21; c-19. Bondage c-11, 12.*

CRIME AND PUNISHMENT (Title inspired by 1935 film)
Lev Gleason Publications: April, 1948 - No. 74, Aug, 1955

	GD	VG	FN	VF	VF/NM	NM-
1-Mr. Crime app. on-c	37	74	111	215	345	475
2	18	36	54	107	169	230
3-Used in **SOTI**, pg. 112; injury-to-eye panel; Fuje-a	20	40	60	118	189	260
4,5	15	30	45	84	127	170
6-10	13	26	39	74	105	135
11-20	11	22	33	64	90	115
21-30	10	20	30	56	76	95
31-38,40-44,46: 46-One pg. Frazetta-a	9	18	27	50	65	80
39-Drug mention story "The 5 Dopes"	14	28	42	76	108	140
45- "Hophead Killer" drug story	14	28	42	76	108	140
47-57,60-65,70-74:	9	18	27	47	61	75
58-Used in **POP**, pg. 79	9	18	27	52	69	85
59-Used in **SOTI**, illo "What comic-book America stands for"	31	62	93	181	291	400
66-Toth-c/a(4); 3-D effect issue (3/54); 1st "Deep Dimension" process	40	80	120	235	380	525
67- "Monkey on His Back" heroin story; 3-D effect issue	37	74	111	215	345	475
68-3-D effect issue; Toth-c (7/54)	30	60	90	174	280	385
69- "The Hot Rod Gang" dope crazy kids	14	28	42	76	108	140

NOTE: ***Biro** c-most. **Everett** a-31. **Fuje** a-2-4, 12, 13, 17, 18, 20, 26, 27. **Guardineer** a-2-4, 10, 14, 17, 18, 20, 26-28, 32, 38-44,54. **Kinstler** c-69. **McWilliams** a-41, 48, 49. **Tuska** a-28, 30, 51, 64, 70.*

CRIME AND PUNISHMENT: MARSHALL LAW TAKES MANHATTAN
Marvel Comics (Epic Comics): 1989 ($4.95, 52 pgs., direct sales only, mature)

	GD	VG	FN	VF	VF/NM	NM-
nn-Graphic album featuring Marshall Law						5.00

CRIME BIBLE: THE FIVE LESSONS (Aftermath of DC's 52 series)
DC Comics: Dec, 2007 - No. 5, Apr, 2008 ($2.99, limited series)

	GD	VG	FN	VF	VF/NM	NM-
1-5-Rucka-s; The Question (Renee Montoya) app. 3-Batwoman app.						3.00
The Question: The Five Books of Blood HC (2008, $19.99) r/#1-5						20.00

CRIME CAN'T WIN (Formerly Cindy Smith)
Marvel/Atlas Comics (TCI 41/CCC 42,43,4-12): No. 41, 9/50 - No. 43, 2/51; No. 4, 4/51 - No. 12, 9/53

	GD	VG	FN	VF	VF/NM	NM-
41(#1)	26	52	78	152	244	335
42(#2)	15	30	45	85	130	175
43(#3)-Horror story	18	36	54	105	165	225
4(4/51),5-12: 10-Possible use in **SOTI**, pg. 161	14	28	42	76	108	140

NOTE: ***Robinson** a-9-11. **Tuska** a-43.*

CRIME CASES COMICS (Formerly Willie Comics)
Marvel/Atlas Comics(CnPC No.24-8/MJMC No.9-12): No. 24, 8/50 - No. 27, 3/51; No. 5, 5/51 - No. 12, 7/52

	GD	VG	FN	VF	VF/NM	NM-
24 (#1, 52 pgs.)-True police cases	18	36	54	103	162	220
25-27(#2-4): 27-Morisi-a	14	28	42	76	108	140
5-12: 11-Robinson-a. 12-Tuska-a	12	24	36	67	94	120

CRIME CLINIC
Ziff-Davis Publishing Co.: No. 10, July-Aug, 1951 - No. 5, Summer, 1952

	GD	VG	FN	VF	VF/NM	NM-
10(#1)-Painted-c; origin Dr. Tom Rogers	28	56	84	162	261	360
11(#2),4,5: 4,5-Painted-c	19	38	57	109	172	235
3-Used in **SOTI**, pg. 18	20	40	60	114	180	245

NOTE: *All have painted covers by **Saunders**. **Starr** a-10.*

CRIME CLINIC
Slave Labor Graphics: May, 1995 - No. 2, Oct, 1995 ($2.95, B&W, limited series)

	GD	VG	FN	VF	VF/NM	NM-
1,2						3.00

CRIME DETECTIVE COMICS
Hillman Periodicals: Mar-Apr, 1948 - V3#8, May-June, 1953

	GD	VG	FN	VF	VF/NM	NM-
V1#1-The Invisible 6, costumed villains app; Fuje-c/a, 15 pgs.	30	60	90	174	280	385
2,5: 5-Krigstein-a	15	30	45	83	124	165
3,4,6,7,10-12: 6-McWilliams-a	13	26	39	72	101	130
8-Kirbyish-a by McCann	13	26	39	72	101	130
9-Used in **SOTI**, pg. 16 & "Caricature of the author in a position comic book publishers wish he were in permanently" illo.	37	74	111	219	352	485
V2#1,4,7-Krigstein-a: 1-Tuska-a	12	24	36	67	94	120
2,3,5,6,8-12 (1-2/52)	10	20	30	56	76	95
V3#1-Drug use-c	10	20	30	56	79	100
2-8	9	18	27	47	61	75

NOTE: ***Briefer** a-11, V3#1. **Kinstlerish**-a by **McCann**-V2#7, V3#2. **Powell** a-10, 11. **Starr** a-10.*

CRIME DETECTOR
Timor Publications: Jan, 1954 - No. 5, Sept, 1954

	GD	VG	FN	VF	VF/NM	NM-
1	21	42	63	123	197	270
2	13	26	39	72	101	130
3,4	11	22	33	60	83	105
5-Disbrow-a (classic)	22	44	66	129	207	285

CRIME DOES NOT PAY (Formerly Silver Streak Comics No. 1-21)
Comic House/Lev Gleason/Golfing: No. 22, June, 1942 - No. 147, July, 1955 (1st crime comic)(Title inspired by film)

	GD	VG	FN	VF	VF/NM	NM-
22 (23 on cover, 22 on indicia)-Origin The War Eagle & only app.; Chip Gardner begins; #22 was rebound in Complete Book of True Crime (Scarce)	300	600	900	1950	3375	4800
23 (Scarce)	173	346	519	1090	1845	2600
24-Intro. & 1st app. Mr. Crime (Scarce)	167	334	501	1052	1776	2500
25,26,28-30: 30-Wood and Biro app.	63	126	189	397	674	950
27-Classic Biro-c	75	150	225	473	799	1125
31,32,34-40	40	80	120	244	397	550
33-Classic Biro Hanging & hatchet-c	60	120	180	378	639	900
41-Origin & 1st app. Officer Common Sense	32	64	96	186	298	410
42-Electrocution-c	40	80	120	239	387	535
43-46,48-50: 44,45,46,50 are 68 pg. issues; 44-"legs" diamond story	21	42	63	125	200	275
47-Electric chair-c	37	74	111	215	345	475
51-70: 63,64-Possible use in **SOTI**, pg. 306. 63-Contains Biro & Gleason's self censorship code of 12 listed restrictions (5/48)	17	34	51	98	154	210
71-99: 87-Chip Gardner begins, ends #100	15	30	45	84	127	170
100	15	30	45	90	140	190
101-104,107-110: 102-Chip Gardner app	13	26	39	72	101	130
105-Used in **POP**, pg. 84	14	28	42	76	108	140
106,114-Frazetta-a, 1 pg.	13	26	39	72	101	130
111-Used in **POP**, pgs. 80 & 81; injury-to-eye sty illo	14	28	42	76	108	140
112,113,115-130	10	20	30	56	76	95
131-140	9	18	27	50	65	80
141,142-Last pre-code issue; Kubert-a(1)	10	20	30	58	79	100
143-Kubert-a in one story	10	20	30	58	79	100
144-146	9	18	27	50	65	80
147-Last issue (scarce); Kubert-a	15	30	45	84	127	170
1(Golfing-1945)	8	16	24	44	57	70
The Best of...(1944, 128 pgs.)-Series contains 4 rebound issues	83	166	249	523	887	1250
...1945 issue	61	122	183	384	652	920
...1946-48 issues	46	92	138	285	473	660
...1949-50 issues	41	82	123	250	413	575
...1951-53 issues	36	72	108	212	341	470

NOTE: *Many issues contain violent covers and stories. Who Dunnit by **Guardineer**-39-42, 44-105, 108-110; Chip Gardner by **Bob Fujitani (Fuje)**-88-103. **Alderman** a-29, 41-44, 49. **Dan Barry** a-67, 75. **Biro** c-1-76, 122, 142.*

Crimefighters #9 © MAR

Crime Mysteries #2 © TM

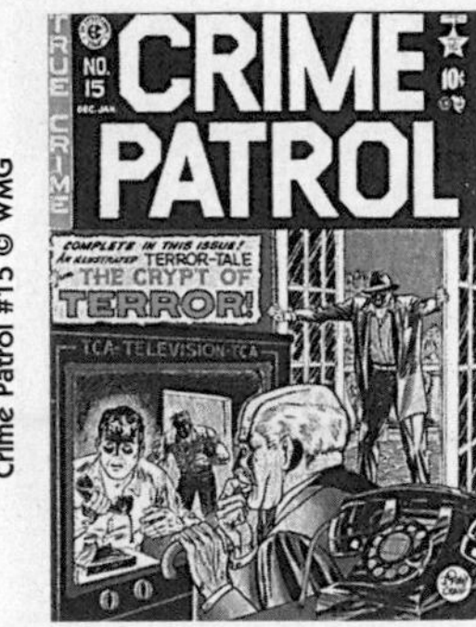

Crime Patrol #15 © WMG

GD 2.0 | VG 4.0 | FN 6.0 | VF 8.0 | VF/NM 9.0 | NM- 9.2

Briefer a-29(2), 30, 31, 33, 37, 39. ***G. Colan*** *a-105.* ***Fuje*** *c-88, 89, 91-94, 96, 98, 99, 102, 103.* ***Guardineer*** *a-51, 57, 67, 68, 71, 74.* ***Kubert*** *c-143.* ***Landau*** *a-118.* ***Maurer*** *a-29, 39, 41, 42.* ***McWilliams*** *a-91, 93, 95, 100-103.* ***Palais*** *a 30, 33, 37, 39, 41-43, 44(2), 46, 49.* ***Powell*** *a-146, 147.* ***Tuska*** *a-48, 50(2), 51, 52, 56, 57(2), 60-64, 66, 67, 68, 71, 74. Painted c-87-102. Bondage c-43, 02, 98.*

CRIME EXPOSED
Marvel Comics (PPI)/Marvel Atlas Comics (PrPI): June, 1948; Dec, 1950 - No. 14, June, 1952

1(6/48) 34 68 102 198 319 440
1(12/50) 20 40 60 115 183 250
2 14 28 42 80 115 150
3-9,11,14 12 24 36 67 94 120
10-Used in **POP**, pg. 81 13 26 39 72 101 130
12-Krigstein & Robinson-a 13 26 39 72 101 130
13-Used in **POP**, pg. 81; Krigstein-a 13 26 39 74 105 135
NOTE: ***Maneely*** *c 8.* ***Robinson*** *a-11, 12.* ***Tuska*** *a-3, 4.*

CRIMEFIGHTERS
Marvel Comics (CmPS 1-3/CCC 4-10): Apr, 1948 - No. 10, Nov, 1949

1-Some copies are undated & could be reprints 25 50 75 145 233 320
2,3: 3-Morphine addict story 14 28 42 82 121 160
4-10: 4-Early John Buscema a. 6-Anti-Wertham editorial. 9,10-Photo-c
13 26 39 74 105 135

CRIME FIGHTERS (...Always Win)
Atlas Comics (CnPC): No. 11, Sept, 1954 - No. 13, Jan, 1955

11-13: 11-Maneely-a,13-Pakula, Reinman, Severin-a
12 24 36 69 97 125

CRIME-FIGHTING DETECTIVE (Shock Detective Cases No. 20 on; formerly Criminals on the Run)
Star Publications: No. 11, Apr-May, 1950 - No. 19, June, 1952 (Based on true crime cases)

11-L. B. Cole-c/a (2 pgs.); L. B. Cole-c on all 18 36 54 107 169 230
12,13,15-19: 17-Young King Cole & Dr. Doom app. 15 30 45 83 124 165
14-L. B. Cole-c/a, r/Law-Crime #2 15 30 45 90 140 190

CRIME FILES
Standard Comics: No. 5, Sept, 1952 - No. 6, Nov, 1952

5-1pg. Alex Toth-a; used in **SOTI**, pg. 4 (text) 23 46 69 133 214 295
6-Sekowsky-a 14 28 42 78 112 145

CRIME ILLUSTRATED (Magazine)
E. C. Comics: Nov-Dec, 1955 - No. 2, Spring, 1956 (25¢, Adult Suspense Stories on-c)

1-Ingels & Crandall-a 18 36 54 103 162 220
2-Ingels & Crandall-a 14 28 42 82 121 160
NOTE: ***Craig*** *a-2.* ***Crandall*** *a-1, 2; c-2.* ***Evans*** *a-1.* ***Davis*** *a-2.* ***Ingels*** *a-1, 2.* ***Krigstein/Crandall*** *a-1.* ***Orlando*** *a-1, 2; c-1.*

CRIME INCORPORATED (Formerly Crimes Incorporated)
Fox Features Syndicate: No. 2, Aug, 1950; No. 3, Aug, 1951

2 26 52 78 152 244 335
3(1951)-Hollingsworth-a 18 36 54 105 165 225

CRIME MACHINE (Magazine reprints pre-code crime and gangster comics)
Skywald Publications: Feb, 1971 - No. 2, May, 1971 (B&W, 68 pgs., roundbound)

1-Kubert-a(2)(r)(Avon); bikini girl in cake-c 6 12 18 39 62 85
2-Torres, Wildey-a; violent-c/a 4 8 12 26 41 55

CRIME MUST LOSE! (Formerly Sports Action?)
Sports Action (Atlas Comics): No. 4, Oct, 1950 - No. 12, April, 1952

4-Ann Brewster-a in all; c-used in N.Y. Legis. Comm. documents
18 36 54 105 165 225
5-12: 9-Robinson-a. 11-Used in **POP**, pg. 89 14 28 42 78 112 145

CRIME MUST PAY THE PENALTY (Formerly Four Favorites; Penalty #47, 48)
Ace Magazines (Current Books): No. 33, Feb, 1948; No. 2, Jun, 1948 - No. 48, Jan, 1956

33(#1, 2/48)-Becomes Four Teeners #34? 37 74 111 215 345 475
2(6/48)-Extreme violence; Palais-a? 22 44 66 129 207 285
3,4,8: 3- "Frisco Mary" story used in Senate Investigation report, pg. 7. 4,8-Transvestism stories 17 34 51 98 154 210
5-7,9,10 13 26 39 74 105 135
11-19 12 24 36 69 97 125
20-Drug story "Dealers in White Death" 15 30 45 90 140 190
21-32,34-40,42-48: 44-Last pre-code 10 20 30 54 72 90
33(7/53)- "Dell Fabry-Junk King" drug story; mentioned in Love and Death
14 28 42 78 112 145
41-reprints "Dealers in White Death" 10 20 30 56 76 95
NOTE: ***Cameron*** *a-29-31, 34, 35, 39-41.* ***Colan*** *a-20, 31.* ***Kremer*** *a-3, 37r.* ***Larsen*** *a-32.* ***Palais*** *a-5?,37.*

CRIME MUST STOP
Hillman Periodicals: October, 1952 (52 pgs.)

V1#1(Scarce)-Similar to Monster Crime; Mort Lawrence, Krigstein-a
80 160 240 504 852 1200

CRIME MYSTERIES (Secret Mysteries #16 on; combined with Crime Smashers #7 on)
Ribage Publ. Corp. (Trojan Magazines): May, 1952 - No. 15, Sept, 1954

1-Transvestism story; crime & terror stories begin 57 114 171 359 610 860
2-Marijuana story (7/52) 40 80 120 244 397 550
3-One pg. Frazetta-a 37 74 111 218 349 480
4-Cover shows girl in bondage having her blood drained; 1 pg. Frazetta-a
57 114 171 359 610 860
5-10 31 62 93 184 295 405
11,12,14 29 58 87 169 272 375
13-(5/54)-Angelo Torres 1st comic work (inks over Check's pencils); Check-a
35 70 105 203 327 450
15-Acid in face-c 41 82 123 250 413 575
NOTE. ***Fass*** *a 13; c-4, 6, 10.* ***Hollingsworth*** *a-10-13, 15; c-2, 12, 13, 15.* ***Kiefer*** *a-4.* ***Woodbridge*** *a-13? Bondage-c-1, 8, 12.*

CRIME ON THE RUN (See Approved Comics #8)

CRIME ON THE WATERFRONT (Formerly Famous Gangsters)
Realistic Publications: No. 4, May, 1952 (Painted cover)

4 28 56 84 162 261 360

CRIME PATROL (Formerly International #1-5; International Crime Patrol #6; becomes Crypt of Terror #17 on)
E. C. Comics: No. 7, Summer, 1948 - No. 16, Feb-Mar, 1950

7-Intro. Captain Crime 72 144 216 454 765 1075
8-14: 12-Ingels-a 62 124 186 391 658 925
15-Intro. of Crypt Keeper (inspired by Witches Tales radio show) & Crypt of Terror (see Tales From the Crypt #33 for origin); used by N.Y. Legis. Comm.; last pg. Feldstein-a
263 526 789 2104 3352 4600
16-2nd Crypt Keeper app.; Roussos-a 170 340 510 1060 2168 2975
NOTE: ***Craig*** *c/a in most issues.* ***Feldstein*** *a-9-16.* ***Kiefer*** *a-8, 10, 11.* ***Moldoff*** *a-7.*

CRIME PATROL
Gemstone Publishing: Apr, 2000 - No. 10, Jan, 2001 ($2.50)

1-10: E.C. reprints 2.50
Volume 1,2 (2000, $13.50) 1-r/#1-5. 2-r/#6-10 14.00

CRIME PHOTOGRAPHER (See Casey...)

CRIME REPORTER
St. John Publ. Co.: Aug, 1948 - No. 3, Dec, 1948 (Indicia shows Oct.)

1-Drug club story 53 106 159 330 553 775
2-Used in **SOTI**: illo- "Children told me what the man was going to do with the red-hot poker;" r/Dynamic #17 with editing; Baker-c; Tuska-a 75 150 225 473 799 1125
3-Baker-c; Tuska-a 41 82 123 250 413 575

CRIMES BY WOMEN
Fox Features Syndicate: June, 1948 - No. 15, Aug, 1951; 1954 (True crime cases)

1-True story of Bonnie Parker 122 244 366 769 1297 1825
2,3: 3-Used in **SOTI**, pg. 234 63 126 189 397 674 950
4,5,7-9,11-15: 8-Used in **POP**. 14-Bondage-c 58 116 174 365 620 875
6-Classic girl fight-c; acid-in-face panel 66 132 198 416 701 985
10-Used in **SOTI**, pg. 72; girl fight-c 59 118 177 372 629 885
54(M.S. Publ.-'54)-Reprint; (formerly My Love Secret)
24 48 72 140 225 310

CRIMES INCORPORATED (Formerly My Past)
Fox Features Syndicate: No. 12, June, 1950 (Crime Incorporated No. 2 on)

12 21 42 63 123 197 270

CRIMES INCORPORATED (See Fox Giants)

CRIME SMASHER (See Whiz #76)
Fawcett Publications: Summer, 1948 (one-shot)

1-Formerly Spy Smasher 41 82 123 253 419 585

CRIME SMASHERS (Becomes Secret Mysteries No. 16 on)
Ribage Publishing Corp.(Trojan Magazines): Oct, 1950 - No. 15, Mar, 1953

1-Used in **SOTI**, pg. 19,20, & illo "A girl raped and murdered;" Sally the Sleuth begins
88 176 264 554 940 1325
2-Kubert-c 47 94 141 291 483 675
3,4 38 76 114 226 363 500
5-Wood-a 45 90 135 279 465 650
6,8-11: 8-Lingerie panel 29 58 87 172 276 380
7-Female heroin junkie story 33 66 99 194 312 430

Crime Suspenstories #16 © WMG

Crimson #1 © Aegis Ent.

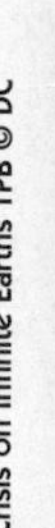
Crisis on Infinite Earths TPB © DC

	GD	VG	FN	VF	VF/NM	NM-
	2.0	4.0	6.0	8.0	9.0	9.2

12-Injury to eye panel; 1 pg. Frazetta-a 32 64 96 188 302 415
13-Used in **POP**, pgs. 79,80; 1 pg. Frazetta-a 32 64 96 188 302 415
14,15 24 48 72 140 225 310
NOTE: ***Hollingsworth** a-14. **Kiefer** a-15. Bondage c-7, 9.*

CRIME SUSPENSTORIES (Formerly Vault of Horror No. 12-14)
E. C. Comics: No. 15, Oct-Nov, 1950 - No. 27, Feb-Mar, 1955

15-Identical to #1 in content; #1 printed on outside front cover. #15 (formerly "The Vault of Horror") printed and blackened out on inside front cover with Vol. 1, No. 1 printed over it. Evidently, several of No. 15 were printed before a decision was made not to drop the Vault of Horror and Haunt of Fear series. The print run was stopped on No. 15 and continued on No. 1. All of the No. 15 issues were changed as described above.
149 298 447 1192 1896 2600
1 114 228 342 912 1456 2000
2 60 120 180 480 765 1050
3-5: 3-Poe adaptation. 3-Old Witch stories begin 41 82 123 328 527 725
6-10: 9-Craig bio. 36 72 108 288 457 625
11,12,14,15: 15-The Old Witch guest stars 28 56 84 224 355 485
13,16-Williamson-a 30 60 90 240 383 525
17-Williamson/Frazetta-a (6 pgs.) Williamson bio. 36 72 108 288 457 625
18,19: 19-Used in **SOTI**, pg. 235 24 48 72 192 309 425
20-Cover used in **SOTI**, illo "Cover of a children's comic book"
31 62 93 248 399 550
21,24-26: 24- "Food For Thought" similar to "Cave In" in Amazing Detective Cases #13 (1952)
17 34 51 136 218 300
22-Used in Senate investigation on juvenile delinquency; Ax decapitation-c
37 74 111 296 473 650
23-Used in Senate investigation on juvenile delinquency
24 48 72 192 309 425
27-Last issue (Low distribution) 21 42 63 168 272 375
NOTE: ***Craig** a-1-21; c-1-18, 20-22. **Crandall** a-18-26. **Davis** a-4, 5, 7, 9-12, 20. **Elder** a-17,18. **Evans** a-15, 19, 21, 23, 25, 27; c-23, 24. **Feldstein** c-19. **Ingels** a-1-12, 14, 15, 27. **Kamen** a-2, 4-18, 20-27; c-25-27. **Krigstein** a-22, 24, 25, 27. **Kurtzman** a-1, 3. **Orlando** a-16, 22, 24, 26. **Wood** a-1, 3. Issues No. 1-3 were printed in Canada as "Weird Suspenstories." Issues No. 11-15 have E. C. "quickie" stories. No. 25 contains the famous "Are You a Red Dupe?" editorial. Ray Bradbury adaptations-15, 17.*

CRIME SUSPENSTORIES
Russ Cochran/Gemstone Publ.: Nov, 1992 - No. 27, May, 1999 ($1.50/$2.00/$2.50)

1-27: Reprints Crime SuspenStories series 3.00

CRIMINAL
Marvel Comics (Icon): Oct, 2006 - No. 10, Oct, 2007 ($2.99)
Volume 2: Feb, 2008 - Present ($3.50)

1-10-Ed Brubaker-s/Sean Phillips-a/c 3.00
Volume 2: 1-5-Brubaker-s/Phillips-a 3.50
... Vol. 1: Coward TPB (2007, $14.99) r/#1-5; intro. by Tom Fontana 15.00
... Vol. 2: Lawless TPB (2007, $14.99) r/#6-10; intro. by Frank Miller 15.00
... Vol. 3. The Dead and the Dying TPB (2008, $11.99) r/V2#1-4; intro. by John Singleton 12.00

CRIMINAL MACABRE: A CAL MCDONALD MYSTERY (Also see Last Train to Deadsville)
Dark Horse Comics: May, 2003 - No. 5, Sept, 2003 ($2.99)

1-5-Niles-s/Templesmith-a 3.00

CRIMINAL MACABRE: (limited series and one-shots)
Dark Horse Comics: ($2.99)

...: Cellblock 666 (9/08 - No. 4)(#25-28 in the series) 1-Niles-s/Stakal-a/Bradstreet-c 3.00
... :Feat of Clay (6/06, $2.99) Niles-s/Hotz-a/c 3.00
...: My Demon Baby (9/07 - No. 4, 4/08)(#21-24 in the series) 1-4-Niles-s/Stakal-a 3.00
...: Two Red Eyes (12/06 - No. 4, 3/07) 1-4-Niles-s/Hotz-a/Bradstreet-c 3.00

CRIMINALS ON THE RUN (Formerly Young King Cole) (Crime Fighting Detective No. 11 on)
Premium Group (Novelty Press): V4#1, Aug-Sep, 1948-#10, Dec-Jan, 1949-50

V4#1-Young King Cole continues 29 58 87 169 272 375
2-6: 6-Dr. Doom app. 25 50 75 145 233 320
7-Classic "Fish in the Face" c by L. B. Cole 53 106 159 330 553 775
V5#1,2 (#8,9),10: 9,10-L. B. Cole-c 22 44 66 129 207 285
NOTE: *Most issues have **L. B. Cole** covers. **McWilliams** a-V4#6, 7, V5#2; c-V4#5.*

CRIMSON (Also see Cliffhanger #0)
Image Comics (Cliffhanger Productions): May, 1998 - No. 7, Dec, 1998;
DC Comics (Cliffhanger Prod.): No. 8, Mar, 1999 - No. 24, Apr, 2001 ($2.50)

1-Humberto Ramos-a/Augustyn-s 5.00
1-Variant-c by Warren 8.00
1-Chromium-c 20.00
2-Ramos-c with street crowd, 2-Variant-c by Art Adams 3.00
2-Dynamic Forces CrimsonChrome cover 15.00
3-7: 3-Ramos Moon background-c. 7-Three covers by Ramos, Madureira, & Campbell 3.50
8-23: 8-First DC issue 2.50
24-($3.50) Final issue; wraparound-c 3.50

	GD	VG	FN	VF	VF/NM	NM-
	2.0	4.0	6.0	8.0	9.0	9.2

DF Premiere Ed. 1998 ($6.95) covers by Ramos and Jae Lee 7.00
Crimson: Scarlet X Blood on the Moon (10/99, $3.95) 4.00
Crimson Sourcebook (11/99, $2.95) Pin-ups and info 3.00
Earth Angel TPB (2001, $14.95) r/#13-18 15.00
Heaven and Earth TPB (1/00, $14.95) r/#7-12 15.00
Loyalty and Loss TPB ('99, $12.95) r/#1-6 13.00
Redemption TPB ('01, $14.95) r/#19-24 15.00

CRIMSON AVENGER, THE (See Detective Comics #20 for 1st app.)(Also see Leading Comics #1 & World's Best/Finest Comics)
DC Comics: June, 1988 - No. 4, Sept, 1988 ($1.00, limited series)

1-4 2.50

CRIMSON DYNAMO
Marvel Comics (Epic): Oct, 2003 - No. 6, Apr, 2004 ($2.50/$2.99)

1-4,6: 1-John Jackson Miller-s/Steve Ellis-a/c 2.50
5-($2.99) Iron Man-c/app. 3.00

CRIMSON PLAGUE
Event Comics: June, 1997 ($2.95, unfinished mini-series)

1-George Perez-a 3.00

CRIMSON PLAGUE (George Pérez's...)
Image Comics (Gorilla): June, 2000 - No. 2, Aug, 2000 ($2.95, mini-series)

1-George Perez-a; reprints 6/97 issue with 16 new pages 3.00
2-($2.50) 2.50

CRISIS AFTERMATH: THE BATTLE FOR BLUDHAVEN (Also see Infinite Crisis)
DC Comics: Jun, 2006 - No. 6, Sept, 2006 ($2.99, limited series)

1-Atomic Knights return; Teen Titans app.; Jurgens-a/Acuna-c 4.00
1-2nd printing with pencil cover 3.00
2-6: 2-Intro S.H.A.D.E. (new Freedom Fighters) 3.00
TPB (2007, $12.99) r/#1-6 13.00

CRISIS AFTERMATH: THE SPECTRE (Also see Infinite Crisis, Gotham Central and Tales of the Unexpected)
DC Comics: Jul, 2006 - No. 3, Sept, 2006 ($2.99, limited series)

1-3-Crispus Allen becomes the Spectre; Pfeifer-s/Chiang-a/c 3.00
TPB (2007, $12.99) r/#1-3 and Tales of the Unexpected #1-3 13.00

CRISIS ON INFINITE EARTHS (Also see Official... Index and Legends of the DC Universe)
DC Comics: Apr, 1985 - No. 12, Mar, 1986 (maxi-series)

1-1st DC app. Blue Beetle & Detective Karp from Charlton; Pérez-c on all
2 4 6 9 13 16
2-6: 6-Intro Charlton's Capt. Atom, Nightshade, Question, Judomaster, Peacemaker & Thunderbolt into DC Universe 1 3 4 6 8 10
7-Double size; death of Supergirl 2 4 6 13 16 22
8-Death of the Flash (Barry Allen) 2 4 6 11 16 20
9-11: 9-Intro. Charlton's Ghost into DC Universe. 10-Intro. Charlton's Banshee, Dr. Spectro, Image, Punch & Jewellee into DC Universe; Starman (Prince Gavyn) dies
1 3 4 6 8 10
12-(52 pgs.)-Deaths of Dove, Kole, Lori Lemaris, Sunburst, G.A. Robin &Huntress; Kid Flash becomes new Flash; 3rd & final DC app. of the 3 Lt. Marvels; Green Fury gets new look (becomes Green Flame in Infinity, Inc. #32) 2 4 6 8 11 14
Slipcased Hardcover (1998, $99.95) Wraparound dust-jacket cover by Pérez and Alex Ross; sketch pages by Pérez; intro by Wolfman 125.00
TPB (2000, $29.95) Wraparound-c by Pérez and Ross 30.00
NOTE: *Crossover issues: All Star Squadron 50-56,60; Amethyst 13; Blue Devil 17,18; DC Comics Presents 78,86-88,95; Detective Comics 558; Fury of Firestorm 41,42; G.I. Combat 274; Green Lantern 194-196,198; Infinity, Inc. 18-25 & Annual 1, Justice League of America 244,245 & Annual 3; Legion of Super-Heroes 16,18; Losers Special 1; New Teen Titans 13,14; Omega Men 31,33; Superman 413-415; Swamp Thing 44,46; Wonder Woman 327-329.*

CRISIS ON MULTIPLE EARTHS
DC Comics: 2002, 2003, 2004 ($14.95, trade paperbacks)

TPB-(2003) Reprints 1st 4 Silver Age JLA/JSA crossovers from J.L.ofA. #21,22; 29,30; 37,38; 46,47; new painted-c by Alex Ross; intro. by Mark Waid 15.00
Volume 2 (2003, $14.95) r/J.L.ofA. #55,56; 64,65; 73,74; 82,83; new Ordway-c 15.00
Volume 3 (2004, $14.95) r/J.L.ofA. #91,92; 100-102; 107,108; 113; Wein intro., Ross-c 15.00
Volume 4 (2006, $14.99) r/J.L.ofA. #123-124 (Earth-Prime),135-137 (Fawcett's Shazam characters), 147-148 (Legion of Super-Heroes); Ross-c 15.00
... The Team-Ups Volume 1 (2005, $14.99) r/Flash #123,129,137,151; Showcase #55,56; Green Lantern #40, Brave and the Bold #61 and Spectre #7; new Ordway-c 15.00

CRITICAL MASS (See A Shadowline Saga: Critical Mass)

CRITTERS (Also see Usagi Yojimbo Summer Special)
Fantagraphics Books: 1986 - No. 50, 1990 ($1.70/$2.00, B&W)

1-Cutey Bunny, Usagi Yojimbo app. 1 3 4 6 8 10
2,4,5,8,9 6.00

Crossing Midnight #13 © Carey & Fern

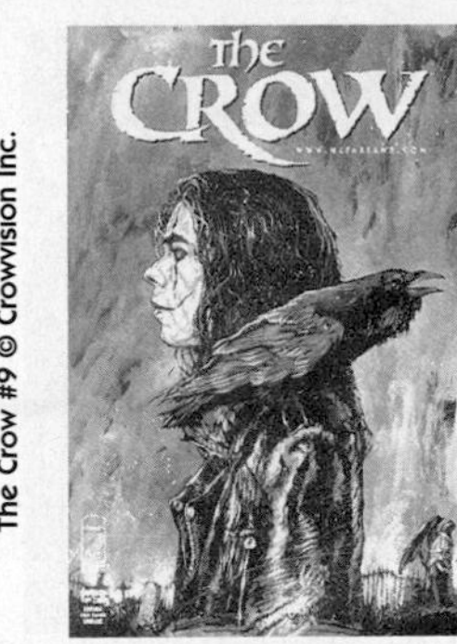

The Crow #9 © Crowvision Inc.

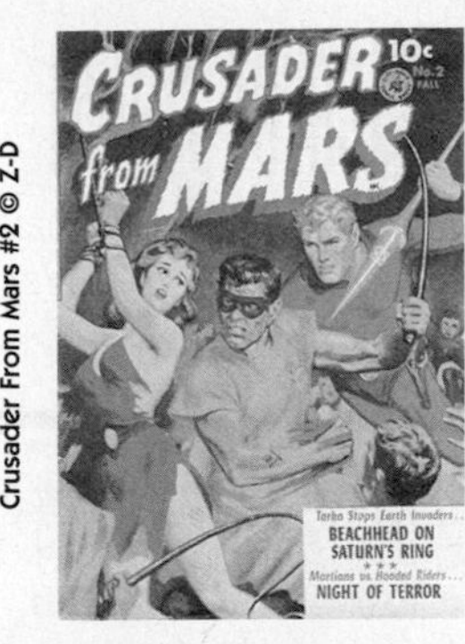

Crusader From Mars #2 © Z-D

	GD 2.0	VG 4.0	FN 6.0	VF 8.0	VF/NM 9.0	NM- 9.2

3,6,7,10-Usagi Yojimbo app. 1 2 3 4 5 7
11-22,24-37,39,40: 11,14-Usagi Yojimbo app. 11-Christmas Special (68 pgs.); Usagi Yojimbo. 22-Watchmen parody; two diff. covers exist 2.50
23-With Alan Moore Flexi-disc ($3.95) 5.00
38-($2.75-c) Usagi Yojimbo app. 3.00
41-49 4.00
50 ($4.95, 84 pgs.)-Neil the Horse, Capt. Jack, Sam & Max & Usagi Yojimbo app.; Quagmire, Shaw-a 1 2 3 4 5 7
Special 1 (1/88, $2.00) 3.00

CROSS
Dark Horse Comics: No. 0, Oct, 1995 - No. 6, Apr, 1995 ($2.95, limited series, mature)
0-6: Darrow-c & Vachss scripts in all 3.00

CROSS AND THE SWITCHBLADE, THE
Spire Christian Comics (Fleming H. Revell Co.): 1972 (35-49¢)
1-Some issues have nn 2 4 6 10 14 18

CROSS BRONX, THE
Image Comics: Sept, 2006 - No. 4, Dec, 2006 ($2.99, limited series)
1-4: 1-Oeming-a/c; Oeming & Brandon-s; Ribic var-c. 2-Johnson var-c. 4-Mack var-c 3.00

CROSSFIRE
Spire Christian Comics (Fleming H. Revell Co.): 1973 (39/49¢)
nn 2 4 6 9 12 15

CROSSFIRE (Also see DNAgents)
Eclipse Comics: 5/84 - No. 17, 3/86; No. 18, 1/87 - No. 26, 2/88 ($1.50, Baxter paper) (#18-26 are B&W)
1-11,14-26: 1-DNAgents x-over; Spiegle-c/a begins 2.50
12,13-Death of Marilyn Monroe. 12-Dave Stevens-c 4.00

CROSSFIRE AND RAINBOW (Also see DNAgents)
Eclipse Comics: June, 1986 - No. 4, Sept, 1986 ($1.25, deluxe format)
1-3: Spiegle-a. 4-Dave Stevens-c 2.50

CROSSGEN...
CrossGeneration Comics
CrossGenesis (1/00) Previews CrossGen universe; cover gallery 3.00
...Primer (1/00) Wizard supplement; intro. to the CrossGen universe 2.50
...Sampler (2/00) Retailer preview book 3.00

CROSSGEN CHRONICLES
CrossGeneration Comics: June, 2000 - No. 8 ($3.95)
1-Intro. to CrossGen characters & company 4.00
1-(no cover price) same contents, customer preview 4.00
2-8: 2-(3/01) George Pérez-c/a. 3-5-Pérez-a/Waid-s. 6,7-Nebres-c/a 4.00

CROSSING MIDNIGHT
DC Comics (Vertigo): Jan, 2007 - No. 19, Jul, 2008 ($2.99)
1-19: 1-Carey-s/Fern-a/Williams III-c. 10-12-Nguyen-a 3.00
...: Cut Here TPB (2007, $9.99) r/#1-5 10.00
...: A Map of Midnight TPB (2008, $14.99) r/#6-12; afterword by Carey 15.00

CROSSING THE ROCKIES (See Classics Illustrated Special Issue)

CROSSOVERS, THE
CrossGeneration Comics: Feb, 2003 - No. 12 ($2.95)
1-12-Robert Rodi-s. 1-6-Mauricet & Ernie Colon-a. 7-Staton-a begins 3.00
Vol. 1: Cross Currents (2003, $9.95) digest-sized reprints #1-6 10.00

CROW, THE (Also see Caliber Presents)
Caliber Press: Feb, 1989 - No. 4, 1989 ($1.95, B&W, limited series)
1-James O'Barr-c/a/scripts 5 10 15 34 55 75
1-3-2nd printing 6.00
2-4 3 6 9 20 30 40
2-3rd printing 4.00

CROW, THE
Tundra Publishing, Ltd.: Jan, 1992 - No. 3, 1992 ($4.95, B&W, 68 pgs.)
1-3: 1-r/#1,2 of Caliber series. 2-r/#3 of Caliber series w/new material. 3-All new material 1 2 3 5 6 8

CROW, THE
Kitchen Sink Press: 1/96 - No. 3, 3/96 ($2.95, B&W)
1-3: James O'Barr-c/scripts 5.00
#0-A Cycle of Shattered Lives (12/98, $3.50) new story by O'Barr 4.00

CROW, THE
Image Comics (Todd McFarlane Prod.): Feb, 1999 - No. 10, Nov, 1999 ($2.50)
1-10: 1-Two covers by McFarlane and Kent Williams; Muth-s in all. 2-6,10-Paul Lee-a 3.00
Book 1 - Vengeance (2000, $10.95, TPB) r/#1-3,5,6 11.00
Book 2 - Evil Beyond Reach (2000, $10.95, TPB) r/#4,7-10 11.00
Todd McFarlane Presents The Crow Magazine 1 (3/00, $4.95) 5.00

CROW, THE: CITY OF ANGELS (Movie)
Kitchen Sink Press: July, 1996 - No. 3, Sept, 1996 ($2.95, limited series)
1-3: Adaptation of film; two-c (photo & illos.). 1-Vincent Perez interview 3.00

CROW, THE: FLESH AND BLOOD
Kitchen Sink Press: May, 1996 - No. 3, July, 1996 ($2.95, limited series)
1-3: O'Barr-c 3.00

CROW, THE: RAZOR - KILL THE PAIN
London Night Studios: Apr, 1998 - No. 3, July, 1998 ($2.95, B&W, lim. series)
1-3-Hartsoe-s/O'Barr-painted-c 3.00
0(10/98) Dorien painted-c, Finale (2/99) 3.00
The Lost Chapter (2/99, $4.95), Tour Book-(12/97) pin-ups; 4 diff.-c 5.00

CROW, THE: WAKING NIGHTMARES
Kitchen Sink Press: Jan, 1997 - No. 4, 1998 ($2.95, B&W, limited series)
1-4-Miran Kim-c 5.00

CROW, THE: WILD JUSTICE
Kitchen Sink Press: Oct, 1996 - No. 3, Dec, 1996 ($2.95, B&W, limited series)
1-3-Prosser-s/Adlard-a 3.00

CROWN COMICS (Also see Vooda)
Golfing/McCombs Publ.: Wint, 1944-45; No. 2, Sum, 1945 - No. 19, July, 1949
1- "The Oblong Box" E.A. Poe adaptation 41 82 123 250 413 575
2,3-Baker-a; 3-Voodah by Baker 29 58 87 169 272 375
4-6-Baker-c/a; Voodah app. #4,5 31 62 93 181 291 400
7-Feldstein, Baker, Kamen-a; Baker-c 30 60 90 176 283 390
8-Baker-a; Voodah app. 25 50 75 145 233 320
9-11,13-19: Voodah in #10-19. 13-New logo 17 34 51 98 154 210
12-Master Marvin by Feldstein, Starr-a; Voodah-c 18 36 54 103 162 220
NOTE: *Bolle a-11, 13-16, 18, 19; c-11p, 15.* ***Powell*** *a-19.* ***Starr*** *a-11-13; c-11i.*

CRUCIBLE
DC Comics (Impact): Feb, 1993 - No. 6, July, 1993 ($1.25, limited series)
1-6: 1-(99¢)-Neon ink-c. 1,2-Quesada-c(p). 1-4-Quesada layouts 2.50

CRUEL AND UNUSUAL
DC Comics (Vertigo): June, 1999 - No. 4, Sept, 1999 ($2.95, limited series)
1-4-Delano & Peyer-s/McCrea-c/a 3.00

CRUSADER FROM MARS (See Tops in Adventure)
Ziff-Davis Publ. Co.: Jan-Mar, 1952 - No. 2, Fall, 1952 (Painted-c)
1-Cover is dated Spring 75 150 225 473 799 1125
2-Bondage-c 53 106 159 330 553 775

CRUSADER RABBIT (TV)
Dell Publishing Co.: No. 735, Oct, 1956 - No. 805, May, 1957
Four Color 735 (#1) 25 50 75 185 343 500
Four Color 805 19 38 57 141 261 380

CRUSADERS, THE (Religious)
Chick Publications: 1974 - Vol. 17, 1988 (39/69¢, 36 pgs.)
Vol.1-Operation Bucharest ('74). Vol.2-The Broken Cross ('74). Vol.3-Scarface ('74). Vol.4-Exorcists ('75). Vol.5-Chaos ('75) 2 4 6 10 14 18
Vol.6-Primal Man? ('76)-(Disputes evolution theory). Vol.7-The Ark-(claims proof of existence, destroyed by Bolsheviks). Vol.8-The Gift-(Life story of Christ). Vol.9-Angel of Light-(Story of the Devil). Vol.10-Spellbound?-(Tells how rock music is Satanic & produced by witches). 11-Sabotage?. 12-Alberto. 13-Double Cross. 14-The Godfathers. (No. 6-14 low in distribution; loaded with religious propaganda.). 15-The Force. 16-The Four Horsemen 2 4 6 10 14 18
Vol. 17-The Prophet (low print run) 2 4 6 11 16 20

CRUSADERS (Southern Knights No. 2 on)
Guild Publications: 1982 (B&W, magazine size)
1-1st app. Southern Knights 2 4 6 8 11 14

CRUSADERS, THE (Also see Black Hood, The Jaguar, The Comet, The Fly, Legend of the Shield, The Mighty... & The Web)
DC Comics (Impact): May, 1992 - No. 8, Dec, 1992 ($1.00/$1.25)
1-8-Contains 3 Impact trading cards 2.50

CRUSADES, THE
DC Comics (Vertigo): 2001 - No. 20, Dec, 2002 ($3.95/$2.50)

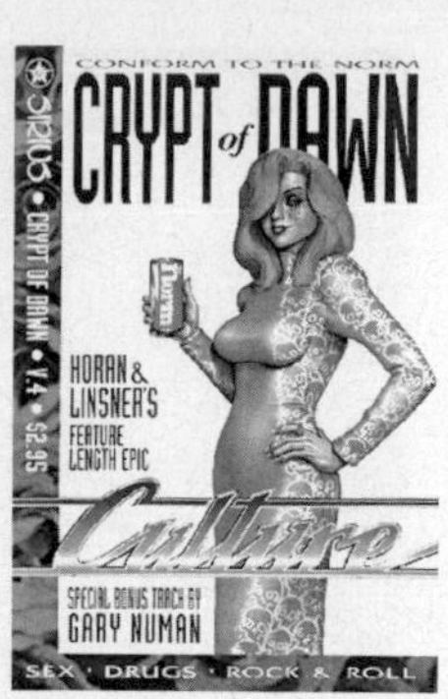

Crypt of Dawn #4 © JM Linsner

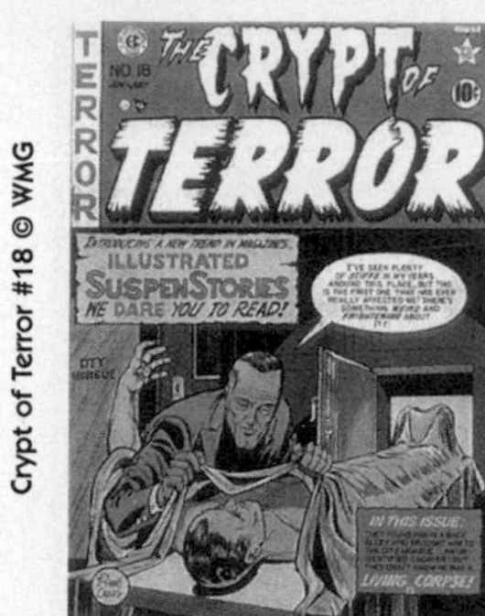

Crypt of Terror #18 © WMG

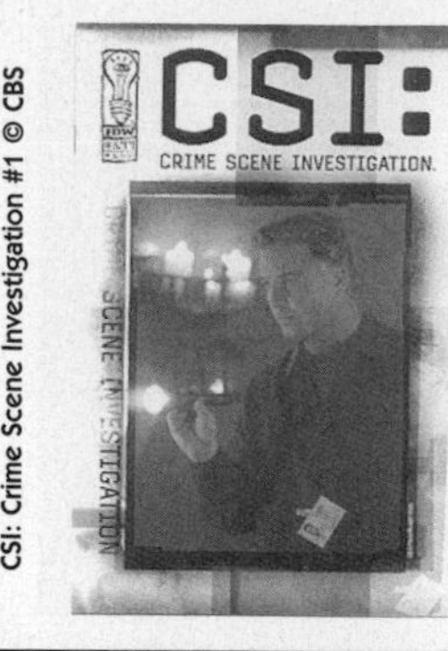

CSI: Crime Scene Investigation #1 © CBS

	GD 2.0	VG 4.0	FN 6.0	VF 8.0	VF/NM 9.0	NM- 9.2

...: Urban Decree ('01, $3.95) Intro. the Knight; Seagle-s/Kelley Jones-c/a 4.00
1-(5/01, $2.50) Sienkiewicz-c 3.00
2-20: 2-Moeller-c. 18-Begin $2.95-c 3.00

CRUSH
Dark Horse Comics: Oct, 2003 - No. 4, Jan, 2004 ($2.99, limited series)

1-4-Jason Hall-s/Sean Murphy-a 3.00

CRUSH, THE
Image Comics (Motown Machineworks): Jan, 1996 - No. 5, July, 1996 ($2.25, limited series)

1-5: Baron scripts 3.00

CRUX
CrossGeneration Comics: May, 2001 - No. 33, Feb, 2004 ($2.95)

1-33: 1-Waid-s/Epting & Magyar-a/c. 6-Pelletier-a. 13-Dixon-s begin. 25-Cover has fake creases and other aging 3.00
Atlantis Rising Vol. 1 TPB (2002, $15.95) r/#1-6 16.00
Test of Time Vol. 2 TPB (12/02, $15.95) r/#7-12 16.00
Vol. 3: Strangers in Atlantis (2003, $15.95) r/#13-18 16.00
Vol. 4: Chaos Reborn (2003, $15.95) r/#19-24 16.00

CRY FOR DAWN
Cry For Dawn Pub.: 1989 - No. 9 ($2.25, B&W, mature)

	GD	VG	FN	VF	VF/NM	NM-
1	7	14	21	49	80	110
1-2nd printing	3	6	9	18	27	35
1-3rd printing	3	6	9	14	20	25
2	5	10	15	30	48	65
2-2nd printing	2	4	6	11	16	20
3	4	8	12	22	34	45
3a-HorrorCon Edition (1990, less than 400 printed, signed inside-c)						200.00
4-6	2	4	6	13	18	22
5-2nd printing	1	2	3	5	6	8
7-9	2	4	6	9	13	16
4-9-Signed & numbered editions	3	6	9	14	20	25

Angry Christ Comix HC (4/03, $29.99) reprints various stories; and 30 pgs. new material 30.00
...Calendar (1993) 35.00

CRYIN' LION COMICS
William H. Wise Co.: Fall, 1944 - No. 3, Spring, 1945

	GD	VG	FN	VF	VF/NM	NM-
1-Funny animal	15	30	45	83	124	165
2-Hitler and Tojo app.	13	26	39	74	105	135
3	10	20	30	56	76	95

CRYPT
Image Comics (Extreme): Aug, 1995 - No.2, Oct. 1995 ($2.50, limited series)

1,2-Prophet app. 2.50

CRYPTIC WRITINGS OF MEGADETH
Chaos! Comics: Sept, 1997 - No. 4, Jun, 1998 ($2.95, quarterly)

1-4-Stories based on song lyrics by Dave Mustaine 3.00

CRYPT OF DAWN (see Dawn)
Sirius: 1996 ($2.95, B&W, limited series)

1-Linsner-c/s; anthology. 5.00
2, 3 (2/98) 4.00
4,5: 4- (6/98), 5-(11/98) 3.00
Ltd. Edition 20.00

CRYPT OF SHADOWS
Marvel Comics Group: Jan, 1973 - No. 21, Nov, 1975 (#1-9 are 20¢)

	GD	VG	FN	VF	VF/NM	NM-
1-Wolverton-r/Advs. Into Terror #7	3	6	9	16	23	30
2-10: 2-Starlin/Everett-c	2	4	6	10	14	18
11-21: 18,20-Kirby-a	2	4	6	9	13	16

NOTE: ***Briefer*** *a-2r.* ***Ditko*** *a-13r, 18-20r.* ***Everett*** *a-6, 14r; c-2i.* ***Heath*** *a-1r.* ***Gil Kane*** *c-1, 6.* ***Mort Lawrence*** *a-1r, 8r.* ***Maneely*** *a-2r.* ***Moldoff*** *a-8.* ***Powell*** *a-12r, 14r.* ***Tuska*** *a-2r.*

CRYPT OF TERROR (Formerly Crime Patrol; Tales From the Crypt No. 20 on)
(Also see EC Archives • Tales From the Crypt)
E. C. Comics: No. 17, Apr-May, 1950 - No. 19, Aug-Sept, 1950

	GD	VG	FN	VF	VF/NM	NM-
17-1st New Trend to hit stands	286	572	858	2288	3644	5000
18,19	166	332	498	1328	2114	2900

NOTE: ***Craig*** *c/a-17-19.* ***Feldstein*** *a-17-19.* ***Ingels*** *a-19.* ***Kurtzman*** *a-18.* ***Wood*** *a-18. Canadian reprints known; see Table of Contents.*

CSI: CRIME SCENE INVESTIGATION (Based on TV series)
IDW Publishing: Jan, 2003 - No. 5, May, 2003 ($3.99, limited series)

1-Two covers (photo & Ashley Wood); Max Allan Collins-s 4.00
2-5 4.00
...: Case Files Vol. 1 TPB (8/06, $19.99) B&W rep/Serial TPB, CSI - Bad Rap and CSI - Demon House limited series 20.00
...: Serial TPB (2003, $19.99) r/#1-5; bonus short story by Collins/Wood 20.00
...: Thicker Than Blood (7/03, $6.99) Mariotte-s/Rodriguez-a 7.00

CSI: CRIME SCENE INVESTIGATION - BAD RAP
IDW Publishing: Aug, 2003 - No. 5, Dec, 2003 ($3.99, limited series)

1-5-Two photo covers; Max Allan Collins-s/Rodriguez-a 4.00
TPB (3/04, $19.99) r/#1-5 20.00

CSI: CRIME SCENE INVESTIGATION - DEMON HOUSE
IDW Publishing: Feb, 2004 - No. 5, Jun, 2004 ($3.99, limited series)

1-5-Photo covers on all; Max Allan Collins-s/Rodriguez-a 4.00
TPB (10/04, $19.99) r/#1-5 20.00

CSI: CRIME SCENE INVESTIGATION - DOMINOS
IDW Publishing: Aug, 2004 - No. 5, Dec, 2004 ($3.99, limited series)

1-5-Photo covers on all; Oprisko-s/Rodriguez-a 4.00

CSI: CRIME SCENE INVESTIGATION - DYING IN THE GUTTERS
IDW Publishing: Aug, 2006 - No. 5, Dec, 2006 ($3.99, limited series)

1-5-"Rich Johnston" murdered; comic creators (Quesada, Rucka, David, Brubaker, Silvestri and others) appear as suspects; Stephen Mooney-a; photo-c 4.00

CSI: CRIME SCENE INVESTIGATION - SECRET IDENTITY
IDW Publishing: Feb, 2005 - No. 5, Jun, 2005 ($3.99, limited series)

1-5-Photo covers on all; Steven Grant-s/Gabriel Rodriguez-a 4.00

CSI: MIAMI
IDW Publishing: Oct, 2003; Apr, 2004 ($6.99, one-shots)

... - Blood Money (9/04)-Oprisko-s/Guedes & Perkins-a 7.00
... - Smoking Gun (10/03)-Mariotte-s/Avilés & Wood-a 7.00
... - Thou Shalt Not... (4/04)-Oprisko-s/Guedes & Wood-a 7.00
TPB (2/05, $19.99) reprints one-shots 20.00

CSI: NY - BLOODY MURDER
IDW Publishing: July, 2005 - No. 5, Nov, 2005 ($3.99, limited series)

1-5-Photo covers on all; Collins-s/Woodward-a 4.00

C-23 (Jim Lee's...) (Based on Wizards of the Coast card game)
Image Comics: Apr, 1998 - No. 8, Nov, 1998 ($2.50)

1-8: 1,2-Choi & Mariotte-s/ Charest-c. 2-Variant-c by Jim Lee. 4-Ryan Benjamin-c. 5,8-Corben var-c. 6-Flip book with Planetary preview; Corben-c 3.00

CUD
Fantagraphics Books: 8/92 - No. 8, 12/94 ($2.25-$2.75, B&W, mature)

1-8: Terry LaBan scripts & art in all. 6-1st Eno & Plum 3.00

CUD COMICS
Dark Horse Comics: Jan, 1995 - No. 8, Sept, 1997 ($2.95, B&W)

1-8: Terry LaBan-c/a/scripts. 5-Nudity; marijuana story 3.00
Eno and Plum TPB (1997, $12.95) r/#1-4, DHP #93-95 13.00

CUPID
Marvel Comics (U.S.A.): Dec, 1949 - No. 2, Mar, 1950

	GD	VG	FN	VF	VF/NM	NM-
1-Photo-c	15	30	45	94	147	200
2-Bettie Page ('50s pin-up queen) photo-c; Powell-a (see My Love #4)	41	82	123	256	428	600

CURIO
Harry 'A' Chesler: 1930's(?) (Tabloid size, 16-20 pgs.)

	GD	VG	FN	VF	VF/NM	NM-
nn	18	36	54	107	169	230

CURLY KAYOE COMICS (Boxing)
United Features Syndicate/Dell Publ. Co.: 1946 - No. 8, 1950; Jan, 1958

	GD	VG	FN	VF	VF/NM	NM-
1 (1946)-Strip-r (Fritzi Ritz); biography of Sam Leff, Kayoe's artist	18	36	54	103	162	220
2	11	22	33	62	86	110
3-8	10	20	30	54	72	90
United Presents...(Fall, 1948)	10	20	30	54	72	90
Four Color 871 (Dell, 1/58)	4	8	12	24	37	50

CURSED
Image Comics (Top Cow): Oct, 2003 - No. 4, Feb, 2004 ($2.99)

1-4-Avery & Blevins-s/Molenaar-a 3.00

CURSE OF DRACULA, THE
Dark Horse Comics: July, 1998 - No. 3, Sept, 1998 ($2.95, limited series)

1-3-Marv Wolfman-s/Gene Colan-a 3.00
TPB (2005, $9.95) r/series; intro. by Marv Wolfman 10.00

Curse of the Spawn #17 © TMP

Cyberforce V2 #3 © TCOW

Cybernary 2.0 #4 © WSP

	GD 2.0	VG 4.0	FN 6.0	VF 8.0	VF/NM 9.0	NM- 9.2

CURSE OF DREADWOLF
Lightning Comics: Sept, 1994 ($2.75, B&W)

1 — 2.75

CURSE OF RUNE (Becomes Rune, 2nd Series)
Malibu Comics (Ultraverse): May, 1995 - No. 4, Aug, 1995 ($2.50, lim. series)

1-4: 1-Two covers form one image — 2.50

CURSE OF THE SPAWN
Image Comics (Todd McFarlane Prod.): Sept, 1996 - No. 29, Mar, 1999 ($1.95)

	GD	VG	FN	VF	VF/NM	NM-
1-Dwayne Turner-a(p)						6.00
1-B&W Edition	2	4	6	9	13	16
2-3						4.00
4-29: 12-Movie photo-c of Melinda Clarke (Priest)						2.50
Blood and Sutures ('99, $9.95, TPB) r/#5-8						10.00
Lost Values ('00, $10.95, TPB) r/#12-14,22; Ashley Wood-c						11.00
Sacrifice of the Soul ('99, $9.95, TPB) r/#1-4						10.00
Shades of Gray ('00, $9.95, TPB) r/#9-11,29						10.00
The Best of the Curse of the Spawn (6/06, $16.99, TPB) B&W r/#1-8,12-16,20-29						17.00

CURSE OF THE WEIRD
Marvel Comics: Dec, 1993 - No. 4, Mar, 1994 ($1.25, limited series)
(Pre-code horror-r)

	GD	VG	FN	VF	VF/NM	NM-
1-4: 1,3,4-Wolverton-r(1-Eye of Doom; 3-Where Monsters Dwell; 4-The End of the World). 2-Orlando-r. 4-Zombie-r by Everett; painted-c	1	2	3	5	6	8

NOTE: *Briefer r-2. Davis a-4r. Ditko a-1r, 2r, 4r; c-1r. Everett r-1. Heath r-1-3. Kubert r-3. Wolverton a-1r, 3r, 4r.*

CUSTER'S LAST FIGHT
Avon Periodicals: 1950

	GD	VG	FN	VF	VF/NM	NM-
nn-Partial reprint of Cowpuncher #1	15	30	45	88	137	185

CUTEY BUNNY (See Army Surplus Komikz Featuring...)

CUTIE PIE
Junior Reader's Guild (Lev Gleason): May, 1955 - No. 3, Dec, 1955; No. 4, Feb, 1956; No. 5, Aug, 1956

	GD	VG	FN	VF	VF/NM	NM-
1	8	16	24	42	54	65
2-5: 4-Misdated 2/55	6	12	18	28	34	40

CUTTING EDGE
Marvel Comics: Dec, 1995 ($2.95)

1-Hulk-c/story; Messner-Loebs scripts — 3.00

CVO: COVERT VAMPIRIC OPERATIONS
IDW Publishing: June, 2003 ($5.99, one-shot)

1-Alex Garner-s/Mindy Lee-a(p) — 6.00
... - Human Touch 1 (8/04, $3.99, one-shot) Hernandez & Garner-a — 4.00
TPB (9/04, $19.99) r/#1 and ... - Artifact #1-3; intro. by Garner — 20.00

CVO: COVERT VAMPIRIC OPERATIONS - AFRICAN BLOOD
IDW Publishing: Sept, 2006 - No. 4, May, 2007 ($3.99, limited series)

1-4-El Torres-s/Luis Czerniawski-a — 4.00

CVO: COVERT VAMPIRIC OPERATIONS - ARTIFACT
IDW Publishing: Oct, 2003 - No. 3, Dec, 2003 ($3.99, limited series)

1-3-Jeff Mariotte-s/Gabriel Hernandez-a/Alex Garner-c — 4.00

CVO: COVERT VAMPIRIC OPERATIONS - ROGUE STATE
IDW Publishing: Nov, 2004 - No. 5, Mar, 2005 ($3.99, limited series)

1-5-Jeff Mariotte-s/Vazquez-a — 4.00
TPB (7/05, $19.99) r/#1-5; cover gallery — 20.00

CYBERELLA
DC Comics (Helix): Sept, 1996 - No. 12, Aug, 1997 ($2.25/$2.50)(1st Helix series)

1-12: 1-5-Chaykin & Cameron-a. 1,2-Chaykin-c. 3-5-Cameron-c — 2.50

CYBERFORCE
Image Comics (Top Cow Productions): Oct, 1992 - No. 4, 1993; No. 0, Sept, 1993 ($1.95, limited series)

1-Silvestri-c/a in all; coupon for Image Comics #0; 1st Top Cow Productions title — 6.00
1-With coupon missing — 2.50
2-4,0: 2-(3/93). 3-Pitt-c/story. 4-Codename: Stryke Force back-up (1st app.); foil-c. 0-(9/93)-Walt Simonson-c/a/scripts — 3.00

CYBERFORCE
Image Comics (Top Cow Productions)/Top Cow Comics No. 28 on: V2#1, Nov, 1993 - No. 35, Sept. 1997 ($1.95)

V2#1-24: 1-7-Marc Silvestri/Keith Williams-c/a. 8-McFarlane-c/a. 10-Painted variant-c exists. 18-Variant-c exists. 23-Velocity-c. — 2.50
1-3: 1-Gold Logo-c. 2-Silver embossed-c. 3-Gold embossed-c — 10.00
1-(99¢, 3/96, 2nd printing) — 2.50
25-($3.95)-Wraparound, foil-c — 4.00
26-35: 28-(11/96)-1st Top Cow Comics iss. Quesada & Palmiotti's Gabriel app. 27-Quesada & Palmiotti's Ash app. — 2.50
Annual 1,2 (3/95, 8/96, $2.50, $2.95) — 3.00
NOTE: *Annuals read Volume One in the indica.*

CYBERFORCE (Volume 2)
Image Comics (Top Cow): Apr, 2006 - No. 6, Nov, 2006 ($2.99)

1-6: 1-Pat Lee-a/Ron Marz-s; three covers by Pat Lee, Marc Silvestri and Dave Finch — 3.00
#0-(6/06, $2.99) reprints origin story from Image Comics Hardcover Vol. 1 — 3.00
.../X-Men 1 (1/07, $3.99) Pat Lee-a/Ron Marz-s; 2 covers by Lee and Silvestri — 4.00
Vol. 1 TPB (12/06, $14.99) r/#1-6, #0 & story from The Cow Quarterly; cover gallery — 15.00

CYBERFORCE ORIGINS
Image Comics (Top Cow Productions): Jan, 1995 - No. 3, Nov, 1995 ($2.50)

1-Cyblade (1/95) — 5.00
1-Cyblade (3/96, 99¢, 2nd printing) — 2.25
1A-Exclusive Ed.; Tucci-c — 4.00
2,3: 2-Stryker (2/95)-1st Mike Turner-a. 3-Impact — 2.50
(#4) Misery (12/95, $2.95) — 3.00

CYBERFORCE/STRYKEFORCE: OPPOSING FORCES (See Codename: Stryke Force #15)
Image Comics (Top Cow Productions): Sept, 1995 - No.2, Oct, 1995 ($2.50, limited series)

1,2: 2-Stryker disbands Strykeforce. — 2.50

CYBERFORCE UNIVERSE SOURCEBOOK
Image Comics (Top Cow Productions): Aug, 1994/Feb, 1995 ($2.50)

1,2-Silvestri-c — 2.50

CYBERFROG
Hall of Heroes: June, 1994 - No. 2, Dec, 1994 ($2.50, B&W, limited series)

1,2 — 3.00

CYBERFROG
Harris Comics: Feb, 1996 - No. 3, Apr, 1996 ($2.95)

0-3: Van Sciver-c/a/scripts. 2-Variant-c exists — 5.00

CYBERFROG: (Title series), **Harris Comics**

--RESERVOIR FROG, 9/96 - No. 2, 10/96 ($2.95) 1,2: Van Sciver-c/a/scripts; wraparound-c — 3.00

--3RD ANNIVERSARY SPECIAL, 1/97 - #2, ($2.50, B&W) 1,2 — 3.00

--VS. CREED, 7/97 ($2.95, B&W)1 — 3.00

CYBERNARY (See Deathblow #1)
Image Comics (WildStorm Productions): Nov, 1995 - No.5, Mar, 1996 ($2.50)

1-5 — 2.50

CYBERNARY 2.0
DC Comics (WildStorm): Sept, 2001 - No. 6, Apr, 2002 ($2.95, limited series)

1-6: Joe Harris-s/Eric Canete-a. 6-The Authority app. — 3.00

CYBERPUNK
Innovation Publishing: Sept, 1989 - No. 2, Oct, 1989 ($1.95, 28 pgs.) Book 2, #1, May, 1990 - No. 2, 1990 ($2.25, 28 pgs.)

1,2, Book 2 #1,2:1,2-Ken Steacy painted-covers (Adults) — 2.50

CYBERPUNK: THE SERAPHIM FILES
Innovation Publishing: Nov, 1990 - No. 2, Dec, 1990 ($2.50, 28 pgs., mature)

1,2: 1-Painted-c; story cont'd from Seraphim — 2.50

CYBERPUNX
Image Comics (Extreme Studios): Mar, 1996 ($2.50)

1 — 3.00

CYBERRAD
Continuity Comics: 1991 - No. 7, 1992 ($2.00)(Direct sale & newsstand-c variations) V2#1, 1993 ($2.50)

1-7: 5-Glow-in-the-dark-c by N. Adams (direct sale only). 6-Contains 4 pg. fold-out poster; N. Adams layouts — 2.50
V2#1-($2.95, direct sale ed.)-Die-cut-c w/B&W hologram on-c; Neal Adams sketches — 3.00
V2#1-($2.50, newsstand ed.)-Without sketches — 2.50

CYBERRAD DEATHWATCH 2000 (Becomes CyberRad w/#2, 7/93)
Continuity Comics: Apr, 1993 - No. 2, 1993 ($2.50)

1,2: 1-Bagged w/2 cards; Adams-c & layouts & plots. 2-Bagged w/card; Adams scripts — 2.50

CYBER 7

Cyclops #3 © MAR

Dagar, Desert Hawk #16 © FOX

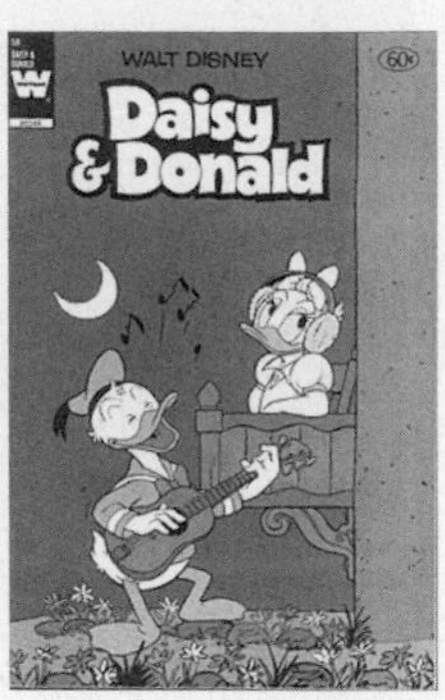

Daisy and Donald #58 © DIS

	GD 2.0	VG 4.0	FN 6.0	VF 8.0	VF/NM 9.0	NM- 9.2

Eclipse Comics: Mar, 1989 - #7, Sept, 1989; V2#1, Oct, 1989 - #10, 1990 ($2.00, B&W)

1-7, Book 2 #1-10: Stories translated from Japanese						2.50

CYBLADE
Image Comics (Top Cow Productions): (one-shots)

.../ Ghost Rider 1 (Marvel/Top Cow, 1/97, $2.95) Devil's Reign pt. 2						4.00
...: Pilot Season 1 (9/07, $2.99) Rick Mays-a						3.00

CYBLADE/SHI (Also see Battle For The Independents & Shi/Cyblade: The Battle For The Independents)
Image Comics (Top Cow Productions): 1995 ($2.95, one-shot)

San Diego Preview	3	6	9	16	20	25
1-($2.95)-1st app. Witchblade	2	4	6	12	16	20
1-($2.95)-variant-c; Tucci-a	2	4	6	10	12	15

CYBRID
Maximum Press: July, 1995; No. 0, Jan, 1997 ($2.95/$3.50)

1-(7/95)						3.50
0-(1/97)-Liefeld-a/script; story cont'd in Avengelyne #4						3.50

CYCLONE COMICS (Also see Whirlwind Comics)
Bilbara Publishing Co.: June, 1940 - No. 5, Nov, 1940

1-Origin Tornado Tom; Volton (the human generator), Tornado Tom, Kingdom of the Moon, Mister Q begin (1st app. of each)	124	248	372	775	1288	1800
2	62	124	186	388	644	900
3-Classic-c (scarce)	103	206	309	649	1100	1550
4	65	130	195	406	673	940
5-(Scarce)	81	162	243	506	846	1185

Ashcan - Not distributed to newsstands, only for in house use. Cover produced on green stock paper. A CGC certified FN (6.0) copy sold for $2,000 in 2006.

CYCLOPS (X-Men)
Marvel Comics: Oct, 2001 - No. 4, Jan, 2002 ($2.50, limited series)

1-4-Texeira-c/a. 1,2-Black Tom and Juggernaut app.						2.50

CYCLOPS: RETRIBUTION
Marvel Comics: 1994 ($5.95, trade paperback)

nn-r/Marvel Comics Presents #17-24						6.00

CY-GOR (See Spawn #38 for 1st app.)
Image Comics (Todd McFarlane Prod.): July, 1999 - No. 6, Dec, 1999 ($2.50)

1-6-Veitch-s						2.50

CYNTHIA DOYLE, NURSE IN LOVE (Formerly Sweetheart Diary)
Charlton Publications: No. 66, Oct, 1962 - No. 74, Feb, 1964

66-74	3	6	9	14	19	24

DAFFY (Daffy Duck No. 18 on)(See Looney Tunes)
Dell Publishing Co./Gold Key No. 31-127/Whitman No. 128 on: #457, 3/53 - #30, 7-9/62; #31, 10-12/62 - #145, 6/84 (No #132,133)

Four Color 457(#1)-Elmer Fudd x-overs begin	10	20	30	71	126	180
Four Color 536,615('55)	6	12	18	41	66	90
4(1-3/56)-11('57)	5	10	15	32	51	70
12-19(1958-59)	4	8	12	24	37	50
20-40(1960-64)	3	6	9	17	25	32
41-60(1964-68)	3	6	9	14	20	25
61-90(1969-74)-Road Runner in most. 76-82-"Daffy Duck and the Road Runner" on-c	2	4	6	10	14	18
91-110	2	4	6	8	10	12
111-127	1	2	3	5	6	8
128,134-141: 139(2/82), 140(2-3/82), 141(4/82)	1	3	4	6	8	10
129(8/80),130,131 (pre-pack?) (scarce). 129-Sherlock Holmes parody-s	3	6	9	20	30	40
142-145(#90029 on-c; nd, nd code, pre-pack): 142(6/83), 143(8/83), 144(3/84), 145(6/84)	3	6	9	14	20	26
Mini-Comic 1 (1976; 3-1/4x6-1/2")	1	2	3	5	6	8

NOTE: *Reprint issues-No.41-46, 48, 50, 53-55, 58, 59, 65, 67, 69, 73, 81, 96, 103-108; 136-142, 144, 145(1/3-2/3-r). (See March of Comics No. 277, 288, 303, 313, 331, 347, 357,375, 387, 397, 402, 413, 425, 437, 460).*

DAFFY DUCK (Digest-size reprints from Looney Tunes)
DC Comics: 2005 - Present ($6.99, digest)

Vol. 1: You're Despicable! - Reprints from Looney Tunes #38,43,45,47,51,53,54,58,61,62,66,70						7.00

DAFFY TUNES COMICS
Four-Star Publications: June, 1947; No. 12, Aug, 1947

nn	9	18	27	50	65	80
12-Al Fago-c/a; funny animal	8	16	24	44	57	70

DAGAR, DESERT HAWK (Captain Kidd No. 24 on; formerly All Great)
Fox Features Syndicate: No. 14, Feb, 1948 - No. 23, Apr, 1949 (No #17,18)

14-Tangi & Safari Cary begin; Good bondage-c/a	78	156	234	491	833	1175
15,16-E. Good-a; 15-Bondage-c	47	94	141	291	488	685
19,20,22: 19-Used in **SOTI**, pg. 180 (Tangi)	42	84	126	260	435	610
21,23: 21-Bondage-c; "Bombs & Bums Away" panel in "Flood of Death" story used in **SOTI**. 23-Bondage-c	46	92	138	285	473	660

NOTE: *Tangi by **Kamen**-14-16, 19, 20; c-20, 21.*

DAGAR THE INVINCIBLE (Tales of Sword & Sorcery...) (Also see Dan Curtis Giveaways & Gold Key Spotlight)
Gold Key: Oct, 1972 - No. 18, Dec, 1976; No. 19, Apr, 1982

1-Origin; intro. Villains Olstellon & Scor	4	8	12	22	34	45
2-5: 3-Intro. Graylin, Dagar's woman; Jarn x-over	2	4	6	13	18	22
6-1st Dark Gods story	2	4	6	9	12	15
7-10: 9-Intro. Torgus. 10-1st Three Witches story	2	4	6	9	12	15
11-18: 13-Durak & Torgus x-over; story continues in Dr. Spektor #15. 14-Dagar's origin retold. 18-Origin retold	1	3	4	6	8	10
19(4/82)-Origin-r/#18						6.00

NOTE: *Durak app. in 7, 12, 13. Tragg app. in 5, 11.*

DAGWOOD (Chic Young's) (Also see Blondie Comics)
Harvey Publications: Sept, 1950 - No. 140, Nov, 1965

1	15	30	45	111	206	300
2	9	18	27	63	107	150
3-10	7	14	21	50	83	115
11-20	6	12	18	41	66	90
21-30	5	10	15	34	55	75
31-50	5	10	15	30	48	65
51-70	4	8	12	22	34	45
71-100	3	6	9	18	27	35
101-121,123-128,130,135	3	6	9	16	23	30
122,129,131-134,136-140-All are 68-pg. issues	4	8	12	22	34	45

NOTE: *Popeye and other one page strips appeared in early issues.*

DAI KAMIKAZE!
Now Comics: June, 1987 - No. 12, Aug, 1988 ($1.75)

1-1st app. Speed Racer; 2nd print exists						4.00
2-12						2.50

DAILY BUGLE (See Spider-Man)
Marvel Comics: Dec, 1996 - No. 3, Feb, 1997 ($2.50, B&W, limited series)

1-3-Paul Grist-s						2.50

DAISY AND DONALD (See Walt Disney Showcase No. 8)
Gold Key/Whitman No. 42 on: May, 1973 - No. 59, July, 1984 (no No. 48)

1-Barks-r/WDC&S #280,308	3	6	9	20	30	40
2-5: 4-Barks-r/WDC&S #224	2	4	6	11	16	20
6-10	2	4	6	9	12	15
11-20	1	3	4	6	8	10
21-41: 32-r/WDC&S #308	1	2	3	5	6	8
42-44 (Whitman)	2	4	6	8	11	14
45 (8/80),46-(pre-pack?)(scarce)	4	8	12	22	34	45
47-(12/80)-Only distr. in Whitman 3-pack (scarce)	5	10	15	35	55	75
48(3/81)-50(8/81): 50-r/#3	2	4	6	10	14	18
51-54: 51-Barks-r/4-Color #1150. 52-r/#2. 53(2/82), 54(4/82)	2	4	6	9	13	16
55-59-(all #90284 on-c, nd, nd code, pre-pack): 55(5/83), 56(7/83), 57(8/83), 58(8/83), 59(7/84)	3	6	9	14	19	24

DAISY & HER PUPS (Dagwood & Blondie's Dogs)(Formerly Blondie Comics #20)
Harvey Publications: No. 21, 7/51 - No. 27, 7/52; No. 8, 9/52 - No. 18, 5/54

21 (#1)-Blondie's dog Daisy and her 5 pups led by Elmer begin. Rags Rabbit app.	6	12	18	41	66	90
22-27 (#2-7): 26 has No. 6 on cover but No. 26 on inside. 23,25-The Little King app. 24-Bringing Up Father by McManus app. 25-27-Rags Rabbit app.	4	8	12	28	44	60
8-18: 8,9-Rags Rabbit app. 8,17-The Little King app. 11-The Flop Family Swan begins. 22-Cookie app. 11-Felix The Cat app. by 17,18-Popeye app.	4	8	12	26	41	55

DAISY DUCK & UNCLE SCROOGE PICNIC TIME (See Dell Giant #33)

DAISY DUCK & UNCLE SCROOGE SHOW BOAT (See Dell Giant #55)

DAISY DUCK'S DIARY (See Dynabrite Comics, & Walt Disney's C&S #298)
Dell Publishing Co.: No. 600, Nov, 1954 - No. 1247, Dec-Fef, 1961-62 (Disney)

Four Color 600 (#1)	7	14	21	47	76	105
Four Color 659, 743 (11/56)	6	12	18	37	59	80

Dale Evans Comics #12 © DC

Dan Dare #1 © Dan Dare Corp.

Danger #10 © Comic Media

	GD	VG	FN	VF	VF/NM	NM-
	2.0	4.0	6.0	8.0	9.0	9.2

Four Color 858 (11/57), 948 (11/58), 1247 (12-2/61-62) 5 10 15 32 51 70
Four Color 1055 (11-1/59-60), 1150 (12-1/60-61)-By Carl Barks 9 18 27 60 100 140

DAISY HANDBOOK
Daisy Manufacturing Co.: 1946; No. 2, 1948 (10¢, pocket-size, 132 pgs.)
1-Buck Rogers, Red Ryder; Wolverton-a (2 pgs.) 29 58 87 167 264 360
2-Captain Marvel & Ibis the Invincible, Red Ryder, Boy Commandos & Robotman; Wolverton-a (2 pgs.); contains 8 pg. color catalog 29 58 87 167 264 360

DAISY MAE (See Oxydol-Dreft)

DAISY'S RED RYDER GUN BOOK
Daisy Manufacturing Co.: 1955 (25¢, pocket-size, 132 pgs.)
nn-Boy Commandos, Red Ryder; 1pg. Wolverton-a 20 40 60 117 184 250

DAKKON BLACKBLADE ON THE WORLD OF MAGIC: THE GATHERING
Acclaim Comics (Armada): June, 1996 ($5.95, one-shot)
1-Jerry Prosser scripts; Rags Morales-c/a. 6.00

DAKOTA LIL (See Fawcett Movie Comics)

DAKTARI (Ivan Tors) (TV)
Dell Publishing Co.: July, 1967 - No. 3, Oct, 1968; No. 4, Oct, 1969
1-Marshall Thompson photo-c on all 4 8 12 24 37 50
2-4 3 6 9 18 27 35

DALE EVANS COMICS (Also see Queen of the West...)(See Boy Commandos #32)
National Periodical Publications: Sept-Oct, 1948 - No. 24, Jul-Aug, 1952 (No. 1-19: 52 pgs.)
1-Dale Evans & her horse Buttermilk begin; Sierra Smith begins by Alex Toth 69 138 207 431 716 1000
2-Alex Toth-a 36 72 108 208 329 450
3-11-Alex Toth-a 22 44 66 120 202 275
12-20: 12-Target-c 15 30 45 83 124 165
21-24 15 30 45 85 130 175
NOTE: *Photo-c-1, 2, 4-14.*

DALGODA
Fantagraphics Books: Aug, 1984 - No. 8, Feb, 1986 (High quality paper)
1,8: 1- Fujitake-c/a in all. 8-Alan Moore story 4.00
2-7: 2,3-Debut Grimwood's Daughter. 2.50

DALTON BOYS, THE
Avon Periodicals: 1951
1-(Number on spine)-Kinstler-c 17 34 51 100 158 215

DAMAGE
DC Comics: Apr, 1994 - No. 20, Jan, 1996 ($1.75/$1.95/$2.25)
1-20: 6-(9/94)-Zero Hour. 0-(10/94). 7-(11/94). 14-Ray app. 3.00

DAMAGE CONTROL (See Marvel Comics Presents #19)
Marvel Comics: 5/89 - No. 4, 8/89; V2#1, 12/89 - No. 4, 2/90 ($1.00)
V3#1, 6/91 - No. 4, 9/91 ($1.25, all are limited series)
V1#1-4,V2#1-4,V3#1-4: V1#4-Wolverine app. V2#2,4-Punisher app. 1-Spider-Man app. 2-New Warriors app. 3,4-Silver Surfer app. 4-Infinity Gauntlet parody 2.50

DAMNED
Image Comics (Homage Comics): June, 1997 - No. 4, Sept, 1997 ($2.50, limited series)
1-4-Steven Grant-s/Mike Zeck-c/a in all 2.50

DAMN NATION
Dark Horse Comics: Feb, 2005 - No. 3, Apr, 2005 ($2.99, limited series)
1-3-J. Alexander-a/Andrew Cosby-s 3.00

DANCES WITH DEMONS (See Marvel Frontier Comics Unlimited)
Marvel Frontier Comics: Sept, 1993 - No. 4, Dec, 1993 ($1.95, limited series)
1-($2.95)-Foil embossed-c; Charlie Adlard & Rod Ramos-a 3.00
2-4 2.50

DAN DARE
Virgin Comics: Nov, 2007 - No. 7, July, 2008 ($2.99/$5.99)
1-6-Ennis-s/Erskine-a. 1-Two covers by Talbot and Horn. 2-6-Two covers on each 3.00
7-($5.99) Double sized finale with wraparound Erskine-c; Gibbons variant-c 6.00

DANDEE: Four Star Publications: 1947 (Advertised, not published)

DAN DUNN (See Crackajack Funnies, Detective Dan, Famous Feature Stories & Red Ryder)

DANDY COMICS (Also see Happy Jack Howard)
E. C. Comics: Spring, 1947 - No. 7, Spring, 1948
1-Funny animal; Vince Fago-a in all; Dandy in all 40 80 120 235 380 525

	GD	VG	FN	VF	VF/NM	NM-
	2.0	4.0	6.0	8.0	9.0	9.2

2 27 54 81 158 254 350
3-7: 3-Intro Handy Andy who is c-feature #3 on 21 42 63 125 200 275

DANGER
Comic Media/Allen Hardy Assoc.: Jan, 1953 - No. 11, Aug, 1954
1-Heck-c/a 25 50 75 149 240 330
2,3,5,7,9-11: 15 30 45 83 124 165
4-Marijuana cover/story 17 34 51 98 154 210
6- "Narcotics" story; begin spy theme 15 30 45 88 137 185
8-Bondage/torture/headlights panels 18 36 54 105 165 225
NOTE: *Morisi a-2, 5, 6(3), 10; c-2. Contains some reprints from Danger & Dynamite.*

DANGER (Formerly Comic Media title)
Charlton Comics Group: No. 12, June, 1955 - No. 14, Oct, 1955
12(#1) 12 24 36 67 94 120
13,14: 14-r/#12 10 20 30 54 72 90

DANGER
Super Comics: 1964
Super Reprint #10-12 (Black Dwarf; #10-r/Great Comics #1 by Novack. #11-r/Johnny Danger #1. #12-r/Red Seal #14), #15-r/Spy Cases #26. #16-Unpublished Chesler material (Yankee Girl), #17-r/Scoop #8 (Capt. Courage & Enchanted Dagger), #18(nd)-r/Guns Against Gangsters #5 (Gun-Master, Annie Oakley, The Chameleon; L.B. Cole-r) 2 4 6 11 16 20

DANGER AND ADVENTURE (Formerly This Magazine Is Haunted; Robin Hood and His Merry Men No. 28 on)
Charlton Comics: No. 22, Feb, 1955 - No. 27, Feb, 1956
22-Ibis the Invincible-c/story; Nyoka app.; last pre-code issue 11 22 33 62 86 110
23-Lance O'Casey-c/sty; Nyoka app.; Ditko-a thru #27 13 26 39 72 101 130
24-27: 24-Mike Danger & Johnny Adventure begin 9 18 27 50 65 80

DANGER GIRL (Also see Cliffhanger #0)
Image Comics (Cliffhanger Productions): Mar, 1998 - No. 4, Dec, 1998;
DC Comics (Cliffhanger Prod.): No. 5, July, 1999 - No. 7, Feb, 2001
Preview-Bagged in DV8 #14 Voyager Pack 4.00
Preview Gold Edition 8.00
1-($2.95) Hartnell & Campbell-s/Campbell/Garner-a 1 2 3 5 6 8
1-($4.95) Chromium cover 45.00
1-American Entertainment Ed. 8.00
1-American Entertainment Gold Ed., 1-Tourbook edition 10.00
1-"Danger-sized" ed.; over-sized format 3 6 9 16 23 30
2-($2.50) 4.00
2-Smoking Gun variant cover, 2-Platinum Ed., 2-Dynamic Forces Omnichrome variant-c 2 4 6 9 13 16
2-Gold foil cover 9.00
2-Ruby red foil cover 90.00
3,4: 3-c by Campbell, Charest and Adam Hughes. 4-Big knife variant-c 3.00
3,5: 3-Gold foil cover. 5-DF Bikini variant-c 5.00
4-6 3.00
7-($5.95) Wraparound gatefold-c; Last issue 6.00
...: Hawaiian Punch (5/03, $4.95) Campbell-c; Phil Noto-a 5.00
...: Odd Jobs TPB (2004, $14.95) r/one-shots Hawaiian Punch, Viva Las Danger & Special; Campbell-c 15.00
San Diego Preview (8/98, B&W) flip book w/Wildcats preview 5.00
Sketchbook (2001, $6.95) Campbell-a; sketches for comics, toys, games 7.00
...Special (2/00, $3.50) art by Campbell, Chiodo, and Art Adams 3.50
... 3-D #1 (4/03, $4.95, bagged with 3-D glasses) r/ Preview & #1 in 3-D 5.00
...: Viva Las Danger (1/04, $4.95) Noto-a/Campbell-c 5.00
... :The Dangerous Collection nn(8/98; r-#1) 6.00
... :The Dangerous Collection 2,3: 2-(11/98, $5.95) r/#2,3. 3-('99) r/#4,5 6.00
... :The Dangerous Collection nn, 2-($10.00) Gold foil logo 10.00
... :The Ultimate Collection HC ($29.95) r/#1-7; intro by Bruce Campbell 30.00
... :The Ultimate Collection SC ($19.95) r/#1-7; intro by Bruce Campbell 20.00

DANGER GIRL: BACK IN BLACK
DC Comics (Cliffhanger): Jan, 2006 - No. 4, Apr, 2006 ($2.99, limited series)
1-4-Hartnell-s/Bradshaw-a. 1-Campbell-c 3.00
TPB (2007, $12.99) r/series & covers 13.00

DANGER GIRL: BODY SHOTS
DC Comics (WildStorm): Jun, 2007 - No. 4, Sept, 2007 ($2.99, limited series)
1-4-Hartnell-s/Bradshaw-a 3.00
TPB (2007, $12.99) r/series & covers 13.00

Dan'l Boone #1 © ME

Daredevil #14 © LEV

Daredevil #7 © MAR

GD VG FN VF VF/NM NM-
2.0 4.0 6.0 8.0 9.0 9.2

DANGER GIRL KAMIKAZE
DC Comics (Cliffhanger): Nov, 2001 - No. 2, Dec., 2001 ($2.95, lim. series)
1,2-Tommy Yune-s/a 3.00

DANGER IS OUR BUSINESS!
Toby Press: 1953(Dec.) - No. 10, June, 1955
1-Captain Comet by Williamson/Frazetta-a, 6 pgs. (science fiction)
44 88 132 273 457 640
2 14 28 42 80 115 150
3-10 12 24 36 67 94 120
I.W. Reprint #9('64)-Williamson/Frazetta-r/#1; Kinstler-c
8 16 24 52 86 120

DANGER IS THEIR BUSINESS (Also see A-1 Comic)
Magazine Enterprises: No. 50, 1952
A-1 50-Powell-a 14 28 42 78 112 145

DANGER MAN (TV)
Dell Publishing Co.: No. 1231, Sept-Nov, 1961
Four Color 1231-Patrick McGoohan photo-c 10 20 30 71 126 180

DANGER TRAIL (Also see Showcase #50, 51)
National Periodical Publ.: July-Aug, 1950 - No. 5, Mar-Apr, 1951 (52 pgs.)
1-King Faraday begins, ends #4; Toth-a in all 125 250 375 788 1332 1875
2 87 174 261 548 924 1300
3-(Rare) one of the rarest early '50s DCs 125 250 375 788 1332 1875
4,5: 5-Johnny Peril-c/story (moves to Sensation Comics #107); new logo (also see Comic Cavalcade #15-29) 67 134 201 422 711 1000

DANGER TRAIL
DC Comics: Apr, 1993 - No. 4, July, 1993 ($1.50, limited series)
1-4: Gulacy-c on all 2.50

DANGER UNLIMITED (See San Diego Comic Con Comics #2 & Torch of Liberty Special)
Dark Horse (Legend): Feb, 1994 - No. 4, May, 1994 ($2.00, limited series)
1-4: Byrne-c/a/scripts in all; origin stories of both original team (Doc Danger, Thermal, Miss Mirage, & Hunk) & future team (Thermal, Belebet, & Caucus). 1-Intro Torch of Liberty & Golgotha (cameo) in back-up story. 4-Hellboy & Torch of Liberty cameo in lead story 2.50
TPB (1995, $14.95)-r/#1-4; includes last pg. originally cut from #4 15.00

DAN HASTINGS (See Syndicate Features)

DANIEL BOONE (See The Exploits of..., Fighting... Frontier Scout...,The Legends of... & March of Comics No. 306)
Dell Publishing Co.: No. 1163, Mar-May, 1961
Four Color 1163-Marsh-a 5 10 15 35 55 75

DANIEL BOONE (TV) (See March of Comics No. 306)
Gold Key: Jan, 1965 - No. 15, Apr, 1969 (All have Fess Parker photo-c)
1-Back-c and last eight pages fold in half to form "Official Handbook Fess Parker as Daniel Boone Trail Blazers Club" 8 16 24 56 93 130
2-Back-c pin-up 5 10 15 32 51 70
3-5-Back-c pin-ups 4 8 12 26 41 55
6-15: 7,8-Back-c pin-up 3 6 9 20 30 40

DAN'L BOONE
Sussex Publ. Co.: Sept, 1955 - No. 8, Sept, 1957
1 14 28 42 80 115 150
2 10 20 30 54 72 90
3-8 8 16 24 40 50 60

DANNY BLAZE (...Firefighter) (Nature Boy No. 3 on)
Charlton Comics: Aug, 1955 - No. 2, Oct, 1955
1-Authentic stories of fire fighting 13 26 39 74 105 135
2 9 18 27 50 65 80

DANNY DINGLE (See Sparkler Comics)
United Features Syndicate: No. 17, 1940
Single Series 17 26 52 78 152 244 335

DANNY THOMAS SHOW, THE (TV)
Dell Publishing Co.: No. 1180, Apr-June, 1961 - No. 1249, Dec-Feb, 1961-62
Four Color 1180-Toth-a, photo-c 15 30 45 107 196 285
Four Color 1249-Manning-a, photo-c 14 28 42 103 184 265

DARBY O'GILL & THE LITTLE PEOPLE (Movie)(See Movie Comics)
Dell Publishing Co.: 1959 (Disney)
Four Color 1024-Toth-a; photo-c. 9 18 27 65 113 160

GD VG FN VF VF/NM NM-
2.0 4.0 6.0 8.0 9.0 9.2

DAREDEVIL ("Daredevil Comics" on cover of #2) (See Silver Streak Comics)
Lev Gleason Publications (Funnies, Inc. No. 1): July, 1941 - No. 134, Sept, 1956 (Charles Biro stories)
1-No. 1 titled "Daredevil Battles Hitler"; The Silver Streak, Lance Hale, Cloud Curtis, Dickey Dean, Pirate Prince team up w/Daredevil and battle Hitler; Daredevil battles the Claw; Origin of Hitler feature story. Hitler photo app. on-c
1216 2432 3648 9120 15,810 22,500
2-London, Pat Patriot (by Reed Crandall), Nightro, Real American No. 1 (by Briefer #2-11), Dickie Dean, Pirate Prince, & Times Square begin; intro. & only app. The Pioneer, Champion of America 318 636 954 2162 3781 5400
3-Origin of 13 240 480 720 1512 2556 3600
4 183 366 549 1153 1952 2750
5-Intro. Sniffer & Jinx; Ghost vs. Claw begins by Bob Wood, ends #20
135 270 405 851 1438 2025
6 113 226 339 712 1206 1700
7-10: 7-(2/42; shows #6 on cover). 8-Nightro ends 92 184 276 580 978 1375
11-London, Pat Patriot end; classic bondage/torture-c
187 334 561 1178 1989 2800
12-Origin of The Claw; Scoop Scuttle by Wolverton begins (2-4 pgs.), ends #22, not in #21 132 264 396 832 1404 1975
13-Intro. of Little Wise Guys (10/42) 107 214 321 674 1137 1600
14 64 128 192 403 682 960
15-Death of Meatball 92 184 276 580 978 1375
16,17 59 118 177 372 629 885
18-New origin of Daredevil (not same as Silver Streak #6). Hitler, Mussolini Tojo and Mickey Mouse app. on-c 117 234 351 737 1244 1750
19,20 53 106 159 334 567 800
21-Reprints cover of Silver Streak #6 (on inside) plus intro. of The Claw from Silver Streak #1 83 166 249 523 887 1250
22-26,28-30 41 82 123 250 413 575
27-Bondage/torture-c 41 82 123 256 428 600
31-Death of The Claw 77 154 231 481 816 1150
32-37,39-41: 35-Two Daredevil stories begin, end #68 (35-41 are 64 pgs.)
31 62 93 181 291 400
38-Origin Daredevil retold from #18 45 90 135 279 465 650
42-50: 42-Intro. Kilroy in Daredevil 26 52 78 152 244 335
51-69-Last Daredevil issue (12/50) 18 36 54 107 169 230
70-Little Wise Guys take over book; McWilliams-a; Hot Rock Flanagan begins, ends #80
13 26 39 72 101 130
71-78,81 10 20 30 54 72 90
79,80: 79-Daredevil returns. 80-Daredevil x-over 10 20 30 56 76 95
82,90,100: 82,90-One pg. Frazetta ad in both 10 20 30 54 72 90
83-89,91-99,101-134 9 18 27 50 65 80
NOTE: ***Biro** c/a-all? **Bolle** a-125. **Maurer** a-75. **McWilliams** a-73, 75, 79, 80.*

DAREDEVIL (...& the Black Widow #92-107 on-c only; see Giant-Size...,Marvel Advs., Marvel Graphic Novel #24, Marvel Super Heroes, '66 & Spider-Man &...)
Marvel Comics Group: Apr, 1964 - No. 380, Oct, 1998
1-Origin/1st app. Daredevil; intro Foggy Nelson & Karen Page; death of Battling Murdock; Bill Everett-c/a; reprinted in Marvel Super Heroes #1 (1966)
272 544 816 2380 4590 6800
2-Fantastic Four cameo; 2nd app. Electro (Spidey villain); Thing guest star
63 126 189 536 1018 1500
3-Origin & 1st app. The Owl (villain) 41 82 123 328 614 900
4-Origin & 1st app. The Purple Man 35 70 105 270 498 725
5-Minor costume change; Wood-a begins 26 52 78 192 359 525
6-Mr. Fear app. 18 36 54 130 240 350
7-Daredevil battles Sub-Mariner & dons red costume for 1st time (4/65)
61 122 183 519 985 1450
8-10: 8-Origin/1st app. Stilt-Man 15 30 45 107 196 285
11-15: 12-1st app. Plunderer; Ka-Zar app. 13-Facts about Ka-Zar's origin; Kirby-a
10 20 30 73 129 185
16,17-Spider-Man x-over. 16-1st Romita-a on Spider-Man (5/66)
17 34 51 120 223 325
18-Origin & 1st app. Gladiator 10 20 30 67 116 165
19,20 8 16 24 54 90 125
21-26,28-30: 24-Ka-Zar app. 6 12 18 41 66 90
27-Spider-Man x-over 7 14 21 47 76 105
31-40: 38-Fantastic Four x-over; cont'd in F.F. #73. 39-1st Exterminator (later becomes Death-Stalker) 5 10 15 34 55 75
41,42,44-49: 41-Death Mike Murdock. 42-1st app. Jester. 45-Statue of Liberty photo-c 5 10 15 30 48 65
43-Daredevil battles Captain America; origin partially retold
6 12 18 41 66 90

Daredevil #98 © MAR

Daredevil #319 © MAR

Daredevil V2 #41 © MAR

GD VG FN VF VF/NM NM-
2.0 4.0 6.0 8.0 9.0 9.2

50-53: 50-52-B. Smith-a. 53-Origin retold; last 12¢ issue
5 10 15 32 51 70
54-56,58-60: 54-Spider-Man cameo. 56-1st app. Death's Head (9/69); story cont'd in #57 (not same as new Death's Head) 3 6 9 21 32 42
57-Reveals i.d. to Karen Page; Death's Head app. 4 8 12 24 37 50
61-76,78-80: 79-Stan Lee cameo. 80-Last 15¢ issue 3 6 9 18 27 35
77-Spider-Man x-over 4 8 12 24 37 50
81-(52 pgs.) Black Widow begins (11/71). 4 8 12 26 41 55
82,84-99: 87-Electro-c/story 3 6 9 14 20 26
83-B. Smith layouts/Weiss-p 3 6 9 16 23 30
100-Origin retold 4 8 12 22 34 45
101-104,106-120: 107-Starlin-c; Thanos cameo. 113-1st brief app. Deathstalker. 114-1st full app. Deathstalker 2 4 6 13 18 22
105-Origin Moondragon by Starlin (12/73); Thanos cameo in flashback (early app.)
3 6 9 14 20 26
121-130,137: 124-1st app. Copperhead; Black Widow leaves. 126-1st new Torpedo
2 4 6 10 14 18
131-Origin/1st app. new Bullseye (see Nick Fury #15) 7 14 21 50 83 115
132-2nd app. new Bullseye (Regular 25¢ edition) 5 10 15 30 48 65
132-(30¢-c variant, limited distribution)(4/76) 8 16 24 56 93 130
133-136-(Regular 25¢ editions). 133-Uri Geller app. 2 4 6 10 14 18
133-136-(30¢-c variants, limited distribution)(5-8/76) 3 6 9 18 27 36
138-Ghost Rider-c/story; Death's Head is reincarnated; Byrne-a
3 6 9 16 22 28
139,140,142-145,147-157: 142-Nova cameo. 147,148-(Reg. 30¢-c). 150-1st app. Paladin. 151-Reveals i.d. to Heather Glenn. 155-Black Widow returns. 156-The '60s Daredevil app.
2 4 6 9 13 16
141,146-Bullseye app. 3 6 9 18 27 35
146-(35¢-c variant, limited distribution) 7 14 21 46 73 100
147,148-(35¢-c variants, limited distribution) 5 10 15 32 51 70
158-Frank Miller art begins (5/79); origin/death of Deathstalker (see Captain America #235 & Spectacular Spider-Man #27 8 16 24 54 90 125
159 4 8 12 28 44 60
160,161-Bullseye app. 4 8 12 22 34 45
162-Ditko-a; no Miller-a 2 4 6 9 13 16
163,164: 163-Hulk cameo. 164-Origin retold 3 6 9 16 23 30
165-167,170 3 6 9 14 20 26
168-Origin/1st app. Elektra; 1st Miller scripts 10 20 30 67 116 165
169-2nd Elektra app. 4 8 12 28 44 60
171-173 3 6 9 14 19 24
174,175-Elektra app. 3 6 9 16 22 28
176-180-Elektra app. 178-Cage app. 179-Anti-smoking issue mentioned in the Congressional Record 3 6 9 14 20 26
181-(52 pgs.)-Death of Elektra; Punisher cameo out of costume
4 8 12 22 34 45
182-184-Punisher app. by Miller (drug issues) 2 4 6 11 16 20
185-191: 187-New Black Widow. 189-Death of Stick. 190-($1.00, 52 pgs.)-Elektra returns, part origin. 191-Last Miller Daredevil 1 3 4 6 8 10
192-195,198,199,201-207,209-218,220-226,234-237: 226-Frank Miller plots begin 3.50
196-Wolverine-c/app. 2 4 6 8 11 14
197-Bullseye-c/app.; 1st app. Yuriko Oyama (who becomes Lady Deathstrike) 5.00
200,238: 200-Bullseye app. 238-Mutant Massacre; Sabretooth app. 6.00
208,219,228-233: 208-Harlan Ellison scripts borrowed from Avengers TV episode "House that Jack Built". 219-Miller-c/script. 228-233-Last Miller scripts 4.00
227-Miller scripts begin 6.00
239,240,242-247 3.00
241-Todd McFarlane-a(p) 5.00
248,249-Wolverine app. 6.00
250,251,253,258: 250-1st app. Bullet. 258-Intro The Bengal (a villain) 3.00
252,260 (52 pgs.): 252-Fall of the Mutants. 260-Typhoid Mary app. 5.00
254-Origin & 1st app. Typhoid Mary (5/88) 1 2 3 4 5 8
255,256,258: 255,256-2nd/3rd app. Typhoid Mary. 259-Typhoid Mary app. 5.00
257-Punisher app. (x-over w/Punisher #10) 1 3 4 6 8 10
261-281,283-294,296-299,301-304,307-318: 270-1st app. Black Heart. 272-Intro Shotgun (villain). 281-Silver Surfer cameo. 283-Capt. America app. 297-Typhoid Mary app.; Kingpin storyline begins. 292-D.G. Chichester scripts begin. 293-Punisher app. 303-Re-intro the Owl. 304-Garney-c/a. 309-Punisher-c.; Terror app. 310-Calypso-c 2.50
282,295,300,305,306: 282-Silver Surfer app. 295-Ghost Rider app. 300-($2.00, 52 pgs.) Kingpin story ends. 305,306-Spider-Man-c 3.00
319-Prologue to Fall From Grace; Elektra returns 6.00
319-2nd printing w/black-c 2.50
320-Fall From Grace Pt 1 5.00
321-Fall From Grace regular ed.; Pt 2; new costume; Venom app. 3.00
321-($2.00)-Wraparound Glow-in-the-dark-c ed. 5.00

GD VG FN VF VF/NM NM-
2.0 4.0 6.0 8.0 9.0 9.2

322-Fall From Grace Pt 3; Eddie Brock app. 4.00
323,324-Fall From Grace Pt. 4 & 5: 323-Vs. Venom-c/story. 324-Morbius-c/story 4.00
325-($2.50, 52 pgs.)-Fall From Grace ends; contains bound-in poster 4.00
326-349,351-353: 326-New logo. 328-Bound-in trading card sheet. 330-Gambit app. 348-1st Cary Nord art in DD (1/96);"Dec" on-c. 353-Karl Kesel scripts; Nord-c/a begins; Mr. Hyde-c/app. 2.50
350-($2.95)-Double-sized 3.00
350-($3.50)-Double-sized; gold ink-c 3.50
354-374,376-379: Kesel scripts, Nord-c/a in all. 354-$1.50-c begins. 355-Larry Hama layouts; Pyro app. 358-Mysterio-c/app. 359-Absorbing Man cameo. 360-Absorbing Man-c/app. 361-Black Widow-c/app. 363,366-370-Gene Colan-a(p). 368-Omega Red-c/app. 372-Ghost Rider-c/app. 376-379-"Flying Blind", DD goes undercover for S.H.I.E.L.D. 2.50
375-($2.99) Wraparound-c; Mr. Fear-c/app. 3.00
380-($2.99) Final issue; flashback story 4.00
Special 1(9/67, 25¢, 68 pgs.)-New art/story 6 12 18 41 66 90
Special 2,3: 2(2/71, 25¢, 52 pgs.)-Entire book has Powell/Wood-r; Wood-c. 3(1/72, 52 pgs.)-Reprints 3 6 9 16 23 30
Annual 4(10/76) 2 4 6 8 10 12
Annual 4(#5)-10: ('89-94 68 pgs.)-5-Atlantis Attacks. 6-Sutton-a. 7-Guice-a (7 pgs.). 8-Deathlok-c/story. 9-Polybagged w/card 3.00
... :Born Again TPB ($17.95)-r/#227-233; Miller-s/Mazzucchelli-a & new-c 20.00
... By Frank Miller and Klaus Janson Omnibus HC (2007, $99.99, dustjacket) r/#158-161, 163-191 and What If...? #28; intros by Miller and Janson; interviews, bonus art 100.00
... By Frank Miller and Klaus Janson Omnibus Companion HC (2007, $59.99, die-cut d.j.) r/#219,226-233, Daredevil: The Man Without Fear #1-5, Daredevil: Love and War, and Peter Parker, the Spect. Spider-Man #27-28; bonus materials 60.00
.../Deadpool- (Annual '97, $2.99)-Wraparound-c 3.00
...:Fall From Grace TPB ($19.95)-r/#319-325 20.00
... :Gang War TPB ($15.95)-r/#169-172,180; Miller-s/a(p) 16.00
...Legends: (Vol. 4) Typhoid Mary TPB (2003, $19.95) r/#254-257,259-263 20.00
... :Love's Labors Lost TPB ($19.99)-r/#215,217,219-222,225,226; Mazzucchelli-c 20.00
.../Punisher TPB (1988, $4.95)-r/D.D. #182-184 (all printings) 5.00
...Visionaries: Frank Miller Vol. 1 TPB ($17.95) r/#158-161,163-167 18.00
...Visionaries: Frank Miller Vol. 2 TPB ($24.95) r/#168-182; new Miller-c 25.00
...Visionaries: Frank Miller Vol. 3 TPB ($24.95) r/#183-191, What If? #28,35 & Bizarre Adventures #28; new Miller-c 25.00
... Vs. Bullseye Vol. 1 TPB (2004, $15.99) r/#131-132,146,169,181,191 16.00
Wizard Ace Edition: Daredevil (Vol. 1) #1 (4/03, $13.99) Acetate Campbell-c 14.00

NOTE: ***Art Adams** c-238p, 239. **Austin** a-191i; c-151i, 200i. **John Buscema** a-136, 137p, 234p, 235p; c-86p, 136i, 137p, 142, 219. **Byrne** c-200p, 201, 203, 223. **Capullo** a-286p. **Colan** a(p)-20-49, 53-82, 84-98, 100, 110, 112, 124, 153, 154, 156, 157, 363, 366-370, Spec. 1p; c(p)-20-42, 44-49, 53-60, 71, 92, 98, 138, 153, 154, 156, 157, Annual 1. **Craig** a-50i, 52i. **Ditko** a-162, 234p, 235p, 264p; c-162. **Everett** c/a-1; inks-21, 83. **Garney** c/a-304. **Gil Kane** a-141p, 146-148p, 151p; c(p)-85, 90, 91, 93, 94, 115, 116, 119, 120, 125-128, 133, 139, 147, 152. **Kirby** c-2-4, 5p, 12p, 13p, 43, 136p. **Layton** c-202. **Miller** scripts-168-182, 183(part), 184-191, 219, 227-233; a-158-161p, 163-184p, 191p; c-158-161p, 163-184p, 185-189, 190p, 191. **Orlando** a-2-4p. **Powell** a-9p, 11p, Special 1r, 2r. **Simonson** c-199, 236p. **B. Smith** a-236p; c-51p, 52p, 217. **Starlin** a-105p. **Steranko** c-44i. **Tuska** a-39i, 145p. **Williamson** a(i)-237, 239, 240, 243, 248-257, 259-282, 283(part), 284, 285, 287, 288(part), 289(part), 293-300; c(i)-237, 243, 244, 248-257, 259-263, 265-278, 280-289, Annual 8. **Wood** a-5-8, 9i, 10, 11i, Spec. 2i; c-5i, 6-11, 164i.*

DAREDEVIL (Volume 2) (Marvel Knights)
Marvel Comics: Nov, 1998 - Present ($2.50/$2.99)

1-Kevin Smith-s/Quesada & Palmiotti-a 12.00
1-($6.95) DF Edition w/Quesada & Palmiotti var.-c 15.00
1-($6.00) DF Sketch Ed. w/B&W-c 10.00
2-Two covers by Campbell and Quesada/Palmiotti 9.00
3-8: 4,5-Bullseye app. 5-Variant-c exists. 8-Spider-Man-c/app.; last Smith-s 6.00
9-15: 9-11-David Mack-s; intro Echo. 12-Begin $2.99-c; Haynes-a. 13,14-Quesada-a 3.00
16-19-Direct editions; Bendis-s/Mack-c/painted-a 3.00
18,19,21,22-Newsstand editions with variant cover logo "Marvel Unlimited Featuring... 3.00
20-($3.50) Gale-s/Winslade-a; back-up by Stan Lee-s/Colan-a; Mack-c 3.50
21-40: 21-25-Gale-s. 26-38-Bendis-s/Maleev-a. 32-Daredevil's ID revealed. 35-Spider-Man-c/app. 38-Iron Fist & Luke Cage app. 40-Dodson-a 3.50
41-(25¢-c) Begins "Lowlife" arc; Maleev-a; intro Milla Donovan 2.50
41-(Newsstand edition with 2.99¢-c) 4.00
42-45-"Lowlife" arc; Maleev-a 2.50
46-50-($2.99). 46-Typhoid Mary returns. 49-Bullseye app. 50-Art panels by various incl. Romita, Colan, Mack, Janson, Oeming, Quesada 3.00
51-64,66-74,76-81: 51-55-Mack-s/a; Echo app. 54-Wolverine-c/app. 61-64-Black Widow app. 71-Decalogue begins. 76-81-The Murdock Papers. 81-Last Bendis-s/Maleev-a 3.00
65-($3.99) 40th Anniversary issue; Land-c; art by Maleev, Horn, Bachalo and others 4.00
75-($3.99) Decalogue ends; Jester app. 4.00
82-99,101-111: 82-Brubaker-s/Lark-a begin; Foggy "killed". 84-86-Punisher app. 87-Other Daredevil ID revealed. 94-Romita-c. 111-Lady Bullseye debut 3.00
82-Variant-c by McNiven 4.00
100-($3.99) Three covers (Djurdjevic, Bermejo and Turner); art by Romita Sr., Colan, Lark, Sienkiewicz, Maleev, Bermejo & Djurdjevic; sketch art gallery; r/Daredevil #90 (1972) 4.00

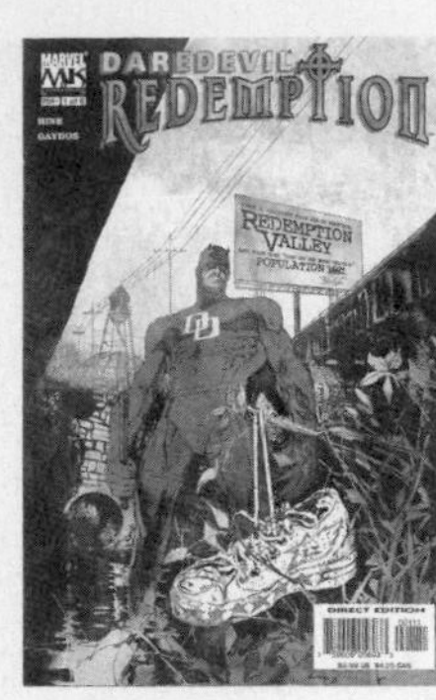

Daredevil: Redemption #1 © MAR

Daredevil: Yellow #2 © MAR

Daring Escapes #1 © Image

GD 2.0 | VG 4.0 | FN 6.0 | VF 8.0 | VF/NM 9.0 | NM- 9.2

Annual #1 (12/07, $3.99) Brubaker-s/Fernandez-a/Djurdjevic-c; Black Tarantula app. 4.00
... Blood of the Tarantula (6/08, $3.99) Parks & Brubaker-s/Samnee-a/Djurdjevic-c 4.00
... By Ed Brubaker Saga (2008, giveaway) synopsis of issues #82-110, preview of #111 1.00
...2099 #1 (11/04, $2.99) Kirkman-s/Moline-a 3.00
TPB ($9.95) r/#1-3 10.00
...Vol. 1 HC (2001, $29.99, with dustjacket) r/#1-11,13-15 30.00
...Vol. 1 HC (2003, $29.99, with dustjacket) r/#1-11,13-15; larger page size 30.00
...Vol. 2 HC (2002, $29.99, with dustjacket) r/#26-37; afterword by Bendis 30.00
...Vol. 3 HC (2004, $29.99, with dustjacket) r/#38-50; Maleev sketch pages 30.00
...Vol. 4 HC (2005, $29.99, with dustjacket) r/#56-65; Vol. 1 #81 (1971) Black Widow 30.00
...Vol. 5 HC (2006, $29.99, with dustjacket) r/#66-75 30.00
...Vol. 6 HC (2006, $34.99, with dustjacket) r/#76-81 & What If Karen Page Had Lived? 35.00
(Vol. 1) Visionaries TPB ($19.95) r/#1-8; Ben Affleck intro. 20.00
(Vol. 2) Parts of a Hole TPB (1/02, $17.95) r/#9-15; David Mack intro. 18.00
(Vol. 3) Wake Up TPB (7/02, $9.99) r/#16-19 10.00
...Vol. 4: Underboss TPB (8/02, $14.99) r/#26-31 15.00
...Vol. 5: Out TPB (2003, $19.99) r/#32-40 20.00
...Vol. 6: Lowlife TPB (2003, $13.99) r/#41-45 14.00
...Vol. 7: Hardcore TPB (2003, $13.99) r/#46-50 14.00
...Vol. 8: Echo - Vision Quest TPB (2004, $13.99) r/#51-55; David Mack-s/a 14.00
...Vol. 9: King of Hell's Kitchen TPB (2004, $13.99) r/#56-60 14.00
...Vol. 10: The Widow TPB (2004, $16.99) r/#61-65 & Vol. 1 #81 17.00
...Vol. 11: Golden Age TPB (2005, $13.99) r/#66-70 14.00
...Vol. 12: Decalogue TPB (2005, $14.99) r/#71-75 15.00
...Vol. 13: The Murdock Papers TPB (2006, $14.99) r/#76-81 15.00
...: The Devil Inside and Out Vol. 1 (2006, $14.99) r/#82-87; Brubaker & Lark interview 15.00
...: The Devil Inside and Out Vol. 2 (2007, $14.99) r/#88-93; Bermejo cover sketches 15.00
...: Hell To Pay Vol. 1 TPB (2007, $14.99) r/#94-99; Djurdjevic cover sketches 15.00
...: Hell To Pay Vol. 2 TPB (2008, $15.99) r/#100-105 16.00

DAREDEVIL/ BATMAN (Also see Batman/Daredevil)
Marvel Comics/ DC Comics: 1997 ($5.99, one-shot)
nn-McDaniel-c/a 6.00

DAREDEVIL BATTLES HITLER (See Daredevil #1[1941 series])

DAREDEVIL: BATTLIN' JACK MURDOCK
Marvel Comics: Aug, 2007 - No. 4, Nov, 2007 ($3.99, limited series)
1-4-Wells-s/DiGiandomenico-a; flashback to the fixed fight 4.00
TPB (2007, $12.99) r/#1-4; page layouts and cover inks 13.00

DAREDEVIL COMICS (Golden Age title) (See Daredevil)

DAREDEVIL/ ELEKTRA: LOVE AND WAR
Marvel Comics: 2003 ($29.99, hardcover with dust jacket)
HC-Larger-size reprints of Daredevil: Love and War (Marvel Graphic Novel #24) & Elektra: Assassin; Frank Miller-s; Bill Sienkiewicz-a 30.00

DAREDEVIL: FATHER
Marvel Comics: June, 2004 - No. 6, Feb, 2007 ($3.50/$2.99, limited series)
1-Quesada-s/a; Isanove-painted color 3.50
1-Director's Cut ($2.99) cover and page development art; partial sketch-c 3.00
2-6: 2-($2.99,10/05). 3-Santerians app. 3.00
HC (2006, $24.99) r/series; Lindelof intro.; sketch pages, cover pencils and bonus art 25.00

DAREDEVIL: NINJA
Marvel Comics: Dec, 2000 - No. 3, Feb, 2001 ($2.99, limited series)
1-3: Bendis-s/Haynes-a 3.00
1-Dynamic Forces foil-c 10.00
TPB (7/01, $12.95) r/#1-3 with cover and sketch gallery 13.00

DAREDEVIL: REDEMPTION
Marvel Comics: Apr, 2005 - No. 6, Aug, 2005 ($2.99, limited series)
1-6-Hine-s/Gaydos-a/Sienkiewicz-c 3.00
TPB (2005, $14.99) r/#1-6 15.00

DAREDEVIL/ SHI (See Shi/ Daredevil)
Marvel Comics/ Crusade Comics: Feb,1997 ($2.95, limited series)
1 3.00

DAREDEVIL/ SPIDER-MAN
Marvel Comics: Jan, 2001 - No. 4, Apr, 2001 ($2.99, limited series)
1-4-Jenkins-s/Winslade-a/Alex Ross-c; Stilt Man app. 3.00
TPB (8/01, $12.95) r/#1-4; Ross-c 13.00

DAREDEVIL THE MAN WITHOUT FEAR
Marvel Comics: Oct, 1993 - No. 5, Feb, 1994 ($2.95, limited series) (foil embossed covers)
1-Miller scripts; Romita, Jr./Williamson-c/a 6.00
2-5 5.00

GD 2.0 | VG 4.0 | FN 6.0 | VF 8.0 | VF/NM 9.0 | NM- 9.2

Hardcover 100.00
Trade paperback 20.00

DAREDEVIL: THE MOVIE (2003 movie adaptation)
Marvel Comics: March, 2003 ($3.50/$12.95, one-shot)
1-Photo-c of Ben Affleck; Bruce Jones-s/Manuel Garcia-a 3.50
TPB ($12.95) r/movie adaptation; Daredevil #32; Ultimate Daredevil & Elektra #1 and Spider-Man's Tangled Web #4; photo-c of Ben Affleck 13.00

DAREDEVIL: THE TARGET (Daredevil Bullseye on cover)
Marvel Comics: Jan, 2003 ($3.50, unfinished limited series)
1-Kevin Smith-s/Glenn Fabry-c/a 3.50

DAREDEVIL VS. PUNISHER
Marvel Comics: Sept, 2005 - No. 6, Jan, 2006 ($2.99, limited series)
1-5-David Lapham-s/a 3.00
TPB (2005, $15.99) r/#1-6 16.00

DAREDEVIL: YELLOW
Marvel Comics: Aug, 2001 - No. 6, Jan, 2002 ($3.50, limited series)
1-6-Jeph Loeb-s/Tim Sale-a/c; origin & yellow costume days retold 3.50
HC (5/02, $29.95) r/#1-6 with dustjacket; intro by Stan Lee; sketch pages 30.00
Daredevil Legends Vol. 1: Daredevil Yellow (2002, $14.99, TPB) r/#1-6 15.00

DARING ADVENTURES (Also see Approved Comics)
St. John Publishing Co.: Nov, 1953 (25¢, 3-D, came w/glasses)
1 (3-D)-Reprints lead story from Son of Sinbad #1 by Kubert 27 54 81 158 254 350

DARING ADVENTURES
I.W. Enterprises/Super Comics: 1963 - 1964
I. W. Reprint #8-r/Fight Comics #53; Matt Baker-a 5 10 15 30 48 65
I.W. Reprint #9-r/Blue Bolt #115; Disbrow-a(3) 5 10 15 32 51 70
Super Reprint #10,11('63)-r/Dynamic #24,16; 11-Marijuana story; Yankee Boy app.; Mac Raboy-a 4 8 12 22 34 45
Super Reprint #12('64)-Phantom Lady from Fox (r/#14 only? w/splash pg. omitted); Matt Baker-a 10 20 30 67 116 165
Super Reprint #15('64)-r/Hooded Menace #1 6 12 18 43 69 95
Super Reprint #16('64)-r/Dynamic #12 3 6 9 20 30 40
Super Reprint #17('64)-r/Green Lama #3 by Raboy 4 8 12 26 41 55
Super Reprint #18-Origin Atlas from unpublished Atlas Comics #1 4 8 12 24 37 50

DARING COMICS (Formerly Daring Mystery) (Jeanie Comics No. 13 on)
Timely Comics (HPC): No. 9, Fall, 1944 - No. 12, Fall, 1945
9-Human Torch, Toro & Sub-Mariner begin 135 270 405 851 1438 2025
10-12: 10-The Angel only app. 11,12-The Destroyer app. 109 218 327 687 1164 1640
NOTE: ***Schomburg*** *c-9-11.* ***Sekowsky*** *c-12? Human Torch, Toro & Sub-Mariner c-9-12.*

DARING CONFESSIONS (Formerly Youthful Hearts)
Youthful Magazines: No. 4, 11/52 - No. 7, 5/53; No. 8, 10/53
4-Doug Wildey-a; Tony Curtis story 16 32 48 92 144 195
5-8: 5-Ray Anthony photo on-c. 6,8-Wildey-a 13 26 39 72 101 130

DARING ESCAPES
Image Comics: Sept, 1998 - No. 4, Mar, 1999 ($2.95/$2.50, mini-series)
1-Houdini; following app. in Spawn #19,20 3.00
2-4-($2.50) 2.50

DARING LOVE (Radiant Love No. 2 on)
Gilmor Magazines: Sept-Oct, 1953
1–Steve Ditko's 1st published work (1st drawn was Fantastic Fears #5)(Also see Black Magic #27)(scarce) 77 154 231 481 816 1150

DARING LOVE (Formerly Youthful Romances)
Ribage/Pix: No. 15, 12/52; No. 16, 2/53-c, 4/53-Indicia; No. 17-4/53-c & indicia
15 12 24 36 69 97 125
16,17: 17-Photo-c 11 22 33 60 83 105
NOTE: ***Colletta*** *a-15.* ***Wildey*** *a-17.*

DARING LOVE STORIES (See Fox Giants)

DARING MYSTERY COMICS (Comedy Comics No. 9 on; title changed to Daring Comics with No. 9)
Timely Comics (TPI 1-6/TCI 7,8): 1/40 - No. 5, 6/40; No. 6, 9/40; No. 7, 4/41 - No. 8, 1/42
1-Origin The Fiery Mask (1st app.) by Joe Simon; Monako, Prince of Magic (1st app.), John Steele, Soldier of Fortune (1st app.), Doc Denton (1st app.) begin; Flash Foster & Barney Mullen, Sea Rover only app; bondage-c

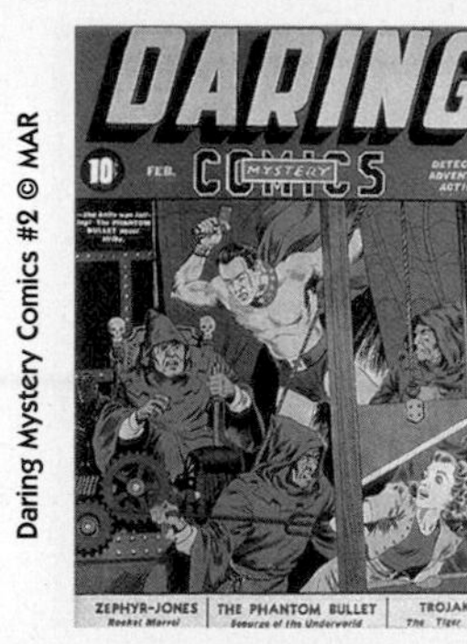

Daring Mystery Comics #2 © MAR

Darkchylde: The Legacy #1 © Randy Queen

Dark Fantasies #1 © Dark Fantasy

	GD	VG	FN	VF	VF/NM	NM-
	2.0	4.0	6.0	8.0	9.0	9.2

1900 3800 5700 14,250 25,625 37,000
2-(Rare)-Origin The Phantom Bullet (1st & only app.); The Laughing Mask & Mr. E only app.; Trojak the Tiger Man begins, ends #6; Zephyr Jones & K-4 & His Sky Devils app., also #4 1100 2200 3300 7800 13,400 19,000
3-The Phantom Reporter, Dale of FBI, Captain Strong only app.; Breeze Barton, Marvex the Super-Robot, The Purple Mask begin 506 1012 1518 3643 6372 9100
4,5: 4-Last Purple Mask; Whirlwind Carter begins; Dan Gorman, G-Man app. 5-The Falcon begins (1st app.); The Fiery Mask, Little Hercules app. by Sagendorf in the Segar style; bondage-c 341 682 1023 2319 4060 5800
6-Origin & only app. Marvel Boy by S&K; Flying Flame, Dynaman, & Stuperman only app.; The Fiery Mask by S&K; S&K-c 423 846 1269 3000 5250 7500
7-Origin and 1st app. The Blue Diamond, Captain Daring by S&K, The Fin by Everett, The Challenger, The Silver Scorpion & The Thunderer by Burgos; Mr. Millions app 353 706 1059 2400 4200 6000
8-Origin Citizen V; Last Fin, Silver Scorpion, Capt. Daring by Borth, Blue Diamond & The Thunderor; Kirby & part solo Simon-c; Rudy the Robot only app.; Citizen V, Fin & Silver Scorpion continue in Comedy #9 300 600 900 1950 3375 4800
NOTE: *Schomburg c-1-4, 7. Simon a-2, 3, 5. Cover features: 1-Fiery Mask; 2-Phantom Bullet; 3-Purple Mask; 4-G-Man; 5-The Falcon; 6-Marvel Boy; 7, 8-Multiple characters.*

DARING NEW ADVENTURES OF SUPERGIRL, THE
DC Comics: Nov, 1982 - No. 13, Nov, 1983 (Supergirl No. 14 on)
1-Origin retold; Lois Lane back-ups in #2-12 1 2 3 5 6 8
2-13: 8,9-Doom Patrol app. 13-New costume; flag-c 4.00
NOTE: *Buckler c-1p, 2p. Giffen c-3p, 4p. Gil Kane c-6,8, 9, 11-13.*

DARK, THE
Continum Comics: Nov, 1990 - No. 4, Feb, 1993; V2#1, May, 1993 - V2#7, Apr?, 1994 ($1.95)
1-4: 1-Bright-p; Panosian, Hanna-i; Stroman-c. 2-(1/92)-Stroman-c/a(p). 4-Perez-c & part-i 3.00
V2#1,V2#2-6: V2#1-Red foil Bart Sears-c. V2#1-Red non-foil variant-c. V2#1 2nd printing w/blue foil Bart Sears-c. V2#2-Stroman/Bryant-a. 3-Perez-c(i). 3-6-Foil-c. 4-Perez-c & part-i, bound-in trading cards. 5,6-(2,3/94)-Perez-c(i). 7-(B&W)-Perez-c(i) 2.50
Convention Book 1,2(Fall/94, 10/94)-Perez-c 2.50

DARK ANGEL (Formerly Hell's Angel)
Marvel Comics UK, Ltd.: No. 6, Dec, 1992 - No. 16, Dec, 1993 ($1.75)
6-8,13-16: 6-Excalibur-c/story. 8-Psylocke app. 2.50
9-12-Wolverine/X-Men app. 3.00

DARK ANGEL: PHOENIX RESURRECTION (Kia Asamiya's...)
Image Comics: May, 2000 - No. 4, Oct, 2001 ($2.95)
1-4-Kia Asamiya-s/a. 3-Van Fleet variant-c 3.00

DARKCHYLDE (Also see Dreams of the Darkchylde)
Maximum Press #1-3/ Image Comics #4 on: June, 1996 - No. 5, Sept, 1997 ($2.95/ $2.50)
1-Randy Queen-c/a/scripts; "Roses" cover 6.00
1-American Entertainment Edition-wraparound-c 6.00
1-"Fashion magazine-style" variant-c 1 2 3 4 5 7
1-Special Comicon Edition (contents of #1) Winged devil variant-c 5.00
1-($2.50)-Remastered Ed.-wraparound-c 4.00
2(Reg-c),2-Spiderweb and Moon variant-c 6.00
3(Reg-c),3-"Kalvin Clein" variant-c by Drew 3.00
4,5(Reg-c), 4-Variant-c 4.00
5-B&W Edition, 5-Dynamic Forces Gold Ed. 8.00
0-(3/98, $2.50) 2.50
0-Remastered (1/01, $2.95) includes Darkchylde: Redemption preview 3.00
1/2-Wizard offer 4.00
1/2 Variant-c 6.00
... The Descent TPB ('98, $19.95) r/#1-5; bagged with Darkchylde The Legacy Preview Special 1998; listed price is for TPB only 20.00

DARKCHYLDE LAST ISSUE SPECIAL
Darkchylde Entertainment: June, 2002 ($3.95)
1-Wraparound-c; cover gallery 4.00

DARKCHYLDE REDEMPTION
Darkchylde Entertainment: Feb, 2001 - No. 2, Dec, 2001 ($2.95)
1,2: 1-Wraparound-c 3.00
1-Dynamic Forces alternate-c 6.00
1-Dynamic Forces chrome-c 16.00

DARKCHYLDE SKETCH BOOK
Image Comics (Dynamic Forces): 1998
1-Regular-c 8.00
1-DarkChrome cover 16.00

DARKCHYLDE SUMMER SWIMSUIT SPECTACULAR
DC Comics (WildStorm): Aug, 1999 ($3.95, one-shot)
1-Pin-up art by various 4.00

DARKCHYLDE SWIMSUIT ILLUSTRATED
Image Comics: 1998 ($2.50, one-shot)
1-Pin-up art by various 2.50
1-(6.95) Variant cover 7.00
1-Chromium cover 15.00

DARKCHYLDE THE DIARY
Image Comics: June, 1997 ($2.50, one-shot)
1-Queen-c/s/ art by various 2.50
1-Variant-c 5.00
1-Holochrome variant-c 8.00

DARKCHYLDE THE LEGACY
Image Comics/DC (WildStorm) #3 on: Aug, 1998 - No. 3, June, 1999 ($2.50)
1-3: 1-Queen-c. 2-Two covers by Queen and Art Adams 2.50

DARK CLAW ADVENTURES
DC Comics (Amalgam): June, 1997 ($1.95, one-shot)
1-Templeton-c/s/a & Burchett-a 2.50

DARK CROSSINGS: DARK CLOUDS RISING
Image Comics (Top Cow): June, 2000; Oct, 2000 ($5.95, limited series)
1-Witchblade, Darkness, Tomb Raider crossover; Dwayne Turner-a 6.00
1-(Dark Clouds Overhead) 6.00

DARK CRYSTAL, THE (Movie)
Marvel Comics Group: April, 1983 - No. 2, May, 1983
1,2-Adaptation of film 3.00

DARK DAYS (See 30 Days of Night)
IDW Publishing: June, 2003 - No. 6, Dec, 2003 ($3.99, limited series)
1-6-Sequel to 30 Days of Night; Niles-s/Templesmith-a 4.00
1-Retailer variant (Diamond/Alliance Fort Wayne 5/03 summit) 15.00
TPB (2004, $19.99) r/#1-6; cover gallery; intro. by Eric Red 20.00

DARKDEVIL (See Spider-Girl)
Marvel Comics: Nov, 2000 - No. 3, Jan, 2001 ($2.99, limited series)
1-3: 1-Origin of Darkdevil; Kingpin-c/app. 3.00

DARK DOMINION
Defiant: Oct, 1993 - No. 10, July, 1994 ($2.50)
1-10-Len Wein scripts begin. 4-Free extra 16 pgs. 7-9-J.G. Jones-c/a. 10-Pre-Schism issue; Shooter/Wein script; John Ridgway-a 2.50

DARKER IMAGE (Also see Deathblow, The Maxx, & Bloodwulf)
Image Comics: Mar, 1993 ($1.95, one-shot)
1-The Maxx by Sam Kieth begins; Bloodwulf by Rob Liefeld & Deathblow by Jim Lee begin (both 1st app.); polybagged w/1 of 3 cards by Kieth, Lee or Liefeld 2.50
1-B&W interior pgs. w/silver foil logo 6.00

DARKEWOOD
Aircel Publishing: 1987 - No. 5, 1988 ($2.00, 28pgs, limited series)
1-5 2.50

DARK FANTASIES
Dark Fantasy: 1994 - No. 8, 1995 ($2.95)
1-Test print Run (3,000)-Linsner-c 1 2 3 5 6 8
1-Linsner-c 5.00
2-8: 2-4 (Deluxe), 2-4 (Regular), 5-8 (Deluxe; $3.95) 4.00
5-8 (Regular; $3.50) 3.50

DARK GUARD
Marvel Comics UK: Oct, 1993 - No. 4, Jan, 1994 ($1.75)
1-($2.95)-Foil stamped-c 3.00
2-4 2.50

DARKHAWK
Marvel Comics: Mar, 1991 - No. 50, Apr, 1995 ($1.00/$1.25/$1.50)
1-Origin/1st app. Darkhawk; Hobgoblin cameo 4.00
2,3,13,14: 2-Spider-Man & Hobgoblin app. 3-Spider-Man & Hobgoblin app. 13,14-Venom-c/story 3.00
4-12,15-24,26-49: 6-Capt. America & Daredevil x-over. 9-Punisher app. 11,12-Tombstone app. 19-Spider-Man & Brotherhood of Evil Mutants-c/story. 20-Spider-Man app. 22-Ghost Rider-c/story. 23-Origin begins, ends #25. 27-New Warriors-c/story. 35-Begin 3 part Venom story. 39-Bound-in trading card sheet 2.50
25,50: (52 pgs.)-Red holo-grafx foil-c w/double gatefold poster; origin of Darkhawk armor 3.00

Dark Horse Comics #2 © DH

Dark Horse Presents #80 © DH

Dark Ivory #1 © JM Linsner & Eva Hopkins

Annual 1-3 ('92-'94,68 pgs.)-1-Vs. Iron Man. 2 -Polybagged w/card 3.00

DARKHOLD: PAGES FROM THE BOOK OF SINS (See Midnight Sons Unlimited)
Marvel Comics (Midnight Sons imprint #15 on): Oct, 1992 - No. 16, Jan, 1994

1-($2.75, 52 pgs.)-Polybagged w/poster by Andy & Adam Kubert; part 4 of Rise of the Midnight Sons storyline 3.00
2-10,12-16: 3-Reintro Modred the Mystic (see Marvel Chillers #1). 4-Sabertooth-c/sty. 5-Punisher & Ghost Rider app. 15-Spot varnish-c. 15,16-Siege of Darkness pt. 4&12 2.50
11-($2.25)-Outer-c is a Darkhold envelope made of black parchment w/gold ink 2.50

DARK HORSE BOOK OF..., THE
Dark Horse Comics: Aug, 2003 - Nov, 2006 ($14.95/$15.95, HC, 9 1/4" x 6 1/4")

... Hauntings (8/03, $14.95)-Short stories by various incl. Mignola (Hellboy), Thompson, Dorkin, Russell; Gianni-c 15.00
... Monsters (11/06, $15.95)-Short-s by Mignola, Thompson, Dorkin, Giffen, Busiek; Gianni-c 16.00
... The Dead (6/05, $14.95)-Short-s by Mignola, Thompson, Dorkin, Powell; Gianni-c 15.00
... Witchcraft (6/04, $14.95)-Short-s by Mignola, Thompson, Dorkin, Millionaire; Gianni-c 15.00

DARK HORSE CLASSICS (Title series), **Dark Horse Comics**
1992 ($3.95, B&W, 52 pgs. nn's): The Last of the Mohicans. 20,000 Leagues Under the Sea 4.00

DARK HORSE CLASSICS, 5/96 ($2.95) 1-r/Predator: Jungle Tales 3.00

--ALIENS VERSUS PREDATOR, 2/97 - No. 6, 7/97 ($2.95,) 1-6: r/Aliens Versus Predator 3.00

--GODZILLA: KING OF THE MONSTERS, 4/98 ($2.95) 1-6: 1-r/Godzilla: Color Special; Art Adams-a 3.00

--STAR WARS: DARK EMPIRE, 3/97 - No. 6, 8/97 ($2.95) 1-6: r/Star Wars: Dark Empire 3.00

--TERROR OF GODZILLA, 8/98 - No. 6, 1/99 ($2.95) 1-6-r/manga Godzilla in color; Art Adams-c 3.00

DARK HORSE COMICS
Dark Horse Comics: Aug, 1992 - No. 25, Sept, 1994 ($2.50)

1-Dorman double gategold painted-c; Predator, Robocop, Timecop (3-part) & Renegade stories begin 3.00
2-6,11-25: 2-Mignola-c. 3-Begin 3-part Aliens story; Aliens-c. 4-Predator-c. 6-Begin 4 part Robocop story. 12-Begin 2-part Aliens & 3-part Predator stories. 13-Thing From Another World begins w/Nino-a(i). 15-Begin 2-part Aliens: Cargo story. 16-Begin 3-part Predator story. 17-Begin 3-part StarWars: Droids story & 3-part Aliens: Alien story; Droids-c. 19-Begin 2-part X story; X cover 2.50
7-Begin Star Wars: Tales of the Jedi 3-part story 1 2 3 4 5 7
8-1st app. X and begins; begin 4-part James Bond 6.00
9,10: 9-Star Wars ends. 10-X ends; Begin 3-part Predator & Godzilla stories 4.00
NOTE: *Art Adams c-11.*

DARK HORSE DOWN UNDER
Dark Horse Comics: June, 1994 - No. 3, Oct, 1994 ($2.50, B&W, limited series)

1-3 2.50

DARK HORSE MAVERICK
Dark Horse Comics: July, 2000; July, 2001; Sept, 2002 (B&W, annual)

2000-($3.95) Short stories by Miller, Chadwick, Sakai, Pearson 4.00
2001-($4.99) Short stories by Sakai, Wagner and others; Miller-c 5.00
...: Happy Endings (9/02, $9.95) Short stories by Bendis, Oeming, Mahfood, Mignola, Miller, Kieth and others; Miller-c 10.00

DARK HORSE MONSTERS
Dark Horse Comics: Feb, 1997 ($2.95, one-shot)

1-reprints 3.00

DARK HORSE PRESENTS
Dark Horse Comics: July, 1986 - No. 157, Sept, 2000 ($1.50-$2.95, B&W)

1-1st app. Concrete by Paul Chadwick 2 4 6 8 11 14
1-2nd printing (1988, $1.50) 2.50
1-Silver ink 3rd printing (1992, $2.25)-Says 2nd printing inside 2.50
2-9: 2-6,9-Concrete app. 6.00
10-1st app. The Mask; Concrete app. 2 4 6 9 12 15
11-19,21-23: 11-19,21-Mask stories. 12,14,16,18,22-Concrete app. 15(2/88). 17-All Roachmill issue 6.00
20-(68 pgs.)-Concrete, Flaming Carrot, Mask 1 3 4 6 8 10
24-Origin Aliens-c/story (11/88); Mr. Monster app. 2 4 6 10 14 18
25-31,33,37-41,44,45,47-49: 28-(52 pgs.)-Concrete app.; Mr. Monster story (homage to Graham Ingels). 33-(44 pgs.). 38-Concrete. 40-(52 pgs.)-1st Argosy story. 44-Crash Ryan. 48,49-Contain 2 trading cards 3.00
32,34,35: 32-(68 pgs.)-Annual; Concrete, American. 34-Aliens-c/story. 35-Predator-c/app. 4.00
36-1st Aliens Vs. Predator story; painted-c, 36-Variant line drawn-c 5.00
42,43,46: 42,43-Aliens-c/stories. 46-Prequel to new Predator II mini-series 3.00
50-S/F story by Perez; contains 2 trading cards 4.00
51-53-Sin City by Frank Miller, parts 2-4; 51,53-Miller-c (see D.H.P. Fifth Anniversary Special for pt. 1) 1 2 3 4 6 8
54-61: 54-(9/91) The Next Men begins (1st app.) by Byrne; Miller-a/Morrow-c. Homocide by Morrow (also in #55). 55-2nd app. The Next Men; parts 5 & 6 of Sin City by Miller; Miller-c. 56-(68 pg. annual)-part 7 of Sin City by Miller; part prologue to Aliens: Genocide; Next Men by Byrne. 57-(52 pgs.)-Part 8 of Sin City by Miller; Next Men by Byrne; Byrne & Miller-c; Alien Fire story; swipes cover to Daredevil #1. 58,59-Alien Fire stories. 58-61- Part 9-12 Sin City by Miller 5.00
62-Last Sin City (entire book by Miller, c/a; 52 pgs.) 1 3 4 6 8 10
63-66,68-79,81-84-($2.25): 64-Dr. Giggles begins (1st app.), ends #66; Boris the Bear story. 66-New Concrete-c/story by Chadwick. 71-Begin 3 part Dominque story by Jim Balent; Balent-c. 72-(3/93)-Begin 3-part Eudaemon (1st app.) story by Nelson 3.00
67-($3.95, 68 pgs.)-Begin 3-part prelude to Predator: Race War mini-series; Oscar Wilde adapt. by Russell 4.00
80-Art Adams-c/a (Monkeyman & O'Brien) 4.00
85-87,92-99: 85-Begin $2.50-c. 92, 93, 95-Too Much Coffee Man 3.00
88-91-Hellboy by Mignola. 6.00
NOTE: *There are 5 different Dark Horse Presents #100 issues*
100-1-Intro Lance Blastoff by Miller; Milk & Cheese by Evan Dorkin 4.00
100-2-Hellboy-c by Wrightson; Hellboy story by Mignola; includes Roberta Gregory & Paul Pope stories 6.00
100-3-100-5: 100-3-Darrow-c, Concrete by Chadwick; Pekar story. 100-4-Gibbons-c: Miller story, Geary story/a. 100-5-Allred-c, Adams, Dorkin, Pope 3.00
101-125: 101-Aliens c/a by Wrightson, story by Pope. 103-Kirby gatefold-c. 106-Big Blown Baby by Bill Wray. 107-Mignola-c/a. 109-Begin $2.95-c; Paul Pope-c. 110-Ed Brubaker-a/s. 114-Flip books begin; Lance Blastoff by Miller; Star Slammers by Simonson. 115-Miller-c. 117-Aliens-c/app. 118-Evan Dorkin-c/a. 119-Monkeyman & O'Brien. 124-Predator. 125-Nocturnals 3.00
126-($3.95, 48 pgs.)-Flip book: Nocturnals, Starship Troopers 4.00
127-134,136-140: 127-Nocturnals. 129-The Hammer. 132-134-Warren-a 3.00
135-($3.50) The Mark 3.50
141-All Buffy the Vampire Slayer issue 4.00
142-149: 142-Mignola-c. 143-Tarzan. 146,147-Aliens vs. Predator. 148-Xena 3.00
150-($4.50) Buffy-c by Green; Buffy, Concrete, Fish Police app. 4.50
151-157: 151-Hellboy-c/app. 153-155-Angel flip c. 156,157-Witch's Son 3.00
Annual 1997 ($4.95, 64 pgs.)-Flip book; Body Bags, Aliens. Pearson-c; stories by Allred & Stephens, Pope, Smith & Morrow 1 2 3 5 6 8
Annual 1998 ($4.95, 64 pgs.) 1st Buffy the Vampire Slayer comic app.; Hellboy story and cover by Mignola 1 2 3 4 5 7
Annual 1999 (7/99, $4.95) Stories of Xena, Hellboy, Ghost, Luke Skywalker, Groo, Concrete, the Mask and Usagi Yojimbo in their youth. 5.00
Annual 2000 ($4.95) Girl sidekicks; Chiodo-c and flip photo Buffy c 5.00
...Aliens Platinum Edition (1992)-r/DHP #24,43,43,56 & Special 11.00
...Fifth Anniversary Special nn (4/91, $9.95)-Part 1 of Sin City by Frank Miller (c/a); Aliens, Aliens vs. Predator, Concrete, Roachmill, Give Me Liberty & The American stories 25.00
The One Trick Rip-off (1997, $12.95, TPB)-r/stories from #101-112 13.00
NOTE: ***Geary** a-59, 60. **Miller** a-Special, 51-53, 55-62; c-59-62, 100-1; c-51, 53, 55, 59-62, 100-1. **Moebius** a-63; c-63, 70. **Vess** a-78; c-75, 78.*

DARK HORSE TWENTY YEARS
Dark Horse Comics: 2006 (25¢, one-shot)

nn-Pin-ups by Dark Horse artists of other artists' Dark Horse characters; Mignola-c 2.50

DARK IVORY
Image Comics: Mar, 2008 - No. 4 ($2.99, limited series)

1-3-Eva Hopkins & Joseph Michael Linsner-s/Linsner-a/c 3.00

DARK KNIGHT (See Batman: The Dark Knight Returns & Legends of the...)

DARK KNIGHT STRIKES AGAIN, THE (Also see Batman: The Dark Knight Returns)
DC Comics: 2001 - No. 3, 2002 ($7.95, prestige format, limited series)

1-Frank Miller-s/a/c; sequel 3 years after Dark Knight Returns; 2 covers 8.00
2,3 8.00
HC (2002, $29.95) intro. by Miller; sketch pages and exclusive artwork; cover has 3 1/4" tall partial dustjacket 30.00
SC (2002, $19.95) intro. by Miller; sketch pages 20.00

DARKLON THE MYSTIC (Also see Eerie Magazine #79,80)
Pacific Comics: Oct, 1983 (one-shot)

1-Starlin-c/a(r) 4.00

DARKMAN (Movie)
Marvel Comics: Sept, 1990; Oct, 1990 - No. 3, Dec, 1990 ($1.50)

1 (9/90, $2.25, B&W mag., 68 pgs.)-Adaptation of film 3.00
1-3: Reprints B&W magazine 2.50

DARKMAN
Marvel Comics: V2#1, Apr, 1993 -No. 6, Sept, 1993 ($2.95, limited series)

Dark Mysteries #4 © Merit Publ.

Darkness #10 © TCOW

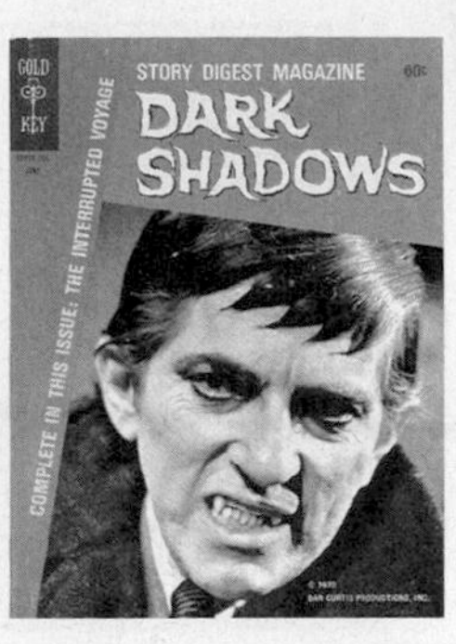

Dark Shadows #3 © Dan Curtis Prods.

	GD 2.0	VG 4.0	FN 6.0	VF 8.0	VF/NM 9.0	NM- 9.2
V2#1 ($3.95, 52 pgs.)						4.00
2-6						3.00

DARKMAN VS. THE ARMY OF DARKNESS (Movie crossover)
Dynamite Entertainment: 2006 - No. 4, 2007 ($3.50)

	GD 2.0	VG 4.0	FN 6.0	VF 8.0	VF/NM 9.0	NM- 9.2
1-4: 1-Busiek & Stern-s/Fry-a; photo-c and Perez and Bradshaw covers						3.50

DARK MANSION OF FORBIDDEN LOVE, THE (Becomes Forbidden Tales of Dark Mansion No. 5 on)
National Periodical Publ.: Sept-Oct, 1971 - No. 4, Mar-Apr, 1972 (52 pgs.)

	GD 2.0	VG 4.0	FN 6.0	VF 8.0	VF/NM 9.0	NM- 9.2
1	17	34	51	126	233	340
2-4: 2-Adams-c. 3-Jeff Jones-c	9	18	27	61	103	145

DARKMINDS
Image Comics (Dreamwave Prod.): July, 1998 - No. 8, Apr, 1999 ($2.50)

	GD 2.0	VG 4.0	FN 6.0	VF 8.0	VF/NM 9.0	NM- 9.2
1-Manga; Pat Lee-s/a; 2 covers	1	3	4	6	8	10
1-2nd printing						2.50
2, 0-(1/99, $5.00) Story and sketch pages						5.00
3-8, 1/2-(5/99, $2.50) Story and sketch pages						2.50
... Collected 1,2 (1/99,3/99; $7.95) 1-r/#1-3. 2-r/#4-6						8.00
... Collected 3 (5/99; $5.95) r/#7,8						6.00

DARKMINDS (Volume 2)
Image Comics (Dreamwave Prod.): Feb, 2000 - No. 10, Apr, 2001 ($2.50)

	GD 2.0	VG 4.0	FN 6.0	VF 8.0	VF/NM 9.0	NM- 9.2
1-10-Pat Lee-c						2.50
0-(7/00) Origin of Mai Murasaki; sketchbook						2.50

DARKMINDS: MACROPOLIS
Image Comics (Dreamwave Prod.): Jan, 2002 - No. 4, Dec, 2002 ($2.95)

	GD 2.0	VG 4.0	FN 6.0	VF 8.0	VF/NM 9.0	NM- 9.2
Preview (8/01) Flip book w/Banished Knights preview						2.50
1-4-Jo Chen-a						3.00

DARKMINDS: MACROPOLIS (Volume 2)
Dreamwave Prod.: Sept, 2003 - No. 4, Jul, 2004 ($2.95)

	GD 2.0	VG 4.0	FN 6.0	VF 8.0	VF/NM 9.0	NM- 9.2
1-4-Chris Sarracini-s/Kwang Mook Lim-a						3.00

DARKMINDS / WITCHBLADE (Also see Witchblade/Dark Minds)
Image Comics (Top Cow/Dreamwave Prod.): Aug, 2000 ($5.95, one-shot)

	GD 2.0	VG 4.0	FN 6.0	VF 8.0	VF/NM 9.0	NM- 9.2
1-Wohl-s/Pat Lee-a; two covers by Silvestri and Lee						6.00

DARK MYSTERIES (Thrilling Tales of Horror & Suspense)
"Master" - "Merit" Publications: June-July, 1951 - No. 24, July, 1955

	GD 2.0	VG 4.0	FN 6.0	VF 8.0	VF/NM 9.0	NM- 9.2
1-Wood-c/a (8 pgs.)	122	244	366	769	1297	1825
2-Wood/Harrison-c/a (8 pgs.)	83	166	249	523	887	1250
3-9: 7-Dismemberment, hypo blood drainage stys	46	92	138	285	475	665
10-Cannibalism story; witch burning-c	49	98	147	304	507	710
11-13,15-18: 11-Severed head panels. 13-Dismemberment-c/story. 17-The Old Gravedigger host	41	82	123	247	404	560
14-Several E.C. Craig swipes	41	82	123	249	410	570
19-Injury-to-eye panel; E.C. swipe; torture-c	49	98	147	304	507	710
20-Female bondage, blood drainage story	44	88	132	273	454	635
21,22: 21-Devil-c. 22-Last pre-code issue, misdated 3/54 instead of 3/55	30	60	90	174	280	385
23,24	22	44	66	129	207	285

NOTE: ***Cameron** a-1, 2. **Myron Fass** c/a-21. **Harrison** a-3, 7; c-3. **Hollingsworth** a-7-17, 20, 21, 23. **Wildey** a-5. Woodish art by **Fleishman**-9; c-10, 14-17. Bondage c-10, 18, 19.*

DARK NEMESIS (VILLAINS) (See Teen Titans)
DC Comics: Feb, 1998 ($1.95, one-shot)

	GD 2.0	VG 4.0	FN 6.0	VF 8.0	VF/NM 9.0	NM- 9.2
1-Jurgens-s/Pearson-c						2.50

DARKNESS, THE (See Witchblade #10)
Image Comics (Top Cow Productions): Dec, 1996 - No. 40, Aug, 2001 ($2.50)

	GD 2.0	VG 4.0	FN 6.0	VF 8.0	VF/NM 9.0	NM- 9.2
Special Preview Edition-(7/96, B&W)-Ennis script; Silvestri-a(p)	2	4	6	9	13	16
0	2	4	6	8	10	12
0-Gold Edition						16.00
1/2	1	3	4	6	8	10
1/2-Christmas-c	3	6	9	14	19	24
1/2-(3/01, $2.95) r/#1/2 w/new 6 pg. story & Silvestri-c						3.00
1-Ennis-s/Silvestri-a, 1-Black variant-c	2	4	6	9	12	15
1-Platinum variant-c						20.00
1-DF Green variant-c						12.00
1,2: 1-Fan Club Ed.	1	3	4	6	8	10
3-5						6.00
6-10: 9,10-Witchblade "Family Ties" x-over pt. 2,3						4.00
7-Variant-c w/concubine	1	2	3	5	7	9
8-American Entertainment						6.00
8-10-American Entertainment Gold Ed.						7.00
11-Regular Ed.; Ennis-s/Silverstri & D-Tron-c						3.00
11-Nine (non-chromium) variant-c (Benitez, Cabrera, the Hildebrandts, Finch, Keown, Peterson, Portacio, Tan, Turner						4.50
11-Chromium-c by Silvestri & Batt						20.00
12-19: 13-Begin Benitez-a(p)						3.00
20-24,26-40: 34-Ripclaw app.						2.50
25-($3.99) Two covers (Benitez, Silvestri)						4.00
25-Chromium-c variant by Silvestri						8.00
.../ Batman (8/99, $5.95) Silvestri, Finch, Lansing-a(p)						6.00
...Collected Editions #1-4 ($4.95,TPB) 1-r/#1,2. 2-r/#3,4. 3- r/#5,6. 4- r/#7,8						6.00
...Collected Editions #5,6 ($5.95, TPB)5- r/#11,12. 6-r/#13,14						6.00
Deluxe Collected Editions #1 (12/98, $14.95, TPB) r/#1-6 & Preview						15.00
...: Heart of Darkness (2001, $14.95, TPB) r/ #7,8, 11-14						15.00
Holiday Pin-up-American Entertainment						5.00
Holiday Pin-up Gold Ed.-American Entertainment						7.00
Infinity #1 (8/99, $3.50) Lobdell-s						3.50
Prelude-American Entertainment						4.00
Prelude Gold Ed.-American Entertainment						9.00
Volume 1 Compendium (2006, $59.99) r/#1-40, V2 #1, Tales of the Darkness #1-4; #1/2, Darkness/Witchblade #1/2, Darkness: Wanted Dead; cover and sketch gallery						60.00
...: Wanted Dead 1 (8/03, $2.99) Texiera-a/Tieri-s						3.00
Wizard ACE Ed.- Reprints #1	2	4	6	8	10	12

DARKNESS (Volume 2)
Image Comics (Top Cow Productions): Dec, 2002 - No. 24, Oct, 2004 ($2.99)

	GD 2.0	VG 4.0	FN 6.0	VF 8.0	VF/NM 9.0	NM- 9.2
1-24: 1-6-Jenkins-s/Keown-a. 17-20-Lapham-s. 23,24-Magdalena app.						3.00
... Black Sails (3/05, $2.99) Marz-s/Cha-a; Hunter-Killer preview						3.00
... and Tomb Raider (4/05, $2.99) r/Darkness Prelude & Tomb Raider/Darkness Special						3.00
...: Resurrection TPB (2/04, $16.99) r/#1-6 & Vol. 1 #40						17.00
.../ The Incredible Hulk (7/04, $2.99) Keown-a/Jenkins-s						3.00
.../ Vampirella (7/05, $2.99) Terry Moore-s; two covers by Basaldua and Moore						3.00
... Vol. 5 TPB (2006, $19.99) r/#7-16 & The Darkness: Wanted Dead #1; cover gallery						20.00
... vs. Mr. Hyde Monster War 2005 (9/05, $2.99) x-over w/Witchblade, Tomb Raider and Magdalena; two covers						3.00
.../ Wolverine (2006, $2.99) Kirkham-a/Tieri-s						3.00

DARKNESS (Volume 3)
Image Comics (Top Cow Productions): Dec, 2007 - Present ($2.99)

	GD 2.0	VG 4.0	FN 6.0	VF 8.0	VF/NM 9.0	NM- 9.2
1-5-Hester-s/Broussard-a. 1-Three covers						3.00
...: Butcher (4/08, $3.99) Story of Butcher Joyce; Levin-s/Broussard-a/c						4.00
... First Look (11/07, 99¢) Previews series; sketch pages						2.25

DARKNESS: LEVEL...
Image Comics (Top Cow): No. 0, Dec, 2006 - No. 5, Aug, 2007 ($2.99, limited series)

	GD 2.0	VG 4.0	FN 6.0	VF 8.0	VF/NM 9.0	NM- 9.2
0-5: 0-Origin of The Darkness in WW1; Jenkins-s. 1-Jackie's origin retold; Sejic-a						3.00

DARKNESS/ PITT
Image Comics (Top Cow): Dec, 2006 - Present ($2.99)

	GD 2.0	VG 4.0	FN 6.0	VF 8.0	VF/NM 9.0	NM- 9.2
...: First Look (12/06) Jenkins script pages with Keown B&W and color art						3.00

DARKNESS/ SUPERMAN
Image Comics (Top Cow Productions): Jan, 2005 - No. 2, Feb, 2005 ($2.99, limited series)

	GD 2.0	VG 4.0	FN 6.0	VF 8.0	VF/NM 9.0	NM- 9.2
1,2-Marz-s/Kirkham & Banning-a/Silvestri-c						3.00

DARKNESS VS. EVA: DAUGHTER OF DRACULA
Dynamite Entertainment: 2008 - No. 4, 2008 ($3.50, limited series)

	GD 2.0	VG 4.0	FN 6.0	VF 8.0	VF/NM 9.0	NM- 9.2
1-4-Leah Moore & John Reppion-s/Salazar-a; three covers on each						3.50

DARKSEID (VILLAINS) (See Jack Kirby's New Gods and New Gods)
DC Comics: Feb, 1998 ($1.95, one-shot)

	GD 2.0	VG 4.0	FN 6.0	VF 8.0	VF/NM 9.0	NM- 9.2
1-Byrne-s/Pearson-c						2.50

DARKSEID VS. GALACTUS: THE HUNGER
DC Comics: 1995 ($4.95, one-shot) (1st DC/Marvel x-over by John Byrne)

	GD 2.0	VG 4.0	FN 6.0	VF 8.0	VF/NM 9.0	NM- 9.2
nn-John Byrne-c/a/script						5.00

DARK SHADOWS
Steinway Comic Publ. (Ajax)(America's Best): Oct, 1957 - No. 3, May, 1958

	GD 2.0	VG 4.0	FN 6.0	VF 8.0	VF/NM 9.0	NM- 9.2
1	27	54	81	156	251	345
2,3	19	38	57	109	172	235

DARK SHADOWS (TV) (See Dan Curtis Giveaways)
Gold Key: Mar, 1969 - No. 35, Feb, 1976 (Photo-c: 1-7)

	GD 2.0	VG 4.0	FN 6.0	VF 8.0	VF/NM 9.0	NM- 9.2
1(30039-903)-With pull-out poster (25¢)	22	44	66	157	291	425
1-With poster missing	8	16	24	56	93	130
2	7	14	21	49	80	110
3-With pull-out poster	10	20	30	68	119	170

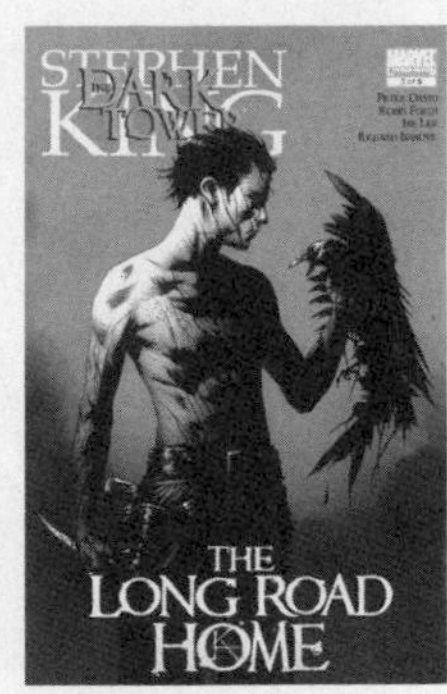

Dark Tower: The Long Road Home #3 © Stephen King

Darling Love #3 © AP

David Cassidy #2 © CC

	GD 2.0	VG 4.0	FN 6.0	VF 8.0	VF/NM 9.0	NM- 9.2
3-With poster missing	6	12	18	41	66	90
4-7: 7-Last photo-c	6	12	18	43	69	95
8-10	5	10	15	32	51	70
11-20	4	8	12	28	44	60
21-35: 30-Last painted-c	4	8	12	24	37	50
Story Digest 1 (6/70, 148pp.)-Photo-c (low print)	8	16	24	54	90	125

DARK SHADOWS (TV) (See Nightmare on Elm Street)
Innovation Publishing: June, 1992 - No. 4, Spring, 1993 ($2.50, limited series, coated stock)

1-Based on 1991 NBC TV mini-series; painted-c 5.00
2-4 4.00

DARK SHADOWS: BOOK TWO
Innovation Publishing: 1993 - No. 4, July, 1993 ($2.50, limited series)

1-4-Painted-c. 4-Maggie Thompson scripts 4.00

DARK SHADOWS: BOOK THREE
Innovation Publishing: Nov, 1993 ($2.50)

1-(Whole #9) 4.00

DARKSTARS, THE
DC Comics: Oct, 1992 - No. 38, Jan, 1996 ($1.75/$1.95)

1-1st app. The Darkstars 3.00
2-24,0,25-38: 5-Hawkman & Hawkwoman app. 18-20-Flash app. 24-(9/94)-Zero Hour. 0-(10/94). 25-(11/94). 30-Green Lantern app. 31-...vs. Darkseid. 32-Green Lantern app. 2.50
NOTE: *Travis Charest a(p)-4-7; c(p)-2-5; c-6-11. Stroman a-1-3; c-1.*

DARK TOWER: THE GUNSLINGER BORN (Based on Stephen King's Dark Tower series)
Marvel Comics: Apr, 2007 - No. 7, Oct, 2007 ($3.99, limited series)

1-Peter David & Robin Furth-s/Jae Lee & Richard Isanove-a; boyhood of Roland Deschain; afterword by Ralph Macchio; map of New Canaan 6.00
1-Variant cover by Quesada 8.00
1-Second printing with variant-c by Quesada 5.00
1-Sketch cover variant by Jae Lee 40.00
2-6-Jae Lee-c 4.00
2-Second printing with variant-c by Immonen 4.00
2-7-Variant covers. 2-Finch-c. 3-Yu-c. 4-McNiven-c. 5-Land-c. 6-Campbell. 7-Coipel 6.00
2-7-B&W sketch-c by Jae Lee 20.00
... Sketchbook (2006, no cover price) pencil art and designs by Lee; coloring process 5.00
Dark Tower: Gunslinger's Guidebook (2007, $3.99) profile pages with Jae Lee-a 4.00
HC (2007, $24.99) r/#1-7; variant covers and sketch pages; Macchio intro. 25.00

DARK TOWER: THE LONG ROAD HOME (Based on Stephen King's Dark Tower series)
Marvel Comics: May, 2008 - No. 5, Sept, 2008 ($3.99, limited series)

1-Peter David & Robin Furth-s/Jae Lee & Richard Isanove-a 4.00
1-Variant cover by Deodato 6.00
1-Sketch cover variant by Jae Lee 40.00
2-5-Jae Lee-c 4.00
2-5: 2-Variant-c by Quesada. 3-Djurdjevic var-c. 4-Garney var-c. 5-Bermejo var-c 6.00
2-5-B&W sketch-c by Jae Lee 20.00
2-Second printing with variant-c by Lee 4.00
Dark Tower: End-World Almanac (2008, $3.99) guide to locations and inhabitants 4.00

DARK TOWER: TREACHERY (Based on Stephen King's Dark Tower series)
Marvel Comics: Nov, 2008 - No. 6 ($3.99, limited series)

1-Peter David & Robin Furth-s/Jae Lee & Richard Isanove-a 4.00
1-Variant cover by Dell'otto 10.00

DARKWING DUCK (TV cartoon) (Also see Cartoon Tales)
Disney Comics: Nov, 1991 - No. 4, Feb, 1992 ($1.50, limited series)

1-4: Adapts hour-long premiere TV episode 3.00

DARLING LOVE
Close Up/Archie Publ. (A Darling Magazine): Oct-Nov, 1949 - No. 11, 1952 (no month) (52 pgs.)(Most photo-c)

	GD	VG	FN	VF	VF/NM	NM-
1-Photo-c	18	36	54	107	169	230
2-Photo-c	12	24	36	67	94	120
3-8,10,11: 3-6-photo-c	10	20	30	56	76	95
9-Krigstein-a	11	22	33	60	83	105

DARLING ROMANCE
Close Up (MLJ Publications): Sept-Oct, 1949 - No. 7, 1951 (All photo-c)

	GD	VG	FN	VF	VF/NM	NM-
1-(52 pgs.)-Photo-c	23	46	69	133	214	295
2	13	26	39	72	101	130
3-7	10	20	30	56	76	95

DARQUE PASSAGES (See Master Darque)
Acclaim (Valiant): April, 1998 ($2.50)

1-Christina Z.-s/Manco-c/a 2.50

DART (Also see Freak Force & Savage Dragon)
Image Comics (Highbrow Entertainment): Feb, 1996 - No. 3, May, 1996 ($2.50, lim. series)

1-3 3.00

DASTARDLY & MUTTLEY (See Fun-In No. 1-4, 6 and Kite Fun Book)

DATE WITH DANGER
Standard Comics: No. 5, Dec, 1952 - No. 6, Feb, 1953

	GD 2.0	VG 4.0	FN 6.0	VF 8.0	VF/NM 9.0	NM- 9.2
5,6-Secret agent stories: 6-Atom bomb story	9	18	27	52	69	85

DATE WITH DEBBI (Also see Debbi's Dates)
National Periodical Publ.: Jan-Feb, 1969 - No. 17, Sept-Oct, 1971; No. 18, Oct-Nov, 1972

	GD	VG	FN	VF	VF/NM	NM-
1-Teenage	6	12	18	39	62	85
2-5,17-(52 pgs) James Taylor sty.	4	8	12	22	34	45
6-12,18-Last issue	3	6	9	20	30	40
13-16-(68 pgs.): 14-1 pg. story on Jack Wild. 15-Marlo Thomas/"That Girl" story	4	8	12	23	36	48

DATE WITH JUDY, A (Radio/TV, and 1948 movie)
National Periodical Publications: Oct-Nov, 1947 - No. 79, Oct-Nov, 1960 (No. 1-25: 52 pgs.)

	GD	VG	FN	VF	VF/NM	NM-
1-Teenage	29	58	87	169	272	375
2	15	30	45	83	124	165
3-10	12	24	36	69	97	125
11-20	9	18	27	52	69	85
21-40	9	18	27	47	61	75
41-45: 45-Last pre-code (2-3/55)	8	16	24	42	54	65
46-79: 79-Drucker-c/a	8	16	24	40	50	60

DATE WITH MILLIE, A (Life With Millie No. 8 on)(Teenage)
Atlas/Marvel Comics (MPC): Oct, 1956 - No. 7, Aug, 1957; Oct, 1959 - No. 7, Oct, 1960

	GD	VG	FN	VF	VF/NM	NM-
1(10/56)-(1st Series)-Dan DeCarlo-a in #1-7	27	54	81	158	254	350
2	15	30	45	85	130	175
3-7	12	24	36	69	97	125
1(10/59)-(2nd Series)	15	30	45	85	130	175
2-7	10	20	30	58	79	100

DATE WITH PATSY, A (Also see Patsy Walker)
Atlas Comics: Sept, 1957 (One-shot)

	GD	VG	FN	VF	VF/NM	NM-
1-Starring Patsy Walker	12	24	36	69	97	125

DAUGHTERS OF THE DRAGON (See Heroes For Hire)
Marvel Comics: 2005; Mar, 2006 - No. 6, Aug, 2006 ($2.99, limited series)

1-6 Palmiotti & Gray-s/Evans-a. 1-Rhino app. 5,6-Iron Fist app. 3.00
... Deadly Hands Special (2005, $3.99) reprints app. from Deadly Hands of Kung Fu #32,33 & Bizarre Adventures #25; Claremont-s/Rogers-a; new Rogers-c & interview 4.00
...: Samurai Bullets TPB (2006, $15.99) r/#1-6 16.00

DAVID AND GOLIATH (Movie)
Dell Publishing Co.: No. 1205, July, 1961

	GD	VG	FN	VF	VF/NM	NM-
Four Color 1205-Photo-c	6	12	18	43	69	95

DAVID BORING (See Eightball)
Pantheon Books: 2000 ($24.95, hardcover w/dust jacket)

Hardcover - reprints David Boring stories from Eightball; Clowes-s/a 25.00

DAVID CASSIDY (TV)(See Partridge Family, Swing With Scooter #33 & Time For Love #30)
Charlton Comics: Feb, 1972 - No. 14, Sept, 1973

	GD	VG	FN	VF	VF/NM	NM-
1-Most have photo covers	6	12	18	41	66	90
2-5	4	8	12	24	37	50
6-14	4	8	12	22	34	45

DAVID LADD'S LIFE STORY (See Movie Classics)

DAVY CROCKETT (See Dell Giants, Fightin..., Frontier Fighters, It's Game Time, Power Record Comics, Western Tales & Wild Frontier)

DAVY CROCKETT (Frontier Fighter...)
Avon Periodicals: 1951

	GD	VG	FN	VF	VF/NM	NM-
nn-Tuska?, Reinman-a; Fawcette-c	18	36	54	105	165	225

DAVY CROCKETT (...King of the Wild Frontier No. 1,2)(TV)
Dell Publishing Co./Gold Key: 5/55 - No. 671, 12/55; No. 1, 12/63; No. 2, 11/69 (Walt Disney)

	GD	VG	FN	VF	VF/NM	NM-
Four Color 631(#1)-Fess Parker photo-c	17	34	51	120	223	325
Four Color 639-Photo-c	14	28	42	102	181	260
Four Color 664,671(Marsh-a)-Photo-c	13	26	39	97	171	245
1(12/63-Gold Key)-Fess Parker photo-c; reprints	8	16	24	54	90	125
2(11/69)-Fess Parker photo-c; reprints	4	8	12	28	44	60

Dawn #2 © J.M. Linsner

DC Comics Presents #3 © DC

DC First: Green Lantern/Green Lantern #1 © DC

	GD	VG	FN	VF	VF/NM	NM-
	2.0	4.0	6.0	8.0	9.0	9.2

DAVY CROCKETT (...Frontier Fighter #1,2; Kid Montana #9 on)
Charlton Comics: Aug, 1955 - No. 8, Jan, 1957

Issue	GD	VG	FN	VF	VF/NM	NM-
1	10	20	30	56	76	95
2	7	14	21	35	43	50
3-8	5	10	15	24	30	35

DAWN
Sirius Entertainment/Image Comics: June, 1995 - No. 6, 1996 ($2.95)

Issue	GD	VG	FN	VF	VF/NM	NM-
1/2-w/certificate	1	2	3	5	6	8
1/2-Variant-c	2	4	6	10	14	18
1-Linsner-c/a	1	2	3	5	6	8
1-Black Light Edition	2	4	6	9	13	16
1-White Trash Edition	3	6	9	16	23	30
1-Look Sharp Edition	3	6	9	19	29	38
2-4: Linsner c/a						4.50
2-Variant-c, 3-Limited Edition	2	4	6	13	18	22
4-6-Vibrato-c						3.50
4, 5-Limited Edition	2	4	6	8	10	12
6-Limited Edition	2	4	6	8	10	12
...Convention Sketchbook (Image Comics, 2002, $2.95) pin-ups						3.00
...2003 Convention Sketchbook (Image Comics, 3/03, $2.95) pin-ups						3.00
...2004 Convention Sketchbook (Image Comics, 4/04, $2.95) pin-ups						3.00
...2005 Convention Sketchbook (Image Comics, 5/05, $2.95) pin-ups						3.00
Genesis Edition ('99, Wizard supplement) previews Return of the Goddess						2.50
Lucifer's Halo TPB (11/97, $19.95) r/Drama, Dawn #1-6 plus 12 pages of new artwork						20.00
...: Tenth Anniversary Special (9/99, $2.95) Interviews						3.00
The Portable Dawn ($9.95, 5"x4", 64 pgs.) Pocket-sized cover gallery						10.00

DAWN OF THE DEAD (George A. Romaro's...)
IDW Publishing: Apr, 2004 - No. 3, Jun, 2004 ($3.99, limited series)

Issue	GD	VG	FN	VF	VF/NM	NM-
1-3-Adaptation of the 2004 movie; Niles-s						4.00
TPB (9/04, $17.99) r/#1-3; intro. by George A. Romero						18.00

DAWN: THE RETURN OF THE GODDESS
Sirius Entertainment: Apr, 1999 - No. 4, July, 2000 ($2.95, limited series)

Issue	GD	VG	FN	VF	VF/NM	NM-
1-4-Linsner-s/a						3.00
TPB (4/02, $12.95) r/#1-4; intro. by Linsner						13.00

DAWN: THREE TIERS
Image Comics: Jun, 2003 - No. 6, Aug, 2005 ($2.95, limited series)

Issue	GD	VG	FN	VF	VF/NM	NM-
1-6-Linsner-s/a. 2-Preview of Vampire's Christmas						3.00

DAYDREAMERS (See Generation X)
Marvel Comics: Aug, 1997 - No. 3, Oct, 1997 ($2.50, limited series)

Issue	GD	VG	FN	VF	VF/NM	NM-
1-3-Franklin Richards, Howard the Duck, Man-Thing app.						2.50

DAY OF JUDGMENT
DC Comics: Nov, 1999 - No. 5, Nov, 1999 ($2.95/$2.50, limited series)

Issue	GD	VG	FN	VF	VF/NM	NM-
1-($2.95) Spectre possessed; Matt Smith-a						3.00
2-5: Parallax returns. 5-Hal Jordan becomes the Spectre						3.00
...Secret Files 1 (11/99, $4.95) Harris-c						5.00

DAY OF VENGEANCE (Prelude to Infinite Crisis)(Also see Birds of Prey #76 for 1st app. of Black Alice)
DC Comics: June, 2005 - No. 6, Nov, 2005 ($2.50, limited series)

Issue	GD	VG	FN	VF	VF/NM	NM-
1-6: 1-Jean Loring becomes Eclipso; Spectre, Ragman, Enchantress, Detective Chimp, Shazam app.; Justiniano-a. 2,3-Capt. Marvel app. 4-6-Black Alice app.						2.50
...: Infinite Crisis Special 1 (3/06, $4.99) Justiniano-a/Simonson-c						5.00
TPB (2005, $12.99) r/series & Action #826, Advs. of Superman #639, Superman #216						13.00

DAYS OF THE DEFENDERS (See Defenders, The)
Marvel Comics: Mar, 2001 ($3.50, one-shot)

Issue	GD	VG	FN	VF	VF/NM	NM-
1-Reprints early team-ups of members, incl. Marvel Feature #1; Larsen-c						3.50

DAYS OF THE MOB (See In the Days of the Mob)

DAZEY'S DIARY
Dell Publishing Co.: June-Aug, 1962

Issue	GD	VG	FN	VF	VF/NM	NM-
01-174-208: Bill Woggon-c/a	4	8	12	28	44	60

DAZZLER, THE (Also see Marvel Graphic Novel & X-Men #130)
Marvel Comics Group: Mar, 1981 - No. 42, Mar, 1986

Issue	GD	VG	FN	VF	VF/NM	NM-
1,22,24,27,28,38,42: 1-X-Men app. 22 (12/82)-vs. Rogue Battle-c/sty. 24-Full app. Rogue w/Powerman (Iron Fist). 27-Rogue app. 28-Full app. Rogue; Mystique app. 38-Wolverine-c/app.; X-Men app. 42-Beast-c/app.						4.00
2-21,23,25,26,29-37,39-41: 2-X-Men app. 10,11-Galactus app. 21-Double size; photo-c. 23-Rogue/Mystique 1 pg. app. 26-Jusko-c. 33-Michael Jackson thriller swipe-c/sty. 40-Secret Wars II						3.00

NOTE: *No. 1 distributed only through comic shops.* **Alcala** *a-1i, 2i.* **Chadwick** *a-38-42p; c(p)-39, 41, 42.* **Guice** *a-38i, 42i; c-38, 40.*

DC CHALLENGE (Most DC superheroes appear)
DC Comics: Nov, 1985 - No. 12, Oct, 1986 ($1.25/$2.00, maxi-series)

Issue	GD	VG	FN	VF	VF/NM	NM-
1-11: 1-Colan-a. 2,8-Batman-c/app. 4-Gil Kane-c/a						2.50
12-($2.00-c) Giant; low print						3.00

NOTE: *Batman app. in 1-4, 6-12. Joker app. in 7.* **Infantino** *a-3.* **Ordway** *c-12.* **Swan/Austin** *c-10.*

DC COMICS PRESENTS
DC Comics: July-Aug, 1978 - No. 97, Sept, 1986 (Superman team-ups in all)

Issue	GD	VG	FN	VF	VF/NM	NM-
1-4th Superman/Flash race	3	6	9	18	27	35
1-(Whitman variant)	3	6	9	20	30	40
2-Part 2 of Superman/Flash race	2	4	6	11	16	20
2-4,9-12,14-16,19,21,22-(Whitman variants, low print run, none have issue # on cover)	2	4	6	11	16	20
3-10: 4-Metal Men. 6-Green Lantern. 8-Swamp Thing. 9-Wonder Woman	1	3	4	6	8	10
11-25,27-40: 13-Legion of Super-Heroes. 19-Batgirl. 31-Robin. 35-Man-Bat						6.00
26-(10/80)-Green Lantern; intro Cyborg, Starfire, Raven (1st app. New Teen Titans in 16 pg. preview); Starlin-c/a; Sargon the Sorcerer back-up	4	8	12	26	41	55
41,72,77,78,97: 41-Superman/Joker-c/story. 72-Joker/Phantom Stranger-c/story. 77,78-Animal Man app. (77-c also), 97-Phantom Zone						5.00
42-46,48-50,52-71,73-76,79-83: 42-Sandman. 43,80-Legion of Super-Heroes. 52 Doom Patrol. 58-Robin. 82-Adam Strange. 83-Batman & Outsiders						4.00
47-He-Man-c/s (1st app. in comics)	2	4	6	10	14	18
51-Preview insert (16 pgs.) of He-Man (2nd app.)	1	2	3	5	6	8
84-Challengers of the Unknown; Kirby-c/s.						6.00
85-Swamp Thing; Alan Moore scripts						6.00
86,88-96: 86-88-Crisis x-over. 88-Creeper						4.00
87-Origin/1st app. Superboy of Earth Prime	1	3	4	6	8	10
Annual 1,4: 1(9/82)-G.A. Superman; 1st app. Alexander Luthor. 4(10/85)-Superwoman						4.00
Annual 2,3: 2(7/83)-Intro/origin Superwoman. 3(9/84)-Shazam						4.00

NOTE: **Adkins** *a-2, 54; c-2.* **Buckler** *a-33, 34; c-30, 33, 34.* **Giffen** *a-39; c-59.* **Gil Kane** *a-28, 35, Annual 3; c-48p, 56, 58, 60, 62, 64, 68, Annual 2, 3.* **Kirby** *c/a-84.* **Kubert** *c/a-66.* **Morrow** *c/a-65.* **Newton** *c/a-54p.* **Orlando** *c-53i.* **Perez** *a-26p, 61p; c-38, 61, 94.* **Starlin** *a-26-29p, 36p, 37p; c-26-29, 36, 37, 93.* **Toth** *a 84.* **Williamson** *i-79, 85, 87.*

DC COMICS PRESENTS: ...(Julie Schwartz tribute series of one-shots based on classic covers)
DC Comics: Sept, 2004 - Oct, 2004 ($2.50)

Issue	GD	VG	FN	VF	VF/NM	NM-
The Atom -(Based on cover of Atom #10) Gibbons-s/Oliffe-a; Waid-s/Jurgens-a; Bolland-c						2.50
Batman -(Batman #183) Johns-s/Infantino-a; Wein-s/Kuhn-a; Hughes-c						2.50
The Flash -(Flash #163) Loeb s/McGuinness-a; O'Neil-s/Mahnke-a; Ross-c						2.50
Green Lantern -(Green Lantern #31) Azzarello-s/Breyfogle-a; Pasko-s/McDaniel-a; Bolland-c						2.50
Hawkman -(Hawkman #6) Bates-s/Byrne-a; Busiek-s/Simonson-a; Garcia-Lopez-c						2.50
Justice League of America -(J.L. of A. #53) Ellison & David-s/Giella-a; Wolfman-s/Nguyen-a; Garcia-Lopez-c						2.50
Mystery in Space -(M.I.S. #82) Maggin-s/Williams-a; Morrison-s/Ordway-a; Ross-c						2.50
Superman -(Superman #264) Stan Lee-s/Cooke-a; Levitz-s/Giffen-a; Hughes-c						2.50

DC COUNTDOWN (To Infinite Crisis)
DC Comics: May, 2005 ($1.00, 80 pages, one-shot)

Issue	GD	VG	FN	VF	VF/NM	NM-
1-Death of Blue Beetle; prelude to OMAC Project, Day of Vengeance, Rann/Thanagar War and Villains United mini-series; s/a by various; Jim Lee/Alex Ross-c						3.00

DC FIRST: ...(series of one-shots)
DC Comics: July, 2002 ($3.50)

Issue	GD	VG	FN	VF	VF/NM	NM-
Batgirl/Joker 1-Sienkiewicz & Terry Moore-a; Nowlan-c						3.50
Green Lantern/Green Lantern 1-Alan Scott & Hal Jordan vs. Krona						3.50
Flash/Superman 1-Superman races Jay Garrick; Abra Kadabra app.						3.50
Superman/Lobo 1-Giffen-s; Nowlan-c						3.50

DC GRAPHIC NOVEL (Also see DC Science Fiction...)
DC Comics: Nov, 1983 - No. 7, 1986 ($5.95, 68 pgs.)

Issue	GD	VG	FN	VF	VF/NM	NM-
1-3,5,7: 1-Star Raiders. 2-Warlords; not from regular Warlord series. 3-The Medusa Chain; Ernie Colon story/a. 5-Me and Joe Priest; Chaykin-c. 7-Space Clusters; Nino-c/a	2	4	6	9	12	15
4-The Hunger Dogs by Kirby; Darkseid kills Himon from Mister Miracle & destroys New Genesis	5	10	15	32	51	70
6-Metalzoic; Sienkiewicz-c ($6.95)	2	4	6	9	12	15

DC INFINITE HALLOWEEN SPECIAL
DC Comics: Dec, 2007 ($5.99, one-shot)

Issue	GD	VG	FN	VF	VF/NM	NM-
1-Halloween short stories by various incl. Dini, Waid, Hairsine, Kelley Jones; Gene Ha-c						6.00

DC/MARVEL: ALL ACCESS (Also see DC Versus Marvel & Marvel Versus DC)
DC Comics: 1996 - No. 4, 1997 ($2.95, limited series)

1-4: 1-Superman & Spider-Man app. 2-Robin & Jubilee app. 3-Dr. Strange & Batman-c/app.,

DC 100 Page Super Spectacular #20 © DC

DC Special #22 © DC

DC Special Series #17 © DC

GD VG FN VF VF/NM NM-
2.0 4.0 6.0 8.0 9.0 9.2

X-Men, JLA app. 4-X-Men vs. JLA-c/app. rebirth of Amalgam 3.00

DC/MARVEL: CROSSOVER CLASSICS
DC Comics: 1998; 2003 ($14.95, TPB)

Vol. II-Reprints Batman/Punisher: Lake of Fire, Punisher/Batman: Deadly Knights, Silver Surfer/Superman, Batman & Capt. America 15.00
Vol. 4 (2003, $14.95) Reprints Green Lantern/Silver Surfer: Unholy Alliances, Darkseid/ Galactus: The Hunger, Batman & Spider-Man, and Superman/Fantastic Four 15.00

DC 100 PAGE SUPER SPECTACULAR
(Title is 100 Page... No. 14 on)(Square bound) (Reprints, 50¢)
National Periodical Publications: No. 4, Summer, 1971 - No. 13, 6/72; No. 14, 2/73 - No. 22, 11/73 (No #1-3)

4-Weird Mystery Tales; Johnny Peril & Phantom Stranger; cover & splashes by Wrightson; origin Jungle Boy of Jupiter 18 36 54 130 240 350
5-Love Stories; Wood inks (7 pgs.)(scarcer) 44 88 132 352 664 975
6- "World's Greatest Super-Heroes"; JLA, JSA, Spectre, Johnny Quick, Vigilante & Hawkman; contains unpublished Wildcat story; N. Adams wrap-around-c; r/JLA #21,22 18 36 54 130 240 350
6-Replica Edition (2004, $6.95) complete reprint w/wraparound-c 7.00
7-(Also listed as Superman #245) Air Wave, Kid Eternity, Hawkman-r; Atom-r/Atom #3 9 18 27 63 107 150
8-(Also listed as Batman #238) Batman, Legion, Aquaman-r; G.A. Atom, Sargon (r/Sensation #57), Plastic Man (r/Police #14) stories; Doom Patrol origin-r; Neal Adams wraparound-c 11 22 33 79 140 200
9-(Also listed as Our Army at War #242) Kubert-c 9 18 27 63 107 150
10-(Also listed as Adventure Comics #416) Golden Age-reprints; r/1st app. Black Canary from Flash #86; no Zatanna 11 22 33 75 133 190
11-(Also listed as Flash #214) origin Metal Men-r/Showcase #37; never before published G.A. Flash story. 8 16 24 56 93 130
12,14: 12-(Also listed as Superboy #185) Legion-c/story; Teen Titans, Kid Eternity (r/Hit #46), Star Spangled Kid-r(S.S. #55). 14-Batman-r/Detective #31,32,156; Atom-r/Showcase #34 7 14 21 49 80 110
13-(Also listed as Superman #252) Ray(r/Smash #17), Black Condor, (r/Crack #18), Hawkman(r/Flash #24); Starman-r/Adv. #67; Dr. Fate & Spectre-r/More Fun #57; Neal Adams-c 10 20 30 68 119 170
15,16,18,19,21,22: 15-r/2nd Boy Commandos/Det. #64. 21-Superboy; r/Brave & the Bold #54. 22-r/All-Flash #13. 6 12 18 37 59 80
17,20: 17-JSA-r/All Star #37 (10-11/47, 38 pgs.), Sandman-r/Adv. #65 (8/41), JLA #23 (11/63) & JLA #43 (3/66). 20-Batman-r/Det. #66,68, Spectre; origin Two-Face 6 12 18 39 62 85
... : Love Stories Replica Edition (2000, $6.95) reprints #5 7.00

NOTE: ***Anderson** r-11, 14, 18i, 22. **B. Baily** r-18, 20. **Burnley** r-18, 20. **Crandall** r-14p, 20. **Drucker** r-4. **Grandenetti** a-22(2)r. **Heath** a-22r. **Infantino** r-17, 20, 22. **G. Kane** r-18. **Kirby** r-15. **Kubert** r-6, 7, 16, 17; c-16, 19. **Manning** a-19r. **Meskin** r-4, 22. **Mooney** r-15, 21. **Toth** r-17, 20.*

DC ONE MILLION (Also see crossover #1,000,000 issues and JLA One Million TPB)
DC Comics: Nov, 1998 - No. 4, Nov, 1998 ($2.95/$1.99, weekly lim. series)

1-($2.95) JLA travels to the 853rd century; Morrison-s 3.00
2-4-($1.99) 2.50
... Eighty-Page Giant (8/99, $4.95) 5.00
TPB ('99, $14.95) r/#1-4 and several x-over stories 15.00

DC SCIENCE FICTION GRAPHIC NOVEL
DC Comics: 1985 - No. 7, 1987 ($5.95)

SF1-SF7: SF1-Hell on Earth by Robert Bloch; Giffen-p. SF2-Nightwings by Robert Silverberg; G. Colan-p. SF3-Frost & Fire by Bradbury. SF4-Merchants of Venus. SF5-Demon With A Glass Hand by Ellison; M. Rogers-a. SF6-The Magic Goes Away by Niven. SF7-Sandkings by George R.R. Martin 2 4 6 8 11 14

DC SILVER AGE CLASSICS
DC Comics: 1992 ($1.00, all reprints)

...Action Comics #252-r/1st Supergirl. Adventure Comics #247-r/1st Legion of Super-Heroes. The Brave and the Bold #28-r/1st JLA. Detective Comics #225-r/1st Martian Manhunter. Detective Comics #327-r/1st new look Batman. Green Lantern #76-r/1st Green Lantern/ Green Arrow. House of Secrets #92-r/1st Swamp Thing. Showcase #4-r/1st S.A. Flash. Showcase #22-r/1st S.A. Green Lantern 2.50
...Sugar and Spike #99; includes 2 unpublished stories 4.00

DC SPECIAL (Also see Super DC Giant)
National Per. Publ.: 10-12/68 - No. 15, 11-12/71; No. 16, Spr/75 - No. 29, 8-9/77

1-All Infantino issue; Flash, Batman, Adam Strange-r; begin 68 pg. issues, end #21 8 16 24 54 90 125
2-Teen humor; Binky, Buzzy, Harvey app. 10 20 30 67 116 165
3-All-Girl issue; unpubl. GA Wonder Woman story 9 18 27 60 100 140
4,11: 4-Horror (1st Abel, brief). 11-Monsters 5 10 15 32 51 70
5-10,12-15: 5-All Kubert issue; Viking Prince, Sgt. Rock-r. 6-Western. 7,9,13-Strangest Sports. 12-Viking Prince; Kubert-c/a (r/B&B almost entirely). 15-G.A. Plastic Man origin-r/Police #1; origin Woozy by Cole; 14,15-(52 pgs.) 4 8 12 26 41 55
16-27: 16-Super Heroes Battle Super Gorillas; r/Capt. Storm #1, 1st Johnny Cloud/All-Amer. Men of War #82. 17-Early S.A. Green Lantern-r. 22-Origin Robin Hood. 26-Enemy Ace. 27-Captain Comet story 3 6 9 16 22 28
28-Earth Shattering Disaster Stories; Legion of Super-Heroes story 3 6 9 16 23 30
29-New "The Untold Origin of the Justice Society"; Staton-a/Neal Adams-c; Hitler app. in story and on cover 3 6 9 21 32 42

NOTE: ***N. Adams** c-3, 4, 6, 11, 29. **Grell** a-20; c-17, 20. **Heath** a-12r. **G. Kane** a-6p, 13r, 17r, 19-21r. **Kirby** a-4,11. **Kubert** a-6r, 12r, 22. **Meskin** a-10. **Moreira** a-10. **Staton** a-29p. **Toth** a-13, 20r. #1-15: 25¢; 16-27: 50¢; 28, 29: 60¢. #1-13, 16-21: 68 pgs.; 14, 15: 52 pgs.; 25-27: oversized.*

DC SPECIAL BLUE RIBBON DIGEST
DC Comics: Mar-Apr, 1980 - No. 24, Aug, 1982

1,2,4,5: 1-Legion reprints. 2-Flash. 4-Green Lantern. 5-Secret Origins; new Zatara and Zatanna 2 4 6 8 11 14
3-Justice Society 2 4 6 10 14 18
6,8-10: 6-Ghosts. 8-Legion. 9-Secret Origins. 10-Warlord-"The Deimos Saga"-Grell-s/c/a 2 4 6 8 11 14
7-Sgt. Rock's Prize Battle Tales 2 4 6 13 18 22
11,16: 11-Justice League. 16-Green Lantern/Green Arrow-r; all Adams-a 2 4 6 11 16 20
12-Haunted Tank; reprints 1st app. 2 4 6 13 18 22
13-15,17-19: 13-Strange Sports Stories. 14-UFO Invaders; Adam Strange app. 15-Secret Origins of Super Villains; JLA app. 17-Ghosts. 18-Sgt. Rock; Kubert front & back-c. 19-Doom Patrol; new Perez-c 2 4 6 9 13 16
20-Dark Mansion of Forbidden Love (scarce) 5 10 15 30 48 65
21-Our Army at War 3 6 9 16 22 28
22-24: 22-Secret Origins. 23-Green Arrow, w/new 7 pg. story. 24-House of Mystery; new Kubert wraparound-c 2 4 6 13 18 22

NOTE: ***N. Adams** a-16(6)r, 17r, 23r; c-16. **Aparo** a-6r, 24r; c-23. **Grell** a-8, 10; c-10. **Heath** a-14. **Infantino** a-15r. **Kaluta** a-17r. **Gil Kane** a-15r, 22r. **Kirby** a-5, 9, 23r. **Kubert** a-3, 18r, 21r; c-7, 12, 14, 17, 18, 21, 24. **Morrow** a-24r. **Orlando** a-17r, 22r; c-1, 20. **Toth** a-21r, 24r. **Wood** a-3, 17r, 24r. **Wrightson** a-16r, 17r, 24r.*

DC SPECIAL: CYBORG (From Teen Titans)
DC Comics: Jul, 2008 - No. 5 ($2.99, limited series)

1-3-Sable-s/Lashley-a. 1-Origin re-told 3.00

DC SPECIAL: RAVEN (From Teen Titans)
DC Comics: May, 2008 - No. 5, Sept, 2008 ($2.99, limited series)

1-5-Marv Wolfman-s/Damion Scott-a 3.00

DC SPECIAL SERIES
National Periodical Publications/DC Comics: 9/77 - No. 16, Fall, 1978; No. 17, 8/79 - No. 27, Fall, 1981 (No. 18, 19, 23, 24 - digest size, 100 pgs.; No. 25-27 - Treasury sized)

1-"5-Star Super-Hero Spectacular 1977"; Batman, Atom, Flash, Green Lantern, Aquaman, in solo stories, Kobra app.; N. Adams-c 4 8 12 22 34 45
2(#1)-"The Original Swamp Thing Saga 1977"-r/Swamp Thing #1&2 by Wrightson; new Wrightson wraparound-c. 2 4 6 9 13 16
3,4,6-8: 3-Sgt Rock. 4-Unexpected. 6-Secret Society of Super Villains, Jones-a. 7-Ghosts Special. 8-Brave and Bold w/ new Batman, Deadman & Sgt Rock team-up 2 4 6 10 14 18
5-"Superman Spectacular 1977"-(84 pg, $1.00)-Superman vs. Brainiac & Lex Luthor, new 63 pg. story 3 6 9 14 19 24
9-Wonder Woman; Ditko-a (11 pgs.) 3 6 9 14 19 24
10-"Secret Origins of Superheroes Special 1978"-(52 pgs.)-Dr. Fate, Lightray & Black Canary on-c/new origin stories; Staton, Newton-a 2 4 6 13 18 22
11-"Flash Spectacular 1978"-(84 pgs.) Flash, Kid Flash, GA Flash & Johnny Quick vs. Grodd; Wood-i on Kid Flash chapter 2 4 6 10 14 18
12-"Secrets of Haunted House Special Spring 1978" 2 4 6 10 14 18
13-"Sgt. Rock Special Spring 1978", 50 pg new story 2 4 6 11 16 20
14,17,20-"Original Swamp Thing Saga", Wrightson-a: 14-Sum '78, r/#3,4. 17-Sum '79 r/#5-7. 20-Jan/Feb '80, r/#8-10 2 4 6 8 10 12
15-"Batman Spectacular Summer 1978", Ra's Al Ghul-app.; Golden-a. Rogers-a/front & back-c 3 6 9 18 27 35
16-"Jonah Hex Spectacular Fall 1978"; death of Jonah Hex, Heath-a; Bat Lash and Scalphunter stories 6 12 18 39 62 85
18,19-Digest size: 18-"Sgt. Rock's Prize Battle Tales Fall 1979". 19-"Secret Origins of Super-Heroes Fall 1979"; origins Wonder Woman (new-a),r/Robin, Batman-Superman team, Aquaman, Hawkman and others 2 4 6 10 14 18
21-"Super-Star Holiday Special Spring 1980", Frank Miller-a in "Batman--Wanted Dead or Alive" (1st Batman story); Jonah Hex, Sgt. Rock, Superboy & LSH and House of Mystery/ Witching Hour-c/stories 4 8 12 22 34 45
22-"G.I. Combat Sept. 1980", Kubert-c. Haunted Tank-s 2 4 6 11 16 20
23,24-Digest size: 23-World's Finest-r. 24-Flash 2 4 6 10 14 18

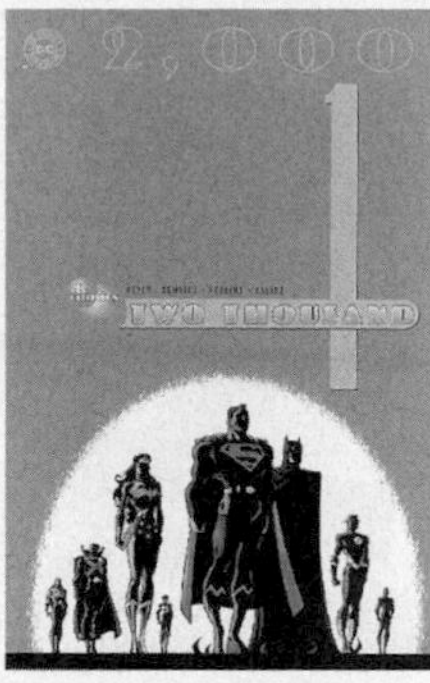

DC 2000 #1 © DC

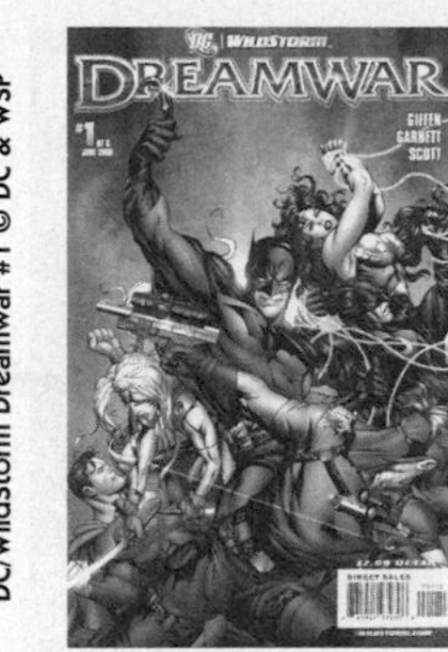

DC/WildStorm Dreamwar #1 © DC & WSP

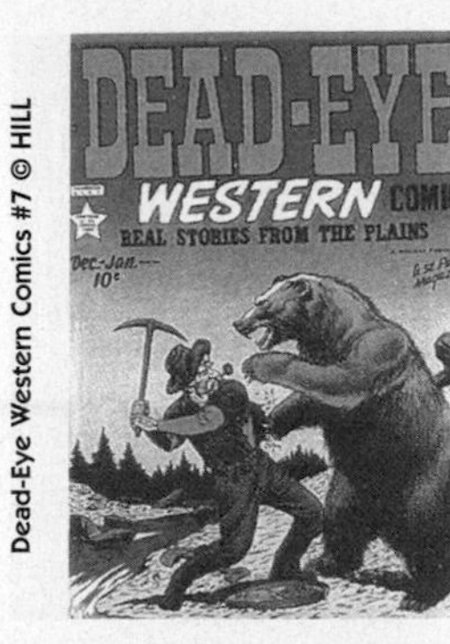

Dead-Eye Western Comics #7 © HILL

GD VG FN VF VF/NM NM-
2.0 4.0 6.0 8.0 9.0 9.2

V5#25-($2.95)-"Superman II, the Adventure Continues Summer 1981"; photos from movie & photo-c (see All-New Coll. Ed. C-62) 3 6 9 14 19 24
26-($2.50)-"Superman and His Incredible Fortress of Solitude Summer 1981" 3 6 9 14 19 24
27-($2.50)-"Batman vs. The Incredible Hulk Fall 1981" 4 8 12 24 37 50
NOTE: ***Aparo** c-8. **Heath** a-12i, 16. **Infantino** a-19r. **Kirby** a-23, 19r. **Kubert** c-13, 19r. **Nasser/Netzer** a-1, 10i, 15. **Newton** a-10. **Nino** a-4, 7. **Starlin** c-12. **Staton** a-1. **Tuska** a-19r. #25 & 26. were advertised as All-New Collectors' Edition C-63, C-64. #26 was originally planned as All-New Collectors' Ed. C-30?; has C-630 & A.N.C.E. on cover.*

DC SPECIAL: THE RETURN OF DONNA TROY
DC Comics: Aug, 2005 - No. 4, Late Oct, 2005 ($2.99, limited series)
1-4-Jimenez-s/Garcia-Lopez-a(p)/Pérez-i 3.00

DC SUPER-STARS
National Periodical Publications/DC Comics: March, 1976 - No. 18, Winter, 1978 (No. 3-18: 52 pgs.)
1-(68 pgs.)-Re-intro Teen Titans (predates T. T. #44 (11/76); tryout iss.) plus r/Teen Titans; W.W. as girl was original Wonder Girl 3 6 9 17 25 32
2-7,9,11,12,16: 2,4,6,8-Adam Strange; 2-(68 pgs.)-r/1st Adam Strange/Hawkman team-up from Mystery in Space #90 plus Atomic Knights origin-r. 3-Legion issue. 4-r/Tales/Unexpected #45 2 4 6 8 10 12
8-r/1st Space Ranger from Showcase #15, Adam Strange-r/Mystery in Space #89 & Star Rovers-r/M.I.S. #80 2 4 6 8 11 14
10-Strange Sports Stories; Batman/Joker-c/story 2 4 6 9 13 16
13-Sergio Aragonés Special 3 6 9 14 19 24
14,15,18: 15-Sgt. Rock 2 4 6 8 11 14
17-Secret Origins of Super-Heroes (origin of The Huntress); origin Green Arrow by Grell; Legion app.; Earth II Batman & Catwoman marry (1st revealed; also see B&B #197 & Superman Family #211) 5 10 15 30 48 65
NOTE: ***M. Anderson** r-2, 4, 6. **Aparo** c-7, 14, 18. **Austin** a-11i. **Buckler** a-14p; c-10. **Grell** a-17. **G. Kane** a-1r, 10r. **Kubert** c-15. **Layton** c/a-16i, 17i. **Mooney** a-4r, 6r. **Morrow** c/a-11r. **Nasser** a-11. **Newton** c/a-16p. **Staton** a-17, c-17. No. 10, 12-18 contain all new material; the rest are reprints. #1 contains new and reprint material.*

DC: THE NEW FRONTIER (Also see Justice League: The New Frontier Special)
DC Comics: Mar, 2004 - No. 6, Nov, 2004 ($6.95, limited series)
1-6-DCU in the 1940s-60s; Darwyn Cooke-c/s/a in all. 1-Hal Jordan and The Losers app. 2-Origin Martian Manhunter; Barry Allen app. 3-Challengers of the Unknown 7.00
...Volume One (2004, $19.95, TPB) r/#1-3; cover gallery & intro. by Paul Levitz 20.00
...Volume Two (2005, $19.99, TPB) r/#4-6; cover gallery & afterword by Cooke 20.00

DC TOP COW CROSSOVERS
DC Comics/Top Cow Productions: 2007 ($14.99, TPB)
SC-r/The Darkness/Batman; JLA/Witchblade; The Darkness/Superman; JLA/Cyberforce 15.00

DC 2000
DC Comics: 2000 - No. 2, 2000 ($6.95, limited series)
1,2-JLA visit 1941 JSA; Semeiks-a 7.00

DCU BRAVE NEW WORLD (See Infinite Crisis and tie-ins)
DC Comics: Aug, 2006 ($1.00, 80 pgs., one-shot)
1-Previews 2006 series Martian Manhunter, OMAC, The Creeper, The All-New Atom, The Trials of Shazam, and Uncle Sam and the Freedom Fighters; the Monitor app. 3.00

DCU HEROES SECRET FILES
DC Comics: Feb, 1999 ($4.95, one-shot)
1-Origin-s and pin-ups; new Star Spangled Kid app. 5.00

DCU INFINITE HOLIDAY SPECIAL
DC Comics: Feb, 2007 ($4.99, one-shot)
1-Christmas anthology by various; Batwoman app.; Porter-c 5.00

DC UNIVERSE CHRISTMAS, A
DC Comics: 2000 ($19.95)
TPB-Reprints DC Christmas stories by various 20.00

DC UNIVERSE HOLIDAY BASH
DC Comics: 1997- 1999 ($3.95)
I,II-(X-mas '96,'97) Christmas stories by various 5.00
III (1999, for Christmas '98, $4.95) 5.00

DC UNIVERSE SPECIAL
DC Comics: July, 2008 - Aug, 2008 ($4.99, collection of reprints related to Final Crisis)
...: Justice League of America (7/08) r/J.L. of A. #111,166-168 & Detective #274; Sook-c 5.00
...: Reign in Hell (8/08) r/Blaze/Satanus War x-over; Sook-c 5.00
...: Superman (7/08) r/Mongul app. in Superman #32, Showcase '95 #7,8, Flash #102 5.00

DC UNIVERSE: THE STORIES OF ALAN MOORE (Also see Across the Universe:...)
DC Comics: 2006 ($19.99)
TPB-Reprints Batman: The Killing Joke, "Whatever Happened to the Man of Tomorrow", "For The Man Who Has Everything, and other classic Moore DC stories; Bolland-c 20.00

DC UNIVERSE: TRINITY
DC Comics: Aug, 1993 - No. 2, Sept, 1993 ($2.95, 52 pgs, limited series)
1,2-Foil-c; Green Lantern, Darkstars, Legion app. 3.50

DCU VILLAINS SECRET FILES
DC Comics: Apr, 1999 ($4.95, one-shot)
1-Origin-s and profile pages 5.00

DC VERSUS MARVEL (See Marvel Versus DC) (Also see Amazon, Assassins, Bruce Wayne: Agent of S.H.I. E. L.D., Bullets & Bracelets, Doctor Strangefate, JLX, Legend of the Dark Claw, Magneto & The Magnetic Men, Speed Demon, Spider-Boy, Super Soldier, X-Patrol)
DC Comics: No. 1, 1996, No. 4, 1996 ($3.95, limited series)
1,4: 1-Marz script, Jurgens-a(p); 1st app. of Access. 4.00
.../Marvel Versus DC ($12.95, trade paperback) r/1-4 13.00

DC/WILDSTORM DREAMWAR
DC Comics: Jun, 2008 - No. 6 ($2.99, limited series)
1-4-Giffen-s; Silver Age JLA, Teen Titans, JSA, Legion app. on WildStorm Earth 3.00
1-Variant-c of Superman & Midnighter by Garbett 6.00

DC: WORLD WAR III (See 52/WWIII)

D-DAY (Also see Special War Series)
Charlton Comics (no No. 3): Sum/63; No. 2, Fall/64; No. 4, 9/66; No. 5, 10/67; No. 6, 11/68
1,2: 1(1963)-Montes/Bache-c. 2(Fall '64)-Wood-a(4) 4 8 12 22 34 45
4-6('66-'68)-Montes/Bache-a #5 3 6 9 14 20 25

DEAD AIR
Slave Labor Graphics: July, 1989 ($5.95, graphic novel)
nn-Mike Allred's 1st published work 6.00

DEAD CORPSE
DC Comics (Helix): Sept, 1998 - No. 4, Dec, 1998 ($2.50, limited series)
1-4-Pugh-a/Hinz-s 2.50

DEAD END CRIME STORIES
Kirby Publishing Co.: April, 1949 (52 pgs.)
nn-(Scarce)-Powell, Roussos-a; painted-c 51 102 153 316 526 735

DEAD ENDERS
DC Comics (Vertigo): Mar, 2000 - No. 16, June, 2001 ($2.50)
1-16-Brubaker-s/Pleece & Case-a 2.50
Stealing the Sun (2000, $9.95, TPB) r/#1-4, Vertigo Winter's Edge #3 10.00

DEAD-EYE WESTERN COMICS
Hillman Periodicals: Nov-Dec, 1948 - V3#1, Apr-May, 1953
V1#1-(52 pgs.)-Krigstein, Roussos-a 19 38 57 112 176 240
V1#2,3-(52 pgs.) 12 24 36 67 94 120
V1#4-12-(52 pgs.) 9 18 27 47 61 75
V2#1,2,5-8,10-12: 1-7-(52 pgs.) 8 16 24 40 50 60
3,4-Krigstein-a 8 16 24 44 57 70
9-One pg. Frazetta ad 8 16 24 40 50 60
V3#1 8 16 24 40 50 60
NOTE: ***Briefer** a-V1#8. Kinstleresque stories by **McCann**-12, V2#1, 2, V3#1. **McWilliams** a-V1#5. **Ed Moore** a-V1#4.*

DEADFACE: DOING THE ISLANDS WITH BACCHUS
Dark Horse Comics: July, 1991 - No. 3, Sept, 1991 ($2.95, B&W, lim. series)
1-3: By Eddie Campbell 3.00

DEADFACE: EARTH, WATER, AIR, AND FIRE
Dark Horse Comics: July, 1992 - No. 4, Oct, 1992 ($2.50, B&W, limited series; British-r)
1-4: By Eddie Campbell 3.00

DEAD IN THE WEST
Dark Horse Comics: Oct, 1993 - No. 2, Mar, 1994 ($3.95, B&W, 52 pgs.)
1,2-Timothy Truman-c 4.00

DEADLANDER (Becomes Dead Rider for #2)
Dark Horse Comics: Oct, 2007 - No. 4, ($2.99, limited series)
1-2-Kevin Ferrara-s/a 3.00

DEADLIEST HEROES OF KUNG FU (Magazine)
Marvel Comics Group: Summer, 1975 (B&W)(76 pgs.)
1-Bruce Lee vs. Carradine painted-c; TV Kung Fu, 4pgs. photos/article; Enter the Dragon, 24 pgs. photos/article w/ Bruce Lee; Bruce Lee photo pinup 4 8 12 24 37 50

DEADLINE

Deadly Hands of Kung Fu #17 © MAR

Deadman: Dead Again #1 © DC

Deadpool (2008 series) #1 © MAR

GD VG FN VF VF/NM NM-
2.0 4.0 6.0 8.0 9.0 9.2

Marvel Comics: June, 2002 - No. 4, Sept, 2002 ($2.99, limited series)

1-4: 1-Intro. Kat Farrell; Bill Rosemann-s/Guy Davis-a; Horn painted-c 3.00
TPB (2002. $9.99) r/#1-4 10.00

DEADLY DUO, THE
Image Comics (Highbrow Entertainment): Nov, 1994 - No. 3, Jan, 1995 ($2.50, lim. series)

1-3: 1-1st app. of Kill Cat 2.50

DEADLY DUO, THE
Image Comics (Highbrow Entertainment): June, 1995 - No. 4, Oct, 1995 ($2.50, lim. series)

1-4: 1-Spawn app. 2-Savage Dragon app. 3-Gen 13 app. 2.50

DEADLY FOES OF SPIDER-MAN (See Lethal Foes of...)
Marvel Comics: May, 1991 - No. 4, Aug, 1991 ($1.00, limited series)

1-4: 1-Punisher, Kingpin, Rhino app. 2.50

DEADLY HANDS OF KUNG FU, THE (See Master of Kung Fu)
Marvel Comics Group: April, 1974 - No. 33, Feb, 1977 (75¢) (B&W, magazine)

1(V1#4 listed in error)-Origin Sons of the Tiger; Shang-Chi, Master of Kung Fu begins (ties w/Master of Kung Fu #17 as 3rd app. Shang-Chi); Bruce Lee painted-c by Neal Adams; 2pg. memorial photo pinup w/8 pgs. photos/articles; TV Kung Fu, 9 pgs. photos/articles; 15 pgs. Starlin-a 5 10 15 34 55 75
2-Adams painted-c; 1st time origin of Shang-Chi, 34 pgs. by Starlin. TV Kung Fu, 6 pgs. photos & article w/2 pg. pinup. Bruce Lee, 11 pgs. ph/a 4 8 12 26 41 55
3,4,7,10: 3-Adams painted-c; Gulacy-a. Enter the Dragon, photos/articles, 8 pgs. 4-TV Kung Fu painted-c by Neal Adams; TV Kung Fu 7 pg. article/art; Fu Manchu; Enter the Dragon, 10 pg. photos/article w/Bruce Lee. 7-Bruce Lee painted-c & 9 pgs. photos/articles-Return of Dragon plus 1 pg. photo pinup. 10-(3/75)-Iron Fist painted-c & 34 pg. sty-Early app. 3 6 9 19 29 38
5,6: 5-1st app. Manchurian, 6 pgs. Gulacy-a. TV Kung Fu, 4 pg. article; reprints books w/Barry Smith-a. Capt. America-sty, 10 pgs. Kirby-a(r). 6-Bruce Lee photos/article, 6 pgs.; 15 pgs. early Perez-a 3 6 9 18 27 35
8,9,11: 9-Iron Fist, 2 pg. Preview pinup; Nebres-a. 11-Billy Jack painted-c by Adams; 17 pgs. photos/article 3 6 9 17 25 32
12,13: 12-James Bond painted-c by Adams; 14 pg. photos/article. 13-16 pgs. early Perez-a; Piers Anthony, 7 pgs. photos/article 3 6 9 16 23 30
14-Classic Bruce Lee painted-c by Adams. Lee pinup by Chaykin. Lee 16 pg. photos/article w/2 pgs. Green Hornet TV 6 12 18 41 66 90
15,19: 15-Sum, '75 Giant Annual #1. 20pgs. Starlin-a. Bruce Lee photo pinup & 3 pg. photos/ article re book; Man-Thing app. Iron Fist-c/sty; Gulacy-a 18pgs. 19-Iron Fist painted-c & series begins; 1st White Tiger 3 6 9 17 25 32
16,18,20: 16-1st app. Corpse Rider, a Samurai w/Sanho Kim-a. 20-Chuck Norris painted-c & 16 pgs. interview w/photos/article; Bruce Lee vs. C. Norris pinup by Ken Barr. Origin The White Tiger, Perez-a 3 6 9 16 22 28
17-Bruce Lee painted-c by Adams; interview w/R. Clouse, director Enter Dragon 7 pgs. w/B. Lee app. 1st Giffen-a (1pg. 11/75) 4 8 12 26 41 55
21-Bruce Lee 1pg. photos/article 3 6 9 16 22 28
22,30-32: 22-1st brief app. Jack of Hearts. 1st Giffen sty-a (along w/Amazing Adv. #35, 3/76). 30-Swordquest-c/sty & conclusion; Jack of Hearts app. 31-Jack of Hearts app; Staton-a. 32-1st Daughters of the Dragon-c/sty, 21 pgs. M. Rogers-a/Claremont-sty; Iron Fist pinup 3 6 9 14 20 26
23-26,29: 23-1st full app. Jack of Hearts. 24-Iron Fist-c & centerfold pinup. early Zeck-a; Shang Chi pinup; 6 pgs. Piers Anthony text sty w/Perez/Austin-a; Jack of Hearts app. early Giffen-a. 25-1st app. Shimuru, "Samurai", 20 pgs. Mantlo-sty/Broderick-a; "Swordquest"-c & begins 17 pg. sty by Sanho Kim; 11 pg. photos/article; partly Bruce Lee. 26-Bruce Lee painted-c & pinup; 16 pgs. interviews w/Kwon & Clouse; talk about Bruce Lee re-filming of Lee legend. 29-Ironfist vs. Shang Chi battle-c/sty; Jack of Hearts app. 3 6 9 17 25 32
27 3 6 9 14 19 24
28-All Bruce Lee Special Issue; (1st time in comics). Bruce Lee painted-c by Ken Barr & pinup. 36 pgs. comics chronicaling Bruce Lee's life; 15 pgs. B. Lee photos/article (Rare in high grade) 7 14 21 49 80 110
33-Shang Chi-c/sty; Classic Daughters of the Dragon, 21 pgs. M. Rogers-a/Claremont-story with nudity; Bob Wall interview, photos/article, 14 pgs. 3 6 9 19 29 38
...Special Album Edition 1(Summer, '74)-Iron Fist-c/story (early app., 3rd?); 10 pgs. Adams-i; Shang Chi/Fu Manchu, 10 pgs.; Sons of Tiger, 11 pgs.; TV Kung Fu, 6 pgs. photos/article 3 6 9 21 32 42

NOTE: ***Bruce Lee**: 1-7, 14, 15, 17, 25, 26, 28. **Kung Fu (TV)**: 1, 2, 4. **Jack of Hearts**: 22, 23, 29-33. **Shang Chi Master of Kung Fu**: 1-9, 11-18, 29, 31, 33. **Sons of Tiger**: 1, 3, 4, 6-14, 16-19. **Swordquest**: 25-27, 29-33. **White Tiger**: 19-24, 26, 27, 29-33. **N. Adams** a-1i(part), 27i; c-1, 2-4, 11, 12, 14, 17. **Giffen** a-22p, 24p. **G. Kane** a-23p. **Kirby** a-5r. **Nasser** a-27p, 28. **Perez** a(p)-6-14, 16, 17, 19, 21. **Rogers** a-26, 32, 33. **Starlin** a-1, 2r, 15r. **Staton** a-28p, 31, 32.*

DEADMAN (See The Brave and the Bold & Phantom Stranger #39)
DC Comics: May, 1985 - No. 7, Nov, 1985 ($1.75, Baxter paper)

GD VG FN VF VF/NM NM-
2.0 4.0 6.0 8.0 9.0 9.2

1-7: 1-Deadman-r by Infantino, N. Adams in all. 5-Batman-c/story-r/Strange Adventures. 7-Batman-r 3.00

DEADMAN
DC Comics: Mar, 1986 - No. 4, June, 1986 (75¢, limited series)

1-4: Lopez-c/a. 4-Byrne-c(p) 3.00

DEADMAN
DC Comics: Feb, 2002 - No. 9, Oct, 2002 ($2.50)

1-9: 1-4-Vance-s/Beroy-a. 3,4-Mignola-c. 5,6-Garcia-Lopez-a 2.50

DEADMAN
DC Comics (Vertigo): Oct, 2006 - No. 13, Oct, 2007 ($2.99)

1-13: 1-Bruce Jones-s/John Watkiss-a/c; intro Brandon Cayce 3.00
...: Deadman Walking TPB (2007, $9.99) r/#1-5 10.00

DEADMAN: DEAD AGAIN (Leads into 2002 series)
DC Comics: Oct, 2001 - No. 5, Oct, 2001 ($2.50, weekly limited series)

1-5: Deadman at the deaths of the Flash, Robin, Superman, Hal Jordan 2.50

DEADMAN: EXORCISM
DC Comics: 1992 - No. 2, 1992 ($4.95, limited series, 52 pgs.)

1,2: Kelley Jones-c/a in both 5.00

DEADMAN: LOVE AFTER DEATH
DC Comics: 1989 - No. 2, 1990 ($3.95, 52 pgs., limited series, mature)

Book One, Two: Kelley Jones-c/a in both. 1-contains nudity 4.00

DEAD OF NIGHT
Marvel Comics Group: Dec, 1973 - No. 11, Aug, 1975

1-Horror reprints 3 6 9 16 23 30
2-10: 10-Kirby-a. 6-Jack the Ripper-c/s 2 4 6 10 14 18
11-Intro Scarecrow; Kane/Wrightson-c 3 6 9 20 30 40

NOTE: ***Ditko** r-7, 10. **Everett** c-2. **Sinnott** r-1.*

DEAD OF NIGHT FEATURING DEVIL-SLAYER
Marvel Comics (MAX): Nov, 2008 - No. 4 ($3.99)

1-Keene-s/Samnee-a/Andrews-c 4.00

DEAD OF NIGHT FEATURING MAN-THING
Marvel Comics (MAX): Apr, 2008 - No. 4, July, 2008 ($3.99)

1-4: 1-Man-Thing origin re-told; Kano-a. 2-4-Jennifer Kale app. 4.00

DEAD OR ALIVE - A CYBERPUNK WESTERN
Image Comics (Shok Studio): Apr, 1998 - No. 4, July, 1998 ($2.50, lim. series)

1-4 3.00

DEADPOOL (See New Mutants #98 for 1st app.)
Marvel Comics: Aug, 1994 - No. 4, Nov, 1994 ($2.50, limited series)

1-4: Mark Waid's 1st Marvel work; Ian Churchill-c/a 4.00

DEADPOOL (... : Agent of Weapon X on cover #57-60) (title becomes Agent X)
Marvel Comics: Jan, 1997 - No. 69, Sept, 2002 ($2.95/$1.95/$1.99)

1-($2.95)-Wraparound-c 1 2 3 4 5 7
2-Begin-$1.95-c. 5.00
3-10,12-22,24: 4-Hulk-c/app. 12-Variant-c. 14-Begin McDaniel-a. 22-Cable app. 5.00
11-($3.99)-Deadpool replaces Spider-Man from Amazing Spider-Man #47; Kraven, Gwen Stacy app. 6.00
23,25-($2.99); 23-Dead Reckoning pt. 1; wraparound-c 4.00
26-40: 27-Wolverine-c/app. 37-Thor app. 3.00
41-53,56-60: 41-Begin $2.25-c. 44-Black Panther-c/app. 46-49-Chadwick-a 51-Cover swipe of Detective #38. 57-60-BWS-c 3.00
54,55-Punisher-c/app. 54-Dillon-c. 55-Bradstreet-c 3.00
61-69: 61-64-Funeral For a Freak on cover. 65-69-Udon Studios-a. 67-Dazzler-c/app. 2.50
#(-1) Flashback (7/97) Lopresti-a; Wade Wilson's early days 3.00
.../Death '98 Annual ($2.99) Kelly-s, ... Team-Up (12/98, $2.99) Widdle Wade-c/app., Baby's First Deadpool Book (12/98, $2.99), Encyclopædia Deadpoolica (12/98, $2.99) Synopses 3.00
.../GLI - Summer Fun Spectacular #1 (9/07, $3.99) short stories; Pelletier-c 4.00
... Classic Vol. 1 TPB (2008, $29.99) r/#1, New Mutants #98, Deadpool: The Circle Chase #1-4 and Deadpool (1994 series) #1-4 30.00
Mission Improbable TPB (9/98, $14.95) r/#1-5 15.00
Wizard #0 ('98, bagged with Wizard #87) 2.50

DEADPOOL
Marvel Comics: Nov, 2008 - Present ($3.99)

1,2: 1-Medina-a; Secret Invasion x-over; 2 covers by Crain & Liefeld 4.00

DEADPOOL: THE CIRCLE CHASE (See New Mutants #98)

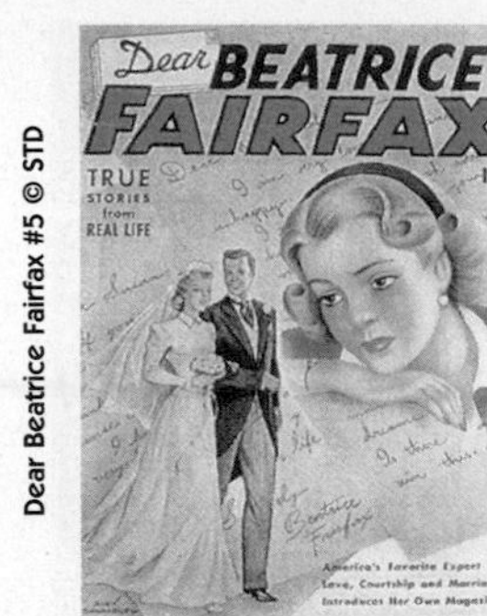
Dear Beatrice Fairfax #5 © STD

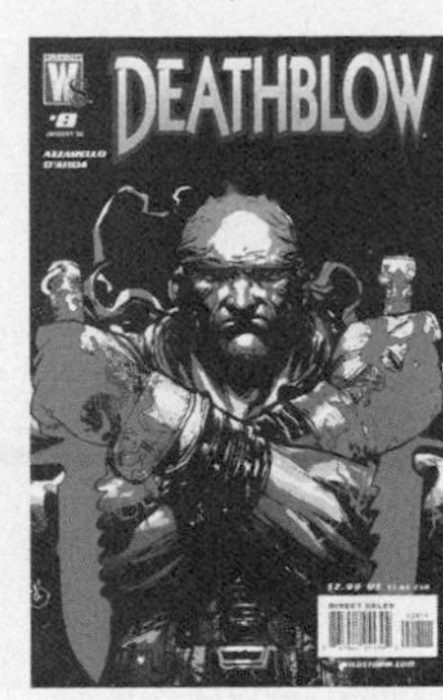

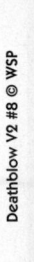

Deathblow V2 #8 © WSP

Deathlok #16 © MAR

	GD 2.0	VG 4.0	FN 6.0	VF 8.0	VF/NM 9.0	NM- 9.2

Marvel Comics: Aug, 1993 - No. 4, Nov, 1993 ($2.00, limited series)

1-($2.50)-Embossed-c 4.00
2-4 3.00

DEAD RIDER (See Deadlander)

DEAD, SHE SAID
IDW Publishing: May, 2008 - Present ($3.99, limited series)

1-3-Bernie Wrightson-a/Steve Niles-s 4.00

DEADSHOT (See Batman #59, Detective Comics #474, & Showcase '93 #8)
DC Comics: Nov, 1988 - No. 4, Feb, 1989 ($1.00, limited series)

1-4 2.50

DEADSHOT
DC Comics: Feb, 2005 - No. 5, June 2005 ($2.95, limited series)

1-5-Zeck-c/Gage-s/Cummings-a. 3-Green Arrow app. 3.00

DEAD SPACE (Based on the Electronics Arts videogame)
Image Comics: Mar, 2008 - No. 6, Sept, 2008 ($2.99, limited series)

1-6-Templesmith-a/Johnston-s 3.00

DEAD WHO WALK, THE (See Strange Mysteries, Super Reprint #15, 16)
Realistic Comics: 1952 (one-shot)

	GD	VG	FN	VF	VF/NM	NM-
nn	53	106	159	332	559	785

DEADWORLD (Also see The Realm)
Arrow Comics/Caliber Comics: Dec, 1986 - No. 26 ($1.50/$1.95/#15 28: $2.50, B&W)

1-4 4.00
5-26-Graphic cover version 4.00
5-26-Tame cover version 3.00
...Archives 1-3 (1992, $2.50) 3.00

DEAN MARTIN & JERRY LEWIS (See Adventures of...)

DEAR BEATRICE FAIRFAX
Best/Standard Comics (King Features): No. 5, Nov, 1950 - No. 9, Sept, 1951 (Vern Greene art)

	GD	VG	FN	VF	VF/NM	NM-
5-All have Schomburg air brush-c	12	24	36	69	97	125
6-9	9	18	27	47	61	75

DEAR HEART (Formerly Lonely Heart)
Ajax: No. 15, July, 1956 - No. 16, Sept, 1956

	GD	VG	FN	VF	VF/NM	NM-
15,16	7	14	21	35	43	50

DEAR LONELY HEART (...Illustrated No. 1-6)
Artful Publications: Mar, 1951; No. 2, Oct, 1951 - No. 8, Oct, 1952

	GD	VG	FN	VF	VF/NM	NM-
1	17	34	51	98	154	210
2	10	20	30	54	72	90
3-Matt Baker Jungle Girl story	20	40	60	115	183	250
4-8	9	18	27	50	65	80

DEAR LONELY HEARTS (Lonely Heart #9 on)
Harwell Publ./Mystery Publ. Co. (Comic Media): Aug, 1953 -No. 8, Oct, 1954

	GD	VG	FN	VF	VF/NM	NM-
1	12	24	36	69	97	125
2-8	9	18	27	47	61	75

DEARLY BELOVED
Ziff-Davis Publishing Co.: Fall, 1952

	GD	VG	FN	VF	VF/NM	NM-
1-Photo-c	17	34	51	100	158	215

DEAR NANCY PARKER
Gold Key: June, 1963 - No. 2, Sept, 1963

	GD	VG	FN	VF	VF/NM	NM-
1-Painted-c on both	4	8	12	23	36	48
2	3	6	9	17	25	32

DEATH: AT DEATH'S DOOR (See Sandman: The Season of Mists)
DC Comics: 2003 ($9.95, graphic novel one-shot, B&W, 7-1/2" x 5")

1-Jill Thompson-s/a/c; manga-style; Morpheus and the Endless app. 10.00

DEATHBLOW (Also see Batman/Deathblow and Darker Image)
Image Comics (WildStorm Productions): May (Apr. inside), 1993 - No. 29, Aug, 1996 ($1.75/$1.95/$2.50)

0-(8/96, $2.95, 32 pgs.)-r/Darker Image w/new story & art; Jim Lee & Trevor Scott-a; new Jim Lee-c 3.00
1-($2.50)-Red foil stamped logo on black varnish-c; Jim Lee-c/a; flip-book side has Cybernary -c/story (#2 also) 3.00
1-($1.95)-Newsstand version w/o foil-c & varnish 2.50
2-29: 2-(8/93)-Lee-a; with bound-in poster. 2-($1.75)-Newsstand version w/o poster. 4-Jim Lee-c/Tim Sale-a begin. 13-W/pinup poster by Tim Sale & Jim Lee. 16-($1.95 Newsstand & $2.50 Direct Market editions)-Wildstorm Rising Pt. 6. 17-Variant "Chicago Comicon" edition exists. 20,21-Gen 13 app. 23-Backlash-c/app. 24,25-Grifter-c/app; Gen 13 & Dane from Wetworks app. 28-Deathblow dies. 29-Memorial issue 2.50
5-Alternate Portacio-c (Forms larger picture when combined with alternate-c for Gen 13 #5, Kindred #3, Stormwatch #10, Team 7 #1, Union #0, Wetworks #2 & WildC.A.T.S #11) 6.00
...:Sinners and Saints TPB ('99, $19.95) r/#1-12; Sale-c 20.00

DEATHBLOW (Volume 2)
DC Comics (WildStorm): Dec, 2006 - No. 9, Apr, 2008 ($2.99)

1-9: 1-Azzarello-s/D'Anda-a; two covers by D'Anda & Platt 3.00

DEATHBLOW BY BLOWS
DC Comics (WildStorm): Nov, 1999 - No. 3, Jan, 2000 ($2.95, limited series)

1-3-Alan Moore-s/Jim Baikie-a 3.00

DEATHBLOW/WOLVERINE
Image Comics (WildStorm Productions)/ Marvel Comics: Sept, 1996 - No. 2, Feb, 1997 ($2.50, limited series)

1,2: Wiesenfeld-s/Bennett-a 2.50
TPB (1997, $8.95) r/#1,2 9.00

DEATHDEALER (Also see Frank Frazetta's...)
Verotik: July, 1995 - No. 4, July, 1997 ($5.95)

	GD	VG	FN	VF	VF/NM	NM-
1-Frazetta-c; Bisley-a	1	2	3	5	6	8
1-2nd print, 2-4-($6.95)-Frazetta-c; embossed logo	1	2	3	4	5	7

DEATH, JR.
Image Comics: Apr, 2005 - No. 3, Aug, 2005 ($4.99, squarebound, limited series)

1-3-Gary Whitta-s/Ted Naifeh-a 5.00
Vol. 1 TPB (2005, $14.99) r/series; concept and promotional art 15.00

DEATH, JR. (Volume 2)
Image Comics: Jul, 2006 - No. 3, May, 2007 ($4.99, squarebound, limited series)

1-3-Gary Whitta-s/Ted Naifeh-a. 1-Dan Brereton-c 5.00
Vol. 2 TPB (2007, $14.99) r/series; Halloween story w/Guy Davis-a; promotional art 15.00

DEATHLOK (Also see Astonishing Tales #25)
Marvel Comics: July, 1990 - No. 4, Oct, 1990 ($3.95, limited series, 52 pgs.)

1-4: 1,2-Guice-a(p). 3,4-Denys Cowan-a, c-4 4.00

DEATHLOK
Marvel Comics: July, 1991 - No. 34, Apr, 1994 ($1.75)

1-Silver ink cover; Denys Cowan-c/a(p) begins 3.00
2-18,20-24,26-34: 2-Forge (X-Men) app. 3-Vs. Dr. Doom. 5-X-Men & F.F. x-over. 6,7-Punisher x-over. 9,10-Ghost Rider-c/story. 16-Infinity War x-over. 17-Jae Lee-c. 22-Black Panther app. 27-Siege app. 2.50
19-($2.25)-Foil-c 3.00
25-($2.95, 52 pgs.)-Holo-grafx foil-c 3.00
Annual 1 (1992, $2.25, 68 pgs.)-Guice-p; Quesada-c(p) 3.00
Annual 2 (1993, $2.95, 68 pgs.)-Bagged w/card; intro Tracer 3.00
NOTE: *Denys Cowan a(p)-9-13, 15, Annual 1; c-9-12, 13p, 14. Guice/Cowan c-8.*

DEATHLOK
Marvel Comics: Sept, 1999 - No. 11, June, 2000 ($1.99)

1-11: 1-Casey-s/Manco-a. 2-Two covers. 4-Canete-a 2.50

DEATHLOK SPECIAL
Marvel Comics: May, 1991 - No. 4, June, 1991 ($2.00, bi-weekly lim. series)

1-4: r/1-4(1990) w/new Guice-c #1,2; Cowan c-3,4 2.50
1-2nd printing w/white-c 2.50

DEATHMASK
Future Comics: Mar, 2003 - No. 3, June, 2003 ($2.99)

1-3-Giordano-a(p)/Michelinie & Layton-s 3.00

DEATHMATE
Valiant (Prologue/Yellow/Blue)/Image Comics (Black/Red/Epilogue): Sept, 1993 - Epilogue (#6), Feb, 1994 ($2.95/$4.95, limited series)

Preview-(7/93, 8 pgs.) 2.25
Prologue (#1)–Silver foil; Jim Lee/Layton-c; B. Smith/Lee-a; Liefeld-a(p) 3.00
Prologue–Special gold foil ed. of silver ed. 4.00
Black (#2)-(9/93, $4.95, 52 pgs.)-Silvestri/Jim Lee-c; pencils by Peterson/Silvestri/Capullo/Jim Lee/Portacio; 1st story app. Gen 13 telling their rebellion against the Troika (see WildC.A.T.S. Trilogy) 6.00
Black-Special gold foil edition 7.00
Yellow (#3)-(10/93, $4.95, 52 pgs)-Yellow foil-c; Indicia says Prologue Sept 1993 by mistake; 3rd app. Ninjak; Thibert-c(i) 5.00

Death of the New Gods #5 © DC

Death: The Time of Your Life #2 © DC

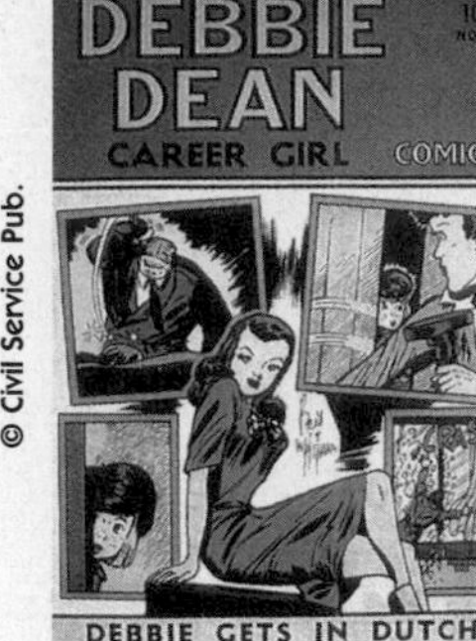

Debbie Dean, Career Girl #2 © Civil Service Pub.

	GD 2.0	VG 4.0	FN 6.0	VF 8.0	VF/NM 9.0	NM- 9.2

Yellow-Special gold foil edition 6.00
Blue (#4)-(10/93, $4.95, 52 pgs.)-Thibert blue foil-c(i); Reese-a(i) 5.00
Blue-Special gold foil edition 6.00
Red (#5), Epilogue (#6)-(2/94, $2.95)-Silver foil Quesada/Silvestri-c; Silvestri-a(p) 3.00

DEATH METAL
Marvel Comics UK: Jan, 1994 - No. 4, Apr, 1994 ($1.95, limited series)
1-4: 1-Silver ink-c. Alpha Flight app. 2.50

DEATH METAL VS. GENETIX
Marvel Comics UK: Dec, 1993 - No. 2, Jan, 1994 (Limited series)
1-($2.95)-Polybagged w/2 trading cards 3.00
2-($2.50)-Polybagged w/2 trading cards 2.50

DEATH OF CAPTAIN MARVEL (See Marvel Graphic Novel #1)

DEATH OF MR. MONSTER, THE (See Mr. Monster #8)

DEATH OF SUPERMAN (See Superman, 2nd Series)

DEATH OF THE NEW GODS (Tie-in to the Countdown series)
DC Comics: Early Dec, 2007 - No. 8, Jun, 2008 ($3.50, limited series)
1-8-Jim Starlin-s/a/c. 1-Barda killed. 6-Orion dies. 7-Scott Free and Metron die 3.50

DEATH RACE 2020
Roger Corman's Cosmic Comics: Apr, 1995 - No. 8, Nov, 1995 ($2.50)
1-8: Sequel to the Movie 2.50

DEATH RATTLE (Formerly an Underground)
Kitchen Sink Press: V2#1, 10/85 - No. 18, 1988, 1994 ($1.95, Baxter paper, mature); V3#1, 11/95 - No. 5, 6/96 ($2.95, B&W)
V2#1-7,9-18: 1-Corben-c. 2-Unpubbed Spirit story by Eisner. 5-Robot Woman-r by Wolverton. 6-B&W issues begin. 10-Savage World-r by by Williamson/Torres/ Krenkel/Frazetta from Witzend #1. 16-Wolverton Spacehawk-r 4.00
8-(12/86)-1st app. Mark Schultz's Xenozoic Tales/Cadillacs & Dinosaurs 1 3 4 6 8 10
8-(1994)-r plus interview w/Mark Schultz 3.00
V3#1-5 ($2.95-c) 3.00

DEATH'S HEAD (See Daredevil #56, Dragon's Claws #5 & Incomplete...)(See Amazing Fantasy (2004) for Death's Head 3.0)
Marvel Comics: Dec, 1988 - No. 10, Sept, 1989 ($1.75)
1-Dragon's Claws spin-off 3.00
2-Fantastic Four app.; Dragon's Claws x-over 3.00
3-10: 8-Dr. Who app. 9-F. F. x-over; Simonson-c(p) 2.50

DEATH'S HEAD II (Also see Battletide)
Marvel Comics UK, Ltd.: Mar, 1992 - No. 4, June (May inside), 1992 ($1.75, color, lim. series)
1-4: 2-Fantastic Four app. 4-Punisher, Spider-Man, Daredevil, Dr. Strange, Capt. America & Wolverine in the year 2020 2.50
1,2-Silver ink 2nd printiings 2.50

DEATH'S HEAD II (Also see Battletide)
Marvel Comics UK, Ltd.: Dec, 1992 - No. 16, Mar, 1994 ($1.75/$1.95)
V2#1-13,15,16: 1-Gatefold-c. 1-4-X-Men app.15-Capt. America & Wolverine app. 2.50
14-($2.95)-Foil flip-c w/Death's Head II Gold #0 3.00
...Gold 1 (1/94, $3.95, 68 pgs.)-Gold foil-c 4.00

DEATH'S HEAD II & THE ORIGIN OF DIE CUT
Marvel Comics UK, Ltd.: Aug, 1993 - No. 2, Sept, 1993 (limited series)
1-($2.95)-Embossed-c 3.00
2 ($1.75) 2.50

DEATHSTROKE: THE TERMINATOR (Deathstroke: The Hunted #0-47; Deathstroke #48-60) (Also see Marvel & DC Present, New Teen Titans #2, New Titans, Showcase '93 #7,9 & Tales of the Teen Titans #42-44)
DC Comics: Aug, 1991 - No. 60, June, 1996 ($1.75-$2.25)
1-New Titans spin-off; Mike Zeck c-1-28 4.00
1-Gold ink 2nd printing ($1.75) 2.50
2 3.00
3-40,0(10/94),41(11/94)-49,51-60: 6,8-Batman cameo. 7,9-Batman-c/story. 9-1st brief app. new Vigilante (female). 10-1st full app. new Vigilante; Perez-i. 13-Vs. Justice League; Team Titans cameo on last pg. 14-Total Chaos, part 1; TeamTitans-c/story cont'd in New Titans #90. 40-(9/94). 0-(10/94)-Begin Deathstroke, The Hunted, ends #47. 2.50
50 ($3.50) 3.50
Annual 1-4 ('92-'95, 68 pgs.): 1-Nightwing & Vigilante app.; minor Eclipso app. 2-Bloodlines Deathstorm; 1st app. Gunfire. 3-Elseworlds story. 4-Year One story 4.00
NOTE: *Golden a-12. Perez a-11i. Zeck c-Annual 1, 2.*

DEATH: THE HIGH COST OF LIVING (See Sandman #8) (Also see the Books of Magic limited & ongoing series)
DC Comics (Vertigo): Mar, 1993 - No. 3, May, 1993 ($1.95, limited series)
1-Bachalo/Buckingham-a; Dave McKean-c; Neil Gaiman scripts in all 6.00
1-Platinum edition 40.00
2 3.50
3-Pgs. 19 & 20 had wrong placement 3.00
3-Corrected version w/pgs. 19 & 20 facing each other; has no-c & ads for Sebastion O & The Geek added 4.00
Death Talks About Life-giveaway about AIDS prevention 5.00
Hardcover (1994, $19.95)-r/#1-3 & Death Talks About Life; intro. by Tori Amos 20.00
Trade paperback (6/94, $12.95, Titan Books)-r/#1-3 & Death Talks About Life; prism-c 13.00

DEATH: THE TIME OF YOUR LIFE (See Sandman #8)
DC Comics (Vertigo): Apr, 1996 - No. 3, July, 1996 ($2.95, limited series)
1-3: Neil Gaiman story & Bachalo/Buckingham-a; Dave McKean-c. 2-(5/96) 3.00
Hardcover (1997, $19.95)-r/#1-3 w/3 new pages & gallery art by various 20.00
TPB (1997, $12.95)-r/#1-3 & Visions of Death gallery; Intro. by Claire Danes 13.00

DEATH 3
Marvel Comics UK: Sept, 1993 - No. 4, Dec, 1993 ($1.75, limited series)
1-($2.95)-Embossed-c 3.00
2-4 2.50

DEATH VALLEY (Cowboys and Indians)
Comic Media: Oct, 1953 - No. 6, Aug, 1954
1-Billy the Kid; Morisi-a; Andru/Esposito-c/a 17 34 51 98 154 210
2-Don Heck-c 11 22 33 62 86 110
3-6: 3,5-Morisi-a. 5-Discount-a 11 22 33 60 83 105

DEATH VALLEY (Becomes Frontier Scout, Daniel Boone No.10-13)
Charlton Comics: No. 7, 6/55 - No. 9, 10/55 (Cont'd from Comic Media series)
7-9: 8-Wolverton-a (half pg.) 9 18 27 50 65 80

DEATHWISH
DC Comics (Milestone Media): Dec, 1994 - No. 4, Mar, 1995 (2.50, lim. series)
1-4 2.50

DEATH WRECK
Marvel Comics UK: Jan, 1994 - No. 4, Apr, 1994 ($1.95, limited series)
1-4: 1-Metallic ink logo; Death's Head II app. 2.50

DEBBIE DEAN, CAREER GIRL
Civil Service Publ.: April, 1945 - No. 2, July, 1945
1,2-Newspaper reprints by Bert Whitman 14 28 42 76 108 140

DEBBI'S DATES (Also see Date With Debbi)
National Periodical Publications: Apr-May, 1969 - No. 11, Dec-Jan, 1970-71
1 6 12 18 39 62 85
2,3,5,7-11: 2-Last 12¢ issue 3 6 9 20 30 40
4-Neal Adams text illo 4 8 12 24 37 50
6-Superman cameo 6 12 18 37 59 80

DECADE OF DARK HORSE, A
Dark Horse Comics: Jul, 1996 - No. 4, Oct, 1996 ($2.95, B&W/color, lim. series)
1-4: 1-Sin City-c/story by Miller; Grendel by Wagner; Predator. 2-Star Wars wraparound-c. 3-Aliens-c/story; Nexus, Mask stories 3.00

DECAPITATOR (Randy Bowen's...)
Dark Horse Comics: Jun, 1998 - No. 4, ($2.95)
1-4-Bowen-s/art by various. 1-Mahnke-c. 3-Jones-c 4.00

DECEPTION, THE
Image Comics (Flypaper Press): 1999 - No. 3, 1999 ($2.95, B&W, mini-series)
1-3-Horley painted-c 3.00

DECIMATION: THE HOUSE OF M
Marvel Comics: Jan, 2006 ($3.99)
... - The Day After (one-shot) Claremont-s/Green-a 4.00

DEEP, THE (Movie)
Marvel Comics Group: Nov, 1977 (Giant)
1-Infantino-c/a 1 3 4 6 8 10

DEEP SLEEPER
Oni Press/Image Comics: Feb, 2004 - No. 4, Sept, 2004 ($3.50/$2.95, B&W, limited series)
1,2-(Oni Press, $3.50)-Hester-s/Huddleston-a 3.50
3,4-(Image Comics, $2.95) 3.00
... Omnibus (Image, 8/04, $5.95) r/#1,2 6.00
... Vol. 1 TPB (2005, $12.95) r/#1-4; cover gallery 13.00

The Defenders #13 © MAR

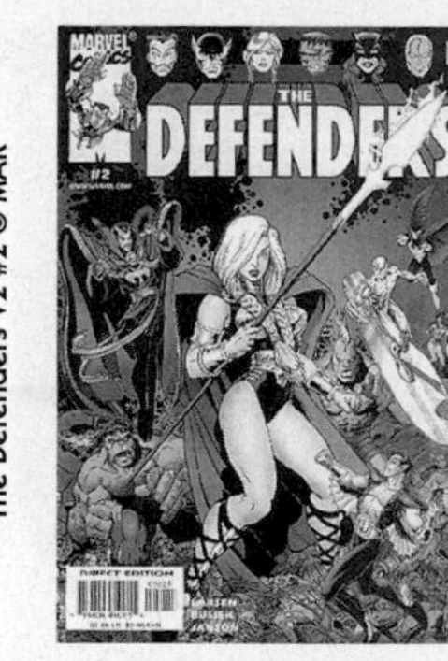

The Defenders V2 #2 © MAR

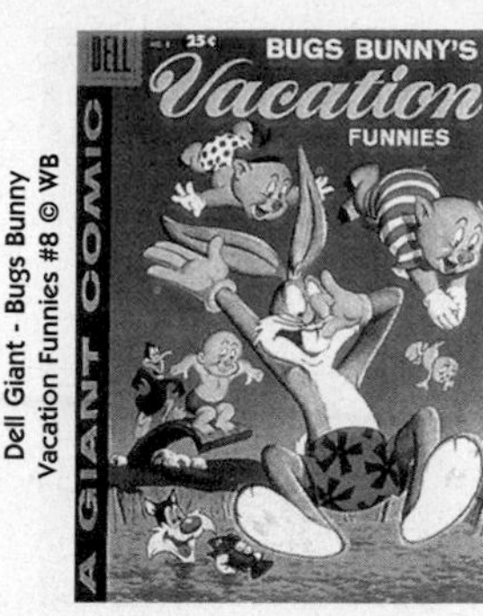

Dell Giant - Bugs Bunny Vacation Funnies #8 © WB

DEFCON 4
Image Comics (WildStorm Productions): Feb, 1996 - No. 4, Sept, 1996 ($2.50, lim. series)

	GD 2.0	VG 4.0	FN 6.0	VF 8.0	VF/NM 9.0	NM- 9.2
1/2	1	2	3	5	7	9
1/2 Gold-(1000 printed)						14.00
1-Main Cover by Mat Broome & Edwin Rosell						3.00
1-Hordes of Cymulants variant-c by Michael Golden						5.00
1-Backs to the Wall variant-c by Humberto Ramos & Alex Garner						5.00
1-Defcon 4-Way variant-c by Jim Lee	1	2	3	4	5	7
2-4						2.50

DEFENDERS, THE (TV)
Dell Publishing Co.: Sept-Nov, 1962 - No. 2, Feb-Apr, 1963

	GD 2.0	VG 4.0	FN 6.0	VF 8.0	VF/NM 9.0	NM- 9.2
12-176-211(#1)	4	8	12	26	41	55
12-176-304(#2)	3	6	9	21	32	42

DEFENDERS, THE (Also see Giant-Size..., Marvel Feature, Marvel Treasury Edition, Secret Defenders & Sub-Mariner #34, 35; The New...#140-on)
Marvel Comics Group: Aug, 1972 - No. 152, Feb, 1986

	GD 2.0	VG 4.0	FN 6.0	VF 8.0	VF/NM 9.0	NM- 9.2
1-The Hulk, Doctor Strange, Sub-Mariner begin	11	22	33	79	140	200
2-Silver Surfer x-over	6	12	18	41	66	90
3-5: 3-Silver Surfer x-over. 4-Valkyrie joins	4	8	12	28	44	60
6,7: 6-Silver Surfer x-over	3	6	9	18	27	35
8,9,11: 8-11-Defenders vs. the Avengers (Crossover with Avengers #115-118)						
8,11-Silver Surfer x-over	4	8	12	22	34	45
10-Hulk vs. Thor battle	7	14	21	50	83	115
12-14: 12-Last 20¢ issue	2	4	6	11	16	20
15,16-Magneto & Brotherhood of Evil Mutants app. from X-Men	2	4	6	13	18	22
17-20: 17-Power Man x-over (11/74)	2	4	6	8	10	12
21-25: 24,25-Son of Satan app.	1	2	3	5	6	8
26-29-Guardians of the Galaxy app. (#26 is 8/75; pre-dates Marvel Presents #3): 28-1st full app. Starhawk (1st brief app. #27). 29-Starhawk joins Guardians	1	3	4	6	8	10
30-33,39-50: 31,32-Origin Nighthawk. 44-Hellcat joins. 45-Dr. Strange leaves. 47-49-Early Moon Knight app. (5/77). 48-50-(Reg. 30¢-c)						5.00
34-38-(Regular 25¢ editions): 35-Intro New Red Guardian						5.00
34-38-(30¢-c variants, limited distribution)(4-8/76)	3	6	9	20	30	40
48-52-(35¢-c variants, limited distribution)(6-10/77)	4	8	12	28	44	60
51-60: 51,52-(Reg. 30¢-c). 53-1st brief app. Lunatik (Lobo lookalike). 55-Origin Red Guardian; Lunatik cameo. 56-1st full Lunatik story						4.00
61-75: 61-Lunatik & Spider-Man app. 70-73-Lunatik (origin #71). 73-75-Foolkiller II app. (Greg Salinger). 74-Nighthawk resigns						3.00
76-93,95,97-99,102-119,123,124,126-149,151: 77-Origin Omega. 78-Original Defenders return thru #101. 104-The Beast joins. 105-Son of Satan joins. 106-Death of Nighthawk. 129-New Mutants cameo (3/84, early x-over)						2.50
94,101,120-122: 94-1st Gargoyle. 101-Silver Surfer-c & app. 120,121-Son of Satan-c/stories. 122-Final app. Son of Satan (2 pgs.)						4.00
96-Ghost Rider app.						4.00
100-(52 pgs.)-Hellcat (Patsy Walker) revealed as Satan's daughter						5.00
125,150: 125-(52 pgs.)-Intro new Defenders. 150-(52 pgs.)-Origin Cloud						4.00
152-(52 pgs.)-Ties in with X-Factor & Secret Wars II						4.00
Annual 1 (1976, 52 pgs.)-New book-length story	3	6	9	17	25	32

NOTE: ***Art Adams** c-142p. **Austin** a-53i; c-65i, 119i, 145i. **Frank Bolle** a-7i, 10i, 11i. **Buckler** c(p)-34, 38, 76, 77, 79-86, 90, 91. **J. Buscema** c-66. **Giffen** a-42-49p, 50, 51-54p. **Golden** a-53p, 54p; c-94, 96. **Guice** c-129. **G. Kane** c(p)-13, 16, 18, 19, 21-26, 31-33, 35-37, 40, 41, 52, 55. **Kirby** c-42-45. **Mooney** a-3i, 31-34i, 62i, 63i, 85i. **Nasser** c-88p. **Perez** c(p)-51, 53, 54. **Rogers** c-98. **Starlin** c-110. **Tuska** a-57p. Silver Surfer in No. 2, 3, 6, 8-11, 92, 98-101, 107, 112-115, 122-125.*

DEFENDERS, THE (Volume 2) (Continues in The Order)
Marvel Comics: Mar, 2001 - No. 12, Feb, 2002 ($2.99/$2.25)

	GD 2.0	VG 4.0	FN 6.0	VF 8.0	VF/NM 9.0	NM- 9.2
1-Busiek & Larsen-s/Larsen & Janson-a/c						3.00
2-11: 2-Two covers by Larsen & Art Adams; Valkyrie app. 4-Frenz-a						2.50
12-($3.50) 'Nuff Said issue; back-up-s Reis-a						3.50

DEFENDERS, THE
Marvel Comics: Sept, 2005 - No. 5, Jan, 2006 ($2.99, limited series)

	GD 2.0	VG 4.0	FN 6.0	VF 8.0	VF/NM 9.0	NM- 9.2
1-5-Giffen & DeMatteis-s/Maguire-a. 2-Dormammu app.						3.00
...: Indefensible HC (2006, $19.99, dust jacket) r/#1-5; Giffen & Maguire sketch page						20.00
...: Indefensible SC (2007, $13.99) r/#1-5; Giffen & Maguire sketch page						14.00

DEFENDERS OF DYNATRON CITY
Marvel Comics: Feb, 1992 - No. 6, July, 1992 ($1.25, limited series)

	GD 2.0	VG 4.0	FN 6.0	VF 8.0	VF/NM 9.0	NM- 9.2
1-6-Lucasarts characters. 2-Origin						3.00

DEFENDERS OF THE EARTH (TV)
Marvel Comics (Star Comics): Jan, 1987 - No. 4, July, 1987

	GD 2.0	VG 4.0	FN 6.0	VF 8.0	VF/NM 9.0	NM- 9.2
1-4: The Phantom, Mandrake The Magician, Flash Gordon begin. 3-Origin Phantom. 4-Origin Mandrake						4.00

DEFEX
Devil's Due Publ.: Oct, 2004 - No. 6, Apr, 2005 ($2.95)

	GD 2.0	VG 4.0	FN 6.0	VF 8.0	VF/NM 9.0	NM- 9.2
1-6: 1-Wolfman-s/Caselli-a. 6-Pérez-c						3.00

DEFIANCE
Image Comics: Feb, 2002 - No. 8, Jun, 2003 ($2.95)

	GD 2.0	VG 4.0	FN 6.0	VF 8.0	VF/NM 9.0	NM- 9.2
Preview Edition (12/01)						2.50
1-8-Barré-s/Kang & Suh-a						3.00

DEFINITIVE DIRECTORY OF THE DC UNIVERSE, THE (See Who's Who...)

DELECTA OF THE PLANETS (See Don Fortune & Fawcett Miniatures)

DELICATE CREATURES
Image Comics (Top Cow): 2001 ($16.95, hardcover with dust jacket)

	GD 2.0	VG 4.0	FN 6.0	VF 8.0	VF/NM 9.0	NM- 9.2
nn-Fairy tale storybook; J. Michael Straczynski-s; Michael Zulli-a						17.00

DELLA VISION (...The Television Queen) (Patty Powers #4 on)
Atlas Comics: April, 1955 - No. 3, Aug, 1955

	GD 2.0	VG 4.0	FN 6.0	VF 8.0	VF/NM 9.0	NM- 9.2
1-Al Hartley-c	15	30	45	92	144	195
2,3	11	22	33	62	86	110

DELL GIANT COMICS

Dell Publishing began to release square bound comics in 1949 with a 132-page issue called Christmas Parade #1. The covers were of a heavier stock to accommodate the increased number of pages. The books proved profitable at 25 cents, but the average number of pages was quickly reduced to 100. Ten years later they were converted to a numbering system similar to the Four Color Comics, for greater ease in distribution and the page counts cut back to mostly 84 pages. The label "Dell Giant" began to appear on the covers in 1954. Because of the size of the books and the heavier, less pliant cover stock, they are rarely found in high grade condition, and with the exception of a small quantity of copies released from Western Publishing's warehouse are almost never found in near mint.

	GD 2.0	VG 4.0	FN 6.0	VF 8.0	VF/NM 9.0	NM- 9.2
Abraham Lincoln Life Story 1(3/58)	8	16	24	64	107	150
Bugs Bunny Christmas Funnies 1(11/50, 116pp)	19	38	57	152	261	370
...Christmas Funnies 2(11/51, 116pp)	11	22	33	88	157	225
...Christmas Funnies 3-5(11/52-11/54,)-Becomes Christmas Party #6	10	20	30	80	138	195
...Christmas Funnies 7-9(12/56-12/58)	9	18	27	72	124	175
...Christmas Party 6(11/55)-Formerly Bugs Bunny Christmas Funnies	9	18	27	72	124	175
...County Fair 1(9/57)	11	22	33	88	149	210
...Halloween Parade 1(10/53)	11	22	33	88	157	225
...Halloween Parade 2(10/54)-Trick 'N' Treat Halloween Fun #3 on	9	18	27	72	129	185
...Trick 'N' Treat Halloween Fun 3,4(10/55-10/56)-Formerly Halloween Parade #2	9	18	27	72	129	185
...Vacation Funnies 1(7/51, 112pp)	18	36	54	144	252	360
...Vacation Funnies 2('52)	13	26	39	104	180	255
...Vacation Funnies 3-5('53-'55)	10	20	30	80	138	195
...Vacation Funnies 6,7,9('56-'59)	9	18	27	72	124	175
...Vacation Funnies 8('58) 1st app. Beep Beep the Road Runner, Wile E. Coyote (1st meeting), Mathilda (Mrs. Beep Beep) and their 3 children who hatch from eggs; one month before Four Color #918	10	20	30	80	140	200
Cadet Gray of West Point 1(4/58)-Williamson-a, 10pgs.; Buscema-a; photo-c	8	16	24	64	107	150
Christmas In Disneyland 1(12/57)-Barks-a, 18 pgs.	25	50	75	200	350	500
Christmas Parade 1(11/49)(132 pgs.)(1st Dell Giant)-Donald Duck (25pgs. by Barks, r-in G.K. Christmas Parade #5); Mickey Mouse & other film oriented stories; Cinderella (prior to movie), 7 Dwarfs, Bambi & Thumper, So Dear To My Heart, Flying Mouse, Dumbo, Cookieland & others	63	126	189	504	877	1250
Christmas Parade 2('50)-Donald Duck (132 pgs.)(25 pgs. by Barks, r-in Gold Key's Christmas Parade #6). Mickey, Pluto, Chip & Dale, etc. Contents shift to a holiday expansion of W.D. C&S type format	42	84	126	336	588	840
Christmas Parade 3-7('51-'55, #3-116pgs; #4-7, 100 pgs.)	14	28	42	112	196	280
Christmas Parade 8(12/56)-Barks-a, 8 pgs.	22	44	66	176	306	435
Christmas Parade 9(12/58)-Barks-a, 20 pgs.	25	50	75	200	350	500
Christmas Treasury, A 1(11/54)	9	18	27	72	126	180
Davy Crockett, King Of The Wild Frontier 1(9/55)-Fess Parker photo-c; Marsh-a	19	38	57	152	269	385
Disneyland Birthday Party 1(10/58)-Barks-a, 16 pgs. r-by Gladstone	25	50	75	200	350	500
Donald and Mickey In Disneyland 1(5/58)	11	22	33	88	157	225

Donald Duck Beach Party 1(7/54)-Has an Uncle Scrooge story (not by Barks) that prefigures the later rivalry with Flintheart Glomgold and tells of Scrooge's wild rivalry with another

Dell Giant - Lone Ranger Western Treasury #1 © Lone Ranger Inc.

Dell Giant - Tom & Jerry Winter Carnival #2 © MGM

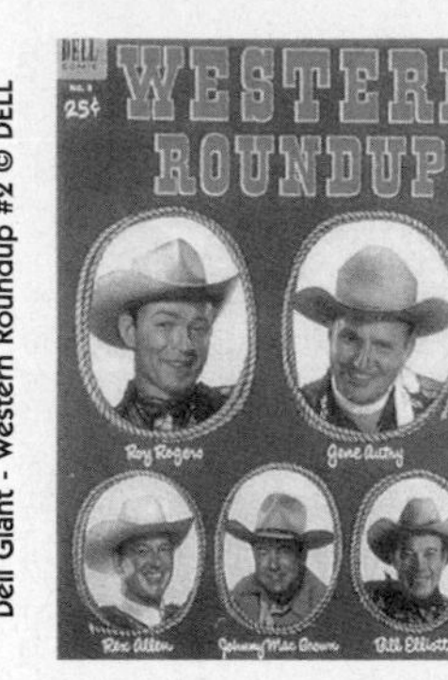

Dell Giant - Western Roundup #2 © DELL

	GD 2.0	VG 4.0	FN 6.0	VF 8.0	VF/NM 9.0	NM- 9.2
millionaire	16	32	48	128	224	320
...Beach Party 2(1955)-Lady & Tramp	11	22	33	88	157	225
...Beach Party 3-5(1956-58)	11	22	33	88	152	215
...Beach Party 6(8/59, 84pp)-Stapled	8	16	24	64	115	165
Donald Duck Fun Book 1,2 (1953 & 10/54)-Games, puzzles, comics & cut-outs (very rare in unused condition)(most copies commonly have defaced interior pgs.)	63	126	189	504	877	1250
Donald Duck In Disneyland 1(9/55)-1st Disneyland Dell Giant	15	30	45	120	210	300
Golden West Rodeo Treasury 1(10/57)	10	20	30	80	135	190
Huey, Dewey and Louie Back To School 1(9/58)	9	18	27	72	126	180
Lady and The Tramp 1(6/55)	17	34	51	136	233	330
Life Stories of American Presidents 1(11/57)-Buscema-a	8	16	24	64	107	150
Lone Ranger Golden West 3(8/55)-Formerly Lone Ranger Western Treasury	18	36	54	144	255	365
Lone Ranger Movie Story nn(3/56)-Origin Lone Ranger in text; Clayton Moore photo-c	36	72	108	288	507	725
...Western Treasury 1(9/53)-Origin Lone Ranger, Silver, & Tonto; painted cover	23	46	69	184	325	465
...Western Treasury 2(8/54)-Becomes Lone Ranger Golden West #3	18	36	54	144	255	365
Marge's Little Lulu & Alvin Story Telling Time 1(3/59)-r/#2,5,3,11,30,10,21,17,8, 14,16; Stanley-a	14	28	42	112	196	280
...& Her Friends 4(3/56)-Tripp-a	14	28	42	112	191	270
...& Her Special Friends 3(3/55)-Tripp-a	15	30	45	120	210	300
...& Tubby At Summer Camp 5,2: 5(10/57)-Tripp-a. 2(10/58)-Tripp-a	13	26	39	104	182	260
...& Tubby Halloween Fun 6,2: 6(10/57)-Tripp-a. 2(10/58)-Tripp-a	13	26	39	104	182	260
...& Tubby In Alaska 1(7/59)-Tripp-a	13	26	39	104	177	250
...On Vacation 1(7/54)-r/4C-110,14,4C-146,5,4C-97,4,4C-158,3,1;Stanley-a	25	50	75	200	350	500
...& Tubby Annual 1(3/53)-r/4C-165,4C-74,4C-146,4C-97,4C-158, 4C-139, 4C-131; Stanley-a (1st Lulu Dell Giant)	30	60	90	240	420	600
...& Tubby Annual 2('54)-r/4C-139,6,4C-115,4C-74,5,4C-97,3,4C-146,18; Stanley-a	25	50	75	200	350	500
Marge's Tubby & His Clubhouse Pals 1(10/56)-1st app. Gran'pa Feeb;1st app. Janie; written by Stanley; Tripp-a	15	30	45	120	210	300
Mickey Mouse Almanac 1(12/57)-Barks-a, 8pgs.	27	54	81	216	378	540
...Birthday Party 1(9/53)-r/entire 48pgs. of Gottfredson's "Mickey Mouse in Love Trouble" from WDC&S 36-39. Quality equal to original. Also reprints one story each from Four Color 27, 79, & 181 plus 6 panels of highlights in the career of Mickey Mouse	31	62	93	248	434	620
...Club Parade 1(12/55)-r/4-Color 16 with some death trap scenes redrawn by Paul Murry & recolored with night turned into day; quality less than original	22	44	66	176	308	440
...In Fantasy Land 1(5/57)	13	26	39	104	180	255
...In Frontier Land 1(5/56)-Mickey Mouse Club iss.	13	26	39	104	180	255
...Summer Fun 1(8/58)-Mobile cut-outs on back-c; becomes Summer Fun with #2	13	26	39	104	180	255
Moses & The Ten Commandments 1(8/57)-Not based on movie; Dell's adaptation; Sekowsky-a	7	14	21	56	98	140
Nancy & Sluggo Travel Time 1(9/58)	8	16	24	64	115	165
Peter Pan Treasure Chest 1(1/53, 212pp)-Disney; contains 54-page movie adaptation & other Peter Pan stories; plus Donald & Mickey stories w/P. Pan; a 32-page retelling of "D. Duck Finds Pirate Gold" with yellow beak, called "Capt. Hook & the Buried Treasure"	120	240	360	960	1680	2400
Picnic Party 6,7(7/55-6/56)(Formerly Vacation Parade)-Uncle Scrooge, Mickey & Donald	12	24	36	96	166	235
Picnic Party 8(7/57)-Barks-a, 6pgs	21	42	63	168	289	410
Pogo Parade 1(9/53)-Kelly-a(r-/Pogo from Animal Comics in this order: #11,13,21,14,27,16,23,9,18,15,17)	25	50	75	200	350	500
Raggedy Ann & Andy 1(2/55)	16	32	48	128	224	320
Santa Claus Funnies 1(11/52)-Dan Noonan -A Christmas Carol adaptation	9	18	27	72	126	180
Silly Symphonies 1(9/52)-Redrawing of Gotfredson's Mickey Mouse strip of "The Brave Little Tailor;" 2 Good Housekeeping pages (from 1943); Lady and the Two Siamese Cats, three years before "Lady & the Tramp;" a retelling of Donald Duck's first app. in "The Wise Little Hen" & other stories based on 1930's Silly Symphony cartoons	29	58	87	232	409	585
Silly Symphonies 2(9/53)-M. Mouse in "The Sorcerer's Apprentice", 2 Good Housekeeping pages (from 1944); The Pelican & the Snipe, Elmer Elephant, Peculiar Penguins, Little Hiawatha, & others	24	48	72	192	336	480

	GD 2.0	VG 4.0	FN 6.0	VF 8.0	VF/NM 9.0	NM- 9.2
Silly Symphonies 3(2/54)-r/Mickey & The Beanstalk (4-Color #157, 39pgs.), Little Minnehaha, Pablo, The Flying Gauchito, Pluto, & Bongo, & 2 Good Housekeeping pages (1944)	20	40	60	160	275	390
Silly Symphonies 4(8/54)-r/Dumbo (4-Color 234), Morris The Midget Moose, The Country Cousin, Bongo, & Clara Cluck	20	40	60	160	275	390
Silly Symphonies 5-8: 5(2/55)-r/Cinderella (4-Color 272), Bucky Bug, Pluto, Little Hiawatha, The 7 Dwarfs & Dumbo, Pinocchio. 6(8/55)-r/Pinocchio (WDC&S 63), The 7 Dwarfs & Thumper (WDC&S 45), M. Mouse "Adventures With Robin Hood" (40 pgs.), Johnny Appleseed, Pluto & Peter Pan, & Bucky Bug; Cut-out on back-c. 7(2/57)-r/Reluctant Dragon, Ugly Duckling, M. Mouse & Peter Pan, Jiminy Cricket, Peter & The Wolf, Brer Rabbit, Bucky Bug; Cut-out on back-c. 8(2/58)-r/Thumper Meets The 7 Dwarfs (4-Color #19), Jiminy Cricket, Niok, Brer Rabbit; Cut-out on back-c	16	32	48	128	224	320
Silly Symphonies 9(2/59)-r/Paul Bunyan, Humphrey Bear, Jiminy Cricket, The Social Lion, Goliath II; cut-out on back-c	15	30	45	120	210	300
Sleeping Beauty 1(4/59)	25	50	75	200	350	500
Summer Fun 2(8/59, 84pp, stapled binding)(Formerly Mickey Mouse...)-Barks-a(2), 24 pgs.	24	48	72	192	336	480
Tarzan's Jungle Annual 1(8/52)-Lex Barker photo on-c of #1,2	15	30	45	120	210	300
...Annual 2(8/53)	11	22	33	88	152	215
...Annual 3-7('54-9/58)(two No. 5s)-Manning-a-No. 3,5-7; Marsh-a in No. 1-7 plus painted-c 1-7	9	18	27	72	124	175
Tom And Jerry Back To School 1(9/56)	12	24	36	96	168	240
...Picnic Time 1(7/58)	10	20	30	80	135	190
...Summer Fun 1(7/54)-Droopy written by Barks	15	30	45	120	205	290
...Summer Fun 2-4(7/55-7/57)	8	16	24	64	107	150
...Toy Fair 1(6/58)	9	18	27	72	126	180
...Winter Carnival 1(12/52)-Droopy written by Barks	20	40	60	160	280	400
...Winter Carnival 2(12/53)-Droopy written by Barks	16	32	48	128	224	320
...Winter Fun 3(12/54)	8	16	24	64	115	165
...Winter Fun 4-7(12/55-11/58)	7	14	21	56	101	145
Treasury of Dogs, A 1(10/56)	7	14	21	56	101	145
Treasury of Horses, A (9/55)	7	14	21	56	101	145
Uncle Scrooge Goes To Disneyland 1(8/57p)-Barks-a, 20pgs.r-by Gladstone	26	52	78	208	359	510
Vacation In Disneyland 1(8/58)	11	22	33	88	157	225
Vacation Parade 1(7/50, 132pp)-Donald Duck & Mickey Mouse; Barks-a, 55 pgs.	90	180	270	720	1260	1800
Vacation Parade 2(7/51,116pp)	25	50	75	200	350	500
Vacation Parade 3-5(7/52-7/54)-Becomes Picnic Party No. 6 on. #4-Robin Hood Advs.	14	28	42	112	194	275
Western Roundup 1(6/52)-Photo-c; Gene Autry, Roy Rogers, Johnny Mack Brown, Rex Allen, & Bill Elliott begin; photo back-c begin, end No. 14,16,18	25	50	75	200	350	500
Western Roundup 2(2/53)-Photo-c	14	28	42	112	196	280
Western Roundup 3-5(7-9/53 - 1-3/54)-Photo-c	11	22	33	88	157	225
Western Roundup 6-10(4-6/54 - 4-6/55)-Photo-c	11	22	33	88	149	210
Western Roundup 11-17,25: 11-17-Photo-c; 11-13,16,17-Manning-a. 11-Flying A's Range Rider, Dale Evans begin	9	18	27	72	129	185
Western Roundup 18-Toth-a; last photo-c; Gene Autry ends	11	22	33	88	149	210
Western Roundup 19-24-Manning-a. 19-Buffalo Bill Jr. begins (7-9/57; early app.). 19,20,22-Toth-a. 21-Rex Allen, Johnny Mack Brown end. 22-Jace Pearson's Texas Rangers, Rin Tin Tin, Tales of Wells Fargo (2nd app., 4-6/58) & Wagon Train (2nd app.) begin	9	18	27	72	129	185
Woody Woodpecker Back To School 1(10/52)	10	20	30	80	140	200
...Back To School 2-4,6('53-10/57)-County Fair No. 5	8	16	24	64	112	160
...County Fair 5(9/56)-Formerly Back To School	8	16	24	64	112	160
...County Fair 2(11/58)	7	14	21	56	101	145

DELL GIANTS (Consecutive numbering)
Dell Publishing Co.: No. 21, Sept, 1959 - No. 55, Sept, 1961 (Most 84 pgs., 25¢)

	GD 2.0	VG 4.0	FN 6.0	VF 8.0	VF/NM 9.0	NM- 9.2
21-(#1)-M.G.M.'s Tom & Jerry Picnic Time (84pp, stapled binding)-Painted-c	11	22	33	88	157	225
22-Huey, Dewey & Louie Back to School (Disney; 10/59, 84pp, square binding begins)	9	18	27	72	129	185
23-Marge's Little Lulu & Tubby Halloween Fun (10/59)-Tripp-a	12	24	36	96	168	240
24-Woody Woodpecker's Family Fun (11/59)(Walter Lantz)	8	16	24	64	112	160
25-Tarzan's Jungle World(11/59)-Marsh-a; painted-c	11	22	33	88	152	215
26-Christmas Parade(Disney; 12/59)-Barks-a, 16pgs.; Barks draws himself on wanted poster on pg. 13	21	42	63	168	289	410
27-Walt Disney's Man in Space (10/59) r-/4-Color 716,866, & 954 (100 pgs., 35¢)(TV)						

Dell Giant #31 © H-B

The Demon #4 © DC

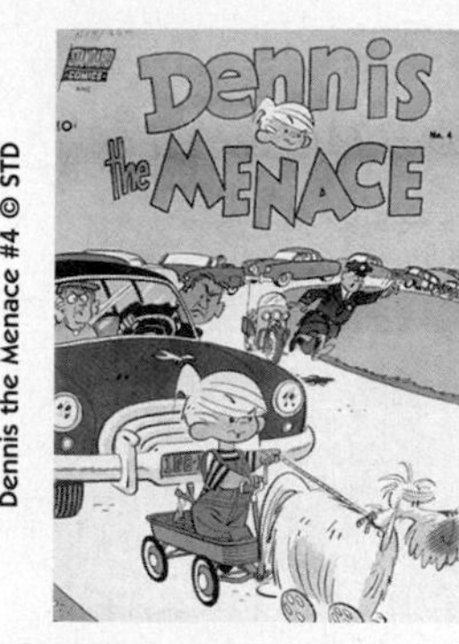

Dennis the Menace #4 © STD

GD 2.0 | VG 4.0 | FN 6.0 | VF 8.0 | VF/NM 9.0 | NM- 9.2

9 18 27 72 129 185
28-Bugs Bunny's Winter Fun (2/60) 9 18 27 72 126 180
29-Marge's Little Lulu & Tubby in Hawaii (4/60)-Tripp-a
12 24 36 96 166 235
30-Disneyland USA(Disney; 6/60) 9 18 27 72 124 175
31-Huckleberry Hound Summer Fun (7/60)(TV)(HannaBarbera)-Yogi Bear & Pixie & Dixie app. 12 24 36 96 173 250
32-Bugs Bunny Beach Party 7 14 21 56 101 145
33-Daisy Duck & Uncle Scrooge Picnic Time (Disney; 9/60)
9 18 27 72 124 175
34-Nancy & Sluggo Summer Camp (8/60) 7 14 21 56 101 145
35-Huey, Dewey & Louie Back to School (Disney; 10/60)-1st app. Daisy Duck's Nieces, April, May & June 12 24 36 96 163 230
36-Marge's Little Lulu & Witch Hazel Halloween Fun (10/60)-Tripp-a
11 22 33 88 157 225
37-Tarzan, King of the Jungle (11/60)-Marsh-a; painted-c
9 18 27 72 129 185
38-Uncle Donald & His Nephews Family Fun (Disney; 11/60)-Cover painting based on a pencil sketch by Barks 12 24 36 96 173 250
39-Walt Disney's Merry Christmas (Disney; 12/60)-Cover painting based on a pencil sketch by Barks 12 24 36 96 173 250
40-Woody Woodpecker Christmas Parade (12/60)(Walter Lantz)
6 12 18 48 87 125
41-Yogi Bear's Winter Sports (12/60)(TV)(Hanna-Barbera)-Huckleberry Hound, Pixie & Dixie, Augie Doggie app. 12 24 36 96 173 250
42-Marge's Little Lulu & Tubby in Australia (4/61) 11 22 33 88 157 225
43-Mighty Mouse in Outer Space (5/61) 18 36 54 144 252 360
44-Around the World with Huckleberry and His Friends (7/61)(TV)(Hanna-Barbera)-Yogi Bear, Pixie & Dixie, Quick Draw McGraw, Augie Doggie app.; 1st app. Yakky Doodle
13 26 39 104 182 260
45-Nancy & Sluggo Summer Camp (8/61) 7 14 21 56 96 135
46-Bugs Bunny Beach Party (8/61) 7 14 21 56 96 135
47-Mickey & Donald in Vacationland (Disney; 8/61) 8 16 24 64 115 165
48-The Flintstones (No. 1)(Bedrock Bedlam)(7/61)(TV)(Hanna-Barbera) 1st app. in comics 19 38 57 152 269 385
49-Huey, Dewey & Louie Back to School (Disney; 9/61)
9 18 27 72 124 175
50-Marge's Little Lulu & Witch Hazel Trick 'N' Treat (10/61)
11 22 33 88 157 225
51-Tarzan, King of the Jungle by Jesse Marsh (11/61)-Painted-c
8 16 24 64 110 155
52-Uncle Donald & His Nephews Dude Ranch (Disney; 11/61)
8 16 24 64 115 165
53-Donald Duck Merry Christmas (Disney; 12/61) 8 16 24 64 112 160
54-Woody Woodpecker's Christmas Party (12/61)-Issued after No. 55
7 14 21 56 98 140
55-Daisy Duck & Uncle Scrooge Showboat (Disney; 9/61)
8 16 24 64 117 170
NOTE: All issues printed with & without ad on back cover.

DELL JUNIOR TREASURY
Dell Publishing Co.: June, 1955 - No. 10, Oct, 1957 (15¢) (All painted-c)
1-Alice in Wonderland; r/4-Color #331 (52 pgs.) 9 18 27 63 107 150
2-Aladdin & the Wonderful Lamp 7 14 21 49 80 110
3-Gulliver's Travels (1/56) 6 12 18 43 69 95
4-Adventures of Mr. Frog & Miss Mouse 7 14 21 45 73 100
5-The Wizard of Oz (7/56) 7 14 21 49 80 110
6-10: 6-Heidi (10/56). 7-Santa and the Angel. 8-Raggedy Ann and the Camel with the Wrinkled Knees. 9-Clementina the Flying Pig. 10-Adventures of Tom Sawyer
6 12 18 43 69 95

DEMOLITION MAN
DC Comics: Nov, 1993 - No. 4, Feb, 1994 ($1.75, color, limited series)
1-4-Movie adaptation 2.50

DEMON, THE (See Detective Comics No. 482-485)
National Periodical Publications: Aug-Sept, 1972 - V3#16, Jan, 1974
1-Origin; Kirby-c/a in all 6 12 18 41 66 90
2-5 4 8 12 22 34 45
6-16 3 6 9 16 23 30

DEMON, THE (1st limited series)(Also see Cosmic Odyssey #2)
DC Comics: Nov, 1986 - No. 4, Feb, 1987 (75¢, limited series)(#2 has #4 of 4 on-c)
1-4: Matt Wagner-a(p) & scripts in all. 4-Demon & Jason Blood become separate entities. 3.00

DEMON, THE (2nd Series)
DC Comics: July, 1990 - No. 58, May, 1995 ($1.50/$1.75/$1.95)
1-Grant scripts begin, ends #39: 1-4-Painted-c 4.00
2-18,20-27,29-39,41,42: 3,8-Batman app. (cameo #4). 12-Bisley painted-c. 12-15,21-Lobo app. (1 pg. cameo #11). 23-Robin app. 29-Superman app. 31,33-39-Lobo app. 2.50
19,28,40: 19-($2.50, 44 pgs.)-Lobo poster stapled inside. 28-Superman-c/story; begin $1.75-c. 40-Garth Ennis scripts begin 4.00
43-45-Hitman app. 1 2 3 5 7 9
46-48 Return of The Haunted Tank-c/s. 48-Begin $1.95-c. 5.00
49,51,0-(10/94),55-58: 51-(9/94) 2.50
50 ($2.95, 52 pgs.) 3.00
52-54-Hitman-s 5.00
Annual 1 (1992, $3.00, 68 pgs.)-Eclipso-c/story 3.00
Annual 2 (1993, $3.50, 68 pgs.)-1st app. of Hitman 2 4 6 9 13 16
NOTE: *Alan Grant scripts in #1-16, 20, 21, 23-25, 30-39, Annual 1.* ***Wagner*** *a/scripts-22.*

DEMON DREAMS
Pacific Comics: Feb, 1984 - No. 2, May, 1984
1,2-Mostly r-/Heavy Metal 2.50

DEMON: DRIVEN OUT
DC Comics: Nov, 2003 - No. 6, Apr, 2004 ($2.50, limited series)
1-6-Dysart-s/Mhan-a 2.50

DEMON-HUNTER
Seaboard Periodicals (Atlas): Sept, 1975
1-Origin/1st app. Demon-Hunter; Buckler-c/a 1 3 4 6 8 10

DEMON KNIGHT: A GRIMJACK GRAPHIC NOVEL
First Publishing: 1990 ($8.95, 52 pgs.)
nn-Flint Henry-a 9.00

DEMONWARS (R.A. Salvatore's...) ("The Demon Awakens" on cover)
Devil's Due Publishing: Jan, 2007 - No. 3, May, 2007 ($4.99/$5.50, limited series)
1-Daab-s/Seeley-a 5.00
2,3-($5.50) 5.50
Volume 2 (The Demon Spirit) (3/08 - Present, $5.50, B&W) 1-Balan-a 5.50

DEMONWARS: EYE FOR AN EYE (R.A. Salvatore's...)
CrossGeneration Comics (Code 6 Comics): Jun, 2003 - No. 5, Nov, 2003 ($2.95, lim. series)
1-5-Ciencln-s/Tocchini-a 3.00

DEMONWARS: TRIAL BY FIRE (R.A. Salvatore's...)
CrossGeneration Comics (Code 6 Comics): Jan, 2003 - No. 5, May, 2003 ($2.95, lim. series)
1-5-Ciencin-s/Wagner-a 3.00
TPB (2003, $9.95) r/#1-5; new short story by Salvatore 10.00

DENNIS THE MENACE (TV with 1959 issues) (Becomes ...Fun Fest Series; See The Best of... & The Very Best of...)(...Fun Fest on-c only to #156-166)
Standard Comics/Pines No.15-31/Hallden (Fawcett) No.32 on: 8/53 - #14, 1/56; #15, 3/56 - #31, 11/58; #32, 1/59 - #166, 11/79
1-1st app. Dennis, Mr. & Mrs. Wilson, Ruff & Dennis' mom & dad; Wiseman-a, written by Fred Toole-most issues 80 160 240 504 852 1200
2 35 70 105 203 327 450
3-10: 8-Last pre-code issue 19 38 57 112 176 240
11-20 14 28 42 80 115 150
21,23-30 10 20 30 58 79 100
22-1st app. Margaret w/blonde hair 13 26 39 72 101 130
31-1st app. Joey 13 26 39 72 101 130
32-38,40(1/60): 37-A-Bomb blast panel 8 16 24 40 50 60
39-1st app. Gina (11/59) 8 16 24 44 57 70
41-60(7/62) 4 8 12 21 30 40
61-80(9/65),100(1/69) 3 6 9 14 19 24
81-99 2 4 6 11 16 20
101-117: 102-Last 12¢ issue 2 4 6 9 12 15
118(1/72)-131 (All 52 pages) 2 4 6 10 14 18
132(1/74)-142,144-160 1 2 3 5 7 9
143(3/76) Olympic-c/s; low print 2 4 6 10 14 18
161-166 1 3 4 6 8 10
NOTE: ***Wiseman*** *c/a-1-46, 53, 68, 69.*

DENNIS THE MENACE (Giants) (No. 1 titled Giant Vacation Special; becomes Dennis the Menace Bonus Magazine No. 76 on)
(#1-8,18,23,25,30,38: 100 pgs.; rest to #41: 84 pgs.; #42-75: 68 pgs.)
Standard/Pines/Hallden(Fawcett): Summer, 1955 - No. 75, Dec, 1969
nn-Giant Vacation Special(Summ/55-Standard) 18 36 54 103 162 220
nn-Christmas issue (Winter '55) 15 30 45 88 137 185

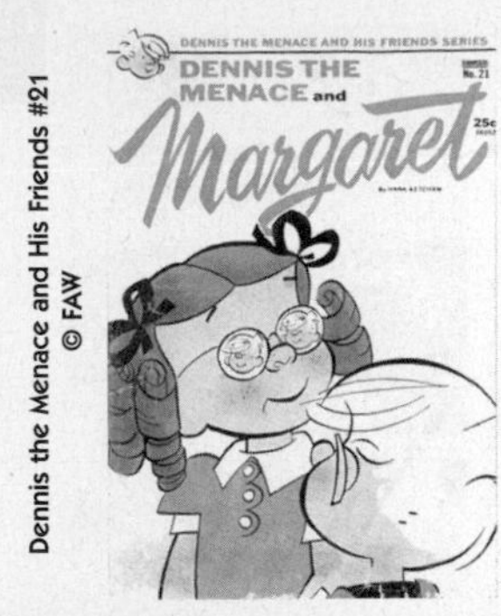

Dennis the Menace and His Friends #21 © FAW

Dennis the Menace Television Special #1 © FAW

Desperado #1 © LEV

	GD 2.0	VG 4.0	FN 6.0	VF 8.0	VF/NM 9.0	NM- 9.2
2-Giant Vacation Special (Summer '56-Pines)	14	28	42	78	112	145
3-Giant Christmas issue (Winter '56-Pines)	13	26	39	72	101	130
4-Giant Vacation Special (Summer '57-Pines)	12	24	36	67	94	120
5-Giant Christmas issue (Winter '57-Pines)	12	24	36	67	94	120
6-In Hawaii (Giant Vacation Special)(Summer '58-Pines)	11	22	33	62	86	110
6-In Hawaii (Summer '59-Hallden)-2nd printing; says 3rd large printing on-c						
6-In Hawaii (Summer '60)-3rd printing; says 4th large printing on-c						
6-In Hawaii (Summer '62)-4th printing; says 5th large printing on-c each....	8	16	24	42	54	65
6-Giant Christmas issue (Winter '58)	11	22	33	62	86	110
7-In Hollywood (Winter '59-Hallden)	5	10	15	32	51	70
7-In Hollywood (Summer '61)-2nd printing	3	6	9	21	32	42
8-In Mexico (Winter '60, 100 pgs.-Hallden/Fawcett)	5	10	15	32	51	70
8-In Mexico (Summer '62, 2nd printing)	3	6	9	21	32	42
9-Goes to Camp (Summer '61, 84 pgs.)-1st CCA approved issue	5	10	15	32	51	70
9-Goes to Camp (Summer '62)-2nd printing	3	6	9	21	32	42
10-12: 10-X-Mas issue (Winter '61), 11-Giant Christmas issue (Winter '62), 12-Triple Feature (Winter '62)	6	12	18	37	59	80
13-17: 13-Best of Dennis the Menace (Spring '63)-Reprints, 14-And His Dog Ruff (Summer '63), 15-In Washington, D.C. (Summer '63), 16-Goes to Camp (Summer '63)-Reprints No. 9, 17-& His Pal Joey (Winter '63)	4	8	12	24	37	50
18-In Hawaii (Reprints No. 6)	3	6	9	20	30	40
19-Giant Christmas issue (Winter '63)	4	8	12	24	37	50
20-Spring Special (Spring '64)	4	8	12	24	37	50
21-40 (Summer '66): 30-r/#6. #35-Xmas spec.Wint,'65	3	6	9	18	27	35
41-60 (Fall '68)	3	6	9	14	19	24
61-75 (12/69): 68-Partial-r/#6	2	4	6	11	16	20

NOTE: *Wiseman c/a-1-8, 12, 14, 15, 17, 20, 22, 27, 28, 31, 35, 36, 41, 49.*

DENNIS THE MENACE
Marvel Comics Group: Nov, 1981 - No. 13, Nov, 1982

	GD	VG	FN	VF	VF/NM	NM-
1-New-a	2	4	6	8	10	12
2-13: 2-New art. 3-Part-r. 4,5-r. 5-X-Mas-c & issue, 7-Spider Kid-c/sty	1	2	3	4	5	7

NOTE: *Hank Ketcham c-most; a-3, 12. Wiseman a-4, 5.*

DENNIS THE MENACE AND HIS DOG RUFF
Hallden/Fawcett: Summer, 1961

	GD	VG	FN	VF	VF/NM	NM-
1-Wiseman-c/a	5	10	15	32	51	70

DENNIS THE MENACE AND HIS FRIENDS
Fawcett Publ.: 1969; No. 5, Jan, 1970 - No. 46, April, 1980 (All reprints)

	GD	VG	FN	VF	VF/NM	NM-
Dennis the Menace & Joey No. 2 (7/69)	2	4	6	13	18	22
Dennis the Menace & Ruff No. 2 (9/69)	2	4	6	13	18	22
Dennis the Menace & Mr. Wilson No. 1 (10/69)	3	6	9	16	22	28
Dennis & Margaret No. 1 (Winter '69)	3	6	9	16	22	28
5-12: 5-Dennis the Menace & Margaret. 6-...& Joey. 7-...& Ruff. 8-...& Mr. Wilson	2	4	6	8	11	14
13-21-(52 pg Giants): 13-(1/72). 21-(1/74)	2	4	6	10	14	18
22-37	1	3	4	6	8	10
38-46 (Digest size, 148 pgs., 4/78, 95¢)	2	4	6	8	11	14

NOTE: *Titles rotate every four issues, beginning with No. 5. Joey issues: #2(7/69),6,10,14,18,22,26,30,34. Ruff issues: #2(9/69), 7,11,15,19,23,27,31,35. Mr. Wilson issues: #1(10/69),8,12,16,20,24,28,32,36. Margaret issues: #1(Wint./69),5,9,13,17,21,25,29,33,37.*

DENNIS THE MENACE AND HIS PAL JOEY
Fawcett Publ.: Summer, 1961 (10¢) (See Dennis the Menace Giants No. 45)

	GD	VG	FN	VF	VF/NM	NM-
1-Wiseman-c/a	5	10	15	34	55	75

DENNIS THE MENACE AND THE BIBLE KIDS
Word Books: 1977 (36 pgs.)

	GD	VG	FN	VF	VF/NM	NM-
1-6: 1-Jesus. 2-Joseph. 3-David. 4-The Bible Girls. 5-Moses. 6-More About Jesus	2	4	6	8	11	14
7-9-Low print run: 7-The Lord's Prayer. 8-Stories Jesus told. 9-Paul, God's Traveller	3	6	9	18	27	35
10-Low print run; In the Beginning	5	10	15	32	51	70

NOTE: *Ketcham c/a in all.*

DENNIS THE MENACE BIG BONUS SERIES
Fawcett Publications: No. 10, Feb, 1980 - No. 11, Apr, 1980

	GD	VG	FN	VF	VF/NM	NM-
10,11	1	2	3	5	6	8

DENNIS THE MENACE BONUS MAGAZINE (Formerly Dennis the Menace Giants Nos. 1-75) (...Big Bonus Series on-c for #174-194)
Fawcett Publications: No. 76, 1/70 - No. 95, 7/71; No. 95, 7/71; No. 97, '71; No. 194, 10/79; (No. 76-124: 68 pgs.; No. 125-163: 52 pgs.; No. 164 on: 36 pgs.)

	GD	VG	FN	VF	VF/NM	NM-
76-90(3/71)	2	4	6	10	14	18
91-95, 97-110(10/72): Two #95's with same date(7/71) A-Summer Games, and B-That's Our Boy. No #96	2	4	6	9	13	16
111-124	2	4	6	8	10	12
125-163-(52 pgs.)	2	4	6	8	10	12
164-194: 166-Indicia printed backwards	1	2	3	4	5	7

DENNIS THE MENACE COMICS DIGEST
Marvel Comics Group: April, 1982 - No. 3, Aug, 1982 ($1.25, digest-size)

	GD	VG	FN	VF	VF/NM	NM-
1-3-Reprints	1	3	4	6	8	10
1-Mistakenly printed with DC emblem on cover	2	4	6	10	12	15

NOTE: *Ketcham c-all. Wiseman a-all. A few thousand #1's were published with a DC emblem on cover.*

DENNIS THE MENACE FUN BOOK
Fawcett Publications/Standard Comics: 1960 (100 pgs.)

	GD	VG	FN	VF	VF/NM	NM-
1-Part Wiseman-a	6	12	18	41	66	90

DENNIS THE MENACE FUN FEST SERIES (Formerly Dennis the Menace #166)
Hallden (Fawcett): No. 16, Jan, 1980 - No. 17, Mar, 1980 (40¢)

	GD	VG	FN	VF	VF/NM	NM-
16,17-By Hank Ketcham	1	2	3	4	5	7

DENNIS THE MENACE POCKET FULL OF FUN!
Fawcett Publications (Hallden): Spring, 1969 - No. 50, March, 1980 (196 pgs.) (Digest size)

	GD	VG	FN	VF	VF/NM	NM-
1-Reprints in all issues	6	12	18	37	59	80
2-10	4	8	12	24	37	50
11-20	3	6	9	16	22	28
21-28	2	4	6	11	16	20
29-50: 35,40,46-Sunday strip-r	2	4	6	8	11	14

NOTE: *No. 1-28 are 196 pgs.; No. 29-36: 164 pgs.; No. 37: 148 pgs.; No. 38 on: 132 pgs. No. 8, 11, 15, 21, 25, 29 all contain strip reprints.*

DENNIS THE MENACE TELEVISION SPECIAL
Fawcett Publ. (Hallden Div.): Summer, 1961 - No. 2, Spring, 1962 (Giant)

	GD	VG	FN	VF	VF/NM	NM-
1	6	12	18	39	62	85
2	4	8	12	22	34	45

DENNIS THE MENACE TRIPLE FEATURE
Fawcett Publications: Winter, 1961 (Giant)

	GD	VG	FN	VF	VF/NM	NM-
1-Wiseman-c/a	6	12	18	39	62	85

DEPUTY, THE (TV)
Dell Publishing Co.: No. 1077, Feb-Apr, 1960 - No. 1225, Oct-Dec, 1961 (all-Henry Fonda photo-c)

	GD	VG	FN	VF	VF/NM	NM-
Four Color 1077 (#1)-Buscema-a	11	22	33	79	140	200
Four Color 1130 (9-11/60)-Buscema-a,1225	9	18	27	63	107	150

DEPUTY DAWG (TV) (Also see New Terrytoons)
Dell Publishing Co./Gold Key: Oct-Dec, 1961 - No. 1299, 1962; No. 1, Aug, 1965

	GD	VG	FN	VF	VF/NM	NM-
Four Color 1238,1299	10	20	30	73	129	185
1(10164-508)(8/65)-Gold Key	10	20	30	73	129	185

DEPUTY DAWG PRESENTS DINKY DUCK AND HASHIMOTO-SAN (TV)
Gold Key: August, 1965

	GD	VG	FN	VF	VF/NM	NM-
1(10159-508)	10	20	30	67	116	165

DESERT GOLD (See Zane Grey 4-Color 467)

DESIGN FOR SURVIVAL (Gen. Thomas S. Power's...)
American Security Council Press: 1968 (36 pgs. in color) (25¢)

	GD	VG	FN	VF	VF/NM	NM-
nn-Propaganda against the Threat of Communism-Aircraft cover; H-Bomb panel	3	6	9	17	25	32
Twin Circle Edition-Cover shows panels from inside	2	4	6	11	16	20

DESOLATION JONES
DC Comics (WildStorm): July, 2005 - Present ($2.95/$2.99)

	GD	VG	FN	VF	VF/NM	NM-
1-8: 1-6-Warren Ellis-s/J.H. Williams-a. 7,8-Zezelj-a						3.00
...: Made in England TPB (2006, $14.99) r/series; cover gallery						15.00

DESPERADO (Becomes Black Diamond Western No. 9 on)
Lev Gleason Publications: June, 1948 - No. 8, Feb, 1949 (All 52 pgs.)

	GD	VG	FN	VF	VF/NM	NM-
1-Biro-c on all; contains inside photo-c of Charles Biro, Lev Gleason & Bob Wood	15	30	45	86	133	180
2	10	20	30	54	72	90
3-Story with over 20 killings	10	20	30	56	76	95
4-8	8	16	24	42	54	65

NOTE: *Barry a-2. Fuje a-4, 8. Guardineer a-5-7. Kida a-3-7. Ed Moore a-4, 6.*

DESPERADO PRIMER
Image Comics (Desperado): Apr, 2005 ($1.99, one-shot)

The Destroyer #1 © Warren Murphy

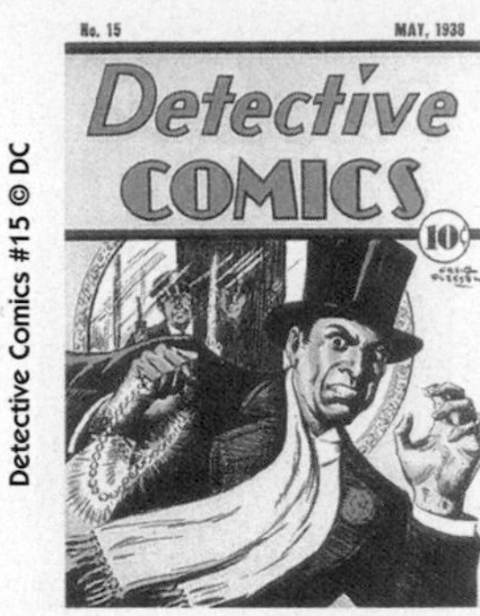

Detective Comics #15 © DC

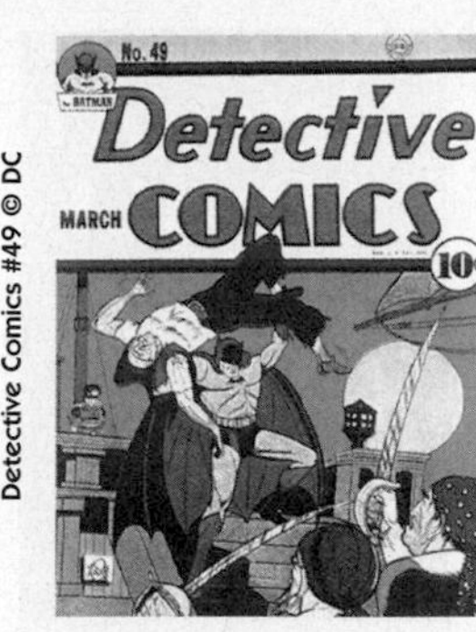

Detective Comics #49 © DC

GD VG FN VF VF/NM NM-
2.0 4.0 6.0 8.0 9.0 9.2

1-Previews of Roundeye, World Traveler, A Mirror To The Soul; Bolland-c 2.50

DESPERADOES
Image Comics (Homage): Sept, 1997 - No. 5, June, 1998 ($2.50/$2.95)

1-5-Mariotte-s/Cassaday-c/a: 1-($2.50-c). 2-5-($2.95) 3.00
...: A Moment's Sunlight TPB ('98, $16.95) r/#1-5 17.00
...: Epidemic! (11/99, $5.95) Mariotte-s 6.00

DESPERADOES: BANNERS OF GOLD
IDW Publishing: Dec, 2004 - No. 5, Apr, 2005 ($3.99, limited series)

1-5: Mariotte-s/Haun-a. 1-Cassaday-c 4.00

DESPERADOES: BUFFALO DREAMS
IDW Publishing: Jan, 2007 - No. 4, Apr, 2007 ($3.99, limited series)

1-4: Mariotte-s/Dose-a/c 4.00

DESPERADOES: QUIET OF THE GRAVE
DC Comics (Homage): Jul, 2001 - No. 5, Nov, 2001 ($2.95)

1-5-Jeff Mariotte-s/John Severin-c/a 3.00
TPB (2002, $14.95) r/#1-5; intro. by Brian Keene 15.00

DESPERATE TIMES (See Savage Dragon)
Image Comics: Jun, 1998 - No. 4, Dec, 1998; Nov, 2000 - No. 4, July, 2001 ($2.95, B&W)

1-4-Chris Eliopoulos-s/a 3.00
(Vol. 2) 1-4 3.00
(Vol. 3) 0-(1/04, $3.50) Pages read sideways 3.50
(Vol. 3) 1-Pages read sideways 3.00

DESTINATION MOON (See Fawcett Movie Comics, Space Adventures #20, 23, & Strange Adventures #1)

DESTINY: A CHRONICLE OF DEATHS FORETOLD (See Sandman)
DC Comics (Vertigo): 1997 - No.3, 1998 ($5.95, limited series)

1-3-Alisa Kwitney-s in all: 1-Kent Williams & Michael Zulli-a, Williams painted-c. 2-Williams & Scott Hampton-painted-c/a. 3-Williams & Guay-a 6.00
TPB (2000, $14.95) r/series 15.00

DESTROY!!
Eclipse Comics: 1986 ($4.95, B&W, magazine-size, one-shot)

1 5.00
3-D Special 1-r-/#1 ($2.50) 5.00

DESTROYER, THE
Marvel Comics: Nov, 1989 - No. 9, Jun, 1990 ($2.25, B&W, magazine, 52 pgs.)

1-Based on Remo Williams movie, paperbacks 6.00
2-9: 2-Williamson part inks. 4-Ditko-a 4.00

DESTROYER, THE
Marvel Comics: V2#1, March, 1991 ($1.95, 52 pgs.)
V3#1, Dec, 1991 - No. 4, Mar, 1992 ($1.95, mini-series)

V2#1,V3#1-4: Based on Remo Williams paperbacks. V3#1-4-Simonson-c. 3-Morrow-a 2.50

DESTROYER, THE (Also see Solar, Man of the Atom)
Valiant: Apr, 1995 ($2.95, color, one-shot)

0-Indicia indicates #1 3.00

DESTROYER DUCK
Eclipse Comics: Feb, 1982 - No. 7, May, 1984 (#2-7: Baxter paper) ($1.50)

1-Origin Destroyer Duck; 1st app. Groo; Kirby-c/a(p) 1 3 4 6 8 10
2-5: 2-Starling back-up begins; Kirby-c/a(p) thru #5 5.00
6,7 4.00

NOTE: ***Neal Adams** c-1i. **Kirby** c/a-1-5p. **Miller** c-7.*

DESTRUCTOR, THE
Atlas/Seaboard: February, 1975 - No. 4, Aug, 1975

1-Origin/1st app.; Ditko/Wood-a; Wood-c(i) 1 3 4 6 8 10
2-4: 2-Ditko/Wood-a. 3,4-Ditko-a(p) 1 2 3 5 6 8

DETECTIVE COMICS (Also see other Batman titles)
National Periodical Publications/DC Comics: Mar, 1937 - Present

1-(Scarce)-Slam Bradley & Spy by Siegel & Shuster, Speed Saunders by Stoner and Flessel, Cosmo, the Phantom of Disguise, Buck Marshall, Bruce Nelson begin; Chin Lung in 'Claws of the Red Dragon' serial begins; Vincent Sullivan-c
10,000 20,000 30,000 70,000 - -
2 (Rare)-Creig Flessel-c begin; new logo 2850 5700 8550 20,000 - -
3 (Rare) 2143 4286 6429 15,000 - -
4,5: 5-Larry Steele begins 1100 2200 3300 6050 8525 11,000
6,7,9,10 780 1560 2340 4290 6045 7800
8-Mister Chang-c; classic-c 1180 2360 3540 6490 9145 11,800
11-17,19: 16-Has interior ad for Action Comics #1. 17-1st app. Fu Manchu in Detective
600 1200 1800 3300 4650 6000
18-Fu Manchu-c; last Flessel-c 960 1920 2880 5280 7440 9600
20-The Crimson Avenger begins (1st app.) 900 1800 2700 4950 6975 9000
21,23-25 480 960 1440 2640 3720 4800
22-1st Crimson Avenger-c by Chambers (12/38) 660 1320 1980 3630 5115 6600
26 450 900 1350 2475 3488 4500
27-The Bat-Man & Commissioner Gordon begin (1st app.), created by Bill Finger & Bob Kane (5/39); Batman-c (1st)(by Kane). Bat-Man's secret identity revealed as Bruce Wayne in 6pg. sty. Signed Rob't Kane (also see Det. Picture Stories #5 & Funny Pages V3#1)
37,000 74,000 111,000 240,000 407,500 575,000
27-Reprint, Oversize 13-1/2x10". WARNING: This comic is an exact duplicate reprint of the original except for its size. DC published it in 1974 with a second cover titling it as Famous First Edition. There have been many reported cases of the outer cover being removed and the interior sold as the original edition. The reprint with the new outer cover removed is practically worthless; see Famous First Edition for value.
28-2nd app. The Batman (6 pg. story); non-Bat-Man-c; signed Rob't Kane
2250 4500 6750 17,000 30,500 44,000
29-1st app. Doctor Death-c/story, Batman's 1st name villain. 1st 2 part story (10 pgs.). 2nd Batman-c by Kane 3700 7400 11,100 27,750 49,875 72,000
30-Dr. Death app. Story concludes from issue #29. Classic Batman splash panel by Kane.
889 1778 2667 6401 11,201 16,000
31-Classic Batman over castle cover; 1st app. The Monk & 1st Julie Madison (Bruce Wayne's 1st love interest); 1st Batplane (Bat-Gyro) and Batarang; 2nd 2-part Batman adventure. Gardner Fox takes over script from Bill Finger. 1st mention of locale (New York City) where Batman lives 4100 8200 12,300 30,500 54,250 78,000
32-Batman story concludes from issue #31. 1st app. Dala (Monk's assistant). Batman uses gun for 1st time to slay The Monk and Dala. This was the 1st time a costumed hero used a gun in comic books. 1st Batman head logo on cover
778 1556 2334 5602 9801 14,000
33-Origin The Batman (2 pgs.)(1st told origin); Batman gun holster-c; Batman w/smoking gun panel at end of story. Batman story now 12 pgs. Classic Batman-c
4350 8700 13,050 32,625 58,812 85,000
34-2nd Crimson Avenger-c by Creig Flessel and last non Batman-c. Story from issue #32 x-over as Bruce Wayne sees Julie Madison off to America from Paris. Classic Batman splash panel used later in Batman #1 for origin story. Steve Malone begins
583 1166 1749 4198 7349 10,500
35-Classic Batman hypodermic needle-c that reflects story in issue #34. Classic Batman with smoking .45 automatic splash panel. Batman-c begin
1533 3066 4600 11,500 20,750 30,000
36-Batman-c that reflects adventure in issue #35. Origin/1st app. of Dr. Hugo Strange (1st major villain, 2/40). 1st finned-gloves worn by Batman
1000 2000 3000 7200 12,600 18,000
37-Last solo Golden-Age Batman adventure in Detective Comics. Panel at end of story reflects solo Batman adventure in Batman #1 that was originally planned for Detective #38. Cliff Crosby begins 861 1722 2583 6199 10,850 15,500
38-Origin/1st app. Robin the Boy Wonder (4/40); Batman and Robin-c begin; cover by Kane & Robinson taken from splash page 4100 8200 12,300 30,750 55,375 80,000
39-Opium story; Clayface app. in 1 panel ad at the end of the Batman story
667 1334 2001 4802 8401 12,000
40-Origin & 1st app. Clayface (Basil Karlo); 1st Joker cover app. (6/40); Joker story intended for this issue was used in Batman #1 instead; cover is similar to splash page in 2nd Joker story in Batman #1 778 1556 2334 5602 9801 14,000
41-Robin's 1st solo 376 752 1128 2444 4322 6200
42-44: 44-Crimson Avenger-new costume 300 600 900 1890 3195 4500
45-1st Joker story in Det. (3rd book app. & 4th story app. over all, 11/40)
394 788 1182 2679 4690 6700
46-50: 46-Death of Hugo Strange. 48-1st time car called Batmobile (2/41); Gotham City 1st mention in Detective (1st mentioned in Wow #1; also see Batman #4).
49-Last Clay Face 280 560 840 1764 2982 4200
51-57 187 374 561 1178 1989 2800
58-1st Penguin app. (12/41); last Speed Saunders; Fred Ray-c
461 922 1383 3319 5810 8300
59,60: 59-Last Steve Malone; 2nd Penguin; Wing becomes Crimson Avenger's aide.
60-Intro. Air Wave; Joker app. (2nd in Det.) 193 386 579 1216 2058 2900
61,63: 63-Last Cliff Crosby; 1st app. Mr. Baffle 173 346 519 1090 1845 2600
62-Joker-c/story (2nd Joker-c, 4/42) 300 600 900 1930 3315 4700
64-Origin & 1st app. Boy Commandos by Simon & Kirby (6/42); Joker app.
394 788 1182 2679 4690 6700
65-1st Boy Commandos-c (S&K-a on Boy Commandos & Ray/Robinson-a on Batman & Robin on-c; 4 artists on one-c) 300 600 900 1930 3315 4700
66-Origin & 1st app. Two-Face 428 856 1284 3082 5391 7700
67-1st Penguin-c (9/42) 300 600 900 1890 3195 4500
68-Two-Face-c/story; 1st Two-Face-c 213 426 639 1342 2271 3200
69-Joker-c/story 233 466 699 1468 2484 3500
70 147 294 441 926 1563 2200
71-Joker-c/story 227 454 681 1430 2415 3400

Detective Comics #108 © DC

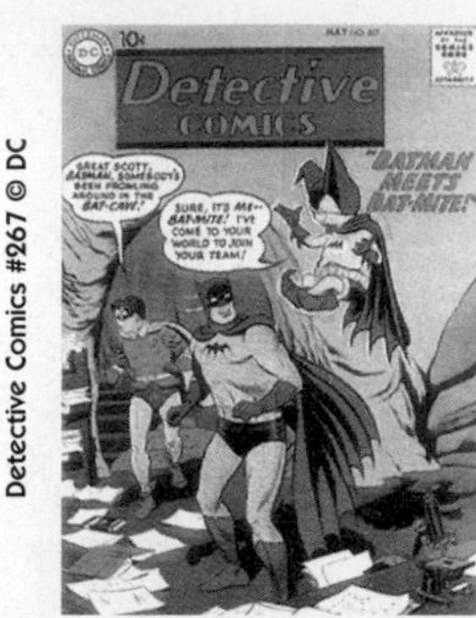

Detective Comics #267 © DC

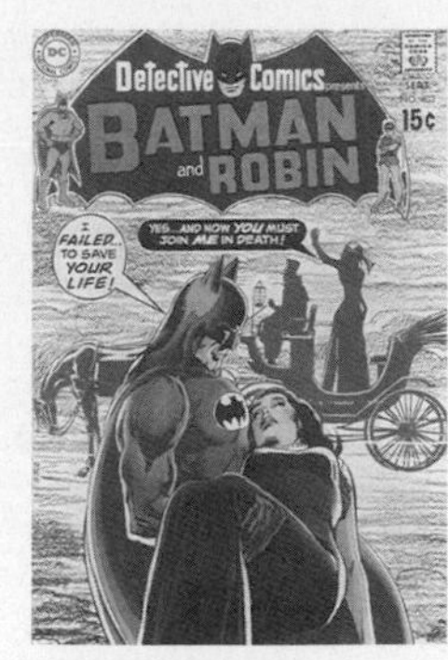

Detective Comics #403 © DC

	GD 2.0	VG 4.0	FN 6.0	VF 8.0	VF/NM 9.0	NM- 9.2
72,74,75: 74-1st Tweedledum & Tweedledee plus-c; S&K-a	127	254	381	800	1350	1900
73-Scarecrow-c/story (1st Scarecrow-c)	167	334	501	1052	1776	2500
76-Newsboy Legion & The Sandman x-over in Boy Commandos; S&K-a; Joker-c/story	200	400	600	1260	2130	3000
77-79: All S&K-a	130	260	390	819	1385	1950
80-Two-Face app.; S&K-a	147	294	441	926	1563	2200
81,82,84,86-90: 81-1st Cavalier-c & app. 89-Last Crimson Avenger; 2nd Cavalier-c & app.	98	196	294	617	1046	1475
83-1st "skinny" Alfred (1/44)(see Batman #21; last S&K Boy Commandos (also #92,128); most issues #84 on signed S&K are not by them	107	214	321	674	1137	1600
85-Joker-c/story; last Spy; Kirby/Klech Boy Commandos	147	294	441	926	1563	2200
91,102-Joker-c/story	140	280	420	882	1491	2100
92-98: 96-Alfred's last name 'Beagle' revealed, later changed to 'Pennyworth' in #214	83	166	249	523	887	1250
99-Penguin-c/story	133	266	399	838	1419	2000
100 (6/45)	122	244	366	769	1297	1825
101,103-108,110-113,115-117,119: 108-1st Bat-signal-c (2/46). 114-1st small logo (8/46)	75	150	225	473	799	1125
109,114,118-Joker-c/stories	123	246	369	775	1313	1850
120-Penguin-c/story	147	294	441	674	1137	2200
121,123,125,127,129,130	72	144	216	454	765	1075
122-1st Catwoman-c (4/47)	173	346	519	1090	1845	2600
124,128-Joker-c/stories	113	226	339	712	1206	1700
126-Penguin-c	110	220	330	693	1172	1650
131-134,136,139: 134-Penguin-c/story	67	134	201	422	711	1000
135-Frankenstein-c/story	85	170	255	536	906	1275
137-Joker-c/story; last Air Wave	93	186	279	586	993	1400
138-Origin Robotman (see Star Spangled #7 for 1st app.); series ends #202	110	220	330	693	1172	1650
140-The Riddler-c/story (1st app., 10/48)	472	944	1416	3398	5949	8500
141,143-148,150: 150-Last Boy Commandos	67	134	201	422	711	1000
142-2nd Riddler-c/story	133	266	399	838	1419	2000
149-Joker-c/story	93	186	279	586	993	1400
151-Origin & 1st app. Pow Wow Smith, Indian lawman (9/49) & begins series	77	154	231	481	816	1150
152,154,155,157-160: 152-Last Slam Bradley	67	134	201	422	711	1000
153-1st app. Roy Raymond TV Detective (11/49); origin The Human Fly	71	142	213	447	754	1060
156(2/50)-The new classic Batmobile	93	186	279	586	993	1400
161-167,169,170,172-176: Last 52 pg. issue	62	124	186	391	658	925
168-Origin the Joker	371	742	1113	2523	4412	6300
171-Penguin-c	90	180	270	567	959	1350
177-179,181-186,188,189,191,192,194-199,201,202,204,206-210,212,214-216: 184-1st app. Fire Fly. 185-Secret of Batman's utility belt. 187-Two-Face app. 202-Last Robotman & Pow Wow Smith. 215-1st app. of Batmen of all Nations. 216-Last precode (2/55)	58	116	174	365	620	875
180,193-Joker-c/story	73	146	219	460	780	1100
187-Two-Face-c/story	67	134	201	422	711	1000
190-Origin Batman retold	82	164	246	517	871	1225
200(10/53), 205: 205-Origin Batcave	76	152	228	479	807	1135
203,211-Catwoman-c/stories	73	146	219	460	780	1100
213-Origin & 1st app. Mirror Man	70	140	210	441	746	1050
217-224: 218-Batman Jr. & Robin Sr. app.	52	104	156	322	536	750
225-(11/55)-1st app. Martian Manhunter (J'onn J'onzz); origin begins; also see Batman #78	377	754	1131	3393	6597	9800
226-Origin Martian Manhunter cont'd (2nd app.)	143	286	429	901	1526	2150
227-229: Martian Manhunter stories in all	57	114	171	359	605	850
230-1st app. Mad Hatter; brief recap origin of Martian Manhunter	63	126	189	397	674	950
231-Brief origin recap Martian Manhunter	47	94	141	291	483	675
232,234,237-240: 239-Early DC grey tone-c	43	86	129	267	446	625
233-Origin & 1st app. Batwoman (7/56)	167	334	501	1052	1776	2500
235-Origin Batman & his costume; tells how Bruce Wayne's father (Thomas Wayne) wore Bat costume & fought crime (reprinted in Batman #255)	70	140	210	441	746	1050
236-1st S.A. issue; J'onn J'onzz talks to parents and Mars-1st since being stranded on Earth; 1st app. Bat-Tank?	45	90	135	279	465	650
241-260: 246-Intro. Diane Meade, John Jones' girl. 249-Batwoman-c/app. 253-1st app. The Terrible Trio. 254-Bat-Hound-c/story. 257-Intro. & 1st app. Whirly Bats. 259-1st app. The Calendar Man	38	76	114	226	363	500
261-264,266,268-271: 261-J. Jones tie-in to sci/fi movie "Incredible Shrinking Man"; 1st app. Dr. Double X. 262-Origin Jackal. 268,271-Manhunter origin recap	30	60	90	174	280	385
265-Batman's origin retold with new facts	41	82	123	250	413	575
267-Origin & 1st app. Bat-Mite (5/59)	45	90	135	279	465	650
272,274,275,277-280	24	48	72	143	229	315
273-J'onn J'onzz i.d. revealed for 1st time	25	50	75	147	236	325
276-2nd app. Bat-Mite	29	58	87	169	272	375
281-292, 294-297: 286,292-Batwoman-c/app. 287-Origin J'onn J'onzz retold. 289-Bat-Mite-c/story. 292-Last Roy Raymond. 297-Last 10¢ issue (11/61)	20	40	60	115	183	250
293-(7/61)-Aquaman begins (pre #1); ends #300	20	40	60	118	189	260
298-(12/61)-1st modern Clayface (Matt Hagen)	24	48	72	176	326	475
299, 300-(2/62)-Aquaman ends	12	24	36	87	156	225
301-(3/62)-J'onn J'onzz returns to Mars (1st time since stranded on Earth six years before)	10	20	30	73	129	185
302-317,319-321,323,324,326,329,330: 302,307-Batwoman-c/app. 311-Intro. Zook in John Jones; 1st app. Cat-Man. 321-2nd Terrible Trio. 326-Last J'onn J'onzz, story cont'd in House of Mystery #143; intro. Idol-Head of Diabolu	9	18	27	63	107	150
318,322,325: 318,325-Cat-Man-c/story (2nd & 3rd app.); also 1st & 2nd app. Batwoman as the Cat-Woman. 322-Bat-Girl's 1st/only app. in Det. (6th in all); Batman cameo in J'onn J'onzz (only hero to app. in series)	9	18	27	64	110	155
327-(5/64)-Elongated Man begins, ends #383; 1st new look Batman with new costume; Infantino/Giella new look-a begins; Batman with gun	13	26	39	90	160	230
328-Death of Alfred; Bob Kane biog, 2 pgs.	12	24	36	82	146	210
331,333-340: 334-1st app. The Outsider	8	16	24	52	86	120
342-358,360,361,366-368: 345-Intro Block Buster. 347-"What If" theme story (1/66). 351-Elongated Man new costume. 355-Zatanna x-over in Elongated Man. 356-Alfred brought back in Batman, early SA app.	7	14	21	45	73	100
332,341,365-Joker-c/stories	9	18	27	63	107	150
359-Intro/origin Batgirl (Barbara Gordon)-c/story (1/67); 1st Silver Age app. Killer Moth	15	30	45	111	206	300
362-364: 362,364-S.A. Riddler app. (early). 363-2nd app. new Batgirl	8	16	24	54	90	125
369(11/67)-N. Adams-a (Elongated Man); 3rd app. S.A. Catwoman (cameo; leads into Batman #197); 4th app. new Batgirl	10	20	30	67	116	165
370-1st Neal Adams-a on Batman (cover only, 12/67)	8	16	24	52	86	120
371-(1/68) 1st new Batmobile from TV show; classic Batgirl-c	9	18	27	60	100	140
372-376,378-386,389,390: 375-New Batmobile-c	6	12	18	37	59	80
377-S.A. Riddler-c/sty	6	12	18	43	69	95
387-r/1st Batman story from #27 (30th anniversary, 5/69); Joker-c; last 12¢ issue	8	16	24	54	90	125
388-Joker-c/story	7	14	21	50	83	115
391-394,396,398,399,401,403,405,406,409: 392-1st app. Jason Bard. 401-2nd Batgirl/Robin team-up. 405-Debut League of Assassins	5	10	15	30	48	65
395,397,402,404,407,408,410-Neal Adams-a. 404-Tribute to Enemy Ace	7	14	21	47	76	105
400-(6/70)-Origin & 1st app. Man-Bat; 1st Batgirl/Robin team-up (cont'd in #401); Neal Adams-a	17	34	51	120	223	325
411-(5/71) Intro. Talia, daughter of Ra's al Ghul (Ra's mentioned, but doesn't appear until Batman #232 (6/71); Bob Brown-a	5	10	15	32	51	70
412-413: 413-Last 15¢ issue	4	8	12	24	37	50
414-424: All-25¢, 52 pgs. 418-Creeper x-over. 424-Last Batgirl.	4	8	12	26	41	55
425-436: 426,430,436-Elongated Man app. 428,434-Hawkman begins, ends #467	3	6	9	17	25	32
437-New Manhunter begins (10-11/73, 1st app.) by Simonson, ends #443	5	10	15	30	48	65
438-445 (All 100 Page Super Spectaculars): 438-Kubert Hawkman-r. 439-Origin Manhunter. 440-G.A. Manhunter(Adv. #79) by S&K, Hawkman, Dollman, Green Lantern; Toth-a. 441-G.A. Plastic Man, Batman, Ibis-r. 442-G.A. Newsboy Legion, Black Canary, Elongated Man, Dr. Fate-r. 443-Origin The Creeper-r; death of Manhunter; G.A. Green Lantern, Spectre-r; Batman-r/Batman #18. 444-G.A. Kid Eternity-r. 445-G.A. Dr. Midnite-r	6	12	18	39	62	85
446-460: 457-Origin retold & updated	3	6	9	14	19	24
461-465,470,480: 480-(44 pgs.). 463-1st app. Black Spider. 464-2nd app. Black Spider 470-Intro. Silver St. Cloud.	2	4	6	11	16	20
466-468,471-474,478,479-Rogers-a in all: 466-1st app. Signalman since Batman #139. 470,471-1st modern app. Hugo Strange. 474-1st app. new Deadshot. 478-1st app. 3rd Clayface (Preston Payne). 479-(44 pgs.)	4	8	12	22	34	45
469-Intro/origin Dr. Phosphorous; Simonson-a	3	6	9	20	30	40
475,476-Joker-c/stories; Rogers-a	6	12	18	41	66	90

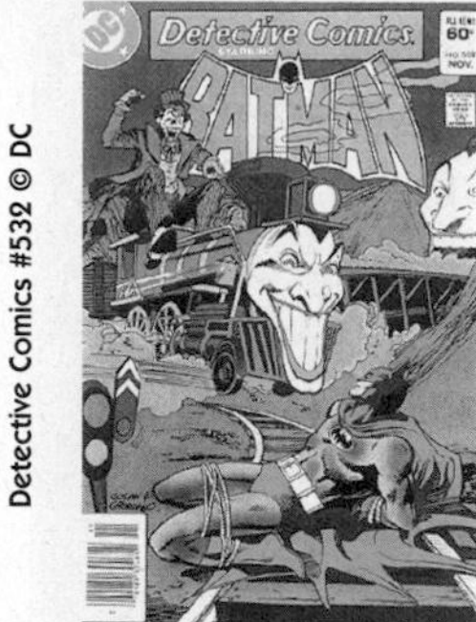

Detective Comics #532 © DC

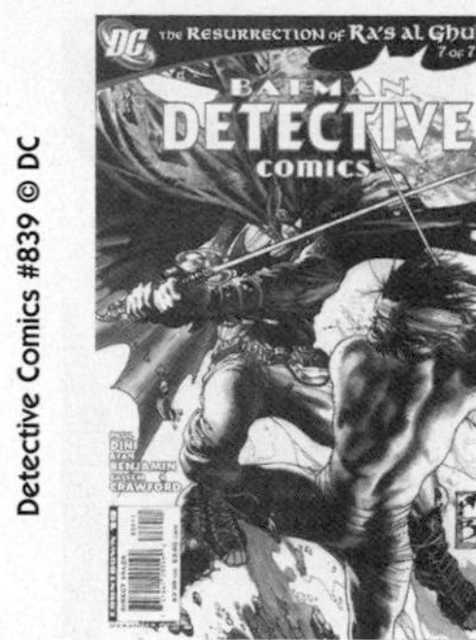

Detective Comics #839 © DC

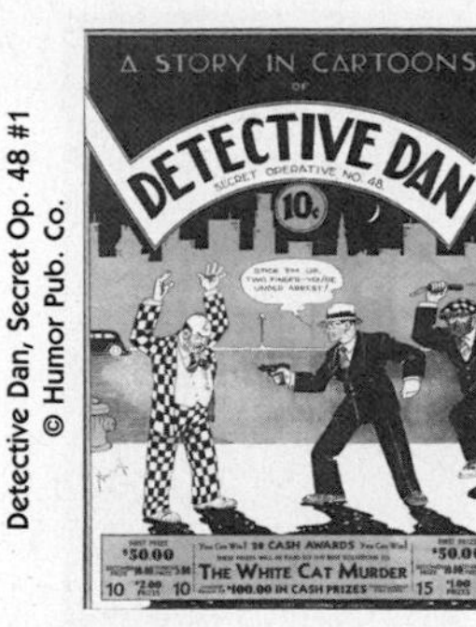

Detective Dan, Secret Op. 48 #1 © Humor Pub. Co.

GD VG FN VF VF/NM NM-
2.0 4.0 6.0 8.0 9.0 9.2

477-Neal Adams-a(r); Rogers-a (3 pgs.) 3 6 9 20 30 40

481-(Combined with Batman Family, 12-1/78-79, begin $1.00, 68 pg. issues, ends #495); 481-495-Batgirl, Robin solo stories 3 6 9 14 19 24

482-Starlin/Russell, Golden-a; The Demon begins (origin-r), ends #485 (by Ditko #483-485) 2 4 6 10 14 18

483-40th Anniversary issue; origin retold; Newton Batman begins 2 4 6 13 18 22

484-495 (68 pgs): 484-Origin Robin. 485-Death of Batwoman. 486-Killer Moth app. 487-The Odd Man by Ditko. 489-Robin/Batgirl team-up. 490-Black Lightning begins. 491-(#492 on inside). 493-Intro. The Swashbuckler 2 4 6 8 10 12

496-499: 496-Clayface app. 1 2 3 5 7 9

500-($1.50, 52 pgs.)-Batman/Deadman team-up with Infantino-a; new Hawkman story by Joe Kubert; incorrectly says 500th Anniv. of Det. 2 4 6 10 14 18

501-503,505-523: 509-Catman-c. 510-Mad Hatter-c. 512-2nd app. new Dr. Death. 519-Last Batgirl. 521-Green Arrow series begins. 523-Solomon Grundy app. 6.00

504-Joker-c/story 2 4 6 8 11 14

524-2nd app. Jason Todd (cameo)(3/83) 1 2 3 5 7 9

525-3rd app. Jason Todd (See Batman #357) 1 2 3 5 7 9

526-Batman's 500th app. in Detective Comics ($1.50, 68 pgs.); Death of Jason Todd's parents, Joker-c/story (55 pgs.); Bob Kane pin-up 2 4 6 13 18 22

527-531,533,534,536-568,571,573: 538-Cat-Man-c/story cont'd from Batman #371. 542-Jason Todd quits as Robin (becomes Robin again #547). 549,550-Alan Moore scripts (Green Arrow). 554-1st new Black Canary (9/85). 566-Batman villains profiled. 567-Harlan Ellison scripts. 5.00

532,569,570-Joker-c/stories 2 4 6 8 10 12

535-Intro new Robin (JasonTodd)-1st appeared in Batman 1 2 3 5 6 8

572-(3/87, $1.25, 60 pgs.)-50th Anniv. of Det. Comics 6.00

574-Origin Batman & Jason Todd retold 1 2 3 5 6 8

575-Year 2 begins, ends #578 2 4 6 13 18 22

576-578: McFarlane-c/a; The Reaper app. 2 4 6 13 18 22

579-597,599,601-610: 579-New bat wing logo. 583-1st app. villains Scarface & Ventriloquist. 589-595-(52 pgs.)-Each contain free 16 pg. Batman stories. 604-607-Mudpack storyline; 604,607-Contain Batman mini-posters. 610-Faked death of Penguin; artists names app. on tombstone on-c 3.00

598-($2.95, 84 pgs.)- "Blind Justice" storyline begins by Batman movie writer Sam Hamm, ends #600 4.00

600-(5/89, $2.95, 84 pgs.)-50th Anniv. of Batman in Det.; 1 pg. Neal Adams pin-up, among other artists 4.00

611-626,628-658: 612-1st new look Cat-Man; Catwoman app. 615- "The Penguin Affair" part 2 (See Batman #448,449). 617-Joker-c/story. 624-1st new Catwoman (w/death) & 1st new Batwoman. 626-Batman's 600th app. in Detective. 642-Return of Scarface, part 2. 644-Last $1.00-c. 652,653-Huntress-c/story w/new costume plus Charest-c on both 3.00

627-($2.95, 84 pgs.)-Batman's 601st app. in Det.; reprints 1st story/#27 plus 3 versions (2 new) of same story 4.00

659-664: 659-Knightfall part 2; Kelley Jones-c. 660-Knightfall part 4; Bane-c by Sam Kieth. 661-Knightfall part 6; brief Joker & Riddler app. 662-Knightfall part 8; Riddler app.; Sam Kieth-c. 663-Knightfall part 10; Kelley Jones-c. 664-Knightfall part 12; Bane-c/story; Joker app.; continued in Showcase 93 #7 & 8; Jones-c 3.00

665-675: 665,666-Knightfall parts 16 & 18; 666-Bane-c/story. 667-Knightquest: The Crusade & new Batman begins (1st app. in Batman #500). 669-Begin $1.50-c; Knightquest, cont'd in Robin #1. 671,673-Joker app. 2.75

675-($2.95)-Collectors edition w/foil-c 3.50

676-($2.50, 52 pgs.)-KnightsEnd pt. 3 3.00

677,678: 677-KnightsEnd pt. 9. 678-(9/94)-Zero Hour tie-in. 2.75

679-685: 679-(11/94). 682-Troika pt. 3 2.75

682-($2.50) Embossed-c Troika pt. 3 3.00

686-699,701-719: 686-Begin $1.95-c. 693,694-Poison Ivy-c/app. 695-Contagion pt. 2; Catwoman, Penguin app. 696-Contagion pt. 8. 698-Two-Face-c/app. 701-Legacy pt. 6; Batman vs. Bane-c/app. 702-Legacy Epilogue. 703-Final Night x-over. 705-707-Riddler-app. 714,715-Martian Manhunter-app. 2.75

700-($4.95, Collectors Edition)-Legacy pt. 1; Ra's Al Ghul-c/app; Talia & Bane app; book displayed at shops in envelope 5.00

700-($2.95, Regular Edition)-Different-c 3.00

720-740: 720,721-Cataclysm pts. 5,14. 723-Green Arrow app. 730-740-No Man's Land stories 2.75

741-($2.50) Endgame; Joker-c/app. 3.00

742-749,751-765: 742-New look Batman begins; 1st app. Crispus Allen (who later becomes the Spectre). 751,752-Poison Ivy app. 756-Superman-c/app. 759-762-Catwoman back-up 2.75

750-($4.95, 64 pgs.) Ra's al Ghul-c 5.00

766-772: 766,767-Bruce Wayne: Murderer pt. 1,8. 769-772-Bruce Wayne: Fugitive pts. 4,8,12,16 3.00

773,774,776-799: 773-Begin $2.75-c; Sienkiewicz-c. 777-784-Sale-c. 784-786-Alan Scott app. 787-Mad Hatter app. 793-Begin $2.95-c. 797-799-War Games 3.00

GD VG FN VF VF/NM NM-
2.0 4.0 6.0 8.0 9.0 9.2

775-($3.50) Sienkiewicz-c 3.50

800-($3.50) Jock-c; aftermath of War Games; back-up by Lapham 3.50

801-816: 801-814-Lapham-s. 804-Mr. Freeze app. 809-War Crimes 3.00

817-847: 817-820: One Year Later 8-part x-over with Batman #651-654; Robinson-s/Bianchi-c 819-Begin $2.99-c. 820-Dini-s/Williams III-a. 825-Doctor Phosperous app. 827-Debut of new Scarface. 831-Harley app.; Dini-s. 833,834-Zatanna & Joker app. 838,839-Resurrection of Ra's al Ghul x-over. 846-847-Batman R.I.P. x-over 3.00

817,818,838,839-2nd printings. 817-Combo-c of #817̳ cover images. 818-Combo-c of #818 and Batman #653 cover images. 838-Andy Kubert variant-c. 839-Red bkgd-c 3.00

#0-(10/94) Zero Hour tie-in 2.75

#1,000,000 (11/98) 853rd Century x-over 2.75

Annual 1 (1988, $1.50) 5.00

Annual 2-7,9 ('89-'94, '96, 68 pgs.)-4-Painted-c. 5-Joker-c/story (54 pgs.) continued in Robin Annual #1; Sam Kieth-c; Eclipso app. 6-Azrael as Batman in new costume; intro Geist the Twilight Man; Bloodlines storyline. 7-Elseworlds story. 9-Legends of the Dead Earth story 3.00

Annual 8 (1995, $3.95, 68 pgs.) Year One story 4.00

Annual 10 (1997, $3.95)-Pulp Heroes story 4.00

NOTE: **Neal Adams** *c-370, 372, 385, 389, 391, 392, 394-422, 439.* **Aparo** *a-437, 438, 444-446, 500, 625-632p, 638-643p; c-430, 437, 440-446, 448, 468-470, 480, 484(back), 492-502,508, 509, 515, 518-522, 641, 716, 719, 722, 724.* **Austin** *a(i)-450, 451, 463-468, 471-476; c(i)-474-476, 478.* **Baily** *a-443r.* **Buckler** *a-434, 446p, 479p; c(p)-467, 482, 505-507, 511, 513-516, 518.* **Burnley** *a(Batman)-65, 75, 78, 83, 100, 103, 125, c-62i, 63i, 64, 73i, 78, 83p, 96p, 103p, 105p, 106, 108, 121p, 123p, 125p.* **Chaykin** *a-441.* **Colan** *a(p)-510, 512, 517, 523, 528-538, 540-546, 555-567; c(p)-510, 512, 528, 530-535, 537, 538, 540, 541, 543-545, 556-558, 560-564.* **J. Craig** *a-488.* **Ditko** *a-443r, 483-485, 487.* **Golden** *a-482p; c-625, 626, 628-631, 633, 644-646.* **Alan Grant** *scripts-584-597, 601-621, 641, 642, Annual 5.* **Grell** *a-445, 455, 463p, 464p; c-455.* **Guardineer** *c-23, 24, 26, 28, 30, 32.* **Gustavson** *a-441r.* **Infantino** *a-354, 442(2)r, 500, 572.* **Infantino/Anderson** *c-333, 337-340, 343, 344, 347, 351, 352, 359, 361-368, 371.* **Kelley Jones** *c-651, 657i, 658i, 659, 661, 663-675.* **Kaluta** *c-423, 424, 426-428, 431, 434, 438, 484, 486, 572.* **Bob Kane** *a-Most early issues #27 on, 297r, 356r, 438-440r, 442r, 443r.* **Kane/Robinson** *c-33.* **Gil Kane** *a(p)-368, 370-374, 384, 385, 388-407, 438r, 439r, 520.* **Kane/Anderson** *c-369.* **Sam Kieth** *c-654-656 (657, 658 w/***Kelley Jones***), 660, 662, Annual #5.* **Kubert** *a-438r, 439r, 500; c-348, 350.* **McFarlane** *c/a(p)-576-578.* **Meskin** *a-420r.* **Mignola** *c-583.* **Moldoff** *c-233-354, 259, 266, 267, 275, 287, 289, 290, 297, 300.* **Moldoff/Giella** *a-328, 330, 332, 334, 336, 338, 340, 342, 344, 346, 348, 350, 352, 354, 356.* **Mooney** *a-444r.* **Moreira** *a-153-300, 419r, 444r, 445r.* **Nasser/Netzer** *a-654, 655, 657, 658.* **Newton** *a(p)-480, 481, 483-499, 501-509, 511, 513-516, 518-520, 524, 526, 539; c-526p.* **Irv Novick** *c-375-377, 383.* **Robbins** *a-426p, 429p.* **Robinson** *a-part: 66, 68, 71-73; all: 74-76, 79, 80; c-62, 64, 66, 68-74, 76, 79, 82, 86, 88, 442r, 443r.* **Rogers** *a-466-468, 471-479p, 481p; c-471p, 472p, 473, 474-479p.* **Roussos** *Airwave-76-105(most); c(i) 71, 72, 74-76, 79, 107.* **Russell** *a-481i, 482i.* **Simon/Kirby** *a-440r, 442r.* **Simonson** *a-437-443, 450, 469, 470, 500.* **Dick Sprang** *c-77, 82, 84, 85, 87, 89-93, 95-100, 102, 103i, 104i, 106, 108, 114, 117, 118, 122, 123, 128, 129, 131, 133, 135, 141, 148, 149, 168, 622-624.* **Starlin** *a-481p, 482p; c-503, 504, 567p.* **Starr** *a-444r.* **Toth** *a-442; r-414, 416, 418, 424, 440-441, 443, 444.* **Tuska** *a-486p, 490p.* **Matt Wagner** *c-647-649.* **Wrightson** *c-425.*

DETECTIVE DAN, SECRET OP. 48 (Also see Adventures of Detective Ace King and Bob Scully, The Two-Fisted Hick Detective)
Humor Publ. Co. (Norman Marsh): 1933 (10¢, 10x13", 36 pgs., B&W, one-shot) (3 color, cardboard-c)

nn-By Norman Marsh, 1st comic w/ original-a; 1st newsstand-c; Dick Tracy look-alike; forerunner of Dan Dunn. (Title and Wu Fang character inspired Detective Comics #1 four years later.) (1st comic of a single theme) 1600 3200 4800 9600 - -

DETECTIVE EYE (See Keen Detective Funnies)
Centaur Publications: Nov, 1940 - No. 2, Dec, 1940

1-Air Man (see Keen Detective) & The Eye Sees begins; The Masked Marvel & Dean Denton app. 230 460 690 1449 2450 3450

2-Origin Don Rance and the Mysticape; Binder-a; Frank Thomas-c 122 244 366 769 1297 1825

DETECTIVE PICTURE STORIES (Keen Detective Funnies No. 8 on?)
Comics Magazine Company: Dec, 1936 - No. 5, Apr, 1937
(1st comic of a single theme)

1 (all issues are very scarce) 560 1120 1680 2968 4284 5600

2-The Clock app. (1/37, early app.) 240 480 720 1272 1836 2400

3,4: 4-Eisner-a 160 320 480 848 1224 1600

5-The Clock-c/story (4/37); 1st detective/adventure art by Bob Kane; Bruce Wayne prototype app.(see Funny Pages V3/1) 185 370 555 981 1416 1850

DETECTIVES, THE (TV)
Dell Publishing Co.: No. 1168, Mar-May, 1961 - No. 1240, Oct-Dec, 1961

Four Color 1168 (#1)-Robert Taylor photo-c 9 18 27 65 113 160

Four Color 1219-Robert Taylor, Adam West photo-c 8 16 24 56 93 130

Four Color 1240-Tufts-a; Robert Taylor photo-c 8 16 24 56 93 130

DETECTIVES, INC. (See Eclipse Graphic Album Series)
Eclipse Comics: Apr, 1985 - No. 2, Apr, 1985 ($1.75, both w/April dates)

1,2: 2-Nudity 2.50

DETECTIVES, INC.: A TERROR OF DYING DREAMS
Eclipse Comics: Jun, 1987 - No. 3, Dec, 1987 ($1.75, B&W& sepia)

1-3: Colan-a 2.50

TPB ('99, $19.95) r/series 20.00

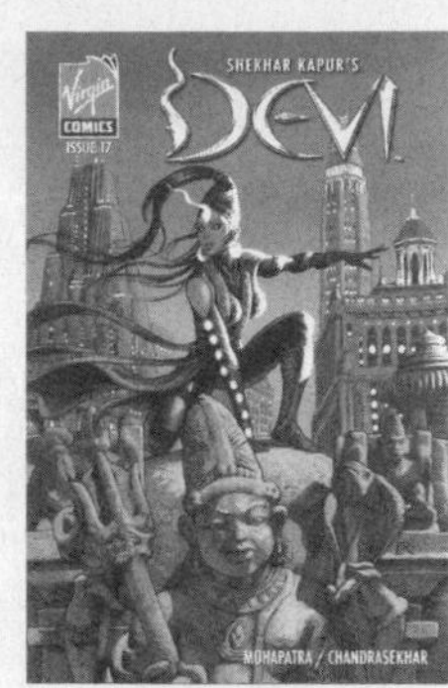

Devi #17 © Virgin Comics

Dexter's Laboratory #14 © CN

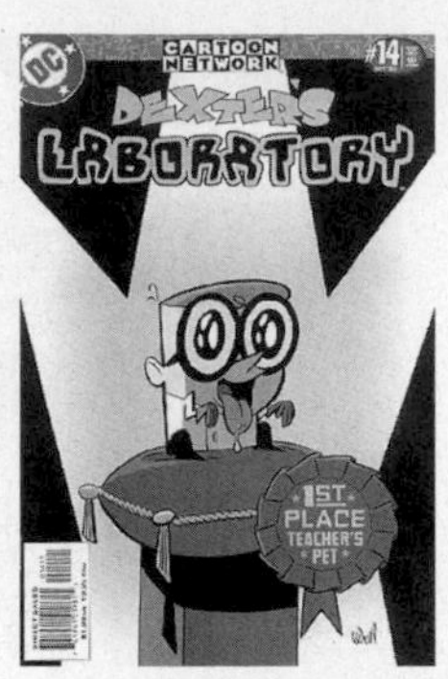

Diary Loves #6 © QUA

	GD 2.0	VG 4.0	FN 6.0	VF 8.0	VF/NM 9.0	NM- 9.2

DETENTION COMICS
DC Comics: Oct, 1996 ($3.50, 56 pgs., one-shot)

1-Robin story by Dennis O'Neil & Norm Breyfogle; Superboy story by Ron Marz & Ron Lim; Warrior story by Ruben Diaz & Joe Phillips; Phillips-c 5.00

DETONATOR (Mike Baron's...)
Image Comics: Nov, 2004 - No. 4 ($2.50/$2.95)

1-4-Mike Baron-s/Mel Rubi-a 3.00

DEVASTATOR
Image Comics/Halloween: 1998 - No. 3 ($2.95, B&W, limited series)

1,2-Hudnall-s/Horn-c/a 3.00

DEVI (Shekhar Kapur's...)
Virgin Comics: July, 2006 - Present ($2.99)

1-20: 1-Mukesh Singh-a/Siddharth Kotian-s. 2-Greg Horn-c 3.00
.../Witchblade (4/08, $2.99) Singh-a/Land-c; continued from Witchblade/Devi 3.00
... Vol. 1 TPB (5/07, $14.99) r/#1-5 and Story from Virgin Comics Preview #0 15.00
... Vol. 2 TPB (9/07, $14.99) r/#6-10; character and cover sketches 15.00

DEVIL CHEF
Dark Horse Comics: July, 1994 ($2.50, B&W, one-shot)

nn 2.50

DEVIL DINOSAUR
Marvel Comics Group: Apr, 1978 - No. 9, Dec, 1978

1-Kirby/Royer-a in all; all have Kirby-c 2 4 6 13 18 22
2-9: 4-7-UFO/sci. fic. 8-Dinoriders-c/sty 2 4 6 8 10 12
... By Jack Kirby Omnibus HC (2007, $29.99, dustjacket) r/#1-9; intro. by Brevoort 30.00

DEVIL DINOSAUR SPRING FLING
Marvel Comics: June, 1997 ($2.99. one-shot)

1-(48pgs.) Moon-Boy-c/app. 3.00

DEVIL-DOG DUGAN (Tales of the Marines No. 4 on)
Atlas Comics (OPI): July, 1956 - No. 3, Nov, 1956

1-Severin-c 14 28 42 76 108 140
2-Iron Mike McGraw x-over; Severin-c 9 18 27 47 61 75
3 8 16 24 42 54 65

DEVIL DOGS
Street & Smith Publishers: 1942

1-Boy Rangers, U.S. Marines 28 56 84 162 261 360

DEVILINA (Magazine)
Atlas/Seaboard: Feb, 1975 - No. 2, May, 1975 (B&W)

1-Art by Reese, Marcos; "The Tempest" adapt. 3 6 9 18 27 35
2 (Low printing) 3 6 9 20 30 40

DEVIL KIDS STARRING HOT STUFF
Harvey Publications (Illustrated Humor): July, 1962 - No. 107, Oct, 1981 (Giant-Size #41-55)

1 (12¢ cover price #1-#41-9/69) 22 44 66 157 291 425
2 11 22 33 79 140 200
3-10 (1/64) 8 16 24 56 93 130
11-20 6 12 18 37 59 80
21-30 4 8 12 26 41 55
31-40: 40-(6/69) 3 6 9 20 30 40
41-50: All 68 pg. Giants 4 8 12 22 34 45
51-55: All 52 pg. Giants 3 6 9 20 30 40
56-70 2 4 6 11 16 20
71-90 2 4 6 8 11 14
91-107 1 2 3 5 6 8

DEVIL'S FOOTPRINTS, THE
Dark Horse Comics: March, 2003 - No. 4, June, 2003 ($2.99, limited series)

1-4-Paul Lee-c/a; Scott Allie-s 3.00

DEXTER COMICS
Dearfield Publ.: Summer, 1948 - No. 5, July, 1949

1-Teen-age humor 11 22 33 60 83 105
2-Junie Prom app. 8 16 24 42 54 65
3-5 7 14 21 35 43 50

DEXTER'S LABORATORY (Cartoon Network)
DC Comics: Sept, 1999 - No. 34, Apr, 2003 ($1.99/$2.25)

1 4.00
2-10: 2-McCracken-s 3.00
11-24, 26-34: 31-Begin $2.25-c. 32-34-Wray-c 2.50
25-(50¢-c) Tartakovsky-s/a; Action Hank-c/app. 2.50

DEXTER THE DEMON (Formerly Melvin The Monster)(See Cartoon Kids & Peter the Little Pest)
Atlas Comics (HPC): No. 7, Sept, 1957

7 8 16 24 42 54 65

DHAMPIRE: STILLBORN
DC Comics (Vertigo): 1996 ($5.95, one-shot, mature)

1-Nancy Collins script; Paul Lee-c/a 6.00

DIARY CONFESSIONS (Formerly Ideal Romance)
Stanmor/Key Publ.(Medal Comics): No. 9, May, 1955 - No. 14, Apr, 1955

9 9 18 27 47 61 75
10-14 7 14 21 35 43 50

DIARY LOVES (Formerly Love Diary #1; G. I. Sweethearts #32 on)
Quality Comics Group: No. 2, Nov, 1949 - No. 31, April, 1953

2-Ward-c/a, 9 pgs. 18 36 54 103 162 220
3 (1/50)-Photo-c begin, end #27? 10 20 30 54 72 90
4-Crandall-a 11 22 33 60 83 105
5-7,10 9 18 27 47 61 75
8,9-Ward-a 6,8 pgs. 8-Gustavson-a; Esther Williams photo-c 14 28 42 76 108 140
11,13,14,17-20 8 16 24 44 57 70
12,15,16-Ward-a 9,7,8 pgs. 12 24 36 69 97 125
21-Ward-a, 7 pgs. 11 22 33 62 86 110
22-31: 31-Whitney-a 8 16 24 442 54 65
NOTE: *Photo c-3-10, 12-27.*

DIARY OF HORROR
Avon Periodicals: December, 1952

1-Hollingsworth-c/a; bondage-c 44 88 132 273 454 635

DIARY SECRETS (Formerly Teen-Age Diary Secrets)(See Giant Comics Ed.)
St. John Publishing Co.: No. 10, Feb, 1952 - No. 30, Sept, 1955

10-Baker-c/a most issues 25 50 75 147 236 325
11-16,18,19 18 36 54 105 165 225
17,20: Kubert-r/Hollywood Confessions #1. 17-r/Teen Age Romances #9 18 36 54 105 165 225
21-30: 22,27-Signed stories by Estrada. 28-Last precode (3/55) 14 28 42 80 115 150
nn-(25¢ giant, nd (1950?)-Baker-c & rebound St. John comics 63 126 189 397 674 950

DICK COLE (Sport Thrills No. 11 on)(See Blue Bolt & Four Most #1)
Curtis Publ./Star Publications: Dec-Jan, 1948-49 - No. 10, June-July, 1950

1-Sgt. Spook; L. B. Cole-c; McWilliams-a; Curt Swan's 1st work 34 68 102 198 319 440
2,5 15 30 45 92 144 195
3,4,6-10: All-L.B. Cole-c. 10-Joe Louis story 23 46 69 133 214 295
Accepted Reprint #7(V1#6 on-c)(1950's)-Reprints #7; L.B. Cole-c 9 18 27 47 61 75
Accepted Reprint #9(nd)-(Reprints #9 & #8-c) 9 18 27 47 61 75
NOTE: ***L. B. Cole** c-1, 3, 4, 6-10. **Al McWilliams** a-6. Dick Cole in 1-9. Baseball c-10. Basketball c-9. Football c-8.*

DICKIE DARE
Eastern Color Printing Co.: 1941 - No. 4, 1942 (#3 on sale 6/15/42)

1-Caniff-a, bondage-c by Everett 60 120 180 378 639 900
2 28 56 84 162 261 360
3,4-Half Scorchy Smith by Noel Sickles who was very influential in Milton Caniff's development 30 60 90 174 280 385

DICK POWELL (Also see A-1 Comics)
Magazine Enterprises: No. 22, 1949 (one shot)

A-1 22-Photo-c 23 46 69 133 214 295

DICK QUICK, ACE REPORTER (See Picture News #10)

DICKS
Caliber Comics: 1997 - No. 4, 1998 ($2.95, B&W)

1-4-Ennis-s/McCrea-c/a; r/Fleetway 3.00
TPB ('98, $12.95) r/series 13.00

DICK'S ADVENTURES
Dell Publishing Co.: No. 245, Sept, 1949

Four Color 245 6 12 18 41 66 90

DICK TRACY (See Famous Feature Stories, Harvey Comics Library, Limited Collectors' Ed., Mammoth Comics, Merry Christmas, The Original..., Popular Comics, Super Book No. 1, 7, 13, 25, Super Comics & Tastee-Freez)

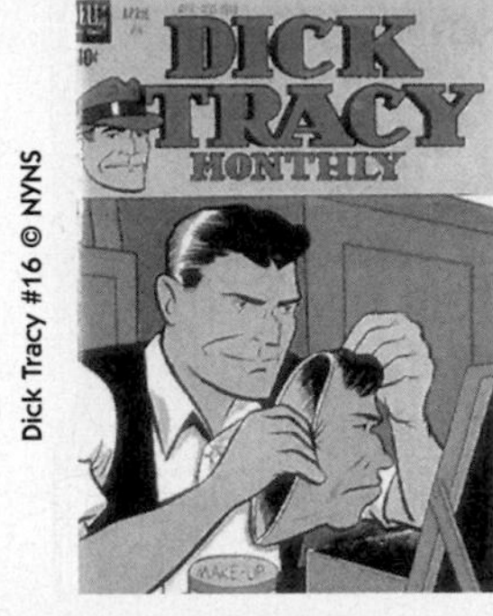

Dick Tracy #16 © NYNS

Dilton's Strange Science #3 © AP

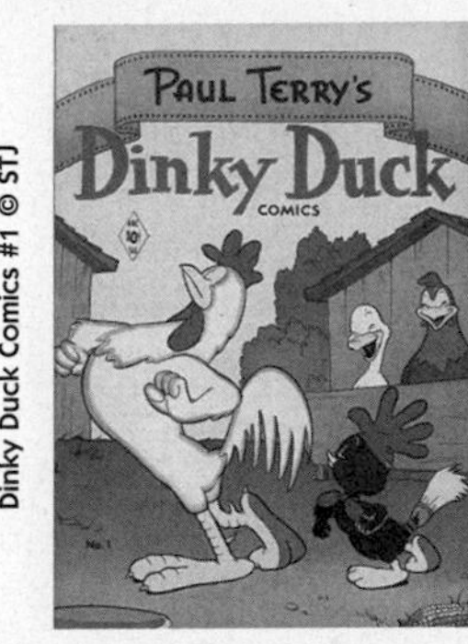

Dinky Duck Comics #1 © STJ

	GD 2.0	VG 4.0	FN 6.0	VF 8.0	VF/NM 9.0	NM- 9.2

DICK TRACY
David McKay Publications: May, 1937 - Jan, 1938

	GD	VG	FN	VF	VF/NM	NM-
Feature Books nn - 100 pgs., partially reprinted as 4-Color No. 1 (appeared before Large Feature Comics, 1st Dick Tracy comic book) (Very Rare-five known copies; two incomplete)	972	1944	2916	6998	12,249	17,500
Feature Books 4 - Reprints nn issue w/new-c	130	260	390	819	1385	1950
Feature Books 6,9	95	190	285	599	1012	1425

DICK TRACY (...Monthly #1-24)
Dell Publishing Co.: 1939 - No. 24, Dec, 1949

	GD	VG	FN	VF	VF/NM	NM-
Large Feature Comic 1 (1939) -Dick Tracy Meets The Blank	180	360	540	1134	1917	2700
Large Feature Comic 4,8	93	186	279	586	993	1400
Large Feature Comic 11,13,15	82	164	246	517	876	1235
Four Color 1(1939)('35-r)	889	1778	2667	6401	11,201	16,000
Four Color 6(1940)('37-r)-(Scarce)	207	414	621	1304	2202	3100
Four Color 8(1940)('38-'39-r)	103	206	309	649	1100	1550
Large Feature Comic 3(1941, Series II)	82	164	246	517	871	1225
Four Color 21('41)('38-r)	78	156	234	491	833	1175
Four Color 34('43)('39-'40-r)	40	80	120	312	581	850
Four Color 56('44)('40-r)	36	72	108	277	514	750
Four Color 96('46)('40-r)	24	48	72	176	326	475
Four Color 133('47)('40-'41-r)	19	38	57	135	250	365
Four Color 163('47)('41-r)	17	34	51	120	223	325
Four Color 215('48)-Titled "Sparkle Plenty", Dick Tracy-r	11	22	33	79	140	200
1(1/48)('34-r)	38	76	114	285	518	750
2,3	20	40	60	150	268	385
4-10	17	34	51	128	227	325
11-18: 13-Bondage-c	14	28	42	99	175	250
19-1st app. Sparkle Plenty, B.O. Plenty & Gravel Gertie in a 3-pg. strip not by Gould	14	28	42	103	184	265
20-1st app. Sam Catchem; c/a not by Gould	13	26	39	95	168	240
21-24-Only 2 pg. Gould-a in each	13	26	39	90	160	230

NOTE: *No. 19-24 have a 2 pg. biography of a famous villain illustrated by **Gould**: 19-Little Face; 20-Flattop; 21-Breathless Mahoney; 22-Measles; 23-Itchy; 24-The Brow.*

DICK TRACY (Continued from Dell series)(...Comics Monthly #25-140)
Harvey Publications: No. 25, Mar, 1950 - No. 145, April, 1961

	GD	VG	FN	VF	VF/NM	NM-
25-Flat Top-c/story (also #26,27)	14	28	42	99	175	250
26-28,30: 28-Bondage-c. 28,29-The Brow-c/stories	10	20	30	73	129	185
29-1st app. Gravel Gertie in a Gould-r	12	24	36	87	156	225
31,32,34,35,37-40: 40-Intro/origin 2-way wrist radio (6/51)	9	18	27	61	103	145
33- "Measles the Teen-Age Dope Pusher"	10	20	30	73	129	185
36-1st app. B.O. Plenty in a Gould-r	10	20	30	73	129	185
41-50	8	16	24	54	90	125
51-56,58-80: 51-2pgs Powell-a	7	14	21	47	76	105
57-1st app. Sam Catchem in a Gould-r	8	16	24	54	90	125
81-99,101-140: 99-109-Painted-c	6	12	18	43	69	95
100, 141-145 (25¢)(titled "Dick Tracy")	7	14	21	47	76	105

NOTE: ***Powell** a(1-2pgs.)-43, 44, 104, 108, 109, 145. No. 110-120, 141-145 are all reprints from earlier issues.*

DICK TRACY ("Reuben Award" series)
Blackthorne Publishing: 12/84 - No. 24, 6/89 (1-12: $5.95; 13-24: $6.95, B&W, 76 pgs.)

	GD	VG	FN	VF	VF/NM	NM-
1-8-1st printings; hard-c ed. ($14.95)						18.00
1-3-2nd printings, 1986; hard-c ed.						18.00
1-12-1st & 2nd printings; squarebound. thick-c						10.00
13-24 ($6.95): 21,22-Regular-c & stapled						10.00

NOTE: ***Gould** daily & Sunday strip-r in all. 1-12 r-12/31/45-4/5/49; 13-24 r-7/13/41-2/20/44.*

DICK TRACY (Disney)
WD Publications: 1990 - No. 3, 1990 (color) (Book 3 adapts 1990 movie)

	GD	VG	FN	VF	VF/NM	NM-
Book One ($3.95, 52pgs.)-Kyle Baker-c/a						6.00
Book Two, Three ($5.95, 68pgs.)-Direct sale						6.00
Book Two, Three ($2.95, 68pgs.)-Newsstand						3.00

DICK TRACY ADVENTURES
Gladstone Publishing: May, 1991 ($4.95, 76 pgs.)

	GD	VG	FN	VF	VF/NM	NM-
1-Reprints strips 2/1/42-4/18/42						5.00

DICK TRACY, EXPLOITS OF
Rosdon Books, Inc.: 1946 ($1.00, hard-c strip reprints)

	GD	VG	FN	VF	VF/NM	NM-
1-Reprints the near complete case of "The Brow" from 6/12/44 to 9/24/44 (story starts a few weeks late)	25	50	75	145	233	320
with dust jacket...	40	80	120	235	380	525

DICK TRACY MONTHLY/WEEKLY
Blackthorne Publishing: May, 1986 - No. 99, 1989 ($2.00, B&W)
(Becomes Weekly #26 on)

	GD	VG	FN	VF	VF/NM	NM-
1-60: Gould-r. 30,31-Mr. Crime app.						3.00
61-90						4.00
91-95						6.00
96-99-Low print	1	2	3	5	7	9

NOTE: *#1-10 reprint strips 3/10/40-7/13/41; #10(pg.8)-51 reprint strips 4/6/49-12/31/55; #52-99 reprint strips 12/26/56-4/26/64.*

DICK TRACY SPECIAL
Blackthorne Publ.: Jan, 1988 - No. 3, Aug. (no month), 1989 ($2.95, B&W)

	GD	VG	FN	VF	VF/NM	NM-
1-3: 1-Origin D. Tracy; 4/strips 10/12/31-3/30/32						3.00

DICK TRACY: THE EARLY YEARS
Blackthorne Publishing: Aug, 1987 - No. 4, Aug (no month) 1989 ($6.95, B&W, 76 pgs.)

	GD	VG	FN	VF	VF/NM	NM-
1-3: 1-4-r/strips 10/12/31(1st daily)-8/31/32 & Sunday strips 6/12/32-8/28/32; Big Boy apps. in #1-3	1	2	3	4	5	7
4 ($2.95, 52pgs.)						3.00

DICK TRACY UNPRINTED STORIES
Blackthorne Publishing: Sept, 1987 - No. 4, June, 1988 ($2.95, B&W)

	GD	VG	FN	VF	VF/NM	NM-
1-4: Reprints strips 1/1/56 12/25/56						3.00

DICK TURPIN (See Legend of Young...)

DIE-CUT
Marvel Comics UK, Ltd: Nov, 1993 - No. 4, Feb, 1994 ($1.75, limited series)

	GD	VG	FN	VF	VF/NM	NM-
1-4: 1-Die-cut-c; The Beast app.						2.50

DIE-CUT VS. G-FORCE
Marvel Comics UK, Ltd: Nov, 1993 - No. 2, Dec, 1993 ($2.75, limited series)

	GD	VG	FN	VF	VF/NM	NM-
1,2-($2.75)-Gold foil-c on both						2.75

DIE, MONSTER, DIE (See Movie Classics)

DIGIMON DIGITAL MONSTERS (TV)
Dark Horse Comics: May, 2000 - No. 12, Nov, 2000 ($2.95/$2.99)

	GD	VG	FN	VF	VF/NM	NM-
1-12						3.00

DIGITEK
Marvel UK, Ltd: Dec, 1992 - No. 4, Mar, 1993 ($1.95/$2.25, mini-series)

	GD	VG	FN	VF	VF/NM	NM-
1-4: 3-Deathlock-c/story						2.50

DILLY (Dilly Duncan from Daredevil Comics; see Boy Comics #57)
Lev Gleason Publications: May, 1953 - No. 3, Sept, 1953

	GD	VG	FN	VF	VF/NM	NM-
1-Teenage; Biro-c	7	14	21	37	46	55
2,3-Biro-c	5	10	15	24	30	35

DILTON'S STRANGE SCIENCE (See Pep Comics #78)
Archie Comics: May, 1989 - No. 5, May, 1990 (75¢/$1.00)

	GD	VG	FN	VF	VF/NM	NM-
1-5						3.00

DIME COMICS
Newsbook Publ. Corp.: 1945; 1951

	GD	VG	FN	VF	VF/NM	NM-
1-Silver Streak-c/sty; L.B. Cole-c; Japanese war-c	87	174	261	548	924	1300
1(1951)	11	22	33	62	86	110

DINGBATS (See 1st Issue Special)

DING DONG
Compix/Magazine Enterprises: Summer?, 1946 - No. 5, 1947 (52 pgs.)

	GD	VG	FN	VF	VF/NM	NM-
1-Funny animal	27	54	81	156	251	345
2 (9/46)	14	28	42	80	115	150
3 (Wint '46-'47) - 5	11	22	33	62	86	110

DINKY DUCK (Paul Terry's...) (See Approved Comics, Blue Ribbon, Giant Comics Edition #5A & New Terrytoons)
St. John Publishing Co./Pines No. 16 on: Nov, 1951 - No. 16, Sept, 1955; No. 16, Fall, 1956; No. 17, May, 1957 - No. 19, Summer, 1958

	GD	VG	FN	VF	VF/NM	NM-
1-Funny animal	13	26	39	72	101	130
2	8	16	24	42	54	65
3-10	6	12	18	29	36	42
11-16(9/55)	6	12	18	27	33	38
16(Fall, '56) - 19	5	10	15	22	26	30

DINKY DUCK & HASHIMOTO-SAN (See Deputy Dawg Presents...)

DINO (TV)(The Flintstones)
Charlton Publications: Aug, 1973 - No. 20, Jan, 1977 (Hanna-Barbera)

	GD	VG	FN	VF	VF/NM	NM-
1	3	6	9	18	27	35

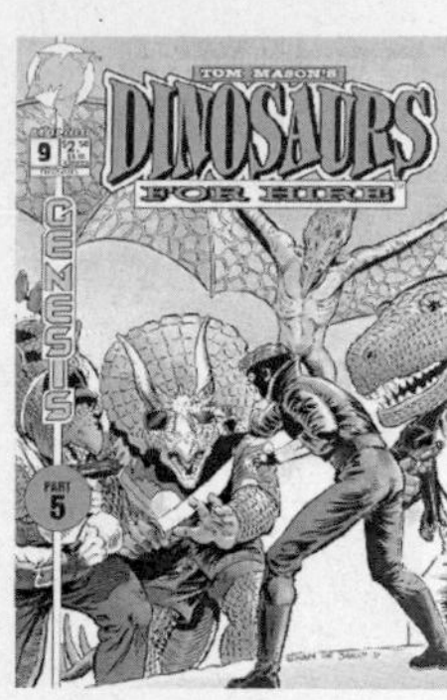

Dinosaurs For Hire #9 © Tom Mason

Dirty Pair II #5 © Haruka Takachiho

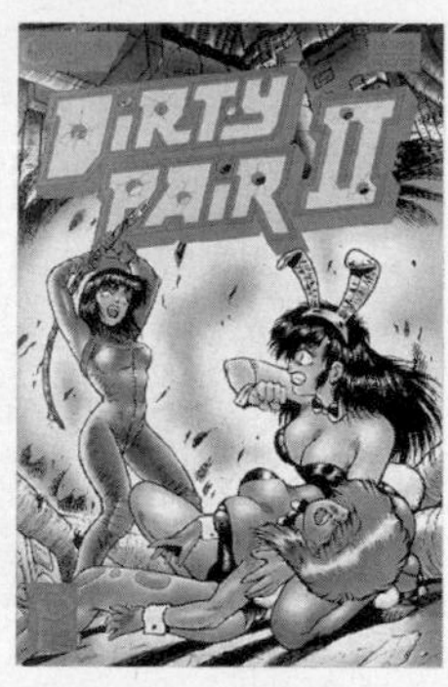

Disney's Aladdin #2 © DIS

GD VG FN VF VF/NM NM-
2.0 4.0 6.0 8.0 9.0 9.2

2-10 2 4 6 10 14 18
11-20 2 4 6 8 10 12
Digest nn (w/Xerox Pub., 1974) (low print run) 2 4 6 11 16 20

DINO ISLAND
Mirage Studios: Feb, 1994 - No. 2, Mar, 1994 ($2.75, limited series)
1,2-By Jim Lawson 2.75

DINO RIDERS
Marvel Comics: Feb, 1989 - No. 3, 1989 ($1.00)
1-3: Based on toys 3.00

DINOSAUR REX
Upshot Graphics (Fantagraphics): 1986 - No. 3, 1986 ($2.00, limited series)
1-3 2.50

DINOSAURS, A CELEBRATION
Marvel Comics (Epic): Oct, 1992 - No. 4, Oct, 1992 ($4.95, lim. series, 52 pgs.)
1-4: 2-Bolton painted-c 5.00

DINOSAURS ATTACK! THE GRAPHIC NOVEL
Eclipse Comics: 1991 ($3.95, coated stock, stiff-c)
Book One- Based on Topps trading cards 4.00

DINOSAURS FOR HIRE
Malibu Comics: Feb, 1993 - No. 12, Feb, 1994 ($1.95/$2.50)
1-12: 1,10-Flip bk. 8-Bagged w/Skycap; Staton-c. 10-Flip book 2.50

DINOSAURS GRAPHIC NOVEL (TV)
Disney Comics: 1992 - No. 2, 1993 ($2.95, 52 pgs.)
1,2-Staton-a; based on Dinosaurs TV show 3.00

DINOSAURUS
Dell Publishing Co.: No. 1120, Aug, 1960
Four Color 1120-Movie, painted-c 8 16 24 56 93 130

DIPPY DUCK
Atlas Comics (OPI): October, 1957
1-Maneely-a; code approved 10 20 30 56 76 95

DIRECTORY TO A NONEXISTENT UNIVERSE
Eclipse Comics: Dec, 1987 ($2.00, B&W)
1 2.50

DIRTY DOZEN (See Movie Classics)

DIRTY PAIR (Manga)
Eclipse Comics: Dec, 1988 - No. 4, Apr, 1989 ($2.00, B&W, limited series)
1-4: Japanese manga with original stories 3.00
...: Start the Violence (Dark Horse, 9/99, $2.95) r/B&W stories in color from Dark Horse Presents #132-134; covers by Warren & Pearson 3.00

DIRTY PAIR: FATAL BUT NOT SERIOUS (Manga)
Dark Horse Comics: July, 1995 - No. 5, Nov, 1995 ($2.95, limited series)
1-5 3.00

DIRTY PAIR: RUN FROM THE FUTURE (Manga)
Dark Horse Comics: Jan, 2000 - No. 4, Mar, 2000 ($2.95, limited series)
1-4-Warren-s/c/a. Var.-c by Hughes(1), Stelfreeze(2), Timm(3), Ramos(4) 3.00

DIRTY PAIR: SIM HELL (Manga)
Dark Horse Comics: May, 1993 - No. 4, Aug, 1993 ($2.50, B&W, limited series)
1-4 3.00
...Remastered #1-4 (5/01 - 8/01) reprints in color, with pin-up gallery 3.00

DIRTY PAIR II (Manga)
Eclipse Comics: June, 1989 - No. 5, Mar, 1990 ($2.00, B&W, limited series)
1-5: 3-Cover is misnumbered as #1 3.00

DIRTY PAIR III, THE (A Plague of Angels) (Manga)
Eclipse Comics: Aug, 1990 - No. 5, Aug, 1991 ($2.00/$2.25, B&W, lim. series)
1-5 3.00

DISHMAN
Eclipse Comics: Sept, 1988 ($2.50, B&W, 52 pgs.)
1 2.50

DISNEY AFTERNOON, THE (TV)
Marvel Comics: Nov, 1994 - No. 10?, Aug, 1995 ($1.50)
1-10: 3-w/bound-in Power Ranger Barcode Card 3.00

DISNEY COMIC ALBUM
Disney Comics: 1990(no month, year) - No. 8, 1991 ($6.95/$7.95)
1,2 ($6.95): 1-Donald Duck and Gyro Gearloose by Barks(r). 2-Uncle Scrooge by Barks(r); Jr. Woodchucks app. 9.00
3-8: 3-Donald Duck-r/F.C. 308 by Barks; begin $7.95-c. 4-Mickey Mouse Meets the Phantom Blot; r/M.M Club Parade (censored 1956 version of story). 5-Chip `n' Dale Rescue Rangers; new-a. 6-Uncle Scrooge. 7-Donald Duck in Too Many Pets; Barks-r(4) including F.C. #29. 8-Super Goof; r/S.G. #1, D.D. #102 9.00

DISNEY COMIC HITS
Marvel Comics: Oct, 1995 - No. 16, Jan, 1997 ($1.50/$2.50)
1-16: 4-Toy Story. 6-Aladdin. 7-Pocahontas. 10-The Hunchback of Notre Dame (Same story in Disney's The Hunchback of Notre Dame). 13-Aladdin and the Forty Thieves 4.00

DISNEY COMICS
Disney Comics: June, 1990
Boxed set of #1 issues includes Donald Duck Advs., Ducktales, Chip 'n Dale Rescue Rangers, Roger Rabbit, Mickey Mouse Advs. & Goofy Advs.; limited to 10,000 sets 2 4 6 9 12 15

DISNEYLAND BIRTHDAY PARTY (Also see Dell Giants)
Gladstone Publishing Co.: Aug, 1985 ($2.50)
1-Reprints Dell Giant with new-photo-c 2 4 6 8 10 12
...Comics Digest #1-(Digest) 2 4 6 8 11 14

DISNEYLAND MAGAZINE
Fawcett Publications: Feb. 15, 1972 - ? (10-1/4"x12-5/8", 20 pgs, weekly)
1-One or two page painted art features on Dumbo, Snow White, Lady & the Tramp, the Aristocats, Brer Rabbit, Peter Pan, Cinderella, Jungle Book, Alice & Pinocchio. Most standard characters app. 3 6 9 16 23 30

DISNEYLAND, USA (See Dell Giant No. 30)

DISNEY MOVIE BOOK
Walt Disney Productions (Gladstone): 1990 ($7.95, 8-1/2"x11", 52 pgs.) (w/pull-out poster)
1-Roger Rabbit in Tummy Trouble; from the cartoon film strips adapted to the comic format. Ron Dias-c 2 4 6 8 10 12

DISNEY'S ACTION CLUB
Acclaim Books: 1997 - No. 4 ($4.50, digest size)
1-4: 1-Hercules. 4-Mighty Ducks 4.50

DISNEY'S ALADDIN (Movie)
Marvel Comics: Oct, 1994 - No. 11, 1995 ($1.50)
1-11 3.00

DISNEY'S BEAUTY AND THE BEAST (Movie)
Marvel Comics: Sept, 1994 - No. 13, 1995 ($1.50)
1-13 3.00

DISNEY'S BEAUTY AND THE BEAST HOLIDAY SPECIAL
Acclaim Books: 1997 ($4.50, digest size, one-shot)
1-Based on The Enchanted Christmas video 4.50

DISNEY'S COLOSSAL COMICS COLLECTION
Disney Comics: 1991 - No. 10, 1993 ($1.95, digest-size, 96/132 pgs.)
1-10: Ducktales, Talespin, Chip 'n Dale's Rescue Rangers. 4-r/Darkwing Duck #1-4. 6-Goofy begins. 8-Little Mermaid 5.00

DISNEY'S COMICS IN 3-D
Disney Comics: 1992 ($2.95, w/glasses, polybagged)
1-Infinity-c; Barks, Rosa, Gottfredson-r 5.00

DISNEY'S ENCHANTING STORIES
Acclaim Books: 1997 - No. 5 ($4.50, digest size)
1-5: 1-Hercules. 2-Pocahontas 4.50

DISNEY'S NEW ADVENTURES OF BEAUTY AND THE BEAST (Also see Beauty and the Beast & Disney's Beauty and the Beast)
Disney Comics: 1992 - No. 2, 1992 ($1.50, limited series)
1,2-New stories based on movie 3.00

DISNEY'S POCAHONTAS (Movie)
Marvel Comics: 1995 ($4.95, one-shot)
1-Movie adaptation 1 2 3 4 5 7

DISNEY'S TALESPIN LIMITED SERIES: "TAKE OFF" (TV) (See Talespin)
W. D. Publications (Disney Comics): Jan, 1991 - No. 4, Apr, 1991 ($1.50, lim. series, 52 pgs.)
1-4: Based on animated series; 4 part origin 2.50

DISNEY'S TARZAN (Movie)

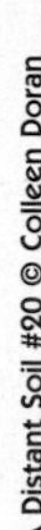
A Distant Soil #20 © Colleen Doran

Dixie Dugan #1 © McNaught Syndicate

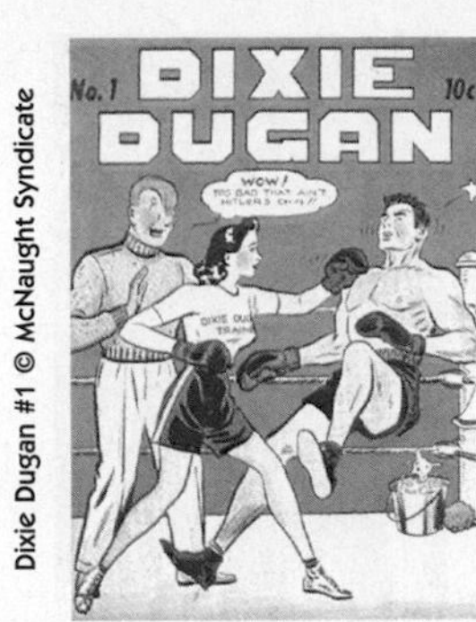

DMZ #27 © Wood & Burchielli

	GD 2.0	VG 4.0	FN 6.0	VF 8.0	VF/NM 9.0	NM- 9.2

Dark Horse Comics: June, 1999 - No. 2, July, 1999 ($2.95, limited series)

	GD	VG	FN	VF	VF/NM	NM-
1,2: Movie adaptation						3.00

DISNEY'S THE LION KING (Movie)
Marvel Comics: July, 1994 - No. 2, July, 1994 ($1.50, limited series)

	GD	VG	FN	VF	VF/NM	NM-
1,2: 2-part movie adaptation						3.00
1-($2.50, 52 pgs.)-Complete story						5.00

DISNEY'S THE LITTLE MERMAID (Movie)
Marvel Comics: Sept, 1994 - No. 12, 1995 ($1.50)

	GD	VG	FN	VF	VF/NM	NM-
1-12						4.00

DISNEY'S THE LITTLE MERMAID LIMITED SERIES (Movie)
Disney Comics: Feb, 1992 - No. 4, May, 1992 ($1.50, limited series)

	GD	VG	FN	VF	VF/NM	NM-
1-4: Peter David scripts						3.00

DISNEY'S THE LITTLE MERMAID: UNDERWATER ENGAGEMENTS
Acclaim Books: 1997 ($4.50, digest size)

	GD	VG	FN	VF	VF/NM	NM-
1-Flip book						4.50

DISNEY'S THE HUNCHBACK OF NOTRE DAME (Movie)(See Disney's Comic Hits #10)
Marvel Comics: July, 1996 ($4.95, squarebound, one-shot)

	GD	VG	FN	VF	VF/NM	NM-
1-Movie adaptation.	1	2	3	4	5	7

NOTE: A different edition of this series was sold at Wal-Mart stores with new covers depicting scenes from the 1989 feature film. Inside contents and price were identical.

DISNEY'S THE THREE MUSKETEERS (Movie)
Marvel Comics: Jan, 1994 - No. 2, Feb, 1994 ($1.50, limited series)

	GD	VG	FN	VF	VF/NM	NM-
1,2-Morrow-c; Spiegle-a; Movie adaptation						2.50

DISNEY'S TOY STORY (Movie)
Marvel Comics: Dec, 1995 ($4.95, one-shot)

	GD	VG	FN	VF	VF/NM	NM-
nn-Adaptation of film	1	2	3	4	5	7

DISTANT SOIL, A (1st Series)
WaRP Graphics: Dec, 1983 - No. 9, Mar 1986 ($1.50, B&W)

	GD	VG	FN	VF	VF/NM	NM-
1-Magazine size						4.00
2-9: 2-4 are magazine size						3.00

NOTE: Second printings exist of #1, 2, 3 & 6.

DISTANT SOIL, A
Donning (Star Blaze): Mar, 1989 ($12.95, trade paperback)

	GD	VG	FN	VF	VF/NM	NM-
nn-new material						13.00

DISTANT SOIL, A (2nd Series)
Aria Press/Image Comics (Highbrow Entertainment) #15 on:
June, 1991 - Present ($1.75/$2.50/$2.95/$3.95, B&W)

	GD	VG	FN	VF	VF/NM	NM-
1-27: 13-$2.95-c begins. 14-Sketchbook. 15-(8/96)-1st Image issue						3.00
29-33,35,37-($3.95)						4.00
34-($4.95, 64 pages) includes sketchbook pages						5.00
36,38-($4.50) 36-Back-up story by Darnall & Doran. 38-Includes sketch pages						4.50
The Aria ('01, $16.95,TPB) r/#26-31						17.00
The Ascendant ('98, $18.95,TPB) r/#13-25						19.00
The Gathering ('97, $18.95,TPB) r/#1-13; intro. Neil Gaiman						19.00
Vol. 4: Coda (2005, $17.99, TPB) r/#32-38						18.00

NOTE: Four separate printings exist for #1 and are clearly marked. Second printings exist of #2-4 and are also clearly marked.

DISTANT SOIL, A: IMMIGRANT SONG
Donning (Star Blaze): Aug, 1987 ($6.95, trade paperback)

	GD	VG	FN	VF	VF/NM	NM-
nn-new material						7.00

DISTRICT X (Also see X-Men titles) (Also see Mutopia X)
Marvel Comics: July, 2004 - No. 14, Aug, 2005 ($2.99)

	GD	VG	FN	VF	VF/NM	NM-
1-14: 1-3-Bishop app.; Yardin-a/Hine-s						3.00
...Vol. 1: Mr. M (2005, $14.99) r/#1-6; sketch page by Yardin						15.00
...Vol. 2: Underground (2005, $19.99) r/#7-14; prologue from X-Men Unlimited #2						20.00

DIVER DAN (TV)
Dell Publishing Co.: Feb-Apr, 1962 - No. 2, June-Aug, 1962

	GD	VG	FN	VF	VF/NM	NM-
Four Color 1254(#1), 2	5	10	15	34	55	75

DIVINE RIGHT
Image Comics (WildStorm Prod.): Sept, 1997 - No. 12, Nov, 1999 ($2.50)

	GD	VG	FN	VF	VF/NM	NM-
Preview						5.00
1,2: 1-Jim Lee-s/a(p)/c, 1-Variant-c by Charest						4.00
1-($3.50)-Voyager Pack w/Stormwatch preview						3.50
1-American Entertainment Ed.						6.00
2-Variant-c of Exotica & Blaze						5.00
3-Chromium-c by Jim Lee						5.00
3-12: 3-5-Fairchild & Lynch app. 4-American Entertainment Ed. 8-Two covers. 9-1st DC issue. 11,12-Divine Intervention pt. 1,4						3.00
5-Pacific Comicon Ed.						6.00
6-Glow in the dark variant-c, European Tour Edition						20.00
...Book One TPB (2002, $17.95) r/#1-7						18.00
...Book Two TPB (2002, $17.95) r/#8-12 & Divine Intervention Gen13, ...Wildcats						18.00
...Collected Edition #1-3 ($5.95, TPB) 1-r/#1,2. 2-r/#3,4. 3-r/#5,6						6.00
Divine Intervention/Gen 13 (11/99, $2.50) Part 3; D'Anda-a						2.50
Divine Intervention/Wildcats (11/99, $2.50) Part 2; D'Anda-a						2.50

DIVISION 13 (See Comic's Greatest World)
Dark Horse Comics: Sept, 1994 - Jan, 1995 ($2.50, color)

	GD	VG	FN	VF	VF/NM	NM-
1-4: Giffen story in all. 1-Art Adams-c						2.50

DIXIE DUGAN (See Big Shot, Columbia Comics & Feature Funnies)
McNaught Syndicate/Columbia/Publication Ent.: July, 1942 - No. 13, 1949
(Strip reprints in all)

	GD	VG	FN	VF	VF/NM	NM-
1-Joe Palooka x-over by Ham Fisher	27	54	81	158	254	350
2	15	30	45	85	130	175
3	12	24	36	69	97	125
4,5(1945-46)-Bo strip-r	10	20	30	54	72	90
6-13(1/47-49): 6-Paperdoll cut-outs	9	18	27	47	61	75

DIXIE DUGAN
Prize Publications (Headline): V3#1, Nov, 1951 - V4#4, Feb, 1954

	GD	VG	FN	VF	VF/NM	NM-
V3#1	10	20	30	54	72	90
2-4	7	14	21	35	43	50
V4#1-4(#5-8)	6	12	18	28	34	40

DIZZY DAMES
American Comics Group (B&M Distr. Co.): Sept-Oct, 1952 - No. 6, Jul-Aug, 1953

	GD	VG	FN	VF	VF/NM	NM-
1-Whitney-c	17	34	51	98	154	210
2	11	22	33	60	83	105
3-6	9	18	27	50	65	80

DIZZY DON COMICS
F. E. Howard Publications/Dizzy Don Ent. Ltd (Canada): 1942 - No. 22, Oct, 1946; No. 3, Apr, 1947 - No. 4, Sept./Oct., 1947 (Most B&W)

	GD	VG	FN	VF	VF/NM	NM-
1 (B&W)	22	44	66	127	204	280
2 (B&W)	14	28	42	80	115	150
4-21 (B&W)	12	24	36	67	94	120
22-Full color, 52 pgs.	22	44	66	127	204	280
3 (4/47), 4 (9-10/47)-Full color, 52 pgs.	22	44	66	127	204	280

DIZZY DUCK (Formerly Barnyard Comics)
Standard Comics: No. 32, Nov, 1950 - No. 39, Mar, 1952

	GD	VG	FN	VF	VF/NM	NM-
32-Funny animal	10	20	30	54	72	90
33-39	6	12	18	31	38	45

DMZ
DC Comics (Vertigo): Jan, 2006 - Present ($2.99)

	GD	VG	FN	VF	VF/NM	NM-
1-Brian Wood-s/Riccardo Burchielli-a						4.00
1-(2008, no cover price) Convention Exclusive promotional edition						3.00
2-33: 2-10-Brian Wood-s/Riccardo Burchielli-a. 11-Donaldson-a. 12-Wood-s/a						3.00
...: Body of a Journalist TPB (2007, $12.99) r/#6-12; intro. by D. Randall Blythe						13.00
...: Friendly Fire TPB (2008, $12.99) r/#18-22; intro. by Sgt. John G. Ford						13.00
...: On the Ground TPB (2006, $9.99) r/#1-5; intro. by Brian Azzarello						10.00
...: Public Works TPB (2007, $12.99) r/#13-17; intro. by Cory Doctorow						13.00

DNAGENTS (The New DNAgents V2/1 on)(Also see Surge)
Eclipse Comics: March, 1983 - No. 24, July, 1985 ($1.50, Baxter paper)

	GD	VG	FN	VF	VF/NM	NM-
1,24: 1-Origin. 4-Amber app. 24-Dave Stevens-c						3.00
2-23: 8-Infinity-c						2.50

DOBERMAN (See Sgt. Bilko's Private...)

DOBIE GILLIS (See The Many Loves of...)

DOC CHAOS: THE STRANGE ATTRACTOR
Vortex Comics: Apr, 1990 - No. 3, 1990 ($3.00, 32 pgs.)

	GD	VG	FN	VF	VF/NM	NM-
1-3: The Lust For Order						3.00

DOC FRANKENSTEIN
Burlyman Entertainment: Nov, 2004 - Present ($3.50)

	GD	VG	FN	VF	VF/NM	NM-
1-6-Wachowski brothers-s/Skroce-a						3.50

DOCK WALLOPER (Ed Burns' ...)
Virgin Comics: Nov, 2007 - No. 5, Jun, 2008 ($2.99)

Doc Savage - Curse of the Fire God #4 © Condé Nast

Doctor Fate #4 © DC

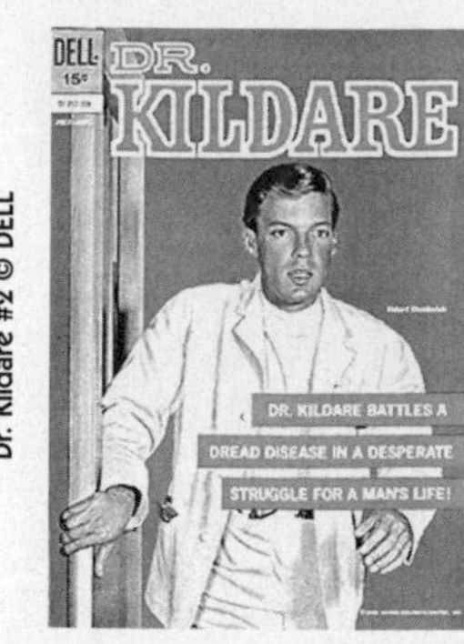

Dr. Kildare #2 © DELL

	GD 2.0	VG 4.0	FN 6.0	VF 8.0	VF/NM 9.0	NM- 9.2

GD 2.0 VG 4.0 FN 6.0 VF 8.0 VF/NM 9.0 NM- 9.2

1-5-Burns & Palmiotti-s/Siju Thomas-a; Prohibition time 3.00

DOC SAMSON (Also see Incredible Hulk)
Marvel Comics: Jan, 1996 - No. 4, Apr, 1996 ($1.95, limited series)
1-4: 1-Hulk c/app. 2-She-Hulk-c/app. 3-Punisher-c/app. 4-Polaris-c/app. 2.50

DOC SAMSON (Incredible Hulk)
Marvel Comics: Mar, 2006 - No. 5, July, 2006 ($2.99, limited series)
1-5: 1-DiFilippo-s/Fiorentino-a. 3-Conner-c 3.00

DOC SAVAGE
Gold Key: Nov, 1966
1-Adaptation of the Thousand-Headed Man; James Bama c-r/1964 Doc Savage paperback 10 20 30 73 129 185

DOC SAVAGE (Also see Giant-Size...)
Marvel Comics Group: Oct, 1972 - No. 8, Jan, 1974
1 3 6 9 18 27 35
2,3-Steranko-c 2 4 6 13 18 22
4-8 2 4 6 8 11 14
NOTE: *Gil Kane c-5, 6.* ***Mooney*** *a-1i. No. 1, 2 adapts pulp story "The Man of Bronze"; No. 3, 4 adapts "Death in Silver"; No. 5, 6 adapts "The Monsters"; No. 7, 8 adapts "The Brand of The Werewolf".*

DOC SAVAGE (Magazine)
Marvel Comics Group: Aug, 1975 - No. 8, Spring, 1977 ($1.00, B&W)
1-Cover from movie poster; Ron Ely photo-c 3 6 9 14 20 25
2-5: 3-Buscema-a. 5-Adams-a(1 pg.), Rogers-a(1 pg) 2 4 6 8 11 14
6-8 2 4 6 9 13 16

DOC SAVAGE
DC Comics: Nov, 1987 - No. 4, Feb, 1988 ($1.75, limited series)
1-4 3.00

DOC SAVAGE
DC Comics: Nov, 1988 - No. 24, Oct, 1990 ($1.75/$2.00: #13-24)
1-16,19-24 3.00
17,18-Shadow x-over 4.00
Annual 1 (1989, $3.50, 68 pgs.) 4.00

DOC SAVAGE COMICS (Also see Shadow Comics)
Street & Smith Publ.: May, 1940 - No. 20, Oct, 1943 (1st app. in Doc Savage pulp, 3/33)
1-Doc Savage, Cap Fury, Danny Garrett, Mark Mallory, The Whisperer, Captain Death, Billy the Kid, Sheriff Pete & Treasure Island begin; Norgil, the Magician app. 489 978 1467 3521 6161 8800
2-Origin & 1st app. Ajax, the Sun Man; Danny Garrett, The Whisperer end; classic sci-fi cover 203 406 609 1279 2165 3050
3 128 256 384 806 1366 1925
4-Treasure Island ends; Tuska-a 103 206 309 649 1100 1550
5-Origin & 1st app. Astron, the Crocodile Queen, not in #9 & 11; Norgi the Magician app.; classic-c 93 186 279 586 993 1400
6-10: 6-Cap Fury ends; origin & only app. Red Falcon in Astron story. 8-Mark Mallory ends; Charlie McCarthy app. on-c plus true life story. 9-Supersnipe app. 10-Origin & only app. The Thunderbolt 61 122 183 384 647 910
11,12 52 104 156 322 536 750
V2#1-6,8(#13-18,20?0): 15-Origin of Ajax the Sun Man; Jack Benny on-c; Hitler app. 16-The Pulp Hero, The Avenger app.; Fanny Brice story. 17-Sun Man ends; Nick Carter begins; Duffy's Tavern part photo-c & story. 18-Huckleberry Finn part-c/story. 19-Henny Youngman part photo-c & life story. 20-Only all funny-c w/Huckleberry Finn 47 94 141 291 483 675
V2#7-Classic Devil-c 52 104 156 322 536 750

DOC SAVAGE: CURSE OF THE FIRE GOD
Dark Horse Comics: Sept, 1995 - No, 4, Dec, 1995 ($2.95, limited series)
1-4 3.00

DOC SAVAGE: THE MAN OF BRONZE
Skylark Pub: Mar, 1979, 68pgs. (B&W comic digest, 5-1/4x7-5/8")(low print)
15406-0: Whitman-a, 60 pgs., new comics 4 8 12 22 34 45

DOC SAVAGE: THE MAN OF BRONZE
Millennium Publications: 1991 - No. 4, 1991 ($2.50, limited series)
1-4: 1-Bronze logo 3.00
...: The Manual of Bronze 1 ($2.50, B&W, color, one-shot)-Unpublished proposed Doc Savage strip in color, B&W strip-r 3.00

DOC SAVAGE: THE MAN OF BRONZE, DOOM DYNASTY
Millennium Publ.: 1992 (Says 1991) - No. 2, 1992 ($2.50, limited series)
1,2 3.00

DOC SAVAGE: THE MAN OF BRONZE - REPEL
Innovation Publishing: 1992 ($2.50)
1-Dave Dorman painted-c 3.00

DOC SAVAGE: THE MAN OF BRONZE THE DEVIL'S THOUGHTS
Millennium Publ.: 1992 (Says 1991) - No. 3, 1992 ($2.50, limited series)
1-3 3.00

DOC STEARN...MR. MONSTER (See Mr. Monster)

DR. ANTHONY KING, HOLLYWOOD LOVE DOCTOR
Minoan Publishing Corp./Harvey Publications No. 4: 1952(Jan) - No. 3, May, 1953; No. 4, May, 1954
1 14 28 42 82 121 160
2-4: 4-Powell-a 9 18 27 52 69 85

DR. ANTHONY'S LOVE CLINIC (See Mr. Anthony's...)

DR. BOBBS
Dell Publishing Co.: No. 212, Jan, 1949
Four Color 212 6 12 18 37 59 80

DOCTOR CYBORG
Attention! Publishing: 1996 - No. 5 ($2.95, B&W)
1-5 3.00
The Clone Conspiracy TPB (1998, $14.95) r/#1-5 15.00

DR. DOOM'S REVENGE
Marvel Comics: 1989 (Came w/computer game from Paragon Software)
V1#1-Spider-Man & Captain America fight Dr. Doom 3.00

DR. FATE (See 1st Issue Special, The Immortal..., Justice League, More Fun #55, & Showcase)

DOCTOR FATE
DC Comics: July, 1987 - No. 4, Oct, 1987 ($1.50, limited series, Baxter paper)
1-4: Giffen-c/a in all 3.00

DOCTOR FATE
DC Comics: Winter, 1988-'89 - No. 41, June, 1992 ($1.25/$1.50 #5 on)
1,15: 15-Justice League app. 3.50
2-14 3.00
16-41: 25-1st new Dr. Fate. 36-Original Dr. Fate returns 2.50
Annual 1(1989, $2.95, 68 pgs.)-Sutton-a 3.50

DOCTOR FATE
DC Comics: Oct, 2003 - No. 5, Feb, 2004 ($2.50, limited series)
1-5-Golden-s/Kramer-a 2.50

DR. FU MANCHU (See The Mask of...)
I.W. Enterprises: 1964
1-r/Avon's "Mask of Dr. Fu Manchu"; Wood-a 7 14 21 49 80 110

DR. GIGGLES (See Dark Horse Presents #64-66)
Dark Horse Comics: Oct, 1992 - No. 2, Oct, 1992 ($2.50, limited series)
1,2-Based on movie 2.50

DOCTOR GRAVES (Formerly The Many Ghosts of...)
Charlton Comics: No. 73, Sept, 1985 - No. 75, Jan, 1986
73-75-Low print run 1 2 3 4 5 7

DR. JEKYLL AND MR. HYDE (See A Star Presentation & Supernatural Thrillers #4)

DR. KILDARE (TV)
Dell Publishing Co.: No. 1337, 4-6/62 - No. 9, 4-6/65 (All Richard Chamberlain photo-c)
Four Color 1337(#1, 1962) 8 16 24 58 97 135
2-9 6 12 18 43 69 95

DR. MASTERS (See The Adventures of Young...)

DOCTOR MID-NITE (Also see All-American #25)
DC Comics: 1999 - No. 3, 1999 ($5.95, square-bound, limited series)
1-3-Matt Wagner-s/John K. Snyder III-painted art 6.00
TPB (2000, $19.95) r/series 20.00

DOCTOR OCTOPUS: NEGATIVE EXPOSURE
Marvel Comics: Dec, 2003 - No. 5, Apr, 2004 ($2.99, limited series)
1-5-Vaughan-s/Staz Johnson-a; Spider-Man app. 3.00
Spider-Man/Doctor Octopus: Negative Exposure TPB (2004, $13.99) r/series 14.00

DR. ROBOT SPECIAL
Dark Horse Comics: Apr, 2000 ($2.95, one-shot)
1-Bernie Mireault-s/a; some reprints from Madman Comics #12-15 3.00

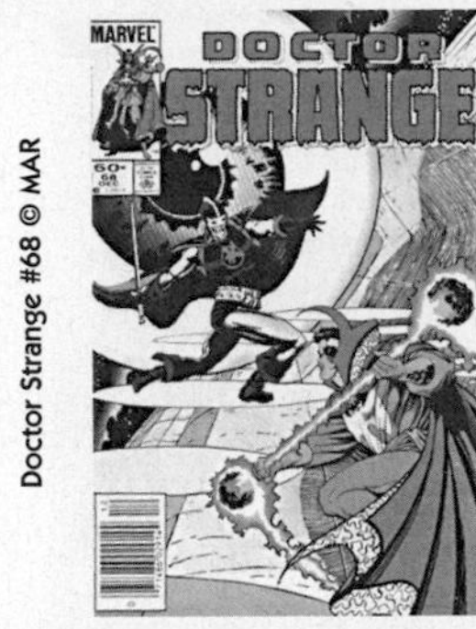
Doctor Strange #68 © MAR

Doctor Strange V2 #1 © MAR

Doctor Who (2008 series) #1 © BBC Worldwide

	GD 2.0	VG 4.0	FN 6.0	VF 8.0	VF/NM 9.0	NM- 9.2

DOCTOR SOLAR, MAN OF THE ATOM (See The Occult Files of Dr. Spektor #14 & Solar)
Gold Key/Whitman No. 28 on: 10/62 - No. 27, 4/69; No. 28, 4/81 - No. 31, 3/82 (1-27 have painted-c)

	GD	VG	FN	VF	VF/NM	NM-
1-(#10000-210)-Origin/1st app. Dr. Solar (1st original Gold Key character)	18	36	54	130	240	350
2-Prof. Harbinger begins	9	18	27	60	100	140
3,4	6	12	18	41	66	90
5-Intro. Man of the Atom in costume	6	12	18	43	69	95
6-10	5	10	15	32	51	70
11-14,16-20	4	8	12	24	37	50
15-Origin retold	4	8	12	26	41	55
21-23: 23-Last 12¢ issue	3	6	9	20	30	40
24-27	3	6	9	19	29	38
28-31: 29-Magnus Robot Fighter begins. 31-(3/82)The Sentinel app.	2	4	6	11	16	20

Hardcover Volume One (Dark Horse Books, 2004, $49.95) r/#1-7; creator bios 50.00
Hardcover Volume Two (Dark Horse Books, 6/05, $49.95) r/#8-14; Jim Shooter foreword 50.00
Hardcover Volume Three (Dark Horse Books, 9/05, $49.95) r/#15-22; Mike Baron foreword 50.00
Hardcover Volume Four (Dark Horse Books, 11/07, $49.95) r/#23-31 and The Occult Files of Dr. Spektor #14; Batton Lash foreword 50.00

NOTE: ***Frank Bolle** a-6-19, 29-31; c-29i, 30i. **Bob Fugitani** a-1-5. **Spiegle** a-29-31. **Al McWilliams** a-20-23.*

DOCTOR SOLAR, MAN OF THE ATOM
Valiant Comics: 1990 - No. 2, 1991 ($7.95, card stock-c, high quality, 96 pgs.)

	GD	VG	FN	VF	VF/NM	NM-
1,2: Reprints Gold Key series	1	2	3	4	5	7

DOCTOR SPECTRUM (See Supreme Power)
Marvel Comics: Oct, 2004 - No. 6, Mar, 2005 ($2.99, limited series)

1-6-Origin; Sara Barnes-s/Travel Foreman-a 3.00
TPB (2005, $16.99) r/#1-6 17.00

DOCTOR SPEKTOR (See The Occult Files of..., & Spine-Tingling Tales)

DOCTOR STRANGE (Formerly Strange Tales #1-168) (Also see The Defenders, Giant-Size..., Marvel Fanfare, Marvel Graphic Novel, Marvel Premiere, Marvel Treasury Edition, Strange & Strange Tales, 2nd Series)
Marvel Comics Group: No. 169, 6/68 - No. 183, 11/69; 6/74 - No. 81, 2/87

	GD	VG	FN	VF	VF/NM	NM-
169(#1)-Origin retold; panel swipe/M.D. #1-c	12	24	36	87	156	225
170-177: 177-New costume	4	8	12	26	41	55
178-183: 178-Black Knight app. 179-Spider-Man story-r. 180-Photo montage-c. 181-Brunner-c(part-i), last 12¢ issue	4	8	12	24	31	50
1(6/74, 2nd series)-Brunner-c/a	6	12	18	43	69	95
2	4	8	12	22	34	45
3-5	3	6	9	14	20	26
6-10	2	4	6	8	11	14
11-13,15-20: 13,15-17-(Regular 25¢ editions)	1	2	3	5	6	8
13,15-17-(30¢-c variants, limited distribution)	4	8	12	22	34	45
14-(5/76) Dracula app.; (regular 25¢ edition)	2	4	6	8	11	14
14-(30¢-c variant, limited distribution)	5	10	15	32	51	70
21-40: 21-Origin-r/Doctor Strange #169. 23-25-(Regular 30¢ editions). 31-Sub-Mariner-c/story						5.00
23-25-(35¢-c variants, limited distribution)(6,8,10/77)	1	3	4	6	8	10
41-57,63-77,79-81: 56-Origin retold						3.50
58-62: 58-Re-intro Hannibal King (cameo). 59-Hannibal King full app. 59-62-Dracula app. (Darkhold storyline). 61,62-Doctor Strange, Blade, Hannibal King & Frank Drake team-up to battle. Dracula. 62-Death of Dracula & Lilith						5.00
78-New costume						4.00
Annual 1(1976, 52 pgs.)-New Russell-a (35 pgs.)	2	4	6	10	14	18
.../Silver Dagger Special Edition 1 (3/83, $2.50)-r/#1,2,4,5; Wrightson-c						3.00
... Vs. Dracula TPB (2006, $19.99) r/#14,58-62 and Tomb of Dracula #44						20.00
...What Is It That Disturbs You, Stephen? #1 (10/97, $5.99, 48 pgs.) Russell-a/Andreyko & Russell-s, retelling of Annual #1 story						6.00

NOTE: ***Adkins** a-169, 170, 171i; c-169-171, 172i, 173. **Adams** a-4i. **Austin** a(i)-48-60, 66, 68, 70, 73; c(i)-38, 47-53, 55, 58-60, 70. **Brunner** a-1-5p; c-1-6, 22, 28-30, 33. **Colan** a(p)-172-178, 180-183, 6-18, 36-45, 47; c(p)-172, 174-183, 11-21, 23, 27, 35, 36, 47. **Ditko** a-179r, 3r. **Everett** c-183i. **Golden** a-46p, 55p; c-42-44, 46, 55p. **G. Kane** c(p)-8-10. **Miller** c-46p. **Nebres** a-20, 22, 23, 24i, 26i, 32i; c-32i, 34. **Rogers** a-48-53p; c-47p-53p. **Russell** a-34i, 46i, Annual 1. **B. Smith** c-179. **Paul Smith** a-54p, 56p, 65, 66p, 68p, 69, 71-73; c-56, 65, 66, 68, 71. **Starlin** a-23p, 26; c-25, 26. **Sutton** a-27-29p, 31i, 33, 34p. Painted c-62, 63.*

DOCTOR STRANGE (Volume 2)
Marvel Comics: Feb, 1999 - No. 4, May, 1999 ($2.99, limited series)

1-4: 1,2-Tony Harris-a/painted cover. 3,4-Chadwick-a 3.00

DOCTOR STRANGE CLASSICS
Marvel Comics Group: Mar, 1984 - No. 4, June, 1984 ($1.50, Baxter paper)

1-4: Ditko-r; Byrne-c. 4-New Golden pin-up 3.00

NOTE: ***Byrne** c-1i, 2-4.*

DOCTOR STRANGEFATE (See Marvel Versus DC #3 & DC Versus Marvel #4)
DC Comics (Amalgam): Apr, 1996 ($1.95)

1-Ron Marz script w/Jose Garcia-Lopez-(p) & Kevin Nowlan-(i). Access & Charles Xavier app 2.50

DOCTOR STRANGE MASTER OF THE MYSTIC ARTS (See Fireside Book Series)

DOCTOR STRANGE, SORCERER SUPREME
Marvel Comics (Midnight Sons imprint #60 on): Nov, 1988 - No. 90, June, 1996 ($1.25/$1.50/$1.75/$1.95, direct sales only, Mando paper)

1 ($1.25) 4.00
2-9,12-14,16-25,27,29-40,42-49,51-64: 3-New Defenders app. 5-Guice-c/a begins. 14-18-Morbius story line. 31-36-Infinity Gauntlet x-overs. 31-Silver Surfer app. 33-Thanos-c & cameo. 36-Warlock app. 37-Silver Surfer app. 40-Daredevil x-over. 41-Wolverine-c/story. 42-47-Infinity War x-overs. 47-Gamora app. 52,53-Morbius-c/stories. 60,61-Siege of Darkness pt. 7 & 15. 60-Spot varnish-c. 61-New Doctor Strange begins (cameo, 1st app.). 62-Dr. Doom & Morbius app. 2.50
10,11,26,28,41: 10-Re-intro Morbius w/new costume (11/89). 11-Hobgoblin app. 26-Werewolf by Night app. 28-Ghost Rider-s cont'd from G.R. #12; published at same time as Doctor Strange/Ghost Rider Special #1(4/91) 3.00
15-Unauthorized Amy Grant photo-c 4.00
50-($2.95, 52 pgs.)-Holo-grafx foil-c; Hulk, Ghost Rider & Silver Surfer app.; leads into new Secret Defenders series 3.00
65-74, 76-90: 65-Begin $1.95-c; bound-in card sheet. 72-Silver ink-c. 80-82- Ellis-s. 84-DeMatteis story begins. 87-Death of Baron Mordo 2.50
75 ($2.50) 3.00
75 ($3.50)-Foil-c 4.00
Annual 2-4 ('92-'94, 68 pgs.)-2-Defenders app. 3-Polybagged w/card 3.00
Ashcan (1995, 75¢) 2.25
.../Ghost Rider Special 1 (4/91, $1.50)-Same book as D.S.S.S. #28 2.50
...Vs. Dracula 1 (3/94, $1.75, 52 pgs.) r/Tomb of Dracula #44 & Dr. Strange #14 2.50

NOTE: ***Colan** c/a-19. **Golden** c-28. **Guice** a-5-10, 18, 20-24; c-5-12, 20-24. See 1st series for Annual #1.*

DOCTOR STRANGE: THE OATH
Marvel Comics: Dec, 2006 - No. 5, Apr, 2007 ($2.99, limited series)

1-5-Vaughan-s/Martin-a; Night Nurse app. 3.00
TPB (2007, $13.99) r/#1-5; sketch pages and promotional art 14.00

DR. TOM BRENT, YOUNG INTERN
Charlton Publications: Feb, 1963 - No. 5, Oct, 1963

	GD	VG	FN	VF	VF/NM	NM-
1	3	6	9	16	23	30
2-5	2	4	6	11	16	20

DR. TOMORROW
Acclaim Comics (Valiant): Sept, 1997 - No. 12 ($2.50)

1-12: 1-Mignola-c 2.50

DR. VOLTZ (See Mighty Midget Comics)

DR. WEIRD
Big Bang Comics: Oct, 1994 - No. 2, May, 1995 ($2.95, B&W)

1,2: 1-Frank Brunner-c 4.00

DR. WEIRD SPECIAL
Big Bang Comics: Feb, 1994 ($3.95, B&W, 68 pgs.)

1-Origin-r by Starlin; Starlin-c. 4.00

DOCTOR WHO (Also see Marvel Premiere #57-60)
Marvel Comics Group: Oct, 1984 - No. 23, Aug, 1986 ($1.50, direct sales, Baxter paper)

1-15-British-r 4.00
16-23 5.00
Graphic Novel Voyager (1985, $8.95) color reprints of B&W comic pages from Doctor Who Magazine #88-99; Colin Baker afterword 12.00

DOCTOR WHO (Based on the 2005 TV series with David Tennant)
IDW Publishing: Jan, 2008 - Present ($3.99)

1-6: 1-Nick Roche-a/Gary Russell-s; two covers 4.00

DR. WHO & THE DALEKS (See Movie Classics)

DOCTOR WHO CLASSICS
IDW Publishing: Nov, 2005 - Present ($3.99)

1-10: Reprints from Doctor Who Weekly (1979); art by Gibbons, Neary and others 4.00

DOCTOR WHO: THE FORGOTTEN (Based on the 2005 TV series with David Tennant)
IDW Publishing: Aug, 2008 - Present ($3.99)

1-Pia Guerra-a/Tony Lee-s; two covers 4.00

DR. WONDER
Old Town Publishing: June, 1996 - No. 5 ($2.95, B&W)

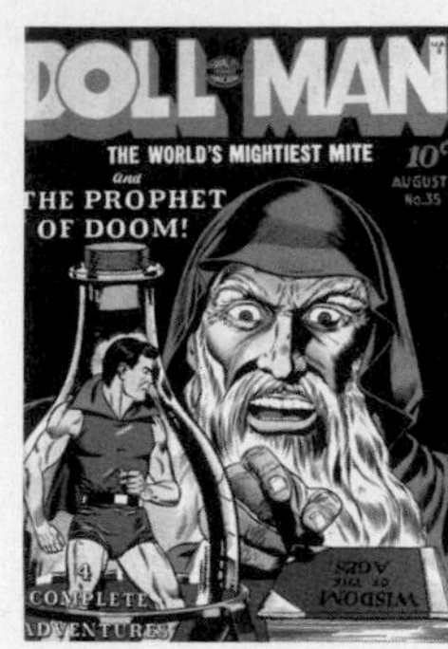

Doll Man #35 © QUA

Dolly #10 © Z-D

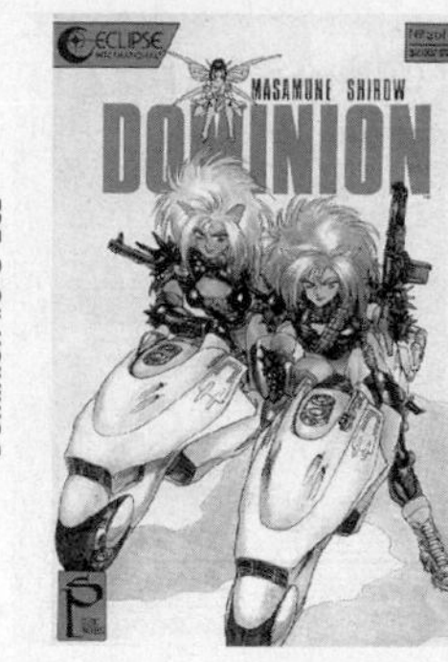

Dominion #3 © ECL

	GD 2.0	VG 4.0	FN 6.0	VF 8.0	VF/NM 9.0	NM- 9.2

1-5: 1-Intro & origin of Dr. Wonder; Dick Ayers-c/a; Irwin Hasen-a 3.00

DOCTOR ZERO
Marvel Comics (Epic Comics): Apr, 1988 - No. 8, Aug, 1989 ($1.25/$1.50)

1-8: 1-Sienkiewicz-c. 6,7-Spiegle-a 2.50
NOTE: ***Sienkiewicz** a-3i, 4i; c-1. **Spiegle** a-6, 7.*

DO-DO (Funny Animal Circus Stories)
Nation-Wide Publishers: 1950 - No. 7, 1951 (5¢, 5x7-1/4" Miniature)

1 (52 pgs.) 26 52 78 152 244 335
2-7 15 30 45 83 124 165

DODO & THE FROG, THE (Formerly Funny Stuff; also see It's Game Time #2)
National Periodical Publications: No. 80, 9-10/54 - No. 88, 1-2/56; No. 89, 8-9/56; No. 90, 10-11/56; No. 91, 9/57; No. 92, 11/57 (See Comic Cavalcade)

80-1st app. Doodles Duck by Sheldon Mayer 20 40 60 117 184 250
81-91: Doodles Duck by Mayer in #81,83-90 14 28 42 76 108 140
92-(Scarce)-Doodles Duck by S. Mayer 18 36 54 105 165 225

DOGFACE DOOLEY
Magazine Enterprises: 1951 - No. 5, 1953

1(A-1 40) 8 16 24 40 50 60
2(A-1 43), 3(A-1 49), 4(A-1 53), 5(A-1 64) 6 12 18 28 34 40
I.W. Reprint #1('64), Super Reprint #17 2 4 6 9 13 16

DOG MOON
DC Comics (Vertigo): 1996 ($6.95, one-shot)

1-Robert Hunter-scripts; Tim Truman-c/a. 7.00

DOG OF FLANDERS, A
Dell Publishing Co.: No. 1088, Mar, 1960

Four Color 1088-Movie, photo-c 5 10 15 30 48 65

DOGPATCH (See Al Capp's... & Mammy Yokum)

DOGS OF WAR (Also see Warriors of Plasm)
Defiant: Apr, 1994 - No. 5, Aug, 1994 ($2.50)

1-5 2.50

DOGS-O-WAR
Crusade Comics: June, 1996 - No. 3, Jan, 1997 ($2.95, B&W, limited series)

1-3: 1,2-Photo-c 3.00

DOLLFACE & HER GANG (Betty Betz'...)
Dell Publishing Co.: No. 309, Jan, 1951

Four Color 309 5 10 15 35 55 75

DOLLMAN (Movie)
Eternity Comics: Sept, 1991 - No. 4, Dec, 1991 ($2.50, limited series)

1-4: Adaptation of film 2.50

DOLL MAN QUARTERLY, THE (Doll Man #17 on; also see Feature Comics #27 & Freedom Fighters)
Quality Comics: Fall, 1941 - No. 7, Fall, '43; No. 8, Spr, '46 - No. 47, Oct, 1953

1-Dollman (by Cassone), Justin Wright begin 329 658 987 2237 3919 5600
2-The Dragon begins; Crandall-a(5) 143 286 429 901 1526 2150
3,4 88 176 264 554 940 1325
5-Crandall-a 85 170 255 536 906 1275
6,7(1943) 53 106 159 334 567 800
8(1946)-1st app. Torchy by Bill Ward 163 326 489 1027 1739 2450
9 53 106 159 330 553 775
10-20 41 82 123 250 413 575
21-30: 28-Vs. The Flame 35 70 105 208 334 460
31-36,38,40: 31-(12/50)-Intro Elmo, the wonder dog (Dollman's faithful dog).
32-34-Jeb Rivers app.; 34 by Crandall(p) 32 64 96 190 305 420
37-Origin & 1st app. Dollgirl; Dollgirl bondage-c 47 94 141 291 483 675
39- "Narcotics...the Death Drug" c-/story 36 72 108 212 341 470
41-47 23 46 69 135 218 300
Super Reprint #11('64, r/#20),15(r/#23),17(r/#28): 15,17-Torchy app.; Andru/Esposito-c
3 6 9 20 30 40
NOTE: ***Ward** Torchy in 8, 9, 11, 12, 14-24, 27; by Fox-#26, 30, 35-47. **Crandall** a-2, 5, 10, 13 & Super #11, 17, 18. **Crandall/Cuidera** c-40-42. **Guardineer** a-3. Bondage c-27, 37, 38, 39.*

DOLLS
Sirius: June, 1996 ($2.95, B&W, one-shot)

1 3.00

DOLLY
Ziff-Davis Publ. Co.: No. 10, July-Aug, 1951 (Funny animal)

10-Painted-c 8 16 24 44 57 70

	GD 2.0	VG 4.0	FN 6.0	VF 8.0	VF/NM 9.0	NM- 9.2

DOLLY DILL
Marvel Comics/Newsstand Publ.: 1945

1 18 36 54 105 165 225

DOLLZ, THE
Image Comics: Apr, 2001 - No. 2, June, 2001 ($2.95)

1,2: 1-Four covers; Sniegoski & Green-s/Green-a 3.00

DOMINATION FACTOR
Marvel Comics: Nov, 1999 - 4.8, Feb, 2000 ($2.50, interconnected mini- series)

1.1, 2.3, 3.5, 4.7-Fantastic Four; Jurgens-s/a 2.50
1.2, 2.4, 3.6, 4.8-Avengers; Ordway-s/a 2.50

DOMINION
Image Comics: Jan, 2003 - No. 2 ($2.95)

1,2-Keith Giffen-s/a 3.00

DOMINION (Manga)
Eclipse Comics: Dec, 1990 - No. 6., July, 1990 ($2.00, B&W, limited series)

1-6 3.00

DOMINION: CONFLICT 1 (Manga)
Dark Horse Comics: Mar, 1996 - No. 6, Aug, 1996 ($2.95, B&W, limited series)

1-6: Shirow-c/a/scripts 3.00

DOMINIQUE: KILLZONE
Caliber Comics: May, 1995 ($2.95, B&W)

1 3.00

DOMINO (See X-Force)
Marvel Comics: Jan, 1997 - No. 3, Mar, 1997 ($1.95, limited series)

1-3: 2-Deathstrike-c/app. 2.50

DOMINO (See X-Force)
Marvel Comics: June, 2003 - No. 4, Aug, 2003 ($2.50, limited series)

1-4-Stelfreeze-c/a; Pruett-s. 2.50

DOMINO CHANCE
Chance Enterprises: May-June, 1982 - No. 9, May, 1985 (B&W)

1-9: 7-1st app. Gizmo, 2 pgs. 8-1st full Gizmo story. 1-Reprint, May, 1985 2.50

DONALD AND MICKEY IN DISNEYLAND (See Dell Giants)

DONALD AND SCROOGE
Disney Comics: 1992 ($8.95, squarebound, 100 pgs.)

nn-Don Rosa reprint special; r/U.S., D.D. Advs. 1 3 4 6 8 10
1-3 (1992, $1.50)-r/D.D. Advs. (Disney) #1,22,24 & U.S. #261-263,269 3.00

DONALD AND THE WHEEL (Disney)
Dell Publishing Co.: No. 1190, Nov, 1961

Four Color 1190-Movie, Barks-c 8 16 24 54 90 125

DONALD DUCK (See Adventures of Mickey Mouse, Cheerios, Donald & Mickey, Ducktales, Dynabrite Comics, Gladstone Comic Album, Mickey & Donald, Mickey Mouse Mag., Story Hour Series, Uncle Scrooge, Walt Disney's Comics & Stories, W. D.'s Donald Duck, Wheaties & Whitman Comic Books, Wise Little Hen, The)

DONALD DUCK
Whitman Publishing Co./Grosset & Dunlap/K.K.: 1935, 1936 (All pages on heavy linen-like finish cover stock in color;1st book ever devoted to Donald Duck; see Advs. of Mickey Mouse for 1st app.) (9-1/2x13")

978(1935)-16 pgs.; Illustrated text story book 285 570 855 1500 2650 3800
nn(1936)-36 pgs.plus hard cover & dust jacket. Story completely rewritten with B&W illos added. Mickey appears and his nephews are named Morty & Monty
Book only 270 540 810 1420 2510 3600
Dust jacket only.... 65 130 195 350 575 700

DONALD DUCK (Walt Disney's) (10¢)
Whitman/K.K. Publications: 1938 (8-1/2x11-1/2", B&W, cardboard-c)
(Has D. Duck with bubble pipe on-c)

nn-The first Donald Duck & Walt Disney comic book; 1936 & 1937 Sunday strip-r(in B&W); same format as the Feature Books; 1st strips with Huey, Dewey & Louie from 10/17/37
380 760 1140 2090 3295 4500

DONALD DUCK (Walt Disney's...#262 on; see 4-Color listings for titles & Four Color No. 1109 for origin story)
Dell Publ. Co./Gold Key #85-216/Whitman #217-245/Gladstone #246 on: 1940 - No. 84, Sept-Nov, 1962; No. 85, Dec, 1962 - No. 245, July, 1984; No. 246, Oct, 1986 - No. 279, May, 1990; No. 280, Sept, 1993 - No. 307, Mar,1998

Four Color 4(1940)-Daily 1939 strip-r by Al Taliaferro
1150 2300 3450 8625 15,812 23,000

Donald Duck #26 © DIS

Donald Duck #253 © DIS

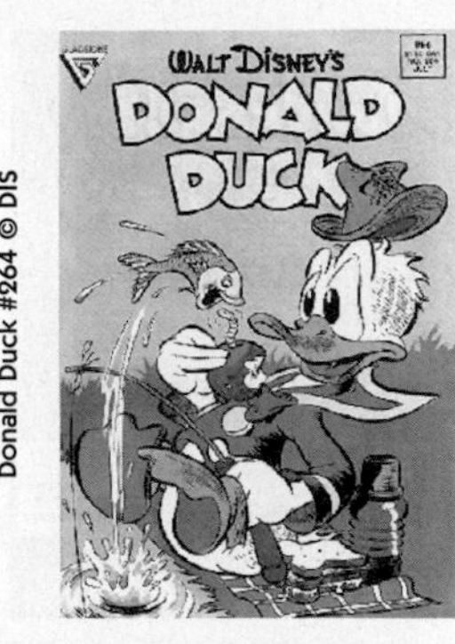

Donald Duck #264 © DIS

	GD 2.0	VG 4.0	FN 6.0	VF 8.0	VF/NM 9.0	NM- 9.2
Large Feature Comic 16(1/41?)-1940 Sunday strips-r in B&W	556	1112	1668	4003	7002	10,000
Large Feature Comic 20('41)-Comic Paint Book, r-single panels from Large Feature #16 at top of each pg. to color; daily strip-r across bottom of each pg.	583	1166	1749	4198	7349	10,500
Four Color 9('42)- "Finds Pirate Gold"; 64 pgs. by Carl Barks & Jack Hannah (pgs. 1,2,5,12-40 are by Barks, his 1st Donald Duck comic book art work; © 8/17/42)	975	1950	2925	7015	12,508	18,000
Four Color 29(9/43)- "Mummy's Ring" by Barks; reprinted in Uncle Scrooge & Donald Duck #1('65), W. D. Comics Digest #44('73) & Donald Duck Advs. #14	711	1422	2133	5119	8960	12,800
Four Color 62(1/45)- "Frozen Gold"; 52 pgs. by Barks, reprinted in The Best of W.D. Comics & Donald Duck Advs. #4	208	416	624	1820	3510	5200
Four Color 108(1946)- "Terror of the River"; 52 pgs. by Carl Barks; reprinted in Gladstone Comic Album #2	152	304	456	1304	2502	3700
Four Color 147(5/47)-in "Volcano Valley" by Barks	104	208	312	884	1692	2500
Four Color 159(8/47)-in "The Ghost of the Grotto";52 pgs. by Carl Barks; reprinted in Best of Uncle Scrooge & Donald Duck #1 ('66) & The Best of W.D. Comics & D.D. Advs. #9; two Barks stories	90	180	270	765	1458	2150
Four Color 178(12/47)-1st app. Uncle Scrooge by Carl Barks; reprinted in Gold Key Christmas Parade #3 & The Best of Walt Disney Comics	121	242	363	1029	1965	2900
Four Color 189(6/48)-by Carl Barks; reprinted in Best of Donald Duck & Uncle Scrooge #1('64) & D.D. Advs. #19	73	146	219	621	1186	1750
Four Color 199(10/48) by Carl Barks; mentioned in Love and Death; r/in Gladstone Comic Album #5	79	158	237	672	1286	1900
Four Color 203(12/48)-by Barks; reprinted as Gold Key Christmas Parade #4	55	110	165	468	897	1325
Four Color 223(4/49)-by Barks; reprinted as Best of Donald Duck #1 & Donald Duck Advs. #3	73	146	219	621	1186	1750
Four Color 238(8/49)-in "Voodoo Hoodoo" by Barks	55	110	165	468	897	1325
Four Color 256(12/49)-by Barks; reprinted in Best of Donald Duck & Uncle Scrooge #2('67), Gladstone Comic Album #16 & W.D. Comics Digest 44('73)	48	96	144	384	717	1050
Four Color 263(2/50)-Two Barks stories; r-in D.D. #278	47	94	141	376	701	1025
Four Color 275(5/50), 282(7/50), 291(9/50), 300(11/50)-All by Carl Barks; 275, 282 reprinted in W.D. Comics Digest #44('73). #275 r/in Gladstone Comic Album #10. #291 r/in D. Duck Advs. #16	45	90	135	360	680	1000
Four Color 308(1/51), 318(3/51)-by Barks; #318-reprinted in W.D. Comics Digest #34 & D.D. Advs. #2,19	43	86	129	344	642	940
Four Color 328(5/51)-by Carl Barks	42	84	126	336	631	925
Four Color 339(7-8/51), 379-2nd Uncle Scrooge-c; art not by Barks.	12	24	36	87	156	225
Four Color 348(9-10/51), 356,394-Barks-c only	20	40	60	148	274	400
Four Color 367(1-2/52)-by Barks; reprinted as Gold Key Christmas Parade #2 & #8	33	66	99	254	477	700
Four Color 408(7-8/52), 422(9-10/52)-All by Carl Barks. #408-r-in Best of Donald Duck & Uncle Scrooge #1('64) & Gladstone Comic Album #13	33	66	99	254	477	700
26(11-12/52)-In "Trick or Treat" (Barks-a, 36pgs.) 1st story r-in Walt Disney Digest #16 & Gladstone C.A. #23	33	66	99	254	477	700
27-30-Barks-c only	12	24	36	87	156	225
31-44,47-50	7	14	21	47	76	105
45-Barks-a (6 pgs.)	14	28	42	103	184	265
46- "Secret of Hondorica" by Barks, 24 pgs.; reprinted in Donald Duck #98 & 154	19	38	57	139	257	375
51-Barks-a,1/2 pg.	7	14	21	47	76	105
52- "Lost Peg-Leg Mine" by Barks, 10 pgs.	14	28	42	104	187	270
53,55-59	6	12	18	41	66	90
54- "Forbidden Valley" by Barks, 26 pgs. (10¢ & 15¢ versions exist)	16	32	48	114	212	310
60- "Donald Duck & the Titanic Ants" by Barks, 20 pgs. plus 6 more pgs.	16	32	48	114	212	310
61-67,69,70	5	10	15	34	55	75
68-Barks-a, 5 pgs.	10	20	30	71	126	180
71-Barks-r, 1/2 pg.	5	10	15	34	55	75
72-78,80,82-97,99,100: 96-Donald Duck Album	5	10	15	32	51	70
79,81-Barks-a, 1pg.	5	10	15	34	55	75
98-Reprints #46 (Barks)	5	10	15	34	55	75
101,103-111,113-135: 120-Last 12¢ issue. 134-Barks-r/#52 & WDC&S 194. 135-Barks-r/WDC&S 198, 19 pgs.	3	6	9	21	32	42
102-Super Goof. 112-1st Moby Duck	4	8	12	22	34	45
136-153,155,156,158: 149-20¢-c begin	3	6	9	14	19	24
154-Barks-r(#46)	3	6	9	16	23	30

	GD 2.0	VG 4.0	FN 6.0	VF 8.0	VF/NM 9.0	NM- 9.2
157,159,160,164: 157-Barks-r(#45); 25¢-c begin. 159-Reprints/WDC&S #192 (10 pgs.). 160-Barks-r(#26). 164-Barks-r(#79)	3	6	9	14	19	24
161-163,165-173,175-187,189-191: 175-30¢-c begin. 187-Barks r/#68.	2	4	6	11	16	20
174,188: 174-r/4-Color #394.	2	4	6	13	18	22
192-Barks-r(40 pgs.) from Donald Duck #60 & WDC&S #226,234 (52 pgs.)	3	6	9	15	21	26
193-200,202-207,209-211,213-216	2	4	6	9	13	16
201,208,212: 201-Barks-r/Christmas Parade #26, 16pgs. 208-Barks-r/#60 (6 pgs.). 212-Barks-r/WDC&S #130	2	4	6	9	13	16
217-219: 217 has 210 on-c. 210 Barks r/WDC&S #106,107, 10 pgs. ea.	2	4	6	10	14	18
220,225-228: 228-Barks-r/F.C. #275	2	4	6	13	18	22
221,223,224: Scarce; only sold in pre-packs. 221(8/80), 223(11/80), 224(12/80)	5	10	15	34	55	75
222-(9-10/80)-(Very low distribution)	16	32	48	114	212	310
229-240: 229-Barks-r/F.C. #282. 230-Barks-r/ #52 & WDC&S #194. 236(2/82), 237(2-3/82), 238(3/82), 239(4/82), 240(5/82)	2	4	6	9	13	16
241-245: 241(4/83), 242(5/83), 243(3/84), 244(4/84), 245(7/84)(low print)	3	6	9	14	19	24
246-(1st Gladstone issue)-Barks-r/FC #422	3	6	9	15	21	26
247-249,251: 248,249-Barks-r/DD #54 & 26. 251-Barks-r/1945 Firestone	2	4	6	9	13	16
250-($1.50, 68 pgs.)-Barks-r/4-Color #9	2	4	6	10	14	18
252-277,280: 254-Barks-r/FC #328. 256-Barks-r/FC #147. 257-($1.50, 52 pgs.)-Barks-r/ Vacaction Parade #1. 261-Barks-r/FC #300. 275-Kelly-r/FC #92. 280 (#1, 2nd Series)	1	2	3	5	6	8
278,279,286: 278,279 ($1.95, 68 pgs.): 278-Rosa-a; Barks-r/FC #263. 279-Rosa-c; Barks-r/MOC #4. 286-Rosa-a	1	2	3	5	7	9
281,282,284	1	2	3	4	5	7
283-Don Rosa-a, part-c & scripts	1	2	3	5	6	8
285,287-307						5.00
286 ($2.95, 68 pgs.)-Happy Birthday, Donald						6.00
Mini-Comic #1(1976)-(3-1/4x6-1/2"); r/D.D. #150	2	4	6	8	11	14

NOTE: ***Carl Barks** wrote all issues he illustrated, but #117, 126, 138 contain his script only. Issues 4-Color #189, 199, 203, 223, 238, 256, 263, 275, 282, 308, 348, 356, 367, 394, 408, 422, 26-30, 35, 44, 46, 52, 55, 57, 60, 65, 70-73, 77-80, 83, 101, 103, 105, 106, 111, 126, 246r, 266r, 268r, 271r, 275r, 278r(F.C. 263) all have **Barks** covers. **Barks** r-263-267, 269-278-282, 284, 285. #96 titled "Comic Album", #99-"Christmas Album". New art issues (not reprints)-106-46, 148-63, 167, 169, 170, 172, 173, 175, 178, 179, 196, 209, 223, 225, 236. **Taliaferro** daily newspaper strips #258-260, 264, 284, 285; Sunday strips #247, 280-283.*

DONALD DUCK ADVENTURES (See Walt Disney's Donald Duck Adventures)

DONALD DUCK ALBUM (See Comic Album No. 1,3 & Duck Album)
Dell Publishing Co./Gold Key: 5-7/59 - F.C. No. 1239, 10-12/61; 1962; 8/63 - No. 2, Oct, 1963

	GD 2.0	VG 4.0	FN 6.0	VF 8.0	VF/NM 9.0	NM- 9.2
Four Color 995 (#1)	6	12	18	43	69	95
Four Color 1099,1140,1239-Barks-c	7	14	21	45	73	100
Four Color 1182, 01204-207 (1962-Dell)	5	10	15	32	51	70
1(8/63-Gold Key)-Barks-c	6	12	18	39	62	85
2(10/63)	5	10	15	30	48	65

DONALD DUCK AND THE BOYS (Also see Story Hour Series)
Whitman Publishing Co.: 1948 (5-1/4x5-1/2", 100pgs., hard-c; art & text)

	GD 2.0	VG 4.0	FN 6.0	VF 8.0	VF/NM 9.0	NM- 9.2
845-(49) new illos by Barks based on his Donald Duck 10-pager in WDC&S #74, Expanded text not written by Barks; Cover not by Barks	50	100	150	350	600	850

(Prices vary widely on this book)

DONALD DUCK AND THE CHRISTMAS CAROL
Whitman Publishing Co.: 1960 (A Little Golden Book, 6-3/8"x7-5/8", 28 pgs.)

	GD 2.0	VG 4.0	FN 6.0	VF 8.0	VF/NM 9.0	NM- 9.2
nn-Story book pencilled by Carl Barks with the intended title "Uncle Scrooge's Christmas Carol." Finished art adapted by Norman McGary. (Rare)-Reprinted in Uncle Scrooge in Color.	30	60	90	150	210	270

DONALD DUCK BEACH PARTY (Also see Dell Giants)
Gold Key: Sept, 1965 (12¢)

	GD 2.0	VG 4.0	FN 6.0	VF 8.0	VF/NM 9.0	NM- 9.2
1(#10158-509)-Barks-r/WDC&S #45; painted-c	6	12	18	43	69	95

DONALD DUCK BOOK (See Story Hour Series)

DONALD DUCK COMICS DIGEST
Gladstone Publishing: Nov, 1986 - No. 5, July, 1987 ($1.25/$1.50, 96 pgs.)

	GD 2.0	VG 4.0	FN 6.0	VF 8.0	VF/NM 9.0	NM- 9.2
1,3: 1-Barks-c/a-r	1	3	4	6	8	10
2,4,5: 4,5-$1.50-c						6.00

DONALD DUCK FUN BOOK (See Dell Giants)

DONALD DUCK IN DISNEYLAND (See Dell Giants)

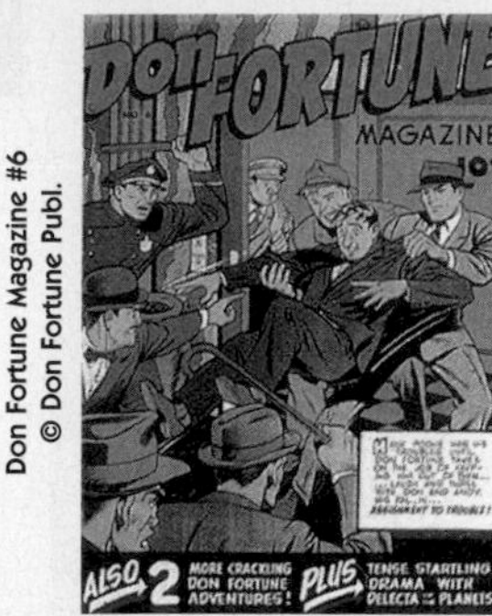

Don Fortune Magazine #6 © Don Fortune Publ.

Don Rosa's Comics and Stories #2 © Don Rosa

Doom Patrol (2nd series) #3 © DC

GD 2.0 | VG 4.0 | FN 6.0 | VF 8.0 | VF/NM 9.0 | NM- 9.2

DONALD DUCK MARCH OF COMICS (See March of Comics #4,20,41,56,69,263)

DONALD DUCK MERRY CHRISTMAS (See Dell Giant No. 53)

DONALD DUCK PICNIC PARTY (See Picnic Party listed under Dell Giants)

DONALD DUCK TELLS ABOUT KITES (See Kite Fun Book)

DONALD DUCK, THIS IS YOUR LIFE (Disney, TV)
Dell Publishing Co.: No. 1109, Aug-Oct, 1960

Four Color 1109-Gyro flashback to WDC&S #141; origin Donald Duck (1st told)
14 28 42 102 181 260

DONALD DUCK XMAS ALBUM (See regular Donald Duck No. 99)

DONALD IN MATHMAGIC LAND (Disney)
Dell Publishing Co.: No. 1051, Oct-Dec, 1959 - No. 1198, May-July, 1961

Four Color 1051 (#1)-Movie 9 18 27 63 107 150
Four Color 1198-Reprint of above 6 12 18 43 69 95

DONATELLO, TEENAGE MUTANT NINJA TURTLE
Mirage Studios: Aug, 1986 ($1.50, B&W, one-shot, 44 pgs.)

1 1 2 3 5 7 9

DONDI
Dell Publishing Co.: No. 1176, Mar-May, 1961 - No. 1276, Dec, 1961

Four Color 1176 (#1)-Movie; origin, photo-c 5 10 15 35 55 75
Four Color 1276 4 8 12 22 34 45

DON FORTUNE MAGAZINE
Don Fortune Publishing Co.: Aug, 1946 - No. 6, Feb, 1947

1-Delecta of the Planets by C.C. Beck in all 26 52 78 152 244 335
2 15 30 45 83 124 165
3-6: 3-Bondage-c 14 28 42 76 108 140

DONKEY KONG (See Blip #1)

DONNA MATRIX
Reactor, Inc.: Aug, 1993 ($2.95, 52 pgs.)

1-Computer generated-c/a by Mike Saenz; 3-D effects 3.00

DON NEWCOMBE
Fawcett Publications: 1950 (Baseball)

nn-Photo-c 43 86 129 267 446 625

DON ROSA'S COMICS AND STORIES
Fantagraphics Books (CX Comics): 1983 ($2.95)

1,2: 1-(68 pgs.) Reprints Rosa's The Pertwillaby Papers episodes #128-133.
2-(60 pgs.) Reprints episodes #134-138 2 4 6 11 16 20

DON SIMPSON'S BIZARRE HEROES (Also see Megaton Man)
Fiasco Comics: May, 1990 - No. 17, Sept, 1996 ($2.50/$2.95, B&W)

1-10,0,11-17: 0-Begin $2.95-c; r/Bizarre Heroes #1. 17-(9/96)-Indicia also reads Megaton Man #0; intro Megaton Man and the Fiascoverse to new readers 3.00

DON'T GIVE UP THE SHIP
Dell Publishing Co.: No. 1049, Aug, 1959

Four Color 1049-Movie, Jerry Lewis photo-c 9 18 27 61 103 145

DON WINSLOW OF THE NAVY
Merwil Publishing Co.: Apr, 1937 - No. 2, May, 1937 (96 pgs.)(A pulp/comic book cross; stapled spine)

V1#1-Has 16 pgs. comics in color. Captain Colorful & Jupiter Jones by Sheldon Mayer; complete Don Winslow novel 653 1306 1959 4900 - -
2-Sheldon Mayer-a 177 354 531 1325 - -

DON WINSLOW OF THE NAVY (See Crackajack Funnies, Famous Feature Stories, Popular Comics & Super Book #5,6)
Dell Publishing Co.: No. 2, Nov, 1939 - No. 22, 1941

Four Color 2 (#1)-Rare 187 374 561 1178 1989 2800
Four Color 22 45 90 135 279 465 650

DON WINSLOW OF THE NAVY (See TV Teens; Movie, Radio, TV) (Fightin' Navy No. 74 on)
Fawcett Publications/Charlton No. 70 on: 2/43 - #64, 12/48; #65, 1/51 - #69, 9/51; #70, 3/55 - #73, 9/55

1-(68 pgs.)-Captain Marvel on cover 116 232 348 725 1200 1675
2 45 90 135 275 450 625
3 36 72 108 208 329 450
4-6: 6-Flag-c 28 56 84 162 256 350
7-10: 8-Last 68 pg. issue? 20 40 60 117 184 250
11-20 15 30 45 90 140 190
21-40 14 28 42 76 108 140
41-43,45-64: 51,60-Singapore Sal (villain) app. 64-(12/48)
12 24 36 67 94 120
44-Classic spider-c 25 50 75 147 236 325
65(1/51)-Flying Saucer attack; photo-c 18 36 54 105 165 225
66 - 69(9/51): All photo-c. 66-sci-fi story 14 28 42 80 115 150
70(3/55)-73: 70-73 r-/#26,58 & 59 9 18 27 50 65 80

DOOM
Marvel Comics: Oct, 2000 - No. 3, Dec, 2000 ($2.99, limited series)

1-3-Dr. Doom; Dixon-s/Manco-a 3.00

DOOM FORCE SPECIAL
DC Comics: July, 1992 ($2.95, 68 pgs., one-shot, mature) (X-Force parody)

1-Morrison scripts; Simonson, Steacy, & others-a; Giffen/Mignola-c 3.00

DOOM PATROL, THE (Formerly My Greatest Adventure No. 1-85; see Brave and the Bold, DC Special Blue Ribbon Digest 19, Official... Index & Showcase No. 94-96)
National Periodical Publ.: No. 86, 3/64 - No. 121, 9-10/68; No. 122, 2/73 - No. 124, 6-7/73

86-1 pg. origin (#86-121 are 12¢ issues) 10 20 30 73 129 185
87-98: 88-Origin The Chief. 91-Intro. Mento 8 16 24 52 86 120
99-Intro. Beast Boy (later becomes the Changeling in New Teen Titans)
9 18 27 63 107 150
100-Origin Beast Boy; Robot-Maniac series begins (12/65)
9 18 27 63 107 150
101-110: 102-Challengers of the Unknown app. 105-Robot-Maniac series ends.
106-Negative Man begins (origin) 6 12 18 37 59 80
111-120 5 10 15 30 48 65
121-Death of Doom Patrol; Orlando-c. 10 20 30 67 116 165
122-124: All reprints 2 4 6 8 10 12

DOOM PATROL
DC Comics (Vertigo imprint #64 on): Oct, 1987 - No, 87, Feb, 1995 (75¢-$1.95, new format)

1-Wraparound-c; Lightle-a 5.00
2-18: 3-1st app. Lodestone. 4-1st app. Karma. 8,15,16-Art Adams-c(i). 18-Invasion tie-in 3.00
19-(2/89)-Grant Morrison scripts begin, ends #63; 1st app Crazy Jane; $1.50-c & new format begins. 1 2 3 5 6 8
20-30: 29-Superman app. 30-Night Breed fold-out 5.00
31-34,37-41,45-49,51-56,58-60: 39-World Without End preview 2.50
35-1st brief app. of Flex Mentallo 5.00
36-1st full app. of Flex Mentallo 6.00
42-44-Origin of Flex Mentallo 4.00
50,57 ($2.50, 52 pgs.) 2.50
61-87: 61,70-Photo-c. 73-Death cameo (2 panels) 3.00
...And Suicide Squad 1 (3/88, $1.50, 52 pgs.)-Wraparound-c 2.50
Annual 1 (1988, $1.50, 52 pgs.) 2.50
Annual 2 (1994, $3.95, 68 pgs.)-Children's Crusade tie-in. 4.00
...: Crawling From the Wreckage TPB (2004, $19.95) r/#19-25; Morrison-s 20.00
...: Down Paradise Way TPB (2005, $19.99) r/#35-41; Morrison-s 20.00
...: Magic Bus TPB (2007, $19.99) r/#51-57; Morrison-s; new Bolland-c 20.00
...: Musclebound TPB (2006, $19.99) r/#42-50; Morrison-s; new Bolland-c 20.00
...: Planet Love TPB (2008, $19.99) r/#58-63 & Doom Force Special #1; Morrison-s 20.00
...: The Painting That Ate Paris TPB (2004, $19.95) r/#26-34; Morrison-s 20.00
NOTE: ***Bisley*** *painted c-26-48, 55-58.* ***Bolland*** *c-64, 75.* ***Dringenberg*** *a-42(p).* ***Steacy*** *a-53.*

DOOM PATROL
DC Comics: Dec, 2001 - No. 22, Sept, 2003 ($2.50)

1-Intro. new team with Robotman; Tan Eng Huat-c/a; John Arcudi-s 3.00
2-22: 4,5-Metamorpho & Elongated Man app. 13,14-Fisher-a. 20-Geary-a 2.50

DOOM PATROL (see JLA #94-99)
DC Comics: Aug, 2004 - No. 18, Jan, 2006 ($2.50)

1-18-John Byrne-s/a. 1-Green Lantern, Batman app. 2.50

DOOM PATROL (See Tangent Comics/ Doom Patrol)

DOOMSDAY
DC Comics: 1995 ($3.95, one-shot)

1-Year One story by Jurgens, L. Simonson, Ordway, and Gil Kane; Superman app. 4.00

DOOMSDAY + 1 (Also see Charlton Bullseye)
Charlton Comics: July, 1975 - No. 6, June, 1976; No. 7, June, 1978 - No. 12, May, 1979

1: #1-5 are 25¢ issues 3 6 9 15 20 25
2-6: 4-Intro Lor. 5-Ditko-a(1 pg.) 6-Begin 30¢-c 2 4 6 10 13 16
V3#7-12 (reprints #1-6) 6.00
5 (Modern Comics reprint, 1977) 4.00
NOTE: ***Byrne*** *c/a-1-12; Painted covers-2-7.*

DOOMSDAY SQUAD, THE
Fantagraphics Books: Aug, 1986 - No. 7, 1987 ($2.00)

Doom 2099 #21 © MAR

Doorway to Nightmare #2 © DC

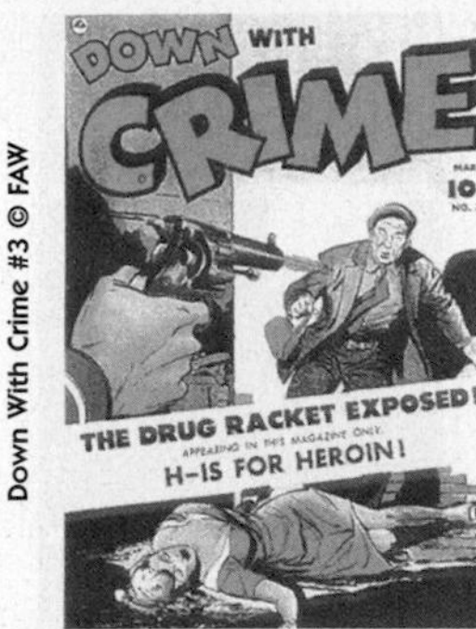

Down With Crime #3 © FAW

	GD 2.0	VG 4.0	FN 6.0	VF 8.0	VF/NM 9.0	NM- 9.2

1-7: Byrne-a in all. 1-3-New Byrne-c. 3-Usagi Yojimbo app. (1st in color). 4-Neal Adams-c. 5-7-Gil Kane-c 3.00

DOOM'S IV
Image Comics (Extreme): July, 1994 - No.4, Oct, 1994 ($2.50, limited series)

1-4-Liefeld story 2.50
1,2-Two alternate Liefeld-c each, 4 covers form 1 picture 5.00

DOOM: THE EMPEROR RETURNS
Marvel Comics: Jan, 2002 - No. 3, Mar, 2002 ($2.50, limited series)

1-3-Dixon-s/Manco-a; Franklin Richards app. 2.50

DOOM 2099 (See Marvel Comics Presents #118 & 2099: World of Tomorrow)
Marvel Comics: Jan, 1993 - No. 44, Aug, 1996 ($1.25/$1.50/$1.95)

1-24,26-44: 1-Metallic foil stamped-c. 4-Ron Lim-c(p). 17-bound-in trading card sheet. 40-Namor & Doctor Strange app. 41-Daredevil app., Namor-c/app. 44-Intro The Emissary; story contin'd in 2099: World of Tomorrow 2.50
1-2nd printing 2.50
18-Variant polybagged with Sega Sub-Terrania poster 4.00
25 ($2.25, 52 pgs.) 2.50
25 ($2.95, 52pgs.) Foil embossed cover 3.00
29 ($3.50)-acetate-c. 3.50

DOORWAY TO NIGHTMARE (See Cancelled Comic Cavalcade)
DC Comics: Jan-Feb, 1978 - No. 5, Sept-Oct, 1978

	GD	VG	FN	VF	VF/NM	NM-
1-Madame Xanadu in all	2	4	6	9	13	16
2-5: 4-Craig-a	1	3	4	6	8	10

NOTE: *Kaluta covers on all. Merged into The Unexpected with No. 190.*

DOPEY DUCK COMICS (Wacky Duck No. 3) (See Super Funnies)
Timely Comics (NPP): Fall, 1945 - No. 2, Apr, 1946

	GD	VG	FN	VF	VF/NM	NM-
1,2-Casper Cat, Krazy Krow	23	46	69	135	218	300

DORK
Slave Labor: June, 1993 - Present ($2.50-$3.50, B&W, mature)

1-7,9-11: Evan Dorkin-c/a/scripts in all. 1(8/95),2(1/96) (2nd printings). 1(3/97) (3rd printing). 1-Milk & Cheese app. 3-Eltingville Club starts. 6-Reprints 1st Eltingville Club app. from Instant Piano #1 3.00
8-($3.50) 3.50
Who's Laughing Now? TPB (2001, $11.95) reprints most of #1-5 12.00
The Collected Dork, Vol. 2: Circling the Drain (6/03, $13.95) r/most of #7-10 & other-s 14.00

DOROTHY LAMOUR (Formerly Jungle Lil)(Stage, screen, radio)
Fox Features Syndicate: No. 2, June, 1950 - No. 3, Aug, 1950

	GD	VG	FN	VF	VF/NM	NM-
2,3-Wood-a(3) each, photo-c	27	54	81	156	251	345

DOT DOTLAND (Formerly Little Dot Dotland)
Harvey Publications: No. 62, Sept, 1974 - No. 63, Nov, 1974

	GD	VG	FN	VF	VF/NM	NM-
62,63	2	4	6	9	12	15

DOTTY (...& Her Boy Friends)(Formerly Four Teeners; Glamorous Romances No. 41 on)
Ace Magazines (A. A. Wyn): No. 35, June, 1948 - No. 40, May, 1949

	GD	VG	FN	VF	VF/NM	NM-
35-Teen-age	9	18	27	47	61	75
36-40: 37-Transvestism story	6	12	18	31	38	45

DOTTY DRIPPLE (Horace & Dotty Dripple No. 25 on)
Magazine Ent.(Life's Romances)/Harvey No. 3 on: 1946 - No. 24, June, 1952 (Also see A-1 No. 1, 3-8, 10)

	GD	VG	FN	VF	VF/NM	NM-
1 (nd) (10¢)	11	22	33	62	86	110
2	7	14	21	37	46	55
3-10: 3,4-Powell-a	6	12	18	31	38	45
11-24	6	12	18	27	33	38

DOTTY DRIPPLE AND TAFFY
Dell Publishing Co.: No. 646, Sept, 1955 - No. 903, May, 1958

	GD	VG	FN	VF	VF/NM	NM-
Four Color 646 (#1)	5	10	15	32	51	70
Four Color 691,718,746,801,903	4	8	12	22	34	45

DOUBLE ACTION COMICS
National Periodical Publications: No. 2, Jan, 1940 (68 pgs., B&W)

2-Contains original stories(?); pre-hero DC contents; same cover as Adventure No. 37. (seven known copies, five in high grade) (not an ashcan) 2000 4000 6000 12,250 15,875 19,500

NOTE: *The cover to this book was probably reprinted from Adventure #37. #1 exists as an ash can copy with B&W cover; contains a coverless comic on inside with 1st & last page missing. There is proof of at least limited newsstand distribution. #2 cover proof only sold in 2005 for $4,000.*

DOUBLE COMICS
Elliot Publications: 1940 - 1944 (132 pgs.)

	GD	VG	FN	VF	VF/NM	NM-
1940 issues; Masked Marvel-c & The Mad Mong vs. The White Flash covers known	247	494	741	1556	2628	3700
1941 issues; Tornado Tim-c, Nordac-c, & Green Light covers known	163	326	489	1027	1739	2450
1942 issues	117	234	351	737	1249	1760
1943,1944 issues	97	194	291	611	1031	1450

NOTE: *Double Comics consisted of an almost endless combination of pairs of remaindered, unsold issues of comics representing most publishers and usually mixed publishers in the same book; e.g., a Captain America with a Silver Streak, or a Feature with a Detective, etc., could appear inside the same cover. The actual contents would have to determine its price. Prices listed are for average contents. Any containing rare origin or first issues are worth much more. Covers also vary in same year. Value would be approximately 50 percent of contents.*

DOUBLE-CROSS (See The Crusaders)

DOUBLE-DARE ADVENTURES
Harvey Publications: Dec, 1966 - No. 2, Mar, 1967 (35¢/25¢, 68 pgs.)

	GD	VG	FN	VF	VF/NM	NM-
1-Origin Bee-Man, Glowing Gladiator, & Magic-Master; Simon/Kirby-a (last S&K art as a team?)	6	12	18	43	69	95
2-Williamson/Crandall-a; r/Alarming Adv. #3('63)	5	10	15	30	48	65

NOTE: *Powell a-1. Simon/Sparling c-1, 2.*

DOUBLE DRAGON
Marvel Comics: July, 1991 - No. 6, Dec, 1991 ($1.00, limited series)

1-6: Based on video game. 2-Art Adams-c 2.50

DOUBLE EDGE
Marvel Comics: Alpha, 1995; Omega, 1995 ($4.95, limited series)

Alpha ($4.95)- Punisher story, Nick Fury app. 5.00
Omega ($4.95)-Punisher, Daredevil, Ghost Rider app. Death of Nick Fury 5.00

DOUBLE IMAGE
Image Comics: Feb, 2001 - No. 5, July, 2001 ($2.95)

1-5: 1-Flip covers of Codeflesh (Casey-s/Adlard-a) and The Bod (Young-s). 2-Two covers. 5-"Trust in Me" begins; Chaudhary-a 3.00

DOUBLE LIFE OF PRIVATE STRONG, THE
Archie Publications/Radio Comics: June, 1959 - No. 2, Aug, 1959

	GD	VG	FN	VF	VF/NM	NM-
1-Origin & re-intro The Shield; Simon & Kirby-c/a, their re-entry into the super-hero genre; intro./1st app. The Fly; 1st S.A. super-hero for Archie Publ.	47	94	141	376	681	985
2-S&K-c/a; Tuska-a; The Fly app. (2nd or 3rd?)	29	58	87	216	388	560

DOUBLE TROUBLE
St. John Publishing Co.: Nov, 1957 - No. 2, Jan-Feb, 1958

	GD	VG	FN	VF	VF/NM	NM-
1,2: Tuffy & Snuffy by Frank Johnson; dubbed "World's Funniest Kids"	6	12	18	31	38	45

DOUBLE TROUBLE WITH GOOBER
Dell Publishing Co.: No. 417, Aug, 1952 - No. 556, May, 1954

	GD	VG	FN	VF	VF/NM	NM-
Four Color 417	4	8	12	28	44	60
Four Color 471,516,556	4	8	12	22	34	45

DOUBLE UP
Elliott Publications: 1941 (Pocket size, 200 pgs.)

	GD	VG	FN	VF	VF/NM	NM-
1-Contains rebound copies of digest sized issues of Pocket Comics, Speed Comics, & Spitfire Comics	80	160	240	504	852	1200

DOVER & CLOVER (See All Funny & More Fun Comics #93)

DOVER BOYS (See Adventures of the...)

DOVER THE BIRD
Famous Funnies Publishing Co.: Spring, 1955

	GD	VG	FN	VF	VF/NM	NM-
1-Funny animal; code approved	7	14	21	35	43	50

DOWN
Image Comics (Top Cow): Dec, 2005 - No. 4, Mar, 2006 ($2.99)

1-4-Warren Ellis-s. 1-Tony Harris-a/c. 2-4-Cully Hamner-a 3.00
Down & Top Cow's Best of Warren Ellis TPB (6/06, $15.99) r/#1-4 & Tales of the Witchblade #3,4; Ellis-s; script for Down #1 with Harris sketch pages 16.00

DOWN WITH CRIME
Fawcett Publications: Nov, 1952 - No. 7, Nov, 1953

	GD	VG	FN	VF	VF/NM	NM-
1	36	72	108	212	341	470
2,4,5: 2,4-Powell-a in each. 5-Bondage-c	18	36	54	107	169	230
3-Used in **POP**, pg. 106; "H is for Heroin" drug story	20	40	60	118	189	260
6,7: 6-Used in **POP**, pg. 80	15	30	45	88	137	185

DO YOU BELIEVE IN NIGHTMARES?
St. John Publishing Co.: Nov, 1957 - No. 2, Jan, 1958

Dracula: Lord of the Undead #2 © MAR

The Dragon #5 © Erik Larsen

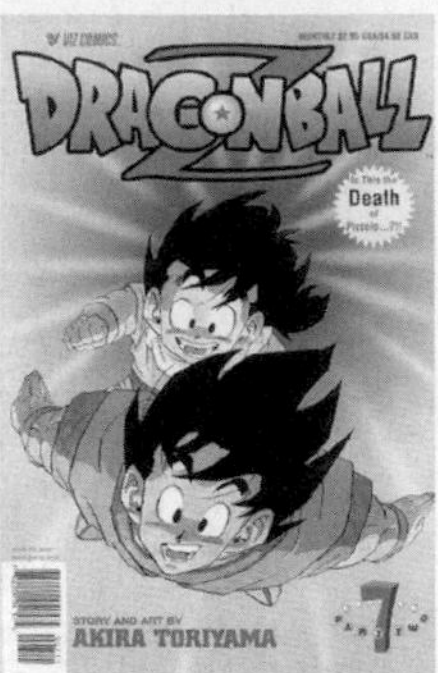
Dragonball Z Part 2 #7 © Bird Studios

	GD 2.0	VG 4.0	FN 6.0	VF 8.0	VF/NM 9.0	NM- 9.2
1-Mostly Ditko-c/a	50	100	150	310	518	725
2-Ayers-a	28	56	84	164	265	365

D.P. 7
Marvel Comics Group (New Universe): Nov, 1986 - No. 32, June, 1989

1-20, Annual #1 (11/87)-Intro. The Witness						2.50
21-32-Low print						4.00
... Classic Vol. 1 TPB (2007, $24.99) r/#1-9; Mark Gruenwald-s/Paul Ryan-a in all						25.00

NOTE: *Williamson a-9i, 11i; c-9i.*

DRACULA (See Bram Stoker's Dracula, Giant-Size..., Little Dracula, Marvel Graphic Novel, Requiem for Dracula, Spider-Man Vs...., Stoker's..., Tomb of... & Wedding of...; also see Movie Classics under Universal Presents as well as Dracula)

DRACULA (See Movie Classics for #1)(Also see Frankenstein & Werewolf)
Dell Publ. Co.: No. 2, 11/66 - No. 4, 3/67; No. 6, 7/72 - No. 8, 7/73 (No #5)

2-Origin & 1st app. Dracula (11/66) (super hero)	4	8	12	28	44	60
3,4: 4-Intro. Fleeta ('67)	3	6	9	19	29	38
6-('72)-r/#2 w/origin	3	6	9	15	21	26
7,8-r/#3, #4	2	4	6	11	16	20

DRACULA (Magazine)
Warren Publishing Co.: 1979 (120 pgs., full color)

Book 1-Maroto art; Spanish material translated into English (mail order only)	6	12	18	39	62	85

DRACULA CHRONICLES
Topps Comics: Apr, 1995 - No. 3, June, 1995 ($2.50, limited series)

1-3-Linsner-c 3.00

DRACULA LIVES! (Magazine)(Also see Tomb of Dracula) (Reprinted in Stoker's Dracula)
Marvel Comics Group: 1973(no month) - No. 13, July, 1975 (75¢, B&W) (76 pgs.)

1-Boris painted-c	7	14	21	47	76	105
2 (7/73)-1st time origin Dracula; Adams, Starlin-a	5	10	15	30	48	65
3-1st app. Robert E. Howard's Soloman Kane; Adams-c/a	5	10	15	30	48	65
4,5: 4-Ploog-a. 5(V2#1)-Bram Stoker's Classic Dracula adapt. begins	4	8	12	22	34	45
6-9: 6-8-Bram Stoker adapt. 9-Bondage-c	4	8	12	22	34	45
10 (1/75)-16 pg. Lilith solo (1st?)	4	8	12	26	41	55
11-13: 11-21 pg. Lilith solo sty. 12-31 pg. Dracula sty	4	8	12	22	34	45
Annual 1(Summer, 1975, $1.25, 92 pgs.)-Morrow painted-c; 6 Dracula stys. 25 pgs. Adams-a(r)	4	8	12	24	37	50

NOTE: ***N. Adams** a-2, 3i, 10i, Annual 1r(2, 3i). **Alcala** a-9. **Buscema** a-3p, 6p, Annual 1p. **Colan** a(p)-1, 2, 5, 6, 8. **Evans** a-7. **Gulacy** a-9. **Heath** a-1r, 13. **Pakula** a-6r. Sutton a-13.**Weiss** r-Annual 1p. 4 **Dracula** stories each in 1, 609; 3 **Dracula** stories each in 2, 4, 5,, 13.*

DRACULA: LORD OF THE UNDEAD
Marvel Comics: Dec, 1998 - No. 3, Dec, 1998 ($2.99, limited series)

1-3-Olliffe & Palmer-a 3.00

DRACULA: RETURN OF THE IMPALER
Slave Labor Graphics: July, 1993 - No. 4, Oct, 1994 ($2.95, limited series)

1-4 3.00

DRACULA'S REVENGE
IDW Publishing: Apr, 2004 - No. 3 ($3.99, limited series)

1,2-Forbeck-s/Kudranski-a 4.00

DRACULA VERSUS ZORRO
Topps Comics: Oct, 1993 - No. 2, Nov, 1993 ($2.95, limited series)

1,2: 1-Spot varnish & red foil-c. 2-Polybagged w/16 pg. Zorro #0 3.00

DRACULA VERSUS ZORRO
Dark Horse Comics: Sept, 1998 - No. 2, Oct, 1998 ($2.95, limited series)

1,2 3.00

DRACULA: VLAD THE IMPALER (Also see Bram Stoker's Dracula)
Topps Comics: Feb, 1993 - No. 3, Apr, 1993 ($2.95, limited series)

1-3-Polybagged with 3 trading cards each; Maroto-c/a 3.00

DRAFT, THE
Marvel Comics: 1988 ($3.50, one-shot, squarebound)

1-Sequel to "The Pitt" 3.50

DRAG 'N' WHEELS (Formerly Top Eliminator)
Charlton Comics: No. 30, Sept, 1968 - No. 59, May, 1973

	GD 2.0	VG 4.0	FN 6.0	VF 8.0	VF/NM 9.0	NM- 9.2
30	4	8	12	28	44	60
31-40-Scot Jackson begins	3	6	9	19	29	38
41-50	3	6	9	17	25	32
51-59: Scot Jackson	2	4	6	13	18	22
Modern Comics Reprint 58('78)						5.00

DRAGON, THE (Also see The Savage Dragon)
Image Comics (Highbrow Ent.): Mar, 1996 - No. 5, July, 1996 (99¢, lim. series)

1-5: Reprints Savage Dragon limited series w/new story & art. 5-Youngblood app; includes 5 pg. Savage Dragon story from 1984 2.50

DRAGON ARCHIVES, THE (Also see The Savage Dragon)
Image Comics: Jun, 1998 - No. 4, Jan, 1999 ($2.95, B&W)

1-4: Reprints early Savage Dragon app. 3.00

DRAGON, THE: BLOOD & GUTS (Also see The Savage Dragon)
Image Comics (Highbrow Entertainment): Mar, 1995 - No. 3, May, 1995 ($2.50, lim. series)

1-3: Jason Pearson-c/a/scripts 2.50

DRAGON BALL
Viz Comics: Mar, 1998 - Part 6: #2, Feb, 2003($2.95, B&W, Manga reprints read right to left)

Part 1: 1-Akira Toriyama-s/a	6.00
2-12	5.00
1-12 (2nd & 3rd printings)	3.00
Part 2: 1-15: 15-($3.50-c)	4.00
Part 3: 1-14	3.00
Part 4: 1-10	3.00
Part 5: 1-7	3.00
Part 6: 1,2	3.50

DRAGON BALL Z
Viz Comics: Mar, 1998 - Part 5: #10, Oct, 2002 ($2.95, B&W, Manga reprints read right to left)

Part 1: 1-Akira Toriyama-s/a	2	4	6	8	10	12
2-9						5.00
1-9 (2nd & 3rd printings)						3.00
Part 2: 1-14						4.00
Part 3: 1-10						3.00
Part 4: 1-15						3.00
Part 5: 1-10						3.00

DRAGON CHIANG
Eclipse Books: 1991 ($3.95, B&W, squarebound, 52 pgs.)

nn-Timothy Truman-c/a(p) 4.00

DRAGONFLIGHT
Eclipse Books: Feb, 1991 - No. 3, 1991 ($4.95, 52 pgs.)

Book One - Three: Adapts 1968 novel 5.00

DRAGONFLY (See Americomics #4)
Americomics: Sum, 1985 - No. 8, 1986 ($1.75/$1.95)

1	3.50
2-8	2.50

DRAGONFORCE
Aircel Publishing: 1988 - No. 13, 1989 ($2.00)

1-Dale Keown-c/a/scripts in #1-12	3.00
2-13: 13-No Keown-a	2.50
...Chronicles Book 1-5 ($2.95, B&W, 60 pgs.): Dale Keown-r/Dragonring & Dragonforce	3.00

DRAGONHEART (Movie)
Topps Comics: May, 1996 - No. 2, June, 1996 ($2.95/$4.95, limited series)

1-($2.95, 24 pgs.)-Adaptation of the film; Hildebrandt Bros-c; Lim-a.	3.00
2-($4.95, 64 pgs.)	5.00

DRAGONLANCE (Also see TSR Worlds)
DC Comics: Dec, 1988 - No. 34, Sept, 1991 ($1.25/$1.50, Mando paper)

1-Based on TSR game	4.00
2-34: Based on TSR game. 30-32-Kaluta-c	3.00

DRAGONLANCE: CHRONICLES
Devil's Due Publ.: Aug, 2005 - No. 8, Mar, 2006 ($2.95)

1-8-Dabb-s/Kurth-a	3.00
...: Dragons of Autumn Twilight TPB (2006, $17.95) r/#1-8	18.00

DRAGONLANCE: CHRONICLES (Volume 2)
Devil's Due Publ.: July, 2006 - No. 4, Jan, 2007 ($4.95/$4.99, 48 pgs.)

1-4-Dragons of Winter Night; Dabb-s/Kurth-a	5.00
...: Dragons of Winter Night TPB (3/07, $18.99) r/#1-4; cover gallery	19.00

DRAGONLANCE: CHRONICLES (Volume 3)
Devil's Due Publ.: Mar, 2007 - No. 12, ($3.50)

1-11-Dragons of Spring Dawning; Dabb-s/Cope-a 3.50

Dragon Prince #1 © Marz, Moder & TCOW

Dreadstar #30 © FC

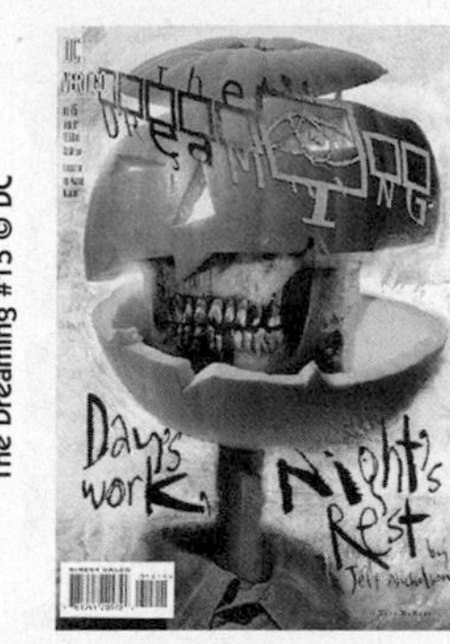

The Dreaming #15 © DC

GD 2.0 | VG 4.0 | FN 6.0 | VF 8.0 | VF/NM 9.0 | NM- 9.2

DRAGONLANCE: THE LEGEND OF HUMA
Devil's Due Publ.: Jan, 2004 - No. 6, Oct, 2005 ($2.95)
1-6-Mike Miller & Rael-a 3.00

DRAGON LINES
Marvel Comics (Epic Comics/Heavy Hitters): May, 1993 - No. 4, Aug, 1993 ($1.95, limited series)
1 ($2.50)-Embossed-c; Ron Lim-c/a in all 3.00
2-4 2.50

DRAGON LINES: WAY OF THE WARRIOR
Marvel Comics (Epic Comics/ Heavy Hitters): Nov, 1993 - No. 2, Jan, 1994 ($2.25, limited series)
1,2-Ron Lim-c/a(p) 2.50

DRAGON PRINCE
Image Comics (Top Cow): Sept, 2008 - Present ($2.99)
1-Marz-s/Moder-a; two covers 3.00

DRAGONQUEST
Silverwolf Comics: Dec, 1986 - No. 2, 1987 ($1.50, B&W, 28 pgs.)
1,2-Tim Vigil-c/a in all 5.00

DRAGONRING
Aircel Publishing: 1986 - V2#15, 1988 ($1.70/$2.00, B&W/color)
1-6: 6-Last B&W issue, V2#1-15($2.00, color) 2.50

DRAGON'S CLAWS
Marvel UK, Ltd.: July, 1988 - No. 10, Apr, 1989 ($1.25/$1.50/$1.75, British)
1-10: 3-Death's Head 1 pg. strip on back-c (1st app.). 4-Silhouette of Death's Head on last pg. 5-1st full app. new Death's Head 2.50

DRAGON'S LAIR: SINGE'S REVENGE (Based on the Don Bluth video game)
CrossGen Comics: Sept, 2003 - No. 3 ($2.95, limited series)
1-3-Mangels-s/Laguna-a 3.00

DRAGONSLAYER (Movie)
Marvel Comics Group: October, 1981 - No. 2, Nov, 1981
1,2-Paramount Disney movie adaptation 3.00

DRAGON'S STAR 2
Caliber Press: 1994 ($2.95, B&W)
1 3.00

DRAGON STRIKE
Marvel Comics: Feb, 1994 ($1.25)
1-Based on TSR role playing game 2.50

DRAGOON WELLS MASSACRE
Dell Publishing Co.: No. 815, June, 1957
Four Color 815-Movie, photo-c 7 14 21 50 83 115

DRAGSTRIP HOTRODDERS (World of Wheels No. 17 on)
Charlton Comics: Sum, 1963; No. 2, Jan, 1965 - No. 16, Aug, 1967
1 7 14 21 49 80 110
2-5 4 8 12 26 41 55
6-16 4 8 12 22 34 45

DRAIN
Image Comics: Nov, 2006 - No. 6, Mar, 2008 ($2.99)
1-6: 1-Cebulski-s/Takeda-a; two covers by Takeda and Finch 3.00

DRAKUUN
Dark Horse Comics: Feb, 1997 - No. 25, Mar, 1999 ($2.95, B&W, manga)
1-25; 1-6- Johji Manabe-s/a in all. Rise of the Dragon Princess series. 7-12-Revenge of Gustav. 13-18-Shadow of the Warlock. 19-25-The Hidden War 3.00

DRAMA
Sirius: June, 1994 ($2.95, mature)
1-1st full color Dawn app. in comics 2 4 6 11 16 20
1-Limited edition (1400 copies); signed & numbered; fingerprint authenticity 4 8 12 24 37 50
NOTE: *Dawn's 1st full color app. was a pin-up in Amazing Heroes' Swimsuit Special #5.*

DRAMA OF AMERICA, THE
Action Text: 1973 ($1.95, 224 pgs.)
1- "Students' Supplement to History" 5.00

DRAWING ON YOUR NIGHTMARES
Dark Horse Comics: Oct, 2003 ($2.99, one-shot)
1-Short stories; The Goon, Criminal Macabre, Tales of the Vampires; Templesmith-c 3.00

DRAX THE DESTROYER
Marvel Comics: Nov, 2005 - No. 4, Feb, 2006 ($2.99, limited series)
1-4-Giffen-s/Breitweiser-a 3.00
...: Earthfall TPB (2006, $10.99) r/#1-4; character design page 11.00

DREADLANDS (Also see Epic)
Marvel Comics (Epic Comics): 1992 - No. 4, 1992 ($3.95, lim. series, 52 pgs.)
1-4: Stiff-c 4.00

DREADSTAR
Marvel Comics (Epic Comics)/First Comics No. 27 on: Nov, 1982 - No. 64, Mar, 1991
1 4.00
2-5,8-49 3.00
6,7,51-64: 6,7-1st app. Interstellar Toybox; 8pgs. ea.; Wrightson-a. 51-64-Lower print run 4.00
50 5.00
Annual 1 (12/83)-r/The Price 4.00

DREADSTAR
Malibu Comics (Bravura): Apr, 1994 - No. 6, Jan, 1995 ($2.50, limited series)
1-6-Peter David scripts: 1,2-Starlin-c 2.50
NOTE: *Issues 1-6 contain Bravura stamps.*

DREADSTAR AND COMPANY
Marvel Comics (Epic Comics): July, 1985 - No. 6, Dec, 1985
1-6: 1,3,6-New Starlin-a: 2-New Wrightson-c; reprints of Dreadstar series 2.50

DREAM BOOK OF LOVE (Also see A-1 Comics)
Magazine Enterprises: No. 106, June-July, 1954 - No. 123, Oct-Nov, 1954
A-1 106 (#1)-Powell, Bolle-a; Montgomery Clift, Donna Reed photo-c 14 28 42 80 115 150
A-1-114 (#2)-Guardineer, Bolle-a; Piper Laurie, Victor Mature photo-c 10 20 30 58 79 100
A-1 123 (#3)-Movie photo-c 10 20 30 54 72 90

DREAM BOOK OF ROMANCE (Also see A-1 Comics)
Magazine Enterprises: No. 92, 1954 - No. 124, Oct-Nov, 1954
A-1 92 (#5)-Guardineer-a; photo-c 14 20 42 76 108 140
A-1 101 (#6)(4-6/54)-Marlon Brando photo-c; Powell, Bolle, Guardineer-a 21 42 63 123 197 270
A-1 109,110,124: 109 (#7)(7-8/54)-Powell-a; movie photo-c. 110 (#8)(1/54)-Movie photo-c. 124 (#8)(10-11/54) 11 22 33 60 83 105

DREAMER, THE
Kitchen Sink Press: 1986 ($6.95, B&W, graphic novel)
nn-Will Eisner-s/a 12.00
DC Comics Reprint ($7.95, 6/00) 8.00

DREAMERY, THE
Eclipse Comics: Dec, 1986 - No. 14, Feb, 1989 ($2.00, B&W, Baxter paper)
1-14: 2-7-Alice In Wonderland adapt. 2.50

DREAMING, THE (See Sandman, 2nd Series)
DC Comics (Vertigo): June, 1996 - No. 60, May, 2001 ($2.50)
1-McKean-c on all.; LaBan scripts & Snejbjerg-a 4.00
2-30,32-60: 2,3-LaBan scripts & Snejbjerg-a. 4-7-Hogan scripts; Parkhouse-a. 8-Zulli-a. 9-11-Talbot-s/Taylor-a(p). 41-Previews Sandman: The Dream Hunters. 50-Hempel, Fegredo, McManus, Totleben-a 2.50
31-($3.95) Art by various 4.00
...Beyond The Shores of Night TPB ('97, $19.95) r/#1-8 20.00
...Special (7/98, $5.95, one-shot) Trial of Cain 6.00
...Through The Gates of Horn and Ivory TPB ('99, $19.95) r/#15-19,22-25 20.00

DREAM OF LOVE
I. W. Enterprises: 1958 (Reprints)
1,2,8: 1-r/Dream Book of Love #1; Bob Powell-a. 2-r/Great Lover's Romances #10. 8-Great Lover's Romances #1; also contains 2 Jon Juan stories by Siegel & Schomburg; Kinstler-c. 2 4 6 10 14 18
9-Kinstler-c; 1pg. John Wayne interview & Frazetta illo from John Wayne Adv. Comics #2 2 4 6 10 14 18

DREAM POLICE
Marvel Comics (Icon): Aug, 2005 ($3.99)
1-Straczynski-s/Deodato-a/c 4.00

DREAMS OF THE DARKCHYLDE
Darkchylde Entertainment: Oct, 2000 - No. 6, Sept, 2001 ($2.95)
1-6-Randy Queen-s in all. 1-Brandon Peterson-c/a 3.00

Droids #4 © LucasFilm

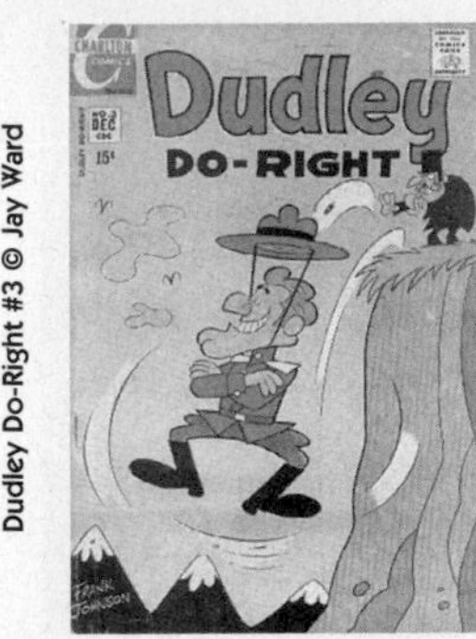

Dudley Do-Right #3 © Jay Ward

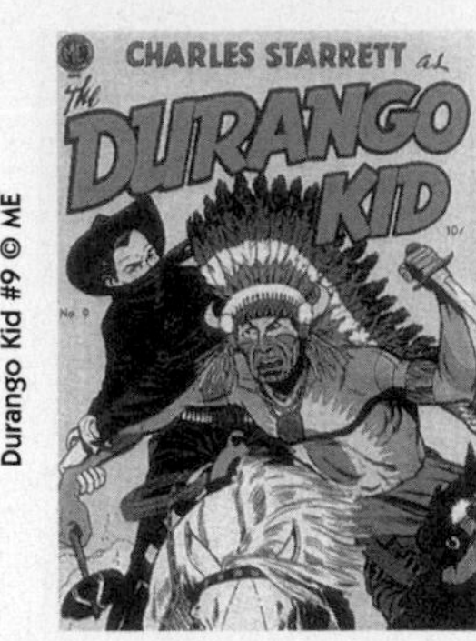

Durango Kid #9 © ME

	GD 2.0	VG 4.0	FN 6.0	VF 8.0	VF/NM 9.0	NM- 9.2

DREAM TEAM (See Battlezones: Dream Team 2)
Malibu Comics (Ultraverse): July, 1995 ($4.95, one-shot)
1-Pin-ups teaming up Marvel & Ultraverse characters by various artists including Allred, Romita, Darrow, Balent, Quesada & Palmiotti 5.00

DREAMWAVE PRODUCTIONS PREVIEW
Dreamwave Productions: May, 2002 ($1.00, one-shot)
nn-Previews Arkanium, Transformers: The War Within and other series 2.50

DRESDEN FILES (See Jim Butcher's...)

DRIFT FENCE (See Zane Grey 4-Color 270)

DRIFT MARLO
Dell Publishing Co.: May-July, 1962 - No. 2, Oct-Dec, 1962
01-232-207 (#1) 5 10 15 32 51 70
2 (12-232-212) 4 8 12 28 44 60

DRISCOLL'S BOOK OF PIRATES
David McKay Publ. (Not reprints): 1934 (B&W, hardcover; 124 pgs, 7x9")
nn-By Montford Amory 25 50 75 144 222 300

DROIDS (Based on Saturday morning cartoon) (Also see Dark Horse Comics)
Marvel Comics (Star Comics): April, 1986 - No. 8, June, 1987
1-R2D2 & C-3PO from Star Wars app. in all 2 4 6 11 16 20
2-8: 2,5,7,8-Williamson-a(i) 2 4 6 8 10 12
NOTE: *Romita a-3p. Sinnott a-3i.*

DROOPY (see Tom & Jerry #60)

DROOPY (Tex Avery's...)
Dark Horse Comics: Oct, 1995 - No. 3, Dec, 1995 ($2.50, limited series)
1-3: Characters created by Tex Avery; painted-c 2.50

DROPSIE AVENUE: THE NEIGHBORHOOD
Kitchen Sink Press: June, 1995 ($15.95/$24.95, B&W)
nn-Will Eisner (softcover) 16.00
nn-Will Eisner (hardcover) 25.00

DROWNED GIRL, THE
DC Comics (Piranha Press): 1990 ($5.95, 52 pgs, mature)
nn 6.00

DRUG WARS
Pioneer Comics: 1989 ($1.95)
1-Grell-c 2.50

DRUID
Marvel Comics: May, 1995 - No. 4, Aug, 1995 ($2.50, limited series)
1-4: Warren Ellis scripts. 3.00

DRUM BEAT
Dell Publishing Co.: No. 610, Jan, 1955
Four Color 610-Movie, Alan Ladd photo-c 8 16 24 56 93 130

DRUMS OF DOOM
United Features Syndicate: 1937 (25¢)(Indian)(Text w/color illos.)
nn-By Lt. F.A. Methot; Golden Thunder app.; Tip Top Comics ad in comic; nice-c
35 70 105 203 327 450

DRUNKEN FIST
Jademan Comics: Aug, 1988 - No. 54, Jan, 1993 ($1.50/$1.95, 68 pgs.)
1 4.00
2-50 3.00
51-54 2.50

DUCK ALBUM (See Donald Duck Album)
Dell Publishing Co.: No. 353, Oct, 1951 - No. 840, Sept, 1957
Four Color 353 (#1)-Barks-c; 1st Uncle Scrooge-c (also appears on back-c).
10 20 30 70 123 175
Four Color 450-Barks-c 7 14 21 49 80 110
Four Color 492,531,560,586,611,649,686, 6 12 18 41 66 90
Four Color 726,782,840 5 10 15 35 55 75

DUCKMAN
Dark Horse Comics: Sept, 1990 ($1.95, B&W, one-shot)
1-Story & art by Everett Peck 4.00

DUCKMAN
Topps Comics: Nov, 1994 - No. 5, May, 1995; No. 0, Feb, 1996 ($2.50)
0 (2/96, $2.95, B&W)-r/Duckman #1 from Dark Horse Comics 4.00

	GD 2.0	VG 4.0	FN 6.0	VF 8.0	VF/NM 9.0	NM- 9.2

1-5: 1-w/ coupon #A for Duckman trading card. 2-w/Duckman 1st season episode guide 3.00

DUCKMAN: THE MOB FROG SAGA
Topps Comics: Nov, 1994 - No. 3, Feb, 1995 ($2.50, limited series)
1-3: 1-w/coupon #B for Duckman trading card, S. Shaw!-c 2.50

DUCKTALES
Gladstone Publ.: Oct, 1988 - No. 13, May, 1990 (1,2,9-11: $1.50; 3-8: 95¢)
1-Barks-r 6.00
2-11: 2-7,9-11-Barks-r 4.00
12,13 ($1.95, 68 pgs.)-Barks-r; 12-r/F.C. #495 5.00
Disney Presents Carl Barks' Greatest DuckTales Stories Vol. 1 (Gemstone Publ., 2006, $10.95) r/stories adapted for the animated TV series including "Back to the Klondike" 11.00
Disney Presents Carl Barks' Greatest DuckTales Stories Vol. 2 (Gemstone Publ., 2006, $10.95) r/stories adapted for the animated TV series; "Robot Robbers" app. 11.00

DUCKTALES (TV)
Disney Comics: June, 1990 - No. 18, Nov, 1991 ($1.50)
1-All new stories; Marv Wolfman-s 3.00
2-18 2.50
Disney's DuckTales by Marv Wolfman: Scrooge's Quest TPB (Gemstone, 9/07, $15.99) r/#1-7; intro. by Wolfman 16.00
The Movie nn (1990, $7.95, 68 pgs.)-Graphic novel adapting animated movie 9.00

DUDLEY (Teen-age)
Feature/Prize Publications: Nov-Dec, 1949 - No. 3, Mar-Apr, 1950
1-By Boody Rogers 15 30 45 83 124 165
2,3 10 20 30 54 72 90

DUDLEY DO-RIGHT (TV)
Charlton Comics: Aug, 1970 - No. 7, Aug, 1971 (Jay Ward)
1 9 18 27 61 103 145
2-7 6 12 18 43 69 95

DUEL MASTERS (Based on a trading card game) (Also see Free Comic Book Day Edition in the Promotional Comics section)
Dreamwave Productions: Nov, 2003 - Present ($2.95)
1-8: 1-Bagged with card; Augustyn-s 3.00

DUKE OF THE K-9 PATROL
Gold Key: Apr, 1963
1 (10052-304) 4 8 12 24 37 50

DUMBO (Disney; see Movie Comics, & Walt Disney Showcase #12)
Dell Publishing Co.: No. 17, 1941 - No. 668, Jan, 1958
Four Color 17 (#1)-Mickey Mouse, Donald Duck, Pluto app.
260 520 780 1638 2769 3900
Large Feature Comic 19 ('41)-Part-r 4-Color 17 293 586 879 1846 3123 4400
Four Color 234 ('49) 14 28 42 99 175 250
Four Color 668 (12/55)-1st of two printings. Dumbo on-c with starry sky. Same-c as #234
10 20 30 70 123 175
Four Color 668 (1/58)-2nd printing. Same cover altered with Timothy Mouse added. Same contents 7 14 21 45 73 100

DUMBO COMIC PAINT BOOK (See Dumbo, Large Feature Comic No. 19)

DUNC AND LOO (#1-3 titled "Around the Block with Dunc and Loo")
Dell Publishing Co.: Oct-Dec, 1961 - No. 8, Oct-Dec, 1963
1 9 18 27 63 107 150
2 7 14 21 47 76 105
3-8 6 12 18 37 59 80
NOTE: *Written by **John Stanley; Bill Williams** art.*

DUNE (Movie)
Marvel Comics: Apr, 1985 - No. 3, June, 1985
1-3-r/Marvel Super Special; movie adaptation 3.00

DURANGO KID, THE (Also see Best of the West, Great Western & White Indian) (Charles Starrett starred in Columbia's Durango Kid movies)
Magazine Enterprises: Oct-Nov, 1949 - No. 41, Oct-Nov, 1955 (All 36 pgs.)
1-Charles Starrett photo-c; Durango Kid & his horse Raider begin; Dan Brand & Tipi (origin) begin by Frazetta & continue through #16 72 144 216 450 750 1050
2-Starrett photo-c. 34 68 102 199 315 430
3-5-All have Starrett photo-c. 30 60 90 174 275 375
6-10: 7-Atomic weapon-c/story 15 30 45 90 140 190
11-16-Last Frazetta issue 14 28 42 76 108 140
17-Origin Durango Kid 15 30 45 90 140 190
18-30: 18-Fred Meagher-a on Dan Brand begins. 19-Guardineer-c/a(3) begins, end #41. 23-Intro. The Red Scorpion 10 20 30 54 72 90

DV8 #6 © WSP

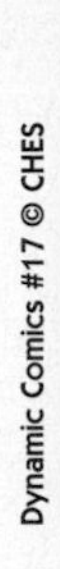
Dynamic Comics #17 © CHES

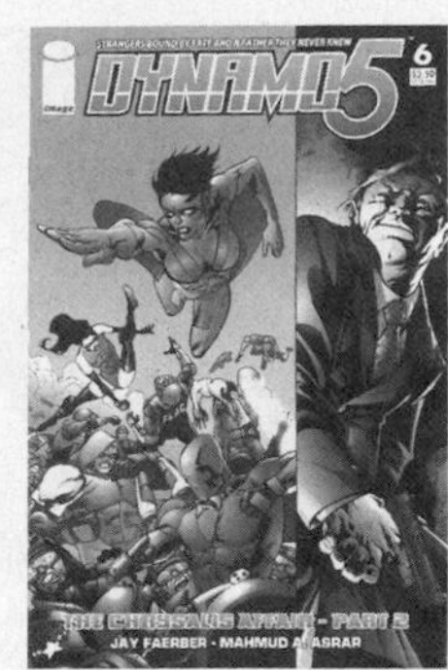

Dynamo 5 #6 © Faerber & Asrar

GD VG FN VF VF/NM NM-
2.0 4.0 6.0 8.0 9.0 9.2

31-Red Scorpion returns 9 18 27 52 69 85
32-41-Bolle/Frazetta*ish*-a (Dan Brand; true in later issues?)
9 18 27 50 65 80
NOTE: *#6, 8, 14, 15 contain* ***Frazetta*** *art not reprinted in White Indian.* ***Ayers*** *c-18.* ***Guardineer*** *a(3)-19-41; c-19-41.* ***Fred Meagher*** *a-18-29 at least.*

DURANGO KID, THE
AC Comics: 1990 - #2, 1990 ($2.50,$2.75, half-color)
1,2: 1-Starrett photo front/back-c; Guardineer-r. 2-B&W)-Starrett photo-c; White Indian-r by Frazetta; Guardineer-r (50th anniversary of films) 3.00

DUSTCOVERS: THE COLLECTED SANDMAN COVERS 1989-1997
DC Comics (Vertigo): 1997 ($39.95, Hardcover)
Reprints Dave McKean's Sandman covers with Gaiman text 40.00
Softcover (1998, $24.95) 25.00

DUSTY STAR
Image Comics (Desperado Studios): No. 0, Apr, 1997 - No. 1 ($2.95, B&W)
0,1-Pruett-s/Robinson-a 3.00

DUSTY STAR
Image Comics (Desperado Publishing): June, 2006 - Present ($3.50)
1-Pruett-s/Robinson-s/a 3.50

DV8 (See Gen 13)
Image Comics (WildStorm Productions): Aug, 1996 - No. 25, Dec, 1998;
DC Comics (WildStorm Prod.): No. 0, Apr, 1999 - No. 32, Nov, 1999 ($2.50)
1/2 6.00
1-Warren Ellis scripts & Humberto Ramos-c/a(p) 4.00
1-(7-variant covers, w/1 by Jim Lee) ...each 4.00
2-4: 3-No Ramos-a 3.00
5-32: 14-Regular-c, 14-Variant-c by Charest. 26-(5/99)-McGuinness-c 2.50
14-($3.50) Voyager Pack w/Danger Girl preview 5.00
0-(4/99, $2.95) Two covers (Rio and McGuinness) 3.00
Annual 1 (1/98, $2.95) 3.00
Annual 1999 ($3.50) Slipstream x-over with Gen13 3.50
Rave-(7/96, $1.75)-Ramos-c; pinups & interviews 3.00
...: Neighborhood Threat TPB (2002, $14.95) r/#1-6 & #1/2; Ellis intro.; Ramos-c 15.00

DV8 VS. BLACK OPS
Image Comics (WildStorm): Oct, 1997 - No. 3, Dec, 1997 ($2.50, lim. series)
1-3-Bury-s/Norton-a 3.00

DWIGHT D. EISENHOWER
Dell Publishing Co.: December, 1969
01-237-912 - Life story 5 10 15 30 48 65

DYNABRITE COMICS
Whitman Publishing Co.: 1978 - 1979 (69¢, 10x7-1/8", 48 pgs., cardboard-c)
(Blank inside covers)
11350 - Walt Disney's Mickey Mouse & the Beanstalk (4-C 157). 11350-1 - Mickey Mouse Album (4-C 1057, 1151,1246). 11351 - Mickey Mouse & His Sky Adventure (4-C 214, 343). 11354 - Goofy: A Gaggle of Giggles. 11354-1 - Super Goof Meets Super Thief. 11356 - (?). 11359 - Bugs Bunny-r. 11360 - Winnie the Pooh Fun and Fantasy (Disney-r).
each.... 2 4 6 8 11 14
11352 - Donald Duck (4-C 408, Donald Duck 45,52)-Barks-a. 11352-1 - Donald Duck (4-C 318, 10 pg. Barks/ WDC&S 125,128)-Barks-c(r). 11353 - Daisy Duck's Diary (4-C 1055,1150) Barks-a. 11355 - Uncle Scrooge (Barks-a/U.S. 12,33). 11355-1 - Uncle Scrooge (Barks-a/U.S. 13,16) - Barks-c(r). 11357 - Star Trek (r/-Star Trek 33,41). 11358 - Star Trek (r/-Star Trek 34,36). 11361 - Gyro Gearloose & the Disney Ducks (r/4-C 1047,1184)-Barks-c(r)
each.... 2 4 6 9 13 16

DYNAMIC ADVENTURES
I. W. Enterprises: No. 8, 1964 - No. 9, 1964
8-Kayo Kirby-r by Baker?/Fight Comics 53. 3 6 9 14 20 25
9-Reprints Avon's "Escape From Devil's Island"; Kinstler-c
3 6 9 16 23 30
nn (no date)-Reprints Risks Unlimited with Rip Carson, Senorita Rio; r/Fight #53
3 6 9 16 22 28

DYNAMIC CLASSICS (See Cancelled Comic Cavalcade)
DC Comics: Sept-Oct, 1978 (44 pgs.)
1-Neal Adams Batman, Simonson Manhunter-r 2 4 6 8 10 12

DYNAMIC COMICS (No #4-7)
Harry 'A' Chesler: Oct, 1941 - No. 3, Feb, 1942; No. 8, Mar, 1944 - No. 25, May, 1948
1-Origin Major Victory by Charles Sultan (reprinted in Major Victory #1), Dynamic Man & Hale the Magician; The Black Cobra only app.; Major Victory & Dynamic Man begin
200 400 600 1260 2130 3000

GD VG FN VF VF/NM NM-
2.0 4.0 6.0 8.0 9.0 9.2

2-Origin Dynamic Boy & Lady Satan; intro. The Green Knight & sidekick Lance Cooper
92 184 276 580 978 1375
3-1st small logo, resumes with #10 90 180 270 567 959 1350
8-Classic-c; Dan Hastings, The Echo, The Master Key, Yankee Boy begin; Yankee Doodle Jones app.; hypo story 102 204 306 643 1084 1525
9-Mr. E begins; Mac Raboy-c 75 150 225 473 799 1125
10-Small logo begins 57 114 171 359 610 860
11-16: 15-The Sky Chief app. 16-Marijuana story 50 100 150 310 518 725
17(1/46)-Illustrated in **SOTI**, "The children told me what the man was going to do with the hot poker," but Wertham saw this in Crime Reporter #2
63 126 189 397 674 950
18-Classic Airplanehead monster-c 53 106 159 334 567 800
19-Classic puppeteer-c by Gattuso 53 106 159 334 567 800
20-Bare-breasted woman-c 78 156 234 491 833 1175
21,22,25: 21-Dinosaur-c; new logo 41 82 123 253 419 585
23,24-(68 pgs.): 23-Yankee Girl app. 40 80 120 244 397 550
I.W. Reprint #1,8('64): 1-r/#23. 8-Exist? 3 7 10 18 27 35
NOTE: ***Kinstler*** *c-IW #1.* ***Tuska*** *art in many issues, #3, 9, 11, 12, 16, 19. Bondage c-16.*

DYNAMITE (Becomes Johnny Dynamite No. 10 on)
Comic Media/Allen Hardy Publ.: May, 1953 - No. 9, Sept, 1954
1-Pete Morisi-a; Don Heck-c; r-as Danger #6 33 66 99 192 309 425
2 17 34 51 98 154 210
3-Marijuana story; Johnny Dynamite (1st app.) begins by Pete Morisi(c/a); Heck text-a; man shot in face at close range 21 42 63 123 197 270
4-Injury-to-eye, prostitution; Morisi-c/a 20 40 60 118 189 260
5-9-Morisi-c/a in all. 7-Prostitute story & reprints 15 30 45 92 144 195

DYNAMO (Also see Tales of Thunder & T.H.U.N.D.E.R. Agents)
Tower Comics: Aug, 1966 - No. 4, June, 1967 (25¢)
1-Crandall/Wood, Ditko/Wood-a; Weed series begins; NoMan & Lightning cameos; Wood-c/a 9 18 27 61 103 145
2-4: Wood-c/a in all 6 12 18 37 59 80
NOTE: ***Adkins/Wood*** *a-2.* ***Ditko*** *a-4?.* ***Tuska*** *a-2, 3.*

DYNAMO 5 (See Noble Causes: Extended Family #2 for debut of Captain Dynamo)
Image Comics: Jan, 2007 - Present ($3.50/$2.99)
1-Intro. the offspring of Captain Dynamo; Faerber-s/Asrar-a 8.00
2 5.00
3-7,11-16: 5-Intro. Synergy. 13-Origin of Myriad 3.50
8-10-($2.99) 3.00
Annual #1 (4/08, $5.99) r/Captain Dynamo app. in Nobel Causes: Extended Family #2 and three new stories by Faerber & various; pin-up gallery 6.00
... Vol. 1: Post-Nuclear Family TPB (2007, $9.99) r/#1-7; Kirkman intro. 10.00
... Vol. 2: Moments of Truth TPB (2008, $14.99) r/#8-13 15.00

DYNAMO JOE (Also see First Adventures & Mars)
First Comics: May, 1986 - No. 15, Jan, 1988 (#12-15: $1.75)
1-15: 4-Cargonauts begin, Special 1(1/87)-Mostly-r/Mars 2.50

DYNOMUTT (TV)(See Scooby-Doo (3rd series))
Marvel Comics Group: Nov, 1977 - No. 6, Sept, 1978 (Hanna-Barbera)
1-The Blue Falcon, Scooby Doo in all 4 8 12 22 34 45
2-6-All newsstand only 3 6 9 16 23 30

EAGLE, THE (1st Series) (See Science Comics & Weird Comics #8)
Fox Features Syndicate: July, 1941 - No. 4, Jan, 1942
1-The Eagle begins; Rex Dexter of Mars app. by Briefer; all issues feature German war covers 180 360 540 1134 1917 2700
2-The Spider Queen begins (origin) 85 170 255 536 906 1275
3,4: 3-Joe Spook begins (origin) 67 134 201 422 711 1000

EAGLE (2nd Series)
Rural Home Publ.: Feb-Mar, 1945 - No. 2, Apr-May, 1945
1-Aviation stories 48 96 144 298 499 700
2-Lucky Aces 26 52 78 152 244 335
NOTE: ***L. B. Cole*** *c/a in each.*

EAGLE
Crystal Comics/Apple Comics #17 on: Sept, 1986 - No. 23, 1989 ($1.50/1.75/1.95, B&W)
1-23: 12-Double size origin issue ($2.50) 2.50
1-Signed and limited 4.00

EARTH 4 (Also see Urth 4)
Continuity Comics: Dec, 1993 - No. 4, Jan, 1994 ($2.50)
1-4: 1-3 all listed as Dec, 1993 in indicia 2.50

EARTH 4 DEATHWATCH 2000

Earth X #4 © MAR

Echo #1 © Terry Moore

Eclipse Graphic Novel Series #1 © MAR

GD VG FN VF VF/NM NM-
2.0 4.0 6.0 8.0 9.0 9.2

GD VG FN VF VF/NM NM-
2.0 4.0 6.0 8.0 9.0 9.2

Continuity Comics: Apr, 1993 - No. 3, Aug, 1993 ($2.50)

1-3 2.50

EARTH MAN ON VENUS (An...) (Also see Strange Planets)
Avon Periodicals: 1951

nn-Wood-a (26 pgs.); Fawcette-c 133 266 399 838 1419 2000

EARTHWORM JIM (TV, cartoon)
Marvel Comics: Dec, 1995 - No. 3, Feb, 1996 ($2.25)

1-3: Based on video game and toys 3.00

EARTH X
Marvel Comics: No. 0, Mar, 1999 - No. 12, Apr, 2000 ($3.99/$2.99, lim. series)

nn- (Wizard supplement) Alex Ross sketchbook; painted-c 6.00
Sketchbook (2/99) New sketches and previews 6.00
0-(3/99)-Prelude; Leon-a(p)/Ross-c 1 2 3 4 5 7
1-(4/99)-Leon-a(p)/Ross-c 1 2 3 4 5 7
1-2nd printing 3.00
2-12 3.50
#1/2 (Wizard) Nick Fury on cover; Reinhold-a 6.00
#X (6/00, $3.99) 4.00
... Trilogy Companion TPB (2008, $29.99) r/#1/2; artwork and content from the Earth X, Paradise X and Universe X series; gallery of variant covers and promotional art 30.00
HC (2005, $49.99) r/#0,1-12, #1/2, X; foreward by Joss Whedon; Ross sketch pages 50.00
TPB (12/00, $24.95) r/#0,1-12, X; foreward by Joss Whedon 25.00

EASTER BONNET SHOP (See March of Comics No. 29)

EASTER WITH MOTHER GOOSE
Dell Publishing Co.: No. 103, 1946 - No. 220, Mar, 1949

Four Color 103 (#1)-Walt Kelly-a 17 34 51 120 223 325
Four Color 140 ('47)-Kelly-a 14 28 42 102 181 260
Four Color 185 ('48),220-Kelly-a 13 26 39 93 164 235

EAST MEETS WEST
Innovation Publishing: Apr, 1990 - No. 2, 1990 ($2.50, limited series, mature)

1,2: 1-Stevens part-i; Redondo-c(i). 2-Stevens-c(i); 1st app. Cheech & Chong in comics 2.50

EC ARCHIVES (Also see EC Sampler in the Promotional Comics section)
Gemstone Publishing: 2006 - Present ($49.95, hardcover with dustjacket)

Crime SuspenStories Vol. 1 - Recolored reprints of #1-6; foreward by Max Allan Collins 50.00
Shock SuspenStories Vol. 1 - Recolored reprints of #1-6; foreward by Steven Spielberg 50.00
Shock SuspenStories Vol. 2 - Recolored reprints of #7-12; foreward by Dean Kamen 50.00
Tales From the Crypt Vol. 1 - Recolored reprints of Crypt of Terror #17-19 and Tales From the Crypt #20-22; foreward by John Carpenter; Al Feldstein behind the-scenes info 50.00
Tales From the Crypt Vol. 2 - Recolored reprints of #23-28; foreward by Joe Dante 50.00
Tales From the Crypt Vol. 3 - Recolored reprints of #29-34; foreward by Bob Overstreet 50.00
Two-Fisted Tales Vol. 1 - Recolored reprints of #18-23; foreward by Stephen Geppi 50.00
Two-Fisted Tales Vol. 2 - Recolored reprints of #24-29; foreward by Rocco Versaci, Ph.D.50.00
Vault of Horror Vol. 1 - Recolored reprints of #12-17; foreward by R.L. Stine 50.00
Weird Science Vol. 1 - Recolored reprints of #1-6; foreward by George Lucas 50.00
Weird Science Vol. 2 - Recolored reprints of #7-12; foreward by Paul Levitz 50.00
Weird Science Vol. 3 - Recolored reprints of #13-18; foreward by Jerry Weist 50.00

E. C. CLASSIC REPRINTS
East Coast Comix Co.: May, 1973 - No. 12, 1976 (E. C. Comics reprinted in color minus ads)

1-The Crypt of Terror #1 (Tales from the Crypt #46) 2 4 6 10 14 18
2-12: 2-Weird Science #15('52). 3-Shock SuspenStories #12. 4-Haunt of Fear #12. 5-Weird Fantasy #13('52). 6-Crime SuspenStories #25. 7-Vault of Horror #26. 8-Shock SuspenStories #6. 9-Two-Fisted Tales #34. 10-Haunt of Fear #23. 11-Weird Science 12(#1). 12-Shock SuspenStories #2 2 4 6 8 10 12

EC CLASSICS
Russ Cochran: Aug, 1985 - No. 12, 1986? (High quality paper; each-r 8 stories in color) (#2-12 were resolicited in 1990)($4.95, 56 pgs., 8x11")

1-12: 1-Tales From the Crypt. 2-Weird Science. 3-Two-Fisted Tales (r/31); Frontline Combat (r/9). 4-Shock SuspenStories. 5-Weird Fantasy. 6-Vault of Horror. 7-Weird Science-Fantasy (r/23,24). 8-Crime SuspenStories (r/17,18). 9-Haunt of Fear (r/14,15). 10-Panic (r/1,2). 11-Tales From the Crypt (r/23,24). 12-Weird Science (r/20,22) 1 2 3 4 5 7

ECHO
Image Comics (Dreamwave Prod.): Mar, 2000 - No. 5, Sept, 2000 ($2.50)

1-5: 1-3-Pat Lee-c 2.50
0-(7/00) 2.50

ECHO
Abstract Studio: Mar, 2008 - Present ($3.50)

1-6-Terry Moore-s/a/c 3.50
Terry Moore's Echo: Moon Lake TPB (2008, $15.95) r/#1-5; Moore sketch pages 16.00

ECHO OF FUTUREPAST
Pacific Comics/Continuity Com.: May, 1984 - No. 9, Jan, 1986 ($2.95, 52 pgs.)

1-9: Neal Adams-c/a in all? 6.00

NOTE: ***N. Adams** a-1-6,7i,9i; c-1-3, 5p,7i,8,9i. **Golden** a-1-6 (Bucky O'Hare); c-6. **Toth** a-6,7.*

ECLIPSE GRAPHIC ALBUM SERIES
Eclipse Comics: Oct, 1978 - 1989 (8-1/2x11") (B&W #1-5)

1-Sabre (10/78, B&W, 1st print.); Gulacy-a; 1st direct sale graphic novel 16.00
1-Sabre (2nd printing, 1/79) 8.00
1-Sabre (3rd printing, $5.95) 6.00
3,4: 3-Detectives, Inc. (5/80, B&W, $6.95)-Rogers-a. 4-Stewart The Rat (1980, B&W) -G. Colan-a 10.00
5-The Price (10/81, B&W)-Starlin-a 16.00
2,6,7,13: 2-Night Music (11/79, B&W)-Russell-a. 6-I Am Coyote (11/84, color)-Rogers-c/a. 7-The Rocketeer (2nd print, $7.95). 7-The Rocketeer (3rd print, 1991, $8.95). 13-The Sisterhood of Steel ('87, $8.95, color) 10.00
7-The Rocketeer (9/85, color)-Dave Stevens-a (r/chapters 1-5)(see Pacific Presents & Starslayer); has 7 pgs. new-a 14.00
7-The Rocketeer, signed & limited HC 60.00
7-The Rocketeer, hardcover (1986, $19.95) 20.00
7-The Rocketeer, unsigned HC (3rd, $32.95) 33.00
8-Zorro In Old California ('86, color) 14.00
8,12-Hardcover 18.00
9,10: 9-Sacred And The Profane ('86)-Steacy-a. 10-Somerset Holmes ('86, $15.95)-Adults, soft-c 16.00
9,10,12-Hardcover ($24.95). 12-signed & #'d 25.00
11-Floyd Farland, Citizen of the Future ('87, $2.95, B&W) Chris Ware-s/a 7.00
12,28,31,35: 12-Silverheels ('87, $7.95, color). 28-Miracleman Book I ($5.95). 31-Pigeons From Hell by R. E. Howard (11/88). 35-Rael: Into The Shadow of the Sun ('88, $7.95)10.00
14,16,18,20,23,24: 14-Samurai, Son of Death ('87, $4.95, B&W). 16,18,20,23-See Airfighters Classics #1-4. 24-Heartbreak ($4.95, B&W) 7.00
14 (2nd pr.),17,21: 14-Samurai, Son of Death ($3.95, 2nd printing). 17-Valkyrie, Prisoner of the Past SC ('88, $3.95, color). 21-XYR-Multiple ending comic ('88, $3.95, B&W) 6.00
15,22,27: 15-Twisted Tales (11/87, color)-Dave Stevens-c. 22-Alien Worlds #1 (5/88, $3.95, 52 pgs.)-Nudity. 27-Fast Fiction (She) ($5.95, B&W) 8.00
17-Valkyrie, Prisoner of the Past S&N Hardcover ('88, $19.95) 20.00
19-Scout: The Four Monsters ('88, $14.95, color)-r/Scout #1-7; soft-c 15.00
25,30,32-34: 25-Alex Toth's Zorro Vol. 1 ,2($10.95, B&W). 30-Brought To Light; Alan Moore scripts ('89). 32-Teenaged Dope Slaves and Reform School Girls. 33-Bogie. 34-Air Fighters Classics #5 12.00
29-Real Love: Best of Simon & Kirby Romance Comics(10/88, $12.95) 15.00
30,31: Limited hardcover ed. ($29.95). 31-signed 30.00
36-Dr. Watchstop: Adventures in Time and Space ('89, $8.95) 10.00

ECLIPSE MAGAZINE (Becomes Eclipse Monthly)
Eclipse Publishing: May, 1981 - No. 8, Jan, 1983 ($2.95, B&W, magazine)

1-8: 1-1st app. Cap'n Quick and a Foozle by Rogers, Ms. Tree by Beatty, and Dope by Trina Robbins. 2-1st app. I Am Coyote by Rogers. 7-1st app. Masked Man by Boyer 3.00

NOTE: ***Colan** a-3, 5, 8. **Golden** c/a-2. **Gulacy** a-6, c-1, 6. **Kaluta** c/a-5. **Mayerik** a-2, 3. **Rogers** a-1-8. **Starlin** a-1. **Sutton** a-6.*

ECLIPSE MONTHLY
Eclipse Comics: Aug, 1983 - No. 10, Jul, 1984 (Baxter paper, $2.00/$1.50/$1.75)

1-10: ($2.00, 52 pgs.)-Cap'n Quick and a Foozle by Rogers, Static by Ditko, Dope by Trina Robbins, Rio by Wildey, The Masked Man by Boyer begin. 3-Ragamuffins begins 2.50

NOTE: ***Boyer** c-6. **Ditko** a-1-3. **Rogers** a-1-4; c-2, 4, 7. **Wildey** a-1, 2, 5, 9, 10; c-5, 10.*

ECLIPSO (See Brave and the Bold #64, House of Secrets #61 & Phantom Stranger, 1987)
DC Comics: Nov, 1992 - No. 18, Apr, 1994 ($1.25)

1-18: 1-Giffen plots/breakdowns begin. 10-Darkseid app. Creeper in #3-6,9,11-13. 18-Spectre-c/s 2.50
Annual 1 (1993, $2.50, 68 pgs.)-Intro Prism 2.50

ECLIPSO: THE DARKNESS WITHIN
DC Comics: July, 1992 - No. 2, Oct, 1992 ($2.50, 68 pgs.)

1,2: 1-With purple gem attached to-c, 1-Without gem; Superman, Creeper app., 2-Concludes Eclipso storyline from annuals 2.50

E. C. 3-D CLASSICS (See Three Dimensional...)

ECTOKID (See Razorline)
Marvel Comics: Sept, 1993 - No. 9, May, 1994 ($1.75/$1.95)

1-($2.50)-Foil embossed-c; created by C. Barker 3.00
2-9: 2-Origin. 5-Saint Sinner x-over 2.50
...: Unleashed! 1 (10/94, $2.95, 52 pgs.) 3.00

Eddie Campbell's Bacchus #37 © Eddie Campbell

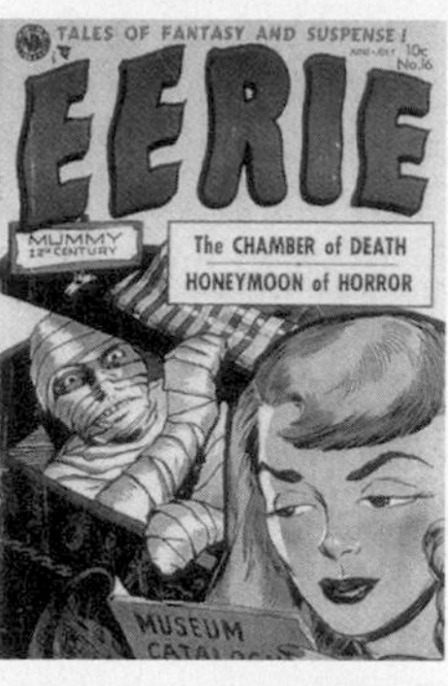

Eerie #16 © AVON

Eerie (Magazine) #6 © WP

ED "BIG DADDY" ROTH'S RATFINK COMIX (Also see Ratfink)
World of Fandom/ Ed Roth: 1991 - No. 3, 1991 ($2.50)

	GD 2.0	VG 4.0	FN 6.0	VF 8.0	VF/NM 9.0	NM- 9.2
1-3: Regular Ed., 1 Limited double cover	1	3	4	6	8	10

EDDIE CAMPBELL'S BACCHUS
Eddie Campbell Comics: May, 1995 - Present ($2.95, B&W)

	GD 2.0	VG 4.0	FN 6.0	VF 8.0	VF/NM 9.0	NM- 9.2
1-Cerebus app.	1	2	3	5	6	8
1-2nd printing (5/97)						3.00
2-10: 9-Alex Ross back-c						5.00
11-60						3.00
Doing The Islands With Bacchus ('97, $17.95)						18.00
Earth, Water, Air & Fire ('98, $9.95)						10.00
King Bacchus ('99, $12.95)						13.00
The Eyeball Kid ('98, $8.50)						8.50

EDDIE STANKY (Baseball Hero)
Fawcett Publications: 1951 (New York Giants)

	GD 2.0	VG 4.0	FN 6.0	VF 8.0	VF/NM 9.0	NM- 9.2
nn-Photo-c	34	68	102	198	319	440

EDEN'S TRAIL
Marvel Comics: Jan, 2003 - No. 6 ($2.99, limited series, Marvelscope-printed sideways)

	GD 2.0	VG 4.0	FN 6.0	VF 8.0	VF/NM 9.0	NM- 9.2
1-5-Chuck Austen-s/Steve Uy-a						3.00

EDGAR ALLAN POE'S - THE FALL OF THE HOUSE OF USHER AND OTHER TALES OF HORROR
Catlan Communications Pub.: Sept. 1985 (hardcover graphic novel)

	GD 2.0	VG 4.0	FN 6.0	VF 8.0	VF/NM 9.0	NM- 9.2
nn-Reprints of Poe story issues from Warren comic mags; all Richard Corben-a; numbered edition of 350 signed by Corben						120.00

EDGAR BERGEN PRESENTS CHARLIE McCARTHY
Whitman Publishing Co. (Charlie McCarthy Co.): No. 764, 1938 (36 pgs.; 15x10-1/2"; color)

	GD 2.0	VG 4.0	FN 6.0	VF 8.0	VF/NM 9.0	NM- 9.2
764	75	150	225	473	799	1125

EDGAR RICE BURROUGHS' TARZAN: A TALE OF MUGAMBI
Dark Horse Comics: 1995 ($2.95, one-shot)

	GD 2.0	VG 4.0	FN 6.0	VF 8.0	VF/NM 9.0	NM- 9.2
1						3.00

EDGAR RICE BURROUGHS' TARZAN: IN THE LAND THAT TIME FORGOT AND THE POOL OF TIME
Dark Horse Comics: 1996 ($12.95, trade paperback)

	GD 2.0	VG 4.0	FN 6.0	VF 8.0	VF/NM 9.0	NM- 9.2
nn-r/Russ Manning-a						13.00

EDGAR RICE BURROUGHS' TARZAN OF THE APES
Dark Horse Comics: May, 1999 ($12.95, trade paperback)

	GD 2.0	VG 4.0	FN 6.0	VF 8.0	VF/NM 9.0	NM- 9.2
nn-reprints						13.00

EDGAR RICE BURROUGHS' TARZAN: THE LOST ADVENTURE
Dark Horse Comics: Jan, 1995 - No. 4, Apr, 1995 ($2.95, B&W, limited series)

	GD 2.0	VG 4.0	FN 6.0	VF 8.0	VF/NM 9.0	NM- 9.2
1-4: ERB's last Tarzan story, adapted by Joe Lansdale						3.00
Hardcover (12/95, $19.95)						20.00
Limited Edition Hardcover ($99.95)-signed & numbered						100.00

EDGAR RICE BURROUGHS' TARZAN: THE RETURN OF TARZAN
Dark Horse Comics: May, 1997 - No. 3, July, 1997 ($2.95, limited series)

	GD 2.0	VG 4.0	FN 6.0	VF 8.0	VF/NM 9.0	NM- 9.2
1-3						3.00

EDGAR RICE BURROUGHS' TARZAN: THE RIVERS OF BLOOD
Dark Horse Comics: Nov, 1999 - No. 4, Feb, 2000 ($2.95, limited series)

	GD 2.0	VG 4.0	FN 6.0	VF 8.0	VF/NM 9.0	NM- 9.2
1-4-Kordey-c/a						3.00

EDGE
Malibu Comics (Bravura): July, 1994 - No. 3, Apr, 1995 ($2.50/$2.95, unfinished lim.series)

	GD 2.0	VG 4.0	FN 6.0	VF 8.0	VF/NM 9.0	NM- 9.2
1,2-S. Grant-story & Gil Kane-c/a; w/Bravura stamp						2.50
3-($2.95-c)						3.00

EDGE (Re-titled as Vector starting with #13)
CrossGeneration Comics: May, 2002 - No. 12, Apr, 2003 ($9.95/$11.95/$7.95, TPB)

	GD 2.0	VG 4.0	FN 6.0	VF 8.0	VF/NM 9.0	NM- 9.2
1-3: Reprints from various CrossGen titles						10.00
4-8-($11.95)						12.00
9-12-($7.95, 8-1/4" x 5-1/2") digest-sized reprints						8.00

EDGE OF CHAOS
Pacific Comics: July, 1983 - No. 3, Jan, 1984 (Limited series)

	GD 2.0	VG 4.0	FN 6.0	VF 8.0	VF/NM 9.0	NM- 9.2
1-3-Morrow c/a; all contain nudity						2.50

ED WHEELAN'S JOKE BOOK STARRING FAT & SLAT (See Fat & Slat)

EERIE (Strange Worlds No. 18 on)
Avon Per.: No. 1, Jan, 1947; No. 1, May-June, 1951 - No. 17, Aug-Sept, 1954

	GD 2.0	VG 4.0	FN 6.0	VF 8.0	VF/NM 9.0	NM- 9.2
1(1947)-1st supernatural comic; Kubert, Fugitani-a; bondage-c	433	866	1299	3118	2184	7800
1(1951)-Reprints story from 1947 #1	73	146	219	460	780	1100
2-Wood-c/a; bondage-c	75	150	225	473	799	1125
3-Wood-c; Kubert, Wood/Orlando-a	75	150	225	473	799	1125
4,5-Wood-c	60	120	180	378	639	900
6,8,13,14: 8-Kinstler-a; bondage-c; Phantom Witch Doctor story	35	70	105	203	327	450
7-Wood/Orlando-c; Kubert-a	41	82	123	247	454	660
9-Kubert-a; Check-c	38	76	114	226	363	500
10,11: 10-Kinstler-a. 11-Kinstlerish-a by McCann	35	70	105	203	327	450
12-Dracula story from novel, 25 pgs.	40	80	120	235	380	525
15-Reprints No. 1('51) minus-c(bondage)	24	48	72	140	225	310
16-Wood-a r-/No. 2	24	48	72	140	225	310
17-Wood/Orlando & Kubert-a; reprints #3 minus inside & outside Wood-c	24	48	72	140	225	310

NOTE: ***Hollingsworth*** *a-9-11; c-10, 11.*

EERIE
I. W. Enterprises: 1964

	GD 2.0	VG 4.0	FN 6.0	VF 8.0	VF/NM 9.0	NM- 9.2
I.W. Reprint #1('64)-Wood-c(r); r-story/Spook #1	4	8	12	22	34	45
I.W. Reprint #2,6,8: 8-Dr. Drew by Grandenetti from Ghost #9	3	6	9	20	30	40
I.W. Reprint #9-r/Tales of Terror #1(Toby); Wood-c	4	8	12	24	37	50

EERIE (Magazine)(See Warren Presents)
Warren Publ. Co.: No. 1, Sept, 1965; No. 2, Mar, 1966 - No. 139, Feb, 1983

1-24 pgs., black & white, small size (5-1/4x7-1/4"), low distribution; cover from inside back cover of Creepy No. 2; stories reprinted from Creepy No. 7, 8. At least three different versions exist.

	GD 2.0	VG 4.0	FN 6.0	VF 8.0	VF/NM 9.0	NM- 9.2
First Printing - B&W, 5-1/4" wide x 7-1/4" high, evenly trimmed. On page 18, panel 5, in the upper left-hand corner, the large rear view of a bald headed man blends into solid black and is unrecognizable. Overall printing quality is poor.	43	86	129	344	647	950
Second Printing - B&W, 5-1/4x7-1/4", with uneven, untrimmed edges (if one of these were trimmed evenly, the size would be less than as indicated). The figure of the bald headed man on page 18, panel 5 is clear and discernible. The staples have a 1/4" blue stripe.	15	30	45	111	206	300

Other unauthorized reproductions for comparison's sake would be practically worthless. One known version was probably shot off a first printing copy with some loss of detail; the finer lines tend to disappear in this version which can be determined by looking at the lower right-hand corner of page one, first story. The roof of the house is shaded with straight lines. These lines are sharp and distinct on original, but broken on this version.

NOTE: ***The Overstreet Comic Book Price Guide*** *recommends that, before buying a 1st issue, you consult an expert.*

	GD 2.0	VG 4.0	FN 6.0	VF 8.0	VF/NM 9.0	NM- 9.2
2-Frazetta-c; Toth-a; 1st app. host Cousin Eerie	10	20	30	70	123	175
3-Frazetta-c & half pg. ad (rerun in #4); Toth, Williamson, Ditko-a	8	16	24	54	90	125
4-7: 4-Frazetta-a (1/2 pg. ad). 5,7-Frazetta-c. Ditko-a in all.	5	10	15	34	55	75
8-Frazetta-c; Ditko-a	6	12	18	39	62	85
9-11,25: 9,10-Neal Adams-a, Ditko-a. 11-Karloff Mummy adapt.-Wood-s/a. 25-Steranko-c	6	12	18	37	59	80
12-16,18-22,24,32-35,40,45: 12,13,20-Poe-s. 12-Bloch-s. 12,15-Jones-a. 13-Lovecraft-s. 14,16-Toth-a. 16,19,24-Stoker-s. 16,32,33,43-Corben-a. 34-Early Boris-c. 35-Early Brunner-a. 35,40-Early Ploog-a. 40-Frankenstein; Ploog-a (6/72, 6 months before Marvel's series)	4	8	12	26	41	55
17-(low distribution)	15	30	45	111	206	300
23-Frazetta-c; Adams-a(reprint)	6	12	18	41	66	90
26-31,36-38,43,44	4	8	12	22	34	45
39,41: 39-1st Dax the Warrior; Maroto-a. 41-(low distribution)	4	8	12	28	44	60
42,51: 42-('73 Annual, 84 pgs.) Spooktacular; Williamson-a. 51-('74 Annual, 76 pgs.) Color poster insert; Toth-a	4	8	12	26	41	55
46,48: 46-Dracula series by Sutton begins; 2pgs. Vampirella. 48-Begin "Mummy Walks" and "Curse of the Werewolf" series (both continue in #49,50,52,53)	4	8	12	22	34	45
47,49,50,52,53: 47-Lilith. 49-Marvin the Dead Thing. 50-Satanna, Daughter of Satan. 52-Hunter by Neary begins. 53-Adams-a	3	6	9	21	32	42
54,55-Color insert Spirit story by Eisner, reprints sections 12/21/47 & 6/16/46 54-Dr. Archaeus series begins	3	6	9	19	29	38
56,57,59,63,69,77,78: All have 8 pg. slick color insert. 56,57,77-Corben-a. 59-(100 pgs.) Summer Special, all Dax issue. 69-Summer Special, all Hunter issue, Neary-a. 78-All Mummy issue	3	6	9	19	29	38
58,60,62,68,72,: 8 pg. slick color insert & Wrightson-a in all. 58,60,62-Corben-a. 60-Summer Giant (9/74, $1.25) 1st Exterminator One; Wood-a. 62-Mummies Walk. 68-Summer Special (84 pgs.)	3	6	9	21	32	42
61,64-67,71: 61-Mummies Walk-s, Wood-a. 64-Corben-a. 64,65,67-Toth-a. 65,66-El Cid. 67-Hunter II. 71-Goblin-c/1st app.	3	6	9	17	25	32

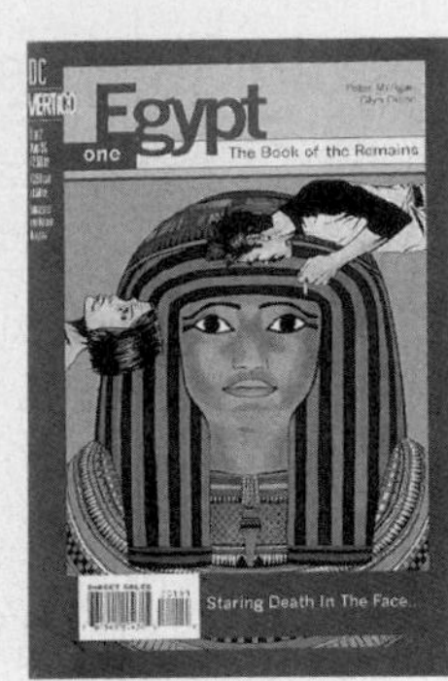

Egypt #1 © Milligan & Dillon

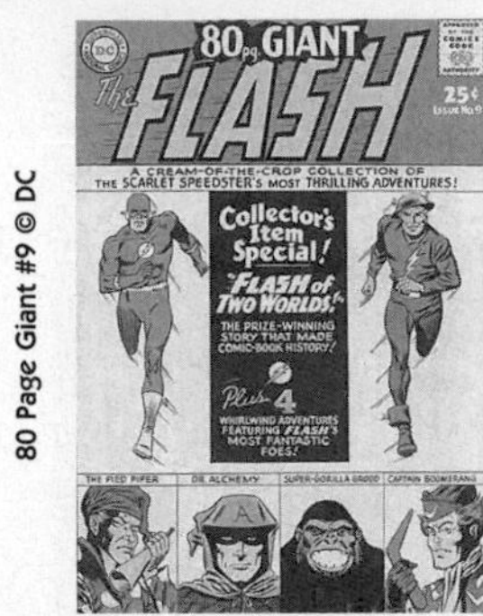

80 Page Giant #9 © DC

El Diablo #1 © DC

GD 2.0 | VG 4.0 | FN 6.0 | VF 8.0 | VF/NM 9.0 | NM- 9.2

70,73-75 3 6 9 14 19 24
76-1st app. Darklon the Mystic by Starlin-s/a 3 6 9 20 30 40
79,80-Origin Darklon the Mystic by Starlin 3 6 9 17 25 32
81,86,97: 81-Frazetta-c, King Kong; Corben-a. 86-(92 pgs.) All Corben issue. 97-Time Travel/ Dinosaur issue; Corben,Adams-a 3 6 9 16 22 28
82-Origin/1st app. The Rook 3 6 9 18 27 35
83,85,88,89,91-93,98,99: 98-Rook (31 pgs.). 99-1st Horizon Seekers. 2 4 6 9 13 16
84,87,90,96,100: 84,100-Starlin-a. 87-Hunter 3; Nino-a. 87,90-Corben-a. 96-Summer Special (92 pgs.). 100-(92 pgs.) Anniversary issue; Rook (30 pgs.) 2 4 6 11 16 20
94,95-The Rook & Vampirella team-up. 95-Vampirella-c; 1st MacTavish 3 6 9 16 23 30
101,106,112,115,118,120,121,128: 101-Return of Hunter II, Starlin-a. 106-Hard John Nuclear Hit Parade Special, Corben-a. 112-All Maroto issue, Luana-s. 115-All José Ortiz issues. 118-1st Haggarth. 120-1st Zud Kamish. 121-Hunter/Darklon. 128-Starlin-a, Hsu-a 2 4 6 9 13 16
102-105,107-111,113,114,116,117,119,122-124,126,127,129: 104-Beast World. 103-105,109-111-Gulacy-a 2 4 6 8 11 14
125-(10/81, 84 pgs.) all Neal Adams issue 2 4 6 13 18 22
130-(76 pgs.) Vampirella-c/sty (54 pgs.); Pantha, Van Helsing, Huntress, Dax, Schreck, Hunter, Exterminator One, Rook app. 3 6 9 16 22 28
131-(Lower distr.); all Wood issue 3 6 9 14 19 24
132-134,136: 132-Rook returns. 133-All Ramon Torrents-a issue. 134,136-Color comic insert 2 4 6 9 13 16
135-(Lower distr., 10/82, 100 pgs.) All Ditko issue 3 6 9 14 19 24
137-139 (lower distr.):137-All Super-Hero issue. 138-Sherlock Holmes. 138,139-Color comic insert 2 4 6 11 16 20
Yearbook '70-Frazetta-c 6 12 18 37 59 80
Annual '71, '72-Reprints in both 4 8 12 26 41 55

NOTE: *The above books contain art by many good artists:* ***N. Adams, Brunner, Corben, Craig (Taycee), Crandall, Ditko, Eisner, Evans, Jeff Jones, Krenkel, McWilliams, Morrow, Orlando, Ploog, Severin, Starlin, Torres, Toth, Williamson, Wood,*** *and* ***Wrightson****; covers by* ***Bode', Corben, Davis, Frazetta, Morrow****, and* ***Orlando****.* ***Frazetta*** *c-2, 3, 7, 8, 23. Annuals from 1973-on are included in regular numbering. 1970-74 Annuals are complete reprints. Annuals from 1975-on are in the format of the regular issues.*

EERIE ADVENTURES (Also see Weird Adventures)
Ziff-Davis Publ. Co.: Winter, 1951 (Painted-c)

1-Powell-a(2), McCann-a; used in **SOTI;** bondage-c; Krigstein back-c 45 90 135 279 465 650

NOTE: *Title dropped due to similarity to Avon's Eerie & legal action.*

EERIE TALES (Magazine)
Hastings Associates: 1959 (Black & White)

1-Williamson, Torres, Tuska-a, Powell(2), & Morrow(2)-a 15 30 45 85 130 175

EERIE TALES
Super Comics: 1963-1964

Super Reprint No. 10,11,12,18: 10('63)-r/Spook #27. Purple Claw in #11,12 ('63); #12-r/Avon's Eerie #1('51)-Kida-r 3 6 9 17 25 32
15-Wolverton-a, Spacehawk-r/Blue Bolt Weird Tales #113; Disbrow-a 5 10 15 30 48 65

EGBERT
Arnold Publications/Quality Comics Group: Spring, 1946 - No. 20, 1950

1-Funny animal; intro Egbert & The Count 20 40 60 114 180 245
2 11 22 33 62 86 110
3-10 9 18 27 47 61 75
11-20 7 14 21 37 46 55

EGON
Dark Horse Comics: Jan, 1998 - No.2, Feb, 1998 ($2.95, limited series)

1,2-Horley-painted-c 3.00

EGYPT
DC Comics (Vertigo): Aug, 1995 - No.7, Feb, 1996 ($2.50, lim. series, mature)

1-7: Milligan scripts in all. 3.00

EH! (...Dig This Crazy Comic) (From Here to Insanity No. 8 on)
Charlton Comics: Dec, 1953 - No. 7, Nov-Dec, 1954 (Satire)

1-Davis-*ish*-c/a by Ayers, Wood-*ish*-a by Giordano; Atomic Mouse app. 37 74 111 215 345 475
2-Ayers-c/a 21 42 63 123 197 270
3,5,7 19 38 57 112 176 240
4,6: Sexual innuendo-c. 6-Ayers-a 20 40 60 117 186 255

EIGHTBALL (Also see David Boring)
Fantagraphics Books: Oct, 1989 - Present ($2.75/$2.95/$3.95, semi-annually, mature)

1 (1st printing) Daniel Clowes-s/a in all 2 4 6 8 10 12
2,3 1 2 3 5 6 8
4-8 6.00
9-19: 17-(8/96) 4.00
20-($4.50) 4.50
21-($4.95) Concludes David Boring 3-parter 5.00
22-($5.95) 29 short stories 6.00
23-($7.00, 9" x 12") The Death Ray 7.00
Twentieth Century Eightball (2002, $19.00) r/Clowes strips 19.00

EIGHTH WONDER, THE
Dark Horse Comics: Nov, 1997 ($2.95, one-shot)

nn-Reprints stories from Dark Horse Presents #85-87 3.00

EIGHT IS ENOUGH KITE FUN BOOK (See Kite Fun Book 1979 in the Promotional Comics section)

EIGHT LEGGED FREAKS
DC Comics (WildStorm): 2002 ($6.95, one-shot, squarebound)

nn-Adaptation of 2002 mutant spider movie; Joe Phillips-a; intro by Dean Devlin 7.00

80 PAGE GIANT (...Magazine No. 2-15)
National Periodical Publications: 8/64 - No. 15, 10/65; No. 16, 11/65 - No. 89, 7/71 (25¢) (All reprints) (#1-56: 84 pgs.; #57-89: 68 pgs.)

1-Superman Annual; originally planned as Superman Annual #9 (8/64) 38 76 114 293 547 800
2-Jimmy Olsen 21 42 63 152 281 410
3,4: 3-Lois Lane. 4-Flash-G.A.-r; Infantino-a 17 34 51 120 223 325
5-Batman; has Sunday newspaper strip; Catwoman-r; Batman's Life Story-r (25th anniversary special) 17 34 51 120 223 325
6-Superman 15 30 45 106 193 280
7-Sgt. Rock's Prize Battle Tales; Kubert-c/a 20 40 60 148 274 400
8-More Secret Origins-origins of JLA, Aquaman, Robin, Atom, & Superman; Infantino-a 30 60 90 222 411 600
9-15: 9-Flash (r/Flash #106,117,123 & Showcase #14); Infantino-a. 10-Superboy. 11-Superman; all Luthor issue. 12-Batman; has Sunday newspaper strip. 13-Jimmy Olsen. 14-Lois Lane. 15-Superman and Batman; Joker-c/story 14 28 42 102 181 260

Continued as part of regular series under each title in which that particular book came out, a Giant being published instead of the regular size. Issues No. 16 to No. 89 are listed for your information. See individual titles for prices. 16-JLA #39 (11/65), 17-Batman #176, 18-Superman #183, 19-Our Army at War #164, 20-Action #334, 21-Flash #160, 22-Superboy #129, 23-Superman #187, 24-Batman #182, 25-Jimmy Olsen #95, 26-Lois Lane #68, 27-Batman #185, 28-World's Finest #161, 29-JLA #48, 30-Batman #187, 31-Superman #193, 32-Our Army at War #177, 33-Action #347, 34-Flash #169, 35-Superboy #138, 36-Superman #197, 37-Batman #193, 38-Jimmy Olsen #104, 39-Lois Lane #77, 40-World's Finest #170, 41-JLA #58, 42-Superman #202, 43-Batman #198, 44-Our Army at War #190, 45-Action #360, 46-Flash #178, 47-Superboy #147, 48-Superman #207, 49-Batman #203, 50-Jimmy Olsen #113, 51-Lois Lane #86, 52-World's Finest #179, 53-JLA #67, 54-Superman #212, 55-Batman #208, 56-Our Army at War #203, 57-Action #373, 58-Flash #187, 59-Superboy #156, 60-Superman #217, 61-Batman #213, 62-Jimmy Olsen #122, 63-Lois Lane #95, 64-World's Finest #188, 65-JLA #76, 66-Superman #222, 67-Batman #218, 68-Our Army at War #216, 69-Adventure #390, 70-Flash #196, 71-Superboy #165, 72-Superman #227, 73-Batman #223, 74-Jimmy Olsen #131, 75-Lois Lane #104, 76-World's Finest #197, 77-JLA #85, 78-Superman #232, 79-Batman #228, 80-Our Army at War #229, 81-Adventure #403, 82-Flash #205, 83-Superboy #174, 84-Superman #239, 85-Batman #233, 86-Jimmy Olsen #140, 87-Lois Lane #113, 88-World's Finest #206, 89-JLA #93.

87TH PRECINCT (TV) (Based on the Ed McBain novels)
Dell Publishing Co.: Apr-June, 1962 - No. 2, July-Sept, 1962

Four Color 1309(#1)-Krigstein-a 9 18 27 65 113 160
2 8 16 24 56 93 130

EL BOMBO COMICS
Standard Comics/Frances M. McQueeny: 1946

nn(1946), 1(no date) 14 28 42 76 108 140

EL CAZADOR
CrossGen Comics: Oct, 2003 - No. 6, Jun, 2004 ($2.95)

1-Dixon-s/Epting-a 5.00
2-6: 5-Lady Death preview 3.00
Collected Edition (2003, $5.95) r/#1-3 6.00
...: The Bloody Ballad of Blackjack Tom 1 (4/04, $2.95, one-shot) Cariello-a 3.00

EL CID
Dell Publishing Co.: No. 1259, 1961

Four Color 1259-Movie, photo-c 7 14 21 47 76 105

EL DIABLO (See All-Star Western #2 & Weird Western Tales #12)
DC Comics: Aug, 1989 - No. 16, Jan, 1991 ($1.50-$1.75, color)

1 ($2.50, 52pgs.)-Masked hero 3.00
2-16 2.50

Elektra V2 #13 © MAR

Elementals #24 © Bill Willingham

Elflord #4 © Barry & Colin Blair

	GD 2.0	VG 4.0	FN 6.0	VF 8.0	VF/NM 9.0	NM- 9.2

EL DIABLO
DC Comics (Vertigo): Mar, 2001 - No. 4, Jun, 2001 ($2.50, limited series)

1-4-Azzarello-s/Zezelj-a/Sale-c 2.50
TPB (2008, $12.99) r/#1-4 13.00

EL DORADO (See Movie Classics)

ELECTRIC UNDERTOW (See Strikeforce Morituri: Electric Undertow)

ELECTRIC WARRIOR
DC Comics: May, 1986 - No. 18, Oct, 1987 ($1.50, Baxter paper)

1-18 2.50

ELECTROPOLIS
Image Comics: May, 2001 - No. 4, Jan, 2003 ($2.95/$5.95)

1-3-Dean Motter-s/a. 3-(12/01) 3.00
4-(1/03, $5.95, 72 pages) The Infernal Machine pts. 4-6 6.00

ELEKTRA (Also see Daredevil #319-325)
Marvel Comics: Mar, 1995 - No. 4, June, 1995 ($2.95, limited series)

1-4-Embossed-c; Scott McDaniel-a 3.00

ELEKTRA (Also see Daredevil)
Marvel Comics: Nov, 1996 - No. 19, Jun, 1998 ($1.95)

1-Peter Milligan scripts; Deodato-c/a 3.00
1-Variant-c 5.00
2-19: 4-Dr. Strange-c/app. 10-Logan-c/app. 2.50
#(-1) Flashback (7/97) Matt Murdock-c/app.; Deodato-c/a 2.50
.../Cyblade (Image, 3/97,$2.95) Devil's Reign pt. 7 3.00

ELEKTRA (Vol. 2) (Marvel Knights)
Marvel Comics: Sept, 2001 - No. 35, Jun, 2004 ($3.50/$2.99)

1-Bendis-s/Austen-a/Horn-c 4.00
2-6: 2-Two covers (Sienkiewicz and Horn) 3,4-Silver Samurai app. 3.00
3-Initial printing with panel of nudity; most copies pulped 18.00
7-35: 7-Rucka-s begin. 9,10,17-Bennett-a. 19-Meglia-a. 23-25-Chen-a; Sienkiewicz-c 3.00
...Vol. 1: Introspect TPB (2002, $16.99) r/#10-15; Marvel Knights: Double Shot #3 17.00
...Vol. 2: Everything Old is New Again TPB (2003, $16.99) r/#16-22 17.00
...Vol. 3: Relentless TPB (2004, $14.99) r/#23-28 15.00
...Vol. 4: Frenzy TPB (2004, $17.99) r/#29-35 18.00

ELEKTRA & WOLVERINE: THE REDEEMER
Marvel Comics: Jan, 2002 - No. 3, Mar, 2002 ($5.95, square-bound, lim. series)

1-3-Greg Rucka-s/Yoshitaka Amano-a/c 6.00
HC (5/02, $29.95, with dustjacket) r/#1-3, interview with Greg Rucka 30.00

ELEKTRA: ASSASSIN (Also see Daredevil)
Marvel Comics (Epic Comics): Aug, 1986 - No. 8, June, 1987 (Limited series, mature)

1,8-Miller scripts in all; Sienkiewicz-c/a. 6.00
2-7 5.00
Signed & numbered hardcover (Graphitti Designs, $39.95, 2000 print run)- reprints 1-8 50.00
TPB (2000, $24.95) 25.00

ELEKTRA: GLIMPSE & ECHO
Marvel Comics: Sept, 2002 - No. 4, Dec, 2002 ($2.99, limited series)

1-4-Scott Morse-s/painted-a 3.00

ELEKTRA LIVES AGAIN (Also see Daredevil)
Marvel Comics (Epic Comics): 1990 ($24.95, oversize, hardcover, 76 pgs.)
(Produced by Graphitti Designs)

nn-Frank Miller-c/a/scripts; Lynn Varley painted-a; Matt Murdock & Bullseye app. 35.00
2nd printing (9/02, $24.99) 25.00

ELEKTRA MEGAZINE
Marvel Comics: Nov, 1996 - No. 2, Dec, 1996 ($3.95, 96 pgs., reprints, limited series)

1,2: Reprints Frank Miller's Elektra stories in Daredevil 4.00

ELEKTRA SAGA, THE
Marvel Comics Group: Feb, 1984 - No. 4, June, 1984 ($2.00, limited series, Baxter paper)

1-4-r/Daredevil 168-190; Miller-c/a 4.00

ELEKTRA: THE HAND
Marvel Comics: Nov, 2004 - No. 5, Feb, 2005 ($2.99, limited series)

1-5-Gossett-a/Sienkiewicz-c/Yoshida-s; origin of the Hand in the 16th century 3.00
TPB (2005, $13.99) r/#1-5 14.00

ELEKTRA: THE MOVIE
Marvel Comics: Feb, 2005 ($5.99)

1-Movie adaptation; McKeever-s/Perkins-a; photo-c 6.00
TPB (2005, $12.95) r/movie adaptation, Daredevil #168, 181 & Elektra #(-1) 13.00

ELEMENTALS, THE (See The Justice Machine & Morningstar Spec.)
Comico The Comic Co. : June, 1984 - No. 29, Sept, 1988; V2#1, Mar, 1989 - No. 28, 1994? ($1.50/$2.50, Baxter paper); V3#1, Dec, 1995 - No. 3 ($2.95)

1-Willingham-c/a, 1-8 5.00
2-29, V2#1-28: 9-Bissette-a(p). 10-Photo-c. V2#6-1st app. Strike Force America. 18-Prelude to Avalon mini-series. 27-Prequel to Strike Force America series 3.00
V3#1-3: 1-Daniel-a(p), bagged w/gaming card 3.00
Lingerie (5/96, $2.95) 3.00
Special 1,2 (3/86, 1/89)-1-Willingham-a(p) 3.00

ELEMENTALS: (Title series), **Comico**

--GHOST OF A CHANCE, 12/95 ($5.95)-graphic novel, nn-Ross-c. 6.00
--HOW THE WAR WAS WON, 6/96 - No. 2, 8/96 ($2.95) 1,2-Tony Daniel-a, & 1-Variant-c; no logo 3.00
--SEX SPECIAL, 1991 - No. 4, Feb, 1993 ($2.95, color) 2 covers for each 3.00
--SEX SPECIAL, 5/97 - No. 2, 6/97 ($2.95, B&W) 1-Tony Daniel, Jeff Moy-a, 2-Robb Phipps, Adam McDaniel-a 3.00
--SWIMSUIT SPECTACULAR 1996, 6/96 ($2.95), 1-pin-ups, 1-Variant-c; no logo 3.00
--THE VAMPIRE'S REVENGE, 6/96 - No. 2 8/96 ($2.95) 1,2-Willingham-s, 1-Variant-c; no logo 3.00

ELEPHANTMEN
Image Comics: July, 2006 - No. 11, Jul, 2007 ($2.99) (Flip covers on most)

1-13: 1-Starkings-s/Moritat-a/Ladronn-c. 6-Campbell flip-c 3.00
...: The Pilot (5/07, $2.99) short stories and pin-ups by various incl. Sale, Jim Lee, Jae Lee 3.00
...: War Toys (11/07 - No. 3, 4/08, $2.99) 1-3-Mappo war; Starkings-s/Moritat-a/Ladronn-c 3.00

1111 (ELEVEN ELEVEN)
Crusade Entertainment: Oct, 1996 ($2.95, B&W, one-shot)

1-Wrightson-c/a 4.00

ELEVEN OR ONE
Sirius: Apr, 1995 ($2.95)

1-Linsner-c/a 1 3 4 6 8 10
1-(6/96) 2nd printing 3.50

ELFLORD
Nightwind Productions: Jun, 1980 - Vol. 2 #1, 1982 (B&W, magazine-size)

1-1st Barry Blair-s/c/a in comics; B&W-c; limited print run for all 11 22 33 79 140 200
2-5-B&W-c 5 10 15 35 55 75
6-14: 9-14-Color-c 4 8 12 28 44 60
Vol. 2 #1 (1982) 4 8 12 24 37 50

ELFLORD
Aircel Publ.: 1986 - No. 6, Oct, 1989 ($1.70, B&W); V2#1- V2#31, 1995 ($2.00)

1 3.00
2-4,V2#1-20,22-30: 4-6: Last B&W issue. V2#1-Color-a begin. 22-New cast. 25-Begin B&W 2.50
1,2-2nd printings 2.50
21-Double size ($4.95) 5.00

ELFLORD
Warp Graphics: Jan, 1997-No.4, Apr, 1997 ($2.95, B&W, mini-series)

1-4 3.00

ELFLORD (CUTS LOOSE) (Vol. 2)
Warp Graphics: Sept, 1997 - No. 7, Apr, 1998 ($2.95, B&W, mini-series)

1-7 3.00

ELFLORD: DRAGON'S EYE
Night Wynd Enterprises: 1993 ($2.50, B&W)

1 2.50

ELFLORD: THE RETURN
Mad Monkey Press: 1996 ($6.95, magazine size)

1 7.00

ELFQUEST (Also see Fantasy Quarterly & Warp Graphics Annual)
Warp Graphics, Inc.: No. 2, Aug, 1978 - No. 21, Feb, 1985 (All magazine size)
No. 1, Apr, 1979

NOTE: *Elfquest* was originally published as one of the stories in **Fantasy Quarterly** #1. When the publisher went out of business, the creative team, Wendy and Richard Pini, formed WaRP Graphics and continued the series, beginning with **Elfquest** #2. **Elfquest** #1, which reprinted the story from **Fantasy Quarterly**, was published about the same time **Elfquest** #4 was released. Thereafter, most issues were reprinted as demand warranted, until Marvel announced it would reprint the entire series under its Epic imprint (Aug., 1985).

1(4/79)-Reprints Elfquest story from Fantasy Quarterly No. 1

Elfquest #14 © Richard and Wendy Pini

Ellery Queen #4 © SUPR

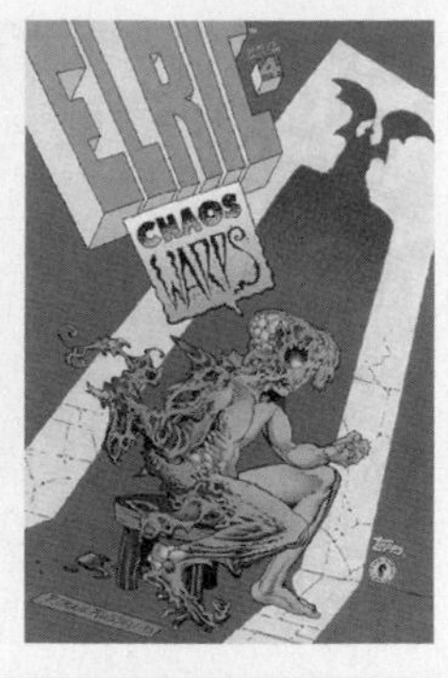

Elric, Stormbringer #4 © Michael Moorcock

	GD 2.0	VG 4.0	FN 6.0	VF 8.0	VF/NM 9.0	NM- 9.2

1st printing ($1.00-c) 4 8 12 22 34 45
2nd printing ($1.25-c) 1 3 4 6 8 10
3rd printings ($1.50-c) 3.00
4th printing; different-c ($1.50-c) 3.00
2(8/78)-5: 1st printings ($1.00-c) 2 4 6 13 18 22
2nd printings ($1.25-c) 4.00
3rd & 4th printings ($1.50-c)(all 4th prints 1989) 3.00
6-9: 1st printings ($1.25-c) 2 4 6 8 10 12
2nd printings ($1.50-c) 3.50
3rd printings ($1.50-c) 3.00
10-21: ($1.50-c); 16-8pg. preview of A Distant Soil 1 2 3 4 6 8
10-14: 2nd printings ($1.50) 3.00

ELFQUEST
Marvel Comics (Epic Comics): Aug, 1985 - No. 32, Mar, 1988

1-Reprints in color the Elfquest epic by Warp Graphics 3.00
2-32 2.50

ELFQUEST
DC Comics: 2003 - Present

Archives Vol. 1 (2003, $49.95, HC) r/#1-5 50.00
Archives Vol. 2 (2005, $49.95, HC) r/#6-10 & Epic Illustrated #1 50.00
25th Anniversary Special (2003, $2.95) r/Elfquest #1 (Apr, 1979); interview w/Pinis 3.00

ELFQUEST (Title series), Warp Graphics
'89 - No. 4, '89 ($1.50, B&W) 1-4: R-original Elfquest series 2.50

ELFQUEST (Volume 2),**Warp Graphics:** V2#1, 5/96 - No. 33, 2/99 ($4.95/$2.95, B&W)
V2#1-31: 1,3,5,8,10,12,13,18,21,23,25-Wendy Pini-c 5.00
32,33-($2.95-c) 3.00

--BLOOD OF TEN CHIEFS, 7/93 - No. 20, 9/95 ($2.00/$2.50) 1-20-By Richard & Wendy Pini 3.00

--HIDDEN YEARS, 5/92 - No. 29, 3/96 ($2.00/$2.25)1-9,9 1/2, 10-29 3.00

--JINK, 11/94 - No. 12, 2/6 ($2.25/$2.50) 1-12-W. Pini/John Byrne-back-c 3.00

--KAHVI, 10/95 - No. 6,3/96 ($2.25, B&W) 1-6 3.00

--KINGS CROSS, 11/97 - No. 2, 12/97 ($2.95, B&W) 1,2 3.00

--KINGS OF THE BROKEN WHEEL, 6/90 - No. 9, 2/92 ($2.00, B&W) (3rd Elfquest saga) 1-9: By R. & W. Pini; 1-Color insert 3.00
1-2nd printing 2.50

--METAMORPHOSIS, 4/96 ($2.95, B&W) 1 3.00

--NEW BLOOD (...Summer Special on-c #1 only), 8/92 - No. 35, 1/96 ($2.00-$2.50, color/ B&W) 1-($3.95, 68 pgs.,...Summer Special on-c)-Byrne-a/scripts (16 pgs.) 4.00
2-35: Barry Blair-a in all 3.00
1993 Summer Special ($3.95) Byrne-a/scripts 4.00

--SHARDS, 8/94 - No. 16, 3/96 ($2.25/$2.50) 1-16 3.00

--SIEGE AT BLUE MOUNTAIN, WaRP Graphics/Apple 3/87 - No. 8, 12/88 (1.75/ $1.95, B&W) 1-Staton-a(i) in all; 2nd Elfquest saga 4.00
1-3-2nd printing, 3-8 2.50
2 3.00

--THE REBELS, 11/94 - No. 12, 3/96 ($2.25/$2.50, B&W/color) 1-12 3.00

--TWO-SPEAR, 10/95 - No. 5, 2/96 ($2.25, B&W) 1-5 3.00

--WAVE DANCERS, 12/93 - No. 6, 3/96, 1-6: 1-Foil-c & poster 3.00
Special 1 ($2.95) 3.00

--WORLDPOOL, 7/97 ($2.95, B&W) 1-Richard Pini-s/Barry Blair-a 3.00

ELFQUEST: THE DISCOVERY
DC Comics: March,2006 - No. 4, Sept, 2006 ($3.99, limited series)

1-4-Wendy Pini-a/Wendy & Richard Pini-s 4.00
TPB (2006, $14.99) r/#1-4 15.00

ELFQUEST: THE GRAND QUEST
DC Comics: 2004 - Present ($9.95/$9.99, B&W, digest-size)

Vol. 1-6 ('04)1-r/Elfquest #1-5; new W. Pini-c. 2-r/#5-8. 3-r/#8-11. 4-r/#11-15. 5-r/#15-18 6-r/#18-20 10.00
Vol. 7-9 ('05) 1-r/Siege At Blue Mountain #1-3. 8-r/SABM #3-5. 9-r/SABM #6-8 10.00
Vol. 10-14 ('05) 10-r/Kings of the Broken Wheel #1-3. 11-KotBW #5-7 & Frazetta Fant. Ill. 12-r/Kings of the Broken Wheel #8&9. 13-r/Elfquest V2 #4-18. 14-r/Hidden Years #4-9 1/2 10.00

ELFQUEST: THE SEARCHER AND THE SWORD
DC Comics: 2004 ($24.95/$14.99, graphic novel)

HC (2004, $24.95, with dust jacket)-Wendy and Richard Pini-s/a/c 25.00
SC (2004, $14.99) 15.00

ELFQUEST: WOLFRIDER
DC Comics: 2003 - Present ($9.95, digest-size)

Volume 1 ('03, $9.95, digest-size) r/Elfquest V2#19,21,23,25,27,29,31; Blood of Ten Chiefs #2; Hidden Years #5; New Blood Special #1; New Blood 1993 Special #1; new W. Pini-c 10.00
Volume 2 ('03, $9.95, digest-size) r/Elfquest V2#33; Blood of Ten Chiefs #10,11,19; Warp Graphics Annual #1 10.00

ELF-THING
Eclipse Comics: March, 1987 ($1.50, B&W, one-shot)

1 2.25

ELIMINATOR (Also see The Solution #16 & The Night Man #16)
Malibu Comics (Ultraverse): Apr, 1995 - No. 3, Jul, 1995 ($2.95/$2.50, lim. series)

0-Mike Zeck-a in all 3.00
1-3-($2.50): 1-1st app. Siren 2.50
1-($3.95)-Black cover edition 4.00

ELIMINATOR FULL COLOR SPECIAL
Eternity Comics: Oct, 1991 ($2.95, one-shot)

1-Dave Dorman painted-c 3.00

ELLA CINDERS (See Comics On Parade, Comics Revue #1,4, Famous Comics Cartoon Book, Giant Comics Editions, Sparkler Comics, Tip Top & Treasury of Comics)

ELLA CINDERS
United Features Syndicate: 1938 - 1940

Single Series 3(1938) 40 80 120 244 397 550
Single Series 21(#2 on-c, #21 on inside), 28('40) 35 70 105 203 327 450

ELLA CINDERS
United Features Syndicate: Mar, 1948 - No. 5, Mar, 1949

1-(#2 on cover) 14 28 42 80 115 150
2 10 20 30 54 72 90
3-5 8 16 24 40 50 60

ELLERY QUEEN
Superior Comics Ltd.: May, 1949 - No. 4, Nov, 1949

1-Kamen-c; L.B. Cole-a; r-in Haunted Thrills 52 104 156 322 536 750
2-4: 3-Drug use stories(2) 40 80 120 235 380 525
NOTE: *Iger shop art in all issues.*

ELLERY QUEEN (TV)
Ziff-Davis Publishing Co.: 1-3/52 (Spring on-c) - No. 2, Summer/52 (Saunders painted-c)

1-Saunders-c 46 92 138 285 475 665
2-Saunders bondage, torture-c 39 78 117 230 370 510

ELLERY QUEEN (Also see Crackajack Funnies No. 23)
Dell Publishing Co.: No. 1165, Mar-May, 1961 - No.1289, Apr, 1962

Four Color 1165 (#1) 10 20 30 70 123 175
Four Color 1243 (11-1/61-61), 1289 8 16 24 56 93 130

ELMER FUDD (Also see Camp Comics, Daffy, Looney Tunes #1 & Super Book #10, 22)
Dell Publishing Co.: No. 470, May, 1953 - No. 1293, Mar-May, 1962

Four Color 470 (#1) 8 16 24 52 86 120
Four Color 558,628,689('56) 5 10 15 30 48 65
Four Color 725,783,841,888,938,977,1032,1081,1131,1171,1222,1293('62) 4 8 12 26 41 55

ELMO COMICS
St. John Publishing Co.: Jan, 1948 (Daily strip-r)

1-By Cecil Jensen 10 20 30 58 79 100

ELONGATED MAN (See Flash #112 & Justice League of America #105)
DC Comics: Jan, 1992 - No. 4, Apr, 1992 ($1.00, limited series)

1-4: 3-The Flash app. 2.50

ELRIC (Of Melnibone)(See First Comics Graphic Novel #6 & Marvel Graphic Novel #2)
Pacific Comics: Apr, 1983 - No. 6, Apr, 1984 ($1.50, Baxter paper)

1-6: Russell-c/a(i) in all 3.00

ELRIC
Topps Comics: 1996 ($2.95, one-shot)

0--One Life: Russell-c/a; adapts Neil Gaiman's short story "One Life--Furnished in Early Moorcock." 3.00

ELRIC, SAILOR ON THE SEAS OF FATE
First Comics: June, 1985 - No. 7, June, 1986 ($1.75, limited series)

1-7: Adapts Michael Moorcock's novel 3.00

ELRIC, STORMBRINGER

Elsie the Cow #3 © DS

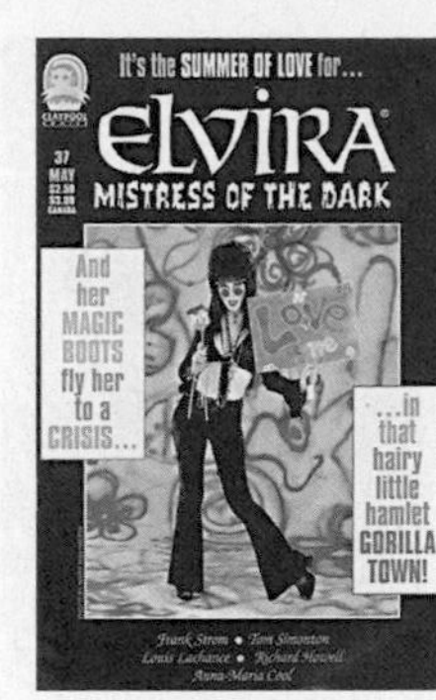

Elvira Mistress of the Dark #37 © Queen B

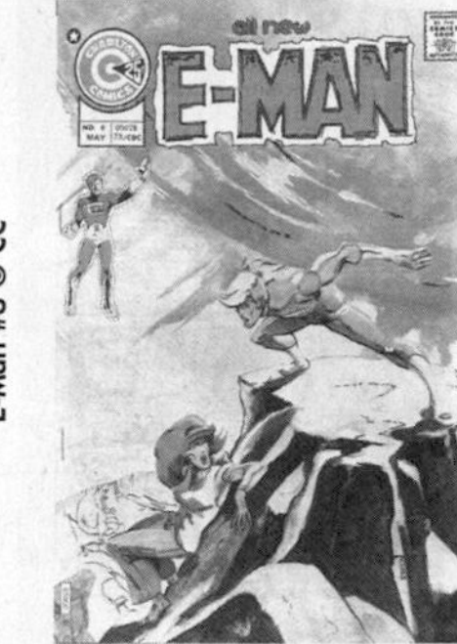

E-Man #8 © CC

GD 2.0 | VG 4.0 | FN 6.0 | VF 8.0 | VF/NM 9.0 | NM- 9.2

Dark Horse Comics/Topps Comics: 1997 - No. 7, 1997($2.95, limited series)
1-7: Russell-c/s/a; adapts Michael Moorcock's novel 3.00

ELRIC: THE BANE OF THE BLACK SWORD
First Comics: Aug, 1988 - No. 6, June, 1989 ($1.75/$1.95, limited series)
1-6: Adapts Michael Moorcock's novel 3.00

ELRIC: THE VANISHING TOWER
First Comics: Aug, 1987 - No. 6, June, 1988 ($1.75, limited series)
1-6: Adapts Michael Moorcock's novel 3.00

ELRIC: WEIRD OF THE WHITE WOLF
First Comics: Oct, 1986 - No. 5, June, 1987 ($1.75, limited series)
1-5: Adapts Michael Moorcock's novel 3.00

EL SALVADOR - A HOUSE DIVIDED
Eclipse Comics: March, 1989 ($2.50, B&W, Baxter paper, stiff-c, 52 pgs.)
1-Gives history of El Salvador 2.50

ELSEWHERE PRINCE, THE (Moebius' Airtight Garage)
Marvel Comics (Epic): May, 1990 - No. 6, Oct, 1990 ($1.95, limited series)
1-6: Moebius scripts & back-up-a in all 3.00

ELSEWORLDS 80-PAGE GIANT
DC Comics: Aug, 1999 ($5.95, one-shot)
1-Most copies destroyed by DC over content of the "Superman's Babysitter" story; some UK shipments sold before recall 10 20 30 70 123 175

ELSEWORLD'S FINEST
DC Comics: 1997 - No. 2, 1997 ($4.95, limited series)
1,2: Elseworld's story-Superman & Batman in the 1920's 5.00

ELSEWORLD'S FINEST: SUPERGIRL & BATGIRL
DC Comics: 1998 ($5.95, one-shot)
1-Haley-a 6.00

ELSIE THE COW
D. S. Publishing Co.: Oct-Nov, 1949 - No. 3, July-Aug, 1950
1-(36 pgs.) 25 50 75 145 233 320
2,3 18 36 54 105 165 225

ELSINORE
Alias Entertainment: Apr, 2005 - Present (75¢/$2.99/$3.25)
1-5: 1-(75¢-c) Brian Denham-a/Kenneth Lillie-Paetz-s. 2-($2.99-c). 4-($3.25-c) 5-Sparacio-a 3.25

ELSON'S PRESENTS
DC Comics: 1981 (100 pgs., no cover price)
Series 1-6: Repackaged 1981 DC comics; 1-DC Comics Presents #29, Flash #303, Batman #331. 2-Superman #335, Ghosts #96, Justice League of America #186. 3-New Teen Titans #3, Secrets of Haunted House #32, Wonder Woman #275. 4-Secrets of the LSH #1, Brave & the Bold #170, New Adv. of Superboy #13. 5-LSH #271, Green Lantern #136, Super Friends #40. 6-Action #515, Mystery in Space #115, Detective #498 2 4 6 10 14 18

ELVEN (Also see Prime)
Malibu Comics (Ultraverse): Oct, 1994 - No. 4, Feb, 1995 ($2.50, lim. series)
0 ($2.95)-Prime app. 3.00
1-4: 2,4-Prime app. 3-Primevil app. 2.50
1-Limited Foil Edition- no price on cover 3.00

ELVIRA MISTRESS OF THE DARK
Marvel Comics: Oct, 1988 ($2.00, B&W, magazine size)
1-Movie adaptation 5.00

ELVIRA MISTRESS OF THE DARK
Claypool Comics (Eclipse): May, 1993 - No. 166, Feb, 2007 ($2.50, B&W)
1-Austin-a(i). Spiegle-a 6.00
2-6: Spiegle-a 4.00
7-99,101-166-Photo-c: 2.50
100-(8/01) Kurt Busiek back-up-s; art by DeCarlo and others 2.50
TPB ($12.95) 13.00

ELVIRA'S HOUSE OF MYSTERY
DC Comics: Jan, 1986 - No. 11, Jan, 1987
1,11: 11-Dave Stevens-c 6.00
2-10: 9-Photo-c, Special 1 (3/87, $1.25) 4.00

ELVIS MANDIBLE, THE
DC Comics (Piranha Press): 1990 ($3.50, 52 pgs., B&W, mature)
nn 3.50

ELVIS PRESLEY (See Career Girl Romances #32, Go-Go, Howard Chaykin's American Flagg #10, Humbug #8, I Love You #60 & Young Lovers #18)

EL ZOMBO FANTASMA
Dark Horse Comics (Rocket Comics): Apr, 2004 - No. 3, June, 2004 ($2.99)
1-3-Wilkins-s&a/Munroe-s 3.00

E-MAN
Charlton Comics: Oct, 1973 - No. 10, Sept, 1975 (Painted-c No. 7-10)
1-Origin & 1st app. E-Man; Staton c/a in all 3 6 9 16 22 28
2-4: 2,4-Ditko-a. 3-Howard-a 2 4 6 8 11 14
5-Miss Liberty Belle app. by Ditko 2 4 6 8 10 12
6-10: 6,7,9,10-Early Byrne-a (#6 is 1/75). 6-Disney parody. 8-Full-length story; Nova begins as E-Man's partner 2 4 6 10 14 18
1-4,9,10 (Modern Comics reprints, '77) 4.00
NOTE: *Killjoy app.-No. 2, 4. Liberty Belle app.-No. 5. Rog 2000 app.-No. 6, 7, 9, 10. Travis app.-No. 3.* ***Sutton*** *a-1.*

E-MAN
Comico: Sept, 1989 ($2.75, one-shot, no ads, high quality paper)
1-Staton-c/a; Michael Mauser story 2.75

E-MAN
Comico: V4#1, Jan, 1990 - No. 3, Mar, 1990 ($2.50, limited series)
1-3: Staton-c/a 2.50

E-MAN
Alpha Productions: Oct, 1993 ($2.75)
V5#1-Staton-c/a; 20th anniversary issue 2.75

E-MAN COMICS (Also see Michael Mauser & The Original E-Man)
First Comics: Apr, 1983 - No. 25, Aug, 1985 ($1.00/$1.25, direct sales only)
1-25: 2-X-Men satire. 3-X-Men/Phoenix satire. 6-Origin retold. 8-Cutey Bunny app. 10-Origin Nova Kane. 24-Origin Michael Mauser 2.50
NOTE: ***Staton*** *a-1-5, 6-25p; c-1-25.*

E-MAN RETURNS
Alpha Productions: 1994 ($2.75, B&W)
1-Joe Staton-c/a(p) 2.75

EMERALD DAWN
DC Comics: 1991 ($4.95, trade paperback)
nn-Reprints Green Lantern: Emerald Dawn #1-6 5.00

EMERALD DAWN II (See Green Lantern...)

EMERGENCY (Magazine)
Charlton Comics: June, 1976 - No. 4, Jan, 1977 (B&W)
1-Neal Adams-c/a; Heath, Austin-a 4 8 12 24 37 50
2,3: 2-N. Adams-c. 3-N. Adams-a. 3 6 9 19 29 38
4-Alcala-a 3 6 9 14 20 25

EMERGENCY (TV)
Charlton Comics: June, 1976 - No. 4, Dec, 1976
1-Staton-c; early Byrne-a (22 pages) 3 6 9 20 30 40
2-4: 2-Staton-c. 2,3-Byrne text illos. 3 6 9 14 20 25

EMERGENCY DOCTOR
Charlton Comics: Summer, 1963 (one-shot)
1 3 6 9 19 29 38

EMIL & THE DETECTIVES (See Movie Comics)

EMISSARY (Jim Valentino's...)
Image Comics (Shadowline): May, 2006 - Present ($3.50)
1-6: 1-Rand-s/Ferreyra-a. 4-6-Long-s 3.50

EMMA FROST
Marvel Comics: Aug, 2003 - No. 18, Feb, 2005 ($2.50/$2.99)
1-7-Emma in high school; Bollers-s/Green-a/Horn-c 2.50
8-18-($2.99) 3.00
... Vol. 1: Higher Learning TPB (2004, $7.99, digest size) r/#1-6 8.00
... Vol. 2: Mind Games TPB (2005, $7.99, digest size) r/#7-12 8.00
... Vol. 3: Bloom TPB (2005, $7.99, digest size) r/#13-18 8.00

EMMA PEEL & JOHN STEED (See The Avengers)

EMPEROR'S NEW CLOTHES, THE
Dell Publishing Co.: 1950 (10¢, 68 pgs., 1/2 size, oblong)
nn - (Surprise Books series) 6 12 18 28 34 40

EMPIRE

Empty Love Stories 1999 © Steve Darnall

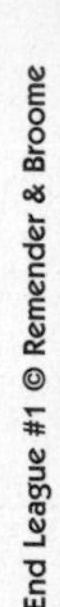

End League #1 © Remender & Broome

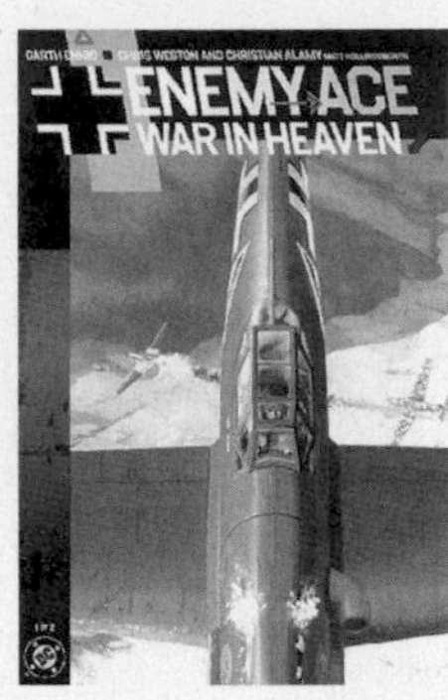

Enemy Ace: War in Heaven #1 © DC

GD VG FN VF VF/NM NM-
2.0 4.0 6.0 8.0 9.0 9.2

Image Comics (Gorilla): May, 2000 - No. 2, Sept, 2000 ($2.50)
DC Comics: No. 0, Aug, 2003; Sept, 2003 - No. 6, Feb, 2004 ($4.95/$2.50, limited series)

1,2: 1 (5/00)-Waid-s/Kitson-a; w/Crimson Plague prologue 2.50
0-(8/03) reprints #1,2 5.00
1-6: 1-(9/03) new Waid-s/Kitson-a/c 2.50
TPB (DC, 2004, $14.95) r/series; Kitson sketch pages; Waid intro. 15.00

EMPIRE STRIKES BACK, THE (See Marvel Comics Super Special #16 & Marvel Special Edition)

EMPTY LOVE STORIES
Slave Labor #1 & 2/Funny Valentine Press: Nov, 1994 - Present ($2.95, B&W)

1,2: Steve Darnall scripts in all. 1-Alex Ross-c. 2-(8/96)-Mike Allred-c 4.00
1,2-2nd printing (Funny Valentine Press) 3.00
... 1999-Jeff Smith-c; Doran-a 3.00
..."Special" (2.95) Ty Templeton-c 3.00

ENCHANTED
Sirius Entertainment: 1997 - No. 3 ($2.50, B&W, limited series)

1-3-Robert Chang-s/a 2.50

ENCHANTED (Volume 2)
Sirius Entertainment: 1998 - No. 3 ($2.95, limited series)

1-Robert Chang-s/a 3.00

ENCHANTED APPLES OF OZ, THE (See First Comics Graphic Novel #5)

ENCHANTER
Eclipse Comics: Apr, 1987 - No. 3, Aug. 1987 ($2.00, B&W, limited series)

1-3 2.50

ENCHANTING LOVE
Kirby Publishing Co.: Oct, 1949 - No. 6, July, 1950 (All 52 pgs.)

1-Photo-c 15 30 45 90 140 190
2-Photo-c; Powell-a 10 20 30 56 76 95
3,4,6: 3-Jimmy Stewart photo-c 10 20 30 54 72 90
5-Ingels-a, 9 pgs.; photo-c 15 30 45 92 144 195

ENCHANTMENT VISUALETTES (Magazine)
World Editions: Dec, 1949 - No. 5, Apr, 1950 (Painted c-1)

1-Contains two romance comic strips each 15 30 45 88 137 185
2 12 24 36 67 94 120
3-5 10 20 30 56 76 95

END LEAGUE, THE
Dark Horse Comics: Dec, 2007 - Present ($2.99)

1-4-Broome-c/a; Remender-s 3.00

ENEMY ACE SPECIAL (Also see Our Army at War #151, Showcase #57, 58 & Star Spangled War Stories #138)
DC Comics: 1990 ($1.00, one-shot)

1-Kubert-r/Our Army #151,153; c-r/Showcase 57 5.00

ENEMY ACE: WAR IDYLL
DC Comics: 1990 (Graphic novel)

Hardcover-George Pratt-s/painted-a/c 30.00
Softcover (1991, $14.95) 15.00

ENEMY ACE: WAR IN HEAVEN
DC Comics: 2001 - No. 2, 2001 ($5.95, squarebound, limited series)

1,2-Ennis-s; Von Hammer in WW2. 1-Weston & Alamy-a. 2-Heath-a 6.00
TPB (2003, $14.95) r/#1,2 & Star Spangled War Stories #139; Jim Dietz-painted-c 15.00

ENGINEHEAD
DC Comics: June, 2004 - No. 6, Nov, 2004 ($2.50, limited series)

1-6-Joe Kelly-s/Ted McKeever-a/c. 6-Metal Men app. 2.50

ENIGMA
DC Comics (Vertigo): Mar, 1993 - No. 8, Oct, 1993 ($2.50, limited series)

1-8: Milligan scripts 2.50
Trade paperback ($19.95)-reprints 20.00

ENO AND PLUM (Also see Cud Comics)
Oni Press: Mar, 1998 ($2.95, B&W)

1-Terry LaBan-s/c/a 3.00

ENSIGN O'TOOLE (TV)
Dell Publishing Co.: Aug-Oct, 1963 - No. 2, 1964

1 3 6 9 20 30 40
2 3 6 9 16 23 30

ENSIGN PULVER (See Movie Classics)

GD VG FN VF VF/NM NM-
2.0 4.0 6.0 8.0 9.0 9.2

EPIC
Marvel Comics (Epic Comics): 1992 - Book 4, 1992 ($4.95, lim. series, 52 pgs.)

Book One-Four: 2-Dorman painted-c 5.00
NOTE: *Alien Legion in #3. Cholly & Flytrap by* ***Burden****(scripts) &* ***Suydam****(art) in 3, 4. Dinosaurs in #4. Dreadlands in #1. Hellraiser in #1. Nightbreed in #2. Sleeze Brothers in #2. Stalkers in #1-4. Wild Cards in #1-4.*

EPIC ANTHOLOGY
Marvel Comics (Epic Comics): Apr, 2004 ($5.99)

1-Short stories by various 6.00

EPIC ILLUSTRATED (Magazine)
Marvel Comics Group: Spring, 1980 - No. 34, Feb, 1986 ($2.00/$2.50, B&W/color, mature)

1-Frazetta-c; Silver Surfer/Galactus-sty; Wendy Pini-s/a; Suydam-s/a; Metamorphosis Odyssey begins (thru #9) Starlin-a 2 4 6 8 10 12
2-10: 2-Bissette/Veitch-a; Goodwin-s. 3-Goodwin-s. 4-Ellison 15 pg. story w/art by Steacy; Hempel-s/a; Veitch-s/a. 5-Hildebrandts-c/interview; Jusko-a; Vess-s/a. 6-Ellison-s (26 pgs). 7-Adams-s/a(16 pgs.); BWS interview. 8-Suydam-s/a; Vess-s/a. 9-Conrad-c. 10-Marada the She-Wolf-c/sty(21 pgs.) by Claremont/Bolton 1 2 3 4 5 7
11-20: 11-Wood-a; Jusko-a. 12-Wolverton Spacehawk-r edited & recolored w/article on him; Muth-a. 13-Blade Runner preview by Williamson. 14-Elric of Melnibone by Russell; Revenge of the Jedi preview. 15-Vallejo-c & interview; 1st Dreadstar story (cont'd in Dreadstar #1). 16-B. Smith-c/a(2); Sim-s/a. 17-Starslammers preview. 18-Go Nagai; Williams-a. 19-Jabberwocky w/Hampton-a; Cheech Wizard-s. 20-The Sacred & the Profane begins by Ken Steacy; Elric by Gould; Williams-a 1 2 3 5 6 8
21-30: 21-Vess-s/a. 22-Frankenstein w/Wrightson-a. 26-Galactus series begins (thru #34); Cerebus the Aardvark story by Dave Sim. 27-Groo. 28-Cerebus. 29-1st Sheeva. 30-Cerebus; History of Dreadstar, Starlin-s/a; Williams-a; Vess-a 1 3 4 6 8 10
31-33: 31-Bolton-c/a. 32-Cerebus portfolio. 2 4 6 8 10 12
34-R.E.Howard tribute by Thomas-s/Plunkett-a; Moore-s/Veitch-a; Cerebus; Cholly & Flytrap w/Suydam-a; BWS-a 2 4 6 10 14 18
Sampler (early 1980 8 pg. preview giveaway) same cover as #1 with "Sampler" text 6.00
NOTE: ***N. Adams*** *a-7; c-6.* ***Austin*** *a-15-20i.* ***Bode*** *a-19, 23, 27r.* ***Bolton*** *a-7, 10-12, 15, 18, 22-25; c-10, 18, 22, 23.* ***Boris*** *c/a-15.* ***Brunner*** *c-12.* ***Buscema*** *a-1p, 9p, 11-13p.* ***Byrne/Austin*** *a-26-34.* ***Chaykin*** *a-2; c-8.* ***Conrad*** *a-2-5, 7-9, 25-34; c-17.* ***Corben*** *a-15; c-2.* ***Frazetta*** *c-1.* ***Golden*** *a-3r.* ***Gulacy*** *c/a-3.* ***Jeff Jones*** *c-25.* ***Kaluta*** *a-17r, 21, 24r, 26; c-4, 28.* ***Nebres*** *a-1.* ***Reese*** *a-12.* ***Russell*** *a-2-4, 9, 14, 33; c-14.* ***Simonson*** *a-17.* ***B. Smith*** *c/a-7, 16.* ***Starlin*** *a-1-9, 14, 15, 34.* ***Steranko*** *c-19.* ***Williamson*** *a-13, 27, 34.* ***Wrightson*** *a-13p, 22, 25, 27, 34; c-30.*

EPIC LITE
Marvel Comics (Epic Comics): Sept, 1991 ($3.95, 52 pgs., one-shot)

1-Bob the Alien, Normalman by Valentino 4.00

EPICURUS THE SAGE
DC Comics (Piranha Press): Vol. 1, 1991 - Vol. 2, 1991 ($9.95, 8-1/8x10-7/8")

Volume 1,2-Sam Kieth-c/a; Messner-Loebs-s 10.00
TPB (2003, $19.95) r/ #1,2, Fast Forward Rising the Sun; new story 20.00

EPILOGUE
IDW Publishing: Sept, 2008 - Present ($3.99)

1-Steve Niles-s/Kyle Hotz-a/c 4.00

ERADICATOR
DC Comics: Aug, 1996 - No. 3, Oct, 1996 ($1.75, limited series)

1-3: Superman app. 3.00

ERNIE COMICS (Formerly Andy Comics #21; All Love Romances #26 on)
Current Books/Ace Periodicals: No. 22, Sept, 1948 - No. 25, Mar, 1949

nn (9/48,11/48; #22,23)-Teenage humor 8 16 24 40 50 60
24,25 6 12 18 28 34 40

ESCAPADE IN FLORENCE (See Movie Comics)

ESCAPE FROM DEVIL'S ISLAND
Avon Periodicals: 1952

1-Kinstler-c; r/as Dynamic Adventures #9 40 80 120 235 380 525

ESCAPE FROM THE PLANET OF THE APES (See Power Record Comics)

ESCAPE TO WITCH MOUNTAIN (See Walt Disney Showcase No. 29)

ESCAPISTS, THE (See Michael Chabon Presents The Amazing Adventures of the Escapist)
Dark Horse Comics: July, 2006 - No. 6, Dec, 2006 ($1.00/$2.99, limited series)

1-($1.00) Frank Miller-c; r/Vaughan story from Michael Chabon...#8 2.50
2-6($2.99) Vaughan-s/Rolston & Alexander-a. 2-James Jean-c. 3-Cassaday-c 3.00

ESPERS (Also see Interface)
Eclipse Comics: July, 1986 - No. 5, Apr, 1987 ($1.25/$1.75, Mando paper)

1-5-James Hudnall story & David Lloyd-a. 3.00

ESPERS
Halloween Comics: V2#1, 1996 - No. 6, 1997 ($2.95, B&W) (1st Halloween Comics series)

ESPers V3 #1 © James Hudnall

Espionage #1 © NBC

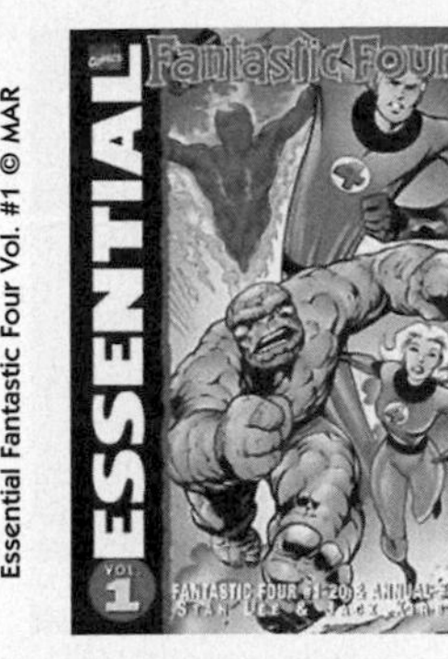

Essential Fantastic Four Vol. #1 © MAR

GD 2.0 VG 4.0 FN 6.0 VF 8.0 VF/NM 9.0 NM- 9.2

V2#1-6: James D. Hudnall scripts 3.00
Undertow TPB ('98, $14.95) r/#1-6 15.00

ESPERS
Image Comics: V3#1, 1997 - Present ($2.95, B&W, limited series)

V3#1-7: James D. Hudnall scripts 3.00
Black Magic TPB ('98, $14.95) r/#1-4 15.00

ESPIONAGE (TV)
Dell Publishing Co.: May-July, 1964 - No. 2, Aug-Oct, 1964

1,2 3 6 9 20 30 40

ESSENTIAL (Title series), **Marvel Comics**

--ANT-MAN, '02 (B&W- r) V1-Reprints app. from Tales To Astonish #27, #35-69; Kirby-c 15.00

--AVENGERS, '98 (B&W- r) V1-R-Avengers #1-24; new Immonen-c 15.00
V2(6/00)-Reprints Avengers #25-46, King-Size Special #1; Immonen-c 15.00
V3(3/01)-Reprints Avengers #47-68, Annual #2; Immonen-c 15.00
V4('04)-Reprints Avengers #69-97, Incredible Hulk #140; Neal Adams-c 17.00
V5('06)-Reprints Avengers #98-119, Daredevil #99, Defenders #8-11 17.00
V6('08)-Reprints Avengers #120-140, Giant Size #1-4, Capt. Marvel #33 & FF #150 17.00

--CAPTAIN AMERICA, '00 (B&W- r) V1-Reprints stories from Tales of Suspense #59-99, Captain America #100-102; new Romita & Milgrom-c 15.00
V2(1/02)-Reprints #103-126; Steranko-c 15.00
V3('06)-Reprints #127-153 17.00
V4('07)-Reprints #157-186 17.00

--CLASSIC X-MEN, '06 - Present (B&W- r) (See Essential Uncanny X-Men for V1)
V2-($16.99) R-X-Men #25-53 & Avengers #53; Gil Kane-c 17.00

--CONAN, '00 (B&W- r) V1-R-Conan the Barbarian#1-25; new Buscema-c 15.00

--DAREDEVIL, '02 - Present (B&W-r)
V1-R-Daredevil #1-25 15.00
V2-($16.99) R-Daredevil #26-48, Special #1, Fantastic Four #73 17.00
V3-($16.99) R-Daredevil #49-74, Iron Man #35-38 17.00
V4-($16.99) R-Daredevil #75-101, Avengers #111 17.00

--DAZZLER, '07 (B&W- r) V1-R/#1-21, X-Men #130-131, Amaz. Spider-Man #203 17.00

--DEFENDERS, '05 (B&W-r) V1-Reprints Doctor Strange #183, Sub-Mariner #22,34,35, Incredible Hulk #126, Marvel Feature #1-3, Defenders #1-14, Avengers #115-118 17.00
V2-($16.99) R- Defenders #15-30, Giant-Size Defenders #1-4, Marvel Two-In-One #6,7, Marvel Team-Up #33-35 and Marvel Treasury Edition #12 17.00
V3-($16.99) R- Defenders #31-60 and Annual #1 17.00

--DOCTOR STRANGE, '04 - Present (B&W-r)
V1-($15.95) Reprints Strange Tales #110,111,114-168 16.00
V1 (2nd printing)-(2006, $16.99) Reprints Strange Tales #110,111,114-168 17.00
V2-($16.99) R-Doctor Strange #169-178,180-183; Avengers #61, Sub-Mariner #22 Marvel Feature #1, Incredible Hulk #126 and Marvel Premiere #3-14 17.00
V3-($16.99) R-Doctor Strange #1-29 & Annual #1;Tomb of Dracula #44,45 17.00

--FANTASTIC FOUR, '98 - Present (B&W-r)
V1-Reprints FF #1-20, Annual #1; new Alan Davis-c; multiple printings exist 17.00
V2-Reprints FF #21-40, Annual #2; Davis and Farmer-c 15.00
V3-Reprints FF #41-63, Annual #3,4; Davis-c 15.00
V4-Reprints FF #64-83, Annual #5,6 17.00
V5-Reprints FF #84-110 17.00
V6-Reprints FF #111-137 17.00

--GHOST RIDER, '05 (B&W-r) V1-Reprints Marvel Spotlight #5-12, Ghost Rider #1-20 and Daredevil #138 17.00
V2-Reprints Ghost Rider #21-50 17.00

--GODZILLA, '06 (B&W-r) V1-Godzilla #1-24 20.00

--HOWARD THE DUCK, '02 (B&W- r) V1-Reprints #1-27, Annual #1; plus stories from Marvel Treasury Ed. #12, Man-Thing #1, Giant-Size Man-Thing #4,5, Fear #19; Bolland-c 15.00

--HULK, '99 (B&W-r) V1-R-Incred. Hulk #1-6, Tales To Astonish stories; new Timm-c 15.00
V2-Reprints Tales To Astonish #102-117, Annual #1 15.00
V3-Reprints Incredible Hulk #118-142, Capt. Marvel #20&21, Avengers #88 17.00
V4-Reprints Incredible Hulk #143-170 17.00

--HUMAN TORCH, '03 (B&W-r) V1-Strange Tales #101-134 & Ann. 2; Kirby-c 15.00

--IRON MAN, '00 - Present (B&W-r)
V1-Reprints Tales Of Suspense #39-72; new Timm-c and back-c 15.00
V2-Reprints Tales Of Suspense #73-99, Tales To Astonish #82 & Iron Man #1-11 17.00
V3-Reprints Iron Man #12-38 & Daredevil #73 17.00

--KILLRAVEN, '05 (B&W-r) V1-Reprints Amazing Adventures V2 #18-39, Marvel Team-Up #45, Marvel Graphic Novel #7, Killraven #1 (2001) 17.00

--LUKE CAGE, POWER MAN, '05 (B&W-r) V1-Hero For Hire #1-16 & Power Man #17-27 17.00
V2-Reprints Power Man #28-49 & Annual #1 17.00

--MAN-THING, '06 (B&W-r) V1-Reprints Savage Tales #1, Astonishing Tales #12-13, Adventure Into Fear #10-19, Man-Thing #1-14, Giant-Size Man-Thing #1-2 & Monsters Unleashed #5,8,9 17.00
V2-R/Man-Thing #15-22 & #1-11 ('79 series), Giant-Size Man-Thing #3-5, Rampaging Hulk #7, Marvel Team-Up #68, Marvel Two-In-One #43 & Doctor Strange #41 17.00

--MARVEL HORROR, '06 (B&W-r) V1-R/#Ghost Rider #1-2, Marvel Spotlight #12-24, Son of Satan #1-8, Marvel Two-In-One #14, Marvel Team-Up #32,80,81, Vampire Tales #2-3, Haunt of Horror #2,4,5, Marvel Premiere #27, & Marvel Preview #7 17.00

--MARVEL SAGA, '08 (B&W-r) V1-R/#1-12 17.00

--MARVEL TEAM-UP, '02 - Present (B&W-r) V1('02, '06)-R/#1-24 17.00
V2-R/#25-51 and Marvel Two-In-One #17 17.00

--MARVEL TWO-IN-ONE, '05 - Present (B&W-r)
V1-Reprints Marvel Feature #11&12, Marvel Two-In-One #1-20,22-25 & Annual #1, Marvel Team-Up #47 and Fantastic Four Ann. #11 17.00
V2-R/#26-52 & Annual #2,3 17.00

--MONSTER OF FRANKENSTEIN, '04 (B&W-r) V1-Reprints Monster of Frankenstein #1-5, Frankenstein Monster #6-18, Giant-Size Werewolf #2, Monsters Unleashed #2,4-10 & Legion of Monsters #1 17.00

--MOON KNIGHT, '06 (B&W-r) V1-Reprints Moon Knight #1-10 and early apps. 17.00
V2-R/#11-30 17.00

--MS. MARVEL, '07 (B&W-r) V1-Reprints Ms. Marvel #1-23, Marvel Super-Heroes Magazine #10,11, and Avengers Annual #10 17.00

--NOVA, '06 (B&W-r) V1-Reprints Nova #1-25, AS-M #175, Marvel Two-In One Ann. #3 17.00

--OFFICIAL HANDBOOK OF THE MARVEL UNIVERSE, '06 (B&W-r) V1-Reprints #1-15 profiling Abomination through Zzzax; dead and inactive characters; weapons & hardware; wraparound-c by Byrne 17.00

--OFFICIAL HANDBOOK OF THE MARVEL UNIVERSE - DELUXE EDITION, '06 (B&W r)
V1-Reprints #1-7 profiling Abomination through Magneto; wraparound-c by Byrne 17.00
V2-Reprints #8-14 profiling Magus through Wolverine; wraparound-c by Byrne 17.00
V3-Reprints #15-20 profiling Wonder Man through Zzzax & Book of the Dead 17.00

--OFFICIAL HANDBOOK OF THE MARVEL UNIVERSE - MASTER EDITION, '08 (B&W-r)
V1-Reprints profiling Abomination through Gargoyle 17.00

--OFFICIAL HANDBOOK OF THE MARVEL UNIVERSE - UPDATE '89, '06 (B&W-r)
V1-Reprints #1-8; wraparound-c by Frenz 17.00

--PETER PARKER, THE SPECTACULAR SPIDER-MAN, '05 (B&W-r) V1-Reprints #1-31 17.00
V2-Reprints #32-53 & Annual #1,2; Amazing Spider-Man Annual #13 17.00
V3-Reprints #54-74 & Annual #3; Frank Miller-c 17.00

--POWER MAN AND IRON FIST, '07 (B&W-r) V1-R/#50-72,74-75 17.00

--PUNISHER, '04, '06 - Present (B&W-r) V1-Reprints early app. in Amazing Spider-Man, Captain America, Daredevil, Marvel Preview and Punisher #1-5 (2 printings) 17.00
V2-Punisher #1-20, Annual #1 and Daredevil #257 17.00

--SAVAGE SHE-HULK, '06 (B&W-r) V1-R/#1-25 17.00

--SILVER SURFER, '98 - Present (B&W-r)
V1-R-material from SS#1-18 and Fantastic Four Ann. #5 15.00
V2-R-SS#1(1982), SS#1-18 & Ann#1(1987), Epic Illustrated #1, Marvel Fanfare #51 17.00

--SPIDER-MAN, '96 - Present (B&W-r)
V1-R-AF #15, Amaz. S-M #1-20, Ann. #1 (2 printings) 15.00
V2-R-Amaz. Spider-Man #21-43, Annual #2,3 15.00
V3-R-Amaz. Spider-Man #44-68 15.00
V4-R-Amaz. Spider-Man #69-89; Annual #4,5; new Timm-f&b-c 15.00
V5-R-Amaz. Spider-Man #90-113; new Romita-c 15.00
V6-R-Amaz. Spider-Man #114-137, Giant-Size Super-Heroes #1 G-S S-M #1,2 17.00
V7-R-Amaz. Spider-Man #138-160, Annual #10; Giant-Size Spider-Man #3-5 17.00
V8-R-Amaz. Spider-Man #161-185, Annual #11; G-S Spider-Man #6; Nova #12 17.00

--SPIDER-WOMAN, '05 (B&W-r) V1-Reprints Marvel Spotlight #32, Marvel Two-In-One #29-33, Spider-Woman #1-25 17.00
V2-R-Spider-Woman #26-50, Marvel Team-Up #97 & Uncanny X-Men #148 17.00

--SUPER-VILLAIN TEAM-UP, '04 (B&W-r) V1-r/S-V T-U #1-14 & 16-17, Giant-Size S-V T-U #1,2; Avengers #154-156; Champions #16, & Astonishing Tales #1-8 17.00

--TALES OF THE ZOMBIE, '06 (B&W-r) V1-($16.99) r/#1-10 & Dracula Lives #1,2 17.00

--THOR, '01 (B&W-r) V1-R-Journey Into Mystery #83-112 15.00
V2-($16.99) R-Thor #113-136 & Annual #1,2 17.00
V3-($16.99) R-Thor #137-166 17.00

--TOMB OF DRACULA, '03 - Present (B&W-r) V1-R-Tomb of Dracula #1-25, Werewolf By Night #15, Giant-Size Chillers #1 15.00

Essential Werewolf By Night Vol. #2 © MAR

Eternals (2008 series) #1 © MAR

Evangeline #5 © FC

GD 2.0 | VG 4.0 | FN 6.0 | VF 8.0 | VF/NM 9.0 | NM- 9.2

V2-($16.99) R-Tomb of Dracula #26-49, Giant-Size Dracula #2-5, Dr. Strange #14 17.00
V3-($16.99) R-Tomb of Dracula #50-70, Tomb of Dracula Magazine #1-4 17.00
V4-($16.99) R/Stories from Tomb of Dracula Magazine #2-6, Dracula Lives! #1-13, and Frankenstein Monster #7-9 17.00

--UNCANNY X-MEN, '99 - Present (B&W reprints) (See Essential Classic X-Men for V2)
V1-Reprints X-Men (1st series) #1-24; Timm-c 15.00

ESSENTIAL VERTIGO: THE SANDMAN
DC Comics (Vertigo): Aug, 1996 - No. 32, Mar, 1999 ($1.95/$2.25, reprints)
1-13,15-31: Reprints Sandman, 2nd series 3.00
14-($2.95) 3.50
32-($4.50) Reprints Sandman Special #1 4.50

ESSENTIAL VERTIGO: SWAMP THING
DC Comics: Nov, 1996 - No. 24, Oct, 1998 ($1.95/$2.25,B&W, reprints)
1-11,13-24: 1-9-Reprints Alan Moore's Swamp Thing stories 3.00
12-($3.50) r/Annual #2 3.50

ESSENTIAL WEREWOLF BY NIGHT
Marvel Comics: 2005 - Present (B&W reprints)
V1-($16.99) r/Marvel Spotlight #2-4, Werewolf By Night 1-23, Marvel Team-Up #12, Tomb of Dracula #18, Giant-Size Creatures #1 17.00
V2-R/#22-43, Giant-Size Werewolf #2-5 and Marvel Premiere #28 17.00

ESSENTIAL WOLVERINE
Marvel Comics: 1999 - Present (B&W reprints)
V1-r/#1-23, V2-r/#24-47, V3-R/#48-69, V4-R/#70-90 17.00

ESSENTIAL X-FACTOR
Marvel Comics: 2005 - Present (B&W reprints)
V1-($16.99) r/X-Factor #1-16 & Annual #1, Avengers #262, Fantastic Four #286, Thor #373&374 and Power Pack #27 17.00
V2-Reprints X-Factor #17-35 & Annual #2, Thor #378 17.00

ESSENTIAL X-MEN
Marvel Comics: 1996 - Present (B&W reprints)
V1-V4: V1-R/Giant Size X-Men #1, X-Men #94-119. V2-R-X-Men #120-144. V3-R-Uncanny X-Men #145-161, Ann. #3-5. V4-Uncanny X-Men #162-179, Ann. #6 15.00
V5-($16.99) R/Uncanny X-Men #180-198, Ann. #7-8 17.00
V6-($16.99) R/Uncanny X-Men #199-213, Ann. #9, New Mutants Special Edition #1, X-Factor #9-11, New Mutants #46, Thor #373-374 and Power Pack #27 17.00
V7-($16.99) R/Uncanny X-Men #214-228, Ann. #10,11, and F.F. vs. The X-Men #1-4 17.00
V8-($16.99) R/Uncanny X-Men #229-243, Ann. #12 & X-Factor #36-39 17.00

ESTABLISHMENT, THE (Also see The Authority and The Monarchy)
DC Comics (WildStorm): Nov, 2001 - No. 13, Nov, 2002 ($2.50)
1-13-Edginton-s/Adlard-a 2.50

ETERNAL, THE
Marvel Comics (MAX): Aug, 2003 - No. 6, Jan, 2004 ($2.99, mature)
1-6-Austen-s/Walker-a 3.00

ETERNAL BIBLE, THE
Authentic Publications: 1946 (Large size) (16 pgs. in color)
1 15 30 45 84 127 170

ETERNALS, THE
Marvel Comics Group: July, 1976 - No. 19, Jan, 1978
1-(Regular 25¢ edition)-Origin & 1st app. Eternals 3 6 9 14 19 24
1-(30¢-c variant, limited distribution) 3 6 9 18 27 36
2-(Reg. 25¢ edition)-1st app. Ajak & The Celestials 2 4 6 8 10 12
2-(30¢-c variant, limited distribution) 2 4 6 10 14 18
3-19: 14,15-Cosmic powered Hulk-c/story 1 3 4 6 8 10
12-16-(35¢-c variants, limited distribution) 2 4 6 9 12 15
Annual 1(10/77) 1 3 4 6 8 10
Eternals by Jack Kirby HC (2006, $75.00, dust jacket) r/#1-19 & Annual #1; intro by Royer; letter pages from #1,2,Annual #1; afterwords by Robert Greenberger 75.00
NOTE: *Kirby c/a(p) in all.*

ETERNALS, THE
Marvel Comics: Oct, 1985 - No. 12, Sept, 1986 (Maxi-series, mando paper)
1,12 (52 pgs.): 12-Williamson-a(i) 3.00
2-11 2.50

ETERNALS
Marvel Comics: Aug, 2006 - No. 7, Mar, 2007 ($3.99, limited series)
1-7-Neil Gaiman-s/John Romita Jr.-a/Rick Berry-c 4.00
1-7-Variant covers by Romita Jr. 4.00

GD 2.0 | VG 4.0 | FN 6.0 | VF 8.0 | VF/NM 9.0 | NM- 9.2

1-Variant cover by Coipel 4.00
... Sketchbook (2006, $1.99, B&W) character sketches and sketch pages from #1 2.25
HC (2007, $29.99, dustjacket) r/#1-7; gallery of variant covers; sketches, Gaiman interview, Gaiman's original proposal; background essay on Kirby's Eternals 30.00

ETERNALS
Marvel Comics: Aug, 2008 - Present ($2.99)
1-4-Acuña-a/c; Knauf-s. 2,4-Iron Man app. 3.00

ETERNALS: THE HEROD FACTOR
Marvel Comics: Nov, 1991 ($2.50, 68 pgs.)
1 2.50

ETERNAL WARRIOR (See Solar #10 & 11)
Valiant/Acclaim Comics (Valiant): Aug, 1992 - No. 50, Mar, 1996 ($2.25/$2.50)
1-Unity x-over; Miller-c; origin Eternal Warrior & Aram (Armstrong) 4.00
1-($2.25-c) Gold logo 5.00
1-Gold foil logo on embossed cover; no cover price 6.00
2-8: 2-Unity x-over; Simonson-c. 3-Archer & Armstrong x-over. 4-1st brief app. Bloodshot (last pg.); see Rai #0 for 1st full app.; Cowan-c. 5-2nd full app. Bloodshot (12/92; see Rai #0). 6,7: 6-2nd app. Master Darque. 8-Flip book w/Archer & Armstrong #8 3.00
9-25,27-34: 9-1st Book of Geomancer. 14-16-Bloodshot app. 18-Doctor Mirage cameo. 19-Doctor Mirage app. 22-W/bound-in trading card. 25-Archer & Armstrong app.; cont'd from A&A #25 2.50
26-($2.75, 44 pgs.)-Flip book w/Archer & Armstrong 2.75
35-50: 35-Double-c; $2.50-c begins. 50-Geomancer app. 2.50
Special 1 (2/96, $2.50)-Wings of Justice; Art Holcomb script 2.50
Yearbook 1 (1993, $3.95), 2(1994, $3.95) 4.00

ETERNAL WARRIORS: BLACKWORKS
Acclaim Comics (Valiant Heroes): Mar, 1998 ($3.50, one-shot)
1 3.50

ETERNAL WARRIORS: DIGITAL ALCHEMY
Acclaim Comics (Valiant Heroes): Vol. 2, Sep, 1997 ($3.95, one-shot, 64 pgs.)
Vol. 2-Holcomb-s/Eaglesham-a(p) 4.00

ETERNAL WARRIORS: FIST AND STEEL
Acclaim Comics (Valiant): May, 1996 - No. 2, June, 1996 ($2.50, lim. series)
1,2: Geomancer app. in both. 1-Indicia reads "June." 2-Bo Hampton-a 2.50

ETERNAL WARRIORS: TIME AND TREACHERY
Acclaim Comics (Valiant Heroes): Vol. 1, Jun, 1997 ($3.95, one-shot, 48 pgs.)
Vol. 1-Reintro Aram, Archer, Ivar the Timewalker, & Gilad the Warmaster; 1st app. Shalla Redburn; Art Holcomb script 4.00

ETERNITY SMITH
Renegade Press: Sept, 1986 - No. 5, May, 1987 ($1.25/$1.50, 36 pgs.)
1-5: 1st app. Eternity Smith. 5-Death of Jasmine 2.50

ETERNITY SMITH
Hero Comics: Sept, 1987 - No. 9, 1988 ($1.95)
V2#1-9: 8-Indigo begins 2.50

ETTA KETT
King Features Syndicate/Standard: No. 11, Dec, 1948 - No. 14, Sept, 1949
11-Teenage 11 22 33 60 83 105
12-14 8 16 24 44 57 70

EVA: DAUGHTER OF THE DRAGON
Dynamite Entertainment: 2007 ($4.99, one-shot)
1-Two covers by Jo Chen and Edgar Salazar; Jerwa-s/Salazar-a 5.00

EVANGELINE (Also see Primer)
Comico/First Comics V2#1 on/Lodestone Publ.: 1984 - #2, 6/84; V2#1, 5/87 - V2#12, Mar, 1989 (Baxter paper)
1,2, V2#1 (5/87) - 12, Special #1 (1986, $2.00)-Lodestone Publ. 2.50

EVA THE IMP
Red Top Comic/Decker: 1957 - No. 2, Nov, 1957
1,2 5 10 14 20 24 28

EVEN MORE FUND COMICS (Benefit book for the Comic Book Legal Defense Fund) (Also see More Fund Comics)
Sky Dog Press: Sept, 2004 ($10.00, B&W, trade paperback)
nn-Anthology of short stories and pin-ups by various; Spider-Man-c by Cho 10.00

E.V.E. PROTOMECHA
Image Comics (Top Cow): Mar, 2000 - No. 6, Sept, 2000 ($2.50)

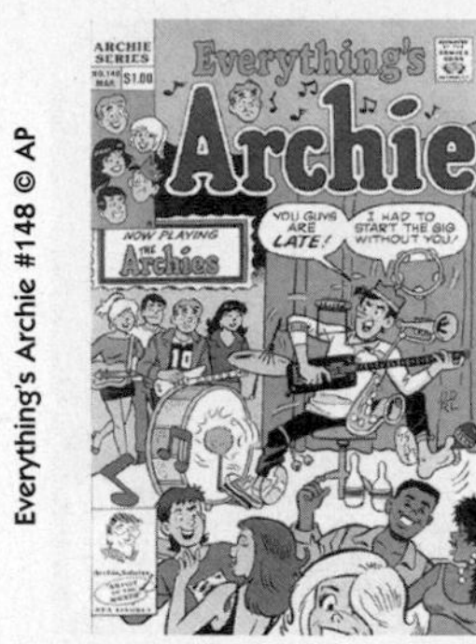

Everything's Archie #148 © AP

The Evil Dead #1 © Sam Raimi

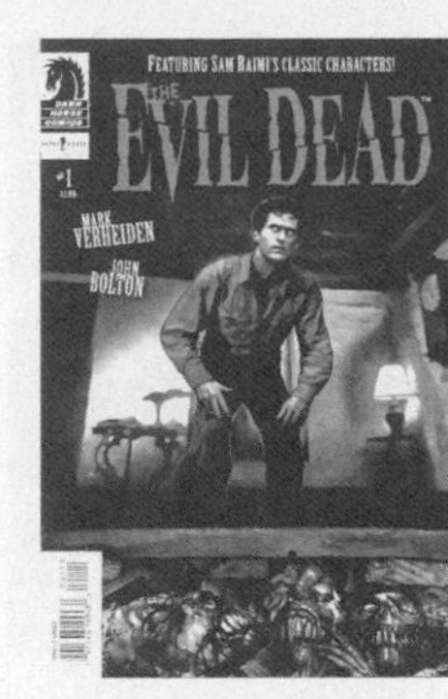

Excalibur #42 © MAR

GD 2.0 | VG 4.0 | FN 6.0 | VF 8.0 | VF/NM 9.0 | NM- 9.2

Preview ($5.95) Flip book w/Soul Saga preview 2 4 6 8 10 12
1-6: 1-Covers by Finch, Madureira, Garza. 2-Turner var-c 3.00
1-Another Universe variant-c 5.00
TPB (5/01, $17.95) r/#1-6 plus cover galley and sketch pages 18.00

EVERQUEST: ...(Based on online role-playing game)
DC Comics (WildStorm): 2002 ($5.95, one-shots)
The Ruins of Kunark - Jim Lee & Dan Norton-a; McQuaid & Lee-s; Lee-c 6.00
Transformations - Philip Tan-a; Devin Grayson-s; Portacio-c 6.00

EVERYBODY'S COMICS (See Fox Giants)

EVERYMAN, THE
Marvel Comics (Epic Comics): Nov, 1991 ($4.50, one-shot, 52 pgs.)
1-Mike Allred-a 1 2 3 4 5 7

EVERYTHING HAPPENS TO HARVEY
National Periodical Publications: Sept-Oct, 1953 - No. 7, Sept-Oct, 1954
1 28 56 84 164 265 365
2 15 30 45 92 144 195
3-7 14 28 42 81 118 155

EVERYTHING'S ARCHIE
Archie Publications: May, 1969 - No. 157, Sept, 1991 (Giant issues No. 1-20)
1-(68 pages) 8 16 24 54 90 125
2-(68 pages) 5 10 15 30 48 65
3-5-(68 pages) 4 8 12 26 41 55
6-13-(68 pages) 3 6 9 18 27 35
14-31-(52 pages) 2 4 6 13 18 22
32 (7/74)-50 (8/76) 2 4 6 8 10 12
51-80 (12/79),100 (4/82) 1 2 3 5 6 8
81-99 6.00
101-120 5.00
121-156: 142,148-Gene Colan-a 4.00
157-Last issue 5.00

EVERYTHING'S DUCKY (Movie)
Dell Publishing Co.: No. 1251, 1961
Four Color 1251 5 10 15 30 48 65

EVIL DEAD, THE (Movie)
Dark Horse Comics: Jan, 2008 - No. 4, Apr, 2008 ($2.99, limited series)
1-4-Adaptation of the Sam Raimi/Bruce Campbell movie; Bolton painted-a/c 3.00

EVIL ERNIE
Eternity Comics: Dec, 1991 - No. 5, 1992 ($2.50, B&W, limited series)
1-1st app. Lady Death by Steven Hughes (12,000 print run); Lady Death app. in all issues
4 8 12 24 37 50
2,3: 2-1st Lady Death-c. 2,3-(7,000 print run) 3 6 9 14 20 25
4-(8,000 print run) 2 4 6 11 16 20
5 2 4 6 9 13 16
Special Edition 1 3 6 9 14 20 25
Youth Gone Wild! ($9.95, trade paperback)-r/#1-5 1 3 4 6 8 10
Youth Gone Wild! Director's Cut ($4.95)-Limited to 15,000, shows the making of the comic 5.00

EVIL ERNIE (Monthly series)
Chaos! Comics: July, 1998 - No. 10, Apr, 1999 ($2.95)
1-10-Pulido & Nutman-s/Brewer-a 3.00
1-($10.00) Premium Ed. 10.00
... Baddest Battles (1/97, $1.50) Pin-ups; 2 covers 2.50
... Pieces of Me (11/00, $2.95, B&W) Flashback story; Pulido-s/Beck-a 3.00
... Relentless (5/02, $4.99, B&W) Pulido-s/Beck, Bonk, & Brewer-a 5.00
... Returns (10/01, $3.99, B&W) Pulido-s/Beck-a 4.00

EVIL ERNIE: DEPRAVED
Chaos! Comics: Jul, 1999 - No. 3, Sept, 1999 ($2.95, limited series)
1-3-Pulido-s/Brewer-a 3.00

EVIL ERNIE: DESTROYER
Chaos! Comics: Oct, 1997 - No. 9, Jun, 1998 ($2.95, limited series)
Preview ($2.50), 1-9-Flip cover 3.00

EVIL ERNIE: IN SANTA FE
Devil's Due Publ.: Sept, 2005 - Mar, 2006 ($2.95, limited series)
1-4-Alan Grant-s/Tommy Castillo-a/Alex Horley-c 3.00

EVIL ERNIE: REVENGE
Chaos! Comics: Oct, 1994 - No. 4, Feb, 1995 ($2.95, limited series)
1-Glow-in-the-dark-c; Lady Death app. 1-3-flip book w. Kilzone Preview (series of 3) 5.00

1-Commemorative-(4000 print run) 1 3 4 6 8 10
2-4 4.00
Trade paperback (10/95, $12.95) 13.00

EVIL ERNIE: STRAIGHT TO HELL
Chaos! Comics: Oct, 1995 - No. 5, May, 1996 ($2.95, limited series)
1-5: 1-fold-out-c 3.00
1,3:1-($19.95) Chromium Ed. 3-Chastity Chase-c-(4000 printed) 20.00
Special Edition (10,000) 20.00

EVIL ERNIE: THE RESURRECTION
Chaos! Comics: 1993 - No. 4, 1994 (Limited series)
0 5.00
1 2 4 6 8 10 12
1A-Gold 3 6 9 16 23 30
2-4 1 2 3 5 6 8

EVIL ERNIE VS. THE MOVIE MONSTERS
Chaos! Comics: Mar, 1997 ($2.95, one-shot)
1 3.00
1-Variant-"Chaos-Scope•Terror Vision" card stock-c 5.00

EVIL ERNIE VS. THE SUPER HEROES
Chaos! Comics: Aug, 1995; Sept, 1998 ($2.95)
1-Lady Death poster 3.00
1-Foil-c variant (limited to 10,000) 2 4 6 11 16 20
1-Limited Edition (1000) 2 4 6 11 16 20
2-(9/98) Ernie vs. JLA and Marvel parodies 3.00

EVIL ERNIE: WAR OF THE DEAD
Chaos! Comics: Nov, 1999 - No. 3, Jan, 2000 ($2.95, limited series)
1-3 Pulido & Kaminski-s/Brewer-a. 3-End of Evil Ernie 3.00

EVIL EYE
Fantagraphics Books: June, 1998 - Present ($2.95/$3.50/$3.95, B&W)
1-7-Richard Sala-s/a 3.00
8-10-($3.50) 3.50
11,12-($3.95) 4.00

EVO (Crossover from Tomb Raider #25 & Witchblade #60)
Image Comics (Top Cow): Feb, 2003 ($2.99, one-shot)
1-Silvestri-c/a(p); Endgame x-over pt. 3; Sara Pezzini & Lara Croft app. 3.00

EWOKS (Star Wars) (TV) (See Star Comics Magazine)
Marvel Comics (Star Comics): June, 1985 - No. 14, Jul, 1987 (75¢/$1.00)
1,10: 10-Williamson-a (From Star Wars) 2 4 6 9 12 15
2-9 2 4 6 8 10 12
11-14: 14-($1.00-c) 2 4 6 8 11 14

EXCALIBUR (Also see Marvel Comics Presents #31)
Marvel Comics: Apr, 1988; Oct, 1988 - No. 125, Oct, 1998 ($1.50/$1.75/$1.99)
Special Edition nn (The Sword is Drawn)(4/88, $3.25)-1st Excalibur comic 6.00
Special Edition nn (4/88)-no price on-c 1 3 4 6 8 10
Special Edition nn (2nd & print, 10/88, 12/89) 3.00
...The Sword is Drawn (Apr, 1992, $4.95) 5.00
1($1.50, 10/88)-X-Men spin-off; Nightcrawler, Shadowcat(Kitty Pryde), Capt. Britain, Phoenix & Meggan begin 5.00
2-4 4.00
5-10 3.00
11-49,51-70,72-74,76: 10,11-Rogers/Austin-a. 21-Intro Crusader X. 22-Iron Man x-over. 24-John Byrne app. in story. 26-Ron Lim-c/a. 27-B. Smith-a(p). 37-Dr. Doom & Iron Man app. 41-X-Men (Wolverine) app.; Cable cameo. 49-Neal Adams c-swipe. 52,57-X-Men (Cyclops, Wolverine) app. 53-Spider-Man-c/story. 58-X-Men (Wolverine, Gambit, Cyclops, etc.)-c/story. 61-Phoenix returns. 68-Starjammers-c/story 2.50
50-($2.75, 56 pgs.)-New logo 3.00
71-($3.95, 52 pgs.)-Hologram on-c; 30th anniversary 5.00
75-($3.50, 52 pgs.)-Holo-grafx foil-c 4.00
75-($2.25, 52 pgs.)-Regular edition 2.50
77-81,83-86: 77-Begin $1.95-c; bound-in trading card sheet. 83-86-Deluxe Editions and Standard Editions. 86-1st app. Pete Wisdom 2.50
82-($2.50)-Newsstand edition 3.00
82-($3.50)-Enhanced edition 4.00
87-89,91-99,101-110: 87-Return from Age of Apocalypse. 92-Colossus-c/app. 94-Days of Future Tense 95-X-Man-c/app. 96-Sebastian Shaw & the Hellfire Club app. 99-Onslaught app. 101-Onslaught tie-in. 102-w/card insert. 103-Last Warren Ellis scripts; Belasco app. 104,105-Hitch & Neary-c/a. 109-Spiral-c/app. 2.50
90,100-($2.95)-double-sized. 100-Onslaught tie-in; wraparound-c 4.00

Exciting Comics #10 © STD

Exiles #75 © MAR

Ex Machina #26 © Vaughan & Harris

	GD 2.0	VG 4.0	FN 6.0	VF 8.0	VF/NM 9.0	NM- 9.2

111-124: 111-Begin $1.99-c, wraparound-c. 119-Calafiore-a 2.50
125-($2.99) Wedding of Capt. Britain and Meggan 4.00
Annual 1,2 ('93, '94, 68 pgs.)-1st app. Khaos. 2-X-Men & Psylocke app. 3.00
#(-1) Flashback (7/97) 2.50
...Air Apparent nn (12/91, $4.95)-Simonson-c 5.00
...Mojo Mayhem nn (12/89, $4.50)-Art Adams/Austin-c/a 5.00
...: The Possession nn (7/91, $2.95, 52 pgs.) 3.00
...: XX Crossing (7/92, 5/92-inside, $2.50)-vs. The X-Men 2.50
...Classic Vol. 1: The Sword is Drawn TPB (2005, $19.99) r/#1-5 & Special Edition nn (The Sword is Drawn) 20.00
...Classic Vol. 2: Two-Edged Sword TPB (2006, $24.99) r/#6-11 25.00
...Classic Vol. 3: Cross-Time Caper Book 1 TPB (2007, $24.99) r/#12-20 25.00
...Classic Vol. 4: Cross-Time Caper Book 2 TPB (2007, $24.99) r/#21-28 25.00

EXCALIBUR
Marvel Comics: Feb, 2001 - No. 4, May, 2001 ($2.99)

1-4-Return of Captain Britain; Raimondi-a 3.00

EXCALIBUR (X-Men Reloaded title) (Leads into House of M series, then New Excalibur)
Marvel Comics: July, 2004 - No. 14, July, 2005 ($2.99)

1-14: 1-Claremont-s/Lopresti-a/Park-c; Magneto returns. 6-11-Beast app. 13,14-Prelude to House of M; Dr. Strange app. 3.00
House of M Prelude: Excalibur TPB (2005, $11.99) r/#11-14 12.00
... Vol. 1: Forging the Sword (2004, $9.99) r/#1-4 10.00
... Vol. 2: Saturday Night Fever (2005, $14.99) r/#5-10 15.00

EXCITING COMICS
Nedor/Better Publications/Standard Comics: Apr, 1940 - No. 69, Sept, 1949

	GD	VG	FN	VF	VF/NM	NM-
1-Origin & 1st app. The Mask, Jim Hatfield, Sgt. Bill King, Dan Williams begin; early Robot-c (see Smash #1)	411	822	1233	2795	4898	7000
2-The Sphinx begins; The Masked Rider app.; Son of the Gods begins, ends #8	170	340	510	1071	1811	2550
3-Robot-c	122	244	366	769	1297	1825
4-6	78	156	234	491	828	1165
7,8	62	124	186	391	663	935
9-Origin/1st app. of The Black Terror & sidekick Tim, begin series (5/41) (Black Terror c-9-21,23-52,54,55)	972	1944	2916	6998	12,249	17,500
10-2nd app. Black Terror	300	600	900	1930	3315	4700
11	153	306	459	964	1632	2300
12,13	102	204	306	643	1084	1525
14-Last Sphinx, Dan Williams	73	146	219	460	780	1100
15-The Liberator begins (origin)	107	214	321	674	1137	1600
16-20: 20-The Mask ends	57	114	171	359	610	860
21,23-25: 25-Robot-c	48	96	144	208	499	700
22-Origin The Eaglet; The American Eagle begins	57	114	171	359	610	860
26-Schomburg-c begin	77	154	231	481	816	1150
27,29,30	67	134	201	422	711	1000
28-(Scarce) Crime Crusader begins, ends #58	113	266	399	838	1419	2000
31-38: 35-Liberator ends, not in 31-33	60	120	180	378	639	900
39-Nazis giving poison candy to kids on cover; origin Kara, Jungle Princess	107	214	321	674	1137	1600
40-50: 42-The Scarab begins. 45-Schomburg Robot-c. 49-Last Kara, Jungle Princess. 50-Last American Eagle	60	120	180	378	639	900
51-Miss Masque begins (1st app.)	63	126	189	397	674	950
52-54: Miss Masque ends. 53-Miss Masque-c	54	108	162	340	575	810
55-58: 55-Judy of the Jungle begins (origin), ends #69; 1 pg. Ingels-a; Judy of the Jungle c-56-66. 57,58-Airbrush-c	54	108	162	340	575	810
59-Frazetta art in Caniff style; signed Frank Frazeta (one t), 9 pgs.	55	110	165	347	584	820
60-66: 60-Rick Howard, the Mystery Rider begins. 66-Robinson/Meskin-a	50	100	150	310	518	725
67-69-All western covers	21	42	63	123	197	270

NOTE: ***Schomburg (Xela)** c-26-68; airbrush c-57-66. Black Terror by **R. Moreira**-#65. **Roussos** a-62. Bondage-c 9, 12, 13, 20, 23, 25, 30, 59.*

EXCITING ROMANCES
Fawcett Publications: 1949 (nd); No. 2, Spring, 1950 - No. 5, 10/50; No. 6 (1951, nd); No. 7, 9/51 -No. 12, 1/53

	GD	VG	FN	VF	VF/NM	NM-
1,3: 1(1949). 3-Wood-a	14	28	42	80	115	150
2,4,5-(1950)	10	20	30	54	72	90
6-12	9	18	27	47	61	75

NOTE: ***Powell** a-8-10. **Marcus Swayze** a-5, 6, 9. Photo c-1-7, 10-12.*

EXCITING ROMANCE STORIES (See Fox Giants)

EXCITING WAR (Korean War)
Standard Comics (Better Publ.): No. 5, Sept, 1952 - No. 8, May, 1953; No. 9, Nov, 1953

	GD	VG	FN	VF	VF/NM	NM-
5	10	20	30	56	76	95
6,7,9	7	14	21	37	46	55
8-Toth-a	8	16	24	44	57	70

EXCITING X-PATROL
Marvel Comics (Amalgam): June, 1997 ($1.95, one-shot)

1-Barbara Kesel-s/ Bryan Hitch-a 2.50

EXECUTIONER, THE (Don Pendleton's...)
IDW Publishing: Apr, 2008 - Present ($3.99)

1-3-Mack Bolan origin re-told; Gallant-a/Wojtowicz-s 4.00

EXILES (Also see Break-Thru)
Malibu Comics (Ultraverse): Aug, 1993 - No. 4, Nov, 1993 ($1.95)

1,2,4: 1,2-Bagged copies of each exist. 4-Team dies; story cont'd in Break-Thru #1 2.50
3-($2.50, 40 pgs.)-Rune flip-c/story by B. Smith (3 pgs.) 2.50
1-Holographic-c edition 1 2 3 5 6 8

EXILES (All New, The) (2nd Series) (Also see Black September)
Malibu Comics (Ultraverse): Sept, 1995 - V2#11, Aug, 1996 ($1.50)

Infinity (9/95, $1.50)-Intro new team including Marvel's Juggernaut & Reaper 2.50
Infinity (2000 signed), V2#1 (2000 signed) 1 3 4 6 8 10
V2#1-4,6-11: 1-(10/95, 64 pgs.)-Reprint of Ultraforce V2#1 follows lead story. 2-1st app. Hellblade. 8-Intro Maxis. 11-Vs. Maxis; Ripfire app.; cont'd in Ultraforce #12 2.50
V2#5-($2.50) Juggernaut returns to the Marvel Universe. 2.50

EXILES (Also see X-Men titles) (Leads into New Exiles series)
Marvel Comics: Aug, 2001 - No. 100, Feb, 2008 ($2.99/$2.25)

1-($2.99) Blink and parallel world X-Men; Winick-s/McKone & McKenna-a 1 2 3 4 5 7
2-10-($2.25) 2-Two covers (McKone & JH Williams III). 5-Alpha Flight app. 3.00
11-24: 22-Blink leaves; Magik joins. 23,24-Walker-a; alternate Weapon-X app. 2.50
25-99: 25-Begin $2.99-c; Inhumans app.; Walker-a. 26-30-Austen-s. 33-Wolverine app. 35-37-Fantastic Four app. 37-Sunfire dies, Blink returns. 38-40-Hyperion app. 69-71-House of M. 77,78-Squadron Supreme app. 85,86-Multiple Wolverines. 90-Claremont-s begin; Psylocke app. 97-Shadowcat joins 3.00
100-($3.99) Last issue; Blink leaves; continues in Exiles (Days of Then and Now); r/#1 4.00
Annual 1 (2/07, $3.99) Bedard-s/Raney-a/c 4.00
Exiles #1 (Days of Then and Now) (3/08, $3.99) short stories by various 4.00
TPB (3/02, $12.95) r/#1-4 13.00
...: A World Apart TPB (7/02, $14.99) r/#5-11 15.00
...: Vol. 3: Out of Time TPB (2003, $17.99) r/#12-19 18.00
...: Vol. 4: Legacy TPB (2003, $12.99) r/#20-25 13.00
...: Vol. 5: Unnatural Instinct TPB (2003, $14.99) r/#26-30 15.00
...: Vol. 6: Fantastic Voyage TPB (2004, $17.99) r/#31-37 18.00
...: Vol. 7: A Blink in Time TPB (2004, $19.99) r/#38-45 20.00
...: Vol. 8: Earn Your Wings TPB (2004, $14.99) r/#46-51 15.00
...: Vol. 9: Bump in the Night TPB (2005, $17.99) r/#52-58 18.00
...: Vol. 10: Age of Apocalypse TPB ('05, $12.99) r/#59-61 & Official Handbook:AoA 2005 13.00
...: Vol. 11: Time Breakers TPB (2006, $17.99) r/#62-68 18.00
...: Vol. 12: World Tour Book 1 TPB (2006, $16.99) r/#69-74 17.00
...: Vol. 13: World Tour Book 2 TPB (2006, $23.99) r/#75-83 24.00
...: Vol. 14: The New Exiles TPB (2007, $14.99) r/#84-89 and Annual #1 15.00
...: Vol. 15: Enemy of the Stars TPB (2007, $13.99) r/#90-94 14.00
...: Vol. 16: Starting Over TPB (2008, $14.99) r/#95-100 & ...: Days of Then and Now 15.00

EXILES VS. THE X-MEN
Malibu Comics (Ultraverse): Oct, 1995 (one-shot)

0-Limited Super Premium Edition; signed w/certificate; gold foil logo, 0-Limited Premium Edition 1 3 4 6 8 10

EX MACHINA
DC Comics: Aug, 2004 - Present ($2.95/$2.99)

1-Intro. Mitchell Hundred; Vaughan-s/Harris-a/c 4.00
2-37: 12-Intro. Automaton. 33-Mitchell meets the Pope 3.00
...: Inside the Machine (4/07, $2.99) script pages and Harris art and cover process 3.00
...: Masquerade Special (10/07, $3.50) John Paul Leon-a; Harris-c 3.50
... Special 1,2 (6/06 - No. 2, 8/06, $2.99) Sprouse-a; flashback to the Great Machine 3.00
...: March To War (2006, $12.99) r/#17-20 and Special #1,2 13.00
...: Power Down (2008, $12.99) r/#26-29 & ...: Inside the Machine 13.00
...: Smoke Smoke (2007, $12.99) r/#21-25 13.00
...: The First Hundred Days (2005, $9.95) r/#1-5; photo reference and sketch pages 10.00
...: Tag (2005, $12.99) r/#6-10; Harris sketch pages 13.00

EX-MUTANTS
Malibu Comics: Nov, 1992 - No. 18, Apr, 1994 ($1.95/$2.25/$2.50)

1-18: 1-Polybagged w/Skycap; prismatic cover 2.50

Exploits of Daniel Boone #6 © QUA

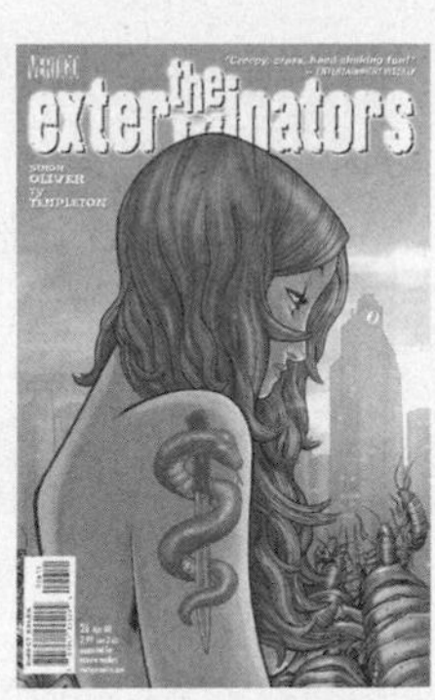

Fables #59 © Bill Willingham & DC

	GD 2.0	VG 4.0	FN 6.0	VF 8.0	VF/NM 9.0	NM- 9.2

EXORCISTS (See The Crusaders)

EXOSQUAD (TV)
Topps Comics: No. 0, Jan, 1994 ($1.25)

0-($1.00, 20 pgs.)-1st app.; Staton-a(p); wraparound-c 2.25

EXOTIC ROMANCES (Formerly True War Romances)
Quality Comics Group (Comic Magazines): No. 22, Oct, 1955-No. 31, Nov, 1956

	GD	VG	FN	VF	VF/NM	NM-
22	12	24	36	67	94	120
23-26,29	8	16	24	42	54	65
27,31-Baker-c/a	15	30	45	83	124	165
28,30-Baker-a	13	26	39	72	101	130

EXPATRIOT
Image Comics: Feb, 2005 - Present ($2.95)

1-4-B. Clay Moore-s/Jason Latour-a. 1,4-Flip-c 3.00

EXPLOITS OF DANIEL BOONE
Quality Comics Group: Nov, 1955 - No. 6, Oct, 1956

	GD	VG	FN	VF	VF/NM	NM-
1-All have Cuidera c(i)	20	40	60	117	184	250
2	14	28	42	82	121	160
3-6	13	26	39	74	105	135

EXPLOITS OF DICK TRACY (See Dick Tracy)

EXPLORER JOE
Ziff-Davis Comic Group (Approved Comics): Win, 1951 - No. 2, Oct-Nov, 1952

	GD	VG	FN	VF	VF/NM	NM-
1-2: Saunders painted covers; 2-Krigstein-a	14	28	42	76	108	140

EXPLORERS OF THE UNKNOWN (See Archie Giant Series #587, 599)
Archie Comics: June, 1990 - No. 6, Apr, 1991 ($1.00)

1-6: Featuring Archie and the gang 3.00

EXPOSED (...True Crime Cases; ...Cases in the Crusade Against Crime #5-9)
D. S. Publishing Co.: Mar-Apr, 1948 - No. 9, July-Aug, 1949

	GD	VG	FN	VF	VF/NM	NM-
1	24	48	72	140	225	310
2-Giggling killer story with excessive blood; two injury-to-eye panels; electrocution panel	30	60	90	174	280	385
3,8,9	14	28	42	78	112	145
4-Orlando-a	14	28	42	81	118	155
5-Breeze Lawson, Sky Sheriff by E. Good	14	28	42	81	118	155
6,7: 6-Ingels-a; used in **SOTI**, illo. "How to prepare an alibi" 7-Illo. in **SOTI**, "Diagram for housebreakers;" used by N.Y. Legis. Committee	34	68	102	198	319	440

EXTERMINATORS, THE
DC Comics (Vertigo): Mar, 2006 - No. 30, Aug, 2008 ($2.99)

1-30: Simon Oliver-s/Tony Moore-a in most. 11,12-Hawthorne-a 3.00
...: Bug Brothers TPB (2006, $9.99) r/#1-5; intro. by screenwriter Josh Olson 10.00
...: Crossfire and Collateral TPB (2008, $14.99) r/#17-23 15.00
...: Insurgency TPB (2007, $12.99) r/#6-10 13.00
...: Lies of Our Fathers TPB (2007, $14.99) r/#11-16 15.00

EXTINCT!
New England Comics Press: Wint, 1991-92 - No. 2, Fall, 1992 ($3.50, B&W)

1,2-Reprints and background info of "perfectly awful" Golden Age stories 3.50

EXTINCTION EVENT
DC Comics (WildStorm): Sept, 2003 - No. 5, Jan, 2004 ($2.50, limited series)

1-5-Booth-a/Weinberg-s 2.50

EXTRA!
E. C. Comics: Mar-Apr, 1955 - No. 5, Nov-Dec, 1955

	GD	VG	FN	VF	VF/NM	NM-
1-Not code approved	19	38	57	152	246	340
2-5	12	24	36	96	156	215

NOTE: *Craig, Crandall, Severin art in all.*

EXTRA!
Gemstone Publishing: Jan, 2000 - No. 5, May, 2000 ($2.50)

1-5-Reprints E.C. series 2.50

EXTRA COMICS
Magazine Enterprises: 1948 (25¢, 3 comics in one)

	GD	VG	FN	VF	VF/NM	NM-
1-Giant; consisting of rebound ME comics. Two versions known; (1)-Funnyman by Siegel & Shuster, Space Ace, Undercover Girl, Red Fox by L.B. Cole, Trail Colt & (2)-All Funnyman	53	106	159	334	567	800

EXTREME
Image Comics (Extreme Studios): Aug, 1993 (Giveaway)

0 3.00

EXTREME DESTROYER
Image Comics (Extreme Studios): Jan, 1996 ($2.50)

Prologue 1-Polybagged w/card; Liefeld-c, Epilogue 1-Liefeld-c 2.50

EXTREME JUSTICE
DC Comics: No. 0, Jan, 1995 - No. 18, July, 1996 ($1.50/$1.75)

0-18 3.00

EXTREMELY YOUNGBLOOD
Image Comics (Extreme Studios): Sept, 1996 ($3.50, one-shot)

1 3.50

EXTREME SACRIFICE
Image Comics (Extreme Studios): Jan, 1995 ($2.50, limited series)

Prelude (#1)-Liefeld wraparound-c; polybagged w/ trading card 2.50
Epilogue (#2)-Liefeld wraparound-c; polybagged w/trading card 2.50
Trade paperback (6/95, $16.95)-Platt-a 17.00

EXTREME SUPER CHRISTMAS SPECIAL
Image Comics (Extreme Studios): Dec, 1994 ($2.95, one-shot)

1 3.00

EXTREMIST, THE
DC Comics (Vertigo): Sept, 1993 - No. 4, Dec, 1993 ($1.95, limited series)

1-4-Peter Milligan scripts; McKeever-c/a 2.50
1-Platinum Edition 5.00

EYE OF THE STORM
Rival Productions: Dec, 1994 - No. 7, June, 1995? ($2.95)

1-7: Computer generated comic 3.00

EYE OF THE STORM
DC Comics (WildStorm): Sept, 2003 ($4.95)

Annual 1-Short stories by various incl. Portacio, Johns, Coker, Pearson, Arcudi 5.00

FABLES
DC Comics (Vertigo): July, 2002 - Present ($2.50/$2.75/$2.99)

1-Willingham-s/Medina-a; two covers by Maleev & Jean 8.00
#1: Special Edition (12/06, 25¢) r/#1 with preview of 1001 Nights of Snowfall 2.50
2-Medina-a 5.00
3-5 4.00
6-37: 6-10-Buckingham-a. 11-Talbot-a. 18-Medley-a. 26-Preview of The Witching 3.00
6-RRP Edition wraparound variant-c; promotional giveaway for retailers (200 printed) 50.00
38-49,51-74: 38-Begin $2.75-c. 49-Begin $2.99-c. 57,58-Allred-a 3.00
50-($3.99) Wedding of Snow White and Bigby Wolf; preview of Jack of Fables series 4.00
Animal Farm (2003, $12.95, TPB) r/#6-10; sketch pages by Buckingham & Jean 13.00
...: Arabian Nights (And Days) (2006, $14.99, TPB) r/#42-47 15.00
...: Homelands (2005, $14.99, TPB) r/#34-41 15.00
Legends in Exile (2002, $9.95, TPB) r/#1-5; new short story Willingham-s/a 10.00
...: March of the Wooden Soldiers (2004, $17.95, TPB) r/#19-21 & ...: The Last Castle 18.00
...: 1001 Nights of Snowfall HC (2006, $19.99) short stories by Willingham with art by various incl. Bolton, Kaluta, Jean, McPherson, Thompson, Vess, Wheatley, Buckingham 20.00
...: 1001 Nights of Snowfall (2008, $14.99, TPB) short stories with art by various 15.00
...: Sons of Empire (2007, $17.99, TPB) r/#52-59 18.00
...: Storybook Love (2004, $14.95, TPB) r/#11-18 15.00
...: The Good Prince (2008, $17.99, TPB) r/#60-69 18.00
...: The Last Castle (2003, $5.95) Hamilton-a/Willingham-s; prequel to title 6.00
...: The Mean Seasons (2005, $14.99, TPB) r/#22,28-33 15.00
...: Wolves (2006, $17.99, TPB) r/#48-51; script to #50 18.00

FACE
DC Comics (Vertigo): Jan, 1995 ($4.95, one-shot)

1 5.00

FACE, THE (Tony Trent, the Face No. 3 on) (See Big Shot Comics)
Columbia Comics Group: 1941 - No. 2, 1943

	GD	VG	FN	VF	VF/NM	NM-
1-The Face; Mart Bailey-c	87	174	261	548	924	1300
2-Bailey-c	50	100	150	310	518	725

FACTOR X
Marvel Comics: Mar, 1995 - No. 4, July, 1995 ($1.95, limited series)

1-Age of Apocalypse 3.00
2-4 2.50

FACULTY FUNNIES
Archie Comics: June, 1989 - No. 5, May, 1990 (75¢/95¢ #2 on)

1-5: 1,2-The Awesome Four app. 3.00

FADE FROM GRACE

Faker #5 © Carey & Simpson

Fallen Son: The Death of Captain America #2 © MAR

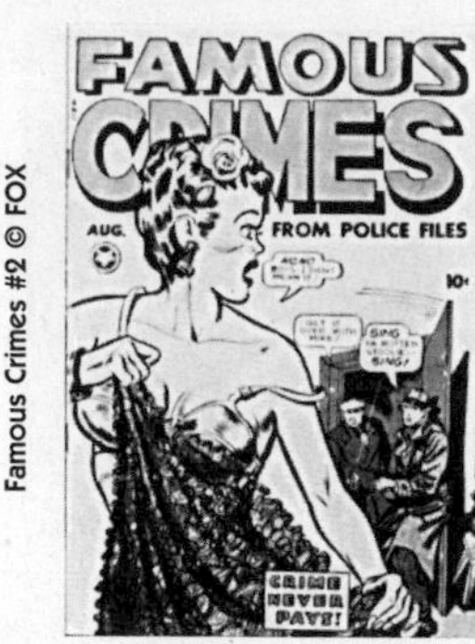

Famous Crimes #2 © FOX

Beckett Comics: Aug, 2004 - No. 5, Mar, 2005 (99¢/$1.99)

	GD 2.0	VG 4.0	FN 6.0	VF 8.0	VF/NM 9.0	NM- 9.2
1-(99¢) Jeff Amano-a/c; Gabriel Benson-s; origin of Fade						2.50
2-5-($1.99)						2.50
TPB (2005, $14.99) r/#1-5; cover gallery, afterword by David Mack						15.00

FAFHRD AND THE GREY MOUSER (Also see Sword of Sorcery & Wonder Woman #202)
Marvel Comics: Oct, 1990 - No. 4, 1991 ($4.50, 52 pgs., squarebound)

	GD 2.0	VG 4.0	FN 6.0	VF 8.0	VF/NM 9.0	NM- 9.2
1-4: Mignola/Williamson-a; Chaykin scripts						4.50

FAGIN THE JAW
Doubleday: Oct, 2003 ($15.95, softcover graphic novel)

	GD 2.0	VG 4.0	FN 6.0	VF 8.0	VF/NM 9.0	NM- 9.2
nn-Will Eisner-s/a; story of Fagin from Dickens' Oliver Twist						16.00

FAIRY TALE PARADE (See Famous Fairy Tales)
Dell Publishing Co.: June-July, 1942 - No. 121, Oct, 1946 (Most by Walt Kelly)

	GD 2.0	VG 4.0	FN 6.0	VF 8.0	VF/NM 9.0	NM- 9.2
1-Kelly-a begins	96	192	288	816	1558	2300
2(8-9/42)	43	86	129	344	647	950
3-5 (10-11/42 - 2-4/43)	31	62	93	239	445	650
6-9 (5-7/43 - 11-1/43-44)	25	50	75	185	343	500
Four Color 50('44),69('45), 87('45)	24	48	72	176	326	475
Four Color 104,114('46)-Last Kelly issue	19	38	57	135	250	365
Four Color 121('46)-Not by Kelly	12	24	36	84	150	215

NOTE: *#1-9, 4-Color #50, 69 have **Kelly** c/a; 4-Color #87, 104, 114-**Kelly** art only. #9 has a redrawn version of The Reluctant Dragon. This series contains all the classic fairy tales from Jack In The Beanstalk to Cinderella.*

FAIRY TALES
Ziff-Davis Publ. Co. (Approved Comics): No. 10, Apr-May, 1951 - No. 11, June-July, 1951

	GD 2.0	VG 4.0	FN 6.0	VF 8.0	VF/NM 9.0	NM- 9.2
10,11-Painted-c	20	40	60	115	183	250

FAITH
DC Comics (Vertigo): Nov, 1999 - No. 5, Mar, 2000 ($2.50, limited series)

	GD 2.0	VG 4.0	FN 6.0	VF 8.0	VF/NM 9.0	NM- 9.2
1-5-Ted McKeever-s/c/a						2.50

FAITHFUL
Marvel Comics/Lovers' Magazine: Nov, 1949 - No. 2, Feb, 1950 (52 pgs.)

	GD 2.0	VG 4.0	FN 6.0	VF 8.0	VF/NM 9.0	NM- 9.2
1,2-Photo-c	11	22	33	62	86	110

FAKER
DC Comics (Vertigo): Sept, 2007 - No. 6, Feb, 2008 ($2.99, limited series)

	GD 2.0	VG 4.0	FN 6.0	VF 8.0	VF/NM 9.0	NM- 9.2
1-6-Mike Carey-s/Jock-a/c						3.00
TPB (2008, $14.99) r/#1-6; Jock sketch pages						15.00

FALCON (See Marvel Premiere #49, Avengers #181 & Captain America #117 & 133)
Marvel Comics Group: Nov, 1983 - No. 4, Feb, 1984 (Mini-series)

	GD 2.0	VG 4.0	FN 6.0	VF 8.0	VF/NM 9.0	NM- 9.2
1-4: 1-Paul Smith-c/a(p). 2-Paul Smith-c/Mark Bright-a. 3-Kupperberg-c						3.00

FALLEN ANGEL
DC Comics: Sept, 2003 - No. 20, July, 2005 ($2.50/$2.95)

	GD 2.0	VG 4.0	FN 6.0	VF 8.0	VF/NM 9.0	NM- 9.2
1-9-Peter David-s/David Lopez-a/Stelfreeze-c; intro. Lee						2.50
10-20: 10-Begin $2.95-c. 13,17-Kaluta-c. 20-Last issue; Pérez-c						3.00
TPB (2004, $12.95) r/#1-6; intro. by Harlan Ellison						13.00
Down to Earth TPB (2007, $14.99) r/#7-12						15.00

FALLEN ANGEL
IDW Publ.: Dec, 2005 - Present ($3.99)

	GD 2.0	VG 4.0	FN 6.0	VF 8.0	VF/NM 9.0	NM- 9.2
1-29: 1-14-Peter David-s/J.K Woodward. Retailer variant-c for each. 15-Donaldson-a. 17-Flip cover with Shi story; Tucci-a. 25-Wraparound-c; character gallery						4.00
...: To Serve in Heaven TPB (8/06, $19.99) r/#1-5; gallery of reg & variant covers						20.00

FALLEN ANGEL ON THE WORLD OF MAGIC: THE GATHERING
Acclaim (Armada): May, 1996 ($5.95, one-shot)

	GD 2.0	VG 4.0	FN 6.0	VF 8.0	VF/NM 9.0	NM- 9.2
1-Nancy Collins story						6.00

FALLEN ANGELS
Marvel Comics Group: April, 1987 - No. 8, Nov, 1987 (Limited series)

	GD 2.0	VG 4.0	FN 6.0	VF 8.0	VF/NM 9.0	NM- 9.2
1-8						2.50

FALLEN SON: THE DEATH OF CAPTAIN AMERICA
Marvel Comics: June, 2007 - No. 5, Aug, 2007 ($2.99, limited series)

	GD 2.0	VG 4.0	FN 6.0	VF 8.0	VF/NM 9.0	NM- 9.2
1-5: Loeb-s in all. 1-Wolverine; Yu-a/c. 2-Avengers; McGuinness-a/c. 3-Captain America; Romita Jr.-a/c; Hawkeye app. 4-Spider-Man; Finch-c/a. 5-Cassaday-c/a						3.00
1-5-Variant covers by Turner						3.00
HC (2007, $19.99, dustjacket) r/#1-5						20.00
TPB (2008, $13.99) r/#1-5						14.00

FALLING IN LOVE
Arleigh Pub. Co./National Per. Pub.: Sept-Oct, 1955 - No. 143, Oct-Nov, 1973

	GD 2.0	VG 4.0	FN 6.0	VF 8.0	VF/NM 9.0	NM- 9.2
1	40	80	120	235	380	525
2	20	40	60	118	189	260
3-10	14	28	42	76	108	140
11-20	11	22	33	64	90	115
21-40	9	18	27	52	69	85
41-47: 47-Last 10¢ issue?	8	16	24	44	57	70
48-70	4	8	12	24	37	50
71-99,108: 108-Wood-a (4 pgs., 7/69)	3	6	9	17	25	32
100	4	8	12	22	34	45
101-107,109-124	2	4	6	13	18	22
134-143	2	4	6	10	14	18
125-133: 52 pgs.	3	6	9	19	29	38

NOTE: ***Colan** c/a-75, 81. 52 pgs.-#125-133.*

FALLING MAN, THE
Image Comics: Feb, 1998 ($2.95)

	GD 2.0	VG 4.0	FN 6.0	VF 8.0	VF/NM 9.0	NM- 9.2
1-McCorkindale-s/Hester-a						3.00

FALL OF THE HOUSE OF USHER, THE (See A Corben Special & Spirit section 8/22/48)

FALL OF THE ROMAN EMPIRE (See Movie Comics)

FAMILY AFFAIR (TV)
Gold Key: Feb, 1970 - No. 4, Oct, 1970 (25¢)

	GD 2.0	VG 4.0	FN 6.0	VF 8.0	VF/NM 9.0	NM- 9.2
1-With pull-out poster; photo-c	6	12	18	39	62	85
1-With poster missing	3	6	9	18	27	35
2-4-Photo-c	3	6	9	21	32	42

FAMILY FUNNIES
Parents' Magazine Institute: No. 9, Aug-Sept, 1946

	GD 2.0	VG 4.0	FN 6.0	VF 8.0	VF/NM 9.0	NM- 9.2
9	5	10	15	24	30	35

FAMILY FUNNIES (Tiny Tot Funnies No. 9)
Harvey Publications: Sept, 1950 - No. 8, Apr, 1951

	GD 2.0	VG 4.0	FN 6.0	VF 8.0	VF/NM 9.0	NM- 9.2
1-Mandrake (has over 30 King Feature strips)	10	20	30	58	79	100
2-Flash Gordon, 1 pg.	8	16	24	40	50	60
3-8: 4,5,7-Flash Gordon, 1 pg.	6	12	18	31	38	45

FAMILY GUY (TV)
Devil's Due Publ.: 2006 - Present ($6.95)

	GD 2.0	VG 4.0	FN 6.0	VF 8.0	VF/NM 9.0	NM- 9.2
nn-101 Ways to Kill Lois; 2-Peter Griffin's Guide to Parenting; 3-Books Don't Taste Very Good						7.00
... A Big Book o' Crap TPB (10/06, $16.95) r/nn,2,3						17.00

FAMILY MATTER
Kitchen Sink Press: 1998 ($24.95/$15.95, graphic novel)

	GD 2.0	VG 4.0	FN 6.0	VF 8.0	VF/NM 9.0	NM- 9.2
Hardcover ($24.95) Will Eisner-s/a						25.00
Softcover ($15.95)						16.00

FAMOUS AUTHORS ILLUSTRATED (See Stories by...)

FAMOUS CRIMES
Fox Features Syndicate/M.S. Dist. No. 51,52: June, 1948 - No. 19, Sept, 1950; No. 20, Aug, 1951; No. 51, 52, 1953

	GD 2.0	VG 4.0	FN 6.0	VF 8.0	VF/NM 9.0	NM- 9.2
1-Blue Beetle app. & crime story-r/Phantom Lady #16	50	100	150	310	518	725
2-Has woman dissolved in acid; lingerie-c/panels	40	80	120	235	380	525
3-Injury-to-eye story used in **SOTI**, pg. 112; has two electrocution stories	48	96	144	298	499	700
4-6	23	46	69	135	218	300
7- "Tarzan, the Wyoming Killer" (**SOTI**, pg. 44)	40	80	120	235	380	525
8-20: 17-Morisi-a. 20-Same cover as #15	18	36	54	103	162	220
51 (nd, 1953)	15	30	45	88	137	185
52 (Exist?)	12	24	36	67	94	120

FAMOUS FEATURE STORIES
Dell Publishing Co.: 1938 (7-1/2x11", 68 pgs.)

	GD 2.0	VG 4.0	FN 6.0	VF 8.0	VF/NM 9.0	NM- 9.2
1-Tarzan, Terry & the Pirates, King of the Royal Mtd., Buck Jones, Dick Tracy, Smilin' Jack, Dan Dunn, Don Winslow, G-Man, Tailspin Tommy, Mutt & Jeff, Little Orphan Annie reprints - all illustrated text	75	140	210	455	710	965

FAMOUS FIRST EDITION (See Limited Collectors' Edition)
National Periodical Publications/DC Comics: ($1.00, 10x13-1/2", 72 pgs.) (No.6-8, 68 pgs.) 1974 - No. 8, Aug-Sept, 1975; C-61, 1979
(Hardbound editions with dust jackets are from Lyle Stuart, Inc.)

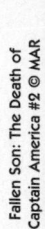

	GD 2.0	VG 4.0	FN 6.0	VF 8.0	VF/NM 9.0	NM- 9.2
C-26-Action Comics #1; gold ink outer-c	4	8	12	28	44	60
C-26-Hardbound edition w/dust jacket	15	30	45	105	190	275
C-28-Detective #27; silver ink outer-c	6	12	18	39	62	85
C-28-Hardbound edition w/dust jacket	17	34	51	124	230	335
C-30-Sensation #1(1974); bronze ink outer-c	4	8	12	28	44	60
C-30-Hardbound edition w/dust jacket	15	30	45	105	190	275

Famous First Edition C-61 © DC

Famous Funnies #124 © EAS

Famous Stars #4 © Z-D

GD VG FN VF VF/NM NM-
2.0 4.0 6.0 8.0 9.0 9.2

F-4-Whiz Comics #2(#1)(10-11/74)-Cover not identical to original (dropped "Gangway for Captain Marvel" from cover); gold ink on outer-c 4 8 12 28 44 60
F-4-Hardbound edition w/dust jacket 15 30 45 105 190 275
F-5-Batman #1(F-6 inside); silver ink on outer-c 5 10 15 32 51 70
F-5-Hardbound edition w/dust jacket 15 30 45 105 190 275
V2#F-6-Wonder Woman #1 4 8 12 28 44 60
F-6-Wonder Woman #1 Hardbound w/dust jacket 15 30 45 105 190 275
F-7-All-Star Comics #3 4 8 12 28 44 60
F-8-Flash Comics #1(8-9/75) 4 8 12 28 44 60
V8#C-61-Superman #1(1979, $2.00) 4 8 12 22 34 45
V8#C-61 (Whitman variant) 4 8 12 24 37 50
V8#C-61 (SC in slipcase, edition of 250 copies) Each signed by Jerry Siegel and Joe Shuster 500.00

Warning: The above books are almost **exact** reprints of the originals that they represent except for the Giant-Size format. None of the originals are Giant-Size. The first five issues and C-61 were printed with two covers. Reprint information can be found on the outside cover, but not on the inside cover which was reprinted exactly like the original (inside and out).

FAMOUS FUNNIES
Eastern Color: 1934; July, 1934 - No. 218, July, 1955

A Carnival of Comics (See Promotional Comics section)

Series 1-(Very rare)(nd-early 1934)(68 pgs.) No publisher given (Eastern Color PrintingCo.); sold in chain stores for 10¢. 35,000 print run. Contains Sunday strip reprints of Mutt & Jeff, Reg'lar Fellers, Nipper, Hairbreadth Harry, Strange As It Seems, Joe Palooka, Dixie Dugan, The Nebbs, Keeping Up With the Jones, and others. Inside front and back covers and pages 1-16 of Famous Funnies Series 1, #s 49-64 reprinted from **Famous Funnies, A Carnival of Comics**, and most of pages 17-48 reprinted from **Funnies on Parade**.
4058 8116 12,174 29,000 - -

No. 1 (Rare)(7/34-on stands 5/34) - Eastern Color Printing Co. First monthly newsstand comic book. Contains Sunday strip reprints of Toonerville Folks, Mutt & Jeff, Hairbreadth Harry, S'Matter Pop, Nipper, Dixie Dugan, The Bungle Family, Connie, Ben Webster, Tailspin Tommy, The Nebbs, Joe Palooka, & others.
3043 6086 9129 22,000 - -
2 (Rare, 9/34) 613 1226 1839 4600 - -
3-Buck Rogers Sunday strip-r by Rick Yager begins, ends #218; not in #191-208; 1st comic book app. of Buck Rogers; the number of the 1st strip reprinted is pg. 190, Series No. 1
800 1000 2400 6000 - -
4 253 506 759 1900 - -
5-1st Christmas-c on a newsstand comic 240 480 720 1800 - -
6-10 170 340 510 1275 - -
11,12,18 Four pgs. of Buck Rogers in each issue, completes stories in Buck Rogers #1 which lacks these pages. 18-Two pgs. of Buck Rogers reprinted in Daisy Comics #1
102 204 306 612 944 1275
13-17,19,20: 14-Has two Buck Rogers panels missing. 17-2nd Christmas-c on a newsstand comic (12/35) 79 158 237 474 730 985
21,23-30: 27-(10/36)-War on Crime begins (4 pgs.); 1st true crime in comics (reprints); part photo-c. 29-X-Mas-c (12/36) 60 120 180 360 560 760
22-Four pgs. of Buck Rogers needed to complete stories in Buck Rogers #1
63 126 189 378 582 785
31,33,34,36,37,39,40: 33-Careers of Baby Face Nelson & John Dillinger traced
42 84 126 252 389 525
32-(3/37) 1st app. the Phantom Magician (costume hero) in Advs. of Patsy
46 92 138 276 426 575
35-Two pgs. Buck Rogers omitted in Buck Rogers #2
46 92 138 276 426 575
38-Full color portrait of Buck Rogers 44 88 132 264 407 550
41-60: 41,53-X-Mas-c. 55-Last bottom panel, pg. 4 in Buck Rogers redrawn in Buck Rogers #3 30 60 90 174 280 385
61,63,64,66,67,69,70 23 46 69 133 214 295
62,65,68,73-78-Two pgs. Kirby-a "Lightnin' & the Lone Rider". 65,77-X-Mas-c
25 50 75 145 233 320
71,79,80: 80-(3/41)-Buck Rogers story continues from Buck Rogers #5
18 36 54 103 162 220
72-Speed Spaulding begins by Marvin Bradley (artist), ends #88. This series was written by Edwin Balmer & Philip Wylie (later appeared as film & book "When Worlds Collide")
20 40 60 117 186 255
81-Origin & 1st app. Invisible Scarlet O'Neil (4/41); strip begins #82, ends #167; 1st non-funny-c (Scarlet O'Neil) 21 42 63 123 197 270
82-Buck Rogers-c 21 42 63 125 200 275
83-87,90: 86-Connie vs. Monsters on the Moon-c (sci/fi). 87 has last Buck Rogers full page-r. 90-Bondage-c 15 30 45 92 144 195
88,89: 88-Buck Rogers in "Moon's End" by Calkins, 2 pgs.(not reprints). Beginning with #88, all Buck Rogers pgs. have rearranged panels. 89-Origin & 1st app. Fearless Flint, the Flint Man 16 32 48 96 151 205
91-93,95,96,98-99,101,103-110: 105-Series 2 begins (Strip Page #1)
15 30 45 83 124 165
94-Buck Rogers in "Solar Holocaust" by Calkins, 3 pgs.(not reprints)
15 30 45 88 137 185

GD VG FN VF VF/NM NM-
2.0 4.0 6.0 8.0 9.0 9.2

97-War Bond promotion, Buck Rogers by Calkins, 2 pgs.(not reprints)
15 30 45 88 137 185
100-1st comic to reach #100; 100th Anniversary cover features 11 major Famous Funnies characters, including Buck Rogers 18 36 54 107 169 230
102-Chief Wahoo vs. Hitler,Tojo & Mussolini-c (1/43) 57 114 171 359 605 850
111-130 (5/45): 113-X-Mas-c 11 22 33 64 90 115
131-150 (1/47): 137-Strip page No. 110 omitted. 144-(7/46) 12th Anniversary cover
10 20 30 58 79 100
151-162,164-168 10 20 30 54 72 90
163-St. Valentine's Day-c 10 20 30 56 76 95
169,170-Two text illos. by Williamson, his 1st comic book work
12 24 36 69 97 125
171-190: 171-Strip pgs. 227,229,230, Series 2 omitted. 172-Strip Pg. 232 omitted. 190-Buck Rogers ends with start of strip pg. 302, Series 2; Oaky Doaks-c/story
9 18 27 50 65 80
191-197,199,201,203,206-208: No Buck Rogers. 191-Barney Carr, Space detective begins, ends #192. 9 18 27 47 61 75
198,200,202,205-One pg. Frazetta ads; no B. Rogers 9 18 27 50 65 80
204-Used in **POP**, pg. 79,99; war-c begin, end #208 9 18 27 52 69 85
209-216: Frazetta-c. 209-Buck Rogers begins (12/53) with strip pg. 480, Series 2; 211-Buck Rogers ads by Anderson begins, ends #217. #215-Contains B. Rogers strip pg. 515-518, series 2 followed by pgs.179-181, Series 3 117 234 351 737 1249 1760
217,218-B. Rogers ends with pg. 199, Series 3. 218-Wee Three-c/story
9 18 27 52 69 85

NOTE: ***Rick Yager*** *did the Buck Rogers Sunday strips reprinted in Famous Funnies. The Sundays were formerly done by Russ Keaton and Lt. Dick Calkins did the dailies, but would sometimes assist Yager on a panel or two from time to time. Strip No. 169 is Yager's first full Buck Rogers page. Yager did the strip until 1958 when* ***Murphy Anderson*** *took over.* ***Tuska*** *art from 4/26/59 - 1965. Virtually every panel was rewritten for Famous Funnies. Not identical to the original Sunday page. The Buck Rogers reprints run continuously through Famous Funnies issue No. 190 (Strip No. 302) with no break in story line. The story line has no continuity after No. 190. The Buck Rogers newspaper strips came out in four series: Series 1, 3/30/30 - 9/21/41 (No. 1 - 600); Series 2, 9/28/41 -10/21/51 (No. 1 -525)(Strip No. 110-1/2 (1/2 pg.) published in only a few newspapers); Series 3, 10/28/51 -2/9/58 (No. 100-428)(No No.1-99), Series 4, 2/16/58 - 6/13/65 (No numbers, dates only).* ***Everett*** *c-86, 86.* ***Moulton*** *a-100, Chief Wahoo c-93, 97, 102, 116, 136, 139, 151. Dickie Dare c-83, 88. Fearless Flint c-89. Invisible Scarlet O'Neil c-81, 87, 95, 121(part), 132. Scorchy Smith c-84, 90.*

FAMOUS FUNNIES
Super Comics: 1964

Super Reprint Nos. 15-18:17-r/Double Trouble #1. 18-Space Comics #?
2 4 6 9 12 15

FAMOUS GANGSTERS (Crime on the Waterfront No. 4)
Avon Periodicals/Realistic No. 3: Apr, 1951 - No. 3, Feb, 1952

1-3: 1-Capone, Dillinger; c-/Avon paperback #329. 2-Dillinger Machine Gun Killer; Wood-c/a (1 pg.); r/Saint #7 & retitled "Mike Strong". 3-Lucky Luciano & Murder, Inc; c-/Avon paperback #66 37 74 111 215 345 475

FAMOUS INDIAN TRIBES
Dell Publishing Co.: July-Sept, 1962; No. 2, July, 1972

12-264-209(#1) (The Sioux) 3 6 9 15 21 26
2(7/72)-Reprints above 1 3 4 6 8 10

FAMOUS STARS
Ziff-Davis Publ. Co.: Nov-Dec, 1950 - No. 6, Spring, 1952 (All have photo-c)

1-Shelley Winters, Susan Peters, Ava Gardner, Shirley Temple; Jimmy Stewart & Shelley Winters photo-c; Whitney-a 37 74 111 215 345 475
2-Betty Hutton, Bing Crosby, Colleen Townsend, Gloria Swanson; Betty Hutton photo-c; Everett-a(2) 23 46 69 135 218 300
3-Farley Granger, Judy Garland's ordeal (life story; she died 6/22/69 at the age of 47), Alan Ladd; Farley Granger photo-c; Whitney-a 29 58 87 169 272 375
4-Al Jolson, Bob Mitchum, Ella Raines, Richard Conte, Vic Damone; Jane Russell and Bob Mitchum photo-c; Crandall-a, 6pgs. 20 40 60 118 189 260
5-Liz Taylor, Betty Grable, Esther Williams, George Brent, Mario Lanza; Liz Taylor photo-c; Krigstein-a 43 86 129 267 446 625
6-Gene Kelly, Hedy Lamarr, June Allyson, William Boyd, Janet Leigh, Gary Cooper; Gene Kelly photo-c 18 36 54 107 169 230

FAMOUS STORIES (...Book No. 2)
Dell Publishing Co.: 1942 - No. 2, 1942

1,2: 1-Treasure Island. 2-Tom Sawyer 30 60 90 174 280 385

FAMOUS TV FUNDAY FUNNIES
Harvey Publications: Sept, 1961 (25¢ Giant)

1-Casper the Ghost, Baby Huey, Little Audrey 6 12 18 37 59 80

FAMOUS WESTERN BADMEN (Formerly Redskin)
Youthful Magazines: No. 13, Dec, 1952 - No. 15, Apr, 1953

13-Redskin story 14 28 42 76 108 140

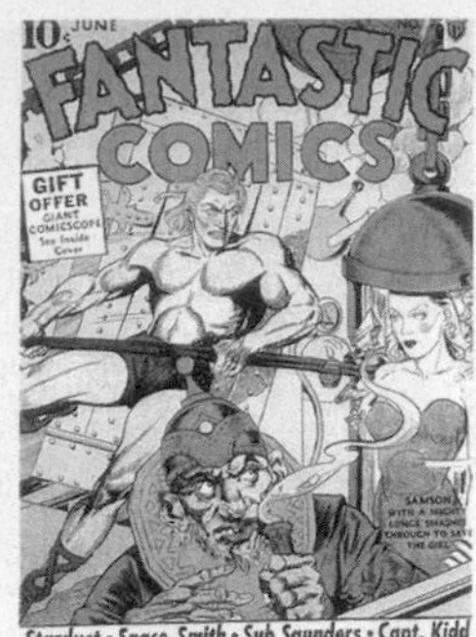

Fantastic Comics
GIFT OFFER
Stardust • Space Smith • Sub Saunders • Capt. Kidd

Fantastic Comics #7 © FOX

Fantastic Five #4 © MAR

Fantastic Four #1 © MAR

GD VG FN VF VF/NM NM-
2.0 4.0 6.0 8.0 9.0 9.2

14,15: 15-The Dalton Boys story 10 20 30 56 76 95

FAN BOY
DC Comics: Mar, 1999 - No. 6, Aug, 1999 ($2.50, limited series)

1-6: 1-Art by Aragonés and various in all. 2-Green Lantern-c/a by Gil Kane. 3-JLA. 4-Sgt. Rock art by Heath, Marie Severin. 5-Batman art by Sprang, Adams, Miller, Timm. 6-Wonder Woman; art by Rude, Grell 2.50
TPB (2001, $12.95) r/#1-6 13.00

FANTASTIC (Formerly Captain Science; Beware No. 10 on)
Youthful Magazines: No. 8, Feb, 1952 - No. 9, Apr, 1952

8-Capt. Science by Harrison 41 82 123 256 428 600
9-Harrison-a; decapitation, shrunken head panels 34 68 102 198 319 440

FANTASTIC ADVENTURES
Super Comics: 1963 - 1964 (Reprints)

9,10,12,15,16,18: 9-r/? 10-r/He-Man #2(Toby). 11-Disbrow-a. 12-Unpublished Chesler material? 15-r/Spook #23. 16-r/Dark Shadows #2(Steinway); Briefer-a.18-r/Superior Stories #1 3 6 9 18 27 35
11-Wood-a; r/Blue Bolt #118 4 8 12 24 37 50
17-Baker-a(2) r/Seven Seas #6 4 8 12 24 37 50

FANTASTIC COMICS
Fox Features Syndicate: Dec, 1939 - No. 23, Nov, 1941

1-Intro/origin Samson; Stardust, The Super Wizard, Sub Saunders (by Kiefer), Space Smith, Capt. Kidd begin 483 966 1449 3478 6089 8700
2-Powell text illos 253 506 759 1594 2697 3800
3-Classic Lou Fine Robot-c; Powell text illos 1300 2600 3900 6500 9750 13,000
4,5: Last Lou Fine-c 200 400 600 1260 2130 3000
6,7-Simon-c 143 286 429 901 1526 2150
8-10: 10-Intro/origin David, Samson's aide 97 194 291 611 1031 1450
11-17,19,20: 16-Stardust ends 78 156 234 491 833 1175
18,23: 18-1st app. Black Fury & sidekick Chuck; ends #23. 23-Origin The Gladiator 80 160 240 504 852 1200
21-The Banshee begins(origin); ends #23; Hitler-c 85 170 255 536 906 1275
22-Hitler-c (likeness of Hitler as furnace on cover) 95 190 285 599 1012 1425
NOTE: *Lou Fine c-1-5.* ***Tuska*** *a-3-5, 8. Bondage c-6, 8, 9. Issue #11 has indicia to Mystery Men Comics #15. All issues feature Samson covers.*

FANTASTIC COMICS (Imagining of a 1941 issue by modern creators in Golden Age style)
Image Comics: No. 24, Jan, 2008 ($5.99, Golden Age sized, one-shot)

24-Samson, Yank Wilson, Stardust, Sub Saunders, Space Smith, Capt. Kidd app.; Larsen-c/a; art by Allred, Sienkiewicz, Yeates, Scioli, Hembeck, Ashley Wood & others 6.00

FANTASTIC COMICS (Fantastic Fears #1-9; Becomes Samson #12)
Ajax/Farrell Publ.: No. 10, Nov-Dec, 1954 - No. 11, Jan-Feb, 1955

10 (#1) 21 42 63 123 197 270
11-Robot-c 26 52 78 152 244 335

FANTASTIC FABLES
Silverwolf Comics: Feb, 1987 - No. 2, 1987 ($1.50, 28 pgs., B&W)

1,2: 1-Tim Vigil-a (6 pgs.). 2-Tim Vigil-a (7 pgs.) 4.00

FANTASTIC FEARS (Formerly Captain Jet) (Fantastic Comics #10 on)
Ajax/Farrell Publ.: No. 7, May, 1953 - No. 9, Sept-Oct, 1954

7(#1, 5/53)-Tales of Stalking Terror 49 98 147 304 507 710
8(#2, 7/53) 36 72 108 212 341 470
3,4 28 56 84 164 265 365
5-(1-2/54)-Ditko story (1st drawn) is written by Bruce Hamilton; r-in Weird V2#8 (1st pro work for Ditko but Daring Love #1 was published 1st) 90 180 240 567 959 1350
6-Decapitation-girl's head w/paper cutter (classic) 56 112 168 353 597 840
7(5-6/54), 9(9-10/54) 28 56 84 164 265 365
8(7-8/54)-Contains story intended for Jo-Jo; name changed to Kaza; decapitation story 23 46 69 135 218 300

FANTASTIC FIVE
Marvel Comics: Oct, 1999 - No. 5, Feb, 2000 ($1.99)

1-5: 1-M2 Universe; recaps origin; Ryan-a. 2-Two covers 2.50
Spider-Girl Presents Fantastic Five: In Search of Doom (2006, $7.99, digest) r/#1-5 8.00

FANTASTIC FIVE
Marvel Comics: Sept, 2007 - No. 5, Nov, 2007 ($2.99, limited series)

1-5-DeFalco-s/Lim-a; Dr. Doom returns vs. the future Fantastic Five 3.00
...: The Final Doom TPB (2007, $13.99) r/#1-5; cover sketches with inks 14.00

FANTASTIC FORCE
Marvel Comics: Nov, 1994 - No. 18, Apr, 1996 ($1.75)

1-($2.50)-Foil wraparound-c; intro Fantastic Force w/Huntara, Delvor, Psi-Lord & Vibraxas 3.00

GD VG FN VF VF/NM NM-
2.0 4.0 6.0 8.0 9.0 9.2

2-18: 13-She-Hulk app. 2.50

FANTASTIC FOUR (See America's Best TV..., Fireside Book Series, Giant-Size..., Giant Size Super-Stars, Marvel Age..., Marvel Collectors Item Classics, Marvel Knights 4, Marvel Milestone Edition, Marvel's Greatest, Marvel Treasury Edition, Marvel Triple Action, Official Marvel Index to..., Power Record Comics & Ultimate...)

FANTASTIC FOUR
Marvel Comics Group: Nov, 1961 - No. 416, Sept, 1996 (Created by Stan Lee & Jack Kirby)

1-Origin & 1st app. The Fantastic Four (Reed Richards: Mr. Fantastic, Johnny Storm: The Human Torch, Sue Storm: The Invisible Girl, & Ben Grimm: The Thing–Marvel's 1st super-hero group since the G.A.; 1st app. S.A. Human Torch); origin/1st app. The Mole Man. 1700 3400 5100 16,000 34,000 52,000
1-Golden Record Comic Set Reprint (1966)-cover not identical to original 17 34 51 124 230 335
with Golden Record 25 50 75 185 343 500
2-Vs. The Skrulls (last 10¢ issue) 365 730 1095 3285 6393 9500
3-Fantastic Four don costumes & establish Headquarters; brief 1pg. origin; intro. The Fantasti-Car; Human Torch drawn w/two left hands on-c 280 560 840 2450 4725 7000
4-1st S. A. Sub-Mariner app. (5/62) 300 600 900 2700 5250 7800
5-Origin & 1st app. Doctor Doom 385 770 1155 3465 6733 10,000
6-Sub-Mariner, Dr. Doom team up; 1st Marvel villain team-up (2nd S.A. Sub-Mariner app. 168 336 504 1470 2835 4200
7-10: 7-1st app. Kurrgo. 8-1st app. Puppet-Master & Alicia Masters. 9-3rd Sub-Mariner app. 10-Stan Lee & Jack Kirby app. in story 115 230 345 978 1864 2750
11-Origin/1st app. The Impossible Man (2/63) 104 208 312 884 1692 2500
12-Fantastic Four vs. The Hulk (1st meeting); 1st Hulk x-over & ties w/Amazing Spider-Man #1 as 1st Marvel x-over; (3/63) 272 544 816 2380 4590 6800
13-Intro. The Watcher; 1st app. The Red Ghost 63 126 189 536 1018 1500
14-19: 14-Sub-Mariner x-over. 15-1st app. Mad Thinker. 16-1st Ant-Man x-over (7/63); Wasp cameo. 18-Origin/1st app. The Super Skrull. 19-Intro. Rama-Tut; Stan Lee & Jack Kirby cameo 48 96 144 384 717 1050
20-Origin/1st app. The Molecule Man 48 96 144 384 717 1050
21-Intro. The Hate Monger; 1st Sgt. Fury x-over (12/63) 43 86 129 344 647 950
22-24: 22-Sue Storm gains more powers 30 60 90 222 411 600
25,26-The Hulk vs. The Thing (their 1st battle). 25-3rd Avengers x-over (1st time w/Captain America)(cameo, 4/64); 2nd S.A. app. Cap (takes place between Avengers #4 & 5.) 26-4th Avengers x-over 54 108 162 459 880 1300
27-1st Doctor Strange x-over (6/64) 35 70 105 270 498 725
28-Early X-Men x-over (7/64); same date as X-Men #6 49 96 147 392 734 1075
29,30: 30-Intro. Diablo 24 48 72 176 326 475
31-40: 31-Early Avengers x-over (10/64). 33-1st app. Attuma; part photo-c. 35-Intro/1st app. Dragon Man. 36-Intro/1st app. Madam Medusa & the Frightful Four (Sandman, Wizard, Paste Pot Pete). 39-Wood inks on Daredevil (early x-over) 20 40 60 143 264 385
41-44,47: 41-43-Frightful Four app. 44-Intro. Gorgon 13 26 39 93 164 235
45-Intro/1st app. The Inhumans (c/story, 12/65); also see Incredible Hulk Special #1 & Thor #146, & 147 20 40 60 148 274 400
46-1st Black Bolt-c (Kirby) & 1st full app. 14 28 42 102 181 260
48-Partial origin/1st app. The Silver Surfer & Galactus (3/66) by Lee & Kirby; Galactus brief app. in last panel; 1st of 3 part story 53 106 159 451 863 1275
49-2nd app./1st cover Silver Surfer & Galactus 37 74 111 284 530 775
50-Silver Surfer battles Galactus; full S.S.-c 40 80 120 319 597 875
51-Classic "This Man...This Monster" story 17 34 51 126 233 340
52-1st app. The Black Panther (7/66) 28 56 84 203 377 550
53-Origin & 2nd app. The Black Panther 15 30 45 111 206 300
54-Inhumans cameo 10 20 30 73 129 185
55-Thing battles Silver Surfer; 4th app. Silver Surfer 17 34 51 126 233 340
56-Silver Surfer cameo 10 20 30 73 129 185
57-60: Dr. Doom steals Silver Surfer's powers (also see Silver Surfer: Loftier Than Mortals). 59,60-Inhumans cameo 9 18 27 65 113 160
61-65,68-71: 61-Silver Surfer cameo; Sandman-c/s 8 16 24 52 86 120
66-Begin 2 part origin of Him (Warlock); does not app. (9/67) 12 24 36 82 146 210
66,67-2nd printings (1994) 2 4 6 8 10 12
67-Origin/1st brief app. Him (Warlock); 1 page; see Thor #165,166 for 1st full app. 12 24 36 82 146 210
72-Silver Surfer-c/story (pre-dates Silver Surfer #1) 11 22 33 79 140 200
73-Spider-Man, D.D., Thor x-over; cont'd from Daredevil #38 10 20 30 73 129 185
74-77: Silver Surfer app.(#77 is same date/S.S. #1) 9 18 27 60 100 140
78-80 6 12 18 41 66 90
81-88: 81-Crystal joins & dons costume. 82,83-Inhumans app. 84-87-Dr. Doom app.

Fantastic Four #197 © MAR

Fantastic Four #307 © MAR

Fantastic Four V2 #4 © MAR

	GD 2.0	VG 4.0	FN 6.0	VF 8.0	VF/NM 9.0	NM- 9.2
88-Last 12¢ issue	6	12	18	37	59	80
89-99,101: 94-Intro. Agatha Harkness.	5	10	15	32	51	70
100 (7/70) F.F. vs Thinker and Puppet-Master	10	20	30	67	116	165
102-104: F.F. vs. Sub-Mariner. 104-Magneto-c/story	5	10	15	34	55	75
105-109,111: 108-Last Kirby issue (not in #103-107)	5	10	15	32	51	70
110-Initial version w/green Thing and blue faces and pink uniforms on-c	6	12	18	37	59	80
110 Corrected-c w/accurately colored faces and uniforms and orange Thing	5	10	15	34	55	75
112-Hulk Vs. Thing (7/71)	14	28	42	99	175	250
113-115: 115-Last 15¢ issue	4	8	12	24	37	50
116 (52 pgs.)	6	12	18	37	59	80
117-120	4	8	12	22	34	45
121-123-Silver Surfer-c/stories. 122,123-Galactus	4	8	12	26	41	55
124,125,127,129-149: 129-Intro. Thundra. 130-Sue leaves F.F. 131-Quicksilver app. 132-Medusa joins. 133-Thundra Vs. Thing. 142-Kirbyish-a by Buckler begins. 143-Dr. Doom-c/story. 147-Sub-Mariner	3	6	9	18	27	35
126-Origin F.F. retold; cover swipe of F.F. #1	3	6	9	20	30	40
128-Four pg. insert of F.F. Friends & Foes	3	6	9	20	30	40
150-Crystal & Quicksilver's wedding	3	6	9	21	32	42
151-154,158-160: 151-Origin Thundra. 159-Medusa leaves; Sue rejoins	2	4	6	11	16	20
155-157: Silver Surfer in all	3	6	9	16	23	30
161-165,168,174-180: 164-The Crusader (old Marvel Boy) revived (origin #165); 1st app. Frankie Raye. 168-170-Cage app. 176-Re-intro Impossible Man; Marvel artists app. 180-r/#101 by Kirby	2	4	6	8	10	12
166,167-vs. Hulk	2	4	6	14	18	28
169-173-(Regular 25¢ edition)(4-8/75)	2	4	6	8	10	12
169-173-(30¢-c, limited distribution)	3	6	9	14	19	30
181-199: 189-G.A. Human Torch app. & origin retold. 190,191-Fantastic Four break up	1	2	3	5	7	9
183-187-(35¢-c variants, limited dist.)(6-10/77)	4	8	12	24	37	50
200-(11/78, 52 pgs.)-F.F. re-united vs. Dr. Doom	2	4	6	9	12	15
201-208,219,222-231: 207 Human Torch vs. Spider-Man-c/story. 211-1st app. Terrax. 224-Contains unused alternate-c for FF #3 and pin-ups						5.00
209-216,218,220,221-Byrne-a. 209-1st Herbie the Robot. 220-Brief origin						6.00
217-Early app. Dazzler (4/80); by Byrne						6.00
232-Byrne-a begins						6.00
233-235,237-249,251-260: All Byrne-a. 238-Origin Frankie Raye. 244-Frankie Raye becomes Nova, Herald of Galactus. 252-Reads sideways; Annihilus app.; contains skin "Tattooz" decals						5.00
236-20th Anniversary issue(11/81, 68 pgs., $1.00)-Brief origin F.F.; Byrne-c/a(p); new Kirby-a(p)						6.00
250-(52 pgs)-Spider-Man x-over; Byrne-a; Skrulls impersonate New X-Men						6.00
261-285: 261-Silver Surfer. 262-Origin Galactus; Byrne writes & draws himself into story. 264-Swipes-c of F.F. #1. 274-Spider-Man's alien costume app. (4th app., 1/85, 2 pgs.)						4.00
286-2nd app. X-Factor continued from Avengers #263; story continues in X-Factor #1						5.00
287-295: 291-Action Comcis #1 cover swipe. 292-Nick Fury app. 293-Last Byrne-a						3.00
296-($1.50)-Barry Smith-c/a; Thing rejoins						4.00
297-318,321-330: 300 Johnny Storm & Alicia Masters wed. 306-New team begins (9/87). 311-Re-intro The Black Panther. 327-Mr. Fantastic & Invisible Girl return						3.00
319,320: 319-Double size. 320-Thing vs. Hulk						4.00
331-346,351-357,359,360: 334-Simonson-c/scripts begin. 337-Simonson-a begins. 342-Spider-Man cameo. 356-F.F. vs. The New Warriors; Paul Ryan-c/a begins. 360-Last $1.00-c						3.00
347-Ghost Rider, Wolverine, Spider-Man, Hulk-c/stories thru #349; Arthur Adams-c/a(p) in each						4.00
347,348-Gold 2nd printing						2.50
348-350: 350-($1.50, 52 pgs.)-Dr. Doom app.						3.00
358-(11/91, $2.25, 88 pgs.)-30th anniversary issue; gives history of F.F.; die cut-c; Art Adams back-up story-a						3.00
361-368,370,372-374,376-380,382-386: 362-Spider-Man app. 367-Wolverine app. (brief). 370-Infinity War x-over; Thanos & Magus app. 374-Secret Defenders (Ghost Rider, Hulk, Wolverine) x-over						2.50
369-Infinity War x-over; Thanos app.						2.50
371-All white embossed-c ($2.00)						4.00
371-All red 2nd printing ($2.00)						2.50
375-($2.95, 52 pgs.)-Holo-grafx foil-c; ann. issue						3.00
376-($2.95)-Variant polybagged w/Dirt Magazine #4 and music tape						5.00
381-Death of Reed Richards (Mister Fantastic) & Dr. Doom						4.00
387-Newsstand ed. ($1.25)						2.25
387-($2.95)-Collector's Ed. w/Die-cut foil-c						3.00
388-393,395-397: 388-bound-in trading card sheet. 394-($1.50-c)						2.50
394,398,399: 394 ($2.95)-Collector's Edition-polybagged w/16 pg. Marvel Action Hour book and acetate print; pink logo. 398,399-Rainbow Foil-c						3.00
400-Rainbow-Foil-c						4.00
401-415: 401,402-Atlantis Rising. 407,408-Return of Reed Richards. 411-Inhumans app. 414-Galactus vs. Hyperstorm. 415-Onslaught tie-in; X-Men app.						2.50
416-($2.50)-Onslaught tie-in; Dr. Doom app.; wraparound-c						3.00
#500-up (See Fantastic Four Vol. 3; series resumed original numbering after Vol. 3 #70)						
Annual 1('63)-Origin F.F.; Ditko-i; early Spidey app.	71	142	213	604	1152	1700
Annual 2('64)-Dr. Doom origin & c/story	38	76	114	293	547	800
Annual 3('65)-Reed & Sue wed; r/#6,11	18	36	54	130	240	350
Special 4(11/66)-G.A. Torch x-over (1st S.A. app.) & origin retold; r/#25,26 (Hulk vs. Thing); Torch vs. Torch battle	12	24	36	84	150	215
Special 5(11/67)-New art; Intro. Psycho-Man, early Black Panther, Inhumans & Silver Surfer (1st solo story) app.	12	24	36	87	156	225
Special 6(11/68)-Intro. Annihilus; birth of Franklin Richards; new 48 pg. movie length epic; last non-reprint annual	8	16	24	56	93	130
Special 7(11/69)-r/F.F. #1,2; Marvel staff photos	4	8	12	28	44	60
Special 8-10: All reprints. 8(12/70)-F.F. vs. Sub-Mariner plus gallery of F.F. foes. 9(12/71). 10('73)	3	6	9	16	23	30
Annual 11-14: 11(1976)-New art begins again. 12(1978). 13(1978). 14(1979)	1	2	3	5	7	9
Annual 15-17: 15('80, 68 pgs.). 17(1983)-Byrne-c/a						5.00
Annual 18-27: 21(1988)-Evolutionary War x-over. 22-Atlantis Attacks x-over; Sub-Mariner & The Avengers app.; Buckler-a. 23 Byrne-c; Guice-p. 24-2 pg. origin recap of Fantastic Four; Guardians of the Galaxy x-over. 25-Moondragon story. 26-Bagged w/card						3.00
Best of the Fantastic Four Vol. 1 HC (2005, $29.99) oversized reprints of classic stories from FF#1,39,40,51,100,116,176,236,267, Ann 2, V3#56,60 and more; Brevoort intro.						30.00
Maximum Fantastic Four HC (2005, $49.99, dust jacket) r/Fantastic Four #1 with super-sized art; historical background from Walter Mosley and Mark Evanier; dust jacket unfolds to a poster: giant FF#1 cover on one side, gallery of interior pages on the other						50.00
...: Monsters Unleashed nn (1992, $5.95)-r/F.F. #347-349 w/new Arthur Adams-c						6.00
...: Nobody Gets Out Alive (1994, $15.95) TPB r/ #387-392						16.00
... Omnibus Vol. 1 HC (2005, $99.99) r/#1-30 & Annual 1 plus letter pages; 3 intros and a 1974 essay by Stan Lee; original plot synopsis for FF #1; essays and Kirby art						100.00
... Omnibus Vol. 2 HC (2007, $99.99) r/#31-60, Annual 2-4 and Not Brand Echh #1 plus letter pages and essays by Stan Lee, Reginald Hudlin, Roy Thomas and others						100.00
Special Edition 1(5/84)-r/Annual #1; Byrne-c/a						3.00
...: The Lost Adventure (4/08, $4.99) Lee & Kirby story partially used in flashback in FF #108 completed with additional art by Frenz & Sinnott; plus reprint of FF #108						5.00
... Visionaries: George Pérez Vol. 1 (2005, $19.99) r/#164-167,170,176-178,184-186						20.00
... Visionaries: George Pérez Vol. 2 (2006, $19.99) r/#187-188,191-192, Annual #14-15, Marvel Two-In-One #60 and back-up story from Adventures of the Thing #3						20.00
... Visionaries (11/01, $19.95) r/#232-240 by John Byrne						20.00
... Visionaries Vol. 2 (2004, $24.99) r/#241-250 by John Byrne						25.00
... Visionaries John Byrne Vol. 3 (2004, $24.99) r/#251-257; Annual #17; Avengers #233 and Thing #2						25.00
... Visionaries John Byrne Vol. 4 (2005, $24.99) r/#258-267; Alpha Flight #4 & Thing #10						25.00
... Visionaries John Byrne Vol. 5 (2005, $24.99) r/#268-275; Annual #18 & Thing #19						25.00
... Visionaries John Byrne Vol. 6 ('06, $24.99) r/#276-284; Secret Wars II #2 & Thing #23						25.00
... Visionaries John Byrne Vol. 7 ('07, $24.99) r/#285,286, Ann. #19, Avengers #263 & Ann. #14, and X-Factor #1						25.00
... Visionaries John Byrne Vol. 8 ('07, $24.99) r/#287-295						25.00
... Visionaries: Walter Simonson Vol. 1 (2007, $19.99) r/#334-341						20.00

NOTE: ***Arthur Adams*** *c/a-347-349p.* ***Austin*** *c(i)-232-236, 238, 240-242, 250i, 286i.* ***Buckler*** *c-151, 168.* ***John Buscema*** *a(p)-107, 108(w/****Kirby, Sinnott & Romita****),109-130, 132, 134-141, 160, 173-175, 202, 296-309p, Annual 11, 13; c(p)-107-122, 124-129, 133-139, 202, Annual 12p, Special 10.* ***Byrne*** *a-209-218p, 220p, 221p, 232-265, 266i, 267-273, 274-293p, Annual 17, 19; c-211-214p, 220p, 232-236p, 237, 238p, 239, 240-242p, 243-249, 250p, 251-267, 269-277, 278-281p, 283p, 284, 285, 286p, 288-293, Annual 17, 18.* ***Ditko*** *a-13i, 14i(w/****Kirby-p****), Annual 16.* ***G. Kane*** *c-145p, 146p, 150p, 160p.* ***Kirby*** *a-1-102p, 108p, 180r, 189r, 236p, Special 1-10; c-1-101, 164, 167, 171-177, 180, 181, 190, 200, Annual 11, Special 1-7, 9.* ***Marcos*** *a-Annual 14i.* ***Mooney*** *a-118i, 152i.* ***Perez*** *a(p)-164-167, 170-172, 176-178, 184-188, 191p, 192p. Annual 14p, 15p; c(p)-183-188, 191, 192, 194-197.* ***Simonson*** *a-337-341, 343, 344p, 345p, 346, 350p, 352-354; c-212, 334-341, 342p, 343-346, 350, 353, 354.* ***Steranko*** *c-130-132p.* ***Williamson*** *c-357i.*

FANTASTIC FOUR (Volume Two)
Marvel Comics: V2#1, Nov, 1996 - No. 13, Nov, 1997 ($2.95/$1.95/$1.99) (Produced by WildStorm Productions)

	GD 2.0	VG 4.0	FN 6.0	VF 8.0	VF/NM 9.0	NM- 9.2
1-($2.95)-Reintro Fantastic Four; Jim Lee-c/a; Brandon Choi scripts; Mole Man app.						5.00
1-($2.95)-Variant-c	1	2	3	4	5	7
2-9: 2-Namor-c/app. 3-Avengers-c/app. 4-Two covers; Dr. Doom cameo						3.00
10,11,13: All $1.99-c. 13-"World War 3"-pt. 1, x-over w/Image						3.00
12-($2.99) "Heroes Reunited"-pt. 1						4.00
...: Heroes Reborn (7/00, $17.95, TPB) r/#1-6						18.00
Heroes Reborn: Fantastic Four (2006, $29.99, TPB) r/#1-12; Jim Lee intro.; pin-ups						30.00

FANTASTIC FOUR (Volume Three)
Marvel Comics: V3#1, Jan, 1998 - Present ($2.99/$1.99/$2.25)

	GD 2.0	VG 4.0	FN 6.0	VF 8.0	VF/NM 9.0	NM- 9.2
1-($2.99)-Heroes Return; Lobdell-s/Davis & Farmer-a						6.00

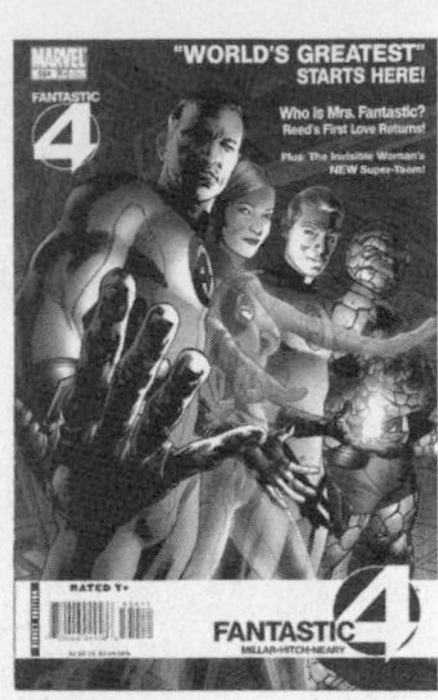

Fantastic Four #554 © MAR

Fantastic Four: Isla De La Muerte! #1 © MAR

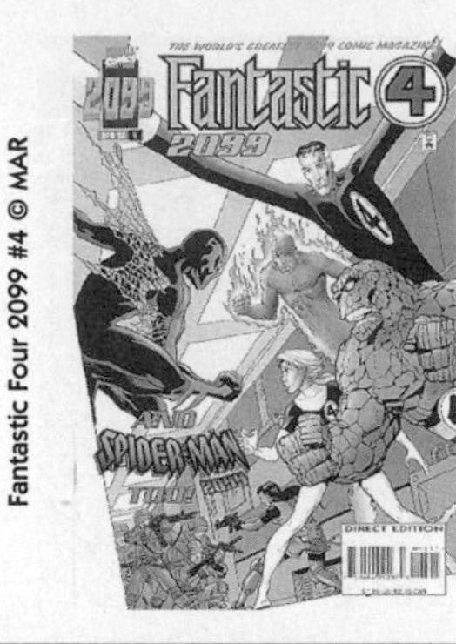

Fantastic Four 2099 #4 © MAR

	GD	VG	FN	VF	VF/NM	NM-
	2.0	4.0	6.0	8.0	9.0	9.2

1-Alternate Heroes Return-c 1 2 3 5 6 8
2-4,12: 2-2-covers. 4-Claremont-s/Larroca-a begin; Silver Surfer c/app.
12-($2.99) Wraparound-c by Larroca 4.00
5-11: 6-Heroes For Hire app. 9-Spider-Man-c/app. 3.50
13-24: 13,14-Ronan-c/app. 3.00
25-($2.99) Dr. Doom returns 3.50
26-49: 27-Dr. Doom marries Sue. 30-Begin $2.25-c. 32,42-Namor-c/app. 35-Regular cover; Pacheco-s/a begins. 37-Super-Skrull-c/app. 38-New Baxter Building 3.00
35-($3.25) Variant foil enhanced-c; Pacheco-s/a begins 3.50
50-($3.99, 64 pgs.) BWS-c; Grummett, Pacheco, Rude, Udon-a 4.00
51-53,55-59: 51-53-Bagley-a(p)/Wieringo-c; Inhumans app. 55,56-Immonen-a 57-59-Warren-s/Grant-a 3.00
54-($3.50, 100 pgs.) Birth of Valeria; r/Annual #6 birth of Franklin 4.00
60-(9¢-c) Waid-s/Wieringo-a begin 3.00
60-($2.25 newsstand edition)(also see Promotional Comics section) 3.00
61-70: 62-64-FF vs. Modulus. 65,66-Buckingham-a. 68-70-Dr. Doom app. 3.00
(After #70 [Aug, 2003] numbering reverted back to original Vol. 1 with #500, Sept, 2003)
500-($3.50) Regular edition; concludes Dr. Doom app.; Dr. Strange app.; Rivera painted-c 4.00
500-($4.99) Director's Cut Edition; chromium-c by Wieringo; sketch and script pages 8.00
501-516: 501,502-Casey Jones-a. 503-508-Porter-a. 509-Wieringo-c/a resumes. 512,513-Spider-Man app. 514-516-Ha-c/Medina-a 3.00
517-537: 517-Begin $2.99-c. 519-523-Galactus app. 527-Straczynski-s begins. 537-Dr. Doom. 3.00
527-Variant Edition with different McKone-c 3.00
527-Wizard World Philadelphia Edition with B&W McKone sketch-c 3.00
536-Variant cover by Bryan Hitch 5.00
537-B&W variant cover 5.00
538-542-Civil War. 538-Don Blake reclaims Thor's hammer 4.00
543-45th Anniversary; Black Panther and Storm replace Reed and Sue; Granov-c 4.00
544-553: 544-546-Silver Surfer app.; Turner-c 3.00
554-560-Millar-s/Hitch-a/c. 558-560-Dr. Doom-c/app. 3.00
554-Variant-c by Bianchi 6.00
554-Variant Skrull-c by Suydam 30.00
...'98 Annual ($3.50) Immonen-a 3.50
...'99 Annual ($3.50) Ladronn-a 3.50
...'00 Annual ($3.50) Larocca-a; Marvel Girl back-up story 3.50
...'01 Annual ($2.99) Maguire-a; Thing back-up w/Yu-a 3.00
... : A Death in the Family (7/06, $3.99, one-shot) Weeks-a/c; and r/F.F. #245 4.00
... By J. Michael Straczynski Vol. 1 (2005, $19.99, HC) r/#527-532 20.00
Civil War: Fantastic Four TPB (2007, $17.99) r/#538-543; 45th Anniversary Toasts 18.00
Fantastic 4th Voyage of Sinbad (9/01, $5.95) Claremont-s/Ferry-a 6.00
Flesh and Stone (8/01, $12.95, TPB) r/#35-39 13.00
... /Inhumans TPB (2007, $19.99) r/#51-54 and Inhumans ('00) #1-4 20.00
...: Isla De La Muerte! (2/08, $3.99) English & Spanish editions; Beland-s/Doe-a 4.00
... Presents: Franklin Richards 1 (11/05, $2.99) r/back-up stories from Power Pack #1-4 plus new 5 pg. story; Sumerak-s/Eliopoulos-a (Also see Franklin Richards) 3.00
...Special (2/06, $2.99) McDuffie-s/Casey Jones-a; dinner with Dr. Doom 3.00
...Tales Vol. 1 (2005, $7.99, digest) r/Marvel Age: FF Tales #1, Tales of the Thing #1-3, and Spider-Man Team-Up Special 8.00
...: The New Fantastic Four HC (2007, $19.99) r/#544-550; variant covers & sketch pgs. 20.00
... : The Wedding Special 1 (1/06, $5.00) 40th Anniversary new story & r/FF Annual #3 5.00
... Vol. 1 HC (2004, $29.99, dust jacket) oversized reprint /#60-70, 500-502; Mark Waid intro and series proposal; cover gallery 30.00
... Vol. 2 HC (2005, $29.99, d.j.) oversized r/#503-513; Waid intro.; deleted scenes 30.00
... Vol. 3 HC (2005, $29.99, d.j.) oversized r/#514-524; Waid commentaries; cover sketches30.00
... Vol. 1: Imaginauts (2003, $17.99, TPB) r/#56,60-66; Mark Waid's series proposal 18.00
... Vol. 2: Unthinkable (2003, $17.99, TPB) r/#67-70,500-502; #500 Director's Cut extras 18.00
... Vol. 3: Authoritative Action (2004, $12.99, TPB) r/#503-508 13.00
... Vol. 4: Hereafter (2004, $11.99, TPB) r/#509-513 12.00
... Vol. 5: Disassembled (2004, $14.99, TPB) r/#514-519 15.00
... Vol. 6: Rising Storm (2005, $13.99, TPB) r/#520-524 14.00
...: The Beginning of the End TPB (2008, $14.99) r/#525,526,551-553 & Fantastic Four: Isla De La Muerte! one-shot 15.00
...: The Life Fantastic TPB (2006, $16.99) r/#533-535; The Wedding Special, Special (2/06) and A Death in the Family one-shots 17.00
Wizard #1/2 -Lim-a 10.00

FANTASTIC FOUR AND POWER PACK
Marvel Comics: Sept, 2007 - No. 4, Dec, 2007 ($2.99, limited series)
1-4-Gurihiru-a/Van Lente-s; the Wizard app. 3.00
...: Favorite Son TPB (2008, $7.99, digest size) r/#1-4 8.00

FANTASTIC FOUR: ATLANTIS RISING
Marvel Comics: June, 1995 - No. 2, July, 1995 ($3.95, limited series)
1,2: Acetate-c 5.00

	GD	VG	FN	VF	VF/NM	NM-
	2.0	4.0	6.0	8.0	9.0	9.2

Collector's Preview (5/95, $2.25, 52 pgs.) 2.50

FANTASTIC FOUR: BIG TOWN
Marvel Comics: Jan, 2001 - No. 4, Apr, 2001 ($2.99, limited series)
1-4:"What If?" story; McKone-a/Englehart-s 3.00

FANTASTIC FOUR: FIREWORKS
Marvel Comics: Jan, 1999 - No. 3, Mar, 1999 ($2.99, limited series)
1-3-Remix; Jeff Johnson-a 3.00

FANTASTIC FOUR: FIRST FAMILY
Marvel Comics: May, 2006 - No. 6, Oct, 2006 ($2.99, limited series)
1-6-Casey-s/Weston-a; flashback to the days after the accident 3.00
TPB (2006, $15.99) r/#1-6 16.00

FANTASTIC FOUR: FOES
Marvel Comics: Mar, 2005 - No. 6, Aug, 2005 ($2.99, limited series)
1-6-Kirkman-s/Rathburn-a. 1-Puppet Master app. 3-Super-Skrull app. 4-Mole Man app. 3.00
TPB (2005, $16.99) r/#1-6 17.00

FANTASTIC FOUR: HOUSE OF M (Reprinted in House of M: Fantastic Four/ Iron Man TPB)
Marvel Comics: Sept, 2005 - No. 3, Nov, 2005 ($2.99, limited series)
1-3: Fearsome Four, led by Doom; Scot Eaton-a 3.00

FANTASTIC FOUR INDEX (See Official...)

FANTASTIC FOUR/ IRON MAN: BIG IN JAPAN
Marvel Comics: Dec, 2005 - No. 4, Mar, 2006 ($3.50, limited series)
1-4-Seth Fisher-a/c; Zeb Wells-s; wraparound-c on each 3.50
TPB (2006, $12.99) r/#1-4 and Seth Fisher illustrated story from Spider-Man Unlimited #8 13.00

FANTASTIC FOUR: 1 2 3 4
Marvel Comics: Oct, 2001 - No. 4, Jan, 2002 ($2.99, limited series)
1-4-Morrison-s/Jae Lee-a. 2-4-Namor-c/app. 3.00
TPB (2002, $9.99) r/#1-4 10.00

FANTASTIC FOUR ROAST
Marvel Comics Group: May, 1982 (75¢, one-shot, direct sales)
1-Celebrates 20th anniversary of F.F.#1; X-Men, Ghost Rider & many others cameo; Golden, Miller, Buscema, Rogers, Byrne, Anderson art; Hembeck/Austin-c 4.00

FANTASTIC FOUR: THE END
Marvel Comics: Jan, 2007 - No. 6, May, 2007 ($2.99, limited series)
1-6-Alan Davis-s/a; last adventure of the future FF. 1-Dr. Doom-c/app. 3.00
Roughcut #1 ($3.99) B&W pencil art for full story and text script; B&W sketch cover 4.00
HC (2007, $19.99, dustjacket) r/#1-6 20.00
SC (2008, $14.99) r/#1-6 15.00

FANTASTIC FOUR: THE LEGEND
Marvel Comics: Oct, 1996 ($3.95, one-shot)
1-Tribute issue 4.00

FANTASTIC FOUR: THE MOVIE
Marvel Comics: Aug, 2005 ($4.99/$12.99, one-shot)
1-($4.99) Movie adaptation; Jurgens-a; behind the scenes feature; Doom origin; photo-c 5.00
TPB-($12.99) Movie adaptation, r/Fantastic Four #5 & 190, and FF Vol. 3 #60, photo-c 13.00

FANTASTIC FOUR: TRUE STORY
Marvel Comics: Sept, 2008 - No. 4 ($2.99, limited series)
1-3-Cornell-s/Domingues-a/Henrichon-c 3.00

FANTASTIC FOUR 2099
Marvel Comics: Jan, 1996 - No. 8, Aug, 1996 ($3.95/$1.95)
1-($3.95)-Chromium-c; X-Nation preview 4.00
2-8: 4-Spider-Man 2099-c/app. 5-Doctor Strange app. 7-Thibert-c 2.50
NOTE: ***Williamson*** *a-1i; c-1i.*

FANTASTIC FOUR UNLIMITED
Marvel Comics: Mar, 1993 - No. 12, Dec, 1995 ($3.95, 68 pgs.)
1-12: 1-Black Panther app. 4-Thing vs. Hulk. 5-Vs. The Frightful Four. 6-Vs. Namor. 7, 9-12-Wraparound-c 4.00

FANTASTIC FOUR UNPLUGGED
Marvel Comics: Sept, 1995 - No. 6, Aug 1996 (99¢, bi-monthly)
1-6 2.50

FANTASTIC FOUR - UNSTABLE MOLECULES
(Indicia for #1 reads STARTLING STORIES: ... ; #2 reads UNSTABLE MOLECULES)
Marvel Comics: Mar, 2003 - No. 4, June, 2003 ($2.99, limited series)
1-4-Guy Davis-c/a 3.00

Fantastic Four: World's Greatest Comics Magazine #6 © MAR

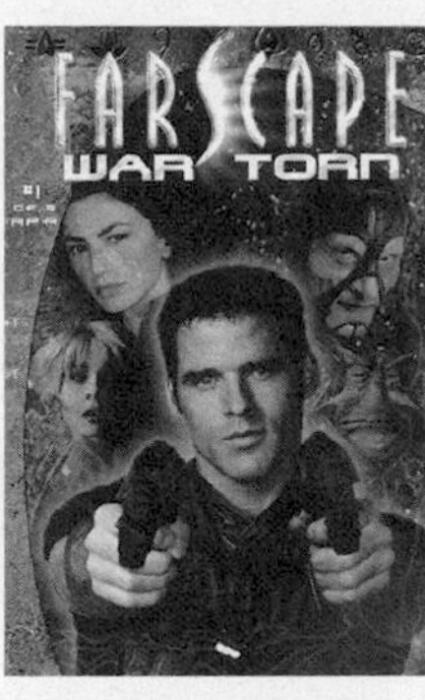

Farscape: War Torn #1 © Jim Henson Co.

Fat Albert #1 © Bill Cosby

	GD 2.0	VG 4.0	FN 6.0	VF 8.0	VF/NM 9.0	NM- 9.2
Fantastic Four Legends Vol. 1 TPB (2003, $13.99) r/#1-4, origin from FF #1 (1963)						14.00
TPB (2005, $13.99) r/#1-4						14.00

FANTASTIC FOUR VS. X-MEN
Marvel Comics: Feb, 1987 - No. 4, June, 1987 (Limited series)

	GD 2.0	VG 4.0	FN 6.0	VF 8.0	VF/NM 9.0	NM- 9.2
1-4: 4-Austin-a(i)						4.00

FANTASTIC FOUR: WORLD'S GREATEST COMICS MAGAZINE
Marvel Comics: Feb, 2001 - No. 12 (Limited series)

	GD 2.0	VG 4.0	FN 6.0	VF 8.0	VF/NM 9.0	NM- 9.2
1-12: Homage to Lee & Kirby era of F.F.; s/a by Larsen & various. 5-Hulk-c/app. 10-Thor app.						3.00

FANTASTIC GIANTS (Formerly Konga #1-23)
Charlton Comics: V2#24, Sept, 1966 (25¢, 68 pgs.)

	GD 2.0	VG 4.0	FN 6.0	VF 8.0	VF/NM 9.0	NM- 9.2
V2#24-Special Ditko issue; origin Konga & Gorgo reprinted plus two new Ditko stories	6	12	18	43	69	95

FANTASTIC TALES
I. W. Enterprises: 1958 (no date) (Reprint, one-shot)

	GD 2.0	VG 4.0	FN 6.0	VF 8.0	VF/NM 9.0	NM- 9.2
1-Reprints Avon's "City of the Living Dead"	3	6	9	20	30	40

FANTASTIC VOYAGE (See Movie Comics)
Gold Key: Aug, 1969 - No. 2, Dec, 1969

	GD 2.0	VG 4.0	FN 6.0	VF 8.0	VF/NM 9.0	NM- 9.2
1 (TV)	4	8	12	28	44	60
2	3	6	9	20	30	40

FANTASTIC VOYAGES OF SINDBAD, THE
Gold Key: Oct, 1965 - No. 2, June, 1967

	GD 2.0	VG 4.0	FN 6.0	VF 8.0	VF/NM 9.0	NM- 9.2
1-Painted-c on both	6	12	18	43	69	95
2	5	10	15	32	51	70

FANTASTIC WORLDS
Standard Comics: No. 5, Sept, 1952 - No. 7, Jan, 1953

	GD 2.0	VG 4.0	FN 6.0	VF 8.0	VF/NM 9.0	NM- 9.2
5-Toth, Anderson-a	36	72	108	212	341	470
6-Toth-c/a	30	60	90	174	280	385
7	20	40	60	115	183	250

FANTASY FEATURES
Americomics: 1987 - No. 2, 1987 ($1.75)

	GD 2.0	VG 4.0	FN 6.0	VF 8.0	VF/NM 9.0	NM- 9.2
1,2						3.00

FANTASY ILLUSTRATED
New Media Publ.: Spring 1982 ($2.95, B&W magazine)

	GD 2.0	VG 4.0	FN 6.0	VF 8.0	VF/NM 9.0	NM- 9.2
1-P. Craig Russell-c/a; art by Ditko, Sekowsky, Sutton; Englehart-s	1	2	3	4	5	7

FANTASY MASTERPIECES (Marvel Super Heroes No. 12 on)
Marvel Comics Group: Feb, 1966 - No. 11, Oct, 1967; V2#1, Dec, 1979 - No. 14, Jan, 1981

	GD 2.0	VG 4.0	FN 6.0	VF 8.0	VF/NM 9.0	NM- 9.2
1-Photo of Stan Lee (12¢-c #1,2)	7	14	21	49	80	110
2-r/1st Fin Fang Foom from Strange Tales #89	5	10	15	30	48	65
3-8: 3-G.A. Capt. America-r begin, end #11; 1st 25¢ Giant; Colan-r. 3-6-Kirby-c(p). 4-Kirby-c(p)(i). 7-Begin G.A. Sub-Mariner, Torch-r/M. Mystery. 8-Torch battles the Sub-Mariner-r/Marvel Mystery #9	5	10	15	32	51	70
9-Origin Human Torch-r/Marvel Comics #1	5	10	15	34	56	75
10,11: 10-r/origin & 1st app. All Winners Squad from All Winners #19. 11-r/origin of Toro (H.T. #1) & Black Knight #1	5	10	15	30	48	65
V2#1(12/79, 75¢, 52 pgs.)-r/origin Silver Surfer from Silver Surfer #1 with editing plus reprints cover; J. Buscema-a						6.00
2-14-Reprints Silver Surfer #2-14 w/covers						4.00

NOTE: *Buscema c-V2#7-9(in part). Ditko r-1-3, 7, 9. Everett r-1,7-9. Matt Fox r-9i. Kirby r-1-11; c(p)-3, 4i, 5, 6. Starlin r-8-13. Some direct sale V2#14's had a 50¢ cover price. #3-11 contain Capt. America-r/Capt. America #3-10. #7-11 contain G.A.Human Torch & Sub-Mariner-r.*

FANTASY QUARTERLY (Also see Elfquest)
Independent Publishers Syndicate: Spring, 1978 (B&W)

	GD 2.0	VG 4.0	FN 6.0	VF 8.0	VF/NM 9.0	NM- 9.2
1-1st app. Elfquest; Dave Sim-a (6 pgs.)	6	12	18	43	69	95

FANTOMAN (Formerly Amazing Adventure Funnies)
Centaur Publications: No. 2, Aug, 1940 - No. 4, Dec, 1940

	GD 2.0	VG 4.0	FN 6.0	VF 8.0	VF/NM 9.0	NM- 9.2
2-The Fantom of the Fair, The Arrow, Little Dynamite-r begin; origin The Ermine by Filchock; Fantoman app. in 2-4; Burgos, J. Cole, Ernst, Gustavson-a	110	220	330	693	1172	1650
3,4: Gustavson-r. 4-Red Blaze story	86	172	258	542	914	1285

FAREWELL MOONSHADOW (See Moonshadow)
DC Comics (Vertigo): Jan, 1997 ($7.95, one-shot)

	GD 2.0	VG 4.0	FN 6.0	VF 8.0	VF/NM 9.0	NM- 9.2
nn-DeMatteis-s/Muth-c/a						8.00

FARGO KID (Formerly Justice Traps the Guilty)(See Feature Comics #47)
Prize Publications: V11#3(#1), June-July, 1958 - V11#5, Oct-Nov, 1958

	GD 2.0	VG 4.0	FN 6.0	VF 8.0	VF/NM 9.0	NM- 9.2
V11#3(#1)-Origin Fargo Kid, Severin-c/a; Williamson-a(2); Heath-a	18	36	54	103	162	220
V11#4,5-Severin-c/a	13	26	39	74	105	135

FARMER'S DAUGHTER, THE
Stanhall Publ./Trojan Magazines: Feb-Mar, 1954 - No. 3, June-July, 1954; No. 4, Oct, 1954

	GD 2.0	VG 4.0	FN 6.0	VF 8.0	VF/NM 9.0	NM- 9.2
1-Lingerie, nudity panel	35	70	105	203	327	450
2-4(Stanhall)	20	40	60	118	189	260

FARSCAPE: WAR TORN (Based on TV series)
DC Comics (WildStorm): Apr, 2002 - No. 2, May, 2002 ($4.95, limited series)

	GD 2.0	VG 4.0	FN 6.0	VF 8.0	VF/NM 9.0	NM- 9.2
1,2-Teranishi-a/Wolfman-s; photo-c						5.00

FASHION IN ACTION
Eclipse Comics: Aug, 1986 - Feb, 1987 (Baxter paper)

	GD 2.0	VG 4.0	FN 6.0	VF 8.0	VF/NM 9.0	NM- 9.2
Summer Special 1 , Winter Special 1, each Snyder III-c/a						2.50

FASTBALL EXPRESS (Major League Baseball)
Ultimate Sports Force: 2000 ($3.95, one-shot)

	GD 2.0	VG 4.0	FN 6.0	VF 8.0	VF/NM 9.0	NM- 9.2
1-Polybagged with poster; Johnson, Maddux, Park, Nomo, Clemens app.						4.00

FASTEST GUN ALIVE, THE (Movie)
Dell Publishing Co.: No. 741, Sept, 1956 (one-shot)

	GD 2.0	VG 4.0	FN 6.0	VF 8.0	VF/NM 9.0	NM- 9.2
Four Color 741-Photo-c	7	14	21	45	73	105

FAST FICTION (...Action) (Stories by Famous Authors Illustrated #6 on)
Seaboard Publ./Famous Authors Ill.: Oct, 1949 - No. 5, Mar, 1950
(All have Kiefer-c)(48 pgs.)

	GD 2.0	VG 4.0	FN 6.0	VF 8.0	VF/NM 9.0	NM- 9.2
1-Scarlet Pimpernel; Jim Lavery-c/a	30	60	90	174	275	375
2-Captain Blood; H. C. Kiefer-c/a	26	52	78	152	239	325
3-She, by Rider Haggard; Vincent Napoli-a	32	64	96	186	293	400
4-(1/50, 52 pgs.)-The 39 Steps; Lavery-c/a	19	38	57	112	176	240
5-Beau Geste; Kiefer-c/a	19	38	57	112	176	240

NOTE: *Kiefer a-2, 5; c-2, 3,5. Lavery c/a-1, 4. Napoli a-3.*

FAST FORWARD
DC Comics (Piranha Press): 1992 - No. 3, 1993 ($4.95, 68 pgs.)

	GD 2.0	VG 4.0	FN 6.0	VF 8.0	VF/NM 9.0	NM- 9.2
1-3: 1-Morrison scripts; McKean-c/a. 3-Sam Kieth-a						5.00

FAST WILLIE JACKSON
Fitzgerald Periodicals, Inc.: Oct, 1976 - No. 7, 1977

	GD 2.0	VG 4.0	FN 6.0	VF 8.0	VF/NM 9.0	NM- 9.2
1	3	6	9	14	19	24
2-7	2	4	6	9	13	16

FAT ALBERT (...& the Cosby Kids) (TV)
Gold Key: Mar, 1974 - No. 29, Feb, 1979

	GD 2.0	VG 4.0	FN 6.0	VF 8.0	VF/NM 9.0	NM- 9.2
1	4	8	12	24	37	50
2-10	3	6	9	14	20	26
11-29	2	4	6	10	14	18

FATALE (Also see Powers That Be #1 & Shadow State #1,2)
Broadway Comics: Jan, 1996 - No. 6, Aug, 1996 ($2.50)

	GD 2.0	VG 4.0	FN 6.0	VF 8.0	VF/NM 9.0	NM- 9.2
1-6: J.G. Jones-c/a in all, Preview Edition 1 (11/95, B&W)						2.50

FAT AND SLAT (Ed Wheelan) (Becomes Gunfighter No. 5 on)
E. C. Comics: Summer, 1947 - No. 4, Spring, 1948

	GD 2.0	VG 4.0	FN 6.0	VF 8.0	VF/NM 9.0	NM- 9.2
1-Intro/origin Voltage, Man of Lightning; "Comics" McCormick, the World's No. 1 Comic Book Fan begins, ends #4	37	74	111	215	345	475
2-4: 4-Comics McCormick-c feature	24	48	72	140	225	310

FAT AND SLAT JOKE BOOK
All-American Comics (William H. Wise): Summer, 1944 (52 pgs., one-shot)

	GD 2.0	VG 4.0	FN 6.0	VF 8.0	VF/NM 9.0	NM- 9.2
nn-by Ed Wheelan	28	56	84	162	261	360

FATE (See Hand of Fate & Thrill-O-Rama)

FATE
DC Comics: Oct, 1994 - No. 22, Sept, 1996 ($1.95/$2.25)

	GD 2.0	VG 4.0	FN 6.0	VF 8.0	VF/NM 9.0	NM- 9.2
0,1-22: 8-Begin $2.25-c. 11-14-Alan Scott (Sentinel) app. 10,14-Zatanna app. 21-Phantom Stranger app. 22-Spectre app.						2.50

FATHOM
Comico: May, 1987 - No. 3, July, 1987 ($1.50, limited series)

	GD 2.0	VG 4.0	FN 6.0	VF 8.0	VF/NM 9.0	NM- 9.2
1-3						2.50

FATHOM
Image Comics (Top Cow Prod.): Aug, 1998 - No. 14, May, 2002 ($2.50)

	GD 2.0	VG 4.0	FN 6.0	VF 8.0	VF/NM 9.0	NM- 9.2
Preview						12.00
0-Wizard supplement						7.00
0-($6.95) DF Alternate						7.00

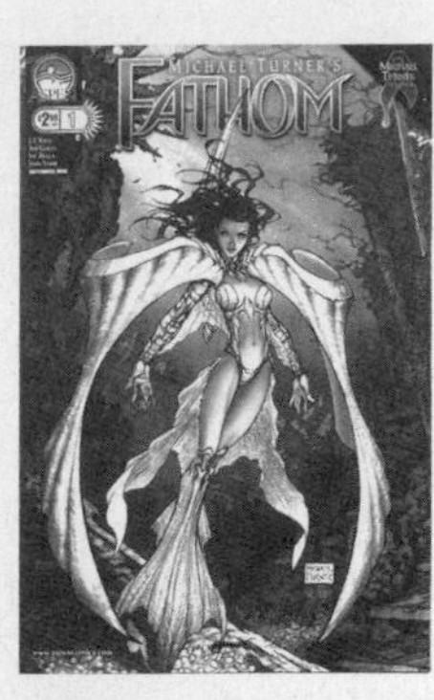

Fathom V3 #1 © Aspen MLT

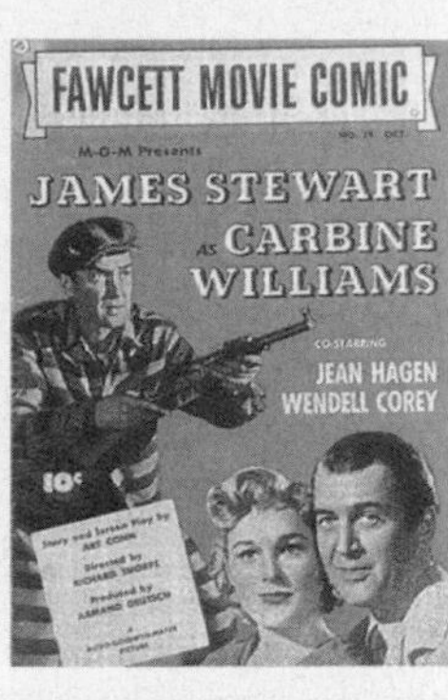

Fawcett Movie Comic #19 © FAW

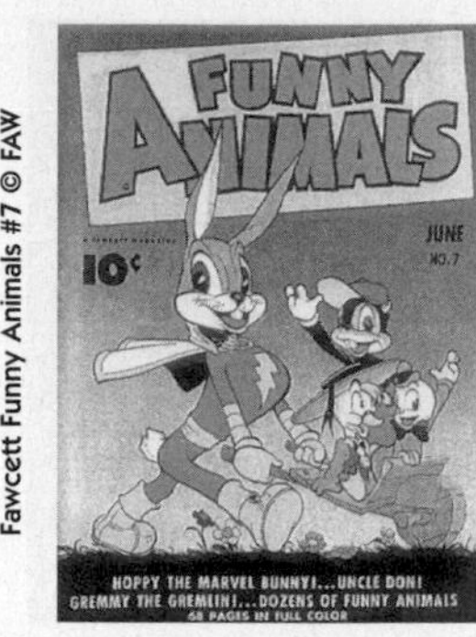

Fawcett Funny Animals #7 © FAW

	GD 2.0	VG 4.0	FN 6.0	VF 8.0	VF/NM 9.0	NM- 9.2
1/2 (Wizard) origin of Cannon; Turner-a						6.00
1/2 (3/03, $2.99) origin of Cannon						3.00
1-Turner-s/a; three covers; alternate story pages						6.00
1-Wizard World Ed.						9.00
2-14: 12-14-Witchblade app. 13,14-Tomb Raider app.						3.00
9-Green foil-c edition						15.00
9,12-Holofoil editions						18.00
12,13-DFE alternate-c						6.00
13,14-DFE Gold edition						8.00
14-DFE Blue						15.00
... Collected Edition 1 (3/99, $5.95) r/Preview & all three #1's						6.00
... Collected Edition 2-4 (3-12/99, $5.95) 2-r/#2,3. 3-r/#4,5. 4-r/#6,7						6.00
... Collected Edition 5 (4/00, $5.95) 5-r/#8,9						6.00
... Swimsuit Special (5/99, $2.95) Pin-ups by various						3.00
... Swimsuit Special 2000 (12/00, $2.95) Pin-ups by various; Turner-c						3.00
Michael Turner's Fathom HC ('01, $39.95) r/#1-9, black-c w/silver foil						40.00
Michael Turner's Fathom SC ('01, $24.95) r/#1-9, new Turner-c						25.00

FATHOM (MICHAEL TURNER'S...) (Volume 2)
Aspen MLT, Inc.: No. 0, Apr, 2005 - No. 11, Dec, 2006 ($2.50/$2.99)

	GD 2.0	VG 4.0	FN 6.0	VF 8.0	VF/NM 9.0	NM- 9.2
0-($2.50) Turnbull-a/Turner-c						2.50
1-11-($2.99) 1-Five covers. 2-Two covers. 4-Six covers						3.00
... Beginnings (2005, $1.99) Two covers; Turnbull-a						2.50
...: Killian's Vessel 1 (7/07, $2.99) 3 covers; Odagawa-a						3.00
... Prelude (6/05, $2.99) Seven covers; Garza-a						3.00

FATHOM (MICHAEL TURNER'S...) (Volume 3)
Aspen MLT, Inc.: No. 0, Jun, 2008 - Present ($2.50/$2.99)

	GD 2.0	VG 4.0	FN 6.0	VF 8.0	VF/NM 9.0	NM- 9.2
0-($2.50) Garza-a/c						2.50
1,2-($2.99) Garza-a; multiple covers on each						3.00

FATHOM: CANNON HAWKE (MICHAEL TURNER'S...)
Aspen MLT, Inc.: Nov, 2005 - No. 5, Feb, 2006 ($2.99)

	GD 2.0	VG 4.0	FN 6.0	VF 8.0	VF/NM 9.0	NM- 9.2
1-5-To-a/Turner-c						3.00
... Prelude (11/05, $2.50) Turner-c						2.50

FATHOM: DAWN OF WAR (MICHAEL TURNER'S...)
Aspen MLT, Inc.: Oct, 2004 - No. 3, Dec, 2004 ($2.99, limited series)

	GD 2.0	VG 4.0	FN 6.0	VF 8.0	VF/NM 9.0	NM- 9.2
0-Caldwell-a						2.50
1-3-Caldwell-a						3.00
...: Cannon Hawke #0 ('04, $2.50) Turner-c						2.50
... The Complete Saga Vol. 1 (2005, $9.99) r/series with cover gallery						10.00

FATHOM: KIANI (MICHAEL TURNER'S...)
Aspen MLT, Inc.: No. 0, Feb, 2007 - No. 4, Dec, 2007 ($2.99, limited series)

	GD 2.0	VG 4.0	FN 6.0	VF 8.0	VF/NM 9.0	NM- 9.2
0-4-Marcus To-a. 1-Six covers						3.00

FATHOM: KILLIAN'S TIDE
Image Comics (Top Cow Prod.): Apr, 2001 - No. 4, Nov, 2001 ($2.95)

	GD 2.0	VG 4.0	FN 6.0	VF 8.0	VF/NM 9.0	NM- 9.2
1-4-Caldwell-a(p); two covers by Caldwell and Turner. 2-Flip-book preview of Universe						3.00
1-DFE Blue, 1-Holographic logo						12.00
4-Foil-c						12.00

FATIMA...CHALLENGE TO THE WORLD
Catechetical Guild: 1951, 36 pgs. (15¢)

	GD 2.0	VG 4.0	FN 6.0	VF 8.0	VF/NM 9.0	NM- 9.2
nn (not same as 'Challenge to the World')	5	10	15	24	30	35

FATMAN, THE HUMAN FLYING SAUCER
Lightning Comics(Milson Publ. Co.): April, 1967 - No. 3, Aug-Sept, 1967 (68 pgs.) (Written by Otto Binder)

	GD 2.0	VG 4.0	FN 6.0	VF 8.0	VF/NM 9.0	NM- 9.2
1-Origin/1st app. Fatman & Tinman by Beck	6	12	18	41	66	90
2-C. C. Beck-a	4	8	12	26	41	55
3-(Scarce)-Beck-a	6	12	18	43	69	95

FAULTLINES
DC Comics (Vertigo): May, 1997 - No. 6, Oct, 1997 ($2.50, limited series)

	GD 2.0	VG 4.0	FN 6.0	VF 8.0	VF/NM 9.0	NM- 9.2
1-6-Lee Marrs-s/Bill Koeb-a in all						2.50

FAUNTLEROY COMICS (Super Duck Presents...)
Close-Up/Archie Publications: 1950; No. 2, 1951; No. 3, 1952

	GD 2.0	VG 4.0	FN 6.0	VF 8.0	VF/NM 9.0	NM- 9.2
1-Super Duck-c/stories by Al Fagaly in all	9	18	27	50	65	80
2,3	6	12	18	31	38	45

FAUST
Northstar Publishing/Rebel Studios #7 on: 1989 - No 11, 1997 ($2.00/$2.25, B&W, mature themes)

	GD 2.0	VG 4.0	FN 6.0	VF 8.0	VF/NM 9.0	NM- 9.2
1-Decapitation-c; Tim Vigil-c/a in all	3	6	9	14	19	24
1-2nd - 4th printings						3.00
2	2	4	6	8	10	12
2-2nd & 3rd printings, 3,5-2nd printing						3.00
3	1	3	4	6	8	10
4-10: 7-Begin Rebel Studios series						5.00
11-($2.25)						3.00

FAWCETT MOTION PICTURE COMICS (See Motion Picture Comics)

FAWCETT MOVIE COMIC
Fawcett Publications: 1949 - No. 20, Dec, 1952 (All photo-c)

	GD 2.0	VG 4.0	FN 6.0	VF 8.0	VF/NM 9.0	NM- 9.2
nn- "Dakota Lil"; George Montgomery & Rod Cameron (1949)	27	54	81	156	246	335
nn- "Copper Canyon"; Ray Milland & Hedy Lamarr (1950)	19	38	58	112	176	240
nn- "Destination Moon" (1950)	72	144	216	450	750	1050
nn- "Montana"; Errol Flynn & Alexis Smith (1950)	19	38	58	112	176	240
nn- "Pioneer Marshal"; Monte Hale (1950)	19	38	58	112	176	240
nn- "Powder River Rustlers"; Rocky Lane (1950)	28	56	84	162	256	350
nn- "Singing Guns"; Vaughn Monroe, Ella Raines & Walter Brennan (1950)	17	34	51	98	154	210
7- "Gunmen of Abilene"; Rocky Lane; Bob Powell-a (1950)	21	42	63	122	191	260
8- "King of the Bullwhip"; Lash LaRue; Bob Powell-a (1950)	31	62	93	178	282	385
9- "The Old Frontier"; Monte Hale; Bob Powell-a (2/51; mis-dated 2/50)	20	40	60	117	184	250
10- "The Missourians"; Monte Hale (4/51)	20	40	60	117	184	250
11- "The Thundering Trail"; Lash LaRue (6/51)	26	52	78	150	235	320
12- "Rustlers on Horseback"; Rocky Lane (8/51)	20	40	60	117	184	250
13- "Warpath"; Edmond O'Brien & Forrest Tucker (10/51)	15	30	45	88	137	185
14- "Last Outpost"; Ronald Reagan (12/51)	34	68	102	197	311	425
15-(Scarce)- "The Man From Planet X"; Robert Clark; Schaffenberger-a (2/52)	241	482	723	1518	2559	3600
16- "10 Tall Men"; Burt Lancaster	14	28	42	78	112	145
17- "Rose of Cimarron"; Jack Buetel & Mala Powers	11	22	33	62	86	110
18- "The Brigand"; Anthony Dexter & Anthony Quinn; Schaffenberger-a	11	22	33	62	86	110
19- "Carbine Williams"; James Stewart; Costanza-a; James Stewart photo-c	12	24	36	69	97	125
20- "Ivanhoe"; Robert Taylor & Liz Taylor photo-c	18	36	54	105	165	225

FAWCETT'S FUNNY ANIMALS (No. 1-26, 80-on titled "Funny Animals"; becomes Li'l Tomboy No. 92 on?)
Fawcett Publications/Charlton Comics No. 84 on: 12/42 - #79, 4/53; #80, 6/53 - #83, 12?/53; #84, 4/54 - #91, 2/56

	GD 2.0	VG 4.0	FN 6.0	VF 8.0	VF/NM 9.0	NM- 9.2
1-Capt. Marvel on cover; intro. Hoppy The Captain Marvel Bunny, cloned from Capt. Marvel; Billy the Kid & Willie the Worm begin	58	116	174	365	620	875
2-Xmas-c	35	70	105	208	334	460
3-5: 3(2/43)-Spirit of '43-c	25	50	75	147	236	325
6,7,9,10	15	30	45	86	133	180
8-Flag-c	15	30	45	90	140	190
11-20: 14-Cover is a 1944 calendar	12	24	36	69	97	125
21-40: 25-Xmas-c. 26-St. Valentine's Day-c	10	20	30	54	72	90
41-86,90,91	9	18	27	47	61	75
87-89(10-54-2/55)-Merry Mailman ish (TV/Radio)-part photo-c	10	20	30	54	72	90

NOTE: *Marvel Bunny in all issues to at least No. 68 (not in 49-54).*

FAZE ONE FAZERS
AC Comics: 1986 - No. 4, Sept, 1986 (Limited series)

	GD 2.0	VG 4.0	FN 6.0	VF 8.0	VF/NM 9.0	NM- 9.2
1-4						2.50

F.B.I., THE
Dell Publishing Co.: Apr-June, 1965

	GD 2.0	VG 4.0	FN 6.0	VF 8.0	VF/NM 9.0	NM- 9.2
1-Sinnott-a	3	6	9	18	27	35

F.B.I. STORY, THE (Movie)
Dell Publishing Co.: No. 1069, Jan-Mar, 1960

	GD 2.0	VG 4.0	FN 6.0	VF 8.0	VF/NM 9.0	NM- 9.2
Four Color 1069-Toth-a; James Stewart photo-c	9	18	27	63	107	150

FEAR (Adventure into...)
Marvel Comics Group: Nov, 1970 - No. 31, Dec, 1975

	GD 2.0	VG 4.0	FN 6.0	VF 8.0	VF/NM 9.0	NM- 9.2
1-Fantasy & Sci-Fi-r in early issues; 68 pg. Giant size; Kirby-a(r)	5	10	15	32	51	70
2-6: 2-4-(68 pgs.). 5,6-(52 pgs.) Kirby-a(r)	3	6	9	19	29	38
7-9-Kirby-a(r)	2	4	6	13	18	22

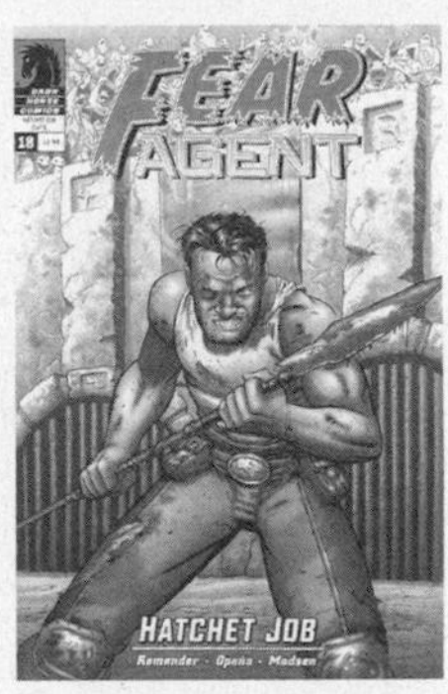

Fear Agent #18 © Remender & Moore

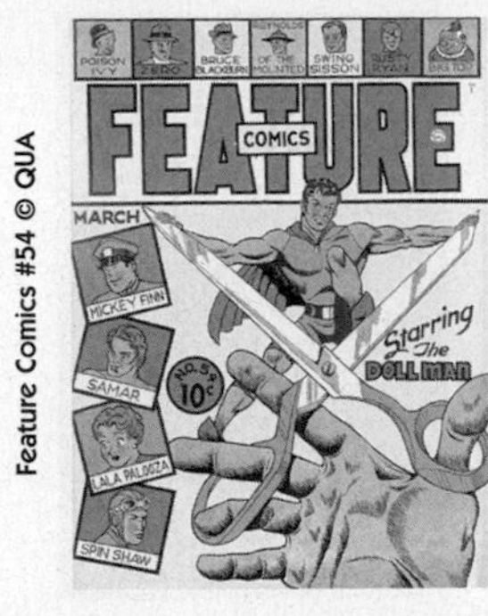

Feature Comics #54 © QUA

Feature Funnies #13 © QUA

	GD 2.0	VG 4.0	FN 6.0	VF 8.0	VF/NM 9.0	NM- 9.2

10-Man-Thing begins (10/72, 4th app.), ends #19; see Savage Tales #1 for 1st app.; 1st solo series; Chaykin/Morrow-c/a; 4 8 12 28 44 60
11,12: 11-N. Adams-c. 12-Starlin/Buckler-a 3 6 9 14 19 24
13,14,16-18: 17-Origin/1st app. Wundarr 2 4 6 11 16 20
15-1st full-length Man-Thing story (8/73) 3 6 9 14 20 26
19-Intro. Howard the Duck; Val Mayerik-a (12/73) 4 8 12 28 44 60
20-Morbius, the Living Vampire begins, ends #31; has history recap of Morbius with X-Men & Spider-Man 4 8 12 28 44 60
21-23,25 2 4 6 11 16 20
24-Blade-c/sty 3 6 9 19 29 38
26-31 2 4 6 9 13 16

NOTE: *Bolle a-13i.* ***Brunner** c-15-17.* ***Buckler** a-11p, 12i.* ***Chaykin** a-10i.* ***Colan** a-23r.* ***Craig** a-10p.* ***Ditko** a-6-8r.* ***Evans** a-30.* ***Everett** a-9, 10i, 21r.* ***Gulacy** a-20p.* ***Heath** a-12r.* ***Heck** a-8r, 13r.* ***Gil Kane** a-21p; c(p)-20, 21, 23-28, 31.* ***Kirby** a-1-9r.* ***Maneely** a-24r.* ***Mooney** a-11i, 26r.* ***Morrow** a-11i.* ***Paul Reinman** a-14r.* ***Robbins** a(p)-25-27, 31.* ***Russell** a-23p, 24p.* ***Severin** c-8.* ***Starlin** c-12p.*

FEAR AGENT
Image Comics.: Oct, 2005 - Present ($2.99)

1-11: 1-Remender-s/Moore-a. 5-Opeña-a begins. 11-Francavilla-a 3.00
... The Last Goodbye 1-4 (6/07 - No. 4, 9/07) (#12-15) 3.00
Tales of the Fear Agent: Twelve Steps in One (#16), 17-23 3.00
... Vol 1.: Re-Ignition TPB (2006, $9.99) r/#1-4 10.00
... Vol 2.: My War TPB (Dark Horse Books, 2007, $14.95) r/#5-10; Opeña sketch pages 15.00

FEAR AGENT: THE LAST GOODBYE
Dark Horse Comics.: June, 2007 - No. 4 ($2.99)

1-Remender-s/Moore-a 3.00

FEARBOOK
Eclipse Comics: April, 1986 ($1.75, one-shot, mature)

1-Scholastic Mag- r; Bissette-a 2.50

FEAR EFFECT (Based on the video game)
Image Comics (Top Cow): May, 2000; March, 2001 ($2.95)

Retro Helix 1 (3/01), Special 1 (5/00) 3.00

FEAR IN THE NIGHT (See Complete Mystery No. 3)

FEARLESS FAGAN
Dell Publishing Co.: No. 441, Dec, 1952 (one-shot)

Four Color 441 4 8 12 24 37 50

FEATURE BOOK (Dell) (See Large Feature Comic)

FEATURE BOOKS (Newspaper-r, early issues)
David McKay Publications: May, 1937 - No. 57, 1948 (B&W)
(Full color, 68 pgs. begin #26 on)

Note: See individual alphabetical listings for prices

nn-Popeye & the Jeep (#1, 100 pgs.); reprinted as Feature Books #3(Very Rare; only 3 known copies, 1-VF, 2-in low grade)
nn-Dick Tracy (#1)-Reprinted as Feature Book #4 (100 pgs.) & in part as 4-Color #1 (Rare, less than 10 known copies)

NOTE: *Above books were advertised together with different covers from Feat. Books #3 & 4.*

1-King of the Royal Mtd. (#1)
2-Popeye (6/37) by Segar
3-Popeye (7/37) by Segar; same as nn issue but a new cover added
4-Dick Tracy (8/37)-Same as nn issue but a new cover added
5-Popeye (9/37) by Segar
6-Dick Tracy (10/37)
7-Little Orphan Annie (#1, 11/37) (Rare)-Reprints strips from 12/31/34 to 7/17/35
8-Secret Agent X-9 (12/37) -Not by Raymond
9-Dick Tracy (1/38)
10-Popeye (2/38)
11-Little Annie Rooney (#1, 3/38)
12-Blondie (#1) (4/38) (Rare)
13-Inspector Wade (5/38)
14-Popeye (6/38) by Segar
15-Barney Baxter (#1) (7/38)
16-Red Eagle (8/38)
17-Gangbusters (#1, 9/38) (1st app.)
18,19-Mandrake
20-Phantom (#1, 12/38)
21-Lone Ranger
22-Phantom
23-Mandrake
24-Lone Ranger (1941)
25-Flash Gordon (#1)-Reprints not by Raymond
26-Prince Valiant (1941)-Hal Foster -c/a; newspaper strips reprinted, pgs. 1-28,30-63; color & 68 pg. issues begin; Foster cover is only original comic book artwork by him
27-29,31,34-Blondie
30-Katzenjammer Kids (#1, 1942)
32,35,41,44-Katzenjammer Kids
33(nn)-Romance of Flying; World War II photos
36('43),38,40('44),42,43, 45,47-Blondie
37-Katzenjammer Kids; has photo & biog. of Harold H. Knerr (1883-1949) who took over strip from Rudolph Dirks in 1914
39-Phantom
46-Mandrake in the Fire World-(58 pgs.)
48-Maltese Falcon by Dashiell Hammett('46)
49,50-Perry Mason; based on Gardner novels
51,54-Rip Kirby; Raymond-c/s; origin-#51
52,55-Mandrake
53,56,57-Phantom

NOTE: *All Feature Books through #25 are over-sized 8-1/2x11-3/8" comics with color covers and black and white interiors. The covers are rough, heavy stock. The page counts, including covers, are as follows: nn, #3, 4-100 pgs.; #1, 2-52 pgs.; #5-25 are all 76 pgs. #33 was found in bound set from publisher.*

FEATURE COMICS (Formerly Feature Funnies)
Quality Comics Group: No. 21, June, 1939 - No. 144, May, 1950

	GD 2.0	VG 4.0	FN 6.0	VF 8.0	VF/NM 9.0	NM- 9.2
21-The Clock, Jane Arden & Mickey Finn continue from Feature Funnies	66	132	198	363	562	760
22-26: 23-Charlie Chan begins (8/39, 1st app.)	46	92	138	253	389	525
26-(nn, nd)-Cover in one color, (10¢, 36 pgs.; issue No. blanked out. Two variations exist, each contain half of the regular #26)	46	92	138	253	389	525
27-(Rare)-Origin/1st app. Doll Man by Eisner (scripts) & Lou Fine (art); Doll Man begins, ends #139	489	978	1467	3521	6161	8800
28-2nd app. Doll Man by Lou Fine	193	386	579	1216	2058	2900
29	103	206	309	649	1100	1550
30-1st Doll Man-c	157	314	471	989	1670	2350
31-Last Clock & Charlie Chan issue (4/40); Charlie Chan moves to Big Shot #1 following month (5/40)	71	142	213	447	756	1065
32,34,36: Dollman covers. 32-Rusty Ryan & Samar begin. 34-Captain Fortune app.	66	132	198	416	701	985
33,35,37: 37-Last Fine Doll Man	47	94	141	291	483	675

NOTE: *A 15¢ Canadian version of Feature Comics #37, made in the US, exists.*

	GD 2.0	VG 4.0	FN 6.0	VF 8.0	VF/NM 9.0	NM- 9.2
38,40-Dollman covers. 38-Origin the Ace of Space. 40-Bruce Blackburn in costume	52	104	156	322	541	760
39,41: 39-Origin The Destroying Demon, ends #40; X-Mas-c.	40	80	120	235	380	525
42,46,48,50-Dollman covers. 42-USA, the Spirit of Old Glory begins. 46-Intro. Boyville Brigadiers in Rusty Ryan. 48-USA ends	40	80	120	244	397	550
43,45,47,49: 47-Fargo Kid begins	29	58	87	169	272	375
44-Doll Man by Crandall begins, ends #63; Crandall-a(2)	52	104	156	322	536	750
51,53,55,57,59: 57-Spider Widow begins	22	44	66	127	204	280
52,54,56,58,60-Dollman covers. 56-Marijuana story in Swing Sisson strip. 60-Raven begins, ends #71	31	62	93	181	291	400
61,63,65,67	20	40	60	115	183	250
62,64,66,68-Dollman covers. 68-(5/43)	27	54	81	158	254	350
69,71-Phantom Lady x-over in Spider Widow	22	44	66	127	204	280
70-Dollman-c; Phantom Lady x-over	30	60	90	174	280	385
72,74,77-80,100-Dollman covers. 72-Spider Widow ends	22	44	66	127	204	280
73,75,76	15	30	45	94	147	200
81-99-All Dollman covers	15	30	45	90	140	190
101-144: 139-Last Doll Man & last Doll Man cover. 140-Intro. Stuntman Stetson (Stuntman Stetson c-140-144)	14	28	42	81	118	155

NOTE: ***Celardo** a-37-43.* ***Crandall** a-44-60, 62, 63-on(most).* ***Gustavson** a-(Rusty Ryan)- 32-134.* ***Powell** a-34, 64-73. The Clock c-25, 28, 29. Doll Man c-30, 32, 34, 36, 38, 40, 42, 44, 46, 48, 50, 52, 54, 56, 58, 60, 62, 64, 66, 68, 70, 72, 74, 77-139. Joe Palooka c-21, 24, 27.*

FEATURE FILMS
National Periodical Publ.: Mar-Apr, 1950 - No. 4, Sept-Oct, 1950 (All photo-c)

	GD 2.0	VG 4.0	FN 6.0	VF 8.0	VF/NM 9.0	NM- 9.2
1- "Captain China" with John Payne, Gail Russell, Lon Chaney & Edgar Bergen	66	132	198	416	701	985
2- "Riding High" with Bing Crosby	69	138	207	435	735	1035
3- "The Eagle & the Hawk" with John Payne, Rhonda Fleming & D. O'Keefe	66	132	198	416	701	985
4- "Fancy Pants"; Bob Hope & Lucille Ball	72	144	216	454	770	1085

FEATURE FUNNIES (Feature Comics No. 21 on)
Harry 'A' Chesler: Oct, 1937 - No. 20, May, 1939

	GD 2.0	VG 4.0	FN 6.0	VF 8.0	VF/NM 9.0	NM- 9.2
1(V9#1-indicia)-Joe Palooka, Mickey Finn (1st app.), The Bungles, Jane Arden, Dixie Dugan (1st app.), Big Top, Ned Brant, Strange As It Seems, & Off the Record strip reprints begin	322	644	966	1770	2635	3500
2-The Hawk app. (11/37); Goldberg-c	150	300	450	825	1213	1600
3-Hawks of Seas begins by Eisner, ends #12; The Clock begins; Christmas-c	117	234	351	644	947	1250
4,5	86	172	258	473	699	925
6-12: 11-Archie O'Toole by Bud Thomas begins, ends #22	67	134	201	369	542	715
13-Espionage, Starring Black X begins by Eisner, ends #20	71	142	213	391	578	765
14-20	50	100	150	275	408	540

NOTE: *Joe Palooka covers 1, 6, 9, 12, 15, 18.*

Felix the Cat #13 © KING

Felon #1 © Greg Rucka & TCOW

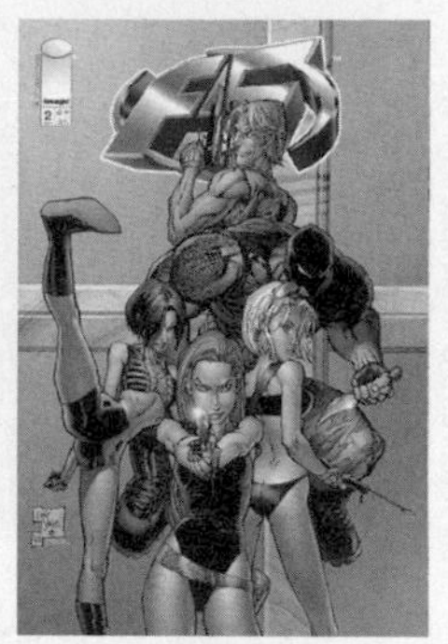
F5 #2 © F5 Entertainment

	GD	VG	FN	VF	VF/NM	NM-
	2.0	4.0	6.0	8.0	9.0	9.2

GD VG FN VF VF/NM NM-
2.0 4.0 6.0 8.0 9.0 9.2

FEATURE PRESENTATION, A (Feature Presentations Magazine #6)
(Formerly Women in Love) (Also see Startling Terror Tales #11)
Fox Features Syndicate: No. 5, April, 1950

5(#1)-Black Tarantula 41 82 123 256 428 600

FEATURE PRESENTATIONS MAGAZINE (Formerly A Feature Presentation #5; becomes Feature Stories Magazine #3 on)
Fox Features Syndicate: No. 6, July, 1950

6(#2)-Moby Dick; Wood-c 32 64 96 186 298 410

FEATURE STORIES MAGAZINE (Formerly Feature Presentations Mag. #6)
Fox Features Syndicate: No. 3, Aug, 1950

3-Jungle Lil, Zegra stories; bondage-c 35 70 105 208 334 460

FEDERAL MEN COMICS
DC Comics: 1936

nn-Ashcan comic, not distributed to newsstands, only for in house use (no known sales)

FEDERAL MEN COMICS (See Adventure Comics #32, The Comics Magazine, New Adventure Comics, New Book of Comics, New Comics & Star Spangled Comics #91)
Gerard Publ. Co.: No. 2, 1945 (DC reprints from 1930's)

2-Siegel/Shuster-a; cover redrawn from Det. #9 38 76 114 222 356 490

FELICIA HARDY: THE BLACK CAT
Marvel Comics: July, 1994 - No. 4, Oct, 1994 ($1.50, limited series)

1-4: 1,4-Spider-Man app. 2.50

FELIX'S NEPHEWS INKY & DINKY
Harvey Publications: Sept, 1957 - No. 7, Oct, 1958

1-Cover shows Inky's left eye with 2 pupils 10 20 30 56 76 95
2-7 7 14 21 35 43 50
NOTE: *Messmer art in 1-6. Oriolo a-1-7.*

FELIX THE CAT (See Cat Tales 3-D, The Funnies, March of Comics #24,36,51, New Funnies & Popular Comics)
Dell Publ. No. 1-19/Toby No. 20-61/Harvey No. 62-118/Dell No. 1-12:
1943 - No. 118, Nov, 1961; Sept-Nov, 1962 - No. 12, July-Sept, 1965

Four Color 15 73 146 219 621 1186 1750
Four Color 46('44) 40 80 120 312 581 850
Four Color 77('45) 38 76 114 293 547 800
Four Color 119('46)-All new stories begin 32 64 96 246 461 675
Four Color 135('46) 23 42 69 167 309 450
Four Color 162(9/47) 17 34 51 124 230 335
1(2-3/48)(Dell) 26 52 78 189 350 510
2 14 28 42 99 175 250
3-5 10 20 30 73 129 185
6-19(2-3/51-Dell) 8 16 24 58 97 135
20-30,32,33,36,38-61(6/55)-All Messmer issues.(Toby): 28-(2/52)-Some copies have #29 on cover, #28 on inside (Rare in high grade) 16 32 48 114 212 310
31,34,35-No Messmer-a; Messmer-c only 31,34 8 16 24 58 97 135
37-(100 pgs., 25 ¢, 1/15/53, X-Mas-c, Toby; daily & Sunday-r (rare)
38 76 114 293 547 800
62(8/55)-80,100 (Harvey) 4 8 12 28 44 60
81-99 4 8 12 24 37 50
101-118(11/61): 101-117-Reprints. 118-All new-a 3 6 9 18 27 35
12-269-211(#1, 9-11/62)(Dell)-No Messmer 5 10 15 30 48 65
2-12(7-9/65)(Dell, TV)-No Messmer 4 8 12 24 37 50
3-D Comic Book 1(1953-One Shot, 25¢)-w/glasses 22 44 66 157 291 425
Summer Annual nn ('53, 25¢, 100 pgs., Toby)-Daily & Sunday-r
31 62 93 239 445 650
Winter Annual 2 ('54, 25¢, 100 pgs., Toby)-Daily & Sunday-r
30 60 90 222 411 600

(Special note: Despite the covers on Toby 37 and the Summer Annual above proclaiming "all new stories," they were actually reformatted newspaper strips)

NOTE: *Otto **Messmer** went to work for Universal Film as an animator in 1915 and then worked for the Pat Sullivan animation studio in 1916. He created a black cat in the cartoon short, Feline Follies in 1919 that became known as Felix in the early 1920s. The Felix Sunday strip began Aug. 14, 1923 and continued until Sept. 19, 1943 whjen **Messmer** took the character to Dell (Western Publishing) and began doing Felix comic books, first adapting strips to the comic format. The first all new Felix comic was Four Color #119 in 1946 (#4 in the Dell run). The daily Felix was begun on May 9, 1927 by another artist, but by the following year, **Messmer** did it too. King Features took the daily away from **Messmer** in 1954 and he began to do some of his most dynamic art for Toby Press. The daily was continued by **Joe Oriolo** who drew it until it was discontinued Jan. 9, 1967. **Oriolo** was **Messmer's** assistant for many years and inked some of **Messmer's** pencils through the Toby run, as well as doing some of the stories by himself. Though **Messmer** continued to work for Harvey, his contiributons were limited, and no all **Messmer** stories appeared after the Toby run until some early Toby reprints were published in the 1990s Harvey revival of the title. 4-Color No. 15, 46, 77 and the Toby Annuals are all daily or Sunday newspaper reprints from the 1930's-1940's drawn by **Otto Messmer**. #101-r/#64; 102-r/#65; 103-r/#67; 104-117-r/#68-81. **Messmer**-a in all Dell/Toby/Harvey issues except #31, 34, 35, 97, 98, 100, 118. **Oriolo** a-20, 31-on.*

FELIX THE CAT (Also see The Nine Lives of...)
Harvey Comics/Gladstone: Sept, 1991 - No. 7, Jan, 1993 ($1.25/$1.50, bi-monthly)

1: 1950s-r/Toby issues by Messmer begins. 1-Inky and Dinky back-up story (produced by Gladstone) 4.00
2-7, Big Book, V2#1 (9/92, $1.95, 52 pgs.) 3.00

FELIX THE CAT AND FRIENDS
Felix Comics: 1992 - No. 5, 1993 ($1.95)

1-5: 1-Contains Felix trading cards 3.00

FELIX THE CAT & HIS FRIENDS (Pat Sullivan's...)
Toby Press: Dec, 1953 - No. 3, 1954 (Indicia title for #2&3 as listed)

1 (Indicia title, "Felix and His Friends," #1 only) 30 60 90 174 280 385
2-3 18 36 54 105 165 225

FELIX THE CAT DIGEST MAGAZINE
Harvey Comics: July, 1992 ($1.75, digest-size, 98 pgs.)

1-Felix, Richie Rich stories 6.00

FELIX THE CAT KEEPS ON WALKIN'
Hamilton Comics: 1991 ($15.95, 8-1/2"x11", 132 pgs.)

nn-Reprints 15 Toby Press Felix the Cat and Felix and His Friends stories in new color 16.00

FELL
Image Comics: Sept, 2005 - Present ($1.99)

1-9-Warren Ellis-s/Ben Templesmith-a 2.50
..., Vol. 1: Feral City TPB (2007, $14.99) r/#1-8 15.00

FELON
Image Comics (Minotaur Press): Nov, 2001 - No. 4, Apr, 2002 ($2.95, B&W)

1-4-Rucka-s/Clark-a/c 3.00

FEM FANTASTIQUE
AC Comics: Aug, 1988 ($1.95, B&W)

V2#1-By Bill Black; Betty Page pin-up 4.00

FEMFORCE (Also see Untold Origin of the Femforce)
Americomics: Apr, 1985 - No. 109 (1.75-/2.95, B&W #16-56)

1-Black-a in most; Nightveil, Ms. Victory begin 1 3 4 6 8 10
2-10 4.00
11-43: 25-Origin/1st app. new Ms. Victory. 28-Colt leaves. 29,30-Camilla-r by Mayo from Jungle Comics. 36-(2.95, 52 pgs.) 4.00
44,64: 44-W/mini-comic, Catman & Kitten #0. 64-Re-intro Black Phantom 5.00
45-63,65-99: 50 (2.95, 52 pgs.)-Contains flexi-disc; origin retold, most AC characters app. 51-Photo-c from movie. 57-Begin color issues. 95-Photo-c 3.00
100-($3.95) 5.00
100-($6.90)-Polybagged 1 2 3 5 6 8
101-109-($4.95) 5.00
Special 1 (Fall, '84)(B&W, 52pgs.)-1st app. Ms. Victory, She-Cat, Blue Bulleteer, Rio Rita & Lady Luger 4.00
Bad Girl Backlash-(12/95, $5.00) 5.00
Frightbook 1 ('92, $2.95, B&W)-Halloween special, In the House of Horror 1 ('89, 2.50, B&W), Night of the Demon 1 ('90, 2.75, B&W), Out of the Asylum Special 1 ('87, B&W, $1.95), Pin-Up Portfolio 3.50
Pin-Up Portfolio (5 issues) 4.00

FEMFORCE UP CLOSE
AC Comics: Apr, 1992 - No. 11, 1995 ($2.75, quarterly)

1-11: 1-Stars Nightveil; inside f/c photo from Femforce movie. 2-Stars Stardust. 3-Stars Dragonfly. 4-Stars She-Cat 3.50

FERDINAND THE BULL (See Mickey Mouse Magazine V4#3)
Dell Publishing Co.: 1938 (10¢, large size, some color w/rest B&W)

nn 19 38 57 112 176 240

FERRET
Malibu Comics: Sept, 1992; May, 1993 - No. 10, Feb, 1994 ($1.95)

1-(1992, one-shot) 3.00
1-10: 1-Die-cut-c. 2-4-Collector's Ed. w/poster. 5-Polybagged w/Skycap 2.50
2-4-($1.95)-Newsstand Edition w/different-c 2.50

F5
Image Comics/Dark Horse: Jan, 2000 - No. 4, Oct, 2000 ($2.50/$2.95)

Preview (1/00, $2.50) Character bios and b&w pages; Daniel-s/a 2.50
1-($2.95, 48 pages) Tony Daniel-s/a 3.00
1-($20.00) Variant bikini-c 20.00
2-4-($2.50) 2.50
F5 Origin (Dark Horse Comics, 11/01, $2.99) w/cove gallery & sketches 3.00

FIBBER McGEE & MOLLY (Radio)(Also see A-1 Comics)

52 #33 © DC

Fight Against Crime #15 © Story Comics

Fight Comics #47 © FH

	GD 2.0	VG 4.0	FN 6.0	VF 8.0	VF/NM 9.0	NM- 9.2

Magazine Enterprises: No. 25, 1949 (one-shot)

A-1 25	11	22	33	64	90	115

FICTION ILLUSTRATED
Byron Preiss Visual Publ./Pyramid: No. 1, Jan, 1975 - No. 4, Jan, 1977 ($1.00, #1,2 are digest size, 132 pgs.; #3,4 are graphic novels for mail order and specialty bookstores only)

1,2; 1-Schlomo Raven; Sutton-a. 2-Starfawn; Stephen Fabian-a.	2	4	6	12	16	20
3-($1.00-c, 4 3/4 x 6 1/2" digest size) Chandler; new Steranko-a	3	6	9	14	19	24
3-($4.95-c, 8 1/2 x 11" graphic novel; low print) same contents and indicia, but "Chandler" is the cover feature title	5	10	15	32	51	70
4-($4.95-c, 8 1/2 x 11" graphic novel; low print) Son of Sherlock Holmes; Reese-a	4	8	12	26	41	55

FIERCE
Dark Horse Comics (Rocket Comics): July, 2004 - No. 4, Dec, 2004 ($2.99, limited series)

1-4-Jeremy Love-s/Robert Love-a 3.00

55 DAYS AT PEKING (See Movie Comics)

52 (Leads into Countdown series)
DC Comics: Week One, July, 2006 - Week Fifty-Two, Jul, 2007 ($2.50, weekly series)

1-Chronicles the year after Infinite Crisis; Johns, Morrison, Rucka & Waid-s; JG Jones-c 4.00
2-10: 2-History of the DC Universe back-up thru #11. 7-Intro. Kate Kane. 10-Supernova 3.00
11-Batwoman debut (single panel cameo in #9) 4.00
12-52: 12-Isis gains powers; back-up 2 pg. origins begin. 15-Booster Gold killed. 17-Lobo returns. 30-Batman-c/Robin & Nightwing app. 37-Booster Gold returns. 38-The Question dies. 42-Ralph Dibny dies. 44-Isis dies. 48 Ronee becomes The Question. 50-World War III. 51-Mister Mind evolves. 52-The Multiverse is re formed; wraparound-c 2.50
...: The Companion TPB (2007, $19.99) r/solo stories of series' prominent characters 20.00
...: Volume One TPB (2007, $19.99) r/#1-13; sample of page development; cover gallery 20.00
...: Volume Two TPB (2007, $19.99) r/#14-26; creator notes and sketches; cover gallery 20.00
...: Volume Three TPB (2007, $19.99) r/#27-39; notes and sketches; cover gallery 20.00
...: Volume Four TPB (2007, $19.99) r/#40-52; creator commentary; cover gallery 20.00

52 AFTERMATH: THE FOUR HORSEMEN (Takes place during 52 Week Fifty)
DC Comics: Oct, 2007 - No. 6, Mar, 2008 ($2.99, limited series)

1-6-Giffen-s/Olliffe-a; Superman, Batman & Wonder Woman app. 2-4,6-Van Sciver-c 3.00
TPB (2008, $19.99) r/#1-6 20.00

52/WWIII (Takes place during 52 Week Fifty)
DC Comics: Part One, Jun, 2007 - Part Four, Jun, 2007 ($2.50, 4 issues came out same day)

Part One - Part Four: Van Sciver-c; heroes vs. Black Adam. 3-Terra dies 2.50
DC: World War III TPB (2007, $17.99) r/Part One - Four and 52 Week 50 18.00

FIGHT AGAINST CRIME (Fight Against the Guilty #22, 23)
Story Comics: May, 1951 - No. 21, Sept, 1954

1-True crime stories #1-4	40	80	120	244	397	550
2	21	42	63	125	200	275
3,5: 5-Frazetta-a, 1 pg.; content change to horror & suspense	19	38	57	109	172	235
4-Drug story "Hopped Up Killers"	20	40	60	115	183	250
6,7: 6-Used in **POP**, pgs. 83,84	17	34	51	98	154	210
8-Last crime format issue	15	30	45	92	144	195

NOTE: *No. 9-21 contain violent, gruesome stories with blood, dismemberment, decapitation, E.C. style plot twists and several E.C. swipes. Bondage c-4, 6, 18, 19.*

9-11,13	38	76	114	226	363	500
12-Morphine drug story "The Big Dope"	40	80	120	244	397	550
14-Tothish art by Ross Andru; electrocution-c	40	80	120	235	380	525
15-B&W & color illos in **POP**	38	76	114	226	363	500
16-E.C. story swipe/Haunt of Fear #19; Tothish-a by Ross Andru; bondage-c	40	80	120	244	397	550
17-Wildey E.C. swipe/Shock SuspenStories #9; knife through neck-c (1/54)	40	80	120	244	397	550
18,19: 19-Bondage/torture-c	37	74	111	219	352	485
20-Decapitation cover; contains hanging, ax murder, blood & violence	65	130	195	410	693	975
21-E.C. swipe	32	64	96	186	298	410

NOTE: ***Cameron** a-4, 5, 8. **Hollingsworth** a-3-7, 9, 10, 13. **Wildey** a-6, 15, 16.*

FIGHT AGAINST THE GUILTY (Formerly Fight Against Crime)
Story Comics: No. 22, Dec, 1954 - No. 23, Mar, 1955

22-Tothish-a by Ross Andru; Ditko-a; E.C. story swipe; electrocution-c (Last pre-code)	32	64	96	186	298	410
23-Hollingsworth-a	21	42	63	123	197	270

FIGHT COMICS
Fiction House Magazines: Jan, 1940 - No. 83, 11/52; No. 84, Wint, 1952-53; No. 85, Spring, 1953; No. 86, Summer, 1954

1-Origin Spy Fighter, Starring Saber; Jack Dempsey life story; Shark Brodie & Chip Collins begin; Fine-c; Eisner-a	335	670	1005	2278	3989	5700
2-Joe Louis life story; Fine/Eisner-c	122	244	366	769	1297	1825
3-Rip Regan, the Power Man begins (3/40)	103	206	309	649	1100	1550
4,5: 4-Fine-c	66	132	198	416	701	985
6-10: 6,7-Powell-c	49	98	147	304	507	710
11-14: Rip Regan ends	46	92	138	285	473	660
15-1st app. Super American plus-c (10/41)	59	118	177	372	629	885
16-Captain Fight begins (12/41); Spy Fighter ends	59	118	177	372	629	885
17,18: Super American ends	46	92	138	285	473	660
19-Captain Fight ends; Senorita Rio begins (6/42, origin & 1st app.); Rip Carson, Chute Trooper begins	48	96	144	298	499	700
20	41	82	123	250	413	575
21-30	38	76	114	226	363	500
31-Classic decapitation-c	73	146	219	460	780	1100
32-Tiger Girl begins (6/44, 1st app.?)	40	80	120	235	380	525
33-50: 44-Capt. Fight returns. 48-Used in Love and Death by Legman. 49-Jungle-c begin, end #81	31	62	93	181	291	400
51-Origin Tiger Girl; Patsy Pin-Up app.	38	76	114	222	356	490
52-60,62-64-Last Baker issue	22	44	66	129	207	285
61-Origin Tiger Girl retold	23	46	69	135	218	300
65-78: 78-Used in **POP**, pg. 99	19	38	57	109	172	235
79-The Space Rangers app.	20	40	60	114	180	245
80-85: 81-Last jungle-c. 82-85-War-c/stories	15	30	45	92	144	195
86-Two Tigerman stories by Evans-r/Rangers Comics #40,41; Moreira-r/Rangers Comics #45	15	30	45	92	144	195

NOTE: *Bondage covers, Lingerie, headlights panels are common. Captain Fight by **Kamen**-51-66. Kayo Kirby by **Baker**-#43-64, 67(not by Baker). Senorita Rio by **Kamen**-#57-64; by **Grandenetti**-#65, 66. Tiger Girl by **Baker**-#36-60, 62-64; **Eisner** c-1-3, 5, 10, 11. **Kamen** a-54?, 57? **Tuska** a-1, 5, 8, 10, 21, 29, 34. **Whitman** c-73-84. **Zolnerwich** c-16, 17, 22. Power Man c-5, 6, 9. Super American c-15-17. Tiger Girl c-49-81.*

FIGHT FOR LOVE
United Features Syndicate: 1952 (no month)

nn-Abbie & Slats newspaper-r	9	18	27	47	61	75

FIGHT FOR TOMORROW
DC Comics (Vertigo): Nov, 2002 - No. 6, Apr, 2003 ($2.50, limited series)

1-6-Denys Cowan-a/Brian Wood-s. 1-Jim Lee-c. 5-Jo Chen-c 2.50
TPB (2008, $14.99) r/#1-6 15.00

FIGHTING AIR FORCE (See United States Fighting Air Force)

FIGHTIN' AIR FORCE (Formerly Sherlock Holmes?; Never Again? War and Attack #54 on)
Charlton Comics: No. 3, Feb, 1956 - No. 53, Feb-Mar, 1966

V1#3	9	18	27	47	61	75
4-10	6	12	18	31	38	45
11(3/58, 68 pgs.)	8	16	24	42	54	65
12 (100 pgs.)-U.S. Nukes Russia	11	22	33	64	90	115
13-30: 13,24-Glanzman-a. 24-Glanzman-c	3	6	9	18	27	35
31-50: 50-American Eagle begins	3	6	9	14	19	24
51-53	2	4	6	11	16	20

FIGHTING AMERICAN
Headline Publ./Prize (Crestwood): Apr-May, 1954 - No. 7, Apr-May, 1955

1-Origin & 1st app. Fighting American & Speedboy (Capt. America & Bucky clones); S&K-c/a(3); 1st super hero satire series	173	346	519	1090	1845	2600
2-S&K-a(3)	80	160	240	504	852	1200
3-5: 3,4-S&K-a(3). 5-S&K-a(2); Kirby/?-a	62	124	186	391	663	935
6-Origin-r (4 pgs.) plus 2 pgs. by S&K	59	118	177	372	629	885
7-Kirby-a	53	106	159	330	553	775

NOTE: ***Simon & Kirby** covers on all. 6 is last pre-code issue.*

FIGHTING AMERICAN
Harvey Publications: Oct, 1966 (25¢)

1-Origin Fighting American & Speedboy by S&K-r; S&K-c/a(3); 1 pg. Neal Adams ad	5	10	15	34	55	75

FIGHTING AMERICAN
DC Comics: Feb, 1994 - No. 6, 1994 ($1.50, limited series)

1-6 2.50

FIGHTING AMERICAN (Vol. 3)
Awesome Entertainment: Aug, 1997 - No. 2, Oct, 1997 ($2.50)

Preview-Agent America (pre-lawsuit)	1	2	3	5	6	7

1-Four covers by Liefeld, Churchill, Platt, McGuinness 2.50
1-Platinum Edition, 1-Gold foil Edition 10.00

Fighting Fronts! #1 © HARV

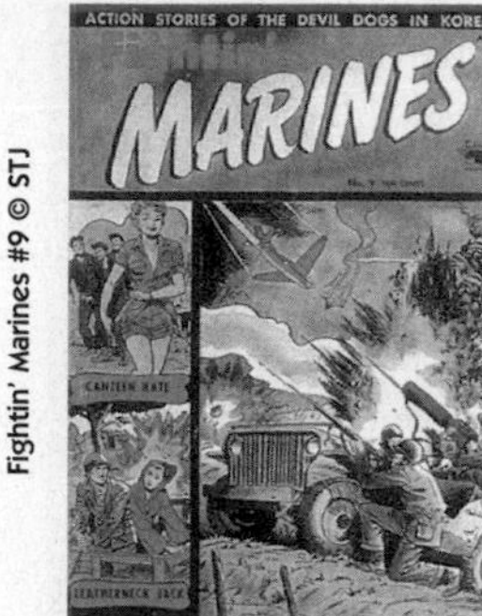

Fightin' Marines #9 © STJ

Fighting Yank #7 © NEDOR

	GD 2.0	VG 4.0	FN 6.0	VF 8.0	VF/NM 9.0	NM- 9.2
1-Comic Cavalcade Edition, 2-American Ent. Spice Ed.						4.00
2-Platt-c, 2-Liefeld variant-c						2.50

FIGHTING AMERICAN: DOGS OF WAR
Awesome-Hyperwerks: Sept, 1998 - No. 3, May, 1999 ($2.50)

Limited Convention Special (7/98, B&W) Platt-a						2.50
1-3-Starlin-s/Platt-a/c						2.50

FIGHTING AMERICAN: RULES OF THE GAME
Awesome Entertainment: Nov, 1997 - No. 3, Mar, 1998 ($2.50, lim. series)

1-3: 1-Loeb-s/McGuinness-a/c. 2-Flip book with Swat! preview						2.50
1-Liefeld SPICE variant-c, 1-Dynamic Forces Ed.; McGuinness-c						2.50
1-Liefeld Fighting American & cast variant-c						2.50

FIGHTIN' ARMY (Formerly Soldier and Marine Comics) (See Captain Willy Schultz)
Charlton Comics: No. 16, 1/56 - No. 127, 12/76; No. 128, 9/77 - No. 172, 11/84

16	9	18	27	47	61	75
17-19,21-23,25-30	6	12	18	31	38	45
20-Ditko-a	9	18	27	47	61	75
24 (3/58, 68 pgs.)	8	16	24	40	50	60
31-45	3	6	9	18	27	35
46-60	3	6	9	16	22	28
61-74	2	4	6	13	18	22
75-1st The Lonely War of Willy Schultz	3	6	9	17	25	32
76-80: 76-92-The Lonely War of Willy Schultz. 79-Devil Brigade	2	4	6	13	18	22
81-88,91,93-99: 82,83-Devil Brigade	2	4	6	9	13	16
89,90,92-Ditko-a	3	6	9	14	19	24
100	2	4	6	11	16	20
101-127	2	4	6	8	11	14
128-140	1	2	3	5	7	9
141-165	1	2	3	4	5	7
166-172-Low print run	1	2	3	5	6	8
108(Modern Comics-1977)-Reprint						4.00

NOTE: *Aparo c-154. **Glanzman** a-77-88. **Montes/Bache** a-48, 49, 51, 69, 75, 76, 170r.*

FIGHTING CARAVANS (See Zane Grey 4-Color 632)

FIGHTING DANIEL BOONE
Avon Periodicals: 1953

nn-Kinstler-c/a, 22 pgs.	18	36	54	105	165	225
I.W. Reprint #1-Reprints #1 above; Kinstler-c/a; Lawrence/Alascia-a	3	6	9	14	19	24

FIGHTING DAVY CROCKETT (Formerly Kit Carson)
Avon Periodicals: No. 9, Oct-Nov, 1955

9-Kinstler-c	10	20	30	54	72	90

FIGHTIN' FIVE, THE (Formerly Space War) (Also see The Peacemaker)
Charlton Comics: July, 1964 - No. 41, Jan, 1967; No. 42, Oct, 1981 - No. 49, Dec, 1982

V2#28-Origin/1st app. Fightin' Five; Montes/Bache-a	6	12	18	39	62	85
29-39,41-Montes/Bache-a in all	3	6	9	21	32	42
40-Peacemaker begins (1st app.)	6	12	18	41	66	90
41-Peacemaker (2nd app.)	4	8	12	28	44	60
42-49: Reprints						5.00

FIGHTING FRONTS!
Harvey Publications: Aug, 1952 - No. 5, Jan, 1953

1	10	20	30	54	72	90
2-Extreme violence; Nostrand/Powell-a	11	22	33	60	83	105
3-5: 3-Powell-a	7	14	21	37	46	55

FIGHTING INDIAN STORIES (See Midget Comics)

FIGHTING INDIANS OF THE WILD WEST!
Avon Periodicals: Mar, 1952 - No. 2, Nov, 1952

1-Geronimo, Chief Crazy Horse, Chief Victorio, Black Hawk begin; Larsen-a; McCann-a(2)	17	34	51	98	154	210
2-Kinstler-c & inside-c only; Larsen, McCann-a	12	24	36	69	97	125
100 Pg. Annual (1952, 25¢)-Contains three comics rebound; Geronimo, Chief Crazy Horse, Chief Victorio; Kinstler-c	34	68	102	198	319	440

FIGHTING LEATHERNECKS
Toby Press: Feb, 1952 - No. 6, Dec, 1952

1- "Duke's Diary"; full pg. pin-ups by Sparling	14	28	42	80	115	150
2-5: 2- "Duke's Diary" full pg. pin-ups. 3-5- "Gil's Gals"; full pg. pin-ups	10	20	30	54	72	90
6-(Same as No. 3-5?)	10	20	30	54	72	90

FIGHTING MAN, THE (War)
Ajax/Farrell Publications(Excellent Publ.): May, 1952 - No. 8, July, 1953

	GD 2.0	VG 4.0	FN 6.0	VF 8.0	VF/NM 9.0	NM- 9.2
1	14	28	42	80	115	150
2	9	18	27	47	61	75
3-8	8	16	24	40	50	60
Annual 1 (1952, 25¢, 100 pgs.)	24	48	72	140	225	310

FIGHTIN' MARINES (Formerly The Texan; also see Approved Comics)
St. John(Approved Comics)/Charlton Comics No. 14 on:
No. 15, 8/51 - No. 12, 3/53; No. 14, 5/55 - No. 132, 11/76; No. 133, 10/77 - No. 176, 9/84 (No #13?) (Korean War #1-3)

15(#1)-Matt Baker c/a "Leatherneck Jack"; slightly large size; Fightin' Texan No. 16 & 17?	43	86	129	267	446	625
2-1st Canteen Kate by Baker; slightly large size; partial Baker-c	50	100	150	310	518	725
3-9,11-Canteen Kate by Baker; Baker c-#2,3,5-11; 4-Partial Baker-c	29	58	87	169	272	375
10-Matt Baker-c	14	28	42	80	115	150
12-No Baker-a; Last St. John issue?	8	16	24	44	57	70
14 (5/55; 1st Charlton issue; formerly?)-Canteen Kate by Baker; all stories reprinted from #2	19	38	57	109	172	235
15-Baker-c	11	22	33	60	83	105
16,18-20-Not Baker-c	7	14	21	35	43	50
17-Canteen Kate by Baker	15	30	45	83	124	165
21-24	6	12	18	31	38	45
25-(68 pgs.)(3/58)-Check-a?	10	20	30	54	72	90
26-(100 pgs.)(8/58)-Check-a(5)	14	28	42	80	115	150
27-50	3	6	9	18	27	35
51-81: 78-Shotgun Harker & the Chicken series begin	3	6	9	16	22	28
82-(100 pgs.)	5	10	15	32	51	70
83-85: 85-Last 12¢ issue	3	6	9	14	20	25
86-94: 94-Last 15¢ issue	2	4	6	10	14	18
95-100,122: 122-(1975) Pilot issue for "War" title (Fightin' Marines Presents War)	2	4	6	9	13	16
101-121	2	4	6	8	10	12
123-140	1	2	3	5	7	9
141-170						6.00
171-176-Low print run	1	2	3	5	6	8
120(Modern Comics reprint, 1977)						4.00

NOTE: *No. 14 & 16 (CC) reprint St. John issues; No. 16 reprints St. John insignia on cover. **Colan** a-3, 7. **Glanzman** c/a-92, 94. **Montes/Bache** a-48, 53, 55, 64, 65, 72-74, 77-83, 176r.*

FIGHTING MARSHAL OF THE WILD WEST (See The Hawk)

FIGHTIN' NAVY (Formerly Don Winslow)
Charlton Comics: No. 74, 1/56 - No. 125, 4-5/66; No. 126, 8/83 - No. 133, 10/84

74	6	12	18	37	59	80
75-81	4	8	12	22	34	45
82-Sam Glanzman-a (68 pg. Giant)	5	10	15	30	48	65
83-(100 pgs.)	6	12	18	41	66	90
84-99,101: 101-UFO-c/story	3	6	9	17	25	32
100	3	6	9	18	27	35
102-105,106-125('66)	3	6	9	14	19	24
126-133 (1984)-Low print run	1	2	3	5	6	8

NOTE: ***Montes/Bache** a-109. **Glanzman** a-82, 92, 96, 98, 100, 131r.*

FIGHTING PRINCE OF DONEGAL, THE (See Movie Comics)

FIGHTIN' TEXAN (Formerly The Texan & Fightin' Marines?)
St. John Publishing Co.: No. 16, Sept, 1952 - No. 17, Dec, 1952

16,17: Tuska-a each. 17-Cameron-c/a	8	16	24	44	57	70

FIGHTING UNDERSEA COMMANDOS (See Undersea Fighting...)
Avon Periodicals: May, 1952 - No. 5, April, 1953 (U.S. Navy frogmen)

1-Cover title is Undersea Fighting... #1 only	15	30	45	84	127	170
2	10	20	30	56	76	95
3-5: 1,3-Ravielli-c. 4-Kinstler-c	9	18	27	50	65	80

FIGHTING WAR STORIES
Men's Publications/Story Comics: Aug, 1952 - No. 5, 1953

1	10	20	30	54	72	90
2-5	6	12	18	31	38	45

FIGHTING YANK (See America's Best Comics & Startling Comics)
Nedor/Better Publ./Standard: Sept, 1942 - No. 29, Aug, 1949

1-The Fighting Yank begins; Mystico, the Wonder Man app; bondage-c	280	560	840	1764	2982	4200

Final Crisis #1 © DC

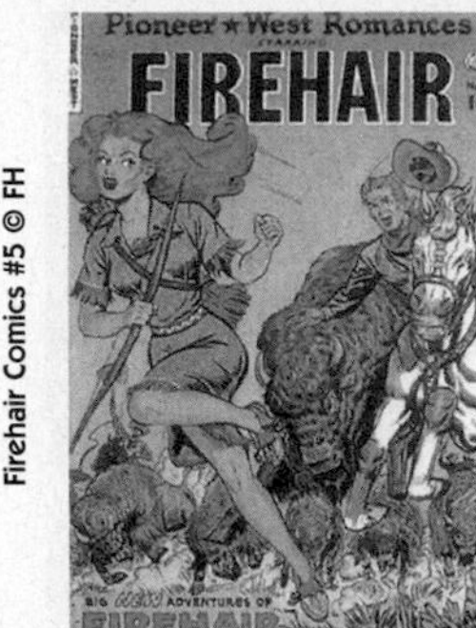

Firehair Comics #5 © FH

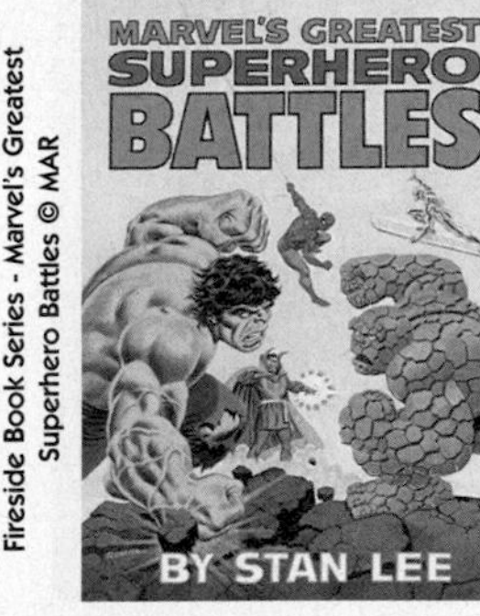

Fireside Book Series - Marvel's Greatest Superhero Battles © MAR

	GD 2.0	VG 4.0	FN 6.0	VF 8.0	VF/NM 9.0	NM- 9.2
2	115	230	345	725	1225	1725
3,4: 4-Schomburg-c begin	83	166	249	523	887	1250
5,6,8-10: 8,10-Bondage/torture-c	65	130	195	410	693	975
7-Hitler special bomb-c; Grim Reaper app.	70	140	210	441	746	1050
11,13-20: 11-The Oracle app. 15-Bondage/torture-c. 18-The American Eagle app.	53	106	159	330	553	775
12-Hirohito bondage-c	73	146	219	460	780	1100
21,24: 21-Kara, Jungle Princess app.; lingerie-c. 24-Miss Masque app.	47	94	141	291	488	685
22-Miss Masque-c/story	53	106	159	330	553	775
23-Classic Schomburg hooded vigilante-c	70	140	210	441	746	1050
25-Robinson/Meskin-a; strangulation, lingerie panel; The Cavalier app.	52	104	156	322	536	750
26-29: All-Robinson/Meskin-a. 28-One pg. Williamson-a	43	86	129	267	446	625

NOTE: *Schomburg (Xela) c-4-29; airbrush-c 28, 29. Bondage c-1, 4, 8, 10, 11, 12, 15, 17.*

FIGHTMAN
Marvel Comics: June, 1993 ($2.00, one-shot, 52 pgs.)

1 — 2.50

FIGHT THE ENEMY
Tower Comics: Aug, 1966 - No. 3, Mar, 1967 (25¢, 68 pgs.)

	GD	VG	FN	VF	VF/NM	NM-
1-Lucky 7 & Mike Manly begin	4	8	12	26	41	55
2-1st Boris Vallejo comic art; McWilliams-a	3	6	9	20	30	40
3-Wood-a (1/2 pg.); McWilliams, Bolle-a	3	6	9	20	30	40

FILM FUNNIES
Marvel Comics (CPC): Nov, 1949 - No. 2, Feb, 1950 (52 pgs.)

	GD	VG	FN	VF	VF/NM	NM-
1-Krazy Krow, Wacky Duck	19	38	57	112	176	240
2-Wacky Duck	14	28	42	82	121	160

FILM STARS ROMANCES
Star Publications: Jan-Feb, 1950 - No. 3, May-June, 1950 (True life stories of movie stars)

	GD	VG	FN	VF	VF/NM	NM-
1-Rudy Valentino & Gregory Peck stories; L. B. Cole-c; lingerie panels	43	86	129	267	446	625
2-Liz Taylor/Robert Taylor photo-c & true life story	53	106	159	334	567	800
3-Douglas Fairbanks story; photo-c	26	52	78	152	244	335

FILTH, THE
DC Comics (Vertigo): Aug, 2002 - No. 13, Oct, 2003 ($2.95, limited series)

1-13-Morrison-s/Weston & Erskine-a — 3.00
TPB (2004, $19.95) r/#1-13 — 20.00

FINAL CRISIS
DC Comics: July, 2008 - No. 7 ($3.99, limited series)

1-Grant Morrison-s/J.G. Jones-a/c; Martian Manhunter killed; 2 covers — 4.00
1-Director's Cut (10/08, $4.99) B&W printing of #1 with creator commentary — 5.00
2,3: 2-Barry Allen-c/cameo; intro Big Science Action; two covers — 4.00
...: Requiem (9/08, $3.99) History, death and funeral of the Martian Manhunter; 2 covers — 4.00
... Sketchbook (7/08, $2.99) Jones development sketches with Morrison commentary — 3.00

FINAL CRISIS: ROGUE'S REVENGE
DC Comics: Sept, 2008 - No. 3 ($3.99, limited series)

1-Johns-s/Kolins-a; Flash's Rogues, Zoom and Inertia app. — 4.00

FINAL NIGHT, THE (See DC related titles and Parallax: Emerald Night)
DC Comics: Nov, 1996 - No. 4, Nov, 1996 ($1.95, weekly limited series)

1-4: Kesel-s/Immonen-a(p) in all. 4-Parallax's final acts — 3.50
Preview — 2.50
TPB-(1998, $12.95) r/#1-4, Parallax: Emerald Night #1, and preview — 13.00

FINALS
DC Comics (Vertigo): Sept, 1999 - No. 4, Dec, 1999 ($2.95, limited series)

1-4-Will Pfeifer-s/Jill Thompson-a — 3.00

FIRE
Caliber Press: 1993 - No. 2, 1993 ($2.95, B&W, limited series, 52 pgs.)

1,2-Brian Michael Bendis-s/a — 3.00
TPB (1999, 2001, $9.95) Restored reprints of series — 10.00

FIREARM (Also see Codename: Firearm, Freex #15, Night Man #4 & Prime #10)
Malibu Comics (Ultraverse): Sept, 1993 - No. 18, Mar, 1995 ($1.95/$2.50)

0 ($14.95)-Came w/ video containing 1st half of story (comic contains 2nd half); 1st app. Duet — 15.00
1,3-6: 1-James Robinson scripts begin; Cully Hamner-a; Chaykin-c; 1st app. Alec Swan. 3-Intro The Sportsmen; Chaykin-c. 4-Break-Thru x-over; Chaykin-c. 5-1st app. Ellen (Swan's girlfriend); 2 pg. origin of Prime. 6-Prime app. (story cont'd in Prime #10); Brereton-c — 2.50
1-($2.50)-Newsstand edition polybagged w/card — 3.00
1-Ultra Limited silver foil-c — 5.00
2 ($2.50, 44 pgs.)-Hardcase app.;Chaykin-c; Rune flip-c/story by B. Smith (3 pgs.) — 3.00
7-10,12-17: 12-The Rafferty Saga begins, ends #18; 1st app. Rafferty. 15-Night Man & Freex app. 17-Swan marries Ellen — 2.50
11-($3.50, 68 pgs.)-Flip book w/Ultraverse Premiere #5 — 3.50
18-Death of Rafferty; Chaykin-c — 3.00

NOTE: ***Brereton** c-6. **Chaykin** c-1-4, 14, 16, 18. **Hamner** a-1-4. **Herrera** a-12. **James Robinson** scripts-0-18.*

FIRE BALL XL5 (See Steve Zodiac & The ...)

FIREBIRDS (See Noble Causes)
Image Comics: Nov, 2004 ($5.95)

1-Faerber-s/Ponce-a/c; intro. Firebird — 6.00

FIREBRAND (Also see Showcase '96 #4)
DC Comics: Feb, 1996 - No. 9, Oct, 1996 ($1.75)

1-9: Brian Augustyn scripts; Velluto-c/a in all. 9-Daredevil #319-c/swipe — 2.50

FIREBREATHER
Image Comics: Jan, 2003 - No. 4, Apr, 2003 ($2.95)

1-4-Hester-s/Kuhn-a — 3.00
...: The Iron Saint (12/04, $6.95, squarebound) Hester-s/Kuhn-a — 7.00
TPB (7/04, $13.95) r/#1-4; foreword by Brad Meltzer; gallery and sketch pages — 14.00

FIREBREATHER
Image Comics: Jun, 2008 - Present ($2.99)

1,2-Hester-s/Kuhn-a — 3.00

FIRE FROM HEAVEN
Image Comics (WildStorm Productions): Mar, 1996 ($2.50)

1,2-Moore-s — 2.50

FIREHAIR COMICS (Formerly Pioneer West Romances #3-6; also see Rangers Comics)
Fiction House Magazines (Flying Stories): Winter/48-49; No. 2, Wint/49-50; No. 7, Spr/51 - No. 11, Spr/52

	GD	VG	FN	VF	VF/NM	NM-
1-Origin Firehair	43	86	129	267	446	625
2-Continues as Pioneer West Romances for #3-6	22	44	66	127	204	280
7-11	15	30	45	92	144	195
I.W. Reprint 8-(nd)-Kinstler-c; reprints Rangers #57; Dr. Drew story by Grandenetti	3	6	9	18	24	30

FIRESIDE BOOK SERIES (Hard and soft cover editions)
Simon and Schuster: 1974 - 1980 (130-260 pgs.), Square bound, color

		GD	VG	FN	VF	VF/NM	NM-
Amazing Spider-Man, The, 1979, 130 pgs., $3.95, Bob Larkin-c	HC	8	16	24	56	93	130
	SC	6	12	18	37	59	80
America At War–The Best of DC War Comics, 1979, $6.95, 260 pgs, Kubert-c	HC	11	22	33	79	140	200
	SC	7	14	21	50	83	115
Best of Spidey Super Stories (Electric Company) 1978, $3.95,	SC	6	12	18	43	69	95
Bring On The Bad Guys (Origins of the Marvel Comics Villains) 1976, $6.95, 260 pgs.; Romita-c	HC	8	16	24	54	90	125
	SC	5	10	15	34	55	75
Captain America, Sentinel of Liberty,1979, 130 pgs., $12.95, Cockrum-c	HC	8	16	24	56	93	130
	SC	6	12	18	37	59	80
Doctor Strange Master of the Mystic Arts, 1980, 130 pgs.	HC	8	16	24	56	93	130
	SC	6	12	18	37	59	80
Fantastic Four, The, 1979, 130 pgs.	HC	8	16	24	54	90	125
	SC	5	10	15	34	55	75
Heart Throbs–The Best of DC Romance Comics, 1979, 260 pgs., $6.,95	HC	16	32	48	114	202	290
	SC	9	18	27	65	113	160
Incredible Hulk, The, 1978, 260 pgs. (8 1/4" x 11")	HC	8	16	24	54	90	125
	SC	5	10	15	34	55	75
Marvel's Greatest Superhero Battles, 1978, 260 pgs., $6.95, Romita-c	HC	10	20	30	67	116	165
	SC	6	12	18	43	69	95
Mysteries in Space, 1980, $7,95, Anderson-c. r-DC sci/fi stories	HC	9	18	27	61	103	145
	SC	6	12	18	39	62	85
Origins of Marvel Comics, 1974, 260 pgs., $5.95. r-covers & origins of Fantastic Four, Hulk, Spider-Man, Thor, & Doctor Strange	HC	8	16	24	54	90	125
	SC	5	10	15	34	55	75
Silver Surfer, The, 1978, 130 pgs., $4.95, Norem-c	HC	8	16	24	56	93	130
	SC	6	12	18	39	62	85

Firestorm, The Nuclear Man #82 © DC

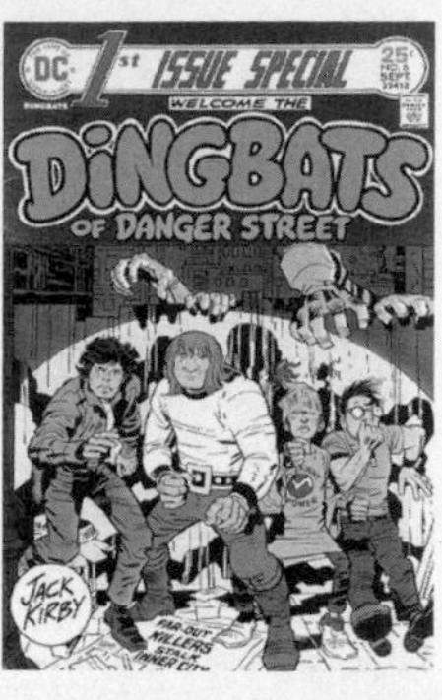

1st Issue Special #6 © DC

First Romance Magazine #2 © HARV

	GD	VG	FN	VF	VF/NM	NM-
	2.0	4.0	6.0	8.0	9.0	9.2

Son of Origins of Marvel Comics, 1975, 260 pgs., $6.95, Romita-c. Reprints covers & origins of X-Men, Iron Man, Avengers, Daredevil, Silver Surfer
HC 8 16 24 54 90 125
SC 5 10 15 34 55 75
Superhero Women, The–Featuring the Fabulous Females of Marvel Comics, 1977, 260 pgs., $6.95, Romita-c
HC 10 20 30 67 116 165
SC 6 12 18 43 69 95
Note: Prices listed are for 1st printings. Later printings have lesser value.

FIRESTAR
Marvel Comics Group: Mar, 1986 - No. 4, June, 1986 (75¢)(From Spider-Man TV series)
1,2: 1-X-Men & New Mutants app. 2-Wolverine-c (not real Wolverine?); Art Adams-a(p) 5.00
3,4: 3-Art Adams/Sienkiewicz-c. 4-B. Smith-c 3.00
X-Men: Firestar Digest (2006, $7.99, digest-size) r/#1-4; profile pages 8.00

FIRESTONE (See Donald And Mickey Merry Christmas)

FIRESTORM (See Cancelled Comic Cavalcade, DC Comics Presents, Flash #289, The Fury of... & Justice League of America #179)
DC Comics: March, 1978 - No. 5, Oct-Nov, 1978
1,5: 1-Origin & 1st app. 1 3 4 6 8 10
2-4: 2-Origin Multiplex. 3-Origin & 1st app. Killer Frost. 4-1st app. Hyena 6.00

FIRESTORM
DC Comics: July, 2004 - No. 35, June, 2007 ($2.50/$2.99)
1-24: 1-Intro. Jason Rusch; Jolley-s/ChrisCross-a. 6-Identity Crisis tie-in. 7-Bloodhound x-over. 8-Killer Frost returns. 9-Ronnie Raymond returns. 17-Villains United tie-in. 21-Infinite Crisis. 24-One Year Later; Killer Frost app. 2.50
25-35: 25-Begin $2.99-c; Mr. Freeze app. 33-35-Mister Miracle & Orion app. 3.00
...: Reborn TPB (2007, $14.99) r/#23-27 15.00

FIRESTORM, THE NUCLEAR MAN (Formerly Fury of Firestorm)
DC Comics: No. 65, Nov, 1987 - No. 100, Aug, 1990
65-99: 66-1st app. Zuggernaut; Firestorm vs. Green Lantern. 71-Death of Capt. X. 67,68-Millennium tie-ins. 83-1st new look 2.50
100-($2.95, 68 pgs.) 4.00
Annual 5 (10/87)-1st app. new Firestorm 3.00

FIRST, THE
CrossGeneration Comics: Jan, 2001 - No. 37, Jan, 2004 ($2.95)
1-3: 1-Barbara Kesel-s/Bart Sears & Andy Smith-a 5.00
4-10 4.00
11-37 3.00
Preview (11/00, free) 8 pg. intro 2.50
Two Houses Divided Vol. 1 TPB (11/01, $19.95) r/#1-7; new Moeller-c 20.00
Magnificent Tension Vol. 2 TPB (2002, $19.95) r/#8-13 20.00
Sinister Motives Vol. 3 TPB (2003, $15.95) r/#14-19 16.00
Vol. 4 Futile Endeavors (2003, $15.95) r/#20-25 16.00
Vol. 5 Liquid Alliances (2003, $15.95) r/#26-31 16.00
Vol. 6 Ragnarok (2004, $15.95) r/#32-37 16.00

FIRST ADVENTURES
First Comics: Dec, 1985 - No. 5, Apr, 1986 ($1.25)
1-5: Blaze Barlow, Whisper & Dynamo Joe in all 2.50

FIRST AMERICANS, THE
Dell Publishing Co.: No. 843, Sept, 1957
Four Color 843-Marsh-a 8 16 24 56 93 130

FIRST BORN (See Witchblade and Darkness titles)
Image Comics (Top Cow): Aug, 2007 - No. 3 ($2.99, limited series)
... First Look (6/07, 99¢) Preview; The Darkness app.; Sejic-a; 2 covers (color & B&W) 2.25
1-3-($2.99) Two covers; Marz-s/Sejic-a. 3-Sara's baby is born 3.00
1-B&W variant Sejic cover 5.00
...: Aftermath (5/08, $3.99) short stories; Magdalena app.; two covers by Sook & Sejic 4.00

FIRST CHRISTMAS, THE (3-D)
Fiction House Magazines (Real Adv. Publ. Co.): 1953 (25¢, 8-1/4x10-1/4", oversize)(Came w/glasses)
nn-(Scarce)-Kelly Freas painted-c; Biblical theme, birth of Christ; Nativity-c
31 62 93 181 291 400

FIRST COMICS GRAPHIC NOVEL
First Comics: Jan, 1984 - No. 21? (52 pgs./176 pgs., high quality paper)
1,2: 1-Beowulf ($5.95)(both printings). 2-Time Beavers 9.00
3($11.95, 100 pgs.)-American Flagg! Hard Times (2nd printing exists) 15.00
4-Nexus ($6.95)-r/B&W 1-3 12.00
5,7: 5-The Enchanted Apples of Oz ($7.95, 52 pgs.)-Intro by Harlan Ellison (1986). 7-The Secret Island Of Oz ($7.95) 10.00
6-Elric of Melnibone ($14.95, 176 pgs.)-Reprints with new color 18.00
8,10,14,18: Teenage Mutant Ninja Turtles Book I -IV ($9.95, 132 pgs.)-8-r/TMNT #1-3 in color w/12 pgs. new-a; origin. 10-r/TMNT #4-6 in color. 14-r/TMNT #7,8 in color plus new 12 pg. story. 18-r/TMNT #10,11 plus 3 pg. fold-out 11.00
9-Time 2: The Epiphany by Chaykin (11/86, $7.95, 52pgs. - indicia says #8) 10.00
11-Sailor On The Sea of Fate ($14.95) 16.00
nn-Time 2: The Satisfaction of Black Mariah (9/87) 10.00
12-American Flagg! Southern Comfort (10/87, $11.95) 14.00
13,16,17,21: 13-The Ice King Of Oz. 16-The Forgotten Forest of Oz ($8.95). 17-Mazinger (68 pgs., $8.95). 21-Elric, The Weird of the White Wolf; r/#1-5 10.00
15,19: 15-Hex Breaker: Badger ($7.95). 19-The Original Nexus Graphic Novel ($7.95, 104 pgs.)-Reprints First Comics Graphic Novel #4 12.00
20-American Flagg!: State of the Union ($11.95, 96 pgs.); r/A.F. #7-9 15.00
NOTE: *Most or all issues have been reprinted.*

1ST FOLIO (The Joe Kubert School Presents...)
Pacific Comics: Mar, 1984 ($1.50, one-shot)
1-Joe Kubert-c/a(2 pgs.); Adam & Andy Kubert-a 3.00

1ST ISSUE SPECIAL
National Periodical Publications: Apr, 1975 - No. 13, Apr, 1976 (Tryout series)
1,6: 1-Intro. Atlas; Kirby-c/a/script. 6-Dingbats 2 4 6 9 12 15
2,12: 2-Green Team (see Cancelled Comic Cavalcade). 12-Origin/1st app. "Blue" Starman (2nd app. in Starman, 2nd Series #3); Kubert-c 1 3 4 6 8 10
3-Metamorpho by Ramona Fradon 1 3 4 6 8 10
4,10,11: 4-Lady Cop. 10-The Outsiders. 11-Code Name: Assassin; Grell-c
1 2 3 5 7 9
5-Manhunter; Kirby-c/a/script 2 4 6 11 16 20
7,9: 7-The Creeper by Ditko (c/a). 9-Dr. Fate; Kubert-c/Simonson-a.
2 4 6 9 13 16
8-Origin/1st app. The Warlord; Grell-c/a (11/75) 3 6 9 18 27 35
13-Return of the New Gods; Darkseid app.; 1st new costume Orion; predates New Gods #12 by more than a year 3 6 9 16 22 28

FIRST KISS
Charlton Comics: Dec, 1957 - No. 40, Jan, 1965
V1#1 4 8 12 28 44 60
V1#2-10 3 6 9 18 27 35
11-40 2 4 6 13 18 22

FIRST LOVE ILLUSTRATED
Harvey Publications(Home Comics)(True Love): 2/49 - No. 9, 6/50; No. 10, 1/51 - No. 86, 3/58; No. 87, 9/58 - No. 88, 11/58; No. 89, 11/62, No. 90, 2/63
1-Powell-a(2) 18 36 54 107 169 230
2-Powell-a 11 22 33 64 90 115
3-"Was I Too Fat To Be Loved" story 13 26 39 74 105 135
4-10 9 18 27 47 61 75
11-30: 13-"I Joined a Teen-age Sex Club" story. 30-Lingerie panel
7 14 21 37 46 55
31-34,37,39-49: 49-Last pre-code (2/55) 7 14 21 35 43 50
35-Used in **SOTI**, illo "The title of this comic book is First Love"
20 40 60 115 183 250
36-Communism story, "Love Slaves" 11 22 33 62 86 110
38-Nostrand-a 8 16 24 44 57 70
50-66,71-90 6 12 18 28 34 40
67-70-Kirby-c 8 16 24 40 50 60
NOTE: ***Disbrow** a-13. **Orlando** c-87. **Powell** a-1, 3-5, 7, 10, 11, 13-17, 19-24, 26-29, 33,35-41, 43, 45, 46, 50, 54, 55, 57, 58, 61-63, 65, 71-73, 76, 79r, 82, 84, 88.*

FIRST MEN IN THE MOON (See Movie Comics)

FIRST ROMANCE MAGAZINE
Home Comics(Harvey Publ.)/True Love: 8/49 - #6, 6/50; #7, 6/51 - #50, 2/58; #51, 9/58 - #52, 11/58
1 16 32 48 94 147 200
2 10 20 30 58 79 100
3-5 9 18 27 47 61 75
6-10,28: 28-Nostrand-a(Powell swipe) 8 16 24 40 50 60
11-20 7 14 21 35 43 50
21-27,29-32: 32-Last pre-code issue (2/55) 6 12 18 31 38 45
33-40,44-52 6 12 18 28 34 40
41-43-Kirby-c 8 16 24 40 50 60
NOTE: ***Powell** a-1-5, 8-10, 14, 18, 20-22, 24, 25, 28, 36, 46, 48, 51.*

FIRST TRIP TO THE MOON (See Space Adventures No. 20)

FIRST WAVE (Based on Sci-Fi Channel TV series)
Andromeda Entertainment: Dec, 2000 - No. 4, Jun, 2001 ($2.99)

Fish Police #18 © Apple Comics

Flaming Carrot Comics #26 © Bob Burden

The Flash #108 © DC

GD 2.0 | VG 4.0 | FN 6.0 | VF 8.0 | VF/NM 9.0 | NM- 9.2

1-4-Kuhoric-s/Parsons-a/Busch-c 3.00

FISH POLICE (Inspector Gill of the...#2, 3)
Fishwrap Productions/Comico V2#5-17/Apple Comics #18 on: Dec, 1985 - No. 11, Nov, 1987 ($1.50, B&W); V2#5, April, 1988 - V2#17, May, 1989 ($1.75, color) No. 18, Aug, 1989 - No. 26, Dec, 1990 ($2.25, B&W)

1-11, 1(5/86),2-2nd print, V2#5-17-(Color): V2#5-11. 12-17, new-a, 18-26 ($2.25-c, B&W). 18-Origin Inspector Gill 2.50
Special 1($2.50, 7/87, Comico) 2.50
Graphic Novel: Hairballs (1987, $9.95, TPB) r/#1-4 in color 10.00

FISH POLICE
Marvel Comics: V2#1, Oct, 1992 - No. 6, Mar, 1993 ($1.25)

V2#1-6: 1-Hairballs Saga begins; r/#1 (1985) 2.50

5 CENT COMICS (Also see Whiz Comics)
Fawcett Publ.: Feb, 1940 (8 pgs., reg. size, B&W)

nn - 1st app. Dan Dare. Ashcan comic, not distributed to newsstands, only for in-house use. A CGC certified 9.6 copy sold for $10,800 in 2003.

5-STAR SUPER-HERO SPECTACULAR (See DC Special Series No. 1)

FLAME, THE (See Big 3 & Wonderworld Comics)
Fox Features Synd.: Sum, 1940 - No. 8, Jan, 1942 (#1,2: 68 pgs; #3-8: 44 pgs.)

1-Flame stories reprinted from Wonderworld #5-9; origin The Flame; Lou Fine-a (36 pgs.), 300 600 900 1980 3440 4900
2-Fine-a(2); Wing Turner by Tuska; r/Wonderworld #3,10 120 240 360 756 1278 1800
3-8: 3-Powell-a 79 158 237 498 842 1185

FLAME, THE (Formerly Lone Eagle)
Ajax/Farrell Publications (Excellent Publ.): No. 5, Dec-Jan, 1954-55 - No. 3, April-May, 1955

5(#1)-1st app. new Flame 45 90 135 279 465 650
2,3 29 58 87 169 272 375

FLAMING CARROT COMICS (Also see Junior Carrot Patrol)
Killian Barracks Press: Summer-Fall, 1981 ($1.95, one shot) (Lg size, 8-1/2x11")

1-Bob Burden-c/a/scripts; serially #'od to 6500 5 10 15 32 51 70

FLAMING CARROT COMICS (See Anything Goes, Cerebus, Teenage Mutant Ninja Turtles/Flaming Carrot Crossover & Visions)
Aardvark-Vanaheim/Renegade Press #6-17/Dark Horse #18-31: May, 1984 - No. 5, Jan, 1985; No. 6, Mar, 1985 - No. 31, Oct, 1994 ($1.70/$2.00, B&W)

1-Bob Burden story/art 4 8 12 28 44 60
2 3 6 9 16 23 30
3 2 4 6 10 16 20
4-6 2 4 6 9 12 15
7-9 1 3 4 6 8 10
10-12 6.50
13-15 4.00
15-Variant without cover price 6.00
16-(6/87) 1st app. Mystery Men 1 2 3 5 6 8
17-20: 18-1st Dark Horse issue 4.00
21-23,25: 25-Contains trading cards; TMNT app. 3.00
24-(2.50, 52 pgs.)-10th anniversary issue 4.00
26-28: 26-Begin $2.25-c. 26,27-Teenage Mutant Ninja Turtles x-over. 27-McFarlane-c 3.00
29-31-(2.50-c) 3.00
Annual 1(1/97, $5.00) 5.00
... & Reid Fleming, World's Toughest Milkman (12/02, $3.99) listed as #32 in indicia 4.00
... :Fortune Favors the Bold (1998, $16.95, TPB) r/#19-24 17.00
... :Men of Mystery (7/97, $12.95, TPB) r/#1-3, + new material 13.00
... 's Greatest Hits (4/98, $17.95, TPB) r/#12-18, + new material 18.00
... :The Wild Shall Wild Remain (1997, $17.95, TPB) r/#4-11, + new s/a 18.00

FLAMING CARROT COMICS
Image Comics (Desperado): Dec, 2004 - Present ($2.95/$3.50, B&W)

1-3-Bob Burden story/art 3.00
4-($3.50-c) 3.50
... Special #1 (3/06, $3.50) All Photo comic 3.50
... Vol. 6 (2006, $14.99) r/1-4 & Special #1; intro. by Brian Bolland 15.00

FLAMING LOVE
Quality Comics Group (Comic Magazines): Dec, 1949 - No. 6, Oct, 1950 (Photo covers #2-6) (52 pgs.)

1-Ward-c/a (9 pgs.) 40 80 120 235 380 525
2 18 36 54 105 165 225
3-Ward-a (9 pgs.); Crandall-a 26 52 78 152 244 335
4-6: 4-Gustavson-a 15 30 45 88 137 185

GD 2.0 | VG 4.0 | FN 6.0 | VF 8.0 | VF/NM 9.0 | NM- 9.2

FLAMING WESTERN ROMANCES (Formerly Target Western Romances)
Star Publications: No. 3, Mar-Apr, 1950

3-Robert Taylor, Arlene Dahl photo on-c with biographies inside; L. B. Cole-c 38 76 114 222 356 490

FLARE (Also see Champions for 1st app. & League of Champions)
Hero Comics/Hero Graphics Vol. 2 on: Nov, 1988 - No. 3, Jan, 1989 ($2.75, color, 52 pgs); V2#1, Nov, 1990 - No. 7, Nov, 1991 ($2.95/$3.50, color, mature, 52 pgs.);V2#8, Oct, 1992 - No. 16, Feb, 1994 ($3.50/$3.95, B&W, 36 pgs.)

V1#1-3, V2#1-16: 5-Eternity Smith returns. 6-Intro The Tigress 4.00
Annual 1(1992, $4.50, B&W, 52 pgs.)-Champions-r 4.50

FLARE ADVENTURES
Hero Graphics: Feb, 1992 - No. 12, 1993? ($3.50/$3.95)

1 (90¢, color, 20 pgs.) 2.50
2-12-Flip books w/Champions Classics 4.00

FLASH, THE (See Adventure Comics, The Brave and the Bold, Crisis On Infinite Earths, DC Comics Presents, DC Special, DC Special Series, DC Super-Stars, The Greatest Flash Stories Ever Told, Green Lantern, Impulse, JLA, Justice League of America, Showcase, Speed Force, Super Team Family, Titans & World's Finest)

FLASH, THE (1st Series)(Formerly Flash Comics)(See Showcase #4,8,13,14)
National Periodical Publ./DC: No. 105, Feb-Mar, 1959 - No. 350, Oct, 1985

105-(2-3/59)-Origin Flash(retold), & Mirror Master (1st app.) 500 1000 1500 4500 9250 14,000
106-Origin Grodd & Pied Piper; Flash's 1st visit to Gorilla City; begin Grodd the Super Gorilla trilogy (Scarce) 176 352 528 1540 2970 4400
107-Grodd trilogy, part 2 100 200 300 850 1625 2400
108-Grodd trilogy ends 83 166 249 706 1353 2000
109-2nd app. Mirror Master 65 130 195 553 1052 1550
110-Intro/origin Kid Flash who later becomes Flash in Crisis On Infinite Earths #12; begin Kid Flash trilogy, ends #112 (also in #114,116,118); 1st app. & origin of The Weather Wizard 150 300 450 1275 2438 3600
111-2nd Kid Flash tryout; Cloud Creatures 50 100 150 400 750 1100
112-Origin & 1st app. Elongated Man (4-5/60); also apps. in #115,119,130 52 104 156 442 846 1250
113-Origin & 1st app. Trickster 48 96 144 384 717 1050
114-Captain Cold app. (see Showcase #8) 40 80 120 312 581 850
115,116,118-120: 119-Elongated Man marries Sue Dearborn. 120-Flash & Kid Flash team-up for 1st time 32 64 96 246 461 675
117-Origin & 1st app. Capt. Boomerang; 1st & only S.A. app. Winky Blinky & Noddy 36 72 108 277 514 750
121,122: 122-Origin & 1st app. The Top 26 52 78 192 359 525
123-(9/61)-Re-intro. Golden Age Flash; origins of both Flashes; 1st mention of an Earth II where DC G. A. heroes live 138 276 414 1173 2237 3300
124-Last 10¢ issue 20 40 60 148 274 400
125-128,130: 127-Return of Grodd-c/story. 128-Origin & 1st app. Abra Kadabra. 130-(7/62)-1st Gauntlet of Super-Villains (Mirror Master, Capt. Cold, The Top, Capt. Boomerang & Trickster) 19 38 57 139 257 375
129-2nd G.A. Flash x-over; J.S.A. cameo in flashback (1st S.A. app. G.A. Green Lantern, Hawkman, Atom, Black Canary & Dr. Mid-Nite. Wonder Woman (1st S.A. app.?) appears) 30 60 90 222 411 600
131-136,138,140: 131-Early Green Lantern x-over (9/62). 135-1st app. of Kid Flash's yellow costume (3/63). 136-1st Dexter Miles. 140-Origin & 1st app. Heat Wave 15 30 45 105 190 275
137-G.A. Flash x-over; J.S.A. cameo (1st S.A. app.)(1st real app. since 2-3/51); 1st S.A. app. Vandal Savage & Johnny Thunder; JSA team decides to re-form 38 76 114 293 547 800
139-Origin & 1st app. Prof. Zoom 15 30 45 111 206 300
141-150: 142-Trickster app. 147-2nd Prof. Zoom 12 24 36 82 146 210
151-Engagement of Barry Allen & Iris West; G.A. Flash vs. The Shade. 13 26 39 93 164 235
152-159: 159-Dr. Mid-Nite cameo 10 20 30 70 123 175
160-(80-Pg. Giant G-21); G.A. Flash & Johnny Quick-r 12 24 36 87 156 225
161-164,166,167: 167-New facts about Flash's origin 8 16 24 58 97 135
165-Barry Allen weds Iris West 9 18 27 61 103 145
168,170: 168-Green Lantern-c/app. 170-Dr. Mid-Nite, Dr. Fate, G.A. Flash x-over 8 16 24 58 97 135
169-(80-Pg. Giant G-34)-New facts about origin 9 18 27 64 110 155
171,172,174,176,177,179,180: 171-JLA, Green Lantern, Atom flashbacks. 174-Barry Allen reveals I.D. to wife. 179-(5/68)-Flash travels to Earth-Prime and meets DC editor Julie Schwartz; 1st unnamed app. Earth-Prime (See Justice League of America #123 for 1st named app. & 3rd app. overall) 7 14 21 50 83 115
173-G.A. Flash x-over 8 16 24 56 93 130
175-2nd Superman/Flash race (12/67) (See Superman #199 & World's Finest #198,199);

The Flash #203 © DC

The Flash (2nd series) #209 © DC

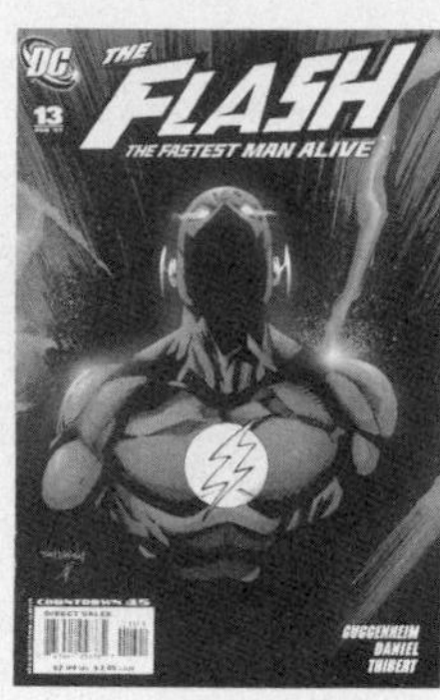
Flash, The Fastest Man Alive #13 © DC

GD VG FN VF VF/NM NM-
2.0 4.0 6.0 8.0 9.0 9.2

JLA cameo; gold kryptonite used (on J'onn J'onzz impersonating Superman)
16 32 48 114 212 310
178-(80-Pg. Giant G-46) 8 16 24 58 97 135
181-186,188,189: 186-Re-intro. Sargon. 189-Last 12¢-c
6 12 18 37 59 80
187,196: (68-Pg. Giants G-58, G-70) 6 12 18 43 69 95
190-195,197-199 4 8 12 26 41 55
200 5 10 15 30 48 65
201-204,206,207: 201-New G.A. Flash story. 206-Elongated Man begins
207-Last 15¢ issue 3 6 9 20 30 40
205-(68-Pg. Giant G-82) 6 12 18 39 62 85
208-213-(52 pg.): 211-G.A. Flash origin-r/#104. 213-Reprints #137
4 8 12 22 34 45
214-DC 100 Page Super Spectacular DC-11; origin Metal Men-r/Showcase #37; never before published G.A. Flash story.
(see DC 100 pg. Super Spec. #11 for price)
215 (52 pgs.)-Flash-r/Showcase #4; G.A. Flash x-over, continued in #216
4 8 12 24 37 50
216,220: 220-1st app. Turtle since Showcase #4 3 6 9 16 23 30
217-219: Neal Adams-a in all. 217-Green Lantern/Green Arrow series begins (9/72); 2nd G.L. & G.A. team-up series (see Green Lantern #76). 219-Last Green Arrow
4 8 12 26 41 55
221-225,227,228,230,231,233: 222-G. Lantern x-over. 228-(7-8/74)-Flash writer Cary Bates travels to Earth-One & meets Flash, Iris Allen & Trickster; 2nd unnamed app. Earth-Prime (See Justice League of America #123 for 1st named app. & 3rd app. overall)
2 4 6 11 16 20
226-Neal Adams-p 3 6 9 16 22 28
229,232-(100 pg. issues)-G.A. Flash-r & new-a 4 8 12 26 41 55
234-250: 235-Green Lantern x-over. 243-Death of The Top. 245-Origin The Floronic Man in Green Lantern back-up, ends #246. 246-Last Green Lantern. 247-Jay Garrick app.
250-Intro Golden Glider 2 4 6 9 12 15
251-274: 256-Death of The Top retold. 265-267-(44 pgs.). 267-Origin of Flash's uniform.
270-Intro The Clown 1 3 4 6 8 10
268,273-276,278,283,286-(Whitman variants; low print run; no issue #s shown on covers
2 4 6 8 10 12
275,276-Iris Allen dies 2 4 6 8 10 12
277-288,290: 286-Intro/origin Rainbow Raider 1 2 3 4 5 7
289-1st Perez DC art (Firestorm); new Firestorm back-up series begins (9/80), ends #304
1 2 3 5 7 9
291-299,301-305: 291-1st app. Saber-Tooth (villain). 295-Gorilla Grodd-c/story. 298-Intro & origin new Shade. 301-Atomic bomb-c. 303-The Top returns. 304-Intro/origin Colonel Computron; 305-G.A. Flash x-over
5.00
300-(52 pgs.)-Origin Flash retold; 25th ann. issue 1 2 3 4 5 7
306-313-Dr. Fate by Giffen. 309-Origin Flash retold 5.00
314-340: 318-323-Creeper back-ups. 323,324-Two part Flash vs. Flash story. 324-Death of Reverse Flash (Professor Zoom). 328-Iris West Allen's death retold. 329-JLA app.
340-Trial of the Flash begins 4.00
341-349: 344-Origin Kid Flash 5.00
350-Double size ($1.25) Final issue 6.00
Annual 1 (10-12/63, 84 pgs.)-Origin Elongated Man & Kid Flash-r; origin Grodd; G.A. Flash-r
36 72 108 277 514 750
Annual 1 Replica Edition (2001, $6.95)-Reprints the entire 1963 Annual 7.00
The Flash Spectacular (See DC Special Series No. 11)
The Life Story of the Flash (1997, $19.95, Hardcover) "Iris Allen's" chronicle of Barry Allen's life; comic panels w/additional text; Waid & Augustyn-s/ Kane & Staton-a/Orbik painted-c
20.00
The Life Story of the Flash (1998, $12.95, Softcover) New Orbik-c 13.00

NOTE: ***N. Adams** c-194, 195, 203, 204, 206-208, 211, 213, 215, 226p, 246. **M. Anderson** c-165, a(i)-195, 200-204, 206-208. **Austin** a-233i, 234i, 246i. **Buckler** a-271p, 272p; c(p)-247-250, 252, 253p, 255, 256p, 258, 262, 265-267, 269-271. **Giffen** a-306-313p; c-310p, 315. **Giordano** a-226i. **Sid Greene** a-167-174i, 229i(r). **Grell** a-237p, 238p, 240-243p; c-236. **Heck** a-198p. **Infantino/Anderson** a-135. c-135, 170-174, 192, 200, 201, 328-330. **Infantino/Giella** c-105-112, 163, 164, 166-168. **G. Kane** a-195p, 197-199p, 229r, 232r; c-197-199, 312p. **Kubert** a-108p, 215i(r); c-189-191. **Lopez** c-272. **Meskin** a-229r, 232r. **Perez** a-289-293p; c-293. **Starlin** a-294-296p. **Staton** c-263p, 264p. Green Lantern x-over-131, 143, 168, 171, 191.*

FLASH (2nd Series)(See Crisis on Infinite Earths #12 and All Flash #1)
DC Comics: June, 1987 - No. 230, Mar, 2006; No. 231, Oct, 2007 - Present (75¢-$2.50)

1-Guice-c/a begins; New Teen Titans app. 1 3 4 6 8 10
2-10: 3-Intro. Kilgore. 5-Intro. Speed McGee. 7-1st app. Blue Trinity. 8,9-Millennium tie-ins. 9-1st app. The Chunk 4.00
11-61: 12-Free extra 16 pg. Dr. Light story. 19-Free extra 16 pg. Flash story. 28-Capt. Cold app. 29-New Phantom Lady app. 40-Dr. Alchemy app. 50-($1.75, 52 pgs.) 3.00
62-78,80: 62-Flash: Year One begins, ends #65. 65-Last $1.00-c. 66-Aquaman app. 69,70-Green Lantern app. 70-Gorilla Grodd story ends. 73-Re-intro Barry Allen & begin saga ("Barry Allen's" true ID revealed in #78). 76-Re-intro of Max Mercury (Quality Comics' Quicksilver), not in uniform until #77. 80-($1.25-c) Regular Edition 4.00

GD VG FN VF VF/NM NM-
2.0 4.0 6.0 8.0 9.0 9.2

79,80 ($2.50): 79-(68 pgs.) Barry Allen saga ends. 80-Foil-c 5.00
81-91,93,94,0,95-99,101: 81,82-Nightwing & Starfire app. 84-Razer app. 94-Zero Hour. 0-(10/94). 95-"Terminal Velocity" begins, ends #100. 96,98,99-Kobra app. 97-Origin Max Mercury; Chillblaine app. 4.00
92-1st Impulse 1 3 4 6 8 10
100 ($2.50)-Newstand edition; Kobra & JLA app. 4.00
100 ($3.50)-Foil-c edition; Kobra & JLA app. 5.00
102-131: 102-Mongul app.; begin-$1.75-c. 105-Mirror Master app. 107-Shazam app. 108-"Dead Heat" begins; 1st app. Savitar. 109-"Dead Heat" Pt. 2 (cont'd in Impulse #10). 110-"Dead Heat" Pt. 4 (cont'd in Impulse #11). 111-"Dead Heat" finale; Savitar disappears into the Speed Force; John Fox cameo (2nd app.). 112-"Race Against Time" begins, ends #118; re-intro John Fox. 113-Tornado Twins app. 119-Final Night x-over. 127-129-Rogue's Gallery & Neron. 128,129-JLA-app.130-Morrison & Millar-s begin 3.50
132-150: 135-GL & GA app. 142-Wally almost marries Linda; Waid-s return. 144-Cobalt Blue origin. 145-Chain Lightning begins.147-Professor Zoom app. 149-Barry Allen app. 150-($2.95) Final showdown with Cobalt Blue 3.00
151-162: 151-Casey-s. 152-New Flash-c. 154-New Flash ID revealed. 159-Wally marries Linda. 162-Last Waid-s. 3.00
163-187,189-196,198,199,201-206: 163-Begin $2.25-c. 164-186-Bolland-c. 183-New Trickster. 196-Winslade-a. 201-Dose-a begins. 205-Batman-c/app. 2.50
188-($2.95) Mirror Master, Weather Wizard, Trickster app. 3.00
197-Origin of Zoom (6/03) 6.00
200-($3.50) Flash vs. Zoom; Barry Allen & Hal Jordan app.; wraparound-c 3.50
207-230: 207-211-Turner-c/Porter-a. 209-JLA app. 210-Nightwing app. 212-Origin Mirror Master. 214-216-Identity Crisis x-over. 219-Wonder Woman app. 220-Rogue War 224-Zoom & Prof. Zoom app. 225-Twins born; Barry Allen app.; last Johns-s 2.50
231-242: 231-(10/07) Waid-s/Acuña-a. 240-Grodd app.; "Dark Side Club" 3.00
#1,000,000 (11/98) 853rd Century x-over 2.50
Annual 1-7,9: 2-('87-'94,'96, 68 pgs), 3-Gives history of G.A.,S.A., & Modern Age Flash in text. 4-Armaggedon 2001. 5-Eclipso-c/story. 7-Elseworlds story. 9-Legends of the Dead Earth story; J.H. Williams-a(p); Mick Gray-a(i) 3.00
Annual 8 (1995, $3.50)-Year One story 3.50
Annual 10 (1997, $3.95)-Pulp Heroes stories 4.00
Annual 11,12 ('98, '99)-11-Ghosts; Wrightson-c. 12-JLApe; Art Adams-c 3.00
Annual 13 ('00, $3.50) Planet DC; Alcatena-c/a 3.50
...: Blitz (2004, $19.95, TPB)-r/#192-200; Kolins-c 20.00
...: Blood Will Run (2002, 2008; $17.95, TPB)-r/#170-176, Secret Files #3, Iron Heights 18.00
...: Crossfire (2004, $17.95, TPB)-r/#183-191 & parts of Flash Secret Files #3 18.00
Dead Heat (2000, $14.95, TPB)-r/#108-111, Impulse #10,11 15.00
...80-Page Giant (8/98, $4.95) Flash family stories by Waid, Millar and others; Mhan-c 5.00
...80-Page Giant 2 (4/99, $4.95) Stories of Flash family, future Kid Flash, original Teen Titans and XS 5.00
...: Ignition (2005, $14.95, TPB)-r/#201-206 15.00
...: Iron Heights (2001, $5.95)-Van Sciver-c/a; intro. Murmur 6.00
...: Our Worlds at War 1 (10/01, $2.95)-Jae Lee-c; Black Racer app. 3.00
...Plus 1 (1/1997, $2.95)-Nightwing-c/app. 3.00
Race Against Time (2001, $14.95, TPB)-r/#112-118 15.00
...: Rogues (2003, $14.95, TPB)-r/#177-182 15.00
...: Rogue War (2006, $17.99, TPB)-r/#1/2,212,218,220-225; cover gallery 18.00
...Secret Files 1 (11/97, $4.95) Origin-s & pin-ups 5.00
...Secret Files 2 (11/99, $4.95) Origin of Replicant 5.00
...Secret Files 3 (11/01; $4.95) Intro. Hunter Zolomon (who later becomes Zoom) 5.00
Special 1 (1990, $2.95, 84 pgs.)-50th anniversary issue; Kubert-c; 1st Flash story by Mark Waid; 1st app. John Fox (27th Century Flash) 3.00
Terminal Velocity (1996, $12.95, TPB)-r/#95-100. 13.00
...: The Greatest Stories Ever Told (2007, $19.99, TPB) reprints; Ross-c/Waid intro. 20.00
The Return of Barry Allen (1996, $12.95, TPB)-r/#74-79 13.00
The Secret of Barry Allen (2005, $19.99, TPB)-r/#207-211,213-217; Turner sketch page 20.00
...: Time Flies (2002, $5.95)-Seth Fisher-c/a; Rozum-s 6.00
TV Special 1 (1991, $3.95, 76 pgs.)-Photo-c plus behind the scenes photos of TV show; Saltares-a, Byrne scripts 4.00
Wizard #1/2 (2005) prelude to Rogue Wars; Justiano-a 10.00
...: Wonderland TPB (2007, $12.99, TPB)-r/#164-169 13.00

NOTE: ***Guice** a-1-9p, 11p, Annual 1p; c-1-9p, Annual 1p. **Perez** c-15-17, Annual 2i. **Charest** c/a-Annual 5p.*

FLASH: THE FASTEST MAN ALIVE (3rd Series)(See Infinite Crisis)
DC Comics: Aug, 2006 - No. 13, Aug, 2007 ($2.99)

1-Bart Allen becomes the Flash; Lashley-a/Bilson & Demeo-s 3.00
1-Variant-c by Joe and Andy Kubert 5.00
2-12: 5-Cyborg app. 7-Inertia returns. 10-Zoom app. 3.00
13-Bart Allen dies; 2 covers 3.00
13-DC Nation Edition from the 2007 San Diego Comic-Con 8.00
...: Full Throttle TPB (2007, $12.99) r/#7-13, All-Flash #1, DCU Infinite Holiday Spec. story 13.00
...: Lightning in a Bottle TPB (2007, $12.99) r/#1-6 13.00

Flash Comics #1 © DC

Flash Comics #83 © DC

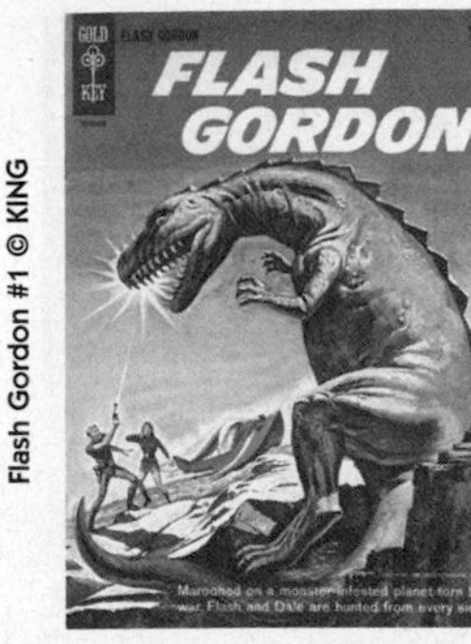

Flash Gordon #1 © KING

GD 2.0 | VG 4.0 | FN 6.0 | VF 8.0 | VF/NM 9.0 | NM- 9.2

FLASH, THE (See Tangent Comics/ The Flash)

FLASH AND GREEN LANTERN: THE BRAVE AND THE BOLD
DC Comics: Oct, 1999 - No. 6, Mar, 2000 ($2.50, limited series)

1-6-Waid & Peyer-s/Kitson-a. 4-Green Arrow app.; Grindberg-a(p) 2.50
TPB (2001, $12.95) r/#1-6 13.00

FLASH COMICS
DC Comics:. Dec. 1939

1-Ashcan comic, not distributed to newsstands, only for in-house use. Cover art is Adventure Comics #41 and interior from All-American Comics #8. A CGC certified 9.6 sold for $11,500 in 2004. A CGC certified 9.4 sold for $6,572.50 in 2008.

FLASH COMICS (Whiz Comics No. 2 on)
Fawcett Publications: Jan, 1940 (12 pgs., B&W, regular size)
(Not distributed to newsstands; printed for in-house use)

NOTE: *Whiz Comics #2 was preceded by two books,* **Flash Comics** *and* **Thrill Comics**, *both dated Jan, 1940, (12 pgs, B&W, regular size) and were not distributed. These two books are identical except for the title, and were sent out to major distributors as ad copies to promote sales. It is believed that the complete 68 page issue of Fawcett's* **Flash** *and* **Thrill Comics** *#1 was finished and ready for publication with the January date. Since DC Comics was also about to publish a book with the same date and title, Fawcett hurriedly printed up the black and white version of* **Flash Comics** *to secure copyright before DC. The inside covers are blank, with the covers and inside pages printed on a high quality uncoated paper stock.The eight page origin story of Captain Thunder is composed of pages 1-7 and 13 of the Captain Marvel story essentially as they appeared in the first issue of* **Whiz Comics**. *The balloon dialogue on page thirteen was relettered to tie the story into the end of page seven in* **Flash** *and* **Thrill Comics** *to produce a shorter version of the origin story for copyright purposes. Obviously, DC acquired the copyright and Fawcett dropped* **Flash** *as well as* **Thrill** *and came out with* **Whiz Comics** *a month later. Fawcett never used the cover to* **Flash** *and* **Thrill** *#1, designing a new cover for* **Whiz Comics**. *Fawcett also must have discovered that Captain Thunder had already been used by another publisher (Captain Terry Thunder by Fiction House). All references to Captain Thunder were relettered to Captain Marvel before appearing in* **Whiz**.

1 (nn on-c, #1 on inside)-Origin & 1st app. Captain Thunder. Cover by C.C. Beck. Eight copies of Flash and three copies of Thrill exist. All 3 copies of Thrill sold in 1986 for between $4,000-$10,000 each. A NM copy of Thrill sold in 1987 for $12,000. A VG copy of Thrill sold in 1987 for $9000 cash. A VF(8.0) copy of Thrill sold in 2003 for $11,400. A CGC certified 9.0 copy of the Flash Comics version sold for $10,117.50 in 2006. A CGC certified 9.0 copy of the Thrill Comics version sold for $8,000 in 2006.

FLASH COMICS (The Flash No. 105 on) (Also see All-Flash)
National Periodical Publ./All-American: Jan, 1940 - No. 104, Feb, 1949

1-The Flash (origin/1st app.) by Harry Lampert, Hawkman (origin/1st app.) by Gardner Fox, The Whip, & Johnny Thunder (origin/1st app.) by Stan Asch; Cliff Cornwall by Moldoff, Flash Picture Novelets (later Minute Movies w/#12) begin; Moldoff (Shelly) cover; 1st app. Shiera Sanders who later becomes Hawkgirl, #24; reprinted in Famous First Edition (on sale 11/10/39); The Flash-c 7100 14,200 21,300 53,000 94,000 135,000

1-Reprint, Oversize 13-1/2x10". **WARNING:** This comic is an exact reprint of the original except for its size. DC published it in 1974 with a second cover titling it as a Famous First Edition. There have been many reported cases of the outer cover being removed and the interior sold as the original edition. The reprint with the new outer cover removed is practically worthless. See Famous First Edition for value.

2-Rod Rian begins, ends #11; Hawkman-c 778 1556 2334 5602 9801 14,000
3-King Standish begins (1st app.), ends #41 (called The King #16-37,39-41); E.E. Hibbard-a begins on Flash 539 1078 1617 3881 6791 9700
4-Moldoff (Shelly) Hawkman begins; The Whip-c 429 858 1287 2917 5109 7300
5-The King-c 353 706 1059 2400 4200 6000
6-2nd Flash-c (alternates w/Hawkman #6 on) 517 1034 1551 3722 6511 9300
7-2nd Hawkman-c; 1st Moldoff Hawkman-c 500 1000 1500 3600 6300 9000
8-New logo begins; classic Moldoff Flash-c 312 624 936 2122 3711 5300
9,10: 9-Moldoff Hawkman-c; 10-Classic Moldoff Flash-c 335 670 1005 2278 3989 5700
11-13,15-20: 12-Les Watts begins; "Sparks" #16 on. 13-Has full page ad for All Star Comics #3. 17-Last Cliff Cornwall 220 440 660 1386 2343 3300
14-World War II cover 260 520 780 1638 2769 3900
21-Classic Hawkman-c 210 420 630 1323 2237 3150
22,23 190 380 570 1197 2024 2850
24-Shiera becomes Hawkgirl (12/41); see All-Star Comics #5 for 1st app. 230 460 690 1449 2450 3450
25-28,30: 28-Last Les Sparks. 123 246 369 775 1313 1850
29-Ghost Patrol begins (origin/1st app.), ends #104 128 256 384 806 1366 1925
31,33-Classic Hawkman-c. 33-Origin Shade 127 254 381 800 1350 1900
32,34-40: 36-1st app. Rag Doll 112 224 336 706 1191 1675
41-50 98 196 294 617 1046 1475
51-61: 52-1st computer in comics, c/s (4/44). 59-Last Minute Movies. 61-Last Moldoff Hawkman 88 176 264 554 940 1325
62-Hawkman by Kubert begins 113 226 339 712 1206 1700
63-85: 66-68-Hop Harrigan in all. 70-Mutt & Jeff app. 80-Atom begins, ends #104 78 156 234 491 833 1175
86-Intro. The Black Canary in Johnny Thunder (8/47); see All-Star #38. 300 600 900 1890 3195 4500
87,88,90: 87-Intro. The Foil. 88-Origin Ghost. 125 250 375 788 1332 1875
89-Intro villain The Thorn 180 360 540 1134 1917 2700
91,93-99: 98-Atom & Hawkman don new costumes 132 264 396 832 1404 1975
92-1st solo Black Canary plus-c; rare in Mint due to black ink smearing on white-c 347 694 1041 2360 4130 5900
100 (10/48),103(Scarce)-52 pgs. each 293 586 879 1846 3123 4400
101,102(Scarce) 253 506 759 1594 2697 3800
104-Origin The Flash retold (Scarce) 667 1314 2001 4802 8401 12,000

NOTE: **Irwin Hasen** *a-Wheaties Giveaway. c-97, Wheaties Giveaway.* **E.E. Hibbard** *c-6, 12, 20, 24, 26, 28, 30, 44, 46, 48, 50, 62, 66, 68, 69, 72, 74, 76, 78, 80, 82.* **Infantino** *a-86p, 90, 93-95, 99-104; c-90, 92, 93, 97, 99, 101, 103.* **Kinstler** *a-87, 89(Hawkman); c-87.* **Chet Kozlak** *c-77, 79, 81.* **Krigstein** *a-94.* **Kubert** *a-62-76, 83, 85, 86, 88-104; c-63, 65, 67, 70, 71, 73, 75, 83, 85, 86, 88, 89, 91, 94, 96, 98, 100, 104.* **Moldoff** *a-3; c-3, 7-11, 13-17, plus odd #'s 19-61.* **Martin Naydell** *c-52, 54, 56, 58, 60, 64, 84.*

FLASH DIGEST, THE (See DC Special Series #24)

FLASH GORDON (See Defenders Of The Earth, Eat Right to Work..., Giant Comic Album, King Classics, King Comics, March of Comics #118, 133, 142, The Phantom #18, Street Comix & Wow Comics, 1st series)

FLASH GORDON
Dell Publishing Co.: No. 25, 1941; No. 10, 1943 - No. 512, Nov, 1953

Feature Books 25 (#1)(1941))-r-not by Raymond 122 244 366 769 1297 1825
Four Color 10(1942)-by Alex Raymond; reprints "The Ice Kingdom" 79 158 237 672 1286 1900
Four Color 84(1945)-by Alex Raymond; reprints "The Fiery Desert" 41 82 123 328 614 900
Four Color 173 19 38 57 135 250 365
Four Color 190-Bondage-c; "The Adventures of the Flying Saucers"; 5th Flying Saucer story (6/48)- see The Spirit 9/28/47(1st), Shadow Comics V7#10 (2nd, 1/48), Captain Midnight #60 (3rd, 2/48) & Boy Commandos #26 (4th, 3-4/48) 20 40 60 148 274 400
Four Color 204,247 15 30 45 105 190 275
Four Color 424 Painted-c 11 22 33 77 136 195
2(5-7/53-Dell)-Painted-c; Evans-a? 8 16 24 58 97 135
Four Color 512-Painted-c 8 16 24 58 97 135

FLASH GORDON (See Tiny Tot Funnies)
Harvey Publications: Oct, 1950 - No. 4, April, 1951

1-Alex Raymond-a; bondage-c; reprints strips from 7/14/40 to 12/8/40 38 76 114 226 363 500
2-Alex Raymond-a; r/strips 12/15/40-4/27/41 23 46 69 135 218 300
3,4-Alex Raymond-a; 3-bondage-c; r/strips 5/4/41-9/21/41. 4-r/strips 10/24/37-3/27/38 21 42 63 125 200 275
5-(Rare)-Small size-5-1/2x8-1/2"; B&W; 32 pgs.; Distributed to some mail subscribers only 60 120 180 378 639 900
(Also see All-New No. 15, Boy Explorers No. 2, and Stuntman No. 3)

FLASH GORDON
Gold Key: June, 1965

1 (1947 reprint)-Painted-c 6 12 18 41 66 90

FLASH GORDON (Also see Comics Reading Libraries in the Promotional Comics section)
King #1-11/Charlton #12-18/Gold Key #19-23/Whitman #28 on:
9/66 - #11, 12/67; #12, 2/69 - #18, 1/70; #19, 9/78 - #37, 3/82 (Painted covers No. 19-30, 34)

1-1st S.A. app Flash Gordon; Williamson c/a(2); E.C. swipe/Incredible S.F. #32; Mandrake story 7 14 21 49 80 110
1-Army giveaway(1968)("Complimentary" on cover)(Same as regular #1 minus Mandrake story & back-c) 4 8 12 28 44 60
2-8: 2-Bolle, Gil Kane-c; Mandrake story. 3-Williamson-c. 4-Secret Agent X-9 begins, Williamson-c/a(3). 5-Williamson-c/a(2). 6,8-Crandall-a. 7-Raboy-a (last in comics?). 8-Secret Agent X-9-r 4 8 12 26 41 55
9-13: 9,10-Raymond-r. 10-Buckler's 1st pro work (11/67). 11-Crandall-a. 12-Crandall-c/a. 13-Jeff Jones-a (15 pgs.) 4 8 12 24 37 50
14,15: 15-Last 12¢ issue 3 6 9 18 27 35
16,17: 17-Brick Bradford story 3 6 9 16 22 28
18-Kaluta-a (3rd pro work?)(see Teen Confessions) 3 6 9 19 29 38
19(9/78, G.K.), 20-26 1 3 4 6 8 10
27-29,34-37: 34-37-Movie adaptation 2 4 6 8 10 12
30 (10/80) (scarce, from Whitman 3-pack only) 3 6 9 18 27 35
30 (7/81; re-issue), 31-33-single issues 2 4 6 8 10 12
31-33 (Bagged 3-pack): Movie adaptation; Williamson-a. 36.00

NOTE: **Aparo** *a-8.* **Bolle** *a-21, 22.* **Boyette** *a-14-18.* **Briggs** *c-10.* **Buckler** *a-10.* **Crandall** *c-6.* **Estrada** *a-3.* **Gene Fawcette** *a-29, 30, 34, 37.* **McWilliams** *a-31-33, 36.*

FLASH GORDON
DC Comics: June, 1988 - No. 9, Holiday, 1988-'89 ($1.25, mini-series)

1-9: 1,5-Painted-c 3.00

Flinch #9 © DC

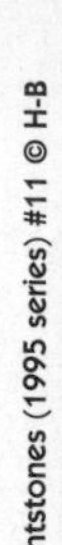

Flintstones (1995 series) #11 © H-B

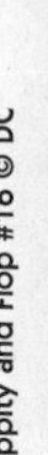

Flippity and Flop #16 © DC

	GD 2.0	VG 4.0	FN 6.0	VF 8.0	VF/NM 9.0	NM- 9.2

FLASH GORDON
Marvel Comics: June, 1995 - No. 2, July, 1995 ($2.95, limited series)

1,2: Schultz scripts; Williamson-a — 3.00

FLASH GORDON
Ardden Entertainment: Aug, 2008 - Present ($3.99)

1-Deneen-s/Green-a; two covers — 4.00

FLASH GORDON THE MOVIE
Western Publishing Co.: 1980 (8-1/4 x 11", $1.95, 68 pgs.)

	GD	VG	FN	VF	VF/NM	NM-
11294-Williamson-c/a; adapts movie	2	4	6	10	14	18
13743-Hardback edition	3	6	9	15	21	26

FLASH/ GREEN LANTERN: FASTER FRIENDS (See Green Lantern/Flash...)
DC Comics: No. 2, 1997 ($4.95, continuation of Green Lantern/Flash: Faster Friends #1)

2-Waid/Augustyn-s — 5.00

FLASHPOINT (Elseworlds Flash)
DC Comics: Dec, 1999 - No. 3, Feb, 2000 ($2.95, limited series)

1-3-Paralyzed Barry Allen; Breyfogle-a/McGreal-s — 3.00

FLAT-TOP
Mazie Comics/Harvey Publ.(Magazine Publ.) No. 4 on: 11/53 - No. 3, 5/54; No. 4, 3/55 - No. 7, 9/55

	GD	VG	FN	VF	VF/NM	NM-
1-Teenage; Flat-Top, Mazie, Mortie & Stevie begin	8	16	24	44	57	70
2,3	5	10	15	24	30	35
4-7	5	10	15	22	26	30

FLESH & BLOOD
Brainstorm Comics: Dec, 1995 ($2.95, B&W, mature)

1-Balent-c; foil-c. — 3.00

FLESH AND BONES
Upshot Graphics (Fantagraphics Books): June, 1986 - No. 4, Dec, 1986 (Limited series)

1-4: Alan Moore scripts (r) & Dalgoda by Fujitake — 3.00

FLESH CRAWLERS
Kitchen Sink Press: Aug, 1993 - No. 3, 1995 ($2.50, B&W, limited series, mature)

1-3 — 2.50

FLEX MENTALLO (Man of Muscle Mystery) (See Doom Patrol, 2nd Series)
DC Comics (Vertigo): Jun, 1996 - No. 4, Sept, 1996 ($2.50, lim. series, mature)

	GD	VG	FN	VF	VF/NM	NM-
1-4: Grant Morrison scripts & Frank Quitely-c/a in all; banned from reprints due to Charles Atlas legal action	2	4	6	8	11	14

FLINCH (Horror anthology)
DC Comics (Vertigo): Jun, 1999 - No. 16, Jan, 2001 ($2.50)

1-16: 1-Art by Jim Lee, Quitely, and Corben. 5-Sale-c. 11-Timm-a — 2.50

FLINTSTONE KIDS, THE (TV) (See Star Comics Digest)
Star Comics/Marvel Comics #5 on: Aug, 1987 - No. 11, Apr, 1989

1-11 — 4.50

FLINTSTONES, THE (TV)(See Dell Giant #48 for No. 1)
Dell Publ. Co./Gold Key No. 7 (10/62) on: No. 2, Nov-Dec, 1961 - No. 60, Sept, 1970 (Hanna-Barbera)

	GD	VG	FN	VF	VF/NM	NM-
2-2nd app. (TV show debuted on 9/30/60); 1st app. of Cave Kids; 15¢-c thru #5	10	20	30	70	123	175
3-6(7-8/62): 3-Perry Gunnite begins. 6-1st 12¢-c	7	14	21	45	73	100
7 (10/62; 1st GK)	7	14	21	45	73	100
8-10	6	12	18	37	59	80
11-1st app. Pebbles (6/63)	8	16	24	58	97	135
12-15,17-20	5	10	15	30	48	65
16-1st app. Bamm-Bamm (1/64)	8	16	24	54	90	125
21-23,25-30,33: 26,27-2nd & 3rd app. The Grusomes. 30-1st app. Martian Mopheads (10/65). 33-Meet Frankenstein & Dracula	4	8	12	28	44	60
24-1st app. The Grusomes	6	12	18	39	62	85
31,32,35-40: 31-Xmas-c. 36-Adaptation of "the Man Called Flintstone" movie. 39-Reprints	4	8	12	24	37	50
34-1st app. The Great Gazoo	6	12	18	39	62	85
41-60: 45-Last 12¢ issue	3	6	9	21	32	42
At N. Y. World's Fair ('64)-J.W. Books (25¢)-1st printing; no date on-c (29¢ version exists, 2nd print?) Most H-B characters app.; including Yogi Bear, Top Cat, Snagglepuss and the Jetsons	5	10	15	34	55	75
At N. Y. World's Fair (1965 on-c; re-issue; Warren Pub.) NOTE: Warehouse find in 1984	2	4	6	10	14	18
Bigger & Boulder 1(#30013-211) (Gold Key Giant, 11/62, 25¢, 84 pgs.)	8	16	24	54	90	125
Bigger & Boulder 2-(1966, 25¢)-Reprints B&B No. 1	5	10	15	32	51	70
...On the Rocks (9/61, $1.00, 6-1/4x9", cardboard-c, high quality paper,116 pgs.) B&W new material	9	18	27	63	107	150
...With Pebbles & Bamm Bamm (100 pgs., G.K.)-30028-511 (paper-c, 25¢) (11/65)	8	16	24	54	90	125

NOTE: *(See Comic Album #16, Bamm-Bamm & Pebbles Flintstone, Dell Giant 48, Golden Comics Digest, March of Comics #229, 243, 271, 289, 299, 317, 327, 341, Pebbles Flintstone, Top Comics #2-4, and Whitman Comic Book.)*

FLINTSTONES, THE (TV)(...& Pebbles)
Charlton Comics: Nov, 1970 - No. 50, Feb, 1977 (Hanna-Barbera)

	GD	VG	FN	VF	VF/NM	NM-
1	8	16	24	52	86	120
2	4	8	12	28	44	60
3-7,9,10	3	6	9	20	30	40
8- "Flintstones Summer Vacation" (Summer, 1971, 52 pgs.)	5	10	15	34	55	75
11-20,36: 36-Mike Zeck illos (early work)	3	6	9	16	23	30
21-35,38-41,43-45	3	6	9	14	19	24
37-Byrne text illos (early work; see Nightmare #20)	3	6	9	16	23	30
42-Byrne-a (2 pgs.)	3	6	9	16	23	30
46-50	2	4	6	13	18	22
Digest nn (1972, B&W, 100 pgs.) (low print run)	3	6	9	20	30	40

(Also see Barney & Betty Rubble, Dino, The Great Gazoo, & Pebbles & Bamm-Bamm)

FLINTSTONES, THE (TV)(See Yogi Bear, 3rd series) (Newsstand sales only)
Marvel Comics Group: October, 1977 - No. 9, Feb, 1979 (Hanna-Barbera)

	GD	VG	FN	VF	VF/NM	NM-
1,7-9: 1-(30¢-c). 7-9-Yogi Bear app.	3	6	9	20	30	40
1-(35¢-c variant, limited distribution)	9	18	27	60	100	140
2,3,5,6: Yogi Bear app.	3	6	9	16	22	28
4-The Jetsons app.	3	6	9	17	25	32

FLINTSTONES, THE (TV)
Harvey Comics: Sept, 1992 - No. 13, Jun, 1994 ($1.25/$1.50) (Hanna-Barbera)

V2#1-13 — 3.00
...Big Book 1,2 (11/92, 3/93; both $1.95, 52 pgs.) — 3.50
...Giant Size 1-3 (10/92, 4/93, 11/93; $2.25, 68 pgs.) — 3.50

FLINTSTONES, THE (TV)
Archie Publications: Sept, 1995 - No. 22, June, 1997 ($1.50)

1-22 — 3.00

FLINTSTONES AND THE JETSONS, THE (TV)
DC Comics: Aug, 1997 - No. 21, May, 1999 ($1.75/$1.95/$1.99)

1 — 6.00
2-21: 19-Bizarro Elroy-c — 3.00

FLINTSTONES CHRISTMAS PARTY, THE (See The Funtastic World of Hanna-Barbera No. 1)

FLIP
Harvey Publications: April, 1954 - No. 2, June, 1954 (Satire)

	GD	VG	FN	VF	VF/NM	NM-
1,2-Nostrand-a each. 2-Powell-a	22	44	66	127	204	280

FLIPPER (TV)
Gold Key: Apr, 1966 - No. 3, Nov, 1967 (All have photo-c)

	GD	VG	FN	VF	VF/NM	NM-
1	7	14	21	45	73	100
2,3	5	10	15	30	48	65

FLIPPITY & FLOP
National Per. Publ. (Signal Publ. Co.): 12-1/51-52 - No. 46, 8-10/59; No. 47, 9-11/60

	GD	VG	FN	VF	VF/NM	NM-
1-Sam dog & his pets Flippity The Bird and Flop The Cat begin; Twiddle and Twaddle begin	27	54	81	156	251	345
2	15	30	45	84	127	170
3-5	14	28	42	76	108	140
6-10	11	22	33	62	86	110
11-20: 20-Last precode (3/55)	10	20	30	56	76	95
21-47	9	18	27	50	65	80

FLOATERS
Dark Horse Comics: Sept, 1993 - No. 5, Jan, 1994 ($2.50, B&W, lim. series)

1-5 — 2.50

FLOYD FARLAND (See Eclipse Graphic Album Series #11)

FLY, THE (Also see Adventures of..., Blue Ribbon Comics & Flyman)
Archie Enterprises, Inc.: May, 1983 - No. 9, Oct, 1984

1,2: 1-Mr. Justice app; origin Shield; Kirby-a; Steranko-c. 2-Ditko-a; Flygirl app. — 5.00
3-5: Ditko-a in all. 4,5-Ditko-c(p) — 4.00
6-9: Ditko-a in all. 6-8-Ditko-c(p) — 5.00

NOTE: ***Ayers** c-9. **Buckler** a-1, 2. **Kirby** a-1. **Nebres** c-3, 4, 5i, 6, 7i. **Steranko** c-1, 2.*

FLY, THE

Flying Cadet #1 © Flying Cadet Publ.

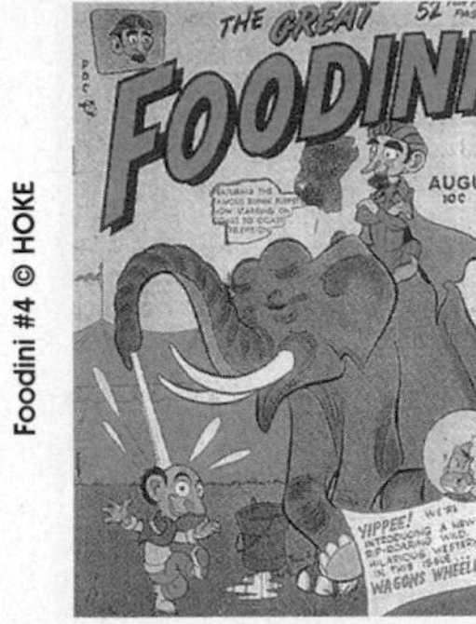

Foodini #4 © HOKE

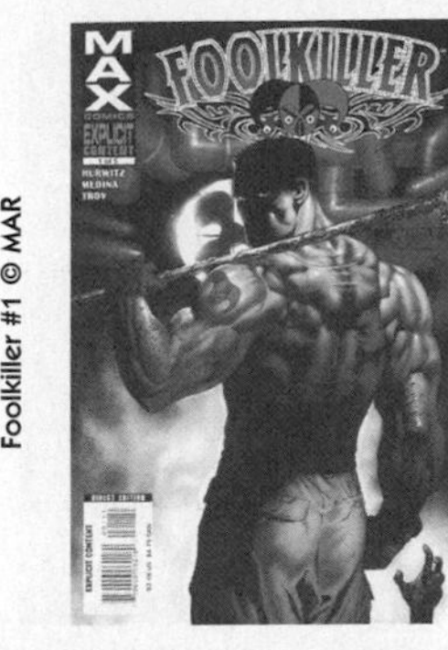

Foolkiller #1 © MAR

Impact Comics (DC): Aug, 1991 - No. 17, Dec, 1992 ($1.00)

	GD 2.0	VG 4.0	FN 6.0	VF 8.0	VF/NM 9.0	NM- 9.2
1						3.00
2-17: 4-Vs. The Black Hood. 9-Trading card inside						2.50
Annual 1 ('92, $2.50, 68 pgs.)-Impact trading card						3.00

FLYBOY (Flying Cadets)(Also see Approved Comics #5)
Ziff-Davis Publ. Co. (Approved): Spring, 1952 - No. 2, Oct-Nov, 1952

	GD 2.0	VG 4.0	FN 6.0	VF 8.0	VF/NM 9.0	NM- 9.2
1-Saunders painted-c	20	40	60	114	180	245
2-(10-11/52)-Saunders painted-c	14	28	42	80	115	150

FLYING ACES (Aviation stories)
Key Publications: July, 1955 - No. 5, Mar, 1956

	GD 2.0	VG 4.0	FN 6.0	VF 8.0	VF/NM 9.0	NM- 9.2
1	8	16	24	40	50	60
2-5: 2 Trapani-a	5	10	15	22	26	30

FLYING A'S RANGE RIDER, THE (TV)(See Western Roundup under Dell Giants)
Dell Publishing Co.: #404, 6-7/52; #2, June-Aug, 1953 - #24, Aug, 1959 (All photo-c)

	GD 2.0	VG 4.0	FN 6.0	VF 8.0	VF/NM 9.0	NM- 9.2
Four Color 404(#1)-Titled "The Range Rider"	10	20	30	71	126	180
2	7	14	21	47	76	105
3-10	6	12	18	39	62	85
11-16,18-24	5	10	15	34	55	75
17-Toth-a	6	12	18	41	66	90

FLYING CADET (WW II Plane Photos)
Flying Cadet Publ. Co.; Jan, 1943 - V2#8, 1944 (Half photos, half comics)

	GD 2.0	VG 4.0	FN 6.0	VF 8.0	VF/NM 9.0	NM- 9.2
V1#1-Painted-c	15	30	45	83	124	165
2	9	18	27	50	65	80
3-8 (Two #6's, Sept. & Oct.): 5,6a,6b-Photo-c	8	16	24	44	57	70
V2#1-7(#10-16)	8	16	24	40	50	60
7(#17 on cover)-Bare-breasted woman-c	18	36	54	103	162	220

FLYING COLORS 10th ANNIVERSARY SPECIAL
Flying Colors Comics: Fall 1998 ($2.95, one-shot)

	GD 2.0	VG 4.0	FN 6.0	VF 8.0	VF/NM 9.0	NM- 9.2
1-Dan Brereton-c; pin-ups by Jim Lee and Jeff Johnson						3.00

FLYIN' JENNY
Pentagon Publ. Co./Leader Enterprises #2: 1946 - No. 2, 1947 (1945 strip-r)

	GD 2.0	VG 4.0	FN 6.0	VF 8.0	VF/NM 9.0	NM- 9.2
nn-Marcus Swayze strip-r (entire insides)	15	30	45	83	124	165
2-Baker-c; Swayze strip reprints	16	32	48	94	147	200

FLYING MODELS
H-K Publ. (Health-Knowledge Publs.): V61#3, May, 1954 (5¢, 16 pgs.)

	GD 2.0	VG 4.0	FN 6.0	VF 8.0	VF/NM 9.0	NM- 9.2
V61#3 (Rare)	9	18	27	50	65	80

FLYING NUN (TV)
Dell Publishing Co.: Feb, 1968 - No. 4, Nov, 1968

	GD 2.0	VG 4.0	FN 6.0	VF 8.0	VF/NM 9.0	NM- 9.2
1-Sally Field photo-c	6	12	18	41	66	90
2-4: 2-Sally Field photo-c	4	8	12	26	41	55

FLYING NURSES (See Sue & Sally Smith...)

FLYING SAUCERS (See The Spirit 9/28/47(1st app.), Shadow Comics V7#10 (2nd, 1/48), Captain Midnight #60 (3rd, 2/48), Boy Commandos #26 (4th, 3-4/48) & Flash Gordon Four Color 190 (5th, 6/48))

FLYING SAUCERS
Avon Periodicals/Realistic: 1950; 1952; 1953

	GD 2.0	VG 4.0	FN 6.0	VF 8.0	VF/NM 9.0	NM- 9.2
1(1950)-Wood-a, 21 pgs.; Fawcette-c	80	160	240	504	852	1200
nn(1952)-Cover altered plus 2 pgs. of Wood-a not in original	46	92	138	285	473	660
nn(1953)-Reprints above	35	70	105	203	327	450

FLYING SAUCERS (Comics)
Dell Publishing Co.: April, 1967 - No. 4, Nov, 1967; No. 5, Oct, 1969

	GD 2.0	VG 4.0	FN 6.0	VF 8.0	VF/NM 9.0	NM- 9.2
1-(12¢-c)	4	8	12	26	41	55
2-5: 5-Has same cover as #1, but with 15¢ price	3	6	9	19	29	38

FLY MAN (Formerly Adventures of The Fly; Mighty Comics #40 on)
Mighty Comics Group (Radio Comics) (Archie): No. 32, July, 1965 - No. 39, Sept, 1966
(Also see Mighty Crusaders)

	GD 2.0	VG 4.0	FN 6.0	VF 8.0	VF/NM 9.0	NM- 9.2
32,33-Comet, Shield, Black Hood, The Fly & Flygirl x-over. 33-Re-intro Wizard, Hangman (1st S.A. appearances)	5	10	15	34	55	75
34-39: 34-Shield begins. 35-Origin Black Hood. 36-Hangman x-over in Shield; re-intro. & origin of Web (1st S.A. app.). 37-Hangman, Wizard x-over in Flyman; last Shield issue. 38-Web story. 39-Steel Sterling (1st S.A. app.)	4	8	12	24	37	50

FOLLOW THE SUN (TV)
Dell Publishing Co.: May-July, 1962 - No. 2, Sept-Nov, 1962 (Photo-c)

	GD 2.0	VG 4.0	FN 6.0	VF 8.0	VF/NM 9.0	NM- 9.2
01-280-207(No.1)	5	10	15	30	48	65
12-280-211(No.2)	5	10	15	30	48	65

FOODANG
Continum Comics: July, 1994 ($1.95, B&W, bi-monthly)

	GD 2.0	VG 4.0	FN 6.0	VF 8.0	VF/NM 9.0	NM- 9.2
1						2.50

FOODINI (TV)(The Great...; see Jingle Dingle & Pinhead &...)
Continental Publ. (Holyoke): March, 1950 - No. 4, Aug, 1950 (All have 52 pgs.)

	GD 2.0	VG 4.0	FN 6.0	VF 8.0	VF/NM 9.0	NM- 9.2
1-Based on TV puppet show (very early TV comic)	22	44	66	127	204	280
2-Jingle Dingle begins	14	28	42	76	108	140
3,4	10	20	30	56	76	95

FOOEY (Magazine) (Satire)
Scoff Publishing Co.: Feb, 1961 - No. 4, May, 1961

	GD 2.0	VG 4.0	FN 6.0	VF 8.0	VF/NM 9.0	NM- 9.2
1	5	10	15	30	48	65
2-4	3	6	9	20	30	40

FOOFUR (TV)
Marvel Comics (Star Comics)/Marvel No. 5 on: Aug, 1987 - No. 6, Jun, 1988

	GD 2.0	VG 4.0	FN 6.0	VF 8.0	VF/NM 9.0	NM- 9.2
1-6						3.00

FOOLKILLER (Also see The Amazing Spider-Man #225, The Defenders #73, Man-Thing #3 & Omega the Unknown #8)
Marvel Comics: Oct, 1990 - No. 10, Oct, 1991 ($1.75, limited series)

	GD 2.0	VG 4.0	FN 6.0	VF 8.0	VF/NM 9.0	NM- 9.2
1-10: 1-Origin 3rd Foolkiller; Greg Salinger app; DoZuniga-a(i) in 1-4. 8-Spider-Man x-over						2.50

FOOLKILLER
Marvel Comics: Dec, 2007 - No. 5, Jul, 2008 ($3.99, limited series)

	GD 2.0	VG 4.0	FN 6.0	VF 8.0	VF/NM 9.0	NM- 9.2
1-5-Hurwitz-s/Medina-a. 2-Origin						4.00

FOOLKILLER: WHITE ANGELS
Marvel Comics: Sept, 2008 - No. 5 ($3.99, limited series)

	GD 2.0	VG 4.0	FN 6.0	VF 8.0	VF/NM 9.0	NM- 9.2
1-3-Hurwitz-s/Azaceta-a						4.00

FOOM (Friends Of Ol' Marvel)
Marvel Comics: 1973 - No. 22, 1979 (Marvel fan magazine)

	GD 2.0	VG 4.0	FN 6.0	VF 8.0	VF/NM 9.0	NM- 9.2
1	7	14	21	49	80	110
2-Hulk-c by Steranko	5	10	15	32	51	70
3,4	5	10	15	30	48	65
5-11: 11-Kirby-a and interview	4	8	12	26	41	55
12-15: 12-Vision-c. 13-Daredevil-c. 14-Conan. 15-Howard the Duck	4	8	12	26	41	55
16-20: 16-Marvel bullpen. 17-Stan Lee issue. 19-Defenders	4	8	12	22	34	45
21-Star Wars	4	8	12	24	37	50
22-Spider-Man-c; low print run final issue	6	12	18	37	59	80

FOOTBALL THRILLS (See Tops In Adventure)
Ziff-Davis Publ. Co.: Fall-Winter, 1951-52 - No. 2, Fall, 1952 (Edited by "Red" Grange)

	GD 2.0	VG 4.0	FN 6.0	VF 8.0	VF/NM 9.0	NM- 9.2
1-Powell a(2); Saunders painted-c; Red Grange, Jim Thorpe stories	27	54	81	156	251	345
2-Saunders painted-c	18	36	54	105	165	225

FOOT SOLDIERS, THE
Dark Horse Comics: Jan, 1996 - No. 4, Apr, 1996 ($2.95, limited series)

	GD 2.0	VG 4.0	FN 6.0	VF 8.0	VF/NM 9.0	NM- 9.2
1-4: Krueger story & Avon Oeming-a. in all. 1-Alex Ross-c. 4-John K. Snyder, III-c						3.00

FOOT SOLDIERS, THE (Volume Two)
Image Comics: Sept, 1997 - No. 5, May, 1998 ($2.95, limited series)

	GD 2.0	VG 4.0	FN 6.0	VF 8.0	VF/NM 9.0	NM- 9.2
1-5: 1-Yeowell-a. 2-McDaniel, Hester, Sienkiewicz, Giffen-a						3.00

FOR A NIGHT OF LOVE
Avon Periodicals: 1951

	GD 2.0	VG 4.0	FN 6.0	VF 8.0	VF/NM 9.0	NM- 9.2
nn-Two stories adapted from the works of Emile Zola; Astarita, Ravielli-a; Kinstler-c	31	62	93	181	291	400

FORBIDDEN KNOWLEDGE: ADVENTURE BEYOND THE DOORWAY TO SOULS WITH RADICAL DREAMER (Also see Radical Dreamer)
Mark's Giant Economy Size Comics: 1996 ($3.50, B&W, one-shot, 48 pgs.)

	GD 2.0	VG 4.0	FN 6.0	VF 8.0	VF/NM 9.0	NM- 9.2
nn-Max Wrighter app.; Wheatley-c/a/script; painted infinity-c						3.50

FORBIDDEN LOVE
Quality Comics Group: Mar, 1950 - No. 4, Sept, 1950 (52 pgs.)

	GD 2.0	VG 4.0	FN 6.0	VF 8.0	VF/NM 9.0	NM- 9.2
1-(Scarce)-Classic photo-c; Crandall-a	76	152	228	479	810	1140
2-(Scarce)-Classic photo-c	63	126	189	397	669	940
3-(Scarce)-Photo-c	40	80	120	240	388	535
4-(Scarce)-Ward/Cuidera-a; photo-c	40	80	120	244	397	550

FORBIDDEN LOVE (See Dark Mansion of...)

FORBIDDEN PLANET
Innovation Publishing: May, 1992 - No. 4, 1992 ($2.50, limited series)

Forbidden Worlds #2 © ACG

Force Works #6 © MAR

Forever People #3 © DC

	GD	VG	FN	VF	VF/NM	NM-
	2.0	4.0	6.0	8.0	9.0	9.2

1-4: Adapts movie; painted-c 2.50

FORBIDDEN TALES OF DARK MANSION (Formerly Dark Mansion of Forbidden Love #1-4)
National Periodical Publ.: No. 5, May-June, 1972 - No. 15, Feb-Mar, 1974

5-(52 pgs.) 5 10 15 34 55 75
6-15: 13-Kane/Howard-a 3 6 9 16 23 30
NOTE: ***N. Adams*** *c-9.* ***Alcala*** *a-9-11, 13.* ***Chaykin*** *a-7,15.* ***Evans*** *a-14.* ***Heck*** *a-5.* ***Kaluta*** *a-7i, 8-12; c-7, 8, 13.* ***G. Kane*** *a-13.* ***Kirby*** *a-6.* ***Nino*** *a-8, 12, 15.* ***Redondo*** *a-14.*

FORBIDDEN WORLDS
American Comics Group: 7-8/51 - No. 34, 10-11/54; No. 35, 8/55 - No. 145, 8/67 (No. 1-5: 52 pgs.; No. 6-8: 44 pgs.)

1-Williamson/Frazetta-a (10 pgs.) 157 314 471 989 1670 2350
2 66 132 198 416 701 985
3-Williamson/Orlando-a (7 pgs.); Wood (2 panels); Frazetta (1 panel)
67 134 201 422 711 1000
4 43 86 129 266 443 620
5-Krenkel/Williamson-a (8 pgs.) 53 106 159 331 558 785
6-Harrison/Williamson-a (8 pgs.) 47 94 141 291 486 680
7,8,10: 7-1st monthly issue 32 64 96 188 302 415
9-A-Bomb explosion story 35 70 105 203 327 450
11-20 21 42 63 125 200 275
21-33: 24-E.C. swipe by Landau 17 34 51 98 154 210
34(10-11/54)(Scarce)(becomes Young Heroes #35 on)-Last pre-code issue;
A-Bomb explosion story 19 38 57 112 176 240
35(8/55)-Scarce 18 36 54 107 169 230
36-62 13 26 39 74 105 135
63,69,76,78-Williamson-a in all; w/Krenkel #69 14 28 42 76 108 140
64,66-68,70-72,74,75,77,79-85,87-90 10 20 30 56 76 95
65- "There's a New Moon Tonight" listed in #114 as holding 1st record fan mail response
14 28 42 76 108 140
73-1st app. Herbie by Ogden Whitney 41 82 123 250 413 575
86-Flying saucer-c by Schaffenberger 11 22 33 62 86 110
91-93,95-100 5 10 15 34 55 75
94-Herbie (2nd app.) 10 20 30 70 123 175
101-109,111-113,115,117-120 4 8 12 28 44 60
110,116-Herbie app. 116-Herbie goes to Hell 7 14 21 45 73 100
114-1st Herbie-c; contains list of editor's top 20 ACG stories
8 16 24 58 97 135
121-123 4 8 12 22 34 45
124,126-130: 124-Magic Agent app. 126-Herbie 4 8 12 24 37 50
125-Magic Agent app.; intro. & origin Magicman series, ends #141; Herbie app.
5 10 15 34 55 75
131-139: 133-Origin/1st app. Dragonia in Magicman (1-2/66); returns in #138.
136-Nemesis x-over in Magicman 4 8 12 22 34 45
140-Mark Midnight app. by Ditko 4 8 12 24 37 50
141-145 3 6 9 20 30 40
NOTE: ***Buscema*** *a-75, 79, 81, 82, 140r.* ***Cameron*** *a-5.* ***Disbrow*** *a-10.* ***Ditko*** *a-137p, 138, 140.* ***Landau*** *a-24, 27-29, 31-34, 48, 86r, 96, 143-45.* ***Lazarus*** *a-18, 23, 24, 57.* ***Moldoff*** *a-27, 31, 139r.* ***Reinman*** *a-93.* ***Whitney*** *a-70, 115, 116, 137; c-40, 46, 57, 60, 68, 70, 78, 79, 90, 93, 94, 100, 102, 103, 106-108, 114, 129.*

FORCE, THE (See The Crusaders)

FORCE MAJEURE: PRAIRIE BAY (Also see Wild Stars)
Little Rocket Publications: May, 2002 ($2.95, B&W)

1-Tierney-s/Gil-c/a 3.00

FORCE OF BUDDHA'S PALM THE
Jademan Comics: Aug, 1988 - No. 55, Feb, 1993 ($1.50/$1.95, 68 pgs.)

1,55-Kung Fu stories in all 3.00
2-54 2.50

FORCE WORKS
Marvel Comics: July, 1994 - No. 22, Apr, 1996 ($1.50)

1-($3.95)-Fold-out pop-up-c; Iron Man, Wonder Man, Spider-Woman, U.S. Agent & Scarlet Witch (new costume) 4.00
2-11, 13-22: 5-Blue logo & pink logo versions. 9-Intro Dreamguard. 13-Avengers app. 2.50
5-Pink logo ($2.95)-polybagged w/ 16pg. Marvel Action Hour Preview & acetate print 3.00
12 ($2.50)-Flip book w/War Machine. 2.50

FORD ROTUNDA CHRISTMAS BOOK (See Christmas at the Rotunda)

FOREIGN INTRIGUES (Formerly Johnny Dynamite; becomes Battlefield Action #16 on)
Charlton Comics: No. 14, 1956 - No. 15, Aug, 1956

14,15-Johnny Dynamite continues 8 16 24 42 54 65

FOREMOST BOYS (See 4Most)

FOREVER AMBER
Image Comics: July, 1999 - Oct, 1999 ($2.95, B&W)

	GD	VG	FN	VF	VF/NM	NM-
	2.0	4.0	6.0	8.0	9.0	9.2

1-4-Don Hudson-s/a 3.00

FOREVER DARLING (Movie)
Dell Publishing Co.: No. 681, Feb, 1956

Four Color 681-w/Lucille Ball & Desi Arnaz; photo-c 11 22 33 79 140 200

FOREVER MAELSTROM
DC Comics: Jan, 2003 - No. 6, Jun, 2003 ($2.95, limited series)

1-6-Chaykin & Tischman-s/Lucas & Barreto-a 3.00

FOREVER PEOPLE, THE
National Periodical Publications: Feb-Mar, 1971 - No. 11, Oct-Nov, 1972 (Fourth World) (#1-3, 10-11 are 36 pgs; #4-9 are 52 pgs.)

1-1st app. Forever People; Superman x-over; Kirby-c/a begins; 1st full app. Darkseid (3rd anywhere, 3 weeks before New Gods #1); Darkseid storyline begins, ends #8 (app. in 1-4,6,8; cameos in 5,11) 7 14 21 49 80 110
2-9: 4-G.A. reprints thru #9. 9,10-Deadman app. 4 8 12 26 41 55
10,11 3 6 9 20 30 40
Jack Kirby's Forever People TPB ('99, $14.95, B&W&Grey) r/#1-11 plus cover gallery 15.00
NOTE: ***Kirby*** *c/a(p)-1-11; #4-9 contain Sandman reprints from Adventure #85, 84, 75, 80, 77, 74 in that order.*

FOREVER PEOPLE
DC Comics: Feb, 1988 - No. 6, July, 1988 ($1.25, limited series)

1-6 3.00

FORGE
CrossGeneration Comics: Feb, 2002 - No. 13, May, 2003 ($9.95/$11.95/$7.95, TPB)

1-3: Reprints from various CrossGen titles 10.00
4-8-($11.95) 12.00
9-13-($7.95, 8-1/4" x 5-1/2") digest-sized reprints 8.00

FOR GIRLS ONLY
Bernard Baily Enterprises: 11/53 - No. 2, 6/54 (100 pgs., digest size, 25¢)

1-25% comic book, 75% articles, illos, games 15 30 45 86 133 180
2-Eddie Fisher photo & story. 11 22 33 62 86 110

FORGOTTEN FOREST OF OZ, THE (See First Comics Graphic Novel #16)

FORGOTTEN REALMS (Also see Avatar & TSR Worlds)
DC Comics: Sept, 1989 - No. 25, Sept, 1991 ($1.50/$1.75)

1, Annual 1 (1990, $2.95, 68 pgs.) 3.00
2-25: Based on TSR role-playing game. 18-Avatar story 2.50

FORGOTTEN REALMS (Based on Wizards of the Coast game)
Devil's Due Publ.: June, 2005 - No. 3, Aug, 2005 ($4.95)

1-3-Salvatore-s/Seeley-a 5.00
...Exile (11/05 - No. 3, 1/06, $4.95) 1-3-Daab-s/Seeley-a. 1-Flip cover 5.00
...: Legacy (2/08 - No. 3, 6/08, $5.50) 1-3-Daab-s/Atkins-a 5.50
The Legend of Drizzt Book II: Exile (2006, $14.95, TPB) r/#1-3 15.00
...Sojourn (3/06 - No. 3, 6/06, $4.95) 1-3-Daab-s/Seeley-a 5.00
...: Streams of Silver (12/06 - No. 3, $5.50) 1-3-Daab-s/Semeiks-a 5.50
...The Crystal Shard (8/06 - No. 3, 12/06, $4.95) 1-3-Daab-s/Semeiks-a 5.00
...The Halfling's Gem (8/07 - No. 3, 12/07, $5.50) 1-3-Daab-s/Seeley-a; two covers 5.50

FORLORN RIVER (See Zane Grey Four Color 395)

FOR LOVERS ONLY (Formerly Hollywood Romances)
Charlton Comics: No. 60, Aug, 1971 - No. 87, Nov, 1976

60 3 6 9 20 30 40
61-80,82-87: 67-Morisi-a 2 4 6 11 16 20
81-Psychedelic cover 3 6 9 14 20 25

FORMERLY KNOWN AS THE JUSTICE LEAGUE
DC Comics: Sept, 2003 - No. 6, Feb, 2004 ($2.50, limited series)

1-Giffen & DeMatteis-s/Maguire-a; Booster Gold, Blue Beetle, Captain Atom, Mary Marvel, Fire, and Elongated Man app. 3.00
2-6: 3,4-Roulette app. 6-JLA app. 2.50
TPB (2004, $12.95) r/#1-6 13.00

FORT: PROPHET OF THE UNEXPLAINED
Dark Horse Comics: June, 2002 - No. 4, Sept, 2002 ($2.99, B&W, limited series)

1-4-Peter Lenkov-s/Frazer Irving-c/a 3.00
TPB (2003, $9.95) r/#1-4 10.00

FORTUNE AND GLORY
Oni Press: Dec, 1999 - No. 3, Apr, 2000 ($4.95, B&W, limited series)

1-3-Brian Michael Bendis in Hollywood 5.00
TPB ($14.95) 15.00

40 BIG PAGES OF MICKEY MOUSE

Four Color Comics Series 1 #17 © DIS

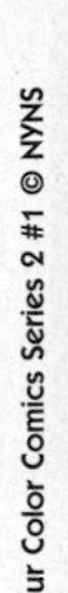
Four Color Comics Series 2 #1 © NYNS

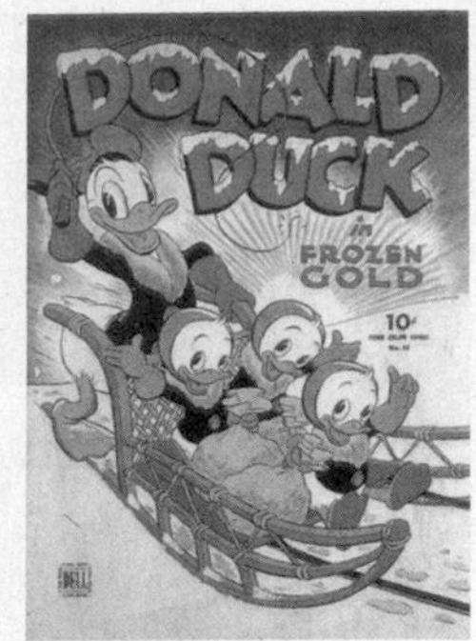

Four Color Comics #62 © DIS

	GD 2.0	VG 4.0	FN 6.0	VF 8.0	VF/NM 9.0	NM- 9.2
Whitman Publ. Co.: No. 945, Jan, 1936 (10-1/4x12-1/2", 44 pgs., cardboard-c)						
945-Reprints Mickey Mouse Magazine #1, but with a different cover; ads were eliminated and some illustrated stories had expanded text. The book is 3/4" shorter than Mickey Mouse Mag. #1, but the reprints are same size (Rare)	164	328	492	1025	1663	2300

40 oz. COLLECTED
Image Comics: Nov, 2003 ($9.95, digest-size, B&W)

Vol. 1-Reprints Jim Mahfood's mini-comics plus 20 pgs. new material; Grrl Scouts app. 10.00

FOR YOUR EYES ONLY (See James Bond...)

FOUNTAIN, THE (Companion graphic novel to the Darren Aronofsky film)
DC Comics (Vertigo): 2005 ($39.99, hardcover with dust jacket)

1-Darren Aronofsky-s/Kent Williams-a 40.00

FOUR (Fantastic Four; See Marvel Knights 4 #28-30)

FOUR COLOR
Dell Publishing Co.: Sept?, 1939 - No. 1354, Apr-June, 1962
(Series I are all 68 pgs.)

NOTE: *Four Color only appears on issues #19-25, 1-99,101. Dell Publishing Co. filed these as Series I, #1-25, and Series II, #1-1354. Issues beginning with #710? were printed with and without ads on back cover. Issues without ads are worth more.*

SERIES I:

	GD 2.0	VG 4.0	FN 6.0	VF 8.0	VF/NM 9.0	NM- 9.2
1(nn)-Dick Tracy	889	1778	2667	6401	11,201	16,000
2(nn)-Don Winslow of the Navy (#1) (Rare) (11/39?)	187	374	561	1178	1989	2800
3(nn)-Myra North (1/40)	95	190	285	599	1012	1425
4-Donald Duck by Al Taliaferro (1940)(Disney)(3/40?)	1150	2300	3450	8625	15,812	23,000
(Prices vary widely on this book)						
5-Smilin' Jack (#1) (5/40?)	71	142	213	447	754	1060
6-Dick Tracy (Scarce)	207	414	621	1304	2202	3100
7-Gang Busters	48	96	144	298	499	700
8-Dick Tracy	103	206	309	649	1100	1550
9-Terry and the Pirates-r/Super #9-29	67	134	201	422	711	1000
10-Smilin' Jack	61	122	183	384	647	910
11-Smitty (#1)	45	90	135	279	465	650
12-Little Orphan Annie; reprints strips from 12/19/37 to 6/4/38	57	114	171	359	605	850
13-Walt Disney's Reluctant Dragon('41)-Contains 2 pgs. of photos from film; 2 pg. foreword to Fantasia by Leopold Stokowski; Donald Duck, Goofy, Baby Weems & Mickey Mouse (as the Sorcerer's Apprentice) app. (Disney)	217	434	651	1367	2309	3250
14-Moon Mullins (#1)	45	90	135	279	465	650
15-Tillie the Toiler (#1)	45	90	135	279	465	650
16-Mickey Mouse (#1) (Disney) by Gottfredson	1250	2500	3750	15,000	-	-
17-Walt Disney's Dumbo, the Flying Elephant (#1)(1941)-Mickey Mouse, Donald Duck, & Pluto app. (Disney)	260	520	780	1638	2769	3900
18-Jiggs and Maggie (#1)(1936-38-r)	48	96	144	298	499	700
19-Barney Google and Snuffy Smith (#1)-(1st issue with Four Color on the cover)	47	94	141	291	483	675
20-Tiny Tim	37	74	111	215	345	475
21-Dick Tracy	78	156	234	491	833	1175
22-Don Winslow	45	90	135	279	465	650
23-Gang Busters	40	80	120	235	380	525
24-Captain Easy	50	100	150	310	518	725
25-Popeye (1942)	83	166	249	523	887	1250

SERIES II:

	GD 2.0	VG 4.0	FN 6.0	VF 8.0	VF/NM 9.0	NM- 9.2
1-Little Joe (1942)	50	100	150	400	750	1100
2-Harold Teen	29	58	87	213	394	575
3-Alley Oop (#1)	43	86	129	344	647	950
4-Smilin' Jack	38	76	114	286	536	785
5-Raggedy Ann and Andy (#1)	45	90	135	360	680	1000
6-Smitty	21	42	63	152	281	410
7-Smokey Stover (#1)	28	56	84	203	377	550
8-Tillie the Toiler	23	46	69	167	309	450
9-Donald Duck Finds Pirate Gold, by Carl Barks & Jack Hannah (Disney) (© 8/17/42)	975	1950	2925	7015	12,508	18,000
10-Flash Gordon by Alex Raymond; reprinted from "The Ice Kingdom"	79	158	237	672	1286	1900
11-Wash Tubbs	28	56	84	203	377	550
12-Walt Disney's Bambi (#1)	50	100	150	400	750	1100
13-Mr. District Attorney (#1)-See The Funnies #35 for 1st app.	27	54	81	198	369	540
14-Smilin' Jack	30	60	90	222	411	600
15-Felix the Cat (#1)	73	146	219	621	1186	1750
16-Porky Pig (#1)(1942)- "Secret of the Haunted House"	81	162	243	689	1320	1950
17-Popeye	42	84	126	336	631	925
18-Little Orphan Annie's Junior Commandos; Flag-c; reprints strips from 6/14/42 to 11/21/42	33	66	99	254	477	700
19-Walt Disney's Thumper Meets the Seven Dwarfs (Disney); reprinted in Silly Symphonies	47	94	141	376	701	1025
20-Barney Baxter	25	50	75	185	343	500
21-Oswald the Rabbit (#1)(1943)	42	84	126	336	631	925
22-Tillie the Toiler	17	34	51	120	223	325
23-Raggedy Ann and Andy	34	68	102	256	483	710
24-Gang Busters	26	52	78	187	349	510
25-Andy Panda (#1) (Walter Lantz)	52	104	156	416	783	1150
26-Popeye	42	84	126	336	631	925
27-Walt Disney's Mickey Mouse and the Seven Colored Terror	76	152	228	646	1236	1825
28-Wash Tubbs	19	38	57	135	250	365
29-Donald Duck and the Mummy's Ring, by Carl Barks (Disney) (9/43)	711	1422	2133	5119	8960	12,800
30-Bambi's Children (1943)-Disney	44	88	132	352	664	975
31-Moon Mullins	17	34	51	120	223	325
32-Smitty	15	30	45	107	196	285
33-Bugs Bunny "Public Nuisance #1"	96	192	288	816	1558	2300
34-Dick Tracy	40	80	120	312	581	850
35-Smokey Stover	16	32	48	114	212	310
36-Smilin' Jack	22	44	66	157	291	425
37-Bringing Up Father	19	38	57	135	250	365
38 Roy Rogers (#1, © 4/44) 1st western comic with photo-c (see Movie Comics #3)	167	334	501	1461	2731	4000
39-Oswald the Rabbit (1944)	29	58	87	213	394	575
40-Barney Google and Snuffy Smith	21	42	63	152	281	410
41-Mother Goose and Nursery Rhyme Comics (#1)-All by Walt Kelly	22	44	66	161	298	435
42-Tiny Tim (1934-r)	16	32	48	114	212	310
43-Popeye (1938-'42-r)	30	60	90	222	411	600
44-Terry and the Pirates (1938-r)	34	68	102	256	483	710
45-Raggedy Ann	29	58	87	213	394	575
46-Felix the Cat and the Haunted Castle	40	80	120	312	581	850
47-Gene Autry (copyright 6/16/44)	39	78	117	293	534	775
48-Porky Pig of the Mounties by Carl Barks (7/44)	88	176	264	748	1424	2100
49-Snow White and the Seven Dwarfs (Disney)	50	100	150	400	750	1100
50-Fairy Tale Parade-Walt Kelly art (1944)	24	48	72	176	326	475
51-Bugs Bunny Finds the Lost Treasure	32	64	96	246	461	675
52-Little Orphan Annie; reprints strips from 6/18/38 to 11/19/38	26	52	78	188	349	510
53-Wash Tubbs	14	28	42	102	181	260
54-Andy Panda	29	58	87	213	394	575
55-Tillie the Toiler	13	26	39	97	171	245
56-Dick Tracy	36	72	108	277	514	750
57-Gene Autry	35	70	105	263	482	700
58-Smilin' Jack	22	44	66	157	291	425
59-Mother Goose and Nursery Rhyme Comics-Kelly-c/a	18	36	54	130	240	350
60-Tiny Folks Funnies	15	30	45	107	196	285
61-Santa Claus Funnies(11/44)-Kelly art	22	44	66	163	302	440
62-Donald Duck in Frozen Gold, by Carl Barks (Disney) (1/45)	208	416	624	1820	3510	5200
63-Roy Rogers; color photo-all 4 covers	41	82	123	328	589	850
64-Smokey Stover	13	26	39	93	164	235
65-Smitty	13	26	39	90	160	230
66-Gene Autry	35	70	105	263	482	700
67-Oswald the Rabbit	17	34	51	120	223	325
68-Mother Goose and Nursery Rhyme Comics, by Walt Kelly	18	36	54	130	240	350
69-Fairy Tale Parade, by Walt Kelly	24	48	72	176	326	475
70-Popeye and Wimpy	22	44	66	157	291	425
71-Walt Disney's Three Caballeros, by Walt Kelly (© 4/45)-(Disney)	62	124	186	527	1006	1485
72-Raggedy Ann	24	48	72	172	319	465
73-The Gumps (#1)	12	24	36	86	153	220
74-Marge's Little Lulu (#1)	121	242	363	1029	1965	2900
75-Gene Autry and the Wildcat	28	56	84	207	374	540
76-Little Orphan Annie; reprints strips from 2/28/40 to 6/24/40						

Four Color Comics #85 © Walter Lantz

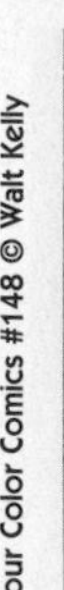
Four Color Comics #148 © Walt Kelly

Four Color Comics #176 © DELL

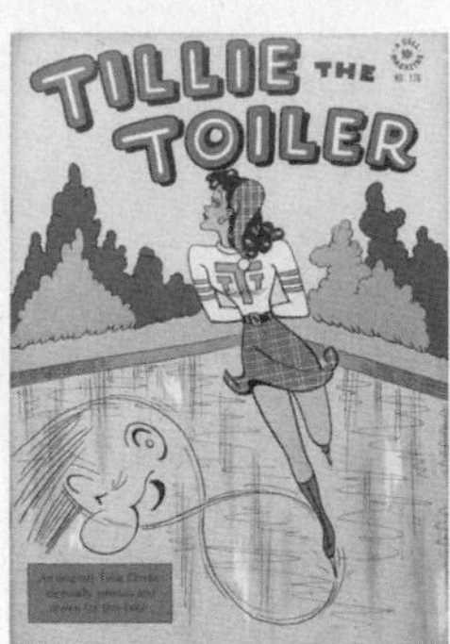

	GD 2.0	VG 4.0	FN 6.0	VF 8.0	VF/NM 9.0	NM- 9.2
	21	42	63	152	281	410
77-Felix the Cat	38	76	114	293	547	800
78-Porky Pig and the Bandit Twins	26	52	78	192	359	525
79-Walt Disney's Mickey Mouse in The Riddle of the Red Hat by Carl Barks (8/45)	92	184	276	782	1491	2200
80-Smilin' Jack	14	28	42	103	184	265
81-Moon Mullins	10	20	30	73	129	185
82-Lone Ranger	38	76	114	286	536	785
83-Gene Autry in Outlaw Trail	28	56	84	207	374	540
84-Flash Gordon by Alex Raymond-Reprints from "The Fiery Desert"	41	82	123	328	614	900
85-Andy Panda and the Mad Dog Mystery	16	32	48	114	212	310
86-Roy Rogers; photo-c	31	62	93	222	404	585
87-Fairy Tale Parade by Walt Kelly; Dan Noonan-c	24	48	72	176	326	475
88-Bugs Bunny's Great Adventure (Sci/fi)	22	44	66	163	302	440
89-Tillie the Toiler	13	26	39	97	171	245
90-Christmas with Mother Goose by Walt Kelly (11/45)	17	34	51	122	226	330
91-Santa Claus Funnies by Walt Kelly (11/45)	17	34	51	120	223	325
92-Walt Disney's The Wonderful Adventures Of Pinocchio (1945); Donald Duck by Kelly, 16 pgs. (Disney)	50	100	150	400	750	1100
93-Gene Autry in The Bandit of Black Rock	25	50	75	187	336	485
94-Winnie Winkle (1945)	12	24	36	87	156	225
95-Roy Rogers Comics; photo-c	31	62	93	222	404	585
96-Dick Tracy	24	48	72	176	326	475
97-Marge's Little Lulu (1946)	51	102	153	434	830	1225
98-Lone Ranger, The	29	58	87	213	394	575
99-Smitty	10	20	30	73	129	185
100-Gene Autry Comics; 1st Gene Autry photo-c	28	56	84	206	371	535
101-Terry and the Pirates	22	44	66	157	291	425

NOTE: No. 101 is last issue to carry "Four Color" logo on cover; all issues beginning with No. 100 are marked "...O. S." (One Shot) which can be found in the bottom left-hand panel on the first page; the numbers following "O. S." relate to the year/month issued.

	GD 2.0	VG 4.0	FN 6.0	VF 8.0	VF/NM 9.0	NM- 9.2
102-Oswald the Rabbit-Walt Kelly art, 1 pg.	14	28	42	102	181	260
103-Easter with Mother Goose by Walt Kelly	17	34	51	120	223	325
104-Fairy Tale Parade by Walt Kelly	19	38	57	135	250	365
105-Albert the Alligator and Pogo Possum (#1) by Kelly (4/46)	51	102	153	434	830	1225
106-Tillie the Toiler (5/46)	10	20	30	68	119	170
107-Little Orphan Annie; reprints strips from 11/16/42 to 3/24/43	18	36	54	130	240	350
108-Donald Duck in The Terror of the River, by Carl Barks (Disney) (© 4/16/46)	152	304	456	1304	2502	3700
109-Roy Rogers Comics; photo-c	23	46	69	171	306	440
110-Marge's Little Lulu	37	74	111	280	528	775
111-Captain Easy	14	28	42	99	175	250
112-Porky Pig's Adventure in Gopher Gulch	16	32	48	114	212	310
113-Popeye; all new Popeye stories begin	14	28	42	102	181	260
114-Fairy Tale Parade by Walt Kelly	19	38	57	135	250	365
115-Marge's Little Lulu	36	72	108	277	514	750
116-Mickey Mouse and the House of Many Mysteries (Disney)	26	52	78	188	349	510
117-Roy Rogers Comics; photo-c	19	38	57	138	244	350
118-Lone Ranger, The	29	58	87	213	394	575
119-Felix the Cat; all new Felix stories begin	32	64	96	246	461	675
120-Marge's Little Lulu	30	60	90	232	434	635
121-Fairy Tale Parade-(not Kelly)	12	24	36	84	150	215
122-Henry (#1) (10/46)	14	28	42	102	181	260
123-Bugs Bunny's Dangerous Venture	15	30	45	110	203	295
124-Roy Rogers Comics; photo-c	19	38	57	138	244	350
125-Lone Ranger, The	20	40	60	143	264	385
126-Christmas with Mother Goose by Walt Kelly (1946)	13	26	39	95	168	240
127-Popeye	14	28	42	102	181	260
128-Santa Claus Funnies- "Santa & the Angel" by Gollub; "A Mouse in the House" by Kelly	14	28	42	102	181	260
129-Walt Disney's Uncle Remus and His Tales of Brer Rabbit (#1) (1946)-Adapted from Disney movie "Song of the South"	26	52	78	191	356	520
130-Andy Panda (Walter Lantz)	12	24	36	82	146	210
131-Marge's Little Lulu	30	60	90	232	434	635
132-Tillie the Toiler (1947)	10	20	30	68	119	170
133-Dick Tracy	19	38	57	135	250	365
134-Tarzan and the Devil Ogre; Marsh-c/a	52	104	156	442	846	1250
135-Felix the Cat	23	42	69	167	309	450

	GD 2.0	VG 4.0	FN 6.0	VF 8.0	VF/NM 9.0	NM- 9.2
136-Lone Ranger, The	20	40	60	143	264	385
137-Roy Rogers Comics; photo-c	19	38	57	138	244	350
138-Smitty	9	18	27	64	110	155
139-Marge's Little Lulu (1947)	30	60	90	225	418	610
140-Easter with Mother Goose by Walt Kelly	14	28	42	102	181	260
141-Mickey Mouse and the Submarine Pirates (Disney)	21	42	63	152	281	410
142-Bugs Bunny and the Haunted Mountain	15	30	45	110	203	295
143-Oswald the Rabbit & the Prehistoric Egg	9	18	27	63	107	150
144-Roy Rogers Comics (1947)-Photo-c	19	38	57	138	244	350
145-Popeye	14	28	42	102	181	260
146-Marge's Little Lulu	30	60	90	225	418	610
147-Donald Duck in Volcano Valley, by Carl Barks (Disney) (5/47)	104	208	312	884	1692	2500
148-Albert the Alligator and Pogo Possum by Walt Kelly (5/47)	43	86	129	342	641	940
149-Smilin' Jack	10	20	30	68	119	170
150-Tillie the Toiler (6/47)	9	18	27	63	107	150
151-Lone Ranger, The	17	34	51	120	223	325
152-Little Orphan Annie; reprints strips from 1/2/44 to 5/6/44	12	24	36	87	156	225
153-Roy Rogers Comics; photo-c	17	34	51	124	220	315
154-Walter Lantz Andy Panda	12	24	36	82	146	210
155-Henry (7/47)	10	20	30	67	116	165
156-Porky Pig and the Phantom	12	24	36	84	150	215
157-Mickey Mouse & the Beanstalk (Disney)	21	42	63	152	281	410
158-Marge's Little Lulu	30	60	90	225	418	610
159-Donald Duck in the Ghost of the Grotto, by Carl Barks (Disney) (8/47)	90	180	270	765	1458	2150
160-Roy Rogers Comics; photo-c	17	34	51	124	220	315
161-Tarzan and the Fires Of Tohr; Marsh-c/a	48	96	144	384	717	1050
162-Felix the Cat (9/47)	17	34	51	124	230	335
163-Dick Tracy	17	34	51	120	223	325
164-Bugs Bunny Finds the Frozen Kingdom	15	30	45	110	203	295
165-Marge's Little Lulu	30	60	90	225	418	610
166-Roy Rogers Comics (52 pgs.)-Photo-c	17	34	51	124	220	315
167-Lone Ranger, The	17	34	51	120	223	325
168-Popeye (10/47)	14	28	42	102	181	260
169-Woody Woodpecker (#1)- "Manhunter in the North"; drug use story	17	34	51	120	223	325
170-Mickey Mouse on Spook's Island (11/47)(Disney)-reprinted in Mickey Mouse #103	18	36	54	130	240	350
171-Charlie McCarthy (#1) and the Twenty Thieves	24	48	72	176	326	475
172-Christmas with Mother Goose by Walt Kelly (11/47)	13	26	39	95	168	240
173-Flash Gordon	19	38	57	135	250	365
174-Winnie Winkle	8	16	24	58	97	135
175-Santa Claus Funnies by Walt Kelly (1947)	14	28	42	102	181	260
176-Tillie the Toiler (12/47)	9	18	27	63	107	150
177-Roy Rogers Comics-(36 pgs.); Photo-c	16	32	48	118	209	300
178-Donald Duck "Christmas on Bear Mountain" by Carl Barks; 1st app. Uncle Scrooge (Disney)(12/47)	121	242	363	1029	1965	2900
179-Uncle Wiggily (#1)-Walt Kelly-c	15	30	45	107	196	285
180-Ozark Ike (#1)	10	20	30	67	116	165
181-Walt Disney's Mickey Mouse in Jungle Magic	18	36	54	130	240	350
182-Porky Pig in Never-Never Land (2/48)	12	24	36	84	150	215
183-Oswald the Rabbit (Lantz)	9	18	27	63	107	150
184-Tillie the Toiler	9	18	27	63	107	150
185-Easter with Mother Goose by Walt Kelly (1948)	13	26	39	93	164	235
186-Walt Disney's Bambi (4/48)-Reprinted as Movie Classic Bambi #3 (1956)	16	32	48	114	212	310
187-Bugs Bunny and the Dreadful Dragon	12	24	36	82	146	210
188-Woody Woodpecker (Lantz, 5/48)	11	22	33	79	140	200
189-Donald Duck in The Old Castle's Secret, by Carl Barks (Disney) (6/48)	73	146	219	621	1186	1750
190-Flash Gordon (6/48); bondage-c; "The Adventures of the Flying Saucers"; 5th Flying Saucer story- see The Spirit 9/28/47(1st), Shadow Comics V7#10 (2nd, 1/48),Captain Midnight #60 (3rd, 2/48) & Boy Commandos #26 (4th, 3-4/48)	20	40	60	148	274	400
191-Porky Pig to the Rescue	12	24	36	84	150	215
192-The Brownies (#1)-by Walt Kelly (7/48)	14	28	42	99	175	250
193-M.G.M. Presents Tom and Jerry (#1)(1948)	22	44	66	161	298	435
194-Mickey Mouse in The World Under the Sea (Disney)-Reprinted in Mickey Mouse #101	18	36	54	130	240	350

Four Color Comics #231 © DIS

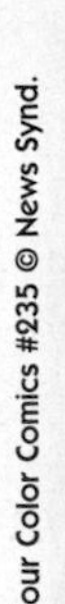
Four Color Comics #235 © News Synd.

Four Color Comics #252 © DIS

	GD 2.0	VG 4.0	FN 6.0	VF 8.0	VF/NM 9.0	NM- 9.2
195-Tillie the Toiler	7	14	21	50	83	115
196-Charlie McCarthy in The Haunted Hide-Out; part photo-c	15	30	45	108	199	290
197-Spirit of the Border (#1) (Zane Grey) (1948)	11	22	33	79	140	200
198-Andy Panda	12	24	36	82	146	210
199-Donald Duck in Sheriff of Bullet Valley, by Carl Barks; Barks draws himself on wanted poster, last page; used in Love & Death (Disney) (10/48)	79	158	237	672	1286	1900
200-Bugs Bunny, Super Sleuth (10/48)	12	24	36	82	146	210
201-Christmas with Mother Goose by W. Kelly	11	22	33	79	140	200
202-Woody Woodpecker	8	16	24	58	97	135
203-Donald Duck in the Golden Christmas Tree, by Carl Barks (Disney) (12/48)	55	110	165	468	897	1325
204-Flash Gordon (12/48)	15	30	45	105	190	275
205-Santa Claus Funnies by Walt Kelly	13	26	39	93	164	235
206-Little Orphan Annie; reprints strips from 11/10/40 to 1/11/41	8	16	24	54	90	125
207-King of the Royal Mounted (#1) (12/48)	14	28	42	99	175	250
208-Brer Rabbit Does It Again (Disney) (1/49)	11	22	33	79	140	200
209-Harold Teen	6	12	18	39	62	85
210-Tippie and Cap Stubbs	5	10	15	32	51	70
211-Little Beaver (#1)	8	16	24	56	93	130
212-Dr. Bobbs	6	12	18	37	59	80
213-Tillie the Toiler	7	14	21	50	83	115
214-Mickey Mouse and His Sky Adventure (2/49)(Disney)-Reprinted in Mickey Mouse #105	14	28	42	102	181	260
215-Sparkle Plenty (Dick Tracy-r by Gould)	11	22	33	79	140	200
216-Andy Panda and the Police Pup (Lantz)	8	16	24	58	97	135
217-Bugs Bunny in Court Jester	12	24	36	82	146	210
218-Three Little Pigs and the Wonderful Magic Lamp (Disney) (3/49)(#1)	10	20	30	71	126	180
219-Swee'pe	8	16	24	56	93	130
220-Easter with Mother Goose by Walt Kelly	13	26	39	93	164	235
221-Uncle Wiggily-Walt Kelly cover in part	9	18	27	63	107	150
222-West of the Pecos (Zane Grey)	7	14	21	47	76	105
223-Donald Duck "Lost in the Andes" by Carl Barks (Disney-4/49) (square egg story)	73	146	219	621	1186	1750
224-Little Iodine (#1), by Hatlo (4/49)	12	24	36	82	146	210
225-Oswald the Rabbit (Lantz)	7	14	21	45	73	100
226-Porky Pig and Spoofy, the Spook	10	20	30	68	119	170
227-Seven Dwarfs (Disney)	9	18	27	65	113	160
228-Mark of Zorro, The (#1) (1949)	20	40	60	143	264	385
229-Smokey Stover	6	12	18	41	66	90
230-Sunset Pass (Zane Grey)	7	14	21	47	76	105
231-Mickey Mouse and the Rajah's Treasure (Disney)	14	28	42	102	181	260
232-Woody Woodpecker (Lantz, 6/49)	8	16	24	58	97	135
233-Bugs Bunny, Sleepwalking Sleuth	12	24	36	82	146	210
234-Dumbo in Sky Voyage (Disney)	14	28	42	99	175	250
235-Tiny Tim	6	12	18	37	59	80
236-Heritage of the Desert (Zane Grey) (1949)	7	14	21	47	76	105
237-Tillie the Toiler	7	14	21	50	83	115
238 Donald Duck in Voodoo Hoodoo, by Carl Barks (Disney) (8/49)	55	110	165	468	897	1325
239-Adventure Bound (8/49)	6	12	18	39	62	85
240-Andy Panda (Lantz)	8	16	24	58	97	135
241-Porky Pig, Mighty Hunter	10	20	30	68	119	170
242-Tippie and Cap Stubbs	4	8	12	26	41	55
243-Thumper Follows His Nose (Disney)	11	22	33	79	140	200
244-The Brownies by Walt Kelly	10	20	30	68	119	170
245-Dick's Adventures (9/49)	6	12	18	41	66	90
246-Thunder Mountain (Zane Grey)	5	10	15	32	51	70
247-Flash Gordon	15	30	45	105	190	275
248-Mickey Mouse and the Black Sorcerer (Disney)	14	28	42	102	181	260
249-Woody Woodpecker in the "Globetrotter" (10/49)	8	16	24	58	97	135
250-Bugs Bunny in Diamond Daze; used in **SOTI**, pg. 309	12	24	36	86	153	220
251-Hubert at Camp Moonbeam	6	12	18	41	66	90
252-Pinocchio (Disney)-not by Kelly; origin	10	20	30	73	129	185
253-Christmas with Mother Goose by W. Kelly	11	22	33	79	140	200
254-Santa Claus Funnies by Walt Kelly; Pogo & Albert story by Kelly (11/49)	13	26	39	93	164	235
255-The Ranger (Zane Grey) (1949)	5	10	15	32	51	70
256-Donald Duck in "Luck of the North" by Carl Barks (Disney) (12/49)-Shows #257 on inside	48	96	144	384	717	1050
257-Little Iodine	8	16	24	56	93	130
258-Andy Panda and the Balloon Race (Lantz)	8	16	24	58	97	135
259-Santa and the Angel (Gollub art-condensed from #128) & Santa at the Zoo (12/49) -two books in one	5	10	15	35	55	75
260-Porky Pig, Hero of the Wild West (12/49)	10	20	30	68	119	170
261-Mickey Mouse and the Missing Key (Disney)	14	28	42	102	181	260
262-Raggedy Ann and Andy	10	20	30	67	116	165
263-Donald Duck in "Land of the Totem Poles" by Carl Barks (Disney) (2/50)-Has two Barks stories	47	94	141	376	701	1025
264-Woody Woodpecker in the Magic Lantern (Lantz)	8	16	24	58	97	135
265-King of the Royal Mounted (Zane Grey)	8	16	24	58	97	135
266-Bugs Bunny on the "Isle of Hercules" (2/50)-Reprinted in Best of Bugs Bunny #1	9	18	27	65	113	160
267-Little Beaver; Harmon-c/a	5	10	15	34	55	75
268-Mickey Mouse's Surprise Visitor (1950)(Disney)	13	26	39	95	168	240
269-Johnny Mack Brown (#1)-Photo-c	22	44	66	157	291	425
270-Drift Fence (Zane Grey) (3/50)	5	10	15	32	51	70
271-Porky Pig in Phantom of the Plains	10	20	30	68	119	170
272-Cinderella (Disney) (4/50)	12	24	36	87	156	225
273-Oswald the Rabbit (Lantz)	7	14	21	45	73	100
274-Bugs Bunny, Hare-brained Reporter	9	18	27	65	113	160
275-Donald Duck in "Ancient Persia" by Carl Barks (Disney) (5/50)	45	90	135	360	680	1000
276-Uncle Wiggily	8	16	24	52	86	120
277-Porky Pig in Desert Adventure (5/50)	10	20	30	68	119	170
278-(Wild) Bill Elliott Comics (#1)-Photo-c	13	26	39	90	160	230
279-Mickey Mouse and Pluto Battle the Giant Ants (Disney); reprinted in Mickey Mouse #102 & 245	10	20	30	71	126	180
280-Andy Panda in The Isle Of Mechanical Men (Lantz)	8	16	24	58	97	135
281-Bugs Bunny in The Great Circus Mystery	9	18	27	65	113	160
282-Donald Duck and the Pixilated Parrot by Carl Barks (Disney) (© 5/23/50)	45	90	135	360	680	1000
283-King of the Royal Mounted (7/50)	8	16	24	58	97	135
284-Porky Pig in The Kingdom of Nowhere	10	20	30	68	119	170
285 Bozo the Clown & His Minikin Circus (#1) (TV)	18	36	54	130	240	350
286-Mickey Mouse in The Uninvited Guest (Disney	10	20	30	71	126	180
287-Gene Autry's Champion in The Ghost Of Black Mountain; photo-c	12	24	36	82	146	210
288-Woody Woodpecker in Klondike Gold (Lantz)	8	16	24	58	97	135
289-Bugs Bunny in "Indian Trouble"	9	18	27	65	113	160
290-The Chief (#1) (8/50)	7	14	21	49	80	110
291-Donald Duck in "The Magic Hourglass" by Carl Barks (Disney) (9/50)	45	90	135	360	680	1000
292-The Cisco Kid Comics (#1)	22	44	66	157	291	425
293-The Brownies-Kelly-c/a	10	20	30	68	119	170
294-Little Beaver	5	10	15	34	55	75
295-Porky Pig in President Porky (9/50)	10	20	30	68	119	170
296-Mickey Mouse in Private Eye for Hire (Disney)	10	20	30	71	126	180
297-Andy Panda In The Haunted Inn (Lantz, 10/50)	8	16	24	58	97	135
298-Bugs Bunny in Sheik for a Day	9	18	27	65	113	160
299-Buck Jones & the Iron Horse Trail (#1)	13	26	39	93	164	235
300-Donald Duck in "Big-Top Bedlam" by Carl Barks (Disney) (11/50)	45	90	135	360	680	1000
301-The Mysterious Rider (Zane Grey)	5	10	15	32	51	70
302-Santa Claus Funnies (11/50)	7	14	21	45	73	100
303-Porky Pig in The Land of the Monstrous Flies	8	16	24	52	86	120
304-Mickey Mouse in Tom-Tom Island (Disney) (12/50)	9	18	27	64	110	155
305-Woody Woodpecker (Lantz)	6	12	18	41	66	90
306-Raggedy Ann	7	14	21	50	83	115
307-Bugs Bunny in Lumber Jack Rabbit	9	18	27	60	100	140
308-Donald Duck in "Dangerous Disguise" by Carl Barks (Disney) (1/51)	43	86	129	344	642	940
309-Betty Betz' Dollface and Her Gang (1951)	5	10	15	35	55	75
310-King of the Royal Mounted (1/51)	6	12	18	43	69	95
311-Porky Pig in Midget Horses of Hidden Valley	8	16	24	52	86	120
312-Tonto (#1)	11	22	33	75	133	190
313-Mickey Mouse in The Mystery of the Double-Cross Ranch (#1) (Disney) (2/51)	9	18	27	64	110	155

Note: Beginning with the above comic in 1951 Dell/Western began adding #1 in small print on the covers of several long running titles with the evident intention of switching these titles to

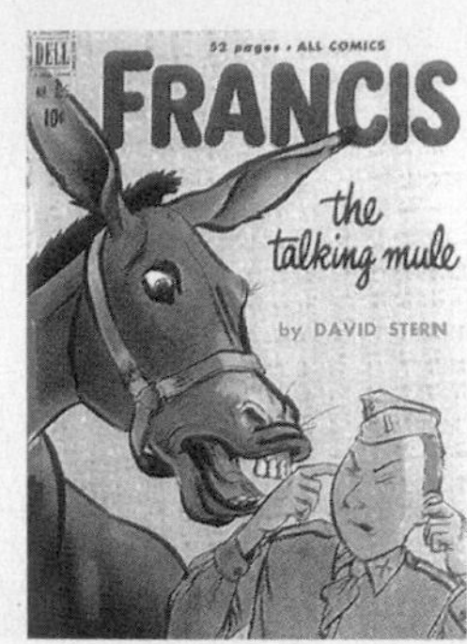

Four Color Comics #335 © David Stern

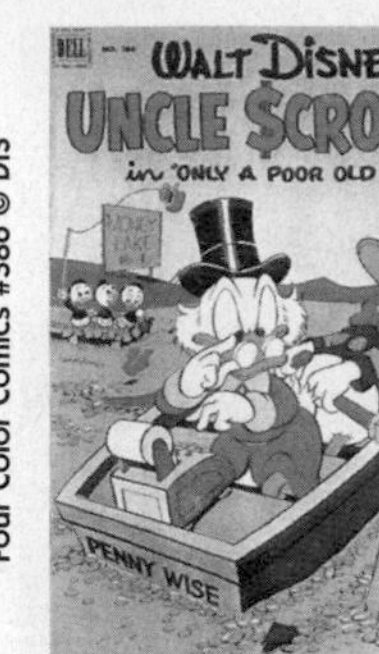

Four Color Comics #386 © DIS

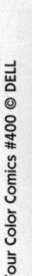

Four Color Comics #400 © DELL

their own monthly numbers, but when the conversions were made, there was no connection. It is thought that the post office may have stepped in and decreed the sequences should commence as though the first four colors printed had each begun with number one, or the first issues sold by subscription. Since the regular series' numbers don't correctly match to the numbers of earlier issues published, it's not known whether or not the numbering was in error.

	GD 2.0	VG 4.0	FN 6.0	VF 8.0	VF/NM 9.0	NM- 9.2
314-Ambush (Zane Grey)	5	10	15	32	51	70
315-Oswald the Rabbit (Lantz)	6	12	18	39	62	85
316-Rex Allen (#1)-Photo-c; Marsh-a	14	28	42	102	181	260
317-Bugs Bunny in Hair Today Gone Tomorrow (#1)	9	18	27	60	100	140
318-Donald Duck in "No Such Varmint" by Carl Barks (#1)-Indicia shows #317 (Disney, © 1/23/51)	43	86	129	344	642	940
319-Gene Autry's Champion; painted-c	7	14	21	45	73	100
320-Uncle Wiggily (#1)	8	16	24	52	86	120
321-Little Scouts (#1) (3/51)	5	10	15	30	48	65
322-Porky Pig in Roaring Rockets (#1 on-c)	8	16	24	52	86	120
323-Susie Q. Smith (#1) (3/51)	5	10	15	32	51	70
324-I Met a Handsome Cowboy (3/51)	8	16	24	56	93	130
325-Mickey Mouse in The Haunted Castle (#2) (Disney) (4/51)	9	18	27	64	110	155
326-Andy Panda (#1) (Lantz)	6	12	18	43	69	95
327-Bugs Bunny and the Rajah's Treasure (#2)	9	18	27	60	100	140
328-Donald Duck in Old California (#2) by Carl Barks-Peyote drug use issue (Disney) (5/51)	42	84	126	336	631	925
329-Roy Roger's Trigger (#1)(5/51)-Painted-c	14	28	42	103	184	265
330-Porky Pig Meets the Bristled Bruiser (#2)	8	16	24	52	86	120
331-Alice in Wonderland (Disney) (1951)	15	30	45	105	190	275
332-Little Beaver	5	10	15	34	55	75
333-Wilderness Trek (Zane Grey) (5/51)	5	10	15	32	51	70
334-Mickey Mouse and Yukon Gold (Disney) (6/51)	9	18	27	64	110	155
335-Francis the Famous Talking Mule (#1, 6/51)-1st Dell non animated movie comic (all issues based on movie)	10	20	30	71	126	180
336-Woody Woodpecker (Lantz)	6	12	18	41	66	90
337-The Brownies-not by Walt Kelly	6	12	18	37	59	80
338-Bugs Bunny and the Rocking Horse Thieves	9	18	27	60	100	140
339-Donald Duck and the Magic Fountain-not by Carl Barks (Disney) (7-8/51)	12	24	36	87	156	225
340-King of the Royal Mounted (7/51)	6	12	18	43	69	95
341-Unbirthday Party with Alice in Wonderland (Disney) (7/51)	15	30	45	105	190	275
342-Porky Pig the Lucky Peppermint Mine; r/in Porky Pig #3	6	12	18	41	66	90
343-Mickey Mouse in The Ruby Eye of Homar-Guy-Am (Disney)-Reprinted in Mickey Mouse #104	8	16	24	54	90	125
344-Sergeant Preston from Challenge of The Yukon (#1) (TV)	12	24	36	82	146	210
345-Andy Panda in Scotland Yard (8-10/51) (Lantz)	6	12	18	43	69	95
346-Hideout (Zane Grey)	5	10	15	32	51	70
347-Bugs Bunny the Frigid Hare (8-9/51)	9	18	27	60	100	140
348-Donald Duck "The Crocodile Collector"; Barks-c only (Disney) (9-10/51)	20	40	60	148	274	400
349-Uncle Wiggily	6	12	18	43	69	95
350-Woody Woodpecker (Lantz)	6	12	18	41	66	90
351-Porky Pig & the Grand Canyon Giant (9-10/51)	6	12	18	41	66	90
352-Mickey Mouse in The Mystery of Painted Valley (Disney)	8	16	24	54	90	125
353-Duck Album (#1)-Barks-c (Disney)	10	20	30	70	123	175
354-Raggedy Ann & Andy	7	14	21	50	83	115
355-Bugs Bunny Hot-Rod Hare	9	18	27	60	100	140
356-Donald Duck in "Rags to Riches"; Barks-c only	20	40	60	148	274	400
357-Comeback (Zane Grey)	4	8	12	28	44	60
358-Andy Panda (Lantz) (11-1/52)	6	12	18	43	69	95
359-Frosty the Snowman (#1)	9	18	27	63	107	150
360-Porky Pig in Tree of Fortune (11-12/51)	6	12	18	41	66	90
361-Santa Claus Funnies	7	14	21	45	73	100
362-Mickey Mouse and the Smuggled Diamonds (Disney)	8	16	24	54	90	125
363-King of the Royal Mounted	6	12	18	39	62	85
364-Woody Woodpecker (Lantz)	5	10	15	34	55	75
365-The Brownies-not by Kelly	6	12	18	37	59	80
366-Bugs Bunny Uncle Buckskin Comes to Town (12-1/52)	9	18	27	60	100	140
367-Donald Duck in "A Christmas for Shacktown" by Carl Barks (Disney) (1-2/52)	33	66	99	254	477	700
368-Bob Clampett's Beany and Cecil (#1)	24	48	72	172	319	465

	GD 2.0	VG 4.0	FN 6.0	VF 8.0	VF/NM 9.0	NM- 9.2
369-The Lone Ranger's Famous Horse Hi-Yo Silver (#1); Silver's origin	10	20	30	71	126	180
370-Porky Pig in Trouble in the Big Trees	6	12	18	41	66	90
371-Mickey Mouse in The Inca Idol Case (1952) (Disney)	8	16	24	54	90	125
372-Riders of the Purple Sage (Zane Grey)	4	8	12	28	44	60
373-Sergeant Preston (TV)	8	16	24	52	86	120
374-Woody Woodpecker (Lantz)	5	10	15	34	55	75
375-John Carter of Mars (E. R. Burroughs)-Jesse Marsh-a; origin	25	50	75	185	343	500
376-Bugs Bunny, "The Magic Sneeze"	9	18	27	60	100	140
377-Susie Q. Smith	4	8	12	26	41	55
378-Tom Corbett, Space Cadet (#1) (TV)-McWilliams-a	16	32	48	114	212	310
379-Donald Duck in "Southern Hospitality"; Not by Barks (Disney)	12	24	36	87	156	225
380-Raggedy Ann & Andy	7	14	21	50	83	115
381-Marge's Tubby (#1)	20	40	60	143	264	385
382-Snow White and the Seven Dwarfs (Disney)-origin; partial reprint of Four Color #49 (Movie)	9	18	27	65	113	160
383-Andy Panda (Lantz)	5	10	15	34	55	75
384-King of the Royal Mounted (3/52)(Zane Grey)	6	12	18	39	62	85
385-Porky Pig in The Isle of Missing Ships (3-4/52)	6	12	18	41	66	90
386-Uncle Scrooge (#1)-by Carl Barks (Disney) in "Only a Poor Old Man" (3/52)	168	336	504	1470	2835	4200
387-Mickey Mouse in High Tibet (Disney) (4-5/52)	8	16	24	54	90	125
388-Oswald the Rabbit (Lantz)	6	12	18	39	62	85
389-Andy Hardy Comics (#1)	5	10	15	34	55	75
390-Woody Woodpecker (Lantz)	5	10	15	34	55	75
391-Uncle Wiggily	6	12	18	43	69	95
392-Hi-Yo Silver	6	12	18	41	66	90
393-Bugs Bunny	9	18	27	60	100	140
394-Donald Duck in Malayalaya-Barks-c only (Disney)	20	40	60	148	274	400
395-Forlorn River(Zane Grey)-First Nevada (5/52)	4	8	12	28	44	60
396-Tales of the Texas Rangers(#1)(TV)-Photo-c	10	20	30	73	129	185
397-Sergeant Preston of the Yukon (TV) (5/52)	8	16	24	52	86	120
398-The Brownies-not by Kelly	6	12	18	37	59	80
399-Porky Pig in The Lost Gold Mine	6	12	18	41	66	90
400-Tom Corbett, Space Cadet (TV)-McWilliams-c/a	10	20	30	68	119	170
401-Mickey Mouse and Goofy's Mechanical Wizard (Disney) (6-7/52)	6	12	18	43	69	95
402-Mary Jane and Sniffles	7	14	21	50	83	115
403-Li'l Bad Wolf (Disney) (6/52)(#1)	7	14	21	47	76	105
404-The Range Rider (#1) (Flying A's...)(TV)-Photo-c	10	20	30	71	126	180
405-Woody Woodpecker (Lantz) (6-7/52)	5	10	15	34	55	75
406-Tweety and Sylvester (#1)	10	20	30	71	126	180
407-Bugs Bunny, Foreign-Legion Hare	7	14	21	50	83	115
408-Donald Duck and the Golden Helmet by Carl Barks (Disney) (7-8/52)	33	66	99	254	477	700
409-Andy Panda (7-9/52)	5	10	15	34	55	75
410-Porky Pig in The Water Wizard (7/52)	6	12	18	41	66	90
411-Mickey Mouse and the Old Sea Dog (Disney) (8-9/52)	6	12	18	43	69	95
412-Nevada (Zane Grey)	4	8	12	28	44	60
413-Robin Hood (Disney-Movie) (8/52)-Photo-c (1st Disney movie Four Color book)	9	18	27	65	113	160
414-Bob Clampett's Beany and Cecil (TV)	15	30	45	105	190	275
415-Rootie Kazootie (#1) (TV)	9	18	27	65	113	160
416-Woody Woodpecker (Lantz)	5	10	15	34	55	75
417-Double Trouble with Goober (#1) (8/52)	4	8	12	28	44	60
418-Rusty Riley, a Boy, a Horse, and a Dog (#1)-Frank Godwin-a (strip reprints) (8/52)	5	10	15	32	51	70
419-Sergeant Preston (TV)	8	16	24	52	86	120
420-Bugs Bunny in The Mysterious Buckaroo (8-9/52)	7	14	21	50	83	115
421-Tom Corbett, Space Cadet(TV)-McWilliams-a	10	20	30	68	119	170
422-Donald Duck and the Gilded Man, by Carl Barks (Disney) (9-10/52) (#423 on inside)	33	66	99	254	477	700
423-Rhubarb, Owner of the Brooklyn Ball Club (The Millionaire Cat) (#1)-Painted cover	6	12	18	39	62	85
424-Flash Gordon-Test Flight in Space (9/52)	11	22	33	77	136	195
425-Zorro, the Return of	12	24	36	82	146	210
426-Porky Pig in The Scalawag Leprechaun	6	12	18	41	66	90
427-Mickey Mouse and the Wonderful Whizzix (Disney) (10-11/52)-Reprinted						

Four Color Comics #481 © Annie Oakley

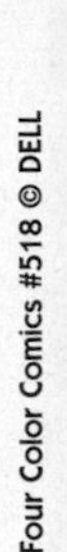
Four Color Comics #518 © DELL

Four Color Comics #530 © Bob Clampett

	GD 2.0	VG 4.0	FN 6.0	VF 8.0	VF/NM 9.0	NM- 9.2
in Mickey Mouse #100	6	12	18	43	69	95
428-Uncle Wiggily	5	10	15	34	55	75
429-Pluto in "Why Dogs Leave Home" (Disney) (10/52)(#1)	9	18	27	64	110	155
430-Marge's Tubby, the Shadow of a Man-Eater	12	24	36	84	150	215
431-Woody Woodpecker (10/52) (Lantz)	5	10	15	34	55	75
432-Bugs Bunny and the Rabbit Olympics	7	14	21	50	83	115
433-Wildfire (Zane Grey) (11-1/52-53)	4	8	12	28	44	60
434-Rin Tin Tin "In Dark Danger" (#1) (TV) (11/52)-Photo-c	14	28	42	102	181	260
435-Frosty the Snowman (11/52)	6	12	18	37	59	80
436-The Brownies-not by Kelly (11/52)	5	10	15	34	55	75
437-John Carter of Mars (E.R. Burroughs)-Marsh-a	15	30	45	111	206	300
438-Annie Oakley (#1) (TV)	14	28	42	103	184	265
439-Little Hiawatha (Disney) (12/52)j(#1)	6	12	18	39	62	85
440-Black Beauty (12/52)	5	10	15	30	48	65
441-Fearless Fagan	4	8	12	24	37	50
442-Peter Pan (Disney) (Movie)	10	20	30	70	123	175
443-Ben Bowie and His Mountain Men (#1)	8	16	24	56	93	130
444-Marge's Tubby	12	24	36	84	150	215
445-Charlie McCarthy	6	12	18	39	62	85
446-Captain Hook and Peter Pan (Disney)(Movie)(1/53)	9	18	27	60	100	140
447-Andy Hardy Comics	4	8	12	26	41	55
448-Bob Clampett's Beany and Cecil (TV)	15	30	45	105	190	275
449-Tappan's Burro (Zane Grey) (2-4/53)	4	8	12	28	44	60
450-Duck Album; Barks-c (Disney)	10	20	30	70	123	175
451-Rusty Riley-Frank Godwin-a (strip-r) (2/53)	4	8	12	26	41	50
452-Raggedy Ann & Andy (1953)	7	14	21	50	83	115
453-Susie Q. Smith (2/53)	4	8	12	26	41	55
454-Krazy Kat Comics; not by Herriman	5	10	15	32	51	70
455-Johnny Mack Brown Comics(3/53)-Photo-c	7	14	21	47	76	105
456-Uncle Scrooge Back to the Klondike (#2) by Barks (3/53) (Disney)	88	176	264	748	1424	2100
457-Daffy (#1)	10	20	30	71	126	180
458-Oswald the Rabbit (Lantz)	5	10	15	32	51	70
459-Rootie Kazootie (TV)	7	14	21	47	76	105
460-Buck Jones (4/53)	6	12	18	41	66	90
461-Marge's Tubby	10	20	30	73	129	185
462-Little Scouts	4	8	12	24	37	50
463-Petunia (4/53)	4	8	12	28	44	60
464-Bozo (4/53)	9	18	27	65	113	160
465-Francis the Famous Talking Mule	6	12	18	41	66	90
466-Rhubarb, the Millionaire Cat; painted-c	5	10	15	34	55	75
467-Desert Gold (Zane Grey) (5-7/53)	4	8	12	28	44	60
468-Goofy (#1) (Disney)	12	24	36	82	146	210
469-Beetle Bailey (#1) (5/53	11	22	33	75	133	190
470-Elmer Fudd	8	16	24	52	86	120
471-Double Trouble with Goober	4	8	12	22	34	45
472-Wild Bill Elliott (6/53)-Photo-c	5	10	15	34	55	75
473-Li'l Bad Wolf (Disney) (6/53)(#2)	5	10	15	32	51	70
474-Mary Jane and Sniffles	7	14	21	47	76	105
475-M.G.M.'s The Two Mouseketeers (#1)	8	16	24	52	86	120
476-Rin Tin Tin (TV)-Photo-c	8	16	24	56	93	130
477-Bob Clampett's Beany and Cecil (TV)	15	30	45	105	190	275
478-Charlie McCarthy	6	12	18	39	62	85
479-Queen of the West Dale Evans (#1)-Photo-c	19	38	57	135	250	365
480-Andy Hardy Comics	4	8	12	26	41	55
481-Annie Oakley And Tagg (TV)	9	18	27	64	110	155
482-Brownies-not by Kelly	5	10	15	34	55	75
483-Little Beaver (7/53)	5	10	15	30	48	65
484-River Feud (Zane Grey) (8-10/53)	4	8	12	28	44	60
485-The Little People-Walt Scott (#1)	8	16	24	52	86	120
486-Rusty Riley-Frank Godwin strip-r	4	8	12	26	41	50
487-Mowgli, the Jungle Book (Rudyard Kipling's)	6	12	18	37	59	80
488-John Carter of Mars (Burroughs)-Marsh-a; painted-c	15	30	45	111	206	300
489-Tweety and Sylvester	6	12	18	41	66	90
490-Jungle Jim (#1)	7	14	21	49	80	110
491-Silvertip (#1) (Max Brand)-Kinstler-a (8/53)	8	16	24	52	86	120
492-Duck Album (Disney)	6	12	18	41	66	90
493-Johnny Mack Brown; photo-c	7	14	21	47	76	105
494-The Little King (#1)	9	18	27	60	100	140
495-Uncle Scrooge (#3) (Disney)-by Carl Barks (9/53)	58	116	174	493	947	1400
496-The Green Hornet; painted-c	23	46	69	167	309	450
497-Zorro (Sword of…)-Kinstler-a	12	24	36	87	156	225
498-Bugs Bunny's Album (9/53)	6	12	18	39	62	85
499-M.G.M.'s Spike and Tyke (#1) (9/53)	6	12	18	43	69	95
500-Buck Jones	6	12	18	41	66	90
501-Francis the Famous Talking Mule	5	10	15	32	51	70
502-Rootie Kazootie (TV)	7	14	21	47	76	105
503-Uncle Wiggily (10/53)	5	10	15	34	55	75
504-Krazy Kat; not by Herriman	5	10	15	32	51	70
505-The Sword and the Rose (Disney) (10/53)(Movie)-Photo-c	8	16	24	56	93	130
506-The Little Scouts	4	8	12	24	37	50
507-Oswald the Rabbit (Lantz)	5	10	15	32	51	70
508-Bozo (10/53)	9	18	27	65	113	160
509-Pluto (Disney) (10/53)	6	12	18	41	66	90
510-Son of Black Beauty	4	8	12	26	41	55
511-Outlaw Trail (Zane Grey)-Kinstler-a	5	10	15	32	51	70
512-Flash Gordon (11/53)	8	16	24	58	97	135
513-Ben Bowie and His Mountain Men	5	10	15	30	48	65
514-Frosty the Snowman (11/53)	6	12	18	37	59	80
515-Andy Hardy	4	8	12	26	41	55
516-Double Trouble With Goober	4	8	12	22	34	45
517-Chip 'N' Dale (#1) (Disney)	10	20	30	73	129	185
518-Rivets (11/53)	4	8	12	24	37	50
519-Steve Canyon (#1)-Not by Milton Caniff	8	16	24	56	93	130
520-Wild Bill Elliott-Photo-c	5	10	15	34	55	75
521-Beetle Bailey (12/53)	6	12	18	43	69	95
522-The Brownies	5	10	15	34	55	75
523-Rin Tin Tin (TV)-Photo-c (12/53)	8	16	24	56	93	130
524-Tweety and Sylvester	6	12	18	41	66	90
525-Santa Claus Funnies	7	14	21	45	73	100
526-Napoleon	4	8	12	24	37	50
527-Charlie McCarthy	6	12	18	39	62	85
528-Queen of the West Dale Evans; photo-c	10	20	30	70	123	175
529-Little Beaver	5	10	15	30	48	65
530-Bob Clampett's Beany and Cecil (TV) (1/54)	15	30	45	105	190	275
531-Duck Album (Disney)	6	12	18	41	66	90
532-The Rustlers (Zane Grey) (2-4/54)	4	8	12	28	44	60
533-Raggedy Ann and Andy	7	14	21	50	83	115
534-Western Marshal(Ernest Haycox's)-Kinstler-a	6	12	18	39	62	85
535-I Love Lucy (#1) (TV) (2/54)-Photo-c	44	88	132	352	664	975
536-Daffy (3/54)	6	12	18	41	66	90
537-Stormy, the Thoroughbred… (Disney-Movie) on top 2/3 of each page; Pluto story on bottom 1/3 of each page (2/54)	5	10	15	30	48	65
538-The Mask of Zorro; Kinstler-a	12	24	36	87	156	225
539-Ben and Me (Disney) (3/54)	4	8	12	26	41	55
540-Knights of the Round Table (3/54) (Movie)-Photo-c	7	14	21	47	76	105
541-Johnny Mack Brown; photo-c	7	14	21	47	76	105
542-Super Circus Featuring Mary Hartline (TV) (3/54)	7	14	21	47	76	105
543-Uncle Wiggily (3/54)	5	10	15	34	55	75
544-Rob Roy (Disney-Movie)-Manning-a; photo-c	7	14	21	50	83	115
545-The Wonderful Adventures of Pinocchio-Partial reprint of Four Color #92 (Disney-Movie)	7	14	21	47	76	105
546-Buck Jones	6	12	18	41	66	90
547-Francis the Famous Talking Mule	5	10	15	32	51	70
548-Krazy Kat; not by Herriman (4/54)	5	10	15	30	48	65
549-Oswald the Rabbit (Lantz)	5	10	15	32	51	70
550-The Little Scouts	4	8	12	24	37	50
551-Bozo (4/54)	9	18	27	65	113	160
552-Beetle Bailey	6	12	18	43	69	95
553-Susie Q. Smith	4	8	12	26	41	55
554-Rusty Riley (Frank Godwin strip-r)	4	8	12	26	41	50
555-Range War (Zane Grey)	4	8	12	28	44	60
556-Double Trouble With Goober (5/54)	4	8	12	22	34	45
557-Ben Bowie and His Mountain Men	5	10	15	30	48	65
558-Elmer Fudd (5/54)	5	10	15	30	48	65
559-I Love Lucy (#2) (TV)-Photo-c	29	58	87	213	394	575
560-Duck Album (Disney) (5/54)	6	12	18	41	66	90
561-Mr. Magoo (5/54)	10	20	30	68	119	170
562-Goofy (Disney)(#2)	7	14	21	47	76	105
563-Rhubarb, the Millionaire Cat (6/54)	5	10	15	34	55	75

Four Color Comics #581 © DIS

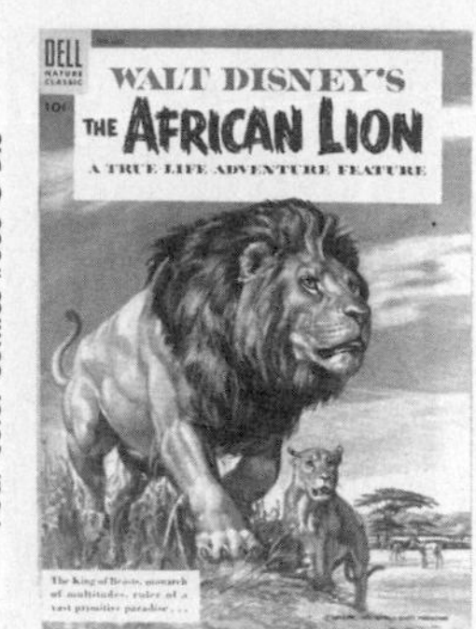

Four Color Comics #665 © DIS

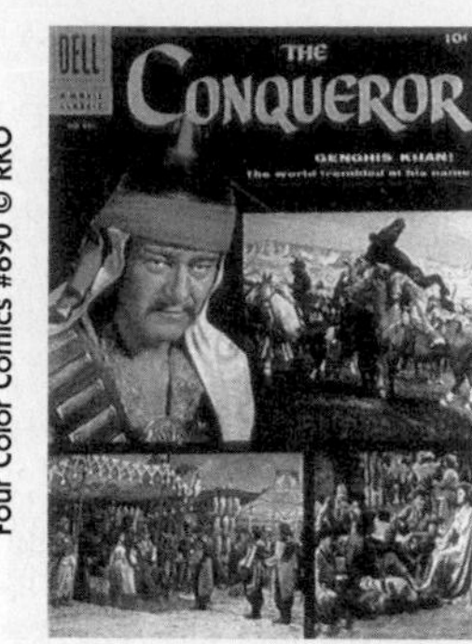

Four Color Comics #690 © RKO

	GD 2.0	VG 4.0	FN 6.0	VF 8.0	VF/NM 9.0	NM- 9.2
564-Li'l Bad Wolf (Disney)(#3)	5	10	15	32	51	70
565-Jungle Jim	5	10	15	30	48	65
566-Son of Black Beauty	4	8	12	26	41	55
567-Prince Valiant (#1)-By Bob Fuje (Movie)-Photo-c	10	20	30	73	129	185
568-Gypsy Colt (Movie) (6/54)	5	10	15	32	51	70
569-Priscilla's Pop	4	8	12	26	41	55
570-Bob Clampett's Beany and Cecil (TV)	15	30	45	105	190	275
571-Charlie McCarthy	6	12	18	39	62	85
572-Silvertip (Max Brand) (7/54); Kinstler-a	5	10	15	30	48	65
573-The Little People by Walt Scott	5	10	15	32	51	70
574-The Hand of Zorro; Kinstler-a	12	24	36	87	156	225
575-Annie Oakley and Tagg (TV)-Photo-c	9	18	27	64	110	155
576-Angel (#1) (8/54)	4	8	12	26	41	55
577-M.G.M.'s Spike and Tyke	4	8	12	28	44	60
578-Steve Canyon (8/54)	5	10	15	34	55	75
579-Francis the Famous Talking Mule	5	10	15	32	51	70
580-Six Gun Ranch (Luke Short-8/54)	4	8	12	28	44	60
581-Chip 'N' Dale (#2) (Disney)	6	12	18	43	69	95
582-Mowgli Jungle Book (Kipling) (8/54)	5	10	15	30	48	65
583-The Lost Wagon Train (Zane Grey)	4	8	12	28	44	60
584-Johnny Mack Brown-Photo-c	7	14	21	47	76	105
585-Bugs Bunny's Album	6	12	18	39	62	85
586-Duck Album (Disney)	6	12	18	41	66	90
587-The Little Scouts	4	8	12	24	37	50
588-King Richard and the Crusaders (Movie) (10/54) Matt Baker-a; photo-c	9	18	27	63	107	150
589-Buck Jones	6	12	18	41	66	90
590-Hansel and Gretel; partial photo-c	6	12	18	43	69	95
591-Western Marshal(Ernest Haycox's)-Kinstler-a	5	10	15	34	55	75
592-Super Circus (TV)	6	12	18	43	69	95
593-Oswald the Rabbit (Lantz)	5	10	15	32	51	70
594-Bozo (10/54)	9	18	27	65	113	160
595-Pluto (Disney)	5	10	15	32	51	70
596-Turok, Son of Stone (#1)	50	100	150	425	813	1200
597-The Little King	5	10	15	34	55	75
598-Captain Davy Jones	5	10	15	30	48	65
599-Ben Bowie and His Mountain Men	5	10	15	30	48	65
600-Daisy Duck's Diary (#1) (Disney) (11/54)	7	14	21	47	76	105
601-Frosty the Snowman	6	12	18	37	59	80
602-Mr. Magoo and Gerald McBoing-Boing	10	20	30	68	119	170
603-M.G.M.'s The Two Mouseketeers	6	12	18	37	59	80
604-Shadow on the Trail (Zane Grey)	4	8	12	28	44	60
605-The Brownies-not by Kelly (12/54)	5	10	15	34	55	75
606-Sir Lancelot (not TV)	7	14	21	49	80	110
607-Santa Claus Funnies	7	14	21	45	73	100
608-Silvertip- "Valley of Vanishing Men" (Max Brand)-Kinstler-a	5	10	15	30	48	65
609-The Littlest Outlaw (Disney-Movie) (1/55)-Photo-c	6	12	18	43	69	95
610-Drum Beat (Movie); Alan Ladd photo-c	8	16	24	56	93	130
611-Duck Album (Disney)	6	12	18	41	66	90
612-Little Beaver (1/55)	5	10	15	30	48	65
613-Western Marshal (Ernest Haycox's) (2/55)-Kinstler-a	5	10	15	34	55	75
614-20,000 Leagues Under the Sea (Disney) (Movie) (2/55)-Painted-c	8	16	24	58	97	135
615-Daffy	6	12	18	41	66	90
616-To the Last Man (Zane Grey)	4	8	12	28	44	60
617-The Quest of Zorro	12	24	36	82	146	210
618-Johnny Mack Brown; photo-c	7	14	21	47	76	105
619-Krazy Kat; not by Herriman	5	10	15	30	48	65
620-Mowgli Jungle Book (Kipling)	5	10	15	30	48	65
621-Francis the Famous Talking Mule (4/55)	4	8	12	28	44	60
622-Beetle Bailey	6	12	18	43	69	95
623-Oswald the Rabbit (Lantz)	4	8	12	28	44	60
624-Treasure Island(Disney-Movie)(4/55)-Photo-c	8	16	24	54	90	125
625-Beaver Valley (Disney-Movie)	6	12	18	41	66	90
626-Ben Bowie and His Mountain Men	5	10	15	30	48	65
627-Goofy (Disney) (5/55)	7	14	21	47	76	105
628-Elmer Fudd	5	10	15	30	48	65
629-Lady and the Tramp with Jock (Disney)	7	14	21	47	76	105
630-Priscilla's Pop	4	8	12	26	41	55
631-Davy Crockett, Indian Fighter (#1) (Disney) (5/55) (TV)-Fess Parker photo-c	17	34	51	120	223	325

	GD 2.0	VG 4.0	FN 6.0	VF 8.0	VF/NM 9.0	NM- 9.2
632-Fighting Caravans (Zane Grey)	4	8	12	28	44	60
633-The Little People by Walt Scott (6/55)	5	10	15	32	51	70
634-Lady and the Tramp Album (Disney) (6/55)	5	10	15	32	51	70
635-Bob Clampett's Beany and Cecil (TV)	15	30	45	105	190	275
636-Chip 'N' Dale (Disney)	6	12	18	43	69	95
637-Silvertip (Max Brand)-Kinstler-a	5	10	15	30	48	65
638-M.G.M.'s Spike and Tyke (8/55)	4	8	12	28	44	60
639-Davy Crockett at the Alamo (Disney) (7/55) (TV)-Fess Parker photo-c	14	28	42	102	181	260
640-Western Marshal(Ernest Haycox's)-Kinstler-a	5	10	15	34	55	75
641-Steve Canyon (1955)-by Caniff	5	10	15	34	55	75
642-M.G.M.'s The Two Mouseketeers	6	12	18	37	59	80
643-Wild Bill Elliott; photo-c	5	10	15	30	48	65
644-Sir Walter Raleigh (5/55)-Based on movie "The Virgin Queen"; photo-c	7	14	21	45	73	100
645-Johnny Mack Brown; photo-c	7	14	21	47	76	105
646-Dotty Dripple and Taffy (#1)	5	10	15	32	51	70
647-Bugs Bunny's Album (9/55)	6	12	18	39	62	85
648-Jace Pearson of the Texas Rangers (TV)-Photo-c	6	12	18	41	66	90
649-Duck Album (Disney)	6	12	18	41	66	90
650-Prince Valiant; by Bob Fuje	7	14	21	50	83	115
651-King Colt (Luke Short) (9/55)-Kinstler-a	4	8	12	28	44	60
652-Buck Jones	5	10	15	32	51	70
653-Smokey the Bear (#1) (10/55)	10	20	30	71	126	180
654-Pluto (Disney)	5	10	15	32	51	70
655-Francis the Famous Talking Mule	4	8	12	28	44	60
656-Turok, Son of Stone (#2) (10/55)	30	60	90	229	427	625
657-Ben Bowie and His Mountain Men	5	10	15	30	48	65
658-Goofy (Disney)	7	14	21	47	76	105
659-Daisy Duck's Diary (Disney)(#2)	6	12	18	37	59	80
660-Little Beaver	5	10	15	30	48	65
661-Frosty the Snowman	6	12	18	37	59	80
662-Zoo Parade (TV)-Marlin Perkins (11/55)	5	10	15	32	51	70
663-Winky Dink (TV)	8	16	24	52	86	120
664-Davy Crockett in the Great Keelboat Race (TV) (Disney) (11/55)-Fess Parker photo-c	13	26	39	97	171	245
665-The African Lion (Disney-Movie) (11/55)	6	12	18	37	59	80
666-Santa Claus Funnies	7	14	21	45	73	100
667-Silvertip and the Stolen Stallion (Max Brand) (12/55)-Kinstler-a	5	10	15	30	48	65
668-Dumbo (Disney) (12/55)-First of two printings. Dumbo on cover with starry sky. Reprints 4-Color #234?; same-c as #234	10	20	30	70	123	175
668-Dumbo (Disney) (1/58)-Second printing. Same cover altered, with Timothy Mouse added. Same contents as above	7	14	21	45	73	100
669-Robin Hood (Disney-Movie) (12/55)-Reprints #413 plus-c; photo-c	6	12	18	37	59	80
670-M.G.M's Mouse Musketeers (#1) (1/56)-Formerly the Two Mouseketeers	5	10	15	35	55	75
671-Davy Crockett and the River Pirates (TV) (Disney) (12/55)-Jesse Marsh-a; Fess Parker photo-c	13	26	39	97	171	245
672-Quentin Durward (1/56) (Movie)-Photo-c	7	14	21	45	73	100
673-Buffalo Bill, Jr. (#1) (TV)-James Arness photo-c	9	18	27	60	100	140
674-The Little Rascals (#1) (TV)	9	18	27	60	100	140
675-Steve Donovan, Western Marshal (#1) (TV)-Kinstler-a; photo-c	8	16	24	52	86	120
676-Will-Yum!	4	8	12	26	41	55
677-Little King	5	10	15	34	55	75
678-The Last Hunt (Movie)-Photo-c	7	14	21	50	83	115
679-Gunsmoke (#1) (TV)-Photo-c	16	32	48	114	212	310
680-Out Our Way with the Worry Wart (2/56)	4	8	12	24	37	50
681-Forever Darling (Movie) with Lucille Ball & Desi Arnaz (2/56)-; photo-c	11	22	33	79	140	200
682-The Sword & the Rose (Disney-Movie)-Reprint of #505; Renamed When Knighthood Was in Flower for the novel; photo-c	7	14	21	47	76	105
683-Hi and Lois (3/56)	5	10	15	30	48	65
684-Helen of Troy (Movie)-Buscema-a; photo-c	9	18	27	65	113	160
685-Johnny Mack Brown; photo-c	7	14	21	47	76	105
686-Duck Album (Disney)	6	12	18	41	66	90
687-The Indian Fighter (Movie)-Kirk Douglas photo-c	7	14	21	50	83	115
688-Alexander the Great (Movie) (5/56)-Buscema-a; photo-c	7	14	21	49	80	110
689-Elmer Fudd (3/56)	5	10	15	30	48	65

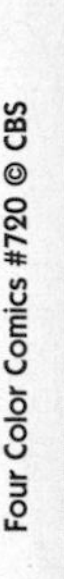
Four Color Comics #720 © CBS

Four Color Comics #777 © DIS

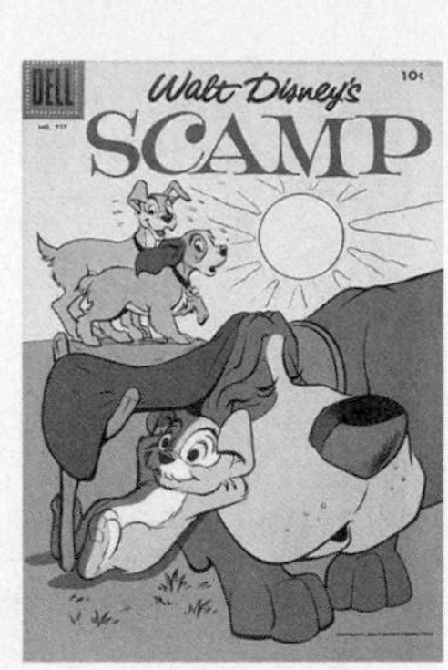

Four Color Comics #793 © DELL

	GD 2.0	VG 4.0	FN 6.0	VF 8.0	VF/NM 9.0	NM- 9.2
690-The Conqueror (Movie) - John Wayne photo-c	15	30	45	108	199	290
691-Dotty Dripple and Taffy	4	8	12	22	34	45
692-The Little People-Walt Scott	5	10	15	32	51	70
693-Song of the South (Disney) (1956)-Partial reprint of #129	8	16	24	56	93	130
694-Super Circus (TV)-Photo-c	6	12	18	43	69	95
695-Little Beaver	5	10	15	30	48	65
696-Krazy Kat; not by Herriman (4/56)	5	10	15	30	48	65
697-Oswald the Rabbit (Lantz)	4	8	12	28	44	60
698-Francis the Famous Talking Mule (4/56)	4	8	12	28	44	60
699-Prince Valiant-by Bob Fuje	7	14	21	50	83	115
700-Water Birds and the Olympic Elk (Disney-Movie) (4/56)	5	10	15	34	55	75
701-Jiminy Cricket (#1) (Disney) (5/56)	8	16	24	56	93	130
702-The Goofy Success Story (Disney)	7	14	21	47	76	105
703-Scamp (#1) (Disney)	8	16	24	58	97	135
704-Priscilla's Pop (5/56)	4	8	12	26	41	55
705-Brave Eagle (#1) (TV)-Photo-c	6	12	18	43	69	95
706-Bongo and Lumpjaw (Disney) (6/56)	6	12	18	37	59	80
707-Corky and White Shadow (Disney) (5/56)-Mickey Mouse Club (TV); photo-c	7	14	21	47	76	105
708-Smokey the Bear	6	12	18	41	66	90
709-The Searchers (Movie) - John Wayne photo-c	23	46	69	167	309	450
710-Francis the Famous Talking Mule	4	8	12	28	44	60
711-M.G.M's Mouse Musketeers	4	8	12	26	41	55
712-The Great Locomotive Chase (Disney-Movie) (9/56)-Photo-c	7	14	21	47	76	105
713-The Animal World (Movie) (8/56)	4	8	12	26	41	55
714-Spin and Marty (#1) (TV) (Disney)-Mickey Mouse Club (6/56); photo-c	12	24	36	87	156	225
715-Timmy (8/56)	5	10	15	30	48	65
716-Man in Space (Disney)(A science feature from Tomorrowland)	8	16	24	56	93	130
717-Moby Dick (Movie)-Gregory Peck photo-c	8	16	24	56	93	130
718-Dotty Dripple and Taffy	4	8	12	22	34	45
719-Prince Valiant; by Bob Fuje (8/56)	7	14	21	50	83	115
720-Gunsmoke (TV)-James Arness photo-c	9	18	27	61	103	145
721-Captain Kangaroo (TV)-Photo-c	15	30	45	108	199	290
722-Johnny Mack Brown-Photo-c	7	14	21	47	76	105
723-Santiago (Movie)-Kinstler-a (9/56); Alan Ladd photo-c	9	18	27	63	107	150
724-Bugs Bunny's Album	5	10	15	34	55	75
725-Elmer Fudd (9/56)	4	8	12	26	41	55
726-Duck Album (Disney) (9/56)	5	10	15	35	55	75
727-The Nature of Things (TV) (Disney)-Jesse Marsh-a	5	10	15	34	55	75
728-M.G.M's Mouse Musketeers	4	8	12	26	41	55
729-Bob Son of Battle (11/56)	4	8	12	24	37	50
730-Smokey Stover	5	10	15	32	51	70
731-Silvertip and The Fighting Four (Max Brand)-Kinstler-a	5	10	15	30	48	65
732-Zorro, the Challenge of (10/56)	12	24	36	82	146	210
733-Buck Jones	5	10	15	32	51	70
734-Cheyenne (#1) (TV) (10/56)-Clint Walker photo-c	15	30	45	107	196	285
735-Crusader Rabbit (#1) (TV)	25	50	75	185	343	500
736-Pluto (Disney)	5	10	15	32	51	70
737-Steve Canyon-Caniff-a	5	10	15	34	55	75
738-Westward Ho, the Wagons (Disney-Movie)-Fess Parker photo-c	9	18	27	63	107	150
739-Bounty Guns (Luke Short)-Drucker-a	4	8	12	26	41	55
740-Chilly Willy (#1) (Walter Lantz)	7	14	21	45	73	100
741-The Fastest Gun Alive (Movie)(9/56)-Photo-c	7	14	21	45	73	105
742-Buffalo Bill, Jr. (TV)-Photo-c	6	12	18	39	62	85
743-Daisy Duck's Diary (Disney) (11/56)	6	12	18	37	59	80
744-Little Beaver	5	10	15	30	48	65
745-Francis the Famous Talking Mule	4	8	12	28	44	60
746-Dotty Dripple and Taffy	4	8	12	22	34	45
747-Goofy (Disney)	7	14	21	47	76	105
748-Frosty the Snowman (11/56)	5	10	15	32	51	70
749-Secrets of Life (Disney-Movie)-Photo-c	5	10	15	32	51	70
750-The Great Cat Family (Disney-TV/Movie)-Pinocchio & Alice app.	6	12	18	43	69	95
751-Our Miss Brooks (TV)-Photo-c	7	14	21	50	83	115

	GD 2.0	VG 4.0	FN 6.0	VF 8.0	VF/NM 9.0	NM- 9.2
752-Mandrake, the Magician	10	20	30	70	123	175
753-Walt Scott's Little People (11/56)	5	10	15	32	51	70
754-Smokey the Bear	6	12	18	41	66	90
755-The Littlest Snowman (12/56)	5	10	15	32	51	70
756-Santa Claus Funnies	7	14	21	45	73	100
757-The True Story of Jesse James (Movie)-Photo-c	8	16	24	58	97	135
758-Bear Country (Disney-Movie)	5	10	15	34	55	75
759-Circus Boy (TV)-The Monkees' Mickey Dolenz photo-c (12/56)	12	24	36	87	156	225
760-The Hardy Boys (#1) (TV) (Disney)-Mickey Mouse Club; photo-c	10	20	30	70	120	175
761-Howdy Doody (TV) (1/57)	10	20	30	71	126	180
762-The Sharkfighters (Movie) (1/57); Buscema-a; photo-c	7	14	21	50	83	115
763-Grandma Duck's Farm Friends (#1) (Disney)	8	16	24	52	86	120
764-M.G.M's Mouse Musketeers	4	8	12	26	41	55
765-Will-Yum!	4	8	12	26	41	55
766-Buffalo Bill, Jr. (TV)-Photo-c	6	12	18	39	62	85
767-Spin and Marty (TV) (Disney)-Mickey Mouse Club (2/57)	9	18	27	63	107	150
768-Steve Donovan, Western Marshal (TV)-Kinstler-a; photo-c	6	12	18	43	69	95
769-Gunsmoke (TV)-James Arness photo-c	9	18	27	61	103	145
770-Brave Eagle (TV)-Photo-c	4	8	12	26	41	55
771-Brand of Empire (Luke Short)(3/57)-Drucker-a	4	8	12	26	41	55
772-Cheyenne (TV)-Clint Walker photo-c	9	18	27	60	100	140
773-The Brave One (Movie)-Photo-c	5	10	15	34	55	75
774-Hi and Lois (3/57)	4	8	12	24	37	50
775-Sir Lancelot and Brian (TV)-Buscema-a; photo-c	9	18	27	65	113	160
776-Johnny Mack Brown; photo-c	7	14	21	47	76	105
777-Scamp (Disney) (3/57)	6	12	18	43	69	95
778-The Little Rascals (TV)	6	12	18	39	62	85
779-Lee Hunter, Indian Fighter (3/57)	5	10	15	34	55	75
780-Captain Kangaroo (TV)-Photo-c	13	26	39	93	164	235
781-Fury (#1) (TV) (3/57)-Photo-c	8	16	24	52	86	120
782-Duck Album (Disney)	5	10	15	35	55	75
783-Elmer Fudd	4	8	12	26	41	55
784-Around the World in 80 Days (Movie) (2/57)-Photo-c	7	14	21	50	83	115
785-Circus Boy (TV) (4/57)-The Monkees' Mickey Dolenz photo-c	10	20	30	70	123	175
786-Cinderella (Disney) (3/57)-Partial-r of #272	7	14	21	45	73	100
787-Little Hiawatha (Disney) (4/57)(#2)	5	10	15	30	48	65
788-Prince Valiant; by Bob Fuje	7	14	21	47	76	105
789-Silvertip-Valley Thieves (Max Brand) (4/57)-Kinstler-a	5	10	15	30	48	65
790-The Wings of Eagles (Movie) (John Wayne)-Toth-a; John Wayne photo-c; 10¢ & 15¢ editions exist	14	28	42	100	178	255
791-The 77th Bengal Lancers (TV)-Photo-c	7	14	21	47	76	105
792-Oswald the Rabbit (Lantz)	4	8	12	28	44	60
793-Morty Meekle	4	8	12	24	37	50
794-The Count of Monte Cristo (5/57) (Movie)-Buscema-a	8	16	24	56	93	130
795-Jiminy Cricket (Disney)(#2)	6	12	18	43	69	95
796-Ludwig Bemelman's Madeleine and Genevieve	4	8	12	24	37	50
797-Gunsmoke (TV)-Photo-c	9	18	27	61	103	145
798-Buffalo Bill, Jr. (TV)-Photo-c	6	12	18	39	62	85
799-Priscilla's Pop	4	8	12	26	41	55
800-The Buccaneers (TV)-Photo-c	7	14	21	47	76	105
801-Dotty Dripple and Taffy	4	8	12	22	34	45
802-Goofy (Disney) (5/57)	7	14	21	47	76	105
803-Cheyenne (TV)-Clint Walker photo-c	9	18	27	60	100	140
804-Steve Canyon-Caniff-a (1957)	5	10	15	34	55	75
805-Crusader Rabbit (TV)	19	38	57	141	261	380
806-Scamp (Disney) (6/57)	6	12	18	43	69	95
807-Savage Range (Luke Short)-Drucker-a	4	8	12	26	41	55
808-Spin and Marty (TV)(Disney)-Mickey Mouse Club; photo-c	9	18	27	63	107	150
809-The Little People (Walt Scott)	5	10	15	32	51	70
810-Francis the Famous Talking Mule	4	8	12	26	41	55
811-Howdy Doody (TV) (7/57)	10	20	30	71	126	180
812-The Big Land (Movie); Alan Ladd photo-c	9	18	27	60	100	140
813-Circus Boy (TV)-The Monkees' Mickey Dolenz photo-c						

Four Color Comics #848 © DIS

Four Color Comics #877 © DELL

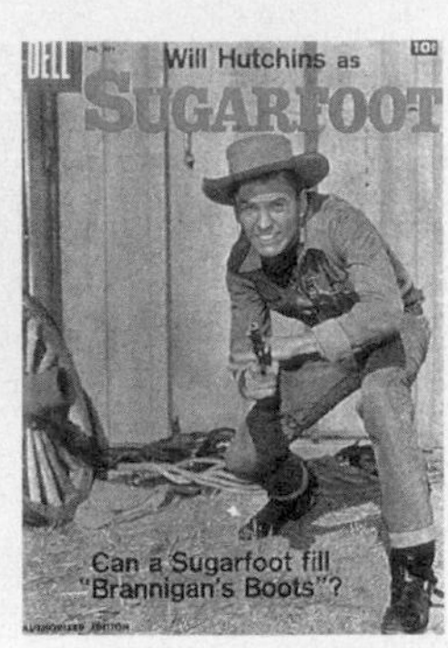

Four Color Comics #907 © WB

	GD 2.0	VG 4.0	FN 6.0	VF 8.0	VF/NM 9.0	NM- 9.2
	10	20	30	70	123	175
814-Covered Wagons, Ho! (Disney)-Donald Duck (TV) (6/57); Mickey Mouse app.	5	10	15	34	55	75
815-Dragoon Wells Massacre (Movie)-photo-c	7	14	21	50	83	115
816-Brave Eagle (TV)-photo-c	4	8	12	26	41	55
817-Little Beaver	5	10	15	30	48	65
818-Smokey the Bear (6/57)	6	12	18	41	66	90
819-Mickey Mouse in Magicland (Disney) (7/57)	6	12	18	39	62	85
820-The Oklahoman (Movie)-Photo-c	8	16	24	58	97	135
821-Wringle Wrangle (Disney)-Based on movie "Westward Ho, the Wagons"; Marsh-a; Fess Parker photo-c	8	16	24	52	86	120
822-Paul Revere's Ride with Johnny Tremain (TV) (Disney)-Toth-a	8	16	24	58	97	135
823-Timmy	4	8	12	26	41	55
824-The Pride and the Passion (Movie) (8/57)-Frank Sinatra & Cary Grant photo-c	9	18	27	63	107	150
825-The Little Rascals (TV)	6	12	18	39	62	85
826-Spin and Marty and Annette (TV) (Disney)-Mickey Mouse Club; Annette Funicello photo-c	22	44	66	157	291	425
827-Smokey Stover (8/57)	5	10	15	32	51	70
828-Buffalo Bill, Jr. (TV)-Photo-c	6	12	18	39	62	85
829-Tales of the Pony Express (TV) (8/57)-Painted-c	5	10	15	30	48	65
830-The Hardy Boys (TV) (Disney)-Mickey Mouse Club (8/57); photo-c	9	18	27	60	100	140
831-No Sleep 'Til Dawn (Movie)-Karl Malden photo-c	6	12	18	43	69	95
832-Lolly and Pepper (#1)	5	10	15	30	48	65
833-Scamp (Disney) (9/57)	6	12	18	43	69	95
834-Johnny Mack Brown; photo-c	7	14	21	47	76	105
835-Silvertip-The False Rider (Max Brand)	5	10	15	30	48	65
836-Man in Flight (Disney) (TV) (9/57)	7	14	21	47	76	105
837-All-American Athlete Cotton Woods	4	8	12	24	37	50
838-Bugs Bunny's Life Story Album (9/57)	5	10	15	34	55	75
839-The Vigilantes (Movie)	7	14	21	47	76	105
840-Duck Album (Disney) (9/57)	5	10	15	35	55	75
841-Elmer Fudd	4	8	12	26	41	55
842-The Nature of Things (Disney-Movie) ('57)-Jesse Marsh-a (TV series)	5	10	15	34	55	75
843-The First Americans (Disney) (TV)-Marsh-a	8	16	24	56	93	130
844-Gunsmoke (TV)-Photo-c	9	18	27	61	103	145
845-The Land Unknown (Movie)-Alex Toth-a	11	22	33	79	140	200
846-Gun Glory (Movie)-by Alex Toth; photo-c	8	16	24	58	97	135
847-Perri (squirrels) (Disney-Movie)-Two different covers published	5	10	15	35	55	75
848-Marauder's Moon (Luke Short)	4	8	12	26	41	55
849-Prince Valiant; by Bob Fuje	7	14	21	47	76	105
850-Buck Jones	5	10	15	32	51	70
851-The Story of Mankind (Movie) (1/58)-Hedy Lamarr & Vincent Price photo-c	7	14	21	47	76	105
852-Chilly Willy (2/58) (Lantz)	5	10	15	30	48	65
853-Pluto (Disney) (10/57)	5	10	15	32	51	70
854-The Hunchback of Notre Dame (Movie)-Photo-c	12	24	36	87	156	225
855-Broken Arrow (TV)-Photo-c	6	12	18	37	59	80
856-Buffalo Bill, Jr. (TV)-Photo-c	6	12	18	39	62	85
857-The Goofy Adventure Story (Disney) (11/57)	7	14	21	47	76	105
858-Daisy Duck's Diary (Disney) (11/57)	5	10	15	32	51	70
859-Topper and Neil (TV) (11/57)	5	10	15	30	48	65
860-Wyatt Earp (#1) (TV)-Manning-a; photo-c	9	18	27	65	113	160
861-Frosty the Snowman	5	10	15	32	51	70
862-The Truth About Mother Goose (Disney-Movie) (11/57)	7	14	21	49	80	110
863-Francis the Famous Talking Mule	4	8	12	26	41	55
864-The Littlest Snowman	5	10	15	32	51	70
865-Andy Burnett (TV) (Disney) (12/57)-Photo-c	8	16	24	58	97	135
866-Mars and Beyond (Disney-TV)(A science feature from Tomorrowland)	8	16	24	56	93	130
867-Santa Claus Funnies	7	14	21	45	73	100
868-The Little People (12/57)	5	10	15	32	51	70
869-Old Yeller (Disney-Movie)-Photo-c	5	10	15	34	55	75
870-Little Beaver (1/58)	5	10	15	30	48	65
871-Curly Kayoe	4	8	12	24	37	50
872-Captain Kangaroo (TV)-Photo-c	13	26	39	93	164	235
873-Grandma Duck's Farm Friends (Disney)	6	12	18	37	59	80
874-Old Ironsides (Disney-Movie with Johnny Tremain) (1/58)	6	12	18	43	69	95
875-Trumpets West (Luke Short) (2/58)	4	8	12	26	41	55
876-Tales of Wells Fargo (#1)(TV)(2/58)-Photo-c	9	18	27	60	100	140
877-Frontier Doctor with Rex Allen (TV)-Alex Toth-a; Rex Allen photo-c	9	18	27	63	107	150
878-Peanuts (#1)-Schulz-c only (2/58)	19	38	57	139	257	375
879-Brave Eagle (TV) (2/58)-Photo-c	4	8	12	26	41	55
880-Steve Donovan, Western Marshal-Drucker-a (TV)-Photo-c	5	10	15	30	48	65
881-The Captain and the Kids (2/58)	4	8	12	28	44	60
882-Zorro (Disney)-1st Disney issue; by Alex Toth (TV) (2/58); photo-c	15	30	45	105	190	275
883-The Little Rascals (TV)	6	12	18	37	59	80
884-Hawkeye and the Last of the Mohicans (TV) (3/58); photo-c	7	14	21	47	76	105
885-Fury (TV) (3/58)-Photo-c	6	12	18	41	66	90
886-Bongo and Lumpjaw (Disney) (3/58)	5	10	15	30	48	65
887-The Hardy Boys (Disney) (TV)-Mickey Mouse Club (1/58)-Photo-c	9	18	27	60	100	140
888-Elmer Fudd (3/58)	4	8	12	26	41	55
889-Clint and Mac (Disney) (TV) (3/58)-Alex Toth-a; photo-c	11	22	33	79	140	200
890-Wyatt Earp (TV)-by Russ Manning; photo-c	7	14	21	49	80	110
891-Light in the Forest (Disney-Movie) (3/58)-Fess Parker photo-c	7	14	21	50	83	115
892-Maverick (#1) (TV) (4/58)-James Garner photo-c	22	44	66	157	291	425
893-Jim Bowie (TV)-Photo-c	6	12	18	39	62	85
894-Oswald the Rabbit (Lantz)	4	8	12	28	44	60
895-Wagon Train (#1) (TV) (3/58)-Photo-c	10	20	30	71	126	180
896-The Adventures of Tinker Bell (Disney)	8	16	24	56	93	130
897-Jiminy Cricket (Disney)	6	12	18	43	69	95
898-Silvertip (Max Brand)-Kinstler-a (5/58)	5	10	15	30	48	65
899-Goofy (Disney) (5/58)	5	10	15	32	51	70
900-Prince Valiant; by Bob Fuje	7	14	21	47	76	105
901-Little Hiawatha (Disney)	5	10	15	30	48	65
902-Will-Yum!	4	8	12	26	41	55
903-Dotty Dripple and Taffy	4	8	12	22	34	45
904-Lee Hunter, Indian Fighter	4	8	12	26	41	55
905-Annette (Disney) (TV) (5/58)-Mickey Mouse Club; Annette Funicello photo-c	26	52	78	192	359	525
906-Francis the Famous Talking Mule	4	8	12	26	41	55
907-Sugarfoot (#1) (TV)Toth-a; photo-c	12	24	36	84	150	215
908-The Little People and the Giant-Walt Scott (5/58)	5	10	15	32	51	70
909-Smitty	4	8	12	24	37	50
910-The Vikings (Movie)-Buscema-a; Kirk Douglas photo-c	8	16	24	54	90	125
911-The Gray Ghost (TV)-Photo-c	8	16	24	56	93	130
912-Leave It to Beaver (#1) (TV)-Photo-c	15	30	45	108	199	290
913-The Left-Handed Gun (Movie) (7/58); Paul Newman photo-c	9	18	27	63	107	150
914-No Time for Sergeants (Movie)-Andy Griffith photo-c; Toth-a	9	18	27	65	113	160
915-Casey Jones (TV)-Alan Hale photo-c	5	10	15	34	55	75
916-Red Ryder Ranch Comics (7/58)	5	10	15	35	55	75
917-The Life of Riley (TV)-Photo-c	10	20	30	70	123	175
918-Beep Beep, the Roadrunner (#1) (7/58)-Published with two different back covers	11	22	33	75	133	190
919-Boots and Saddles (#1) (TV)-Photo-c	7	14	21	50	83	115
920-Zorro (Disney) (TV) (6/58)Toth-a; photo-c	11	22	33	80	143	205
921-Wyatt Earp (TV)-Manning-a; photo-c	7	14	21	49	80	110
922-Johnny Mack Brown by Russ Manning; photo-c	7	14	21	45	73	100
923-Timmy	4	8	12	26	41	55
924-Colt .45 (#1) (TV) (8/58)-W. Preston photo-c	10	20	30	70	123	175
925-Last of the Fast Guns (Movie) (8/58)-Photo-c	7	14	21	47	76	105
926-Peter Pan (Disney)-Reprint of #442	4	8	12	28	44	60
927-Top Gun (Luke Short) Buscema-a	4	8	12	26	41	55
928-Sea Hunt (#1) (9/58) (TV)-Lloyd Bridges photo-c	11	22	33	79	140	200
929-Brave Eagle (TV)-Photo-c	4	8	12	26	41	55
930-Maverick (TV) (7/58)-James Garner photo-c	11	22	33	75	133	190
931-Have Gun, Will Travel (#1) (TV)-Photo-c	13	26	39	95	168	240
932-Smokey the Bear (His Life Story)	6	12	18	41	66	90
933-Zorro (Disney, 9/58) (TV)-Alex Toth-a; photo-c	11	22	33	80	143	205
934-Restless Gun (#1) (TV)-Photo-c	10	20	30	71	126	180

Four Color Comics #968 © Overland Prods.

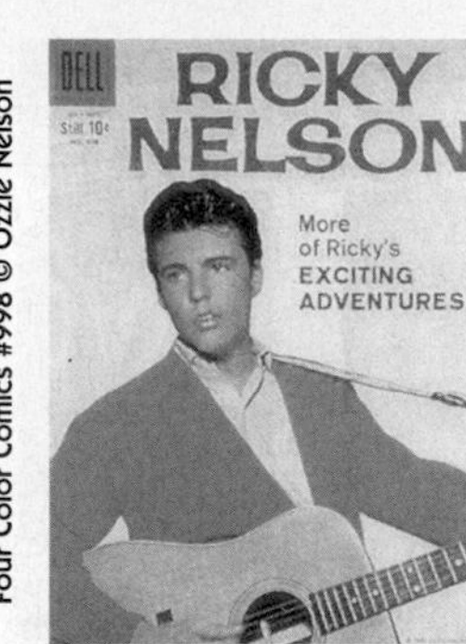

Four Color Comics #998 © Ozzie Nelson

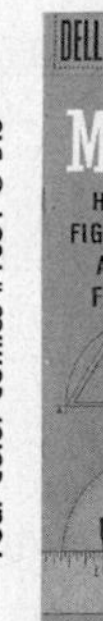
Four Color Comics #1051 © DIS

	GD 2.0	VG 4.0	FN 6.0	VF 8.0	VF/NM 9.0	NM- 9.2
935-King of the Royal Mounted	4	8	12	28	44	60
936-The Little Rascals (TV)	6	12	18	37	59	80
937-Ruff and Reddy (#1) (9/58) (TV) (1st Hanna-Barbera comic book)	12	24	36	84	150	215
938-Elmer Fudd (9/58)	4	8	12	26	41	55
939-Steve Canyon - not by Caniff	5	10	15	34	55	75
940-Lolly and Pepper (10/58)	4	8	12	22	34	45
941-Pluto (Disney) (10/58)	4	8	12	28	44	60
942-Pony Express (Tales of the ...) (TV)	5	10	15	30	48	65
943-White Wilderness (Disney-Movie) (10/58)	6	12	18	43	69	95
944-The 7th Voyage of Sinbad (Movie) (9/58)-Buscema-a; photo-c	12	24	36	87	156	225
945-Maverick (TV)-James Garner/Jack Kelly photo-c	11	22	33	75	133	190
946-The Big Country (Movie)-Photo-c	7	14	21	47	76	105
947-Broken Arrow (TV)-Photo-c (11/58)	5	10	15	32	51	70
948-Daisy Duck's Diary (Disney) (11/58)	5	10	15	32	51	70
949-High Adventure(Lowell Thomas')(TV)-Photo-c	6	12	18	37	59	80
950-Frosty the Snowman	5	10	15	32	51	70
951-The Lennon Sisters Life Story (TV)-Toth-a, 32 pgs.; photo-c	13	26	39	95	168	240
952-Goofy (Disney) (11/58)	5	10	15	32	51	70
953-Francis the Famous Talking Mule	4	8	12	26	41	55
954-Man in Space-Satellites (TV)	7	14	21	47	76	105
955-Hi and Lois (11/58)	4	8	12	24	37	50
956-Ricky Nelson (#1) (TV)-Photo-c	17	34	51	120	223	325
957-Buffalo Bee (#1) (TV)	8	16	24	58	97	135
958-Santa Claus Funnies	6	12	18	41	66	90
959-Christmas Stories-(Walt Scott's Little People) (1951-56 strip reprints)	5	10	15	32	51	70
960-Zorro (Disney) (TV) (12/58)-Toth art; photo-c	11	22	33	80	143	205
961-Jace Pearson's Tales of the Texas Rangers (TV)-Spiegle-a; photo-c	6	12	18	37	59	80
962-Maverick (TV) (1/59)-James Garner/Jack Kelly photo-c	11	22	33	75	133	190
963-Johnny Mack Brown; photo-c	7	14	21	47	76	105
964-The Hardy Boys (TV) (Disney) (1/59)-Mickey Mouse Club; photo-c	9	18	27	60	100	140
965-Grandma Duck's Farm Friends (Disney)(1/59)	5	10	15	32	51	70
966-Tonka (starring Sal Mineo; Disney-Movie)-Photo-c	8	16	24	58	97	135
967-Chilly Willy (2/59) (Lantz)	5	10	15	30	48	65
968-Tales of Wells Fargo (TV)-Photo-c	8	16	24	56	93	130
969-Peanuts (2/59)	12	24	36	87	156	225
970-Lawman (#1) (TV)-Photo-c	12	24	36	87	156	225
971-Wagon Train (TV)-Photo-c	7	14	21	45	73	100
972-Tom Thumb (Movie)-George Pal (1/59)	8	16	24	58	97	135
973-Sleeping Beauty and the Prince(Disney)(5/59)	11	22	33	75	133	190
974-The Little Rascals (TV) (3/59)	6	12	18	37	59	80
975-Fury (TV)-Photo-c	6	12	18	41	66	90
976-Zorro (Disney) (TV)-Toth-a; photo-c	11	22	33	80	143	205
977-Elmer Fudd (3/59)	4	8	12	26	41	55
978-Lolly and Pepper	4	8	12	22	34	45
979-Oswald the Rabbit (Lantz)	4	8	12	28	44	60
980-Maverick (TV) (4-6/59)-James Garner/Jack Kelly photo-c	11	22	33	75	133	190
981-Ruff and Reddy (TV) (Hanna-Barbera)	8	16	24	52	86	120
982-The New Adventures of Tinker Bell (TV) (Disney)	8	16	24	52	86	120
983-Have Gun, Will Travel (TV) (4-6/59)-Photo-c	9	18	27	60	100	140
984-Sleeping Beauty's Fairy Godmothers (Disney)	9	18	27	61	103	145
985-Shaggy Dog (Disney-Movie)-Photo-all four covers; Annette on back-c(5/59)	7	14	21	50	83	115
986-Restless Gun (TV)-Photo-c	8	16	24	52	86	120
987-Goofy (Disney) (7/59)	5	10	15	32	51	70
988-Little Hiawatha (Disney)	5	10	15	30	48	65
989-Jiminy Cricket (Disney) (5-7/59)	6	12	18	43	69	95
990-Huckleberry Hound (#1)(TV)(Hanna-Barbera); 1st app. Huck, Yogi Bear, & Pixie & Dixie & Mr. Jinks	12	24	36	86	153	220
991-Francis the Famous Talking Mule	4	8	12	26	41	55
992-Sugarfoot (TV)-Toth-a; photo-c	11	22	33	77	136	195
993-Jim Bowie (TV)-Photo-c	5	10	15	35	55	75
994-Sea Hunt (TV)-Lloyd Bridges photo-c	8	16	24	54	90	125
995-Donald Duck Album (Disney) (5-7/59)(#1)	6	12	18	43	69	95
996-Nevada (Zane Grey)	4	8	12	28	44	60

	GD 2.0	VG 4.0	FN 6.0	VF 8.0	VF/NM 9.0	NM- 9.2
997-Walt Disney Presents-Tales of Texas John Slaughter (#1) (TV) (Disney)-Photo-c; photo of W. Disney inside-c	7	14	21	49	80	110
998-Ricky Nelson (TV)-Photo-c	17	34	51	120	223	325
999-Leave It to Beaver (TV)-Photo-c	13	26	39	95	168	240
1000-The Gray Ghost (TV) (6-8/59)-Photo-c	8	16	24	56	93	130
1001-Lowell Thomas' High Adventure (TV) (8-10/59)-Photo-c	5	10	15	34	55	75
1002-Buffalo Bee (TV)	7	14	21	45	73	100
1003-Zorro (TV) (Disney)-Toth-a; photo-c	11	22	33	80	143	205
1004-Colt .45 (TV) (6-8/59)-Photo-c	8	16	24	56	93	130
1005-Maverick (TV)-James Garner/Jack Kelly photo-c	11	22	33	75	133	190
1006-Hercules (Movie)-Buscema-a; photo-c	9	18	27	60	100	140
1007-John Paul Jones (Movie)-Robert Stack photo-c	5	10	15	35	55	75
1008-Beep Beep, the Road Runner (7-9/59)	6	12	18	43	69	95
1009-The Rifleman (#1) (TV)-Photo-c	21	42	63	152	281	410
1010-Grandma Duck's Farm Friends (Disney)-by Carl Barks	12	24	36	87	156	225
1011-Buckskin (#1) (TV)-Photo-c	7	14	21	47	76	105
1012-Last Train from Gun Hill (Movie) (7/59)-Photo-c	8	16	24	56	93	130
1013-Bat Masterson (#1) (TV) (8/59)-Gene Barry photo-c	11	22	33	79	140	200
1014-The Lennon Sisters (TV)-Toth-a; photo-c	12	24	36	87	156	225
1015-Peanuts-Schulz-c	12	24	36	87	156	225
1016-Smokey the Bear Nature Stories	4	8	12	28	44	60
1017-Chilly Willy (Lantz)	5	10	15	30	48	65
1018-Rio Bravo (Movie)(6/59)-John Wayne; Toth-a; John Wayne, Dean Martin & Ricky Nelson photo-c	22	44	66	157	291	425
1019-Wagon Train (TV)-Photo-c	7	14	21	45	73	100
1020-Jungle Jim-McWilliams-a	4	8	12	26	41	55
1021-Jace Pearson's Tales of the Texas Rangers (TV)-Photo-c	6	12	18	37	59	80
1022-Timmy	4	8	12	26	41	55
1023-Tales of Wells Fargo (TV)-Photo-c	8	16	24	56	93	130
1024-Darby O'Gill and the Little People (Disney-Movie)-Toth-a; photo-c	9	18	27	65	113	160
1025-Vacation in Disneyland (8-10/59)-Carl Barks-a(24pgs.) (Disney)	16	32	48	112	209	305
1026-Spin and Marty (TV) (Disney) (9-11/59)-Mickey Mouse Club; photo-c	8	16	24	52	86	120
1027-The Texan (#1)(TV)-Photo-c	8	16	24	56	93	130
1028-Rawhide (#1) (TV) (9-11/59)-Clint Eastwood photo-c; Tufts-a	22	44	66	157	291	425
1029-Boots and Saddles (TV) (9/59)-Photo-c	5	10	15	34	55	75
1030-Spanky and Alfalfa, the Little Rascals (TV)	6	12	18	37	59	80
1031-Fury (TV)-Photo-c	6	12	18	41	66	90
1032-Elmer Fudd	4	8	12	26	41	55
1033-Steve Canyon-not by Caniff; photo-c	5	10	15	34	55	75
1034-Nancy and Sluggo Summer Camp (9-11/59)	5	10	15	32	51	70
1035-Lawman (TV)-Photo-c	8	16	24	54	90	125
1036-The Big Circus (Movie)-Photo-c	6	12	18	43	69	95
1037-Zorro (Disney) (TV)-Tufts-a; Annette Funicello photo-c	14	28	42	100	178	255
1038-Ruff and Reddy (TV)(Hanna-Barbera)(1959)	8	16	24	52	86	120
1039-Pluto (Disney) (11-1/60)	4	8	12	28	44	60
1040-Quick Draw McGraw (#1) (TV) (Hanna-Barbera) (12-2/60)	13	26	39	95	168	240
1041-Sea Hunt (TV) (10-12/59)-Toth-a; Lloyd Bridges photo-c	8	16	24	54	90	125
1042-The Three Chipmunks (Alvin, Simon & Theodore) (#1) (TV) (10-12/59)	8	16	24	52	86	120
1043-The Three Stooges (#1)-Photo-c	25	50	75	185	343	500
1044-Have Gun, Will Travel (TV)-Photo-c	9	18	27	60	100	140
1045-Restless Gun (TV)-Photo-c	8	16	24	52	86	120
1046-Beep Beep, the Road Runner (11-1/60)	6	12	18	43	69	95
1047-Gyro Gearloose (#1) (Disney)-All Barks-c/a	17	34	51	120	223	325
1048-The Horse Soldiers (Movie) (John Wayne)-Sekowsky-a; painted cover featuring John Wayne	13	26	39	95	168	240
1049-Don't Give Up the Ship (Movie) (8/59)-Jerry Lewis photo-c	9	18	27	61	103	145
1050-Huckleberry Hound (TV) (Hanna-Barbera) (10-12/59)	8	16	24	56	93	130
1051-Donald in Mathmagic Land (Disney-Movie)	9	18	27	63	107	150
1052-Ben-Hur (Movie) (11/59)-Manning-a	10	20	30	67	116	165

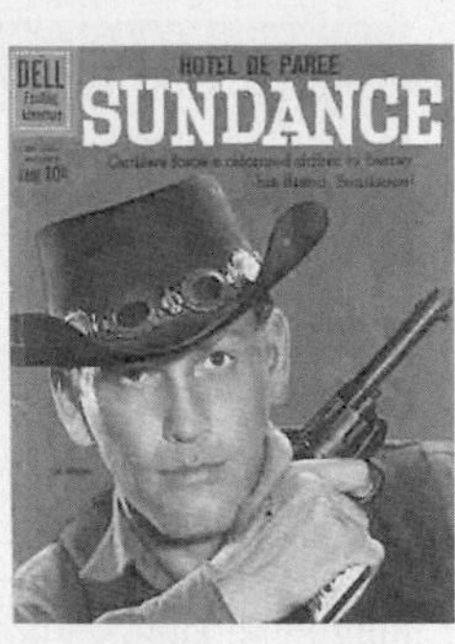

Four Color Comics #1126 © DELL

Four Color Comics #1130 © DELL

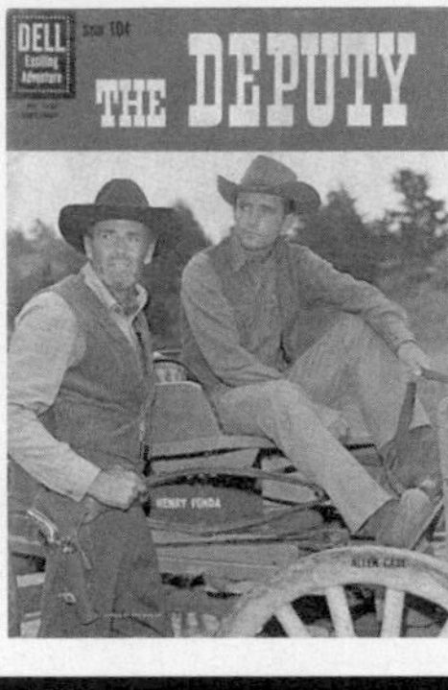

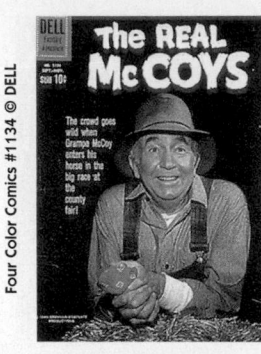

Four Color Comics #1134 © DELL

	GD 2.0	VG 4.0	FN 6.0	VF 8.0	VF/NM 9.0	NM- 9.2
1053-Goofy (Disney) (11-1/60)	5	10	15	32	51	70
1054-Huckleberry Hound Winter Fun (TV) (Hanna-Barbera) (12/59)	8	16	24	56	93	130
1055-Daisy Duck's Diary (Disney)-by Carl Barks (11-1/60)	9	18	27	60	100	140
1056-Yellowstone Kelly (Movie)-Clint Walker photo-c	6	12	18	37	59	80
1057-Mickey Mouse Album (Disney)	5	10	15	34	55	75
1058-Colt .45 (TV)-Photo-c	8	16	24	56	93	130
1059-Sugarfoot (TV)-Photo-c	8	16	24	58	97	135
1060-Journey to the Center of the Earth (Movie)-Pat Boone & James Mason photo-c	10	20	30	73	129	185
1061-Buffalo Bee (TV)	7	14	21	45	73	100
1062-Christmas Stories (Walt Scott's Little People strip-r)	5	10	15	32	51	70
1063-Santa Claus Funnies	6	12	18	41	66	90
1064-Bugs Bunny's Merry Christmas (12/59)	5	10	15	34	55	75
1065-Frosty the Snowman	5	10	15	32	51	70
1066-77 Sunset Strip (#1) (TV)-Toth-a (1-3/60)-Efrem Zimbalist, Jr. & Edd "Kookie" Byrnes photo-c	10	20	30	71	126	180
1067-Yogi Bear (#1) (TV) (Hanna-Barbera)	10	20	30	71	126	180
1068-Francis the Famous Talking Mule	4	8	12	26	41	55
1069-The FBI Story (Movie)-Toth-a; James Stewart photo on-c	9	18	27	63	107	150
1070-Solomon and Sheba (Movie)-Sekowsky-a; photo-c	8	16	24	58	97	135
1071-The Real McCoys (#1) (TV) (1-3/60)-Toth-a; Walter Brennan photo-c	9	18	27	60	100	140
1072-Blythe (Marge's)	5	10	15	34	55	75
1073-Grandma Duck's Farm Friends-Barks-c/a (Disney)	12	24	36	87	156	225
1074-Chilly Willy (Lantz)	5	10	15	30	48	65
1075-Tales of Wells Fargo (TV)-Photo-c	8	16	24	56	93	130
1076-The Rebel (#1) (TV)-Sekowsky-a; photo-c	9	18	27	65	113	160
1077-The Deputy (#1) (TV)-Buscema-a; Henry Fonda photo-c	11	22	33	79	140	200
1078-The Three Stooges (2-4/60)-Photo-c	14	28	42	99	175	250
1079-The Little Rascals (TV) (Spanky & Alfalfa)	6	12	18	37	59	80
1080-Fury (TV) (2-4/60)-Photo-c	6	12	18	41	66	90
1081-Elmer Fudd	4	8	12	26	41	55
1082-Spin and Marty (Disney) (TV)-Photo-c	8	16	24	52	86	120
1083-Men into Space (TV)-Anderson-a; photo-c	5	10	15	34	55	75
1084-Speedy Gonzales	5	10	15	34	55	75
1085-The Time Machine (H.G. Wells) (Movie) (3/60)-Alex Toth-a; Rod Taylor photo-c	14	28	42	100	178	255
1086-Lolly and Pepper	4	8	12	22	34	45
1087-Peter Gunn (TV)-Photo-c	8	16	24	58	97	135
1088-A Dog of Flanders (Movie)-Photo-c	5	10	15	30	48	65
1089-Restless Gun (TV)-Photo-c	8	16	24	52	86	120
1090-Francis the Famous Talking Mule	4	8	12	26	41	55
1091-Jacky's Diary (4-6/60)	5	10	15	30	48	65
1092-Toby Tyler (Disney-Movie)-Photo-c	6	12	18	43	69	95
1093-MacKenzie's Raiders (Movie/TV)-Richard Carlson photo-c from TV show	6	12	18	43	69	95
1094-Goofy (Disney)	5	10	15	32	51	70
1095-Gyro Gearloose (Disney)-All Barks-c/a	9	18	27	65	113	160
1096-The Texan (TV)-Rory Calhoun photo-c	8	16	24	52	86	120
1097-Rawhide (TV)-Manning-a; Clint Eastwood photo-c	14	28	42	102	181	260
1098-Sugarfoot (TV)-Photo-c	8	16	24	58	97	135
1099-Donald Duck Album (Disney) (5-7/60)-Barks-c	7	14	21	45	73	100
1100-Annette's Life Story (Disney-Movie) (5/60)-Annette Funicello photo-c	22	44	66	157	291	425
1101-Robert Louis Stevenson's Kidnapped (Disney-Movie) (5/60); photo-c	6	12	18	43	69	95
1102-Wanted: Dead or Alive (#1) (TV) (5-7/60); Steve McQueen photo-c	12	24	36	87	156	225
1103-Leave It to Beaver (TV)-Photo-c	13	26	39	95	168	240
1104-Yogi Bear Goes to College (TV) (Hanna-Barbera) (6-8/60)	7	14	21	49	80	110
1105-Gale Storm (Oh! Susanna) (TV)-Toth-a; photo-c	11	22	33	77	136	195
1106-77 Sunset Strip(TV)(6-8/60)-Toth-a; photo-c	8	16	24	58	97	135
1107-Buckskin (TV)-Photo-c	6	12	18	43	69	95
1108-The Troubleshooters (TV)-Keenan Wynn photo-c	5	10	15	34	55	75
1109-This Is Your Life, Donald Duck (Disney) (TV) (8-10/60)-Gyro flashback to WDC&S #141; origin Donald Duck (1st told)	14	28	42	102	181	260
1110-Bonanza (#1) (TV) (6-8/60)-Photo-c	31	62	93	239	445	650
1111-Shotgun Slade (TV)-Photo-c	6	12	18	41	66	90
1112-Pixie and Dixie and Mr. Jinks (#1) (TV) (Hanna-Barbera) (7-9/60)	7	14	21	50	83	115
1113-Tales of Wells Fargo (TV)-Photo-c	8	16	24	56	93	130
1114-Huckleberry Finn (Movie) (7/60)-Photo-c	5	10	15	34	55	75
1115-Ricky Nelson (TV)-Manning-a; photo-c	14	28	42	102	181	260
1116-Boots and Saddles (TV) (8/60)-Photo-c	5	10	15	34	55	75
1117-Boy and the Pirates (Movie)-Photo-c	6	12	18	43	69	95
1118-The Sword and the Dragon (Movie) (6/60)-Photo-c	7	14	21	50	83	115
1119-Smokey the Bear Nature Stories	4	8	12	28	44	60
1120-Dinosaurus (Movie)-Painted-c	8	16	24	56	93	130
1121-Hercules Unchained (Movie) (8/60)-Crandall/Evans-a	9	18	27	60	100	140
1122-Chilly Willy (Lantz)	5	10	15	30	48	65
1123-Tombstone Territory (TV)-Photo-c	8	16	24	56	93	130
1124-Whirlybirds (#1) (TV)-Photo-c	8	16	24	56	93	130
1125-Laramie (#1) (TV)-Photo-c; G. Kane/Heath-a	8	16	24	58	97	135
1126-Hotel Deparee - Sundance (TV) (8-10/60)-Earl Holliman photo-c	6	12	18	43	69	95
1127-The Three Stooges-Photo-c (8-10/60)	14	28	42	99	175	250
1128-Rocky and His Friends (#1) (TV) (Jay Ward) (8-10/60)	29	58	87	213	394	575
1129-Pollyanna (Disney-Movie)-Hayley Mills photo-c	7	14	21	50	83	115
1130-The Deputy (TV)-Buscema-a; Henry Fonda photo-c	9	18	27	63	107	150
1131-Elmer Fudd (9-11/60)	4	8	12	26	41	55
1132-Space Mouse (Lantz) (8-10/60)	4	8	12	28	44	60
1133-Fury (TV)-Photo-c	6	12	18	41	66	90
1134-Real McCoys (TV)-Toth-a; photo-c	9	18	27	60	100	140
1135-M.G.M.'s Mouse Musketeers (9-11/60)	4	8	12	24	37	50
1136-Jungle Cat (Disney-Movie)-Photo-c	6	12	18	43	69	95
1137-The Little Rascals (TV)	6	12	18	37	59	80
1138-The Rebel (TV)-Photo-c	8	16	24	56	93	130
1139-Spartacus (Movie) (11/60)-Buscema-a; Kirk Douglas photo-c	12	24	36	87	156	225
1140-Donald Duck Album (Disney)-Barks-c	7	14	21	45	73	100
1141-Huckleberry Hound for President (TV) (Hanna-Barbera) (10/60)	8	16	24	52	86	120
1142-Johnny Ringo (TV)-Photo-c	7	14	21	47	76	105
1143-Pluto (Disney) (11-1/61)	4	8	12	28	44	60
1144-The Story of Ruth (Movie)-Photo-c	8	16	24	58	97	135
1145-The Lost World (Movie)-Gil Kane-a; photo-c; 1 pg. Conan Doyle biography by Torres	9	18	27	64	110	155
1146-Restless Gun (TV)-Photo-c; Wildey-a	8	16	24	52	86	120
1147-Sugarfoot (TV)-Photo-c	8	16	24	58	97	135
1148-I Aim at the Stars-the Wernher Von Braun Story (Movie) (11-1/61)-Photo-c	7	14	21	47	76	105
1149-Goofy (Disney) (11-1/61)	5	10	15	32	51	70
1150-Daisy Duck's Diary (Disney) (12-1/61) by Carl Barks	9	18	27	60	100	140
1151-Mickey Mouse Album (Disney) (11-1/61)	5	10	15	34	55	75
1152-Rocky and His Friends (TV) (Jay Ward) (12-2/61)	18	36	54	133	247	360
1153-Frosty the Snowman	5	10	15	32	51	70
1154-Santa Claus Funnies	6	12	18	41	66	90
1155-North to Alaska (Movie)-John Wayne photo-c	16	32	48	112	209	305
1156-Walt Disney Swiss Family Robinson (Movie) (12/60)-Photo-c	7	14	21	49	80	110
1157-Master of the World (Movie) (7/61)	7	14	21	45	73	100
1158-Three Worlds of Gulliver (2 issues exist with different covers) (Movie)-Photo-c	7	14	21	45	73	100
1159-77 Sunset Strip (TV)-Toth-a; photo-c	8	16	24	58	97	135
1160-Rawhide (TV)-Clint Eastwood photo-c	14	28	42	102	181	260
1161-Grandma Duck's Farm Friends (Disney) by Carl Barks (2-4/61)	12	24	36	87	156	225
1162-Yogi Bear Joins the Marines (TV) (Hanna-Barbera) (5-7/61)	7	14	21	49	80	110
1163-Daniel Boone (3-5/61); Marsh-a	5	10	15	35	55	75
1164-Wanted: Dead or Alive (TV)-Steve McQueen photo-c						

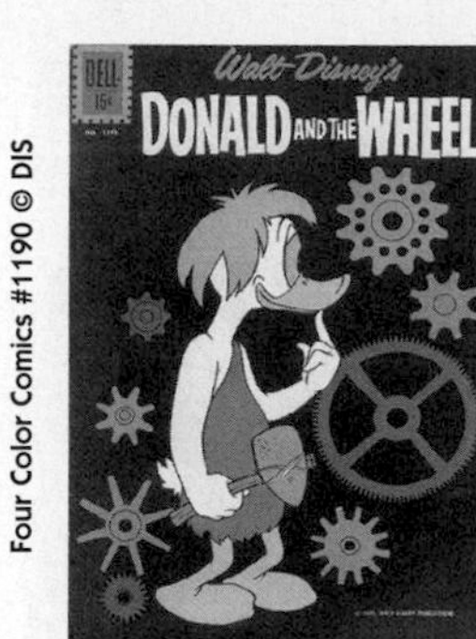

Four Color Comics #1190 © DIS

Four Color Comics #1235 © DELL

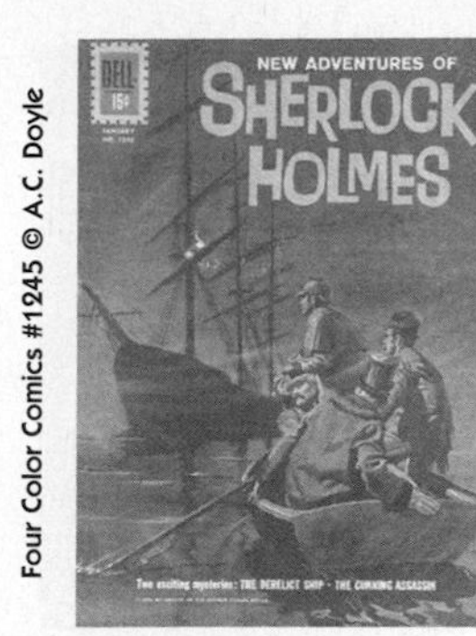

Four Color Comics #1245 © A.C. Doyle

	GD 2.0	VG 4.0	FN 6.0	VF 8.0	VF/NM 9.0	NM- 9.2
	9	18	27	63	107	150
1165-Ellery Queen (#1) (3-5/61)	10	20	30	70	123	175
1166-Rocky and His Friends (TV) (Jay Ward)	18	36	54	133	247	360
1167-Tales of Wells Fargo (TV)-Photo-c	8	16	24	52	86	120
1168-The Detectives (TV)-Robert Taylor photo-c	9	18	27	65	113	160
1169-New Adventures of Sherlock Holmes	14	28	42	102	181	260
1170-The Three Stooges (3-5/61)-Photo-c	14	28	42	99	175	250
1171-Elmer Fudd	4	8	12	26	41	55
1172-Fury (TV)-Photo-c	6	12	18	41	66	90
1173-The Twilight Zone (#1) (TV) (5/61)-Crandall/Evans-c/a; Crandall tribute to Ingles	21	42	63	152	281	410
1174-The Little Rascals (TV)	5	10	15	30	48	65
1175-M.G.M.'s Mouse Musketeers (3-5/61)	4	8	12	24	37	50
1176-Dondi (Movie)-Origin; photo-c	5	10	15	35	55	75
1177-Chilly Willy (Lantz) (4-6/61)	5	10	15	30	48	65
1178-Ten Who Dared (Disney-Movie) (12/60)-Painted-c; cast member photo on back-c	7	14	21	49	80	110
1179-The Swamp Fox (TV) (Disney)-Leslie Nielsen photo-c	8	16	24	56	93	130
1180-The Danny Thomas Show (TV)-Toth-a; photo-c	15	30	45	107	196	285
1181-Texas John Slaughter (TV) (Walt Disney Presents...) (4-6/61)-Photo-c	7	14	21	47	76	105
1182-Donald Duck Album (Disney) (5-7/61)	5	10	15	32	51	70
1183-101 Dalmatians (Disney-Movie) (3/61)	9	18	27	65	113	160
1184-Gyro Gearloose; All Barks-c/a (Disney) (5-7/61) Two variations exist	9	18	27	65	113	160
1185-Sweetie Pie	5	10	15	30	48	65
1186-Yak Yak (#1) by Jack Davis (2 versions - one minus 3-pg. Davis-c/a)	8	16	24	58	97	135
1187-The Three Stooges (6-8/61)-Photo-c	14	28	42	99	175	250
1188-Atlantis, the Lost Continent (Movie) (5/61)-Photo-c	10	20	30	68	119	170
1189-Greyfriars Bobby (Disney-Movie) (11/61)-Photo-c (scarce)	7	14	21	47	76	105
1190-Donald and the Wheel (Disney-Movie) (11/61); Barks-c	8	16	24	54	90	125
1191-Leave It to Beaver (TV)-Photo-c	13	26	39	95	168	240
1192-Ricky Nelson (TV)-Manning-a; photo-c	14	28	42	102	181	260
1193-The Real McCoys (TV) (6-8/61)-Photo-c	8	16	24	56	93	130
1194-Pepe (Movie) (4/61)-Photo-c	4	8	12	24	37	50
1195-National Velvet (#1) (TV)-Photo-c	7	14	21	49	80	110
1196-Pixie and Dixie and Mr. Jinks (TV) (Hanna-Barbera) (7-9/61)	6	12	18	37	59	80
1197-The Aquanauts (TV) (5-7/61)-Photo-c	7	14	21	47	76	105
1198-Donald in Mathmagic Land (Disney-Movie)-Reprint of #1051	6	12	18	43	69	95
1199-The Absent-Minded Professor (Disney-Movie) (4/61)-Photo-c	8	16	24	56	93	130
1200-Hennessey (TV) (8-10/61)-Gil Kane-a; photo-c	7	14	21	47	76	105
1201-Goofy (Disney) (8-10/61)	5	10	15	32	51	70
1202-Rawhide (TV)-Clint Eastwood photo-c	14	28	42	102	181	260
1203-Pinocchio (Disney) (3/62)	5	10	15	34	55	75
1204-Scamp (Disney)	4	8	12	28	44	60
1205-David and Goliath (Movie) (7/61)-Photo-c	6	12	18	43	69	95
1206-Lolly and Pepper (9-11/61)	4	8	12	22	34	45
1207-The Rebel (TV)-Sekowsky-a; photo-c	8	16	24	56	93	130
1208-Rocky and His Friends (Jay Ward) (TV)	18	36	54	133	247	360
1209-Sugarfoot (TV)-Photo-c (10-12/61)	8	16	24	58	97	135
1210-The Parent Trap (Disney-Movie) (8/61)-Hayley Mills photo-c	9	18	27	60	100	140
1211-77 Sunset Strip (TV)-Manning-a; photo-c	8	16	24	54	90	125
1212-Chilly Willy (Lantz) (7-9/61)	5	10	15	30	48	65
1213-Mysterious Island (Movie)-Photo-c	8	16	24	56	93	130
1214-Smokey the Bear	4	8	12	28	44	60
1215-Tales of Wells Fargo (TV) (10-12/61)-Photo-c	8	16	24	52	86	120
1216-Whirlybirds (TV)-Photo-c	8	16	24	52	86	120
1218-Fury (TV)-Photo-c	6	12	18	41	66	90
1219-The Detectives (TV)-Robert Taylor & Adam West photo-c	8	16	24	56	93	130
1220-Gunslinger (TV)-Photo-c	8	16	24	56	93	130
1221-Bonanza (TV) (9-11/61)-Photo-c	17	34	51	120	223	325
1222-Elmer Fudd (9-11/61)	4	8	12	26	41	55
1223-Laramie (TV)-Gil Kane-a; photo-c	6	12	18	43	69	95
1224-The Little Rascals (TV) (10-12/61)	5	10	15	30	48	65
1225-The Deputy (TV)-Henry Fonda photo-c	9	18	27	63	107	150
1226-Nikki, Wild Dog of the North (Disney-Movie) (9/61)-Photo-c	5	10	15	34	55	75
1227-Morgan the Pirate (Movie)-Photo-c	7	14	21	50	83	115
1229-Thief of Baghdad (Movie)-Crandall/Evans-a; photo-c	7	14	21	45	73	100
1230-Voyage to the Bottom of the Sea (#1) (Movie)-Photo insert on-c	10	20	30	71	126	180
1231-Danger Man (TV) (9-11/61)-Patrick McGoohan photo-c	10	20	30	71	126	180
1232-On the Double (Movie)	5	10	15	30	48	65
1233-Tammy Tell Me True (Movie) (1961)	6	12	18	43	69	95
1234-The Phantom Planet (Movie) (1961)	7	14	21	47	76	105
1235-Mister Magoo (#1) (12-2/62)	8	16	24	56	93	130
1235-Mister Magoo (3-5/65) 2nd printing; reprint of 12-2/62 issue	6	12	18	41	66	90
1236-King of Kings (Movie)-Photo-c	7	14	21	50	83	115
1237-The Untouchables (#1) (TV)-Not by Toth; photo-c	20	40	60	143	264	385
1238-Deputy Dawg (TV)	10	20	30	73	129	185
1239-Donald Duck Album (Disney) (10-12/61)-Barks-c	7	14	21	45	73	100
1240-The Detectives (TV)-Tufts-a; Robert Taylor photo-c	8	16	24	56	93	130
1241-Sweetie Pie	4	8	12	24	37	50
1242-King Leonardo and His Short Subjects (#1) (TV) (11-1/62)	12	24	36	84	150	215
1243-Ellery Queen	8	16	24	56	93	130
1244-Space Mouse (Lantz) (11-1/62)	4	8	12	28	44	60
1245-New Adventures of Sherlock Holmes	13	26	39	90	160	230
1246-Mickey Mouse Album (Disney)	5	10	15	34	55	75
1247-Daisy Duck's Diary (Disney) (12-2/62)	5	10	15	32	51	70
1248-Pluto (Disney)	4	8	12	28	44	60
1249-The Danny Thomas Show (TV)-Manning-a; photo-c	15	30	45	107	196	285
1250-The Four Horsemen of the Apocalypse (Movie)-Photo-c	6	12	18	43	69	95
1251-Everything's Ducky (Movie) (1961)	5	10	15	30	48	65
1252-The Andy Griffith Show (TV)-Photo-c; 1st show aired 10/3/60	35	70	105	270	498	725
1253-Space Man (#1) (1-3/62)	7	14	21	49	80	110
1254- "Diver Dan" (#1) (TV) (2-4/62)-Photo-c	5	10	15	34	55	75
1255-The Wonders of Aladdin (Movie) (1961)	6	12	18	43	69	95
1256-Kona, Monarch of Monster Isle (#1) (2-4/62)-Glanzman-a	9	18	27	63	107	150
1257-Car 54, Where Are You? (#1) (TV) (3-5/62)-Photo-c	8	16	24	56	93	130
1258-The Frogmen (#1)-Evans-a	8	16	24	52	86	120
1259-El Cid (Movie) (1961)-Photo-c	7	14	21	47	76	105
1260-The Horsemasters (TV, Movie) (Disney) (12-2/62)-Annette Funicello photo-c	12	24	36	87	156	225
1261-Rawhide (TV)-Clint Eastwood photo-c	14	28	42	102	181	260
1262-The Rebel (TV)-Photo-c	8	16	24	56	93	130
1263-77 Sunset Strip (TV) (12-2/62)-Manning-a; photo-c	8	16	24	54	90	125
1264-Pixie and Dixie and Mr. Jinks (TV) (Hanna-Barbera)	6	12	18	37	59	80
1265-The Real McCoys (TV)-Photo-c	8	16	24	56	93	130
1266-M.G.M.'s Spike and Tyke (12-2/62)	4	8	12	24	37	50
1267-Gyro Gearloose; Barks-c/a, 4 pgs. (Disney) (12-2/62)	8	16	24	54	90	125
1268-Oswald the Rabbit (Lantz)	4	8	12	28	44	60
1269-Rawhide (TV)-Clint Eastwood photo-c	14	28	42	102	181	260
1270-Bullwinkle and Rocky (#1) (TV) (Jay Ward) (3-5/62)	18	36	54	133	247	360
1271-Yogi Bear Birthday Party (TV) (Hanna-Barbera) (11/61) (Given away for 1 box top from Kellogg's Corn Flakes)	6	12	18	37	59	80
1272-Frosty the Snowman	5	10	15	32	51	70
1273-Hans Brinker (Disney-Movie)-Photo-c (2/62)	6	12	18	43	69	95
1274-Santa Claus Funnies (12/61)	6	12	18	41	66	90
1275-Rocky and His Friends (TV) (Jay Ward)	18	36	54	133	247	360
1276-Dondi	4	8	12	22	34	45
1278-King Leonardo and His Short Subjects (TV)	12	24	36	84	150	215

Four Color Comics #1297
© Hal Roach Studios

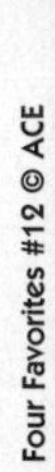
Four Favorites #12 © ACE

4-Most V5 #4 © Premium Services

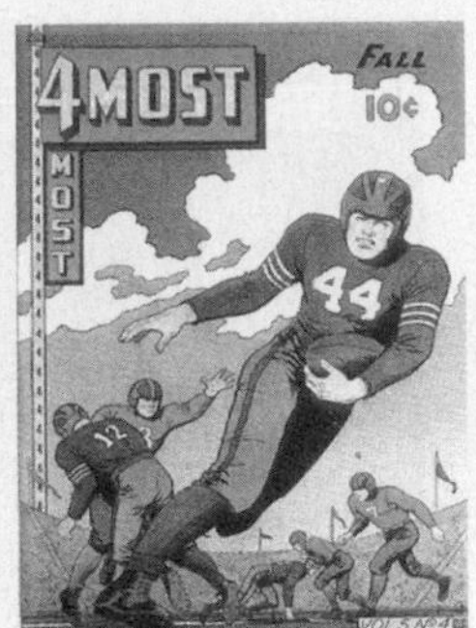

	GD 2.0	VG 4.0	FN 6.0	VF 8.0	VF/NM 9.0	NM- 9.2
1279-Grandma Duck's Farm Friends (Disney)	5	10	15	32	51	70
1280-Hennesey (TV)-Photo-c	6	12	18	43	69	95
1281-Chilly Willy (Lantz) (4-6/62)	5	10	15	30	48	65
1282-Babes in Toyland (Disney-Movie) (1/62); Annette Funicello photo-c	14	28	42	99	175	250
1283-Bonanza (TV) (2-4/62)-Photo-c	17	34	51	120	223	325
1284-Laramie (TV)-Heath-a; photo-c	6	12	18	43	69	95
1285-Leave It to Beaver (TV)-Photo-c	13	26	39	95	168	240
1286-The Untouchables (TV)-Photo-c	14	28	42	102	181	260
1287-Man from Wells Fargo (TV)-Photo-c	6	12	18	37	59	80
1288-Twilight Zone (TV) (4/62)-Crandall/Evans-c/a	12	24	36	87	156	225
1289-Ellery Queen	8	16	24	56	93	130
1290-M.G.M.'s Mouse Musketeers	4	8	12	24	37	50
1291-77 Sunset Strip (TV)-Manning-a; photo-c	8	16	24	54	90	125
1293-Elmer Fudd (3-5/62)	4	8	12	26	41	55
1294-Ripcord (TV)	7	14	21	47	76	105
1295-Mister Ed, the Talking Horse (#1) (TV) (3-5/62)-Photo-c	12	24	36	87	156	225
1296-Fury (TV) (3-5/62)-Photo-c	6	12	18	41	66	90
1297-Spanky, Alfalfa and the Little Rascals (TV)	5	10	15	30	48	65
1298-The Hathaways (TV)-Photo-c	5	10	15	30	48	65
1299-Deputy Dawg (TV)	10	20	30	73	129	185
1300-The Comancheros (Movie) (1961)-John Wayne photo-c	15	30	45	105	188	270
1301-Adventures in Paradise (TV) (2-4/62)	6	12	18	39	62	85
1302-Johnny Jason, Teen Reporter (2-4/62)	4	8	12	24	37	50
1303-Lad: A Dog (Movie)-Photo-c	4	8	12	28	44	60
1304-Nellie the Nurse (3-5/62)-Stanley-a	7	14	21	47	76	105
1305-Mister Magoo (3-5/62)	8	16	24	56	93	130
1306-Target: The Corruptors (#1) (TV) (3-5/62)-Photo-c	6	12	18	37	59	80
1307-Margie (TV) (3-5/62)	6	12	18	37	59	80
1308-Tales of the Wizard of Oz (TV) (3-5/62)	11	22	33	79	140	200
1309-87th Precinct (#1) (TV) (4-6/62)-Krigstein-a; photo-c	9	18	27	65	113	160
1310-Huck and Yogi Winter Sports (TV) (Hanna-Barbera) (3/62)	8	16	24	56	93	130
1311-Rocky and His Friends (TV) (Jay Ward)	18	36	54	133	247	360
1312-National Velvet (TV)-Photo-c	4	8	12	28	44	60
1313-Moon Pilot (Disney-Movie)-Photo-c	7	14	21	47	76	105
1328-The Underwater City (Movie) (1961)-Evans-a; photo-c	7	14	21	47	76	105
1329-See Gyro Gearloose #01329-207						
1330-Brain Boy (#1)-Gil Kane-a	11	22	33	79	140	200
1332-Bachelor Father (TV)	7	14	21	50	83	115
1333-Short Ribs (4-6/62)	5	10	15	34	55	75
1335-Aggie Mack (4-6/62)	4	8	12	28	44	60
1336-On Stage; not by Leonard Starr	5	10	15	30	48	65
1337-Dr. Kildare (#1) (TV) (4-6/62)-Photo-c	8	16	24	58	97	135
1341-The Andy Griffith Show (TV) (4-6/62)-Photo-c	32	64	96	246	461	675
1348-Yak Yak (#2)-Jack Davis-c/a	8	16	24	52	86	120
1349-Yogi Bear Visits the U.N. (TV) (Hanna-Barbera) (1/62)-Photo-c	8	16	24	58	97	135
1350-Comanche (Disney-Movie)(1962)-Reprints 4-Color #966 (title change from "Tonka" to "Comanche") (4-6/62)-Sal Mineo photo-c	5	10	15	35	55	75
1354-Calvin & the Colonel (#1) (TV) (4-6/62)	8	16	24	56	93	130

NOTE: *Missing numbers probably do not exist.*

4-D MONKEY, THE (Adventures of... #? on)
Leung's Publications: 1988 - No. 11, 1990 ($1.80/$2.00, 52 pgs.)

1-11: 1-Karate Pig, Ninja Flounder & 4-D Monkey (48 pgs., centerfold is a Christmas card). 2-4 (52 pgs.) 2.50

FOUR FAVORITES (Crime Must Pay the Penalty No. 33 on)
Ace Magazines: Sept, 1941 - No. 32, Dec, 1947

	GD 2.0	VG 4.0	FN 6.0	VF 8.0	VF/NM 9.0	NM- 9.2
1-Vulcan, Lash Lightning (formerly Flash Lightning in Sure-Fire), Magno the Magnetic Man & The Raven begin; flag/Hitler-c	177	354	531	1115	1883	2650
2-The Black Ace only app.	62	124	186	391	663	935
3-Last Vulcan	52	104	156	322	536	750
4,5: 4-The Raven & Vulcan end; Unknown Soldier begins (see Our Flag), ends #28. 5-Captain Courageous begins (5/42), ends #28 (moves over from Captain Courageous #6); not in #6	45	90	135	279	465	650
6-8: 6-The Flag app.; Mr. Risk begins (7/42)	41	82	123	256	428	600
9-Kurtzman-a (Lash Lightning); robot-c	46	92	138	285	473	660
10-Classic Kurtzman-c/a (Magno & Davey)	53	106	159	330	553	775
11-Kurtzman-a; Hitler, Mussolini, Hirohito-c; L.B. Cole-a; Unknown Soldier by Kurtzman	77	154	231	481	816	1150
12-L.B. Cole-a	39	78	117	230	370	510
13-20: 18,20-Palais-c/a	34	68	102	198	319	440
21-No Unknown Soldier; The Unknown app.	23	46	69	135	218	300
22-26: 22-Captain Courageous drops costume. 23-Unknown Soldier drops costume. 25-29-Hap Hazard app. 26-Last Magno	23	46	69	135	218	300
27-29: Hap Hazard app. in all	19	38	57	112	176	240
30-32: 30-Funny-c begin (teen humor), end #32	14	28	42	82	121	160

NOTE: ***Dave Berg** c-5. **Jim Mooney** a-6; c-1-3. **Palais** a-18-20; c-18-25. Torture chamber c-5.*

FOUR HORSEMEN, THE (See The Crusaders)

FOUR HORSEMEN
DC Comics (Vertigo): Feb, 2000 - No. 4, May, 2000 ($2.50, limited series)

1-4-Essad Ribic-c/a; Robert Rodi-s 2.50

FOUR HORSEMEN OF THE APOCALYPSE, THE (Movie)
Dell Publishing Co.: No. 1250, Jan-Mar, 1962 (one-shot)

	GD 2.0	VG 4.0	FN 6.0	VF 8.0	VF/NM 9.0	NM- 9.2
Four Color 1250-Photo-c	6	12	18	43	69	95

4MOST (Foremost Boys No. 32-40; becomes Thrilling Crime Cases #41 on)
Novelty Publications/Star Publications No. 37-on:
Winter, 1941-42 - V8#5(#36), 9-10/49; #37, 11-12/49 - #40, 4-5/50

	GD 2.0	VG 4.0	FN 6.0	VF 8.0	VF/NM 9.0	NM- 9.2
V1#1-The Target by Sid Greene, The Cadet & Dick Cole begin with origins retold; produced by Funnies Inc.; quarterly issues begin, end V6#3	152	304	456	958	1617	2275
2-Last Target (Spr/42); WWII cover	62	124	186	391	665	935
3-Dan'l Flannel begins; flag-c	47	94	141	291	483	675
4-1pg. Dr. Seuss (signed) (Aut/42); fish in the face-c	49	98	147	304	507	710
V2#1-3	19	38	57	112	176	240
4-Hitler, Tojo & Mussolini app. as pumpkins on-c	40	80	120	235	380	525
V3#1-4	15	30	45	88	137	185
V4#1-4: 2-Walter Johnson-c	13	26	39	74	105	135
V5#1-4: 1-The Target & Targeteers app.	11	22	33	64	90	115
V6#1-4	10	20	30	56	76	95
5-L. B. Cole-c	20	40	60	114	180	245
V7#1,3,5, V8#1, 37	10	20	30	56	76	95
2,4,6-L. B. Cole-c. 6-Last Dick Cole	20	40	60	114	180	245
V8#2,3,5-L. B. Cole-c/a	23	46	69	133	214	295
4-L. B. Cole-a	15	30	45	83	124	165
38-40: 38-Johnny Weismuller (Tarzan) life story & Jim Braddock (boxer) life story. 38-40-L.B. Cole-c. 40-Last White Rider	17	34	51	98	154	210
Accepted Reprint 38-40 (nd): 40-r/Johnny Weismuller life story; all have L.B. Cole-c	10	20	30	56	76	95

411
Marvel Comics: June, 2003 - No. 3 ($3.50, limited series)

1,2-Tributes to peacemakers; s/a by various. 1-Millar, Quitely, Mack, Winslade & others-s/a. 2-Harris, Phillips, Manco, Bruce Jones. 3.50

FOUR-STAR BATTLE TALES
National Periodical Publications: Feb-Mar, 1973 - No. 5, Nov-Dec, 1973

	GD 2.0	VG 4.0	FN 6.0	VF 8.0	VF/NM 9.0	NM- 9.2
1-Reprints begin	3	6	9	16	23	30
2-5	2	4	6	10	14	18

NOTE: ***Drucker** r-1, 3-5. **Heath** r-2, 5; c-1. **Krigstein** r-5. **Kubert** r-4; c-2.*

FOUR STAR SPECTACULAR
National Periodical Publications: Mar-Apr, 1976 - No. 6, Jan-Feb, 1977

	GD 2.0	VG 4.0	FN 6.0	VF 8.0	VF/NM 9.0	NM- 9.2
1-Includes G.A. Flash story with new art	2	4	6	10	14	18
2-6: Reprints in all. 2-Infinity cover	1	3	4	6	8	10

NOTE: *All contain DC Superhero reprints. #1 has 68 pgs.; #2-6, 52 pgs.. #1, 4-Hawkman app.; #2-Kid Flash app.; #3-Green Lantern app; #2, 4, 5-Wonder Woman, Superboy app; #5-Green Arrow, Vigilante app; #6-Blackhawk G.A.-r.*

FOUR TEENERS (Formerly Crime Must Pay The Penalty; Dotty No. 35 on)
A. A. Wyn: No. 34, April, 1948 (52 pgs.)

	GD 2.0	VG 4.0	FN 6.0	VF 8.0	VF/NM 9.0	NM- 9.2
34-Teen-age comic; Dotty app.; Curly & Jerry continue from Four Favorites	8	16	24	42	54	65

FOURTH WORLD GALLERY, THE (Jack Kirby's...)
DC Comics: 1996 (9/96) ($3.50, one-shot)

nn-Pin-ups of Jack Kirby's Fourth World characters (New Gods, Forever People & Mister Miracle) by John Byrne, Rick Burchett, Dan Jurgens, Walt Simonson & others 3.50

FOUR WOMEN
DC Comics (Homage): Dec, 2001 - No. 5, Apr, 2002 ($2.95, limited series)

Fox Giant - March of Crime © FOX

Foxhole #1 © Mainline

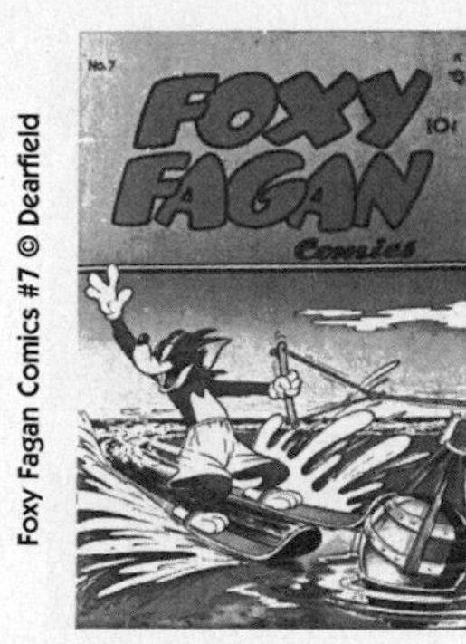

Foxy Fagan Comics #7 © Dearfield

	GD 2.0	VG 4.0	FN 6.0	VF 8.0	VF/NM 9.0	NM- 9.2
1-5-Sam Kieth-s/a						3.00
TPB (2002, $17.95) r/series; foreward by Kieth						18.00

FOX AND THE CROW (Stanley & His Monster No. 109 on) (See Comic Cavalcade & Real Screen Comics)
National Periodical Publications: Dec-Jan, 1951-52 - No. 108, Feb-Mar, 1968

	GD 2.0	VG 4.0	FN 6.0	VF 8.0	VF/NM 9.0	NM- 9.2
1	117	234	351	737	1249	1760
2(Scarce)	53	106	159	334	567	800
3-5	37	74	111	215	345	475
6-10	26	52	78	152	244	335
11-20	19	38	57	112	176	240
21-30: 22-Last precode issue (2/55)	14	28	42	82	121	160
31-40	12	24	36	69	97	125
41-60	6	12	18	43	69	95
61-80	5	10	15	34	55	75
81-94: 94-(11/65)-The Brat Finks begin	4	8	12	26	41	55
95-Stanley & His Monster begins (origin & 1st app)	5	10	15	35	55	75
96-99,101-108	3	6	9	20	30	40
100 (10-11/66)	4	8	12	22	34	45

NOTE: *Many later covers by **Mort Drucker**.*

FOX AND THE HOUND, THE (Disney)(Movie)
Whitman Publishing Co.: Aug, 1981 - No. 3, Oct, 1981

	GD 2.0	VG 4.0	FN 6.0	VF 8.0	VF/NM 9.0	NM- 9.2
11292- Golden Press Graphic Novel	2	4	6	8	10	12
1-3-Based on animated movie	1	2	3	5	7	9

FOXFIRE (See The Phoenix Resurrection)
Malibu Comics (Ultraverse): Feb, 1996 - No. 4, May, 1996 ($1.50)

	GD 2.0	VG 4.0	FN 6.0	VF 8.0	VF/NM 9.0	NM- 9.2
1-4: Sludge, Ultraforce app. 4-Punisher app.						2.50

FOX GIANTS (Also see Giant Comics Edition)
Fox Features Syndicate: 1944 - 1950 (25¢, 132 - 196 pgs.)

	GD 2.0	VG 4.0	FN 6.0	VF 8.0	VF/NM 9.0	NM- 9.2
Album of Crime nn(1949, 132p)	50	100	150	310	518	725
Album of Love nn(1949, 132p)	47	94	141	291	483	675
All Famous Crime Stories nn('49, 132p)	50	100	150	310	518	725
All Good Comics 1(1944, 132p)(R.W. Voigt)-The Bouncer, Purple Tigress, Rick Evans, Puppeteer, Green Mask; Infinity-c	40	80	120	244	397	550
All Great nn(1944, 132p)-Capt. Jack Terry, Rick Evans, Jaguar Man	40	80	120	244	397	550
All Great nn(Chicago Nite Life News)(1945, 132p)-Green Mask, Bouncer, Puppeteer, Rick Evans, Rocket Kelly	40	80	120	244	397	550
All-Great Confessions nn(1949, 132p)	45	90	135	279	465	650
All Great Crime Stories nn('49, 132p)	50	100	150	310	518	725
All Great Jungle Adventures nn('49, 132p)	53	106	159	334	567	800
All Real Confession Magazine 3 (3/49, 132p)	45	90	135	279	465	650
All Real Confession Magazine 4 (4/49, 132p)	45	90	135	279	465	650
All Your Comics 1(1944, 132p)-The Puppeteer, Red Robbins, & Merciless the Sorcerer	40	80	120	244	397	550
Almanac Of Crime nn(1948, 148p)-Phantom Lady	55	110	165	347	586	825
Almanac Of Crime 1(1950, 132p)	49	98	147	304	510	715
Book Of Love nn(1950, 132p)	43	86	129	267	446	625
Burning Romances 1(1949, 132p)	52	104	156	322	536	750
Crimes Incorporated nn(1950, 132p)	45	90	135	279	465	650
Daring Love Stories nn(1950, 132p)	43	86	129	267	446	625
Everybody's Comics 1(1944, 50¢, 196p)-The Green Mask, The Puppeteer, The Bouncer, Rocket Kelly, Rick Evans	45	90	135	279	465	650
Everybody's Comics 1(1946, 196p)-Green Lama, The Puppeteer	40	80	120	235	380	525
Everybody's Comics 1(1946, 196p)-Same as 1945 Ribtickler	31	62	93	181	291	400
Everybody's Comics nn(1947, 132p)-Jo-Jo, Purple Tigress, Cosmo Cat, Bronze Man	40	80	120	238	387	535
Exciting Romance Stories nn(1949, 132p)	47	94	141	291	483	675
Famous Love nn(1950, 132p)	43	86	129	267	446	625
Intimate Confessions nn(1950, 132p)	43	86	129	267	446	625
Journal Of Crime nn(1949, 132p)	50	100	150	310	518	725
Love Problems nn(1949, 132p)	45	90	135	279	465	650
Love Thrills nn(1950, 132p)	44	88	132	273	457	640
March of Crime nn('48, 132p)-Female w/rifle-c	48	96	144	298	499	700
March of Crime nn('49, 132p)-Cop w/pistol-c	47	94	141	291	483	675
March of Crime nn(1949, 132p)-Coffin & man w/machine-gun-c	47	94	141	291	483	675
Revealing Love Stories nn(1950, 132p)	43	86	129	267	446	625
Ribtickler nn(1945, 50¢, 196p)-Chicago Nite Life News; Marvel Mutt, Cosmo Cat, Flash Rabbit, The Nebbs app.	40	80	120	235	380	525
Romantic Thrills nn(1950, 132p)	43	86	129	267	446	625
Secret Love Stories nn(1949, 132p)	47	94	141	291	483	675
Strange Love nn(1950, 132p)-Photo-c	50	100	150	310	518	725
Sweetheart Scandals nn(1950, 132p)	43	86	129	267	446	625
Teen-Age Love nn(1950, 132p)	43	86	129	267	446	625
Throbbing Love nn(1950, 132p)-Photo-c, used in **POP**, pg. 107	50	100	150	310	518	725
Truth About Crime nn(1949, 132p)	50	100	150	310	518	725
Variety Comics 1(1946, 132p)-Blue Beetle, Jungle Jo	41	82	123	250	413	575
Variety Comics nn(1950, 132p)-Jungle Jo, My Secret Affair(w/Harrison/Wood-a), Crimes by Women & My Story	40	80	120	244	397	550
Western Roundup nn('50, 132p)-Hoot Gibson; Cody of the Pony Express app.	40	80	120	235	380	525

NOTE: *Each of the above usually contain four remaindered Fox books minus covers. Since these missing covers often had the first page of the first story, most Giants therefore are incomplete. Approximate values are listed. Books with appearances of Phantom Lady, Rulah, Jo-Jo, etc. could bring more.*

FOXHOLE (Becomes Never Again #8?)
Mainline/Charlton No. 5 on: 9-10/54 - No. 4, 3-4/55; No. 5, 7/55 - No. 7, 3/56

	GD 2.0	VG 4.0	FN 6.0	VF 8.0	VF/NM 9.0	NM- 9.2
1-Classic Kirby-c	48	96	144	298	499	700
2-Kirby-c/a(2); Kirby scripts based on his war time experiences	35	70	105	203	327	450
3-5-Kirby-c only	21	42	63	123	197	270
6-Kirby-c/a(2)	30	60	90	176	283	390
7	12	24	36	67	94	120
Super Reprints #10,15-17: 10-r/? 15,16-r/United States Marines #5,8. 17-r/Monty Hall #?	2	4	6	11	16	20
11,12,18-r/Foxhole #1,2,3; Kirby-c	3	6	9	17	25	32

NOTE: ***Kirby** a(r)-Super #11, 12. **Powell** a(r)-Super #15, 16. Stories by actual veterans.*

FOXY FAGAN COMICS (Funny Animal)
Dearfield Publishing Co.: Dec, 1946 - No. 7, Summer, 1948

	GD 2.0	VG 4.0	FN 6.0	VF 8.0	VF/NM 9.0	NM- 9.2
1-Foxy Fagan & Little Buck begin	13	26	39	72	101	130
2	8	16	24	42	54	65
3-7: 6-Rocket ship-c	7	14	21	37	46	55

FRACTION
DC Comics (Focus): June, 2004 - No. 6, Nov, 2004 ($2.50, limited series)

	GD 2.0	VG 4.0	FN 6.0	VF 8.0	VF/NM 9.0	NM- 9.2
1-6-David Tischman-s/Timothy Green II-a						2.50

FRACTURED FAIRY TALES (TV)
Gold Key: Oct, 1962 (Jay Ward)

	GD 2.0	VG 4.0	FN 6.0	VF 8.0	VF/NM 9.0	NM- 9.2
1 (10022-210)-From Bullwinkle TV show	10	20	30	71	126	180

FRAGGLE ROCK (TV)
Marvel Comics (Star Comics)/Marvel V2#1 on: Apr, 1985 - No. 8, Sept, 1986; V2#1, Apr, 1988 - No. 5, Aug, 1988

	GD 2.0	VG 4.0	FN 6.0	VF 8.0	VF/NM 9.0	NM- 9.2
1-6 (75¢-c)						5.00
7,8						6.00
V2#1-5-($1.00): Reprints 1st series						2.50

FRANCIS, BROTHER OF THE UNIVERSE
Marvel Comics Group: 1980 (75¢, 52 pgs., one-shot)

	GD 2.0	VG 4.0	FN 6.0	VF 8.0	VF/NM 9.0	NM- 9.2
nn-John Buscema/Marie Severin-a; story of Francis Bernadone celebrating his 800th birthday in 1982						4.00

FRANCIS THE FAMOUS TALKING MULE (All based on movie)
Dell Publishing Co.: No. 335 (#1), June, 1951 - No. 1090, March, 1960

	GD 2.0	VG 4.0	FN 6.0	VF 8.0	VF/NM 9.0	NM- 9.2
Four Color 335 (#1)	10	20	30	71	126	180
Four Color 465	6	12	18	41	66	90
Four Color 501,547,579	5	10	15	32	51	70
Four Color 621,655,698,710,745	4	8	12	28	44	60
Four Color 810,863,906,953,991,1068,1090	4	8	12	26	41	55

FRANK
Nemesis Comics (Harvey): Apr (Mar inside), 1994 - No. 4, 1994 ($1.75/$2.50, limited series)

	GD 2.0	VG 4.0	FN 6.0	VF 8.0	VF/NM 9.0	NM- 9.2
1-4-($2.50, direct sale): 1-Foil-c Edition						3.00
1-4-($1.75)-Newsstand Editions; Cowan-a in all						2.50

FRANK
Fantagraphics Books: Sept, 1996 ($2.95, B&W)

	GD 2.0	VG 4.0	FN 6.0	VF 8.0	VF/NM 9.0	NM- 9.2
1-Woodring-c/a/scripts						3.00

FRANK BUCK (Formerly My True Love)
Fox Features Syndicate: No. 70, May, 1950 - No. 3, Sept, 1950

	GD 2.0	VG 4.0	FN 6.0	VF 8.0	VF/NM 9.0	NM- 9.2
70-Wood a(p)(3 stories)-Photo-c	32	64	96	186	298	410
71-Wood-a (9 pgs.); photo/painted-c	17	3	51	100	158	215
3: 3-Photo/painted-c	14	28	42	80	115	150

Frankenstein #1 © MAR

Frankenstein Comics #1 © PRIZE

Fray #4 © Joss Whedon

	GD 2.0	VG 4.0	FN 6.0	VF 8.0	VF/NM 9.0	NM- 9.2

NOTE: *Based on "Bring 'Em Back Alive" TV show.*

FRANKENSTEIN (See Dracula, Movie Classics & Werewolf)
Dell Publishing Co.: Aug-Oct, 1964; No. 2, Sept, 1966 - No. 4, Mar, 1967

	GD	VG	FN	VF	VF/NM	NM-
1(12-283-410)(1964)(2nd printing; see Movie Classics for 1st printing)	5	10	15	34	55	75
2-Intro. & origin super-hero character (9/66)	4	8	12	26	41	55
3,4	3	6	9	18	27	35

FRANKENSTEIN (The Monster of...; also see Monsters Unleashed #2, Power Record Comics, Psycho & Silver Surfer #7)
Marvel Comics Group: Jan, 1973 - No. 18, Sept, 1975

	GD	VG	FN	VF	VF/NM	NM-
1-Ploog-c/a begins, ends #6	6	12	18	43	69	95
2	4	8	12	24	37	50
3-5	3	6	9	18	27	35
6,7,10: 7-Dracula cameo	3	6	9	16	22	28
8,9-Dracula c/sty. 9-Death of Dracula	4	8	12	26	41	55
11-17	2	4	6	13	18	22
18-Wrightson-c(i)	3	6	9	14	20	26

NOTE: ***Adkins** c-17i. **Buscema** a-7-10p. **Ditko** a-12r. **G. Kane** c-15p. **Orlando** a-8r. **Ploog** a-1-3, 4p, 5p, 6; c-1-6. **Wrightson** c-18i.*

FRANKENSTEIN (Mary Wollstonecraft Shelley's...; A Marvel Illustrated Novel)
Marvel Pub.: 1983 ($8.95, B&W, 196 pgs., 8x11" TPB)

	GD	VG	FN	VF	VF/NM	NM-
nn-Wrightson-a; 4 pg. intro. by Stephen King	4	8	12	28	44	60
Limited HC Edition						165.00

FRANKENSTEIN COMICS (Also See Prize Comics)
Prize Publ. (Crestwood/Feature): Sum, 1945 - V5#5(#33), Oct-Nov, 1954

	GD	VG	FN	VF	VF/NM	NM-
1-Frankenstein begins by Dick Briefer (origin); Frank Sinatra parody	120	240	360	756	1278	1800
2	55	110	165	347	586	825
3-5	41	82	123	256	428	600
6-10: 7-S&K a(r)/Headline Comics. 8(7-8/47)-Superman satire	38	76	114	226	363	500
11-17(1-2/49)-11-Boris Karloff parody-c/story. 17-Last humor issue	33	66	99	194	312	430
18(3/52)-New origin, horror series begins	41	82	123	256	428	600
19,20(V3#4, 8-9/52)	28	56	84	164	265	365
21(V3#5), 22(V3#6), 23(V4#1) - #28(V4#6)	26	52	78	154	247	340
29(V5#1) - #33(V5#5)	25	50	75	149	240	330

NOTE: ***Briefer** c/a-all. **Meskin** a-21, 29.*

FRANKENSTEIN/DRACULA WAR, THE
Topps Comics: Feb, 1995 - No. 3, May, 1995 ($2.50, limited series)

	GD	VG	FN	VF	VF/NM	NM-
1-3						3.00

FRANKENSTEIN, JR. (...& the Impossibles) (TV)
Gold Key: Jan, 1966 (Hanna-Barbera)

	GD	VG	FN	VF	VF/NM	NM-
1-Super hero (scarce)	11	22	33	77	136	195

FRANKENSTEIN MOBSTER
Image Comics: No. 0, Oct, 2003 - No. 7, Dec, 2004 ($2.95)

	GD	VG	FN	VF	VF/NM	NM-
0-7: 0-Two covers by Wheatley and Hughes; Wheatley-s/a. 1-Variant-c by Wieringo						3.00

FRANKENSTEIN: OR THE MODERN PROMETHEUS
Caliber Press: 1994 ($2.95, one-shot)

	GD	VG	FN	VF	VF/NM	NM-
1						3.00

FRANK FRAZETTA FANTASY ILLUSTRATED (Magazine)
Quantum Cat Entertainment: Spring 1998 - No. 8 ($5.95, quarterly)

	GD	VG	FN	VF	VF/NM	NM-
1-Anthology; art by Corben, Horley, Jusko	1	2	3	4	5	7
1-Linsner variant-c						10.00
2-Battle Chasers by Madureira; Harris-a						8.00
2-Madureira Battle Chasers variant-c						12.00
3-8-Frazetta-c						6.00
3-Tony Daniel variant-c						15.00
5,6-Portacio variant-c, 7,8-Alex Nino variant-c						10.00
8-Alex Ross Chicago Comicon variant-c						10.00

FRANK FRAZETTA'S DEATH DEALER
Image Comics: Mar, 2007 - No. 6, Jan, 2008 ($3.99)

	GD	VG	FN	VF	VF/NM	NM-
1-6-Nat Jones-a; 3 covers (Frazetta, Jones, Jones sketch)						4.00

FRANK FRAZETTA'S...
Fantagraphics Books/Image Comics: one-shots

	GD	VG	FN	VF	VF/NM	NM-
... Creatures 1 (Image Comics, 7/08, $3.99) Bergting-a; covers by Frazetta & Bergting						4.00
... Dark Kingdom 1 (Image, 4/08, $3.99) Tim Vigil-a; covers by Frazetta & Vigil						4.00
... Dracula Meets the Wolfman 1 (Image, 8/08, $3.99) Francavilla-a; 2 covers						4.00
... Swamp Demon 1 (Image, 7/08, $3.99) Medors-a; covers by Frazetta & Medors						4.00
... Thun'da Tales 1 (Fantagraphics Books, 1987, $2.00) Frazetta-r						6.00
... Untamed Love 1 (Fantagraphics Books, 11/87, $2.00) r/1950's romance comics						6.00

FRANKIE COMICS (...& Lana No. 13-15) (Formerly Movie Tunes; becomes Frankie Fuddle No. 16 on)
Marvel Comics (MgPC): No. 4, Wint, 1946-47 - No. 15, June, 1949

	GD	VG	FN	VF	VF/NM	NM-
4-Mitzi, Margie, Daisy app.	15	30	45	85	130	175
5-9	10	20	30	56	76	95
10-15: 13-Anti-Wertham editorial	9	18	27	52	69	85

FRANKIE DOODLE (See Sparkler, both series)
United Features Syndicate: No. 7, 1939

	GD	VG	FN	VF	VF/NM	NM-
Single Series 7	33	66	99	192	309	425

FRANKIE FUDDLE (Formerly Frankie & Lana)
Marvel Comics: No. 16, Aug, 1949 - No. 17, Nov, 1949

	GD	VG	FN	VF	VF/NM	NM-
16,17	9	18	27	52	69	85

FRANKLIN RICHARDS (Fantastic Four)
Marvel Comics: April, 2006 - Present ($2.99, one-shots)

	GD	VG	FN	VF	VF/NM	NM-
...: Collected Chaos (2008, $8.99, digest) reprints various one-shots						8.00
...: Fall Football Fiasco (1/08, $2.99) Eliopoulos-a/Sumerak-s						3.00
...: Happy Franksgiving (1/07, $2.99) Thanksgiving stories by Eliopoulos-a/Sumerak-s						3.00
...: Lab Brat (2007, $7.99, digest) reprints one-shots and Masked Marvel back-ups						8.00
...: March Madness (5/07, $2.99) More science gone wrong by Eliopoulos-a/Sumerak-s						3.00
...: Monster Mash (11/07, $2.99) Science mishaps by Eliopoulos-a/Sumerak-s						3.00
...: Not-So-Secret Invasion (7/08, $2.99) Skrull cover; The Wizard app.						3.00
... One Shot (4/06, $2.99) short stories by Eliopoulos-a/Sumerak-s						3.00
...: Spring Break (5/08, $2.99) short stories by Eliopoulos-a/Sumerak-s						3.00
...: Summer Smackdown (10/08, $2.99) short stories by Eliopoulos-a/Sumerak-s						3.00
...: Super Summer Spectacular (9/06, $2.99) short stories by Eliopoulos-a/Sumerak-s						3.00
...: World Be Warned (8/07, $2.99) short stories by Eliopoulos-a/Sumerak-s; Hulk app.						3.00

FRANK LUTHER'S SILLY PILLY COMICS (See Jingle Dingle...)
Children's Comics (Maltex Cereal): 1950 (10¢)

	GD	VG	FN	VF	VF/NM	NM-
1-Characters from radio, records, & TV	8	16	24	44	57	70

FRANK MERRIWELL AT YALE (Speed Demons No. 5 on?)
Charlton Comics: June, 1955 - No. 4, Jan, 1956 (Also see Shadow Comics)

	GD	VG	FN	VF	VF/NM	NM-
1	7	14	21	37	46	55
2-4	5	10	15	24	30	35

FRANTIC (Magazine) (See Ratfink & Zany)
Pierce Publishing Co.: Oct, 1958 - V2#2, Apr, 1959 (Satire)

	GD	VG	FN	VF	VF/NM	NM-
V1#1	12	24	36	69	97	125
2	9	18	27	52	69	85
V2#1,2: 1-Burgos-a, Severin-c/a; Powell-a?	8	16	24	42	54	65

FRAY
Dark Horse Comics: June, 2001 - No. 8, July, 2003 ($2.99, limited series)

	GD	VG	FN	VF	VF/NM	NM-
1-Joss Whedon-s/Moline & Owens-a	1	2	3	5	6	8
1-DF Gold edition	2	4	6	9	12	15
2-8: 6-(3/02). 7-(4/03)						4.00
TPB (11/03, $19.95) r/#1-8; intros by Whedon & Loeb; Moline sketch pages						20.00

FREAK FORCE (Also see Savage Dragon)
Image Comics (Highbrow Ent.): Dec, 1993 - No. 18, July, 1995 ($1.95/$2.50)

	GD	VG	FN	VF	VF/NM	NM-
1-18-Superpatriot & Mighty Man in all; Erik Larsen scripts in all. 4-Vanguard app. 8-Begin $2.50-c. 9-Cyberforce-c & app. 13-Variant-c						3.00

FREAK FORCE (Also see Savage Dragon)
Image Comics: Apr, 1997 - No. 3, July, 1997 ($2.95)

	GD	VG	FN	VF	VF/NM	NM-
1-3-Larsen-s						3.00

FREAK OUT, USA (See On the Scene Presents...)

FREAK SHOW
Image Comics (Desperado): 2006 ($5.99, B&W, one-shot)

	GD	VG	FN	VF	VF/NM	NM-
nn-Bruce Jones-s/Bernie Wrightson-c/a						6.00

FREAKS OF THE HEARTLAND
Dark Horse Comics: Jan, 2004 - No. 6, Nov, 2004 ($2.99)

	GD	VG	FN	VF	VF/NM	NM-
1-6-Steve Niles-s/Greg Ruth-a						3.00

FRECKLES AND HIS FRIENDS (See Crackajack Funnies, Famous Comics Cartoon Book, Honeybee Birdwhistle... & Red Ryder)

FRECKLES AND HIS FRIENDS
Standard Comics/Argo: No. 5, 11/47 - No. 12, 8/49; 11/55 - No. 4, 6/56

Freckles and His Friends #7 © STD

Freddy vs. Jason vs. Ash #1 © New Line & MGM

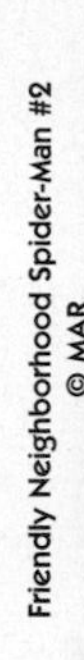
Friendly Neighborhood Spider-Man #2 © MAR

GD VG FN VF VF/NM NM-
2.0 4.0 6.0 8.0 9.0 9.2

5-Reprints 9 18 27 50 65 80
6-12-Reprints. 7-9-Airbrush-c (by Schomburg?). 11-Lingerie panels
7 14 21 35 43 50

NOTE: *Some copies of No. 8 & 9 contain a printing oddity. The negatives were elongated in the engraving process, probably to conform to page dimensions on the filler pages. Those pages only look normal when viewed at a 45 degree angle.*

1(Argo,'55)-Reprints (NEA Service) 6 12 18 28 34 40
2-4 4 8 12 18 22 25

FREDDY (Formerly My Little Margie's Boy Friends) (Also see Blue Bird)
Charlton Comics: V2#12, June, 1958 - No. 47, Feb, 1965

V2#12 4 8 12 22 34 45
13-15 3 6 9 16 22 28
16-47 2 4 6 11 16 20

FREDDY
Dell Publishing Co.: May-July, 1963 - No. 3, Oct-Dec, 1964

1 3 6 9 19 29 38
2,3 3 6 9 14 20 26

FREDDY KRUEGER'S A NIGHTMARE ON ELM STREET
Marvel Comics: Oct, 1989 - No. 2, Dec, 1989 ($2.25, B&W, movie adaptation, magazine)

1,2: Origin Freddy Krueger; Buckler/Alcala-a 6.00

FREDDY'S DEAD: THE FINAL NIGHTMARE
Innovation Publishing: Oct, 1991 - No. 3, Dec 1991 ($2.50, color mini-series, adapts movie)

1-3: Dismukes (film poster artist) painted-c 3.00

FREDDY VS. JASON VS. ASH (Freddy Krueger, Friday the 13th, Army of Darkness)
DC Comics (WildStorm): Early Jan, 2008 - No. 6, May, 2008 ($2.99, limited series)

1-Three covers by J. Scott Campbell; Kuhoric-s/Craig-a 5.00
1-Second printing with 3 covers combined sideways 4.00
2-6: 2-4-Eric Powell-c. 5,6-Richard Friend-c 3.00
2-4 Second printings with B&W covers 3.00

FRED HEMBECK DESTROYS THE MARVEL UNIVERSE
Marvel Comics: July, 1989 ($1.50, one-shot)

1-Punisher app.; Staton-i (5 pgs.) 3.00

FRED HEMBECK SELLS THE MARVEL UNIVERSE
Marvel Comics: Oct, 1990 ($1.25, one-shot)

1-Punisher, Wolverine parodies; Hembeck/Austin-c 3.00

FREEDOM AGENT (Also see John Steele)
Gold Key: Apr, 1963 (12¢)

1 (10054-304)-Painted-c 4 8 12 26 41 55

FREEDOM FIGHTERS (See Justice League of America #107,108)
National Periodical Publ./DC Comics: Mar-Apr, 1976 - No. 15, July-Aug, 1978

1-Uncle Sam, The Ray, Black Condor, Doll Man, Human Bomb, & Phantom Lady begin (all former Quality characters) 2 4 6 13 18 22
2-9: 4,5-Wonder Woman x-over. 7-1st app. Crusaders 2 4 6 8 11 14
10-15: 10-Origin Doll Man; Cat-Man-c/story (4th app; 1st revival since Detective #325). 11-Origin The Ray. 12-Origin Firebrand. 13-Origin Black Condor. 14-Batgirl & Batwoman app. 15-Batgirl & Batwoman app.; origin Phantom Lady
2 4 6 9 12 15

NOTE: ***Buckler** c-5-11p, 13p, 14p.*

FREEDOM FORCE
Image Comics: Jan, 2005 - No. 6, June, 2005 ($2.95)

1-6-Eric Dieter-s/Tom Scioli-a 3.00

FREEMIND
Future Comics: No. 0, Aug, 2002; Nov, 2002 - No. 7, June, 2003 ($3.50)

0-($2.25) Giordano-c 2.50
0-($2.25) Variant-c by Layton 2.50
1-7 ($3.50) 1-Two covers by Giordano & Layton; Giordano-a thru #3. 4,5-Leeke-a 3.50

FREEX
Malibu Comics (Ultraverse): July, 1993 - No. 18, Mar, 1995 ($1.95)

1-3,5-14,16-18: 1-Polybagged w/trading card. 2-Some were polybagged w/card. 6-Nightman-c/story. 7-2 pg. origin Hardcase by Zeck. 17-Rune app. 2.50
1-Holographic-c edition 6.00
1-Ultra 5,000 limited silver ink-c 3.00
4-($2.50, 48 pgs.)-Rune flip-c/story by B. Smith (3 pgs.); 3 pg. Night Man preview 2.50
15 ($3.50)-w/Ultraverse Premiere #9 flip book; Alec Swan & Rafferty app. 3.50
Giant Size 1 (1994, $2.50)-Prime app. 2.50

NOTE: ***Simonson** c-1.*

FRENZY (Magazine) (Satire)

GD VG FN VF VF/NM NM-
2.0 4.0 6.0 8.0 9.0 9.2

Picture Magazine: Apr, 1958 - No. 6, Mar, 1959

1 13 26 39 72 101 130
2-6 8 16 24 44 57 70

FRESHMEN
Image Comics: Jul, 2005 - No. 6, Mar, 2006 ($2.99)

1-Sterbakov-s/Kirk-a; co-created by Seth Green; covers by Pérez, Migliari, Linsner 3.00
2-6-Migliari-c 3.00
... Yearbook (1/06, $2.99) profile pages of characters; art by various incl. Chaykin, Kirk 3.00
... Vol. 1 (3/06, $16.99, TPB) r/#1-6 & Yearbook; cover gallery with concept art 17.00

FRESHMEN (Volume 2)
Image Comics: Nov, 2006 - No. 6, Aug, 2007 ($2.99)

1-6: 1-Sterbakov-s/Conrad-a; 4 covers 3.00
...: Summer Vacation Special (7/08, $4.99) Sterbakov-s; bonus pin-ups by various 5.00
... Vol. 2 Fundamentals of Fear (6/07, $16.99, TPB) r/#1-6; cover gallery, journals 17.00

FRIDAY FOSTER
Dell Publishing Co.: October, 1972

1 3 6 9 20 30 40

FRIDAY THE 13TH (Based on the horror movie franchise)
DC Comics (WildStorm): Feb, 2007 - No. 6, July, 2007 ($2.99, mature)

1-6: 1-Two covers by Sook and Bradstreet; Gray & Palmiotti-s 3.00
...: Abuser and The Abused (6/08, $3.50) Fialkov-s/Andy B. -a 3.50
.... Bad Land 1,2 (3/08 - No. 2, 4/08, $2.99) Marz-s/Huddleston-a/McKone-c 3.00
...: How I Spent My Summer Vacation 1,2 (11/07 - No. 2, 12/07, $2.99) Aaron-s/Archer-a 3.00
...: Pamela's Tale 1,2 (9/07 - No. 2, 10/07, $2.99) Andreyko-s/Moll-a/Nguyen-c 3.00

FRIENDLY GHOST, CASPER, THE (Becomes Casper... #254 on)
Harvey Publications: Aug, 1958 - No. 224, Oct, 1982; No. 225, Oct, 1986 - No. 253, June, 1990

1-Infinity-c 33 66 99 254 477 700
2 15 30 45 111 206 300
3-10: 6-X-Mas-c 9 18 27 64 110 155
11-20: 18-X-Mas-c 7 14 21 40 80 110
21-30 5 10 15 32 51 70
31-50 4 8 12 24 37 50
51-70,100: 54-X-Mas-c 3 6 9 20 30 40
71-99 3 6 9 16 23 30
101-131: 131-Last 12¢ issue 3 6 9 14 20 26
132-159 2 4 6 11 16 20
160-163: All 52 pg. Giants 3 6 9 14 20 26
164-199: 173,179,185-Cub Scout Specials 2 4 6 8 10 12
200 2 4 6 8 11 14
201-224 1 2 3 5 7 9
225-237: 230-X-mas-c. 232-Valentine's-c 5.00
238-253: 238-Begin $1.00-c. 238,244-Halloween-c. 243-Last new material 4.00

FRIENDLY NEIGHBORHOOD SPIDER-MAN
Marvel Comics: Dec, 2005 - No. 24, Nov, 2007 ($2.99)

1-Evolve or Die pt. 1; Peter David-s/Mike Wieringo-a; Morlun app. 4.00
1-Variant Wieringo-c with regular costume 3.00
2-4: 2-New Avengers app. 3-Spider-Man dies 3.00
2-4-var-c: 2-Bag-Head Fantastic Four costume. 3-Captain Universe. 4-Wrestler 5.00
5-23: 6-Red & gold costume. 8-10-Uncle Ben app. 17-Black costume; Sandman app. 3.00
24-($3.99) "One More Day" part 2; Quesada-a; covers by Quesada & Djurdjevic 4.00
Annual 1 (7/07, $3.99) Origin of The Sandman; back-up w/Doran-a 4.00
... Vol. 1: Derailed (2006, $14.99) r/#5-10; Wieringo sketch pages 15.00
... Vol. 2: Mystery Date (2007, $13.99) r/#11-16 14.00

FRIENDS OF MAXX (Also see Maxx)
Image Comics (I Before E): Apr, 1996 - No. 3, Mar, 1997 ($2.95)

1-3: Sam Kieth-c/a/scripts. 1-Featuring Dude Japan 3.00

FRIGHT
Atlas/Seaboard Periodicals: June, 1975 (Aug. on inside)

1-Origin/1st app. The Son of Dracula; Frank Thorne-c/a
2 4 6 8 10 12

FRIGHT NIGHT
Now Comics: Oct, 1988 - No. 22, 1990 ($1.75)

1-22: 1,2 Adapts movie. 8, 9-Evil Ed horror photo-c from movie 2.50

FRIGHT NIGHT II
Now Comics: 1989 ($3.95, 52 pgs.)

1-Adapts movie sequel 4.00

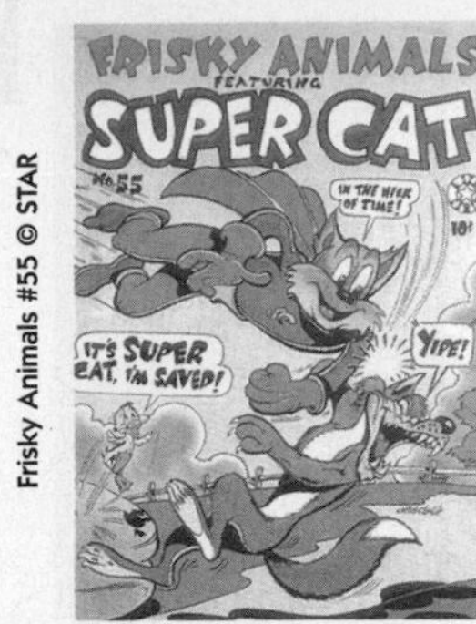

Frisky Animals #55 © STAR

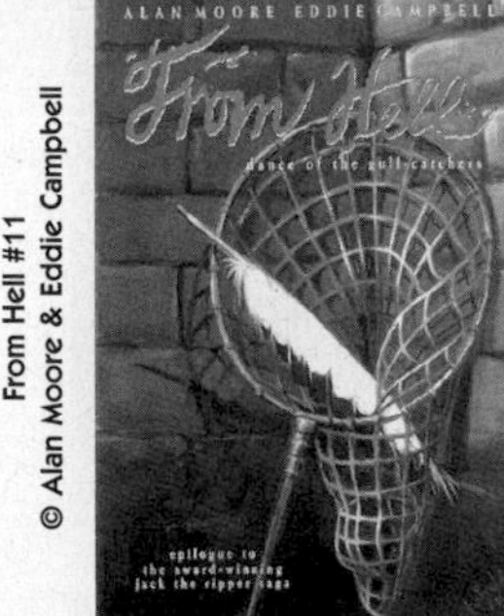

From Hell #11 © Alan Moore & Eddie Campbell

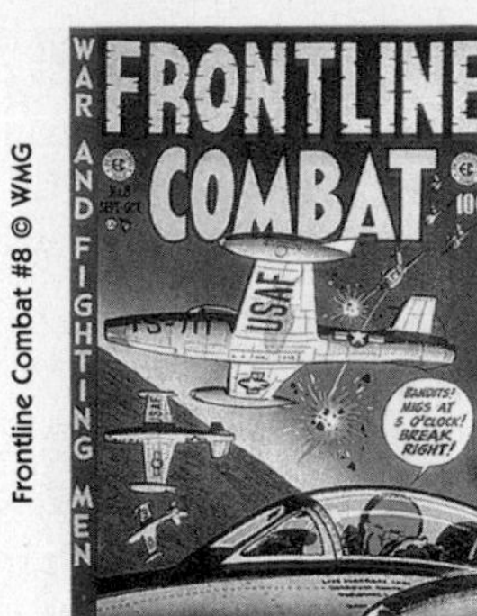

Frontline Combat #8 © WMG

FRISKY ANIMALS (Formerly Frisky Fables; Super Cat #56 on)
Star Publications: No. 44, Jan, 1951 - No. 55, Sept, 1953

	GD 2.0	VG 4.0	FN 6.0	VF 8.0	VF/NM 9.0	NM- 9.2
44-Super Cat; L.B. Cole	23	46	69	130	205	280
45-Classic L. B. Cole-c	32	64	96	186	293	400
46-51,53-55: Super Cat. 54-Super Cat-c begin	21	42	63	122	191	260
52-L. B. Cole-c/a, 3 1/2 pgs.; X-Mas-c	23	46	69	130	205	280

NOTE: *All have* ***L. B. Cole****-c. No. 47-No Super Cat.* ***Disbrow*** *a-49, 52.* ***Fago*** *a-51.*

FRISKY ANIMALS ON PARADE (Formerly Parade Comics; becomes Superspook)
Ajax-Farrell Publ. (Four Star Comic Corp.): Sept, 1957 - No. 3, Dec-Jan, 1957-1958

	GD 2.0	VG 4.0	FN 6.0	VF 8.0	VF/NM 9.0	NM- 9.2
1-L. B. Cole-c	19	38	57	109	172	235
2-No L. B. Cole-c	10	20	30	56	76	95
3-L. B. Cole-c	6	32	48	92	144	195

FRISKY FABLES (Frisky Animals No. 44 on)
Premium Group/Novelty Publ./Star Publ. V5#4 on: Spring, 1945 - No. 43, Oct, 1950

	GD 2.0	VG 4.0	FN 6.0	VF 8.0	VF/NM 9.0	NM- 9.2
V1#1-Funny animal; Al Fago-c/a #1-38	22	44	66	127	204	280
2,3(Fall & Winter, 1945)	13	26	39	72	101	130
V2#1(#4, 4/46) - 9,11,12(#15, 3/47): 4-Flag-c	10	20	30	56	76	95
10-Christmas-c. 12-Valentine's-c	10	20	30	58	79	100
V3#1(#16, 4/47) - 12(#27, 3/48): 4-Flag-c. 7,9-Infinity-c. 10-X-Mas-c. 12-Washington crossing the Delaware parody-c	9	18	27	47	61	75
V4#1(#28, 4/48) - 7(#34, 2-3/49)	8	16	24	44	57	70
V5#1(#35, 4-5/49) - 4(#38, 10-11/49)	8	16	24	44	57	70
39-43-L. B. Cole-c; 40-Xmas-c	22	44	66	127	204	280
Accepted Reprint No. 43 (nd); L.B. Cole-c	10	20	30	54	72	90

FRITZI RITZ (See Comics On Parade, Single Series #5, 1(reprint), Tip Top & United Comics)

FRITZI RITZ (United Comics No. 8-26) (Also see Tip Topper for early Peanuts by Schulz)
United Features Synd./St. John No. 37-55/Dell No. 56 on:
1939; Fall, 1948; No. 3, 1949 - No. 7, 1949; No. 27, 3-4/53 - No. 36, 9-10/54; No. 37 - No. 55, 9-11/57; No. 56, 12-2/57-58 - No. 59, 9-11/58

	GD 2.0	VG 4.0	FN 6.0	VF 8.0	VF/NM 9.0	NM- 9.2
Single Series #5 (1939)	32	64	96	186	298	410
nn(1948)-Special Fall issue; by Ernie Bushmiller	17	34	51	100	158	215
3(#1)	12	24	36	69	97	125
4-7(1949): 6-Abbie & Slats app.	9	18	27	52	69	85
27(1953)-33,37-50,57-59-Early Peanuts (1-4 pgs.) by Schulz. 29-Five pg. Abbie & Slats; 1 pg. Mamie by Russell Patterson. 38(9/55)-41(4/56)-Low print run	9	18	27	52	69	85
34-36,51-56: 36-1 pg. Mamie by Patterson	8	16	24	42	54	65

NOTE: *Abbie & Slats in #6,7, 27-31. Li'l Abner in #32-36.*

FROGMAN COMICS
Hillman Periodicals: Jan-Feb, 1952 - No. 11, May, 1953

	GD 2.0	VG 4.0	FN 6.0	VF 8.0	VF/NM 9.0	NM- 9.2
1	15	30	45	84	127	170
2	9	18	27	52	69	85
3,4,6-11: 4-Meskin-a	8	16	24	40	50	60
5-Krigstein-a	8	16	24	44	57	70

FROGMEN, THE
Dell Publishing Co.: No. 1258, Feb-Apr, 1962 - No. 11, Nov-Jan, 1964-65 (Painted-c)

	GD 2.0	VG 4.0	FN 6.0	VF 8.0	VF/NM 9.0	NM- 9.2
Four Color 1258(#1)-Evans-a	8	16	24	52	86	120
2,3-Evans-a; part Frazetta inks in #2,3	6	12	18	37	59	80
4,6-11	4	8	12	24	37	50
5-Toth-a	4	8	12	28	44	60

FROM BEYOND THE UNKNOWN
National Periodical Publications: 10-11/69 - No. 25, 11-12/73

	GD 2.0	VG 4.0	FN 6.0	VF 8.0	VF/NM 9.0	NM- 9.2
1	5	10	15	34	55	75
2-6	3	6	9	19	29	38
7-11: (64 pgs.) 7-Intro Col. Glenn Merrit	3	6	9	21	32	42
12-17: (52 pgs.) 13-Wood-a(i)(r). 17-Pres. Nixon-c	3	6	9	17	25	32
18-25: Star Rovers-r begin #18,19. Space Museum in #23-25	2	4	6	11	16	20

NOTE: ***N. Adams*** *c-3, 6, 8, 9.* ***Anderson*** *c-2, 4, 5, 10, 11i, 15-17, 22; reprints-3, 4, 6-8, 10, 11, 13-16, 24, 25.* ***Infantino*** *r-1-5, 7-19, 23-25; c-11p.* ***Kaluta*** *c-18, 19.* ***Gil Kane*** *a-9r.* ***Kubert*** *c-1, 7, 12-14.* ***Toth*** *a-2r.* ***Wood*** *a-13i. Photo c-22.*

FROM DUSK TILL DAWN (Movie)
Big Entertainment: 1996 ($4.95, one-shot)

	GD 2.0	VG 4.0	FN 6.0	VF 8.0	VF/NM 9.0	NM- 9.2
nn-Adaptation of the film; Brereton-c						5.00
nn-($9.95)Deluxe Ed. w/ new material						10.00

FROM HELL
Mad Love/Tundra Publishing/Kitchen Sink: 1991 - No. 11, Sept, 1998 (B&W)

	GD 2.0	VG 4.0	FN 6.0	VF 8.0	VF/NM 9.0	NM- 9.2
1-Alan Moore and Eddie Campbell's Jack The Ripper story collected from the Taboo anthology series	2	4	6	11	16	20
1-(2nd printing)	2	4	6	8	10	12
1-(3rd printing)	1	2	3	4	5	7
2	1	2	3	5	6	8
2-(2nd printing)						6.00
2-(3rd printing)						4.00
3-1st Kitchen Sink Press issue	1	2	3	5	6	8
3-(2nd printing)						5.00
4-10: 10-(8/96)	1	2	3	4	5	7
11-Dance of the Gull Catchers (9/98, $4.95) Epilogue	2	4	6	9	12	15
Tundra Publishing reprintings 1-5 ('92)	1	2	3	4	5	7
HC						125.00
HC Ltd. Edition of 1,000 (signed and numbered)						225.00
TPB-1st printing (11/99)						60.00
TPB-2nd printing (3/00)						50.00
TPB-3rd printing (11/00)						40.00
TPB-4th printing (7/01) Regular and movie covers						35.00
TPB-5th printing - Regular and movie covers						35.00

FROM HERE TO INSANITY (Satire) (Formerly Eh! #1-7) (See Frantic & Frenzy)
Charlton Comics: No. 8, Feb, 1955 - V3#1, 1956

	GD 2.0	VG 4.0	FN 6.0	VF 8.0	VF/NM 9.0	NM- 9.2
8	17	34	51	100	158	215
9	15	30	45	90	140	190
10-Ditko-c/a (3 pgs.)	23	46	69	135	218	300
11,12-All Kirby except 4 pgs.	33	66	99	192	309	425
V3#1(1956)-Ward-c/a(2) (signed McCartney); 5 pgs. Wolverton-a; 3 pgs. Ditko-a; magazine format (cover says "Crazy, Man, Crazy" and becomes Crazy, Man, Crazy with V2#2)	40	80	120	240	390	540

FROM THE PIT
Fantagor Press: 1994 ($4.95, one-shot, mature)

	GD 2.0	VG 4.0	FN 6.0	VF 8.0	VF/NM 9.0	NM- 9.2
1-R. Corben-a; HP Lovecraft back-up story	1	2	3	5	6	8

FRONTIER DOCTOR (TV)
Dell Publishing Co.: No. 877, Feb, 1958 (one-shot)

	GD 2.0	VG 4.0	FN 6.0	VF 8.0	VF/NM 9.0	NM- 9.2
Four Color 877-Toth-a, Rex Allen photo-c	9	18	27	63	107	150

FRONTIER FIGHTERS
National Periodical Publications: Sept-Oct, 1955 - No. 8, Nov-Dec, 1956

	GD 2.0	VG 4.0	FN 6.0	VF 8.0	VF/NM 9.0	NM- 9.2
1-Davy Crockett, Buffalo Bill (by Kubert), Kit Carson begin (Scarce)	55	110	165	347	586	825
2	37	74	111	215	345	475
3-8	34	68	102	198	319	440

NOTE: *Buffalo Bill by* ***Kubert*** *in all.*

FRONTIER ROMANCES
Avon Periodicals/I. W.: Nov-Dec, 1949 - No. 2, Feb-Mar, 1950 (Painted-c)

	GD 2.0	VG 4.0	FN 6.0	VF 8.0	VF/NM 9.0	NM- 9.2
1-Used in **SOTI**, pg. 180 (General reference) & illo. "Erotic spanking in a western comic book"	48	96	144	298	499	700
2 (Scarce)-Woodish-a by Stallman	37	74	111	215	345	475
I.W. Reprint #1-Reprints Avon's #1	4	8	12	22	34	45
I.W. Reprint #9-Reprints ?	3	6	9	16	22	28

FRONTIER SCOUT: DAN'L BOONE (Formerly Death Valley; The Masked Raider No. 14 on)
Charlton Comics: No. 10, Jan, 1956 - No. 13, Aug, 1956; V2#14, Mar, 1965

	GD 2.0	VG 4.0	FN 6.0	VF 8.0	VF/NM 9.0	NM- 9.2
10	10	20	30	54	72	90
11-13(1956)	6	12	18	31	38	45
V2#14(3/65)	5	10	14	20	24	28

FRONTIER TRAIL (The Rider No. 1-5)
Ajax/Farrell Publ.: No. 6, May, 1958

	GD 2.0	VG 4.0	FN 6.0	VF 8.0	VF/NM 9.0	NM- 9.2
6	6	12	18	28	34	40

FRONTIER WESTERN
Atlas Comics (PrPI): Feb, 1956 - No. 10, Aug, 1957

	GD 2.0	VG 4.0	FN 6.0	VF 8.0	VF/NM 9.0	NM- 9.2
1	19	38	57	109	172	235
2,3,6-Williamson-a, 4 pgs. each	14	28	42	80	115	150
4,7,9,10: 10-Check-a	10	20	30	56	76	95
5-Crandall, Baker, Davis-a; Williamson text illos	14	28	42	76	108	140
8-Crandall, Morrow, & Wildey-a	10	20	30	58	79	100

NOTE: ***Baker*** *a-9.* ***Colan*** *a-2, 6.* ***Drucker*** *a-3, 4.* ***Heath*** *c-5.* ***Maneely*** *c/a-2, 7, 9.* ***Maurera*** *a-2.* ***Romita*** *a-7.* ***Severin*** *c-6, 8, 10.* ***Tuska*** *a-2.* ***Wildey*** *a-5, 8. Ringo Kid in No. 4.*

FRONTLINE COMBAT
E. C. Comics: July-Aug, 1951 - No. 15, Jan, 1954

	GD 2.0	VG 4.0	FN 6.0	VF 8.0	VF/NM 9.0	NM- 9.2
1-Severin/Kurtzman-a	66	132	198	528	844	1160
2	36	72	108	288	459	630
3	28	56	84	224	357	490

4-Used in **SOTI**, pg. 257; contains "Airburst" by Kurtzman which is his personal all-time

Fugitives From Justice #1 © STJ

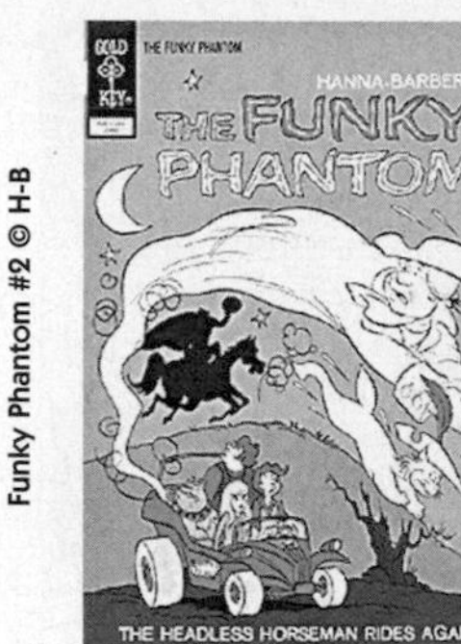

Funky Phantom #2 © H-B

The Funnies #51 © DELL

	GD 2.0	VG 4.0	FN 6.0	VF 8.0	VF/NM 9.0	NM- 9.2
favorite story	26	52	78	208	332	455
5-John Severin and Bill Elder bios.	22	44	66	176	281	385
6-10: 6-Kurtzman bio.	19	38	57	152	244	335
11-15	15	30	45	120	188	255

NOTE: ***Davis** a-in all; c-11, 12. **Evans** a-10-15. **Heath** a-1. **Kubert** a-14. **Kurtzman** a-1-5; c-1-9. **Severin** a-5-7, 9, 13, 15. **Severin/Elder** a-2-11; c-10. **Toth** a-8, 12. **Wood** a-1-4, 6-10, 12-15; c-13-15. Special issues: No. 7 (Iwo Jima), No. 9 (Civil War), No. 12 (Air Force).*

(Canadian reprints known; see Table of Contents.)

FRONTLINE COMBAT
Russ Cochran/Gemstone Publishing: Aug, 1995 - No. 14 ($2.00/$2.50)

	GD	VG	FN	VF	VF/NM	NM-
1-14-E.C. reprints in all						3.00

FRONT PAGE COMIC BOOK
Front Page Comics (Harvey): 1945

	GD	VG	FN	VF	VF/NM	NM-
1-Kubert-a; intro. & 1st app. Man in Black by Powell; Fuje-c	40	80	120	240	390	540

FROST AND FIRE (See DC Science Fiction Graphic Novel)

FROSTY THE SNOWMAN
Dell Publishing Co.: No. 359, Nov, 1951 - No. 1272, Dec-Feb?/1961-62

	GD	VG	FN	VF	VF/NM	NM-
Four Color 359 (#1)	9	18	27	63	107	150
Four Color 435,514,601,661	6	12	18	37	59	80
Four Color 748,861,950,1065,1153,1272	5	10	15	32	51	70

FRUITMAN SPECIAL
Harvey Publications: Dec, 1969 (68 pgs.)

	GD	VG	FN	VF	VF/NM	NM-
1-Funny super hero	4	8	12	22	34	45

F-TROOP (TV)
Dell Publishing Co.: Aug, 1966 - No. 7, Aug, 1967 (All have photo-c)

	GD	VG	FN	VF	VF/NM	NM-
1	9	18	27	64	110	155
2-7	6	12	18	39	62	85

FUGITIVES FROM JUSTICE
St. John Publishing Co.: Feb, 1952 - No. 5, Oct, 1952

	GD	VG	FN	VF	VF/NM	NM-
1	22	44	66	127	204	280
2-Matt Baker-r/Northwest Mounties #2; Vic Flint strip reprints begin	22	44	66	127	204	280
3-Reprints panel from Authentic Police Cases that was used in **SOTI** with changes; Tuska-a	21	42	63	123	197	270
4	12	24	36	69	97	125
5-Last Vic Flint-r; bondage-c	14	28	42	78	112	145

FUGITOID
Mirage Studios: 1985 (B&W, magazine size, one-shot)

	GD	VG	FN	VF	VF/NM	NM-
1-Ties into Teenage Mutant Ninja Turtles #5	1	2	3	4	5	7

FULL OF FUN
Red Top (Decker Publ.)(Farrell)/I. W. Enterprises: Aug, 1957 - No. 2, Nov, 1957; 1964

	GD	VG	FN	VF	VF/NM	NM-
1(1957)-Funny animal; Dave Berg-a	7	14	21	37	46	55
2-Reprints Bingo, the Monkey Doodle Boy	5	10	15	22	26	30
8-I.W. Reprint('64)	2	4	6	9	12	15

FUN AT CHRISTMAS (See March of Comics No. 138)

FUN CLUB COMICS (See Interstate Theatres...)

FUN COMICS (Formerly Holiday Comics #1-8; Mighty Bear #13 on)
Star Publications: No. 9, Jan, 1953 - No. 12, Oct, 1953

	GD	VG	FN	VF	VF/NM	NM-
9-(25¢ Giant)-L. B. Cole X-Mas-c; X-Mas issue	23	46	69	133	214	295
10-12-L. B. Cole-c. 12-Mighty Bear-c/story	18	36	54	105	165	225

FUNDAY FUNNIES (See Famous TV..., and Harvey Hits No. 35,40)

FUN-IN (TV)(Hanna-Barbera)
Gold Key: Feb, 1970 - No. 10, Jan, 1972; No. 11, 4/74 - No. 15, 12/74

	GD	VG	FN	VF	VF/NM	NM-
1-Dastardly & Muttley in Their Flying Machines; Perils of Penelope Pitstop in #1-4; It's the Wolf in all	7	14	21	45	73	100
2-4,6-Cattanooga Cats in 2-4	4	8	12	22	34	45
5,7-Motormouse & Autocat, Dastardly & Muttley in both; It's the Wolf in #7	4	8	12	24	37	50
8,10-The Harlem Globetrotters, Dastardly & Muttley in #10	4	8	12	24	37	50
9-Where's Huddles?, Dastardly & Muttley, Motormouse & Autocat app.	4	8	12	24	37	50
11-Butch Cassidy	3	6	9	20	30	40
12-15: 12,15-Speed Buggy. 13-Hair Bear Bunch. 14-Inch High Private Eye	3	6	9	20	30	40

FUNKY PHANTOM, THE (TV)
Gold Key: Mar, 1972 - No. 13, Mar, 1975 (Hanna-Barbera)

	GD	VG	FN	VF	VF/NM	NM-
1	5	10	15	32	51	75
2-5	3	6	9	18	27	38
6-13	3	6	9	15	21	28

FUNLAND
Ziff-Davis (Approved Comics): No date (1940s) (25¢)

	GD	VG	FN	VF	VF/NM	NM-
nn-Contains games, puzzles, cut-outs, etc.	18	36	54	105	165	225

FUNLAND COMICS
Croyden Publishers: 1945

	GD	VG	FN	VF	VF/NM	NM-
1-Funny animal	15	30	45	85	130	175

FUNNIES, THE (New Funnies No. 65 on)
Dell Publishing Co.: Oct, 1936 - No. 64, May, 1942

	GD	VG	FN	VF	VF/NM	NM-
1-Tailspin Tommy, Mutt & Jeff, Alley Oop (1st app?), Capt. Easy (1st app.), Don Dixon begin	400	800	1200	2300	3550	4800
2 (11/36)-Scribbly by Mayer begins (see Popular Comics #6 for 1st app.)	179	358	537	1029	1590	2150
3	123	246	369	707	1091	1475
4,5: 4(1/37)-Christmas-c	92	184	276	529	815	1100
6-10	70	140	210	403	622	840
11-20: 16-Christmas-c	65	130	195	374	580	785
21-29: 25-Crime Busters by McWilliams(4pgs.)	52	104	156	299	462	625
30-John Carter of Mars (origin/1st app.) begins by Edgar Rice Burroughs; Warner Bros.' Bosko-c (4/39)	147	294	441	926	1563	2200
31-34,36-44: 33-John Coleman Burroughs art begins on John Carter. 34-Last funny-c.	78	156	234	491	833	1175
35-(9/39)-Mr. District Attorney begins; based on radio show; 1st cover app. John Carter of Mars	83	166	249	523	887	1250
45-Origin/1st app. Phantasmo, the Master of the World (Dell's 1st super-hero, 7/40) & his sidekick Whizzer McGee	92	184	276	580	978	1375
46-50: 46-The Black Knight begins, ends #62	55	110	165	347	586	825
51-56-Last ERB John Carter of Mars	47	94	141	291	483	675
57-Intro. & origin Captain Midnight (7/41)	347	694	1041	2360	4130	5900
58-60: 58-Captain Midnight-c begin, end #63	87	174	261	548	924	1300
61-Andy Panda begins by Walter Lantz	95	190	285	599	1012	1425
62,63: 63-Last Captain Midnight-c; bondage-c	67	134	201	422	711	1000
64-Format change; Oswald the Rabbit, Felix the Cat, Li'l Eight Ball app.; origin & 1st app. Woody Woodpecker in Oswald; last Capt. Midnight; Oswald, Andy Panda, Li'l Eight Ball-c	137	274	411	863	1457	2050

NOTE: ***Mayer** c-26, 48. **McWilliams** art in many issues on "Rex King of the Deep". Alley Oop c-17, 20. Captain Midnight c-57(i/2), 58-63. John Carter c-35-37, 40. Phantasmo c-45-56, 57(1/2), 58-61(part). Rex King c-38, 39, 42. Tailspin Tommy c-41.*

FUNNIES ANNUAL, THE
Avon Periodicals: 1959 ($1.00, approx. 7x10", B&W; tabloid-size)

	GD	VG	FN	VF	VF/NM	NM-
1-(Rare)-Features the best newspaper comic strips of the year: Archie, Snuffy Smith, Beetle Bailey, Henry, Blondie, Steve Canyon, Buz Sawyer, The Little King, Hi & Lois, Popeye, & others. Also has a chronological history of the comics from 2000 B.C. to 1959.	43	86	129	267	446	625

FUNNIES ON PARADE (See Promotional Comics section)

FUNNY ANIMALS (See Fawcett's Funny Animals)
Charlton Comics: Sept, 1984 - No. 2, Nov, 1984

	GD	VG	FN	VF	VF/NM	NM-
1,2-Atomic Mouse-r; low print						6.00

FUNNYBONE (... The Laugh-Book of Comical Comics)
La Salle Publishing Co.: 1944 (25¢, 132 pgs.)

	GD	VG	FN	VF	VF/NM	NM-
nn	29	58	87	169	272	375

FUNNY BOOK (...Magazine for Young Folks) (Hocus Pocus No. 9)
Parents' Magazine Press (Funny Book Publishing Corp.):
Dec, 1942 - No. 9, Aug-Sept, 1946 (Comics, stories, puzzles, games)

	GD	VG	FN	VF	VF/NM	NM-
1-Funny animal; Alice In Wonderland app.	15	30	45	84	127	170
2-Gulliver in Giant-Land	10	20	30	54	72	90
3-9: 4-Advs. of Robin Hood. 9-Hocus-Pocus strip	8	16	24	44	57	70

FUNNY COMICS
Modern Store Publ.: 1955 (7¢, 5x7", 36 pgs.)

	GD	VG	FN	VF	VF/NM	NM-
1-Funny animal	4	8	12	22	34	45

FUNNY COMIC TUNES (See Funny Tunes)

FUNNY FABLES
Decker Publications (Red Top Comics): Aug, 1957 - V2#2, Nov, 1957

	GD	VG	FN	VF	VF/NM	NM-
V1#1	6	12	18	31	38	45
V1#2,V2#1,2: V1#2 (11/57)-Reissue of V1#1	5	10	14	20	24	28

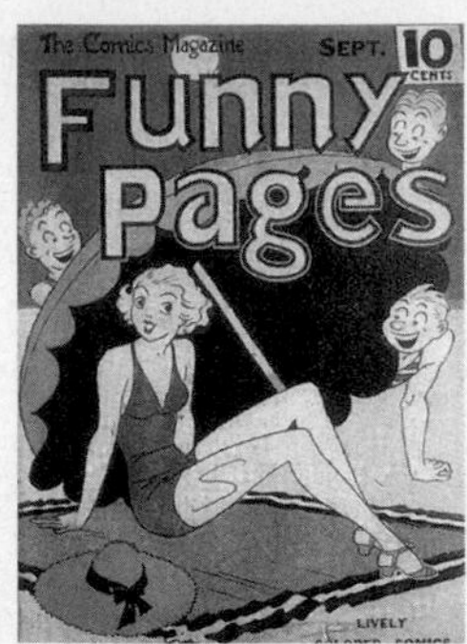

Funny Pages #5 © CEN

Funny Tunes #2 © AVON

Funtastic World of Hanna-Barbera #3 © H-B

	GD 2.0	VG 4.0	FN 6.0	VF 8.0	VF/NM 9.0	NM- 9.2

GD VG FN VF VF/NM NM- 2.0 4.0 6.0 8.0 9.0 9.2

FUNNY FILMS (Features funny animal characters from films)
American Comics Group(Michel Publ./Titan Publ.): Sept-Oct, 1949 - No. 29, May-June, 1954 (No. 1-4: 52 pgs.)

1-Puss An' Boots, Blunderbunny begin 18 36 54 105 165 225
2 11 22 33 62 86 110
3-10: 3-X-Mas-c 9 18 27 47 61 75
11-20 7 14 21 35 43 50
21-29 6 12 18 28 34 40

FUNNY FOLKS
DC Comics: Feb, 1946

nn-Ashcan comic, not distributed to newsstands, only for in house use (no known sales)

FUNNY FOLKS (Hollywood... on cover only No. 16-26; becomes Hollywood Funny Folks No. 27 on)
National Periodical Publ.: April-May, 1946 - No. 26, June-July, 1950 (52 pgs., #15 on)

1-Nutsy Squirrel begins (1st app.) by Rube Grossman;
Grossman-a in most issues 40 80 120 235 380 525
2 20 40 60 114 180 245
3-5: 4-1st Nutsy Squirrel-c 15 30 45 84 127 170
6-10: 6,9-Nutsy Squirrel-c begin 11 22 33 62 86 110
11-26: 15-Begin 52 pg. issues (8-9/48) 10 20 30 54 72 90

NOTE: ***Sheldon Mayer** a-in some issues. **Post** a-18. Christmas c-12.*

FUNNY FROLICS
Timely/Marvel Comics (SPI): Summer, 1945 - No. 5, Dec, 1946

1-Sharpy Fox, Puffy Pig, Krazy Krow 25 50 75 145 233 320
2 14 28 42 82 121 160
3,4 12 24 36 67 94 120
5-Kurtzman-a 13 26 39 74 105 135

FUNNY FUNNIES
Nedor Publishing Co.: April, 1943 (68 pgs.)

1-Funny animals; Peter Porker app. 19 38 57 109 172 235

FUNNYMAN (Also see Cisco Kid Comics & Extra Comics)
Magazine Enterprises: Dec, 1947; No. 1, Jan, 1948 - No. 6, Aug, 1948

nn(12/47)-Prepublication B&W undistributed copy by Siegel & Shuster-(5-3/4x8"), 16 pgs.;
Sold at auction in 1997 for $575.00
1-Siegel & Shuster-a in all; Dick Ayers 1st pro work (as assistant) on 1st few issues
45 90 135 279 465 650
2 27 54 81 158 254 350
3-6 23 46 69 133 214 295

FUNNY MOVIES (See 3-D Funny Movies)

FUNNY PAGES (Formerly The Comics Magazine)
Comics Magazine Co./Ultem Publ.(Chesler)/Centaur Publications: No. 6, Nov, 1936 - No. 42, Oct, 1940

V1#6 (nn, nd)-The Clock begins (2 pgs., 1st app.), ends #11; The Clock is the 1st masked
comic book hero 260 520 780 1638 2769 3900
7-11 98 196 294 617 1046 1475
V2#1-V2#3: V2#1 (9/37)(V2#2 on-c; V2#1 in indicia). V2#2 (10/37)(V2#3 on-c; V2#2 in indicia).
V2#3(11/37)-5 68 136 204 428 727 1025
6(1st Centaur, 3/38) 92 184 276 580 978 1375
7-9 68 136 204 428 727 1025
10(Scarce, 9/38)-1st app. of The Arrow by Gustavson (Blue costume)
347 694 1041 2360 4130 5900
11,12 122 244 366 769 1297 1825
V3#1-Bruce Wayne prototype in "Case of the Missing Heir," by Bob Kane, 3 months before
app. Batman (See Det. Pic. Stories #5) 128 256 384 806 1366 1925
2-6,8: 6,8-Last funny covers 110 220 330 693 1172 1650
7-1st Arrow-c (9/39) 293 586 879 1846 3123 4400
9-Tarpe Mills jungle-c 122 244 366 769 1297 1825
10-2nd Arrow-c 240 480 720 1512 2556 3600
V4#1(1/40, Arrow-c)-(Rare)-The Owl & The Phantom Rider app.; origin Mantoka, Maker of
Magic by Jack Cole. Mad Ming begins, ends #42; Tarpe Mills-a
280 560 840 1764 2982 4200
35-Classic Arrow-c 280 560 840 1764 2982 4200
36-38-Mad Ming-c 118 236 354 743 1259 1775
39-41-Arrow-c 200 400 600 1260 2130 3000
42 (Scarce,10/40)-Last Arrow; Arrow-c 207 414 621 1304 2202 3100

NOTE: ***Biro** c-V2#9. **Burgos** c-V3#10. **Jack Cole** a-V2#3, 7, 8, 10, 11, V3#2, 6, 9, 10, V4#1, 37; c-V3#2, 4. **Eisner** a-V1#7, 8?, 10. **Ken Ernst** a-V1#7, 8. **Everett** a-V2#11 (illos). **Filchock** c-V2#10, V3#6. **Gill Fox** a-V2#11. **Sid Greene** a-39. **Guardineer** a-V2#2, 3, 5. **Gustavson** a-V2#5, 11, 12, V3#1-10, 35, 38-42; c-V3#7, 35, 39-42. **Bob Kane** a-V3#1. **McWilliams** a-V2#12, V3#1, 3-6. **Tarpe Mills** a-V3#8-10, V4#1; c-V3#9. **Ed Moore Jr.** a-V2#12. **Schwab** c-V3#1. **Bob Wood** a-V2#2, 3, 8, 11, V3#6, 9, 10; c-V2#6, 7. Arrow c-V3#7, 10, V4#1, 35, 40-42.*

FUNNY PICTURE STORIES (Comic Pages V3#4 on)
Comics Magazine Co./Centaur Publications: Nov, 1936 - V3#3, May, 1939

V1#1-The Clock begins (c-feature)(see Funny Pages for 1st app.)
347 694 1041 2360 4130 5900
2 125 250 375 788 1332 1875
3-7(6/37): 4-Eisner-a; X-Mas-c. 7-Racial humor-c 83 166 249 523 887 1250
V2#1 (9/37; V1#10 on-c; V2#1 in indicia)-Jack Strand begins
53 106 159 334 567 800
2 (10/37; V1#11 on-c; V2#2 in indicia) 53 106 159 334 567 800
3-5,7-11(11/38): 4-Xmas-c 48 96 144 298 499 700
6-(1st Centaur, 3/38) 79 158 237 498 842 1185
V3#1(1/39)-3 47 94 141 291 483 675

NOTE: ***Biro** c-V2#1, 8, 9, 11. **Guardineer** a-V1#11; c-V2#6, V3#5. **Bob Wood** c/a-V1#11, V2#2; c-V2#3, 5.*

FUNNY STUFF (Becomes The Dodo & the Frog No. 80)
All-American/National Periodical Publications No. 7 on: Summer, 1944 - No. 79, July-Aug, 1954 (#1-7 are quarterly)

1-The Three Mouseketeers (ends #28) & The "Terrific Whatzit" begin;
Sheldon Mayer-a; Grossman-a in most issues 88 176 264 554 940 1325
2-Sheldon Mayer-a 42 84 126 260 435 610
3-5: 3-Flash parody. 5-All Mayer-a/scripts issue 30 60 90 174 280 385
6-10 10-(6/46) 20 40 60 115 183 250
11-17,19 15 30 45 90 140 190
18-The Dodo & the Frog (2/47, 1st app?) begin?; X-Mas-c
27 54 81 158 254 350
19-1st Dodo & the Frog-c (3/47) 18 36 54 105 165 225
20-2nd Dodo & the Frog-c (4/47) 14 28 42 80 115 150
21,23-30: 24-Infinity-c. 30-Christmas-c 11 22 33 62 86 110
22-Superman cameo 38 76 114 222 356 490
31-79: 70-1st Bo Bunny by Mayer & begins 10 20 30 56 76 95

NOTE: ***Mayer** a-1-8, 55, ,57, 58, 61, 62, 64, 65, 68, 70, 72, 74-79; c-2, 5, 6, 8.*

FUNNY STUFF STOCKING STUFFER
DC Comics: Mar, 1985 ($1.25, 52 pgs.)

1-Almost every DC funny animal featured 4.00

FUNNY 3-D
Harvey Publications: December, 1953 (25¢, came with 2 pair of glasses)

1-Shows cover in 3-D on inside 11 22 33 62 86 110

FUNNY TUNES (Animated Funny Comic Tunes No. 16-22; Funny Comic Tunes No. 23, on covers only; Oscar No. 24 on)
U.S.A. Comics Magazine Corp. (Timely): No. 16, Summer, 1944 - No. 23, Fall, 1946

16-Silly Seal, Ziggy Pig, Krazy Krow begin 15 30 45 90 140 190
17 (Fall/44)-Becomes Gay Comics #18 on? 14 28 42 76 108 140
18-22: 21-Super Rabbit app. 11 22 33 64 90 115
23-Kurtzman-a 13 26 39 72 101 130

FUNNY TUNES (Becomes Space Comics #4 on)
Avon Periodicals: July, 1953 - No. 3, Dec-Jan, 1953-54

1-Space Mouse, Peter Rabbit, Merry Mouse, Spotty the Pup, Cicero the Cat begin;
all continue in Space Comics 11 22 33 60 83 105
2,3 8 16 24 44 57 70

FUNNY WORLD
Marbak Press: 1947 - No. 3, 1948

1-The Berrys, The Toodles & other strip-r begin 9 18 27 47 61 75
2,3 6 12 18 31 38 45

FUNTASTIC WORLD OF HANNA-BARBERA, THE (TV)
Marvel Comics Group: Dec, 1977 - No. 3, June, 1978 ($1.25, oversized)

1-3: 1-The Flintstones Christmas Party(12/77). 2-Yogi Bear's Easter Parade(3/78).
3-Laff-a-lympics(6/78) 4 8 12 24 37 50

FUN TIME
Ace Periodicals: Spring, 1953; No. 2, Sum, 1953; No. 3(nn), Fall, 1953; No. 4, Wint, 1953-54

1-(25¢, 100 pgs.)-Funny animal 18 36 54 105 165 225
2-4 (All 25¢, 100 pgs.) 15 30 45 85 130 175

FUN WITH SANTA CLAUS (See March of Comics No. 11, 108, 325)

FURTHER ADVENTURES OF CYCLOPS AND PHOENIX (Also see Adventures of Cyclops and Phoenix, Uncanny X-Men & X-Men)
Marvel Comics: June, 1996 - No. 4, Sept, 1996 ($1.95, limited series)

1-4: Origin of Mr. Sinister; Milligan scripts; John Paul Leon-c/a(p). 2-4-Apocalypse app. 3.00
Trade Paperback (1997, $14.99) r/1-4 15.00

FURTHER ADVENTURES OF INDIANA JONES, THE (Movie) (Also see

Further Adventures of Indiana Jones #10 © LucasFilm

Futurama Comics #35 © Bongo

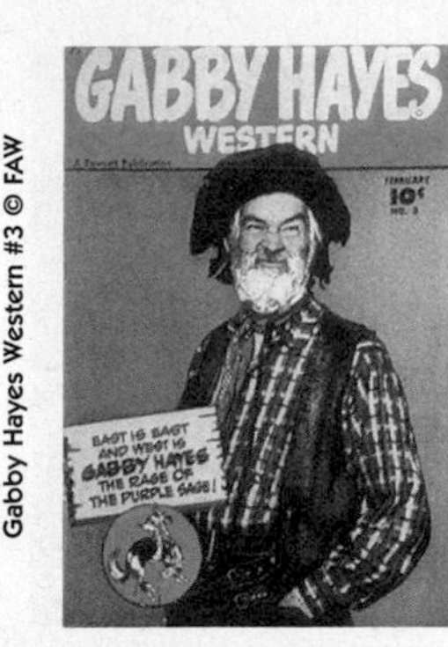

Gabby Hayes Western #3 © FAW

	GD 2.0	VG 4.0	FN 6.0	VF 8.0	VF/NM 9.0	NM- 9.2

GD VG FN VF VF/NM NM-
2.0 4.0 6.0 8.0 9.0 9.2

Indiana Jones and the Last Crusade & Indiana Jones and the Temple of Doom)
Marvel Comics Group: Jan, 1983 - No. 34, Mar, 1986

1-Byrne/Austin-a; Austin-c 5.00
2-34: 2-Byrne/Austin-c/a 3.00
NOTE: ***Austin*** *a-1i, 2i, 6i, 9i; c-1, 2i, 6i, 9i.* ***Byrne*** *a-1p, 2p; c-2p.* ***Chaykin*** *a-6p; c-6p, 8p-10p.* ***Ditko*** *a-21p, 25-28, 34.* ***Golden*** *c-24, 25.* ***Simonson*** *c-9. Painted c-14.*

FURTHER ADVENTURES OF NYOKA, THE JUNGLE GIRL, THE (See Nyoka)
AC Comics: 1988 - No. 5, 1989 ($1.95, color; $2.25/$2.50, B&W)

1-5 : 1,2-Bill Black-a plus reprints. 3-Photo-c. 5-(B&W)-Reprints plus movie photos 2.50

FURY (Straight Arrow's Horse...) (See A-1 No. 119)

FURY (TV) (See March Of Comics #200)
Dell Publishing Co./Gold Key: No. 781, Mar, 1957 - Nov, 1962 (All photo-c)

	GD	VG	FN	VF	VF/NM	NM-
Four Color 781	8	16	24	52	86	120
Four Color 885,975,1031,1080,1133,1172,1218,1296	6	12	18	41	66	90
01292-208(#1-'62), 10020-211(11/62-G.K.)	6	12	18	37	59	80

FURY
Marvel Comics: May, 1994 ($2.95, one-shot)

1-Iron Man, Red Skull, FF, Hatemonger, Logan app.; Origin Nick Fury 3.00

FURY (Volume 3)
Marvel Comics (MAX): Nov, 2001 - No. 6, Apr, 2002 ($2.99, mature content)

1-6-Ennis-s/Robertson-a 3.00

FURY/ AGENT 13
Marvel Comics: June, 1998 - No. 2, July, 1998 ($2.99, limited series)

1,2-Nick Fury returns 3.00

FURY OF FIRESTORM, THE (Becomes Firestorm The Nuclear Man on cover with #50, in indicia with #65) (Also see Firestorm)
DC Comics: June, 1982 - No. 64, Oct, 1987 (75¢ on)

1-Intro The Black Bison; brief origin 6.00
2-40,43-64: 4-JLA x-over. 17-1st app. Firehawk. 21-Death of Killer Frost. 22-Origin. 23-Intro Byte. 24-(6/84)-1st app. Blue Devil & Bug (origin); origin Byte. 34-1st app./origin Killer Frost II. 39-Weasel's ID revealed. 48-Intro. Moonbow. 53-Origin/1st app. Silver Shade. 55,56-Legends x-over. 58-1st app./origin new Parasite 2.50
41,42-Crisis x-over 3.00
61-Test cover variant; Superman logo 4 8 12 22 34 45
Annual 1-4: 1(1983), 2(1984), 3(1985), 4(1986) 3.00
NOTE: ***Colan*** *a-19p, Annual 4p.* ***Giffen*** *a-Annual 4p.* ***Gil Kane*** *c-30.* ***Nino*** *a-37.* ***Tuska*** *a-(p)-17, 18, 32, 45.*

FURY OF SHIELD
Marvel Comics: Apr, 1995 - No. 4, July, 1995 ($2.50/$1.95, limited series)

1 ($2.50)-Foil-c 3.00
2-4: 4-Bagged w/ decoder 2.50

FURY: PEACEMAKER
Marvel Comics: Apr, 2006 - No. 6, Sept, 2006 ($3.50, limited series)

1-6-Flashback to WW2; Ennis-s/Robertson-a. 1-Deodato-c. 2-Texeira-c. 5-Dillon-c 3.50
TPB (2006, $17.99) r/#1-6 18.00

FUSED
Image Comics: Mar, 2002 - No. 4, Jan, 2003 ($2.95)

1-4-Steve Niles-s. 1,2-Paul Lee-a. 3-Brad Rader-a. 4-Templesmith-a 3.00
Canned Heat TPB (Dark Horse, 6/04, $12.95) r/series; Dan Wickline intro. 13.00

FUSED
Dark Horse Comics: Dec, 2003 - No. 4, Mar, 2004 ($2.95)

1-4-Steve Niles-s/Josh Medors-a. 1-Powell-c 3.00

FUSION
Eclipse Comics: Jan, 1987 - No. 17, Oct, 1989 ($2.00, B&W, Baxter paper)

1-17: 11-The Weasel Patrol begins (1st app.?) 2.50

FUTURAMA (TV)
Bongo Comics: 2000 - Present ($2.50/$2.99, bi-monthly)

1-Based on the FOX-TV animated series; Groening/Morrison-c 3.50
1-San Diego Comic-Con Premiere Edition 5.00
2-38: 8-CGC cover spoof; X-Men parody 3.00
Futurama Adventures TPB (2004, $14.95) r/#5-9 15.00
Futurama Conquers the Universe TPB (2007, $14.95) r/#10-13 15.00
Futurama-O-Rama TPB (2002, $12.95) r/#1-4; sketch pages of Fry's development 13.00
...: The Time Bender Trilogy TPB (2006, $14.95) r/#16-19; cover gallery 15.00

FUTURAMA/SIMPSONS INFINITELY SECRET CROSSOVER CRISIS (TV) (See Simpsons/Futurama Crossover Crisis II for sequel)
Bongo Comics: 2002 - No. 2, 2002 ($2.50, limited series)

1,2-Evil Brain Spawns put Futurama crew into the Simpsons' Springfield 2.50

FUTURE COMICS
David McKay Publications: June, 1940 - No. 4, Sept, 1940

1-(6/40, 64 pgs.)-Origin The Phantom (1st in comics) (4 pgs.); The Lone Ranger (8 pgs.) & Saturn Against the Earth (4 pgs.) begin

	GD	VG	FN	VF	VF/NM	NM-
1	287	574	861	1808	3054	4300
2	122	244	366	769	1297	1825
3,4	87	174	261	548	924	1300

FUTURE COP L.A.P.D. (Electronic Arts video game) (Also see Promotional Comics section)
DC Comics (WildStorm): Jan, 1999 ($4.95, magazine sized)

1-Stories & art by various 5.00

FUTURE WORLD COMICS
George W. Dougherty: Summer, 1946 - No. 2, Fall, 1946

1,2: H. C. Kiefer-c; preview of the World of Tomorrow 31 62 93 178 282 385

FUTURE WORLD COMIX (Warren Presents...)
Warren Publications: Sept, 1978 (B&W magazine, 84 pgs.)

1-Corben, Maroto, Morrow, Nino, Sutton-a; Todd-c/a; contains nudity panels 2 4 6 8 10 12

FUTURIANS, THE (See Marvel Graphic Novel #9)
Lodestone Publishing/Eternity Comics: Sept, 1985 - No. 3, 1985 ($1.50)

1-3: Indicia title "Dave Cockrum's..." 2.25
Graphic Novel 1 ($9.95, Eternity)-r/#1-3, plus never published #4 issue 10.00

FX
IDW Publishing: Mar, 2008 - No. 6, Aug, 2008 ($3.99)

1-6-John Byrne-a/c; Wayne Osborne-s 4.00

G-8 (Listed at G-Eight)

GABBY (Formerly Ken Shannon) (Teen humor)
Quality Comics Group: No. 11, Jul, 1953; No. 2, Sep, 1953 - No. 9, Sep, 1954

	GD	VG	FN	VF	VF/NM	NM-
11(#1)(7/53)	9	18	27	47	61	75
2	6	12	18	31	38	45
3-9	5	10	15	24	30	35

GABBY GOB (See Harvey Hits No. 85, 90, 94, 97, 100, 103, 106, 109)

GABBY HAYES ADVENTURE COMICS
Toby Press: Dec, 1953

1-Photo-c 15 30 45 88 137 185

GABBY HAYES WESTERN (Movie star)(See Monte Hale, Real Western Hero & Western Hero)
Fawcett Publications/Charlton Comics No. 51 on: Nov, 1948 - No. 50, Jan, 1953; No. 51, Dec, 1954 - No. 59, Jan, 1957

1-Gabby & his horse Corker begin; photo front/back-c begin

	GD	VG	FN	VF	VF/NM	NM-
1	41	82	123	256	416	575
2	21	42	63	124	195	265
3-5	15	30	45	88	137	185
6-10: 9-Young Falcon begins	14	28	42	78	112	145
11-20: 19-Last photo back-c	11	22	33	64	90	115
21-49: 20,22,24,26,28,29-(52 pgs.)	9	18	27	52	69	85
50-(1/53)-Last Fawcett issue; last photo-c?	10	20	30	58	79	100
51-(12/54)-1st Charlton issue; photo-c	11	22	33	60	83	105
52-59(1955-57): 53,55-Photo-c. 58-Swayze-a	8	16	24	42	54	65

GAGS
United Features Synd./Triangle Publ. No. 9 on: Jul, 1937 - V3#10, Oct, 1944 (13-3/4x10-3/4")

1(7/37)-52 pgs.; 20 pgs. Grin & Bear It, Fellow Citizen

	GD	VG	FN	VF	VF/NM	NM-
1(7/37)	10	20	30	54	72	90
V1#9 (36 pgs.) (7/42)	6	12	18	28	34	40
V3#10	5	10	15	24	30	35

GALACTICA: THE NEW MILLENNIUM
Realm Press: Sept, 1999 ($2.99)

1-Stories by Shooter, Braden, Kuhoric 3.00

GALACTIC GUARDIANS
Marvel Comics: July, 1994 - No. 4, Oct, 1994 ($1.50, limited series)

1-4 2.50

GALACTIC WARS COMIX (Warren Presents... on cover)
Warren Publications: Dec, 1978 (B&W magazine, 84 pgs.)

nn-Wood, Williamson-r; Battlestar Galactica/Flash Gordon photo/text stories 2 4 6 8 10 12

Gambit V2 #16 © MAR

Gandy Goose #4 © STJ

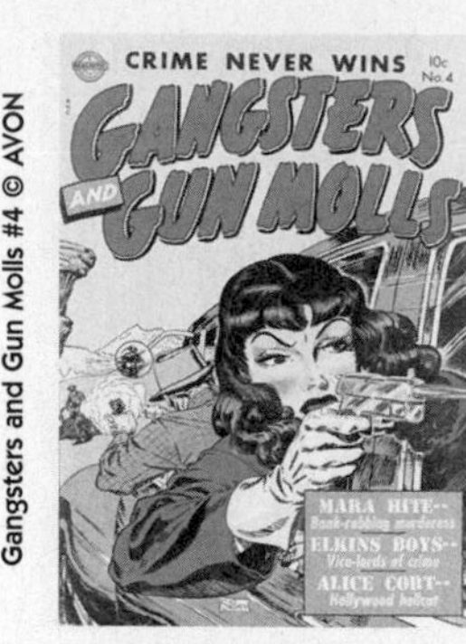

Gangsters and Gun Molls #4 © AVON

	GD 2.0	VG 4.0	FN 6.0	VF 8.0	VF/NM 9.0	NM- 9.2

GALACTUS THE DEVOURER
Marvel Comics: Sept, 1999 - No. 6, Mar, 2000 ($3.50/$2.50, limited series)

	GD	VG	FN	VF	VF/NM	NM-
1-($3.50) L. Simonson-s/Muth & Sienkiewicz-a						3.50
2-5-($2.50) Buscema & Sienkiewicz-a						2.50
6-($3.50) Death of Galactus; Buscema & Sienkiewicz-a						3.50

GALAXIA (Magazine)
Astral Publ.: 1981 ($2.50, B&W, 52 pgs.)

	GD	VG	FN	VF	VF/NM	NM-
1-Buckler/Giordano-c; Texeira/Guice-a; 1st app. Astron, Sojourner, Bloodwing, Warlords; Buckler-s/a	2	4	6	8	11	14

GALAXY QUEST: GLOBAL WARNING! (Based on the 1999 movie)
IDW Publishing: Aug, 2008 - Present ($3.99)

	GD	VG	FN	VF	VF/NM	NM-
1,2-Lobdell-s/Kyriazis-a						4.00

GALLANT MEN, THE (TV)
Gold Key: Oct, 1963 (Photo-c)

	GD	VG	FN	VF	VF/NM	NM-
1(1008-310)-Manning-a	4	8	12	22	34	45

GALLEGHER, BOY REPORTER (Disney, TV)
Gold Key: May, 1965

	GD	VG	FN	VF	VF/NM	NM-
1(10149-505)-Photo-c	3	6	9	18	27	35

GAMBIT (See X-Men #266 & X-Men Annual #14)
Marvel Comics: Dec, 1993 - No. 4, Mar, 1994 ($2.00, limited series)

	GD	VG	FN	VF	VF/NM	NM-
1-($2.50)-Lee Weeks-c/a in all; gold foil stamped-c.						5.00
1 (Gold)	2	4	6	9	12	15
2-4						3.00

GAMBIT
Marvel Comics: Sept, 1997 - No. 4, Dec, 1997 ($2.50, limited series)

	GD	VG	FN	VF	VF/NM	NM-
1-4-Janson-a/Mackie & Kavanagh-s						3.00

GAMBIT
Marvel Comics: Feb, 1999 - No. 25, Feb, 2001 ($2.99/$1.99)

	GD	VG	FN	VF	VF/NM	NM-
1-($2.99) Five covers; Nicieza-a/Skroce-a						4.00
2-11,13-16-($1.99): 2-Two covers (Skroce & Adam Kubert)						2.50
12-($2.99)						3.50
17-24: 17-Begin $2.25-c. 21-Mystique-c/app.						2.50
25-($2.99) Leads into "Gambit & Bishop"						3.00
...1999 Annual ($3.50) Nicieza-s/McDaniel-a						3.50
...2000 Annual ($3.50) Nicieza-s/Derenick & Smith-a						3.50

GAMBIT
Marvel Comics: Nov, 2004 - No. 12, Aug, 2005 ($2.99)

	GD	VG	FN	VF	VF/NM	NM-
1-12: 1-Jeanty-a/Land-c/Layman-s. 5-Wolverine-c/app. 9-Brother Voodoo-c/app.						3.00
...: Hath No Fury TPB (2005, $14.99) r/#7-12						15.00
...: House of Cards TPB (2005, $14.99) r/#1-6; Land cover sketches; unused covers						15.00

GAMBIT & BISHOP (... : Sons of the Atom on cover)
Marvel Comics: Feb, 2001 - No. 6, May, 2001 ($2.25, bi-weekly limited series)

	GD	VG	FN	VF	VF/NM	NM-
Alpha (2/01) Prelude to series; Nord-a						2.50
1-6-Jeanty-a/Williams-c						2.50
Genesis (3/01, $3.50) reprints their first apps. and first meeting						3.50

GAMBIT AND THE X-TERNALS
Marvel Comics: Mar, 1995 - No. 4, July, 1995 ($1.95, limited series)

	GD	VG	FN	VF	VF/NM	NM-
1-4-Age of Apocalypse						2.50

GAMEBOY (Super Mario covers on all)
Valiant: 1990 - No. 5 ($1.95, coated-c)

	GD	VG	FN	VF	VF/NM	NM-
1-5: 3,4-Layton-c. 4-Morrow-a. 5-Layton-c(i)						4.00

GAMEKEEPER (Guy Ritchie's...)
Virgin Comics: Mar, 2007 - No. 5, Sept, 2007; Mar, 2008 - Present ($2.99)

	GD	VG	FN	VF	VF/NM	NM-
1-5-Andy Diggle-s/Mukesh Singh-a; 2 covers on each						3.00
1-Extended Edition (6/07, $2.99) r/#1 with script excerpt and sketch art						3.00
Series 2 (3/08 - Present) 1-5-Parker-s/Randle-a						3.00
Vol. 1 TPB (10/07, $14.99) r/#1-5; script and sketch pages; Guy Ritchie intro.						15.00

GAMERA
Dark Horse Comics: Aug, 1996 - No. 4, Nov, 1996 ($2.95, limited series)

	GD	VG	FN	VF	VF/NM	NM-
1-4						3.00

GAMMARAUDERS
DC Comics: Jan, 1989 - No. 10, Dec, 1989 ($1.25/$1.50/$2.00)

	GD	VG	FN	VF	VF/NM	NM-
1-10-Based on TSR game						2.50

GAMORRA SWIMSUIT SPECIAL

	GD 2.0	VG 4.0	FN 6.0	VF 8.0	VF/NM 9.0	NM- 9.2

Image Comics (WildStorm Productions): June, 1996 ($2.50, one-shot)

	GD	VG	FN	VF	VF/NM	NM-
1-Campbell wraparound-c; pinups						2.50

GANDY GOOSE (Movies/TV)(See All Surprise, Giant Comics Edition #5A &10, Paul Terry's Comics & Terry-Toons)
St. John Publ. Co./Pines No. 5,6: Mar, 1953 - No. 5, Nov, 1953; No. 5, Fall, 1956 - No. 6, Sum/58

	GD	VG	FN	VF	VF/NM	NM-
1-All St. John issues are pre-code	10	20	30	58	79	100
2	7	14	21	35	43	50
3-5(1953)(St. John)	6	12	18	31	38	45
5,6(1956-58)(Pines)-CBS Television Presents...	5	10	15	24	30	35

GANG BUSTERS (See Popular Comics #38)
David McKay/Dell Publishing Co.: 1938 - 1943

	GD	VG	FN	VF	VF/NM	NM-
Feature Books 17(McKay)('38)-1st app.	65	130	195	410	693	975
Large Feature Comic 10('39)-(Scarce)	65	130	195	410	693	975
Large Feature Comic 17('41)	45	90	135	279	465	650
Four Color 7(1940)	48	96	144	298	499	700
Four Color 23('42)	40	80	120	235	380	525
Four Color 24('43)	26	52	78	187	349	510

GANG BUSTERS (Radio/TV)(Gangbusters #14 on)
National Periodical Publ.: Dec-Jan, 1947-48 - No. 67, Dec-Jan, 1958-59 (No. 1-23: 52 pgs.)

	GD	VG	FN	VF	VF/NM	NM-
1	83	166	249	523	887	1250
2	40	80	120	235	380	525
3-5	28	56	84	164	265	365
6-10: 9-Dan Barry-a. 9,10-Photo-c	21	42	63	123	197	270
11-13-Photo-c	17	34	51	100	158	215
14,17-Frazetta-a, 8 pgs. each. 14-Photo-c	36	72	108	212	341	470
15,16,18-20,26: 26-Kirby-a	15	30	45	85	130	175
21-25,27-30	14	28	42	76	108	140
31-44: 44-Last Pre-code (2-3/55)	12	24	36	67	94	120
45-67	10	20	30	54	72	90

NOTE: *Barry a-6, 8, 10. Drucker a-51. Moreira a-48, 50, 59. Roussos a-8.*

GANGLAND
DC Comics (Vertigo): Jun, 1998 - No. 4, Sept, 1998 ($2.95, limited series)

	GD	VG	FN	VF	VF/NM	NM-
1-4:Crime anthology by various. 2-Corben-a						3.00
TPB-(2000, $12.95) r/#1-4; Bradstreet-c						13.00

GANGSTERS AND GUN MOLLS
Avon Per./Realistic Comics: Sept, 1951 - No. 4, June, 1952 (Painted c-1-3)

	GD	VG	FN	VF	VF/NM	NM-
1-Wood-a, 1 pg; c-/Avon paperback #292	49	98	147	304	507	710
2-Check-a, 8 pgs.; Kamen-a; Bonnie Parker story	40	80	120	235	380	525
3-Marijuana mentioned; used in **POP**, pg. 84,85	38	76	114	222	356	490
4-Syd Shores-c	29	58	87	169	272	375

GANGSTERS CAN'T WIN
D. S. Publishing Co.: Feb-Mar, 1948 - No. 9, June-July, 1949 (All 52 pgs?)

	GD	VG	FN	VF	VF/NM	NM-
1-True crime stories	36	72	108	212	341	470
2	19	38	57	109	172	235
3,5,6	17	34	51	98	154	210
4-Acid in face story	21	42	63	123	197	270
7-9	14	28	42	81	118	155

NOTE: *Ingles a-5, 6. McWilliams a-5, 7, 8. Reinman c-6.*

GANG WORLD
Standard Comics: No. 5, Nov, 1952 - No. 6, Jan, 1953

	GD	VG	FN	VF	VF/NM	NM-
5-Bondage-c	19	38	57	109	172	235
6	15	30	45	83	124	165

GARGOYLE (See The Defenders #94)
Marvel Comics Group: June, 1985 - No. 4, Sept, 1985 (75¢, limited series)

	GD	VG	FN	VF	VF/NM	NM-
1-Wrightson-c; character from Defenders						3.50
2-4						2.50

GARGOYLES (TV cartoon)
Marvel Comics: Feb, 1995 - No. 11, Dec, 1995 ($2.50)

	GD	VG	FN	VF	VF/NM	NM-
1-11: Based on animated series						3.00

GARRISON'S GORILLAS (TV)
Dell Publishing Co.: Jan, 1968 - No. 4, Oct, 1968; No. 5, Oct, 1969 (Photo-c)

	GD	VG	FN	VF	VF/NM	NM-
1	5	10	15	30	48	65
2-5: 5-Reprints #1	3	6	9	20	30	40

GARY GIANNI'S THE MONSTERMEN
Dark Horse Comics: Aug, 1999 ($2.95, one-shot)

	GD	VG	FN	VF	VF/NM	NM-
1-Gianni-s/c/a; back-up Hellboy story by Mignola						3.00

Gay Comics #1 © MAR

Geeksville V2 #3 © Koslowski & Sassaman

Gene Autry Comics #58 © Gene Autry

GD VG FN VF VF/NM NM-
2.0 4.0 6.0 8.0 9.0 9.2

GASM
Stories, Layouts & Press, Inc.: Nov, 1977 - nn(No. 4), Jun, 1978 (B&W/color)

1-Mark Wheatley-s/a; Gene Day-s/a; Workman-a 2 4 6 13 18 22
nn(#2, 2/78) Day-s/a; Wheatley-a; Workman-a 2 4 6 9 13 16
nn(#3, 4/78) Day-s/a; Wheatley-a; Corben-a 3 6 9 14 19 24
nn(#4, 6/78) Hempel-a; Howarth-a; Corben-a 3 6 9 14 20 26

GASOLINE ALLEY (Top Love Stories No. 3 on?)
Star Publications: Sept-Oct, 1950 - No. 2, Dec, 1950 (Newspaper-r)

1-Contains 1 pg. intro. history of the strip (The Life of Skeezix); reprints 15 scenes of highlights from 1921-1935, plus an adventure from 1935 and 1936 strips; a 2-pg. filler is included on the life of the creator Frank King, with photo of the cartoonist.
21 42 63 120 188 255
2-(1936-37 reprints)-L. B. Cole-c 23 46 69 135 213 290
(See Super Book No. 21)

GASP!
American Comics Group: Mar, 1967 - No. 4, Aug, 1967 (12¢)

1 5 10 15 30 48 65
2-4 3 6 9 20 30 40

GATECRASHER
Black Bull Entertainment: Mar, 2000 - No. 4, Jun, 2000 ($2.50, limited series)

1,2-Waid-s/Conner & Palmiotti-c/a; 1,2-variant-c by J.G. Jones 2.50
3,4: 3-Jusko var-c. 4-Linsner-c 2.50
... Ring of Fire TPB (11/00, $12.95) r/#1-4; Hughes-c; Ennis intro. 13.00

GATECRASHER (Regular series)
Black Bull Entertainment: Aug, 2000 - No. 6, Jan, 2001 ($2.50, limited series)

1-6-Waid-s/Conner & Palmiotti-c/a; 1-3-Variant-c by Fabry. 4-Hildebrandts variant c. 5-Art Adams var-c. 6-Texeira var-c 2.50

GAY COMICS (Honeymoon No. 41)
Timely Comics/USA Comic Mag. Co. No. 18-24: Mar, 1944 (no month); No. 18, Fall, 1944 - No. 40, Oct, 1949

1-Wolverton's Powerhouse Pepper; Tessie the Typist begins; 1st app. Willie (one shot)
53 106 159 334 567 800
18-(Formerly Funny Tunes #17?)-Wolverton-a 37 74 111 215 345 475
19-29: Wolverton-a in all. 21,24-6 pg., 7 pg. Powerhouse Pepper; additional 2 pg. story in 24) 23-7 pg Wolverton story & 2 two pg stories(total of 11pgs.). 24,29-Kurtzman-a (24-"Hey Look"(2)) 33 66 99 192 309 425
30,33,36,37-Kurtzman's "Hey Look" 14 28 42 80 115 150
31-Kurtzman's "Hey Look" (1), Giggles 'N' Grins (1-1/2)
14 28 42 80 115 150
32,35,38-40: 35-Nellie The Nurse begins? 13 26 39 74 105 135
34-Three Kurtzman's "Hey Look" 14 28 42 82 121 160

GAY COMICS (Also see Smile, Tickle, & Whee Comics)
Modern Store Publ.: 1955 (7¢, 5x7-1/4", 52 pgs.)

1 4 8 12 22 34 45

GAY PURR-EE (See Movie Comics)

GAZILLION
Image Comics: Nov, 1998 ($2.50, one-shot)

1-Howard Shum-s/ Keron Grant-a 2.50

GEAR STATION, THE
Image Comics: Mar, 2000 - No. 5, Nov, 2000 ($2.50)

1-Four covers by Ross, Turner, Pat Lee, Fraga 2.50
1-($6.95) DF Cover 7.00
2-5: 2-Two covers by Fraga and Art Adams 2.50

GEEK, THE (See Brother Power... & Vertigo Visions)

GEEKSVILLE (Also see 3 Geeks, The)
3 Finger Prints/ Image: Aug, 1999 - No. 6, Mar, 2001 ($2.75/$2.95, B&W)

1,2,4-6-The 3 Geeks by Koslowski; Innocent Bystander by Sassaman 3.00
3-Includes "Babes & Blades" mini-comic 5.00
0-(3/00) First Image issue 3.00
(Vol. 2) 1-4-($2.95) 3-Mini-comic insert by the Geeks. 4-Steve Borock app. 3.00

G-8 AND HIS BATTLE ACES (Based on pulps)
Gold Key: Oct, 1966

1 (10184-610)-Painted-c 4 8 12 26 41 55

G-8 AND HIS BATTLE ACES
Blazing Comics: 1991 ($1.50, one-shot)

1-Glanzman-a; Truman-c 2.50
NOTE: *Flip book format with "The Spider's Web" #1 on other side w/**Glanzman**-a, **Truman**-c.*

GEISHA (Also see Oni Press Summer Vacation Supercolor Fun Special)
Oni Press: Sept, 1998 - No. 4, Dec, 1998 ($2.95, limited series)

1-4-Andi Watson-s/a. 2-Adam Warren-c 3.00
...One Shot (5/00, $4.50) 4.50
The Complete Geisha TPB (5/03, $15.95, digest size) r/#1-4, One Shot & story from Oni Press Summer Vacation Supercolor Fun Special 16.00

GEM COMICS
Spotlight Publishers: Apr, 1945 (52 pgs)

1-Little Mohee, Steve Strong app.; Jungle bondage-c
48 96 144 298 499 700

GEMINAR
Image Comics: July, 2000 ($4.95, B&W)

1-(72-Page Special) Terry Collins-s/Al Bigley-a 5.00

GEMINI BLOOD
DC Comics (Helix): Sept, 1996 - No. 9, May, 1997 ($2.25, limited series)

1-9: 5-Simonson-c 2.50

GEN ACTIVE
DC Comics (WildStorm): May, 2000 - No. 6, Aug, 2001 ($3.95)

1-6: 1-Covers by Campbell and Madureira; Gen 13 & DV8 app. 5-Mahfood-a; Quitely and Stelfreeze-c. 6-Portacio-a/c 4.00

GENE AUTRY (See March of Comics No. 25, 28, 39, 54, 78, 90, 104, 120, 135, 150 in the Promotional Comics section & Western Roundup under Dell Giants)

GENE AUTRY COMICS (Movie, Radio star; singing cowboy)
Fawcett Publications: 1941 (On sale 12/31/41) - No. 10, 1943 (68 pgs.) (Dell takes over with No. 11)

1 (Rare)-Gene Autry & his horse Champion begin
629 1258 1887 4400 7700 11,000
2-(1942) 138 276 414 863 1432 2000
3-5: 3-(11/1/42) 80 166 249 519 860 1200
6-10 62 124 186 388 644 900

GENE AUTRY COMICS (...& Champion No. 102 on)
Dell Publishing Co.: No. 11, 1943 - No. 121, Jan-Mar, 1959 (TV - later issues)

11 (1943, 60 pgs.)-Continuation of Fawcett series; photo back-c; first Dell issue
42 84 126 336 606 875
12 (2/44, 60 pgs.) 39 78 117 293 534 775
Four Color 47 (1944, 60 pgs.) 39 78 117 293 534 775
Four Color 57 (11/44),66('45)(52 pgs. each) 35 70 105 263 482 700
Four Color 75,83 ('45, 36 pgs. each) 28 56 84 207 374 540
Four Color 93 ('45, 36 pgs.) 25 50 75 187 336 485
Four Color 100 ('46, 36 pgs.) First Gene Autry photo-c
28 56 84 206 371 535
1 (5-6/46, 52 pgs.) 39 78 117 293 534 775
2 (7-8/46)-Photo-c begin, end #111 20 40 60 146 261 375
3-5: 4-Intro Flapjack Hobbs 15 30 45 107 191 275
6-10 13 26 39 95 168 240
11-20: 20-Panhandle Pete begins 11 22 33 79 140 200
21-29 (36 pgs.) 10 20 30 67 116 165
30-40 (52 pgs.) 9 18 27 60 100 140
41-56 (52 pgs.) 7 14 21 50 83 115
57-66 (36 pgs.): 58-X-mas-c 6 12 18 43 69 95
67-80 (52 pgs.): 70-X-mas-c 6 12 18 43 69 95
81-90 (52 pgs.): 82-X-mas-c. 87-Blank inside-c 6 12 18 39 62 85
91-99 (36 pgs. No. 91-on). 94-X-mas-c 5 10 15 35 55 75
100 6 12 18 37 59 80
101-111-Last Gene Autry photo-c 5 10 15 32 51 70
112-121-All Champion painted-c, most by Savitt 5 10 15 30 48 65
NOTE: *Photo back covers 4-18, 20-45, 48-65.* ***Manning** a-118.* ***Jesse Marsh** art: 4-Color No. 66, 75, 93, 100, No. 1-25, 27-37, 39, 40.*

GENE AUTRY'S CHAMPION (TV)
Dell Publ. Co.: No. 287, 8/50; No. 319, 2/51; No. 3, 8-10/51 - No. 19, 8-10/55

Four Color 287(#1)('50, 52 pgs.)-Photo-c 12 24 36 82 146 210
Four Color 319(#2, '51), 3: 2-Painted-c begin, most by Sam Savitt
7 14 21 45 73 100
4-19: 19-Last painted-c 5 10 15 34 55 75

GENE COLAN TRIBUTE BOOK (Produced for The Hero Initiative)
Marvel Comics: 2008 ($9.99, one-shot)

1-Spotlighted stories from Tales of Suspense #89,90, Doctor Strange #174 and others 10.00

Generation X #2 © MAR

GeNext #1 © MAR

Gen13 #13A © WSP

GD VG FN VF VF/NM NM-
2.0 4.0 6.0 8.0 9.0 9.2

GENE DOGS
Marvel Comics UK: Oct, 1993 - No. 4, Jan, 1994 ($1.75, limited series)
1-($2.75)-Polybagged w/4 trading cards 3.00
2-4: 2-Vs. Genetix 2.50

GENE POOL
IDW Publishing: Oct, 2003 ($6.99, squarebound)
nn-Wein & Wolfman-s/Cummings-a 7.00

GENERAL DOUGLAS MACARTHUR
Fox Features Syndicate: 1951
nn-True life story 20 40 60 115 183 250

GENERIC COMIC, THE
Marvel Comics Group: Apr, 1984 (one-shot)
1 3.00

GENERATION HEX
DC Comics (Amalgam): June, 1997 ($1.95, one-shot)
1-Milligan-s/ Pollina & Morales-a 2.50

GENERATION M (Follows House of M x-over)
Marvel Comics: Jan, 2006 - No. 5, May, 2006 ($2.99, limited series)
1-5-Jenkins-s/Bachs-a. 1-Chamber app. 2-Jubilee app. 3-Blob-c. 4-Angel-c 3.00
Decimation: Generation M TPB (2006, $13.99) r/#1-5 14.00

GENERATION NEXT
Marvel Comics: Mar, 1995 - No. 4, June, 1995 ($1.95, limited series)
1-4-Age of Apocalypse; Scott Lobdell scripts & Chris Bachalo-c/a 2.50

GENERATION X (See Gen 13/ Generation X)
Marvel Comics: Oct, 1994 - No. 75, June, 2001 ($1.50/$1.95/$1.99/$2.25)
Collectors Preview ($1.75), "Ashcan" Edition 2.25
-1(7/97) Flashback story 3.00
1/2 (San Diego giveaway) 2 4 6 8 10 12
1-($3.95)-Wraparound chromium-c; Scott Lobdell scripts & Chris Bachalo-a begins 6.00
2-($1.95)-Deluxe edition, Bachalo-a 4.00
3,4-($1.95)-Deluxe Edition; Bachalo-a 3.00
2-10: 2-4-Standard Edition. 5-Returns from "Age of Apocalypse," begin $1.95-c. 6-Bachalo-a(p) ends, returns #17. 7-Roger Cruz-a(p). 10-Omega Red-c/app. 3.00
11-24, 26-28: 13,14-Bishop-app. 17-Stan Lee app. (Stan Lee scripts own dialogue); Bachalo/Buckingham-a; Onslaught update. 18-Toad cameo. 20-Franklin Richards app; Howard the Duck cameo. 21-Howard the Duck app. 22-Nightmare app. 2.50
25-($2.99)-Wraparound-c. Black Tom, Howard the Duck app. 3.50
29-37: 29-Begin $1.99-c, "Operation Zero Tolerance". 33-Hama-s 2.50
38-49: 38-Dodson-a begins. 40-Penance ID revealed. 49-Maggott app. 2.50
50,57-($2.99): 50-Crossover w/X-Man #50 3.50
51-56, 58-62: 59-Avengers & Spider-Man app. 2.50
63-74: 63-Ellis-s begin. 64-Begin $2.25-c. 69-71-Art Adams-c 2.50
75-($2.99) Final issue; Chamber joins the X-Men; Lim-a 3.00
'95 Special-($3.95) 4.00
'96 Special-($2.95)-Wraparound-c; Jeff Johnson-c/a 3.50
'97 Special-($2.99)-Wraparound-c; 3.50
'98 Annual-($3.50)-vs. Dracula 3.50
'99 Annual-($3.50)-Monet leaves 3.50
75¢ Ashcan Edition 3.00
...Holiday Special 1 (2/99, $3.50) Pollina-a 3.50
...Underground Special 1 (5/98, $2.50, B&W) Mahfood-a 2.50

GENERATION X/ GEN 13 (Also see Gen 13/ Generation X)
Marvel Comics: 1997 ($3.99, one-shot)
1-Robinson-s/Larroca-a(p) 4.00

GENE RODDENBERRY'S LOST UNIVERSE
Tekno Comix: Apr, 1995 - No. 7, Oct, 1995 ($1.95)
1-7: 1-3-w/ bound-in game piece & trading card. 4-w/bound-in trading card 2.50

GENE RODDENBERRY'S XANDER IN LOST UNIVERSE
Tekno Comix: No. 0, Nov, 1995; No. 1, Dec, 1995 - No. 8, July, 1996 ($2.25)
0,1-8: 1-5-Jae Lee-c. 4-Polybagged. 8-Pt. 5 of The Big Bang x-over 2.50

GENESIS (See DC related titles)
DC Comics: Oct, 1997 - No. 4, Oct, 1997 ($1.95, weekly limited series)
1-4: Byrne-s/Wagner-a(p) in all. 3.00

GENESIS: THE #1 COLLECTION (WildStorm Archives)
WildStorm Productions: 1998 ($9.99, TPB, B&W)
nn-Reprints #1 issues of WildStorm titles and pin-ups 10.00

GD VG FN VF VF/NM NM-
2.0 4.0 6.0 8.0 9.0 9.2

GENETIX
Marvel Comics UK: Oct, 1993 - No. 6, Mar, 1994 ($1.75, limited series)
1-($2.75)-Polybagged w/4 cards; Dark Guard app. 3.00
2-6: 2-Intro Tektos. 4-Vs. Gene Dogs 2.50

GENEXT (Next generation of X-Men)
Marvel Comics: July, 2008 - No. 5, Nov, 2008 ($3.99, limited series)
1-5: 1-Claremont-s/Scherberger-a; character profile pages 4.00

GEN 12 (Also see Gen 13 and Team 7)
Image Comics (WildStorm Productions): Feb, 1998 - No. 5, June, 1998 ($2.50, lim. series)
1-5: 1-Team 7 & Gen 13 app.; wraparound-c 3.00

GEN 13 (Also see Wild C.A.T.S. #1 & Deathmate Black #2)
Image Comics (WildStorm Productions): Feb, 1994 - No. 5, July 1994 ($1.95, limited series)
0 (8/95, $2.50)-Ch. 1 w/Jim Lee-p; Ch.4 w/Charest-p 3.00
1/2 1 2 3 4 5 7
1-($2.50)-Created by Jim Lee 1 3 4 6 8 10
1-2nd printing 2.50
1-"3-D" Edition (9/97, $4.95)-w/glasses 5.00
2-($2.50) 1 2 3 4 5 7
3-Pitt-c & story 4.00
4-Pitt-c & story; wraparound-c 3.00
5 4.00
5-Alternate Portacio-c; see Deathblow #5 6.00
...Collected Edition ('94, $12.95)-r/#1-5 13.00
...Rave ($1.50, 3/95)-wraparound-c 3.00
...: Who They Are And How They Came To Be... (2006, $14.99) r/#1-5; sketch gallery 15.00
NOTE: *Issues 1-4 contain coupons redeemable for the ashcan edition of Gen 13 #0. Price listed is for a complete book.*

GEN 13
Image Comics (WildStorm Productions): Mar, 1995 - No. 36, Dec, 1998;
DC Comics (WildStorm): No. 37, Mar, 1999 - No. 77, Jul, 2002 ($2.95/$2.50)
1-A (Charge)-Campbell/Garner-c 4.50
1-B (Thumbs Up)-Campbell/Garner-c 4.50
1-C-1-F,1-I-1-M: 1-C (Lil' GEN 13)-Art Adams-c. 1-D (Barbari-GEN)-Simon Bisley-c. 1-E (Your Friendly Neighborhood Grunge)-Cleary-c. 1-F (GEN 13 Goes Madison Ave.)-Golden-c. 1-I (That's the way we became GEN 13)-Campbell/Gibson-c. 1-J (All Dolled Up)-Campbell/ McWeeney-c. 1-K (Verti-GEN)-Dunn-c. 1-L (Picto-Fiction). 1-M (Do it Yourself Cover) 1 2 3 4 5 7
1-G (Lin-GEN-re) Michael Lopez-c 2 4 6 8 10 12
1-H (GEN-et Jackson)-Jason Pearson-c 2 4 6 8 10 12
1-Chromium-c by Campbell 4 8 12 28 44 60
1-Chromium-c by Jim Lee 6 12 18 37 59 80
1-"3-D" Edition (2/98, $4.95)-w/glasses 5.00
2 ($1.95, Newsstand)-WildStorm Rising Pt. 4; bound-in card 2.50
2-12: 2-($2.50, Direct Market)-WildStorm Rising Pt. 4, bound-in card. 6,7-Jim Lee-c/a(p). 9-Ramos-a. 10,11-Fire From Heaven Pt. 3. & Pt.9 3.00
11-($4.95)-Special European Tour Edition; chromium-c 2 4 6 10 14 18
13A,13B,13C-($1.30, 13 pgs.): 13A-Archie & Friends app. 13B-Bone-c/app.; Teenage Mutant Ninja Turtles, Madman, Spawn & Jim Lee app. 3.00
14-24: 20-Last Campbell-a 2.50
25-($3.50)-Two covers by Campbell and Charest 3.50
25-($3.50)-Voyager Pack w/Danger Girl preview 4.50
25-Foil-c 10.00
26-32,34: 26-Arcudi-s/Frank-a begins. 34-Back-up story by Art Adams 2.50
33-Flip book w/Planetary preview 4.00
35-49: 36,38,40-Two covers. 37-First DC issue. 41-Last Frank-a 2.50
50-($3.95) Two covers by Lee and Benes; art by various 4.00
51-76: 51-Moy-a; Fairchild loses her powers. 60-Warren-s/a. 66-Art by various incl. Campbell (3 pgs.). 70,75,76-Mays-a. 76-Original team dies 2.50
77-($3.50) Mays, Andrews, Warren-a 3.50
Annual 1 (1997, $2.95) Ellis-s/ Dillon-c/a. 3.50
Annual 1999 ($3.50, DC) Slipstream x-over w/ DV8 3.50
Annual 2000 ($3.50) Devil's Night x-over w/WildStorm titles; Bermejo-c 3.50
...: A Christmas Caper (1/00, $5.95, one-shot) McWeeney-s/a 6.00
... Archives (4/98, $12.99) B&W reprints of mini-series, #0,1/2,1-13ABC; includes cover gallery and sourcebook 13.00
...: Carny Folk (2/00, $3.50) Collect back-up stories 3.50
... European Vacation TPB ($6.95) r/#6,7 7.00
.../ Fantastic Four (2001, $5.95) Maguire-s/c/a(p) 6.00
...: Going West (6/99, $2.50, one-shot) Pruett-s 2.50
...: Grunge Saves the World (5/99, $5.95, one-shot) Altieri-c/a 6.00
... I Love New York TPB ($9.95) r/part #25, 26-29; Frank-c 10.00

Gen 13 (2nd series) #7 © WSP

Georgie Comics #9 © MAR

Get Smart #8 © Talent Associates

	GD 2.0	VG 4.0	FN 6.0	VF 8.0	VF/NM 9.0	NM- 9.2

... London, New York, Hell TPB ($6.95) r/Annual #1 & Bootleg Ann. #1 7.00
... Lost in Paradise TPB ($6.95) r/#3-5 7.00
.../ Maxx (12/95, $3.50, one-shot) Messner-Loebs-s, 1st Coker-c/a. 3.50
...: Meanwhile (2003, $17.95) r/#43,44,66-70; all Warren-s; art by various 18.00
...: Medicine Song (2001, $5.95) Brent Anderson-c/a(p)/Raab-s 6.00
... Science Friction (2001, $5.95) Haley & Lopresti-a 6.00
... Starting Over TPB ($14.95) r/#1-7 15.00
... Superhuman Like You TPB ($12.95) r/#60-65; Warren-c 13.00
... #13 A,B&C Collected Edition ($6.95, TPB) r/#13A,B&C 7.00
... 3-D Special (1997, $4.95, one-shot) Art Adams-s/a(p) 5.00
...: The Unreal World (7/96, $2.95, one-shot) Humberto Ramos-c/a 3.00
... We'll Take Manhattan TPB ($14.95) r/#45-50; new Benes-c 15.00
...: Wired (4/99, $2.50, one-shot) Richard Bennett-c/a 2.50
... Yearbook 1997 (6/97, $2.50) College-themed stories and pin-ups by various 2.50
...: 'Zine (12/96, $1.95, B&W, digest size) Campbell/Garner-c 2.50
Variant Collection-Four editions (all 13 variants w/Chromium variant-limited, signed) 100.00

GEN 13
DC Comics (WildStorm): No. 0, Sept, 2002 - No. 16, Feb, 2004 ($2.95)

0-(13¢-c) Intro. new team; includes previews of 21 Down & The Resistance 2.50
1-Claremont-s/Garza-c/a; Fairchild app. 3.00
2-16: 8-13-Bachs-a. 16-Original team returns 3.00
...: September Song TPB (2003, $19.95) r/#0-6; Garza sketch pages 20.00

GEN 13 (Volume 4)
DC Comics (WildStorm): Dec, 2006 - Present ($2.99)

1-20: 1-Simone-s/Caldwell-a; re-intro the original team; Caldwell-c. 8-The Authority app. 3.00
1-Variant-c by J. Scott Campbell 5.00
...: Armageddon (1/08, $2.99) Gage-s/Meyers-a; future Gen13 app. 3.00
...: Boot of a Bad Lot TPB (2007, $14.99) r/#1-6 15.00
...: Road Trip TPB (2008, $14.99) r/#7-13 15.00

GEN 13 BOOTLEG
Image Comics (WildStorm): Nov, 1996 - No. 20, Jul, 1998 ($2.50)

1-Alan Davis-a; alternate costumes-c 2.50
1-Team falling variant-c 3.00
2-7: 2-Alan Davis-a. 5,6-Terry Moore-s. 7-Robinson-s/Scott Hampton-a 2.50
8-10-Adam Warren-s/a 4.00
11-20: 11,12-Lopresti-s/a & Simonson-s. 13-Wieringo-s/a. 14-Mariotte-s/Phillips-a. 15,16-Strnad-s/Shaw-a. 18-Altieri-s/a(p)/c, 18-Variant-c by Bruce Timm 2.50
Annual 1 (2/98, $2.95) Ellis-s/Dillon-c/a 3.00
... Grunge: The Movie (12/97, $9.95) r/#8-10, Warren-c 10.00
...Vol. 1 TPB (10/98, $11.95) r/#1-4 12.00

GEN 13/ GENERATION X (Also see Generation X / Gen 13)
Image Comics (WildStorm Publications): July, 1997 ($2.95, one-shot)

1-Choi-s/ Art Adams-p/Garner-i. Variant covers by Adams/Garner and Campbell/McWeeney 3.00
1-($4.95) 3-D Edition w/glasses; Campbell-c 5.00

GEN 13 INTERACTIVE
Image Comics (WildStorm): Oct, 1997 - No. 3, Dec, 1997 ($2.50, lim. series)

1-3-Internet voting used to determine storyline 2.50
... Plus! (7/98, $11.95) r/series & 3-D Special (in 2-D) 12.00

GEN 13 : MAGICAL DRAMA QUEEN ROXY
Image Comics (WildStorm): Oct, 1998 - No. 3, Dec, 1998 ($3.50, lim. series)

1-3-Adam Warren-s/c/a; manga style, 2-Variant-c by Hiroyuki Utatane 3.50
1-($6.95) Dynamic Forces Ed. w/Variant Warren-c 7.00

GEN 13 /MONKEYMAN & O'BRIEN
Image Comics (WildStorm): Jun, 1998 - No. 2, July, 1998 ($2.50, lim. series)

1,2-Art Adams-s/a(p); 1-Two covers 2.50
1-($4.95) Chromium-c 5.00
1-($6.95) Dynamic Forces Ed. 7.00

GEN 13: ORDINARY HEROES
Image Comics (WildStorm Publications): Feb, 1996 - No. 2, July, 1996 ($2.50, lim. series)

1,2-Adam Hughes-c/a/scripts 3.00
TPB (2004, $14.95) r/series, Gen13 Bootleg #1&2 and Wildstorm Thunderbook; new Hughes-c and art pages 15.00

GENTLE BEN (TV)
Dell Publishing Co.: Feb, 1968 - No. 5, Oct, 1969 (All photo-c)

1 4 8 12 26 41 55
2-5: 5-Reprints #1 3 6 9 16 23 30

GEOMANCER (Also see Eternal Warrior: Fist & Steel)
Valiant: Nov, 1994 - No. 8, June, 1995 ($3.75/$2.25)

1 ($3.75)-Chromium wraparound-c; Eternal Warrior app. 3.75
2-8 2.50

GEORGE OF THE JUNGLE (TV)(See America's Best TV Comics)
Gold Key: Feb, 1969 - No. 2, Oct, 1969 (Jay Ward)

1 9 18 27 65 113 160
2 6 12 18 41 66 90

GEORGE PAL'S PUPPETOONS (Funny animal puppets)
Fawcett Publications: Dec, 1945 - No. 18, Dec, 1947; No. 19, 1950

1-Captain Marvel-c 42 84 126 261 436 610
2 23 46 69 135 218 300
3-10 15 30 45 86 133 180
11-19 13 26 39 74 105 135

GEORGIE COMICS (...& Judy Comics #20-35?; see All Teen & Teen Comics)
Timely Comics/GPI No. 1-34: Spr, 1945 - No. 39, Oct, 1952 (#1-3 are quarterly)

1-Dave Berg-a 30 60 90 74 280 385
2 15 30 45 90 140 190
3-5,7,8 14 28 42 82 121 160
6-Georgie visits Timely Comics 15 30 45 90 140 190
9,10-Kurtzman's "Hey Look" (1 & ?); Millie the Model & Margie app. 15 30 45 83 124 165
11,12: 11-Margie, Millie app. 11 22 33 64 90 115
13-Kurtzman's "Hey Look", 3 pgs. 12 24 36 69 97 125
14-Wolverton-a(1 pg.); Kurtzman's "Hey Look" 13 26 39 74 105 135
15,16,18-20 11 22 33 60 83 105
17,29-Kurtzman's "Hey Look", 1 pg. 11 22 33 64 90 115
21-24,27,28,30-39: 21-Anti-Wertham editorial. 33-38-Hy Rosen-c 10 20 30 56 76 95
25-Painted-c by classic pin-up artist Peter Driben 13 26 39 74 105 135
26-Logo design swipe from Archie Comics 10 20 30 58 79 100

GERALD McBOING-BOING AND THE NEARSIGHTED MR. MAGOO (TV) (Mr. Magoo No. 6 on)
Dell Publishing Co.: Aug-Oct, 1952 - No. 5, Aug-Oct, 1953

1 11 22 33 75 133 190
2-5 9 18 27 63 107 150

GERONIMO (See Fighting Indians of the Wild West!)
Avon Periodicals: 1950 - No. 4, Feb, 1952

1-Indian Fighter; Maneely-a; Texas Rangers-r/Cowpuncher #1; Fawcette-c 19 38 57 109 172 235
2-On the Warpath; Kit West app.; Kinstler-c/a 13 26 39 74 105 135
3-And His Apache Murderers; Kinstler-c/a(2); Kit West-r/Cowpuncher #6 13 26 39 74 105 135
4-Savage Raids of; Kinstler-c & inside front-c; Kinstlerish-a by McCann(3) 12 24 36 69 97 125

GERONIMO JONES
Charlton Comics: Sept, 1971 - No. 9, Jan, 1973

1 2 4 6 11 16 20
2-9 1 3 4 6 8 10
Modern Comics Reprint #7('78) 4.00

GETALONG GANG, THE (TV)
Marvel Comics (Star Comics): May, 1985 - No. 6, Mar, 1986

1-6: Saturday morning TV stars 3.00

GET LOST
Mikeross Publications/New Comics: Feb-Mar, 1954 - No. 3, June-July, 1954 (Satire)

1-Andru/Esposito-a in all? 31 62 93 181 291 400
2-Andru/Esposito-c; has 4 pg. E.C. parody featuring "The Sewer Keeper" 21 42 63 123 197 270
3-John Wayne 'Hondo' parody 17 34 51 98 154 210
1,2 (10,12/87-New Comics)-B&W r-original 2.50

GET SMART (TV)
Dell Publ. Co.: June, 1966 - No. 8, Sept, 1967 (All have Don Adams photo-c)

1 10 20 30 68 119 170
2,3-Ditko-a 7 14 21 47 76 105
4-8: 8-Reprints #1 (cover and insides) 6 12 18 37 59 80

GHOST (...Comics #9)
Fiction House Magazines: 1951(Winter) - No. 11, Summer, 1954

1-Most covers by Whitman 77 154 231 481 816 1150

Ghost Special #2 © DH

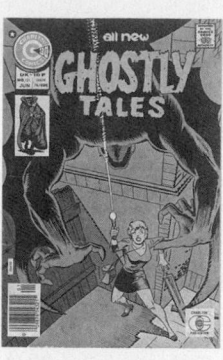

Ghostly Tales #121 © CC

Ghost Manor #57 © CC

	GD 2.0	VG 4.0	FN 6.0	VF 8.0	VF/NM 9.0	NM- 9.2
2-Ghost Gallery & Werewolf Hunter stories	40	80	120	244	397	550
3-9: 3,6,7,9-Bondage-c. 9-Abel, Discount-a	34	68	102	198	319	440
10,11-Dr. Drew by Grandenetti in each, reprinted from Rangers; 11-Evans-r/ Rangers #39; Grandenetti-r/Rangers #49	29	58	87	169	272	375

GHOST (See Comic's Greatest World)
Dark Horse Comics: Apr, 1995 - No. 36, Apr, 1998 ($2.50/$2.95)

	GD 2.0	VG 4.0	FN 6.0	VF 8.0	VF/NM 9.0	NM- 9.2
1-Adam Hughes-a	1	2	3	5	6	8
2,3-Hughes-a						4.00
4-24: 4-Barb Wire app. 5,6-Hughes-c. 12-Ghost/Hellboy preview. 15,21-X app. 18,19-Barb Wire app.						3.00
25-($3.50)-48 pgs. special						3.50
26-36: 26-Begin $2.95-c. 29-Flip book w/Timecop. 33-36-Jade Cathedral; Harris painted-c						3.00
Special 1 (7/94, $3.95, 48 pgs.)	1	2	3	4	5	7
Special 2 (6/98, $3.95) Barb Wire app.						4.00
...Black October (1/99, $14.95, trade paperback)-r/#6-9,26,27						15.00
...Nocturnes (1996, $9.95, trade paperback)-r/#1-3 & 5						10.00
...Stories (1995, $9.95, trade paperback)-r/Early Ghost app.						10.00

GHOST (Volume 2)
Dark Horse Comics: Sept, 1998 - No. 22, Aug, 2000 ($2.95)

	GD 2.0	VG 4.0	FN 6.0	VF 8.0	VF/NM 9.0	NM- 9.2
1-22: 1-4-Ryan Benjamin-c/Zanier-a						3.00
Handbook (8/99, $2.95) guide to issues and characters						3.00
Special 3 (12/98, $3.95)						4.00

GHOST AND THE SHADOW
Dark Horse Comics: Dec, 1995 ($2.95, one-shot)

	GD 2.0	VG 4.0	FN 6.0	VF 8.0	VF/NM 9.0	NM- 9.2
1-Moench scripts						3.00

GHOST/BATGIRL
Dark Horse Comics: Aug, 2000 - No. 4, Dec, 2000 ($2.95, limited series)

	GD 2.0	VG 4.0	FN 6.0	VF 8.0	VF/NM 9.0	NM- 9.2
1-4-New Batgirl; Oracle & Bruce Wayne app.; Benjamin-c/a						3.00

GHOST/HELLBOY
Dark Horse Comics: May, 1996 - No. 2, June, 1996 ($2.50, limited series)

	GD 2.0	VG 4.0	FN 6.0	VF 8.0	VF/NM 9.0	NM- 9.2
1,2: Mike Mignola-c/scripts & breakdowns; Scott Benefiel finished-a						3.00

GHOST BREAKERS (Also see Racket Squad in Action, Red Dragon & (CC) Sherlock Holmes Comics)
Street & Smith Publications: Sept, 1948 - No. 2, Dec, 1948 (52 pgs.)

	GD 2.0	VG 4.0	FN 6.0	VF 8.0	VF/NM 9.0	NM- 9.2
1-Powell-c/a(3); Dr. Neff (magician) app.	41	82	123	256	428	600
2-Powell-c/a(2); Maneely-a	34	68	102	198	319	440

GHOSTBUSTERS (TV) (Also, see Real...and Slimer)
First Comics: Feb, 1987 - No. 6, Aug, 1987 ($1.25)

	GD 2.0	VG 4.0	FN 6.0	VF 8.0	VF/NM 9.0	NM- 9.2
1-6: Based on new animated TV series						3.00

GHOSTBUSTERS: LEGION (Movie)
88 MPH Studios: Feb, 2004 - No. 4, May, 2004 ($2.95/$3.50)

	GD 2.0	VG 4.0	FN 6.0	VF 8.0	VF/NM 9.0	NM- 9.2
1-4-Steve Kurth-a/Andrew Dabb-s						3.00
1-3-($3.50) Brereton variant-c						3.50

GHOSTBUSTERS II
Now Comics: Oct, 1989 - No. 3, Dec, 1989 ($1.95, mini-series)

	GD 2.0	VG 4.0	FN 6.0	VF 8.0	VF/NM 9.0	NM- 9.2
1-3: Movie Adaptation						3.00

GHOST CASTLE (See Tales of...)

GHOSTING
Platinum Studios: 2007 - No. 5 ($2.99, limited series)

	GD 2.0	VG 4.0	FN 6.0	VF 8.0	VF/NM 9.0	NM- 9.2
1-3-Van Lente-s/Carvalho-a/Wolfe-c						3.00

GHOST IN THE SHELL (Manga)
Dark Horse: Mar, 1995 - No. 8, Oct, 1995 ($3.95, B&W/color, lim. series)

	GD 2.0	VG 4.0	FN 6.0	VF 8.0	VF/NM 9.0	NM- 9.2
1,2	2	4	6	13	18	22
3	2	4	6	8	10	12
4-8	1	2	3	5	6	8

GHOST IN THE SHELL 2: MAN-MADE INTERFACE (Manga)
Dark Horse Comics: Jan, 2003 - No. 11, Dec, 2003 ($3.50, color/B&W, lim. series)

	GD 2.0	VG 4.0	FN 6.0	VF 8.0	VF/NM 9.0	NM- 9.2
1-11-Masamune Shirow-s/a. 5-B&W						3.50

GHOSTLY HAUNTS (Formerly Ghost Manor)
Charlton Comics: #20, 9/71 - #53, 12/76; #54, 9/77 - #55, 10/77; #56, 1/78 - #58, 4/78

	GD 2.0	VG 4.0	FN 6.0	VF 8.0	VF/NM 9.0	NM- 9.2
20	3	6	9	17	25	32
21	2	4	6	10	14	18
22-25,27,31-34,36,37-Ditko-c/a. 27-Dr. Graves x-over. 32-New logo. 33-Back to old logo	2	4	6	13	18	22
26,29,30,35-Ditko-c	2	4	6	9	13	16
28,38-40-Ditko-a. 39-Origin & 1st app. Destiny Fox	2	4	6	9	13	16
41,42: 41-Sutton-c; Ditko-a. 42-Newton-c/a	2	4	6	10	14	18
43-46,48,50,52-Ditko-a	2	4	6	9	12	15
47,54,56-Ditko-c/a. 56-Ditko-a(r).	2	4	6	10	14	18
49,51,53,55,57	1	3	4	6	8	10
58 (4/78) Last issue	2	4	6	10	14	18
40,41(Modern Comics-r, 1977, 1978)						4.00

NOTE: ***Ditko** a-22-25, 27, 28, 31-34, 36-41, 43-48, 50, 52, 54, 56r; c-22-27, 29, 30, 33-37, 47, 54, 56. **Glanzman** a-20. **Howard** a-27, 30, 35, 40-43, 48, 54, 57. **Kim** a-38, 41, 57. **Larson** a-48, 50. **Newton** c/a-42. **Staton** a-32, 35; c-28, 46. **Sutton** c-33, 37, 39, 41.*

GHOSTLY TALES (Formerly Blue Beetle No. 50-54)
Charlton Comics: No. 55, 4-5/66 - No. 124, 12/76; No. 125, 9/77 - No. 169, 10/84

	GD 2.0	VG 4.0	FN 6.0	VF 8.0	VF/NM 9.0	NM- 9.2
55-Intro. & origin Dr. Graves; Ditko-a	6	12	18	43	69	95
56-58,60,61,70,71-Ditko-a. 70-Dr. Graves ends. 71-Last 12¢ issue	4	8	12	22	34	45
59,62-66,68	3	6	9	16	23	30
67,69-Ditko-c/a	4	8	12	24	37	50
72,75,76,79-82,85-Ditko-a	2	4	6	13	18	22
73,77,78,83,84,86-90,92-95,97,99-Ditko-c/a	3	6	9	16	22	28
74,91,98,119,123,124,127-130: 127,130-Sutton-a	2	4	6	8	11	14
96-Ditko-c	2	4	6	11	16	20
100-Ditko-c; Sutton-a	2	4	6	11	16	20
101,103-105-Ditko-a	2	4	6	10	14	18
102,109-Ditko-c/a	2	4	6	13	18	22
110,113-Sutton-c; Ditko-a	2	4	6	10	14	18
106-Ditko & Sutton-a; Sutton-c	2	4	6	10	14	18
107-Ditko, Wood, Sutton-a	2	4	6	11	16	20
108,116,117,126-Ditko-a	2	4	6	10	14	18
111,118,120-122,125-Ditko-c/a	2	4	6	13	18	22
112,114,115: 112,114-Ditko, Sutton-a. 114-Newton-a. 115-Newton, Ditko-a.	2	4	6	10	14	18
131-134,151,157,163-Ditko-c/a	2	4	6	9	13	16
135,142,145-150,153,154,156,158-160	1	2	3	5	6	8
136-141,143,144,152,155-Ditko-a	1	3	4	6	8	10
161,162,164-168-Lower print run. 162-Nudity panel	2	4	6	8	11	14
169 (10/84) Last issue; lower print run	2	4	6	10	14	18

NOTE: ***Aparo** a-65, 66, 68, 72, 137, 141r, 142r; c-71, 72, 74-76, 81, 146r, 149. **Ditko** a-55-58, 60, 61, 67, 69-73, 75-90, 92-95, 97, 99-118, 120-122, 125r, 126r, 131-141r, 143r, 144r, 146, 147, 149-152, 154-157, 159-161, 163; c-67, 69, 73, 77, 78, 83, 84, 86-90, 92-97, 99, 102, 109, 111, 118, 120-122, 125, 131-133, 147, 148, 151, 157-160, 163. **Glanzman** a-167. **Howard** a-95, 98, 99, 108, 117, 129, 131; c-98, 107, 120, 121, 161. **Larson** a-117, 119, 136, 159; c-136. **Morisi** a-83, 84, 86. **Newton** a-114; c-115(painted). **Palais** a-61. **Staton** a-161; c-117. **Sutton** a-106, 107, 111-114, 127, 130, 162; c-100, 106, 110, 113(painted). **Wood** a-107.*

GHOSTLY WEIRD STORIES (Formerly Blue Bolt Weird)
Star Publications: No. 120, Sept, 1953 - No. 124, Sept, 1954

	GD 2.0	VG 4.0	FN 6.0	VF 8.0	VF/NM 9.0	NM- 9.2
120-Jo-Jo-r	40	80	120	240	390	540
121-124: 121-Jo-Jo-r. 122-The Mask-r/Capt. Flight #5; Rulah-r; has 1pg. story 'Death and the Devil Pills'-r/Western Outlaws #17. 123-Jo-Jo; Disbrow-a(2). 124-Torpedo Man	37	74	111	215	345	475

NOTE: ***Disbrow** a-120-124. **L. B. Cole** covers-all issues (#122 is a sci-fi cover).*

GHOST MANOR (Ghostly Haunts No. 20 on)
Charlton Comics: July, 1968 - No. 19, July, 1971

	GD 2.0	VG 4.0	FN 6.0	VF 8.0	VF/NM 9.0	NM- 9.2
1	5	10	15	34	55	75
2-6: 6-Last 12¢ issue	3	6	9	19	29	38
7-12,17: 17-Morisi-a	3	6	9	16	23	30
13,14,16-Ditko-a	3	6	9	19	29	38
15,18,19-Ditko-c/a	4	8	12	22	34	45

GHOST MANOR (2nd Series)
Charlton Comics: Oct, 1971-No. 32, Dec, 1976; No. 33, Sept, 1977-No. 77, 11/84

	GD 2.0	VG 4.0	FN 6.0	VF 8.0	VF/NM 9.0	NM- 9.2
1	4	8	12	28	44	60
2,3,5-7,9-Ditko-c	3	6	9	16	22	28
4,10-Ditko-c/a	3	6	9	18	27	35
8-Wood, Ditko-a; Sutton-c	3	6	9	18	27	35
11,14-Ditko-c/a	3	6	9	15	21	26
12,17,27,30	2	4	6	8	11	14
13,15,16,23-26,29: 13-Ditko-a. 15,16-Ditko-c. 23-Sutton-a. 24-26,29-Ditko-a. 26-Early Zeck-a; Boyette-c	2	4	6	10	14	18
18-(3/74) Newton 1st pro art; Ditko-a; Sutton-c	3	6	9	14	20	25
19-21: 19-Newton, Sutton-a; nudity panels. 20-Ditko-a. 21-E-Man, Blue Beetle, Capt. Atom cameos; Ditko-a.	2	4	6	10	14	18
22-Newton-c/a; Ditko-a	2	4	6	11	16	20
25,28,31,37,38-Ditko-c/a: 28-Nudity panels	2	4	6	11	16	20
32-36,39,41,45,48-50,53: 34-Black Cat by Kim	1	2	3	5	7	9
40-Ditko-a; torture & drug use	2	4	6	10	14	18

Ghost Rider #1 © MAR

Ghost Rider V2 #6 © MAR

Ghost Rider (2006 series) #16 © MAR

	GD 2.0	VG 4.0	FN 6.0	VF 8.0	VF/NM 9.0	NM- 9.2
42,43,46,47,51,52,60,62,69-Ditko-c/a	2	4	6	9	13	16
44,54,71-Ditko-a	2	4	6	8	10	12
55,56,58,59,61,63,65-68,70	1	2	3	4	5	7
57-Wood, Ditko, Howard-a	2	4	6	8	11	14
64-Ditko & Newton-a	2	4	6	8	10	12
71-76 (low print)	1	2	3	5	6	8
77-(11/84) Last issue Aparo-r/Space Adventures V3#60 (Paul Mann)	2	4	6	9	13	16
19 (Modern Comics reprint, 1977)						4.00

NOTE: ***Ditko** a-4, 8, 10, 11(2), 13, 14, 18, 20-22, 24-26, 28, 29, 31, 37r, 38r, 40r, 42-44r, 46r, 47, 51r, 52r, 54r, 57, 60, 62(4). 64r, 69, 71; c-2-7, 9-11, 14-16, 28, 31, 37, 38, 42, 43, 46, 47, 51, 52, 60, 62, 64. **Howard** a-4, 8, 12, 17, 19-21, 31, 41, 45, 57. **Newton** a-18-20, 22, 64; c-22. **Staton** a-13, 38, 44, 45. **Sutton** a-19, 23, 25, 45;c-8, 18.*

GHOST RIDER (See A-1 Comics, Best of the West, Black Phantom, Bobby Benson, Great Western, Red Mask & Tim Holt)
Magazine Enterprises: 1950 - No. 14, 1954

NOTE: *The character was inspired by Vaughn Monroe's "Ghost Riders in the Sky", and Disney's movie "The Headless Horseman".*

	GD	VG	FN	VF	VF/NM	NM-
1(A-1 #27)-Origin Ghost Rider	112	224	336	706	1191	1675
2-5: 2(A-1 #29), 3(A-1 #31), 4(A-1 #34), 5(A-1 #37)-All Frazetta-c only	72	144	216	454	770	1085
6,7: 6(A-1 #44)-Loco weed story, 7(A-1 #51)	32	64	96	190	305	420
8,9: 8(A-1 #57)-Drug use story, 9(A-1 #69)	28	56	84	162	261	360
10(A-1 #71) Vs. Frankenstein	30	60	90	174	280	385
11-14: 11(A-1 #75). 12(A-1 #80)-Bondage-c; one-eyed Devil-c. 13(A-1 #84). 14(A-1 #112)	24	48	72	143	229	315

NOTE: ***Dick Ayers** art in all; c-1, 6-14.*

GHOST RIDER, THE (See Night Rider & Western Gunfighters)
Marvel Comics Group: Feb, 1967 - No. 7, Nov, 1967 (Western hero)(12¢)

	GD	VG	FN	VF	VF/NM	NM-
1-Origin & 1st app. Ghost Rider; Kid Colt-reprints begin	8	16	24	58	97	135
2	5	10	15	32	51	70
3-7: 6-Last Kid Colt-r; All Ayers-c/a(p)	4	8	12	28	44	60

GHOST RIDER (See The Champions, Marvel Spotlight #5, Marvel Team-Up #15, 58, Marvel Treasury Edition #18, Marvel Two-In-One #8, The Original Ghost Rider & The Original Ghost Rider Rides Again)
Marvel Comics Group: Sept, 1973 - No. 81, June, 1983 (Super-hero)

	GD	VG	FN	VF	VF/NM	NM-
1-Johnny Blaze, the Ghost Rider begins; 1st brief app. Daimon Hellstrom (Son of Satan)	13	26	39	95	168	240
2-1st full app. Daimon Hellstrom; gives glimpse of costume (1 panel); story continues in Marvel Spotlight #12	6	12	18	37	59	80
3-5: 3-Ghost Rider gains power to make cycle of fire; Son of Satan app.	4	8	12	26	41	55
6-10: 10-Reprints origin/1st app. from Marvel Spotlight #5; Ploog-a	3	6	9	19	29	38
11-16	2	4	6	11	16	20
17,19-(Reg. 25¢ editions)(4,8/76)	2	4	6	11	16	20
17,19-(30¢-c variants, limited distribution)	4	8	12	28	44	60
18-(Reg. 25¢ edition)(6/76). Spider-Man-c & app.	2	4	6	13	18	22
18-(30¢-c variant, limited distribution)	5	10	15	32	51	70
20-Daredevil x-over; ties into D.D. #138; Byrne-a	3	6	9	16	23	30
21-30: 22-1st app. Enforcer. 29,30-Vs. Dr. Strange	2	4	6	8	10	12
24-26-(35¢-c variants, limited distribution)	4	8	12	26	41	55
31-34,36-49	1	2	3	5	7	9
35-Death Race classic; Starlin-c/a/sty	2	4	6	8	11	14
50-Double size	1	3	4	6	8	10
51-76,78-80: 80-Brief origin recap. 68,77-Origin retold						6.00
81-Death of Ghost Rider (Demon leaves Blaze)	2	4	6	11	16	20
... Team Up TPB (2007, $15.99) r/#27, 50, Marvel Team-Up #91, Marvel Two-In-One #80, Avengers #214 and Marvel Premiere #28; Night Rider app.; coveer gallery						16.00

NOTE: ***Anderson** c-64p. **Infantino** a(p)-43, 44, 51. **G. Kane** a-21p; c(p)-1, 2, 4, 5, 8, 9, 11-13, 19, 20, 24, 25. **Kirby** c-21-23. **Mooney** a-2-9p, 30i. **Nebres** c-26i. **Newton** a-23i. **Perez** c-26p. **Shores** a-2i. J. **Sparling** a-62p, 64p, 65p. **Starlin** a(p)-35. **Sutton** a-1p, 44i, 64i, 65i, 66, 67i. **Tuska** a-13p, 14p, 16p.*

GHOST RIDER (Volume 2) (Also see Doctor Strange/Ghost Rider Special, Marvel Comics Presents & Midnight Sons Unlimited)
Marvel Comics (Midnight Sons imprint #44 on): V2#1, May, 1990 - No. 93, Feb, 1998 ($1.50/$1.75/$1.95)

	GD	VG	FN	VF	VF/NM	NM-
1-($1.95, 52 pgs.)-Origin/1st app. new Ghost Rider; Kingpin app.						6.00
1-2nd printing (not gold)						2.50
2-5: 3-Kingpin app. 5-Punisher app.; Jim Lee-c						3.00
5-Gold background 2nd printing						2.50
6-14,16-24,29,30,32-39: 6-Punisher app. 6,17-Spider-Man/Hobgoblin-c/story. 9-X-Factor app. 10-Reintro Johnny Blaze on the last pg. 11-Stroman-c/a(p). 12,13-Dr. Strange x-over cont'd in D.S. #28. 13-Painted-c. 14-Johnny Blaze vs. Ghost Rider; origin recap 1st Ghost Rider (Blaze). 18-Painted-c by Nelson. 29-Wolverine-c/story. 32-Dr. Strange x-over; Johnny Blaze app. 34-Williamson-a(i). 36-Daredevil app. 37-Archangel app.						3.00
15-Glow in the dark-c						3.00
25-27: 25-($2.75)-Contains pop-up scene insert. 26,27-X-Men x-over; Lee/Williams-c on both						3.00
28,31-($2.50, 52 pgs.)-Polybagged w/poster; part 1 & part 6 of Rise of the Midnight Sons storyline (see Ghost Rider/Blaze #1)						3.00
40-Outer-c is Darkhold envelope made of black parchment w/gold ink; Midnight Massacre; Demogoblin app.						3.00
41-48; 41-Lilith & Centurious app.; begin $1.75-c. 41-43-Neon ink-c. 43-Has free extra 16 pg. insert on Siege of Darkness. 44,45-Siege of Darkness parts 2 & 10. 44-Spot varnish-c. 46-Intro new Ghost Rider. 48-Spider-Man app.						2.50
49,51-60,62-74: 49-Begin $1.95-c; bound-in trading card sheet; Hulk app. 55-Werewolf by Night app. 65-Punisher app. 67,68-Gambit app. 68-Wolverine app. 73,74-Blaze, Vengeance app.						2.50
50,61: 50-($2.50, 52 pgs.)-Regular edition						3.00
50-($2.95, 52 pgs.)-Collectors Ed. die cut foil-c						3.00
75-89: 76-Vs. Vengeance. 77,78-Dr. Strange-app. 78-New costume						2.50
90-92						5.00
93-($2.99)-Last issue; Saltares & Texeira-a	1	2	3	5	6	8
(#94, see Ghost Rider Finale for unpublished story)						
#(-1) Flashback (7/97) Saltares-a						2.50
Annual 1,2 ('93, '94, $2.95, 68 pgs.) 1-Bagged w/card						3.00
...And Cable 1 (9/92, $3.95, stiff-c, 68 pgs.)-Reprints Marvel Comics Presents #90-98 w/new Kieth-c						4.00
...:Crossroads (11/95, $3.95) Die cut cover; Nord-a						5.00
... Finale (2007, $3.99) r/#93 and the story meant for the unpublished #94; Saltares-a						4.00
Highway to Hell (2001, $3.50) Reprints origin from Marvel Spotlight #5						3.50
...: Resurrected TPB (2001, $12.95) r/#1-7						13.00

NOTE: ***Andy & Joe Kubert** c/a-28-31. **Quesada** c-21. **Williamson** a(i)-33-35; c-33i.*

GHOST RIDER (Volume 3)
Marvel Comics: Aug, 2001 - No. 6, Jan, 2002 ($2.99, limited series)

1-6-Grayson-s/Kaniuga-a/c	3.00
...: The Hammer Lane TPB (6/02, $15.95) r/#1-6	16.00

GHOST RIDER
Marvel Comics: Nov, 2005 - No. 6, Apr, 2006 ($2.99, limited series)

1-6-Garth Ennis-s/Clayton Crain-a/c. 1-Origin retold	3.00
1 (Director's Cut) (2005, $3.99) r/#1 with Ennis pitch and script and Crain art process	4.00
...: Road to Damnation HC (2006, $19.99, dust jacket) r/#1-6; variant covers & concept-a	20.00
...: Road to Damnation SC (2007, $14.99) r/#1-6; variant covers & concept-a	15.00

GHOST RIDER
Marvel Comics: Sept, 2006 - Present ($2.99)

1-11: 1-Daniel Way-s/Saltares & Texeira-a. 2-4-Dr. Strange app. 6,7-Corben-a	3.00
12-27: 12,13-World War Hulk x-over; Saltares-a/Dell'Otto-c. 23-Danny Ketch returns	3.00
Annual 1 (1/08, $3.99) Ben Oliver-a/c/Stuart Moore-s	4.00
Annual 2 (10/08, $3.99) Spurrier-s/Robinson-a; r/Ghost Rider #35 (1979)	4.00
... Vol. 1: Vicious Cycle TPB (2007, $13.99) r/#1-5	14.00
... Vol. 2: The Life and Death of Johnny Blaze TPB (2007, $13.99) r/#6-11	14.00
... Vol. 3: Apocalypse Soon TPB (2008, $10.99) r/#12,13 & Annual #1	11.00
... Vol. 4: Revelations TPB (2008, $14.99) r/#14-19	15.00

GHOST RIDER/BALLISTIC
Marvel Comics: Feb, 1997 ($2.95, one-shot)

1-Devil's Reign pt. 3	3.00

GHOST RIDER/BLAZE: SPIRITS OF VENGEANCE (Also see Blaze)
Marvel Comics (Midnight Sons imprint #17 on): Aug, 1992 - No. 23, June, 1994 ($1.75)

1-($2.75, 52 pgs.)-Polybagged w/poster; part 2 of Rise of the Midnight Sons storyline; Adam Kubert-c/a begins	3.00
2-11,14-21: 4-Art Adams & Joe Kubert-p. 5,6-Spirits of Venom parts 2 & 4 cont'd from Web of Spider-Man #95,96 w/Demogoblin. 14-17-Neon ink-c. 15-Intro Blaze's new costume & power. 17,18-Siege of Darkness parts 8 & 13. 17-Spot varnish-c	2.50
12-($2.95)-Glow-in-the-dark-c	3.00
13-($2.25)-Outer-c is Darkhold envelope made of black parchment w/gold ink; Midnight Massacre x-over	3.00
22,23: 22-Begin $1.95-c; bound-in trading card sheet	2.50

NOTE: ***Adam & Joe Kubert** c-7, 8. **Adam Kubert/Steacy** c-6. **J. Kubert** a-13p(6 pgs.)*

GHOST RIDER/CAPTAIN AMERICA: FEAR
Marvel Comics: Oct, 1992 ($5.95, 52 pgs.)

nn-Wraparound gatefold-c; Williamson inks	6.00

GHOST RIDER: TRAIL OF TEARS
Marvel Comics: Apr, 2007 - No. 6, Sept, 2007 ($2.99, limited series)

Ghosts #72 © DC

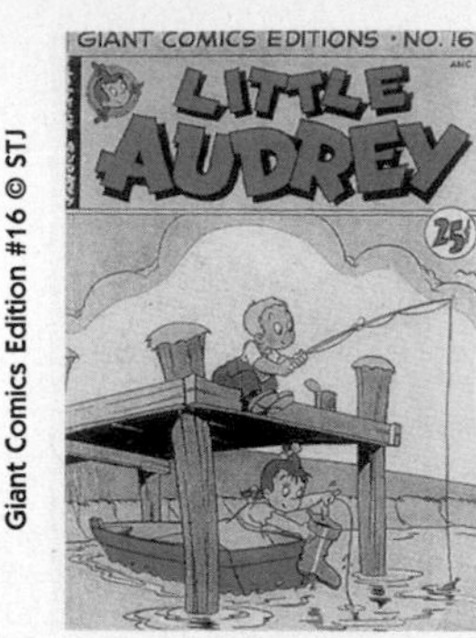

Giant Comics Edition #16 © STJ

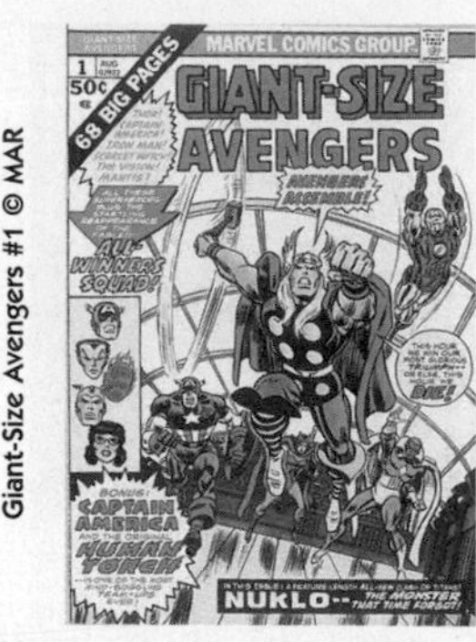

Giant-Size Avengers #1 © MAR

GD VG FN VF VF/NM NM-
2.0 4.0 6.0 8.0 9.0 9.2

GD VG FN VF VF/NM NM-
2.0 4.0 6.0 8.0 9.0 9.2

1-6-Garth Ennis-s/Clayton Crain-a/c; Civil War era tale 3.00
HC (2007, $19.99) r/series 20.00
SC (2008, $14.99) r/series 15.00

GHOST RIDER 2099
Marvel Comics: May, 1994 - No. 25, May, 1996 ($1.50/$1.95)

1 ($2.25)-Collector's Edition w/prismatic foil-c 3.00
1 ($1.50)-Regular Edition; bound-in trading card sheet 2.50
2-24: 7-Spider-Man 2099 app. 2.50
2-(Variant; polybagged with Sega Sub-Terrania poster) 5.00
25 ($2.95) 3.00

GHOST RIDER, WOLVERINE, PUNISHER: THE DARK DESIGN
Marvel Comics: Dec, 1994 ($5.95, one-shot)

nn-Gatefold-c 6.00

GHOST RIDER; WOLVERINE; PUNISHER: HEARTS OF DARKNESS
Marvel Comics: Dec, 1991 ($4.95, one-shot, 52 pgs.)

1-Double gatefold-c; John Romita, Jr.-c/a(p) 5.00

GHOSTS (Ghost No. 1)
National Periodical Publications/DC Comics: Sept-Oct, 1971 - No. 112, May, 1982 (No. 1-5: 52 pgs.)

1-Aparo-a 13 26 39 90 160 230
2-Wood-a(i) 7 14 21 49 80 110
3-5-(52 pgs.) 6 12 18 41 66 90
6-10 3 6 9 20 40 60
11-20 3 6 9 14 20 25
21-39 2 4 6 9 13 16
40-(68 pgs.) 3 6 9 16 23 30
41-60 1 3 4 6 8 10
61-96 1 2 3 4 5 7
97-99-The Spectre vs. Dr. 13 by Aparo. 97,98-Spectre-c by Aparo.
2 4 6 9 13 16
100-Infinity-c 1 2 3 5 7 9
101-112 1 2 3 4 5 7

NOTE: ***B. Baily** a-77. **Buckler** c-99, 100. **J. Craig** a-108. **Ditko** a-77, 111. **Giffen** a-104p, 106p, 111p. **Glanzman** a-2. **Golden** a-88. **Infantino** a-8. **Kaluta** c-7, 93, 101. **Kubert** a-8; c-89, 105-108, 111. **Mayer** a-111. **McWilliams** a-99. **Win Mortimer** a-89, 91, 94. **Nasser/Netzer** a-97. **Newton** a-92p, 94p. **Nino** a-35, 37, 57. **Orlando** a-74i; c-80. **Redondo** a-8, 13, 45. **Sparling** a(p)-90, 93, 94. **Spiegle** a-103, 105. **Tuska** a-2i. Dr. 13, the Ghostbreaker back-ups in 95-99, 101.*

GHOSTS SPECIAL (See DC Special Series No. 7)

GHOST STORIES (See Amazing Ghost Stories)

GHOST STORIES
Dell Publ. Co.: Sept-Nov, 1962; No. 2, Apr-June, 1963 - No. 37, Oct, 1973

12-295-211(#1)-Written by John Stanley 6 12 18 43 69 95
2 4 8 12 23 36 48
3-10: Two No. 6's exist with different c/a(12-295-406 & 12-295-503)
#12-295-503 is actually #9 with indicia to #6 3 6 9 20 30 40
11-21: 21-Last 12¢ issue 3 6 9 16 23 30
22-37 2 4 6 11 16 20

NOTE: *#21-34, 36, 37 all reprint earlier issues.*

GHOST WHISPERER (Based on the CBS television series)
IDW Publishing: Mar, 2008 - No. 5, July, 2008 ($3.99)

1-5: 1-Two covers by Casagrande & Ho; Casagrande-a 4.00

GHOUL TALES (Magazine)
Stanley Publications: Nov, 1970 - No. 5, July, 1971 (52 pgs.) (B&W)

1-Aragon pre-code reprints; Mr. Mystery as host; bondage-c
7 14 21 49 80 110
2,3: 2-(1/71)Reprint/Climax #1. 3-(3/71) 4 8 12 26 41 55
4-(5/71)Reprints story "The Way to a Man's Heart" used in **SOTI**
5 10 15 30 48 65
5-ACG reprints 4 8 12 22 34 45

NOTE: *No. 1-4 contain pre-code Aragon reprints.*

GIANT BOY BOOK OF COMICS (Also see Boy Comics)
Newsbook Publications (Gleason): 1945 (240 pgs., hard-c)

1-Crimebuster & Young Robin Hood; Biro-c 93 186 279 586 993 1400

GIANT COMIC ALBUM
King Features Syndicate: 1972 (59¢, 11x14", 52 pgs., B&W, cardboard-c)

Newspaper reprints: Barney Google, Little Iodine, Katzenjammer Kids, Henry, Beetle Bailey, Blondie, & Snuffy Smith each... 3 6 9 18 27 36
Flash Gordon ('68-69 Dan Barry) 4 8 12 24 37 50
Mandrake the Magician ('59 Falk), Popeye 4 8 12 22 34 45

GIANT COMICS
Charlton Comics: Summer, 1957 - No. 3, Winter, 1957 (25¢, 100 pgs.)

1-Atomic Mouse, Hoppy app. 21 42 63 123 197 270
2,3: 2-Romance. 3-Christmas Book; Atomic Mouse, Atomic Rabbit, Li'l Genius, Li'l Tomboy & Atom the Cat stories 15 30 45 88 137 185

NOTE: *The above may be rebound comics; contents could vary.*

GIANT COMICS (See Wham-O Giant Comics)

GIANT COMICS EDITION (See Terry-Toons) (Also see Fox Giants)
St. John Publishing Co.: 1947 - No. 17, 1950 (25¢, 100-164 pgs.)

1-Mighty Mouse 50 100 150 310 518 725
2-Abbie & Slats 27 54 81 158 254 350
3-Terry-Toons Album; 100 pgs. 40 80 120 240 390 540
4-Crime comics; contains Red Seal No. 16, used & illo. in **SOTI**
55 110 165 347 584 820
5-Police Case Book (4/49, 132 pgs.)-Contents varies; contains remaindered St. John books - some volumes contain 5 copies rather than 4, with 160 pages; Matt Baker-c
54 108 162 340 575 810
5A-Terry-Toons Album (132 pgs.)-Mighty Mouse, Heckle & Jeckle, Gandy Goose & Dinky stories 37 74 111 215 345 475
6-Western Picture Stories; Baker-c/a(3); Tuska-a; The Sky Chief, Blue Monk, Ventrilo app., 132 pgs. 52 104 156 322 536 750
7-Contains a teen-age romance plus 3 Mopsy comics
34 68 102 198 319 440
8-The Adventures of Mighty Mouse (10/49) 37 74 111 215 345 475
9-Romance and Confession Stories; Kubert-a(4); Baker-a; photo-c (132 pgs.)
67 134 201 422 711 1000
10-Terry-Toons Album (132 pgs.)-Mighty Mouse, Heckle & Jeckle, Gandy Goose stories
37 74 111 215 345 475
11-Western Picture Stories-Baker-c/a(4); The Sky Chief, Desperado, & Blue Monk app.; another version with Son of Sinbad by Kubert (132 pgs.)
52 104 156 322 536 750
12-Diary Secrets; Baker prostitute-c; 4 St. John romance comics; Baker-a
187 374 561 1178 1989 2800
13-Romances; Baker, Kubert-a 57 114 171 359 605 850
14-Mighty Mouse Album (132 pgs.) 36 72 108 212 341 470
15-Romances (4 love comics)-Baker-c 63 126 189 397 674 950
16-Little Audrey; Abbott & Costello, Casper 40 80 120 235 380 525
17(nn)-Mighty Mouse Album (nn, no date, but did follow No. 16); 100 pgs. on cover but has 148 pgs. 36 72 108 212 341 470

NOTE: *The above books contain remaindered comics and contents could vary with each issue. No. 11, 12 have part photo magazine insides.*

GIANT COMICS EDITIONS
United Features Syndicate: 1940's (132 pgs.)

1-Abbie & Slats, Abbott & Costello, Jim Hardy, Ella Cinders, Iron Vic, Gordo, & Bill Bumlin 40 80 120 235 380 525
2-Jim Hardy, Ella Cinders, Elmo & Gordo 27 54 81 158 254 350

NOTE: *Above books contain rebound copies; contents can vary.*

GIANT GRAB BAG OF COMICS (See Archie All-Star Specials under Archie Comics)

GIANTKILLER
DC Comics: Aug, 1999 - No. 6, Jan, 2000 ($2.50, limited series)

1-6-Story and painted art by Dan Brereton 2.50
...A to Z: A Field Guide to Big Monsters (8/99) 2.50
...Vol. 1 TPB (Image Comics, 2006, $14.99) r/#1-6 & A-Z; gallery of concept art 15.00

GIANTS (See Thrilling True Story of the Baseball...)

GIANT-SIZE...
Marvel Comics Group: May, 1974 - Dec, 1975 (35/50¢, 52/68 pgs.)
(Some titles quarterly) (Scarce in strict NM or better due to defective cutting, gluing and binding; warping, splitting and off-center pages are common)

Avengers 1(8/74)-New-a plus G.A. H. Torch-r; 1st modern app. The Whizzer; 1st & only modern app. Miss America; 2nd app. Invaders; Kang, Rama-Tut, Mantis app.
5 10 15 32 51 70
Avengers 2,3,5: 2(11/74)-Death of the Swordsman; origin of Rama-Tut. 3(2/75).
5(12/75)-Reprints Avengers Special #1 3 6 9 20 30 40
Avengers 4 (6/75)-Vision marries Scarlet Witch. 4 8 12 26 41 55
Captain America 1(12/75)-r/stories T.O.S. 59-63 by Kirby (#63 reprints origin)
4 8 12 22 34 45
Captain Marvel 1(12/75)-r/Capt. Marvel #17, 20, 21 by Gil Kane (p)
3 6 9 19 29 38
Chillers 1(6/74, 52 pgs)-Curse of Dracula; origin/1st app. Lilith, Dracula's daughter; Heath-r, Colan-c/a(p); becomes Giant-Size Dracula #2 on 5 10 15 34 55 75

Giant-Size Iron Man #1 © MAR

Giant-Size Astonishing X-Men #1 © MAR

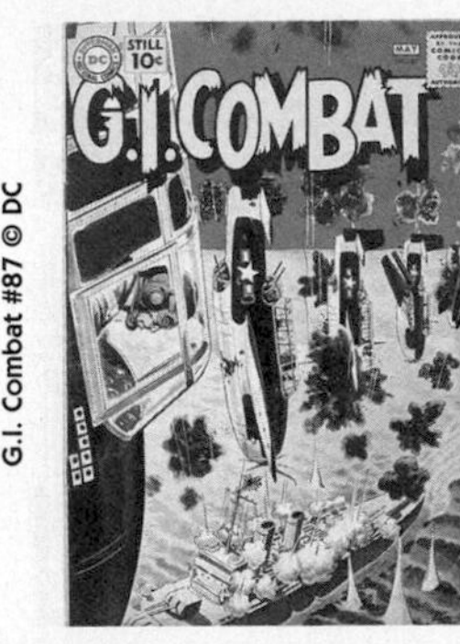

G.I. Combat #87 © DC

	GD 2.0	VG 4.0	FN 6.0	VF 8.0	VF/NM 9.0	NM- 9.2
Chillers 1(2/75, 50¢, 68 pgs.)-Alcala-a	3	6	9	19	29	38
Chillers 2(5/75)-All-r; Everett-r from Advs. into Weird Worlds	3	6	9	16	23	30
Chillers 3(8/75)-Wrightson c(new)/a(r); Colan, Kirby, Smith-r	3	6	9	19	29	38
Conan 1(9/74)-B. Smith-r/#3; start adaptation of Howard's "Hour of the Dragon" (ends #4); 1st app. Belit; new-a begins	3	6	9	21	32	42
Conan 2(12/74)-B. Smith-r/#5; Sutton-a(i)(#1 also); Buscema-c	3	6	9	17	25	32
Conan 3-5: 3(4/75)-B. Smith-r/#6; Sutton-a(i). 4(6/75)-B. Smith-r/#7. 5(1975)-B. Smith-r/#14,15; Kirby-c	3	6	9	16	22	28
Creatures 1(5/74, 52 pgs.)-Werewolf app; 1st app. Tigra (formerly Cat); Crandall-r; becomes Giant-Size Werewolf w/#2	4	8	12	26	41	55
Daredevil 1(1975)-Reprints Daredevil Annual #1	3	6	9	18	27	35
Defenders 1(7/74)-Silver Surfer app.; Starlin-a; Ditko, Everett & Kirby reprints	4	8	12	26	41	55
Defenders 2(10/74, 68 pgs.)-New G. Kane-c/a(p); Son of Satan app.; Sub-Mariner-r by Everett; Ditko-r/Strange Tales #119 (Dr. Strange); Maneely-r	3	6	9	18	27	35
Defenders 3-5: 3(1/75)-1st app. Korvac.; Newton, Starlin-a; Ditko, Everett-r. 4(4/75)-Ditko, Everett-r; G. Kane-c. 5-(7/75)-Guardians app.	3	6	9	16	23	30
Doc Savage 1(1975, 68 pgs.)-r/#1,2; Mooney-r	3	6	9	14	20	26
Doctor Strange 1(11/75)-Reprints stories from Strange Tales #164-168; Lawrence, Tuska-r	3	6	9	16	23	30
Dracula 2(9/74, 50¢)-Formerly Giant-Size Chillers	3	6	9	19	29	38
Dracula 3(12/74)-Fox-r/Uncanny Tales #6	3	6	9	18	27	35
Dracula 4(3/75)-Ditko-r(2)	3	6	9	18	27	35
Dracula 5(6/75)-1st Byrne art at Marvel	5	10	15	30	48	65
Fantastic Four 2-4: 2(8/74)-Formerly Giant-Size Super-Stars; Ditko-r. 3(11/74). 4(2/75)-1st Madrox; 2-4-All have Buscema-a	3	6	9	20	30	40
Fantastic Four 5,6: 5(5/75)-All-r; Kirby, G. Kane-r. 6(10/75)-All-r; Kirby-r	3	6	9	16	23	30
Hulk 1(1975) r/Hulk Special #1	3	6	9	20	30	40
Invaders 1(6/75, 50¢, 68 pgs.)-Origin; G.A. Sub-Mariner-r/Sub-Mariner #1; intro Master Man	4	8	12	22	34	45
Iron Man 1(1975)-Ditko reprint	3	6	9	19	29	38
Kid Colt 1-3: 1(1/75). 2(4/75). 3(7/75)-new Ayers-a	7	14	21	45	73	100
Man-Thing 1(8/74)-New Ploog-c/a (25 pgs.); Ditko-r/Amazing Adv. #11; Kirby-r/Strange Tales Ann. #2 & T.O.S. #15; (#1-5 all have new Man-Thing stories, pre-hero-r & are 68 pgs.)	4	8	12	23	36	48
Man-Thing 2,3: 2(11/74)-Buscema-c/a(p); Kirby, Powell-r. 3(2/75)-Alcala-a; Ditko, Kirby, Sutton-r; Gil Kane-c	3	6	9	17	25	32
Man-Thing 4,5: 4(5/75)-Howard the Duck by Brunner-c/a; Ditko-r. 5(8/75)-Howard the Duck by Brunner (p); Dracula cameo in Howard the Duck; Buscema-a(p); Sutton-a(i); G. Kane-c	4	8	12	22	34	45
Marvel Triple Action 1,2: 1(5/75). 2(7/75)	3	6	9	14	20	26
Master of Kung Fu 1(9/74)-Russell-a; Yellow Claw-r in #1-4; Gulacy-a in #1,2	3	6	9	21	32	42
Master of Kung Fu 2-4: 2-(12/74)-r/Yellow Claw #1. 3(3/75)-Gulacy-a; Kirby-a. 4(6/75)-Kirby-a	3	6	9	17	25	32
Power Man 1(1975)	3	6	9	16	23	30
Spider-Man 1(7/74)-Spider-Man /Human Torch-r by Kirby/Ditko; Byrne-r plus new-a (Dracula-c/story)	6	12	18	43	69	95
Spider-Man 2,3: 2(10/74)-Shang-Chi-c/app. 3(1/75)-Doc Savage-c/app.; Daredevil/Spider-Man-r w/Ditko-a	4	8	12	26	41	55
Spider-Man 4(4/75)-3rd Punisher app.; Byrne, Ditko-r	10	20	30	71	126	180
Spider-Man 5,6: 5(7/75)-Man-Thing/Lizard-c. 6(9/75)	4	8	12	22	34	45
Super-Heroes Featuring Spider-Man 1(6/74, 35¢, 52 pgs.)-Spider-Man vs. Man-Wolf; Morbius, the Living Vampire app.; Ditko-r; G. Kane-a(p); Spidey villains app.	6	12	18	41	66	90
Super-Stars 1(5/74, 35¢, 52 pgs.)-Fantastic Four; Thing vs. Hulk; Kirbyish-c/a by Buckler/Sinnott; F.F. villains profiled; becomes Giant-Size Fantastic Four #2 on	5	10	15	34	55	75
Super-Villain Team-Up 1(3/75, 68 pgs.)-Craig-r(i) (Also see Fantastic Four #6 for 1st super-villain team-up)	3	6	9	19	29	38
Super-Villain Team-Up 2(6/75, 68 pgs.)-Dr. Doom, Sub-Mariner app.; Spider-Man-r from Amazing Spider-Man #8 by Ditko; Sekowsky-a(p)	3	6	9	16	23	30
Thor 1(7/75)	4	8	12	22	34	45
Werewolf 2(10/74, 68 pgs.)-Formerly Giant-Size Creatures; Ditko-r; Frankenstein app.	3	6	9	18	27	35
Werewolf 3,5: 3(1/75, 68 pgs.). 5(7/75, 68 pgs.)	3	6	9	18	27	35
Werewolf 4(4/75, 68 pgs.)-Morbius the Living Vampire app.	3	6	9	20	30	40
X-Men 1(Summer, 1975, 50¢, 68 pgs.)-1st app. new X-Men; intro. Nightcrawler, Storm, Colossus & Thunderbird; 2nd full app. Wolverine after Incredible Hulk #181	52	104	156	442	846	1250
X-Men 2 (11/75)-N. Adams-r (51 pgs)	8	16	24	58	97	135
Giant Size Marvel TPB (2005, $24.99) reprints stories from Giant-Size Avengers #1, G-S Fantastic Four #4, G-S Defenders #4, G-S Super-Heroes #1, G-S Invaders #1, G-S X-Men #1 and Giant-Size Creatures #1						25.00

GIANT-SIZE...
Marvel Comics: 2005 - Present ($4.99/$3.99)

	GD 2.0	VG 4.0	FN 6.0	VF 8.0	VF/NM 9.0	NM- 9.2
Astonishing X-Men 1 (7/08, $4.99) Concludes story from Astonishing X-Men #24; Whedon-s/Cassaday-a/wraparound-c; Spider-Man, FF, Dr. Strange app.; variant cover gallery						5.00
Astonishing X-Men 1 (7/08, $4.99) Variant B&W cover						5.00
Avengers 1 (2/08, $4.99) new short stories and r/Avengers #58, 201; Hitch-c						5.00
Avengers/Invaders 1 ('08, $3.99) r/Avengers #71; Invaders #10, Ann. 1 & G-S #2						4.00
Hulk 1 (8/06, $4.99)-2 new stories; Planet Hulk (David-s/Santacruz-a) & Hulk vs. The Champions (Pak-s/Lopresti-a; r/Incredible Hulk: The End						5.00
Incredible Hulk 1 (7/08, $3.99)-1 new story; r/Incredible Hulk Annual #7; Frank-c						4.00
Invaders 2 ('05, $4.99)-new Thomas-s/Weeks-a; r/Invaders #1&2 & All-Winners #1&2						5.00
Marvel Adventures The Avengers (9/07, $3.99) Agents of Atlas and Kang app.; Kirk-a: reprint of 1st Namora app. from Marvel Mystery Comics #82; reprint from Venus #1						4.00
Spider-Woman ('05, $4.99)-new Bendis-s/Mays-a; r/Marvel Spotlight #32 & S-W #1,37,38						5.00
Wolverine (12/06, $4.99)-new Lapham-s/Aja-a; r/X-Men #6,7						5.00
X-Men 3 ('05, $4.99)-new Whedon-s/N. Adams-a; r/team-ups; Cockrum & Cassaday-c						5.00

GIANT SPECTACULAR COMICS (See Archie All-Star Special under Archie Comics)

GIANT SUMMER FUN BOOK (See Terry-Toons...)

G. I. COMBAT
Quality Comics Group: Oct, 1952 - No. 43, Dec, 1956

	GD 2.0	VG 4.0	FN 6.0	VF 8.0	VF/NM 9.0	NM- 9.2
1-Crandall-c; Cuidera a-1-43i	73	146	219	460	780	1100
2	37	74	111	219	352	485
3-5,10-Crandall-c/a	32	64	96	190	305	420
6-Crandall-a	28	56	84	164	265	365
7-9	24	48	72	143	229	315
11-20	19	38	57	109	172	235
21-31,33,35-43: 41-1st S.A. issue	17	34	51	98	154	210
32-Nuclear attack-c/story "Atomic Rocket Assault"	20	40	60	114	180	245
34-Crandall-a	18	36	54	105	165	225

G. I. COMBAT (See DC Special Series #22)
National Periodical Publ./DC Comics: No. 44, Jan, 1957 - No. 288, Mar, 1987

	GD 2.0	VG 4.0	FN 6.0	VF 8.0	VF/NM 9.0	NM- 9.2
44-Grey tone-c	52	104	156	442	846	1250
45	29	58	87	213	394	575
46-50	24	48	72	176	326	475
51-Grey tone-c	29	58	87	213	394	575
52-54,59,60	22	44	66	157	291	425
55-Minor Sgt. Rock prototype by Finger	22	44	66	163	302	440
56-Sgt. Rock prototype by Kanigher/Kubert	26	52	78	192	359	525
57,58-Pre-Sgt. Rock Easy Co. stories	25	50	75	185	343	500
61-65,70-74: 74-American flag-c	15	30	45	111	206	300
66-Pre-Sgt. Rock Easy Co. story	23	46	69	167	309	450
67-1st Tank Killer	29	58	87	213	394	575
68-(1/59) Introduces "The Rock", Sgt. Rock prototype by Kanigher/Kubert, once considered his actual 1st app. (see Our Army at War #82,83)	75	150	225	638	1219	1800
69-Grey tone-c	23	46	69	167	309	450
75-80: 75-Grey tone-c begin, end #109	23	46	69	167	309	450
81,82,84-86	19	38	57	139	257	375
83-1st Big Al, Little Al, & Charlie Cigar; grey tone-c	22	44	66	157	291	425
87-(4-5/61) 1st Haunted Tank; series begins; classic Heath washtone-c	77	154	231	655	1253	1850
88-(6-7/61) 2nd Haunted Tank	29	58	87	213	394	575
89,90: 90-Last 10¢ issue	19	38	57	135	250	365
91-(12/61-1/62)1st Haunted Tank-c	29	58	87	213	394	575
92-95,99-Grey tone-c	16	32	48	116	216	315
96-98	15	30	45	106	193	280
100,108: 100-(6-7/63). 108-1st Sgt. Rock x-over	15	30	45	111	206	300
101-103,105-107	13	26	39	93	164	235
104,109-Grey tone-c	14	28	42	99	175	250
110-112,115-118,120	11	22	33	75	133	190
113-Grey tone-c	13	26	39	95	168	240
114-Origin Haunted Tank	22	44	66	157	291	425
119-Grey tone-c	12	24	36	87	156	225
121-136: 121-1st app. Sgt. Rock's father. 125-Sgt. Rock app. 136-Last 12¢ issue	7	14	21	47	76	105
137,139,140	4	8	12	28	44	60

G.I. Combat #217 © DC

Giggle Comics #32 © ACG

G.I. Joe V2 #29 © HASBRO

GD VG FN VF VF/NM NM-
2.0 4.0 6.0 8.0 9.0 9.2

138-Intro. The Losers (Capt. Storm, Gunner/Sarge, Johnny Cloud) in Haunted Tank (10-11/69) 9 18 27 65 113 160
141-143 3 6 9 18 27 35
144-148 (68 pgs.) 4 8 12 24 37 50
149,151-154 (52 pgs.): 151-Capt. Storm story. 151,153-Medal of Honor series by Maurer 3 6 9 18 27 35
150- (52 pgs.) Ice Cream Soldier story (tells how he got his name); Death of Haunted Tank-c/s 4 8 12 24 37 50
155-167,169,170 2 4 6 10 14 18
168-Neal Adams-c 3 6 9 14 20 26
171-192,194-199: 195-Haunted Tank & War That Time Forgot 2 4 6 8 11 14
193-(10/76) Haunted Tank meets War That Time Forgot; Dinosaur-c/s; Kubert-a 2 4 6 10 14 18
200-(3/77) Haunted Tank-c/s; Sgt. Rock and the Losers app.; Kubert-c 2 4 6 13 18 22
201,202 ($1.00 size) Neal Adams-c 2 4 6 13 18 22
203-210 ($1.00 size) 2 4 6 10 14 18
211-230 ($1.00 size) 2 4 6 8 11 14
231-259 ($1.00 size).232-Origin Kana the Ninja. 244-Death of Slim Stryker; 1st app. The Mercenaries. 246-(76 pgs., $1.50)-30th Anniversary issue. 257-Intro. Stuart's Raiders 1 3 4 6 8 10
260-281: 260-Begin $1.25, 52 pg. issues, end #281. 264-Intro Sgt. Bullet; origin Kana. 269-Intro. The Bravos of Vietnam. 274-Cameo of Monitor from Crisis on Infinite Earths 6.00
282-288 (75¢): 282-New advs. begin 6.00

NOTE: ***N. Adams** c-168, 201, 202. **Check** a-168, 173. **Drucker** a-48, 61, 63, 66, 71, 72, 76, 134, 140, 141, 144, 147, 148, 153. **Evans** a-135, 138, 158, 164, 166, 201, 202, 204, 205, 215, 256. **Giffen** a-267. **Glanzman** a-most issues. **Kubert/Heath** a-most issues; **Kubert** covers most issues. **Morrow** a-159-161(2 pgs.). **Redondo** a-189, 240i, 243i. **Sekowsky** a-162p. **Severin** a-147, 152, 154. **Simonson** c-169. **Thorne** a-152, 156. **Wildey** a-153. Johnny Cloud app.-112, 115, 120. Mlle. Marie app.-123, 132, 200. Sgt. Rock app.-111-113, 115, 120, 125, 141, 146, 147, 149, 200. USS Stevens by **Glanzman**-145, 150-153, 157. **Grandenetti** c-44-48.*

GIDGET (TV)
Dell Publishing Co.: Apr, 1966 - No. 2, Dec, 1966

1-Sally Field photo-c 9 18 27 60 100 140
2 6 12 18 43 69 95

GIFT COMICS
Fawcett Publications: 1942 - No. 4, 1949 (50¢/25¢, 324 pgs./152 pgs.)

1-Captain Marvel, Bulletman, Golden Arrow, Ibis the Invincible, Mr. Scarlet, & Spy Smasher begin; not rebound, remaindered comics, printed at same time as originals; 50¢-c & 324 pgs. begin, end #3. 280 560 840 1764 2982 4200
2-Commando Yank, Phantom Eagle, others app. 167 334 501 1052 1776 2500
3-(50¢, 324 pgs.) 113 226 339 712 1206 1700
4-(25¢, 152 pgs.)-The Marvel Family, Captain Marvel, etc.; each issue can vary in contents 70 140 210 441 746 1050

GIFTS FROM SANTA (See March of Comics No. 137)

GIFTS OF THE NIGHT
DC Comics (Vertigo): Feb, 1999 - No. 4, May, 1999 ($2.95, limited series)

1-4-Bolton-c/a; Chadwick-s 3.00

GIGGLE COMICS (Spencer Spook No. 100) (Also see Ha Ha Comics)
Creston No.1-63/American Comics Group No. 64 on; Oct, 1943 - No. 99, Jan-Feb, 1955

1-Funny animal 34 68 102 198 319 440
2 17 34 51 98 154 210
3-5: Ken Hultgren-a begins? 14 28 42 78 112 145
6-10: 9-1st Superkatt (6/44) 11 22 33 62 86 110
11-20 10 20 30 54 72 90
21-40: 32-Patriotic-c. 37,61-X-Mas-c 9 18 27 47 61 75
41-54,56-59,61-99: Spencer Spook app. in many 8 16 24 42 54 65
55,60-Milt Gross-a 10 20 30 54 72 90

G-I IN BATTLE (G-I No. 1 only)
Ajax-Farrell Publ./Four Star: Aug, 1952 - No. 9, July, 1953; Mar, 1957 - No. 6, May, 1958

1 12 24 36 69 97 125
2 8 16 24 40 50 60
3-9 7 14 21 37 46 55
Annual 1(1952, 25¢, 100 pgs.) 25 50 75 145 233 320
1(1957-Ajax) 8 16 24 42 54 65
2-6 6 12 18 28 34 40

G. I. JANE
Stanhall/Merit No. 11: May, 1953 - No. 11, Mar, 1955 (Misdated 3/54)

1-PX Pete begins; Bill Williams-c/a 14 28 42 76 108 140
2-7(5/54) 8 16 24 44 57 70
8-10(12/54, Stanhall) 8 16 24 40 50 60
11 (3/55, Merit) 7 14 21 37 46 55

G. I. JOE (Also see Advs. of..., Showcase #53, 54 & The Yardbirds)
Ziff-Davis Publ. Co. (Korean War): No. 10, 1950; No. 11, 4-5/51 - No. 51, 6/57(52pgs.: 10-14,6-17?)

10(#1, 1950)-Saunders painted-c begin 16 32 48 94 147 200
11-14(#2-5, 10/51): 11-New logo. 12-New logo 11 22 33 64 90 115
V2#6(12/51)-17-(11/52; Last 52 pgs.?) 10 20 30 56 76 95
18-(25¢, 100 pg. Giant, 12-1/52-53) 25 50 75 145 233 320
19-30: 20-22,24,28-31-The Yardbirds app. 9 18 27 50 65 80
31-47,49-51 9 18 27 47 61 75
48-Atom bomb story 9 18 27 50 65 80

NOTE: ***Powell** a-V2#7, 8, 11. **Norman Saunders** painted c-10-14, V2#6-14, 26, 30, 31, 35, 38, 39. **Tuska** a-7. Bondage c-29, 35, 38.*

G. I. JOE (America's Movable Fighting Man)
Custom Comics: 1967 (5-1/8x8-3/8", 36 pgs.)

nn-Schaffenberger-a; based on Hasbro toy 3 6 9 20 30 40

G.I. JOE
Dark Horse Comics: Dec, 1995 - No. 4, Apr, 1996 ($1.95, limited series)

1-4: Mike W. Barr scripts. 1-Three Frank Miller covers with title logos in red, white and blue. 2-Breyfogle-c. 3-Simonson-c 3.00

G.I. JOE
Dark Horse Comics: V2#1, June, 1996 - V2#4, Sept, 1996 ($2.50)

V2#1-4: Mike W. Barr scripts. 4-Painted-c 3.00

G.I. JOE
Image Comics/Devil's Due Publishing: 2001 - No. 43, May, 2005 ($2.95)

1-Campbell-c; back-c painted by Beck; Blaylock-s 2 4 6 8 10 12
1-2nd printing with front & back covers switched 6.00
2,3 5.00
4-($3.50) 4.00
5-20,22-41: 6-SuperPatriot preview. 18-Brereton-c. 31-33-Wraith back-up; Caldwell-a 3.00
21-Silent issue; Zeck-a; two covers by Campbell and Zeck 3.00
42,43-($4.50)-Dawn of the Red Shadows; leads into G.I. Joe Vol. 2 4.50
...:Cobra Reborn (1/04, $4.95) Bradstreet-c/Jenkins-s 5.00
...:G.I. Joe Reborn (2/04, $4.95) Bradstreet-c/Bennett & Saltares-a 5.00
...: Malfunction (2003, $15.95) r/#11-15 16.00
... M. I. A. (2002, $4.95) r/#1&2; Beck back-c from #1 on cover 5.00
...: Players & Pawns (11/04, $12.95) r/#28-33; cover gallery 13.00
...: Reborn (2004, $9.95) r/Cobra Reborn & G.I. Joe Reborn 10.00
...: Reckonings (2002, $12.95) r/#6-9; Zeck-c 13.00
...: Reinstated (2002, $14.95) r/#1-4 15.00
...: The Return of Serpentor (9/04, $12.95) r/#16,22-25; cover gallery 13.00
...Vol. 8: The Rise of the Red Shadows (1/06, $14.95) r/#42,43 & prologue pgs. from #37-41 15.00

G.I. JOE (Volume 2) (Also see Snake Eyes: Declassified)
Devil's Due Publishing: No. 0, June, 2005 - No. 36, June, 2008 (25¢/$2.95/$3.50/$4.50)

0-(25¢-c) Casey-s/Caselli-a 2.50
1-4,7-19 ($2.95): 1-Four covers; Casey-s/Caselli-a. 4-R. Black-c 3.00
5,6-($4.50) 6-Wraparound-c 4.50
20-29,31-35-($3.50) 25-Wraparound-c World War III part 1 3.50
30,36-($5.50) 30-Double-sized World War III part 6. 36-Double-sized WW III part 12 5.50
...America's Elite Vol. 1: The Newest War TPB ('06, $14.95) r/#0-5; cover gallery 15.00
...America's Elite Vol. 2: The Ties That Bind TPB (8/06, $15.95) r/#6-12; cover gallery 16.00
...America's Elite Vol. 3: In Sheep's Clothing TPB (2007, $18.99) r/#13-18; cover gallery 19.00
...America's Elite Vol. 4: Truth and Consequences TPB (9/07, $18.99) r/#19-24; covers 19.00
... Data Desk Handbook (10/05, $2.95) character profile pages 3.00
... Data Desk Handbook A-M (10/07, $5.50) character profile pages 5.50
... Data Desk Handbook N-Z (11/07, $3.50) character profile pages 3.50
... :Scarlett: Declassified (7/06, $4.95) Scarlett's childhood and training; Noto-c/a 5.00
... Special Missions (2/06, $4.95) short stories and profile pages by various 5.00
... Special Missions Antarctica (12/06, $4.95) short stories and profile pages by various 5.00
... Special Missions Brazil (4/07, $5.50) short stories and profile pages by various 5.50
... Special Missions: The Enemy (9/07, $5.50) two stories and profile pages by various 5.50
... Special Missions Tokyo (9/06, $4.95) short stories and profile pages by various 5.00
...: The Hunt For Cobra Commander (5/06, 25¢) short story and character profiles 2.50

G. I. JOE AND THE TRANSFORMERS
Marvel Comics Group: Jan, 1987 - No. 4, Apr, 1987 (Limited series)

1-4 6.00

G. I. JOE, A REAL AMERICAN HERO (...Starring Snake-Eyes on-c #135 on)
Marvel Comics Group: June, 1982 - No. 155, Dec, 1994

1-Printed on Baxter paper; based on Hasbro toy 3 6 9 18 27 35

G.I. Joe, A Real American Hero #2 © HASBRO

Ginger #9 © AP

Girl Comics #1 © MAR

GD VG FN VF VF/NM NM-
2.0 4.0 6.0 8.0 9.0 9.2

2-Printed on regular paper; 1st app. Kwinn 3 6 9 17 25 32
3-10: 6-1st app. Oktobor Guard 2 4 6 13 18 22
11-20: 11-Intro Airborne. 13-1st Destro (cameo). 14-1st full app. Doctro. 15-1st app. Major Blood. 16-1st app. Cover Girl and Trip-Wire 2 4 6 9 13 16
21-1st app. Storm Shadow; silent issue 3 6 9 18 27 35
22-1st app. Duke and Roadblock 2 4 6 9 13 16
23-25,28-30,60: 25-1st full app. Zartan, 1st app of Cutter, Deep Six, Mutt and Junkyard, and The Dreadnoks. 60-Todd McFarlane-a 1 2 3 5 7 9
26,27-Origin Snake-Eyes parts 1 & 2 2 4 6 11 16 20
31-50: 31-1st Spirit Iron-Knife. 32-1st Blowtorch, Lady J, Recondo, Ripcord. 33-New headquarters. 40-1st app. of Shipwreck, Barbecue. 48-1st app. Sgt. Slaughter. 49-1st app. of Lift-Ticket, Slipstream, Leatherneck, Serpentor 5.00
51-59,61-90 4.00
91,92,94-99: 94 06-Snake Fyes Trilogy 5.00
93-Snake-Eyes' face first revealed 2 4 6 10 14 18
100,135-138: 135-138-($1.75)-Bagged w/trading card. 138-Transformers app. 2 4 6 8 11 14
101-134: 101-New Oktober Guard app. 110-1st Garney-a. 117- Debut G.I. Joe Ninja Force 1 2 3 5 7 9
139-142-New Transformers app. 2 4 6 11 16 20
143,145-149: 145-Intro. G.I. Joe Star Brigade 2 4 6 9 12 15
144 Origin Snake-Eyes 2 4 6 13 18 22
150-Low print thru #155 3 6 9 18 27 35
151-154: 152-30th Anniversary (of doll) issue, original G.I. Joe General Joseph Colton app. (also app. in #151) 3 6 9 17 25 32
155-Last issue 4 8 12 26 41 55
All 2nd printings 2.50
Special #1 (2/95, $1.50) r/#60 w/McFarlane a. Cover swipe from Spider-Man #1 4 8 12 24 37 50
Special Treasury Edition (1982)-r/#1 3 6 9 17 25 32
Volume 1 TPB (4/02, $24.95) r/#1-10; new cover by Michael Golden 25.00
Volume 2 TPB (6/02, $24.95) r/#11-20; new cover by J. Scott Campbell 25.00
Volume 3 TPB (2002, $24.99) r/#21-30; new cover by J. Scott Campbell 25.00
Volume 4 TPB (2002, $25.99) r/#31-40; new cover by J. Scott Campbell 26.00
Volume 5 TPB (2002, $24.99) r/#42-50; new cover by J. Scott Campbell 25.00
Yearbook 1-4. (3/85 3/88)-r/#1; Golden-c. 2-Golden-c/a 5.00
NOTE: *Garney a(p)-110. Golden c-23, 29, 34, 36. Heath a-24. Rogers a(p)-75, 77-82, 84, 86; c-77.*

G.I. JOE: BATTLE FILES
Image Comics: 2002 - No. 3, 2002 ($5.95)
1-3-Profile pages of characters and history; Beck-c 6.00

G. I. JOE COMICS MAGAZINE
Marvel Comics Group: Dec, 1986 - No. 13, 1988 ($1.50, digest-size)
1-13: G.I. Joe-r 2 4 6 8 10 12

G.I. JOE DECLASSIFIED
Devil's Due Publishing: June, 2006 - No. 3 ($4.95, bi-monthly)
1-3-New "early" adventures of the team; Hama-s; Quinn & DeLandro-a; var-c for each 5.00
TPB (1/07, $18.99) r/#1-3; cover gallery 19.00

G.I. JOE DREADNOKS: DECLASSIFIED
Devil's Due Publishing: Nov, 2006 - No. 3, Mar, 2007 ($4.95/$4.99/$5.50, bi-monthly)
1,2-Secret history of the team; Blaylock-s; var-c for each 5.00
3-($5.50) 5.50

G.I. JOE EUROPEAN MISSIONS (Action Force in indicia) (Series reprints Action Force)
Marvel Comics Ltd. (British): Jun, 1988 - No. 15, Dec, 1989 ($1.50/$1.75)
1,3-Snake Eyes & Storm Shadow-c/s 1 2 3 5 7 9
2,4-15 6.00

G.I. JOE: FRONT LINE
Image Comics: 2002 - No. 18, Dec, 2003 ($2.95)
1-18: 1-Jurgens-a/Hama-s. 1-Two covers by Dorman & Sharpe. 7,8-Harris-c 3.00
...Vol. 1 - The Mission That Never Was TPB (2003, $14.95) r/ #1-4; script pages 15.00
...Vol. 2 - Icebound TPB (3/04, $12.95) r/ #5-8 13.00
...Vol. 3 - History Repeating TPB (4/04, $9.95) r/#11-14 10.00
...Vol. 4 - One-Shots TPB (5/04, $15.95) r/#9,10,15-18 16.00

G.I. JOE: MASTER & APPRENTICE
Image Comics: May, 2004 - No. 4, Aug, 2004 ($2.95)
1-4-Caselli-a/Jerwa-s 3.00

G.I. JOE: MASTER & APPRENTICE 2
Image Comics: Feb, 2005 - No. 4, May, 2005 ($2.95, limited series)
1-4: Stevens & Vedder-a/Jerwa-s 3.00

G. I. JOE ORDER OF BATTLE, THE
Marvel Comics Group: Dec, 1986 - No. 4, Mar, 1987 (limited series)
1-4 6.00

G.I. JOE: RELOADED
Image Comics: Mar, 2004 -No. 14, Apr, 2005 ($2.95)
1-14: 1-3-Granov-c/Ney Rieber-s. 5,6-Rieber-s/Saltares-a. 8-Origin of the Baroness 3.00
Vol. 1 In the Name of Patriotism (11/04, $12.95) r/#1-6; cover gallery 13.00

G.I. JOE SIGMA 6 (Based on the cartoon TV series)
Devil's Due Publishing: Dec, 2005 - No. 6, May, 2006 ($2.95, limited series)
1-6-Andrew Daab-s 3.00
TPB Vol. 1 (10/06, $10.95, 8-1/4" x 5-3/4") r/#1-6; cover gallery 11.00

G. I. JOE SPECIAL MISSIONS (Indicia title: Special Missions)
Marvel Comics Group: Oct, 1986 - No. 28, Dec, 1989 ($1.00)
1-20 4.00
21-28 5.00

G.I. JOE VS. THE TRANSFORMERS
Image Comics: Jun, 2003 - No. 6, Nov, 2003 ($2.95, limited series)
1-Blaylock-s/Mike Miller-a; three covers by Miller, Campbell & Andrews 3.00
1-2nd printing; black cover with logo; back-c by Campbell 3.00
2-6: 2-Two covers by Miller & Brooks 3.00
TPB (3/04, $15.95) r/series; sketch pages 16.00

G.I. JOE VS. THE TRANSFORMERS (Volume 2)
Devil's Due Publ.: Sept, 2004 - No. 4, Dec, 2004 ($4.95/$2.95, limited series)
1-($4.95) Three covers; Jolley-s/Su & Seeley-a 5.00
2-4-($2.95) Two covers by Su & Pollina 3.00
Vol. 2 TPB (4/05, $14.95) r/series; interview with creators; sketch pages and covers 15.00

G.I. JOE VS. THE TRANSFORMERS (Volume 3) THE ART OF WAR
Devil's Due Publ.: Mar, 2006 - No. 5, July, 2006 ($2.95, limited series)
1-5: 1-Three covers; Seeley-s/Ng-a 3.00
TPB (8/06, $14.95) r/series; cover gallery 15.00

G.I. JOE VS. THE TRANSFORMERS (Volume 4) BLACK HORIZON
Devil's Due Publ.: Jan, 2007 - No. 2, July, 2006 ($5.50, limited series)
1,2: 1-Three covers; Seeley-s/Wildman-a. 2-Two covers 5.50

G. I. JUNIORS (See Harvey Hits No. 86,91,95,98,101,104,107,110,112,114,116,118,120,122)

GILGAMESH II
DC Comics: 1989 - No. 4, 1989 ($3.95, limited series, prestige format, mature)
1-4: Starlin-c/a/scripts 4.00

GIL THORP
Dell Publishing Co.: May-July, 1963
1-Caniff-*ish* art 4 8 12 24 37 50

GINGER
Archie Publications: 1951 - No. 10, Summer, 1954
1-Teenage humor 15 30 45 84 127 170
2-(1952) 9 18 27 52 69 85
3-6: 6 (Sum/53) 8 16 24 44 57 70
7-10-Katy Keene app. 10 20 30 56 76 95

GINGER FOX (Also see The World of Ginger Fox)
Comico: Sept, 1988 - No. 4, Dec, 1988 ($1.75, limited series)
1-4: Part photo-c on all 2.50

G.I. R.A.M.B.O.T.
Wonder Color Comics/Pied Piper #2: Apr, 1987 - No. 2? ($1.95)
1,2: 2-Exist? 2.50

GIRL
DC Comics (Vertigo Verite): Jul, 1996 - No. 3, 1996 ($2.50, lim. series, mature)
1-3: Peter Milligan scripts; Fegredo-c/a 2.50

GIRL COMICS (Becomes Girl Confessions No. 13 on)
Marvel/Atlas Comics(CnPC): Oct, 1949 - No. 12, Jan, 1952 (#1-4: 52 pgs.)
1-Photo-c 23 46 69 135 218 300
2-Kubert-a; photo-c 14 28 42 80 115 150
3-Everett-a; Liz Taylor photo-c 29 58 87 169 272 375
4-11: 4-Photo-c. 10-12-Sol Brodsky-c 11 22 33 64 90 115
12-Krigstein-a; Al Hartley-c 12 24 36 69 97 125

GIRL CONFESSIONS (Formerly Girl Comics)
Atlas Comics (CnPC/ZPC): No. 13, Mar, 1952 - No. 35, Aug, 1954
13-Everett-a 14 28 42 76 108 140

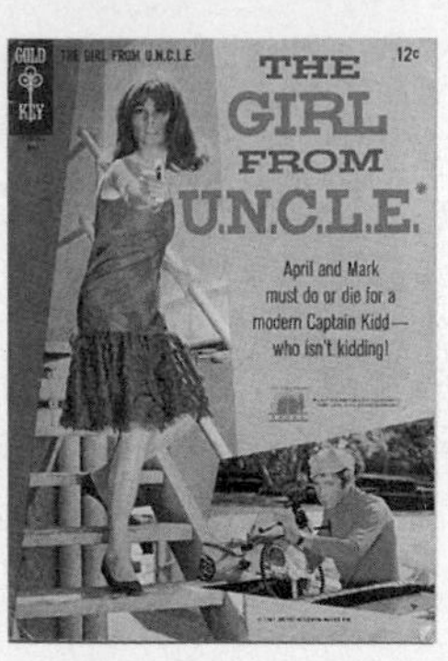

The Girl From U.N.C.L.E. #3 © GK

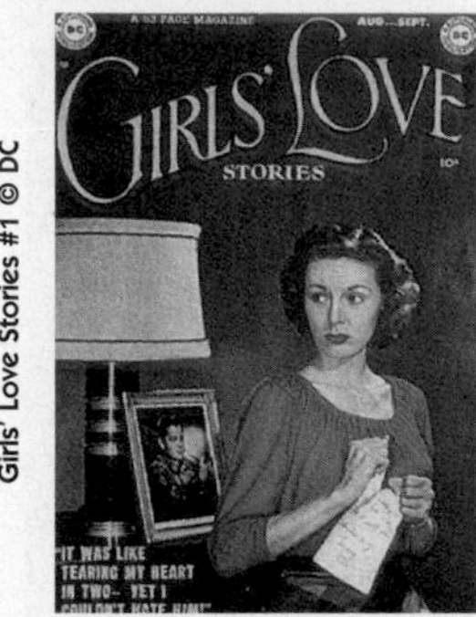

Girls' Love Stories #1 © DC

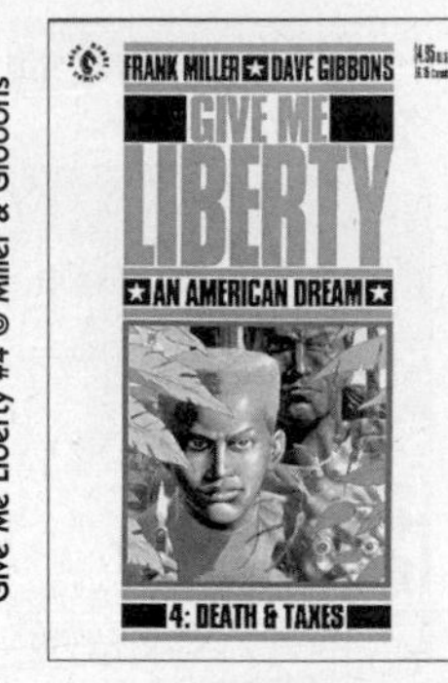

Give Me Liberty #4 © Miller & Gibbons

	GD 2.0	VG 4.0	FN 6.0	VF 8.0	VF/NM 9.0	NM- 9.2
14,15,19,20	10	20	30	56	76	95
16-18-Everett-a	11	22	33	64	90	115
21-35: Robinson-a	9	18	27	47	61	75

GIRL CRAZY
Dark Horse Comics: May, 1996 - No. 3, July, 1996 ($2.95, B&W, limited series)

	GD 2.0	VG 4.0	FN 6.0	VF 8.0	VF/NM 9.0	NM- 9.2
1-3: Gilbert Hernandez-a/scripts.						3.00

GIRL FROM U.N.C.L.E., THE (TV) (Also see The Man From...)
Gold Key: Jan, 1967 - No. 5, Oct, 1967

	GD 2.0	VG 4.0	FN 6.0	VF 8.0	VF/NM 9.0	NM- 9.2
1-McWilliams-a; Stephanie Powers photo front/back-c & pin-ups (no ads, 12¢)	8	16	24	52	86	120
2-5-Leonard Swift-Courier No. 5. 4-Back-c pin-up	6	12	18	37	59	80

GIRLS
Image Comics: May, 2005 - No. 24, Apr, 2007 ($2.95/$2.99)

	GD 2.0	VG 4.0	FN 6.0	VF 8.0	VF/NM 9.0	NM- 9.2
1-Luna Brothers-s/a/c						4.00
2-24						3.00
... Vol. 1: Conception TPB (2005, $14.99) r/#1-6						15.00
... Vol. 2: Emergence TPB (2006, $14.99) r/#7-12						15.00
... Vol. 3: Survival TPB (2006, $14.99) r/#13-18						15.00
... Vol. 4: Extinction TPB (2007, $14.99) r/#19-24						15.00

GIRLS' FUN & FASHION MAGAZINE (Formerly Polly Pigtails)
Parents' Magazine Institute: V5#44, Jan, 1950 - V5#48, Sept., 1950

	GD 2.0	VG 4.0	FN 6.0	VF 8.0	VF/NM 9.0	NM- 9.2
V5#44	7	14	21	35	43	50
45-48	5	10	15	24	30	35

GIRLS IN LOVE
Fawcett Publications: May, 1950 - No. 2, July, 1950

	GD 2.0	VG 4.0	FN 6.0	VF 8.0	VF/NM 9.0	NM- 9.2
1-Photo-c	12	24	36	69	97	125
2-Photo-c	10	20	30	54	72	90

GIRLS IN LOVE (Formerly G. I. Sweethearts No. 45)
Quality Comics Group: No. 46, Sept, 1955 - No. 57, Dec, 1956

	GD 2.0	VG 4.0	FN 6.0	VF 8.0	VF/NM 9.0	NM- 9.2
46	9	18	27	50	65	80
47-53,55,56	7	14	21	37	46	55
54- 'Commie' story	9	18	27	47	61	75
57-Matt Baker-c/a	13	26	39	72	101	130

GIRLS IN WHITE (See Harvey Comics Hits No. 58)

GIRLS' LIFE (Patsy Walker's Own Magazine For Girls!)
Atlas Comics (BFP): Jan, 1954 - No. 6, Nov, 1954

	GD 2.0	VG 4.0	FN 6.0	VF 8.0	VF/NM 9.0	NM- 9.2
1	14	28	42	76	108	140
2-Al Hartley-c	8	16	24	44	57	70
3-6	8	16	24	40	50	60

GIRLS' LOVE STORIES
National Comics(Signal Publ. No. 9-65/Arleigh No. 83-117): Aug-Sept, 1949 - No. 180, Nov-Dec, 1973 (No. 1-13: 52 pgs.)

	GD 2.0	VG 4.0	FN 6.0	VF 8.0	VF/NM 9.0	NM- 9.2
1-Toth, Kinstler-a, 8 pgs. each; photo-c	54	108	162	340	575	810
2-Kinstler-a?	31	62	93	181	291	400
3-10: 1-9-Photo-c	21	42	63	123	197	270
11-20	16	32	48	94	147	200
21-33: 21-Kinstler-a. 33-Last pre-code (1-2/55)	13	26	39	72	101	130
34-50	11	22	33	60	83	105
51-70	10	20	30	54	72	90
71-99: 83-Last 10¢ issue	5	10	15	32	51	70
100	5	10	15	34	55	75
101-146: 113-117-April O'Day app.	3	6	9	20	30	40
147-151- "Confessions" serial. 150-Wood-a	3	6	9	21	32	42
152-160,171-179	3	6	9	16	22	28
161-170 (52 pgs.)	4	8	12	22	34	45
180 Last issue	3	6	9	20	30	40
Ashcan (8-9/49) not distributed to newsstands, only for in house use			(no known sales)			

GIRLS' ROMANCES
National Periodical Publ.(Signal Publ. No. 7-79/Arleigh No. 84): Feb-Mar, 1950 - No. 160, Oct, 1971 (No. 1-11: 52 pgs.)

	GD 2.0	VG 4.0	FN 6.0	VF 8.0	VF/NM 9.0	NM- 9.2
1-Photo-c	53	106	159	330	553	775
2-Photo-c; Toth-a	30	60	90	174	280	385
3-10: 3-6-Photo-c	21	42	63	123	197	270
11,12,14-20	15	30	45	86	133	180
13-Toth-c	15	30	45	90	140	190
21-31: 31-Last pre-code (2-3/55)	13	26	39	72	101	130
32-50	7	14	21	45	73	100
51-99: 80-Last 10¢ issue	5	10	15	32	51	70
100	5	10	15	34	55	75
101-108,110-120	3	6	9	20	30	40
109-Beatles-c/story	13	26	39	90	160	230
121-133,135-140	3	6	9	18	27	35
134-Neal Adams-c (splash pg. is same as-c)	5	10	15	32	51	70
141-158	3	6	9	16	22	28
159,160-52 pgs.	4	8	12	22	34	45

GIRL WHO WOULD BE DEATH, THE
DC Comics (Vertigo): Dec, 1998 - No. 4, March, 1999 ($2.50, lim. series)

	GD 2.0	VG 4.0	FN 6.0	VF 8.0	VF/NM 9.0	NM- 9.2
1-4-Kiernan-s/Ormston-a						2.50

G. I. SWEETHEARTS (Formerly Diary Loves; Girls In Love #46 on)
Quality Comics Group: No. 32, June, 1953 - No. 45, May, 1955

	GD 2.0	VG 4.0	FN 6.0	VF 8.0	VF/NM 9.0	NM- 9.2
32	10	20	30	54	72	90
33-45: 44-Last pre-code (3/55)	8	16	24	40	50	60

G.I. TALES (Formerly Sgt. Barney Barker No. 1-3)
Atlas Comics (MCI): No. 4, Feb, 1957 - No. 6, July, 1957

	GD 2.0	VG 4.0	FN 6.0	VF 8.0	VF/NM 9.0	NM- 9.2
4-Severin-a(4)	10	20	30	54	72	90
5	8	16	24	40	50	60
6-Orlando, Powell, & Woodbridge-a	8	16	24	42	54	65

GIVE ME LIBERTY (Also see Dark Horse Presents Fifth Anniversary Special, Dark Horse Presents #100-4, Happy Birthday Martha Washington, Martha Washington Goes to War, Martha Washington Stranded In Space & San Diego Comicon Comics #2)
Dark Horse Comics: June, 1990 - No. 4, 1991 ($4.95, limited series, 52 pgs.)

	GD 2.0	VG 4.0	FN 6.0	VF 8.0	VF/NM 9.0	NM- 9.2
1-4: 1st app. Martha Washington; Frank Miller scripts, Dave Gibbons-c/a in all						5.00

G. I. WAR BRIDES
Superior Publishers Ltd.: Apr, 1954 - No. 8, June, 1955

	GD 2.0	VG 4.0	FN 6.0	VF 8.0	VF/NM 9.0	NM- 9.2
1	10	20	30	54	72	90
2	7	14	21	35	43	50
3-8: 4-Kamen*esque*-a; lingerie panels	6	12	18	31	38	45

G. I. WAR TALES
National Periodical Publications: Mar-Apr, 1973 - No. 4, Oct-Nov, 1973

	GD 2.0	VG 4.0	FN 6.0	VF 8.0	VF/NM 9.0	NM- 9.2
1-Reprints in all; dinosaur-c/s	3	6	9	17	25	32
2-N. Adams-a(r)	2	4	6	11	16	20
3,4: 4-Krigstein-a(r)	2	4	6	10	14	18

NOTE: ***Drucker** a-3r, 4r. **Heath** a-4r. **Kubert** a-2, 3; c-4r.*

GIZMO (Also see Domino Chance)
Chance Ent.: May-June, 1985 (B&W, one-shot)

	GD 2.0	VG 4.0	FN 6.0	VF 8.0	VF/NM 9.0	NM- 9.2
1						6.00

GIZMO
Mirage Studios: 1986 - No. 6, July, 1987 ($1.50, B&W)

	GD 2.0	VG 4.0	FN 6.0	VF 8.0	VF/NM 9.0	NM- 9.2
1-6						2.50

G.L.A. (Great Lakes Avengers)(Also see GLX-Mas Special)
Marvel Comics: June, 2005 - No. 4, Sept, 2005 ($2.99, limited series)

	GD 2.0	VG 4.0	FN 6.0	VF 8.0	VF/NM 9.0	NM- 9.2
1-4-Slott-s/Pelletier-a						3.00
...: Misassembled TPB (2005, $14.99) r/#1-4, West Coast Avengers #46 (1st app.) and Marvel Super-Heroes #8 (1st app. Squirrel Girl; Ditko-a)						15.00

GLADSTONE COMIC ALBUM
Gladstone: 1987 - No. 28, 1990 ($5.95/$9.95, 8-1/2x11")(All Mickey Mouse albums are by Gottfredson)

	GD 2.0	VG 4.0	FN 6.0	VF 8.0	VF/NM 9.0	NM- 9.2
1-10: 1-Uncle Scrooge; Barks-r; Beck-c. 2-Donald Duck; r/F.C. #108 by Barks. 3-Mickey Mouse-r by Gottfredson. 4-Uncle Scrooge; r/F.C. #456 by Barks w/unedited story. 5-Donald Duck Advs.; r/F.C. #199. 6-Uncle Scrooge-r by Barks. 7-Donald Duck-r by Barks. 8-Mickey Mouse-r. 9-Bambi; r/F.C. #186? 10-Donald Duck Advs.; r/F.C. #275	1	3	4	6	8	10
11-20: 11-Uncle Scrooge; r/U.S. #4. 12-Donald And Daisy; r/F.C. #1055, WDC&S. 13-Donald Duck Advs.; r/F.C. #408. 14-Uncle Scrooge; Barks-r/U.S #21. 15-Donald And Gladstone; Barks-r. 16-Donald Duck Advs.; r/F.C. #238. 17-Mickey Mouse strip-r (The World of Tomorrow, The Pirate Ghost Ship). 18-Donald Duck and the Junior Woodchucks; Barks-r. 19-Uncle Scrooge; r/U.S. #12; Rosa-c. 20-Uncle Scrooge; r/F.C. #386; Barks-c/a(r)	1	3	4	6	8	10
21-25: 21-Donald Duck Family; Barks-c/a(r). 22-Mickey Mouse strip-r. 23-Donald Duck; Barks-r/D.D. #26 w/unedited story. 24-Uncle Scrooge; Barks-r; Rosa-c. 25-D. Duck; Barks-c/a-r/F.C. #367	1	3	4	6	8	10
26-28: All have $9.95-c. 26-Mickey & Donald; Gottfredson-c/a(r). 27-Donald Duck; r/WDC&S by Barks; Barks painted-c. 28-Uncle Scrooge & Donald Duck; Rosa-c/a (4 stories)	1	3	4	6	8	10

Special 1-7: 1 ('89-'90, $9.95/13.95)-1-Donald Duck Finds Pirate Gold; r/F.C. #9. 2 ('89, $8.95)-Uncle Scrooge and Donald Duck; Barks-r/Uncle Scrooge #5; Rosa-c. 3 ('89, $8.95)-Mickey

Glamourous Romances #60 © ACE

Glamourpuss #1 © Dave Sim

Godland #22 © Casey & Scioli

GD 2.0 | VG 4.0 | FN 6.0 | VF 8.0 | VF/NM 9.0 | NM- 9.2

GD 2.0 | VG 4.0 | FN 6.0 | VF 8.0 | VF/NM 9.0 | NM- 9.2

Mouse strip-r. 4 ('89, $11.95)-Uncle Scrooge; Rosa-c/a-r/Son of the Sun from U.S. #219 plus Barks-r/U.S. 5 ('90, $11.95)-Donald Duck Advs.; Barks-r/F.C. #282 & 422 plus Barks painted-c. 6 ('90, $12.95)-Uncle Scrooge; Barks-c/a-r/Uncle Scrooge. 7 ('90, $13.95)-Mickey Mouse; Gottfredson strip-r 2 4 6 9 11 14

GLADSTONE COMIC ALBUM (2nd Series)(Also see The Original Dick Tracy)
Gladstone Publishing: 1990 ($5.95, 8-1/2 x 11," stiff-c, 52 pgs.)

1,2-The Original Dick Tracy. 2-Origin of the 2-way wrist radio 6.00
3-D Tracy Meets the Mole-r by Gould ($6.95). 1 2 3 5 6 8

GLAMOROUS ROMANCES (Formerly Dotty)
Ace Magazines (A. A. Wyn): No. 41, July, 1949 - No. 90, Oct, 1956 (Photo-c 68-90)

41-Dotty app. 11 22 33 60 83 105
42-72,74-80: 44-Begin 52 pg. issues. 45,50-61-Painted-c. 80-Last pre-code (2/55) 8 16 24 44 57 70
73-L.B. Cole-r/All Love #27 9 18 27 47 61 75
81-90 8 16 24 42 54 65

GLAMOURPUSS
Aardvark-Vanahelm Inc.: Apr, 2008 - Present ($3.00, B&W)

1-3: 1-Two covers; Dave Sim-s/a/c 3.00
1-Comics Industry Preview Edition (Diamond Dateline supplement) 3.00

GLOBAL FREQUENCY
DC Comics (WildStorm): Dec, 2002 - No. 12, Aug, 2004 ($2.95, limited series)

1-12-Warren Ellis-s. 1-Leach-a. 2-Fabry a. 3 Dillon-a. 5-Muth-a. 7-Bisley-a. 12-Ha-a 3.00
1-RRP Edition variant-c; promotional giveaway for retailers (200 printed) 10.00
...: Detonation Radio TPB (2005, $14.95) r/#7-12 15.00
...: Planet Ablaze TPB (2003, $14.95) r/#1-6 15.00

GLORY
Image Comics (Extreme Studios)/Maximum Press: Mar, 1995 - No. 22, Apr, 1997 ($2.50)

0-Deodato-c/a, 1-(3/95)-Deodato-a 2.50
1A-Variant-c 4.00
2-11,13-22: 4-Variant-c by Quesada & Palmiotti. 5-Bagged w/Youngblood gaming card. 7,8-Deodato-c/a(p). 8-Babewatch x-over. 9-Cruz-c; Extreme Destroyer Pt. 5; polybagged w/card. 10-Angela-c/app. 11 Deodato-c. 2.50
12-($3.50)-Photo-c 3.50
... & Friends Christmas Special (12/95, $2.50) Deodato-c 2.50
... & Friends Lingerie Special (9/95, $2.95) Pin-ups w/photos; photo-c; varant-c exists 3.00
... /Angela: Angels in Hell (4/96, $2.50) Flip book w/Darkchylde #1 2.50
... /Avengelyne (10/95, $3.95) 1-Chromium-c, 1-Regular-c 4.00
Trade Paperback (1995, $9.95)-r/#1-4 10.00

GLORY
Awesome Comics: Mar, 1999 ($2.50)

0-Liefeld-c; story and sketch pages 2.50

GLORY (ALAN MOORE'S...)
Avatar Press: Dec, 2001 - No. 2 ($3.50)

Preview-(9/01, $1.99) B&W pages and cover art; Alan Moore-s 2.50
0-Four regular covers 3.50
1,2: 1-Alan Moore-s/Mychaels & Gebbie-a; nine covers by various. 2-Five covers 3.50

GLORY & FRIENDS BIKINI FEST
Image Comics (Extreme): Sept, 1995 - No. 2, Oct, 1995 ($2.50, limited series)

1,2: 1-Photo-c; centerfold photo; pin-ups 2.50

GLORY/CELESTINE: DARK ANGEL
Image Comics/Maximum Press (Extreme Studios): Sept, 1996 - No. 3, Nov, 1996 ($2.50, limited series)

1-3 2.50

GLX-MAS SPECIAL (Great Lakes Avengers)
Marvel Comics: Feb, 2006 ($3.99, one-shot)

1-Christmas themed stories by various incl. Haley, Templeton, Grist, Wieringo 4.00

GNOME MOBILE, THE (See Movie Comics)

GOBBLEDYGOOK
Mirage Studios: 1984 - No. 2, 1984 (B&W)(1st Mirage comics, published at same time)

1-(24 pgs.)-(distribution of approx. 50) Teenage Mutant Ninja Turtles app. on full page back-c ad; Teenage Mutant Ninja Turtles do not appear inside. 1st app of Fugitoid 50 100 150 400 750 1100
2-(24 pgs.)-Teenage Mutant Ninja Turtles on full page back-c ad 33 66 99 254 477 700

NOTE: Counterfeit copies exist. Originals feature both black & white covers and interiors. Signed and numbered copies do not exist.

GOBBLEDYGOOK
Mirage Studios: Dec, 1986 ($3.50, B&W, one-shot, 100 pgs.)

1-New 8 pg. TMNT story plus a Donatello/Michaelangelo 7 pg. story & a Gizmo story; Corben-i(r)/TMNT #7 1 2 3 4 5 7

GOBLIN, THE
Warren Publishing Co.: June, 1982 - No. 3, Dec, 1982 ($2.25, B&W magazine with 8 pg. color insert comic in all)

1-The Gremlin app. Philo Photon & the Troll Patrol, Micro-Buccaneers & Wizard Wormglow begin & app. in all. Tin Man app. Golden-a(p). Nebres-c/a in all 2 4 6 13 18 22
2,3: 2-1st Hobgoblin. 3-Tin Man app. 2 4 6 9 12 15

NOTE: *Bermejo a-1-3. Elias a-1-3. Laxamana a-1-3. Nino a-3.*

GODDESS
DC Comics (Vertigo): June, 1995 - No. 8, Jan, 1996 ($2.95, limited series)

1-Garth Ennis scripts; Phil Winslade-c/a in all 5.00
2-8 4.00
TPB (2002, $19.95) r/#1-8; foreword and sketch pages by Winslade 20.00

GODFATHERS, THE (See The Crusaders)

GOD IS
Spire Christian Comics (Fleming H. Revell Co.): 1973, 1975 (35-49¢)

nn-(1973) By Al Hartley 2 4 6 8 11 14
nn-(1975) 1 3 4 6 8 10

GODLAND
Image Comics: July, 2005 - Present ($2.99)

1-15,17-25-Joe Casey-s; Kirby-esque art by Tom Scioli. 13-Var-c by Giffen & Larsen 3.00
16-(60¢-c) Re-cap/origin issue 2.25
...: Celestial Edition One HC (2007, $34.99) r/#1-12 and story from Image Holiday Special; intro. by Grant Morrison; cover gallery, developmental art and original story pitches 35.00
... Vol. 1: Hello Cosmic! TPB (1/06, $14.99) r/#1-6; sketch development pages 15.00
... Vol. 2: Another Sunny Delight TPB (8/06, $14.99) r/#7-12; early Christmas story 15.00
... Vol. 3: Proto-Plastic Party TPB (2007, $14.99) r/#13-18 15.00

GOD SAVE THE QUEEN
DC Comics (Vertigo): 2007 ($19.99, hardcover with dustjacket, graphic novel)

HC-Mike Carey-s/John Bolton-painted art 20.00
SC-(2008, $12.99) Different Bolton painted-c 13.00

GOD'S COUNTRY (Also see Marvel Comics Presents)
Marvel Comics: 1994 ($6.95)

nn-P. Craig Russell-a; Colossus story; r/Marvel Comics Presents #10-17 7.00

GOD'S HEROES IN AMERICA
Catechetical Guild Educational Society: 1956 (nn) (25¢/35¢, 68 pgs.)

307 3 6 9 16 23 30

GOD'S SMUGGLER (Religious)
Spire Christian Comics/Fleming H. Revell Co.: 1972 (35¢/39¢/40¢)

1-Three variations exist 2 4 6 8 11 14

GODWHEEL
Malibu Comics (Ultraverse): No. 0, Jan, 1995 - No. 3, Feb, 1995 ($2.50, limited series)

0-3: 0-Flip-c. 1-1st app. of Primevil; Thor cameo (1 panel). 3-Perez-a in Chapter 3, Thor app. 2.50

GODZILLA (Movie)
Marvel Comics : August, 1977 - No. 24, July, 1979 (Based on movie series)

1-(Regular 30¢ edition)-Mooney-i 3 6 9 18 27 35
1-(35¢-c variant, limited distribution) 6 12 18 37 59 80
2-(Regular 30¢ edition)-Tuska-i. 2 4 6 8 11 14
2,3-(35¢-c variant, limited distribution) 3 6 9 20 30 40
3-(30¢-c) Champions app.(w/o Ghost Rider) 2 4 6 9 13 16
4-10: 4,5-Sutton-a 2 4 6 8 10 12
11-23: 14-Shield app. 20-F.F. app. 21,22-Devil Dinosaur app. 1 3 4 6 8 10
24-Last issue 2 4 6 8 11 14

GODZILLA (Movie)
Dark Horse Comics: May, 1988 - No. 6, 1988 ($1.95, B&W, limited series) (Based on movie series)

1 6.00
2-6 4.00
...Collection (1990, $10.95)-r/1-6 with new-c 11.00
...Color Special 1 (Sum, 1992, $3.50, color, 44 pgs.)-Arthur Adams wraparound-c/a &

Godzilla #14 © Toho Co. Ltd.

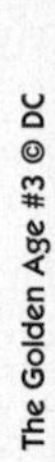

The Golden Age #3 © DC

Golden Lad #3 © Spark

GD 2.0 | VG 4.0 | FN 6.0 | VF 8.0 | VF/NM 9.0 | NM- 9.2

part scripts 5.00
...King Of The Monsters Special (8/87, $1.50)-Origin; Bissette-c/a 4.00
...Vs. Barkley nn (12/93, $2.95, color)-Dorman painted-c 4.00

GODZILLA (King of the Monsters) (Movie)
Dark Horse Comics: May, 1995 - No. 16, Sept, 1996 ($2.50) (Based on movies)

0-16: 0-r/Dark Horse Comics #10,11. 1-3-Kevin Maguire scripts. 3-8-Art Adams-c 4.00
...Vs. Hero Zero ($2.50) 3.00

GOG (VILLAINS) (See Kingdom Come)
DC Comics: Feb, 1998 ($1.95, one-shot)

1-Waid-s/Ordway-a(p)/Pearson-c 3.00

GO GIRL!
Image Comics: Aug, 2000 - No. 5 ($3.50, B&W, quarterly)

1-5-Trina Robbins-s/Anne Timmons-a; pin-up gallery 3.50

GO-GO
Charlton Comics: June, 1966 - No. 9, Oct, 1967

1-Miss Bikini Luv begins w/Jim Aparo's 1st published work; Rolling Stones, Beatles, Elvis, Sonny & Cher, Bob Dylan, Sinatra, parody; Herman's Hermits pin-ups; D'Agostino-c/a in #1-8 8 16 24 54 90 125
2-Ringo Starr, David McCallum & Beatles photos on cover; Beatles story and photos 8 16 24 54 90 125
3,4: 3-Blooperman begins, ends #6; 1 pg. Batman & Robin satire; full pg. photo pin-ups Lovin' Spoonful & The Byrds 5 10 15 32 51 70
5,7,9: 5 (2/67)-Super Hero & TV satire by Jim Aparo & Grass Green begins. 6-8-Aparo-a. 7-Photo of Brian Wilson of Beach Boys on-c & Beach Boys photo inside f/b-c. 9-Aparo-c/a 5 10 15 32 51 70
6-Parody of JLA & DC heroes vs. Marvel heroes; Aparo-a; Elvis parody; Petula Clark photo-c 6 12 18 37 59 80
8-Monkees photo on-c & photo inside f/b-c 6 12 18 41 66 90

GO-GO AND ANIMAL (See Tippy's Friends...)

GOING STEADY (Formerly Teen-Age Temptations)
St. John Publ. Co.: No. 10, Dec, 1954 - No. 13, June, 1955; No. 14, Oct, 1955

10(1954)-Matt Baker-c/a 27 54 81 158 254 350
11(2/55, last precode), 12(4/55)-Baker-c 15 30 45 94 147 200
13(6/55)-Baker-c/a 21 42 63 125 200 275
14(10/55)-Matt Baker-c/a, 25 pgs. 25 50 75 147 236 325

GOING STEADY (Formerly Personal Love)
Prize Publications/Headline: V3#3, Feb, 1960 - V3#6, Aug, 1960; V4#1, Sept-Oct, 1960

V3#3-6, V4#1 3 6 9 16 23 30

GOING STEADY WITH BETTY (Becomes Betty & Her Steady No. 2)
Avon Periodicals: Nov-Dec, 1949

1 15 30 45 86 133 180

GOLDEN AGE, THE (TPB also reprinted in 2005 as JSA: The Golden Age)
DC Comics (Elseworlds): 1993 - No. 4, 1994 ($4.95, limited series)

1-4: James Robinson scripts; Paul Smith-c/a; gold foil embossed-c 6.00
Trade Paperback (1995, $19.95) intro by Howard Chaykin 20.00

GOLDEN AGE SECRET FILES
DC Comics: Feb, 2001 ($4.95, one-shot)

1-Origins and profiles of JSA members and other G.A. heroes; Lark-c 5.00

GOLDEN ARROW (See Fawcett Miniatures, Mighty Midget & Whiz Comics)

GOLDEN ARROW (...Western No. 6)
Fawcett Publications: Spring, 1942 - No. 6, Spring, 1947 (68 pgs.)

1-Golden Arrow begins 69 138 207 431 716 1000
2-(1943) 36 72 108 208 329 450
3-5: 3-(Win/45-46). 4-(Spr/46). 5-(Fall/46) 25 50 75 148 232 315
6-Krigstein-a 26 52 78 152 239 325
Ashcan (1942) not distributed to newsstands, only for in house use. A CGC certified 9.0 sold for $3,734.38 in 2008.

GOLDEN COMICS DIGEST
Gold Key: May, 1969 - No. 48, Jan, 1976

NOTE: *Whitman editions exist of many titles and are generally valued the same.*

1-Tom & Jerry, Woody Woodpecker, Bugs Bunny 6 12 18 37 59 80
2-Hanna-Barbera TV Fun Favorites; Space Ghost, Flintstones, Atom Ant, Jetsons, Yogi Bear, Banana Splits, others app. 7 14 21 49 80 110
3-Tom & Jerry, Woody Woodpecker 3 6 9 17 25 32
4-Tarzan; Manning & Marsh-a 5 10 15 30 48 65
5,8-Tom & Jerry, W. Woodpecker, Bugs Bunny 3 6 9 16 23 30
6-Bugs Bunny 3 6 9 16 23 30
7-Hanna-Barbera TV Fun Favorites 6 12 18 37 59 80
9-Tarzan 5 10 15 30 48 65
10,12-17: 10-Bugs Bunny. 12-Tom & Jerry, Bugs Bunny, W. Woodpecker Journey to the Sun. 13-Tom & Jerry. 14-Bugs Bunny Fun Packed Funnies. 15-Tom & Jerry, Woody Woodpecker, Bugs Bunny. 16-Woody Woodpecker Cartoon Special. 17-Bugs Bunny 3 6 9 16 23 30
11-Hanna-Barbera TV Fun Favorites 6 12 18 39 62 85
18-Tom & Jerry; Barney Bear-r by Barks 3 6 9 17 25 32
19-Little Lulu 4 8 12 26 41 55
20-22: 20-Woody Woodpecker Falltime Funtime. 21-Bugs Bunny Showtime. 22-Tom & Jerry Winter Wingding 3 6 9 16 23 30
23-Little Lulu & Tubby Fun Fling 4 8 12 26 41 55
24-26,28: 24-Woody Woodpecker Fun Festival. 25-Tom & Jerry. 26-Bugs Bunny Halloween Hulla-Boo-Loo; Dr. Spektor article, also #25. 28-Tom & Jerry 3 6 9 14 20 26
27-Little Lulu & Tubby in Hawaii 4 8 12 25 39 52
29-Little Lulu & Tubby 4 8 12 25 39 52
30-Bugs Bunny Vacation Funnies 3 6 9 14 20 26
31-Turok, Son of Stone; r/4-Color #596,656; c-r/#9 4 8 12 28 44 60
32-Woody Woodpecker Summer Fun 3 6 9 14 20 26
33,36: 33-Little Lulu & Tubby Halloween Fun; Dr. Spektor app. 36-Little Lulu & Her Friends 4 8 12 25 39 52
34,35,37-39: 34-Bugs Bunny Winter Funnies. 35-Tom & Jerry Snowtime Funtime. 37-Woody Woodpecker County Fair. 39-Bugs Bunny Summer Fun 3 6 9 14 20 26
38-The Pink Panther 3 6 9 17 25 32
40,43: 40-Little Lulu & Tubby Trick or Treat; all by Stanley. 43-Little Lulu in Paris 4 8 12 25 39 52
41,42,44,47: 41-Tom & Jerry Winter Carnival. 42-Bugs Bunny. 44-Woody Woodpecker Family Fun Festival. 47-Bugs Bunny 3 6 9 14 20 25
45-The Pink Panther 3 6 9 17 25 32
46-Little Lulu & Tubby 4 8 12 22 34 45
48-The Lone Ranger 3 6 9 18 27 35
NOTE: *#1-30, 164 pgs.; #31 on, 132 pgs..*

GOLDEN LAD
Spark/Fact & Fiction Publ.: July, 1945 - No. 5, June, 1946 (#4, 5: 52 pgs.)

1-Origin & 1st app. Golden Lad & Swift Arrow; Sandusky and the Senator begins 64 128 192 400 663 925
2-Mort Meskin-c/a 32 64 96 186 293 400
3,4-Mort Meskin-c/a 29 58 87 167 264 360
5-Origin & 1st app. Golden Girl; Shaman & Flame app. 32 64 96 186 293 400

NOTE: *All have* ***Robinson,*** *and* ***Roussos*** *art plus* ***Meskin*** *covers and art.*

GOLDEN LEGACY
Fitzgerald Publishing Co.: 1966 - 1972 (Black History) (25¢)

1-12,14-16: 1-Toussaint L'Ouverture (1966), 2-Harriet Tubman (1967), 3-Crispus Attucks & the Minutemen (1967), 4-Benjamin Banneker (1968), 5-Matthew Henson (1969), 6-Alexander Dumas & Family (1969), 7-Frederick Douglass, Part 1 (1969), 8-Frederick Douglass, Part 2 (1970), 9-Robert Smalls (1970), 10-J. Cinque & the Amistad Mutiny (1970), 11-Men in Action: White, Marshall J. Wilkins (1970), 12-Black Cowboys (1972), 14-The Life of Alexander Pushkin (1971), 15-Ancient African Kingdoms (1972), 16-Black Inventors (1972) each.... 3 6 9 16 23 30
13-The Life of Martin Luther King, Jr. (1972) 3 6 9 20 30 40
1-10,12,13,15,16(1976)-Reprints 1 2 3 5 7 9

GOLDEN LOVE STORIES (Formerly Golden West Love)
Kirby Publishing Co.: No. 4, April, 1950

4-Powell-a; Glenn Ford/Janet Leigh photo-c 15 30 45 92 144 200

GOLDEN PICTURE CLASSIC, A
Western Printing Co. (Simon & Shuster): 1956-1957 (Text stories w/illustrations in color; 100 pgs. each)

CL-401: Treasure Island 11 22 33 62 86 110
CL-402,403: 402: Tom Sawyer. 403: Black Beauty 9 18 27 52 69 85
CL-404, 405: CL-404: Little Women. CL-405: Heidi 9 18 27 52 69 85
CL-406: Ben Hur 8 16 24 42 54 65
CL-407: Around the World in 80 Days 8 16 24 42 54 65
CL-408: Sherlock Holmes 9 18 27 47 61 75
CL-409: The Three Musketeers 8 16 24 42 54 65
CL-410: The Merry Advs. of Robin Hood 8 16 24 42 54 65
CL-411,412: 411: Hans Brinker. 412: The Count of Monte Cristo 9 18 27 47 61 75
(Both soft & hardcover editions are valued the same)

Golden Picture Story Book #3 © DIS

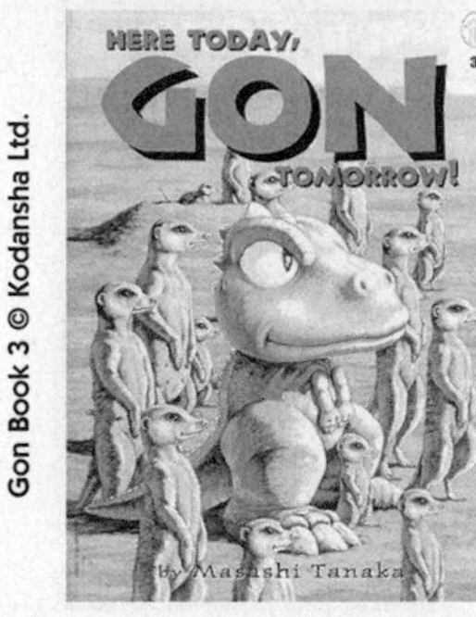

Gon Book 3 © Kodansha Ltd.

Goofy Comics #9 © STD

	GD 2.0	VG 4.0	FN 6.0	VF 8.0	VF/NM 9.0	NM- 9.2

NOTE: *Recent research has uncovered new information. Apparently #s 1-6 were issued in 1956 and #7-12 in 1957. But they can be found in five different series listings: CL-1 to CL-12 (softbound); CL-401 to CL-412 (also softbound); CL-101 to CL-112 (hardbound), plus two new series discoveries: A Golden Reading Adventure, publ. by Golden Press; edited down to 60 pages and reduced in size to 6x9"; only #s discovered so far are #381 (CL-4), #382 (CL-6) & #387 (CL-3). They have no reorder list and some have covers different from GPC. There have also been found British hardbound editions of GPC with dust jackets. Copies of all five listed series vary from scarce to very rare. Some editions of some series have not yet been found at all.*

GOLDEN PICTURE STORY BOOK
Racine Press (Western): Dec, 1961 (50¢, Treasury size, 52 pgs.) (All are scarce)

ST-1-Huckleberry Hound (TV); Hokey Wolf, Pixie & Dixie, Quick Draw McGraw, Snooper and Blabber, Augie Doggie app. 17 34 51 124 230 335
ST-2-Yogi Bear (TV); Snagglepuss, Yakky Doodle, Quick Draw McGraw, Snooper and Blabber, Augie Doggie app. 17 34 51 124 230 335
ST-3-Babes in Toyland (Walt Disney's...)-Annette Funicello photo-c 22 44 66 157 291 425
ST-4-(...of Disney Ducks)-Walt Disney's Wonderful World of Ducks (Donald Duck, Uncle Scrooge, Donald's Nephews, Grandma Duck, Ludwig Von Drake, & Gyro Gearloose stories) 22 44 66 157 291 425

GOLDEN RECORD COMIC (See Amazing Spider-Man #1, Avengers #4, Fantastic Four #1, Journey Into Mystery #83)

GOLDEN STORY BOOKS
Western Printing Co. (Simon & Shuster): 1949 (Heavy covers, digest size, 128 pgs.) (Illustrated text in color)

7-Walt Disney's Mystery in Disneyville, a book-length adventure starring Donald and Nephews, Mickey and Nephews, and with Minnie, Daisy and Goofy. Art by Dick Moores & Manuel Gonzales (scarce) 30 60 90 174 280 385
10-Bugs Bunny's Treasure Hunt, a book-length adventure starring Bugs & Porky Pig, with Petunia Pig & Nephew, Cicero. Art by Tom McKimson (scarce) 21 42 63 123 197 270

GOLDEN WEST LOVE (Golden Love Stories No. 4)
Kirby Publishing Co.: Sept-Oct, 1949 - No. 3, Feb, 1950 (All 52 pgs.)

1-Powell-a in all; Roussos-a; painted-c 22 44 66 127 204 280
2,3: Photo-c 15 30 45 94 147 200

GOLDEN WEST RODEO TREASURY (See Dell Giants)

GOLDFISH (See A.K.A. Goldfish)

GOLDILOCKS (See March of Comics No. 1)

GOLD KEY CHAMPION
Gold Key: Mar, 1978 - No. 2, May, 1978 (50¢, 52pgs.)

1,2: 1-Space Family Robinson; half-r. 2-Mighty Samson; half-r 1 3 4 6 8 10

GOLD KEY SPOTLIGHT
Gold Key: May, 1976 - No. 11, Feb, 1978

1-Tom, Dick & Harriet 2 4 6 8 11 14
2-11: 2-Wacky Advs. of Cracky. 3-Wacky Witch. 4-Tom, Dick & Harriet. 5-Wacky Advs. of Cracky. 6-Dagar the Invincible; Santos-a; origin Demonomicon. 7-Wacky Witch & Greta Ghost. 8-The Occult Files of Dr. Spektor, Simbar, Lu-sai; Santos-a. 9-Tragg. 10-O. G. Whiz. 11-Tom, Dick & Harriet 2 4 6 8 10 12

GOLD MEDAL COMICS
Cambridge House: 1945 (25¢, one-shot, 132 pgs.)

nn-Captain Truth by Fugitani as well as Stallman and Howie Post, Crime Detector, The Witch of Salem, Luckyman, others app. 30 60 90 174 280 385

GOMER PYLE (TV)
Gold Key: July, 1966 - No. 3, Jan, 1967

1-Photo front/back-c 8 16 24 54 90 125
2,3 6 12 18 39 62 85

GON
DC Comics (Paradox Press): July, 1996 - No. 4, Oct, 1996; No. 5, 1997 ($5.95, B&W, digest-size, limited series)

1-5: Misadventures of baby dinosaur; 1-Gon. 2-Gon Again. 3-Gon: Here Today, Gone Tomorrow. 4-Gon: Going, Going...Gon. 5-Gon Swimmin'. Tanaka-c/a/scripts in all 1 2 3 5 6 8

GON COLOR SPECTACULAR
DC Comics (Paradox Press): 1998 ($5.95, square-bound)

nn-Tanaka-c/a/scripts 1 2 3 5 6 8

GON ON SAFARI
DC Comics (Paradox Press): 2000 ($7.95, B&W, digest-size)

nn-Tanaka-c/a/scripts 1 2 3 5 6 8

GON UNDERGROUND
DC Comics (Paradox Press): 1999 ($7.95, B&W, digest-size)

nn-Tanaka-c/a/scripts 1 2 3 5 6 8

GON WILD
DC Comics (Paradox Press): 1997 ($9.95, B&W, digest-size)

nn-Tanaka-c/a/scripts in all. (Rep. Gon #3,4) 1 3 4 6 8 10

GOODBYE, MR. CHIPS (See Movie Comics)

GOOD GIRL ART QUARTERLY
AC Comics: Summer, 1990 - No. 15, Spring, 1994 (B&W/color, 52 pgs.)

1,3-15 ($3.50)-All have one new story (often FemForce) & rest reprints by Baker, Ward & other "good girl" artists 4.00
2 ($3.95) 4.00

GOOD GIRL COMICS (Formerly Good Girl Art Quarterly)
AC Comics: No. 16, Summer, 1994 - No. 18, 1995 (B&W)

16-18 4.00

GOOD GUYS, THE
Defiant: Nov, 1993 - No. 9, July, 1994 ($2.50/$3.25/$3.50)

1-($3.50, 52 pgs.)-Glory x-over from Plasm 3.50
2,3,5-9: 9-Pre-Schism issue 2.50
4-($3.25, 52 pgs.) 3.25

GOOD TRIUMPHS OVER EVIL! (Also see Narrative Illustration)
M.C. Gaines: 1943 (12 pgs., 7-1/4"x10", B&W) (not a comic book) (Rare)

nn-A pamphlet, sequel to Narrative Illustration 100 200 300 630 1065 1500
NOTE: ***Print, A Quarterly Journal of the Graphic Arts** Vol. 3 No. 3 (64 pg. square bound) features 1st printing of Good Triumphs Over Evil! A VG copy sold for $350 in 2005.*

GOOFY (Disney)(See Dynabrite Comics, Mickey Mouse Magazine V4#7, Walt Disney Showcase #35 & Wheaties)
Dell Publishing Co.: No. 468, May, 1953 - Sept-Nov, 1962

Four Color 468 (#1) 12 24 36 82 146 210
Four Color 562,627,658,702,747,802,857 7 14 21 47 76 105
Four Color 899,952,987,1053,1094,1149,1201 5 10 15 32 51 70
12-308-211(Dell, 9-11/62) 5 10 15 32 51 70

GOOFY ADVENTURES
Disney Comics: June, 1990 - No. 17, 1991 ($1.50)

1-17: Most new stories. 2-Joshua Quagmire-a w/free poster. 7-WDC&S-r plus new-a. 9-Gottfredson-r. 14-Super Goof story. 15-All Super Goof issue. 17-Gene Colan-a(p) 3.00

GOOFY ADVENTURE STORY (See Goofy No. 857)

GOOFY COMICS (Companion to Happy Comics)(Not Disney)
Nedor Publ. Co. No. 1-14/Standard No. 14-48: June, 1943 - No. 48, 1953 (Animated Cartoons)

1-Funny animal; Oriolo-c 29 58 87 169 272 375
2 15 30 45 88 137 185
3-10 14 28 42 76 108 140
11-19 10 20 30 58 79 100
20-35-Frazetta text illos in all 11 22 33 64 90 115
36-48 9 18 27 50 65 80

GOOFY SUCCESS STORY (See Goofy No. 702)

GOON, THE
Avatar Press: Mar, 1999 - No. 3, July, 1999 ($3.00, B&W)

1- Eric Powell-s/a 20.00
2 12.00
3 8.00
...: Rough Stuff (Albatross, 1/03, $15.95) r/Avatar Press series #1-3 16.00
...: Rough Stuff (Dark Horse, 2/04, $12.95) r/Avatar Press series #1-3 newly colored 13.00

GOON, THE (2nd series)
Albatross Exploding Funny Books: Oct, 2002 - No. 4, Feb, 2003 ($2.95)

1- Eric Powell-s/a 10.00
2-4 6.00
...Color Special 1 (8/02) 10.00
...: Nothin' But Misery Vol. 1 (Dark Horse, 7/03, $15.95, TPB) - Reprints The Goon #1-4 (Albatross series), Color Special, and story from DHP #157 16.00

GOON, THE (3rd series)
Dark Horse Comics: June, 2003 - Present ($2.99)

1-Eric Powell-s/a in all 6.00
2-4 4.00
5-28: 7-Hellboy-c/app; framing seq. by Mignola 14-Two covers 3.00

The Goon #24 © Eric Powell

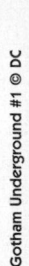

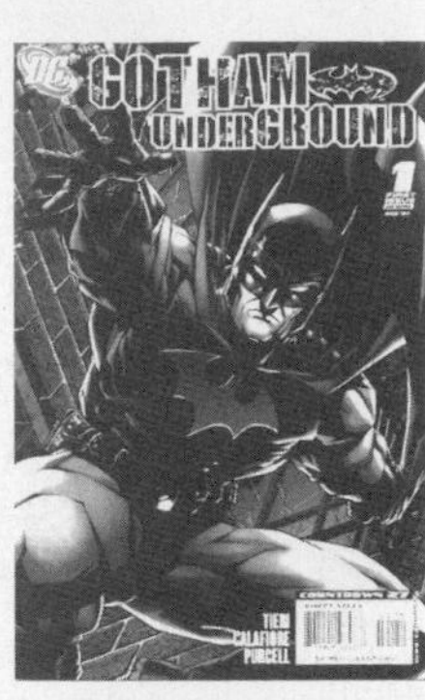

Gotham Underground #1 © DC

Great Action Comics #8 © I.W. Ent.

GD 2.0 | VG 4.0 | FN 6.0 | VF 8.0 | VF/NM 9.0 | NM- 9.2

... 25¢ Edition (9/05, 25¢) 2.50
...: Chinatown and the Mystery of Mr. Wicker HC (11/07, $19.95) original GN; Powell-s/a 20.00
...: Fancy Pants Edition HC (10/05, $24.95, dust jacket) r/#1,2 of 2nd series & #1,3,5,9 of 3rd series; Powell intro.; sketch pages and cover gallery 25.00
...: Heaps of Ruination (5/05, $12.95, TPB) r/#5-8; intro. by Frank Darabont 13.00
...: My Murderous Childhood (And Other Grievous Yarns) (5/04, $13.95, TPB) r/#1-4 and short story from Drawing on Your Nightmares one-shot; intro. by Frank Cho 14.00
...: Virtue and the Grim Consequences Thereof (2/06, $16.95) r/#9-13 17.00
...: Wicked Inclinations (12/06, $14.95) r/#14-18; intro. by Mike Allred 15.00

GOON NOIR, THE (Dwight T. Albatross's...)
Dark Horse Comics: Sept, 2006 - No. 3, Jan, 2007 ($2.99, B&W, limited series)
1-3-Anthology 1-Oswalt-s/Ploog-a; Sniegoski-s/Powell-a; Morrison-s/a; Niles-s/Sook-a. 2-Nowlan, Barta-a. 3-Ramos, Guy Davis-a; Nelson, Posehn, Thomas Lennon-s 3.00
TPB (7/07, $12.95) r/#1-3; sketch pages; intros by "Dwight" 13.00

GOOSE (Humor magazine)
Cousins Publ. (Fawcett): Sept, 1976 - No. 3, 1976 (75¢, 52 pgs., B&W)
1-Nudity in all 3 6 9 14 20 25
2,3: 2-(10/76) Fonz-c/s; Lone Ranger story. 3-Wonder Woman, King Kong, Six Million Dollar Man stories 2 4 6 10 14 18

GORDO (See Comics Revue No. 5 & Giant Comics Edition)

GORGO (Based on M.G.M. movie) (See Return of...)
Charlton Comics: May, 1961 - No. 23, Sept, 1965
1-Ditko-a, 22 pgs. 22 44 66 159 295 430
2,3-Ditko-c/a 12 24 36 84 150 215
4-Ditko-c 8 16 24 56 93 130
5-11,13-16: 11,13-16-Ditko-a 7 14 21 49 80 110
12,17-23: 12-Reptisaurus x-over; Montes/Bache-a-No. 17-23. 20-Giordano-c 5 10 15 32 51 70
Gorgo's Revenge('62)-Becomes Return of... 6 12 18 39 62 85

GOSPEL BLIMP, THE
Spire Christian Comics (Fleming H. Revell Co.): 1973,1975 (35¢/39¢, 36 pgs.)
nn-(1973) 2 4 6 8 11 14
nn-(1975) 1 3 4 6 8 10

GOTHAM BY GASLIGHT (A Tale of the Batman)(See Batman: Master of...)
DC Comics: 1989 ($3.95, one-shot, squarebound, 52 pgs.)
nn-Mignola/Russell-a; intro by Robert Bloch 4.00

GOTHAM CENTRAL
DC Comics: Early Feb, 2003 - No. 40, Apr, 2006 ($2.50)
1-40-Stories of Gotham City Police. 1-Brubaker & Rucka-s/Lark-c/a. 10-Two-Face app. 13,15-Joker-c. 18-Huntress app. 27-Catwoman-c. 32-Poison Ivy app. 34-Teen Titans-c/app. 38-Crispus Allen killed (becomes The Spectre in Infinite Crisis #5) 2.50
...: Dead Robin (2007, $17.99, TPB) r/#33-40; cover gallery 18.00
...: Half a Life (2005, $14.99, TPB) r/#6-10, Batman Chronicles #16 and Detective #747 15.00
...: In The Line of Duty (2004, $9.95, TPB) r/#1-5, cover gallery & sketch pages 10.00
...: The Quick and the Dead TPB (2006, $14.99) r/#23-25,28-31 15.00
...: Unresolved Targets (2006, $14.99, TPB) r/#12-15,19-22, cover gallery 15.00

GOTHAM GIRLS
DC Comics: Oct, 2002 - No. 5, Feb, 2003 ($2.25, limited series)
1-5-Catwoman, Batgirl, Poison Ivy, Harley Quinn from animated series 2.50

GOTHAM NIGHTS (See Batman: Gotham Nights II)
DC Comics: Mar, 1992 - No. 4, June, 1992 ($1.25, limited series)
1-4: Featuring Batman 2.50

GOTHAM UNDERGROUND
DC Comics: Dec, 2007 - No. 9, Aug, 2008 ($2.99, limited series)
1-9-Nine covers interlock for single image; Tieri-s/Calafiore-a/c. 7,8-Vigilante app. 3.00

GOTHIC ROMANCES
Atlas/Seaboard Publ.: Dec, 1974 (75¢, B&W, magazine, 76 pgs.)
1-Text w/ illos by N. Adams, Chaykin, Heath (2 pgs. ea.); painted cover (scarce) 19 38 57 139 257 375

GOTHIC TALES OF LOVE (Magazine)
Marvel Comics: Apr, 1975 - No. 3, 1975 (B&W, 76 pgs.)
1-3-Painted-c/a (scarce) 23 46 69 167 309 450

GOVERNOR & J. J., THE (TV)
Gold Key: Feb, 1970 - No. 3, Aug, 1970 (Photo-c)
1 4 8 12 26 41 55
2,3 3 6 9 19 29 38

GD 2.0 | VG 4.0 | FN 6.0 | VF 8.0 | VF/NM 9.0 | NM- 9.2

GRACKLE, THE
Acclaim Comics: Jan, 1997 - No. 4, Apr, 1997 ($2.95, B&W)
1-4: Mike Baron scripts & Paul Gulacy-c/a. 1-4-Doublecross 3.00

GRAFIK MUSIK
Caliber Press: Nov, 1990 - No. 4, Aug, 1991 ($3.50/$2.50)
1-($3.50, 48 pgs., color) Mike Allred-c/a/scripts-1st app. in color of Frank Einstein (Madman) 3 6 9 14 20 25
2-($2.50, 24 pgs., color) 2 4 6 9 12 15
3,4-($2.50, 24 pgs., B&W) 2 4 6 8 10 12

GRANDMA DUCK'S FARM FRIENDS(See Walt Disney's C&S 293 & Wheaties)
Dell Publishing Co.: No. 763, Jan, 1957 - No. 1279, Feb, 1962 (Disney)
Four Color 763 (#1) 8 16 24 52 86 120
Four Color 873 6 12 18 37 59 80
Four Color 965,1279 5 10 15 32 51 70
Four Color 1010,1073,1161-Barks-a; 1073,1161-Barks c/a 12 24 36 87 156 225

GRAND PRIX (Formerly Hot Rod Racers)
Charlton Comics: No. 16, Sept, 1967 - No. 31, May, 1970
16-Features Rick Roberts 4 8 12 22 34 45
17-20 3 6 9 17 26 34
21-31 3 6 9 16 23 30

GRAPHIQUE MUSIQUE
Slave Labor Graphics: Dec, 1989 - No. 3, May, 1990 ($2.95, 52 pgs.)
1-Mike Allred-c/a/scripts 3 6 9 20 30 40
2,3 3 6 9 16 23 30

GRAVESLINGER
Image Comics (Shadowline): Oct, 2007 - No. 4, Mar, 2008 ($3.50, limited series)
1-4-Denton & Mariotte-s/Cboins-a 3.50

GRAVE TALES
Hamilton Comics: Oct, 1991 - No. 3, Feb, 1992 ($3.95, B&W, mag., 52 pgs.)
1-Staton-c/a 1 2 3 5 6 8
2,3: 2-Staton-a; Morrow-c 6.00

GRAVITY (Also see Beyond! limited series)
Marvel Comics: Aug, 2005 - No. 5, Dec, 2005 ($2.99, limited series)
1-5: 1-Intro. Gravity; McKeever-s/Norton-a. 2-Rhino-c/app. 5-Spider-Man app 3.00
...: Big-City Super Hero (2005, $7.99, digest) r/#1-5 8.00

GRAY AREA, THE
Image Comics: Jun, 2004 - No. 3, Oct, 2004 ($5.95/$3.95, limited series)
1,3-($5.95) Romita, Jr.-a/Brunswick-s; sketch pages and script pages. 3-Pin-up pages 6.00
2-($3.95) 4.00
...Vol. 1: All Of This Can Be Yours (2005, $14.95) r/series & sketch,script & pin-up pages 15.00

GRAY GHOST, THE
Dell Publishing Co.: No. 911, July, 1958; No. 1000, June-Aug, 1959
Four Color 911 (#1), 1000-Photo-c each 8 16 24 56 93 130

GREAT ACTION COMICS
I. W. Enterprises: 1958 (Reprints with new covers)
1-Captain Truth reprinted from Gold Medal #1 3 6 9 16 23 30
8,9-Reprints Phantom Lady #15 & 23 7 14 21 49 80 110

GREAT AMERICAN COMICS PRESENTS - THE SECRET VOICE
Peter George 4-Star Publ./American Features Syndicate: 1945 (10¢)
1-Anti-Nazi; "What Really Happened to Hitler" 37 74 111 215 345 475

GREAT AMERICAN WESTERN, THE
AC Comics: 1987 - No. 4, 1990? ($1.75/$2.95/$3.50, B&W with some color)
1-4: 1-Western-r plus Bill Black-a. 2-Tribute to ME comics; Durango Kid photo-c 3-Tribute to Tom Mix plus Roy Rogers, Durango Kid; Billy the Kid-r by Severin; photo-c. 4- ($3.50, 52 pgs., 16 pgs. color)-Tribute to Lash LaRue; photo-c & interior photos; Fawcett-r 4.00
...Presents 1 (1991, $5.00) New Sunset Carson; film history 5.00

GREAT CAT FAMILY, THE (Disney-TV/Movie)
Dell Publishing Co.: No. 750, Nov, 1956 (one-shot)
Four Color 750-Pinocchio & Alice app. 6 12 18 43 69 95

GREAT COMICS
Great Comics Publications: Nov, 1941 - No. 3, Jan, 1942
1-Origin/1st app. The Great Zarro; Madame Strange & Guy Gorham, Wizard of Science & The Great Zarro begin 125 250 375 788 1332 1875
2-Buck Johnson, Jungle Explorer app.; X-Mas-c 65 130 195 410 693 975

Greatest Joker Stories Ever Told © DC

Great Lover Romances #6 © TOBY

Green Arrow #55 © DC

GD 2.0 VG 4.0 FN 6.0 VF 8.0 VF/NM 9.0 NM- 9.2

3-Futuro Takes Hitler to Hell-c/s; "The Lost City" movie story (starring William Boyd); continues in Choice Comics #3 324 648 972 2203 3852 5500

GREAT COMICS
Novack Publishing Co./Jubilee Comics/Knockout/Barrel O' Fun: 1945
1-(Four publ. variations: Barrel O-Fun, Jubilee, Knockout & Novack)-The Defenders, Capt. Power app.; L. B. Cole-c 32 64 96 186 298 410
1-(Jubilee)-Same cover; Boogey Man, Satanas, & The Sorcerer & His Apprentice 26 52 78 152 244 335
1-(Barrel O' Fun)-L. B. Cole-c; Barrel O' Fun overprinted in indicia; Li'l Cactus, Cuckoo Sheriff (humorous) 18 36 54 105 165 225

GREAT DOGPATCH MYSTERY (See Mammy Yokum & the...)

GREATEST BATMAN STORIES EVER TOLD, THE
DC Comics
Hardcover ($24.95) 50.00
Softcover ($15.95) "Greatest DC Stories Vol. 2" on spine 20.00
Vol. 2 softcover (1992, $16.95) "Greatest DC Stories Vol. 7" on spine 20.00

GREATEST FLASH STORIES EVER TOLD, THE
DC Comics: 1991
nn-Hardcover ($29.95); Infantino-c 45.00
nn-Softcover ($14.95) 20.00

GREATEST GOLDEN AGE STORIES EVER TOLD, THE
DC Comics: 1990 ($24.95, hardcover)
nn-Ordway-c 60.00

GREATEST JOKER STORIES EVER TOLD, THE (See Batman)
DC Comics: 1983
Hardcover ($19.95)-Kyle Baker painted-c 45.00
Softcover ($14.95) 20.00
Stacked Deck...Expanded Edition (1992, $29.95)-Longmeadow Press Publ. 32.00

GREATEST 1950s STORIES EVER TOLD, THE
DC Comics: 1990
Hardcover ($29.95)-Kubert-c 55.00
Softcover ($14.95) "Greatest DC Stories Vol. 5" on spine 22.00

GREATEST TEAM-UP STORIES EVER TOLD, THE
DC Comics: 1989
Hardcover ($24.95)-DeVries and Infantino painted-c 55.00
Softcover ($14.95) "Greatest DC Stories Vol. 4" on spine; Adams-c 22.00

GREATEST SUPERMAN STORIES EVER TOLD, THE
DC Comics: 1987
Hardcover ($24.95) 50.00
Softcover ($15.95) 22.00

GREAT EXPLOITS
Decker Publ./Red Top: Oct, 1957
1-Krigstein-a(2) (re-issue on cover); reprints Daring Advs. #6 by Approved Comics 6 12 18 31 38 45

GREAT FOODINI, THE (See Foodini)

GREAT GAZOO, THE (The Flintstones)(TV)
Charlton Comics: Aug, 1973 - No. 20, Jan, 1977 (Hanna-Barbera)
1 4 8 12 24 37 50
2-10 3 6 9 14 19 24
11-20 2 4 6 10 14 18

GREAT GRAPE APE, THE (TV)(See TV Stars #1)
Charlton Comics: Sept, 1976 - No. 2, Nov, 1976 (Hanna-Barbera)
1 3 6 9 20 30 40
2 2 4 6 13 18 22

GREAT LOCOMOTIVE CHASE, THE (Disney)
Dell Publishing Co.: No. 712, Sept, 1956 (one-shot)
Four Color 712-Movie, photo-c 7 14 21 47 76 105

GREAT LOVER ROMANCES (Young Lover Romances #4,5)
Toby Press: 3/51; #2, 1951(nd); #3, 1952 (nd); #6, Oct?, 1952 - No. 22, May, 1955 (Photo-c #1-5, 10 ,13, 15, 17) (no #4, 5)
1-Jon Juan story-r/Jon Juan #1 by Schomburg; Dr. Anthony King app. 18 36 54 103 162 220
2-Jon Juan, Dr. Anthony King app. 11 22 33 62 86 110
3,7,9-14,16-22: 10-Rita Hayworth photo-c. 17-Rita Hayworth & Aldo Ray photo-c 9 18 27 47 61 75
6-Kurtzman-a (10/52) 11 22 33 60 83 105
8-Five pgs. of "Pin-Up Pete" by Sparling 11 22 33 60 83 105
15-Liz Taylor photo-c 30 60 90 174 280 385

GREAT RACE, THE (See Movie Classics)

GREAT SCOTT SHOE STORE (See Bulls-Eye)

GREAT SOCIETY COMIC BOOK, THE (Political parody)
Pocket Books Inc./Parallax Pub.: 1966 ($1.00, 36 pgs., 7"x10", one-shot)
nn-Super-LBJ-c/story; 60s politicians app. as super-heroes; Tallarico-a 3 6 9 16 23 30

GREAT WEST (Magazine)
M. F. Enterprises: 1969 (B&W, 52 pgs.)
V1#1 2 4 6 10 14 18

GREAT WESTERN
Magazine Enterprises: No. 8, Jan-Mar, 1954 - No. 11, Oct-Dec, 1954
8(A-1 93)-Trail Colt by Guardineer; Powell Red Hawk-r/Straight Arrow begins, ends #11; Durango Kid story 18 36 54 103 162 220
9(A-1 105), 11(A-1 127)-Ghost Rider, Durango Kid app. in each. 9-Red Mask-c, but no app. 15 30 45 83 124 165
10(A-1 113)-The Calico Kid by Guardineer-r/Tim Holt #8; Straight Arrow, Durango Kid app. 12 24 36 69 97 125
I.W. Reprint #1,2 9: 1,2-r/Straight Arrow #36,42. 9-r/Straight Arrow #? 3 6 9 16 22 28
I.W. Reprint #8-Origin Ghost Rider(r/Tim Holt #11); Tim Holt app.; Bolle-a 3 6 9 17 25 32
NOTE: *Guardineer c-8. Powell a(r)-8-11 (from Straight Arrow).*

GREEN ARROW (See Action #440, Adventure, Brave & the Bold, DC Super Stars #17, Detective #521, Flash #217, Green Lantern #76, Justice League of America #4, Leading Comics, More Fun #73 (1st app.), Showcase '95 #9 & World's Finest Comics)

GREEN ARROW
DC Comics: May, 1983 - No. 4, Aug, 1983 (limited series)
1-Origin; Speedy cameo; Mike W. Barr scripts, Trevor Von Eeden-c/a 5.00
2-4 4.00

GREEN ARROW
DC Comics: Feb, 1988 - No. 137, Oct, 1998 ($1.00-$2.50) (Painted-c #1-3)
1-Mike Grell scripts begin, ends #80 5.00
2-49,51-74,76-86: 27,28-Warlord app. 35-38-Co-stars Black Canary; Bill Wray-i. 40-Grell-a. 47-Begin $1.50-c. 63-No longer has mature readers on-c. 63-66-Shado app. 81-Aparo-a begins, ends #100; Nuklon app. 82-Intro & death of Rival. 83-Huntress-c/story. 84, 85-Deathstroke app. 86-Catwoman-c/story w/Jim Balent layouts 2.50
50,75-($2.50, 52 pgs.): Anniversary issues. 75-Arsenal (Roy Harper) & Shado app. 3.00
0,87-96: 87-$1.95-c begins. 88-Guy Gardner, Martian Manhunter, & Wonder Woman-c/app.; Flash-c. 89-Anarky app. 90-(9/94)-Zero Hour tie-in. 0-(10/94)-1st app. Connor Hawke; Aparo-a(p). 91-(11/94). 93-1st app. Camorouge. 95-Hal Jordan cameo. 96-Intro new Force of July; Hal Jordan (Parallax) app; Oliver Queen learns that Connor Hawke is his son 2.50
97-99,102-109: 97-Begin $2.25-c; no Aparo-a. 97-99-Arsenal app. 102,103-Underworld Unleashed x-over. 104-GL(Kyle Rayner)-c/app. 105-Robin-c/app. 107-109-Thorn app. 109-Lois Lane cameo; Weeks-c. 2.50
100-($3.95)-Foil-c; Superman app. 1 3 4 6 8 10
101-Death of Oliver Queen; Superman app. 3 6 9 16 23 30
110,111-124: 110,111-GL x-over. 110-Intro Hatchet. 114-Final Night. 115-117-Black Canary & Oracle app. 2.50
125-($3.50, 48 pgs)-GL x-over cont. in GL #92 3.50
126-136: 126-Begin $2.50-c. 130-GL & Flash x-over. 132,133-JLA app. 134,135-Brotherhood of the Fist pts. 1,5. 136-Hal Jordan-c/app. 2.50
137-Last issue; Superman app.; last panel cameo of Oliver Queen 2 4 6 9 12 15
#1,000,000 (11/98) 853rd Century x-over 2.50
Annual 1-6 ('88-'94, 68 pgs.)-1-No Grell scripts. 2-No Grell scripts; recaps origin Green Arrow, Speedy, Black Canary & others. 3-Bill Wray-a. 4-50th anniversary issue. 5-Batman, Eclipso app. 6-Bloodlines; Hook app. 3.50
Annual 7-('95, $3.95)-Year One story 4.00
NOTE: *Aparo a-0, 81-85, 86 (partial),87p, 88p, 91-95, 96i, 98-100p, 109p; c-81,98-100p. Austin c-96i. Balent layouts-86. Burchett c-91-95. Campanella a-100-108i, 110-113i; c-99i, 101-108i,110-113i. Denys Cowan a-39p, 41-43p, 47p, 48p, 60p; c-41-43. Damaggio a(p)-97p, 100-108p, 110-112p; c-97-99p, 101-108p, 110-113p. Mike Grell c-1-4, 10p, 11, 39, 40, 44, 45, 47-80, Annual 4, 5. Nasser/Netzer a-89, 96. Sienkiewicz a-109i. Springer a-67, 68. Weeks c-109.*

GREEN ARROW
DC Comics: Apr, 2001 - No. 75, Aug, 2007 ($2.50/$2.99)
1-Oliver Queen returns; Kevin Smith-s/Hester-a/Wagner-painted-c 2 4 6 9 13 16
1-2nd-4th printings 3.00

Green Arrow V2 #4 © DC

Green Arrow: Year One #6 © DC

Green Lama #3 © Spark

	GD 2.0	VG 4.0	FN 6.0	VF 8.0	VF/NM 9.0	NM- 9.2

2-Batman cameo 1 2 3 4 5 7
2-2nd printing 2.50
3-5: 4-JLA app. 5.00
6-15: 7-Barry Allen & Hal Jordan app. 9,10-Stanley & his Monster app. 10-Oliver regains his soul. 12-Hawkman-c/app. 3.00
16-25: 16-Brad Meltzer-s begin; The Shade app. 18-Solomon Grundy-c/app. 19-JLA app. 22-Beatty-s; Count Vertigo app. 23-25-Green Lantern app.; Raab-s/Adlard-a 2.50
26-49: 26-Winick-s begin. 35-37-Riddler app. 43-Mia learns she's HIV+. 45-Mia becomes the new Speedy. 46-Teen Titans app. 49-The Outsiders app. 2.50
50-($3.50) Green Arrow's team and the Outsiders vs. The Riddler and Drakon 3.50
51-59: 51-Anarky app. 52-Zatanna-c/app. 55-59-Dr. Light app. 2.50
60-74: 60-One Year Later starts. 62-Begin $2.99-c; Deathstroke app. 69-Batman app. 3.00
75-($3.50) Ollie proposes to Dinah (see Black Canary mini-series); JLA app. 3.50
...: City Walls SC (2005, $17.95) r/#32, 34-39 18.00
...: Crawling Through the Wreckage SC (2007, $12.99) r/#60-65 13.00
...: Heading Into the Light SC (2006, $12.99) r/#52,54-59 13.00
...: Moving Targets SC (2006, $17.99) r/#40-50 18.00
...: Quiver HC (2002, $24.95) r/#1-10; Smith intro. 25.00
...: Quiver SC (2003, $17.95) r/#1-10; Smith intro. 18.00
...: Road to Jericho SC (2007, $17.99) r/#66-75 18.00
...Secret Files & Origins 1-(12/02, $4.95) Origin stories & profiles; Wagner-c 5.00
...: Sounds of Violence HC (2003, $19.95) r/#11-15; Hester intro. & sketch pages 20.00
...: Sounds of Violence SC (2003, $12.95) r/#11-15; Hester intro. & sketch pages 13.00
...: Straight Shooter SC (2004, $12.95) r/#26-31 13.00
...: The Archer's Quest HC (2003, $19.95) r/#16-21; pitch, script and sketch pages 20.00
...: The Archer's Quest SC (2004, $14.95) r/#16-21; pitch, script and sketch pages 15.00

GREEN ARROW/BLACK CANARY
DC Comics: Dec, 2007 - Present ($3.50/$2.99)
1-($3.50) Connor Hawke & Black Canary; follows Wedding Special; Winick-s/Chang-a 3.50
2-10-($2.99) 3-Two covers; Connor shot. 5-Dinah & Ollie's real wedding 3.00
... Wedding Special 1 (11/07, $3.99) Winick-s/Conner-a/c; Dinah & Ollie's "wedding" 4.00
... Wedding Special 1 (11/07, $3.99) 2nd printing with Ryan Sook variant-c 4.00

GREEN ARROW: THE LONG BOW HUNTERS
DC Comics: Aug, 1987 - No. 3, Oct, 1987 ($2.95, limited series, mature)
1-Grell-c/a in all 6.00
1,2-2nd printings 3.00
2,3 4.00
Trade paperback (1989, $12.95)-r/#1-3 13.00

GREEN ARROW: THE WONDER YEAR
DC Comics: Feb, 1993 - No. 4, May, 1993 ($1.75, limited series)
1-4: Mike Grell-a(p)/scripts & Gray Morrow-a(i) 2.50

GREEN ARROW: YEAR ONE
DC Comics: Early Sept, 2007 - No. 6, Late Nov, 2007 ($2.99, bi-weekly limited series)
1-6-Origin re-told; Diggle-s/Jock-a 3.00
HC (2008, $24.99) r/#1-6; intro. by Brian K. Vaughan; script and sketch pages 25.00

GREEN BERET, THE (See Tales of...)

GREEN GIANT COMICS (Also see Colossus Comics)
Pelican Publ. (Funnies, Inc.): 1940 (No price on cover; distributed in New York City only)
1-Dr. Nerod, Green Giant, Black Arrow, Mundoo & Master Mystic app.; origin Colossus (Rare) 1075 2150 3225 8170 14,585 21,000

NOTE: *The idea for this book came from George Kapitan. Printed by Moreau Publ. of Orange, N.J. as an experiment to see if they could profitably use the idle time of their 40-page Hoe color press. The experiment failed due to the difficulty of obtaining good quality color registration and Mr. Moreau believes the book never reached the stands. The book has no price or date which lends credence to this. Contains five pages reprinted from Motion Picture Funnies Weekly.*

GREEN GOBLIN
Marvel Comics: Oct, 1995 - No. 13, Oct, 1996 ($2.95/$1.95)
1-($2.95)-Scott McDaniel-c/a begins, ends #7; foil-c 3.50
2-13: 2-Begin $1.95-c. 4-Hobgoblin-c/app; Thing app. 6-Daredevil-c/app. 8-Robertson-a; McDaniel-c. 12,13-Onslaught x-over. 13-Green Goblin quits; Spider-Man app. 2.50

GREENHAVEN
Aircel Publishing: 1988 - No. 3, 1988 ($2.00, limited series, 28 pgs.)
1-3 2.50

GREEN HORNET, THE (TV)
Dell Publishing Co./Gold Key: Sept, 1953; Feb, 1967 - No. 3, Aug, 1967
Four Color 496-Painted-c. 23 46 69 167 309 450
1-Bruce Lee photo-c and back-c pin-up 17 34 51 120 223 325
2,3-Bruce Lee photo-c 12 24 36 82 146 210

GREEN HORNET, THE (Also see Kato of the... & Tales of the...)
Now Comics: Nov, 1989 - No. 14, Feb, 1991 ($1.75)
V2#1, Sept, 1991 - V2#40, Jan, 1995 ($1.95)
1 ($2.95, double-size)-Steranko painted-c; G.A. Green Hornet 5.00
1,2: 1-2nd printing ('90, $3.95)-New Butler-c 4.00
3-14: 5-Death of original ('30s) Green Hornet. 6-Dave Dorman painted-c. 11-Snyder-c 3.00
V2#1-11,13-21,24-26,28-30,32-37: 1-Butler painted-c. 9-Mayerik-c 2.50
12-($2.50)-Color Green Hornet button polybagged inside 4.00
22,23-($2.95)-Bagged w/color hologravure card 4.00
27-($2.95)-Newsstand ed. polybagged w/multi-dimensional card (1993 Anniversary Special on cover), 27-($2.95)-Direct Sale ed. polybagged w/multi-dimensional card; cover variations 3.00
31,38: 31-($2.50)-Polybagged w/trading card 2.50
39,40-Low print run 6.00
1-($2.50)-Polybagged w/button (same as #12) 3.00
2,3-($1.95)-Same as #13 & 14 2.50
Annual 1 (12/92, $2.50), Annual 1994 (10/94, $2.95) 3.50

GREEN HORNET: DARK TOMORROW
Now Comics: Jun, 1993 - No. 3, Aug, 1993 ($2.50, limited series)
1-3: Future Green Hornet 3.00

GREEN HORNET: SOLITARY SENTINEL, THE
Now Comics: Dec, 1992 - No. 3, 1993 ($2.50, limited series)
1-3 3.00

GREEN HORNET COMICS (...Racket Buster #44) (Radio, movies)
Helnit Publ. Co.(Holyoke) No. 1-6/Family Comics(Harvey) No. 7-on:
Dec, 1940 - No. 47, Sept, 1949 (See All New #13,14)(Early issues: 68 pgs.)
1-1st app. Green Hornet & Kato; origin of Green Hornet on inside front-c; intro the Black Beauty (Green Hornet's car); painted-c 511 1022 1533 3679 6440 9200
2-Early issues based on radio adventures 217 434 651 1367 2309 3250
3 150 300 450 945 1598 2250
4-6: 6-(8/41) 122 244 366 769 1297 1825
7 (6/42)-Origin The Zebra & begins; Robin Hood, Spirit of '76, Blonde Bomber & Mighty Midgets begin; new logo 100 200 300 630 1065 1500
8,10 85 170 255 536 906 1275
9-Kirby-c 105 210 315 662 1119 1575
11,12-Mr. Q in both 82 164 246 517 871 1225
13-1st Nazi-c; shows Hitler poster on-c 92 184 276 580 978 1375
14-19 65 130 195 410 693 975
20-Classic-c 80 160 240 504 852 1200
21-23,25-30 47 94 141 291 488 685
24-Sci-Fi-c 53 106 159 330 553 775
31-The Man in Black Called Fate begins (11-12/45, early app.) 49 98 147 304 507 710
32-36 36 72 108 212 341 470
37,38: Shock Gibson app. by Powell. 37-S&K Kid Adonis reprinted from Stuntman #3. 38-Kid Adonis app. 36 72 108 212 341 470
39-Stuntman story by S&K 40 80 120 238 387 535
40-47: 42-47-Kerry Drake in all. 45-Boy Explorers on-c only. 46- "Case of the Marijuana Racket" cover/story; Kerry Drake app. 28 56 84 162 261 360

NOTE: *Fuje a-23, 24, 26.* ***Henkle*** *c-7-9.* ***Kubert*** *a-20, 30.* ***Powell*** *a-7-10, 12, 14, 16-21, 30, 31(2), 32(3), 33, 34(3), 35, 36, 37(2), 38.* ***Robinson*** *a-27.* ***Schomburg*** *c-15, 17-23. Kirbyish c-7, 15. Bondage c-8, 14, 18, 26, 36.*

GREEN JET COMICS, THE (See Comic Books, Series 1)

GREEN LAMA (Also see Comic Books, Series 1, Daring Adventures #17 & Prize Comics #7)
Spark Publications/Prize No. 7 on: Dec, 1944 - No. 8, Mar, 1946
1-Intro. Lt. Hercules & The Boy Champions; Mac Raboy-c/a #1-8 115 230 345 725 1225 1725
2-Lt. Hercules borrows the Human Torch's powers for one panel 62 124 186 391 663 935
3-5,8: 4-Dick Tracy take-off in Lt. Hercules story by H. L. Gold (science fiction writer). 5-Lt. Hercules story; Little Orphan Annie, Smilin' Jack & Snuffy Smith take-off (5/45) 50 100 150 310 518 725
6-Classic Raboy swastica-c 52 104 156 322 536 750
7-X-mas-c; Raboy craft tint-c/a (note: a small quantity of NM copies surfaced) 34 68 102 198 319 440

NOTE: ***Robinson*** *a-3-5, 8.* ***Roussos*** *a-8. Formerly a pulp hero who began in 1940.*

GREEN LANTERN (1st Series) (See All-American, All Flash Quarterly, All Star Comics, The Big All-American & Comic Cavalcade)
National Periodical Publications/All-American: Fall, 1941 - No. 38, May-June, 1949 (#1-18 are quarterly)
1-Origin retold; classic Purcell-c 3000 6000 9000 22,000 38,000 61,000
2-1st book-length story 667 1334 2001 4802 8401 12,000
3-Classic German war-c by Mart Nodell 528 1056 1584 3802 6651 9500

Green Lantern #7 © DC

Green Lantern (2nd series) #110 © DC

Green Lantern (3rd series) #86 © DC

	GD 2.0	VG 4.0	FN 6.0	VF 8.0	VF/NM 9.0	NM- 9.2
4-Green Lantern & Doiby Dickles join the Army	394	788	1182	2679	4690	6700
5	300	600	900	1950	3375	4800
6,8: 8-Hop Harrigan begins; classic-c	240	480	720	1512	2556	3600
7-Robot-c.	253	506	759	1504	2697	3800
9,10: 10-Origin/1st app. Vandal Savage	213	426	639	1342	2271	3200
11-15: 12-Origin/1st app. Gambler	157	314	471	989	1670	2350
16-Classic jungle-c (scarce in high grade)	163	326	489	1027	1739	2450
17,19,20	132	264	396	832	1404	1975
18-Christmas-c	180	360	540	1134	1917	2700
21-26,28	120	240	360	756	1278	1800
27-Origin/1st app. Sky Pirate	128	256	384	806	1366	1925
29-All Harlequin issue; classic Harlequin-c	132	264	396	832	1404	1975
30-Origin/1st app. Streak the Wonder Dog by Toth (2-3/48) (scarce)	227	454	681	1430	2415	3400
31-35: 35-Kubert-c. 35-38-New logo	107	214	321	674	1137	1600
36-38: 37-Sargon the Sorcerer app.	123	240	360	775	1313	1850

NOTE: *Book-length stories #2-7.* ***Mayer/Moldoff** c-9.* ***Mayer/Purcell** c-8.* ***Purcell** c-1.* ***Mart Nodell** c-2, 3, 7.* ***Paul Reinman** c-11, 12, 15-22.* ***Toth** a-28, 30, 31, 34-38; c-28, 30, 34p, 36-38p. Cover to #8 says Fall while the indicia says Summer Issue. Streak the Wonder Dog c-30 (w/Green Lantern), 34, 36, 38.*

GREEN LANTERN (See Action Comics Weekly, Adventure Comics, Brave & the Bold, Day of Judgment, DC Special, DC Special Series, Flash, Guy Gardner, Guy Gardner Reborn, JLA, JSA, Justice League of America, Parallax: Emerald Night, Showcase, Showcase '93 #12 & Tales of The...Corps)

GREEN LANTERN (2nd Series)(Green Lantern Corps #206 on) (See Showcase #22-24)
National Periodical Publ./DC Comics: Jul/Aug, 1960 - No. 89, Apr/May 1972; No. 90, Aug/Sept. 1976 - No. 205, Oct, 1986

	GD 2.0	VG 4.0	FN 6.0	VF 8.0	VF/NM 9.0	NM- 9.2
1-(7-8/60)-Origin retold; Gil Kane-c/a continues; 1st app. Guardians of the Universe	365	730	1095	3285	6393	9500
2-1st Pieface	75	150	225	638	1219	1800
3-Contains readers poll	45	90	135	360	680	1000
4,5: 5-Origin/1st app. Hector Hammond	37	74	111	286	536	785
6-Intro Tomar-Re the alien G.L.	33	66	99	254	477	700
7-Origin/1st app. Sinestro (7-8/61)	32	64	96	246	461	675
8-1st 5700 A.D. story; grey tone-c	29	58	87	213	394	575
9,10: 9-1st Jordan Brothers; last 10¢ issue	26	52	78	192	359	525
11,12	19	38	57	135	250	365
13-Flash x-over	30	60	90	229	427	625
14-20: 14-Origin/1st app. Sonar. 16-Origin & 1st app. (Silver Age) Star Sapphire. 20-Flash x-over	15	30	45	111	206	300
21-30: 21-Origin & 1st app. Dr. Polaris. 23-1st Tattooed Man. 24-Origin & 1st app. Shark. 29-JLA cameo; 1st Blackhand	12	24	36	87	156	225
31-39: 37-1st app. Evil Star (villain)	11	22	33	77	136	195
40-Origin of Infinite Earths (10/65); 2nd solo G.A. Green Lantern in Silver Age (see Showcase #55); origin The Guardians; Doiby Dickles app.	43	86	129	344	647	950
41-44,46-50: 42-Zatanna x-over. 43-Flash x-over	9	18	27	64	110	155
45-2nd S.A. app. G.A. Green Lantern in title (6/66)	14	28	42	102	181	260
51,53-58	8	16	24	52	86	120
52-G.A. Green Lantern x-over; Sinestro app.	9	18	27	63	107	150
59-1st app. Guy Gardner (3/68)	15	30	45	108	199	290
60,62-69: 69-Wood inks; last 12¢ issue	6	12	18	39	62	85
61-G.A. Green Lantern x-over	7	14	21	47	76	105
70-75	5	10	15	32	51	70
76-(4/70)-Begin Green Lantern/Green Arrow series (by Neal Adams #76-89) ends #122 (see Flash #217 for 2nd series)	38	76	114	304	752	1200
77	10	20	30	67	116	165
78-80	8	16	24	58	97	135
81-84: 82-Wrightson-i(1 pg.). 83-G.L. reveals i.d. to Carol Ferris. 84-N. Adams/Wrightson-a (22 pgs.); last 15¢-c; partial photo-c	7	14	21	49	80	110
85,86-(52 pgs.)-Anti-drug issues. 86-G.A. Green Lantern-r; Toth-a	9	18	27	64	110	155
87-(52 pgs.): 2nd app. Guy Gardner (cameo); 1st app. John Stewart (12-1/71-72) (becomes 3rd Green Lantern in #182)	7	14	21	45	73	100
88-(2-3/72, 52 pgs.)-Unpubbed G.A. Green Lantern story; Green Lantern-r/Showcase #23. N. Adams-c/a (1 pg.)	5	10	15	32	51	70
89-(4-5/72, 52 pgs.)-G.A. Green Lantern-r; Green Lantern & Green Arrow move to Flash #217 (2nd team-up series)	7	14	21	45	73	100
90 (8-9/76)-Begin 3rd Green Lantern/Green Arrow team-up series; Mike Grell-c/a begins, ends #111	2	4	6	13	18	22
91-99	2	4	6	8	10	12
100-(1/78, Giant)-1st app. Air Wave II	2	4	6	11	16	20
101-107,111,113-115,117-119: 107-1st Tales of the G.L. Corps story	1	2	3	5	7	9
108-110-(44 pgs)-G.A. Green Lantern back-ups in each. 111-Origin retold; G.A. Green Lantern app.	1	3	4	6	8	10
112-G.A. Green Lantern origin retold	2	4	6	9	13	16
116-1st app. Guy Gardner as a G.L. (5/79)	4	8	12	22	34	45
116-Whitman variant; issue # on cover	4	8	12	28	44	60
117-119,121-(Whitman variants; low print run; none have issue # on cover)	2	4	6	8	11	14
120-122,124-150: 22-Last Green Lantern/Green Arrow team-up. 130-132-Tales of the G.L. Corps. 132-Adam Strange series begins, ends147. 136,137-1st app. Citadel; Space Ranger app. 141-1st app. Omega Men (6/81). 142,143-Omega Men app.;Perez-c. 144-Omega Men cameo. 148-Tales of the G.L. Corps begins, ends #173. 150-Anniversary issue, 52 pgs.; no G.L. Corps						6.00
123-Green Lantern back to solo action; 2nd app. Guy Gardner as Green Lantern	1	3	4	6	8	10
151-180,183,184,186,187: 159-Origin Evil Star. 160,161-Omega Men app.						4.00
181,182,185,188: 181-Hal Jordan resigns as G.L. 182-John Stewart becomes new G.L.; origin recap of Hal Jordan as G.L. 185-Origin new G.L. (John Stewart).188-I.D. revealed; Alan Moore back-up scripts.						5.00
189-193,196-199,201-205: 191-Re-intro Star Sapphire (cameo). 192-Re-intro & origin of Star Sapphire (1st full app.). 194,198-Crisis x-over. 199-Hal Jordan returns as a member of G.L. Corps (3 G.L.s now). 201-Green Lantern Corps begins (is cover title, says premiere issue), intro. Kilowog						3.50
194-Hal Jordan/Guy Gardner battle; Guardians choose Guy Gardner to become new Green Lantern						6.00
195-Guy Gardner becomes Green Lantern; Crisis on Infinite Earths x-over	2	4	6	8	10	12
200-Double-size						4.00
Annual 1 (Listed as Tales Of The Green Lantern Corps Annual 1)						
Annual 2,3 (See Green Lantern Corps Annual #2,3)						3.50
Special 1 (1988), 2 (1989)-(Both $1.50, 52 pgs.)						3.50

NOTE: ***N. Adams** a-76, 77-87p, 89; c-63, 76-89.* ***M. Anderson** a-137i.* ***Austin** a-93i, 94i, 171i.* ***Chaykin** c-196.* ***Greene** a-39-49i, 58-63i; c-54-58i.* ***Grell** a-90-100, 106, 108-111; c-90-106, 108-112.* ***Heck** a-120-122p.* ***Infantino** a-137p, 145-147p, 151, 152p.* ***Gil Kane** a-1-49p, 50-57, 58-61p, 68-75p, 85p(r), 87p(r), 88p(r), 156, 177, 184p; c-1-52, 54-61p, 67-75, 123, 154, 156, 165-171, 177, 184.* ***Newton** a-148p, 149p, 181.* ***Perez** c-132p, 141-144.* ***Sekowsky** a-65p, 170p.* ***Simonson** c-200.* ***Sparling** a-63p.* ***Starlin** c-129, 133.* ***Staton** a-117p, 123-127p, 128, 129-131p, 132-139, 140p, 141-146, 147p, 148-150, 151-155p; c-107p, 117p, 135(i), 136p, 145p, 146, 147, 148-152p, 155p.* ***Toth** a-86r, 171p.* ***Tuska** a-166-168p, 170p.*

GREEN LANTERN (3rd Series)
DC Comics: June, 1990 - No. 181, Nov, 2004 ($1.00/$1.25/$1.50/$1.75/$1.95/$1.99/$2.25)

	NM- 9.2
1-Hal Jordan, John Stewart & Guy Gardner return; Batman & JLA app.	5.00
2-26: 9-12-Guy Gardner solo story. 13-(52 pgs.). 18-Guy Gardner solo story. 19-($1.75, 52 pgs.)-50th anniversary issue; Mart Nodell (original G.A. artist) part-p on G.A. Gr.Lantern; G. Kane-c. 25-($1.75, 52 pgs.)-Hal Jordan/Guy Gardner battle	4.00
27-45,47: 30,31-Gorilla Grodd-c/story(see Flash #69). 38,39-Adam Strange-c/story. 42-Deathstroke-c/s. 47-Green Arrow x-over	3.00
46,48,49,50: 46-Superman app. cont'd in Superman #82. 48-Emerald Twilight part 1. 50-($2.95, 52 pgs.)-Glow-in-the-dark-c	6.00
0, 51-62: 51-1st app. New Green Lantern (Kyle Rayner) with new costume. 53-Superman-c/story. 55-(9/94)-Zero Hour. 0-(10/94). 56-(11/94)	4.00
63,64-Kyle Rayner vs. Hal Jordan.	4.00
65-80,82-92: 63-Begin $1.75-c. 65-New Titans app. 66,67-Flash app. 71-Batman & Robin app. 72-Shazam!-c/app. 73-Wonder Woman-c/app. 73-75-Adam Strange app. 76,77-Green Arrow x-over. 80-Final Night. 87-JLA app. 91-Genesis x-over. 92-Green Arrow x-over	3.00
81-(Regular Ed.)-Memorial for Hal Jordan (Parallax); most DC heroes app.	5.00
81-($3.95, Deluxe Edition)-Embossed prism-c	6.00
93-99: 93-Begin $1.95-c; Deadman app. 94-Superboy app. 95-Starlin-a(p). 98,99-Legion of Super-Heroes-c/app.	2.50
100-($2.95) Two covers (Jordan & Rayner); vs. Sinestro	5.00
101-106: 101-106-Hal Jordan-c/app. 103-JLA-c/app. 104-Green Arrow app. 105,106-Parallax app.	3.00
107-126: 107-Jade becomes a Green Lantern. 119-Hal Jordan/Spectre app. 125-JLA app.	2.50
127-149: 127-Begin $2.25-c. 129-Winick-s begin. 134-136-JLA-c/app. 143-Joker: Last Laugh; Lee-c. 145-Kyle becomes The Ion. 149-Superman-c/app.	2.50
150-($3.50) Jim Lee-c; Kyle becomes Green Lantern again; new costume	3.50
151-181: 151-155-Jim Lee-c: 154-Terry attacked. 155-Spectre-c/app. 162-164-Crossover with Green Arrow #23-25. 165-Raab-s begin. 169-Kilowog returns	2.50
#1,000,000 (11/98) 853rd Century x-over; Hitch & Neary-a/c	3.00
Annual 1-3: ('92-'94, 68 pgs.)-1-Eclipso app. 2 -Intro Nightblade. 3-Elseworlds story	3.50
Annual 4 (1995, $3.50)-Year One story	4.00
Annual 5,7,8 ('96, '98, '99, $2.95): 5-Legends of the Dead Earth. 7-Ghosts; Wrightson-c. 8-JLApe; Art Adams-c	3.00
Annual 6 (1997, $3.95)-Pulp Heroes story	5.00
Annual 9 (2000, $3.50) Planet DC	3.50
...80 Page Giant (12/98, $4.95) Stories by various	5.00
...80 Page Giant 2 (6/99, $4.95) Team-ups	5.00
...80 Page Giant 3 (8/00, $5.95) Darkseid vs. the GL Corps	6.00
...: 1001 Emerald Nights (2001, $6.95) Elseworlds; Guay-a/c; LaBan-s	7.00
...3-D #1 (12/98, $3.95) Jeanty-a	4.00

Green Lantern (4th series) #21 © DC

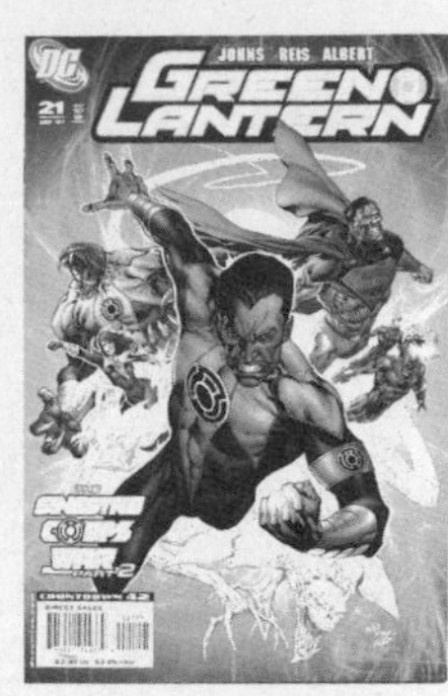

Green Lantern Corps #19 © DC

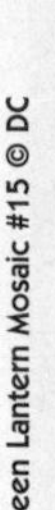
Green Lantern Mosaic #15 © DC

GD	VG	FN	VF	VF/NM	NM-
2.0	4.0	6.0	8.0	9.0	9.2

...: A New Dawn TPB (1998, $9.95)-r/#50-55 10.00
...: Baptism of Fire TPB (1999, $12.95)-r/#59,66,67,70-75 13.00
...: Brother's Keeper (2003, $12.95)-r/#151-155; Green Lantern Secret Files #3 13.00
...: Emerald Allies TPB (2000, $14.95)-r/GL/GA team-ups 15.00
...: Emerald Knights TPB (1998, $12.95)-r/Hal Jordan's return 13.00
...: Emerald Twilight nn (1994, $5.95)-r/#48-50 6.00
...: Emerald Twilight/New Dawn TPB (2003, $19.95)-r/#48-55 20.00
...: Ganthet's Tale nn (1992, $5.95, 68 pgs.)-Silver foil logo; Niven scripts; Byrne-c/a 6.00
.../Green Arrow Vol. 1 (2004, $12.95) -r/GL #76-82; intro. by O'Neil 13.00
.../Green Arrow Vol. 2 (2004, $12.95) -r/GL #83-87,89 & Flash #217-219, 226; cover gallery with 1983-84 GL/GA covers #1-7; intro. by Giordano 13.00
.../Green Arrow Collection, Vol. 2-r/GL #84-87,89 & Flash #217-219 & GL/GA #5-7 by O'Neil/Adams/Wrightson 13.00
...: New Journey, Old Path TPB (2001, $12.95)-r/#129-136 13.00
... : Our Worlds at War (8/01, $2.95) Jae Lee-c; prelude to x-over 3.00
...: Passing The Torch (2004, $12.95, TPB) r/#156,158-161 & GL Secret Files #2 13.00
...Plus 1 (12/1996, $2.95)-The Ray & Polaris-c/app. 3.00
...Secret Files 1-3 (7/98-7/02, $4.95)1-Origin stories & profiles. 2-Grell-c 5.00
.../Superman: Legend of the Green Flame (2000, $5.95) 1988 unpub. Neil Gaiman story of Hal Jordan with new art by various; Frank Miller-c 6.00
...: The Power of Ion (2003, $14.95, TPB) r/#142-150 15.00
...The Road Back nn (1992, $8.95)-r/1-8 w/covers 9.00
...: Traitor TPB (2001, $12.95) r/Legends of the DCU #20,21,28,29,37,38 13.00
...: Willworld (2001, $24.95, HC) Seth Fisher-a/J.M. DeMatteis-s; Hal Jordan 25.00
...: Willworld (2003, $17.95, SC) Seth Fisher-a/J.M. DeMatteis-s; Hal Jordan 18.00
NOTE: *Staton a(p)-9-12; c-9-12.*

GREEN LANTERN (See Tangent Comics/ Green Lantern)

GREEN LANTERN (4th Series) (Follows Hal Jordan's return in Green Lantern: Rebirth)
DC Comics: July, 2005 - Present ($3.50/$2.99)

1-($3.50) Two covers by Pacheco and Ross; Johns-s/Van Sciver and Pacheco-a 5.00
2-20-($2.99) 2-4-Manhunters app. 6-Bianchi-a. 7,8-Green Arrow app. 8-Bianchi-c. 9-Batman app.; two covers by Bianchi and Van Sciver. 10,11-Reis-a. 17-19-Star Sapphire returns. 18-Acuna-a; Sinestro Corps back-ups begin 3.00
8-Variant-c by Neal Adams 8.00
21-Sinestro Corps War pt. 2 5.00
21-2nd printing with variant green hued background-c 3.00
22-24: 22-Sinestro Corps War pt. 4; green hued-c. 23-Part 6. 24-Part 8 4.00
22,23-2nd printings. 22-Yellow hued-c. 23-B&W Hal Jordan with colored rings 3.00
25-($4.99) Sinestro Corps War conclusion; Ivan Reis-c 6.00
25-($4.99) Variant cover by Gary Frank; Sinestro Corps War conclusion 8.00
26-33: 26-Alpha Lanterns. 29-32-Childhood & origin re-told. 32,33-Sinestro app. 3.00
...Secret Files and Origins 2005 (6/05, $4.99) Johns-s/Cooke & Van Sciver-a; profiles with art by various incl. Chaykin, Gibbons, Gleason, Igle; Pacheco-c 5.00
.../Sinestro Corps: Secret Files 1 (2/08, $4.99) Profiles of Green Lanterns and Corps info 5.00
...: No Fear HC (2006, $24.99) r/#1-6 & Secret Files and Origins 25.00
...: No Fear SC (2008, $12.99) r/#1-6 & Secret Files and Origins 13.00
...: Revenge of the Green Lanterns HC (2006, $19.99) r/#7-13; variant cover gallery 20.00
...: Tales of the Sinestro Corps HC (2008, $29.99, d.j.) r/back-up stories from #18-20, Tales of the Sinestro Corps series, Green Lantern: Sinestro Corps Special and Sinestro Corps: Secret Files 30.00
...: The Sinestro Corps War Vol. 1 HC (2008, $24.99, d.j.) r/#21-23, Green Lantern Corps #14-15 and Green Lantern: Sinestro Corps Special 25.00
...: The Sinestro Corps War Vol. 2 HC (2008, $24.99, d.j.) r/#24,25, Green Lantern Corps #16-19; interview with the creators and sketch art 25.00
... - Wanted: Hal Jordan HC (2007, $19.99) r/#14-20 without Sinestro Corps back-ups 20.00

GREEN LANTERN ANNUAL NO. 1, 1963
DC Comics: 1998 ($4.95, one-shot)

1-Reprints Golden Age & Silver Age stories in 1963-style 80 pg. Giant format; new Gil Kane sketch art 5.00

GREEN LANTERN: BRIGHTEST DAY; BLACKEST NIGHT
DC Comics: 2002 ($5.95, squarebound, one-shot)

nn-Alan Scott vs. Solomon Grundy in 1944; Snyder III-c/a; Seagle-s 6.00

GREEN LANTERN: CIRCLE OF FIRE
DC Comics: Early Oct, 2000 - No. 2, Late Oct, 2000 (limited series)

1-($4.95) Intro. other Green Lanterns 5.00
2-($3.75) 4.00
Green Lantern (x-overs)- .../Adam Strange; .../Atom; .../Firestorm; ... /Green Lantern, Winick-s; .../Power Girl (all $2.50-c) 2.50
TPB (2002, $17.95) r/#1,2 & x-overs 18.00

GREEN LANTERN CORPS, THE (Formerly Green Lantern; see Tales of...)
DC Comics: No. 206, Nov, 1986 - No. 224, May, 1988

206-223: 212-John Stewart marries Katma Tui. 220,221-Millennium tie-ins 3.00
224-Double-size last issue 4.00
...Corps Annual 2,3- (12/86,8/87) 1-Formerly Tales of ...Annual #1; Alan Moore scripts. 3-Indicia says Green Lantern Annual #3; Moore scripts; Byrne-a 3.00
NOTE: *Austin a-Annual 3i. **Gil Kane** a-223, 224p; c-223, 224, Annual 2. **Russell** a-Annual 3i. **Staton** a-207-213p, 217p, 221p, 222p, Annual 3; c-207-213p, 217p, 221p, 222p. **Willingham** a-213p, 219p, 220p, 218p, 219p, Annual 2, 3p; c-218p, 219p.*

GREEN LANTERN CORPS
DC Comics: Aug, 2006 - Present ($2.99)

1-13: 1-6,10,11-Gibbons-s. 9-Darkseid app. 3.00
14-19-Sinestro Corps War pts. 3,5,7,9,10, Epilogue 3.00
20-26: 20-Mongul app. 3.00
20-Second printing with sketch-c 3.00
...: The Dark Side of Green TPB (2007, $12.99) r/#7-13 13.00
...: To Be a Lantern TPB (2007, $12.99) r/#1-6 13.00

GREEN LANTERN CORPS QUARTERLY
DC Comics: Summer, 1992 - No. 8, Spring, 1994 ($2.50/$2.95, 68 pgs.)

1,7,8: 1-G.A. Green Lantern story; Staton-a(p). 7-Painted-c; Tim Vigil-a. 8-Lobo-c/s 3.50
2-6: 2-G.A. G.L.-c/story; Austin-c(i); Gulacy-a(p). 3-G.A. G.L. story. 4-Austin-i 3.00

GREEN LANTERN CORPS: RECHARGE
DC Comics: Nov, 2005 - No. 5, Mar, 2006 ($3.50/$2.99, limited series)

1-($3.50) Kyle Rayner, Guy Gardner & Kilowog app.; Gleason-a 3.50
2-5-($2.99) 3.00
TPB (2006, $12.99) r/series 13.00

GREEN LANTERN: DRAGON LORD
DC Comics: 2001 - No. 3, 2001 ($4.95, squarebound, limited series)

1-3: A G.L. in ancient China; Moench-s/Gulacy-c/a 5.00

GREEN LANTERN: EMERALD DAWN (Also see Emerald Dawn)
DC Comics: Dec, 1989 - No. 6, May, 1990 ($1.00, limited series)

1-Origin retold; Giffen plots in all 5.00
2-6: 4-Re-intro. Tomar-Re 4.00

GREEN LANTERN: EMERALD DAWN II (Emerald Dawn II #1 & 2)
DC Comics: Apr, 1991 - No. 6, Sept, 1991 ($1.00, limited series)

1-6 2.50
TPB (2003, $12.95) r/#1-6; Alan Davis-c 13.00

GREEN LANTERN: EVIL'S MIGHT (Elseworlds)
DC Comics: 2002 - No. 3 ($5.95, squarebound, limited series)

1-3-Kyle Rayner in 19th century NYC; Rogers-a; Chaykin & Tischman-s 6.00

GREEN LANTERN: FEAR ITSELF
DC Comics: 1999 (Graphic novel)

Hardcover ($24.95) Ron Marz-s/Brad Parker painted-a 25.00
Softcover ($14.95) 15.00

GREEN LANTERN/FLASH: FASTER FRIENDS (See Flash/Green Lantern...)
DC Comics: 1997 ($4.95, limited series)

1-Marz-s 5.00

GREEN LANTERN GALLERY
DC Comics: Dec, 1996 ($3.50, one-shot)

1-Wraparound-c; pin-ups by various 3.50

GREEN LANTERN/GREEN ARROW (Also see The Flash #217)
DC Comics: Oct, 1983 - No. 7, April, 1984 (52-60 pgs.)

1-7- r-Green Lantern #76-89 4.00
NOTE: ***Neal Adams** r-1-7; c-1-4. **Wrightson** r-4, 5.*

GREEN LANTERN · LEGACY: THE LAST WILL & TESTAMENT OF HAL JORDAN
DC Comics: 2002 ($24.95, hardcover graphic novel)

Hardcover-Anderson & Sienkiewicz-a/c; Kelly-s; Return of Oa 25.00
Softcover (2004, $17.95) 18.00

GREEN LANTERN: MOSAIC (Also see Cosmic Odyssey #2)
DC Comics: June, 1992 - No. 18, Nov, 1993 ($1.25)

1-18: Featuring John Stewart. 1-Painted-c by Cully Hamner 2.50

GREEN LANTERN: REBIRTH
DC Comics: Dec, 2004 - No. 6, May, 2005 ($2.95, limited series)

1-Johns-s/Van Sciver-a; Hal Jordan as The Spectre on-c 8.00
1-2nd printing; Hal Jordan as Green Lantern on-c 4.00
1-3rd printing; B&W-c version of 1st printing 3.00
2-Guy Gardner becomes a Green Lantern again; JLA app. 5.00
2-2nd & 3rd printings 3.00

Green Mask #7 © FOX

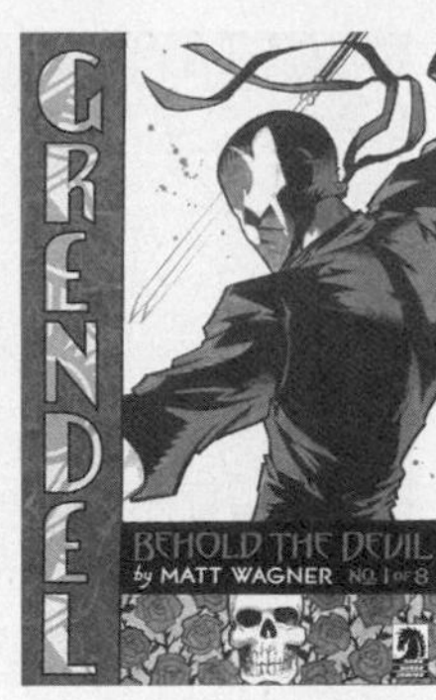

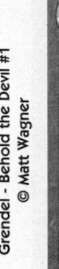

Grendel - Behold the Devil #1 © Matt Wagner

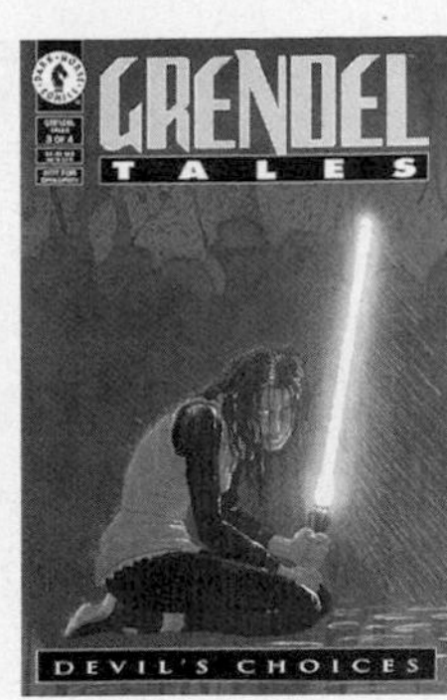

Grendel Tales: Devil's Choices #3 © Matt Wagner

GD VG FN VF VF/NM NM-
2.0 4.0 6.0 8.0 9.0 9.2

3-6: 3-Sinestro returns. 4-6-JLA & JSA app. 3.00
HC (2005, $24.99, dust jacket) r/series & Wizard preview; intro. by Brad Meltzer 25.00
SC (2007, $14.99) r/series & Wizard preview; intro. by Brad Meltzer 15.00

GREEN LANTERN/SENTINEL: HEART OF DARKNESS
DC Comics: Mar, 1998 - No. 3, May, 1998 ($1.95, limited series)
1-3-Marz-s/Pelletier-a 3.00

GREEN LANTERN/SILVER SURFER: UNHOLY ALLIANCES
DC Comics: 1995 ($4.95, one-shot)(Prelude to DC Versus Marvel)
nn-Hal Jordan app. 5.00

GREEN LANTERN SINESTRO CORPS SPECIAL (Continues in Green Lantern #21)
DC Comics: Aug, 2007 ($4.99, one-shot)
1-Kyle Rayner becomes Parallax; Cyborg Superman & Earth-Prime Superboy app.; Johns-s; Van Sciver-a/c; back-up story origin of Sinestro; Gibbons-a; Sinestro on cover 8.00
1-(2nd printing) Kyle Rayner as Parallax on cover 6.00
1-(3rd printing) Sinestro cover with muted colors 5.00

GREEN LANTERN: THE GREATEST STORIES EVER TOLD
DC Comics: 2006 ($19.99, TPB)
SC-Reprints Showcase #22; G.L. #1,31,74,87,172; ('90 series) #3, and others; Ross-c 20.00

GREEN LANTERN: THE NEW CORPS
DC Comics:1999 - No. 2, 1999 ($4.95, limited series)
1,2-Kyle recruits new GLs; Eaton-a 5.00

GREEN LANTERN VS. ALIENS
Dark Horse Comics: Sept, 2000 - No. 4, Dec, 2000 ($2.95, limited series)
1-4: 1-Hal Jordan and GL Corps vs. Aliens; Leonardi-p. 2-4-Kyle Rayner 3.00

GREEN MASK, THE (See Mystery Men)
Summer, 1940 - No. 9, 2/42; No. 10, 8/44 - No. 11, 11/44;
Fox Features Syndicate: V2#1, Spring, 1945 - No. 6, 10-11/46

	GD	VG	FN	VF	VF/NM	NM-
V1#1-Origin The Green Mask & Domino; reprints/Mystery Men #1-3,5-7; Lou Fine-c	335	670	1005	2278	3989	5700
2-Zanzibar The Magician by Tuska	132	264	396	832	1404	1975
3-Powell-a; Marijuana story	83	166	249	523	887	1250
4-Navy Jones begins, ends #6	65	130	195	410	693	975
5	53	106	159	330	553	775
6-The Nightbird begins, ends #9; bondage/torture-c	45	90	135	279	465	650
7-9: 9(2/42)-Becomes The Bouncer #10(nn) on? & Green Mask #10 on	39	78	117	227	369	510
10,11: 10-Origin One Round Hogan & Rocket Kelly	30	60	90	176	283	390
V2#1	23	46	69	135	218	300
2-6	19	38	57	112	176	240

GREEN PLANET, THE
Charlton Comics: 1962 (one-shot) (12¢)
nn-Giordano-c; sci-fi 6 12 18 43 69 95

GREEN TEAM (See Cancelled Comic Cavalcade & 1st Issue Special)

GREETINGS FROM SANTA (See March of Comics No. 48)

GRENDEL (Also see Primer #2, Mage and Comico Collection)
Comico: Mar, 1983 - No. 3, Feb, 1984 ($1.50, B&W)(#1 has indicia to Skrog #1)

	GD	VG	FN	VF	VF/NM	NM-
1-Origin Hunter Rose	10	20	30	71	126	180
2,3: 2-Origin Argent	8	16	24	52	86	120

GRENDEL
Comico: Oct, 1986 - No. 40, Feb, 1990 ($1.50/$1.95/$2.50, mature)
1 1 2 3 5 7 9
1,2: 2nd printings 3.00
2,3,5-15: 13-15-Ken Steacy-c. 4.00
4,16: 4-Dave Stevens-c(i). 16-Re-intro Mage (series begins, ends #19) 6.00
17-40: 24-25,27-28,30-31-Snyder-c/a 3.00
Devil by the Deed (Graphic Novel, 10/86, $5.95, 52 pgs.)-r/Grendel back-ups/ Mage 6-14; Alan Moore intro. 1 2 3 4 5 7
Devil's Legacy ($14.95, 1988, Graphic Novel) 2 4 6 9 12 15
Devil's Vagary (10/87, B&W & red)-No price; included in Comico Collection 2 4 6 8 10 12

GRENDEL (Title series): **Dark Horse Comics**
--ARCHIVES, 5/07 ($14.95, HC) r/1st apps. in Primer #2 and Grendel #1-3; Wagner intro. 15.00
--BEHOLD THE DEVIL, No. 0, 7/07 - No. 8, 6/08 ($3.50/50¢, B&W&Red)
0-(50¢-c) Prelude to series; Matt Wagner-s/a; interview with Wagner 2.25

GD VG FN VF VF/NM NM-
2.0 4.0 6.0 8.0 9.0 9.2

1-8-Matt Wagner-s/a/c in all 3.50
--BLACK, WHITE, AND RED, 11/98 - No. 4, 2/99 ($3.95, anthology)
1-Wagner-s in all. Art by Sale, Leon and others 5.00
2-4: 2-Mack, Chadwick-a. 3-Allred, Kristensen-a. 4-Pearson, Sprouse-a 4.00
--CLASSICS, 7/95 - 8/95 ($3.95, mature) 1,2-reprints; new Wagner-c 4.00
--CYCLE, 10/95 ($5.95) 1-nn-history of Grendel by M. Wagner & others 6.00
--DEVIL BY THE DEED, 7/93 ($3.95, varnish-c) 1-nn-M. Wagner-c/a/scripts; r/Grendel back-ups from Mage #6-14 4.00
Reprint (12/97, $3.95) w/pin-ups by various 4.00
Hardcover (2007, $12.95) reprint recolored to B&W&red; includes covers and intros from previously reprinted editions 13.00
--DEVIL CHILD, 6/99 - No. 2, 7/99 ($2.95, mature) 1,2-Sale & Kristiansen-a/Schutz-s 3.00
--DEVIL QUEST, 11/95 ($4.95) 1-nn-Prequel to Batman/Grendel II; M. Wagner story & art; r/back-up story from Grendel Tales series. 5.00
--DEVILS AND DEATHS, 10/94 - 11/94 ($2.95, mature) 1,2 3.00
: DEVIL'S LEGACY, 3/00 - No. 12, 2/01 ($2.95, reprints 1986 series, recolored)
1-12-Wagner-s/c; Pander Bros.-a 3.00
: DEVIL'S REIGN, 5/04 - No. 7, 12/04 ($3.50, repr. 1989 series #34-40, recolored)
1-7-Sale-c/a. 3.50
: GOD AND THE DEVIL, No. 0, 1/03 - No. 10, 12/03 ($3.50/$4.99, repr. 1986 series, recolored)
0-9: 0-Sale-c/a; r/#23. 1-9-Snyder-c 3.50
10-($4.99) Double-sized; Snyder-c 5.00
--RED, WHITE & BLACK, 9/02 - No. 4, 12/02 ($4.99, anthology)
1-4-Wagner-s in all. 1-Art by Thompson, Sakai, Mahfood and others. 2-Kelley Jones, Watson, Brereton, Hester & Parks-a. 3-Oeming, Noto, Cannon, Ashley Wood, Huddleston-a 4-Chiang, Dalrymple, Robertson, Snyder III and Zulli-a 5.00
TPB (2005, $19.95) r/#1-4; cover gallery, artist bios 20.00
--TALES: DEVIL'S CHOICES, 3/95 - 6/95 ($2.95, mature) 1-4 3.00
--TALES: FOUR DEVILS, ONE HELL, 8/93 - 1/94 ($2.95, mature)
1-6-Wagner painted-c 3.00
TPB (12/94, $17.95) r/#1-6 18.00
--TALES: HOMECOMING, 12/94 - 2/95 ($2.95, mature) 1-3 3.00
--TALES: THE DEVIL IN OUR MIDST, 5/94 - 9/95 ($2.95, mature) 1-5-Wagner painted-c 3.00
--TALES: THE DEVIL MAY CARE, 12/95 - No. 6, 5/96 ($2.95, mature)
1-6-Terry LaBan scripts. 5-Batman/Grendel II preview 3.00
--TALES: THE DEVIL'S APPRENTICE, 9/97 - No. 3, 11/97 ($2.95, mature)
1-3 3.00
: THE DEVIL INSIDE, 9/01 - No. 3, 11/01 ($2.99)
1-3-r/#13-15 with new Wagner-c 3.00
: WAR CHILD, 8/92 - No. 10, 6/93 ($2.50, lim. series, mature)
1-9: 1-4-Bisley painted-c; Wagner-i & scripts in all 3.00
10-($3.50, 52 pgs.) Wagner-c 4.00
Limited Edition Hardcover ($99.95) 100.00

GREYFRIARS BOBBY (Disney)(Movie)
Dell Publishing Co.: No. 1189, Nov, 1961 (one-shot)
Four Color 1189-Photo-c (scarce) 7 14 21 47 76 105

GREYLORE
Sirius: 12/85 - No. 5, Sept, 1986 ($1.50/$1.75, high quality paper)
1-5: Bo Hampton-a in all 2.50

GREYSHIRT: INDIGO SUNSET (Also see Tomorrow Stories)
America's Best Comics: Dec, 2001 - No. 6, Aug, 2002 ($3.50, limited series)
1-6-Veitch-s/a. 4-Back-up w/John Severin-a. 6-Cho-a 3.50
TPB (2002, $19.95) r/#1-6; preface by Alan Moore 20.00

GRIDIRON GIANTS
Ultimate Sports Ent.: 2000 - No. 2 ($3.95, cardstock covers)
1,2-NFL players Sanders, Marino, Plummer, T. Davis battle evil 4.00

GRIFFIN, THE
DC Comics: 1991 - No. 6, 1991 ($4.95, limited series, 52 pgs.)
Book 1-6: Matt Wagner painted-c 5.00

GRIFTER (Also see Team 7 & WildC.A.T.S)
Image Comics (WildStorm Prod.): May, 1995 - No. 10, Mar, 1996 ($1.95)
1 ($1.95, Newsstand)-WildStorm Rising Pt. 5 2.50
1-10:1 ($2.50, Direct)-WildStorm Rising Pt. 5, bound-in trading card 3.00
...: One Shot (1/95, $4.95) Flip-c 5.00

Grifter #3 © WSP

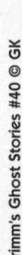

Grimm's Ghost Stories #40 © GK

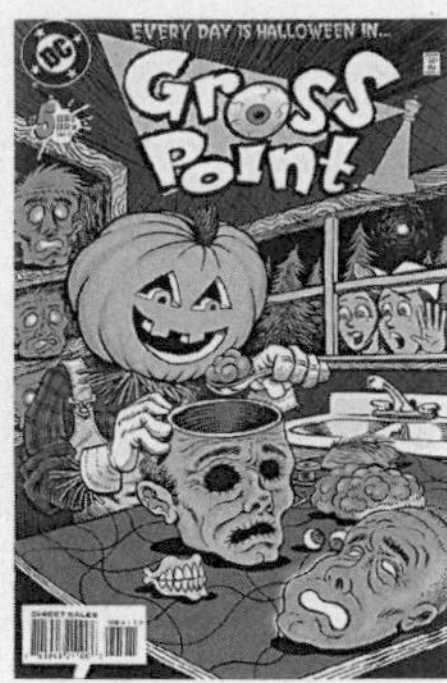

Gross Point #5 © DC

GD VG FN VF VF/NM NM-
2.0 4.0 6.0 8.0 9.0 9.2

GRIFTER
Image Comics (WildStorm Prod.): V2#1, July, 1996 - No. 14, Aug, 1997 ($2.50)
V2#1-14: Steven Grant scripts 3.00

GRIFTER & MIDNIGHTER
DC Comics (WildStorm Prod.): May, 2007 - No. 6, Oct, 2007 ($2.99, limited series)
1-6-Dixon-s/Benjamin-a/c. 1,3-The Authority app. 3.00
TPB (2008, $17.99) r/#1-6 18.00

GRIFTER AND THE MASK
Dark Horse Comics: Sept, 1996 - No. 2, Oct, 1996 ($2.50, limited series)
(1st Dark Horse Comics/Image x-over)
1,2: Steve Seagle scripts 3.00

GRIFTER/BADROCK (Also see WildC.A.T.S & Youngblood)
Image Comics (Extreme Studios): Oct, 1995 - No.2, Nov, 1995 ($2.50, unfinished lim. series)
1,2: 2-Flip book w/Badrock #2 2.50

GRIFTER/SHI
Image Comics (WildStorm Productions): Apr, 1996 - No. 2, May, 1996 ($2.95, limited series)
1,2: 1-Jim Lee-c/a(p); Travis Charest-a(p). 2-Billy Tucci-c/a(p); Travis Charest-a(p) 3.00

GRIM GHOST, THE
Atlas/Seaboard Publ.: Jan, 1975 - No. 3, July, 1975
1-3: Fleisher-s in all. 1-Origin. 2-Son of Satan; Colan-a. 3-Heath-c
1 3 4 6 8 10

GRIMJACK (Also see Demon Knight & Starslayer)
First Comics: Aug, 1984 - No. 81, Apr, 1991 ($1.00/$1.95/$2.25)
1-John Ostrander scripts & Tim Truman-c/a begins. 3.00
2-25: 20-Sutton-c/a begins. 22-Bolland-a. 2.50
26-2nd color Teenage Mutant Ninja Turtles 4.00
27-74,76-81 (Later issues $1.95, $2.25): 30-Dynamo Joe x-over; 31-Mandrake-c/a begins. 73,74-Kelley Jones-a 2.50
75-($5.95, 52 pgs.)-Fold-out map; coated stock 6.00
The Legend of Grimjack Vol. 1 (IDW Publishing, 2004, $19.99) r/Starslayer #10-18; 8 new pages & art 20.00
The Legend of Grimjack Vol. 2 (IDW, 2005, $19.99) r/#1-7; unpublished art 20.00
The Legend of Grimjack Vol. 3 (IDW, 2005, $19.99) r/#8-14; cover gallery 20.00
The Legend of Grimjack Vol. 4 (IDW, 2005, $24.99) r/#15-21; cover gallery 25.00
The Legend of Grimjack Vol. 5 (IDW, 5/06, $24.99) r/#22-30; cover gallery 25.00
The Legend of Grimjack Vol. 6 (IDW, 1/07, $24.99) r/#31-37; cover gallery 25.00
The Legend of Grimjack Vol. 7 (IDW, 4/07, $24.99) r/#38-46; covers; "Rough Trade" 25.00
NOTE: *Truman c/a-1-17.*

GRIMJACK CASEFILES
First Comics: Nov, 1990 - No. 5, Mar, 1991 ($1.95, limited series)
1-5 Reprints 1st stories from Starslayer #10 on 2.50

GRIMJACK: KILLER INSTINCT
IDW Publ.: Jan, 2005 - No. 6, June, 2005 ($3.99, limited series)
1-6-Ostrander-s/Truman-a 4.00

GRIMM'S GHOST STORIES (See Dan Curtis)
Gold Key/Whitman No. 55 on: Jan, 1972 - No. 60, June, 1982 (Painted-c #1-42,44,46-56)
1 4 8 12 22 34 45
2-5,8: 5,8-Williamson-a 2 4 6 13 18 22
6,7,9,10 2 4 6 11 16 20
11-20 2 4 6 8 11 14
21-42,45-54: 32,34-Reprints. 45-Photo-c 1 3 4 6 8 10
43,44,55-60: 43,44-(52 pgs.). 43-Photo-c. 58(2/82). 59(4/82)-Williamson-a(r/#8). 60(6/82)
2 4 6 8 11 14
Mini-Comic No. 1 (3-1/4x6-1/2", 1976) 1 3 4 6 8 10
NOTE: *Reprints-#32?, 34?, 39, 43, 44, 47?, 53; 56-60(1/3).* ***Bolle*** *a-8, 17, 22-25, 27, 29(2), 33, 35, 41, 43r, 45(2), 48(2), 50, 52, 57.* ***Celardo*** *a-17, 26, 28p, 30, 31, 43(2), 45.* ***Lopez*** *a-24, 25.* ***McWilliams*** *a-33, 44r, 48, 54(2), 57, 58.* ***Win Mortimer*** *a-31, 33, 49, 51, 55, 56, 58(2), 59, 60.* ***Roussos*** *a-25, 30.* ***Sparling*** *a-23, 24, 28, 30, 31, 33, 43r, 44, 45, 51(2), 52, 56-58, 59(2), 60.* ***Spiegle*** *a-44.*

GRIN (The American Funny Book) (Satire)
APAG House Pubs: Nov, 1972 - No. 3, April, 1973 (Magazine, 52 pgs.)
1-Parodies-Godfather, All in the Family 3 6 9 16 23 30
2,3 2 4 6 10 14 18

GRIN & BEAR IT (See Gags)
Dell Publishing Co.: No. 28, 1941
Large Feature Comic 28 16 32 48 94 147 200

GRIPS (Extreme violence)
Silverwolf Comics: Sept, 1986 - No. 4, Dec, 1986 ($1.50, B&W, mature)
1-Tim Vigil-c/a in all 6.00
2-4 4.00

GRIP: THE STRANGE WORLD OF MEN
DC Comics (Vertigo): Jan, 2002 - No. 5, May, 2002 ($2.50, limited series)
1-4-Gilbert Hernandez-s/a 2.50

GRIT GRADY (See Holyoke One-Shot No. 1)

GROO (Sergio Aragonés'...)
Image Comics: Dec, 1994 - No. 12, Dec, 1995 ($1.95)
1-12: 2-Indicia reads #1, Jan, 1995; Aragonés-c/a in all 3.50

GROO (Sergio Aragonés'...)
Dark Horse Comics: Jan, 1998 - No. 4, Apr, 1998 ($2.95)
1-4: Aragonés-c/a in all 4.00

GROO CHRONICLES, THE (Sergio Aragonés)
Marvel Comics (Epic Comics): June, 1989 - No. 6, Feb, 1990 ($3.50)
Book 1-6: Reprints early Pacific issues 3.50

GROO SPECIAL
Eclipse Comics: Oct, 1984 ($2.00, 52 pgs., Baxter paper)
1-Aragonés-c/a 3 6 9 14 20 26

GROO THE WANDERER (See Destroyer Duck #1 & Starslayer #5)
Pacific Comics: Dec, 1982 - No. 8, Apr, 1984
1-Aragonés-c/a(p) in all; Aragonés bio., photo 2 4 6 11 16 20
2-5: 5-Deluxe paper (1.00-c) 2 4 6 8 11 14
6-8 2 4 6 9 13 16

GROO THE WANDERER (Sergio Aragonés'...) (See Marvel Graphic Novel #32)
Marvel Comics (Epic Comics): March, 1985 - No. 120, Jan, 1995
1-Aragonés-c/a in all 2 4 6 9 13 16
2-10 1 2 3 5 6 8
11-20,50-($1.50, double size) 5.00
21-49,51-99: 87-direct sale only, high quality paper 3.00
100-($2.95, 52 pgs.) 5.00
101-120 4.00
Groo Carnival, The (12/91, $8.95)-r/#9-12 11.00
Groo Garden, The (4/94, $10.95)-r/#25-28 11.00

GROOVY (Cartoon Comics - not CCA approved)
Marvel Comics Group: March, 1968 - No. 3, July, 1968
1-Monkees, Ringo Starr, Sonny & Cher, Mamas & Papas photos
8 16 24 58 97 135
2,3 6 12 18 39 62 85

GROSS POINT
DC Comics: Aug, 1997 - No. 14, Aug, 1998 ($2.50)
1-14: 1-Waid/Augustyn-s 2.50

GROUNDED
Image Comics: July, 2005 - No. 6, May, 2006 ($2.95/$2.99, limited series)
1-6-Mark Sable-s/Paul Azaceta-a. 1-Mike Oeming-c 3.00
Vol. 1: Powerless TPB (2006, $14.99) r/#1-6; sketch pages and creator bios 15.00

GRRL SCOUTS (Jim Mahfood's...) (Also see 40 oz. Collected)
Oni Press: Mar,1999 - No. 4, Dec, 1999 ($2.95, B&W, limited series)
1-4-Mahfood-s/c/a 3.00
TPB (2003, $12.95) r/#1-4; pin-ups by Warren, Winick, Allred, Fegredo and others 13.00

GRRL SCOUTS: WORK SUCKS
Image Comics: Feb, 2003 - No. 4, May, 2003 ($2.95, B&W, limited series)
1-4-Mahfood-s/c/a 3.00
TPB (2004, $12.95) r/#1-4; pin-ups by Oeming, Dwyer, Tennapel and others 13.00

GUADALCANAL DIARY (See American Library)

GUARDIAN ANGEL
Image Comics: May, 2002 - No. 2, July, 2002 ($2.95)
1,2-Peterson-s/Wiesenfeld-a 3.00

GUARDIANS
Marvel Comics: Sept, 2004 - No. 5, Dec, 2004 ($2.99, limited series)
1-5-Sumerak-s/Casey Jones-a 3.00

GUARDIANS OF JUSTICE & THE O-FORCE
Shadow Comics: 1990 (no date) ($1.50, 7-1/2 x10-1/4)
1-Super-hero group 2.50

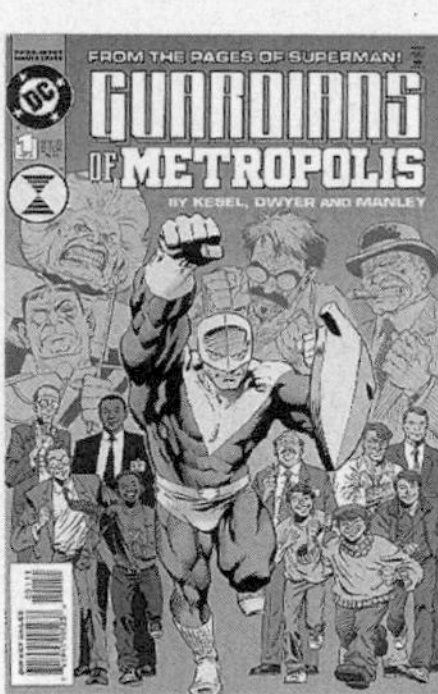

Guardians of Metropolis #1 © DC

Guns Against Gangsters #1 © NOVP

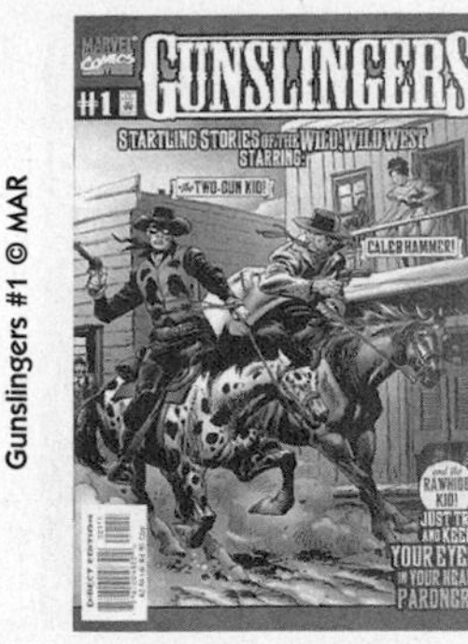

Gunslingers #1 © MAR

	GD	VG	FN	VF	VF/NM	NM-
	2.0	4.0	6.0	8.0	9.0	9.2

GUARDIANS OF METROPOLIS
DC Comics: Nov, 1995 - Feb, 1995 ($1.50, limited series)

1-4: 1-Superman & Granny Goodness app. 2.50

GUARDIANS OF THE GALAXY (Also see The Defenders #26, Marvel Presents #3, Marvel Super-Heroes #18, Marvel Two-In-One #5)
Marvel Comics: June, 1990 - No. 62, July, 1995 ($1.00/$1.25)

1-Valentino-c/a(p) begin. 3.00
2-16: 2-Zeck-c(i). 5-McFarlane-c(i). 7-Intro Malevolence (Mephisto's daughter); Perez-c(i). 8-Intro Rancor (descendant of Wolverine) in cameo. 9-1st full app. Rancor; Rob Liefeld-c(i). 10-Jim Lee-c(i). 13,14-1st app. Spirit of Vengeance (futuristic Ghost Rider). 14-Spirit of Vengeance vs. The Guardians. 15-Starlin-c(i). 16-($1.50, 52 pgs.)-Starlin-c(i) 2.50
17-24,26-38,40-47: 17-20-31st century Punishers storyline. 20-Last $1.00-c. 21-Rancor app. 22-Reintro Starhawk. 24-Silver Surfer-c/story; Ron Lim-c. 26-Origin retold. 27-28-Infinity War x-over, 27-Inhumans app. 43-Intro Wooden (son of Thor) 2.50
25-($2.50)-Prism foil-c; Silver Surfer/Galactus-c/s 3.00
25-($2.50)-Without foil-c; newsstand edition 2.50
39-($2.95, 52 pgs.)-Embossed & holo-grafx foil-c; Dr. Doom vs. Rancor 3.00
48,49,51-62: 48-bound-in trading card sheet 2.50
50-($2.00, 52 pgs.)-Newsstand edition 2.75
50-($2.95, 52 pgs.)-Collectors ed. w/foil embossed-c 3.00
Annual 1-4: ('91-'94, 68 pgs.)-1-Origin. 2-Spirit of Vengeance-c/story. 3,4-Bagged w/card 3.00

GUARDIANS OF THE GALAXY (See Annihilation series)
Marvel Comics: July, 2008 - Present ($2.99)

1-5: 1-Pelletier-a/Abnett & Lanning-s; 2nd printing exists 3.00

GUERRILLA WAR (Formerly Jungle War Stories)
Dell Publishing Co.: No. 12, July-Sept, 1965 - No. 14, Mar, 1966

12-14 3 6 9 16 22 28

GUILTY (See Justice Traps the Guilty)

GULLIVER'S TRAVELS (See Dell Jr. Treasury No. 3)
Dell Publishing Co.: Sept-Nov, 1965 - No. 3, May, 1966

1 5 10 15 34 55 75
2,3 4 8 12 24 37 50

GUMBY
Wildcard Ink: July, 2006 - Present ($3.99)

1-3-Bob Burden & Rick Geary-s&a 4.00

GUMBY'S SUMMER FUN SPECIAL
Comico: July, 1987 ($2.50)

1-Art Adams-c/a; B. Burden scripts 3.00

GUMBY'S WINTER FUN SPECIAL
Comico: Dec, 1988 ($2.50, 44 pgs.)

1-Art Adams-c/a 3.00

GUMPS, THE (See Merry Christmas..., Popular & Super Comics)
Dell Publ. Co./Bridgeport Herald Corp.: No. 73, 1945; Mar-Apr, 1947 - No. 5, Nov-Dec, 1947

Four Color 73 (Dell)(1945) 12 24 36 86 153 220
1 (3-4/47) 15 30 45 88 137 185
2-5 11 22 33 60 83 105

GUN CANDY (Also see The Ride)
Image Comics: July, 2005 - Present ($5.99)

1,2-Stelfreeze-c/a; flip book with The Ride (1-Pearson-c. 2-Noto-c) 6.00

GUNFIGHTER (Fat & Slat #1-4) (Becomes Haunt of Fear #15 on)
E. C. Comics (Fables Publ. Co.): No. 5, Sum, 1948 - No. 14, Mar-Apr, 1950

5,6-Moon Girl in each 53 106 159 334 567 800
7-14: 14-Bondage-c 40 80 120 244 397 550

NOTE: ***Craig & H. C. Kiefer*** *art in most issues.* ***Craig*** *c-5, 6, 13, 14.* ***Feldstein/Craig*** *a-10.* ***Feldstein*** *a-7-11.* ***Harrison/Wood*** *a-13, 14.* ***Ingels*** *a-5-14; c-7-12.*

GUNFIGHTERS, THE
Super Comics (Reprints): 1963 - 1964

10-12,15,16,18: 10,11-r/Billy the Kid #s? 12-r/The Rider #5(Swift Arrow). 15-r/Straight Arrow #42; Powell-r. 16-r/Billy the Kid #?(Toby). 18-r/The Rider #3; Severin-c 2 4 6 10 14 18

GUNFIGHTERS, THE (Formerly Kid Montana)
Charlton Comics: No. 51, 10/66 - No. 52, 10/67; No. 53, 6/79 - No. 85, 7/84

51,52 2 4 6 11 16 20
53,54,56:53,54-Williamson/Torres-r/Six Gun Heroes #47,49. 56-Williamson/Severin-c; Severin-r/Sheriff of Tombstone #1 1 3 4 6 8 10
55,57-80 6.00
81-84-Lower print run 1 2 3 5 6 8
85-S&K-r/1955 Bullseye 1 3 4 6 8 10

GUNFIRE (See Deathstroke Annual #2 & Showcase 94 #1,2)
DC Comics: May, 1994 - No. 13, June, 1995 ($1.75/$2.25)

1-5,0,6-13: 2-Ricochet-c/story. 5-(9/94). 0-(10/94). 6-(11/94) 2.50

GUN GLORY (Movie)
Dell Publishing Co.: No. 846, Oct, 1957 (one-shot)

Four Color 846-Toth-a, photo-c. 8 16 24 58 97 135

GUNHAWK, THE (Formerly Whip Wilson)(See Wild Western)
Marvel Comics/Atlas (MCI): No. 12, Nov, 1950 - No. 18, Dec, 1951 (Also see Two-Gun Western #5)

12 18 36 54 105 165 225
13-18: 13-Tuska-a. 16-Colan-a. 18-Maneely-c 14 28 42 76 108 140

GUNHAWKS (Gunhawk No. 7)
Marvel Comics Group: Oct, 1972 - No. 7, October, 1973

1,6: 1-Reno Jones, Kid Cassidy; Shores-c/a(p). 6-Kid Cassidy dies 3 6 9 15 21 26
2-5,7: 7-Reno Jones solo 2 4 6 10 14 18

GUNMASTER (Becomes Judo Master #89 on)
Charlton Comics: 9/64 - No. 4, 1965; No. 84, 7/65 - No. 88, 3-4/66; No. 89, 10/67

V1#1 4 8 12 22 34 45
2,4, V5#84-86: 84-Formerly Six-Gun Heroes 3 6 9 16 22 28
V5#87-89 2 4 6 11 16 20

NOTE: *Vol. 5 was originally cancelled with #88 (3-4/66). #89 on, became Judo Master, then later in 1967, Charlton issued #89 as a Gunmaster one-shot.*

GUN RUNNER
Marvel Comics UK: Oct, 1993 - No. 6, Mar, 1994 ($1.75, limited series)

1-($2.75)-Polybagged w/4 trading cards; Spirits of Vengeance app. 3.00
2-6: 2-Ghost Rider & Blaze app. 2.50

GUNS AGAINST GANGSTERS (True-To-Life Romances #8 on)
Curtis Publications/Novelty Press: Sept-Oct, 1948 - No. 6, July-Aug, 1949; V2#1, Sept-Oct, 1949

1-Toni & Greg Gayle begins by Schomburg; L.B. Cole-c 40 80 120 235 380 525
2-L.B. Cole-c 28 56 84 162 261 360
3-6, V2#1: 6-Toni Gayle-c by Cole 25 50 75 145 233 320

NOTE: ***L. B. Cole*** *c-1-6, V2#1, 2; a-1, 2, 3(2), 4-6.*

GUNSLINGER
Dell Publishing Co.: No. 1220, Oct-Dec, 1961 (one-shot)

Four Color 1220-Photo-c 8 16 24 56 93 130

GUNSLINGER (Formerly Tex Dawson...)
Marvel Comics Group: No. 2, Apr, 1973 - No. 3, June, 1973

2,3 2 4 6 13 18 22

GUNSLINGERS
Marvel Comics: Feb, 2000 ($2.99)

1-Reprints stories of Two-Gun Kid, Rawhide Kid and Caleb Hammer 3.00

GUNSMITH CATS: (Title series), **Dark Horse Comics**

--BAD TRIP (Manga), 6/98 - No. 6, 11/98 ($2.95, B&W) 1-6 3.00
--BEAN BANDIT (Manga), 1/99 - No. 9 ($2.95, B&W, limited series) 1-9 3.00
--GOLDIE VS. MISTY (Manga), 11/97 - No. 7, 5/98 ($2.95, B&W) 1-7 3.00
--KIDNAPPED (Manga), 11/99 - No. 10, 8/00 ($2.95, B&W) 1-10 3.00
--MISTER V (Manga), 10/00 - No. 11, 8/01 ($3.50/$2.99), B&W) 1-7,9-11 3.50
8-($2.99) 3.00
--THE RETURN OF GRAY (Manga), 8/96 - No. 7, 2/97 ($2.95, B&W) 1-7 3.00
--SHADES OF GRAY (Manga), 5/97 - No. 5, 9/97 ($2.95, B&W) 1-5 3.00
--SPECIAL (Manga) Nov, 2001 ($2.99, B&W, one-shot) 3.00

GUNSMOKE (Blazing Stories of the West)
Western Comics (Youthful Magazines): Apr-May, 1949 - No. 16, Jan, 1952

1-Gunsmoke & Masked Marvel begin by Ingels; Ingels bondage-c 45 90 135 279 465 650
2-Ingels-c/a(2) 29 58 87 172 276 380
3-Ingels bondage-c/a 25 50 75 147 236 325
4-6: Ingels-c 20 40 60 115 183 250

Gunsmoke Western #68 © MAR

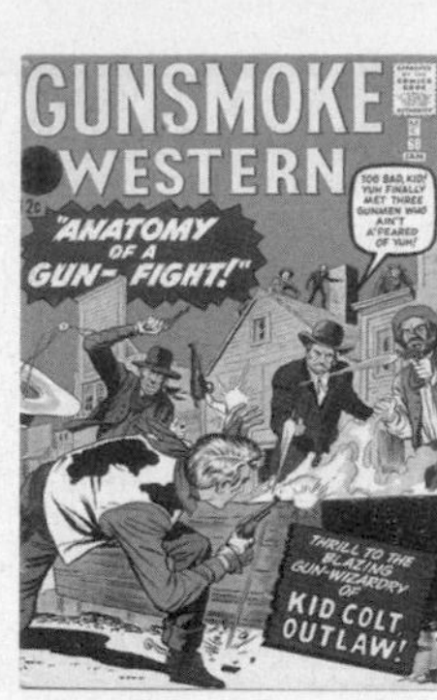

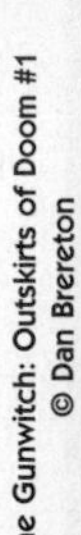

The Gunwitch: Outskirts of Doom #1 © Dan Brereton

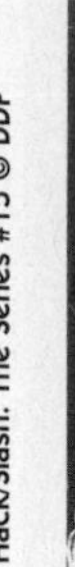

Hack/Slash: The Series #15 © DDP

GD 2.0 VG 4.0 FN 6.0 VF 8.0 VF/NM 9.0 NM- 9.2

7-10 13 26 39 74 105 135
11-16: 15,16-Western/horror stories 12 24 36 69 97 125
NOTE: *Stallman a-11, 14. Wildey a-15, 16.*

GUNSMOKE (TV)
Dell Publishing Co./Gold Key (All have James Arness photo-c): No. 679, Feb, 1956 - No. 27, Feb, 1969 - No. 6, Feb, 1970
Four Color 679(#1) 16 32 48 114 212 310
Four Color 720,769,797,844 (#2-5),6(11-1/57-58) 9 18 27 61 103 145
7,8,9,11,12-Williamson-a in all, 4 pgs. each 9 18 27 63 107 150
10-Williamson/Crandall-a, 4 pgs. 9 18 27 63 107 150
13-27 8 16 24 52 86 120
1 (Gold Key) 6 12 18 41 66 90
2-6('69-70) 4 8 12 22 34 45

GUNSMOKE TRAIL
Ajax-Farrell Publ./Four Star Comic Corp.: June, 1957 - No. 4, Dec, 1957
1 11 22 33 60 83 105
2-4 7 14 21 35 43 50

GUNSMOKE WESTERN (Formerly Western Tales of Black Rider)
Atlas Comics No. 32-35(CPS/NPI); Marvel No. 36 on: No. 32, Dec, 1955 - No. 77, July, 1963
32-Baker & Drucker-a 17 34 51 100 158 215
33,35,36-Williamson-a in each: 5,6 & 4 pgs. plus Drucker-a #33. 33-Kinstler-a? 14 28 42 81 118 155
34-Baker-a, 4 pgs.; Kirby-c 14 28 42 78 112 145
37-Davis-a(2); Williamson text illo 12 24 36 67 94 120
38,39: 39-Williamson text illo (unsigned) 10 20 30 54 72 90
40-Williamson/Mayo-a (4 pgs.) 10 20 30 58 79 100
41,42,45,46,48,49,52-54,57,58,60: 49,52-Kid from Texas story. 57-1st Two Gun Kid by Severin. 60-Sam Hawk app. in Kid Colt 8 16 24 44 57 70
43,44-Torres-a 8 16 24 44 57 70
47,51,59,61: 47,51,59-Kirby-a. 61-Crandall-a 9 18 27 52 69 85
50-Kirby, Crandall-a 10 20 30 58 79 100
55,56-Matt Baker-a 10 20 30 58 79 100
62-67,69,71-73,77-Kirby-a. 72-Origin Kid Colt 5 10 15 35 55 75
68,70,74-76: 68-(10¢-c) 4 8 12 28 44 60
68-(10¢ cover price blacked out, 12¢ printed on) 8 16 24 52 86 120
NOTE: ***Colan** a-35-37, 39, 72, 76. **Davis** a-37, 52, 54, 55; c-50, 54. **Ditko** a-66; c-56p. **Drucker** a-.32-34. **Heath** c-33. **Jack Keller** a-35, 40, 60, 72; c-72. **Kirby** a-47, 50, 51, 59, 62(3), 63-67, 69, 71, 73, 77; c-56(w/**Ditko**),57, 58, 60, 61(w/**Ayers**), 62, 63, 66, 68, 69, 71-77. **Robinson** a-35. **Severin** a-35, 59-61; c-34, 35, 39, 42, 43. **Tuska** a-34. **Wildey** a-10, 37, 42, 56, 57. Kid Colt in all. Two-Gun Kid in No. 57, 59, 60-63. Wyatt Earp in No. 45, 48, 49, 52, 54, 55, 58.*

GUNS OF FACT & FICTION (Also see A-1 Comics)
Magazine Enterprises: No. 13, 1948 (one-shot)
A-1 13-Used in **SOTI**, pg. 19; Ingels & J. Craig-a 27 54 81 158 254 350

GUNS OF THE DRAGON
DC Comics: Oct, 1998 - No. 4, Jan, 1999 ($2.50, limited series)
1-4-DCU in the 1920's; Enemy Ace & Bat Lash app. 2.50

GUN THEORY
Marvel Comics (Epic): Oct, 2003 - No. 4 ($2.50, limited series)
1,2-Daniel Way-s/Jon Proctor-a 2.50

GUNWITCH, THE : OUTSKIRTS OF DOOM (See The Nocturnals)
Oni Press: June, 2001 - No. 3, Oct, 2001 ($2.95, B&W, limited series)
1-3-Brereton-s/painted-c/Naifeh-s 3.00

GUY GARDNER (Guy Gardner: Warrior #17 on)(Also see Green Lantern #59)
DC Comics: Oct, 1992 - No. 44, July, 1996 ($1.25/$1.50/$1.75)
1-24,0,26-30: 1-Staton-c/a(p) begins. 6-Guy vs. Hal Jordan. 8-Vs. Lobo-c/story. 15-JLA x-over, begin $1.50-c. 18-Begin 4-part Emerald Fallout story; splash page x-over GL #50. 18-21-Vs. Hal Jordan. 24-(9/94)-Zero Hour. 0-(10/94) 2.50
25 (11/94, $2.50, 52 pgs.) 3.00
29 ($2.95)-Gatefold-c 3.50
29-Variant-c (Edward Hopper's Nighthawks) 2.50
31-44: 31-$1.75-c begins. 40-Gorilla Grodd-c/app. 44-Parallax-app. (1 pg.) 2.50
Annual 1 (1995, $3.50)-Year One story 4.00
Annual 2 (1996, $2.95)-Legends of the Dead Earth story 3.00

GUY GARDNER: COLLATERAL DAMAGE
DC Comics: 2006 - No. 2 ($5.99, square-bound, limited series)
1,2-Howard Chaykin-s/a 6.00

GUY GARDNER REBORN
DC Comics: 1992 - Book 3, 1992 ($4.95, limited series)
1-3: Staton-c/a(p). 1-Lobo-c/cameo. 2,3-Lobo-c/s 5.00

GYPSY COLT
Dell Publishing Co.: No. 568, June, 1954 (one-shot)
Four Color 568--Movie 5 10 15 32 51 70

GYRO GEARLOOSE (See Dynabrite Comics, Walt Disney's C&S #140 &Walt Disney Showcase #18)
Dell Publishing Co.: No. 1047, Nov-Jan/1959-60 - May-July, 1962 (Disney)
Four Color 1047 (No. 1)-All Barks-c/a 17 34 51 120 223 325
Four Color 1095,1184-All by Carl Barks 9 18 27 65 113 160
Four Color 1267-Barks c/a, 4 pgs. 8 16 24 54 90 125
01329-207 (#1, 5-7/62)-Barks-c only (intended as 4-Color 1329?) 6 12 18 41 66 90

HACKER FILES, THE
DC Comics: Aug, 1992 - No. 12, July, 1993 ($1.95)
1-12: 1-Sutton-a(p) begins; computer generated-c 2.50

HACK/SLASH
Devil's Due Publishing: Apr. 2004 - Present ($3.25/$4.95)
1-Seeley-s/Caselli-a/c 5.00
...: (The Series) 1-15 (5/07-Present, $3.50) Flashack to Cassie's childhood and origin. 12-Milk & Cheese cameo. 15-Re-Animator app. 3.50
...: Comic Book Carnage (3/05) Manfredi-a/Seeley-s; Robert Kirkman & Steve Niles app. 5.00
...: First Cut TPB (10/05, $14.95) r/one-shots with sketch pages , designs, interviews 15.00
...: Girls Gone Dead (10/04, $4.95) Manfredi-a/Seeley-s 5.00
...: Land of Lost Toys 1-3 (11/05 - No. 3, 1/06, $3.25) Crossland-a/Seeley-s 3.25
...: The Final Revenge of Evil Ernie (6/05, $4.95) Salman-a/Seeley-s; two covers 5.00
...: Trailers (2/05, $3.25) short stories by Seeley; art by various; three covers 3.25
...: Slice Hard (12/05, $4.95) Seeley-s 5.00
...: Slice Hard Pre-Sliced 25¢ Special (2/06, 25¢) origin story by Seeley; sketch pages 2.25
...: Vs Chucky (3/07, $5.50) Seeley-s/Merhoff-a; 3 covers 5.50
...: Vol. 2 Death By Sequel TPB (1/07, $18.99) r/Land of Lost Toys #1-3, Trailers, Slice Hard 19.00
...: Vol. 3 Friday the 31st TPB (10/07, $18.99) r/The Series #1-4 & ... Vs Chucky 19.00

HAGAR THE HORRIBLE (See Comics Reading Libraries in the Promotional Comics section)

HA HA COMICS (Teepee Tim No. 100 on; also see Giggle Comics)
Scope Mag.(Creston Publ.) No. 1-80/American Comics Group: Oct, 1943 - No. 99, Jan, 1955
1-Funny animal 35 70 105 203 327 450
2 17 34 51 100 158 215
3-5: Ken Hultgren-a begins? 14 28 42 80 115 150
6-10 11 22 33 64 90 115
11-20: 14-Infinity-c 10 20 30 54 72 90
21-40 9 18 27 50 65 80
41-94,96-99: 49,61-X-Mas-c 8 16 24 44 57 70
95-3-D effect-c 15 30 45 88 137 185

HAIR BEAR BUNCH, THE (TV) (See Fun-In No. 13)
Gold Key: Feb, 1972 - No. 9, Feb, 1974 (Hanna-Barbera)
1 4 8 12 24 37 50
2-9 3 6 9 17 25 32

HALF DEAD
Marvel Comics (Dabel Brothers Prods.): March, 2007 ($10.99, softcover, graphic novel)
SC-Barb Lien-Cooper & Park Cooper-s/Jimmy Bott-a 11.00

HALLELUJAH TRAIL, THE (See Movie Classics)

HALL OF FAME FEATURING THE T.H.U.N.D.E.R. AGENTS
JC Productions(Archie Comics Group): May, 1983 - No. 3, Dec, 1983
1-3: Thunder Agents-r(Crandall, Kane, Tuska, Wood-a). 2-New Ditko-c 3.00

HALLOWEEN (Movie)
Chaos! Comics: Nov, 2000; Apr, 2001 ($2.95/$2.99, one-shots)
1-Brewer-a; Michael Myers childhood at the Sanitarium 3.00
...II: The Blackest Eyes (4/01, $2.99) Beck-a 3.00
...III: The Devil's Eyes (11/01, $2.99) Justiniano-a 3.00

HALLOWEEN (Halloween Nightdance on cover)(Movie)
Devils Due Publishing: Mar, 2008 - No. 4, May, 2008 ($3.50, limited series)
1-4-Seeley-a/Hutchinson-s; multiple covers on each 3.50
...: 30 Years of Terror (8/08, $5.50) short stories by various incl. Seeley 5.50

HALLOWEEN HORROR
Eclipse Comics: Oct, 1987 (Seduction of the Innocent #7)($1.75)
1-Pre-code horror-r 3.00

Halo: Uprising #1 © Microsoft

The Hand of Fate #24 © ACE

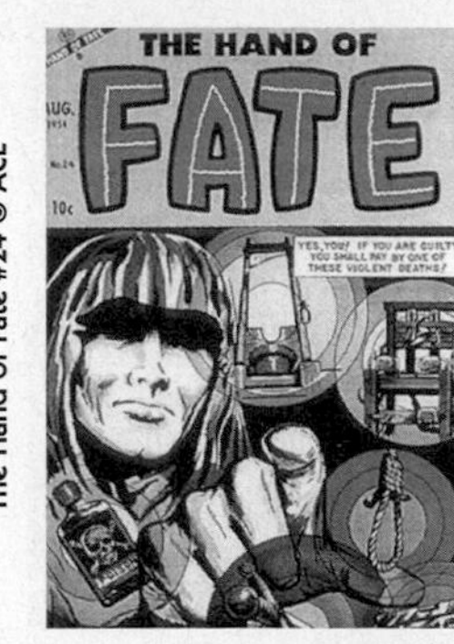

Hangman Comics #7 © MLJ

HALLOWEEN MEGAZINE
Marvel Comics: Dec, 1996 ($3.95, one-shot, 96 pgs.)

	GD 2.0	VG 4.0	FN 6.0	VF 8.0	VF/NM 9.0	NM- 9.2
1-Reprints Tomb of Dracula						4.00

HALO GRAPHIC NOVEL (Based on video game)
Marvel Publishing Inc.: 2006 ($24.99, hardcover with dust jacket)

	GD 2.0	VG 4.0	FN 6.0	VF 8.0	VF/NM 9.0	NM- 9.2
HC-Anthology set in the Halo universe; art by Bisley, Moebius and others; pin-up gallery by various incl. Darrow, Pratt, Williams and Van Fleet; Phil Hale painted-c						25.00

HALO: UPRISING (Based on video game) (Also see Marvel Spotlight: Halo)
Marvel Comics: Oct, 2007 - No. 4 ($3.99, limited series)

	GD 2.0	VG 4.0	FN 6.0	VF 8.0	VF/NM 9.0	NM- 9.2
1-3-Bendis-s/Maleev-a; takes pllace between the *Halo 2* and *Halo 3* video games						4.00

HALO JONES (See The Ballad of...)

HAMMER, THE
Dark Horse Comics: Oct, 1997 - No. 4, Jan, 1998 ($2.95, limited series)

	GD 2.0	VG 4.0	FN 6.0	VF 8.0	VF/NM 9.0	NM- 9.2
1-4-Kelley Jones-s/c/a, ...: Uncle Alex (8/98, $2.95)						3.00

HAMMER, THE: THE OUTSIDER
Dark Horse Comics: Feb, 1999 - No. 3, Apr, 1999 ($2.95, limited series)

	GD 2.0	VG 4.0	FN 6.0	VF 8.0	VF/NM 9.0	NM- 9.2
1-3-Kelley Jones-s/c/a						3.00

HAMMERLOCKE
DC Comics: Sept, 1992 - No. 9, May, 1993 ($1.75, limited series)

	GD 2.0	VG 4.0	FN 6.0	VF 8.0	VF/NM 9.0	NM- 9.2
1-($2.50, 52 pgs.)-Chris Sprouse-c/a in all						3.00
2-9						2.50

HAMMER OF GOD (Also see Nexus)
First Comics: Feb, 1990 - No. 4, May, 1990 ($1.95, limited series)

	GD 2.0	VG 4.0	FN 6.0	VF 8.0	VF/NM 9.0	NM- 9.2
1-4						2.50

HAMMER OF GOD: BUTCH
Dark Horse Comics: May, 1994 - No. 4, Aug, 1994 ($2.50, limited series)

	GD 2.0	VG 4.0	FN 6.0	VF 8.0	VF/NM 9.0	NM- 9.2
1-3						2.50

HAMMER OF GOD: PENTATHLON
Dark Horse Comics: Jan, 1994 ($2.50, one shot)

	GD 2.0	VG 4.0	FN 6.0	VF 8.0	VF/NM 9.0	NM- 9.2
1-Character from Nexus						2.50

HAMMER OF GOD: SWORD OF JUSTICE
First Comics: Feb 1991 - Mar 1991 ($4.95, lim. series, squarebound, 52 pgs.)

	GD 2.0	VG 4.0	FN 6.0	VF 8.0	VF/NM 9.0	NM- 9.2
V2#1,2						5.00

HAMMER OF THE GODS
Insight Studio Groups: 2001 - No. 5, 2001 ($2.95, limited series)

	GD 2.0	VG 4.0	FN 6.0	VF 8.0	VF/NM 9.0	NM- 9.2
1-Michael Oeming & Mark Wheatley-s/a; Frank Cho-c						6.00
2-5: 3-Hughes-c. 5-Dave Johnson-c						3.00
The ColorSaga (2002, $4.95) r/"Enemy of the Gods" internet strip						5.00
Mortal Enemy TPB (2002, $18.95) r/#1-5; intro. by Peter David; afterword by Raven						19.00

HAMMER OF THE GODS: HAMMER HITS CHINA
Image Comics: Feb, 2003 - No. 3, Sept, 2003 ($2.95, limited series)

	GD 2.0	VG 4.0	FN 6.0	VF 8.0	VF/NM 9.0	NM- 9.2
1-3-Oeming & Wheatley-s/a; Oeming-c. 2-Frankenstein Mobster by Wheatley						3.00

HANDBOOK OF THE CONAN UNIVERSE, THE
Marvel Comics: June, 1985; Jan, 1986 ($1.25, one-shot)

	GD 2.0	VG 4.0	FN 6.0	VF 8.0	VF/NM 9.0	NM- 9.2
1-(6/85) Kaluta-c (2 printings)						4.00
1-(1/86) Kaluta-c						6.00
nn-(no date, circa '87-88, B&W, 36 pgs.) reprints '86 with changes; new painted cover	1	2	3	5	6	8

HAND OF FATE (Formerly Men Against Crime)
Ace Magazines: No. 8, Dec, 1951 - No. 25, Dec, 1954 (Weird/horror stories) (Two #25's)

	GD 2.0	VG 4.0	FN 6.0	VF 8.0	VF/NM 9.0	NM- 9.2
8-Surrealistic text story	41	82	123	256	428	600
9,10,21-Necronomicon sty; drug belladonna used	25	50	75	147	236	325
11-18,20,22,23	21	42	63	123	197	270
19-Bondage, hypo needle scenes	22	44	66	131	211	290
24-Electric chair-c	31	62	93	181	291	400
25a(11/54), 25b(12/54)-Both have Cameron-a	17	34	51	98	154	210

NOTE: ***Cameron** a-9, 10, 19-25a, 25b; c-13. **Sekowsky** a-8, 9, 13, 14.*

HAND OF FATE
Eclipse Comics: Feb, 1988 - No. 3, Apr, 1988 ($1.75/$2.00, Baxter paper)

	GD 2.0	VG 4.0	FN 6.0	VF 8.0	VF/NM 9.0	NM- 9.2
1-3; 3-B&W						2.50

HANDS OF THE DRAGON
Seaboard Periodicals (Atlas): June, 1975

	GD 2.0	VG 4.0	FN 6.0	VF 8.0	VF/NM 9.0	NM- 9.2
1-Origin/1st app.; Craig-a(p)/Mooney inks	2	4	6	8	10	12

HANGMAN COMICS (Special Comics No. 1; Black Hood No. 9 on)
(Also see Flyman, Mighty Comics, Mighty Crusaders & Pep Comics)
MLJ Magazines: No. 2, Spring, 1942 - No. 8, Fall, 1943

	GD 2.0	VG 4.0	FN 6.0	VF 8.0	VF/NM 9.0	NM- 9.2
2-The Hangman, Boy Buddies begin	200	400	600	1260	2130	3000
3-Beheading splash pg.; 1st Nazi war-c	133	266	399	838	1419	2000
4-8: 5-1st Japan war-c. 8-2nd app. Super Duck (ties w/Jolly Jingles #11)	115	230	345	725	1225	1725

NOTE: ***Fuje** a-7(3), 8(3); c-3. **Reinman** c/a-3. Bondage c-3. **Sahle** c-6.*

HANK
Pentagon Publishing Co.: 1946

	GD 2.0	VG 4.0	FN 6.0	VF 8.0	VF/NM 9.0	NM- 9.2
nn-Coulton Waugh's newspaper reprint	8	16	24	44	57	70

HANNA-BARBERA (See Golden Comics Digest No. 2, 7, 11)

HANNA-BARBERA ALL-STARS
Archie Publications: Oct, 1995 - No. 4, Apr, 1996 ($1.50, bi-monthly)

	GD 2.0	VG 4.0	FN 6.0	VF 8.0	VF/NM 9.0	NM- 9.2
1-4						3.00

HANNA-BARBERA BANDWAGON (TV)
Gold Key: Oct, 1962 - No. 3, Apr, 1963

	GD 2.0	VG 4.0	FN 6.0	VF 8.0	VF/NM 9.0	NM- 9.2
1-Giant, 84 pgs. 1-Augie Doggie app.; 1st app. Lippy the Lion, Touché Turtle & Dum Dum, Wally Gator, Loopy de Loop,	12	24	36	87	156	225
2-Giant, 84 pgs.; Mr. & Mrs. J. Evil Scientist (1st app.) in Snagglepuss story; Yakky Doodle, Ruff and Reddy and others app.	9	18	27	60	100	140
3-Regular size; Mr. & Mrs. J. Evil Scientist app. (pre-#1), Snagglepuss, Wally Gator and others app.	7	14	21	47	76	105

HANNA-BARBERA GIANT SIZE
Harvey Comics: Oct, 1992 - No. 3 ($2.25, 68 pgs.)

	GD 2.0	VG 4.0	FN 6.0	VF 8.0	VF/NM 9.0	NM- 9.2
V2#1-3:Flintstones, Yogi Bear, Magilla Gorilla, Huckleberry Hound, Quick Draw McGraw, Yakky Doodle & Chopper, Jetsons & others						5.00

HANNA-BARBERA HI-ADVENTURE HEROES (See Hi-Adventure...)

HANNA-BARBERA PARADE (TV)
Charlton Comics: Sept, 1971 - No. 10, Dec, 1972

	GD 2.0	VG 4.0	FN 6.0	VF 8.0	VF/NM 9.0	NM- 9.2
1	7	14	21	49	80	110
2,4-10	4	8	12	26	41	55
3-(52 pgs.)- "Summer Picnic"	6	12	18	37	59	80

NOTE: *No. 4 (1/72) went on sale late in 1972 with the January 1973 issues.*

HANNA-BARBERA PRESENTS
Archie Publications: Nov, 1995 - No. 6 ($1.50, bi-monthly)

	GD 2.0	VG 4.0	FN 6.0	VF 8.0	VF/NM 9.0	NM- 9.2
1-8: 1-Atom Ant & Secret Squirrel. 2-Wacky Races. 3-Yogi Bear. 4-Quick Draw McGraw & Magilla Gorilla. 5-A Pup Named Scooby-Doo. 6-Superstar Olympics. 7-Wacky Races. 8-Frankenstein Jr. & the Impossibles						3.00

HANNA-BARBERA SPOTLIGHT (See Spotlight)

HANNA-BARBERA SUPER TV HEROES (TV)
Gold Key: Apr, 1968 - No. 7, Oct, 1969 (Hanna-Barbera)

	GD 2.0	VG 4.0	FN 6.0	VF 8.0	VF/NM 9.0	NM- 9.2
1-The Birdman, The Herculoids(ends #6; not in #3), Moby Dick, Young Samson & Goliath (ends #2,4), and The Mighty Mightor begin; Spiegle-a in all	14	28	42	99	175	250
2-The Galaxy Trio app.; Shazzan begins; 12¢ & 15¢ versions exist	9	18	27	65	113	160
3,6,7-The Space Ghost app.	9	18	27	60	100	140
4,5	8	16	24	52	86	120

NOTE: *Birdman in #1,2,4,5. Herculoids in #2,4-7. Mighty Mightor in #1,2,4-7. Moby Dick in all. Shazzan in #2-5. Young Samson & Goliath in #1,3.*

HANNA-BARBERA TV FUN FAVORITES (See Golden Comics Digest #2,7,11)

HANNA-BARBERA (TV STARS) (See TV Stars)

HANS BRINKER (Disney)
Dell Publishing Co.: No. 1273, Feb, 1962 (one-shot)

	GD 2.0	VG 4.0	FN 6.0	VF 8.0	VF/NM 9.0	NM- 9.2
Four Color 1273-Movie, photo-c	6	12	18	43	69	95

HANS CHRISTIAN ANDERSEN
Ziff-Davis Publ. Co.: 1953 (100 pgs., Special Issue)

	GD 2.0	VG 4.0	FN 6.0	VF 8.0	VF/NM 9.0	NM- 9.2
nn-Danny Kaye (movie)-Photo-c; fairy tales	16	32	48	94	147	200

HANSEL & GRETEL
Dell Publishing Co.: No. 590, Oct, 1954 (one-shot)

	GD 2.0	VG 4.0	FN 6.0	VF 8.0	VF/NM 9.0	NM- 9.2
Four Color 590-Partial photo-c	6	12	18	43	69	95

HANSI, THE GIRL WHO LOVED THE SWASTIKA
Spire Christian Comics (Fleming H. Revell Co.): 1973, 1976 (39¢/49¢)

	GD 2.0	VG 4.0	FN 6.0	VF 8.0	VF/NM 9.0	NM- 9.2
1973 edition with 39¢-c	5	10	15	32	51	70
1976 edition with 49¢-c	3	6	9	20	30	40

Happy Comics #7 © STD

Harbinger #35 © Voyager Comm.

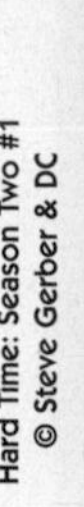
Hard Time: Season Two #1 © Steve Gerber & DC

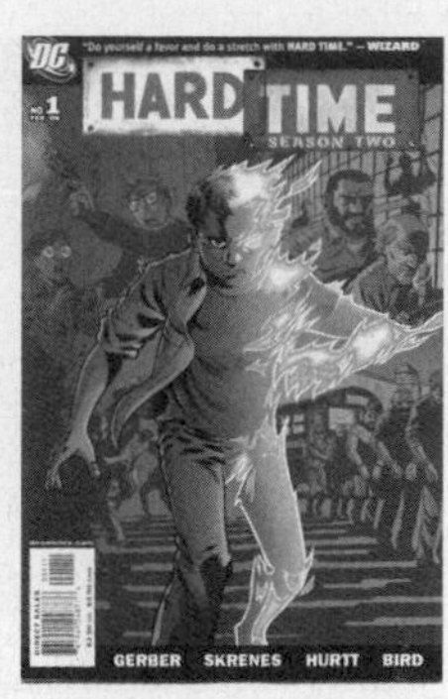

GD VG FN VF VF/NM NM-
2.0 4.0 6.0 8.0 9.0 9.2

HAP HAZARD COMICS (Real Love No. 25 on)
Ace Magazines (Readers' Research): Summer, 1944 - No. 24, Feb, 1949
(#1-6 are quarterly issues)

	GD 2.0	VG 4.0	FN 6.0	VF 8.0	VF/NM 9.0	NM- 9.2
1	15	30	45	84	127	170
2	9	18	27	52	69	85
3-10	8	16	24	44	57	70
11-13,15-24	8	16	24	40	50	60
14-Feldstein-c (4/47)	10	20	30	56	76	95

HAP HOPPER (See Comics Revue No. 2)

HAPPIEST MILLIONAIRE, THE (See Movie Comics)

HAPPI TIM (See March of Comics No. 182)

HAPPY BIRTHDAY MARTHA WASHINGTON (Also see Give Me Liberty, Martha Washington Goes To War, & Martha Washington Stranded In Space)
Dark Horse Comics: Mar, 1995 ($2.95, one-shot)

1-Miller script; Gibbons-c/a 3.00

HAPPY COMICS (Happy Rabbit No. 41 on)
Nedor Publ./Standard Comics (Animated Cartoons): Aug, 1943 - No. 40, Dec, 1950
(Companion to Goofy Comics)

	GD 2.0	VG 4.0	FN 6.0	VF 8.0	VF/NM 9.0	NM- 9.2
1-Funny animal	27	54	81	158	254	350
2	15	30	45	85	130	175
3-10	11	22	33	64	90	115
11-19	10	20	30	54	72	90
20-31,34-37-Frazetta text illos in all (2 in #34&35, 3 in #27,28,30). 27-Al Fago-a	11	22	33	64	90	115
32-Frazetta-a, 7 pgs. plus 2 text illos; Roussos-a	20	40	60	117	186	255
33-Frazetta-a(2), 6 pgs. each (Scarce)	28	56	84	162	261	360
38-40	9	18	27	47	61	75

HAPPYDALE: DEVILS IN THE DESERT
DC Comics (Vertigo): 1999 - No. 2, 1999 ($6.95, limited series)

1,2-Andrew Dabb-s/Seth Fisher-a 7.00

HAPPY DAYS (TV)(See Kite Fun Book)
Gold Key: Mar, 1979 - No. 6, Feb, 1980

	GD 2.0	VG 4.0	FN 6.0	VF 8.0	VF/NM 9.0	NM- 9.2
1-Photo-c of TV cast; 35¢-c	3	6	9	16	23	30
2-6-(40¢-c)	2	4	6	9	12	15

HAPPY HOLIDAY (See March of Comics No. 181)

HAPPY HOULIHANS (Saddle Justice No. 3 on; see Blackstone, The Magician Detective)
E. C. Comics: Fall, 1947 - No. 2, Winter, 1947-48

	GD 2.0	VG 4.0	FN 6.0	VF 8.0	VF/NM 9.0	NM- 9.2
1-Origin Moon Girl (same date as Moon Girl #1)	54	108	162	340	575	810
2	31	62	93	181	291	400

HAPPY JACK
Red Top (Decker): Aug, 1957 - No. 2, Nov, 1957

	GD 2.0	VG 4.0	FN 6.0	VF 8.0	VF/NM 9.0	NM- 9.2
V1#1,2	5	10	15	22	26	30

HAPPY JACK HOWARD
Red Top (Farrell)/Decker: 1957

	GD 2.0	VG 4.0	FN 6.0	VF 8.0	VF/NM 9.0	NM- 9.2
nn-Reprints Handy Andy story from E. C. Dandy Comics #5, renamed "Happy Jack"	5	10	15	22	26	30

HAPPY RABBIT (Formerly Happy Comics)
Standard Comics (Animated Cartoons): No. 41, Feb, 1951 - No. 48, Apr, 1952

	GD 2.0	VG 4.0	FN 6.0	VF 8.0	VF/NM 9.0	NM- 9.2
41-Funny animal	8	16	24	42	54	65
42-48	6	12	18	31	38	45

HARBINGER (Also see Unity)
Valiant: Jan, 1992 - No. 41, June, 1995 ($1.95/$2.50)

	GD 2.0	VG 4.0	FN 6.0	VF 8.0	VF/NM 9.0	NM- 9.2
0-Prequel to the series; available by redeeming coupons in #1-6; cover image has pink sky; title logo is blue	4	8	12	24	37	50
0-(2nd printing) cover has blue sky & red logo						5.00
1-1st app.	2	4	6	8	10	12
2-4: 4-Low print run	1	2	3	5	7	9
5,6: 5-Solar app. 6-Torque dies	1	2	3	4	5	7
7-10: 8,9-Unity x-overs. 8-Miller-c. 9-Simonson-c. 10-1st app. H.A.R.D Corps (10/92)						5.00
11-24,26-41: 14-1st app. Stronghold. 18-Intro Screen. 19-1st app. Stunner. 22-Archer & Armstrong app. 24-Cover similar to #1. 26-Intro New Harbingers. 29-Bound-in trading card. 30-H.A.R.D. Corps app. 32-Eternal Warrior app. 33-Dr. Eclipse app.						2.50
25-($3.50, 52 pgs.)-Harada vs. Sting						3.50
...Files 1,2 (8/94,2/95 $2.50)						2.50
...: The Beginning HC (2007, $24.95) recolored reprints #0-7 and Story of Harada from coupons from #1-6; new "Origin of Harada" story by Shooter and Bob Hall						25.00
Trade paperback nn (11/92, $9.95)-Reprints #1-4 & comes polybagged with a copy of Harbinger #0 w/new-c. Price for TPB only						10.00

NOTE: *Issues 1-6 have coupons with origin of Harada and are redeemable for Harbinger #0.*

HARD BOILED
Dark Horse Comics: Sept, 1990 - No. 3, Mar, 1992 ($4.95/$5.95, 8 1/2x11", lim. series)

	GD 2.0	VG 4.0	FN 6.0	VF 8.0	VF/NM 9.0	NM- 9.2
1-3-Miller-s; Darrow-c/a; sexually explicit & violent	1	2	3	4	5	7
TPB (5/93, $15.95)						16.00
Big Damn Hard Boiled (12/97, $29.95, B&W) r/#1-3						30.00

HARDCASE (See Break Thru, Flood Relief & Ultraforce, 1st Series)
Malibu Comics (Ultraverse): June, 1993 - No. 26, Aug, 1995 ($1.95/$2.50)

1-Intro Hardcase; Dave Gibbons-c; has coupon for Ultraverse Premiere #0; Jim Callahan-a(p) begin, ends #3 3.00
1-With coupon missing 2.25
1-Platinum Edition 4.00
1-Holographic Cover Edition; 1st full-c holograph tied w/Prime 1 & Strangers 1 7.00
1-Ultra Limited silver foil-c 4.00
2,3-Callahan-a, 2-($2.50)-Newsstand edition bagged w/trading card 2.50
4,6-15, 17-19: 4-Strangers app. 7-Break-Thru x-over. 8-Solution app. 9-Vs. Turf. 12-Silver foil logo, wraparound-c. 17-Prime app. 2.50
5-($2.50, 48 pgs.)-Rune flip-c/story by B. Smith (3 pgs.) 2.50
16 ($3.50, 68 pgs.)-Rune pin-up 3.50
20-26: 23-Loki app. 2.50

NOTE: *Perez a-8(2); c-20i.*

HARDCORE STATION
DC Comics: July, 1998 - No. 6, Dec, 1998 ($2.50, limited series)

1-6-Starlin-s/a(p). 3-Green Lantern-c/app. 5,6-JLA-c/app. 3.00

H.A.R.D. CORPS, THE (See Harbinger #10)
Valiant: Dec, 1992 - No. 30, Feb, 1995 ($2.25) (Harbinger spin-off)

1-($2.50)-Gatefold-c by Jim Lee & Bob Layton 3.00
1-Gold variant 5.00
2-30: 5-Bloodshot-c/story cont'd from Bloodshot #3. 5-Variant edition; came w/Comic Defense System. 10-Turok app. 17-vs. Armorines. 18-Bound-in trading card. 20-Harbinger app. 2.50

HARD TIME
DC Comics (Focus): Apr, 2004 - No. 12, Mar, 2005 ($2.50)

1-12-Gerber-s/Hurtt-a; 1-Includes previews of other DC Focus series 2.50
...: 50 to Life (2004, $9.95, TPB) r/#1-6; cover gallery with sketches 10.00

HARD TIME: SEASON TWO
DC Comics: Feb, 2006 - No. 7, Aug, 2006 ($2.50/$2.99)

1-5-Gerber-s/Hurtt-a 2.50
6,7-($2.99) 7-Ethan paroled in 2053 3.00

HARDWARE
DC Comics (Milestone): Apr, 1993 - No. 50, Apr, 1997 ($1.50/$1.75/$2.50)

1-($2.95)-Collector's Edition polybagged w/poster & trading card (direct sale only) 4.00
1-Platinum Edition 6.00
1-15,17-19: 11-Shadow War x-over. 11,14-Simonson-c. 12-Buckler-a(p). 17-Worlds Collide Pt. 2. 18-Simonson-c; Worlds Collide Pt. 9. 15-1st Humberto Ramos DC work 2.50
16,50-($3.95, 52 pgs.)-16-Collector's Edition w/gatefold 2nd cover by Byrne; new armor; Icon app. 4.00
16,20-24,26-49: 16-($2.50, 52 pgs.)-Newsstand Ed. 49-Moebius-c 2.50
25-($2.95, 52 pgs.) 3.00

HARDY BOYS, THE (Disney
Dell Publ. Co.: No. 760, Dec, 1956 - No. 964, Jan, 1959 (Mickey Mouse Club)

	GD 2.0	VG 4.0	FN 6.0	VF 8.0	VF/NM 9.0	NM- 9.2
Four Color 760 (#1)-Photo-c	10	20	30	70	123	175
Four Color 830(8/57), 887(1/58), 964-Photo-c	9	18	27	60	100	140

HARDY BOYS, THE (TV)
Gold Key: Apr, 1970 - No. 4, Jan, 1971

	GD 2.0	VG 4.0	FN 6.0	VF 8.0	VF/NM 9.0	NM- 9.2
1	4	8	12	28	44	60
2-4	3	6	9	18	27	35

HARLAN ELLISON'S DREAM CORRIDOR
Dark Horse Comics: Mar, 1995 - No. 5, July, 1995 ($2.95, anthology)

1-5: Adaptation of Ellison stories. 1-4-Byrne-a. 3.00
Special (1/95, $4.95) 5.00
Trade paperback-(1996, $18.95, 192 pgs)-r/#1-5 & Special #1 19.00

HARLAN ELLISON'S DREAM CORRIDOR QUARTERLY
Dark Horse Comics: V2#1, Aug, 1996 ($5.95, anthology, squarebound)

V2#1-Adaptations of Ellison's stories w/new material; Neal Adams-a 6.00
Volume 2 TPB (3/07, $19.95) r/V2#1 and unpublished material incl. last Swan-a 20.00

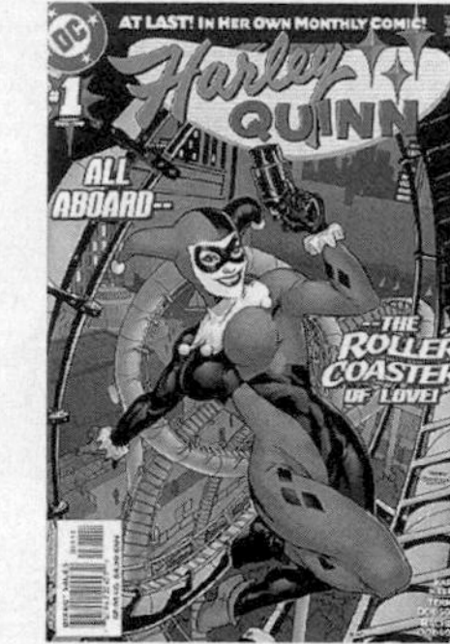

Harley Quinn #1 © DC

Harvey Comics Hits #57 © KING

Harvey Hits #2 © HARV

HARLEM GLOBETROTTERS (TV) (See Fun-In No. 8, 10)
Gold Key: Apr, 1972 - No. 12, Jan, 1975 (Hanna-Barbera)

	GD 2.0	VG 4.0	FN 6.0	VF 8.0	VF/NM 9.0	NM- 9.2
1	4	8	12	26	41	55
2-5	3	6	9	16	22	28
6-12	2	4	6	13	18	22

NOTE: *#4, 8, and 12 contain 16 extra pages of advertising.*

HARLEQUIN ROMANCE
Dark Horse Comics: Nov, 2001 ($10.95, hardcover, one-shot)

	GD 2.0	VG 4.0	FN 6.0	VF 8.0	VF/NM 9.0	NM- 9.2
nn-Neil Gaiman-s; painted-a/c by John Bolton						11.00

HARLEY QUINN
DC Comics: Dec, 2000 - No. 38, Jan, 2004 ($2.95/$2.25/$2.50)

	GD 2.0	VG 4.0	FN 6.0	VF 8.0	VF/NM 9.0	NM- 9.2
1-Joker and Poison Ivy app.; Terry & Rachel Dodson-a/c						4.00
2-11-($2.25). 2-Two-Face-c/app. 3-Slumber party. 6,7-Riddler app.						2.50
12-($2.95) Batman app.						3.00
13-38: 13-Joker: Last Laugh. 17,18-Bizarro-c/app. 23-Begin $2.50-c. 23,24-Martian Manhunter app. 25,32-Joker-c/app.						2.50
Harley & Ivy: Love on the Lam (2001, $5.95) Winick-s/Chiodo-c/a						6.00
...: Our Worlds at War (10/01, $2.95) Jae Lee-c; art by various						3.00

HAROLD TEEN (See Popular Comics, & Super Comics)
Dell Publishing Co.: No. 2, 1942 - No. 209, Jan, 1949

	GD 2.0	VG 4.0	FN 6.0	VF 8.0	VF/NM 9.0	NM- 9.2
Four Color 2	29	58	87	213	394	575
Four Color 209	6	12	18	39	62	85

HARROWERS, THE (See Clive Barker's...)

HARSH REALM (Inspired 1999 TV series)
Harris Comics: 1993- No. 6, 1994 ($2.95, limited series)

	GD 2.0	VG 4.0	FN 6.0	VF 8.0	VF/NM 9.0	NM- 9.2
1-6: Painted-c. Hudnall-s/Paquette & Ridgway-a						3.50
TPB (2000, $14.95) r/series						15.00

HARVEY
Marvel Comics: Oct, 1970; No. 2, 12/70; No. 3, 6/72 - No. 6, 12/72

	GD 2.0	VG 4.0	FN 6.0	VF 8.0	VF/NM 9.0	NM- 9.2
1	9	18	27	63	107	150
2-6	6	12	18	41	66	90

HARVEY COLLECTORS COMICS (Titled Richie Rich Collectors Comics on cover of #6-on)
Harvey Publ.: Sept, 1975 - No. 15, Jan, 1978; No. 16, Oct, 1979 (52 pgs.)

	GD 2.0	VG 4.0	FN 6.0	VF 8.0	VF/NM 9.0	NM- 9.2
1-Reprints Richie Rich #1,2	2	4	6	13	18	22
2-10: 7-Splash pg. shows cover to Friendly Ghost Casper #1	2	4	6	8	11	14
11-16: 16-Sad Sack-r	1	2	3	5	7	9

NOTE: *All reprints: Casper-#2, 7, Richie Rich-#1, 3, 5, 6, 8-15, Sad Sack-#16. Wendy-#4.*

HARVEY COMICS HITS (Formerly Joe Palooka #50)
Harvey Publications: No. 51, Oct, 1951 - No. 62, Apr, 1953

	GD 2.0	VG 4.0	FN 6.0	VF 8.0	VF/NM 9.0	NM- 9.2
51-The Phantom	31	62	93	181	291	400
52-Steve Canyon's Air Power(Air Force sponsored)	13	26	39	72	101	130
53-Mandrake the Magician	20	40	60	115	183	250
54-Tim Tyler's Tales of Jungle Terror	13	26	39	74	105	135
55-Love Stories of Mary Worth	11	22	33	62	86	110
56-The Phantom; bondage-c	26	52	78	152	244	335
57-Rip Kirby Exposes the Kidnap Racket; entire book by Alex Raymond	15	30	45	85	130	175
58-Girls in White (nurses stories)	11	22	33	62	86	110
59-Tales of the Invisible featuring Scarlet O'Neil	12	24	36	67	94	120
60-Paramount Animated Comics #1 (9/52) (3rd app. Baby Huey); 2nd Harvey app. Baby Huey & Casper the Friendly Ghost (1st in Little Audrey #25 (8/52)); 1st app. Herman & Catnip (c/story) & Buzzy the Crow	41	82	123	256	428	600
61-Casper the Friendly Ghost #6 (3rd Harvey Casper, 10/52)-Casper-c	47	94	141	291	483	675
62-Paramount Animated Comics #2; Herman & Catnip, Baby Huey & Buzzy the Crow	17	34	51	98	154	210

HARVEY COMICS LIBRARY
Harvey Publications: Apr, 1952 - No. 2, 1952

	GD 2.0	VG 4.0	FN 6.0	VF 8.0	VF/NM 9.0	NM- 9.2
1-Teen-Age Dope Slaves as exposed by Rex Morgan, M.D.; drug propaganda story; used in **SOTI,** pg. 27	153	306	459	964	1632	2300
2-Dick Tracy Presents Sparkle Plenty in "Blackmail Terror"	20	40	60	115	183	250

HARVEY COMICS SPOTLIGHT
Harvey Comics: Sept, 1987 - No. 4, Mar, 1988 (75¢/$1.00)

	GD 2.0	VG 4.0	FN 6.0	VF 8.0	VF/NM 9.0	NM- 9.2
1-New material; begin 75ç, ends #3; Sand Sack						5.00
2-4: 2,4-All new material. 2-Baby Huey. 3-Little Dot; contains reprints w/5 pg. new story. 4-$1.00-c; Little Audrey						4.00

NOTE: No. 5 was advertised but not published.

HARVEY HITS (Also see Tastee-Freez Comics in the Promotional Comics section)
Harvey Publications: Sept, 1957 - No. 122, Nov, 1967

	GD 2.0	VG 4.0	FN 6.0	VF 8.0	VF/NM 9.0	NM- 9.2
1-The Phantom	25	50	75	185	343	500
2-Rags Rabbit (10/57)	5	10	15	32	51	70
3-Richie Rich (11/57)-r/Little Dot; 1st book devoted to Richie Rich; see Little Dot for 1st app.	125	250	375	1063	2032	3000
4-Little Dot's Uncles (12/57)	16	32	48	114	212	310
5-Stevie Mazie's Boy Friend (1/58)	4	8	12	26	41	55
6-The Phantom (2/58); Kirby-c; 2pg. Powell-a	17	34	51	120	223	325
7-Wendy the Good Little Witch (3/58, pre-dates Wendy #1; 1st book devoted to Wendy)	26	52	78	192	359	525
8-Sad Sack's Army Life; George Baker-c	7	14	21	49	80	110
9-Richie Rich's Golden Deeds; (2nd book devoted to Richie Rich) reprints Richie Rich story from Tastee-Freez #1	50	100	150	425	813	1200
10-Little Lotta's Lunch Box	11	22	33	77	136	195
11-Little Audrey Summer Fun (7/58)	8	16	24	50	87	135
12-The Phantom; Kirby-c; 2pg. Powell-a (8/58)	14	28	42	102	181	260
13-Little Dot's Uncles (9/58); Richie Rich 1pg.	11	22	33	77	136	195
14-Herman & Katnip (10/58, TV/movies)	4	8	12	26	41	55
15-The Phantom (12/58)-1 pg. origin	14	28	42	102	181	260
16-Wendy the Good Little Witch (1/59); Casper app.	11	22	33	79	140	210
17-Sad Sack's Army Life (2/59)	6	12	18	39	62	85
18-Buzzy & the Crow	4	8	12	26	41	55
19-Little Audrey (4/59)	6	12	18	37	59	80
20-Casper & Spooky	8	16	24	52	86	120
21-Wendy the Witch	8	16	24	52	86	120
22-Sad Sack's Army Life	5	10	15	30	48	65
23-Wendy the Witch (8/59)	8	16	24	52	86	120
24-Little Dot's Uncles (9/59); Richie Rich 1pg.	9	18	27	60	100	140
25-Herman & Katnip (10/59)	4	8	12	22	34	45
26-The Phantom (11/59)	10	20	30	73	129	185
27-Wendy the Good Little Witch (12/59)	7	14	21	50	83	115
28-Sad Sack's Army Life (1/60)	4	8	12	26	41	55
29-Harvey-Toon (No.1)('60); Casper, Buzzy	5	10	15	34	55	75
30-Wendy the Witch (3/60)	7	14	21	50	83	115
31-Herman & Katnip (4/60)	3	6	9	20	30	40
32-Sad Sack's Army Life (5/60)	4	8	12	22	34	45
33-Wendy the Witch (6/60)	7	14	21	47	76	105
34-Harvey-Toon (7/60)	4	8	12	24	37	50
35-Funday Funnies (8/60)	3	6	9	20	30	40
36-The Phantom (1960)	10	20	30	68	119	170
37-Casper & Nightmare	6	12	18	37	59	80
38-Harvey-Toon	4	8	12	24	37	50
39-Sad Sack's Army Life (12/60)	3	6	9	21	32	42
40-Funday Funnies (1/61)	3	6	9	17	25	32
41-Herman & Katnip	3	6	9	17	25	32
42-Harvey-Toon (3/61)	3	6	9	19	29	38
43-Sad Sack's Army Life (4/61)	3	6	9	19	29	38
44-The Phantom (5/61)	9	18	27	65	113	160
45-Casper & Nightmare	5	10	15	30	48	65
46-Harvey-Toon (7/61)	3	6	9	17	25	32
47-Sad Sack's Army Life (8/61)	3	6	9	17	25	32
48-The Phantom (9/61)	9	18	27	65	113	160
49-Stumbo the Giant (1st app. in Hot Stuff)	9	18	27	65	113	160
50-Harvey-Toon (11/61)	3	6	9	16	23	30
51-Sad Sack's Army Life (12/61)	3	6	9	16	23	30
52-Casper & Nightmare	4	8	12	28	44	60
53-Harvey-Toons (2/62)	3	6	9	16	23	30
54-Stumbo the Giant	5	10	15	34	55	75
55-Sad Sack's Army Life (4/62)	3	6	9	16	23	30
56-Casper & Nightmare	4	8	12	26	41	55
57-Stumbo the Giant	5	10	15	34	55	75
58-Sad Sack's Army Life	3	6	9	16	23	30
59-Casper & Nightmare (7/62)	4	8	12	26	41	55
60-Stumbo the Giant (9/62)	5	10	15	34	55	75
61-Sad Sack's Army Life	3	6	9	16	22	28
62-Casper & Nightmare	4	8	12	23	36	48
63-Stumbo the Giant	4	8	12	28	44	60
64-Sad Sack's Army Life (1/63)	3	6	9	16	22	28
65-Casper & Nightmare	4	8	12	23	36	48
66-Stumbo The Giant (3/63)	4	8	12	28	44	60
67-Sad Sack's Army Life (4/63)	3	6	9	16	22	28
68-Casper & Nightmare	4	8	12	23	36	48

Hate #26 © Peter Bagge

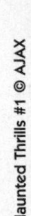

Haunted Thrills #1 © AJAX

Haunt of Fear #12 © WMG

	GD 2.0	VG 4.0	FN 6.0	VF 8.0	VF/NM 9.0	NM- 9.2
69-Stumbo the Giant (6/63)	4	8	12	28	44	60
70-Sad Sack's Army Life (7/63)	3	6	9	16	22	28
71-Casper & Nightmare (8/63)	3	6	9	21	32	42
72-Stumbo the Giant	4	8	12	28	44	60
73-Little Sad Sack (10/63)	3	6	9	16	22	28
74-Sad Sack's Muttsy... (11/63)	3	6	9	16	22	28
75-Casper & Nightmare	3	6	9	19	29	38
76-Little Sad Sack	3	6	9	16	22	28
77-Sad Sack's Muttsy...	3	6	9	16	22	28
78-Stumbo the Giant (3/64); JFK caricature	4	8	12	28	44	60
79-87: 79-Little Sad Sack (4/64). 80-Sad Sack's Muttsy... (5/64). 81-Little Sad Sack. 82-Sad Sack's Muttsy... 83-Little Sad Sack(8/64). 84-Sad Sack's Muttsy... 85-Gabby Gob (#1) (10/64). 86-G. I. Juniors (#1)(11/64). 87-Sad Sack's Muttsy... (12/64)	3	6	9	16	22	28
88-Stumbo the Giant (1/65)	4	8	12	28	44	60
89-122: 89-Sad Sack's Muttsy... 90-Gabby Gob. 91-G. I. Juniors. 92-Sad Sack's Muttsy... (5/65). 93-Sadie Sack (6/65). 94-Gabby Gob. 95-G. I. Juniors (8/65). 96-Sad Sack's Muttsy... (9/65). 97-Gabby Gob (10/65). 98-G. I. Juniors (11/65). 99-Sad Sack's Muttsy... (12/65). 100-Gabby Gob(1/66). 101-G. I. Juniors (2/66). 102-Sad Sack's Muttsy... (3/66). 103-Gabby Gob. 104- G. I. Juniors. 105-Sad Sack's Muttsy... 106-Gabby Gob (7/66). 107-G. I. Juniors (8/66). 108-Sad Sack's Muttsy...109-Gabby Gob. 110-G. I. Juniors (11/66). 111-Sad Sack's Muttsy... (12/66). 112-G. I. Juniors. 113-Sad Sack's Muttsy... 114-G. I. Juniors. 115-Sad Sack's Muttsy... 116-G. I. Juniors (5/67). 117-Sad Sack's Muttsy... 118-G. I. Juniors. 119-Sad Sack's Muttsy... (8/67). 120-G. I. Juniors (9/67). 121-Sad Sack's Muttsy... (10/67). 122-G. I. Juniors (11/67)	2	4	6	10	14	18

HARVEY HITS COMICS
Harvey Publications: Nov, 1986 - No. 6, Oct, 1987

	GD	VG	FN	VF	VF/NM	NM-
1-Little Lotta, Little Dot, Wendy & Baby Huey	1	2	3	4	5	7
2-6: 3-Xmas-c						4.50

HARVEY POP COMICS (Rock Happening) (Teen Humor)
Harvey Publications: Oct, 1968 - No. 2, Nov, 1969 (Both are 68 pg. Giants)

	GD	VG	FN	VF	VF/NM	NM-
1-The Cowsills	6	12	18	37	59	80
2-Bunny	5	10	15	32	51	70

HARVEY 3-D HITS (See Sad Sack)

HARVEY-TOON (...S) (See Harvey Hits No. 29, 34, 38, 42, 46, 50, 53)

HARVEY WISEGUYS (...Digest #? on)
Harvey Comics: Nov, 1987; #2, Nov, 1988; #3, Apr, 1989 - No. 4, Nov, 1989 (98 pgs., digest-size, $1.25/$1.75)

	GD	VG	FN	VF	VF/NM	NM-
1-Hot Stuff, Spooky, etc.	1	2	3	5	6	8
2-4: 2 (68 pgs.)						6.00

HATARI (See Movie Classics)

HATE
Fantagraphics Books: Spr, 1990 - No. 30, 1998 ($2.50/$2.95, B&W/color)

	GD	VG	FN	VF	VF/NM	NM-
1	2	4	6	10	12	15
2-3	1	2	3	5	6	8
4-10						5.00
11-20: 16- color begins						4.00
21-29						3.00
30-($3.95) Last issue						4.00
Annual 1 (2/01, $3.95) Peter Bagge-s/a						4.00
Annual 2-7 (12/01-Present; $4.95) Peter Bagge-s/a						5.00
Buddy Bites the Bullet! (2001, $16.95) r/Buddy stories in color						17.00
Buddy Go Home! (1997, $16.95) r/Buddy stories in color						17.00
Hate-Ball Special Edition ($3.95, giveaway)-reprints						4.00
Hate Jamboree (10/98, $4.50) old & new cartoons						4.50

HATHAWAYS, THE (TV)
Dell Publishing Co.: No. 1298, Feb-Apr, 1962 (one-shot)

	GD	VG	FN	VF	VF/NM	NM-
Four Color 1298-Photo-c	5	10	15	30	48	65

HAUNTED (See This Magazine Is Haunted)

HAUNTED (Baron Weirwulf's Haunted Library on-c #21 on)
Charlton Comics: 9/71 - No. 30, 11/76; No. 31, 9/77 - No. 75, 9/84

	GD	VG	FN	VF	VF/NM	NM-
1-All Ditko issue	5	10	15	30	48	65
2-7-Ditko-c/a	3	6	9	17	25	32
8,12,28-Ditko-a	2	4	6	11	16	20
9,19	2	4	6	8	11	14
10,20,15,18: 10,20-Sutton-a. 15-Sutton-c	2	4	6	8	11	14
11,13,14,16-Ditko-c/a	2	4	6	11	16	20
17-Sutton-c/a; Newton-a	2	4	6	9	12	15
21-Newton-c/a; Sutton-a; 1st Baron Weirwulf	3	6	9	16	22	28
22-Newton-c/a; Sutton-a	2	4	6	9	13	16
23,24-Sutton-c; Ditko-a	2	4	6	9	13	16
25-27,29,32,33	1	3	4	6	8	10
30,41,47,49-52,60,74-Ditko-c/a: 51-Reprints #1	2	4	6	9	13	16
31,35,37,38-Sutton-a	1	3	4	6	8	10
34,36,39,40,42,57-Ditko-a	2	4	6	8	10	12
43-46,48,53-56,58,59,61-73: 59-Newton-a. 64-Sutton-c. 71-73-Low print	1	2	3	5	6	8
75-(9/84) Last issue; low print	2	4	6	9	13	16

NOTE: ***Aparo** c-45. **Ditko** a-1-8, 11-16, 18, 23, 24, 28, 30, 34r, 36r, 39-42r, 47r, 49-52r, 57, 60, 74. c-1-7, 11, 13, 14, 16, 30, 41, 47, 49-52, 74. **Howard** a-6, 9, 18, 22, 25, 32. **Kim** a-9, 19. **Morisi** a-13. **Newton** a-17, 21, 59r; c-21, 22(painted). **Staton** a-11, 12, 18, 21, 22, 30, 33, 35, 38; c-18, 33, 38. **Sutton** a-10, 17, 20-22, 31, 35, 37, 38; c-15, 17, 18, 23(painted), 24(painted), 27, 64r. #49 reprints Tales of the Mysterious Traveler #4.*

HAUNTED, THE
Chaos! Comics: Jan, 2002 - No. 4, Apr, 2002 ($2.99, limited series)

	GD	VG	FN	VF	VF/NM	NM-
1-4-Peter David-s/Nat Jones-a						3.00
...: Gray Matters (7/02, $2.99) David-s/Jones-a						3.00

HAUNTED LOVE
Charlton Comics: Apr, 1973 - No. 11, Sept, 1975

	GD	VG	FN	VF	VF/NM	NM-
1-Tom Sutton-a (16 pgs.)	5	10	15	32	51	70
2,3,6,7,10,11	3	6	9	17	25	32
4,5-Ditko-a	3	6	9	20	30	40
8,9-Newton-c	3	6	9	17	25	32
Modern Comics #1(1978)	2	4	6	9	12	15

NOTE: ***Howard** a-8i. **Kim** a-7-9. **Newton** c-8, 9. **Staton** a-1-6. **Sutton** a-1, 3-5, 10, 11.*

HAUNTED MAN, THE
Dark Horse Comics: Mar, 2000 ($2.95, unfinished limited series)

	GD	VG	FN	VF	VF/NM	NM-
1-Gerald Jones-s/Mark Badger-a						3.00

HAUNTED THRILLS (Tales of Horror and Terror)
Ajax/Farrell Publications: June, 1952 - No. 18, Nov-Dec, 1954

	GD	VG	FN	VF	VF/NM	NM-
1-r/Ellery Queen #1	57	114	171	359	605	850
2-L. B. Cole-a r-/Ellery Queen #1	40	80	120	235	380	525
3-5: 3-Drug use story	35	70	105	203	327	450
6-10,12: 7-Hitler story.	30	60	90	176	283	390
11-Nazi death camp story	32	64	96	186	298	410
13-18: 18-Lingerie panels. 14-Jesus Christ apps. in story by Webb. 15-Jo-Jo-r	25	50	75	145	233	320

NOTE: ***Kamenish** art in most issues. **Webb** a-12.*

HAUNT OF FEAR (Formerly Gunfighter)
E. C. Comics: No. 15, May-June, 1950 - No. 28, Nov-Dec, 1954

	GD	VG	FN	VF	VF/NM	NM-
15(#1, 1950)(Scarce)	286	572	858	2288	3644	5000
16-1st app. "The Witches Cauldron" & the Old Witch (by Kamen); begin series as hostess of Haunt of Fear	120	240	360	960	1530	2100
17-Origin of Crypt of Terror, Vault of Horror, & Haunt of Fear; used in **SOTI**, pg. 43; last pg. Ingels-a used by N.Y. Legis. Comm.; story "Monster Maker" based on Frankenstein. Old Witch by Feldstein	120	240	360	960	1530	2100
4-Ingles becomes regular artist for Old Witch. 1st Vault Keeper & Crypt Keeper app. in HOF; begin series	75	150	225	600	955	1310
5-Injury-to-eye panel, pg. 4 of Wood story	59	118	177	472	749	1025
6,7,9,10: 6-Crypt Keeper by Feldstein begins. 9-Crypt Keeper by Davis begins. 10-Ingels biog.	44	88	132	352	559	765
8-Classic Feldstein Shrunken Head-c	47	94	141	376	596	815
11,12: Classic Ingels-c; 11-Kamen biog. 12-Feldstein biog.	36	72	108	288	457	625
13,15,16,20: 16-Ray Bradbury adaptation. 20-Feldstein-r/Vault of Horror #12	34	68	102	272	431	590
14-Origin Old Witch by Ingels; classic-Ingels-c	49	98	147	392	621	850
17-Classic Ingels-c	36	72	108	288	457	625
18-Old Witch-c; Ray Bradbury adaptation & biography	36	72	108	288	457	625
19-Used in **SOTI**, ill. "A comic book baseball game" & Senate investigation on juvenile delinq. bondage/decapitation-c	44	88	132	352	559	765
21-27: 23-EC version of the Hansel and Gretel story; **SOTI**, pg. 241 discusses the original Grimm tale in relation to comics. 24-Used in Senate Investigative Report, pg.8. 26-Contains anti-censorship editorial, 'Are you a Red Dupe?' 27-Cannibalism story; Vault Keeper shown reading **SOTI**	24	48	72	192	309	425
28-Low distribution	32	64	96	256	408	560

NOTE: *(Canadian reprints known; see Table of Contents). **Craig** a-15-17, 5, 7, 10, 12, 13; c-15-17, 5-7. **Crandall** a-20, 21, 26, 27. **Davis** a-4-26, 28. **Evans** a-15-19, 22-25, 27. **Feldstein** a-15-17, 20; c-4, 8-10. **Ingels** a-16, 17, 4-28; c-11-28. **Kamen** a-16, 4, 6, 7, 9-11, 13-19, 21-28. **Krigstein** a-28. **Kurtzman** a-15(#1), 17(#3). **Orlando** a-9, 12. **Wood** a-15, 16, 4-6.*

HAUNT OF FEAR, THE

Haunt of Horror #4 © MAR

Hawk & Dove ('89 series) #9 © DC

Hawkman #7 © DC

GD VG FN VF VF/NM NM-
2.0 4.0 6.0 8.0 9.0 9.2

GD VG FN VF VF/NM NM-
2.0 4.0 6.0 8.0 9.0 9.2

Gladstone Publishing: May, 1991 - No. 2, July, 1991 ($2.00, 68 pgs.)
1,2: 1 Ghastly Ingels-c(r); 2-Craig-c(r) 3.00

HAUNT OF FEAR
Russ Cochran/Gemstone Publ.: Sept, 1991 - No. 5, 1992 ($2.00, 68 pgs.); Nov, 1992 - No. 28, Aug, 1998 ($1.50/$2.00/$2.50)
1-28: 1-Ingels-c(r). 1-3-r/HOF #15-17 with original-c. 4,5-r/HOF #4,5 with original-c 2.50
Annual 1-5: 1- r/#1-5. 2- r/#6-10. 3- r/#11-15. 4- r/#16-20. 5- r/#21-25 14.00
Annual 6-r/#26-28 9.00

HAUNT OF HORROR, THE (Digest)
Marvel Comics: Jun, 1973 - No. 2, Aug, 1973 (164 pgs.; text and art)
1-Morrow painted skull-c; stories by Ellison, Howard, and Leiber; Brunner-a 4 8 12 22 34 45
2-Kelly Freas painted bondage-c; stories by McCaffrey, Goulart, Leiber, Ellison; art by Simonson, Brunner, and Buscema 3 6 9 16 23 30

HAUNT OF HORROR, THE (Magazine)
Cadence Comics Publ. (Marvel): May, 1974 - No. 5, Jan, 1975 (75¢) (B&W)
1,2: 2-Origin & 1st app. Gabriel the Devil Hunter; Satana begins 3 6 9 14 20 26
3-5: 4-Neal Adams-a. 5-Evans-a(2) 3 6 9 18 27 35
NOTE: *Alcala a-2. Colan a-2p. Heath r-1. Krigstein r-3. Reese a-1. Simonson a-1.*

HAUNT OF HORROR: EDGAR ALLAN POE
Marvel Comics (MAX): July, 2006 - No. 3, Sept, 2006 ($3.99, B&W, limited series)
1-3- Poe-inspired/adapted stories with Richard Corben-a 4.00
HC (2006, $19.99) r/series; cover sketches 20.00

HAUNT OF HORROR: LOVECRAFT
Marvel Comics (MAX): Aug, 2008 - No. 3, Oct, 2008 ($3.99, B&W, limited series)
1-3-Lovecraft-inspired/adapted stories with Richard Corben-a 4.00

HAVE GUN, WILL TRAVEL (TV)
Dell Publishing Co.: No. 931, 8/58 - No. 14, 7-9/62 (All Richard Boone photo-c)
Four Color 931 (#1) 13 26 39 95 168 240
Four Color 983,1044 (#2,3) 9 18 27 60 100 140
4 (1-3/60) - 10 8 16 24 54 90 125
11-14 8 16 24 52 86 120

HAVEN: THE BROKEN CITY (See JLA/Haven: Arrival and JLA/Haven: Anathema)
DC Comics: Feb, 2002 - No. 9, Oct, 2002 ($2.50, limited series)
1-9-Olivetti-c/a: 1- JLA app. Series concludes in JLA/Haven: Anathema 2.50

HAVOK & WOLVERINE - MELTDOWN (See Marvel Comics Presents #24)
Marvel Comics (Epic Comics): Mar, 1989 - No. 4, Oct, 1989 ($3.50, mini-series, square-bound, mature)
1-4: Art by Kent Williams & Jon J. Muth; story by Walt & Louise Simonson 4.00

HAWAIIAN DICK
Image Comics: Dec, 2002 - No. 3, Feb, 2003 ($2.95, limited series)
1-3-B. Clay Moore-s/Steven Griffin-a 3.00
...: Byrd of Paradise TPB (8/03, $14.95) r/#1-3, script & sketch pages 15.00

HAWAIIAN DICK: SCREAMING BLACK THUNDER
Image Comics: Nov, 2007 - No. 4, May, 2008 ($2.99, limited series)
1-4-B. Clay Moore-s/Scott Chantler-a 3.00

HAWAIIAN DICK: THE LAST RESORT
Image Comics: Aug, 2004 - No. 4, June, 2006 ($2.95/$2.99, limited series)
1-4-B. Clay Moore-s/Steven Griffin-a 3.00
Vol. 2 TPB (10/06, $14.99) r/#1-4 & the original series pitch 15.00

HAWAIIAN EYE (TV)
Gold Key: July, 1963 (Troy Donahue, Connie Stevens photo-c)
1 (10073-307) 5 10 15 34 55 75

HAWAIIAN ILLUSTRATED LEGENDS SERIES
Hogarth Press: 1975 (B&W)(Cover printed w/blue, yellow, and green)
1-Kalelealuaka, the Mysterious Warrior 5.00

HAWK, THE (Also see Approved Comics #1, 7 & Tops In Adventure)
Ziff-Davis/St. John Publ. Co. No. 4 on: Wint/51 - No. 3, 11-12/52; No. 4, 1-2/53; No. 8, 9/54 - No. 12, 5/55 (Painted c-1-4)(#5-7 don't exist)
1-Anderson-a 20 40 60 115 183 250
2 (Sum, '52)-Kubert, Infantino-a 12 24 36 69 97 125
3-4,11: 11-Buckskin Belle & The Texan app. 10 20 30 56 76 95
8-10,12: 8(9/54)-Reprints #3 w/different-c by Baker. 9-Baker-c/a; Kubert-a(r)/#2. 10-Baker-c/a; r/one story from #2. 12-Baker-c/a; Buckskin Belle app. 15 30 45 85 130 175
3-D 1(11/53, 25¢)-Came w/glasses; Baker-c 32 64 96 186 298 410
NOTE: *Baker c-8-12. Larsen a-10. Tuska a-1, 9, 12. Painted c-1, 4, 7.*

HAWK AND THE DOVE, THE (See Showcase #75 & Teen Titans) (1st series)
National Periodical Publications: Aug-Sept, 1968 - No. 6, June-July, 1969
1-Ditko-c/a 8 16 24 54 90 125
2-6: 5-Teen Titans cameo 5 10 15 32 51 70
NOTE: *Ditko c/a-1, 2. Gil Kane a-3p, 4p, 5, 6p; c-3-6.*

HAWK AND DOVE (2nd Series)
DC Comics: Oct, 1988 - No. 5, Feb, 1989 ($1.00, limited series)
1-Rob Liefeld-c/a(p) in all 4.00
2-5 3.00
Trade paperback ('93, $9.95)-Reprints #1-5 10.00

HAWK AND DOVE
DC Comics: June, 1989 - No. 28, Oct, 1991 ($1.00)
1-28 2.50
Annual 1,2 ('90, '91; $2.00) 1-Liefeld pin-up. 2-Armageddon 2001 x-over 3.00

HAWK AND DOVE
DC Comics: Nov, 1997 - No. 5, Mar, 1998 ($2.50, limited series)
1-5-Baron-s/Zachary & Giordano-a 2.50

HAWK AND WINDBLADE (See Elflord)
Warp Graphics: Aug, 1997 - No.2, Sept, 1997 ($2.95, limited series)
1,2-Blair-s/Chan-c/a 3.00

HAWKEYE (See The Avengers #16 & Tales Of Suspense #57)
Marvel Comics Group: Sept, 1983 - No. 4, Dec, 1983 (limited series)
1-4: Mark Gruenwald-a/scripts. 1-Origin Hawkeye. 3-Origin Mockingbird. 4-Hawkeye & Mockingbird elope 3.00

HAWKEYE
Marvel Comics: Jan, 1994 - No. 4, Apr, 1994 ($1.75, limited series)
1-4 2.50

HAWKEYE (Volume 2)
Marvel Comics: Dec, 2003 - No. 8, Aug, 2004 ($2.99)
1-8: 1-6-Nicieza-s/Raffaele-a. 7,8-Bennett-a; Black Widow app. 3.00

HAWKEYE & THE LAST OF THE MOHICANS (TV)
Dell Publishing Co.: No. 884, Mar, 1958 (one-shot)
Four Color 884-Photo-c 7 14 21 47 76 105

HAWKEYE: EARTH'S MIGHTIEST MARKSMAN
Marvel Comics: Oct, 1998 ($2.99, one-shot)
1-Justice and Firestar app.; DeFalco-s 3.00

HAWKGIRL (Title continued from Hawkman #49, Apr, 2006)
DC Comics: No. 50, May, 2006 - No. 66, Sept, 2007 ($2.50/$2.99)
50-66: 50-Chaykin-a/Simonson-s begin; One Year Later. 52-Begin $2.99-c. 57,58-Bennett-a. 59-Blackfire app. 63-Batman app. 64-Superman app. 3.00
...: Hath-Set TPB (2008, $17.99) r/#61-66 18.00
...: Hawkman Returns TPB (2007, $17.99) r/#57-60 & JSA Classified #21,22 18.00
...: The Maw TPB (2007, $17.99) r/#50-56 18.00

HAWKMAN (See Atom & Hawkman, The Brave & the Bold, DC Comics Presents, Detective Comics, Flash Comics, Hawkworld, JSA, Justice League of America #31, Legend of the Hawkman, Mystery in Space, Shadow War Of..., Showcase, & World's Finest #256)

HAWKMAN (1st Series) (Also see The Atom #7 & Brave & the Bold #34-36, 42-44, 51)
National Periodical Publications: Apr-May, 1964 - No. 27, Aug-Sept, 1968
1-(4-5/64)-Anderson-c/a begins, ends #21 52 104 156 442 846 1250
2 22 44 66 161 298 435
3,5: 5-2nd app. Shadow Thief 15 30 45 105 190 275
4-Origin & 1st app. Zatanna (10-11/64) 17 34 51 126 233 340
6 11 22 33 79 140 200
7 9 18 27 65 113 165
8-10: 9-Atom cameo; Hawkman & Atom learn each other's I.D.; 3rd app. Shadow Thief 9 18 27 60 100 140
11-15 7 14 21 45 73 100
16,17-27: 18-Adam Strange x-over (cameo #19). 25-G.A. Hawkman-r by Moldoff. 26-Kirby-a(r). 27-Kubert-c 5 10 15 34 55 75

HAWKMAN (2nd Series)
DC Comics: Aug, 1986 - No. 17, Dec, 1987
1-17: 10-Byrne-c, Special #1 (1986, $1.25) 2.50
Trade paperback (1989, $19.95)-r/Brave and the Bold #34-36,42-44 by Kubert; Kubert-c 20.00

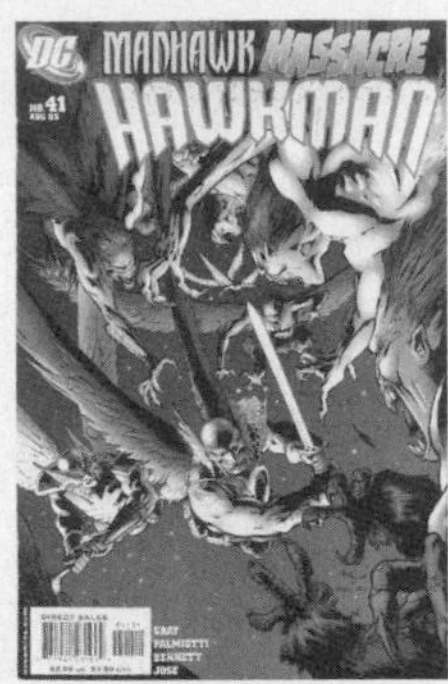

Hawkman #41 © DC

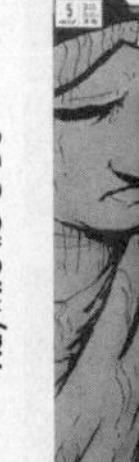

Haywire #5 © DC

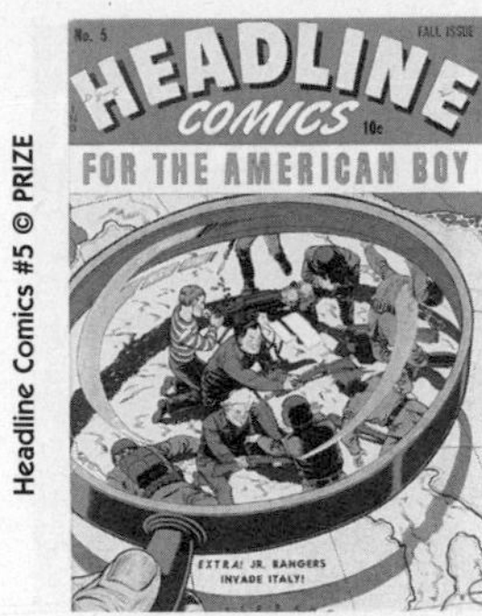

Headline Comics #5 © PRIZE

	GD	VG	FN	VF	VF/NM	NM-
	2.0	4.0	6.0	8.0	9.0	9.2

HAWKMAN (4th Series)(See both Hawkworld limited & ongoing series)
DC Comics: Sept, 1993 - No. 33, July, 1996 ($1.75/$1.95/$2.25)

1-($2.50)-Gold foil embossed-c; storyline cont'd from Hawkworld ongoing series; new costume & powers. 3.00
2-13,0,14-33: 2-Green Lantern x-over. 3-Airstryke app. 4,6-Wonder Woman app. 13-(9/94)-Zero Hour. 0-(10/94). 14-(11/94). 15-Aquaman-c & app. 23-Wonder Woman app. 25-Kent Williams-c. 29,30-Chaykin-c. 32-Breyfogle-c 2.50
Annual 1 (1993, $2.50, 68 pgs.)-Bloodlines Earthplague 3.00
Annual 2 (1995, $3.95)-Year One story 4.00

HAWKMAN (Title continues as Hawkgirl #50-on) (See JSA #23 for return)
DC Comics: May, 2002 - No. 49, Apr, 2006 ($2.50)

1-Johns & Robinson-s/Morales-a 5.00
1-2nd printing 2.50
2-40: 2-4-Shadow Thief app. 5,6-Green Arrow-c/app. 8-Atom-c/app. 13-Van Sciver-a. 14-Gentleman Ghost app. 15-Hawkwoman app. 16-Byth returns. 23-25-Black Reign x-over with JSA #56-58. 26-Byrne-c/a. 29,30-Land-c. 37-Golden Eagle returns 2.50
41-49: 41-Hawkman killed. 43-Golden Eagle origin. 46-49-Adam Kubert-c 2.50
...: Allies & Enemies TPB (2004, $14.95) r/#7-14 & pages from Secret Files and Origins 15.00
...: Endless Flight TPB (2003, $12.95) r/#1-6 & Secret Files and Origins 13.00
...: Rise of the Golden Eagle TPB (2006, $17.99) r/#37-45 18.00
... Secret Files and Origins (10/02, $4.95) profiles and pin-ups by various 5.00
... Special 1 (10/08, $3.50) Tie-in to Rann-Thanagar Holy War series; Starlin-s/a(p) 3.50
...: Wings of Fury TPB (2005, $17.99) r/#15-22 18.00

HAWKMOON: THE JEWEL IN THE SKULL
First Comics: May, 1986 - No. 4, Nov, 1986 ($1.75, limited series, Baxter paper)

1-4: Adapts novel by Michael Moorcock 2.50

HAWKMOON: THE MAD GOD'S AMULET
First Comics: Jan, 1987 - No. 4, July, 1987 ($1.75, limited series, Baxter paper)

1-4: Adapts novel by Michael Moorcock 2.50

HAWKMOON: THE RUNESTAFF
First Comics: Jun, 1988 -No. 4, Dec, 1988 ($1.75-$1.95, lim. series, Baxter paper)

1-4: ($1.75) Adapts novel by Michael Moorcock. 3,4 ($1.95) 2.50

HAWKMOON: THE SWORD OF DAWN
First Comics: Sept, 1987 - No. 4, Mar, 1988 ($1.75, lim. series, Baxter paper)

1-4: Dorman painted-c; adapts Moorcock novel 2.50

HAWKS OF THE SEAS (WILL EISNER'S...)
Dark Horse Comics: July, 2003 ($19.95, B&W, hardcover)

nn-Reprints 1937-1939 weekly Pirate serial by Will Eisner; Williamson Intro. 20.00

HAWKWORLD
DC Comics: 1989 - No. 3, 1989 ($3.95, prestige format, limited series)

Book 1-3: 1-Tim Truman story & art in all; Hawkman dons new costume; reintro Byth 4.00
TPB (1991, $16.95) r/#1-3 17.00

HAWKWORLD (3rd Series)
DC Comics: June, 1990 - No. 32, Mar, 1993 ($1.50/$1.75)

1-Hawkman spin-off; story cont'd from limited series. 3.00
2-32: 15,16-War of the Gods x-over. 22-J'onn J'onzz app. 2.50
Annual 1-3 ('90-'92, $2.95, 68 pgs.), 2-2nd printing with silver ink-c 3.00
NOTE: *Truman a-30-32; c-27-32, Annual 1.*

HAYWIRE
DC Comics: Oct, 1988 - No. 13, Sept, 1989 ($1.25, mature)

1-13 2.50

HAZARD
Image Comics (WildStorm Prod.): June, 1996 - No. 7, Nov, 1996 ($1.75)

1-7: 1-Intro Hazard; Jeff Mariotte scripts begin; Jim Lee-c(p) 3.00

HEADHUNTERS
Image Comics: Apr, 1997 - No. 3, June, 1997 ($2.95, B&W)

1-3: Chris Marrinan-s/a 3.00

HEADLINE COMICS
DC Comics: Jan. 1942

nn - Ashcan comic, not distributed to newsstands, only for in-house use. Cover art is More Fun Comics #73 with interior being Star Spangled Comics #2 (no known sales)

HEADLINE COMICS (...For the American Boy) (...Crime No. 32-39)
Prize Publ./American Boys' Comics: Feb, 1943 - No. 22, Nov-Dec, 1946; No. 23, 1947 - No. 77, Oct, 1956

	GD	VG	FN	VF	VF/NM	NM-
	2.0	4.0	6.0	8.0	9.0	9.2

	GD	VG	FN	VF	VF/NM	NM-
1-Junior Rangers-c/stories begin; Yank & Doodle x-over in Junior Rangers (Junior Rangers are Uncle Sam's nephews)	57	114	171	359	610	860
2	34	68	102	198	319	440
3-Used in **POP**, pg. 84	23	46	69	135	218	300
4-7,9,10: 4,9,10-Hitler stories in each	20	40	60	115	183	250
8-Classic Hitler-c	83	166	249	523	887	1250
11,12	18	36	54	103	162	220
13-15-Blue Streak in all	19	38	57	109	172	235
16-Origin & 1st app. Atomic Man (11-12/45)	27	54	81	158	254	350
17,18,20,21: 21-Atomic Man ends (9-10/46)	15	30	45	90	140	190
19-S&K-a	31	62	93	181	291	400
22-Last Junior Rangers; Kiefer-c	14	28	42	80	115	150
23,24: (All S&K-a). 23-Valentine's Day Massacre story; content changes to true crime. 24-Dope-crazy killer story	30	60	90	174	280	385
25-35-S&K-c/a. 25-Powell-a	27	54	81	158	254	350
36-S&K-a; photo-c begin	21	42	63	123	197	270
37-1 pg. S&K, Severin-a; rare Kirby photo-c app.	21	42	63	123	197	270
38,40-Meskin-a	10	20	30	58	79	100
39,41-43,46-50,52-55: 41-J. Edgar Hoover 26th Anniversary Issue with photo on-c. 43,49-Meskin-a	9	18	27	50	65	80
44-S&K-c; Severin/Elder, Meskin-a	15	30	45	83	124	165
45-Kirby-a	13	26	39	72	101	130
51-Kirby-c	11	22	33	62	86	110
56-S&K-a	14	28	42	81	118	155
57-77: 72-Meskin-c/a(i)	8	16	24	42	54	65

NOTE: ***Hollingsworth** a-30. Photo c-36-43. **H. C. Kiefer** c-12-16, 22. Atomic Man c-17-19.*

HEADMAN
Innovation Publishing: 1990 ($2.50, mature)

1-Sci/fi 2.50

HEAP, THE
Skywald Publications: Sept, 1971 (52 pgs.)

	GD	VG	FN	VF	VF/NM	NM-
1-Kinstler-r/Strange Worlds #8; new-s w/Sutton-a	3	6	9	20	30	40

HEART AND SOUL
Mikeross Publications: April-May, 1954 - No. 2, June-July, 1954

	GD	VG	FN	VF	VF/NM	NM-
1,2	8	16	24	44	57	70

HEARTBREAKERS (Also see Dark Horse Presents)
Dark Horse Comics: Apr, 1996 - No. 4, July, 1996 ($2.95, limited series)

1-4: 1-W/paper doll & pin-up. 2-Alex Ross pin-up. 3-Evan Dorkin pin-ups. 4-Brereton-c; Matt Wagner pin-up 3.00
...Superdigest (7/98, $9.95, digest-size) new stories 10.00

HEARTLAND (See Hellblazer)
DC Comics (Vertigo): Mar, 1997 ($4.95, one-shot, mature)

1-Garth Ennis-s/Steve Dillon-c/a 5.00

HEART OF DARKNESS
Hardline Studios: 1994 ($2.95)

1-Brereton-c 3.00

HEART OF EMPIRE
Dark Horse Comics: Apr, 1999 - No. 9, Dec, 1999 ($2.95, limited series)

1-9-Bryan Talbot-s/a 3.00

HEART OF THE BEAST, THE
DC Comics (Vertigo): 1994 ($19.95, hardcover, mature)

1-Dean Motter scripts 20.00

HEARTS OF DARKNESS (See Ghost Rider; Wolverine; Punisher: Hearts of...)

HEART THROBS (Love Stories No. 147 on)
Quality Comics/National Periodical #47(4-5/57) on (Arleigh #48-101): 8/49 - No. 8, 10/50; No. 9, 3/52 - No. 146, Oct, 1972

	GD	VG	FN	VF	VF/NM	NM-
1-Classic Ward-c, Gustavson-a, 9 pgs.	42	84	126	260	435	610
2-Ward-c/a (9 pgs); Gustavson-a	26	52	78	152	244	335
3-Gustavson-a	13	26	39	72	101	130
4,6,8-Ward-a, 8-9 pgs.	15	30	45	88	137	185
5,7	10	20	30	58	79	100
9-Robert Mitchum, Jane Russell photo-c	14	28	42	76	108	140
10,15-Ward-a	14	28	42	76	108	140
11-14,16-20: 12 (7/52)	9	18	27	52	69	85
21-Ward-c	12	24	36	69	97	125
22,23-Ward-a(p)	10	20	30	56	76	95
24-33: 33-Last pre-code (3/55)	9	18	27	50	65	80
34-39,41-44,46 (12/56; last Quality issue)	9	18	27	47	61	75
40-Ward-a; r-7 pgs./#21	9	18	27	52	69	85

Heart Throbs #5 © QUA

Heckle and Jeckle #25 © CBS

Hellblazer #238 © DC

	GD 2.0	VG 4.0	FN 6.0	VF 8.0	VF/NM 9.0	NM- 9.2
45-Baker-a	6	12	18	39	62	85
47-(4-5/57; 1st DC issue)	21	42	63	152	281	410
48-60, 100	9	18	27	60	100	140
61-70	6	12	18	43	69	95
71-99: 74-Last 10 cent issue	6	12	18	37	59	80
101-The Beatles app. on-c	14	28	42	99	175	250
102-120: 102-123-(Serial)-Three Girls, Their Lives, Their Loves	3	6	9	20	30	40
121-132,143-146	3	6	9	17	25	32
133-142-(52 pgs.)	4	8	12	22	34	45

NOTE: *Gustavson a-8. Tuska a-128. Photo c-4, 5, 8-10, 15, 17.*

HEART THROBS - THE BEST OF DC ROMANCE COMICS (See Fireside Book Series)

HEART THROBS
DC Comics (Vertigo): Jan, 1999 - No. 4, Apr, 1999 ($2.95, lim. series)

1-4-Romance anthology. 1-Timm-c. 3-Corben-a						3.00

HEATHCLIFF (See Star Comics Magazine)
Marvel Comics (Star Comics)/Marvel Comics No. 23 on: Apr, 1985 - No. 56, Feb, 1991 (#16-on, $1.00)

1-Post-a most issues						6.00
2-10,47: 47-Batman parody (Catman vs. the Soaker)						4.00
11-46,48-56: 43-X-Mas issue						3.00
Annual 1 ('87)						3.00

HEATHCLIFF'S FUNHOUSE
Marvel Comics (Star Comics)/Marvel No. 6 on: May, 1987 - No. 10, 1988

1						4.00
2-10						3.00

HEAVEN'S DEVILS
Image Comics: Sept, 2003 - No. 4, July, 2004 ($2.95/$3.50, B&W, limited series)

1-3-($2.95) Jai Nitz-s/Zach Howard-a						3.00
4-($3.50) Kevin Sharpe-a						3.50

HEAVY HITTERS
Marvel Comics (Epic Comics): 1993 ($3.75, 68 pgs.)

1-Bound w/trading card; Lawdog, Feud, Alien Legion, Trouble With Girls, & Spyke						3.75

HEAVY LIQUID
DC Comics (Vertigo): Oct, 1999 - No. 5, Feb, 2000 ($5.95, limited series)

1-5-Paul Pope-s/a; flip covers						6.00
TPB (2001, $29.95) r/#1-5						30.00

HECKLE AND JECKLE (Paul Terry's...)(See Blue Ribbon, Giant Comics Edition #5A & 10, Paul Terry's, Terry-Toons Comics)
St. John Publ. Co. No. 1-24/Pines No. 25 on: No. 3, 2/52 - No. 24, 10/55; No. 25, Fall/56 - No. 34, 6/59

3(#1)-Funny animal	24	48	72	140	225	310
4(6/52), 5	13	26	39	74	105	135
6-10(4/53)	9	18	27	50	65	80
11-20	8	16	24	40	50	60
21-34: 25-Begin CBS Television Presents on-c	7	14	21	35	43	50

HECKLE AND JECKLE (TV) (See New Terrytoons)
Gold Key/Dell Publ. Co.: 11/62 - No. 4, 8/63; 5/66; No. 2, 10/66; No. 3, 8/67

1 (11/62; Gold Key)	6	12	18	43	69	95
2-4	4	8	12	22	34	45
1 (5/66; Dell)	4	8	12	26	41	55
2,3	3	6	9	19	29	38

(See March of Comics No. 379, 472, 484)

HECKLE AND JECKLE 3-D
Spotlight Comics: 1987 - No. 2?, 1987 ($2.50)

1,2						5.00

HECKLER, THE
DC Comics: Sept, 1992 - No. 6, Feb, 1993 ($1.25)

1-6-T&M Bierbaum-s/Keith Giffen-c/a						2.50

HECTIC PLANET
Slave Labor Graphics 1998 ($12.95/$14.95)

Book 1,2-r-Dorkin-s/a from Pirate Corp$ Vol. 1 & 2						15.00

HECTOR COMICS (The Keenest Teen in Town)
Key Publications: Nov, 1953 - No. 3, 1954

1-Teen humor	6	12	18	31	38	45
2,3	4	8	12	18	22	25

HECTOR HEATHCOTE (TV)
Gold Key: Mar, 1964

1 (10111-403)	7	14	21	47	76	105

HECTOR THE INSPECTOR (See Top Flight Comics)

HEDGE KNIGHT, THE
Image Comics: Aug, 2003 - No. 6, Apr, 2004 ($2.95, limited series)

1-6-George R.R. Martin-s/Mike S. Miller-a. 1-Two covers by Kaluta and Miller						3.00
George R.R. Martin's The Hedge Knight HC (Marvel, 2006, $19.99) r/series; 2 covers						20.00
George R.R. Martin's The Hedge Knight SC (Marvel, 2007, $14.99) r/series						15.00
TPB (2004, $14.95) r/series plus new short story						15.00

HEDGE KNIGHT II: SWORN SWORD
Marvel Comics (Dabel Brothers): Jun, 2007 - No. 6, Jun, 2008 ($2.99, limited series)

1-6-George R.R. Martin-s/Mike Miller-a. 1-Two covers by Yu & Miller, plus Miller B&W-c						3.00

HEDY DEVINE COMICS (Formerly All Winners #21? or Teen #22?(6/47); Hedy of Hollywood #36 on; also see Annie Oakley, Comedy & Venus)
Marvel Comics (RCM)/Atlas #50: No. 22, Aug, 1947 - No. 50, Sept, 1952

22-1st app. Hedy Devine (also see Joker #32)	29	58	87	169	272	375
23,24,27-30: 23-Wolverton-a, 1 pg; Kurtzman's "Hey Look", 2 pgs. 24,27-30- "Hey Look" by Kurtzman, 1-3 pgs.	19	38	57	109	172	235
25-Classic "Hey Look" by Kurtzman, "Optical Illusion"	20	40	60	118	189	260
26- "Giggles 'n' Grins" by Kurtzman	15	30	45	88	137	185
31-34,36-50: 32-Anti-Wertham editorial	12	24	36	69	97	125
35-Four pgs. "Rusty" by Kurtzman	15	30	45	90	140	190

HEDY-MILLIE-TESSIE COMEDY (See Comedy Comics)

HEDY WOLFE (Also see Patsy & Hedy & Miss America Magazine V1#2)
Atlas Publishing Co. (Emgee): Aug, 1957

1-Patsy Walker's rival; Al Hartley-c	12	24	36	67	94	120

HEE HAW (TV)
Charlton Press: July, 1970 - No. 7, Aug, 1971

1	4	8	12	28	44	60
2-7	3	6	9	19	29	30

HEIDI (See Dell Jr. Treasury No. 6)

HELEN OF TROY (Movie)
Dell Publishing Co.: No. 684, Mar, 1956 (one-shot)

Four Color 684-Buscema-a, photo-c	9	18	27	65	113	160

HELL
Dark Horse Comics: July, 2003 - No. 4, Mar, 2004 ($2.99, limited series)

1-4-Augustyn-s/Demong-a/Meglia-c						3.00

HELLBLAZER (John Constantine) (See Saga of Swamp Thing #37) (Also see Books of Magic limited series)
DC Comics (Vertigo #63 on): Jan, 1988 - Present ($1.25-$2.99)

1-(44 pgs.)-John Constantine; McKean-c thru #21	2	4	6	8	10	12
2-5	1	2	3	4	5	7
6-8,10: 10-Swamp Thing cameo						5.00
9,19: 9-X-over w/Swamp Thing #76. 19-Sandman app.						6.00
11-18,20						5.00
21-26,28-30: 22-Williams-c. 24-Contains bound-in Shocker movie poster. 25,26-Grant Morrison scripts.						5.00
27-Gaiman scripts; Dave McKean-a; low print run	2	4	6	10	12	15
31-39: 36-Preview of World Without End.						4.00
40-($2.25, 52 pgs.)-Dave McKean-a & colors; preview of Kid Eternity						4.00
41-Ennis scripts begin; ends #83						5.00
42-120: 44,45-Sutton-a(i). 50-($3.00, 52 pgs.). 52-Glenn Fabry painted-c begin. 62-Special Death insert by McKean. 63-Silver metallic ink on-c. 77-Totleben-c. 84-Sean Phillips-c/a begins; Delano story. 85-88-Eddie Campbell story. 75-($2.95, 52 pgs.). 89-Paul Jenkins scripts begin. 100,120 ($3.50,48 pgs.). 108-Adlard-a.						3.50
121-199, 201-246: 129-Ennis-s. 141-Bradstreet-a. 146-150-Corben-a 151-Azzarello-s begin. 175-Carey-s begin; Dillon-a. 176-Begin $2.75-c. 182,183-Bermejo-a. 216-Mina-s begins. 220-Begin $2.99-c. 229-Carey-s/Leon-a. 234-Initial printing (white title logo) has missing text; corrected printing has lt. blue title logo						3.00
200-($4.50) Carey-s/Dillon, Frusin, Manco-a						4.50
Annual 1 (1989, $2.95, 68 pgs.)-Bryan Talbot's 1st work in American comics						5.00
Special 1 (1993, $3.95, 68 pgs.)-Ennis story; w/pin-ups.						4.00
...Black Flowers (2005, $14.99, TPB) r/#181-186						15.00
...Bloodlines (2007, $19.99, TPB) r/#47-50,52-55,59-61						20.00
...Damnation's Flame (1999, $16.95, TPB) r/#72-77						17.00

Hellboy, Jr. #1 © DH

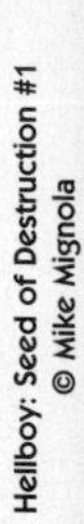
Hellboy: Seed of Destruction #1 © Mike Mignola

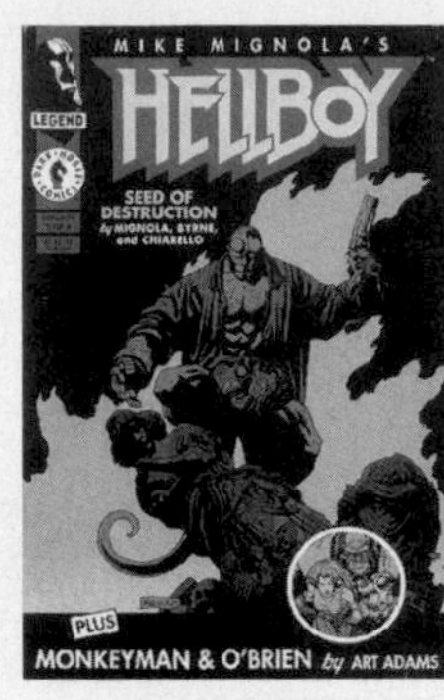

Hellboy: The Crooked Man #1 © Mike Mignola

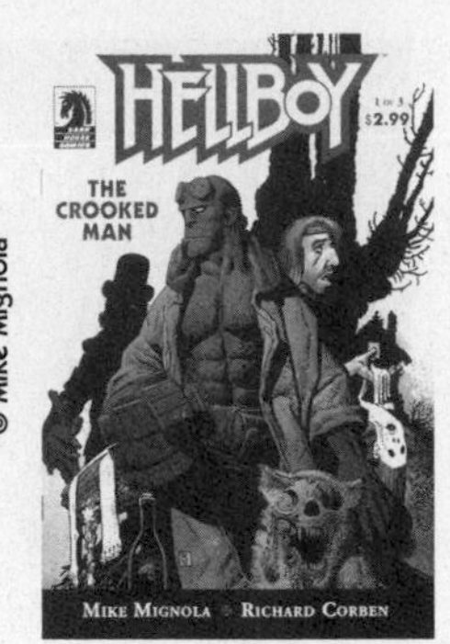

GD VG FN VF VF/NM NM-
2.0 4.0 6.0 8.0 9.0 9.2

...Dangerous Habits (1997, $14.95, TPB) r/#41-46 15.00
...Fear and Loathing (1997, $14.95, TPB) r/#62-67 18.00
...Fear and Loathing (2nd printing, $17.95) 18.00
...: Freezes Over (2003, $14.95, TPB) r/#157-163 15.00
...Good Intentions (2002, $12.95, TPB) r/#151-156 13.00
...Hard Time (2001, $9.95, TPB) r/#146-150 10.00
...Haunting (2003, $12.95, TPB) r/#134-139 13.00
...Highwater (2004, $19.95, TPB) r/#164-174 20.00
John Constantine Hellblazer: All His Engines HC (2005, $24.95, with dustjacket) new graphic novel; Mike Carey-s/Leonardo Manco-a 25.00
John Constantine Hellblazer: All His Engines SC (2006, $14.99) new graphic novel 15.00
John Constantine Hellblazer: Empathy is the Enemy SC (2006, $14.99) r/#216-222 15.00
John Constantine Hellblazer: Joyride SC (2008, $14.99) r/#230-237 15.00
John Constantine Hellblazer: The Devil You Know SC (2007, $19.99) r/#10-13, Annual #1 and The Horrorist miniseries #1,2 20.00
John Constantine Hellblazer: The Fear Machine SC (2008, $19.99, TPB) r/#14-22 20.00
John Constantine Hellblazer: The Red Right Hand SC (2007, $14.99) r/#223-228 15.00
...Original Sins (1993, $19.95, TPB) r/#1-9 20.00
...Rake at the Gates of Hell (2003, $19.95, TPB) r/#78-83; Heartland #1 20.00
...: Rare Cuts (2005, $14.95, TPB) r/#11,25,26,35,56,84 & Vertigo Secret Files: Hellblazer 15.00
...: Reasons To Be Cheerful (2007, $14.99, TPB) r/#201-206 15.00
...: Red Sepulchre (2005, $12.99, TPB) r/#175-180 13.00
...: Setting Sun (2004, $12.95, TPB) r/#140-143 13.00
...: Son of Man (2004, $12.95, TPB) r/#129-133 13.00
...: Stations of the Cross (2006, $14.99, TPB) r/#194-200 15.00
...: Staring At The Wall (2005, $14.99, TPB) r/#187-193 15.00
...Tainted Love (1998, $16.95, TPB) r/#68-71, Vertigo Jam #1 and Hellblazer Special #1 17.00

NOTE: ***Alcala** a-8i, 9i, 18-22i. **Gaiman** scripts-27. **McKean** a-27,40; c-1-21. **Sutton** a-44i, 45i. **Talbot** a-Annual 1.*

HELLBLAZER SPECIAL: BAD BLOOD
DC Comics (Vertigo): Sept, 2000 - No. 4, Dec, 2000 ($2.95, mini-series)
1-4-Delano-s/Bond-a; Constantine in 2025 London 3.00

HELLBLAZER SPECIAL: CHAS
DC Comics (Vertigo): Sept, 2008 - No. 5 ($2.99, mini-series)
1,2-Story of Constantine's cab driver; Oliver-s/Sudzuka-a/Fabry-c 3.00

HELLBLAZER SPECIAL: LADY CONSTANTINE
DC Comics (Vertigo): Feb, 2003 - No. 4, May, 2003 ($2.95, mini-series)
1-4-Story of Johanna Constantine in 1785; Diggle-s/Sudzuka-a/Noto-c 3.00

HELLBLAZER/THE BOOKS OF MAGIC
DC Comics (Vertigo): Dec, 1997 - No. 2, Jan, 1998 ($2.50, mini-series)
1,2-John Constantine and Tim Hunter 2.50

HELLBOY (Also see Batman/Hellboy/Starman, Danger Unlimited #4, Dark Horse Presents, Free Comic Book Day edition in the Promotional section, Gen^{13} #13B, Ghost/Hellboy, John Byrne's Next Men, San Diego Comic Con #2, & Savage Dragon)

HELLBOY: ALMOST COLOSSUS
Dark Horse Comics (Legend): Jun, 1997 - No. 2, Jul, 1997 ($2.95, lim. series)
1,2-Mignola-s/a 3.50

HELLBOY: BOX FULL OF EVIL
Dark Horse Comics: Aug, 1999 - No. 2, Sept, 1999 ($2.95, lim. series)
1,2-Mignola-s/a; back-up story w/ Matt Smith-a 3.50

HELLBOY CHRISTMAS SPECIAL
Dark Horse Comics: Dec, 1997 ($3.95, one-shot)
nn-Christmas stories by Mignola, Gianni, Darrow, Purcell 4.50

HELLBOY: CONQUEROR WORM
Dark Horse Comics: May, 2001 - No. 4, Aug, 2001 ($2.99, lim. series)
1-4-Mignola-s/a/c 3.00

HELLBOY: DARKNESS CALLS
Dark Horse Comics: Apr, 2007 - No. 6, Nov, 2007 ($2.99, lim. series)
1-6-Mignola-s/Fegredo-a 3.00

HELLBOY, JR.
Dark Horse Comics: Oct, 1999 - No. 2, Nov, 1999 ($2.95, limited series)
1,2-Stories and art by various 3.50
TPB (1/04, $14.95) r/#1&2, Halloween; sketch pages; intro. by Steve Niles; Bill Wray-c 15.00

HELLBOY, JR., HALLOWEEN SPECIAL
Dark Horse Comics: Oct, 1997 ($3.95, one-shot)
nn-"Harvey" style renditions of Hellboy characters; Bill Wray, Mike Mignola & various-s/a; wraparound-c by Wray 4.50

HELLBOY: MAKOMA, OR A TALE TOLD...
Dark Horse Comics: Feb, 2006 - No. 2, Mar, 2006 ($2.99, lim. series)
1,2-Mignola-s/c; Mignola & Corben-a 3.00

HELLBOY PREMIERE EDITION
Dark Horse Comics (Wizard): 2004 (no price, one-shot)
nn- Two covers by Mignola & Davis; Mignola-s/a; BPRD story w/Arcudi-s/Davis-a 5.00
Wizard World Los Angeles-Movie photo-c; Mignola-s/a; BPRD story w/Arcudi-s/Davis-a 10.00

HELLBOY: SEED OF DESTRUCTION
Dark Horse Comics (Legend): Mar, 1994 - No. 4, Jun, 1994 ($2.50, lim. series)
1-4-Mignola-c/a w/Byrne scripts; Monkeyman & O'Brien back-up story (origin) by Art Adams. 5.00
Trade paperback (1994, $17.95)-collects all four issues plus r/Hellboy's 1st app. in San Diego Comic Con #2 & pin-ups 18.00
Limited edition hardcover (1995, $99.95)-includes everything in trade paperback plus additional material. 100.00

HELLBOY STRANGE PLACES
Dark Horse Books: Apr, 2006 ($17.95, TPB)
SC - Reprints Hellboy: The Third Wish #1,2 and Hellboy: The Island #1,2; sketch pages 18.00

HELLBOY: THE CHAINED COFFIN AND OTHERS
Dark Horse Comics (Legend): Aug, 1998 ($17.95, TPB)
nn-Mignola-c/a/s; reprints out-of-print one shots; pin-up gallery 18.00

HELLBOY: THE COMPANION
Dark Horse Books: May, 2008 ($14.95, 9"x6", TPB)
nn-Overview of Hellboy history, characters, stories, mythology; text with Mignola panels 15.00

HELLBOY: THE CORPSE
Dark Horse Comics: Mar, 2004 (25¢, one-shot)
nn-Mignola-c/a/scripts; reprints "The Corpse" serial from Capitol City's Advance Comics catalog; development sketches and photos of the Corpse from the Hellboy movie 2.50

HELLBOY: THE CORPSE AND THE IRON SHOES
Dark Horse Comics (Legend): Jan, 1996 ($2.95, one-shot)
nn-Mignola-c/a/scripts; reprints "The Corpse" serial w/new story 3.50

HELLBOY: THE CROOKED MAN
Dark Horse Comics: Jul, 2008 - No. 3 ($2.99, lim. series)
1,2-Mignola-s/Corben-a/c 3.00

HELLBOY: THE GOLDEN ARMY
Dark Horse Comics: Jan, 2008 (no cover price)
nn-Prelude to the 2008 movie; Del Toro & Mignola-s/Velasco-a; 3 photo covers 2.25

HELLBOY: THE ISLAND
Dark Horse Comics: June, 2005 - No. 2, July, 2005 ($2.99, lim. series)
1,2: Mignola-c/a & scripts 3.00

HELLBOY: THE RIGHT HAND OF DOOM
Dark Horse Comics (Legend): Apr, 2000 ($17.95, TPB)
nn-Mignola-c/a/s; reprints 18.00

HELLBOY: THE THIRD WISH
Dark Horse Comics (Maverick): July, 2002 - No. 2, Aug, 2002 ($2.99, limited series)
1,2-Mignola-c/a/s 3.00

HELLBOY THE TROLL WITCH AND OTHERS
Dark Horse Books: Nov, 2007 ($17.95, TPB)
SC - Reprints Hellboy: Makoma, Hellboy Premiere Edition and stories from Dark Horse Book of Hauntings, DHB of Witchcraft, DHB of the Dead, DHB of Monsters 18.00

HELLBOY: THE WOLVES OF ST. AUGUST
Dark Horse Comics (Legend): 1995 ($4.95, squarebound, one-shot)
nn-Mignola--c/a/scripts; r/Dark Horse Presents #88-91 with additional story 5.00

HELLBOY: WAKE THE DEVIL (Sequel to Seed of Destruction)
Dark Horse Comics (Legend): Jun, 1996 - No. 5, Oct, 1996 ($2.95, lim. series)
1-5: Mignola-c/a & scripts; The Monstermen back-up story by Gary Gianni 4.00
TPB (1997, $17.95) r/#1-5 18.00

HELLBOY: WEIRD TALES
Dark Horse Comics: Feb, 2003 - No. 8, Apr, 2004 ($2.99, limited series, anthology)
1-8-Hellboy stories from other creators. 1-Cassaday-c/s/a; Watson-s/a. 6-Cho-c 3.00
... Vol. 1 (2004, 17.95) r/#1-4 18.00
... Vol. 2 (2004, 17.95) r/#5-8 and Lobster Johnson serial from #1-8 18.00

HELLCAT

Hell's Angel #2 © MAR

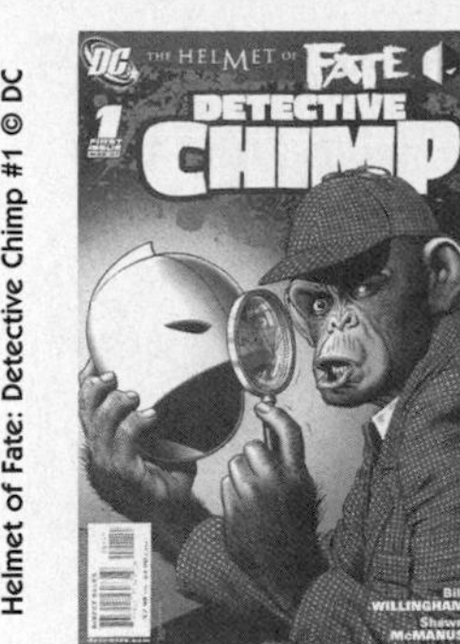

Helmet of Fate: Detective Chimp #1 © DC

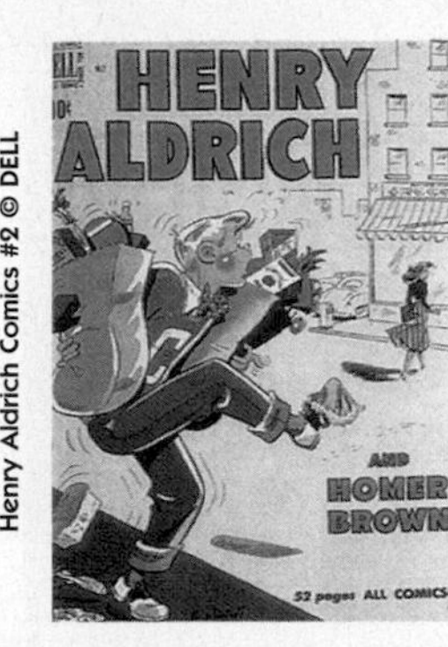

Henry Aldrich Comics #2 © DELL

GD VG FN VF VF/NM NM-
2.0 4.0 6.0 8.0 9.0 9.2

Marvel Comics: Sept, 2000 - No. 3, Nov, 2000 ($2.99)
1-3-Englehart-s/Breyfogle-a; Hedy Wolfe app. 3.00

HELLCOP
Image Comics (Avalon Studios): Aug, 1998 - No. 4, Mar, 1999 ($2.50)
1-4: 1-(Oct. on-c) Casey-s 2.50

HELL ETERNAL
DC Comics (Vertigo Verité): 1998 ($6.95, squarebound, one-shot)
1-Delano-s/Phillips-a 7.00

HELLGATE: LONDON (Based on the video game)
Dark Horse Comics: No. 0, May 2006 - No. 3, Mar, 2007 ($2.99)
0-3-Edginton-s/Pugh-a/Briclot-c 3.00

HELLHOUNDS (...: Panzer Cops #3-6)
Dark Horse Comics: 1994 - No. 6, July, 1994 ($2.50, B&W, limited series)
1-6: 1-Hamner-c. 3-(4/94). 2-Joe Phillips-c 3.00

HELLHOUND, THE REDEMPTION QUEST
Marvel Comics (Epic Comics): Dec, 1993 - No. 4, Mar, 1994 ($2.25, lim. series, coated stock)
1-4 2.50

HELLO, I'M JOHNNY CASH
Spire Christian Comics (Fleming H. Revell Co.): 1976 (39¢/49¢)

	GD	VG	FN	VF	VF/NM	NM-
nn-(39¢-c)	2	4	6	13	18	22
nn-(49¢-c)	2	4	6	8	11	14

HELL ON EARTH (See DC Science Fiction Graphic Novel)

HELLO PAL COMICS (Short Story Comics)
Harvey Publications: Jan, 1943 - No. 3, May, 1943 (Photo-c)

	GD	VG	FN	VF	VF/NM	NM-
1-Rocketman & Rocketgirl begin; Yankee Doodle Jones app.; Mickey Rooney photo-c	62	124	186	391	663	935
2-Charlie McCarthy photo-c (scarce)	54	108	162	340	575	810
3-Bob Hope photo-c (scarce)	60	120	180	378	639	900

HELLRAISER/NIGHTBREED – JIHAD (Also see Clive Barker's...)
Epic Comics (Marvel Comics): 1991 - Book 2, 1991 ($4.50, 52 pgs.)
Book 1,2 4.50

HELL-RIDER (Motorcycle themed magazine)
Skywald Publications: Aug, 1971 - No. 2, Oct, 1971 (B&W, 68 pgs.)

	GD	VG	FN	VF	VF/NM	NM-
1-Origin & 1st app.; Butterfly & the Wild Bunch begin; 1st Hell-Rider by Andru, Esposito and Friedrich	6	12	18	39	62	85
2-Andru, Ayers, Buckler, Shores-a	4	8	12	26	41	55

NOTE: *#3 advertised in Psycho #5 but did not come out.* ***Buckler*** *a-1, 2.* ***Rosenbaum*** *c-1,2.*

HELL'S ANGEL (Becomes Dark Angel #6 on)
Marvel Comics UK: July, 1992 - No. 5, Nov, 1993 ($1.75)
1-5: X-Men (Wolverine, Cyclops)-c/stories. 1-Origin. 3-Jim Lee cover swipe 2.50

HELLSHOCK
Image Comics: July, 1994 - No. 4, Nov, 1994 ($1.95, limited series)
1-4-Jae Lee-c/a & scripts. 4-Variant-c. 2.50

HELLSHOCK
Image Comics: Jan, 1997 - No. 3, Jan, 1998 ($2.95/$2.50, limited series)
1-($2.95)-Jae Lee-c/s/a, Villarrubia-painted-a 4.00
2-($2.50) 2.50
Book 3: The Science of Faith (1/98, $2.50) Jae Lee-c/s/a, Villarrubia-painted-a 2.50
Vol. 1 HC (2006, $49.99) r/#1-3 re-colored, with unpublished 22 pg. conclusion; cover gallery and sketches; alternate opening art; intro. by Jim Lee 50.00

HELLSPAWN
Image Comics: Aug, 2000 - No. 16, Apr, 2003 ($2.50)
1-Bendis-s/Ashley Wood-c/a; Spawn and Clown app. 2.50
2-9: 6-Last Bendis-s; Mike Moran (Miracleman app.). 7-Niles-s 2.50
10-16-Templesmith-a 2.50
...: The Ashley Wood Collection Vol. 1 (4/06, $24.95, TPB) r/#1-10; sketch & cover gallery 25.00

HELLSTORM: PRINCE OF LIES (See Ghost Rider #1 & Marvel Spotlight #12)
Marvel Comics: Apr, 1993 - No. 21, Dec, 1994 ($2.00)
1-($2.95)-Parchment-c w/red thermographic ink 3.00
2-21: 14-Bound-in trading card sheet. 18-P. Craig Russell-c 2.50

HELLSTORM: SON OF SATAN
Marvel Comics (MAX): Dec, 2006 - No. 5, Apr, 2007 ($3.99, limited series)
1-5-Suydam-c/Irvine-s/Braun & Janson-a 4.00

GD VG FN VF VF/NM NM-
2.0 4.0 6.0 8.0 9.0 9.2

... - Equinox TPB (2007, $17.99) r/#1-5; interviews with the creators 18.00

HELMET OF FATE, THE (Series of one-shots following Doctor Fate's helmet)
DC Comics: Mar, 2007 - May 2007 ($2.99, one-shots)
...: Black Alice (5/07) Simone-s/Rouleau-a/c 3.00
...: Detective Chimp (3/07) Willingham-s/McManus-a/Bolland-c 3.00
...: Ibis the Invincible (3/07) Williams-s/Winslade-a; the Ibistick returns 3.00
...: Sargon the Sorcerer (4/07) Niles-s/Scott Hampton-s; debut new Sargon 3.00
...: Zauriel (4/07) Gerber-s/Snejbjerg-a/Kaluta-c; leads into new Doctor Fate series 3.00
TPB (2007, $14.99) r/one-shots 15.00

HE-MAN (See Masters Of The Universe)

HE-MAN (Also see Tops In Adventure)
Ziff-Davis Publ. Co. (Approved Comics): Fall, 1952

	GD	VG	FN	VF	VF/NM	NM-
1-Kinstler painted-c; Powell-a	16	32	48	92	144	195

HE-MAN
Toby Press: May, 1954 - No. 2, July, 1954 (Painted-c by B. Safran)

	GD	VG	FN	VF	VF/NM	NM-
1	15	30	45	88	137	185
2-Shark-c	15	30	45	85	130	175

HENNESSEY (TV)
Dell Publishing Co.: No. 1200, Aug-Oct, 1961 - No. 1280, Mar-May, 1962

	GD	VG	FN	VF	VF/NM	NM-
Four Color 1200-Gil Kane-a, photo-c	7	14	21	47	76	105
Four Color 1280-Photo-c	6	12	18	43	69	95

HENRY (Also see Little Annie Rooney)
David McKay Publications: 1935 (52 pgs.) (Daily B&W strip reprints)(10"x10" cardboard-c)

	GD	VG	FN	VF	VF/NM	NM-
1-By Carl Anderson	40	80	120	235	380	525

HENRY (See King Comics & Magic Comics)
Dell Publishing Co.: No. 122, Oct, 1946 - No. 65, Apr-June, 1961

	GD	VG	FN	VF	VF/NM	NM-
Four Color 122-All new stories begin	14	28	42	102	181	260
Four Color 155 (7/47), 1 (1-3/48)-All new stories	10	20	30	67	116	165
2	6	12	18	41	66	90
3-10	5	10	15	34	55	75
11-20: 20-Infinity-c	4	8	12	26	41	55
21-30	3	6	9	21	32	42
31-40	3	6	9	18	27	35
41-65	3	6	9	16	22	28

HENRY (See Giant Comic Album and March of Comics No. 43, 58, 84, 101, 112, 129, 147, 162, 178, 189)

HENRY ALDRICH COMICS (TV)
Dell Publishing Co.: Aug-Sept, 1950 - No. 22, Sept-Nov, 1954

	GD	VG	FN	VF	VF/NM	NM-
1-Part series written by John Stanley; Bill Williams-a	9	18	27	65	113	160
2	6	12	18	37	59	80
3-5	5	10	15	30	48	65
6-10	4	8	12	26	41	55
11-22	4	8	12	22	34	45

HENRY BREWSTER
Country Wide (M.F. Ent.): Feb, 1966 - V2#7, Sept, 1967 (All 25¢ Giants)

	GD	VG	FN	VF	VF/NM	NM-
1	3	6	9	18	27	35
2-6(12/66), V2#7-Powell-a in most	2	4	6	11	16	20

HEPCATS
Antarctic Press: Nov, 1996 - No. 12 ($2.95, B&W)
0-12-Martin Wagner-c/s/a: 0-color 3.00
0-($9.95) CD Edition 10.00

HERBIE (See Forbidden Worlds #73,94,110,114,116 & Unknown Worlds #20)
American Comics Group: April-May, 1964 - No. 23, Feb, 1967 (All 12¢)

	GD	VG	FN	VF	VF/NM	NM-
1-Whitney-c/a in most issues	16	32	48	114	212	310
2-4	9	18	27	64	110	155
5-Beatles parody (10 pgs.), Dean Martin, Frank Sinatra app. (10-11/64)	10	20	30	71	126	180
6,7,9,10	8	16	24	54	90	125
8-Origin & 1st app. The Fat Fury	9	18	27	63	107	150
11-23: 14-Nemesis & Magicman app. 17-r/2nd Herbie from Forbidden Worlds #94. 23-r/1st Herbie from F.W. #73	6	12	18	41	66	90

... Archives Volume One HC (Dark Horse, 8/08, $49.95, dust jacket) r/earliest apps. in Forbidden Worlds, Unknown Worlds, and Herbie #1-5; Scott Shaw intro. 50.00

HERBIE
Dark Horse Comics: Oct, 1992 - No. 12, 1993 ($2.50, limited series)
1-Whitney-r plus new-c/a in all; Byrne-c/a & scripts 3.00

Hercules #11 © CC

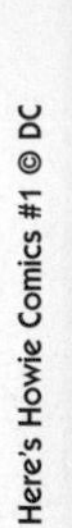
Here's Howie Comics #1 © DC

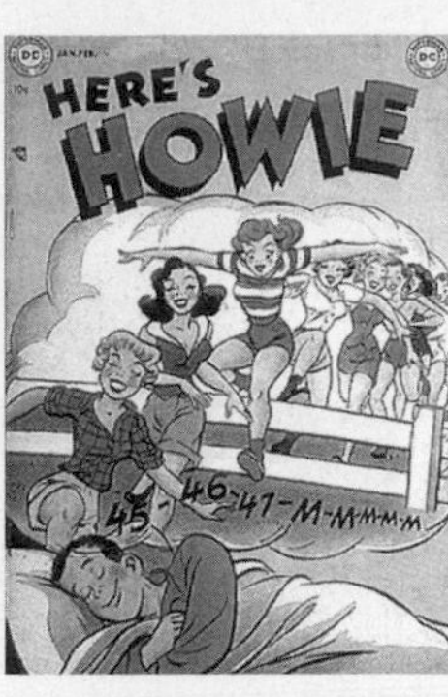

Heroes For Hire #15 © MAR

GD VG FN VF VF/NM NM-
2.0 4.0 6.0 8.0 9.0 9.2

2-6: 3-Bob Burden-c/a. 4-Art Adams-c 2.50

HERBIE GOES TO MONTE CARLO, HERBIE RIDES AGAIN (See Walt Disney Showcase No. 24, 41)

HERCULES (See Hit Comics #1-21, Journey Into Mystery Annual, Marvel Graphic Novel #37, Marvel Premiere #26 & The Mighty...)

HERCULES (See Charlton Classics)
Charlton Comics: Oct, 1967 - No. 13, Sept, 1969; Dec, 1968

1-Thane of Bagarth begins; Glanzman-a in all 4 8 12 24 37 50
2-13: 1-5,7-10-Aparo-a. 8-(12¢-c) 3 6 9 16 22 28
8-(Low distribution)(12/68, 35¢, B&W); magazine format; new Hercules story plus-r story/#1; Thane-r/#1-3 5 10 15 34 55 75
Modern Comics reprint 10('77), 11('78) 6.00

HERCULES (Prince of Power) (Also see The Champions)
Marvel Comics Group: V1#1, Sept, 1982 - V1#4, Dec, 1982; V2#1, Mar, 1984 - V2#4, Jun, 1984 (color, both limited series)

1-4, V2#1-4: Layton-c/a. 4-Death of Zeus. 3.00
NOTE: *Layton a-1, 2, 3p, 4p, V2#1-4; c-1-4, V2#1-4.*

HERCULES
Marvel Comics: Jun, 2005 - No. 5, Sept, 2005 ($2.99, limited series)

1-5-Texeira-a/c; Tieri-s. 4-Capt. America, Wolverine and New Avengers app. 3.00
...: New Labors of Hercules TPB (2005, $13.99) r/#1-5 14.00

HERCULES: HEART OF CHAOS
Marvel Comics: Aug, 1997 - No. 3, Oct, 1997 ($2.50, limited series)

1-3-DeFalco-s, Frenz-a 2.50

HERCULES: OFFICIAL COMICS MOVIE ADAPTION
Acclaim Books: 1997 ($4.50, digest size)

nn-Adaption of the Disney animated movie 4.50

HERCULES: THE LEGENDARY JOURNEYS (TV)
Topps Comics: June, 1996 - No. 5, Oct, 1996 ($2.95)

1-2: 1-Golden-c. 3.00
3-Xena-c/app. 1 2 3 4 5 7
3-Variant-c 2 4 6 9 12 15
4,5: Xena-c/app. 5.00

HERCULES UNBOUND
National Periodical Publications: Oct-Nov, 1975 - No. 12, Aug-Sept, 1977

1-Wood-i begins 2 4 6 8 11 14
2-12: 7-Adams ad. 10-Atomic Knights x-over 1 2 3 5 6 8
NOTE: ***Buckler** c-7p. **Layton** inks-No. 9, 10. **Simonson** a-7-10p, 11, 12; c- 8p, 9-12. **Wood** a-1-8i; c-7i, 8i.*

HERCULES (...Unchained #1121) (Movie)
Dell Publishing Co.: No. 1006, June-Aug, 1959 - No.1121, Aug, 1960

Four Color 1006-Buscema-a, photo-c 9 18 27 60 100 140
Four Color 1121-Crandall/Evans-a 9 18 27 60 100 140

HERE COMES SANTA (See March of Comics No. 30, 213, 340)

HERE'S HOWIE COMICS
National Periodical Publications: Jan-Feb, 1952 - No. 18, Nov-Dec, 1954

1 27 54 81 158 254 350
2 15 30 45 85 130 175
3-5: 5-Howie in the Army issues begin (9-10/52) 13 26 39 72 101 130
6-10 11 22 33 60 83 105
11-18 10 20 30 56 76 95
Ashcan (1,2/51) not distributed to newsstands, only for in house use (no known sales)

HERETIC, THE
Dark Horse (Blanc Noir): Nov, 1996 - No. 4, Mar, 1997 ($2.95, lim. series)

1-4:-w/back-up story 3.00

HERITAGE OF THE DESERT (See Zane Grey, 4-Color 236)

HERMAN & KATNIP (See Harvey Comics Hits #60 & 62, Harvey Hits #14,25,31,41 & Paramount Animated Comics #1)

HERMES VS. THE EYEBALL KID
Dark Horse Comics: Dec, 1994 - No. 3,Feb, 1995 ($2.95, B&W, limited series)

1-3: Eddie Campbell-c/a/scripts 3.00

H-E-R-O (Dial H For HERO)
DC Comics: Apr, 2003 - No. 22, Jan, 2005 ($2.50)

1-Will Pfeiffer-s/Kano-a/Van Fleet-c 3.00
2-22: 2-6-Kano-a. 7,8-Gleason-a. 12-14-Kirk-a. 15-22-Robby Reed app. 2.50
...: Double Feature (6/03, $4.95) r/#1&2 5.00
...: Powers and Abilities (2003, $9.95) r/#1-6; intro. by Geoff Johns 10.00

GD VG FN VF VF/NM NM-
2.0 4.0 6.0 8.0 9.0 9.2

HERO (Warrior of the Mystic Realms)
Marvel Comics: May, 1990 - No. 6, Oct, 1990 ($1.50, limited series)

1-6: 1-Portacio-i 2.50

HERO ALLIANCE, THE
Sirius Comics: Dec, 1985 - No. 2, Sept, 1986 (B&W)

1,2: 2-($1.50), Special Edition 1 (7/86, color) 2.50

HERO ALLIANCE
Wonder Color Comics: May, 1987 ($1.95)

1-Ron Lim-a 2.50

HERO ALLIANCE
Innovation Publishing: V2#1, Sept, 1989 - V2#17, Nov, 1991 ($1.95, 28 pgs.)

V2#1-17: 1,2-Ron Lim-a 2.50
Annual 1 (1990, $2.75, 36 pgs.)-Paul Smith-c/a 2.75
Special 1 (1992, $2.50, 32 pgs.)-Stuart Immonen-a (10 pgs.) 2.50

HERO ALLIANCE: END OF THE GOLDEN AGE
Innovation Publ.: July, 1989 - No. 3, Aug, 1989 ($1.75, bi-weekly lim. series)

1-3: Bart Sears & Ron Lim-c/a; reprints & new-a 2.50

HEROES
Marvel Comics: Dec, 2001 ($3.50, magazine-size, one-shot)

1-Pin-up tributes to the rescue workers of the Sept. 11 tragedy; art and text by various; cover by Alex Ross 3.50
1-2nd and 3rd printings 3.50

HEROES (Also see Shadow Cabinet & Static)
DC Comics (Milestone): May, 1996 - No. 6, Nov, 1996 ($2.50, limited series)

1-6: 1-Intro Heroes (Iota, Donner, Blitzen, Starlight, Payback & Static) 2.50

HEROES AGAINST HUNGER
DC Comics: 1986 ($1.50; one-shot for famine relief)

1-Superman, Batman app.; Neal Adams-c(p); includes many artists work; Jeff Jones assist (2 pg.) on B. Smith-a; Kirby-a 4.00

HEROES ALL CATHOLIC ACTION ILLUSTRATED
Heroes All Co.: 1943 - V6#5, Mar 10, 1948 (paper covers)

V1#1-(16 pgs., 8x11") 24 48 72 140 225 310
V1#2-(16 pgs., 8x11") 19 38 57 109 176 240
V2#1(1/44)-3(3/44)-(16 pgs., 8x11") 15 30 45 94 147 200
V3#1(1/45)-10(12/45)-(16 pgs., 8x11") 15 30 45 84 127 170
V4#1-35 (12/20/46)-(16 pgs.) 14 28 42 80 115 150
V5#1(1/10/47)-8(2/28/47)-(16 pgs.), V5#9(3/7/47)-20(11/25/47)-(32 pgs.), V6#1(1/10/48)-5(3/10/48)-(32 pgs.) 12 24 36 67 94 120

HEROES ANONYMOUS
Bongo Comics: 2003 - No. 6, 2004 ($2.99, limited series)

1-6-($2.99)-Bill Morrison-c. 2-Guerra-a. 3-Pepoy-a 3.00

HEROES FOR HIRE
Marvel Comics: July, 1997 - No. 19, Jan, 1999 ($2.99/$1.99)

1-($2.99)-Wraparound cover 5.00
2-19: 2-Variant cover. 7-Thunderbolts app. 9-Punisher-c/app. 10,11-Deadpool-c/app. 18,19-Wolverine-c/app. 3.00
.../Quicksilver '98 Annual ($2.99) Siege of Wundagore pt.5 3.00

HEROES FOR HIRE
Marvel Comics: Oct, 2006 - No. 15, Dec, 2007 ($2.99)

1-5-Tucci-a/c; Black Cat, Shang-Chi, Tarantula, Humbug & Daughters of the Dragon app. 3.00
6-15: 6-8-Sparacio-c. 9,10-Golden-c. 11-13-World War Hulk x-over. 13-Takeda-c 3.00
... Vol. 1: Civil War (2007, $13.99) r/#1-5 14.00
... Vol. 2: Ahead of the Curve (2007, $13.99) r/#6-10 14.00
... Vol. 3: World War Hulk (2008, $13.99) r/#11-15 14.00

HEROES FOR HOPE STARRING THE X-MEN
Marvel Comics Group: Dec, 1985 ($1.50, one-shot, 52 pgs., proceeds donated to famine relief)

1-Stephen King scripts; Byrne, Miller, Corben-a; Wrightson/J. Jones-a (3 pgs.); Art Adams-c; Starlin back-c 5.00

HEROES, INC. PRESENTS CANNON
Wally Wood/CPL/Gang Publ.:1969 - No. 2, 1976 (Sold at Army PX's)

nn-Ditko, Wood-a; Wood-c; Reese-a(p) 2 4 6 9 12 15
2-Wood-c; Ditko, Byrne, Wood-a; 8-1/2x10-1/2"; B&W; $2.00 2 4 6 13 18 22
NOTE: *First issue not distributed by publisher; 1,800 copies were stored and 900 copies were stolen from warehouse. Many copies have surfaced in recent years.*

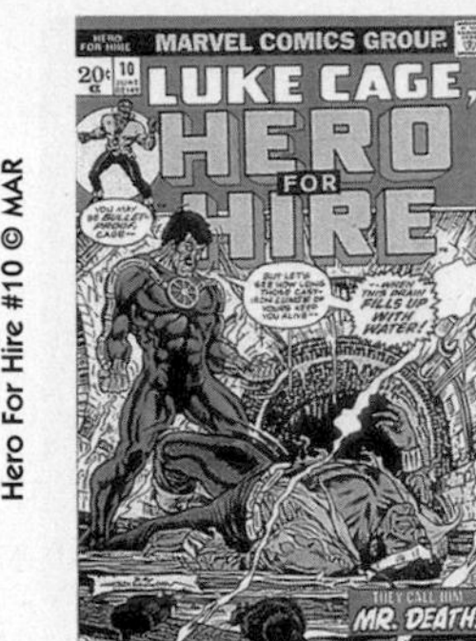

Hero For Hire #10 © MAR

Heroic Comics #17 © EAS

Highlander #3 © Davis•Panzer Prods.

GD VG FN VF VF/NM NM-
2.0 4.0 6.0 8.0 9.0 9.2

HEROES OF THE WILD FRONTIER (Formerly Baffling Mysteries)
Ace Periodicals: No. 27, Jan, 1956 - No. 2, Apr, 1956

27(#1),2-Davy Crockett, Daniel Boone, Buffalo Bill 6 12 18 29 36 42

HEROES REBORN (one-shots)
Marvel Comics: Jan, 2000 ($1.99)

...:Ashema; ...:Doom; ...:Doomsday; ...:Masters of Evil; ...:Rebel; ...:Remnants;
...:Young Allies 2.50

HEROES REBORN: THE RETURN (Also see Avengers, Fantastic Four, Iron Man & Captain America titles for issues and TPBs)
Marvel Comics: Dec, 1997 - No. 4 ($2.50, weekly mini-series)

1-4-Avengers, Fantastic Four, Iron Man & Captain America rejoin regular Marvel Universe; Peter David-s/Larocca-c/a 4.00
1-4-Variant-c for each 6.00
Wizard 1/2 1 2 3 5 7 9
Return of the Heroes TPB ('98, $14.95) r/#1-4 15.00

HERO FOR HIRE (Power Man No. 17 on; also see Cage)
Marvel Comics Group: June, 1972 - No. 16, Dec, 1973

1-Origin & 1st app. Luke Cage; Tuska-a(p) 9 18 27 60 100 140
2-Tuska-a(p) 4 8 12 28 44 60
3-5: 3-1st app. Mace. 4-1st app. Phil Fox of the Bugle 3 6 9 20 30 40
6-10: 8,9-Dr. Doom app. 9-F.F. app. 3 6 9 14 20 25
11-16: 14-Origin retold. 15-Everett Sub-Mariner-r('53). 16-Origin Stilletto; death of Rackham 2 4 6 9 13 16

HERO HOTLINE (1st app. in Action Comics Weekly #637)
DC Comics: April, 1989 - No. 6, Sept, 1989 ($1.75, limited series)

1-6: Super-hero humor; Schaffenberger-i 2.50

HEROIC ADVENTURES (See Adventures)

HEROIC COMICS (Reg'lar Fellers...#1-15; New Heroic #41 on)
Eastern Color Printing Co./Famous Funnies(Funnies, Inc. No. 1): Aug, 1940 - No. 97, June, 1955

1-Hydroman (origin) by Bill Everett, The Purple Zombie (origin) & Mann of India by Tarpe Mills begins (all 1st apps.) 193 386 579 1216 2058 2900
2 80 160 240 504 852 1200
3,4 52 104 156 322 536 750
5,6 43 86 129 267 446 625
7-Origin & 1st app. Man O'Metal (1 pg.) 46 92 138 285 473 660
8-10: 10-Lingerie panels 35 70 105 203 327 450
11,13 32 64 96 188 302 415
12-Music Master (origin/1st app.) begins by Everett, ends No. 31; last Purple Zombie & Mann of India 36 72 108 212 341 470
14,15-Hydroman x-over in Rainbow Boy. 14-Origin & 1st app. Rainbow Boy (super hero). 15-1st app. Downbeat 35 70 105 203 327 450
16-20: 16-New logo. 17-Rainbow Boy x-over in Hydroman. 19-Rainbow Boy x-over in Hydroman & vice versa 24 48 72 140 225 310
21-30:25-Rainbow Boy x-over in Hydroman. 28-Last Man O'Metal. 29-Last Hydroman 18 36 54 103 162 220
31,34,38 9 18 27 47 61 75
32,36,37-Toth-a (3-4 pgs. each) 10 20 30 54 72 90
33,35-Toth-a (8 & 9 pgs.) 10 20 30 56 76 95
39-42-Toth, Ingels-a 10 20 30 56 76 95
43,46,47,49-Toth-a (2-4 pgs.). 47-Ingels-a 9 18 27 52 69 85
44,45,50-Toth-a (6-9 pgs.) 10 20 30 54 72 90
48,53,54 8 16 24 44 57 70
51-Williamson-a 10 20 30 54 72 90
52-Williamson-a (3 pg. story) 9 18 27 47 61 75
55-Toth-a 9 18 27 52 69 85
56-60: 60-Everett-a 9 18 27 47 61 75
61-Everett-a 8 16 24 44 57 70
62,64-Everett-c/a 9 18 27 47 61 75
63-Everett-c 8 16 24 44 57 70
65-Williamson/Frazetta-a; Evans-a (2 pgs.) 11 22 33 64 90 115
66,75,94-Frazetta-a (2 pgs. each) 9 18 27 47 61 75
67,73-Frazetta-a (4 pgs. each) 10 20 30 54 72 90
68,74,76-80,84,85,88-93,95-97: 95-Last pre-code 8 16 24 42 54 65
69,72-Frazetta-a (6 & 8 pgs. each); 1st (?) app. Frazetta Red Cross ad 11 22 33 64 90 115
70,71,86,87-Frazetta, 3-4 pgs. each; 1 pg. ad by Frazetta in #70 9 18 27 50 65 80
81,82-Frazetta art (1 pg. each): 81-1st (?) app. Frazetta Boy Scout ad (tied w/ Buster Crabbe #9 8 16 24 44 57 70

GD VG FN VF VF/NM NM-
2.0 4.0 6.0 8.0 9.0 9.2

83-Frazetta-a (1/2 pg.) 8 16 24 44 57 70

NOTE: ***Evans*** *a-64, 65.* ***Everett*** *a-(Hydroman-c/a-No. 1-9), 44, 60-64; c-1-9, 62-64.* ***Harvey Fuller*** *c-28-35.* ***Sid Greene*** *a-38-43, 46.* ***Guardineer*** *a-42(3), 43, 44, 45(2), 49(3), 50, 60, 61(2), 65, 67(2) 70-72.* ***Ingels*** *c-41.* ***Kiefer*** *a-46, 48; c-19-22, 24, 44, 46, 48, 51-53, 65, 67-69, 71-74, 76, 77, 79, 80, 82, 85, 86, 88, 89, 94, 95.* ***Mort Lawrence*** *a-45.* ***Tarpe Mills*** *a-2(2), 3(2), 10.* ***Ed Moore*** *a-49, 52-54, 56-63, 65-69, 72-74, 76, 77.* ***H.G. Peter*** *a-58-74, 76, 77, 87.* ***Paul Reinman*** *a-49.* ***Rico*** *a-31. Captain Tootsie by* ***Beck****-31, 32. Painted c #16 on. Hydroman c-1-11. Music Master c-12, 13, 15. Rainbow Boy c-14.*

HERO INITIATIVE: MIKE WIERINGO BOOK
Marvel Comics: Aug, 2008 ($4.99)

1-The "What If" Fantastic Four story with Wieringo-a (7 pgs.) finished by other artists after his passing; art by Davis, Immonen, Ramos, Kitson and others; written tributes 5.00

HERO ZERO (Also see Comics' Greatest World & Godzilla Versus Hero Zero)
Dark Horse Comics: Sept, 1994 ($2.50)

0 2.50

HEX (Replaces Jonah Hex)
DC Comics: Sept, 1985 - No. 18, Feb, 1987 (Story cont'd from Jonah Hex # 92)

1-Hex in post-atomic war world; origin 1 2 3 5 6 8
2-18: 6-Origin Stiletta. 11-13: All contain future Batman storyline. 13-Intro The Dogs of War (origin #15) 5.00

NOTE: ***Giffen*** *a(p)-15-18; c(p)-15,17,18.* ***Texeira*** *a-1, 2p, 3p, 5-7p, 9p, 11-14p; c(p)-1, 2, 4-7, 12.*

HEXBREAKER (See First Comics Graphic Novel #15)

HEY THERE, IT'S YOGI BEAR (See Movie Comics)

HI-ADVENTURE HEROES (TV)
Gold Key: May, 1969 - No. 2, Aug, 1969 (Hanna-Barbera)

1-Three Musketeers, Gulliver, Arabian Knights 5 10 15 32 51 70
2-Three Musketeers, Micro-Venture, Arabian Knights 4 8 12 28 44 60

HI AND LOIS
Dell Publishing Co.: No. 683, Mar, 1956 - No. 955, Nov, 1958

Four Color 683 (#1) 5 10 15 30 48 65
Four Color 774(3/57),955 4 8 12 24 37 50

HI AND LOIS
Charlton Comics: Nov, 1969 - No. 11, July, 1971

1 3 6 9 14 20 25
2-11 2 4 6 9 12 15

HICKORY (See All Humor Comics)
Quality Comics Group: Oct, 1949 - No. 6, Aug, 1950

1-Sahl-c/a in all; Feldstein?-a 19 38 57 112 176 240
2 12 24 36 67 94 120
3-6 10 20 30 56 76 95

HIDDEN CREW, THE (See The United States Air Force Presents:...)

HIDE-OUT (See Zane Grey, Four Color No. 346)

HIDING PLACE, THE
Spire Christian Comics (Fleming H. Revell Co.): 1973 (39¢/49¢)

nn 2 4 6 8 10 12

HIGH ADVENTURE
Red Top(Decker) Comics (Farrell): Oct, 1957

1-Krigstein-r from Explorer Joe (re-issue on-c) 5 10 15 23 28 32

HIGH ADVENTURE (TV)
Dell Publishing Co.: No. 949, Nov, 1958 - No. 1001, Aug-Oct, 1959 (Lowell Thomas)

Four Color 949 (#1)-Photo-c 6 12 18 37 59 80
Four Color 1001-Lowell Thomas'...(#2) 5 10 15 34 55 75

HIGH CHAPPARAL (TV)
Gold Key: Aug, 1968 (Photo-c)

1 (10226-808)-Tufts-a 5 10 15 32 51 70

HIGHLANDER
Dynamite Entertainment: No. 0, 2006 - No. 12, 2007 (25¢/$2.99)

0-(25¢-c) Takes place after the first movie; photo-c and Dell'Otto painted-c 2.25
1-12: 1-($2.99) Three covers; Moder-a/Jerwa & Oeming-s. 2-Three covers 3.00
...: Way of the Sword (2007 - No. 4, 2008, $3.50) Two interlocking covers for each 3.50

HIGH ROADS
DC Comics (Cliffhanger): June, 2002 - No. 6, Nov, 2002 ($2.95, limited series)

1-6-Leinil Yu-c/a; Lobdell-s 3.00
TPB (2003, $14.95) r/#1-6; sketch pages 15.00

HIGH SCHOOL CONFIDENTIAL DIARY (Confidential Diary #12 on)

Highwaymen #1 © WSP

Hit Comics #1 © QUA

Hitman #2 © DC

Charlton Comics: June, 1960 - No. 11, Mar, 1962

	GD 2.0	VG 4.0	FN 6.0	VF 8.0	VF/NM 9.0	NM- 9.2
1	4	8	12	26	41	55
2-11	3	6	9	17	25	32

HIGHWAYMEN
DC Comics (WildStorm): Aug, 2007 - No. 5, Dec, 2007 ($2.99)

	GD 2.0	VG 4.0	FN 6.0	VF 8.0	VF/NM 9.0	NM- 9.2
1-5-Bernardin & Freeman-s/Garbett-a						3.00
TPB (2008, $17.99) r/#1-5						18.00

HI HI PUFFY AMIYUMI (Based on Cartoon Network animated series)
DC Comics: Apr, 2006 - No. 3 ($2.25, limited series)

	GD 2.0	VG 4.0	FN 6.0	VF 8.0	VF/NM 9.0	NM- 9.2
1,2-Phil Moy-a						2.50

HI-HO COMICS
Four Star Publications: nd (2/46?) - No. 3, 1946

	GD 2.0	VG 4.0	FN 6.0	VF 8.0	VF/NM 9.0	NM- 9.2
1-Funny Animal; L. B. Cole-c	38	76	114	222	356	490
2,3: 2-L. B. Cole-c	21	42	63	123	197	270

HI-JINX (Teen-age Animal Funnies)
La Salle Publ. Co./B&I Publ. Co. (American Comics Group)/Creston: 1945; July-Aug, 1947 - No. 7, July-Aug, 1948

	GD 2.0	VG 4.0	FN 6.0	VF 8.0	VF/NM 9.0	NM- 9.2
nn-(© 1945, 25 cents, 132 Pgs.)(La Salle)	24	48	72	140	225	310
1-Teen-age, funny animal	17	34	51	98	154	210
2,3	11	22	33	64	90	115
4-7-Milt Gross. 4-X-Mas-c	15	30	45	90	140	190

HI-LITE COMICS
E. R. Ross Publishing Co.: Fall, 1945

	GD 2.0	VG 4.0	FN 6.0	VF 8.0	VF/NM 9.0	NM- 9.2
1-Miss Shady	20	40	60	114	180	245

HILLBILLY COMICS
Charlton Comics: Aug, 1955 - No. 4, July, 1956 (Satire)

	GD 2.0	VG 4.0	FN 6.0	VF 8.0	VF/NM 9.0	NM- 9.2
1-By Art Gates	9	18	27	52	69	85
2-4	7	14	21	35	43	50

HILLY ROSE'S SPACE ADVENTURES
Astro Comics: May, 1995 - No. 9 ($2.95, B&W)

	GD 2.0	VG 4.0	FN 6.0	VF 8.0	VF/NM 9.0	NM- 9.2
1	1	2	3	5	7	9
2-5						5.00
6-9						3.00
Trade Paperback (1996, $12.95)-r/#1-5						13.00

HIP FLASK UNNATURAL SELECTION
Active Images: Sept, 2002 ($2.99)

	GD 2.0	VG 4.0	FN 6.0	VF 8.0	VF/NM 9.0	NM- 9.2
1-Casey & Starkings-s/Ladronn-a; var.-c by Madureira, Campbell, Churchill						3.00

HIP-IT-TY HOP (See March of Comics No. 15)

HIRE, THE (BMWfilms.com's...)
Dark Horse Comics: July, 2004 - No. 6 ($2.99)

	GD 2.0	VG 4.0	FN 6.0	VF 8.0	VF/NM 9.0	NM- 9.2
1-4: 1-Matt Wagner-s/Wagner & Velasco-a. 2-Bruce Campbell-s/Plunkett-a. 3-Waid-s						3.00
TPB (4/06, $17.95) r/#1-4						18.00

HI-SCHOOL ROMANCE (...Romances No. 41 on)
Harvey Publ./True Love(Home Comics): Oct, 1949 - No. 5, June, 1950; No. 6, Dec, 1950 - No. 73, Mar, 1958; No. 74, Sept, 1958 - No. 75, Nov, 1958

	GD 2.0	VG 4.0	FN 6.0	VF 8.0	VF/NM 9.0	NM- 9.2
1-Photo-c	15	30	45	88	137	185
2-Photo-c	10	20	30	54	72	90
3-9: 3-5-Photo-c	8	16	24	44	57	70
10-Rape story	10	20	30	54	72	90
11-20	7	14	21	37	46	55
21-31	6	12	18	29	36	42
32- "Unholy passion" story	9	18	27	47	61	75
33-36: 36-Last pre-code (2/55)	6	12	18	28	34	40
37-53,59-72,74,75	5	10	15	23	28	32
54-58,73-Kirby-c	6	12	18	28	34	40

NOTE: ***Powell** a-1-3, 5, 8, 12-16, 18, 21-23, 25-27, 30-34, 36, 37, 39, 45-48, 50-52, 57, 58, 60, 64, 65, 67, 69.*

HI-SCHOOL ROMANCE DATE BOOK
Harvey Publications: Nov, 1962 - No. 3, Mar, 1963 (25¢ Giants)

	GD 2.0	VG 4.0	FN 6.0	VF 8.0	VF/NM 9.0	NM- 9.2
1-Powell, Baker-a	6	12	18	39	62	85
2,3	3	6	9	20	30	40

HIS NAME IS SAVAGE (Magazine format)
Adventure House Press: June, 1968 (35¢, 52 pgs.)

	GD 2.0	VG 4.0	FN 6.0	VF 8.0	VF/NM 9.0	NM- 9.2
1-Gil Kane-a	5	10	15	32	51	70

HI-SPOT COMICS (Red Ryder No. 1 & No. 3 on)
Hawley Publications: No. 2, Nov, 1940

	GD 2.0	VG 4.0	FN 6.0	VF 8.0	VF/NM 9.0	NM- 9.2
2-David Innes of Pellucidar; art by J. C. Burroughs; written by Edgar Rice Burroughs	128	256	384	806	1366	1925

HISTORY OF THE DC UNIVERSE (Also see Crisis on Infinite Earths)
DC Comics: Sept, 1986 - No. 2, Nov, 1986 ($2.95, limited series)

	GD 2.0	VG 4.0	FN 6.0	VF 8.0	VF/NM 9.0	NM- 9.2
1,2: 1-Perez-c/a						3.00
Limited Edition hardcover	4	8	12	26	41	55
Softcover (2002, $9.95) new Alex Ross wraparound-c						10.00

HISTORY OF VIOLENCE, A (Inspired the 2005 movie)
DC Comics (Paradox Press) 1997 ($9.95, B&W graphic novel)

	GD 2.0	VG 4.0	FN 6.0	VF 8.0	VF/NM 9.0	NM- 9.2
nn-Paperback ($9.95) John Wagner-s/Vince Locke-a						10.00

HITCHHIKERS GUIDE TO THE GALAXY (See Life, the Universe and Everything & Restaurant at the End of the Universe)
DC Comics: 1993 - No. 3, 1993 ($4.95, limited series)

	GD 2.0	VG 4.0	FN 6.0	VF 8.0	VF/NM 9.0	NM- 9.2
1-3: Adaptation of Douglas Adams book						5.00
TPB (1997, $14.95) r/#1-3						15.00

HIT COMICS
Quality Comics Group: July, 1940 - No. 65, July, 1950

	GD 2.0	VG 4.0	FN 6.0	VF 8.0	VF/NM 9.0	NM- 9.2
1-Origin/1st app. Neon, the Unknown & Hercules; intro. The Red Bee; Bob & Swab, Blaze Barton, the Strange Twins, X-5 Super Agent, Casey Jones & Jack & Jill (ends #7) begin	667	1334	2001	4802	8401	12,000
2-The Old Witch begins, ends #14	273	546	819	1720	2910	4100
3-Casey Jones ends; transvestism story "Jack & Jill"	260	520	780	1638	2769	3900
4-Super Agent (ends #17), & Betty Bates (ends #65) begin; X-5 ends	230	460	690	1449	2450	3450
5-Classic Lou Fine cover	583	1166	1749	4198	7349	10,500
6-10: 10-Old Witch by Crandall (4 pgs.); 1st work in comics (4/41)	193	386	579	1216	2058	2900
11-Classic cover	187	374	561	1178	1989	2800
12-17: 13-Blaze Barton ends. 17-Last Neon; Crandall Hercules in all; Last Lou Fine-c	122	244	366	769	1297	1825
18-Origin & 1st app. Stormy Foster, the Great Defender (12/41); The Ghost of Flanders begins; Crandall-c	127	254	381	800	1350	1900
19,20	98	196	294	617	1046	1475
21-24: 21-Last Hercules. 24-Last Red Bee & Strange Twins	95	190	285	599	1012	1425
25-Origin & 1st app. Kid Eternity and begins by Moldoff (12/42); 1st app. The Keeper (Kid Eternity's aide)	183	366	549	1153	1952	2750
26-Blackhawk x-over in Kid Eternity	97	194	291	611	1031	1450
27-29	49	98	147	304	507	710
30,31- "Bill the Magnificent" by Kurtzman, 11 pgs. in each	45	90	135	279	465	650
32-40: 32-Plastic Man x-over. 34-Last Stormy Foster	30	60	90	176	283	390
41-50	21	42	63	125	200	275
51-60-Last Kid Eternity	20	40	60	118	189	260
61-63-Crandall-c/a; 61-Jeb Rivers begins	21	42	63	123	197	270
64,65-Crandall-a	20	40	60	118	189	260

NOTE: ***Crandall** a-11-17(Hercules), 23, 24(Stormy Foster); c-18-20, 23, 24. **Fine** c-1-14, 16, 17(most). **Ward** c-33. Bondage c-7, 64. Hercules c-3, 10-17. Jeb Rivers c-61-65. Kid Eternity c-25-60 (w/Keeper-28-34, 36, 39-43, 45-55). Neon the Unknown c-2, 4, 8, 9. Red Bee c-1, 5-7. Stormy Foster c-18-24.*

HITLER'S ASTROLOGER (See Marvel Graphic Novel #35)

HITMAN (Also see Bloodbath #2, Batman Chronicles #4, Demon #43-45 & Demon Annual #2)
DC Comics: May, 1996 - No. 60, Apr, 2001 ($2.25/$2.50)

	GD 2.0	VG 4.0	FN 6.0	VF 8.0	VF/NM 9.0	NM- 9.2
1-Garth Ennis-s & John McCrea-c/a begin; Batman app.	1	2	3	5	7	9
2-Joker-c;Two Face, Mad Hatter, Batman app.						6.00
3-5: 3-Batman-c/app.; Joker app. 4-1st app. Nightfist						4.00
6-20: 8-Final Night x-over. 10-GL cameo. 11-20: 11,12-GL-c/app. 15-20-"Ace of Killers". 16-18-Catwoman app. 17-19-Demon-app.						3.00
21-59: 34-Superman-c/app.						2.50
60-($3.95) Final issue; includes pin-ups by various						4.00
#1,000,000 (11/98) Hitman goes to the 853rd Century						2.50
Annual 1 (1997, $3.95) Pulp Heroes						4.00
.../Lobo: That Stupid Bastich (7/00, $3.95) Ennis-s/Mahnke-a						4.00
TPB-(1997, $9.95) r/#1-3, Demon Ann. #2, Batman Chronicles #4						10.00
Ace of Killers TPB ('00, $17.95) r/#15-22						18.00
Local Heroes TPB ('99, $17.95) r/#9-14 & Annual #1						18.00
10,000 Bullets TPB ('98, $9.95) r/#4-8						10.00
Who Dares Wins TPB ('01, $12.95) r/#23-28						13.00

HI-YO SILVER (See Lone Ranger's Famous Horse... and The Lone Ranger; and March of Comics No. 215 in

Hogan's Heroes #3 © Bing Crosby Prods.

Hollywood Diary #2 © QUA

Holyoke One-Shot #9 © HOKE

	GD 2.0	VG 4.0	FN 6.0	VF 8.0	VF/NM 9.0	NM- 9.2

the Promotional Comics section)

HOBBIT, THE
Eclipse Comics: 1989 - No. 3, 1990 ($4.95, squarebound, 52 pgs.)

Book 1-3: Adapts novel; Wenzel-a 7.00
Book 1-Second printing 5.00
Graphic Novel (1990, Ballantine)-r/#1-3 20.00

HOCUS POCUS (See Funny Book #9)

HOGAN'S HEROES (TV)
Dell Publishing Co.: June, 1966 - No. 8, Sept, 1967; No. 9, Oct, 1969

1: #1-7 photo-c 8 16 24 56 93 130
2,3-Ditko-a(p) 6 12 18 37 59 80
4-9: 9-Reprints #1 5 10 15 30 48 65

HOKUM & HEX (See Razorline)
Marvel Comics (Razorline): Sept, 1993 - No. 9, May, 1994 ($1.75/$1.95)

1-($2.50)-Foil embossed-c; by Clive Barker 3.00
2-9: 5-Hyperkind x-over 2.50

HOLIDAY COMICS
Fawcett Publications: 1942 (25¢, 196 pgs.)

1-Contains three Fawcett comics plus two page portrait of Captain Marvel; Capt. Marvel, Jungle Girl #1, & Whiz. Not rebound, remaindered comics; printed at the same time as originals 200 400 600 1250 2075 2900

HOLIDAY COMICS (Becomes Fun Comics #9-12)
Star Publications: Jan, 1951 - No. 8, Oct, 1952

1-Funny animal contents (Frisky Fables) in all; L. B. Cole X-Mas-c 34 68 102 195 308 420
2-Classic L. B. Cole-c 36 72 108 208 329 450
3-8: 5,8-X-Mas-c; all L.B. Cole-c 20 40 60 117 184 250
Accepted Reprint 4 (nd) L.B. Cole-c 10 20 30 58 79 100

HOLIDAY DIGEST
Harvey Comics: 1988 ($1.25, digest size)

1 1 2 3 5 7 9

HOLIDAY PARADE (Walt Disney's...)
W. D. Publications (Disney): Winter, 1990-91(no year given) - No. 2, Winter, 1990-91 ($2.95, 68 pgs.)

1-Reprints 1947 Firestone by Barks plus new-a 4.00
2-Barks-r plus other stories 4.00

HOLI-DAY SURPRISE (Formerly Summer Fun)
Charlton Comics: V2#55, Mar, 1967 (25¢ Giant)

V2#55 4 8 12 22 34 45

HOLLYWOOD COMICS
New Age Publishers: Winter, 1944 (52 pgs.)

1-Funny animal 18 36 54 105 165 225

HOLLYWOOD CONFESSIONS
St. John Publishing Co.: Oct, 1949 - No. 2, Dec, 1949

1-Kubert-c/a (entire book) 32 64 96 188 302 415
2-Kubert-c/a (entire book) (Scarce) 34 68 102 198 319 440

HOLLYWOOD DIARY
Quality Comics Group: Dec, 1949 - No. 5, July-Aug, 1950

1-No photo-c 21 42 63 123 197 270
2-Photo-c 14 28 42 81 118 155
3-5-Photo-c. 5-June Allyson/Peter Lawford photo-c 13 26 39 72 101 130

HOLLYWOOD FILM STORIES
Feature Publications/Prize: April, 1950 - No. 4, Oct, 1950 (All photo-c; "Fumetti" type movie comic)

1-June Allyson photo-c 20 40 60 115 183 250
2-4: 2-Lizabeth Scott photo-c. 3-Barbara Stanwick photo-c. 4-Betty Hutton photo-c 15 30 45 83 124 165

HOLLYWOOD FUNNY FOLKS (Formerly Funny Folks; Becomes Nutsy Squirrel #61 on)
National Periodical Publ.: No. 27, Aug-Sept, 1950 - No. 60, July-Aug, 1954

27 14 28 42 76 108 140
28-40 10 20 30 54 72 90
41-60 9 18 27 47 61 75

NOTE: *Rube Grossman a-most issues. Sheldon Mayer a-27-35, 37-40, 43-46, 48-51, 53, 56, 57, 60.*

HOLLYWOOD LOVE DOCTOR (See Doctor Anthony King...)

HOLLYWOOD PICTORIAL (...Romances on cover)
St. John Publishing Co.: No. 3, Jan, 1950

3-Matt Baker-a; photo-c 27 54 81 158 254 350
(Becomes a movie magazine - Hollywood Pictorial Western with No. 4.)

HOLLYWOOD ROMANCES (Formerly Brides In Love; becomes For Lovers Only #60 on)
Charlton Comics: V2#46, 11/66; #47, 10/67; #48, 11/68;V3#49,11/69-V3#59, 6/71

V2#46-Rolling Stones-c/story 9 18 27 63 107 150
V2#47-V3#59: 56- "Born to Heart Break" begins 2 4 6 13 18 22

HOLLYWOOD SECRETS
Quality Comics Group: Nov, 1949 - No. 6, Sept, 1950

1-Ward-c/a (9 pgs.) 34 68 102 198 319 440
2-Crandall-a, Ward-c/a (9 pgs.) 23 46 69 133 214 295
3-6: All photo-c. 5-Lex Barker (Tarzan)-c 14 28 42 76 108 140
...of Romance, I.W. Reprint #9; r/#2 above w/Kinstler-c 2 4 6 10 14 18

HOLLYWOOD SUPERSTARS
Marvel Comics (Epic Comics): Nov, 1990 - No. 5, Apr, 1991 ($2.25)

1-($2.95, 52 pgs.)-Spiegle-c/a in all; Aragones-a, inside front-c plus 2-4 pgs. 3.00
2-5 ($2.25) 2.50

HOLO-MAN (See Power Record Comics)

HOLYOKE ONE-SHOT
Holyoke Publishing Co. (Tem Publ.): 1944 - No. 10, 1945 (All reprints)

1,2: 1-Grit Grady (on cover only), Miss Victory, Alias X (origin)-All reprints from Captain Fearless. 2-Rusty Dugan (Corporal); Capt. Fearless (origin), Mr. Miracle (origin) app. 20 40 60 115 183 250
3-Miss Victory; r/Crash #4; Cat Man (origin), Solar Legion by Kirby app.; Miss Victory on cover only (1945) 32 64 96 186 298 410
4,6,8: 4-Mr. Miracle; The Blue Streak app. 6-Capt. Fearless, Alias X, Capt. Stone (splash used as-c to #10); Diamond Jim & Rusty Dugan (splash from cover of #2). 8-Blue Streak, Strong Man (story matches cover to #7)-Crash reprints 17 34 51 100 158 215
5,7: 5-U.S. Border Patrol Comics (Sgt. Dick Carter of the...), Miss Victory (story matches cover to #3), Citizen Smith, & Mr. Miracle app. 7-Secret Agent Z-2, Strong Man, Blue Streak (story matches cover to #8); Reprints from Crash #2 19 38 57 112 176 240
9-Citizen Smith, The Blue Streak, Solar Legion by Kirby & Strongman, the Perfect Human app.; reprints from Crash #4 & 5; Citizen Smith on cover only from story in #5 (1944-before #3) 21 42 63 125 200 275
10-Captain Stone; r/Crash; Solar Legion by S&K 21 42 63 125 200 275

HOLY TERROR
Image Comics: Aug, 2002 - Present ($2.95)

1,2-Phil Hester-a/c; Jason Caskey-s 3.00

HOMER COBB (See Adventures of...)

HOMER HOOPER
Atlas Comics: July, 1953 - No. 4, Dec, 1953

1-Teenage humor 10 20 30 58 79 100
2-4 8 16 24 40 50 60

HOMER, THE HAPPY GHOST (See Adventures of...)
Atlas(ACI/PPI/WPI)/Marvel: 3/55 - No. 22, 11/58; V2#1, 11/69 - V2#4, 5/70

V1#1-Dan DeCarlo-c/a begins, ends #22 22 44 66 127 204 280
2-1st code approved issue 14 28 42 76 108 140
3-10 12 24 36 67 94 120
11-22 10 20 30 58 79 100
V2#1 (11/69) 10 20 30 71 126 180
2-4 6 12 18 41 66 90

HOME RUN (Also see A-1 Comics)
Magazine Enterprises: No. 89, 1953 (one-shot)

A-1 89 (#3)-Powell-a; Stan Musial photo-c 14 28 42 76 108 140

HOMICIDE (Also see Dark Horse Presents)
Dark Horse Comics: Apr, 1990 ($1.95, B&W, one-shot)

1-Detective story 2.50

HONEYMOON (Formerly Gay Comics)
A Lover's Magazine(USA) (Marvel): No. 41, Jan, 1950

41-Photo-c; article by Betty Grable 11 22 33 62 86 110

HONEYMOONERS, THE (TV)
Lodestone: Oct, 1986 ($1.50)

1-Photo-c 4.00

The Hood #1 © MAR

Hopalong Cassidy #3 © FAW

Horrific #11 © Comic Media

HONEYMOONERS, THE (TV)
Triad Publications: Sept, 1987 - No. 13? ($2.00)

	GD 2.0	VG 4.0	FN 6.0	VF 8.0	VF/NM 9.0	NM- 9.2
1-13						4.00

HONEYMOON ROMANCE
Artful Publications (Canadian): Apr, 1950 - No. 2, July, 1950 (25¢, digest size)

	GD 2.0	VG 4.0	FN 6.0	VF 8.0	VF/NM 9.0	NM- 9.2
1,2-(Rare)	40	80	120	244	397	550

HONEY WEST (TV)
Gold Key: Sept, 1966 (Photo-c)

	GD 2.0	VG 4.0	FN 6.0	VF 8.0	VF/NM 9.0	NM- 9.2
1 (10186-609)	9	18	27	60	100	140

HONG KONG PHOOEY (TV)
Charlton Comics: June, 1975 - No. 9, Nov, 1976 (Hanna-Barbera)

	GD 2.0	VG 4.0	FN 6.0	VF 8.0	VF/NM 9.0	NM- 9.2
1	5	10	15	34	55	75
2	3	6	9	19	29	38
3-9	3	6	9	16	22	28

HONG ON THE RANGE
Image/Flypaper Press: Dec, 1997 - No. 3, Feb, 1998 ($2.50, lim. series)

	GD 2.0	VG 4.0	FN 6.0	VF 8.0	VF/NM 9.0	NM- 9.2
1-3: Wu-s/Lafferty-a						2.50

HOOD, THE
Marvel Comics (MAX): Jul, 2002 - No. 6, Dec, 2002 ($2.99, limited series)

	GD 2.0	VG 4.0	FN 6.0	VF 8.0	VF/NM 9.0	NM- 9.2
1-6-Vaughan-s/Hotz-c/a						3.00
Vol. 1 Blood From Stones HC (2007, $19.99, dustjacket) r/#1-6; production sketch art						20.00
Vol. 1 Blood From Stones TPB (2003, $14.99) r/#1-6						15.00

HOODED HORSEMAN, THE (Formerly Blazing West)
American Comics Group (Michel Publ.): No. 21, 1-2/52 - No. 27, 1-2/54; No. 18, 12-1/54-55 - No. 22, 8-9/55

	GD 2.0	VG 4.0	FN 6.0	VF 8.0	VF/NM 9.0	NM- 9.2
21(1-2/52)-Hooded Horseman, Injun Jones cont.	15	30	45	83	124	165
22	10	20	30	56	76	95
23,24,27(1-2/54)	9	18	27	50	65	80
25 (9-10/53)-Cowboy Sahib on cover only; Hooded Horseman i.d. revealed	9	18	27	52	69	85
26-Origin/1st app. Cowboy Sahib by L. Starr	11	22	33	62	86	110
18(12-1/54-55)(Formerly Out of the Night)	10	20	30	54	72	90
19,21,22: 19-Last precode (1-2/55)	8	16	24	44	57	70
20-Origin Johnny Injun	9	18	27	50	65	80

NOTE: ***Whitney** c/a-21('52), 20-22.*

HOODED MENACE, THE (Also see Daring Adventures)
Realistic/Avon Periodicals: 1951 (one-shot)

	GD 2.0	VG 4.0	FN 6.0	VF 8.0	VF/NM 9.0	NM- 9.2
nn-Based on a band of hooded outlaws in the Pacific Northwest, 1900-1906; reprinted in Daring Advs. #15	48	96	144	298	499	700

HOODS UP (See the Promotional Comics section)

HOOK (Movie)
Marvel Comics: Early Feb, 1992 - No. 4, Late Mar, 1992 ($1.00, limited series)

	GD 2.0	VG 4.0	FN 6.0	VF 8.0	VF/NM 9.0	NM- 9.2
1-4: Adapts movie; Vess-c; 1-Morrow-a(p)						2.50
nn (1991, $5.95, 84 pgs.)-Contains #1-4; Vess-c						6.00
1 (1991, $2.95, magazine, 84 pgs.)-Contains #1-4; Vess-c (same cover as nn issue)						3.00

HOOT GIBSON'S WESTERN ROUNDUP (See Western Roundup under Fox Giants)

HOOT GIBSON WESTERN (Formerly My Love Story)
Fox Features Syndicate: No. 5, May, 1950 - No. 3, Sept, 1950

	GD 2.0	VG 4.0	FN 6.0	VF 8.0	VF/NM 9.0	NM- 9.2
5,6(#1,2): 5-Photo-c. 6-Photo/painted-c	22	44	66	126	198	270
3-Wood-a; painted-c	23	46	69	135	213	290

HOPALONG CASSIDY (Also see Bill Boyd Western, Master Comics, Real Western Hero, Six Gun Heroes & Western Hero; Bill Boyd starred as Hopalong Cassidy in movies, radio & TV)
Fawcett Publications: Feb, 1943; No. 2, Summer, 1946 - No. 85, Nov, 1953

	GD 2.0	VG 4.0	FN 6.0	VF 8.0	VF/NM 9.0	NM- 9.2
1 (1943, 68 pgs.)-H. Cassidy & his horse Topper begin (on sale 1/8/43)-Captain Marvel app. on-c	480	960	1440	3360	5880	8400
2-(Sum, '46)	72	144	216	450	750	1050
3,4: 3-(Fall, '46, 52 pgs. begin)	38	76	114	219	347	475
5- "Mad Barber" story mentioned in **SOTI**, pgs. 308,309; photo-c	28	56	84	162	256	350
6-10: 8-Photo-c	21	42	63	122	191	260
11-19: 11,13-19-Photo-c	15	30	45	90	140	190
20-29 (52 pgs.)-Painted/photo-c	14	28	42	80	115	150
30,31,33,34,37-39,41 (52 pgs.)-Painted-c	11	22	33	64	90	115
32,40 (36pgs.)-Painted-c	10	20	30	58	79	100
35,42,43,45-47,49-51,53,54,56 (52 pgs.)-Photo-c	11	22	33	60	83	105
36,44,48 (36 pgs.)-Photo-c	10	20	30	56	76	95
52,55,57-70 (36 pgs.)-Photo-c	9	18	27	52	69	85
71-84-Photo-c	8	16	24	44	57	70
85-Last Fawcett issue; photo-c	10	20	30	54	72	90

NOTE: *Line-drawn c-1-4, 6, 7, 9, 10, 12.*

	GD 2.0	VG 4.0	FN 6.0	VF 8.0	VF/NM 9.0	NM- 9.2
... & The 5 Men of Evil (AC Comics, 1991, $12.95) r/newspaper strips and Fawcett story "Signature of Death"						13.00

HOPALONG CASSIDY
National Periodical Publications: No. 86, Feb, 1954 - No. 135, May-June, 1959 (All-36 pgs.)

	GD 2.0	VG 4.0	FN 6.0	VF 8.0	VF/NM 9.0	NM- 9.2
86-Gene Colan-a begins, ends #117; photo covers continue	38	76	114	223	354	485
87	21	42	63	122	191	260
88-91: 91-1 pg. Superboy-sty (7/54)	15	30	45	83	124	165
92-99 (98 has #93 on-c; last precode issue, 2/55). 95-Reversed photo-c to #52. 98-Reversed photo-c to #61. 99-Reversed photo-c to #60	14	28	42	76	108	140
100-Same cover as #50	15	30	45	83	124	165
101-108: 105-Same photo-c as #54. 107-Same photo-c as #51. 108-Last photo-c	7	14	21	45	73	100
109-130: 118-Gil Kane-a begins. 123-Kubert-a (2 pgs.). 124-Painted-c	6	12	18	41	66	90
131-135	6	12	18	43	69	95

HOPELESS SAVAGES (Also see Too Much Hopeless Savages; and the Promotional Comics section for Free Comic Book Day edition)
Oni Press: Aug, 2001 - No. 4, Nov, 2001 ($2.95, B&W, limited series)

	GD 2.0	VG 4.0	FN 6.0	VF 8.0	VF/NM 9.0	NM- 9.2
1-4-Van Meter-s/Norrie-a/Clugston-Major-a/Watson-c						3.00
TPB (2002, $13.95, 8" x 5.75") r/#1-4; plus color stories; Watson-c						14.00

HOPELESS SAVAGES: GROUND ZERO
Oni Press: June, 2002 - No. 4, Oct, 2002 ($2.95, B&W, limited series)

	GD 2.0	VG 4.0	FN 6.0	VF 8.0	VF/NM 9.0	NM- 9.2
1-4-Van Meter-s/O'Malley-a/Dodson-c. 1-Watson-a						3.00
TPB (2003, $11.95, 8" x 5.75") r/#1-4; Dodson-c						12.00

HOPE SHIP
Dell Publishing Co.: June-Aug, 1963

	GD 2.0	VG 4.0	FN 6.0	VF 8.0	VF/NM 9.0	NM- 9.2
1	3	6	9	16	22	28

HOPPY THE MARVEL BUNNY (See Fawcett's Funny Animals)
Fawcett Publications: Dec, 1945 - No. 15, Sept, 1947

	GD 2.0	VG 4.0	FN 6.0	VF 8.0	VF/NM 9.0	NM- 9.2
1	28	56	84	162	261	360
2	14	28	42	82	121	160
3-15: 7-Xmas-c	12	24	36	67	94	120

HORACE & DOTTY DRIPPLE (Dotty Dripple No. 1-24)
Harvey Publications: No. 25, Aug, 1952 - No. 43, Oct, 1955

	GD 2.0	VG 4.0	FN 6.0	VF 8.0	VF/NM 9.0	NM- 9.2
25-43	4	9	13	18	22	26

HORIZONTAL LIEUTENANT, THE (See Movie Classics)

HOROBI
Viz Premiere Comics: 1990 - No. 8, 1990 ($3.75, B&W, mature readers, 84 pgs.) V2#1, 1990 - No. 7, 1991 ($4.25, B&W, 68 pgs.)

	GD 2.0	VG 4.0	FN 6.0	VF 8.0	VF/NM 9.0	NM- 9.2
1-8: Japanese manga, Part Two, #1-7						4.50

HORRIFIC (Terrific No. 14 on)
Artful/Comic Media/Harwell/Mystery: Sept, 1952 - No. 13, Sept, 1954

	GD 2.0	VG 4.0	FN 6.0	VF 8.0	VF/NM 9.0	NM- 9.2
1	58	116	174	365	620	875
2	37	72	111	220	353	485
3-Bullet in head-c	65	130	195	410	693	975
4,5,7,9,10: 4-Shrunken head-c. 7-Guillotine-c	32	64	96	190	305	420
6-Jack The Ripper story	33	66	99	196	316	435
8-Origin & 1st app. The Teller (E.C. parody)	37	74	111	220	353	485
11-13: 11-Swipe/Witches Tales #6,27; Devil-c	26	52	78	152	244	335

NOTE: ***Don Heck** a-8; c-3-13. **Hollingsworth** a-4. **Morisi** a-8. **Palais** a-5, 7-12.*

HORRORCIDE
IDW Publishing: Sept, 2004 ($6.99)

	GD 2.0	VG 4.0	FN 6.0	VF 8.0	VF/NM 9.0	NM- 9.2
1-Steve Niles short stories; art by Templesmith, Medors and Chee						7.00

HORROR FROM THE TOMB (Mysterious Stories No. 2 on)
Premier Magazine Co.: Sept, 1954

	GD 2.0	VG 4.0	FN 6.0	VF 8.0	VF/NM 9.0	NM- 9.2
1-Woodbridge/Torres, Check-a; The Keeper of the Graveyard is host	41	82	123	256	428	600

HORRORIST, THE (Also see Hellblazer)
DC Comics (Vertigo): Dec, 1995 - No. 2, Jan, 1996 ($5.95, lim. series, mature)

	GD 2.0	VG 4.0	FN 6.0	VF 8.0	VF/NM 9.0	NM- 9.2
1,2: Jamie Delano scripts, David Lloyd-c/a; John Constantine (Hellblazer) app.						6.00

HORROR OF COLLIER COUNTY
Dark Horse Comics: Oct, 1999 - No. 5, Feb, 2000 ($2.95, B&W, limited series)

Hot Rod King #1 © Z-D

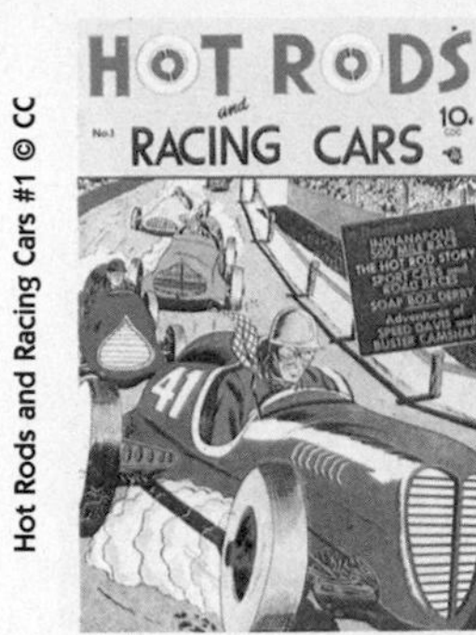

Hot Rods and Racing Cars #1 © CC

Hot Stuff Sizzlers #36 © HARV

	GD 2.0	VG 4.0	FN 6.0	VF 8.0	VF/NM 9.0	NM- 9.2
1-5-Rich Tommaso-s/a						3.00

HORRORS, THE (Formerly Startling Terror Tales #10)
Star Publications: No. 11, Jan, 1953 - No. 15, Apr, 1954

	GD	VG	FN	VF	VF/NM	NM-
11-Horrors of War; Disbrow-a(2)	30	60	90	174	280	385
12-Horrors of War; color illo in **POP**	28	56	84	162	261	360
13-Horrors of Mystery; crime stories	26	52	78	152	244	335
14,15-Horrors of the Underworld; crime stories	28	56	84	162	261	360

NOTE: *All have **L. B. Cole** covers; a-12. **Hollingsworth** a-13. **Palais** a-13r.*

HORROR TALES (Magazine)
Eerie Publications: V1#7, 6/69 - V6#6, 12/74; V7#1, 2/75; V7#2, 5/76 - V8#5, 1977; V9#1-3, 8/78; V10#1(2/79) (V1-V6: 52 pgs.; V7, V8#2: 112 pgs.; V8#4 on: 68 pgs.) (No V5#3, V8#1,3)

	GD	VG	FN	VF	VF/NM	NM-
V1#7	6	12	18	37	59	80
V1#8,9	4	8	12	26	41	55
V2#1-6('70), V3#1-6('71), V4#1-3,5-7('72)	4	8	12	22	34	45
V4#4-LSD story reprint/Weird V3#5	5	10	15	30	48	65
V5#1,2,4,5(6/73),5(10/73),6(12/73),V6#1-6('74),V7#1,2,4('76),V7#3('76)-Giant issue, V8#2,4,5('77)	4	8	12	22	34	45
V9#1-3(11/78, $1.50), V10#1(2/79)	4	8	12	24	37	50

NOTE: *Bondage-c-V6#1, 3, V7#2.*

HORSE FEATHERS COMICS
Lev Gleason Publ.: Nov, 1945 - No. 4, July(Summer on-c), 1948 (52 pgs.) (#2,3 are oversized)

	GD	VG	FN	VF	VF/NM	NM-
1-Wolverton's Scoop Scuttle, 2 pgs.	19	38	57	109	172	235
2	11	22	33	60	83	105
3,4: 3-(5/48)	9	18	27	47	61	75

HORSEMAN
Crusade Comics/Kevlar Studios: Mar, 1996 - No. 3, Nov, 1997 ($2.95)

	GD	VG	FN	VF	VF/NM	NM-
0-1st Kevlar Studios issue, 1-(3/96)-Crusade issue; Shi c/app., 1-(11/96)-3-(11/97)-Kevlar Studios						3.00

HORSEMASTERS, THE (Disney)(TV, Movie)
Dell Publishing Co.: No. 1260, Dec-Feb, 1961/62

	GD	VG	FN	VF	VF/NM	NM-
Four Color 1260-Annette Funicello photo-c	12	24	36	87	156	225

HORSE SOLDIERS, THE
Dell Publishing Co.: No. 1048, Nov-Jan, 1959/60 (John Wayne movie)

	GD	VG	FN	VF	VF/NM	NM-
Four Color 1048-Painted-c, Sekowsky-a	13	26	39	95	168	240

HORSE WITHOUT A HEAD, THE (See Movie Comics)

HOT DOG
Magazine Enterprises: June-July, 1954 - No. 4, Dec-Jan, 1954-55

	GD	VG	FN	VF	VF/NM	NM-
1(A-1 #107)	9	18	27	47	61	75
2,3(A-1 #115),4(A-1 #136)	6	12	18	31	38	45

HOT DOG (See Jughead's Pal, Hotdog)

HOTEL DEPAREE - SUNDANCE (TV)
Dell Publishing Co.: No. 1126, Aug-Oct, 1960 (one-shot)

	GD	VG	FN	VF	VF/NM	NM-
Four Color 1126-Earl Holliman photo-c	6	12	18	43	69	95

HOT ROD AND SPEEDWAY COMICS
Hillman Periodicals: Feb-Mar, 1952 - No. 5, Apr-May, 1953

	GD	VG	FN	VF	VF/NM	NM-
1	27	54	81	158	254	350
2-Krigstein-a	18	36	54	105	165	225
3-5	12	24	36	69	97	125

HOT ROD COMICS (...Featuring Clint Curtis) (See XMas Comics)
Fawcett Publications: Nov, 1951 (no month given) - V2#7, Feb, 1953

	GD	VG	FN	VF	VF/NM	NM-
nn (V1#1)-Powell-c/a in all	29	58	87	169	272	375
2 (4/52)	15	30	45	90	140	190
3-6, V2#7	13	26	39	72	101	130

HOT ROD KING (Also see Speed Smith the Hot Rod King)
Ziff-Davis Publ. Co.: Fall, 1952

	GD	VG	FN	VF	VF/NM	NM-
1-Giacoia-a; Saunders painted-c	25	50	75	145	233	320

HOT ROD RACERS (Grand Prix No. 16 on)
Charlton Comics: Dec, 1964 - No. 15, July, 1967

	GD	VG	FN	VF	VF/NM	NM-
1	8	16	24	54	90	125
2-5	5	10	15	32	51	70
6-15	4	8	12	24	37	50

HOT RODS AND RACING CARS
Charlton Comics (Motor Mag. No. 1): Nov, 1951 - No. 120, June, 1973

	GD	VG	FN	VF	VF/NM	NM-
1-Speed Davis begins; Indianapolis 500 story	28	56	84	162	261	360
2	15	30	45	86	133	180
3-10	12	24	36	67	94	120
11-20	10	20	30	54	72	90
21-33,36-40	8	16	24	44	57	70
34, 35 (? & 6/58, 68 pgs.)	11	22	33	60	83	105
41-60	7	14	21	37	46	55
61-80	3	6	9	19	29	38
81-100	3	6	9	16	22	28
101-120	2	4	6	13	18	22

HOT SHOT CHARLIE
Hillman Periodicals: 1947 (Lee Elias)

	GD	VG	FN	VF	VF/NM	NM-
1	11	22	33	60	83	105

HOT SHOTS: AVENGERS
Marvel Comics: Oct, 1995 ($2.95, one-shot)

	GD	VG	FN	VF	VF/NM	NM-
nn-pin-ups						3.00

HOTSPUR
Eclipse Comics: Jun, 1987 - No. 3, Sep, 1987 ($1.75, lim. series, Baxter paper)

	GD	VG	FN	VF	VF/NM	NM-
1-3						3.00

HOT STUFF (See Stumbo Tinytown)
Harvey Comics: V2#1, Sept, 1991 - No. 12, June, 1994 ($1.00)

	GD	VG	FN	VF	VF/NM	NM-
V2#1-Stumbo back-up story						4.00
2-12 ($1.50)						3.00
...Big Book 1 (11/92), 2 (6/93) (Both $1.95, 52 pgs.)						4.00

HOT STUFF CREEPY CAVES
Harvey Publications: Nov, 1974 - No. 7, Nov, 1975

	GD	VG	FN	VF	VF/NM	NM-
1	4	8	12	22	34	45
2-7	3	6	9	15	21	26

HOT STUFF DIGEST
Harvey Comics: July, 1992 - No. 5, Nov, 1993 ($1.75, digest-size)

	GD	VG	FN	VF	VF/NM	NM-
V2#1-Hot Stuff, Stumbo, Richie Rich stories						6.00
2-5						4.00

HOT STUFF GIANT SIZE
Harvey Comics: Oct, 1992 - No. 3, Oct, 1993 ($2.25, 68 pgs.)

	GD	VG	FN	VF	VF/NM	NM-
V2#1-Hot Stuff & Stumbo stories						4.50
2,3						3.50

HOT STUFF SIZZLERS
Harvey Publications: July, 1960 - No. 59, Mar, 1974; V2#1, Aug, 1992

	GD	VG	FN	VF	VF/NM	NM-
1- 84 pgs. begin, ends #5; Hot Stuff, Stumbo begin	15	30	45	107	196	285
2-5	8	16	24	56	93	130
6-10: 6-68 pgs. begin, ends #45	6	12	18	41	66	90
11-20	4	8	12	28	44	60
21-45	3	6	9	20	30	40
46-52: 52 pgs. begin	3	6	9	16	23	30
53-59	2	4	6	10	14	18
V2#1-(8/92, $1.25)-Stumbo back-up						5.00

HOT STUFF, THE LITTLE DEVIL (Also see Devil Kids & Harvey Hits)
Harvey Publications (Illustrated Humor): 10/57 - No. 141, 7/77; No. 142, 2/78 - No. 164, 8/82; No. 165, 10/86 - No. 171, 11/87; No. 172, 11/88; No. 173, Sept, 1990 - No. 177, 1/91

	GD	VG	FN	VF	VF/NM	NM-
1	50	100	150	400	750	1100
2-Stumbo-like giant 1st app. (12/57)	24	48	72	176	326	475
3-5: 3-Stumbo the Giant debut (2/58)	18	36	54	130	240	350
6-10	11	22	33	79	140	200
11-20	9	18	27	60	100	140
21-40	6	12	18	39	62	85
41-60	4	8	12	26	41	55
61-80	3	6	9	20	30	40
81-105	3	6	9	16	22	28
106-112: All 52 pg. Giants	3	6	9	18	27	35
113-125	2	4	6	9	12	15
126-141	1	2	3	5	7	9
142-177: 172-177-($1.00)						6.00
Harvey Comics Classics Vol. 3 TPB (Dark Horse Books, 3/08, $19.95) Reprints Hot Stuff's earliest appearances in this title and Devil Kids, mostly B&W with some color stories; history, early concept drawings; foreword by Mark Arnold						20.00

HOT WHEELS (TV)
National Periodical Publications: Mar-Apr, 1970 - No. 6, Jan-Feb, 1971

	GD	VG	FN	VF	VF/NM	NM-
1	9	18	27	63	107	150
2,4,5	5	10	15	35	55	75
3-Neal Adams-c	6	12	18	41	66	90

Hourman #2 © DC

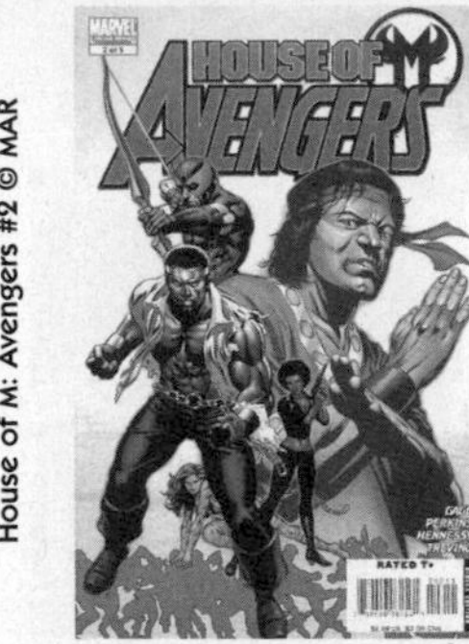

House of M: Avengers #2 © MAR

House of Mystery #204 © DC

	GD 2.0	VG 4.0	FN 6.0	VF 8.0	VF/NM 9.0	NM- 9.2
6-Neal Adams-c/a	7	14	21	50	83	115

NOTE: *Toth a-1p, 2-5; c-1p, 5.*

HOURMAN (Justice Society member, see Adventure Comics #48)

HOURMAN (See JLA and DC One Million)
DC Comics: Apr, 1999 - No. 25, Apr, 2001 ($2.50)

	GD 2.0	VG 4.0	FN 6.0	VF 8.0	VF/NM 9.0	NM- 9.2
1-25: 1-JLA app.; McDaniel-c. 2-Tomorrow Woman-c/app. 6,7-Amazo app. 11-13-Justice Legion A app. 16-Silver Age flashback. 18,19-JSA-c/app. 22-Harris-c/a. 24-Hourman Vs. Rex Tyler						2.50

HOUSE OF M (Also see miniseries with Fantastic Four, Iron Man and Spider-Man)
Marvel Comics: Aug, 2005 - No. 8, Dec, 2005 ($2.99, limited series)

	GD 2.0	VG 4.0	FN 6.0	VF 8.0	VF/NM 9.0	NM- 9.2
1-Bendis-s/Coipel-a/Ribic-c; Scarlet Witch changes reality; Quesada variant-c						3.00
2-8-Variant covers for each. 3-Hawkeye returns						3.00
Secrets Of The House Of M (2005, $3.99, one-shot) profile pages and background info						4.00
... Sketchbook (6/05) B&W preview sketches by Coipel, Davis, Hairsine, Quesada						2.50
TPB (2006, $24.99) r/#1-8 and The Pulse: House of M Special Edition newspaper						25.00
...: Fantastic Four/ Iron Man TPB (2006, $13.99) r/ both House of M mini-series						14.00
...: World of M Featuring Wolverine TPB (2006, $13.99) r/2005 x-over issues Wolverine #33-35, Black Panther #7, Captain America #10 and The Pulse #10						14.00
HC (2008, $29.99, oversized with d.j.) r/#1-8, The Pulse: House of M Special Edition newspaper and Secrets Of The House Of M one-shot; script pages; cover gallery						30.00

HOUSE OF M: AVENGERS
Marvel Comics: Jan, 2008 - No. 5, Apr, 2008 ($2.99, limited series)

	GD 2.0	VG 4.0	FN 6.0	VF 8.0	VF/NM 9.0	NM- 9.2
1-5-Gage-s/Perkins-a; Luke Cage, Iron Fist, Hawkeye, Tigra, Misty Knight, Shang-Chi						3.00

HOUSE OF MYSTERY
DC Comics: Dec/Jan. 1951

nn - Ashcan comic, not distributed to newsstands, only for in-house use. Cover art is Danger Trail #3 with interior being Star Spangled Comics #109. A VG+ copy sold for $2,357.50 in 2002.

HOUSE OF MYSTERY (See Brave and the Bold #93, Elvira's House of Mystery, Limited Collectors' Edition & Super DC Giant)

HOUSE OF MYSTERY, THE
National Periodical Publications/DC Comics: Dec-Jan, 1951-52 - No. 321, Oct, 1983 (No. 194-203: 52 pgs.)

	GD 2.0	VG 4.0	FN 6.0	VF 8.0	VF/NM 9.0	NM- 9.2
1-DC's first horror comic	243	486	729	1531	2591	3650
2	93	186	279	586	993	1400
3	65	130	195	410	693	975
4,5	52	104	156	322	536	750
6-10	45	90	135	279	465	650
11-15	40	80	120	235	380	525
16(7/53)-25	31	62	93	181	291	400
26-35(2/55)-Last pre-code issue; 30-Woodish-a	24	48	72	140	225	310
36-50: 50-Text story of Orson Welles' War of the Worlds broadcast	14	28	42	99	175	250
51-60: 55-1st S.A. issue	11	22	33	79	140	200
61,63,65,66,69,70,72,76,85-Kirby-a	13	26	39	90	160	230
62,64,67,68,71,73-75,77-83,86-99	10	20	30	68	119	170
84-Prototype of Negative Man (Doom Patrol)	13	26	39	90	160	230
100 (7/60)	10	20	30	73	129	185
101-116: 109-Toth, Kubert-a. 116-Last 10¢ issue	9	18	27	63	107	150
117-130: 117-Swipes-c to HOS #20. 120-Toth-a	8	16	24	56	93	130
131-142	7	14	21	49	80	110
143-J'onn J'onzz, Manhunter begins (6/64), ends #173; story continues from Detective #326; intro. Idol-Head of Diabolu	19	38	57	135	250	365
144	8	16	24	58	97	135
145-155,157-159: 149-Toth-a. 155-The Human Hurricane app. (12/65), Red Tornado prototype. 158-Origin Diabolu Idol-Head	6	12	18	39	62	85
156-Robby Reed begins (origin/1st app.), ends #173	7	14	21	50	83	115
160-(7/66)-Robby Reed becomes Plastic Man in this issue only; 1st S.A. app. Plastic Man; intro Marco Xavier (Martian Manhunter) & Vulture Crime Organization; ends #173	9	18	27	63	107	150
161-173: 169-Origin/1st app. Gem Girl	4	8	12	28	44	60
174-Mystery format begins.	10	20	30	68	119	170
175-1st app. Cain (House of Mystery host)	7	14	21	49	80	110
176,177	7	14	21	45	73	100
178-Neal Adams-a (2/69)	7	14	21	50	83	115
179-N. Adams/Orlando, Wrightson-a (1st pro work, 3 pgs.)	9	18	27	63	107	150
180,181,183: Wrightson-a (3,10, & 3 pgs.). 180-Last 12¢ issue; Kane/Wood-a(2). 183-Wood-a	7	14	21	45	73	100
182,184: 182-Toth-a. 184-Kane/Wood, Toth-a	5	10	15	30	48	65
185-Williamson/Kaluta-a; Howard-a (3 pgs.)	5	10	15	34	55	75
186-N. Adams-c/a; Wrightson-a (10 pgs.)	7	14	21	49	80	110
187,190: Adams-c. 187-Toth-a. 190-Toth-a(r)	4	8	12	28	44	60
188-Wrightson-a (8 & 3pgs.); Adams-c	6	12	18	37	59	80
189,192,197: Adams-c on all. 189-Wood-a(i). 192-Last 15¢-c	4	8	12	28	44	60
191-Wrightson-a (8 & 3pgs.); Adams-c	6	12	18	37	59	80
193-Wrightson-c	4	8	12	28	44	60
194-Wrightson-c; 52 pgs begin, end #203; Toth,Kirby-a	6	12	18	37	59	80
195: Wrightson-c. Swamp creature story by Wrightson similar to Swamp Thing (10 pgs.)(10/71)	7	14	21	49	80	110
196,198	4	8	12	24	37	50
199-Adams-c; Wood-a(8pgs.); Kirby-a	5	10	15	32	51	70
200-(25¢, 52 pgs.)-One third-r (3/72)	5	10	15	32	51	70
201-203-(25¢, 52 pgs.)-One third-r	4	8	12	24	37	50
204-Wrightson-c/a, 9 pgs.	4	8	12	23	36	48
205,206,208,210,212,215,216,218	3	6	9	16	22	28
207-Wrightson-c/a; Starlin, Redondo-a	4	8	12	23	36	48
209,211,213,214,217-Wrightson-c	3	6	9	20	30	40
219,220,222,223	3	6	9	14	19	24
221-Wrightson/Kaluta-a(8 pgs.)	3	6	9	21	32	42
224-229: 224-Wrightson-r from Spectre #9; Dillin/Adams-r from House of Secrets #82; begin 100 pg. issues; Phantom Stranger-r. 225,227-(100 pgs.): 225-Spectre app. 226-Wrightson/Redondo-a Phantom Stranger-r. 228-N. Adams inks; Wrightson-r. 229-Wrightson-a(r); Toth-r; last 100 pg. issue	5	10	15	34	55	75
230,232-235,237-250	2	4	6	10	14	18
231-Classic Wrightson-c	4	8	12	22	34	45
236-Wrightson-c; Ditko-a(p); N. Adams-i	3	6	9	16	23	30
251-254-(84 pgs.)-Adams-c. 251-Wood-a	3	6	9	18	27	35
255,256-(84 pgs.)-Wrightson-c	3	6	9	18	27	35
257-259-(84 pgs.)	3	6	9	14	20	25
260-289: 282-(68 pgs.)-Has extra story "The Computers That Saved Metropolis" Radio Shack giveaway by Jim Starlin	1	2	3	5	7	9
290-1st "I, Vampire"	3	6	9	14	19	24
291-299: 291,293,295-299- "I, Vampire"	2	4	6	8	11	14
300,319,321: Death of "I, Vampire"	2	4	6	9	13	16
301-318,320: 301-318-"I, Vampire"	2	4	6	8	11	14
Welcome to the House of Mystery (7/98, $5.95) reprints stories with new framing story by Gaiman and Aragonés						6.00

NOTE: ***Neal Adams** a-236i; c-175-192, 197, 199, 251-254. **Alcala** a-209, 217, 219, 224, 227. **M. Anderson** a-212; c/a-37. **Aparo** a-209. **Aragones** a-185, 186, 194, 196, 200, 202, 229, 251. **Baily** a-279p. **Cameron** a-76, 79. **Colan** a-202r. **Craig** a-263, 275, 295, 300. **Dillin/Adams** r-224. **Ditko** a-236p, 247, 254, 258, 276; c-277. **Drucker** a-37. **Evans** c-218. **Fradon** a-251. **Giffen** a-284. **Giunta** a-199, 227r. **Golden** a-257, 259. **Heath** a-194r; c-203. **Howard** a-182, 185, 187, 196, 229r, 247i, 254, 279i. **Kaluta** a-195, 200, 250r; c-200-202, 210, 212, 233, 260, 261, 263, 265, 267, 268, 273, 276, 284, 287, 288, 293-295, 300, 302, 304, 305, 309-319, 321. **Bob Kane** a-84. **Gil Kane** a-196p, 253p, 300p. **Kirby** a-194r, 199r; c-65, 76, 78, 79, 85. **Kubert** c-282, 283, 285, 286, 289-292, 297-299, 301, 303, 306-308. **Maneely** a-68, 227r. **Mayer** a-317p. **Meskin** a-52-144 (most), 195r, 224r, 229r; c-63, 66, 124, 127. **Mooney** a-24, 159, 160. **Moreira** a-3, 4, 20-50, 58, 59, 62, 68, 77, 79, 90, 108, 113, 123, 201r, 228; c-4-28, 44, 47, 50, 54, 59, 62, 64, 68, 70, 73. **Morrow** a-192, 196, 255, 320i. **Mortimer** a-204(3 pgs.). **Nasser** a-276. **Newton** a-259, 272. **Nino** a-204, 212, 213, 220, 224, 225, 245, 250, 252-256, 283. **Orlando** a-175(2 pgs.), 178, 240i; c-240, 258p, 262, 264p, 270p, 271, 272, 274, 275, 278, 296i. **Redondo** a-194, 195, 197, 202, 203, 207, 211, 214, 217, 219, 226, 227, 229, 235, 241, 287(layout), 302p, 303i, 308; c-229. **Reese** a-195, 200, 205i. **Rogers** a-254, 274, 277. **Roussos** a-65, 84, 224i. **Sekowsky** a-282p. **Sparling** a-203. **Starlin** a-207(2 pgs.), 282p; c-281. **Leonard Starr** a-9. **Staton** a-300p. **Sutton** a-189, 271, 290, 291, 293, 295, 297-299, 302, 303, 306-309, 310-313i, 314. **Tuska** a-293p, 294p, 316p. **Wrightson** c-193-195, 204, 207, 209, 211, 213, 214, 217, 219, 221, 231, 236, 255, 256; r-224.*

HOUSE OF MYSTERY
DC Comics (Vertigo): Jul, 2008 - Present ($2.99)

	GD 2.0	VG 4.0	FN 6.0	VF 8.0	VF/NM 9.0	NM- 9.2
1-4: 1-Cain and Abel app.; Rossi-a/Weber-c; short story by Willingham						3.00
1-Variant-c by Bernie Wrightson						5.00

HOUSE OF SECRETS (Combined with The Unexpected after #154)
National Periodical Publications/DC Comics: 11-12/56 - No. 80, 9-10/66; No. 81, 8-9/69 - No. 140, 2-3/76; No. 141, 8-9/76 - No. 154, 10-11/78

	GD 2.0	VG 4.0	FN 6.0	VF 8.0	VF/NM 9.0	NM- 9.2
1-Drucker-a; Moreira-c	110	220	330	935	1793	2650
2-Moreira-a	42	84	126	319	597	875
3-Kirby-c/a	35	70	105	270	498	725
4-Kirby-a	25	50	75	185	343	500
5-7	18	36	54	130	240	350
8-Kirby-a	20	40	60	145	268	390
9-11: 11-Lou Cameron-a (unsigned)	16	32	48	112	209	305
12-Kirby-c/a; Lou Cameron-a	17	38	51	122	226	330
13-15: 14-Flying saucer-c	12	24	36	87	156	225
16-20	11	22	33	79	140	200
21,22,24-30	10	20	30	68	119	170
23-1st app. Mark Merlin & begin series (8/59)	11	22	33	75	133	190
31-50: 48-Toth-a. 50-Last 10¢ issue	9	18	27	63	107	150
51-60: 58-Origin Mark Merlin	8	16	24	52	86	120

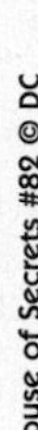
House of Secrets #82 © DC

Howard the Duck #26 © MAR

Howdy Doody #5 © Cal. Nat. Prods.

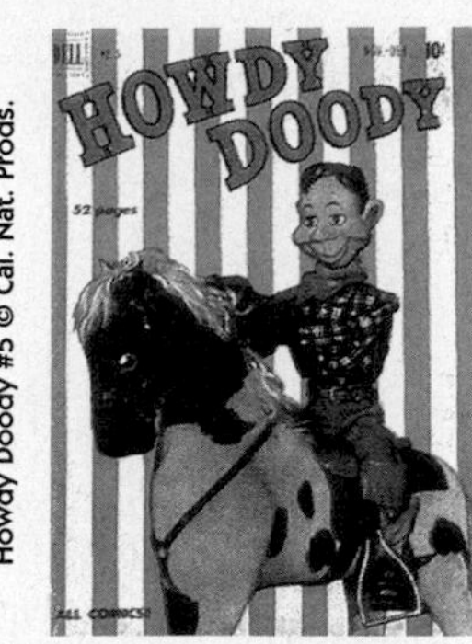

	GD 2.0	VG 4.0	FN 6.0	VF 8.0	VF/NM 9.0	NM- 9.2
61-First Eclipso (7-8/63) and begin series	15	30	45	105	190	275
62	8	16	24	54	90	125
63-65-Toth-a on Eclipso (see Brave and the Bold #64)	6	12	18	43	69	95
66-1st Eclipso-c (also #67,70,78,79); Toth-a	8	16	24	54	90	125
67,73: 67-Toth-a on Eclipso. 73-Mark Merlin becomes Prince Ra-Man (1st app.)	6	12	18	43	69	95
68-72,74-80: 76-Prince Ra-Man vs. Eclipso. 80-Eclipso, Prince Ra-Man end	6	12	18	39	62	85
81-Mystery format begins; 1st app. Abel (House Of Secrets host); (cameo in DC Special #4)	10	20	30	68	119	170
82-84: 82-Neal Adams-c(i)	6	12	18	37	59	80
85,90: 85-N. Adams-a(i). 90-Buckler (early work)/N. Adams-a(i)	6	12	18	39	62	85
86,88,89,91	5	10	15	30	48	65
87-Wrightson & Kaluta-a	6	12	18	41	66	90
92-1st app. Swamp Thing-c/story (8 pgs.)(6-7/71) by Berni Wrightson(p) w/JeffJones/Kaluta/Weiss ink assists; classic-c.	48	96	144	384	717	1050
93,94,96-(52 pgs.)-Wrightson-c. 94-Wrightson-a(i); 96-Wood-a	5	10	15	32	51	70
95,97,98-(52 pgs.)	4	8	12	28	44	60
99-Wrightson splash pg.	4	8	12	26	41	55
100-Classic Wrightson-c	6	12	18	39	62	85
101,102,104,105,108-120: 112-Grey tone-c	3	6	9	14	20	25
103,106,107-Wrightson-c	3	6	9	21	32	42
121-133	2	4	6	9	13	16
134-136,139-Wrightson-a	3	6	9	16	22	28
137,138,141-153	1	3	4	6	8	10
140-1st solo origin of the Patchworkman (see Swamp Thing #3)	3	6	9	16	22	20
154 (10-11/78, 44 pgs.) Last issue	2	4	6	8	11	14

NOTE: ***Neal Adams*** *c-81, 82, 84-88, 90, 91.* ***Alcala*** *a-104-107.* ***Anderson*** *a-91. Aparo a-93, 97, 105.* ***B. Bailey*** *a-107.* ***Cameron*** *a-13, 15.* ***Colan*** *a-63.* ***Ditko*** *a-139p, 148.* ***Elias*** *a-58.* ***Evans*** *a-118.* ***Finlay*** *a-7(Real Fact?).* ***Glanzman*** *a-91.* ***Golden*** *a-151.* ***Heath*** *a-31.* ***Heck*** *a-85.* ***Kaluta*** *a-87, 98, 99; c-98, 99, 101, 102, 105, 149, 151, 154.* ***Bob Kane*** *a-18, 21.* ***G. Kane*** *a-85p.* ***Kirby*** *c-3, 11, 12.* ***Kubert*** *a-39.* ***Meskin*** *a-2-68 (most), 94r; c-55-60.* ***Moreira*** *a-7, 8, 51, 54, 102-104, 106, 108, 113, 116, 118, 121, 123, 127; c-1, 2, 4-10, 13-20.* ***Morrow*** *a-86, 89, 90; c-89, 146-148.* ***Nino*** *a-101, 103, 106, 109, 115, 117, 126, 128, 131, 147, 153.* ***Redondo*** *a-95, 99, 102, 104p, 113, 116, 134, 136, 139, 140.* ***Reese*** *a-85.* ***Severin*** *a-91.* ***Starlin*** *c-150.* ***Sutton*** *a-154.* ***Toth*** *a-63-67, 83, 93r, 94r, 96r-98r, 123.* ***Tuska*** *a-90, 104.* ***Wrightson*** *a-134; c-92-94, 96, 100, 103, 106, 107, 135, 136, 139.*

HOUSE OF SECRETS
DC Comics (Vertigo): Oct, 1996 - No. 25, Dec, 1998 ($2.50) (Creator-owned series)

1-Steven Seagle-s/Kristiansen-c/a.						3.50
2-25: 5,7-Kristiansen-c/a. 6-Fegrado-a						3.00
TPB-(1997, $14.95) r/1-5						15.00

HOUSE OF SECRETS: FACADE
DC Comics (Vertigo): 2001 - No. 2, 2001 ($5.95, limited series)

1,2-Steven Seagle-s/Teddy Kristiansen-c/a.						6.00

HOUSE OF TERROR (3-D)
St. John Publishing Co.: Oct, 1953 (25¢, came w/glasses)

1-Kubert, Baker-a	27	54	81	158	254	350

HOUSE OF YANG, THE (See Yang)
Charlton Comics: July, 1975 - No. 6, June, 1976; 1978

1-Sanho Kim-a in all	2	4	6	11	16	20
2-6	1	3	4	6	8	10
Modern Comics #1,2(1978)						4.00

HOUSE ON THE BORDERLAND
DC Comics (Vertigo): 2000 ($29.95, hardcover, one-shot)

HC-Adaptation of William Hope Hodgson book; Corben-a						30.00
SC (2003, $19.95)						20.00

HOUSE II: THE SECOND STORY
Marvel Comics: Oct, 1987 (One-shot)

1-Adapts movie						2.50

HOWARD CHAYKIN'S AMERICAN FLAGG (See American Flagg!)
First Comics: V2#1, May, 1988 - V2#12, Apr, 1989 ($1.75/$1.95, Baxter paper)

V2#1-9,11,12-Chaykin-c(p) in all						2.50
10-Elvis Presley photo-c						3.00

HOWARD THE DUCK (See Bizarre Adventures #34, Crazy Magazine, Fear, Man-Thing, Marvel Treasury Edition & Sensational She-Hulk #14-17)
Marvel Comics Group: Jan, 1976 - No. 31, May, 1979; No. 32, Jan, 1986; No. 33, Sept, 1986

1-Brunner-c/a; Spider-Man x-over (low distr.)	3	6	9	20	30	40
2-Brunner-c/a	2	4	6	10	14	18
3,4-(Regular 25¢ edition). 3-Buscema-a(p), (7/76)	2	4	6	8	10	12
3,4-(30¢-c, limited distribution)	3	6	9	14	19	24
5	2	4	6	8	10	12
6-11: 8-Howard The Duck for president. 9-1st Sgt. Preston Dudley of RCMP. 10-Spider-Man-c/sty	1	2	3	5	6	8
12-1st brief app. Kiss (3/77)	3	6	9	20	30	40
13-(30¢-c) 1st full app. Kiss (6/77); Daimon Hellstrom app. plus cameo of Howard as Son of Satan	4	8	12	22	34	45
13 (35¢-c, limited distribution)	9	18	27	65	113	160
14-32: 14-17-(Regular 30¢-c). 14-Howard as Son of Satan-c/story; Son of Satan app. 16-Album issue; 3 pgs. comics. 22,23-Man-Thing-c/stories; Star Wars parody. 30,32-P. Smith-a						4.00
14-17-(35¢-c, limited distribution)	3	6	9	14	20	25
33-Last issue; low print run	1	2	3	4	5	7
Annual 1(1977, 52 pgs.)-Mayerik-a	1	2	3	5	7	9
... Omnibus HC (2008, $99.99, dustjacket) r/#1-33 & Annual #1, Adventure Into Fear #19, Man-Thing #1, Giant-Size Man-Thing #4&5, Marvel Treasury Ed. #12, Marvel Team-Up #96 and FOOM #15; Gerber foreword; creator interviews; bonus art; 2 covers						100.00

NOTE: ***Austin*** *c-29i.* ***Bolland*** *c-33.* ***Brunner*** *a-1p, 2p; c-1, 2.* ***Buckler*** *c-3p.* ***Buscema*** *a-3p.* ***Colan*** *a(p)-4-15, 17-20, 24-27, 30, 31; c(p)-4-31, Annual 1p.* ***Leialoha*** *a-1-13i; c(i)-3-5, 8-11.* ***Mayerik*** *a-22, 23, 33.* ***Paul Smith*** *a-30p, 32. Man-Thing app. in #22, 23.*

HOWARD THE DUCK (Magazine)
Marvel Comics Group: Oct, 1979 - No. 9, Mar, 1981 (B&W, 68 pgs.)

1-Art by Colan, Janson, Golden. Kidney Lady app.	1	3	4	6	8	10
2,3,5-9 (nudity in most): 2-Mayerick-c. 3-Xmas issue; Jack Davis-c; Duck World flashback. 5-Dracula app. 6-1st Street People back-up story. 7-Has pin-up by Byrne; Man-Thing-c/s (46 pgs.). 8-Batman parody w/Marshall Rogers-a; Dave Sim-a (1 pg.). 9-Marie Severin-a; John Pound painted-c						5.00
4-Beatles, John Lennon, Elvis, Kiss & Devo cameos; Hitler app.	2	4	6	8	10	12

NOTE: ***Buscema*** *a-4p.* ***Colan*** *a-1-5p, 7-9p.* ***Jack Davis*** *c-3.* ***Golden*** *a(p)-1, 5, 6(51pgs.).* ***Rogers*** *a-7, 8.* ***Simonson*** *a-7.*

HOWARD THE DUCK (Volume 2)
Marvel Comics: Mar, 2002 - No. 6, Aug, 2002 ($2.99)

1-Gerber-s/Winslade-a/Fabry-c						4.00
2-6: 2,4-6-Gerber-s/Winslade-a/Fabry-c. 3-Fabry-a/c						3.00
TPB (9/02, $14.99) r/#1-6						15.00

HOWARD THE DUCK (Volume 3)
Marvel Comics: Dec, 2007 - No. 4, Feb, 2008 ($2.99, limited series)

1-4-Templeton-s/Bobillo-a/c; She-Hulk app.						3.00
...: Media Duckling TPB (2008, $11.99) r/#1-4; Howard the Duck #1 (1/76) and pages from Civil War: Choosing Sides						12.00

HOWARD THE DUCK HOLIDAY SPECIAL
Marvel Comics: Feb, 1997 ($2.50, one-shot)

1-Wraparound-c; Hama-s						2.50

HOWARD THE DUCK: THE MOVIE
Marvel Comics Group: Dec, 1986 - No. 3, Feb, 1987 (Limited series)

1-3: Movie adaptation; r/Marvel Super Special						2.50

HOW BOYS AND GIRLS CAN HELP WIN THE WAR
The Parents' Magazine Institute: 1942 (10¢, one-shot)

1-All proceeds used to buy war bonds	26	52	78	152	244	335

HOWDY DOODY (TV)(See Jackpot of Fun-- & Poll Parrot)
Dell Publishing Co.: 1/50 - No. 38, 7-9/56; No. 761, 1/57; No. 811, 7/57

1-(Scarce)-Photo-c; 1st TV comic	79	158	237	672	1286	1900
2-Photo-c	38	76	114	293	547	800
3-5: All photo-c	22	44	66	161	298	435
6-Used in **SOTI**, pg. 309; classic-c; painted covers begin	23	46	69	167	309	450
7-10	14	28	42	104	187	270
11-20: 13-X-Mas-c	12	24	36	87	156	225
21-38, Four Color 761,811	10	20	30	71	126	180

HOW IT BEGAN
United Features Syndicate: No. 15, 1939 (one-shot)

Single Series 15	34	68	102	198	319	440

HOW SANTA GOT HIS RED SUIT (See March of Comics No. 2)

HOW THE WEST WAS WON (See Movie Comics)

HOW TO DRAW FOR THE COMICS
Street and Smith: No date (1942?) (10¢, 64 pgs., B&W & color, no ads)

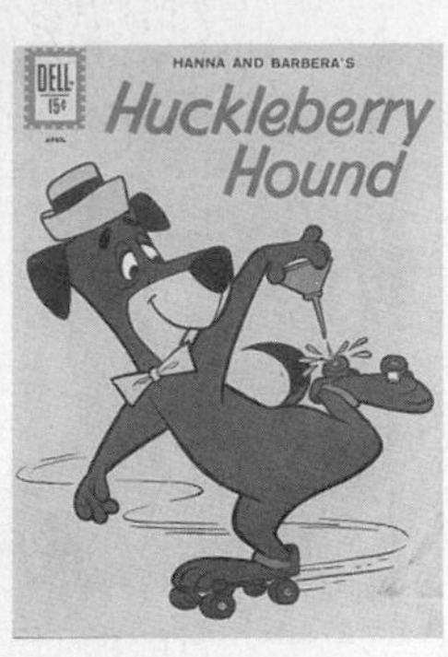

Huckleberry Hound #16 © H-B

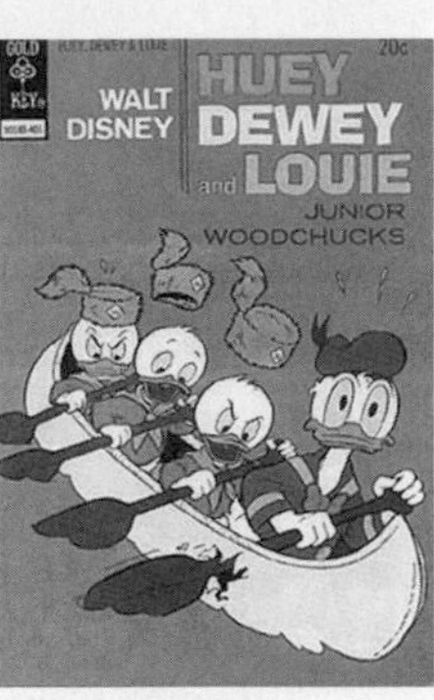

Huey, Dewey, and Louie Junior Woodchucks #24 © DIS

Hulk (2008 series) #1 © MAR

GD 2.0 | VG 4.0 | FN 6.0 | VF 8.0 | VF/NM 9.0 | NM- 9.2

nn-Art by Robert Winsor McCay (recreating his father's art), George Marcoux (Supersnipe artist), Vernon Greene (The Shadow artist), Jack Binder (with biog.), Thorton Fisher, Jon Small, & Jack Farr; has biographies of each artist 29 58 87 169 272 375

H. P. LOVECRAFT'S CTHULHU
Millennium Publications: Dec, 1991 - No. 3, May, 1992 ($2.50, limited series)
1-3: 1-Contains trading cards on thin stock 3.00

H. R. PUFNSTUF (TV) (See March of Comics #360)
Gold Key: Oct, 1970 - No. 8, July, 1972
1-Photo-c 15 30 45 105 190 275
2-8-Photo-c on all. 6-8-Both Gold Key and Whitman editions exist 9 18 27 65 113 160

HUBERT AT CAMP MOONBEAM
Dell Publishing Co.: No. 251, Oct, 1949 (one shot)
Four Color 251 6 12 18 41 66 90

HUCK & YOGI JAMBOREE (TV)
Dell Publishing Co.: Mar, 1961 ($1.00, 6-1/4x9", 116 pgs., cardboard-c, high quality paper) (B&W original material)
nn (scarce) 9 18 27 63 107 150

HUCK & YOGI WINTER SPORTS (TV)
Dell Publishing Co.: No. 1310, Mar, 1962 (Hanna-Barbara) (one-shot)
Four Color 1310 8 16 24 56 93 130

HUCK FINN (See The New Adventures of... & Power Record Comics)

HUCKLEBERRY FINN (Movie)
Dell Publishing Co.: No. 1114, July, 1960
Four Color 1114-Photo-c 5 10 15 34 55 75

HUCKLEBERRY HOUND (See Dell Giant #31,44, Golden Picture Story Book, Kite Fun Book, March of Comics #199, 214, 235, Spotlight #1 & Whitman Comic Books)

HUCKLEBERRY HOUND (TV)
Dell/Gold Key No. 18 (10/62) on: No. 990, 5-7/59 - No. 43, 10/70 (Hanna-Barbera)
Four Color 990(#1)-1st app. Huckleberry Hound, Yogi Bear, & Pixie & Dixie & Mr. Jinks 12 24 36 86 153 220
Four Color 1050,1054 (12/59) 8 16 24 56 93 130
3(1-2/60) - 7 (9-10/60), Four Color 1141 (10/60) 8 16 24 52 86 120
8-10 6 12 18 43 69 95
11,13-17 (6-8/62) 5 10 15 32 51 70
12-1st Hokey Wolf & Ding-a-Ling 6 12 18 37 59 80
18,19 (84pgs.; 18-20 titled ...Chuckleberry Tales) 8 16 24 52 86 120
20-Titled Chuckleberry Tales 5 10 15 30 48 65
21-30: 28-30-Reprints 4 8 12 24 37 50
31-43: 31,32,35,37-43-Reprints 3 6 9 20 30 40

HUCKLEBERRY HOUND (TV)
Charlton Comics: Nov, 1970 - No. 8, Jan, 1972 (Hanna-Barbera)
1 5 10 15 32 51 70
2-8 3 6 9 18 27 35

HUEY, DEWEY, & LOUIE (See Donald Duck, 1938 for 1st app. Also see Mickey Mouse Magazine V4#2, V5#7 & Walt Disney's Junior Woodchucks Limited Series)

HUEY, DEWEY, & LOUIE BACK TO SCHOOL (See Dell Giant #22, 35, 49 & Dell Giants)

HUEY, DEWEY, AND LOUIE JUNIOR WOODCHUCKS (Disney)
Gold Key No. 1-61/Whitman No. 62 on: Aug, 1966 - No. 81, July, 1984 (See Walt Disney's Comics & Stories #125)
1 6 12 18 39 62 85
2,3(12/68) 4 8 12 22 34 45
4,5(4/70)-r/two WDC&S D.Duck stories by Barks 3 6 9 20 30 40
6-17 3 6 9 18 27 35
18,27-30 3 6 9 15 21 26
19-23,25-New storyboarded scripts by Barks, 13-25 pgs. per issue 3 6 9 19 29 38
24,26: 26-r/Barks Donald Duck WDC&S stories 3 6 9 16 23 30
31-57,60,61: 35,41-r/Barks J.W. scripts 2 4 6 8 11 14
58,59: 58-r/Barks Donald Duck WDC&S stories 2 4 6 9 13 16
62-64 (Whitman) 2 4 6 9 13 16
65-(9/80), 66 (Pre-pack? scarce) 3 6 9 20 30 40
67 (1/81),68 2 4 6 9 13 16
69-74: 72(2/82), 73(2-3/82), 74(3/82) 2 4 6 8 11 14
75-81 (all #90183; pre-pack; nd, nd code; scarce): 75(4/83), 76(5/83), 77(7/83), 78(8/83), 79(4/84), 80(5/84), 81(7/84) 3 6 9 14 20 25

HUGGA BUNCH (TV)
Marvel Comics (Star Comics): Oct, 1986 - No. 6, Aug, 1987
1-6 4.00

HULK (Magazine)(Formerly The Rampaging Hulk)(Also see The Incredible Hulk)
Marvel Comics: No. 10, Aug., 1978 - No. 27, June, 1981 ($1.50)
10-18: 10-Bill Bixby interview. 11-Moon Knight begins. 12-15,17,18-Moon Knight stories. 12-Lou Ferrigno interview. 2 4 6 10 14 18
19-27: 20-Moon Knight story. 23-Last full color issue; Banner is attacked. 24-Part color, Lou Ferrigno interview. 25-Part color. 26,27-are B&W 2 4 6 8 10 12

NOTE: #10-20 have fragile spines which split easily. ***Alcala** a(i)-15, 17-20, 22, 24-27. **Buscema** a-23; c-26. **Chaykin** a-21-25. **Colan** a(p)-11, 19, 24-27. **Jusko** painted c-12. **Nebres** a-16. **Severin** a-19i. Moon Knight by **Sienkiewicz** in 13-15, 17, 18, 20. **Simonson** a-27; c-23. Dominic Fortune appears in #21-24.*

HULK (Becomes Incredible Hulk Vol. 2 with issue #12) (Also see Marvel Age Hulk)
Marvel Comics: Apr, 1999 - No. 11, Feb, 2000 ($2.99/$1.99)
1-($2.99) Byrne-s/Garney-a 5.00
1-Variant-c 9.00
1-DFE Remarked-c 50.00
1-Gold foil variant 10.00
2-7-($1.99): 2-Two covers. 5-Art by Jurgens, Buscema & Texeira. 7-Avengers app. 4.00
8-Hulk battles Wolverine 7.00
9-11: 11-She-Hulk app. 3.00
1999 Annual ($3.50) Chapter One story; Byrne-s/Weeks-a 3.50
Hulk Vs. The Thing (12/99, $3.99, TPB) reprints their notable battles 4.00

HULK (Also see King-Size Hulk)
Marvel Comics: Mar, 2008 - Present ($2.99)
1-Red Hulk app.; Abomination killed; Loeb-s/McGuinness-a/c 5.00
1-Variant-c by Acuña 10.00
1-Variant-c with Incredible Hulk #1 cover swipe by McGuinness 20.00
1,2-2nd printings with wraparound McGuinness variant-c 3.00
2-6: Iron Man app.; Rick Jones becomes the new Abomination. 4,6-Red Hulk vs. green Hulk; two covers (each Hulk); Thor app. 3.00
2,3: 2-Variant-c by Djurdjevic. 3-Var-c by Finch. 5-Var-c by Coipel. 6-Var-c by Turner 5.00
...: Raging Thunder 1 (8/08, $3.99) Hulk vs. Thundra; Breitweiser-a; r/FF #133; Land-c 4.00
... Vs. Fin Fang Foom (2/08, $3.99) new re-telling of first meeting; r/Strange Tales #89 4.00
... Vs. Hercules (6/08, $3.99) Djurdjevic-c; new story w/art by various; r/Tales To Ast. #79 4.00

HULK AND POWER PACK (All ages series)
Marvel Comics: May, 2007 - No. 4, Aug, 2007 ($2.99, limited series)
1-4-Sumerak-s. 1,2,4-Williams-a. 1-Absorbing Man app. 3-Kuhn-a; Abomination app. 3.00
...: Pack Smash! (2007, $6.99, digest) r/#1-4 7.00

HULK & THING: HARD KNOCKS
Marvel Comics: Nov, 2004 - No. 4, Feb, 2005 ($3.50, limited series)
1-4-Bruce Jones-s/Jae Lee-a/c 3.50
TPB (2005, $13.99) r/#1-4 and Giant-Size Super-Stars #1 14.00

HULK CHRONICLES: WWH
Marvel Comics: Oct, 2008 - Present ($4.99, limited series)
1-3-Reprints stories from World War Hulk x-over. 1-R/Inc. Hulk #106 & WWH Prologue 5.00

HULK: DESTRUCTION
Marvel Comics: Sept, 2005 - No. 4, Dec, 2005 ($2.99, limited series)
1-4-Origin of the Abomination; Peter David-s/Jim Muniz-a 3.00

HULK: FUTURE IMPERFECT
Marvel Comics: Jan, 1993 - No. 2, Dec, 1992 (In error) ($5.95, 52 pgs., squarebound, limited series)
1,2: Embossed-c; Peter David story & George Perez-c/a. 1-1st app. Maestro. 1 2 3 5 6 8

HULK: GRAY
Marvel Comics: Dec, 2003 - No. 6, Apr, 2004 ($3.50, limited series)
1-6-Hulk's origin & early days; Loeb-s/Sale-a/c 3.50
HC (2004, $21.99, with dust jacket) oversized r/#1-6 22.00
SC (2005, $19.99) r/#1-6 20.00

HULK: NIGHTMERICA
Marvel Comics: Aug, 2003 - No. 6, May, 2004 ($2.99, limited series)
1-6-Brian Ashmore painted-a/c 3.00

HULK/ PITT
Marvel Comics: 1997 ($5.99, one-shot)
1-David-s/Keown-c/a 6.00

HULK SMASH

Human Fly #9 © MAR

Human Torch #10 © MAR

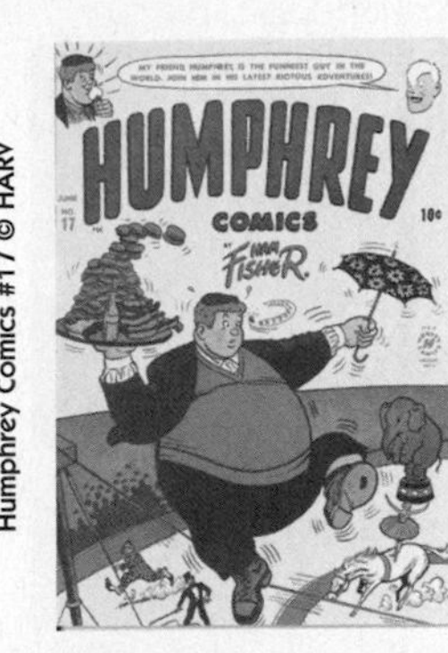

Humphrey Comics #17 © HARV

GD 2.0 | VG 4.0 | FN 6.0 | VF 8.0 | VF/NM 9.0 | NM- 9.2

Marvel Comics: Mar, 2001 - No. 2, Apr, 2001 ($2.99, limited series)

1,2-Ennis-s/McCrea & Janson-a/Nowlan painted-c 3.00

HULK: THE MOVIE
Marvel Comics

...Adaptation (8/03, $3.50) Bruce Jones-s/Bagley-a/Keown-c 3.50
TPB (2003, $12.99) r/Adaptation, Ultimates #5, Inc. Hulk #34, Ult. Marvel Team-Up #2&3 13.00

HULK 2099
Marvel Comics: Dec, 1994 - No. 10, Sept, 1995 ($1.50/$1.95)

1-($2.50)-Green foil-c 3.00
2-10: 2-A. Kubert-c 2.50

HULK/WOLVERINE: 6 HOURS
Marvel Comics: Mar, 2003 - No. 4, May, 2003 ($2.99, limited series)

1-4-Bruce Jones-s/Scott Kolins-a; Bisley-c 3.00
Hulk Legends Vol. 1: Hulk/Wolverine: 6 Hours (2003, $13.99, TPB) r/#1-4 & 1st Wolverine app. from Incredible Hulk #181 14.00

HUMAN DEFENSE CORPS
DC Comics: Jul, 2003 - No. 6, Dec, 2003 ($2.50, limited series)

1-6-Ty Templeton-s/Sauve, Jr & Vlasco-a. 1-Lois Lane app. 2.50

HUMAN FLY
I.W. Enterprises/Super: 1963 - 1964 (Reprints)

I.W. Reprint #1-Reprints Blue Beetle #44('46) 2 4 6 13 18 22
Super Reprint #10-R/Blue Beetle #46('47) 2 4 6 13 18 22

HUMAN FLY, THE
Marvel Comics Group: Sept, 1977 - No. 19, Mar, 1979

1,2,9,19: 1,2-(Regular 30¢-c). 1-Origin; Spider-Man x-over. 2-Ghost Rider app. 9-Daredevil x-over; Byrne-c(p). 19-Last issue 1 2 3 5 6 8
1,2-(35¢-c, limited distribution) 3 6 9 20 30 40
3-8,10-18 4.00
NOTE: ***Austin*** *c-4i, 9i.* ***Elias*** *a-1, 3p, 4p, 7p, 10-12p, 15p, 18p, 19p.* ***Layton*** *c-19.*

HUMANKIND
Image Comics (Top Cow): Sept, 2004 - No. 5, Mar, 2005 ($2.99, limited series)

1-5-Tony Daniel-a. 1-Three covers by Daniel, Silvestri, and Land 3.00

HUMAN RACE, THE
DC Comics: May, 2005 - No. 7, Nov, 2005 ($2.99, limited series)

1-7-Raab-s/Justiniano-a/c 3.00

HUMAN TARGET
DC Comics (Vertigo): Apr, 1999 - No. 4, July, 1999 ($2.95, limited series)

1-4-Milligan-s/Bradstreet-c/Biuković-a 3.00
TPB (2000, $12.95) new Bradstreet-c 13.00

HUMAN TARGET
DC Comics (Vertigo): Oct, 2003 - No. 21, June, 2005 ($2.95)

1-21: 1-5 Milligan-s/Pulido-a/c. 6-Chiang-a 3.00
...: Living in Amerika TPB (2004, $14.95) r/#6-10; Chiang sketch pages 15.00
...: Strike Zones TPB (2004, $9.95) r/#1-5 10.00

HUMAN TARGET: FINAL CUT
DC Comics (Vertigo): 2002 ($29.95/$19.95, graphic novel)

Hardcover (2002, $29.95) Milligan-s/Pulido-a/c 30.00
Softcover (2003, $19.95) 20.00

HUMAN TARGET SPECIAL (TV)
DC Comics: Nov, 1991 ($2.00, 52 pgs., one-shot)

1 3.00

HUMAN TORCH, THE (Red Raven #1)(See All-Select, All Winners, Marvel Mystery, Men's Adventures, Mystic Comics (2nd series), Sub-Mariner, USA & Young Men)
Timely/Marvel Comics (TP 2,3/TCI 4-9/SePI 10/SnPC 11-25/CnPC 26-35/Atlas Comics (CPC 36-38)): No. 2, Fall, 1940 - No. 15, Spring, 1944; No. 16, Fall, 1944 - No. 35, Mar, 1949 (Becomes Love Tales #36 on); No. 36, April, 1954 - No. 38, Aug, 1954

2(#1)-Intro & Origin Toro; The Falcon, The Fiery Mask, Mantor the Magician, & Microman only app.; Human Torch by Burgos, Sub-Mariner by Everett begin (origin of each in text) 3100 6200 9300 23,250 42,625 62,000
3(#2)-40 pg. H.T. story; H.T. & S.M. battle over who is best artist in text-Everett or Burgos 556 1112 1668 4003 7002 10,000
4(#3)-Origin The Patriot in text; last Everett Sub-Mariner; Sid Greene-a 433 866 1299 3118 5459 7800
5(#4)-The Patriot app; Angel x-over in Sub-Mariner (Summer, 1941); 1st Nazi war-c this title 371 742 1113 2523 4412 6300
5-Human Torch battles Sub-Mariner (Fall, '41); 60 pg. story 556 1112 1668 4003 7002 10,000
6,9 293 586 879 1846 3123 4400
7-1st Japanese war-c 300 600 900 1890 3195 4500
8-Human Torch battles Sub-Mariner; 52 pg. story; Wolverton-a, 1 pg. 382 764 1146 2598 4549 6500
10-Human Torch battles Sub-Mariner, 45 pg. story; Wolverton-a, 1 pg. 312 624 936 2122 3711 5300
11,13-15: 14-1st Atlas Globe logo (Winter, 1943-44; see All Winners #11 also) 223 446 669 1405 2378 3350
12-Classic-c 341 682 1023 2319 4060 5800
16-20: 20-Last War issue 153 306 459 964 1632 2300
21,22,24-30: 27-2nd app. (1st-c) Asbestos Lady (see Capt. America Comics #63 for 1st app.) 133 266 399 838 1419 2000
23 (Sum/46)-Becomes Junior Miss 24? Classic Schomburg Robot-c 160 320 480 1008 1704 2400
31,32: 31-Namora x-over in Sub-Mariner (also #30); last Toro. 32-Sungirl, Namora app.; Sungirl-c 113 226 339 712 1200 1700
33-Capt. America x-over 118 236 354 743 1259 1775
34-Sungirl solo 107 214 321 674 1137 1600
35-Captain America & Sungirl app. (1949) 113 226 339 712 1206 1700
36-38(1954)-Sub-Mariner in all 93 186 279 586 993 1400
NOTE: ***Ayers*** *Human Torch in 36(3).* ***Brodsky*** *c-25, 31-33?, 37, 38,* ***Burgos*** *c-36.* ***Everett*** *a-1-3, 27, 28, 30, 37, 38.* ***Powell*** *a-36(Sub-Mariner).* ***Schomburg*** *c-1-3, 5-8, 10-23.* ***Sekowsky*** *c-28, 34?, 35?* ***Shores*** *c-24, 26, 27, 29, 30.* ***Mickey Spillane*** *text 4-6. Bondage c-2, 12, 19.*

HUMAN TORCH, THE (Also see Avengers West Coast, Fantastic Four, The Invaders, Saga of the Original... & Strange Tales #101)
Marvel Comics Group: Sept, 1974 - No. 8, Nov, 1975

1: 1-8-r/stories from Strange Tales #101-108 2 4 6 11 16 20
2-8: 1st H.T. title since G.A. 7-vs. Sub-Mariner 2 4 6 8 10 12
NOTE: *Golden Age & Silver Age Human Torch-r #1-8.* ***Ayers*** *r-6, 7.* ***Kirby/Ayers*** *r-1-5, 8.*

HUMAN TORCH (From the Fantastic Four)
Marvel Comics: June, 2003 - No. 12, Jun, 2004 ($2.50/$2.99)

1-7-Skottie Young-c/a; Karl Kesel-s 2.50
8-12-($2.99) 8,10-Dodd-a. 9-Young-a. 11-Porter-a. 12-Medina-a 3.00
... Vol. 1: Burn TPB (2005, $7.99, digest size) r/#1-6 8.00

HUMBUG (Satire by Harvey Kurtzman)
Humbug Publications: Aug, 1957 - No. 9, May, 1958; No. 10, June, 1958; No. 11, Oct, 1958

1-Wood-a (intro pgs. only) 27 54 81 158 254 350
2 15 30 45 84 127 170
3-9: 8-Elvis in Jailbreak Rock 14 28 42 76 108 140
10,11-Magazine format. 10-Photo-c 15 30 45 90 140 190
Bound Volume(#1-9)(extremely rare) 65 130 195 410 693 975
NOTE: ***Davis*** *a-1-11.* ***Elder*** *a-2-4, 6-9, 11.* ***Heath*** *a-2, 4-8, 10.* ***Jaffee*** *a-2, 4-9.* ***Kurtzman*** *a-11.*

HUMDINGER (Becomes White Rider and Super Horse #3 on?)
Novelty Press/Premium Group: May-June, 1946 - V2#2, July-Aug, 1947

1-Jerkwater Line, Mickey Starlight by Don Rico, Dink begin 36 72 108 212 341 470
2 16 32 48 89 137 200
3-6, V2#1,2 12 24 36 67 94 125

HUMONGOUS MAN
Alternative Press (Ikon Press): Sept, 1997 -No. 3 ($2.25, B&W)

1-3-Stopp & Harrison-c/s/a. 2.50

HUMOR (See All Humor Comics)

HUMPHREY COMICS (Joe Palooka Presents...; also see Joe Palooka)
Harvey Publications: Oct, 1948 - No. 22, Apr, 1952

1-Joe Palooka's pal (r); (52 pgs.)-Powell-a 14 28 42 80 115 150
2,3: Powell-a 9 18 27 47 61 75
4-Boy Heroes app.; Powell-a 9 18 27 50 65 80
5-8,10: 5,6-Powell-a. 7-Little Dot app. 8 16 24 40 50 60
9-Origin Humphrey 9 18 27 47 61 75
11-22 7 14 21 37 46 55

HUNCHBACK OF NOTRE DAME, THE
Dell Publishing Co.: No. 854, Oct, 1957 (one shot)

Four Color 854-Movie, photo-c 12 24 36 87 156 225

HUNGER, THE
Speakeasy Comics: May, 2005 - Present ($2.99)

1-Andy Bradshaw-s/a; Eric Powell-c 3.00

HUNGER DOGS, THE (See DC Graphic Novel #4)

Hunter-Killer #12 © TCOW

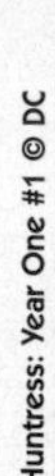

Huntress: Year One #1 © DC

Icon #17 © Milestone

	GD 2.0	VG 4.0	FN 6.0	VF 8.0	VF/NM 9.0	NM- 9.2

HUNK
Charlton Comics: Aug, 1961 - No. 11, 1963

	GD 2.0	VG 4.0	FN 6.0	VF 8.0	VF/NM 9.0	NM- 9.2
1	4	8	12	24	37	50
2-11	3	6	9	14	20	25

HUNTED (Formerly My Love Memoirs)
Fox Features Syndicate: No. 13, July, 1950; No. 2, Sept, 1950

	GD 2.0	VG 4.0	FN 6.0	VF 8.0	VF/NM 9.0	NM- 9.2
13(#1)-Used in **SOTI**, pg. 42 & illo. "Treating police contemptuously" (lower left); Hollingsworth bondage-c	36	72	108	212	341	470
2	17	34	51	98	154	210

HUNTER-KILLER
Image Comics (Top Cow): Nov, 2004 - No. 12, Mar, 2007 ($2.99)

0-(11/04, 25¢) Prelude with Silvestri sketch page and Waid afterword 2.25
1-12: 1-(3/05, $2.99) Waid-s/Silvestri-a; four covers. 2-Linsner variant-c 3.00
... Collected Edition Vol. 1 (9/05, $4.99) r/#0-3 5.00
...Dossier 1 (9/05, $2.99) character profiles with art by various; Migliari-c 3.00
... Volume 1 TPB (1/08, $24.99) r/#0-12; Dossier and Script Book; variant covers 25.00

HUNTER: THE AGE OF MAGIC (See Books of Magic)
DC Comics (Vertigo): Sept, 2001 - No. 25, Sept, 2003 ($2.50/$2.75)

1-25: Horrocks-s/Case-a. 1-8-Bolton-c. 14-Begin $2.75-c. 19-Bachalo-c 2.75

HUNTRESS, THE (See All-Star Comics #69, Batman Family, DC Super Stars #17, Detective #652, Infinity, Inc. #1 & Wonder Woman #271)
DC Comics: Apr, 1989 - No. 19, Oct, 1990 ($1.00, mature)

1-16: Staton-c/a(p) in all 2.50
17-19-Batman-c/stories 3.00
..: Darknight Daughter TPB (2006, $19.99) r/origin & early apps. in DC Super Stars #17, Batman Family #18-20 & Wonder Woman #271-287,289,290,294,295; Bolland-c 20.00

HUNTRESS, THE
DC Comics: June, 1994 - No. 4, Sept, 1994 ($1.50, limited series)

1-4-Netzer-c/a: 2-Batman app. 2.25

HUNTRESS: YEAR ONE
DC Comics: Early July, 2008 - No. 6, Late Sept, 2008 ($2.99, limited series)

1-6-Origin re-told; Cliff Richards-a/Ivory Madison-s 3.00

HURRICANE COMICS
Cambridge House: 1945 (52 pgs.)

	GD 2.0	VG 4.0	FN 6.0	VF 8.0	VF/NM 9.0	NM- 9.2
1-(Humor, funny animal)	23	46	69	133	214	295

HYBRIDS
Continunity Comics: Jan, 1994 ($2.50, one-shot)

1-Neal Adams-c(p) & part-a(i); embossed-c. 3.50

HYBRIDS DEATHWATCH 2000
Continuity Comics: Apr, 1993 - No. 3, Aug, 1993 ($2.50)

0-(Giveaway)-Foil-c; Neal Adams-c(i) & plots (also #1,2) 3.50
1-3: 1-Polybagged w/card; die-cut-c. 2-Thermal-c. 3-Polybagged w/card; indestructible-c; Adams plot 3.00

HYBRIDS ORIGIN
Continunity Comics: 1993 - No. 5, Jan, 1994 ($2.50)

1-5: 2,3-Neal Adams-c. 4,5-Valeria the She-Bat app. Adams-c(i) 3.25

HYDE
IDW Publ.: Oct, 2004 ($7.49, one-shot)

1-Steve Niles-s/Nick Stakal 7.50

HYDE-25
Harris Publications: Apr, 1995 ($2.95, one-shot)

0-coupon for poster; r/Vampirella's 1st app. 3.00

HYDROMAN (See Heroic Comics)

HYPERKIND (See Razorline)
Marvel Comics: Sept, 1993 - No. 9, May, 1994 ($1.75/$1.95)

1-($2.50)-Foil embossed-c; by Clive Barker 3.00
2-9 2.50

HYPERKIND UNLEASED
Marvel Comics: Aug, 1994 ($2.95, 52 pgs., one-shot)

1 3.00

HYPER MYSTERY COMICS
Hyper Publications: May, 1940 - No. 2, June, 1940 (68 pgs.)

	GD 2.0	VG 4.0	FN 6.0	VF 8.0	VF/NM 9.0	NM- 9.2
1-Hyper, the Phenomenal begins; Calkins-a	207	414	621	1304	2202	3100
2	103	206	309	649	1100	1550

HYPERSONIC
Dark Horse Comics: Nov, 1997 - No. 4, Feb, 1998 ($2.95, limited series)

1-4: Abnett & White/Erskine-a 3.00

I AIM AT THE STARS (Movie)
Dell Publishing Co.: No. 1148, Nov-Jan/1960-61 (one-shot)

	GD 2.0	VG 4.0	FN 6.0	VF 8.0	VF/NM 9.0	NM- 9.2
Four Color 1148-The Werner Von Braun Sty-photo-c	7	14	21	47	76	105

I AM COYOTE (See Eclipse Graphic Album Series & Eclipse Magazine #2)

I AM LEGEND
Eclipse Books: 1991 - No. 4, 1991 ($5.95, B&W, squarebound, 68 pgs.)

1-4: Based on 1954 novel by Richard Matheson 6.00

IBIS, THE INVINCIBLE (See Fawcett Miniatures, Mighty Midget & Whiz)
Fawcett Publications: 1942 (Fall?); #2, Mar.,1943; #3, Wint, 1945 - #5, Fall, 1946; #6, Spring, 1948

	GD 2.0	VG 4.0	FN 6.0	VF 8.0	VF/NM 9.0	NM- 9.2
1-Origin Ibis; Raboy-c; on sale 1/2/43	233	466	699	1468	2484	3500
2-Bondage-c (on sale 2/5/43)	100	200	300	630	1065	1500
3-Wolverton-a #3-6 (4 pgs. each)	73	146	219	460	780	1100
4-6: 5-Bondage-c	49	98	147	304	507	710

NOTE: *Mac Raboy c(p)-3-5. Schaffenberger c-6.*

I-BOTS (See Isaac Asimov's I-BOTS)

ICE AGE ON THE WORLD OF MAGIC: THE GATHERING (See Magic The Gathering)

ICE KING OF OZ, THE (See First Comics Graphic Novel #13)

ICEMAN (Also see The Champions & X-Men #94)
Marvel Comics Group: Dec, 1984 - No. 4, June, 1985 (Limited series)

1,2,4: Zeck covers on all 3.50
3-The Defenders, Champions (Ghost Rider) & the original X-Men x-over 4.00

ICEMAN (X-Men)
Marvel Comics: Dec, 2001 - No. 4, Mar, 2002 ($2.50, limited series)

1-4-Abnett & Lanning-s/Kerschl-a 3.00

ICON
DC Comics (Milestone): May, 1993 - No. 42, Feb, 1997($1.50/$1.75/$2.50)

1-($2.95)-Collector's Edition polybagged w/poster & trading card (direct sale only) 3.00
1-24,30-42: 9-Simonson-c. 15,16-Worlds Collide Pt. 4 & 11. 15-Superboy app. 16-Superman-c/story. 40-Vs. Blood Syndicate 2.50
25-($2.95, 52 pgs.) 3.00

IDAHO
Dell Publishing Co.: June-Aug, 1963 - No. 8, July-Sept, 1965

	GD 2.0	VG 4.0	FN 6.0	VF 8.0	VF/NM 9.0	NM- 9.2
1	3	6	9	17	25	32
2-8: 5-7-Painted-c	2	4	6	9	13	16

IDEAL (... a Classical Comic) (2nd Series) (Love Romances No. 6 on)
Timely Comics: July, 1948 - No. 5, March, 1949 (Feature length stories)

	GD 2.0	VG 4.0	FN 6.0	VF 8.0	VF/NM 9.0	NM- 9.2
1-Antony & Cleopatra	37	74	111	215	345	475
2-The Corpses of Dr. Sacotti	31	62	93	181	291	400
3-Joan of Arc; used in **SOTI**, pg. 310 'Boer War'	29	58	87	169	272	375
4-Richard the Lion-hearted; titled "...the World's Greatest Comics"; The Witness story	40	80	120	244	397	550
5-Ideal Love & Romance; change to love; photo-c	20	40	60	115	183	250

IDEAL COMICS (1st Series) (Willie Comics No. 5 on)
Timely Comics (MgPC): Fall, 1944 - No. 4, Spring, 1946

	GD 2.0	VG 4.0	FN 6.0	VF 8.0	VF/NM 9.0	NM- 9.2
1-Funny animal; Super Rabbit in all	25	50	75	145	233	320
2	14	28	42	82	121	160
3,4	14	28	42	80	115	150

IDEAL LOVE & ROMANCE (See Ideal, A Classical Comic)

IDEAL ROMANCE (Formerly Tender Romance)
Key Publ.: No. 3, April, 1954 - No. 8, Feb, 1955 (Diary Confessions No. 9 on)

	GD 2.0	VG 4.0	FN 6.0	VF 8.0	VF/NM 9.0	NM- 9.2
3-Bernard Baily-c	10	20	30	54	72	90
4-8: 4-6-B. Baily-c	7	14	21	37	46	55

IDEALS (Secret Stories)
Ideals Publ., USA: 1981 (68 pgs, graphic novels, 7x10", stiff-c)

	GD 2.0	VG 4.0	FN 6.0	VF 8.0	VF/NM 9.0	NM- 9.2
Captain America - Star Spangled Super Hero	3	6	9	18	27	35
Fantastic Four - Cosmic Quartet	3	6	9	18	27	35
Incredible Hulk - Gamma Powered Goliath	3	6	9	18	27	35
Spider-Man - World Famous Wall Crawler	4	8	12	22	34	45

IDENTITY CRISIS
DC Comics: Aug, 2004 - No. 7, Feb, 2005 ($3.95, limited series)

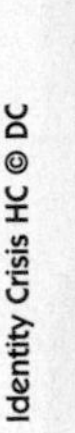

I Love Lucy #10 © Desilu

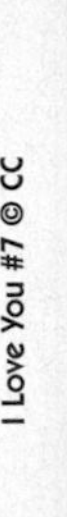

	GD 2.0	VG 4.0	FN 6.0	VF 8.0	VF/NM 9.0	NM- 9.2
1-Meltzer-s/Morales-a/Turner-c in all; Sue Dibny murdered						6.00
1-(Second printing) black-c with white sketch lines						4.00
1-(Third printing) Bloody broken photo glass image-c by Morales						4.00
1-Diamond Retailer Summit Edition with sketch-c						125.00
2-7: 2-4-Deathstroke app. 5-Firestorm, Jack Drake, Capt. Boomerang killed						4.00
2-(Second printing) new Morales sketch-c						4.00
Final printings for all issues with red background variant covers						4.00
HC (2005, $24.99, dust jacket) r/series; Director's Cut extras; cover gallery; Whedon intro.; 2 covers: Direct Market-c by Turner, Bookstore-c with Morales-a						25.00
SC (2006, $14.99) r/series; Director's Cut extras; cover gallery; Whedon intro						15.00

IDENTITY DISC
Marvel Comics: Aug, 2004 - No. 5, Dec, 2004 ($2.99, limited series)

	GD	VG	FN	VF	VF/NM	NM-
1-5-Sabretooth, Bullseye, Sandman, Vulture, Deadpool, Juggernaut app.; Higgins-a						4.00
TPB (2004, $13.99) r/#1-5						14.00

I DIE AT MIDNIGHT (Vertigo V2K)
DC Comics (Vertigo): 2000 ($6.95, prestige format, one-shot)

	GD	VG	FN	VF	VF/NM	NM-
1-Kyle Baker-s/a						7.00

IDOL
Marvel Comics (Epic Comics): 1992 - No. 3, 1992 ($2.95, mini-series, 52 pgs.)

	GD	VG	FN	VF	VF/NM	NM-
Book 1-3						3.00

I DREAM OF JEANNIE (TV)
Dell Publishing Co.: Apr, 1965 - No. 2, Dec, 1966 (Photo-c)

	GD	VG	FN	VF	VF/NM	NM-
1-Barbara Eden photo-c, each	14	28	42	102	181	260
2	11	22	33	77	136	195

I FEEL SICK
Slave Labor Graphics: Aug, 1999 - No. 2, May, 2000 ($3.95, limited series)

	GD	VG	FN	VF	VF/NM	NM-
1,2-Jhonen Vasquez-s/a						4.00

I (heart) MARVEL
Marvel Comics: Apr, 2006; May, 2006 ($2.99, one-shots)

	GD	VG	FN	VF	VF/NM	NM-
...: Marvel AI 1 (4/06) Cebulski-s; manga art by various; Vision, Daredevil, Elektra app.						3.00
...: Masked Intentions 1 (5/06) Squirrel Girl, Speedball, Firestar, Justice app.; Nicieza-s						3.00
...: My Mutant Heart 1 (4/06) Wolverine, Cannonball, Doop app.						3.00
...: Outlaw Love 1 (4/06) Bullseye, The Answer, Ruby Thursday app.; Nicieza-s						3.00
...: Web of Romance 1 (4/06) Spider-Man, Mary Jane, The Avengers app.						3.00

ILLUMINATOR
Marvel Comics/Nelson Publ.: 1993 - No. 4, 1993 ($4.99/$2.95, 52 pgs.)

	GD	VG	FN	VF	VF/NM	NM-
1,2-($4.99) Religious themed						5.00
3,4						3.00

ILLUSTRATED GAGS
United Features Syndicate: No. 16, 1940

	GD	VG	FN	VF	VF/NM	NM-
Single Series 16	16	32	48	94	147	200

ILLUSTRATED LIBRARY OF..., AN (See Classics Illustrated Giants)

ILLUSTRATED STORIES OF THE OPERAS
Baily (Bernard) Publ. Co.: 1943 (16 pgs.; B&W) (25 cents) (cover-B&W & red)

	GD	VG	FN	VF	VF/NM	NM-
nn-(Rare)(4 diff. issues)-Faust (part-r in Cisco Kid #1), nn-Aida, nn-Carmen; Baily-a, nn-Rigoleito	55	110	165	347	586	825

ILLUSTRATED STORY OF ROBIN HOOD & HIS MERRY MEN, THE (See Classics Giveaways, 12/44)

ILLUSTRATED TARZAN BOOK, THE (See Tarzan Book)

I LOVED (Formerly Rulah; Colossal Features Magazine No. 33 on)
Fox Features Syndicate: No. 28, July, 1949 - No. 32, Mar, 1950

	GD	VG	FN	VF	VF/NM	NM-
28	13	26	39	74	105	135
29-32	10	20	30	54	72	90

I LOVE LUCY
Eternity Comics : 6/90 - No. 6, 1990;V2#1, 11/90 - No. 6, 1991 ($2.95, B&W, mini-series)

	GD	VG	FN	VF	VF/NM	NM-
1-6: Reprints 1950s comic strip; photo-c						4.00
Book II #1-6: Reprints comic strip; photo-c						4.00
...In Full Color 1 (1991, $5.95, 52 pgs.)-Reprints I Love Lucy Comics #4,5,8,16; photo-c with embossed logo (2 versions exist, one with pgs. 18 & 19 reversed, the other corrected)	1	2	3	5	6	8
...In 3-D 1 (1991, $3.95, w/glasses)-Reprints I Love Lucy Comics; photo-c; bagged						6.00

I LOVE LUCY COMICS (TV) (Also see The Lucy Show)
Dell Publishing Co.: No. 535, Feb, 1954 - No. 35, Apr-June, 1962 (Lucille Ball photo-c on all)

	GD	VG	FN	VF	VF/NM	NM-
Four Color 535(#1)	44	88	132	352	664	975
Four Color 559(#2, 5/54)	29	58	87	213	394	575
3 (8-10/54) - 5	17	34	51	120	223	325
6-10	14	28	42	102	181	260
11-20	10	20	30	73	129	185
21-35	9	18	27	63	107	150

I LOVE NEW YORK
Linsner.com: 2002 ($2.95, B&W, one-shot)

	GD	VG	FN	VF	VF/NM	NM-
1-Linsner-s/a; benefit book for the Sept. 11 charities						3.00

I LOVE YOU
Fawcett Publications: June, 1950 (one-shot)

	GD	VG	FN	VF	VF/NM	NM-
1-Photo c	15	30	45	83	124	165

I LOVE YOU (Formerly In Love)
Charlton Comics: No. 7, 9/55 - No. 121, 12/76; No. 122, 3/79 - No. 130, 5/80

	GD	VG	FN	VF	VF/NM	NM-
7-Kirby-c; Powell-a	9	18	27	63	107	150
8-10	5	10	15	32	51	70
11-16,18-20	4	8	12	28	44	60
17-(68 pg. Giant)	7	14	21	49	80	110
21-50: 26-No Torres-a	3	6	9	21	32	42
51-59	3	6	9	16	23	30
60-(1/66)-Elvis Presley line drawn c/story	15	30	45	107	196	285
61-85	2	4	6	11	16	20
86-90,92-110: 99-David Cassidy pin-up	2	4	6	8	10	12
91-(5/71) Ditko-a (5 pgs.)	2	4	6	11	16	20
111-113,115-130	1	2	3	5	7	9
114-Psychedelic cover	2	4	6	9	12	15

I, LUSIPHUR (Becomes Poison Elves, 1st series #8 on)
Mulehide Graphics: 1991 - No. 7, 1992 (B&W, magazine size)

	GD	VG	FN	VF	VF/NM	NM-
1-Drew Hayes-c/a/scripts	4	8	12	26	41	55
2,4,5	3	6	9	14	20	25
3-Low print run	4	8	12	28	44	60
6,7	2	4	6	8	11	14
Poison Elves: Requiem For An Elf (Sirius Ent., 6/96, $14.95, trade paperback) -Reprints I, Lusiphur #1,2 as text, and 3-6						15.00

I'M A COP
Magazine Enterprises: 1954 - No. 3, 1954

	GD	VG	FN	VF	VF/NM	NM-
1(A-1 #111)-Powell-c/a in all	15	30	45	88	137	185
2(A-1 #126), 3(A-1 #128)	10	20	30	56	76	95

IMAGE COMICS HARDCOVER
Image Comics: 2005 ($24.99, hardcover with dust jacket)

	GD	VG	FN	VF	VF/NM	NM-
Vol. 1-New Spawn by McFarlane-s/a; Savage Dragon origin by Larsen; CyberForce by Silvestri; ShadowHawk by Valentino; intro by Marder; Image timeline						25.00

IMAGE FIRST
Image Comics: 2005 ($6.99, TPB)

	GD	VG	FN	VF	VF/NM	NM-
Vol. 1 (2005) r/Strange Girl #1, Sea of Red #1, The Walking Dead #1 and Girls #1						7.00

IMAGE GRAPHIC NOVEL
Image Int.: 1984 ($6.95)(Advertised as Pacific Comics Graphic Novel #1)

	GD	VG	FN	VF	VF/NM	NM-
1-The Seven Samuroid; Brunner-c/a						7.00

IMAGE HOLIDAY SPECIAL 2005
Image Comics: 2005 ($9.99, TPB)

	GD	VG	FN	VF	VF/NM	NM-
nn-Holiday-themed short stories by various incl. Larsen, Kurtz, Kirkman, Valentino						10.00

IMAGE INTRODUCES...
Image Comics: Oct, 2001 - June, 2002 ($2.95, anthology)

	GD	VG	FN	VF	VF/NM	NM-
Believer #1-Schamberger-s/Thurman & Molder-a; Legend of Isis preview						3.00
Cryptopia #1-Raab-s/Quinn-a						3.00
Dog Soldiers #1-Hunter-s/Pachoumis-a						3.00
Legend of Isis #1-Valdez-a						3.00
Primate #1-Two covers; Beau Smith & Bernhardt-s/Byrd-a						3.00

IMAGES OF A DISTANT SOIL
Image Comics: Feb, 1997 ($2.95, B&W, one-shot)

	GD	VG	FN	VF	VF/NM	NM-
1-Sketches by various						3.00

IMAGES OF SHADOWHAWK (Also see Shadowhawk)
Image Comics: Sept, 1993 - No. 3, 1994 ($1.95, limited series)

	GD	VG	FN	VF	VF/NM	NM-
1-3: Keith Giffen-c/a; Trencher app.						2.50

IMAGE TWO-IN-ONE
Image Comics: Mar, 2001 ($2.95, 48 pgs., B&W, one-shot)

	GD	VG	FN	VF	VF/NM	NM-
1-Two stories; 24 pages produced in 24 hrs. by Larsen and Eliopoulos						3.00

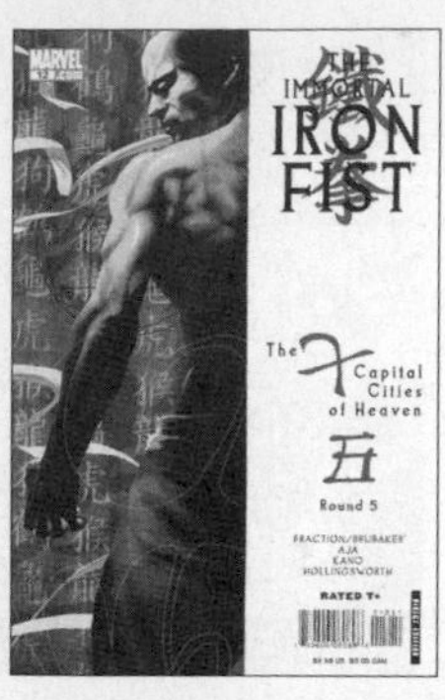

Immortal Iron Fist #12 © MAR

Impulse #70 © DC

Incredible Hercules #113 © MAR

GD VG FN VF VF/NM NM-
2.0 4.0 6.0 8.0 9.0 9.2

IMAGE ZERO
Image Comics: 1993 (Received through mail w/coupons from Image books)
0-Savage Dragon, StormWatch, Shadowhawk, Strykeforce; 1st app. Troll; 1st app. McFarlane's Freak, Blotch, Sweat and Bludd 5.00

IMAGINARIES, THE
Image Comics: Mar, 2005 - No. 4, June, 2005 ($2.95, limited series)
1-4-Mike S. Miller & Ben Avery-s; Miller & Titus-a 3.00

I'M DICKENS - HE'S FENSTER (TV)
Dell Publishing Co.: May-July, 1963 - No. 2, Aug-Oct, 1963 (Photo-c)
1 6 12 18 37 59 80
2 5 10 15 32 51 70

I MET A HANDSOME COWBOY
Dell Publishing Co.: No. 324, Mar, 1951
Four Color 324 8 16 24 56 93 130

IMMORTAL DOCTOR FATE, THE
DC Comics: Jan, 1985 - No. 3, Mar, 1985 ($1.25, limited series)
1-3: 1-Simonson-c/a. 2-Giffen-c/a(p) 4.00

IMMORTAL IRON FIST, THE (Also see Iron Fist)
Marvel Comics: Jan, 2007 - Present ($2.99)
1-Brubaker & Fraction-s/Aja-c/a; origin retold; intro. Orson Randall 5.00
1-Variant-c by Dell'Otto 8.00
1-Director's Cut ($3.99) r/#1 and 8-page story from Civil War: Choosing Sides; script excerpt; character designs; sketch and inks art; cover variant and concepts 4.00
2-13,15-18: 6,17,18-Flashback-a by Heath 3.00
14-($3.99) Heroes For Hire app. 4.00
Annual 1 (11/07, $3.99) Brubaker & Fraction-s/Chaykin, Brereton & J. Djurdjevic-a 4.00
... Orson Randall and the Death Queen of California (11/08, $3.99) art by Camuncoli 4.00
... Orson Randall and the Green Mist of Death (4/08, $3.99) art by Heath and various 4.00
...: The Origin of Danny Rand (2008, $3.99) r/Marvel Premiere #15-16 recolored 4.00
... Vol. 1: The Last Iron Fist Story HC (2007, $19.99, dustjacket) r/#1-6, story from Civil War: Choosing Sides; sketch pages 20.00
... Vol. 1: The Last Iron Fist Story SC (2007, $14.99) same content as HC 15.00

IMMORTALIS (See Mortigan Goth: Immortalis)

IMMORTAL II
Image Comics: Apr, 1997 - No. 5, Feb, 1998 ($2.50, B&W&Grey, limited series)
1-5: 1-B&W w/ color pull-out poster 2.50

IMPACT
E. C. Comics: Mar-Apr, 1955 - No. 5, Nov-Dec, 1955
1-Not code approved 17 34 51 136 218 300
2 10 20 30 80 130 180
3-5: 4-Crandall-a 9 18 27 72 116 160
NOTE: ***Crandall** a-1-4. **Davis** a-2-4; c-1-5. **Evans** a-1, 4, 5. **Ingels** a-in all. **Kamen** a-3. **Krigstein** a-1, 5. **Orlando** a-2, 5.*

IMPACT
Gemstone Publishing: Apr, 1999 - No. 5, Aug, 1999 ($2.50)
1-5-Reprints E.C. series 2.50

IMPACT CHRISTMAS SPECIAL
DC Comics (Impact Comics): 1991 ($2.50, 68 pgs.)
1-Gift of the Magi by Infantino/Rogers; The Black Hood, The Fly, The Jaguar, & The Shield stories 2.50

IMPERIAL GUARD
Marvel Comics: Jan, 1997 - No. 3, Mar, 1997 ($1.95, limited series)
1-3: Augustyn-s in all; 1-Wraparound-c 2.50

IMPOSSIBLE MAN SUMMER VACATION SPECTACULAR, THE
Marvel Comics: Aug, 1990; No. 2, Sept, 1991 ($2.00, 68 pgs.) (See Fantastic Four#11)
1-Spider Man, Quasar, Dr. Strange, She-Hulk, Punisher & Dr. Doom stories; Barry Crain, Guice-a; Art Adams-c(i) 2.50
2-Ka Zar & Thor app.; Cable Wolverine-c app. 2.50

IMPULSE (See Flash #92, 2nd Series for 1st app.) (Also see Young Justice)
DC Comics: Apr, 1995 - No. 89, Oct, 2002 ($1.50/$1.75/$1.95/$2.25/$2.50)
1-Mark Waid scripts & Humberto Ramos-c/a(p) begin; brief retelling of origin 6.00
2-12: 9-XS from Legion (Impulse's cousin) comes to the 20th Century, returns to the 30th Century in #12. 10-Dead Heat Pt. 3 (cont'd in Flash #110). 11-Dead Heat Pt. 4 (cont'd in Flash #111); Johnny Quick dies. 3.00
13-25: 14-Trickster app. 17-Zatanna-c/app. 21-Legion-c/app. 22-Jesse Quick-c/app. 24-Origin; Flash app. 25-Last Ramos-a. 2.50
26-55: 26-Rousseau-a begins. 28-1st new Arrowette (see World's Finest #113). 30-Genesis x-over. 47-Superman-c/app. 50-Batman & Joker-c/app. Van Sciver-a begins 2.50
56-62: 56-Young Justice app. 2.50
63-89: 63-Begin $2.50-c. 66-JLA,JSA-c/app. 68,69-Adam Strange, GL app. 77-Our Worlds at War x-over; Young Justice-c/app. 85-World Without Young Justice x-over pt. 2. 2.50
#1,000,000 (11/98) John Fox app. 2.50
Annual 1 (1996, $2.95)-Legends of the Dead Earth; Parobeck-a 4.00
Annual 2 (1997, $3.95)-Pulp Heroes stories; Orbik painted-c 4.00
.../Atom Double-Shot 1(2/98, $1.95) Jurgens-s/Mhan-a 3.00
...: Bart Saves the Universe (4/99, $5.95) JSA app. 6.00
...Plus(9/97, $2.95) w/Gross Out (Scare Tactics)-c/app. 3.00
...Reckless Youth (1997, $14.95, TPB) r/Flash #92-94, Impulse #1-6 15.00

INCAL, THE
Marvel Comics (Epic): Nov, 1988 - No. 3, Jan, 1989 ($10.95/$12.95, mature)
1-3: Moebius-c/a in all; sexual content 16.00

INCOGNEGRO
DC Comics (Vertigo): 2008 ($19.99, B&W, hardcover graphic novel with dustjacket)
HC-Mat Johnson-s/Warren Pleece-a 20.00

INCOMPLETE DEATH'S HEAD (Also see Death's Head)
Marvel Comics UK: Jan, 1993 - No. 12, Dec, 1993 ($1.75, limited series)
1-($2.95, 56 pgs.)-Die-cut cover 3.00
2-11: 2-Re-intro original Death's Head. 3-Original Death's Head vs. Dragon's Claws 2.50
12-($2.50, 52 pgs.)-She Hulk app. 2.50

INCREDIBLE HERCULES (Continued from Incredible Hulk #112, Jan, 2008)
Marvel Comics: No. 113, Feb, 2008 - Present ($2.99)
113-121: 113-Ares and Wonder Man app.; Art Adams-c. 116-Romita Jr-c; Eternals app. 3.00
113-Variant-c by Pham 5.00

INCREDIBLE HULK, THE (See Aurora, The Avengers #1, The Defenders #1, Giant-Size..., Hulk, Marvel Collectors Item Classics, Marvel Comics Presents #26, Marvel Fanfare, Marvel Treasury Edition, Power Record Comics, Rampaging Hulk, She-Hulk, 2099 Unlimited & World War Hulk)

INCREDIBLE HULK, THE
Marvel Comics: May, 1962 - No. 6, Mar, 1963; No. 102, Apr, 1968 - No. 474, Mar, 1999
1-Origin & 1st app. (skin is grey colored); Kirby pencils begin, end #5 1000 2000 3000 10,000 21,000 32,000
2-1st green skinned Hulk; Kirby/Ditko-a 258 516 744 2258 4229 6200
3-Origin retold; 1st app. Ringmaster (9/62) 154 308 462 1348 2524 3700
4,5: 4-Brief origin retold 140 296 444 1258 2329 3400
6-(3/63) Intro. Teen Brigade; all Ditko-a 163 326 489 1426 2663 3900
102-(4/68) (Formerly Tales to Astonish)-Origin retold; story continued from Tales to Astonish #101 20 40 60 146 261 375
103 9 18 27 63 107 150
104-Rhino app. 9 18 27 63 107 150
105-108: 105-1st Missing Link. 107-Mandarin app.(9/68). 108-Mandarin & Nick Fury app. (10/68) 6 12 18 43 69 95
109,110: 109-Ka-Zar app. 5 10 15 35 55 75
111-117: 117-Last 12¢ issue 4 8 12 28 44 60
118-Hulk vs. Sub-Mariner 6 12 18 39 62 85
119-121,123-125 4 8 12 22 34 45
122-Hulk battles Thing (12/69) 7 14 21 49 80 110
126-1st Barbara Norriss (Valkyrie) 4 8 12 24 37 50
127-139: 131-Hulk vs. Iron Man; 1st Jim Wilson, Hulk's new sidekick. 136-1st Xeron, The Star-Slayer 3 6 9 17 25 32
140-Written by Harlan Ellison; 1st Jarella, Hulk's love 3 6 9 18 27 35
140-2nd printing (1994) 2 4 6 8 10 12
141-1st app. Doc Samson (7/71) 8 16 24 58 97 135
142-144: 144-Last 15¢ issue 3 6 9 16 23 30
145-(52 pgs.)-Origin retold 4 8 12 24 37 50
146-160: 149-1st app. The Inheritor. 155-1st app. Shaper. 158-Warlock cameo(12/72) 3 6 9 14 20 25
161-The Mimic dies; Beast app. 4 8 12 22 34 45
162-1st app. The Wendigo (4/73); Beast app. 6 12 18 41 66 90
163-171,173-176: 163-1st app. The Gremlin. 164-1st Capt. Omen & Colonel John D. Armbruster. 166-1st Zzzax. 168-1st The Harpy; nudity panels of Betty Ross. 169-1st app. Bi-Beast.176-Warlock cameo (2 panels only); same date as Strange Tales #178 (6/74) 2 4 6 11 16 20
172-X-Men cameo; origin Juggernaut retold 4 8 12 22 34 45
177-1st actual death of Warlock (last panel only) 2 4 6 13 18 22
178-Rebirth of Warlock 2 4 6 13 18 22
179 2 4 6 9 12 15
180-(10/74)-1st brief app. Wolverine (last pg.) 15 30 45 111 198 285
181-(11/74)-1st full Wolverine story; Trimpe-a 90 180 270 700 1075 1450

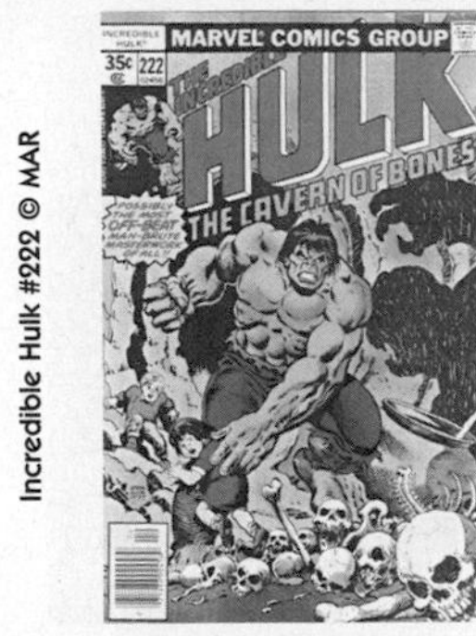

Incredible Hulk #222 © MAR

Incredible Hulk #418 © MAR

Incredible Hulk (2nd series) #106 © MAR

GD 2.0 | VG 4.0 | FN 6.0 | VF 8.0 | VF/NM 9.0 | NM- 9.2

182-Wolverine cameo; see Giant-Size X-Men #1 for next app.; 1st Crackajack Jackson 10 20 30 70 123 175
183-199: 185-Death of Col. Armbruster. 195,196-Abomination app. 197,198-Man-Thing-c/s 2 4 6 8 10 12
198,199, 201,202-(30¢-c variants, lim. distribution) 3 6 9 16 23 30
200-(25¢-c) Silver Surfer app.; anniversary issue 3 6 9 17 25 32
200-(30¢-c variant, limited distribution)(6/76) 5 10 15 32 51 70
201-220: 201-Conan swipe-c/sty. 212-1st app. The Constrictor 6.00
212-216-(35¢-c variant, limited distribution) 3 6 9 20 30 40
221-249: 227-Original Avengers app. 232-Capt. America x-over from C.A. #230. 233-Marvel Man app. 234-(4/79)-1st app. Quasar (formerly called Marvel Man. 243-Cage app. 5.00
250-Giant size; Silver Surfer app. 2 4 6 8 10 12
251-277,280-299: 271-Rocket Raccoon app. 272-Sasquatch & Wendigo app.; Wolverine & Alpha Flight cameo in flashback. 282-284-She-Hulk app. 293-F.F. app. 4.00
278,279-Most Marvel characters app. (Wolverine in both). 279-X-Men & Alpha Flight cameos 5.00
300-(11/84, 52 pgs.)-Spider-Man app in new black costume on-c & 2 pg. cameo 6.00
301-313: 312-Origin Hulk retold 3.00
314-Byrne-c/a begins, ends #319 5.00
315-319: 319-Bruce Banner & Betty Talbot wed 4.00
320-323,325,327-329 3.00
324-1st app. Grey Hulk since #1 (c-swipe of #1) 2 4 6 8 10 12
326-Grey vs. Green Hulk 5.00
330,331: 330-1st McFarlane ish (4/87); Thunderbolt Ross dies. 331-Grey Hulk series begins 3 6 9 14 20 25
332-334,336-339: 336,337-X-Factor app. 2 4 6 8 11 14
335-No McFarlane-a 5.00
340-Hulk battles Wolverine by McFarlane 4 8 12 22 34 45
341-346: 345-($1.50, 52 pgs.). 346-Last McFarlane issue 1 2 3 5 6 8
347-349,351-358,360-366: 347-1st app. Marlo 3.00
350-Hulk/Thing battle 6.00
359-Wolverine app. (illusion only) 3.00
367,372,377: 367-1st Dale Keown-a on Hulk (3/90). 372-Green Hulk app.;Keown-c/a. 377-1st all new Hulk; fluorescent-c; Keown-c/a 1 2 3 5 6 8
368-371,373-376: 368-Sam Kieth-c/a, 1st app. Pantheon. 369,370-Dale Keown-c/a. 370,371-Original Defenders app. 371,373-376: Keown-c/a. 376-Green vs. Grey Hulk 5.00
377-Fluorescent green logo 2nd printing 3.00
378,380,389: No Keown-a. 380-Doc Samson app. 3.00
379,381-388,390-392-Keown-a. 385-Infinity Gauntlet x-over. 389-Last $1.00-c. 392-X-Factor app. 4.00
393-($2.50, 72 pgs.)-30th anniversary issue; green foil stamped-c; swipes-c to #1; has pin-ups of classic battles; Keown-c/a 5.00
393-2nd printing 2.50
394-399: 394-No Keown-c/a; intro Trauma. 395,396-Punisher-c/stories; Keown-c/a. 397-Begin "Ghost of the Past" 4-part sty; Keown c/a. 398-Last Keown-c/a 2.50
400-($2.50, 68 pgs.)-Holo-grafx foil-c & r/TTA #63 3.00
400-416: 400-2nd print-Diff. color foil-c. 402-Return of Doc Samson 2.50
417-424: 417-Begin $1.50-c; Rick Jones' bachelor party; Hulk returns from "Future Imperfect"; bound-in trading card sheet. 418-(Regular edition)-Rick Jones marries Marlo; includes cameo apps of various Marvel characters as well as DC's Death & Peter David. 420-Death of Jim Wilson 2.50
418-($2.50)-Collector's Edition w/gatefold die-cut-c 3.00
425 ($2.25, 52 pgs.) 2.50
425 ($3.50, 52 pgs.)-Holographic-c 4.00
426-434, 436-442: 426-Begin $1.95-c. 427, 428-Man-Thing app. 431,432-Abomination app. 434-Funeral for Nick Fury. 436-Ghosts of the Future begins, ends #440. 439-Hulk becomes Maestro, Avengers app. 440-Thor-c/app. 441,442-She-Hulk-c/app. 2.50
435 ($2.50)-Rhino-app; excerpt from "What Savage Beast" 3.00
443,446-448: 443-Begin $1.50-c; re-app. of Hulk. 446-w/card insert. 447-Begin Deodato-c/a(p) 2.50
444,445: 444-Cable-c/app.; "Onslaught". 445-"Onslaught" 4.00
447-Variant cover 4.00
449-1st app. Thunderbolts 6.00
450-($2.95)-Thunderbolts app.; 2 stories; Heroes Reborn-c/app. 5.00
451-470: 455-X-Men-c/app. 460-Bruce Banner returns. 464-Silver Surfer-c/app. 466,467: Betty dies. 467-Last Peter David-s/Kubert-a. 468-Casey-s/Pulido-a begin 2.50
471-473 3.00
474-($2.99) Last issue; Abomination app. 4.00
#(-1) Flashback (7/97) Kubert-a 2.50
Special 1 (10/68, 25¢, 68 pg.)-New 51 pg. story, Hulk battles The Inhumans (early app.); Steranko-c. 10 20 30 67 116 165
Special 2 (10/69, 25¢, 68 pg.)-Origin retold 6 12 18 37 59 80
Special 3,4: 3-(1/71, 25¢, 68 pg.). 4-(1/72, 52pgs.) 3 6 9 18 27 35
Annual 5 (1976) 2 4 6 9 13 16
Annual 6-8 ('77-79)-7-Byrne/Layton-c/a; Iceman & Angel app. in book-length story. 8-Book-length Sasquatch-c/sty 2 4 6 8 10 12
Annual 9,10: 9('80). 10 ('81) 6.00
Annual 11('82)-Doc Samson back-up by Miller(p)(5 pgs.); Spider-Man & Avengers app. Buckler-a(p) 6.00
Annual 12-17: 12 ('83). 13('84). 14('85). 15('86). 16('90, $2.00, 68 pgs.)-She-Hulk app. 17(1991, $2.00)-Origin retold 3.50
Annual 18-20 ('92-'94 68 pgs.)-18-Return of the Defenders, Pt. I; no Keown-c/a 19-Bagged w/card 3.00
...'97 ($2.99) Pollina-c 3.00
...And Wolverine 1 (10/86, $2.50)-r/1st app. (#180-181) 1 3 4 6 8 10
...: Beauty and the Behemoth ('98, $19.95, TPB) r/Bruce & Betty stories 20.00
...Ground Zero ('95, $12.95) r/#340-346 13.00
...Hercules Unleashed (10/96, $2.50) David-s/Deodato-c/a 2.50
... Omnibus Vol. 1 HC (2008, $99.99, dustjacket) r/#1-6 & 102, Tales To Astonish #59-101 bonus art, cover reprints; afterword by Peter David; 2 covers (Kirby & Ross swipe) 100.00
.../Sub-Mariner '98 Annual ($2.99) 3.00
...Versus Quasimodo 1 (3/83, one-shot)-Based on Saturday morning cartoon 4.00
...Vs. Superman 1 (7/99, $5.95, one-shot)-painted-c by Rude 6.00
...Versus Venom 1 (4/94, $2.50, one-shot)-Embossed-c; red foil logo 3.00
... Visionaries: Peter David Vol. 1 (2005, $19.99) r/#331-339 written by Peter David 20.00
... Visionaries: Peter David Vol. 2 (2005, $19.99) r/#340-348 20.00
... Visionaries: Peter David Vol. 3 (2006, $19.99) r/#349-354, Web of Spider-Man #44, and Fantastic Four #320 20.00
... Visionaries: Peter David Vol. 4 (2007, $19.99) r/#355-363 and Marvel Comics Presents #26,45 20.00
... Visionaries: Peter David Vol. 5 (2008, $19.99) r/#364-372 and Annual #16 20.00
Wizard #1 Ace Edition - Reprints #1 with new Andy Kubert-c 14.00
Wizard #181 Ace Edition - Reprints #181 with new Chen-c 14.00

(Also see titles listed under **Hulk**)

NOTE: ***Adkins*** *a-111-116i.* ***Austin*** *a(i)-350, 351, 353, 354; c-302i, 350i.* ***Ayers*** *a-3-5i.* ***Buckler*** *a-Annual 5; c-252.* ***John Buscema*** *c-202p.* ***Byrne*** *a-314-319p; c-314-316, 318, 319, 359, Annual 14i.* ***Colan*** *c-363.* ***Ditko*** *a-2i, 6, 249, Annual 2r(5), 3r, 9p; c-2i, 6, 235, 249.* ***Everett*** *c-133i.* ***Golden*** *c-248, 251.* ***Kane*** *c(p)-193, 194, 196, 198.* ***Dale Keown*** *a(p)-367, 369-377, 379, 381-388, 390-393, 395-398; c-369-377p, 381, 382p, 384, 385, 386, 387p, 388, 390p, 391-393, 395p, 396, 397p, 398.* ***Kirby*** *a-1-5p, Special 2, 3p, Annual 5p; c-1-5, Annual 5.* ***McFarlane*** *a-330-334p, 336-339p, 340-343, 344-346p; c-330p, 340p, 341-343, 344p, 345, 346p.* ***Mignola*** *c-302, 305, 313.* ***Miller*** *c-258p, 261, 264, 268.* ***Mooney*** *a-230p, 287i, 288i.* ***Powell*** *a-Special 3r(2).* ***Romita*** *a-Annual 17p.* ***Severin*** *a(i)-108-110, 131-133, 141-151, 153-155; c(i)-109, 110, 132, 142, 144-155.* ***Simonson*** *c-283, 364-367.* ***Starlin*** *a-222p; c-217.* ***Staton*** *a(i)-187-189, 191-209.* ***Tuska*** *a-102i, 105i, 106i, 218p.* ***Williamson*** *a-310i; c-310i, 311i.* ***Wrightson*** *c-197.*

INCREDIBLE HULK (Vol. 2) (Formerly Hulk #1-11; becomes Incredible Hercules with #113) (Also see World War Hulk)
Marvel Comics: No. 12, Mar, 2000 - No. 112, Jan, 2008 ($1.99-$3.50)

12-Jenkins-s/Garney & McKone-a 3.00
13,14-($1.99) Garney & Buscema-a 2.50
15-24,26-32: 15-Begin $2.25-c. 21-Maximum Security x-over. 24-($1.99-c) 2.50
25-($2.99) Hulk vs. The Abomination; Romita Jr.-a 3.00
33-($3.50, 100 pgs.) new Bogdanove-a/Priest-s; reprints 3.50
34-Bruce Jones-s begin; Romita Jr.-a 5.00
35-49,51-54: 35-39 Jones-s/Romita Jr.-a. 40-43-Weeks-a. 44-49-Immonen-a 3.00
50-($3.50) Deodato-a begins; Abomination app. thru #54 3.50
55-74,77-91: 55(25¢-c) Absorbing Man returns; Fernandez-a. 60-65,70-72-Deodato-a. 66-69-Braithwaite-a. 71-74-Iron Man app. 77-($2.99-c) Peter David-s begin/Weeks-a. 80-Wolverine-c. 82-Jae Lee-c/a. 83-86-House of M x-over. 87-Scorpion app. 3.00
75,76-($3.50) The Leader app. 75-Robertson-a/Frank-c. 76-Braithwaite-a 3.50
92-Planet Hulk begins; Ladronn-c 5.00
92-2nd printing with variant-c by Bryan Hitch 4.00
93-99,101-105 Planet Hulk; Ladronn-c 3.00
100-($3.99) Planet Hulk continues; back-up w/Frank-a; r/#152,153; Ladronn-c 4.00
100-($3.99) Green Hulk variant-c by Michael Turner 10.00
100-($3.99) Gray Hulk variant-c by Michael Turner 30.00
106-World War Hulk begins; Gary Frank-a/c 5.00
106-2nd printing with new cover of Hercules and Angel 3.00
107-112: 107-Hercules vs. Hulk. 108-Rick Jones app. 112-Art Adams-c 3.00
Annual 2000 ($3.50) Texeira-a/Jenkins-s; Avengers app. 3.50
Annual 2001 ($2.99) Thor-c/app.; Larsen-s/Williams III-c 3.00
... : Boiling Point (Volume 2, 2002, $8.99, TPB) r/#40-43; Andrews-c 9.00
Dogs of War (6/01, $19.95, TPB) r/#12-20 20.00
House of M (2006, $13.99) r/House of M tie-in issues Incredible Hulk #83-87 14.00
Hulk: Planet Hulk HC (2007, $39.99, dustjacket) oversized r/#92-105, Planet Hulk: Gladiator Guidebook, stories from Amazing Fantasy (2004) #15 and Giant-Size Hulk #1 40.00
Hulk: Planet Hulk SC (2008, $34.99) same content as HC 35.00

Indiana Jones and the Kingdom of the Crystal Skull #1 © LucasFilm

Indians #3 © FH

Inferior Five #7 © DC

	GD 2.0	VG 4.0	FN 6.0	VF 8.0	VF/NM 9.0	NM- 9.2

Planet Hulk: Gladiator Guidebook (2006, $3.99) bios of combatants and planet history 4.00
...: Prelude to Planet Hulk (2006, $13.99, TPB) r/#88-91 & Official Handbook: Hulk 2004 14.00
...: Return of the Monster (7/02, $12.99, TPB) r/#34-39 13.00
...: The End (8/02, $5.95) David-s/Keown-a; Hulk in the far future 6.00
...: The End HC (2008, $19.99, dustjacket) r/The End and Hulk: Future Imperfect #1-2 20.00
...Volume 1 HC (2002, $29.99, oversized) r/#34-43 & Startling Stories: Banner #1-4 30.00
...Volume 2 HC (2003, $29.99, oversized) r/#44-54; sketch pages and cover gallery 30.00
Volume 3: Transfer of Power (2003, $12.99, TPB) r/#44-49 13.00
Volume 4: Abominable (2003, $11.99, TPB) r/#50-54; Abomination app.; Deodato-a 12.00
Volume 5: Hide in Plain Sight (2003, $11.99, TPB) r/#55-59; Fernandez-a 12.00
Volume 6: Split Decisions (2004, $12.99, TPB) r/#60-65; Deodato-a 13.00
Volume 7: Dead Like Me (2004, $12.99, TPB) r/#66-69 & Hulk Smash #1&2 13.00
Volume 8: Big Things (2004, $17.99, TPB) r/#70-76; Iron Man app. 18.00
Volume 9: Tempest Fugit (2005, $14.99, TPB) r/#77-82 15.00

INCREDIBLE MR. LIMPET, THE (See Movie Classics)

INCREDIBLES, THE
Image Comics: Nov, 2004 - No. 4, Feb, 2005 ($2.99, limited series)

1-4-Adaptation of 2004 Pixar movie; Ricardo Curtis-a 3.00
TPB (2005, $12.95) r/#1-4; cover gallery 13.00

INCREDIBLE SCIENCE FICTION (Formerly Weird Science-Fantasy)
E. C. Comics: No. 30, July-Aug, 1955 - No. 33, Jan-Feb, 1956

Issue	GD	VG	FN	VF	VF/NM	NM-
30-Davis-c begin, end #32	39	78	117	312	486	660
31-Williamson/Krenkel-a, Wood-a(2)	40	80	120	320	498	675
32-Williamson/Krenkel-a	40	80	120	320	498	675
33-Classic Wood-c; "Judgment Day" story-r/Weird Fantasy #18; final issue & last E.C. comic book	41	82	123	328	509	690

NOTE: *Davis a-30, 32, 33; c-30-32. Krigstein a-in all. Orlando a-30, 32, 33. Wood a-30, 31, 33; c-33.*

INCREDIBLE SCIENCE FICTION (Formerly Weird Science-Fantasy)
Russ Cochran/Gemstone Publ.: No. 8, Aug, 1994 - No. 11, May, 1995 ($2.00)

8-11: Reprints #30-33 of E.C. series 2.50

INDEPENDENCE DAY (Movie)
Marvel Comics: No. 0, June, 1996 - No. 2, Aug, 1996 ($1.95, limited series)

0-Special Edition; photo-c 5.00
0-2 2.50

INDIANA JONES (Title series), **Dark Horse Comics**
--ADVENTURES, 6/08 ($6.95, digest-sized) Vol. 1 - new all-ages adventures; Beavers-a 7.00
--AND THE ARMS OF GOLD, 2/94 - 5/94 ($2.50) 1-4 2.50
--AND THE FATE OF ATLANTIS, 3/91 - 9/91 ($2.50) 1-4-Dorman painted-c on all; contain trading cards (#1 has a 2nd printing, 10/91) 2.50
--AND THE GOLDEN FLEECE, 6/94 - 7/94 ($2.50) 1,2
2.50
--AND THE IRON PHOENIX, 12/94 - 3/95 ($2.50) 1-4 2.50

INDIANA JONES AND THE KINGDOM OF THE CRYSTAL SKULL
Dark Horse Comics: May, 2008 - No. 2, May, 2008 ($5.99, limited series, movie adaptation)

1,2-Luke Ross-a/John Jackson Miller-adapted-s; two covers by Struzan & Fleming 6.00
TPB (5/08, $12.95) r/#1,2; Struzan-c 13.00

INDIANA JONES AND THE LAST CRUSADE
Marvel Comics: 1989 - No. 4, 1989 ($1.00, limited series, movie adaptation)

1-4: Williamson-i assist 3.00
1-(1989, $2.95, B&W mag., 80 pgs.) 4.00

--AND THE SHRINE OF THE SEA DEVIL: Dark Horse, 9/94 ($2.50, one shot)
1-Gary Gianni-a 2.50
--AND THE SARGASSO PIRATES: Dark Horse, 12/95 - 3/96 ($2.50) 1-4: 1,2-Ross-c 2.50
--AND THE SPEAR OF DESTINY: Dark Horse, 4/95 - 8/95 ($2.50) 1-4 2.50
--AND THE TOMB OF THE GODS, 6/08 - No. 4 ($2.99) 1-Tony Harris-c 3.00
--THUNDER IN THE ORIENT: Dark Horse, 9/93 - '94 ($2.50)
1-6: Dan Barry story & art in all; 1-Dorman painted-c 2.50

INDIANA JONES AND THE TEMPLE OF DOOM
Marvel Comics Group: Sept, 1984 - No. 3, Nov, 1984 (Movie adaptation)

1-3-r/Marvel Super Special; Guice-a 3.00

INDIANA JONES OMNIBUS
Dark Horse Books: Feb, 2008; June 200 8 ($24.95, digest-size)

Volume One - Reprints Indiana Jones and the Fate of Atlantis, Indiana Jones: Thunder in the Orient; and Indiana Jones and the Arms of Gold mini-series 25.00
Volume Two - Reprints I.J. and the Golden Fleece, IJ. and the Shrine of the Sea Devil, I.J. and the Iron Phoenix, I.J. and the Spear of Destiny, I.J. and the Sargasso Pirates 25.00

INDIAN BRAVES (Baffling Mysteries No. 5 on)
Ace Magazines: March, 1951 - No. 4, Sept, 1951

Issue	GD	VG	FN	VF	VF/NM	NM-
1-Green Arrowhead begins, ends #3	14	28	42	82	121	160
2	9	18	27	50	65	80
3,4	8	16	24	44	57	70
I.W. Reprint #1 (nd)-r/Indian Braves #4	2	4	6	9	13	16

INDIAN CHIEF (White Eagle...) (Formerly The Chief, Four Color 290)
Dell Publ. Co.: No. 3, July-Sept, 1951 - No. 33, Jan-Mar, 1959 (All painted-c)

Issue	GD	VG	FN	VF	VF/NM	NM-
3	5	10	15	35	55	75
4-11: 6-White Eagle app.	4	8	12	28	44	60
12-1st White Eagle(10-12/53)-Not same as earlier character	5	10	15	35	55	75
13-29	4	8	12	23	36	48
30-33-Buscema-a	4	8	12	24	37	50

INDIAN CHIEF (See March of Comics No. 94, 110, 127, 140, 159, 170, 187)

INDIAN FIGHTER, THE (Movie)
Dell Publishing Co.: No. 687, May, 1956 (one-shot)

Issue	GD	VG	FN	VF	VF/NM	NM-
Four Color 687-Kirk Douglas photo-c	7	14	21	50	83	115

INDIAN FIGHTER
Youthful Magazines: May, 1950 - No. 11, Jan, 1952

Issue	GD	VG	FN	VF	VF/NM	NM-
1	14	28	42	82	121	160
2-Wildey-a/c(bondage)	10	20	30	58	79	100
3-11: 3,4-Wildey-a	8	16	24	44	57	70

NOTE: *Hollingsworth a-5. Walter Johnson c-1, 3, 4, 6. Palais a-10. Stallman a-5-8. Wildey a-2-4; c-2, 5.*

INDIAN LEGENDS OF THE NIAGARA (See American Graphics)

INDIANS
Fiction House Magazines (Wings Publ. Co.): Spring, 1950 - No. 17, Spr, 1953 (1-8: 52 pgs.)

Issue	GD	VG	FN	VF	VF/NM	NM-
1-Manzar The White Indian, Long Bow & Orphan of the Storm begin	30	60	90	174	275	375
2-Starlight begins	15	30	45	88	137	185
3-5: 5-17-Most-c by Whitman	14	28	42	80	115	150
6-10	12	24	36	69	97	125
11-17	11	22	33	60	83	105

INDIANS OF THE WILD WEST
I. W. Enterprises: Circa 1958? (no date) (Reprints)

Issue	GD	VG	FN	VF	VF/NM	NM-
9-Kinstler-c; Whitman-a; r/Indians #?	2	4	6	10	14	18

INDIANS ON THE WARPATH
St. John Publishing Co.: No date (Late 40s, early 50s) (132 pgs.)

Issue	GD	VG	FN	VF	VF/NM	NM-
nn-Matt Baker-c; contains St. John comics rebound. Many combinations possible	37	74	111	213	339	465

INDIAN TRIBES (See Famous Indian Tribes)

INDIAN WARRIORS (Formerly White Rider and Super Horse; becomes Western Crime Cases #9)
Star Publications: No. 7, June, 1951 - No. 8, Sept, 1951

Issue	GD	VG	FN	VF	VF/NM	NM-
7-White Rider & Superhorse continue; "Last of the Mohicans" serial begins; L.B. Cole-c	18	36	54	105	165	225
8-L. B. Cole-c	17	34	51	98	154	210
3-D 1(12/53, 25¢)-Came w/glasses; L. B. Cole-c	35	70	105	204	322	440
Accepted Reprint(nn)(inside cover shows White Rider & Superhorse #11)-r/cover to #7; origin White Rider &...; L. B. Cole-c	7	14	21	37	46	55
Accepted Reprint #8 (nd); L.B. Cole-c (r-cover to #8)	7	14	21	37	46	55

INDOORS-OUTDOORS (See Wisco)

INDOOR SPORTS
National Specials Co.: nd (6x9", 64 pgs., B&W-r, hard-c)

Issue	GD	VG	FN	VF	VF/NM	NM-
nn-By Tad	5	10	15	24	30	35

INDUSTRIAL GOTHIC
DC Comics (Vertigo): Dec, 1995 - No. 5, Apr, 1996 ($2.50, limited series)

1-5: Ted McKeever-c/a/scripts 2.50

INFERIOR FIVE, THE (Inferior 5 #11, 12) (See Showcase #62, 63, 65)
National Periodical Publications (#1-10: 12¢): 3-4/67 - No. 10, 9-10/68; No. 11, 8-9/72 - No. 12, 10-11/72

Issue	GD	VG	FN	VF	VF/NM	NM-
1-(3-4/67)-Sekowsky-a(p); 4th app.	5	10	15	35	55	75
2-5: 2-Plastic Man, F.F. app. 4-Thor app.	3	6	9	19	29	38
6-9: 6-Stars DC staff	3	6	9	16	22	28

10-Superman x-over; F.F., Spider-Man & Sub-Mariner app.

Infinite Crisis #5 © DC

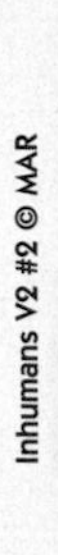

Infinity Inc. #7 © DC

Inhumans V2 #2 © MAR

	GD 2.0	VG 4.0	FN 6.0	VF 8.0	VF/NM 9.0	NM- 9.2
	3	6	9	18	27	35
11,12: Orlando-c/a; both r/Showcase #62,63	2	4	6	11	16	20

INFERNO
Caliber Comics: 1995 - No. 5 ($2.95, B&W)
1-5 3.00

INFERNO (See Legion of Super-Heroes)
DC Comics: Oct, 1997 - No. 4, Feb, 1998 ($2.50, limited series)
1-Immonen-s/c/a in all 4.00
2-4 3.00

INFERNO: HELLBOUND
Image Comics (Top Cow): Jan, 2002 - No. 3 ($2.50/$2.99)
1,2: 1-Seven covers; Silvestri-a/Silvestri and Wohl-s 2.50
3 ($2.99) Tan-a 3.00
#0 (7/02, $3.00) Tan-a 3.00
Wizard #0- Previews series; bagged with Wizard Top Cow Special mag 2.25

INFINITE CRISIS
DC Comics: Dec, 2005 - No. 7, Jun, 2006 ($3.99, limited series)
1-Johns-s/Jimenez-a; two covers by Jim Lee and George Pérez 5.00
1-RRP Edition with Jim Lee sketch-c 275.00
2-7: 4-New Spectre; Earth-2 returns. 5-Earth-2 Lois dies; new Blue Beetle debut. 6-Superboy killed, new Earth formed. 7-Earth-2 Superman dies 4.00
HC (2006, $24.99, dustjacket) r/#1-7; DiDio intro.; sketch cover gallery; Interview/commentary with Johns, Jimenez and editors; sketch art 25.00
... Companion TPB (2006, $14.99) r/Day of Vengeance: Infinite Crisis Special #1, Rann-Thanagar War: ICS #1, The Omac Project: ICS #1, Villains United: ICS #1 15.00
... Secret Files 2006 (4/06, $5.99) tie-in story with Earth-2 Lois and Superman, Earth-Prime Superboy and Alexander Luthor; art by various; profile pages 6.00

INFINITE CRISIS AFTERMATH (See Crisis Aftermath:...)

INFINITE HORIZON
Image Comics: Dec, 2007 - No. 6 ($2.99)
1-3-Re-imagining of Homer's The Odyssey in modern times; Noto-a/Duggan-s 3.00

INFINITY ABYSS (Also see Marvel Universe: The End)
Marvel Comics: Aug, 2002 - No. 6 ($2.99, limited series)
1-5-Starlin-s/a; Thanos, Captain Marvel, Spider-Man, Dr. Strange app. 3.00
6-($3.50) 3.50
Thanos Vol. 2: Infinity Abyss TPB (2003, $17.99) r/ #1-6 18.00

INFINITY CRUSADE
Marvel Comics: June, 1993 - No. 6, Nov, 1993 ($2.50, limited series, 52 pgs.)
1-6: By Jim Starlin & Ron Lim 2.50

INFINITY GAUNTLET (The... #2 on; see Infinity Crusade, The Infinity War & Warlock & the Infinity Watch)
Marvel Comics: July, 1991 - No. 6, Dec, 1991 ($2.50, limited series)
1-6:Thanos-c/stories in all; Starlin scripts in all; 5,6-Ron Lim-c/a 3.00
TPB (4/99, $24.95) r/#1-6 25.00
NOTE: *Lim a-3p(part), 5p, 6p; c-5i, 6i. Perez a-1-3p, 4p(part); c-1(painted), 2-4, 5i, 6i.*

INFINITY, INC. (See All-Star Squadron #25)
DC Comics: Mar, 1984 - No. 53, Aug, 1988 ($1.25, Baxter paper, 36 pgs.)
1-Brainwave, Jr., Fury, The Huntress, Jade, Northwind, Nuklon, Obsidian, Power Girl, Silver Scarab & Star Spangled Kid begin 4.00
2-13,38-49,51-53: 2-Dr. Midnite, G.A. Flash, W. Woman, Dr. Fate, Hourman, Green Lantern, Wildcat app. 5-Nudity panels. 46,47-Millennium tie-ins 3.00

	GD 2.0	VG 4.0	FN 6.0	VF 8.0	VF/NM 9.0	NM- 9.2
14-Todd McFarlane-a (5/85, 2nd full story)	1	2	3	6	8	9

15-37-McFarlane-a (20,23,24: 5 pgs. only; 33: 2 pgs.); 18-24-Crisis x-over. 21-Intro new Hourman & Dr. Midnight. 26-New Wildcat app. 31-Star Spangled Kid becomes Skyman. 32-Green Fury becomes Green Flame. 33-Origin Obsidian. 35-1st modern app. G.A. Fury 4.00
50 ($2.50, 52 pgs.) 3.00
Annual 1,2: 1(12/85)-Crisis x-over. 2('88, $2.00), Special 1 ('87, $1.50) 3.00
NOTE: *Kubert r-4. McFarlane a-14-37p, Annual 1p; c(p)-14-19, 22, 25, 26, 31-33, 37, Annual 1. Newton a-12p, 13p(last work 4/85). Tuska a-11p. JSA app. 3-10.*

INFINITY, INC. (See 52)
DC Comics: Nov, 2007 - No. 12, Oct, 2008 ($2.99)
1-12: 1-Milligan-s; Steel app. 3.00
...: Luthor's Monsters TPB (2008, $14.99) r/#1-5 15.00

INFINITY WAR, THE (Also see Infinity Gauntlet & Warlock and the Infinity...)
Marvel Comics: June, 1992 - No. 6, Nov, 1992 ($2.50, mini-series)
1-Starlin scripts, Lim-c/a(p), Thanos app. in all 2.50
2-6: All have wraparound gatefold covers 2.50
TPB (2006, $29.99) r/#1-6, Marvel Comics Presents #108-111, Warlock and the Infinity Watch #7-10; cover gallery and synopses of Infinity War crossovers 30.00

INFORMER, THE
Feature Television Productions: April, 1954 - No. 5, Dec, 1954

	GD 2.0	VG 4.0	FN 6.0	VF 8.0	VF/NM 9.0	NM- 9.2
1-Sekowsky-a begins	12	24	36	69	97	125
2	9	18	27	47	61	75
3-5	8	16	24	42	54	65

IN HIS STEPS
Spire Christian Comics (Fleming H. Revell Co.): 1973, 1977 (39/49¢)

	GD 2.0	VG 4.0	FN 6.0	VF 8.0	VF/NM 9.0	NM- 9.2
nn	2	4	6	8	10	12

INHUMANOIDS, THE (TV)
Marvel Comics (Star Comics): Jan, 1987 - No. 4, July 1987
1-4: Based on Hasbro toys 3.00

INHUMANS, THE (See Amazing Adventures, Fantastic Four #54 & Special #5, Incredible Hulk Special #1, Marvel Graphic Novel & Thor #146)
Marvel Comics Group: Oct, 1975 - No. 12, Aug, 1977

	GD 2.0	VG 4.0	FN 6.0	VF 8.0	VF/NM 9.0	NM- 9.2
1: #1-4,6 are 25¢ issues	2	4	6	13	18	22
2-4-Peréz-a	1	3	4	6	8	10
5-12: 9-Reprints Amazing Adventures #1,2('70). 12-Hulk app.	1	2	3	5	7	9
4-(30¢-c variant, limited distribution)(4/76) Peréz-a	2	4	6	10	14	18
6-(30¢-c variant, limited distribution)(8/76)	2	4	6	10	14	18
11,12-(35¢-c variants, limited distribution)	2	4	6	10	14	18

Special 1(4/90, $1.50, 52 pgs.)-F.F. cameo 3.00
...: The Great Refuge (5/95, $2.95) 3.00
NOTE: *Buckler c-2-4p, 5. Gil Kane a-5-7p; c-1p, 7p, 8p. Kirby a-9r. Mooney a-11i. Perez a-1-4p, 8p.*

INHUMANS (Marvel Knights)
Marvel Comics: Nov, 1998 - No. 12, Oct, 1999 ($2.99, limited series)
1-Jae Lee-c/a; Paul Jenkins-s 10.00
1-($6.95) DF Edition; Jae Lee variant-c 7.00
2-Two covers by Lee and Darrow 4.00
3-12 3.00
TPB (10/00, $24.95) r/#1-12 25.00

INHUMANS (Volume 3)
Marvel Comics: Jun, 2000 - No. 4, Oct, 2000 ($2.99, limited series)
1-4-Ladronn-c/Pacheco & Marin-s. 1-3-Ladronn-a. 4-Lucas-a 3.00

INHUMANS (Volume 6)
Marvel Comics: Jun, 2003 - No. 12, Jun, 2004 ($2.50/$2.99)
1-12: 1-6-McKeever-s/Clark-a/JH Williams III-c. 7-Begin $2.99-c. 7,8-Teranishi-a 3.00
Vol. 1: Culture Shock (2005, $7.99, digest) r/#1-6; story pitch and sketch pages 8.00

INHUMANS 2099
Marvel Comics: Nov, 2004 ($2.99, one-shot)
1-Kirkman-s/Rathburn-a/Pat Lee-c 3.00

INKY & DINKY (See Felix's Nephews...)

IN LOVE (...Magazine on-c; I Love You No. 7 on)
Mainline/Charlton No. 5 (5/55)-on: Aug-Sept, 1954 - No. 6, July, 1955 ('Adult Reading' on-c)

	GD 2.0	VG 4.0	FN 6.0	VF 8.0	VF/NM 9.0	NM- 9.2
1-Simon & Kirby-a; book-length novel in all issues	40	80	120	235	368	500
2,3-S&K-a. 3-Last pre-code (12-1/54-55)	23	46	69	135	213	290
4-S&K-a.(Rare)	26	52	78	150	235	320
5-S&K-c only	13	26	39	72	101	130
6-No S&K-a	9	18	27	47	61	75

INNOVATION SPECTACULAR
Innovation Publishing: 1991 - No. 2, 1991 ($2.95, squarebound, 100 pgs.)
1,2: Contains rebound comics w/o covers 3.00

INNOVATION SUMMER FUN SPECIAL
Innovation Publishing: 1991 ($3.50, B&W/color, squarebound)
1-Contains rebound comics (Power Factory) 3.50

IN SEARCH OF THE CASTAWAYS (See Movie Comics)

INSIDE CRIME (Formerly My Intimate Affair)
Fox Features Syndicate (Hero Books): No. 3, July, 1950 - No. 2, Sept, 1950

	GD 2.0	VG 4.0	FN 6.0	VF 8.0	VF/NM 9.0	NM- 9.2
3-Wood-a (10 pgs.); L. B. Cole-c	30	60	90	174	275	375
2-Used in **SOTI**, pg. 182,183; r/Spook #24	23	46	69	132	209	285
nn(no publ. listed, nd)	11	22	33	60	83	105

INSPECTOR, THE (TV) (Also see The Pink Panther)

Interface #4 © James D. Hudnall

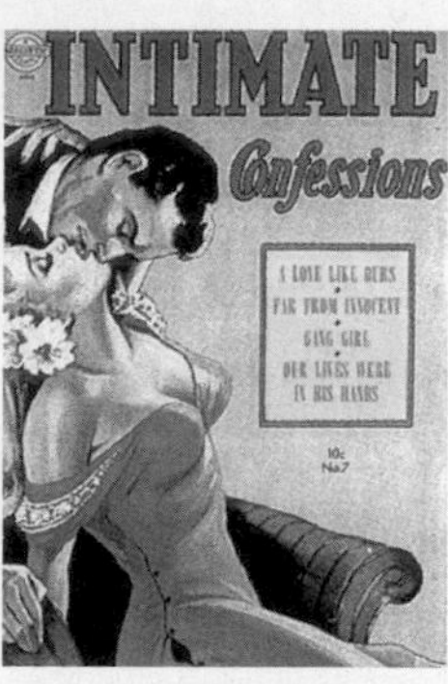

Intimate Confessions #7 © Realistic

Invaders #4 © MAR

	GD 2.0	VG 4.0	FN 6.0	VF 8.0	VF/NM 9.0	NM- 9.2
Gold Key: July, 1974 - No. 19, Feb, 1978						
1	3	6	9	19	29	38
2-5	2	4	6	13	18	22
6-9	2	4	6	10	14	18
10-19: 11-Reprints	2	4	6	8	10	12
INSPECTOR GILL OF THE FISH POLICE (See Fish Police)						
INSPECTOR WADE						
David McKay Publications: No. 13, May, 1938						
Feature Books 13	29	58	87	167	264	360
INSTANT PIANO						
Dark Horse Comics: Aug, 1994 - No. 4, Feb, 1995 ($3.95, B&W, bimonthly, mature)						
1-4						4.00
INTERFACE						
Marvel Comics (Epic Comics): Dec, 1989 - No. 8, Dec, 1990 ($1.95, mature, coated paper)						
1-8: Cont. from 1st ESPers series; painted-c/a						2.50
Espers: Interface TPB ('98, $16.95) r/#1-6						17.00
INTERNATIONAL COMICS (...Crime Patrol No. 6)						
E. C. Comics: Spring, 1947 - No. 5, Nov-Dec, 1947						
1-Schaffenberger-a begins, ends #4	62	124	186	388	644	900
2	43	86	129	263	431	600
3-5	40	80	120	239	380	520
INTERNATIONAL CRIME PATROL (Formerly International Comics #1-5; becomes Crime Patrol No. 7 on)						
E. C. Comics: No. 6, Spring, 1948						
6-Moon Girl app.	62	124	186	388	644	900
IN THE BLOOD						
Boom! Studios: Feb, 2006 - Present ($3.99)						
1-Steve Niles-s/Josh Medors-a						3.00
IN THE DAYS OF THE MOB (Magazine)						
Hampshire Dist. Ltd. (National): Fall, 1971 (B&W)						
1-Kirby-a; John Dillinger wanted poster inside (1/2 value if poster is missing)	7	14	21	49	80	110
IN THE PRESENCE OF MINE ENEMIES						
Spire Christian Comics/Fleming H. Revell Co.: 1973 (35/49¢)						
nn	2	4	6	8	10	12
IN THE SHADOW OF EDGAR ALLAN POE						
DC Comics (Vertigo): 2002 (Graphic novel)						
Hardcover (2002, $24.95) Fuqua-s/Phillips and Parke photo-a						25.00
Softcover (2003, $17.95)						18.00
INTIMATE						
Charlton Comics: Dec, 1957 - No. 3, May, 1958						
1	6	12	18	28	34	40
2,3	4	8	12	18	22	25
INTIMATE CONFESSIONS (See Fox Giants)						
INTIMATE CONFESSIONS						
Country Press Inc.: 1942						
nn-Ashcan comic, not distributed to newsstands, only for in house use. A VF copy sold for $1,000 in 2007, and a VF+ copy sold for $1,525 in 2007.						
INTIMATE CONFESSIONS						
Realistic Comics: July-Aug, 1951 - No. 7, Aug, 1952; No. 8, Mar, 1953 (All painted-c)						
1-Kinstler-c/a; c/Avon paperback #222	86	172	258	538	894	1250
2	23	46	69	130	205	280
3-c/Avon paperback #250; Kinstler-c/a	27	54	81	156	246	335
4-8: 4-c/Avon paperback #304; Kinstler-c. 6-c/Avon paperback #120. 8-c/Avon paperback #375; Kinstler-a	23	46	69	130	205	280
INTIMATE CONFESSIONS						
I. W. Enterprises/Super Comics: 1964						
I.W. Reprint #9,10, Super Reprint #10,12,18	2	4	6	10	14	18
INTIMATE LOVE						
Standard Comics: No. 5, 1950 - No. 28, Aug, 1954						
5-8: 6-8-Severin/Elder-a	10	20	30	54	72	90
9	8	16	24	40	50	60
10-Jane Russell, Robert Mitchum photo-c	13	26	39	74	105	135
11-18,20,23,25,27,28	7	14	21	37	46	55

	GD 2.0	VG 4.0	FN 6.0	VF 8.0	VF/NM 9.0	NM- 9.2
19,21,22,24,26-Toth-a	8	16	24	44	57	70
NOTE: ***Celardo*** *a-8, 10.* ***Colletta*** *a-23.* ***Moreira*** *a-13(2). Photo-c-6, 7, 10, 12, 14, 15, 18-20, 24, 26, 27.*						
INTIMATES, THE						
DC Comics (WildStorm): Jan, 2005 - No. 12, Dec, 2005 ($2.95/$2.99)						
1-12: 1-Joe Casey-s/Jim Lee-c/Lee and Giuseppe Camuncoli-a						3.00
INTIMATE SECRETS OF ROMANCE						
Star Publications: Sept, 1953 - No. 2, Apr, 1954						
1,2-L. B. Cole-c	19	38	57	109	172	235
INTIMIDATORS (Jim Valentino's...)						
Image Comics (Shadowline): Dec, 2005 - Present ($3.50)						
1-4: 1-Montenegro-a/Kleid-s. 4-Oeming-c						3.50
INTRIGUE						
Quality Comics Group: Jan, 1955						
1-Horror; Jack Cole reprint/Web of Evil	34	68	102	195	308	420
INTRIGUE						
Image Comics: Aug, 1999 - No. 3, Feb, 2000 ($2.50/$2.95)						
1,2: 1-Two covers (Andrews, Wieringo); Shum-s/Andrews-a						2.50
3-($2.95)						3.00
INTRUDER						
TSR, Inc.: 1990 - No. 10, 1991 ($2.95, 44 pgs.)						
1-10						3.00
INVADERS, THE (TV)						
Gold Key: Oct, 1967 - No. 4, Oct, 1968 (All have photo-c)						
1-Spiegle-a in all	9	18	27	60	100	140
2-4: 2-Pin-up on back-c	6	12	18	41	66	90
INVADERS, THE (Also see The Avengers #71 & Giant-Size Invaders)						
Marvel Comics Group: August, 1975 - No. 40, May, 1979; No. 41, Sept, 1979						
1-Captain America & Bucky, Human Torch & Toro, & Sub-Mariner begin; cont'd. from Giant Size Invaders #1; #1-7 are 25¢ issues	5	10	15	32	51	70
2-5: 2-1st app. Brain-Drain. 3-Battle issue; Cap vs. Namor vs. Torch; intro U-Man	3	6	9	15	21	26
6-10: 6,7-(Regular 25¢ edition). 6-(7/76) Liberty Legion app. 7-Intro Baron Blood & intro/1st app. Union Jack; Human Torch origin retold. 8-Union Jack-c/story. 9-Origin Baron Blood. 10-G.A. Capt. America-r/C.A #22	2	4	6	9	12	15
6,7-(30¢-c variants, limited distribution)	3	6	9	20	30	40
11-19: 11-Origin Spitfire; intro The Blue Bullet. 14-1st app. The Crusaders. 16-Re-intro The Destroyer. 17-Intro Warrior Woman. 18-Re-intro The Destroyer w/new origin. 19-Hitler-c/story	1	3	4	6	8	10
17-19,21-(35¢-c variants, limited distribution)	4	8	12	24	37	50
20-(Regular 30¢-c) Reprints origin/1st app. Sub-Mariner from Motion Picture Funnies Weekly with color added & brief write-up about MPFW; 1st app. new Union Jack II	2	4	6	9	12	15
20-(35¢-c variant, limited distribution)	4	8	12	28	44	60
21-(Regular 30¢ edition)-r/Marvel Mystery #10 (battle issue)	2	4	6	8	10	12
22-30,34-40: 22-New origin Toro. 24-r/Marvel Mystery #17 (team-up issue; all-r). 25-All new-a begins. 28-Intro new Human Top & Golden Girl. 29-Intro Teutonic Knight. 34-Mighty Destroyer joins. 35-The Whizzer app.	1	2	3	4	5	7
31-33: 31-Frankenstein-c/sty. 32,33-Thor app.	1	3	4	6	8	10
41-Double size last issue	2	4	6	10	14	18
Annual 1 (9/77)-Schomburg, Rico stories (new); Schomburg-c/a (1st for Marvel in 30 years); Avengers app.; re-intro The Shark & The Hyena	4	8	12	26	41	55
... Classic Vol. 1 TPB (2007, $24.99) r/#1-9, Giant-Size Invaders #1 and Marvel Premiere #29,30; cover pencils and cover inks						25.00
NOTE: ***Buckler*** *a-5.* ***Everett*** *r-20('39), 21(1940), 24, Annual 1.* ***Gil Kane*** *c(p)-13, 17, 18, 20-27.* ***Kirby*** *c(p)-3-12, 14-16, 32, 33.* ***Mooney*** *a-5i, 16, 22.* ***Robbins*** *a-1-4, 6-9, 10(3 pg.), 11-15, 17-21, 23, 25-28; c-28.*						
INVADERS (See Namor, the Sub-Mariner #12)						
Marvel Comics Group: May, 1993 - No. 4, Aug, 1993 ($1.75, limited series)						
1-4						2.50
INVADERS (2004 title - see New Invaders)						
INVADERS FROM HOME						
DC Comics (Piranha Press): 1990 - No. 6, 1990 ($2.50, mature)						
1-6						2.50
INVASION						
DC Comics: Holiday, 1988-'89 - No. 3, Jan, 1989 ($2.95, lim. series, 84 pgs.)						
1-3:1-McFarlane/Russell-a. 2-McFarlane/Russell & Giffen/Gordon-a						3.00
INVINCIBLE (Also see The Pact #4)						

Invincible #51 © Kirkman & Walker

The Invisibles #12 © Grant Morrison

Iron Fist #10 © MAR

	GD 2.0	VG 4.0	FN 6.0	VF 8.0	VF/NM 9.0	NM- 9.2

Image Comics: Jan, 2003 - Present ($2.95/$2.99)

1-Kirkman-s/Walker-a 40.00
2-8-Kirkman-s/Walker-a. 4-Preview of The Moth 12.00
9-14: 11-Origin of Omni-Man. 14-Cho-c 6.00
15-24,26-41,43-49: 33-Tie-in w/Marvel Team-Up #14 3.00
25-($4.95) Science Dog app.; back-up stories w/origins of Science Dog and teammates 5.00
42-($1.99) Includes re-cap of the entire series 2.25
50-(6/08, $4.99) Two covers; back-up origin of Cecil Stedman; Science Dog app. 5.00
51,52: 51-Jim Lee-c; new costumes 3.00
#0-(4/05, 50¢) Origin of Invincible; Ottley-a 2.25
Official Handbook of the Invincible Universe 1,2 (11/06, 1/07, $4.99) profile pages 5.00
Official Handbook of the Invincible Universe Vol. 1 (2007, $12.99) r/#1-2; sketch pages 13.00
... Presents Atom Eve 1,2 (12/07, 3/08, $2.99) origin of Atom Eve; Bellegarde-a 5.00
... Universe Primer 1 (5/08, $5.99) r/Invincible #1, Brit #1, Astounding Wolf-Man #1 6.00
The Complete Invincible Library Vol. 1 Slipcase HC (2006, $125.00) oversized r/#1-24, #0 and story from Image Comics Summer Special (FCBD 2004); sketch pages; script for #1 125.00
..., Ultimate Collection Vol. 1 HC (2005, $34.95) oversized r/#1-13; sketch pages 35.00
..., Ultimate Collection Vol. 2 HC (2006, $34.99) oversized r/#14-24, #0 and story from Image Comics Summer Special (FCBD 2004); sketch pages and script for #23; intro by Damon Lindelof; afterword by Robert Kirkman 35.00
..., Ultimate Collection Vol. 3 HC (2007, $34.95) oversized r/#25-35 & The Pact #4; sketch pages and script for #28; afterword by Robert Kirkman 35.00
..., Ultimate Collection Vol. 4 HC (2008, $34.99) oversized r/#36-47; sketch & script pgs. 35.00
Vol. 1: Family Matters TPB (8/03, $12.95) r/#1-4; intro. by Busiek; sketch pages 13.00
Vol. 2: Eight in Enough TPB (3/04, $12.95) r/#5-8; intro. by Larsen; sketch pages 13.00
Vol. 3: Perfect Strangers TPB (2004, $12.95) r/#9-12; intro. by Brevoort; sketch pages 13.00
Vol. 4: Head of the Class TPB (1/05, $14.95) r/#14-19; intro. by Waid; sketch pages 15.00
Vol. 5: The Facts of Life TPB (2005, $14.99) r/#0,20-24; intro. by Wieringo; sketch pages 15.00
Vol. 6: A Different World TPB (2006, $14.99) r/#25-30; intro. by Brubaker; sketch pages 15.00
Vol. 7: Three's Company TPB (2006, $14.99) r/#31-35 & The Pact #4; sketch pages 15.00
Vol. 8: My Favorite Martian TPB (2007, $14.99) r/#36-41; sketch pages 15.00
Vol. 9: Out of This World TPB (2008, $14.99) r/#42-47; sketch pages 15.00

INVINCIBLE FOUR OF KUNG FU & NINJA
Leung Publications: April, 1988 - No. 6, 1989 ($2.00)

1-($2.75) 3.00
2-6: 2-Begin $2.00-c 2.50

INVINCIBLE IRON MAN
Marvel Comics: July, 2008 - Present ($2.99)

1-Fraction-s/Larroca-a; covers by Larroca & Quesada 3.00
1-Downey movie photo wraparound 6.00
1-Secret Movie Variant white-c with movie cast 50.00
2-5: 2-War Machine and Thor app. 3.00

INVISIBLE BOY (See Approved Comics)

INVISIBLE MAN, THE (See Superior Stories #1 & Supernatural Thrillers #2)

INVISIBLE PEOPLE
Kitchen Sink Press: 1992 (B&W, lim. series)

Book One: Sanctum; Book Two: "The Power": Will Eisner-s/a in all 2.50
Book Three: "Mortal Combat" 4.00
Hardcover ($34.95) 35.00
TPB (DC Comics, 9/00, $12.95) reprints series 13.00

INVISIBLES, THE (1st Series)
DC Comics (Vertigo): Sept, 1994 - No. 25, Oct, 1996 ($1.95/$2.50, mature)

1-($2.95, 52 pgs.)-Intro King Mob, Ragged Robin, Boy, Lord Fanny & Dane (Jack Frost); Grant Morrison scripts in all 6.00
2-8: 4-Includes bound-in trading cards. 5-1st app. Orlando; brown paper-c 4.00
9-25: 10-Intro Jim Crow. 13-15-Origin Lord Fanny. 19-Origin King Mob; polybagged. 20-Origin Boy. 21-Mister Six revealed. 25-Intro Division X 2.50
Apocalipstick (2001, $19.95, TPB)-r/#9-16; Bolland-c 20.00
Entropy in the U.K. (2001, $19.95, TPB)-r/#17-25; Bolland-c 20.00
Say You Want A Revolution (1996, $17.50, TPB)-r/#1-8 18.00
NOTE: ***Buckingham** a-25p. **Rian Hughes** c-1, 5. **Phil Jimenez** a-17p-19p. **Paul Johnson** a-16, 21. **Sean Phillips** c-2-4, 6-25. **Weston** a-10p. **Yeowell** a-1p-4p, 22p-24p.*

INVISIBLES, THE (2nd Series)
DC Comics (Vertigo): V2#1, Feb, 1997 - No. 22, Feb, 1999 ($2.50, mature)

1-Intro Jolly Roger; Grant Morrison scripts, Phil Jimenez-a, & Brian Bolland-c begins 4.00
2-22: 9,14-Weston-a 2.50
Bloody Hell in America TPB ('98, $12.95) r/#1-4 13.00
Counting to None TPB ('99, $19.95) r/#5-13 20.00
Kissing Mr. Quimper TPB ('00, $19.95) r/#14-22 20.00

INVISIBLES, THE (3rd Series) (Issue #'s go in reverse from #12 to #1)
DC Comics (Vertigo): V3#12, Apr, 1999 - No. 1, June, 2000 ($2.95, mature)

1-12-Bolland-c; Morrison-s on all. 1-Quitely-a. 2-4-Art by various. 5-8-Phillips-a. 9-12-Phillip Bond-a. 3.00
The Invisible Kingdom TPB ('02, $19.95) r/#12-1; new Bolland-c 20.00

INVISIBLE SCARLET O'NEIL (Also see Famous Funnies #81 & Harvey Comics Hits #59)
Famous Funnies (Harvey): Dec, 1950 - No. 3, Apr, 1951 (2-3 pgs. of Powell-a in each issue.)

	GD 2.0	VG 4.0	FN 6.0	VF 8.0	VF/NM 9.0	NM- 9.2
1	15	30	45	86	133	180
2,3	12	24	36	67	94	120

ION (Green Lantern Kyle Rayner) (See Countdown)
DC Comics: Jun, 2006 - No. 12, May, 2007 ($2.99)

1-12: 1-Marz-s/Tocchini-a. 3-Mogo app. 9,10-Tangent Green Lantern app. 12-Monitor app. 3.00
...: The Torchbearer TPB (2007, $14.99) r/#1-6 15.00

I, PAPARAZZI
DC Comics (Vertigo): 2001 ($29.95, HC, digitally manipulated photographic art)

nn-Pat McGreal-s/Steven Parke-digital-a/Stephen John Phillips-photos 30.00

IRON AND THE MAIDEN
Aspen MLT: Sept, 2007 - No. 4, Dec, 2007 ($3.99)

1-4: 1-Two covers by Manapul and Madureira/Matsuda; Jason Rubin-s 4.00
...: Brutes, Bims and the City (2/08, $2.99) character backgrounds/development art 3.00

IRON CORPORAL, THE (See Army War Heroes #22)
Charlton Comics: No. 23, Oct, 1985 - No. 25, Feb, 1986

23-25: Glanzman-a(r); low print 5.00

IRON FIST (See Immortal Iron Fist, Deadly Hands of Kung Fu, Marvel Premiere & Power Man)
Marvel Comics: Nov, 1975 - No. 15, Sept, 1977

	GD 2.0	VG 4.0	FN 6.0	VF 8.0	VF/NM 9.0	NM- 9.2
1-Iron Fist battles Iron Man (#1-6: 25¢)	6	12	18	37	59	80
2	3	6	9	20	30	40
3-10: 4-6-(Regular 25¢ edition)(4-6/76). 8-Origin retold	3	6	9	16	23	30
4-6-(30¢-c variant, limited distribution)	5	10	15	32	51	70
11,13: 13-(30¢-c)	3	6	9	14	19	24
12-Capt. America app.	3	6	9	16	23	30
13-(35¢-c variant, limited distribution)	7	14	21	45	73	100
14-1st app. Sabretooth (8/77)(see Power Man)	12	24	36	87	156	225
14-(35¢-c variant, limited distribution)	52	104	156	442	821	1200
15-(Regular 30¢ ed.) X-Men app., Byrne-a	6	12	18	39	62	85
15-(35¢-c variant, limited distribution)	19	38	57	138	244	350

NOTE: ***Adkins** a-8p, 10i, 13i; c-8i. **Byrne** a-1-15p; c-8p, 15p. **G. Kane** c-4-6p. **McWilliams** a-1i.*

IRON FIST
Marvel Comics: Sept, 1996 - No. 2, Oct, 1996 ($1.50, limited series)

1,2 3.00

IRON FIST
Marvel Comics: Jul, 1998 - No. 3, Sept, 1998 ($2.50, limited series)

1-3: Jurgens-s/Guice-a 2.50

IRON FIST (Also see Immortal Iron Fist)
Marvel Comics: May, 2004 - No. 6, Oct, 2004 ($2.99)

1-6: 1-4,6-Kevin Lau c/a. 5-Mays-c/a 3.00

IRON FIST: WOLVERINE
Marvel Comics: Nov, 2000 - No. 4, Feb, 2001 ($2.99, limited series)

1-4-Igle-c/a; Kingpin app. 2-Iron Man app. 3,4-Capt. America app. 3.00

IRON GHOST
Image Comics: Apr, 2005 - No. 6, Mar, 2006 ($2.95/$2.99, limited series)

1-6-Chuck Dixon-s/Sergio Cariello-a; flip cover on each 3.00

IRONHAND OF ALMURIC (Robert E. Howard's...)
Dark Horse Comics: Aug, 1991 - No. 4, 1991 ($2.00, B&W, mini-series)

1-4: 1-Conrad painted-c 2.25

IRON HORSE (TV)
Dell Publishing Co.: March, 1967 - No. 2, June, 1967

	GD 2.0	VG 4.0	FN 6.0	VF 8.0	VF/NM 9.0	NM- 9.2
1-Dale Robertson photo covers on both	3	6	9	18	27	35
2	3	6	9	15	21	26

IRONJAW (Also see The Barbarians)
Atlas/Seaboard Publ.: Jan, 1975 - No. 4, July, 1975

	GD 2.0	VG 4.0	FN 6.0	VF 8.0	VF/NM 9.0	NM- 9.2
1,2-Neal Adams-c. 1-1st app. Iron Jaw; Sekowsky-a(p); Fleisher-s	2	4	6	8	10	12
3,4-Marcos. 4-Origin	1	2	3	4	5	7

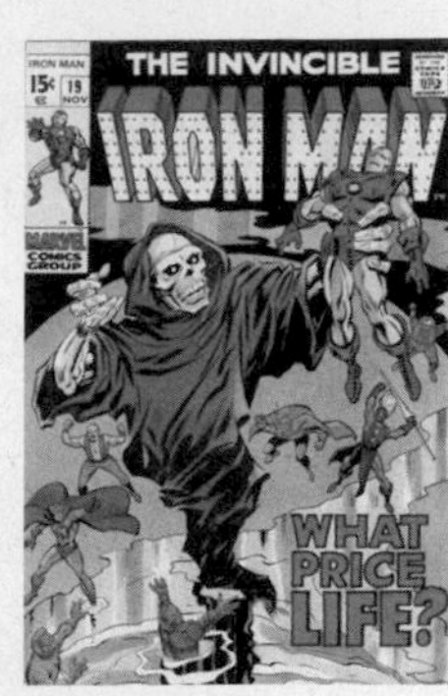

Iron Man #19 © MAR

Iron Man #262 © MAR

Iron Man V3 #50 © MAR

GD VG FN VF VF/NM NM-
2.0 4.0 6.0 8.0 9.0 9.2

IRON LANTERN
Marvel Comics (Amalgam): June, 1997 ($1.95, one-shot)

1-Kurt Busiek-s/Paul Smith & Al Williamson-a 2.50

IRON MAN (Also see The Avengers #1, Giant-Size..., Marvel Collectors Item Classics, Marvel Double Feature, Marvel Fanfare & Tales of Suspense #39)
Marvel Comics: May, 1968 - No. 332, Sept, 1996

1-Origin; Colan-c/a(p); story continued from Iron Man & Sub-Mariner #1 32 64 96 240 445 650
2 12 24 36 86 153 220
3 8 16 24 58 97 135
4,5 7 14 21 49 80 110
6-10: 9-Iron Man battles green Hulk-like android 6 12 18 39 62 85
11-15: 15-Last 12¢ issue 5 10 15 32 51 70
16-20 4 8 12 26 41 55
21-24,26-30: 22-Death of Janice Cord. 27-Intro Firebrand 3 6 9 19 29 38
25-Iron Man battles Sub-Mariner 4 8 12 22 34 45
31-42: 33-1st app. Spymaster. 35-Nick Fury & Daredevil x-over. 42-Last 15¢ issue 3 6 9 15 21 26
43-Intro The Guardsman; 25¢ giant (52 pgs.) 4 8 12 22 34 45
44-46,48-50: 43-Giant-Man back-up by Ayers. 44-Ant-Man by Tuska. 46-The Guardsman dies. 50-Princess Python app. 2 4 6 11 16 20
47-Origin retold; Barry Smith-a(p) 3 6 9 17 25 32
51-53: 53-Starlin part pencils 2 4 6 9 13 16
54-Iron Man battles Sub-Mariner; 1st app. Moondragon (1/73) as Madame MacEvil; Everett part-c 4 8 12 24 37 50
55-1st app. Thanos, Drax the Destroyer, Mentor, Starfox & Kronos (2/73); Starlin-c/a 13 26 39 93 164 235
56-Starlin-a 4 8 12 24 37 50
57-65,67-70: 59-Firebrand returns. 65-Origin Dr. Spectrum. 67-Last 20¢ issue. 68-Sunfire & Unicorn app.; origin retold; Starlin-c 2 4 6 9 12 15
66-Iron Man vs. Thor. 3 6 9 16 22 28
71-84: 72-Cameo portraits of N. Adams. 73-Rename Stark Industries to Stark International; Brunner. 76-r/#9. 2 4 6 8 10 12
85-89-(Regular 25¢ editions): 86-1st app. Blizzard. 87-Origin Blizzard. 88-Thanos app. 89-Daredevil app.; last 25¢-c 2 4 6 8 10 12
85-89-(30¢-c variants, limited distribution)(4-8/76) 3 6 9 20 30 40
90-99: 96-1st app. new Guardsman 1 3 4 6 8 10
99,101-103-(35¢-c variants, limited dist.) 4 8 12 26 41 55
100-(7/77)-Starlin-c 3 6 9 16 23 30
100-(35¢-c variant, limited dist.) 8 16 24 56 93 130
101-117: 101-Intro DreadKnight. 109-1st app. new Crimson Dynamo; 1st app. Vanguard. 110-Origin Jack of Hearts retold; death of Count Nefaria. 114-Avengers app. 1 2 3 5 6 8
118-Byrne-a(p); 1st app. Jim Rhodes 2 4 6 8 10 12
119-127: 120,121-Sub-Mariner x-over. 122-Origin. 123-128-Tony Stark treated for alcohol problem. 125-Ant-Man app. 1 3 4 6 8 10
128-Classic Tony Stark alcoholism cover 2 4 6 10 14 18
129,130,133-149 6.00
131,132-Hulk x-over 1 2 3 5 6 8
150-Double size 1 2 3 5 7 9
151-168: 152-New armor. 161-Moon Knight app. 167-Tony Stark alcohol problem resurfaces 4.00
169-New Iron Man (Jim Rhodes replaces Tony Stark) 6.00
170,171 4.00
172-199: 172-Captain America x-over. 186-Intro Vibro. 190-Scarlet Witch app. 191-198-Tony Stark returns as original Iron Man. 192-Both Iron Men battle 3.00
200-(11/85, $1.25, 52 pgs.)-Tony Stark returns as new Iron Man (red & white armor) thru #230 5.00
201-213,215-224: 213-Intro new Dominic Fortune 3.00
214,225,228,231,234,247: 214-Spider-Woman app. in new black costume (1/87). 225-Double size ($1.25). 228-vs. Capt. America. 231-Intro new Iron Man. 234-Spider-Man x-over. 247-Hulk x-over 4.00
226,227,229,230,232,233,235-243,245,246,248,249: 233-Ant-Man app. 243-Tony Stark loses use of legs 2.50
244-($1.50, 52 pgs.)-New Armor makes him walk 3.00
250-($1.50, 52 pgs.)-Dr. Doom-c/story 3.00
251-274,276-281,283,285-287,289,291-299: 258-277-Byrne scripts. 271-Fin Fang Foom app. 276-Black Widow-c/story; last $1.00-c. 281-1st brief app. War Machine. 283-2nd full app. War Machine 2.50
275-($1.50, 52 pgs.) 3.00
282-1st full app. War Machine (7/92) 4.00
284-Death of Iron Man (Tony Stark) 4.00

GD VG FN VF VF/NM NM-
2.0 4.0 6.0 8.0 9.0 9.2

288-($2.50, 52pg.)-Silver foil stamped-c; Iron Man's 350th app. in comics 3.00
290-($2.95, 52pg.)-Gold foil stamped-c; 30th ann. 3.00
300-($3.95, 68 pgs.)-Collector's Edition w/embossed foil-c; anniversary issue; War Machine-c/story 4.00
300-($2.50, 68 pgs.)-Newsstand Edition 2.50
301-303: 302-Venom-c/story (cameo #301) 2.50
304-316,318-324,326-331: 304-Begin $1.50-c; bound-in trading card sheet; Thunderstrike-c/story. 310-Orange logo. 312-w/bound-in Power Ranger Card. 319-Prologue to "The Crossing." 326-New Tony Stark; Pratt-c. 330-War Machine & Stockpile app; return of Morgan Stark 2.50
310,325: 310 ($2.95)-Polybagged w/ 16 pg. Marvel Action Hour preview & acetate print; white logo. 325-($2.95)-Wraparound-c 3.00
317-($2.50)-Flip book 2.50
332-Onslaught x-over 4.00
Special 1 (8/70)-Sub-Mariner x-over; Everett-c 4 8 12 26 41 55
Special 2 (11/71, 52 pgs.)-r/TOS #81,82,91 (all-r) 3 6 9 16 23 30
Annual 3 (1976)-Man-Thing app. 2 4 6 10 14 18
King Size 4 (8/77)-The Champions (w/Ghost Rider) app.; Newton-a(i) 2 4 6 9 12 15
Annual 5 ('82) New-a 6.00
Annual 6-8: ('83-'85) 6-New Iron Man (J. Rhodes) app. 8-X-Factor app. 5.00
Annual 9-15: ('86-'94) 10-Atlantis Attacks x-over; P. Smith-a; Layton/Guice-a; Sub-Mariner app. 11-(1990)-Origin of Mrs. Arbogast by Ditko (p&i). 12-1 pg. origin recap; Ant-Man back-up-s. 13-Darkhawk & Avengers West Coast app.; Colan/Williamson-a. 14-Bagged w/card 3.00
...: Armor Wars TPB (2007, $24.99) r/#225-232; Michelinie intro. 25.00
Manual 1 (1993, $1.75)-Operations handbook 2.50
Graphic Novel: Crash (1988, $12.95, Adults, 72 pgs.)-Computer generated art & color; violence & nudity 13.00
...Collector's Preview 1(11/94, $1.95)-wraparound-c; text & illos-no comics 2.50
...: Demon in a Bottle HC (2008, $24.99) r/#120-128; two covers 25.00
...: Demon in a Bottle TPB (2006, $24.99) r/#120-128 25.00
...: Many Armors of Iron Man (2008, $24.99) r/#47, 142-144, 152-153, 200, 218 25.00
...Vs. Dr. Doom (12/94, $12.95)-r/#149-150, 249,250. Julie Bell-c 13.00
...Vs. Dr. Doom: Doomquest HC (2008, $19.99, dustjacket)-r/#149-150, 249,250; new Micelinie intro.; bonus art 20.00
The Invincible Iron Man Omnibus Vol. 1 HC (2008, $99.99, dustjacket) r/Iron Man stories from Tales of Suspense #39-83 & Tales To Astonish #82; 1992 intro. by Stan Lee; 1975 essay by Lee; 2008 essay by Layton; gallery of original art and covers; creator bios 100.00

NOTE: ***Austin*** *c-105i, 109-111i, 151i.* ***Byrne*** *a-118p; c-109p, 197, 253.* ***Colan*** *a-1p, 253, Special 1p(3); c-1p.* ***Craig*** *a-1i, 2-4, 5-13i, 14, 15-19i, 24p, 25p, 26-28i; c-2-4.* ***Ditko*** *a-160p.* ***Everett*** *c-29.* ***Guice*** *a-233-241p.* ***G. Kane*** *c(p)-52-54, 63, 67, 72-75, 77-79, 88, 98.* ***Kirby*** *a-Special 1p; c-13, 80p, 90, 92-95.* ***Mooney*** *a-40i, 43i, 47i.* ***Perez*** *c-103p.* ***Simonson*** *c-Annual 8.* ***B. Smith*** *a-232p, 243i; c-232.* ***P. Smith*** *a-159p, 245p, Annual 10p; c-159.* ***Starlin*** *a-53p(part), 55p, 56p; c-55p, 100, 163.* ***Tuska*** *a-5-13p, 15-23p, 24i, 32p, 38-46p, 48-54p, 57-61p, 63-69p, 70-72p, 78p, 86-92p, 95-106p, Annual 4p.* ***Wood*** *a-Special 1i.*

IRON MAN (The Invincible...) (Volume Two)
Marvel Comics: Nov, 1996 - No. 13, Nov, 1997 ($2.95/$1.95/$1.99)
(Produced by WildStorm Productions)

V2#1-3-Heroes Reborn begins; Scott Lobdell scripts & Whilce Portacio-c/a begin; new origin Iron Man & Hulk. 2-Hulk app. 3-Fantastic Four app. 4.00
1-Variant-c 5.00
4-11: 4-Two covers. 6-Fantastic Four app.; Industrial Revolution; Hulk app. 7-Return of Rebel. 11-($1.99) Dr. Doom-c/app. 3.00
12-($2.99) "Heroes Reunited"-pt. 3; Hulk-c/app. 3.50
13-($1.99) "World War 3"-pt. 3, x-over w/Image 3.00
Heroes Reborn: Iron Man (2006, $29.99, TPB) r/#1-12; Heroes Reborn #1/2; pin-ups 30.00

IRON MAN (The Invincible...) (Volume Three)
Marvel Comics: Feb, 1998 - No. 89, Dec, 2004 ($2.99/$1.99/$2.25)

V3#1-($2.99)-Follows Heroes Return; Busiek scripts & Chen-c/a begin; Deathsquad app. 5.00
1-Alternate Ed. 1 2 3 5 6 8
2-12: 2-Two covers. 6-Black Widow-c/app. 7-Warbird-c/app. 8-Black Widow app. 9-Mandarin returns 3.00
13-($2.99) battles the Controller 3.50
14-24: 14-Fantastic Four-c/app. 3.00
25-($2.99) Iron Man and Warbird battle Ultimo; Avengers app. 3.00
26-30-Quesada-s. 28-Whiplash killed. 29-Begin $2.25-c. 2.50
31-45,47-49,51-54: 35-Maximum Security x-over; FF-c/app. 41-Grant-a begins. 44-New armor debut. 48-Ultron-c/app. 2.50
46-($3.50, 100 pgs.) Sentient armor returns; r/V1#78,140,141 3.50
50-($3.50) Grell-s begin; Black Widow app. 3.50
55-($3.50) 400th issue; Asamiya-c; back-up story Stark reveals ID; Grell-a 3.50
56-66: 56-Reis-a. 57,58-Ryan-a. 59-61-Grell-c/a. 62,63-Ryan-a. 64-Davis-a; Thor-c/app. 2.50
67-89: 67-Begin $2.99-c; Gene Ha-c. 75-83-Granov-c. 84-Avengers Disassembled prologue 85-89-Avengers Disassembled. 85-88-Harris-a. 86-89-Pat Lee-c. 87-Rumiko killed 3.00
.../Captain America '98 Annual ($3.50) vs. Modok 3.50

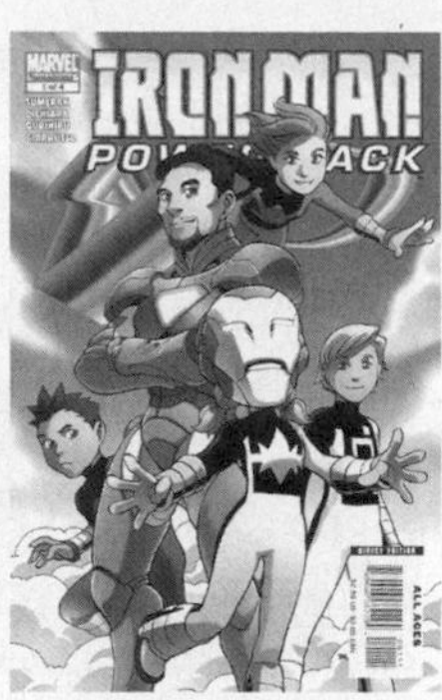

Iron Man and Power Pack #1 © MAR

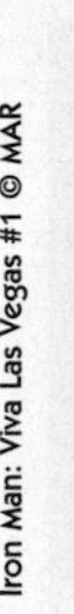

Iron Man: Viva Las Vegas #1 © MAR

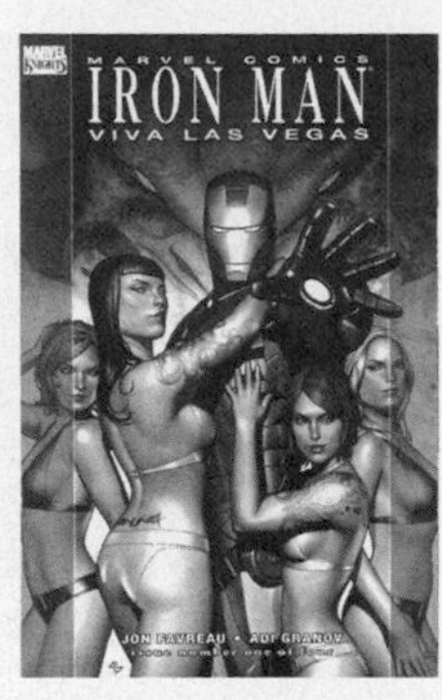

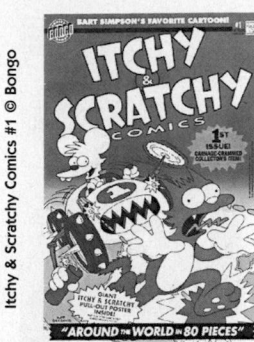

Itchy & Scratchy Comics #1 © Bongo

	GD	VG	FN	VF	VF/NM	NM-
	2.0	4.0	6.0	8.0	9.0	9.2

1999, 2000 Annual ($3.50) 3.50
2001 Annual ($2.99) Claremont-s/Ryan-a 3.00
Avengers Disassembled: Iron Man TPB (2004, $14.99) r/#84-89 15.00
Mask in the Iron Man (5/01, $14.95, TPB) r/#26-30, #1/2 15.00

IRON MAN (The Invincible...)
Marvel Comics: Jan, 2005 - Present ($3.50/$2.99)

1-($3.50-c) Warren Ellis-s/Adi Granov-c/a 3.50
2-14-($2.99) 5-Flashback to origin; Stark gets new abilities. 7-Knauf-s/Zircher-a 13,14-Civil War 3.00
15-24,26,27,29-33: 15-Stark becomes Director of S.H.I.E.L.D. 19,20-World War Hulk. 33-Secret Invasion; War Machine app. 3.00
25,28-($3.99) 25-Includes movie preview & armor showcase. 28-Red & white armor 4.00
All-New Iron Manual (2/08, $4.99) Handbook-style guide to characters & armor suits 5.00
...: Director of S.H.I.E.L.D. Annual 1 (1/08, $3.99) Madame Hydra app.; Cheung-c 4.00
...Golden Avenger 1 (11/08, $2.99) Santacruz-a; movie photo-c 3.00
Civil War: Iron Man TPB (2007, $11.99) r/#13,14, .../Captain America: Casualities of War, and Civil War: The Confession 12.00
.../Captain America: Casualities of War (2/07, $3.99) two covers; flashbacks 4.00
HC (2006, $19.99, dust jacket) r/#1-6 and Granov covers from Iron Man V3 #75-83 20.00
...: Director of S.H.I.E.L.D. TPB (2007, $14.99) r/#15-18; Strange Tales #135 (1965) and Iron Man #129; profile pages for Iron Man and S.H.I.E.L.D.; creator interviews 15.00
...: Extremis SC (2007, $14.99) r/#1-6 and Granov covers from Iron Man V3 #75-83 15.00
...: Execute Program SC (2007, $14.99) r/#7-12; cover layouts and sketches 15.00

IRON MAN AND POWER PACK
Marvel Comics: Jan, 2008 - No. 4, Apr, 2008 ($2.99, limited series)

1-4-Gurihiru-c/Sumerak-s; Puppet Master app.; Mini Marvels back-ups in each 3.00

IRON MAN & SUB-MARINER
Marvel Comics Group: Apr, 1968 (12¢, one-shot) (Pre-dates Iron Man #1 & Sub-Mariner #1)

1-Iron Man story by Colan/Craig continued from Tales of Suspense #99 & continued in Iron Man #1; Sub-Mariner story by Colan continued from Tales to Astonish #101 & continued in Sub-Mariner #1; Colan/Everett-c 14 28 42 99 175 250

IRON MAN: BAD BLOOD
Marvel Comics: Sept, 2000 - No. 4, Dec, 2000 ($2.99, limited series)

1-4-Micheline-s/Layton-a 3.00

IRON MAN: ENTER THE MANDARIN
Marvel Comics: Nov, 2007 - No. 6, Apr, 2008 ($2.99, limited series)

1-6-Casey-s/Canete-a; retells first meeting 3.00

IRON MAN: HOUSE OF M (Also see House of M and related x-overs)
(Reprinted in House of M: Fantastic Four/ Iron Man TPB)
Marvel Comics: Sept, 2005 - No. 3, Nov, 2005 ($2.99, limited series)

1-3-Pat Lee-a/c; Greg Pak-s 3.00

IRON MAN: HYPERVELOCITY
Marvel Comics: Mar, 2007 - No. 6, Aug, 2007 ($2.99, limited series)

1-6-Adam Warren-s/Brian Denham-a/c 3.00
TPB (2007, $14.99) r/#1-6; layout pages and armor design sketches 15.00

IRON MAN: INEVITABLE
Marvel Comics: Feb, 2006 - No. 6, July, 2006 ($2.99, limited series)

1-6-Joe Casey-s/Frazer Irving; Spymaster and the Living Laser app. 3.00
TPB (2006, $14.99) r/#1-6; cover sketches 15.00

IRON MAN: LEGACY OF DOOM
Marvel Comics: Jun, 2008 - No. 4, Sept, 2008 ($2.99, limited series)

1-4-Michelinie-s/Lim & Layton-a; Dr. Doom app. 3.00

IRON MAN: THE IRON AGE
Marvel Comics: Aug, 1998 - No. 2, Sept, 1998 ($5.99, limited series)

1,2-Busiek-s; flashback story from gold armor days 6.00

IRON MAN: THE LEGEND
Marvel Comics: Sept, 1996 ($3.95, one-shot)

1-Tribute issue 4.50

IRON MAN 2020 (Also see Machine Man limited series)
Marvel Comics: June, 1994 ($5.95, one-shot)

nn 6.00

IRON MAN: VIVA LAS VEGAS
Marvel Comics: Jul, 2008 - No. 4 ($3.99, limited series)

1,2-Jon Favreau-s/Adi Granov-a/c 4.00

IRON MAN/X-O MANOWAR: HEAVY METAL (See X-O Manowar/Iron Man: In Heavy Metal)
Marvel Comics: Sept, 1996 ($2.50, one-shot) (1st Marvel/Valiant x-over)

1-Pt. II of Iron Man/X-O Manowar x-over; Fabian Nicieza scripts; 1st app. Rand Banion 2.50

IRON MARSHALL
Jademan Comics: July, 1990 - No. 32, Feb, 1993 ($1.75, plastic coated-c)

1,32: Kung Fu stories. 1-Poster centerfold 2.50
2-31-Kung Fu stories in all 2.50

IRON VIC (See Comics Revue No. 3 & Giant Comics Editions)
United Features Syndicate/St. John Publ. Co.: 1940

Single Series 22 34 68 102 195 308 420

IRONWOLF
DC Comics: 1986 ($2.00, one shot)

1-r/Weird Worlds 8-10; Chaykin story & art 2.50

IRONWOLF: FIRES OF THE REVOLUTION (See Weird Worlds #8-10)
DC Comics: 1992 ($29.95, hardcover)

nn-Chaykin/Moore story, Mignola-a w/Russell inks. 30.00

IRREDEEMABLE ANT-MAN, THE
Marvel Comics: Dec, 2006 - No. 12, Nov, 2007 ($2.99)

1-12-Kirkman-s/Hester-a/c; intro. Eric O'Grady as the new Ant-Man. 7-Ms. Marvel app. 10-World War Hulk x-over 3.00
... Vol. 1: Lowlife (2007, $9.99, digest) r/#1-6 10.00
... Vol. 2: Small-Minded (2007, $9.99, digest) r/#7-12 10.00

ISAAC ASIMOV'S I-BOTS
Tekno Comix: Dec, 1995 - No. 7, May, 1996 ($1.95)

1-7: 1-6-Perez-c/a. 2-Chaykin variant-c exists. 3-Polybagged. 7-Lady Justice-c/app. 2.50

ISAAC ASIMOV'S I-BOTS
BIG Entertainment: V2#1, June, 1996 - No. 9, Feb, 1997 ($2.25)

V2#1-9: 1-Lady Justice-c/app. 6-Gil Kane-c 2.50

ISIS (TV) (Also see Shazam)
National Per.l Publ./DC Comics: Oct-Nov, 1976 - No. 8, Dec-Jan, 1977-78

1-Wood inks 2 4 6 9 13 16
2-8: 5-Isis new look. 7-Origin 1 2 3 5 7 9

ISLAND AT THE TOP OF THE WORLD (See Walt Disney Showcase #27)

ISLAND OF DR. MOREAU, THE (Movie)
Marvel Comics Group: Oct, 1977 (52 pgs.)

1-Gil Kane-c 1 2 3 5 6 8

I SPY (TV)
Gold Key: Aug, 1966 - No. 6, Sept, 1968 (All have photo-c)

1-Bill Cosby, Robert Culp photo covers 15 30 45 107 191 275
2-6: 3,4-McWilliams-a. 5-Last 12¢-c 9 18 27 65 113 160

IT! (See Astonishing Tales No. 21-24 & Supernatural Thrillers No. 1)

ITCHY & SCRATCHY COMICS (The Simpsons TV show)
Bongo Comics: 1993 - No. 3, 1993 ($1.95)

1-3: 1-Bound-in jumbo poster. 3-w/decoder screen trading card 4.00
Holiday Special ('94, $1.95) 4.00

IT GIRL (Also see Atomics, and Madman Comics)
Oni Press: May, 2002 ($2.95, one-shot)

1-Allred-s/Clugston-Major-c/a; Atomics and Madman app. 3.00

IT REALLY HAPPENED
William H. Wise No. 1,2/Standard (Visual Editions): 1944 - No. 11, Oct, 1947

1-Kit Carson & Ben Franklin stories 23 46 69 139 205 280
2 14 28 42 76 108 140
3,4,6,9,11: 4-D-Day story. 6-Joan of Arc story. 9-Captain Kidd & Frank Buck stories 11 22 33 64 90 115
5-Lou Gehrig & Lewis Carroll stories 16 32 48 94 147 200
7-Teddy Roosevelt story 14 28 42 76 108 140
8-Story of Roy Rogers 16 32 48 94 147 200
10-Honus Wagner & Mark Twain stories 14 28 42 82 121 160
NOTE: *Guardineer a-7(2), 8(2), 10, 11. Schomburg c-1-7, 9-11.*

IT RHYMES WITH LUST (Also see Bold Stories & Candid Tales)
St. John Publishing Co.: 1950 (Digest size, 128 pgs.)

nn (Rare)-Matt Baker & Ray Osrin-a 76 152 228 475 788 1100

IT'S A BIRD...
DC Comics: 2004 ($24.95, hardcover with dust jacket)

Jackie Gleason #2 © STJ

Jack of Fables #20 © Bill Willingham & DC

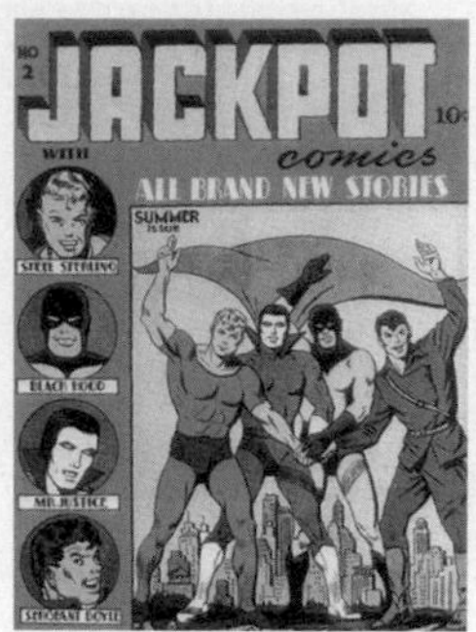

Jackpot Comics #2 © MLJ

	GD 2.0	VG 4.0	FN 6.0	VF 8.0	VF/NM 9.0	NM- 9.2
HC-Semi-autobiographical story of Steven Seagle writing Superman; Kristiansen-a						25.00
SC-($17.95)						18.00

IT'S ABOUT TIME (TV)
Gold Key: Jan, 1967

	GD	VG	FN	VF	VF/NM	NM-
1 (10195-701)-Photo-c	4	8	12	28	44	60

IT'S A DUCK'S LIFE
Marvel Comics/Atlas(MMC): Feb, 1950 - No. 11, Feb, 1952

	GD	VG	FN	VF	VF/NM	NM-
1-Buck Duck, Super Rabbit begin	15	30	45	86	133	180
2	10	20	30	54	72	90
3-11	9	18	27	50	65	80

IT'S GAMETIME
National Periodical Publications: Sept-Oct, 1955 - No. 4, Mar-Apr, 1956

	GD	VG	FN	VF	VF/NM	NM-
1-(Scarce)-Infinity-c; Davy Crockett app. in puzzle	79	158	237	494	822	1150
2,3 (Scarce): 2-Dodo & The Frog	60	120	180	375	625	875
4 (Rare)	63	126	189	394	657	920

IT'S LOVE, LOVE, LOVE
St. John Publishing Co.: Nov, 1957 - No. 2, Jan, 1958 (10¢)

	GD	VG	FN	VF	VF/NM	NM-
1,2	6	12	18	31	38	45

IVANHOE (See Fawcett Movie Comics No. 20)

IVANHOE
Dell Publishing Co.: July-Sept, 1963

	GD	VG	FN	VF	VF/NM	NM-
1 (12-373-309)	3	6	9	21	32	42

IWO JIMA (See Spectacular Features Magazine)

JACE PEARSON OF THE TEXAS RANGERS (Radio/TV)(4-Color #396 is titled Tales of the Texas Rangers; ...'s Tales of ... #11-on)(See Western Roundup under Dell Giants)
Dell Publishing Co.: No. 396, 5/52 - No. 1021, 8-10/59 (No #10) (All-Photo-c)

	GD	VG	FN	VF	VF/NM	NM-
Four Color 396 (#1)	10	20	30	73	129	185
2(5-7/53) - 9(2-4/55)	7	14	21	47	76	105
Four Color 648(#10, 9/55)	6	12	18	41	66	90
11(11-2/55-56) - 14,17-20(6-8/58)	6	12	18	37	59	80
15,16-Toth-a	6	12	18	39	62	85
Four Color 961,1021: 961-Spiegle-a	6	12	18	37	59	80

NOTE: *Joel McCrea photo c-1-9, F.C. 648 (starred on radio show only); Willard Parker photo c-11-on (starred on TV series).*

JACK ARMSTRONG (Radio)(See True Comics)
Parents' Institute: Nov, 1947 - No. 9, Sept, 1948; No. 10, Mar, 1949 - No. 13, Sept, 1949

	GD	VG	FN	VF	VF/NM	NM-
1-(Scarce) (odd size) Cast intro. inside front-c; Vic Hardy's Crime Lab begins	43	86	129	262	431	600
2	20	40	60	115	180	245
3-5	15	30	45	83	124	165
6-13	13	26	39	72	101	130

JACK CROSS
DC Comics: Oct, 2005 - No. 4, Jan, 2006 ($2.50)

1-4-Warren Ellis-s/Gary Erskine-a 2.50

JACK HUNTER
Blackthorne Publishing: July, 1987 - No. 3 ($1.25)

1-3 2.50

JACKIE CHAN'S SPARTAN X
Topps Comics: May, 1997 - No. 3 ($2.95, limited series)

1-3-Michael Golden-s/a; variant photo-c 3.00

JACKIE CHAN'S SPARTAN X: HELL BENT HERO FOR HIRE
Image Comics (Little Eva Ink): Mar, 1998 - No. 3 ($2.95, B&W)

1-3-Michael Golden-s/a: 1-variant photo-c 3.00

JACKIE GLEASON (TV) (Also see The Honeymooners)
St. John Publishing Co.: Sept, 1955 - No. 4, Dec, 1955?

	GD	VG	FN	VF	VF/NM	NM-
1(1955)(TV)-Photo-c	62	124	186	388	644	900
2-4	41	82	123	256	416	575

JACKIE GLEASON AND THE HONEYMOONERS (TV)
National Periodical Publications: June-July, 1956 - No. 12, Apr-May, 1958

	GD	VG	FN	VF	VF/NM	NM-
1-1st app. Ralph Kramden	90	180	270	563	932	1300
2	53	106	159	323	537	750
3-11	41	82	123	256	416	575
12 (Scarce)	60	120	180	375	625	875

JACKIE JOKERS (Became Richie Rich &...)
Harvey Publications: March, 1973 - No. 4, Sept, 1973 (#5 was advertised, but not published)

	GD	VG	FN	VF	VF/NM	NM-
1-1st app.	3	6	9	16	22	28
2-4: 2-President Nixon app.	2	4	6	8	11	14

JACKIE ROBINSON (Famous Plays of...) (Also see Negro Heroes #2 & Picture News #4)
Fawcett Publications: May, 1950 - No. 6, 1952 (Baseball hero) (All photo-c)

	GD	VG	FN	VF	VF/NM	NM-
nn	97	194	291	606	1003	1400
2	55	110	165	344	572	800
3-6	46	92	138	281	466	650

JACK IN THE BOX (Formerly Yellowjacket Comics #1-10; becomes Cowboy Western Comics #17 on)
Frank Comunale/Charlton Comics No. 11 on: Feb, 1946; No. 11, Oct, 1946 - No. 16, Nov-Dec, 1947

	GD	VG	FN	VF	VF/NM	NM-
1-Stitches, Marty Mouse & Nutsy McKrow	17	34	51	98	154	210
11-Yellowjacket (early Charlton comic)	20	40	60	117	184	250
12,14,15	11	22	33	64	90	115
13-Wolverton-a	21	42	63	122	191	260
16-12 pg. adapt. of Silas Marner; Kiefer-a	13	26	39	74	105	135

JACK KIRBY'S FOURTH WORLD (See Mister Miracle & New Gods, 3rd Series)
DC Comics: Mar, 1997 - No. 20, Oct, 1998 ($1.95/$2.25)

1-20: 1-Byrne-a/scripts & Simonson-c begin; story cont'd from New Gods, 3rd Series #15; retells "The Pact" (New Gods, 1st Series #7); 1st brief DC app. Thor. 2-Thor vs. Big Barda; "Apokolips Then" back-up begins; Kirby-c/swipe (Thor #126) 8-Genesis x-over. 10-Simonson-s/a 13-Simonson back-up story. 20-Superman-c/app. 2.50

JACK KIRBY'S FOURTH WORLD OMNIBUS
DC Comics: 2007 - Vol. 4, 2008 ($49.99, hardcovers with dustjackets)

Vol. 1 ('07) Recolored reprints in chronological order of Superman's Pal, Jimmy Olsen #133-139, Forever People #1-3, New Gods #1-3, and Mister Miracle #1-3; Morrison intro, bonus art 50.00
Vol. 2 ('07) r/Jimmy Olsen #141-145, F.P. #4-6, N.G. #4-6 & M.M. #4-6; bonus art 50.00
Vol. 3 ('07) r/Jimmy Olsen #146-148, F.P. #7-10, N.G. #7-10 & M.M. #7-9; bonus art 50.00
Vol. 4 ('08) r/F.P. #11, M.M. #10-18, N.G. #11 & reprint series #6, & DC Graphic Novel #6 (The Hunger Dogs); Levitz intro.; Evanier afterword; character profile pages 50.00

JACK KIRBY'S GALACTIC BOUNTY HUNTERS
Marvel Comics (Icon): July, 2006 - No. 6, Nov, 2007 ($3.99)

1-6-Based on a Kirby concept; Mike Thibodeaux-a; Lisa Kirby, Thibodeaux and others-s 4.00
HC (2007, $24.99) r/series; pin-ups and supplemental art and interviews 25.00

JACK KIRBY'S SECRET CITY SAGA
Topps Comics (Kirbyverse): No. 0, Apr, 1993; No. 1, May, 1993 - No. 4, Aug, 1993 ($2.95, limited series)

0-(No cover price, 20 pgs.)-Simonson-c/a 3.00
0-Red embossed-c (limited ed.) 5.00
1-4-Bagged w/3 trading cards; Ditko-c/a: 1-Ditko/Art Adams-c. 2-Ditko/Byrne-c; has coupon for Pres. Clinton holo-foil trading card. 3-Dorman poster; has coupon for Gore holo-foil trading card. 4-Ditko/Perez-c 3.00

NOTE: *Issues #1-4 contain coupons redeemable for Kirbychrome version of #1*

JACK KIRBY'S SILVER STAR (Also see Silver Star)
Topps Comics (Kirbyverse): Oct, 1993 ($2.95)(Intended as a 4-issue limited series)

1-Silver ink-c; Austin-c/a(i); polybagged w/3 cards 3.00

JACK KIRBY'S TEENAGENTS (See Satan's Six)
Topps Comics (Kirbyverse): Aug, 1993 - No. 4, Nov, 1993 ($2.95, limited series)

1-4: Bagged with/3 trading cards; Busiek-s/Austin-c(i): 3-Liberty Project app. 3.00

JACK OF FABLES (See Fables)
DC Comics (Vertigo): Sept, 2006 - Present ($2.99)

1-24: 1-Willingham & Sturges-s/Akins-a 3.00
...: Jack of Hearts TPB (2007, $14.99) r/#6-11 15.00
...: The Bad Prince TPB (2008, $14.99) r/#12-16 15.00
...: The (Nearly) Great Escape TPB (2007, $14.99) r/#1-5; Akins sketch pages 15.00

JACK OF HEARTS (Also see The Deadly Hands of Kung Fu #22 & Marvel Premiere #44)
Marvel Comics Group: Jan, 1984 - No. 4, Apr, 1984 (60¢, limited series)

1-4 2.50

JACKPOT COMICS (Jolly Jingles #10 on)
MLJ Magazines: Spring, 1941 - No. 9, Spring, 1943

	GD	VG	FN	VF	VF/NM	NM-
1-The Black Hood, Mr. Justice, Steel Sterling & Sgt. Boyle begin; Biro-c	321	642	963	2087	3694	5300
2-S. Cooper-c	145	290	435	906	1503	2100
3-Hubbell-c	110	220	330	688	1144	1600
4-Archie begins (Win/41; on sale 12/41)-(also see Pep Comics #22); 1st app. Mrs. Grundy, the principal; Novick-c	429	858	1287	3000	5250	7500

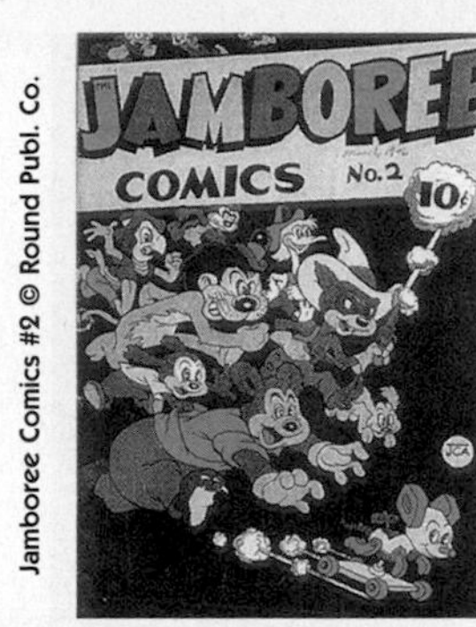

Jamboree Comics #2 © Round Publ. Co.

Jann of the Jungle #10 © MAR

Jeanie Comics #22 © MAR

GD VG FN VF VF/NM NM-
2.0 4.0 6.0 8.0 9.0 9.2

GD VG FN VF VF/NM NM-
2.0 4.0 6.0 8.0 9.0 9.2

5-Hitler, Tojo, Mussolini-c by Montana; 1st definitive Mr. Weatherbee; 1st brief app. Reggie in 1 panel 172 344 516 1075 1788 2500
6-9: 6,7-Bondage-c by Novick. 8,9-Sahle-c 110 220 330 688 1144 1600

JACK Q FROST (See Unearthly Spectaculars)

JACK STAFF (Vol. 2; previously published in Britain)
Image Comics: Feb, 2003 - Present ($2.95/$3.50)
1-5-Paul Grist-s/a 3.00
6-18-($3.50) 6-Flashback to the WW2 Freedom Fighters 3.50
... Special 1 (1/08, $3.50) Molachi the Immortal app. 0.60
The Weird World of Jack Staff King Size Special 1 (7/07, $5.99, B&W) r/story serialized in Comics International magazine; afterword by Grist 6.00
Vol. 1: Everything Used to Be Black and White TPB (12/03, $19.95) r/British issues 20.00
Vol. 2: Soldiers TPB (2005, $15.95) r/#1-5; cover gallery 16.00
Vol. 3: Echoes of Tomorrow TPB (2006, $16.99) r/#6 12; cover gallery 17.00

JACK THE GIANT KILLER (See Movie Classics)

JACK THE GIANT KILLER (New Adventures of...)
Bimfort & Co.: Aug-Sept, 1953
V1#1-H. C. Kiefer-c/a 24 48 72 139 220 300

JACKY'S DIARY
Dell Publishing Co.: No. 1091, Apr-June, 1960 (one-shot)
Four Color 1091 5 10 15 30 48 65

JADEMAN COLLECTION
Jademan Comics: Dec, 1989 - No. 3, 1990 ($2.50, plastic coated-c, 68 pgs.)
1-3: 1 Wraparound-c w/fold-out poster 2.50

JADEMAN KUNG FU SPECIAL
Jademan Comics: 1988 ($1.50, 64 pgs.)
1 2.50

JADE WARRIORS (Mike Deodato's...)
Image Comics (Glass House Graphics): Nov, 1999 - No. 3, 2000 ($2.50)
1-3-Deodato-a 2.50
1-Variant-c 2.50

JAGUAR, THE (Also see The Adventures of...)
Impact Comics (DC): Aug, 1991 - No. 14, Oct, 1992 ($1.00)
1-14: 4-The Black Hood x-over. 7-Sienkiewicz-c. 9-Contains Crusaders trading card 2.50
Annual 1 (1992, $2.50, 68 pgs.)-With trading card 2.50

JAGUAR GOD
Verotik: Mar, 1995 - No. 7, June, 1997 ($2.95, mature)
0 (2/96, $3.50)-Embossed Frazetta-c; Bisley-a; w/pin-ups. 4.00
1-Frazetta-c. 4.00
2-7: 2-Frazetta-c. 3-Bisley-c. 4-Emond-c. 7-($2.95)-Frazetta-c 3.00

JAKE THRASH
Aircel Publishing: 1988 - No. 3, 1988 ($2.00)
1-3 2.50

JAM, THE (...Urban Adventure)
Slave Labor Nos. 1-5/Dark Horse Comics Nos. 6-8/Caliber Comics No. 9 on: Nov, 1989 - No. 14, 1997 ($1.95/$2.50/$2.95, B&W)
1-14: Bernie Mireault-c/a/scripts. 6-1st Dark Horse issue. 9-1st Caliber issue 3.00

JAMBOREE
Round Publishing Co.: Feb, 1946(no month given) - No. 3, Apr, 1946
1-Funny animal 25 50 75 148 232 315
2,3 15 30 45 88 137 185

JAMES BOND 007: A SILENT ARMAGEDDON
Dark Horse Comics/Acme Press: Mar, 1993 - Apr 1993 (limited series)
1,2 3.50

JAMES BOND 007: GOLDENEYE (Movie)
Topps Comics: Jan, 1996 ($2.95, unfinished limited series of 3)
1-Movie adaptation; Stelfreeze-c 3.00

JAMES BOND 007: SERPENT'S TOOTH
Dark Horse Comics/Acme Press: July 1992 - Aug 1992 ($4.95, limited series)
1-3-Paul Gulacy-c/a 5.00

JAMES BOND 007: SHATTERED HELIX
Dark Horse Comics: Jun 1994 - July 1994 ($2.50, limited series)
1,2 3.00

JAMES BOND 007: THE QUASIMODO GAMBIT
Dark Horse Comics: Jan 1995 - May 1995 ($3.95, limited series)
1-3 4.50

JAMES BOND FOR YOUR EYES ONLY
Marvel Comics Group: Oct, 1981 - No. 2, Nov, 1981
1,2-Movie adapt.; r/Marvel Super Special #19 3.00

JAMES BOND JR. (TV)
Marvel Comics: Jan, 1992 - No. 12, Dec, 1992 (#1: $1.00, #2-on: $1.25)
1-12: Based on animated TV show 2.50

JAMES BOND: LICENCE TO KILL (See Licence To Kill)

JAMES BOND: PERMISSION TO DIE
Eclipse Comics/ACME Press: 1989 - No. 3, 1991 ($3.95, lim. series, squarebound, 52 pgs.)
1-3: Mike Grell-c/a/scripts in all. 3-($4.95) 5.00

JAM, THE: SUPER COOL COLOR INJECTED TURBO ADVENTURE #1 FROM HELL!
Comico: May, 1988 ($2.50, 44 pgs., one-shot)
1 2.50

JANE ARDEN (See Feature Funnies & Pageant of Comics)
St. John (United Features Syndicate): Mar, 1948 - No. 2, June, 1948
1-Newspaper reprints 15 30 45 88 137 185
2 12 24 36 67 94 120

JANN OF THE JUNGLE (Jungle Tales No. 1-7)
Atlas Comics (CSI): No. 8, Nov, 1955 - No. 17, June, 1957
8(#1) 36 72 108 208 329 450
9,11-15 20 40 60 115 180 245
10 Williamson/Colletta-c 20 40 60 117 184 250
16,17-Williamson/Mayo-a(3), 5 pgs. each 21 42 63 122 191 260
NOTE: *Everett c-15-17. Heck a-8, 15, 17. Maneely c-11. Shores a-8.*

JASON & THE ARGOBOTS
Oni Press: Aug, 2002 - No. 4, Dec, 2002 ($2.95, B&W, limited series)
1-4-Torres-s/Norton-c/a 3.00
Vol. 1 Birthquake TPB (6/03, $11.95, digest size) r/#1-4, Sunday comic strips 12.00
Vol. 2 Machina Ex Deus TPB (9/03, $11.95, digest size) new story 12.00

JASON & THE ARGONAUTS (See Movie Classics)

JASON GOES TO HELL: THE FINAL FRIDAY (Movie)
Topps Comics: July, 1993 - No. 3, Sept, 1993 ($2.95, limited series)
1-3: Adaptation of film. 1-Glow-in-the-dark-c 3.00

JASON'S QUEST (See Showcase #88-90)

JASON VS. LEATHERFACE
Topps Comics: Oct, 1995 - No. 3, Jan, 1996 ($2.95, limited series)
1-3: Collins scripts; Bisley-c 3.00

JAWS 2 (See Marvel Comics Super Special, A)

JAY & SILENT BOB (See Clerks, Oni Double Feature, and Tales From the Clerks)
Oni Press: July, 1998 - No. 4, Oct, 1999 ($2.95, B&W, limited series)
1-Kevin Smith-s/Fegredo-a; photo-c & Quesada/Palmiotti-c 8.00
1-San Diego Comic Con variant covers (2 different covers, came packaged with action figures) 10.00
1-2nd & 3rd printings, 2-4: 2-Allred-c. 3-Flip-c by Jaime Hernandez 3.00
Chasing Dogma TPB (1999, $11.95) r/#1-4; Alanis Morissette intro. 12.00
Chasing Dogma TPB (2001, $12.95) r/#1-4 in color; Morissette intro. 13.00
Chasing Dogma HC (1999, $69.95, S&N) r/#1-4 in color; Morissette intro. 70.00

JCP FEATURES
J.C. Productions (Archie): Feb, 1982-c; Dec, 1981-indicia ($2.00, one-shot, B&W magazine)
1-T.H.U.N.D.E.R. Agents; Black Hood by Morrow & Neal Adams; Texeira-a; 2 pgs. S&K-a from Fly #1 1 3 4 6 8 10

JEANIE COMICS (Formerly All Surprise; Cowgirl Romances #28)
Marvel Comics/Atlas(CPC): No. 13, April, 1947 - No. 27, Oct, 1949
13-Mitzi, Willie begin 21 42 63 122 191 260
14,15 15 30 45 84 127 170
16-Used in Love and Death by Legman; Kurtzman's "Hey Look" 16 32 48 94 147 200
17-19,21,22-Kurtzman's "Hey Look" (1-3 pgs. each) 14 28 42 76 108 140
20,23-27 12 24 36 69 97 125

JEEP COMICS (Also see G.I. Comics and Overseas Comics)
R. B. Leffingwell & Co.: Winter, 1944 - No. 3, Mar-Apr, 1948

Jesse James #8 © AVON

Jet Aces #1 © FH

Jezebelle #1 © WSP

	GD 2.0	VG 4.0	FN 6.0	VF 8.0	VF/NM 9.0	NM- 9.2
1-Capt. Power, Criss Cross & Jeep & Peep (costumed) begin	59	118	177	369	615	860
2	40	80	120	235	368	500
3-L. B. Cole dinosaur-c	47	94	141	287	474	660
JEFF JORDAN, U.S. AGENT						
D. S. Publishing Co.: Dec, 1947 - Jan, 1948						
1	15	30	45	84	127	170
JEMM, SON OF SATURN						
DC Comics: Sept, 1984 - No. 12, Aug, 1985 (Maxi-series, mando paper)						
1-12: 3-Origin						2.50
NOTE: *Colan a-1-12p; c-1-5, 7-12p.*						
JENNY FINN						
Oni Press: June, 1999 - No. 2, Sept, 1999 ($2.95, B&W, unfinished lim. series)						
1,2-Mignola & Nixey-s/Nixey-a/Mignola-c						3.00
...: Doom (Atomeka, 2005, $6.99, TPB) r/#1 & 2 with new supplemental material						7.00
JENNY SPARKS: THE SECRET HISTORY OF THE AUTHORITY						
DC Comics (WildStorm): Aug, 2000 - No. 5, Mar, 2001 ($2.50, limited series)						
1-Millar-s/McCrea & Hodgkins-a/Hitch & Neary-c						3.50
1-Variant-c by McCrea	1	3	4	6	8	10
2-5: 2-Apollo & Midnighter. 3-Jack Hawksmoor. 4-Shen. 5-Engineer						3.00
TPB (2001, $14.95) r/#1-5; Ellis intro.						15.00
JEREMIAH HARM						
Boom! Studios: Feb, 2006 - Present ($3.99)						
1-5: 1-Giffen & Grant-s/Lyra-a						4.00
JERRY DRUMMER (Formerly Soldier & Marine V2#9)						
Charlton Comics: V2#10, Apr, 1957 - V3#12, Oct, 1957						
V2#10, V3#11,12: 11-Whitman-c/a	6	12	18	29	36	42
JERRY IGER'S... (All titles, Blackthorne/First)(Value: cover or less)						
JERRY LEWIS (See The Adventures of...)						
JESSE JAMES (The True Story Of..., also seeThe Legend of...)						
Dell Publishing Co.: No. 757, Dec, 1956 (one shot)						
Four Color 757-Movie, photo-c	8	16	24	58	97	135
JESSE JAMES (See Badmen of the West & Blazing Sixguns)						
Avon Periodicals: 8/50 - No. 9, 11/52; No. 15, 10/53 - No. 29, 8-9/56						
1-Kubert Alabam-r/Cowpuncher #1	17	34	51	98	154	210
2-Kubert-a(3)	14	28	42	80	115	150
3-Kubert Alabam-r/Cowpuncher #2	14	28	42	76	108	140
4,9-No Kubert	8	16	24	44	57	70
5,6-Kubert Jesse James-a(3); 5-Wood-a(1pg.)	14	28	42	76	108	140
7-Kubert Jesse James-a(2)	12	24	36	67	94	120
8-Kinstler-a(3)	9	18	27	50	65	80
15-Kinstler-r/#3	8	16	24	40	50	60
16-Kinstler-r/#3 & story-r/Butch Cassidy #1	8	16	24	42	54	65
17-19,21: 17-Jesse James-r/#4; Kinstler-c idea from Kubert splash in #6. 18-Kubert Jesse James-r/#5. 19-Kubert Jesse James-r/#6. 21-Two Jesse James-r/#4, Kinstler-r/#4	7	14	21	37	46	55
20-Williamson/Frazetta-a; r/Chief Vic. Apache Massacre; Kubert Jesse James-r/#6; Kit West story by Larsen	14	28	42	80	115	150
22-29: 22,23-No Kubert. 24-New McCarty strip by Kinstler; Kinstler-r. 25-New McCarty Jesse James strip by Kinstler; Jesse James-r/#7,9. 26,27-New McCarty Jesse James strip plus a Kinstler/McCann Jesse James-r. 28-Reprints most of Red Mountain, Featuring Quantrells Raiders	7	14	21	37	46	55
Annual nn (1952; 25¢, 100 pgs.)- "...Brings Six-Gun Justice to the West"- 3 earlier issues rebound; Kubert, Kinstler-a(3)	28	56	84	162	256	350
NOTE: *Mostly reprints #10 on.* ***Fawcette*** *c-1, 2.* ***Kida*** *a-5.* ***Kinstler*** *a-3, 4, 7-9, 15r, 16r(2), 21-27; c-3, 4, 9, 17-27. Painted c-5-8. 22 has 2 stories r/Sheriff Bob Dixon's Chuck Wagon #1 with name changed to Sheriff Bob Trent.*						
JESSE JAMES						
Realistic Publications: July, 1953						
nn-Reprints Avon's #1; same-c, colors different	9	18	27	52	69	85
JEST (Formerly Snap; becomes Kayo #12)						
Harry 'A' Chesler: No. 10, 1944; No. 11, 1944						
10-Johnny Rebel & Yankee Boy app. in text	17	34	51	98	154	210
11-Little Nemo in Adventure Land	17	34	51	98	154	210
JESTER						
Harry 'A' Chesler: No. 10, 1945						
10	15	30	45	86	133	180

	GD 2.0	VG 4.0	FN 6.0	VF 8.0	VF/NM 9.0	NM- 9.2
JESUS						
Spire Christian Comics (Fleming H. Revell Co.): 1979 (49¢)						
nn	2	4	6	9	12	15
JET (See Jet Powers)						
JET (Crimson from Wildcore & Backlash)						
DC Comics (WildStorm): Nov, 2000 - No. 4, Feb, 2001 ($2.50, limited series)						
1-4-Nguyen-a/Abnett & Lanning-s						2.50
JET ACES						
Fiction House Magazines: 1952 - No. 4, 1953						
1	16	32	48	94	147	200
2-4	11	22	33	60	83	105
JETCAT CLUBHOUSE (Also see Land of Nod, The)						
Oni Press: Apr, 2001 - No. 3, Aug, 2001 ($3.25)						
1-3-Jay Stephens-s/a. 1-Wraparound-c						3.25
TPB (8/02, $10.95, 8 3/4" x 5 3/4") r/#1-3 & stories from Nickelodeon mag. & other						11.00
JET DREAM (...and Her Stunt-Girl Counterspies)(See The Man from Uncle #7)						
Gold Key: June, 1968 (12¢)						
1-Painted-c	4	8	12	22	34	45
JET FIGHTERS (Korean War)						
Standard Magazines: No. 5, Nov, 1952 - No. 7, Mar, 1953						
5,7-Toth-a. 5-Toth-c	12	24	36	69	97	125
6-Celardo-a	8	16	24	40	50	60
JET POWER						
I.W. Enterprises: 1963						
I.W. Reprint 1,2-r/Jet Powers #1,2	3	6	9	17	25	32
JET POWERS (American Air Forces No. 5 on)						
Magazine Enterprises: 1950 - No. 4, 1951						
1(A-1 #30)-Powell-c/a begins	38	76	114	219	347	475
2(A-1 #32) Classic Powell dinosaur-c/a	38	76	114	219	347	475
3(A-1 #35)-Williamson/Evans-a	40	80	120	243	389	535
4(A-1 #38)-Williamson/Wood-a; "The Rain of Sleep" drug story	40	80	120	243	389	535
JET PUP (See 3-D Features)						
JETSONS, THE (TV) (See March of Comics #276, 330, 348 & Spotlight #3)						
Gold Key: Jan, 1963 - No. 36, Oct, 1970 (Hanna-Barbera)						
1-1st comic book app.	23	46	69	171	306	440
2	12	24	36	82	146	210
3-10	9	18	27	60	100	140
11-22	7	14	21	47	76	105
23-36-Reprints	6	12	18	37	59	80
JETSONS, THE (TV) (Also see Golden Comics Digest)						
Charlton Comics: Nov, 1970 - No. 20, Dec, 1973 (Hanna-Barbera)						
1	8	16	24	56	93	130
2	5	10	15	30	48	65
3-10	3	6	9	21	32	42
11-20	3	6	9	17	25	32
nn (1973, digest, 60¢, 100 pgs.) B&W one page gags	4	8	12	24	37	50
JETSONS, THE (TV)						
Harvey Comics: V2#1, Sept, 1992 - No. 5, Nov, 1993 ($1.25/$1.50) (Hanna-Barbera)						
V2#1-5						4.00
...Big Book V2#1,2,3 ($1.95, 52 pgs.): 1-(11/92). 2-(4/93). 3-(7/93)						4.00
...Giant Size 1,2,3 ($2.25, 68 pgs): 1-(10/92). 2-(4/93). 3-(10/93)						4.00
JETSONS, THE (TV)						
Archie Comics: Sept, 1995 - No. 8, Apr, 1996 ($1.50)						
1-8						3.00
JETTA OF THE 21ST CENTURY						
Standard Comics: No. 5, Dec, 1952 - No. 7, Apr, 1953 (Teen-age Archie type)						
5-Dan DeCarlo-a	23	46	69	135	213	290
6,7: 6-Robot-c	14	28	42	80	121	160
TPB (Airwave Publ., 2006, $9.99) B&W reprint of series; Bill Morrison intro./back-c						10.00
JEZEBEL JADE (Hanna-Barbara)						
Comico: Oct, 1988 - No. 3, Dec, 1988 ($2.00, mini-series)						
1-3: Johnny Quest spin-off						3.00
JEZEBELLE (See Wildstorm 2000 Annuals)						

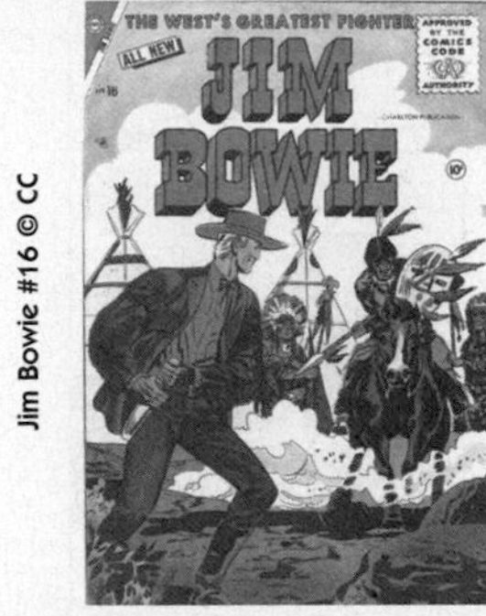

Jim Bowie #16 © CC

Jimmy Wakely #7 © DC

Jingle Jangle Comics #10 © EAS

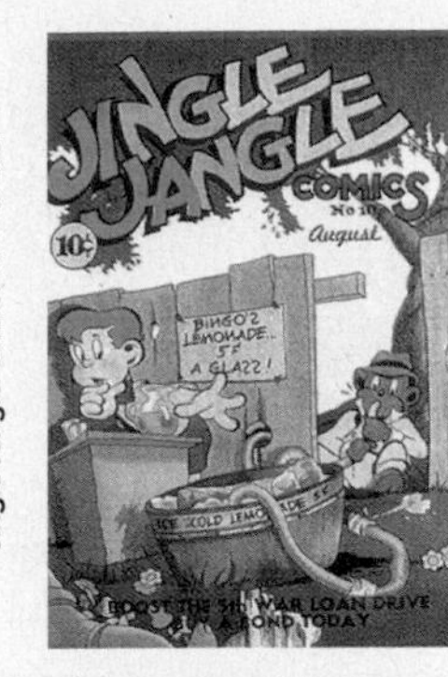

	GD 2.0	VG 4.0	FN 6.0	VF 8.0	VF/NM 9.0	NM- 9.2

DC Comics (WildStorm): Mar, 2001 - No. 6, Aug, 2001 ($2.50, limited series)

1-6-Ben Raab-s/Steve Ellis-a 2.50

JIGGS & MAGGIE
Dell Publishing Co.: No. 18, 1941 (one shot)

	GD	VG	FN	VF	VF/NM	NM-
Four Color 18 (#1)-(1936-38-r)	48	96	144	293	484	675

JIGGS & MAGGIE
Standard Comics/Harvey Publications No. 22 on: No. 11, 1949(June) - No. 21, 2/53; No. 22, 4/53 - No. 27, 2-3/54

	GD	VG	FN	VF	VF/NM	NM-
11	14	28	42	80	115	150
12-15,17-21	9	18	27	50	65	80
16-Wood text illos.	10	20	30	54	72	90
22-24-Little Dot app.	10	20	30	54	72	90
25,27	9	18	27	52	69	85
26-Four pgs. partially in 3-D	14	28	42	78	112	145

NOTE: *Sunday page reprints by McManus loosely blended into story continuity. Based on Bringing Up Father strip. Advertised on covers as "All New."*

JIGSAW (Big Hero Adventures)
Harvey Publ. (Funday Funnies): Sept, 1966 - No. 2, Dec, 1966 (36 pgs.)

	GD	VG	FN	VF	VF/NM	NM-
1-Origin & 1st app.; Crandall-a (5 pgs.)	3	6	9	20	30	40
2-Man From S.R.A.M.	3	6	9	14	20	25

JIGSAW OF DOOM (See Complete Mystery No. 2)

JIM BOWIE (Formerly Danger?; Black Jack No. 20 on)
Charlton Comics: No. 16, Mar, 1956 - No. 19, Apr, 1957

	GD	VG	FN	VF	VF/NM	NM-
16	8	16	24	42	54	65
17-19: 18-Giordano-c	6	12	18	29	36	42

JIM BOWIE (TV, see Western Tales)
Dell Publishing Co.: No. 893, Mar, 1958 - No. 993, May-July, 1959

	GD	VG	FN	VF	VF/NM	NM-
Four Color 893 (#1)	6	12	18	39	62	85
Four Color 993-Photo-c	5	10	15	35	55	75

JIM BUTCHER'S THE DRESDEN FILES: WELCOME TO THE JUNGLE (Based on the Dresden Files novel series)
Dabel Bros. Productions: Mar, 2008 (Apr. on-c) - No. 4, Jul, 2008 ($3.99, limited series)

1-Jim Butcher-s/Ardian Syaf-a; Ardian Syaf-c 5.00
1-Variant-c by Chris McGrath 8.00
1-New York Comic-Con 2008 variant-c 15.00
1-Second printing 4.00
2-4-Two covers on each 4.00

JIM DANDY
Dandy Magazine (Lev Gleason): May, 1956 - No. 3, Sept, 1956 (Charles Biro)

	GD	VG	FN	VF	VF/NM	NM-
1-Biro-c	9	18	27	47	61	75
2,3	6	12	18	29	36	42

JIM HARDY (See Giant Comics Eds., Sparkler & Treasury of Comics #2 & 5)
United Features Syndicate/Spotlight Publ.: 1939; 1942; 1947 - No. 2, 1947

	GD	VG	FN	VF	VF/NM	NM-
Single Series 6 ('39)	41	82	123	256	416	575
Single Series 27('42)	36	72	108	208	329	450
1('47)-Spotlight Publ.	15	30	45	85	130	175
2	10	20	30	54	72	90

JIM HARDY
Spotlight/United Features Synd.: 1944 (25¢, 132 pgs.) (Tip Top, Sparkler-r)

	GD	VG	FN	VF	VF/NM	NM-
nn-Origin Mirror Man; Triple Terror app.	40	80	120	235	368	500

JIMINY CRICKET (Disney,, see Mickey Mouse Mag. V5#3 & Walt Disney Showcase #37)
Dell Publishing Co.: No. 701, May, 1956 - No. 989, May-July, 1959

	GD	VG	FN	VF	VF/NM	NM-
Four Color 701	8	16	24	56	93	130
Four Color 795, 897, 989	6	12	18	43	69	95

JIM LEE SKETCHBOOK
DC Comics (WildStorm): 2002 (no price, 16 pgs.)

nn-Various DC and WildStorm character sketches by Lee 2.50

JIMMY CORRIGAN (See Acme Novelty Library)

JIMMY DURANTE (Also see A-1 Comics)
Magazine Enterprises: No. 18, 1949 - No. 20, 1949

	GD	VG	FN	VF	VF/NM	NM-
A-1 18,20-Photo-c	42	84	126	256	421	585

JIMMY OLSEN (See Superman's Pal...)

JIMMY OLSEN: ADVENTURES BY JACK KIRBY
DC Comics: 2003, 2004 ($19.95, TPB)

nn-(2003) Reprints Jack Kirby's early issues of Superman's Pal Jimmy Olsen #133-139,141; Mark Evanier intro.; cover by Kirby and Steve Rude 20.00
Vol. 2 (2004) Reprints #142-148; Evanier intro.; cover gallery and sketch pages 20.00

JIMMY WAKELY (Cowboy movie star)
National Per. Publ.: Sept-Oct, 1949 - No. 18, July-Aug, 1952 (1-13: 52pgs.)

	GD	VG	FN	VF	VF/NM	NM-
1-Photo-c, 52 pgs. begin; Alex Toth-a; Kit Colby Girl Sheriff begins	90	180	270	563	932	1300
2-Toth-a	40	80	120	235	368	500
3,4,6,7-Frazetta-a in all, 3 pgs. each; Toth-a in all. 7-Last photo-c. 4-Kurtzman "Pot-Shot Pete", 1 pg; Toth-a	41	82	123	256	416	575
5,8-15-Toth-a; 12,14-Kubert-a (3 & 2 pgs.)	31	62	93	178	282	385
16-18	26	52	78	152	239	325

NOTE: ***Gil Kane** c-10-19p.*

JIM RAY'S AVIATION SKETCH BOOK
Vital Publishers: Mar-Apr, 1946 - No. 2, May-June, 1946

	GD	VG	FN	VF	VF/NM	NM-
1-Picture stories about planes and pilots	40	80	120	235	368	500
2	26	52	78	150	235	320

JIM SOLAR (See Wisco/Klarer in the Promotional Comics section)

JINGLE BELLE (Paul Dini's...)
Oni Press: Nov, 1999 - No. 2, Dec, 1999 ($2.95, B&W, limited series)

1,2-Paul Dini-s. 2-Alex Ross flip-c 3.00
Jingle Belle: Dash Away All (12/03, $11.95, digest-size) Dini-s/Garibaldi-a 12.00
Jingle Belle's Cool Yule (11/02, $13.95,TPB) r/All-Star Holiday Hullabaloo, The Mighty Elves, and Jubilee; internet strips and a color section w/DeStefano-a 14.00
Paul Dini's Jingle Belle Jubilee (11/01, $2.95) Dini-s; art by Rolston, DeCarlo, Morrison and Bone; pin-ups by Thompson and Aragonés 3.00
Paul Dini's Jingle Belle's All-Star Holiday Hullabaloo (11/00, $4.95) stories by various including Dini, Aragonés, Jeff Smith, Bill Morrison; Frank Cho-c 5.00
Paul Dini's Jingle Belle: The Fight Before Christmas (12/05, $2.99) Dini-s/Bone & others-a 3.00
Paul Dini's Jingle Belle: The Mighty Elves (7/01, $2.95) Dini-s/Bone-a 3.00
Paul Dini's Jingle Belle Winter Wingding (11/02, $2.95) Dini-s/Clugston-Major-c 3.00
The Bakers Meet Jingle Belle (12/06, $2.99) Dini-s/Kyle Baker-a 3.00
TPB (10/00, $8.95) r/#1&2, and app. from Oni Double Feature #13 9.00

JINGLE BELLE (Paul Dini's...)
Dark Horse Comics: Nov, 2004 - No. 4, Apr, 2005 ($2.99, limited series)

1-4-Paul Dini-s/Jose Garibaldi-a 3.00
TPB (9/05, $12.95) r/#1-4 13.00

JINGLE BELLS (See March of Comics No. 65)

JINGLE DINGLE CHRISTMAS STOCKING COMICS (See Foodini #2)
Stanhall Publications: V2#1, 1951 (no date listed) (25¢, 100 pgs.; giant-size) (Publ. annually)

	GD	VG	FN	VF	VF/NM	NM-
V2#1-Foodini & Pinhead, Silly Pilly plus games & puzzles	19	38	57	109	172	235

JINGLE JANGLE COMICS (Also see Puzzle Fun Comics)
Eastern Color Printing Co.: Feb, 1942 - No. 42, Dec, 1949

	GD	VG	FN	VF	VF/NM	NM-
1-Pie-Face Prince of Old Pretzleburg, Jingle Jangle Tales by George Carlson, Hortense, & Benny Bear begin	46	92	138	281	461	640
2-4: 2,3-No Pie-Face Prince. 4-Pie-Face Prince-c	21	42	63	124	195	265
5	19	38	57	112	176	240
6-10: 8-No Pie-Face Prince	15	30	45	85	130	175
11-15	12	24	36	69	97	125
16-30: 17,18-No Pie-Face Prince. 24,30-XMas-c	10	20	30	56	76	95
31-42: 36,42-Xmas-c	9	18	27	52	69	85

NOTE: ***George Carlson** a-(2) in all except No. 2, 3, 8; c-1-6. **Carlson** 1 pg. puzzles in 9, 10, 12-15, 18, 20. **Carlson** illustrated a series of Uncle Wiggily books in 1930's.*

JING PALS
Victory Publishing Corp.: Feb, 1946 - No. 4, Aug?, 1946 (Funny animal)

	GD	VG	FN	VF	VF/NM	NM-
1-Wishing Willie, Puggy Panda & Johnny Rabbit begin	15	30	45	84	127	170
2-4	9	18	27	52	69	85

JINKS, PIXIE, AND DIXIE (See Kite Fun Book & Whitman Comic Books)

JINX
Caliber Press: 1996 - No. 7, 1996 ($2.95, B&W, 32 pgs.)

1-7: Brian Michael Bendis-c/a/scripts. 2-Photo-c 3.00

JINX (Volume 2)
Image Comics: 1997 - No. 5, 1998 ($2.95, B&W, bi-monthly)

1-4: Brian Michael Bendis-c/a/scripts. 3.00
5-($3.95) Brereton-c 4.00
...Buried Treasures ('98, $3.95) short stories, ...Confessions ('98, $3.95) short stories,

JLA #16 © DC

JLA #29 © DC

JLA: Classified #50 © DC

	GD 2.0	VG 4.0	FN 6.0	VF 8.0	VF/NM 9.0	NM- 9.2

...Pop Culture Hoo-Hah ('98, $3.95) humor shorts 4.00
TPB (1997, $10.95) r/Vol 1,#1-4 11.00
...: The Definitive Collection ('01, $24.95) remastered #1-5, sketch pages, art gallery, script excerpts, Mack intro. 25.00

JINX: TORSO
Image Comics: 1998 - No. 6, 1999 ($3.95/$4.95, B&W)

1-6-Based on Eliot Ness' pursuit of America's first serial killer; Brian Michael Bendis & Marc Andreyko-s/Bendis-a. 3-6-($4.95) 5.00
Softcover (2000, $24.95) r/#1-6; intro. by Greg Rucka; photo essay of the actual murders and police documents 25.00
Hardcover (2000, $49.95) signed & numbered 50.00

JLA (See Justice League of America and Justice Leagues)
DC Comics: Jan, 1997 - No. 125, Apr, 2006 ($1.95/$1.99/$2.25/$2.50)

	GD	VG	FN	VF	VF/NM	NM-
1-Morrison-s/Porter & Dell-a. The Hyperclan app.	2	4	6	9	12	15
2	1	3	4	6	8	10
3,4	1	2	3	5	7	9

5-Membership drive; Tomorrow Woman app. 6.00
6-9: 8-Green Arrow joins. 6.00
10-21: 10-Rock of Ages begins. 11-Joker and Luthor-c/app. 15-($2.95) Rock of Ages concludes. 16-New members join; Prometheus app. 17,20-Jorgensen-a. 18-21-Waid-s. 20,21-Adam Strange c/app. 5.00
22-40: 22-Begin $1.99-c; Sandman (Daniel) app. 27-Amazo app. 28-31-JSA app. 35-Hal Jordan/Spectre app. 36-40-World War 3 2.50
41-($2.99) Conclusion of World War 3; last Morrison-s 3.00
42-46: 43-Waid-s; Ra's al Ghul app. 44-Begin $2.25-c. 46-Batman leaves 2.50
47-49: 47-Hitch & Neary-a begins; JLA battles Queen of Fables 2.50
50-($3.75) JLA vs. Dr. Destiny; art by Hitch & various 3.75
51-74: 52-55-Hitch-a. 59-Joker: Last Laugh. 61-68-Kelly-s/Mahnke-a. 69-73-Hunt for Aquaman;
bi-monthly with alternating art by Mahnke and Guichet 2.50
75-(1/03, $3.95) leads into Aquaman (4th series) #1 4.00
76-93: 76-Firestorm app. 77-Banks-a. 79-Kanjar Ro app. 91-93-O'Neil-s/Huat-a 2.50
94-99-Byrne & Ordway-a/Claremont-s; Doom Patrol app. 2.50
100-($3.50) Intro. Vera Black; leads into Justice League Elite #1 3.50
101-114: 101-106-Austen-s/Garney-a/c. 107-114-Crime Syndicate app.; Busiek-s 2.25
115-125: 115-Begin $2.50-c; Johns & Heinberg-s;Secret Society of Super-Villains app. 2.50
#1,000,000 (11/98) 853rd Century x-over 2.50
Annual 1 (1997, $3.95) Pulp Heroes; Augustyn-s/Olivetti & Ha-a 4.00
Annual 2 (1998, $2.95) Ghosts; Wrightson-c 4.00
Annual 3 (1999, $2.95) JLApe; Art Adams-c 3.00
Annual 4 (2000, $3.50) Planet DC x-over; Steve Scott-c/a 3.50
... American Dreams (1998, $7.95, TPB) r/#5-9 8.00
...: Crisis of Conscience TPB (2006, $12.99) r/#115-119 13.00
.../ Cyberforce (DC/Top Cow, 2005, $5.99) Kelly-s/Mahnke-a/Silvestri-c 6.00
Divided We Fall (2001, $17.95, TPB) r/#47-54 18.00
...80-Page Giant 1 (7/98, $4.95) stories & art by various 6.00
...80-Page Giant 2 (11/99, $4.95) Green Arrow & Hawkman app. Hitch-c 6.00
...80-Page Giant 3 (10/00, $5.95) Pariah & Harbinger; intro. Moon Maiden 6.00
...Foreign Bodies (1999, $5.95, one-shot) Kobra app.; Semeiks-a 6.00
...Gallery (1997, $2.95) pin-ups by various; Quitely-c 3.00
...God & Monsters (2001, $6.95, one-shot) Benefiel-a/c 7.00
Golden Perfect (2003, $12.95, TPB) r/#61-65 13.00
.../ Haven: Anathema (2002, $6.95) Concludes the Haven: The Broken City series 7.00
.../ Haven: Arrival (2001, $6.95) Leads into the Haven: The Broken City series 7.00
...In Crisis Secret Files 1 (11/98, $4.95) recap of JLA in DC x-overs 5.00
...: Island of Dr. Moreau, The (2002, $6.95, one-shot) Elseworlds; Pugh-c/a; Thomas-s 7.00
.../ JSA Secret Files & Origins (1/03, $4.95) prelude to JLA/JSA: Virtue & Vice; short stories and pin-ups by various; Pacheco-c 5.00
.../ JSA: Virtue and Vice HC (2002, $24.95) Teams battle Despero & Johnny Sorrow; Goyer & Johns-s/Pacheco-a/c 25.00
.../ JSA: Virtue and Vice SC (2003, $17.95) 18.00
Justice For All (1999, $14.95, TPB) r/#24-33 15.00
New World Order (1997, $5.95, TPB) r/#1-4 6.00
...: Obsidian Age Book One, The (2003, $12.95) r/#66-71 13.00
...: Obsidian Age Book Two, The (2003, $12.95) r/#72-76 13.00
One Million (2004, $19.95, TPB) r/#DC One Million #1-4 and other #1,000,000 x-overs 20.00
...: Our Worlds at War (9/01, $2.95) Jae Lee-c; Aquaman presumed dead 3.00
...: Pain of the Gods (2005, $12.99) r/#101-106 13.00
...Primeval (1999, $5.95, one-shot) Abnett & Lanning-s/Olivetti-a 6.00
...: Riddle of the Beast HC (2001, $24.95) Grant-s/painted-a by various; Sweet-c 25.00
...: Riddle of the Beast SC (2003, $14.95) Grant-s/painted-a by various; Kaluta-c 15.00
Rock of Ages (1998, $9.95, TPB) r/#10-15 10.00
Rules of Engagement (2004, $12.95, TPB) r/#77-82 13.00
...: Seven Caskets (2000, $5.95, one-shot) Brereton-s/painted-c/a 6.00
...: Shogun of Steel (2002, $6.95, one-shot) Elseworlds; Justiniano-c/a 7.00
...Showcase 80-Page Giant (2/00, $4.95) Hitch-c 5.00
Strength in Numbers (1998, $12.95, TPB) r/#16-23, Secret Files #2 and Prometheus #1 13.00
...Superpower (1999, $5.95, one-shot) Arcudi-s/Eaton-a; Mark Antaeus joins 6.00
Syndicate Rules (2005, $17.99, TPB) r/#107-114, Secret Files #4 18.00
Terror Incognita (2002, $12.95, TPB) r/#55-60 13.00
The Tenth Circle (2004, $12.95, TPB) r/#94-99 13.00
...: The Greatest Stories Ever Told TPB (2006, $19.99) r/Justice League of America #19,71,122, 166-168,200, Justice League #1, JLA Secret Files #1 and JLA #61; Alex Ross-c 20.00
Tower of Babel (2001, $12.95, TPB) r/#42-46, Secret Files #3, 80-Page Giant #1 13.00
Trial By Fire (2004, $12.95, TPB) r/#84-89 13.00
...Vs. Predator (DC/Dark Horse, 2000, $5.95, one-shot) Nolan-c/a 6.00
...: Welcome to the Working Week (2003, $6.95, one-shot) Patton Oswalt-s 7.00
...: World War III (2000, $12.95, TPB) r/#34-41 13.00
...: World Without a Justice League (2006, $12.99, TPB) r/#120-125 13.00
...: Zatanna's Search (2003, $12.95, TPB) rep. Zatanna's early app. & origin; Bolland-c 13.00

JLA: ACT OF GOD
DC Comics: 2000 - No. 3, 2001 ($4.95, limited series)

1-3-Elseworlds; metahumans lose their powers; Moench-s/Dave Ross-a 5.00

JLA: AGE OF WONDER
DC Comics: 2003 - No. 2, 2003 ($5.95, limited series)

1,2-Elseworlds; Superman and the League of Science during the Industrial Revolution 6.00

JLA: A LEAGUE OF ONE
DC Comics: 2000 (Graphic novel)

Hardcover ($24.95) Christopher Moeller-s/painted-a 25.00
Softcover (2002, $14.95) 15.00

JLA/AVENGERS (See Avengers/JLA for #2 & #4)
Marvel Comics: Sept, 2003; No. 3, Dec, 2003 ($5.95, limited series)

1-Busiek-s/Pérez-a; wraparound-c; Krona, Starro, Grandmaster, Terminus app. 6.00
3-Busiek-s/Pérez-a; wraparound-c; Phantom Stranger app. 6.00

JLA: BLACK BAPTISM
DC Comics: May, 2001 - No. 4, Aug, 2001 ($2.50, limited series)

1-4-Saiz-a(p)/Bradstreet-c; Zatanna app. 2.50

JLA: CLASSIFIED
DC Comics: Jan, 2005 - No. 54, May, 2008 ($2.95/$2.99)

1-3-Morrison-s/McGuinness-a/c; Ultramarines app. 3.00
4-9-"I Can't Believe It's Not The Justice League," Giffen & DeMatteis-s/Maguire-a 3.00
10-31,33-54: 10-15-New Maps of Hell; Ellis-s/Guice-a. 16-21-Garcia-Lopez-a. 22-25-Detroit League & Royal Flush Gang app.; Englehart-s. 26-28-Chaykin-s. 37-41-Kid Amazo. 50-54-Byrne-a/Middleston-c 3.00
32-($3.99) Dr. Destiny app.; Jurgens-a 4.00
I Can't Believe It's Not The Justice League TPB (2005, $12.99) r/#4-9 13.00
...: Kid Amazo TPB (2007, $12.99) r/#37-41 13.00
...: New Maps of Hell TPB (2006, $12.99) r/#10-15 13.00
...: The Hypothetical Woman TPB (2008, $12.99) r/#16-21 13.00
...: Ultramarine Corps TPB (2007, $14.99) r/#1-3, JLA/WildC.A.T.s #1 and JLA Secret Files 2004 #1 15.00

JLA CLASSIFIED: COLD STEEL
DC Comics: 2005 - No. 2, 2006 ($5.99, limited series, prestige format)

1,2-Chris Moeller-s/a; giant robot Justice League 6.00

JLA: CREATED EQUAL
DC Comics: 2000 - No. 2, 2000 ($5.95, limited series, prestige format)

1,2-Nicieza-s/Maguire-a; Elseworlds-Superman as the last man on Earth 6.00

JLA: DESTINY
DC Comics: 2002 - No. 4, 2002 ($5.95, prestige format, limited series)

1-4-Elseworlds; Arcudi-s/Mandrake-a 6.00

JLA: EARTH 2
DC Comics: 2000 (Graphic novel)

Hardcover ($24.95) Morrison-s/Quitely-a; Crime Syndicate app. 25.00
Softcover ($14.95) 15.00

JLA: GATEKEEPER
DC Comics: 2001 - No. 3, 2001 ($4.95, prestige format, limited series)

1-3-Truman-s/a 5.00

JLA: HEAVEN'S LADDER
DC Comics: 2000 ($9.95, Treasury-size one-shot)

JLA: Year One #5 © DC

Joe Palooka #18 © HARV

Joe Yank #5 © STD

	GD 2.0	VG 4.0	FN 6.0	VF 8.0	VF/NM 9.0	NM- 9.2

nn-Bryan Hitch & Paul Neary-c/a; Mark Waid-s 10.00

JLA/HITMAN (Justice League/Hitman in indicia)
DC Comics: Nov, 2007 - No. 2, Dec, 2007 ($3.99, limited series)

1,2-Ennis-s/McCrea-a; Bloodlines creatures return 4.00

JLA: INCARNATIONS
DC Comics: Jul, 2001 - No. 7, Feb, 2002 ($3.50, limited series)

1-7-Ostrander-s/Semeiks-a; different eras of the Justice League 3.50

JLA: LIBERTY AND JUSTICE
DC Comics: Nov, 2003 ($9.95, Treasury-size one-shot)

nn-Alex Ross-c/a; Paul Dini-s; story of the classic Justice League 10.00

JLA PARADISE LOST
DC Comics: Jan, 1998 - No. 3, Mar, 1998 ($1.95, limited series)

1-3-Millar-s/Olivetti-a 2.50

JLA: SCARY MONSTERS
DC Comics: May, 2003 - No. 6, Oct, 2003 ($2.50, limited series)

1-6-Claremont-s/Art Adams-c 2.50

JLA SECRET FILES
DC Comics: Sept, 1997 - Present ($4.95)

1-Standard Ed. w/origin-s & pin-ups 5.00
1-Collector's Ed. w/origin-s & pin-ups; cardstock-c 6.00
2,3: 2-(8/98) origin-s of JLA #16's newer members. 3-(12/00) 5.00
... 2004 (11/04) Justice League Elite app.; Mahnke & Byrne-a; Crime Syndicate app. 5.00

JLA: SECRET ORIGINS
DC Comics: Nov, 2002 ($7.95, Treasury-size one-shot)

nn-Alex Ross 2-page origins of Justice League members; text by Paul Dini 8.00

JLA: SECRET SOCIETY OF SUPER-HEROES
DC Comics: 2000 - No. 2, 2000 ($5.95, limited series, prestige format)

1,2-Elseworlds JLA, Chaykin and Tischman-s/McKone-a 6.00

JLA /SPECTRE: SOUL WAR
DC Comics: 2003 - No. 2, 2003 ($5.95, limited series, prestige format)

1,2-DeMatteis-s/Banks & Neary-a 6.00

JLA: THE NAIL (Elseworlds) (Also see Justice League of America: Another Nail)
DC Comics: Aug, 1998 - No. 3, Oct, 1998 ($4.95, prestige format)

1-3-JLA in a world without Superman; Alan Davis-s/a(p) 5.00
TPB ('98, $12.95) r/series w/new Davis-c 13.00

JLA / TITANS
DC Comics: Dec, 1998 - No. 3, Feb, 1999 ($2.95, limited series)

1-3-Grayson-s; P. Jimenez-c/a 3.00
...:The Technis Imperative ('99, $12.95, TPB) r/#1-3; Titans Secret Files 13.00

JLA: TOMORROW WOMAN (Girlfrenzy)
DC Comics: June, 1998 ($1.95, one-shot)

1-Peyer-s; story takes place during JLA #5 2.50

JLA / WILDC.A.T.S
DC Comics: 1997 ($5.95, one-shot, prestige format)

1-Morrison-s/Semeiks & Conrad-a 6.00

JLA /WITCHBLADE
DC Comics/Top Cow: 2000 ($5.95, prestige format, one-shot)

1-Pararillo-c/a 6.00

JLA / WORLD WITHOUT GROWN-UPS (See Young Justice)
DC Comics: Aug, 1998 - No. 2, Sept, 1998 ($4.95, prestige format)

1,2-JLA, Robin, Impulse & Superboy app.; Ramos & McKone-a 6.00
TPB ('98, $9.95) r/series & Young Justice: The Secret #1 10.00

JLA: YEAR ONE
DC Comics: Jan, 1998 - No. 12, Dec, 1998 ($2.95/$1.95, limited series)

1-($2.95)-Waid & Augustyn-s/Kitson-a 5.00
1-Platinum Edition 10.00
2-8-($1.95): 5-Doom Patrol-c/app. 7-Superman app. 4.00
9-12 3.00
TPB ('99, $19.95) r/#1-12; Busiek intro. 20.00

JLA-Z
DC Comics: Nov, 2003 - No. 3, Jan, 2004 ($2.50, limited series)

1-3-Pin-ups and info on current and former JLA members and villains; art by various 2.50

JLX
DC Comics (Amalgam): Apr, 1996 ($1.95, one-shot)

1-Mark Waid scripts 2.50

JLX UNLEASHED
DC Comics (Amalgam): June, 1997 ($1.95, one-shot)

1-Priest-s/ Oscar Jimenez & Rodriquez/a 2.50

JOAN OF ARC (Also see A-1 Comics & Ideal a Classical Comic)
Magazine Enterprises: No. 21, 1949 (one shot)

A-1 21-Movie adaptation; Ingrid Bergman photo-covers & interior photos; Whitney-a 29 58 87 170 268 365

JOE COLLEGE
Hillman Periodicals: Fall, 1949 - No. 2, Wint, 1950 (Teen-age humor, 52 pgs.)

1-Powell-a; Briefer-a 12 24 36 67 94 120
2-Powell-a 10 20 30 54 72 90

JOE JINKS
United Features Syndicate: No. 12, 1939

Single Series 12 31 62 93 178 282 385

JOE LOUIS (See Fight Comics #2, Picture News #6 & True Comics #5)
Fawcett Publications: Sept, 1950 - No. 2, Nov, 1950 (Photo-c) (Boxing champ) (See Dick Cole #10)

1-Photo-c; life story 55 110 165 344 572 800
2-Photo-c 40 80 120 235 368 500

JOE PALOOKA (1st Series)(Also see Big Shot Comics, Columbia Comics & Feature Funnies)
Columbia Comic Corp. (Publication Enterprises): 1942 - No. 4, 1944

1-1st to portray American president; gov't permission required 98 196 294 613 1019 1425
2 (1943) Hitler-c 57 114 171 356 591 825
3-Nazi Sub-c 40 80 120 235 368 500
4 34 68 102 195 308 420

JOE PALOOKA (2nd Series) (Battle Adv. #68-74; ...Advs. #75, 77-81, 83-85, 87; Champ of the Comics #76, 82, 86, 89-93) (See All-New)
Harvey Publications: Nov, 1945 - No. 118, Mar, 1961

1 49 98 147 299 492 685
2 25 50 75 145 228 310
3,4,6,7-1st Flyin' Fool, ends #25 15 30 45 90 140 190
5-Boy Explorers by S&K (7-8/46) 21 42 63 122 191 260
8-10 14 28 42 80 115 150
11-14,16,18-20: 14-Black Cat text-s(2). 18-Powell-a.; Little Max app. 19-Freedom Train-c 11 22 33 64 90 115
15-Origin & 1st app. Humphrey (12/47); Super-heroine Atoma app. by Powell 15 30 45 90 140 190
17-Humphrey vs. Palooka-c/s; 1st app. Little Max 15 30 45 90 140 190
21-26,29,30: 22-Powell-a. 30-Nude female painting 10 20 30 56 76 95
27-Little Max app.; Howie Morenz-s 10 20 30 58 79 100
28-Babe Ruth 4 pg. sty. 10 20 30 58 79 100
31,39,51: 31-Dizzy Dean 4 pg. sty. 39-(12/49) Humphrey & Little Max begin; Sonny Baugh football-s; Sherlock Max-s. 51-Babe Ruth 2 pg. sty; Jake Lamotta 1/2 pg. sty 9 18 27 50 65 80
32-38,40-50,52-61: 35-Little Max-c/story(4 pgs.); Joe Louis 1 pg. sty. 36-Humphrey story. 41-Bing Crosby photo on-c. 44-Palooka marries Ann Howe. 50-(11/51)-Becomes Harvey Comics Hits #51 8 16 24 44 57 70
62-S&K Boy Explorers-r 9 18 27 50 65 80
63-65,73-80,100: 79-Story of 1st meeting with Ann 8 16 24 40 50 60
66,67-'Commie' torture story "Drug-Diet Horror" 9 18 27 52 69 85
68,70-72: 68,70-Joe vs. "Gooks"-c. 71-Bloody bayonets-c. 72-Tank-c 9 18 27 50 65 80
69-1st "Battle Adventures" issue; torture & bondage 9 18 27 52 69 85
81-99,101-115: 104,107-Humphrey & Little Max-s 7 14 21 37 46 55
116-S&K Boy Explorers-r (Giant, '60) 9 18 27 47 61 75
117-(84 pg. Giant) r/Commie issues #66,67; Powell-a 9 18 27 50 65 80
118-(84 pg. Giant) Jack Dempsey 2 pg. sty, Powell-a 9 18 27 47 61 75
...Visits the Lost City nn (1945)(One Shot)(50¢)-164 page continuous story strip reprint. Has biography & photo of Ham Fisher; possibly the single longest comic book story published in that era (159 pgs.?) 179 358 537 1119 1860 2600

NOTE: ***Nostrand/Powell** a-73. **Powell** a-7, 8, 10, 12, 14, 17, 19, 26-45, 47-53, 70, 73 at least. Black Cat text stories #8, 12, 13, 19.*

JOE PSYCHO & MOO FROG
Goblin Studios: 1996 - No. 5, 1997 ($2.50, B&W)

1-5: 4-Two covers 2.50
...Full Color Extravagarbonzo ($2.95, color) 3.00

John Byrne's Next Men #5 © John Byrne

John Law Detective #1 © Will Eisner

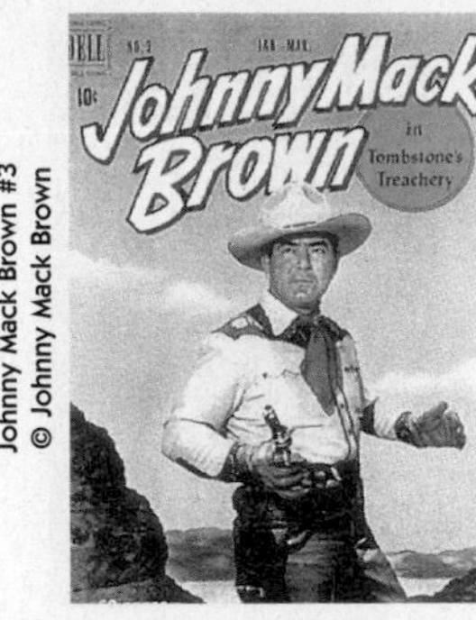

Johnny Mack Brown #3 © Johnny Mack Brown

	GD 2.0	VG 4.0	FN 6.0	VF 8.0	VF/NM 9.0	NM- 9.2

JOE YANK (Korean War)
Standard Comics (Visual Editions): No. 5, Mar, 1952 - No. 16, 1954

5-Toth, Celardo, Tuska-a	10	20	30	54	72	90
6-Toth, Severin/Elder-a	9	18	27	52	69	85
7-Pinhead Perkins by Dan DeCarlo (in all?)	7	14	21	37	46	55
8-Toth-c	8	16	24	42	54	65
9-16: 9-Andru-c. 12-Andru-a	7	14	21	35	43	50

JOHN BOLTON'S HALLS OF HORROR
Eclipse Comics: June, 1985 - No. 2, June, 1985 ($1.75, limited series)

1,2-British-r; Bolton-c/a 3.00

JOHN BOLTON'S STRANGE WINK
Dark Horse Comics: Mar, 1998 - No. 3, May, 1998 ($2.95, B&W, limited series)

1-3-Anthology; Bolton-s/c/a 3.00

JOHN BYRNE'S NEXT MEN (See Dark Horse Presents #54)
Dark Horse Comics (Legend imprint #19 on): Jan, 1992 - No. 30, Dec, 1994 ($2.50, mature)

1-Silver foil embossed-c; Byrne-c/a/scripts in all 4.00
1-4: 1-2nd printing with gold ink logo 2.50
0-(2/92)-r/chapters 1-4 from DHP w/new Byrne-c 2.50
5-20,22-30: 7-10-MA #1-4 mini-series on flip side. 16-Origin of Mark IV. 17-Miller-c. 19-22-Faith storyline. 23-26-Power storyline. 27-30-Lies storyline Pt. 1-4 2.50
21-(12/93) 1st Hellboy; cover and Hellboy pages by Mike Mignola; Byrne other pages 3 6 9 18 27 35
...Parallel, Book 2 ($16.95)-TPB; r/#7-12 17.00
...Fame, Book 3($16.95)-TPB r/#13-18 17.00
...Faith, Book 4($14.95)-TPB r/#19-22 15.00

NOTE: *Issues 1 through 6 contain certificates redeemable for an exclusive Next Men trading card set by Byrne. Prices are for complete books.* ***Cody*** *painted c-23-26.* ***Mignola*** *a-21(part); c-21.*

JOHN BYRNE'S 2112
Dark Horse Comics (Legend): Oct, 1994 ($9.95, TPB)

1-Byrne-c/a/s 10.00

JOHN CARTER OF MARS (See The Funnies & Tarzan #207)
Dell Publishing Co.: No. 375, Mar-May, 1952 - No. 488, Aug-Oct, 1953 (Edgar Rice Burroughs)

Four Color 375 (#1)-Origin; Jesse Marsh-a	25	50	75	186	333	480
Four Color 437, 488-Painted-c	15	30	45	111	198	285

JOHN CARTER OF MARS
Gold Key: Apr, 1964 - No. 3, Oct, 1964

1(10104-404)-r/4-Color #375; Jesse Marsh-a	6	12	18	41	66	90
2(407), 3(410)-r/4-Color #437 & 488; Marsh-a	4	8	12	28	44	60

JOHN CARTER OF MARS
House of Greystroke: 1970 (10-1/2x16-1/2", 72 pgs., B&W, paper-c)

1941-42 Sunday strip-r; John Coleman Burroughs-a	3	6	9	20	30	40

JOHN CARTER, WARLORD OF MARS (Also see Weird Worlds)
Marvel Comics: June, 1977 - No. 28, Oct, 1979

1,18: 1-Origin. 18-Frank Miller-a(p)(1st publ. Marvel work)	1	2	3	5	7	9
1-(35¢-c variant, limited dist.)	3	6	9	20	30	40
2-5-(35¢-c variants, limited dist.)	3	6	9	16	23	30
2-17,19-28: 11-Origin Dejah Thoris						4.00
Annuals 1-3: 1(1977). 2(1978). 3(1979)-All 52 pgs. with new book-length stories						5.00

NOTE: ***Austin*** *c-24i.* ***Gil Kane*** *a-1-10p; c-1p, 2p, 3, 4-9p, 10, 15p, Annual 1p.* ***Layton*** *a-17i.* ***Miller*** *c-25, 26p.* ***Nebres*** *a-2-4i, 8-16i; c(i)-6-9, 11-22, 25, Annual 1.* ***Perez*** *c-24p.* ***Simonson*** *a-15p.* ***Sutton*** *a-7i.*

JOHN CONSTANTINE - HELLBLAZER SPECIAL: PAPA MIDNITE
DC Comics (Vertigo): April, 2005 - No. 5, Aug, 2005 ($2.95/$2.99, limited series)

1-5-Origin of Papa Midnite; Akins-a/Johnson-s 3.00

JOHN F. KENNEDY, CHAMPION OF FREEDOM
Worden & Childs: 1964 (no month) (25¢)

nn-Photo-c	7	14	21	49	80	110

JOHN F. KENNEDY LIFE STORY
Dell Publishing Co.: Aug-Oct, 1964; Nov, 1965; June, 1966 (12¢)

12-378-410-Photo-c	6	12	18	41	66	90
12-378-511 (reprint, 11/65)	3	6	9	21	32	42
12-378-606 (reprint, 6/66)	3	6	9	19	29	38

JOHN FORCE (See Magic Agent)

JOHN HIX SCRAP BOOK, THE
Eastern Color Printing Co. (McNaught Synd.): Late 1930's (no date) (10¢, 68 pgs., regular size)

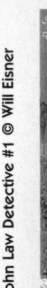

	GD 2.0	VG 4.0	FN 6.0	VF 8.0	VF/NM 9.0	NM- 9.2

1-Strange As It Seems (resembles Single Series books)	40	80	120	235	368	500
2-Strange As It Seems	26	52	78	152	239	325

JOHN JAKES' MULLKON EMPIRE
Tekno Comix: Sept, 1995 - No. 6, Feb, 1996 ($1.95)

1-6 2.50

JOHN LAW DETECTIVE (See Smash Comics #3)
Eclipse Comics: April, 1983 ($1.50, Baxter paper)

1-Three Eisner stories originally drawn in 1948 for the never published John Law #1; original cover pencilled in 1948 & inked in 1982 by Eisner 3.00

JOHN McCAIN (See Presidential Material: John McCain)

JOHNNY APPLESEED (See Story Hour Series)

JOHNNY CASH (See Hello, I'm...)

JOHNNY DANGER (See Movie Comics, 1946)
Toby Press: 1950 (Based on movie serial)

1-Photo-c; Sparling-a	17	34	51	100	158	215

JOHNNY DANGER PRIVATE DETECTIVE
Toby Press: Aug, 1954 (Reprinted in Danger #11 by Super)

1-Photo-c; Opium den story	14	28	42	78	112	145

JOHNNY DELGADO IS DEAD
Image Comics: Sept, 2007 - Present ($3.99)

1,2-Chris Moreno-a/John Leekley & Michael D. Olmos-s 4.00

JOHNNY DYNAMITE (Formerly Dynamite #1-9; Foreign Intrigues #14 on)
Charlton Comics: No. 10, June, 1955 - No. 12, Oct, 1955

10-12	11	22	33	60	83	105

JOHNNY DYNAMITE
Dark Horse Comics: Sept, 1994 - Dec, 1994 ($2.95, B&W & red, limited series)

1-4: Max Allan Collins scripts in all; Terry Beatty-a 3.00
...: Underworld GN (AiT/Planet Lar, 3/03, $12.95, B&W) r/#1-4 in B&W without red 13.00

JOHNNY HAZARD
Best Books (Standard Comics) (King Features): No. 5, Aug, 1948 - No. 8, May, 1949; No. 35, date?

5-Strip reprints by Frank Robbins (c/a)	18	36	54	105	165	225
6,8-Strip reprints by Frank Robbins	15	30	45	88	137	185
7,35: 7-New art, not Robbins	12	24	36	67	94	120

JOHNNY JASON (...Teen Reporter)
Dell Publishing Co.: Feb-Apr, 1962 - No. 2, June-Aug, 1962

Four Color 1302, 2(01380-208)	4	8	12	24	37	50

JOHNNY LAW, SKY RANGER
Good Comics (Lev Gleason): Apr, 1955 - No. 3, Aug, 1955; No. 4, Nov, 1955

1-Edmond Good-c/a	10	20	30	56	76	95
2-4	7	14	21	35	43	50

JOHNNY MACK BROWN (Western star; see Western Roundup under Dell Giants)
Dell Publishing Co.: No. 269, Mar, 1950 - No. 963, Feb, 1959 (All Photo-c)

Four Color 269(#1)(3/50, 52pgs.)-Johnny Mack Brown & his horse Rebel begin; photo front/back-c begin; Marsh-a in #1-9	22	44	66	160	285	410
2(10-12/50, 52pgs.)	11	22	33	79	140	200
3(1-3/51, 52pgs.)	9	18	27	63	107	150
4-10 (9-11/52)(36pgs.), Four Color 455,493,541,584,618,645,685,722,776,834,963	7	14	21	47	76	105
Four Color 922-Manning-a	7	14	21	45	73	100

JOHNNY NEMO
Eclipse Comics: Sept, 1985 - No. 3, Feb, 1986 (Mini-series)

1-3 2.50

JOHNNY PERIL (See Comic Cavalcade #15, Danger Trail #5, Sensation Comics #107 & Sensation Mystery)

JOHNNY RINGO (TV)
Dell Publishing Co.: No. 1142, Nov-Jan, 1960/61 (one shot)

Four Color 1142-Photo-c	7	14	21	47	76	105

JOHNNY STARBOARD (See Wisco)

JOHNNY THE HOMICIDAL MANIAC (Also see Squee)
Slave Labor Graphics: Aug, 1995 - No. 7, Jan, 1997 ($2.95, B&W, lim. series)

1-Jhonen Vasquez-c/s/a	1	3	4	6	8	10
1-Signed & numbered edition	2	4	6	9	12	15

John Wayne Adventure Comics #5 © TOBY

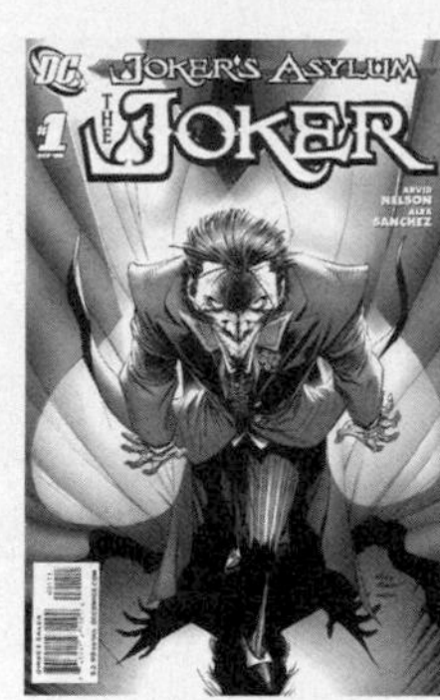
Joker's Asylum: Joker #1 © DC

Jonah Hex (2006 series) #1 © DC

GD VG FN VF VF/NM NM-
2.0 4.0 6.0 8.0 9.0 9.2

2,3: 2-(11/95). 3-(2/96) 6.00
4-7: 4-(5-96). 5-(8/96) 4.00
Hardcover-($29.95) r/#1-7 30.00
TPB-($19.95) 20.00

JOHNNY THUNDER
National Periodical Publications: Feb-Mar, 1973 - No. 3, July-Aug, 1973
1-Johnny Thunder & Nighthawk-r. in all 2 4 6 11 16 20
2,3: 2-Trigger Twins app. 2 4 6 8 10 12
NOTE: *All contain 1950s DC reprints from All-American Western.* **Drucker** *r-2, 3.* **G. Kane** *r-2, 3.* **Moreira** *r-1.* **Toth** *r-1, 3; c-1r, 3r. Also see All-American, All-Star Western, Flash Comics, Western Comics, World's Best & World's Finest.*

JOHN PAUL JONES
Dell Publishing Co.: No. 1007, July-Sept, 1959 (one-shot)
Four Color 1007-Movie, Robert Stack photo-c 5 10 15 35 55 75

JOHN ROMITA JR. 30TH ANNIVERSARY SPECIAL
Marvel Comics: 2006 ($3.99, one-shot)
nn-r/1st story in Amazing Spider-Man Annual #11; timeline, sketch pages, interviews 4.00

JOHN STEED & EMMA PEEL (See The Avengers, Gold Key series)

JOHN STEELE SECRET AGENT (Also see Freedom Agent)
Gold Key: Dec, 1964
1-Freedom Agent 6 12 18 37 59 80

JOHN WAYNE ADVENTURE COMICS (Movie star; See Big Tex, Oxydol-Dreft, Tim McCoy, & With The Marines...#1)
Toby Press: Winter, 1949-50 - No. 31, May, 1955 (Photo-c: 1-12,17,25-on)
1 (36pgs.)-Photo-c begin (1st time in comics on-c) 162 324 486 1013 1682 2350
2-4: 2-(4/50, 36pgs.)-Williamson/Frazetta-a(2) 6 & 2 pgs. (one story-r/Billy the Kid #1); photo back-c. 3-(36pgs.)-Williamson/Frazetta-a(2), 16 pgs. total; photo back-c. 4-(52pgs.)-Williamson/Frazetta-a(2), 16 pgs. total 71 142 213 444 735 1025
5 (52pgs.)-Kurtzman-a-(Alfred "L" Newman in Potshot Pete) 52 104 156 317 521 725
6 (52pgs.)-Williamson/Frazetta-a (10 pgs.); Kurtzman-a "Pot-Shot Pete", (5 pgs.); & "Genius Jones", (1 pg.) 61 122 183 381 633 885
7 (52pgs.)-Williamson/Frazetta-a (10 pgs.) 53 106 159 329 545 760
8 (36pgs.)-Williamson/Frazetta-a(2) (12 & 9 pgs.) 66 132 198 413 682 950
9-11: Photo western-c 39 78 117 225 355 485
12,14-Photo war-c. 12-Kurtzman-a(2 pg.) "Genius" 39 78 117 225 355 485
13,15: 13,15-Line-drawn-c begin, end #24 33 66 99 190 300 410
16-Williamson/Frazetta-r/Billy the Kid #1 36 72 108 208 329 450
17-Photo-c 36 72 108 208 329 450
18-Williamson/Frazetta-a (r/#4 & 8, 19 pgs.) 40 80 120 235 368 500
19-24: 23-Evans-a? 29 58 87 170 268 365
25-Photo-c resume; end #31; Williamson/Frazetta-r/Billy the Kid #3 40 80 120 235 368 500
26-28,30-Photo-c 33 66 99 190 300 410
29,31-Williamson/Frazetta-a in each (r/#4, 2) 38 76 114 222 351 480
NOTE: *Williamsonish art in later issues by* **Gerald McCann.**

JO-JO COMICS (...Congo King #7-29; My Desire #30 on)(Also see Fantastic Fears and Jungle Jo)
Fox Feature Syndicate: 1945 - No. 29, July, 1949 (Two No.7's; no #13)
nn(1945)-Funny animal, humor 16 32 48 92 144 195
2(Sum,'46)-6(4-5/47): Funny animal. 2-Ten pg. Electro story (Fall/46) 10 20 30 56 76 95
7(7/47)-Jo-Jo, Congo King begins (1st app.); Bronze Man & Purple Tigress app. 90 180 270 563 932 1300
7(#8) (9/47) 66 132 198 413 682 950
8-10(#9-11): 8-Tanee begins 54 108 162 338 557 775
11,12(#12,13),14,16: 11,16-Kamen bondage-c 48 96 144 293 484 675
15,17: 15-Cited by Dr. Wertham in 5/47 Saturday Review of Literature. 17-Kamen bondage-c 50 100 150 305 503 700
18-20 48 96 144 293 484 675
21-29: 21-Hollingsworth-a(4 pgs.; 23-1 pg.) 40 80 120 244 392 540
NOTE: *Many bondage-c/a by* **Baker/Kamen/Feldstein/Good.** *No. 7's have Princesses Gwenna, Geesa, Yolda, & Safra before settling down on Tanee.*

JOKEBOOK COMICS DIGEST ANNUAL (...Magazine No. 5 on)
Archie Publications: Oct, 1977 - No. 13, Oct, 1983 (Digest Size)
1(10/77)-Reprints; Neal Adams-a 2 4 6 13 18 22
2(4/78)-5 2 4 6 9 12 15
6-13 1 3 4 6 8 10

JOKER, THE (See Batman #1, Batman: The Killing Joke, Brave & the Bold, Detective, Greatest Joker Stories & Justice League Annual #2)
National Periodical Publications: May, 1975 - No. 9, Sept-Oct, 1976
1-Two-Face app. 5 10 15 32 51 70
2,3: 3-The Creeper app. 3 6 9 18 27 35
4-9: 4-Green Arrow-c/sty. 6-Sherlock Holmes-c/sty. 7-Lex Luthor-c/story. 8-Scarecrow-c/story. 9-Catwoman-c/story 3 6 9 15 21 26
...: The Greatest Stories Ever Told TPB (2008, $19.99) r/Batman #1 and other apps. 20.00

JOKER, THE (See Tangent Comics/ The Joker)

JOKER COMICS (Adventures Into Terror No. 43 on)
Timely/Marvel Comics No. 36 on (TCI/CDS): Apr, 1942 - No. 42, Aug, 1950
1-(Rare)-Powerhouse Pepper (1st app.) begins by Wolverton; Stuporman app. from Daring Comics 297 594 891 1856 3078 4300
2-Wolverton-a; 1st app. Tessie the Typist & begin series 95 190 285 594 985 1375
3-5-Wolverton-a 54 108 162 338 562 785
6-10-Wolverton-a. 6-Tessie-c begin 41 82 123 256 416 575
11-20-Wolverton-a 40 80 120 235 368 500
21,22,24-27,29,30-Wolverton cont'd. & Kurtzman's "Hey Look" in #23-27 34 68 102 197 311 425
23-1st "Hey Look" by Kurtzman; Wolverton-a 36 72 108 208 329 450
28,32,34,37-41: 28-Millie the Model begins. 32-Hedy begins. 41-Nellie the Nurse app. 14 28 42 82 121 160
31-Last Powerhouse Pepper; not in #28 26 52 78 150 235 320
33,35,36-Kurtzman's "Hey Look" 15 30 45 84 127 170
42-Only app. 'Patty Pinup,' clone of Millie the Model 15 30 45 83 124 165

JOKER: DEVIL'S ADVOCATE
DC Comics: 1996 ($24.95/$12.95, one-shot)
nn-(Hardcover)-Dixon scripts/Nolan & Hanna-a 25.00
nn-(Softcover) 13.00

JOKER: LAST LAUGH (See Batman: The Joker's Last Laugh for TPB)
DC Comics: Dec, 2001 - No. 6, Jan, 2002 ($2.95, weekly limited series)
1-6: 1,6-Bolland-c 3.00
...Secret Files (12/01, $5.95) Short stories by various, Simonson-c 6.00

JOKER / MASK
Dark Horse Comics: May, 2000 - No. 4, Aug, 2000 ($2.95, limited series)
1-4-Batman, Harley Quinn, Poison Ivy app. 3.00

JOKER'S ASYLUM
DC Comics: Sept, 2008 ($2.99, weekly limited series of one-shots)
...: Joker - Andy Kubert-c, Sanchez-a; ...: Penguin - Pearson-c/a; ...: Poison Ivy - Guillem March-c/a; ...: Scarecrow - Juan Doe-c/a; ...: Two-Face - Andy Clarke-c/a 3.00

JOLLY CHRISTMAS, A (See March of Comics No. 269)

JOLLY COMICS: **Four Star Publishing Co.:** 1947 (Advertised, not published)

JOLLY JINGLES (Formerly Jackpot Comics)
MLJ Magazines: No. 10, Sum, 1943 - No. 16, Wint, 1944/45
10-Super Duck begins (origin & 1st app.); Woody The Woodpecker begins (not same as Lantz character) 40 80 120 235 368 500
11 (Fall, '43)-2nd Super Duck(see Hangman #8) 20 40 60 117 184 250
12-Hitler-c 28 56 84 162 256 350
13-16: 13-Sahle-c. 15,16-Vigoda-c 14 28 42 80 115 150

JONAH HEX (See All-Star Western, Hex and Weird Western Tales)
National Periodical Pub./DC Comics: Mar-Apr, 1977 - No. 92, Aug, 1985
1 9 18 27 63 107 150
2 5 10 15 35 55 75
3,4,9: 9-Wrightson-c. 4 8 12 28 44 60
5,6,10: 5-Rep. 1st app. from All-Star Western #10 4 8 12 24 37 50
7,8-Explains Hex's face disfigurement (origin) 5 10 15 30 48 65
11-20: 12-Starlin-c 3 6 9 16 23 30
21-32: 31,32-Origin retold 2 4 6 9 13 16
33-50 1 3 4 6 8 10
51-80 6.00
81-91: 89-Mark Texeira-a. 91-Cover swipe from Superman #243 (hugging a mystery woman) 1 2 3 4 5 7
92-Story cont'd in Hex #1 3 6 9 14 19 24
NOTE: **Ayers** *a(p)-35-37, 40, 41, 44-53, 56, 58-82.* **Buckler** *a-11; c-11, 13-16.* **Kubert** *c-43-46.* **Morrow** *a-90-92; c-10.* **Spiegle(Tothish)** *a-34, 38, 40, 49, 52.* **Texeira** *a-89p. Batlash back-ups in 49, 52. El Diablo back-ups in 48, 56-60, 73-75. Scalphunter back-ups in 40, 41, 45-47.*

JONAH HEX
DC Comics: Jan, 2006 - Present ($2.99)
1-Justin Gray & Jimmy Palmiotti-s/Luke Ross-a/Quitely-c 5.00

Jonah Hex: Shadows West #1 © DC

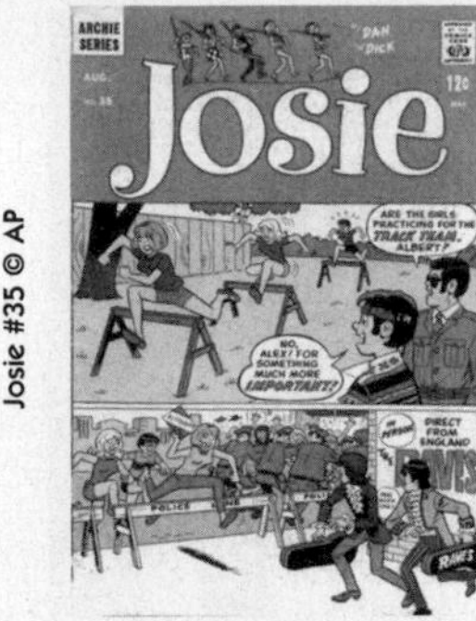

Josie #35 © AP

Journey Into Mystery #67 © MAR

GD VG FN VF VF/NM NM-
2.0 4.0 6.0 8.0 9.0 9.2

2-34: 3-Bat Lash app. 10,16,17,19,20,22-Noto-a. 11-El Diablo app.; Beck-a. 13-15-Origin retold. 21,23,27,30,32-Bernet-a. 33-Darwyn Cooke-a/c. 34-Sparacio-a 3.00
...: Face Full of Violence TPB (2006, $12.99) r/#1-6 13.00
...: Guns of Vengeance TPB (2007, $12.99) r/#7-12 13.00
...: Only the Good Die Young TPB (2008, $12.99) r/#19-24 13.00
...: Origins TPB (2007, $12.99) r/#13-18 13.00

JONAH HEX AND OTHER WESTERN TALES (Blue Ribbon Digest)
DC Comics: Sept-Oct, 1979 - No. 3, Jan-Feb, 1980 (100 pgs.)

1-3: 1-Origin Scalphunter-r, Ayers/Evans, Neal Adams-a.; painted-c. 2-Weird Western Tales-r; Neal Adams, Toth, Aragones-a. 3-Outlaw-r, Scalphunter-r; Gil Kane, Wildey-a
2 4 6 10 14 18

JONAH HEX: RIDERS OF THE WORM AND SUCH
DC Comics (Vertigo): Mar, 1995 - No. 5, July, 1995 ($2.95, limited series)

1-5-Lansdale story, Truman -a 4.00

JONAH HEX: SHADOWS WEST
DC Comics (Vertigo): Feb, 1999 - No. 3, Apr, 1999 ($2.95, limited series)

1-3-Lansdale-s/Truman -a 4.00

JONAH HEX SPECTACULAR (See DC Special Series No. 16)

JONAH HEX: TWO-GUN MOJO
DC Comics (Vertigo): Aug, 1993 - No. 5, Dec, 1993 ($2.95, limited series)

1-Lansdale scripts in all; Truman/Glanzman-a in all w/Truman-c 6.00
1-Platinum edition with no price on cover 20.00
2-5 4.00
TPB-(1994, $12.95) r/#1-5 13.00

JONESY (Formerly Crack Western)
Comic Favorite/Quality Comics Group: No. 85, Aug, 1953; No. 2, Oct, 1953 - No. 8, Oct, 1954

85(#1)-Teen-age humor 8 16 24 44 57 70
2 6 12 18 27 33 38
3-8 5 10 15 23 28 32

JON JUAN (Also see Great Lover Romances)
Toby Press: Spring, 1950

1-All Schomburg-a (signed Al Reid on-c); written by Siegel; used in **SOTI**, pg. 38 (Scarce)
64 128 192 400 663 925

JONNI THUNDER (...A.K.A. Thunderbolt)
DC Comics: Feb, 1985 - No. 4, Aug, 1985 (75¢, limited series)

1-4: 1-Origin & 1st app. 2.50

JONNY DOUBLE
DC Comics (Vertigo): Sept, 1998 - No. 4, Dec, 1998 ($2.95, limited series)

1-4-Azzarello-s 3.00
TPB (2002, $12.95) r/#1-4; Chiarello-c 13.00

JONNY QUEST (TV)
Gold Key: Dec, 1964 (Hanna-Barbera)

1 (10139-412) 34 68 102 255 465 675

JONNY QUEST (TV)
Comico: June 1986 - No. 31, Dec, 1988 ($1.50/$1.75)(Hanna-Barbera)

1 5.00
2,3,5: 3,5-Dave Stevens-c 4.00
4,6-31: 30-Adapts TV episode 3.00
Special 1(9/88, $1.75), 2(10/88, $1.75) 4.00
NOTE: ***M. Anderson*** *a-9.* ***Mooney*** *a-Special 1.* ***Pini*** *a-2.* ***Quagmire*** *a-31p.* ***Rude*** *a-1; c-2i.* ***Sienkiewicz*** *c-11.* ***Spiegle*** *a-7, 12, 21; c-21* ***Staton*** *a-2i, 11p.* ***Steacy*** *c-8.* ***Stevens*** *a-4i; c-3,5.* ***Wildey*** *a-1, c-1, 7, 12.* ***Williamson*** *a-4i; c-4i.*

JONNY QUEST CLASSICS (TV)
Comico: May, 1987 - No. 3, July, 1987 ($2.00) (Hanna-Barbera)

1-3: Wildey-c/a; 3-Based on TV episode 3.00

JON SABLE, FREELANCE (Also see Mike Grell's Sable & Sable)
First Comics: 6/83 - No. 56, 2/88 (#1-17, $1; #18-33, $1.25, #34-on, $1.75)

1-Mike Grell-c/a/scripts 3.00
2-56: 3-5-Origin, parts 1-3. 6-Origin, part 4. 11-1st app. of Maggie the Cat. 14-Mando paper begins. 16-Maggie the Cat. app. 25-30-Shatter app. 34-Deluxe format begins ($1.75) 2.50
The Complete Jon Sable, Freelance: Vol. 1 (IDW, 2005, $19.99) r/#1-6 20.00
The Complete Jon Sable, Freelance: Vol. 2 (IDW, 2005, $19.99) r/#7-11 20.00
The Complete Jon Sable, Freelance: Vol. 3 (IDW, 2005, $19.99) r/#12-16 20.00
The Complete Jon Sable, Freelance: Vol. 4 (IDW, 2005, $19.99) r/#17-21 20.00
NOTE: ***Aragones*** *a-33; c-33(part).* ***Grell*** *a-1-43;c-1-52, 53p, 54-56.*

JON SABLE, FREELANCE: BLOODTRAIL
IDW Publ.: Apr, 2005 - No. 6, Nov, 2005 ($3.99, limited series)

1-6-Mike Grell-c/a/scripts 4.00
TPB (4/06, $19.99) r/#1-6; cover gallery 20.00

JOSEPH & HIS BRETHREN (See The Living Bible)

JOSIE (She's... #1-16) (...& the Pussycats #45 on) (See Archie's Pals 'n' Gals #23 for 1st app.) (Also see Archie Giant Series Magazine #528, 540, 551, 562, 571, 584, 597, 610, 622)
Archie Publ./Radio Comics: Feb, 1963; No. 2, Aug, 1963 - No. 106, Oct, 1982

1 15 30 45 109 195 280
2 9 18 27 60 100 140
3-5 6 12 18 43 69 95
6-10 4 8 12 28 44 60
11-20 3 6 9 21 32 42
21, 23-30 3 6 9 17 25 32
22 (9/66)-Mighty Man & Mighty (Josie Girl) app. 4 8 12 23 36 48
31-44 3 6 9 15 21 26
45 (12/69)-Josie and the Pussycats begins (Hanna Barbera TV cartoon); 1st app. of the Pussycats 10 20 30 70 123 175
46-2nd app./1st cover Pussycats 7 14 21 49 80 110
47-3rd app. of the Pussycats 5 10 15 32 51 70
48,49-Pussycats band-c/s 6 12 18 37 59 80
50-J&P-c; go to Hollywood, meet Hanna & Barbera 6 12 18 43 69 95
51-54 3 6 9 17 25 32
55-74 (2/74)(52 pg. issues) 3 6 9 17 25 32
75-90(8/76) 2 4 6 10 14 18
91-99 2 4 6 9 12 15
100 (10/79) 2 4 6 11 16 20
101-106 2 4 6 10 14 18

JOSIE & THE PUSSYCATS (TV)
Archie Comics: 1993 - No. 2, 1994 ($2.00, 52 pgs.)(Published annually)

1,2-Bound-in pull-out poster in each. 2-(Spr/94) 5.00

JOURNAL OF CRIME (See Fox Giants)

JOURNEY
Aardvark-Vanaheim #1-14/Fantagraphics Books #15-on: 1983 - No. 14, Sept, 1984; No. 15, Apr, 1985 - No. 27, July, 1986 (B&W)

1 3.00
2-27: 20-Sam Kieth-a 2.50

JOURNEY INTO FEAR
Superior-Dynamic Publications: May, 1951 - No. 21, Sept, 1954

1-Baker-r(2) 66 132 198 413 682 950
2 46 92 138 281 466 640
3,4 40 80 120 235 368 500
5-10,15: 15-Used in **SOTI**, pg. 389 29 38 87 167 264 360
11-14,16-21 26 52 78 154 242 330
NOTE: *Kamenish 'headlight'-a most issues.* ***Robinson*** *a-10.*

JOURNEY INTO MYSTERY (1st Series) (Thor Nos. 126-502)
Atlas(CPS No. 1-48/AMI No. 49-68/Marvel No. 69 (6/61) on): 6/52 - No. 48, 8/57; No. 49, 11/58 - No. 125, 2/66; 503, 11/96 - No. 521, June, 1998

1-Weird/horror stories begin 300 600 900 1970 3485 5000
2 109 218 327 681 1128 1575
3,4 81 162 243 506 841 1175
5-11 54 108 162 338 562 785
12-20,22: 15-Atomic explosion panel. 22-Davis*esque*-a; last pre-code issue (2/55)
44 88 132 268 439 610
21-Kubert-a; Tothish-a by Andru 44 88 132 273 447 620
23-32,35-38,40: 24-Torres?-a. 38-Ditko-a 34 68 102 195 308 420
33-Williamson-a; Ditko-a (his 1st for Atlas?) 36 72 108 208 329 450
34,39: 34-Krigstein-a. 39-1st S.A. issue; Wood-a 34 68 102 197 311 425
41-Crandall-a; Frazetta*esque*-a by Morrow 19 38 57 141 251 360
42,46,48: 42,48-Torres-a. 46-Torres & Krigstein-a 19 38 57 138 244 350
43,44-Williamson/Mayo-a in both. 43-Invisible Woman prototype
19 38 57 141 251 360
45,47,50,52-54: 50-Davis-a. 54-Williamson-a 18 36 54 134 237 340
49-Matt Fox, Check-a 19 38 57 138 244 350
51-Kirby/Wood-a 20 40 60 150 268 385
55-61,63-65,67-69,71,72,74,75: 74-Contents change to Fantasy. 75-Last 10¢ issue
19 38 57 138 244 350
62-Prototype ish. (The Hulk); 1st app. Xemnu (Titan) called "The Hulk"
29 58 87 212 381 550
66-Prototype ish. (The Hulk)-Return of Xemnu "The Hulk"

Journey Into Mystery #517 © MAR

Journey Into Unknown Worlds #14 © MAR

JSA #24 © DC

GD 2.0 VG 4.0 FN 6.0 VF 8.0 VF/NM 9.0 NM- 9.2

25 50 75 184 330 475
70-Prototype ish. (The Sandman)(7/61); similar to Spidey villain
24 48 72 175 313 450
73-Story titled "The Spider" where a spider is exposed to radiation & gets powers of a human and shoots webbing; a reverse prototype of Spider-Man's origin
36 72 108 270 498 725
76,77,80-82: 80-Anti-communist propaganda story 15 30 45 107 191 275
76-(10¢ cover price blacked out, 12¢ printed on) 36 72 108 270 498 725
78-The Sorceror (Dr. Strange prototype) app. (3/62) 24 48 72 175 313 450
79-Prototype issue. (Mr. Hyde) 20 40 60 146 261 375
83-Origin & 1st app. The Mighty Thor by Kirby (8/62) and begin series; Thor-c also begin
600 1200 1800 5500 10,250 15,000
83-Reprint from the Golden Record Comic Set 15 30 45 109 195 280
With the record (1966) 22 44 66 164 292 420
84-2nd app. Thor 158 316 474 1383 2592 3800
85-1st app. Loki & Heimdall; 1st brief app. Odin (1 panel); 1st app. Asgard
102 204 306 867 1609 2350
86-1st full app. Odin 63 126 189 536 993 1450
87-89: 89-Origin Thor retold 50 100 150 413 757 1100
90-No Kirby-a 41 82 123 328 589 850
91,92,94,96-Sinnott-a 34 68 102 255 465 675
93,97-Kirby-a; Tales of Asgard series begins #97 (origin which concludes in #99); origin/1st app. Lava Man 40 80 120 300 550 800
95-Sinnott-a 38 76 114 285 518 750
98,99-Kirby/Heck-a. 98-Origin/1st app. The Human Cobra. 99-1st app. Surtur & Mr. Hyde
29 58 87 212 381 550
100-Kirby/Heck-a; Thor battles Mr. Hyde 29 58 87 212 381 550
101,108: 101-(2/64)-2nd Avengers x-over (w/o Capt. America); see Tales Of Suspense #49 for 1st x-over. 108-(9/64) Early Dr. Strange & Avengers x-over; ten extra pgs. Kirby-a
19 38 57 138 244 350
102,104-107,110: 102-Intro Sif. 105-109-Ten extra pgs. Kirby-a in each.
107-1st app. Grey Gargoyle 18 36 54 130 230 330
103-1st app. Enchantress 20 40 60 148 264 380
109-Magneto-c & app. (1st x-over, 10/64) 39 78 117 293 534 775
111,113: 113-Origin Loki 15 30 45 105 188 270
112-Thor Vs. Hulk (1/65); Origin Loki 45 90 135 360 655 950
114-Origin/1st app. Absorbing Man 20 40 60 148 264 380
115-Detailed origin of Loki 18 36 54 134 237 340
116-123,125: 118-1st app. Destroyer. 119-Intro Hogun, Fandral, Volstagg
12 24 36 87 156 225
124-Hercules-c/story 13 26 39 95 168 240
503-521: 503-(11/96, $1.50)-The Lost Gods begin; Tom DeFalco scripts & Deodato Studios-c/a.
505-Spider-Man-c/app. 509-Loki-c/app. 514-516-Shang-Chi 2.50
#(-1) Flashback (7/97) Tales of Asgard Donald Blake app. 2.50
Annual 1(1965, 25¢, 72 pgs.)-New Thor vs. Hercules(1st app.)-c/story (see Incredible Hulk #3); Kirby-c/a; r/#85,93,95,97 21 42 63 156 278 400

NOTE: ***Ayers** a-14, 39, 64i, 71i, 74i, 80i. **Bailey** a-43. **Briefer** a-5, 12. **Cameron** a-35. **Check** a-17. **Colan** a-23, 81; c-14. **Ditko** a-33, 38, 50-96; c-58, 67, 71, 88i. **Kirby/Ditko** a-50-83. **Everett** a-20, 48; c-4-7, 9, 36, 37, 39-42, 44, 45, 47. **Forte** a-19, 35, 40, 53. **Heath** a-4-6, 11, 14; c-1, 8, 11, 15, 51. **Heck** a-53, 73. **Kirby** a(p)-51, 52, 56, 57-60, 62-64, 66, 67, 69-89, 93, 97, 98, 100(w/**Heck**), 101-125; c-50-57, 59-66, 68-70, 72-82, 88(w/**Ditko**), 83 & 84(w/**Sinnott**), 85-96(w/**Ayers**), 97-125p. **Leiber/Fox** a-93, 98-102. **Maneely** c-20-22. **Morisi** a-42. **Morrow** a-41, 42. **Orlando** a-30, 45, 57. **Mac Pakula** (Tothish) a-9, 35, 41. **Powell** a-20, 27, 34. **Reinman** a-39, 87, 92, 96i. **Robinson** a-9. **Roussos** a-39. **Robert Sale** a-14. **Severin** a-27; c-30. **Sinnott** a-41; c-50. **Tuska** a-11. **Wildey** a-16.*

JOURNEY INTO MYSTERY (2nd Series)
Marvel Comics: Oct, 1972 - No. 19, Oct, 1975

1-Robert Howard adaptation; Starlin/Ploog-a 3 6 9 18 27 35
2-5: 2,3,5-Bloch adapt. 4-H. P. Lovecraft adapt. 3 6 9 14 19 24
6-19: Reprints 2 4 6 10 14 18

NOTE: ***N. Adams** a-2i. **Ditko** r-7, 10, 12, 14, 15, 19; c-10. **Everett** r-9, 14. **G. Kane** a-1p, 2p; c-1-3p. **Kirby** r-7, 13, 15, 18, 19; c-7. **Mort Lawrence** r-2. **Maneely** r-3. **Orlando** r-16. **Reese** a-1, 2i. **Starlin** a-1p, 3p. **Torres** r-16. **Wildey** r-9, 14.*

JOURNEY INTO UNKNOWN WORLDS (Formerly Teen)
Atlas Comics (WFP): No. 36, Sept, 1950 - No. 38, Feb, 1951;
No. 4, Apr, 1951 - No. 59, Aug, 1957

36(#1)-Science fiction/weird; "End Of The Earth" c/story
255 510 765 1594 2647 3700
37(#2)-Science fiction; "When Worlds Collide" c/story; Everett-c/a; Hitler story
103 206 309 644 1072 1500
38(#3)-Science fiction 88 176 264 550 913 1275
4-6,8,10-Science fiction/weird 54 108 162 338 557 775
7-Wolverton-a "Planet of Terror", 6 pgs; electric chair c-inset/story
90 180 270 563 932 1300
9-Giant eyeball story 66 132 198 415 688 960
11,12-Krigstein-a 43 86 129 243 389 535
13,16,17,20 36 72 108 208 329 450
14-Wolverton-a "One of Our Graveyards Is Missing", 4 pgs; Tuska-a
66 132 198 413 682 950
15-Wolverton-a "They Crawl by Night", 5 pgs.; 2 pg. Maneely s/f story
66 132 198 413 682 950
18,19-Matt Fox-a 43 86 129 243 389 535
21-33: 21-Decapitation-c. 24-Sci/fic story. 26-Atom bomb panel. 27-Sid Check-a.
33-Last pre-code (2/55) 26 52 78 152 239 325
34-Kubert, Torres-a 21 42 63 120 188 255
35-Torres-a 18 36 54 107 169 230
36-45,48,50,53,55,59: 43-Krigstein-a. 44-Davis-a. 45,55,59-Williamson-a in all; with Mayo #55,59. 55-Crandall-a. 48,53-Crandall-a (4 pgs. #48). 48-Check-a. 50-Davis, Crandall-a
18 36 54 103 162 220
46,47,49,52,54,56-58: 54-Torres-a 16 32 48 92 144 195
51-Ditko, Wood-a 20 40 60 115 180 245

NOTE: ***Ayers** a-24, 43, **Berg** a-38(#3), 43. **Lou Cameron** a-33. **Colan** a-37(#2), 6, 17, 19, 20, 23, 39. **Ditko** a-45, 51. **Drucker** a-35, 58. **Everett** a-37(#2), 11, 14, 41, 55, 56; c-37(#2), 11, 13, 14, 17, 22, 47, 48, 50, 53-55, 59. **Forte** a-49. **Fox** a-21i. **Heath** a-36(#1), 4, 6-8, 17, 20, 22, 36i; c-18. **Keller** a-15. **Mort Lawrence** a-38, 39. **Maneely** a-7, 8, 15, 16, 22, 49, 58; c-19, 25, 52. **Morrow** a-48. **Orlando** a-44, 57. **Pakula** a-36. **Powell** a-42, 53, 54. **Reinman** a-8. **Rico** a-21. **Robert Sale** a-24, 49. **Sekowsky** a-4, 5, 9. **Severin** a-38, 51; c-38, 48i, 56. **Sinnott** a-9, 21, 24. **Tuska** a-38(#3), 14. **Wildey** a-25, 43, 44.*

JOURNEYMAN
Image Comics: Aug, 1999 - No. 3, Oct, 1999 ($2.95, B&W, limited series)

1-3-Brandon McKinney-s/a 3.00

JOURNEY TO THE CENTER OF THE EARTH (Movie)
Dell Publishing Co.: No. 1060, Nov-Jan, 1959/60 (one-shot)

Four Color 1060-Pat Boone & James Mason photo-c 10 20 30 73 129 185

JSA (Justice Society of America) (Also see All Star Comics)
DC Comics: Aug, 1999 - No. 87, Sept, 2006 ($2.50/$2.99)

1-Robinson and Goyer-s; funeral of Wesley Dodds 2 4 6 8 10 12
2-5: 4-Return of Dr. Fate 6.00
6-24: 6-Black Adam-c/app. 11,12-Kobra. 16-20-JSA vs. Johnny Sorrow. 19,20-Spectre app. 22-Hawkgirl origin. 23-Hawkman returns 4.00
25-($3.75) Hawkman rejoins the JSA 1 2 3 5 7 9
26-36, 38-49: 27-Capt. Marvel app. 29-Joker: Last Laugh. 31,32-Snejbjerg-a. 33-Ultra-Humanite. 34-Intro. new Crimson Avenger and Hourman. 42-G.A. Mr. Terrific and the Freedom Fighters app. 46-Eclipso returns 3.00
37-($3.50) Johnny Thunder merges with the Thunderbolt; origin new Crimson Avenger 3.50
50-($3.95) Wraparound-c by Pacheco; Sentinel becomes Green Lantern again 4.00
51-74,76-82: 51-Kobra killed. 54-JLA app. 55-Ma Hunkle (Red Tornado) app. 56-58-Black Reign x-over with Hawkman #23-25. 64-Sand returns. 67-Identity Crisis tie-in; Gibbons-a. 68,69,72-81-Ross-c. 73,74-Day of Vengeance tie-in. 76-OMAC tie-in. 82-Infinite Crisis x-over; Levitz-s/Perez-a 2.50
75-($2.99) Day of Vengeance tie-in; Alex Ross Spectre-c 3.00
83-87: One Year Later; Pérez-c. 83-85,87-Morales-a; Gentleman Ghost app. 85-Begin $2.99-c; Earth-2 Batman, Atom, Sandman, Mr. Terrific app. 86,87-Ordway-a. 3.00
Annual 1 (10/00, $3.50) Planet DC; intro. Nemesis 3.50
...: Black Reign TPB (2005, $12.99) r/#56-58, Hawkman #23-25; Watson cover gallery 13.00
...: Black Vengeance TPB (2006, $19.99) r/#66-75 20.00
...: Darkness Falls TPB (2002, $19.95) r/#6-15 20.00
...: Fair Play TPB (2003, $14.95) r/#26-31 & Secret Files #2 15.00
...: Ghost Stories TPB (2006, $14.99) r/#82-87 15.00
...: Justice Be Done TPB (2000, $14.95) r/Secret Files & #1-5 15.00
...: Lost TPB (2005, $19.99) r/#59-67 20.00
...: Mixed Signals TPB (2006, $14.99) r/#76-81 15.00
...: Our Worlds at War 1 (9/01, $2.95) Jae Lee-c; Saltares-a 3.00
...: Princes of Darkness TPB (2005, $19.95) r/#46-55 20.00
...: Savage Times TPB (2004, $14.95) r/#39-45 15.00
... Secret Files 1 (8/99, $4.95) Origin stories and pin-ups; death of Wesley Dodds (G.A. Sandman); intro new Hawkgirl 5.00
... Secret Files 2 (9/01, $4.95) Short stories and profile pages 5.00
...: Stealing Thunder TPB (2003, $14.95) r/#32-38; JSA vs. The Ultra-Humanite 15.00
...: The Golden Age TPB (2005, $19.99) r/"The Golden Age" Elseworlds mini-series 20.00
...: The Return of Hawkman TPB (2002, $19.95) r/#16-26 & Secret Files #1 20.00

JSA: ALL STARS
DC Comics: July, 2003 - No. 8, Feb, 2004 ($2.50/$3.50, limited series, back-up stories in Golden Age style)

1-6,8-Goyer & Johns-s/Cassaday-c. 1-Velluto-a; intro. Legacy. 2-Hawkman by Loeb/Sale 3-Dr. Fate by Cooke. 4-Starman by Robinson/Harris. 5-Hourman by Chaykin. 6-Dr. Mid-nite by Azzarello/Risso 2.50
7-($3.50) Mr. Terrific back-up story by Chabon; Lark-a 3.50

Judge Dredd Movie Adaptation © DC

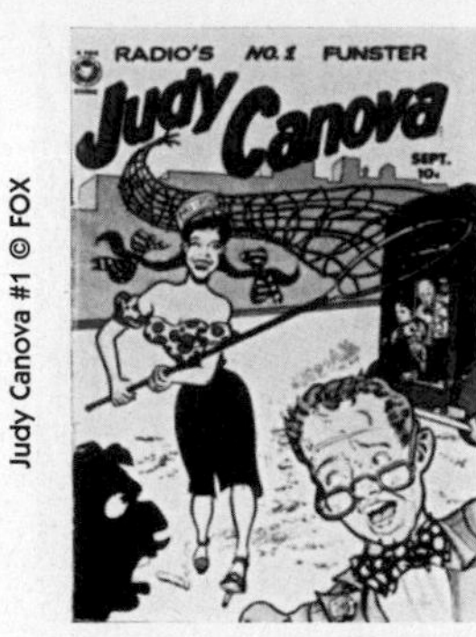

Judy Canova #1 © FOX

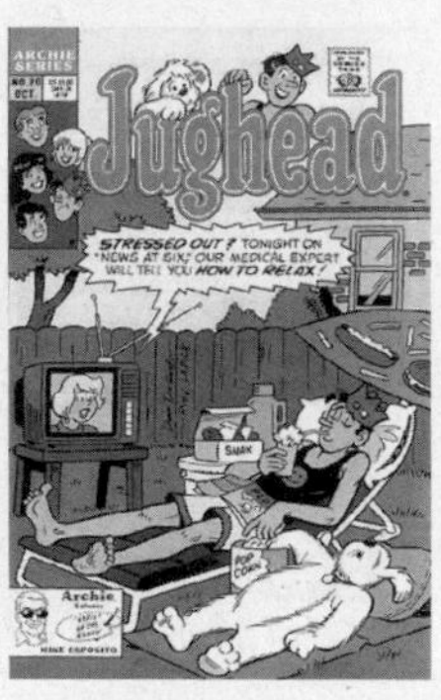

Jughead #20 © AP

GD VG FN VF VF/NM NM-
2.0 4.0 6.0 8.0 9.0 9.2

TPB (2004, $14.95) r/#1-8 15.00

JSA: CLASSIFIED (Issues #1-4 reprinted in Power Girl TPB)
DC Comics: Sept, 2005 - No. 39, Aug, 2008 ($2.50/$2.99)
1-(1st printing) Conner-c/a; origin of Power Girl 3.00
1-(1st printing) Adam Hughes variant-c 5.00
1-(2nd & 3rd printings) 2nd-Hughes B&W sketch-c. 3rd-Close-up of Conner-c 2.50
2-11: 2-LSH app. 4-Leads into Infinite Crisis #2. 5-7-Injustice Society app. 10-13-Vandal Savage origin retold; Gulacy-a/c 2.50
12-39: 12-Begin $2.99-c. 17,18-Bane app. 19,20-Morales-a. 21,22-Simonson-s/a 3.00
...: Honor Among Thieves TPB (2007, $14.99) r/#5-9 15.00

JSA STRANGE ADVENTURES
DC Comics: Oct, 2004 - No. 6, Mar, 2005 ($3.50, limited series)
1-6-Johnny Thunder as pulp writer; Kitson-a/Watson-c/ Kevin Anderson-s 3.50

JSA: THE LIBERTY FILE (Elseworlds)
DC Comics: Feb, 2000 - No. 2, Mar, 2000 ($6.95, limited series)
1,2-Batman, Dr. Mid-Nite and Hourman vs. WW2 Joker; Tony Harris-c/a 7.00
JSA: The Liberty Files TPB (2004, $19.95) r/The Liberty File and The Unholy Three series 20.00

JSA: THE UNHOLY THREE (Elseworlds)(Sequel to JSA: The Liberty File)
DC Comics: 2003 - No. 2, 2003 ($6.95, limited series)
1,2-Batman, Superman and Hourman; Tony Harris-c/a 7.00

J2 (Also see A-Next and Juggernaut)
Marvel Comics: Oct, 1998 - No. 12, Sept, 1999 ($1.99)
1-12:1-Juggernaut's son; Lim-a. 2-Two covers; X-People app. 3-J2 battles the Hulk 2.50
Spider-Girl Presents Juggernaut Jr. Vol.1: Secrets & Lies (2006, $7.99, digest) r/#1-6 8.00

JUBILEE (X-Men)
Marvel Comics: Nov, 2004 - No. 6, Apr, 2005 ($2.99)
1-6: 1-Jubilee in a Los Angeles high school; Kirkman-s; Casey Jones-c 3.00

JUDENHASS
Aardvark-Vanaheim Press: 2008 ($4.00, B&W, squarebound)
nn-Dave Sim-writer/artist; The Shoah and Jewish persecution through history 4.00

JUDE, THE FORGOTTEN SAINT
Catechetical Guild Education Soc.: 1954 (16 pgs.; 8x11"; full color; paper-c)
nn 5 10 15 22 26 30

J.U.D.G.E.: THE SECRET RAGE
Image Comics: Mar, 2000 - No. 3, May, 2000 ($2.95)
1-3-Greg Horn-s/c/a 3.00

JUDGE COLT
Gold Key: Oct, 1969 - No. 4, Sept, 1970
1 3 6 9 16 23 30
2-4 2 4 6 9 13 16

JUDGE DREDD (...Classics #62 on; also see Batman - Judge Dredd, The Law of Dredd & 2000 A.D. Monthly)
Eagle Comics/IPC Magazines Ltd./Quality Comics #34-35, V2#1-37/ Fleetway #38 on: Nov, 1983 - No. 35, 1986; V2#1, Oct, 1986 - No. 77, 1993
1-Bolland-c/a 6.00
2-35 3.00
V2#1-77: 1-('86)-New look begins. 20-Begin $1.50-c. 21/22, 23/24-Two issue numbers in one. 28-1st app. Megaman (super-hero). 39-Begin $1.75-c. 51-Begin $1.95-c. 53-Bolland-a. 57-Reprints 1st published Judge Dredd story 2.50
Special 1 2.50
NOTE: *Bolland a-1-6, 8, 10; c-1-10, 15. Guice c-V2#23/24, 26, 27.*

JUDGE DREDD (3rd Series)
DC Comics: Aug, 1994 - No. 18, Jan, 1996 ($1.95)
1-18: 12-Begin $2.25-c 2.50
nn ($5.95)-Movie adaptation, Sienkiewicz-c 6.00

JUDGE DREDD'S CRIME FILE
Eagle Comics: Aug, 1989 - No. 6, Feb, 1986 ($1.25, limited series)
1-6: 1-Byrne-a 2.50

JUDGE DREDD: LEGENDS OF THE LAW
DC Comics: Dec, 1994 - No. 13, Dec, 1995 ($1.95)
1-13: 1-5-Dorman-c 2.50

JUDGE DREDD: THE EARLY CASES
Eagle Comics: Feb, 1986 - No. 6, Jul, 1986 ($1.25, Mega-series, Mando paper)
1-6: 2000 A.D.-r 2.50

GD VG FN VF VF/NM NM-
2.0 4.0 6.0 8.0 9.0 9.2

JUDGE DREDD: THE JUDGE CHILD QUEST (Judge Child in indicia)
Eagle Comics: Aug, 1984 - No. 5, Oct, 1984 ($1.25, Lim. series, Baxter paper)
1-5: 2000A.D.-r; Bolland-c/a 2.50

JUDGE DREDD: THE MEGAZINE
Fleetway/Quality: 1991 - Present ($4.95, stiff-c, squarebound, 52 pgs.)
1-3 5.00

JUDGE DREDD VS. ALIENS: INCUBUS
Dark Horse Comics: March, 2003 - No. 4, June, 2003 ($2.99, limited series)
1-4-Flint-a/Wagner & Diggle-s 3.00

JUDGE PARKER
Argo: Feb, 1956 - No. 2, 1956
1-Newspaper strip reprints 7 14 21 35 43 50
2 5 10 15 24 30 35

JUDGMENT DAY
Awesome Entertainment: June, 1997 - No. 3, Oct, 1997 ($2.50, limited series)
1-3: 1 Alpha-Moore-s/Liefeld-c/a(p) flashback art by various in all. 2 Omega. 3 Final Judgment. All have a variant cover by Dave Gibbons 2.50
...Aftermath-($3.50) Moore-s/Kane-a; Youngblood, Glory, New Men, Maximage, Allies and Spacehunter short stories. Also has a variant cover by Dave Gibbons 3.50
TPB (Checker Books, 2003, $16.95) r/series 17.00

JUDO JOE
Jay-Jay Corp.: Aug, 1953 - No. 3, Dec, 1953 (Judo lessons in each issue)
1-Drug ring story 10 20 30 58 79 100
2,3: 3-Hypo needle story 8 16 24 40 50 60

JUDOMASTER (Gun Master #84-89) (Also see Crisis on Infinite Earths, Sarge Steel #6 & Special War Series)
Charlton Comics: No. 89, May-June, 1966 - No. 98, Dec, 1967 (Two No. 89's)
89-3rd app. Judomaster 4 8 12 24 37 50
90-Origin of Thunderbolt 4 8 12 22 34 45
91-Sarge Steel begins 3 6 9 21 32 42
92-98: 93-Intro. Tiger 3 6 9 20 30 40
93,94,96,98 (Modern Comics reprint, 1977) 4.00
NOTE: *Morisi Thunderbolt #90. #91 has 1 pg. biography on writer/artist Frank McLaughlin.*

JUDY CANOVA (Formerly My Experience) (Stage, screen, radio)
Fox Features Syndicate: No. 23, May, 1950 - No. 3, Sept, 1950
23(#1)-Wood-c,a(p)? 23 46 69 130 205 280
24-Wood-a(p) 22 44 66 126 198 270
3-Wood-c; Wood/Orlando-a 24 48 72 139 220 300

JUDY GARLAND (See Famous Stars)

JUDY JOINS THE WAVES
Toby Press: 1951 (For U.S. Navy)
nn 7 14 21 35 43 50

JUGGERNAUT (See X-Men)
Marvel Comics: Apr, 1997, Nov, 1999 ($2.99, one-shots)
1-(4/97) Kelly-s/ Rouleau-a 3.00
1-(11/99) Casey-s; Eighth Day x-over; Thor, Iron Man, Spidey app. 3.00

JUGHEAD (Formerly Archie's Pal...)
Archie Publications: No. 127, Dec, 1965 - No. 352, June, 1987
127-130: 129-LBJ on cover 3 6 9 16 23 30
131,133,135-160(9/68) 3 6 9 14 19 24
132,134: 132-Shield-c; The Fly & Black Hood app.; Shield cameo. 134-Shield-c 3 6 9 20 30 40
161-180 2 4 6 10 14 18
181-199 2 4 6 8 11 14
200(1/72) 2 4 6 9 13 16
201-240(5/75) 1 3 4 6 8 10
241-270(11/77) 1 2 3 5 6 8
271-299 1 2 3 4 5 7
300(5/80)-Anniversary issue; infinity-c 1 2 3 5 6 8
301-320(1/82) 5.00
321-324,326-352 4.00
325-(10/82) Cheryl Blossom app. (not on cover); same month as intro. (cover & story) in Archie's Girls, Betty & Veronica #320; Jason Blossom app.; DeCarlo-a 3 6 9 18 27 35

JUGHEAD (2nd Series)(Becomes Archie's Pal Jughead Comics #46 on)
Archie Enterprises: Aug, 1987 - No. 45, May, 1993 (.75/$1.00/$1.25)

Jughead's Double Digest #78 © AP

Jumbo Comics #123 © FH

Jumper: Jumpscars © 20th Century Fox

GD VG FN VF VF/NM NM-
2.0 4.0 6.0 8.0 9.0 9.2

1 1 2 3 4 5 7
2-10 4.00
11-45: 4-X-Mas issue. 17-Colan-c/a 3.00

JUGHEAD & FRIENDS DIGEST MAGAZINE
Archie Publ.: June, 2005 - Present ($2.39/$2.49, digest-size)
1-30: 1-That Wilkin Boy app. 2.50

JUGHEAD AS CAPTAIN HERO (See Archie as Pureheart the Powerful, Archie Giant Series Magazine #142 & Life With Archie)
Archie Publications: Oct, 1966 - No. 7, Nov, 1967
1-Super hero parody 6 12 18 43 69 95
2 4 8 12 28 44 60
3-7 4 8 12 24 37 50

JUGHEAD JONES COMICS DIGEST, THE (...Magazine No. 10-64; Jughead Jones Digest Magazine #65)
Archie Publ.: June, 1977 - No. 100, May, 1996 ($1.35/$1.50/$1.75, digest-size, 128 pgs.)
1-Neal Adams-a; Capt. Hero-r 3 6 9 20 30 40
2(9/77)-Neal Adams-a 3 6 9 15 21 26
3-6,8-10 2 4 6 10 14 18
7-Origin Jaguar-r; N. Adams-a 2 4 6 11 16 20
11-20: 13-r/1957 Jughead's Folly 1 3 4 6 8 10
21-50 1 2 3 4 5 7
51-70 5.00
71-100 3.00

JUGHEAD'S BABY TALES
Archie Comics: Spring, 1994 - No. 2, Wint. 1994 ($2.00, 52 pgs.)
1,2: 1-Bound-in pull-out poster 4.00

JUGHEAD'S DINER
Archie Comics: Apr, 1990 - No. 7, Apr, 1991 ($1.00)
1 4.00
2-7 2.50

JUGHEAD'S DOUBLE DIGEST (...Magazine #5)
Archie Comics: Oct, 1989 - Present ($2.25 - $3.69)
1 2 4 6 8 10 12
2-10: 2,5-Capt. Hero stories 1 2 3 5 6 8
11-25 5.00
26-146: 58-Begin $2.99-c. 66-Begin $3.19-c. 75-Begin $3.29-c. 91-Begin $3.59-c. 138-Reprints entire Jughead #1 (1949). 139-142-"New Look" Jughead; Staton-a 3.75

JUGHEAD'S EAT-OUT COMIC BOOK MAGAZINE (See Archie Giant Series Magazine No. 170)

JUGHEAD'S FANTASY
Archie Publications: Aug, 1960 - No. 3, Dec, 1960
1 16 32 48 118 209 300
2 10 20 30 71 126 180
3 8 16 24 58 97 135

JUGHEAD'S FOLLY
Archie Publications (Close-Up): 1957 (36 pgs.)(one-shot)
1-Jughead a la Elvis (Rare) (1st reference to Elvis in comics?)
50 100 150 305 503 700

JUGHEAD'S JOKES
Archie Publications: Aug, 1967 - No. 78, Sept, 1982
(No. 1-8, 38 on: reg. size; No. 9-23: 68 pgs.; No. 24-37: 52 pgs.)
1 6 12 18 41 66 90
2 4 8 12 22 34 45
3-8 3 6 9 16 23 30
9,10 (68 pgs.) 3 6 9 18 27 35
11-23(4/71) (68 pgs.) 3 6 9 16 22 28
24-37(1/74) (52 pgs.) 2 4 6 10 14 18
38-50(9/76) 1 2 3 5 7 9
51-78 6.00

JUGHEAD'S PAL HOT DOG (See Laugh #14 for 1st app.)
Archie Comics: Jan, 1990 - No. 5, Oct, 1990 ($1.00)
1 4.00
2-5 2.50

JUGHEAD'S SOUL FOOD
Spire Christian Comics (Fleming H. Revell Co.): 1979 (49¢/59¢)
nn-Low print run 2 4 6 9 13 16

JUGHEAD'S TIME POLICE
Archie Comics: July, 1990 - No. 6, May, 1991 ($1.00, bi-monthly)
1 4.00
2-6: Colan a-3-6p; c-3-6 2.50

JUGHEAD WITH ARCHIE DIGEST (...Plus Betty & Veronica & Reggie Too No. 1,2; ...Magazine #33-?, 101-on; ...Comics Digest Mag.)
Archie Pub.: Mar, 1974 - No. 200, May, 2005 ($1.00-$2.39)
1 5 10 15 32 51 70
2 4 8 12 22 34 45
3-10 3 6 9 17 25 32
11-13,15-17,19,20: Capt. Hero-r in #14-16; Capt. Pureheart #17,19
2 4 6 9 13 16
14,18,21,22-Pureheart the Powerful in #18,21,222 4 6 10 14 18
23-30: 29-The Shield-r. 30-The Fly-r 1 3 4 6 8 10
31-50,100 1 2 3 5 6 8
51-99 1 2 3 4 5 7
101-121 4.00
122-200: 156-Begin $2.19-c. 180-Begin $2.39-c 2.50

JUKE BOX COMICS
Famous Funnies: Mar, 1948 - No. 6, Jan, 1949
1-Toth-c/a; Hollingsworth-a 40 80 120 235 368 500
2-Transvestism story 24 48 72 139 220 300
3-6: 3-Peggy Lee story. 4-Jimmy Durante line drawn-c. 6-Features Desi Arnaz plus Arnaz line drawn-c 18 36 54 105 165 225

JUMBO COMICS (Created by S.M. Iger)
Fiction House Magazines (Real Adv. Publ. Co.): Sept, 1938 - No. 167, Mar, 1953 (No. 1-3: 68 pgs.; No. 4-8: 52 pgs.)(No. 1-8 oversized-10-1/2x14-1/2"; black & white)
1-(Rare)-Sheena Queen of the Jungle(1st app.) by Meskin, Hawks of the Seas (The Hawk #10 on; see Feature Funnies #3) by Eisner, The Hunchback by Dick Briefer (ends #8), Wilton of the West (ends #24), Inspector Dayton (ends #67) & ZX-5 (ends #140) begin; 1st comic art by Jack Kirby (Count of Monte Cristo & Wilton of the West); Mickey Mouse appears (1 panel) with brief biography of Walt Disney; 1st app. Peter Pupp by Bob Kane. Note: Sheena was created by Iger for publication in England as a newspaper strip. The early issues of Jumbo contain Sheena strip-r; multiple panel-c 1,2,7
2150 4300 6450 21,500 - -
2-(Rare)-Origin Sheena. Diary of Dr. Hayward by Kirby (also #3) plus 2 other stories; contains strip from Universal Film featuring Edgar Bergen & Charlie McCarthy plus-c (preview of film) 700 1400 2100 7000 - -
3-Last Kirby issue 500 1000 1500 5000 - -
4-(Scarce)-Origin The Hawk by Eisner; Wilton of the West by Fine (ends #14)(1st comic work); Count of Monte Cristo by Fine (ends #15); The Diary of Dr. Hayward by Fine (cont'd #8,9) 460 920 1380 4600 - -
5-Christmas-c 395 790 1185 3950 - -
6-8-Last B&W issue. #8 was a 1939 N. Y. World's Fair Special Edition; Frank Buck's Jungleland story 355 710 1065 3550 - -
9-Stuart Taylor begins by Fine (ends #140); Fine-c; 1st color issue (8-9/39)-1st Sheena (jungle) cover; 8-1/4x10-1/4" (oversized in width only)
335 670 1005 3350 - -
10-Regular size 68 pg. issues begin; Sheena dons new costume w/origin costume; Stuart Taylor sci/fi-c; classic Lou Fine-c. 200 400 600 1250 2075 2900
11-13: 12-The Hawk-c by Eisner. 13-Eisner-c 131 262 393 819 1360 1900
14-Intro. Lightning (super-hero) on-c only 134 268 402 838 1394 1950
15,17-20: 15-1st Lightning story and begins, ends #41. 17-Lightning part-c
83 166 249 519 860 1200
16-Lightning-c 98 196 294 613 1019 1425
21-30: 22-1st Tom, Dick & Harry; origin The Hawk retold. 25-Midnight the Black Stallion begins, ends #65 62 124 186 388 644 900
31-40: 31-(9/41)-1st app. Mars God of War in Stuart Taylor story (see Planet Comics #15. 35-Shows V2#11 (correct number does not appear)
52 104 156 317 521 725
41-50: 42-Ghost Gallery begins, ends #167 40 80 120 244 392 540
51-60: 52-Last Tom, Dick & Harry 36 72 108 208 329 450
61-70: 68-Sky Girl begins, ends #130; not in #79 28 56 84 162 256 350
71-93,95-99: 89-ZX5 becomes a private eye. 23 46 69 132 209 285
94-Used in Love and Death by Legman 25 50 75 145 228 310
100 25 50 75 145 228 310
101-121 21 42 63 122 191 260
121-140,150-158: 155-Used in **POP**, pg. 98 18 36 54 105 165 225
141-149-Two Sheena stories. 141-Long Bow, Indian Boy begins, ends #160
19 38 57 109 172 235
159-163: Space Scouts serial in all. 160-Last jungle-c (6/52). 161-Ghost Gallery covers begin, end #167. 163-Suicide Smith app. 16 32 48 94 147 200
164-The Star Pirate begins, ends #165 16 32 48 94 147 200

Jungle Action #14 © MAR

Jungle Comics #26 © FH

Jungle Girl #1 © Jungle Girl, LLC

	GD 2.0	VG 4.0	FN 6.0	VF 8.0	VF/NM 9.0	NM- 9.2

165-167: 165,167-Space Rangers app. 16 32 48 94 147 200

NOTE: *Bondage covers, negligee panels, torture, etc. are common in this series. Hawks of the Seas, Inspector Dayton, Spies in Action, Sports Shorts, & Uncle Otto by Eisner, #1-7. Hawk by* **Eisner***-#10-15.* **Eisner** *c-1-8, 12-14. 1pg. Patsy pin-ups in 92-97, 99-101. Sheena by* **Meskin***-#1, 4; by* **Powell***-#2, 3, 5-28;* **Powell** *c-14, 16, 17, 19.* **Powell/Eisner** *c-15. Sky Girl by* **Matt Baker***-#69-78, 80-130. ZX-5 & Ghost Gallery by* **Kamen***-#90-130.* **Bailey** *a-3-8.* **Briefer** *a-1-8, 10.* **Fine** *a-14; c-9-11.* **Kamen** *a-101, 105, 123, 132; c-105, 121-145.* **Bob Kane** *a-1-8.* **Whitman** *c-146-167(most). Jungle c-9, 13, 15, 17 on.*

JUMPER: JUMPSCARS
Oni Press: Jan, 2008 ($14.95, graphic novel)

SC-Prelude to 2008 movie Jumper; Brian Hurtt-a/c 15.00

JUNGLE ACTION
Atlas Comics (IPC): Oct, 1954 - No. 6, Aug, 1955

1-Leopard Girl begins by Al Hartley (#1,3); Jungle Boy by Forte; Maneely-a in all
37 74 111 214 340 465
2-(3-D effect cover) 37 74 111 214 340 465
3-6: 3-Last precode (2/55) 23 46 69 132 209 285

NOTE: **Maneely** *c-1, 2, 5, 6.* **Romita** *a-3, 6.* **Shores** *a-3, 6; c-3, 4?.*

JUNGLE ACTION (...& Black Panther #18-21?)
Marvel Comics Group: Oct, 1972 - No. 24, Nov, 1976

1-Lorna, Jann-r (All reprints in 1-4) 2 4 6 11 16 20
2-4 2 4 6 8 10 12
5-Black Panther begins (r/Avengers #62) 3 6 9 16 23 30
6-New solo Black Panther stories begin 3 6 9 15 21 26
7,9,10: 9-Contains pull-out centerfold ad by Mark Jewelers
2 4 6 8 11 14
8-Origin Black Panther 2 4 6 11 16 20
11-20,23,24: 19-23-KKK x-over. 23-r/#22. 24-1st Wind Eagle; story contd in Marvel Premiere #51-#53 1 2 3 5 7 9
21,22-(Regular 25¢ edition)(5,7/76) 1 2 3 5 7 9
21,22-(30¢-c variant, limited distribution) 3 6 9 14 20 25

NOTE: **Buckler** *a-6-9p, 22; c-8p, 12p.* **Buscema** *a-5p; c-22.* **Byrne** *c-23.* **Gil Kane** *a-8p; c-2, 4, 10p, 11p, 13-17, 19, 24.* **Kirby** *c-18.* **Maneely** *r-1.* **Russell** *a-13i.* **Starlin** *c-3p.*

JUNGLE ADVENTURES
Super Comics: 1963 - 1964 (Reprints)

10,12,15,17,18: 10-r/Terrors of the Jungle #4 & #10(Rulah). 12-r/Zoot #14(Rulah).15-r/Kaanga from Jungle #152 & Tiger Girl. 17-All Jo-Jo-r. 18-Reprints/White Princess of the Jungle #1; no Kinstler-a; origin of both White Princess & Cap'n Courage
3 6 9 19 29 38

JUNGLE ADVENTURES
Skywald Comics: Mar, 1971 - No. 3, June, 1971 (25¢, 52 pgs.) (Pre-code reprints & new-s)

1-Zangar origin; reprints of Jo-Jo, Blue Gorilla(origin)/White Princess #3, Kinstler-r/White Princess #2 3 6 9 16 22 28
2,3: 2-Zangar, Sheena-r/Sheena #17 & Jumbo #162, Jo-Jo, origin Slave Girl-r. 3-Zangar, Jo-Jo, White Princess, Rulah-r 2 4 6 10 14 18

JUNGLE BOOK (See King Louie and Mowgli, Movie Comics, Mowgli..., Walt Disney Showcase #45 & Walt Disney's The Jungle Book)

JUNGLE CAT (Disney)
Dell Publishing Co.: No. 1136, Sept-Nov, 1960 (one shot)

Four Color 1136-Movie, photo-c 6 12 18 43 69 95

JUNGLE COMICS
Fiction House Magazines: 1/40 - No. 157, 3/53; No. 158, Spr, 1953 - No. 163, Summer, 1954

1-Origin The White Panther, Kaanga, Lord of the Jungle, Tabu, Wizard of the Jungle; Wambi, the Jungle Boy, Camilla & Capt. Terry Thunder begin (all 1st app.). Lou Fine-c
457 914 1371 3200 5600 8000
2-Fantomah, Mystery Woman of the Jungle begins, ends #51; The Red Panther begins, ends #26 166 332 498 1038 1719 2400
3,4 134 268 402 838 1394 1950
5-Classic Eisner-c 150 300 450 938 1557 2175
6-10: 7,8-Powell-c 79 158 237 494 822 1150
11-20: 13-Tuska-c 54 108 162 338 557 775
21-30: 25-Shows V2#1 (correct number does not appear). #27-New origin Fantomah, Daughter of the Pharoahs; Camilla dons new costume
45 90 135 275 455 635
31-40 37 74 111 213 337 460
41,43-50 32 64 96 186 293 400
42-Kaanga by Crandall, 12 pgs. 34 68 102 195 308 420
51-60 28 56 84 162 256 350
61-70: 67-Cover swipes Crandall splash pg. in #42 25 50 75 145 228 310
71-80: 79-New origin Tabu 22 44 66 128 202 275
81-97,99 21 42 63 122 191 260
98-Used in **SOTI**, pg. 185 & illo "In ordinary comic books, there are pictures within pictures for children who know how to look;" used by N.Y. Legis. Comm.
33 66 99 190 300 410
100 25 50 75 145 228 310
101-110: 104-In Camilla story, villain is Dr. Wertham 20 40 60 117 184 250
111-120: 118-Clyde Beatty app. 19 38 57 112 176 240
121-130 18 36 54 105 165 225
131-163: 135-Desert Panther begins in Terry Thunder (origin), not in #137; ends (dies) #138. 139-Last 52 pg. issue. 141-Last Tabu. 143,145-Used in **POP**, pg. 99. 151-Last Camilla & Terry Thunder. 152-Tiger Girl begins. 158-Last Wambi; Sheena app.
16 32 48 94 147 200
I.W. Reprint #1,9: 1-r/? 9-r/#151 3 6 9 17 25 32

NOTE: *Bondage covers, negligee panels, torture, etc. are common to this series. Camilla by* **Fran Hopper***-#70-92; by* **Baker***-#69, 100-113, 115, 116; by* **Lubbers***-#97-99 by* **Tuska***-#63, 65. Kaanga by* **John Celardo***-#80-113; by* **Larsen***-#71, 75-79; by* **Moreira***-#58, 60, 61, 63-70, 72-74; by* **Tuska***-#37, 62; by* **Whitman***-#114-163. Tabu by* **Larsen***-#59-75, 82-92; by* **Whitman***-#93-115. Terry Thunder by* **Hopper***-#71, 72; by* **Celardo***-#78, 79; by* **Lubbers***-#80-85. Tiger Girl-r by* **Baker***-#152, 153, 155-157, 159. Wambi by* **Baker***-#62-67, 74.* **Astarita** *c-45, 46.* **Celardo** *a-78; c-98-113.* **Crandall** *c-67 from splash pg.* **Eisner** *c-2, 5, 6.* **Fine** *c-1.* **Larsen** *a-65, 66, 71, 72, 74, 75, 79, 83, 84, 87-90.* **Moreira** *c-43, 44.* **Morisi** *a-51.* **Powell** *c-7, 8.* **Sultan** *c-3, 4.* **Tuska** *c-13.* **Whitman** *c-132-163(most).* **Zolnerowich** *c-11, 12, 18-41.*

JUNGLE COMICS
Blackthorne Publishing: May, 1988 - No. 4 ($2.00, B&W/color)

1-Dave Stevens-c; B. Jones scripts in all. 3.00
2-4: 2-B&W-a begins 2.50

JUNGLE GIRL (See Lorna, the...)

JUNGLE GIRL (Nyoka, Jungle Girl No. 2 on)
Fawcett Publications: Fall, 1942 (one-shot)(No month listed)

1-Bondage-c; photo of Kay Aldridge who played Nyoka in movie serial app. on-c. Adaptation of the classic Republic movie serial Perils of Nyoka. 1st comic to devote entire contents to a movie serial adaptation 124 248 372 775 1288 1800

JUNGLE GIRL
Dynamite Entertainment: No. 0, 2007 - Present (25¢/$2.99)

0-(25¢-c) Eight page preview; preview of Superpowers w/Alex Ross-a 2.25
1-5-Frank Cho-plot/cover; Batista-a/variant-c 3.00

JUNGLE GIRLS
AC Comics: 1989 - No. 16, 1993 (B&W)

1-16: 1-4,10,13-16-New story & "good girl" reprints. 5-9,11,12-All g.g. reprints (Baker, Powell, Lubbers, others) 3.00

JUNGLE JIM (Also see Ace Comics)
Standard Comics (Best Books): No. 11, Jan, 1949 - No. 20, Apr, 1951

11 11 22 33 62 86 110
12-20 8 16 24 42 54 65

JUNGLE JIM
Dell Publishing Co.: No. 490, 8/53 - No. 1020, 8-10/59 (Painted-c)

Four Color 490(#1) 7 14 21 49 80 110
Four Color 565(#2, 6/54) 5 10 15 30 48 65
3(10-12/54)-5 4 8 12 28 44 60
6-19(1-3/59), Four Color 1020(#20) 4 8 12 26 41 55

JUNGLE JIM
King Features Syndicate: No. 5, Dec, 1967

5-Reprints Dell #5; Wood-c 2 4 6 10 14 18

JUNGLE JIM (Continued from Dell series)
Charlton Comics: No. 22, Feb, 1969 - No. 28, Feb, 1970 (#21 was an overseas edition only)

22-Dan Flagg begins; Ditko/Wood-a 3 6 9 21 32 42
23-26: 23-Last Dan Flagg; Howard-c. 24-Jungle People begin
3 6 9 15 21 26
27,28: 27-Ditko/Howard-a. 28-Ditko-a 3 6 9 17 25 32

NOTE: *Ditko cover of #22 reprints story panels*

JUNGLE JO
Fox Feature Syndicate (Hero Books): Mar, 1950 - No. 3, Sept, 1950

nn-Jo-Jo blanked out in titles of interior stories, leaving Congo King; came out after Jo-Jo #29 (intended as Jo-Jo #30?) 48 96 144 293 484 675
1-Tangi begins; part Wood-a 50 100 150 305 503 700
2,3 40 80 120 235 368 500

JUNGLE LIL (Dorothy Lamour #2 on; also see Feature Stories Magazine)
Fox Feature Syndicate (Hero Books): April, 1950

1 40 80 120 240 383 525

JUNGLE TALES (Jann of the Jungle No. 8 on)

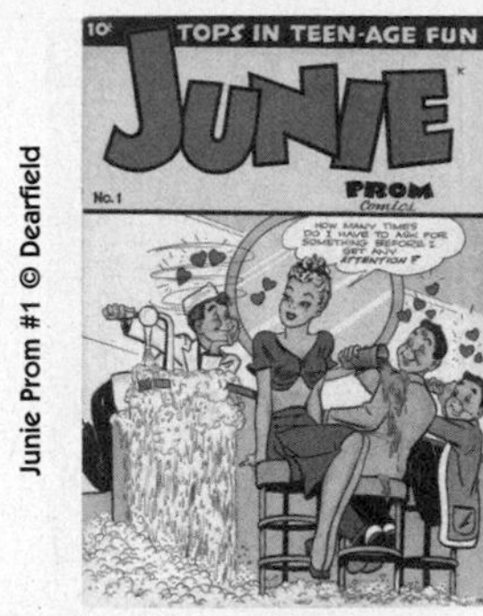

Junie Prom #1 © Dearfield

Junior Miss #33 © MAR

Justice #1 © DC

GD 2.0 | VG 4.0 | FN 6.0 | VF 8.0 | VF/NM 9.0 | NM- 9.2

Atlas Comics (CSI): Sept, 1954 - No. 7, Sept, 1955
1-Jann of the Jungle 39 78 117 225 355 485
2-7: 3-Last precode (1/55) 26 52 78 152 239 325
NOTE: *Heath c-5. Heck a-6, 7. Maneely a-2; c-1, 3. Shores a-5-7; c-4, 6. Tuska a-2.*

JUNGLE TALES OF TARZAN
Charlton Comics: Dec, 1964 - No. 4, July, 1965
1 6 12 18 37 59 80
2-4 4 8 12 24 37 50
NOTE: *Giordano c-3p. Glanzman a-1-3. Montes/Bache a-4.*

JUNGLE TERROR (See Harvey Comics Hits No. 54)

JUNGLE THRILLS (Formerly Sports Thrills; Terrors of the Jungle #17 on)
Star Publications: No. 16, Feb, 1952; Dec, 1953; No. 7, 1954
16-Phantom Lady & Rulah story-reprint/All Top No. 15; used in **POP**, pg. 98,99; L. B. Cole-c 49 98 147 299 492 685
3-D 1(12/53, 25¢)-Came w/glasses; Jungle Lil & Jungle Jo appear; L. B. Cole-c 49 98 147 299 492 685
7-Titled 'Picture Scope Jungle Adventures;' (1954, 36 pgs, 15¢)-3-D effect c/stories; story & coloring book; Disbrow-a/script; L.B. Cole-c 49 98 147 299 492 685

JUNGLE TWINS, THE (Tono & Kono)
Gold Key/Whitman No. 18: Apr, 1972 - No. 17, Nov, 1975; No. 18, May, 1982
1 3 6 9 14 19 24
2-5 2 4 6 8 10 12
6-18: 18(Whitman, 5/82)-Reprints 1 2 3 5 6 8
NOTE: *UFO c/story No. 13. Painted-c No. 1-17. Spiegle c-18.*

JUNGLE WAR STORIES (Guerrilla War No. 12 on)
Dell Publishing Co.: July-Sept, 1962 - No. 11, Apr-June, 1965 (Painted-c)
01-384-209 (#1) 4 8 12 22 34 45
2-11 3 6 9 16 23 30

JUNIE PROM (Also see Dexter Comics)
Dearfield Publishing Co.: Winter, 1947-48 - No. 7, Aug, 1949
1-Teen-age 14 28 42 80 115 150
2 9 18 27 47 61 75
3-7 8 16 24 40 50 60

JUNIOR
Fantagraphics Books: June, 2000 - No. 5, Jan, 2001 ($2.95, B&W)
1-5-Peter Bagge-s/a 3.00

JUNIOR CARROT PATROL (Jr. Carrot Patrol #2)
Dark Horse Comics: May, 1989; No. 2, Nov, 1990 ($2.00, B&W)
1,2-Flaming Carrot spin-off. 1-Bob Burden-c(i) 2.50

JUNIOR COMICS (Formerly Li'l Pan; becomes Western Outlaws with #17)
Fox Feature Syndicate: No. 9, Sept, 1947 - No. 16, July, 1948
9-Feldstein-c/a; headlights-c 110 220 330 688 1144 1600
10-16-Feldstein-c/a; headlights-c on all 100 200 300 625 1038 1450

JUNIOR FUNNIES (Formerly Tiny Tot Funnies No. 9)
Harvey Publ. (King Features Synd.): No. 10, Aug, 1951 - No. 13, Feb, 1952
10-Partial reprints in all; Blondie, Dagwood, Daisy, Henry, Popeye, Felix, Katzenjammer Kids 6 12 18 28 34 40
11-13 5 10 15 24 30 35

JUNIOR HOPP COMICS
Stanmor Publ.: Feb, 1952 - No. 3, July, 1952
1-Teenage humor 10 20 30 54 72 90
2,3: 3-Dave Berg-a 6 12 18 31 38 45

JUNIOR MEDICS OF AMERICA, THE
E. R. Squire & Sons: No. 1359, 1957 (15¢)
1359 4 8 12 17 21 24

JUNIOR MISS
Timely/Marvel (CnPC): Wint, 1944; No. 24, Apr, 1947 - No. 39, Aug, 1950
1-Frank Sinatra & June Allyson life story 31 62 93 178 282 385
24-Formerly The Human Torch #23? 15 30 45 84 127 170
25-38: 29,31,34-Cindy-c/stories (others?) 9 18 27 52 69 85
39-Kurtzman-a 11 22 33 60 83 105
NOTE: *Painted-c 35-37. 35, 37-all romance. 36, 38-mostly teen humor. Louise Alston c-36.*

JUNIOR PARTNERS (Formerly Oral Roberts' True Stories)
Oral Roberts Evangelistic Assn.: No. 120, Aug, 1959 - V3#12, Dec, 1961
120(#1) 4 8 12 24 37 50
2(9/59) 3 6 9 17 25 32
3-12(7/60) 2 4 6 13 18 22
V2#1(8/60)-5(12/60) 2 4 6 9 13 16
V3#1(1/61)-12 2 4 6 8 10 12

JUNIOR TREASURY (See Dell Junior...)

JUNIOR WOODCHUCKS GUIDE (Walt Disney's...)
Danbury Press: 1973 (8-3/4"x5-3/4", 214 pgs., hardcover)
nn-Illustrated text based on the long-standing J.W. Guide used by Donald Duck's nephews Huey, Dewey & Louie by Carl Barks. The guidebook was a popular plot device to enable the nephews to solve problems facing their uncle or Scrooge McDuck (scarce) 5 10 15 35 55 75

JUNIOR WOODCHUCKS LIMITED SERIES (Walt Disney's...)
W. D. Publications (Disney): July, 1991 - No. 4, Oct, 1991 ($1.50, limited series; new & reprint-a)
1-4: 1-The Beagle Boys app.; Barks-r 2.50

JUNIOR WOODCHUCKS (See Huey, Dewey & Louie...)

JURASSIC PARK
Topps Comics: June, 1993 - No. 4, Aug, 1993; No. 5, Oct, 1994 - No. 10, Feb, 1995
1-($2.50)-Newsstand Edition; Kane/Perez-a in all; 1-4: movie adaptation 2.50
1-($2.95)-Collector's Ed.; polybagged w/3 cards 4.00
1-Amberchrome Edition w/no price or ads 1 2 3 4 5 7
2-4-($2.50)-Newsstand Edition 2.50
2,3-($2.95)-Collector's Ed.; polybagged w/3 cards 3.00
4-10: 4-($2.95)-Collector's Ed.; polybagged w/1 of 4 different action hologram trading card; Gil Kane/Perez-a. 5-becomes Advs. of 3.00
Annual 1 ($3.95, 5/95) 4.00
Trade paperback (1993, $9.95)-r/#1-4; bagged w/#0 10.00

JURASSIC PARK: RAPTOR
Topps Comics: Nov, 1993 - No. 2, Dec, 1993 ($2.95, limited series)
1,2: 1-Bagged w/3 trading cards & Zorro #0; Golden c-1,2 3.00

JURASSIC PARK: RAPTORS ATTACK
Topps Comics: Mar, 1994 - No. 4, June, 1994 ($2.50, limited series)
1-4-Michael Golden-c/frontispiece 2.50

JURASSIC PARK: RAPTORS HIJACK
Topps Comics: July, 1994 - No. 4, Oct, 1994 ($2.50, limited series)
1-4: Michael Golden-c/front piece 2.50

JUST A PILGRIM
Black Bull Entertainment: May, 2001 - No. 5, Sept, 2001 ($2.99)
Limited Preview Edition (12/00, $7.00) Ennis & Ezquerra interviews 7.00
1-Ennis-s/Ezquerra-a; two covers by Texeira & JG Jones 3.00
2-5: 2-Fabry-c. 3-Nowlan-c. 4-Sienkiewicz-c 3.00
TPB (11/01, $12.99) r/#1-5; Waid intro. 13.00

JUST A PILGRIM: GARDEN OF EDEN
Black Bull Entertainment: May, 2002 - No. 4, Aug, 2002 ($2.99, limited series)
Limited Preview Ed. (1/02, $7.00) Ennis & Ezquerra interviews; Jones-c 7.00
1-4-Ennis-s/Ezquerra-a 3.00
TPB (11/02, $12.99) r/#1-4; Gareb Shamus intro. 13.00

JUSTICE
Marvel Comics Group (New Universe): Nov, 1986 - No. 32, June, 1989
1-32: 26-32-$1.50-c (low print run) 2.50

JUSTICE
DC Comics: Oct, 2005 - No. 12, Aug, 2007 ($2.99/$3.50/$3.99, bi-monthly maxi-series)
1-Classic Justice League vs. The Legion of Doom; Alex Ross & Doug Braithwaite-a; Jim Krueger-s; two covers by Ross; Ross sketch pages 5.00
1-2nd & 3rd printings 4.00
2-($3.50) 4.00
2 (2nd printing), 3-11-($3.50) 3.50
12-($3.99) Two covers (Heroes & Villains) 4.00
... Volume One HC (2006, $19.99, dustjacket) r/#1-4; Krueger intro.; sketch pages 20.00
... Volume One SC (2008, $14.99) r/#1-4; Krueger intro.; sketch pages 15.00
... Volume Two HC (2007, $19.99, dustjacket) r/#5-8; Krueger intro.; sketch pages 20.00
... Volume Three HC (2007, $19.99, dustjacket) r/#9-12; Krueger intro.; sketch pages 20.00

JUSTICE COMICS (Formerly Wacky Duck; Tales of Justice #53 on)
Marvel/Atlas Comics (NPP 7-9,4-19/CnPC 20-23/MjMC 24-38/Male 39-52: No. 7, Fall/47 - No. 9, 6/48; No. 4, 8/48 - No. 52, 3/55
7(#1, 1947) 30 60 90 174 275 375
8(#2)-Kurtzman-a "Giggles 'n' Grins" (3) 20 40 60 117 184 250

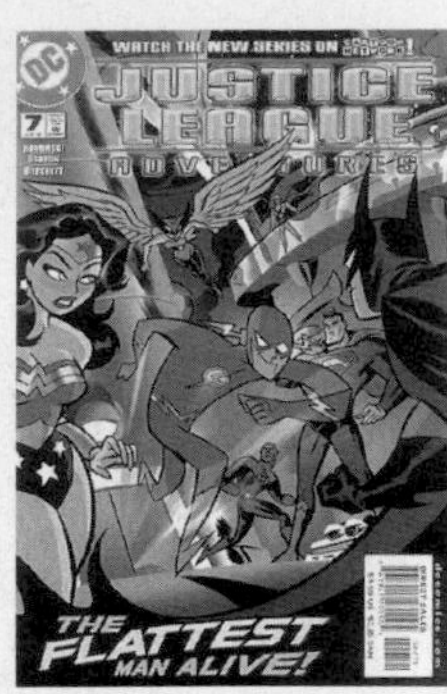

Justice League Adventures #7 © DC

Justice League Europe #23 © DC

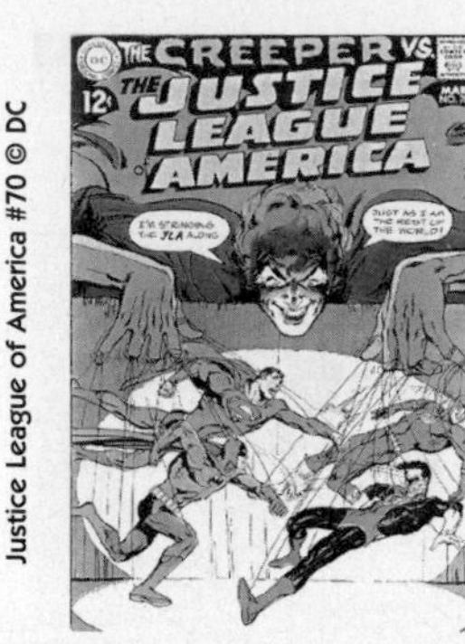

Justice League of America #70 © DC

GD VG FN VF VF/NM NM-
2.0 4.0 6.0 8.0 9.0 9.2

9(#3, 6/48) 18 36 54 103 162 220
4 16 32 48 92 144 195
5(9/48)-9: 8-Anti-Wertham editorial 14 28 42 82 121 160
10-15-Photo-c 12 24 36 69 97 125
16-30 11 22 33 60 83 105
31-40,42-52: 35-Gene Colan-a. 48-Last precode; Pakula & Tuska-a.
10 20 30 56 76 95
41-Electrocution-c 16 32 48 94 147 200

NOTE: ***Heath** a-24. **Maneely** c-44, 52. **Pakula** a-43, 45, 48. **Louis Ravielli** a-39. **Robinson** a-22, 25, 41. **Shores** c-7(#1), 8(#2)? **Tuska** a-48. **Wildey** a-52.*

JUSTICE: FOUR BALANCE
Marvel Comics: Sept, 1994 - No. 4, Dec, 1994 ($1.75, limited series)

1-4: 1-Thing & Firestar app. 2.50

JUSTICE, INC. (The Avenger) (Pulp)
National Periodical Publications: May-June, 1975 - No. 4, Nov-Dec, 1975

1-McWilliams-a, Kubert-c; origin 2 4 6 9 13 16
2-4: 2-4-Kirby-a(p), c-2,3p. 4-Kubert-c 2 4 6 9 12 15

NOTE: *Adapted from Kenneth Robeson novel, creator of Doc Savage.*

JUSTICE, INC. (Pulp)
DC Comics: 1989 - No. 2, 1989 ($3.95, 52 pgs., squarebound, mature)

1,2: Re-intro The Avenger; Andrew Helfer scripts & Kyle Baker-c/a 4.00

JUSTICE LEAGUE (...International #7-25; ...America #26 on)
DC Comics: May, 1987 - No. 113, Aug, 1996 (Also see Legends #6)

1-Batman, Green Lantern (Guy Gardner), Blue Beetle, Mr. Miracle, Capt. Marvel & Martian Manhunter begin 1 2 3 4 5 7
2,3: 3-Regular-c (white background) 5.00
3-Limited-c (yellow background, Superman logo) 4 8 12 24 37 50
4-10: 4-Booster Gold joins. 5-Origin Gray Man; Batman vs. Guy Gardner; Creeper app. 7-($1.25, 52 pgs.)-Capt. Marvel & Dr. Fate resign; Capt. Atom & Rocket Red join. 9,10-Millennium x-over 3.00
11-17,22,23,25-49,51-68,71-82: 16-Bruce Wayne-c/story. 31,32-J. L. Europe x-over. 58-Lobo app. 61-New team begins; swipes-c to J.L. of A. #1('60). 70-Newsstand version w/o outer-c. 71-Direct sales version w/black outer-c. 71-Newsstand version w/o outer-c. 80-Intro new Booster Gold. 82,83-Guy Gardner-c/stories 2.50
18-21,24,50: 18-21-Lobo app. 24-($1.50)-1st app. Justice League Europe. 50-($1.75, 52 pgs.) 3.00
69-Doomsday tie-in; takes place between Superman: The Man of Steel #18 & Superman #74 5.00
69,70-2nd printings 2.50
70-Funeral for a Friend part 1; red 3/4 outer-c 4.00
83-99,101-113: 92-(9/94)-Zero Hour x-over; Triumph app. 113-Green Lantern, Flash & Hawkman app. 2.50
100 ($3.95)-Foil-c; 52 pgs. 4.00
100 ($2.95)-Newstand 3.00
#0-(10/94) Zero Hour (publ between #92 & #93); new team begins (Hawkman, Flash, Wonder Woman, Metamorpho, Nuklon, Crimson Fox, Obsidian & Fire) 2.50
Annual 1-8,10 ('87-'94, '96, 68 pgs.): 2-Joker-c/story; Batman cameo. 5-Armageddon 2001 x-over; Silver ink 2nd print. 7-Bloodlines x-over. 8-Elseworlds story. 10-Legends of the Dead Earth 3.00
Annual 9 (1995, $3.50)-Year One story 3.50
Special 1,2 ('90,'91, 52 pgs.): 1-Giffen plots. 2-Staton-a(p) 3.00
Spectacular 1 (1992, $1.50, 52 pgs.)-Intro new JLI & JLE teams; ties into JLI #61 & JLE #37; two interlocking covers by Jurgens 3.00
A New Beginning Trade Paperback (1989, $12.95)-r/#1-7 13.00
... International Vol. 1 HC (2008, $24.99) r/#1-7; new intro. by Giffen 25.00
... International Vol. 2 HC (2008, $24.99) r/#8-13, Annual #1 and Suicide Squad #13 25.00

NOTE: ***Anderson** c-61i. **Austin** a-1i, 60i; c-1i. **Giffen** a-13; c-21p. **Guice** a-62i. **Maguire** a-1-12, 16-19, 22, 23. **Russell** a-Annual 1i; c-54i. **Willingham** a-30p, Annual 2.*

JUSTICE LEAGUE ADVENTURES (Based on Cartoon Network series)
DC Comics: Jan, 2002 - No. 34, Oct, 2004 ($1.99/$2.25)

1-Timm & Ross-c 3.00
2-32: 3-Nicieza-s. 5-Starro app. 10-Begin $2.25-c. 14-Includes 16 pg. insert for VERB with Haberlin CG-art. 15,29-Amancio-a. 16-McCloud-s. 20-Psycho Pirate app. 25,26-Adam Strange-c/app. 28-Legion of Super-Heroes app. 30-Kamandi app. 2.50
Free Comic Book Day giveaway - (See Promotional Comics section)
TPB (2003, $9.95) r/#1,3,6,10-13; Timm/Ross-c from #1 10.00
...Vol. 1: The Magnificent Seven (2004, $6.95) digest-size reprints #3,6,10-12 7.00
...Vol. 2: Friends and Foes (2004, $6.95) digest-size reprints #13,14,16,19,20 7.00

JUSTICE LEAGUE: A MIDSUMMER'S NIGHTMARE
DC Comics: Sept, 1996 - No. 3, Nov, 1996 ($2.95, limited series, 38 pgs.)

1-3: Re-establishes Superman, Batman, Green Lantern, The Martian Manhunter, Flash, Aquaman & Wonder Woman as the Justice League; Mark Waid & Fabian Nicieza co-scripts; Jeff Johnson & Darick Robertson-a(p); Kevin Maguire-c 5.00
TPB-(1997, $8.95) r/1-3 9.00

GD VG FN VF VF/NM NM-
2.0 4.0 6.0 8.0 9.0 9.2

JUSTICE LEAGUE ELITE (See JLA #100 and JLA Secret Files 2004)
DC Comics: Sept, 2004 - No. 12, Aug, 2005 ($2.50)

1-12-Flash, Green Arrow, Vera Black and others; Kelly-s/Mahnke-a. 5,6-JSA app. 2.50
JL Elite TPB (2005, $19.99) r/#1-4, Action #775, JLA #100, JLA Secret Files 2004 20.00
... Vol. 2 TPB (2007, $19.99) r/#5-12 20.00

JUSTICE LEAGUE EUROPE (Justice League International #51 on)
DC Comics: Apr, 1989 - No. 68, Sept., 1994 (75¢/ $1.00/$1.25/$1.50)

1-Giffen plots in all, breakdowns in #1-8,13-30; Justice League #1-c/swipe 3.00
2-10: 7-9-Batman app. 7,8-JLA x-over. 8,9-Superman app. 2.50
11-49: 12-Metal Men app. 20-22-Rogers-c/a(p). 33,34-Lobo vs. Despero. 37-New team begins; swipes-c to JLA #9; see JLA Spectacular 2.50
50-($2.50, 68 pgs.)-Battles Sonar 3.00
51-68: 68-Zero Hour x-over; Triumph joins Justice League Task Force (See JLTF #17) 2.50
Annual 1-5 ('90-'94, 68 pgs.)-1-Return of the Global Guardians; Giffen plots/breakdowns. 2-Armageddon 2001; Giffen-a(p); Rogers-a(p); Golden-a(i). 3-Eclipso app. 4-Intro Lionheart. 5-Elseworlds story 3.00

NOTE: ***Phil Jimenez** a-68p. **Rogers** c/a-20-22. **Sears** a-1-12, 14-19, 23-29; c-1-10, 12, 14-19, 23-29.*

JUSTICE LEAGUE INTERNATIONAL (See Justice League Europe)

JUSTICE LEAGUE OF AMERICA (See Brave & the Bold #28-30, Mystery In Space #75 & Official... Index) (See Crisis on Multiple Earths TPBs for reprints of JLA/JSA crossovers)
National Periodical Publ./DC Comics: Oct-Nov, 1960 - No. 261, Apr, 1987 (#91-99,139-157: 52 pgs.)

1-(10-11/60)-Origin & 1st app. Despero; Aquaman, Batman, Flash, Green Lantern, J'onn J'onzz, Superman & Wonder Woman continue from Brave and the Bold
400 800 1200 3600 6800 10,000
2 100 200 300 850 1575 2300
3-Origin/1st app. Kanjar Ro (see Mystery in Space #75)(scarce in high grade due to black-c)
83 166 249 706 1303 1900
4-Green Arrow joins JLA 52 104 156 442 821 1200
5-Origin & 1st app. Dr. Destiny 50 100 150 400 725 1050
6-8,10: 6-Origin & 1st app. Prof. Amos Fortune. 7-(10-11/61)-Last 10¢ issue. 10-(3/62)-Origin & 1st app. Felix Faust; 1st app. Lord of Time 39 78 117 293 534 775
9-(2/62)-Origin JLA (1st origin) 45 90 135 360 655 950
11-15: 12-(6/62)-Origin & 1st app. Dr. Light. 13-(8/62)-Speedy app. 14-(9/62)-Atom joins JLA. 24 48 72 175 313 450
16-20: 17-Adam Strange flashback 20 40 60 146 261 375
21-(8/63)-"Crisis on Earth-One"; re-intro. of JSA in this title (see Flash #129) (1st S.A. app. Hourman & Dr. Fate) 35 70 105 263 482 700
22- "Crisis on Earth-Two"; JSA x-over (story continued from #21)
30 60 90 225 413 600
23-28: 24-Adam Strange app. 27-Robin app. 15 30 45 107 191 275
29-JSA x-over; 1st S.A. app. Starman; "Crisis on Earth-Three"
17 34 51 128 227 325
30-JSA x-over 16 32 48 118 209 300
31-Hawkman joins JLA, Hawkgirl cameo (11/64) 12 24 36 86 153 220
32,34: 32-Intro & Origin Brain Storm. 34-Joker-c/sty 10 20 30 67 116 165
33,35,36,40,41: 40-3rd S.A. Penguin app. 41-Intro & origin The Key
9 18 27 63 107 150
37-39: 37,38-JSA x-over. 37-1st S.A. app. Mr. Terrific; Batman cameo. 38-"Crisis on Earth-A". 39-Giant G-16; r/B&B #28,30 & JLA #5 11 22 33 79 140 200
42-45: 42-Metamorpho app. 43-Intro. Royal Flush Gang
7 14 21 50 83 115
46-JSA x-over; 1st S.A. app. Sandman; 3rd S.A. app. of G.A. Spectre (8/66)
11 22 33 79 140 200
47-JSA x-over; 4th S.A. app of G.A. Spectre. 8 16 24 58 97 135
48-Giant G-29; r/JLA #2,3 & B&B #29 8 16 24 54 90 125
49-54,57,59,60 6 12 18 43 69 95
55-Intro. Earth 2 Robin (1st G.A. Robin in S.A.) 8 16 24 56 93 130
56-JLA vs. JSA (1st G.A. Wonder Woman in S.A.) 7 14 21 49 80 110
58-Giant G-41; r/JLA #6,8,1 7 14 21 49 80 110
61-63,66,68-72: 69-Wonder Woman quits. 71-Manhunter leaves. 72-Last 12¢ issue
5 10 15 32 51 70
64,65-JSA story. 64-(8/68)-Origin/1st app. S.A. Red Tornado
6 12 18 37 59 80
67-Giant G-53; r/JLA #4,14,31 7 14 21 47 76 105
73-1st S.A. app. of G.A. Superman 6 12 18 39 62 85
74-Black Canary joins; Larry Lance dies; 1st meeting of G.A. & S.A. Superman; Neal Adams-c 6 12 18 39 62 85
75-2nd app. Green Arrow in new costume (see Brave & the Bold #85)

Justice League of America #111 © DC

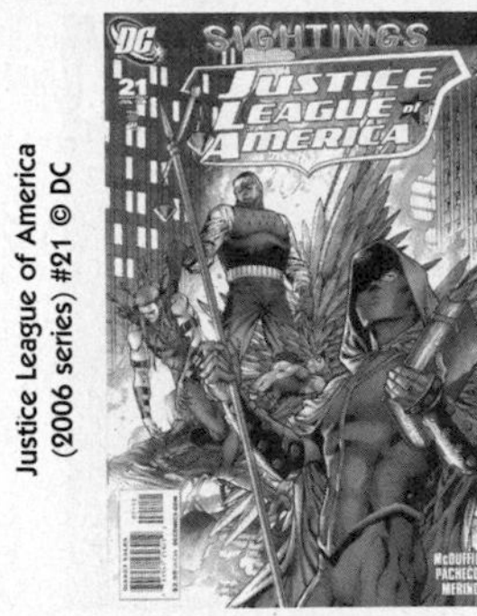

Justice League of America (2006 series) #21 © DC

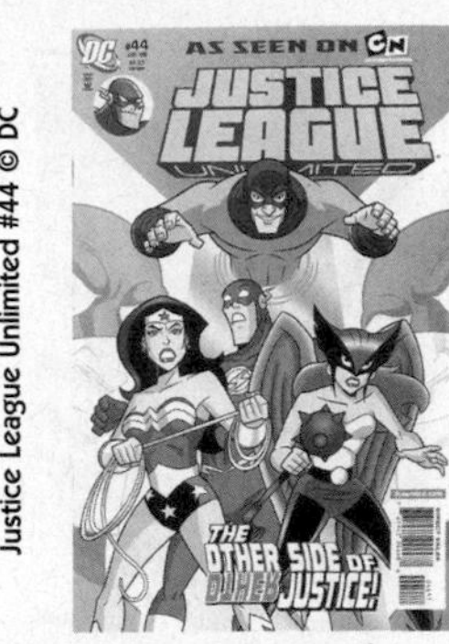

Justice League Unlimited #44 © DC

GD 2.0 | VG 4.0 | FN 6.0 | VF 8.0 | VF/NM 9.0 | NM- 9.2

6 12 18 37 59 80
76-Giant G-65 6 12 18 37 59 80
77-80: 78-Re-intro Vigilante (1st S.A. app?) 4 8 12 22 34 45
81-84,86-90: 82-1st S.A. app. of G.A. Batman (cameo). 83-Apparent death of The Spectre. 90-Last 15¢ issue 3 6 9 20 30 40
85,93-(Giant G-77,G-89; 68 pgs.) 4 8 12 28 44 60
91,92: 91-1st meeting of the G.A. & S.A. Robin; begin 25¢, 52 pgs. issues, ends #99. 92-S.A. Robin tries on costume that is similar to that of G.A. Robin in All Star Comics #58 4 8 12 24 37 50
94-Reprints 1st Sandman story (Adv. #40) & origin/1st app. Starman (Adventure #61); Deadman x-over; N. Adams-a (4 pgs.) 8 16 24 52 86 120
95,96: 95-Origin Dr. Fate & Dr. Midnight -r/ More Fun #67, All-American #25). 96-Origin Hourman (Adv. #48); Wildcat-r 4 8 12 26 41 55
97-99: 97-Origin JLA retold; Sargon, Starman-r. 98 G.A. Sargon, Starman-r. 99-G.A. Sandman, Atom-r; last 52 pg. issue 4 8 12 22 34 45
100-(8/72)-1st meeting of G.A. & S.A. W. Woman 4 8 12 26 41 55
101,102: JSA x-overs. 102-Red Tornado dies 3 6 9 21 32 42
103-106,109: 103-Rutland Vermont Halloween x-over; Phantom Stranger joins. 105-Elongated Man joins. 106-New Red Tornado joins. 109-Hawkman resigns 3 6 9 15 21 26
107,108 JSA x-over; 1st revival app. of G.A. Uncle Sam, Black Condor, The Ray, Dollman, Phantom Lady & The Human Bomb 3 6 9 16 23 30
110,112-116: All 100 pgs. 112-Amazo app; Crimson Avenger, Vigilante r; origin Starman-r/ Adv. #81. 115-Martian Manhunter app. 4 8 12 28 41 55
111-JLA vs. Injustice Gang; intro. Libra (re-appears in 2008's Final Crisis); Shining Knight, Green Arrow-r 4 8 12 26 41 55
117-122,125-134: 117-Hawkman rejoins. 120,121-Adam Strange app. 125,126-Two-Face-app. 128-Wonder Woman rejoins. 129-Destruction of Red Tornado 2 4 6 11 16 20
123-(10/75),124: JLA/JSA x-over. DC editor Julie Schwartz & JLA writers Cary Bates & Elliot S! Maggin appear in story as themselves. 1st named app. Earth-Prime (3rd app. after Flash, 1st Series #179 & 228) 3 6 9 14 19 24
135-136: 135-137-G.A. Bulletman, Bulletgirl, Spy Smasher, Mr. Scarlet, Pinky & Ibis x-over, 1st appearances since G.A. 3 6 9 14 19 24
137-Superman battles G.A. Capt. Marvel 3 6 9 16 22 28
138-Adam Strange app. w/c by Neal Adams; 1st app. Green Lantern of the 73rd Century 2 4 6 11 16 20
139-157: 139-157-(52 pgs.): 139-Adam Strange app. 144-Origin retold; origin J'onn J'onzz. 145-Red Tornado resurrected. 147,148-Legion of Super-Heroes x-over 2 4 6 9 13 16
158-160-(44 pgs.) 2 4 6 8 10 12
158,160-162,169,171,172,173,176-179,181-(Whitman variants; low print run, none show issue # on cover) 2 4 6 9 13 16
161-165,169-182: 161-Zatanna joins & new costume. 171,172-JSA x-over. 171-Mr. Terrific murdered. 178-Cover similar to #1; J'onn J'onzz app. 179-Firestorm joins. 181-Green Arrow leaves JLA 1 2 3 4 5 7
166-168- "Identity Crisis (2004)" precursor; JSA app. vs. Secret Society of Super-Villains 2 4 6 10 14 18
166-168-Whitman variants (no issue # on covers) 3 6 9 18 27 35
183-185-JSA/New Gods/Darkseid/Mr. Miracle x-over 1 2 3 5 7 9
186-194,198,199: 192,193-Real origin Red Tornado. 193-1st app. All-Star Squadron as free 16 pg. insert 6.00
195-197-JSA app. vs. Secret Society of Super-Villains 1 2 3 4 5 7
200 ($1.50, Anniversary issue, 76 pgs.)-JLA origin retold; Green Arrow rejoins; Bolland, Aparo, Giordano, Gil Kane, Infantino, Kubert-a; Perez-c/a 1 2 3 4 5 7
201-206,209-243,246-259: 203-Intro/origin new Royal Flush Gang. 219,220-True origin Black Canary. 228-Re-intro Martian Manhunter. 228-230-War of the Worlds storyline; JLA Satellite destroyed by Martians. 233-Story cont'd from Annual #2. 243-Aquaman leaves. 250-Batman rejoins. 253-Origin Despero. 258-Death of Vibe. 258-261-Legends x-over 4.00
207,208-JSA, JLA, & All-Star Squadron team-up 6.00
244,245-Crisis x-over 5.00
260-Death of Steel 6.00
261-Last issue 1 2 3 5 6 8
Annual 1-3 ('83-'85), 2-Intro new J.L.A. (Aquaman, Martian Manhunter, Steel, Gypsy, Vixen, Vibe, Elongated Man & Zatanna). 3-Crisis x-over 4.00
... Hereby Elects (2006, $14.99, TPB) reprints issues where new members joined; JLofA #4,75,105,106,146,161,173&174; roster of various incarnations; Ordway-c 15.00

NOTE: ***Neal Adams** c-63, 66, 67, 70, 74, 79, 81, 82, 86-89, 91, 92, 94, 96-98, 138, 139. **M. Anderson** c-1-4, 6, 7, 10, 12-14. **Aparo** a-200. **Austin** a-200i. **Baily** a-96r. **Bolland** a-200. **Buckler** c-158, 163, 164. **Burnley** r-94, 98, 99. **Greene** a-46-61i, 64-73i, 110i(r). **Grell** c-117, 122. **Kaluta** c-154p. **Gil Kane** a-200. **Krigstein** a-96(r/Sensation #84). **Kubert** a-200; c-72, 73. **Nino** a-228i, 230i. **Orlando** c-151i. **Perez** a-184-186p, 192-197p, 200p; c-184p, 186, 192-195, 196p, 197p, 199, 200, 201p, 202, 203-205p, 207-209, 212-215, 217, 219, 220. **Reinman** r-97. **Roussos** a-62i. **Sekowsky** a-37, 38, 44-63p, 110-112p(r); c-46-48p, 51p. **Sekowsky/Anderson** c-5, 8, 9, 11, 15. **B. Smith** c-185i. **Starlin** c-178-180, 183, 185p. **Staton** a-244p; c-157p, 244p. **Toth** r-110. **Tuska** a-153, 228p, 241-243p. JSA x-overs-21, 22, 29, 30, 37, 38, 46, 47, 55, 56, 64, 65, 73, 74, 82, 83, 91, 92, 100, 101, 102, 107, 108, 110, 113, 115, 123, 124, 135-137, 147, 148, 159, 160, 171, 172, 183-185, 195-197, 207-209, 219, 220, 231, 232, 244.*

JUSTICE LEAGUE OF AMERICA
DC Comics: No. 0, Sept, 2006 - Present ($2.99)
0-Meltzer-s; history of the JLA; art by various incl. Lee, Giordano, Benes; Turner-c 5.00
0-Variant-c by Campbell 12.00
1-($3.99) Two interlocking covers by Benes; Benes-a 5.00
1-Variant-c by Turner 8.00
1 RRP Edition; sideways composite of both Benes covers 80.00
1-Second printing, Benes cover image between black bars 4.00
2-5-($2.99) Turner-c 3.00
2-5: Variant-c: 2-Jimenez. 3-Sprouse. 4-JG Jones. 5-Art Adams 5.00
6,7-($3.50) 6-JLA vs. Amazo; covers by Turner and Hughes. 7-Roster picked, new HQs; two Benes covers and Turner cover. 3.50
8-11,13-23-($2.99) 8-11-JLA/JSA team-up; covers by Turner & Jimenez. 10-Wally West returns. 13-Two covers. 13-15-Injustice Gang. 16-Tangent Flash. 20-Queen Bee app. 21-Libra app.; leads into Final Crisis #1 3.00
12-($3.50) Two Ross covers; origin retold with Wight-a; Benes-a 3.50
Justice League Wedding Special 1 (11/07, $3.99) McKone-a; Injustice League forms 4.00
...: The Injustice Gang HC (2008, $19.99, dustjacket) r/#13-16; Wedding Special 20.00
...: The Lightning Saga HC (2008, $24.99, dustjacket) r/#0,8 12 & Justice Society of America #5,6; intro. by Patton Oswalt 25.00
...: The Tornado's Path HC (2007, $24.99, dustjacket) r/#1-7; variant cover gallery; Lindelof intro.; commentary by Meltzer & Benes 25.00

JUSTICE LEAGUE OF AMERICA : ANOTHER NAIL (Elseworlds) (Also see JLA: The Nail)
DC Comics: 2004 - No. 3, 2004 ($5.95, prestige format)
1-3-Sequel to JLA: The Nail; Alan Davis-s/a(p) 6.00
TPB (2004, $12.95) r/series 13.00

JUSTICE LEAGUE OF AMERICA SUPER SPECTACULAR
DC Comics: 1999 ($5.95, mimics format of DC 100 Page Super Spectaculars)
1-Reprints Silver Age JLA and Golden Age JSA 6.00

JUSTICE LEAGUE QUARTERLY (...International Quarterly #6 on)
DC Comics: Winter, 1990-91 - No. 17, Winter, 1994 ($2.95/$3.50, 84 pgs.)
1-12,14-17: 1-Intro The Conglomerate (Booster Gold, Praxis, Gypsy, Vapor, Echo, Maxi-Man, & Reverb); Justice League #1-c/swipe. 1,2-Keith Giffen plots/breakdowns. 3-Giffen plot; 72 pg. story. 4-Rogers/Russell-a in back-up. 5,6-Mark Waid scripts. 8,17-Global Guardians app. 3.50
13-Linsner-c 6.00
NOTE: ***Phil Jimenez** a-17p. **Sprouse** a-1p.*

JUSTICE LEAGUES...
DC Comics: Mar, 2001 ($2.50, limited series)
JL?, Justice League of Amazons, Justice League of Atlantis, Justice League of Arkham, Justice League of Aliens, JLA: JLA split by the Advance Man; Perez-c in all; s&a by various 2.50

JUSTICE LEAGUE TASK FORCE
DC Comics: June, 1993 - No. 37, Aug, 1996 ($1.25/$1.50/$1.75)
1-16,0,17-37: Aquaman, Nightwing, Flash, J'onn J'onzz, & Gypsy form team. 5,6-Knight-quest tie-ins (new Batman cameo #5, 1 pg.). 15-Triumph cameo. 16-(9/94)-Zero Hour x-over; Triumph app. 0-(10/94). 17-(11/94)-Triumph becomes part of Justice League Task Force (See JLE #68). 26-Impulse app. 35-Warlord app. 37-Triumph quits team 2.50

JUSTICE LEAGUE: THE NEW FRONTIER SPECIAL (Also see DC: The New Frontier)
DC Comics: May, 2008 ($4.99, one-shot)
1-Short stories by Darwyn Cooke, J.Bone and Dave Bullock; bonus storyboards from the movie 5.00

JUSTICE LEAGUE UNLIMITED (Based on Cartoon Network animated series) (Also see Free Comic Book Day Edition in the Promotional Comics section)
DC Comics: Nov, 2004 - No. 46, Aug, 2008 ($2.25)
1-46: 1-Zatanna app. 2,23,42-Royal Flush Gang app. 4-Adam Strange app. 10-Creeper app. 17-Freedom Fighters app. 18-Space Cabby app. 27-Black Lightning app. 34-Zod app. 2.50
Jam Packed Action (2005, $7.99, digest) adaptations of two TV episodes 8.00
... Vol. 1: United They Stand (2005, $6.99, digest) r/#1-5 7.00
... Vol. 2: World's Greatest Heroes (2006, $6.99, digest) r/#6-10 7.00
... Vol. 3: Champions of Justice (2006, $6.99, digest) r/#11-15 7.00
...: The Ties That Bind (2008, $12.95, full-size) r/#16-22 13.00

JUSTICE MACHINE, THE
Noble Comics: June, 1981 - No. 5, Nov, 1983 ($2.00, nos. 1-3 are mag. size)
1-Byrne-c(p) 3 6 9 15 21 26
2-Austin-c(i) 2 4 6 9 12 15

Justice Society of America (2007 series) #11 © DC

Ka'a'nga Comics #2 © FH

Kaboom #1 © Jeff Matsuda

	GD 2.0	VG 4.0	FN 6.0	VF 8.0	VF/NM 9.0	NM- 9.2
3	1	3	4	6	8	10

4,5, Annual 1: Ann. 1-(1/84, 68 pgs.)(published by Texas Comics); 1st app. The Elementals; Golden-c(p); new Thunder Agents story (43 pgs.) 6.00

JUSTICE MACHINE (Also see The New Justice Machine)
Comico/Innovation Publishing: Jan, 1987 - No. 29, May 1989 ($1.50/$1.75)

1-29 2.50
Annual 1(6/89, $2.50, 36 pgs.)-Last Comico ish. 3.00
Summer Spectacular 1 ('89, $2.75)-Innovation Publ.; Byrne/Gustovich-c 3.00

JUSTICE MACHINE, THE
Innovation Publishing: 1990 - No. 4, 1990 ($1.95/$2.25, deluxe format, mature)

1-4: Gustovich-c/a in all 2.50

JUSTICE MACHINE FEATURING THE ELEMENTALS
Comico: May, 1986 - No. 4, Aug, 1986 ($1.50, limited series)

1-4 2.50

JUSTICE RIDERS
DC Comics: 1997 ($5.95, one-shot, prestige format)

1-Elseworlds; Dixon-s/Williams & Gray-a 6.00

JUSTICE SOCIETY
DC Comics: 2006; 2007 ($14.99, TPB)

Vol. 1 - Rep. from 1976 revival in All Star Comics #58-67 & DC Special #29; Bolland-c 15.00
Vol. 2 - R/All Star Comics #68-74 & Adventure Comics #461-466; new Bolland-c 15.00

JUSTICE SOCIETY OF AMERICA (See Adventure #461 & All-Star #3)
DC Comics: April, 1991 - No. 8, Nov, 1991 ($1.00, limited series)

1-8: 1-Flash. 2-Black Canary. 3-Green Lantern. 4-Hawkman. 5-Flash/Hawkman. 6-Green Lantern/Black Canary. 7-JSA 2.50

JUSTICE SOCIETY OF AMERICA (Also see Last Days of the... Special)
DC Comics: Aug, 1992 - No. 10, May, 1993 ($1.25)

1-10 2.50

JUSTICE SOCIETY OF AMERICA (Follows JSA series)
DC Comics: Feb, 2007 - Present ($3.99/$2.99)

1-($3.99) New team selected; intro. Maxine Hunkle; Alex Ross-c 4.00
1-Variant-c by Eaglesham 6.00
2-17: Covers by Ross and Eaglesham. 3,4-Vandal Savage app. 5,6-JLA/JSA team-up. 9-17-Kingdom Come Superman app. 3.00
JSA Annual 1 (9/08, $3.99) Power Girl on Earth-2; Ross-c/Ordway-a 4.00
...: Thy Kingdom Come Part One HC (2008, $19.99, d.j.) r/#7-12; Ross sketch pages 20.00

JUSTICE SOCIETY OF AMERICA 100-PAGE SUPER SPECTACULAR
DC Comics: 2000 ($6.95, mimics format of DC 100 Page Super Spectaculars)

1-"1975 Issue" reprints Flash team-up and Golden Age JSA 7.00

JUSTICE SOCIETY RETURNS, THE (See All Star Comics (1999) for related titles)
DC Comics: 2003 ($19.95, TPB)

TPB-Reprints 1999 JSA x-over from All-Star Comics #1,2 and related one-shots 20.00

JUSTICE TRAPS THE GUILTY (Fargo Kid V11#3 on)
Prize/Headline Publications: Oct-Nov, 1947 - V11#2(#92), Apr-May, 1958 (True FBI Cases)

	GD 2.0	VG 4.0	FN 6.0	VF 8.0	VF/NM 9.0	NM- 9.2
V2#1-S&K-c/a; electrocution-c	58	116	174	363	599	835
2-S&K-c/a	35	70	105	204	322	440
3-5-S&K-c/a	32	64	96	186	293	400
6-S&K-c/a; Feldstein-a	34	68	102	197	311	425
7,9-S&K-c/a. 7-9-V2#1-3 in indicia; #7-9 on-c	28	56	84	164	260	355
8-Krigstein-a; S&K-c	27	54	81	158	249	340
10-Krigstein-a; S&K-c/a	28	56	84	164	260	355
11,18,19-S&K-c	15	30	45	86	133	180
12,14-17,20-No S&K. 14-Severin/Elder-a (8pg.)	10	20	30	56	76	95
13-Used in **SOTI**, pg. 110-111	11	22	33	62	86	110
21,30-S&K-c/a	15	30	45	86	133	180
22,23-S&K-c	12	24	36	67	94	120
24-26,27,29,31-50: 32-Meskin story	9	18	27	52	69	85
28-Kirby-c	11	22	33	62	86	110
51-55,57,59-70	9	18	27	47	61	75
56-Ben Oda, Joe Simon, Joe Genola, Mort Meskin & Jack Kirby app. in police line-up on classic-c	12	24	36	69	97	125
58-Illo. in **SOTI**, "Treating police contemptuously" (top left); text on heroin	25	50	75	145	228	310
71-92: 76-Orlando-a	8	16	24	40	50	60

NOTE: ***Bailey** a-12, 13. **Elder** a-8. **Kirby** a-19p. **Meskin** a-22, 27, 63, 64; c-45, 46. **Robinson/Meskin** a-5, 19. **Severin** a-8, 11p. Photo c-12, 15-17.*

JUST IMAGINE STAN LEE WITH... (Stan Lee re-invents DC icons)
DC Comics: 2001 - 2002 ($5.95, prestige format, one-shots)
(Adam Hughes back-c on all)(Michael Uslan back-up stories in all, diff. artists)

Scott McDaniel Creating **Aquaman**- Back-up w/Fradon-a 6.00
Joe Kubert Creating **Batman**- Back-up w/Kaluta-a 6.00
Chris Bachalo Creating **Catwoman**- Back-up w/Cooke & Allred-a 6.00
John Cassaday Creating **Crisis**- no back-up story 6.00
Kevin Maguire Creating **The Flash**- Back-up w/Aragonés-a 6.00
Dave Gibbons Creating **Green Lantern**- Back-up w/Giordano-a 6.00
Jerry Ordway Creating **JLA** 6.00
John Byrne Creating **Robin**- Back-up w/John Severin-a 6.00
Walter Simonson Creating **Sandman**- Back-up w/Corben-a 6.00
Gary Frank Creating **Shazam!**- Back-up w/Kano-a 6.00
John Buscema Creating **Superman**- Back-up w/Kyle Baker-a 6.00
Jim Lee Creating **Wonder Woman**- Back-up w/Gene Colan-a 6.00
Secret Files and Origins #1 (3/02, $4.95) Crisis prologue; Jurgens-a 5.00
TPB -Just Imagine Stan Lee Creating the DC Universe: Book One (2002, $19.95) r/Batman, Wonder Woman, Superman, Green Lantern 20.00
TPB -Just Imagine Stan Lee Creating the DC Universe: Book Two (2003, $19.95) r/Flash, JLA, Secret Files and Origins, Robin, Shazam; sketch pages 20.00
TPB -Just Imagine Stan Lee Creating the DC Universe: Book Three (2004, $19.95) r/Aquaman, Catwoman, Sandman, Crisis; profile pages 20.00

JUST MARRIED
Charlton Comics: January, 1958 - No. 114, Dec, 1976

	GD 2.0	VG 4.0	FN 6.0	VF 8.0	VF/NM 9.0	NM- 9.2
1	6	12	18	39	62	85
2	3	6	9	21	32	42
3-10	3	6	9	17	25	32
11-30	3	6	9	14	19	24
31-50	2	4	6	10	14	18
51-70	2	4	6	9	12	15
71-78,80-90: 90-Susan Dey and David Cassidy full page poster	2	4	6	8	10	12
79-Ditko-a (7 pages)	2	4	6	9	13	16
91-114	1	3	4	6	8	10

KA'A'NGA COMICS (...Jungle King)(See Jungle Comics)
Fiction House Magazines (Glen-Kel Publ. Co.): Spring, 1949 - No. 20, Summer, 1954

	GD 2.0	VG 4.0	FN 6.0	VF 8.0	VF/NM 9.0	NM- 9.2
1-Ka'a'nga, Lord of the Jungle begins	52	104	156	317	521	725
2 (Winter, '49-'50)	30	60	90	170	275	375
3,4	22	44	66	128	202	275
5-Camilla app.	17	34	51	98	154	210
6-10: 7-Tuska-a. 9-Tabu, Wizard of the Jungle app. 10-Used in **POP**, pg. 99	15	30	45	85	130	175
11-15: 15-Camilla-r by Baker/Jungle #106	14	28	42	76	108	140
16-Sheena app.	14	28	42	80	115	150
17-20	12	24	36	69	97	125
I.W. Reprint #1,8: 1-r/#18; Kinstler-c. 8-r/#10	3	6	9	14	20	25

NOTE: ***Celardo** c-1. **Whitman** c-8-20(most).*

KABOOM
Awesome Entertainment: Sept, 1997 - No. 3, Nov, 1997 ($2.50)

1-3: 1-Matsuda-a/Loeb-s; 4 covers exist (Matsuda, Sale, Pollina and McGuinness), 1-Dynamic Forces Edition, 2-Regular, 2-Alicia Watcher variant-c, 2-Gold logo variant-c, 3-Two covers by Liefeld & Matsuda, 3-Dynamic Forces Ed., Prelude Ed. 2.50
Prelude Gold Edition 4.00

KABOOM (2nd series)
Awesome Entertainment: July, 1999 - No. 3, Dec, 1999 ($2.50)

1-3: 1-Grant-a(p); at least 4 variant covers 2.50

KABUKI
Caliber: Nov, 1994 ($3.50, B&W, one-shot)

	GD 2.0	VG 4.0	FN 6.0	VF 8.0	VF/NM 9.0	NM- 9.2
nn-(Fear The Reaper) 1st app.; David Mack-c/a/s	1	2	3	5	6	8

Color Special (1/96, $2.95)-Mack-c/a/scripts; pin-ups by Tucci, Harris & Quesada 4.00
Gallery (8/95, $2.95)- pinups from Mack, Bradstreet, Paul Pope & others 3.00

KABUKI
Image Comics: Oct, 1997 - No. 9, Mar, 2000 ($2.95, color)

1-David Mack-c/s/a 5.00

	GD 2.0	VG 4.0	FN 6.0	VF 8.0	VF/NM 9.0	NM- 9.2
1-($10.00)-Dynamic Forces Edition	1	3	4	6	8	10

2-5 4.00
6-9 3.00
#1/2 (9/01, $2.95) r/Wizard 1/2; Eklipse Mag. article; bio 3.00
...Classics (2/99, $3.95) Reprints Fear the Reaper 4.00
...Classics 2 (3/99, $3.95) Reprints Dance of Dance 4.00
...Classics 3-5 (3-6/99, $4.95) Reprints Circle of Blood-Acts 1-3 5.00

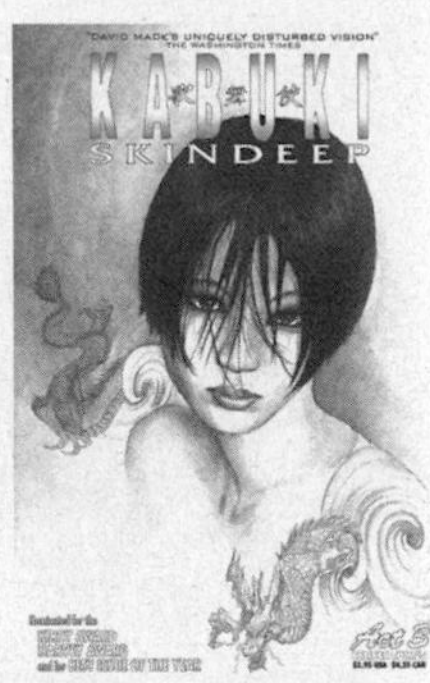

Kabuki: Skin Deep #3 © DC

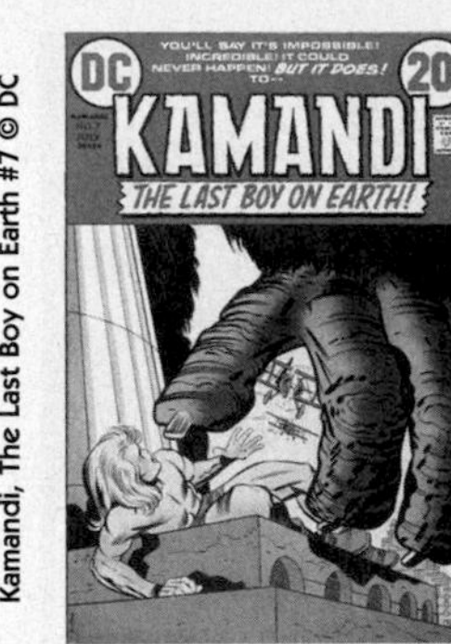

Kamandi, The Last Boy on Earth #7 © DC

Kathy #1 © MAR

	GD 2.0	VG 4.0	FN 6.0	VF 8.0	VF/NM 9.0	NM- 9.2
...Classics 6-12 (7/99-3/00, $3.25) Various reprints						3.25
...Images (6/98, $4.95) r/#1 with new pin-ups						5.00
...Images 2 (1/99, $4.95) r/#1 with new pin-ups						5.00
...Metamorphosis TPB (10/00, $24.95) r/#1-9; Sienkiewicz intro.; 2nd printing exists						25.00
...Reflections 1-4 (7/98-5/02; $4.95) new story plus art techniques						5.00
... The Ghost Play (11/02, $2.95) new story plus interview						3.00

KABUKI
Marvel Comics (Icon): July, 2004 - Present ($2.99, color)

1-9: 1-David Mack-c/s/a in all; variant-c by Alex Maleev. 4-Variant-c by Adam Hughes. 6-Variant-c by Mignola. 8-Variant-c by Kent Williams. 9-Allred var-c						3.00
... Reflections 5-10 (7/05-4/07, $5.99) paintings & sketches of recent work; photos						6.00

KABUKI AGENTS (SCARAB)
Image Comics: Aug, 1999 - No. 8, Aug, 2001 ($2.95, B&W)

1-8-David Mack-s/Rick Mays-a						3.00
Lost in Translation HC (3/02, $29.95) r/#1-8; intro. by Paul Pope						30.00
Lost in Translation SC (3/02, $19.95) r/#1-8; intro. by Paul Pope						20.00

KABUKI: CIRCLE OF BLOOD
Caliber Press: Jan, 1995 - No. 6, Nov, 1995 ($2.95, B&W)

1-David Mack story/a in all						5.00
2-6: 3-#1 on inside indicia.						3.00
6-Variant-c						3.00
TPB ($16.95) r/#1-6, intro. by Steranko						17.00
TPB (1997, $17.95) Image Edition-r/#1-6, intro. by Steranko						18.00
TPB ($24.95) Deluxe Edition						25.00

KABUKI: DANCE OF DEATH
London Night Studios: Jan, 1995 ($3.00, B&W, one-shot)

1-David Mack-c/a/scripts	1	2	3	5	6	8

KABUKI: DREAMS
Image Comics: Jan, 1998 ($4.95, TPB)

nn-Reprints Color Special & Dreams of the Dead						5.00

KABUKI: DREAMS OF THE DEAD
Caliber: July, 1996 ($2.95, one-shot)

nn-David Mack-c/a/scripts						3.00

KABUKI FAN EDITION
Gemstone Publ./Caliber: Feb, 1997 (mail-in offer, one-shot)

nn-David Mack-c/a/scripts						4.00

KABUKI: MASKS OF THE NOH
Caliber: May, 1996 - No. 4, Feb, 1997 ($2.95, limited series)

1-4: 1-Three-c (1A-Quesada, 1B-Buzz, &1C-Mack). 3-Terry Moore pin-up						3.00
TPB-(4/98, $10.95) r/#1-4; intro by Terry Moore						11.00

KABUKI: SKIN DEEP
Caliber Comics: Oct, 1996 - No. 3, May, 1997 ($2.95)

1-3:David Mack-c/a/scripts. 2-Two-c (1-Mack, 1-Ross) 3.00						
TPB-(5/98, $9.95) r/#1-3; intro by Alex Ross						10.00

KAMANDI: AT EARTH'S END
DC Comics: June, 1993 - No. 6, Nov, 1993 ($1.75, limited series)

1-6: Elseworlds storyline						2.50

KAMANDI, THE LAST BOY ON EARTH (Also see Alarming Tales #1, Brave and the Bold #120 & 157 & Cancelled Comic Cavalcade)
National Periodical Publ./DC Comics: Oct-Nov, 1972 - No. 59, Sept-Oct, 1978

1-Origin & 1st app. Kamandi	7	14	21	47	76	105
2,3	4	8	12	26	41	55
4,5: 4-Intro. Prince Tuftan of the Tigers	4	8	12	22	34	45
6-10	3	6	9	17	25	32
11-20	2	4	6	13	18	22
21-28,30,31,33-40: 24-Last 20¢ issue. 31-Intro Pyra.	2	4	6	11	16	20
29,32: 29-Superman x-over. 32-(68 pgs.)-r/origin from #1 plus one new story; 4 pg. biog. of Jack Kirby with B&W photos	3	6	9	14	19	24
41-57	2	4	6	9	13	16
58-(44 pgs.)-Karate Kid x-over from LSH	2	4	6	13	18	22
59-(44 pgs.)-Cont'd in B&B #157; The Return of Omac back-up by Starlin-c/a(p)	2	4	6	13	18	22

NOTE: *Ayers a(p)-48-59 (most). **Giffen** a-44p, 45p. **Kirby** a-1-40p; c-1-33. **Kubert** c-34-41. **Nasser** a-45p, 46p. **Starlin** a-59p; c-57, 59p.*

KAMUI (Legend Of...#2 on)
Eclipse Comics/Viz Comics: May 12, 1987 - No. 37, Nov. 15, 1988 ($1.50, B&W, bi-weekly)

1-37: 1-3 have 2nd printings						2.50

KAOS MOON (Also see Negative Burn #34)
Caliber Comics: 1996 - No. 4, 1997 ($2.95, B&W)

1-4-David Boller-s/a						3.00
3,4-Limited Alternate-c						4.00
3,4-Gold Alternate-c, Full Circle TPB ($5.95) r/#1,2						6.00

KARATE KID (See Action, Adventure, Legion of Super-Heroes, & Superboy)
National Periodical Publications/DC Comics: Mar-Apr, 1976 - No. 15, July-Aug, 1978 (Legion of Super-Heroes spin-off)

1,15: 1-Meets Iris Jacobs; Estrada/Staton-a. 15-Continued into Kamandi #58	2	4	6	9	11	14
2-14: 2-Major Disaster app. 14-Robin x-over	1	2	3	5	6	8

NOTE: ***Grell** c-1-4, 5p, 6p, 7, 8. **Staton** a-1-9i. Legion x-over-No. 1, 2, 4, 6, 10, 12, 13. Princess Projectra x-over-#8, 9.*

KATHY
Standard Comics: Sept, 1949 - No. 17, Sept, 1955

1-Teen-age	14	28	42	82	121	160
2-Schomburg-c	11	22	33	60	83	105
3-5	8	16	24	44	57	70
6-17: 17-Code approved	8	16	24	40	50	60

KATHY (The Teenage Tornado)
Atlas Comics/Marvel (ZPC): Oct, 1959 - No. 27, Feb, 1964 (most issues contain paper dolls and pin-up pages)

1-The Teen-age Tornado; Goldberg-c/a in all	7	14	21	49	80	110
2	4	8	12	28	44	60
3-15	4	8	12	22	34	45
16-23,25,27	3	6	9	16	23	30
24 (8/63) Frank Sinatra, Cary Grant, Ed Sullivan & Liz Taylor-c	3	6	9	18	27	35
26-(12/63) Kathy becomes a model; Millie app.	3	6	9	18	27	35

KAT KARSON
I. W. Enterprises: No date (Reprint)

1-Funny animals	2	4	6	10	12	15

KATO OF THE GREEN HORNET (Also see The Green Hornet)
Now Comics: Nov, 1991 - No. 4, Feb, 1992 ($2.50, mini-series)

1-4: Brent Anderson-c/a						2.50

KATO OF THE GREEN HORNET II (Also see The Green Hornet)
Now Comics: Nov, 1992 - No. 2, Dec, 1993 ($2.50, mini-series)

1,2-Baron-s/Mayerik & Sherman-a						2.50

KATY KEENE (Also see Kasco Komics, Laugh, Pep, Suzie, & Wilbur)
Archie Publ./Close-Up/Radio Comics: 1949 - No. 4, 1951; No. 5, 3/52 - No. 62, Oct, 1961 (50-53-Adventures of...on-c) (Cut and missing pages are common)

1-Bill Woggon-c/a begins; swipes-c to Mopsy #1	138	276	414	863	1432	2000
2-(1950)	59	118	177	369	610	850
3-5: 3-(1951). 4-(1951)	46	92	138	281	466	650
6-10	37	74	111	213	337	460
11,13-21: 21-Last pre-code issue (3/55)	30	60	90	174	275	375
12-(Scarce)	36	72	108	208	329	450
22-40	21	42	63	122	191	260
41-60: 54-Wedding Album plus wedding pin-up	16	32	48	94	147	200
61,62: 62-Robot-c	18	36	54	105	165	225
Annual 1('54, 25¢)-All new stories; last pre-code	53	106	159	323	537	750
Annual 2-6('55-59, 25¢)-All new stories	31	62	93	178	282	385
3-D 1(1953, 25¢, large size)-Came w/glasses	39	78	117	224	355	485
Charm 1(9/58)-Woggon-c/a; new stories, and cut-outs	29	58	87	170	268	365
Glamour 1(1957)-Puzzles, games, cut-outs	29	58	87	170	268	365
Spectacular 1('56)	30	60	90	172	271	370

NOTE: *Debby's Diary in #45, 47-49, 52, 57.*

KATY KEENE COMICS DIGEST MAGAZINE
Close-Up, Inc. (Archie Ent.): 1987 - No. 10, July, 1990 ($1.25/$1.35/$1.50, digest size)

1	2	4	6	9	13	16
2-10	1	2	3	5	7	9

NOTE: *Many used copies are cut-up inside.*

KATY KEENE FASHION BOOK MAGAZINE
Radio Comics/Archie Publications: 1955 - No. 13, Sum, '56 - N. 23, Wint, '58-59 (nn 3-10)

1-Bill Woggon-c/a	52	104	156	317	521	725
2	30	60	90	174	275	375

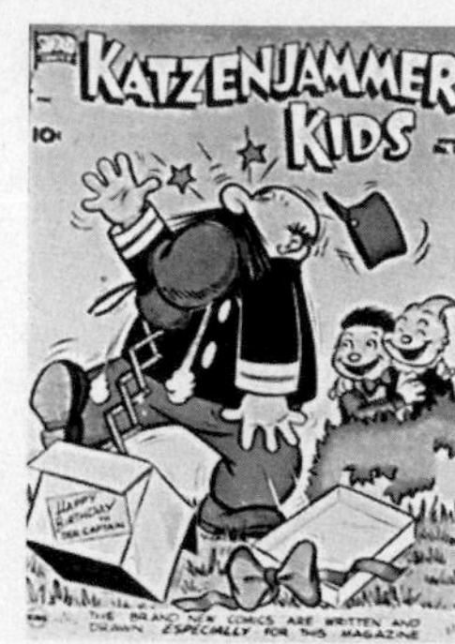

Katzenjammer Kids #16 © STD

Kazar V2 #16 © MAR

Keen Detective Funnies V2 #4 © CEN

	GD 2.0	VG 4.0	FN 6.0	VF 8.0	VF/NM 9.0	NM- 9.2
11-18: 18-Photo Bill Woggon	22	44	66	126	198	270
19-23	18	36	54	103	162	220

KATY KEENE HOLIDAY FUN (See Archie Giant Series Magazine No. 7, 12)

KATY KEENE MODEL BEHAVIOR
Archie Comic Publications: 2008 ($10.95, TPB)

	GD 2.0	VG 4.0	FN 6.0	VF 8.0	VF/NM 9.0	NM- 9.2
Vol. 1 - New story and reprinted apps./pin-ups from Archie & Friends #101-112						11.00

KATY KEENE PINUP PARADE
Radio Comics/Archie Publications: 1955 - No. 15, Summer, 1961 (25¢)
(Cut-out & missing pages are common)

	GD 2.0	VG 4.0	FN 6.0	VF 8.0	VF/NM 9.0	NM- 9.2
1-Cut-outs in all?; last pre-code issue	52	104	156	317	521	725
2-(1956)	30	60	90	174	275	375
3-5: 3-(1957)	26	52	78	150	235	320
6-10,12-14: 8-Mad parody. 10-Bill Woggon photo	21	42	63	122	191	260
11-Story of how comics get CCA approved, narrated by Katy	26	52	78	152	239	325
15(Rare)-Photo artist & family	40	80	120	243	389	535

KATY KEENE SPECIAL (Katy Keene #7 on; see Laugh Comics Digest)
Archie Ent.: Sept, 1983 - No. 33, 1990 (Later issues published quarterly)

	GD 2.0	VG 4.0	FN 6.0	VF 8.0	VF/NM 9.0	NM- 9.2
1-10: 1-Woggon-r; new Woggon-c. 3-Woggon-r						5.00
11-25: 12-Spider-Man parody						6.00
26-32-(Low print run)	1	2	3	5	7	9
33	2	4	6	8	10	12

KATZENJAMMER KIDS, THE (See Captain & the Kids & Giant Comic Album)
David McKay Publ./Standard No. 12-21(Spring/'50 - 53)/Harvey No. 22, 4/53 on: 1945-1946; Summer, 1947 - No. 27, Feb-Mar, 1954

	GD 2.0	VG 4.0	FN 6.0	VF 8.0	VF/NM 9.0	NM- 9.2
Feature Books 30	20	40	60	117	184	250
Feature Books 32,35('45),41,44('46)	18	36	54	103	162	220
Feature Book 37-Has photos & biography of Harold Knerr	19	38	57	109	172	235
1(1947)-All new stories begin	19	38	57	109	172	235
2	11	22	33	64	90	115
3-11	9	18	27	52	69	85
12-14(Standard)	8	16	24	42	54	65
15-21(Standard)	8	16	24	40	50	60
22-25,27(Harvey): 22-24-Henry app.	7	14	21	35	43	50
26-Half in 3-D	16	32	48	94	147	200

KAYO (Formerly Bullseye & Jest; becomes Carnival Comics)
Harry 'A' Chesler: No. 12, Mar, 1945

	GD 2.0	VG 4.0	FN 6.0	VF 8.0	VF/NM 9.0	NM- 9.2
12-Green Knight, Capt. Glory, Little Nemo (not by McCay)	17	34	51	98	154	210

KA-ZAR (Also see Marvel Comics #1, Savage Tales #6 & X-Men #10)
Marvel Comics Group: Aug, 1970 - No. 3, Mar, 1971 (Giant-Size, 68 pgs.)

	GD 2.0	VG 4.0	FN 6.0	VF 8.0	VF/NM 9.0	NM- 9.2
1-Reprints earlier Ka-Zar stories; Avengers x-over in Hercules; Daredevil, X-Men app.; hidden profanity-c	3	6	9	21	32	42
2,3-Daredevil-r. 2-r/Daredevil #13 w/Kirby layouts; Ka-Zar origin, Angel-r from X-Men by Tuska. 3-Romita & Heck-a (no Kirby)	3	6	9	16	22	28

NOTE: ***Buscema** r-2. **Colan** a-1p(r). **Kirby** c/a-1, 2. #1-Reprints X-Men #10 & Daredevil #24*

KA-ZAR
Marvel Comics Group: Jan, 1974 - No. 20, Feb, 1977 (Regular Size)

	GD 2.0	VG 4.0	FN 6.0	VF 8.0	VF/NM 9.0	NM- 9.2
1	2	4	6	10	14	18
2-10	1	2	3	5	7	9
11-14,16,18-20						6.00
15,17-(Regular 25¢ edition)(8/76)						6.00
15,17-(30¢-c variants, limited distribution)	2	4	6	10	14	18

NOTE: ***Alcala** a-6i, 8i. **Brunner** c-4. **J. Buscema** a-6-10p; c-1, 5, 7. **Heath** a-12. **G. Kane** c(p)-3, 5, 8-11, 15, 20. **Kirby** c-12p. **Reinman** a-1p.*

KA-ZAR (Volume 2)
Marvel Comics: May, 1997 - No. 20, Dec, 1998 ($1.95/$1.99)

	GD 2.0	VG 4.0	FN 6.0	VF 8.0	VF/NM 9.0	NM- 9.2
1-Waid-s/Andy Kubert-c/a. thru #4						3.00
1-2nd printing; new cover						2.50
2,4: 2-Two-c						2.50
3-Alpha Flight #1 preview						3.00
5-13,15-20: 8-Includes Spider-Man Cybercomic CD-ROM. 9-11-Thanos app. 15-Priest-s/Martinez & Rodriguez-a begin; Punisher app.						2.50
14-($2.99) Last Waid/Kubert issue; flip book with 2nd story previewing new creative team of Priest-s/Martinez & Rodriguez-a						3.00
'97 Annual ($2.99)-Wraparound-c						3.00

KA-ZAR OF THE SAVAGE LAND
Marvel Comics: Feb, 1997 ($2.50, one-shot)

	GD 2.0	VG 4.0	FN 6.0	VF 8.0	VF/NM 9.0	NM- 9.2
1-Wraparound-c						2.50

KA-ZAR: SIBLING RIVALRY
Marvel Comics: July, 1997 ($1.95, one-shot)

	GD 2.0	VG 4.0	FN 6.0	VF 8.0	VF/NM 9.0	NM- 9.2
(# -1) Flashback story w/Alpha Flight #1 preview						2.50

KA-ZAR THE SAVAGE (See Marvel Fanfare)
Marvel Comics Group: Apr, 1981 - No. 34, Oct, 1984 (Regular size)(Mando paper #10 on)

	GD 2.0	VG 4.0	FN 6.0	VF 8.0	VF/NM 9.0	NM- 9.2
1						4.00
2-20,24,27,28,30-34: 11-Origin Zabu. 12-One of two versions with panel missing on pg. 10. 20-Kraven the Hunter-c/story (also apps. in #21)						2.50
12-Version with panel on pg. 10 (1600 printed)						6.00
21-23, 25,26-Spider-Man app. 26-Photo-c.						3.00
29-Double size; Ka-Zar & Shanna wed						3.00

NOTE: ***B. Anderson** a-1-15p, 18, 19; c-1-17, 18p, 20(back). **G. Kane** a(back-up)-11, 12, 14.*

KEEN DETECTIVE FUNNIES (Formerly Detective Picture Stories?)
Centaur Publications: No. 8, July, 1938 - No. 24, Sept, 1940

	GD 2.0	VG 4.0	FN 6.0	VF 8.0	VF/NM 9.0	NM- 9.2
V1#8-The Clock continues-r/Funny Picture Stories #1; Roy Crane-a (1st?)	241	482	723	1506	2503	3500
9-Tex Martin by Eisner; The Gang Buster app.	88	176	264	550	913	1275
10,11: 11-Dean Denton story (begins?)	79	158	237	494	822	1150
V2#1,2-The Eye Sees by Frank Thomas begins; ends #23(Not in V2#3&5). 2-Jack Cole-a	73	146	219	456	758	1060
3-6: 3-TNT Todd begins. 4-Gabby Flynn begins. 5,6-Dean Denton story	69	138	207	431	716	1000
7-The Masked Marvel by Ben Thompson begins (7/39, 1st app.)(scarce)	248	496	744	1550	2575	3600
8-Nudist ranch panel w/four girls	88	176	264	550	913	1275
9-11	78	156	234	488	807	1125
12(12/39)-Origin The Eye Sees by Frank Thomas; death of Masked Marvel's sidekick ZL	95	190	285	594	985	1375
V3#1,2	69	138	207	431	716	1000
18,19,21,22: 18-Bondage/torture-c	69	138	207	431	716	1000
20-Classic Eye Sees-c by Thomas	105	210	315	656	1091	1525
23-Air Man begins (intro); Air Man-c	97	194	291	606	1003	1400
24-(scarce) Air Man-c	103	206	309	644	1072	1500

NOTE: ***Burgos** a-V2#2. **Jack Cole** a-V2#2. **Eisner** a-10, V2#6r. **Ken Ernst** a-V2#4-7, 9, 10, 19, 21; c-V2#4. **Everett** a-V2#6, 7, 9, 11, 12, 20. **Guardineer** a-V2#5, 66. **Gustavson** a-V2#4-6. **Simon** c-V3#1. **Thompson** c-V2#7, 9, 10, 22.*

KEEN KOMICS
Centaur Publications: V2#1, May, 1939 - V2#3, Nov, 1939

	GD 2.0	VG 4.0	FN 6.0	VF 8.0	VF/NM 9.0	NM- 9.2
V2#1(Large size)-Dan Hastings (s/f), The Big Top, Bob Phantom the Magician, The Mad Goddess app.	97	194	291	606	1003	1400
V2#2(Reg. size)-The Forbidden Idol of Machu Picchu; Cut Carson by Burgos begins	62	124	186	388	644	900
V2#3-Saddle Sniffl by Jack Cole, Circus Pays, Kings Revenge app.	62	124	186	388	644	900

NOTE: ***Binder** a-V2#2. **Burgos** a-V2#2, 3. **Ken Ernst** a-V2#3. **Gustavson** a-V2#2. **Jack Cole** a-V2#3.*

KEEN TEENS (Girls magazine)
Life's Romances Publ./Leader/Magazine Ent.: 1945 - No. 6, Aug-Sept, 1947

	GD 2.0	VG 4.0	FN 6.0	VF 8.0	VF/NM 9.0	NM- 9.2
nn (#1)-14 pgs. Claire Voyant (cont'd. in other nn issue) movie photos, Dotty Dripple, Gertie O'Grady & Sissy; Van Johnson, Frank Sinatra photo-c	40	80	120	235	368	500
nn (#2, 1946)-16 pgs. Claire Voyant & 16 pgs. movie photos	28	56	84	162	256	350
3-6: 4-Glenn Ford photo-c. 5-Perry Como-c	14	28	42	82	121	160

KELLYS, THE (Formerly Rusty Comics; Spy Cases No. 26 on)
Marvel Comics (HPC): No. 23, Jan, 1950 - No. 25, June, 1950 (52 pgs.)

	GD 2.0	VG 4.0	FN 6.0	VF 8.0	VF/NM 9.0	NM- 9.2
23-Teenage	13	26	39	74	105	135
24,25: 24-Margie app.	9	18	27	50	65	80

KEN MAYNARD WESTERN (Movie star)(See Wow Comics, 1936)
Fawcett Publ.: Sept, 1950 - No. 8, Feb, 1952 (All 36 pgs; photo front/back-c)

	GD 2.0	VG 4.0	FN 6.0	VF 8.0	VF/NM 9.0	NM- 9.2
1-Ken Maynard & his horse Tarzan begin	50	100	150	305	490	675
2	30	60	90	173	267	360
3-8: 6-Atomic bomb explosion panel	22	44	66	125	193	260

KEN SHANNON (Becomes Gabby #11 on) (Also see Police Comics #103)
Quality Comics Group: Oct, 1951 - No. 10, Apr, 1953 (A private eye)

	GD 2.0	VG 4.0	FN 6.0	VF 8.0	VF/NM 9.0	NM- 9.2
1-Crandall-a	40	80	120	235	368	500
2-Crandall c/a(2)	29	58	87	167	264	360
3-Horror-c; Crandall-a	24	48	72	139	220	300
4,5-Crandall-a	21	42	63	122	191	260
6-Crandall-c/a; "The Weird Vampire Mob"-c/s	24	48	72	139	220	300

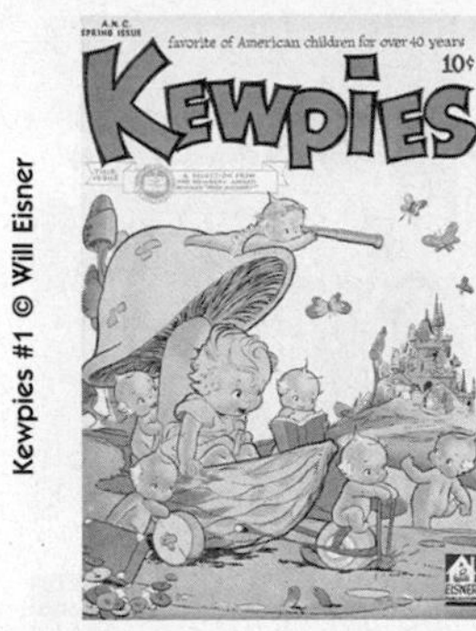

Kewpies #1 © Will Eisner

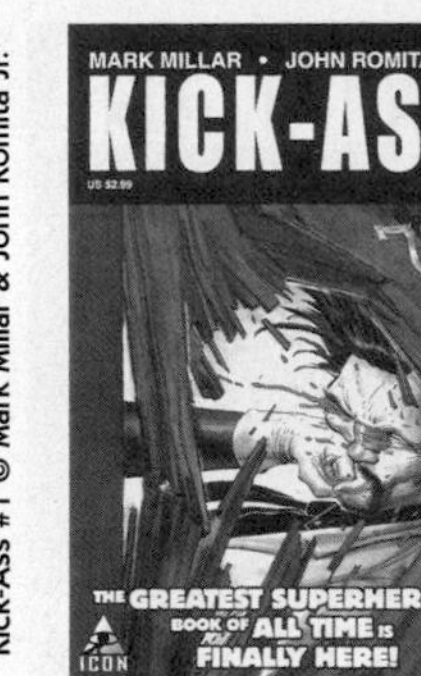

Kick-Ass #1 © Mark Millar & John Romita Jr.

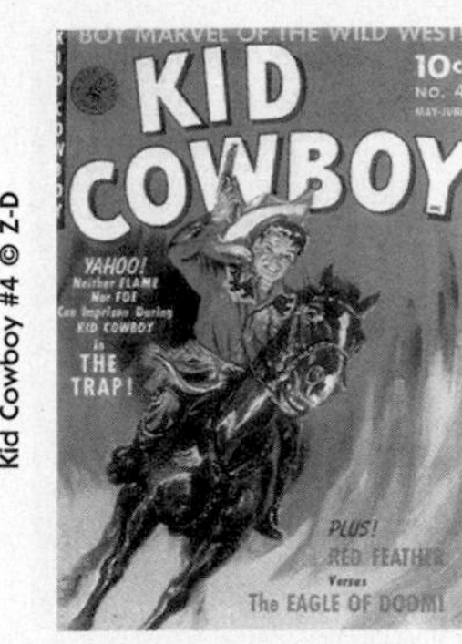

Kid Cowboy #4 © Z-D

	GD 2.0	VG 4.0	FN 6.0	VF 8.0	VF/NM 9.0	NM- 9.2

7,10: 7-Crandall-a. 10-Crandall-c 18 36 54 103 162 220
8,9: 8-Opium den drug use story 17 34 51 98 154 210
NOTE: ***Crandall/Cuidera** c-1-10. **Jack Cole** a-1-9. #1-15 published after title change to Gabby.*

KEN STUART
Publication Enterprises: Jan, 1949 (Sea Adventures)
1-Frank Borth-c/a 10 20 30 54 72 90

KENT BLAKE OF THE SECRET SERVICE (Spy)
Marvel/Atlas Comics(20CC): May, 1951 - No. 14, July, 1953
1-Injury to eye, bondage, torture; Brodsky-c 21 42 63 122 191 260
2-Drug use w/hypo scenes; Brodsky-c 15 30 45 85 130 175
3-14: 8-R.Q. Sale-a (2 pgs.) 10 20 30 56 76 95
NOTE: ***Heath** c-5, 7, 8. **Infantino** c-12. **Maneely** c-3. **Sinnott** a-2(3). **Tuska** a-8(3pg.).*

KENTS, THE
DC Comics: Aug, 1997 - No. 12, July, 1998 ($2.50, limited series)
1-12-Ostrander-s/art by Truman and Bair (#1-8), Mandrake (#9-12) 3.00
TPB ($19.95) r/#1-12 20.00

KERRY DRAKE (Also see A-1 Comics)
Argo: Jan, 1956 - No. 2, March, 1956
1,2-Newspaper-r 8 16 24 44 57 70

KERRY DRAKE DETECTIVE CASES (...Racket Buster No. 32,33)
(Also see Chamber of Clues & Green Hornet Comics #42-47)
Life's Romances/Com/Magazine Ent. No.1-5/Harvey No.6 on: 1944 - No. 5, 1944; No. 6, Jan, 1948 - No. 33, Aug, 1952
nn(1944)(A-1 Comics)(slightly over-size) 30 60 90 174 275 375
2 18 36 54 105 165 225
3-5(1944) 15 30 45 88 137 185
6,8(1948): Lady Crime by Powell. 8-Bondage-c 12 24 36 67 94 120
7-Kubert-a; biog of Andriola (artist) 13 26 39 74 105 135
9,10-Two-part marijuana story; Kerry smokes marijuana in #10
15 30 45 88 137 185
11-15 10 20 30 58 79 100
16-33 9 18 27 50 65 80
NOTE: ***Andiola** c-6-9. **Berg** a-5. **Powell** a-10-23, 28, 29.*

KEWPIES
Will Eisner Publications: Spring, 1949
1-Feiffer-a; Kewpie Doll ad on back cover; used in **SOTI**, pg. 35
46 92 138 281 466 650

KEY COMICS
Consolidated Magazines: Jan, 1944 - No. 5, Aug, 1946
1-The Key, Will-O-The-Wisp begin 41 82 123 256 416 575
2 (3/44) 23 46 69 132 209 285
3,4: 4-(5/46)-Origin John Quincy The Atom (begins); Walter Johnson c-3-5
20 40 60 115 180 245
5-4pg. Faust Opera adaptation; Kiefer-a; back-c advertises "Masterpieces Illustrated" by Lloyd Jacquet after he left Classic Comics (no copies of Masterpieces Illustrated known)
25 50 75 145 228 310

KEY RING COMICS
Dell Publishing Co.: 1941 (16 pgs.; two colors) (sold 5 for 10¢)
1-Sky Hawk, 1-Viking Carter, 1-Features Sleepy Samson, 1-Origin Greg Gilday-r/War Comics #2 9 18 27 47 61 75
1-Radior (Super hero) 10 20 30 54 72 90
NOTE: *Each book has two holes in spine to put in binder.*

KICK-ASS
Marvel Comics (Icon): April, 2008 - Present ($2.99)
1-Mark Millar-s/John Romita Jr.-a/c 10.00
1-Red variant cover by McNiven 15.00
1-2nd printing 4.00
1-Director's Cut (8/08, $3.99) r/#1 with script and sketch pages; Millar afterword 4.00
2-4 4.00
NOTE: *Multiple printings exist for most issues.*

KID CARROTS
St. John Publishing Co.: September, 1953
1-Funny animal 8 16 24 42 54 65

KID COLT OUTLAW (Kid Colt #1-4; ...Outlaw #5-on)(Also see All Western Winners, Best Western, Black Rider, Giant-Size..., Two-Gun Kid, Two-Gun Western, Western Winners, Wild Western, Wisco)
Marvel Comics(LCC) 1-16; Atlas(LMC) 17-102; Marvel 103-on: 8/48 - No. 139, 3/68; No. 140, 11/69 - No. 229, 4/79
1-Kid Colt & his horse Steel begin. 110 220 330 688 1144 1600
2 53 106 159 323 537 750
3-5: 4-Anti-Wertham editorial; Tex Taylor app. 5-Blaze Carson app.
42 84 126 256 421 585
6-8: 6-Tex Taylor app; 7-Nimo the Lion begins, ends #10
30 60 90 174 275 375
9,10 (52 pgs.) 30 60 90 174 275 375
11-Origin 35 70 105 201 318 435
12-20 20 40 60 117 184 250
21-32 16 32 48 94 147 200
33-45: Black Rider in all 14 28 42 80 115 150
46,47,49,50 12 24 36 67 94 120
48-Kubert-a 12 24 36 69 97 125
51-53,55,56 10 20 30 56 76 95
54-Williamson/Maneely-c 11 22 33 60 83 105
57-60,66: 4-pg. Williamson-a in all 7 14 21 49 80 110
61-63,67-78,80-86: 70-Severin-c. 69,73-Maneely-c. 86-Kirby-a(r).
6 12 18 37 59 80
64,65-Crandall-a 6 12 18 39 62 85
79,87: 79-Origin retold. 87-Davis-a(r) 6 12 18 39 62 85
88,89-Williamson-a in both (4 pgs.). 89-Redrawn Matt Slade #2
6 12 18 41 66 90
90-99,101-106,108,109: 91-Kirby/Ayers-c. 95-Kirby/Ayers-c/story. 102-Last 10¢ issue
5 10 15 32 51 70
100 5 10 15 35 55 75
107-Only Kirby sci-fi cover of title; Kirby -a. 6 12 18 41 66 90
110-(5/63)-1st app. Iron Mask (Iron Man type villain) 6 12 18 39 62 85
111-120: 114-(1/64)-2nd app. Iron Mask 4 8 12 26 41 55
121-129,133-139: 121-Rawhide Kid x-over. 125-Two-Gun Kid x-over. 139-Last 12¢ issue
3 6 9 20 30 40
130-132 (68 pgs.)-one new story each. 130-Origin 4 8 12 28 44 60
140-155: 140-Reprints begin (later issues mostly-r). 155-Last 15¢ issue
2 4 6 11 16 20
156-Giant; reprints (52 pgs.) 3 6 9 16 23 30
157-180,200: 170-Origin retold. 2 4 6 9 13 16
181-199 2 4 6 8 10 12
201-229: 201-New material w/Rawhide Kid app; Kane-c. 229-Rawhide Kid-r
1 3 4 6 8 10
205-209-(30¢-c variants, limited dist.) 5 10 15 30 48 65
218-220-(35¢-c variants, limited dist.) 7 14 21 47 76 105
...Album (no date; 1950's; Atlas Comics)-132 pgs.; random binding, cardboard cover, B&W stories; contents can vary (Rare) 86 172 258 538 894 1250
NOTE: ***Ayers** a-many. **Colan** a-52, 53; c(p)-223, 228, 229. **Crandall** a-140r, 167r. **Everett** a-90, 137i, 225i(r). **Heath** a-8(2); c-34, 35, 39, 44, 46, 48, 49, 57, 64. **Heck** a-135, 139. **Jack Keller** a-25(2), 26-68(3-4), 78, 94p, 98, 99, 108, 110, 130, 132, 140-150r. **Kirby** a-86r, 93, 96, 107, 119, 176(part); c-87, 92-95, 97, 99-112, 114-117, 121-123, 197r; w/**Ditko** c-89. **Maneely** a-12, 68, 81; c-17, 19, 40-43, 47, 52, 53, 62, 65, 68, 78, 81, 142r, 150r. **Morrow** a-173r, 216r. **Rico** a-13, 18. **Severin** c-58, 59, 143, 148, 149i. **Shores** a-39, 41-43, 143r; c-1-10(most), 24. **Sutton** a-136, 137p, 225p(r). **Wildey** a-47, 54, 82, 144r. **Williamson** r-147, 170, 172, 216. **Woodbridge** a-64, 81. Black Rider in #33-45, 74, 86. Iron Mask in #110, 114, 121, 127. Sam Hawk in #80, 84, 101, 111, 121, 146, 174, 181, 188.*

KID COWBOY (Also see Approved Comics #4 & Boy Cowboy)
Ziff-Davis Publ./St. John (Approved Comics) #11,14: 1950 - No. 11, Wint, '52-'53; No. 13, April 1953; No. 14, June, 1954 (No #12) (Painted covers #1-10,13,14)
1-Lucy Belle & Red Feather begin 16 32 48 94 147 200
2-Maneely-c 11 22 33 62 86 110
3-11,13,14: (#3, spr. '51). 5-Berg-a. 14-Code approved
10 20 30 56 76 95

KID DEATH & FLUFFY HALLOWEEN SPECIAL
Event Comics: Oct, 1997 ($2.95, B&W, one-shot)
1-Variant-c by Cebollero & Quesada/Palmiotti 3.00

KID DEATH & FLUFFY SPRING BREAK SPECIAL
Event Comics: July, 1996 ($2.50, B&W, one-shot)
1-Quesada & Palmiotti-c/scripts 2.50

KIDDIE KAPERS
Kiddie Kapers Co., 1945/Decker Publ. (Red Top-Farrell): 1945?(nd); Oct, 1957; 1963 - 1964
1(nd, 1945-46?, 36 pgs.)-Infinity-c; funny animal 10 20 30 54 72 90
1(10/57)(Decker)-Little Bit-r from Kiddie Karnival 5 10 15 22 26 30
Super Reprint #7, 10('63), 12, 14('63), 15,17('64), 18('64): 10, 14-r/Animal Adventures #1. 15-Animal Advs. #? 17-Cowboys 'N' Injuns #? 2 4 6 8 11 14

KIDDIE KARNIVAL
Ziff-Davis Publ. Co. (Approved Comics): 1952 (25¢, 100 pgs.) (One Shot)

Kid Komics #5 © MAR

Killraven #1 © MAR

The Kilroys #7 © ACG

	GD 2.0	VG 4.0	FN 6.0	VF 8.0	VF/NM 9.0	NM- 9.2
nn-Rebound Little Bit #1,2; painted-c	36	72	108	208	329	450

KID ETERNITY (Becomes Buccaneers) (See Hit Comics)
Quality Comics Group: Spring, 1946 - No. 18, Nov, 1949

	GD	VG	FN	VF	VF/NM	NM-
1	103	206	309	644	1072	1500
2	41	82	123	250	400	550
3-Mac Raboy-a	41	82	123	253	409	565
4-10	25	50	75	145	228	310
11-18	19	38	57	109	172	235

KID ETERNITY
DC Comics: 1991 - No. 3, Nov, 1991 ($4.95, limited series)

	GD	VG	FN	VF	VF/NM	NM-
1-3: Grant Morrison scripts/Duncan Fegredo-a/c						6.00
TPB (2006, $14.99) r/#1-3						15.00

KID ETERNITY
DC Comics (Vertigo): May, 1993 - No. 16, Sept, 1994 ($1.95, mature)

	GD	VG	FN	VF	VF/NM	NM-
1-16: 1-Gold ink-c. 6-Photo-c. All Sean Phillips-c/a except #15 (Phillips-c/i only)						2.50

KID FROM DODGE CITY, THE
Atlas Comics (MMC): July, 1957 - No. 2, Sept, 1957

	GD	VG	FN	VF	VF/NM	NM-
1-Don Heck-c	10	20	30	56	76	95
2-Everett-c	7	14	21	37	46	55

KID FROM TEXAS, THE (A Texas Ranger)
Atlas Comics (CSI): June, 1957 - No. 2, Aug, 1957

	GD	VG	FN	VF	VF/NM	NM-
1-Powell-a; Severin-c	10	20	30	56	76	95
2	7	14	21	37	46	55

KID KOKO
I. W. Enterprises: 1958

	GD	VG	FN	VF	VF/NM	NM-
Reprint #1,2-(r/M.E.'s Koko & Kola #4, 1947)	2	4	6	8	11	14

KID KOMICS (Kid Movie Komics No. 11)
Timely Comics (USA 1,2/FCI 3-10): Feb, 1943 - No. 10, Spring, 1946

	GD	VG	FN	VF	VF/NM	NM-
1-Origin Captain Wonder & sidekick Tim Mullrooney, & Subbie; intro the Sea-Going Lad, Pinto Pete, & Trixie Trouble; Knuckles & Whitewash Jones (from Young Allies) app.; Wolverton-a (7 pgs.)	423	846	1269	2855	5028	7200
2-The Young Allies, Red Hawk, & Tommy Tyme begin; last Captain Wonder & Subbie	200	400	600	1250	2075	2900
3-The Vision, Daredevils & Red Hawk app.	152	304	456	950	1575	2200
4-The Destroyer begins; Sub-Mariner app.; Red Hawk & Tommy Tyme end	128	256	384	800	1325	1850
5,6: 5-Tommy Tyme begins, ends #10	97	194	291	606	1003	1400
7-10: 7,10-The Whizzer app. Destroyer not in #7,8. 10-Last Destroyer, Young Allies & Whizzer	86	172	258	538	894	1250

NOTE: *Brodsky c-5.* ***Schomburg*** *c-2-4, 6-10.* ***Shores*** *c-1. Captain Wonder c-1, 2. The Young Allies c-3-10.*

KID MONTANA (Formerly Davy Crockett Frontier Fighter; The Gunfighters No. 51 on)
Charlton Comics: V2#9, Nov, 1957 - No. 50, Mar, 1965

	GD	VG	FN	VF	VF/NM	NM-
V2#9 (#1)	4	8	12	28	44	60
10	3	6	9	20	30	40
11,12,14-20	3	6	9	16	22	28
13-Williamson-a	3	6	9	20	30	40
21-35: 25,31-Giordano-c. 32-Origin Kid Montana. 34-Geronimo-c/s. 35-Snow Monster-c/s	2	4	6	11	16	20
36-50: 36-Dinosaur-c/s. 37,48-Giordano-c	2	4	6	9	12	15

NOTE: *Title change to Montana Kid on cover only #44 & 45; remained Kid Montana on inside.* ***Chasal*** *a-29,30.* ***Giordano*** *c-25,31,37,48.* ***Giordano/Alascia*** *c-12.* ***Mastroserio*** *a-9,11,13,14,22; c-11,14.* ***Masulli/Mastroserio*** *c-13.* ***Montes/Bache*** *c-42.* ***Morisi*** *c-16,32-34,36?,40,41,44,46; a-13,15;16,31-50.* ***Nicholas/Alascia*** *a-44,48.*

KID MOVIE KOMICS (Formerly Kid Komics; Rusty Comics #12 on)
Timely Comics: No. 11, Summer, 1946

	GD	VG	FN	VF	VF/NM	NM-
11-Silly Seal & Ziggy Pig; 2 pgs. Kurtzman "Hey Look" plus 6 pg. "Pigtales" story	27	54	81	158	249	340

KIDNAPPED (Robert Louis Stevenson's...also see Movie Comics)(Disney)
Dell Publishing Co.: No. 1101, May, 1960

	GD	VG	FN	VF	VF/NM	NM-
Four Color 1101-Movie, photo-c	6	12	18	43	69	95

KIDNAP RACKET (See Harvey Comics Hits No. 57)

KID SLADE GUNFIGHTER (Formerly Matt Slade...)
Atlas Comics (SPI): No. 5, Jan, 1957 - No. 8, July, 1957

	GD	VG	FN	VF	VF/NM	NM-
5-Maneely, Roth, Severin-a in all; Maneely-c	13	26	39	72	101	130
6,8-Severin-c	8	16	24	44	57	70
7-Williamson/Mayo-a, 4 pgs.	10	20	30	56	76	95

KID SUPREME (See Supreme)
Image Comics (Extreme Studios): Mar, 1996 - No. 3, July, 1996 ($2.50)

	GD	VG	FN	VF	VF/NM	NM-
1-3: Fraga-a/scripts. 3-Glory-c/app.						2.50

KID TERRIFIC
Image Comics: Nov, 1998 ($2.95, B&W)

	GD	VG	FN	VF	VF/NM	NM-
1-Snyder & Diliberto-s/a						3.00

KID ZOO COMICS
Street & Smith Publications: July, 1948 (52 pgs.)

	GD	VG	FN	VF	VF/NM	NM-
1-Funny Animal	29	58	87	170	268	365

KILL ALL PARENTS
Image Comics: June, 2008 ($3.99, one-shot)

	GD	VG	FN	VF	VF/NM	NM-
1-Marcelo Di Chiara-a/Mark Andrew Smith-s						4.00

KILLER (...Tales By Timothy Truman)
Eclipse Comics: March, 1985 ($1.75, one-shot, Baxter paper)

	GD	VG	FN	VF	VF/NM	NM-
1-Timothy Truman-c/a						2.50

KILLER INSTINCT (Video game)
Acclaim Comics: June, 1996 - No. 6 ($2.50, limited series)

	GD	VG	FN	VF	VF/NM	NM-
1-6: 1-Bart Sears-a(p). 4-Special #1. 5-Special #2. 6-Special #3						3.00

KILLERS, THE
Magazine Enterprises: 1947 - No. 2, 1948 (No month)

	GD	VG	FN	VF	VF/NM	NM-
1-Mr. Zin, the Hatchet Killer; mentioned in **SOTI**, pgs. 179,180; used by N.Y. Legis. Comm.; L. B. Cole-c	114	228	342	713	1182	1650
2-(Scarce)-Hashish smoking story; "Dying, Dying, Dead" drug story; Whitney, Ingels-a; Whitney hanging-c	93	186	279	581	966	1350

KILLING GIRL
Image Comics: Aug, 2007 - No. 5, Dec, 2007 ($2.99, limited series)

	GD	VG	FN	VF	VF/NM	NM-
1-5: 1-Frank Espinosa-a/Glen Brunswick-s; covers by Espinosa and Frank Cho						3.00

KILLING JOKE, THE (See Batman: The Killing Joke under Batman one-shots)

KILLPOWER: THE EARLY YEARS
Marvel Comics UK: Sept, 1993 - No. 4, Dec, 1993 ($1.75, mini-series)

	GD	VG	FN	VF	VF/NM	NM-
1-($2.95)-Foil embossed-c						3.00
2-4: 2-Genetix app. 3-Punisher app.						2.25

KILLRAVEN (See Amazing Adventures #18 (5/73))
Marvel Comics: Feb, 2001 ($2.99, one-shot)

	GD	VG	FN	VF	VF/NM	NM-
1-Linsner-s/a/c						3.00

KILLRAVEN
Marvel Comics: Dec, 2002 - No. 6, May, 2003 ($2.99, limited series)

	GD	VG	FN	VF	VF/NM	NM-
1-6-Alan Davis-s/a(p)/Mark Farmer-i						3.00
HC (2007, $19.99) r/#1-6; cover gallery, pencil art; foreward by Alan Davis						20.00

KILLRAZOR
Image Comics (Top Cow Productions): Aug, 1995 ($2.50, one-shot)

	GD	VG	FN	VF	VF/NM	NM-
1						2.50

KILL YOUR BOYFRIEND
DC Comics (Vertigo): June, 1995 ($4.95, one-shot)

	GD	VG	FN	VF	VF/NM	NM-
1-Grant Morrison story						6.00
1 ($5.95, 1998) 2nd printing						6.00

KILROY (Volume 2)
Caliber Press: 1998 ($2.95, B&W)

	GD	VG	FN	VF	VF/NM	NM-
1-Pruett-s						3.00

KILROY IS HERE
Caliber Press: 1995 ($2.95, B&W)

	GD	VG	FN	VF	VF/NM	NM-
1-10						3.00

KILROYS, THE
B&I Publ. Co. No. 1-19/American Comics Group: June-July, 1947 - No. 54, June-July, 1955

	GD	VG	FN	VF	VF/NM	NM-
1	22	44	66	126	198	270
2	13	26	39	74	105	135
3-5: 5-Gross-a	11	22	33	62	86	110
6-10: 8-Milt Gross's Moronica	9	18	27	52	69	85
11-20: 14-Gross-a	9	18	27	47	61	75
21-30	8	16	24	42	54	65
31-47,50-54	8	16	24	40	50	60
48,49-(3-D effect-c/stories)	17	34	51	98	154	210

KILROY: THE SHORT STORIES
Caliber Press: 1995 ($2.95, B&W)

	GD	VG	FN	VF	VF/NM	NM-
1						3.00

King (magazine) #1 © Skywald

King Comics #47 © DMP

The Kingdom: Kid Flash #1 © DC

	GD 2.0	VG 4.0	FN 6.0	VF 8.0	VF/NM 9.0	NM- 9.2

KIN
Image Comics (Top Cow): Mar, 2000 - No. 6, Sept, 2000 ($2.95)

1-5-Gary Frank-s/c/a 3.00
1-($6.95) DF Alternate footprint cover 7.00
6-($3.95) 4.00
... Descent of Man TPB (2002, $19.95) r/ #1-6 20.00

KINDRED, THE
Image Comics (WildStorm Productions): Mar, 1994 - No. 4, July, 1995 ($1.95, lim. series)

1-($2.50)-Grifter & Backlash app. in all; bound-in trading card 2.50
2-4 2.50
2,3: 2-Variant-c. 3-Alternate-c by Portacio, see Deathblow #5 4.00
Trade paperback (2/95, $9.95) 10.00
NOTE: *Booth c/a-1-4. The first four issues contain coupons redeemable for a Jim Lee Grifter/Backlash print.*

KINDRED II, THE
DC Comics (WildStorm): Mar, 2002 - No. 4, June, 2002 ($2.50, limited series)

1-4-Booth-s/Booth & Regla-a 2.50

KINETIC
DC Comics (Focus): May, 2004 - No. 8, Dec, 2004 ($2.50)

1-8-Puckett-s/Pleece-a/c 2.50
TPB (2005, $9.99) r/#1-8; cover gallery and sketch pages 10.00

KING (Magazine)
Skywald Publ.: Mar, 1971 - No. 2, July, 1971

	GD	VG	FN	VF	VF/NM	NM-
1-Violence; semi-nudity; Boris Vallejo-a (2 pgs.)	5	10	15	32	51	70
2-Photo-c	3	6	9	20	30	40

KING ARTHUR AND THE KNIGHTS OF JUSTICE
Marvel Comics UK: Dec, 1993 - No. 3, Feb, 1994 ($1.25, limited series)

1-3: TV adaptation 2.50

KING CLASSICS
King Features : 1977 (36 pgs., cardboard-c) (Printed in Spain for U.S. distr.)

1-Connecticut Yankee, 2-Last of the Mohicans, 3-Moby Dick, 4-Robin Hood, 5-Swiss Family Robinson, 6-Robinson Crusoe, 7-Treasure Island, 8 20,000 Leagues, 9-Christmas Carol, 10-Huck Finn, 11-Around the World in 80 Days, 12-Davy Crockett, 13-Don Quixote, 14-Gold Bug, 15-Ivanhoe, 16-Three Musketeers, 17-Baron Munchausen, 18-Alice in Wonderland, 19-Black Arrow, 20-Five Weeks in a Balloon, 21-Great Expectations, 22-Gulliver's Travels, 23-Prince & Pauper, 24-Lawrence of Arabia (Originals, 1977-78)

	GD	VG	FN	VF	VF/NM	NM-
each....	2	4	6	9	13	16
Reprints (1979; HRN-24)	1	3	4	6	8	10

NOTE: *The first eight issues were not numbered. Issues No. 25-32 were advertised but not published. The 1977 originals have HRN 32a; the 1978 originals have HRN 32b.*

KING COLT (See Luke Short's Western Stories)

KING COMICS (Strip reprints)
David McKay Publications/Standard #156-on: 4/36 - No. 155, 11-12/49; No. 156, Spr/50 - No. 159, 2/52 (Winter on-c)

	GD	VG	FN	VF	VF/NM	NM-
1-1st app. Flash Gordon by Alex Raymond; Brick Bradford (1st app.), Popeye, Henry (1st app.) & Mandrake the Magician (1st app.) begin; Popeye-c begin	1250	2500	3750	10,000	-	-
2	360	720	1080	1980	2790	3600
3	245	490	735	1348	1899	2450
4	190	380	570	1045	1473	1900
5	140	280	420	770	1085	1400
6-10: 9-X-Mas-c	95	190	285	523	737	950
11-20	75	150	225	413	582	750
21-30: 21-X-Mas-c	55	110	165	303	427	550
31-40: 33-Last Segar Popeye	45	90	135	248	349	450
41-50: 46-Text illos by Marge Buell contain characters similar to Lulu, Alvin & Tubby. 50-The Lone Ranger begins	32	64	96	186	298	410
51-60: 52-Barney Baxter begins?	23	46	69	133	214	295
61-The Phantom begins	24	48	72	140	225	310
62-80: 76-Flag-c. 79-Blondie begins	17	34	51	98	154	210
81-99	14	28	42	81	118	155
100	16	32	48	92	144	195
101-114: 114-Last Raymond issue (1 pg.); Flash Gordon by Austin Briggs begins, ends #155	14	28	42	76	108	140
115-145: 117-Phantom origin retold	10	20	30	56	76	95
146,147-Prince Valiant in both	9	18	27	50	65	80
148-155: 155-Flash Gordon ends (11-12/49)	9	18	27	50	65	80
156-159: 156-New logo begins (Standard)	9	18	27	47	61	75

NOTE: *Marge Buell text illos in No. 24-46 at least.*

KING CONAN (Conan The King No. 20 on)
Marvel Comics Group: Mar, 1980 - No. 19, Nov, 1983 (52 pgs.)

1 6.00
2-19: 4-Death of Thoth Amon. 7-1st Paul Smith-a, 1 pg. pin-up (9/81) 4.00
NOTE: ***J. Buscema** a-1-9p, 17p; c(p)-1-5, 7-9, 14, 17. **Kaluta** c-19. **Nebres** a-17i, 18, 19i. **Severin** c-18. **Simonson** c-6.*

KING DAVID
DC Comics (Vertigo): 2002 ($19.95, 8 1/2" x 11")

nn-Story of King David; Kyle Baker-s/a 20.00

KINGDOM, THE
DC Comics: Feb, 1999 - No. 2, Feb, 1999 ($2.95/$1.99, limited series)

1,2-Waid-s; sequel to Kingdom Come; introduces Hypertime 4.00
...: Kid Flash 1 (2/99, $1.99) Waid-s/Pararillo-a, ...: Nightstar 1 (2/99, $1.99) Waid-s/Haley-a, ...: Offspring 1 (2/99, $1.99) Waid-s/Quitely-a, ...: Planet Krypton 1 (2/99, $1.99) Waid-s/Kitson-a, ...: Son of the Bat 1 (2/99, $1.99) Waid-s/Apthorp-a 2.50

KINGDOM COME
DC Comics: 1996 - No. 4, 1996 ($4.95, painted limited series)

	GD	VG	FN	VF	VF/NM	NM-
1-Mark Waid scripts & Alex Ross-painted c/a in all; tells the last days of the DC Universe; 1st app. Magog	1	2	3	5	6	8
2-Superman forms new Justice League	1	2	3	4	5	7
3-Return of Captain Marvel						5.00
4-Final battle of Superman and Captain Marvel	1	2	3	4	5	7

Deluxe Slipcase Edition-($89.95) w/Revelations companion book, 12 new story pages, foil stamped covers, signed and numbered 120.00
Hardcover Edition-($29.95)-Includes 12 new story pages and artwork from Revelations, new cover artwork with gold foil inlay 35.00
Hardcover 2nd printing 30.00
Softcover Ed.-($14.95)-Includes 12 new story pgs. & artwork from Revelations, new c-artwork 15.00

KING KONG (See Movie Comics)

KING KONG: THE 8TH WONDER OF THE WORLD (Adaptation of 2005 movie)
Dark Horse Comics: Dec, 2005 ($3.99, planned limited series completed in TPB)

1-Photo-c; Dustin Weaver-a/Christian Gossett-s 4.00
TPB (11/06, $12.95) r/#1 and unpublished parts 2&3; photo-c; Dorman paintings 13.00

KING LEONARDO & HIS SHORT SUBJECTS (TV)
Dell Publishing Co./Gold Key: Nov-Jan, 1961-62 - No. 4, Sept, 1963

	GD	VG	FN	VF	VF/NM	NM-
Four Color 1242,1278	12	24	36	84	150	215
01390-207(5-7/62)(Dell)	9	18	27	61	103	145
1 (10/62)	10	20	30	71	126	180
2-4	8	16	24	56	93	130

KING LOUIE & MOWGLI (See Jungle Book under Movie Comics)
Gold Key: May, 1968 (Disney)

	GD	VG	FN	VF	VF/NM	NM-
1 (#10223-805)-Characters from Jungle Book	3	6	9	20	30	40

KING OF DIAMONDS (TV)
Dell Publishing Co.: July-Sept, 1962

	GD	VG	FN	VF	VF/NM	NM-
01-391-209-Photo-c	4	8	12	26	41	55

KING OF KINGS (Movie)
Dell Publishing Co.: No. 1236, Oct-Nov, 1961

	GD	VG	FN	VF	VF/NM	NM-
Four Color 1236-Photo-c	7	14	21	50	83	115

KING OF THE BAD MEN OF DEADWOOD
Avon Periodicals: 1950 (See Wild Bill Hickok #16)

	GD	VG	FN	VF	VF/NM	NM-
nn-Kinstler-c; Kamen/Feldstein-r/Cowpuncher #2	15	30	45	94	147	200

KING OF THE ROYAL MOUNTED (See Famous Feature Stories, King Comics, Red Ryder #3 & Super Book #2, 6)

KING OF THE ROYAL MOUNTED (Zane Grey's...)
David McKay/Dell Publishing Co.: No. 1, May, 1937; No. 9, 1940; No. 207, Dec, 1948 - No. 935, Sept-Nov, 1958

	GD	VG	FN	VF	VF/NM	NM-
Feature Books 1 (5/37)(McKay)	87	174	261	548	924	1300
Large Feature Comic 9 (1940)	47	94	141	291	483	675
Four Color 207(#1, 12/48)	14	28	42	99	175	250
Four Color 265,283	8	16	24	58	97	135
Four Color 310,340	6	12	18	43	69	95
Four Color 363,384, 8(6-8/52)-10	6	12	18	39	62	85
11-20	5	10	15	34	55	75
21-28(3-5/58), Four Color 935(9-11/58)	4	8	12	28	44	60

NOTE: *4-Color No. 207, 265, 283, 310, 340, 363, 384 are all newspaper reprints with **Jim Gary** art. No. 8 on are all Dell originals. Painted c-No. 9-on.*

KINGPIN
Marvel Comics: Nov, 1997 ($5.99, squarebound, one-shot)

nn-Spider-Man & Daredevil vs. Kingpin; Stan Lee-s/ John Romita Sr.-a 6.00

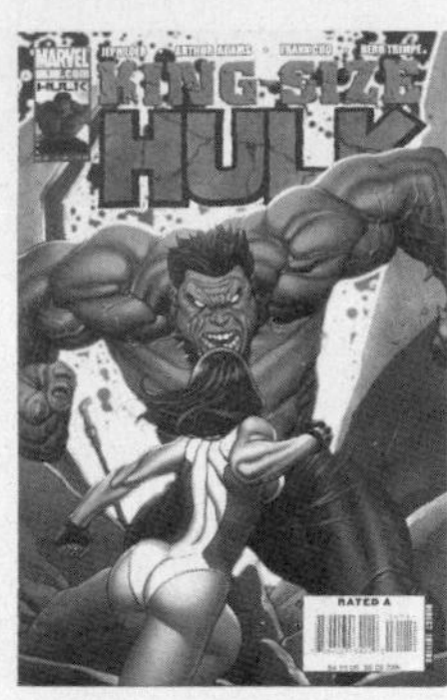

King-Size Hulk #1 © MAR

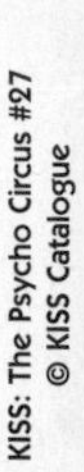
KISS: The Psycho Circus #27 © KISS Catalogue

Kit Carson #7 © AVON

GD 2.0 | VG 4.0 | FN 6.0 | VF 8.0 | VF/NM 9.0 | NM- 9.2

KINGPIN
Marvel Comics: Aug, 2003 - No. 7, Jan, 2004 ($2.50/$2.99, limited series)
1-6-Bruce Jones-s/Sean Phillips & Klaus Janson-a 2.50
7-($2.99) 3.00

KING RICHARD & THE CRUSADERS
Dell Publishing Co.: No. 588, Oct, 1954
Four Color 588-Movie, Matt Baker-a, photo-c 9 18 27 63 107 150

KING-SIZE CABLE SPECTACULAR (Takes place between Cable (2008 series) #6 & #7)
Marvel Comics: Nov, 2008 ($4.99, one-shot)
1-Lashley-a; Deadpool #1 preview; cover gallery of variants from 2008 series 5.00

KING-SIZE HULK (Takes place between Hulk (2008 series) #3 & #4)
Marvel Comics: July, 2008 ($4.99, one-shot)
1-Art Adams, Frank Cho, & Herb Trimpe-a; double-c by Cho & Adams; Red Hulk, She-Hulk & Wendigo app.; origin Abomination; r/Incr. Hulk #180,181 & Avengers #83 5.00

KING-SIZE SPIDER-MAN SUMMER SPECIAL
Marvel Comics: Oct, 2008 ($4.99, one-shot)
1-Short stories by various; Falcon app.; Burchett, Giarrusso & Coover-a 5.00

KINGS OF THE NIGHT
Dark Horse Comics: 1990 - No. 2, 1990 ($2.25, limited series)
1,2-Robert E. Howard adaptation; Bolton-c 2.50

KING SOLOMON'S MINES (Movie)
Avon Periodicals: 1951
nn (#1 on 1st page) 40 80 120 235 380 525

KIPLING, RUDYARD (See Mowgli, The Jungle Book)

KISS (See Crazy Magazine, Howard the Duck #12, 13, Marvel Comics Super Special #1, 5, Rock Fantasy Comics #10 & Rock N' Roll Comics #9)

KISS
Dark Horse Comics: June, 2002 - No. 13, Sept, 2003 ($2.99, limited series)
1-Photo-c and J. Scott Campbell-c; Casey-s 4.00
2-13: 2-Photo-c and J. Scott Campbell-c. 3-Photo-c and Leinil Yu-c 3.00
...: Men and Monsters TPB (9/03, $12.95) r/#7-10 13.00
...: Rediscovery TPB (2003, $9.95) r/#1-3 10.00
...: Return of the Phantom TPB (2003, $9.95) r/#4-6 10.00
...: Unholy War TPB (2004, $9.95) r/#11-13 10.00

KISS 4K
Platinum Studios Comics: May, 2007 - Present ($3.99/$2.99)
1-Sprague-s/Crossley & Campos-a/Migliari-c 4.00
1-B&W sketch-c 6.00
1-Destroyer Edition ($50.00, 30"x18", edition of 5000) 50.00
2-6-($2.99) 3.00
KISSMAS (12/07, $4.99) Christmas-themed issue; re-cap of issues #1-4 5.00

KISS: THE PSYCHO CIRCUS
Image Comics: Aug, 1997 - No. 31, June, 2000 ($1.95/$2.25/$2.50)
1-Holguin-s/Medina-a(p) 1 2 3 5 6 8
1-2nd & 3rd printings 2.50
2 5.00
3,4: 4-Photo-c 4.00
5-8: 5-Begin $2.25-c 3.00
9-29 2.50
30,31: 30-Begin $2.50-c 2.50
Book 1 TPB ('98, $12.95) r/#1-6 13.00
Book 2 Destroyer TPB (8/99, $9.95) r/#10-13 10.00
Book 3 Whispered Scream TPB ('00, $9.95) r/#7-9,18 10.00
...Magazine 1 ($6.95) r/#1-3 plus interviews 7.00
...Magazine 2-5 ($4.95) 2-r/#4,5 plus interviews. 3-r/#6,7. 4-r/#8,9 5.00
Wizard Edition ('98, supplement) Bios, tour preview and interviews 2.50

KISSING CHAOS
Oni Press: Sept, 2001 - No. 8, Mar, 2002 ($2.25, B&W, 6" x 9", limited series)
1-8-Arthur Dela Cruz-s/a 2.50
...: Nine Lives (12/03, $2.99, regular comic-sized) 3.00
...: 1000 Words (7/03, $2.99, regular comic-sized) 3.00
TPB (9/02, $17.95) r/#1-8 18.00

KISSING CHAOS: NONSTOP BEAUTY
Oni Press: Oct, 2002 - No. 4, March, 2003 ($2.95, B&W, 6" x 9", limited series)
1-4-Arthur Dela Cruz-s/a 3.00
TPB (9/03, $11.95) r/#1-4 12.00

KISS KISS BANG BANG
CrossGen Comics: Feb, 2004 - No. 5, Jun, 2004 ($2.95)
1-5-Bedard-s/Perkins-a 3.00

KISSYFUR (TV)
DC Comics: 1989 (Sept.) ($2.00, 52 pgs., one-shot)
1-Based on Saturday morning cartoon 4.00

KIT CARSON (Formerly All True Detective Cases No. 4; Fighting Davy Crockett No. 9; see Blazing Sixguns & Frontier Fighters)
Avon Periodicals: 1950; No. 2, 8/51 - No. 3, 12/51; No. 5, 11-12/54 - No. 8, 9/55 (No #4)
nn(#1) (1950)- "...Indian Scout"; r-Cowboys 'N' Injuns #? 14 28 42 76 108 140
2(8/51) 10 20 30 56 76 95
3(12/51)- "...Fights the Comanche Raiders" 9 18 27 50 65 80
5-6,8(11-12/54-9/55): 5-Formerly All True Detective Cases (last pre-code); titled "...and the Trail of Doom" 9 18 27 47 61 75
7-McCann-a? 9 18 27 47 61 75
I.W. Reprint #10('63)-r/Kit Carson #1; Severin-c 2 4 6 11 16 20
NOTE: *Kinstler c-1-3, 5-8.*

KIT CARSON & THE BLACKFEET WARRIORS
Realistic: 1953
nn-Reprint; Kinstler-c 9 18 27 52 69 85

KIT KARTER
Dell Publishing Co.: May-July, 1962
1 3 6 9 19 29 38

KITTY
St. John Publishing Co.: Oct, 1948
1-Teenage; Lily Renee-c/a 8 16 24 44 57 70

KITTY PRYDE, AGENT OF S.H.I.E.L.D. (Also see Excalibur and Mekanix)
Marvel Comics: Dec, 1997 - No. 3, Feb, 1998 ($2.50, limited series)
1-3-Hama-s 2.50

KITTY PRYDE AND WOLVERINE (Also see Uncanny X-Men & X-Men)
Marvel Comics Group: Nov, 1984 - No. 6, Apr, 1985 (Limited series)
1-6: Characters from X-Men 4.50

KLARER GIVEAWAYS (See Wisco in the Promotional Comics section)

KNIGHTHAWK
Acclaim Comics (Windjammer): Sept, 1995 - No. 6, Nov, 1995 ($2.50, lim. series)
1-6: 6-origin 2.50

KNIGHTMARE
Antarctic Press: July, 1994 - May, 1995 ($2.75, B&W, mature readers)
1-6 2.75

KNIGHTMARE
Image Comics (Extreme Studios): Feb, 1995 - No. 5, June, 1995 ($2.50)
0 ($3.50) 3.50
1-5: 4-Quesada & Palmiotti variant-c, 5-Flip book w/Warcry 2.50

KNIGHTS 4 (See Marvel Knights 4)

KNIGHTS OF PENDRAGON, THE (Also see Pendragon)
Marvel Comics Ltd.: July, 1990 - No. 18, Dec, 1991 ($1.95)
1-18: 1-Capt. Britain app. 2,8-Free poster inside. 9,10-Bolton-c. 11,18-Iron Man app. 2.50

KNIGHTS OF THE ROUND TABLE
Dell Publishing Co.: No. 540, Mar, 1954
Four Color 540-Movie, photo-c 7 14 21 47 76 105

KNIGHTS OF THE ROUND TABLE
Pines Comics: No. 10, April, 1957
10 5 10 15 24 30 35

KNIGHTS OF THE ROUND TABLE
Dell Publishing Co.: Nov-Jan, 1963-64
1 (12-397-401)-Painted-c 3 6 9 21 32 42

KNIGHTSTRIKE (Also see Operation: Knightstrike)
Image Comics (Extreme Studios): Jan, 1996 ($2.50)
1-Rob Liefeld & Eric Stephenson story; Extreme Destroyer Part 6. 2.50

KNIGHT WATCHMAN (See Big Bang Comics & Dr. Weird)
Image Comics: June, 1998 - No. 4, Oct, 1998 ($2.95/$3.50, B&W, lim. series)
1-3-Ben Torres-c/a in all 3.00

Kobra #5 © DC

Konga #2 © CC

Korak, Son of Tarzan #52 © ERB

	GD 2.0	VG 4.0	FN 6.0	VF 8.0	VF/NM 9.0	NM- 9.2
4-($3.50)						3.50
KNIGHT WATCHMAN: GRAVEYARD SHIFT						
Caliber Press: 1994 ($2.95, B&W)						
1,2-Ben Torres-a						3.00
KNOCK KNOCK (...Who's There?)						
Dell Publ./Gerona Publications: No. 801, 1936 (52 pgs.) (8x9", B&W)						
801-Joke book; Bob Dunn-a	10	20	30	54	72	90
KNOCKOUT ADVENTURES						
Fiction House Magazines: Winter, 1953-54						
1-Reprints Fight Comics #53 w/Rip Carson-c/s	14	28	42	76	108	140
KNUCKLES (Spin-off of Sonic the Hedgehog)						
Archie Publications: Apr, 1997 - Present ($1.50/$1.75/$1.79)						
1-29						2.50
KNUCKLES' CHAOTIX						
Archie Publications: Jan, 1996 ($2.00, annual)						
1						3.00
KOBALT						
DC Comics (Milestone): June, 1994 - No. 16, Sept, 1995 ($1.75/$2.50)						
1-16: 1-Byrne-c. 4-Intro Page. 16-Kent Williams-c						2.50
KOBRA (Unpublished #8 appears in DC Special Series No. 1)						
National Periodical Publications: Feb-Mar, 1976 - No. 7, Mar-Apr, 1977						
1-1st app.; Kirby-a redrawn by Marcos; only 25¢-c	2	4	6	8	10	12
2-7: (All 30¢ issues) 3-Giffen a	1	2	3	4	5	7
NOTE: *Austin a-3i. Buckler a-5p, c-5p. Kubert c-4. Nasser a-6p, 7, c-7.*						
KOKEY KOALA (...and the Magic Button)						
Toby Press: May, 1952						
1	11	22	33	62	86	110
KOKO AND KOLA (Also see A-1 Comics #16 & Tick Tock Tales)						
Com/Magazine Enterprises: Fall, 1946 - No. 5, May, 1947; No. 6, 1950						
1-Funny animal	12	24	36	67	94	120
2-X-Mas-c	8	16	24	44	57	70
3-6: 6(A-1 28)	8	16	24	40	50	60
KO KOMICS						
Gerona Publications: Oct, 1945 (scarce)						
1-The Duke of Darkness & The Menace (hero)	73	146	219	460	780	1100
KOLCHAK: THE NIGHT STALKER (TV)						
Moonstone: 2002 - Present ($6.50/$6.95)						
1-($6.50) Jeff Rice-s/Gordon Purcell-a						6.50
... Black & White & Read All Over (2005, $4.95) short stories by various; 2 covers						5.00
... Devil in the Details (2003, $6.95) Trevor Von Eeden-a						7.00
... Eve of Terror (2005, $5.95) Gentile-s/Figueroa-a/ Beck-c						6.00
... Fever Pitch (2002, $6.95) Christopher Jones-a						7.00
... Get of Belial (2002, $6.95) Art Nichols-a						7.00
... Lambs to the Slaughter (2003, $6.95) Trevor Von Eeden-a						7.00
... Pain Most Human (2004, $6.95) Greg Scott-a						7.00
... Tales: The Frankenstein Agenda 1 (2007 - No. 3, $3.50) Michelinie-s						3.50
... Tales of the Night Stalker 1-7 (2003-Present, $3.50) two covers by Moore & Ulanski						3.50
TPB (2004, $17.95) r/#1, Get of Belial & Fever Pitch						18.00
Vol. 2: Terror Within TPB (2006, $16.95) r/Pain Most Human, Pain Without Tears & Devil in the Details						17.00
KOMIC KARTOONS						
Timely Comics (EPC): Fall, 1945 - No. 2, Winter, 1945						
1,2-Andy Wolf, Bertie Mouse	20	40	60	118	189	260
KOMIK PAGES (Formerly Snap; becomes Bullseye #11)						
Harry 'A' Chesler, Jr. (Our Army, Inc.): Apr, 1945 (All reprints)						
10(#1 on inside)-Land O' Nod by Rick Yager (2 pgs.), Animal Crackers, Foxy GrandPa, Tom, Dick & Mary, Cheerio Minstrels, Red Starr plus other 1-2 pg. strips; Cole-a	23	46	69	135	218	300
KONA (...Monarch of Monster Isle)						
Dell Publishing Co.: Feb-Apr, 1962 - No. 21, Jan-Mar, 1967 (Painted-c)						
Four Color 1256 (#1)	9	18	27	63	107	150
2-10: 4-Anak begins. 6-Gil Kane-c	5	10	15	34	55	75
11-21	4	8	12	28	44	60
NOTE: *Glanzman a-all issues.*						

	GD 2.0	VG 4.0	FN 6.0	VF 8.0	VF/NM 9.0	NM- 9.2
KONGA (Fantastic Giants No. 24) (See Return of...)						
Charlton Comics: 1960; No. 2, Aug, 1961 - No. 23, Nov, 1965						
1(1960)-Based on movie; Giordano-c	23	46	69	167	309	450
2-5: 2-Giordano-c; no Ditko-a	11	22	33	75	133	190
6-15	9	18	27	61	103	145
16-23	6	12	18	41	66	90
NOTE: *Ditko a-1, 3-15; c-4, 6-9. Glanzman a-12. Montes & Bache a-16-23.*						
KONGA'S REVENGE (Formerly Return of...)						
Charlton Comics: No. 2, Summer, 1963 - No. 3, Fall, 1964; Dec, 1968						
2,3: 2-Ditko-c/a	6	12	18	41	66	90
1(12/68)-Reprints Konga's Revenge #3	3	6	9	17	25	32
KONG THE UNTAMED						
National Periodical Publications: June-July, 1975 - V2#5, Feb-Mar, 1976						
1-1st app. Kong; Wrightson-c; Alcala-a	2	4	6	9	12	15
2-Wrightson c; Alcala-a	2	4	6	8	10	12
3-5: 3-Alcala-a	1	2	3	4	5	7
KOOKIE						
Dell Publishing Co.: Feb-Apr, 1962 - No. 2, May-July, 1962 (15 cents)						
1-Written by John Stanley; Bill Williams-a	8	16	24	54	90	125
2	7	14	21	49	80	110
KOOSH KINS						
Archie Comics: Oct, 1991 - No. 3, Feb, 1992 ($1.00, bi-monthly, limited series)						
1-3						2.50
NOTE: *No. 4 was planned, but cancelled.*						
KORAK, SON OF TARZAN (Edgar Rice Burroughs)(See Tarzan #139)						
Gold Key: Jan, 1964 - No. 45, Jan, 1972 (Painted-c No. 1-?)						
1-Russ Manning-a	9	18	27	63	107	150
2-5-Russ Manning-a	5	10	15	34	55	75
6-11-Russ Manning-a	4	8	12	28	44	65
12-23: 12,13-Warren Tufts-a. 14-Jon of the Kalahari ends. 15-Mabu, Jungle Boy begins. 21-Manning-a. 23-Last 12¢ issue	4	8	12	26	41	55
24-30	3	6	9	20	30	40
31-45	3	6	9	16	23	30
KORAK, SON OF TARZAN (Tarzan Family #60 on; see Tarzan #230)						
National Periodical Publications: V9#46, May-June, 1972 - V12#56, Feb-Mar, 1974; No. 57, May-June, 1975 - No. 59, Sept-Oct, 1975 (Edgar Rice Burroughs)						
46-(52 pgs.)-Carson of Venus begins (origin), ends #56; Pellucidar feature; Weiss-a	3	6	9	14	20	25
47-59: 49-Origin Korak retold	2	4	6	8	10	12
NOTE: *All have covers by Joe Kubert. Manning strip reprints-No. 57-59. Murphy Anderson a-52. Michael Kaluta a-46-56. Frank Thorne a-46-51.*						
KORE						
Image Comics: Apr, 2003 - No. 5, Sept, 2003 ($2.95)						
1-5: 1-Two covers by Capullo and Seeley; Seeley-a (p)						3.00
KORG: 70,000 B. C. (TV)						
Charlton Publications: May, 1975 - No. 9, Nov, 1976 (Hanna-Barbera)						
1,2: 1-Boyette-c/a. 2-Painted-c; Byrne text illos	2	4	6	11	16	20
3-9	2	4	6	8	11	14
KORNER KID COMICS: Four Star Publications: 1947 (Advertised, not pub.)						
KOSMIC KAT ACTIVITY BOOK (See Deity)						
Image Comics: Aug, 1999 ($2.95, one-shot)						
1-Stories and games by various						3.00
KRAZY KAT						
Holt: 1946 (Hardcover)						
Reprints daily & Sunday strips by Herriman	56	112	168	353	597	840
dust jacket only	43	86	129	267	446	625
KRAZY KAT (See Ace Comics & March of Comics No. 72, 87)						
KRAZY KAT COMICS (...& Ignatz the Mouse early issues)						
Dell Publ. Co./Gold Key: May-June, 1951 - F.C. #696, Apr, 1956; Jan, 1964 (None by Herriman)						
1(1951)	9	18	27	60	100	140
2-5 (#5, 8-10/52)	5	10	15	35	55	75
Four Color 454,504	5	10	15	32	51	70
Four Color 548,619,696 (4/56)	5	10	15	30	48	65
1(10098-401)(1/64-Gold Key)(TV)	4	8	12	26	41	55
KRAZY KOMICS (1st Series) (Cindy Comics No. 27 on) (Also see Ziggy Pig)						

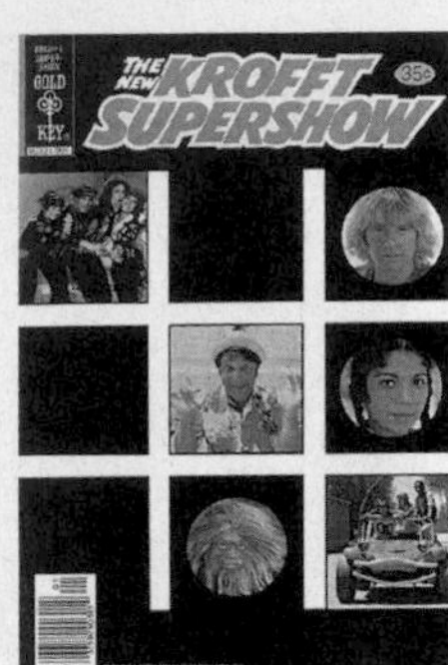

Krofft Supershow #6 © Sid & Marty Krofft

Krusty Comics #3 © Bongo

Kull the Destroyer #18 © MAR

GD 2.0 | VG 4.0 | FN 6.0 | VF 8.0 | VF/NM 9.0 | NM- 9.2

Timely Comics (USA No. 1-21/JPC No. 22-26): July, 1942 - No. 26, Spr, 1947
1-Toughy Tomcat, Ziggy Pig (by Jaffee) & Silly Seal begin
67 134 201 422 711 1000
2 31 62 93 181 291 400
3-8,10 21 42 63 125 200 275
9-Hitler parody 22 44 66 129 207 285
11,13,14 15 30 45 94 147 200
12-Timely's entire art staff drew themselves into a Creeper story
26 52 78 154 247 340
15-(8-9/44)-Has "Super Soldier" by Pfc. Stan Lee 15 30 45 94 147 200
16-24,26: 16-(10-11/44). 26-Super Rabbit-c/story 14 28 42 82 121 160
25-Wacky Duck-c/story & begin; Kurtzman-a (6pgs.) 15 30 45 94 147 200

KRAZY KOMICS (2nd Series)
Timely/Marvel Comics: Aug, 1948 - No. 2, Nov, 1948
1-Wolverton (10 pgs.) & Kurtzman (8 pgs.)-a; Eustice Hayseed begins (Li'l Abner swipe)
43 86 129 267 446 625
2-Wolverton-a (10 pgs.); Powerhouse Pepper cameo
32 64 96 186 298 410

KRAZY KROW (Also see Dopey Duck, Film Funnies, Funny Frolics & Movie Tunes)
Marvel Comics (ZPC): Summer, 1945 - No. 3, Wint, 1945/46
1 22 44 66 127 204 280
2,3 15 30 45 83 124 165
I.W. Reprint #1('57), 2('58), 7 2 4 6 11 16 20

KRAZYLIFE (Becomes Nutty Life #2)
Fox Feature Syndicate: 1945 (no month)
1-Funny animal 20 40 60 115 183 250

KREE/SKRULL WAR STARRING THE AVENGERS, THE
Marvel Comics: Sept, 1983 - No. 2, Oct, 1983 ($2.50, 68 pgs., Baxter paper)
1,2 4.00
*NOTE: **Neal Adams** p-1r, 2. **Buscema** a-1r, 2r. **Simonson** a-1p; c-1p.*

KROFFT SUPERSHOW (TV)
Gold Key: Apr, 1978 - No. 6, Jan, 1979
1-Photo-c 3 6 9 17 25 32
2-6: 6-Photo-c 2 4 6 13 18 22

KRULL
Marvel Comics Group: Nov, 1983 - No. 2, Dec, 1983
1,2-Adaptation of film; r/Marvel Super Special. 1-Photo-c from movie 2.50

KRUSTY COMICS (TV)(See Simpsons Comics)
Bongo Comics: 1995 - No. 3, 1995 ($2.25, limited series)
1-3 2.50

KRYPTON CHRONICLES
DC Comics: Sept, 1981 - No. 3, Nov, 1981
1-3: 1-Buckler-c(p) 4.00

KRYPTO THE SUPERDOG (TV)
DC Comics: Nov, 2006 - No. 6, Apr, 2007 ($2.25)
1-6-Based on Cartoon Network series. 1-Origin retold 2.50

KULL AND THE BARBARIANS
Marvel Comics: May, 1975 - No. 3, Sept, 1975 ($1.00, B&W, magazine)
1-(84 pgs.) Andru/Wood-r/Kull #1; 2 pgs. Neal Adams; Gil Kane(p), Marie & John Severin-a(r); Krenkel text illo. 3 6 9 16 22 28
2,3: 2-(84 pgs.) Red Sonja by Chaykin begins; Solomon Kane by Weiss/Adams; Gil Kane-a; Solomon Kane pin-up by Wrightson. 3-(76 pgs.) Origin Red Sonja by Chaykin; Adams-a; Solomon Kane app. 2 4 6 11 16 20

KULL THE CONQUEROR (...the Destroyer #11 on; see Conan #1, Creatures on the Loose #10, Marvel Preview, Monsters on the Prowl)
Marvel Comics Group: June, 1971 - No. 2, Sept, 1971; No. 3, July, 1972 - No. 15, Aug, 1974; No. 16, Aug, 1976 - No. 29, Oct, 1978
1-Andru/Wood-a; 2nd app. & origin Kull; 15¢ issue 5 10 15 34 55 75
2-5: 2-3rd Kull app. Last 15¢ iss. 3-13: 20¢ issues. 3-Thulsa Doom-c/app.
3 6 9 16 23 30
6-10: 7-Thulsa Doom-c/app 2 4 6 9 13 16
11-15: 11-15-Ploog-a. 14,15: 25¢ issues 2 4 6 8 10 12
16-(Regular 25¢ edition)(8/76) 1 2 3 5 7 9
16-(30¢-c variant, limited distribution) 3 6 9 14 20 25
17-29: 21-23-(Reg. 30¢ editions) 1 2 3 5 7 9
21-23-(35¢-c variants, limited distribution) 3 6 9 20 40 60
*NOTE: No. 1, 2, 7-9, 11 are based on Robert E. Howard stories. **Alcala** a-17p, 18-20i; c-24. **Ditko** a-12r, 15r. **Gil Kane** c-15p, 21. **Nebres** a-22i-27i; c-25i, 27i. **Ploog** c-11, 12p, 13. **Severin** a-2-9i; c-2-10i, 19. **Starlin** c-14.*

GD 2.0 | VG 4.0 | FN 6.0 | VF 8.0 | VF/NM 9.0 | NM- 9.2

KULL THE CONQUEROR
Marvel Comics Group: Dec, 1982 - No. 2, Mar, 1983 (52 pgs., Baxter paper)
1,2: 1-Buscema-a(p) 4.00

KULL THE CONQUEROR (No. 9,10 titled "Kull")
Marvel Comics Group: 5/83 - No. 10, 6/85 (52 pgs., Baxter paper)
V3#1-10: Buscema-a in #1-3,5-10 3.00
NOTE: Bolton a-4. Golden painted c-3-8. Guice a-4p. Sienkiewicz a-4; c-2.

KUNG FU (See Deadly Hands of..., & Master of...)

KUNG FU FIGHTER (See Richard Dragon...)

KURT BUSIEK'S ASTRO CITY (Limited series) (Also see Astro City: Local Heroes)
Image Comics (Juke Box Productions): Aug, 1995 - No. 6, Jan, 1996 ($2.25)
1-Kurt Busiek scripts, Brent Anderson-a & Alex Ross front & back-c begins; 1st app. Samaritan & Honor Guard (Cleopatra, MHP, Beautie, The Black Rapier, Quarrel & N-Forcer) 2 4 6 8 10 12
2-6: 2-1st app. The Silver Agent, The Old Soldier, & the "original" Honor Guard (Max O'Millions, Starwoman, the "original" Cleopatra, the "original" N-Forcer, the Bouncing Beatnik, Leopardman & Kitkat). 3-1st app. Jack-in-the-Box & The Deacon. 4-1st app. Winged Victory (cameo), The Hanged Man & The First Family. 5-1st app. Crackerjack, The Astro City Irregulars, Nightingale & Sunbird. 6-Origin Samaritan; 1st full app. Winged Victory 1 3 4 6 8 10
Life In The Big City-(8/96, $19.95, trade paperback)-r/Image Comics limited series w/sketchbook & cover gallery; Ross-c 20.00
Life In The Big City-(8/96, $49.95, hardcover, 1000 print run)-r/Image Comics limited series w/sketchbook & cover gallery; Ross-c 50.00

KURT BUSIEK'S ASTRO CITY (1st Homage Comics series)
Image Comics (Homage Comics): V2#1, Sept, 1996 - No. 15, Dec, 1998;
DC Comics (Homage Comics): No. 16, Mar, 1999 - No. 22, Aug, 2000 ($2.50)
1/2-(10/96)-The Hanged Man story; 1st app. The All-American & Slugger, The Lamplighter, The Time-Keeper & Eterneon 1 3 4 6 8 10
1/2-(1/98) 2nd printing w/new cover 2.50
1- Kurt Busiek scripts, Alex Ross-c, Brent Anderson-p & Will Blyberg-i begin; intro The Gentleman, Thunderhead & Helia. 1 2 3 5 6 8
1-(12/97, $4.95) "3-D Edition" w/glasses 5.00
2-Origin The First Family; Astra story 1 2 3 4 5 7
3-5: 4-1st app. The Crossbreed, Ironhorse, Glue Gun & The Confessor (cameo) 6.00
6-10 5.00
11-22: 14-20-Steeljack story arc. 16-(3/99) First DC issue 2.50
TPB-($19.95) Ross-c, r/#4-9, #1/2 w/sketchbook 20.00
Family Album TPB ($19.95) r/#1-3,10-13 20.00
The Tarnished Angel HC ($29.95) r/#14-20; new Ross dust jacket; sketch pages by Anderson & Ross; cover gallery with reference photos 30.00
The Tarnished Angel SC ($19.95) r/#14-20; new Ross-c 20.00

LABMAN
Image Comics: Nov, 1996 ($3.50, one-shot)
1-Allred-c 4.00

LAB RATS
DC Comics: June, 2002 - No. 8, Jan, 2003 ($2.50)
1-8-John Byrne-s/a. 5,6-Superman app. 2.50

LABYRINTH
Marvel Comics Group: Nov, 1986 - No. 3, Jan, 1987 (Limited series)
1-3: David Bowie movie adaptation; r/Marvel Super Special #40 4.00

LA COSA NOSTROID (See Scud: The Disposible Assassin)
Fireman Press: Mar, 1996 - No. 9, 1998 ($2.95, B&W)
1-9-Dan Harmon-s/Rob Schrab-c/a 3.00

LAD: A DOG (Movie)
Dell Publishing Co.: 1961 - No. 2, July-Sept, 1962
Four Color 1303 4 8 12 28 44 60
2 4 8 12 24 37 50

LADY AND THE TRAMP (Disney, See Dell Giants & Movie Comics)
Dell Publishing Co.: No. 629, May, 1955 - No. 634, June, 1955
Four Color 629 (#1)-..with Jock 7 14 21 47 76 105
Four Color 634-...Album 5 10 15 32 51 70

LADY COP (See 1st Issue Special)

LADY DEATH (See Evil Ernie)
Chaos! Comics: Jan, 1994 - No. 3, Mar, 1994 ($2.75, limited series)

Lab Rats #1 © John Byrne

Lady Death #7 © Chaos!

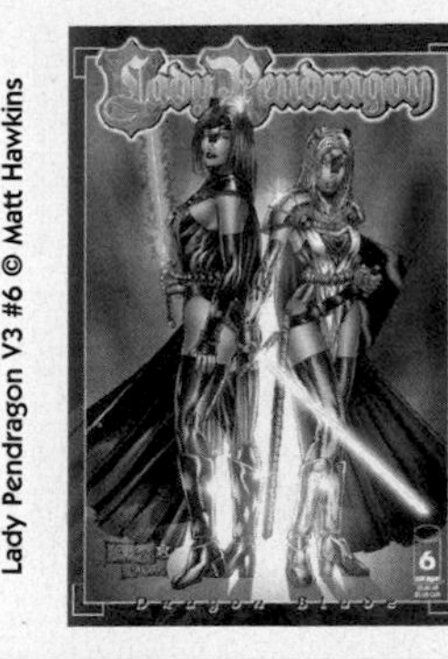

Lady Pendragon V3 #6 © Matt Hawkins

	GD 2.0	VG 4.0	FN 6.0	VF 8.0	VF/NM 9.0	NM- 9.2
1/2-S. Hughes-c/a in all, 1/2 Velvet	1	2	3	4	5	7
1/2 Gold	1	3	4	6	8	10
1/2 Signed Limited Edition	2	4	6	8	10	12
1-($3.50)-Chromium-c	2	4	6	10	14	18
1-Commemorative	2	4	6	9	13	16
1-(9/96, $2.95) "Encore Presentation"; r/#1						3.00
2	1	2	3	5	6	8
3						5.00
... And Jade (4/02, $2.99) Augustyn-s/Reis-a						3.00
...And The Women of Chaos! Gallery #1 (11/96, $2.25) pin-ups by various						3.00
.../Bad Kitty (9/01, $2.99) Mota-c/a						3.00
.../Bedlam (6/02, $2.99) Augustyn-s/Reis-c						3.00
...By Steven Hughes (6/00, $2.95) Tribute issue to Steven Hughes						3.00
...By Steven Hughes Deluxe Edition(6/00, $15.95)						16.00
.../Chastity (1/02, $2.99) Mota-c/a; Augustyn-s						3.00
...Death Becomes Her #0 (11/97, $2.95) Hughes-c/a						3.00
...FAN Edition: All Hallow's Eve #1 (1/97, mail-in)						5.00
...In Lingerie #1 (8/95, $2.95) pin-ups, wraparound-c						3.00
...In Lingerie #1-Leather Edition (10,000)						12.00
...In Lingerie #1-Micro Premium Edition; Lady Demon-c (2,000)						35.00
...: Love Bites (3/01, $2.99) Kaminski-s/Luke Ross-a						3.00
.../Medieval Witchblade (8/01, $3.50) covers by Molenaar and Silvestri						3.50
.../Medieval Witchblade Preview Ed. (8/01, $1.99) Molenaar-c						2.50
...: Mischief Night (11/01, $2.99) Ostrander-s/Reis-a						3.00
...: Re-Imagined (7/02, $2.99) Gossett-c						3.00
...: River of Fear (4/01, $2.99) Bennett-a(p)/Cleavenger-c						3.00
...Swimsuit Special #1-($2.50)-Wraparound-c						3.00
...Swimsuit Special #1-Red velvet-c						14.00
...Swimsuit 2001 #1-(2/01, $2.99)-Reis-c; art by various						3.00
...: The Reckoning (7/94, $6.95)-r/#1-3						7.00
...: The Reckoning (8/95, $12.95)- new printing including Lady Death 1/2 & Swimsuit Special #1						13.00
.../Vampirella (3/99, $3.50) Hughes-c/a						3.50
.../Vampirella 2 (3/00, $3.50) Deodato-c/a						3.50
... Vs. Purgatori (12/99, $3.50) Deodato-a						3.50
... Vs. Vampirella Preview (2/00, $1.00) Deodato-a/c						2.50

LADY DEATH (Ongoing series)
Chaos! Comics: Feb, 1998 - No. 16, May, 1999 ($2.95)

1-16: 1-4: Pulido-s/Hughes-c/a. 5-8,13-16-Deodato-a. 9-11-Hughes-a						3.00
...Retribution (8/98, $2.95) Jadsen-a						3.00
...Retribution Premium Ed.						6.00

LADY DEATH: ALIVE
Chaos! Comics: May, 2001 - No. 4, Aug, 2001 ($2.99, limited series)

1-4-Ivan Reis-a; Lady Death becomes mortal — 3.00

LADY DEATH: A MEDIEVAL TALE (Brian Pulido's...)
CG Entertainment: Mar, 2003 - No. 12, Apr, 2004 ($2.95)

1-12: 1-Brian Pulido-s/Ivan Reis-a; Lady Death in the CrossGen Universe — 3.00
Vol.1 TPB (2003, $9.95) digest-sized reprint of #1-6 — 10.00

LADY DEATH: DARK ALLIANCE
Chaos! Comics: July, 2002 - No. 5, ($2.99, limited series)

1-3-Reis-a/Ostrander-s — 3.00

LADY DEATH: DARK MILLENNIUM
Chaos! Comics: Feb, 2000 - No. 3, Apr, 2000 ($2.95, limited series)

Preview (6/00, $5.00) — 5.00
1-3-Ivan Reis-a — 3.00

LADY DEATH: GODDESS RETURNS
Chaos! Comics: Jun, 2002 - No. 2, Aug, 2002 ($2.99, limited series)

1,2-Mota-a/Ostrander-s — 3.00

LADY DEATH: HEARTBREAKER
Chaos! Comics: Mar, 2002 - No. 4, ($2.99, limited series)

1-Molenaar-a/Ostrander-s — 3.00

LADY DEATH: JUDGEMENT WAR
Chaos! Comics: Nov, 1999 - No. 3, Jan, 2000 ($2.95, limited series)

Prelude (10/99) two covers — 3.00
1-3-Ivan Reis-a — 3.00

LADY DEATH: LAST RITES
Chaos! Comics: Oct, 2001 - No. 4, Feb, 2001 ($2.99, limited series)

1-4-Ivan Reis-a/Ostrander-s — 3.00

LADY DEATH: THE CRUCIBLE
Chaos! Comics: Nov, 1996 - No. 6, Oct, 1997 ($3.50/$2.95, limited series)

1/2 — 4.00
1/2 Cloth Edition — 8.00
1-Wraparound silver foil embossed-c — 4.00
2-6-($2.95) — 3.00

LADY DEATH: THE GAUNTLET
Chaos! Comics: Apr, 2002 - No. 2, May, 2002 ($2.99, limited series)

1,2: 1-J. Scott Campbell-c/redesign of Lady Death's outfit; Mota-a — 3.00

LADY DEATH: THE ODYSSEY
Chaos! Comics: Apr, 1996 - No. 4, Aug, 1996 ($3.50/$2.95)

	GD 2.0	VG 4.0	FN 6.0	VF 8.0	VF/NM 9.0	NM- 9.2
1-($1.50)-Sneak Peek Preview						2.50
1-($1.50)-Sneak Peek Preview Micro Premium Edition (2500 print run)	2	4	6	8	10	12
1-($3.50)-Embossed, wraparound goil foil-c						5.00
1-Black Onyx Edition (200 print run)	6	12	18	37	59	80
1-($19.95)-Premium Edition (10,000 print run)						20.00
2-4-($2.95)						3.00

LADY DEATH: THE RAPTURE
Chaos! Comics: Jun, 1999 - No. 4, Sept, 1999 ($2.95, limited series)

1-4-Ivan Reis-c/a; Pulido-s — 3.00

LADY DEATH: THE WILD HUNT (Brian Pulido's...)
CG Entertainment: Apr, 2004 - No. 2, May, 2005 ($2.95)

1-2: 1-Brian Pulido-s/Jim Cheung-a — 3.00

LADY DEATH: TRIBULATION
Chaos! Comics: Dec, 2000 - No. 4, Mar, 2001 ($2.95, limited series)

1-4-Ivan Reis-a; Kaminski-s — 3.00

LADY DEATH II: BETWEEN HEAVEN & HELL
Chaos! Comics: Mar, 1995 - No. 4, July, 1995 ($3.50, limited series)

	GD 2.0	VG 4.0	FN 6.0	VF 8.0	VF/NM 9.0	NM- 9.2
1-Chromium wraparound-c; Evil Ernie cameo						5.00
1-Commemorative (4,000), 1-Black Velvet-c	2	4	6	10	14	18
1-Gold	1	3	4	6	8	10
1-"Refractor" edition (5,000)	2	4	6	11	16	20
2-4						3.50
4-Lady Demon variant-c	1	2	3	5	7	9
Trade paperback-($12.95)-r/#1-4						13.00

LADY DEMON
Chaos! Comics: Mar, 2000 - No. 3, May, 2000 ($2.95, limited series)

1-3-Kaminski-s/Brewer-a — 3.00
1-Premium Edition — 10.00

LADY FOR A NIGHT (See Cinema Comics Herald)

LADY JUSTICE (See Neil Gaiman's...)

LADY LUCK (Formerly Smash #1-85) (Also see Spirit Sections #1)
Quality Comics Group: No. 86, Dec, 1949 - No. 90, Aug, 1950

	GD 2.0	VG 4.0	FN 6.0	VF 8.0	VF/NM 9.0	NM- 9.2
86(#1)	92	184	276	580	978	1375
87-90	66	132	198	416	701	985

LADY PENDRAGON
Maximum Press: Mar, 1996 ($2.50)

1-Matt Hawkins script — 2.50

LADY PENDRAGON
Image Comics: Nov, 1998 - No. 3, Jan, 1999 ($2.50, mini-series)

Preview (6/98) Flip book w/ Deity preview — 3.00
1-3: 1-Matt Hawkins-s/Stinsman-a — 3.00
1-($6.95) DF Ed. with variant-c by Jusko — 7.00
2-($4.95)Variant edition — 5.00
0-(3/99) Origin; flip book — 2.50

LADY PENDRAGON (Volume 3)
Image Comics: Apr, 1999 - No. 9, Mar, 2000 ($2.50, mini-series)

1,2,4-6,8-10: 1-Matt Hawkins-s/Stinsman-a. 2-Peterson-c — 2.50
3-Flip book w/Alley Cat preview (1st app.) — 3.00
7-($3.95) Flip book; Stinsman-a/Cleavenger painted-a — 4.00
Gallery Edition (10/99, $2.95) pin-ups — 3.00
...Merlin (1/00, $2.95) Stinsman-a — 3.00
.../ More Than Mortal (5/99, $2.50) Scott-s/Norton-a; 2 covers by Norton & Finch — 2.50
.../ More Than Mortal Preview (2/99) Diamond Dateline supplement — 2.50
Pilot Season: Lady Pendragon (5/08, $3.99) Hawkins-s/Eru-a; wraparound-c by Struzan — 4.00

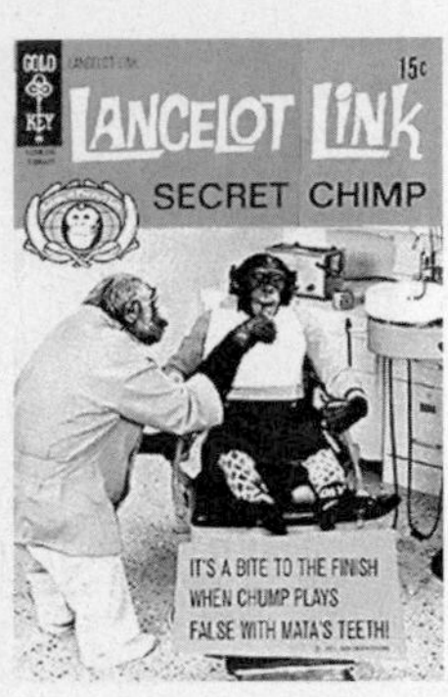

Lancelot Link, Secret Chimp #4 © GK

The Land of Nod #2 © Jay Stephens

Large Feature Comic #19 © DIS

	GD 2.0	VG 4.0	FN 6.0	VF 8.0	VF/NM 9.0	NM- 9.2

LADY RAWHIDE
Topps Comics: July, 1995 - No. 5, Mar, 1996 ($2.95, bi-monthly, limited series)

	GD	VG	FN	VF	VF/NM	NM-
1-5: Don McGregor scripts & Mayhew-a. in all. 2-Stelfreeze-c. 3-Hughes-c. 4-Golden-c. 5-Julie Bell-c.						3.00
It Can't Happen Here TPB (8/99, $16.95) r/#1-5						17.00
Mini Comic 1 (7/95) Maroto-a; Zorro app.						2.50
Special Edition 1 (6/95, $3.95)-Reprints						4.00

LADY RAWHIDE (Volume 2)
Topps Comics: Oct, 1996 -No. 5, June, 1997 ($2.95, limited series)

	GD	VG	FN	VF	VF/NM	NM-
1-5: 1-Julie Bell-c.						3.00

LADY RAWHIDE OTHER PEOPLE'S BLOOD (ZORRO'S ...)
Image Comics: Mar, 1999 - No. 5, July, 1999 ($2.95, B&W)

	GD	VG	FN	VF	VF/NM	NM-
1-5-Reprints Lady Rawhide series in B&W						3.00

LADY SUPREME (See Asylum)(Also see Supreme & Kid Supreme)
Image Comics (Extreme): May, 1996 - No. 2, June, 1996 ($2.50, limited series)

	GD	VG	FN	VF	VF/NM	NM-
1,2-Terry Moore -s: 1-Terry Moore-c. 2-Flip book w/Newmen preview						2.50

LAFF-A-LYMPICS (TV)(See The Funtastic World of Hanna-Barbera)
Marvel Comics: Mar, 1978 - No. 13, Mar, 1979 (Newsstand sales only)

	GD	VG	FN	VF	VF/NM	NM-
1-Yogi Bear, Scooby Doo, Pixie & Dixie, etc.	3	6	9	17	25	32
2-8	2	4	6	13	18	22
9-13: 11-Jetsons x-over; 1 pg. illustrated bio of Mighty Mightor, Herculoids, Shazzan, Galaxy Trio & Space Ghost	3	6	9	16	22	28

LAFFY-DAFFY COMICS
Rural Home Publ. Co.: Feb, 1945 - No. 2, Mar, 1945

	GD	VG	FN	VF	VF/NM	NM-
1,2-Funny animal	10	20	30	56	76	95

LANA (Little Lana No. 8 on)
Marvel Comics (MjMC): Aug, 1948 - No. 7, Aug, 1949 (Also see Annie Oakley)

	GD	VG	FN	VF	VF/NM	NM-
1-Rusty, Millie begin	22	44	66	129	207	285
2-Kurtzman's "Hey Look" (1); last Rusty	14	28	42	81	118	155
3-7: 3-Nellie begins	11	22	33	62	86	110

LANCELOT & GUINEVERE (See Movie Classics)

LANCELOT LINK, SECRET CHIMP (TV)
Gold Key: Apr, 1971 - No. 8, Feb, 1973

	GD	VG	FN	VF	VF/NM	NM-
1-Photo-c	6	12	18	41	66	90
2-8: 2-Photo-c	4	8	12	24	37	50

LANCELOT STRONG (See The Shield)

LANCE O'CASEY (See Mighty Midget & Whiz Comics)
Fawcett Publications: Spring, 1946 - No. 3, Fall, 1946; No. 4, Summer, 1948

	GD	VG	FN	VF	VF/NM	NM-
1-Captain Marvel app. on-c	30	60	90	174	280	385
2	19	38	57	112	176	240
3,4	15	30	45	86	133	180

NOTE: *The cover for the 1st issue was done in 1942 but was not published until 1946. The cover shows 68 pages but actually has only 36 pages.*

LANCER (TV)(Western)
Gold Key: Feb, 1969 - No. 3, Sept, 1969 (All photo-c)

	GD	VG	FN	VF	VF/NM	NM-
1	4	8	12	24	37	50
2,3	3	6	9	18	27	35

LAND OF NOD, THE
Dark Horse Comics: July, 1997 - No. 3, Feb, 1998 ($2.95, B&W)

	GD	VG	FN	VF	VF/NM	NM-
1-3-Jetcat; Jay Stephens-s/a						3.00

LAND OF OZ
Arrow Comics: 1998 - No. 9 ($2.95, B&W)

	GD	VG	FN	VF	VF/NM	NM-
1-9-Bishop-s/Bryan-s/a						3.00

LAND OF THE DEAD (George A. Romaro's...)
IDW Publishing: Aug, 2005 - No. 5 ($3.99, limited series)

	GD	VG	FN	VF	VF/NM	NM-
1-4-Adaptation of 2005 movie; Ryall-s/Rodriguez-a						4.00
TPB (3/06, $19.99) r/#1-5; cover gallery						20.00

LAND OF THE GIANTS (TV)
Gold Key: Nov, 1968 - No. 5, Sept, 1969 (All have photo-c)

	GD	VG	FN	VF	VF/NM	NM-
1	6	12	18	43	69	95
2-5	4	8	12	26	41	55

LAND OF THE LOST COMICS (Radio)
E. C. Comics: July-Aug, 1946 - No. 9, Spring, 1948

	GD	VG	FN	VF	VF/NM	NM-
1	39	78	117	230	370	510
2	24	48	72	140	225	310
3-9	20	40	60	118	189	260

LAND UNKNOWN, THE (Movie)
Dell Publishing Co.: No. 845, Sept, 1957

	GD	VG	FN	VF	VF/NM	NM-
Four Color 845-Alex Toth-a	11	22	33	79	140	200

LA PACIFICA
DC Comics (Paradox Press): 1994/1995 ($4.95, B&W, limited series, digest size, mature readers)

	GD	VG	FN	VF	VF/NM	NM-
1-3						5.00

LARAMIE (TV)
Dell Publishing Co.: Aug, 1960 - July, 1962 (All photo-c)

	GD	VG	FN	VF	VF/NM	NM-
Four Color 1125-Gil Kane/Heath-a	8	16	24	58	97	135
Four Color 1223,1284, 01-418-207 (7/62)	6	12	18	43	69	95

LAREDO (TV)
Gold Key: June, 1966

	GD	VG	FN	VF	VF/NM	NM-
1 (10179-606)-Photo-c	4	8	12	22	34	45

LARGE FEATURE COMIC (Formerly called Black & White in previous guides)
Dell Publishing Co.: 1939 - No. 13, 1943

Note: See individual alphabetical listings for prices

1 (Series I)-Dick Tracy Meets the Blank
2-Terry and the Pirates (#1)
3-Heigh-Yo Silver! The Lone Ranger (text & ill.)(76 pgs.); also exists as a Whitman #710; based on radio
4-Dick Tracy Gets His Man
5-Tarzan of the Apes (#1) by Harold Foster (origin); reprints 1st Tarzan dailies from 1929
6-Terry & the Pirates & The Dragon Lady; reprints dailies from 1936
7-(Scarce, 52 pgs.)-Hi-Yo Silver the Lone Ranger to the Rescue; also exists as a Whitman #715, based on radio program
8-Dick Tracy the Racket Buster
9-King of the Royal Mounted (Zane Grey's...)
10-(Scarce)-Gang Busters (No. appears on inside front cover); first slick cover (based on radio program)
11-Dick Tracy Foils the Mad Doc Hump
12-Smilin' Jack; no number on-c
13-Dick Tracy and Scottie of Scotland Yard
14-Smilin' Jack Helps G-Men Solve a Case!
15-Dick Tracy and the Kidnapped Princes
16-Donald Duck; 1st app. Daisy Duck on back cover (6/41-Disney)
17-Gang Busters (1941)
18-Phantasmo (see The Funnies #45)
19-Dumbo Comic Paint Book (Disney); partial-r from 4-Color #17
20-Donald Duck Comic Paint Book (rarer than #16) (Disney)
21,22: 21-Private Buck. 22-Nuts & Jolts
23-The Nebbs
24-Popeye in "Thimble Theatre" by Segar
25-Smilin' Jack-1st issue to show title on-c
26-Smitty
27-Terry and the Pirates; Caniff-c/a
28-Grin and Bear It
29-Moon Mullins
30-Tillie the Toiler
1 (Series II)-Peter Rabbit by Harrison Cady; arrival date-3/27/42
2-Winnie Winkle (#1)
3-Dick Tracy
4-Tiny Tim (#1)
5-Toots and Casper
6-Terry and the Pirates; Caniff-a
7-Pluto Saves the Ship (#1) (Disney)-Written by Carl Barks, Jack Hannah, & Nick George (Barks' 1st comic book work)
8-Bugs Bunny (#1)('42)
9-Bringing Up Father
10-Popeye (Thimble Theatre)
11-Barney Google and Snuffy Smith
12-Private Buck
13-(nn)-1001 Hours Of Fun; puzzles & games; by A. W. Nugent. This book was bound as #13 with Large Feature Comics in publisher's files

NOTE: *The Black & White Feature Books are oversized 8-1/2x11-3/8" comics with color covers and black and white interiors. The first nine issues all have rough, heavy stock covers and, except for #7, all have 76 pages, including covers. #7 and #10-on all have 52 pages. Beginning with #10 the covers are slick and thin and, because of their size, are difficult to handle without damaging. For this reason, they are seldom found in fine to mint condition. The paper stock, unlike Wow #1 and Capt. Marvel #1, is itself not unstable ...just thin. Issues #2,6, and 27 were reprinted in the early 1980s, identical except for the copyright notice on the first page.*

LARRY DOBY, BASEBALL HERO
Fawcett Publications: 1950 (Cleveland Indians)

	GD	VG	FN	VF	VF/NM	NM-
nn-Bill Ward-a; photo-c	77	154	231	481	816	1150

LARRY HARMON'S LAUREL AND HARDY (...Comics)
National Periodical Publ.: July-Aug, 1972 (Digest advertised, not published)

	GD	VG	FN	VF	VF/NM	NM-
1-Low print run	8	16	24	58	97	135

LARS OF MARS
Ziff-Davis Publishing Co.: No. 10, Apr-May, 1951 - No. 11, July-Aug, 1951 (Painted-c) (Created by Jerry Siegel, editor)

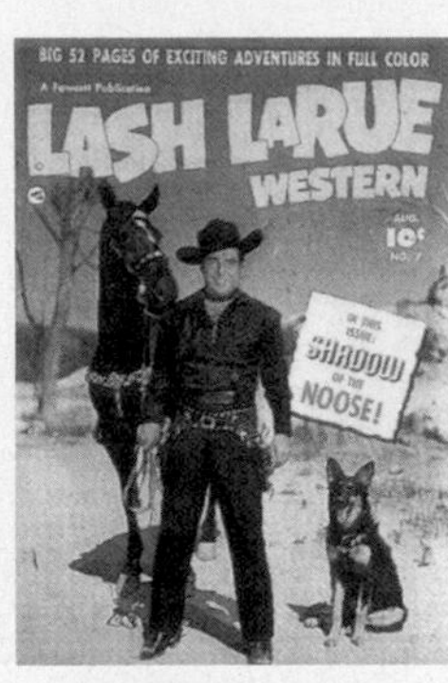

Lash Larue Western #7 © FAW

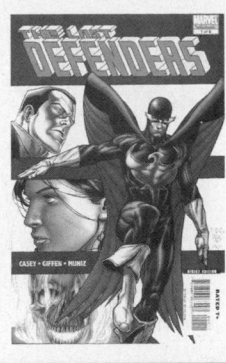

The Last Defenders #1 © MAR

Last Shot: First Draw #1 © Studio XD

GD VG FN VF VF/NM NM-
2.0 4.0 6.0 8.0 9.0 9.2

10-Origin; Anderson-a(3) in each; classic robot-c 83 166 249 523 887 1250
11-Gene Colan-a; classic-c 66 132 198 416 701 985

LARS OF MARS 3-D
Eclipse Comics: Apr, 1987 ($2.50)
1-r/Lars of Mars #10,11 in 3-D plus new story 4.00
2-D limited edition (B&W, 100 copies) 6.00

LASER ERASER & PRESSBUTTON (See Axel Pressbutton & Miracle Man 9)
Eclipse Comics: Nov, 1985 - No. 6, 1987 (95¢/$2.50, limited series)
1-6: 5,6-(95¢) 2.50
...In 3-D 1 (8/86, $2.50) 4.00
2-D 1 (B&W, limited to 100 copies signed & numbered) 8.00

LASH LARUE WESTERN (Movie star; King of the bullwhip)(See Fawcett Movie Comic, Motion Picture Comics & Six-Gun Heroes)
Fawcett Publications: Sum, 1949 - No. 46, Jan, 1954 (36 pgs., 1-6,9,13,16-on)
1-Lash & his horse Black Diamond begin; photo front/back-c begin 86 172 258 538 894 1250
2(11/49) 40 80 120 235 368 500
3-5 32 64 96 186 293 400
6,9: 6-Last photo back-c; Intro. Frontier Phantom (Lash's twin brother) 26 52 78 150 235 320
7,8,10 (52pgs.) 27 54 81 156 246 335
11,12,14,15 (52pgs.) 18 36 54 103 162 220
13,16-20 (36pgs.) 16 32 48 94 147 200
21-30: 21-The Frontier Phantom app. 15 30 45 84 127 170
31-45 14 28 42 76 108 140
46-Last Fawcett issue & photo-c 14 28 42 80 115 150

LASH LARUE WESTERN (Continues from Fawcett series)
Charlton Comics: No. 47, Mar-Apr, 1954 - No. 84, June, 1961
47-Photo-c 16 32 48 94 147 200
48 14 28 42 80 115 150
49-60, 67,68-(68 pgs.). 68-Check-a 11 22 33 62 86 110
61-66,69,70: 52-r/#8; 53-r/#22 10 20 30 54 72 90
71-83 8 16 24 44 57 70
84-Last issue 10 20 30 54 72 90

LASH LARUE WESTERN
AC Comics: 1990 ($3.50, 44 pgs) (24 pgs. of color, 16 pgs. of B&W)
1-Photo covers; r/Lash #6; r/old movie posters 3.50
Annual 1 (1990, $2.95, B&W, 44 pgs.)-Photo covers 3.00

LASSIE (TV)(M-G-M's... #1-36; see Kite Fun Book)
Dell Publ. Co./Gold Key No. 59 (10/62) on: June, 1950 - No. 70, July, 1969
1 (52 pgs.)-Photo-c; inside lists One Shot #282 in error 15 30 45 107 195 285
2-Painted-c begin 8 16 24 58 97 135
3-10 6 12 18 43 69 95
11-19: 12-Rocky Langford (Lassie's master) marries Gerry Lawrence. 15-1st app. Timbu 5 10 15 34 55 75
20-22-Matt Baker-a 6 12 18 39 62 85
23-38: 33-Robinson-a. 5 10 15 32 51 70
39-1st app. Timmy as Lassie picks up her TV family; photo-c 6 12 18 43 69 95
40-50-Photo-c on all 5 10 15 32 51 70
51-58-Photo-c on all 5 10 15 30 48 65
59 (10/62)-1st Gold Key 5 10 15 32 51 70
60-70: 63-Last Timmy (10/63). 64-r/#19. 65-Forest Ranger Corey Stuart begins, ends #69. 70-Forest Rangers Bob Ericson & Scott Turner app. (Lassie's new masters) 4 8 12 26 41 55
11193(1978, $1.95, 224 pgs., Golden Press)-Baker-r (92 pgs.) 4 8 12 28 44 60
NOTE: *Also see March of Comics #210, 217, 230, 254, 266, 278, 296, 308, 324,334, 346, 358, 370, 381, 394, 411, 432.*

LAST AMERICAN, THE
Marvel Comics (Epic): Dec, 1990 - No. 4, March, 1991 ($2.25, mini-series)
1-4: Alan Grant scripts 2.50

LAST AVENGERS STORY, THE (Last Avengers #1)
Marvel Comics: Nov, 1995 - No. 2, Dec, 1995 ($5.95, painted, limited series) (Alterniverse)
1,2: Peter David story; acetate-c in all. 1-New team (Hank Pym, Wasp, Human Torch, Cannonball, She-Hulk, Hotshot, Bombshell, Tommy Maximoff, Hawkeye & Mockingbird) forms to battle Ultron 59, Kang the Conqueror, The Grim Reaper & Oddball 6.00

LAST CHRISTMAS, THE

GD VG FN VF VF/NM NM-
2.0 4.0 6.0 8.0 9.0 9.2

Image Comics: May, 2006 - No. 5, Oct, 2006 ($2.99, limited series)
1-5-Gerry Duggan & Brian Posehn-s/Rick Remender & Hilary Barta-a 3.00
TPB (2006, $14.99) r/#1-5; Patton Oswalt intro.; sketch pages and art 15.00

LAST DAY IN VIETNAM
Dark Horse Books: July, 2000 ($10.95, graphic novel)
nn-Will Eisner-s/a/c 11.00

LAST DAYS OF THE JUSTICE SOCIETY SPECIAL
DC Comics: 1986 ($2.50, one-shot, 68 pgs.)
1-62 pg. JSA story plus unpubbed G.A. pg. 1 3 4 6 8 10

LAST DEFENDERS, THE
Marvel Comics: May, 2008 - No. 6, Oct, 2008 ($2.99, limited series)
1-6-Nighthawk, She-Hulk, Colossus, and Blazing Skull; Muniz-a. 2-Deodato-c 3.00

LAST FANTASTIC FOUR STORY, THE
Marvel Comics: Oct, 2007 ($4.99, one-shot)
1-Stan Lee-s/John Romita, Jr.-a/c; Galactus app. 5.00

LAST GENERATION, THE
Black Tie Studios: 1986 - No. 5, 1989 ($1.95, B&W, high quality paper)
1-5 2.50
Book 1 (1989, $6.95)-By Caliber Press 7.00

LAST HERO STANDING (Characters from Spider-Girl's M2 universe)
Marvel Comics: Aug, 2005 - No. 5, Aug, 2005 ($2.99, weekly limited series)
1-5: 1-DeFalco-s/Olliffe-a. 4-Thor app. 5-Capt. America dies 3.00
TPB (2005, $13.99) r/#1-5 14.00

LAST HUNT, THE
Dell Publishing Co.: No. 678, Feb, 1956
Four Color 678-Movie, photo-c 7 14 21 50 83 115

LAST KISS
ACME Press (Eclipse): 1988 ($3.95, B&W, squarebound, 52 pgs.)
1-One story adapts E.A. Poe's The Black Cat 4.00

LAST OF THE COMANCHES (Movie) (See Wild Bill Hickok #28)
Avon Periodicals: 1953
nn-Kinstler-c/a, 21pgs.; Ravielli-a 15 30 45 88 137 185

LAST OF THE ERIES, THE (See American Graphics)

LAST OF THE FAST GUNS, THE
Dell Publishing Co.: No. 925, Aug, 1958
Four Color 925-Movie, photo-c 7 14 21 47 76 105

LAST OF THE MOHICANS (See King Classics & White Rider and...)

LAST OF THE VIKING HEROES, THE (Also see Silver Star #1)
Genesis West Comics: Mar, 1987 - No. 12 ($1.50/$1.95)
1-4,5A,5B,6-12: 4-Intro The Phantom Force, 1-Signed edition ($1.50), 5A-Kirby/Stevens-c. 5B,6 ($1.95). 7-Art Adams-c. 8-Kirby back-c. 4.00
Summer Special 1-3: 1-(1988)-Frazetta-c & illos. 2 (1990, $2.50)-A TMNT app. 3 (1991, $2.50)-Teenage Mutant Ninja Turtles 4.00
Summer Special 1-Signed edition (sold for $1.95) 4.00
NOTE: ***Art Adams** c-7. **Byrne** c-3. **Kirby** c-1p, 5p. **Perez** c-2i. **Stevens** c-5Ai.*

LAST ONE, THE
DC Comics (Vertigo): July, 1993 - No. 6, Dec, 1993 ($2.50, lim. series, mature)
1-6 2.50

LAST PLANET STANDING
Marvel Comics: July, 2006 - No. 5, Sept, 2006 ($2.99, limited series)
1-5-Galactus threatens Spider-Girl & Fantastic Five's M2 Earth; Avengers app.; Olliffe-a 3.00
TPB (2006, $13.99) r/series 14.00

LAST SHOT
Image Comics: Aug, 2001 - No. 4, Mar, 2002 ($2.95, limited series)
1-4: 1-Wraparound-c; by Studio XD 3.00
...: First Draw (5/01, $2.95) Introductory one-shot 3.00

LAST STARFIGHTER, THE
Marvel Comics Group: Oct, 1984 - No. 3, Dec, 1984 (75¢, movie adaptation)
1-3: r/Marvel Super Special; Guice-c 2.50

LAST TEMPTATION, THE
Marvel Comics: 1994 - No. 3, 1994 ($4.95, limited series)
1-3-Alice Cooper story; Neil Gaiman scripts; McKean-c; Zulli-a: 1-Two covers 5.00
HC (Dark Horse Comics, 2005, $14.95) r/#1-3; Gaiman intro. 15.00

Laugh #14 © AP

Laurel and Hardy #1 © STJ

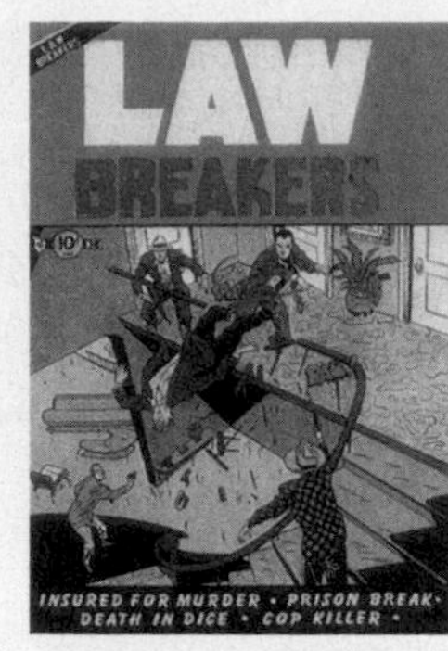

Lawbreakers #8 © CC

	GD 2.0	VG 4.0	FN 6.0	VF 8.0	VF/NM 9.0	NM- 9.2

LAST TRAIN FROM GUN HILL
Dell Publishing Co.: No. 1012, July, 1959

Four Color 1012-Movie, photo-c	8	16	24	56	93	130

LAST TRAIN TO DEADSVILLE: A CAL McDONALD MYSTERY (See Criminal Macabre)
Dark Horse Comics: May, 2004 - No. 4, Sept, 2004 ($2.99, limited series)

1-4-Steve Niles-s/Kelley Jones-a/c						3.00
TPB (2005, $14.95) r/series						15.00

LATEST ADVENTURES OF FOXY GRANDPA (See Foxy Grandpa)

LATEST COMICS (Super Duper No. 3?)
Spotlight Publ./Palace Promotions (Jubilee): Mar, 1945 - No. 2, 1945?

1-Super Duper	16	32	48	94	147	200
2-Bee-29 (nd); Jubilee in indicia blacked out	14	28	42	76	108	140

LAUGH
Archie Enterprises: June, 1987 - No. 29, Aug, 1991 (75¢/$1.00)

V2#1						5.00
2-10,14,24: 5-X-Mas issue. 14-1st app. Hot Dog. 24-Re-intro Super Duck						4.00
11-13,15-23,25-29: 19-X-Mas issue						3.00

LAUGH COMICS (Teenage) (Formerly Black Hood #9-19) (Laugh #226 on)
Archie Publications (Close-Up): No. 20, Fall, 1946 - No. 400, Apr, 1987

20-Archie begins; Katy Keene & Taffy begin by Woggon; Suzie & Wilbur also begin; Archie covers begin	67	134	201	422	711	1000
21-23,25	37	74	111	218	349	480
24- "Pipsy" by Kirby (6 pgs.)	38	76	114	222	356	490
26-30	22	44	66	127	204	280
31-40	15	30	45	94	147	200
41-60: 41,54-Debbi by Woggon	14	28	42	76	108	140
61-80: 67-Debbi by Woggon	10	20	30	56	76	95
81-99	5	10	15	34	55	75
100	6	12	18	37	59	80
101-105,110,112,114-126: 125-Debbi app.	4	8	12	26	41	55
106-109,111,113-Neal Adams-a (1 pg.) in each	4	8	12	28	44	60
127-144: Super-hero app. in all (see note)	5	10	15	32	51	70
145-(4/63) Josie by DeCarlo begins	5	10	15	34	55	75
146-149-early Josie app. by DeCarlo	4	8	12	24	37	50
150,162,163,165,167,169,170-No Josie	3	6	9	17	25	32
151-161,164,168-Josie app. by DeCarlo	4	8	12	22	34	45
166-Beatles-c (1/65)	5	10	15	34	55	75
171-180, 200 (12/67)	3	6	9	16	23	30
181-199	3	6	9	14	19	24
201-240(3/71)	2	4	6	10	14	18
241-280(7/74)	2	4	6	9	12	15
281-299	2	4	6	8	10	12
300(3/76)	2	4	6	8	11	14
301-340 (7/79)	1	2	3	5	7	9
341-370 (1/82)	1	2	3	4	5	7
371-380,385-399: 380-Cheryl Blossom app.						5.00
381-384,400: 381-384-Katy Keene app.; by Woggon-381,382						6.00

NOTE: *The Fly app. in 128, 129, 132, 134, 138, 139. Flygirl app. in 136, 137, 143. Flyman app. in 137. The Jaguar app. in 127, 130, 131, 133, 135, 140-142, 144. Josie app. in 145-149, 151-161, 164, 168. Katy Keene app. in 20-125, 129, 130, 133. Horror/Sci-Fi covers on 128-135, 137, 139. Many issues contain paper dolls.* ***Al Fagaly*** *c-20-29.* ***Montana*** *c-33, 36, 37, 42.* ***Bill Vigoda*** *c-30, 50.*

LAUGH COMICS DIGEST (...Magazine #23-89; Laugh Digest Mag. #90 on)
Archie Publ. (Close-Up No. 1, 3 on): 8/74; No. 2, 9/75; No. 3, 3/76 - No. 200, Apr, 2005 (Digest-size) (Josie and Sabrina app. in most issues)

1-Neal Adams-a	5	10	15	32	51	70
2,7,8,19-Neal Adams-a	3	6	9	19	29	38
3-6,9,10	3	6	9	16	22	28
11-18,20	2	4	6	11	16	20
21-40	2	4	6	9	13	16
41-60	1	3	4	6	8	10
61-80	1	2	3	5	6	8
81-99						5.00
100						6.00
101-138						3.00
139-200: 139-Begin $1.95-c. 148-Begin $1.99-c. 156-Begin $2.19-c. 180-Begin $2.39-c						2.50

NOTE: *Katy Keene in 23, 25, 27, 32-38, 40, 45-48, 50. The Fly-r in 19, 20. The Jaguar-r in 25, 27. Mr. Justice-r in 21. The Web-r in 23.*

LAUGH COMIX (Laugh Comics inside)(Formerly Top Notch Laugh; Suzie Comics No. 49 on)
MLJ Magazines: No. 46, Summer, 1944 - No. 48, Winter, 1944-45

46-Wilbur & Suzie in all; Harry Sahle-c	23	46	69	133	214	295
47,48: 47-Sahle-c. 48-Bill Vigoda-c	15	30	45	90	140	190

LAUGH-IN MAGAZINE (TV)(Magazine)
Laufer Publ. Co.: Oct, 1968 - No. 12, Oct, 1969 (50¢) (Satire)

V1#1	5	10	15	32	51	70
2-12	4	8	12	22	34	45

LAUREL & HARDY (See Larry Harmon's... & March of Comics No. 302, 314)

LAUREL AND HARDY (...Comics)
St. John Publ. Co.: 3/49 - No. 3, 9/49; No. 26, 11/55 - No. 28, 3/56 (No #4-25)

1	72	144	216	454	770	1085
2	40	80	120	240	390	540
3	31	62	93	181	291	400
26-28 (Reprints)	15	30	45	92	144	195

LAUREL AND HARDY (TV)
Dell Publishing Co.: Oct, 1962 - No. 4, Sept-Nov, 1963

12-423-210 (8-10/62)	6	12	18	43	69	95
2-4 (Dell)	4	8	12	28	44	60

LAUREL AND HARDY (Larry Harmon's...)
Gold Key: Jan, 1967 - No. 2, Oct, 1967

1-Photo back-c	4	8	12	28	44	60
2	4	8	12	22	34	45

LAUREL AND HARDY DIGEST: DC Comics. 1972 (Advertised, not published)

L.A.W., THE (LIVING ASSAULT WEAPONS)
DC Comics: Sept, 1999 - No. 6, Feb, 2000 ($2.50, limited series)

1-6-Blue Beetle, Question, Judomaster, Capt. Atom app.; Giordano-a. 5-JLA app.						2.50

LAW AGAINST CRIME (Law-Crime on cover)
Essenkay Publishing Co.: April, 1948 - No. 3, Aug, 1948 (Real Stories from Police Files)

1-(#1-3 are half funny animal, half crime stories)-L. B. Cole-c/a in all; electrocution-c	73	146	219	460	780	1100
2-L. B. Cole-c/a	54	108	162	340	575	810
3-Used in **SOTI**, pg. 180,181 & illo "The wish to hurt or kill couples in lovers' lanes;" reprinted in All-Famous Crime #9	68	136	204	428	727	1025

LAW AND ORDER
Maximum Press: Sept, 1995 - No. 2, 1995 ($2.50, unfinished limited series)

1,2						2.50

LAWBREAKERS (...Suspense Stories No. 10 on)
Law and Order Magazines (Charlton): Mar, 1951 - No. 9, Oct-Nov, 1952

1	41	82	123	247	404	560
2	23	46	69	135	218	300
3,5,6,8,9	20	40	60	114	180	245
4- "White Death" junkie story	25	50	75	45	233	320
7- "The Deadly Dopesters" drug story	25	50	75	45	233	320

LAWBREAKERS ALWAYS LOSE!
Marvel Comics (CBS): Spring, 1948 - No. 10, Oct, 1949

1-2pg. Kurtzman-a, "Giggles 'n' Grins"	36	72	108	212	341	470
2	20	40	60	114	180	245
3-5: 4-Vampire story	15	30	45	88	137	185
6(2/49)-Has editorial defense against charges of Dr. Wertham	17	34	51	95	154	210
7-Used in **SOTI**, illo "Comic-book philosophy"	31	62	93	181	291	400
8-10: 9,10-Photo-c	14	28	42	82	121	160

NOTE: ***Brodsky*** *c-4, 5.* ***Shores*** *c-1-3, 6-8.*

LAWBREAKERS SUSPENSE STORIES (Formerly Lawbreakers; Strange Suspense Stories No. 16 on)
Capitol Stories/Charlton Comics: No. 10, Jan, 1953 - No. 15, Nov, 1953

10	41	82	123	247	404	560
11 (3/53)-Severed tongues-c/story & woman negligee scene	127	254	381	800	1350	1900
12-14: 13-Giordano-c begin, end #15	26	52	78	154	247	340
15-Acid-in-face-c/story; hands dissolved in acid story	55	110	165	347	586	825

LAW-CRIME (See Law Against Crime)

LAWDOG
Marvel Comics (Epic Comics): May, 1993 - No. 10, Feb, 1993

1-10						2.50

LAWDOG/GRIMROD: TERROR AT THE CROSSROADS
Marvel Comics (Epic Comics): Sept, 1993 ($3.50)

Leading Comics #6 © DC

Leave It To Binky #3 © DC

Leave It To Chance #9 © Robinson & Smith

	GD	VG	FN	VF	VF/NM	NM-
	2.0	4.0	6.0	8.0	9.0	9.2

GD VG FN VF VF/NM NM-
2.0 4.0 6.0 8.0 9.0 9.2

1 3.50

LAWMAN (TV)
Dell Publishing Co.: No. 970, Feb, 1959 - No. 11, Apr-June, 1962 (All photo-c)

Four Color 970(#1) 12 24 36 87 156 225
Four Color 1035('60), 3(2-4/60)-Toth-a 8 16 24 54 90 125
4-11 6 12 18 43 69 95

LAW OF DREDD, THE (Also see Judge Dredd)
Quality Comics/Fleetway #8 on: 1989 - No. 33, 1992 ($1.50/$1.75)

1-33: Bolland a-1-6,8,10-12,14(2 pg),15,19 2.50

LAWRENCE (See Movie Classics)

LAZARUS CHURCHYARD
Tundra Publishing: June, 1992 - No. 3, 1992 ($3.95, 44 pgs., coated stock)

1-3 4.00
The Final Cut (Image, 1/01, $14.95, TPB) Reprints Ellis/D'Israeli strips 15.00

LAZARUS FIVE
DC Comics: July, 2000 - No. 5, Nov, 2000 ($2.50, limited series)

1-5-Harris-c/Abell-a(p) 2.50

LEADING COMICS
DC Comics: Jan. 1942

nn - Ashcan comic, not distributed to newsstands, only for in-house use. Cover art is Detective Comics #57 with interior being Star Spangled Comics #2 (no known sales)

LEADING COMICS (...Screen Comics No. 42 on)
National Periodical Publications: Winter, 1941-42 - No. 41, Feb-Mar, 1950

1-Origin The Seven Soldiers of Victory; Crimson Avenger, Green Arrow & Speedy, Shining Knight, The Vigilante, Star Spangled Kid & Stripesy begin; The Dummy (Vigilante villain) 1st app. 446 892 1338 3122 5461 7800
2-Meskin-a; Fred Ray-c 159 318 477 994 1647 2300
3 121 242 363 756 1253 1750
4,5 86 172 258 538 889 1240
6-10 66 132 198 413 682 950
11,12,14(Spring, 1945) 48 96 144 293 484 675
13-Classic robot-c 93 186 279 581 966 1350
15-(Sum,'45)-Contents change to funny animal 28 56 84 162 256 350
16-22,24-30: 16-Nero Fox-c begin, end #22 14 28 42 80 115 150
23-1st app. Peter Porkchops by Otto Feuer & begins 28 56 84 162 256 350
31,32,34-41: 34-41-Leading Screen... on-c only 12 24 36 67 94 120
33-(Scarce) 20 40 60 117 184 250
NOTE: *Otto Feuer-a most #15-on; Rube Grossman-a most #15-on;c-15-41. Post a-23-37, 39, 41.*

LEADING MAN
Image Comics: June, 2006 - No. 5, Feb, 2007 ($3.50, limited series)

1-5-B. Clay Moore-s/Jeremy Haun-a 3.50
TPB (2/07, $14.95) r/#1-5; sketch gallery 15.00

LEADING SCREEN COMICS (Formerly Leading Comics)
National Periodical Publ.: No. 42, Apr-May, 1950 - No. 77, Aug-Sept, 1955

42-Peter Porkchops-c/stories continue 12 24 36 67 94 120
43-77 11 22 33 60 83 105
NOTE: *Grossman a-most. Mayer a-45-48, 50, 54-57, 60, 62-74, 75(3), 76, 77.*

LEAGUE OF CHAMPIONS, THE (Also see The Champions)
Hero Graphics: Dec, 1990 - No. 12, 1992 ($2.95, 52 pgs.)

1-12: 1-Flare app. 2-Origin Malice 3.00

LEAGUE OF EXTRAORDINARY GENTLEMEN, THE
America's Best Comics: Mar, 1999 - No. 6, Sept, 2000 ($2.95, limited series)

1-Alan Moore-s/Kevin O'Neill-a 2 4 6 8 10 12
1-DF Edition ($10.00) O'Neill-c 2 4 6 9 12 15
2,3 6.00
4-6: 5-Revised printing with "Amaze 'Whirling Spray' Syringe" parody ad 4.00
5-Initial printing recalled because of "Marvel Co. Syringe" parody ad 250.00
... Compendium 1,2: 1-r/#1,2. 2-r/#3,4 6.00
Hardcover (2000, $24.95) r/#1-6 plus cover gallery 25.00

LEAGUE OF EXTRAORDINARY GENTLEMEN, THE (Volume 2)
America's Best Comics: Sept, 2002 - No. 6, Nov, 2003 ($3.50, limited series)

1-6-Alan Moore-s/Kevin O'Neill-a 4.00
... Bumper Compendium 1,2: 1-r/#1,2. 2-r/#3,4 6.00

LEAGUE OF JUSTICE
DC Comics (Elseworlds): 1996 - No. 2, 1996 ($5.95, 48 pgs., squarebound)

1,2: Magic-based alternate DC Universe story; Giordano-i 6.00

LEATHERFACE
Arpad Publishing: May (April on-c), 1991 - No. 4, May, 1992 ($2.75, painted-c)

1-4-Based on Texas Chainsaw movie; Dorman-c 1 2 3 5 6 8

LEATHERNECK THE MARINE (See Mighty Midget Comics)

LEAVE IT TO BEAVER (TV)
Dell Publishing Co.: No. 912, June, 1958; May-July, 1962 (All photo-c)

Four Color 912 15 30 45 108 199 290
Four Color 999,1103,1191,1285, 01-428-207 13 26 39 95 168 240

LEAVE IT TO BINKY (Binky No. 72 on) (Super DC Giant) (No. 1-22: 52 pgs.)
National Periodical Publications: 2-3/48 - #60, 10/58; #61, 6-7/68 - #71, 2-3/70 (Teen-age humor)

1-Lucy wears Superman costume 36 72 108 212 341 470
2 19 38 57 112 176 240
3,4 14 28 42 76 108 140
5-Superman cameo 18 36 54 105 165 225
6-10 11 22 33 64 90 115
11-14,16-22: Last 52 pg. issue 10 20 30 58 79 100
15-Scribbly story by Mayer 12 24 36 67 94 120
23-28,30-45: 45-Last pre-code (2/55) 9 18 27 50 65 80
29-Used in **POP**, pg. 78 9 18 27 52 69 85
46-60: 60-(10/58) 5 10 15 34 55 75
61 (6-7/68) 1950's reprints with art changes 6 12 18 39 62 85
62-69: 67-Last 12¢ issue 4 8 12 28 44 60
70-7pg. app. Bus Driver who looks like Ralph from Honeymooners 5 10 15 32 51 70
71-Last issue 5 10 15 30 48 65
NOTE: *Aragones-a-61, 62, 67. Drucker a-28. Mayer a-1, 2, 15. Created by Mayer.*

LEAVE IT TO CHANCE (Also see Promotional Comics section for FCBD Ed.)
Image Comics (Homage Comics): Sept, 1996 - No. 11, Sept, 1998; No. 13, July, 2002
DC Comics (Homage Comics): No. 12, Jun, 1999 ($2.50/$2.95/$4.95)

1-3: 1-Intro Chance Falconer & St. George; James Robinson scripts & Paul Smith-c/a 5.00
4-12: 12-(6/99) 3.00
13-(7/02, $4.95) includes sketch pages and pin-ups 5.00
Shaman's Rain TPB (1997, $9.95) r/#1-4 10.00
Shaman's Rain HC (2002, $14.95, over-sized 8 1/4" x 12") r/#1-4 15.00
Trick or Threat TPB (1997, $12.95) r/#5-8 13.00
Trick or Threat HC (2002, $14.95, over-sized 8 1/4" x 12") r/#5-8 15.00
Vol. 3: Monster Madness and Other Stories HC (2003, $14.95, 8 1/4" x 12") r/#9-11 15.00

LEE HUNTER, INDIAN FIGHTER
Dell Publishing Co.: No. 779, Mar, 1957; No. 904, May, 1958

Four Color 779 (#1) 5 10 15 34 55 75
Four Color 904 4 8 12 26 41 55

LEFT-HANDED GUN, THE (Movie)
Dell Publishing Co.: No. 913, July, 1958

Four Color 913-Paul Newman photo-c 9 18 27 63 107 150

LEGACY
Majestic Entertainment: Oct, 1993 - No. 2, Nov, 1993; No. 0, 1994 ($2.25)

1-2,0: 1-Glow-in-the-dark-c. 0-Platinum 2.50

LEGACY
Image Comics: May, 2003 - No. 4, Feb, 2004 ($2.95)

1-4: 1-Francisco-a/Treffiletti-s 3.00

LEGACY OF KAIN (Based on the Eidos video game)
Top Cow Productions: Oct, 1999; Jan, 2004 ($2.99)

...Defiance 1 (1/04, $2.99) Cha-c; Kirkham-a 3.00
...Soul Reaver 1 (10/99, Diamond Dateline supplement) Benitez-c 2.50

LEGEND
DC Comics (WildStorm): Apr, 2005 - No. 4, July, 2005 ($5.95/$5.99, limited series)

1-4-Howard Chaykin-s/Russ Heath-a; inspired by Philip Wylie's novel "Gladiator" 6.00

LEGEND OF CUSTER, THE (TV)
Dell Publishing Co.: Jan, 1968

1-Wayne Maunder photo-c 3 6 9 18 27 35

LEGEND OF ISIS
Alias Entertainment: May, 2005 - Present ($2.99)

1-5: 1-Three covers; Ottney-s/Fontana-a 3.00
...: Beginnings TPB (5/05, $9.99) Ottney-s 10.00

LEGEND OF JESSE JAMES, THE (TV)

Legend of Mother Sarah: City of the Children #3 © DH

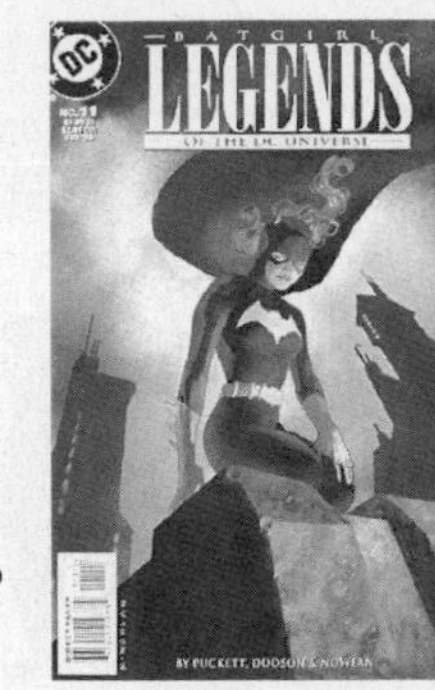

Legends of the DC Universe #11 © DC

Legends of the Legion #2 © DC

	GD	VG	FN	VF	VF/NM	NM-
	2.0	4.0	6.0	8.0	9.0	9.2

Gold Key: Feb, 1966

10172-602-Photo-c	3	6	9	18	27	35

LEGEND OF KAMUI, THE (See Kamui)

LEGEND OF LOBO, THE (See Movie Comics)

LEGEND OF MOTHER SARAH (Manga)
Dark Horse Comics: Apr, 1995 - No. 8, Nov, 1995 ($2.50, limited series)

1-8: Katsuhiro Otomo scripts 4.00

LEGEND OF MOTHER SARAH: CITY OF THE ANGELS (Manga)
Dark Horse Comics: Oct, 1996 - No. 9 ($3.95, B&W, limited series)

1(10/96), 2(12/97),3-9: Otomo scripts 4.00

LEGEND OF MOTHER SARAH: CITY OF THE CHILDREN (Manga)
Dark Horse Comics: Jan, 1996 - No. 7, July, 1996 ($3.95, B&W, limited series)

1-7:Otomo scripts 4.00

LEGEND OF SUPREME
Image Comics (Extreme): Dec, 1994 - No. 3, Feb, 1995 ($2.50, limited series)

1-3 2.50

LEGEND OF THE ELFLORD
DavDez Arts: July, 1998 - No. 2, Sept, 1998 ($2.95)

1,2-Barry Blair & Colin Chin-s/a 3.00

LEGEND OF THE HAWKMAN
DC Comics: 2000 - No. 3, 2000 ($4.95, limited series)

1-3-Raab-s/Lark-c/a 5.00

LEGEND OF THE SHIELD, THE
DC Comics (Impact Comics): July, 1991 - No. 16, Oct, 1992 ($1.00)

1-16: 6,7-The Fly x-over. 12-Contains trading card 2.50
Annual 1 (1992, $2.50, 68 pgs.)-Snyder-a; w/trading card 2.50

LEGEND OF WONDER WOMAN, THE
DC Comics: May, 1986 - No. 4, Aug, 1986 (75¢, limited series)

1-4 4.00

LEGEND OF YOUNG DICK TURPIN, THE (Disney)(TV)
Gold Key: May, 1966

1 (10176-605)-Photo/painted-c	3	6	9	18	27	35

LEGEND OF ZELDA, THE (Link: The Legend... in indicia)
Valiant Comics: 1990 - No. 4, 1990 ($1.95, coated stiff-c) V2#1, 1990 - No. 5, 1990 ($1.50)

1-4: 4-Layton-c(i) 3.00
V2#1-5 3.00

LEGENDS
DC Comics: Nov, 1986 - No. 6, Apr, 1987 (75¢, limited series)

1-5: 1-Byrne-c/a(p) in all; 1st app. new Capt. Marvel. 3-1st app. new Suicide Squad; death of Blockbuster 4.00
6-1st app. new Justice League 6.00

LEGENDS OF DANIEL BOONE, THE (...Frontier Scout)
National Periodical Publications: Oct-Nov, 1955 - No. 8, Dec-Jan, 1956-57

1 (Scarce)-Nick Cardy c-1-8	56	112	168	353	594	835
2 (Scarce)	41	82	123	250	413	575
3-8 (Scarce)	35	70	105	203	327	450

LEGENDS OF NASCAR, THE
Vortex Comics: Nov, 1990 - No. 14, 1992? (#1 3rd printing (1/91) says 2nd printing inside)

1-Bill Elliott biog.; Trimpe-a ($1.50) 5.00
1-2nd printing (11/90, $2.00) 2.50
1-3rd print; contains Maxx racecards ($3.00) 3.00
2-14: 2-Richard Petty. 3-Ken Schrader (7/91). 4-Bobby Allison; Spiegle-a(p); Adkins part-i. 5-Sterling Marlin. 6-Bill Elliott. 7-Junior Johnson; Spiegle-c/a. 8-Benny Parsons; Heck-a3.00
1-13-Hologram cover versions. 2-Hologram shows Bill Elliott's car by mistake (all are numbered & limited) 5.00
2-Hologram corrected version 5.00
Christmas Special ($5.95) 6.00

LEGENDS OF THE DARK CLAW
DC Comics (Amalgam): Apr, 1996 ($1.95)

1-Jim Balent-c/a 3.00

LEGENDS OF THE DARK KNIGHT (See Batman: ...)

LEGENDS OF THE DC UNIVERSE
DC Comics: Feb, 1998 - No. 41, June, 2001 ($1.95/$1.99/$2.50)

1-13,15-21: 1-3-Superman; Robinson-s/Semeiks-a/Orbik-painted-c. 4,5-Wonder Woman; Deodato-a/Rude painted-c. 8-GL/GA, O'Neil-s. 10,11-Batgirl; Dodson-a. 12,13-Justice League. 15-17-Flash. 18-Kid Flash; Guice-a. 19-Impulse; prelude to JLApe Annuals. 20,21-Abin Sur 3.00
14-($3.95) Jimmy Olsen; Kirby-esque-c by Rude 4.00
22-27,30: 22,23-Superman; Rude-c/Ladronn-a. 26,27-Aquaman/Joker 2.50
28,29: Green Lantern & the Atom; Gil Kane-a; covers by Kane and Ross 2.50
31,32: 32-Begin $2.50-c; Wonder Woman; Texeira-c 2.50
33-36-Hal Jordan as The Spectre; DeMatteis-s/Zulli-a; Hale painted-c 2.50
37-41: 37,38-Kyle Rayner. 39-Superman. 40,41-Atom; Harris-c 2.50
... Crisis on Infinite Earths 1 (2/99, $4.95) Untold story during and after Crisis on Infinite Earths #4; Wolfman-s/Ryan-a/Orbik-c 5.00
... 80 Page Giant 1 (9/98, $4.95) Stories and art by various incl. Ditko, Perez, Gibbons, Mumy; Joe Kubert-c 5.00
... 80 Page Giant 2 (1/00, $4.95) Stories and art by various incl. Challengers by Art Adams; Sean Phillips-c 5.00
... 3-D Gallery (12/98, $2.95) Pin-ups w/glasses 3.00

LEGENDS OF THE LEGION (See Legion of Super-Heroes)
DC Comics: Feb, 1998 - No. 4, May, 1998 ($2.25, limited series)

1-4:1-Origin-s of Ultra Boy. 2-Spark. 3-Umbra. 4-Star Boy 3.00

LEGENDS OF THE STARGRAZERS (See Vanguard Illustrated #2)
Innovation Publishing: Aug, 1989 - No. 6, 1990 ($1.95, limited series, mature)

1-6: 1-Redondo part inks 2.50

LEGENDS OF THE WORLD'S FINEST (See World's Finest)
DC Comics: 1994 - No. 3, 1994 ($4.95, squarebound, limited series)

1-3: Simonson scripts; Brereton-c/a; embossed foil logos 6.00
TPB-(1995, $14.95) r/#1-3 15.00

L.E.G.I.O.N. (The # to right of title represents year of print)(Also see Lobo & R.E.B.E.L.S.)
DC Comics: Feb, 1989 - No. 70, Sept, 1994 ($1.50/$1.75)

1-Giffen plots/breakdowns in #1-12,28 5.00
2-22,24-47: 3-Lobo app. #3 on. 4-1st Lobo-c this title. 5-Lobo joins L.E.G.I.O.N. 13-Lar Gand app. 16-Lar Gand joins L.E.G.I.O.N., leaves #19. 31-Capt. Marvel app. 35-L.E.G.I.O.N. '92 begins 3.00
23,70-($2.50, 52 pgs.)-L.E.G.I.O.N. '91 begins. 70-Zero Hour 4.00
48,49,51-69: 48-Begin $1.75-c. 63-L.E.G.I.O.N. '94 begins; Superman x-over 3.00
50-($3.50, 68 pgs.) 4.00
Annual 1-5 ('90-94, 68 pgs.): 1-Lobo, Superman app. 2-Alan Grant scripts. 5-Elseworlds story; Lobo app. 4.00
NOTE: *Alan Grant scripts in #1-39, 51, Annual 1, 2.*

LEGION, THE (Continued from Legion Lost & Legion Worlds)
DC Comics: Dec, 2001 - No. 38, Oct, 2004 ($2.50)

1-Abnett & Lanning-s; Coipel & Lanning-c/a 4.00
2-24: 3-8-Ra's al Ghul app. 5-Snejbjerg-a. 9-DeStefano-a. 12-Legion vs. JLA. 16-Fatal Five app.; Walker-a 17,18-Ra's al Ghul app. 20-23-Universo app. 2.50
25-($3.95) Art by Harris, Cockrum, Rivoche; teenage Clark Kent app.; Harris-c 4.00
26-38-Superboy in classic costume. 26-30-Darkseid app. 31-Giffen-a. 35-38-Jurgens-a 2.50
...Secret Files 3003 (1/04, $4.95) Kirk-a, Harris-c/a; Superboy app. 5.00
...Foundations TPB (2004, $19.95) r/#25-30 & Secret Files 3003; Harris-c 20.00

LEGION LOST (Continued from Legion of Super-Heroes [4th series] #125)
DC Comics: May, 2000 - No. 12, Apr, 2001 ($2.50, limited series)

1-Abnett & Lanning-s. Coipel & Lanning-c/a	1	2	3	4	5	7

2-12-Abnett & Lanning-s. Coipel & Lanning-c/a in most. 4,9-Alixe-a 3.00

LEGIONNAIRES (See Legion of Super-Heroes #40, 41 & Showcase 95 #6)
DC Comics: Apr, 1992 - No. 81, Mar, 2000 ($1.25/$1.50/$2.25)

0-(10/94)-Zero Hour restart of Legion; released between #18 & #19 2.50
1-49,51-77: 1-(4/92)-Chris Sprouse-c/a; polybagged w/SkyBox trading card. 11-Kid Quantum joins. 18-(9/94)-Zero Hour. 19(11/94). 37-Valor (Lar Gand) becomes M'onel (5/96). 43-Legion tryouts; reintro Princess Projectra, Shadow Lass & others. 47-Forms one cover image with LSH #91. 60-Karate Kid & Kid Quantum join. 61-Silver Age & 70's Legion app. 76-Return of Wildfire. 79,80-Coipel-c/a; Legion vs. the Blight 2.50
50-($3.95) Pullout poster by Davis/Farmer 4.00
#1,000,000 (11/98) Sean Phillips-a 2.50
Annual 1,3 ('94,'96 $2.95)-1-Elseworlds-s. 3-Legends of the Dead Earth-s 3.00
Annual 2 (1995, $3.95)-Year One-s 4.50

LEGIONNAIRES THREE
DC Comics: Jan, 1986 - No. 4, May, 1986 (75¢, limited series)

1-4 3.00

LEGION OF MONSTERS (Also see Marvel Premiere #28 & Marvel Preview #8)
Marvel Comics Group: Sept, 1975 ($1.00, B&W, magazine, 76 pgs.)

Legion of Monsters Werewolf By Night #1 © MAR

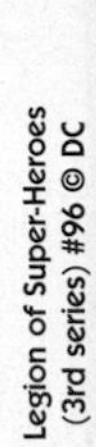
Legion of Super-Heroes (3rd series) #96 © DC

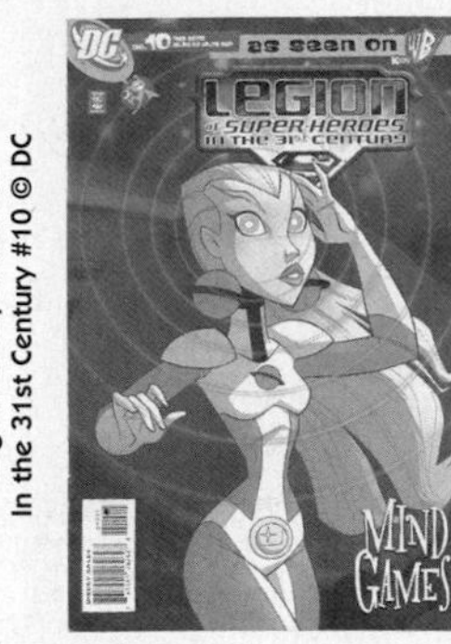

Legion of Super-Heroes In the 31st Century #10 © DC

GD VG FN VF VF/NM NM-
2.0 4.0 6.0 8.0 9.0 9.2

GD VG FN VF VF/NM NM-
2.0 4.0 6.0 8.0 9.0 9.2

1-Origin & 1st app. Legion of Monsters; Neal Adams-c; Morrow-a; origin & only app. The Manphibian; Frankenstein by Mayerik; Bram Stoker's Dracula adaptation; Reese-a; painted-c (#2 was advertised with Morbius & Satana, but was never published) 5 10 15 30 48 65

LEGION OF MONSTERS (One-shots)
Marvel Comics: Apr, 2007 - Sept, 2007 ($2.99)

... Man-Thing (5/07) Huston-s/Janson-a/Land-c; Simon Garth: Zombie by Ted McKeever 3.00
... Morbius (9/07) Cahill-s/Gaydos-a/Land-c; Dracula w/Finch-a/Cebulski-s 3.00
... Satana (8/07) Furth-s/Andrasofszky-a/Land-c; Living Mummy by Hickman 3.00
... Werewolf By Night (4/07) Carey-s/Land-a/c; Monster of Frankenstein by Skottie Young 3.00
HC (2007, $24.99, dustjacket) oversized r/series and classic stories; sketch pages 25.00

LEGION OF NIGHT, THE
Marvel Comics: Oct, 1991 - No. 2, Oct, 1991 ($4.95, 52 pgs.)

1,2-Whilce Portacio-c/a(p) 5.00

LEGION OF SUBSTITUTE HEROES SPECIAL (See Adventure Comics #306)
DC Comics: July, 1985 ($1.25, one-shot, 52 pgs.)

1-Giffen-c/a(p) 3.00

LEGION OF SUPER-HEROES (See Action Comics, Adventure, All New Collectors Edition, Legionnaires, Legends of the Legion, Limited Collectors Edition, Secrets of the..., Superboy & Superman)
National Periodical Publications: Feb, 1973 - No. 4, July-Aug, 1973

1-Legion & Tommy Tomorrow reprints begin 3 6 9 17 25 32
2-4: 2-Forte-r. 3-r/Adv. #340. Action #240. 4-r/Adv. #341, Action #233; Mooney-r 2 4 6 10 14 18

LEGION OF SUPER-HEROES, THE (Formerly Superboy and...; Tales of The Legion No. 314 on)
DC Comics: No. 259, Jan, 1980 - No. 313, July, 1984

259(#1)-Superboy leaves Legion 2 4 6 8 11 14
260-270,285-289: 265-Contains 28 pg. insert "Superman & the TRS-80 computer"; origin Tyroc; Tyroc leaves Legion 6.00
261,263,264,266-(Whitman variants; low print run; no cover #'s) 2 4 6 8 11 14
271-284: 272-Blok joins; origin; 20 pg. insert-Dial 'H' For Hero. 277-Intro. Reflecto. 280-Superboy re-joins Legion. 282-Origin Reflecto. 283-Origin Wildfire 6.00
290-294-Great Darkness saga. 294-Double size (52 pgs.) 1 2 3 5 7 9
295-299,301-313: 297-Origin retold. 298-Free 16 pg. Amethyst preview. 306-Brief origin Star Boy (Swan art). 311-Colan-a 3.00
300-(68 pgs., Mando paper)-Anniversary issue; has c/a by almost everyone at DC 5.00
Annual 1-3(82-84, 52 pgs.)-1-Giffen-c/a; 1st app./origin new Invisible Kid who joins Legion. 2-Karate Kid & Princess Projectra wed & resign 3.00
...The Great Darkness Saga (1989, $17.95, 196 pgs.)-r/LSH #287,290-294 & Annual #3; Giffen-c/a 2 4 6 10 14 18

NOTE: ***Aparo*** *c-282, 283, 300(part).* ***Austin*** *c-268i.* ***Buckler*** *c-273p, 274p, 276p.* ***Colan*** *a-311p.* ***Ditko*** *a(p)-267, 268, 272, 274, 276, 281.* ***Giffen*** *a-285-313p, Annual 1p; c-287p, 288p, 289, 290p, 291p, 292, 293, 294-299p, 300, 301-313p, Annual 1p, 2p.* ***Perez*** *c-268p, 277-280, 281p.* ***Starlin*** *a-265.* ***Staton*** *a-259p, 260p, 280.* ***Tuska*** *a-308p.*

LEGION OF SUPER-HEROES (3rd Series) (Reprinted in Tales of the Legion)
DC Comics: Aug, 1984 - No. 63, Aug, 1989 ($1.25/$1.75, deluxe format)

1-Silver ink logo 5.00
2-36,39-44,46-49,51-62: 4-Death of Karate Kid. 5-Death of Nemesis Kid. 12-Cosmic Boy, Lightning Lad, & Saturn Girl resign. 14-Intro new members: Tellus, Sensor Girl, Quislet. 15-17-Crisis tie-ins. 18-Crisis x-over. 25-Sensor Girl i.d. revealed as Princess Projectra. 35-Saturn Girl rejoins. 42,43-Millennium tie-ins. 44-Origin Quislet 3.00
37,38-Death of Superboy 2 4 6 8 11 14
45,50: 45 ($2.95, 68 pgs.)-Anniversary ish. 50-Double size ($2.50-c) 4.00
63-Final issue 4.00
Annual 1-4 (10/85-'88, 52 pgs.)-1-Crisis tie-in 3.00
...: An Eye For An Eye TPB (2007, $17.99)-r/#1-6; intro by Paul Levitz; cover gallery 18.00

NOTE: ***Byrne*** *c-36p.* ***Giffen*** *a(p)-1, 2, 50-55, 57-63, Annual 1p, 2; c-1-5p, 54p, Annual 1.* ***Orlando*** *a-6p.* ***Steacy*** *c-45-50, Annual 3.*

LEGION OF SUPER-HEROES (4th Series)
DC Comics: Nov, 1989 - No. 125, Mar, 2000 ($1.75/$1.95/$2.25)

0-(10/94)-Zero Hour restart of Legion; released between #61 & #62 2.50
1-Giffen-c/a(p)/scripts begin (4 pg.-a only #18) 4.00
2-20,26-49,51-53,55-58: 4-Mon-El (Lar Gand) destroys Time Trapper, changes reality. 5-Alt. reality story where Mordru rules all; Ferro Lad app. 6-1st app. of Laurel Gand (Lar Gand's cousin). 8-Origin. 13-Free poster by Giffen showing new costumes. 15-(2/91)-1st reference of Lar Gand as Valor. 26-New map of headquarters. 34-Six pg. preview of Timber Wolf mini-series. 40-Minor Legionnaires app. 41-(3/93)-SW6 Legion renamed Legionnaires w/new costumes and some new code-names 3.00
21-25: 21-24-Lobo & Darkseid storyline. 24-Cameo SW6 younger Legion duplicates. 25-SW6 Legion full intro. 3.50
50-($3.50, 68 pgs.) 4.00
54-($2.95)-Die-cut & foil stamped-c 4.00
59-99: 61-(9/94)-Zero Hour. 62-(11/94). 75-XS travels back to the 20th Century (cont'd in Impulse #9). 77-Origin of Brainiac 5. 81-Reintro Sun Boy. 85-Half of the Legion sent to the 20th century, Superman-c/app. 86-Final Night. 87-Deadman-c/app. 88-Impulse-c/app. Adventure Comics #247 cover swipe. 91-Forms one cover image with Legionnaires #47. 96-Wedding of Ultra Boy and Apparition. 99-Robin, Impulse, Superboy app. 2.50
100-($5.95, 96 pgs.)-Legionnaires return to the 30th Century; gatefold-c; 5 stories-art by Simonson, Davis and others 1 2 3 4 5 7
101-121: 101-Armstrong-a(p) begins. 105-Legion past & present vs. Time Trapper. 109-Moder-a. 110-Thunder joins. 114,115-Bizarro Legion. 120,121-Fatal Five. 2.50
122-124: 122,123-Coipel-c/a. 124-Coipel-c 3.00
125-Leads into "Legion Lost" maxi-series; Coipel-c 5.00
#1,000,000 (11/98) Giffen-a 2.50
Annual 1-5 (1990-1994, $3.50, 68 pgs.): 4-Bloodlines. 5-Elseworlds story 3.50
Annual 6 (1995,$3.95)-Year One story 4.00
Annual 7 (1996, $3.50, 48 pgs.)-Legends of the Dead Earth story; intro 75th Century Legion of Super-Heroes; Wildfire app. 3.50
Legion: Secret Files 1 (1/98, $4.95) Retold origin & pin-ups 5.00
Legion: Secret Files 2 (6/99, $4.95) Story and profile pages 5.00
The Beginning of Tomorrow TPB ('99, $17.95) r/post Zero Hour reboot 18.00

NOTE: ***Giffen*** *a-1-24; breakdowns-26-32, 34-36; c-1-7, 8(part), 9-24.* ***Brandon Peterson*** *a(p)-15(1st for DC), 16, 18, Annual 2(54 pgs.); c-Annual 2p.* ***Swan/Anderson*** *c-8(part).*

LEGION OF SUPER-HEROES (5th Series) (Title becomes Supergirl and the Legion of Super-Heroes #16-36) (Intro. in Teen Titans/Legion Special)
DC Comics: Feb, 2005 - No. 15, Apr, 2006; No. 37, Feb, 2008 - No. 50 ($2.95/$2.99)

1-15: 1-Waid-s/Kitson-a/c. 4-Kirk & Gibbons-a. 9-Jeanty-a. 15-Dawnstar, Tyroc, Blok-c 3.00
37-44: 37-Shooter-s/Manapul-a begin; two interlocking covers 3.00
44-Variant-c by Neal Adams 5.00
... Death of a Dream TPB ('06, $14.99) r/#7-13 15.00
...: 1050 Years of the Future TPB ('08, $19.99) r/greatest tales of their 50 year history 20.00
... Teenage Revolution TPB ('05, $14.99) r/#1-6 & Teen Titans/Legion Spec.; sketch pages 15.00

LEGION OF SUPER-HEROES IN THE 31ST CENTURY (Based on the animated series)
DC Comics: June, 2007 - Present ($2.25)

1-16: 1-Chynna Clugston-a; Fatal Five app. 6-Green Lantern Corps app. 15-Impulse app. 2.25
...: Tomorrow's Heroes (2008, $14.99) r/#1-7; cover gallery 15.00

LEGION: SCIENCE POLICE (See Legion of Super-Heroes)
DC Comics: Aug, 1998 - No. 4, Nov, 1998 ($2.25, limited series)

1-4-Ryan-a 2.50

LEGION WORLDS (Follows Legion Lost series)
DC Comics: Jun, 2001 - No. 6, Nov, 2001 ($3.95, limited series)

1-6-Abnett & Lanning-s; art by various. 5-Dillon-a. 6-Timber Wolf app. 4.00

LEMONADE KID, THE (See Bobby Benson's B-Bar-B Riders)
AC Comics: 1990 ($2.50, 28 pgs.)

1-Powell-c(r); Red Hawk-r by Powell; Lemonade Kid-r/Bobby Benson by Powell (2 stories) 2.50

LENNON SISTERS LIFE STORY, THE
Dell Publishing Co.: No. 951, Nov, 1958 - No. 1014, Aug, 1959

Four Color 951 (#1)-Toth-a, 32pgs, photo-c 13 26 39 95 168 240
Four Color 1014-Toth-a, photo-c 12 24 36 87 156 225

LENORE
Slave Labor Graphics: Feb, 1998 - Present ($2.95/$3.95, B&W, color #13-on)

1-12: 1-Roman Dirge-s/a, 1,2-2nd printing 3.00
13-($3.95, color) 4.00
...: Noogies TPB ($11.95) r/#1-4 12.00
...: Wedgies TPB (2000, $13.95) r/#5-8 14.00
...: Cooties TPB (3/06, $13.95) r/#9-12; pin-ups by various 14.00

LEONARD NIMOY'S PRIMORTALS
Tekno Comix: Mar, 1995 - No. 15, May, 1996 ($1.95)

1-15: Concept by Leonard Nimoy & Isaac Asimov 1-3-w/bound-in game piece & trading card. 4-w/Teknophage Steel Edition coupon. 13,14-Art Adams-c. 15-Simonson-c 2.50

LEONARD NIMOY'S PRIMORTALS
BIG Entertainment: V2#0, June, 1996 - No. 8, Feb, 1997 ($2.25)

V2#0-8: 0-Includes Pt. 9 of "The Big Bang" x-over. 0,1-Simonson-c. 3-Kelley Jones-c 2.50

LEONARD NIMOY'S PRIMORTALS ORIGINS
Tekno Comix: Nov, 1995 - No. 2, Dec, 1995 ($2.95, limited series)

Lethargic Lad #1 © Greg Hyland

Liberty Meadows #9 © Creators Syndicate

Lidsville #1 © GK

	GD 2.0	VG 4.0	FN 6.0	VF 8.0	VF/NM 9.0	NM- 9.2

1,2: Nimoy scripts; Art Adams-c; polybagged 3.00

LEONARDO (Also see Teenage Mutant Ninja Turtles)
Mirage Studios: Dec, 1986 ($1.50, B&W, one-shot)

1 6.00

LEO THE LION
I. W. Enterprises: No date(1960s) (10¢)

1-Reprint 2 4 6 9 13 16

LEROY (Teen-age)
Standard Comics: Nov, 1949 - No. 6, Nov, 1950

1 14 28 42 80 115 150
2-Frazetta text illo. 10 20 30 56 76 95
3-6: 3-Lubbers-a 9 18 27 50 65 80

LETHAL (Also see Brigade)
Image Comics (Extreme Studios): Feb, 1996 ($2.50, unfinished limited series)

1-Marat Mychaels-c/a. 2.50

LETHAL FOES OF SPIDER-MAN (Sequel to Deadly Foes of Spider-Man)
Marvel Comics: Sept, 1993 - No. 4, Dec, 1993 ($1.75, limited series)

1-4 2.50

LETHARGIC LAD
Crusade Ent.: June, 1996 - No. 3, Sept, 1996 ($2.95, B&W, limited series)

1,2 3.00
3-Alex Ross-c/swipe (Kingdom Come) 4.00
...Jumbo Sized Annual #1 (Summer 2002, $3.99) prints comic stories from internet 4.00

LETHARGIC LAD ADVENTURES
Crusade Ent./Destination Ent.#3 on: Oct, 1997 - No. 12, Sept./Oct. 1999 ($2.95, B&W)

1-12-Hyland-s/a. 9-Alex Ross sketch page & back-c 3.00

LET'S PRETEND (CBS radio)
D. S. Publishing Co.: May-June, 1950 - No. 3, Sept-Oct, 1950

1 18 36 54 103 162 220
2,3 14 28 42 81 118 155

LET'S READ THE NEWSPAPER
Charlton Press: 1974

nn-Features Quincy by Ted Sheares 1 3 4 6 8 10

LET'S TAKE A TRIP (TV) (CBS Television Presents)
Pines Comics: Spring, 1958

1-Marv Levy-c/a 5 10 15 23 28 32

LETTERS TO SANTA (See March of Comics No. 228)

LEX LUTHOR: MAN OF STEEL
DC Comics: May, 2005 - No. 5, Sept, 2005 ($2.99, limited series)

1-5: 1-Azzarello-s/Bermejo-a/c in all. 3-Batman-c/app. 3.00
TPB (2005, $12.99) r/series 13.00

LEX LUTHOR: THE UNAUTHORIZED BIOGRAPHY
DC Comics: 1989 ($3.95, 52 pgs., one-shot, squarebound)

1-Painted-c; Clark Kent app. 4.00

LIBERTY COMICS (Miss Liberty No. 1)
Green Publishing Co.: No. 5, May, '46 - No. 15, July, 1946 (MLJ & other-r)

5 (5/46)-The Prankster app; Starr-a 21 42 63 123 197 270
10-Hangman & Boy Buddies app.; reprints 3 Hangman stories, incl. Hangman #8
22 44 66 129 207 285
11 (V2#2, 1/46)-Wilbur in women's clothes 17 34 51 100 158 215
12 (V2#4)-Black Hood & Suzie app.; classic Skull-c 58 116 174 365 620 875
14,15-Patty of Airliner; Starr-a in both 15 30 45 88 137 185

LIBERTY COMICS (The CBLDF Presents...)
Image Comics: July, 2008 ($3.99, benefit book for the Comic Book Legal Defense Fund)

1-Two covers by Campbell & Mignola; art by Cooke, Aragones, A. Adams & others 4.00

LIBERTY COMICS
Heroic Publishing: Sept, 2007 - Present ($4.50)

1-Mark Sparacio-c 4.50

LIBERTY GIRL
Heroic Publishing: Aug, 2006 - Present ($3.25/$2.99)

1-3-Mark Sparacio-c/a 3.25

LIBERTY GUARDS
Chicago Mail Order: No date (1946?)

nn-Reprints Man of War #1 with cover of Liberty Scouts #1; Gustavson-c
35 70 105 203 327 450

LIBERTY MEADOWS
Insight Studios Group/Image Comics #27 on: 1999 - Present ($2.95, B&W)

1-Frank Cho-s/a; reprints newspaper strips 3 6 9 14 20 25
2,3 2 4 6 8 11 14
4-10 1 2 3 4 5 7
11-25,27-37: 20-Adam Hughes-c. 22-Evil Brandy vs. Brandy. 27-1st Image issue, printed sideways 3.00
..., Cover Girl HC (Image, 2006, $24.99, with dustjacket) r/color covers of #1-19,21-37 along with B&W inked versions, sketches and pin-up art 25.00
...: Eden Book 1 SC (Image, 2002, $14.95) r/#1-9; sketch gallery 15.00
...: Eden Book 1 SC 2nd printing (Image, 2004, $19.95) r/#1-9; sketch gallery 20.00
...: Eden Book 1 HC (Image, 2003, $24.95, with dustjacket) r/#1-9; sketch gallery 25.00
...: Creature Comforts Book 2 HC (Image, 2004, $24.95, with d.j.) r/#10-18; sketch gallery 25.00
...: Creature Comforts Book 2 SC (Image, 12/04, $14.95) r/#10-18; sketch gallery 15.00
...Book 3: Summer of Love HC (Image, 12/04, $24.95) r/#19-27; sketch gallery 25.00
...Book 3: Summer of Love SC (Image, 7/05, $14.95) r/#19-27; sketch gallery 15.00
...Book 4: Cold, Cold Heart HC (Image, 9/05, $24.95) r/#28-36; sketch gallery 25.00
...Book 4: Cold, Cold Heart SC (Image, 2006, $14.99) r/#28-36; sketch gallery 15.00
... Sourcebook (5/04, $4.95) character info and unpublished strips 5.00
... Wedding Album (#26) (2002, $2.95) 3.00

LIBERTY PROJECT, THE
Eclipse Comics: June, 1987 - No. 8, May, 1988 ($1.75, color, Baxter paper)

1-8: 6-Valkyrie app. 2.50

LIBERTY SCOUTS (See Liberty Guards & Man of War)
Centaur Publications: No. 2, June, 1941 - No. 3, Aug, 1941

2(#1)-Origin The Fire-Man, Man of War; Vapo-Man & Liberty Scouts begin; intro Liberty Scouts; Gustavson-c/a in both 128 256 384 806 1366 1925
3(#2)-Origin & 1st app. The Sentinel 90 180 270 567 959 1350

LICENCE TO KILL (James Bond 007) (Movie)
Eclipse Comics: 1989 ($7.95, slick paper, 52 pgs.)

nn-Movie adaptation; Timothy Dalton photo-c 1 2 3 5 6 8
Limited Hardcover ($24.95) 25.00

LIDSVILLE (TV)
Gold Key: Oct, 1972 - No. 5, Oct, 1973

1-Photo-c 5 10 15 35 55 75
2-5 4 8 12 22 34 45

LIEUTENANT, THE (TV)
Dell Publishing Co.: April-June, 1964

1-Photo-c 3 6 9 18 27 35

LIEUTENANT BLUEBERRY (Also see Blueberry)
Marvel Comics (Epic Comics): 1991 - No. 3, 1991 (Graphic novel)

1,2 ($8.95)-Moebius-a in all 2 4 6 10 14 18
3 ($14.95) 3 6 9 14 20 25

LT. ROBIN CRUSOE, U.S.N. (See Movie Comics & Walt Disney Showcase #26)

LIFE EATERS, THE
DC Comics (WildStorm): 2003 ($29.95, hardcover with dust jacket)

HC-David Brin-s; Scott Hampton-painted-a/c; Norse Gods team with the Nazis 30.00
SC-(2004, $19.95) 20.00

LIFE OF CAPTAIN MARVEL, THE
Marvel Comics Group: Aug, 1985 - No. 5, Dec, 1985 ($2.00, Baxter paper)

1-5: 1-All reprint Starlin issues of Iron Man #55, Capt. Marvel #25-34 plus Marvel Feature #12 (all with Thanos). 4-New Thanos back-c by Starlin 3.00

LIFE OF CHRIST, THE
Catechetical Guild Educational Society: No. 301, 1949 (35¢, 100 pgs.)

301-Reprints from Topix(1949)-V5#11,12 9 18 27 50 65 80

LIFE OF CHRIST: THE CHRISTMAS STORY, THE
Marvel Comics/Nelson: Feb, 1993 ($2.99, slick stock)

nn 5.00

LIFE OF CHRIST: THE EASTER STORY, THE
Marvel Comics/Nelson: 1993 ($2.99, slick stock)

nn 5.00

LIFE OF CHRIST VISUALIZED
Standard Publishers: 1942 - No. 3, 1943

Life Story #19 © FAW

Life With Archie #283 © AP

Lightning Comics #4 © ACE

	GD 2.0	VG 4.0	FN 6.0	VF 8.0	VF/NM 9.0	NM- 9.2
1-3: All came in cardboard case, each...	8	16	24	44	57	70
Case only.....	10	20	30	54	72	90

LIFE OF CHRIST VISUALIZED
The Standard Publ. Co.: 1946? (48 pgs. in color)

nn	6	12	18	31	38	45

LIFE OF ESTHER VISUALIZED
The Standard Publ. Co.: No. 2062, 1947 (48 pgs. in color)

2062	6	12	18	31	38	45

LIFE OF JOSEPH VISUALIZED
The Standard Publ. Co.: No. 1054, 1946 (48 pgs. in color)

1054	6	12	18	31	38	45

LIFE OF PAUL (See The Living Bible)

LIFE OF POPE JOHN PAUL II, THE
Marvel Comics Group: Jan, 1983 ($1.50/$1.75)

1	1	3	4	6	8	10

LIFE OF RILEY, THE (TV)
Dell Publishing Co.: No. 917, July, 1958

Four Color 917-Photo-c	10	20	30	70	123	175

LIFE ON ANOTHER PLANET
Kitchen Sink Press: 1978 (B&W, graphic novel, magazine size)

nn-Will Eisner-s/a						13.00
Reprint (DC Comics, 5/00, $12.95)						13.00

LIFE'S LIKE THAT
Croyden Publ. Co.: 1945 (25¢, B&W, 68 pgs.)

nn-Newspaper Sunday strip-r by Neher	7	14	21	35	43	50

LIFE STORIES OF AMERICAN PRESIDENTS (See Dell Giants)

LIFE STORY
Fawcett Publications: Apr, 1949 - V8#46, Jan, 1953; V8#47, Apr, 1953 (All have photo-c?)

V1#1	15	30	45	84	127	170
2	9	18	27	52	69	85
3-6, V2#7-12	8	16	24	44	57	70
V3#13-Wood-a	15	30	45	84	127	170
V3#14-18, V4#19-24, V5#25-30, V6#31-35	8	16	24	40	50	60
V6#36- "I sold drugs" on-c	10	20	30	56	76	95
V7#37,40-42, V8#44,45	7	14	21	37	46	55
V7#38, V8#43-Evans-a	8	16	24	40	50	60
V7#39-Drug Smuggling & Junkie story	9	18	27	50	65	80
V8#46,47 (Scarce)	9	18	27	50	65	80

NOTE: ***Powell** a-13, 23, 24, 26, 28, 30, 32, 39. **Marcus Swayze** a-1-3, 10-12, 15, 16, 20, 21, 23-25, 31, 35, 37, 40, 44, 46.*

LIFE, THE UNIVERSE AND EVERYTHING (See Hitchhikers Guide to the Galaxy & Restaurant at the End of the Universe)
DC Comics: 1996 - No. 3, 1996 ($6.95, squarebound, limited series)

1-3: Adaptation of novel by Douglas Adams.	1	2	3	4	5	7

LIFE WITH ARCHIE
Archie Publications: Sept, 1958 - No. 286, Sept, 1991

1	25	50	75	185	343	500
2-(9/59)	13	26	39	97	171	245
3-5: 3-(7/60)	9	18	27	64	110	155
6-8,10	7	14	21	50	83	115
9,11-Horror/SciFi-c	8	16	24	56	93	130
12-20	6	12	18	39	62	85
21(7/63)-30	5	10	15	30	48	65
31-34,36-38,40,41	4	8	12	24	37	50
35,39-Horror/Sci-Fi-c	5	10	15	30	48	65
42-Pureheart begins (1st app.-c/s, 10/65)	7	14	21	49	80	110
43,44	5	10	15	32	51	70
45(1/66) 1st Man From R.I.V.E.R.D.A.L.E.	6	12	18	41	66	90
46-Origin Pureheart	5	10	15	32	51	70
47-49	4	8	12	24	37	50
50-United Three begin: Pureheart (Archie), Superteen (Betty), Captain Hero (Jughead)	5	10	15	32	51	70
51-59: 59-Pureheart ends	4	8	12	24	37	50
60-Archie band begins, ends #66	5	10	15	32	51	70
61-66: 61-Man From R.I.V.E.R.D.A.L.E.-c/s	4	8	12	22	34	45
67-80	3	6	9	14	20	26
81-99	3	6	9	14	19	24
100 (8/70), 113-Sabrina & Salem app.	3	6	9	17	26	34
101-112, 114-130(2/73), 139(11/73)-Archie Band c/s	2	4	6	10	14	18
131,134-138,140-146,148-161,164-170(6/76)	2	4	6	8	11	14
132,133,147,163-all horror-c/s	2	4	6	13	18	22
162-UFO c/s	2	4	6	13	18	22
171,173-175,177-184,186,189,191-194,196	1	2	3	5	7	9
172,185,197 : 172-(9/77)-Bi-Cent. spec. ish, 185-2nd 24th cent.-c/s, 197-Time machine/SF-c/s	1	3	4	6	8	10
176(12/76)-1st app. Capt. Archie of Starship Rivda, in 24th century c/s; 1st app. Stella the Robot	2	4	6	13	18	22
187,188,195,198,199-all horror-c/s	2	4	6	8	11	14
190-1st Dr. Doom-c/s	2	4	6	8	11	14
200 (12/78) Maltese Pigeon-s	2	4	6	8	10	12
201-203,205-237,239,240(1/84): 208-Reintro Veronica	1	2	3	4	5	7
204-Flying saucer-c/s	1	2	3	5	7	9
238-(9/83)-25th anniversary issue; Ol' Betsy (jalopy) replaced	1	2	3	5	6	8
241-278,280-285: 250-Comic book convention-s						5.00
279,286: 279-Intro Mustang Sally ($1.00, 7/90)						6.00

NOTE: ***Gene Colan** a-272-279, 285, 286. Horror/Sci-Fi-c 9, 11, 35, 39, 162.*

LIFE WITH MILLIE (Formerly A Date With Millie) (Modeling With Millie #21 on)
Atlas/Marvel Comics Group: No. 8, Dec, 1960 - No. 20, Dec, 1962

8-Teenage	8	16	24	54	90	125
9-11	6	12	18	39	62	85
12-20	5	10	15	34	55	75

LIFE WITH SNARKY PARKER (TV)
Fox Feature Syndicate: Aug, 1950

1-Early TV comic; photo-c from TV puppet show	27	54	81	158	254	350

LIGHT AND DARKNESS WAR, THE
Marvel Comics (Epic Comics): Oct, 1988 - No. 6, Dec, 1989 ($1.95, lim. series)

1-6						2.50

LIGHT BRIGADE, THE
DC Comics: 2004 - No. 4, 2004 ($5.95, limited series)

1-4-Archangels in World War II; Tomasi-s/Snejbjerg-a						6.00
TPB (2005, $19.99) r/series; cover galery						20.00

LIGHT FANTASTIC, THE (Terry Pratchett's)
Innovation Publishing: June, 1992 - No. 4, Sept, 1992 ($2.50, mini-series)

1-4: Adapts 2nd novel in Discworld series						2.50

LIGHT IN THE FOREST (Disney)
Dell Publishing Co.: No. 891, Mar, 1958

Four Color 891-Movie, Fess Parker photo-c	7	14	21	50	83	115

LIGHTNING COMICS (Formerly Sure-Fire No. 1-3)
Ace Magazines: No. 4, Dec, 1940 - No. 13(V3#1), June, 1942

4-Characters continue from Sure-Fire	100	200	300	630	1065	1500
5,6: 6-Dr. Nemesis begins	68	136	204	428	727	1025
V2#1-6: 2- "Flash Lightning" becomes "Lash..."	54	108	162	340	575	810
V3#1-Intro. Lightning Girl & The Sword	54	108	162	340	575	810

NOTE: ***Anderson** a-V2#6. **Mooney** c-V1#5, 6, V2#1-6, V3#1. Bondage c-V2#6. Lightning-c on all.*

LIGHTNING COMICS PRESENTS
Lightning Comics: May, 1994 ($3.50)

1-Red foil-c distr. by Diamond Distr., 1-Black/yellow/blue-c distrib. by Capital Distr., 1-Red/yellow-c distributed by H. World, 1-Platinum						3.50

LI'L ... (See Little ...)

LILI
Image Comics: No. 0, 1999 ($4.95, B&W)

0-Bendis & Yanover-s						5.00

LILLITH (See Warrior Nun...)
Antarctic Press: Sept, 1996 - No. 3, Feb, 1997 ($2.95, limited series)

1-3: 1-Variant-c						3.00

LIMITED COLLECTORS' EDITION (See Famous First Edition, Marvel Treasury #28, Rudolph The Red-Nosed Reindeer, & Superman Vs. The Amazing Spider-Man; becomes All-New Collectors' Edition)
National Periodical Publications/DC Comics:
(#21-34,51-59: 84 pgs.; #35-41: 68 pgs.; #42-50: 60 pgs.)
C-21, Summer, 1973 - No. C-59, 1978 ($1.00) (10x13-1/2")

(Rudolph...C-20 (implied), 12/72)-See Rudolph The Red-Nosed Reindeer
C-21: Shazam (TV); r/Captain Marvel Jr. #11 by Raboy; C.C. Beck-c, biog. & photo

Limited Collectors' Edition C-41 © DC

Lionheart #1 © Awesome

Li'l Abner #81 © TOBY

	GD 2.0	VG 4.0	FN 6.0	VF 8.0	VF/NM 9.0	NM- 9.2
	3	6	9	20	30	40
C-22: Tarzan; complete origin reprinted from #207-210; all Kubert-c/a; Joe Kubert biography & photo inside	3	6	9	17	25	32
C-23: House of Mystery; Wrightson, N. Adams/Orlando, G. Kane/Wood, Toth, Aragones, Sparling reprints	4	8	12	24	37	50
C-24: Rudolph The Red-Nosed Reindeer	7	14	21	45	73	100
C-25: Batman; Neal Adams-c/a(r); G.A. Joker-r; Batman/Enemy Ace-r; Novick-a(r); has photos from TV show	4	8	12	26	41	55
C-26: See Famous First Edition C-26 (same contents)						
C-27,C-29,C-31: C-27: Shazam (TV); G.A. Capt. Marvel & Mary Marvel-r; Beck-r. C-29: Tarzan; reprints "Return of Tarzan" from #219-223 by Kubert; Kubert-c. C-31: Superman; origin-r; Giordano-a; photos of George Reeves from 1950s TV show on inside b/c; Burnley, Boring-r	3	6	9	16	23	30
C-32: Ghosts (new-a)	4	8	12	22	34	45
C-33: Rudolph The Red-Nosed Reindeer(new-a)	6	12	18	41	66	90
C-34: Christmas with the Super-Heroes; unpublished Angel & Ape story by Oksner & Wood; Batman & Teen Titans-r	3	6	9	16	23	30
C-35: Shazam (TV); photo cover features TV's Captain Marvel, Jackson Bostwick; Beck-r; TV photos inside b/c	3	6	9	16	22	28
C-36: The Bible; all new adaptation beginning with Genesis by Kubert, Redondo & Mayer; Kubert-c	3	6	9	16	22	28
C-37: Batman; r-1946 Sundays; inside b/c photos of Batman TV show villains (all villain issue; r/G.A. Joker, Catwoman, Penguin, Two-Face, & Scarecrow stories plus 1946 Sundays-r)	3	6	9	18	27	35
C-38: Superman; 1 pg. N. Adams; part photo-c; photos from TV show on inside back-c	3	6	9	16	22	28
C-39: Secret Origins of Super-Villains; N. Adams-i(r); collection reprints 1950's Joker origin, Luthor origin from Adv. Comics #271, Captain Cold origin from Showcase #8 among others; G.A. Batman-r; Beck-r	3	6	9	16	22	28
C-40: Dick Tracy by Gould featuring Flattop; newspaper-r from 12/21/43 - 5/17/44; biog. of Chester Gould	3	6	9	16	22	28
C-41: Super Friends (TV); JLA-r(1965); Toth-c/a	3	6	9	16	23	30
C-42: Rudolph	4	8	12	28	44	60
C-43-C-47: C-43: Christmas with the Super-Heroes; Wrightson, S&K, Neal Adams-a. C-44: Batman; N. Adams-p(r) & G.A.-r; painted-c. C-45: More Secret Origins of Super-Villains; Flash-r/#105; G.A. Wonder Woman & Batman/Catwoman-r. C-46: Justice League of America(1963-r); 3 pgs. Toth-a C-47: Superman Salutes the Bicentennial (Tomahawk interior); 2 pgs. new-a	3	6	9	14	20	26
C-48,C-49: C-48: Superman Vs. The Flash (Superman/Flash race); swipes-c to Superman #199; r/Superman #199 & Flash #175; 6 pgs. Neal Adams-a. C-49: Superboy & the Legion of Super-Heroes	3	6	9	16	23	30
C-50: Rudolph The Red-Nosed Reindeer; contains poster (1/2 price if poster is missing)	4	8	12	28	44	60
C-51: Batman; Neal Adams-c/a	3	6	9	17	25	32
C-52,C-57: C-52: The Best of DC; Neal Adams-c/a; Toth, Kubert-a. C-57: Welcome Back, Kotter-r(TV)(5/78) includes unpublished #11	3	6	9	16	22	28
C-53 thru C-56, C-58, C-60 thru C-62 (See All-New Collectors' Edition)						
C-59: Batman's Strangest Cases; N. Adams-r; Wrightson-r/Swamp Thing #7; N. Adams/Wrightson-c	3	6	9	16	22	28

NOTE: *All-r with exception of some special features and covers.* **Aparo** *a-52r; c-37.* **Grell** *c-49.* **Infantino** *a-25, 39, 44, 45, 52.* **Bob Kane** *r-25.* **Robinson** *r-25, 44.* **Sprang** *r-44. Issues #21-31, 35-39, 45, 48 have back cover cut-outs.*

LINDA (Everybody Loves...) (Phantom Lady No. 5 on)
Ajax-Farrell Publ. Co.: Apr-May, 1954 - No. 4, Oct-Nov, 1954

	GD	VG	FN	VF	VF/NM	NM-
1-Kamenish-a	15	30	45	85	130	175
2-Lingerie panel	13	26	39	72	101	130
3,4	10	20	30	56	76	95

LINDA CARTER, STUDENT NURSE
Atlas Comics (AMI): Sept, 1961 - No. 9, Jan, 1963

	GD	VG	FN	VF	VF/NM	NM-
1-Al Hartley-c	6	12	18	41	66	90
2-9	4	8	12	28	44	60

LINDA LARK
Dell Publishing Co.: Oct-Dec, 1961 - No. 8, Aug-Oct, 1963

	GD	VG	FN	VF	VF/NM	NM-
1	3	6	9	19	29	38
2-8	3	6	9	14	19	24

LINUS, THE LIONHEARTED (TV)
Gold Key: Sept, 1965

	GD	VG	FN	VF	VF/NM	NM-
1 (10155-509)	7	14	21	49	80	110

LION, THE (See Movie Comics)

LIONHEART
Awesome Comics: Sept, 1999 - No. 2 ($2.99/$2.50)

	GD	VG	FN	VF	VF/NM	NM-
1-Ian Churchill-story/a, Jeph Loeb-s; Coven app.						3.00
2-Flip book w/Coven #4						2.50

LION OF SPARTA (See Movie Classics)

LIPPY THE LION AND HARDY HAR HAR (TV)
Gold Key: Mar, 1963 (12¢) (See Hanna-Barbera Band Wagon #1)

	GD	VG	FN	VF	VF/NM	NM-
1 (10049-303)	9	18	27	63	107	150

LISA COMICS (TV)(See Simpsons Comics)
Bongo Comics: 1995 ($2.25)

	GD	VG	FN	VF	VF/NM	NM-
1-Lisa in Wonderland						3.00

LI'L ABNER (See Comics on Parade, Sparkle, Sparkler Comics, Tip Top Comics & Tip Topper)
United Features Syndicate: 1939 - 1940

	GD	VG	FN	VF	VF/NM	NM-
Single Series 4 ('39)	76	152	228	479	810	1140
Single Series 18 ('40) (#18 on inside, #2 on-c)	59	118	177	372	629	885

LI'L ABNER (Al Capp's; continued from Comics on Parade #58)
Harvey Publ. No. 61-69 (2/49)/Toby Press No. 70 on: No. 61, Dec, 1947 - No. 97, Jan, 1955 (See Oxydol-Dreft in Promotional Comics section)

	GD	VG	FN	VF	VF/NM	NM-
61(#1)-Wolverton & Powell-a	31	62	93	178	282	385
62-65: 63-The Wolf Girl app. 65-Powell-a	17	34	51	98	154	210
66,67,69,70	15	30	45	90	140	190
68-Full length Fearless Fosdick-c/story	16	32	48	94	147	200
71-74,76,80	14	28	42	80	115	150
75,77-79,86,91-All with Kurtzman art; 86-Sadie Hawkins Day. 91-r/#77	15	30	45	90	140	190
81-85,87-90,92-94,96,97: 83-Evil-Eye Fleegle & Double Whammy app. 88-Cousin Weakeyes goes hunting. 94-Six lessons from Adam Lazonga. 96-Football issue	14	28	42	76	108	140
95-Full length Fearless Fosdick story	14	28	42	82	121	160

LI'L ABNER
Toby Press: 1951

	GD	VG	FN	VF	VF/NM	NM-
1	18	36	54	103	162	220

LI'L ABNER'S DOGPATCH (See Al Capp's...)

LITTLE AL OF THE F.B.I.
Ziff-Davis Publications: No. 10, 1950 (no month) - No. 11, Apr-May, 1951 (Saunders painted-c)

	GD	VG	FN	VF	VF/NM	NM-
10(1950)	16	32	48	94	147	200
11(1951)	14	28	42	78	112	145

LITTLE AL OF THE SECRET SERVICE
Ziff-Davis Publications: No. 10, 7-8/51; No, 2, 9-10/51; No. 3, Winter, 1951 (Saunders painted-c)

	GD	VG	FN	VF	VF/NM	NM-
10(#1)	16	32	48	92	144	195
2,3	14	28	42	76	108	140

LITTLE AMBROSE
Archie Publications: September, 1958

	GD	VG	FN	VF	VF/NM	NM-
1-Bob Bolling-c	15	30	45	84	127	170

LITTLE ANGEL
Standard (Visual Editions)/Pines: No. 5, Sept, 1954; No. 6, Sept, 1955 - No. 16, Sept, 1959

	GD	VG	FN	VF	VF/NM	NM-
5-Last pre-code issue	8	16	24	40	50	60
6-16	5	10	15	24	30	35

LITTLE ANNIE ROONEY (Also see Henry)
David McKay Publ.: 1935 (25¢, B&W dailies, 48 pgs.)(10"x10", cardboard-c)

	GD	VG	FN	VF	VF/NM	NM-
Book 1-Daily strip-r by Darrell McClure	38	76	114	222	356	490

LITTLE ANNIE ROONEY (See King Comics & Treasury of Comics)
David McKay/St. John/Standard: 1938; Aug, 1948 - No. 3, Oct, 1948

	GD	VG	FN	VF	VF/NM	NM-
Feature Books 11 (McKay, 1938)	39	78	117	230	370	510
1 (St. John)	15	30	45	88	137	185
2,3	10	20	30	54	72	90

LITTLE ARCHIE (The Adventures of... #13-on) (See Archie Giant Series Mag. #527, 534, 538, 545, 549, 556, 560, 566, 570, 583, 594, 596, 607, 609, 619)
Archie Publications: 1956 - No. 180, Feb, 1983 (Giants No. 3-84)

	GD	VG	FN	VF	VF/NM	NM-
1-(Scarce)	54	108	162	459	880	1300
2 (1957)	24	48	72	174	322	470
3-5: 3-(1958)-Bob Bolling-c & giant issues begin	14	28	42	104	187	270
6-10	10	20	30	73	129	185
11-17,19,21 (84 pgs.)	8	16	24	54	90	125
18,20,22 (84 pgs.)-Horror/Sci-Fi-c	9	18	27	63	107	150
23-39 (68 pgs.)	6	12	18	41	66	90
40 (Fall/66)-Intro. Little Pureheart-c/s (68 pgs.)	7	14	21	45	73	100

Little Archie Digest Magazine #17 © AP

Little Audrey #2 © HARV

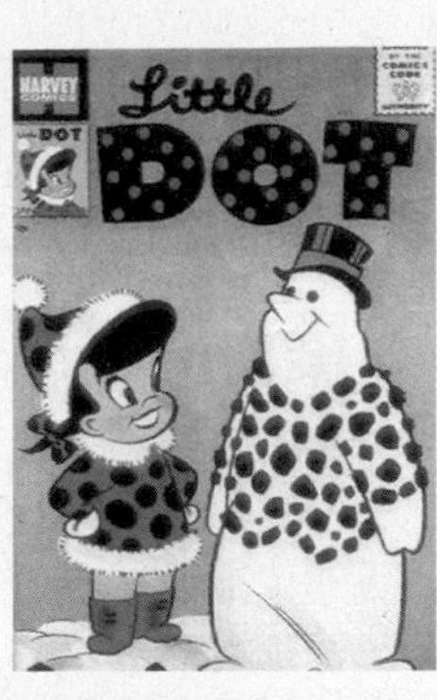

Little Dot #15 © HARV

	GD 2.0	VG 4.0	FN 6.0	VF 8.0	VF/NM 9.0	NM- 9.2
41,44-Little Pureheart (68 pgs.)	6	12	18	39	62	85
42-Intro The Little Archies Band, ends #66 (68 pgs.)	6	12	18	43	69	95
43-1st Boy From R.I.V.E.R.D.A.L.E. (68 pgs.)	6	12	18	41	66	90
45-58 (68 pgs.)	5	10	15	30	48	65
59 (68 pgs.)-Little Sabrina begins	8	16	24	52	86	120
60-66 (68 pgs.)	4	8	12	25	39	52
67(9/71)-84: 84-Last 52pg. Giant-Size (2/74)	3	6	9	16	23	30
85-99	2	4	6	9	12	15
100	2	4	6	10	14	18
101-112,114-116,118-129	1	3	4	6	8	10
113,117,130: 113-Halloween Special issue(12/76). 117-Donny Osmond-c cameo 130-UFO cover (5/78)	2	4	6	8	11	14
131-150(1/80), 180(Last issue, 2/83)	1	2	3	5	6	8
151-179						5.00
...In Animal Land 1 (1957)	13	26	39	95	168	240
...In Animal Land 17 (Winter, 1957-58)-19 (Summer,1958)-Formerly Li'l Jinx	8	16	24	52	86	120
Archie Classics - The Adventures of Little Archie Vol. 1 TPB (2004, $10.95) reprints						11.00
Vol. 2 TPB (2008, $9.95) reprints plus new 22 pg. story with Bolling-s/a						10.00

NOTE: *Little Archie Band app. 42-66. Little Sabrina in 59-78,80-180*

LITTLE ARCHIE CHRISTMAS SPECIAL (See Archie Giant Series #581)

LITTLE ARCHIE COMICS DIGEST ANNUAL (...Magazine #5 on)
Archie Publications: 10/77 - No. 48, 5/91 (Digest-size, 128 pgs., later issues $1.35-$1.50)

	GD	VG	FN	VF	VF/NM	NM-
1(10/77)-Reprints	3	6	9	20	30	40
2(4/78,3(11/78)-Neal Adams-a. 3-The Fly-r by S&K	3	6	9	14	20	26
4(4/79) - 10	2	4	6	10	14	18
11-20	2	4	6	8	10	12
21-30: 28-Christmas-c	1	2	3	5	6	8
31-48: 40,46-Christmas-c						5.00

NOTE: *Little Archie, Little Jinx, Little Jughead & Little Sabrina in most issues*

LITTLE ARCHIE DIGEST MAGAZINE
Archie Comics: July, 1991 - No. 21, Mar, 1998 ($1.50/$1.79/$1.89, digest size, bi-annual)

	GD	VG	FN	VF	VF/NM	NM-
V2#1						6.00
2-10						3.50
11-21						2.50

LITTLE ARCHIE MYSTERY
Archie Publications: Aug, 1963 - No. 2, Oct, 1963 (12¢ issues)

	GD	VG	FN	VF	VF/NM	NM-
1	10	20	30	73	129	185
2	6	12	18	43	69	95

LITTLE ASPIRIN (See Little Lenny & Wisco)
Marvel Comics (CnPC): July, 1949 - No. 3, Dec, 1949 (52 pgs.)

	GD	VG	FN	VF	VF/NM	NM-
1-Oscar app.; Kurtzman-a (4 pgs.)	17	34	51	98	154	210
2-Kurtzman-a (4 pgs.)	11	22	33	60	83	105
3-No Kurtzman-a	9	18	27	47	61	75

LITTLE AUDREY (Also see Playful...)
St. John Publ.: Apr, 1948 - No. 24, May, 1952

	GD	VG	FN	VF	VF/NM	NM-
1-1st app. Little Audrey	48	96	144	298	499	700
2	26	52	78	152	244	335
3-5	17	34	51	100	158	215
6-10	14	28	42	80	115	150
11-20: 16-X-Mas-c	10	20	30	58	79	100
21-24	9	18	27	52	69	85

LITTLE AUDREY (See Harvey Hits #11, 19)
Harvey Publications: No. 25, Aug, 1952 - No. 53, April, 1957

	GD	VG	FN	VF	VF/NM	NM-
25-(Paramount Pictures Famous Star... on-c); 1st Harvey Casper and Baby Huey (1 month earlier than Harvey Comic Hits #60(9/52))	13	26	39	93	164	235
26-30: 26-28-Casper app.	7	14	21	50	83	115
31-40: 32-35-Casper app.	6	12	18	43	69	95
41-53	5	10	15	32	51	70
...Clubhouse 1 (9/61, 68 pg. Giant)-New stories & reprints	8	16	24	58	97	135

LITTLE AUDREY
Harvey Comics: Aug, 1992 - No. 8, July, 1994 ($1.25/$1.50)

	GD	VG	FN	VF	VF/NM	NM-
V2#1						3.00
2-8						2.50

LITTLE AUDREY (...Yearbook)
St. John Publishing Co.: 1950 (50¢, 260 pgs.)

Contains 8 complete 1949 comics rebound; Casper, Alice in Wonderland, Little Audrey, Abbott & Costello, Pinocchio, Moon Mullins, Three Stooges (from Jubilee), Little Annie Rooney app. (Rare)

	GD	VG	FN	VF	VF/NM	NM-
	80	160	240	504	852	1200

(Also see All Good & Treasury of Comics)

NOTE: *This book contains remaindered St. John comics; many variations possible.*

LITTLE AUDREY & MELVIN (Audrey & Melvin No. 62)
Harvey Publications: May, 1962 - No. 61, Dec, 1973

	GD	VG	FN	VF	VF/NM	NM-
1	10	20	30	67	116	165
2-5	6	12	18	39	62	85
6-10	5	10	15	30	48	65
11-20	3	6	9	19	29	38
21-40: 22-Richie Rich app.	3	6	9	14	20	26
41-50,55-61	2	4	6	11	16	20
51-54: All 52 pg. Giants	3	6	9	14	20	26

LITTLE AUDREY TV FUNTIME
Harvey Publ.: Sept, 1962 - No. 33, Oct, 1971 (#1-31: 68 pgs.; #32,33: 52 pgs.)

	GD	VG	FN	VF	VF/NM	NM-
1-Richie Rich app.	10	20	30	67	116	165
2,3: Richie Rich app.	6	12	18	39	62	85
4,5: 5-25¢ & 35¢ issues exist	5	10	15	32	51	70
6-10	3	6	9	21	32	42
11-20	3	6	9	16	23	28
21-33	3	6	9	14	19	24

LITTLE BAD WOLF (Disney; seeWalt Disney's C&S #52, Walt Disney Showcase #21 & Wheatles)
Dell Publishing Co.: No. 403, June, 1952 - No. 564, June, 1954

	GD	VG	FN	VF	VF/NM	NM-
Four Color 403 (#1)	7	14	21	47	76	105
Four Color 473 (6/53), 564	5	10	15	32	51	70

LITTLE BEAVER
Dell Publishing Co.: No. 211, Jan, 1949 - No. 870, Jan, 1958 (All painted-c)

	GD	VG	FN	VF	VF/NM	NM-
Four Color 211('49)-All Harman-a	8	16	24	56	93	130
Four Color 267,294,332(5/51)	5	10	15	34	55	75
3(10-12/51)-8(1-3/53)	5	10	15	32	51	70
Four Color 483(8-10/53),529	5	10	15	30	48	65
Four Color 612,660,695,744,817,870	5	10	15	30	48	65

LITTLE BIT
Jubilee/St. John Publishing Co.: Mar, 1949 - No. 2, June, 1949

	GD	VG	FN	VF	VF/NM	NM-
1	9	18	27	52	69	85
2	7	14	21	37	46	55

LITTLE DOT (See Humphrey, Li'l Max, Sad Sack, and Tastee-Freez Comics)
Harvey Publications: Sept, 1953 - No. 164, Apr, 1976

	GD	VG	FN	VF	VF/NM	NM-
1-Intro./1st app. Richie Rich & Little Lotta	280	560	840	1764	2982	4200
2-1st app. Freckles & Pee Wee (Richie Rich's poor friends)	93	186	279	586	993	1400
3	57	114	171	359	605	850
4	52	104	156	322	536	750
5-Origin dots on Little Dot's dress	57	114	171	359	605	850
6-Richie Rich, Little Lotta, & Little Dot all on cover; 1st Richie Rich cover featured	57	114	171	359	605	850
7-10: 9-Last pre-code issue (1/55)	37	74	111	215	345	475
11-20	25	50	75	147	236	325
21-30	15	30	45	94	147	200
31-40	13	26	39	74	105	135
41-50	10	20	30	56	76	95
51-60	8	16	24	44	57	70
61-80	4	8	12	24	37	50
81-100	3	6	9	18	27	35
101-141	3	6	9	15	21	26
142-145: All 52 pg. Giants	3	6	9	16	23	30
146-164	2	4	6	10	14	18

NOTE: *Richie Rich & Little Lotta in all.*

LITTLE DOT
Harvey Comics: Sept, 1992 - No. 7, June, 1994 ($1.25/$1.50)

	GD	VG	FN	VF	VF/NM	NM-
V2#1-Little Dot, Little Lotta, Richie Rich in all						3.00
2-7 ($1.50)						2.50

LITTLE DOT DOTLAND (Dot Dotland No. 62, 63)
Harvey Publications: July, 1962 - No. 61, Dec, 1973

	GD	VG	FN	VF	VF/NM	NM-
1-Richie Rich begins	12	24	36	86	153	220
2,3	7	14	21	49	80	110
4,5	6	12	18	39	62	85
6-10	5	10	15	30	48	65
11-20	4	8	12	22	34	45

Little Eva #1 © STJ

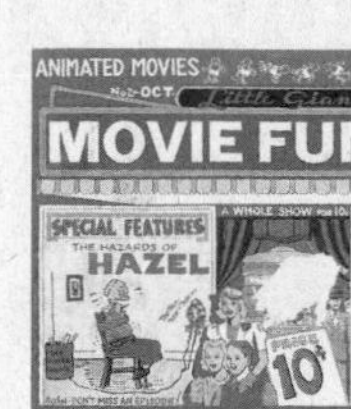

Little Giant Movie Funnies #2 © CEN

Little Lizzie #4 © MAR

	GD 2.0	VG 4.0	FN 6.0	VF 8.0	VF/NM 9.0	NM- 9.2
21-30	3	6	9	17	25	32
31-50	3	6	9	16	22	28
51-54: All 52 pg. Giants	3	6	9	17	25	32
55-61	2	4	6	10	14	18

LITTLE DOT'S UNCLES & AUNTS (See Harvey Hits No. 4, 13, 24)
Harvey Enterprises: Oct, 1961; No. 2, Aug, 1962 - No. 52, Apr, 1974

	GD 2.0	VG 4.0	FN 6.0	VF 8.0	VF/NM 9.0	NM- 9.2
1-Richie Rich begins; 68 pgs. begin	14	28	42	103	184	265
2,3	8	16	24	56	93	130
4,5	6	12	18	39	62	85
6-10	5	10	15	32	51	70
11-20	4	8	12	23	36	48
21-37: Last 68 pg. issue	3	6	9	18	27	35
38-52: All 52 pg. Giants	3	6	9	16	22	28

LITTLE DRACULA
Harvey Comics: Jan, 1992 - No. 3, May, 1992 ($1.25, quarterly, mini-series)

	GD 2.0	VG 4.0	FN 6.0	VF 8.0	VF/NM 9.0	NM- 9.2
1-3						3.00

LITTLE ENDLESS STORYBOOK, THE (See The Sandman titles)
DC Comics: 2001 ($5.95, Prestige format, one-shot)

	GD 2.0	VG 4.0	FN 6.0	VF 8.0	VF/NM 9.0	NM- 9.2
nn-Jill Thompson-s/painted-a/c; puppy Barnabas searches for Delirium						20.00

LITTLE EVA
St. John Publishing Co.: May, 1952 - No. 31, Nov, 1956

	GD 2.0	VG 4.0	FN 6.0	VF 8.0	VF/NM 9.0	NM- 9.2
1	15	30	45	90	140	190
2	10	20	30	54	72	90
3-5	8	16	24	44	57	70
6-10	8	16	24	40	50	60
11-31	7	14	21	35	43	50
3-D 1,2(10/53, 11/53, 25¢)-Both came w/glasses. 1-Infinity-c	18	36	54	107	169	230
I.W. Reprint #1-3,6-8: 1-r/Little Eva #28. 2-r/Little Eva #29. 3-r/Little Eva #24	2	4	6	8	11	14
Super Reprint #10,12('63),14,16,18('64): 18-r/Little Eva #25.	2	4	6	8	11	14

LI'L GENIUS (Formerly Super Brat; Summer Fun No. 54) (See Blue Bird & Giant Comics #3)
Charlton Comics: 1954 - No. 52, 1/65; No. 53, 10/65; No. 54, 10/85 - No. 55, 1/86

	GD 2.0	VG 4.0	FN 6.0	VF 8.0	VF/NM 9.0	NM- 9.2
5(#1?)	11	22	33	62	86	110
6-10	7	14	21	37	46	55
11-15,19,20	6	12	18	29	36	42
16,17-(68 pgs.)	8	16	24	40	50	60
18-(100 pgs., 10/58)	11	22	33	60	83	105
21-35	3	6	9	16	22	28
36-53	2	4	6	10	14	18
54,55 (Low print)						5.00

LI'L GHOST
St. John Publ. Co./Fago No. 1 on: 2/58; No. 2,1/59 - No. 3, Mar, 1959

	GD 2.0	VG 4.0	FN 6.0	VF 8.0	VF/NM 9.0	NM- 9.2
1(St. John)	9	18	27	50	65	80
2,3	6	12	18	28	34	40

LITTLE GIANT COMICS
Centaur Publications: 7/38 - No. 3, 10/38; No. 4, 2/39 (132 pgs.) (6-3/4x4-1/2")

	GD 2.0	VG 4.0	FN 6.0	VF 8.0	VF/NM 9.0	NM- 9.2
1-B&W with color-c; stories, puzzles, magic	97	194	291	611	1031	1450
2,3-B&W with color-c	63	126	189	397	674	950
4 (6-5/8x9-3/8")(68 pgs., B&W inside)	63	126	189	397	674	950

NOTE: *Filchock c-2, 4.* ***Gustavson*** *a-1.* ***Pinajian*** *a-4.* ***Bob Wood*** *a-1.*

LITTLE GIANT DETECTIVE FUNNIES
Centaur Publ.: Oct, 1938; No. 4, Jan, 1939 (6-3/4x4-1/2", 132 pgs., B&W)

	GD 2.0	VG 4.0	FN 6.0	VF 8.0	VF/NM 9.0	NM- 9.2
1-B&W with color-c	97	194	291	611	1031	1450
4(1/39, B&W; color-c; 68 pgs., 6-1/2x9-1/2")-Eisner-r	63	126	189	397	674	950

LITTLE GIANT MOVIE FUNNIES
Centaur Publ.: Aug, 1938 - No. 2, Oct, 1938 (6-3/4x4-1/2", 132 pgs., B&W)

	GD 2.0	VG 4.0	FN 6.0	VF 8.0	VF/NM 9.0	NM- 9.2
1-Ed Wheelan's "Minute Movies" reprints	97	194	291	611	1031	1450
2-Ed Wheelan's "Minute Movies" reprints	63	126	189	397	674	950

LITTLE GROUCHO (...the Red-Headed Tornado; ...Grouchy No. 2)
Reston Publ. Co.: No. 16; Feb-Mar, 1955 - No. 2, June-July, 1955 (See Tippy Terry)

	GD 2.0	VG 4.0	FN 6.0	VF 8.0	VF/NM 9.0	NM- 9.2
16, 1 (2-3/55)	8	16	24	42	54	65
2(6-7/55)	6	12	18	27	33	38

LITTLE HIAWATHA (Disney; see Walt Disney's C&S #143)
Dell Publishing Co.: No. 439, Dec, 1952 - No. 988, May-July, 1959

	GD 2.0	VG 4.0	FN 6.0	VF 8.0	VF/NM 9.0	NM- 9.2
Four Color 439 (#1)	6	12	18	39	62	85
Four Color 787 (4/57), 901 (5/58), 988	5	10	15	30	48	65

LITTLE IKE
St. John Publishing Co.: April, 1953 - No. 4, Oct, 1953

	GD 2.0	VG 4.0	FN 6.0	VF 8.0	VF/NM 9.0	NM- 9.2
1	10	20	30	54	72	90
2	6	12	18	31	38	45
3,4	5	10	15	24	30	35

LITTLE IODINE (See Giant Comic Album)
Dell Publ. Co.: No. 224, 4/49 - No. 257, 1949: 3-5/50 - No. 56, 4-6/62 (1-4-52pgs.)

	GD 2.0	VG 4.0	FN 6.0	VF 8.0	VF/NM 9.0	NM- 9.2
Four Color 224-By Jimmy Hatlo	12	24	36	82	146	210
Four Color 257	8	16	24	56	93	130
1(3-5/50)	9	18	27	65	113	160
2-5	6	12	18	37	59	80
6-10	4	8	12	28	44	60
11-20	4	8	12	22	34	45
21-30: 27-Xmas-c	3	6	9	20	30	40
31-40	3	6	9	18	27	35
41-56	3	6	9	16	23	30

LITTLE JACK FROST
Avon Periodicals: 1951

	GD 2.0	VG 4.0	FN 6.0	VF 8.0	VF/NM 9.0	NM- 9.2
1	11	22	33	62	86	110

LI'L JINX (Little Archie in Animal Land #17) (Also see Pep Comics #62)
Archie Publications: No. 1(#11), Nov, 1956 - No. 16, Sept, 1957

	GD 2.0	VG 4.0	FN 6.0	VF 8.0	VF/NM 9.0	NM- 9.2
1(#11)-By Joe Edwards; "First Issue" on cover	14	28	42	76	108	140
12(1/57)-16	10	20	30	54	72	90

LI'L JINX (See Archie Giant Series Magazine No. 223)

LI'L JINX CHRISTMAS BAG (See Archie Giant Series Mag. No. 195, 206, 219)

LI'L JINX GIANT LAUGH-OUT (See Archie Giant Series Mag. No. 176, 185)
Archie Publications: No. 33, Sept, 1971 - No. 43, Nov, 1973 (52 pgs.)

	GD 2.0	VG 4.0	FN 6.0	VF 8.0	VF/NM 9.0	NM- 9.2
33-43 (52 pgs.)	2	4	6	13	18	22

LITTLE JOE (See Popular Comics & Super Comics)
Dell Publishing Co.: No. 1, 1942

	GD 2.0	VG 4.0	FN 6.0	VF 8.0	VF/NM 9.0	NM- 9.2
Four Color 1	50	100	150	400	750	1100

LITTLE JOE
St. John Publishing Co.: Apr, 1953

	GD 2.0	VG 4.0	FN 6.0	VF 8.0	VF/NM 9.0	NM- 9.2
1	5	10	15	24	30	35

LI'L KIDS (Also see Li'l Pals)
Marvel Comics Group: 8/70 - No. 2, 10/70; No. 3, 11/71 - No. 12, 6/73

	GD 2.0	VG 4.0	FN 6.0	VF 8.0	VF/NM 9.0	NM- 9.2
1	7	14	21	45	73	100
2-9	4	8	12	24	37	50
10-12-Calvin app.	4	8	12	26	41	55

LITTLE KING
Dell Publishing Co.: No. 494, Aug, 1953 - No. 677, Feb, 1956

	GD 2.0	VG 4.0	FN 6.0	VF 8.0	VF/NM 9.0	NM- 9.2
Four Color 494 (#1)	9	18	27	60	100	140
Four Color 597, 677	5	10	15	34	55	75

LITTLE LANA (Formerly Lana)
Marvel Comics (MjMC): No. 8, Nov, 1949; No. 9, Mar, 1950

	GD 2.0	VG 4.0	FN 6.0	VF 8.0	VF/NM 9.0	NM- 9.2
8,9	11	22	33	60	83	110

LITTLE LENNY
Marvel Comics (CDS): June, 1949 - No. 3, Nov, 1949

	GD 2.0	VG 4.0	FN 6.0	VF 8.0	VF/NM 9.0	NM- 9.2
1-Little Aspirin app.	13	26	39	72	101	130
2,3	8	16	24	44	57	70

LITTLE LIZZIE
Marvel Comics (PrPl)/Atlas (OMC): 6/49 - No. 5, 4/50; 9/53 - No. 3, Jan, 1954

	GD 2.0	VG 4.0	FN 6.0	VF 8.0	VF/NM 9.0	NM- 9.2
1	14	28	42	80	115	150
2-5	9	18	27	47	61	75
1 (9/53, 2nd series by Atlas)-Howie Post-c	10	20	30	54	72	90
2,3	8	16	24	40	50	60

LITTLE LOTTA (See Harvey Hits No. 10)
Harvey Publications: 11/55 - No. 110, 11/73; No. 111, 9/74 - No. 120, 5/76
V2#1, Oct, 1992 - No. 4, July, 1993 ($1.25)

	GD 2.0	VG 4.0	FN 6.0	VF 8.0	VF/NM 9.0	NM- 9.2
1-Richie Rich (r) & Little Dot begin	36	72	108	277	514	750
2,3	16	32	48	118	219	320
4,5	11	22	33	75	133	190
6-10	8	16	24	54	90	125

Little Lulu Vol. 17 The Valentine © Marjorie Buell

Little Max Comics #14 © HARV

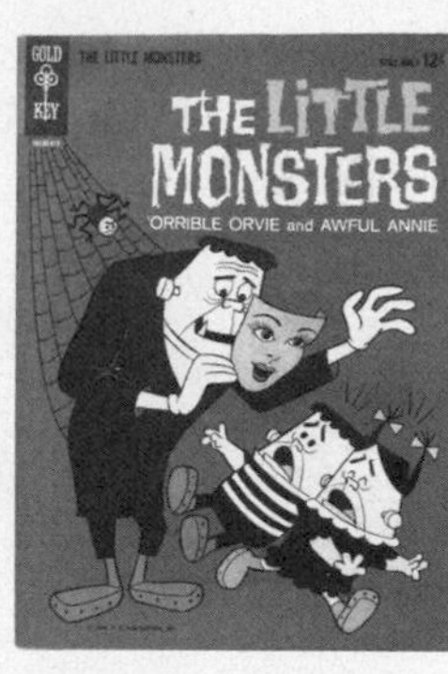

Little Monsters #1 © GK

	GD 2.0	VG 4.0	FN 6.0	VF 8.0	VF/NM 9.0	NM- 9.2
11-20	6	12	18	39	62	85
21-40	4	8	12	24	37	50
41-60	3	6	9	19	29	38
61-80: 62-1st app. Nurse Jenny	3	6	9	16	22	28
81-99	2	4	6	11	16	20
100-103: All 52 pg. Giants	3	6	9	14	19	24
104-120	2	4	6	8	10	12
V2#1-4 (1992-93)						3.00

NOTE: *No. 121 was advertised, but never released.*

LITTLE LOTTA FOODLAND
Harvey Publications: 9/63 - No. 14, 10/67; No. 15, 10/68 - No. 29, Oct, 1972

	GD 2.0	VG 4.0	FN 6.0	VF 8.0	VF/NM 9.0	NM- 9.2
1-Little Lotta, Little Dot, Richie Rich, 68 pgs. begin	13	26	39	95	168	240
2,3	9	18	27	60	100	140
4,5	6	12	18	43	69	95
6-10	5	10	15	32	51	70
11-20	3	6	9	20	30	40
21-26: 26-Last 68 pg. issue	3	6	9	16	23	30
27,28: Both 52 pgs.	3	6	9	14	19	24
29-(36 pgs.)	2	4	6	9	13	16

LITTLE LULU (Formerly Marge's Little Lulu)
Gold Key 207-257/Whitman 258 on: No. 207, Sept, 1972 - No. 268, Mar, 1984

	GD 2.0	VG 4.0	FN 6.0	VF 8.0	VF/NM 9.0	NM- 9.2
207,209,220-Stanley-r. 207-1st app. Henrietta	2	4	6	11	16	20
208,210-219: 208-1st app. Snobbly, Wilbur's butler	2	4	6	9	12	15
221-240,242-249, 250(r/#166), 251-254(r/#206)	1	3	4	6	8	10
241,263-Stanley-r	2	4	6	8	10	12
255-257(Gold Key): 256-r/#212	1	2	3	5	7	9
258,259,262(50¢-c),264(2/82),265(3/82) (Whitman)	2	4	6	8	11	14
260-(9/80)(Whitman pre-pack only - low distribution)	14	28	42	99	175	250
261-(11/80)(Whitman pre-pack only)	4	8	12	24	37	50
262-(1/81) Variant 40¢-c price error (reg. ed. 50¢-c)	2	4	6	11	16	20
266-268 (All #00028 on-c; no date, no date code; 3-pack): 266(7/83). 267(8/83). 268(3/84)-Stanley-r	3	6	9	15	21	26

LITTLE LULU
Dark Horse Books: Nov, 2004 - Present ($9.95/$10.95, B&W, digest-size TPB)

	NM- 9.2
Vol. 1 -B&W reprints of Marge's Little Lulu #6-12; John Stanley-s/a & Irving Tripp-a	10.00
...: (Vol. 2) Lulu Takes a Trip (2/05) -B&W r/Marge's Little Lulu #13-16	10.00
...: (Vol. 3) My Dinner With Lulu (4/05) -B&W r/Four Color #74,97,110,115,120	10.00
...: (Vol. 4) Sunday Afternoon (6/05) -B&W r/Four Color #131,139,146,158	10.00
...: (Vol. 5) Lulu in the Doghouse (8/05) -B&W r/Four Color #165 & Marge's Little Lulu #1-5	10.00
...: (Vol. 6) Letters to Santa (10/05) -B&W r/Marge's Little Lulu #18-22	10.00
...: (Vol. 7) Lulu's Umbrella Service (12/05) -B&W r/Marge's Little Lulu #23-27	10.00
...: (Vol. 8) Late For School (2/06) -B&W r/Marge's Little Lulu #28-32	10.00
...: (Vol. 9) Lucky Lulu (4/06) -B&W r/Marge's Little Lulu #33-37	10.00
...: (Vol. 10) All Dressed Up (6/06) -B&W r/Marge's Little Lulu #38-42	10.00
...: (Vol. 11) April Fools (8/06) -B&W r/Marge's Little Lulu #43-48	10.00
...: (Vol. 12) Leave It to Lulu (10/06) -B&W r/Marge's Little Lulu #49-53	10.00
...: (Vol. 13) Too Much Fun (12/06) -B&W r/Marge's Little Lulu #54-58	10.00
...: (Vol. 14) Queen Lulu (2/07) -B&W r/Marge's Little Lulu #59-63	10.00
...: (Vol. 15) The Explorers (4/07) -B&W r/Marge's Little Lulu #64-68	10.00
...: (Vol. 16) A Handy Kid (7/07, $10.95) -B&W r/Marge's Little Lulu #69-74	11.00
...: (Vol. 17) The Valentine (10/07, $10.95) -B&W r/Marge's Little Lulu #75-81	11.00
...: (Vol. 18) The Expert (1/08, $10.95) -B&W r/Marge's Little Lulu #82-87	11.00
Color Special (9/06, $13.95, standard size) r/various stories from Marge's Little Lulu	14.00

LITTLE MARY MIXUP (See Comics On Parade)
United Features Syndicate: No. 10, 1939, - No. 26, 1940

	GD 2.0	VG 4.0	FN 6.0	VF 8.0	VF/NM 9.0	NM- 9.2
Single Series 10, 26	34	68	102	198	319	440

LITTLE MAX COMICS (Joe Palooka's Pal; see Joe Palooka)
Harvey Publications: Oct, 1949 - No. 73, Nov, 1961

	GD 2.0	VG 4.0	FN 6.0	VF 8.0	VF/NM 9.0	NM- 9.2
1-Infinity-c; Little Dot begins; Joe Palooka on-c	22	44	66	127	204	280
2-Little Dot app.; Joe Palooka on-c	14	28	42	76	108	140
3-Little Dot app.; Joe Palooka on-c	10	20	30	56	76	95
4-10: 5-Little Dot app., 1pg.	8	16	24	44	57	70
11-20	8	16	24	40	50	60
21-40: 23-Little Dot app. 38-r/#20	6	12	18	31	38	45
41-62,66	3	6	9	18	27	35
63-65,67-73-Include new five pg. Richie Rich stories. 70-73-Little Lotta app.	3	6	9	19	29	38

LI'L MENACE
Fago Magazine Co.: Dec, 1958 - No. 3, May, 1959

	GD 2.0	VG 4.0	FN 6.0	VF 8.0	VF/NM 9.0	NM- 9.2
1-Peter Rabbit app.	8	16	24	44	57	70
2-Peter Rabbit (Vincent Fago's)	7	14	21	35	43	50
3	6	12	18	28	34	40

LITTLE MERMAID, THE (Walt Disney's...; also see Disney's...)
W. D. Publications (Disney): 1990 (no date given)($5.95, no ads, 52 pgs.)

	GD 2.0	VG 4.0	FN 6.0	VF 8.0	VF/NM 9.0	NM- 9.2
nn-Adapts animated movie	1	2	3	4	5	7
nn-Comic version ($2.50)						3.00

LITTLE MERMAID, THE
Disney Comics: 1992 - No. 4, 1992 ($1.50, mini-series)

	GD 2.0	VG 4.0	FN 6.0	VF 8.0	VF/NM 9.0	NM- 9.2
1-4: Based on movie						3.00
1-4: 2nd printings sold at Wal-Mart w/different-c						2.25

LITTLE MISS MUFFET
Best Books (Standard Comics)/King Features Synd.: No. 11, Dec, 1948 - No. 13, March, 1949

	GD 2.0	VG 4.0	FN 6.0	VF 8.0	VF/NM 9.0	NM- 9.2
11-Strip reprints; Fanny Cory-c/a	9	18	27	50	65	80
12,13-Strip reprints; Fanny Cory-c/a	7	14	21	35	43	50

LITTLE MISS SUNBEAM COMICS
Magazine Enterprises/Quality Bakers of America: June-July, 1950 - No. 4, Dec-Jan, 1950-51

	GD 2.0	VG 4.0	FN 6.0	VF 8.0	VF/NM 9.0	NM- 9.2
1	15	30	45	94	147	200
2-4	10	20	30	56	76	95
...Advs. In Space ('55)	7	14	21	35	43	50

LITTLE MONSTERS, THE (See March of Comics #423, Three Stooges #17)
Gold Key: Nov, 1964 - No. 44, Feb, 1978

	GD 2.0	VG 4.0	FN 6.0	VF 8.0	VF/NM 9.0	NM- 9.2
1	6	12	18	37	59	80
2	3	6	9	20	30	40
3-10	3	6	9	17	25	32
11-20	3	6	9	15	21	26
21-30: 19-21-Reprints	2	4	6	11	16	20
31-44: 34-39,43-Reprints	2	4	6	8	11	14

LITTLE MONSTERS (Movie)
Now Comics: 1989 - No. 6, June, 1990 ($1.75)

	GD 2.0	VG 4.0	FN 6.0	VF 8.0	VF/NM 9.0	NM- 9.2
1-6: Photo-c from movie						2.50

LITTLE NEMO (See Cocomalt, Future Comics, Help, Jest, Kayo, Punch, Red Seal, & Superworld; most by Winsor McCay Jr., son of famous artist) (Other McCay books: see Little Sammy Sneeze & Dreams of the Rarebit Fiend)

LITTLE NEMO (...in Slumberland)
McCay Features/Nostalgia Press('69): 1945 (11x7-1/4", 28 pgs., B&W)

	GD 2.0	VG 4.0	FN 6.0	VF 8.0	VF/NM 9.0	NM- 9.2
1905 & 1911 reprints by Winsor McCay	10	20	30	56	76	95
1969-70 (Exact reprint)	2	4	6	9	12	15

LITTLE ORPHAN ANNIE (See Annie, Famous Feature Stories, Marvel Super Special, Merry Christmas..., Popular Comics, Super Book #7, 11, 23 & Super Comics)

LITTLE ORPHAN ANNIE
David McKay Publ./Dell Publishing Co.: No. 7, 1937 - No. 3, Sept-Nov, 1948; No. 206, Dec, 1948

	GD 2.0	VG 4.0	FN 6.0	VF 8.0	VF/NM 9.0	NM- 9.2
Feature Books(McKay) 7-(1937) (Rare)	97	194	291	611	1031	1450
Four Color 12(1941)	57	114	171	359	605	850
Four Color 18(1943)-Flag-c	33	66	99	254	477	700
Four Color 52(1944)	26	52	78	188	349	510
Four Color 76(1945)	21	42	63	152	281	410
Four Color 107(1946)	18	36	54	130	240	350
Four Color 152(1947)	12	24	36	87	156	225
1(3-5/48)-r/strips from 5/7/44 to 7/30/44	12	24	36	86	153	220
2-r/strips from 7/21/40 to 9/9/40	9	18	27	60	100	140
3-r/strips from 9/10/40 to 11/9/40	9	18	27	60	100	140
Four Color 206(12/48)	8	16	24	54	90	125

LI'L PALS (Also see Li'l Kids)
Marvel Comics Group: Sept, 1972 - No. 5, May, 1973

	GD 2.0	VG 4.0	FN 6.0	VF 8.0	VF/NM 9.0	NM- 9.2
1	6	12	18	37	59	80
2-5	4	8	12	24	37	50

LI'L PAN (Formerly Rocket Kelly; becomes Junior Comics with #9)
Fox Features Syndicate: No. 6, Dec-Jan, 1946-47 - No. 8, Apr-May, 1947
(Also see Wotalife Comics)

	GD 2.0	VG 4.0	FN 6.0	VF 8.0	VF/NM 9.0	NM- 9.2
6	10	20	30	58	79	100
7,8: 7-Atomic bomb story; robot-c	8	16	24	44	57	70

LITTLE PEOPLE (Also see Darby O'Gill & the...)
Dell Publishing Co.: No. 485, Aug-Oct, 1953 - No. 1062, Dec, 1959 (Walt Scott's)

	GD 2.0	VG 4.0	FN 6.0	VF 8.0	VF/NM 9.0	NM- 9.2
Four Color 485 (#1)	8	16	24	52	86	120
Four Color 573(7/54), 633(6/55)	5	10	15	32	51	70

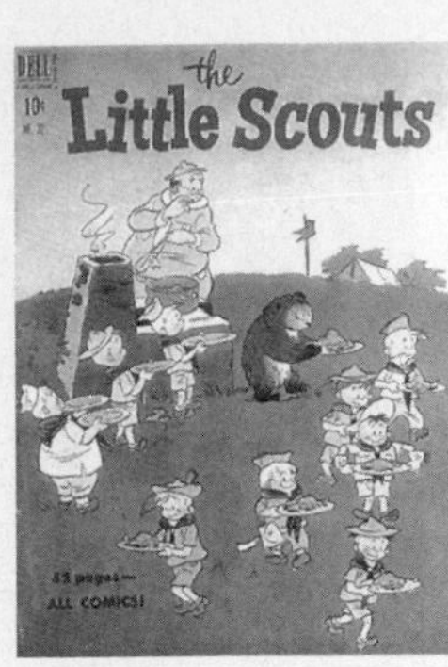

Little Scouts FC #321 © Roland Coe

Living With The Dead #1 © DH

Lobo #50 © DC

	GD 2.0	VG 4.0	FN 6.0	VF 8.0	VF/NM 9.0	NM- 9.2
Four Color 692(3/56),753(11/56),809(7/57),868(12/57),908(5/58), 959(12/58), 1062	5	10	15	32	51	70

LITTLE RASCALS
Dell Publishing Co.: No. 674, Jan, 1956 - No. 1297, Mar-May, 1962

	GD	VG	FN	VF	VF/NM	NM-
Four Color 674 (#1)	9	18	27	60	100	140
Four Color 778(3/57),825(8/57)	6	12	18	39	62	85
Four Color 883(3/58),936(9/58),974(3/59),1030(9/59),1079(2-4/60),1137(9-11/60)	6	12	18	37	59	80
Four Color 1174(3-5/61),1224(10-12/61),1297	5	10	15	30	48	65

LI'L RASCAL TWINS (Formerly Nature Boy)
Charlton Comics: No. 6, 1957 - No. 18, Jan, 1960

	GD	VG	FN	VF	VF/NM	NM-
6-Li'l Genius & Tomboy in all	6	12	18	29	36	42
7-18: 7-Timmy the Timid Ghost app.	4	8	12	18	22	25

LITTLE RED HOT: (CHANE OF FOOLS)
Image Comics: Feb, 1999 - No. 3, Apr, 1999 ($2.95/$3.50, B&W, limited series)

	GD	VG	FN	VF	VF/NM	NM-
1-3-Dawn Brown-s/a. 2,3-($3.50-c)						3.50
The Foolish Collection TPB ($12.95) r/#1-3						13.00

LITTLE RED HOT: BOUND
Image Comics: July, 2001 - No. 3, Nov, 2001 ($2.95, color, limited series)

	GD	VG	FN	VF	VF/NM	NM-
1-3-Dawn Brown-s/a.						3.00

LITTLE ROQUEFORT COMICS (See Paul Terry's Comics #105)
St. John Publishing Co.(all pre-code)/Pines No. 10: June, 1952 - No. 9, Oct, 1953; No. 10, Summer, 1958

	GD	VG	FN	VF	VF/NM	NM-
1-By Paul Terry	10	20	30	54	72	90
2	6	12	18	31	38	45
3-10: 10-CBS Television Presents on-c	5	10	15	24	30	35

LITTLE SAD SACK (See Harvey Hits No. 73, 76, 79, 81, 83)
Harvey Publications: Oct, 1964 - No. 19, Nov, 1967

	GD	VG	FN	VF	VF/NM	NM-
1-Richie Rich app. on cover only	5	10	15	32	51	70
2-10	3	6	9	18	27	35
11-19	3	6	9	16	22	28

LITTLE SCOUTS
Dell Publishing Co.: No. 321, Mar, 1951 - No. 587, Oct, 1954

	GD	VG	FN	VF	VF/NM	NM-
Four Color 321 (#1, 3/51)	5	10	15	30	48	65
2(10-12/51) - 6(10-12/52)	4	8	12	24	37	50
Four Color 462,506,550,587	4	8	12	24	37	50

LITTLE SHOP OF HORRORS SPECIAL (Movie)
DC Comics: Feb, 1987 ($2.00, 68 pgs.)

	GD	VG	FN	VF	VF/NM	NM-
1-Colan-c/a						4.00

LITTLE SPUNKY
I. W. Enterprises: No date (1963?) (10¢)

	GD	VG	FN	VF	VF/NM	NM-
1-r/Frisky Fables #1	2	4	6	8	11	14

LITTLE STAR
Oni Press: Feb, 2005 - No. 6, Dec, 2005 ($2.99, B&W, limited series)

	GD	VG	FN	VF	VF/NM	NM-
1-6-Andi Watson-s/a						3.00
TPB (4/06, $19.95) r/#1-6						20.00

LITTLE STOOGES, THE (The Three Stooges' Sons)
Gold Key: Sept, 1972 - No. 7, Mar, 1974

	GD	VG	FN	VF	VF/NM	NM-
1-Norman Maurer cover/stories in all	3	6	9	18	27	35
2-7	2	4	6	11	16	20

LITTLEST OUTLAW (Disney)
Dell Publishing Co.: No. 609, Jan, 1955

	GD	VG	FN	VF	VF/NM	NM-
Four Color 609-Movie, photo-c	6	12	18	43	69	95

LITTLEST SNOWMAN, THE
Dell Publishing Co.: No. 755, 12/56; No. 864, 12/57; 12-2/1963-64

	GD	VG	FN	VF	VF/NM	NM-
Four Color 755,864, 1(1964)	5	10	15	32	51	70

LI'L TOMBOY (Formerly Fawcett's Funny Animals; see Giant Comics #3)
Charlton Comics: V14#92, Oct, 1956; No. 93, Mar, 1957 - No. 107, Feb, 1960

	GD	VG	FN	VF	VF/NM	NM-
V14#92	6	12	18	27	33	38
93-107: 97-Atomic Bunny app.	5	10	14	20	24	28

LI'L WILLIE COMICS (Formerly & becomes Willie Comics #22 on)
Marvel Comics (MgPC): No. 20, July, 1949 - No. 21, Sept, 1949

	GD	VG	FN	VF	VF/NM	NM-
20,21: 20-Little Aspirin app.	13	26	39	74	105	135

LITTLE WOMEN (See Power Record Comics)

LIVE IT UP
Spire Christian Comics (Fleming H. Revell Co.): 1973, 1974 (39-49 cents)

	GD	VG	FN	VF	VF/NM	NM-
nn-1973 Edition	2	4	6	8	11	14
nn-1974 Edition	1	3	4	6	8	10

LIVEWIRES
Marvel Comics: Apr, 2005 - No. 6, Sept, 2005 ($2.99, limited series)

	GD	VG	FN	VF	VF/NM	NM-
1-6-Adam Warren-s/c; Rick Mays-a						3.00
...: Clockwork Thugs, Yo (2005, $7.99, digest) r/#1-6						8.00

LIVING BIBLE, THE
Living Bible Corp.: Fall, 1945 - No. 3, Spring, 1946

	GD	VG	FN	VF	VF/NM	NM-
1-The Life of Paul; all have L. B. Cole-c	39	78	117	230	370	510
2-Joseph & His Brethren; Jonah & the Whale	27	54	81	158	254	350
3-Chaplains At War (classic-c)	40	80	120	244	397	550

LIVING WITH THE DEAD
Dark Horse Comics: Oct, 2007 - No. 3, Nov, 2007 ($2.99, limited series)

	GD	VG	FN	VF	VF/NM	NM-
1-3-Zombies; Mike Richardson-s/Ben Stenbeck-a/Richard Corben-c						3.00

LOADED BIBLE
Image Comics: Apr, 2006; May, 2007; Feb, 2008 ($4.99)

	GD	VG	FN	VF	VF/NM	NM-
...: Jesus vs. Vampires (4/06) Tim Seeley-s/Nate Bellegarde-a						5.00
...2: Blood of Christ (5/07) Seeley-s/Mike Norton-a. ...3: Communion (2/08)						5.00

LOBO
Dell Publishing Co.: Dec, 1965; No. 2, Oct, 1966

	GD	VG	FN	VF	VF/NM	NM-
1-1st black character to have his own title	4	8	12	26	41	55
2	3	6	9	19	29	38

LOBO (Also see Action #650, Adventures of Superman, Demon (2nd series), Justice League, L.E.G.I.O.N., Mister Miracle, Omega Men #3 & Superman #41)
DC Comics: Nov, 1990 - No. 4, Feb, 1991 ($1.50, color, limited series)

	GD	VG	FN	VF	VF/NM	NM-
1-(99¢)-Giffen plots/Breakdowns in all						4.00
1-2nd printing						2.50
2-4: 2-Legion '89 spin-off. 1-4 have Bisley painted covers & art						2.50
...: Blazing Chain of Love 1 (9/92, $1.50)-Denys Cowan-c/a; Alan Grant scripts, ...Convention Special 1 (1993, $1.75), ...Paramilitary Christmas Special 1 (1991, $2.39, 52 pgs.) -Bisley-c/a, ...: Portrait of a Victim 1 (1993, $1.75)						2.50
...: Portrait of a Bastich TPB (2008, $19.99) r/#1-4 & Lobo's Back #1-4						20.00

LOBO (Also see Showcase '95 #9)
DC Comics: Dec, 1993 - No. 64, Jul, 1999 ($1.75/$1.95/$2.25/$2.50, mature)

	GD	VG	FN	VF	VF/NM	NM-
1 ($2.95)-Foil onhanced-c, Alan Grant scripts begin						3.00
2-9,0,10-64: 2-7-Alan Grant scripts. 9-(9/94). 0-(10/94)-Origin retold. 50-Lobo vs. the DCU. 58-Giffen-a						2.50
#1,000,000 (11/98) 853rd Century x-over						2.50
Annual 1 (1993, $3.50, 68 pgs.)-Bloodlines x-over						3.50
Annual 2 (1994, $3.50)-21 artists (20 listed on-c); Alan Grant script; Elseworlds story						3.50
Annual 3 (1995, $3.95)-Year One story						4.00
.../Authority: Holiday Hell TPB (2006, $17.99) r/Lobo Paramilitary Christmas Special; Authority/Lobo: Jingle Hell and Spring Break Massacre; WildStorm Winter Special						18.00
...Big Babe Spring Break Special (Spr, '95, $1.95)-Balent-a						2.50
...Bounty Hunting for Fun and Profit ('95)-Bisley-c						5.00
... Chained (5/97, $2.50)-Alan Grant story						2.50
.../Deadman: The Brave And The Bald (2/95, $3.50)						3.50
.../Demon: Helloween (12/96, $2.25)-Giarrano-a						2.50
...Fragtastic Voyage 1 ('97, $5.95)-Mejia painted-c/a						6.00
...Gallery (9/95, $3.50)-pin-ups.						3.50
...In the Chair 1 (8/94, $1.95, 36 pgs.), ...I Quit-(12/95, $2.25)						2.50
.../Judge Dredd ('95, $4.95).						5.00
...Lobocop 1 (2/94, $1.95)-Alan Grant scripts; painted-c						2.50

LOBO: (Title Series), DC Comics

	GD	VG	FN	VF	VF/NM	NM-
--A CONTRACT ON GAWD, 4/94 - 7/94 (mature) 1-4: Alan Grant scripts. 3-Groo cameo						2.50
--DEATH AND TAXES, 10/96 - No. 4, 1/97, 1-4-Giffen/Grant scripts						2.50
--GOES TO HOLLYWOOD, 8/96 ($2.25), 1-Grant scripts						2.50
--INFANTICIDE, 10/92 - 1/93 ($1.50, mature), 1-4-Giffen-c/a; Grant scripts						2.50
--/ MASK, 2/97 - No. 2, 3/97 ($5.95), 1,2						6.00
--'S BACK, 5/92 - No. 4, 11/92 ($1.50, mature), 1-4: 1-Has 3 outer covers. Bisley painted-c 1,2; a-1-3. 3-Sam Kieth-c; all have Giffen plots/breakdown & Grant scripts						2.50
Trade paperback (1993, $9.95)-r/1-4						10.00
--THE DUCK, 6/97 ($1.95), 1-A. Grant-s/V. Semeiks & R. Kryssing-a						2.50

--UNAMERICAN GLADIATORS, 6/93 - No. 4, 9/93 ($1.75, mature), 1-4-Mignola-c;

Logan #2 © MAR

Lone Gunmen #1 © 20th Century Fox

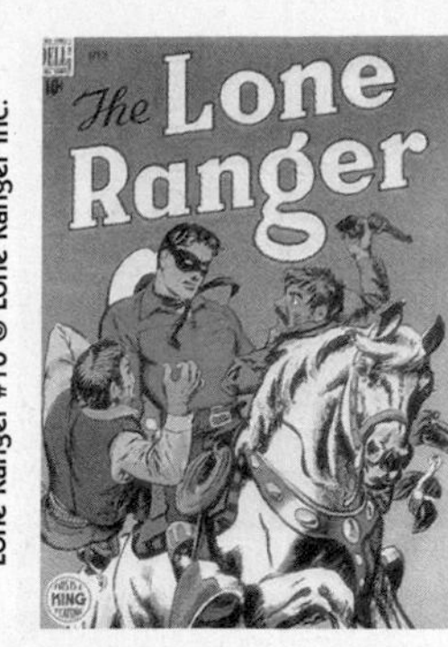

Lone Ranger #10 © Lone Ranger Inc.

GD 2.0 | VG 4.0 | FN 6.0 | VF 8.0 | VF/NM 9.0 | NM- 9.2

Grant/Wagner scripts 2.50
--UNBOUND, 8/03 - No. 6, 5/04 ($2.95), 1-6-Giffen-s/Horley-c/a. 4-6-Ambush Bug app. 3.00

LOBSTER JOHNSON: THE IRON PROMETHEUS (See B.P.R.D. and Hellboy titles)
Dark Horse Comics: Sept, 2007 - No. 5, Jan, 2000 ($2.99, limited series)
1-5-Mignola-s/c; Armstrong-a 3.00

LOCKE & KEY
IDW Publ.: Feb, 2008 - No. 6 ($3.99, limited series)
1-Joe Hill-s/Gabriel Rodriguez-a 10.00
1-Second printing 4.00
2-6 4.00

LOCO (Magazine) (Satire)
Satire Publications: Aug, 1958 - V1#3, Jan, 1959
V1#1-Chic Stone-a 9 18 27 47 61 75
V1#2,3 Sovorin-a, 2 pgs. Davis; 3-Heath-a 7 14 21 35 43 50

LOGAN (Wolverine)
Marvel Comics: May, 2008 - No. 3, Jul, 2008 ($3.99, limited series)
1-3-Vaughan-s/Risso-a/c; regular & B&W editions for each 4.00

LOGAN: PATH OF THE WARLORD
Marvel Comics: Feb, 1996 ($5.95, one-shot)
1-John Paul Leon-a 6.00

LOGAN: SHADOW SOCIETY
Marvel Comics: 1996 ($5.95, one-shot)
1 6.00

LOGAN'S RUN
Marvel Comics Group: Jan, 1977 - No. 7, July, 1977
1: 1-5-Based on novel & movie 1 3 4 6 8 10
2-5,7: 6,7-New stories adapted from novel 6.00
6-1st Thanos (also see Iron Man #55) solo story (back-up) by Zeck (6/77)
3 6 9 10 27 35
6-(35¢-c variant, limited distribution) 8 16 24 52 86 120
7-(35¢-c variant, limited distribution) 3 6 9 20 30 40
NOTE: *Austin a-6i. Gulacy c-6. Kane c-7p. Perez a-1-5p; c-1-5p. Sutton a-6p, 7p.*

LOIS & CLARK, THE NEW ADVENTURES OF SUPERMAN
DC Comics: 1994 ($9.95, one-shot)
1-r/Man of Steel #2, Superman Ann. 1, Superman #9 & 11, Action #600 & 655, Adventures of Superman #445, 462 & 466 1 3 4 6 8 10

LOIS LANE (Also see Daring New Adventures of Supergirl, Showcase #9,10 & Superman's Girlfriend...)
DC Comics: Aug, 1986 - No. 2, Sept, 1986 ($1.50, 52 pgs.)
1,2-Morrow-c/a in each 4.00

LOKI (Thor)
Marvel Comics: Sept, 2004 - No. 4, Nov, 2004 ($3.50)
1-4-Rodi-s/Ribic-a/c 3.50
HC (2005, $17.99, with dustjacket) oversized r/#1-4; original proposal and sketch pages 18.00
SC (2007, $12.99) r/#1-4; original proposal and sketch pages 13.00

LOLLY AND PEPPER
Dell Publishing Co.: No. 832, Sept, 1957 - July, 1962
Four Color 832(#1) 5 10 15 30 48 65
Four Color 940,978,1086,1206 4 8 12 22 34 45
01-459-207 (7/62) 3 6 9 18 27 35

LOMAX (See Police Action)

LONDON'S DARK
Escape/Titan: 1989 ($8.95, B&W, graphic novel)
nn-James Robinson script; Paul Johnson-c/a 1 2 3 5 7 9

LONE
Dark Horse Comics: Sept, 2003 - No. 6, Mar, 2004 ($2.99)
1-6-Stuart Moore-s/Jerome Opeña-a/Templesmith-c 3.00

LONE EAGLE (The Flame No. 5 on)
Ajax/Farrell Publications: Apr-May, 1954 - No. 4, Oct-Nov, 1954
1 13 26 39 74 105 135
2-4: 3-Bondage-c 9 18 27 50 65 80

LONE GUNMEN, THE (From the X-Files)
Dark Horse Comics: June, 2001 ($2.99, one-shot)
1-Paul Lee-a; photo-c 3.00

GD 2.0 | VG 4.0 | FN 6.0 | VF 8.0 | VF/NM 9.0 | NM- 9.2

LONELY HEART (Formerly Dear Lonely Hearts; Dear Heart #15 on)
Ajax/Farrell Publ. (Excellent Publ.): No. 9, Mar, 1955 - No. 14, Feb, 1956
9-Kamenesque-a; (Last precode) 10 20 30 54 72 90
10-14 7 14 21 37 46 55

LONE RANGER, THE (See Ace Comics, Aurora, Dell Giants, Future Comics, Golden Comics Digest #48, King Comics, Magic Comics & March of Comics #165, 174, 193, 208, 225, 238, 310, 322, 338, 350)

LONE RANGER, THE
Dell Publishing Co.: No. 3, 1939 - No. 167, Feb, 1947
Large Feature Comic 3(1939)-Heigh-Yo Silver; text with illus. by Robert Weisman; also exists as a Whitman #710 167 334 501 1052 1776 2500
Large Feature Comic 7(1939)-Illustr. by Henry Vallely; Hi-Yo Silver the Lone Ranger to the Rescue; also exists as a Whitman #715 153 306 459 964 1632 2300
Feature Book 21(1940), 24(1941) 87 174 261 548 924 1300
Four Color 82(1945) 38 76 114 286 536 785
Four Color 98(1945),118(1946) 29 58 87 213 394 575
Four Color 125(1946),136(1947) 20 40 60 143 264 385
Four Color 151,167(1947) 17 34 51 120 223 325

LONE RANGER, THE (Movie, radio & TV; Clayton Moore starred as Lone Ranger in the movies; No. 1-37: strip reprints)(See Dell Giants)
Dell Publishing Co.: Jan-Feb, 1948 - No. 145, May-July, 1962
1 (36 pgs.)-The Lone Ranger, his horse Silver, companion Tonto & his horse Scout begin
52 104 156 442 846 1250
2 (52 pgs. begin, end #41) 27 54 81 200 370 540
3-5 20 40 60 148 274 400
6,7,9,10 17 34 51 122 226 330
8-Origin retold; Indian back-c begin, end #35 20 40 60 143 264 385
11-20: 11- "Young Hawk" Indian boy serial begins, ends #145
13 26 39 90 160 230
21,22,24-31: 51-Reprint. 31-1st Mask logo 10 20 30 71 126 180
23-Origin retold 13 26 39 93 164 235
32-37: 32-Painted-c begin. 36-Animal photo back-c begin, end #49. 37-Last newspaper-r issue; new outfit; red shirt becomes blue; most known copies show the blue shirt on-c & inside 9 18 27 63 107 150
37-Variant issue; Long Ranger wears a red shirt on-c and inside. A few copies of the red shirt outfit were printed before catching the mistake and changing the color to blue (rare)
15 30 45 111 206 300
38-41 (All 52 pgs.) 38-Paul S. Newman-s (wrote most of the stories #38-on)
9 18 27 60 100 140
42-50 (36 pgs.) 7 14 21 50 83 115
51-74 (52 pgs.): 56-One pg. origin story of Lone Ranger & Tonto. 71-Blank inside-c
7 14 21 49 80 110
75,77-99: 79-X-mas-c 7 14 21 45 73 100
76-Classic flag-c 7 14 21 49 80 110
100 8 16 24 52 86 120
101-111: Last painted-c 6 12 18 43 69 95
112-Clayton Moore photo-c begin, end #145 17 34 51 120 223 325
113-117: 117-10¢ &15¢-c exist 10 20 30 70 123 175
118-Origin Lone Ranger, Tonto, & Silver retold; Special anniversary issue
22 44 66 157 291 425
119-140: 139-Fran Striker-s 9 18 27 64 110 155
141-145 10 20 30 67 116 165
NOTE: *Hank Hartman painted c(signed)-65, 66, 70, 75, 82; unsigned-64?, 67-69?, 71, 72, 73?, 74?, 76-78, 80, 81, 83-91, 92?, 93-111. Ernest Nordli painted c(signed)-42, 50, 52, 53, 56, 59, 60; unsigned-39-41, 44-49, 51, 54, 55, 57, 58, 61-63?*

LONE RANGER, THE
Gold Key (Reprints in #13-20): 9/64 - No. 16, 12/69; No. 17, 11/72; No. 18, 9/74 - No. 28, 3/77
1-Retells origin 6 12 18 41 66 90
2 4 8 12 22 34 45
3-10: Small Bear-r in #6-12. 10-Last 12¢ issue 3 6 9 20 30 40
11-17 3 6 9 16 22 28
18-28 2 4 6 11 16 20
Golden West 1(30029-610, 10/66)-Giant; r/most Golden West #3 including Clayton Moore photo front/back-c 7 14 21 45 73 100

LONE RANGER
Dynamite Entertainment: 2006 - Present ($2.99)
1-Retells origin; Carriello-a/Matthews-s; badge cover by Cassaday 3.00
1-Variant mask cover by Cassaday 5.00
1-Baltimore Comic-Con 2006 variant cover with masked face and horse silhouette 12.00
1-Directors' Cut ($4.99) r/#1 with comments at page bottoms, script and sketches 5.00
2-13: 2-Origin continues; Tonto app. 3.00
... and Tonto 1 (2008, $4.99) Cassaday-c 5.00

Lone Rider #14 © Farrell

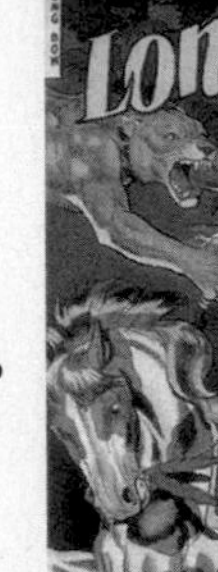

Long Bow #4 © FH

Looney Tunes #106 © WB

GD 2.0 | VG 4.0 | FN 6.0 | VF 8.0 | VF/NM 9.0 | NM- 9.2

... Volume 1: Now and Forever TPB (2007, $19.99) r/#1-6; sketch pages 20.00

LONE RANGER AND TONTO, THE
Topps Comics: Aug, 1994 - No. 4, Nov, 1994 ($2.50, limited series)
1-4: 3-Origin of Lone Ranger; Tonto leaves; Lansdale story, Truman-c/a in all. 2.50
1-4: Silver logo. 1-Signed by Lansdale and Truman 6.00
Trade paperback (1/95, $9.95) 10.00

LONE RANGER'S COMPANION TONTO, THE (TV)
Dell Publishing Co.: No. 312, Jan, 1951 - No. 33, Nov-Jan/58-59 (All painted-c)
Four Color 312(#1, 1/51) 11 22 33 75 133 190
2(8-10/51),3: (#2 titled "Tonto") 6 12 18 43 69 95
4-10 6 12 18 37 59 80
11-20 5 10 15 32 51 70
21-33 4 8 12 28 44 60
NOTE: ***Ernest Nordli*** *painted c(signed)-2, 7; unsigned-3-6, 8-11, 12?, 13, 14, 18?, 22-24? See Aurora Comic Booklets.*

LONE RANGER'S FAMOUS HORSE HI-YO SILVER, THE (TV)
Dell Publishing Co.: No. 369, Jan, 1952 - No. 36, Oct-Dec, 1960 (All painted-c, most by Sam Savitt) (Lone Ranger appears in most issues)
Four Color 369(#1)-Silver's origin as told by The Lone Ranger
10 20 30 71 126 180
Four Color 392(#2, 4/52) 6 12 18 41 66 90
3(7-9/52)-10(4-6/52) 5 10 15 35 55 75
11-36 4 8 12 28 44 60

LONE RIDER (Also see The Rider)
Superior Comics(Farrell Publ.): Apr, 1951 - No. 26, Jul, 1955 (#3-on: 36 pgs.)
1 (52 pgs.)-The Lone Rider & his horse Lightnin' begin; Kamenish-a begins
31 62 93 181 291 400
2 (52 pgs.)-The Golden Arrow begins (origin) 15 30 45 94 147 200
3-6: 6-Last Golden Arrow 15 30 45 90 140 190
7-Golden Arrow becomes Swift Arrow; origin of his shield
15 30 45 94 147 200
8-Origin Swift Arrow 17 34 51 98 154 210
9,10 11 22 33 64 90 115
11-14 10 20 30 54 72 90
15-Golden Arrow origin-r from #2, changing name to Swift Arrow
10 20 30 58 79 100
16-20,22-26: 23-Apache Kid app. 9 18 27 50 65 80
21-3-D effect-c 15 30 45 90 140 190

LONERS, THE
Marvel Comics: June, 2007 - No. 6, Jan, 2008 ($2.99, limited series)
1-6-Cebulski-s/Moline-a/Pearson-c; Lightspeed, Spider-Woman, Ricochet app. 3.00
...: The Secret Lives of Super Heroes TPB (2008, $14.99) r/#1-6; sketch pages 15.00

LONE WOLF AND CUB
First Comics: May, 1987 - No. 45, Apr, 1991 ($1.95-$3.25, B&W, deluxe size)
1-Frank Miller-c & intro.; reprints manga series by Koike & Kojima
1 2 3 6 8 10
1-2nd print, 3rd print, 2-2nd print 3.25
2-12: 6-72 pgs. origin issue 5.50
13-38,40: 40-Ploog-c 4.00
39-($5.95, 120 pgs.)-Ploog-c 6.50
41-44: 41-($3.95, 84 pgs.)-Ploog-c. 42-Ploog-c 6.00
45-Last issue; low print 1 3 4 6 8 10
Deluxe Edition ($19.95, B&W) 20.00
NOTE: ***Sienkiewicz*** *c-13-24.* ***Matt Wagner*** *c-25-30.*

LONE WOLF AND CUB (Trade paperbacks)
Dark Horse Comics: Aug, 2000 - No. 28 ($9.95, B&W, 4" x 6", approx. 300 pgs.)
1-Collects First Comics reprint series; Frank Miller-c 18.00
1-(2nd printing) 12.00
1-(3rd-5th printings) 10.00
2,3-(1st printings) 12.00
2,3-(2nd printings) 10.00
4-28 10.00

LONE WOLF 2100 (Also see Reveal)
Dark Horse Comics: May, 2002 - No. 11, Dec, 2003 ($2.99, color)
1-New homage to Lone Wolf and Cub; Kennedy-s/Velasco-a 4.00
2-11 3.00
...: The Red File (1/03, $2.99) character and story background files 3.00
... Vol. 1 - Shadows on Saplings TPB (2003, $12.95, 6" x 9") r/#1-4 13.00
... Vol. 2 - The Language of Chaos TPB (2003, $12.95, 6" x 9") r/#5-8, Dirty Tricks short story from Reveal 13.00

LONG BOW (...Indian Boy)(See Indians & Jumbo Comics #141)
Fiction House Mag. (Real Adventures Publ.): 1951 - No. 9, Wint, 1952/53
1-Most covers by Maurice Whitman 17 34 51 98 154 210
2 11 22 33 60 83 105
3-9 10 20 30 54 72 90

LONG HOT SUMMER, THE
DC Comics (Milestone): Jul, 1995 - No. 3, Sept, 1995 ($2.95/$2.50, lim. series)
1-3: 1-($2.95-c). 2,3-($2.50-c) 3.00

LONG JOHN SILVER & THE PIRATES (Formerly Terry & the Pirates)
Charlton Comics: No. 30, Aug, 1956 - No. 32, March, 1957 (TV)
30-32: Whitman-c 10 20 30 54 72 90

LONGSHOT (Also see X-Men, 2nd Series #10)
Marvel Comics: Sept, 1985 - No. 6, Feb, 1986 (60¢, limited series)
1-6: 1-Art Adams/Whilce Portacio-c/a in all. 4-Spider-Man app. 6-Double size
1 2 3 4 5 7
Trade Paperback (1989, $16.95)-r/#1-6 17.00

LONGSHOT
Marvel Comics: Feb, 1998 ($3.99, one-shot)
1-DeMatteis-s/Zulli-a 4.00

LOOKING GLASS WARS: HATTER M
Image Comics (Desperado): Dec, 2005 - No. 4, Nov, 2006 ($3.99)
1-4-Templesmith-a/c 4.00

LOONEY TUNES (2nd Series) (TV)
Gold Key/Whitman: April, 1975 - No. 47, June, 1984
1-Reprints 3 6 9 20 30 40
2-10: 2,4-reprints 2 4 6 11 16 20
11-20: 16-reprints 2 4 6 8 11 14
21-30 1 2 3 5 7 9
31,32,36-42(2/82) 1 2 3 4 5 7
33-(8/80)-35 (Whitman pre-pack only, scarce) 3 6 9 16 23 30
43(4/82),44(6/83) (low distribution) 2 4 6 8 11 14
45-47 (All #90296 on-c; nd, nd code, pre-pack) 45(8/83), 46(3/84), 47(6/84)
3 6 9 14 19 24

LOONEY TUNES (3rd Series) (TV)
DC Comics: Apr, 1994 - Present ($1.50/$1.75/$1.95/$1.99/$2.25)
1-10,120: 1-Marvin Martian-c/sty; Bugs Bunny, Roadrunner, Daffy begin. 120-($2.95-C) 3.00
11-119,121-165: 23-34-($1.75-c). 35-43-($1.95-c). 44-Begin $1.99-c. 93-Begin $2.25-c. 100-Art by various incl. Kyle Baker, Marie Severin, Darwyn Cooke, Jill Thompson 2.50
...Back In Action Movie Adaptation (12/03, $3.95) photo-c 4.00

LOONEY TUNES AND MERRIE MELODIES COMICS ("Looney Tunes" #166(8/55) on)
(Also see Porky's Duck Hunt)
Dell Publishing Co.: 1941 - No. 246, July-Sept, 1962
1-Porky Pig, Bugs Bunny, Daffy Duck, Elmer Fudd, Mary Jane & Sniffles, Pat Patsy and Pete begin (1st comic book app. of each). Bugs Bunny story by Win Smith (early Mickey Mouse artist) 1075 2150 3225 8200 14,600 21,000
2 (11/41) 152 304 456 1330 2565 3800
3-Kandi the Cave Kid begins by Walt Kelly; also in #4-6,8,11,15
110 220 330 935 1793 2650
4-Kelly-a 110 220 330 935 1793 2650
5-Bugs Bunny The Super-Duper Rabbit story (1st funny animal super hero, 3/42; also see Coo Coo); Kelly-a 83 166 249 706 1353 2000
6,8-Kelly-a 64 128 192 544 1035 1525
7,9,10: 9-Painted-c. 10-Flag-c 50 100 150 406 766 1125
11,15-Kelly-a; 15-X-Mas-c 50 100 150 400 750 1100
12-14,16-19 39 78 117 300 563 825
20-25: Pat, Patsy & Pete by Walt Kelly in all. 20-War Bonds-c
32 64 96 250 468 685
26-30 25 50 75 185 343 500
31-40: 33-War Bonds-c. 39-X-Mas-c 20 40 60 148 274 400
41-50: 45-War Bonds-c 15 30 45 111 206 300
51-60 13 26 39 93 164 235
61-80 9 18 27 63 107 150
81-99: 87-X-Mas-c 8 16 24 54 90 125
100 8 16 24 58 97 135
101-120 7 14 21 45 73 100
121-150 6 12 18 39 62 85
151-200: 159-X-Mas-c 5 10 15 34 55 75

Lords of Avalon: Sword of Darkness #1 © Sherilyn Kenyon

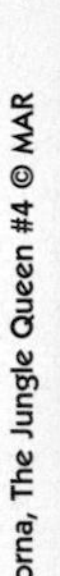
Lorna, The Jungle Queen #4 © MAR

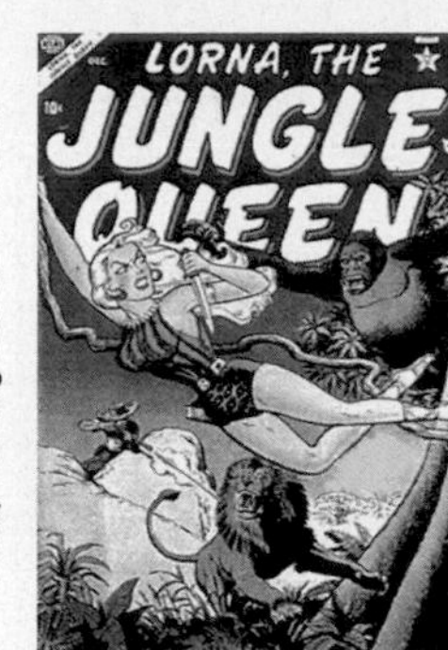

Love and Rockets V2 #1 © Fantagraphics

	GD 2.0	VG 4.0	FN 6.0	VF 8.0	VF/NM 9.0	NM- 9.2
201-240	5	10	15	32	51	70
241-246	5	10	15	34	55	75
LOONY SPORTS (Magazine)						
3-Strikes Publishing Co.: Spring, 1975 (68 pgs.)						
1-Sports satire	2	4	6	8	11	14
LOOSE CANNON (Also see Action Comics Annual #5 & Showcase '94 #5)						
DC Comics: June, 1995 - No. 4, Sept, 1995 ($1.75, limited series)						
1-4: Adam Pollina-a. 1-Superman app.						2.50
LOOY DOT DOPE						
United Features Syndicate: No. 13, 1939						
Single Series 13	30	60	90	174	280	385
LORD JIM (See Movie Comics)						
LORD PUMPKIN						
Malibu Comics (Ultraverse): Oct, 1994 ($2.50, one-shot)						
0-Two covers						2.50
LORD PUMPKIN/NECROMANTRA						
Malibu Comics (Ultraverse): Apr, 1995 - No. 4, July, 1995 ($2.95, limited series, flip book)						
1-4						3.00
LORDS OF AVALON: SWORD OF DARKNESS						
Marvel Comics: Apr, 2000 - No. 6, Sept, 2006 ($3.99/$2.99, limited series)						
1-($3.99)-Adaptation of Sherrilyn Kenyon's Arthurian fantasy; Ohtsuka-a/c						4.00
2-6-($2.99)						3.00
HC (2008, $19.99) r/#1-6; two covers						20.00
LORNA THE JUNGLE GIRL (...Jungle Queen #1-5)						
Atlas Comics (NPI 1/OMC 2-11/NPI 12-26): July, 1953 - No. 26, Aug, 1957						
1-Origin & 1st app.	40	80	120	235	380	525
2-Intro. & 1st app. Greg Knight	20	40	60	115	183	250
3-5	17	34	51	98	154	210
6-11: 11-Last pre-code (1/55)	15	30	45	84	127	170
12-17,19-26: 14-Colletta & Maneely-c	14	28	42	76	108	140
18-Williamson/Colletta-c	14	28	42	80	115	150
NOTE: *Brodsky c-1-3, 5, 9. Everett c-21, 23-26. Heath c-6, 7. Maneely c-12, 15. Romita a-20, 22, 24, 26. Shores a-14-16, 24, 26; c-11, 13, 16. Tuska a-6.*						
LOSERS						
DC Comics (Vertigo): Aug, 2003 - No. 32, Mar, 2006 ($2.95/$2.99)						
1-Andy Diggle-s/Jock-a						4.00
2-32: 15-Bagged with Sky Captain CD. 20-Oliver-a. 27-Wilson-a						3.00
...: Ante Up TPB (2004, $9.95) r/#1-6						10.00
...: Close Quarters TPB (2005, $14.99) r/#20-25						15.00
...: Double Down TPB (2004, $12.95) r/#7-12						13.00
...: Endgame TPB (2006, $14.99) r/#26-32						15.00
...: Trifecta TPB (2005, $14.99) r/#13-19						15.00
LOSERS SPECIAL (See Our Fighting Forces #123)(Also see G.I. Combat & Our Fighting Forces)						
DC Comics: Sept, 1985 ($1.25, one-shot)						
1-Capt. Storm, Gunner & Sarge; Crisis x-over						5.00
LOST, THE						
Chaos! Comics: Dec, 1997 - No. 3 ($2.95, B&W, unfinished limited series)						
1-3-Andreyko-script: 1-Russell back-c						3.00
LOST BOYS: REIGN OF FROGS (Based on the 1987 vampire movie)						
DC Comics (WildStorm): Jul, 2008 - No. 4 ($3.50, limited series)						
1-3-Rodionoff-s/Gomez-a; Edgar Frog app.						3.50
LOST CONTINENT						
Eclipse Int'l: Sept, 1990 - No. 6, 1991 ($3.50, B&W, squarebound, 60 pgs.)						
1-6: Japanese story translated to English						3.50
LOST IN SPACE (Movie)						
Dark Horse Comics: Apr, 1998 - No. 3, July, 1998 ($2.95, limited series)						
1-3-Continuation of 1998 movie; Erskine-c						3.00
LOST IN SPACE (TV)(Also see Space Family Robinson)						
Innovation Publishing: Aug, 1991 - No. 12, Jan, 1993 ($2.50, limited series)						
1-12: Bill Mumy (Will Robinson) scripts in #1-9. 9-Perez-c						3.00
1,2-Special Ed.; r/#1,2 plus new art & new-c						3.00
Annual 1,2 (1991, 1992, $2.95, 52 pgs.)						3.00
...: Project Robinson (11/93, $2.50) 1st & only part of intended series						3.00
LOST IN SPACE: VOYAGE TO THE BOTTOM OF THE SOUL						

	GD 2.0	VG 4.0	FN 6.0	VF 8.0	VF/NM 9.0	NM- 9.2
Innovation Publishing: No. 13, Aug, 1993 - No. 18, 1994 ($2.50, limited series)						
13(V1#1, $2.95)-Embossed silver logo edition; Bill Mumy scripts begin; painted-c						3.00
13(V1#1, $4.95)-Embossed gold logo edition bagged w/poster						5.00
14-18: Painted-c						3.00
NOTE: *Originally intended to be a 12 issue limited series.*						
LOST ONES, THE						
Image Comics: Mar, 2000 ($2.95)						
1-Ken Penders-s/a						3.00
LOST PLANET						
Eclipse Comics: 5/87 - No. 5, 2/88; No. 6, 3/89 (Mini-series, Baxter paper)						
1-6-Bo Hampton-c/a in all						2.50
LOST WAGON TRAIN, THE (See Zane Grey Four Color 583)						
LOST WORLD, THE						
Dell Publishing Co.: No. 1145, Nov-Jan, 1960-61						
Four Color 1145-Movie, Gil Kane-a, photo-c; 1pg. Conan Doyle biography by Torres	9	18	27	64	110	155
LOST WORLD, THE (See Jurassic Park)						
Topps Comics: May, 1997 - No. 4, Aug, 1997 ($2.95, limited series)						
1-4-Movie adaption						3.00
LOST WORLDS (Weird Tales of the Past and Future)						
Standard Comics: No. 5, Oct, 1952 - No. 6, Dec, 1952						
5- "Alice in Terrorland" by Alex Toth; J. Katz-a	43	86	129	267	446	625
6-Toth-a	36	72	108	212	341	470
LOTS 'O' FUN COMICS						
Robert Allen Co.: 1940's? (5¢, heavy stock, blue covers)						
nn-Contents can vary; Felix, Planet Comics known; contents would determine value. Similar to Up-To-Date Comics. Remainders - re-packaged.						
LOU GEHRIG (See The Pride of the Yankees)						
LOVE ADVENTURES (Actual Confessions #13)						
Marvel (IPS)/Atlas Comics (MPI): Oct, 1949; No. 2, Jan, 1950; No. 3, Feb, 1951 - No. 12, Aug, 1952						
1-Photo-c	17	34	51	98	154	210
2-Powell-a; Tyrone Power, Gene Tierney photo-c	15	30	45	84	127	170
3-8,10-12: 8-Robinson-a	10	20	30	54	72	90
9-Everett-a	10	20	30	56	76	95
LOVE AND MARRIAGE						
Superior Comics Ltd. (Canada): Mar, 1952 - No. 16, Sept, 1954						
1	14	28	42	82	121	160
2	9	18	27	47	61	75
3-10	8	16	24	42	54	65
11-16	7	14	21	37	46	55
I.W. Reprint #1,2,8,11,14: 8-r/Love and Marriage #3. 11-r/Love and Marriage #11	2	4	6	9	13	16
Super Reprint #10('63),15,17('64):15-Love and Marriage #?	2	4	6	9	13	16
NOTE: *All issues have **Kamenish** art.*						
LOVE AND ROCKETS						
Fantagraphics Books: July, 1982 - No. 50, May, 1996 ($2.95/$2.50/$4.95, B&W, mature)						
1-B&W-c (6/82, $2.95; small size, publ. by Hernandez Bros.)(800 printed)	6	12	18	39	62	85
1 (Fall, '82; color-c)	4	8	12	22	34	45
1-2nd & 3rd printing, 2-11,29-31: 2nd printings						3.00
2	2	4	6	10	14	18
3-10	1	3	4	6	8	10
11-49: 30 ($2.95, 52 pgs.)						5.00
50-($4.95)						6.00
LOVE AND ROCKETS (Volume 2)						
Fantagraphics Books: Spring, 2001 - Present ($3.95-$7.99, B&W, mature)						
1-9-Gilbert, Jaime and Mario Hernandez-s/a						4.00
10-($5.95)						6.00
11-19-($4.50)						4.50
20-($7.99)						8.00
LOVE AND ROMANCE						
Charlton Comics: Sept, 1971 - No. 24, Sept, 1975						
1	3	6	9	17	25	32
2-10: 6-David Cassidy pin-up; grey-tone cover	2	4	6	9	13	16

Love Confessions #47 © QUA

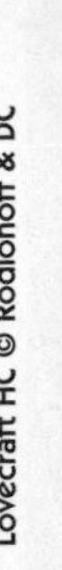

Lovecraft HC © Rodionoff & DC

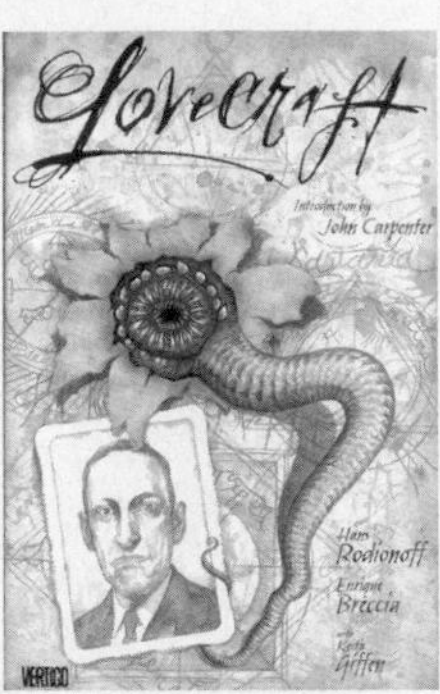

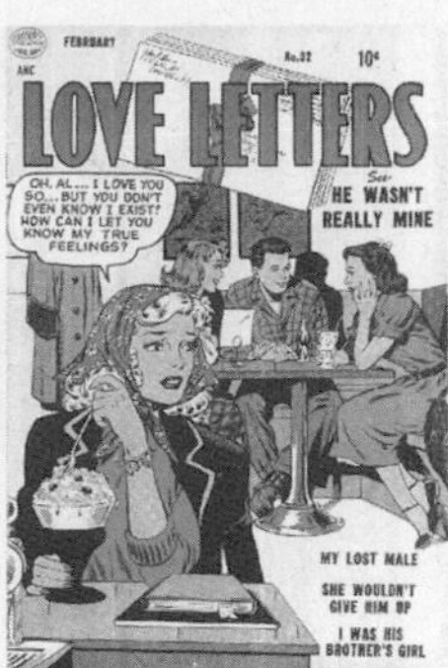

Love Letters #32 © QUA

	GD 2.0	VG 4.0	FN 6.0	VF 8.0	VF/NM 9.0	NM- 9.2
11,13-24	1	3	4	6	8	10
12-Susan Dey poster	2	4	6	9	12	15

LOVE AT FIRST SIGHT
Ace Magazines (RAR Publ. Co./Periodical House): Oct, 1949 - No. 43, Nov, 1956 (Photo-c: 18-42)

	GD 2.0	VG 4.0	FN 6.0	VF 8.0	VF/NM 9.0	NM- 9.2
1-Painted-c	15	30	45	90	140	190
2-Painted-c	10	20	30	56	76	95
3-10: 4,7-Painted-c	9	18	27	47	61	75
11-20	8	16	24	44	57	70
21-33: 33-Last pre-code	8	16	24	42	54	65
34-43	8	16	24	40	50	60

LOVE BUG, THE (See Movie Comics)

LOVEBUNNY AND MR. HELL
Devil's Due Publ./Image Comics: 2002 - 2004 ($2.95, B&W, one-shots)

	GD 2.0	VG 4.0	FN 6.0	VF 8.0	VF/NM 9.0	NM- 9.2
1-Tim Seeley-s						3.00
...: A Day in the Lovelife (Image, 2003) Blaylock-a						3.00
...: Savage Love (Image, 2003) Seeley-s/a; Savage Dragon app.; Seeley & Larsen-c						3.00
TPB (4/04, $9.95, digest-sized) reprints						10.00

LOVE CLASSICS
A Lover's Magazine/Marvel: Nov, 1949 - No. 2, Feb, 1950 (Photo-c, 52 pgs.)

	GD 2.0	VG 4.0	FN 6.0	VF 8.0	VF/NM 9.0	NM- 9.2
1,2: 2-Virginia Mayo photo-c; 30 pg. story "I Turned Into a Small-Town Flirt"	15	30	45	86	133	180

LOVE CONFESSIONS
Quality Comics: Oct, 1949 - No. 54, Dec, 1956 (Photo-c: 3,4,6,7,9,11-18,21,24,25)

	GD 2.0	VG 4.0	FN 6.0	VF 8.0	VF/NM 9.0	NM- 9.2
1-Ward-c/a, 9 pgs; Gustavson-a	31	62	93	181	291	400
2-Gustavson-a; Ward-c	15	30	45	88	137	185
3	11	22	33	60	83	105
4-Crandall-a	12	24	36	67	94	120
5-Ward-a, 7 pgs.	14	28	42	76	108	140
6,7,9,11-13,15,16,18: 7-Van Johnson photo-c. 8-Robert Mitchum & Jane Russell photo-c	9	18	27	50	65	80
8,10-Ward-a (2 stories in #10)	14	28	42	76	108	140
14,17,19,22-Ward-a; 17-Faith Domerque photo-c	13	26	39	72	101	130
20-Ward-a(2)	14	28	42	76	108	140
21,23-28,30-38,40-42: Last precode, 4/55	8	16	24	42	54	65
29-Ward-a	12	24	36	67	94	120
39,53-Matt Baker-a	10	20	30	58	79	100
43,44,46,47,50-52,54: 47-Ward-c?	8	16	24	40	50	60
45,48-Ward-a	9	18	27	50	65	80
49-Baker-c/a	12	24	36	69	97	125

LOVECRAFT
DC Comics: 2003 (graphic novel)

	GD 2.0	VG 4.0	FN 6.0	VF 8.0	VF/NM 9.0	NM- 9.2
Hardcover ($24.95) Rodionoff & Giffen-s/Breccia-a; intro. by John Carpenter						25.00
Softcover ($17.95)						18.00

LOVE DIARY
Our Publishing Co./Toytown/Patches: July, 1949 - No. 48, Oct, 1955 (Photo-c: 1-24,27-29) (52 pgs. #1-11?)

	GD 2.0	VG 4.0	FN 6.0	VF 8.0	VF/NM 9.0	NM- 9.2
1-Krigstein-a	20	40	60	115	183	250
2,3-Krigstein & Mort Leav-a in each	14	28	42	80	115	150
4-8	10	20	30	54	72	90
9,10-Everett-a	10	20	30	56	76	95
11-15,17-20	9	18	27	47	61	75
16- Mort Leav-a, 3 pg. Baker-sty. Leav-a	9	18	27	50	65	80
21-30,32-48: 45-Leav-a. 47-Last precode(12/54)	8	16	24	44	57	70
31-John Buscema headlights-c	9	18	27	52	69	85

LOVE DIARY (Diary Loves #2 on; title change due to previously published title)
Quality Comics Group: Sept, 1949

	GD 2.0	VG 4.0	FN 6.0	VF 8.0	VF/NM 9.0	NM- 9.2
1-Ward-c/a, 9 pgs.	31	62	93	181	291	400

LOVE DIARY
Charlton Comics: July, 1958 - No. 102, Dec, 1976

	GD 2.0	VG 4.0	FN 6.0	VF 8.0	VF/NM 9.0	NM- 9.2
1	10	20	30	56	76	95
2	7	14	21	35	43	50
3-5,7-10: 10-Photo-c	6	12	18	28	34	40
6-Torres-a	6	12	18	31	38	45
11-20: 20-Photo-c	3	6	9	16	23	30
21-40	3	6	9	14	19	24
41-60	2	4	6	10	14	18
61-80,100-102: 79-David Cassidy pin-up	2	4	6	8	11	14
81-99: 82-Partridge Family poster. 85-Danny poster	1	3	4	6	8	10

LOVE DOCTOR (See Dr. Anthony King...)

LOVE DRAMAS (True Secrets No. 3 on?)
Marvel Comics (IPS): Oct, 1949 - No. 2, Jan, 1950

	GD 2.0	VG 4.0	FN 6.0	VF 8.0	VF/NM 9.0	NM- 9.2
1-Jack Kamen-a; photo-c	18	36	54	107	169	230
2-Photo-c	14	28	42	78	112	145

LOVE EXPERIENCES (Challenge of the Unknown No. 6)
Ace Periodicals (A.A. Wyn/Periodical House): Oct, 1949 - No. 5, June, 1950; No. 6, Apr, 1951 - No. 38, June, 1956

	GD 2.0	VG 4.0	FN 6.0	VF 8.0	VF/NM 9.0	NM- 9.2
1-Painted-c	15	30	45	86	133	180
2	10	20	30	54	72	90
3-5: 5-Painted-c	9	18	27	47	61	75
6-10	8	16	24	44	57	70
11-30: 30-Last pre-code (2/55)	8	16	24	40	50	60
31-38: 38-Indicia date-6/56; c-date-8/56	7	14	21	35	43	50

NOTE: *Anne Brewster a-15. Photo c-4, 15-35, 38.*

LOVE FIGHTS (Also see Free Comic Book Day Edition in the Promotional Comics section)
Oni Press: June, 2003 - No. 12, Aug, 2004 ($2.99, B&W)

	GD 2.0	VG 4.0	FN 6.0	VF 8.0	VF/NM 9.0	NM- 9.2
1-12-Andi Watson-s/a						3.00
Vol. 1 TPB (4/04, $14.95, digest-size) r/#1-6						15.00

LOVE JOURNAL
Our Publishing Co.: No. 10, Oct, 1951 - No. 25, July, 1954

	GD 2.0	VG 4.0	FN 6.0	VF 8.0	VF/NM 9.0	NM- 9.2
10	13	26	39	72	101	130
11-15,17-25: 19-Mort Leav-a	9	18	27	47	61	75
16-Buscema headlight-c	9	18	27	52	69	85

LOVELAND
Mutual Mag./Eye Publ. (Marvel): Nov, 1949 - No. 2, Feb, 1950 (52 pgs.)

	GD 2.0	VG 4.0	FN 6.0	VF 8.0	VF/NM 9.0	NM- 9.2
1,2-Photo-c	13	26	39	72	101	130

LOVELESS
DC Comics: Dec, 2005 - No. 24, Jun, 2008 ($2.99)

	GD 2.0	VG 4.0	FN 6.0	VF 8.0	VF/NM 9.0	NM- 9.2
1-24: 1-Azzarello-s/Frusin-a. 6-8,15,22,23,24-Zezelj-a. 11,12,16-21-Dell'Edera-a						3.00
...: A Kin of Homecoming TPB (2006, $9.99) r/#1-5						10.00
...: Thicker Than Blackwater TPB (2007, $14.99) r/#6-12						15.00

LOVE LESSONS
Harvey Comics/Key Publ. No. 5: Oct, 1949 - No. 5, June, 1950

	GD 2.0	VG 4.0	FN 6.0	VF 8.0	VF/NM 9.0	NM- 9.2
1-Metallic silver-c printed over the cancelled covers of Love Letters #1; indicia title is "Love Letters"	15	30	45	85	130	175
2-Powell-a; photo-c	9	18	27	52	69	85
3-5: 3,4-Photo-c	8	16	24	42	54	65

LOVE LETTERS (10/49, Harvey; advertised but never published; covers were printed before cancellation and were used as the cover to Love Lessons #1)

LOVE LETTERS (Love Secrets No. 32 on)
Quality Comics: 11/49 - #6, 9/50; #7, 3/51 - #31, 6/53; #32, 2/54 - #51, 12/56

	GD 2.0	VG 4.0	FN 6.0	VF 8.0	VF/NM 9.0	NM- 9.2
1-Ward-c, Gustavson-a	25	50	75	145	233	320
2-Ward-c, Gustavson-a	20	40	60	117	186	255
3-Gustavson-a	15	30	45	83	124	165
4-Ward-a, 9 pgs.; photo-c	19	38	57	109	172	235
5-8,10	10	20	30	56	76	95
9-One pg. Ward "Be Popular with the Opposite Sex"; Robert Mitchum photo-c	11	22	33	62	86	110
11-Ward-r/Broadway Romances #2 & retitled	11	22	33	62	86	110
12-15,18-20	9	18	27	50	65	80
16,17-Ward-a; 16-Anthony Quinn photo-c. 17-Jane Russell photo-c	14	28	42	81	118	155
21-29	9	18	27	47	61	75
30,31(6/53)-Ward-a	10	20	30	56	76	95
32(2/54)-39: 37-Ward-a. 38-Crandall-a. 39-Last precode (4/55)	8	16	24	42	54	65
40-48	8	16	24	40	50	60
49,50-Baker-a	12	24	36	67	94	120
51-Baker-c	11	22	33	62	86	110

NOTE: *Photo-c on most 3-28.*

LOVE LIFE
P. L. Publishing Co.: Nov, 1951

	GD 2.0	VG 4.0	FN 6.0	VF 8.0	VF/NM 9.0	NM- 9.2
1	10	20	30	56	76	95

LOVELORN (Confessions of the Lovelorn #52 on)
American Comics Group (Michel Publ./Regis Publ.): Aug-Sept, 1949 - No. 51, July, 1954 (No. 1-26: 52 pgs.)

	GD 2.0	VG 4.0	FN 6.0	VF 8.0	VF/NM 9.0	NM- 9.2
1	15	30	45	90	140	190

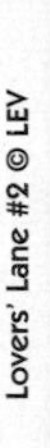

Lovers' Lane #2 © LEV

Love Secrets #1 © MAR

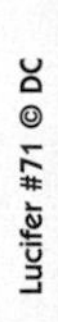

Lucifer #71 © DC

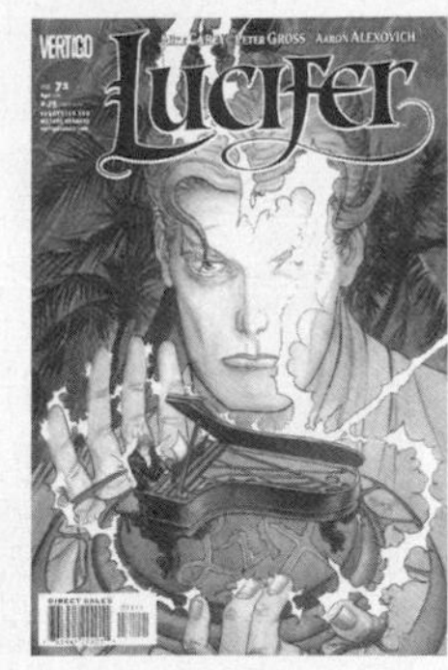

	GD 2.0	VG 4.0	FN 6.0	VF 8.0	VF/NM 9.0	NM- 9.2
2	10	20	30	56	76	95
3-10	9	18	27	47	61	75
11-20,22-48: 18-Drucker-a(2 pgs.). 46-Lazarus-a	8	16	24	40	50	60
21-Prostitution story	9	18	27	50	65	80
49-51-Has 3-D effect-c/stories	15	30	45	90	140	190

LOVE MEMORIES
Fawcett Publications: 1949 (no month) - No. 4, July, 1950 (All photo-c)

	GD 2.0	VG 4.0	FN 6.0	VF 8.0	VF/NM 9.0	NM- 9.2
1	15	30	45	88	137	185
2-4: 2-(Win/49-50)	10	20	30	56	76	95

LOVE ME TENDERLOIN: A CAL McDONALD MYSTERY
Dark Horse Comics: Jan, 2004 ($2.99, one-shot)

	GD 2.0	VG 4.0	FN 6.0	VF 8.0	VF/NM 9.0	NM- 9.2
1-Niles-s/Templesmith-a/c						3.00

LOVE MYSTERY
Fawcett Publications: June, 1950 - No. 3, Oct, 1950 (All photo-c)

	GD 2.0	VG 4.0	FN 6.0	VF 8.0	VF/NM 9.0	NM- 9.2
1-George Evans-a	22	44	66	127	204	280
2,3-Evans-a. 3-Powell-a	16	32	48	92	144	195

LOVE PROBLEMS (See Fox Giants)

LOVE PROBLEMS AND ADVICE ILLUSTRATED (see True Love...)

LOVE ROMANCES (Formerly Ideal #5)
Timely/Marvel/Atlas(TCI No. 7-71/Male No. 72-106): No. 6, May, 1949 - No. 106, July, 1963

	GD 2.0	VG 4.0	FN 6.0	VF 8.0	VF/NM 9.0	NM- 9.2
6-Photo-c	17	34	51	98	154	210
7-Photo-c; Kamen-a	11	22	33	64	90	115
8-Kubert-a; photo-c	11	22	33	64	90	115
9-20: 9-12-Photo-c	10	20	30	58	79	100
21,24-Krigstein-a	11	22	33	60	83	105
22,23,25-35,37,39,40	10	20	30	56	76	95
36,38-Krigstein-a	10	20	30	58	79	100
41-44,46,47: Last precode (2/55)	10	20	30	54	72	90
45,57-Matt Baker-a	11	22	33	64	90	115
48,50-52,54-56,58-74	5	10	15	34	55	75
49,53-Toth-a, 6 & ? pgs.	6	12	18	39	62	85
75,77,82-Matt Baker-a	7	14	21	47	76	105
76,78-81,86,88-90,92-95: 80-Heath-c. 95-Last 10¢-c?	5	10	15	32	51	70
83,84,87,91-Kirby-c. 83-Severin-a	6	12	18	43	69	95
85,96,97,99-106-Kirby-c/a. 97-10¢ cover price blacked out, 12¢ printed on cover	7	14	21	50	83	115
98-Kirby-c/a	8	16	24	52	86	120

NOTE: ***Anne Brewster** a-67, 72. **Colletta** a-37, 40, 42, 44, 67(2); c-42, 44, 49, 54, 80. **Everett** c-70. **Hartley** c-20, 21, 30, 31. **Heath** a-87. **Kirby** c-80, 85, 88. **Robinson** a-29.*

LOVERS (Formerly Blonde Phantom)
Marvel Comics No. 23,24/Atlas No. 25 on (ANC): No. 23, May, 1949 - No. 86, Aug?, 1957

	GD 2.0	VG 4.0	FN 6.0	VF 8.0	VF/NM 9.0	NM- 9.2
23-Photo-c begin, end #29	18	36	54	103	162	220
24-Toth-*ish* plus Robinson-a	11	22	33	62	86	110
25,30-Kubert-a; 7, 10 pgs.	11	22	33	64	90	115
26-29,31-36,39,40: 35-Maneely-c	10	20	30	56	76	95
37,38-Krigstein-a	11	22	33	62	86	110
41-Everett-a(2)	11	22	33	62	86	110
42,44-65: 65-Last pre-code (1/55)	9	18	27	47	61	75
43-Frazetta 1 pg. ad	9	18	27	50	65	80
66,68-80,82-86	8	16	24	44	57	70
67-Toth-a	9	18	27	50	65	80
81-Baker-a	9	18	27	50	65	80

NOTE: ***Anne Brewster** a-86. **Colletta** a-54, 59, 62, 64, 65, 69, 85; c-61, 64, 65, 75. **Hartley** c-37, 53, 54. **Heath** a-61. **Maneely** a-57. **Powell** a-27, 30. **Robinson** a-42, 54, 56.*

LOVERS' LANE
Lev Gleason Publications: Oct, 1949 - No. 41, June, 1954 (No. 1-18: 52 pgs.)

	GD 2.0	VG 4.0	FN 6.0	VF 8.0	VF/NM 9.0	NM- 9.2
1-Biro-c	14	28	42	82	121	160
2-Biro-c	9	18	27	52	69	85
3-20: 3,4-Painted-c. 20-Frazetta 1 pg. ad	9	18	27	47	61	75
21-38,40,41	8	16	24	40	50	60
39-Story narrated by Frank Sinatra	9	18	27	52	69	85

NOTE: ***Briefer** a-6, 13, 21. **Esposito** a-5. **Fuje** a-4, 16; c-many. **Guardineer** a-1, 3. **Kinstler** c-41. **Sparling** a-3. **Tuska** a-6. Painted c-3-18. Photo c-19-22, 26-28.*

LOVE SCANDALS
Quality Comics: Feb, 1950 - No. 5, Oct, 1950 (Photo-c #2-5) (All 52 pgs.)

	GD 2.0	VG 4.0	FN 6.0	VF 8.0	VF/NM 9.0	NM- 9.2
1-Ward-c/a, 9 pgs.	26	52	78	152	244	335
2,3: 2-Gustavson-a	13	26	39	74	105	135
4-Ward-a, 18 pgs; Gil Fox-a	20	40	60	118	189	260
5-C. Cuidera-a; tomboy story "I Hated Being a Woman"	14	28	42	76	108	140

LOVE SECRETS
Marvel Comics(IPC): Oct, 1949 - No. 2, Jan, 1950 (52 pgs., photo-c)

	GD 2.0	VG 4.0	FN 6.0	VF 8.0	VF/NM 9.0	NM- 9.2
1	15	30	45	90	140	190
2	11	22	33	62	86	110

LOVE SECRETS (Formerly Love Letters #31)
Quality Comics Group: No. 32, Aug, 1953 - No. 56, Dec, 1956

	GD 2.0	VG 4.0	FN 6.0	VF 8.0	VF/NM 9.0	NM- 9.2
32	12	24	36	69	97	125
33,35-39	9	18	27	47	61	75
34-Ward-a	12	24	36	69	97	125
40-Matt Baker-c	11	22	33	62	86	110
41-43: 43-Last precode (3/55)	9	18	27	47	61	75
44,47-50,53,54	8	16	24	40	50	60
45-Ward-a	10	20	30	56	76	95
46-Ward-a; Baker-a	11	22	33	62	86	110
51,52-Ward(r). 52-r/Love Confessions #17	9	18	27	47	61	75
55,56: 55-Baker-a. 56-Baker-c	10	20	30	56	76	95

LOVE STORIES (See Top Love Stories)

LOVE STORIES (Formerly Heart Throbs)
National Periodical Publ.: No. 147, Nov, 1972 - No. 152, Oct-Nov, 1973

	GD 2.0	VG 4.0	FN 6.0	VF 8.0	VF/NM 9.0	NM- 9.2
147-152	3	6	9	14	19	24

LOVE STORIES OF MARY WORTH (See Harvey Comics Hits #55 & Mary Worth)
Harvey Publications: Sept, 1949 - No. 5, May, 1950

	GD 2.0	VG 4.0	FN 6.0	VF 8.0	VF/NM 9.0	NM- 9.2
1-1940's newspaper reprints-#1-4	9	18	27	47	61	75
2-5: 3-Kamen/Baker-a?	6	12	18	31	38	45

LOVE TALES (Formerly The Human Torch #35)
Marvel/Atlas Comics (ZPC No. 36-50/MMC No. 67-75): No. 36, 5/49 - No. 58, 8/52; No. 59, date? - No. 75, Sept, 1957

	GD 2.0	VG 4.0	FN 6.0	VF 8.0	VF/NM 9.0	NM- 9.2
36-Photo-c	16	32	48	94	147	200
37	10	20	30	56	79	100
38-44,46-50: 39-41-Photo-c	10	20	30	54	72	90
45,51,52,69: 45-Powell-a. 51,69-Everett-a. 52-Krigstein-a	10	20	30	56	76	95
53-60: 60-Last pre-code (2/55)	8	16	24	44	57	70
61-68,70-75: 75-Brewster, Cameron, Colletta-a	8	16	24	42	54	65

LOVE THRILLS (See Fox Giants)

LOVE TRAILS (Western romance)
A Lover's Magazine (CDS)(Marvel): Dec, 1949 - No. 2, Mar, 1950 (52 pgs.)

	GD 2.0	VG 4.0	FN 6.0	VF 8.0	VF/NM 9.0	NM- 9.2
1,2: 1-Photo-c	15	30	45	85	130	175

LOWELL THOMAS' HIGH ADVENTURE (See High Adventure)

LT. (See Lieutenant)

LUCIFER (See The Sandman #4)
DC Comics (Vertigo): Jun, 2000 - No. 75, Aug, 2006 ($2.50/$2.75)

	GD 2.0	VG 4.0	FN 6.0	VF 8.0	VF/NM 9.0	NM- 9.2
1-Carey-s/Weston-a/Fegredo-c						8.00
2,3-Carey-s/Weston-a/Fegredo-c						5.00
4-10: 4-Pleece-a. 5-Gross-a						4.00
11-49,51-73: 16-Moeller-c begin. 25,26-Death app. 45-Naifeh-a. 53-Kaluta-c begin. 62-Doran-a. 63-Begin $2.75-c						2.75
50-($3.50) P. Craig Russell-a; Mazikeen app.						3.50
74-($2.99) Kaluta-c						3.00
75-($3.99) Last issue; Lucifer's origins retold; Morpheus app.; Gross-a/Moeller-c						4.00
Preview-16 pg. flip book w/Swamp Thing Preview						3.00
...: A Dalliance With the Damned TPB ('02, $14.95) r/#14-20						15.00
...: Children and Monsters TPB ('01, $17.95) r/#5-13						18.00
...: Crux TPB (2006, $14.99) r/#55-61						15.00
...: Devil in the Gateway TPB ('01, $14.95) r/#1-4 & Sandman Presents:..#1-3						15.00
...: Evensong TPB (2007, $14.99) r/#70-75 & Lucifer: Nirvana one-shot						15.00
...: Exodus TPB (2005, $14.95) r/#42-44,46-49						15.00
...: Inferno TPB (2003, $14.95) r/#29-35						15.00
...: Mansions of the Silence TPB (2004, $14.95) r/#36-41						15.00
...: Morningstar TPB (2006, $14.99) r/#62-69						15.00
...: Nirvana (2002, $5.95) Carey-s/Muth-painted-c/a; Daniel app.						6.00
...: The Divine Comedy TPB (2003, $17.95) r/#21-28						18.00
...: The Wolf Beneath the Tree TPB (2005, $14.99) r/#45,50-54						15.00

LUCIFER'S HAMMER (Larry Niven & Jerry Pournelle's...)
Innovation Publishing: Nov, 1993 - No. 6, 1994 ($2.50, painted, limited series)

	GD 2.0	VG 4.0	FN 6.0	VF 8.0	VF/NM 9.0	NM- 9.2
1-6: Adaptatin of novel, painted-c & art						2.50

Lucky Duck #6 © STD

The Lucy Show #1 © Desilu

Machine Man 2020 #2 © MAR

	GD 2.0	VG 4.0	FN 6.0	VF 8.0	VF/NM 9.0	NM- 9.2

LUCKY COMICS
Consolidated Magazines: Jan, 1944; No. 2, Sum, 1945 - No. 5, Sum, 1946

	GD	VG	FN	VF	VF/NM	NM-
1-Lucky Starr & Bobbie begin	22	44	66	127	204	280
2-5: 5-Devil-c by Walter Johnson	14	28	42	78	112	145

LUCKY DUCK
Standard Comics (Literary Ent.): No. 5, Jan, 1953 - No. 8, Sept, 1953

	GD	VG	FN	VF	VF/NM	NM-
5-Funny animal; Irving Spector-a	11	22	33	60	83	105
6-8-Irving Spector-a	10	20	30	54	72	90

NOTE: *Harvey Kurtzman tried to hire Spector for Mad #1.*

LUCKY "7" COMICS
Howard Publishers Ltd.: 1944 (No date listed)

	GD	VG	FN	VF	VF/NM	NM-
1-Pioneer, Sir Gallagher, Dick Royce, Congo Raider, Punch Powers; bondage-c	40	80	120	235	380	525

LUCKY STAR (Western)
Nation Wide Publ. Co.: 1950 - No. 7, 1951; No. 8, 1953 - No. 14, 1955 (5x7-1/4"; full color, 5¢)

	GD	VG	FN	VF	VF/NM	NM-
nn (#1)-(5¢, 52 pgs.)-Davis-a	18	36	54	105	165	225
2,3-(5¢, 52 pgs.)-Davis-a	12	24	36	67	94	120
4-7-(5¢, 52 pgs.)-Davis-a	11	22	33	60	83	105
8-14-(36 pgs.)(Exist?)	9	18	27	50	65	80
Given away with Lucky Star Western Wear by the Juvenile Mfg. Co.	7	14	21	35	43	50

LUCY SHOW, THE (TV) (Also see I Love Lucy)
Gold Key: June, 1963 - No. 5, June, 1964 (Photo-c: 1,2)

	GD	VG	FN	VF	VF/NM	NM-
1	12	24	36	87	156	225
2	7	14	21	49	80	110
3-5: Photo back c-1,2,4,5	6	12	18	43	69	95

LUCY, THE REAL GONE GAL (Meet Miss Pepper #5 on)
St. John Publishing Co.: June, 1953 - No. 4, Dec, 1953

	GD	VG	FN	VF	VF/NM	NM-
1-Negligee panels	14	28	42	82	121	160
2	9	18	27	50	65	80
3,4: 3-Drucker-a	8	16	24	44	57	70

LUDWIG BEMELMAN'S MADELEINE & GENEVIEVE
Dell Publishing Co.: No. 796, May, 1957

	GD	VG	FN	VF	VF/NM	NM-
Four Color 796	4	8	12	24	37	50

LUDWIG VON DRAKE (TV)(Disney)(See Walt Disney's C&S #256)
Dell Publishing Co.: Nov-Dec, 1961 - No. 4, June-Aug, 1962

	GD	VG	FN	VF	VF/NM	NM-
1	7	14	21	45	73	100
2-4	5	10	15	32	51	70

LUFTWAFFE: 1946 (Volume 1)
Antarctic Press: July, 1996 - No. 4, Jan, 1997 ($2.95, B&W, limited series)

	NM-
1-4-Ben Dunn & Ted Nomura-s/a, ...Special Ed.	3.00

LUFTWAFFE: 1946 (Volume 2)
Antarctic Press: Mar, 1997 - No. 18 ($2.95/$2.99, B&W, limited series)

	NM-
1-18: 8-Reviews Tigers of Terra series	3.00
Annual 1 (4/98, $2.95)-Reprints early Nomura pages	3.00
...Color Special (4/98)	3.00
...Technical Manual 1,2 (2/98, 4/99)	4.00

LUGER
Eclipse Comics: Oct, 1986 - No. 3, Feb, 1987 ($1.75, miniseries, Baxter paper)

	NM-
1-3: Bruce Jones scripts; Yeates-c/a	2.50

LUKE CAGE (See Cage & Hero for Hire)

LUKE SHORT'S WESTERN STORIES
Dell Publishing Co.: No. 580, Aug, 1954 - No. 927, Aug, 1958

	GD	VG	FN	VF	VF/NM	NM-
Four Color 580(8/54), 651(9/55)-Kinstler-a	4	8	12	28	44	60
Four Color 739,771,807,848,875,927	4	8	12	26	41	55

LUNATIC FRINGE, THE
Innovation Publishing: July, 1989 - No. 2, 1989 ($1.75, deluxe format)

	NM-
1,2	2.50

LUNATICKLE (Magazine) (Satire)
Whitstone Publ.: Feb, 1956 - No. 2, Apr, 1956

	GD	VG	FN	VF	VF/NM	NM-
1,2-Kubert-a (scarce)	8	16	24	40	50	60

LUNATIK
Marvel Comics: Dec, 1995 - No. 3, Feb, 1996 ($1.95, limited series)

	NM-
1-3	2.50

LURKERS, THE
IDW Publ.: Oct, 2004 - No. 4, Jan, 2005 ($3.99)

	NM-
1-4-Niles-s/Casanova-a	4.00

LUST FOR LIFE
Slave Labor Graphics: Feb, 1997 - No. 4, Jan, 1998 ($2.95, B&W)

	NM-
1-4: 1-Jeff Levin-s/a	3.00

LYCANTHROPE LEO
Viz Communications: 1994 - No. 7($2.95, B&W, limited series, 44 pgs.)

	NM-
1-7	3.00

LYNCH (See Gen [13])
Image Comics (WildStorm Productions): May, 1997 ($2.50, one-shot)

	NM-
1-Helmut-c/app.	2.50

LYNCH MOB
Chaos! Comics: June, 1994 - No. 4, Sept, 1994 ($2.50, limited series)

	NM-
1-4	2.50
1-Special edition full foil-c	5.00

LYNDON B. JOHNSON
Dell Publishing Co.: Mar, 1965

	GD	VG	FN	VF	VF/NM	NM-
12-445-503-Photo-c	3	6	9	20	30	40

M
Eclipse Books: 1990 - No. 4, 1991 ($4.95, painted, 52 pgs.)

	NM-
1-Adapts movie; contains flexi-disc ($5.95)	6.00
2-4	5.00

MACE GRIFFIN BOUNTY HUNTER (Based on video game)
Image Comics (Top Cow): May, 2003 ($2.99, one-shot)

	NM-
1-Nocon-a	3.00

MACHINE, THE
Dark Horse Comics: Nov, 1994 - No. 4, Feb, 1995 ($2.50, limited series)

	NM-
1-4	2.50

MACHINE MAN (Also see 2001, A Space Odyssey)
Marvel Comics Group: Apr, 1978 - No. 9, Dec, 1978; No. 10, Aug, 1979 - No. 19, Feb, 1981

	GD	VG	FN	VF	VF/NM	NM-
1-Jack Kirby-c/a/scripts begin; end #9	2	4	6	11	16	20
2-9-Kirby-c/a/s. 9-(12/78)	1	3	4	6	8	10
10-17: 10-(8/79) Marv Wolfman scripts & Ditko-a begins						6.00
18-Wendigo, Alpha Flight-ties into X-Men #140	2	4	6	11	16	20
19-Intro/1st app. Jack O'Lantern (Macendale), later becomes 2nd Hobgoblin	2	4	6	9	13	16

NOTE: ***Austin** c-7i, 19i. **Buckler** c-17p, 18p. **Byrne** c-14p. **Ditko** a-10-19; c-10-13, 14i, 15, 16. **Kirby** a-1-9p; c-1-5, 7-9p. **Layton** c-7i. **Miller** c-19p. **Simonson** c-6.*

MACHINE MAN (Also see X-51)
Marvel Comics Group: Oct, 1984 - No. 4, Jan, 1985 (limited series)

	NM-
1-4-Barry Smith-c/a(i) & colors in all	4.00
TPB (1988, $6.95)-r/ #1-4; Barry Smith-c	7.00
.../Bastion '98 Annual ($2.99) wraparound-c	3.00

MACHINE MAN 2020
Marvel Comics: Aug, 1994 - Nov, 1994 ($2.00, 52 pgs., limited series)

	NM-
1-4: Reprints Machine Man limited series; Barry Windsor-Smith-c/i(r)	2.50

MACHINE TEEN
Marvel Comics: July, 2005 - No. 5, Nov, 2005 ($2.99, limited series)

	NM-
1-5-Sumerak-s/Hawthorne-a. 1-James Jean-c	3.00
...: History (2005, $7.99, digest) r/#1-5	8.00

MACK BOLAN: THE EXECUTIONER (Don Pendleton's...)
Innovation Publishing: July, 1993 ($2.50)

	NM-
1-3-($2.50)	2.50
1-($3.95)-Indestructible Cover Edition	4.00
1-($2.95)-Collector's Gold Edition; foil stamped	3.00
1-($3.50)-Double Cover Edition; red foil outer-c	3.50

MACKENZIE'S RAIDERS (Movie, TV)
Dell Publishing Co.: No. 1093, Apr-June, 1960

	GD	VG	FN	VF	VF/NM	NM-
Four Color 1093-Richard Carlson photo-c from TV show	6	12	18	43	69	95

MACROSS (Becomes Robotech: The Macross Saga #2 on)
Comico: Dec, 1984 ($1.50)(Low print run)

	GD	VG	FN	VF	VF/NM	NM-
1-Early manga app.	3	6	9	14	20	25

Mad #2 © E.C. Publ.

Mad #189 © E.C. Publ.

Madame Mirage #2 © Paul Dini & TCOW

MACROSS II
Viz Select Comics: 1992 - No. 10, 1993 ($2.75, B&W, limited series)

	GD 2.0	VG 4.0	FN 6.0	VF 8.0	VF/NM 9.0	NM- 9.2
1-10: Based on video series						2.75

MAD (Tales Calculated to Drive You...)
E. C. Comics (Educational Comics): Oct-Nov, 1952 - Present (No. 24-on are magazine format) (Kurtzman editor No. 1-28, Feldstein No. 29 - No. ?)

	GD 2.0	VG 4.0	FN 6.0	VF 8.0	VF/NM 9.0	NM- 9.2
1-Wood, Davis, Elder start as regulars	414	828	1242	3312	5281	7250
2-Dick Tracy cameo	109	218	327	872	1386	1900
3,4: 3-Stan Lee mentioned. 4-Reefer mention story "Flob Was a Slob" by Davis; Superman parody	76	152	228	608	967	1325
5-Low distr.; W.M. Gaines biog.	153	306	459	1224	1950	2675
6-11: 6-Popeye cameo. 7,8- "Hey Look" reprints by Kurtzman. 11-Wolverton-a; Davis story was-r/Crime Suspenstories #12 w/new Kurtzman dialogue	59	118	177	472	754	1035
12-15: 15,18-Pot Shot Pete-r by Kurtzman	47	94	141	376	601	825
16-23(5/55): 18-Alice in Wonderland by Jack Davis. 21-1st app. Alfred E. Neuman on-c in fake ad. 22-All by Elder plus photo-montages by Kurtzman. 23-Special cancel announcement	40	80	120	320	510	700
24(7/55)-1st magazine issue (25¢); Kurtzman logo & border on-c; 1st "What? Me Worry?" on-c; 2nd printing exists	94	188	282	752	1201	1650
25-Jaffee starts as regular writer	44	88	132	352	564	775
26,27: 27-Jaffee starts as story artist; new logo	39	78	117	312	499	685
28-Last issue edited by Kurtzman; (three cover variations exist with different wording on contents banner on lower right of cover; value of each the same)	37	74	111	231	358	485
29-Kamen-a; Don Martin starts as regular; Feldstein editing begins	37	74	111	231	358	485
30-1st A. E. Neuman cover by Mingo; last Elder-a; Bob Clarke starts as regular; Disneyland & Elvis Presley spoof	57	114	171	356	546	735
31-Freas starts as regular; last Davis-a until #99	34	68	102	213	324	435
32,33: 32-Orlando, Drucker, Woodbridge start as regulars; Wood back-c. 33-Orlando back-c	29	58	87	181	276	370
34-Berg starts as regular	23	46	69	144	222	300
35-Mingo wraparound-c; Crandall-a	23	46	69	144	222	300
36-40 (7/58): 39-Beall-c	17	34	51	106	166	225
41-50: 42-Danny Kaye-s. 44-Xmas-c. 47-49-Sid Caesar-s. 48-Uncle Sam-c. 50 (10/59)-Peter Gunn-s	15	30	45	94	142	190
51-59: 52-Xmas-c; 77 Sunset Strip. 53-Rifleman-s. 54-Jaffee-a begins. 55-Sid Caesar-s. 59-Strips of Superman, Flash Gordon, Donald Duck & others. 59-Halloween/Headless Horseman-c	12	24	36	75	113	150
60 (1/61)-JFK/Nixon flip-c; 1st Spy vs. Spy by Prohias, who starts as regular	14	28	42	88	134	180
61-70: 64-Rickard starts as regular. 65-JFK-s. 66-JFK-c. 68-Xmas-c by Martin. 70-Route 66-s	9	18	27	56	83	110
71-75,77-80 (7/63): 72-10th Anniv. special; 1/3 pg. strips of Superman, Tarzan & others. 73-Bonanza-s. 74-Dr. Kildare-s	5	10	15	34	55	75
76-Aragonés starts as regular	6	12	18	39	62	85
81-85: 81-Superman strip. 82-Castro-c. 85-Lincoln-c	5	10	15	30	48	65
86-1st Fold-in; commonly creased back covers makes these and later issues scarcer in NM	6	12	18	37	59	80
87,88	5	10	15	34	55	75
89,90: 89-One strip by Walt Kelly; Frankenstein-c; Fugitive-s. 90-Ringo back-c by Frazetta; Beatles app.	6	12	18	37	59	80
91,94,96,100: 94-King Kong-c. 96-Man From U.N.C.L.E. 100-(1/66)-Anniversary issue	5	10	15	30	48	65
92,93,95,97-99: 99-Davis-a resumes	4	8	12	28	44	60
101,104,106,108,114,115,119,121: 101-Infinity-c; Voyage to the Bottom of the Sea-s. 104-Lost in Space-s. 106-Tarzan back-c by Frazetta; 2 pg. Batman by Aragonés. 108-Hogan's Heroes by Davis. 114-Rat Patrol-s. 115-Star Trek. 119-Invaders (TV). 121-Beatles-c; Ringo pin-up; flip-c of Sik-Teen; Flying Nun-s	3	6	9	21	32	42
102,103,107,109-113,116-118,120(7/68): 118-Beatles cameo	3	6	9	19	29	38
105-Batman-c/s, TV show parody (9/66)	4	8	12	24	37	50
122,124,126,128,129,131-134,136,137,139,140: 122-Ronald Reagan photo inside; Drucker & Mingo-c. 126-Family Affair-s. 128-Last Orlando. 131-Reagan photo back-c. 132-Xmas-c. 133-John Wayne/True Grit. 136-Room 222	3	6	9	16	22	28
123-Four different covers	3	6	9	16	23	30
125,127,130,135,138: 125-2001 Space Odyssey; Hitler back-c. 127-Mod Squad-c/s. 130-Land of the Giants-s; Torres begins as reg. 135-Easy Rider-c by Davis. 138-Snoopy-c; MASH-s	3	6	9	17	25	32
141-149,151-156,158-165,167-170: 141-Hawaii Five-0. 147-All in the Family-s. 153-Dirty Harry-s. 155-Godfather-c/s. 156-Columbo-s. 159-Clockwork Orange-c/s. 161-Tarzan-s. 164-Kung Fu (TV)-s. 165-James Bond-s; Dean Martin-c. 169-Drucker-c; McCloud-s. 170-Exorcist-s	3	6	9	14	19	24
150-(4/72) Partridge Family-s	3	6	9	15	21	26
157-(3/73) Planet of the Apes-c/s	3	6	9	16	23	30
166-(4/74) Classic finger-c	3	6	9	16	23	30
171-185,187,189-192,194,195,198,199: 172-Six Million Dollar Man-s; Hitler back-c. 178-Godfather II-c/s. 180-Jaws-c/s (1/76). 182-Bob Jones starts as regular. 185-Starsky & Hutch-s. 187-Fonz/Happy Days-c/s; Harry North starts as regular. 189-Travolta/Kotter-c/s. 190-John Wayne-c/s. 192-King Kong-c/s. 194-Rocky-c/s; Laverne & Shirley-s. 199-James Bond-s	2	4	6	10	14	18
186,188,197,200: 186-Star Trek-c/s. 188-Six Million Dollar Man/ Bionic Woman. 197-Spock-s; Star Wars-s. 200-Close Encounters	2	4	6	13	18	22
193,196: 193-Farrah/Charlie's Angels-c/s. 196-Star Wars-c/s	3	6	9	14	19	24
201,203,205,220: 201-Sat. Night Fever-c/s. 203-Star Wars. 205-Travolta/Grease. 220-Yoda-c, Empire Strikes Back-s	2	4	6	9	13	16
202,204,206,207,209,211-219,221-227,229,230: 204-Hulk TV show. 206-Tarzan. 208-Superman movie. 209 Mork & Mindy. 212-Spider-Man-s; Alien (movie)-s. 213-James Bond, Dracula, Rocky II-s 216-Star Trek. 219-Martin-c. 221-Shining-s. 223-Dallas-c/s. 225-Popeye. 226-Superman II. 229-James Bond. 230-Star Wars	1	3	4	6	8	10
208,228: 208-Superman movie-c/s; Battlestar Galactica-s. 228-Raiders of the Lost Ark-c/s	2	4	6	9	12	15
210-Lord of the Rings	2	4	6	9	13	16
231-235,237-241,243-249,251-260: 233-Pac-Man-c. 234-MASH-c/s. 235-Flip-c with Rocky III & Conan; Boris-a. 239-Mickey Mouse-c. 241-Knight Rider-s. 243-Superman III. 245- Last Rickard-a. 247-Seven Dwarfs-c. 253-Supergirl movie-s; Prince/Purple Rain-s. 254-Rock stars-s. 255-Reagan-c; Cosby-s. 256-Last issue edited by Feldstein; Dynasty, Bev. Hills Cop. 259-Rambo. 260-Back to the Future-c/s; Honeymooners-s	1	2	3	5	6	8
236,242,250: 236-E.T.-c/s;Star Trek II-s. 242-Star Wars/A-Team-c/s. 250-Temple of Doom-c/s; Tarzan-s	1	2	3	5	7	9
261-267,269-276,278-288,290-297: 261-Miami Vice. 262-Rocky IV-c/s, Leave It To Beaver-s. 263-Young Sherlock Holmes-s. 264-Hulk Hogan-c; Rambo-s. 267-Top Gun. 271-Star Trek IV-c/s. 272-ALF-c, Get Smart-s. 273-Pee Wee Herman-c/s. 274-Last Martin-a. 281-California Raisins-c. 282-Star Trek:TNG-s; ALF-s. 283-Rambo III-c/s. 284-Roger Rabbit-c/s. 285-Hulk Hogan-c. 287-3 pgs. Eisner-a. 291-TMNT-c; Indiana Jones-s. 292-Super Mario Bros.-c; Married with Children-s. 295-Back to the Future II. 297-Mike Tyson-c	1	2	3	4	5	7
268,277,289,298-300: 268-Aliens-c/s. 277-Michael Jackson-c/s; Robocop-s. 289-Batman movie parody. 298-Gremlins II-c/s; Robocop II. Batman-s. 299-Simpsons-c/story, Total Recall-s. 300(1/91) Casablanca-s, Dick Tracy-s, Wizard of Oz-s, Gone With The Wind-s	1	2	3	5	6	8
300-303 (1/91-6/91)-Special Hussein Asylum Editions; only distributed to the troops in the Middle East (see Mad Super Spec.)	2	4	6	13	18	22
301-310,312,313,315-320,322,324,326-334,337-349: 303-Home Alone-c/s. 305-Simpsons-s. 306-TMNT II movie. 308-Terminator II. 315-Tribute to William Gaines. 316-Photo-c. 319-Dracula-c/s. 320-Disney's Aladdin-s. 322-Batman Animated series. 327-Seinfeld-s; X-Men-s. 331-Flintstones-c/s. 332-O.J. Simpson-c/s; Simpsons app. in Lion King. 334-Frankenstein-c/s. 338-Judge Dredd-c by Frazetta. 341-Pocahontas-s. 345-Beatles app. (1 pg.) 347-Broken Arrow & Mission Impossible						5.00
311,314,321,323,325,335,336,350,354,358: 311-Addams Family-c/story, Home Improvement-s. 314-Batman Returns-c/story. 321-Star Trek DS9-c/s. 323-Jurassic Park-c/s. 325,336-Beavis & Butthead-c/s. 335-X-Files-s; Pulp Fiction-s; Interview with the Vampire-s. 336-Lois & Clark-s. 350-Polybagged w/CD Rom. 354-Star Wars; Beavis & Butthead-s. 358-X-Files						6.00
351-353,355-357,359-400						4.00
401-494						4.00
Mad About Super Heroes (2002, $9.95) r/super hero app.; Alex Ross-c						10.00

NOTE: ***Aragones*** *c-210, 293.* ***Beall*** *c-39.* ***Davis*** *c-2, 27, 135, 139, 173, 178, 212, 213, 219, 246, 260, 296, 308.* ***Drucker*** *a-35-62; c-122, 169, 176, 225, 234, 264, 266, 274, 280, 285, 297, 299, 303, 314, 315, 321.* ***Elder*** *c-5, 259, 261, 268.* ***Elder/Kurtzman*** *a-258-274.* ***Jules Feiffer*** *a(r)-42.* ***Freas*** *c-40-59, 62-67, 69-70, 72, 74.* ***Heath*** *a-14, 27.* ***Jaffee*** *c-199, 217, 224, 258.* ***Kamen*** *a-29.* ***Krigstein*** *a-12, 17, 24, 26.* ***Kurtzman*** *c-1, 3, 4, 6-10, 13, 16, 18.* ***Martin*** *a-29-62; c-68, 165, 229.* ***Mingo*** *c-30-37, 61, 71, 75-80, 82-114, 117-124, 126, 129, 131, 133, 134, 136, 140, 143-148, 150-162, 164, 166-168, 171, 172, 174, 175, 177, 179, 181, 183, 185, 198, 206, 209, 211, 214, 218, 221, 222, 300.* ***John Severin*** *a-1-6, 9, 10.* ***Wolverton*** *c-11; a-11, 17, 29, 31, 36, 40, 82, 137.* ***Wood*** *a-1-21, 23-62; c-26, 28, 29.* ***Woodbridge*** *a-35-62. Issues 1-23 are 36 pgs.; 24-28 are 58 pgs.; 29 on are 52 pgs.*

MAD (See Mad Follies, ...Special, More Trash from..., and The Worst from...)

MAD ABOUT MILLIE (Also see Millie the Model)
Marvel Comics Group: April, 1969 - No. 16, Nov, 1970

	GD 2.0	VG 4.0	FN 6.0	VF 8.0	VF/NM 9.0	NM- 9.2
1-Giant issue	9	18	27	60	100	140
2,3 (Giants)	6	12	18	39	62	85
4-10	4	8	12	26	41	55
11-16: 16-r	4	8	12	24	37	50
Annual 1(11/71, 52 pgs.)	4	8	12	26	41	55

MADAME MIRAGE

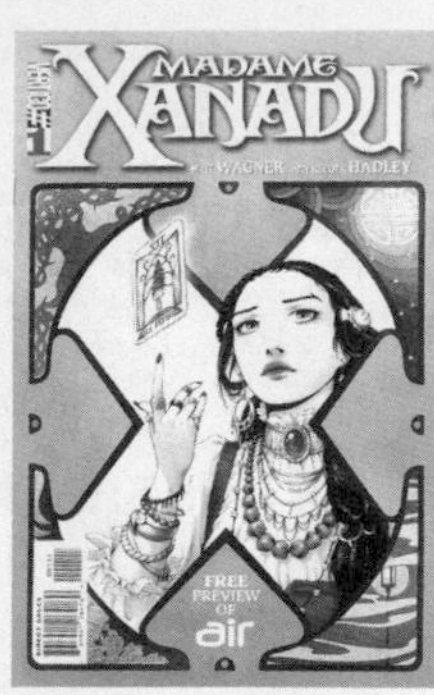

Madame Xanadu #1 © DC

Mad Follies #6 © E.C. Publ.

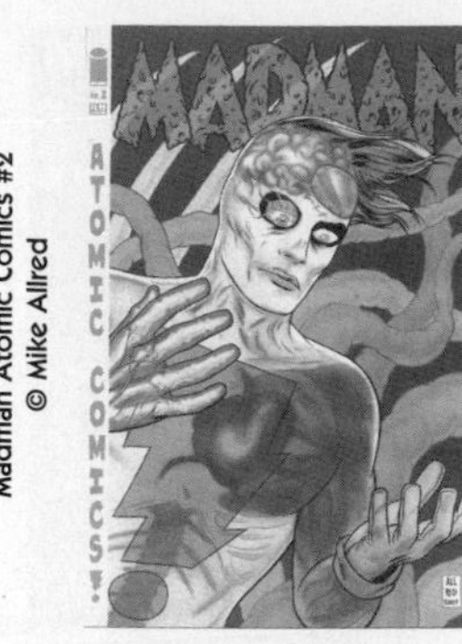

Madman Atomic Comics #2 © Mike Allred

GD VG FN VF VF/NM NM-
2.0 4.0 6.0 8.0 9.0 9.2

Image Comics (Top Cow): June, 2007 - No. 6, May, 2008 ($2.99)
1-6: 1-Paul Dini-s/Kenneth Rocafort-a; two covers by Horn and Rocafort 3.00
... First Look (5/07, 99¢) preview of series; Dini interview; cover gallery 2.25
Volume 1 TPB (7/08, $14.99) r/#1-6; cover gallery; cover and design sketches 15.00

MADAME XANADU
DC Comics: July, 1981 ($1.00, no ads, 36 pgs.)
1-Marshall Rogers-a(25 pgs.); Kaluta-c/a(2pgs.); pin-up 5.00

MADAME XANADU
DC Comics (Vertigo): Aug, 2008 - Present ($2.99)
1,2-Matt Wagner-s/Amy Reeder Hadley-a/c; Phantom Stranger app. 3.00

MADBALLS
Star Comics/Marvel Comics #9 on: Sept, 1986 - No. 3, Nov, 1986; No. 4, June, 1987 - No. 10, June, 1988
1-10: Based on toys. 9-Post-a 4.00

MAD DISCO
E.C. Comics: 1980 (one-shot, 36 pgs.)
1-Includes 30 minute flexi-disc of Mad disco music 2 4 6 11 16 20

MAD-DOG
Marvel Comics: May, 1993 - No. 6, Oct, 1993 ($1.25)
1-6-Flip book w/2nd story "created" by Bob Newhart's character from his TV show "Bob" set at a comic book company; actual s/a-Ty Templeton 2.50

MAD DOGS
Eclipse Comics: Feb, 1992 - No. 3, July, 1992 ($2.50, B&W, limited series)
1-3 2.50

MAD 84 (Mad Extra)
E.C. Comics: 1984 (84 pgs.)
1 1 3 4 6 8 10

MAD FOLLIES (Special)
E. C. Comics: 1963 - No. 7, 1969
nn(1963)-Paperback book covers 22 44 66 157 291 425
2(1964)-Calendar 17 34 51 120 223 325
3(1965)-Mischief Stickers 14 28 42 99 175 250
4(1966)-Mobile; Frazetta-r/back-c Mad #90 10 20 30 67 116 165
5,6: 5(1967)-Stencils. 6(1968)-Mischief Stickers 8 16 24 52 86 120
7(1969)-Nasty Cards 8 16 24 52 86 120
(If bonus is missing, issue is half price)
NOTE: *Clarke c-4. Frazetta r-4, 6 (1 pg. ea.). Mingo c-1-3. Orlando a-5.*

MAD HATTER, THE (Costumed Hero)
O. W. Comics Corp.: Jan-Feb, 1946; No. 2, Sept-Oct, 1946
1-Freddy the Firefly begins; Giunta-c/a 76 152 228 479 810 1140
2-Has ad for E.C.'s Animal Fables #1 40 80 120 244 397 550

MADHOUSE
Ajax/Farrell Publ. (Excellent Publ./4-Star): 3-4/54 - No. 4, 9-10/54; 6/57 - No. 4, Dec?, 1957
1(1954) 31 62 93 181 291 400
2,3 17 34 51 98 154 210
4-Surrealistic-c 23 46 69 135 218 300
1(1957, 2nd series) 14 28 42 80 115 150
2-4 (#4 exist?) 10 20 30 54 72 90

MAD HOUSE (Formerly Madhouse Glads; ...Comics #104? on)
Red Circle Productions/Archie Publications: No. 95, 9/74 - No. 97, 1/75; No. 98, 8/75 - No. 130, 10/82
95,96-Horror stories through #97; Morrow-c 2 4 6 10 14 18
97-Intro. Henry Hobson; Morrow-a/c, Thorne-a 2 4 6 8 11 14
98,99,101-120-Satire/humor stories. 110-Sabrina app.,1pg.
1 3 4 6 8 10
100 1 3 4 6 8 11
121-129 1 3 4 6 8 11
130 2 4 6 9 13 16
Annual 8(1970-71)-Formerly Madhouse Ma-ad Annual; Sabrina app. (6 pgs.)
4 8 12 22 34 45
Annual 9-12(1974-75): 11-Wood-a(r) 2 4 6 11 16 20
...Comics Digest 1('75-76) 2 4 6 10 14 18
2-8(8/82)(...Mag. #5 on)-Sabrina in many 2 4 6 8 11 14
NOTE: *B. Jones a-96. McWilliams a-97. Wildey a-95, 96. See Archie Comics Digest #1, 13.*

MADHOUSE GLADS (Formerly ...Ma-ad; Madhouse #95 on)
Archie Publ.: No. 73, May, 1970 - No. 94, Aug, 1974 (No. 78-92: 52 pgs.)
73-77,93,94: 74-1 pg. Sabrina 2 4 6 9 13 16
78-92 (52 pgs.) 2 4 6 11 16 20

MADHOUSE MA-AD (...Jokes #67-70; ...Freak-Out #71-74)
(Formerly Archie's Madhouse) (Becomes Madhouse Glads #73 on)
Archie Publications: No. 67, April, 1969 - No. 72, Jan, 1970
67-71: 70-1 pg. Sabrina 2 4 6 13 18 22
72-6 pgs. Sabrina 4 8 12 22 34 45
...Annual 7(1969-70)-Formerly Archie's Madhouse Annual; becomes Madhouse Annual; 6 pgs. Sabrina 4 8 12 22 34 45

MADMAN (See Creatures of the Id #1)
Tundra Publishing: Mar, 1992 - No. 3, 1992 ($3.95, duotone, high quality, lim. series, 52 pgs.)
1-Mike Allred-c/a in all 2 4 6 8 10 12
1-2nd printing 4.00
2,3 6.00

MADMAN ADVENTURES
Tundra Publishing: 1992 - No. 3, 1993 ($2.95, limited series)
1-Mike Allred-c/a in all 1 2 3 5 7 9
2,3 5.00
TPB (Oni Press, 2002, $14.95) r/#1-3 & first app. of Frank Einstein from Creatures of the Id in color; gallery pages 15.00

MADMAN ATOMIC COMICS (Also see The Atomics)
Image Comics: Apr, 2007 - Present ($2.99)
1-10-Mike Allred-s/c/a. 1-Origin re-told; pin-ups by Rivoche and Powell. 3-Sale back-c 3.00
... Vol. 1 (2008, $19.99) r/#1-7; bonus art; Jamie Rich intro. 20.00

MADMAN COMICS (Also see The Atomics)
Dark Horse Comics (Legend No. 2 on): Apr, 1994 - No. 20, Dec, 2000 ($2.95/$2.99)
1-Allred-c/a; F. Miller back-c. 1 2 3 5 6 8
2-3: 3-Alex Toth back-c. 5.00
4-11: 4-Dave Stevens back-c. 6,7-Miller/Darrow's Big Guy app. 6-Bruce Timm back-c. 7-Darrow back-c. 8-Origin?; Bagge back-c. 10-Allred/Ross-c; Ross back-c. 11-Frazetta back-c 4.00
12-16: 12-(4/99) 3.00
17-20: 17-The G-Men From Hell #1 on cover; Brereton back-c. 18-(#2). 19,20-($2.99-c). 20-Clowes back-c 3.00
... Boogaloo TPB (6/99, $8.95) r/Nexus Meets Madman & Madman/The Jam 9.00
... Gargantua! (2007, $125.00, HC with dustjacket) r/Madman#1-3, Madman Adventures #1-3, Madman Comics #1-20 and Madman King-Size Super Groovy Special; pin-ups 125.00
Ltd. Ed. Slipcover (1997, $99.95, signed and numbered) w/Vol. I & Vol. 2.
Vol.1- reprints #1-5; Vol. 2- reprints #6-10 100.00
The Complete Madman Comics: Vol. 2 (11/96, $17.95, TPB) r/#6-10 plus new material 18.00
Madman King-Size Super Groovy Special (Oni Press, 7/03, $6.95) new short stories by Allred, Derington, Krall and Weissman 7.00
Madman Picture Exhibition No. 1-4 (4-7/02, $3.95) pin-ups by various 4.00
Madman Picture Exhibition Limited Edition (10/02, $29.95) Hardcover collects MPE #1-4 30.00
... Volume 2 SC (2007, $17.99) r/#1-11; Erik Larsen intro. 18.00
... Volume 3 SC (2007, $17.99) r/#12-20 and story from King-Size Groovy; Allred intro. 18.00
Yearbook '95 (1996, $17.95, TPB)-r/#1-5, intro by Teller 18.00

MADMAN / THE JAM
Dark Horse Comics: Jul, 1998 - No. 2, Aug, 1998 ($2.95, mini-series)
1,2-Allred & Mireault-s/a 3.00

MAD MONSTER PARTY (See Movie Classics)

MADNESS IN MURDERWORLD
Marvel Comics: 1989 (Came with computer game from Paragon Software)
V1#1-Starring The X-Men 2.50

MADRAVEN HALLOWEEN SPECIAL
Hamilton Comics: Oct, 1995 ($2.95, one-shot)
nn-Morrow-a 3.00

MADROX (from X-Factor)
Marvel Comics (Marvel Knights): Nov, 2004 - No. 5, Mar, 2005 ($2.99)
1-5-Peter David-s/Pablo Raimondi-a; Strong Guy app. 3.00
...: Multiple Choice TPB (2005, $13.99) r/#1-5 14.00
X-Factor: Madrox - Multiple Choice HC (2008, $19.99) r/#1-5 20.00

MAD SPECIAL (...Super Special)
E. C. Publications, Inc.: Fall, 1970 - Present (84 - 116 pgs.)
(If bonus is missing, issue is one half price)
Fall 1970(#1)-Bonus-Voodoo Doll; contains 17 pgs. new material
10 20 30 68 119 170

Mad Super Special #94 © E.C. Publ.

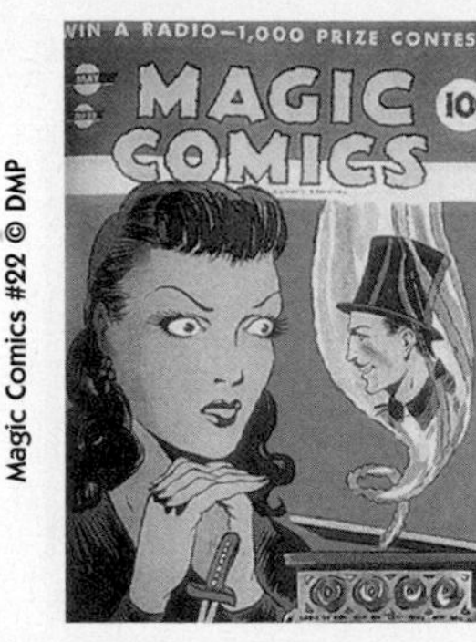

Magic Comics #22 © DMP

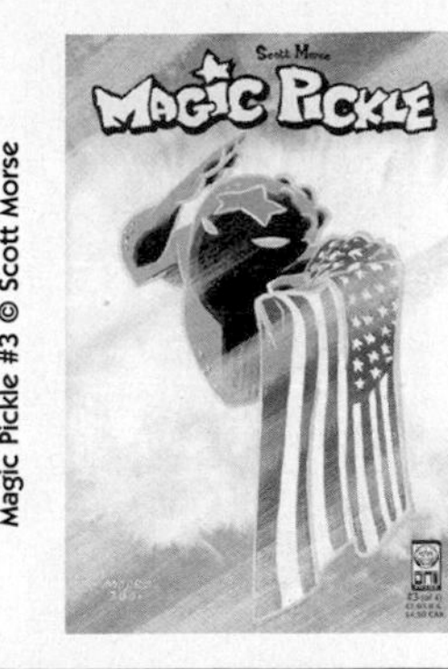

Magic Pickle #3 © Scott Morse

	GD 2.0	VG 4.0	FN 6.0	VF 8.0	VF/NM 9.0	NM- 9.2
Spring 1971(#2)-Wall Nuts; 17 pgs. new material	6	12	18	37	59	80
3-Protest Stickers	6	12	18	37	59	80
4-8: 4-Mini Posters. 5-Mad Flag. 6-Mad Mischief Stickers. 7-Presidential candidate posters, Wild Shocking Message posters. 8-TV Guise	5	10	15	32	51	70
9(1972)-Contains Nostalgic Mad #1 (28 pgs.)	4	8	12	26	41	55
10-13: 10-Nonsense Stickers (Don Martin). 13-Sickie Stickers; 3 pgs. Wolverton-r/Mad #137. 11-Contains 33-1/3 RPM record. 12-Contains Nostalgic Mad #2 (36 pgs.); Davis, Wolverton-a	3	6	9	20	30	40
14,16-21,24: 4-Vital Message posters & Art Depreciation paintings. 16-Mad-hesive Stickers. 17-Don Martin posters. 20-Martin Stickers. 10 Contains Nostalgic Mad #4 (36 pgs.). 21,24-Contains Nostalgic Mad #5 (28 pgs.) & #6 (28 pgs.)	3	6	9	16	23	30
15-Contains Nostalgic Mad #3 (28 pgs.)	3	6	9	17	25	32
22,23,25,27-29,30: 22-Diplomas. 23-Martin Stickers. 25-Martin Posters. 27-Mad Shock-Sticks. 28-Contains Nostalgic Mad #7 (36 pgs.). 29-Mad Collectable-Connectables Posters. 30-The Movies	2	4	6	9	13	16
26-Has 33-1/3 RPM record	2	4	6	13	18	22
31,33-35,37-50	2	4	6	8	11	14
32-Contains Nostalgic Mad #8. 36-Has 96 pgs. of comic book & comic strip spoofs: titles "The Comics" on-c	2	4	6	9	13	16
51-70	1	3	4	6	8	10
71-88,90-100: 71-Batman parodies-r by Wood, Drucker. 72-Wolverton-c r-from 1st panel in Mad #11; Wolverton-s r/new dialogue. 83-All Star Trek spoof issue	1	2	3	5	6	8
76-(Fall, 1991)-Special Hussein Asylum Edition; distributed only to the troops in the Middle East (see Mad #300-303)	2	4	6	13	18	22
89-($3.95)-Polybaged w/1st of 3 Spy vs. Spy hologram trading cards (direct sale only issue) (other cards came w/card set)	1	3	4	6	8	10
101-135: 117-Sci-Fi parodies-r.						4.00

NOTE: #28-30 have no number on cover. Freas c-76. Mingo c-9, 11, 15, 19, 23.

MAGDALENA, THE (See The Darkness #15-18)
Image Comics (Top Cow): Apr, 2000 - No. 3, Jan, 2001 ($2.50)

Preview Special ('00, $4.95) Flip book w/Blood Legacy preview	5.00
1-Benitez-c/a; variant covers by Silvestri & Turner	2.50
2,3: 2-Two covers	2.50
.../Angelus #1/2 (11/01, $2.95) Benitez-c/Ching-a	3.00
...Blood Divine (2002, $9.95) r/#1-3 & #1/2; cover gallery	10.00
.../Vampirella (7/03, $2.99) Wohl-s/Benitez-a; two covers	3.00

MAGDALENA, THE (Volume 2)
Image Comics (Top Cow): Aug, 2003 - No. 4 ($2.99)

Preview (6/03) B&W preview; Wizard World East logo on cover	2.50
1-4-Holguin-s/Basaldua-a	3.00
1-Variant-c by Jim Silke benefitting ACTOR charity	5.00
TPB Volume 1 (12/06, $19.99) r/both series, Darkness #15-18 & Magdalena/Angelus	20.00
.../Daredevil (5/08, $3.99) Phil Hester-s/a; Hester & Sejic-c	4.00
.../Vampirella (12/04, $2.99) Kirkman-s/Manapul-a; two covers by Manapul and Bachalo	3.00
... Vs. Dracula Monster War 2005 (6/05, $2.99) four covers; Joyce Chin-a	3.00

MAGE (The Hero Discovered...; also see Grendel #16)
Comico: Feb, 1984 (no month) - No. 15, Dec, 1986 ($1.50, Mando paper)

	GD	VG	FN	VF	VF/NM	NM-
1-Comico's 1st color comic	2	4	6	8	11	14
2-5: 3-Intro Edsel						6.00
6-Grendel begins (1st in color)	3	6	9	14	20	25
7-1st new Grendel story	2	4	6	8	10	12
8-14: 13-Grendel dies. 14-Grendel story ends						6.00
15-($2.95) Double size w/pullout poster	1	2	3	5	6	8
TPB Volume 1-4 (Image, $5.95) 1- r/#1,2. 2- r/#3,4. 3- r/#5,6. 4- r/#7,8						7.00
TPB Volume 5-7 (Image, $6.95) 5- r/#9,10. 6- r/#11,12. 7- r/#13,14						7.00
TPB Volume 8 (Image, 9/99, $7.50) r/#15						7.50
..., Vol. 1 TPB (Image, 2004, $29.99) r/#1-15; cover gallery, promo artwork, bonus art						30.00

MAGE (The Hero Defined) (Volume 2)
Image Comics: July, 1997 - No. 15, Oct, 1999 ($2.50)

0-(7/97, $5.00) American Ent. Ed.	5.00
1-14:Matt Wagner-c/s/a in all. 13-Three covers	2.50
1-"3-D Edition" (2/98, $4.95) w/glasses	5.00
15-($5.95) Acetate cover	6.00
Volume 1,2 TPB ('98,'99, $9.95) 1- r/#1-4. 2-r/#5-8	10.00
Volume 3 TPB ('00, $12.95) r/#9-12	13.00
Volume 4 TPB ('01, $14.95) r/#13-15	15.00
Hardcover Vol. 2 (2005, $49.95) r/#1-15; cover gallery, character design & sketch pages	50.00

MAGE KNIGHT: STOLEN DESTINY (Based on the fantasy game Mage Knight)
Idea + Design Works: Oct, 2002 - No. 5, Feb, 2003 ($3.50, limited series)

1-5: 1-J. Scott Campbell-c; Cabrera-a/Dezago-s, 2-Dave Johnson-c	3.50

MAGGIE AND HOPEY COLOR SPECIAL (See Love and Rockets)
Fantagraphics Books: May, 1997 ($3.50, one-shot)

1	3.50

MAGGIE THE CAT (Also see Jon Sable, Freelance #11 & Shaman's Tears #12)
Image Comics (Creative Fire Studio): Jan, 1996 - No. 2, Feb, 1996 ($2.50, unfinished limited series)

1,2: Mike Grell-c/a/scripts	2.50

MAGICA DE SPELL (See Walt Disney Showcase #30)

MAGIC AGENT (See Forbidden Worlds & Unknown Worlds)
American Comics Group: Jan-Feb, 1962 - No. 3, May-June, 1962

	GD	VG	FN	VF	VF/NM	NM-
1-Origin & 1st app. John Force	4	8	12	26	41	55
2,3	3	6	9	19	29	38

MAGICAL POKÉMON JOURNEY
Viz Comics: 2000 - Present ($4.95, B&W, magazine-size)

1-4	5.00
Part 2: 1-3; Part 3: 1-4: 1-Includes color poster; Part 4: 1-4; Part 5: 1-4; Part 6: 1-4	5.00

MAGIC COMICS
David McKay Publications: Aug, 1939 - No. 123, Nov-Dec, 1949

	GD	VG	FN	VF	VF/NM	NM-
1-Mandrake the Magician, Henry, Popeye, Blondie, Barney Baxter, Secret Agent X-9 (not by Raymond), Bunky by Billy DeBeck & Thornton Burgess text stories illustrated by Harrison Cady begin; Henry covers begin	348	696	1044	1949	2975	4000
2	124	248	372	694	1060	1425
3	91	182	273	510	780	1050
4	72	144	216	403	614	825
5	59	118	177	330	503	675
6-10: 8-11,21-Mandrake/Henry-c	47	94	141	263	402	540
11-16,18,20: 12-Mandrake-c begin.	39	78	117	218	334	450
17-The Lone Ranger begins	44	88	132	246	373	500
19-Classic robot-c	67	134	201	375	575	775
21-30: 25-Only Blondie-c. 26-Dagwood-c begin	26	52	78	152	244	335
31-40: 36-Flag-c	18	36	54	105	165	225
41-50	15	30	45	83	124	165
51-60	13	26	39	72	101	130
61-70	11	22	33	60	83	105
71-99, 107,108-Flash Gordon app; not by Raymond	9	18	27	52	69	85
100	10	20	30	56	76	95
101-106,109-123: 123-Last Dagwood-c	9	18	27	47	61	75

MAGIC FLUTE, THE (See Night Music #9-11)

MAGICIAN: APPRENTICE
Dabel Brothers/Marvel Comics (Dabel Brothers) #3 on: Mar, 2007 - No. 12, Dec, 2007 ($2.95/$2.99)

1-12-Adaptation of the Raymond E. Feist Riftwar Saga series	3.00
1,2-($5.95) 1-Wraparound variant-c by Maitz. 2-Wraparound variant-c by Booth	6.00
Collected Edition (10/06, $3.99) r/#1&2	4.00
Vol. 1 HC (2007, $19.99, dustjacket) r/#1-6; foreword by Feist	20.00
Vol. 1 SC (2007, $15.99) r/#1-6; foreword by Feist	16.00
Vol. 2 HC (2008, $19.99, dustjacket) r/#7-12	20.00

MAGIC PICKLE
Oni Press: Sept, 2001 - No. 4, Dec, 2001 ($2.95, limited series)

1-4-Scott Morse-s/a; Mahfood-a (2 pgs.)	3.00

MAGIC SWORD, THE (See Movie Classics)

MAGIC THE GATHERING (Title Series), **Acclaim Comics (Armada)**

...ANTIQUITIES WAR, 11/95 - 2/96 ($2.50), 1-4-Paul Smith-a(p)	2.50
...ARABIAN NIGHTS, 12/95 - 1/96 ($2.50), 1,2	2.50
...COLLECTION, '95 ($4.95), 1,2-polybagged	5.00
...CONVOCATIONS, '95 ($2.50), 1-nn-pin-ups	2.50
...ELDER DRAGONS, '95 ($2.50), 1,2-Doug Wheatley-a	2.50
...FALLEN ANGEL, '95 ($5.95), nn	6.00
...FALLEN EMPIRES, 9/95 - 10/95 ($2.75), 1,2	3.00
...Collection ($4.95)-polybagged	5.00
...HOMELANDS, '95 ($5.95), nn-polybagged w/card; Hildebrandts-c	6.00
... ICE AGE (On The World of...), 7/5 -11/95 ($2.50), 1-4: 1,2-bound-in Magic Card. 3,4-bound-in insert	2.50
...LEGEND OF JEDIT OJANEN, '96 ($2.50), 1,2	2.50

Magneto #1 © MAR

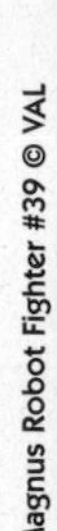
Magnus Robot Fighter #39 © VAL

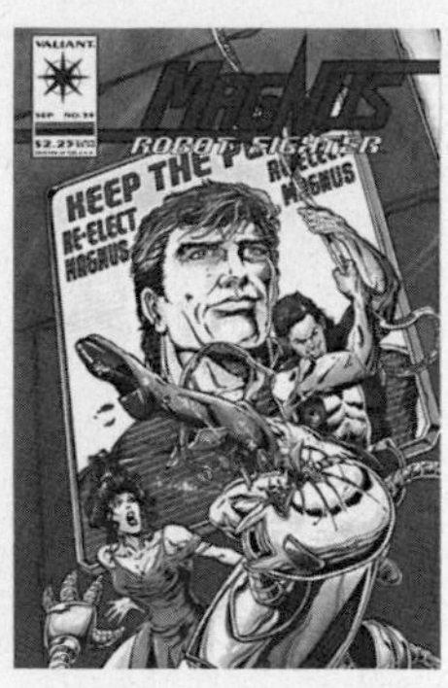

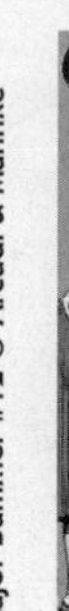
Major Bummer #12 © Arcudi & Mahnke

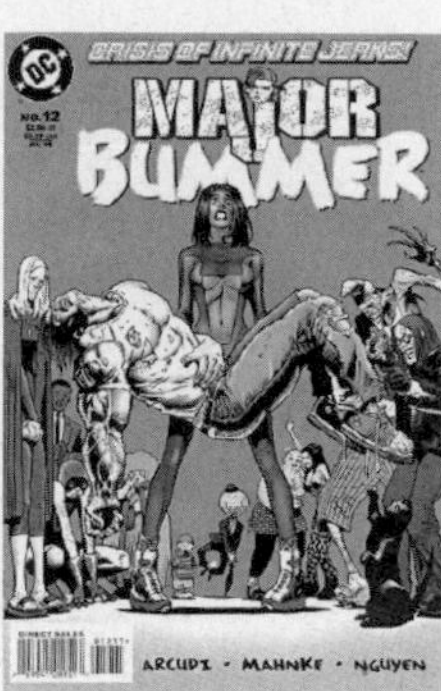

	GD	VG	FN	VF	VF/NM	NM-
	2.0	4.0	6.0	8.0	9.0	9.2

...**NIGHTMARE**, '95 ($2.50, one shot), 1 — 2.50
...**THE SHADOW MAGE**, 7/95 - 10/95 ($2.50), 1-4-bagged w/Magic The Gathering card — 2.50
...Collection 1,2 (1995, $4.95)-Trade paperback; polybagged — 5.00
...**SHANDALAR** ,'96 ($2.50), 1,2 — 2.50
...**WAYFARER** ,11/95 - 2/96 ($2.50), 1-5 — 2.50

MAGIC: THE GATHERING: GERRARD'S QUEST
Dark Horse Comics: Mar, 1998 - No. 4, June, 1998 ($2.95, limited series)
1-4: Grell-s/Mhan-a — 3.00

MAGIK (Illyana and Storm Limited Series)
Marvel Comics Group: Dec, 1983 - No. 4, Mar, 1984 (60¢, limited series)
1-4: 1-Characters from X-Men; Inferno begins; X-Men cameo (Buscema pencils in #1,2; c-1p. 2-4: 2-Nightcrawler app. & X-Men cameo — 3.00

MAGIK (See Black Sun mini-series)
Marvel Comics: Dec, 2000 - No. 4, Mar, 2001 ($2.99, limited series)
1-4-Liam Sharp-a/Abnett & Lanning-s; Nightcrawler app. — 3.00

MAGILLA GORILLA (TV) (See Kite Fun Book)
Gold Key: May, 1964 - No. 10, Dec, 1968 (Hanna-Barbera)
1-1st comic app. — 9 18 27 65 113 160
2-4: 3-Vs. Yogi Bear for President. 4-1st Punkin Puss & Mushmouse, Ricochet Rabbit & Droop-a-Long — 6 12 18 37 59 80
5-10: 10-Reprints — 5 10 15 30 48 65

MAGILLA GORILLA (TV)(See Spotlight #4)
Charlton Comics: Nov, 1970 - No. 5, July, 1971 (Hanna-Barbera)
1 — 5 10 15 34 55 75
2-5 — 4 8 12 22 34 45

MAGNETIC MEN FEATURING MAGNETO
Marvel Comics (Amalgam): June, 1997 ($1.95, one-shot)
1-Tom Peyer-s/Barry Kitson & Dan Panosian-a — 2.50

MAGNETO (See X-Men #1)
Marvel Comics: nd (Sept, 1993) (Giveaway) (one-shot)
0-Embossed foil-c by Sienkiewicz; r/Classic X-Men #19 & 12 by Bolton — 5.00

MAGNETO
Marvel Comics: Nov, 1996 - No. 4, Feb, 1997 ($1.95, limited series)
1-4: Peter Milligan scripts & Kelley Jones-a(p) — 2.50

MAGNETO AND THE MAGNETIC MEN
Marvel Comics (Amalgam): Apr, 1996 ($1.95, one-shot)
1-Jeff Matsuda-a(p) — 2.50

MAGNETO ASCENDANT
Marvel Comics: May, 1999 ($3.99, squarebound one-shot)
1-Reprints early Magneto appearances — 4.00

MAGNETO: DARK SEDUCTION
Marvel Comics: Jun, 2000 - No. 4, Sept, 2000 ($2.99, limited series)
1-4: Nicieza-s/Cruz-a. 3,4-Avengers-c/app. — 3.00

MAGNETO REX
Marvel Comics: Apr, 1999 - No. 3, July, 1999 ($2.50, limited series)
1-3-Rogue, Quicksilver app.; Peterson-a(p) — 2.50

MAGNUS, ROBOT FIGHTER (...4000 A.D.)(See Doctor Solar)
Gold Key: Feb, 1963 - No. 46, Jan, 1977 (All painted covers except #5,30,31)
1-Origin & 1st app. Magnus; Aliens (1st app.) series begins — 22 44 66 157 291 425
2,3 — 10 20 30 70 123 175
4-10: 10-Simonson fan club illo (5/65, 1st-a?) — 7 14 21 47 76 105
11-20 — 5 10 15 32 51 70
21,24-28: 28-Aliens ends — 4 8 12 22 34 45
22,23: 22-Origin-r/#1; last 12¢ issue — 4 8 12 23 36 48
29-46-Mostly reprints — 2 4 6 11 16 20
Russ Manning's Magnus Robot Fighter - Vol. 1 HC (Dark Horse, 2004, $49.95) r/#1-7 — 50.00
Russ Manning's Magnus Robot Fighter - Vol. 2 HC (DH, 6/05, $49.95) r/#8-14; forward by Steve Rude — 50.00
Russ Manning's Magnus Robot Fighter - Vol. 3 HC (Dark Horse, 10/06, $49.95) r/#15-21 — 50.00
NOTE: ***Manning** a-1-22, 28-43(r). **Spiegle** a-23, 44r.*

MAGNUS ROBOT FIGHTER (Also see Vintage Magnus)
Valiant/Acclaim Comics: May, 1991 - No. 64, Feb, 1996 ($1.75/$1.95/$2.25/$2.50)
1-Nichols/Layton-c/a; 1-8 have trading cards — 1 2 3 5 6 8

	GD	VG	FN	VF	VF/NM	NM-
	2.0	4.0	6.0	8.0	9.0	9.2

2-8: 4-Rai cameo. 5-Origin & 1st full app. Rai (10/91); 5-8 are in flip book format and back-c & half of book are Rai #1-4 mini-series. 6-1st Solar x-over. 7-Magnus vs. Rai-c/story; 1st X-O Armor — 6.00
0-Origin issue; Layton-a; ordered through mail w/coupons from 1st 8 issues plus 50¢; B. Smith trading card — 2 4 6 11 16 20
0-Sold thru comic shops without trading card — 2 4 6 8 10 12
9-11 — 3.00
12-(3.25, 44 pgs.)-Turok-c/story (1st app. in Valiant universe, 5/92); has 8 pg. Magnus story insert — 1 3 4 6 8 10
13-24,26-48: 14-1st app. Isak. 15,16-Unity x-overs. 15-Miller-c. 16-Birth of Magnus. 21-New direction & new logo. 21-Gold ink variant. 24-Story cont'd in Rai & the Future Force #9. 33-Timewalker app.36-Bound-in trading cards. 37-Rai & Starwatchers app. 44-Bound-in sneak peek card. — 2.50
25-($2.95)-Embossed silver foil-c; new costume — 3.00
49-63 — 3.00
64-($2.50): 64-Magnus dies? — 4.00
...Invasion (1994, $9.95)-r/Rai #1-4 & Magnus #5-8 — 10.00
Magnus Steel Nation (1994, $9.95) r/#1-4 — 10.00
Yearbook (1994, $3.95, 52 pgs.) — 4.00
NOTE: ***Ditko/Reese** a-18. **Layton** a(i)-5; c-6-9i, 25; back(i)-5-8. **Reese** a(i)-22, 25, 28; c(i)-22, 24, 28. **Simonson** c-16. Prices for issues 1-8 are for trading cards and coupons intact.*

MAGNUS ROBOT FIGHTER
Acclaim Comics (Valiant Heroes): V2#1, May, 1997 - No. 18, Jun, 1998 ($2.50)
1-18: 1-Reintro Magnus; Donavon Wylie (X-O Manowar) cameo; Tom Peyer scripts & Mike McKone-c/a begin; painted variant-c exists — 2.50

MAGNUS ROBOT FIGHTER/NEXUS
Valiant/Dark Horse Comics: Dec, 1993 - No. 2, Apr, 1994 ($2.95, lim. series)
1,2: Steve Rude painted-c & pencils in all — 3.00

MAID OF THE MIST (See American Graphics)

MAI, THE PSYCHIC GIRL
Eclipse Comics: May, 1987 - No. 28, July, 1989 ($1.50, B&W, bi-weekly, 44pgs.)
1-28, 1,2-2nd print — 2.50

MAJESTIC (Mr. Majestic from WildCATS)
DC Comics: Oct, 2004 - No. 4, Jan, 2005 ($2.95, limited series)
1-4-Kerschl-a/Abnett & Lanning-s. 1-Superman app.; Superman #1 cover swipe — 3.00
...: Strange New Visitor TPB (2005, $14.99) r/#1-4 & Action #811, Advs. of Superman #624 & Superman #201 — 15.00

MAJESTIC (Mr. Majestic from WildCATS)
DC Comics (WildStorm): Mar, 2005 - No. 17, July, 2006 ($2.95/$2.99)
1-17: 1-Googe-a/Abnett & Lanning-s; Superman app. 9-Jeanty-a; Zealot app. — 3.00
...: Meanwhile, Back on Earth... TPB (2006, $14.99) r/#8-12 — 13.00
...: The Final Cut TPB (2007, $14.99) r/#13-17 & story fro WildStorm Winter Special — 15.00
...: While You Were Out TPB (2006, $12.99) r/#1-7 — 13.00

MAJOR BUMMER
DC Comics: Aug, 1997 - No. 15, Oct, 1998 ($2.50)
1-15: 1-Origin and 1st app. Major Bummer — 2.50

MAJOR HOOPLE COMICS (See Crackajack Funnies)
Nedor Publications: nd (Jan, 1943)
1-Mary Worth, Phantom Soldier app. by Moldoff — 38 76 114 219 352 485

MAJOR VICTORY COMICS (Also see Dynamic Comics)
H. Clay Glover/Service Publ./Harry 'A' Chesler: 1944 - No. 3, Summer, 1945
1-Origin Major Victory (patriotic hero) by C. Sultan (reprint from Dynamic #1); 1st app. Spider Woman — 64 128 192 403 682 960
2-Dynamic Boy app. — 40 80 120 235 380 525
3-Rocket Boy app. — 37 74 111 215 345 475

MALIBU ASHCAN: RAFFERTY (See Firearm #12)
Malibu Comics (Ultraverse): Nov, 1994 (99¢, B&W w/color-c; one-shot)
1-Previews "The Rafferty Saga" storyline in Firearm; Chaykin-c — 2.50

MALTESE FALCON
David McKay Publications: No. 48, 1946
Feature Books 48-by Dashiell Hammett — 82 164 246 517 871 1225

MALU IN THE LAND OF ADVENTURE
I. W. Enterprises: 1964 (See White Princess of Jungle #2)
1-r/Avon's Slave Girl Comics #1; Severin-c — 5 10 15 30 48 65

MAMMOTH COMICS
Whitman Publishing Co.(K. K. Publ.): 1938 (84 pgs.) (B&W, 8-1/2x11-1/2")

Man-Bat (2006 series) #1 © DC

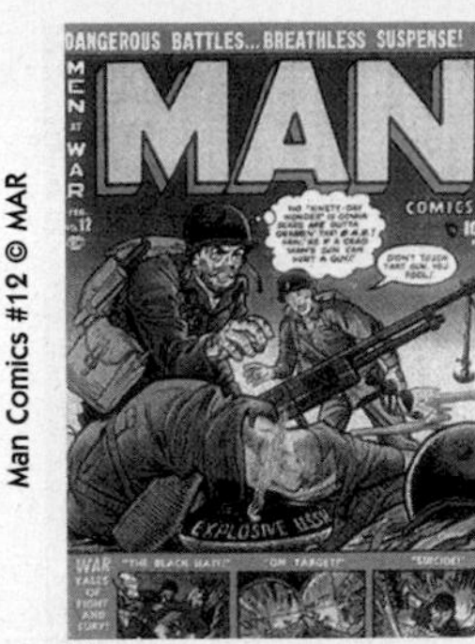

Man Comics #12 © MAR

Manhunter (2004 series) #12 © DC

GD VG FN VF VF/NM NM-
2.0 4.0 6.0 8.0 9.0 9.2

GD VG FN VF VF/NM NM-
2.0 4.0 6.0 8.0 9.0 9.2

1-Alley Oop, Terry & the Pirates, Dick Tracy, Little Orphan Annie, Wash Tubbs, Moon Mullins, Smilin' Jack, Tailspin Tommy, Don Winslow, Dan Dunn, Smokey Stover & other reprints (scarce) 200 400 600 1260 2130 3000

MAN AGAINST TIME
Image Comics (Motown Machineworks): May, 1996 - No. 4, Aug, 1996 ($2.25, lim. series)
1-4: 1-Simonson-c. 2,3-Leon-c. 4-Barreto & Leon-c 2.50

MAN-BAT (See Batman Family, Brave & the Bold, & Detective #400)
National Periodical Publ./DC Comics: Dec-Jan, 1975-76 - No. 2, Feb-Mar, 1976; Dec, 1984
1-Ditko-a(p); Aparo-c; Batman app.; 1st app. She-Bat? 2 4 6 11 16 20
2-Aparo-c 2 4 6 8 10 12
1 (12/84)-N. Adams-r(3)/Det.(Vs. Batman on-c) 4.00

MAN-BAT
DC Comics: Feb, 1996 - No. 3, Apr, 1996 ($2.25, limited series)
1-3: Dixon scripts in all. 2-Killer Croc-c/app. 2.50

MAN-BAT
DC Comics: Jun, 2006 - No. 5, Oct, 2006 ($2.99, limited series)
1-5: Bruce Jones-s/Mike Huddleston-a/c. 1 Hush app. 3.00

MAN CALLED A-X, THE
Malibu Comics (Bravura): Nov, 1994 - No. 4, Jun, 1995 ($2.95, limited series)
0-4: Marv Wolfman scripts & Shawn McManus-c/a. 0-(2/95). 1-"1A" on cover 3.00

MAN CALLED A-X, THE
DC Comics: Oct, 1997 - No. 8, May, 1998 ($2.50)
1-8: Marv Wolfman scripts & Shawn McManus-c/a. 2.50

MAN CALLED KEV, A (See The Authority)
DC Comics (WildStorm): Sept, 2006 - No. 5, Feb, 2007 ($2.99, limited series)
1-5-Ennis-s/Ezquerra-a/Fabry-c 3.00
TPB (2007, $14.99) r/#1-5; cover gallery 15.00

MAN COMICS
Marvel/Atlas Comics (NPI): Dec, 1949 - No. 28, Sept, 1953 (#1-6: 52 pgs.)
1-Tuska-a 23 46 69 135 218 300
2-Tuska-a 14 28 42 82 121 160
3-6 12 24 36 67 94 120
7,8 11 22 33 62 86 110
9-13,15: 9-Format changes to war 9 18 27 52 69 85
14-Henkel (3 pgs.); Pakula-a 10 20 30 54 72 90
16-21,23-28: 28-Crime issue (Bob Brant) 9 18 27 47 61 75
22-Krigstein-a, 5 pgs. 10 20 30 56 76 95
NOTE: *Berg a-14, 15, 19. Colan a-9, 21, 23. Everett a-8, 22; c-22, 25. Heath a-11, 13, 17, 21. Kubertish a-by Bob Brown-3. Maneely a-11-13; c-10, 11. Reinman a-11. Robinson a-7, 10, 14. Robert Sale a-9, 11. Sinnott a-22, 23. Tuska a-14, 23.*

MANDRAKE THE MAGICIAN (See Defenders Of The Earth, 123, 46, 52, 55, Giant Comic Album, King Comics, Magic Comics, The Phantom #21, Tiny Tot Funnies & Wow Comics, '36)

MANDRAKE THE MAGICIAN (See Harvey Comics Hits #53)
David McKay Publ./Dell/King Comics (All 12¢): 1938 - 1948; Sept, 1966 - No. 10, Nov, 1967
Feature Books 18,19,23 (1938) 65 130 195 410 693 975
Feature Books 46 45 90 135 279 465 650
Feature Books 52,55 38 76 114 226 363 500
Four Color 752 (11/56) 10 20 30 70 123 175
1-Begin S.O.S. Phantom, ends #3 6 12 18 37 59 80
2-7,9: 4-Girl Phantom app. 5-Flying Saucer-c/story. 5,6-Brick Bradford app. 7-Origin Lothar. 9-Brick Bradford app. 4 8 12 22 34 45
8-Jeff Jones-a (4 pgs.) 4 8 12 24 37 50
10-Rip Kirby app.; Raymond-a (14 pgs.) 4 8 12 28 44 60

MANDRAKE THE MAGICIAN
Marvel Comics: Apr, 1995 - No. 2, May, 1995 ($2.95, unfinished limited series)
1,2: Mike Barr scripts 3.00

MAN-EATING COW (See Tick #7,8)
New England Comics: July, 1992 - No. 10, 1994? ($2.75, B&W, limited series)
1-10 3.00
Man-Eating Cow Bonanza (6/96, $4.95, 128 pgs.)-r/#1-4. 5.00

MAN FROM ATLANTIS (TV)
Marvel Comics: Feb, 1978 - No. 7, Aug, 1978
1-(84 pgs.)-Sutton-a(p), Buscema-c; origin & cast photos 1 3 4 6 8 10
2-7 4.00

MAN FROM PLANET X, THE
Planet X Productions: 1987 (no price; probably unlicensed)
1-Reprints Fawcett Movie Comic 2.50

MAN FROM U.N.C.L.E., THE (TV) (Also see The Girl From Uncle)
Gold Key: Feb, 1965 - No. 22, Apr, 1969 (All photo-c)
1 13 26 39 95 168 240
2-Photo back c-2-8 7 14 21 50 83 115
3-10: 7-Jet Dream begins (1st app., also see Jet Dream) (all new stories) 6 12 18 37 59 80
11-22: 19-Last 12¢ issue. 21,22-Reprint #10 & 7 5 10 15 32 51 70

MAN FROM U.N.C.L.E., THE (TV)
Entertainment Publishing: 1987 - No. 11 ($1.50/$1.75, B&W)
1-7 ($1.50), 8-11 ($1.75) 3.00

MAN FROM WELLS FARGO (TV)
Dell Publishing Co.: No. 1287, Feb-Apr, 1962 - May-July, 1962 (Photo-c)
Four Color 1287, #01-495-207 6 12 18 37 59 80

MANGA DARKCHYLDE (Also see Darkchylde titles)
Dark Horse Comics: Feb, 2005 - No. 5 ($2.99, limited series)
1,2-Randy Queen-s/a; manga-style pre-teen Ariel Chylde 3.00

MANGA SHI (See Tomoe)
Crusade Entertainment: Aug, 1996 ($2.95)
1-Printed backwards (manga-style) 3.00

MANGA SHI 2000
Crusade Entertainment: Feb, 1997 - No. 3, June, 1997 ($2.95, mini-series)
1-3: 1-Two covers 3.00

MANGA ZEN (Also see Zen Intergalactic Ninja)
Zen Comics (Fusion Studios): 1996 - No. 3, 1996 ($2.50, B&W)
1-3 2.50

MANGAZINE
Antarctic Press: Aug, 1985 - No. 4, Sept, 1986 (B&W)
1-Soft paper-c 2 4 6 11 16 20
2-4 2 4 6 8 11 14

MANGLE TANGLE TALES
Innovation Publishing: 1990 ($2.95, deluxe format)
1-Intro by Harlan Ellison 3.00

MANHUNT! (Becomes Red Fox #15 on)
Magazine Enterprises: 10/47 - No. 11, 8/48; #13,14, 1953 (no #12)
1-Red Fox by L. B. Cole, Undercover Girl by Whitney, Space Ace begin (1st app.); negligee panels 50 100 150 310 518 725
2-Electrocution-c 40 80 120 235 380 525
3-6: 6-Bondage-c 32 64 96 186 298 410
7-10: 7-Space Ace ends. 8-Trail Colt begins (intro/1st app., 5/48) by Guardineer; Trail Colt-c. 10-G. Ingels-a 28 56 84 162 261 360
11(8/48)-Frazetta-a, 7 pgs.; The Duke, Scotland Yard begin 40 80 120 244 397 550
13(A-1 #63)-Frazetta, r-/Trail Colt #1, 7 pgs. 40 80 120 235 380 525
14(A-1 #77)-Bondage/hypo-c; last L. B. Cole Red Fox; Ingels-a 40 80 120 235 380 525
NOTE: *Guardineer a-1-5; c-8. Whitney a-2-14; c-1-6, 10. Red Fox by L. B. Cole-#1-14. #15 was advertised but came out as Red Fox #15.*

MANHUNTER (See Adventure #58, 73, Brave & the Bold, Detective Comics, 1st Issue Special, House of Mystery #143 and Justice League of America)
DC Comics: 1984 ($2.50, 76 pgs; high quality paper)
1-Simonson-c/a(r)/Detective; Batman app. 3.50

MANHUNTER
DC Comics: July, 1988 - No. 24, Apr, 1990 ($1.00)
1-24: 8,9-Flash app. 9-Invasion. 17-Batman-c/sty 2.50

MANHUNTER
DC Comics: No. 0, Nov, 1994 - No. 12, Nov, 1995 ($1.95/$2.25)
0-12 2.50

MANHUNTER
DC Comics: Oct, 2004 - Present ($2.50/$2.99)
1-21: 1-Intro. Kate Spencer; Saiz-a/Jae Lee-c/Andreyko-s. 2,3 Shadow Thief app. 13,14-Omac x-over. 20-One Year Later 2.50
22-30: 22-Begin $2.99-c. 23-Sandra Knight app. 27-Chaykin-c. 28-Batman app. 3.00
31-33: 31-(8/08) Gaydos-a. 33-Suicide Squad app. 3.00

Man in Black #1 © HARV

Man-Thing #4 © MAR

Many Ghosts of Dr. Graves #49 © CC

	GD	VG	FN	VF	VF/NM	NM-
	2.0	4.0	6.0	8.0	9.0	9.2

...: Origins (2007, $17.99) r/#15-23 18.00
...: Street Justice (2005, $12.99) r/#1-5; Andreyko intro. 13.00
...: Trial By Fire (2007, $17.99) r/#6-14 18.00
...: Unleashed (2008, $17.99) r/#24-30 18.00

MANHUNTER: ...
DC Comics: 1979, 1999
The Complete Saga TPB (1979) Reprints stories from Detective Comics #437-443 by Goodwin and Simonson 40.00
The Special Edition TPB (1999, $9.95) r/stories from Detective Comics #437-443 10.00

MANIFEST ETERNITY
DC Comics: Aug, 2006 - No. 6, Jan, 2007 ($2.99)
1-6-Lobdell-s/Nguyen-a/c 3.00

MAN IN BLACK (See Thrill-O-Rama) (Also see All New Comics, Front Page, Green Hornet #31, Strange Story & Tally-Ho Comics)
Harvey Publications: Sept, 1957 - No. 4, Mar, 1958
1-Bob Powell-c/a 18 36 54 105 165 225
2-4: Powell-c/a 14 28 42 80 115 150

MAN IN BLACK
Lorne-Harvey Publications (Recollections): 1990 - No. 2, July, 1991 (B&W)
1,2 3.00

MAN IN FLIGHT (Disney, TV)
Dell Publishing Co.: No. 836, Sept, 1957
Four Color 836 7 14 21 47 76 105

MAN IN SPACE (Disney, TV, see Dell Giant #27)
Dell Publishing Co.: No. 716, Aug, 1956 - No. 954, Nov, 1958
Four Color 716-A science feat. from Tomorrowland 8 16 24 56 93 130
Four Color 954-Satellites 7 14 21 47 76 105

MANKIND (WWF Wrestling)
Chaos Comics: Sept, 1999 ($2.95, one-shot)
1-Regular and photo-c 3.00
1-Premium Edition ($10.00) Dwayne Turner & Danny Miki-c 10.00

MANN AND SUPERMAN
DC Comics: 2000 ($5.95, prestige format, one-shot)
nn-Michael T. Gilbert-s/a 6.00

MAN OF STEEL, THE (Also see Superman: The Man of Steel)
DC Comics: 1986 (June release) - No. 6, 1986 (75¢, limited series)
1-6: 1-Silver logo; Byrne-c/a/scripts in all; origin, 1-Alternate-c for newsstand sales,1-Distr. to toy stores by So Much Fun, 2-6: 2-Intro. Lois Lane, Jimmy Olsen. 3-Intro/origin Magpie; Batman-c/story. 4-Intro. new Lex Luthor 4.00
1-6-Silver Editions (1993, $1.95)-r/1-6 3.00
...The Complete Saga nn-Contains #1-6, given away in contest 35.00
Limited Edition, softcover 4 8 12 28 44 60
NOTE: *Issues 1-6 were released between Action #583 (9/86) & Action #584 (1/87) plus Superman #423 (9/86) & Advs. of Superman #424 (1/87).*

MAN OF THE ATOM (See Solar, Man of the Atom Vol. 2)

MAN OF WAR (See Liberty Guards & Liberty Scouts)
Centaur Publications: Nov, 1941 - No. 2, Jan, 1942
1-The Fire-Man, Man of War, The Sentinel, Liberty Guards, & Vapo-Man begin; Gustavson-c/a; Flag-c 167 334 501 1052 1776 2500
2-Intro The Ferret; Gustavson-c/a 122 244 366 769 1297 1825

MAN OF WAR
Eclipse Comics: Aug, 1987 - No. 3, Feb, 1988 ($1.75, Baxter paper)
1-3: Bruce Jones scripts 2.50

MAN OF WAR (See The Protectors)
Malibu Comics: 1993 - No, 8, Feb, 1994 ($1.95/$2.50/$2.25)
1-5 ($1.95)-Newsstand Editions w/different-c 2.50
1-8: 1-5-Collector's Edi. w/poster. 6-8 ($2.25): 6-Polybagged w/Skycap. 8-Vs. Rocket Rangers 3.00

MAN O' MARS
Fiction House Magazines: 1953; 1964
1-Space Rangers; Whitman-c 45 90 135 279 465 650
I.W. Reprint #1-r/Man O'Mars #1 & Star Pirate; Murphy Anderson-a 5 10 15 35 55 75

MANTECH ROBOT WARRIORS
Archie Enterprises, Inc.: Sept, 1984 - No. 4, Apr, 1985 (75¢)
1-4: Ayers-c/a(p). 1-Buckler-c(i) 3.00

	GD	VG	FN	VF	VF/NM	NM-
	2.0	4.0	6.0	8.0	9.0	9.2

MAN-THING (See Fear, Giant-Size..., Marvel Comics Presents, Marvel Fanfare, Monsters Unleashed, Power Record Comics & Savage Tales)
Marvel Comics Group: Jan, 1974 - No. 22, Oct, 1975; V2#1, Nov, 1979 - V2#11, July, 1981
1-Howard the Duck(2nd app.) cont'd/Fear #19 5 10 15 34 55 75
2 3 6 9 16 22 28
3-1st app. original Foolkiller 2 4 6 13 18 22
4-Origin Foolkiller; last app. 1st Foolkiller 2 4 6 11 16 20
5-11-Ploog-a. 11-Foolkiller cameo (flashback) 2 4 6 11 16 20
12-22: 19-1st app. Scavenger. 20-Spidey cameo. 21-Origin Scavenger, Man-Thing. 22-Howard the Duck cameo 2 4 6 8 10 12
V2#1(1979) 1 2 3 5 6 8
V2#2-11: 4-Dr. Strange-c/app. 11-Mayerik-a 4.00
NOTE: ***Alcala** a-14. **Brunner** c-1. **J. Buscema** a-12p, 13p, 16p. **Gil Kane** c-4p, 10p, 12-20p, 21. **Mooney** a-17, 18, 19p, 20-22, V2#1-3p. **Ploog** Man-Thing-5p, 6p, 7, 8, 9-11p; c-5, 6, 8, 9, 11. **Sutton** a-13i. No. 19 says #10 in indicia.*

MAN-THING (Volume Three, continues in Strange Tales #1 (9/98))
Marvel Comics: Dec, 1997 - No. 8, July, 1998 ($2.99)
1-8-DeMatteis-s/Sharp-a. 2-Two covers. 6-Howard the Duck-c/app. 3.00

MAN-THING (Prequel to 2005 movie)
Marvel Comics: Sept, 2004 - No. 3, Nov, 2004 ($2.99, limited series)
1-3-Hans Rodionoff-s/Kyle Hotz-a 3.00
...: Whatever Knows Fear... (2005, $12.99, TPB) r/#1-3, Savage Tales #1, Adv. Into Fear #16 13.00

MANTRA
Malibu Comics (Ultraverse): July, 1993 - No. 24, Aug, 1995 ($1.95/$2.50)
1-Polybagged w/trading card & coupon 3.00
1-Newsstand edition w/o trading card or coupon 2.50
1-Full cover holographic edition 1 3 4 6 8 10
1-Ultra-limited silver foil-c 5.00
2-9,11-24: 3-Intro Warstrike & Kismet. 6-Break-Thru x-over. 2-($2.50-Newsstand edition bagged w/card. 4-($2.50, 48 pgs.)-Rune flip-c/story by B. Smith (3 pgs.). 7-Prime app.; origin Prototype by Jurgens/Austin (2 pgs.). 11-New costume. 17-Intro NecroMantra & Pinnacle; prelude to Godwheel 2.50
10-($3.50, 68 pgs.)-Flip-c w/Ultraverse Premiere #2 3.50
Giant Size 1 (7/94, $2.50, 44 pgs.) 2.50
...Spear of Destiny 1,2 (4/95, $2.50, 36pgs.) 2.50

MANTRA (2nd Series) (Also See Black September)
Malibu Comics (Ultraverse): Infinity, Sept, 1995 - No. 7, Apr, 1996 ($1.50)
Infinity (9/95, $1.50)-Black September x-over, Intro new Mantra 2.50
1-7: 1-(10/95). 5-Return of Eden (original Mantra). 6,7-Rush app. 2.50

MAN WITH NO NAME, THE (Based on the Clint Eastwood gunslinger character)
Dynamite Entertainment: 2008 - Present ($3.50)
1-3-Gage-s/Dias-a/Isanove-c 3.50

MAN WITH THE SCREAMING BRAIN (Based on screenplay by Bruce Campbell & David Goodman)
Dark Horse Comics: Apr, 2005 - No. 4, July, 2005 ($2.99, limited series)
1-4-Campbell & Goodman-s; Remender-a/c. 1-Variant-c by Noto. 3-Powell var-c. 4-Mignola var-c 3.00
TPB (11/05, $13.95) r/#1-4; David Goodman intro.; cover gallery 14.00

MAN WITH THE X-RAY EYES, THE (See X,... under Movie Comics)

MANY GHOSTS OF DR. GRAVES, THE (Doctor Graves #73 on)
Charlton Comics: 5/67 - No. 60, 12/76; No. 61, 9/77 - No. 62, 10/77; No. 63, 2/78 - No. 65, 4/78; No. 66, 6/81 - No. 72, 5/82
1-Ditko-a; Palais-a; early issues 12¢-c 6 12 18 37 59 80
2-6,8,10 3 6 9 18 27 35
7,9-Ditko-a 3 6 9 20 30 40
11-13,16-18-Ditko-c/a 3 6 9 16 22 28
14,19,23,25 2 4 6 8 11 14
15,20,21-Ditko-a 2 4 6 10 14 18
22,24,26,27,29-35,38,40-Ditko-c/a 2 4 6 11 16 20
28-Ditko-c 2 4 6 10 14 18
36,46,56,57,59,61,66,67,69,71 1 2 3 5 7 9
37,41,43,51,60-Ditko-a 2 4 6 8 10 12
39,58-Ditko-c. 39-Sutton-a. 58-Ditko-a 2 4 6 8 10 12
42,44,53-Sutton-c; Ditko-a. 42-Sutton-a 2 4 6 8 10 12
45-(5/74) 2nd Newton comic work (8 pgs.); new logo; Sutton-c 2 4 6 9 13 16
47-Newton, Sutton, Ditko-a 2 4 6 8 11 14
48-Ditko, Sutton-a 2 4 6 8 10 12

Many Loves of Dobie Gillis #13 © DC

Marge's Little Lulu #10 © Marjorie Buell

Margie Comics #40 © MAR

	GD 2.0	VG 4.0	FN 6.0	VF 8.0	VF/NM 9.0	NM- 9.2
49-Newton-c/a; Sutton-a.	1	3	4	6	8	10
50-Sutton-a	1	2	3	5	7	9
52-Newton-c; Ditko-a	2	4	6	8	10	12
54-Early Byrne-c; Ditko-a	2	4	6	8	10	12
55-Ditko-c; Sutton-a	2	4	6	8	10	12
62-65,68-Ditko-c/a. 65-Sutton-a	2	4	6	9	13	16
70,72-Ditko-a	2	4	6	8	11	14
Modern Comics Reprint 12,25 (1978)						4.00

NOTE: ***Aparo** a-4, 5, 7, 8, 66r, 69r; c-8, 14, 19, 66r, 67r. **Byrne** c-54. **Ditko** a-1, 7, 9, 11-13, 15-18, 20-22, 24, 26, 27, 29, 30-35, 37, 38, 40-44, 47, 48, 51-54, 58, 60r-65r, 70, 72; c-11-13, 16-18, 22, 24, 26-35, 38, 40, 55, 58, 62-65. **Howard** a-38, 39, 45i, 65; c-48. **Kim** a-36, 46, 52. **Larson** a-58. **Morisi** a-10, 14, 23, 26. **Newton** a-45, 47p, 49p; c-49, 52. **Staton** a-36, 37, 41, 43. **Sutton** a-39, 42, 47-50, 55, 65; c-42, 44, 45; painted c-53. **Zeck** a-56, 59.*

MANY LOVES OF DOBIE GILLIS (TV)
National Periodical Publications: May-June, 1960 - No. 26, Oct, 1964

	GD	VG	FN	VF	VF/NM	NM-
1-Most covers by Bob Oskner	22	44	66	157	291	425
2-5	12	24	36	87	156	225
6-10: 10-Last 10¢-c	9	18	27	60	100	140
11-26: 20-Drucker-a. 24-(3-4/64). 25-(9/64)	8	16	24	54	90	125

MANY WORLDS OF TESLA STRONG, THE (Also see Tom Strong)
America's Best Comics: July, 2003 ($5.95, one-shot)

1-Two covers by Timm & Art Adams; art by various incl. Campbell, Cho, Noto, Hughes 6.00

MARAUDER'S MOON (See Luke Short, Four Color #848)

MARCH OF COMICS (See Promotional Comics section)

MARCH OF CRIME (Formerly My Love Affair #1-6) (See Fox Giants)
Fox Features Synd.: No. 7, July, 1950 - No. 2, Sept, 1950; No. 3, Sept, 1951

	GD	VG	FN	VF	VF/NM	NM-
7(#1)(7/50)-True crime stories; Wood-a	40	80	120	244	397	550
2(9/50)-Wood-a (exceptional)	40	80	120	235	380	525
3(9/51)	19	38	57	112	176	240

MARCO POLO
Charlton Comics Group: 1962 (Movie classic)

	GD	VG	FN	VF	VF/NM	NM-
nn (Scarce)-Glanzman-c/a (25 pgs.)	10	20	30	67	116	165

MARC SILVESTRI SKETCHBOOK
Image Comics (Top Cow): Jan, 2004 ($2.99, one-shot)

1-Character sketches, concept artwork, storyboards of Witchblade, Darkness & others 3.00

MARC SPECTOR: MOON KNIGHT (Also see Moon Knight)
Marvel Comics: June, 1989 - No. 60, Mar, 1994 ($1.50/$1.75, direct sales)

1-24,26-49,51-54,58,59: 4-Intro new Midnight. 8,9-Punisher app. 15-Silver Sable app. 19-21-Spider-Man & Punisher app. 25-(52 pgs.)-Ghost Rider app. 32,33-Hobgoblin II (Macendale) & Spider-Man (in black costume) app. 35-38-Punisher story. 42-44-Infinity War x-over. 46-Demogoblin app. 51,53-Gambit app. 55-New look. 57-Spider-Man-c/story. 60-Moon Knight dies 2.50
50-(56 pgs.)-Special die-cut-c 3.00
55-57,60-Platt a 3.50
...: Divided We Fall ($4.95, 52 pgs.) 5.00
Special 1 (1992, $2.50) 2.50

NOTE: *Cowan c(p) 20-23. Guice c-20. Heath c/a-4. Platt -a 55-57,60; c-55-60.*

MARGARET O'BRIEN (See The Adventures of...)

MARGE'S LITTLE LULU (Continues as Little Lulu from #207 on)
Dell Publishing Co./Gold Key #165-206: No. 74, 6/45 - No. 164, 7-9/62; No. 165, 10/62 - No. 206, 8/72

Marjorie Henderson Buell, born in Philadelphia, Pa., in 1904, created Little Lulu, a cartoon character that appeared weekly in the Saturday Evening Post from Feb. 23, 1935 through Dec. 30, 1944. She was not responsible for any of the comic books. **John Stanley** did pencils only on all Little Lulu comics through at least #135 (1959). He did pencils and inks on Four Color #74 & 97. **Irving Tripp** began inking stories from #1 on, and remained the comic's illustrator throughout its entire run. **Stanley** did storyboards (layouts), pencils, and scripts in all cases and inking only on covers. His word balloons were written in cursive. **Tripp** and occasionally other artists at Western Publ. in Poughkeepsie, N.Y. blew up the pencilled pages, inked the blowups, and lettered them. **Arnold Drake** did storyboards, pencils and scripts starting with #197 (1970) on, amidst reprinted issues. **Buell** sold her rights exclusively to Western Publ. in Dec., 1971. The earlier issues had to be approved by **Buell** prior to publication.

	GD	VG	FN	VF	VF/NM	NM-
Four Color 74('45)-Intro Lulu, Tubby & Alvin	121	242	363	1029	1965	2900
Four Color 97(2/46)	51	102	153	434	830	1225
(Above two books are all John Stanley - cover, pencils, and Inks.)						
Four Color 110('46)-1st Alvin Story Telling Time; 1st app. Willy; variant cover exists	37	74	111	280	528	775
Four Color 115-1st app. Boys' Clubhouse	36	72	108	277	514	750
Four Color 120, 131: 120-1st app. Eddie	30	60	90	232	434	635
Four Color 139('47),146,158	30	60	90	225	418	610
Four Color 165 (10/47)-Smokes doll hair & has wild hallucinations. 1st Tubby detective story	30	60	90	225	418	610
1(1-2/48)-Lulu's Diary feature begins	63	126	189	536	1018	1500
2-1st app. Gloria; 1st Tubby story in a L.L. comic; 1st app. Miss Feeny	30	60	90	229	427	625
3-5	28	56	84	207	384	560
6-10: 7-1st app. Annie; Xmas-c	23	46	69	167	309	450
11-20: 18-X-Mas-c. 19-1st app. Wilbur. 20-1st app. Mr. McNabbem	18	36	54	130	240	350
21-30: 26-r/F.C. 110. 30-Xmas-c	15	30	45	111	206	300
31-38,40: 35-1st Mumday story	13	26	39	93	164	235
39-Intro. Witch Hazel in "That Awful Witch Hazel"	13	26	39	95	168	240
41-60: 42-Xmas-c. 45-2nd Witch Hazel app. 49-Gives Stanley & others credit	11	22	33	79	140	200
61-80: 63-1st app. Chubby (Tubby's cousin). 68-1st app. Prof. Cleff. 78-Xmas-c. 80-Intro. Little Itch (2/55)	9	18	27	63	107	150
81-99: 90-Xmas-c	8	16	24	52	86	120
100	8	16	24	56	93	130
101-130: 123-1st app. Fifi	6	12	18	41	66	90
131-164: 135-Last Stanley-p	5	10	15	34	55	75
165-Giant; ...in Paris ('62)	10	20	30	71	126	180
166-Giant; ...Christmas Diary (1962 - '63)	10	20	30	71	126	180
167-169	4	8	12	28	44	60
170,172,175,176,178-196,198-200-Stanley-r. 182-1st app. Little Scarecrow Boy	3	6	9	16	23	30
171,173,174,177,197	3	6	9	14	19	24
201,203,206-Last issue to carry Marge's name	2	4	6	13	18	22
202,204,205-Stanley-r	3	6	9	14	19	24
...& Tubby in Japan (12¢)(5-7/62) 01476-207	7	14	21	50	83	115
...Summer Camp 1(8/67-G.K.-Giant) '57-58-r	6	12	18	41	66	90
...Trick 'N' Treat 1(12¢)(12/62-Gold Key)	7	14	21	45	73	100

NOTE: *See Dell Giant Comics #23, 29, 36, 42, 50, & Dell Giants for annuals. All Giants not by Stanley from L.L. on Vacation (7/54) on. Irving Tripp a-#1-on. Christmas c-7, 18, 30, 42, 78, 90, 126, 166, 250. Summer Camp issues #173, 177, 181, 189, 197, 201, 206.*

MARGE'S LITTLE LULU (See Golden Comics Digest #10, 23, 27, 29, 33, 36, 40, 43, 46, & March of Comics #251, 267, 275, 293, 307, 323, 335, 349, 355, 369, 385, 400, 417, 427, 430, 456, 468, 475, 488)

MARGE'S TUBBY (Little Lulu)(See Dell Giants)
Dell Publishing Co./Gold Key: No. 381, Aug, 1952 - No. 49, Dec-Feb, 1961-62

	GD	VG	FN	VF	VF/NM	NM-
Four Color 381(#1)-Stanley script; Irving Tripp-a	20	40	60	143	264	385
Four Color 430,444 Stanley-a	12	24	36	84	150	215
Four Color 461 (4/53)-1st Tubby & Men From Mars story; Stanley-a	10	20	30	73	129	185
5 (7-9/53)-Stanley-a	9	18	27	60	100	140
6-10	7	14	21	50	83	115
11-20	6	12	18	37	59	80
21-30	5	10	15	30	48	65
31-49	4	8	12	26	41	55
...& the Little Men From Mars No. 30020-410(10/64-G.K.)-25¢, 68 pgs.	8	16	24	52	86	120

NOTE: ***John Stanley** did all storyboards & scripts through at least #35 (1959). **Lloyd White** did all art except F.C. 381, 430, 444, 461 & #5.*

MARGIE (See My Little...)

MARGIE (TV)
Dell Publ. Co.: No. 1307, Mar-May, 1962 - No. 2, July-Sept, 1962 (Photo-c)

	GD	VG	FN	VF	VF/NM	NM-
Four Color 1307(#1)	6	12	18	37	59	80
2	5	10	15	30	48	65

MARGIE COMICS (Formerly Comedy Comics; Reno Browne #50 on)
(Also see Cindy Comics & Teen Comics)
Marvel Comics (ACI): No. 35, Winter, 1946-47 - No. 49, Dec, 1949

	GD	VG	FN	VF	VF/NM	NM-
35	18	36	54	103	162	220
36-38,42,45,47-49	11	22	33	62	86	110
39,41,43(2),44,46-Kurtzman's "Hey Look"	12	24	36	69	97	125
40-Three "Hey Looks", three "Giggles 'n' Grins" by Kurtzman	14	28	42	78	112	145

MARINES (See Tell It to the...)

MARINES ATTACK
Charlton Comics: Aug, 1964 - No. 9, Feb-Mar, 1966

	GD	VG	FN	VF	VF/NM	NM-
1-Glanzman-a begins	4	8	12	22	34	45
2-9	3	6	9	14	19	24

MARINES AT WAR (Formerly Tales of the Marines #4)
Atlas Comics (OPI): No. 5, Apr, 1957 - No. 7, Aug, 1957

	GD	VG	FN	VF	VF/NM	NM-
5-7	10	20	30	54	72	90

NOTE: ***Colan** a-5. **Drucker** a-5. **Everett** a-5. **Maneely** a-5. **Orlando** a-7. **Severin** c-5.*

MARINES IN ACTION
Atlas News Co.: June, 1955 - No. 14, Sept, 1957

Marmaduke Mouse #6 © QUA

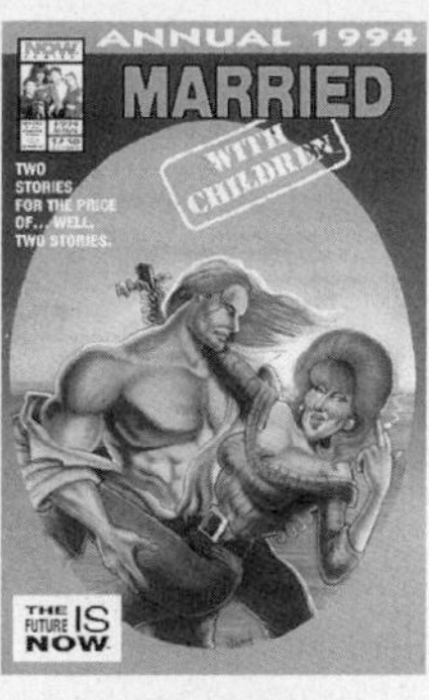

Married With Children 1994 Annual © ELP

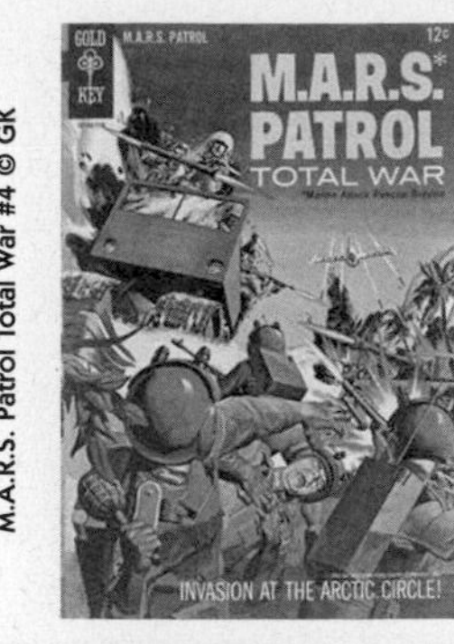

M.A.R.S. Patrol Total War #4 © GK

	GD 2.0	VG 4.0	FN 6.0	VF 8.0	VF/NM 9.0	NM- 9.2
1-Rock Murdock, Boot Camp Brady begin	13	26	39	74	105	135
2-14	10	20	30	54	72	90

NOTE: ***Berg** a-2, 8, 9, 11, 14. **Heath** c-2, 9. **Maneely** c-1. **Severin** a-4; c-7-11, 14.*

MARINES IN BATTLE
Atlas Comics (ACI No. 1-12/WPI No. 13-25): Aug, 1954 - No. 25, Sept, 1958

	GD	VG	FN	VF	VF/NM	NM-
1-Heath-c; Iron Mike McGraw by Heath; history of U.S. Marine Corps. begins	21	42	63	123	197	270
2-Heath-c	13	26	39	74	105	135
3-6,8-10: 4-Last precode (2/55)	10	20	30	58	79	100
7-Kubert/Moskowitz-a (6 pgs.)	11	22	33	60	83	105
11-16,18-21,24	10	20	30	54	72	90
17-Williamson-a (3 pgs.)	11	22	33	62	86	110
22,25-Torres-a	10	20	30	56	76	95
23-Crandall-a; Mark Murdock app.	10	20	30	58	79	100

NOTE: ***Berg** a-22. **G. Colan** a-22, 23. **Drucker** a-6. **Everett** a-4, 15; c-21. **Heath** c-1, 2, 4. **Maneely** c-23, 24. **Orlando** a-14. **Pakula** a-6, 23. **Powell** a-16. **Severin** a-22; c-12. **Sinnott** a-23. **Tuska** a-15.*

MARINE WAR HEROES (Charlton Premiere #19 on)
Charlton Comics: Jan, 1964 - No. 18, Mar, 1967

	GD	VG	FN	VF	VF/NM	NM-
1-Montes/Bache-c/a	4	8	12	23	36	48
2-18: 14,18-Montes/Bache-a	3	6	9	14	20	26

MARK, THE (Also see Mayhem)
Dark Horse Comics: Dec, 1993 - No. 4, Mar, 1994 ($2.50, limited series)

1-4						2.50

MARK HAZZARD: MERC
Marvel Comics Group: Nov, 1986 - No. 12, Oct, 1987 (75¢)

1-12: Morrow-a, Annual 1 (11/87, $1.25)						2.50

MARK OF CHARON (See Negation)
CG Entertainment: Apr, 2003 - No. 5, Aug, 2003 ($2.95, limited series)

1-5-Bedard-s/Bennett-a						3.00

MARK OF ZORRO (See Zorro, Four Color #228)

MARK 1 COMICS (Also see Shaloman)
Mark 1 Comics: Apr, 1988 - No. 3, Mar, 1989 ($1.50)

1-3: Early Shaloman app. 2-Origin						2.50

MARKSMAN, THE (Also see Champions)
Hero Comics: Jan, 1988 - No. 5, 1988 ($1.95)

1-5: 1-Rose begins. 1-3-Origin The Marksman						2.50
Annual 1 ('88, $2.75, 52pgs)-Champions app.						2.75

MARK TRAIL
Standard Magazines (Hall Syndicate)/Fawcett Publ. No. 5: Oct, 1955; No. 5, Summer, 1959

	GD	VG	FN	VF	VF/NM	NM-
1(1955)-Sunday strip-r	7	14	21	37	46	55
5(1959)	5	10	15	22	26	30
...Adventure Book of Nature 1 (Summer, 1958, 25¢, Pines)-100 pg. Giant; Special Camp Issue; contains 78 Sunday strip-r	9	18	27	52	69	85

MARMADUKE MONK
I. W. Enterprises/Super Comics: No date; 1963 (10¢)

	GD	VG	FN	VF	VF/NM	NM-
I.W. Reprint 1 (nd)	2	4	6	8	11	14
Super Reprint 14 (1963)-r/Monkeyshines Comics #?	2	4	6	8	10	12

MARMADUKE MOUSE
Quality Comics Group (Arnold Publ.): Spring, 1946 - No. 65, Dec, 1956 (Early issues: 52 pgs.)

	GD	VG	FN	VF	VF/NM	NM-
1-Funny animal	17	34	51	98	154	210
2	11	22	33	60	83	105
3-10	9	18	27	47	61	75
11-30	7	14	21	35	43	50
31-65: Later issues are 36 pgs.	6	12	18	28	34	40
Super Reprint #14(1963)	2	4	6	9	12	15

MARQUIS, THE
Oni Press

...: A Sin of One ($2.99, 5/03) Guy Davis-s/a; Michael Gaydos-c						3.00
...: Intermezzo TPB ($11.95, 12/03) r/A Sin of One and Hell's Courtesan #1,2						12.00

MARQUIS, THE: DANSE MACABRE
Oni Press: May, 2000 - No. 5, Feb, 2001 ($2.95, B&W, limited series)

1-5-Guy Davis-s/a. 1-Wagner-c. 2-Mignola-c. 3-Vess-c. 5-K. Jones-c						3.00
TPB (8/2001, $18.95) r/1-5 & Les Preludes; Seagle intro.						19.00

MARQUIS, THE: DEVIL'S REIGN: HELL'S COURTESAN
Oni Press: Feb, 2002 - No. 2, Apr, 2002 ($2.95, B&W, limited series)

	GD 2.0	VG 4.0	FN 6.0	VF 8.0	VF/NM 9.0	NM- 9.2
1,2-Guy Davis-s/a						3.00

MARRIAGE OF HERCULES AND XENA, THE
Topps Comics: July, 1998 ($2.95, one-shot)

1-Photo-c; Lopresti-a; Alex Ross pin-up, 1-Alex Ross painted-c						3.00
1-Gold foil logo-c						5.00

MARRIED ... WITH CHILDREN (TV)(Based on Fox TV show)
Now Comics: June, 1990 - No. 7, Feb, 1991(12/90 inside) ($1.75)
V2#1, Sept, 1991 - No. 12, 1992 ($1.95)

1-7: 2-Photo-c, 1,2-2nd printing, V2#1-12: 1,4,5,9-Photo-c						2.50
...Buck's Tale (6/94, $1.95)						2.50
...1994 Annual nn (2/94, $2.50, 52 pgs.)-Flip book format						3.00
Special 1 (7/92, $1.95)-Kelly Bundy photo-c/poster						2.50

MARRIED ... WITH CHILDREN: KELLY BUNDY
Now Comics: Aug, 1992 - No. 3, Oct, 1992 ($1.95, limited series)

1-3: Kelly Bundy photo-c & poster in each						2.50

MARRIED ... WITH CHILDREN: QUANTUM QUARTET
Now Comics: Oct, 1993 - No. 4, 1994, ($1.95, limited series)

1-4: Fantastic Four parody						2.50

MARRIED ... WITH CHILDREN: 2099
Now Comics: June, 1993 - No. 3, Aug, 1993 ($1.95, limited series)

1-3						2.50

MARS
First Comics: Jan, 1984 - No. 12, Jan, 1985 ($1.00, Mando paper)

1-12: Marc Hempel & Mark Wheatley story & art. 2-The Black Flame begins. 10-Dynamo Joe begins						2.50
TPB (IDW Publ., 8/05, $39.99) r/#1-12, creator commentary; bonus art; new Hempel-c						40.00

MARS & BEYOND (Disney, TV)
Dell Publishing Co.: No. 866, Dec, 1957

	GD	VG	FN	VF	VF/NM	NM-
Four Color 866-A Science feat. from Tomorrowland	8	16	24	56	93	130

MARS ATTACKS
Topps Comics: May, 1994 - No. 5, Sept, 1994 ($2.95, limited series)

	GD	VG	FN	VF	VF/NM	NM-
1-5-Giffen story; flip books						4.50
Special Edition	2	4	6	8	10	12
Trade paperback (12/94, $12.95)-r/limited series plus new 8 pg. story						13.00

MARS ATTACKS
Topps Comics: V2#1, 8/95 - V2#3, 10/95; V2#4, 1/96 - No. 7, 5/96($2.95, bi-monthly #6 on)

V2#1-7: 1-Counterstrike storyline begins. 4-(1/96). 5-(1/96). 5,7-Brereton-c. 6-(3/96)-Simonson-c. 7-Story leads into Baseball Special #1						3.00
Baseball Special 1 (6/96, $2.95)-Bisley-c.						3.00

MARS ATTACKS HIGH SCHOOL
Topps Comics: May, 1997 - No. 2, Sept, 1997 ($2.95, B&W, limited series)

1,2-Stelfreeze-c						3.00

MARS ATTACKS IMAGE
Topps Comics: Dec, 1996 - No. 4, Mar, 1997 ($2.50, limited series)

1-4-Giffen-s/Smith/Sienkiewicz-a						3.00

MARS ATTACKS THE SAVAGE DRAGON
Topps Comics: Dec, 1996 - No. 4, Mar, 1997 ($2.95, limited series)

1-4: 1-w/bound-in card						3.00

MARSHAL BLUEBERRY (See Blueberry)
Marvel Comics (Epic Comics): 1991 ($14.95, graphic novel)

	GD	VG	FN	VF	VF/NM	NM-
1-Moebius-a	2	4	6	13	18	22

MARSHAL LAW (Also see Crime And Punishment: Marshall Law...)
Marvel Comics (Epic Comics): Oct, 1987 - No. 6, May, 1989 ($1.95, mature)

1-6						2.50

M.A.R.S. PATROL TOTAL WAR (Formerly Total War #1,2)
Gold Key: No. 3, Sept, 1966 - No. 10, Aug, 1969 (All-Painted-c except #7)

	GD	VG	FN	VF	VF/NM	NM-
3-Wood-a; aliens invade USA	6	12	18	39	62	85
4-10	4	8	12	23	36	48
Wally Wood's M.A.R.S. Patrol Total War TPB (Dark Horse, 9/04, $12.95) r/#3 & Total War #1&2; foreward by Batton Lash; afterword by Dan Adkins						13.00

MARTHA WASHINGTON (Also see Dark Horse Presents Fifth Anniversary Special, Dark Horse Presents #100-4, Give Me Liberty, Happy Birthday Martha Washington & San Diego Comicon Comics #2)

MARTHA WASHINGTON... (one-shots)
Dark Horse Comics (Legend): ($2.95/$3.50, one-shots)

Martian Manhunter #29 © DC

Marvel Adventures Fantastic Four #0 © MAR

Marvel Adventures Hulk #4 © MAR

... Dies (7/07, $3.50) Miller-s/Gibbons-a; r/Miller's original outline for Give Me Liberty 3.50
... Stranded in Space (11/95, $2.95) Miller-s/Gibbons-a; Big Guy app. 3.00

MARTHA WASHINGTON GOES TO WAR
Dark Horse Comics (Legend): May, 1994 - No. 5, Sep, 1994 ($2.95, lim. series)
1-5-Miller scripts; Gibbons-c/a 3.00
TPB ($17.95) r/#1-5 18.00

MARTHA WASHINGTON SAVES THE WORLD
Dark Horse Comics: Dec, 1997 - No. 3, Feb, 1998 ($2.95/$3.95, lim. series)
1,2-Miller scripts; Gibbons-c/a in all 3.00
3-($3.95) 4.00

MARTHA WAYNE (See The Story of...)

MARTIAN MANHUNTER (See Detective Comics & Showcase '95 #9)
DC Comics: May, 1988 - No. 4, Aug,. 1988 ($1.25, limited series)
1-4: 1,4-Batman app. 2-Batman cameo 2.50
Special 1-(1996, $3.50) 3.50

MARTIAN MANHUNTER (See JLA)
DC Comics: No. 0, Oct, 1998 - No. 36, Nov, 2001 ($1.99)
0-(10/98) Origin retold; Ostrander-s/Mandrake-c/a 3.00
1-36: 1-(12/98). 6-9-JLA app. 18,19-JSA app. 24-Mahnke-a 2.50
#1,000,000 (11/98) 853rd Century x-over 2.50
Annual 1,2 (1998,1999; $2.95) 1-Ghosts, Wrightson c. 2-JLApe 3.00

MARTIAN MANHUNTER (See DCU Brave New World)
DC Comics: Oct, 2006 - No. 8, May, 2007 ($2.99, limited series)
1-8-Lieberman-s/Barrionuevo-a/c 3.00
: The Others Among Us TPB (2007, $19.99) r/#1-8 & story from DCU Brave New World 20.00

MARTIAN MANHUNTER: AMERICAN SECRETS
DC Comics: 1992 - Book Three, 1992 ($4.95, limited series, prestige format)
1-3: Barreto-a 5.00

MARTIN KANE (William Gargan as... Private Eye)(Stage/Screen/Radio/TV)
Fox Features Syndicate (Hero Books): No. 4, June, 1950 - No. 2, Aug, 1950 (Formerly My Secret Affair)
4(#1)-True crime stories; Wood-c/a(2); used in **SOTI**, pg. 160; photo back-c 31 62 93 181 291 400
2-Wood/Orlando story, 5 pgs; Wood-a(2) 23 46 69 135 218 300

MARTIN MYSTERY
Dark Horse (Bonelli Comics): Mar, 1999 - No. 6, Aug, 1999 ($4.95, B&W, digest size)
1-6-Reprints Italian series in English; Gibbons-c on #1-3 5.00

MARTY MOUSE
I. W. Enterprises: No date (1958?) (10¢)
1-Reprint 2 4 6 9 12 15

MARVEL ACTION HOUR FEATURING IRON MAN (TV cartoon)
Marvel Comics: Nov, 1994 - No. 8, June, 1995 ($1.50/$2.95)
1-8: Based on cartoon series 2.50
1 ($2.95)-Polybagged w/16 pg Marvel Action Hour Preview & acetate print 3.00

MARVEL ACTION HOUR FEATURING THE FANTASTIC FOUR (TV cartoon)
Marvel Comics: Nov, 1994 - No. 8, June, 1995 ($1.50/$2.95)
1-8: Based on cartoon series 2.50
1-($2.95)-Polybagged w/ 16 pg. Marvel Action Hour Preview & acetate print 3.00

MARVEL ACTION UNIVERSE (TV cartoon)
Marvel Comics: Jan, 1989 ($1.00, one-shot)
1-r/Spider-Man And His Amazing Friends 4.00

MARVEL ADVENTURES
Marvel Comics: Apr, 1997 - No. 18, Sept, 1998 ($1.50)
1-18-"Animated style": 1,4,7-Hulk-c/app. 2,11-Spider-Man. 3,8,15-X-Men. 5-Spider-Man & X-Men. 6-Spider-Man & Human Torch. 9,12-Fantastic Four. 10,16-Silver Surfer. 13-Spider-Man & Silver Surfer. 14-Hulk & Dr. Strange. 18-Capt. America 2.50

MARVEL ADVENTURES FANTASTIC FOUR (All ages title)
Marvel Comics: No. 0, July, 2005 - Present ($1.99/$2.50/$2.99)
0-($1.99) Movie version characters; Dr. Doom app.; Eaton-a 2.50
1-10-($2.50) 1-Skrulls app.; Pagulayan-a. 7-Namor app. 2.50
11-40-($2.99) 12-Dr. Doom app. 24-Namor app. 26,28-Silver Surfer app. 3.00
... Vol. 1: Family of Heroes (2005, $6.99, digest) r/#1-4 7.00
... Vol. 2: Fantastic Voyages (2006, $6.99, digest) r/#5-8 7.00
... Vol. 3: World's Greatest (2006, $6.99, digest) r/#9-12 7.00
... Vol. 4: Cosmic Threats (2006, $6.99, digest) r/#13-16 7.00
... Vol. 5: All 4 One, 4 For All (2007, $6.99, digest) r/#17-20 7.00
... Vol. 6: Monsters & Mysteries (2007, $6.99, digest) r/#21-24 7.00
... Vol. 7: The Silver Surfer (2007, $6.99, digest) r/#25-28 7.00

MARVEL ADVENTURES FLIP MAGAZINE (All ages title)
Marvel Comics: Aug, 2005 - Present ($3.99/$4.99)
1-11: 1-10-Rep. Marvel Advs. Fantastic Four and Marvel Advs. Spider-Man in flip format 4.00
12-14-($4.99) Reprints Marvel Advs. Spider-Man & X-Men/Power Pack in flip format 5.00
15-26-Rep. Marvel Advs. Fantastic Four and Marvel Advs. Spider-Man in flip format 5.00

MARVEL ADVENTURES HULK (All ages title)
Marvel Comics: Sept, 2007 - Present ($2.99)
1-15: 1-New version of Hulk's origin; Pagulayan-c. 2-Jamie Madrox app. 13-Mummies 3.00
... Vol. 1: Misunderstood Monster (2007, $6.99, digest) r/#1-4 7.00

MARVEL ADVENTURES IRON MAN (All ages title)
Marvel Comics: July, 2007 - Present ($2.99)
1-13: 1-4-Michael Golden c. 1-New version of Iron Man's origin. 2-Intro. the Mandarin 3.00
... Vol. 1: Heart of Steel (2007, $6.99, digest) r/#1-4 7.00
... Vol. 2: Iron Armory (2008, $7.99, digest) r/#5-8 8.00

MARVEL ADVENTURES SPIDER-MAN (All ages title)
Marvel Comics: May, 2005 - Present ($2.50/$2.99)
1-13-Lee & Ditko stories retold with new art. 13-Conner-c 2.50
14-43: 14-Begin $2.99-c. 14-16-Conner-c. 22,23-Black costume. 35-Venom app. 3.00
... Vol. 1 HC (2006, $19.99, with dustjacket) r/#1-8; plot for #7; sketch pages from #6,8 20.00
... Vol. 1: The Sinister Six (2005, $6.99, digest) r/#1-4 7.00
... Vol. 2: Power Struggle (2005, $6.99, digest) r/#5-8 7.00
... Vol. 3: Doom With a View (2006, $6.99, digest) r/#9-12 7.00
... Vol. 4: Concrete Jungle (2006, $6.99, digest) r/#13-16 7.00
... Vol. 5: Monsters on the Prowl (2007, $6.99, digest) r/#17-20 7.00
... Vol. 6: The Black Costume (2007, $6.99, digest) r/#21-24 7.00
... Vol. 7: Secret Identity (2007, $6.99, digest) r/#25-28 7.00
... Vol. 8: Forces of Nature (2008, $7.99, digest) r/#29-32 8.00
... Vol. 9: Fiercest Foes (2008, $7.99, digest) r/#33-36 8.00

MARVEL ADVENTURES STARRING DAREDEVIL (...Adventure #3 on)
Marvel Comics Group: Dec, 1975 - No. 6, Oct, 1976
1 1 3 4 6 8 10
2-6-r/Daredevil #22-27 by Colan. 3-5-(25¢-c) 6.00
3-5-(30¢-c variants, limited distribution)(4,6,8/76) 2 4 6 11 16 20

MARVEL ADVENTURES SUPER HEROES (All ages title)
Marvel Comics: Sept, 2008 - Present ($2.99)
1-3-Spider-Man, Hulk and Iron Man team-ups; Hercules app. 3.00

MARVEL ADVENTURES THE AVENGERS (All ages title)
Marvel Comics: July, 2006 - Present ($2.99)
1-28-Spider-Man, Wolverine, Hulk, Iron Man, Capt. America, Storm, Giant-Girl app. 3.00
... Vol. 1: Heroes Assembled (2006, $6.99, digest) r/#1-4 7.00
... Vol. 2: Mischief (2007, $6.99, digest) r/#5-8 7.00
... Vol. 3: Bizarre Adventures (2007, $6.99, digest) r/#9-12 7.00
... Vol. 4: The Dream Team (2007, $6.99, digest) r/#13-15 & Giant-Size #1 7.00
... Vol. 5: Some Assembling Required (2008, $7.99, digest) r/#16-19 8.00

MARVEL ADVENTURES TWO-IN-ONE
Marvel Comics: Oct, 2007 - Present ($4.99, bi-weekly)
1-15: 1-9-Reprints Marvel Adventures Spider-Man and Fantastic Four stories. 10-Hulk 5.00

MARVEL AGE FANTASTIC FOUR (All ages title)
Marvel Comics: Jun, 2004 - No. 12, Mar, 2005 ($2.25)
1-12-Lee & Kirby stories retold with new art by various. 11-Impossible Man app. 2.50
...Tales (4/05, $2.25) retells first meeting with the Black Panther; O'Hare & Lim-a 2.50
Vol. 1: All For One TPB (2004, $5.99, digest size) r/#1-4 6.00
Vol. 2: Doom TPB (2004, $5.99, digest size) r/#5-8 6.00
Vol. 3: The Return of Doctor Doom TPB (2005, $5.99, digest size) r/#9-12 6.00

MARVEL AGE HULK (All ages title)
Marvel Comics: Nov, 2004 - No. 4, Feb, 2005 ($1.75)
1-3-Lee & Kirby stories retold with new art by various 2.50
Vol. 1: Incredible TPB (2005, $5.99, digest size) r/#1-4 6.00
Vol. 2: Defenders (2008, $7.99, digest) r/#5-8 8.00

MARVEL AGE SPIDER-MAN (All ages title) (Also see Free Comic Book Day edition in the Promotional Comics section)
Marvel Comics: May, 2004 - No. 20, Mar, 2005 ($2.25)
1-20-Lee & Ditko stories retold with new art. 4-Doctor Doom app. 5-Lizard app. 2.50
Vol. 1 TPB (2004, $5.99, digest) 1-r/#1-4 6.00

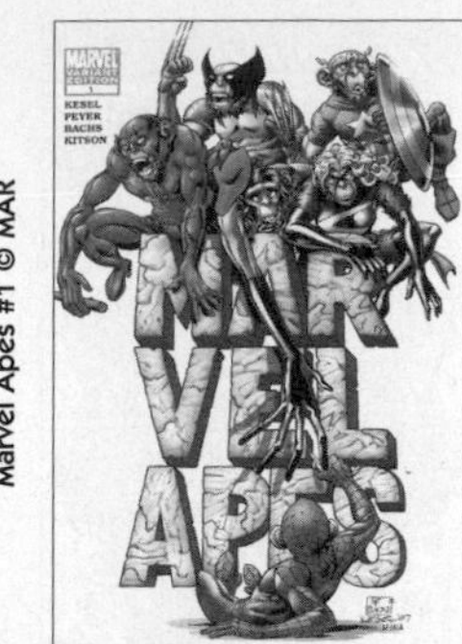

Marvel Apes #1 © MAR

Marvel Comics #1 © MAR

Marvel Comics Presents #2 © MAR

GD VG FN VF VF/NM NM-
2.0 4.0 6.0 8.0 9.0 9.2

GD VG FN VF VF/NM NM-
2.0 4.0 6.0 8.0 9.0 9.2

Vol. 2: Everyday Hero TPB (2004, $5.99, digest) r/#5-8 6.00
Vol. 3: Swingtime TPB (2004, $5.99, digest) r/#9-12 6.00
Spidey Strikes Back TPB (2005, 5.99, digest) r/#17-20 6.00

MARVEL AGE TEAM-UP (All ages Spider-Man team-ups) (Also see Free Comic Book Day edition in the Promotional Comics section)
Marvel Comics: Nov, 2004 - No. 5, Apr, 2005 ($1.75)

1-5-Stories retold with new art by various. 1-Fantastic Four app. 3-Kitty Pryde app. 2.50
... Vol. 1: A Little Help From My Friends (2005, $7.99, digest) r/#1-5 8.00

MARVEL AND DC PRESENT FEATURING THE UNCANNY X-MEN AND THE NEW TEEN TITANS
Marvel Comics/DC Comics: 1982 ($2.00, 68 pgs., one-shot, Baxter paper)

1-3rd app. Deathstroke the Terminator; Darkseid app.; Simonson/Austin-c/a
2 4 6 11 16 20

MARVEL APES
Marvel Comics: Nov, 2008 - No. 4 ($3.99, limited series)

1,2: 1-Kesel-s/Bachs-a; back-up history story with Peyer-s/Kitson-a; two covers 4.00

MARVEL ATLAS (Styled after the Official Marvel Handbooks)
Marvel Comics: 2007 - No. 2, 2008 ($3.99, limited series)

1,2-Profiles and maps of countries in the Marvel Universe 4.00

MARVEL BOY (Astonishing #3 on; see Marvel Super Action #4)
Marvel Comics (MPC): Dec, 1950 - No. 2, Feb, 1951

1-Origin Marvel Boy by Russ Heath 112 224 336 706 1191 1675
2-Everett-a 78 156 234 491 833 1175

MARVEL BOY (Marvel Knights)
Marvel Comics: Aug, 2000 - No. 6, Mar, 2001 ($2.99, limited series)

1-Intro. Marvel Boy; Morrison-s/J.G. Jones-c/a 3.50
1-DF Variant-c 5.00
2-6 3.00
TPB (6/01, $15.95) 16.00

MARVEL CHILLERS (Also see Giant-Size Chillers)
Marvel Comics Group: Oct, 1975 - No. 7, Oct, 1976 (All 25¢ issues)

1-Intro. Modred the Mystic, ends #2; Kane-c(p) 2 4 6 9 13 16
2,4,5,7: 4-Kraven app. 5,6-Red Wolf app. 7-Kirby-c; Tuska-p
1 3 4 6 8 10
3-Tigra, the Were-Woman begins (origin), ends #7 (see Giant-Size Creatures #1). Chaykin/Wrightson-c. 3 6 9 14 19 24
4-6-(30¢-c variants, limited distribution)(4-8/76) 3 6 9 18 27 35
6-Byrne-a(p); Buckler-c(p) 2 4 6 8 11 14
NOTE: *Bolle a-1. Buckler c-2. Kirby c-7.*

MARVEL CLASSICS COMICS SERIES FEATURING...
(Also see Pendulum Illustrated Classics)
Marvel Comics Group: 1976 - No. 36, Dec, 1978 (52 pgs., no ads)

1-Dr. Jekyll and Mr. Hyde 2 4 6 10 14 18
2-10,28: 28-1st Golden-c/a; Pit and the Pendulum 2 4 6 8 10 12
11-27,29-36 1 2 3 5 7 9
NOTE: ***Adkins** c-1i, 4i, 12i. **Alcala** a-34i; c-34. **Bolle** a-35. **Buscema** c-17p, 19p, 26p. **Golden** c/a-28. **Gil Kane** c-1-16p, 21p, 22p, 24p, 32p. **Nebres** a-5; c-24i. **Nino** a-2, 8, 12. **Redondo** a-1, 9. No. 1-12 were reprinted from Pendulum Illustrated Classics.*

MARVEL COLLECTIBLE CLASSICS: AVENGERS
Marvel Comics: 1998 ($10.00, reprints with chromium wraparound-c)

1-Reprints Avengers Vol.3, #1; Perez-c 10.00

MARVEL COLLECTIBLE CLASSICS: SPIDER-MAN
Marvel Comics: 1998 ($10.00, reprints with chromium wraparound-c)

1-Reprints Amazing Spider-Man #300; McFarlane-c 10.00
2-Reprints Spider-Man #1; McFarlane-c 10.00

MARVEL COLLECTIBLE CLASSICS: X-MEN
Marvel Comics: 1998 ($10.00, reprints with chromium wraparound-c)

1-6: 1-Reprints (Uncanny) X-Men #1 & 2; Adam Kubert-c. 2-Reprints Uncanny X-Men #141 & 142; Byrne-c. 3-Reprints (Uncanny) X-Men #137; Larroca-c. 4-Reprints X-Men #25; Andy Kubert-c. 5-Reprints Giant Size X-Men #1; Gary Frank-c. 6-Reprints X-Men V2#1; Ramos-c 10.00

MARVEL COLLECTOR'S EDITION
Marvel Comics: 1992 (Ordered thru mail with Charleston Chew candy wrapper)

1-Flip-book format; Spider-Man, Silver Surfer, Wolverine (by Sam Kieth), & Ghost Rider stories; Wolverine back-c by Kieth 3.00

MARVEL COLLECTORS' ITEM CLASSICS (Marvel's Greatest #23 on)
Marvel Comics Group(ATF): Feb, 1965 - No. 22, Aug, 1969 (25¢, 68 pgs.)

1-Fantastic Four, Spider-Man, Thor, Hulk, Iron Man-r begin
10 20 30 71 126 180
2 (4/66) 6 12 18 41 66 90
3,4 5 10 15 32 51 70
5-10 4 8 12 28 44 60
11-22: 22-r/The Man in the Ant Hill/TTA #27 4 8 12 24 37 50
NOTE: *All reprints; **Ditko, Kirby** art in all.*

MARVEL COMICS (Marvel Mystery Comics #2 on)
Timely Comics (Funnies, Inc.): Oct, Nov, 1939

NOTE: The first issue was originally dated October 1939. Most copies have a black circle stamped over the date (on cover and inside) with "November" printed over it. However, some copies do not have the November overprint and could have a higher value. Most No. 1's have printing defects, i.e., tilted pages which caused trimming into the panels usually on right side and bottom. Covers exist with and without gloss finish.

1-Origin Sub-Mariner by Bill Everett(1st newsstand app.); 1st 8 pgs. were produced for Motion Picture Funnies Weekly #1 which was probably not distributed outside of advance copies; intro Human Torch by Carl Burgos, Kazar the Great (1st Tarzan clone), & Jungle Terror(only app.); intro. The Angel by Gustavson, The Masked Raider & his horse Lightning (ends #12); cover by sci/fi pulp illustrator Frank R. Paul
23,000 46,000 69,000 155,000 270,000 460,000

MARVEL COMICS PRESENTS
Marvel Comics (Midnight Sons imprint #143 on): Early Sept, 1988 - No. 175, Feb, 1995 ($1.25/$1.50/$1.75, bi-weekly)

1-Wolverine by Buscema in #1-10 6.00
2-5 4.00
6-10: 6-Sub-Mariner app. 10-Colossus begins 3.00
11-47,51-71: 17-Cyclops begins. 19-1st app. Damage Control. 24-Havok begins. 25-Origin/1st app. Nth Man. 26-Hulk begins by Rogers. 29-Quasar app. 31-Excalibur begins by Austin (i). 32-McFarlane-a(p). 33-Capt. America; Jim Lee-a. 37-Devil-Slayer app. 38-Wolverine begins by Buscema; Hulk app. 39-Spider-Man app. 46-Liefeld Wolverine-c. 51-53-Wolverine by Rob Liefeld. 54-61-Wolverine/Hulk story: 54-Werewolf by Night begins; The Shroud by Ditko. 58-Iron Man by Ditko. 59-Punisher. 62-Deathlok & Wolverine stories 63-Wolverine. 64-71-Wolverine/Ghost Rider 8-part story. 70-Liefeld Ghost Rider/ Wolverine-c 2.50
48-50-Wolverine & Spider-Man team-up by Erik Larsen-c/a. 48-Wasp app. 49,50-Savage Dragon prototype app. by Larsen. 50-Silver Surfer. 50-53-Comet Man; Mumy scripts 4.00
72-Begin 13-part Weapon-X story (Wolverine origin) by B. Windsor-Smith (prologue) 5.00
73-Weapon-X part 1; Black Knight, Sub-Mariner 4.00
74-84: 74-Weapon-X part 2; Black Knight, Sub-Mariner. 76-Death's Head story. 77-Mr. Fantastic story. 78-Iron Man by Steacy. 80,81-Capt. America by Ditko/Austin. 81-Daredevil by Rogers/Williamson. 82-Power Man. 83-Human Torch by Ditko(a&scripts); $1.00-c direct, $1.25 newsstand. 84-Last Weapon-X (24 pg. conclusion) 3.00
85-Begin 8-part Wolverine story by Sam Kieth (c/a); 1st Kieth-a on Wolverine; begin 8-part Beast story by Jae Lee(p) with Liefeld part pencils #85,86; 1st Jae Lee-a (assisted w/Liefeld, 1991) 4.00
86-90: 86-89-Wolverine, Beast stories continue. 90-Begin 8-part Ghost Rider & Cable story, ends #97; begin flip book format w/two-c 3.00
91-175: 93-Begin 6-part Wolverine story, ends #98. 98-Begin 2-part Ghost Rider story. 99-Spider-Man story. 100-Full-length Ghost Rider/Wolverine story by Sam Kieth w/Tim Vigil assists; anniversary issue, non flip-book. 101-Begin 6-part Ghost Rider/Dr. Strange story & begin 8-part Wolverine/Nightcrawler story by Colan/Williamson; Punisher story. 107-Begin 6-part Ghost Rider/Werewolf by Night story. 109-Begin 8 part Wolverine/Typhoid Mary story. 111-Iron Fist. 113-Begin 6-part Giant-Man & begin 6-part Ghost Rider/Iron Fist stories. 117-Preview of Ravage 2099 (1st app.); begin 6 part Wolverine/Venom story w/Kieth-a. 118-Preview of Doom 2099 (1st app.). 119-Begin Ghost Rider/Cloak & Dagger by Colan. 120,136,138-Spider-Man. 123-Begin 8-part Ghost Rider/Typhoid Mary story; begin 4-part She Hulk story; begin 8-part Wolverine/Lynx story. 125-Begin 6-part Iron Fist story. 130-Begin 6-part Ghost Rider/ Cage story. 136-Daredevil. 137-Begin 6-part Wolverine story & 6-part Ghost Rider story. 147-Begin 2-part Vengeance-c/story w/new Ghost Rider. 149-Vengeance-c/story w/new Ghost Rider. 150-Silver ink-c; begin 2-part Bloody Mary story w/Typhoid Mary,Wolverine, Daredevil, new Ghost Rider; intro Steel Raven. 152-Begin 4-part Wolverine, 4-part War Machine, 4-part Vengeance, 3-part Moon Knight stories; same date as War Machine #1. 143-146: Siege of Darkness parts 3,6,11,14; all have spot-varnished-c. 143-Ghost Rider/Scarlet Witch; intro new Werewolf. 144-Begin 2-part Morbius story. 145-Begin 2-part Nightstalkers story. 153-155-Bound-in Spider-Man trading card sheet 2.50
...Colossus: God's Country (1994, $6.95) r/#10-17 1 2 3 4 5 7
....: Wolverine Vol. 1 TPB (2005, $12.99) r/Wolverine stories from #1-10 13.00
....: Wolverine Vol. 2 TPB (2006, $12.99) r/from #39-50 and Marvel Age Annual #4 13.00
....: Wolverine Vol. 3 TPB (2006, $12.99) r/from #51-61 13.00
....: Wolverine Vol. 4 TPB (2006, $12.99) r/from #62-71 13.00
NOTE: ***Austin** a-31-37i; c(i)-48, 50, 99, 122. **Buscema** a-1-10, 38-47; c-6. **Byrne** a-79; c-71. **Colan** a(p)-36, 37. **Colan/Williamson** a-101-108. **Ditko** a-7p, 10, 56p, 58, 80, 81, 83. **Guice** a-62. **Sam Kieth** a-85-92, 117-122; c-85-98, 99p, 100-108, 117, 118, 120-122; back c-109-113, 117. **Jae Lee** c-129(back). **Liefeld** a-51, 52, 53p(2), 85p; c-46, 70. **McFarlane** c-32. **Mooney** a-73. **Rogers** a-26, 38, 46i, 81p. **Russell** a-10-14,16,17i; c-4,19, 30,31i.*

Marvel Double Feature #21 © MAR

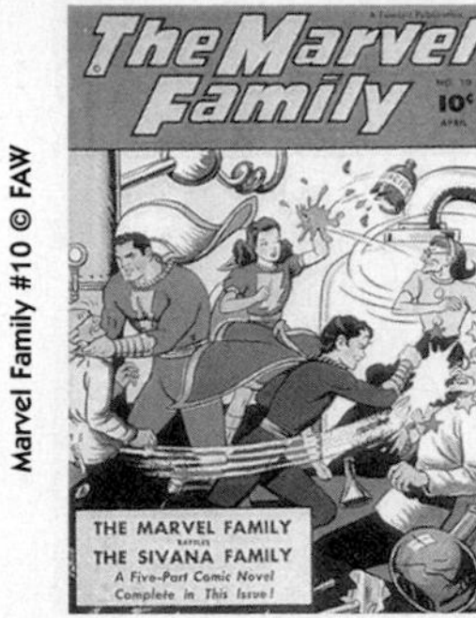

Marvel Family #10 © FAW

Marvel Feature (2nd series) #6 © MAR

GD VG FN VF VF/NM NM-
2.0 4.0 6.0 8.0 9.0 9.2

Saltares a-8p(early), 38-45p. ***Simonson*** *c-1.* ***B. Smith*** *a-72-84; c-72-84.* ***P. Smith*** *c-34.* ***Sparling*** *a-33.* ***Starlin*** *a-89i.* ***Staton*** *a-74.* ***Steacy*** *a-78.* ***Sutton*** *a-101-105.* ***Williamson*** *c-62i. Two Gun Kid by* ***Gil Kane*** *in #116, 122.*

MARVEL COMICS PRESENTS
Marvel Comics: Nov, 2007 - No. 12, Oct, 2008 ($3.99)

1-12-Short stories by various. 1-Wraparound-c by Campbell 4.00

MARVEL COMICS SUPER SPECIAL, A (Marvel Super Special #5 on)
Marvel Comics: Sept, 1977 - No. 41(?), Nov, 1986 (nn 7) ($1.50, magazine)

1-Kiss, 40 pgs. comics plus photos & features; John Buscema-a(p); also see Howard the Duck #12; ink contains real KISS blood; Dr. Doom, Spider-Man, Avengers, Fantastic Four, Mephisto app. 11 22 33 77 136 195
2-Conan (1978) 2 4 6 13 18 22
3-Close Encounters of the Third Kind (1978); Simonson-a 2 4 6 9 12 15
4-The Beatles Story (1978)-Perez/Janson-a; has photos & articles 4 8 12 20 41 60
5-Kiss (1978)-Includes poster 11 22 33 77 136 195
6-Jaws II (1978) 2 4 6 9 12 15
7-Sgt. Pepper; Beatles movie adaptation; withdrawn from U.S. distribution (French ed. exists)
8-Battlestar Galactica; tabloid size ($1.50, 1978); adapts TV show 2 4 6 11 16 20
8-Modern-r of tabloid size 2 4 6 10 14 18
8-Battlestar Galactica; publ. in regular magazine format; low distribution ($1.50, 8-1/2x11") 2 4 6 13 18 22
9-Conan 2 4 6 10 14 18
10-Star-Lord 2 4 6 8 11 14
11-13-Weirdworld begins #11; 25 copy special press run of each with gold seal and signed by artists (Proof quality), Spring-June, 1979 7 14 21 50 83 115
11-15: 11-13-Weirdworld (regular issues): 11-Fold-out centerfold. 14-Miller-c(p); adapts movie "Meteor." 15-Star Trek with photos & pin-ups ($1.50-c) 1 3 4 6 8 10
15-With $2.00 price; the price was changed at tail end of a 200,000 press run 2 4 6 0 10 12
16-Empire Strikes Back adaption; Williamson-a 2 4 6 8 11 14
17-20 (Movie adaptations):17-Xanadu. 18-Raiders of the Lost Ark. 19-For Your Eyes Only (James Bond). 20-Dragonslayer 6.00
21-26,28-30 (Movie adaptations): 21-Conan. 22-Blade Runner; Williamson-a; Steranko-c. 23-Annie. 24-The Dark Crystal. 25-Rock and Rule-w/photos; artwork is from movie. 26-Octopussy (James Bond). 28-Krull; photo-c. 29-Tarzan of the Apes (Greystoke movie). 30-Indiana Jones and the Temple of Doom 1 2 3 4 5 7
27,31-41: 27-Return of the Jedi. 31-The Last Star Fighter. 32-The Muppets Take Manhattan. 33-Buckaroo Banzai. 34-Sheena. 35-Conan The Destroyer. 36-Dune. 37-2010. 38-Red Sonja. 39-Santa Claus:The Movie. 40-Labyrinth. 41-Howard The Duck 1 2 3 5 7 9

NOTE: ***J. Buscema*** *a-1, 2, 9, 11-13, 18p, 21, 35, 40; c-11(part), 12.* ***Chaykin*** *a-9, 19p; c-18, 19.* ***Colan*** *a(p)-6, 10, 14.* ***Morrow*** *a-34; c-1i, 34.* ***Nebres*** *a-11.* ***Spiegle*** *a-29.* ***Stevens*** *a-27.* ***Williamson*** *a-27. #22-28 contain photos from movies.*

MARVEL COMICS: 2001
Marvel Comics: 2001 (no cover price, one-shot)

1-Previews new titles for Fall 2001; Wolverine-c 2.50

MARVEL DABEL BROTHERS SAMPLER
Marvel Comics: Dec, 2006 (no cover price, one-shot)

1-Profiles and sample pages of Anita Blake, Magician: Apprentice, Red Prophet, Ptolus 2.50

MARVEL DOUBLE FEATURE
Marvel Comics Group: Dec, 1973 - No. 21, Mar, 1977

1-Capt. America, Iron Man-r/T.O.S. begin 2 4 6 9 13 16
2-10: 3-Last 20¢ issue 1 3 4 6 8 10
11-17,20,21:17-Story-r/Iron Man & Sub-Mariner #1; last 25¢ issue 6.00
15-17-(30¢-c variants, limited distribution)(4,6,8/76) 1 3 4 6 8 10
18,19-Colan/Craig-r from Iron Man #1 in both 1 2 3 5 6 8

NOTE: ***Colan*** *r-1-19p.* ***Craig*** *r-17-19i.* ***G. Kane*** *r-15p; c-15p.* ***Kirby*** *r-1-16p, 20, 21; c-17-20.*

MARVEL DOUBLE SHOT
Marvel Comics: Jan, 2003 - No. 4, April, 2003 ($2.99, limited series)

1-4: 1-Hulk by Haynes; Thor w/Asamiya-a; Jusko-c. 2-Dr. Doom by Rivera; Simpsons-style Avengers by Bill Morrison 3.00

MARVEL FAMILY (Also see Captain Marvel Adventures No. 18)
Fawcett Publications: Dec, 1945 - No. 89, Jan, 1954

1-Origin Captain Marvel, Captain Marvel Jr., Mary Marvel, & Uncle Marvel retold; origin/1st app. Black Adam 173 346 519 1090 1895 2700
2-The 3 Lt. Marvels & Uncle Marvel app. 78 156 234 491 833 1175
3 54 108 162 340 575 810
4,5 45 90 135 279 465 650

GD VG FN VF VF/NM NM-
2.0 4.0 6.0 8.0 9.0 9.2

6-10: 7-Shazam app. 39 78 117 230 370 510
11-20 29 58 87 169 272 375
21-30 25 50 75 145 233 320
31-40 20 40 60 118 189 260
41-46,48-50 17 34 51 98 154 210
47-Flying Saucer-c/story (5/50) 23 46 69 135 218 300
51-76 15 30 45 92 144 195
77-Communist Threat-c 26 52 78 152 244 335
78,81-Used in **POP**, pg. 92,93. 18 36 54 107 169 230
79,80,82-89: 79-Horror satire-c 18 36 54 103 162 220

MARVEL FANFARE (1st Series)
Marvel Comics Group: Mar, 1982 - No. 60, Jan, 1992 ($1.25/$2.25, slick paper, direct sales)

1-Spider-Man/Angel team-up; 1st Paul Smith-a (1st full story; see King Conan #7); Daredevil app. (many copies were printed missing the centerfold) 1 2 3 5 6 8
2-Spider-Man, Ka-Zar, The Angel. F.F. origin retold 6.00
3,4-X-Men & Ka-Zar. 4-Deathlok, Spidey app. 5.00
5-14: 5-Dr. Strange, Capt. America. 6-Spider-Man, Scarlet Witch. 7-Incredible Hulk; D.D. back-up(also 15). 8-Dr. Strange; Wolf Boy begins. 9-Man-Thing. 10-13-Black Widow. 14-The Vision 3.00
15,24,33: 15-The Thing by Barry Smith, c/a. 24-Weirdworld; Wolverine back-up. 33-X-Men, Wolverine app.; Punisher pin-up 4.00
16-23,25-32,34-44,46-50: 16,17-Skywolf. 16-Sub-Mariner back-up. 17-Hulk back-up. 18-Capt. America by Miller. 19-Cloak and Dagger. 20-Thing/Dr. Strange. 21-Thing/Dr. Strange /Hulk. 22,23-Iron Man vs. Dr. Octopus. 25,26-Weirdworld. 27-Daredevil/Spider-Man. 28-Alpha Flight. 29-Hulk. 30-Moon Knight. 31,32-Captain America. 34-37-Warriors Three. 38-Moon Knight/Dazzler. 39-Moon Knight/Hawkeye. 40-Angel/Rogue & Storm. 41-Dr. Strange. 42-Spider-Man. 43-Sub-Mariner/Human Torch. 44-Iron Man vs. Dr. Doom by Ken Steacy. 46-Fantastic Four. 47-Hulk. 48-She-Hulk/Vision. 49-Dr. Strange/Nick Fury. 50-X-Factor 2.50
45-All pin-up issue by Steacy, Art Adams & others 4.00
51-($2.95, 52 pgs.)-Silver Surfer; Fantastic Four & Capt. Marvel app.; 51,52-Colan/Williamson back-up (Dr. Strange) 3.00
52,53,56-60: 52,53-Black Knight; 53-Iron Man back up. 56-59-Shanna the She-Devil. 58-Vision & Scarlet Witch back-up. 60-Black Panther/Rogue/Daredevil stories 2.50
54,55-Wolverine back-ups. 54-Black Knight. 55-Power Pack 4.00
... Vol. 1 TPB (2008, $24.99) r/#1-7 25.00

NOTE: ***Art Adams*** *c-13.* ***Austin*** *a-1i, 4i, 33i, 38i; c-8i, 33i.* ***Buscema*** *a-51p.* ***Byrne*** *a-1p, 29, 48; c-29.* ***Chiodo*** *painted c-56-59.* ***Colan*** *a-51p.* ***Cowan/Simonson*** *c/a-60.* ***Golden*** *a-1, 2, 4p, 47; c-1, 2, 47.* ***Infantino*** *c/a(p)-8* ***Gil Kane*** *a-8-11p.* ***Miller*** *a-18; c-1(Back-c), 18.* ***Perez*** *a-10, 11p, 12, 13p; c-10-13p.* ***Rogers*** *a-5p; c-5p.* ***Russell*** *a-5i, 6i, 8-11i, 43i; c-5i, 6.* ***Paul Smith*** *a-1p, 4p, 32, 60; c-4p. Staton c/a-50(p).* ***Williamson*** *a-30i, 51i.*

MARVEL FANFARE (2nd Series)
Marvel Comics: Sept, 1996 - No. 6, Feb, 1997 (99¢)

1-6: 1-Capt. America & The Falcon-c/story; Deathlok app. 2-Wolverine & Hulk-c/app. 3-Ghost Rider & Spider-Man-c/app. 5-Longshot-c/app. 6-Sabretooth, Power Man, & Iron Fist-c/app 2.50

MARVEL FEATURE (See Marvel Two-In-One)
Marvel Comics Group: Dec, 1971 - No. 12, Nov, 1973 (1,2: 25¢, 52 pg. giants) (#1-3: quarterly)

1-Origin/1st app. The Defenders (Sub-Mariner, Hulk & Dr. Strange); see Sub-Mariner #34,35 for prequel; Dr. Strange solo story (predates Dr.Strange #1) plus 1950s Sub-Mariner-r; Neal Adams-c 15 30 45 111 206 300
2-2nd app. Defenders; 1950s Sub-Mariner-r. Rutland, Vermont Halloween x-over 8 16 24 58 97 135
3-Defenders ends 6 12 18 41 66 90
4-Re-intro Antman (1st app. since 1960s), begin series; brief origin; Spider-Man app. 3 6 9 20 30 40
5-7,9,10: 6-Wasp app. & begins team-ups. 9-Iron Man app. 10-Last Antman 2 4 6 13 18 22
8-Origin Antman & Wasp-r/TTA #44; Kirby-a 3 6 9 14 20 25
11-Thing vs. Hulk; 1st Thing solo book (9/73); origin Fantastic Four retold 7 14 21 45 73 100
12-Thing/Iron Man; early Thanos app.; occurs after Capt. Marvel #33; Starlin-a(p) 4 8 12 28 44 60

NOTE: ***Bolle*** *a-9i.* ***Everett*** *a-1i, 3i.* ***Hartley*** *r-10.* ***Kane*** *c-3p, 7p.* ***Russell*** *a-7-10p.* ***Starlin*** *a-8, 11, 12; c-8.*

MARVEL FEATURE (Also see Red Sonja)
Marvel Comics: Nov, 1975 - No. 7, Nov, 1976 (Story cont'd in Conan #68)

1,7: 1-Red Sonja begins (pre-dates Red Sonja #1); adapts Howard short story; Adams-r/Savage Sword of Conan #1. 7-Battles Conan 1 3 4 6 8 10
2-6: Thorne-c/a in #2-7. 4,5-(Regular 25¢ edition)(5,7/76) 6.00
4,5-(30¢-c variants, limited distribution) 3 6 9 14 20 25

MARVEL FRONTIER COMICS UNLIMITED

Marvel Graphic Novel #18 © MAR

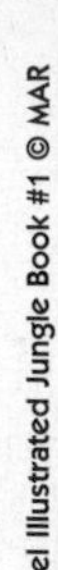

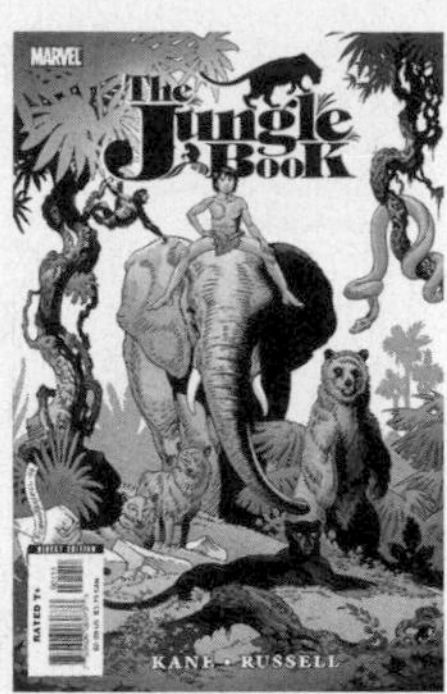

Marvel Illustrated Jungle Book #1 © MAR

Marvel Illustrated: Moby Dick #1 © MAR

GD VG FN VF VF/NM NM-
2.0 4.0 6.0 8.0 9.0 9.2

Marvel Frontier Comics: Jan, 1994 ($2.95, 68 pgs.)
1-Dances with Demons, Immortalis, Children of the Voyager, Evil Eye, The Fallen stories 3.00

MARVEL FUMETTI BOOK
Marvel Comics Group: Apr, 1984 ($1.00, one-shot)
1-All photos; Stan Lee photo-c; Art Adams touch-ups 4.00

MARVEL FUN & GAMES
Marvel Comics Group: 1979/80 (color comic for kids)
1,11: 1-Games, puzzles, etc. 11-X-Men-c 1 2 3 5 7 9
2-10,12,13: (beware marked pages) 6.00

MARVEL GRAPHIC NOVEL
Marvel Comics Group (Epic Comics): 1982 - No. 38, 1990? ($5.95/$6.95)
1-Death of Captain Marvel (2nd Marvel graphic novel); Capt. Marvel battles Thanos by Jim Starlin (c/a/scripts) 3 6 9 14 19 24
1 (2nd & 3rd printings) 1 2 3 5 6 8
2-Elric: The Dreaming City 2 4 6 8 10 12
3-Dreadstar; Starlin-c/a, 52 pgs. 2 4 6 8 11 14
4-Origin/1st app. The New Mutants (1982) 2 4 6 8 11 14
4,5-2nd printings 1 2 3 4 5 7
5-X-Men; book-length story (1982) 3 6 9 14 20 25
6-15,20,23,25,30,31: 6-The Star Slammers. 7-Killraven. 8-Super Boxers; Byrne scripts. 9-The Futurians. 10-Heartburst. 11-Void Indigo. 12-Dazzler. 13-Starstruck. 14-The Swords Of The Swashbucklers. 15-The Raven Banner (a Tale of Asgard). 20-Greenberg the Vampire. 23-Dr. Strange. 25-Alien Legion. 30-A Sailor's Story. 31-Wolfpack 1 2 3 5 7 9
16,17,21,29: 16-The Aladdin Effect (Storm, Tigra, Wasp, She-Hulk). 17-Revenge Of The Living Monolith (Spider-Man, Avengers, FF app.). 21-Marada the She-Wolf. 29-The Big Chance (Thing vs. Hulk) 1 2 3 5 7 9
18,19,26-28: 18-She Hulk. 19-Witch Queen of Acheron (Conan). 26-Dracula. 27-Avengers (Emperor Doom). 28-Conan the Reaver 2 4 6 9 11 13
22-Amaz. Spider-Man in Hooky by Wrightson 2 4 6 9 12 15
24-Love and War (Daredevil); Miller scripts 2 4 6 8 11 14
32-Death of Groo 2 4 6 9 12 15
32-2nd printing ($5.95) 1 2 3 5 6 8
33,34,36,37: 33-Thor. 34-Predator & Prey (Cloak & Dagger). 36-Willow (movie adapt.). 37-Hercules 1 3 4 6 8 10
35-Hitler's Astrologer (The Shadow, $12.95, HC) 2 4 6 9 13 16
35-Soft-c reprint (1990, $10.95) 2 4 6 8 10 12
38-Silver Surfer (Judgement Day)($14.95, HC) 2 4 6 10 14 18
38-Soft-c reprint (1990, $10.95) 2 4 6 8 11 14
nn-Abslom Daak: Dalak Killer (1990, $8.95) Dr. Who 1 3 4 6 8 10
nn-Arena by Bruce Jones (1989, $5.95) Dinosaurs 1 2 3 5 6 8
nn- A-Team Storybook Comics Illustrated (1983) r/ A-Team mini-series #1-3 1 3 4 6 8 10
nn-Ax (1988, $5.95) Ernie Colan-s/a 1 3 4 6 8 10
nn-Black Widow Coldest War (4/90, $9.95) 2 4 6 8 10 12
nn-Chronicles of Genghis Grimtoad (1990, $8.95)-Alan Grant-s 1 3 4 6 8 10
nn-Conan the Barbarian in the Horn of Azoth (1990, $8.95) 2 4 6 8 11 16
nn-Conan of Isles ($8.95) 2 4 6 8 11 16
nn-Conan Ravagers of Time (1992, $9.95) Kull & Red Sonja app. 2 4 6 8 11 16
nn-Conan -The Skull of Set 2 4 6 8 11 16
nn-Doctor Strange and Doctor Doom Triumph and Torment (1989, $17.95, HC) 2 4 6 13 18 22
nn-Dreamwalker (1989, $6.95)-Morrow-a 1 2 3 5 7 9
nn-Excalibur Weird War III (1990, $9.95) 2 4 6 8 10 12
nn-G.I. Joe - The Trojan Gambit (1983, 68 pgs.) 2 4 6 8 10 12
nn-Harvey Kurtzman Strange Adventures (Epic, $19.95, HC) Aragonés, Crumb 3 6 9 14 20 25
nn-Hearts and Minds (1990, $8.95) Heath-a 1 3 4 6 8 10
nn-Inhumans (1988, $7.95)-Williamson-i 1 2 3 5 7 9
nn-Jhereg (Epic, 1990, $8.95) 1 3 4 6 8 10
nn-Kazar-Guns of the Savage Land (7/90, $8.95) 1 3 4 6 8 10
nn-Kull-The Vale of Shadow ('89, $6.95) 2 4 6 8 10 12
nn-Last of the Dragons (1988, $6.95) Austin-a(i) 1 2 3 4 5 7
nn-Nightraven: House of Cards (1991, $14.95) 2 4 6 9 12 15
nn-Nightraven: The Collected Stories (1990, $9.95) Bolton-r/British Hulk mag.; David Lloyd-c/a 2 4 6 8 10 12
nn-Original Adventures of Cholly and Flytrap (Epic, 1991, $9.95) Suydam-s/c/a 2 4 6 9 12 15
nn-Rick Mason Agent (1989, $9.95) 1 3 4 6 8 10

GD VG FN VF VF/NM NM-
2.0 4.0 6.0 8.0 9.0 9.2

nn-Roger Rabbit In The Resurrection Of Doom (1989, $8.95) 1 3 4 6 8 10
nn-A Sailor's Story Book II: Winds, Dreams and Dragons ('86, $6.95, softcover) Glansman-s/c/a 1 3 4 6 8 10
nn-Squadron Supreme: Death of a Universe (1989, $9.95) Gruenwald-s; Ryan & Williamson-a 3 6 9 14 20 25
nn-Who Framed Roger Rabbit (1989, $6.95) 1 3 4 6 8 10
NOTE: ***Aragones** a-27, 32. **Buscema** a-38. **Byrne** c/a-18. **Heath** a-35i. **Kaluta** a-13, 35p; c-13. **Miller** a-24p. **Simonson** a-6; c-6. **Starlin** c/a-1,3. **Williamson** a-34. **Wrightson** c-29i.*

MARVEL-HEROES & LEGENDS
Marvel Comics: Oct, 1996; 1997 ($2.95)
nn-Wraparound-c, ...1997 ($2.99) -Original Avengers story 3.00

MARVEL HEROES FLIP MAGAZINE
Marvel Comics: Aug, 2005 - No. 26, Sept, 2007 ($3.99/$4.99)
1-11-Reprints New Avengers and Captain America (2005 series) in flip format thru #13 4.00
12-26: 14-19-Reprints New Avengers and Young Avengers in flip format. 20-Ghost Rider 5.00

MARVEL HOLIDAY SPECIAL
Marvel Comics: No. 1, 1991 ($2.25, 84 pgs.) - Present
1-X-Men, Fantastic Four, Punisher, Thor, Capt. America, Ghost Rider, Capt. Ultra, Spidey stories; Art Adams-c/a 3.00
nn (1/93)-Wolverine, Thanos (by Starlin/Lim/Austin) 3.00
nn (1994)-Capt. America, X-Men, Silver Surfer 3.00
...1996-Spider-Man by Waid & Olliffe; X-Men, Silver Surfer 3.00
...2004-Spider-Man by DeFalco & Miyazawa; X-Men, Fantastic Four 3.00
...2004 TPB ($15.99) r/M.H.S. 2004 & past Christmas-themed stories 16.00
1 (1/06, $3.99) new Christmas-themed stories by various; Immonen-c 4.00
....2006 (2/07, $3.99) Fin Fang Foom, Hydra, AIM app.; gallery of past covers; Irving-c 4.00
....2007 (2/08, $3.99) Spider-Man & Wolverine stories; Hembeck-a 4.00
Marvel Holiday (2006, $7.99, digest) reprints from M.H.S. 2004, 2006 & TPB 8.00
NOTE: ***Art Adams** c-'93. **Golden** a-'93. **Perez** c-'94.*

MARVEL ILLUSTRATED...
Marvel Comics: 2007 ($2.99)
...Jungle Book - reprints from Marvel Fanfare #8-11; Gil Kane-s/a(p); P. Craig Russell-i 3.00

MARVEL ILLUSTRATED: LAST OF THE MOHICANS
Marvel Comics: July, 2007 - No. 6, Dec, 2007 ($2.99, limited series)
1-6-Adaptation of the Cooper novel; Roy Thomas-s/Steve Kurth-a. 1-Jo Chen-c 3.00
HC (2008, $19.99) r/#1-6 20.00

MARVEL ILLUSTRATED: MOBY DICK
Marvel Comics: Apr, 2008 - No. 6, Sept, 2008 ($2.99, limited series)
1-6-Adaptation of the Melville novel; Roy Thomas-s/Alixe-a/Watson-c 3.00

MARVEL ILLUSTRATED: PICTURE OF DORIAN GRAY
Marvel Comics: Jan, 2008 - No. 6, July, 2008 ($2.99, limited series)
1-6-Adaptation of the Wilde novel; Roy Thomas-s/Fiumara-a. 1-Parel-c 3.00

MARVEL ILLUSTRATED: SWIMSUIT ISSUE (Also see Marvel Swimsuit Special)
Marvel Comics: 1991 ($3.95, magazine, 52 pgs.)
V1#1-Parody of Sports Illustrated swimsuit issue; Mary Jane Parker centerfold pin-up by Jusko; 2nd print exists 1 3 4 6 8 10

MARVEL ILLUSTRATED: THE ILIAD
Marvel Comics: Feb, 2008 - No. 8, Sept, 2008 ($2.99, limited series)
1-8-Adaptation of Homer's Epic Poem; Roy Thomas-s/Sepulveda-a/Rivera-c 3.00

MARVEL ILLUSTRATED: THE MAN IN THE IRON MASK
Marvel Comics: Sept, 2007 - No. 6, Feb, 2008 ($2.99, limited series)
1-6-Adaptation of the Dumas novel; Roy Thomas-s/Hugo Petrus-a. 1-Djurdjevic-c 3.00
HC (2008, $19.99) r/#1-6 20.00

MARVEL ILLUSTRATED: THE ODYSSEY
Marvel Comics: Nov, 2008 - No. 8 ($2.99, limited series)
1-Adaptation of Homer's Epic Poem; Roy Thomas-s/Greg Tocchini-a/c 3.00

MARVEL ILLUSTRATED: THE THREE MUSKETEERS
Marvel Comics: Aug, 2008 - No. 6, ($3.99, limited series)
1-4-Adaptation of the Dumas novel; Roy Thomas-s/Hugo Petrus-a/Parel-c 4.00

MARVEL ILLUSTRATED: TREASURE ISLAND
Marvel Comics: Aug, 2007 - No. 6, Jan, 2008 ($2.99, limited series)
1-6-Adaptation of the Stevenson novel; Roy Thomas-s/Mario Gully-a/Greg Hildebrandt-c 3.00
HC (2008, $19.99) r/#1-6 20.00

MARVEL KNIGHTS (See Black Panther, Daredevil, Inhumans, & Punisher)
Marvel Comics: 1998 (Previews for upcoming series)

Marvel Knights Magazine #3 © MAR

Marvel Mangaverse #1 © MAR

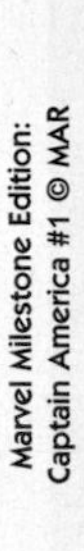

Marvel Milestone Edition: Captain America #1 © MAR

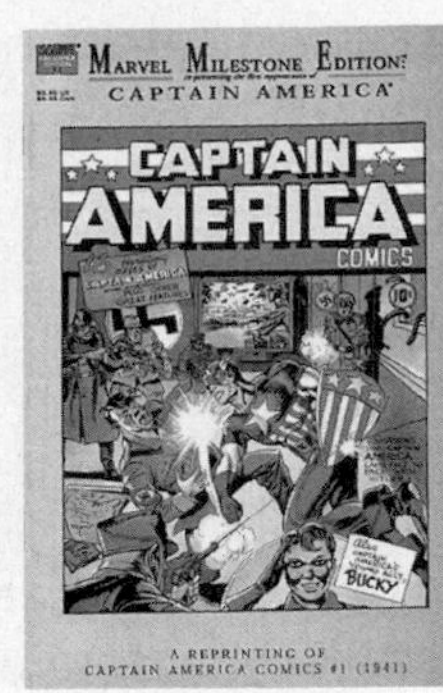

	GD	VG	FN	VF	VF/NM	NM-
	2.0	4.0	6.0	8.0	9.0	9.2

Sketchbook-Wizard suppl.; Quesada & Palmiotti-c 3.00
Tourbook-($2.99) Interviews and art previews 3.00

MARVEL KNIGHTS
Marvel Comics: July, 2000 - No. 15, Sept, 2001 ($2.99)

1-Daredevil, Punisher, Black Widow, Shang-Chi, Dagger app. 4.00
2-15: 2-Two covers by Barreto & Quesada 3.00
.../Marvel Boy Genesis Edition (6/00) Sketchbook preview 2.50
...: Millennial Visions (2/02, $3.99) Pin-ups by various; Harris-c 4.00

MARVEL KNIGHTS (Volume 2)
Marvel Comics: May, 2002 - No. 6, Oct, 2002 ($2.99)

1-6-Daredevil, Punisher, Black Widow app.; Ponticelli-a 3.00

MARVEL KNIGHTS: DOUBLE SHOT
Marvel Comics: June, 2002 - No. 4 ($2.99, limited series)

1-5: 1-Punisher by Ennis & Quesada; Daredevil by Haynes; Fabry-c 3.00

MARVEL KNIGHTS 4 (Fantastic Four) (Issues #1&2 are titled **Knights 4**) (#28-30 titled **Four**)
Marvel Comics: Apr, 2004 - No. 30, July, 2006 ($2.99)

1-30: 1-7-McNiven-c/a; Aguirre-Sacasa-a. 8,9-Namor app. 13-Cho-c. 14-Land-c. 21-Flashback meeting with Black Panther. 30-Namor app. 3.00
...Vol. 1: The Wolf at the Door (2004, $16.99, TPB) r/#1-7 17.00
...Vol. 2: The Stuff of Nightmares (2005, $13.99, TPB) r/#8-12 14.00
...Vol. 3: Divine Time (2005, $14.99, TPB) r/#13-18 15.00
...Vol. 4: Impossible Things Happen Every Day (2006, $14.99, TPB) r/#19-24 15.00
Fantastic Four: The Resurrection of Nicholas Scratch TPB (2006, $14.99) r/#25-30 15.00

MARVEL KNIGHTS MAGAZINE
Marvel Comics: May, 2001 - No. 6, Oct, 2001 ($3.99, magazine size)

1-6-Reprints of recent Daredevil, Punisher, Black Widow, Inhumans 4.00

MARVEL KNIGHTS SPIDER-MAN (Title continues in Sensational Spider-Man #23)
Marvel Comics: Jun, 2004 - No. 22, Mar, 2006 ($2.99)

1-Wraparound-c by Dodson; Millar-s/Dodson-a; Green Goblin app. 3.00
2-12: 2-Avengers app. 2,3-Vulture & Electro app. 5,8-Cho-c/a. 6-8-Venom app. 3.00
13-18-Reginald Hudlin-s/Billy Tan-a. 13,14,18-New Avengers app. 15-Punisher app. 3.00
19-22-The Other x-over pts. 2,5,8,11; Pat Lee-a 3.00
19-22-var-c: 19-Black costume. 20-Scarlet Spider. 21-Spider-Armor. 22-Peter Parker 5.00
... Vol. 1 HC (2005, $29.99, over-sized with d.j.) r/#1-12; Stan Lee intro.; Dodson & Cho sketch pages 30.00
... Vol. 1: Down Among the Dead Men (2004, $9.99, TPB) r/#1-4 10.00
... Vol. 2: Venomous (2005, $9.99, TPB) r/#5-8 10.00
... Vol. 3: The Last Stand (2005, $9.99, TPB) r/#9-12 10.00
... Vol. 4: Wild Blue Yonder (2005, $14.99, TPB) r/#13-18 15.00

MARVEL KNIGHTS 2099
Marvel Comics: 2005 ($13.99, TPB)

nn-Reprints one shots: Daredevil 2099, Punisher 2099, Black Panther 2099, Inhumans 2099 and Mutant 2099; Pat Lee-c 14.00

MARVEL LEGACY: ...
Marvel Comics: 2006, 2007 ($4.99, one-shots)

... The 1960s Handbook - Profiles of 1960s iconic and minor characters; info thru 1969 5.00
... The 1970s Handbook - Profiles of 1970s iconic and minor characters; info thru 1979 5.00
... The 1980s Handbook - Profiles of 1980s iconic and minor characters; info thru 1989 5.00
... The 1990s Handbook - Profiles of 1990s iconic and minor characters; Lim-c 5.00
...: The 1960s-1990s Handbook TPB (207, $19.99) r/one-shots 20.00

MARVEL MANGAVERSE:... (one-shots)
Marvel Comics: March, 2002 ($2.25, manga-inspired one-shots)

Avengers Assemble! - Udon Studio-s/a 2.50
Eternity Twilight ($3.50) - Ben Dunn-s/a/wrap-around-c 3.50
Fantastic Four - Adam Warren-s/Keron Grant-a 2.50
Ghost Riders - Chuck Austen-s/a 2.50
Punisher - Peter David-s/Lea Hernandez-a 2.50
Spider-Man - Kaare Andrews-s/a 2.50
X-Men - C.B. Cebulski-s/Jeff Matsuda-a 2.50

MARVEL MANGAVERSE (Manga series)
Marvel Comics: June, 2002 - No. 6, Nov., 2002 ($2.25)

1-6: 1-Ben Dunn-s/a; intro. manga Captain Marvel 2.50
Vol. 1 TPB (2002, $24.95) r/one-shots 25.00
Vol. 2 TPB (2002, $12.99) r/#1-6 13.00
Vol. 3: Spider-Man-Legend of the Spider-Clan (2003, $11.99, TPB) r/series 12.00

MARVEL MASTERPIECES COLLECTION, THE
Marvel Comics: May, 1993 - No. 4, Aug, 1993 ($2.95, coated paper, lim. series)

1-4-Reprints Marvel Masterpieces trading cards w/ new Jusko paintings in each; Jusko painted-c/a 3.00

MARVEL MASTERPIECES 2 COLLECTION, THE
Marvel Comics: July, 1994 - No. 3, Sept, 1994 ($2.95, limited series)

1-3: 1-Kaluta-c; r/trading cards; new Steranko centerfold 3.00

MARVEL MILESTONE EDITION
Marvel Comics: 1991 - 1999 ($2.95, coated stock)(r/originals with original ads w/silver ink-c)

...: X-Men #1-Reprints X-Men #1 (1991) 3.00
...: Giant Size X-Men #1-(1991, $3.95, 68 pgs.) 4.00
...: Fantastic Four #1 (11/91), ...: Incredible Hulk #1 (3/92, says 3/91 by error), ...: Amazing Fantasy #15 (3/92), ...: Fantastic Four #5 (11/92), ...: Amazing Spider-Man #129 (11/92), ...: Iron Man #55 (11/92), ...: Iron Fist #14 (11/92), ...: Amazing Spider-Man #1 (1/93), ...: Amazing Spider-Man #1 (1/93) variation- no price on-c, ...: Tales of Suspense #39 (3/93), ...: Avengers #1 (9/93), ...: X-Men #9 (10/93), ...: Avengers #16 (10/93), ...:Amazing Spider-Man #149 (11/94, $2.95), ...:X-Men #28 (11/94, $2.95) 3.00
...:Captain America #1 (3/95, $3.95) 4.00
...:Amazing Spider-Man #3 (3/95, $2.95), ...:Avengers #4 (3/95, $2.95), ...:Strange Tales-r/Dr. Strange stories from #110, 111, 114, & 115 3.00
....:Hulk #181 (8/99, $2.99) 3.00

MARVEL MILESTONES
Marvel Comics: 2005 - Present ($3.99, coated stock)(r/originals w/silver ink-c)

...: Beast & Kitty Pryde-r/from Amazing Adventures #11 & Uncanny X-Men #153 4.00
...: Black Panther, Storm & Ka-Zar-r/from Black Panther #26, Marvel Team-Up #100 and Marvel Mystery Comics #7 4.00
...: Blade, Man-Thing & Satana-r/from Tomb of Dracula #10, Adv. Into Fear #16 and Vampire Tales #2 4.00
...: Captain Britain, Psylocke & Sub-Mariner-r/from Spect. Spidey #114, Uncanny X-Men #213 and Human Torch #2 4.00
...: Doom, Sub-Marinor & Red Skull -r/from FF Ann. #2, Sub-Mariner Comics #1, Captain America Comics #1 4.00
...: Dragon Lord, Speedball and The Man in the Sky -r/from Marvel Spotlight #5, Speedball #1 and Amazing Adult Fantasy #14; Ditko-a on all 4.00
...: Dr. Strange, Silver Surfer, Sub-Mariner, & Hulk -r/from Marvel Premiere #3, FF Ann. #5, Marvel Comics #1, Incredible Hulk #3 4.00
...: Ghost Rider, Black Widow & Iceman -r/from Marvel Spotlight #5, Daredevil #81, X-Men #47 4.00
...: Iron Man, Ant-Man & Captain America -r/from TOS #39,40, TTA #27, Capt. America #1 4.00
...: Legion of Monsters, Spider Man and Brother Voodoo -r/Marvel Premiere #28 & others 4.00
...: Millie the Model & Patsy Walker-r/from Millie the Model #100, Defenders #65 4.00
...: Onslaught -r/Onslaught: Marvel; wraparound-c 4.00
...: Rawhide Kid & Two-Gun Kid-r/Two-Gun Kid #60 and Rawhide Kid #17 4.00
...: Special: Bloodstone, X-51 & Captain Marvel II ($4.99) -r/from Marvel Presents #1, Machine Man #1, Amazing Spider-Man Ann. #19, and Bloodstone #1 5.00
...: Star Brand & Quasar -r/from Star Brand #1 & Quasar #1 4.00
...: Ultimate Spider-Man, Ult. X-Men, Microman & Mantor -r/from Ultimate Spider-Man #1/2, Ultimate X-Men #1/2 and Human Torch #2 4.00
...: Venom & Hercules -r/Marvel S-H Secret Wars #8, Journey Into Mystery Ann. #1 4.00
...: Wolverine, X-Men & Tuk: Caveboy -r/from Marvel Comics Presents #1, Uncanny X-Men #201, Capt. America Comics #1,2 4.00
...: (Jim Lee and Chris Claremont) X-Men and the Starjammers Pt. 1 -r/Unc. X-Men #275 4.00
...: X-Men and the Starjammers Pt. 2 -r/Unc. X-Men #276,277 4.00

MARVEL MINI-BOOKS (See Promotional Comics section)

MARVEL MONSTERS:... (one-shots)
Marvel Comics: Dec, 2005 ($3.99)

...Devil Dinosaur 1 - Hulk app.; Eric Powell-c/a; Sniegoski-s; r/Journey Into Mystery #62 4.00
...Fin Fang Four 1 - FF app.; Powell-c; Langridge-s/Gray-a; r/Strange Tales #89 4.00
...From the Files of Ulysses Bloodstone 1 - Guide to classic Marvel monsters; Powell-c 4.00
...Monsters on the Prowl 1 - Niles-s/Fegredo-a/Powell-c; Thing, Hulk, Giant-Man & Beast app. 4.00
...Where Monsters Dwell 1 - Giffen-s/a; David-s/Pander-a; Parker-s/Braun-s; Powell-c 4.00
HC (2006, $20.99, dust jacket) r/one-shots 21.00

MARVEL MOVIE PREMIERE (Magazine)
Marvel Comics Group: Sept, 1975 (B&W, one-shot)

	GD	VG	FN	VF	VF/NM	NM-
1-Burroughs' "The Land That Time Forgot" adapt.	2	4	6	8	11	14

MARVEL MOVIE SHOWCASE FEATURING STAR WARS
Marvel Comics Group: Nov, 1982 - No. 2, Dec, 1982 ($1.25, 68 pgs.)

1,2-Star Wars movie adaptation; reprints Star Wars #1-6 by Chaykin; 1-Reprints-c to Star Wars #1. 2-Stevens-r 4.00

MARVEL MOVIE SPOTLIGHT FEATURING RAIDERS OF THE LOST ARK
Marvel Comics Group: Nov, 1982 ($1.25, 68 pgs.)

1-Edited-r/Raiders of the Lost Ark #1-3; Buscema-c/a(p); movie adapt. 3.00

Marvel Mystery Comics #37 © MAR

Marvel 1985 #1 © MAR

Marvel Premiere #36 © MAR

GD 2.0 | VG 4.0 | FN 6.0 | VF 8.0 | VF/NM 9.0 | NM- 9.2

GD 2.0 | VG 4.0 | FN 6.0 | VF 8.0 | VF/NM 9.0 | NM- 9.2

MARVEL MUST HAVES (Reprints of recent sold-out issues)
Marvel Comics: Dec, 2001 - Present ($2.99/$3.99/$4.99)

1,2,4-6: 1-r/Wolverine: Origin #1, Startling Stories: Banner #1, Tangled Web #4 and Cable #97. 2-Amazing Spider-Man #36 and others. 4-Truth #1, Capt. America V4 #1, and The Ultimates #1. 5-r/Ultimate War #1, Ult. X-Men #26, Ult Spider-Man #33. 6-Ult. Spider-Man #33-36 4.00
3-r/Call of Duty: The Brotherhood #1 & Daredevil #32,33 3.00
Amazing Spider-Man #30-32; Incredible Hulk #34-36; The Ultimates #1-3; Ultimate Spider-Man #1-3; Ultimate X-Men #1-3; (New) X-Men #114-116 each.... 4.00
NYX #1-3; NYX #4-5 with sketch & cover gallery; Ultimates 2 #1-3 each... 5.00
Spider-Man and the Black Cat #1-3; preview of #4 5.00

MARVEL MYSTERY COMICS (Formerly Marvel Comics) (Becomes Marvel Tales No. 93 on)
Timely /Marvel Comics (TP #2-17/TCI #18-54/MCI #55-92): No. 2, Dec, 1939 - No. 92, June, 1949 (Some material from #8-10 reprinted in 2004's Marvel 65th Anniversary Special #1)

2-(Rare)-American Ace begins, ends #3; Human Torch (blue costume) by Burgos, Sub-Mariner by Everett continue; 2 pg. origin recap of Human Torch 3000 6000 9000 22,500 41,250 60,000
3-New logo from Marvel pulp begins; 1st app. of television in comics? in Human Torch story (1/40) 1675 3350 5025 12,550 22,775 33,000
4-Intro. Electro, the Marvel of the Age (ends #19), The Ferret, Mystery Detective (ends #9); 1st Sub-Mariner-c by Schomburg; 2nd German swastika on-c of a comic (2/40); one month after Top-Notch Comics #2 1333 2666 4000 10,000 18,000 26,000
5 Classic Schomburg-c (Scarce) 2500 5000 7500 18,250 34,375 50,000
6,7: 6-Gustavson Angel story 861 1722 2583 6199 10,850 15,500
8-1st Human Torch & Sub-Mariner battle(6/40) 1200 2400 3600 8500 15,250 22,000
9-(Scarce)-Human Torch & Sub-Mariner battle (cover/story); classic-c 3000 6000 9000 22,500 40,250 58,000
10-Human Torch & Sub-Mariner battle, conclusion; Terry Vance, the Schoolboy Sleuth begins, ends #57 1000 2000 3000 7400 13,200 19,000
11 394 788 1182 2679 4690 6700
12-Classic Kirby-c 428 856 1284 3082 5391 7700
13-Intro. & 1st app. The Vision by S&K (11/40); Sub-Mariner dons new costume, ends #15 556 1112 1668 4003 7002 10,000
14-16: 14-Shows-c to Human Torch #1 on-c (12/40). 15-S&K Vision, Gustavson Angel story 300 600 900 1950 3375 4800
17-Human Torch/Sub-Mariner team-up by Burgos/Everett; pin-up on back-c; shows-c to Human Torch #2 on-c 330 660 990 2079 3690 5300
18 300 600 900 1890 3195 4500
19,20: 19-Origin Toro in text; shows-c to Sub-Mariner #1 on-c. 20-Origin The Angel in text 300 600 900 1910 3255 4600
21-The Patriot begins, (intro. in Human Torch #4 (#3)); not in #46-48; pin-up on back-c (7/41) 300 600 900 1890 3195 4500
22-25: 23-Last Gustavson Angel; origin The Vision in text. 24-Injury-to-eye story 287 574 861 1808 3054 4300
26-30: 27-Ka-Zar ends; last S&K Vision who battles Satan. 28-Jimmy Jupiter in the Land of Nowhere begins, ends #48; Sub-Mariner vs. The Flying Dutchman. 30-1st Japanese war-c 260 520 780 1638 2769 3900
31-33,35,36,38,39: 31-Sub-Mariner by Everett ends, resumes #84. 32-1st app. The Boboes 233 466 699 1468 2484 3500
34-Everett, Burgos, Martin Goodman, Funnies, Inc. office appear in story & battles Hitler; last Burgos Human Torch 260 520 780 1638 2769 3900
37-Classic Hitler-c 267 534 801 1682 2841 4000
40-Classic Zeppelin-c 260 520 780 1638 2769 3900
41-43,45,47,48: 48-Last Vision; flag-c 193 386 579 1216 2058 2900
44-Classic Super Plane-c 230 460 690 1449 2450 3450
46-Classic Hitler-c 227 454 681 1430 2415 3400
49-Origin Miss America 217 434 651 1367 2309 3250
50-Mary becomes Miss Patriot (origin) 193 386 579 1216 2058 2900
51-60: 54-Bondage-c 167 334 501 1052 1776 2500
61,62,64-Last German war-c 160 320 480 1008 1704 2400
63-Classic Hitler War-c; The Villainess Cat-Woman only app. 190 380 570 1197 2024 2850
65,66-Last Japanese War-c 160 320 480 1008 1704 2400
67-78: 74-Last Patriot. 75-Young Allies begin. 76-Ten Chapter Miss America serial begins, ends #85 127 254 381 800 1350 1900
79-New cover format; Super Villains begin on cover; last Angel 133 266 399 838 1419 2000
80-1st app. Capt. America in Marvel Comics 153 306 459 964 1632 2300
81-Captain America app. 125 250 375 788 1332 1875
82-Origin & 1st app. Namora (5/47); 1st Sub-Mariner/Namora team-up; Captain America app. 293 586 879 1846 3123 4400
83,85: 83-Last Young Allies. 85-Last Miss America; Blonde Phantom app. 112 224 336 706 1191 1675
84-Blonde Phantom begins (on-c of #84,88,89); Sub-Mariner by Everett begins; Captain America app. 153 306 459 964 1632 2300
86-Blonde Phantom i.d. revealed; Captain America app.; last Bucky app. 120 240 360 756 1278 1800
87-1st Capt. America/Golden Girl team-up; last Toro app. (8/48) 130 260 390 819 1385 1950
88-Golden Girl, Namora, & Sun Girl (1st in Marvel Comics) x-over; Captain America, Blonde Phantom app. 122 244 366 769 1297 1825
89-1st Human Torch/Sun Girl team-up; 1st Captain America solo; Blonde Phantom app. 120 240 360 756 1278 1800
90,91: 90-Blonde Phantom un-masked; Captain America app. 91-Capt. America app.; Blonde Phantom & Sub-Mariner end; early Venus app. (4/49) (scarce) 163 326 489 1027 1739 2450
92-Feature story on the birth of the Human Torch and the death of Professor Horton (his creator); 1st app. The Witness in Marvel Comics; Captain America app. (scarce) 329 658 987 2237 3919 5600
132 Pg. issue, B&W, 25¢ (1943-44)-printed in N. Y.; square binding, blank inside covers); has Marvel No. 33-c in color; contains Capt. America #18 & Marvel Mystery Comics #33; same contents as Captain America Annual (Less than 5 copies known to exist) 5333 10,666 16,000 32,000 - -
132 Pg. issue (with variant contents), B&W, 25¢ (1942-'43)- square binding, blank inside covers; has same Marvel No. 33-c in color but contains Capt. America #22 & Marvel Mystery Comics #41 instead (possibly scarcer than other version) (a VG+ copy sold in 2007 for $29,000)

NOTE: ***Brodsky** c-49, 72, 86, 88-92. **Crandall** a-26i. **Everett** c-7-9, 27, 84. **Gabrielle** c-30-32. **Schomburg** c-3-11, 13-29, 33-36, 39-48, 50-59, 63-69, 74, 76, 132 pg. issue. **Shores** c-37, 38, 75p, 77, 78p, 79p, 80, 81p, 82-84, 85p, 87p. **Sekowsky** c-73. Bondage covers-3, 4, 7, 12, 28, 29, 49, 50, 52, 56, 57, 58, 59, 65. Angel c-2, 3, 8, 12. Remember Pearl Harbor issues-#30-32.*

MARVEL MYSTERY COMICS
Marvel Comics: Dec, 1999 ($3.95, reprints)

1-Reprints original 1940s stories; Schomburg-c from #74 4.00

MARVEL NEMESIS: THE IMPERFECTS (EA Games characters)
Marvel Comics: July, 2005 - No. 6, Dec, 2005 ($2.99, limited series)

1-6-Jae Lee-c/Greg Pak-s/Renato Arlem-a; Spider-Man, Thing, Wolverine, Elektra app 3.00
Digest (2005, $7.99) r/#1-6 3.00

MARVEL 1985
Marvel Comics: July, 2008 - No. 6, ($3.99, limited series)

1-5: 1-Marvel villains come to the real world; Millar-s/Edwards-a; three covers 4.00

MARVEL NO-PRIZE BOOK, THE (The Official... on-c)
Marvel Comics Group: Jan, 1983 (one-shot, direct sales only)

1-Golden-c; Kirby-a 4.00

MARVELOUS ADVENTURES OF GUS BEEZER
Marvel Comics: May, 2003; Feb, 2004 ($2.99, one-shots)

...: Gus Beezer & Spider-Man 1 - (5/03) Gurihiru-a 3.00
...: Hulk 1 - (5/03) Simone-s/Lethcoe-a; She-Hulk app. 3.00
...: Spider-Man 1 - (5/03) Simone-s/Lethcoe-a; The Lizard & Dr. Doom app. 3.00
...: X-Men 1 - (5/03) Simone-s/Lethcoe-a 3.00

MARVEL PREMIERE
Marvel Comics Group: April, 1972 - No. 61, Aug, 1981 (A tryout book for new characters)

1-Origin Warlock (pre-#1) by Gil Kane/Adkins; origin Counter-Earth; Hulk & Thor cameo (#1-14 are 20¢-c) 7 14 21 45 73 100
2-Warlock ends; Kirby Yellow Claw-r 4 8 12 22 34 45
3-Dr. Strange series begins (pre #1, 7/72), B. Smith-c/a(p) 6 12 18 41 66 90
4-Smith/Brunner-a 3 6 9 18 27 35
5-9: 8-Starlin-c/a(p) 3 6 9 14 20 25
10-Death of the Ancient One 3 6 9 16 23 30
11-14: 11-Dr. Strange origin-r by Ditko. 14-Last Dr. Strange (3/74), gets own title 3 months later 2 4 6 9 13 16
15-Origin/1st app. Iron Fist (5/74), ends #25 8 16 24 56 93 130
16,25: 16-2nd app. Iron Fist; origin cont'd from #15; Hama's 1st Marvel-a. 25-1st Byrne Iron Fist (moves to own title next) 4 8 12 24 37 50
17-24: Iron Fist in all 3 6 9 17 25 32
26-Hercules. 1 2 3 5 7 9
27-Satana 2 4 6 8 10 12
28-Legion of Monsters (Ghost Rider, Man-Thing, Morbius, Werewolf) 3 6 9 16 22 28
29-46,49: 29,30-The Liberty Legion. 29-1st modern app. Patriot. 31-1st app. Woodgod; last 25¢ issue. 32-1st app. Monark Starstalker. 33,34-1st color app. Solomon Kane (Robert E. Howard adaptation "Red Shadows".) 35-Origin/1st app. 3-D Man. 36,37-3-D Man. 38-1st Weirdworld. 39,40-Torpedo. 41-1st Seeker 3000! 42-Tigra. 43-Paladin. 44-Jack of

Marvel Romance Redux: I Should Have Been a Blonde © MAR

Marvels #3 © MAR

Marvels of Science #2 © CC

GD 2.0 | VG 4.0 | FN 6.0 | VF 8.0 | VF/NM 9.0 | NM- 9.2

Hearts (1st solo book, 10/78). 45,46-Man-Wolf. 49-The Falcon (1st solo book, 8/79) 4.00
29-31-(30¢-c variants, limited distribution)(4,6,8/76) 2 4 6 11 16 20
36-38-(35¢-c variants, limited distribution)(6,8,10/77) 3 6 9 18 27 35
47,48-Byrne-a: 47-Origin/1st app. new Ant-Man. 48-Ant-Man
2 4 6 8 10 12
50-1st app. Alice Cooper; co-plotted by Alice 2 4 6 9 12 15
51-56,58-61: 51-53-Black Panther. 54-1st Caleb Hammer. 55-Wonder Man. 56-1st color app. Dominic Fortune. 58-60-Dr. Who. 61-Star Lord 4.00
57-Dr. Who (2nd U.S. app.-see Movie Classics) 6.00
NOTE: **N. Adams** *(Crusty Bunkers) part inks-10, 12, 10.* **Austin** *a-60i, 56i; c-46i, 50i, 56i, 58.* **Brunner** *a-4i, 6p, 9-14p; c-9-14.* **Byrne** *a-47p, 48p.* **Chaykin** *a-32-34; c-32, 33, 56.* **Giffen** *a-31p, 44p; c-44.* **Gil Kane** *a(p)-1, 2, 10, c(p)-1, 2, 15, 16, 22-24, 27, 36, 37.* **Kirby** *c-26, 29-31, 35.* **Layton** *a-47i, 48i; c-47.* **McWilliams** *a-25i.* **Miller** *c-49p, 53p, 58p.* **Nebres** *a-44i; c-38i.* **Nino** *a-38i.* **Perez** *c/a-38p, 45p, 46p.* **Ploog** *a-38; c-5-7.* **Russell** *a-7p.* **Simonson** *a-60(2pgs.); c-57.* **Starlin** *a-8p; c-8.* **Sutton** *a-41, 43, 50p, 61; c-50p, 61. #57-60 publ'd w/two different prices on-c.*

MARVEL PRESENTS
Marvel Comics: October, 1975 - No. 12, Aug, 1977 (#1-6 are 25¢ issues)

1-Origin & 1st app. Bloodstone 2 4 6 8 11 14
2-Origin Bloodstone continued; Kirby-c 1 2 3 5 6 8
3-Guardians of the Galaxy (1st solo book, 2/76) begins, ends #12
2 4 6 10 14 18
4-7,9-12: 9,10-Origin Starhawk 1 2 3 5 7 9
4-6-(30¢-c variants, limited distribution)(4-8/76) 3 6 9 16 23 30
8-r/story from Silver Surfer #2 plus 4 pgs. new-a 1 2 3 5 7 9
11,12-(35¢-c variants, limited distribution)(6,8/77) 4 8 12 24 37 50
NOTE: **Austin** *a-6i.* **Buscema** *r-8p.* **Chaykin** *a-5p.* **Kane** *c-1p.* **Starlin** *layouts-10.*

MARVEL PREVIEW (Magazine) (Bizarre Adventures #25 on)
Marvel Comics: Feb (no month), 1975 - No. 24, Winter, 1980 (B&W) ($1.00)

1-Man-Gods From Beyond the Stars; Crusty Bunkers (Neal Adams)-a(i) & cover; Nino-a
3 6 9 14 19 24
2-1st origin The Punisher (see Amaz. Spider-Man #129 & Classic Punisher); 1st app. Dominic Fortune; Morrow-c 10 20 30 67 116 165
3,8,10: 3-Blade the Vampire Slayer. 8-Legion of Monsters; Morbius app. 10-Thor the Mighty; Starlin frontispiece 3 6 9 16 22 28
4,5: 4-Star-Lord & Sword in the Star (origins & 1st app.). 5,6-Sherlock Holmes.
2 4 6 11 16 20
6,9: 6-Sherlock Holmes; N. Adams frontispiece. 9-Man-God; origin Star Hawk, ends #20
2 4 6 9 13 16
7-Satana, Sword in the Star app. 2 4 6 10 14 18
11,12,16,19: 11-Star-Lord; Byrne-a; Starlin frontispiece. 12-Haunt of Horror. 16-Masters of Terror. 19-Kull 1 3 4 6 8 10
13-15,17,18,20-24: 14,15-Star-Lord. 14-Starlin painted-c. 17-Blackmark by G. Kane (see SSOC #1-3). 18-Star-Lord; Sienkiewicz-a; Veitch & Bissette-a. 20-Bizarre Advs. 21-Moon Knight (Spr/80)-Predates Moon Knight #1; The Shroud by Ditko. 22-King Arthur. 23-Bizarre Advs.; Miller-a. 24-Debut Paradox 1 2 3 4 5 7
NOTE: **N. Adams** *(C. Bunkers) r-20i.* **Buscema** *a-22, 23.* **Byrne** *a-11.* **Chaykin** *a-20r; c-20 (new).* **Colan** *a-8, 16p(3), 18p, 23p; c-16p.* **Elias** *a-18.* **Giffen** *a-7.* **Infantino** *a-14p.* **Kaluta** *a-12; c-15.* **Miller** *a-23.* **Morrow** *a-8i; c-2-4.* **Perez** *a-20p.* **Ploog** *a-8.* **Starlin** *c-13, 14. Nudity in some issues*

MARVEL RIOT
Marvel Comics: Dec, 1995 ($1.95, one-shot)

1-"Age of Apocalypse" spoof; Lobdell script 2.50

MARVEL ROMANCE
Marvel Comics: 2006 ($19.99, TPB)

nn-Reprints romance stories from 1960-1972; art by Kirby, Buscema, Colan, Romita 20.00

MARVEL ROMANCE REDUX (Humor stories using art reprinted from Marvel romance comics)
Marvel Comics: Apr, 2006 - Aug, 2006 ($2.99, one-shots)

...: But I Thought He Loved Me Too (4/06) art by Kirby, Colan, Buscema & Romita; Giffen-c 3.00
...: Guys & Dolls (5/06) art by Starlin, Heck, Colan & Buscema; Conner-c 3.00
...: I Should Have Been a Blonde (7/06) art by Brodsky Colletta & Colan; Cho-c 3.00
...: Love is a Four Letter Word (8/06) art by Kirby, Buscema, Colan & Heck; Land-c 3.00
...: Restraining Orders are For Other Girls (6/06) art by Giordano, Kirby; Baker-c 3.00
...: Another Kind of Love TPB (2007, $13.99) r/one-shots 14.00

MARVELS
Marvel Comics: Jan, 1994 - No. 4, Apr, 1994 ($5.95, painted lim. series)
No. 1 (2nd Printing), Apr, 1996 - No. 4 (2nd Printing), July, 1996 ($2.95)

1-4: Kurt Busiek scripts & Alex Ross painted-c/a in all; double-c w/acetate overlay
1 2 3 5 6 8
Marvel Classic Collectors Pack ($11.90)-Issues #1 & 2 boxed (1st printings).
2 4 6 9 13 16
0-(8/94, $2.95)-no acetate overlay. 4.00
1-4-(2nd printing): r/original limited series w/o acetate overlay 3.00
Hardcover (1994, $59.95)-r/#0-4; w/intros by Stan Lee, John Romita, Sr., Kurt Busiek & Scott McCloud. 60.00
...: 10th Anniversary Edition (2004, $49.99, hardcover w/dustjacket) r/#0-4; scripts and commentaries; Ross sketch pages, cover gallery, behind the scenes art 50.00
Trade paperback ($19.95) 20.00

MARVEL SAGA, THE
Marvel Comics Group: Dec, 1985 - No. 25, Dec, 1987

1,21-25 2.50
2-20 2.50
NOTE: **Williamson** *a(i)-9, 10; c(i)-7, 10-12, 14, 16.*

MARVELS COMICS: (Marvel-type comics read in the Marvel Universe)
Marvel Comics: Jul, 2000 ($2.25, one-shots)

...Captain America #1 -Frenz & Sinnott-a; ...Daredevil #1 -Isabella-s/Newell-a; ...Fantastic Four #1 -Kesel-s/Paul Smith-a; Spider-Man #1 -Oliff-a; ...Thor #1 -Templeton-s/Aucoin-a 2.50
...X-Men #1 -Millar-s/ Sean Phillips & Duncan Fegredo-a 2.50
The History of Marvels Comics (no cover price)-Faux history; previews titles 2.50

MARVEL SELECT FLIP MAGAZINE
Marvel Comics: Aug, 2005 - Present ($3.99/$4.99)

1-11-Reprints Astonishing X-Men and New X-Men: Academy X in flip format 4.00
12-24-($4.99) Reprints recent X-Men mini-series in flip format 5.00

MARVEL SELECTS:
Marvel Comics: Jan, 2000 - No. 6, June, 2000 ($2.75/$2.99, reprints)

...Fantastic Four 1-6: Reprints F.F. #107-112; new Davis-c 2.75
...Spider-Man 1,2,4-6: Reprints AS-M #100,101,103,104,93; Wieringo-c 2.75
...Spider-Man 3 ($2.99): Reprints AS-M #102; new Wieringo-c 3.00

MARVEL'S GREATEST COMICS (Marvel Collectors' Item Classics #1-22)
Marvel Comics Group: No. 23, Oct, 1969 - No. 96, Jan, 1981

23-34 (Giants). Begin Fantastic Four-r/#30s?-116 3 6 9 16 22 28
35-37-Silver Surfer-r/Fantastic Four #48-50 2 4 6 8 10 12
38-50: 42-Silver Surfer-r/F.F.(others?) 1 2 3 5 6 8
51-70: 63,64-(25¢ editions) 5.00
63,64-(30¢-c variants, limited distribution)(5,7/76) 2 4 6 11 16 20
71-96: 71-73-(30¢ editions) 4.00
71-73-(35¢-c variants, limited distribution)(7,9-10/77) 3 6 9 18 27 35
...: Fantastic Four #52 (2006, $2.99) reprints entire comic with ads and letter column 3.00
NOTE: *Dr. Strange, Fantastic Four, Iron Man, Watcher-#23, 24. Capt. America, Dr. Strange, Iron Man, Fantastic Four-#25-28. Fantastic Four-#38-96.* **Buscema** *r-85-92; c-87-92r.* **Ditko** *r-23-28.* **Kirby** *r-23-82; c-75, 77p, 80p. #81 reprints Fantastic Four #100.*

MARVEL'S GREATEST SUPERHERO BATTLES (See Fireside Book Series)

MARVEL: SHADOWS AND LIGHT
Marvel Comics: Feb, 1997 ($2.95, B&W, one-shot)

1-Tony Daniel-c 3.00

MARVEL 1602
Marvel Comics: Nov, 2003 - No. 8, June, 2004 ($3.50, limited series)

1-8-Neil Gaiman-s; Andy Kubert & Richard Isanove-a 3.50
HC (2004, $24.99) r/series; script pages for #1, sketch pages and Gaiman afterword 25.00
SC (2005, $19.99) 20.00

MARVEL 1602: FANTASTICK FOUR
Marvel Comics: Nov, 2006 - No. 5, Mar, 2007s ($3.50, limited series)

1-5-Peter David-s/Pascal Alixe-a/Leinil Yu-c 3.50
TPB (2007, $14.99) r/#1-5; sketch page 15.00

MARVEL 1602: NEW WORLD
Marvel Comics: Oct, 2005 - No. 5, Jan, 2006 ($3.50, limited series)

1-5-Greg Pak-s/Greg Tocchini-a; "Hulk" and "Iron Man" app. 3.50
TPB (2006, $14.99) r/#1-5 15.00

MARVEL 65TH ANNIVERSARY SPECIAL
Marvel Comics: 2004 ($4.99, one-shot)

1-Reprints Sub-Mariner & Human Torch battle from Marvel Mystery Comics #8-10 5.00

MARVELS OF SCIENCE
Charlton Comics: March, 1946 - No. 4, June, 1946

1-A-Bomb story 23 46 69 133 214 295
2-4 14 28 42 80 115 150

MARVEL SPECIAL EDITION FEATURING... (Also see Special Collectors' Ed.)
Marvel Comics Group: 1975 - 1978 (84 pgs.) (Oversized)

1-The Spectacular Spider-Man ($1.50); r/Amazing Spider-Man #6,35, Annual 1; Ditko-a(r) 3 6 9 18 27 35
1,2-Star Wars ('77,'78; r/Star Wars #1-3 & #4-6; regular edition and Whitman variant exist
2 4 6 10 14 18

Marvel Spectacular #2 © MAR

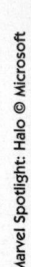

Marvel Spotlight: Halo © Microsoft

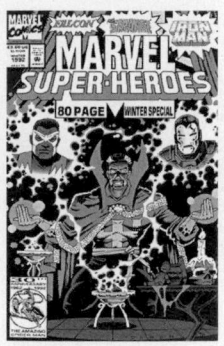

Marvel Super-Heroes (2nd series) #12 © MAR

3-Star Wars ('78, $2.50, 116 pgs.); r/S. Wars #1-6; regular edition and Whitman variant exist
3 6 9 14 19 24
3-Close Encounters of the Third Kind (1978, $1.50, 56 pgs.)-Movie adaptation;
Simonson-a(p) 2 4 6 9 13 16
V2#2(Spring, 1980, $2.00, oversized)- "Star Wars: The Empire Strikes Back";
r/Marvel Comics Super Special #16 3 6 9 16 23 30
NOTE: ***Chaykin** c/a(r)-1(1977), 2, 3. **Stevens** a(r)-2i, 3i. **Williamson** a(r)-V2#2.*

MARVEL SPECTACULAR
Marvel Comics Group: Aug, 1973 - No. 19, Nov, 1975
1-Thor-r from mid-sixties begin by Kirby 2 4 6 8 10 12
2-19 6.00

MARVELS: PORTRAITS
Marvel Comics: Mar, 1995 - No. 4, June, 1995 ($2.95, limited series)
1-4:Different artists renditions of Marvel characters 3.00

MARVEL SPOTLIGHT (...& Son of Satan #19, 20, 23, 24)
Marvel Comics Group: Nov, 1971 - No. 33, Apr, 1977; V2#1, July, 1979 - V2#11, Mar, 1981
(A try-out book for new characters)
1-Origin Red Wolf (western hero)(1st solo book, pre-#1); Wood inks, Neal Adams-c;
only 15¢ issue 5 10 15 34 55 75
2-(25¢, 52 pgs.)-Venus-r by Everett; origin/1st app. Werewolf By Night (begins) by Ploog;
N. Adams-c 19 38 57 139 257 375
3,4: 4-Werewolf By Night ends (6/72); gets own title 9/72
6 12 18 43 69 95
5-Origin/1st app. Ghost Rider (8/72) & begins 23 46 69 167 309 450
6-8: 6-Origin G.R. retold. 8-Last Ploog issue 7 14 21 47 76 105
9-11-Last Ghost Rider (gets own title next mo.) 5 10 15 34 55 75
12-Origin & 2nd full app. The Son of Satan (10/73); story cont'd from Ghost Rider #2 & into
#3; series begins, ends #24 4 8 12 24 37 50
13-24: 13-Partial origin Son of Satan. 14-Last 20¢ issue. 22-Ghost Rider-c & cameo
(5 panels). 24-Last Son of Satan (10/75); gets own title 12/75
2 4 6 8 11 14
25,27,30,31: 27-(Regular 25¢-c), Sub-Mariner app. 30-The Warriors Three. 31-Nick Fury 6.00
26-Scarecrow 1 3 4 6 8 10
27-(30¢-c variant, limited distribution) 2 4 6 13 18 22
28-(Regular 25¢-c) 1st solo Moon Knight app. 3 6 9 18 27 35
28-(30¢-c variant, limited distribution) 8 16 24 54 90 125
29,32: 29-(Regular 25¢-c) (8/76) Moon Knight app.; last 25¢ issue. 32-1st app./partial origin
Spider-Woman (2/77); Nick Fury app. 3 6 9 14 19 24
29-(30¢-c variant, limited distribution) 6 12 18 41 66 90
33-Deathlok; 1st app. Devil-Slayer 1 2 3 5 6 8
V2#1-7,9-11: 1-4-Capt. Marvel. 5-Dragon Lord. 6,7-StarLord; origin #6. 9-11-Capt. Universe
(see Micronauts #0) 3.00
1-Variant copy missing issue #1 on cover 2 4 6 8 10 12
8-Capt. Marvel; Miller-c/a(p) 6.00
NOTE: ***Austin** c-V2#2i, 8. **J. Buscema** c/a-30p. **Chaykin** a-31; c-26, 31. **Colan** a-18p, 19p. **Ditko** a-V2#4, 5, 9-11; c-V2#4, 9-11. **Kane** c-21p, 32p. **Kirby** c-29p. **McWilliams** a-20i. **Miller** a-V2#8p; c(p)-V2#2, 5, 7, 8. **Mooney** a-8i, 10i, 14p, 15, 16p, 17p, 24p, 27, 32i. **Nasser** a-33p. **Ploog** a-2-5, 6-8p; c-3-9. **Romita** c-13. **Sutton** a-9-11p, V2#6, 7. #29-25¢ & 30¢ issues exist.*

MARVEL SPOTLIGHT (Most issues spotlight one Marvel artist and one Marvel writer)
Marvel Comics: 2005 - Present ($2.99)
...Brian Bendis/Mark Bagley; Daniel Way/Olivier Coipel; David Finch/Roberto Aguirre-Sacasa;
Ed Brubaker/Billy Tan; John Cassaday/Sean McKeever; Joss Whedon/Michael Lark;
Laurell K. Hamilton/George R.R. Martin; Neil Gaiman/Salvador Larroca; Robert Kirkman/
Greg Land; Stan Lee/Jack Kirby; Warren Ellis/Jim Cheung each... 3.00
...Steve McNiven/Mark Millar - Civil War 10.00
...: Captain America Remembered (2007) character features; creator interviews 3.00
...: Civil War Aftermath (2007) Top 10 Moments, casualty list, previews of upcoming series 3.00
...: Dark Tower (2007) previews the Stephen King adaptation; creator interviews 5.00
...: Fantastic Four and Silver Surfer (2007) character features; creator interviews 3.00
...: Ghost Rider (2007) character and movie features; creator interviews 3.00
...: Halo (2007) a World of Halo feature; Bendis & Maleev interviews 3.00
...: Heroes Reborn/Onslaught Reborn (2006) 3.00
...: Hulk Movie (2008) character and movie features; comic & movie creator interviews 3.00
...: Iron Man Movie (2008) character and movie features; Terrence Howard interview 3.00
...: Marvel Knights 10th Anniversary (2008) Quesada interview; series synopsies 3.00
...: Marvel Zombies/Mystic Arcana (2008) character features; creator interviews 3.00
...: Secret Invasion (2008) features on the Skrulls; Bendis, Reed & Yu interviews 3.00
...: Spider-Man (2007) character features; creator interviews; Ditko art showcase 3.00
...: Spider-Man - Brand New Day (2008) storyline features; Romitas interviews 3.00
...: Spider-Man-One More Day/Brand New Day (2008) storyline features; interviews 3.00
...: Thor (2007) character features; Straczynski interview; Romita Jr. art showcase 3.00
...: Ultimates 3 (2008) character features; Loeb & Madureira interviews 3.00
...: Uncanny X-Men 500 Issues Celebration (2008) creator interviews; timeline 3.00
...: World War Hulk (2007) character features; creator interviews; early art showcase 3.00
...: X-Men: Messiah Complex (2008) X-Men crossover features; creator interviews 3.00

MARVEL SUPER ACTION (Magazine)
Marvel Comics Group: Jan, 1976 (B&W, 76 pgs.)
1-2nd app. Dominic Fortune (see Marvel Preview); early Punisher app.; Weird World &
The Huntress; Evans, Ploog-a 7 14 21 49 80 110

MARVEL SUPER ACTION
Marvel Comics Group: May, 1977 - No. 37, Nov, 1981
1-Reprints Capt. America #100 by Kirby 2 4 6 8 10 12
2-13: 2,3,5-13 reprint Capt. America #101,102,103-111. 4-Marvel Boy-r(origin)/M. Boy #1.
11-Origin-r. 12,13-Classic Steranko-c/a(r). 1 2 3 5 6 8
2,3-(35¢-c variants, limited distribution)(6,8/77) 4 8 12 22 34 45
14-20: r/Avengers #55,56, Annual 2, others 5.00
21-37: 30-r/Hulk #6 from U.K. 4.00
NOTE: ***Buscema** a(r)-14p, 15p; c-18-20, 22, 35r-37. **Everett** a-4. **Heath** a-4r. **Kirby** r-1-3, 5-11. **B. Smith** a-27r, 28r. **Steranko** a(r)-12p, 13p; c-12r, 13r.*

MARVEL SUPER HERO CONTEST OF CHAMPIONS
Marvel Comics Group: June, 1982 - No. 3, Aug, 1982 (Limited series)
1-3: Features nearly all Marvel characters currently appearing in their comics;
1st Marvel limited series 1 2 3 5 6 8

MARVEL SUPER HEROES
Marvel Comics Group: October, 1966 (25¢, 68 pgs.) (1st Marvel one-shot)
1-r/origin Daredevil from D.D. #1; r/Avengers #2; G.A. Sub-Mariner-r/Marvel Mystery #8
(Human Torch app.). Kirby-a 11 22 33 75 133 190

MARVEL SUPER-HEROES (Formerly Fantasy Masterpieces #1-11)
(Also see Giant-Size Super Heroes) (#12-20: 25¢, 68 pgs.)
Marvel Comics: No. 12, 12/67 - No. 31, 11/71; No. 32, 9/72 - No. 105, 1/82
12-Origin & 1st app. Capt. Marvel of the Kree; G.A. Human Torch, Destroyer, Capt. America,
Black Knight, Sub-Mariner-r (#12-20 all contain new stories and reprints)
12 24 36 87 156 225
13-2nd app. Capt. Marvel; G.A. Black Knight, Torch, Vision, Capt. America, Sub-Mariner-r
7 14 21 49 80 110
14-Amazing Spider-Man (5/68, new-a by Andru/Everett); G.A. Sub-Mariner, Torch, Mercury
(1st Kirby-a at Marvel), Black Knight, Capt. America reprints
9 18 27 65 113 160
15-17: 15-Black Bolt cameo in Medusa (new-a); Black Knight, Sub-Mariner, Black Marvel,
Capt. America-r. 16-Origin & 1st app. S. A. Phantom Eagle; G.A. Torch, Capt. America,
Black Knight, Patriot, Sub-Mariner-r. 17-Origin Black Knight (new-a); G.A. Torch,
Sub-Mariner-r; reprint from All-Winners Squad #21 (cover & story)
4 8 12 28 44 60
18-Origin/1st app. Guardians of the Galaxy (1/69); G.A. Sub-Mariner, All-Winners Squad-r
6 12 18 43 69 95
19-Ka-Zar (new-a); G.A. Torch, Marvel Boy, Black Knight, Sub-Mariner reprints; Smith-c(p);
Tuska-a(r) 4 8 12 22 34 45
20-Doctor Doom (5/69); r/Young Men #24 w/-c 4 8 12 26 41 55
21-31: All-r issues. 21-X-Men, Daredevil, Iron Man-r begin, end #31. 31-Last Giant issue
3 6 9 14 19 24
32-50: 32-Hulk/Sub-Mariner-r begin from TTA. 1 2 3 5 6 8
51-70,100: 56-r/origin Hulk/Inc. Hulk #102; Hulk-r begin 5.00
57,58-(30¢-c variants, limited distribution)(5,7/76) 2 4 6 11 16 20
65,66-(35¢-c variants, limited distribution)(7,9/77) 3 6 9 17 25 32
71-99,101-105 4.00
NOTE: ***Austin** a-104. **Colan** a(p)-12, 13, 15, 18; c-12, 13, 15, 18. **Everett** a-14i(new); r-14, 15i, 18, 19, 33; c-85(r). New **Kirby** c-22, 27, 54. **Maneely** r-14, 15, 19. **Severin** r-83-85i, 100-102; c-100-102r. **Starlin** c-47. **Tuska** a-19p. Black Knight-r by **Maneely** in 12-16, 19. Sub-Mariner-r by **Everett** in 12-20.*

MARVEL SUPER-HEROES
Marvel Comics: May, 1990 - V2#15, Oct, 1993 ($2.95/$2.50, quart., 68-84 pgs.)
1-Moon Knight, Hercules, Black Panther, Magik, Brother Voodoo, Speedball (by Ditko)
& Hellcat; Hembeck-a 3.00
2,4,5,V2#3,6-15: 2-Summer Special(7/90); Rogue, Speedball (by Ditko), Iron Man, Falcon,
Tigra & Daredevil. 4-Spider-Man/Nick Fury, Daredevil,Speedball, Wonder Man, Spitfire &
Black Knight; Byrne-c. 5-Thor, Dr. Strange, Thing & She-Hulk; Speedball by Ditko(p).
V2#3-Retells origin Capt. America w/new facts; Blue Shield, Capt. Marvel,Speedball, Wasp;
Hulk by Ditko/Rogers V2#6-9: 6-8-$2.25-c. 6,7-X-Men, Cloak & Dagger, The Shroud (by
Ditko) & Marvel Boy in each. 8-X-Men, Namor & Iron Man (by Ditko); Larsen-c. 9-West
Coast Avengers, Iron Man app.; Kieth-c(p). V2#10-Ms. Marvel/Sabretooth-c/story
(intended for Ms. Marvel #24; shows-c to #24); Namor, Vision, Scarlet Witch stories.
V2#11,12 :11-Original Ghost Rider-c/story; Giant-Man, Ms. Marvel stories. 12-Dr. Strange,
Falcon, Iron Man. V2#13-15 ($2.75, 84 pgs.): 13-All Iron Man 30th anniversary.
15-Iron Man/Thor/Volstagg/Dr. Druid 2.75

MARVEL SUPER-HEROES MEGAZINE

Marvel Tales #123 © MAR

Marvel Tales (2nd series) #233 © MAR

Marvel Team-Up #21 © MAR

GD VG FN VF VF/NM NM-
2.0 4.0 6.0 8.0 9.0 9.2

Marvel Comics: Oct, 1994 - No. 6, Mar, 1995 ($2.95, 100 pgs.)
1-6: 1-r/FF #232, DD #159, Iron Man #115, Incred. Hulk #314 3.00

MARVEL SUPER-HEROES SECRET WARS (See Secret Wars II)
Marvel Comics Group: May, 1984 - No. 12, Apr, 1985 (limited series)
1 1 2 3 5 6 8
1-3-(2nd printings, sold in multi-packs) 2.50
2-6,9-11: 6-The Wasp dies 6.00
7,12: 7-Intro. new Spider-Woman. 12-($1.00, 52 pgs.) 1 2 3 4 5 7
8-Spider-Man's new black costume explained as alien costume (1st app. Venom as alien costume) 3 6 9 17 25 32
NOTE: ***Zeck** a-1-12; c-1,3,8-12. Additional artists (John Romita Sr., Art Adams and others) had uncreditted art in #12.*

MARVEL SUPER SPECIAL, A (See Marvel Comics Super...)

MARVEL SWIMSUIT SPECIAL (Also see Marvel Illustrated...)
Marvel Comics: 1992 - No. 4, 1995 ($3.95/$4.50, magazine, 52 pgs.)
1-4-Silvestri-c; pin-ups by diff. artists. 2-Jusko-c. 3-Hughes-c 1 3 4 6 8 10

MARVEL TAILS STARRING PETER PORKER THE SPECTACULAR SPIDER-HAM (Also see Peter Porker...)
Marvel Comics Group: Nov, 1983 (one-shot)
1-Peter Porker, the Spectacular Spider-Ham, Captain Americat, Goose Rider, Hulk Bunny app. 4.00

MARVEL TALES (Formerly Marvel Mystery Comics #1-92)
Marvel/Atlas Comics (MCI): No. 93, Aug, 1949 - No. 159, Aug, 1957
93-Horror/weird stories begin 147 294 441 926 1563 2200
94-Everett-a 93 186 279 586 993 1400
95-New logo 69 138 207 435 735 1035
96,99,101,103,105 59 118 177 372 629 885
97-Sun Girl, 2 pgs; Kirbyish-a; one story used in N.Y. State Legislative document 77 154 231 481 816 1150
98,100: 98-Krigstein-a 60 120 180 378 639 900
102-Wolverton-a "The End of the World", (6 pgs.) 83 166 249 523 887 1250
104-Wolverton-a "Gateway to Horror", (6 pgs.) 83 166 249 523 887 1250
106,107-Krigstein-a. 106-Decapitation story 48 96 144 298 499 700
108-120: 116-(7/53) Werewolf By Night story. 118-Hypo-c/panels in End of World story. 120-Jack Katz-a 37 74 111 215 345 475
121,123-131: 128-Flying Saucer-c. 131-Last precode (2/55) 28 56 84 164 265 365
122-Kubert-a 29 58 87 169 272 375
132,133,135-141,143,145 21 42 63 125 200 275
134-Krigstein, Kubert-a; flying saucer-c 23 46 69 135 218 300
142-Krigstein-a 22 44 66 129 207 285
144-Williamson/Krenkel-a, 3 pgs. 22 44 66 129 207 285
146,148-151,154-156,158: 150-1st S.A. issue. 156-Torres-a 17 34 51 98 154 210
147,152: 147-Ditko-a. 152-Wood, Morrow-a 20 40 60 114 180 245
153-Everett End of World c/story 21 42 63 125 200 275
157,159-Krigstein-a 18 36 54 105 165 225
NOTE: ***Andru** a-103. **Briefer** a-118. **Check** a-147. **Colan** a-102, 105, 107, 118, 120, 121, 127, 131. **Drucker** a-127, 135, 141, 146, 150. **Everett** a-98, 104, 106(2), 108(2), 131, 148, 151, 153, 155; c-107, 109, 111, 112, 114, 117, 127, 143, 147-151, 153, 155, 156. **Forte** a-119, 125, 130. **Heath** a-110, 113, 118, 119; c-104-106, 110, 130. **Gil Kane** a-117. **Lawrence** a-130. **Maneely** a-111, 126, 129; c-108, 116, 120, 129, 152. **Mooney** a-114. **Morisi** a-153. **Morrow** a-150, 152, 156. **Orlando** a-149, 151, 157. **Pakula** a-119, 121, 135, 144, 150, 152, 156. **Powell** a-136, 137, 150, 154. **Ravielli** a-117. **Rico** a-97, 99. **Romita** a-108. **Sekowsky** a-96-98. **Shores** a-110; c-96. **Sinnott** a-105, 116. **Tuska** a-114. **Whitney** a-107. **Wildey** a-126, 138.*

MARVEL TALES (...Annual #1,2; ...Starring Spider-Man #123 on)
Marvel Comics Group (NPP earlier issues): 1964 - No. 291, Nov, 1994 (No. 1-32: 72 pgs.)
(#1-3 have Canadian variants; back & inside-c are blank, same value)
1-Reprints origins of Spider-Man/Amazing Fantasy #15, Hulk/Inc. Hulk#1, Ant-Man/T.T.A. #35, Giant Man/T.T.A. #49, Iron Man/T.O.S. #39,48, Thor/J.I.M. #83 & r/Sgt. Fury #1 30 60 90 217 401 585
2 ('65)-r/X-Men #1(origin), Avengers #1(origin), origin Dr. Strange-r/Strange Tales #115 & origin Hulk(Hulk #3) 10 20 30 73 129 185
3 (7/66)-Spider-Man, Strange Tales (H. Torch), Journey into Mystery (Thor), Tales to Astonish (Ant-Man)-r begin (r/Strange Tales #101) 6 12 18 43 69 95
4,5 5 10 15 30 48 65
6-8,10: 10-Reprints 1st Kraven/Amaz. S-M #15 3 6 9 20 30 40
9-r/Amazing Spider-Man #14 w/cover 4 8 12 22 34 45
11-33: 11-Spider-Man battles Daredevil-r/Amaz. Spider-Man #16. 13-Origin Marvel Boy-r from M. Boy #1. 22-Green Goblin-c/story-r/Amaz. Spider-Man #27. 30-New Angel story (x-over w/Ka-Zar #2,3). 32-Last 72 pg. iss. 33-(52 pgs.) Kraven-r 3 6 9 16 22 28

GD VG FN VF VF/NM NM-
2.0 4.0 6.0 8.0 9.0 9.2

34-50: 34-Begin regular size issues 1 2 3 5 7 9
51-65 5.00
66-70-(Regular 25¢ editions)(4-8/76) 4.00
66-70-(30¢-c variants, limited distribution) 2 4 6 11 16 20
71-105: 75-Origin Spider-Man-r. 77-79-Drug issues-r/Amaz. Spider-Man #96-98. 98-Death of Gwen Stacy-r/Amaz. Spider-Man #121 (Green Goblin). 99-Death Green Goblin r/Amaz. Spider-Man #122. 100-(52 pgs.)-New Hawkeye/Two Gun Kid story. 101-105-All Spider-Man-r 3.00
80-84-(35¢-c variants, limited distribution)(6-10/77) 3 6 9 16 23 30
106-r/1st Punisher-Amazing Spider-Man #129 1 2 3 5 6 8
107-136: 107-133-All Spider-Man-r. 111,112-r/Spider-Man #134,135 (Punisher). 113,114-r/Spider-Man #136,137(Green Goblin). 126-128-r/Clone story from Amazing Spider-Man #149-151. 134-136-Dr. Strange-r begin; SpM stories continue. 134-Dr. Strange-r/Strange Tales #110 3.00
137-Origin-r Dr. Strange; shows original unprinted-c & origin Spider-Man/Amazing Fantasy #15 6.00
137-Nabisco giveaway 1 2 3 4 5 7
138-Reprints all Amazing Spider-Man #1; begin reprints of Spider-Man with covers similar to originals 5.00
139-144: r/Amazing Spider-Man #2-7 3.00
145-149,151-190,193-199: Spider-Man-r continue w/#8 on. 149-Contains skin "Tattooz" decals. 153-r/1st Kraven/Spider-Man #15. 155-r/2nd Green Goblin/Spider-Man #17. 161,164,165-Gr. Goblin-c/stories-r/Spider-Man #23,26,27. 178,179-Green Goblin-c/story-r/Spider-Man #39,40. 187,189-Kraven-r. 193-Byrne-r/Marvel Team-Up begin w/scripts 2.50
150,191,192,200: 150-($1.00, 52pgs.)-r/Spider-Man Annual #1(Kraven app.). 191-($1.50, 68 pgs.)-r/Spider-Man #96-98. 192-($1.25, 52 pgs.)-r/Spider-Man #121,122. 200-Double size ($1.25)-Miller-c & r/Annual #14 4.00
201-257: 208-Last Byrne-r. 210,211-r/Spidey #134,135. 212,213-r/Giant-Size Spidey #4. 213-r/1st solo Silver Surfer story/F.F. Annual #5. 214,215-r/Spidey #161,162. 222-Reprints origin Punisher/Spectacular Spider-Man #83; last Punisher reprint. 209-Reprints 1st app. The Punisher/Amazing Spider-Man #129, Punisher reprints begin, end #222. 223-McFarlane-c begins, end #239. 233-Spider-Man/X-Men team ups begin; r/X-Men #35. 234-r/Marvel Team-Up #4. 235,236-r/M. Team-Up Annual #1. 237,238-r/M. Team-Up #150. 239,240-r/M. Team-Up #38,90(Beast). 242-r/M.Team-Up #89. 243-r/M. Team-Up #117 (Wolverine). 250-($1.50, 52pgs.)-r/1st Karma/M. Team-Up #100. 251-r/Spider-Man #100 (Green Goblin-c/story). 252-r/1st app. Morbius/Amaz. Spider-Man #101. 253-($1.50, 52 pgs.) -r/Amaz. S-M #102254-r/M. Team-Up #15(Ghost Rider); new painted-c. 255,256-Spider-Man & Ghost Rider-r/Marvel Team-Up #58,91. 257-Hobgoblin-r begin (r/Amazing Spider-Man #238) 2.50
258-291: 258-261-r/A. Spider-Man #239,249-251(Hobgoblin). 262,263-r/Marv. Team-Up #53,54. 262-New X-Men vs. Sunstroke story. 263-New Woodgod origin story. 264,265-r/Amazing Spider-Man Annual 5. 266-273-Reprints alien costume stories/A. S-M 252-259. 277-r/1st Silver Sable/A. S-M 265. 283-r/A. S-M 275 (Hobgoblin). 284-r/A. S-M 276 (Hobgoblin) 2.50
285-variant w/Wonder-Con logo on c-no price-giveaway 2.50
286-($2.95)-p/bagged w/16 page insert & animation print 3.00
NOTE: *All contain reprints; some have new art. #89-97-r/Amazing Spider-Man #110-118; #98-136-r/#121-159; #137-150-r/Amazing Fantasy #15, #1-12 & Annual 1; #151-167-r/#13-28 & Annual 2; #168-186-r/#29-46. **Austin** a-100i; c-272i, 273i. **Byrne** a(r)-193-198p, 201-208p. **Ditko** a-1-30, 83, 100, 137-155. **G. Kane** a-71, 81, 98-101p, 249r; c-125-127p, 130p, 137-155. **Sam Kieth** c-255, 262, 263. **Ron Lim** c-266p-281p, 283p-285p. **McFarlane** c-223-239. **Mooney** a-63, 95-97i, 103(i). **Nasser** a-100p. **Nebres** a-242i. **Perez** c-259-261. **Rogers** c-240, 241, 243-252.*

MARVEL TALES FLIP MAGAZINE
Marvel Comics: Sept, 2005 - No. 25, Sept, 2007 ($3.99/$4.99)
1-6-Reprints Amazing Spider-Man #30-up and Amazing Fantasy (2004) in flip format 4.00
7-10-Reprints Amazing Spider-Man #36-up and Runaways Vol. 2 in flip format 4.00
11-25-($4.99) Reprints Amazing Spider-Man #36-up and Runaways Vol. 2 in flip format 5.00

MARVEL TAROT, THE
Marvel Comics: 2007 ($3.99, one-shot)
1-Marvel characters featured in Tarot deck images; Djurdjevic-c 4.00

MARVEL TEAM-UP (See Marvel Treasury Edition #18 & Official Marvel Index To...) (Replaced by Web of Spider-Man)
Marvel Comics Group: March, 1972 - No. 150, Feb, 1985
NOTE: *Spider-Man team-ups in all but Nos. 18, 23, 26, 29, 32, 35, 97, 104, 105, 137.*
1-Human Torch 13 26 39 95 168 240
2-Human Torch 6 12 18 37 59 80
3-Spider-Man/Human Torch vs. Morbius (part 1); 3rd app. of Morbius (7/72) 6 12 18 43 69 95
4-Spider-Man/X-Men vs. Morbius (part 2 of story); 4th app. of Morbius 6 12 18 43 69 95
5-10: 5-Vision. 6-Thing. 7-Thor. 8-The Cat (4/73, came out between The Cat #3 & 4). 9-Iron Man. 10-H-T 3 6 9 19 29 38
11,13,14,16-20: 11-Inhumans. 13-Capt. America. 14-Sub-Mariner. 16-Capt. Marvel. 17-Mr. Fantastic. 18-H-T/Hulk. 19-Ka-Zar. 20-Black Panther; last 20¢ issue

Marvel Team-Up #141 © MAR

Marvel Treasury Edition #24 © MAR

Marvel Triple Action #11 © MAR

GD 2.0 VG 4.0 FN 6.0 VF 8.0 VF/NM 9.0 NM- 9.2

2 4 6 10 14 18
12-Werewolf (By Night) (8/73) 3 6 9 19 29 38
15-1st Spider-Man/Ghost Rider team-up (11/73) 3 6 9 19 29 38
21-30: 21-Dr. Strange. 22-Hawkeye. 23-H-T/Iceman (X-Men cameo). 24-Brother Voodoo. 25-Daredevil. 26-H-T/Thor. 27-Hulk. 28-Hercules. 29-H-T/Iron Man. 30-Falcon 2 4 6 8 10 12
31-45,47-50: 31-Iron Fist. 32-H-T/Son of Satan. 33-Nighthawk. 34-Valkyrie. 35-H-T/Dr. Strange. 36-Frankenstein. 37-Man-Wolf. 38-Beast. 39-H-T. 40-Sons of the Tiger/H-T. 41-Scarlet Witch. 42-The Vision. 43-Dr. Doom; retells origin. 44-Moondragon. 45-Killraven. 47-Thing. 48-Iron Man; last 25¢ issue. 49-Dr. Strange; Iron Man app. 50-Iron Man; Dr. Strange app. 1 2 3 5 6 8
44-48-(30¢-c variants, limited distribution)(4-8/76) 3 6 9 20 30 40
46-Spider-Man/Deathlok team-up 1 2 3 5 7 9
51,52,56,57: 51-Iron Man; Dr. Strange app. 52-Capt. America. 56-Daredevil. 57-Black Widow 1 2 3 4 5 7
53-Hulk; Woodgod & X-Men app., 1st Byrne-a on X-Men (1/77) 3 6 9 17 26 34
54,55,58-60: 54,59,60: 54-Hulk; Woodgod app. 59-Yellowjacket/The Wasp. 60-The Wasp (Byrne-a in all). 55-Warlock-c/story; Byrne-a. 58-Ghost Rider 1 2 3 5 7 9
58-62-(35¢-c variants, limited distribution)(6-10/77) 5 10 15 30 48 65
61-70: All Byrne-a; 61-H-T. 62-Ms. Marvel; last 30¢ issue. 63-Iron Fist. 64-Daughters of the Dragon. 65-Capt. Britain (1st U.S. app.). 66-Capt. Britain; 1st app. Arcade. 67-Tigra; Kraven the Hunter app. 68-Man-Thing. 69-Havok (from X-Men). 70-Thor 1 2 3 5 6 8
71-74,76-78,80: 71-Falcon. 72-Iron Man. 73-Daredevil. 74-Not Ready for Prime Time Players (Belushi). 76-Dr. Strange. 77-Ms. Marvel. 78-Wonder Man. 80-Dr. Strange/Clea; last 35¢ issue 5.00
75,79,81: Byrne-a(p). 75-Power Man; Cage app. 79-Mary Jane Watson as Red Sonja; Clark Kent cameo (1 panel, 3/79). 81-Death of Satana 1 2 3 4 5 7
82-99: 82-Black Widow. 83-Nick Fury. 84-Shang-Chi. 86-Guardians of the Galaxy. 89-Nightcrawler (from X-Men). 91-Ghost Rider. 92-Hawkeye. 93-Werewolf by Night. 94-Spider-Man vs. The Shroud. 95-Mockingbird (intro.); Nick Fury app. 96-Howard the Duck; last 40¢ issue. 97-Spider-Woman/ Hulk. 98-Black Widow. 99-Machine Man. 85-Shang-Chi/ Black Widow/Nick Fury. 87-Black Panther. 88-Invisible Girl. 90-Beast 4.00
100-(Double-size)-Fantastic Four/Storm/Black Panther; origin/1st app. Karma, one of the New Mutants; origin Storm; X-Men x-over; Miller-c/a(p); Byrne-a (on X-Men app. only) 1 2 3 5 6 8
101-116: 101-Nighthawk(Ditko-a). 102-Doc Samson. 103-Ant-Man. 104-Hulk/Ka-Zar. 105-Hulk/Powerman/Iron Fist. 106-Capt. America. 107-She-Hulk. 108-Paladin; Dazzler cameo. 109-Dazzler; Paladin app. 110-Iron Man. 111-Devil-Slayer. 112-King Kull; last 50¢ issue. 113-Quasar. 114-Falcon. 115-Thor. 116-Valkyrie 4.00
117-Wolverine-c/story 2 4 6 8 10 12
118-140,142-149: 118-Professor X; Wolverine app. (4 pgs.); X-Men cameo. 119-Gargoyle. 120-Dominic Fortune. 121-Human Torch. 122-Man-Thing. 123-Daredevil. 124-The Beast. 125-Tigra. 126-Hulk & Powerman/Son of Satan. 127-The Watcher. 128-Capt. America; Spider-Man/Capt. America photo-c. 129-The Vision. 130-Scarlet Witch. 131-Frogman. 132-Mr. Fantastic. 133-Fantastic Four. 134-Jack of Hearts. 135-Kitty Pryde; X-Men cameo. 136-Wonder Man. 137-Aunt May/Franklin Richards. 138-Sandman. 139-Nick Fury. 140-Black Widow. 142-Capt. Marvel. 143-Starfox. 144-Moon Knight. 145-Iron Man. 146-Nomad. 147-Human Torch; Spider-Man back to old costume. 148-Thor. 149-Cannonball 3.00
141-Daredevil; SpM/Black Widow app. (Spidey in new black costume; ties w/ Amazing Spider-Man #252 for 1st black costume) 2 4 6 8 10 12
150-X-Men ($1.00, double-size); B. Smith-c 5.00
Annual 1 (1976)-Spider-Man/X-Men (early app.) 3 6 9 19 29 38
Annual 2 (1979)-Spider-Man/Hulk 1 3 4 6 8 10
Annuals 3,4: 3 (1980)-Hulk/Power Man/Machine Man/Iron Fist; Miller-c(p). 4 (1981)-Spider-Man /Daredevil/Moon Knight/Power Man/Iron Fist; brief origins of each; Miller-c; Miller scripts on Daredevil 1 2 3 4 5 7
Annuals 5-7: 5 (1982)-SpM/The Thing/Scarlet Witch/Dr. Strange/Quasar. 6 (1983)-Spider-Man/ New Mutants (early app.), Cloak & Dagger. 7(1984)-Alpha Flight; Byrne-c(i) 6.00

NOTE: ***Art Adams*** *c-141p.* ***Austin*** *a-79i; c-76i, 79i, 96i, 101i, 112i, 130i.* ***Bolle*** *a-9i.* ***Byrne*** *a(p)-53-55, 59-70, 75, 79, 100; c-68p, 70p, 72p, 75, 76p, 79p, 129i, 133i.* ***Colan*** *a-87p.* ***Ditko*** *a-101.* ***Kane*** *a(p)-4-6, 13, 14, 16-19, 23; c(p)-4, 13, 14, 17-19, 23, 25, 26, 32-35, 37, 41, 44, 45, 47, 53, 54.* ***Miller*** *a-100p; c-95p, 99p, 100p, 102p, 106.* ***Mooney*** *a-2i, 7i, 8, 10p, 11p, 16i, 24-31p, 72, 93i, Annual 5i.* ***Nasser*** *a-89p; c-101p.* ***Simonson*** *c-99i, 148.* ***Paul Smith*** *c-131, 132.* ***Starlin*** *c-27.* ***Sutton*** *a-93p. "H-T" means Human Torch; "SpM" means Spider-Man; "S-M" means Sub-Mariner.*

MARVEL TEAM-UP (2nd Series)
Marvel Comics: Sept, 1997 - No. 11, July, 1998 ($1.99)

1-11: 1-Spider-Man team-ups begin, Generation x-app. 2-Hercules-c/app.; two covers. 3-Sandman. 4-Man-Thing. 7-Blade. 8-Namor team-ups begin, Dr. Strange app. 9-Capt. America. 10-Thing. 11-Iron Man 2.50

MARVEL TEAM-UP
Marvel Comics: Jan, 2005 - No. 25, Dec, 2006 ($2.25/$2.99)

1-7,9: 1,2-Spider-Man & Wolverine; Kirkman-s/Kolins-a. 5,6-X-23 app. 2.50
8,10-25 ($2.99-c) 10-Spider-Man & Daredevil. 12-Origin of Titannus. 14-Invincible app. 3.00
... Vol. 1: The Golden Child TPB (2005, $12.99) r/#1-6 13.00
... Vol. 2: Master of the Ring TPB (2005, $17.99) r/#7-13 18.00
... Vol. 3: League of Losers TPB (2006, $13.99) r/#14-18 14.00
... Vol. 4: Freedom Ring TPB (2007, $17.99) r/#19-25 18.00

MARVEL: THE LOST GENERATION
Marvel Comics: No. 12, Mar, 2000 - No. 1, Feb, 2001 ($2.99, issue #s go in reverse)

1-12-Stern-s/Byrne-s/a; untold story of The First Line. 5-Thor app. 3.00

MARVEL/ TOP COW CROSSOVERS
Image Comics (Top Cow): Nov, 2005 ($24.99, TPB)

Vol. 1-Reprints crossovers with Wolverine, Witchblade, Hulk, Darkness; Devil's Reign 25.00

MARVEL TREASURY EDITION
Marvel Comics Group/Whitman #17,18: 1974; #2, Dec, 1974 - #28, 1981 ($1.50/$2.50, 100 pgs., oversized, new-a &-r)(Also see Amazing Spider-Man, The, Marvel Spec. Ed. Feat.--, Savage Fists of Kung Fu, Superman Vs. , & 2001, A Space Odyssey)

1-Spectacular Spider-Man; story-r/Marvel Super-Heroes #14; Romita-c/a(r); G. Kane, Ditko-r; Green Goblin/Hulk-r 5 10 15 34 55 75
1-1,000 numbered copies signed by Stan Lee & John Romita on front-c & sold thru mail for $5.00; these were the1st 1,000 copies off the press 10 20 30 71 126 180
2-10: 2-Fantastic Four-r/F.F. 6,11,48-50(Silver Surfer). 3-The Mighty Thor-r/Thor #125-130. 4-Conan the Barbarian; Barry Smith-c/a(r)/Conan #11. 5-The Hulk (origin-r/Hulk #3). 6-Dr. Strange. 7-Mighty Avengers. 8-Giant Superhero Holiday Grab-Bag; Spider-Man, Hulk, Nick Fury. 9-Giant; Super-hero Team-up. 10-Thor; r/Thor #154-157 3 6 9 16 23 30
11-20: 11-Fantastic Four. 12-Howard the Duck (r/#H. the Duck #1 & G.S. Man-Thing #4,5) plus new Defenders story. 13-Giant Super-Hero Holiday Grab-Bag. 14-The Sensational Spider-Man; r/1st Morbius from Amazing S-M #101,102 plus #100 & r/Not Brand Echh #6. 15-Conan; B. Smith, Neal Adams-i; r/Conan #24. 16-The Defenders (origin) & Valkyrie; r/Defenders #1,4,13,14. 17-The Hulk. 18-The Astonishing Spider-Man; r/Spider-Man's 1st team-ups with Iron Fist, The X-Men, Ghost Rider & Werewolf by Night; inside back-c has photos from 1978 Spider-Man TV show. 19-Conan the Barbarian. 20-Hulk 2 4 6 11 16 20
21-24,27: 21-Fantastic Four. 22-Spider-Man. 23-Conan. 24-Rampaging Hulk. 27-Spider-Man 2 4 6 11 16 20
25-Spider-Man vs. The Hulk new story 3 6 9 14 20 26
26-Thc Hulk; 6 pg. new Wolverine/Hercules-s 3 6 9 14 19 24
28-Spider-Man/Superman; (origin of each) 4 8 12 28 44 60

NOTE: *Reprints-2, 3, 5, 7-9, 13, 14, 16, 17.* ***Neal Adams*** *a(i)-6, 15.* ***Brunner*** *a-6, 12; c-6.* ***Buscema*** *a-15, 19, 28; c-28.* ***Colan*** *a-6r; c-12p.* ***Ditko*** *a-1, 6.* ***Gil Kane*** *c-16p.* ***Kirby*** *a-1-3, 5, 7, 9-11; c-7.* ***Perez*** *a-26.* ***Romita*** *c-1, 5.* ***B. Smith*** *a-4, 15, 19; c-4, 19.*

MARVEL TREASURY OF OZ FEATURING THE MARVELOUS LAND OF OZ
Marvel Comics Group: 1975 ($1.50, oversized) (See MGM's Marvelous...)

1-Roy Thomas-s/Alfredo Alcala-a; Romita-c & bk-c 3 6 9 16 22 28

MARVEL TREASURY SPECIAL (Also see 2001: A Space Odyssey)
Marvel Comics Group: 1974; 1976 ($1.50, oversized, 84 pgs.)

Vol. 1-Spider-Man, Torch, Sub-Mariner, Avengers "Giant Superhero Holiday Grab-Bag"; Wood, Colan/Everett, plus 2 Kirby-r; reprints Hulk vs. Thing from Fantastic Four #25,26 3 6 9 16 22 28
Vol. 1-... Featuring Captain America's Bicentennial Battles (6/76)-Kirby-a; B. Smith inks, 11 pgs. 3 6 9 16 23 30

MARVEL TRIPLE ACTION (See Giant-Size...)
Marvel Comics Group: Feb, 1972 - No. 24, Mar, 1975; No. 25, Aug, 1975 - No. 47, Apr, 1979

1-(25¢ giant, 52 pgs.)-Dr. Doom, Silver Surfer, The Thing begin, end #4 ('66 reprints from Fantastic Four) 3 6 9 20 30 40
2-5 2 4 6 10 14 18
6-10 1 2 3 5 6 8
11-47: 45-r/X-Men #45. 46-r/Avengers #53(X-Men) 5.00
29,30-(30¢-c variants, limited distribution)(5,7/76) 3 6 9 14 20 25
36,37-(35¢-c variants, limited distribution)(7,9/77) 3 6 9 20 30 40

NOTE: *#5-44, 46, 47 reprint Avengers #11 thru ?. #40-r/Avengers #48(1st Black Knight).* ***Buscema*** *a(r)-35p, 36p, 38p, 39p, 41, 42, 43p, 44p, 46p, 47p.* ***Ditko*** *a-2r; c-47.* ***Kirby*** *a(r)-1-4p; c-1-4, 9-19, 22, 24, 29.* ***Starlin*** *c-7.* ***Tuska*** *a(r)-40p, 43i, 46i, 47i. #2 through #17 are 20¢-c.*

MARVEL TWO-IN-ONE (...Featuring ... #82 on; also see The Thing)
Marvel Comics Group: January, 1974 - No. 100, June, 1983

1-Thing team-ups begin; Man-Thing 6 12 18 43 69 95
2,3: 2-Sub-Mariner; last 20¢ issue. 3-Daredevil 3 6 9 18 27 35

Marvel Two-In-One #39 © MAR

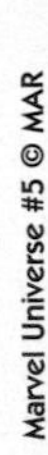
Marvel Universe #5 © MAR

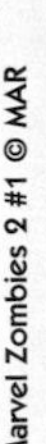
Marvel Zombies 2 #1 © MAR

GD VG FN VF VF/NM NM-
2.0 4.0 6.0 8.0 9.0 9.2

4-6: 4-Capt. America. 5-Guardians of the Galaxy (9/74, 2nd app.?). 6-Dr. Strange (11/74) 3 6 9 14 20 25
7,9,10 2 4 6 9 13 16
8-Early Ghost Rider app. (3/75) 3 6 9 14 20 25
11-14,19,20: 13-Power Man. 14-Son of Satan (early app.) 1 3 4 6 8 10
15-18-(Regular 25¢ editions)(5-7/76) 17-Spider-Man. 1 3 4 6 8 10
15-18-(30¢-c variants, limited distribution) 3 6 9 18 27 35
21-29: 27-Deathlok. 29-Master of Kung Fu; Spider-Woman cameo 1 2 3 4 5 7
28,29,31-(35¢-c variants, limited distribution) 4 8 12 24 37 50
30-2nd full app. Spider-Woman (see Marvel Spotlight #32 for 1st app.) 2 4 6 8 10 12
30-(35¢-c variant, limited distribution)(8/77) 5 10 15 32 51 70
31-33-Spider-Woman app. 1 3 4 6 8 10
34-40: 39-Vision 1 2 3 4 5 7
41,42,44,45,47-49: 42-Capt. America. 45-Capt. Marvel 5.00
43,50,53,55-Byrne-a(p). 53-Quasar(7/79, 2nd app.) 1 2 3 4 5 7
46-Thing battles Hulk-c/story 2 4 6 8 10 12
51-The Beast, Nick Fury, Ms. Marvel; Miller-p 1 2 3 5 7 9
52-Moon Knight app. 4.00
54-Death of Deathlok; Byrne-a 2 4 6 8 10 12
56-60,64-74,76-79,81,82: 60-Intro. Impossible Woman. 68-Angel. 69-Guardians of the Galaxy. 71-1st app. Maelstrom. 76-Iceman 4.00
61-63: 61-Starhawk (from Guardians); "The Coming of Her" storyline begins, ends #63; cover similar to F.F. #67 (Him-c). 62-Moondragon; Thanos & Warlock cameo in flashback; Starhawk app. 63-Warlock revived shortly; Starhawk & Moondragon app. 5.00
75-Avengers (52 pgs.) 5.00
80,90,100: 80 Ghost Rider. 90-Spider-Man. 100-Double size, Byrne-s 5.00
83-89,91-99: 83-Sasquatch. 84 Alpha Flight app. 93-Jocasta dies. 98-X-Men-c & cameo 4.00
Annual 1(1976, 52 pgs.)-Thing/Liberty Legion; Kirby-c 2 4 6 8 11 14
Annual 2(1977, 52 pgs.)-Thing/Spider-Man; 2nd death of Thanos; end of Thanos saga; Warlock app.; Starlin-c/a 4 8 12 28 44 60
Annual 3,4 (1978-79, 52 pgs.): 3-Nova. 4-Black Bolt 1 2 3 4 5 7
Annual 5-7 (1980-82, 52 pgs.): 5-Hulk. 6-1st app. American Eagle. 7-The Thing/Champion; Sasquatch, Colossus app.; X-Men cameo (1 pg.) 5.00

NOTE: ***Austin*** *c(i)-42, 54, 56, 58, 61, 63, 66.* ***John Buscema*** *a-30p, 45; c-30p.* ***Byrne*** *(p)-43, 50, 53-55; c-43, 53p, 56p, 98i, 99i.* ***Gil Kane*** *a 1p, 2p; c(p)-1-3, 9, 11, 14, 28.* ***Kirby*** *c-10, 12, 19p, 20, 25, 27.* ***Mooney*** *a-18i, 38i, 90i.* ***Nasser*** *a-70p.* ***Perez*** *a(p)-56-58, 60, 64, 65; c(p)-32, 33, 42, 50-52, 54, 55, 57, 58, 61-66, 70.* ***Roussos*** *a-Annual 1i.* ***Simonson*** *c-43i, 97p, Annual 6i.* ***Starlin*** *c-6, Annual 1.* ***Tuska*** *a-6p.*

MARVEL TWO-IN-ONE
Marvel Comics: Sept, 2007 - Present ($4.99, 64 pgs.)

1-8,13-15-Reprints Marvel Adventures Avengers and X-Men: First Class stories 5.00
9-12-Reprints Marvel Adventures Iron Man and Avengers stories 5.00

MARVEL UNIVERSE (See Official Handbook Of The...)

MARVEL UNIVERSE (Title on variant covers for newsstand editions of some 2001 Marvel titles. See indicia for actual titles and issue numbers)

MARVEL UNIVERSE
Marvel Comics: June, 1998 - No. 7, Dec, 1998 ($2.99/$1.99)

1-($2.99)-Invaders stories from WW2; Stern-s 3.00
2-7-($1.99): 2-Two covers. 4-7-Monster Hunters; Manley-a/Stern-s 2.50

MARVEL UNIVERSE: MILLENNIAL VISIONS
Marvel Comics: Feb, 2002 ($3.99, one-shot)

1-Pin-ups by various; wraparound-c by JH Williams & Gray 4.00

MARVEL UNIVERSE: THE END (Also see Infinity Abyss)
Marvel Comics: May, 2003 - No. 6, Aug, 2003 ($3.50/$2.99, limited series)

1-($3.50)-Thanos, X-Men, FF, Avengers, Spider-Man, Daredevil app.; Starlin-s/a(p) 3.50
2-6-($2.99) Akhenaten, Eternity, Living Tribunal app. 3.00
Thanos Vol. 3: Marvel Universe - The End (2003, $16.99) r/#1-6 17.00

MARVEL UNLIMITED (Title on variant covers for newsstand editions of some 2001 Daredevil issues. See indicia for actual titles and issue numbers)

MARVEL VALENTINE SPECIAL
Marvel Comics: Mar, 1997 ($2.99, one-shot)

1-Valentine stories w/Spider-Man, Daredevil, Cyclops, Phoenix 3.00

MARVEL VERSUS DC (See DC Versus Marvel) (Also see Amazon, Assassins, Bruce Wayne: Agent of S.H.I.E.L.D., Bullets & Bracelets, Doctor Strangefate, JLX, Legend of the Dark Claw, Magneto & The Magnetic Men, Speed Demon, Spider-Boy, Super Soldier, & X-Patrol)
Marvel Comics: No. 2, 1996 - No. 3, 1996 ($3.95, limited series)

2,3: 2-Peter David script. 3-Ron Marz script; Dan Jurgens-a(p). 1st app. of Super Soldier, Spider-Boy, Dr. Doomsday, Doctor Strangefate, The Dark Claw, Nightcreeper, Amazon, Wraith & others. Storyline continues in Amalgam books. 4.00

MARVEL VISIONARIES
Marvel Comics: 2002 - Present (various prices, HC and TPB)

...: Chris Claremont (2005, $29.99) r/X-Men #137, Uncanny X-Men #153,205,268 & Ann. #12, Iron Fist #14, Wolverine #3, New Mutants #21 and other highlights 30.00
...: Gil Kane (8/02, $24.95) r/Amazing Spider-Man #99, Marvel Premiere #1,#15, TOA #76 & others; plus sketch pages and a cover gallery 25.00
...: Jack Kirby HC (2004, $29.99) r/career highlights- Red Raven Comics #1 (1st work), Captain America Comics #1, Avengers #4, Fantastic Four #48-50 and more 30.00
...: Jack Kirby Vol. 2 HC (2006, $34.99) r/career highlights- Captain America, Two-Gun Kid, Fantastic Four, Thor, Fin Fang Foom, Devil Dinosaur, romance and more 35.00
...: Jim Steranko (9/02, $14.95) r/Captain America #110,111,113; X-Men #50,51 and stories from Tower of Shadows #1 and Our Love Story #5; plus a cover gallery 15.00
...: John Buscema (2007, $34.99) r/career highlights-Avengers, Silver Surfer, Thor, FF, Hulk, Wolverine and others; Roy Thomas intro.; sketch pages and pin-up art 35.00
...: John Romita Jr. (2005, $29.99) r/various stories 1977-2002; debut in AS-M Ann. #11; Iron Man #128, AS-M V2 #36, issues of Hulk, Daredevil: The Man Without Fear, Punisher; sketch pages; intro. by John Romita Sr. 30.00
...: John Romita Sr. (2005, $29.99) r/various stories 1951-1997 including Young Men #24&26, Daredevil #16, ASM #39,42,50; sketch pages; intro. by John Romita Jr. 30.00
...: Roy Thomas (2006, $34.99) r/career highlights; Intro. by Stan Lee 35.00
...: Steve Ditko (2005, $29.99) r/various stories 1961-1992; intro. by Blake Bell 30.00
...: Stan Lee HC (2005, $29.99) r/career highlights- Captain America Comics #3 (1st work), and various Spider-Man, FF, Thor, Daredevil stories; 1940-1995; Roy Thomas intro. 30.00

MARVEL WEDDINGS
Marvel Comics: 2005 ($19.99, TPB)

TPB-Reprints weddings of Peter & Mary Jane, Reed & Sue, Scott & Jean, and others 20.00

MARVEL WESTERNS: ...
Marvel Comics: 2006 ($3.99, one shots)

... Kid Colt and the Arizona Girl 1 (9/06) 2 short stories & 3 Kirby/Ayers reps.; Powell-c 4.00
... Outlaw Files-Profiles and essays about Marvel western characters 4.00
... Strange Westerns Starring The Black Rider 1 (10/06) Englehart-s/Rogers-a & 2 Kirby Rawhide Kid reprints; Rogers-c 4.00
... The Two-Gun Kid 1 (8/06) 2 short stories & a Kirby/Ayers reprint; Powell-c 4.00
... Western Legends 1 (9/06) 2 short stories & r/Hawkhide Kid origin by Kirby; Powell-c 4.00
HC (2006, $20.99, dustjacket) r/one-shots 21.00

MARVEL X-MEN COLLECTION, THE
Marvel Comics: Jan, 1994 - No. 3, Mar, 1994 ($2.95, limited series)

1-3-r/X-Men trading cards by Jim Lee 3.00

MARVEL - YEAR IN REVIEW (Magazine)
Marvel Comics: 1989 - No. 3, 1991 (52 pgs.)

1-3: 1-Spider-Man-c by McFarlane. 2-Capt. America-c. 3-X-Men/Wolverine-c 5.00

MARVEL: YOUR UNIVERSE SAGA
Marvel Comics: 2008 (no cover price)

nn-Re-caps of crossovers from Secret War through Secret Invasion; wraparound-c 2.25

MARVEL ZOMBIES (See Ultimate Fantastic Four #21-23, 30-32)
Marvel Comics: Feb, 2006 - No. 5, June, 2006 ($2.99, limited series)

1-Zombies vs. Magneto; Kirkman-s/Phillips-a/Suydam-c swipe of A.F. #15 15.00
1-(2nd-4th printings) Variant Suydam-c swipes of Spider-Man #1, Amazing Spider-Man #50 and Incredible Hulk #1 5.00
2-Avengers #4 cover swipe by Suydam 8.00
3-5: 3-Inc. Hulk #340 c-swipe. 4-X-Men #1 c-swipe. 5-AS-M Ann. #21 c-swipe 5.00
3-5-(2nd printings) 3-Daredevil #179 c-swipe. 4-AS-M #39 c-swipe. 5-Silver Surfer #1 3.00
...: Dead Days (7/07, $3.99) Early days of the plaque; Kirkman-s/Phillips-a/Suydam-c 4.00
...: Dead Days HC (2008, $29.99, oversized) r/Dead Days one-shot, Ultimate Fantastic Four #21-23, 30-32, and Black Panther #28-30 30.00
...: The Book of Angels, Demons and Various Monstrosities (2007, $3.99) profile pages 4.00
...: The Covers HC (2007, $19.99, d.j.) Suydam's covers with originals and commentary 20.00
HC (2006, $19.99) r/#1-5; Kirkman foreword; cover gallery with variants 20.00

MARVEL ZOMBIES 2
Marvel Comics: Dec, 2007 - No. 5, Apr, 2008 ($2.99, limited series)

1-5-Kirkman-s/Phillips-a/Suydam zombie-fied cover swipes 3.00
HC (2008, $19.99) r/#1-5; cover swipe gallery 20.00

MARVEL ZOMBIES / ARMY OF DARKNESS
Marvel Comics/Dynamite Entertainment: May, 2007 - No. 5, Aug, 2007($2.99, limited series)

1-Zombies vs. Ash during the start of the plaque; Layman-s/Neves-a/Suydam-c 5.00
1-Second printing with Suydam zombie-fied Captain America Comics #1 cover swipe 3.00
2-5-Suydam zombie-fied cover swipes on all 3.00

Mary Marvel Comics #4 © FAW

The Mask World Tour #2 © DH

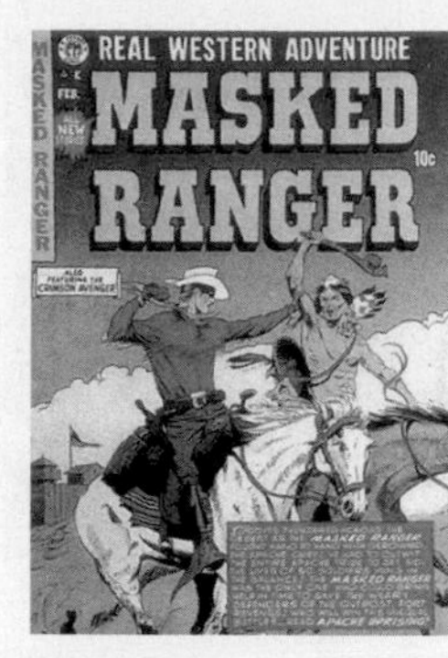

Masked Ranger #6 © CC

GD VG FN VF VF/NM NM-
2.0 4.0 6.0 8.0 9.0 9.2

HC (2007, $19.99) r/#1-5; cover gallery with variants and non-zombied original covers 20.00

MARVILLE
Marvel Comics: Nov, 2002 - No. 7, Jul, 2003 ($2.25, limited series)
1-6-Satire on DC/AOL-Time-Warner; Jemas-a/Bright-a/Horn-c 2.50
1-($3.95) Variant foil cover by Udon Studios; bonus sketch pages and Jemas afterword 4.00
7-($2.99) Intro. to Epic Comics line with submission guidelines 3.00

MARVIN MOUSE
Atlas Comics (BPC): September, 1957
1-Everett-c/a; Maneely-a 14 28 42 80 115 150

MARY JANE (Spider-Man) (Also see Spider-Man Loves Mary Jane)
Marvel Comics: Aug, 2004 - No. 4, Nov, 2004 ($2.25, limited series)
1-4-Marvel Age series with teen-age MJ Watson; Miyazawa-c/a; McKeever-s 2.50
... Vol. 1: Circle of Friends (2004, $5.99, digest-size) r/#1-4 6.00

MARY JANE & SNIFFLES (See Looney Tunes)
Dell Publishing Co.: No. 402, June, 1952 - No. 474, June, 1953
Four Color 402 (#1) 7 14 21 50 83 115
Four Color 474 7 14 21 47 76 105

MARY JANE: HOMECOMING (Spider-Man)
Marvel Comics: May, 2005 - No. 4, Aug, 2005 ($2.99, limited series)
1-4-Teen-age MJ Watson in high school; Miyazawa-c/a; McKeever-s 3.00
... Vol. 2 (2005, $6.99, digest-size) r/#1-4 7.00

MARY MARVEL COMICS (Monte Hale #29 on) (Also see Captain Marvel #18, Marvel Family, Shazam, & Wow Comics)
Fawcett Publications: Dec, 1945 - No. 28, Sept, 1948
1-Captain Marvel introduces Mary on-c; intro/origin Georgia Sivana
223 446 669 1405 2378 3350
2 80 160 240 504 852 1200
3,4: 3-New logo 53 106 159 330 553 775
5-8: 8-Bulletgirl x-over in Mary Marvel; X-Mas-c 40 80 120 240 390 540
9,10 37 74 111 215 345 475
11-20 25 50 75 147 236 325
21-28: 28-Western-c 21 42 63 123 197 270

MARY POPPINS (See Movie Comics & Walt Disney Showcase No. 17)

MARY SHELLEY'S FRANKENSTEIN
Topps Comics: Oct, 1994 - Jan, 1995 ($2.95, limited series)
1-4-polybagged w/3 trading cards 3.00
1-4 ($2.50)-Newstand ed. 2.50

MARY WORTH (See Harvey Comics Hits #55 & Love Stories of...)
Argo: March, 1956 (Also see Romantic Picture Novelettes)
1 8 16 24 42 54 65

MASK (TV)
DC Comics: Dec, 1985 - No. 4, Mar, 1986; Feb, 1987 - No. 9, Oct, 1987
1-4; 1-9 (2nd series)-Sat. morning TV show. 2.50

MASK, THE (Also see Mayhem)
Dark Horse Comics: Aug, 1991 - No. 4, Oct, 1991; No. 0, Dec, 1991 ($2.50, 36 pgs., limited series)
1-4: 1-1st app. Lt. Kellaway as The Mask (see Dark Horse Presents #10 for 1st app.) 5.00
0-(12/91, B&W, 56 pgs.)-r/Mayhem #1-4 4.00
...Omnibus Vol. 1 (8/08, $24.95) r/#1-4, Mask Returns and Mask Strikes Back series 25.00
...: **HUNT FOR GREEN OCTOBER** July, 1995 - Oct, 1995 ($2.50, lim. series)
1-4-Evan Dorkin scripts 2.50
../ **MARSHALL LAW** Feb, 1998 - No. 2, Mar, 1998 ($2.95, lim. series)
1,2-Mills-s/O'Neill-a 3.00
...: **OFFICIAL MOVIE ADAPTATION** July, 1994 - Aug, 1994 ($2.50, lim. series)
1,2 2.50
... **RETURNS** Oct, 1992 - No. 4, Mar, 1993 ($2.50, limited series)
1-4 4.00
... **SOUTHERN DISCOMFORT** Mar, 1996 - No. 4, July, 1996 ($2.50, lim. series)
1-4 2.50
... **STRIKES BACK** Feb, 1995 - No. 5, Jun, 1995 ($2.50, limited series)
1-5 2.50
... **SUMMER VACATION** July, 1995 ($10.95, one shot, hard-c)
1-nn-Rick Geary-c/a 11.00
... **TOYS IN THE ATTIC** Aug, 1998 - No. 4, Nov, 1998 ($2.95, limited series)
1-4-Fingerman-s 3.00

GD VG FN VF VF/NM NM-
2.0 4.0 6.0 8.0 9.0 9.2

... **VIRTUAL SURREALITY** July, 1997 ($2.95, one shot)
nn-Mignola, Aragonés, and others-s/a 3.00
... **WORLD TOUR** Dec, 1995 - No. 4, Mar, 1996 ($2.50, limited series)
1-4: 3-X & Ghost-c/app. 2.50

MASK COMICS
Rural Home Publ.: Feb-Mar, 1945 - No. 2, Apr-May, 1945; No. 2, Fall, 1945
1-Classic L. B. Cole Satan-c/a; Palais-a 300 600 900 1910 3255 4600
2-(Scarce)-Classic L. B. Cole Satan-c; Black Rider, The Boy Magician, & The Collector app.
187 374 561 1178 1989 2800
2-(Fall, 1945)-No publ.-same as regular #2; L. B. Cole-c
150 300 450 945 1598 2250

MASKED BANDIT, THE
Avon Periodicals: 1952
nn-Kinstler-a 16 32 48 94 147 200

MASKED MAN, THE
Eclipse Comics: 12/84 - #10, 4/86; #11, 10/87; #12, 4/88 ($1.75/$2.00, color/B&W #9 on, Baxter paper)
1-12: 1-Origin retold. 3-Origin Aphid-Man; begin $2.00-c 2.50

MASKED MARVEL (See Keen Detective Funnies)
Centaur Publications: Sept, 1940 - No. 3, Dec, 1940
1-The Masked Marvel begins 167 334 501 1052 1776 2500
2,3: 2-Gustavson, Tarpe Mills-a 110 220 330 693 1172 1650

MASKED RAIDER, THE (Billy The Kid #9 on; Frontier Scout, Daniel Boone #10-13) (Also see Blue Bird)
Charlton Comics: June, 1955 - No. 8, July, 1957; No. 14, Aug, 1958 - No. 30, June, 1961
1-Masked Raider & Talon the Golden Eagle begin; painted-c
13 26 39 72 101 130
2 8 16 24 42 54 65
3-8,15: 8-Billy The Kid app. 15-Williamson-a, 7 pgs. 6 12 18 31 38 45
14,16-30: 22-Rocky Lane app. 5 10 15 24 30 35

MASKED RANGER
Premier Magazines: Apr, 1954 - No. 9, Aug, 1955
1-The Masked Ranger, his horse Streak, & The Crimson Avenger (origin) begin, end #9; Woodbridge/Frazetta-a 40 80 120 239 380 520
2,3 15 30 45 85 130 175
4-8-All Woodbridge-a. 5-Jesse James by Woodbridge. 6-Billy The Kid by Woodbridge. 7-Wild Bill Hickok by Woodbridge. 8-Jim Bowie's Life Story
15 30 45 86 133 180
9-Torres-a; Wyatt Earp by Woodbridge; Says Death of Masked Ranger on-c
16 32 48 92 144 195
NOTE: *Check a-1. Woodbridge c/a-1, 4-9.*

MASK OF DR. FU MANCHU, THE (See Dr. Fu Manchu)
Avon Periodicals: 1951
1-Sax Rohmer adapt.; Wood-c/a (26 pgs.); Hollingsworth-a
93 186 279 586 993 1400

MASK OF ZORRO, THE
Image Comics: Aug, 1998 - No. 4, Dec, 1998 ($2.95, limited series)
1-4-Movie adapt. Photo variant-c 3.00

MASKS: TOO HOT FOR TV!
DC Comics (WildStorm): Feb, 2004 ($4.95)
1-Short stories by various incl. Thompson, Brubaker, Mahnke, Conner; Fabry-c 5.00

MASQUE OF THE RED DEATH (See Movie Classics)

MASTER COMICS (Combined with Slam Bang Comics #7 on)
Fawcett Publications: Mar, 1940 - No. 133, Apr, 1953 (No. 1-6: oversized issues) (#1-3: 15¢, 52 pgs.; #4-6: 10¢, 36 pgs.; #7-Begin 68 pg. issues)
1-Origin & 1st app. Master Man; The Devil's Dagger, El Carim, Master of Magic, Rick O'Say, Morton Murch, White Rajah, Shipwreck Roberts, Frontier Marshal, Streak Sloan, Mr. Clue begin (all features end #6) 778 1556 2334 5602 9801 14,000
2 243 486 729 1531 2591 3650
3-6: 6-Last Master Man 173 346 519 1090 1845 2600
NOTE: *#1-6 rarely found in near mint or very fine condition due to large-size format.*
7-(10/40)-Bulletman, Zoro, the Mystery Man (ends #22), Lee Granger, Jungle King, & Buck Jones begin; only app. The War Bird & Mark Swift & the Time Retarder; Zoro, Lee Granger, Jungle King & Mark Swift all continue from Slam Bang; Bulletman moves from Nickel
293 586 879 1846 3123 4400
8-The Red Gaucho (ends #13), Captain Venture (ends #22) & The Planet Princess begin
157 314 471 989 1670 2350

Master Comics #26 © FAW

Master of Kung Fu #79 © MAR

Masters of the Universe #1 © Mattel

GD VG FN VF VF/NM NM-
2.0 4.0 6.0 8.0 9.0 9.2

9,10: 10-Lee Granger ends 122 244 366 769 1297 1825
11-Origin & 1st app. Minute-Man (2/41) 263 526 789 1657 2804 3950
12 128 256 384 806 1366 1925
13-Origin & 1st app. Bulletgirl; Hitler-c 207 414 621 1304 2202 3100
14-16: 14-Companions Three begins, ends #31 110 220 330 693 1172 1650
17-20: 17-Raboy-a on Bulletman begins. 20-Captain Marvel cameo app. in Bulletman
100 200 300 630 1065 1500
21-(12/41; Scarce)-Captain Marvel & Bulletman team up against Capt. Nazi; origin & 1st app. Capt. Marvel Jr's most famous nemesis Captain Nazi who will cause creation of Capt. Marvel Jr. in Whiz #25. Part I of trilogy origin of Capt. Marvel Jr.; 1st Mac Raboy-c for Fawcett; Capt. Nazi-c 506 1012 1518 3643 6372 9100
22-(1/42)-Captain Marvel Jr. moves over from Whiz #25 & teams up with Bulletman against Captain Nazi; part III of trilogy origin of Capt. Marvel Jr. & his 1st cover and adventure
453 906 1359 3262 5706 8150
23-Capt. Marvel Jr. c/stories begin (1st solo story); fights Capt. Nazi by himself.
287 574 861 1808 3054 4300
24,25 100 200 300 630 1065 1500
26-28,30-Captain Marvel Jr. vs. Capt. Nazi. 28-Liberty Bell-c. 30-Flag-c
92 184 276 580 978 1375
29-Hitler & Hirohito-c 118 236 354 743 1259 1775
31-33,35: 32-Last El Carim & Buck Jones; intro Balbo, the Boy Magician in El Carim story; classic Eagle-c by Raboy. 33-Balbo, the Boy Magician (ends #47), Hopalong Cassidy (ends #49) begins 67 134 201 422 711 1000
34-Capt. Marvel Jr. vs. Capt. Nazi-c/story 75 150 225 473 799 1125
36-40: 40-Flag-c 60 120 180 378 639 900
41-(8/43)-Bulletman, Capt. Marvel Jr. & Bulletgirl x-over in Minute-Man; only app. Crime Crusaders Club (Capt. Marvel Jr., Minute-Man, Bulletman & Bulletgirl)
64 128 192 403 682 960
42-47,49: 47-Hitler becomes Corpl. Hitler Jr. 49-Last Minute-Man
42 84 126 252 409 565
48-Intro. Bulletboy; Capt. Marvel cameo in Minute-Man
46 92 138 285 475 665
50-Intro Radar & Nyoka the Jungle Girl & begin series (5/44); Radar also intro in Captain Marvel #35 (same date); Capt. Marvel x-over in Radar; origin Radar; Capt. Marvel & Capt. Marvel, Jr. introduce Radar on-c 41 82 123 253 419 585
51-58 24 48 72 140 225 310
59-62: Nyoka serial "Terrible Tiara" in all; 61-Capt. Marvel Jr. 1st meets Uncle Marvel
26 52 78 152 244 335
63-80 19 38 57 109 172 235
81,83-87,89-91,95-99: 88-Hopalong Cassidy begins (ends #94). 95-Tom Mix begins (cover only in #123, ends #133) 16 32 48 96 151 205
82,88,92-94-Krigstein-a 17 34 51 100 158 215
100 17 34 51 100 158 215
101-106-Last Bulletman (not in #104) 15 30 45 92 144 195
107-120: 118-Mary Marvel 15 30 45 88 137 185
121-131-(lower print run): 123-Tom Mix-c only 15 30 45 94 147 200
132-B&W and color illos in **POP**; last Nyoka 16 32 48 96 151 205
133-Bill Battle app. 22 44 66 127 204 280
NOTE: ***Mac Raboy*** *a-15-39, 40(part), 42, 58. c-21-49, 51, 52, 54, 56, 58, 68(part), 69(part). Bulletman c-7-11, 13(half), 15, 18(part), 19, 20, 21(w/Capt. Marvel & Capt. Nazi), 22(w/Capt. Marvel, Jr.). Capt. Marvel, Jr. c-23-133. Master Man c-1-6. Minute Man c-12, 13(half), 14, 16, 17, 18(part).*

MASTER DARQUE
Acclaim Comics (Valiant): Feb, 1998 ($3.95)
1-Manco-a/Christina Z.-s 4.00

MASTER DETECTIVE
Super Comics: 1964 (Reprints)
17-r/Criminals on the Loose V4 #2; r/Young King Cole #?; McWilliams-r
2 4 6 8 11 14

MASTER OF KUNG FU (Formerly Special Marvel Edition; see Deadly Hands of Kung Fu & Giant-Size...)
Marvel Comics Group: No. 17, April, 1974 - No. 125, June, 1983
17-Starlin-a; intro Black Jack Tarr; 3rd Shang-Chi (ties w/Deadly Hands #1)
3 6 9 20 30 40
18,20 2 4 6 11 16 20
19-Man-Thing-c/story 3 6 9 14 19 24
21-23,25-30 2 4 6 8 11 14
24-Starlin, Simonson-a 2 4 6 9 13 16
31-50: 33-1st Leiko Wu. 43-Last 25¢ issue 1 2 3 5 6 8
39-43-(30¢-c variants, limited distribution)(5-7/76) 3 6 9 16 22 28
51-99 4.00
53-57-(35¢-c variants, limited distribution)(6-10/77) 3 6 9 18 27 35
100,118,125-Double size 5.00
101-117,119-124 3.00
Annual 1(4/76)-Iron Fist app. 3 6 9 16 22 28
NOTE: ***Austin*** *c-63i, 74i.* ***Buscema*** *c-44p.* ***Gulacy*** *a(p)-18-20, 22, 25, 29-31, 33-35, 38, 39, 40(p&i), 42-50, 53r(#20); c-51, 55, 64, 67.* ***Gil Kane*** *c(p)-20, 38, 39, 42, 45, 59, 63.* ***Nebres*** *c-73i.* ***Starlin*** *a-17p, 24; c-54.* ***Sutton*** *a-42i. #53 reprints #20.*

MASTER OF KUNG-FU, SHANG-CHI:... (2002 series, see Shang Chi:...)

MASTER OF KUNG-FU: BLEEDING BLACK
Marvel Comics: Feb, 1991 ($2.95, 84 pgs., one-shot)
1-The Return of Shang-Chi 3.00

MASTER OF THE WORLD
Dell Publishing Co.: No. 1157, July, 1961
Four Color 1157-Movie based on Jules Verne's "Master of the World" and "Robur the Conqueror" novels; with Vincent Price & Charles Bronson 7 14 21 45 73 100

MASTERS OF TERROR (Magazine)
Marvel Comics Group: July, 1975 - No. 2, Sept, 1975 (B&W) (All reprints)
1-Brunner, Barry Smith-a; Morrow/Steranko-c; Starlin-a(p); Gil Kane-a
3 6 9 16 23 30
2-Reese, Kane, Mayerik-a; Adkins/Steranko-c 2 4 6 11 16 20

MASTERS OF THE UNIVERSE (See DC Comics Presents #47 for 1st app.)
DC Comics: Dec, 1982 - No. 3, Feb, 1983 (Mini-series)
1 6.00
2,3: 2-Origin He-Man & Ceril 4.00
NOTE: ***Alcala*** *a-1i,, 2i.* ***Tuska*** *a-1-3p; c-1-3p. #2 has 75 & 95 cent cover price.*

MASTERS OF THE UNIVERSE (Comic Album)
Western Publishing Co.: 1984 (8-1/2x11", $2.95, 64 pgs.)
11362-Based on Mattel toy & cartoon 2 4 6 10 14 18

MASTERS OF THE UNIVERSE
Star Comics/Marvel #7 on: May 1986 - No. 13, May, 1988 (75¢/$1.00)
1 1 2 3 4 5 7
2-11: 8-Begin $1.00-c 5.00
12-Death of He-Man (1st Marvel app.) 2 4 6 8 10 12
13-Return of He-Man & death of Skeletor 2 4 6 8 10 12
The Motion Picture (11/87, $2.00)-Tuska-p 6.00

MASTERS OF THE UNIVERSE
Image Comics: Nov, 2002 - No. 4, March, 2003 ($2.95, limited series)
1-($2.95) Two covers by Santalucia and Campbell; Santalucia-a 3.00
1-($5.95) Variant-c by Norem w/gold foil logo 6.00
2-4($2.95) 2-Two covers by Santalucia and Manapul. 3,4-Two covers 3.00
TPB (CrossGen, 2003, $9.95, 8-1/4" x 5-1/2") digest-sized reprints #1-4 10.00

MASTERS OF THE UNIVERSE (Volume 2)
Image Comics: March, 2003 - No. 6, Aug, 2003 ($2.95)
1-6-($2.95) 1-Santalucia-c. 2-Two covers by Santalucia & JJ Kirby 3.00
1-($5.95) Wraparound variant-c by Struzan w/silver foil logo 6.00
3,4-($5.95) Wraparound variant holofoil-c. 3-By Edwards 4-By Boris Vallejo & Julie Bell 6.00
Volume 2 Dark Reflections TPB (2004, $18.95) r/#1-6 19.00

MASTERS OF THE UNIVERSE (Volume 3)
MVCreations: Apr, 2004 - No. 8, Dec, 2004 ($2.95)
1-8: 1-Santalucia-c 3.00

MASTERS OF THE UNIVERSE...
CrossGen Comics
...Rise of the Snake-Men (Nov, 2003 - No. 3, $2.95) Meyers-a 3.00
...The Power of Fear (12/03, $2.95, one-shot) Santalucia-a 3.00

MASTERS OF THE UNIVERSE, ICONS OF EVIL
Image Comics/CrossGen Comics: 2003 ($4.95, one-shots)
...Beastman -(Image) Origin of Beast Man; Tony Moore-a 5.00
...Mer-Man -(CrossGen) 5.00
...Trapjaw -(CrossGen) 5.00
...Tri-Klops -(CrossGen) Walker-c 5.00
TPB (3/04, $18.95, MVCreations) r/one-shots; sketch pages 19.00

MASTERWORKS SERIES OF GREAT COMIC BOOK ARTISTS, THE
Sea Gate Dist./DC Comics: May, 1983 - No. 3, Dec, 1983 (Baxter paper)
1-3: 1,2-Shining Knight by Frazetta r-/Adventure. 2-Tomahawk by Frazetta-r. 3-Wrightson-c/a(r) 5.00

MATADOR
DC Comics (WildStorm): July, 2005 - No. 6, May, 2006 ($2.99, limited series)
1-6-Devin Grayson-s/Brian Stelfreeze-a/c 3.00

MATRIX COMICS, THE (Movie)

Maverick #13 © DELL

Mazie #18 © HARV

McCandless & Company #1 © J.C. Vaughn

GD VG FN VF VF/NM NM-
2.0 4.0 6.0 8.0 9.0 9.2

Burlyman Entertainment: 2003; 2004 ($21.95, trade paperback)
nn-Short stories by various incl. Wachowskis, Darrow, Gaiman, Sienkiewicz, Bagge 22.00
...Volume One Preview (7/03, no cover price) bios of creators; Chadwick-s/a 2.50
Volume 2-(2004) Short stories by various incl. Wachowskis, Sale, McKeever, Dorman 22.00

MATT SLADE GUNFIGHTER (Kid Slade Gunfighter #5 on; See Western Gunfighters)
Atlas Comics (SPI): May, 1956 - No. 4, Nov, 1956
1-Intro Matt & horse Eagle; Williamson/Torres-a 18 36 54 107 169 230
2-Williamson-a 13 26 39 74 105 135
3,4 10 20 30 56 76 95
NOTE: ***Maneely** a-1, 3, 4; c-1, 2, 4. **Roth** a-2-4. **Severin** a-1, 3, 4. **Maneely** c/a-1. Issue #s stamped on cover after printing.*

MAUS: A SURVIVOR'S TALE (First graphic novel to win a Pulitzer Prize)
Pantheon Books: 1986, 1991 (B&W)
Vol. 1-(...: My Father Bleeds History)(1986) Art Spiegelman-s/a; recounts stories of Spiegelman's father in 1930s-40s Nazi-occupied Poland; collects first six stories serialized in Raw Magazine from 1980-1985 20.00
Vol. 2-(...: And Here My Troubles Began)(1991) 20.00
Complete Maus Survivor's Tale -HC Vols. 1& 2 w/slipcase 35.00
Hardcover Vol. 1 (1991) 24.00
Hardcover Vol. 2 (1991) 24.00
TPB (1992, $14.00) Vols. 1& 2 14.00

MAVERICK (TV)
Dell Publishing Co.: No. 892, 4/58 - No. 19, 4-6/62 (All have photo-c)
Four Color 892 (#1)-James Garner photo-c begin 22 44 66 157 291 425
Four Color 930,945,962,980,1005 (6-8/59): 945-James Garner/Jack Kelly photo-c begin 11 22 33 75 133 190
7 (10-12/59) - 14: Last Garner/Kelly-c 9 18 27 63 109 150
15-18: Jack Kelly/Roger Moore photo-c 8 16 24 52 86 120
19-Jack Kelly photo-c (last issue) 8 16 24 54 90 125

MAVERICK (See X-Men)
Marvel Comics: Jan, 1997 ($2.95, one-shot)
1-Hama-s 3.00

MAVERICK (See X-Men)
Marvel Comics: Sept, 1997 - No. 12, Aug, 1998 ($2.99/$1.99)
1,12: 1-($2.99)-Wraparound-c. 12-($2.99) Battles Omega Red 4.00
2-11: 2-Two covers. 4-Wolverine app. 6,7-Sabretooth app. 3.00

MAVERICK MARSHAL
Charlton Comics: Nov, 1958 - No. 7, May, 1960
1 6 12 18 33 41 48
2-7 5 10 15 23 28 32

MAVERICKS
Daggar Comics Group: Jan, 1994 - No. 5, 1994 (#1-$2.75, #2-5-$2.50)
1-5: 1-Bronze. 1-Gold. 1-Silver 2.75

MAX BRAND (See Silvertip)

MAX HAMM FAIRY TALE DETECTIVE
Nite Owl Comix: 2002 - 2004 ($4.95, B&W, 6 1/2" x 8")
1-(2002) Frank Cammuso-s/a 5.00
Vol. 2 #1-3 (2003-2004) Frank Cammuso-s/a 5.00

MAXIMAGE
Image Comics (Extreme Studios): Dec, 1995 - No. 7, June 1996 ($2.50)
1-7: 1-Liefeld-c. 2-Extreme Destroyer Pt. 2; polybagged w/card. 4-Angela & Glory-c/app. 2.50

MAXIMO
Dreamwave Prods.: Jan, 2004 ($3.95, one-shot)
1-Based on the Capcom video game 4.00

MAXIMUM SECURITY (Crossover)
Marvel Comics: Oct, 2000 - No. 3, Jan, 2001 ($2.99)
1-3-Busiek-s/Ordway-a; Ronan the Accuser, Avengers app. 3.00
...Dangerous Planet 1: Busiek-s/Ordway-a; Ego, the Living Planet 3.00
Thor vs. Ego (11/00, $2.99) Reprints Thor #133,160,161; Kirby-a 3.00

MAXX (Also see Darker Image, Primer #5, & Friends of Maxx)
Image Comics (I Before E): Mar, 1993 - No. 35, Feb, 1998 ($1.95)
1/2 1 3 4 6 8 10
1/2 (Gold) 20.00
1-Sam Kieth-c/a/scripts 4.00
1-Glow-in-the-dark variant 2 4 6 8 10 12
1-"3-D Edition" (1/98, $4.95) plus new back-up story 5.00

GD VG FN VF VF/NM NM-
2.0 4.0 6.0 8.0 9.0 9.2

2-12: 6-Savage Dragon cameo(1 pg.). 7,8-Pitt-c & story 2.50
13-16 2.50
17-35: 21-Alan Moore-s 2.50
Volume 1 TPB (DC/WildStorm, 2003, $17.95) r/#1-6 18.00
Volume 2 TPB (DC/WildStorm, 2004, $17.95) r/#7-13 18.00
Volume 3 TPB (DC/WildStorm, 2004, $17.95) r/#14-20 18.00
Volume 4 TPB (DC/WildStorm, 2005, $17.95) r/#21-27 18.00
Volume 5 TPB (DC/WildStorm, 2005, $19.99) r/#28-35 20.00
Volume 6 TPB (DC/WildStorm, 2006, $19.99) r/Friends of Maxx #1-3 & The Maxx 3-D 20.00

MAYA (See Movie Classics)
Gold Key: Mar, 1968
1 (10218-803)(TV) 3 6 9 17 25 32

MAYHEM
Dark Horse Comics: May, 1989 - No. 4, Sept, 1989 ($2.50, B&W, 52 pgs.)
1- Four part Stanley Ipkiss/Mask story begins; Mask-c 1 3 4 6 8 10
2-4: 2-Mask 1/2 back-c. 4-Mask-c 1 2 3 5 7 9

MAZE AGENCY, THE
Comico/Innovation Publ. #8 on: Dec, 1988 - No. 20, 1991 ($1.95-$2.50, color)
1-20: 9-Ellery Queen app. 7 ($2.50)-Last Comico issue 2.50
Annual 1 (1990, $2.75)-Ploog-c; Spirit tribute ish 2.75
Special 1 (1989, $2.75)-Staton-p (Innovation) 2.75
TPB (IDW Publ., 11/05, $24.99) r/#1-5 25.00

MAZE AGENCY, THE (Vol. 2)
Caliber Comics: July, 1997 - No. 3, 1998 ($2.95, B&W)
1-3: 1-Barr-s/Gonzales-a(p). 3-Hughes-c 3.00

MAZE AGENCY, THE
Caliber Comics: Nov, 2005 - No. 3, Jan, 2006 ($3.99, limited series)
1-3-Barr-s/Padilla-a(p)/c 4.00

MAZIE (...& Her Friends) (See Flat-Top, Mortie, Stevie & Tastee-Freez)
Mazie Comics(Magazine Publ.)/Harvey Publ. No. 13-on: 1953 - #12, 1954; #13, 12/54 - #22, 9/56; #23, 9/57 - #28, 8/58
1-(Teen-age)-Stevie's girlfriend 10 20 30 58 79 100
2 7 14 21 35 43 50
3-10 6 12 18 31 38 45
11-28 5 10 15 24 30 35

MAZIE
Nation Wide Publishers: 1950 - No. 7, 1951 (5¢) (5x7-1/4"-miniature)(52 pgs.)
1-Teen-age 15 30 45 94 147 200
2-7 10 20 30 58 79 100

MAZINGER (See First Comics Graphic Novel #17)

'MAZING MAN
DC Comics: Jan, 1986 - No. 12, Dec, 1986
1-11: 7,8-Hembeck-a 2.50
12-Dark Knight part-c by Miller 3.00
Special 1 ('87), 2 (4/88), 3 ('90)-All $2.00, 52pgs. 2.50

McCANDLESS & COMPANY
Mandalay Books: 2001 ($7.95)
...: Dead Razor - J.C. Vaughn-s/Busch & Sheehan-a; 3 covers 8.00
Crime Scenes: A McCandless & Company Reader TPB (Spring 2006, $17.95) Vaughn-s 18.00

McHALE'S NAVY (TV) (See Movie Classics)
Dell Publ. Co.: May-July, 1963 - No. 3, Nov-Jan, 1963-64 (All have photo-c)
1 7 14 21 45 73 100
2,3 5 10 15 32 51 70

McKEEVER & THE COLONEL (TV)
Dell Publishing Co.: Feb-Apr, 1963 - No. 3, Aug-Oct, 1963
1-Photo-c 6 12 18 39 62 85
2,3 5 10 15 30 48 65

McLINTOCK (See Movie Comics)

MD
E. C. Comics: Apr-May, 1955 - No. 5, Dec-Jan, 1955-56
1-Not approved by code; Craig-c 14 28 42 112 181 250
2-5 9 18 27 72 119 165
NOTE: ***Crandall, Evans, Ingels, Orlando** art in all issues; **Craig** c-1-5.*

MD

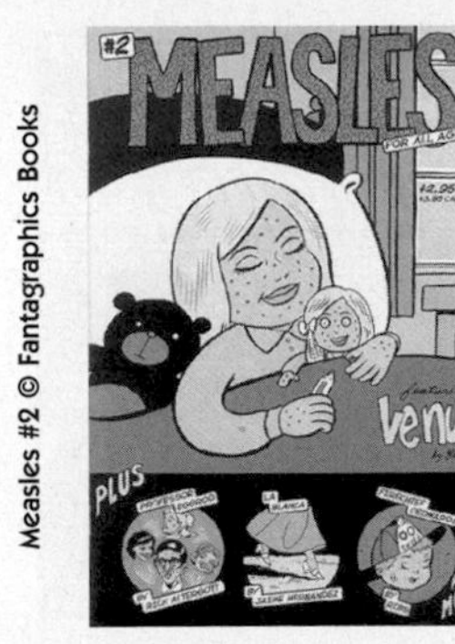

Measles #2 © Fantagraphics Books

Meet Corliss Archer #2 © FOX

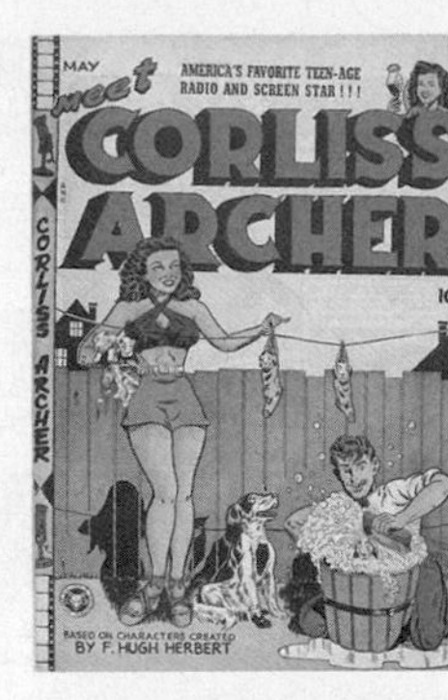

Megalith #1 © Continuity

GD VG FN VF VF/NM NM-
2.0 4.0 6.0 8.0 9.0 9.2

Russ Cochran/Gemstone Publishing: Sept, 1999 - No. 5, Jan, 2000 ($2.50)
1-5-Reprints original EC series 2.50
Annual 1 (1999, $13.50) r/#1-5 14.00

MEASLES
Fantagraphics Books: Christmas 1998 - Present ($2.95, B&W, quarterly)
1-8-Anthology: 1-Venus-s by Hernandez 3.00

MECHA (Also see Mayhem)
Dark Horse Comics: June, 1987 - No. 6, 1988 ($1.50/$1.95, color/B&W)
1-6: 1,2 ($1.95, color), 3,4-($1.75, B&W), 5,6-($1.50, B&W) 2.50

MECHANIC, THE
Image Comics: 1998 ($5.95, one-shot, squarebound)
1-Chiodo-painted art; Peterson-s 6.00
1-($10.00) DF Alternate Cover Ed. 10.00

MECHA SPECIAL
Dark Horse Comics: May, 1995 ($2.95, one-shot)
1 3.00

MECH DESTROYER
Image Comics: Apr, 2001 - No. 4, Sept, 2001 ($2.95, limited series)
1-4-Jae Kim-c/a; Robert Chong-s 3.00

MEDAL FOR BOWZER, A
American Visuals: 1966 (8 pgs.)
nn-Eisner-c/script 27 54 81 158 254 350

MEDAL OF HONOR COMICS
A. S. Curtis: Spring, 1946
1-War stories 13 26 39 74 105 135

MEDAL OF HONOR SPECIAL
Dark Horse Comics: 1994 ($2.50, one-shot)
1-Kubert-c/a (first story) 2.50

MEDIA STARR
Innovation Publ.: July, 1989 - No. 3, Sept, 1989 ($1.95, mini-series, 28 pgs.)
1-3: Deluxe format 2.50

MEDIEVAL SPAWN/WITCHBLADE
Image Comics (Top Cow Productions): May, 1996 - No. 3, June, 1996 ($2.95, limited series)
1-3-Garth Ennis scripts in all 6.00
1-Platinum foil-c (500 copies from Pittsburgh Con) 35.00
1-Gold 10.00
1-ETM Exclusive Edition; gold foil logo 7.00
TPB ($9.95) r/#1-3 10.00

MEET ANGEL (Formerly Angel & the Ape)
National Periodical Publications: No. 7, Nov-Dec, 1969
7-Wood-a(i) 3 6 9 19 29 38

MEET CORLISS ARCHER (Radio/Movie)(My Life #4 on)
Fox Features Syndicate: Mar, 1948 - No. 3, July, 1948
1-(Teen-age)-Feldstein-c/a; headlight-c 107 214 321 674 1137 1600
2 55 110 165 347 586 825
3-Part Feldstein-c only 52 104 156 322 536 750
NOTE: *No. 1-3 used in Seduction of the Innocent, pg. 39.*

MEET HERCULES (See Three Stooges)

MEET MERTON
Toby Press: Dec, 1953 - No. 4, June, 1954
1-(Teen-age)-Dave Berg-c/a 9 18 27 52 69 85
2-Dave Berg-c/a 6 12 18 29 36 42
3,4-Dave Berg-c/a 6 12 18 27 33 38
I.W. Reprint #9, Super Reprint #11('63), 18 2 4 6 8 11 14

MEET MISS BLISS (Becomes Stories Of Romance #5 on)
Atlas Comics (LMC): May, 1955 - No. 4, Nov, 1955
1-Al Hartley-c/a 14 28 42 80 115 150
2-4 9 18 27 52 69 85

MEET MISS PEPPER (Formerly Lucy, The Real Gone Gal)
St. John Publishing Co.: No. 5, April, 1954 - No. 6, June, 1954
5-Kubert/Maurer-a 21 42 63 123 197 270
6-Kubert/Maurer-a; Kubert-c 18 36 54 103 162 220

MEGACITY909

GD VG FN VF VF/NM NM-
2.0 4.0 6.0 8.0 9.0 9.2

Devil's Due Publ.: Sept, 2004 - No. 8, Aug, 2005 ($2.95)
1-8-Kano Kang & Zack Suh-a 3.00

MEGA DRAGON & TIGER
Image Comics: Mar, 1999 - No. 5 ($2.95)
1-5-Tony Wong-s/a 3.00

MEGAHURTZ
Image Comics: Aug, 1997 - No. 3, Oct, 1997 ($2.95, B&W)
1-3-St. Pierre-s 3.00

MEGALITH (Megalith Deathwatch 2000 #1,2 of second series)
Continuity: 1989 - No. 9, Mar, 1992; No. 0, Apr, 1993 - No. 7, Jan, 1994
1-9-($2.00-c) 1-Neal Adams & Mark Texiera-c/Texiera & Nebres-a 3.00
2nd series: 0-(4/93)-Foil-c; no c-price, giveaway; Adams plot 3.00
1-7: 1-3-Bagged w/card: 1-Gatefold-c by Nebres; Adams plot. 2-Fold-out-c; Adams plot. 3-Indestructible-c. 4-7-Embossed-c: 4-Adams/Nebres-c; Adams part-i. 5-Sienkiewicz-i. 6-Adams part-i. 7-Adams-c(p); Adams plot 3.00

MEGAMAN
Dreamwave Productions: Sept, 2003 - No. 4, Dec, 2003 ($2.95)
1-4-Brian Augustyn-s/Mic Fong-a 3.00
1-($5.95) Chromium wraparound variant-c 6.00

MEGA MORPHS
Marvel Comics: Oct, 2005 - No. 4, Dec, 2005 ($2.99, limited series)
1-4-Giant robots based on action figures; McKeever-s; Kang-a 3.00
Digest (2006, $7.99) r/#1-4 plus mini-comics 8.00

MEGATON (A super hero)
Megaton Publ.: Nov, 1983; No. 2, Oct, 1985 - No. 8, Aug, 1987 (B&W)
1-($2.00, 68 pgs.)-Erik Larsen's 1st pro work; Vanguard by Larsen begins (1st app.), ends #4; 1st app. Megaton, Berzorkor, & Ethrian; Guice-c/a(p); Gustovich-a(p) in #1,2 2 4 6 10 14 18
2-($2.00, 68 pgs.)-1st brief app. The Dragon (1 pg.) by Larsen (later The Savage Dragon in Image Comics); Guice-c/a(p) 2 4 6 9 12 15
3-(44 pgs.)-1st full app. Savage Dragon-c/story by Larsen; 1st comic book work by Angel Medina (pin-up) 2 4 6 13 18 22
4-(52 pgs.)-2nd full app. Savage Dragon by Larsen; 4,5-Wildman by Grass Green 2 4 6 8 10 12
5-1st Liefeld published-a (inside f/c, 6/86) 1 2 3 5 7 9
6,7: 6-Larsen-c 1 2 3 4 5 7
8-1st Liefeld story-a (7 pg. super hero story) plus 1 pg. Youngblood ad 1 3 4 6 8 10
...Explosion (6/87, 16 pg. color giveaway)-1st app. Youngblood by Rob Liefeld (2 pg. spread); shows Megaton heroes 3 6 9 14 20 25
...Holiday Special 1 (1994, $2.95, color, 40 pgs., publ. by Entity Comics)-Gold foil logo; bagged w/Kelley Jones card; Vanguard, Megaton plus shows unpublished-c to 1987 Youngblood #1 by Liefeld/Ordway 5.00
NOTE: *Copies of Megaton Explosion were also released in early 1992 all signed by Rob Liefeld and were made available to retailers.*

MEGATON MAN (See Don Simpson's Bizarre Heroes)
Kitchen Sink Enterprises: Nov, 1984 - No. 10, 1986
1-10, 1-2nd printing (1989) 3.00
...Meets The Uncategorizable X-Thems 1 (4/89, $2.00) 3.00

MEGATON MAN: BOMB SHELL
Image Comics: Jul, 1999 - No. 2 ($2.95, B&W, mini-series)
1-Reprints stories from Megaton Man internet site 3.00

MEGATON MAN: HARD COPY
Image Comics: Feb, 1999 - No. 2, Apr, 1999 ($2.95, B&W, mini-series)
1,2-Reprints stories from Megaton Man internet site 3.00

MEGATON MAN VS. FORBIDDEN FRANKENSTEIN
Fiasco Comics: Apr, 1996 ($2.95, B&W, one-shot)
1-Intro The Tomb Team (Forbidden Frankenstein, Drekula, Bride of the Monster, & Moon Wolf). 3.00

MEK (See Reload/Mek flipbook for TPB reprint)
DC Comics (Homage): Jan, 2003 - No. 3, Mar, 2003 ($2.95, limited series)
1-3-Warren Ellis-s/Steve Rolston-a 3.00

MEKANIX (See X-Men titles) (See X-Treme X-Men Vol. 4 for TPB)
Marvel Comics: Dec, 2002 - No. 6, May, 2003 ($2.99, limited series)
1-6-Kitty Pryde in college; Claremont-s/Bobillo & Sosa-a 3.00

MEL ALLEN SPORTS COMICS (The Voice of the Yankees)

Menace #3 © MAR

Men in Action #4 © MAR

Men's Adventures #16 © MAR

GD 2.0 | VG 4.0 | FN 6.0 | VF 8.0 | VF/NM 9.0 | NM- 9.2

Standard Comics: No. 5, Nov, 1949; No. 6, June, 1950
5(#1 on inside)-Tuska-a 23 46 69 133 214 295
6(#2)-Lou Gehrig story 15 30 45 92 144 195

MELTDOWN
Image Comics: Dec, 2006 - No. 2, Jan, 2007 ($5.95, squarebound, limited series)
1,2-Schwartz-s/Wang-a. 1-Bachalo-c. 2-Horn-c 6.00

MELVIN MONSTER
Dell Publishing Co.: Apr-June, 1965 - No. 10, Oct, 1969
1-By John Stanley 9 18 27 65 113 160
2-10-All by Stanley. #10-r/#1 7 14 21 49 80 110

MELVIN THE MONSTER (See Peter, the Little Pest & Dexter The Demon #7)
Atlas Comics (HPC): July, 1956 - No. 6, July, 1957
1-Maneely-c/a 14 28 42 80 115 150
2-6: 4-Maneely-c/a 10 20 30 54 72 90

MENACE
Atlas Comics (HPC): Mar, 1953 - No. 11, May, 1954
1-Horror & sci/fi stories begin; Everett-c/a 73 146 219 460 780 1100
2-Post-atom bomb disaster by Everett; anti-Communist propaganda/torture scenes; Sinnott sci/fi story "Rocket to the Moon" 50 100 150 310 518 725
3,4,6-Everett-a. 4-Sci/fi story "Escape to the Moon". 6-Romita sci/fi story "Science Fiction" 41 82 123 250 413 575
5-Origin & 1st app. The Zombie by Everett (reprinted in Tales of the Zombie #1)(7/53); 5-Sci/fi story "Rocket Ship" 57 114 171 359 605 850
7,8,10,11: 7-Frankenstein story. 8-End of world story; Heath 3-D art(3 pgs.). 10-H-Bomb panels 33 66 99 192 309 425
9-Everett-a r-in Vampire Tales #1 37 74 111 215 345 475
NOTE: ***Brodsky*** *c-7, 8, 11.* ***Colan*** *a-6; c-9.* ***Everett*** *a-1-6, 9; c-1-6.* ***Heath*** *a-1-8; c-10.* ***Katz*** *a-11.* ***Maneely*** *a-3, 5, 7-9.* ***Powell*** *a-11.* ***Romita*** *a-3, 6, 8, 11.* ***Shelly*** *a-10.* ***Shores*** *a-7.* ***Sinnott*** *a-2, 7.* ***Tuska*** *a-1, 2, 5.*

MENACE
Awesome-Hyperwerks: Nov, 1998 ($2.50)
1-Jada Pinkett Smith-s/Fraga-a 2.50

MEN AGAINST CRIME (Formerly Mr. Risk; Hand of Fate #8 on)
Ace Magazines: No. 3, Feb, 1951 - No. 7, Oct, 1951
3-Mr. Risk app. 11 22 33 60 83 105
4-7: 4-Colan-a; entire book-r as Trapped! #4. 5-Meskin-a 8 16 24 44 57 70

MEN, GUNS, & CATTLE (See Classics Illustrated Special Issue)

MEN IN ACTION (Battle Brady #10 on)
Atlas Comics (IPS): April, 1952 - No. 9, Dec, 1952 (War stories)
1-Berg, Reinman-a 17 34 51 98 154 210
2,3: 3-Heath-c/a 11 22 33 60 83 105
4-6,8,9 10 20 30 54 72 90
7-Krigstein-a; Heath-c 11 22 33 60 83 105
NOTE: ***Brodsky*** *c-1, 4-6.* ***Maneely*** *c-5.* ***Pakula*** *a-1, 6.* ***Robinson*** *c-8.* ***Shores*** *c-9.* ***Sinnott*** *a-6.*

MEN IN ACTION
Ajax/Farrell Publications: April, 1957 - No. 6, 1958
1 9 18 27 52 69 85
2 6 12 18 33 41 48
3-6 6 12 18 28 34 40

MEN IN BLACK, THE (1st series)
Aircel Comics (Malibu): Jan, 1990 - No. 3 Mar, 1990 ($2.25, B&W, lim. series)
1-Cunningham-s/a in all 4 8 12 24 37 50
2,3 3 6 9 16 22 28
Graphic Novel (Jan, 1991) r/#1-3 3 6 9 14 20 25

MEN IN BLACK (2nd series)
Aircel Comics (Malibu): May, 1991 - No. 3, Jul, 1991 ($2.50, B&W, lim. series)
1-Cunningham-s/a in all 3 6 9 16 22 28
2,3 2 4 6 8 11 14

MEN IN BLACK: FAR CRY
Marvel Comics: Aug, 1997 ($3.99, color, one-shot)
1-Cunningham-s 4.00

MEN IN BLACK: RETRIBUTION
Marvel Comics: Dec, 1997 ($3.99, color, one-shot)
1-Cunningham-s; continuation of the movie 4.00

MEN IN BLACK: THE MOVIE
Marvel Comics: Oct, 1997 ($3.99, one-shot, movie adaptation)

GD 2.0 | VG 4.0 | FN 6.0 | VF 8.0 | VF/NM 9.0 | NM- 9.2

1-Cunningham-s 4.00

MEN INTO SPACE
Dell Publishing Co.: No. 1083, Feb-Apr, 1960
Four Color 1083-Anderson-a, photo-c 5 10 15 34 55 75

MEN OF BATTLE (Also see New Men of Battle)
Catechetical Guild: V1#5, March, 1943 (Hardcover)
V1#5-Topix reprints 6 12 18 28 34 40

MEN OF WAR
DC Comics, Inc.: August, 1977 - No. 26, March, 1980 (#9,10: 44 pgs.)
1-Enemy Ace, Gravedigger (origin #1,2) begin 2 4 6 13 18 22
2-4,8-10,12-14,19,20: All Enemy Ace stories. 4-1st Dateline Frontline. 9-Unknown Soldier app. 2 4 6 8 10 12
5-7,11,15-18,21-25: 17-1st app. Rosa 1 2 3 5 7 9
26-Sgt. Rock & Easy Co.-c/s 2 4 6 10 14 18
NOTE: ***Chaykin*** *a-9, 10, 12-14, 19, 20.* ***Evans*** *c-25.* ***Kubert*** *c-2-23, 24p, 26.*

MEN'S ADVENTURES (Formerly True Adventures)
Marvel/Atlas Comics (CCC): No. 4, Aug, 1950 - No. 28, July, 1954
4(#1)(52 pgs.) 32 64 96 190 305 420
5-Flying Saucer story 21 42 63 123 197 270
6-8: 7-Buried alive story. 8-Sci/fic story 19 38 57 112 176 240
9-20: All war format 14 28 42 76 108 140
21,22,24,26: All horror format 22 44 66 127 204 280
23-Crandall-a; Fox-a(i); horror format 22 44 66 131 211 290
25-Shrunken head-c 35 70 105 203 327 450
27,28-Human Torch & Toro-c/stories; Captain America & Sub-Mariner stories in each (also see Young Men #24-28) 113 226 339 712 1206 1700
NOTE: ***Ayers*** *a-20, 27(H. Torch).* ***Berg*** *a-15, 16.* ***Brodsky*** *c-4-9, 11, 12, 16-18, 24.* ***Burgos*** *c-27, 28(Human Torch).* ***Colan*** *a-13, 14, 19.* ***Everett*** *a-10, 14, 22, 25, 28; c-14, 21-23.* ***Heath*** *a-8, 11, 24; c-13, 20, 26.* ***Lawrence*** *a-23; 27(Captain America).* ***Maneely*** *a-24; c-10, 15.* ***Mac Pakula*** *a-15, 25.* ***Post*** *a-23.* ***Powell*** *a-27(Sub-Mariner).* ***Reinman*** *a-11, 12.* ***Robinson*** *c-19.* ***Romita*** *a-22.* ***Shores*** *c-25.* ***Sinnott*** *a-13, 21.* ***Tuska*** *a-24. Adventure-#4-8; War-#9-20; Weird/Horror-#21-26.*

MENZ INSANA
DC Comics (Vertigo): 1997 ($7.95, one-shot)
nn-Fowler-s/Bolton painted art 1 2 3 5 6 8

MEPHISTO VS... (See Silver Surfer #3)
Marvel Comics Group: Apr, 1987 - No. 4, July, 1987 ($1.50, mini-series)
1-4: 1-Fantastic Four; Austin-i. 2-X-Factor. 3-X-Men. 4-Avengers 3.00

MERC (See Mark Hazzard: Merc)

MERCENARIES (Based on the Pandemic video game)
Dynamite Entertainment: 2007 - No. 3, 2008 ($3.99, limited series)
1-3-Michael Turner-c; Brian Reed-s/Edgar Salazar-a 4.00

MERCHANTS OF DEATH
Acme Press (Eclipse): Jul, 1988 - No. 4, Nov, 1988 ($3.50, B&W/16 pgs. color, 44 pg. mag.)
1-4: 4-Toth-c 3.50

MERIDIAN
CrossGeneration Comics: Jul, 2000 - No. 44, Apr, 2004 ($2.95)
1-44: Barbara Kesel-s 3.00
Flying Solo Vol. 1 TPB (2001, $19.95) r/#1-7; cover by Steve Rude 20.00
Going to Ground Vol. 2 TPB (2002, $19.95) r/#8-14 20.00
Taking the Skies Vol. 3 TPB (2002, $15.95) r/#15-20 16.00
Vol. 4: Coming Home (12/02, $15.95) r/#21-26 16.00
Vol. 5: Minister of Cadador (7/03, $15.95) r/#27-32 16.00
Vol. 6: Changing Course (1/04, $15.95) r/#33-38 16.00
Traveler Vol. 1-4 ($9.95): Digest-size reprints of TPBs 10.00

MERLIN JONES AS THE MONKEY'S UNCLE (See Movie Comics and The Misadventures of... under Movie Comics)

MERRILL'S MARAUDERS (See Movie Classics)

MERRY CHRISTMAS (See A Christmas Adventure, Donald Duck..., Dell Giant #39, & March of Comics #153 in the Promotional Comics section)

MERRY COMICS
Carlton Publishing Co.: Dec, 1945 (10¢)
nn-Boogeyman app. 20 40 60 115 183 250

MERRY COMICS: Four Star Publications: 1947 (Advertised, not published)

MERRY-GO-ROUND COMICS
LaSalle Publ. Co./Croyden Publ./Rotary Litho.: 1944 (25¢, 132 pgs.); 1946; 9-10/47 - No. 2, 1948
nn(1944)(LaSalle)-Funny animal; 29 new features 18 36 54 105 165 225

Metal Men (2007 series) #3 © DC

Metamorpho: Year One #1 © DC

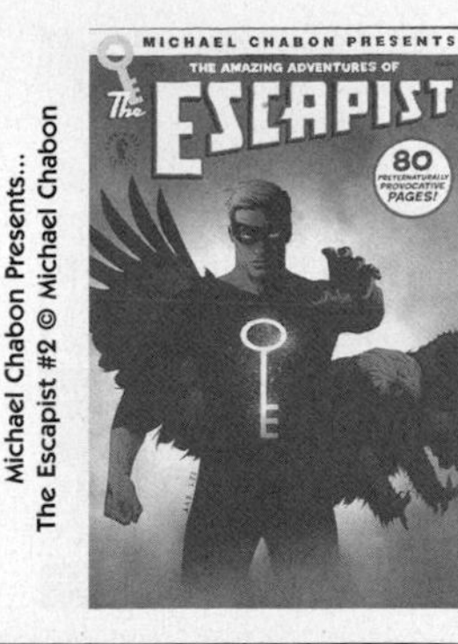

Michael Chabon Presents... The Escapist #2 © Michael Chabon

	GD 2.0	VG 4.0	FN 6.0	VF 8.0	VF/NM 9.0	NM- 9.2
21 (Publisher?)	9	18	27	47	61	75
1(1946)(Croyden)-Al Fago-c; funny animal	11	22	33	60	83	105
V1#1,2(1947-48; 52 pgs.)(Rotary Litho. Co. Ltd., Canada); Ken Hultgren-a	9	18	27	47	61	75

MERRY MAILMAN (See Fawcett's Funny Animals #87-89)

MERRY MOUSE (Also see Funny Tunes & Space Comics)
Avon Periodicals: June, 1953 - No. 4, Jan-Feb, 1954

	GD	VG	FN	VF	VF/NM	NM-
1-1st app.; funny animal; Frank Carin-c/a	10	20	30	54	72	90
2-4	7	14	21	35	43	50

MERV PUMPKINHEAD, AGENT OF D.R.E.A.M. (See The Sandman)
DC Comics (Vertigo): 2000 ($5.95, one-shot)

1-Buckingham-a(p); Nowlan painted-c 6.00

META-4
First Comics: Feb, 1991 - No. 4, 1991 ($2.25)

1-($3.95, 52pgs.) 4.00
2-4 2.50

METAL GEAR SOLID (Based on the video game)
IDW Publ.: Sept, 2004 - No. 12, Aug, 2005 ($3.99)

1-12: 1-Two covers; Ashley Wood-a/Kris Oprisko-s 4.00
1-Retailer edition with foil cover 20.00

METAL GEAR SOLID: SONS OF LIBERTY
IDW Publ.: Sept, 2005 - Present ($3.99)

#0 (9/05) profile pages on characters; Ashley Wood-a 4.00
1-9: 1-Two covers; Ashley Wood-a/Alex Garner-s 4.00

METALLIX
Future Comics: Dec, 2002 - No. 6, June, 2003 ($3.50)

0-6-Ron Lim-a. 0-(6/03) Origin. 1-Layton-c 3.50
1-Collector's Edition with variant cover by Lim 3.50
1-Free Comic Book Day Edition (4/03) Layton-c 2.50

METAL MEN (See Brave & the Bold, DC Comics Presents, and Showcase #37-40)
National Periodical Publications/DC Comics: 4-5/63 - No. 41, 12-1/69-70; No. 42, 2-3/73 - No. 44, 7-8/73; No. 45, 4-5/76 - No. 56, 2-3/78

	GD	VG	FN	VF	VF/NM	NM-
1-(4-5/63)-5th app. Metal Men	52	104	156	442	846	1250
2	22	44	66	157	291	425
3-5	14	28	42	104	187	270
6-10	9	18	27	65	113	160
11-20: 12-Beatles cameo (2-3/65)	8	16	24	52	86	120
21-Batman, Robin & Flash x-over	6	12	18	41	66	90
22-26,28-30	6	12	18	37	59	80
27-Origin Metal Men retold	7	14	21	49	80	110
31-41(1968-70): 38-Last 12¢ issue. 41-Last 15¢	5	10	15	32	51	70
42-44(1973)-Reprints	2	4	6	9	12	15
45('76)-49-Simonson-a in all: 48,49-Re-intro Eclipso	2	4	6	8	10	12
50-56: 50-Part-r. 54,55-Green Lantern x-over	2	4	6	8	10	12

NOTE: ***Andru/Esposito** c-1-30. **Aparo** c-53-56. **Giordano** c-45, 46. **Kane/Esposito** a-30, 31; c-31. **Simonson** a-45-49; c-47-52. **Staton** a-50-56.*

METAL MEN (Also see Tangent Comics/ Metal Men)
DC Comics: Oct, 1993 - No. 4, Jan, 1994 ($1.25, mini-series)

1-($2.50)-Multi-colored foil-c 4.00
2-4: 2-Origin 2.50

METAL MEN (Also see 52)
DC Comics: Oct, 2007 - No. 8, Jul, 2008 ($2.99, limited series)

1-8-Duncan Rouleau-s/a; origin re-told. 3-Chemo returns 3.00

METAMORPHO (See Action Comics #413, Brave & the Bold #57,58, 1st Issue Special, & World's Finest #217)
National Periodical Publications: July-Aug, 1965 - No. 17, Mar-Apr, 1968 (All 12¢ issues)

	GD	VG	FN	VF	VF/NM	NM-
1-(7-8/65)-3rd app. Metamorpho	13	26	39	90	160	230
2,3	7	14	21	49	80	110
4-6,10:10-Origin & 1st app. Element Girl (1-2/67)	6	12	18	41	66	90
7-9	5	10	15	34	55	75
11-17: 17-Sparling-c/a	5	10	15	30	48	65

NOTE: ***Ramona Fradon** a-B&B 57, 58, 1-4. **Orlando** a-5, 6; c-5-9, 11. **Trapani** a(p)-7-16; i-16.*

METAMORPHO
DC Comics: Aug, 1993 - No. 4, Nov, 1993 ($1.50, mini-series)

1-4 2.50

METAMORPHO: YEAR ONE
DC Comics: Early Dec, 2007 - No. 6, Late Feb, 2008 ($2.99, limited series)

1-6-Origin re-told; Jurgens-s/Jurgens & Delperdang-a/Nowlan-c. 6-Justice League app. 3.00
TPB ('08, $14.99) r/#1-6 15.00

METAPHYSIQUE
Malibu Comics (Bravura): Apr, 1995 - No. 6, Oct, 1995 ($2.95, limited series)

1-6: Norm Breyfogle-c/a/scripts 3.00

METEOR COMICS
L. L. Baird (Croyden): Nov, 1945

	GD	VG	FN	VF	VF/NM	NM-
1-Captain Wizard, Impossible Man, Race Wilkins app.; origin Baldy Bean, Capt. Wizard's sidekick; bare-breasted mermaids story	40	80	120	235	380	525

METEOR MAN
Marvel Comics: Aug, 1993 - No. 6, Jan, 1994 ($1.25, limited series)

1-6: 1-Regular unbagged. 4-Night Thrasher-c/story. 6-Terry Austin-c(i) 2.50
1-Polybagged w/button & rap newspaper 4.00
...: The Movie (4/93 [7/93 on cover], $2.25) movie adaptation 2.50

METROPOL (See Ted McKeever's...)

METROPOL A.D. (See Ted McKeever's...)

METROPOLIS S.C.U. (Also see Showcase '96 #1)
DC Comics: Nov, 1995 - No. 4, Feb, 1996 ($1.50, limited series)

1-4:1-Superman-c & app. 2.50

MEZZ: GALACTIC TOUR 2494 (Also See Nexus)
Dark Horse Comics: May, 1994 ($2.50, one-shot)

1 2.50

MGM'S MARVELOUS WIZARD OF OZ (See Marvel Treasury of Oz)
Marvel Comics Group/National Periodical Publications: 1975 ($1.50, 84 pgs.; oversize)

	GD	VG	FN	VF	VF/NM	NM-
1-Adaptation of MGM's movie; J. Buscema-a	3	6	9	16	22	28

M.G.M'S MOUSE MUSKETEERS (Formerly M.G.M.'s The Two Mouseketeers)
Dell Publishing Co.: No. 670, Jan, 1956 - No. 1290, Mar-May, 1962

	GD	VG	FN	VF	VF/NM	NM-
Four Color 670 (#4)	5	10	15	35	55	75
Four Color 711,728,764	4	8	12	26	41	55
8 (4-6/57) - 21 (3-5/60)	4	8	12	24	37	50
Four Color 1135,1175,1290	4	8	12	24	37	50

M.G.M.'S SPIKE AND TYKE (also see Tom & Jerry #79)
Dell Publishing Co.: No. 499, Sept, 1953 - No. 1266, Dec-Feb, 1961-62

	GD	VG	FN	VF	VF/NM	NM-
Four Color 499 (#1)	6	12	18	43	69	95
Four Color 577,638	4	8	12	28	44	60
4(12-2/55-56)-10	4	8	12	24	37	50
11-24(12-2/60-61)	3	6	9	21	32	42
Four Color 1266	4	8	12	24	37	50

M.G.M.'S THE TWO MOUSKETEERS
Dell Publishing Co.: No. 475, June, 1953 - No. 642, July, 1955

	GD	VG	FN	VF	VF/NM	NM-
Four Color 475 (#1)	8	16	24	52	86	120
Four Color 603 (11/54), 642	6	12	18	37	59	80

MICE TEMPLAR, THE
Image Comics: Sept, 2007 - Present ($3.99/$2.99)

1-($3.99)-Bryan Glass-s/Michael Avon Oeming-a/c 4.00
2-5-($2.99) 3.00

MICHAELANGELO CHRISTMAS SPECIAL (See Teenage Mutant Ninja Turtles Christmas Special)

MICHAELANGELO, TEENAGE MUTANT NINJA TURTLE
Mirage Studios: 1986 (One shot) ($1.50, B&W)

1 5.00
1-2nd printing ('89, $1.75)-Reprint plus new-a 2.50

MICHAEL CHABON PRESENTS THE AMAZING ADVENTURES OF THE ESCAPIST
Dark Horse Comics: Feb, 2004 - Present ($8.95, squarebound)

1-5,7,8-Short stories by Chabon and various incl. Chaykin, Starlin, Brereton, Baker 9.00
6-Includes 6 pg. Spirit & Escapist story (Will Eisner's last work); Spirit on cover 9.00
... Vol. 1 (5/04, $17.95, digest-size) r/#1&2; wraparound-c by Chris Ware 18.00
... Vol. 2 (11/04, $17.95, digest-size) r/#3&4; wraparound-c by Matt Kindt 18.00
... Vol. 3 (4/06, $14.95, digest-size) r/#5&6; Tim Sale-c 15.00

MICHAEL MOORCOCK'S ELRIC: THE MAKING OF A SORCEROR
DC Comics: 2004 - No. 4, 2006 ($5.95, prestige format, limited series)

1-4-Moorcock-s/Simonson-a 6.00
TPB (2007, $19.99) r/#1-4 20.00

MICHAEL MOORCOCK'S MULTIVERSE
DC Comics (Helix): Nov, 1997 - No. 12, Oct, 1998 ($2.50, limited series)

Mickey Finn #5 © McNaught Synd.

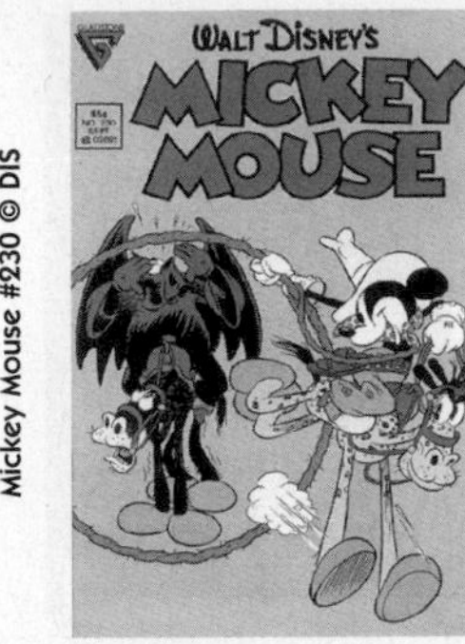

Mickey Mouse #230 © DIS

Mickey Mouse Magazine #3 © DIS

GD 2.0 VG 4.0 FN 6.0 VF 8.0 VF/NM 9.0 NM- 9.2

1-12: Simonson, Reeve & Ridgway-a 2.50
TPB (1999, $19.95) r/#1-12 20.00

MICHAEL TURNER PRESENTS: ASPEN (See Aspen)

MICKEY AND DONALD (See Walt Disney's...)

MICKEY AND DONALD IN VACATIONLAND (See Dell Giant No. 47)

MICKEY & THE BEANSTALK (See Story Hour Series)

MICKEY & THE SLEUTH (See Walt Disney Showcase #38, 39, 42)

MICKEY FINN (Also see Big Shot Comics #74 & Feature Funnies)
Eastern Color 1-4/McNaught Synd. #5 on (Columbia)/Headline V3#2:
Nov?, 1942 - V3#2, May, 1952

1 30 60 90 174 280 385
2 15 30 45 90 140 190
3-Charlie Chan story 12 24 36 69 97 125
4 10 20 30 56 76 95
5-10 9 18 27 47 61 75
11-15(1949): 12-Sparky Watts app. 8 16 24 40 50 60
V3#1,2(1952) 6 12 18 31 38 45

MICKEY MALONE
Hale Nass Corp.: 1936 (Color, punchout-c) (B&W-a on back)

nn-1pg. of comics 190 380 760 - - -

MICKEY MANTLE (See Baseball's Greatest Heroes #1)

MICKEY MOUSE (See Adventures of Mickey Mouse, The Best of Walt Disney Comics, Cheerios giveaways, Donald and ..., Dynabrite Comics, 40 Big Pages..., Gladstone Comic Album, Merry Christmas From..., Walt Disney's Mickey and Donald, Walt Disney's Comics & Stories, Walt Disney's..., & Wheaties)

MICKEY MOUSE (...Secret Agent #107-109; Walt Disney's... #148-205?)
(See Dell Giants for annuals) (#204 exists from both G.K. & Whitman)
Dell Publ. Co./Gold Key #85-204/Whitman #204-218/Gladstone #219 on:
#16, 1941 - #84, 7-9/62; #85, 11/62 - #218, 6/84; #219, 10/86 - #256, 4/90

Four Color 16(1941)-1st Mickey Mouse comic book; "...vs. the Phantom Blot" by Gottfredson 1250 2500 3750 15,000 - -
Four Color 27(1943)- "7 Colored Terror" 76 152 228 646 1236 1825
Four Color 79(1945)-By Carl Barks (1 story) 92 184 276 782 1491 2200
Four Color 116(1946) 26 52 78 188 349 510
Four Color 141,157(1947) 21 42 63 152 281 410
Four Color 170,181,194('48) 18 36 54 130 240 350
Four Color 214('49),231,248,261 14 28 42 102 181 260
Four Color 268-Reprints/WDC&S #22-24 by Gottfredson ("Surprise Visitor") 13 26 39 95 168 240
Four Color 279,286,296 10 20 30 71 126 180
Four Color 304,313(#1),325(#2),334 9 18 27 64 110 155
Four Color 343,352,362,371,387 8 16 24 54 90 125
Four Color 401,411,427(10-11/52) 6 12 18 43 69 95
Four Color 819-Mickey Mouse in Magicland 6 12 18 39 62 85
Four Color 1057,1151,1246(1959-61)-Album; #1057 has 10¢ & 12¢ editions; back covers are different 5 10 15 34 55 75
28(12-1/52-53)-32,34 6 12 18 37 59 80
33-(Exists with 2 dates, 10-11/53 & 12-1/54) 6 12 18 37 59 80
35-50 5 10 15 32 51 70
51-73,75-80 4 8 12 26 41 55
74-Story swipe "The Rare Stamp Search" from 4-Color #422- "The Gilded Man" 4 8 12 28 44 60
81-105: 93,95-titled "Mickey Mouse Club Album". 100-105: Reprint 4-Color #427,194,279, 170,343,214 in that order 3 6 9 21 32 42
106-120 3 6 9 16 23 30
121-130 2 4 6 13 18 22
131-146 2 4 6 11 16 20
147,148: 147-Reprints "The Phantom Fires" from WDC&S #200-202.148-Reprints "The Mystery of Lonely Valley" from WDC&S #208-210 2 4 6 11 16 20
149-158 2 4 6 8 11 14
159-Reprints "The Sunken City" from WDC&S #205-207 2 4 6 8 11 14
160-178: 162-165,167-170-r 2 4 6 9 13 16
179-(52 pgs.) 1 3 4 6 8 10
180-203: 200-r/Four Color #371 1 2 3 5 7 9
204-(Whitman or G.K.), 205,206 2 4 6 8 11 14
207(8/80), 209(pre-pack?) 4 8 12 22 34 45
208-(8-12/80)-Only distr. in Whitman 3-pack 9 18 27 60 100 140
210(2/81),211-214 2 4 6 8 11 14
215-218: 215(2/82), 216(4/82), 217(3/84), 218(misdated 8/82; actual date 7/84) 2 4 6 9 13 16
219-1st Gladstone issue; The Seven Ghosts serial-r begins by Gottfredson 2 4 6 10 14 18
220,221 1 2 3 5 7 9
222-225: 222-Editor-in Grief strip-r 4.00
226-230 4.00
231-243,246-254: 240-r/March of Comics #27. 245-r/F.C. #279. 250-r/F.C. #248 3.00
244 (1/89, $2.95, 100 pgs.)-Squarebound 60th anniversary issue; gives history of Mickey 4.00
245, 256: 245-r/F.C. #279. 256-$1.95, 68 pgs. 4.00
255 ($1.95, 68 pgs.) 3.00
NOTE: *Reprints #195-197, 198(2/3), 199(1/3), 200-208, 211(1/2), 212, 213, 215(1/3), 216-on.* ***Gottfredson*** *Mickey Mouse serials in #219-239, 241-244, 246-249, 251-253, 255.*
Album 01-518-210(Dell), 1(10082-309)(9/63-Gold Key) 3 6 9 20 30 40
...Club 1(1/64-Gold Key)(TV) 3 6 9 21 32 42
Mini Comic 1(1976)(3-1/4x6-1/2")-Reprints 158 1 2 3 5 6 8
Surprise Party 1(30037-901, G.K.)(1/69)-40th Anniversary (see Walt Disney Showcase #47) 3 6 9 21 32 42
Surprise Party 1(1979)-r/1969 issue 1 2 3 5 6 8

MICKEY MOUSE ADVENTURES
Disney Comics: June, 1990 - No. 18, Nov, 1991 ($1.50)

1,8,9: 1-Bradbury, Murry-r/M.M. #45,73 plus new-a. 8-Byrne-c. 9-Fantasia 50th ann. issue w/new adapt. of movie 3.00
2-7,10-18: 2-Begin all new stories. 10-r/F.C. #214 2.50

MICKEY MOUSE CLUB FUN BOOK
Golden Press: 1977 (1.95, 228 pgs.)(square bound)

11190-1950s-r; 20,000 Leagues, M. Mouse Silly Symphonys, The Reluctant Dragon, etc. 4 8 12 26 41 55

MICKEY MOUSE CLUB MAGAZINE (See Walt Disney...)

MICKEY MOUSE COMICS DIGEST
Gladstone: 1986 - No. 5, 1987 (96 pgs.)

1 ($1.25-c) 1 2 3 5 6 8
2-5: 3-5 ($1.50-c) 5.00

MICKEY MOUSE IN COLOR
Another Rainbow/Pantheon: 1988 (Deluxe, 13"x17", hard-c, $250.00)
(Trade, 9-7/8"x11-1/2", hard-c, $39.95)

Deluxe limited edition of 3,000 copies signed by Floyd Gottfredson and Carl Barks, designated as the "Official Mickey Mouse 60th Anniversary" book. Mickey Sunday and daily reprints, plus Barks "Riddle of the Red Hat" from Four Color #79. Comes with 45 r.p.m. record interview with Gottfredson and Barks. 240 pgs. 15 30 45 105 190 275
Deluxe, limited to 100 copies, as above, but with a unique colored pencil original drawing of Mickey Mouse by Carl Barks. Add value of art to book price. 800.00
Pantheon trade edition, edited down & without Barks, 192 pgs. 3 6 9 20 30 40

MICKEY MOUSE MAGAZINE (Becomes Walt Disney's Comics & Stories)(Also see 40 Big Pages of Mickey Mouse)
K. K. Publ./Western Publishing Co.: Summer, 1935 (June-Aug, indicia) - V5#12, Sept, 1940; V1#1-5, V3#11,12, V4#1-3 are 44 pgs; V2#3-100 pgs; V5#12-68 pgs; rest are 36 pgs.(No V3#1, V4#6)

V1#1 (Large size, 13-1/4x10-1/4"; 25¢)-Contains puzzles, games, cels, stories & comics of Disney characters. Promotional magazine for Disney cartoon movies and paraphernalia 1400 2800 4200 9000 18,500 -
Note: *Some copies were autographed by the editors & given away with all early one year subscriptions.*
2 (Size change, 11-1/2x8-1/2"; 10/35; 10¢)-High quality paper begins; Messmer-a 270 540 810 2300 - -
3,4: 3-Messmer-a 147 294 441 1250 - -
5-1st Donald Duck solo-c; 2nd cover app. ever; last 44 pg. & high quality paper issue 259 518 777 2200 - -
6-9: 6-36 pg. issues begin; Donald becomes editor. 8-2nd Donald solo-c.
9-1st Mickey/Minnie-c 135 270 405 1150 - -
10-12, V2#1,2: 11-1st Pluto/Mickey-c; Donald fires himself and appoints Mickey as editor 129 258 387 1100 - -
V2#3-Special 100 pg. Christmas issue (25¢); Messmer-a; Donald becomes editor of Wise Quacks 429 858 1287 3650 - -
4-Mickey Mouse Comics & Roy Ranger (adventure strip) begin; both end V2#9; Messmer-a 109 218 327 925 - -
5-9: 5-Ted True (adventure strip, ends V2#9) & Silly Symphony Comics (ends V3#3) begin. 6-1st solo Minnie-c. 6-9-Mickey Mouse Movies cut-out in each 53 106 159 331 561 790
10-1st full color issue; Mickey Mouse (by Gottfredson; ends V3#12) & Silly Symphony (ends V3#3) full color Sunday-r, Peter The Farm Detective (ends V5#8)

Mickey Mouse Magazine V4 #2 © DIS

Micronauts #41 © MEGO Corp.

Midnighter #16 © WSP

	GD 2.0	VG 4.0	FN 6.0	VF 8.0	VF/NM 9.0	NM- 9.2
& Ole Of The North (ends V3#3) begins	80	160	240	504	852	1200
11-13: 12-Hiawatha-c & feature story	53	106	159	329	547	765
V3#2-Big Bad Wolf Halloween-c	60	120	180	378	639	900
3 (12/37)-1st app. Snow White & The Seven Dwarfs (before release of movie) (possibly 1st in print); Mickey X-Mas-c	107	214	321	674	1137	1600
4 (1/38)-Snow White & The Seven Dwarfs serial begins (on stands before release of movie); Ducky Symphony (ends V3#11) begins	88	176	264	554	940	1325
5-1st Snow White & Seven Dwarfs-c (St. Valentine's Day)	107	214	321	674	1137	1600
6-Snow White serial ends; Lonesome Ghosts app. (2 pp.)	59	118	177	372	629	885
7-Seven Dwarfs Easter-c	55	110	165	347	586	825
8-10: 9-Dopey-c. 10-1st solo Goofy-c	48	96	144	298	499	700
11,12 (44 pgs; 8 more pgs. color added). 11-Mickey the Sheriff serial (ends V4#3) & Donald Duck strip-r (ends V3#12) begin. Color feature on Snow White's Forest Friends	52	104	156	322	536	750
V4#1 (10/38; 44 pgs.)-Brave Little Tailor-c/feature story, nominated for Academy Award; Bobby & Chip by Otto Messmer (ends V4#2) & The Practical Pig (ends V4#2) begin	52	104	156	322	536	750
2 (44 pgs.)-1st Huey, Dewey & Louie-c	53	106	159	330	553	775
3 (12/38, 44 pgs.)-Ferdinand The Bull-c/feature story, Academy Award winner; Mickey Mouse & The Whalers serial begins, ends V4#12	52	104	156	322	536	750
4-Spotty, Mother Pluto strip-r begin, end V4#8	48	96	144	298	499	700
5-St. Valentine's day-c. 1st Pluto solo-c	53	106	159	334	567	800
7 (3/39)-The Ugly Duckling-c/feature story, Academy Award winner	52	104	156	322	536	750
7 (4/39)-Goofy & Wilbur The Grasshopper classic-c/feature story from 1st Goofy solo cartoon movie; Timid Elmer begins, ends V5#5	52	104	156	322	536	750
8-Big Bad Wolf-c from Practical Pig movie poster; Practical Pig feature story	52	104	156	322	536	750
9-Donald Duck & Mickey Mouse Sunday-r begin; The Pointer feature story, nominated for Academy Award	52	104	156	322	536	750
10-Classic July 4th drum & fife-c; last Donald Sunday-r	62	124	186	391	663	935
11-1st slick-c; last over-sized issue	48	96	144	298	499	700
12 (9/39; format change, 10-1/4x8-1/4")-1st full color, cover to cover issue; Donald's Penguin-c/feature story	55	110	165	347	586	825
V5#1-Black Pete-c; Officer Duck-c/feature story; Autograph Hound feature story; Robinson Crusoe serial begins	54	108	162	340	575	810
2-Goofy-c; 1st brief app. Pinocchio	71	142	213	447	754	1060
3 (12/39)-Pinocchio Christmas-c (Before movie release). 1st app. Jiminy Cricket; Pinocchio serial begins	83	166	249	523	887	1250
4,5: 5-Jiminy Cricket-c; Pinocchio serial ends; Donald's Dog Laundry feature story	54	108	162	340	575	810
6,7: 6-Tugboat Mickey feature story; Rip Van Winkle feature begins, ends V5#8. 7-2nd Huey, Dewey & Louie-c	53	106	159	331	558	785
8-Last magazine size issue; 2nd solo Pluto-c; Figaro & Cleo feature story	54	108	162	340	575	810
9-11: 9 (6/40; change to comic book size)-Jiminy Cricket feature story; Donald-c & Sunday-r begin. 10-Special Independence Day issue. 11-Hawaiian Holiday & Mickey's Trailer feature stories; last 36 pg. issue	59	118	177	372	629	885
12 (Format change)-The transition issue (68 pgs.) becoming a comic book. With only a title change to follow, becomes Walt Disney's Comics & Stories #1 with the next issue	461	922	1383	3319	5810	8300

NOTE: *Otto Messmer-a is in many issues of the first two-three years. The following story titles and issues have gags created by **Carl Barks**: V4#3(12/38)-'Donald's Better Self' & 'Donald's Golf Game;' V4#4(1/39)-'Donald's Lucky Day;' V4#7(3/39)-'Hockey Champ;' V4#7(4/39)-'Donald's Cousin Gus;' V4#9(6/39)-'Sea Scouts;' V4#12(9/39)-'Donald's Penguin;' V5#9 (6/40)-'Donald's Vacation;' V5#10(7/40)-'Bone Trouble;' V5#12(9/40)-'Window Cleaners.'*

MICKEY MOUSE MAGAZINE (Russian Version)
May 16, 1991 (1st Russian printing of a modern comic book)

1-Bagged w/gold label commemoration in English — 10.00

MICKEY MOUSE MARCH OF COMICS (See March of Comics #8,27,45,60,74)

MICKEY MOUSE'S SUMMER VACATION (See Story Hour Series)

MICKEY MOUSE SUMMER FUN (See Dell Giants)

MICKEY SPILLANE'S MIKE DANGER
Tekno Comix: Sept, 1995 - No. 11, May, 1996 ($1.95)

1-11: 1-Frank Miller-c. 7-polybagged; Simonson-c. 8,9-Simonson-c — 2.50

MICKEY SPILLANE'S MIKE DANGER
Big Entertainment: V2#1, June, 1996 - No. 10, Apr, 1997 ($2.25)

V2#1-10: Max Allan Collins scripts — 2.50

MICKEY'S TWICE UPON A CHRISTMAS (Disney)
Gemstone Publishing: 2004 ($3.95, square-bound, one-shot)

nn-Christmas short stories with Mickey, Minnie, Donald, Uncle Scrooge, Goofy and others 4.00

MICROBOTS, THE
Gold Key: Dec, 1971 (one-shot)

	GD 2.0	VG 4.0	FN 6.0	VF 8.0	VF/NM 9.0	NM- 9.2
1 (10271-112)	3	6	9	16	22	28

MICRONAUTS (Toys)
Marvel Comics Group: Jan, 1979 - No. 59, Aug, 1984 (Mando paper #53 on)

1-Intro/1st app. Baron Karza — 5.00
2-10,35,37,57: 7-Man-Thing app. 8-1st app. Capt. Universe (8/79). 9-1st app. Cilicia. 35-Double size; origin Microverse; intro Death Squad; Dr. Strange app. 37-Nightcrawler app.; X-Men cameo (2 pgs.). 57-(52 pgs.) — 3.00
11-34,36,38-56,58,59: 13-1st app. Jasmine. 15-Death of Microtron. 15-17-Fantastic Four app. 17-Death of Jasmine. 20-Ant-Man app. 21-Microverse series begins. 25-Origin Baron Karza. 25-29-Nick Fury app. 27-Death of Biotron. 34-Dr. Strange app. 38-First direct sale. 40-Fantastic Four app. 48-Early Guice-a begins. 59-Golden painted-c — 2.50
nn-Blank UPC; diamond on top — 2.50
Annual 1,2 (12/79,10/80)-Ditko-c/a — 3.00
NOTE: *#38-on distributed only through comic shops. **N. Adams** c-7i. **Chaykin** a-13-18p. **Ditko** a-39p. **Giffen** a-36p, 37p(part). **Golden** a-1-12p; c-2-7p, 8-23, 24p, 38, 39, 59. **Guice** a-48-58p; c-49-58. **Gil Kane** a-38, 40-45p; c-40-45. **Layton** c-33-37. **Miller** c-31.*

MICRONAUTS (Micronauts: The New Voyages on cover)
Marvel Comics Group: Oct, 1984 - No. 20, May, 1986

V2#1-20 — 2.50
NOTE: ***Kelley Jones** a-1; c-1, 6. **Guice** a-4p; c-2p.*

MICRONAUTS
Image Comics: 2002 - No. 11, Sept, 2003 ($2.95)

2002 Convention Special (no cover price, B&W) previews series — 2.50
1-11: 1-3-Hanson-a; Dave Johnson-c. 4-Su-a; 2 covers by Linsner & Hanson — 3.00
...Vol. 1: Revolution (2003, $12.95, digest size) r/#1-5 — 13.00

MICRONAUTS (Volume 2)
Devil's Due Publishing: Mar, 2004 - No. 3, May, 2004 ($2.95)

1-3-Jolley-s/Broderick-a — 3.00

MICRONAUTS: KARZA
Image Comics: Feb, 2003 - No. 4, May, 2003 ($2.95)

1-4-Krueger-s/Kurth-a — 3.00

MICRONAUTS SPECIAL EDITION
Marvel Comics Group: Dec, 1983 - No. 5, Apr, 1984 ($2.00, limited series, Baxter paper)

1-5: r-/original series 1-12; Guice-c(p)-all — 3.00

MIDGET COMICS (Fighting Indian Stories)
St. John Publishng Co.: Feb, 1950 - No. 2, Apr, 1950 (5-3/8x7-3/8", 68 pgs.)

	GD 2.0	VG 4.0	FN 6.0	VF 8.0	VF/NM 9.0	NM- 9.2
1-Fighting Indian Stories; Matt Baker-c	18	36	54	107	169	230
2-Tex West, Cowboy Marshal (also in #1)	10	20	30	58	79	100

MIDNIGHT (See Smash Comics #18)

MIDNIGHT
Ajax/Farrell Publ. (Four Star Comic Corp.): Apr, 1957 - No. 6, June, 1958

	GD 2.0	VG 4.0	FN 6.0	VF 8.0	VF/NM 9.0	NM- 9.2
1-Reprints from Voodoo & Strange Fantasy with some changes	15	30	45	85	130	175
2-6	10	20	30	56	76	95

MIDNIGHTER (See The Authority)
DC Comics (WildStorm): Jan, 2007 - No. 20, Aug, 2008 ($2.99)

1-20: 1-Ennis-s/Sprouse-a/c. 6-Fabry-a. 7-Vaughan-s. 8-Gage-s. 9-Stelfreeze-a — 3.00
1-4-Variant covers. 1-Michael Golden. 2-Art Adams 3-Jason Pearson. 4-Glenn Fabry — 4.00
...: Armageddon (12/07, $2.99) Gage-s/Coleby-a/McKone-c — 3.00
...: Killing Machine TPB (2008, $14.99) r/#1-6 — 15.00

MIDNIGHT MASS
DC Comics (Vertigo): Jun, 2002 - No. 8, Jan, 2003 ($2.50)

1-8-Rozum-s/Saiz & Palmiotti-a — 2.50

MIDNIGHT MASS: HERE THERE BE MONSTERS
DC Comics (Vertigo): March, 2004 - No. 6, Aug, 2004 ($2.95, limited series)

1-6-Rozum-s/Paul Lee-a — 3.00

MIDNIGHT MEN
Marvel Comics (Epic Comics/Heavy Hitters): June, 1993 - No. 4, Sept, 1993 ($2.50/$1.95,

Mighty Avengers #1 © MAR

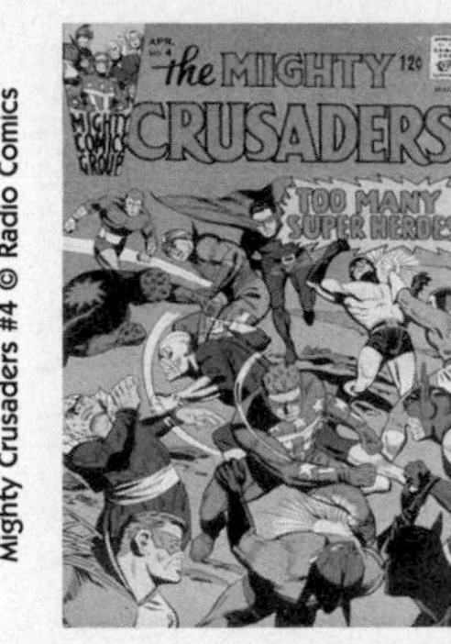

Mighty Crusaders #4 © Radio Comics

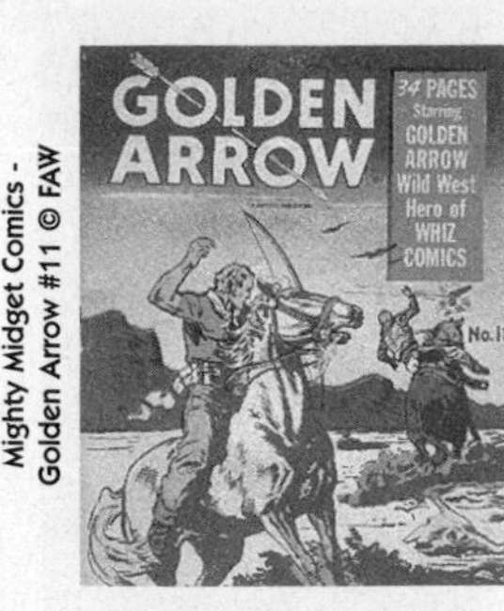

Mighty Midget Comics - Golden Arrow #11 © FAW

GD VG FN VF VF/NM NM-
2.0 4.0 6.0 8.0 9.0 9.2

GD VG FN VF VF/NM NM-
2.0 4.0 6.0 8.0 9.0 9.2

limited series)
1-($2.50)-Embossed-c; Chaykin-c/a & scripts in all 3.00
2-4 2.50

MIDNIGHT MYSTERY
American Comics Group: Jan-Feb, 1961 - No. 7, Oct, 1961
1-Sci/Fi story 8 16 24 52 86 120
2-7: 7-Gustavson-a 4 8 12 28 44 60
NOTE: *Reinman a-1, 3. Whitney a-1, 4-6; c-1-3, 5, 7.*

MIDNIGHT NATION
Image Comics (Top Cow): Oct, 2000 - No. 12, July, 2002 ($2.50/$2.95)
1-Straczynski-s/Frank-a; 2 covers 3.00
2-11: 9-Twin Towers cover 2.50
12-($2.95)Last issue 3.00
Wizard #1/2 (2001) Michael Zulli-a; two covers by Frank 3.00
Vol. 1 ('03, $29.99, TPB) r/#1-12 & Wizard #1/2; cover gallery; afterword by Straczynski 30.00

MIDNIGHT SONS UNLIMITED
Marvel Comics (Midnight Sons imprint #4 on): Apr, 1993 - No. 9, May, 1995 ($3.95, 68 pgs.)
1-9: Blaze, Darkhold (by Quesada #1), Ghost Rider, Morbius & Nightstalkers in all. 1-Painted-c. 3-Spider-Man app. 4-Siege of Darkness part 17; new Dr. Strange & new Ghost Rider app.; spot varnish-c 4.00
NOTE: *Sears a-2.*

MIDNIGHT TALES
Charlton Press: Dec, 1972 - No. 18, May, 1976
V1#1 2 4 6 13 18 22
2-10 2 4 6 8 11 14
11-18: 11-14-Newton-a(p) 1 3 4 6 8 10
12,17(Modern Comics reprint, 1977) 5.00
NOTE: *Adkins a-12i, 13i. Ditko a-12. Howard (Wood imitator) a-1-15, 17, 18; c-1-18. Don Newton a-11-14p. Staton a-1, 3-11, 13. Sutton a-3-10.*

MIGHTY ATOM, THE (...& the Pixies #6) (Formerly The Pixies #1-5)
Magazine Enterprises: No. 6, 1949; Nov, 1957 - No. 6, Aug-Sept, 1958
6(1949-M.E.)-no month (1st Series) 7 14 21 35 43 50
1-6(2nd Series)-Pixies-r 4 8 12 18 22 25
I.W. Reprint #1(nd) 2 4 6 8 11 14

MIGHTY AVENGERS
Marvel Comics: May, 2007 - Present ($3.99/$2.99)
1-($3.99) Iron Man, Ms. Marvel select new team; Bendis-s/Cho-a/c; Mole Man app. 5.00
2-6-($2.99) Ultron returns 3.00
7-15: 7-Bagley-a begins; Venom on-c. 9-11-Dr. Doom app. 3.00
12-18-Secret Invasion: 12,13-Maleev-a. 15-Romita Jr.-a. 16-Elektra 3.00
...: Most Wanted Files (2007, $3.99) profiles of members, accomplices & adversaries 4.00
... Vol. 1: The Ultron Initiative HC (2008, $19.99) r/#1-6; variant covers and sketch art 20.00
... Vol. 2: Venom Bomb HC (2008, $19.99) r/#7-11; B&W cover art 20.00

MIGHTY BEAR (Formerly Fun Comics; becomes Unsane #15)
Star Publ. No. 13,14/Ajax-Farrell (Four Star): No. 13, Jan, 1954 - No. 14, Mar, 1954; 9/57 - No. 3, 2/58
13,14-L. B. Cole-c 18 36 54 103 162 220
1-3('57-58)Four Star; becomes Mighty Ghost #4 7 14 21 35 43 50

MIGHTY COMICS (...Presents) (Formerly Flyman)
Radio Comics (Archie): No. 40, Nov, 1966 - No. 50, Oct, 1967 (All 12¢ issues)
40-Web 4 8 12 26 41 55
41-50: 41-Shield, Black Hood. 42-Black Hood. 43-Shield, Web & Black Hood. 44-Black Hood, Steel Sterling & The Shield. 45-Shield & Hangman; origin Web retold. 46-Steel Sterling, Web & Black Hood. 47-Black Hood & Mr. Justice. 48-Shield & Hangman; Wizard x-over in Shield. 49-Steel Sterling & Fox; Black Hood x-over in Steel Sterling. 50-Black Hood & Web; Inferno x-over in Web 4 8 12 24 37 50
NOTE: *Paul Reinman a-40-50.*

MIGHTY CRUSADERS, THE (Also see Adventures of the Fly, The Crusaders & Fly Man)
Mighty Comics Group (Radio Comics): Nov, 1965 - No. 7, Oct, 1966 (All 12¢)
1-Origin The Shield 7 14 21 45 73 100
2-Origin Comet 4 8 12 26 41 55
3,5-7: 3-Origin Fly-Man. 5-Intro. Ultra-Men (Fox, Web, Capt. Flag) & Terrific Three (Jaguar, Mr. Justice, Steel Sterling). 7-Steel Sterling feature; origin Fly-Girl 4 8 12 24 37 50
4-1st S.A. app. Fireball, Inferno & Fox; Firefly, Web, Bob Phantom, Blackjack, Hangman, Zambini, Kardak, Steel Sterling, Mr. Justice, Wizard, Capt. Flag, Jaguar x-over 4 8 12 26 41 55
Volume 1: Origin of a Super Team TPB (2003, $12.95) r/#1 & Fly Man #31-33 13.00
NOTE: *Reinman a-6.*

MIGHTY CRUSADERS, THE (All New Advs. of...#2)
Red Circle Prod./Archie Ent. No. 6 on: Mar, 1983 - No. 13, Sept, 1985 ($1.00, 36 pgs, Mando paper)
1-Origin Black Hood, The Fly, Fly Girl, The Shield, The Wizard, The Jaguar, Pvt. Strong & The Web. 6.00
2-10: 2-Mister Midnight begins. 4-Darkling replaces Shield. 5-Origin Jaguar, Shield begins. 7-Untold origin Jaguar. 10-Veitch-a 4.00
11-13-Lower print run 5.00
NOTE: *Buckler a-1-3, 4i, 5p, 7p, 8i, 9i; c-1-10p.*

MIGHTY GHOST (Formerly Mighty Bear #1-3)
Ajax/Farrell Publ.: No. 4, June, 1958
4 7 14 21 35 43 50

MIGHTY HERCULES, THE (TV)
Gold Key: July, 1963 - No. 2, Nov, 1963
1 (10072-307) 14 28 42 100 178 255
2 (10072-311) 13 26 39 95 168 240

MIGHTY HEROES, THE (TV) (Funny)
Dell Publishing Co.: Mar, 1967 - No. 4, July, 1967
1-Also has a 1957 Heckle & Jeckle-r 13 26 39 95 168 240
2-4: 4-Has two 1958 Mighty Mouse-r 9 18 27 63 107 150

MIGHTY HEROES
Spotlight Comics: 1987 (B&W, one-shot)
1-Heckle & Jeckle backup 5.00

MIGHTY HEROES
Marvel Comics: Jan, 1998 ($2.99, one-shot)
1-Origin of the Mighty Heroes 3.00

MIGHTY LOVE
DC Comics: 2003 ($24.99/$17.95, graphic novel)
HC-($24.95) Howard Chaykin-s/a; intro. Skylark and the Iron Angel 25.00
SC-($17.95) 18.00

MIGHTY MAN (From Savage Dragon titles)
Image Comics: Dec, 2004 ($7.95, one-shot)
1-Reprints seriaizedl back-up from Savage Dragon #109-118 8.00

MIGHTY MARVEL TEAM-UP THRILLERS
Marvel Comics: 1983 ($5.95, trade paperback)
1-Reprints team-up stories 38.00

MIGHTY MARVEL WESTERN, THE
Marvel Comics Group (LMC earlier issues): Oct, 1968 - No. 46, Sept, 1976 (#1-14: 68 pgs.; #15,16: 52 pgs.)
1-Begin Kid Colt, Rawhide Kid, Two-Gun Kid-r 5 10 15 34 55 75
2-5: (2-14 are 68 pgs.) 4 8 12 24 37 50
6-16: (15,16 are 52 pgs.) 4 8 12 22 34 45
17-20 2 4 6 13 18 22
21-30,32,37: 24-Kid Colt-r end. 25-Matt Slade-r begin. 32-Origin-r/Rawhide Kid #23; Williamson-r/Kid Slade #7. 37-Williamson, Kirby-r/Two-Gun Kid 51 2 4 6 9 13 16
31,33-36,38-46: 31-Baker-r. 2 4 6 8 11 14
45-(30¢-c variant, limited distribution)(6/76) 4 8 12 26 41 55
NOTE: *Jack Davis a(r)-21-24. Keller r-1-13, 22. Kirby a(r)-1-3, 6, 9, 12-14, 16, 25-29, 32-38, 40, 41, 43-46; c-29. Maneely a(r)-22. Severin c-3i, 9. No Matt Slade-#43.*

MIGHTY MIDGET COMICS, THE (Miniature)
Samuel E. Lowe & Co.: No date; circa 1942-1943 (Sold 2 for 5¢, B&W and red, 36 pgs, approx. 5x4")
Bulletman #11(1943)-r/cover/Bulletman #3 18 36 54 107 169 230
Captain Marvel Adventures #11 18 36 54 107 169 230
Captain Marvel #11 (Same as above except for full color ad on back cover; this issue was glued to cover of Captain Marvel #20 and is not found in fine-mint condition) 340 680 1020 - - -
Captain Marvel Jr. #11 (Same-c as Master #27 18 36 54 107 169 230
Captain Marvel Jr. #11 (Same as above except for full color ad on back-c; this issue was glued to cover of Captain Marvel #21 and is not found in fine-mint condition) 340 680 1020 - - -
Golden Arrow #11 16 32 48 92 144 200
Golden Arrow #11 (Same as above except for full color ad on back-c; this issue was glued to cover of Captain Marvel #21 and is not found in fine-mint condition) 280 560 840 - - -
Ibis the Invincible #11(1942)-Origin; reprints cover to Ibis #1 (Predates Fawcett's Ibis the Invincible #1). 18 36 54 107 169 230

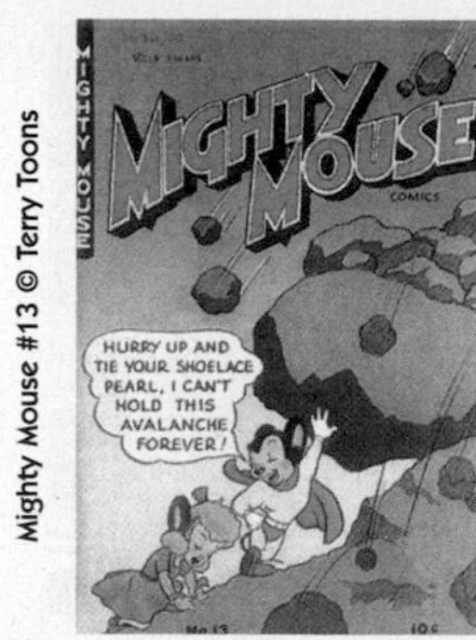

Mighty Mouse #13 © Terry Toons

Mighty Samson #21 © WEST

Mike Barnett, Man Against Crime #3 © FAW

	GD 2.0	VG 4.0	FN 6.0	VF 8.0	VF/NM 9.0	NM- 9.2
Spy Smasher #11(1942)	18	36	54	107	169	230

NOTE: *The above books came in a box called "box full of books" and was distributed with other Samuel Lowe puzzles, paper dolls, coloring books, etc. They are not titled Mighty Midget Comics. All have a war bond seal on back cover which is otherwise blank. These books came in a "Mighty Midget" flat cardboard counter display rack.*

	GD 2.0	VG 4.0	FN 6.0	VF 8.0	VF/NM 9.0	NM- 9.2
Balbo, the Boy Magician #12 (1943)-1st book devoted entirely to character.	11	22	33	62	86	110
Bulletman #12	14	28	42	81	118	155
Commando Yank #12 (1943)-Only comic devoted entirely to character.	11	22	33	64	90	115
Dr. Voltz the Human Generator (1943)-Only comic devoted entirely to character.	11	22	33	62	86	110
Lance O'Casey #12 (1943)-1st comic devoted entirely to character (Predates Fawcett's Lance O'Casey #1).	11	22	33	62	86	110
Leatherneck the Marine (1943)-Only comic devoted entirely to character.	11	22	33	62	86	110
Minute Man #12	14	28	42	80	115	150
Mister "Q" (1943)-Only comic devoted entirely to character.	11	22	33	62	86	110
Mr. Scarlet and Pinky #12 (1943)-Only comic devoted entirely to character.	13	26	39	72	101	130
Pat Wilton and His Flying Fortress (1943)-1st comic devoted entirely to character.	11	22	33	62	86	110
The Phantom Eagle #12 (1943)-Only comic devoted entirely to character.	11	22	33	62	86	110
State Trooper Stops Crime (1943)-Only comic devoted entirely to character.	11	22	33	62	86	110
Tornado Tom (1943)-Origin, r/from Cyclone #1-3; only comic devoted entirely to character.	11	22	33	62	86	110

MIGHTY MORPHIN' POWER RANGERS: THE MOVIE (Also see Saban's Mighty Morphin' Power Rangers)
Marvel Comics: Sept, 1995 ($3.95, one-shot)

nn-Adaptation of movie 4.00

MIGHTY MOUSE (See Adventures of..., Dell Giant #43, Giant Comics Edition, March of Comics #205, 237, 247, 257, 447, 459, 471, 483, Oxydol-Dreft, Paul Terry's, & Terry-Toons Comics)

MIGHTY MOUSE (1st Series)
Timely/Marvel Comics (20th Century Fox): Fall, 1946 - No. 4, Summer, 1947

	GD 2.0	VG 4.0	FN 6.0	VF 8.0	VF/NM 9.0	NM- 9.2
1	160	320	480	1008	1704	2400
2	65	130	195	410	693	975
3,4	41	82	123	253	419	585

MIGHTY MOUSE (2nd Series) (Paul Terry's... #62-71)
St. John Publishing Co./Pines No. 68 (3/56) on (TV issues #72 on): Aug, 1947 - No. 67, 11/55; No. 68, 3/56 - No. 83, 6/59

	GD 2.0	VG 4.0	FN 6.0	VF 8.0	VF/NM 9.0	NM- 9.2
5(#1)	40	80	120	235	380	525
6-10: 10-Over-sized issue	20	40	60	118	189	260
11-19	14	28	42	80	115	150
20 (11/50) - 25-(52 pg. editions)	11	22	33	62	86	110
20-25-(36 pg. editions)	10	20	30	54	72	90
26-37: 35-Flying saucer-c	9	18	27	50	65	80
38-45-(100 pgs.)	18	36	54	107	169	230
46-83: 62-64,67-Painted-c. 82-Infinity-c	9	18	27	47	61	75
Album nn (nd, 1952/53?, St. John)(100 pgs.)(Rebound issues w/new cover)	22	44	66	127	204	280
Album 1(10/52, 25¢, 100 pgs., St. John)-Gandy Goose app.	28	56	84	162	261	360
Album 2,3(11/52 & 12/52, St. John) (100 pgs.)	22	44	66	127	204	280
Fun Club Magazine 1(Fall, 1957-Pines, 25¢, 100 pgs.) (CBS TV)-Tom Terrific, Heckle & Jeckle, Dinky Duck, Gandy Goose	15	30	45	90	140	190
Fun Club Magazine 2-6(Winter, 1958-Pines)	11	22	33	62	86	110
3-D 1-(1st printing-9/53, 25¢)(St. John)-Came w/glasses; stiff covers; says World's First! on-c; 1st 3-D comic	28	56	84	162	261	360
3-D 1-(2nd printing-10/53, 25¢)-Came w/glasses; slick, glossy covers, slightly smaller	20	40	60	115	183	250
3-D 2,3(11/53, 12/53, 25¢)-(St. John)-With glasses	20	40	60	115	183	250

MIGHTY MOUSE (TV)(3rd Series)(Formerly Adventures of Mighty Mouse)
Gold Key/Dell Publ. Co. No. 166-on: No. 161, Oct, 1964 - No. 172, Oct, 1968

	GD 2.0	VG 4.0	FN 6.0	VF 8.0	VF/NM 9.0	NM- 9.2
161(10/64)-165(9/65)-(Becomes Adventures of... No. 166 on)	5	10	15	30	48	65
166(3/66), 167(6/66)-172	3	6	9	21	32	42

MIGHTY MOUSE (TV)
Spotlight Comics: 1987 - No. 2, 1987 ($1.50, color)

1,2-New stories 3.00

...And Friends Holiday Special (11/87, $1.75) 3.00

MIGHTY MOUSE (TV)
Marvel Comics: Oct, 1990 - No. 10, July, 1991 ($1.00)(Based on Sat. cartoon)

1-10: 1-Dark Knight-c parody. 2-10: 3-Intro Bat-Bat; Byrne-c. 4,5-Crisis-c/story parodies w/Perez-c. 6-Spider-Man-c parody. 7-Origin Bat-Bat 2.50

MIGHTY MOUSE ADVENTURE MAGAZINE
Spotlight Comics: 1987 ($2.00, B&W, 52 pgs., magazine size, one-shot)

1-Deputy Dawg, Heckle & Jeckle backup stories 5.00

MIGHTY MOUSE ADVENTURES (Adventures of... #2 on)
St. John Publishing Co.: November, 1951

	GD 2.0	VG 4.0	FN 6.0	VF 8.0	VF/NM 9.0	NM- 9.2
1	34	68	102	198	319	440

MIGHTY MOUSE ADVENTURE STORIES (Paul Terry's... on-c only)
St. John Publishing Co.: 1953 (50¢, 384 pgs.)

	GD 2.0	VG 4.0	FN 6.0	VF 8.0	VF/NM 9.0	NM- 9.2
nn-Rebound issues	43	86	129	267	446	625

MIGHTY MUTANIMALS (See Teenage Mutant Ninja Turtles Adventures #19)
May, 1991 - No. 3, July, 1991 ($1.00, limited series)
Archie Comics: Apr, 1992 - No. 8, June, 1993 ($1.25)

	GD 2.0	VG 4.0	FN 6.0	VF 8.0	VF/NM 9.0	NM- 9.2
1-3: 1-Story cont'd from TMNT Advs. #19.						5.00
1-4 (1992)						5.00
5-8: 7-1st app. Merdude	1	2	3	5	6	8

MIGHTY SAMSON (Also see Gold Key Champion)
Gold Key/Whitman #32: July, 1964 - No. 20, Nov, 1969; No. 21, Aug, 1972; No. 22, Dec, 1973 - No. 31, Mar, 1976; No. 32, Aug, 1982 (Painted-c #1-31)

	GD 2.0	VG 4.0	FN 6.0	VF 8.0	VF/NM 9.0	NM- 9.2
1-Origin/1st app.; Thorne-a begins	8	16	24	54	90	125
2-5	5	10	15	30	48	65
6-10: 7-Tom Morrow begins, ends #20	3	6	9	20	30	40
11-20	3	6	9	16	23	30
21-31: 21,22-r	2	4	6	11	16	20
32(Whitman, 8/82)-r	2	4	6	8	10	12

MIGHTY THOR (See Thor)

MIKE BARNETT, MAN AGAINST CRIME (TV)
Fawcett Publications: Dec, 1951 - No. 6, Oct, 1952

	GD 2.0	VG 4.0	FN 6.0	VF 8.0	VF/NM 9.0	NM- 9.2
1	19	38	57	109	172	235
2	13	26	39	72	101	130
3,4,6	10	20	30	58	79	100
5- "Market for Morphine" cover/story	14	28	42	80	115	150

MIKE DANGER (See Mickey Spillane's...)

MIKE DEODATO'S...
Caliber Comics: 1996, ($2.95, B&W)

...FALLOUT 3000 #1, **...JONAS** (mag. size) #1,**...PRIME CUTS** (mag. size) #1, **...PROTHEUS** #1,2, **...RAMTHAR** #1,**...RAZOR NIGHTS** #1 3.00

MIKE GRELL'S SABLE (Also see Jon Sable & Sable)
First Comics: Mar, 1990 - No. 10, Dec, 1990 ($1.75)

1-10: r/Jon Sable Freelance #1-10 by Grell 2.50

MIKE MIST MINUTE MIST-ERIES (See Ms. Tree/Mike Mist in 3-D)
Eclipse Comics: April, 1981 ($1.25, B&W, one-shot)

1 2.50

MIKE SHAYNE PRIVATE EYE
Dell Publishing Co.: Nov-Jan, 1962 - No. 3, Sept-Nov, 1962

	GD 2.0	VG 4.0	FN 6.0	VF 8.0	VF/NM 9.0	NM- 9.2
1	4	8	12	24	37	50
2,3	3	6	9	17	25	32

MILITARY COMICS (Becomes Modern Comics #44 on)
Quality Comics Group: Aug, 1941 - No. 43, Oct, 1945

	GD 2.0	VG 4.0	FN 6.0	VF 8.0	VF/NM 9.0	NM- 9.2
1-Origin/1st app. Blackhawk by C. Cuidera (Eisner scripts); Miss America, The Death Patrol by Jack Cole (also #2-7,27-30), & The Blue Tracer by Guardineer; X of the Underground, The Yankee Eagle, Q-Boat & Shot & Shell, Archie Atkins, Loops & Banks by Bud Ernest (Bob Powell)(ends #13) begin	743	1486	2229	5200	9100	13,000
2-Secret War News begins (by McWilliams #2-16); Cole-a; new uniform with yellow circle & hawk's head for Blackhawk	228	456	684	1425	2363	3300
3-Origin/1st app. Chop Chop (9/41)	193	386	579	1206	2003	2800
4	155	310	465	969	1610	2250
5-The Sniper begins; Miss America in costume #4-7	131	262	393	819	1360	1900
6-9: 8-X of the Underground begins (ends #13). 9-The Phantom Clipper begins (ends #16)	90	180	270	563	932	1300
10-Classic Eisner-c	103	206	309	644	1072	1500

Military Comics #38 © QUA

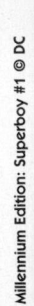

Millennium Edition: Superboy #1 © DC

Millie the Model #3 © MAR

	GD 2.0	VG 4.0	FN 6.0	VF 8.0	VF/NM 9.0	NM- 9.2
11-Flag-c	79	158	237	494	822	1150
12-Blackhawk by Crandall begins, ends #22	90	180	270	563	932	1300
13-15: 14-Private Dogtag begins (ends #83)	66	132	198	413	682	950
16-20: 16-Blue Tracer ends. 17-P.T. Boat begins	59	118	177	369	610	850
21-31: 22-Last Crandall Blackhawk. 23-Shrunken head-c. 27-Death Patrol revived	50	100	150	305	503	700
32-43	43	86	129	262	431	600

NOTE: ***Berg** a-6. **Al Bryant** c-31-34, 38, 40-43. **J. Cole** a-1-3, 27-32. **Crandall** a-12-22; c-13-20. **Cuidera** c-2-9. **Eisner** c-1, 2(part), 9, 10. **Kotsky** c-21-29, 35, 37, 39. **McWilliams** a-2-16. **Powell** a-1-13. **Ward** Blackhawk-30, 31(15 pgs. each); c-30.*

MILK AND CHEESE (Also see Cerebus Bi-Weekly #20)
Slave Labor: 1991 - Present ($2.50, B&W)

	GD	VG	FN	VF	VF/NM	NM-
1-Evan Dorkin story & art in all	4	8	12	24	37	50
1-2nd-6th printings						4.00
2-"Other #1"	3	6	9	16	23	30
2-reprint						3.00
3-"Third #1"	2	4	6	11	16	20
4-"Fourth #1", 5-"First Second Issue"	1	3	4	6	8	10
6,7: 6-"#666"						5.00

NOTE: *Multiple printings of all issues exist and are worth cover price unless listed here.*

MILKMAN MURDERS, THE
Dark Horse Comics: Jun, 2004 - No. 4, Aug, 2004 ($2.99, limited series)

1-4-Casey-s/Parkhouse-a 3.00

MILLENNIUM
DC Comics: Jan, 1988 - No. 8, Feb, 1988 (Weekly limited series)

1-Staton c/a(p) begins 3.00
2-8 2.50

MILLENNIUM EDITION:... (Reprints of classic DC issues)
DC Comics: Feb, 2000 - Feb, 2001 (gold foil cover stamps)

Action Comics #1, Adventure Comics #61, All Star Comics #3, All Star Comics #8, Batman #1, Detective Comics #1, Detective Comics #27, Detective Comics #38, Flash Comics #1, Military Comics #1, More Fun Comics #73, Police Comics #1, Sensation Comics #1, Superman #1, Whiz Comics #2, Wonder Woman #1 -($3.95-c) 4.00
Action Comics #252, Adventure Comics #247, Brave and the Bold #28, Brave and the Bold #85, Crisis on Infinte Earths #1, Detective #225, Detective #327, Detective #359, Detective #395, Flash #123, Gen13 #1, Green Lantern #76, House of Mystery #1, House of Secrets #92, JLA #1, Justice League #1, Mad #1, Man of Steel #1, Mysterious Suspense #1, New Gods, #1, New Teen Titans #1, Our Army at War #81, Plop! #1, Saga of the Swamp Thing #21, Shadow #1, Showcase #4, Showcase #9, Showcase #22, Superman #233, Superman (2nd) #75, Superman's Pal Jimmy Olsen #1, Watchmen #1, WildC.A.T.s #1, Wonder Woman (2nd) #1, World's Finest #71 -($2.50-c) 2.50
All-Star Western #10, Hellblazer #1, More Fun Comics #101, Preacher #1, Sandman #1, Spirit #1, Superboy #1, Superman #76, Young Romance #1-($2.95-c) 3.00
Batman: The Dark Knight Returns #1, Kingdom Come #1 -($5.95-c) 6.00
All Star Comics #3, Batman #1, Justice League #1: Chromium cover 10.00
Crisis on Infinite Earths #1 Chromium cover 20.00

MILLENNIUM FEVER
DC Comics (Vertigo): Oct, 1995 - No.4, Jan, 1996 ($2.50, limited series)

1-4: Duncan Fegredo-c/a 2.50

MILLENNIUM INDEX
Independent Comics Group: Mar, 1988 - No. 2, Mar, 1988 ($2.00)

1,2 2.50

MILLENNIUM 2.5 A.D.
ACG Comics: No. 1, 2000 ($2.95)

1-Reprints 1934 Buck Rogers daily strips #1-48 3.00

MILLIE, THE LOVABLE MONSTER
Dell Publishing Co.: Sept-Nov, 1962 - No. 6, Jan, 1973

	GD	VG	FN	VF	VF/NM	NM-
12-523-211	5	10	15	34	55	75
2(8-10/63)-Bill Woggon c/a	5	10	15	30	48	65
3(8-10/64)	4	8	12	26	41	55
4(7/72), 5(10/72), 6(1/73)	3	6	9	14	19	24

NOTE: ***Woggon** a-3-6; c-3-6. 4 reprints 1; 5 reprints 2; 6 reprints 3.*

MILLIE THE MODEL (See Comedy Comics, A Date With..., Joker Comics #28, Life With..., Mad About..., Marvel Mini-Books, Misty & Modeling With...)
Marvel/Atlas/Marvel Comics(CnPC #1)(SPI/Male/VPI):1945 - No. 207, Dec, 1973

	GD	VG	FN	VF	VF/NM	NM-
1-Origin	90	180	270	567	959	1350
2 (10/46)-Millie becomes The Blonde Phantom to sell Blonde Phantom perfume; a pre-Blonde Phantom app. (see All-Select #11, Fall, 1946)	41	82	123	256	428	600
3-8,10: 4-7-Willie app. 7-Willie smokes extra strong tobacco. 8,10-Kurtzman's "Hey Look".	31	62	93	181	291	400
8-Willie & Rusty app.						
9-Powerhouse Pepper by Wolverton, 4 pgs.	35	70	105	203	327	450
11-Kurtzman-a, "Giggles 'n' Grins"	21	42	63	123	197	270
12,15,17,19,20: 12-Rusty & Hedy Devine app.	15	30	45	94	147	200
13,14,16,18: 13,14,16-Kurtzman's "Hey Look". 13-Hedy Devine app. 18-Dan DeCarlo-a begins	17	34	51	98	154	210
21-30	14	28	42	76	108	140
31-40	7	14	21	50	83	115
41-60	6	12	18	43	69	95
61-99	5	10	15	34	55	75
100	6	12	18	39	62	85
101-130: 107-Jack Kirby app. in story	5	10	15	30	48	65
131-134,136,138-153: 141-Groovy Gears-c/s	4	8	12	24	37	50
135-(2/66) 1st app. Groovy Gears	5	10	15	30	48	65
137-2nd app. Groovy Gears	4	8	12	26	41	55
154-New Millie begins (10/67)	5	10	15	34	55	75
155-190	4	8	12	24	37	50
191,193-199,201-206	3	6	9	20	30	40
192-(52 pgs.)	4	8	12	24	37	50
200,207(Last issue)	4	8	12	24	37	50
(Beware: cut-up pages are common in all Annuals)						
Annual 1(1962)-Early Marvel annual (2nd?)	19	38	57	135	250	365
Annual 2(1963)	13	26	39	95	168	240
Annual 3-5 (1964-1966)	9	18	27	60	100	140
Annual 6-10(1967-11/71)	7	14	21	47	76	105
Queen-Size 11(9/74), 12(1975)	6	12	18	41	66	90

NOTE: ***Dan DeCarlo** a-18-93.*

MILLION DOLLAR DIGEST (Richie Rich... #23 on; also see Richie Rich...)
Harvey Publications: 11/86 - No. 7, 11/87; No. 8, 4/88 - No. 34, Nov, 1994 ($1.25/$1.75, digest size)

	GD	VG	FN	VF	VF/NM	NM-
1	1	2	3	5	6	8
2-8: 8-(68 pgs.)						6.00
9-20: 9-Begin $1.75-c. 14-May not exist	1	2	3	4	5	7
21-34	1	3	4	6	8	10

MILT GROSS FUNNIES (Also see Picture News #1)
Milt Gross, Inc. (ACG?): Aug, 1947 - No. 2, Sept, 1947

	GD	VG	FN	VF	VF/NM	NM-
1	21	42	63	123	197	270
2	15	30	45	85	130	175

MILTON THE MONSTER & FEARLESS FLY (TV)
Gold Key: May, 1966

	GD	VG	FN	VF	VF/NM	NM-
1 (10175-605)	9	18	27	63	107	150

MINIMUM WAGE
Fantagraphics Books: V1#1, July, 1995 ($9.95, B&W, graphic novel, mature)
V2#1, 1995 - Present ($2.95, B&W, mature)

	GD	VG	FN	VF	VF/NM	NM-
V1#1-Bob Fingerman story & art	1	3	4	6	8	10
V2#1-9($2.95): Bob Fingerman story & art. 2-Kevin Nowlan back-c. 4-w/pin-ups. 5-Mignola back-c						3.00
Book Two TPB ('97, $12.95) r/V2#1-5						13.00

MINISTRY OF SPACE
Image Comics: Apr, 2001 - No. 3, Apr, 2004 ($2.95, limited series)

1-3-Warren Ellis-s/Chris Weston-a 3.00
...Vol. 1 Omnibus (3/04, $4.95) r/1&2 5.00
TPB (12/04, $12.95) r/series; sketch & design pages; intro by Mark Millar 13.00

MINOR MIRACLES
DC Comics: 2000 ($12.95, B&W, squarebound)

nn-Will Eisner-s/a 13.00

MINUTE MAN (See Master Comics & Mighty Midget Comics)
Fawcett Publications: Summer, 1941 - No. 3, Spring, 1942 (68 pgs.)

	GD	VG	FN	VF	VF/NM	NM-
1	207	414	621	1304	2202	3100
2,3	123	246	369	775	1308	1840

MINX, THE
DC Comics (Vertigo): Oct, 1998 - No. 8, May, 1999 ($2.50, limited series)

1-8-Milligan-s/Phillips-c/a 3.00

MIRACLE COMICS
Hillman Periodicals: Feb, 1940 - No. 4, Mar, 1941

	GD	VG	FN	VF	VF/NM	NM-
1-Sky Wizard Master of Space, Dash Dixon, Man of Might, Pinkie Parker, Dusty Doyle, The Kid Cop, K-7, Secret Agent, The Scorpion, & Blandu, Jungle Queen begin; Masked Angel only app. (all 1st app.)	187	374	561	1178	1989	2800

Miracleman #12 © ECL

Miss America Magazine #4 © MAR

Miss Fury Comics #1 © MAR

	GD 2.0	VG 4.0	FN 6.0	VF 8.0	VF/NM 9.0	NM- 9.2
2	93	186	279	586	993	1400
3,4: 3-Bill Colt, the Ghost Rider begins. 4-The Veiled Prophet & Bullet Bob (by Burnley) app.	80	160	240	504	852	1200

MIRACLEMAN
Eclipse Comics: Aug, 1985 - No. 15, Nov, 1988; No. 16, Dec, 1989 - No. 24, 1994

	GD	VG	FN	VF	VF/NM	NM-
1-r/British Marvelman series; Alan Moore scripts in #1-16	1	2	3	5	7	9
1-Gold variant (edition of 400, signed by Alan Moore, came with signed & #'d certificate of authenticity)	63	126	189	536	1018	1500
1-Blue variant (edition of 600, came with signed certificate of authenticity)	38	76	114	293	547	800
2-12: 8-Airboy preview. 9,10-Origin Miracleman. 9-Shows graphic scenes of childbirth. 10-Snyder-c	1	2	3	5	6	8
13,14	2	4	6	10	14	18
15-($1.75-c, scarce) end of Kid Miracleman	6	12	18	37	59	80
16-Last Alan Moore-s; 1st $1.95-c (low print)	3	6	9	14	20	25
17,18-($1.95): 17-"The Golden Age" begins, ends #22. Dave McKean-c begins, end #22; Neil Gaiman scripts in #17-24	2	4	6	9	13	16
19-23-($2.50); 23-"The Silver Age" begins; BWS-c	1	3	4	6	8	10
24-Last issue; B. Smith-c	2	4	6	10	14	18
3-D 1 (12/85)	1	2	3	5	7	9

NOTE: Miracleman 3-D #1 (12/85) (2D edition) Interior is the same as the 3-D version except in non 3-D format. Indicia are the same for both versions of the book with only the non 3-D art distinguishing this book from the standard 3-D version. Standard 3-D edition has house ad mentioning the non 3-D edition. Two known copies exist, one in the Michigan State University Special Collection Department. (No known sales)

Book One: A Dream of Flying (1988, $9.95, TPB) r/#1-5; Leach-c	22.00
Book One: A Dream of Flying-Hardcover (1988, $29.95) r/#1-5	70.00
Book Two: The Red King Syndrome (1990, $12.95, TPB) r/#6-10; Bolton-c	22.00
Book Two: The Red King Syndrome-Hardcover (1990, $30.95) r/#6-10	85.00
Book Three: Olympus (1990, $12.95, TPB) r/#11-16	120.00
Book Three: Olympus-Hardcover (1990, $30.95) r/#11-16	260.00
Book Four: The Golden Age (1992, $15.95, TPB) r/#17-22	30.00
Book Four: The Golden Age Hardcover (1992, $33.95) r/#17-22	50.00
Book Four: The Golden Age (1993, $12.99, TPB) new McKean-c	15.00

NOTE: Eclipse archive copies exist for #4,5,8,17,23. Each has a small Miracleman image foil-stamped on the cover. ***Chaykin** c-3.* ***Gulacy** c-7.* ***McKean** c-17-22.* ***B. Smith** c-23, 24.* ***Starlin** c-4.* ***Totleben** a-11-13; c-9, 11-13.* ***Truman** c-6.*

MIRACLEMAN: APOCRYPHA
Eclipse Comics: Nov, 1991 - No. 3, Feb, 1992 ($2.50, limited series)

	GD	VG	FN	VF	VF/NM	NM-
1-3: 1-Stories by Neil Gaiman, Mark Buckingham, Alex Ross & others. 3-Stories by James Robinson, Kelley Jones, Matt Wagner, Neil Gaiman, Mark Buckingham & others	1	2	3	4	5	7
TPB (12/92, $15.95) r/#1-3; Buckingham-c						20.00

MIRACLEMAN FAMILY
Eclipse Comics: May, 1988 - No. 2, Sept, 1988 ($1.95, lim. series, Baxter paper)

1,2: 2-Gulacy-c — 5.00

MIRACLE OF THE WHITE STALLIONS, THE (See Movie Comics)

MIRACLE SQUAD, THE
Upshot Graphics (Fantagraphics Books): Aug, 1986 - No. 4, 1987 ($2.00)

1-4 — 2.50

MIRACLE SQUAD: BLOOD AND DUST, THE
Apple Comics: Jan, 1989 - No. 4, July, 1989 ($1.95, B&W, limited series)

1-4 — 2.50

MISADVENTURES OF MERLIN JONES, THE (See Movie Comics & Merlin Jones as the Monkey's Uncle under Movie Comics)

MISPLACED
Image Comics: May, 2003 - No. 4, Dec, 2004 ($2.95)

1-4: 1-Three covers by Blaylock, Green and Clugston-Major; Blaylock-s/a	3.00
... @17 (12/04, $4.95) Nara from "Dead @17 " app.; Blaylock-s/a	5.00
Somewhere Under the Rainbow TPB (12/04, $10.99, digest size) r/#1-4	11.00

MISS AMERICA COMICS (Miss America Magazine #2 on; also see Blonde Phantom & Marvel Mystery Comics)
Marvel Comics (20CC): 1944 (one-shot)

	GD	VG	FN	VF	VF/NM	NM-
1-2 pgs. pin-ups	187	374	561	1178	1989	2800

MISS AMERICA MAGAZINE (Formerly Miss America; Miss America #51 on)
Miss America Publ. Corp./Marvel/Atlas (MAP): V1#2, Nov, 1944 - No. 93, Nov, 1958

	GD	VG	FN	VF	VF/NM	NM-
V1#2-Photo-c of teenage girl in Miss America costume; Miss America, Patsy Walker (intro.) comic stories plus movie reviews & stories; intro. Buzz Baxter & Hedy Wolfe; 1 pg. origin Miss America	140	280	420	882	1491	2100
3-5-Miss America & Patsy Walker stories	57	114	171	359	605	850
6-Patsy Walker only	29	58	87	169	272	375
V2#1(4/45)-6(9/45)-Patsy Walker continues	14	28	42	80	115	150
V3#1(10/45)-6(4/46)	12	24	36	69	97	125
V4#1(5/46),2,5(9/46)	11	22	33	62	86	110
V4#3(7/46)-Liz Taylor photo-c	27	54	81	158	254	350
V4#4 (8/46; 68 pgs.), V4#6 (10/46; 92 pgs.)	10	20	30	58	79	100
V5#1(11/46)-6(4/47), V6#1(5/47)-3(7/47)	10	20	30	58	79	100
V7#1(8/47)-23(#56, 6/49)	10	20	30	56	76	95
V7#24(#57, 7/49) Kamen-a (becomes Best Western #58 on?)	10	20	30	58	79	100
V7#25(8/49), 27-44(3/52), VII,nn(5/52)	10	20	30	54	72	90
V7#26(9/49)-All comics	10	20	30	58	79	100
V1,nn(7/52)-V1,nn(1/53)(#46-49), V7#50(Spring '53), V1#51-V7?#54(7/53), 55-93	9	18	27	52	69	85

NOTE: Photo-c #1, 4, V2#1, 4, 5, V3#5, V4#3, 4, 6, V7#15, 16, 24, 26, 34, 37, 38. Painted c-3. ***Powell** a-V7#31.*

MISS BEVERLY HILLS OF HOLLYWOOD (See Adventures of Bob Hope)
National Periodical Publ.: Mar-Apr, 1949 - No. 9, July-Aug, 1950 (52 pgs.)

	GD	VG	FN	VF	VF/NM	NM-
1 (Meets Alan Ladd)	60	120	180	378	639	900
2-William Holden photo on-c	44	88	132	273	454	635
3-5: 2-9-Part photo-c. 5-Bob Hope photo on-c	40	80	120	236	383	530
6,7,9: 6-Lucille Ball photo on-c	36	72	108	212	341	470
8-Reagan photo on-c	40	80	120	244	397	550

NOTE: Beverly meets Alan Ladd in #1, Eve Arden #2, Betty Hutton #4, Bob Hope #5.

MISS CAIRO JONES
Croyden Publishers: 1945

	GD	VG	FN	VF	VF/NM	NM-
1-Bob Oksner daily newspaper-r (1st strip story); lingerie panels	20	40	60	115	180	245

MISS FURY COMICS (Newspaper strip reprints)
Timely Comics (NPI 1/CmPI 2/MPC 3-8): Winter, 1942-43 - No. 8, Winter, 1946 (Published twice a year)

	GD	VG	FN	VF	VF/NM	NM-
1-Origin Miss Fury by Tarpe' Mills (68 pgs.) in costume w/paper dolls with cut-out costumes	394	788	1182	2679	4690	6700
2-(60 pgs.)-In costume w/paper dolls	203	406	609	1270	2165	3050
3-(60 pgs.)-In costume w/paper dolls; Hitler-c	157	314	471	989	1670	2350
4-(52 pgs.)-In costume, 2 pgs. w/paper dolls	122	244	366	769	1297	1825
5-(52 pgs.)-In costume w/paper dolls	103	206	309	649	1100	1550
6-(52 pgs.)-Not in costume in inside stories, w/paper dolls	93	186	279	586	993	1400
7,8-(36 pgs.)-In costume 1 pg. each; no paper dolls	82	164	246	517	871	1225

NOTE: ***Schomburg** c-1, 5, 6.*

MISS FURY
Adventure Comics: 1991 - No. 4, 1991 ($2.50, limited series)

1-4: 1-Origin; granddaughter of original Miss Fury	3.00
1-Limited ed. ($4.95)	5.00

MISSION IMPOSSIBLE (TV)
Dell Publ. Co.: May, 1967 - No. 4, Oct, 1968; No. 5, Oct, 1969 (All have photo-c)

	GD	VG	FN	VF	VF/NM	NM-
1	8	16	24	58	97	135
2-5: 5-Reprints #1	6	12	18	41	66	90

MISSION IMPOSSIBLE (Movie)
Marvel Comics (Paramount Comics): May, 1996 ($2.95, one-shot)
(1st Paramount Comics book)

1-Liefeld-c & back-up story — 3.00

MISS LIBERTY (Becomes Liberty Comics)
Burten Publishing Co.: 1945 (MLJ reprints)

	GD	VG	FN	VF	VF/NM	NM-
1-The Shield & Dusty, The Wizard, & Roy, the Super Boy app.; r/Shield-Wizard #13	28	56	84	162	261	360

MISS MELODY LANE OF BROADWAY (See The Adventures of Bob Hope)
National Periodical Publ.: Feb-Mar, 1950 - No. 3, June-July, 1950 (52 pgs.)

	GD	VG	FN	VF	VF/NM	NM-
1-Movie stars photos app. on all-c.	60	120	180	378	639	900
2,3: 3-Ed Sullivan photo on-c.	40	80	120	235	380	525

MISS PEACH
Dell Publishing Co.: Oct-Dec, 1963; 1969

	GD	VG	FN	VF	VF/NM	NM-
1-Jack Mendelsohn-a/script	8	16	24	52	86	120
...Tells You How to Grow (1969; 25¢)-Mel Lazarus-a; also given away (36 pgs.)	5	10	15	32	51	70

MISS PEPPER (See Meet Miss Pepper)

MISS SUNBEAM (See Little Miss...)

MISS VICTORY (See Captain Fearless #1,2, Holyoke One-Shot #3, Veri Best Sure Fire &

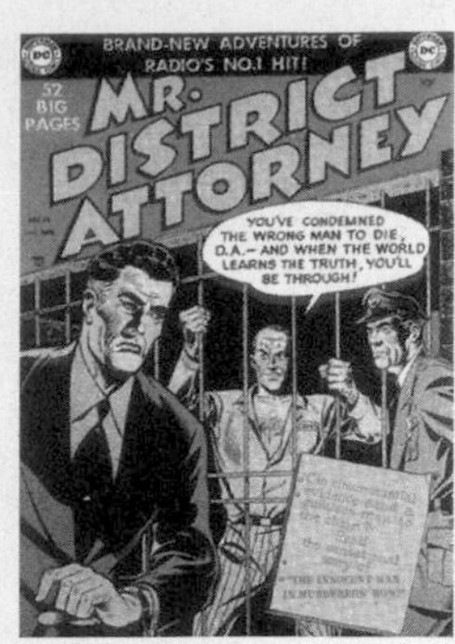

Mr. District Attorney #14 © DC

Mister Miracle #1 © DC

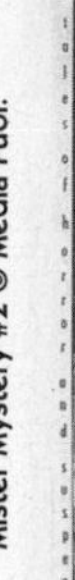

Mister Mystery #2 © Media Publ.

Veri Best Sure Shot Comics)

MISTER AMERICA
Endeavor Comics: Apr, 1994 - No. 2, May, 1994 ($2.95, limited series)

	GD 2.0	VG 4.0	FN 6.0	VF 8.0	VF/NM 9.0	NM- 9.2
1,2						3.00

MR. & MRS. BEANS
United Features Syndicate: No. 11, 1939

	GD 2.0	VG 4.0	FN 6.0	VF 8.0	VF/NM 9.0	NM- 9.2
Single Series 11	35	70	105	203	327	450

MR. & MRS. J. EVIL SCIENTIST (TV)(See The Flintstones & Hanna-Barbera Band Wagon #3)
Gold Key: Nov, 1963 - No. 4, Sept, 1966 (Hanna-Barbera, all 12¢)

	GD 2.0	VG 4.0	FN 6.0	VF 8.0	VF/NM 9.0	NM- 9.2
1	6	12	18	41	66	90
2-4	4	8	12	24	37	50

MR. ANTHONY'S LOVE CLINIC (Based on radio show)
Hillman Periodicals: Nov, 1949 - No. 5, Apr-May, 1950 (52 pgs.)

	GD 2.0	VG 4.0	FN 6.0	VF 8.0	VF/NM 9.0	NM- 9.2
1-Photo-c on all	15	30	45	86	133	180
2	10	20	30	58	79	100
3-5	10	20	30	54	72	90

MISTER BLANK
Amaze Ink: No. 0, Jan, 1996 - No. 14, May, 2000 ($1.75/$2.95, B&W)

	GD 2.0	VG 4.0	FN 6.0	VF 8.0	VF/NM 9.0	NM- 9.2
0-($1.75, 16 pgs.) Origin of Mr. Blank						2.25
1-14-($2.95) Chris Hicks-s/a						3.00

MR. DISTRICT ATTORNEY (Radio/TV)
National Per. Publ.: Jan-Feb, 1948 - No. 67, Jan-Feb, 1959 (1-23: 52 pgs.)

	GD 2.0	VG 4.0	FN 6.0	VF 8.0	VF/NM 9.0	NM- 9.2
1-Howard Purcell c-5-23 (most)	87	174	261	548	924	1300
2	41	82	123	250	413	575
3-5	29	58	87	169	272	375
6-10	23	46	69	133	214	295
11-20	17	34	51	98	154	210
21-43: 43-Last pre-code (1-2/55)	14	28	42	76	108	140
44-67	11	22	33	62	86	110

MR. DISTRICT ATTORNEY (SeeThe Funnies #35)
Dell Publishing Co.: No. 13, 1942

	GD 2.0	VG 4.0	FN 6.0	VF 8.0	VF/NM 9.0	NM- 9.2
Four Color 13-See The Funnies #35 for 1st app.	27	54	81	198	369	540

MISTER E (Also see Books of Magic limited series)
DC Comics: Jun, 1991- No. 4, Sept, 1991($1.75, limited series)

	GD 2.0	VG 4.0	FN 6.0	VF 8.0	VF/NM 9.0	NM- 9.2
1-4-Snyder III-c/a; follow-up to Books of Magic limited series						3.00

MISTER ED, THE TALKING HORSE (TV)
Dell Publishing Co./Gold Key: Mar-May, 1962 - No. 6, Feb, 1964 (All photo-c; photo back-c: 1-6)

	GD 2.0	VG 4.0	FN 6.0	VF 8.0	VF/NM 9.0	NM- 9.2
Four Color 1295	12	24	36	87	156	225
1(11/62) (Gold Key)-Photo-c	9	18	27	60	100	140
2-6: Photo-c	6	12	18	37	59	80

(See March of Comics #244, 260, 282, 290)

MR. GUM (From The Atomics)
Oni Press: April, 2003 ($2.99, one-shot)

	GD 2.0	VG 4.0	FN 6.0	VF 8.0	VF/NM 9.0	NM- 9.2
1-Mike Allred-s/J. Bone-a; Madman & The Atomics app.						3.00

MR. HERO, THE NEWMATIC MAN (See Neil Gaiman's...)

MR. MAGOO (TV) (The Nearsighted..., ...& Gerald McBoing Boing 1954 issues; formerly Gerald McBoing-Boing And ...)
Dell Publishing Co.: No. 6, Nov-Jan, 1953-54; 5/54 - 3-5/62; 9-11/63 - 3-5/65

	GD 2.0	VG 4.0	FN 6.0	VF 8.0	VF/NM 9.0	NM- 9.2
6	10	20	30	68	119	170
Four Color 561(5/54),602(11/54)	10	20	30	68	119	170
Four Color 1235(#1, 12-2/62),1305(#2, 3-5/62)	8	16	24	56	93	130
3(9-11/63) - 5	7	14	21	50	83	115
Four Color 1235(12-536-505)(3-5/65)-2nd Printing	6	12	18	41	66	90

MR. MAJESTIC (See WildC.A.T.S.)
DC Comics (WildStorm): Sept, 1999 - No. 9, May, 2000 ($2.50)

	GD 2.0	VG 4.0	FN 6.0	VF 8.0	VF/NM 9.0	NM- 9.2
1-9: 1-McGuinness-a/Casey & Holguin-s. 2-Two covers						2.50

TPB (2002, $14.95) r/#1-6 & Wildstorm Spotlight #1

MISTER MIRACLE (1st series) (See Cancelled Comic Cavalcade)
National Periodical Publications/DC Comics: 3-4/71 - V4#18, 2-3/74; V5#19, 9/77 - V6#25, 8-9/78; 1987 (Fourth World)

	GD 2.0	VG 4.0	FN 6.0	VF 8.0	VF/NM 9.0	NM- 9.2
1-1st app. Mr. Miracle (#1-3 are 15¢)	8	16	24	54	86	120
2,3: 2-Intro. Granny Goodness. 3-Last 15¢ issue	4	8	12	28	44	60
4-8: 4-Intro. Barda; Boy Commandos-r begin; all 52 pgs.	4	8	12	28	44	60
9-18: 9-Origin Mr. Miracle; Darkseid cameo. 15-Intro/1st app. Shilo Norman. 18-Barda & Scott Free wed; New Gods app. & Darkseid cameo; Last Kirby issue.	3	6	9	16	22	28
19-25 (1977-78)	1	2	3	6	8	10
Special 1(1987, $1.25, 52 pgs.)						3.00
Jack Kirby's Fourth World TPB ('01, $12.95) B&W&Grey-toned reprint of #11-18; Mark Evanier intro.						13.00
Jack Kirby's Mister Miracle TPB ('98, $12.95) B&W&Grey-toned reprint of #1-10; David Copperfield intro.						13.00

NOTE: **Austin** a-19i. **Ditko** a-6r. **Golden** a-23-25p; c-25p. **Heath** a-24i, 25i; c-25i. **Kirby** a(p)/c-1-18. **Nasser** a-19i. **Rogers** a-19-22p; c-19, 20p, 21p, 22-24. 4-8 contain **Simon & Kirby** Boy Commandos reprints from Detective 82,76, Boy Commandos 1, 3 & Detective 64 in that order.

MISTER MIRACLE (2nd Series) (See Justice League)
DC Comics: Jan, 1989 - No. 28, June, 1991 ($1.00/$1.25)

	GD 2.0	VG 4.0	FN 6.0	VF 8.0	VF/NM 9.0	NM- 9.2
1-28: 13,14-Lobo app. 22-1st new Mr. Miracle w/new costume						2.50

MISTER MIRACLE (3rd Series)
DC Comics: Apr, 1996 - No. 7, Oct, 1996 ($1.95)

	GD 2.0	VG 4.0	FN 6.0	VF 8.0	VF/NM 9.0	NM- 9.2
1-7: 2-Vs. JLA. 6-Simonson-c						2.50

MR. MIRACLE (See Capt. Fearless #1 & Holyoke One-Shot #4)

MR. MONSTER (1st Series)(Doc Stearn... #7 on; See Airboy-Mr. Monster Special, Dark Horse Presents, Super Duper Comics & Vanguard Illustrated #7)
Eclipse Comics: Jan, 1985 - No. 10, June, 1987 ($1.75, Baxter paper)

	GD 2.0	VG 4.0	FN 6.0	VF 8.0	VF/NM 9.0	NM- 9.2
1-3: 1-1st story-r from Vanguard Ill. #7(1st app.). 2-Dave Stevens-c. 3-Alan Moore scripts; Wolverton-r/Weird Mysteries #5.						5.00
4-10: 6-Ditko-r/Fantastic Fears #5 plus new Giffen-a. 10- "6-D" issue						4.00

MR. MONSTER
Dark Horse Comics: Feb, 1988 - No. 8, July, 1991 ($1.75, B&W)

	GD 2.0	VG 4.0	FN 6.0	VF 8.0	VF/NM 9.0	NM- 9.2
1-7						3.00
8-($4.95, 60 pgs.)-Origins conclusion						5.00

MR. MONSTER ATTACKS! (Doc Stearn...)
Tundra Publ.: Aug, 1992 - No. 3, Oct, 1992 ($3.95, limited series, 32 pgs.)

	GD 2.0	VG 4.0	FN 6.0	VF 8.0	VF/NM 9.0	NM- 9.2
1-3: Michael T. Gilbert-a/scripts; Gilbert/Dorman painted-c						4.00

MR. MONSTER PRESENTS (CRACK-A-BOOM!)
Caliber Comics: 1997 - No. 3, 1997 ($2.95, B&W&Red, limited series)

	GD 2.0	VG 4.0	FN 6.0	VF 8.0	VF/NM 9.0	NM- 9.2
1-3: Michael T. Gilbert-a/scripts: 1-Wraparound-c						3.00

MR. MONSTER'S GAL FRIDAY...KELLY!
Image Comics: Jan, 2000 - No. 3, May, 2004 ($3.50, B&W)

	GD 2.0	VG 4.0	FN 6.0	VF 8.0	VF/NM 9.0	NM- 9.2
1-3-Michael T. Gilbert-c; story & art by various. 3-Alan Moore-s						3.50

MR. MONSTER'S SUPER-DUPER SPECIAL
Eclipse Comics: May, 1986 - No. 8, July, 1987

	GD 2.0	VG 4.0	FN 6.0	VF 8.0	VF/NM 9.0	NM- 9.2
1-(5/86)...3-D High Octane Horror #1						5.00
1-(5/86)...2-D version, 100 copies	2	4	6	9	13	16
2-(8/86)...High Octane Horror #1, 3-(9/86)...True Crime #1, 4-(11/86)...True Crime #2, 5-(1/87)...Hi-Voltage Super Science #1, 6-(3/87)...High Shock Schlock #1, 7-(5/87)...High Shock Schlock #2, 8-(7/87)...Weird Tales Of The Future #1						4.00

NOTE: **Jack Cole** r-3, 4. **Evans** a-2r. **Kubert** a-1r. **Powell** a-5r. **Wolverton** a-2r, 7r, 8r.

MR. MONSTER VS. GORZILLA
Image Comics: July, 1998 ($2.95, one-shot)

	GD 2.0	VG 4.0	FN 6.0	VF 8.0	VF/NM 9.0	NM- 9.2
1-Michael T. Gilbert-a						3.00

MR. MONSTER: WORLDS WAR TWO
Atomeka Press: 2004 ($6.99, one-shot)

	GD 2.0	VG 4.0	FN 6.0	VF 8.0	VF/NM 9.0	NM- 9.2
nn-Michael T. Gilbert-s/George Freeman-a; two covers by Horley & Dorman						7.00

MR. MUSCLES (Formerly Blue Beetle #18-21)
Charlton Comics: No. 22, Mar, 1956; No. 23, Aug, 1956

	GD 2.0	VG 4.0	FN 6.0	VF 8.0	VF/NM 9.0	NM- 9.2
22,23	8	16	24	44	57	70

MR. MXYZPTLK (VILLAINS)
DC Comics: Feb, 1998 ($1.95, one-shot)

	GD 2.0	VG 4.0	FN 6.0	VF 8.0	VF/NM 9.0	NM- 9.2
1-Grant-s/Morgan-a/Pearson-c						2.50

MISTER MYSTERY (Tales of Horror and Suspense)
Mr. Publ. (Media Publ.) No. 1-3/SPM Publ./Stanmore (Aragon): Sept, 1951 - No. 19, Oct, 1954

	GD 2.0	VG 4.0	FN 6.0	VF 8.0	VF/NM 9.0	NM- 9.2
1-Kurtzman*esque* horror story	93	186	279	586	993	1400
2,3-Kurtzman*esque* story. 3-Anti-Wertham edit.	62	124	186	391	658	925
4,6: Bondage-c; 6-Torture	62	124	186	391	658	925
5,8,10	56	112	168	353	594	835

Mr. T and the T-Force #1 © NOW

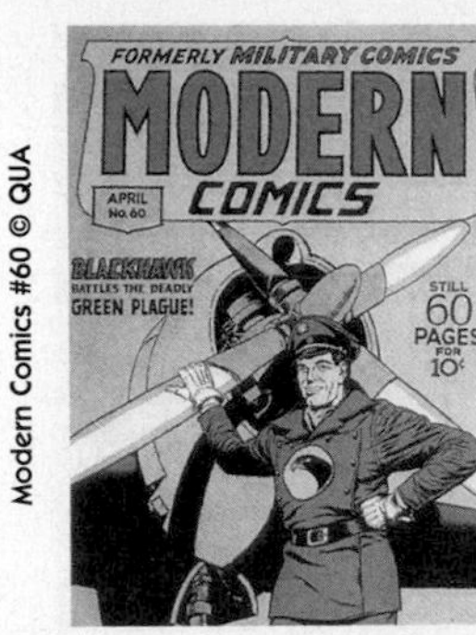

Modern Comics #60 © QUA

Mod Wheels #14 © GK

	GD 2.0	VG 4.0	FN 6.0	VF 8.0	VF/NM 9.0	NM- 9.2
7- "The Brain Bats of Venus" by Wolverton; partially re-used in Weird Tales of the Future #7	125	250	375	788	1332	1875
9-Nostrand-a	56	112	168	353	594	835
11-Wolverton "Robot Woman" story/Weird Mysteries #2, cut up, rewritten & partially redrawn	85	170	255	536	906	1275
12-Classic injury to eye-c	133	266	399	838	1419	2000
13-17,19: 15- "Living Dead" junkie story. 16-Bondage-c. 17-Severed heads-c. 19-Reprints	44	88	132	273	454	635
18- "Robot Woman" by Wolverton reprinted from Weird Mysteries #2; decapitation, bondage-c	63	126	189	397	674	950

NOTE: *Andru a-1, 2p, 3p.* ***Andru/Esposito*** *c-1-3.* ***Baily*** *c-10-18(most).* ***Mortellaro*** *c-5-7. Bondage c-7, 16. Some issues have graphic dismemberment scenes.*

MR. PUNCH
DC Comics (Vertigo): 1994 ($24.95, one-shot)

	GD 2.0	VG 4.0	FN 6.0	VF 8.0	VF/NM 9.0	NM- 9.2
nn (Hard-c) Gaiman scripts; McKean-c/a						40.00
nn (Soft-c)						15.00

MISTER Q (See Mighty Midget Comics & Our Flag Comics #5)

MR. RISK (Formerly All Romances; Men Against Crime #3 on)(Also see Our Flag Comics & Super-Mystery Comics)
Ace Magazines: No. 7, Oct, 1950; No. 2, Dec, 1950

	GD 2.0	VG 4.0	FN 6.0	VF 8.0	VF/NM 9.0	NM- 9.2
7,2	10	20	30	54	72	90

MR. SCARLET & PINKY (See Mighty Midget Comics)

MR. T
APComics: May, 2005 ($3.50)

	GD 2.0	VG 4.0	FN 6.0	VF 8.0	VF/NM 9.0	NM- 9.2
1-Chris Bunting-s/Neil Edwards-a						3.50

MR. T AND THE T-FORCE
Now Comics: June, 1993 - No. 10, May, 1994 ($1.95, color)

	GD 2.0	VG 4.0	FN 6.0	VF 8.0	VF/NM 9.0	NM- 9.2
1-10-Newsstand editions: 1-7-polybagged with photo trading card in each. 1,2-Neal Adams-c/a(p). 3-Dave Dorman painted-c						2.50
1-10-Direct Sale editions polybagged w/line drawn trading cards. 1-Contains gold foil trading card by Neal Adams						2.50

MISTER UNIVERSE (Professional wrestler)
Mr. Publications Media Publ. (Stanmor, Aragon): July, 1951; No. 2, Oct, 1951 - No. 5, April, 1952

	GD 2.0	VG 4.0	FN 6.0	VF 8.0	VF/NM 9.0	NM- 9.2
1	22	44	66	127	204	280
2- "Jungle That Time Forgot", (24 pg. story); Andru/Esposito-c	14	28	42	80	115	150
3-Marijuana story	14	28	42	80	115	150
4,5- "Goes to War" cover/stories	11	22	33	60	83	105

MISTER X (See Vortex)
Mr. Publications/Vortex Comics/Caliber V3#1 on: 6/84 - No. 14, 8/88 ($1.50/$2.25, direct sales, coated paper);V2#1, Apr, 1989 - V2#12, Mar, 1990 ($2.00/$2.50, B&W, newsprint) V3#1, 1996 - Present ($2.95, B&W)

	GD 2.0	VG 4.0	FN 6.0	VF 8.0	VF/NM 9.0	NM- 9.2
1-14: 11-Dave McKean story & art (6 pgs.)						4.00
V2 #1-12: 1-11 (Second Coming, B&W): 1-Four diff.-c. 10-Photo-c						3.00
V3 #1-4						3.00
Return of... ($11.95, graphic novel)-r/V1#1-4						12.00
Return of... ($34.95, hardcover limited edition)-r/1-4						35.00
Special (no date, 1990?)						3.00

MISTY
Marvel Comics (Star Comics): Dec, 1985 - No. 6, May, 1986 (Limited series)

	GD 2.0	VG 4.0	FN 6.0	VF 8.0	VF/NM 9.0	NM- 9.2
1-6: Millie The Model's niece						3.00

MITZI COMICS (Becomes Mitzi's Boy Friend #2-7)(See All Teen)
Timely Comics: Spring, 1948 (one-shot)

	GD 2.0	VG 4.0	FN 6.0	VF 8.0	VF/NM 9.0	NM- 9.2
1-Kurtzman's "Hey Look" plus 3 pgs. "Giggles 'n' Grins"	26	52	78	154	247	340

MITZI'S BOY FRIEND (Formerly Mitzi Comics; becomes Mitzi's Romances)
Marvel Comics (TCI): No. 2, June, 1948 - No. 7, April, 1949

	GD 2.0	VG 4.0	FN 6.0	VF 8.0	VF/NM 9.0	NM- 9.2
2	15	30	45	83	124	165
3-7	13	26	39	72	101	130

MITZI'S ROMANCES (Formerly Mitzi's Boy Friend)
Timely/Marvel Comics (TCI): No. 8, June, 1949 - No. 10, Dec, 1949

	GD 2.0	VG 4.0	FN 6.0	VF 8.0	VF/NM 9.0	NM- 9.2
8-Becomes True Life Tales #8 (10/49) on?	14	28	42	76	108	140
9,10: 10-Painted-c	11	22	33	62	86	110

MNEMOVORE
DC Comics (Vertigo): Jun, 2005 - No. 6, Nov, 2005 ($2.99, limited series)

	GD 2.0	VG 4.0	FN 6.0	VF 8.0	VF/NM 9.0	NM- 9.2
1-6-Rodionoff & Fawkes-s/Huddleston-a/c						3.00

MOBY DICK (See Feature Presentations #6, and King Classics)
Dell Publishing Co.: No. 717, Aug, 1956

	GD 2.0	VG 4.0	FN 6.0	VF 8.0	VF/NM 9.0	NM- 9.2
Four Color 717-Movie, Gregory Peck photo-c	8	16	24	56	93	130

MOBY DUCK (See Donald Duck #112 & Walt Disney Showcase #2,11)
Gold Key (Disney): Oct, 1967 - No. 11, Oct, 1970; No. 12, Jan, 1974 - No. 30, Feb, 1978

	GD 2.0	VG 4.0	FN 6.0	VF 8.0	VF/NM 9.0	NM- 9.2
1	3	6	9	21	32	42
2-5	2	4	6	11	16	20
6-11	2	4	6	9	13	16
12-30: 21,30-r	1	3	4	6	8	10

MODEL FUN (With Bobby Benson)
Harle Publications: No. 2, Fall, 1954 - No. 5, July, 1955

	GD 2.0	VG 4.0	FN 6.0	VF 8.0	VF/NM 9.0	NM- 9.2
2-Bobby Benson	7	14	21	35	43	50
3-5-Bobby Benson	5	10	15	23	28	32

MODELING WITH MILLIE (Formerly Life With Millie)
Atlas/Marvel Comics (Male Publ.): No. 21, Feb, 1963 - No. 54, June, 1967

	GD 2.0	VG 4.0	FN 6.0	VF 8.0	VF/NM 9.0	NM- 9.2
21	8	16	24	56	93	130
22-30	5	10	15	32	51	70
31-53	4	8	12	26	41	55
54-Last issue; Gears-c & 6 pg. story; Beatles swipe imitators; FF #63 comic appears in story; "Millie the Marvel" 6 pg. story as super-hero	4	8	12	28	44	60

MODERN COMICS (Formerly Military Comics #1-43)
Quality Comics Group: No. 44, Nov, 1945 - No. 102, Oct, 1950

	GD 2.0	VG 4.0	FN 6.0	VF 8.0	VF/NM 9.0	NM- 9.2
44-Blackhawk continues	53	106	159	337	556	775
45-52: 49-1st app. Fear, Lady Adventuress	40	80	120	238	374	510
53-Torchy by Ward begins (9/46)	42	84	126	258	422	585
54-60: 55-J. Cole-a	35	70	105	201	318	435
61-Classic-c	38	76	114	219	347	475
62-77,79,80: 73-J. Cole-a	33	66	99	190	300	410
78-1st app. Madame Butterfly	36	72	108	208	329	450
81-99,101: 82,83-One pg. J. Cole-a. 83-Last 52 pg. issue 99-Blackhawks on the moon-c/story	31	62	93	178	282	385
100	33	66	99	190	300	410
102-(Scarce) J. Cole-a; Spirit by Eisner app.	40	80	120	235	368	500

NOTE: ***Al Bryant*** *c-44-51, 54, 55, 66, 69.* ***Jack Cole*** *a-55, 73.* ***Crandall*** *Blackhawk-#46, 47, 50, 51, 54, 56, 58-60, 64, 67-70, 73, 74, 76-78, 80-83; c-60-65, 67, 68, 70-95.* ***Crandall/Cuidera*** *c-56-59, 96-102.* ***Gustavson*** *a-4/, 49.* ***Ward*** *Blackhawk-#52, 53, 55 (15 pgs. each). Torchy in #53-102; by* ***Ward*** *only in #53-89(9/49); by* ***Gil Fox*** *#92, 93, 102.*

MODERN LOVE
E. C. Comics: June-July, 1949 - No. 8, Aug-Sept, 1950

	GD 2.0	VG 4.0	FN 6.0	VF 8.0	VF/NM 9.0	NM- 9.2
1-Feldstein, Ingels-a	75	150	234	491	833	1175
2-Craig/Feldstein-c/s	50	100	150	310	518	725
3	45	90	135	279	465	650
4-6 (Scarce): 4-Bra/panties panels	55	110	165	347	586	825
7,8	45	90	135	279	465	650

NOTE: ***Craig*** *a-3.* ***Feldstein*** *a-in most issues; c-1, 2i, 3-8.* ***Harrison*** *a-4.* ***Iger*** *a-6-8.* ***Ingels*** *a-1, 2, 4-7.* ***Palais*** *a-5.* ***Wood*** *a-7.* ***Wood/Harrison*** *a-5-7. (Canadian reprints known; see Table of Contents.)*

MOD LOVE
Western Publishing Co.: 1967 (50¢, 36 pgs.)

	GD 2.0	VG 4.0	FN 6.0	VF 8.0	VF/NM 9.0	NM- 9.2
1-(Low print)	6	12	18	37	59	80

MODNIKS, THE
Gold Key: Aug, 1967 - No. 2, Aug, 1970

	GD 2.0	VG 4.0	FN 6.0	VF 8.0	VF/NM 9.0	NM- 9.2
10206-708(#1)	4	8	12	22	34	45
2	3	6	9	16	22	28

MOD SQUAD (TV)
Dell Publishing Co.: Jan, 1969 - No. 3, Oct, 1969 - No. 8, April, 1971

	GD 2.0	VG 4.0	FN 6.0	VF 8.0	VF/NM 9.0	NM- 9.2
1-Photo-c	7	14	21	45	73	100
2-4: 2-4-Photo-c	4	8	12	28	44	60
5-8: 8-Photo-c; Reprints #2	4	8	12	24	37	50

MOD WHEELS
Gold Key: Mar, 1971 - No. 19, Jan, 1976

	GD 2.0	VG 4.0	FN 6.0	VF 8.0	VF/NM 9.0	NM- 9.2
1	4	8	12	26	41	55
2-9	3	6	9	16	23	30
10-19: 11,15-Extra 16 pgs. ads	3	6	9	14	19	24

MOE & SHMOE COMICS
O. S. Publ. Co.: Spring, 1948 - No. 2, Summer, 1948

	GD 2.0	VG 4.0	FN 6.0	VF 8.0	VF/NM 9.0	NM- 9.2
1	9	18	27	47	61	75
2	6	12	18	31	38	45

MOEBIUS (Graphic novel)

The Monarchy #1 © DC

Monster Hunters #11 © CC

Monster Pile-Up #1 © Image

GD 2.0 | VG 4.0 | FN 6.0 | VF 8.0 | VF/NM 9.0 | NM- 9.2

Marvel Comics (Epic Comics): Oct, 1987 - No. 6, 1988; No. 7, 1990; No. 8, 1991 ($9.95, 8x11", mature)

1,2,4-6,8: (#2, 2nd printing, $9.95) 3 6 9 14 20 25
3,7,0: 3-(1st & 2nd printings, $12.95). 0 (1990, $12.95) 3 6 9 16 23 30
Moebius I-Signed & #'d hard-c ($45.95, Graphitti Designs, 1,500 copies printed)-r/#1-3 5 10 15 32 51 70

MOEBIUS COMICS
Caliber: May, 1996 - No. 6 ($2.95, B&W)

1-6: Moebius-c/a. 1-William Stout-a 4.00

MOEBIUS: THE MAN FROM CIGURI
Dark Horse Comics: 1996 ($7.95, digest-size)

nn-Moebius-c/a 1 2 3 5 7 9

MOLLY MANTON'S ROMANCES (Romantic Affairs #3)
Marvel Comics (SePI): Sept, 1949 - No. 2, Dec, 1949 (52 pgs.)

1-Photo-c (becomes Blaze the Wonder Collie #2 (10/49) on? & Molly Manton's Romances #2 17 34 51 98 154 210
2-Titled "Romances of..."; photo-c 13 26 39 72 101 130

MOLLY O'DAY (Super Sleuth)
Avon Periodicals: February, 1945 (1st Avon comic)

1-Molly O'Day, The Enchanted Dagger by Tuska (r/Yankee #1), Capt'n Courage, Corporal Grant app. 55 110 165 347 586 825

MOMENT OF SILENCE
Marvel Comics: Feb, 2002 ($3.50, one-shot)

1-Tributes to the heroes and victims of Sept. 11; s/a by various 3.50

MONARCHY, THE (Also see The Authority and StormWatch)
DC Comics (WildStorm): Apr, 2001 - No. 12, May, 2002 ($2.50)

1-12: 1-McCrea & Leach-a/Young-s 2.50
Bullets Over Babylon TPB (2001, $12.95) r/#1-4, Authority #21 13.00

MONKEES, THE (TV)(Also see Circus Boy, Groovy, Not Brand Echh #3, Teen-Age Talk, Teen Beam & Teen Beat)
Dell Publishing Co.: March, 1967 - No. 17, Oct, 1969

1-Photo-c 10 20 30 68 119 170
2-17: All photo-c. 17-Reprints #1 6 12 18 41 66 90

MONKEY AND THE BEAR, THE
Atlas Comics (ZPC): Sept, 1953 - No. 3, Jan, 1954

1-Howie Post-c/a in all; funny animal 9 18 27 52 69 85
2,3 7 14 21 37 46 55

MONKEYMAN AND O'BRIEN (Also see Dark Horse Presents #80, 100-5, Gen^{13}/..., Hellboy: Seed of Destruction, & San Diego Comic Con #2)
Dark Horse Comics (Legend): Jul, 1996 - No. 3, Sept, 1996 ($2.95, lim. series)

1-3: New stories; Art Adams-c/a/scripts 3.50
nn-(2/96, $2.95)-r/back-up stories from Hellboy: Seed of Destruction; Adams-c/a/scripts 3.50

MONKEYSHINES COMICS
Ace Periodicals/Publishers Specialists/Current Books/Unity Publ.: Summer, 1944 - No. 27, July, 1949

1-Funny animal 14 28 42 82 121 160
2-(Aut/44) 9 18 27 50 65 80
3-10: 3-(Win/44) 8 16 24 44 57 70
11-18,20-27: 23,24-Fago-c/a 8 16 24 40 50 60
19-Frazetta-a 9 18 27 50 65 80

MONKEY'S UNCLE, THE (See Merlin Jones As... under Movie Comics)

MONOLITH, THE
DC Comics: Apr, 2004 - No. 12, Mar, 2005 ($3.50/$2.95)

1-($3.50) Palmiotti & Gray-s/Winslade-a 3.50
2-12-($2.95): 6-8-Batman app.; Coker-a 3.00

MONROES, THE (TV)
Dell Publishing Co.: Apr, 1967

1-Photo-c 3 6 9 18 27 35

MONSTER
Fiction House Magazines: 1953 - No. 2, 1953

1-Dr. Drew by Grandenetti; reprint from Rangers Comics #48; Whitman-c 52 104 156 322 536 750
2-Whitman-c 40 80 120 235 380 525

MONSTER CRIME COMICS (Also see Crime Must Stop)
Hillman Periodicals: Oct, 1952 (15¢, 52 pgs.)

1 (Scarce) 147 294 441 926 1563 2200

MONSTER HOUSE (Companion to the 2006 movie)
IDW Publishing: June, 2006 ($7.99, one-shot)

nn-Two stories about Bones and Skull by Joshua Dysart and Simeon Wilkins 8.00

MONSTER HOWLS (Magazine)
Humor-Vision: December, 1966 (Satire) (35¢, 68 pgs.)

1 6 12 18 39 62 85

MONSTER HUNTERS
Charlton Comics: Aug, 1975 - No. 9, Jan, 1977; No. 10, Oct, 1977 - No. 18, Feb, 1979

1-Howard-a; Newton-c; 1st Countess Von Bludd and Colonel Whiteshroud 3 6 9 17 25 32
2-Sutton-c/a; Ditko-a 2 4 6 13 18 22
3,4,5,7: 4-Sutton-c/a 2 4 6 8 11 14
6,8,10: 6,8,10-Ditko-a 2 4 6 9 13 16
9,11,12 1 3 4 6 8 10
13,15,18-Ditko-c/a. 18-Sutton-a 2 4 6 9 13 16
14-Special all-Ditko issue 3 6 9 16 23 30
16,17-Sutton-a 1 2 3 5 7 9
1,2 (Modern Comics reprints, 1977) 4.00

NOTE: ***Ditko** a-2, 6, 8, 10, 13-15r, 18r; c-13-15, 18. **Howard** a-1, 3, 17; r-13. **Morisi** a-1. **Staton** a-1, 13. **Sutton** a-2, 4; c-2, 4; r-16-18. **Zeck** a-4-9. Reprints in #12-18.*

MONSTER MADNESS (Magazine)
Marvel Comics: 1972 - No. 3, 1973 (60¢, B&W)

1-3: Stories by "Sinister" Stan Lee 4 8 12 24 37 50

MONSTER MAN
Image Comics (Action Planet): Sept, 1997 ($2.95, B&W)

1-Mike Manley-c/s/a 3.00

MONSTER MASTERWORKS
Marvel Comics: 1989 ($12.95, TPB)

nn-Reprints 1960's monster stories; art by Kirby, Ditko, Ayers, Everett 18.00

MONSTER MATINEE
Chaos! Comics: Oct, 1997 - No. 3, Oct, 1997 ($2.50, limited series)

1-3: pin-ups 2.50

MONSTER MENACE
Marvel Comics: Dec, 1993 - No. 4, Mar, 1994 ($1.25, limited series)

1-4: Pre-code Atlas horror reprints. 6.00

NOTE: ***Ditko**-r & **Kirby**-r in all.*

MONSTER OF FRANKENSTEIN (See Frankenstein and Essential Monster of Frankenstein)

MONSTER PILE-UP
Image Comics: Aug, 2008 - Present ($1.99)

1-New short stories of Astounding Wolf-Man, Firebreather, Perhapanauts, Proof 2.25

MONSTERS ATTACK (Magazine)
Globe Communications Corpse: Sept, 1989 - No. 5, Dec, 1990 (B&W)

1-5-Ditko, Morrow, J. Severin-a. 5-Toth, Morrow-a 1 2 3 4 5 7

MONSTERS ON THE PROWL (Chamber of Darkness #1-8)
Marvel Comics Group (No. 13,14: 52 pgs.): No. 9, 2/71 - No. 27, 11/73; No. 28, 6/74 - No. 30, 10/74

9-Barry Smith inks 4 8 12 22 34 45
10-12,15: 12-Last 15¢ issue 3 6 9 14 20 26
13,14-(52 pgs.) 3 6 9 17 25 32
16-(4/72)-King Kull 4th app.; Severin-c 3 6 9 17 25 32
17-30 2 4 6 11 16 20

NOTE: ***Ditko** r-9, 14, 16. **Kirby** r-10-17, 21, 23, 25, 27, 28, 30; c-9, 25. **Kirby/Ditko** r-14, 17-20, 22, 24, 26, 29. **Marie/John Severin** a-16(Kull). 9-13, 15 contain one new story. Woodish art by **Reese**-11. King Kull created by Robert E. Howard.*

MONSTERS TO LAUGH WITH (Magazine) (Becomes Monsters Unlimited #4)
Marvel Comics Group: 1964 - No. 3, 1965 (B&W)

1-Humor by Stan Lee 7 14 21 45 73 100
2,3 4 8 12 26 41 55

MONSTERS UNLEASHED (Magazine)
Marvel Comics Group: July, 1973 - No. 11, Apr, 1975; Summer, 1975 (B&W)

1-Soloman Kane sty; Werewolf app. 5 10 15 30 48 65
2-4: 2-The Frankenstein Monster begins, ends #10. 3-Neal Adams-c/a; The Man-Thing begins (origin-r); Son of Satan preview. 4-Werewolf app. 4 8 12 24 37 50

Monte Hale Western #33 © FAW

Moon Girl #3 © WMG

Moon Knight (4th series) #7 © MAR

GD VG FN VF VF/NM NM-
2.0 4.0 6.0 8.0 9.0 9.2

5-7: Werewolf in all. 5-Man-Thing. 7-Williamson-a(r) 3 6 9 18 27 35
8-11: 8-Man-Thing; N. Adams-r. 9-Man-Thing; Wendigo app. 10-Origin Tigra
3 6 9 19 29 38
Annual 1 (Summer,1975, 92 pgs.)-Kane-a 3 6 9 18 27 35
NOTE: ***Boris*** *c-2, 6.* ***Brunner*** *a-2; c-11.* ***J. Buscema*** *a-2p, 4p, 5p.* ***Colan*** *a-1, 4r.* ***Davis*** *a-3r.* ***Everett*** *a-2r.* ***G. Kane*** *a-3.* ***Krigstein*** *r-4.* ***Morrow*** *a-3; c-1.* ***Perez*** *a-8.* ***Ploog*** *a-6.* ***Reese*** *a-1, 2.* ***Tuska*** *a-3p.* ***Wildey*** *a-1r.*

MONSTERS UNLIMITED (Magazine) (Formerly Monsters To Laugh With)
Marvel Comics Group: No. 4, 1965 - No. 7, 1966 (B&W)

4-7 4 8 12 26 41 55

MONSTER WORLD
DC Comics (WildStorm): Jul, 2001 - No. 4, Oct, 2001 ($2.50, limited series)

1-4-Lobdell-s/Meglia-c/a 2.50

MONTANA KID, THE (See Kid Montana)

MONTE HALE WESTERN (Movie star; Formerly Mary Marvel #1-28; also see Fawcett Movie Comic, Motion Picture Comics, Picture News #8, Real Western Hero, Six-Gun Heroes, Western Hero & XMas Comics)
Fawcett Publ./Charlton No. 83 on: No. 29, Oct, 1948 - No. 88, Jan, 1956

29-(#1, 52 pgs.)-Photo-c begin, end #82; Monte Hale & his horse Pardner begin
36 72 108 208 329 450
30-(52 pgs.)-Big Bow and Little Arrow begin, end #34; Captain Tootsie by Beck
16 32 48 94 147 200
31-36,38-40-(52 pgs.): 34-Gabby Hayes begins, ends #80. 39-Captain Tootsie by Beck
14 28 42 81 118 155
37,41,45,49-(36 pgs.) 11 22 33 64 90 115
42-44,46-48,50-(52 pgs.): 47-Big Bow & Little Arrow app.
13 26 39 72 101 130
51,52,54-56,58,59-(52 pgs.) 11 22 33 60 83 105
53,57-(36 pgs.): 53-Slim Pickens app. 9 18 27 52 69 85
60-81: 36 pgs. #60-on. 80-Gabby Hayes ends 9 18 27 50 65 80
82-Last Fawcett issue (6/53) 10 20 30 58 79 100
83-1st Charlton issue (2/55); B&W photo back-c begin. Gabby Hayes returns, ends #86
11 22 33 64 90 115
84 (4/55) 9 18 27 52 69 85
85-86 9 18 27 50 65 80
87,88: 87-Wolverton-r, 1/2 pg. 88-Last issue 9 18 27 52 69 85
NOTE: ***Gil Kane*** *a-33?, 34? Rocky Lane 1 pg. (Carnation ad)-38, 40, 41, 43, 44, 46, 55.*

MONTY HALL OF THE U.S. MARINES (See With the Marines...)
Toby Press: Aug, 1951 - No. 11, Apr, 1953

1 12 24 36 69 97 125
2 8 16 24 42 54 65
3-5 8 16 24 40 50 60
6-11 7 14 21 37 46 55
NOTE: *Full page pin-ups (Pin-Up Pete) by* ***Jack Sparling*** *in #1-9.*

MOON, A GIRL...ROMANCE, A (Becomes Weird Fantasy #13 on; formerly Moon Girl #1-8)
E. C. Comics: No. 9, Sept-Oct, 1949 - No. 12, Mar-Apr, 1950

9-Moon Girl cameo 78 156 234 491 833 1175
10,11 65 130 195 410 693 975
12 (Scarce) 78 156 234 491 833 1175
NOTE: ***Feldstein, Ingels*** *art in all.* ***Feldstein*** *c-9-12.* ***Wood/Harrison*** *a-10-12. Canadian reprints known; see Table of Contents.*

MOON GIRL AND THE PRINCE (#1) (Moon Girl #2-6; Moon Girl Fights Crime #7, 8; becomes A Moon, A Girl, Romance #9 on)(Also see Animal Fables #7, Int. Crime Patrol #6, Happy Houlihans & Tales From The Crypt #22)
E. C. Comics: Fall, 1947 - No. 8, Summer, 1949

1-Origin Moon Girl (see Happy Houlihans #1). Intro Santana, Queen of the Underworld
105 210 315 662 1119 1575
2-Moon Girl battles Futureman 60 120 180 378 639 900
3,4: 3-Santana, Queen of the Underworld returns. 4-Moon Girl vs. a vampire
53 106 159 328 547 765
5-E.C.'s 1st horror story, "Zombie Terror" 115 230 345 725 1225 1725
6-8 (Scarce): 7-Origin Star (Moongirl's sidekick) 60 120 180 378 639 900
NOTE: ***Craig*** *a-2, 5; c-1, 2.* ***Moldoff*** *a-1-8; c-3-8 (Shelly).* ***Wheelan's*** *Fat and Slat app. in #3, 4, 6. #2 & #3 are 52 pgs., #4 on, 36 pgs. Canadian reprints known; (see Table of Contents.)*

MOON KNIGHT (Also see The Hulk, Marc Spector..., Marvel Preview #21, Marvel Spotlight & Werewolf by Night #32)
Marvel Comics Group: Nov, 1980 - No. 38, Jul, 1984 (Mando paper #33 on)

1-Origin resumed in #4 5.00
2-15,25,35: 4-Intro Midnight Man. 25-Double size. 35-($1.00, 52 pgs.)-X-Men app.; F.F. cameo 3.00
16-24,26-28,30-34,36-38: 16-The Thing app. 2.50
29,30-Werewolf By Night app. 4.00

GD VG FN VF VF/NM NM-
2.0 4.0 6.0 8.0 9.0 9.2

NOTE: ***Austin*** *c-27i, 31i.* ***Cowan*** *a-16; c-16, 17.* ***Kaluta*** *c-36-38; back c-35.* ***Miller*** *c-9, 12p, 13p, 15p, 27p.* ***Ploog*** *back c-35.* ***Sienkiewicz*** *a-1-15, 17-20, 22-26, 28-30, 33i, 36(4), 37; c-1-5, 7, 8, 10, 11, 14-16, 18-26, 28-30, 31p, 33, 34.*

MOON KNIGHT
Marvel Comics Group: June, 1985 - V2#6, Dec, 1985

V2#1-6: 1-Double size; new costume. 6-Sienkiewicz painted-c 2.50

MOON KNIGHT
Marvel Comics: Jan, 1998 - No. 4, Apr, 1998 ($2.50, limited series)

1-4-Moench-s/Edwards-c/a 2.50

MOON KNIGHT (Volume 3)
Marvel Comics: Jan, 1999 - No. 4, Feb, 1999 ($2.99, limited series)

1-4-Moench-s/Texeira-a(p) 3.00

MOON KNIGHT (Fourth series)
Marvel Comics: June, 2006 - Present ($2.99, limited series)

1-Finch-a/c; Huston-s 4.00
1-B&W sketch variant-c 6.00
2-19,21,22: 7-Spider-Man app. 9,10-Punisher app. 13-22-Suydam-c 3.00
20-($3.99) Deodato-a; back-up r/1st app. in Werewolf By Night #32,33 4.00
Annual 1 (1/08, $3.99) Swierczynski-s/Palo-a 4.00
... Vol. 1: The Bottom HC (2006, $19.99) r/#1-6; Huston afterword; 2 covers 20.00
... Vol. 1: The Bottom SC (2007, $14.99) r/#1-6; Huston afterword 15.00
... Vol. 2: Midnight Sun HC (2008, $19.99) r/#7-13 & Annual #1 20.00
... Vol. 2: Midnight Sun SC (2008, $14.99) r/#7-13 & Annual #1 15.00

MOON KNIGHT: DIVIDED WE FALL
Marvel Comics: 1992 ($4.95, 52 pgs.)

nn-Denys Cowan-c/a(p) 5.00

MOON KNIGHT SPECIAL
Marvel Comics: Oct, 1992 ($2.50, 52 pgs.)

1-Shang Chi, Master of Kung Fu-c/story 2.50

MOON KNIGHT SPECIAL EDITION
Marvel Comics Group: Nov, 1983 - No. 3, Jan, 1984 ($2.00, limited series, Baxter paper)

1-3: Reprints from Hulk mag. by Sienkiewicz 3.00

MOON MULLINS (See Popular Comics, Super Book #3 & Super Comics)
Dell Publishing Co.: 1941 - 1945

Four Color 14(1941) 45 90 135 279 465 650
Large Feature Comic 29(1941) 36 72 108 212 341 470
Four Color 31(1943) 17 34 51 120 223 325
Four Color 81(1945) 10 20 30 73 129 185

MOON MULLINS
Michel Publ. (American Comics Group)#1-6/St. John #7,8: Dec-Jan, 1947-48 - No. 8, 1949 (52 pgs)

1-Alternating Sunday & daily strip-r 22 44 66 127 204 280
2 14 28 42 76 108 140
3-8: 7,8-St. John Publ. 8-...Featuring Kayo on-c 13 26 39 72 101 130
NOTE: ***Milt Gross*** *a-2-6, 8.* ***Frank Willard*** *r-all.*

MOON PILOT
Dell Publishing Co.: No. 1313, Mar-May, 1962

Four Color 1313-Movie, photo-c 7 14 21 47 76 105

MOONSHADOW (Also see Farewell, Moonshadow)
Marvel Comics (Epic Comics): 5/85 - #12, 2/87 ($1.50/$1.75, mature)
(1st fully painted comic book)

1-Origin; J. M. DeMatteis scripts & Jon J. Muth painted-c/a. 6.00
2-12: 11-Origin 4.00
Trade paperback (1987?)-r/#1-12 14.00
Signed & numbered hard-c ($39.95, 1,200 copies)-r/#1-12
4 8 12 28 44 60

MOONSHADOW
DC Comics (Vertigo): Oct, 1994 - No. 12, Aug, 1995 ($2.25/$2.95)

1-11: Reprints Epic series. 2.50
12 ($2.95)-w/expanded ending 3.00
The Complete Moonshadow TPB ('98, $39.95) r/#1-12 and Farewell Moonshadow; new Muth painted-c 40.00

MOON-SPINNERS, THE (See Movie Comics)

MOONSTONE MONSTERS
Moonstone: 2003 - 2005 ($2.95, B&W)

...: Demons ($2.95) - Short stories by various; Frenz-c 3.00

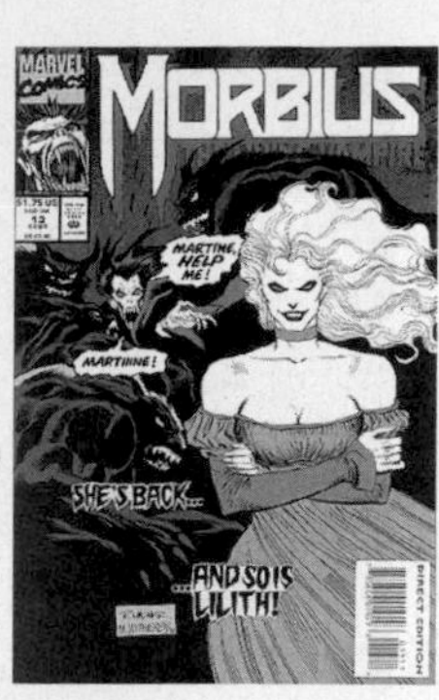

Morbius, The Living Vampire #13 © MAR

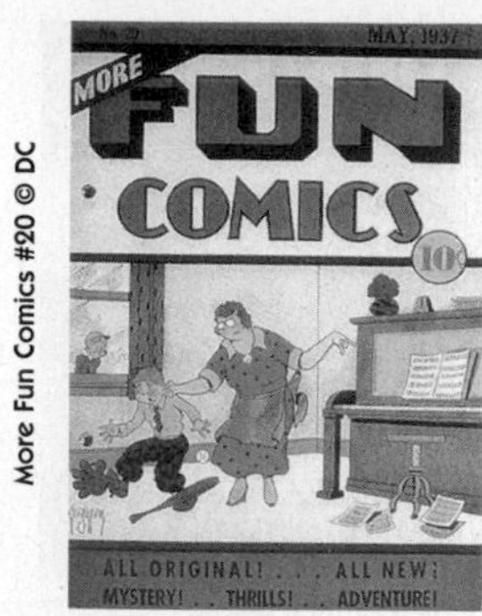

More Fun Comics #20 © DC

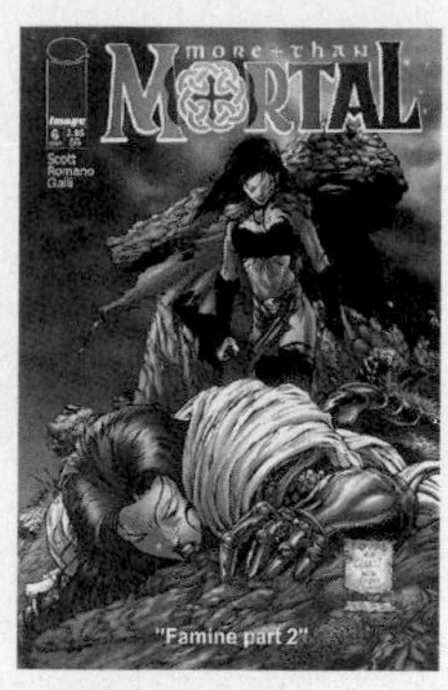

More Than Mortal #6 © Sharon Scott

	GD	VG	FN	VF	VF/NM	NM-
	2.0	4.0	6.0	8.0	9.0	9.2

...: Ghosts ($2.95) - Short stories by various; Frenz-c 3.00
...: Sea Creatures ($2.95) - Short stories by various; Frenz-c 3.00
...: Witches ($2.95) - Short stories by various; Frenz-c 3.00
...: Zombies ($2.95) - Short stories by various; Frenz-c 3.00
Volume 1 (2004, $16.95, TPB) r/short stories from series; Wolak-c 17.00

MOONSTONE NOIR
Moonstone: 2003 - Present ($2.95/$4.95/$5.50, B&W)

...: Bulldog Drummond (2004, $4.95) - Messner-Loebs-s/Barkley-a 5.00
...: Johnny Dollar ($4.95) - Gallaher-s/Theriault-a 5.00
...: Mr. Keen, Tracer of Lost Persons 1,2 ($2.95, limited series) - Ferguson-a 3.00
...: Mysterious Traveler (2003, $5.50) - Trevor Von Eeden-a/Joe Gentile-s 5.50
...: Mysterious Traveler Returns (2004, $4.95) - Trevor Von Eeden-a/Joe Gentile-s 5.00
...: The Lone Wolf ($4.95) - Jolley-s/Croall-a 5.00

MOPSY (See Pageant of Comics & TV Teens)
St. John Publ. Co.: Feb, 1948 - No. 19, Sept, 1953

1-Part-r; reprints "Some Punkins" by Neher 18 36 54 103 162 220
2 11 22 33 62 86 110
3-10(1953): 8-Lingerie panels 10 20 30 56 76 95
11-19: 19-Lingerie-c 9 18 27 52 69 85
NOTE: *#1-7, 13, 18, 19 have paper dolls.*

MORBIUS REVISITED
Marvel Comic: Aug, 1993 - No. 5, Dec, 1993 ($1.95, mini-series)

1-5-Reprints Fear #27-31 2.50

MORBIUS: THE LIVING VAMPIRE (Also see Amazing Spider-Man #101,102, Fear #20, Marvel Team-Up #3, 4, Midnight Sons Unl. & Vampire Tales)
Marvel Comics (Midnight Sons imprint #16 on): Sep, 1992 - No. 32, Apr, 1995 ($1.75/$1.95)

1-($2.75, 52 pgs.)-Polybagged w/poster; Ghost Rider & Johnny Blaze x-over (part 3 of Rise of the Midnight Sons) 3.00
2-11,13-24,26-32: 3,4-Vs. Spider-Man-c/s.15-Ghost Rider app. 16-Spot varnish-c. 16,17-Siege of Darkness,parts 5 &13. 18-Deathlok app. 21-Bound-in Spider-Man trading card sheet; Spider-Man app. 2.50
12-($2.25)-Outer-c is a Darkhold envelope made of black parchment w/gold ink; Midnight Massacre x-over 2.50
25-($2.50, 52 pgs.)-Gold foil logo 2.50

MORE FUN COMICS (Formerly New Fun Comics #1-6)
National Periodical Publications: No. 7, Jan, 1936 - No. 127, Nov-Dec, 1947 (No. 7,9-11: paper-c)

7(1/36)-Oversized, paper-c; 1 pg. Kelly-a 787 1574 2361 6200 - -
8(2/36)-Oversized (10x12"), paper-c; 1 pg. Kelly-a; Sullivan-c 787 1574 2361 6200 - -
9(3-4/36)(Very rare, 1st standard-sized comic book with original material)-Last multiple panel-c 947 1894 2841 7400 - -
10,11(7/36): 10-Last Henri Duval by Siegel & Shuster. 11-1st "Calling All Cars" by Siegel & Shuster; new classic logo begins 547 1094 1641 4400 - -
12(8/36)-Slick-c begin 433 866 1299 3450 - -
V2#1(9/36, #13) 1 pg. Fred Astaire photo/bio 397 794 1191 3150 - -
2(10/36, #14)-Dr. Occult in costume (1st in color)(Superman proto-type; 1st DC appearance) continues from The Comics Magazine, ends #17 1867 3734 5601 14,500 - -
V2#3(11/36, #15), 17(V2#5) 760 1520 2280 5900 - -
16(V2#4)-Cover numbering begins; ties with New Comics #11 as 1st DC Christmas-c; last Superman tryout issue 775 1550 2325 6100 - -
18-20(V2#8, 5/37) 300 600 900 2500 - -
21(V2#9)-24(V2#12, 9/37) 276 552 828 1518 2209 2900
25(V3#1, 10/37)-27(V3#3, 12/37): 27-Xmas-c 276 552 828 1518 2209 2900
28-30: 30-1st non-funny cover 250 500 750 1375 1988 2600
31-Has ad for Action Comics #1 265 530 795 1458 2104 2750
32-35: 32-Last Dr. Occult 250 500 750 1375 1988 2600
36-40: 36-(10/38)-The Masked Ranger & sidekick Pedro begins; Ginger Snap by Bob Kane (2 pgs.; 1st-a?). 39-Xmas-c 250 500 750 1375 1988 2600
41-50: 41-Last Masked Ranger 212 424 636 1166 1758 2350
51-The Spectre app. (in costume) in one panel ad at end of Buccaneer story 741 1482 2223 4076 5888 7700
52-(2/40)-Origin/1st app. The Spectre (in costume splash panel only), part 1 by Bernard Baily (parts 1 & 2 written by Jerry Siegel; Spectre's costume changes color from purple & blue to green & grey; last Wing Brady; Spectre-c 6500 13,000 19,500 48,750 86,875 125,000
53-Origin The Spectre (in costume at end of story), part 2; Capt. Desmo begins; Spectre-c 3000 6000 9000 21,500 43,250 65,000
54-The Spectre in costume; last King Carter; classic-Spectre-c 1500 3000 4500 11,250 20,125 29,000

	GD	VG	FN	VF	VF/NM	NM-
	2.0	4.0	6.0	8.0	9.0	9.2

55-(Scarce, 5/40)-Dr. Fate begins (1st app.); last Bulldog Martin; Spectre-c 1500 3000 4500 11,250 20,125 29,000
56-1st Dr. Fate-c (classic), origin continues. Congo Bill begins (6/40), 1st app.; 778 1556 2334 5602 9801 14,000
57-60-All Spectre-c 423 846 1269 2917 5109 7300
61,65: 61-Classic Dr. Fate-c. 65-Classic Spectre-c 400 800 1200 2720 4760 6800
62-64,66: 63-Last Lt. Bob Neal. 64-Lance Larkin begins; all Spectre-c 318 636 954 2162 3781 5400
67-(5/41)-Origin (1st) Dr. Fate; last Congo Bill & Biff Bronson (Congo Bill continues in Action Comics #37, 6/41)-Spectre-c 778 1556 2334 5602 9801 14,000
68-70: 68-Clip Carson begins. 70-Last Lance Larkin; all Dr. Fate-c 280 560 840 1764 2982 4200
71-Origin & 1st app. Johnny Quick by Mort Weisinger (9/41); classic sci/fi Dr. Fate-c 528 1056 1584 3802 6651 9500
72-Dr. Fate's new helmet; last Sgt. Carey, Sgt. O'Malley & Captain Desmo; German submarine-c (only German war-c) 273 546 819 1720 2910 4100
73-Origin & 1st app. Aquaman (11/41) by Paul Norris; intro. Green Arrow & Speedy; Dr. Fate-c 1475 2950 4425 11,000 19,500 28,000
74-2nd Aquaman; 1st Percival Popp, Supercop; Dr. Fate-c 300 600 900 1930 3315 4700
75,76: 75-New origin Spectre; Nazi spy ring cover w/Hitler's photo. 76-Last Dr. Fate-c; Johnny Quick (by Meskin #76-97) begins, ends #107; last Clip Carson 253 506 759 1594 2697 3800
77-80: 77-Green Arrow-c begin 200 400 600 1260 2130 3000
81-83,85,88,90: 81-Last large logo. 82-1st small logo. 135 270 405 851 1438 2025
84-Green Arrow Japanese war-c 138 276 414 869 1472 2075
86,87-Johnny Quick-c. 87-Last Radio Squad 135 270 405 851 1438 2025
89-Origin Green Arrow & Speedy Team-up 143 286 429 901 1526 2150
91-97,99: 91-1st bi-monthly issue. 93-Dover & Clover begin (1st app., 9-10/43). 97-Kubert-a 90 180 270 567 959 1350
98-Last Dr. Fate (scarce) 110 220 330 693 1172 1650
100 (11-12/44)-Johnny Quick-c 122 244 366 769 1297 1825
101-Origin & 1st app. Superboy (1-2/45)(not by Siegel & Shuster); last Spectre issue; Green Arrow-c 889 1778 2667 6401 11,201 16,000
102-2nd Superboy app; 1st Dover & Clover-c 140 280 420 882 1491 2100
103-3rd Superboy app; last Green Arrow-c 100 200 300 630 1065 1500
104-1st Superboy-c w/Dover & Clover 87 174 261 548 924 1300
105,106-Superboy-c 80 160 240 504 852 1200
107-Last Johnny Quick & Superboy 80 160 240 504 852 1200
108-120: 108-Genius Jones begins; 1st c-app. (3-4/46; cont'd from Adventure Comics #102) 25 50 75 147 236 325
121-124,126: 121-123,126-Post funny animal (Jimminy & the Magic Book)-c 23 46 69 135 218 300
125-Superman c-app.w/Jimminy 80 160 240 504 852 1200
127-(Scarce)-Post-c/a 38 76 114 222 356 490
NOTE: *All issues are scarce to rare. Cover features: The Spectre-#52-55, 57-60, 62-67. Dr. Fate-#56, 61, 68-76. The Green Arrow & Speedy-#77-85, 88-97, 99, 101 (w/Dover & Clover-#98, 103). Johnny Quick-#86, 87, 100. Dover & Clover-#102, (104, 106 w/Superboy), 107, 108(w/Genius Jones), 110, 112, 114, 117, 119. Genius Jones-#109, 111, 113, 115, 116, 118, 120.* ***Baily*** *a-45, 52-on; c-52-55, 57-60, 62-67.* ***Al Capp*** *a-45(signed Koppy).* ***Ellsworth*** *c-7.* ***Craig Flessel*** *c-30, 31, 35-48(most).* ***Guardineer*** *c-47, 49, 50.* ***Kiefer*** *a-20.* ***Meskin*** *c-86, 87, 100?* ***Moldoff*** *c-51.* ***George Papp*** *c-77-85.* ***Post*** *c-121-127.* ***Vincent Sullivan*** *c-8-28, 32-34.*

MORE FUND COMICS (Benefit book for the Comic Book Legal Defense Fund) (Also see Even More Fund Comics)
Sky Dog Press: Sept, 2003 ($10.00, B&W, trade paperback)

nn-Anthology of short stories and pin-ups by various; Hulk-c by Pérez 10.00

MORE SEYMOUR (See Seymour My Son)
Archie Publications: Oct, 1963

1-DeCarlo-a? 3 6 9 18 27 35

MORE THAN MORTAL (Also see Lady Pendragon/...)
Liar Comics: June, 1997 - No. 4, Apr, 1998 ($2.95, limited series)
Image Comics: No. 5, Dec, 1999 - Present ($2.95)

1-Blue forest background-c, 1-Variant-c 4.00
1-White-c 6.00
1-2nd printing; purple sky cover 3.00
2-4: 3-Silvestri-c, 4-Two-c, one by Randy Queen 3.00
5,6: 5-1st Image Comics issue 3.00

MORE THAN MORTAL: OTHERWORLDS
Image Comics: July, 1999 - No. 4, Dec, 1999 ($2.95, limited series)

1-4-Firchow-a. 1-Two covers 3.00

MORE THAN MORTAL SAGAS
Liar Comics: Jun, 1998 - No. 3, Dec, 1998 ($2.95, limited series)

Morlocks #1 © MAR

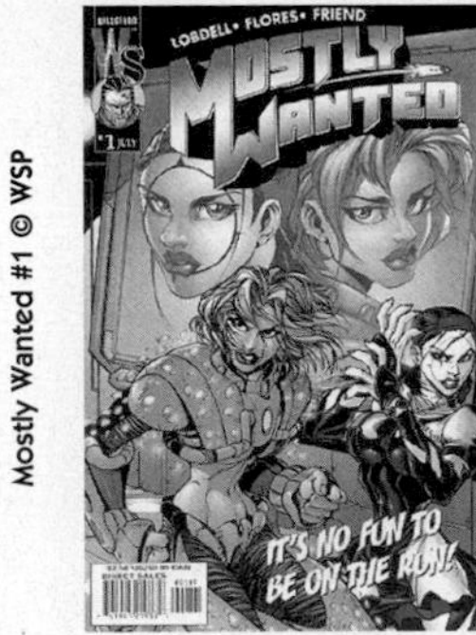

Mostly Wanted #1 © WSP

Movie Classics - Bon Voyage © DIS

GD VG FN VF VF/NM NM-
2.0 4.0 6.0 8.0 9.0 9.2

1,2-Painted art by Romano. 2-Two-c, one by Firchow 3.00
1-Variant-c by Linsner 5.00

MORE THAN MORTAL TRUTHS AND LEGENDS
Liar Comics: Aug, 1998 - No. 6, Apr, 1999 ($2.95)
1-6-Firchow-a(p) 3.00
1-Variant-c by Dan Norton 4.50

MORE TRASH FROM MAD (Annual)
E. C. Comics: 1958 - No. 12, 1969
(Note: Bonus missing = half price)
nn(1958)-8 pgs. color Mad reprint from #20 19 38 57 135 250 365
2(1959)-Market Product Labels 14 28 42 99 175 250
3(1960)-Text book covers 12 24 36 87 156 225
4(1961)-Sing Along with Mad booklet 12 24 36 87 156 225
5(1962)-Window Stickers; r/from Mad #39 9 18 27 63 107 150
6(1963)-TV Guise booklet 9 18 27 63 107 150
7(1964)-Alfred E. Neuman commemorative stamps 8 16 24 52 86 120
8(1965)-Life size poster-Alfred E. Neuman 6 12 18 41 66 90
9-12: 9,10(1966-67)-Mischief Sticker. 11(1968)-Campaign poster & bumper sticker. 12(1969)-Pocket medals 6 12 18 41 66 90
NOTE: *Kelly Freas c-1, 2, 4. Mingo c-3, 5-9, 12.*

MORGAN THE PIRATE (Movie)
Dell Publishing Co.: No. 1227, Sept-Nov, 1961
Four Color 1227-Photo-c 7 14 21 50 83 115

MORLOCKS
Marvel Comics: June, 2002 - No. 4, Sept, 2002 ($2.50, limited series)
1-4-Johns-s/Martinbrough-c/a 2.50

MORLOCK 2001
Atlas/Seaboard Publ.: Feb, 1975 - No. 3, July, 1975
1,2: 1 (Super-hero)-Origin & 1st app.; Milgrom-c 1 3 4 6 8 10
3-Ditko/Wrightson-a; origin The Midnight Man & The Mystery Men 2 4 6 8 10 12

MORNINGSTAR SPECIAL
Comico: Apr, 1990 ($2.50)
1-From the Elementals; Willingham-c/a/scripts 3.00

MORTAL KOMBAT
Malibu Comics: July, 1994 - No. 6, Dec, 1994 ($2.95)
1-6: 1-Two diff. covers exist 3.00
1-Limited edition gold foil embossed-c 4.00
0 (12/94), Special Edition 1 (11/94) 3.00
Tournament Edition I12/94, $3.95), II('95)($3.95) 4.00
...: **BARAKA** ,June, 1995 ($2.95, one-shot) #1; ...**BATTLEWAVE** ,2/95 - No. 6, 7/95 , #1-6; ...**GORO, PRINCE OF PAIN** ,9/94 - No. 3, 11/94, #1-3; ...**KITANA AND MILEENA** ,8/95 , ...**KUNG LAO** ,7/95 , #1; ... **RAYDON & KANO** ,3/95 - No. 3, 5/95, #1-3: ...(all $2.95-c) 3.00
...: **U.S. SPECIAL FORCES** ,1/95 - No. 2, ($3.50), #1,2 3.50

MORTIE (Mazie's Friend; also see Flat Top)
Magazine Publishers: Dec, 1952 - No. 4, June, 1953?
1 9 18 27 50 65 80
2-4 6 12 18 28 34 40

MORTIGAN GOTH: IMMORTALIS (See Marvel Frontier Comics Unlimited)
Marvel Comics: Sept, 1993 - No. 4, Mar, 1994 ($1.95, mini-series)
1-($2.95)-Foil-c 3.00
2-4 2.50

MORT THE DEAD TEENAGER
Marvel Comics: Nov, 1993 - No. 4, Mar, 1994 ($1.75, mini-series)
1-4 2.50

MORTY MEEKLE
Dell Publishing Co.: No. 793, May, 1957
Four Color 793 4 8 12 24 37 50

MOSES & THE TEN COMMANDMENTS (See Dell Giants)

MOSTLY WANTED
DC Comics (WildStorm): Jul, 2000 - No. 4, Nov, 2000 ($2.50, limited series)
1-4-Lobdell-s/Flores-a 2.50

MOTH, THE (Also see Promotional Comics section for Free Comic Book Day edition)
Dark Horse Comics: Apr, 2004 - No. 4 ($2.99)

GD VG FN VF VF/NM NM-
2.0 4.0 6.0 8.0 9.0 9.2

1-4-Steve Rude-c/a; Gary Martin-s 3.00
... Special (3/04, $4.95) 5.00
TPB (5/05, $12.95) r/#1-4 and Special; gallery of extras 13.00

MOTHER GOOSE AND NURSERY RHYME COMICS (See Christmas With Mother Goose)
Dell Publishing Co.: No. 41, 1944 - No. 862, Nov, 1957
Four Color 41-Walt Kelly-c/a 22 44 66 161 298 435
Four Color 59, 68-Kelly c/a 18 36 54 130 240 350
Four Color 862-The Truth About..., Movie (Disney) 7 14 21 49 80 110

MOTHER TERESA OF CALCUTTA
Marvel Comics Group: 1984
1-(52 pgs.) No ads 4.00

MOTION PICTURE COMICS (See Fawcett Movie Comics)
Fawcett Publications: No. 101, 1950 - No. 114, Jan, 1953 (All-photo-c)
101- "Vanishing Westerner"; Monte Hale (1950) 23 46 69 132 209 285
102- "Code of the Silver Sage"; Rocky Lane (1/51) 20 40 60 117 184 250
103- "Covered Wagon Raid"; Rocky Lane (3/51) 20 40 60 117 184 250
104- "Vigilante Hideout"; Rocky Lane (5/51)-Book length Powell-a 20 40 60 117 184 250
105- "Red Badge of Courage"; Audie Murphy; Bob Powell-a (7/51) 26 52 78 152 239 325
106- "The Texas Rangers"; George Montgomery (9/51) 20 40 60 117 184 250
107- "Frisco Tornado"; Rocky Lane (11/51) 18 36 54 105 165 225
108- "Mask of the Avenger"; John Derek 15 30 45 85 130 175
109- "Rough Rider of Durango"; Rocky Lane 19 38 57 109 172 235
110- "When Worlds Collide"; George Evans-a (5/52); Williamson & Evans drew themselves in story; (also see Famous Funnies No. 72-88) 93 186 279 581 966 1350
111- "The Vanishing Outpost"; Lash LaRue 23 46 69 132 209 285
112- "Brave Warrior"; Jon Hall & Jay Silverheels 15 30 45 83 124 165
113- "Walk East on Beacon"; George Murphy; Schaffenberger-a 12 24 36 69 97 125
114- "Cripple Creek"; George Montgomery (1/53) 13 26 39 74 105 135

MOTION PICTURE FUNNIES WEEKLY (See Promotional Comics section)

MOTORHEAD (See Comic's Greatest World)
Dark Horse Comics: Aug, 1995 - No. 6, Jan, 1996 ($2.50)
1-6: Bisley-c on all. 1-Predator app. 2.50
Special 1 (3/94, $3.95, 52pgs.)-Jae Lee-c; Barb Wire, The Machine & Wolf Gang app. 4.00

MOTORMOUTH (... & Killpower #7? on)
Marvel Comics UK: June, 1992 - No. 12, May, 1993 ($1.75)
1-13: 1,2-Nick Fury app. 3-Punisher-c/story. 5,6-Nick Fury & Punisher app. 6-Cable cameo. 7-9-Cable app. 2.50

MOUNTAIN MEN (See Ben Bowie)

MOUSE MUSKETEERS (See M.G.M.'s...)

MOUSE ON THE MOON, THE (See Movie Classics)

MOVIE CARTOONS
DC Comics: Dec, 1944 (cover only ashcan)
nn-Ashcan comic, not distributed to newsstands, only for in house use. Covers were produced, but not the rest of the book. A copy sold in 2006 for $500.

MOVIE CLASSICS
Dell Publishing Co.: Apr, 1956; May-Jul, 1962 - Dec, 1969
(Before 1963, most movie adaptations were part of the 4-Color series)
(Disney movie adaptations after 1970 are in Walt Disney Showcase)
Around the World Under the Sea 12-030-612 (12/66) 3 6 9 20 30 40
Bambi 3(4/56)-Disney; r/4-Color #186 4 8 12 24 37 50
Battle of the Bulge 12-056-606 (6/66) 3 6 9 21 32 42
Beach Blanket Bingo 12-058-509 7 14 21 47 76 105
Bon Voyage 01-068-212 (12/62)-Disney; photo-c 4 8 12 22 34 45
Castilian, The 12-110-401 3 6 9 20 30 40
Cat, The 12-109-612 (12/66) 3 6 9 19 29 38
Cheyenne Autumn 12-112-506 (4-6/65) 5 10 15 34 55 75
Circus World, Samuel Bronston's 12-115-411; John Wayne app.; John Wayne photo-c 9 18 27 65 113 160
Countdown 12-150-710 (10/67)-James Caan photo-c 3 6 9 21 32 42
Creature, The 1 (12-142-302) (12-2/62-63) 8 16 24 56 93 130
Creature, The 12-142-410 (10/64) 5 10 15 32 51 70
David Ladd's Life Story 12-173-212 (10-12/62)-Photo-c 7 14 21 47 76 105
Die, Monster, Die 12-175-603 (3/66)-Photo-c 5 10 15 34 55 75

Movie Classics - Lawrence © DELL

Movie Comics #1 © FH

Movie Comics - Big Red © DIS

	GD 2.0	VG 4.0	FN 6.0	VF 8.0	VF/NM 9.0	NM- 9.2
Dirty Dozen 12-180-710 (10/67)	4	8	12	28	44	60
Dr. Who & the Daleks 12-190-612 (12/66)-Peter Cushing photo-c; 1st U.S. app. of Dr. Who	10	20	30	71	126	180
Dracula 12-231-212 (10-12/62)	7	14	21	50	83	115
El Dorado 12-240-710 (10/67)-John Wayne; photo-c	11	22	33	79	140	200
Ensign Pulver 12-257-410 (8-10/64)	3	6	9	19	29	38
Frankenstein 12-283-305 (3-5/63)(see Frankenstein 8-10/64 for 2nd printing)	8	16	24	52	86	120
Great Race, The 12-299-603 (3/66)-Natallie Wood, Tony Curtis photo-c	4	8	12	28	44	60
Hallelujah Trail, The 12-307-602 (2/66) (Shows 1/66 inside); Burt Lancaster, Lee Remick photo-c	5	10	15	30	48	65
Hatari 12-340-301 (1/63)-John Wayne	8	16	24	52	86	120
Horizontal Lieutenant, The 01-348-210 (10/62)	3	6	9	19	29	38
Incredible Mr. Limpet, The 12-370-408; Don Knotts photo-c	5	10	15	30	48	65
Jack the Giant Killer 12-374-301 (1/63)	8	16	24	52	86	120
Jason & the Argonauts 12-376-310 (8-10/63)-Photo-c	9	18	27	61	103	145
Lancelot & Guinevere 12-416-310 (10/63)	5	10	15	32	51	70
Lawrence 12-426-308 (8/63)-Story of Lawrence of Arabia; movie ad on back-c; not exactly like movie	5	10	15	32	51	70
Lion of Sparta 12-439-301 (1/63)	4	8	12	22	34	45
Mad Monster Party 12-460-801 (9/67)-Based on Kurtzman's screenplay	8	16	24	56	93	130
Magic Sword, The 01-496-209 (9/62)	5	10	15	35	55	75
Masque of the Red Death 12-490-410 (8-10/64)-Vincent Price photo-c	6	12	18	41	66	90
Maya 12-495-612 (12/66)-Clint Walker & Jay North part photo-c	4	8	12	24	37	50
McHale's Navy 12-500-412 (10-12/64)	4	8	12	28	44	60
Merrill's Marauders 12-510-301 (1/63)-Photo-c	3	6	9	19	29	38
Mouse on the Moon, The 12-530-312 (10/12/63)-Photo-c	4	8	12	22	34	45
Mummy, The 12-537-211 (9-11/62) 2 versions with different back-c	8	16	24	54	90	125
Music Man, The 12-538-301 (1/63)	3	6	9	20	30	40
Naked Prey, The 12-545-612 (12/66)-Photo-c	5	10	15	34	55	75
Night of the Grizzly, The 12-558-612 (12/66)-Photo-c	4	8	12	22	34	45
None But the Brave 12-565-506 (4-6/65)	5	10	15	34	55	75
Operation Bikini 12-597-310 (10/63)-Photo-c	3	6	9	20	30	40
Operation Crossbow 12-590-512 (10-12/65)	3	6	9	20	30	40
Prince & the Pauper, The 01-654-207 (5-7/62)-Disney	4	8	12	22	34	45
Raven, The 12-680-309 (9/63)-Vincent Price photo-c	6	12	18	39	62	85
Ring of Bright Water 01-701-910 (10/69) (inside shows #12-701-909)	4	8	12	22	34	45
Runaway, The 12-707-412 (10-12/64)	3	6	9	19	29	38
Santa Claus Conquers the Martians #? (1964)-Photo-c	9	18	27	65	113	160
Santa Claus Conquers the Martians 12-725-603 (3/66, 12¢)-Reprints 1964 issue; photo-c	7	14	21	47	76	105
Another version given away with a Golden Record, SLP 170, nn, no price (3/66)-Complete with record	12	24	36	87	156	225
Six Black Horses 12-750-301 (1/63)-Photo-c	3	6	9	20	30	40
Ski Party 12-743-511 (9-11/65)-Frankie Avalon photo-c; photo inside-c; Adkins-a	5	10	15	30	48	65
Smoky 12-746-702 (2/67)	3	6	9	19	29	38
Sons of Katie Elder 12-748-511 (9-11/65); John Wayne app.; photo-c	11	22	33	79	140	200
Tales of Terror 12-793-302 (2/63)-Evans-a	5	10	15	34	55	75
Three Stooges Meet Hercules 01-828-208 (8/62)-Photo-c	9	18	27	60	100	140
Tomb of Ligeia 12-830-506 (4-6/65)	5	10	15	34	55	75
Treasure Island 01-845-211 (7-9/62)-Disney; r/4-Color #624	3	6	9	20	30	40
Twice Told Tales (Nathaniel Hawthorne) 12-840-401 (11-1/63-64); Vincent Price photo-c	6	12	18	37	59	80
Two on a Guillotine 12-850-506 (4-6/65)	4	8	12	22	34	45
Valley of Gwangi 01-880-912 (12/69)	9	18	27	60	100	140
War Gods of the Deep 12-900-509 (7-9/65)	3	6	9	20	30	40
War Wagon, The 12-533-709 (9/67); John Wayne app.	8	16	24	54	90	125
Who's Minding the Mint? 12-924-708 (8/67)	3	6	9	19	29	38

	GD 2.0	VG 4.0	FN 6.0	VF 8.0	VF/NM 9.0	NM- 9.2
Wolfman, The 12-922-308 (6-8/63)	8	16	24	52	86	120
Wolfman, The 1(12-922-410)(8-10/64)-2nd printing; r/#12-922-308	4	8	12	23	36	48
Zulu 12-950-410 (8-10/64)-Photo-c	7	14	21	49	80	110

MOVIE COMICS (See Cinema Comics Herald & Fawcett Movie Comics)

MOVIE COMICS
National Periodical Publications/Picture Comics: April, 1939 - No. 6, Sept-Oct, 1939 (Most all photo-c)

	GD	VG	FN	VF	VF/NM	NM-
1- "Gunga Din", "Son of Frankenstein", "The Great Man Votes", "Fisherman's Wharf", & "Scouts to the Rescue" part 1; Wheelan "Minute Movies" begin	353	706	1059	2400	4200	6000
2- "Stagecoach", "The Saint Strikes Back", "King of the Turf","Scouts to the Rescue" part 2, "Arizona Legion", Andy Devine photo-c	243	486	729	1531	2591	3650
3- "East Side of Heaven", "Mystery in the White Room", "Four Feathers", "Mexican Rose" with Gene Autry, "Spirit of Culver", "Many Secrets", "The Mikado" (1st Gene Autry photo cover)	173	346	519	1090	1845	2600
4- "Captain Fury", Gene Autry in "Blue Montana Skies", "Streets of N.Y." with Jackie Cooper, "Oregon Trail" part 1 with Johnny Mack Brown, "Big Town Czar" with Barton MacLane, & "Star Reporter" with Warren Hull	147	294	441	926	1563	2200
5- "The Man in the Iron Mask", "Five Came Back", "Wolf Call", "The Girl & the Gambler", "The House of Fear", "The Family Next Door", "Oregon Trail" part 2	160	320	480	1008	1704	2400
6- "The Phantom Creeps", "Chumps at Oxford", & "The Oregon Trail" part 3; 2nd Robot-c	200	400	600	1260	2130	3000

NOTE: *Above books contain many original movie stills with dialogue from movie scripts. All issues are scarce.*

MOVIE COMICS
Fiction House Magazines: Dec, 1946 - No. 4, 1947

	GD	VG	FN	VF	VF/NM	NM-
1-Big Town (by Lubbers), Johnny Danger begin; Celardo-a; Mitzi of the Movies by Fran Hopper	47	94	141	291	483	675
2-(2/47)- "White Tie & Tails" with William Bendix; Mitzi of the Movies begins	36	72	108	212	341	470
3-(6/47)-Andy Hardy starring Mickey Rooney	36	72	108	212	341	470
4-Mitzi In Hollywood by Matt Baker; Merton of the Movies with Red Skelton; Yvonne DeCarlo & George Brent in "Slave Girl"	41	82	123	250	413	575

MOVIE COMICS
Gold Key/Whitman: Oct, 1962 - 1984

	GD	VG	FN	VF	VF/NM	NM-
Alice in Wonderland 10144-503 (3/65)-Disney; partial reprint of 4-Color #331	4	8	12	22	34	45
Alice In Wonderland #1 (Whitman pre-pack, 3/84)	2	4	6	10	14	18
Aristocats, The 1 (30045-103)(3/71)-Disney; with pull-out poster (25¢) (No poster = half price)	7	14	21	47	76	105
Bambi 1 (10087-309)(9/63)-Disney; r/4-C #186	4	8	12	24	37	50
Bambi 2 (10087-607)(7/66)-Disney; r/4-C #186	3	6	9	20	30	40
Beneath the Planet of the Apes 30044-012 (12/70)-with pull-out poster; photo-c (No poster = half price)	9	18	27	61	103	145
Big Red 10026-211 (11/62)-Disney; photo-c	3	6	9	20	30	40
Big Red 10026-503 (3/65)-Disney; reprints 10026-211; photo-c	3	6	9	16	23	30
Blackbeard's Ghost 10222-806 (6/68)-Disney	3	6	9	19	29	38
Bullwhip Griffin 10181-706 (6/67)-Disney; Spiegle-a; photo-c	4	8	12	22	34	45
Captain Sindbad 10077-309 (9/63)-Manning-a; photo-c	6	12	18	41	66	90
Chitty Chitty Bang Bang 1 (30038-902)(2/69)-with pull-out poster; Disney; photo-c (No poster = half price)	6	12	18	43	69	95
Cinderella 10152-508 (8/65)-Disney; r/4-C #786	4	8	12	26	41	55
Darby O'Gill & the Little People 10251-001(1/70)-Disney; reprints 4-Color #1024 (Toth-a); photo-c	5	10	15	30	48	65
Dumbo 1 (10090-310)(10/63)-Disney; r/4-C #668	3	6	9	21	32	42
Emil & the Detectives 10120-502 (11/64)-Disney; photo-c & back-c photo pin-up	3	6	9	20	30	40
Escapade in Florence 1 (10043-301)(1/63)-Disney; starring Annette Funicello	8	16	24	52	86	120
Fall of the Roman Empire 10118-407 (7/64); Sophia Loren photo-c	4	8	12	24	37	50
Fantastic Voyage 10178-702 (2/67)-Wood/Adkins-a; photo-c	6	12	18	37	59	80
55 Days at Peking 10081-309 (9/63)-Photo-c	3	6	9	20	30	40
Fighting Prince of Donegal, The 10193-701 (1/67)-Disney	3	6	9	19	29	38
First Men in the Moon 10132-503 (3/65)-Fred Fredericks-a; photo-c	4	8	12	24	37	50

Movie Comics - King Kong © RKO

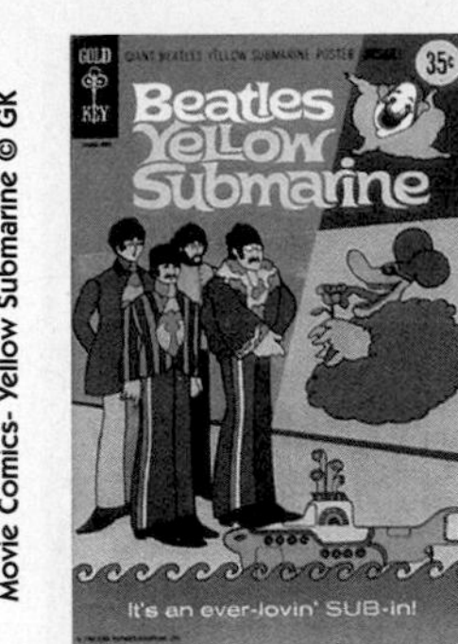

Movie Comics- Yellow Submarine © GK

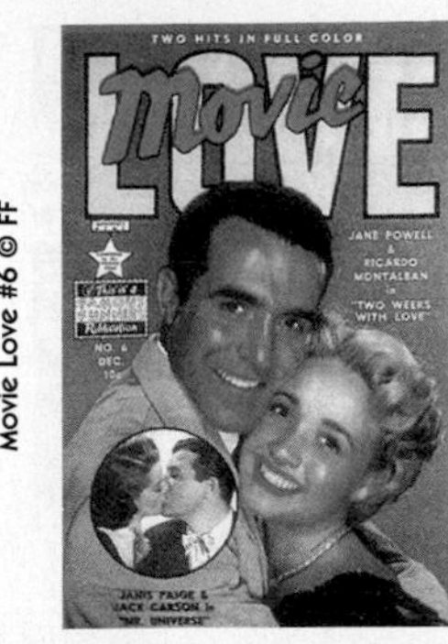

Movie Love #6 © FF

	GD 2.0	VG 4.0	FN 6.0	VF 8.0	VF/NM 9.0	NM- 9.2
Gay Purr-ee 30017-301(1/63, 84 pgs.)	5	10	15	32	51	70
Gnome Mobile, The 10207-710 (10/67)-Disney; Walter Brennan photo-c & back-c photo pin-up	4	8	12	22	34	45
Goodbye, Mr. Chips 10246-006 (6/70)-Peter O'Toole photo-c	3	6	9	20	30	40
Happiest Millionaire, The 10221-804 (4/68)-Disney	4	8	12	22	34	45
Hey There, It's Yogi Bear 10122-409 (9/64)-Hanna-Barbera	6	12	18	43	69	95
Horse Without a Head, The 10109-401 (1/64)-Disney	3	6	9	19	29	38
How the West Was Won 10074-307 (7/63)-Based on the L'Amour novel; Tufts-a	4	8	12	28	44	60
In Search of the Castaways 10048-303 (3/63)-Disney; Hayley Mills photo-c	6	12	18	43	69	95
Jungle Book, The 1 (6022-801)(1/68-Whitman)-Disney; large size (10x13-1/2"); 59¢	6	12	18	43	69	95
Jungle Book, The 1 (30033-803)(3/68, 68 pgs.)-Disney; same contents as Whitman #1	4	8	12	24	37	50
Jungle Book, The 1 (6/78, $1.00 tabloid)	3	6	9	16	23	30
Jungle Book (7/84)-r/Giant; Whitman pre-pack	2	4	6	10	14	18
Kidnapped 10080-306 (6/63)-Disney; reprints 4-Color #1101; photo-c	3	6	9	20	30	40
King Kong 30036-809(9/68-68 pgs.)-painted-c	4	8	12	26	41	55
King Kong nn-Whitman Treasury($1.00, 68 pgs.,1968), same cover as Gold Key issue	5	10	15	34	55	75
King Kong 11299(#1-786, 10x13-1/4", 68 pgs., $1.00, 1978)	3	6	9	18	27	35
Lady and the Tramp 10042-301 (1/63)-Disney; r/4-Color #629	3	6	9	21	32	42
Lady and the Tramp 1 (1967-Giant; 25¢)-Disney; reprints part of Dell #1	5	10	15	34	55	75
Lady and the Tramp 2 (10042-203)(3/72)-Disney; r/4-Color #629	3	6	9	16	23	30
Legend of Lobo, The 1 (10059-303)(3/63)-Disney; photo-c	3	6	9	16	23	30
Lt. Robin Crusoe, U.S.N. 10191-610 (10/66)-Disney; Dick Van Dyke photo-c & back-c photo pin-up	3	6	9	18	27	35
Lion, The 10035-301 (1/63)-Photo-c	3	6	9	17	25	32
Lord Jim 10156-509 (9/65)-Photo-c	3	6	9	17	25	32
Love Bug, The 10237-906 (6/69)-Disney; Buddy Hackett photo-c	4	8	12	22	34	45
Mary Poppins 10136-501 (1/65)-Disney; photo-c	5	10	15	30	48	65
Mary Poppins 30023-501 (1/65-68 pgs.)-Disney; photo-c	7	14	21	47	76	105
McLintock 10110-403 (3/64); John Wayne app.; John Wayne & Maureen O'Hara photo-c	12	24	36	82	146	210
Merlin Jones as the Monkey's Uncle 10115-510 (10/65)-Disney; Annette Funicello front/back photo-c	6	12	18	39	62	85
Miracle of the White Stallions, The 10065-306 (6/63)-Disney	3	6	9	19	29	38
Misadventures of Merlin Jones, The 10115-405 (5/64)-Disney; Annette Funicello photo front/back-c	6	12	18	39	62	85
Moon-Spinners, The 10124-410 (10/64)-Disney; Hayley Mills photo-c	6	12	18	43	69	95
Mutiny on the Bounty 1 (10040-302)(2/63)-Marlon Brando photo-c	4	8	12	22	34	45
Nikki, Wild Dog of the North 10141-412 (12/64)-Disney; reprints 4-Color #1226	3	6	9	16	23	30
Old Yeller 10168-601 (1/66)-Disney; reprints 4-Color #869; photo-c	3	6	9	16	23	30
One Hundred & One Dalmations 1 (10247-002) (2/70)-Disney; reprints Four Color #1183	3	6	9	18	27	35
Peter Pan 1 (10086-309)(9/63)-Disney; reprints Four Color #442	3	6	9	21	32	42
Peter Pan 2 (10086-909)(9/69)-Disney; reprints Four Color #442	3	6	9	16	23	30
Peter Pan 1 (3/84)-r/4-Color #442; Whitman pre-pack	2	4	6	11	16	20
P.T. 109 10123-409 (9/64)-John F. Kennedy	5	10	15	30	48	65
Rio Conchos 10143-503(3/65)	4	8	12	22	34	45
Robin Hood 10163-506 (6/65)-Disney; reprints Four Color #413	3	6	9	17	25	32
Shaggy Dog & the Absent-Minded Professor 30032-708 (8/67-Giant, 68 pgs.) Disney; reprints 4-Color #985,1199	5	10	15	32	51	70
Sleeping Beauty 1 (30042-009)(9/70)-Disney; reprints Four Color #973; with pull-out poster (No poster = half price)	6	12	18	43	69	95
Snow White & the Seven Dwarfs 1 (10091-310)(10/63)-Disney; reprints Four Color #382	3	6	9	20	30	40
Snow White & the Seven Dwarfs 10091-709 (9/67)-Disney; reprints Four Color #382	3	6	9	16	23	30
Snow White & the Seven Dwarfs 90091-204 (2/84)-Reprints Four Color #382; Whitman pre-pack	2	4	6	11	16	20
Son of Flubber 1 (10057-304)(4/63)-Disney; sequel to "The Absent-Minded Professor"	4	8	12	22	34	45
Summer Magic 10076-309 (9/63)-Disney; Hayley Mills photo-c; Manning-a	6	12	18	43	69	95
Swiss Family Robinson 10236-904 (4/69)-Disney; reprints Four Color #1156; photo-c	3	6	9	18	27	35
Sword in the Stone, The 30019-402 (2/64-Giant, 68 pgs.)-Disney (see March of Comics #258 & Wart and the Wizard	6	12	18	43	69	95
That Darn Cat 10171-602 (2/66)-Disney; Hayley Mills photo-c	6	12	18	43	69	95
Those Magnificent Men in Their Flying Machines 10162-510 (10/65); photo-c	3	6	9	20	30	40
Three Stooges in Orbit 30016-211 (11/62-Giant, 32 pgs.)-All photos from movie; stiff-photo-c	9	18	27	65	113	160
Tiger Walks, A 10117-406 (6/64)-Disney; Torres?, Tufts-a; photo-c	4	8	12	24	37	50
Toby Tyler 10142-502 (2/65)-Disney; reprints Four Color #1092; photo-c	3	6	9	18	27	35
Treasure Island 1 (10200-703)(3/67)-Disney; reprints Four Color #624; photo-c	3	6	9	16	23	30
20,000 Leagues Under the Sea 1 (10095-312)(12/63)-Disney; reprints Four Color #614	3	6	9	18	27	35
Wonderful Adventures of Pinocchio, The 1 (10089-310)(10/63)-Disney; reprints Four Color #545 (see Wonderful Advs. of...)	3	6	9	21	32	42
Wonderful Adventures of Pinocchio, The 10089-109 (9/71)-Disney; reprints Four Color #545	3	6	9	16	23	30
Wonderful World of the Brothers Grimm 1 (10008-210)(10/62)	4	8	12	28	44	60
X, the Man with the X-Ray Eyes 10083-309 (9/63)-Ray Milland photo on-c	7	14	21	49	80	110
Yellow Submarine 35000-902 (2/69-Giant, 68 pgs.)-With pull-out poster; The Beatles cartoon movie; Paul S. Newman-s	21	42	63	152	281	410
Without poster	9	18	27	63	107	150

MOVIE FABLES
DC Comics: Dec, 1944 (cover only ashcan)

nn-Ashcan comic, not distributed to newsstands, only for in house use. Covers were produced, but not the rest of the book. A copy sold in 2006 for $500.

MOVIE GEMS
DC Comics: Dec, 1944 (cover only ashcan)

nn-Ashcan comic, not distributed to newsstands, only for in house use. Covers were produced, but not the rest of the book. A copy sold in 2006 for $500.

MOVIE LOVE (Also see Personal Love)
Famous Funnies: Feb, 1950 - No. 22, Aug, 1953 (All photo-c)

	GD 2.0	VG 4.0	FN 6.0	VF 8.0	VF/NM 9.0	NM- 9.2
1-Dick Powell, Evelyn Keyes, & Mickey Rooney photo-c	17	34	51	98	154	210
2-Myrna Loy photo-c	11	22	33	60	83	105
3-7,9: 6-Ricardo Montalban photo-c. 9-Gene Tierney, John Lund, Glenn Ford, & Rhonda Fleming photo-c.	10	20	30	56	76	95
8-Williamson/Frazetta-a, 6 pgs.	45	90	135	279	465	650
10-Frazetta-a, 6 pgs.	46	92	138	285	473	660
11,14-16: 14-Janet Leigh photo-c	10	20	30	54	72	90
12-Dean Martin & Jerry Lewis photo-c (12/51, pre-dates Advs. of Dean Martin & Jerry Lewis comic)	18	36	54	107	169	230
13-Ronald Reagan photo-c with 1 pg. biog.	25	50	75	145	233	320
17-Leslie Caron & Ralph Meeker photo-c; 1 pg. Frazetta ad	10	20	30	56	76	95
18-22: 19-John Derek photo-c. 20-Donald O'Connor & Debbie Reynolds photo-c. 21-Paul Henreid & Patricia Medina photo-c. 22-John Payne & Coleen Gray photo-c	9	18	27	52	69	85

NOTE: *Each issue has a full-length movie adaptation with photo covers.*

MOVIE THRILLERS (Movie)
Magazine Enterprises: 1949

	GD 2.0	VG 4.0	FN 6.0	VF 8.0	VF/NM 9.0	NM- 9.2
1-Adaptation of "Rope of Sand" w/Burt Lancaster; Burt Lancaster photo-c	28	56	84	162	261	360

MOVIE TOWN ANIMAL ANTICS (Formerly Animal Antics; becomes Raccoon Kids #52 on)

Ms. Marvel (2006 series) #22 © MAR

Munsters #2 © TV Comics

Murder Incorporated #4 © FOX

GD 2.0 | VG 4.0 | FN 6.0 | VF 8.0 | VF/NM 9.0 | NM- 9.2

National Periodical Publ.: No. 24, Jan-Feb, 1950 - No. 51, July-Aug, 1954

	GD	VG	FN	VF	VF/NM	NM-
24-Raccoon Kids continue	12	24	36	67	94	120
25-51	10	20	30	54	72	90

NOTE: ***Sheldon Mayer** a-28-33, 35, 37-41, 43, 44, 47, 49-51.*

MOVIE TUNES COMICS (Formerly Animated...; Frankie No. 4 on)
Marvel Comics (MgPC): No. 3, Fall, 1946

	GD	VG	FN	VF	VF/NM	NM-
3-Super Rabbit, Krazy Krow, Silly Seal & Ziggy Pig	14	28	42	82	121	160

MOWGLI JUNGLE BOOK (Rudyard Kipling's...)
Dell Publ. Co.: No. 487, Aug-Oct, 1953 - No. 620, Apr, 1955

	GD	VG	FN	VF	VF/NM	NM-
Four Color 487 (#1)	6	12	18	37	59	80
Four Color 582 (8/54), 620	5	10	15	30	48	65

MR. (See Mister)

M. REX
Image Comics: July, 1999 - No. 2, Dec, 1999 ($2.95)

Preview ($5.00) B&W pages and sketchbook; Rouleau-a 5.00
1,2-($2.95) 1-Joe Kelly-s/Rouleau-a/Anacleto-c. 2-Rouleau-c 3.00

MS. MARVEL (Also see The Avengers #183)
Marvel Comics Group: Jan, 1977 - No. 23, Apr, 1979

	GD	VG	FN	VF	VF/NM	NM-
1-1st app. Ms. Marvel; Scorpion app. in #1,2	2	4	6	8	11	14
2-10: 2-Origin. 5-Vision app. 6-10-(Reg. 30¢-c). 10-Last 30¢ issue	1	2	3	4	5	7
6-10-(35¢-c variants, limited dist.)(6/77)	4	8	12	22	34	45
11-15,19-23: 19-Capt. Marvel app. 20-New costume. 23-Vance Astro (leader of the Guardians) app.						6.00
16,17-1st brief app. Mystique	3	6	9	14	20	25
18-1st full app. Mystique; Avengers x-over	4	8	12	26	41	55

NOTE: ***Austin** c-14i, 16i, 17i, 22i. **Buscema** a-1-3p; c(p)-2, 4, 6, 7, 15. **Infantino** a-14p, 19p. **Gil Kane** c-8. **Mooney** a-4-8p, 13p, 15-18p. **Starlin** c-12.*

MS. MARVEL (Also see New Avengers)
Marvel Comics: May, 2006 - Present ($2.99)

1-24: 1-Cho-c/Reed-s/De La Torre-a; Stilt-Man app. 4,5-Dr. Strange app. 6,7-Araña app. 3.00
1-Variant cover by Michael Turner 5.00
25-($3.99) Two covers by Horn and Dodson; Secret Invasion 4.00
26-31-Secret Invasion 3.00
... Annual 1 (11/08, $3.99) Spider-Man app.; Horn-c 3.00
... Special (3/07, $2.99) Reed-s/Camuncoli-a/c 3.00
... Vol. 1: Best of the Best HC (2006, $19.99) r/#1-5 & Giant-Size Ms. Marvel #1 20.00
... Vol. 1: Best of the Best SC (2007, $14.99) r/#1-5 & Giant-Size Ms. Marvel #1 15.00
... Vol. 2: Civil War HC (2007, $19.99) r/#6-10 & Ms. Marvel Special #1 20.00
... Vol. 2: Civil War SC (2007, $14.99) r/#6-10 & Ms. Marvel Special #1 15.00
... Vol. 3: Operation Lightning Storm HC (2007, $19.99) r/#11-17 20.00
... Vol. 4: Monster Smash HC (2008, $19.99) r/#18-24 20.00

MS. MYSTIC
Pacific Comics: Oct, 1982 - No. 2, Feb, 1984 ($1.00/$1.50)

1,2: Neal Adams-c/a/script. 1-Origin; intro Erth, Ayre, Fyre & Watr 4.00

MS. MYSTIC
Continuity Comics: 1988 - No. 9, May, 1992 ($2.00)

1-9: 1,2-Reprint Pacific Comics issues 3.00

MS. MYSTIC
Continuity Comics: V2#1, Oct, 1993 - V2#4, Jan, 1994 ($2.50)

V2#1-4: 1-Adams-c(i)/part-i. 2-4-Embossed-c. 2-Nebres part-i. 3-Adams-c(i)/plot. 4-Adams-c(p)/plot 2.50

MS. MYSTIC DEATHWATCH 2000 (Ms. Mystic #3)
Continuity: May, 1993 - No. 3, Aug, 1993 ($2.50)

1-3-Bagged w/card; Adams plots 2.50

MS. TREE QUARTERLY / SPECIAL
DC Comics: Summer, 1990 -No. 10, 1992 ($3.95/$3.50, 84 pgs, mature)

1-10: 1-Midnight story; Batman text story, Grell-a. 2,3-Midnight stories; The Butcher text stories 4.00

NOTE: ***Cowan** c-2. **Grell** c-1, 6. **Infantino** a-8.*

MS. TREE'S THRILLING DETECTIVE ADVS (Ms. Tree #4 on; also see The Best of Ms. Tree) (Baxter paper #4-9)
Eclipse Comics/Aardvark-Vanaheim 10-18/Renegade Press 19 on: 2/83 - #9, 7/84; #10, 8/84 - #18, 5/85; #19, 6/85 - #50, 6/89

1 3.00
2-49: 2-Schythe begins. 9-Last Eclipse & last color issue. 10,11-two-tone 2.50
50-Contains flexi-disc ($3.95, 52 pgs.) 4.00

Summer Special 1 (8/86) 3.00
1950s 3-D Crime (7/87, no glasses)-Johnny Dynamite in 3-D 3.00
Mike Mist in 3-D (8/85)-With glasses 3.00

NOTE: ***Miller** pin-up 1-4. Johnny Dynamite-r begin #36 by **Morisi**.*

MS. VICTORY SPECIAL(Also see Capt. Paragon & Femforce)
Americomics: Jan, 1985 (nd)

1 2.50

MUCHA LUCHA (Based on Kids WB animated TV show)
DC Comics: Jun, 2003 - No. 3, Aug, 2003 ($2.25, limited series)

1-3-Rikochet, Buena Girl and The Flea app. 2.50

MUGGSY MOUSE (Also see Tick Tock Tales)
Magazine Enterprises: 1951 - No. 3, 1951; No. 4, 1954 - No. 5, 1954; 1963

	GD	VG	FN	VF	VF/NM	NM-
1(A-1 #33)	9	18	27	50	65	80
2(A-1 #36)-Racist-c	13	26	39	72	101	130
3(A-1 #39), 4(A-1 #95), 5(A-1 #99)	7	14	21	37	46	55
Super Reprint #14(1963), I.W. Reprint #1,2 (nd)	2	4	6	8	11	14

MUGGY-DOO, BOY CAT
Stanhall Publ.: July, 1953 - No. 4, Jan, 1954

	GD	VG	FN	VF	VF/NM	NM-
1-Funny animal; Irving Spector-a	9	18	27	47	61	75
2-4	6	12	18	27	33	38
Super Reprint #12('63), 16('64)	2	4	6	8	11	14

MULLKON EMPIRE (See John Jake's...)

MUMMY, THE (See Universal Presents... under Dell Giants & Movie Classics)

MUMMY, THE: THE RISE AND FALL OF XANGO'S AX (Based on the Brendan Fraser movies)
IDW Publishing: Apr, 2008 - No. 4, July, 2008 ($3.99, limited series)

1-4-Prequel to '08 movie The Mummy: Tomb of the Dragon Emperor; Stephen Mooney-a 4.00

MUNDEN'S BAR ANNUAL
First Comics: Apr, 1988; 1989 ($2.95/$5.95)

1-($2.95)-r/from Grimjack; Fish Police story; Ordway-c 3.00
2-($5.95)-Teenage Mutant Ninja Turtles app. 6.00

MUNSTERS, THE (TV)
Gold Key: Jan, 1965 - No. 16, Jan, 1968 (All photo-c)

	GD	VG	FN	VF	VF/NM	NM-
1 (10134-501)	17	34	51	120	223	325
2	9	18	27	65	113	160
3-5	8	16	24	54	90	125
6-16	7	14	21	47	76	105

MUNSTERS, THE (TV)
TV Comics!: Aug, 1997 - No. 4 ($2.95, B&W)

1-4-All have photo-c 3.00
1,4-($7.95)-Variant-c 8.00
2-Variant-c w/Beverly Owens as Marilyn 3.00
Special Comic Con Ed. (7/97, $9.95) 10.00

MUPPET BABIES, THE (TV)(See Star Comics Magazine)
Marvel Comics (Star Comics)/Marvel #18 on: Aug, 1985 - No. 26, July, 1989 (Children's book)

1-26 3.00

MUPPETS TAKE MANHATTAN, THE
Marvel Comics (Star Comics): Nov, 1984 - No. 3, Jan, 1985

1-3-Movie adapt. r-/Marvel Super Special 3.00

MURCIELAGA, SHE-BAT
Heroic Publishing: Jan, 1993 - No. 2, 1993 (B&W)

1-($1.50, 28 pgs.) 2.50
2-($2.95, 36 pgs.)-Coated-c 3.00

MURDER CAN BE FUN
Slave Labor Graphics: Feb, 1996 - No. 12 ($2.95, B&W)

1-12: 1-Dorkin-c. 2-Vasquez-c. 3.00

MURDER INCORPORATED (My Private Life #16 on)
Fox Feature Syndicate: 1/48 - No. 15, 12/49; (2 No.9's); 6/50 - No. 3, 8/51

	GD	VG	FN	VF	VF/NM	NM-
1 (1st Series); 1,2 have 'For Adults Only' on-c	50	100	150	310	518	725
2-Electrocution story	40	80	120	235	380	525
3-7,9(4/49),10(5/49),11-15	23	46	69	133	214	295
8-Used in **SOTI**, pg. 160	25	50	75	147	236	325
9(3/49)-Possible use in **SOTI**, pg. 145; r/Blue Beetle #56('48)	23	46	69	133	214	295

5(#1, 6/50)(2nd Series)-Formerly My Desire #4; bondage-c.

Murder Me Dead #3 © David Lapham

Mutopia X #1 © MAR

My Experience #21 © FOX

	GD 2.0	VG 4.0	FN 6.0	VF 8.0	VF/NM 9.0	NM- 9.2
	19	38	57	109	172	235
2(8/50)-Morisi-a	16	32	48	96	151	205
3(8/51)-Used in **POP**, pg. 81; Rico-a; lingerie-c/panels	18	36	54	105	165	225

MURDER ME DEAD
El Capitán Books: July, 2000 - No. 9, Oct, 2001 ($2.95/$4.95, B&W)

	GD 2.0	VG 4.0	FN 6.0	VF 8.0	VF/NM 9.0	NM- 9.2
1-8-David Lapham-s/a						3.00
9-($4.95)						5.00

MURDEROUS GANGSTERS
Avon Per./Realistic No. 3 on: Jul, 1951; No. 2, Dec, 1951 - No. 4, Jun, 1952

	GD 2.0	VG 4.0	FN 6.0	VF 8.0	VF/NM 9.0	NM- 9.2
1-Pretty Boy Floyd, Leggs Diamond; 1 pg. Wood-a	45	90	135	279	465	650
2-Baby-Face Nelson; 1 pg. Wood-a; painted-c	29	58	87	169	272	375
3-Painted-c	24	48	72	140	225	310
4- "Murder by Needle" drug story; Mort Lawrence-a; Kinstler-c	30	60	90	174	280	385

MURDER MYSTERIES (Neil Gaiman's...)
Dark Horse Comics: 2002 ($13.95, HC, one-shot)

	GD 2.0	VG 4.0	FN 6.0	VF 8.0	VF/NM 9.0	NM- 9.2
HC-Adapts Gaiman story; P. Craig Russell-script/art						14.00

MURDER TALES (Magazine)
World Famous Publications: V1#10, Nov, 1970 - V1#11, Jan, 1971 (52 pgs.)

	GD 2.0	VG 4.0	FN 6.0	VF 8.0	VF/NM 9.0	NM- 9.2
V1#10-One pg. Frazetta ad	4	8	12	26	41	55
11-Guardineer-r; bondage-c	4	8	12	22	34	45

MUSHMOUSE AND PUNKIN PUSS (TV)
Gold Key: September, 1965 (Hanna-Barbera)

	GD 2.0	VG 4.0	FN 6.0	VF 8.0	VF/NM 9.0	NM- 9.2
1 (10153-509)	8	16	24	58	97	135

MUSIC MAN, THE (See Movie Classics)

MUTANT CHRONICLES (Video game)
Acclaim Comics (Armada): May, 1996 - No. 4, Aug, 1996 ($2.95, lim. series)

	GD 2.0	VG 4.0	FN 6.0	VF 8.0	VF/NM 9.0	NM- 9.2
1-4: Simon Bisley-c on all, Sourcebook (#5)						3.00

MUTANT EARTH (Stan Winston's...)
Image Comics: April, 2002 - No. 4, Jan, 2003 ($2.95)

	GD 2.0	VG 4.0	FN 6.0	VF 8.0	VF/NM 9.0	NM- 9.2
1-4-Flip book w/Realm of the Claw						3.00
Trakk...His Adventures in Mutant Earth TPB (2003, $16.95) r/#1-4; Winston interview						17.00

MUTANT MISADVENTURES OF CLOAK AND DAGGER, THE
(Becomes Cloak and Dagger #14 on)
Marvel Comics: Oct, 1988 - No. 19, Aug, 1991 ($1.25/$1.50)

	GD 2.0	VG 4.0	FN 6.0	VF 8.0	VF/NM 9.0	NM- 9.2
1-8,10-15: 1-X-Factor app. 10-Painted-c. 12-Dr. Doom app. 14-Begin new direction						2.50
9,16-19: 9-(52 pgs.) The Avengers x-over; painted-c. 16-18-Spider-Man x-over. 18-Infinity Gauntlet x-over; Thanos cameo; Ghost Rider app. 19-(52 pgs.) Origin Cloak & Dagger						3.00

NOTE: ***Austin** a-12i; c(i)-4, 12, 13; scripts-all. **Russell** a-2i. **Williamson** a-14i-16i; c-15i.*

MUTANTS & MISFITS
Silverline Comics (Solson): 1987 - No. 3, 1987 ($1.95)

	GD 2.0	VG 4.0	FN 6.0	VF 8.0	VF/NM 9.0	NM- 9.2
1-3						2.50

MUTANTS VS. ULTRAS
Malibu Comics (Ultraverse): Nov, 1995 ($6.95, one-shot)

	GD 2.0	VG 4.0	FN 6.0	VF 8.0	VF/NM 9.0	NM- 9.2
1-r/Exiles vs. X-Men, Night Man vs. Wolverine, Prime vs. Hulk						7.00

MUTANT, TEXAS: TALES OF SHERIFF IDA RED (Also see Jingle Belle)
Oni Press: May, 2002 - No. 4, Nov, 2002 ($2.95, B&W, limited series)

	GD 2.0	VG 4.0	FN 6.0	VF 8.0	VF/NM 9.0	NM- 9.2
1-4-Paul Dini-s/J. Bone-c/a						3.00
TPB (2003, $11.95) r/#1-4; intro. by Joe Lansdale						12.00

MUTANT 2099
Marvel Comics (Marvel Knights): Nov, 2004 ($2.99, one-shot)

	GD 2.0	VG 4.0	FN 6.0	VF 8.0	VF/NM 9.0	NM- 9.2
1-Kirkman-s/Pat Lee-c						3.00

MUTANT X (See X-Factor)
Marvel Comics: Nov, 1998 - No. 32, June, 2001 ($2.99/$1.99/$2.25)

	GD 2.0	VG 4.0	FN 6.0	VF 8.0	VF/NM 9.0	NM- 9.2
1-($2.99) Alex Summers with alternate world's X-Men						3.00
2-11,13-19-($1.99): 2-Two covers. 5-Man-Spider-c/app.						2.50
12,25-($2.99): 12-Pin-up gallery by Kaluta, Romita, Byrne						3.00
20-24,26-32: 20-Begin $2.25-c. 28-31-Logan-c/app. 32-Last issue						2.50
Annual '99, '00 (5/99,'00, $3.50) '00-Doran-a(p)						3.50
Annual 2001 ($2.99) Story oocurs between #31 & #32; Dracula app.						3.00

MUTANT X (Based on TV show)
Marvel Comics: May, 2002 - Present ($3.50)

	GD 2.0	VG 4.0	FN 6.0	VF 8.0	VF/NM 9.0	NM- 9.2
...: Dangerous Decisions (6/02) -Kuder-s/Immonen-a						3.50
...: Origin (5/02) -Tischman & Chaykin-s/Ferguson-a						3.50

MUTATIS
Marvel Comics (Epic Comics): 1992 - No. 3, 1992 ($2.25, mini-series)

	GD 2.0	VG 4.0	FN 6.0	VF 8.0	VF/NM 9.0	NM- 9.2
1-3: Painted-c						2.50

MUTIES
Marvel Comics: Apr, 2002 - No. 6, Sept, 2002 ($2.50)

	GD 2.0	VG 4.0	FN 6.0	VF 8.0	VF/NM 9.0	NM- 9.2
1-6: 1-Bollars-s/Ferguson-a. 2-Spaziante-a. 3-Haspiel-a. 4-Kanuiga-a						2.50

MUTINY (Stormy Tales of the Seven Seas)
Aragon Magazines: Oct, 1954 - No. 3, Feb, 1955

	GD 2.0	VG 4.0	FN 6.0	VF 8.0	VF/NM 9.0	NM- 9.2
1	16	32	48	92	144	195
2,3: 2-Capt. Mutiny. 3-Bondage-c	14	28	42	76	108	140

MUTINY ON THE BOUNTY (See Classics Illustrated #100 & Movie Comics)

MUTOPIA X (Also see House of M and related titles)
Marvel Comics: Sept, 2005 - No. 5, Jan, 2006 ($2.99, limited series)

	GD 2.0	VG 4.0	FN 6.0	VF 8.0	VF/NM 9.0	NM- 9.2
1-5-Medina-a/Hine-s						3.00
House of M: Mutopia X (2006, $13.99, TPB) r/series						14.00

MUTT AND JEFF (See All-American, All-Flash #18, Cicero's Cat, Comic Cavalcade, Famous Feature Stories, The Funnies, Popular & Xmas Comics)
All American/National 1-103(6/58)/Dell 104(10/58)-115 (10-12/59)/ Harvey 116(2/60)-148: Summer, 1939 (nd) - No. 148, Nov, 1965

	GD 2.0	VG 4.0	FN 6.0	VF 8.0	VF/NM 9.0	NM- 9.2
1(nn)-Lost Wheels	140	280	420	882	1491	2100
2(nn)-Charging Bull (Summer, 1940, nd; on sale 6/20/40)	68	136	204	428	727	1025
3(nn)-Bucking Broncos (Summer, 1941, nd)	49	98	147	304	507	710
4(Winter, '41), 5(Summer, '42)	45	90	135	279	465	650
6-10: 6-Includes Minute Man Answers the Call	26	52	78	154	247	340
11-20: 20-X-Mas-c	19	38	57	109	172	235
21-30	15	30	45	83	124	165
31-50: 32-X-Mas-c	12	24	36	69	97	125
51-75-Last Fisher issue. 53-Last 52 pgs.	10	20	30	56	76	95
76-99,101-103: 76-Last pre-code issue(1/55)	5	10	15	34	55	75
100	6	12	18	37	59	80
104-115,132-148	4	8	12	24	44	60
116-131-Richie Rich app.	5	10	15	30	48	65
...Jokes 1-3(8/60-61, Harvey)-84 pgs.; Richie Rich in all; Little Dot in #2,3; Lotta in #2	5	10	15	30	48	65
...New Jokes 1-4(10/63-11/65, Harvey)-68 pgs.; Richie Rich in #1-3; Stumbo in #1	4	8	12	24	37	50

NOTE: *Most all issues by **Al Smith**. Issues from 1963 on have **Fisher** reprints. Clarification: early issues signed by Fisher are mostly drawn by Smith.*

MY BROTHERS' KEEPER
Spire Christian Comics (Fleming H. Revell Co.): 1973 (35/49¢, 36 pgs.)

	GD 2.0	VG 4.0	FN 6.0	VF 8.0	VF/NM 9.0	NM- 9.2
nn	2	4	6	8	10	12

MY CONFESSIONS (My Confession #7&8; formerly Western True Crime; A Spectacular Feature Magazine #11)
Fox Feature Syndicate: No. 7, Aug, 1949 - No. 10, Jan-Feb, 1950

	GD 2.0	VG 4.0	FN 6.0	VF 8.0	VF/NM 9.0	NM- 9.2
7-Wood-a (10 pgs.)	24	48	72	140	225	310
8,9: 8-Harrison/Wood-a (19 pgs.). 9-Wood-a	22	44	66	127	204	280
10	12	24	36	69	97	125

MY DATE COMICS (Teen-age)
Hillman Periodicals: July, 1947 - V1#4, Jan, 1948 (2nd Romance comic; see Young Romance)

	GD 2.0	VG 4.0	FN 6.0	VF 8.0	VF/NM 9.0	NM- 9.2
1-S&K-c/a	38	76	114	226	363	500
2-4-S&K-c/a; Dan Barry-a	26	52	78	152	244	335

MY DESIRE (Formerly Jo-Jo Comics; becomes Murder, Inc. #5 on)
Fox Feature Syndicate: No. 30, Aug, 1949 - No. 4, April, 1950

	GD 2.0	VG 4.0	FN 6.0	VF 8.0	VF/NM 9.0	NM- 9.2
30(#1)	17	34	51	100	158	215
31 (#2, 10/49),3(2/50),4	14	28	42	76	108	140
31 (Canadian edition)	8	16	24	44	57	70
32(12/49)-Wood-a	21	42	63	123	197	270

MY DIARY (Becomes My Friend Irma #3 on?)
Marvel Comics (A Lovers Mag.): Dec, 1949 - No. 2, Mar, 1950

	GD 2.0	VG 4.0	FN 6.0	VF 8.0	VF/NM 9.0	NM- 9.2
1,2-Photo-c	15	30	45	85	130	175

MY EXPERIENCE (Formerly All Top; becomes Judy Canova #23 on)
Fox Feature Syndicate: No. 19, Sept, 1949 - No. 22, Mar, 1950

	GD 2.0	VG 4.0	FN 6.0	VF 8.0	VF/NM 9.0	NM- 9.2
19,21: 19-Wood-a. 21-Wood-a(2)	26	52	78	152	244	335
20	14	28	42	76	108	140
22-Wood-a (9 pgs.)	22	44	66	127	204	280

MY FAITH IN FRANKIE

My Greatest Adventure #17 © DC

My Life #9 © FOX

My Love Secret #26 © FOX

DC Comics (Vertigo): March, 2004 - No. 4, June, 2004 ($2.95, limited series)

	GD 2.0	VG 4.0	FN 6.0	VF 8.0	VF/NM 9.0	NM- 9.2
1-4-Mike Carey-s/Sonny Liew & Marc Hempel-a						3.00
TPB (2004, $6.95, digest-size) r/series in B&W; Dead Boy Detectives preview						7.00

MY FAVORITE MARTIAN (TV)
Gold Key: 1/64; No.2, 7/64 - No. 9, 10/66 (No. 1,3-9 have photo-c)

	GD 2.0	VG 4.0	FN 6.0	VF 8.0	VF/NM 9.0	NM- 9.2
1-Russ Manning-a	12	24	36	87	156	225
2	7	14	21	49	80	110
3-9	6	12	18	41	66	90

MY FRIEND IRMA (Radio/TV) (Formerly My Diary? and/or Western Life Romances?)
Marvel/Atlas Comics (BFP): No. 3, June, 1950 - No. 47, Dec, 1954; No. 48, Feb, 1955

	GD 2.0	VG 4.0	FN 6.0	VF 8.0	VF/NM 9.0	NM- 9.2
3-Dan DeCarlo-a in all; 52 pgs. begin, end ?	19	38	57	112	176	240
4-Kurtzman-a (10 pgs.)	19	38	57	109	172	235
5- "Egghead Doodle" by Kurtzman (4 pgs.)	15	30	45	85	130	175
6,8-10: 9-Paper dolls, 1 pg; Millie app. (5 pgs.)	12	24	36	69	97	125
7-One pg. Kurtzman-a	13	26	39	72	101	130
11-23: 23-One pg. Frazetta-a	9	18	27	52	69	85
24-48: 41,48-Stan Lee & Dan DeCarlo app.	8	16	24	44	57	70

MY GIRL PEARL
Atlas Comics: 4/55 - #4, 10/55; #5, 7/57 - #6, 9/57; #7, 8/60 - #11, ?/61

	GD 2.0	VG 4.0	FN 6.0	VF 8.0	VF/NM 9.0	NM- 9.2
1-Dan DeCarlo-c/a in #1-6	15	30	45	86	133	180
2	10	20	30	54	72	90
3-6	8	16	24	44	57	70
7-11	4	8	12	28	44	60

MY GREATEST ADVENTURE (Doom Patrol #86 on)
National Periodical Publications: Jan-Feb, 1955 - No. 85, Feb, 1964

	GD 2.0	VG 4.0	FN 6.0	VF 8.0	VF/NM 9.0	NM- 9.2
1-Before CCA	121	242	363	1029	1963	2900
2	47	94	141	376	701	1025
3-5	34	68	102	256	483	710
6-10: 6-Science fiction format begins	28	56	84	207	384	560
11-14: 12-1st S.A. issue	20	40	60	148	274	400
15-17: Kirby-a in all	22	44	66	161	298	435
18-Kirby-c/a	25	50	75	185	343	500
19,22-25	17	34	51	124	230	335
20,21,28-Kirby-a	20	40	60	148	274	400
26,27,29,30	14	28	42	99	175	250
31-40	11	22	33	79	140	200
41,42,44-57,59	9	18	27	65	113	160
43-Kirby-a	10	20	30	70	123	175
58,60,61-Toth-a; Last 10¢ issue	10	20	30	67	116	165
62-76,78,79: 79-Promotes "Legion of the Strange" for next issue; renamed Doom Patrol for #80	7	14	21	50	83	115
77-Toth-a; Robotman prototype	8	16	24	52	86	120
80-(6/63)-Intro/origin Doom Patrol and begin series; origin & 1st app. Negative Man, Elasti-Girl & S.A. Robotman	48	96	144	384	717	1050
81,85-Toth-a	18	36	54	130	240	350
82-84	17	34	51	120	223	325

NOTE: ***Anderson** a-42. **Cameron** a-24. **Colan** a-77. **Meskin** a-25, 26, 32, 39, 45, 50, 56, 57, 61, 64, 70, 73, 74, 76, 79; c-76. **Moreira** a-11, 12, 15, 17, 20, 23, 25, 27, 37, 40-43, 46, 48, 55-57, 59, 60, 62-65, 67, 69, 70; c-1-4, 7-10. **Roussos** c/a-71-73. **Wildey** a-32.*

MY GREAT LOVE (Becomes Will Rogers Western #5)
Fox Feature Syndicate: Oct, 1949 - No. 4, Apr, 1950

	GD 2.0	VG 4.0	FN 6.0	VF 8.0	VF/NM 9.0	NM- 9.2
1	15	30	45	88	137	185
2-4	10	20	30	56	76	95

MY INTIMATE AFFAIR (Inside Crime #3)
Fox Feature Syndicate: Mar, 1950 - No. 2, May, 1950

	GD 2.0	VG 4.0	FN 6.0	VF 8.0	VF/NM 9.0	NM- 9.2
1	15	30	45	88	137	185
2	10	20	30	56	76	95

MY LIFE (Formerly Meet Corliss Archer)
Fox Feature Syndicate: No. 4, Sept, 1948 - No. 15, July, 1950

	GD 2.0	VG 4.0	FN 6.0	VF 8.0	VF/NM 9.0	NM- 9.2
4-Used in **SOTI**, pg. 39; Kamen/Feldstein-a	40	80	120	244	397	550
5-Kamen-a	24	48	72	140	225	310
6-Kamen/Feldstein-a	26	52	78	152	244	335
7-Wood-a; wash cover	21	42	63	123	197	270
8,9,11-15	12	24	36	69	97	125
10-Wood-a	19	38	57	112	176	240

MY LITTLE MARGIE (TV)
Charlton Comics: July, 1954 - No. 54, Nov, 1964

	GD 2.0	VG 4.0	FN 6.0	VF 8.0	VF/NM 9.0	NM- 9.2
1-Photo front/back-c	37	74	111	215	345	475
2-Photo front/back-c	18	36	54	105	165	225
3-7,10	12	24	36	67	94	120
8,9-Infinity-c	12	24	36	69	97	125
11-14: Part-photo-c (#13, 8/56)	10	20	30	58	79	100
15-19	10	20	30	54	72	90
20-(25¢, 100 pg. issue)	15	30	45	85	130	175
21-40: 40-Last 10¢ issue	5	10	15	32	51	70
41-53	4	8	12	28	44	60
54-(11/64) Beatles on cover; lead story spoofs the Beatle haircut craze of the 1960's; Beatles app. (scarce)	16	32	48	114	212	310

NOTE: *Doll cut-outs in 32, 33, 40, 45, 50.*

MY LITTLE MARGIE'S BOY FRIENDS (TV) (Freddy V2#12 on)
Charlton Comics: Aug, 1955 - No. 11, Apr?, 1958

	GD 2.0	VG 4.0	FN 6.0	VF 8.0	VF/NM 9.0	NM- 9.2
1-Has several Archie swipes	15	30	45	84	127	170
2	9	18	27	52	69	85
3-11	8	16	24	44	57	70

MY LITTLE MARGIE'S FASHIONS (TV)
Charlton Comics: Feb, 1959 - No. 5, Nov, 1959

	GD 2.0	VG 4.0	FN 6.0	VF 8.0	VF/NM 9.0	NM- 9.2
1	14	28	42	76	108	140
2-5	8	16	24	44	57	70

MY LOVE (Becomes Two Gun Western #5 (11/50) on?)
Marvel Comics (CLDS): July, 1949 - No. 4, Apr, 1950 (All photo-c)

	GD 2.0	VG 4.0	FN 6.0	VF 8.0	VF/NM 9.0	NM- 9.2
1	15	30	45	90	140	190
2,3	11	22	33	60	83	105
4-Bettie Page photo-c (see Cupid #2)	40	80	120	235	380	525

MY LOVE
Marvel Comics Group: Sept, 1969 - No. 39, Mar, 1976

	GD 2.0	VG 4.0	FN 6.0	VF 8.0	VF/NM 9.0	NM- 9.2
1	7	14	21	45	73	100
2-9: 4-6-Colan-a	4	8	12	24	37	50
10-Williamson-r/My Own Romance #71; Kirby-a	4	8	12	26	41	55
11-13,15-19	3	6	9	20	30	40
14-(52 pgs.)-Woodstock-c/sty; Morrow-c/a; Kirby/Colletta-r	5	10	15	34	55	75
20-Starlin-a	4	8	12	22	34	45
21,22,24-27,29-38: 38-Reprints	3	6	9	18	27	35
23-Steranko-r/Our Love Story #5	4	8	12	22	34	45
28-Kirby-a	3	6	9	19	29	38
39-Last issue; reprints	3	6	9	19	29	38
Special 1 (12/71)(52 pgs.)	5	10	15	30	48	65

NOTE: ***John Buscema** a-1-7, 10, 18-21, 22r(2), 24r, 25r, 29r, 34r, 36r, 37r, Spec. (r)(4); c-13, 15, 25, 27, Spec. **Colan** a-4, 5, 6, 8, 9, 16, 17, 20, 21, 22, 24r, 27r, 30r, 35r, 39r. **Colan/Everett** a-13, 15, 16, 27(r/#13). **Kirby** a-(r)-10, 14, 26, 28. **Romita** a-1-3, 19, 20, 25, 34, 38; c-1-3, 15.*

MY LOVE AFFAIR (March of Crime #7 on)
Fox Feature Syndicate: July, 1949 - No. 6, May, 1950

	GD 2.0	VG 4.0	FN 6.0	VF 8.0	VF/NM 9.0	NM- 9.2
1	15	30	45	88	137	185
2	10	20	30	56	76	95
3-6-Wood-a. 5-(3/50)-Becomes Love Stories #6	18	36	54	107	169	230

MY LOVE LIFE (Formerly Zegra)
Fox Feature Synd.: No. 6, June, 1949 - No. 13, Aug, 1950; No. 13, Sept, 1951

	GD 2.0	VG 4.0	FN 6.0	VF 8.0	VF/NM 9.0	NM- 9.2
6-Kamenish-a	15	30	45	88	137	185
7-13	10	20	30	58	79	100
13 (9/51)(Formerly My Story #12)	10	20	30	54	72	90

MY LOVE MEMOIRS (Formerly Women Outlaws; Hunted #13 on)
Fox Feature Syndicate: No. 9, Nov, 1949 - No. 12, May, 1950

	GD 2.0	VG 4.0	FN 6.0	VF 8.0	VF/NM 9.0	NM- 9.2
9,11,12-Wood-a	18	36	54	107	169	230
10	10	20	30	58	79	100

MY LOVE SECRET (Formerly Phantom Lady; Animal Crackers #31)
Fox Feature Syndicate/M. S. Distr.: No. 24, June, 1949 - No. 30, June, 1950; No. 53, 1954

	GD 2.0	VG 4.0	FN 6.0	VF 8.0	VF/NM 9.0	NM- 9.2
24-Kamen/Feldstein-a	19	38	57	109	172	235
25-Possible caricature of Wood on-c?	13	26	39	74	105	135
26,28-Wood-a	18	36	54	107	169	230
27,29,30: 30-Photo-c	11	22	33	62	86	110
53-(Reprint, M.S. Distr.) 1954? nd given; formerly Western Thrillers; becomes Crimes by Women #54; photo-c	7	14	21	35	43	50

MY LOVE STORY (Hoot Gibson Western #5 on)
Fox Feature Syndicate: Sept, 1949 - No. 4, Mar, 1950

	GD 2.0	VG 4.0	FN 6.0	VF 8.0	VF/NM 9.0	NM- 9.2
1	15	30	45	88	137	185
2	10	20	30	56	76	95
3,4-Wood-a	18	36	54	107	169	230

MY LOVE STORY

My Own Romance #74 © MAR

My Secret Life #22 © FOX

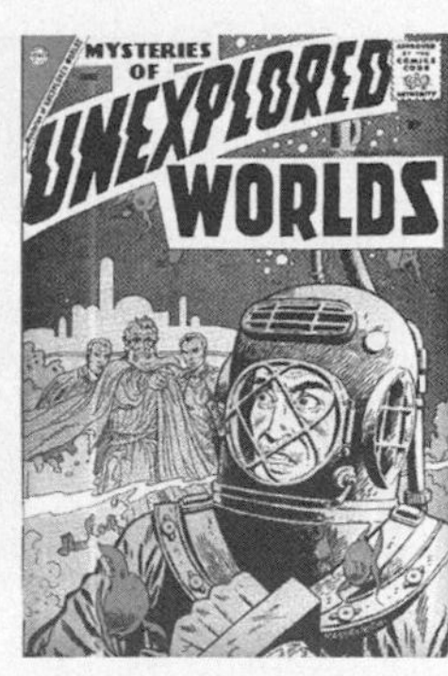

Mysteries of Unexplored Worlds #8 © CC

	GD 2.0	VG 4.0	FN 6.0	VF 8.0	VF/NM 9.0	NM- 9.2

Atlas Comics (GPS): April, 1956 - No. 9, Aug, 1957

	GD	VG	FN	VF	VF/NM	NM-
1	14	28	42	76	108	140
2	8	16	24	44	57	70
3,7: Matt Baker-a. 7-Toth-a	10	20	30	58	79	100
4-6,8,9	8	16	24	42	54	65

NOTE: ***Brewster** a-3. **Colletta** a-1(2), 3, 4(2), 5; c-3.*

MY NAME IS CHAOS
DC Comics: 1992 - No. 4, 1992 ($4.95, limited series, 52 pgs.)

Book 1-4: Tom Veitch scripts; painted-c						5.00

MY NAME IS HOLOCAUST
DC Comics: May, 1995 - No. 5, Sept, 1995 ($2.50, limited series)

1-5						2.50

MY ONLY LOVE
Charlton Comics: July, 1975 - No. 9, Nov, 1976

	GD	VG	FN	VF	VF/NM	NM-
1	3	6	9	14	19	24
2,4-9	2	4	6	9	13	16
3-Toth-a	2	4	6	11	16	20

MY OWN ROMANCE (Formerly My Romance; Teen-Age Romance #77 on)
Marvel/Atlas (MjPC/RCM No. 4-59/ZPC No. 60-76): No. 4, Mar, 1949 - No. 76, July, 1960

	GD	VG	FN	VF	VF/NM	NM-
4-Photo-c	15	30	45	90	140	190
5-10: 5,6,8-10-Photo-c	11	22	33	60	83	105
11-20: 14-Powell-a	10	20	30	54	72	90
21-42,55: 42-Last precode (2/55). 55-Toth-a	9	18	27	50	65	80
43-54,56-60	5	10	15	30	48	65
61-70,72,73,75,76	4	8	12	26	41	55
71-Williamson-a	5	10	15	32	51	70
74-Kirby-a	5	10	15	32	51	70

NOTE: ***Brewster** a-59. **Colletta** a-45(2), 48, 50, 55, 57(2), 59; c-58i, 59, 61. **Everett** a-25; c-58p. **Kirby** c-71, 75, 76. **Morisi** a-18. **Orlando** a-61. **Romita** a-36. **Tuska** a-10.*

MY PAL DIZZY (See Comic Books, Series I)

MY PAST (...Confessions) (Formerly Western Thrillers)
Fox Feature Syndicate: No. 7, Aug, 1949 - No. 11, Apr, 1950 (Crimes Inc. #12)

	GD	VG	FN	VF	VF/NM	NM-
7	15	30	45	88	137	185
8-10	10	20	30	56	76	95
11-Wood-a	18	36	54	107	169	230

MY PERSONAL PROBLEM
Ajax/Farrell/Steinway Comic: 11/55; No. 2, 2/56; No. 3, 9/56 - No. 4, 11/56; 10/57 - No. 3, 5/58

	GD	VG	FN	VF	VF/NM	NM-
1	9	18	27	52	69	85
2-4	7	14	21	35	43	50
1-3('57-'58)-Steinway	6	12	18	28	34	40

MY PRIVATE LIFE (Formerly Murder, Inc.; becomes Pedro #18)
Fox Feature Syndicate: No. 16, Feb, 1950 - No. 17, April, 1950

	GD	VG	FN	VF	VF/NM	NM-
16,17	14	28	42	78	112	145

MYRA NORTH (See The Comics, Crackajack Funnies & Red Ryder)
Dell Publishing Co.: No. 3, Jan, 1940

	GD	VG	FN	VF	VF/NM	NM-
Four Color 3	95	190	285	599	1012	1425

MY REAL LOVE
Standard Comics: No. 5, June, 1952 (Photo-c)

	GD	VG	FN	VF	VF/NM	NM-
5-Toth-a, 3 pgs.; Tuska, Cardy, Vern Greene-a	14	28	42	76	108	140

MY ROMANCE (Becomes My Own Romance #4 on)
Marvel Comics (RCM): Sept, 1948 - No. 3, Jan, 1949

	GD	VG	FN	VF	VF/NM	NM-
1	18	36	54	105	165	225
2,3: 2-Anti-Wertham editorial (11/48)	12	24	36	69	97	125

MY ROMANTIC ADVENTURES (Formerly Romantic Adventures)
American Comics Group: No. 68, 8/56 - No. 115, 12/60; No. 116, 7/61 - No. 138, 3/64

	GD	VG	FN	VF	VF/NM	NM-
68	8	16	24	40	50	60
69-85	6	12	18	31	38	45
86-Three pg. Williamson-a (2/58)	8	16	24	42	54	65
87-100	3	6	9	18	27	35
101-138	3	6	9	15	21	26

NOTE: ***Whitney** art in most issues.*

MY SECRET (Becomes Our Secret #4 on)
Superior Comics, Ltd.: Aug, 1949 - No. 3, Oct, 1949

	GD	VG	FN	VF	VF/NM	NM-
1	15	30	45	88	137	185
2,3	12	24	36	67	94	120

MY SECRET AFFAIR (Becomes Martin Kane #4)
Hero Book (Fox Feature Syndicate): Dec, 1949 - No. 3, April, 1950

	GD	VG	FN	VF	VF/NM	NM-
1-Harrison/Wood-a (10 pgs.)	23	46	69	133	214	295
2,3-Wood-a	18	36	54	107	169	230

MY SECRET CONFESSION
Sterling Comics: September, 1955

	GD	VG	FN	VF	VF/NM	NM-
1-Sekowsky-a	9	18	27	50	65	80

MY SECRET LIFE (Formerly Western Outlaws; Romeo Tubbs #26 on)
Fox Feature Syndicate: No. 22, July, 1949 - No. 27, July, 1950; No. 27, 9/51

	GD	VG	FN	VF	VF/NM	NM-
22	13	26	39	72	101	130
23,26-Wood-a, 6 pgs.	18	36	54	107	169	230
24,25,27	11	22	33	62	86	110
27 (9/51)	10	20	30	54	72	90

NOTE: *The title was changed to Romeo Tubbs after #25 even though #26 & 27 did come out.*

MY SECRET LIFE (Formerly Young Lovers; Sue & Sally Smith #48)
Charlton Comics: No. 19, Aug, 1957 - No. 47, Sept, 1962

	GD	VG	FN	VF	VF/NM	NM-
19	4	8	12	24	37	50
20-35	3	6	9	16	22	28
36-47: 44-Last 10¢ issue	3	6	9	14	19	24

MY SECRET MARRIAGE
Superior Comics, Ltd.: May, 1953 - No. 24, July, 1956 (Canadian)

	GD	VG	FN	VF	VF/NM	NM-
1	14	28	42	76	108	140
2	8	16	24	44	57	70
3-24	7	14	21	37	46	55
I.W. Reprint #9	2	4	6	8	11	14

NOTE: *Many issues contain **Kamen-ish** art.*

MY SECRET ROMANCE (Becomes A Star Presentation #3)
Hero Book (Fox Feature Syndicate): Jan, 1950 - No. 2, March, 1950

	GD	VG	FN	VF	VF/NM	NM-
1	15	30	45	86	133	180
2-Wood-a	18	36	54	107	169	230

MY SECRETS (Magazine)
Atlas/Seaboard: Feb, 1975 (B&W, 68 pgs.)

	GD	VG	FN	VF	VF/NM	NM-
Vol. 1 #1	6	12	18	37	59	80

MY SECRET STORY (Formerly Captain Kidd #25; Sabu #30 on)
Fox Feature Syndicate: No. 26, Oct, 1949 - No. 29, April, 1950

	GD	VG	FN	VF	VF/NM	NM-
26	15	30	45	84	127	170
27-29	10	20	30	54	72	90

MYSPACE DARK HORSE PRESENTS
Dark Horse Books: Sept, 2008 ($19.95, TPB)

Vol. 1 - Short stories previously appearing on Dark Horse's MySpace.com webpage; s/a by various incl. Whedon, Bá, Bagge, Mignola, Moon, Nord, Trimpe, Warren, Way						20.00

MYSTERIES (...Weird & Strange)
Superior/Dynamic Publ. (Randall Publ. Ltd.): May, 1953 - No. 11, Jan, 1955

	GD	VG	FN	VF	VF/NM	NM-
1-All horror stories	41	82	123	250	413	575
2-A-Bomb blast story	26	52	78	154	247	340
3-11: 10-Kamenish-c/a reprinted from Strange Mysteries #2; cover is from a panel in Strange Mysteries #2	23	46	69	135	218	300

MYSTERIES IN SPACE (See Fireside Book Series)

MYSTERIES OF SCOTLAND YARD (Also see A-1 Comics)
Magazine Enterprises: No. 121, 1954 (one shot)

	GD	VG	FN	VF	VF/NM	NM-
A-1 121-Reprinted from Manhunt (5 stories)	15	30	45	85	130	175

MYSTERIES OF UNEXPLORED WORLDS (See Blue Bird)(Becomes Son of Vulcan V2#49 on)
Charlton Comics: Aug, 1956; No. 2, Jan, 1957 - No. 48, Sept, 1965

	GD	VG	FN	VF	VF/NM	NM-
1	37	74	111	218	349	480
2-No Ditko	15	30	45	90	140	190
3,4,8,9 Ditko-a. 3-Ditko c/a (4). 4-Ditko c/a (2).	29	58	87	172	276	380
5,6,10,11: 5,6-Ditko-c/a (all). 10-Ditko-c/a(4). 11-Ditko-c/a(3); signed J. Kotdi	31	62	93	181	291	400
7-(2/58, 68 pgs.) 4 stories w/Ditko-a	34	68	102	198	319	440
12,19,21-24,26-Ditko-a. 12-Ditko sty (3); Baker story "The Charm Bracelet."	23	46	69	133	214	295
13-18,20	10	20	30	56	76	95
25,27-30	5	10	15	32	51	70
31-45	4	8	12	26	41	55
46(5/65)-Son of Vulcan begins (origin/1st app.)	4	8	12	28	44	60
47,48	4	8	12	23	34	45

NOTE: ***Ditko** c-3-6, 10, 11, 19, 21-24. Covers to #19, 21-24 reprint story panels.*

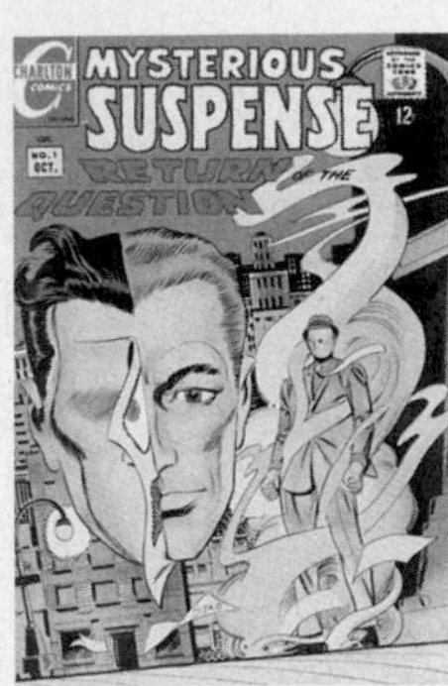

Mysterious Suspense #1 © CC

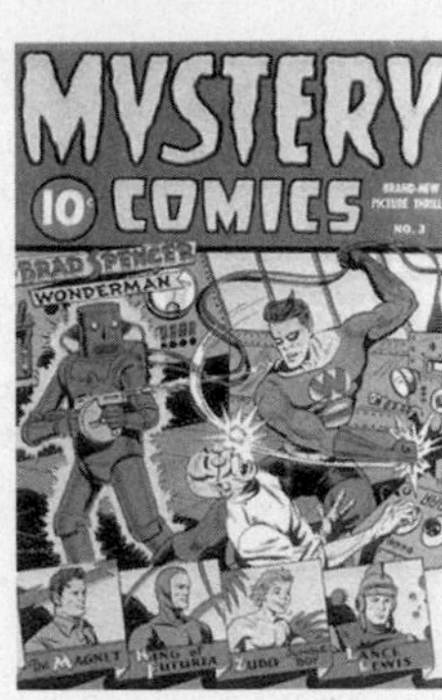

Mystery Comics #3 © WHW

Mystery Men Comics #2 © FOX

	GD 2.0	VG 4.0	FN 6.0	VF 8.0	VF/NM 9.0	NM- 9.2
MYSTERIOUS ADVENTURES						
Story Comics: Mar, 1951 - No. 24, Mar, 1955; No. 25, Aug, 1955						
1-All horror stories	70	140	210	441	746	1050
2-(6/51)	40	80	120	239	387	535
3,4,6,10	38	76	114	226	363	500
5-Bondage-c	40	80	120	239	387	535
7-Dagger in eye panel; dismemberment stories	43	86	129	267	446	625
8-Eyeball story	50	100	150	310	518	725
9-Extreme violence (8/52)	42	84	126	248	404	560
11-(12/52)-Used in **SOTI**, pg. 84	42	84	126	248	404	560
12,14: 14-E.C. Old Witch swipe	38	76	114	226	363	500
13-Classic skull-c	43	86	129	267	446	625
15-21: 18-Used in Senate Investigative report, pgs. 5,6; E.C. swipe/TFTC #35; The Coffin-Keeper & Corpse (hosts). 20-Used by Wertham in the Senate hearings. 21-Bondage/beheading-c	41	82	123	253	419	585
22- "Cinderella" parody	38	76	114	226	363	500
23-Disbrow-a (6 pgs.); E.C. swipe "The Mystery Keeper's Tale" (host) and "Mother Ghoul's Nursery Tale"	38	76	114	226	363	500
24,25	26	52	78	154	247	340

NOTE: *Tothish art by* ***Ross Andru****-#22, 23.* ***Bache*** *a-8.* ***Cameron*** *a-5-7.* ***Harrison*** *a-12.* ***Hollingsworth*** *a-3-8, 12.* ***Schaffenberger*** *a-24, 25.* ***Wildey*** *a-15, 17.*

	GD 2.0	VG 4.0	FN 6.0	VF 8.0	VF/NM 9.0	NM- 9.2
MYSTERIOUS ISLAND						
Dell Publishing Co.: No. 1213, July-Sept, 1961						
Four Color 1213-Movie, photo-c	8	16	24	56	93	130
MYSTERIOUS ISLE						
Dell Publishing Co.: Nov-Jan, 1963/64 (Jules Verne)						
1	4	8	12	22	34	45

MYSTERIOUS RIDER, THE (See Zane Grey, 4-Color 301)

	GD 2.0	VG 4.0	FN 6.0	VF 8.0	VF/NM 9.0	NM- 9.2
MYSTERIOUS STORIES (Formerly Horror From the Tomb #1)						
Premier Magazines: No. 2, Dec-Jan, 1954-1955 - No. 7, Dec, 1955						
2-Woodbridge-c; last pre-code issue	48	96	144	298	499	700
3-Woodbridge-c/a	34	68	102	198	319	440
4-7: 5-Cinderella parody. 6-Woodbridge-c	31	62	93	181	291	400

NOTE: *Hollingsworth a-2, 4.*

MYSTERIOUS STRANGER
DC Comics: Aug/Sept. 1952

nn-Ashcan comic, not distributed to newsstands, only for in-house use. Cover art is All Star Western #60 with interior being Sensation Comics #100. A FN/VF copy sold for $2,357.50 in 2002.

	GD 2.0	VG 4.0	FN 6.0	VF 8.0	VF/NM 9.0	NM- 9.2
MYSTERIOUS SUSPENSE (Also see Blue Beetle #1 (1967))						
Charlton Comics: Oct, 1968 (12¢)						
1-Return of the Question by Ditko (c/a)	7	14	21	47	76	105

MYSTERIOUS TRAVELER (See Tales of the...)

	GD 2.0	VG 4.0	FN 6.0	VF 8.0	VF/NM 9.0	NM- 9.2
MYSTERIOUS TRAVELER COMICS (Radio)						
Trans-World Publications: Nov, 1948						
1-Powell-c/a(2); Poe adaptation, "Tell Tale Heart"	57	114	171	359	610	860
MYSTERY COMICS						
William H. Wise & Co.: 1944 - No. 4, 1944 (No months given)						
1-The Magnet, The Silver Knight, Brad Spencer, Wonderman, Dick Devins, King of Futuria, & Zudo the Jungle Boy begin (all 1st app.); Schomburg-c on all	122	244	366	769	1297	1825
2-Bondage-c	69	138	207	435	738	1040
3,4: 3-Lance Lewis, Space Detective begins (1st app.); Robot-c. 4(V2#1 inside)	63	126	189	397	669	940
MYSTERY COMICS DIGEST						
Gold Key/Whitman?: Mar, 1972 - No. 26, Oct, 1975						
1-Ripley's Believe It or Not; reprint of Ripley's #1 origin Ra-Ka-Tep the Mummy; Wood-a	4	8	12	26	41	55
2-9: 2-Boris Karloff Tales of Mystery; Wood-a; 1st app. Werewolf Count Wulfstein. 3-Twilight Zone (TV); Crandall, Toth & George Evans-a; 1st app. Tragg & Simbar the Lion Lord; (2) Crandall/Frazetta-r/Twilight Zone #1 4-Ripley's Believe It or Not; 1st app. Baron Tibor, the Vampire. 5-Boris Karloff Tales of Mystery; 1st app. Dr. Spektor. 6-Twilight Zone (TV); 1st app. U.S. Marshal Reid & Sir Duane; Evans-r. 7-Ripley's Believe It or Not; origin The Lurker in the Swamp; 1st app. Duroc. 8-Boris Karloff Tales of Mystery; McWilliams-r; Orlando-r. 9-Twilight Zone (TV); Williamson, Crandall, McWilliams-a; 2nd Tragg app.;Torres, Evans, Heck/Tuska-r	3	6	9	20	30	40
10-26: 10,13-Ripley's Believe It or Not: 13-Orlando-r. 11,14-Boris Karloff Tales of Mystery. 14-1st app. Xorkon. 12,15-Twilight Zone (TV). 16,19,22,25-Ripley's Believe It or Not. 17-Boris Karloff Tales of Mystery; Williamson-r; Orlando-r. 18,21,24-Twilight Zone (TV). 20,23,26-Boris Karloff Tales of Mystery	3	6	9	16	23	30

NOTE: *Dr. Spektor app.-#5, 10-12, 21. Durak app.-#15. Duroc app.-#14 (later called Durak). King George 1st app.-#8.*

	GD 2.0	VG 4.0	FN 6.0	VF 8.0	VF/NM 9.0	NM- 9.2
MYSTERY IN SPACE (Also see Fireside Book Series and Pulp Fiction Library: ...)						
National Periodical Pub.: 4-5/51 - No. 110, 9/66; No. 111, 9/80 - No. 117, 3/81 (#1-3: 52 pgs.)						
1-Frazetta-a, 8 pgs.; Knights of the Galaxy begins, ends #8	240	480	720	2100	4050	6000
2	85	170	255	723	1387	2050
3	67	134	201	570	1085	1600
4,5	55	110	165	468	897	1325
6-10: 7-Toth-a	44	88	132	352	656	960
11-15	35	70	105	273	504	735
16-18,20-25: Interplanetary Insurance feature by Infantino in all. 21-1st app. Space Cabbie. 24-Last pre-code issue	30	60	90	232	434	635
19-Virgil Finlay-a	32	64	96	250	468	685
26-40: 26-Space Cabbie feature begins. 34-1st S.A. issue	25	50	75	185	343	500
41-52: 47-Space Cabbie feature ends	19	38	57	139	257	375
53-Adam Strange begins (8/59, 10pg. sty); robot-c	152	304	456	1330	2565	3800
54	44	88	132	352	664	975
55-Grey tone-c	40	80	120	312	581	850
56-60: 59-Kane/Anderson-a	23	46	69	167	309	450
61-71: 61-1st app. Adam Strange foe Ulthoon. 62-1st app. A.S. foe Mortan. 63-Origin Vandor. 66-Star Rovers begin (1st app.). 68-1st app. Dust Devils (6/61). 69-1st Mailbag. 70-2nd app. Dust Devils. 71-Last 10¢ issue	18	36	54	130	240	350
72-74,76-80	13	26	39	93	164	235
75-JLA x-over in Adam Strange (5/62)(sequel to J.L.A. #3, 2nd app. of Kanjar Ro)	23	46	69	170	315	460
81-86	10	20	30	71	126	180
87-(11/63)-Adam Strange/Hawkman double feat begins; 3rd Hawkman tryout series	17	34	51	120	223	325
88-Adam Strange & Hawkman stories	15	30	45	107	196	285
89-Adam Strange & Hawkman stories	15	30	45	105	190	275
90-Book-length Adam Strange & Hawkman story; 1st team-up (3/64); Hawkman moves to own title next month; classic-c	17	34	51	120	223	325
91-102: 91-End Infantino art on Adam Strange; double-length Adam Strange story. 92-Space Ranger begins (6/64), ends #103. 92-94,96,98-Space Ranger-c. 94,98-Adam Strange/ Space Ranger team-up. 102-Adam Strange ends (no Space Ranger)	6	12	18	43	69	95
103-Origin Ultra, the Multi-Alien; last Space Ranger	6	12	18	39	62	85
104-110: 110-(9/66)-Last 12¢ issue	5	10	15	30	48	65
V17#111(9/80)-117: 117-Newton-a(3 pgs.)	1	3	4	6	8	10

NOTE: ***Anderson*** *a-2, 4, 8-10, 12-17, 19, 45-48, 51, 57, 59i, 61-64, 70, 76, 87-91; c-9, 10, 15-25, 87, 89, 105-108, 110.* ***Aparo*** *a-111.* ***Austin*** *a-112i.* ***Bolland*** *a-115.* ***Craig*** *a-114, 116.* ***Ditko*** *a-111, 114-116.* ***Drucker*** *a-13, 14.* ***Elias*** *a-98, 102, 103.* ***Golden*** *a-113p.* ***Sid Greene*** *a-78, 91.* ***Infantino*** *a-1-8, 11, 14-25, 27-46, 48, 49, 51, 53-91, 103, 117; c-60-86, 88, 90, 91, 105, 107.* ***Gil Kane*** *a-14p, 15p, 18p, 19p, 26p, 29-59p(most), 100-102; c-52, 101.* ***Kubert*** *a-113; c-111-115.* ***Moreira*** *c-27, 28.* ***Rogers*** *a-111.* ***Sekowsky*** *a-52.* ***Simon & Kirby*** *a-4(2 pgs.).* ***Spiegle*** *a-111, 114.* ***Starlin*** *c-116.* ***Sutton*** *a-112.* ***Tuska*** *a-115p, 117p.*

MYSTERY IN SPACE
DC Comics: Nov, 2006 - No. 8, Jul, 2007 ($3.99, limited series)

	NM- 9.2
1-8: 1-Captain Comet's rebirth; Starlin-s/Shane Davis-a; The Weird by Starlin	4.00
1-Variant cover by Neal Adams	10.00
Volume One TPB (2007, $17.99) r/#1-5	18.00
Volume Two TPB (2007, $17.99) r/#6-8 and The Weird #1-4	18.00

	GD 2.0	VG 4.0	FN 6.0	VF 8.0	VF/NM 9.0	NM- 9.2
MYSTERY MEN COMICS						
Fox Features Syndicate: Aug, 1939 - No. 31, Feb, 1942						
1-Intro. & 1st app. The Blue Beetle, The Green Mask, Rex Dexter of Mars by Briefer, Zanzibar by Tuska, Lt. Drake, D-13-Secret Agent by Powell, Chen Chang, Wing Turner, & Captain Denny Scott	1000	2000	3000	7200	12,600	18,000
2-Robot & sci/fi-c (2nd Robot-c w/Movie #6)	335	670	1005	2278	3989	5700
3 (10/39)-Classic Lou Fine-c	423	846	1269	3000	5250	7500
4,5: 4-Capt. Savage begins (11/39)	267	534	801	1682	2841	4000
6-Tuska-c	223	446	669	1405	2378	3350
7-1st Blue Beetle-c app.	280	560	840	1764	2982	4200
8-Lou Fine bondage-c	253	506	759	1594	2697	3800
9-The Moth begins; Lou Fine-c	127	254	381	800	1350	1900
10-12: All Joe Simon-c. 10-Wing Turner by Kirby; Simon bondage-c. 11-Intro. Domino	103	206	309	649	1100	1550
13-Intro. Lynx & sidekick Blackie (8/40)	66	132	198	416	701	985
14-18	62	124	186	391	663	935
19-Intro. & 1st app. Miss X (ends #21)	66	132	198	416	701	985
20-31: 26-The Wraith begins	60	120	180	378	639	900

NOTE: ***Briefer*** *a-1-15, 20, 24; c-9.* ***Cuidera*** *a-22.* ***Lou Fine*** *c-1-5,8,9.* ***Powell*** *a-1-15, 24.* ***Simon*** *c-10-12.* ***Tuska*** *a-1-16, 22, 24, 27; c-6. Bondage-c 1, 3, 7, 8, 10, 25, 27-29, 31. Blue Beetle c-7, 8, 10-31. D-13 Secret Agent c-6.*

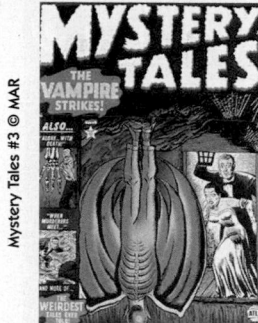

Mystery Tales #3 © MAR

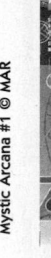

Mystic Arcana #1 © MAR

Mystic Comics #2 © MAR

GD VG FN VF VF/NM NM-
2.0 4.0 6.0 8.0 9.0 9.2

Green Mask c-1, 3-5. Rex Dexter of Mars c-2, 9.

MYSTERY MEN MOVIE ADAPTION
Dark Horse Comics: July, 1999 - No. 2, Aug, 1999 ($2.95, mini-series)

1,2-Fingerman-s; photo-c 3.00

MYSTERY PLAY, THE
DC Comics (Vertigo): 1994 ($19.95, one-shot)

nn-Hardcover-Morrison-s/Muth-painted art 25.00
Softcover ($9.95)-New Muth cover 10.00

MYSTERY TALES
Atlas Comics (20CC): Mar, 1952 - No. 54, Aug, 1957

1-Horror/weird stories in all 88 176 264 554 940 1325
2-Krigstein-a 47 94 141 291 483 675
3-10: 6-A-Bomb panel. 10-Story similar to "The Assassin" from Shock SuspenStories
41 82 123 256 428 600
11,13-21: 14-Maneely s/f story. 20-Electric chair issue. 21-Matt Fox-a;
decapitation story 30 60 90 176 283 390
12,22: 12-Matt Fox-a. 22-Forte/Matt Fox-c; a(i) 34 68 102 198 319 440
23-26 (2/55)-Last precode issue 24 48 72 143 229 315
27,29-35,37,38,41-43,48,49. 43-Morisi story contains Frazetta art swipes from Untamed Love
20 40 60 114 180 245
28,36,39,40,45: 28-Jack Katz-a. 36,39-Krigstein-a. 40,45-Ditko-a (#45 is 3 pgs. only)
20 40 60 117 186 255
44,51-Williamson/Krenkel-a 21 42 63 123 197 270
46-Williamson/Krenkel-a; Crandall text illos 21 42 63 123 197 270
47-Crandall, Ditko, Powell-a 21 42 63 123 197 270
50,52,53: 50-Torres, Morrow-a 20 40 60 114 180 245
54-Crandall, Check-a 20 40 60 117 186 255

NOTE: ***Ayers** a-18, 49, 52. **Berg** a-17, 51. **Colan** a-1, 3, 18, 35, 43. **Collotta** a-18. **Drucker** a-41. **Everett** a-2, 29, 33, 35, 41; c-8-11, 14, 38, 39, 41, 43, 44, 46, 48-51, 53. **Fass** a-16. **Forte** a-21, 22, 45, 46. **Matt Fox** a-12?, 21, 22; c-22. **Heath** a-3; c-3, 15, 17, 26. **Heck** a-25. **Kinstler** a-15. **Mort Lawrence** a-26, 32, 34. **Maneely** a-1, 9, 14, 22, c-12, 20, 24, 27. **Mooney** a-3, 40. **Morisi** a-43, 49, 52. **Morrow** a-50. **Orlando** a-51. **Pakula** a-16. **Powell** a-21, 29, 37, 38, 47. **Reinman** a-1, 14, 17. **Robinson** a-7p, 42. **Romita** a-37. **Roussos** a-4, 44. **R.Q. Sale** a-45, 46, 49. **Severin** c-52. **Shores** a-17, 45. **Tuska** a-10, 12, 14. **Whitney** a-2. **Wildey** a-37.*

MYSTERY TALES
Super Comics: 1964

Super Reprint #16,17('64): 16-r/Tales of Horror #2. 17-r/Eerie #14(Avon),
18-Kubert-r/Strange Terrors #4 3 6 9 14 20 25

MYSTERY TRAIL
DC Comics: Feb/Mar 1950

nn - Ashcan comic, not distributed to newsstands, only for in-house use. Cover art is Danger Trail #3 with interior being Star Spangled Comics #109. A FN/VF copy sold for $2,357.50 in 2002.

MYSTIC (3rd Series)
Marvel/Atlas Comics (CLDS 1/CSI 2-21/OMC 22-35/CSI 35-61): March, 1951 - No. 61, Aug, 1957

1-Atom bomb panels; horror/weird stories in all 93 186 279 586 993 1400
2 50 100 150 310 518 725
3-Eyes torn out 45 90 135 279 465 650
4- "The Devil Birds" by Wolverton (6 pgs.) 80 160 240 504 852 1200
5,7-10 37 74 111 215 345 475
6- "The Eye of Doom" by Wolverton (7 pgs.) 80 160 240 504 852 1200
11-20: 16-Bondage/torture c/story 30 60 90 174 280 385
21-25,27-36-Last precode (3/55). 25-E.C. swipe 24 48 72 143 229 315
26-Atomic War story; severed head story/cover 27 54 81 158 254 350
37-51,53-56,61 20 40 60 117 186 255
52-Wood-a; Crandall-a? 22 44 66 127 204 280
57-Story "Trapped in the Ant-Hill" (1957) is very similar to "The Man in the Ant Hill" in TTA #27
23 46 69 135 218 300
58,59-Krigstein-a 20 40 60 118 189 260
60-Williamson/Mayo-a (4 pgs.) 20 40 60 118 189 260

NOTE: ***Andru** a-23, 25. **Ayers** a-35, 53; c-8. **Berg** a-49. **Cameron** a-49, 51. **Check** a-31, 60. **Colan** a-3, 7, 12, 21, 37, 60. **Colletta** a-29. **Drucker** a-46, 52, 56. **Everett** a-8, 9, 17, 40, 44, 57; c-13, 18, 21, 42, 47, 49, 51-55, 57-59, 61. **Forte** a-35, 52, 58. **Fox** a-24i. **Al Hartley** a-35. **Heath** a-10; c-10, 20, 22, 23, 25, 30. **Infantino** a-12. **Kane** a-8, 24p. **Jack Katz** a-31, 33. **Mort Law.rence** a-19, 37. **Maneely** a-22, 24, 58; c-7, 15, 28, 29, 31. **Moldoff** a-29. **Morisi** a-48, 49, 52. **Morrow** a-51. **Orlando** a-57, 61. **Pakula** a-52, 57, 59. **Powell** a-52, 54-56. **Robinson** a-5. **Romita** a-11, 15. **R.Q. Sale** a-35, 53, 58. **Sekowsky** a-1, 2, 4, 5. **Severin** c-56, 60. **Tuska** a-15. **Whitney** a-33. **Wildey** a-28, 30. **Ed Win** a-17, 20. Canadian reprints known-title 'Startling.'*

MYSTIC (Also see CrossGen Chronicles)
CrossGeneration Comics: Jul, 2000 - No. 43, Jan, 2004 ($2.95)

1-43: 1-Marz-s/Peterson & Dell-a. 15-Cameos by DC & Marvel characters 3.00
...: Rite of Passage Vol. 1 TPB (5/01, $19.95) r/#1-7; Linsner-c 20.00
...: The Demon Queen Vol. 2 TPB (2002, $19.95) r/#8-14 20.00
...: Siege of Scales Vol. 3 TPB (2002, $15.95) r/#15-20 16.00
...: Out All Night Vol.4 TPB (2003, $15.95) r/#21-26 16.00
Vol. 5: Master Class (2003, $15.95) r/#27-32 16.00

MYSTICAL TALES
Atlas Comics (CCC 1/EPI 2-8): June, 1956 - No. 8, Aug, 1957

1-Everett-c/a 48 96 144 298 499 700
2-4: 2-Berg-a. 3,4-Crandall-a. 26 52 78 152 244 335
5-Williamson-a (4 pgs.) 28 56 84 162 261 360
6-Torres, Krigstein-a 25 50 75 145 233 320
7-Bolle, Forte, Torres, Orlando-a 24 48 72 140 225 310
8-Krigstein, Check-a 25 50 75 145 233 320

NOTE: ***Everett** a-1; c-1-4, 6, 7. **Orlando** a-1, 2, 7. **Pakula** a-3. **Powell** a-1, 4.*

MYSTIC ARCANA
Marvel Comics: Aug, 2007 - Jan, 2008 ($2.99)

1 Magik on-c; art by Scott and Nguyen; Ian McNee and Dani Moonstar app. 3.00
(#2)...: Black Knight 1 (9/07, $2.99) Djurdjevic-c/Grummett & Hanna-a; origin retold 3.00
3-("Scarlet Witch" on cover)(10/07, $2.99) Djurdjevic-c/Santacruz-a; childhood 3.00
(#4)...: Sister Grimm 1 (1/08, $2.99) Nico Minoru from Runaways; Djurdjevic-c/Noto-a 3.00
...: The Book of Marvel Magic ('07, $3.99) Official Handbook profiles of the magic-related 4.00
HC (2007, $24.99, d.j.) r/series and ...: The Book of Marvel Magic 25.00

MYSTIC COMICS (1st Series)
Timely Comics (TPI 1-5/TCI 8-10): March, 1940 - No. 10, Aug, 1942

1-Origin The Blue Blaze, The Dynamic Man, & Flexo the Rubber Robot; Zephyr Jones, 3X's & Deep Sea Demon app.; The Magician begins (all 1st app.);
c-from Spider pulp V18#1, 6/39 1367 2734 4100 10,300 18,150 26,000
2-The Invisible Man & Master Mind Excello begin; Space Rangers, Zara of the Jungle,
Taxi Taylor app. (scarce) 472 944 1416 3398 5949 8500
3-Origin Hercules, who last appears in #4 341 682 1023 2319 4060 5800
4-Origin The Thin Man & The Black Widow; Merzak the Mystic app.; last Flexo, Dynamic Man, Invisible Man & Blue Blaze (some issues have date sticker on cover; others have July w/August overprint in silver color); Roosevelt assassination-c
365 730 1095 2482 4341 6200
5-(3/41)-Origin The Black Marvel, The Blazing Skull, The Sub-Earth Man, Super Slave & The Terror; The Moon Man & Black Widow app.; 5 German war-c begin, end #10
341 682 1023 2319 4060 5800
6-(10/41)-Origin The Challenger & The Destroyer (1st app.?; also see All-Winners #2, Fall, 1941) 411 822 1233 2795 4898 7000
7-The Witness begins (12/41, origin & 1st app.); origin Davey & the Demon; last Black Widow; Hitler opens his trunk of terror-c by Simon & Kirby (classic-c)
423 846 1269 2958 5179 7400
8,10: 10-Father Time, World of Wonder, & Red Skeleton app.; last Challenger & Terror
267 534 801 1682 2841 4000
9-Gary Gaunt app.; last Black Marvel, Mystic & Blazing Skull; Hitler-c
287 574 861 1808 3054 4300

NOTE: ***Gabrielle** c-8-10. **Kirby/Schomburg** c-6. **Rico** a-9(2). **Schomburg** a-1-4; c-1-5. **Sekowsky** a-9. **Sekowsky/Klein** a-8(Challenger). Bondage c-1, 2, 9.*

MYSTIC COMICS (2nd Series)
Timely Comics (ANC): Oct, 1944 - No. 3, Win, 1944-45; No. 4, Mar, 1945

1-The Angel, The Destroyer, The Human Torch, Terry Vance the Schoolboy Sleuth,
& Tommy Tyme begin 273 546 819 1720 2910 4100
2-(Fall/44)-Last Human Torch & Terry Vance; bondage/hypo-c
140 280 420 882 1491 2100
3-Last Angel (two stories) & Tommy Tyme 127 254 381 800 1350 1900
4-The Young Allies-c & app.; Schomburg-c 115 230 345 725 1225 1725

MYSTIC EDGE (Manga)
Antarctic Press: Oct, 1998 ($2.95, one-shot)

1-Ryan Kinnaird-s/a/c 3.00

MYSTIQUE (See X-Men titles)
Marvel Comics: June, 2003 - No. 24, Apr, 2005 ($2.99)

1-24: 1-6-Linsner-c/Vaughan-s/Lucas-a. 7-Ryan-a begins. 8-Horn-c. 9-24-Mayhew-c
23-Wolverine & Rogue app. 3.00
... Vol. 1: Drop Dead Gorgeous TPB (2004, $14.99) r/#1-6 15.00
... Vol. 2: Tinker, Tailor, Mutant, Spy TPB (2004, $17.99) r/#7-13 18.00
... Vol. 3: Unnatural TPB (2004, $13.99) r/#14-18 14.00

MYSTIQUE & SABRETOOTH (Sabretooth and Mystique on-c)
Marvel Comics: Dec, 1996 - No. 4, Mar, 1997 ($1.95, limited series)

1-4: Characters from X-Men 3.00

MY STORY (...True Romances in Pictures #5,6; becomes My Love Life #13) (Formerly Zago)
Hero Books (Fox Features Syndicate): No. 5, May, 1949 - No. 12, Aug, 1950

Mythos: Spider-Man #1 © MAR

The 'Nam #7 © MAR

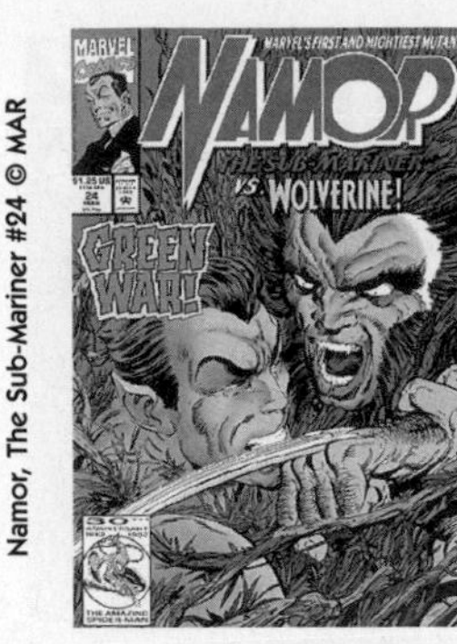

Namor, The Sub-Mariner #24 © MAR

GD VG FN VF VF/NM NM-
2.0 4.0 6.0 8.0 9.0 9.2

5-Kamen/Feldstein-a 20 40 60 120 193 265
6-8,11,12: 12-Photo-c 12 24 36 67 94 120
9,10-Wood-a 18 36 54 107 169 230

MYTHOS
Marvel Comics: Mar, 2006 - Dec, 2007 ($3.99)

1-Retelling of X-Men #1 with painted-a by Paolo Rivera; Paul Jenkins-s 4.00
...: Captain America 1 (8/08) Retelling of origin; painted-a by Rivera; Jenkins-s 4.00
...: Fantastic Four 1 (12/07) Retelling of Fantastic Four #1; painted-a by Rivera; Jenkins-s 4.00
...: Ghost Rider 1 (3/07) Retelling of Marvel Spotlight #5; painted-a by Rivera; Jenkins-s 4.00
...: Hulk 1 (10/06) Retelling of Incredible Hulk #1; painted-a by Rivera; Jenkins-s 4.00
...: Spider-Man 1 (8/07) Retelling of Amazing Fantasy #15; painted-a by Rivera; Jenkins-s 4.00

MYTHOS: THE FINAL TOUR
DC Comics/Vertigo: Dec, 1996 - No. 3, Feb, 1997 ($5.95, limited series)

1-3: 1-Ney Rieber-s/Amaro-a. 2-Snejbjerg-a; Constantine-app. 3-Kristiansen-a; Black Orchid-app. 6.00

MYTHSTALKERS
Image Comics: Mar, 2003 - No. 8, Mar, 2004 ($2.95)

1-8-Jiro-a 3.00

MY TRUE LOVE (Formerly Western Killers #64; Frank Buck #70 on)
Fox Features Syndicate: No. 65, July, 1949 - No. 69, March, 1950

65 16 32 48 94 147 200
66,68,69: 69-Morisi-a 12 24 36 67 94 120
67-Wood-a 18 36 54 107 169 230

NAIL, THE
Dark Horse Comics: June, 2004 - No. 4, Oct, 2004 ($2.99, limited series)

1-4-Rob Zombie & Steve Niles-s/Nat Jones-a/Simon Bisley-c 3.00
TPB (2005, $12.95) r/series 13.00

NAKED BRAIN (Marc Hempel's...)
Insight Studios Group: 2002 - No. 3, 2002 ($2.95, B&W, limited series)

1-3-Marc Hempel cartoons and sketches; Tug & Buster app. 3.00

NAKED PREY, THE (See Movie Classics)

'NAM, THE (See Savage Tales #1, 2nd series & Punisher Invades...)
Marvel Comics Group: Dec, 1986 - No. 84, Sept, 1993

1-Golden a(p)/c begins, ends #13 5.00
1 (2nd printing) 2.50
2-7,9-19,21-66,70-74: 7-Golden-a (2 pgs.). 32-Death R. Kennedy. 52,53-Frank Castle (The Punisher) app. 52,53-Gold 2nd printings. 58-Silver logo. 65-Heath-c/a. 70-Lomax scripts begin 3.00
8-1st app. Fudd Verzyl, Tunnel Rat 4.00
20-2nd app. Fudd Verzyl, Tunnel Rat 3.50
67-69,76-84: 67-69-Punisher 3 part story 3.00
75-($2.25, 52 pgs.) 6.00
Trade Paperback 1,2: 1-r/#1-4. 2-r/#5-8 5.00
TPB ('99, $14.95) r/#1-4; recolored 15.00

'NAM MAGAZINE, THE
Marvel Comics: Aug, 1988 - No. 10, May, 1989 ($2.00, B&W, 52pgs.)

1-10: Each issue reprints 2 issues of the comic 2.50

NAMELESS, THE
Image Comics: May, 1997 - No. 5, Sept, 1997 ($2.95, B&W)

1-5: Pruett/Hester-s/a 3.00
...: The Director's Cut TPB (2006, $15.99) r/#1-5; original proposal by Pruett 16.00

NAMES OF MAGIC, THE (Also see Books of Magic)
DC Comics (Vertigo): Feb, 2001 - No. 5, June, 2001 ($2.50, limited series)

1-5: Bolton painted-c on all; Case-a; leads into Hunter: The Age of Magic 2.50
TPB (2002, $14.95) r/#1-5 15.00

NAME OF THE GAME, THE
DC Comics: 2001 ($29.95, graphic novel)

Hardcover ($29.95) Will Eisner-s/a 30.00

NAMOR (Volume 2)
Marvel Comics: June, 2003 - No. 12, May, 2004 (25¢/$2.25/$2.99)

1-(25¢-c)Young Namor in the 1920s; Larroca-c/a 2.50
2-6-($2.25) Larroca-a 2.50
7-12-($2.99): 7-Olliffe-a begins 3.00

NAMORA (See Marvel Mystery Comics #82 & Sub-Mariner Comics)
Marvel Comics (PrPl): Fall, 1948 - No. 3, Dec, 1948

1-Sub-Mariner x-over in Namora; Namora by Everett(2), Sub-Mariner by Rico (10 pgs.) 273 546 819 1720 2910 4100
2-The Blonde Phantom & Sub-Mariner story; Everett-a 140 280 420 882 1491 2100
3-(Scarce)-Sub-Mariner app.; Everett-a 147 294 441 926 1563 2200

NAMOR, THE SUB-MARINER (See Prince Namor & Sub-Mariner)
Marvel Comics: Apr, 1990 - No. 62, May, 1995 ($1.00/$1.25/$1.50)

1-Byrne-c/a/scripts in 1-25 (scripts only #26-32) 4.00
2-5: 5-Iron Man app. 3.00
6-11,13-23,25,27-49,51-62: 16-Re-intro Iron Fist (8-cameo only). 18-Punisher cameo (1 panel); 21-23,25-Wolverine cameos. 22,23-Iron Fist app. 28-Iron Fist-c/story. 31-Dr. Doom-c/story. 33,34-Iron Fist cameo. 35-New Tiger Shark-c/story. 37-Aqua holografx foil-c. 48-The Thing app. 2.50
12,24: 12-(52pgs.)-Re-intro. The Invaders. 24-Namor vs. Wolverine 3.00
26-Namor w/new costume; 1st Jae Lee-c/a this title (5/92) & begins 3.50
50-($1.75, 52 pgs.)-Newsstand ed.; w/bound-in S-M trading card sheet (both versions) 2.50
50-($2.95, 52 pgs.)-Collector edition w/foil-c 3.00
Annual 1-4 ('91-94, 68 pgs.): 1-3 pg. origin recap. 2-Return/Defenders. 3-Bagged w/card. 4-Painted-c 3.00

NOTE: *Jae Lee a-26-30p, 31-37, 38p, 39, 40; c-26-40.*

NANCY AND SLUGGO (See Comics On Parade & Sparkle Comics)
United Features Syndicate: No. 16, 1949 - No. 23, 1954

16(#1) 10 20 30 58 79 100
17-23 8 16 24 40 50 60

NANCY & SLUGGO (Nancy #146-173; formerly Sparkler Comics)
St. John/Dell #146-187/Gold Key #188 on: No. 121, Apr, 1955-No. 192, Oct, 1963

121(4/55)(St. John) 10 20 30 54 72 90
122-145(7/57)(St. John) 8 16 24 44 57 70
146(9/57)-Peanuts begins, ends #192 (Dell) 7 14 21 49 80 110
147-161 (Dell) Peanuts in all 6 12 18 41 66 90
162-165,177-180-John Stanley-a 7 14 21 49 80 110
166-176-Oona & Her Haunted House series; Stanley-a 8 16 24 54 90 125
181-187(3-5/62)(Dell) 6 12 18 37 59 80
188(10/62)-192 (Gold Key) 6 12 18 37 59 80
Four Color 1034(9-11/59)-Summer Camp 5 10 15 32 51 70
(See Dell Giant #34, 45 & Dell Giants)

NANNY AND THE PROFESSOR (TV)
Dell Publishing Co.: Aug, 1970 - No. 2, Oct, 1970 (Photo-c)

1-(01-546-008) 5 10 15 32 51 70
2 4 8 12 26 41 55

NAPOLEON
Dell Publishing Co.: No. 526, Dec, 1953

Four Color 526 4 8 12 24 37 50

NAPOLEON & SAMANTHA (See Walt Disney Showcase No. 10)

NAPOLEON & UNCLE ELBY (See Clifford McBride's...)
Eastern Color Printing Co.: July, 1942 (68 pgs.) (One Shot)

1 43 86 129 267 446 625
1945-American Book-Strafford Press (128 pgs.) (8x10-1/2"; B&W reprints; hardcover) 15 30 45 83 124 165

NARRATIVE ILLUSTRATION, THE STORY OF THE COMICS (Also see Good Triumphs Over Evil!)
M.C. Gaines: Summer, 1942 (32 pgs., 7-1/4"x10", B&W w/color inserts)

nn-16 pgs. text with illustrations of ancient art, strips and comic covers; 4 pg. WWII War Bond promo, "The Minute Man Answers the Call" color comic drawn by Shelly and a special 8-page color comic insert of "The Story of Saul" (from Picture Stories from the Bible #10 or soon to appear in PS #10) or "Noah and His Ark" or "The Story of Ruth". Insert has special title page indicating it was part of a Sunday newspaper supplement insert series that had already run in a New England "Sunday Herald." Another version exists with insert from Picture Stories from the Bible #7. (very rare) Estimated value... 1500.00

NOTE: *Print, A Quarterly Journal of the Graphic Arts Vol. 3 No. 2 (88 pg., square bound) features the 1st printing of Narrative Illustration, The Story of The Comics. A VG+ copy sold for $750 in 2005.*

NASCAR HEROES (Also see Promotional Comics section for Free Comic Book Day edition)
Starbridge Media: 2007 - Present ($3.95)

1-3: 1-Origin of fictional racer Jimmy Dash. 3-Origin of the Daytona 500; DeStefano-s 4.00

NASH (WCW Wrestling)
Image Comics: July, 1999 - No. 2, July, 1999 ($2.95)

NASCAR Heroes #3 © Starbridge

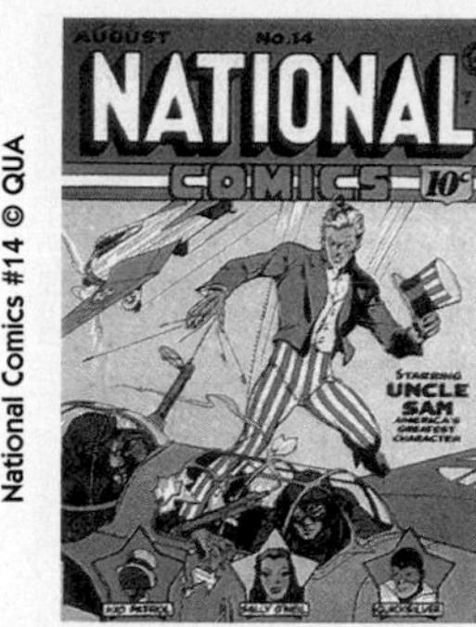

National Comics #14 © QUA

Navy Heroes #1 © Almanac

	GD 2.0	VG 4.0	FN 6.0	VF 8.0	VF/NM 9.0	NM- 9.2
1,2-Regular and photo-c						3.00
1-($6.95) Photo-split-cover Edition						7.00

NATHANIEL DUSK
DC Comics: Feb, 1984 - No. 4, May, 1984 ($1.25, mini-series, direct sales, Baxter paper)

	GD 2.0	VG 4.0	FN 6.0	VF 8.0	VF/NM 9.0	NM- 9.2
1-4: 1-Intro/origin; Gene Colan-c/a in all						2.50

NATHANIEL DUSK II
DC Comics: Oct, 1985 - No. 4, Jan, 1986 ($2.00, mini-series, Baxter paper)

	GD 2.0	VG 4.0	FN 6.0	VF 8.0	VF/NM 9.0	NM- 9.2
1-4: Gene Colan-c/a in all						2.50

NATIONAL COMICS
Quality Comics Group: July, 1940 - No. 75, Nov, 1949

	GD 2.0	VG 4.0	FN 6.0	VF 8.0	VF/NM 9.0	NM- 9.2
1-Uncle Sam begins (1st app.); origin sidekick Buddy by Eisner; origin Wonder Boy & Kid Dixon; Merlin the Magician (ends #45); Cyclone, Kid Patrol, Sally O'Neil Policewoman, Pen Miller (by Klaus Nordling; ends #22), Prop Powers (ends #26), & Paul Bunyan (ends #22) begin	517	1034	1551	3722	6511	9300
2	242	484	726	1525	2575	3625
3-Last Eisner Uncle Sam	167	334	501	1052	1776	2500
4-Last Cyclone	132	264	396	832	1404	1975
5-(11/40)-Quicksilver begins (1st app.; 3rd w/lightning speed?; re-intro'd by DC in 1993 as Max Mercury in Flash #76, 2nd series); origin Uncle Sam; bondage-c	150	300	450	945	1598	2250
6,8-11: 8-Jack & Jill begins (ends #22). 9-Flag-c	125	250	375	788	1332	1875
7-Classic Lou Fine-c	243	486	729	1531	2591	3650
12	85	170	255	536	906	1275
13-16-Lou Fine-a	87	174	261	548	924	1300
17,19-22: 21-Classic Nazi swastika cover. 22-Last Pen Miller (moves to Crack #23)	67	134	201	422	711	1000
18-(12/41)-Shows Asians attacking Pearl Harbor; on stands one month before actual event	130	260	390	819	1385	1950
23-The Unknown & Destroyer 171 begin	68	136	204	428	727	1025
24-Japanese War-c	68	136	204	428	727	1025
25-30: 25-Nazi drug usage/hypodermic needle in story. 26-Wonder Boy ends. 27- G-2 the Unknown begins (ends #46). 29-Origin The Unknown	47	94	141	291	488	685
31-33: 33-Chic Carter begins (ends #47)	43	86	129	267	446	625
34-37,40: 35-Last Kid Patrol	39	78	117	229	370	510
38-Hitler, Tojo, Mussolini-c	53	106	159	330	553	775
39-Hitler-c	53	106	159	334	567	800
41,43-50: 48-Origin The Whistler	26	52	78	152	244	335
42-The Barker begins (1st app?, 5/44); The Barker covers begin	37	74	111	215	345	475
51-Sally O'Neil by Ward, 8 pgs. (12/45)	29	58	87	169	272	375
52-60	20	40	60	115	183	250
61-67: 67-Format change; Quicksilver app.	15	30	45	86	133	180
68-75: The Barker ends	14	28	42	80	115	150

NOTE: ***Cole*** *Quicksilver-13; Barker-43; c-43, 46, 47, 49-51.* ***Crandall*** *Uncle Sam-11-13 (with* ***Fine****), 25, 26; c-24-26, 30-33, 43.* ***Crandall*** *Paul Bunyan-10-13.* ***Fine*** *Uncle Sam-13 (w/****Crandall****), 17, 18; c-1-14, 16, 18, 21.* ***Gill Fox*** *c-69-74.* ***Guardineer*** *Quicksilver-27, 35.* ***Gustavson*** *Quicksilver-14-26.* ***McWilliams*** *a-23-28, 55, 57. Uncle Sam c-1-41. Barker c-42-75.*

NATIONAL COMICS (Also see All Star Comics 1999 crossover titles)
DC Comics: May, 1999 ($1.99, one-shot)

	GD 2.0	VG 4.0	FN 6.0	VF 8.0	VF/NM 9.0	NM- 9.2
1-Golden Age Flash and Mr. Terrific; Waid-s/Lopresti-a						2.50

NATIONAL CRUMB, THE (Magazine-Size)
Mayfair Publications: August, 1975 (52 pgs., B&W) (Satire)

	GD 2.0	VG 4.0	FN 6.0	VF 8.0	VF/NM 9.0	NM- 9.2
1-Grandenetti-c/a, Ayers-a	2	4	6	11	16	20

NATIONAL VELVET (TV)
Dell Publishing Co./Gold Key: May-July, 1961 - No. 2, Mar, 1963 (All photo-c)

	GD 2.0	VG 4.0	FN 6.0	VF 8.0	VF/NM 9.0	NM- 9.2
Four Color 1195 (#1)	7	14	21	49	80	110
Four Color 1312, 01-556-207, 12-556-210 (Dell)	4	8	12	28	44	60
1,2: 1(12/62) (Gold Key). 2(3/63)	4	8	12	28	44	60

NATION OF SNITCHES
Piranha Press (DC): 1990 ($4.95, color, 52 pgs.)

	GD 2.0	VG 4.0	FN 6.0	VF 8.0	VF/NM 9.0	NM- 9.2
nn						5.00

NATURE BOY (Formerly Danny Blaze; Li'l Rascal Twins #6 on)
Charlton Comics: No. 3, March, 1956 - No. 5, Feb, 1957

	GD 2.0	VG 4.0	FN 6.0	VF 8.0	VF/NM 9.0	NM- 9.2
3-Origin; Blue Beetle story; Buscema-c/a	23	46	69	133	214	295
4,5	15	30	45	92	144	195

NOTE: ***John Buscema*** *a-3, 4p, 5; c-3.* ***Powell*** *a-4.*

NATURE OF THINGS (Disney, TV/Movie)
Dell Publishing Co.: No. 727, Sept, 1956 - No. 842, Sept, 1957

	GD 2.0	VG 4.0	FN 6.0	VF 8.0	VF/NM 9.0	NM- 9.2
Four Color 727 (#1), 842-Jesse Marsh-a	5	10	15	34	55	75

NAUSICAA OF THE VALLEY OF WIND
Viz Comics: 1988 - No. 7, 1989; 1989 - No. 4, 1990 ($2.50, B&W, 68pgs.)

	GD 2.0	VG 4.0	FN 6.0	VF 8.0	VF/NM 9.0	NM- 9.2
Book 1-7: 1-Contains Moebius poster						3.25
Part II, Book 1-4 ($2.95)						3.25

NAVY ACTION (Sailor Sweeney #12-14)
Atlas Comics (CDS): Aug, 1954 - No. 11, Apr, 1956; No. 15, 1/57 - No. 18, 8/57

	GD 2.0	VG 4.0	FN 6.0	VF 8.0	VF/NM 9.0	NM- 9.2
1-Powell-a	19	38	57	112	176	240
2-Lawrence-a	12	24	36	67	94	120
3-11: 4-Last precode (2/55)	10	20	30	54	72	90
15-18	9	18	27	52	69	85

NOTE: ***Berg*** *a-7, 9.* ***Colan*** *a-8.* ***Drucker*** *a-7, 17.* ***Everett*** *a-3, 7, 16; c-16, 17.* ***Heath*** *c-1, 2, 6.* ***Maneely*** *a-7, 8, 18; c-9, 11.* ***Pakula*** *a-2, 3, 9.* ***Reinman*** *a-17.*

NAVY COMBAT
Atlas Comics (MPI): June, 1955 - No. 20, Oct, 1958

	GD 2.0	VG 4.0	FN 6.0	VF 8.0	VF/NM 9.0	NM- 9.2
1-Torpedo Taylor begins by Don Heck	19	38	57	112	176	240
2	12	24	36	67	94	120
3-10	10	20	30	54	72	90
11,13-16,18-20: 14-Torres-a	9	18	27	52	69	85
12-Crandall-a	10	20	30	58	79	100
17-Williamson-a, 4 pgs.; Torres-a	10	20	30	56	76	95

NOTE: ***Berg*** *a-10, 11.* ***Colan*** *a-11.* ***Drucker*** *a-7.* ***Everett*** *a-3, 20; c-8 & 9 w/****Tuska****, 10, 13-16.* ***Heck*** *a-11(2).* ***Maneely*** *c-1, 6, 11, 17.* ***Morisi*** *a-8.* ***Pakula*** *a-7.* ***Powell*** *a-20.*

NAVY HEROES
Almanac Publishing Co.: 1945

	GD 2.0	VG 4.0	FN 6.0	VF 8.0	VF/NM 9.0	NM- 9.2
1-Heavy in propaganda	13	26	39	74	105	135

NAVY PATROL
Key Publications: May, 1955 - No. 4, Nov, 1955

	GD 2.0	VG 4.0	FN 6.0	VF 8.0	VF/NM 9.0	NM- 9.2
1	8	16	24	44	57	70
2-4	6	12	18	28	34	40

NAVY TALES
Atlas Comics (CDS): Jan, 1957 - No. 4, July, 1957

	GD 2.0	VG 4.0	FN 6.0	VF 8.0	VF/NM 9.0	NM- 9.2
1-Everett-c; Berg, Powell-a	16	32	48	90	147	200
2-Williamson/Mayo-a(5 pgs); Crandall-a	14	28	42	80	115	150
3,4-Reinman-a; Severin-c. 4-Crandall-a	12	24	36	69	97	125

NOTE: ***Colan*** *a-4.* ***Maneely*** *c-2.* ***Sinnott*** *a-4.*

NAVY TASK FORCE
Stanmor Publications/Aragon Mag. No. 4-8: Feb, 1954 - No. 8, April, 1956

	GD 2.0	VG 4.0	FN 6.0	VF 8.0	VF/NM 9.0	NM- 9.2
1	9	18	27	50	65	80
2	6	12	18	31	38	45
3-8: #8-r/Navy Patrol #1	6	12	18	28	34	40

NAVY WAR HEROES
Charlton Comics: Jan, 1964 - No. 7, Mar-Apr, 1965

	GD 2.0	VG 4.0	FN 6.0	VF 8.0	VF/NM 9.0	NM- 9.2
1	3	6	9	20	30	40
2-7	3	6	9	14	19	24

NAZA (Stone Age Warrior)
Dell Publishing Co.: Nov-Jan, 1963-64 - No. 9, March, 1966

	GD 2.0	VG 4.0	FN 6.0	VF 8.0	VF/NM 9.0	NM- 9.2
12-555-401 (#1)-Painted-c	5	10	15	34	55	75
2-9: 2-4-Painted-c	4	8	12	24	37	50

NEBBS, THE (Also see Crackajack Funnies)
Dell Publishing Co./Croydon Publishing Co.: 1941; 1945

	GD 2.0	VG 4.0	FN 6.0	VF 8.0	VF/NM 9.0	NM- 9.2
Large Feature Comic 23(1941)	21	42	63	123	197	270
1(1945, 36 pgs.)-Reprints	13	26	39	74	105	135

NECESSARY EVIL
Desperado Publishing: Oct, 2007 - Present ($3.99)

	GD 2.0	VG 4.0	FN 6.0	VF 8.0	VF/NM 9.0	NM- 9.2
1-7: 1-Joshua Williamson-s/Marcus Harris-a/Dustin Nguyen-c						4.00

NECROMANCER
Image Comics (Top Cow): Sept, 2005 - No. 6, July 2006 ($2.99)

	GD 2.0	VG 4.0	FN 6.0	VF 8.0	VF/NM 9.0	NM- 9.2
1-6: 1-Manapul-a/Ortega-s; three covers by Manapul, Horn & Bachalo						3.00
... Pilot Season Vol. 1 #1 (11/07, $2.99) Ortega-s/Meyers-a/Manapul-c						3.00

NECROMANCER: THE GRAPHIC NOVEL
Marvel Comics (Epic Comics): 1989 ($8.95)

	GD 2.0	VG 4.0	FN 6.0	VF 8.0	VF/NM 9.0	NM- 9.2
nn						9.00

NECROWAR
Dreamwave Productions: July, 2003 - No. 3, Sept, 2003 ($2.95)

	GD 2.0	VG 4.0	FN 6.0	VF 8.0	VF/NM 9.0	NM- 9.2
1-3-Furman-s/Granov-digital art						3.00

Negative Burn V2 #18 © P,P, & M

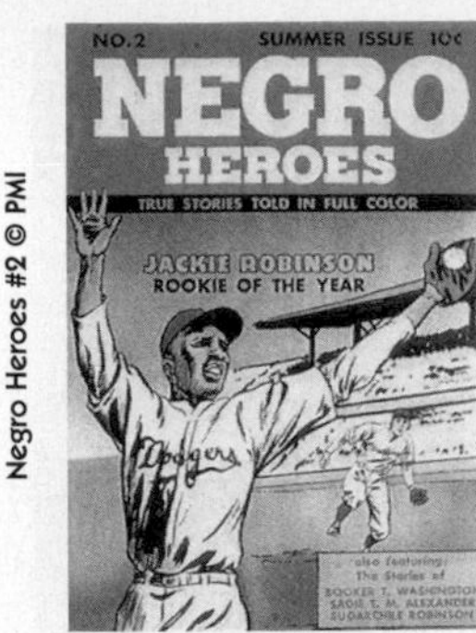

Negro Heroes #2 © PMI

Neil Gaiman's Lady Justice #4 © BIG Ent.

GD VG FN VF VF/NM NM-
2.0 4.0 6.0 8.0 9.0 9.2

GD VG FN VF VF/NM NM-
2.0 4.0 6.0 8.0 9.0 9.2

NEGATION
CrossGeneration Comics: Dec, 2001 - No. 27, Mar, 2004 ($2.95)

Prequel (12/01) 3.00
1-27: 1-(1/02) Pelletier-a/Bedard & Waid-s 3.00
... Lawbringer (11/02, $2.95) Nebres-a 3.00
Vol. 1: Bohica! (10/02, $19.95, TPB) r/ Prequel & #1-6 20.00
Vol. 2: Baptism of Fire (5/03, $15.95, TPB) r/#7-12 16.00
Vol. 3: Hounded (12/03, $15.95, TPB) r/#13-18 16.00

NEGATION WAR
CrossGeneration Comics: Apr, 2004 - No. 6 ($2.95)

1-4-Bedard-s/Pelletier-a 3.00

NEGATIVE BURN
Caliber: 1993 - No. 50, 1997 ($2.95, B&W, anthology)

1,2,4-12,14-47: Anthology by various including Bolland, Burden, Doran, Gaiman, Moebius, Moore, & Pope 4.00
3,13: 3-Bone story. 13-Strangers in Paradise story 2 4 6 8 10 12
48,49-($4.95) 5.00
50-($6.95, 96 pgs.)-Gaiman, Robinson, Bolland 7.00
...Summer Special 2005 (Image, 2005, $9.99) new short stories by various 10.00
...: The Best From 1993-1998 (Image, 1/05, $19.95) r/short stories by various 20.00
...Winter Special 2005 (Image, 2005, $9.95) new short stories by various 10.00

NEGATIVE BURN
Image Comics (Desperado): May, 2006 - Present ($5.99, B&W, anthology)

1-21: 1-Art by Bolland, Powell, Luna, Smith, Hester. 2-Milk & Cheese by Dorkin 6.00

NEGRO (See All-Negro)

NEGRO HEROES (Calling All Girls, Real Heroes, & True Comics reprints)
Parents' Magazine Institute: Spring, 1947 - No. 2, Summer, 1948

1 97 194 291 611 1031 1450
2-Jackie Robinson-c/story 103 206 309 649 1100 1550

NEGRO ROMANCE (Negro Romances #4)
Fawcett Publications: June, 1950 - No. 3, Oct, 1950 (All photo-c)

1-Evans-a 123 246 369 775 1313 1850
2,3 97 194 291 611 1031 1450

NEGRO ROMANCES (Formerly Negro Romance; Romantic Secrets #5 on)
Charlton Comics: No. 4, May, 1955

4-Reprints Fawcett #2 67 134 201 422 711 1000

NEIL GAIMAN AND CHARLES VESS' STARDUST
DC Comics (Vertigo): 1997 - No. 4, 1998 ($5.95/$6.95, square bound, lim. series)

1-4: Gaiman text with Vess paintings in all 7.00
Hardcover (1998, $29.95) r/series with new sketches 35.00
Softcover (1999, $19.95) oversized; new Vess-c 20.00

NEIL GAIMAN'S LADY JUSTICE
Tekno Comix: Sept, 1995 - No. 11, May, 1996 ($1.95/$2.25)

1-11: 1-Sienkiewicz-c; pin-ups. 1-5-Brereton-c. 7-Polybagged. 11-The Big Bang Pt. 7 2.50

NEIL GAIMAN'S LADY JUSTICE
BIG Entertainment: V2#1, June, 1996 - No. 9, Feb, 1997 ($2.25)

V2#1-9: Dan Brereton-c on all. 6-8-Dan Brereton script 2.50

NEIL GAIMAN'S MIDNIGHT DAYS
DC Comics (Vertigo): 1999 ($17.95, trade paperback)

nn-Reprints Gaiman's short stories; new Swamp Thing w/ Bissette-a 18.00

NEIL GAIMAN'S MR. HERO-THE NEWMATIC MAN
Tekno Comix: Mar, 1995 - No. 17, May, 1996 ($1.95/$2.25)

1-17: 1-Intro Mr. Hero & Teknophage; bound-in game piece and trading card. 4-w/Steel edition Neil Gaiman's Teknophage #1 coupon. 13-Polybagged 2.50

NEIL GAIMAN'S MR. HERO-THE NEWMATIC MAN
BIG Entertainment: V2#1, June, 1996 ($2.25)

V2#1-Teknophage destroys Mr. Hero; includes The Big Bang Pt. 10 2.50

NEIL GAIMAN'S NEVERWHERE
DC Comics (Vertigo): Aug, 2005 - No. 9, Sept, 2006 ($2.99, limited series)

1-9-Adaptation of Gaiman novel; Carey-s/Fabry-a/c 3.00
TPB (2007, $19.99) r/series; intro. by Carey 20.00

NEIL GAIMAN'S PHAGE-SHADOWDEATH
BIG Entertainment: June, 1996 - No. 6, Nov, 1996 ($2.25, limited series)

1-6: Bryan Talbot-c & scripts in all. 1-1st app. Orlando Holmes 2.50

NEIL GAIMAN'S TEKNOPHAGE
Tekno Comix: Aug, 1995 - No. 10, Mar, 1996 ($1.95/$2.25)

1-6-Rick Veitch scripts & Bryan Talbot-c/a. 2.50
1-Steel Edition 4.00
7-10: Paul Jenkins scripts in all. 8-polybagged 2.50

NEIL GAIMAN'S WHEEL OF WORLDS
Tekno Comix: Apr, 1995 - No. 1, May, 1996 ($2.95/$3.25)

0-1st app. Lady Justice; 48 pgs.; bound-in poster 3.25
0-Regular edition 2.50
1 ($3.25, 5/96)-Bruce Jones scripts; Lady Justice & Teknophage app.; CGI photo-c 3.25

NEIL THE HORSE (See Charlton Bullseye #2)
Aardvark-Vanaheim #1-10/Renegade Press #11 on: 2/83 - No. 10, 12/84; No. 11, 4/85 - #15, 1985 (B&W)

1($1.40) 4.00
1-2nd print 2.50
2-13: 13-Double size; 11,13-w/paperdolls 2.50
14,15: Double size ($3.00). 15 is a flip book(2-c) 3.00

NELLIE THE NURSE (Also see Gay Comics & Joker Comics)
Marvel/Atlas Comics (SPI/LMC): 1945 - No. 36, Oct, 1952; 1957

1-(1945) 41 82 123 256 428 600
2-(Spring/46) 21 42 63 125 200 275
3,4: 3-New logo (9/46) 17 34 51 98 154 210
5-Kurtzman's "Hey Look" (3); Georgie app. 18 36 54 105 165 225
6-8,10: 7,8-Georgie app. 10-Millie app. 15 30 45 92 144 195
9-Wolverton-a (1 pg.); Mille the Model app. 15 30 45 94 147 200
11,14-16,18-Kurtzman's "Hey Look" 16 32 48 96 151 205
12- "Giggles 'n' Grins" by Kurtzman 15 30 45 92 144 195
13,17,19,20: 17-Annie Oakley app. 14 28 42 76 108 140
21-30: 28-Mr. Nexdoor-r (3 pgs.) by Kurtzman/Rusty #22
12 24 36 67 94 120
31-36: 36-Post-c 10 20 30 58 79 100
1('57)-Leading Mag. (Atlas)-Everett-a, 20 pgs 11 22 33 62 86 110

NELLIE THE NURSE
Dell Publishing Co.: No. 1304, Mar-May, 1962

Four Color 1304-Stanley-a 7 14 21 47 76 105

NEMESIS ARCHIVES (Listed with Adventures Into the Unknown)

NEMESIS THE WARLOCK (Also see Spellbinders)
Eagle Comics: Sept, 1984 - No. 7, Mar, 1985 (limited series, Baxter paper)

1-7: 2000 A.D. reprints 2.50

NEMESIS THE WARLOCK
Quality Comics/Fleetway Quality #2 on: 1989 - No. 19, 1991 ($1.95, B&W)

1-19 2.50

NEUTRO
Dell Publishing Co.: Jan, 1967

1-Jack Sparling-c/a (super hero); UFO-s 4 8 12 26 41 55

NEVADA (See Zane Grey's Four Color 412, 996 & Zane Grey's Stories of the West #1)

NEVADA (Also see Vertigo Winter's Edge #1)
DC Comics (Vertigo): May, 1998 - No. 6, Oct, 1998 ($2.50, limited series)

1-6-Gerber-s/Winslade-c/a 2.50
TPB-(1999, $14.95) r/#1-6 & Vertigo Winter's Edge preview 15.00

NEVER AGAIN (War stories; becomes Soldier & Marine V2#9)
Charlton Comics: Aug, 1955; No. 8, July, 1956 (No #2-7)

1 9 18 27 50 65 80
8-(Formerly Foxhole?) 6 12 18 28 34 40

NEVERMEN, THE (See Dark Horse Presents #148-150)
Dark Horse Comics: May, 2000 - No. 4, Aug, 2000 ($2.95, limited series)

1-4-Phil Amara-s/Guy Davis-a 3.00

NEVERMEN, THE: STREETS OF BLOOD
Dark Horse Comics: Jan, 2003 - No. 3, Apr, 2003 ($2.99, limited series)

1-3-Phil Amara-s/Guy Davis-a 3.00
TPB (7/03, $9.95) r/#1-3; Paul Jenkins intro.; Davis sketch pages 10.00

NEW ADVENTURE COMICS (Formerly New Comics; becomes Adventure Comics #32 on; V1#12 indicia says NEW COMICS #12)
National Periodical Publications: V1#12, Jan, 1937 - No. 31, Oct, 1938

V1#12-Federal Men by Siegel & Shuster continues; Jor-L mentioned;

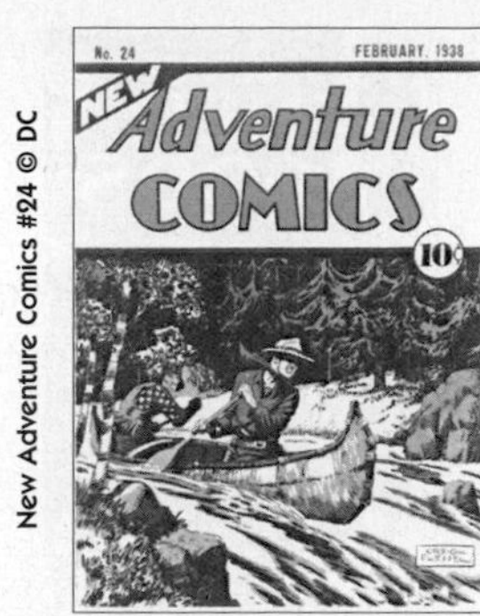

New Adventure Comics #24 © DC

New Avengers #28 © MAR

New Dynamix #1 © WSP

	GD	VG	FN	VF	VF/NM	NM-
	2.0	4.0	6.0	8.0	9.0	9.2

Whitney Ellsworth-c begin, end #14 533 1066 1600 4100 – –
V2#1(2/37, #13)-(Rare) 507 1014 1521 3900 – –
V2#2 (#14) 450 900 1350 3500 – –
15(V2#3)-20(V2#8): 15-1st Adventure logo; Creig Flessel-c begin, end #31. 16-1st non-funny cover. 17-Nadir, Master of Magic begins, ends #30
360 720 1080 1980 3040 4100
21(V2#9),22(V2#10, 2/37): 22-X-Mas-c 320 640 960 1760 2730 3700
23-25,27-31: 27(6/38) has house ad for Action Comics #1 showing B&W image of cover (early published image of Superman) 270 540 810 1485 2343 3200
26(5/38) (scarce) has house ad for Action Comics #1 showing B&W image of cover (early published image of Superman)(prices vary widely on this book) (A CGC 5.0 sold in 2006 for $5377.50)

NEW ADVENTURES OF ABRAHAM LINCOLN, THE
Image Comics (Homage): 1998 ($19.95, one-shot)

1-Scott McCloud-s/computer art 20.00

NEW ADVENTURES OF CHARLIE CHAN, THE (TV)
National Periodical Publications: May-June, 1958 - No. 6, Mar-Apr, 1959

1 (Scarce)-John Broome-s/Sid Greene-a in all 72 144 216 454 765 1075
2 (Scarce) 46 92 138 285 473 660
3-6 (Scarce)-Greene/Giella-a 40 80 120 239 387 535

NEW ADVENTURES OF HUCK FINN, THE (TV)
Gold Key: December, 1968 (Hanna-Barbera)

1- "The Curse of Thut"; part photo-c 4 8 12 22 34 45

NEW ADVENTURES OF PINOCCHIO (TV)
Dell Publishing Co.: Oct-Dec, 1962 - No. 3, Sept-Nov, 1963

12-562-212(#1) 8 16 24 56 93 130
2,3 7 14 21 45 73 100

NEW ADVENTURES OF ROBIN HOOD (See Robin Hood)

NEW ADVENTURES OF SHERLOCK HOLMES (Also see Sherlock Holmes)
Dell Publishing Co.: No. 1169, Mar-May, 1961 - No. 1245, Nov-Jan, 1961/62

Four Color 1169(#1) 14 28 42 102 181 260
Four Color 1245 13 26 39 90 160 230

NEW ADVENTURES OF SPEED RACER
Now Comics: Dec, 1993 - No. 7, 1994? ($1.95)

1-7 2.50
0-(Premiere)-3-D cover 3.00

NEW ADVENTURES OF SUPERBOY, THE (Also see Superboy)
DC Comics: Jan, 1980 - No. 54, June, 1984

1 5.00
2-6,8-10 4.00
11-49,51-54: 11-Superboy gets new power. 14-Lex Luthor app. 15-Superboy gets new parents. 28-Dial "H" For Hero begins, ends #49. 45-47-1st app. Sunburst. 48-Begin 75¢-c.
3.00
1,2,5,6,8 (Whitman variants; low print run; no issue # shown on cover)
2 4 6 8 10 12
7,50: 7-Has extra story "The Computers That Saved Metropolis" by Starlin (Radio Shack giveaway w/indicia). 50-Legion app. 5.00
NOTE: *Buckler a-9p; c-36p. Giffen a-50; c-50. 40i. Gil Kane c-32p, 33p, 35, 39, 41-49. Miller c-51. Starlin a-7. Krypto back-ups in 17, 22. Superbaby in 11, 14, 19, 24.*

NEW ADVENTURES OF THE PHANTOM BLOT, THE (See The Phantom Blot)

NEW AMERICA
Eclipse Comics: Nov, 1987 - No. 4, Feb, 1988 ($1.75, Baxter paper)

1-4: Scout limited series 2.50

NEW ARCHIES, THE (TV)
Archie Comic Publications: Oct, 1987 - No. 22, May, 1990 (75¢)

1 5.00
2-10: 3-Xmas issue 4.00
11-22: 17-22 (95¢-$1.00): 21-Xmas issue 3.00

NEW ARCHIES DIGEST (TV)(...Comics Digest Magazine #4?-10; ...Digest Magazine #11 on)
Archie Comics: May, 1988 - No. 14, July, 1991 ($1.35/$1.50, quarterly)

1 6.00
2-14: 6-Begin $1.50-c 3.50

NEW AVENGERS, THE (Also see Promotional section for military giveaway)
Marvel Comics: Jan, 2005 - Present ($2.25/$2.50/$2.99)

1-Bendis-s/Finch-a; Spider-Man app.; re-intro The Sentry; 4 covers by McNiven, Quesada & Finch; variants from #1-6 combine for one team image 5.00
1-Director's Cut ($3.99) includes alternate covers, script, villain gallery 4.00
2-20: 2-6-Finch-a. 5-Wolverine app. 7-10-Origin of the Sentry; McNiven-a. 11-Debut of Ronin. 14,15-Cho-c/a. 17-20-Deodato-a 3.00
21-44: 21-26-Civil War. 21-Chaykin-a/c. 26-Maleev-a. 27-31-Yu-a; Echo & "Elektra" app. 33-37-The Hood app. 38-Gaydos-a. 39-Mack-a. 40-44-Secret Invasion 3.00
Annual 1 (6/06, $3.99) Wedding of Luke Cage and Jessica Jones; Bendis-s/Coipel-a 4.00
Annual 2 (2/08, $3.99) Avengers vs. The Hood's gang; Bendis-s/Pagulayan-a 4.00
...: Illuminati (5/06, $3.99) Bendis-s/Maleev-a; leads into Planet Hulk; Civil War preview 4.00
... Most Wanted Files (2006, $3.99) profile pages of Avenger villains 4.00
... Vol. 1: Breakout HC (2005, $19.99) r/#1-6; gallery of variant covers 20.00
... Vol. 1: Breakout SC (2006, $14.99) r/#1-6; gallery of variant covers 15.00
... Vol. 2: Sentry HC (2006, $19.99) r/#7-10 & ... Most Wanted Files 20.00
... Vol. 2: Sentry SC (2006, $14.99) r/#7-10 & ... Most Wanted Files 15.00
... Vol. 3: Secrets and Lies HC (2006, $19.99) r/#11-15 & Giant-Size Spider-Woman #1 20.00
... Vol. 3: Secrets and Lies SC (2006, $14.99) r/#11-15 & Giant-Size Spider-Woman #1 15.00
... Vol. 4: The Collective HC (2006, $19.99) r/#16-20 20.00
... Vol. 4: The Collective SC (2007, $14.99) r/#16-20 15.00
... Vol. 5: Civil War HC (2007, $19.99) r/#21-25 20.00
... Vol. 5: Civil War SC (2007, $14.99) r/#21-25 15.00
... Vol. 6: Revolution HC (2007, $19.99) r/#26-31 20.00
... Vol. 6: Revolution SC (2007, $14.99) r/#26-31 15.00
... Volume 1 HC (2007, $29.99) oversized r/#1-10, ... Most Wanted Files, and ... Guest Starring the Fantastic Four (militiary giveaway); new intro. by Bendis; script & sketch pages 30.00
... Volume 2 HC (2008, $29.99) oversized r/#11-20, ... Annual #1, and story from Giant-Size Spider-Woman; variant covers & sketch pages 30.00

NEW AVENGERS: ILLUMINATI (Also see Civil War and Secret Invasion)
Marvel Comics: Feb, 2007 - No. 5, Jan, 2008 ($2.99, limited series)

1-5-Bendis & Reed-s/Cheung-a. 3-Origin of The Beyonder. 5-Secret Invasion 3.00
HC (2008, $19.99, dustjacket) r/#1-5; cover sketch art 20.00

NEW AVENGERS/TRANSFORMERS
Marvel Comics: Sept, 2007 - No. 4, Dec, 2007 ($2.99, limited series)

1-4-Kirkham-a; Capt. America app. 1-Cheung-c. 2-Pearson-c 3.00
TPB (2008, $10.99) r/#1-4 11.00

NEW BOOK OF COMICS (Also see Big Book Of Fun)
National Periodical Publ.: 1937; No. 2, Spring, 1938 (100 pgs. each) (Reprints)

1(Rare)-1st regular size comic annual; 2nd DC annual; contains r/New Comics #1-4 & More Fun #9; r/Federal Men (8 pgs.), Henri Duval (1 pg.), & Dr. Occult in costume (1 pg.) by Siegel & Shuster; Moldoff, Sheldon Mayer (15 pgs.)-a
1850 3700 5550 12,000 21,000 30,000
2-Contains-r/More Fun #15 & 16; r/Dr. Occult in costume (a Superman prototype), & Calling All Cars (4 pgs.) by Siegel & Shuster 950 1900 2850 6175 11,088 16,000

NEW COMICS (New Adventure #12 on)
National Periodical Publ.: 12/35 - No. 11, 12/36 (No. 1-6: paper cover) (No. 1-5: 84 pgs.)

V1#1-Billy the Kid, Sagebrush 'n' Cactus, Jibby Jones, Needles, The Vikings, Sir Loin of Beef, Now-When I Was a Boy, & other 1-2 pg. strips; 2 pgs. Kelly art(1st)-(Gulliver's Travels); Sheldon Mayer-a(1st)(2 2pg. strips); Vincent Sullivan-c(1st)
2786 5572 8358 19,500 – –
2-1st app. Federal Men by Siegel & Shuster & begins (also see The Comics Magazine #2); Mayer, Kelly-a (Rare)(1/36) 1171 2342 3513 8200 – –
3-6: 3,4-Sheldon Mayer-a which continues in The Comics Magazine #1. 3-Vincent Sullivan-c. 4-Dickens' "A Tale of Two Cities" adaptation begins. 5-Junior Federal Men Club; Kiefer-a. 6- "She" adaptation begins 829 1658 2487 5800 – –
7-10 593 1186 1779 4150 – –
11-Ties with More Fun #16 as DC's 1st Christmas-c 621 1242 1863 4350 – –
NOTE: *#1-6 rarely occur in mint condition. Whitney Ellsworth c-4-11.*

NEW DEFENDERS (See Defenders)

NEW DNAGENTS, THE (Formerly DNAgents)
Eclipse Comics: V2#1, Oct, 1985 - V2#17, Mar, 1987 (Whole #s 25-40; Mando paper)

V2#1-17: 1-Origin recap. 7-Begin 95 cent-c. 9,10-Airboy preview 2.50
3-D 1 (1/86, $2.25) 2.50
2-D 1 (1/86)-Limited ed. (100 copies) 10.00

NEW DYNAMIX
DC Comics (WildStorm): May, 2008 - No. 5, Sept, 2008 ($2.99, limited series)

1-5-Warner-s/J.J. Kirby-a/c. 1-Variant-c by Jim Lee. 1-Convention Ed. with Lee-c 3.00

NEW ETERNALS: APOCALYPSE NOW (Also see Eternals, The)
Marvel Comics: Feb, 2000 ($3.99, one-shot)

1-Bennett & Hanna-a; Ladronn-c 4.00

NEW EXCALIBUR
Marvel Comics: Jan, 2006 - No. 24, Dec, 2007 ($2.99)

1-24: 1-Claremont-s/Ryan-a; Dazzler app. 3-Juggernaut app. 4-Lionheart app. 3.00

New Exiles #1 © MAR

New Funnies #67 © DELL

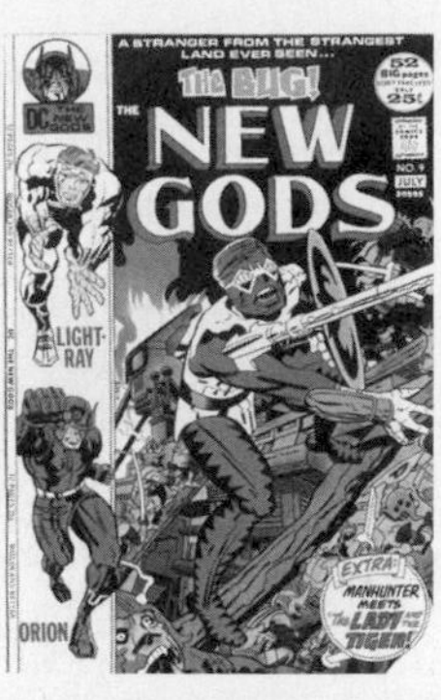
New Gods #9 © DC

... Vol. 1: Defenders of the Realm TPB (2006, $17.99) r/#1-7 18.00
... Vol. 2: Last Days of Camelot TPB (2007, $19.99) r/#8-15 20.00
... Vol. 3: Battle for Eternity TPB (2007, $24.99) r/#16-24; sketch pages 25.00

NEW EXILES (Continued from Exiles #100 and Exiles - Days of Then and Now)
Marvel Comics: Mar, 2008 - Present ($2.99)

1-11: 1-Claremont-s/Grummett-a; 2 covers by Land & Golden; new team 3.00
1-2nd printing with Grummett-c 3.00

NEWFORCE (Also see Newmen)
Image Comics (Extreme Studios): Jan, 1996-No. 4, Apr, 1996 ($2.50, lim. series)

1-4: 1-"Extreme Destroyer" Pt. 8; polybagged w/gaming card. 4-Newforce disbands 2.50

NEW FUN COMICS (More Fun #7 on; see Big Book of Fun Comics)
National Periodical Publications: Feb, 1935 - No. 6, Oct, 1935 (10x15", No. 1-4,: slick-c) (No. 1-5: 36 pgs; 40 pgs. No. 6)

V1#1 (1st DC comic); 1st app. Oswald The Rabbit; Jack Woods (cowboy) begins
7143 14,286 21,429 50,000 – –
2(3/35)-(Very Rare) 3071 6142 9213 21,500 – –
3-5(8/35): 3-Don Drake on the Planet Soro-c/story (sci/fi, 4/35); early (maybe 1st) DC letter column. 5-Soft-c 1714 3428 5142 12,000 – –
6(10/35)-1st Dr. Occult by Siegel & Shuster (Leger & Reuths); last "New Fun" title. "New Comics" #1 begins in Dec. which is reason for title change to More Fun; Henri Duval (ends #10) by Siegel & Shuster begins; paper-c
3357 6714 10,071 23,500 – –

NEW FUNNIES (The Funnies #1-64; Walter Lantz...#109 on; New TV... #259, 260, 272, 273; TV Funnies #261-271)
Dell Publishing Co.: No. 65, July, 1942 - No. 288, Mar-Apr, 1962

65(#1)-Andy Panda in a world of real people, Raggedy Ann & Andy, Oswald the Rabbit (with Woody Woodpecker x-overs), Li'l Eight Ball & Peter Rabbit begin; Bugs Bunny and Elmer app. 69 138 207 587 1119 1650
66-70: 66-Felix the Cat begins. 67-Billy & Bonny Bee by Frank Thomas begins. 69-Kelly-a (2 pgs.); The Brownies begin (not by Kelly) 32 64 96 246 461 675
71-75: 72-Kelly illos. 75-Brownies by Kelly? 21 42 63 155 288 420
76-Andy Panda (Carl Barks & Pabian-a); Woody Woodpecker x-over in Oswald ends
73 146 219 621 1186 1750
77,78: 77-Kelly-c. 78-Andy Panda in a world with real people ends
21 42 63 155 288 420
79-81 15 30 45 105 190 275
82-Brownies by Kelly begins; Homer Pigeon begins 15 30 45 110 203 295
83-85-Brownies by Kelly in ea. 83-X-mas-c; Homer Pigeon begins. 85-Woody Woodpecker, 1 pg. strip begins 15 30 45 108 199 290
86-90: 87-Woody Woodpecker stories begin 12 24 36 82 146 210
91-99 9 18 27 65 113 160
100 (6/45) 10 20 30 68 119 170
101-120: 119-X-Mas-c 8 16 24 52 86 120
121-150: 131,143-X-Mas-c 7 14 21 45 73 100
151-200: 155-X-Mas-c. 167-X-Mas-c. 182-Origin & 1st app. Knothead & Splinter. 191-X-Mas-c 6 12 18 39 62 85
201-240 5 10 15 34 55 75
241-288: 270,271-Walter Lantz c-app. 281-1st story swipes/WDC&S #100
5 10 15 30 48 65

NOTE: *Early issues written by **John Stanley**.*

NEW GODS, THE (1st Series)(New Gods #12 on)(See Adventure #459, DC Graphic Novel #4, 1st Issue Special #13 & Super-Team Family)
National Periodical Publications/DC Comics: 2-3/71 - V2#11, 10-11/72; V3#12, 7/77 - V3#19, 7-8/78 (Fourth World)

1-Intro/1st app. Orion; 4th app. Darkseid (cameo; 3 weeks after Forever People #1) (#1-3 are 15¢ issues) 8 16 24 56 93 130
2-Darkseid-c/story (2nd full app., 4-5/71) 4 8 12 28 44 60
3-1st app. Black Racer; last 15¢ issue 3 6 9 20 30 40
4-9: (25¢, 52 pg. giants): 4-Darkseid cameo; origin Manhunter-r. 5,7,8-Young Gods feature. 7-Darkseid app. (2-3/72); origin Orion; 1st origin of all New Gods as a group. 9-1st app. Forager 3 6 9 20 30 40
10,11: 11-Last Kirby issue. 3 6 9 16 23 30
12-19: Darkseid storyline w/minor apps. 12-New costume Orion (see 1st Issue Special #13 for 1st new costume). 19-Story continued in Adventure Comics #459,460
1 3 4 6 8 10
Jack Kirby's New Gods TPB ('98, $11.95, B&W&Grey) r/#1-11 plus cover gallery of original series and "84 reprints 12.00

NOTE: *#4-9(25¢, 52 pgs.) contain Manhunter-r by **Simon & Kirby** from Adventure #73, 74, 75, 76, 77, 78 with covers in that order. **Adkins** i-12-14, 17-19. **Buckler** a(p)-15. **Kirby** c/a-1-11p. **Newton** a(p)-12-14, 16-19. **Starlin** c-17. **Staton** c-19p.*

NEW GODS (Also see DC Graphic Novel #4)
DC Comics: June, 1984 - No. 6, Nov, 1984 ($2.00, Baxter paper)

1-5: New Kirby-c; r/New Gods #1-10. 4.00
6-Reprints New Gods #11 w/48 pgs of new Kirby story & art; leads into DC Graphic Novel #4
2 4 6 8 10 12

NEW GODS (2nd Series)
DC Comics: Feb, 1989 - No. 28, Aug, 1991 ($1.50)

1-28 2.50

NEW GODS (3rd Series) (Becomes Jack Kirby's Fourth World) (Also see Showcase '94 #1 & Showcase '95 #7)
DC Comics: Oct, 1995 - No. 15, Feb, 1997 ($1.95)

1-11,13-15: 9-Giffen-a(p). 10,11-Superman app. 13-Takion, Mr. Miracle & Big Barda app. 13-15-Byrne-a(p)/scripts & Simonson-c. 15-Apokolips merged w/ New Genesis; story cont'd in Jack Kirby's Fourth World 2.50
12-(11/96, 99¢)-Byrne-a(p)/scripts & Simonson-c begin; Takion cameo; indicia reads October 1996 2.50
...Secret Files 1 (9/98, $4.95) Origin-s 5.00

NEW GUARDIANS, THE
DC Comics: Sept, 1988 - No. 12, Sept, 1989 ($1.25)

1-($2.00, 52 pgs)-Staton-c/a in #1-9 3.00
2-12 2.50

NEW HEROIC (See Heroic)

NEW INVADERS (Titled Invaders for #0 & #1) (See Avengers V3#83,84)
Marvel Comics: No. 0, Aug, 2004 - No. 9, June, 2005 ($2.99)

0-9-Roster of U.S. Agent, Sub-Mariner, Blazing Skull and others. 0-Avengers app. 3.00

NEW JUSTICE MACHINE, THE (Also see The Justice Machine)
Innovation Publishing: 1989 - No. 3, 1989 ($1.95, limited series)

1-3 2.50

NEW KIDS ON THE BLOCK, THE (Also see Richie Rich and...)
Harvey Comics: Dec, 1990 - No. 8, Dec, 1991 ($1.25)

1-8 2.50
...**Back Stage Pass** 1(12/90) - 7(11/91) **Chillin'** 1(12/90) - 7(12/91): 1-Photo-c ...**Comic Tour** '90/91 1 (12/90) - 7(12/91) **Digest** 1(1/91) - 5(1/92) **Hanging Tough** 1 (2/91) **Magic Summer Tour** 1 (Fall/90) **Magic Summer Tour** nn (Fall/90, sold at concerts) **Step By Step** 1 (Fall/90, one-shot) **Valentine Girl** 1 (Fall/90, one-shot)-Photo-c 2.50

NEW LINE CINEMA'S TALES OF HORROR (Anthology)
DC Comics (WildStorm): Nov, 2007 - Present ($2.99)

1-Freddy Krueger and Leatherface app.; Darick Robertson-c 3.00

NEW LOVE (See Love & Rockets)
Fantagraphics Books: Aug, 1996 - No. 6, Dec, 1997 ($2.95, B&W, lim. series)

1-6: Gilbert Hernandez-s/a 3.00

NEWMAN
Image Comics (Extreme Studios): Jan, 1996 - No. 4, Apr, 1996 ($2.50, lim. series)

1-4: 1-Extreme Destroyer Pt. 3; polybagged w/card. 4-Shadowhunt tie-in; Eddie Collins becomes new Shadowhawk 2.50

NEW MANGVERSE (Also see Marvel Mangaverse)
Marvel Comics: Mar, 2006 - No. 5, July, 2006 ($2.99, lim. series)

1-5: Cebulski-s/Ohtsuka-a; The Hand and Elektra app. 3.00
...: The Rings of Fate (2006, $7.99, digest) r/#1-5 8.00

NEWMEN (becomes The Adventures Of The...#22)
Image Comics (Extreme Studios): Apr, 1994 - No. 20, Nov, 1995; No. 21, Nov, 1996 ($1.95/$2.50)

1-21: 1-5: Matsuda-c/a. 10-Polybagged w/trading card. 11-Polybagged. 20-Has a variant-c; Babewatch! x-over. 21-(11/96)-Series relaunch; Chris Sprouse-a begins; pin-up. 16-Has a variant-c by Quesada & Palmiotti 2.50
TPB-(1996, $12.95) r/#1-4 w/pin-ups 13.00

NEW MEN OF BATTLE, THE
Catechetical Guild: 1949 (nn) (Carboard-c)

nn(V8#1-3,5,6)-192 pgs.; contains 5 issues of Topix rebound
9 18 27 47 61 75
nn(V8#7-V8#11)-160 pgs.; contains 5 iss. of Topix 9 18 27 47 61 75

NEW MUTANTS, THE (See Marvel Graphic Novel #4 for 1st app.)(Also see X-Force & Uncanny X-Men #167)
Marvel Comics Group: Mar, 1983 - No. 100, Apr, 1991

1 5.00
2-10: 3,4-Ties into X-Men #167. 10-1st app. Magma 3.00

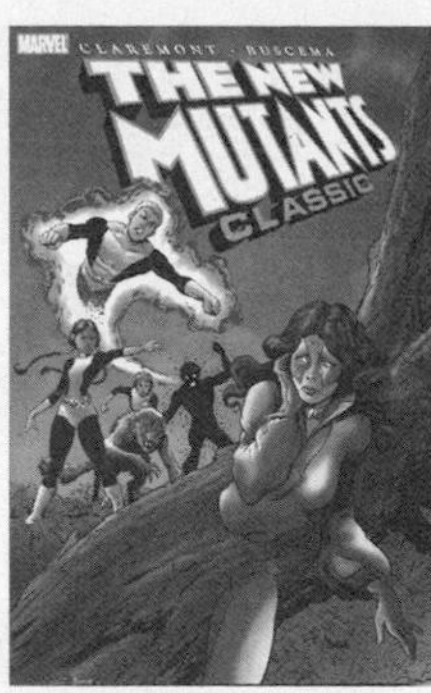
New Mutants Classic Vol. 2 TPB © MAR

New Romances #7 © STD

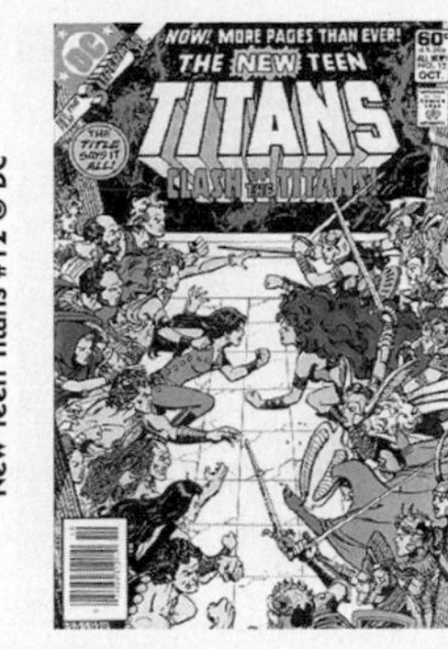

New Teen Titans #12 © DC

GD VG FN VF VF/NM NM-
2.0 4.0 6.0 8.0 9.0 9.2

11-17,19,20: 13-Kitty Pryde app. 16-1st app. Warpath (w/out costume); see X-Men #193 2.50
18,21: 18-Intro. new Warlock. 21-Double size; origin new Warlock; newsstand version has cover price written in by Sienkiewicz 3.00
22-24,27-30: 23-25-Cloak & Dagger app. 2.50
25,26: 25-1st brief app. Legion. 26-1st full Legion app. 4.00
31-58: 35-Magneto intro'd as new headmaster. 43-Portacio-i. 50-Double size. 58-Contains pull-out mutant registration form 2.50
59-61: Fall of The Mutants series. 60(52 pgs.) 3.00
62-85: 68-Intro Spyder. 63-X-Men & Wolverine clones app. 73-(52 pgs.). 76-X-Factor & X-Terminator app. 85-Liefeld-c begin 2.50
86-Rob Liefeld-a begins; McFarlane-c(i) swiped from Ditko splash pg.; 1st brief app. Cable (last page teaser) 6.00
87-1st full app. Cable (3/90) 2 4 6 11 16 20
87-2nd printing; gold metallic ink-c ($1.00) 2.50
88-2nd app. Cable 1 2 3 4 5 7
92-No Liefeld-a; Liefeld-c 4.00
89,90,91,93-100: 89-3rd app. Cable. 90-New costumes. 90,91-Sabretooth app. 93,94-Cable vs. Wolverine. 95-97-X-Tinction Agenda x-over. 95-Death of new Warlock. 97-Wolverine & Cable-c, but no app. 98-1st app. Deadpool, Gideon & Domino (2/91); 2nd Shatterstar (cameo). 99-1st app. of Feral (of X-Force); Byrne-c/swipe (X-Men, 1st Series #138). 100-(52 pgs.)-1st brief app. X-Force. 5.00
95,100-Gold 2nd printing. 100-Silver ink 3rd printing 2.50
Annual 1 (1984) 4.00
Annual 2 (1986, $1.25)-1st Psylocke 1 2 3 5 6 8
Annual 3,4,6,7 ('87, '88,'90,'91, 68 pgs.): 4-Evolutionary War x-over. 6-1st new costumes by Liefeld (3 pgs.); 1st brief app. Shatterstar (of X-Force). 7-Liefeld pin-up only; X-Terminators back-up story; 2nd app. X-Force (cont'd in New Warriors Annual #1) 3.00
Annual 5 (1989, $2.00, 68 pgs.)-Atlantis Attacks; 1st Liefeld-a on New Mutants 4.00
... Classic Vol. 1 TPB (2006, $24.99) r/#1-7, Marvel Graphic Novel #4, Uncanny X-Men #167 25.00
... Classic Vol. 2 TPB (2007, $24.99) r/#8-17 25.00
... Classic Vol. 3 TPB (2008, $24.99) r/#18-25 & Annual #1 25.00
Special 1-Special Edition ('85, 68 pgs.)-Ties in w/X-Men Alpha Flight limited series; cont'd in X-Men Annual #9; Art Adams/Austin-a 5.00
Summer Special 1(Sum/90, $2.95, 84 pgs.) 3.00
NOTE: ***Art Adams** c-38, 39. **Austin** c-57i. **Byrne** c/a-75p. **Liefeld** a-86-91p, 93-96p, 98-100, Annual 5p, 6(3 pgs.); c-85-91p, 92, 93p, 94, 95, 96p, 97-100, Annual 5, 6p. **McFarlane** c-85-89i, 93i. **Portacio** a(i)-43. **Russell** a-48i. **Sienkiewicz** a-18-31, 35-38i; c-17-31, 35i, 37i, Annual 1. **Simonson** c-11p. **B. Smith** c-36, 40-48. **Williamson** a(i)-69, 71-73, 78-80, 82, 83; c(i)-69, 72, 73, 78i.*

NEW MUTANTS (Continues as New X-Men (Academy X))
Marvel Comics: July, 2003 - No. 13, June, 2004 ($2.50/$2.99)

1-7: 1-6-Josh Middleton-c. 7-Bachalo-c 2.50
8-13 ($2.99) 8-11-Bachalo-c 3.00
... Vol. 1: Back To School TPB (2005, $16.99) r/#1-6; new Middleton-c 17.00

NEW MUTANTS, THE: TRUTH OR DEATH
Marvel Comics: Nov, 1997 - No. 3, Jan, 1998 ($2.50, limited series)

1-3-Raab-s/Chang-a(p) 2.50

NEW ORDER, THE
CFD Publishing: Nov, 1994 ($2.95)

1 3.00

NEW PEOPLE, THE (TV)
Dell Publishing Co.: Jan, 1970 - No. 2, May, 1970

1 3 6 9 17 25 32
2 3 6 9 15 21 26

NEW ROMANCES
Standard Comics: No. 5, May, 1951 - No. 21, May, 1954

5-Photo-c 15 30 45 84 127 170
6-9: 6-Barbara Bel Geddes, Richard Basehart "Fourteen Hours" photo-c. 7-Ray Milland & Joan Fontaine photo-c. 9-Photo-c from '50s movie 10 20 30 54 72 90
10,14,16,17-Toth-a 10 20 30 58 79 100
11-Toth-a; Liz Taylor, Montgomery Cliff photo-c 27 54 81 158 254 350
12,13,15,18-21 9 18 27 50 65 80
NOTE: ***Celardo** a-9. **Moreira** a-6. **Tuska** a-7, 20. Photo c-5-16.*

NEW SHADOWHAWK, THE (Also see Shadowhawk & Shadowhunt)
Image Comics (Shadowline Ink): June, 1995 - No. 7, Mar, 1996 ($2.50)

1-7: Kurt Busiek scripts in all 3.00

NEW STATESMEN, THE
Fleetway Publications (Quality Comics): 1989 - No. 5, 1990 ($3.95, limited series, mature readers, 52pgs.)

GD VG FN VF VF/NM NM-
2.0 4.0 6.0 8.0 9.0 9.2

1-5: Futuristic; squarebound; 3-Photo-c 4.00

NEWSTRALIA
Innovation Publ.: July, 1989 - No. 5, 1989 ($1.75, color)(#2 on, $2.25, B&W)

1-5: 1,2: Timothy Truman-c/a; Gustovich-i 2.50

NEW TALENT SHOWCASE (Talent Showcase #16 on)
DC Comics: Jan, 1984 - No. 19, Oct, 1985 (Direct sales only)

1-19: Features new strips & artists. 18-Williamson-c(i) 2.50

NEW TEEN TITANS, THE (See DC Comics Presents #26, Marvel and DC Present & Teen Titans; Tales of the Teen Titans #41 on)
DC Comics: Nov, 1980 - No. 40, Mar, 1984

1-Robin, Kid Flash, Wonder Girl, The Changeling (1st app.), Starfire, The Raven, Cyborg begin; partial origin 2 4 6 10 14 18
2-1st app. Deathstroke the Terminator 3 6 9 19 29 38
3-10: 3-Origin Starfire; Intro The Fearsome Five. 4-Origin continues; J.L.A. app. 6-Origin Raven. 7-Cyborg origin. 8-Origin Kid Flash retold. 9-Minor app. Deathstroke on last pg. 10-2nd app. Deathstroke the Terminator (see Marvel & DC Present for 3rd app.); origin Changeling retold 1 2 3 4 5 7
11-20: 13-Return of Madame Rouge & Capt. Zahl; Robotman revived. 14-Return of Mento; origin Doom Patrol. 15-Death of Madame Rouge & Capt. Zahl; intro. new Brotherhood of Evil. 16-1st app. Captain Carrot (free 16 pg. preview). 18-Return of Starfire. 19-Hawkman teams-up 5.00
21-40: 21-Intro Night Force in free 16 pg. insert; intro Brother Blood. 23-1st app. Vigilante (not in costume), & Blackfire. 24-Omega Men app. 25-Omega Men cameo; free 16 pg. preview Masters of the Universe. 26-1st app. Terra. 27-Free 16 pg. preview Atari Force. 29-The New Brotherhood of Evil & Speedy app. 30-Terra joins the Titans. 34-4th app. Deathstroke the Terminator.37-Batman & The Outsiders x-over. 38-Origin Wonder Girl. 39-Last Dick Grayson as Robin; Kid Flash quits 4.00
Annual 1(11/82)-Omega Men app. 5.00
Annual V2#2(9/83)-1st app. Vigilante in costume; 1st app. Lyla 4.00
Annual 3 (See Tales of the Teen Titans Annual #3)
...: Terra Incognito TPB (2006, $19.99) r/#26,28-34 & Annual #2 20.00
...: The Judas Contract TPB (2003, $19.95) r/#39,40 plus Tales of the Teen Titans #41-44 & Annual #3 20.00
...: Who is Donna Troy? TPB (2005, $19.99) r/#38,Tales of the Teen Titans #50, New Titans #50-55 and Teen Titans/Outsiders Secret Files 2003 20.00
NOTE: ***Perez** a-1-4p, 6-34p, 37-40p, Annual 1p, 2p; c-1-12, 13-17p, 18-21, 22p, 23p, 24-37, 38, 39(painted), 40, Annual 1, 2.*

NEW TEEN TITANS, THE (Becomes The New Titans #50 on)
DC Comics: Aug, 1984 - No. 49, Nov, 1988 ($1.25/$1.75; deluxe format)

1-New storyline; Perez-c/a begins 6.00
2,3: 2-Re-intro Lilith 5.00
4-10: 5-Death of Trigon. 7-9-Origin Lilith. 8-Intro Kole. 10-Kole joins 4.00
11-49: 13,14-Crisis x-over. 20-Robin (Jason Todd) joins; original Teen Titans return. 38-Infinity, Inc. x-over. 47-Origin of all Titans; Titans (East & West) pin-up by Perez 3.00
Annual 1-4 (9/85-'88): 1-Intro. Vanguard. 2-Byrne c/a(p); origin Brother Blood; intro new Dr. Light. 3-Intro. Danny Chase. 4-Perez-c 3.50
...: The Terror of Trigon TPB (2003, $17.95) r/#1-5; new cover by Phil Jimenez 18.00
NOTE: ***Buckler** c-10. **Kelley Jones** a-47, Annual 4. **Erik Larsen** a-33. **Orlando** c-33p. **Perez** a-1-5; c-1-7, 19-23, 43. **Steacy** c-47.*

NEW TERRYTOONS (TV)
Dell Publishing Co./Gold Key: 6-8/60 - No. 8, 3-5/62; 10/62 - No. 54, 1/79

1(1960-Dell)-Deputy Dawg, Dinky Duck & Hashimoto-San begin (1st app. of each) 9 18 27 60 100 140
2-8(1962) 5 10 15 34 55 75
1(30010-210)(10/62-Gold Key, 84 pgs.)-Heckle & Jeckle begins 9 18 27 61 103 145
2(30010-301)-84 pgs. 8 16 24 54 90 125
3-5 4 8 12 26 41 55
6-10 3 6 9 21 32 42
11-20 3 6 9 16 22 28
21-30 2 4 6 9 13 16
31-43 1 3 4 6 8 10
44-54: Mighty Mouse-c/s in all 2 4 6 8 11 14
NOTE: *Reprints: #4-12, 38, 40, 47. (See March of Comics #379, 393, 412, 435)*

NEW TESTAMENT STORIES VISUALIZED
Standard Publishing Co.: 1946 - 1947

"New Testament Heroes–Acts of Apostles Visualized, Book I"
"New Testament Heroes–Acts of Apostles Visualized, Book II"
"Parables Jesus Told" Set.... 16 32 48 94 147 200
NOTE: *All three are contained in a cardboard case, illustrated on front and info about the set.*

NEW THUNDERBOLTS (Continues in Thunderbolts #100)

New Titans #55 © DC

New Warriors #70 © MAR

New X-Men #43 © MAR

	GD 2.0	VG 4.0	FN 6.0	VF 8.0	VF/NM 9.0	NM- 9.2

Marvel Comics: Jan, 2005 - No. 18, Apr, 2006 ($2.99)

1-18: 1-Grummett-a/Nicieza-s. 1-Captain Marvel app. 2-Namor app. 4-Wolverine app. 3.00
... Vol. 1: One Step Forward (2005, $14.99) r/#1-6 15.00
... Vol. 2: Modern Marvels (2005, $14.99) r/#7-12 15.00
... Vol. 3: Right of Power (2006, $17.99) r/#13-18 & Thunderbolts #100 18.00

NEW TITANS, THE (Formerly The New Teen Titans)
DC Comics: No. 50, Dec, 1988 - No. 130, Feb, 1996 ($1.75/$2.25)

50-Perez-c/a begins; new origin Wonder Girl 6.00
51-59: 50-55-Painted-c. 55-Nightwing (Dick Grayson) forces Danny Chase to resign; Batman app. in flashback, Wonder Girl becomes Troia 3.00
60,61: 60-A Lonely Place of Dying Part 2 continues from Batman #440; new Robin tie-in; Timothy Drake app. 61-A Lonely Place of Dying Part 4 3.00
62-99,101-124,126-130: 62-65: Deathstroke the Terminator app. 65-Tim Drake (Robin) app. 70-1st Deathstroke solo cover/sty. 71-(44 pgs.)-10th anniversary issue; Deathstroke cameo. 72-79-Deathstroke in all: 74-Intro. Pantha. 79-Terra brought back to life; 1 panel cameo Team Titans (1st app.). Deathstroke in #80-84,86. 80-2nd full app. Team Titans. 83,84-Deathstroke kills his son, Jericho. 85-Team Titans app. 86-Deathstroke vs. Nightwing-c/story; last Deathstroke app. 87-New costume Nightwing. 90-92-Parts 2,5,8 Total Chaos (Team Titans). 115-(11/94) 2.50
100-($3.50, 52 pgs.)-Holo-grafx foil-c 3.50
125 (3.50)-wraparound-c 3.50
#0-(10/94) Zero Hour, released between #114 & 115 2.50
Annual 5-10 ('89-'94, 68 pgs.. 7-Armaggedon 2001 x-over; 1st full app. Teen (Team) Titans (new group). 8-Deathstroke app.; Eclipso app. (minor). 10-Elseworlds story 3.50
Annual 11 (1995, $3.95)-Year One story 4.00
NOTE: *Perez a-50-55p, 57,60p, 58,59,61(layouts); c-50-61, 62-67i, Annual 5i; co-plots-66.*

NEW TV FUNNIES (See New Funnies)

NEW TWO-FISTED TALES, THE
Dark Horse Comics/Byron Preiss: 1993 ($4.95, limited series, 52 pgs.)

1-Kurtzman-r & new-a 5.00
NOTE: ***Eisner** c-1i. **Kurtzman** c-1p, 2.*

NEWUNIVERSAL
Marvel Comics: Feb, 2007 - No. 6, July, 2007 ($2.99)

1-6-Warren Ellis-s/Salvador Larroca-a. 1,2-Variant covers by Ribic 3.00
...: 1959 (9/08, $3.99) Aftermath of the White Event of 1953; Tony Stark app. 4.00
...: Conqueror (10/08, $3.99) The White Event of 2689 B.C.; Eric Nguyen-a 4.00
... : Everything Went White HC (2007, $19.99) r/#1-6; sketch pages 20.00
... : Everything Went White SC (2008, $14.99) r/#1-6; sketch pages 15.00

NEWUNIVERSAL: SHOCKFRONT
Marvel Comics: Jul, 2008 - Present ($2.99)

1,2-Warren Ellis-s/Steve Kurth-a 3.00

NEW WARRIORS, THE (See Thor #411,412)
Marvel Comics: July, 1990 - No. 75, 1996 ($1.00/$1.25/$1.50)

1-Williamson-i; Bagley-c/a(p) in 1-13, Annual 1 5.00
1-Gold 2nd printing (7/91) 2.50
2-5: 1,3-Guice-c(i). 2-Williamson-c/a(i). 3.00
6-24,26-49,51-75: 7-Punisher cameo (last pg.). 8,9-Punisher app. 14-Darkhawk & Namor x-over. 17-Fantastic Four & Silver Surfer x-over. 19-Gideon (of X-Force) app. 28-Intro Turbo & Cardinal. 31-Cannonball & Warpath app. 42-Nova vs. Firelord. 46-Photo-c. 47-Bound-in S-M trading card sheet. 52-12 pg. ad insert. 62-Scarlet Spider-c/app. 70-Spider-Man-c/app. 72-Avengers-c/app. 2.50
25-($2.50, 52 pgs.)-Die-cut cover 3.00
40,60: 40-($2.25)-Gold foil collector's edition 3.00
50-($2.95, 52 pgs.)-Glow in the dark-c 3.00
Annual 1-4('91-'94,68 pgs.)-1-Origins all members; 3rd app. X-Force (cont'd from New Mutants Ann. #7 & cont'd in X-Men Ann. #15); x-over before X-Force #1. 3-Bagged w/card 3.00

NEW WARRIORS, THE
Marvel Comics: Oct, 1999 - No. 10, July, 2000 ($2.99/$2.50)

0-Wizard supplement; short story and preview sketchbook 2.25
1-($2.99) 3.00
2-11: 2-Two covers. 5-Generation X app. 9-Iron Man-c 2.50

NEW WARRIORS (See Civil War #1)
Marvel Comics: Aug, 2005 - No. 6, Feb, 2006 ($2.99, limited series)

1-6-Scottie Young-a 3.00
...: Reality Check TPB (2006, $14.99) r/#1-6 15.00

NEW WARRIORS (The Initiative)
Marvel Comics: Aug, 2007 - Present ($2.99)

1-16: 1-Medina-a; new team is formed. 2-Jubilee app. 14-16-Secret Invasion 3.00
...: Defiant TPB (2008, $14.99) r/#1-6 15.00

NEW WAVE, THE
Eclipse Comics: 6/10/86 - No. 13, 3/87 (#1-8: bi-weekly, 20pgs; #9-13: monthly)

1-13:1-Origin, concludes #5. 6-Origin Megabyte. 8,9-The Heap returns. 13-Snyder-c 2.50
...Versus the Volunteers 3-D #1,2(4/87): 1-Snyder-c 3.00

NEW WEST, THE
Black Bull Comics: Mar, 2005 - No. 2, Jun, 2005 ($4.99, limited series)

1,2-Phil Noto-a/c; Jimmy Palmiotti-s 5.00

NEW WORLD (See Comic Books, series I)

NEW WORLDS
Caliber: 1996 - No. 6 ($2.95/$3.95, 80 pgs., B&W, anthology)

1-6: 1-Mister X & other stories 4.00

NEW X-MEN (See X-Men *2nd series* #114-156)

NEW X-MEN (Academy X) (Continued from New Mutants)
Marvel Comics: July, 2004 - Present ($2.99)

1-46: 1,2-Green-c/a. 16-19-House of M. 20,21-Decimation. 40-Endangered Species back-ups begin. 44-46-Messiah Complex x-over; Ramos-a 3.00
Yearbook 1 (12/05, $3.99) new story and profile pages 4.00
...: Childhood's End Vol. 1 TPB (2006, $10.99) r/#20-23 11.00
...: Childhood's End Vol. 2 TPB (2006, $10.99) r/#24-27 11.00
...: Childhood's End Vol. 3 TPB (2006, $10.99) r/#28-32 11.00
...: Childhood's End Vol. 4 TPB (2007, $10.99) r/#33-36 11.00
...: Childhood's End Vol. 5 TPB (2007, $17.99) r/#37-43 18.00
House of M: New X-Men TPB (2006, $13.99) r/#16-19 and selections from Secrets Of The House of M one-shot 14.00
... Vol. 1: Choosing Sides TPB (2004, $14.99) r/#1-6 15.00
... Vol. 2: Haunted TPB (2005, $14.99) r/#7-12 15.00
... Vol. 3: X-Posed TPB (2006, $14.99) r/#12-15 & Yearbook Special 15.00

NEW X-MEN: HELLIONS
Marvel Comics: July, 2005 - No. 4, Oct, 2005 ($2.99, limited series)

1-4-Henry-a/Weir & DeFilippis-s 3.00
TPB (2006, $9.99) r/#1-4 10.00

NEW YORK GIANTS (See Thrilling True Story of the Baseball Giants)

NEW YORK STATE JOINT LEGISLATIVE COMMITTEE TO STUDY THE PUBLICATION OF COMICS, THE
N.Y. State Legislative Document: 1951, 1955

This document was referenced by Wertham for **Seduction of the Innocent.** Contains numerous repros from comics showing violence, sadism, torture, and sex. 1955 version (196p, No. 37, 2/23/55) - Sold for $180 in 1986.

NEW YORK, THE BIG CITY
Kitchen Sink Press: 1986 ($10.95, B&W); **DC Comics:** July, 2000 ($12.95, B&W)

nn-Will Eisner-s/a 13.00

NEW YORK WORLD'S FAIR (Also see Big Book of Fun & New Book of Fun)
National Periodical Publ.: 1939, 1940 (100 pgs.; cardboard covers) (DC's 4th & 5th annuals)

1939-Scoop Scanlon, Superman (blond haired Superman on-c), Sandman, Zatara, Slam Bradley, Ginger Snap by Bob Kane begin; 1st published app. The Sandman (see Adventure #40 for his 1st drawn story); Vincent Sullivan-c; cover background by Guardineer 1700 3400 5100 12,750 29,000 –
1940-Batman, Hourman, Johnny Thunderbolt, Red, White & Blue & Hanko (by Creig Flessel) app.; Superman, Batman & Robin-c (1st time they all appear together); early Robin app.; 1st Burnley-c/a (per Burnley) 922 1844 2766 6915 15,500 –
NOTE: *The 1939 edition was published 4/29/39 and released 4/30/39, the day the fair opened, at 25¢, and was first sold only at the fair. Since all other comics were 10¢, it didn't sell. Remaining copies were advertised beginning in the August issues of most DC comics for 25¢, but soon the price was dropped to 15¢. Everyone that sent a quarter through the mail for it received a free Superman #1 or a #2 to make up the dime difference. 15¢ stickers were placed over the 25¢ price. Four variations on the 15¢ stickers are known. The 1940 edition was published 5/11/40 and was priced at 15¢. It was a precursor to World's Best #1.*

NEW YORK: YEAR ZERO
Eclipse Comics: July, 1988 - No. 4, Oct, 1988 ($2.00, B&W, limited series)

1-4 2.50

NEXT, THE
DC Comics: Sept, 2006 - No. 6, Feb, 2007 ($2.99, limited series)

1-6-Tad Williams-s/Dietrich Smith-a; Superman app. 3.00

NEXT MEN (See John Byrne's...)

NEXT NEXUS, THE
First Comics: Jan, 1989 - No. 4, April, 1989 ($1.95, limited series, Baxter paper)

1-4: Mike Baron scripts & Steve Rude-c/a. 2.50
TPB (10/89, $9.95) r/series 10.00

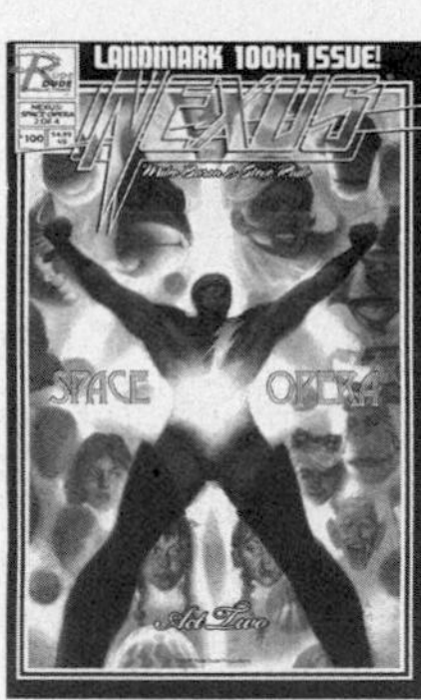

Nexus #100 © Baron & Rude

Nickel Comics #6 © FAW

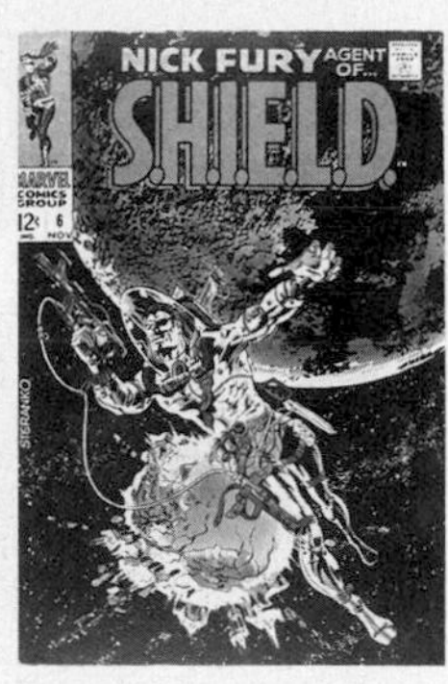

Nick Fury, Agent of S.H.I.E.L.D. #6 © MAR

GD	VG	FN	VF	VF/NM	NM-
2.0	4.0	6.0	8.0	9.0	9.2

NEXTWAVE: AGENTS OF H.A.T.E
Marvel Comics: Mar, 2006 - No. 12, Mar, 2007 ($2.99)

1-12-Warren Ellis-s/Stuart Immonen-a. 2-Fin Fang Foom app. 12-Devil Dinosaur app. 3.00
Vol. 1 - This Is What They Want HC (2006, $19.99) r/#1-6; Ellis original pitch 20.00
Vol. 1 - This Is What They Want SC (2007, $14.99) r/#1-6; Ellis original pitch 15.00
Vol. 2 - I Kick Your Face HC (2007, $19.99) r/#7-12 20.00
Vol. 2 - I Kick Your Face SC (2008, $14.99) r/#7-12 15.00

NEXUS (See First Comics Graphic Novel #4, 19 & The Next Nexus)
Capital Comics/First Comics No. 7 on: June, 1981 - No. 6, Mar, 1984; No. 7, Apr, 1985 - No. 80?, May, 1991 (Direct sales only, 36 pgs.; V2#1('83)-printed on Baxter paper)

1-B&W version; mag. size; w/double size poster 3 6 9 14 20 26
1-B&W 1981 limited edition; 500 copies printed and signed; same as above except this version has a 2-pg. poster & a pencil sketch on paperboard by Steve Rude
4 8 12 24 37 50
2-B&W, magazine size 2 4 6 11 16 20
3-B&W, magazine size; Brunner back-c; contains 33-1/3 rpm record ($2.95 price)
2 4 6 9 13 16
V2#1-Color version 4.00
2-49,51-80: 2-Nexus' origin begins. 67-Snyder-c/a 2.50
50-($3.50, 52 pgs.) 3.50
Hardcover Volume One (Dark Horse Books, 11/05, $49.95) r/#1-3 & V2 #1-4; creator bios 50.00
HC Volume Two (Dark Horse Books, 3/06, $49.95) r/V2 #5-11; creator bios 50.00
HC Volume Three (Dark Horse Books, 5/06, $49.95) r/V2 #12-18; Marz forward 50.00
HC Volume Four (Dark Horse Books, 8/06, $49.95) r/V2 #19-25; Powell forward 50.00
HC Volume Five (Dark Horse Books, 2/07, $49.95) r/V2 #26-32; Brubaker forward 50.00
HC Volume Six (Dark Horse Books, 2/07, $49.95) r/V2 #33-39; Evanier forward 50.00
HC Volume Seven (Dark Horse Books, 2/08, $49.95) r/V2 #40-46; Brunning forward 50.00
NOTE: ***Bissette*** *c-V2#29.* ***Giffen*** *c/a-V2#23.* ***Gulacy*** *c-1 (B&W), 2(B&W).* ***Mignola*** *c/a-V2#28.* ***Rude*** *c-3(B&W), V2#1-22, 24-27, 33-36, 39-42, 45-48, 50, 58-60, 75; a-1-3, V2#1-7, 8-16p, 18-22p, 24-27p, 33-36p, 39-42p, 45-48p, 50, 58, 59p, 60.* ***Paul Smith*** *a-V2#37, 38, 43, 44, 51-55p; c-V2#37, 38, 43, 44, 51-55.*

NEXUS
Rude Dude Productions: No. 99, July, 2007 - Present ($2.99)

99-Mike Baron scripts & Steve Rude-c/a 3.00
100-($4.99) Part 2 of Space Opera; back-up feature: History of Nexus 5.00
... Greatest Hits (8/07, $1.99) Excerpts from previous issues and preview of #99 2.25
...: The Origin (11/07, $3.99) reprints the 7/96 one-shot 4.00

NEXUS: ALIEN JUSTICE
Dark Horse Comics: Dec, 1992 - No. 3, Feb, 1993 ($3.95, limited series)

1-3: Mike Baron scripts & Steve Rude-c/a 4.00

NEXUS: EXECUTIONER'S SONG
Dark Horse Comics: June, 1996 - No. 4, Sept, 1996 ($2.95, limited series)

1-4: Mike Baron scripts & Steve Rude-c/a 3.00

NEXUS FILES
First Comics: 1989 ($4.50, color/16pgs. B&W, one-shot, squarebound, 52 pgs.)

1-New Rude-a; info on Nexus 4.50

NEXUS: GOD CON
Dark Horse Comics: Apr, 1997 - No. 2, May, 1997 ($2.95, limited series)

1,2-Baron-s/Rude-c/a 3.00

NEXUS LEGENDS
First Comics: May, 1989 - No. 23, Mar, 1991 ($1.50, Baxter paper)\

1-23: R/1-3(Capital) & early First Comics issues w/new Rude covers #1-6,9,10 2.50

NEXUS MEETS MADMAN (...Special)
Dark Horse Comics: May, 1996 ($2.95, one-shot)

nn-Mike Baron & Mike Allred scripts, Steve Rude-c/a. 3.00

NEXUS: NIGHTMARE IN BLUE
Dark Horse Comics: July, 1997 - No. 4, Oct, 1997 ($2.95, limited series)

1-4: 1,2,4-Adam Hughes-c 3.00

NEXUS: THE LIBERATOR
Dark Horse Comics: Aug, 1992 - No. 4, Nov, 1992 ($2.95, limited series)

1-4 3.00

NEXUS: THE ORIGIN
Dark Horse Comics: July, 1996 ($3.95, one-shot)

nn-Mike Baron- scripts, Steve Rude-c/a. 4.00

NEXUS: THE WAGES OF SIN
Dark Horse Comics: Mar, 1995 - No. 4, June, 1995 ($2.95, limited series)

1-4 3.00

NFL SUPERPRO
Marvel Comics: Oct, 1991 - No. 12, Sept, 1992 ($1.00)

1-12: 1-Spider-Man-c/app. 2.50
Special Edition (9/91, $2.00) Jusko painted-c 3.00
Super Bowl Edition (3/91, squarebound) Jusko painted-c 4.00

NICKEL COMICS
Dell Publishing Co.: 1938 (Pocket size - 7-1/2x5-1/2")(68 pgs.)

1- "Bobby & Chip" by Otto Messmer, Felix the Cat artist. Contains some English reprints
80 160 240 504 852 1200

NICKEL COMICS
Fawcett Publications: Feb 1940

nn - Ashcan comic, not distributed to newsstands, only for in-house use. A CGC certified 9.6 copy sold for $7,200 in 2003. In 2008, a CGC certified 8.5 sold for $2,390 and an uncertified Near Mint copy sold for $3,100.

NICKEL COMICS
Fawcett Publications: May, 1940 - No. 8, Aug, 1940 (36 pgs.; Bi-Weekly; 5¢)

1-Origin/1st app. Bulletman 365 730 1095 2482 4341 6200
2 115 230 345 725 1225 1725
3 83 166 249 523 887 1250
4-The Red Gaucho begins 67 134 201 422 711 1000
5-7 66 132 198 416 701 985
8-World's Fair-c; Bulletman moved to Master Comics #7 in October (scarce)
87 174 261 548 924 1300
NOTE: ***Beck*** *c-5-8.* ***Jack Binder*** *c-1-4. Bondage c-5. Bulletman c-1-8.*

NICK FURY, AGENT OF SHIELD (See Fury, Marvel Spotlight #31 & Shield)
Marvel Comics Group: 6/68 - No. 15, 11/69; No. 16, 11/70 - No. 18, 3/71

1 11 22 33 79 140 200
2-4: 4-Origin retold 7 14 21 45 73 100
5-Classic-c 7 14 21 49 80 110
6,7: 7-Salvador Dali painting swipe 6 12 18 41 66 90
8-11,13: 9-Hate Monger begins, ends #11. 10-Smith layouts/pencil. 11-Smith-c. 13-1st app. Super-Patriot; last 12¢ issue 4 8 12 24 37 50
12-Smith-c/a 4 8 12 26 41 55
14-Begin 15¢ issues 3 6 9 21 32 42
15-1st app. & death of Bullseye-c/story(11/69); Nick Fury shot & killed; last 15¢ issue
7 14 21 49 80 110
16-18-(25¢, 52 pgs.) r/Str. Tales #135-143 3 6 9 17 25 32
TPB (May 2000, $19.95) r/ Strange Tales #150-168 20.00
...: Who is Scorpio? TPB (11/00, $12.95) r/#1-3,5; Steranko-c 13.00
NOTE: ***Adkins*** *a-3i.* ***Craig*** *a-10i.* ***Sid Greene*** *a-12i.* ***Kirby*** *a-16-18r.* ***Springer*** *a-4, 6, 7, 8p, 9, 10p, 11; c-8, 9.* ***Steranko*** *a(p)-1-3, 5; c-1-7.*

NICK FURY AGENT OF SHIELD (Also see Strange Tales #135)
Marvel Comics: Dec, 1983 - No. 2, Jan, 1984 (2.00, 52 pgs., Baxter paper)

1,2-r/Nick Fury #1-4; new Steranko-c 3.50

NICK FURY, AGENT OF S.H.I.E.L.D.
Marvel Comics: Sept, 1989 - No. 47, May, 1993 ($1.50/$1.75)

V2#1-26,30-47: 10-Capt. America app. 13-Return of The Yellow Claw. 15-Fantastic Four app. 30,31-Deathlok app. 36-Cage app. 37-Woodgod c/story. 38-41-Flashes back to pre-Shield days after WWII. 44-Capt. America-c/s. 45-Viper-c/s. 46-Gideon x-over 2.50
27-29-Wolverine-c/stories 3.00
NOTE: ***Alan Grant*** *scripts-11.* ***Guice*** *a(p)-20-23, 25, 26; c-20-28.*

NICK FURY'S HOWLING COMMANDOS
Marvel Comics: Dec, 2005 -No. 6, May, 2006 ($2.99)

1-6: 1-Giffen-s/Francisco-a 3.00
1-Director's Cut ($3.99) r/#1 with original script and sketch design pages 4.00

NICK FURY VS. S.H.I.E.L.D.
Marvel Comics: June, 1988 - No. 6, Nov, 1988 ($3.50, 52 pgs, deluxe format)

1,2: 1-Steranko-c. 2-(Low print run) Sienkiewicz-c 5.00
3-6 4.00

NICK HALIDAY (Thrill of the Sea)
Argo: May, 1956

1-Daily & Sunday strip-r by Petree 8 16 24 44 57 70

NIGHT AND THE ENEMY (Graphic Novel)
Comico: 1988 (8-1/2x11") ($11.95, color, 80 pgs.)

1-Harlan Ellison scripts/Ken Steacy-c/a; r/Epic Illustrated & new-a (1st & 2nd printings) 12.00
1-Limited edition ($39.95) 40.00

NIGHT BEFORE CHRISTMAS, THE (See March of Comics No. 152 in the Promotional Comics section)

Nightcrawler V2 #1 © MAR

Night Man #6 © MAL

Nightmare (1994 series) #1 © MAR

	GD 2.0	VG 4.0	FN 6.0	VF 8.0	VF/NM 9.0	NM- 9.2

NIGHT BEFORE CHRISTMASK, THE
Dark Horse Comics: Nov, 1994 ($9.95, one-shot)

nn-Hardcover book; The Mask; Rick Geary-c/a 10.00

NIGHTBREED (See Clive Barker's Nightbreed)

NIGHT CLUB
Image Comics: Apr, 2005 - No. 4, Dec, 2006 ($2.95/$2.99, limited series)

1-4: 1-Mike Baron-s/Mike Norton-a 3.00

NIGHTCRAWLER (X-Men)
Marvel Comics Group: Nov, 1985 - No. 4, Feb, 1986 (Mini-series from X-Men)

1-4: 1-Cockrum-c/a 3.50

NIGHTCRAWLER (Volume 2)
Marvel Comics: Feb, 2002 - No. 4, May, 2002 ($2.50, limited series)

1-4-Matt Smith-a 2.50

NIGHTCRAWLER
Marvel Comics: Nov, 2004 - No. 12, Jan, 2006 ($2.99)

1-12: 1-6-Robertson-a/Land-c. 2-Magik app. 8-Wolverine app. 10-Man-Thing app. 3.00
...: The Devil Inside TPB (2005, $14.99) r/#1-6 15.00
...: The Winding Way TPB (2006, $14.99) r/#7-12 15.00

NIGHTFALL: THE BLACK CHRONICLES
DC Comics (Homage): Dec, 1999 - No. 3, Feb, 2000 ($2.95, limited series)

1-3-Coker-a/Gilmore-s 3.00

NIGHT FORCE, THE (See New Teen Titans #21)
DC Comics: Aug, 1982 - No. 14, Sept, 1983 (60¢)

1 4.00
2-14: 13-Origin Baron Winter. 14-Nudity panels 3.00
NOTE: ***Colan** c/a-1-14p. **Giordano** c-1i, 2i, 4i, 5i, 7i, 12i.*

NIGHT FORCE
DC Comics: Dec, 1996 - No. 12, Nov, 1997 ($2.25)

1-12: 1-3-Wolfman-s/Anderson-a(p). 8-"Convergence" part 2 2.50

NIGHT GLIDER
Topps Comics (Kirbyverse): April, 1993 ($2.95, one-shot)

1-Kirby c-1, Heck-a; polybagged w/Kirbychrome trading card 3.00

NIGHTHAWK
Marvel Comics: Sept, 1998 - No. 3, Nov, 1998 ($2.99, mini-series)

1-3-Krueger-s; Daredevil app. 3.00

NIGHTINGALE, THE
Henry H. Stansbury Once-Upon-A-Time Press, Inc.: 1948 (10¢, 7-1/4x10-1/4", 14 pgs., 1/2 B&W)

(Very Rare)-Low distribution; distributed to Westchester County & Bronx, N.Y. only; used in **Seduction of the Innocent**, pg. 312,313 as the 1st and only "good" comic book ever published. Ill. by Dong Kingman; 1,500 words of text, printed on high quality paper & no word balloons. Copyright registered 10/22/48, distributed week of 12/5/48. (By Hans Christian Andersen)
Estimated value........ $250

NIGHT MAN, THE (See Sludge #1)
Malibu Comics (Ultraverse): Oct, 1993 - No. 23, Aug, 1995 ($1.95/$2.50)

1-($2.50, 48 pgs.)-Rune flip-c/story by B. Smith (3 pgs.) 2.50
1-Ultra-Limited silver foil-c 6.00
2-15, 17: 3-Break-Thru x-over; Freex app. 4-Origin Firearm (2 pgs.) by Chaykin. 6-TNTNT app. 8-1st app. Teknight 2.50
16 ($3.50)-flip book (Ultraverse Premiere #11) 3.50
...:The Pilgrim Conundrum Saga (1/95, $3.95, 68 pgs.)-Strangers app. 4.00
18-23: 22-Loki-c/a 2.50
Infinity ($1.50) 2.50
...Vs. Wolverine #0-Kelley Jones-c; mail in offer 1 3 4 6 8 10
NOTE: ***Zeck** a-16.*

NIGHT MAN, THE
Malibu Comics (Ultraverse): Sept, 1995 - No.4, Dec, 1995 ($1.50, lim. series)

1-4: Post Black September storyline 2.50

NIGHT MAN, THE /GAMBIT
Malibu Comics (Ultraverse): Mar, 1996 - No. 3, May, 1996 ($1.95, lim. series)

0-Limited Premium Edition 4.00
1-3: David Quinn scripts in all. 3-Rhiannon discovered to be The Night Man's mother 2.50

NIGHTMARE
Ziff-Davis (Approved Comics)/St. John No. 3: Summer, 1952 - No. 3, Winter, 1952, 53 (Painted-c)

1-1 pg. Kinstler-a; Tuska-a(2) 53 106 159 334 567 800
2-Kinstler-a-Poe's "Pit & the Pendulum" 40 80 120 235 380 525
3-Kinstler-a 35 70 105 203 327 450

NIGHTMARE (Weird Horrors #1-9) (Amazing Ghost Stories #14 on)
St. John Publishing Co.: No. 10, Dec, 1953 - No. 13, Aug, 1954

10-Reprints Ziff-Davis Weird Thrillers #2 w/new Kubert-c plus 2 pgs. Kinstler-a; Anderson, Colan & Toth-a 53 106 159 330 553 775
11-Krigstein-a; painted-c; Poe adapt., "Hop Frog" 40 80 120 235 380 525
12-Kubert bondage-c; adaptation of Poe's "The Black Cat"; Cannibalism story 38 76 114 226 363 500
13-Reprints Z-D Weird Thrillers #3 with new cover; Powell-a(2), Tuska-a; Baker-c 27 54 81 158 254 350

NIGHTMARE (Magazine) (Also see Psycho)
Skywald Publishing Corp.: Dec, 1970 - No. 23, Feb, 1975 (B&W, 68 pgs.)

1-Everett-a; Heck-a; Shores-a 9 18 27 63 107 150
2-5,8,9: 2,4-Decapitation story. 5-Nazi-s; Boris Karloff 4 pg. photo/text-s. 8-Features E.C. movie "Tales From the Crypt"; reprints some E.C. comics panels. 9-Wrightson-a; bondage-c; 1st Lovecraft Saggoth Chronicles/Cthulhu 5 10 15 34 55 75
6-Kaluta-a; Jeff Jones-c, photo & interview; 1st Living Gargoyle; Love Witch-s w/nudity; Boris Karloff-s 6 12 18 37 59 80
7 4 8 12 28 44 60
10-Wrightson-a (1 pg.); Princess of Earth-c/s; Edward & Mina Sartyros, the Human Gargoyles series continues from Psycho #8 6 12 18 37 59 80
11-19: 12-Excessive gore, severed heads. 13-Lovecraft-s. 15-Dracula-c/s. 17-Vampires issue; Autobiography of a Vampire series begins 4 8 12 22 34 45
20-John Byrne's 1st artwork (2 pgs.)(8/74); severed head-c; Hitler app. 7 14 21 47 76 105
21-23: 21-(1974 Summer Special)-Kaluta-a. 22-Tomb of Horror issue. 23-(1975 Winter Special) 4 8 12 26 41 55
Annual 1(1972)-Squarebound; B. Jones-a 4 8 12 26 41 55
Winter Special 1(1973)-All new material 4 8 12 22 34 45
Yearbook nn(1974)-B. Jones, Reese, Wildey-a 4 8 12 22 34 45
NOTE: ***Adkins** a-5. **Boris** c-2, 3, 5 (#4 is not by Boris). **Buckler** a-3, 15. **Byrne** a-20p. **Everett** a-1, 2, 4, 5, 12. **Jeff Jones** a-6, 21r(Psycho #6); c-6. **Katz** a-3, 5, 21. **Reese** a-4, 5. **Wildey** a-4, 5, 6, 21, '74 Yearbook. **Wrightson** a-9, 10.*

NIGHTMARE (Alex Nino's)
Innovation Publishing: 1989 ($1.95)

1-Alex Nino-a 2.50

NIGHTMARE
Marvel Comics: Dec, 1994 - No. 4, Mar, 1995 ($1.95, limited series)

1-4 2.50

NIGHTMARE & CASPER (See Harvey Hits #71) (Casper & Nightmare #6 on) (See Casper The Friendly Ghost #19)
Harvey Publications: Aug, 1963 - No. 5, Aug, 1964 (25¢)

1-All reprints? 8 16 24 54 90 125
2-5: All reprints? 5 10 15 32 51 70

NIGHTMARE ON ELM STREET, A (Also see Freddy Krueger's...)
DC Comics (WildStorm): Dec, 2006 - Present ($2.99)

1-8: 1-Two covers by Harris & Bradstreet; Dixon-s/West-a 3.00

NIGHTMARES (See Do You Believe in Nightmares)

NIGHTMARES
Eclipse Comics: May, 1985 - No. 2, May, 1985 ($1.75, Baxter paper)

1,2 3.00

NIGHTMARE THEATER
Chaos! Comics: Nov, 1997 - No. 4, Nov, 1997 ($2.50, mini-series)

1-4-Horror stories by various; Wrightson-a 2.50

NIGHTMARK: BLOOD & HONOR
Alpha Productions: 1994 - No. 3, 1994 ($2.50, B&W, mini-series)

1,2 2.50

NIGHTMARK MYSTERY SPECIAL
Alpha Productions: Jan, 1994 ($2.50, B&W)

1 2.50

NIGHTMASK
Marvel Comics Group: Nov, 1986 - No. 12, Oct, 1987

1-12 2.50

NIGHT MASTER
Silverwolf: Feb, 1987 ($1.50, B&W)

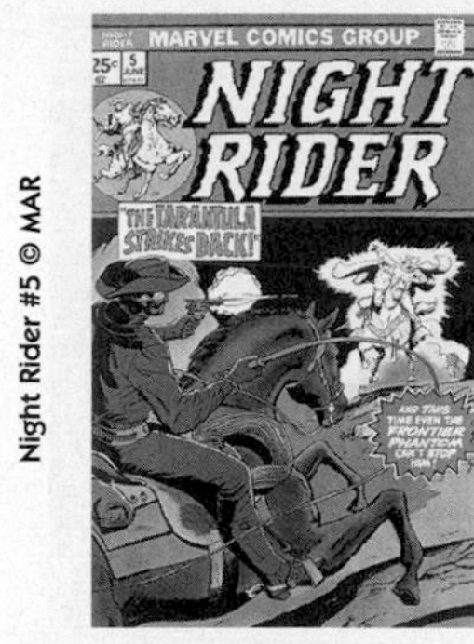

Night Rider #5 © MAR

Night Thrasher #14 © MAR

Nightwing Annual #2 © DC

GD 2.0 | VG 4.0 | FN 6.0 | VF 8.0 | VF/NM 9.0 | NM- 9.2

1-Tim Vigil-c/a 3.00

NIGHT MUSIC (See Eclipse Graphic Album Series, The Magic Flute)
Eclipse Comics: Dec, 1984 - No. 11, 1990 ($1.75/$3.95/$4.95, Baxter paper)

1-7: 3-Russell's Jungle Book adapt. 4,5-Pelleas And Melisando (double titled) 6-Salomé (double titled). 7-Red Dog #1 2.50

8-($3.95) Ariane and Bluebeard 4.00

9-11-($4.95) The Magic Flute; Russell adapt. 5.00

NIGHT NURSE
Marvel Comics Group: Nov, 1972 - No. 4, May, 1973

1 10 20 30 73 129 185

2-4 8 16 24 54 90 125

NIGHT OF MYSTERY
Avon Periodicals: 1953 (no month) (one-shot)

nn-1 pg. Kinstler-a, Hollingsworth-c 45 90 135 279 465 650

NIGHT OF THE GRIZZLY, THE (See Movie Classics)

NIGHTRAVEN (See Marvel Graphic Novel)

NIGHT RIDER (Western)
Marvel Comics Group: Oct, 1974 - No. 6, Aug, 1975

1: 1-6 reprint Ghost Rider #1-6 (#1-origin) 2 4 6 9 13 16

2-6 1 3 4 6 8 10

NIGHT'S CHILDREN: THE VAMPIRE
Millenium: July, 1995 - No. 2, Aug, 1995 ($2.95, B&W)

1,2: Wendy Snow-Lang story & art 3.00

NIGHTSIDE
Marvel Comics: Dec, 2001 - No. 4, Mar, 2002 ($2.99)

1-4: 1-Weinberg-s/Derenick-a; intro Sydney Taine 3.00

NIGHTS INTO DREAMS (Based on video game)
Archie Comics: Feb, 1998 -No. 6, Oct, 1998 ($1.75, limited series)

1-6 2.50

NIGHTSTALKERS (Also see Midnight Sons Unlimited)
Marvel Comics (Midnight Sons #14 on): Nov, 1992 - No. 18, Apr, 1994 ($1.75)

1-($2.75, 52 pgs.)-Polybagged w/poster; part 5 of Rise of the Midnight Sons storyline; Garney/Palmer-c/a begins; Hannibal King, Blade & Frank Drake begin (see Tomb of Dracula for & Dr. Strange) 3.00

2-9,11-18: 5-Punisher app. 7-Ghost Rider app. 8,9-Morbius app. 14-Spot varnish-c. 14,15-Siege of Darkness Pts 1 & 9 2.50

10-($2.25)-Outer-c is a Darkhold envelope made of black parchment w/gold ink; Midnight Massacre part 1 2.75

NIGHT TERRORS,THE
Chanting Monks Studios: 2000 ($2.75, B&W)

1-Bernie Wrightson-c; short stories, one by Wrightson-s/a 2.75

NIGHT THRASHER (Also see The New Warriors)
Marvel Comics: Aug, 1993 - No. 21, Apr, 1995 ($1.75/$1.95)

1-($2.95, 52 pgs.)-Red holo-grafx foil-c; origin 3.00

2-21: 2-Intro Tantrum. 3-Gideon (of X-Force) app. 10-Bound-in trading card sheet; Iron Man app. 15-Hulk app. 2.50

NIGHT THRASHER: FOUR CONTROL
Marvel Comics: Oct, 1992 - No. 4, Jan, 1993 ($2.00, limited series)

1-4: 2-Intro Tantrum. 3-Gideon (of X-Force) app. 2.50

NIGHT TRIBES
DC Comics (WildStorm): July, 1999 ($4.95, one-shot)

1-Golden & Sniegoski-s/Chin-a 5.00

NIGHTVEIL (Also see Femforce)
Americomics/AC Comics: Nov, 1984 - No. 7, 1987 ($1.75)

1-7 2.50

...'s Cauldron Of Horror 1 (1989, B&W)-Kubert, Powell, Wood-r plus new Nightveil story 3.00

...'s Cauldron Of Horror 2 (1990, $2.95, B&W)-Pre-code horror-r by Kubert & Powell 3.00

...'s Cauldron Of Horror 3 (1991) 3.00

Special 1 ('88, $1.95)-Kaluta-c 2.50

One Shot ('96, $5.95)-Flip book w/ Colt 6.00

NIGHTWATCH
Marvel Comics: Apr, 1994 - No. 12, Mar, 1995 ($1.50)

1-($2.95)-Collectors edition; foil-c; Ron Lim-c/a begins; Spider-Man app. 3.00

1-12-Regular edition. 2-Bound-in S-M trading card sheet; 5,6-Venom-c & app.

7,11-Cardiac app. 2.50

NIGHTWING (Also see New Teen Titans, New Titans, Showcase '93 #11,12, Tales of the New Teen Titans & Teen Titans Spotlight)
DC Comics: Sept, 1995 - No. 4, Dec, 1995 ($2.25, limited series)

1-Dennis O'Neil story/Greg Land-a in all 5.00

2-4 4.00

...: Alfred's Return (7/95, $3.50) Giordano-a 4.00

...Ties That Bind (1997, $12.95, TPB) r/mini-series & Alfred's Return 13.00

NIGHTWING
DC Comics: Oct, 1996 - Present ($1.95/$1.99/$2.25/$2.50/$2.99)

1-Chuck Dixon scripts & Scott McDaniel-c/a 2 4 6 9 11 12

2,3 6.00

4-10: 6-Robin-c/app. 4.00

11-20: 13-15-Batman app. 19,20-Cataclysm pts. 2,11 3.00

21-49,51-64: 23-Green Arrow app. 26-29-Huntress-c/app. 30-Superman-c/app. 35-39-No Man's Land. 41-Land/Geraci-a begins. 46-Begin $2.25-c. 47-Texiera-c. 52-Catwoman-c/app. 54-Shrike app. 2.50

50-($3.50) Nightwing battles Torque 3.50

65-74,76-99: 65,66-Bruce Wayne: Murderer x-over pt. 3,9. 68,69: B.W.: Fugitive pt. 6,9. 70-Last Dixon-s. 71-Devin Grayson-s begin. 81-Batgirl vs. Deathstroke. 93-Blockbuster killed. 94-Copperhead app. 96-Bagged w/CD. 96-98-War Games 2.50

75-(1/03, $2.95) Intro. Tarantula 3.00

100-(2/05, $2.95) Tarantula app. 3.00

101-117: 101-Year One begins. 103-Jason Todd & Deadman app. 107-110-Hester-a. 109-Begin $2.50-c. 109,110-Villains United tie-ins. 112-Deathstroke app. 2.50

118-147: 118-One Year Later; Jason Todd as 2nd Nightwing. 120-Begin $2.99-c. 138,139-Resurrection of Ra's al Ghul x-over. 138-2nd printing. 147-Two-Face app. 3.00

#1,000,000 (11/98) teams with future Batman 2.50

Annual 1(1997, $3.95) Pulp Heroes 4.00

Annual 2 (6/07, $3.99) Dick Grayson and Barbara Gordon's shared history 4.00

...Eighty Page Giant 1 (12/00, $5.95) Intro. of Hella; Dixon-s/Haley-c 6.00

...: Big Guns (2004, $14.95, TPB) r/#47-50; Secret Files 1, Eighty Page Giant 1 15.00

...: Brothers in Blood (2007, $14.99, TPB) r/#118-124 15.00

...: A Darker Shade of Justice (2001, $19.95, TPB) r/#30-39, Secret Files #1 20.00

...: A Knight in Blüdhaven (1998, $14.95, TPB) r/#1-8 15.00

...: Love and Bullets (2000, $17.95, TPB) r/#1/2, 19,21,22,24-29 18.00

...: Love and War (2007, $14.99, TPB) r/#125-132 15.00

...: On the Razor's Edge (2005, $14.99, TPB) r/#52,54-60 15.00

...: Our Worlds at War (9/01, $2.95) Jae Lee-c 3.00

...: Renegade TPB (2006, $17.95) r/#112-117 18.00

...: Rough Justice (1999, $17.95, TPB) r/#9-18 18.00

Secret Files 1 (10/99, $4.95) Origin-s and pin-ups 5.00

...: The Hunt for Oracle (2003, $14.95, TPB) r/#41-46 & Birds of Prey #20,21 15.00

...: The Lost Year (2008, $14.99) r/#133-137 & Annual #2 15.00

...: The Target (2001, $5.95) McDaniel-c/a 6.00

Wizard 1/2 (Mail offer) 5.00

...: Year One (2005, $14.99) r/#101-106 15.00

NIGHTWING (See Tangent Comics/ Nightwing)

NIGHTWING AND HUNTRESS
DC Comics: May, 1998 - No. 4, Aug, 1998 ($1.95, limited series)

1-4-Grayson-s/Land & Sienkiewicz-a 2.50

TPB (2003, $9.95) r/#1/4; cover gallery 10.00

NIGHTWINGS (See DC Science Fiction Graphic Novel)

NIKKI, WILD DOG OF THE NORTH (Disney, see Movie Comics)
Dell Publishing Co.: No. 1226, Sept, 1961

Four Color 1226-Movie, photo-c 5 10 15 34 55 75

9-11 - ARTISTS RESPOND
Dark Horse Comics: 2002 ($9.95, TPB, proceeds donated to charities)

Volume 1-Short stories about the September 11 tragedies by various Dark Horse, Chaos! and Image writers and artists; Eric Drooker-c 10.00

9-11: EMERGENCY RELIEF
Alternative Comics: 2002 ($14.95, TPB, proceeds donated to the Red Cross)

nn-Short stories by various inc. Pekar, Eisner, Hester, Oeming, Noto; Cho-c 15.00

9-11 - THE WORLD'S FINEST COMIC BOOK WRITERS AND ARTISTS TELL STORIES TO REMEMBER
DC Comics: 2002 ($9.95, TPB, proceeds donated to charities)

Volume 2-Short stories about the September 11 tragedies by various DC, MAD, and WildStorm writers and artists ; Alex Ross-c 10.00

NINE RINGS OF WU-TANG

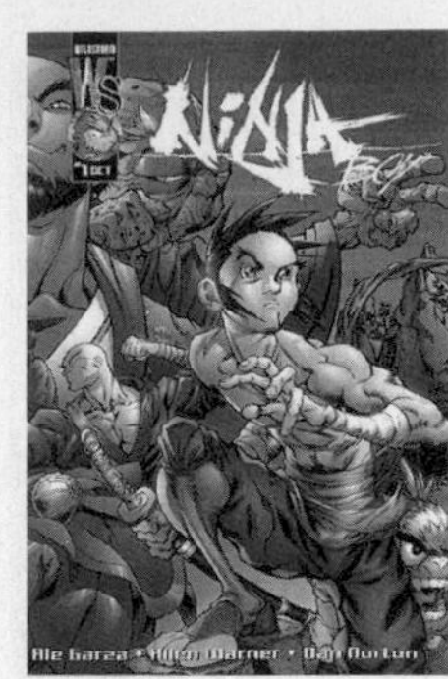

Ninja Boy #1 © Ale Garza

Noble Causes #33 © Jay Faerber

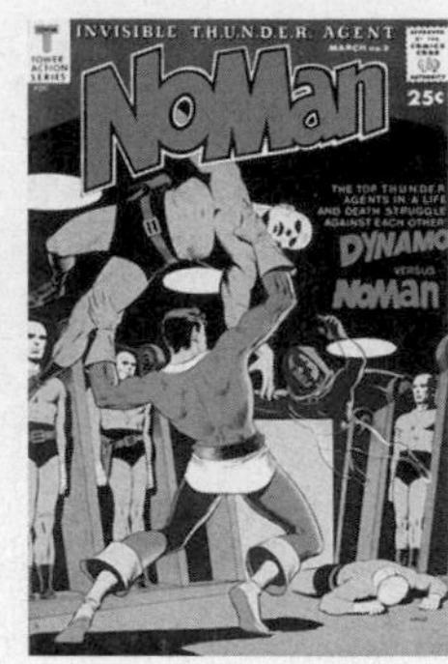

Noman #2 © Tower

GD VG FN VF VF/NM NM-
2.0 4.0 6.0 8.0 9.0 9.2

Image Comics: July, 1999 - No. 5, July, 2000 ($2.95)
Preview (7/99, $5.00, B&W) 5.00
1-5: 1-(11/99, $2.95) Clayton Henry-a 3.00
Tower Records Variant-c 5.00
Wizard #0 Prelude 2.50
TPB (1/01, $19.95) r/#1-5, Preview & Prelude; sketchbook & cover gallery 20.00

1963
Image Comics (Shadowline Ink): Apr, 1993 - No. 6, Oct, 1993 ($1.95, lim. series)
1-6: Alan Moore scripts; Veitch, Bissette & Gibbons-a(p) 2.50
1-Gold 3.00
*NOTE: **Bissette** a-2-4; **Gibbons** a-1i, 2i, 6i; c-2.*

1984 (Magazine) (1994 #11 on)
Warren Publishing Co.: June, 1978 - No. 10, Jan, 1980 ($1.50, B&W with color inserts, mature content with nudity; 84 pgs. except #4 has 92 pgs.)
1-Nino-a in all; Mutant World begins by Corben 3 6 9 14 19 24
2-10: 4-Rex Havoc begins. 7-1st Ghita of Alizarr by Thorne. 9-1st Starfire 2 4 6 9 13 16
NOTE: ***Alcala** a-1-3,5,7i. **Corben** a-1-8; c-1,2. **Nebres** a-1-8,10. **Thorne** a-7,8,10. **Wood** a-1,2,5i.*

1994 (Formerly 1984) (Magazine)
Warren Publishing Co.: No. 11, Feb, 1980 - No. 29, Feb, 1983 (B&W with color; mature; #11-(84 pgs.); #12-16,18-21,24-(76 pgs.); #17,22,23,25-29-(68 pgs.)
11,17,18,20,22,23,29: 11,17-8 pgs. color insert. 18-Giger-c. 20-1st Diana Jacklighter Manhuntress by Maroto. 22-1st Sigmund Pavlov by Nino; 1st Ariel Hart by Hsu. 23-All Nino issue 2 4 6 8 11 14
12-16,19,21,24-28: 21-1st app. Angel by Nebres. 27-The Warhawks return 1 3 4 6 8 10
NOTE: ***Corben** c-26. **Maroto** a-20, 21, 24-28. **Nebres** a-11-13, 15, 16, 18, 21, 22, 25, 28. **Nino** a-11-19, 20(2), 21, 25, 26, 28; c-21. **Redondo** c-20. **Thorne** a-11-14, 17-21, 24-26, 28, 29.*

NINJA BOY
DC Comics (WildStorm): Oct, 2001 - No. 6, Mar, 2002 ($3.50/$2.95)
1-($3.50) Ale Garza-a/c 3.50
2-6-($2.95) 3.00
...: Faded Dreams TPB (2003, $14.95) r/#1-6; sketch pages 15.00

NINJA HIGH SCHOOL (1st series)
Antarctic Press: 1986 - No. 3, Aug, 1987 (B&W)
1-Ben Dunn-s/c/a; early Manga series 2 4 6 9 12 15
2,3 1 3 4 6 8 10

NINJAK (See Bloodshot #6, 7 & Deathmate)
Valiant/Acclaim Comics (Valiant) No. 16 on: Feb, 1994 - No. 26, Nov. 1995 ($2.25/$2.50)
1 ($3.50)-Chromium-c; Quesada c/a(p) in #1-3 3.50
1-Gold 5.00
2-13: 3-Batman, Spawn & Random (from X-Factor) app. as costumes at party (cameo). 4-w/bound-in trading card. 5,6-X-O app. 2.50
0,00,14-26: 14-(4/95)-Begin $2.50-c. 0-(6/95, $2.50). 00-(6/95, $2.50) 2.50
Yearbook 1 (1994, $3.95) 4.00

NINJAK
Acclaim Comics (Valiant Heroes): V2#1, Mar, 1997 -No. 12, Feb, 1998 ($2.50)
V2#1-12: 1-Intro new Ninjak; 1st app. Brutakon; Kurt Busiek scripts begin; painted variant-c exists. 2-1st app. Karnivor & Zeer. 3-1st app. Gigantik, Shurikai, & Nixie. 4-Origin; 1st app. Yasuiti Motomiya; intro The Dark Dozen; Colin King cameo. 9-Copycat-c 2.50

NINJA SCROLL
DC Comics (WildStorm): Nov, 2006 - Present ($2.99)
1-12: 1-J. Torres-s/Michael Chang Ting Yu-a/c. 11-Puckett-s/Meyers-a 3.00
1-3-Variant covers by Jim Lee 5.00
TPB (2007, $19.99) r/#1-3,5-7 20.00

NINTENDO COMICS SYSTEM (Also see Adv. of Super Mario Brothers)
Valiant Comics: Feb, 1990 - No. 9, Oct, 1991 ($4.95, card stock-c, 68pgs.)
1-9: 1-Featuring Game Boy, Super Mario, Clappwall. 3-Layton-c. 5-8-Super Mario Bros. 9-Dr. Mario 1st app. 5.00

NOAH'S ARK
Spire Christian Comics/Fleming H. Revell Co.: 1973 (35/49¢)
nn-By Al Hartley 2 4 6 8 10 12

NOBLE CAUSES
Image Comics: July, 2001; Jan, 2002 - No. 4, May, 2002 ($2.95)
...First Impressions (7/01) Intro. the Noble family; Faerber-s 3.00
1-4: 1-(1/02) Back-up-s with Conner-a. 2-Igle back-up-a. 2-4-Two covers 3.00
...: Extended Family (5/03, $6.95) short stories by various 7.00
...: Extended Family 2 (6/04, $7.95) short stories by various 8.00
Vol. 1: In Sickness and in Health (2003, $12.95) r/#1-4 & ...First Impresssions 13.00

NOBLE CAUSES (Volume 3)
Image Comics: July, 2004 - Present ($3.50)
1-24,26-36-Faerber-s. 1-Two covers. 2-Venture app. 5-Invincible app. 3.50
25-($4.99) Art by various; Randolph-c 5.00
Vol. 4: Blood and Water (2005, $14.95) r/#1-6 15.00
Vol. 5: Betrayals (2006, $14.99) r/#7-12 & The Pact V2 #2 15.00
Vol. 6: Hidden Agendas (2006, $15.99) r/#13-18 and Image Holiday Spec. 2005 story 16.00
Vol. 7: Powerless (2007, $15.99) r/#19-25; Wieringo sketch page 16.00

NOBLE CAUSES: DISTANT RELATIVES
Image Comics: Jul, 2003 - No. 4, Oct, 2003 ($2.95, B&W, limited series)
1-4-Faerber-s/Richardson & Ponce-a 3.00
Vol. 3: Distant Relatives (1/05, $12.95) r/#1-4; intro. by Joe Casey 13.00

NOBLE CAUSES: FAMILY SECRETS
Image Comics: Oct, 2002 - No. 4, Jan, 2003 ($2.95, limited series)
1-4-Faerber-s/Oeming-c. 1-Variant cover by Walker. 2,3-Valentino var-c. 4-Hester var-c 3.00
Vol. 2: Family Secrets (2004, $12.95) r/#1-4; sketch pages 13.00

NOBODY (Amado, Cho & Adlard's...)
Oni Press: Nov, 1998 - No. 4, Feb, 1999 ($2.95, B&W, mini-series)
1-4 3.00

NOCTURNALS, THE
Malibu Comics (Bravura): Jan, 1995 - No. 6, Aug, 1995 ($2.95, limited series)
1-6: Dan Brereton painted-c/a & scripts 3.00
1-Glow-in-the-Dark premium edition 5.00

NOCTURNALS, THE
Dark Horse Comics/Image Comics/Oni Press: one-shots and trade paperbacks
Black Planet TPB (Oni Press, 1998, $19.95) r/#1-6 (Malibu Comics series) 20.00
Black Planet and Other Stories HC (Olympian Publ.; 7/07, $39.95) r/Black Planet & Witching Hour contents; cover & sketch gallery with Brereton interviews 40.00
Carnival of Beasts (Image, 7/08, $6.99) short stories; Brereton-s/Brereton & others-a 7.00
Troll Bridge (Oni Press, 2000, $4.95, B&W & orange) Brereton-s/painted-c; art by Brereton, Chin, Art Adams, Sakai, Timm, Warren, Thompson, Purcell, Stephens and others 5.00
Unhallowed Eve TPB (Oni Press, 10/02, $9.95) r/Witching Hour & Troll Bridge one-shots 10.00
Witching Hour (Dark Horse, 5/98, $4.95) Brereton-s/a; reprints DHP stories + 8 new pgs. 5.00

NOCTURNALS: THE DARK FOREVER
Oni Press: Jul, 2001 -No. 3, Feb, 2002 ($2.95, limited series)
1-3-Brereton-s/painted-a/c 3.00
TPB (5/02, $9.95) r/#1-3; afterword & pin-ups by Alex Ross 10.00

NOCTURNE
Marvel Comics: June, 1995 - No. 4, Sept. 1995 ($1.50, limited series)
1-4 2.50

NO ESCAPE (Movie)
Marvel Comics: June, 1994 - No. 3, Aug, 1994 ($1.50)
1-3: Based on movie 2.50

NO HONOR
Image Comics (Top Cow): Feb, 2001 - No. 4, July, 2001 ($2.50)
Preview (12/00, B&W) Silvestri-c 2.50
1-4-Avery-s/Crain-a 2.50
TPB (8/03, $12.99) r/#1-4; intro. by Straczynski 13.00

NOMAD (See Captain America #180)
Marvel Comics: Nov, 1990 - No. 4, Feb, 1991 ($1.50, limited series)
1-4: 1,4-Captain America app. 2.50

NOMAD
Marvel Comics: V2#1, May, 1992 - No. 25, May, 1994 ($1.75)
V2#1-25: 1-Has gatefold-c w/map/wanted poster. 4-Deadpool x-over. 5-Punisher vs. Nomad-c/story. 6-Punisher & Daredevil-c/story cont'd in Punisher War Journal #48. 7-Gambit-c/story. 10-Red Wolf app. 21-Man-Thing-c/story. 25-Bound-in trading card sheet 2.50

NOMAN (See Thunder Agents)
Tower Comics: Nov, 1966 - No. 2, March, 1967 (25¢, 68 pgs.)
1-Wood/Williamson-c; Lightning begins; Dynamo cameo; Kane-a(p) & Whitney-a 9 18 27 61 103 145
2-Wood-c only; Dynamo x-over; Whitney-a 6 12 18 37 59 80

NONE BUT THE BRAVE (See Movie Classics)

NOODNIK COMICS (See Pinky the Egghead)

Northlanders #2 © Brian Wood & DC

Nova (2007 series) #7 © MAR

Nursery Rhymes #10 © Z-D

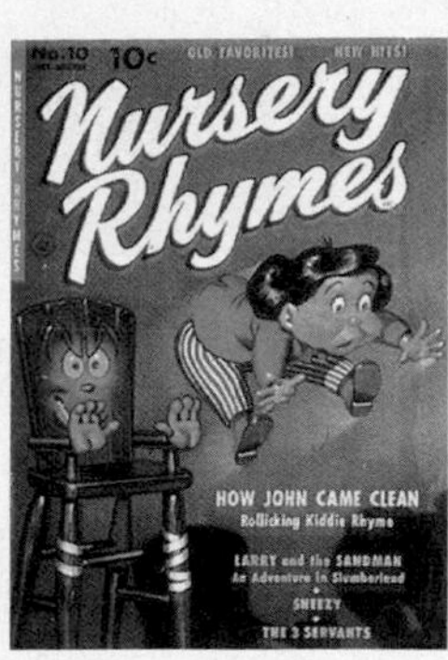

GD 2.0 | VG 4.0 | FN 6.0 | VF 8.0 | VF/NM 9.0 | NM- 9.2

Comic Media/Mystery/Biltmore: Dec, 1953; No. 2, Feb, 1954 - No. 5, Aug, 1954
3-D(1953, 25¢; Comic Media)(#1)-Came w/glasses 29 58 87 169 272 375
2-5 9 18 27 50 65 80

NORMALMAN (See Cerebus the Aardvark #55, 56)
Aardvark-Vanaheim/Renegade Press #6 on: Jan, 1984 - No. 12, Dec, 1985 ($1.70/$2.00)
1-12: 1-Jim Valentino-c/a in all. 6-12 ($2.00, B&W): 10-Cerebus cameo; Sim-a (2 pgs.) 2.50
...- Megaton Man Special 1 (Image Comics, 8/94, $2.50) 3.00
...3-D 1 (Annual, 1986, $2.25) 2.50
...Twentieth Anniversary Special (7/04, $2.95) 3.00

NORTH AVENUE IRREGULARS (See Walt Disney Showcase #49)

NORTHLANDERS
DC Comics (Vertigo): Feb, 2008 - Present ($2.99)
1-8-Vikings in 980 A.D.; Wood-s/Gianfelice-a; covers by Carnivale 3.00
1,2-Variant covers. 1-Adam Kubert. 2-Andy Kubert 6.00

NORTHSTAR
Marvel Comics: Apr, 1994 - No. 4, July, 1994 ($1.75, mini-series)
1-4: Character from Alpha Flight 2.50

NORTH TO ALASKA
Dell Publishing Co.: No. 1155, Dec, 1960
Four Color 1155-Movie, John Wayne photo-c 16 32 48 112 209 305

NORTHWEST MOUNTIES (Also see Approved Comics #12)
Jubilee Publications/St. John: Oct, 1948 - No. 4, July, 1949
1-Rose of the Yukon by Matt Baker; Walter Johnson-a; Lubbers-c
47 94 141 291 483 675
2-Baker-a; Lubbers-c. Ventrilo app. 38 76 114 226 363 500
3-Dondagc o, Baker-a; Sky Chief, K-9 app. 40 00 120 235 380 525
4-Baker-c/a(2 pgs.); Blue Monk & The Desperado app.
41 82 123 246 403 560

NO SLEEP 'TIL DAWN
Dell Publishing Co.: No. 831, Aug, 1957
Four Color 831-Movie, Karl Malden photo-c 6 12 18 43 69 95

NOSTALGIA ILLUSTRATED
Marvel Comics: Nov, 1974 - V2#8, Aug, 1975 (B&W, 76 pgs.)
V1#1 3 6 9 20 30 40
V1#2, V2#1-8 3 6 9 14 20 25

NOT BRAND ECHH (Brand Echh #1-4; See Crazy, 1973)
Marvel Comics Group (LMC): Aug, 1967 - No. 13, May, 1969
(1st Marvel parody book)
1: 1-8 are 12¢ issues 6 12 18 39 62 85
2-8: 3-Origin Thor, Hulk & Capt. America; Monkees, Alfred E. Neuman cameo. 4-X-Men app. 5-Origin/intro. Forbush Man. 7-Origin Fantastical-4 & Stuporman. 8-Beatles cameo; X-Men satire; last 12¢-c 4 8 12 22 34 45
9-13 (25¢, 68 pgs., all Giants) 9-Beatles cameo. 10-All-r; The Old Witch, Crypt Keeper & Vault Keeper cameos. 12,13-Beatles cameo 4 8 12 28 44 60
NOTE: *Colan a(p)-4, 5, 8, 9, 13. Everett a-1i. Kirby a(p)-1, 3, 5-7, 10r; c-1p. J. Severin a-1; c-3, 6-8, 11. M. Severin a-1-13; c-2, 9, 10, 12, 13. Sutton a-3, 4, 5i, 6i, 8, 9, 10r, 11-13; c-5. Archie satire in #9. Avengers satire in #8, 12.*

NOTHING CAN STOP THE JUGGERNAUT
Marvel Comics: 1989 ($3.95)
1-r/Amazing Spider-Man #229 & 230 4.00

NO TIME FOR SERGEANTS (TV)
Dell Publ. Co.: No. 914, July, 1958; Feb-Apr, 1965 - No. 3, Aug-Oct, 1965
Four Color 914 (Movie)-Toth-a; Andy Griffith photo-c 9 18 27 65 113 160
1(2-4/65) (TV): Photo-c 6 12 18 39 62 85
2,3 (TV): Photo-c 5 10 15 30 48 65

NOVA (The Man Called... No. 22-25)(See New Warriors)
Marvel Comics Group: Sept, 1976 - No. 25, May, 1979
1-Origin/1st app. Nova 2 4 6 11 16 20
2-4,12: 4-Thor x-over. 12-Spider-Man x-over 1 3 4 6 8 10
5-11 1 2 3 4 5 7
10,11-(35¢-c variants, limited distribution)(6,7/77) 4 8 12 26 41 55
12-(35¢-c variant, limited distribution)(8/77) 5 10 15 32 51 70
13,14-(Regular 30¢ editions)(9/77) 13-Intro Crime-Buster. 6.00
13,14-(35¢-c variants, limited distribution) 4 8 12 24 37 50
15-24: 18-Yellow Claw app. 19-Wally West (Kid Flash) cameo 6.00
25-Last issue 1 2 3 5 6 8
NOTE: *Austin c-21i, 23i. John Buscema a(p)-1-3, 8, 21; c-1p, 2, 15. Infantino a(p)-15-20, 22-25; c-17-20, 21p, 23p, 24p. Kirby c-4p, 5, 7. Nebres c-25i. Simonson a-23i.*

NOVA
Marvel Comics: Jan, 1994 - June, 1995 ($1.75/$1.95) (Started as 4-part mini-series)
1-($2.95, 52 pgs.)-Collector's Edition w/gold foil-c; new Nova costume 3.00
1-($2.25, 52 pgs.)-Newsstand Edition w/o foil c 2.50
2-18: 3-Spider-Man-c/story. 5-Stan Lee app. 5-Bound-in card sheet. 13-Firestar & Night Thrasher app.14-Darkhawk 2.50

NOVA
Marvel Comics: May, 1999 - No. 7, Nov, 1999 ($2.99/$1.99)
1-($2.99) Larsen-s/Bennett-a; wraparound-c by Larsen 3.00
2-7-($1.99): 2-Two covers; Capt. America app. 5-Spider-Man. 7-Venom 2.50

NOVA
Marvel Comics: June, 2007 - Present ($2.99)
1-17: 1-Sean Chen-a/Granov-c. 2,3-Iron Man app. 3-Thunderbolts app. 14,15-Silver Surfer & Galactus app. 16,17-Secret Invasion 3.00
... Annual 1 (4/08, $3.99) Origin retold; Annihilation: Conquest tie-in 4.00
... Vol. 1: Annihilation - Conquest TPB (2007, $17.99) r/#1-7; cover sketches 18.00

NOW AGE ILLUSTRATED (See Pendulum Illustrated Classics)

NOW AGE BOOKS ILLUSTRATED (See Pendulum Illustrated Classics)

NTH MAN THE ULTIMATE NINJA (See Marvel Comics Presents #25)
Marvel Comics: Aug, 1989 - No. 16, Sept, 1990 ($1.00)
1-16-Ninja mercenary. 8-Dale Keown's 1st Marvel work (1/90, pencils) 2.50

NUCLEUS (Also see Cerebus)
Heiro-Graphic Publications: May, 1979 ($1.50, B&W, adult fanzine)
1-Contains "Demonhorn" by Dave Sim; early app. of Cerebus The Aardvark (4 pg. story)
5 10 15 32 51 70

NUKLA
Dell Publishing Co.: Oct-Dec, 1965 - No. 4, Sept, 1966
1-Origin & 1st app. Nukla (super hero) 4 8 12 28 44 60
2,3 3 6 9 19 29 38
4-Ditko-a, c(p) 4 8 12 23 36 48

NUMBER OF THE BEAST
DC Comics (WildStorm): June, 2008 - No. 8, Sept, 2008 ($2.99, limited series)
1-8-Beatty-s/Sprouse-a/c. 1-Variant-c by Mahnke. 6-The Authority app. 3.00

NURSE BETSY CRANE (Formerly Teen Secret Diary) (Also see Registered Nurse for reprints)
Charlton Comics: V2#12, Aug, 1961 - V2#27, Mar, 1964 (See Soap Opera Romances)
V2#12-27 3 6 9 16 23 30

NURSE HELEN GRANT (See The Romances of...)

NURSE LINDA LARK (See Linda Lark)

NURSERY RHYMES
Ziff-Davis Publ. Co. (Approved Comics): No. 10, July-Aug, 1951 - No. 2, Winter, 1951 (Painted-c)
10 (#1), 2: 10-Howie Post-a 16 32 48 94 147 200

NURSES, THE (TV)
Gold Key: April, 1963 - No. 3, Oct, 1963 (Photo-c: #1,2)
1 4 8 12 24 37 50
2,3 3 6 9 18 27 35

NUTS! (Satire)
Premiere Comics Group: March, 1954 - No. 5, Nov, 1954
1-Hollingsworth-a 30 60 90 174 280 385
2,4,5: 5-Capt. Marvel parody 20 40 60 115 183 250
3-Drug "reefers" mentioned 20 40 60 115 183 250

NUTS (Magazine) (Satire)
Health Knowledge: Feb, 1958 - No. 2, April, 1958
1 9 18 27 52 69 85
2 7 14 21 35 43 50

NUTS & JOLTS
Dell Publishing Co.: No. 22, 1941
Large Feature Comic 22 17 34 51 100 158 215

NUTSY SQUIRREL (Formerly Hollywood Funny Folks)(See Comic Cavalcade)
National Periodical Publications: #61, 9-10/54 - #69, 1-2/56; #70, 8-9/56 - #71, 10-11/56; #72, 11/57
61-Mayer-a; Grossman-a in all 14 28 42 76 108 140
62-72: Mayer a-62,65,67-72 10 20 30 54 72 90

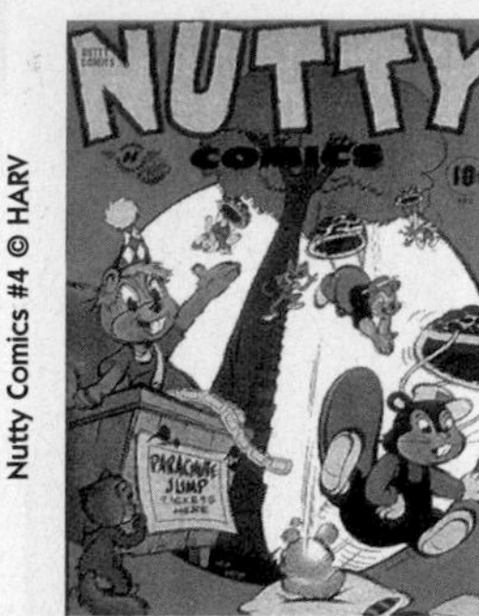

Nutty Comics #4 © HARV

NYX #7 © MAR

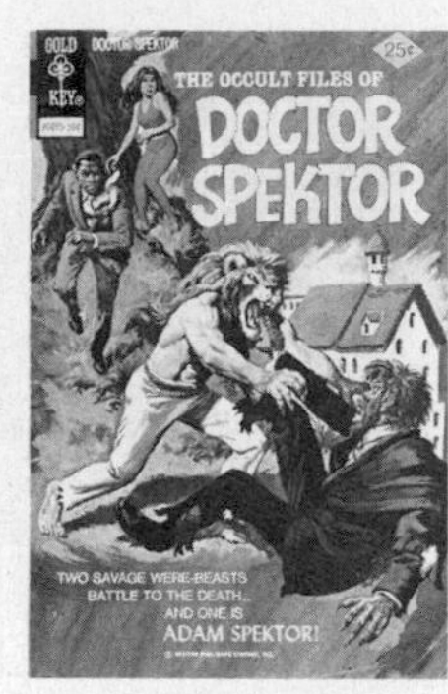

Occult Files of Dr. Spektor #13 © GK

	GD	VG	FN	VF	VF/NM	NM-
	2.0	4.0	6.0	8.0	9.0	9.2

NUTTY COMICS
Fawcett Publications: Winter, 1946

1-Capt. Kidd story; 1 pg. Wolverton-a 14 28 42 80 115 150

NUTTY COMICS
Home Comics (Harvey Publications): 1945; No. 4, May-June, 1946 - No. 8, June-July, 1947 (No #2,3)

nn-Helpful Hank, Bozo Bear & others (funny animal) 9 18 27 50 65 80
4 7 14 21 37 46 55
5-Rags Rabbit begins(1st app.); infinity-c 8 16 24 40 50 60
6-8 6 12 18 31 38 45

NUTTY LIFE (Formerly Krazy Life #1; becomes Wotalife Comics #3 on)
Fox Features Syndicate: No. 2, Summer, 1946

2 15 30 45 85 130 175

NYOKA, THE JUNGLE GIRL (Formerly Jungle Girl; see The Further Adventures of..., Master Comics #50 & XMas Comics)
Fawcett Publications: No. 2, Winter, 1945 - No. 77, June, 1953 (Movie serial)

2 54 108 162 340 575 810
3 32 64 96 186 298 410
4,5 26 52 78 152 244 335
6-11,13,14,16-18-Krigstein-a: 17-Sam Spade ad by Lou Fine
19 38 57 112 176 240
12,15,19,20 17 34 51 100 158 215
21-30: 25-Clayton Moore photo-c? 14 28 42 76 108 140
31-40 11 22 33 62 86 110
41-50 10 20 30 56 76 95
51-60 9 18 27 50 65 80
61-77 8 16 24 44 57 70
NOTE: *Photo-c from movies 25, 30-70, 72, 75-77. Bondage c-4, 5, 7, 8, 14, 24.*

NYOKA, THE JUNGLE GIRL (Formerly Zoo Funnies; Space Adventures #23 on)
Charlton Comics: No. 14, Nov, 1955 - No. 22, Nov, 1957

14 11 22 33 62 86 110
15-22 9 18 27 52 69 85

NYX (Also see X-23 title)
Marvel Comics: Nov, 2003 - No. 7, Oct, 2005 ($2.99)

1,2: 1-Quesada-s/Middleton-a/c; intro. Kiden Nixon 3.00
3-1st app. X-23 1 3 4 6 8 10
4-6: 5,6-Teranishi-a 3.00
7-($3.99) Teranishi-a 4.00
NYX X-23 (2005, $34.99, oversized with d.j.) r/X-23 #1-6 & NYX #1-7; intro by Craig Kyle; sketch pages, development art and unused covers 35.00
...: Wannabe TPB (2006, $19.99) r/#1-7; development art and unused covers 20.00

NYX: NO WAY HOME
Marvel Comics: Oct, 2008 - No. 6 ($3.99)

1,2: 1-Andrasofszky-a/Liu-s/Urusov-c; sketch pages, character and cover design art 4.00

OAKLAND PRESS FUNNYBOOK, THE
The Oakland Press: 9/17/78 - 4/13/80 (16 pgs.) (Weekly)
Full color in comic book form; changes to tabloid size 4/20/80-on

Contains Tarzan by Manning, Marmaduke, Bugs Bunny, etc. (low distribution); 9/23/79 - 4/13/80 contain Buck Rogers by Gray Morrow & Jim Lawrence 2.50

OAKY DOAKS (See Famous Funnies #190)
Eastern Color Printing Co.: July, 1942 (One Shot)

1 35 70 105 203 327 450

OBERGEIST: RAGNAROK HIGHWAY
Image Comics (Top Cow/Minotaur): May, 2001 - No. 6, Nov, 2001 ($2.95, limited series)

Preview ('01, B&W, 16 pgs.) Harris painted-c 2.25
1-6-Harris-c/a/Jolley-s. 1-Three covers 3.00
... :The Directors' Cut (2002, $19.95, TPB) r/#1-6; Bruce Campbell intro. 20.00
... :The Empty Locket (3/02, $2.95, B&W) Harris & Snyder-a 3.00

OBIE
Store Comics: 1953 (6¢)

1 6 12 18 28 34 40

OBJECTIVE FIVE
Image Comics: July, 2000 - No. 6, Jan, 2001($2.95)

1-6-Lizalde-a 3.00

OBLIVION
Comico: Aug, 1995 - No. 3, May, 1996 ($2.50)

1-3: 1-Art Adams-c. 2-(1/96)-Bagged w/gaming card. 3-(5/96)-Darrow-c 2.50

OBNOXIO THE CLOWN (Character from Crazy Magazine)
Marvel Comics Group: April, 1983 (one-shot)

1-Vs. the X-Men 4.00

OCCULT CRIMES TASKFORCE
Image Comics: July, 2006 - No. 4, May, 2007 ($2.99, limited series)

1-4-Rosario Dawson & David Atchison-s/Tony Shasteen-a 3.00
... Vol. 1 TPB (2007, $14.99) r/#1-4; sketch and cover development art 15.00

OCCULT FILES OF DR. SPEKTOR, THE
Gold Key/Whitman No. 25: Apr, 1973 - No. 24, Feb, 1977; No. 25, May, 1982 (Painted-c #1-24)

1-1st app. Lakota; Baron Tibor begins 5 10 15 30 48 65
2-5: 3-Mummy-c/s. 5-Jekyll & Hyde-c/s 3 6 9 17 25 32
6-10: 6,9-Frankenstein. 8,9-Dracula c/s. 9.-Jekyll & Hyde c/s. 9,10-Mummy-c/s
2 4 6 13 18 22
11-13,15-17,19-22,24: 11-1st app. Spektor as Werewolf. 11-13-Werewolf-c/s. 12,16-Frankenstein c/s. 17-Zombie/Voodoo-c. 19-Sea monster-c/s. 20-Mummy-s. 21-Swamp monster-c/s. 24-Dragon-c/s 2 4 6 9 12 15
14-Dr. Solar app. 3 6 9 16 22 28
18,23-Dr. Solar cameo 2 4 6 10 14 18
22-Return of the Owl c/s 2 4 6 10 14 18
25(Whitman, 5/82)-r/#1 with line drawn-c 2 4 6 8 10 12
NOTE: *Also see Dan Curtis, Golden Comics Digest 33, Gold Key Spotlight, Mystery Comics Digest 5, & Spine Tingling Tales.*

OCEAN
DC Comics (WildStorm): Dec, 2005 - No. 6, Sept, 2005 ($2.95/$2.99/$3.99, limited series)

1-5-Warren Ellis-s/Chris Sprouse-a 3.00
6-($3.99) Conclusion 4.00

ODELL'S ADVENTURES IN 3-D (See Adventures in 3-D)

OFFCASTES
Marvel Comics (Epic Comics/Heavy Hitters): July, 1993 - No. 3, Sept, 1993 ($1.95, limited series)

1-3: Mike Vosburg-c/a/scripts in all 2.50

OFFICIAL CRISIS ON INFINITE EARTHS INDEX, THE
Independent Comics Group (Eclipse): Mar, 1986 ($1.75)

1 5.00

OFFICIAL CRISIS ON INFINITE EARTHS CROSSOVER INDEX, THE
Independent Comics Group (Eclipse): July, 1986 ($1.75)

1-Perez c. 5.00

OFFICIAL DOOM PATROL INDEX, THE
Independent Comics Group (Eclipse): Feb, 1986 - No. 2, Mar, 1986 ($1.50, limited series)

1,2: Byrne-c. 4.00

OFFICIAL HANDBOOK OF THE CONAN UNIVERSE (See Handbook of...)

OFFICIAL HANDBOOK OF THE MARVEL UNIVERSE, THE
Marvel Comics Group: Jan, 1983 - No. 15, May, 1984 (Limited series)

1-Lists Marvel heroes & villains (letter A) 5.00
2-15: 2 (B-C, 3-(C-D). 4-(D-G). 5-(H-J), 6-(K-L). 7-(M). 8-(N-P); Punisher-c. 9-(Q-S), 10-(S). 11-(S-U). 12-(V-Z); Wolverine-c. 13,14-Book of the Dead. 15-Weaponry catalogue 4.00
NOTE: ***Bolland** a-8. **Byrne** c/a(p)-1-14; c-15p. **Grell** a-6, 9. **Kirby** a-1, 3. **Layton** a-2, 5, 7. **Mignola** a-3, 4, 5, 6, 8, 12. **Miller** a-4-6, 8, 10. **Nebres** a-3, 4, 8. **Redondo** a-3, 4, 8, 13, 14. **Simonson** a-1, 4, 6-13. **Paul Smith** a-1-12. **Starlin** a-5, 7, 8, 10, 13, 14. **Steranko** a-8p. **Zeck**-2-14.*

OFFICIAL HANDBOOK OF THE MARVEL UNIVERSE, THE
Marvel Comics Group: Dec, 1985 - No. 20, Feb, 1988 ($1.50, maxi-series)

V2#1-Byrne-c 4.00
2-20: 2,3-Byrne-c 3.00
Trade paperback Vol. 1-10 ($6.95) 1 3 4 6 8 10
NOTE: ***Art Adams** a-7, 8, 11, 12, 14. **Bolland** a-8, 10, 13. **Buckler** a-1, 3, 5, 10. **Buscema** a-1, 5, 8, 9, 10, 13, 14. **Byrne** a-1-14; c-1-11. **Ditko** a-1, 2, 4, 6, 7, 11, 13. a-7, 11. **Mignola** a-2, 4, 9, 11, 13. **Miller** a-2, 4, 12. **Simonson** a-1, 2, 4-13, 15. **Paul Smith** a-1-5, 7-12, 14. **Starlin** a-6, 8, 9, 12, 16. **Zeck** a-1-4, 6, 7, 9-14, 16.*

OFFICIAL HANDBOOK OF THE MARVEL UNIVERSE, THE
Marvel Comics: July, 1989 - No. 8, Mid-Dec, 1990 ($1.50, lim. series, 52 pgs.)

V3#1-8: 1-McFarlane-a (2 pgs.) 3.00

OFFICIAL HANDBOOK OF THE MARVEL UNIVERSE, THE (Also see Spider-Man)
Marvel Comics: 2004 - Present ($3.99, one-shots)

...: Alternate Universes 2005 - Profile pages of 1602, MC2, 2099, Earth X, Mangaverse, Days of Future Past, Squadron Supreme, Spider-Ham's Larval Earth and others 4.00
...: Avengers 2004 - Profile pages; art by various; lists of character origins and 1st apps. 4.00
...: Avengers 2005 - Profile pages and info for New Avengers, Young Avengers & others 4.00

Official Marvel Index to the Avengers #1 © MAR

O. G. Whiz #2 © GK

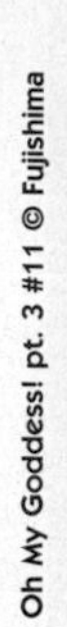
Oh My Goddess! pt. 3 #11 © Fujishima

GD 2.0 | VG 4.0 | FN 6.0 | VF 8.0 | VF/NM 9.0 | NM- 9.2

...: Book of the Dead 2004 - Profile pages of deceased Marvel characters; art by various; 4.00
...: Daredevil 2004 - Profile pages; art by various; lists of character origins and 1st apps. 4.00
...: Fantastic Four 2005 - Profile pages of members, friends & enemies 4.00
...: Golden Age 2005 - Profile pages; art by various; lists of character origins and 1st apps. 4.00
...: Horror 2005 - Profile pages; art by various; lists of character origins and 1st apps. 4.00
...: Hulk 2004 - Profile pages; art by various; lists of character origins and 1st apps. 4.00
...: Marvel Knights 2005 - Profile pages of characters from Marvel Knights line 4.00
...: Spider-Man 2004 - Profile pages; art by various; lists of character origins and 1st apps. 4.00
...: Spider-Man 2005 - Profile pages of Spidey's friends and foes, emphasizing the recent 4.00
...: Wolverine 2004 - Profile pages; art by various; lists of character origins and 1st apps. 4.00
...: Teams 2005 - Profile pages of Avengers, X-Men and other teams 4.00
...: Women of Marvel 2005 - Profile pages; art by various; Greg Land-c 4.00
...: X-Men 2004 - Profile pages; art by various; lists of character origins and 1st apps. 4.00
...: X-Men 2005 - Profile pages; art by various; lists of character origins and 1st apps. 4.00
...: X-Men - The Age of Apocalypse 2005 - Profile pages of characters plus Exiles 4.00
HC A-Z Vol. 1 (2008, $24.99, dustjacket) editied & updated pages for characters A-B 25.00
HC A-Z Vol. 2 (2008, $24.99, dustjacket) editied & updated pages for characters B-C 25.00
HC A-Z Vol. 3 (2008, $24.99, dustjacket) editied & updated pages for characters C-E 25.00

OFFICIAL HANDBOOK OF THE ULTIMATE MARVEL UNIVERSE, THE
Marvel Comics: 2005 ($3.99, one-shots)
... 2005: The Fantastic Four and Spider-Man - Profile pages; art by various 4.00
... The Ultimates and X-Men 2005 - Profile pages; art by various; Bagley-c 4.00

OFFICIAL HAWKMAN INDEX, THE
Independent Comics Group: Nov, 1986 - No. 2, Dec, 1986 ($2.00)
1,2 4.00

OFFICIAL JUSTICE LEAGUE OF AMERICA INDEX, THE
Independent Comics Group (Eclipse): April, 1986 - No. 8, Mar, 1987 ($2.00, Baxter paper)
1-8: 1,2-Perez-c. 6.00

OFFICIAL LEGION OF SUPER-HEROES INDEX, THE
Independent Comics Group (Eclipse): Dec, 1986 - No. 5, 1987 ($2.00, limited series)
(No Official in Title #2 on)
1-5: 4-Mooney-c 6.00

OFFICIAL MARVEL INDEX TO MARVEL TEAM-UP
Marvel Comics Group: Jan, 1986 - No. 6, 1987 ($1.25, limited series)
1-6 4.00

OFFICIAL MARVEL INDEX TO THE AMAZING SPIDER-MAN
Marvel Comics Group: Apr, 1985 - No. 9, Dec, 1985 ($1.25, limited series)
1 ($1.00)-Byrne-c. 4.00
2-9: 5,6,8,9-Punisher-c. 3.00

OFFICIAL MARVEL INDEX TO THE AVENGERS, THE
Marvel Comics: Jun, 1987 - No. 7, Aug, 1988 ($2.95, limited series)
1-7 5.00

OFFICIAL MARVEL INDEX TO THE AVENGERS, THE
Marvel Comics: V2#1, Oct, 1994 - V2#6, 1995 ($1.95, limited series)
V2#1-#6 3.00

OFFICIAL MARVEL INDEX TO THE FANTASTIC FOUR
Marvel Comics Group: Dec, 1985 - No. 12, Jan, 1987 ($1.25, limited series)
1-12: 1-Byrne-c. 1,2-Kirby back-c (unpub. art) 3.00

OFFICIAL MARVEL INDEX TO THE X-MEN, THE
Marvel Comics: May, 1987 - No. 7, July, 1988 ($2.95, limited series)
1-7 5.00

OFFICIAL MARVEL INDEX TO THE X-MEN, THE
Marvel Comics: V2#1, Apr, 1994 - V2#5, 1994 ($1.95, limited series)
V2#1-5: 1-Covers X-Men #1-51. 2-Covers #52-122,Special #1,2,Giant-Size #1,2. 3-Byrne-c; covers #123-177, Annuals 3-7, Spec. Ed. #1. 4-Covers Uncanny X-Men #178-234, Annuals 8-12. 5-Covers #235-287, Annuals 13-15 3.00

OFFICIAL SOUPY SALES COMIC (See Soupy Sales)

OFFICIAL TEEN TITANS INDEX, THE
Indep. Comics Group (Eclipse): Aug, 1985 - No. 5, 1986 ($1.50, lim. series)
1-5 4.00

OFFICIAL TRUE CRIME CASES (Formerly Sub-Mariner #23; All-True Crime Cases #26 on)
Marvel Comics (OCI): No. 24, Fall, 1947 - No. 25, Winter, 1947-48
24(#1)-Burgos-a; Syd Shores-c 23 46 69 133 214 295
25-Syd Shores-c; Kurtzman's "Hey Look" 18 36 54 105 165 225

OF SUCH IS THE KINGDOM
George A. Pflaum: 1955 (15¢, 36 pgs.)
nn-Reprints from 1951 Treasure Chest 4 7 10 14 17 20

O.G. WHIZ (See Gold Key Spotlight #10)
Gold Key: 2/71 - No. 6, 5/72; No. 7, 5/78 - No. 11, 1/79 (No. 7: 52 pgs.)
1-John Stanley script 5 10 15 34 55 75
2-John Stanley script 4 8 12 24 37 50
3-6(1972) 3 6 9 18 27 35
7-11(1978-79)-Part-r: 9-Tubby issue 2 4 6 9 12 15

OH, BROTHER! (Teen Comedy)
Stanhall Publ.: Jan, 1953 - No. 5, Oct, 1953
1-By Bill Williams 8 16 24 44 57 70
2-5 6 12 18 28 34 40

OH MY GODDESS! (Manga)
Dark Horse Comics: Aug, 1994 - Present ($2.50-$3.99, B&W)
1-6-Kosuke Fujishima-s/a in all 3.00
... PART II 2/95 - No. 9, 9/95 ($2.50, B&W, lim.series) #1-9 3.00
... PART III 11/95 - No. 11, 9/96 ($2.95, B&W, lim. series) #1-11 3.00
... PART IV 12/96 - No. 8, 7/97 ($2.95, B&W, lim. series) #1-8 3.00
... PART V 9/97 - No. 12, 8/98 ($2.95, B&W, lim. series)
1,2,5,8: 5-Ninja Master pt. 1 3.00
3,4,6,7,10-12-($3.95, 48 pgs.) 10-Fallen Angel. 11-Play The Game 4.00
9-($3.50) "It's Lonely At The Top" 3.50
... PART VI 10/98 - No. 5, 3/99 ($3.50/$2.95, B&W, lim. series)
1-($3.50) 3.50
2-6-($2.95)-6-Super Urd one-shot 3.00
... PART VII 5/99 - No. 8, 12/99 ($2.95, B&W, lim. series) #1-3 3.00
4-8-($3.50) 3.50
... PART VIII 1/00 - No. 6, 6/00 ($3.50, B&W, lim. series) #1-3,5,7 3.50
4 ($2.95) "Hail To The Chief" begins 3.00
... PART IX 7/00 - No. 7, 1/01 ($3.50/$2.99) #1-4: 3-Queen Sayoko 3.50
5-7-($2.99) 3.00
... PART X 2/01 - No. 5, 6/01 ($3.50) #1-5 3.50
... PART XI 10/01 - No. 10, 3/02 ($3.50) #1,2,7,8 3.50
3-6,9-($2.99) Mystery Child 3.00
10-($3.99) 4.00
(Series adapts new numbering) 88-90-($3.50) Learning to Love 3.50
91-94,96-103,105,107-110: 91-94 ($2.99) Traveler. 96-98-The Phantom Racer 3.00
95,104,106-($3.50) 95-Traveler pt. 5 3.50
111,112-($3.99) 4.00

OH SUSANNA (TV)
Dell Publishing Co.: No. 1105, June-Aug, 1960 (Gale Storm)
Four Color 1105-Toth-a, photo-c 11 22 33 77 136 195

OKAY COMICS
United Features Syndicate: July, 1940
1-Captain & the Kids & Hawkshaw the Detective reprints 45 90 135 279 465 650

O.K. COMICS
Hit Publications: May, 1940 (ashcan)
nn-Ashcan comic, not distributed to newsstands, only for in house use. A CGC certified 8.0 copy sold in 2003 for $1,000.

O.K. COMICS
United Features Syndicate/Hit Publications: July, 1940 - No. 2, Oct, 1940
1-Little Giant (w/super powers), Phantom Knight, Sunset Smith, & The Teller Twins begin 73 146 219 460 780 1100
2 (Rare)-Origin Mister Mist by Chas. Quinlan 75 150 225 473 799 1125

OKLAHOMA KID
Ajax/Farrell Publ.: June, 1957 - No. 4, 1958
1 11 22 33 60 83 105
2-4 7 14 21 37 46 55

OKLAHOMAN, THE
Dell Publishing Co.: No. 820, July, 1957
Four Color 820-Movie, photo-c 8 16 24 58 97 135

OKTANE
Dark Horse Comics: Aug, 1995 - Nov, 1995 ($2.50, color, limited series)
1-4-Gene Ha-a 2.50

OKTOBERFEST COMICS
Now & Then Publ.: Fall 1976 (75¢, Canadian, B&W, one-shot)

Omac #2 © DC

Omega the Unknown (2007 series) #1 © MAR

100 Bullets #73 © Azzarello, Risso & DC

GD 2.0 | VG 4.0 | FN 6.0 | VF 8.0 | VF/NM 9.0 | NM- 9.2

1-Dave Sim-s/a; Gene Day-a; 1st app. Uncle Hans & Natter P. Bombast; The Beavers sty; 1st Cap'n Riverrat, Sim-s/Day-a 3 6 9 14 20 25

OLD GLORY COMICS
DC Comics: 1941

nn - Ashcan comic, not distributed to newsstands, only for in-house use. Cover art is Flash Comics #12 with interior being Action Comics #37 (no known sales)

OLD IRONSIDES (Disney)
Dell Publishing Co.: No. 874, Jan, 1958

Four Color 874-Movie w/Johnny Tremain 6 12 18 43 69 95

OLD YELLER (Disney, see Movie Comics, and Walt Disney Showcase #25)
Dell Publishing Co.: No. 869, Jan, 1958

Four Color 869-Movie, photo-c 5 10 15 34 55 75

OMAC (One Man Army; ...Corps. #4 on; also see Kamandi #59 & Warlord)
(See Cancelled Comic Cavalcade)
National Periodical Publications: Sept-Oct, 1974 - No. 8, Nov-Dec, 1975

1-Origin 5 10 15 32 51 70
2-8: 8-2 pg. Neal Adams ad 3 6 9 16 23 30
Jack Kirby's Omac: One Man Army Corps HC (2008, $24.99, d.j.) r/#1-8; Evanier intro. 25.00
NOTE: *Kirby a-1-8p; c-1-7p. Kubert c-8.*

OMAC (See DCU Brave New World)
DC Comics: Sept, 2006 - No. 8, Apr, 2007 ($2.99, limited series)

1-8: 1-Bruce Jones-s/Renato Guedes-a. 1-3-Firestorm & Cyborg app. 8-Superman app. 3.00

OMAC: ONE MAN ARMY CORPS
DC Comics: 1991 - No. 4, 1991 ($3.95, B&W, mini-series, mature, 52 pgs.)

Book One - Four: John Byrne-c/a & scripts 4.00

OMAC PROJECT, THE
DC Comics: June, 2005 - No. 6, Nov, 2005 ($2.50, limited series)

1-6-Prelude to Infinite Crisis x-over; Rucka-s/Saiz-a 2.50
...: Infinite Crisis Special 1 (5/06, $4.99) Rucka-s/Saiz-a; follows destruction of satellite 5.00
TPB (2005, $14.99) r/#1-6, Countdown to Infinite Crisis, Wonder Woman #219 15.00

O'MALLEY AND THE ALLEY CATS
Gold Key: April, 1971 - No. 9, Jan, 1974 (Disney)

1 3 6 9 16 23 30
2-9 2 4 6 9 13 16

OMEGA ELITE
Blackthorne Publishing: 1987 ($1.25)

1-Starlin-c 3.00

OMEGA FLIGHT
Marvel Comics: Jun, 2007 - No. 5, Oct, 2007 ($2.99, limited series)

1-Oeming-s/Kolins-a; Wrecking Crew app. 4.00
1-Second printing with Sasquatch variant-c 3.00
2-5: 5-Beta Ray Bill app. 3.00
...: Alpha to Omega TPB ('07, $13.99) r/#1-5, USAgent story/Civil War: Choosing Sides 14.00

OMEGA MEN, THE (See Green Lantern #141)
DC Comics: Dec, 1982 - No. 38, May, 1986 ($1.00/$1.25/$1.50; Baxter paper)

1,20: 20-2nd full Lobo story 3.00
2,4-9,11-19,21-25,28-30,32,33,36,38: 2-Origin Broot. 5,9-2nd & 3rd app. Lobo (cameo, 2 pgs. each). 7-Origin The Citadel. 19-Lobo cameo. 30-Intro new Primus 2.50
3-1st app. Lobo (5 pgs.)(6/83); Lobo-c 1 2 3 4 5 7
10-1st full Lobo story 5.00
26,27,31,34,35: 26,27-Alan Moore scripts. 31-Crisis x-over. 34,35-Teen Titans x-over 3.00
37-1st solo Lobo story (8 pg. back-up by Giffen) 4.00
Annual 1(11/84, 52 pgs.), 2(11/85) 3.00
NOTE: *Giffen c/a-1-6p. Morrow a-24r. Nino c/a-16, 21; a-Annual 1i.*

OMEGA MEN, THE
DC Comics: Dec, 2006 - No. 6, May, 2007 ($2.99, limited series)

1-6: 1-Superman, Wonder Girl, Green Lantern app.; Flint-a/Gabrych-s 3.00

OMEGA THE UNKNOWN
Marvel Comics Group: March, 1976 - No. 10, Oct, 1977

1-1st app. Omega 2 4 6 8 11 14
2,3-(Regular 25¢ editions). 2-Hulk-c/story. 3-Electro-c/story. 1 2 3 5 6 8
2,3-(30¢-c variants, limited distribution) 3 6 9 18 27 35
4-10: 8-1st brief app. 2nd Foolkiller (Greg Salinger), 1 panel only. 9,10-(Reg. 30¢ editions). 9-1st full app. 2nd Foolkiller 1 2 3 4 5 7
9,10-(35¢-c variants, limited distribution) 4 8 12 22 34 45

GD 2.0 | VG 4.0 | FN 6.0 | VF 8.0 | VF/NM 9.0 | NM- 9.2

... Classic TPB (2005, $29.99) r/#1-10 30.00
NOTE: *Kane c(p)-3, 5, 8, 9. Mooney a-1-3, 4p, 5, 6p, 7, 8i, 9, 10.*

OMEGA: THE UNKNOWN
Marvel Comics: Dec, 2007 - No. 10, Sept, 2008 ($2.99, limited series)

1-10-Jonathan Lethem-s/Farel Dalrymple-a 3.00

OMEN
Northstar Publishing: 1989 - No. 3, 1989 ($2.00, B&W, mature)

1-Tim Vigil-c/a in all 1 2 3 5 7 9
1, (2nd printing) 3.00
2,3 6.00

OMEN, THE
Chaos! Comics: May, 1998 - No. 5, Sept, 1998 ($2.95, limited series)

1-5: 1-Six covers, ...: Vexed (10/98, $2.95) Chaos! characters appear 3.00

OMNI MEN
Blackthorne Publishing: 1987 - No. 3, 1987 ($1.25)

1-3 2.50
Graphic Novel (1989, $3.50) 3.50

ONE, THE
Marvel Comics (Epic Comics): July, 1985 - No. 6, Feb, 1986 (Limited series, mature)

1-6: Post nuclear holocaust super-hero. 2-Intro The Other 2.50

ONE-ARM SWORDSMAN, THE
Victory Prod./Lueng's Publ. #4 on: 1987 - No. 12, 1990 ($2.75/$1.80, 52 pgs.)

1-3 ($2.75) 2.75
4-12: 4-6-$1.80-c. 7-12-$2.00-c 2.50

ONE HUNDRED AND ONE DALMATIANS (Disney, see Cartoon Tales, Movie Comics, and Walt Disney Showcase #9, 51)
Dell Publishing Co.: No. 1183, Mar, 1961

Four Color 1183-Movie 9 18 27 65 113 160

101 DALMATIONS (Movie)
Disney Comics: 1991 (52 pgs., graphic novel)

nn-($4.95, direct sales)-r/movie adaptation & more 5.00
1-($2.95, newsstand edition) 3.00

101 WAYS TO END THE CLONE SAGA (See Spider-Man)
Marvel Comics: Jan, 1997 ($2.50, one-shot)

1 2.50

100 BULLETS
DC Comics (Vertigo): Aug, 1999 - Present ($2.50/$2.75/$2.99)

1-Azzarello-s/Risso-a/Dave Johnson-c 4.00
2-5 3.00
6-49,51-61: 26-Series summary; art by various. 45-Preview of Losers 2.50
50-($3.50) History of the Trust 3.50
62-71: 62-Begin $2.75-c. 64-Preview of Loveless 2.75
72-93: 72-Begin $2.99-c 3.00
...: A Foregone Tomorrow TPB (2002, $17.95) r/#20-30 18.00
...: Decayed TPB (2006, $14.99) r/#68-75; Darwyn Cooke intro. 15.00
...: First Shot, Last Call TPB (2000, $9.95) r/#1-5, Vertigo Winter's Edge #3 10.00
...: Hang Up on the Hang Low TPB (2001, $9.95) r/#15-19; Jim Lee intro. 10.00
...: Once Upon a Crime TPB (2007, $12.99) r/#76-83 13.00
...: Samurai TPB (2003, $12.95) r/#43-49 13.00
...: Six Feet Under the Gun TPB (2003, $12.95) r/#37-42 13.00
...: Split Second Chance TPB (2001, $14.95) r/#6-14 15.00
...: Strychnine Lives TPB (2006, $14.99) r/#59-67; Manuel Ramos intro. 15.00
...: The Counterfifth Detective TPB (2003, $12.95) r/#31-36 13.00
...: The Hard Way TPB (2005, $14.99) r/#50-58 15.00

100 GREATEST MARVELS OF ALL TIME
Marvel Comics: Dec, 2001 ($7.50/$3.50, limited series)

1-5-Reprints top #6-#25 stories voted by poll for Marvel's 40th ann. 7.50
6-($3.50) (#5 on-c) Reprints X-Men (2nd series) #1 3.50
7-($3.50) (#4 on-c) Reprints Giant-Size X-Men #1 3.50
8-($3.50) (#3 on-c) Reprints (Uncanny) X-Men #137 (Death of Jean Grey) 3.50
9-($3.50) (#2 on-c) Reprints Fantastic Four #1 3.50
10-($3.50) (#1 on-c) Reprints Amazing Fantasy #15 (1st app. Spider-Man) 3.50

100 PAGES OF COMICS
Dell Publishing Co.: 1937 (Stiff covers, square binding)

101(Found on back cover)-Alley Oop, Wash Tubbs, Capt. Easy, Og Son of Fire, Apple Mary, Tom Mix, Dan Dunn, Tailspin Tommy, Doctor Doom

Oni Double Feature #13 © Oni

Onslaught Reborn #5 © MAR

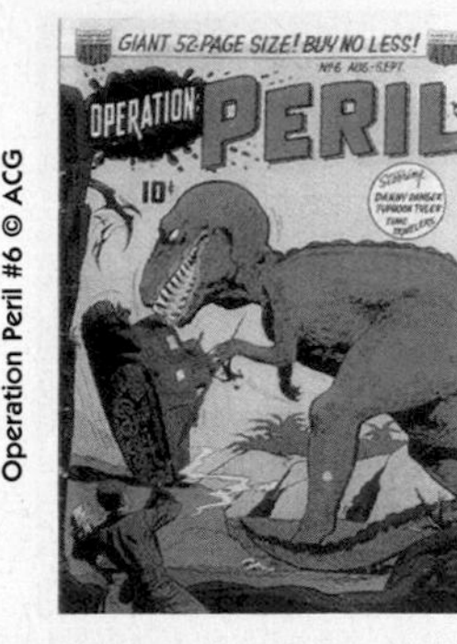

Operation Peril #6 © ACG

	GD 2.0	VG 4.0	FN 6.0	VF 8.0	VF/NM 9.0	NM- 9.2
	145	290	435	914	1545	2175

100 PAGE SUPER SPECTACULAR (See DC 100 Page Super Spectacular)

100%
DC Comics (Vertigo): Aug, 2002 - No. 5, July, 2003 ($5.95, B&W, limited series)

1-5-Paul Pope-s/a 6.00
TPB (2005, $24.99) r/#1-5; sketch pages and background info 25.00

100% TRUE?
DC Comics (Paradox Press): Summer 1996 - No. 2 ($4.95, B&W)

1,2-Reprints stories from various Paradox Press books. 5.00

$1,000,000 DUCK (See Walt Disney Showcase #5)

ONE MILLION YEARS AGO (Tor #2 on)
St. John Publishing Co.: Sept, 1953

1-Origin & 1st app. Tor; Kubert-c/a; Kubert photo inside front cover
18 36 54 105 165 225

ONE PLUS ONE
Oni Press: Sept, 2002 - No. 5, March, 2003 ($2.95, B&W, limited series)

1-5-Shaffer-s/Krall-a 3.00
TPB (9/03, $14.95, digest-size) r/#1-5 & story from Oni Press Color Special 2002 15.00

ONE SHOT (See Four Color...)

1001 HOURS OF FUN
Dell Publishing Co.: No. 13, 1943

Large Feature Comic 13 (nn)-Puzzles & games; by A.W. Nugent. This book was bound as #13 w/Large Feature Comics in publisher's files 28 56 84 162 261 360

ONE TRICK RIP OFF, THE (See Dark Horse Presents)

ONI (Adaption of video game)
Dark Horse Comics: Feb, 2001 - No. 3, Apr, 2001 ($2.99, limited series)

1-3-Sunny Lee-a(p) 3.00

ONI DOUBLE FEATURE (See Clerks: The Comic Book and Jay & Silent Bob)
Oni Press: Jan, 1998 - No. 13, Sept, 1999 ($2.95, B&W)

1-Jay & Silent Bob; Kevin Smith-s/Matt Wagner-a 1 3 4 6 8 10
1-2nd printing 3.00
2-11,13: 2,3-Paul Pope-s/a. 3,4-Nixey-s/a. 4,5-Sienkowicz-s/a. 6,7-Gaiman-s. 9-Bagge-c. 13-All Paul Dini-s; Jingle Belle 3.00
12-Jay & Silent Bob as Bluntman & Chronic; Smith-s/Allred-a 5.00

ONI PRESS COLOR SPECIAL
Oni Press: Jun, 2001; Jul, 2002 ($5.95, annual)

...2001-Oeming "Who Killed Madman?" cover; stories & art by various 6.00
...2002-Allred wraparound-c; stories & art by various 6.00

ONSLAUGHT: EPILOGUE
Marvel Comics: Feb, 1997 ($2.95, one-shot)

1-Hama-s/Green-a; Xavier-c; Bastion-app. 3.00

ONSLAUGHT: MARVEL
Marvel Comics: Oct, 1996 ($3.95, one-shot)

1-Conclusion to Onslaught x-over; wraparound-c 1 2 3 4 5 7

ONSLAUGHT REBORN
Marvel Comics: Jan, 2007 - No. 5, Feb, 2008 ($2.99, limited series)

1-5-Loeb-s/Liefeld-a; female Bucky app. 2-Variant-c by Joe Madureira. 3-McGuiness var-c. 4-Campbell var-c. 5-Bianchi var-c; female Bucky goes to regular Marvel Universe 3.00
1-Variant-c by Michael Turner 4.00
HC (2008, $19.99) r/#1-5; sketch pages; foreword by Liefeld 20.00

ONSLAUGHT: X-MEN
Marvel Comics: Aug, 1996 ($3.95, one-shot)

1-Waid & Lobdell script; Fantastic Four & Avengers app.; Xavier as Onslaught 5.00
1-Variant-c 2 4 6 8 10 12

ON STAGE
Dell Publishing Co.: No. 1336, Apr-June, 1962

Four Color 1336-Not by Leonard Starr 5 10 15 30 48 65

ON THE DOUBLE (Movie)
Dell Publishing Co.: No. 1232, Sept-Nov, 1961

Four Color 1232 5 10 15 30 48 65

ON THE ROAD TO PERDITION (Movie)
DC Comics (Paradox Press): 2003 - Book 3, 2004 ($7.95, 8"x5 1/2", B&W, limited series)

...: Oasis, Book 1-Max Allan Collins-s/José Luis García-López-a/David Beck-c 8.00
...: Sanctuary, Book 2-Max Allan Collins-s/Steve Lieber-a/José Luis García-López-c 8.00
...: Detour, Book 3-Max Allan Collins-s/José Luis García-López-a/Steve Lieber-c/a(i) 8.00
Road to Perdition 2: On the Road (2004, $14.95) r/series; Collins intro. 15.00

ON THE ROAD WITH ANDRAE CROUCH
Spire Christian Comics (Fleming H. Revell): 1973, 1974 (39¢)

nn-1973 Edition 2 4 6 8 11 14
nn-1974 Edition 1 3 4 6 8 10

ON THE SCENE PRESENTS:...
Warren Publishing Co.: Oct, 1966 - No. 2, 1967 (B&W magazine, two #1 issues)

#1 "Super Heroes" (68 pgs.) Batman 1966 movie photo-c/s; has articles/photos/comic art from serials on Superman, Flash Gordon, Capt. America, Capt. Marvel and The Phantom
4 8 12 28 44 60
#1 "Freak Out, USA" (Fall/1966, 60 pgs.) (lower print run) articles on musicians like Zappa, Jefferson Airplane, Supremes 5 10 15 30 48 65
#2 "Freak Out, USA" (2/67, 52 pgs.) Beatles, Country Joe, Doors/Jim Morrison, Bee Gees
5 10 15 30 48 65

ON THE SPOT (Pretty Boy Floyd...)
Fawcett Publications: Fall, 1948

nn-Pretty Boy Floyd photo on-c; bondage-c 34 68 102 198 319 440

ONYX OVERLORD
Marvel Comics (Epic): Oct, 1992 - No. 4, Jan, 1993 ($2.75, mini-series)

1-4: Moebius scripts 2.75

OPEN SPACE
Marvel Comics: Mid-Dec, 1989 - No. 4, Aug, 1990 ($4.95, bi-monthly, 68 pgs.)

1-4: 1-Bill Wray-a; Freas-c 5.00
0-(1999) Wizard supplement; unpubl. early Alex Ross-a; new Ross-c 2.50

OPERATION BIKINI (See Movie Classics)

OPERATION BUCHAREST (See The Crusaders)

OPERATION CROSSBOW (See Movie Classics)

OPERATION: KNIGHTSTRIKE (See Knightstrike)
Image Comics (Extreme Studios): May, 1995 - No.3, July, 1995 ($2.50)

1-3 2.50

OPERATION PERIL
American Comics Group (Michel Publ.): Oct-Nov, 1950 - No. 16, Apr-May, 1953 (#1-5: 52 pgs.)

1-Time Travelers, Danny Danger (by Leonard Starr) & Typhoon Tyler (by Ogden Whitney) begin 40 80 120 235 380 525
2-War-c 23 46 69 133 214 295
3-War-c; horror story 20 40 60 118 189 260
4,5-Sci/fi-c/story 23 46 69 133 214 295
6-10: 6,8,9,10-Sci/fi-c. 6-Dinosaur-c. 7-Sabretooth-c 20 40 60 115 183 250
11,12-War-c; last Time Travelers 14 28 42 80 115 150
13-16: All war format 10 20 30 56 76 95

NOTE: *Starr a-2, 5. Whitney a-1, 2, 5-10, 12; c-1, 3, 5, 8, 9.*

OPERATION: STORMBREAKER
Acclaim Comics (Valiant Heroes): Aug, 1997 ($3.95, one-shot)

1-Waid/Augustyn-s, Braithwaite-a 4.00

OPTIC NERVE
Drawn and Quarterly: Apr, 1995 - Present ($2.95-$3.95, bi-annual)

1-7: Adrian Tomine-c/a/scripts in all 3.00
8-11: 8-($3.50). 9-11-($3.95) 4.00
32 Stories-($9.95, trade paperback)-r/Optic Nerve mini-comics 10.00
32 Stories-($29.95, hardcover)-r/Optic Nerve mini-comics; signed & numbered 30.00

ORAL ROBERTS' TRUE STORIES (Junior Partners #120 on)
TelePix Publ. (Oral Roberts' Evangelistic Assoc./Healing Waters): 1956 (no month) - No. 119, 7/59 (15¢)(No. 102: 25¢)

V1#1(1956)-(Not code approved)- "The Miracle Touch"
19 38 57 109 172 235
102-(Only issue approved by code, 10/56) "Now I See"
13 26 39 74 105 135
103-119: 115-(114 on inside) 10 20 30 54 72 90

NOTE: *Also see Happiness & Healing For You.*

ORANGE BIRD, THE
Walt Disney Educational Media Co.: No date (1980) (36 pgs.; in color; slick cover)

nn-Included with educational kit on foods, ...in Nutrition Adventures nn (1980) ...and the Nutrition Know-How Revue nn (1983) 3.00

ORB (Magazine)

The Order #9 © MAR

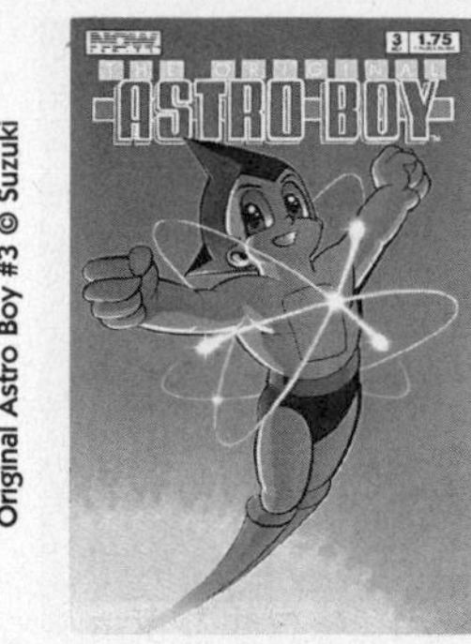

Original Astro Boy #3 © Suzuki

Oscar Comics #7 © MAR

	GD 2.0	VG 4.0	FN 6.0	VF 8.0	VF/NM 9.0	NM- 9.2

Orb Publishing: 1974 - No. 6, Mar/Apr 1976 (B&W/color)

	GD	VG	FN	VF	VF/NM	NM-
1-1st app. Northern Light & Kadaver, both series begin	5	10	15	30	48	65
2,3 (72 pgs.)	3	6	9	16	22	28
4-6 (60 pgs.): 4,5-origin Northern Light	2	4	6	10	14	18

NOTE: ***Allison** a-1-3. **Gene Day** a-1-6. **P. Hsu** a-4-6. **Steacy** s/a-3,4.*

ORBIT
Eclipse Books: 1990 - No. 3, 1990 ($4.95, 52 pgs., squarebound)

1-3: Reprints from Isaac Asimov's Science Fiction Magazine; 1-Dave Stevens-c, Bolton-a. 3-Bolton-c/a, Yeates-a — 5.00

ORBITER
DC Comics (Vertigo): 2003 ($24.95, hardcover with dust jacket)

HC-Warren Ellis-s/Colleen Doran-a — 25.00
SC-(2004, $17.95) Warren Ellis-s/Colleen Doran-a — 18.00

ORDER, THE (cont'd from Defenders V2#12)
Marvel Comics: Apr, 2002 - No. 6, Sept, 2002 ($2.25, limited series)

1-6: 1-Haley-a/Duffy & Busiek-s. 3-Avengers-c/app. 4-Jurgens-a — 2.50

ORDER, THE (The Initiative following Civil War)
Marvel Comics: Sept, 2007 - No. 10, Jun, 2008 ($2.99)

1-10-California's Initiative team; Fraction-s/Kitson-a/c — 3.00
... Vol. 1: The Next Right Thing TPB (2008, $14.99) r/#1-7 — 15.00

ORIENTAL HEROES
Jademan Comics: Aug, 1988 - No. 55, Feb, 1993 ($1.50/$1.95, 68 pgs.)

1,55 — 2.50
2-54 — 2.50

ORIGINAL ADVENTURES OF CHOLLY & FLYTRAP, THE
Image Comics: Feb, 2006 - No. 2, June, 2006 ($5.99, limited series)

1,2-Arthur Suydam-s/a; interview with Suydam and art pages — 6.00

ORIGINAL ASTRO BOY, THE
Now Comics: Sept, 1987 - No. 20, Jun, 1989 ($1.50/$1.75)

1-20-All have Ken Steacy painted-c/a — 3.00

ORIGINAL BLACK CAT, THE
Recollections: Oct. 6, 1988 - No. 9, 1992 ($2.00, limited series)

1-9: Elias-r; 1-Bondage-c. 2-Murphy Anderson-c — 4.00

ORIGINAL DICK TRACY, THE
Gladstone Publishing: Sept, 1990 - No. 5, 1991 ($1.95, bi-monthly, 68pgs.)

1-5: 1-Vs. Pruneface. 2-& the Evil influence; begin $2.00-c — 2.50

NOTE: *#1 reprints strips 7/16/43 - 9/30/43. #2 reprints strips 12/1/46 - 2/2/47. #3 reprints 8/31/46 - 11/14/46. #4 reprints 9/17/45 - 12/23/45. #5 reprints 6/10/46 - 8/28/46.*

ORIGINAL DOCTOR SOLAR, MAN OF THE ATOM, THE
Valiant: Apr, 1995 ($2.95, one-shot)

1-Reprints Doctor Solar, Man of the Atom #1,5; Bob Fugitani-r; Paul Smith-c; afterword by Seaborn Adamson — 4.00

ORIGINAL E-MAN AND MICHAEL MAUSER, THE
First Comics: Oct, 1985 - No. 7, April, 1986 ($1.75, Baxter paper)

1-7: 1-Has r-/Charlton's E-Man, Vengeance Squad. 2-Shows #4 in indicia by mistake. 7-($2.00, 44pgs.)-Staton-a — 2.50

ORIGINAL GHOST RIDER, THE
Marvel Comics: July, 1992 - No. 20, Feb, 1994 ($1.75)

1-20: 1-7-r/Marvel Spotlight #5-11 by Ploog w/new-c. 3-New Phantom Rider (former Night Rider) back-ups begin by Ayers. 4-Quesada-c(p). 8-Ploog-c. 8,9-r/Ghost Rider #1,2. 10-r/Marvel Spotlight #12. 11-18,20-r/Ghost Rider #3-12. 19-r/Marvel Two-in-One #8 — 2.50

ORIGINAL GHOST RIDER RIDES AGAIN, THE
Marvel Comics: July, 1991 - No. 7, Jan, 1992, ($1.50, limited series, 52 pgs.)

1-7: 1-r/Ghost Rider #68(origin),69 w/covers. 2-7: R/ G.R. #70-81 w/covers — 2.50

ORIGINAL MAGNUS ROBOT FIGHTER, THE
Valiant: Apr, 1995 ($2.95, one-shot)

1-Reprints Magnus, Robot Fighter 4000 #2; Russ Manning-r; Rick Leonardi-c; afterword by Seaborn Adamson — 4.00

ORIGINAL NEXUS GRAPHIC NOVEL (See First Comics Graphic Novel #19)

ORIGINALS, THE
DC Comics (Vertigo): 2004 ($24.95/$17.99, B&W graphic novel)

HC (2004, $24.95) Dave Gibbons-s/a — 25.00
SC (2005, $17.99) — 18.00

ORIGINAL SHIELD, THE
Archie Enterprises, Inc.: Apr, 1984 - No. 4, Oct, 1984

1-4: 1,2-Origin Shield; Ayers p-1-4, Nebres c-1,2 — 4.00

ORIGINAL SWAMP THING SAGA, THE (See DC Special Series #2, 14, 17, 20)

ORIGINAL TUROK, SON OF STONE, THE
Valiant: Apr, 1995 - No. 2, May, 1995 ($2.95, limited series)

1,2: 1-Reprints Turok, Son of Stone #24,25,42; Alberto Gioletti-r; Rags Morales-c; afterword by Seaborn Adamson. 2-Reprints Turok, Son of Stone #24,33; Gioletti-r; McKone-c — 4.00

ORIGIN OF GALACTUS (See Fantastic Four #48-50)
Marvel Comics: Feb, 1996 ($2.50, one-shot)

1-Lee & Kirby reprints w/pin-ups — 2.50

ORIGIN OF THE DEFIANT UNIVERSE, THE
Defiant Comics: Feb, 1994 ($1.50, 20 pgs., one-shot)

1-David Lapham, Adam Pollina & Alan Weiss-a; Weiss-c — 5.00

NOTE: *The comic was originally published as Defiant Genesis and was distributed at the 1994 Philadelphia ComicCon.*

ORIGINS OF MARVEL COMICS (See Fireside Book Series)

ORION (Manga)
Dark Horse Comics: Sept, 1992 - No. 6, July, 1993 ($2.95/$3.95, B&W, bimonthly, lim. series)

1-6:1,2,6-Squarebound): 1-Masamune Shirow-c/a/s in all — 4.00

ORION (See New Gods)
DC Comics: June, 2000 - No. 25, June, 2002 ($2.50)

1-14-Simonson-s/a. 3-Back-up story w/Miller-a. 4-Gibbons-a back-up. 7-Chaykin back-up. 8-Loeb/Liefeld back-up. 10-A. Adams back-up-a 12-Jim Lee back-up-a. 13-JLA-c/app.; Byrne-a — 2.50
15-($3.95) Black Racer app.; back-up story w/J.P. Leon-a — 4.00
16-24-Simonson-s/a: 19-Joker: Last Laugh x-over — 2.50
25-($3.95) Last issue; Mister Miracle-c/app. — 4.00
The Gates of Apocalypse (2001, $12.95, TPB) r/#1-5 & various short-s — 13.00

ORORO: BEFORE THE STORM (Storm from X-Men)
Marvel Comics: Aug, 2005 - No. 4, Nov, 2005 ($2.99, limited series)

1-4-Barberi-a/Sumerak-s; young Storm in Egypt — 3.00
... Digest (2006, $6.99) r/#1-4 — 7.00

OSBORNE JOURNALS (See Spider-Man titles)
Marvel Comics: Feb, 1997 ($2.95, one-shot)

1-Hotz-c/a — 3.00

OSCAR COMICS (Formerly Funny Tunes; Awful...#11 & 12) (Also see Cindy Comics)
Marvel Comics: No. 24, Spring, 1947 - No. 10, Apr, 1949; No. 13, Oct, 1949

	GD	VG	FN	VF	VF/NM	NM-
24(#1, Spring, 1947)	18	36	54	107	169	230
25(#2, Sum, 1947)-Wolverton-a plus Kurtzman's "Hey Look"	20	40	60	115	183	250
26(#3)-Same as regular #3 except #26 was printed over in black ink with #3 appearing on-c below the over print	14	28	42	76	108	140
3-9,13: 8-Margie app.	14	28	42	76	108	140
10-Kurtzman's "Hey Look"	14	28	42	82	121	160

OSWALD THE RABBIT (Also see New Fun Comics #1)
Dell Publishing Co.: No. 21, 1943 - No. 1268, 12-2/61-62 (Walter Lantz)

	GD	VG	FN	VF	VF/NM	NM-
Four Color 21(1943)	42	84	126	336	631	925
Four Color 39(1943)	29	58	87	213	394	575
Four Color 67(1944)	17	34	51	120	223	325
Four Color 102(1946)-Kelly-a, 1 pg.	14	28	42	102	181	260
Four Color 143,183	9	18	27	63	107	150
Four Color 225,273	7	14	21	45	73	100
Four Color 315,388	6	12	18	39	62	85
Four Color 458,507,549,593	5	10	15	32	51	70
Four Color 623,697,792,894,979,1268	4	8	12	28	44	60

OSWALD THE RABBIT (See The Funnies, March of Comics #7, 38, 53, 67, 81, 95, 111, 126, 141, 156, 171, 186, New Funnies & Super Book #8, 20)

OTHER SIDE, THE
DC Comics (Vertigo): Dec, 2006 - No. 5, Apr, 2007 ($2.99, limited series)

1-5-Soldiers from both sides of the Vietnam War; Aaron-s/Stewart-a/c — 3.00
TPB (2007, $12.99) r/#1-5; sketch pages, Stewart's travelogue to Saigon — 13.00

OTHERWORLD
DC Comics (Vertigo): May, 2005 - No. 7, Nov, 2005 ($2.99)

1-7-Phil Jimenez-s/a(p) — 3.00
...: Book One TPB (2006, $19.99) r/#1-7; cover gallery — 20.00

Our Army at War #125 © DC

Our Army at War #280 © DC

Our Fighting Forces #4 © DC

OUR ARMY AT WAR (Becomes Sgt. Rock #302 on; also see Army At War)
National Periodical Publications: Aug, 1952 - No. 301, Feb, 1977

	GD 2.0	VG 4.0	FN 6.0	VF 8.0	VF/NM 9.0	NM- 9.2
1	152	304	456	1330	2565	3800
2	69	138	207	587	1119	1650
3,4: 4-Krigstein-a	50	100	150	425	813	1200
5-7	43	86	129	344	642	940
8-11,14-Krigstein-a	40	80	120	318	597	875
12,15-20	35	70	105	270	498	725
13-Krigstein-c/a; flag-c	41	82	123	328	614	900
21-31: Last precode (2/55)	24	48	72	179	332	485
32-40	20	40	60	143	264	385
41-60: 51-1st S.A. issue	17	34	51	126	233	340
61-70: 61-(8/57) Pre-Sgt. Rock Easy Co.-c/s. 67-Minor Sgt. Rock prototype						
	15	30	45	108	199	290
71-80	14	28	42	100	178	255
81-(4/59)-Sgt. Rocky of Easy Co. app. by Andru & Esposito-a/ Haney-s;						
(the last Sgt. Rock prototype)	220	440	660	1925	3713	5500
82-1st Sgt. Rock app., in name only, in Easy Co. story (6 panels) by Kanigher & Drucker						
	56	112	168	476	913	1350
83-(6/59)-1st true Sgt. Rock app. in "The Rock and the Wall" by Kubert & Kanigher;						
(most similar to prototype in G.I. Combat #68)	180	360	540	1575	3038	4500
84-Kubert-c	35	70	105	270	408	725
85-Origin & 1st app. Ice Cream Soldier	40	80	120	321	603	885
86,87-Early Sgt. Rock; Kubert-a	32	64	96	250	468	685
88-1st Sgt. Rock-c; Kubert-c/a	40	80	120	312	581	850
89	29	58	87	213	394	575
90-Kubert-c/a; How Rock got his stripes	37	74	111	284	530	775
91-All-Sgt. Rock issue; Grandenetti-c/Kubert-a	73	146	219	621	1186	1750
92,94,96-99: 97-Regular Kubert-c begin	19	38	57	139	257	375
93-1st Zack Nolan	20	40	60	145	268	390
95,100: 95-1st app. Bulldozer	20	40	60	148	274	400
101,105,108,113,115: 101-1st app. Buster. 105-1st app. Junior. 113-1st app. Wildman & Jackie Johnson. 115-Rock revealed as orphan; 1st x-over Mlle. Marie. 1st Sgt. Rock's battle family						
	15	30	45	111	206	300
102-104,106,107,109,110,114,116-120: 104-Nurse Jane-c/s. 109-Pre Easy Co. Sgt. Rock-s.						
118-Sunny injured	14	28	42	103	184	265
111-1st app. Wee Willie & Sunny	18	36	54	130	240	350
112-Classic Easy Co. roster-c	20	40	60	148	274	400
121-125,130-133,135-139,141-150: 138-1st Sparrow. 141-1st Shaker.						
147,148-Rock becomes a General	10	20	30	70	123	175
126-1st app. Canary; grey tone-c	11	22	33	79	140	200
127-2nd all-Sgt. Rock issue; 1st app. Little Sure Shot	15	30	45	105	190	275
128-Training & origin Sgt. Rock; 1st Sgt. Krupp	30	60	90	222	411	600
129,134	10	20	30	73	129	185
140-3rd all-Sgt. Rock issue	12	24	36	87	156	225
151-Intro. Enemy Ace by Kubert (2/65), black-c	39	78	117	300	563	825
152-4th all-Sgt. Rock issue	11	22	33	79	140	200
153-2nd app. Enemy Ace (4/65)	17	34	51	124	230	335
154,156,157,159-161,165-167: 157-2 pg. pin-up: 159-1st Nurse Wendy Winston-c/s.						
165-2nd Iron Major	8	16	24	54	90	125
155-3rd app. Enemy Ace (6/65)(see Showcase)	13	26	39	93	164	235
158-Origin & 1st app. Iron Major(9/65), formerly Iron Captain						
	9	18	27	64	110	155
162,163-Viking Prince x-over in Sgt. Rock	9	18	27	61	103	145
164-Giant G-19	14	28	42	102	181	260
168-1st Unknown Soldier app.; referenced in Star-Spangled War Stories #157;						
(Sgt. Rock x-over) (6/66)	14	28	42	99	175	250
169,170	7	14	21	47	76	105
171-176,178-181: 171-1st Mad Emperor	6	12	18	43	69	95
177-(80 pg. Giant G-32)	9	18	27	63	107	150
182,183,186-Neal Adams-a. 186-Origin retold	7	14	21	47	76	105
184-Wee Willie dies	8	16	24	54	90	125
185,187,188,193-195,197-199	6	12	18	37	59	80
189,191,192,196: 189-Intro. The Teen-age Underground Fighters of Unit 3. 196-Hitler cameo						
	6	12	18	39	62	85
190-(80 pg. Giant G-44)	7	14	21	50	83	115
200-12 pg. Rock story told in verse; Evans-a	6	12	18	41	66	90
201,202,204-207: 201-Krigstein-r/#14. 204,205-All reprints; no Sgt. Rock. 207-Last 12¢ cover						
	4	8	12	26	41	55
203-(80 pg. Giant G-56)-All-r, Sgt. Rock story	6	12	18	43	69	95
208-215	3	6	9	20	30	40
216,229-(80 pg. Giants G-68, G-80): 216-Has G-58 on-c by mistake						
	6	12	18	39	62	85
217-219: 218-1st U.S.S. Stevens	3	6	9	18	27	35
220-Classic dinosaur/Sgt. Rock-c/s	3	6	9	20	30	40
221-228,230-234: 231-Intro/death Rock's brother. 234-Last 15¢ issue						
	3	6	9	16	22	28
235-239,241: 52 pg. Giants	3	6	9	20	30	40
240-Neal Adams-a; 52 pg. Giant	4	8	12	26	41	55
242-Also listed as **DC 100 Page Super Spectacular #9**; see for price						
243-246: (All 52 pgs.) 244-No Adams-a	3	6	9	19	29	38
247-250,254-268,270: 247-Joan of Arc	2	4	6	11	16	20
251-253-Return of Iron Major	3	6	9	14	19	24
269,275-(100 pgs.)	4	8	12	28	44	60
271-274,276-279: 273-Crucifixion-c	2	4	6	10	14	18
280-(68 pgs.)-200th app. Sgt. Rock; reprints Our Army at War #81,83						
	3	6	9	18	27	35
281-299,301: 295-Bicentennial cover	2	4	6	9	13	16
300-Sgt. Rock-s by Kubert (2/77)	2	4	6	11	16	20

NOTE ***Alcala*** *a-251.* ***Drucker*** *a-27, 67, 68, 79, 82, 83, 96, 164, 177, 203, 212, 243r, 244, 269r, 275r, 280r.* ***Evans*** *a-165-175, 200, 266, 269, 270, 274, 276, 278, 280.* ***Glanzman*** *a-218, 220, 222, 223, 225, 227, 230-232, 238-241, 244, 247, 248, 256-259, 261, 265-267, 271, 282, 283, 298.* ***Grandenetti*** *c-91,120.* ***Grell*** *a-287.* ***Heath*** *a-50, 164, & most 176-281.* ***Kubert*** *a-38, 59, 67, 68 & most issues from 83-165, 171, 233, 236, 267, 275, 300; c-84, 280.* ***Maurer*** *a-233, 237, 239, 240, 45, 280, 284, 288, 290, 291, 295.* ***Severin*** *a-236, 252, 265, 267, 269r, 272.* ***Toth*** *a-235, 241, 254.* ***Wildey*** *a-283-285, 287p.* ***Wood*** *a-249.*

OUR FIGHTING FORCES
National Per. Publ./DC Comics: Oct-Nov, 1954 - No. 181, Sept-Oct, 1978

	GD 2.0	VG 4.0	FN 6.0	VF 8.0	VF/NM 9.0	NM- 9.2
1-Grandenetti-c/a	104	208	312	884	1692	2500
2	43	86	129	344	642	940
3-Kubert-c; last precode issue (3/55)	36	72	108	276	508	740
4,5	30	60	90	217	404	590
6-9: 7-1st S.A. issue	24	48	72	179	332	485
10-Wood-a	25	50	75	184	340	495
11-19	21	42	63	152	281	410
20-Grey tone-c (4/57)	27	54	81	197	366	535
21-30	16	32	48	114	212	310
31-40	15	30	45	106	193	280
41-Unknown Soldier tryout	17	34	51	124	230	335
42-44	14	28	42	102	181	260
45-Gunner & Sarge begins, end #94	41	82	123	328	614	900
46	17	34	51	124	230	335
47	14	28	42	102	181	260
48,50	12	24	36	87	156	225
49-1st Pooch	16	32	48	114	212	310
51-Grey tone-c	15	30	45	105	190	275
52-64: 64-Last 10¢ issue	10	20	30	68	119	170
65-70	8	16	24	54	90	125
71-Grey tone-c	10	20	30	67	116	165
72-80	7	14	21	47	76	105
81-90	6	12	18	39	62	85
91-98: 95-Devil-Dog begins, ends #98.	5	10	15	30	48	65
99-Capt. Hunter begins, ends #106	5	10	15	32	51	70
100	5	10	15	32	51	70
101-105,107-120: 116-Mlle. Marie app. 120-Last 12¢ issue						
	4	8	12	24	37	50
106-Hunters Hellcats begin	4	8	12	26	41	55
121,122: 121-Intro. Heller	3	6	9	21	32	42
123-The Losers (Capt. Storm, Gunner & Sarge, Johnny Cloud) begin						
	6	12	18	43	69	95
124-132: 132-Last 15¢ issue	3	6	9	16	23	30
133-137 (Giants). 134-Toth-a	3	6	9	19	29	38
138-145,147-150	2	4	6	11	16	20
146-Classic "Burma Sky" story; Toth-a/Goodwin-s	3	6	9	14	19	24
151-162-Kirby a(p)	3	6	9	14	20	26
163-180	2	4	6	9	13	16
181-Last issue	2	4	6	11	16	20

NOTE: ***N. Adams*** *c-147.* ***Drucker*** *a-28, 37, 39, 42-44, 49, 53, 133r.* ***Evans*** *a-149, 164-174, 177-181.* ***Glanzman*** *a-125-128, 132, 134, 138-141, 143, 144.* ***Heath*** *a-2, 16, 18, 28, 41, 44, 49, 114, 135-138r; c-51.* ***Kirby*** *a-151-162p; c-152-159.* ***Kubert*** *c/a in many issues.* ***Maurer*** *a-135.* ***Redondo*** *a-166.* ***Severin*** *a-123-130, 131i, 132-150.*

OUR FIGHTING MEN IN ACTION (See Men In Action)

OUR FLAG COMICS
Ace Magazines: Aug, 1941 - No. 5, April, 1942

	GD 2.0	VG 4.0	FN 6.0	VF 8.0	VF/NM 9.0	NM- 9.2
1-Captain Victory, The Unknown Soldier (intro.) & The Three Cheers begin						
	257	514	771	1619	2735	3850
2-Origin The Flag (patriotic hero); 1st app?	110	220	330	693	1172	1650
3-5: 5-Intro & 1st app. Mr. Risk	83	166	249	523	887	1250

NOTE: ***Anderson*** *a-1, 4.* ***Mooney*** *a-1, 2; c-2.*

OUR GANG COMICS (With Tom & Jerry #39-59; becomes Tom & Jerry #60 on;

Our Gang Comics #7 © Loew's Inc.

Outer Space #23 © CC

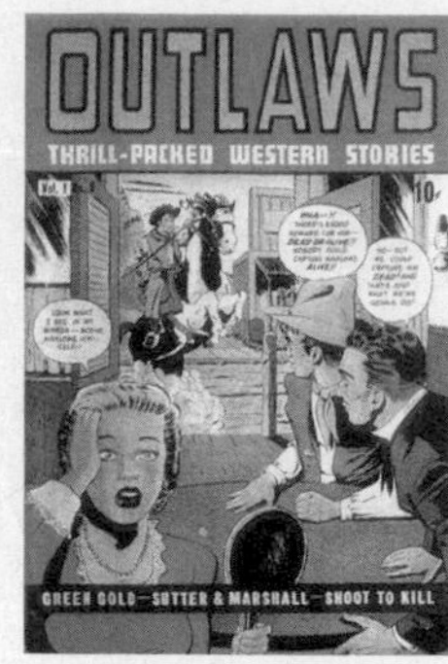

Outlaws #9 © DS

based on film characters)
Dell Publishing Co.: Sept-Oct, 1942 - No. 59, June, 1949

1-Our Gang & Barney Bear by Kelly, Tom & Jerry, Pete Smith, Flip & Dip, The Milky Way begin (all 1st app.) 70 140 210 595 1135 1675
2-Benny Burro begins (#2 by Kelly) 37 74 111 284 530 775
3-5 26 52 78 187 349 510
6-Bumbazine & Albert only app. by Kelly 34 68 102 260 485 710
7-No Kelly story 19 38 57 139 257 375
8-Benny Burro begins by Barks 43 86 129 344 647 950
9-Barks-a(2): Benny Burro & Happy Hound; no Kelly story
40 80 120 308 574 840
10-Benny Burro by Barks 30 60 90 222 411 600
11-1st Barney Bear & Benny Burro by Barks (5-6/44); Happy Hound by Barks
40 80 120 308 574 840
12-20 19 38 57 135 250 365
21-30: 30-X-Mas-c 14 28 42 100 178 255
31-36-Last Barks issue 11 22 33 77 136 195
37-40 8 16 24 52 86 120
41-50 7 14 21 45 73 100
51-57 6 12 18 41 66 90
58,59-No Kelly art or Our Gang stories 6 12 18 37 59 80
Our Gang Volume 1 (Fantagraphics Books, 2006, $12.95, TPB) r/Our Gang stories written and by Walt Kelly from #1-8; Leonard Maltin intro.; Jeff Smith-c 13.00
Our Gang Volume 2 (Fantagraphics Books, 2007, $12.95, TPB) r/Our Gang stories written and by Walt Kelly from #9-15; Steve Thompson intro.; Jeff Smith-c 13.00
Our Gang Volume 3 (Fantagraphics Books, 2008, $14.99, TPB) r/Our Gang stories written and by Walt Kelly from #16-23; Steve Thompson intro.; Jeff Smith-c 15.00
NOTE: ***Barks** art in part only. **Barks** did not write Barney Bear stories #30-34. (See March of Comics #3, 26). Early issues have photo back-c.*

OUR LADY OF FATIMA
Catechetical Guild Educational Society: 3/11/55 (15¢) (36 pgs.)
395 6 12 18 28 34 40

OUR LOVE (True Secrets #3 on? or Romantic Affairs #3 on?)
Marvel Comics (SPC): Sept, 1949 - No. 2, Jan, 1950
1-Photo-c 15 30 45 90 140 190
2-Photo-c 11 22 33 62 86 110

OUR LOVE STORY
Marvel Comics Group: Oct, 1969 - No. 38, Feb, 1976
1 7 14 21 45 73 100
2-4,6-8,10,11 4 8 12 22 34 45
5-Steranko-a 9 18 27 61 103 145
9,12-Kirby-a 4 8 12 24 37 50
13-(10/71, 52 pgs.) 4 8 12 28 44 60
14-New story by Gary Fredrich & Tarpe' Mills 4 8 12 24 37 50
15-20,27:27-Colan/Everett-a(r?); Kirby/Colletta-r 3 6 9 17 25 32
21-26,28-37 3 6 9 14 20 26
38-Last issue 3 6 9 18 27 35
NOTE: ***J. Buscema** a-1-3, 5-7, 9, 13r, 16r, 19r(2), 21r, 22r(2), 23r, 34r, 35r; c-11, 13, 16, 22, 23, 24, 27, 35. **Colan** a-3-6, 21r(#6), 22r, 23r(#3), 24r(#4), 27; c-19. **Katz** a-17. **Maneely** a-13r. **Romita** a-13r; c-1, 2, 4-6. **Weiss** a-16, 17, 29r(#17).*

OUR MEN AT WAR
DC Comics: Aug/Sept 1952
nn - Ashcan comic, not distributed to newsstands, only for in-house use. Cover art is All Star Western #60 with interior being Detective Comics #181 (no known sales)

OUR MISS BROOKS
Dell Publishing Co.: No. 751, Nov, 1956
Four Color 751-Photo-c 7 14 21 50 83 115

OUR SECRET (Exciting Love Stories)(Formerly My Secret)
Superior Comics Ltd.: No. 4, Nov, 1949 - No. 8, Jun, 1950
4-Kamen-a; spanking scene 18 36 54 107 169 230
5,6,8 11 22 33 64 90 115
7-Contains 9 pg. story intended for unpublished Ellery Queen #5; lingerie panels
12 24 36 69 97 125

OUTBREED 999
Blackout Comics: May, 1994 - No. 6, 1994 ($2.95)
1-6: 4-1st app. of Extreme Violet in 7 pg. backup story 3.00

OUTCAST, THE
Valiant: Dec, 1995 ($2.50, one-shot)
1-Breyfogle-a. 2.50

OUTCASTS
DC Comics: Oct, 1987 - No. 12, Sept, 1988 ($1.75, limited series)
1-12: John Wagner & Alan Grant scripts in all 2.50

OUTER LIMITS, THE (TV)
Dell Publishing Co.: Jan-Mar, 1964 - No. 18, Oct, 1969 (Most painted-c)
1 12 24 36 86 153 220
2-5 7 14 21 49 80 110
6-10 6 12 18 41 66 90
11-18: 17-Reprints #1. 18-r/#2 5 10 15 34 55 75

OUTER SPACE (Formerly This Magazine Is Haunted, 2nd Series)
Charlton Comics: No. 17, May, 1958 - No. 25, Dec, 1959; Nov, 1968
17-Williamson/Wood style art; not by them (Sid Check?)
14 28 42 80 115 150
18-20-Ditko-a 23 46 69 133 214 295
21-Ditko-c 17 34 51 98 154 210
22-25 14 28 42 80 115 150
V2#1(11/68)-Ditko-a, Boyette-c 5 10 15 32 51 70

OUT FOR BLOOD
Dark Horse: Sept, 1999 - No. 4, Dec, 1999 ($2.95, B&W, limited series)
1-4-Kelley Jones-c; Erskine-a 3.00

OUTLANDERS (Manga)
Dark Horse Comics: Dec, 1988 - No. 33, Sept,1991 ($2.00-$2.50, B&W, 44 pgs.)
1-33: Japanese Sci-fi manga 2.50

OUTLAW (See Return of the...)

OUTLAW FIGHTERS
Atlas Comics (IPC): Aug, 1954 - No. 5, Apr, 1955
1-Tuska-a 14 28 42 76 108 140
2-5: 5-Heath-c/a, 7 pgs. 9 18 27 50 65 80
NOTE: ***Heath** c/a-5. **Maneely** c-2. **Pakula** a-2. **Reinman** a-2. **Tuska** a-1, 2.*

OUTLAW KID, THE (1st Series; see Wild Western)
Atlas Comics (CCC No. 1-11/EPI No. 12-29): Sept, 1954 - No. 19, Sept, 1957
1-Origin; The Outlaw Kid & his horse Thunder begin; Black Rider app.
27 54 81 158 254 350
2-Black Rider app. 14 28 42 80 115 150
3-7,9: 3-Wildey-a(3) 12 24 36 69 97 125
8-Williamson/Woodbridge-a, 4 pgs. 13 26 39 74 105 135
10-Williamson-a 13 26 39 74 105 135
11-17,19: 13-Baker text illo. 15-Williamson text illo (unsigned)
9 18 27 52 69 85
18-Williamson/Mayo-a 10 20 30 56 76 95
NOTE: ***Berg** a-4, 7, 13. **Maneely** c-1-3, 5-8, 11-13, 15, 16, 18. **Pakula** a-3. **Severin** c-10, 17, 19. **Shores** a-1. **Wildey** a-1(3), 2-8, 10, 11, 12(4), 13(4), 15-19(4 each); c-4.*

OUTLAW KID, THE (2nd Series)
Marvel Comics Group: Aug, 1970 - No. 30, Oct, 1975
1-Reprints; 1-Orlando-r, Wildey-r(3) 3 6 9 19 29 38
2,3,9: 2-Reprints. 3,9-Williamson-a(r) 2 4 6 11 16 20
4-7: 7-Last 15¢ issue 2 4 6 10 14 18
8-Double size (52 pgs.); Crandall-r 3 6 9 16 23 30
10-Origin 3 6 9 19 29 38
11-20: new-a in #10-16 2 4 6 11 16 20
21-30: 27-Origin-r/#10 2 4 6 8 11 14
NOTE: ***Ayers** a-10, 27r. **Berg** a-7, 25r. **Everett** a-2(2 pgs.). **Gil Kane** c-10, 11, 15, 27r, 28. **Roussos** a-10i, 27i(r). **Severin** c-1, 9, 20, 25. **Wildey** r-1-4, 6-9, 19-22, 25, 26. **Williamson** a-28r. **Woodbridge/Williamson** a-9r.*

OUTLAW NATION
DC Comics (Vertigo): Nov, 2000 - No. 19, May, 2002 ($2.50)
1-19-Fabry painted-c/Delano-s/Sudzuka-a 2.50
TPB (Image Comics, 11/06, $15.99) B&W reprint of #1-19; Delano intro. 16.00

OUTLAWS
D. S. Publishing Co.: Feb-Mar, 1948 - No. 9, June-July, 1949
1-Violent & suggestive stories 34 68 102 198 319 440
2-Ingels-a; Baker-a 34 68 102 198 319 440
3,5,6: 3-Not Frazetta. 5-Sky Sheriff by Good app. 6-McWilliams-a
15 30 45 92 144 195
4-Orlando-a 17 34 51 98 154 210
7,8-Ingels-a in each 24 48 72 143 229 315
9-(Scarce)-Frazetta-a (7 pgs.) 47 94 141 291 483 675
NOTE: *Another #3 was printed in Canada with **Frazetta** art "Prairie Jinx," 7 pgs.*

OUTLAWS, THE (Formerly Western Crime Cases)

Out of the Shadows #7 © STD

Outsiders #50 © DC

Out There #1 © Ramos & Augustyn

	GD 2.0	VG 4.0	FN 6.0	VF 8.0	VF/NM 9.0	NM- 9.2

Star Publishing Co.: No. 10, May, 1952 - No. 13, Sep, 1953; No. 14, Apr, 1954

10-L. B. Cole-c 21 42 63 123 197 270
11-14-L. B. Cole-c. 14-Reprints Western Thrillers #4 (Fox) w/new L.B. Cole-c; Kamen, Feldstein-r 16 32 48 92 144 195

OUTLAWS
DC Comics: Sept, 1991 - No. 8, Apr, 1992 ($1.95, limited series)

1-8: Post-apocalyptic Robin Hood. 2.50

OUTLAWS OF THE WEST (Formerly Cody of the Pony Express #10)
Charlton Comics: No. 11, 7/57 - No. 81, 5/70; No. 82, 7/79 - No. 88, 4/80

11 8 16 24 44 57 70
12,13,15-17,19,20 6 12 18 27 33 38
14-(68 pgs., 2/58) 9 18 27 50 65 80
18-Ditko-a 10 20 30 56 76 95
21-30 3 6 9 16 23 30
31-50: 34-Gunmaster app. 2 4 6 13 18 22
51-63,65,67-70: 54-Kid Montana app. 2 4 6 10 14 18
64,66: 64-Captain Doom begins (1st app.). 68-Kid Montana series begins 2 4 6 13 18 22
71-79: 73-Origin & 1st app. The Sharp Shooter, last app. #74. 75-Last Capt. Doom 2 4 6 9 12 15
80,81-Ditko-a 2 4 6 13 18 22
82-88 6.00
64,79(Modern Comics-r, 1977, '78) 4.00

OUTLAWS OF THE WILD WEST
Avon Periodicals: 1952 (25¢, 132 pgs.) (4 rebound comics)

1-Wood back-c; Kubert-a (3 Jesse James-r) 34 68 102 198 319 440

OUTLAW TRAIL (See Zane Grey 4-Color 511)

OUT OF SANTA'S BAG (See March of Comics #10 in the Promotional Comics section)

OUT OF THE NIGHT (The Hooded Horseman #18 on)
Amer. Comics Group (Creston/Scope): Feb-Mar, 1952 - No. 17, Oct-Nov, 1954

1-Williamson/LeDoux-a (9 pgs.) 66 132 198 416 701 985
2-Williamson-a (5 pgs.) 47 94 141 291 483 675
3,5-10: 9-Sci/Fic story 29 58 87 169 272 375
4-Williamson-a (7 pgs.) 40 80 120 240 388 535
11-17: 13-Nostrand-a? 17-E.C. Wood swipe 22 44 66 127 204 280
NOTE: *Landau a-14, 16, 17. Shelly a-12.*

OUT OF THE SHADOWS
Standard Comics/Visual Editions: No. 5, July, 1952 - No. 14, Aug, 1954

5-Toth-p; Moreira, Tuska-a; Roussos-c 54 108 162 340 575 810
6-Toth/Celardo-a; Katz-a(2) 40 80 120 235 380 525
7,9: 7-Jack Katz-c/a(2). 9-Crandall-a(2) 32 64 96 186 298 410
8-Katz shrunken head-c 52 104 156 322 536 750
10-Spider-c; Sekowsky-a 32 64 96 186 298 410
11-Toth-a, 2 pgs.; Katz-a; Andru-c 32 64 96 186 298 410
12-Toth/Peppe-a(2); Katz-a 40 80 120 235 380 525
13-Cannabalism story; Sekowsky-a; Roussos-c 37 74 111 219 352 485
14-Toth-a 32 64 96 186 298 410

OUT OF THE VORTEX (Comics' Greatest World:... #1-4)
Dark Horse Comics: Oct., 1993 - No. 12, Oct, 1994 ($2.00, limited series)

1-11: 1-Foil logo. 4-Dorman-c(p). 6-Hero Zero x-over 2.50
12 ($2.50) 2.50
NOTE: *Art Adams c-7. Golden c-8. Mignola c-2. Simonson c-3. Zeck c-10.*

OUT OF THIS WORLD
Charlton Comics: Aug, 1956 - No. 16, Dec, 1959

1 26 52 78 154 247 340
2 15 30 45 83 124 165
3-6-Ditko-c/a (3) each 31 62 93 181 291 400
7-(2/58, 15¢, 68 pgs.)-Ditko-c/a(4) 33 66 99 192 309 425
8-(5/58, 15¢, 68 pgs.)-Ditko-a(2) 29 58 87 169 272 375
9,10,12,16-Ditko-a 22 44 66 129 207 285
11-Ditko c/a (3) 26 52 78 152 244 335
13-15 12 24 36 67 94 120
NOTE: *Ditko c-3-12, 16. Reinman a-10.*

OUT OF THIS WORLD
Avon Periodicals: June, 1950; Aug, 1950

1-Kubert-a(2) (one reprinted/Eerie #1, 1947) plus Crom the Barbarian by Gardner Fox & John Giunta (origin); Fawcette-c 73 146 219 460 780 1100
1-(8/50) Reprint; no month on cover 45 90 135 279 465 650

OUT OF THIS WORLD ADVENTURES
Avon Periodicals: July, 1950 - No. 2, Apr, 1951 (25¢ sci-fi pulp magazine with 32-page color comic insert)

1-Kubert-a(2); Crom the Barbarian by Fox & Giunta; text stories by Cummings, Van Vogt, del Rey, Chandler 67 134 201 422 711 1000
2-Kubert-a plus The Spider God of Akka by Gardner Fox & John Giunta pulp magazine w/comic insert; Wood-a (21 pgs.) 47 94 141 291 483 675

OUT OUR WAY WITH WORRY WART
Dell Publishing Co.: No. 680, Feb, 1956

Four Color 680 4 8 12 24 37 50

OUTPOSTS
Blackthorne Publishing: June, 1987 - No. 4, 1987 ($1.25)

1-4: 1-Kaluta-c(p) 2.50

OUTSIDERS, THE
DC Comics: Nov, 1985 - No. 28, Feb, 1988

1 3.00
2-17 2.50
18-28: 18-26-Batman returns. 21-Intro. Strike Force Kobra; 1st app. Clayface IV 22-E.C. parody; Orlando-a. 21- 25-Atomic Knight app. 27,28-Millennium tie-ins 2.50
Annual 1 (12/86, $2.50), Special 1 (7/87, $1.50) 2.50
NOTE: *Aparo a-1-7, 9-14, 17-22, 25, 26; c-1-7, 9-14, 17, 19-26. Byrne a-11. Bolland a-6, 18; c-16. Ditko a-13p. Erik Larsen a-24, 27 28; c-27, 28. Morrow a-12.*

OUTSIDERS
DC Comics: Nov, 1993 - No. 24, Nov, 1995 ($1.75/$1.95/$2.25)

1-11,0,12-24: 1-Alpha; Travis Charest-c. 1-Omega; Travis Charest-c. 5-Atomic Knight app. 8-New Batman-c/story. 11-(9/94)-Zero Hour. 0-(10/94).12-(11/94). 21-Darkseid cameo. 22-New Gods app. 2.50

OUTSIDERS (See Titans/Young Justice: Graduation Day)(Leads into Batman and the Outsiders)
DC Comics: Aug, 2003 - No. 50, Nov, 2007 ($2.50/$2.99)

1-Nightwing, Arsenal, Metamorpho app.; Winick-s/Raney-a 5.00
2 Joker and Grodd app. 3.00
3-33: 3-Joker-c. 5,6-ChrisCross-a. 8-Huntress app. 9,10-Capt. Marvel Jr. app. 24,25-X-over with Teen Titans. 26,27-Batman & old Outsiders 2.50
34-50: 34-One Year Later. 36-Begin $2.99-c. 37-Superman app. 44-Red Hood app. 3.00
Annual 1 (6/07, $3.99) McDaniel-a; Black Lightning app. 4.00
.../Checkmate: Checkout TPB (2008, $14.99) r/#47-49 & Checkmate #13-15 15.00
... Double Feature (10/03, $4.95) r/#1,2 5.00
...: Crisis Intervention TPB (2006, $12.99) r/#29-33 13.00
...: Looking For Trouble TPB (2004, $12.95) r/#1-7 & Teen Titans/Outsiders Secret Files & Origins 2003; intro. by Winick 13.00
...: Pay As You Go TPB (2007, $14.99) r/#42-46 & Annual #1 15.00
...: Sum of All Evil TPB (2004, $14.95) r/#8-15 15.00
...: The Good Fight TPB (2006, $14.99) r/#34-41 15.00
...: Wanted TPB (2005, $14.99) r/#16-23 15.00

OUTSIDERS: FIVE OF A KIND (Bridges Outsiders #49 & 50)
DC Comics: Oct, 2007 ($2.99, weekly limited series)

...Katana/Shazam! (part 2 of 5) - Barr-s/Sharpe-a 3.00
...Metamorpho/Aquaman (part 4 of 5) - Wilson-s/Middleton-a 3.00
...Nightwing/Captain Boomerang (part 1 of 5) - DeFilippis & Weir-s/Willams-a 3.00
...Thunder/Martian Manhunter (part 3 of 5) - Bedard-s/Turnbull-a; Grayven app. 3.00
...Wonder Woman/Grace (part 5 of 5) - Andreyko-s/Richards-a 3.00
TPB (2008, $14.99) r/series & Outsiders #50 15.00

OUT THERE
DC Comics(Cliffhanger): July, 2001 - No. 18, Aug, 2003 ($2.50/$2.95)

1-Humberto Ramos-c/a; Brian Augustyn-s 3.00
1-Variant-c by Carlos Meglia 4.00
2-8: 3-Variant-c by Bruce Timm 2.50
9-18: 9-Begin $2.95-c 3.00
...: The Evil Within TPB (2002, $12.95) r/#1-6; Ramos sketch pages 13.00

OVERKILL: WITCHBLADE/ ALIENS/ DARKNESS/ PREDATOR
Image Comics/Dark Horse Comics: Dec, 2000 - No. 2, 2001 ($5.95)

1,2-Jenkins-s/Lansing, Ching & Benitez-a 6.00

OVER THE EDGE
Marvel Comics: Nov, 1995 - No. 10, Aug, 1996 (99¢)

1-10: 1,6,10-Daredevil-c/story. 2,7-Dr. Strange-c/story. 3-Hulk-c/story. 4,9-Ghost Rider-c/story. 5-Punisher-c/story. 8-Elektra-c/story 2.50

OWL, THE (See Crackajack Funnies #25, Popular Comics #72 and Occult Files of Dr. Spektor #22)

Ozzie and Harriet #2 © DC

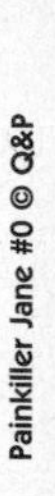

Painkiller Jane #0 © Q&P

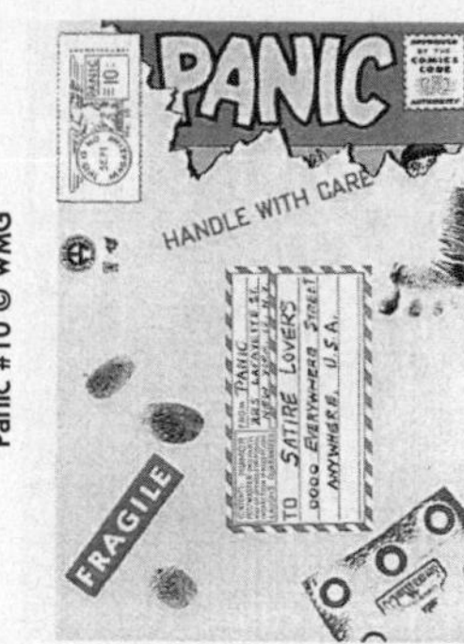

Panic #10 © WMG

	GD 2.0	VG 4.0	FN 6.0	VF 8.0	VF/NM 9.0	NM- 9.2
Gold Key: April, 1967; No. 2, April, 1968						
1-Written by Jerry Siegel; '40s super hero	6	12	18	39	62	85
2	5	10	15	30	48	65
OZ (See First Comics Graphic Novel, Marvel Treaury Of Oz & MGM's Marvelous...)						
OZ						
Caliber Press: 1994 - 1997 ($2.95, B&W)						
0-20: 0-Released between #10 & #11						3.00
1 ($5.95)-Limited Edition; double-c						6.00
...Specials: Freedom Fighters. Lion. Scarecrow. Tin Man						3.00
OZARK IKE						
Dell Publishing Co./Standard Comics B11 on: Feb, 1948; Nov, 1948 - No. 24, Dec, 1951; No. 25, Sept, 1952						
Four Color 180(1948-Dell)	10	20	30	67	116	165
B11, B12, 13-15	10	20	30	54	72	90
16-25	9	18	27	47	61	75
OZ: DAEMONSTORM						
Caliber Press: 1997 ($3.95, B&W, one-shot)						
1						4.00
OZ: ROMANCE IN RAGS						
Caliber Press: 1996 ($2.95, B&W, limited series)						
1-3, ..Special						3.00
OZ SQUAD						
Brave New Worlds/Patchwork Press: 1992 - No. 4, 1994 ($2.50/$2.75, B&W)						
1-4-Patchwork Press						3.00
OZ SQUAD						
Patchwork Press: Dec, 1995 - No. 10, 1996 ($3.95/$2.95, B&W)						
1-($3.95)						4.00
2-10						3.00
OZ: STRAW AND SORCERY						
Caliber Press: 1997 ($2.95, B&W, limited series)						
1-3						3.00
OZ-WONDERLAND WARS, THE						
DC Comics: Jan, 1986 - No. 3, March, 1986 (Mini-series)(Giants)						
1-3-Capt. Carrot app.; funny animals						4.00
OZZIE & BABS (TV Teens #14 on)						
Fawcett Publications: Dec, 1947 - No. 13, Fall, 1949						
1-Teen-age	10	20	30	54	72	90
2	6	12	18	31	38	45
3-13	6	12	18	27	33	38
OZZIE AND HARRIET (The Adventures of... on cover) (Radio)						
National Periodical Publications: Oct-Nov, 1949 - No. 5, June-July, 1950						
1-Photo-c	93	186	279	586	993	1400
2	47	94	141	291	483	675
3-5	40	80	120	235	380	525
OZZY OSBOURNE (Todd McFarlane Presents)						
Image Comics (Todd McFarlane Prod.): June, 1999 ($4.95, magazine-sized)						
1-Bio, interview and comic story; Ormston painted-a; Ashley Wood-c						5.00
PACIFIC COMICS GRAPHIC NOVEL (See Image Graphic Novel)						
PACIFIC PRESENTS (Also see Starslayer #2, 3)						
Pacific Comics: Oct, 1982 - No. 2, Apr, 1983; No. 3, Mar, 1984 - No. 4, Jun, 1984						
1-Chapter 3 of The Rocketeer; Stevens-c/a; Bettie Page model	1	2	3	4	5	7
2-Chapter 4 of The Rocketeer (4th app.); nudity; Stevens-c/a	1	2	3	4	5	7
3,4: 3-1st app. Vanity						3.00
NOTE: ***Conrad** a-3, 4; c-3. **Ditko** a-1-3; c-1(1/2). **Dave Stevens** a-1, 2; c-1(1/2), 2.*						
PACT, THE						
Image Comics: Feb, 1994 - No. 3, June, 1994 ($1.95, limited series)						
1-3: Valentino co-scripts & layouts						2.50
PACT, THE						
Image Comics: Apr, 2005 - No. 4, Jan, 2006 ($2.99/$2.95)						
1-4: Invincible, Shadowhawk, Firebreather & Zephyr team-up. 1-Valentino-s/a						3.00
PAGEANT OF COMICS (See Jane Arden & Mopsy)						
Archer St. John: Sept, 1947 - No. 2, Oct, 1947						

	GD 2.0	VG 4.0	FN 6.0	VF 8.0	VF/NM 9.0	NM- 9.2
1,2: 1-Mopsy strip-r. 2-Jane Arden strip-r	10	20	30	54	72	90
PAINKILLER JANE						
Event Comics: June, 1997 - No. 5, Nov, 1997 ($3.95/$2.95)						
1-Augustyn/Waid-s/Leonardi/Palmiotti-a, variant-c						4.00
2-5: Two covers (Quesada, Leonardi)						3.00
0-(1/99, $3.95) Retells origin; two covers						4.00
Essential Painkiller Jane TPB (2007, $19.99) r/#0-5; cover gallery and pin-ups						20.00
PAINKILLER JANE						
Dynamite Entertainment: 2006 - No. 3, 2006 ($2.99)						
1-3-Quesada & Palmiotti-s/Moder-a. 1-Four covers by Q&P, Moder, Tan and Conner						3.00
Volume #1 TPB (2007, $9.99) r/#1-3; cover gallery and Palmiotti interview						10.00
PAINKILLER JANE						
Dynamite Entertainment: No. 0, 2007 - Present ($3.50)						
0-(25¢) Quesada & Palmiotti-s/Moder-a						2.25
1-5-($3.50) 1-Continued from #0; 5 covers. 4,5-Crossover with Terminator 2 #6,7						3.50
Volume #2 TPB (2007, $11.99) r/#0-3; cover gallery						12.00
PAINKILLER JANE / DARKCHYLDE						
Event Comics: Oct, 1998 ($2.95, one-shot)						
Preview-($6.95) DF Edition, 1-($6.95) DF Edition						7.00
1-Three covers; J.G. Jones-a						3.00
PAINKILLER JANE / HELLBOY						
Event Comics: Aug, 1998 ($2.95, one-shot)						
1-Leonardi & Palmiotti-a						3.00
PAINKILLER JANE VS. THE DARKNESS						
Event Comics: Apr, 1997 ($2.95, one-shot)						
1-Ennis-s; four variant-c (Conner, Hildebrandts, Quesada, Silvestri)						3.50
PAKKINS' LAND						
Caliber Comics (Tapestry): Oct, 1996 - No. 6, July, 1997 ($2.95, B&W)						
1-Gary and Rhoda Shipman-s/a						6.00
2,3						4.00
1-3-2nd printing						3.00
4-6						3.00
0-(6/97, $1.95)						3.00
PAKKINS' LAND						
Alias Enterprises: Apr, 2005 - No. 2 ($2.99)						
1,2-Gary Shipman-s/a						3.00
PAKKINS' LAND: FORGOTTEN DREAMS						
Caliber Comics/Image Comics #4: Apr, 1998 - No. 4, Mar, 2000 ($2.95, B&W)						
1-4-Gary and Rhoda Shipman-s/a						3.00
PAKKINS' LAND: QUEST FOR KINGS						
Caliber Comics: Aug, 1997 - No. 6, Mar, 1998 ($2.95, B&W)						
1-6: 1-Gary and Rhoda Shipman-s/a; Jeff Smith var-c						3.00
PANCHO VILLA						
Avon Periodicals: 1950						
nn-Kinstler-c	23	46	69	133	214	295
PANHANDLE PETE AND JENNIFER (TV) (See Gene Autry #20)						
J. Charles Laue Publishing Co.: July, 1951 - No. 3, Nov, 1951						
1	10	20	30	54	72	90
2,3: 2-Interior photo-cvrs	7	14	21	37	46	55
PANIC (Companion to Mad)						
E. C. Comics (Tiny Tot Comics): Feb-Mar, 1954 - No. 12, Dec-Jan, 1955-56						
1-Used in Senate Investigation hearings; Elder draws entire E. C. staff; Santa Claus & Mickey Spillane parody	31	62	93	248	399	550
2	15	30	45	120	190	260
3,4: 3-Senate Subcommittee parody; Davis draws Gaines, Feldstein & Kelly, 1 pg.; Old King Cole smokes marijuana. 4-Infinity-c; John Wayne parody	12	24	36	96	153	210
5-11: 8-Last pre-code issue (5/55). 9-Superman, Smilin' Jack & Dick Tracy app. on-c; has photo of Walter Winchell on-c. 11-Wheedies cereal box-c	11	22	33	88	142	195
12 (Low distribution; thousands were destroyed)	14	28	42	112	181	250
NOTE: ***Davis** a-1-12; c-12. **Elder** a-1-12. **Feldstein** c-1-3, 5. **Kamen** a-1. **Orlando** a-1-9. **Wolverton** c-4, panel-3. **Wood** a-2-9, 11, 12.*						
PANIC (Magazine) (Satire)						
Panic Publ.: July, 1958 - No. 6, July, 1959; V2#10, Dec, 1965 - V2#12, 1966						

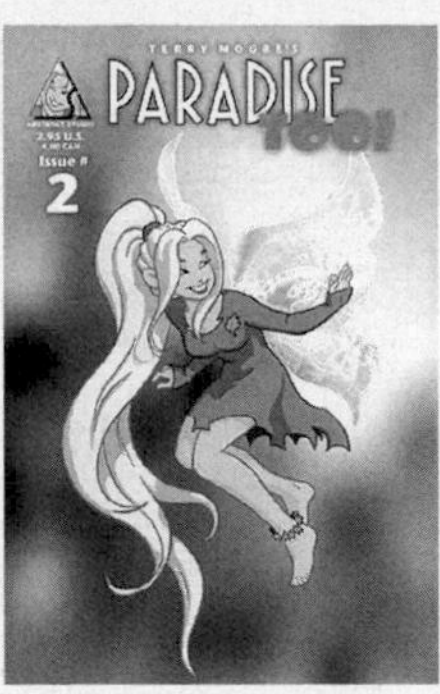

Paradise Too! #2 © Terry Moore

Parts of a Hole #1 © Bendis

The Path #1 © CRO

GD VG FN VF VF/NM NM-
2.0 4.0 6.0 8.0 9.0 9.2

1 13 26 39 74 105 135
2-6 9 18 27 47 61 75
V2#10-12: Reprints earlier issues 3 6 9 18 27 35
NOTE: *Davis a-3(2 pgs.), 4, 5, 10; c-10.* ***Elder*** *a-5.* ***Powell*** *a-V2#10, 11.* ***Torres*** *a-1-5.* ***Tuska*** *a-V2#11.*

PANIC
Gemstone Publishing: March, 1997 - No. 12, Dec, 1999 ($2.50, quarterly)
1-12: E.C. reprints 2.50

PANTHA (See Vampirella-The New Monthly #16,17)

PANTHA: HAUNTED PASSION (Also see Vampirella Monthly #0)
Harris Comics: May, 1997 ($2.95, B&W, one-shot)
1-r/Vampirella #30,31 3.00

PAPA MIDNITE (See John Constantine - Hellblazer Special:...)

PARADE (See Hanna-Barbera...)

PARADE COMICS (See Frisky Animals on Parade)

PARADE OF PLEASURE
Derric Verschoyle Ltd., London, England: 1954 (192 pgs.) (Hardback book)
By Geoffrey Wagner. Contains section devoted to the censorship of American comic books with illustrations in color and black and white. (Also see **Seduction of the Innocent**).
Distributed in USA by Library Publishers, N. Y. 50 100 150 275 438 600
with dust jacket.... 105 210 315 578 889 1200

PARADISE TOO!
Abstract Studios: 2000 - No. 14, 2003 ($2.95, B&W)
1-14-Terry Moore's unpublished newspaper strips and sketches 3.00
...: Checking For Weirdos TPB (4/03, $14.95) r/#8-12 15.00
...: Drunk Ducks! TPB (7/02, $15.95) r/#1-7 16.00

PARADISE X (Also see Earth X and Universe X)
Marvel Comics: Apr, 2002 - No. 11, July, 2003 ($4.50/$2.99)
0-Ross-c; Braithwaite-a 4.50
1-11-($2.99) Ross-c; Braithwaite-a. 7-Punisher on-c. 10-Kingpin on-c 3.00
...:A (10/03, $2.99) Braithwaite-a; Ross-c 3.00
...:Devils (11/02, $4.50) Sadowski-a; Ross-c 4.50
...:Ragnarok 1,2 (3/02, 4/03; $2.99) Yeates-a; Ross-c 3.00
...:X (11/03, $2.99) Braithwaite-a; Ross-c; conclusion of story 3.00
...:Xen (7/02, $4.50) Yeowell & Sienkiewicz-a; Ross-c 4.50
Earth X Vol. 4: Paradise X Book 1 (2003, $29.99, TPB) r/#0,1-5, ...: Xen; Heralds #1-3 30.00
Vol. 5: Paradise X Book 2 (2004, $29.99, TPB) r/#6-12, Ragnarok #1&2; Devils, A & X 30.00

PARADISE X: HERALDS (Also see Earth X and Universe X)
Marvel Comics: Dec, 2001 - No. 3, Feb, 2002 ($3.50)
1-3-Prelude to Paradise X series; Ross-c; Pugh-a 3.50
Special Edition (Wizard preview) Ross-c 2.50

PARADOX
Dark Visions Publ: June, 1994 - No. 2, Aug, 1994 ($2.95, B&W, mature)
1,2: 1-Linsner-c. 2-Boris-c. 3.00

PARALLAX: EMERALD NIGHT (See Final Night)
DC Comics: Nov, 1996 ($2.95, one-shot, 48 pgs.)
1-Final Night tie-in; Green Lantern (Kyle Rayner) app. 4.00

PARAMOUNT ANIMATED COMICS (See Harvey Comics Hits #60, 62)
Harvey Publications: No. 3, Feb, 1953 - No. 22, July, 1956
3-Baby Huey, Herman & Katnip, Buzzy the Crow begin
23 46 69 133 214 295
4-6 13 26 39 74 105 135
7-Baby Huey becomes permanent cover feature; cover title becomes Baby Huey with #9
22 44 66 127 204 280
8-10: 9-Infinity-c 12 24 36 69 97 125
11-22 10 20 30 54 72 90

PARENT TRAP, THE (Disney)
Dell Publishing Co.: No. 1210, Oct-Dec, 1961
Four Color 1210-Movie, Hayley Mills photo-c 9 18 27 60 100 140

PARLIAMENT OF JUSTICE
Image Comics: Mar, 2003 ($5.95, B&W, one-shot, square-bound)
1-Michael Avon Oeming-c/s; Neil Vokes-a 6.00

PARODY
Armour Publishing: Mar, 1977 - No. 3, Aug, 1977 (B&W humor magazine)
1 2 4 6 13 18 22
2,3: 2-King Kong, Happy Days. 3-Charlie's Angels, Rocky
2 4 6 9 13 16

PAROLE BREAKERS
Avon Periodicals/Realistic #2 on: Dec, 1951 - No. 3, July, 1952
1(#2 on inside)-r-c/Avon paperback #283 (painted-c)
43 86 129 267 446 625
2-Kubert-a; r-c/Avon paperback #114 (photo-c) 30 60 90 174 280 385
3-Kinstler-c 27 54 81 158 254 350

PARTRIDGE FAMILY, THE (TV)(Also see David Cassidy)
Charlton Comics: Mar, 1971 - No. 21, Dec, 1973
1 (2 versions: B&W photo-c & tinted color photo-c) 7 14 21 45 73 100
2-4,6-10 4 8 12 24 37 50
5-Partridge Family Summer Special (52 pgs.); The Shadow, Lone Ranger, Charlie McCarthy, Flash Gordon, Hopalong Cassidy, Gene Autry & others app.
7 14 21 50 83 115
11-21 3 6 9 21 32 42

PARTS OF A HOLE
Caliber Press: 1991 ($2.50, B&W)
1-Short stories & cartoons by Brian Michael Bendis 3.00

PARTS UNKNOWN
Eclipse Comics/FX: July, 1992 - No. 4, Oct, 1992 ($2.50, B&W, mature)
1-4: All contain FX gaming cards 2.50

PARTS UNKNOWN
Image Comics: May, 2000 - Present ($2.95, B&W)
...: Killing Attractions 1 (5/00) Beau Smith-s/Brad Gorby-a 3.00
...: Hostile Takeover 1-4 (6-9/00) 3.00

PASSION, THE
Catechetical Guild: No. 394, 1955
394 6 12 18 28 34 40

PASSOVER (See Avengelyne)
Maximum Press: Dec, 1996 ($2.99, one-shot)
1 3.00

PAT BOONE (TV)(Also see Superman's Girlfriend Lois Lane #9)
National Per. Publ.: Sept-Oct, 1959 - No. 5, May-Jun, 1960 (All have photo-c)
1 45 90 135 275 450 625
2-5: 3-Fabian, Connie Francis & Paul Anka photos on-c. 4-Previews "Journey To The Center Of The Earth". 4-Johnny Mathis & Bobby Darin photos on-c. 5-Dick Clark & Frankie Avalon photos on-c 36 72 108 208 329 450

PATCHES
Rural Home/Patches Publ. (Orbit): Mar-Apr, 1945 - No. 11, Nov, 1947
1-L. B. Cole-c 40 80 120 240 383 525
2 15 30 45 88 137 185
3,4,6,8-11: 6-Henry Aldrich story. 8-Smiley Burnette-c/s (6/47); pre-dates Smiley Burnette #1. 9-Mr. District Attorney story (radio). Leav/Keigstein-a (16 pgs.). 9-11-Leav-c. 10-Jack Carson (radio) c/story; Leav-c. 11-Red Skelton story 15 30 45 85 130 175
5-Danny Kaye-c/story; L.B. Cole-c. 21 42 63 120 188 255
7-Hopalong Cassidy-c/story 18 36 54 103 162 220

PATH, THE (Also see Negation War)
CrossGeneration Comics: Apr, 2002 - No. 23, Apr, 2004 ($2.95)
1-23: 1-Ron Marz-s/Bart Sears-a. 13-Matthew Smith-a begins 3.00
Vol. 1: Crisis of Faith (2002, $15.95, TPB) r/#1-6 16.00
Vol. 2: Blood on Snow (5/03, $15.95, TPB) r/#7-12 16.00
Vol. 3: Death and Dishonor ('03, $15.95, TPB) r/#13-18 16.00

PATHWAYS TO FANTASY
Pacific Comics: July, 1984
1-Barry Smith-c/a; Jeff Jones-a (4 pgs.) 4.00

PATIENT ZERO
Image Comics: Mar, 2004 - No. 4, Jun, 2004 ($2.95, limited series)
1-4-Brent White-a/John McLean-Foreman-s 3.00

PATORUZU (See Adventures of...)

PATRIOTS, THE
DC Comics (WildStorm): Jan, 2000 - No. 10, Oct, 2000 ($2.50)
1-10-Choi and Peterson-s/Ryan-a 2.50

PATSY & HEDY (Teenage)(Also see Hedy Wolfe)
Atlas Comics/Marvel (GPI/Male): Feb, 1952 - No. 110, Feb, 1967
1-Patsy Walker & Hedy Wolfe; Al Jaffee-c 23 46 69 135 218 300

Patsy Walker: Hellcat #1 © MAR

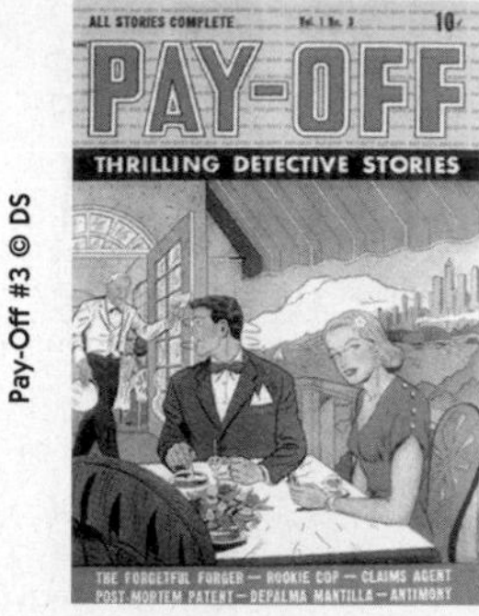

Pay-Off #3 © DS

Peanuts #9 © UFS

	GD 2.0	VG 4.0	FN 6.0	VF 8.0	VF/NM 9.0	NM- 9.2
2	14	28	42	80	115	150
3-10: 3,7,8,9-Al Jaffee-c	11	22	33	64	90	115
11-20: 17,19,20-Al Jaffee-c	10	20	30	56	76	95
21-40	9	18	27	47	61	75
41-50	5	10	15	30	48	65
51-60	4	8	12	28	44	60
61-80,100: 88-Lingerie panel	4	8	12	24	37	50
81-87,89-99,101-110	4	8	12	22	34	45
Annual 1(1963)-Early Marvel annual	9	18	27	60	100	140

PATSY & HER PALS (Teenage)
Atlas Comics (PPI): May, 1953 - No. 29, Aug, 1957

	GD	VG	FN	VF	VF/NM	NM-
1-Patsy Walker	18	36	54	105	165	225
2	11	22	33	62	86	110
3-10	10	20	30	56	76	95
11-29: 24-Everett-c	9	18	27	47	61	75

PATSY WALKER (See All Teen, A Date With Patsy, Girls' Life, Miss America Magazine, Patsy & Hedy, Patsy & Her Pals & Teen Comics)
Marvel/Atlas Comics (BPC): 1945 (no month) - No. 124, Dec, 1965

	GD	VG	FN	VF	VF/NM	NM-
1-Teenage	53	106	159	323	567	800
2	30	60	90	174	280	385
3,4,6-10	23	46	69	135	218	300
5-Injury-to-eye-c	26	52	78	154	247	340
11,12,15,16,18	15	30	45	85	130	175
13,14,17,19-22-Kurtzman's "Hey Look"	15	30	45	88	137	185
23,24	13	26	39	74	105	135
25-Rusty by Kurtzman; painted-c	15	30	45	88	137	185
26-29,31: 26-31: 52 pgs.	11	22	33	62	86	110
30(52 pgs.)-Egghead Doodle by Kurtzman (1 pg.)	12	24	36	67	94	120
32-57: Last precode (3/55)	9	18	27	52	69	85
58-80,100	5	10	15	30	48	65
81-99: 92,98-Millie x-over. 99-Linda Carter x-over	4	8	12	26	41	55
101-124	4	8	12	24	37	50
Fashion Parade 1(1966, 68 pgs.) (Beware cut-out & marked pages)	8	16	24	54	90	125

NOTE: *Painted c-25-28. Anti-Wertham editorial in #21. Georgie app. in #8, 11. Millie app. in #10, 92, 98. Mitzi app. in #11. Rusty app. in #12, 25. Willie app. in #12.* ***Al Jaffee*** *c-44, 47, 49, 57, 58.*

PATSY WALKER: HELLCAT
Marvel Comics: Sept, 2008 - No. 5 ($2.99, limited series)

	GD	VG	FN	VF	VF/NM	NM-
1-3-Lafuente-a/Kathryn Immonen-s/Stuart Immonen-c; Hellcat joins The Initiative						3.00

PAT THE BRAT (Adventures of Pipsqueak #34 on)
Archie Publications (Radio): June, 1953; Summer, 1955 - No. 4, 5/56; No. 15, 7/56 - No. 33, 7/59

	GD	VG	FN	VF	VF/NM	NM-
nn(6/53)	14	28	42	76	108	140
1(Summer, 1955)	10	20	30	54	72	90
2-4-(5/56) (#5-14 not published). 3-Early Bolling-a	7	14	21	37	46	55
15-(7/56)-33: 18-Early Bolling-a	4	8	12	22	34	45

PAT THE BRAT COMICS DIGEST MAGAZINE
Archie Publications: October, 1980

	GD	VG	FN	VF	VF/NM	NM-
1-Li'l Jinx & Super Duck app.	2	4	6	9	12	15

PATTY CAKE
Permanent Press: Mar, 1995 - No. 9, Jul, 1996 ($2.95, B&W)

	GD	VG	FN	VF	VF/NM	NM-
1-9: Scott Roberts-s/a						3.00

PATTY CAKE
Caliber Press (Tapestry): Oct, 1996 - No. 3, Apr, 1997 ($2.95, B&W)

	GD	VG	FN	VF	VF/NM	NM-
1-3: Scott Roberts-s/a, ...Christmas (12/96)						3.00

PATTY CAKE & FRIENDS
Slave Labor Graphics: Nov, 1997 - Present ($2.95, B&W)

	GD	VG	FN	VF	VF/NM	NM-
Here There Be Monsters (10/97), 1-14: Scott Roberts-s/a						3.00
Volume 2 #1 (11/00, $4.95)						5.00

PATTY POWERS (Formerly Della Vision #3)
Atlas Comics: No. 4, Oct, 1955 - No. 7, Oct, 1956

	GD	VG	FN	VF	VF/NM	NM-
4	10	20	30	58	79	100
5-7	7	14	21	35	43	50

PAT WILTON (See Mighty Midget Comics)

PAUL
Spire Christian Comics (Fleming H. Revell Co.): 1978 (49¢)

	GD	VG	FN	VF	VF/NM	NM-
nn	2	4	6	8	10	12

PAULINE PERIL (See The Close Shaves of...)

PAUL REVERE'S RIDE (TV, Disney, see Walt Disney Showcase #34)
Dell Publishing Co.: No. 822, July, 1957

	GD 2.0	VG 4.0	FN 6.0	VF 8.0	VF/NM 9.0	NM- 9.2
Four Color 822-w/Johnny Tremain, Toth-a	8	16	24	58	97	135

PAUL TERRY (See Heckle and Jeckle)

PAUL TERRY'S ADVENTURES OF MIGHTY MOUSE (See Adventures of...)

PAUL TERRY'S COMICS (Formerly Terry-Toons Comics; becomes Adventures of Mighty Mouse No. 126 on)
St. John Publishing Co.: No. 85, Mar, 1951 - No. 125, May, 1955

	GD	VG	FN	VF	VF/NM	NM-
85,86-Same as Terry-Toons #85, & 86 with only a title change; published at same time?; Mighty Mouse, Heckle & Jeckle & Gandy Goose continue from Terry-Toons	12	24	36	67	94	120
87-99	9	18	27	50	65	80
100	10	20	30	54	72	90
101-104,107-125: 121,122,125-Painted-c	9	18	27	47	61	75
105,106-Giant Comics Edition (25¢, 100 pgs.) (9/53 & ?). 105-Little Roquefort-c/story	18	36	54	105	165	225

PAUL TERRY'S MIGHTY MOUSE (See Mighty Mouse)

PAUL TERRY'S MIGHTY MOUSE ADVENTURE STORIES (See Mighty Mouse Adventure Stories)

PAUL THE SAMURAI (See The Tick #4)
New England Comics: July, 1992 - No. 6, July, 1993 ($2.75, B&W)

	GD	VG	FN	VF	VF/NM	NM-
1-6						2.75

PAWNEE BILL
Story Comics (Youthful Magazines?): Feb, 1951 - No. 3, July, 1951

	GD	VG	FN	VF	VF/NM	NM-
1-Bat Masterson, Wyatt Earp app.	13	26	39	72	101	130
2,3: 3-Origin Golden Warrior; Cameron-a	8	16	24	42	54	65

PAY-OFF (This Is the..., ...Crime, ...Detective Stories)
D. S. Publishing Co.: July-Aug, 1948 - No. 5, Mar-Apr, 1949 (52 pgs.)

	GD	VG	FN	VF	VF/NM	NM-
1-True Crime Cases #1,2	26	52	78	152	244	335
2	15	30	45	94	147	200
3-5-Thrilling Detective Stories	14	28	42	82	121	160

PEACEMAKER, THE (Also see Fightin' Five)
Charlton Comics: V3#1, Mar, 1967 - No. 5, Nov, 1967 (All 12¢ cover price)

	GD	VG	FN	VF	VF/NM	NM-
1-Fightin' Five begins	5	10	15	34	55	75
2,3,5	3	6	9	21	32	42
4-Origin The Peacemaker	4	8	12	26	41	55
1,2(Modern Comics reprint, 1978)						5.00

PEACEMAKER (Also see Crisis On Infinite Earths & Showcase '93 #7,9,10)
DC Comics: Jan, 1988 - No. 4, Apr, 1988 ($1.25, limited series)

	GD	VG	FN	VF	VF/NM	NM-
1-4						2.50

PEANUTS (Charlie Brown) (See Fritzi Ritz, Nancy & Sluggo, Sparkle & Sparkler, Tip Top, Tip Topper & United Comics)
United Features Syndicate/Dell Publishing Co./Gold Key: 1953-54; No. 878, 2/58 - No. 13, 5-7/62; 5/63 - No. 4, 2/64

	GD	VG	FN	VF	VF/NM	NM-
1(U.F.S.)(1953-54)-Reprints United Features' Strange As It Seems, Willie, Ferdnand	12	24	36	82	146	210
Four Color 878(#1) (Dell) Schulz-s/a, with assistance from Dale Hale and Jim Sasseville thru #4	19	38	57	139	257	375
Four Color 969,1015('59)	12	24	36	87	156	225
4(2-4/60) Schulz-s/a; one story by Anthony Pocrnich, Schulz's assistant cartoonist	10	20	30	73	129	185
5-13-Schulz-c only; s/a by Pocrnich	9	18	27	63	107	150
1(Gold Key, 5/63)	10	20	30	71	126	180
2-4	7	14	21	49	80	110

PEBBLES & BAMM BAMM (TV) (See Cave Kids #7, 12)
Charlton Comics: Jan, 1972 - No. 36, Dec, 1976 (Hanna-Barbera)

	GD	VG	FN	VF	VF/NM	NM-
1-From the Flintstones; "Teen Age..." on cover	5	10	15	30	48	65
2-10	3	6	9	17	25	32
11-20	2	4	6	13	18	22
21-36	2	4	6	9	13	16
nn (1973, digest, 100 pgs.) B&W one page gags	3	6	9	18	27	35

PEBBLES & BAMM BAMM (TV)
Harvey Comics: Nov, 1993 - No. 3, Mar, 1994 ($1.50) (Hanna-Barbera)

	GD	VG	FN	VF	VF/NM	NM-
V2#1-3						3.00
...Giant Size 1 (10/93, $2.25, 68 pgs.)("Summer Special" on-c)						4.00

PEBBLES FLINTSTONE (TV) (See The Flintstones #11)

Penance: Relentless #3 © MAR

Penny Century #6 © Jaime Hernandez

Pep Comics #39 © AP

GD VG FN VF VF/NM NM-
2.0 4.0 6.0 8.0 9.0 9.2

Gold Key: Sept, 1963 (Hanna-Barbera)
1 (10088-309)-Early Pebbles app. 9 18 27 60 100 140

PEDRO (Formerly My Private Life #17; also see Romeo Tubbs)
Fox Features Syndicate: No. 18, June, 1950 - No. 2, Aug, 1950?
18(#1)-Wood-c/a(p) 22 44 66 129 207 285
2-Wood-a? 15 30 45 88 137 185

PEE-WEE PIXIES (See The Pixies)

PELLEAS AND MELISANDE (See Night Music #4, 5)

PENALTY (See Crime Must Pay the...)

PENANCE: RELENTLESS (See Civil War, Thunderbolts and related titles)
Marvel Comics: Nov, 2007 - No. 5 ($2.99)
1-5-Speedball/Penance; Jenkins-s/Gulacy-a. 3-Wolverine app. 3.00
TPB (2008, $13.99) r/#1-5 14.00

PENDRAGON (Knights of... #5 on; also see Knights of...)
Marvel Comics UK, Ltd.: July, 1992 - No. 15, Sept, 1993 ($1.75)
1-15: 1-4-Iron Man app. 6-8-Spider-Man app. 2.50

PENDULUM ILLUSTRATED BIOGRAPHIES
Pendulum Press: 1979 (B&W)

19-355x-George Washington/Thomas Jefferson, 19-3495-Charles Lindbergh/Amelia Earhart, 19-3509-Harry Houdini/Walt Disney, 19-3517-Davy Crockett/Daniel Boone-Redondo-a, 19-3525-Elvis Presley/Beatles, 19-3533-Benjamin Franklin/Martin Luther King Jr, 19-3541-Abraham Lincoln/Franklin D. Roosevelt, 19-3568-Marie Curie/Albert Einstein-Redondo-a, 19-3576-Thomas Edison/Alexander Graham Bell-Redondo-a, 19-3584-Vince Lombardi/Pele, 19-3592-Babe Ruth/Jackie Robinson, 19-3606-Jim Thorpe/Althea Gibson
Softback 3.00
Hardback 5.00
NOTE: *Above books still available from publisher.*

PENDULUM ILLUSTRATED CLASSICS (Now Age Illustrated)
Pendulum Press: 1973 - 1978 (75¢, 62pp, B&W, 5-3/8x8")
(Also see Marvel Classics)

64-100x(1973)-Dracula-Redondo art, 64-131x-The Invisible Man-Nino art, 64-0968-Dr. Jekyll and Mr. Hyde-Redondo art, 64-1005-Black Beauty, 64-1010-Call of the Wild, 64-1020-Frankenstein, 64-1025-Hucklebury Finn, 64-1030-Moby Dick-Nino-a, 64-1040-Red Badge of Courage, 64-1045-The Time Machine-Nino-a, 64-1050-Tom Sawyer, 64-1055-Twenty Thousand Leagues Under the Sea, 64-1069-Treasure Island, 64 1328(1974)-Kidnapped, 64-1336-Three Musketeers-Nino art, 64-1344-A Tale of Two Cities, 64-1352-Journey to the Center of the Earth, 64-1360-The War of the Worlds-Nino-a, 64-1379-The Greatest Advs. of Sherlock Holmes-Redondo art, 64-1387-Mysterious Island, 64-1395-Hunchback of Notre Dame, 64-1409-Helen Keller-story of my life, 64-1417-Scarlet Letter, 64-1425-Gulliver's Travels, 64-2618(1977)-Around the World in Eighty Days, 64-2626-Captains Courageous, 64-2634-Connecticut Yankee, 64-2642-The Hound of the Baskervilles, 64-2650-The House of Seven Gables, 64-2669-Jane Eyre, 64-2677-The Last of the Mohicans, 64-2685-The Best of O'Henry, 64-2693-The Best of Poe-Redondo-a, 64-2707-Two Years Before the Mast, 64-2715-White Fang, 64-2723-Wuthering Heights, 64-3126(1978)-Ben Hur-Redondo art, 64-3134-A Christmas Carol, 64-3142-The Food of the Gods, 64-3150-Ivanhoe, 64-3169-The Man in the Iron Mask, 64-3177-The Prince and the Pauper, 64-3185-The Prisoner of Zenda, 64-3193-The Return of the Native, 64-3207-Robinson Crusoe, 64-3215-The Scarlet Pimpernel, 64-3223-The Sea Wolf, 64-3231-The Swiss Family Robinson, 64-3851-Billy Budd, 64-386x-Crime and Punishment, 64-3878-Don Quixote, 64-3886-Great Expectations, 64-3894-Heidi, 64-3908-The Iliad, 64-3916-Lord Jim, 64-3924-The Mutiny on Board H.M.S. Bounty, 64-3932-The Odyssey, 64-3940-Oliver Twist, 64-3959-Pride and Prejudice, 64-3967-The Turn of the Screw
Softback 3.00
Hardback 5.00

NOTE: *All of the above books can be ordered from the publisher; some were reprinted as Marvel Classic Comics #1-12. In 1972 there was another brief series of 12 titles which contained Classics Ill. artwork. They were entitled* ***Now Age Books*** *Illustrated, but can be easily distinguished from later series by the small Classics Illustrated logo at the top of the front cover. The format is the same as the later series. The 48 pg. C.I. art was stretched out to make 62 pgs. After Twin Circle Publ. terminated the Classics Ill. series in 1971, they made a one year contract with Pendulum Press to print these twelve titles of C.I. art. Pendulum was unhappy with the contract, and at the end of 1972 began their own art series, utilizing the talents of the Filipino artist group. One detail which makes this rather confusing is that when they redid the art in 1973, they gave it the same identifying no. as the 1972 series. All 12 of the 1972 C.I. editions have new covers, taken from internal art panels. In spite of their recent age, all of the 1972 C.I. series are very rare. Mint copies would fetch at least $50. Here is a list of the 1972 series, with C.I. title no. counterpart:*

64-1005 (CI#60-A2) 64-1010 (CI#91) 64-1015 (CI-Jr #503) 64-1020 (CI#26)
64-1025 (CI#19-A2) 64-1030 (CI#5-A2) 64-1035 (CI#169) 64-1040 (CI#98)
64-1045 (CI#133) 64-1050 (CI#50-A2) 64-1055 (CI#47) 64-1060 (CI-Jr#535)

PENDULUM ILLUSTRATED ORIGINALS
Pendulum Press: 1979 (In color)
94-4254-Solarman: The Beginning (See Solarman) 6.00

PENDULUM'S ILLUSTRATED STORIES
Pendulum Press: 1990 - No. 72, 1990? (No cover price ($4.95), squarebound, 68 pgs.)
1-72: Reprints Pendulum Ill. Classics series 5.00

PENNY
Avon Comics: 1947 - No. 6, Sept-Oct, 1949 (Newspaper reprints)
1-Photo & biography of creator 15 30 45 90 140 190
2-5 10 20 30 54 72 90

GD VG FN VF VF/NM NM-
2.0 4.0 6.0 8.0 9.0 9.2

6-Perry Como photo on-c 10 20 30 58 79 100

PENNY CENTURY (See Love and Rockets)
Fantagraphics Books: Dec, 1997 - Present ($2.95, B&W, mini-series)
1-7-Jaime Hernandez-s/a 3.00

PEP COMICS (See Archie Giant Series #576, 589, 601, 614, 624)
MLJ Magazines/Archie Publications No. 56 (3/46) on: Jan, 1940 - No. 411, Mar, 1987
1-Intro. The Shield (1st patriotic hero) by Irving Novick; origin & 1st app. The Comet by Jack Cole, The Queen of Diamonds & Kayo Ward; The Rocket, The Press Guardian (The Falcon #1 only), Sergeant Boyle, Fu Chang, & Bentley of of Scotland Yard; Robot-c; Shield-c begin
972 1944 2916 6998 12,249 17,500
2-Origin The Rocket 260 520 780 1638 2769 3900
3 193 386 579 1216 2058 2900
4-Wizard cameo; early robot-s 153 306 459 964 1632 2300
5-Wizard cameo in Shield story 153 306 459 964 1632 2300
6-10: 8-Last Cole Comet; no Cole-a in #6,7 127 254 381 800 1350 1900
11-Dusty, Shield's sidekick begins (1st app.); last Press Guardian, Fu Chang
130 260 390 819 1385 1950
12-Origin & 1st app. Fireball (2/41); last Rocket & Queen of Diamonds; Danny in Wonderland begins 150 300 450 945 1598 2250
13-15 103 206 309 649 1100 1550
16-Origin Madam Satan; blood drainage-c 163 326 489 1027 1739 2450
17-Origin/1st app. The Hangman (7/41); death of The Comet; Comet is revealed as Hangman's brother 382 764 1146 2598 4549 6500
18,19,21: 21-Last Madam Satan 97 194 291 611 1031 1450
20-Classic Nazi swastika-c; last Fireball 133 266 399 838 1419 2000
22-Intro. & 1st app. Archie, Betty, & Jughead(12/41); (also see Jackpot)
2100 4200 6300 16,000 27,000 38,000
23 240 480 720 1512 2556 3600
24,25: 24-Coach Kleets app. (unnamed until Archie #94); bondage/torture-c. 25-1st app. Archie's jalopy; 1st skinny Mr. Weatherbee prototype 160 320 480 1008 1704 2400
26-1st app. Veronica Lodge (4/42); "Remember Pearl Harbor!" cover caption
247 494 741 1556 2628 3700
27,29,30: 27-Bill of Rights-c. 29-Origin Shield retold; 30-Capt. Commando begins; bondage/torture-c; 1st Miss Grundy (definitive version); see Jackpot #4
123 246 369 775 1313 1850
28-Classic swastika/Hangman-c 130 260 390 819 1385 1950
31-35: 31-MLJ offices & artists are visited in Sgt. Boyle story; 1st app. Mr. Lodge. 32-Shield dons new costume. 34-Bondage/Hypo-c. 33-Pre-Moose tryout (see Jughead #1)
100 200 300 630 1065 1500
36-1st Archie-c (2/43) w/Shield & Hangman 267 534 801 1682 2841 4000
37-40 70 140 210 441 746 1050
41-50: 41-Archie-c begin. 47-Last Hangman issue; infinity-c. 48-Black Hood begins (5/44); ends #51,59,60 48 96 144 298 499 700
51-60: 52-Suzie begins; 1st Mr Weatherbee-c. 56-Last Capt. Commando. 59-Black Hood not in costume; lingerie panels; Archie dresses as his aunt; Suzie ends. 60-Katy Keene begins(3/47), ends #154 33 66 99 192 309 425
61-65-Last Shield. 62-1st app. Li'l Jinx (7/47) 27 54 81 158 254 350
66-80: 66-G-Man Club becomes Archie Club (2/48); Nevada Jones by Bill Woggon. 78-1st app. Dilton 15 30 45 94 147 200
81-99 14 28 42 80 115 150
100 15 30 45 90 140 190
101-130 10 20 30 54 72 90
131(2/59)-140: 138-140-Neal Adams-a (1 pg.) in each 5 10 15 32 51 70
141-149(9/61) 4 8 12 26 41 55
150-160-Super-heroes app. in each (see note). 150 (10/61?)-2nd or 3rd app. The Jaguar? 151-154,156-158-Horror/Sci/Fi-c. 157-Li'l Jinx 6 12 18 39 62 85
161(3/63)-167,169-180: 161-Early Josie stories w/DeCarlo-a begin (see Note for others)
3 6 9 20 30 40
168,200: 168-(1/64)-Jaguar app. 200-(12/66) 4 8 12 22 34 45
181(5/65)-199: 187-Pureheart try-out story. 192-UFO-c. 198-Giantman-c(only)
3 6 9 16 23 30
201-217,219-226,228-240(4/70) 3 6 9 14 19 24
218,227-Archies Band-c only 3 6 9 16 22 28
241-270(10/72) 2 4 6 10 14 18
271-297,299 2 4 6 8 10 12
298, 300: 298-Josie and the Pussycats-c. 300(4/75) 2 4 6 10 14 18
301-340(8/78) 1 2 3 5 7 9
341-382 6.00
383(4/82),393(3/84): 383-Marvelous Maureen begins (Sci/fi). 393-Thunderbunny begins
1 2 3 4 5 7
384-392,394-399,401-410: 396-Early Cheryl Blossom-c 4.00
400(5/85),411: 400-Story featuring Archie staff (DeCarlo-a) 6.00
NOTE: ***Biro*** *a-2, 4, 5.* ***Jack Cole*** *a-1-5, 8.* ***Al Fagaly*** *c-55-72.* ***Fuje*** *a-39, 45, 47; c-34.* ***Meskin*** *a-2, 4, 5, 11(2).*

Perfect Crime #26 © Cross Publ.

Personal Love #2 © FF

Peter Parker: Spider-Man V2 #29 © MAR

Montana c-30, 32, 33, 36, 73-87(most). ***Novick*** *c-1-28, 29(w/****Schomburg****), 31i.* ***Harry Sahle*** *c-35, 39-50.* ***Schomburg*** *c-38.* ***Bob Wood*** *a-2, 4-6, 11. The Fly app. in 151, 154, 160. Flygirl app. in 153, 155, 156, 158. Jaguar app. in 150, 152, 157, 159, 168. Josie by* ***DeCarlo*** *in 161-166, 168-171, 173, 175-177, 179, 181. Katy Keene by* ***Bill Woggon*** *in 73-126. Bondage c-7, 12, 13, 15, 18, 21, 31, 32. Cover features: Shield #1-16; Shield/Hangman #17-27, 29-41; Hangman #28. Archie #36, 41-on.*

PEPE
Dell Publishing Co.: No. 1194, Apr, 1961

	GD 2.0	VG 4.0	FN 6.0	VF 8.0	VF/NM 9.0	NM- 9.2
Four Color 1194-Movie, photo-c	4	8	12	24	37	50

PERFECT CRIME, THE
Cross Publications: Oct, 1949 - No. 33, May, 1953 (#2-12, 52 pgs.)

	GD 2.0	VG 4.0	FN 6.0	VF 8.0	VF/NM 9.0	NM- 9.2
1-Powell-a(2)	35	70	105	203	327	450
2 (4/50)	19	38	57	109	172	235
3-10: 7-Steve Duncan begins, ends #30. 10-Flag-c	16	32	48	94	147	200
11-Used in **SOTI**, pg. 159	18	36	54	105	165	225
12-14	15	30	45	88	137	185
15- "The Most Terrible Menace" 2 pg. drug editorial	16	32	48	94	147	200
16,17,19-25,27-29,31-33	13	26	39	74	105	135
18-Drug cover, heroin drug propaganda story, plus 2 pg. anti-drug editorial	25	50	75	147	236	325
26-Drug-c with hypodermic needle; drug propaganda story	26	52	78	154	247	340
30-Strangulation cover	25	50	75	149	240	330

NOTE: ***Powell*** *a-No. 1, 2, 4.* ***Wildey*** *a-1, 5. Bondage c-11.*

PERFECT LOVE
Ziff-Davis(Approved Comics)/St. John No. 9 on: #10, 8-9/51 (cover date; 5-6/51 indicia date); #2, 10-11/51 - #10, 12/53

	GD 2.0	VG 4.0	FN 6.0	VF 8.0	VF/NM 9.0	NM- 9.2
10(#1)(8-9/51)-Painted-c	21	42	63	123	197	270
2(10-11/51)	15	30	45	84	127	170
3,5-7: 3-Painted-c. 5-Photo-c	13	26	39	74	105	135
4,8 (Fall, 1952)-Kinstler-a; last Z-D issue	14	28	42	76	108	140
9,10 (10/53, 12/53, St. John): 9-Painted-c. 10-Photo-c	13	26	39	72	101	130

PERHAPANAUTS, THE
Dark Horse Comics: Nov, 2005 - No. 4, Feb, 2006 ($2.99, limited series)

	GD 2.0	VG 4.0	FN 6.0	VF 8.0	VF/NM 9.0	NM- 9.2
1-4-Todd Dezago-s/Craig Rousseau-a/c						3.00
... Annual #1 (2/08, $3.50) Two covers by Rousseau and Allred						3.50
(2nd series) (4/08 - Present, $3.50) 1-4: 1-Two covers by Art Adams and Rousseau						3.50

PERHAPANAUTS: SECOND CHANCES, THE
Dark Horse Comics: Oct, 2006 - No. 4, Jan, 2007 ($2.99, limited series)

	GD 2.0	VG 4.0	FN 6.0	VF 8.0	VF/NM 9.0	NM- 9.2
1-4-Todd Dezago-s/Craig Rousseau-a/c						3.00

PERRI (Disney)
Dell Publishing Co.: No. 847, Jan, 1958

	GD 2.0	VG 4.0	FN 6.0	VF 8.0	VF/NM 9.0	NM- 9.2
Four Color 847-Movie, w/2 diff-c publ.	5	10	15	35	55	75

PERRY MASON
David McKay Publications: No. 49, 1946 - No. 50, 1946

	GD 2.0	VG 4.0	FN 6.0	VF 8.0	VF/NM 9.0	NM- 9.2
Feature Books 49, 50-Based on Gardner novels	31	62	93	181	291	400

PERRY MASON MYSTERY MAGAZINE (TV)
Dell Publishing Co.: June-Aug, 1964 - No. 2, Oct-Dec, 1964

	GD 2.0	VG 4.0	FN 6.0	VF 8.0	VF/NM 9.0	NM- 9.2
1	6	12	18	39	62	85
2-Raymond Burr photo-c	5	10	15	32	51	70

PERSONAL LOVE (Also see Movie Love)
Famous Funnies: Jan, 1950 - No. 33, June, 1955

	GD 2.0	VG 4.0	FN 6.0	VF 8.0	VF/NM 9.0	NM- 9.2
1-Photo-c	20	40	60	118	189	260
2-Kathryn Grayson & Mario Lanza photo-c	13	26	39	72	101	130
3-7,10: 7-Robert Walker & Joanne Dru photo-c. 10-Loretta Young & Joseph Cotton photo-c	11	22	33	64	90	115
8,9: 8-Esther Williams & Howard Keel photo-c. 9-Debra Paget & Louis Jourdan photo-c	12	24	36	67	94	120
11-Toth-a; Glenn Ford & Gene Tierney photo-c	14	28	42	78	112	145
12,16,17-One pg. Frazetta each. 17-Rock Hudson & Yvonne DeCarlo photo-c	11	22	33	64	90	115
13-15,18-23: 12-Jane Greer & William Lundigan photo-c. 14-Kirk Douglas photo-c. 15-Dale Robertson & Joanne Dru photo-c. 18-Gregory Peck & Susan Hayworth photo-c. 19-Anthony Quinn & Suzan Ball photo-c. 20-Robert Wagner & Kathleen Crowley photo-c. 21-Roberta Peters & Byron Palmer photo-c. 22-Dale Robertson photo-c. 23-Rhonda Fleming-c	11	22	33	60	83	105
24,27,28-Frazetta-a in each (8,8&6 pgs.). 27-Rhonda Fleming & Fernando Lamas photo-c. 28-Mitzi Gaynor photo-c	43	86	129	267	446	625
25-Frazetta-a (tribute to Bettie Page, 7 pg. story); Tyrone Power/Terry Moore photo-c from "King of the Khyber Rifles"	53	106	159	334	567	800
26,29,30,33: 26-Constance Smith & Byron Palmer photo-c. 29-Charlton Heston & Nicol Morey photo-c. 30-Johnny Ray & Mitzi Gaynor photo-c. 33-Dana Andrews & Piper Laurie photo-c	11	22	33	60	83	105
31-Marlon Brando & Jean Simmons photo-c; last pre-code (2/55)	13	26	39	74	105	135
32-Classic Frazetta-a (8 pgs.); Kirk Douglas & Bella Darvi photo-c	58	116	174	365	620	875

NOTE: *All have photo-c. Many feature movie stars.* ***Everett*** *a-5, 9, 10, 24.*

PERSONAL LOVE (Going Steady V3#3 on)
Prize Publ. (Headline): V1#1, Sept, 1957 - V3#2, Nov-Dec, 1959

	GD 2.0	VG 4.0	FN 6.0	VF 8.0	VF/NM 9.0	NM- 9.2
V1#1	10	20	30	54	72	90
2	7	14	21	35	43	50
3-6(7-8/58)	6	12	18	29	36	42
V2#1(9-10/58)-V2#6(7-8/59)	6	12	18	27	33	38
V3#1-Wood?/Orlando-a	6	12	18	31	38	45
2	5	10	15	24	30	35

PETER CANNON - THUNDERBOLT (See Crisis on Infinite Earths)(Also see Thunderbolt)
DC Comics: Sept, 1992 - No. 12, Aug, 1993 ($1.25)

	GD 2.0	VG 4.0	FN 6.0	VF 8.0	VF/NM 9.0	NM- 9.2
1-12						2.50

PETER COTTONTAIL
Key Publications: Jan, 1954; Feb, 1954 - No. 2, Mar, 1954 (Says 3/53 in error)

	GD 2.0	VG 4.0	FN 6.0	VF 8.0	VF/NM 9.0	NM- 9.2
1(1/54)-Not 3-D	9	18	27	50	65	80
1(2/54)-(3-D, 25¢)-Came w/glasses; written by Bruce Hamilton	21	42	63	123	197	270
2-Reprints 3-D #1 but not in 3-D	6	12	18	31	38	45

PETER GUNN (TV)
Dell Publishing Co.: No. 1087, Apr-June, 1960

	GD 2.0	VG 4.0	FN 6.0	VF 8.0	VF/NM 9.0	NM- 9.2
Four Color 1087-Photo-c	8	16	24	58	97	135

PETE ROSE: HIS INCREDIBLE BASEBALL CAREER
Masstar Creations Inc.: 1995

	GD 2.0	VG 4.0	FN 6.0	VF 8.0	VF/NM 9.0	NM- 9.2
1-John Tartaglione-a						2.50

PETER PAN (Disney) (See Hook, Movie Classics & Comics, New Adventures of... & Walt Disney Showcase #36)
Dell Publishing Co.: No. 442, Dec, 1952 - No. 926, Aug, 1958

	GD 2.0	VG 4.0	FN 6.0	VF 8.0	VF/NM 9.0	NM- 9.2
Four Color 442 (#1)-Movie	10	20	30	70	123	175
Four Color 926-Reprint of 442	4	8	12	28	44	60

PETER PAN
Disney Comics: 1991 ($5.95, graphic novel, 68 pgs.)(Celebrates video release)

	GD 2.0	VG 4.0	FN 6.0	VF 8.0	VF/NM 9.0	NM- 9.2
nn-r/Peter Pan Treasure Chest from 1953						7.00

PETER PANDA
National Periodical Publications: Aug-Sept, 1953 - No. 31, Aug-Sept, 1958

	GD 2.0	VG 4.0	FN 6.0	VF 8.0	VF/NM 9.0	NM- 9.2
1-Grossman-c/a in all	47	94	141	291	483	675
2	24	48	72	140	225	310
3,4,6-8,10	20	40	60	118	189	260
5-Classic-c (scarce)	53	106	159	334	567	800
9-Robot-c	25	50	75	147	236	325
11-31	14	28	42	82	121	160

PETER PAN RECORDS (See Power Records)

PETER PAN TREASURE CHEST (See Dell Giants)

PETER PARKER (See The Spectacular Spider-Man)

PETER PARKER: SPIDER-MAN
Marvel Comics: Jan, 1999 - No. 57, Aug, 2003 ($2.99/$1.99/$2.25)

	GD 2.0	VG 4.0	FN 6.0	VF 8.0	VF/NM 9.0	NM- 9.2
1-Mackie-s/Romita Jr.-a; wraparound-c						3.00
1-($6.95) DF Edition w/variant cover by the Romitas						7.00
2-11,13-17-($1.99): 2-Two covers; Thor app. 3-Iceman-c/app. 4-Marrow-c/app. 5-Spider-Woman app. 7,8-Blade app. 9,10-Venom app. 11-Iron Man & Thor-c/app.						2.50
12-($2.99) Sinister Six and Venom app.						3.00
18-24,26-43: 18-Begin $2.25-c. 20-Jenkins-s/Buckingham-a start. 23-Intro Typeface. 24-Maximum Security x-over. 29-Rescue of MJ. 30-Ramos-c. 42,43-Mahfood-a						2.50
25-($2.99) Two covers; Spider-Man & Green Goblin						3.00
44-47-Humberto Ramos-c/a; Green Goblin-c/app.						3.00
48,49,51-57: 48,49-Buckingham-c/a. 51,52-Herrera-a. 56,57-Kieth-a; Sandman returns						2.50
50-($3.50) Buckingham-c/a						3.50
...'99 Annual (8/99, $3.50) Man-Thing app.						3.50
...'00 Annual ($3.50) Bounty app.; Joe Bennett-a; Black Cat back-up story						3.50
...'01 Annual ($2.99) Avery-s						3.00

Peter Porkchops #9 © DC

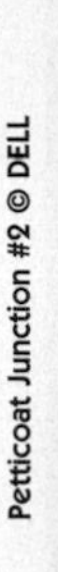

Petticoat Junction #2 © DELL

The Phantom #53 © KING

	GD 2.0	VG 4.0	FN 6.0	VF 8.0	VF/NM 9.0	NM- 9.2
...: A Day in the Life TPB (5/01, $14.95) r/#20-22,26; Webspinners #10-12						15.00
...: One Small Break TPB (2002, $16.95) r/#27,28,30-34; Andrews-c						17.00
Spider-Man: Return of the Goblin TPB (2002, $8.99) r/#44-47; Ramos-c						9.00
...Vol. 4: Trials & Tribulations TPB (2003, $11.99) r/#35,37,48-50; Cho-c						12.00

PETER PAT
United Features Syndicate: No. 8, 1939

	GD 2.0	VG 4.0	FN 6.0	VF 8.0	VF/NM 9.0	NM- 9.2
Single Series 8	36	72	108	212	341	470

PETER PAUL'S 4 IN 1 JUMBO COMIC BOOK
Capitol Stories (Charlton): No date (1953)

	GD 2.0	VG 4.0	FN 6.0	VF 8.0	VF/NM 9.0	NM- 9.2
1-Contains 4 comics bound; Space Adventures, Space Western, Crime & Justice, Racket Squad in Action	40	80	120	235	380	525

PETER PIG
Standard Comics: No. 5, May, 1953 - No. 6, Aug, 1953

	GD 2.0	VG 4.0	FN 6.0	VF 8.0	VF/NM 9.0	NM- 9.2
5,6	7	14	21	35	43	50

PETER PORKCHOPS (See Leading Comics #23)
National Periodical Publications: 11-12/49 - No. 61, 9-11/59; No. 62, 10-12/60 (1-11: 52 pgs.)

	GD 2.0	VG 4.0	FN 6.0	VF 8.0	VF/NM 9.0	NM- 9.2
1	34	68	102	198	319	440
2	15	30	45	90	140	190
3-10: 6- "Peter Rockets to Mars!" c/story	13	26	39	74	105	135
11-30	10	20	30	56	76	95
31-62	9	18	27	47	61	75

NOTE: *Otto Feuer a-all. Rube Grossman-a most issues. Sheldon Mayer a-30-38, 40-44, 46-52, 61.*

PETER PORKER, THE SPECTACULAR SPIDER-HAM
Star Comics (Marvel): May, 1985 - No. 17, Sept, 1987 (Also see Marvel Tails)

	GD 2.0	VG 4.0	FN 6.0	VF 8.0	VF/NM 9.0	NM- 9.2
1-Michael Golden-c						5.00
2-17: 12-Origin/1st app. Bizarro Phil. 13-Halloween issue						4.00

NOTE: *Back-up features: 2-X-Bugs. 3-Iron Mouse. 4-Croctor Strange. 5-Thrr, Dog of Thunder.*

PETER POTAMUS (TV)
Gold Key: Jan, 1965 (Hanna-Barbera)

	GD 2.0	VG 4.0	FN 6.0	VF 8.0	VF/NM 9.0	NM- 9.2
1-1st app. Peter Potamus & So-So, Breezly & Sneezly	9	18	27	63	107	150

PETER RABBIT (See New Funnies #65 & Space Comics)
Dell Publishing Co.: No. 1, 1942

	GD 2.0	VG 4.0	FN 6.0	VF 8.0	VF/NM 9.0	NM- 9.2
Large Feature Comic 1	60	120	180	378	639	900

PETER RABBIT (Adventures of...; New Advs. of... #9 on)(Also see Funny Tunes & Space Comics)
Avon Periodicals: 1947 - No. 34, Aug-Sept, 1956

	GD 2.0	VG 4.0	FN 6.0	VF 8.0	VF/NM 9.0	NM- 9.2
1(1947)-Reprints 1943-44 Sunday strips; contains a biography & drawing of Cady	35	70	105	203	327	450
2 (4/48)	24	48	72	140	225	310
3 ('48) - 6(7/49)-Last Cady issue	21	42	63	123	197	270
7-10(1950-8/51): 9-New logo	10	20	30	58	79	100
11(11/51)-34('56)-Avon's character	9	18	27	50	65	80
...Easter Parade (1952, 25¢, 132 pgs.)	19	38	57	112	176	240
...Jumbo Book (1954-Giant Size, 25¢)-Jesse James by Kinstler (6 pgs.); space ship-c	23	46	69	133	214	295

PETER RABBIT 3-D
Eternity Comics: April, 1990 ($2.95, with glasses; sealed in plastic bag)

	GD 2.0	VG 4.0	FN 6.0	VF 8.0	VF/NM 9.0	NM- 9.2
1-By Harrison Cady (reprints)						3.00

PETER, THE LITTLE PEST (#4 titled Petey)
Marvel Comics Group: Nov, 1969 - No. 4, May, 1970

	GD 2.0	VG 4.0	FN 6.0	VF 8.0	VF/NM 9.0	NM- 9.2
1	6	12	18	39	62	85
2-4-r-Dexter the Demon & Melvin the Monster	4	8	12	28	44	60

PETE'S DRAGON (See Walt Disney Showcase #43)

PETE THE PANIC
Stanmor Publications: November, 1955

	GD 2.0	VG 4.0	FN 6.0	VF 8.0	VF/NM 9.0	NM- 9.2
nn-Code approved	5	10	15	24	30	35

PETEY (See Peter, the Little Pest)

PETTICOAT JUNCTION (TV, inspired Green Acres)
Dell Publ. Co.: Oct-Dec, 1964 - No. 5, Oct-Dec, 1965 (#1-3, 5 have photo-c)

	GD 2.0	VG 4.0	FN 6.0	VF 8.0	VF/NM 9.0	NM- 9.2
1	7	14	21	47	76	105
2-5	5	10	15	32	51	70

PETUNIA (Also see Looney Tunes and Porky Pig)
Dell Publishing Co.: No. 463, Apr, 1953

	GD 2.0	VG 4.0	FN 6.0	VF 8.0	VF/NM 9.0	NM- 9.2
Four Color 463	4	8	12	28	44	60

PHAGE (See Neil Gaiman's Teknophage & Neil Gaiman's Phage-Shadowdeath)

PHANTACEA
McPherson Publishing Co.: Sept, 1977 - No. 6, Summer, 1980 (B&W)

	GD 2.0	VG 4.0	FN 6.0	VF 8.0	VF/NM 9.0	NM- 9.2
1-Early Dave Sim-a (32 pgs.)	3	6	9	20	40	60
2-Dave Sim-a(10 pgs.)	2	4	6	13	18	22
3-6: 3-Flip-c w/Damnation Bridge. 4-Gene Day-a	2	4	6	9	13	16

PHANTASMO (See The Funnies #45)
Dell Publishing Co.: No. 18, 1941

	GD 2.0	VG 4.0	FN 6.0	VF 8.0	VF/NM 9.0	NM- 9.2
Large Feature Comic 18	38	76	114	222	356	490

PHANTOM, THE
David McKay Publishing Co.: 1939 - 1949

	GD 2.0	VG 4.0	FN 6.0	VF 8.0	VF/NM 9.0	NM- 9.2
Feature Books 20	90	180	270	567	959	1350
Feature Books 22	65	130	195	410	693	975
Feature Books 39	50	100	150	310	518	725
Feature Books 53,56,57	40	80	120	244	397	550

PHANTOM, THE (See Ace Comics, Defenders Of The Earth, Eat Right to Work and Win, Future Comics, Harvey Comics Hits #51,56, Harvey Hits #1, 6, 12, 15, 26, 36, 44, 48, & King Comics)

PHANTOM, THE (nn (#29)-Published overseas only) (Also see Comics Reading Libraries in the Promotional Comics section)
Gold Key(#1-17)/King(#18-28)/Charlton(#30 on): Nov, 1962 - No. 17, Jul, 1966; No. 18, Sept, 1966 - No. 28, Dec, 1967; No. 30, Feb, 1969 - No. 74, Jan, 1977

	GD 2.0	VG 4.0	FN 6.0	VF 8.0	VF/NM 9.0	NM- 9.2
1-Origin revealed on inside-c & back-c	16	32	48	114	212	310
2-King, Queen & Jack begins, ends #11	9	18	27	63	107	150
3-5	8	16	24	54	90	125
6-10	7	14	21	45	73	100
11-17: 12-Track Hunter begins	6	12	18	37	59	80
18-Flash Gordon begins; Wood-a	5	10	15	30	48	65
19-24: 20-Flash Gordon ends (both by Gil Kane). 21-Mandrake begins. 20,24-Girl Phantom app.	4	8	12	28	44	60
25-28: 25-Jeff Jones-a(4 pgs.); 1 pg. Williamson ad. 26-Brick Bradford app. 28(nn)-Brick Bradford app.	4	8	12	22	34	45
30-33: 33-Last 12¢ issue	3	6	9	17	25	32
34-40: 36,39-Ditko-a	3	6	9	16	23	30
41-66: 46-Intro. The Piranha. 62-Bolle-c	3	6	9	14	19	24
67-Origin retold; Newton-c/a	3	6	9	17	25	32
68-73-Newton-c/a	2	4	6	13	18	22
74-Classic flag-c by Newton; Newton-a;	3	6	9	16	23	30

NOTE: *Aparo a-31-34, 36-38; c-31-38, 60, 61. Painted c-1-17.*

PHANTOM, THE
DC Comics: May, 1988 - No. 4, Aug, 1988 ($1.25, mini-series)

	GD 2.0	VG 4.0	FN 6.0	VF 8.0	VF/NM 9.0	NM- 9.2
1-4: Orlando-c/a in all						3.00

PHANTOM, THE
DC Comics: Mar, 1989 - No. 13, Mar, 1990 ($1.50)

	GD 2.0	VG 4.0	FN 6.0	VF 8.0	VF/NM 9.0	NM- 9.2
1-13: 1-Brief origin						3.00

PHANTOM, THE
Wolf Publishing: 1992 - No. 8, 1993 ($2.25)

	GD 2.0	VG 4.0	FN 6.0	VF 8.0	VF/NM 9.0	NM- 9.2
1-8						2.50

PHANTOM, THE
Moonstone: 2003 - Present ($3.50/$3.99)

	GD 2.0	VG 4.0	FN 6.0	VF 8.0	VF/NM 9.0	NM- 9.2
1-21: 1-Cassaday-c/Raab-s/Quinn-a						4.00
... Annual #1 (2007, $6.50) Blevins-c; stroy and art by various incl. Nolan						6.50

PHANTOM BLOT, THE (#1 titled New Adventures of...)
Gold Key: Oct, 1964 - No. 7, Nov, 1966 (Disney)

	GD 2.0	VG 4.0	FN 6.0	VF 8.0	VF/NM 9.0	NM- 9.2
1 (Meets The Mysterious Mr. X)	6	12	18	41	66	90
2-1st Super Goof	5	10	15	34	55	75
3-7	4	8	12	22	34	45

PHANTOM EAGLE (See Mighty Midget, Marvel Super Heroes #16 & Wow #6)

PHANTOM FORCE
Image Comics/Genesis West #0, 3-7: 12/93 - #2, 1994; #0, 3/94; #3, 5/94 - #8, 10/94 ($2.50/$3.50, limited series)

	GD 2.0	VG 4.0	FN 6.0	VF 8.0	VF/NM 9.0	NM- 9.2
0 (3/94, $2.50)-Kirby/Jim Lee-c; Kirby-p pgs. 1,5,24-29.						3.00
1 (12/93, $2.50)-Polybagged w/trading card; Kirby Liefeld-c; Kirby plots/pencils w/inks by Liefeld, McFarlane, Jim Lee, Silvestri, Larsen, Williams, Ordway & Miki						3.00
2 ($3.50)-Kirby-a(p); Kirby/Larson-c						3.50
3-8: 3-(5/94, $2.50)-Kirby/McFarlane-c 4-(5/94)-Kirby-c(p). 5-(6/94)						3.00

PHANTOM GUARD
Image Comics (WildStorm Productions): Oct, 1997 - No. 6, Mar, 1998 ($2.50)

Phantom Lady #19 © FOX

Phantom Stranger #33 © DC

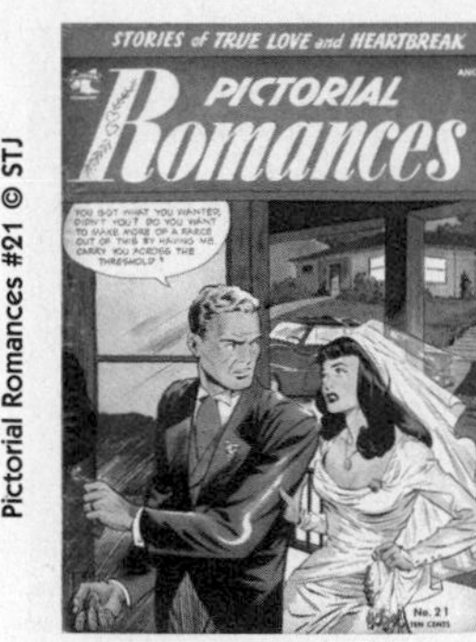

Pictorial Romances #21 © STJ

GD VG FN VF VF/NM NM-
2.0 4.0 6.0 8.0 9.0 9.2

1-6: 1-Two covers 3.00
1-($3.50)-Voyager Pack w/Wildcore preview 3.50

PHANTOM JACK
Image Comics: Mar, 2004 - No. 5, July, 2004 ($2.95)
1-5-Mike San Giacomo-s/Mitchell Breitweiser-a. 4-Initial printings with errors exist 3.00
The Collected Edition (Speakeasy Comics, 2005, $17.99) r/series; Bendis intro 18.00

PHANTOM LADY (1st Series) (My Love Secret #24 on) (Also see All Top, Daring Adventures, Freedom Fighters, Jungle Thrills, & Wonder Boy)
Fox Features Syndicate: No. 13, Aug, 1947 - No. 23, Apr, 1949
13(#1)-Phantom Lady by Matt Baker begins (see Police Comics #1 for 1st app.); Blue Beetle story 423 846 1269 3000 5250 7500
14-16: 14(#2)-Not Baker-c. 15-P.L. injected with experimental drug. 16-Negligee-c, panels; true crime stories begin 260 520 780 1638 2769 3900
17-Classic bondage cover; used in **SOTI**, illo "Sexual stimulation by combining 'headlights' with the sadist's dream of tying up a woman" 639 1278 1917 4601 8051 11,500
18,19 180 360 540 1134 1917 2700
20-22 150 300 450 945 1598 2250
23-Bondage-c 160 320 480 1008 1704 2400
NOTE: ***Matt Baker** a-in all; c-13, 15-21. **Kamen** a-22, 23.*

PHANTOM LADY (2nd Series) (See Terrific Comics) (Formerly Linda)
Ajax/Farrell Publ.: V1#5, Dec-Jan, 1954/1955 - No. 4, June, 1955
V1#5(#1)-By Matt Baker 117 234 351 737 1244 1750
V1#2-Last pre-code 87 174 261 548 924 1300
3,4-Red Rocket. 3-Heroin story 68 136 204 428 727 1025

PHANTOM LADY
Verotik Publications: 1994 ($9.95)
1-Reprints G. A. stories from Phantom Lady and All Top Comics; Adam Hughes-c 10.00

PHANTOM PLANET, THE
Dell Publishing Co.: No. 1234, 1961
Four Color 1234-Movie 7 14 21 47 76 105

PHANTOM STRANGER, THE (1st Series)(See Saga of Swamp Thing)
National Periodical Publications: Aug-Sept, 1952 - No. 6, June-July, 1953
1(Scarce)-1st app. 200 400 600 1260 2130 3000
2 (Scarce) 110 220 330 693 1172 1650
3-6 (Scarce) 95 190 285 599 1012 1425
Ashcan (8,9/52) Not distributed to newsstands, only for in house use (no known sales)

PHANTOM STRANGER, THE (2nd Series) (See Showcase #80) (See Showcase Presents for B&W reprints)
National Periodical Publications: May-June, 1969 - No. 41, Feb-Mar, 1976
1-2nd S.A. app. P. Stranger; only 12¢ issue 11 22 33 75 133 190
2,3 6 12 18 39 62 85
4-1st new look Phantom Stranger; N. Adams-a 6 12 18 41 66 90
5-7 5 10 15 30 48 65
8-14: 14-Last 15¢ issue 3 6 9 20 30 40
15-19: All 25¢ giants (52 pgs.) 4 8 12 22 34 45
20-Dark Circle begins, ends #24. 3 6 9 14 20 26
21,22 2 4 6 11 16 20
23-Spawn of Frankenstein begins by Kaluta 4 8 12 22 34 45
24,25,27-30-Last Spawn of Frankenstein 3 6 9 18 27 35
26- Book-length story featuring Phantom Stranger, Dr. 13 & Spawn of Frankenstein 3 6 9 19 29 38
31-The Black Orchid begins (6-7/74). 3 6 9 18 27 35
32,34-38: 34-Last 20¢ issue (#35 on are 25¢) 2 4 6 10 14 18
33,39-41: 33-Deadman-c/story. 39-41-Deadman app. 2 4 6 13 18 22
NOTE: ***N. Adams** a-4; c-3-19. **Anderson** a-4, 5i. **Aparo** a-7-17, 19-26; c-20-24, 33-41. **B. Bailey** a-27-30. **DeZuniga** a-12-16, 18, 19, 21, 22, 31, 34. **Grell** a-33. **Kaluta** a-23-25; c-26. **Meskin** r-15, 16, 18, 19. **Redondo** a-32, 35, 36. **Sparling** a-20. **Starr** a-17r. **Toth** a-15r. Black Orchid by **Carrilo**-38-41. Dr. 13 solo in-13, 18, 19, 20, 21, 34. Frankenstein by **Kaluta**-23-25; by **Baily**-27-30. No Black Orchid-33, 34, 37.*

PHANTOM STRANGER (See Justice League of America #103)
DC Comics: Oct, 1987 - No. 4, Jan, 1988 (75¢, limited series)
1-4-Mignola/Russell-c/a & Eclipso app. in all. 3,4-Eclipso-c 3.00

PHANTOM STRANGER (See Vertigo Visions-The Phantom Stranger)

PHANTOM: THE GHOST WHO WALKS
Marvel Comics: Feb, 1995 - No. 3, Apr, 1995 ($2.95, limited series)
1-3 4.00

PHANTOM: THE GHOST WHO WALKS
Moonstone: 2003 ($16.95, TPB)
nn-Three new stories by Raab, Goulart, Collins, Blanco and others; Klauba painted-c 17.00

GD VG FN VF VF/NM NM-
2.0 4.0 6.0 8.0 9.0 9.2

PHANTOM 2040 (TV cartoon)
Marvel Comics: May, 1995 - No. 4, Aug, 1995 ($1.50)
1-4-Based on animated series; Ditko-a(p) in all 3.00

PHANTOM WITCH DOCTOR (Also see Durango Kid #8 & Eerie #8)
Avon Periodicals: 1952
1-Kinstler-c/a (7 pgs.) 47 94 141 291 488 685

PHANTOM ZONE, THE (See Adventure #283 & Superboy #100, 104)
DC Comics: January, 1982 - No. 4, April, 1982
1-4-Superman app. in all. 2-4: Batman, Green Lantern app. 3.00
NOTE: ***Colan** a-1-4p; c-1-4p. **Giordano** c-1-4i.*

PHAZE
Eclipse Comics: Apr, 1988 - No. 2, Oct, 1988 ($2.25)
1,2: 1-Sienkiewicz-c. 2-Gulacy painted-c 2.50

PHIL RIZZUTO (Baseball Hero)(See Sport Thrills, Accepted reprint)
Fawcett Publications: 1951 (New York Yankees)
nn-Photo-c 69 138 207 435 738 1040

PHOENIX
Atlas/Seaboard Publ.: Jan, 1975 - No. 4, Oct, 1975
1-Origin; Rovin-s/Amendola-a 1 3 4 6 8 10
2-4: 3-Origin & only app. The Dark Avenger. 4-New origin/costume The Protector (formerly Phoenix) 1 2 3 5 7 9
NOTE: ***Infantino** appears in #1, 2. **Austin** a-3i. **Thorne** c-3.*

PHOENIX (...The Untold Story)
Marvel Comics Group: April, 1984 ($2.00, one-shot)
1-Byrne/Austin-r/X-Men #137 with original unpublished ending 2 4 6 8 10 12

PHOENIX RESURRECTION, THE
Malibu Comics (Ultraverse): 1995 - 1996 ($3.95)
Genesis #1 (12/95)-X-Men app; wraparound-c, Revelations #1 (12/95)-X-Men app; wraparound-c, Aftermath #1 (1/96)-X-Men app. 4.00
0-($1.95)-r/series 2.50
0-American Entertainment Ed. 4.00

PICNIC PARTY (See Dell Giants)

PICTORIAL CONFESSIONS (Pictorial Romances #4 on)
St. John Publishing Co.: Sept, 1949 - No. 3, Dec, 1949
1-Baker-c/a(3) 45 90 135 279 465 650
2-Baker-a; photo-c 24 48 72 143 229 315
3-Kubert, Baker-a; part Kubert-c 26 52 78 154 247 340

PICTORIAL LOVE STORIES (Formerly Tim McCoy)
Charlton Comics: No. 22, Oct, 1949 - No. 26, July, 1950 (all photo-c)
22-26: All have "Me-Dan Cupid". 25-Fred Astaire-c 19 38 57 112 176 240

PICTORIAL LOVE STORIES
St. John Publishing Co.: October, 1952
1-Baker-c 31 62 93 181 291 400

PICTORIAL ROMANCES (Formerly Pictorial Confessions)
St. John Publ. Co.: No. 4, Jan, 1950; No. 5, Jan, 1951 - No. 24, Mar, 1954
4-Baker-a; photo-c 31 62 93 181 291 400
5,10-All Matt Baker issues. 5-Reprints all stories from #4 w/new Baker-c 27 54 81 158 254 350
6-9,12,13,15,16-Baker-c, 2-3 stories 23 46 69 135 218 300
11-Baker-c/a(3); Kubert-r/Hollywood Confessions #1 28 56 84 162 261 360
14,21-24: Baker-c/a each. 21,24-Each has signed story by Estrada 22 44 66 131 211 290
17-20(7/53, 25¢, 100 pgs.): Baker-c/a; each has two signed stories by Estrada 41 82 123 256 428 600
NOTE: ***Matt Baker** art in most issues. **Estrada** a-17-20(2), 21, 24.*

PICTURE NEWS
Lafayette Street Corp.: Jan, 1946 - No. 10, Jan-Feb, 1947
1-Milt Gross begins, ends No. 6; 4 pg. Kirby-a; A-Bomb-c/story 41 82 123 250 413 575
2-Atomic explosion panels; Frank Sinatra/Perry Como story 22 44 66 127 204 280
3-Atomic explosion panels; Frank Sinatra, June Allyson, Benny Goodman stories 19 38 57 112 176 240
4-Atomic explosion panels; "Caesar and Cleopatra" movie adapt. w/Claude Raines &

Picture Stories From the Bible #3 © WMG

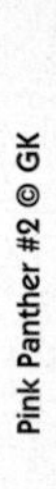

Pink Panther #2 © GK

Pinky and the Brain #7 © WB

	GD 2.0	VG 4.0	FN 6.0	VF 8.0	VF/NM 9.0	NM- 9.2

Vivian Leigh; Jackie Robinson story 21 42 63 123 197 270
5-7: 5-Hank Greenberg story; Atomic explosion panel. 6-Joe Louis-c/story
15 30 45 94 147 200
8,10: 8-Monte Hale story (9-10/46; 1st?). 10-Dick Quick; A-Bomb story; Krigstein, Gross-a
17 34 51 98 154 210
9-A-Bomb story; "Crooked Mile" movie adaptation; Joe DiMaggio story.
19 38 57 112 176 240

PICTURE PARADE (Picture Progress #5 on)
Gilberton Company (Also see A Christmas Adventure): Sept, 1953 - V1#4, Dec, 1953 (28 pgs.)

V1#1-Andy's Atomic Adventures; A-bomb blast-c; (Teachers version distributed to schools exists) 20 40 60 115 183 250
2-Around the World with the United Nations 12 24 36 69 97 125
3-Adventures of the Lost One(The American Indian), 4-A Christmas Adventure (r-under same title in 1969) 12 24 36 69 97 125

PICTURE PROGRESS (Formerly Picture Parade)
Gilberton Corp.: V1#5, Jan, 1954 - V3#2, Oct, 1955 (28-36 pgs.)

V1#5-9,V2#1-9: 5-News in Review 1953. 6-The Birth of America. 7-The Four Seasons. 8-Paul Revere's Ride. 9-The Hawaiian Islands(5/54). V2#1-The Story of Flight(9/54). 2-Vote for Crazy River (The Meaning of Elections). 3-Louis Pasteur. 4-The Star Spangled Banner. 5-News in Review 1954. 6-Alaska: The Great Land. 7-Life in the Circus. 8-The Time of the Cave Man. 9-Summer Fun(5/55) 9 18 27 47 61 75
V3#1,2: 1-The Man Who Discovered America. 2-The Lewis & Clark Expedition
8 16 24 44 57 70

PICTURE SCOPE JUNGLE ADVENTURES (See Jungle Thrills)

PICTURE STORIES FROM AMERICAN HISTORY
National/All-American/E. C. Comics: 1945 - No. 4, Sum, 1947 (#1,2: 10¢, 56 pgs.; #3,4: 15¢, 52 pgs.)

1 30 60 90 174 280 385
2-4 24 48 72 140 225 310

PICTURE STORIES FROM SCIENCE
E.C. Comics: Spring, 1947 - No. 2, Fall, 1947

1-(15¢) 30 60 90 174 280 385
2-(10¢) 24 48 72 140 225 310

PICTURE STORIES FROM THE BIBLE (See Narrative Illustration, the Story of the Comics by M.C. Gaines)
National/All-American/E.C. Comics: 1942 - No. 4, Fall, 1943; 1944-46

1-4('42-Fall, '43)-Old Testament (DC) 24 48 72 140 225 310
Complete Old Testament Edition, (12/43-DC, 50¢, 232 pgs.);-1st printing; contains #1-4; 2nd - 8th (1/47) printings exist; later printings by E.C. some with 65¢-c
27 54 81 158 254 350
Complete Old Testament Edition (1945-publ. by Bible Pictures Ltd.)-232 pgs., hardbound, in color with dust jacket 27 54 81 158 254 350
NOTE: *Both Old and New Testaments published in England by Bible Pictures Ltd. in hardback, 1943, in color, 376 pgs. (2 vols.: O.T. 232 pgs. & N.T. 144 pgs.), and were also published by Scarf Press in 1979 (Old Test., $9.95) and in 1980 (New Test., $7.95)*
1-3(New Test.; 1944-46, DC)-52 pgs. ea. 19 38 57 109 172 235
The Complete Life of Christ Edition (1945, 25¢, 96 pgs.)-Contains #1&2 of the New Testament Edition 27 54 81 158 254 350
1,2(Old Testament-r in comic book form)(E.C., 1946; 52 pgs.)
19 38 57 109 172 235
1(DC),2(AA),3(EC)(New Testament-r in comic book form)(E.C., 1946; 52 pgs.)
19 38 57 109 172 235
Complete New Testament Edition (1945-E.C., 40¢, 144 pgs.)-Contains #1-3
1946 printing has 50¢-c 27 54 81 158 254 350
NOTE: *Another British series entitled **The Bible Illustrated** from 1947 has recently been discovered, with the same internal artwork. This eight edition series (5-OT, 3-NT) is of particular interest to Classics Ill. collectors because it exactly copied the C.I. logo format. The British publisher was Thorpe & Porter, who in 1951 began publishing the British Classics Ill. series. All editions of The Bible Ill. have new British painted covers. While this market is still new, and not all editions have as yet been found, current market value is about the same as the first U.S. editions of Picture Stories From The Bible.*

PICTURE STORIES FROM WORLD HISTORY
E.C. Comics: Spring, 1947 - No. 2, Summer, 1947 (52, 48 pgs.)

1-(15¢) 30 60 90 174 280 385
2-(10¢) 24 48 72 140 225 310

PINHEAD
Marvel Comics (Epic Comics): Dec, 1993 - No. 6, May, 1994 ($2.50)

1-($2.95)-Embossed foil-c by Kelley Jones; Intro Pinhead & Disciples (Snakeoil, Hangman, Fan Dancer & Dixie) 3.00
2-6 2.50

PINHEAD & FOODINI (TV)(Also see Foodini & Jingle Dingle Christmas...)
Fawcett Publications: July, 1951 - No. 4, Jan, 1952 (Early TV comic)

1-(52 pgs.)-Photo-c; based on TV puppet show 32 64 96 186 298 410
2,3-Photo-c 16 32 48 92 144 195
4 14 28 42 78 112 145

PINHEAD VS. MARSHALL LAW (Law in Hell)
Marvel Comics (Epic): Nov, 1993 - No. 2, Dec, 1993 ($2.95, lim. series)

1,2: 1-Embossed red foil-c. 2-Embossed silver foil-c 3.00

PINK DUST
Kitchen Sink Press: 1998 ($3.50, B&W, mature)

1-J. O'Barr-s/a 3.50

PINK PANTHER, THE (TV)(See The Inspector & Kite Fun Book)
Gold Key #1-70/Whitman #71-87: April, 1971 - No. 87, Mar, 1984

1-The Inspector begins 5 10 15 34 55 75
2-5 3 6 9 18 27 35
6-10 3 6 9 14 19 24
11-30: Warren Tufts-a #16-on 2 4 6 9 13 16
31-60 2 4 6 8 11 14
61-70 1 2 3 5 7 9
71-74,81-83: 81(2/82), 82(3/82), 83(4/82) 2 4 6 8 10 12
75(8/80)-77 (Whitman pre-pack) (scarce) 3 6 9 19 29 38
78(1/81)-80 (Whitman pre-pack) (not as scarce) 2 4 6 10 14 18
78 (1/81, 40¢-c) Cover price error variant 3 6 9 14 20 26
84-87(All #90266 on-c, no date or date code): 84(6/83), 85(8/83), 87(3/84)
3 6 9 14 20 26
Mini-comic No. 1(1976)(3-1/4x6-1/2") 1 3 4 6 8 10
NOTE: *Pink Panther began as a movie cartoon. (See Golden Comics Digest #38, 45 and March of Comics #376, 384, 390, 409, 418, 429, 441, 449, 461, 473, 486); #37, 72, 80-85 contain reprints.*

PINK PANTHER SUPER SPECIAL (TV)
Harvey Comics: Oct, 1993 ($2.25, 68 pgs.)

V2#1-The Inspector & Wendy Witch stories also 4.00

PINK PANTHER, THE
Harvey Comics: Nov, 1993 - No. 9, July, 1994 ($1.50)

V2#1-9 3.00

PINKY & THE BRAIN (See Animaniacs)
DC Comics: July, 1996 - No. 27, Nov, 1998 ($1.75/$1.95/$1.99)

1-27, ...Christmas Special (1/96, $1.50) 3.00

PINKY LEE (See Adventures of...)

PINKY THE EGGHEAD
I.W./Super Comics: 1963 (Reprints from Noodnik)

I.W. Reprint #1,2(nd) 2 4 6 8 11 14
Super Reprint #14-r/Noodnik Comics #4 2 4 6 8 11 14

PINOCCHIO (See 4-Color #92, 252, 545, 1203, Mickey Mouse Mag. V5#3, Movie Comics under Wonderful Advs. of..., New Advs. of..., Thrilling Comics #2, Walt Disney Showcase, Walt Disney's..., Wonderful Advs. of..., & World's Greatest Stories #2)
Dell Publishing Co.: No. 92, 1945 - No. 1203, Mar, 1962 (Disney)

Four Color 92-The Wonderful Adventures of...; 16 pg. Donald Duck story ; entire book by Kelly 50 100 150 400 750 1100
Four Color 252 (10/49)-Origin, not by Kelly 10 20 30 73 129 185
Four Color 545 (3/54)-The Wonderful Advs. of...; part-r of 4-Color #92; Disney-movie
7 14 21 47 76 105
Four Color 1203 (3/62) 5 10 15 34 55 75

PINOCCHIO AND THE EMPEROR OF THE NIGHT
Marvel Comics: Mar, 1988 ($1.25, 52 pgs.)

1-Adapts film 3.00

PINOCCHIO LEARNS ABOUT KITES (See Kite Fun Book)

PIN-UP PETE (Also see Great Lover Romances & Monty Hall...)
Toby Press: 1952

1-Jack Sparling pin-ups 18 36 54 103 162 220

PIONEER MARSHAL (See Fawcett Movie Comics)

PIONEER PICTURE STORIES
Street & Smith Publications: Dec, 1941 - No. 9, Dec, 1943

1-The Legless Air Ace begins 31 62 93 181 291 400
2 -True life story of Errol Flynn 15 30 45 90 140 200
3-9 14 28 42 82 121 165

PIONEER WEST ROMANCES (Firehair #1,2,7-11)

Pitt #11 © Dale Keown

Planetary #25 © WSP

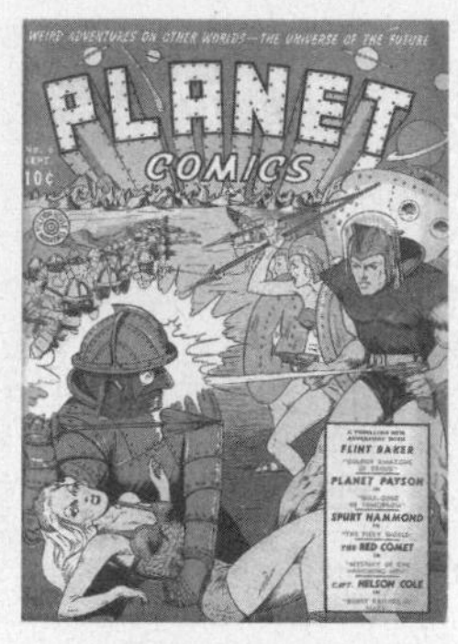

Planet Comics #8 © FH

GD VG FN VF VF/NM NM-
2.0 4.0 6.0 8.0 9.0 9.2

Fiction House Magazines: No. 3, Spring, 1950 - No. 6, Winter, 1950-51
3-(52 pgs.)-Firehair continues 19 38 57 109 172 235
4-6 19 38 57 109 172 235

PIPSQUEAK (See The Adventures of...)

PIRACY
E. C. Comics: Oct-Nov, 1954 - No. 7, Oct-Nov, 1955
1-Williamson/Torres-a 27 54 81 216 343 470
2-Williamson/Torres-a 17 34 51 136 218 300
3-7: 5-7-Comics Code symbol on cover 13 26 39 104 170 235
NOTE: ***Crandall** a-in all; c-2-4. **Davis** a-1, 2, 6. **Evans** a-3-7; c-7. **Ingels** a-3-7. **Krigstein** a-3-5, 7; c-5, 6. **Wood** a-1, 2; c-1.*

PIRACY
Gemstone Publishing: March, 1998 - No. 7, Sept, 1998 ($2.50)
1-7: E.C. reprints 2.50
Annual 1 ($10.95) Collects #1-4 11.00
Annual 2 ($7.95) Collects #5-7 8.00

PIRANA (See The Phantom #46 & Thrill-O-Rama #2, 3)

PIRATE CORP$, THE (See Hectic Planet)
Eternity Comics/Slave Labor Graphics: 1987 - No. 4, 1988 ($1.95)
1-4: 1,2-Color. 3,4-B&W 2.50
Special 1 ('89, B&W)-Slave Labor Publ. 2.50

PIRATE CORP$, THE (Volume 2)
Slave Labor Graphics: 1989 - No. 6, 1992 ($1.95)
1-6-Dorkin-s/a 2.50

PIRATE OF THE GULF, THE (See Superior Stories #2)

PIRATES COMICS
Hillman Periodicals: Feb-Mar, 1950 - No. 4, Aug-Sept, 1950 (All 52 pgs.)
1 24 48 72 140 225 310
2-Dave Berg-a 17 34 51 98 154 210
3,4-Berg-a 15 30 45 88 137 185

PIRATES OF CONEY ISLAND, THE
Image Comics: Oct, 2006 - No. 8 ($2.99)
1-6-Rick Spears-s/Vasilis Lolos-a; two covers. 2-Cloonan var-c 3.00

PIRATES OF DARK WATER, THE (Hanna Barbera)
Marvel Comics: Nov, 1991 - No. 9, Aug, 1992 ($1.95)
1-9: 9-Vess-c 3.00

P.I.'S: MICHAEL MAUSER AND MS. TREE, THE
First Comics: Jan, 1985 - No. 3, May, 1985 ($1.25, limited series)
1-3: Staton-c/a(p) 2.50

PITT, THE (Also see The Draft & The War)
Marvel Comics: Mar, 1988 ($3.25, 52 pgs., one-shot)
1-Ties into Starbrand, D.P.7 3.50

PITT (See Youngblood #4 & Gen 13 #3,#4)
Image Comics #1-9/Full Bleed #1/2,10-on: Jan, 1993 - No. 20 ($1.95, intended as a four part limited series)
1/2-(12/95)-1st Full Bleed issue 4.00
1-Dale Keown-c/a. 1-1st app. The Pitt 4.00
2-13: All Dale Keown-c/a. 3 (Low distribution). 10 (1/96)-Indicia reads "January 1995" 3.00
14-20: 14-Begin $2.50-c, pullout poster 2.50
TPB-(1997, $9.95) r/#1/2, 1-4 10.00
TPB 2-(1999, $11.95) r/#5-9 12.00

PITT CREW
Full Bleed Studios: Aug, 1998 - No. 5, Dec, 1999 ($2.50)
1-5: 1-Richard Pace-s/Ken Lashley-a. 2-4-Scott Lee-a 2.50

PITT IN THE BLOOD
Full Bleed Studios: Aug, 1996 ($2.50, one-shot)
nn-Richard Pace-a/script 2.50

PIXIE & DIXIE & MR. JINKS (TV)(See Jinks, Pixie, and Dixie & Whitman Comic Books)
Dell Publishing Co./Gold Key: July-Sept, 1960 - Feb, 1963 (Hanna-Barbera)
Four Color 1112 7 14 21 50 83 115
Four Color 1196,1264, 01-631-207 (Dell, 7/62) 6 12 18 37 59 80
1(2/63-Gold Key) 6 12 18 43 69 95

PIXIE PUZZLE ROCKET TO ADVENTURELAND
Avon Periodicals: Nov, 1952

GD VG FN VF VF/NM NM-
2.0 4.0 6.0 8.0 9.0 9.2

1 14 28 42 80 115 150

PIXIES, THE (Advs. of...)(The Mighty Atom and ...#6 on)(See A-1 Comics #16)
Magazine Enterprises: Winter, 1946 - No. 4, Fall?, 1947; No. 5, 1948
1-Mighty Atom 9 18 27 50 65 80
2-5-Mighty Atom 6 12 18 28 34 40
I.W. Reprint #1(1958), 8-(Pee-Wee Pixies), 10-I.W. on cover, Super on inside 2 4 6 8 10 12

PIZZAZZ
Marvel Comics: Oct, 1977 - No. 16, Jan, 1979 (slick-color kids mag. w/puzzles, games, comics)
1-Star Wars photo-c/article; origin Tarzan; KISS photos/article; Iron-On bonus; 2 pg. pin-up calendars thru #8 3 6 9 18 27 35
2-Spider-Man-c; Beatles pin-up calendar 2 4 6 11 16 20
3-8: 3-Close Encounters-s; Bradbury-s. 4-Alice Cooper, Travolta; Charlie's Angels/Fonz/Hulk/Spider-Man-c. 5-Star Trek quiz. 6-Asimov-s. 7-James Bond; Spock/Darth Vader-c. 8-TV Spider-Man photo-c/article 2 4 6 10 14 18
9-14: 9-Shaun Cassidy-c. 10-Sgt. Pepper-c/s. 12-Battlestar Galactica-s; Spider-Man app. 13-TV Hulk-c/s. 14-Meatloaf-c/s 2 4 6 9 12 15
15,16: 15-Battlestar Galactica-s. 16-Movie Superman photo-c/s, Hulk. 2 4 6 10 14 18
NOTE: ***Star Wars** comics in all (1-6:Chaykin-a, 7-9: DeZuniga-a, 10-13:Simonson/Janson-a. 14-16:Cockrum-a). **Tarzan** comics, 1pg.-#1-8. 1pg. "Hey Look" by Kurtzman #12-16.*

PLANETARY (See Preview in flip book Gen13 #33)
DC Comics (WildStorm Prod.): Apr, 1999 - Present ($2.50/$2.95/$2.99)
1-Ellis-s/Cassaday-a/c 1 3 4 6 8 10
2-5 6.00
6-10 5.00
11-15: 12-Fourth Man revealed 4.00
16-26: 16-Begin $2.95-c. 23-Origin of The Drummer 3.00
...: All Over the World and Other Stories (2000, $14.95) r/#1-6 & Preview 15.00
...: All Over the World and Other Stories-Hardcover (2000, $24.95) r/#1-6 & Preview; with dustjacket 25.00
.../Batman: Night on Earth 1 (8/03, $5.95) Ellis-s/Cassaday-a 6.00
...: Crossing Worlds (2004, $14.95) r/Batman, JLA, and The Authority x-overs 15.00
.../JLA: Terra Occulta (11/02, $5.95) Elseworlds; Ellis-s/Ordway-a 6.00
...: Leaving the 20th Century -HC (2004, $24.95) r/#13-18 25.00
...: Leaving the 20th Century -SC (2004, $14.99) r/#13-18 25.00
.../The Authority: Ruling the World (8/00, $5.95) Ellis-s/Phil Jimenez-a 6.00
...: The Fourth Man -Hardcover (2001, $24.95) r/#7-12 25.00
...: The Planetary Reader (8/03, $5.95) r/#13-15 6.00

PLANETARY BRIGADE (Also see Hero Squared)
Boom Studios: Feb, 2006 - Present ($2.99)
1,2-Giffen & DeMatteis-s/art by various; Haley-c 3.00
... Origins 1-3 (10/06-4/07, $3.99) Giffen & DeMatteis-s/Julia Bax-a 4.00

PLANET COMICS
Fiction House Magazines: 1/40 - No. 62, 9/49; No. 63, Wint, 1949-50; No. 64, Spring, 1950; No. 65, 1951(nd); No. 66-68, 1952(nd); No. 69, Wint, 1952-53; No. 70-72, 1953(nd); No. 73, Winter, 1953-54
1-Origin Auro, Lord of Jupiter by Briefer (ends #61); Flint Baker & The Red Comet begin; Eisner/Fine-c 1200 2400 3600 9000 16,000 23,000
2-Lou Fine-c (Scarce) 428 856 1284 3082 5391 7700
3-Eisner-c 300 600 900 2010 3505 5000
4-Gale Allen and the Girl Squadron begins 283 566 849 1783 3017 4250
5,6-(Scarce): 5-Eisner/Fine-c 273 546 819 1720 2910 4100
7-12: 8-Robot-c. 12-The Star Pirate begins 210 420 630 1323 2237 3150
13,14: 13-Reff Ryan begins 153 306 459 964 1632 2300
15-(Scarce)-Mars, God of War begins (11/41); see Jumbo Comics #31 for 1st app. 300 600 900 2010 3505 5000
16-20,22 140 280 420 882 1491 2100
21-The Lost World & Hunt Bowman begin 147 294 441 926 1563 2200
23-26: 26-Space Rangers begin (9/43), end #71 128 256 384 806 1366 1925
27-30 103 206 309 649 1100 1550
31-35: 33-Origin Star Pirates Wonder Boots, reprinted in #52. 35-Mysta of the Moon begins, ends #62 88 176 264 554 940 1325
36-45: 38-1st Mysta of the Moon-c. 41-New origin of "Auro, Lord of Jupiter". 42-Last Gale Allen. 43-Futura begins 82 164 246 517 871 1225
46-60: 48-Robot-c. 53-Used in **SOTI**, pg. 32 64 128 192 403 682 960
61-68,70: 64,70-Robot-c. 65-70-All partial-r of earlier issues. 70-r/stories from #41 48 96 144 298 499 700
69-Used in **POP**, pgs. 101,102 48 96 144 298 499 700
71-73-No series stories. 71-Space Rangers strip 40 80 120 235 380 525

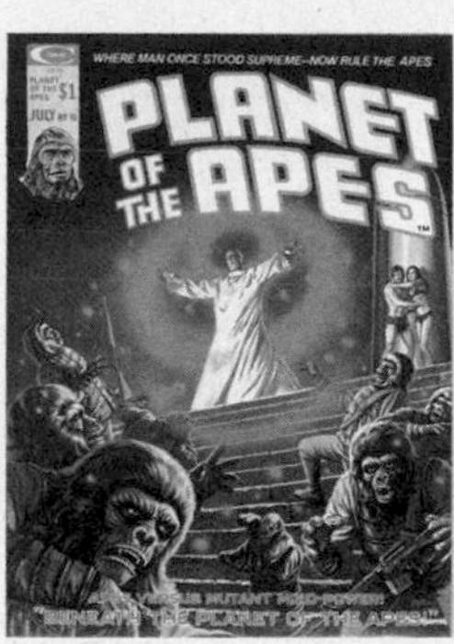

Planet of the Apes #10 © MAR

Plastic Man #33 © QUA

Playful Little Audrey #92 © HARV

GD VG FN VF VF/NM NM-
2.0 4.0 6.0 8.0 9.0 9.2

I.W. Reprint 1,8,9: 1(nd)-r/#70; cover-r from Attack on Planet Mars. 8 (r/#72), 9-r/#73 7 14 21 50 83 115

NOTE: ***Anderson*** *a-33-38, 40-51 (Star Pirate).* ***Matt Baker*** *a-53-59 (Mysta of the Moon).* ***Celardo*** *c-12.* ***Bill Discount*** *a-71 (Space Rangers).* ***Elias*** *c-70.* ***Evans*** *a-46-49 (Auro, Lord of Jupiter), 50-64 (Lost World).* ***Fine*** *c-2, 5.* ***Hopper*** *a-31, 35 (Gale Allen), 41, 42, 48, 49 (Mysta of the Moon).* ***Ingels*** *a-24-31 (Lost World), 56-61 (Auro, Lord of Jupiter).* ***Lubbers*** *a-44-47 (Space Rangers); c-40, 41.* ***Moreira*** *a-43, 44 (Mysta of the Moon).* ***Renee*** *a-40-49 (Lost World); c-33, 35, 39.* ***Tuska*** *a-30 (Star Pirate).* ***M. Whitman*** *a-50-52 (Mysta of the Moon), 53-58 (Star Pirate); c-71-73.* ***Starr*** *a-59.* ***Zolnerwich*** *c-10. 13-25. Bondage c-53.*

PLANET COMICS
Pacific Comics: 1984 ($5.95)

1-Reprints Planet Comics #1(1940) 1 2 3 5 6 8

PLANET COMICS
Blackthorne Publishing: Apr, 1988 - No. 3 ($2.00, color/B&W #3)

1-3: New stories. 1-Dave Stevens-c 3.00

PLANET HULK (See Incredible Hulk and Giant-Size Hulk #1 (2006))

PLANET OF THE APES (Magazine) (Also see Adventures on the... & Power Record Comics)
Marvel Comics Group: Aug, 1974 - No. 29, Feb, 1977 (B&W) (Based on movies)

1-Ploog-a 4 8 12 22 34 45
2-Ploog-a 3 6 9 16 22 28
3-10 2 4 6 13 18 22
11-20 3 6 9 14 19 24
21-28 (low distribution) 3 6 9 16 22 28
29 (low distribution) 5 10 15 30 48 65

NOTE: ***Alcala*** *a-7-11, 17-22, 24.* ***Ploog*** *a-1-4, 6, 8, 11, 13, 14, 19.* ***Sutton*** *a-11, 12, 15, 17, 19, 20, 23, 24, 29.* ***Tuska*** *a-1-6.*

PLANET OF THE APES
Adventure Comics: Apr, 1990 - No. 24, 1992 ($2.50, B&W)

1-New movie tie-in; comes w/outer-c (3 colors) 4.00
1-Limited serial numbered edition ($5.00) 5.00
1-2nd printing (no outer-c, $2.50) 2.50
2-24 3.00
Annual 1 ($3.50) 4.00
...Urchak's Folly 1-4 ($2.50, mini-series) 3.00

PLANET OF THE APES (The Human War)
Dark Horse Comics: Jun, 2001 - No. 3, Aug, 2001 ($2.99, limited series)

1-3-Follows the 2001 movie; Edginton-s 3.00

PLANET OF THE APES
Dark Horse Comics: Sept, 2001 - No. 6, Feb, 2002 ($2.99, ongoing series)

1-6: 1-3-Edginton-s. 1-Photo & Wagner covers. 2-Plunkett & photo-c 3.00

PLANET OF VAMPIRES
Seaboard Publications (Atlas): Feb, 1975 - No. 3, July, 1975

1-Neal Adams-c(i); 1st Broderick-c/a(p); Hama-s 2 4 6 8 11 14
2,3: 2-Neal Adams-c. 3-Heath-c/a 1 3 4 6 8 10

PLANET TERRY
Marvel Comics (Star Comics)/Marvel: April, 1985 - No. 12, March, 1986 (Children's comic)

1-12 3.00
1-Variant with "Star Chase" game on last page & inside back-c 10.00

PLASM (See Warriors of Plasm)
Defiant Comics: June, 1993

0-Came bound into Diamond Previews V3#6 (6/93); price is for complete Previews with comic still attached 3.00
0-Comic only removed from Previews 2.50

PLASMER
Marvel Comics UK: Nov, 1993 - No. 4, Feb, 1994 ($1.95, limited series)

1-($2.50)-Polybagged w/4 trading cards 2.75
2-4: Capt. America & Silver Surfer app. 2.50

PLASTIC FORKS
Marvel Comis (Epic Comics): 1990 - No. 5, 1990 ($4.95, 68 pgs., limited series, mature)

Book 1-5: Squarebound 5.00

PLASTIC MAN (Also see Police Comics & Smash Comics #17)
Vital Publ. No. 1,2/Quality Comics No. 3 on: Sum, 1943 - No. 64, Nov, 1956

nn(#1)- "In The Game of Death"; Skull-c; Jack Cole-c/a begins; ends-#64? 429 858 1287 2917 5109 7300
nn(#2, 2/44)- "The Gay Nineties Nightmare" 180 360 540 1134 1917 2700
3 (Spr, '46) 117 234 351 737 1249 1760
4 (Sum, '46) 88 176 264 554 940 1325
5 (Aut, '46) 72 144 216 454 770 1085
6-10 59 118 177 372 629 885
11-15,17-20 53 106 159 330 553 775
16-Classic-c 57 114 171 359 605 850
21-30: 26-Last non-r issue? 41 82 123 250 413 575
31-40: 40-Used in POP, pg. 91 34 68 102 198 319 440
41-64: 53-Last precode issue. 54-Robot-c 26 52 78 152 244 335
Super Reprint 11,16,18: 11('63)-r/#16. 16-r/#18 & #21; Cole-a. 18('64)-Spirit-r by Eisner from Police #95 4 8 12 24 37 50

NOTE: ***Cole*** *r-44, 49, 56, 58, 59 at least.* ***Cuidera*** *c-32-64i.*

PLASTIC MAN (See DC Special #15 & House of Mystery #160)
National Periodical Publications/DC Comics: 11-12/66 - No. 10, 5-6/68; V4#11, 2-3/76 - No. 20, 10-11/77

1-Real 1st app. Silver Age Plastic Man (House of Mystery #160 is actually tryout); Gil Kane-c/a; 12¢ issues begin 9 18 27 63 107 150
2-5: 4-Infantino-c; Mortimer-a 5 10 15 30 48 65
6-10('68): 7-G.A. Plastic Man & Woozy Winks (1st S.A. app.) app.; origin retold. 10-Sparling-a, last 12¢ issue 4 8 12 24 37 50
V4#11('76)-20: 11-20-Fradon-p. 17-Origin retold 1 3 4 6 8 10
...80-Page Giant (2003, $6.95) reprints origin and other stories in 80-Pg. Giant format 7.00
...Special 1 (8/99, $3.95) 4.00

PLASTIC MAN
DC Comics: Nov, 1988 - No. 4, Feb, 1989 ($1.00, mini-series)

1-4: 1-Origin; Woozy Winks app. 2.50

PLASTIC MAN
DC Comics: Feb, 2004 - No. 20, Mar, 2006 ($2.95/$2.99)

1-20-Kyle Baker-s/a in most. 1-Retells origin. 7,12-Scott Morse-s/a. 8-JLA cameo 3.00
...: On the Lam TPB (2004, $14.95) r/#1-6 15.00
...: Rubber Bandits TPB (2005, $14.99) r/#8-11,13,14 15.00

PLASTRON CAFE
Mirage Studios: Dec, 1992 - No. 4, July, 1993 ($2.25, B&W)

1-4: 1-Teenage Mutant Ninja Turtles app.; Kelly Freas-c. 2-Hildebrandt painted-c. 4-Spaced & Alien Fire stories 2.50

PLAYFUL LITTLE AUDREY (TV)(Also see Little Audrey #25)
Harvey Publications: 6/57 - No. 110, 11/73; No. 111, 8/74 - No. 121, 4/76

1 23 46 69 167 309 450
2 12 24 36 82 146 210
3-5 9 18 27 60 100 140
6-10 7 14 21 47 76 105
11-20 5 10 15 34 55 75
21-40 4 8 12 26 41 55
41-60 3 6 9 20 30 40
61-84: 84-Last 12¢ issue 3 6 9 16 22 28
85-99 2 4 6 11 16 20
100-52 pg. Giant 3 6 9 16 23 30
101-103: 52 pg. Giants 3 6 9 14 20 25
104-121 1 3 4 6 8 10
...In 3-D (Spring, 1988, $2.25, Blackthorne #66) 4.00

PLOP! (Also see The Best of DC #60)
National Periodical Publications: Sept-Oct, 1973 - No. 24, Nov-Dec, 1976

1-Sergio Aragonés-a begins; Wrightson-a 4 8 12 22 34 45
2-4,6-20 3 6 9 14 19 24
5-Wrightson-a 3 6 9 14 20 26
21-24 (52 pgs.). 23-No Aragonés-a 3 6 9 16 22 28

NOTE: ***Alcala*** *a-1-3.* ***Anderson*** *a-5.* ***Aragonés*** *a-1-22, 24.* ***Ditko*** *a-16p.* ***Evans*** *a-1.* ***Mayer*** *a-1.* ***Orlando*** *a-21, 22; c-21.* ***Sekowsky*** *a-5, 6p.* ***Toth*** *a-11.* ***Wolverton*** *r-4, 22-24(1 pg.ea.); c-1-12, 14, 17, 18.* ***Wood*** *a-14, 16i, 18-24; c-13, 15, 16, 19.*

PLUTO (See Cheerios Premiums, Four Color #537, Mickey Mouse Magazine, Walt Disney Showcase #4, 7, 13, 20, 23, 33 & Wheaties)
Dell Publ. Co.: No. 7, 1942; No. 429, 10/52 - No. 1248, 11-1/61-62 (Disney)

Large Feature Comic 7(1942)-Written by Carl Barks, Jack Hannah, & Nick George (Barks' 1st comic book work) 160 320 480 1008 1704 2400
Four Color 429 (#1) 9 18 27 64 110 155
Four Color 509 6 12 18 41 66 90
Four Color 595,654,736,853 5 10 15 32 51 70
Four Color 941,1039,1143,1248 4 8 12 28 44 60

POCKET CLASSICS
Academic Inc. Publications: 1984 (B&W, 4 1/4" x 6 3/4", 68 pages)

C1(Black Beauty. C2(The Call of the Wild). C3(Dr. Jekyll and Mr. Hyde). C4(Dracula). C5(Frankenstein). C6(Huckleberry Finn). C7(Moby Dick). C8(The Red Badge of Courage). C9(The Time Machine). C10(Tom Sawyer). C11(Treasure Island). C12(20,000

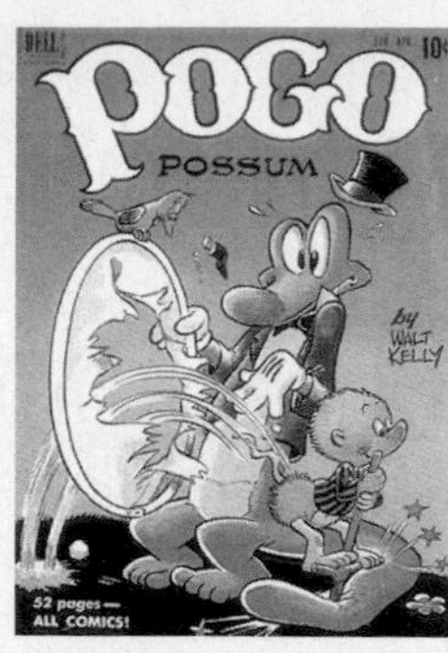

Pogo Possum #4 © Oskar Lebeck

Poison Elves #80 © Sirius

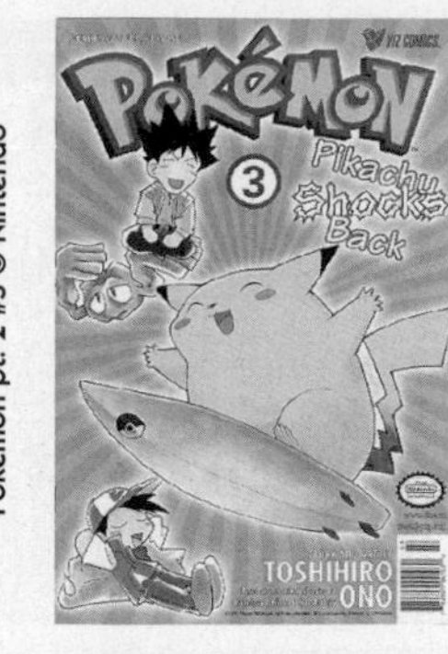

Pokémon pt. 2 #3 © Nintendo

GD 2.0 | VG 4.0 | FN 6.0 | VF 8.0 | VF/NM 9.0 | NM- 9.2

Leagues Under the Sea). C13(The Great Adventures of Sherlock Holmes). C14(Gulliver's Travels). C15(The Hunchback of Notre Dame). C16(The Invisible Man). C17(Journey to the Center of the Earth). C18(Kidnapped). C19(The Mysterious Island). C20(The Scarlet Letter). C21(The Story of My Life). C22(A Tale of Two Cities). C23(The Three Musketeers). C24(The War of the Worlds). C25(Around the World in Eighty Days). C26(Captains Courageous). C27(A Connecticut Yankee in King Arthur's Court). C28(Sherlock Holmes - The Hound of the Baskervilles). C29(The House of the Seven Gables). C30(Jane Eyre). C31(The Last of the Mohicans). C32(The Best of O. Henry). C33(The Best of Poe). C34(Two Years Before the Mast). C35(White Fang). C36(Wuthering Heights). C37(Ben Hur). C38(A Christmas Carol). C39(The Food of the Gods). C40(Ivanhoe). C41(The Man in the Iron Mask). C42(The Prince and the Pauper). C43(The Prisoner of Zenda). C44(The Return of the Native). C45(Robinson Crusoe). C46(The Scarlet Pimpernel). C47(The Sea Wolf). C48(The Swiss Family Robinson). C49(Billy Budd). C50(Crime and Punishment). C51(Don Quixote). C52(Great Expectations). C53(Heidi). C54(The Illiad). C55(Lord Jim). C56(The Mutiny on Board H.M.S. Bounty). C57(The Odyssey). C58(Oliver Twist). C59(Pride and Prejudice). C60(The Turn of the Screw) each... 8.00

Shakespeare Series:
S1(As You Like It). S2(Hamlet). S3(Julius Caesar). S4(King Lear). S5(Macbeth). S6(The Merchant of Venice). S7(A Midsummer Night's Dream). S8(Othello). S9(Romeo and Juliet). S10(The Taming of the Shrew). S11(The Tempest). S12(Twelfth Night) each... 9.00

POCKET COMICS (Also see Double Up)
Harvey Publications: Aug, 1941 - No. 4, Jan, 1942 (Pocket size; 100 pgs.) (1st Harvey comic)

1-Origin & 1st app. The Black Cat, Cadet Blakey the Spirit of '76, The Red Blazer, The Phantom, Sphinx, & The Zebra; Phantom Ranger, British Agent #99, Spin Hawkins, Satan, Lord of Evil begin (1st app. of each); Simon-c/a in #1-3 — 100 200 300 630 1065 1500
2 (9/41)-Black Cat on-c #2-4 — 65 130 195 410 693 975
3,4 — 50 100 150 310 518 725

POE
Cheese Comics: Sept, 1996 - No. 6, Apr, 1997 ($2.00, B&W)

1-6-Jason Asala-s/a 3.00

POE
Sirius Entertainment (Dogstar Press): Oct, 1997 - No. 24 ($2.50/$2.95, B&W)

1-24-Jason Asala-s/a. 20-24 ($2.95) 3.00
... Color Special (12/98, $2.95) Linsner-c 3.00

POGO PARADE (See Dell Giants)

POGO POSSUM (Also see Animal Comics & Special Delivery)
Dell Publishing Co.: No. 105, 4/46 - No. 148, 5/47; 10-12/49 - No. 16, 4-6/54

Four Color 105(1946)-Kelly-c/a — 51 102 153 434 830 1225
Four Color 148-Kelly-c/a — 43 86 129 342 641 940
1-(10-12/49)-Kelly-c/a in all — 38 76 114 289 540 790
2 — 26 52 78 192 359 525
3-5 — 18 36 54 133 247 360
6-10: 10-Infinity-c — 16 32 48 114 212 310
11-16: 11-X-Mas-c — 12 24 36 87 156 225

NOTE: *#1-4, 9-13: 52 pgs.; #5-8, 14-16: 36 pgs.*

POINT BLANK (See Wildcats)
DC Comics (WildStorm): Oct, 2002 - No. 5, Feb, 2003 ($2.95, limited series)

1-5-Brubaker-s/Wilson-a/Bisley-c. 1-Variant-c by Wilson; Grifter and John Lynch app. 3.00
TPB (2003, $14.95) r/#1-5 15.00

POISON ELVES (Formerly I, Lusiphur)
Mulehide Graphics: No. 8, 1993- No. 20, 1995 (B&W, magazine/comic size, mature readers)

8-Drew Hayes-c/a/scripts. — 2 4 6 8 10 12
9-11: 11-1st comic size issue — 2 4 6 8 10 12
12,14,16 — 1 2 3 5 6 8
13,15-(low print) — 2 4 6 8 11 14
15-2nd print 4.00
17-20 — 1 2 3 5 6 8
...Desert of the Third Sin-(1997, $14.95, TPB)-r/#13-18 15.00
...Patrons-($4.95, TPB)-r/#19,20 5.00
...Traumatic Dogs-(1996, $14.95,TPB)-Reprints I, Lusiphur #7, Poison Elves #8-12 15.00

POISON ELVES (See I, Lusiphur)
Sirius Entertainment: June, 1995 - No. 79, Sept, 2004 ; No. 80, Nov, 2007 ($2.50/$2.95, B&W, mature readers)

1-Linsner-c; Drew Hayes-a/scripts in all. 5.00
1-2nd print 2.50
2-25: 12-Purple Marauder-c/app. 3.00
26-45, 47-49 2.50
46,50-79: 61-Fillbăch Brothers-s/a. 74-Art by Crilley (3 pgs.) 3.00
80-($3.50) Tribute issue to Drew Hayes; sketchbook and notebook art with commentary 3.50
... Baptism By Fire-(2003, $19.95, TPB)-r/#48-59 20.00
... Color Special #1 (12/98, $2.95) 5.00
... Companion (12/02, $3.50) Back-story and character bios 3.50
... : Dark Wars TPB Vol. 1 (2005, $15.95) r/#60,62-68 16.00
... FAN Edition #1 mail-in offer; Drew Hayes-c/s/a — 1 2 3 5 6 8
... Rogues-(2002, $15.95, TPB)-r/#40-47 16.00
...Salvation-(2001, $19.95, TPB)-r/#26-39 20.00
...Sanctuary-(1999, $14.95, TPB)-r/#1-12 15.00

POISON ELVES: DOMINION
Sirius Entertainment: Sept, 2005 - No. 6, Sept, 2006 ($3.50, B&W, limited series)

1-6-Keith Davidsen-s/Scott Lewis-a 3.50

POISON ELVES: HYENA
Sirius Entertainment: Sept, 2004 - No. 4, Feb, 2005 ($2.95, B&W, limited series)

1-4-Keith Davidsen-s/Scott Lewis-a 3.00
Ventures TPB Vol. 1: The Hyena Collection (2006, $14.95) r/#1-4 & 2 short stories 15.00

POISON ELVES: LOST TALES
Sirius Entertainment: Jan, 2006 - Present ($2.95, B&W, limited series)

1-11-Aaron Bordner-a; Bordner & Davidsen-s 3.00

POISON ELVES: LUSIPHUR & LIRILITH
Sirius Entertainment: 2001 - No. 4, 2001 ($2.95, B&W, limited series)

1-4-Drew Hayes-s/Jason Alexander-a 3.00
TPB (2002, $11.95) r/#1-4 12.00

POISON ELVES: PARINTACHIN
Sirius Entertainment: 2001 - No. 3, 2002 ($2.95, B&W, limited series)

1-3-Drew Hayes-c/Fillbăch Brothers-s/a 3.00
TPB (2003, $8.95) r/#1-3 9.00

POISON ELVES VENTURES
Sirius Entertainment: May, 2005 - No. 4, Apr, 2006 ($3.50, B&W, limited series)

... #1: Cassanova; ...#2: Lynn; ...#3: The Purple Marauder; #4: Jace - Bordner-a 3.50

POKÉMON (TV) (Also see Magical Pokémon Journey)
Viz Comics: Nov, 1998 - Present ($3.25/$3.50, B&W)

...Part 1: The Electric Tale of Pikachu
1-Toshiro Ono-s/a — 1 3 4 6 8 10
1-4 (2nd through current printings) 3.50
2 6.00
3,4 4.00
TPB ($12.95) 13.00

...Part 2: Pikachu Strikes Back
1 5.00
2-4 4.00
TPB 13.00

...Part 3: Electric Pikachu Boogaloo
1 4.00
2-4 ($2.95-c) 3.50
TPB 13.00

...Part 4: Surf's Up Pikachu
1,3,4 4.00
2 ($2.95-c) 3.50
TPB 13.00

NOTE: Multiple printings exist for most issues

POKÉMON ADVENTURES
Viz Comics: Sept, 1999 - No. 4 ($5.95, B&W, magazine-size)

1-4-Includes stickers bound in 6.00

POKÉMON ADVENTURES
Viz Comics: 2000 - Present ($2.95/$4.95, B&W)

Part 2 (2/00-7/00) 1-6-Includes stickers bound in 3.50
Part 3 (8/00-2/01) 1-7 3.50
Part 4 (3/00-6/01) 1-4 5.00
Part 5 (7/01-10/01) 1-4 5.00
Part 6 - 1-4, Part 7 1-5 5.00

POKÉMON: THE FIRST MOVIE
Viz Comics: 1999 ($3.95)

Mewtwo Strikes Back 1-4 4.00
Pikachu's Vacation 4.00

POKÉMON: THE MOVIE 2000

Police Academy #6 © WB

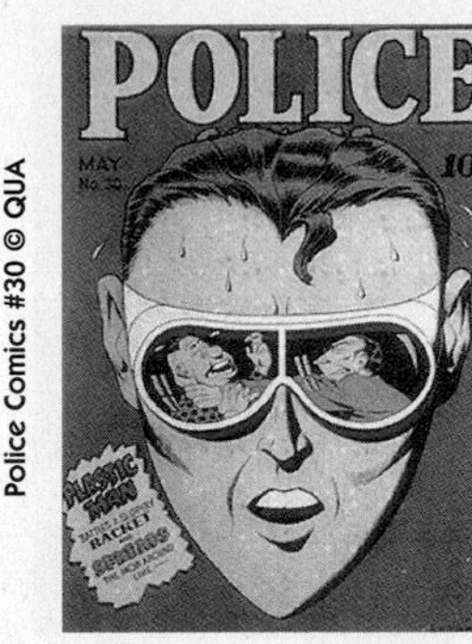

Police Comics #30 © QUA

Polly Pigtails #1 © PMI

GD 2.0 VG 4.0 FN 6.0 VF 8.0 VF/NM 9.0 NM- 9.2

Viz Comics: 2000 ($3.95)
1-Official movie adaption 4.00
Pikachu's Rescue Adventure 4.00
...:The Power of One (mini-series) 1-3 4.00

POLICE ACADEMY (TV)
Marvel Comics: Nov, 1989 - No. 6, Feb, 1990 ($1.00)
1-6: Based on TV cartoon; Post-c/a(p) in all 2.50

POLICE ACTION
Atlas News Co.: Jan, 1954 - No. 7, Nov, 1954
1-Violent-a by Robert Q. Sale 21 42 63 123 197 270
2 12 24 36 69 97 125
3-7: 7-Powell-a 11 22 33 62 86 110
NOTE: *Ayers a-4, 5. Colan a-1. Forte a-1, 2. Mort Lawrence a-5. Maneely a-3; c-1, 5. Reinman a-6, 7.*

POLICE ACTION
Atlas/Seaboard Publ.: Feb, 1975 - No. 3, June, 1975
1-3: 1-Lomax, N.Y.P.D., Luke Malone begin; McWilliams-a. 2-Origin Luke Malone, Manhunter; Ploog-a 1 3 4 6 8 10
NOTE: *Ploog art in all. Sekowsky/McWilliams a-1-3. Thorne c-3.*

POLICE AGAINST CRIME
Premiere Magazines: April, 1954 - No. 9, Aug, 1955
1-Disbrow-a; extreme violence (man's face slashed with knife); Hollingsworth-a 27 54 81 158 254 350
2-Hollingsworth-a 15 30 45 86 133 180
3-9 14 28 42 76 108 140

POLICE BADGE #479 (Formerly Spy Thrillers #1-4)
Atlas Comics (PrPI): No. 5, Sept, 1955
5-Maneely-c/a (6 pgs.); Heck-a 11 22 33 60 83 105

POLICE CASE BOOK (See Giant Comics Editions)

POLICE CASES (See Authentic... & Record Book of...)

POLICE COMICS
Quality Comics Group (Comic Magazines): Aug, 1941 - No. 127, Oct, 1953
1-Origin/1st app. Plastic Man by Jack Cole (r-in DC Special #15), The Human Bomb by Gustavson, & No. 711; intro. The Firebrand by Reed Crandall, The Mouthpiece by Guardineer, Phantom Lady, & The Sword; Chic Carter by Eisner app.; Firebrand-c 1-4 778 1556 2334 5602 9801 14,000
2-Plastic Man smuggles opium 300 600 900 2040 3570 5100
3 227 454 681 1430 2415 3400
4 190 380 570 1197 2024 2850
5-Plastic Man-c begin; Plastic Man forced to smoke marijuana; Plastic Man covers begin, end #102 220 440 660 1386 2343 3300
6,7 168 336 504 1058 1792 2525
8-Manhunter begins (origin/1st app.) (3/42) 193 386 579 1216 2058 2900
9,10 133 266 399 838 1419 2000
11-The Spirit strip reprints begin by Eisner (origin-strip #1); 1st comic book app. The Spirit & 1st cover app. (9/42) 267 534 801 1682 2841 4000
12-Intro. Ebony 153 306 459 964 1632 2300
13-Intro. Woozy Winks; last Firebrand 150 300 450 945 1598 2250
14-19: 15-Last No. 711; Destiny begins 95 190 285 599 1012 1425
20-The Raven x-over in Phantom Lady; features Jack Cole himself 95 190 285 599 1012 1425
21,22: 21-Raven & Spider Widow x-over in Phantom Lady (cameo in #22) 80 160 240 504 852 1200
23-30: 23-Last Phantom Lady. 24-26-Flatfoot Burns by Kurtzman in all 75 150 225 473 799 1125
31-41: 37-1st app. Candy by Sahle & begins (12/44). 41-Last Spirit-r by Eisner 52 104 156 322 536 750
42,43-Spirit-r by Eisner/Fine 51 102 153 316 528 740
44-Fine Spirit-r begin, end #88,90,92 51 102 153 314 525 735
45-50: 50-(#50 on-c, #49 on inside, 1/46) 40 80 120 244 397 550
51-60: 58-Last Human Bomb 33 66 99 192 309 425
61-88,90,92: 63-(Some issues have #65 printed on cover, but #63 on inside) Kurtzman-a, 6 pgs. 90,92-Spirit by Fine 25 50 75 145 233 320
89,91,93-No Spirit stories 23 46 69 133 214 295
94-99,101,102: Spirit by Eisner in all; 101-Last Manhunter. 102-Last Spirit & Plastic Man by Jack Cole 32 64 96 186 298 410
100 38 76 114 222 356 490
103-Content change to crime; Ken Shannon & T-Man begin (1st app. of each, 12/50) 27 54 81 158 254 350
104-112,114-127: Crandall-a most issues (not in 104,105,122,125-127). 109-Atomic bomb story. 112-Crandall-a 19 38 57 112 176 240
113-Crandall-c/a(2), 9 pgs. each 21 42 63 123 197 270
NOTE: *Most Spirit stories signed by Eisner are not by him; all are reprints.* ***Crandall*** *Firebrand-1-8. Spirit by* ***Eisner*** *1-41, 94-102; by* ***Eisner/Fine****-42, 43; by* ***Fine****-44-88, 90, 92. 103, 109.* ***Al Bryant*** *c-33, 34.* ***Cole*** *c-17-32, 35-102(most).* ***Crandall*** *c-13, 14.* ***Crandall/Cuidera*** *c-105-127.* ***Eisner*** *c-4i.* ***Gill Fox*** *c-1-3, 4p, 5-12, 15. Bondage c-103, 109, 125.*

POLICE LINE-UP
Avon Periodicals/Realistic Comics #3,4: Aug, 1951 - No. 4, July, 1952 (Painted-c #1-3)
1-Wood-a, 1 pg. plus part-c; spanking panel-r/Saint #5 39 78 117 230 370 510
2-Classic story "The Religious Murder Cult", drugs, perversion; r/Saint #5; c-r/Avon paperback #329 27 54 81 158 254 350
3,4: 3-Kubert-a(r?)/part-c; Kinstler-a (inside-c only) 20 40 60 118 189 260

POLICE TRAP (Public Defender In Action #7 on)
Mainline #1-4/Charlton #5,6: 8-9/54 - No. 4, 2-3/55; No. 5, 7/55 - No. 6, 9/55
1-S&K covers-all issues; Meskin-a; Kirby scripts 31 62 93 181 291 400
2-4 20 40 60 115 183 250
5,6-S&K-c/a 25 50 75 147 236 325

POLICE TRAP
Super Comics: No. 11, 1963; No. 16-18, 1964
Reprint #11,16-18: 11-r/Police Trap #3. 16-r/Justice Traps the Guilty #? 17-r/Inside Crime #3 & r/Justice Traps The Guilty #83; 18-r/Inside Crime #3 2 4 6 9 13 16

POLLY & HER PALS (See Comic Monthly #1)

POLLY & THE PIRATES
Oni Press: Sept, 2005 - No. 6, June, 2006 ($2.99, B&W, limited series)
1-6-Ted Naifeh-s/a; Polly is shanghaied by the pirate ship Titania 3.00
TPB (7/06, $11.95, digest) r/#1-6 12.00

POLLYANNA (Disney)
Dell Publishing Co.: No. 1129, Aug-Oct, 1960
Four Color 1129-Movie, Hayley Mills photo-c 7 14 21 50 83 115

POLLY PIGTAILS (Girls' Fun & Fashion Magazine #44 on)
Parents' Magazine Institute/Polly Pigtails: Jan, 1946 - V4#43, Oct-Nov, 1949
1-Infinity-c; photo-c 15 30 45 84 127 170
2-Photo-c 9 18 27 52 69 85
3-5: 3,4-Photo-c 9 18 27 47 61 75
6-10: 7-Photo-c 8 16 24 42 54 65
11-30: 22-Photo-c 7 14 21 37 46 55
31-43 6 12 18 31 38 45

PONY EXPRESS (See Tales of the...)

PONYTAIL (Teen-age)
Dell Publishing Co./Charlton No. 13 on: 7-9/62 - No. 12, 10-12/65; No. 13, 11/69 - No. 20, 1/71
12-641-209(#1) 4 8 12 24 37 50
2-12 3 6 9 18 27 35
13-20 3 6 9 14 19 24

POP COMICS
Modern Store Publ.: 1955 (36 pgs.; 5x7"; in color) (7¢)
1-Funny animal 6 12 18 28 34 40

POPEYE (See Comic Album #7, 11, 15, Comics Reading Libraries *in the Promotional Comics section,* Eat Right to Work and Win, Giant Comic Album, King Comics, Kite Fun Book, Magic Comics, March of Comics #37,52, 66, 80, 96, 117, 134, 148, 157, 169, 194, 246, 264, 274, 294, 453, 465, 477 & Wow Comics, 1st series)

POPEYE
David McKay Publications: 1937 - 1939 (All by Segar)
Feature Books nn (100 pgs.) (Very Rare) 700 1400 2100 5000 8000 11,000
Feature Books 2 (52 pgs.) 90 180 270 567 959 1350
Feature Books 3 (100 pgs.)-r/nn issue with a new-c 83 166 249 523 887 1250
Feature Books 5,10 (76 pgs.) 75 150 225 473 799 1125
Feature Books 14 (76 pgs.) (Scarce) 82 164 246 517 871 1225

POPEYE (Strip reprints through 4-Color #70)
Dell #1-65/Gold Key #66-80/King #81-92/Charlton #94-138/Gold Key #139-155/Whitman #156 on: 1941 - 1947; #1, 2-4/48 - #65, 7-9/62; #66, 10/62 - #80, 5/66; #81, 8/66 - #92, 12/67; #94, 2/69 - #138, 1/77; #139, 5/78 - #171, 6/84 (no #93,160,161)
Large Feature Comic 24('41)-Half by Segar 68 136 204 428 727 1025
Four Color 25('41)-by Segar 83 166 249 523 887 1250
Large Feature Comic 10('43) 55 110 165 347 586 825
Four Color 17('43),26('43)-by Segar 42 84 126 336 631 925
Four Color 43('44) 30 60 90 222 411 600

Popular Comics #2 © DELL

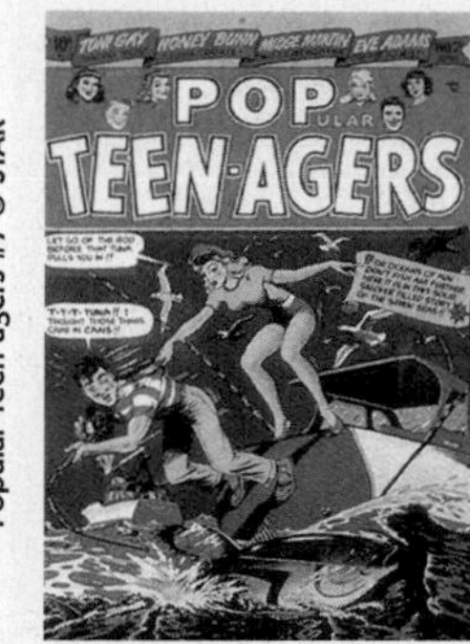

Popular Teen-agers #7 © STAR

Porky Pig FC #303 © WB

	GD 2.0	VG 4.0	FN 6.0	VF 8.0	VF/NM 9.0	NM- 9.2
Four Color 70('45)-Title: ...& Wimpy	22	44	66	157	291	425
Four Color 113('46-original strips begin),127,145('47),168	14	28	42	102	181	260
1(2-4/48)(Dell)-All new stories continue	26	52	78	192	359	525
2	14	28	42	99	175	250
3-10: 5-Popeye on moon w/rocket-c	11	22	33	79	140	200
11-20	9	18	27	60	115	150
21-40,46: 46-Origin Swee' Pee	8	16	24	52	86	120
41-45,47-50	6	12	18	43	69	95
51-60	6	12	18	37	59	80
61-65 (Last Dell issue)	5	10	15	32	51	70
66,67-Both 84 pgs. (Gold Key)	7	14	21	47	76	105
68-80	4	8	12	25	39	52
81-92,94-97 (no #93): 97-Last 12¢ issue	3	6	9	21	32	42
98,99,101-138	3	6	9	14	19	24
100	3	6	9	18	27	35
139-155: 144-50th Anniversary issue	2	4	6	8	10	12
156,157,162-167(Whitman)(no #160,161).167(3/82)	2	4	6	10	14	18
158(9/80),159(11/80)-pre-pack only	4	8	12	22	34	45
168-171:(All #90069 on-c; pre-pack) 168(6/83). 169(#168 on-c)(8/83). 170(3/84). 171(6/84)	3	6	9	16	22	28

NOTE: *Reprints-#145, 147, 149, 151, 153, 155, 157, 163-168(1/3), 170.*

POPEYE
Harvey Comics: Nov, 1993 - No. 7, Aug, 1994 ($1.50)

	GD 2.0	VG 4.0	FN 6.0	VF 8.0	VF/NM 9.0	NM- 9.2
V2#1-7						3.00
...Summer Special V2#1-(10/93, $2.25, 68 pgs.)-Sagendorf-r & others						4.00

POPEYE SPECIAL
Ocean Comics: Summer, 1987 - No. 2, Sept, 1988 ($1.75/$2.00)

	GD 2.0	VG 4.0	FN 6.0	VF 8.0	VF/NM 9.0	NM- 9.2
1,2: 1-Origin						4.00

POPPLES (TV, movie)
Star Comics (Marvel): Dec, 1986 - No. 4, Jun, 1987

	GD 2.0	VG 4.0	FN 6.0	VF 8.0	VF/NM 9.0	NM- 9.2
1-4-Based on toys						4.00

POPPO OF THE POPCORN THEATRE
Fuller Publishing Co. (Publishers Weekly): 10/29/55 - No. 13, 1956 (weekly)

	GD 2.0	VG 4.0	FN 6.0	VF 8.0	VF/NM 9.0	NM- 9.2
1	9	18	27	52	69	85
2-5	7	14	21	37	46	55
6-13	6	12	18	31	38	45

NOTE: *By **Charles Biro.** 10¢ cover, given away by supermarkets such as IGA.*

POP-POP COMICS
R. B. Leffingwell Co.: No date (Circa 1945) (52 pgs.)

	GD 2.0	VG 4.0	FN 6.0	VF 8.0	VF/NM 9.0	NM- 9.2
1-Funny animal	13	26	39	74	105	135

POPULAR COMICS
Dell Publishing Co.: Feb, 1936 - No. 145, July-Sept, 1948

	GD 2.0	VG 4.0	FN 6.0	VF 8.0	VF/NM 9.0	NM- 9.2
1-Dick Tracy (1st comic book app.), Little Orphan Annie, Terry & the Pirates, Gasoline Alley, Don Winslow (1st app.), Harold Teen, Little Joe, Skippy, Moon Mullins, Mutt & Jeff, Tailspin Tommy, Smitty, Smokey Stover, Winnie Winkle & The Gumps begin (all strip-r)	771	1542	2313	5400	-	-
2	257	514	771	1800	-	-
3	193	386	579	1350	-	-
4-6(7/36): 5-Tom Mix begins. 6-1st app. Scribbly	150	300	450	1050	-	-
7-10: 8,9-Scribbly & Reglar Fellers app.	121	242	363	850	-	-
11-20: 12-X-Mas-c	83	166	249	477	739	1000
21-27: 27-Last Terry & the Pirates, Little Orphan Annie, & Dick Tracy	63	126	189	362	556	750
28-37: 28-Gene Autry app. 31,32-Tim McCoy app. 35-Christmas-c; Tex Ritter app.	49	98	147	282	434	585
38-43: Tarzan in text only. 38-(4/39)-Gang Busters (Radio, 2nd app.) & Zane Grey's Tex Thorne begins? 43-The Masked Pilot app.; 1st non-funny-c?	47	94	141	270	415	560
44,45: 45-Hurricane Kid-c	36	72	108	207	321	435
46-Origin/1st app. Martan, the Marvel Man(12/39)	46	92	138	265	408	550
47-50	35	70	105	201	311	420
51-Origin The Voice (The Invisible Detective) strip begins (5/40)	37	74	111	213	327	440
52-Robot-c	42	84	126	242	371	500
53-59: 55-End of World story	33	66	99	190	295	400
60-Origin/1st app. Professor Supermind and Son (2/41)	34	68	102	196	303	410
61-71: 63-Smilin' Jack begins	26	52	78	150	230	310
72-The Owl & Terry & the Pirates begin (2/42); Smokey Stover reprints begin	42	84	126	242	371	500
73-75	29	58	87	167	259	350
76-78-Capt. Midnight in all (see The Funnies #57)	40	80	120	230	358	485
79-85-Last Owl	27	54	81	155	238	320
86-99: 98-Felix the Cat, Smokey Stover-r begin	18	36	54	104	157	210
100	20	40	60	115	175	235
101-130	10	20	30	58	89	120
131-145: 142-Last Terry & the Pirates	9	18	27	52	79	105

NOTE: *Martan, the Marvel Man c-47-49, 52, 57-59. Professor Supermind c-60-63, 64(1/2), 65, 66. The Voice c-53.*

POPULAR FAIRY TALES (See March of Comics #6, 18)

POPULAR ROMANCE
Better-Standard Publications: No. 5, Dec, 1949 - No. 29, July, 1954

	GD 2.0	VG 4.0	FN 6.0	VF 8.0	VF/NM 9.0	NM- 9.2
5	14	28	42	76	108	140
6-9: 7-Palais-a; lingerie panels	10	20	30	56	76	95
10-Wood-a (2 pgs.)	11	22	33	64	90	115
11,12,14-16,18-21,28,29	9	18	27	47	61	75
13,17-Severin/Elder-a (3&8 pgs.)	9	18	27	52	69	85
22-27-Toth-a	10	20	30	58	79	100

NOTE: *All have photo-c. **Tuska** art in most issues.*

POPULAR TEEN-AGERS (Secrets of Love) (School Day Romances #1-4)
Star Publications: No. 5, Sept, 1950 - No. 23, Nov, 1954

	GD 2.0	VG 4.0	FN 6.0	VF 8.0	VF/NM 9.0	NM- 9.2
5-Toni Gay, Midge Martin & Eve Adams continue from School Day Romances; Ginger Bunn (formerly Ginger Snapp & becomes Honey Bunn #6 on) begins; all features end #8	27	54	81	156	251	345
6-8 (7/51)-Honey Bunn begins; all have L. B. Cole-c; 6-Negligee panels	22	44	66	127	204	280
9-(...Romances; 1st romance issue, 10/51)	18	36	54	105	165	225
10-(...Secrets of Love thru #23)	17	34	51	98	154	210
11,16,18,19,22,23	15	30	45	83	124	165
12,13,17,20,21-Disbrow-a	15	30	45	88	137	185
14-Harrison/Wood-a	21	42	63	123	197	270
15-Wood?, Disbrow-a	16	32	48	94	147	200
Accepted Reprint 5,6 (nd); L.B. Cole-c	9	18	27	47	61	75

NOTE: *All have **L. B. Cole** covers.*

PORKY PIG (See Bugs Bunny &..., Kite Fun Book, Looney Tunes, March of Comics #42, 57, 71, 89, 99, 113, 130, 143, 164, 175, 192, 209, 218, 367, and Super Book #6, 18, 30)

PORKY PIG (...& Bugs Bunny #40-69)
Dell Publishing Co./Gold Key No. 1-93/Whitman No. 94 on: No. 16, 1942 - No. 81, Mar-Apr, 1962; Jan, 1965 - No. 109, June, 1984

	GD 2.0	VG 4.0	FN 6.0	VF 8.0	VF/NM 9.0	NM- 9.2
Four Color 16(#1, 1942)	81	162	243	689	1320	1950
Four Color 48(1944)-Carl Barks-a	88	176	264	748	1424	2100
Four Color 78(1945)	26	52	78	192	359	525
Four Color 112(7/46)	16	32	48	114	212	310
Four Color 156,182,191('49)	12	24	36	84	150	215
Four Color 226,241('49),260,271,277,284,295	10	20	30	68	119	170
Four Color 303,311,322,330: 322-Sci/fi-c/story	8	16	24	52	86	120
Four Color 342,351,360,370,385,399,410,426	6	12	18	41	66	90
25 (11-12/52)-30	5	10	15	34	55	75
31-40	5	10	15	30	48	65
41-60	4	8	12	24	37	50
61-81(3-4/62)	3	6	9	20	30	40
1(1/65-Gold Key)(2nd Series)	5	10	15	32	51	70
2,4,5-r/4-Color 226,284 & 271 in that order	3	6	9	19	29	38
3,6-10: 3-r/Four Color #342	3	6	9	16	23	30
11-30	2	4	6	13	18	22
31-54	2	4	6	9	13	16
55-70	2	4	6	8	10	12
71-93(Gold Key)	1	2	3	5	7	9
94-96	1	3	4	6	8	10
97(9/80),98-pre-pack only (99 known not to exist)	3	6	9	20	30	40
100	2	4	6	9	13	16
101-105: 104(2/82). 105(4/82)	2	4	6	8	10	12
106-109 (All #90140 on-c, no date or date code): 106(7/83), 107(8/83), 108(2/84), 109(6/84) low print run	3	6	9	14	19	24

NOTE: *Reprints-#1-8, 9-35(2/3); 36-46(1/4-1/2), 58, 67, 69-74, 76, 78, 102-109(1/3-1/2).*

PORKY PIG'S DUCK HUNT
Saalfield Publishing Co.: 1938 (12pgs.)(large size)(heavy linen-like paper)

	GD 2.0	VG 4.0	FN 6.0	VF 8.0	VF/NM 9.0	NM- 9.2
2178-1st app. Porky Pig & Daffy Duck by Leon Schlesinger. Illustrated text story book written in verse. 1st book ever devoted to these characters. (see Looney Tunes #1 for their 1st comic book app.)	75	150	225	473	799	1125

PORTENT, THE

Power & Glory #2 © Howard Chaykin

Powerless #1 © MAR

Power of Shazam! #4 © DC

GD VG FN VF VF/NM NM-
2.0 4.0 6.0 8.0 9.0 9.2

Image Comics: Feb, 2006 - No. 4, Aug, 2006 ($2.99)

1-4-Peter Bergting-s/a 3.00
Vol. 1: Duende TPB (2006, 12.99) r/#1-4; pin-up art; intro. by Kaluta 13.00

PORTIA PRINZ OF THE GLAMAZONS
Eclipse Comics: Dec, 1986 - No. 6, Oct, 1987 ($2.00, B&W, Baxter paper)

1-6 2.50

POSSESSED, THE
DC Comics (Cliffhanger): Sept, 2003 - No. 6, March, 2004 ($2.95, limited series)

1-6-Johns & Grimminger-s/Sharp-a 3.00
TPB (2004, $14.95) r/#1-6; promo art and sketch pages 15.00

POST GAZETTE (See Meet the New... in the Promotional Comics section)

POWDER RIVER RUSTLERS (See Fawcett Movie Comics)

POWER & GLORY (See American Flagg! & Howard Chaykin's American Flagg!
Malibu Comics (Bravura): Feb, 1994 - No. 4, May, 1994 ($2.50, limited series, mature)

1A, 1B-By Howard Chaykin; w/Bravura stamp 2.50
1-Newsstand ed. (polybagged w/children's warning on bag), Gold ed., Silver-foil ed., Blue-foil ed.(print run of 10,000), Serigraph ed. (print run of 3,000)($2.95)-Howard Chaykin-c/a begin 3.00
2-4-Contains Bravura stamp 2.50
Holiday Special (Win '94, $2.95) 3.00

POWER COMICS
Holyoke Publ. Co./Narrative Publ.: 1944 - No. 4, 1945

	GD	VG	FN	VF	VF/NM	NM-
1-L. B. Cole-c	138	276	414	869	1472	2075
2-Hitler, Hirohito-c (scarce)	140	280	420	882	1491	2100
3-Classic L.B. Cole-c; Dr. Mephisto begins?	167	334	501	1052	1776	2500
4-L.B. Cole-c; Miss Espionage app. #3,4; Leav-a	138	276	414	869	1472	2075

POWER COMICS
Power Comics Co.: 1977 - No. 5, Dec, 1977 (B&W)

	GD	VG	FN	VF	VF/NM	NM-
1- "A Boy And His Aardvark" by Dave Sim; first Dave Sim aardvark (not Cerebus)	2	4	6	13	18	22
1-Reprint (3/77, black-c)	1	2	3	5	6	8
2-Cobalt Blue by Gustovich	1	3	4	6	8	10
3-5: 3-Nightwitch. 4-Northern Light. 5-Bluebird	1	3	4	6	8	10

POWER COMICS
Eclipse Comics (Acme Press): Mar, 1988 - No. 4, Sept, 1988 ($2.00, B&W, mini-series)

1-4: Bolland, Gibbons-r in all 2.50

POWER COMPANY, THE
DC Comics: Apr, 2002 - No. 18, Sep, 2003 ($2.50/$2.75)

1-6-Busiek-s/Grummett-a. 6-Green Arrow & Black Canary-c/app. 2.50
7-18: 7:Begin $2.75-c. 8,9-Green Arrow app. 11-Firestorm joins. 15-Batman app. 2.75
...Bork (3/02) Busiek-s/Dwyer-a; Batman & Flash (Barry Allen) app. 2.50
...Josiah Power (3/02) Busiek-s/Giffen-a; Superman app. 2.50
...Manhunter (3/02) Busiek-s/Jurgens-a; Nightwing app. 2.50
...Sapphire (3/02) Busiek-s/Bagley-a; JLA & Kobra app. 2.50
...Skyrocket (3/02) Busiek-s/Staton-a; Green Lantern (Hal Jordan) app. 2.50
...Striker Z (3/02) Busiek-s/Bachs-a; Superboy app. 2.50
...Witchfire (3/02) Busiek-s/Haley-a; Wonder Woman app. 2.50

POWER FACTOR
Wonder Color Comics #1/Pied Piper #2: May, 1987 - No. 2, 1987 ($1.95)

1,2: Super team. 2-Infantino-c 2.50

POWER FACTOR
Innovation Publishing: Oct, 1990 - No. 3, 1991 ($1.95/$2.25)

1-3: 1-R-/1st story + new-a, 2-r/2nd story + new-a. 3-Infantino-a 2.50

POWER GIRL (See All-Star #58, Infinity, Inc., JSA Classified, Showcase #97-99)
DC Comics: June, 1988 - No. 4, Sept, 1988 ($1.00, color, limited series)

1-4 3.00
TPB (2006, $14.99) r/Showcase #97-99; Secret Origins #11; JSA Classified #1-4 and pages from JSA #32,39; cover gallery 15.00

POWERHOUSE PEPPER COMICS (See Gay Comics, Joker Comics & Tessie the Typist)
Marvel Comics (20CC): No. 1, 1943; No. 2, May, 1948 - No. 5, Nov, 1948

	GD	VG	FN	VF	VF/NM	NM-
1-(60 pgs.)-Wolverton-a in all; c-2,3	207	414	621	1304	2202	3100
2	88	176	264	554	940	1325
3,4	82	164	246	517	871	1225
5-(Scarce)	93	186	279	586	993	1400

POWERLESS
Marvel Comics: Aug, 2004 - No. 6, Jan, 2005 ($2.99, limited series)

GD VG FN VF VF/NM NM-
2.0 4.0 6.0 8.0 9.0 9.2

1-6-Peter Parker, Matt Murdock and Logan without powers; Gaydos-a 3.00
TPB (2005, $14.99) r/series; sketch page by Gaydos 15.00

POWER LINE
Marvel Comics (Epic Comics): May, 1988 - No. 8, Sept, 1989 ($1.25/$1.50)

1-8: 2-Williamson-i. 3-Dr. Zero app. 4-7-Morrow-a. 8-Williamson-i 2.50

POWER LORDS
DC Comics: Dec, 1983 - No. 3, Feb, 1984 (Limited series, Mando paper)

1-3: Based on Revell toys 2.50

POWER MAN (Formerly Hero for Hire; ...& Iron Fist #50 on; see Cage & Giant-Size...)
Marvel Comics Group: No. 17, Feb, 1974 - No. 125, Sept, 1986

	GD	VG	FN	VF	VF/NM	NM-
17-Luke Cage continues; Iron Man app.	2	4	6	11	16	20
18-20: 18-Last 20¢ issue	2	4	6	8	11	14
21-30	1	2	3	5	7	9
30-(30¢-c variant, limited distribution)(4/76)	3	6	9	17	25	32
31-46: 31-Part Neal Adams-i. 34-Last 25¢ issue. 36-r/Hero For Hire #12. 41-1st app. Thunderbolt. 45-Starlin-c.	1	2	3	5	6	8
31-34-(30¢-c variants, limited distribution)(5-8/76)	3	6	9	17	25	32
44-46-(35¢-c variants, limited distribution)(6-8/77)	4	8	12	22	34	45
47-Barry Smith-a	1	3	4	6	8	10
47-(35¢-c variant, limited distribution)(10/77)	4	8	12	26	41	55
48-50-Byrne-a(p); 48-Power Man/Iron Fist 1st meet. 50-Iron Fist joins Cage	2	4	6	8	11	14
51-56,58-65,67-77: 58-Intro El Aguila. 75-Double size. 77-Daredevil app.						4.00
57-New X-Men app. (6/79)	3	6	9	20	30	40
66-2nd app. Sabretooth (see Iron Fist #14)	4	8	12	28	44	60
78,84: 78-3rd app. Sabretooth (cameo under cloak). 84-4th app. Sabretooth	3	6	9	18	27	35
79-83,85-99,101-124: 87-Moon Knight app. 109-The Reaper app.						3.00
100,125-Double size: 100-Origin K'un L'un. 125-Death of Iron Fist						4.00
Annual 1(1976)-Punisher cameo in flashback	2	4	6	10	14	18

NOTE: ***Austin*** *c-102i.* ***Byrne*** *a-48-50; c-102, 104, 106, 107, 112-116.* ***Kane*** *c(p)-24, 25, 28, 48.* ***Miller*** *a-68, 76(2 pgs.); c-66-68, 70-74, 80i.* ***Mooney*** *a-38i, 53i, 55i.* ***Nebres*** *a-76p.* ***Nino*** *a-42i, 43i.* ***Perez*** *a-27.* ***B. Smith*** *a-47i.* ***Tuska*** *a(p)-17, 20, 24, 26, 28, 29, 36, 47. Painted c-75, 100.*

POWER OF PRIME
Malibu Comics (Ultraverse): July, 1995 - No. 4, Nov, 1995 ($2.50, lim. series)

1-4 2.50

POWER OF SHAZAM!, THE (See SHAZAM!)
DC Comics: 1994 (Painted graphic novel) (Prequel to new series)

	GD	VG	FN	VF	VF/NM	NM-
Hardcover-($19.95)-New origin of Shazam!; Ordway painted-c/a & script	3	6	9	14	20	25
Softcover-($7.50), Softcover-($9.95)-New-c.	2	4	6	8	10	12

POWER OF SHAZAM!, THE
DC Comics: Mar, 1995 - No. 47, Mar, 1999 ($1.50/$1.75/$1.95/$2.50)

1-Jerry Ordway scripts begin 4.00
2-20: 4-Begin $1.75-c. 6-Re-intro of Capt. Nazi. 8-Re-intro of Spy Smasher, Bulletman & Minuteman; Swan-a (7 pgs.). 11-Re-intro of Ibis, Swan-a(2 pgs.). 14-Gil Kane-a(p). 20-Superman-c/app.; "Final Night" 3.00
21-47: 21-Plastic Man-c/app. 22-Batman-c/app. 35,36-X-over w/Starman #39,40. 38-41-Mr. Mind. 43-Bulletman app. 45-JLA-c/app. 2.50
#1,000,000 (11/98) 853rd Century x-over; Ordway-c/s/a 3.00
Annual 1 (1996, $2.95)-Legends of the Dead Earth story; Jerry Ordway-c; Mike Manley-a 4.00

POWER OF STRONGMAN, THE (Also see Strongman)
AC Comics: 1989 ($2.95)

1-Powell G.A.-r 3.00

POWER OF THE ATOM (See Secret Origins #29)
DC Comics: Aug, 1988 - No. 18, Nov, 1989 ($1.00)

1-18: 6-Chronos returns; Byrne-p. 9-JLI app. 2.50

POWER PACHYDERMS
Marvel Comics: Sept, 1989 ($1.25, one-shot)

1-Elephant super-heroes; parody of X-Men, Elektra, & 3 Stooges 2.50

POWER PACK
Marvel Comics Group: Aug, 1984 - No. 62, Feb, 1991

1-($1.00, 52 pgs.)-Origin & 1st app. Power Pack 3.00
2-18,20-26,28,30-45,47-62 2.50
19-(52 pgs.)-Cloak & Dagger, Wolverine app. 3.00
27-Mutant massacre; Wolverine & Sabretooth app. 5.00
29,46: 29-Spider-Man & Hobgoblin app. 46-Punisher app. 2.75
Graphic Novel: Power Pack & Cloak & Dagger: Shelter From the Storm ('89, SC, $7.95)

Power Pack: Day One #1 © MAR

Powers V2 #26 © Jinxworld

Preacher #54 © Ennis & Dillon

GD 2.0 | VG 4.0 | FN 6.0 | VF 8.0 | VF/NM 9.0 | NM- 9.2

Velluto/Farmer-a 10.00
...Holiday Special 1 (2/92, $2.25, 68 pgs.) 2.50
NOTE: ***Austin** scripts-53. **Mignola** c-20. **Morrow** a-51. **Spiegle** a-55i. **Williamson** a(i)-43, 50, 52.*

POWER PACK (Volume 2)
Marvel Comics: Aug, 2000 - No. 4, Nov, 2000 ($2.99, limited series)
1-4-Doran & Austin-c/a 3.00

POWER PACK
Marvel Comics: June, 2005 - No. 4, Aug, 2005 ($2.99, limited series)
1-4-Sumerak-s/Gurihiru-a; back-up Franklin Richards story. 3-Fantastic Four app. 3.00
... Digest (2006, $6.99) r/#1-4 7.00

POWER PACK: DAY ONE
Marvel Comics: May, 2008 - No. 4, Aug, 2008($2.99, limited series)
1-4-Van Lente-s/Gurihiru-a; origin retold; Coover-a back-ups. 1-Fantastic Four cameo 3.00

POWERPUFF GIRLS, THE (Also see Cartoon Network Starring... #1)
DC Comics: May, 2000 - No. 70, Mar, 2006 ($1.99/$2.25)
1 4.00
2-55,57-70: 25-Pin-ups by Allred, Byrne, Baker, Mignola, Hernandez, Warren 2.50
56-($2.95) Bonus pages; Mojo Jojo-c 3.00
...Double Whammy (12/00, $3.95) r/#1,2 & a Dexter's Lab story 4.00
...Movie: The Comic (9/02, $2.95) Movie adaptation; Phil Moy & Chris Cook-a 3.00

POWER RANGERS ZEO (TV)(Saban's...)(Also see Saban's Mighty Morphin Power Rangers)
Image Comics (Extreme Studios): Aug, 1996 ($2.50)
1-Based on TV show 2.50

POWER RECORD COMICS (Named Peter Pan Record Comics for #34-47)
Marvel Comics/Power Records: 1974 - 1978 ($1.49, 7x10" comics, 20 pgs. with 45 R.P.M. record) (Clipped corners - reduce value 20%) (Comic alone - 50%; record alone - 50%)
PR10-Spider-Man-r/from #124,125; Man-Wolf app. PR18-Planet of the Apes-r. PR19-Escape From the Planet of the Apes-r. PR20-Beneath the Planet of the Apes-r. PR21-Battle for the Planet of the Apes-r. PR24-Spider-Man II-New-a begins. PR27-Batman "Stacked Cards"; N. Adams-a(p). PR30-Batman; N. Adams-r/Det.(7 pgs.).
With record; each... 5 10 15 30 48 65
PR11-Hulk-r. PR12-Captain America-r/#168. PR13-Fantastic Four-r/#126. PR14-Frankenstein -Ploog-r/#1. PR15-Tomb of Dracula-Colan-r/#2. PR16-Man-Thing-Ploog-r/#5. PR17-Werewolf By Night-Ploog-r/Marvel Spotlight #2. PR28-Superman "Alien Creatures". PR29-Space: 1999 "Breakaway". PR31-Conan-N. Adams-a; reprinted in Conan #116. PR32-Space: 1999 "Return to the Beginning". PR33-Superman-G.A. origin, Buckler-a(p). PR34-Superman. PR35-Wonder Woman-Buckler-a(p)
With record; each... 4 8 12 26 41 55
PR11-(1981 Peter Pan records re-issue) new Abomination & Rhino c
With record 4 8 12 28 44 60
PR25-Star Trek "Passage to Moauv". PR26-Star Trek "Crier in Emptiness." PR36-Holo-Man. PR37-Robin Hood. PR39-Huckleberry Finn. PR40-Davy Crockett. PR41-Robinson Crusoe. PR42-20,000 Leagues Under the Sea. PR45-Star Trek "Dinosaur Planet". PR46-Star Trek "The Robot Masters". PR47-Little Women
With record; each... 4 8 12 22 34 45
NOTE: *Peter Pan re-issues exist for #25-34 and are valued the same.*

POWERS
Image Comics: 2000 - No. 37, Feb, 2004 ($2.95)
1-Bendis-s/Oeming-a; murder of Retro Girl 1 3 4 6 8 10
2-6: 6-End of Retro Girl arc. 5.00
7-14: 7-Warren Ellis app. 12-14-Death of Olympia 3.50
15-37: 31-36-Origin of the Powers 3.00
Annual 1 (2001, $3.95) 4.00
...: Anarchy TPB (11/03, $14.95) r/#21-24; interviews, sketchbook, cover gallery 15.00
...Coloring/Activity Book (2001, $1.50, B&W, 8 x 10.5") Oeming-a 2.50
...: Forever TPB (2005, $19.95) r/#31-37; script for #31, sketchbook, cover gallery 20.00
...: Little Deaths TPB (2002, $19.95) r/#7,12-14, Ann. #1, Coloring/Activity Book; sketch pages, cover gallery 20.00
...: Roleplay TPB (2001, $13.95) r/#8-11; sketchbook, cover gallery 14.00
... Scriptbook (2001, $19.95) scripts for #1-11; Oeming sketches 20.00
...: Supergroup TPB (2003, $19.95) r/#15-20; sketchbook, cover gallery 20.00
...: The Definitive Collection Vol. 1 HC (2006, $29.99, dust jacket) r/#1-11 & Coloring/Activity Book, script for #1, sketch pages and covers, interviews, letter column highlights 30.00
...: Who Killed Retro Girl TPB (2000, $21.95) r/#1-6; sketchbook, cover gallery, and promotional strips from Comic Shop News 22.00

POWERS
Marvel Comics (Icon): Jul, 2004 - Present ($2.95/$3.95)
1-11,13-24-Bendis-s/Oeming-a. 14-Cover price error 3.00
12-($3.95, 64 pages) 2 covers; Bendis & Oeming interview 4.00
25-30-($3.95, 40 pages) 25-Two covers; Bendis interview 4.00
Annual 2008 (5/08, $4.95) Bendis-s/Oeming-a; interview with Brubaker, Simone, others 5.00
...: Legends TPB (2005, $17.95) r/#1-6; sketchbook, cover gallery 18.00
...: Psychotic TPB (1/06, $19.95) r/#7-12; Bendis & Oeming interview, cover gallery 20.00
...: Cosmic TPB (10/07, $19.95) r/#13-18; script and sketch pages 20.00
...: Secret Identity TPB (12/07, $19.95) r/#19-24; script pages 20.00

POWERS THAT BE (Becomes Star Seed No.7 on)
Broadway Comics: Nov, 1995 - No. 6, June, 1996 ($2.50)
1-6: 1-Intro of Fatale & Star Seed. 6-Begin $2.95-c. 3.00
Preview Editions 1-3 (9/95 - 11/95, B&W) 2.50

POW MAGAZINE (Bob Sproul's) (Satire Magazine)
Humor-Vision: Aug, 1966 - No. 3, Feb, 1967 (30¢)
1,2: 2-Jones-a 4 8 12 28 44 60
3-Wrightson-a 6 12 18 37 59 80

PREACHER
DC Comics (Vertigo): Apr, 1995 - No. 66, Oct, 2000 ($2.50, mature)
nn-Preview 2 4 6 11 16 20
1 ($2.95)-Ennis scripts, Dillon-a & Fabry-c in all; 1st app. Jesse, Tulip, & Cassidy
2 4 6 8 11 14
2,3: 2-1st app. Saint of Killers. 1 2 3 5 7 9
4,5 1 2 3 4 5 7
6-10 5.00
11-20: 12-Polybagged w/videogame w/Ennis text. 13-Hunters storyline begins; ends #17. 19-Saint of Killers app.; begin "Crusaders", ends #24 4.00
21-25: 21-24-Saint of Killers app. 25-Origin of Cassidy. 3.00
26-49,52-64: 52-Tulip origin 2.50
50-($3.75) Pin-ups by Jim Lee, Bradstreet, Quesada and Palmiotti 3.75
51-Includes preview of 100 Bullets; Tulip origin 4.00
65,66-($3.75) 65-Almost everyone dies. 66-Final issue 5.00
Alamo (2001, $17.95, TPB) r/#59-66; Fabry-c 18.00
All Hell's a-Coming (2000, $17.95, TPB)-r/#51-58, ...:Tall in the Saddle 18.00
...: Dead or Alive HC (2000, $29.95) Gallery of Glenn Fabry's cover paintings for every Preacher issue; commentary by Fabry & Ennis 30.00
...: Dead or Alive SC (2003, $19.95) 20.00
Dixie Fried (1998, $14.95, TPB)-r/#27-33, Special: Cassidy 15.00
Gone To Texas (1996, $14.95, TPB)-r/#1-7; Fabry-c 15.00
Proud Americans (1997, $14.95, TPB)-r/#18-26; Fabry-c 15.00
Salvation (1999, $14.95, TPB)-r/#41-50; Fabry-c 15.00
Until the End of the World (1996, $14.95, TPB)-r/#8-17; Fabry-c 15.00
War in the Sun (1999, $14.95, TPB)-r/#34-40 15.00

PREACHER SPECIAL: CASSIDY: BLOOD & WHISKEY
DC Comics (Vertigo): 1998 ($5.95, one-shot)
1-Ennis-scripts/Fabry-c /Dillon-a 6.00

PREACHER SPECIAL: ONE MAN'S WAR
DC Comics (Vertigo): Mar, 1998 ($4.95, one-shot)
1-Ennis-scripts/Fabry-c /Snejbjerg-a 5.00

PREACHER SPECIAL: SAINT OF KILLERS
DC Comics (Vertigo): Aug, 1996 - No. 4, Nov, 1996 ($2.50, lim. series, mature)
1-4: Ennis-scripts/Fabry-c. 1,2-Pugh-a. 3,4-Ezquerra-a 3.00
1-Signed & numbered 20.00

PREACHER SPECIAL: THE GOOD OLD BOYS
DC Comics (Vertigo): Aug, 1997 ($4.95, one-shot, mature)
1-Ennis-scripts/Fabry-c /Esquerra-a 5.00

PREACHER SPECIAL: THE STORY OF YOU-KNOW-WHO
DC Comics (Vertigo): Dec, 1996 ($4.95, one-shot, mature)
1-Ennis-scripts/Fabry-c/Case-a 5.00

PREACHER: TALL IN THE SADDLE
DC Comics (Vertigo): 2000 ($5.95, one-shot)
1-Ennis-scripts/Fabry-c/Dillon-a; early romance of Tulip and Jesse 6.00

PREDATOR (Also see Aliens Vs. ..., Batman vs. ..., Dark Horse Comics, & Dark Horse Presents)
Dark Horse Comics: June, 1989 - No. 4, Mar, 1990 ($2.25, limited series)
1-Based on movie; 1st app. Predator 1 2 3 4 5 7
1-2nd printing 3.00
2 5.00
3,4 4.00
Trade paperback (1990, $12.95)-r/#1-4 13.00
... Omnibus Volume 1 (8/07, $24.95, 6" x 9") r/#1-4, ... Cold War, ... Dark River, ...Bloody Sands

Predator Vs. Magnus Robot Fighter #2 © DH & VAL

Presidential Material: Barack Obama © IDW

Primer #2 © Comico

GD 2.0 | VG 4.0 | FN 6.0 | VF 8.0 | VF/NM 9.0 | NM- 9.2

of Time mini-series and stories from Dark Horse Comics #1,2,4-7,10-12 25.00
... Omnibus Volume 2 (2/08, $24.95, 6" x 9") r/ ... Big Game, ... Race War, ...Invaders From The, Fourth Dimension mini-series and stories from Dark Horse Comics #16-18,20,21; Dark Horse Presents #46 and A Decade of Dark Horse 25.00
... Omnibus Volume 3 (6/08, $24.95, 6" x 9") r/ ... Bad Blood, ... Kindred, ...Hell and Hot Water, ... Strange Roux mini-series and stories from Dark Horse Comics #12-14 and Dark Horse Presents #119 & 124 25.00

PREDATOR: (title series) **Dark Horse Comics**
--BAD BLOOD, 12/93 - No. 4, 1994 ($2.50) 1-4 3.00
--BIG GAME, 3/91 - No. 4, 6/91 ($2.50) 1-4: 1-3-Contain 2 Dark Horse trading cards 3.00
--BLOODY SANDS OF TIME, 2/92 - No. 2, 2/92 ($2.50) 1,2-Dan Barry-c/a(p)/scripts 3.00
--CAPTIVE, 4/98 ($2.95, one-shot) 1 3.00
--COLD WAR, 9/91 - No. 4, 12/91 ($2.50) 1-4: All have painted-c 3.00
--DARK RIVER, 7/96 - No.4, 10/96 ($2.95)1-4: Miran Kim-c 3.00
--HELL & HOT WATER, 4/97 - No. 3, 6/97 ($2.95) 1-3 3.00
--HELL COME A WALKIN', 2/98 - No. 2, 3/98 ($2.95) 1,2-In the Civil War 3.00
--HOMEWORLD, 3/99 - No. 4, 6/99 ($2.95) 1-4 3.00
--INVADERS FROM THE FOURTH DIMENSION, 7/94 ($3.95, one-shot, 52 pgs.) 1 4.00
--JUNGLE TALES, 3/95 ($2.95) 1-r/Dark Horse Comics 3.00
--KINDRED, 12/96 - No. 4, 3/97 ($2.50) 1-4 3.00
--NEMESIS, 12/97 - No. 2, 1/98 ($2.95) 1,2-Predator in Victorian England; Taggart-c 3.00
--PRIMAL, 7/97 - No. 2, 8/97 ($2.95) 1,2 3.00
--RACE WAR (See Dark Horse Presents #67), 2/93 - No. 4,10/93 ($2.50, color)
1-4,0: 1-4-Dorman painted-c #1-4, 0(4/93) 3.00
--STRANGE ROUX, 11/96 ($2.95, one-shot) 1 3.00
--XENOGENESIS (Also see Aliens Xenogenesis), 8/99 - No. 4, 11/99 ($2.95)
1,2-Edginton-s 3.00

PREDATOR 2
Dark Horse Comics: Feb, 1991 - No. 2, June, 1991 ($2.50, limited series)
1,2: 1-Adapts movie; both w/trading cards & photo-c 3.00

PREDATOR VS. JUDGE DREDD
Dark Horse Comics: Oct, 1997 - No. 3 ($2.50, limited series)
1-3-Wagner-s/Alcatena-a/Bolland-c 3.00

PREDATOR VS. MAGNUS ROBOT FIGHTER
Dark Horse/Valiant: Oct, 1992 - No. 2, 1993 ($2.95, limited series)
(1st Dark Horse/Valiant x-over)
1,2: (Reg.)-Barry Smith-c; Lee Weeks-a. 2-w/trading cards 3.00
1 (Platinum edition, 11/92)-Barry Smith-c 10.00

PREHISTORIC WORLD (See Classics Illustrated Special Issue)

PRELUDE TO INFINITE CRISIS
DC Comics: 2005 ($5.99, squarebound)
nn-Reprints stories and panels with commentary leading into Infinite Crisis series 6.00

PREMIERE (See Charlton Premiere)

PRESIDENTIAL MATERIAL
IDW Publishing: Oct, 2008 ($3.99/$7.99)
...: Barack Obama - Biography of the candidate; Mariotte-s/Morgan-a/Campbell-c 4.00
...: John McCain - Biography of the candidate; Helfer-s/Thompson-a/Campbell-c 4.00
Flipbook ($7.99) Both issues in flipbook format 8.00

PRESTO KID, THE (See Red Mask)

PRETTY BOY FLOYD (See On the Spot)

PREZ (See Cancelled Comic Cavalcade, Sandman #54 & Supergirl #10)
National Periodical Publications: Aug-Sept, 1973 - No. 4, Feb-Mar, 1974
1-Origin; Joe Simon scripts 3 6 9 17 25 32
2-4 2 4 6 11 16 20

PRICE, THE (See Eclipse Graphic Album Series)

PRIDE & JOY
DC Comics (Vertigo): July, 1997 - No. 4, Oct, 1997 ($2.50, limited series)
1-4-Ennis-s 2.50
TPB (2004, $14.95) r/#1-4 15.00

PRIDE AND THE PASSION, THE
Dell Publishing Co.: No. 824, Aug, 1957
Four Color 824-Movie, Frank Sinatra & Cary Grant photo-c
9 18 27 63 107 150

PRIDE OF BAGHDAD
DC Comics (Vertigo): 2006 ($19.99, hardcover with dustjacket)
HC-A pride of lions escaping from the Baghdad zoo in 2003, Vaughan-s/Henrichon-a 20.00
SC-(2007, $12.99) 13.00

PRIDE OF THE YANKEES, THE (See Real Heroes & Sport Comics)
Magazine Enterprises: 1949 (The Life of Lou Gehrig)
nn-Photo-c; Ogden Whitney-a 82 164 246 517 871 1225

PRIEST (Also see Asylum)
Maximum Press: Aug, 1996 - No. 2, Oct, 1996 ($2.99)
1,2 3.00

PRIMAL FORCE
DC Comics: No. 0, Oct, 1994 - No. 14, Dec, 1995 ($1.95/$2.25)
0-14: 0- Teams Red Tornado, Golem, Jack O'Lantern, Meridian & Silver Dragon. 9-begin $2.25-c 2.50

PRIMAL MAN (See The Crusaders)

PRIMAL RAGE
Sirius Entertainment: 1996 ($2.95)
1-Dark One-c; based of video game 3.00

PRIME (See Break-Thru, Flood Relief & Ultraforce)
Malibu Comics (Ultraverse): June, 1993 - No. 26, Aug, 1995 ($1.95/$2.50)
1-1st app. Prime; has coupon for Ultraverse Premiere #0 3.00
1-With coupon missing 2.00
1-Full cover holographic edition; 1st of kind w/Hardcase #1 & Strangers #1 6.00
1-Ultra 5,000 edition w/silver ink-c 4.00
2-11,14-26: 2-Polybagged w/card & coupon for U. Premiere #0. 3,4-Prototype app. 4-Direct sale w/o card.4-($2.50)-Newsstand ed. polybagged w/card. 5-($2.50, 48 pgs.)-Rune flip-c/ story part B by Barry Smith; see Sludge #1 for 1st app. Rune; 3-pg. Night Man preview. 6-Bill & Chelsea Clinton app 115-Intro Papa Verite; Perez-c/a. 16-Intro Turbo Charge 2.50
12-($3.50, 68 pgs.)-Flip book w/Ultraverse Premiere #3; silver foil logo 3.50
13-($2.95, 52 pgs.)-Variant covers 3.00
...: Gross and Disgusting 1 (10/94, $3.95)-Boris-c; "Annual" on cover, published monthly in indicia 4.00
...Month "Ashcan" (8/94, 75¢)-Boris-c 2.50
... Time: A Prime Collection (1994, $9.95)-r/1-4 10.00
...Vs. The Incredible Hulk (1995)-mail away limited edition 10.00
...Vs. The Incredible Hulk Premium edition 10.00
...Vs. The Incredible Hulk Super Premium edition 15.00
NOTE: *Perez a-15; c-15, 16.*

PRIME (Also see Black September)
Malibu Comics (Ultraverse): Infinity, Sept, 1995 - V2#15, Dec, 1996 ($1.50)
Infinity, V2#1-8: Post Black September storyline. 6-8-Solitaire app. 9-Breyfogle-c/a. 10-12-Ramos-c. 15-Lord Pumpkin app. 2.50
Infinity Signed Edition (2,000 printed) 5.00

PRIME/CAPTAIN AMERICA
Malibu Comics: Mar, 1996 ($3.95, one-shot)
1-Norm Breyfogle-a 4.00

PRIME8: CREATION
Two Morrows Publishing: July, 2001 ($3.95, B&W)
1-Neal Adams-c 4.00

PRIMER (Comico...)
Comico: Oct (no month), 1982 - No. 6, Feb, 1984 (B&W)
1 (52 pgs.) 2 4 6 9 13 16
2-1st app. Grendel & Argent by Wagner 9 18 27 60 100 140
3,4 2 4 6 8 10 12
5-1st Sam Kieth art in comics ('83) & 1st The Maxx 3 6 9 20 30 40
6-Intro & 1st app. Evangeline 2 4 6 10 14 18

PRIMORTALS (Leonard Nimoy's...)

PRIMUS (TV)
Charlton Comics: Feb, 1972 - No. 7, Oct, 1972
1-Staton-a in all 2 4 6 11 16 20
2-7: 6-Drug propaganda story 2 4 6 8 11 14

PRINCE NAMOR, THE SUB-MARINER (Also see Namor ...)
Marvel Comics Group: Sept, 1984 - No. 4, Dec, 1984 (Limited-series)
1-4 2.50

Prince Valiant #3 © KING

Prison Break! #2 © AVON

Prize Comics #58 © Prize

	GD	VG	FN	VF	VF/NM	NM-
	2.0	4.0	6.0	8.0	9.0	9.2

PRINCESS SALLY (Video game)
Archie Publications: Apr, 1995 - No. 3, June, 1995 ($1.50, limited series)

1-3: Spin-off from Sonic the Hedgehog 4.00

PRINCE VALIANT (See Ace Comics, Comics Reading Libraries *in the Promotional Comics section,* & King Comics #146, 147)
David McKay Publ./Dell: No. 26, 1941; No. 67, June, 1954 - No. 900, May, 1958

Feature Books 26 ('41)-Harold Foster-c/a; newspaper strips reprinted, pgs. 1-28,30-63; color & 68 pgs; Foster cover is only original comic book artwork by him
100 200 300 630 1065 1500
Four Color 567 (6/54)(#1)-By Bob Fuje-Movie, photo-c
10 20 30 73 129 185
Four Color 650 (9/55), 699 (4/56), 719 (8/56),-Fuje-a 7 14 21 50 83 115
Four Color 788 (4/57), 849 (1/58), 900-Fuje-a 7 14 21 47 76 105

PRINCE VALIANT
Marvel Comics: Dec, 1994 - No. 4, Mar, 1995 ($3.95, limited series)

1-4; Kaluta-c in all. 4.00

PRINCE VANDAL
Triumphant Comics: Nov, 1993 - Apr?, 1994 ($2.50)

1-6: 1,2-Triumphant Unleashed x-over 2.50

PRIORITY: WHITE HEAT
AC Comics: 1986 - No. 2, 1986 ($1.75, mini-series)

1,2-Bill Black-a 3.00

PRISCILLA'S POP
Dell Publishing Co.: No. 569, June, 1954 - No. 799, May, 1957

Four Color 569 (#1), 630 (5/55), 704 (5/56),799 4 8 12 26 41 55

PRISON BARS (See Behind...)

PRISON BREAK!
Avon Per./Realistic No. 3 on: Sept, 1951 - No. 5, Sept, 1952 (Painted c-3)

1-Wood-c & 1 pg.; has-r/Saint #7 retitled Michael Strong Private Eye
41 82 123 250 413 575
2-Wood-c; Kubert-a; Kinstler inside front-c 30 60 90 174 280 385
3-Orlando, Check-a; c-/Avon paperback #179 24 48 72 140 225 310
4,5: 4-Kinstler-c & inside f/c; Lawrence, Lazarus-a. 5-Kinstler-c; Infantino-a
21 42 63 123 197 270

PRISONER, THE (TV)
DC Comics: 1988 - No. 4, 1989 ($3.50, squarebound, mini-series)

1-4 (Books a-d) 3.50

PRISON RIOT
Avon Periodicals: 1952

1-Marijuana Murders-1 pg. text; Kinstler-c; 2 Kubert illos on text pages
28 56 84 162 261 360

PRISON TO PRAISE
Logos International: 1974 (35¢) (Religious, Christian)

nn-True Story of Merlin R. Carothers 2 4 6 9 12 15

PRIVATE BUCK
Dell Publishing Co.: No. 21, 1941 - No. 12, 1942

Large Feature Comic 21 (#1)(1941)(Series I), 22 (1941)(Series I), 12 (1942)(Series II)
17 34 51 98 154 210

PRIVATE EYE (Cover title: Rocky Jorden...#6-8)
Atlas Comics (MCI): Jan, 1951 - No. 8, March, 1952

1-Cover title: Crime Cases... #1-5 21 42 63 123 197 270
2,3-Tuska c/a(3) 14 28 42 76 108 140
4-8 11 22 33 60 83 105
NOTE: *Henkel a-6(3), 7; c-7.* ***Sinnott*** *a-6.*

PRIVATE EYE (See Mike Shayne...)

PRIVATE SECRETARY
Dell Publishing Co.: Dec-Feb, 1962-63 - No. 2, Mar-May, 1963

1 3 6 9 21 32 42
2 3 6 9 17 25 32

PRIVATE STRONG (See The Double Life of...)

PRIZE COMICS (...Western #69 on) (Also see Treasure Comics)
Prize Publications: March, 1940 - No. 68, Feb-Mar, 1948

1-Origin Power Nelson, The Futureman & Jupiter, Master Magician; Ted O'Neil, Secret Agent M-11, Jaxon of the Jungle, Bucky Brady & Storm Curtis begin (1st app. of each)
273 546 819 1720 2910 4100
2-The Black Owl begins (1st app.) 118 236 354 743 1259 1775
3 103 206 309 649 1100 1550
4-Classic robot-c 113 226 339 712 1206 1700
5,6: Dr. Dekkar, Master of Monsters app. in each 90 180 270 567 959 1350
7-(Scarce)-1st app. The Green Lama (12/40); Black Owl by S&K; origin/1st app. Dr. Frost & Frankenstein; Capt. Gallant, The Great Voodini & Twist Turner begin;
220 440 660 1386 2343 3300
8,9-Black Owl & Ted O'Neil by S&K 100 200 300 630 1065 1500
10-12,14,15: 11-Origin Bulldog Denny. 14-War-c 72 144 216 454 770 1085
13-Yank & Doodle begin (8/41, origin/1st app.) 79 158 237 498 842 1185
16-20: 16-Spike Mason begins 66 132 198 416 701 985
21-24: 21-War-c. 22-Statue of Liberty Japanese attack war-c. 23-Uncle Sam patriotic war-c. 24-Lincoln statue patriotic-c 52 104 156 322 536 750
25-30: 25-28 War-c. 26-Liberty Bell-c 37 74 111 219 352 485
31-33: 31-Japanese war-c 33 66 99 192 309 425
34-Origin Airmale, Yank & Doodle; The Black Owl joins army, Yank & Doodle's father assumes Black Owl's role 35 70 105 203 327 450
35-36,38-40: 35-Flying Fist & Bingo begin 25 50 75 147 236 325
37-Intro. Stampy, Airmale's sidekick; Hitler-c 40 80 120 235 380 525
41-50: 45-Yank & Doodle learn Black Owl's I.D. (their father). 48-Prince Ra begins
20 40 60 118 189 260
51-62,64,67,68: 53-Transvestism story. 55-No Frankenstein. 57-X-Mas-c. 64-Black Owl retires 15 30 45 90 140 190
63-Simon & Kirby c/a 19 38 57 112 176 240
65,66-Frankenstein-c by Briefer 17 34 51 98 154 210
NOTE: ***Briefer*** *a 7-on; c-65, 66.* ***J. Binder*** *a-16; c-21-29.* ***Guardineer*** *a-62.* ***Kiefer*** *c-62.* ***Palais*** *c-68.* ***Simon & Kirby*** *c-63, 75, 83.*

PRIZE COMICS WESTERN (Formerly Prize Comics #1-68)
Prize Publications (Feature): No. 69(V7#2), Apr-May, 1948 - No. 119, Nov-Dec, 1956 (No. 69-84: 52 pgs.)

69(V7#2) 14 28 42 80 115 150
70-75: 74-Kurtzman-a (8 pgs.) 12 24 36 67 94 120
76-Randolph Scott photo-c; "Canadian Pacific" movie adaptation
13 26 39 72 101 130
77-Photo-c; Severin/Elder, Mart Bailey-a; "Streets of Laredo" movie adaptation
12 24 36 67 94 120
78-Photo-c; S&K-a, 10 pgs.; Severin, Mart Bailey-a; "Bullet Code", & "Roughshod" movie adaptations 15 30 45 90 140 190
79-Photo-c; Kurtzman-a, 8 pgs.; Severin/Elder, Severin, Mart Bailey-a; "Stage To Chino" movie adaptation w/George O'Brien 15 30 45 90 140 190
80-82-Photo-c; 80,81-Severin/Elder-a(2). 82-1st app. The Preacher by Mart Bailey; Severin/Elder-a(3) 13 26 39 72 101 130
83,84 10 20 30 58 79 100
85-1st app. American Eagle by John Severin & begins (V9#6, 1-2/51)
19 38 57 112 176 240
86,101-105, 109-Severin/Williamson-a 11 22 33 64 90 115
87-99,110,111-Severin/Elder-a(2-3) each 12 24 36 69 97 125
100 13 26 39 74 105 135
106-108,112 9 18 27 47 61 75
113-Williamson/Severin-a(2)/Frazetta? 12 24 36 69 97 125
114-119: Drifter series in all; by Mort Meskin #114-118
8 16 24 42 54 65
NOTE: ***Fass*** *a-81.* ***Severin & Elder*** *c-84-99.* ***Severin*** *a-72, 75, 77-79, 83-86, 96, 97, 100-105; c-92,100-109(most), 110-119.* ***Simon & Kirby*** *c-75, 83.*

PRIZE MYSTERY
Key Publications: May, 1955 - No. 3, Sept, 1955

1 11 22 33 60 83 105
2,3 8 16 24 44 57 70

PRO, THE
Image Comics: July, 2002 ($5.95, squarebound, one-shot)

1-Ennis-s/Conner & Palmiotti-a; prostitute gets super-powers 8.00
1-Second printing with different cover 6.00
Hardcover Edition (10/04, $14.95) oversized reprint plus new 8 pg. story; sketch pages 15.00

PROFESSIONAL FOOTBALL (See Charlton Sport Library)

PROFESSOR COFFIN
Charlton Comics: No. 19, Oct, 1985 - No. 21, Feb, 1986

19-21: Wayne Howard-a(r); low print run 1 2 3 5 6 8

PROFESSOR OM
Innovation Publishing: May, 1990 - No. 2, 1990 ($2.50, limited series)

1,2-East Meets West spin-off 2.50

PROFESSOR XAVIER AND THE X-MEN (Also see X-Men, 1st series)

The Programme #7 © Milligan & Smith

Proposition Player #5 © William Willingham

Psycho #14 © Skywald

	GD	VG	FN	VF	VF/NM	NM-
	2.0	4.0	6.0	8.0	9.0	9.2

Marvel Comics: Nov, 1995 - No. 18 (99¢)

1-18: Stories featuring the Original X-Men. 2-vs. The Blob. 5-Vs. the Original Brotherhood of Evil Mutants. 10-Vs. The Avengers 2.50

PROGRAMME, THE
DC Comics (WildStorm): Sept, 2007 - No. 12, Aug, 2008 ($2.99, limited series)

1-12: 1-Milligan-s/C.P. Smith-a; covers by Smith & Van Sciver 3.00
Book One TPB (2008, $17.99) r/#1-6; cover sketches 18.00

PROJECT A-KO (Manga)
Malibu Comics: Mar, 1994 - No. 4, June, 1994 ($2.95)

1-4-Based on anime film 3.00

PROJECT A-KO 2 (Manga)
CPM Comics: May, 1995 - No. 3, Aug, 1995 ($2.95, limited series)

1-3 3.00

PROJECT A-KO VERSUS THE UNIVERSE (Manga)
CPM Comics: Oct, 1995 - No. 5, June, 1996 ($2.95, limited series, bi-monthly)

1-5 3.00

PROJECT SUPERPOWERS
Dynamite Entertainment: 2008 - Present ($1.00/$3.50/$2.99)

0-($1.00) Two connecting covers by Alex Ross; re-intro of Golden Age heroes 3.00
0-($1.00) Variant cover by Michael Turner 5.00
1-($3.50) Covers by Ross and Turner; Jim Krueger-s/Carlos Paul-a 3.50
2-6-($2.99) 3.00

PROMETHEA
America's Best Comics: Aug, 1999 - No. 32, Apr, 2005 ($3.50/$2.95)

1-Alan Moore-s/Williams III & Gray-a; Alex Ross painted-c 3.50
1-Variant-c by Williams III & Gray 3.50
2-31-($2.95): 7-Villarrubia photo-a. 10-"Sex, Stars & Serpents". 26-28-Tom Strong app. 27-Cover swipe of Superman vs. Spider-Man treasury ed. 3.00
32-($3.95) Final issue; pages can be cut & assembled into a 2-sided poster 4.00
32-Limited edition of 1000; variant issue printed as 2-sided poster, signed by Moore and Williams; each came with a 48 page book of Promethea covers 120.00
Book 1 Hardcover ($24.95, dust jacket) r/#1-6 25.00
Book 1 TPB ($14.95) r/#1-6 15.00
Book 2 Hardcover ($24.95, dust jacket) r/#7-12 25.00
Book 2 TPB ($14.95) r/#7-12 15.00
Book 3 Hardcover ($24.95, dust jacket) r/#13-18 25.00
Book 3 TPB ($14.95) r/#13-18 15.00
Book 4 Hardcover ($24.95, dust jacket) r/#19-25 25.00
Book 4 TPB ($14.99) r/#19-25 15.00
Book 5 Hardcover ($24.95, d.j.) r/#26-32; includes 2-sided poster image from #32 25.00
Book 5 TPB ($14.99) r/#26-32; includes 2-sided poster image from #32 15.00

PROMETHEUS (VILLAINS) (Leads into JLA #16,17)
DC Comics: Feb, 1998 ($1.95, one-shot)

1-Origin & 1st app.; Morrison-s/Pearson-c 3.00

PROPELLERMAN
Dark Horse Comics: Jan, 1993 - No. 8, Mar, 1994 ($2.95, limited series)

1-8: 2,4,8-Contain 2 trading cards 3.00

PROPHET (See Youngblood #2)
Image Comics (Extreme Studios): Oct, 1993 - No. 10, 1995 ($1.95)

1-($2.50)-Liefeld/Panosian-c/a; 1st app. Mary McCormick; Liefeld scripts in 1-4; #1-3 contain coupons for Prophet #0 2.50
1-Gold foil embossed-c edition rationed to dealers 4.00
2-10: 2-Liefeld-c(p). 3-1st app. Judas. 4-1st app. Omen; Black and White Pt. 3 by Thibert. 4-Alternate-c by Stephen Platt. 5,6-Platt-c/a. 7-(9/94, $2.50)-Platt-c/a. 8-Bloodstrike app. 10-Polybagged w/trading card; Platt-c. 2.50
0-(7/94, $2.50)-San Diego Comic Con ed. (2200 copies) 3.00

PROPHET
Image Comics (Extreme Studios): V2#1, Aug, 1995 - No. 8 ($3.50)

V2#1-8: Dixon scripts in all. 1-4-Platt-a. 1-Boris-c; F. Miller variant-c. 4-Newmen app. 5,6-Wraparound-c 3.50
Annual 1 (9/95, $2.50)-Bagged w/Youngblood gaming card; Quesada-c 2.50
Babewatch Special 1 (12/95, $2.50)-Babewatch tie-in 2.50
1995 San Diego Edition-B&W preview of V2#1. 3.00
TPB-(1996, $12.95) r/#1-7 13.00

PROPHET (Volume 3)
Awesome Comics: Mar, 2000 ($2.99)

1-Flip-c by Jim Lee and Liefeld 3.00

PROPHET/CABLE
Image Comics (Extreme): Jan, 1997 - No. 2, Mar, 1997 ($3.50, limited series)

1,2-Liefeld-c/a: 2-#1 listed on cover 3.50

PROPHET/CHAPEL: SUPER SOLDIERS
Image Comics (Extreme): May, 1996 - No. 2, June, 1996 ($2.50, limited series)

1,2: 1-Two covers exist 2.50
1-San Diego Edition; B&W-c 2.50

PROPOSITION PLAYER
DC Comics (Vertigo): Dec, 1999 - No. 6, May, 2000 ($2.50, limited series)

1-6-Willingham-s/Guinan-a/Bolton-c 2.50
TPB (2003, $14.95) r/#1-6; intro. by James McManus 15.00

PROTECTORS (Also see The Ferret)
Malibu Comics: Sept, 1992 - No. 20, May, 1994 ($1.95-$2.95)

1-20 ($2.50, direct sale)-With poster & diff-c: 1-Origin; has 3/4 outer-c. 3-Polybagged w/Skycap 2.50
1-12 ($1.95, newsstand)-Without poster 2.25

PROTOTYPE (Also see Flood Relief & Ultraforce)
Malibu Comics (Ultraverse): Aug, 1993 - No. 18, Feb, 1995 ($1.95/$2.50)

1-Holo-c 6.00
1-Ultra Limited silver foil-c 4.00
1-12,0,14-18: 3-($2.50, 48 pgs.)-Rune flip-c/story by B. Smith (3 pgs.). 4-Intro Wrath. 5-Break-Thru & Strangers x-over. 6-Arena cameo. 7,8-Arena-c/story. 12-(7/94). 0-(8/94, $2.50, 44 pgs.), 14(10/94) 2.50
13 (8/94, $3.50)-Flip book(Ultraverse Premiere #6) 3.50
Giant Size 1 (10/94, $2.50, 44 pgs.) 2.50

PRUDENCE & CAUTION (Also see Dogs of War & Warriors of Plasm)
Defiant: May, 1994 - No. 2, June, 1994 ($3.50/$2.50)(Spanish versions exist)

1-($3.50, 52 pgs.)-Chris Claremont scripts in all 3.50
2-($2.50) 2.50

PRYDE AND WISDOM (Also see Excalibur)
Marvel Comics: Sept, 1996 - No. 3, Nov, 1996 ($1.95, limited series)

1-3: Warren Ellis scripts; Terry Dodson & Karl Story-c/a 2.50

PSI-FORCE
Marvel Comics Group: Nov, 1986 - No. 32, June, 1989 (75¢/$1.50)

1-25: 11-13-Williamson-i 2.50
26-32 2.50
Annual 1 (10/87) 3.00

PSI-JUDGE ANDERSON
Fleetway Publications (Quality): 1989 - No. 15, 1990 ($1.95, B&W)

1-15 2.50

PSI-LORDS
Valiant: Sept, 1994 - No. 10, June, 1995 ($2.25)

1-($3.50)-Chromium wraparound-c 3.50
1-Gold 5.00
2-10: 3-Chaos Effect Epsilon Pt. 2 2.50

PSYBA-RATS (Also see Showcase '94 #3,4)
DC Comics: Apr, 1995-No. 3, June, 1995 ($2.50, limited series)

1-3 2.50

PSYCHO (Magazine) (Also see Nightmare)
Skywald Publ. Corp.: Jan, 1971 - No. 24, Mar, 1975 (68 pgs.; B&W)

	GD	VG	FN	VF	VF/NM	NM-
1-All reprints	8	16	24	56	93	130
2-Origin & 1st app. The Heap, series begins	6	12	18	39	62	85
3-Frankenstein series by Adkins begins	6	12	18	37	59	80
4,7,9,10: 4-7-Squarebound. 4-1st Out of Chaos/Satan-c/s	5	10	15	32	51	70
8-(Squarebound)1st app. Edward & Mina Sartyros, the Human Gargoyles	6	12	18	37	59	80
11-18: 13-Cannabalism; 3 pgs of Christopher Lee as Dracula photos. 18-Injury to eye-c.	4	8	12	24	37	50
19-Origin Dracula.	4	8	12	26	41	55
20-Severed Head-c	5	10	15	30	48	65
21-24: 22-1974 Fall Special; Reese, Wildey-a(r). 24-1975 Winter Special; Dave Sim scripts (1st pro work)	4	8	12	28	44	60
Annual 1 (1972)(68 pgs.) Dracula & the Heap app.	4	8	12	28	44	60
Yearbook (1974-nn)-Everett, Reese-a	4	8	12	24	37	50

NOTE: *Boris c-3, 5. Buckler a-2, 4, 5. Gene Day a-21, 23, 24. Everett a-3-6. B. Jones a-4. Jeff Jones a-6, 7, 9; c-12. Kaluta a-13. Katz/Buckler a-3. Kim a-24. Morrow a-1. Reese a-5. Dave Sim s-24. Sutton a-3. Wildey*

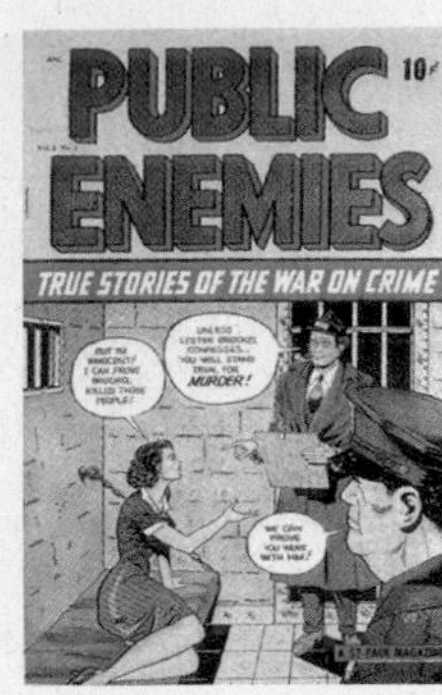
Public Enemies #3 © DS

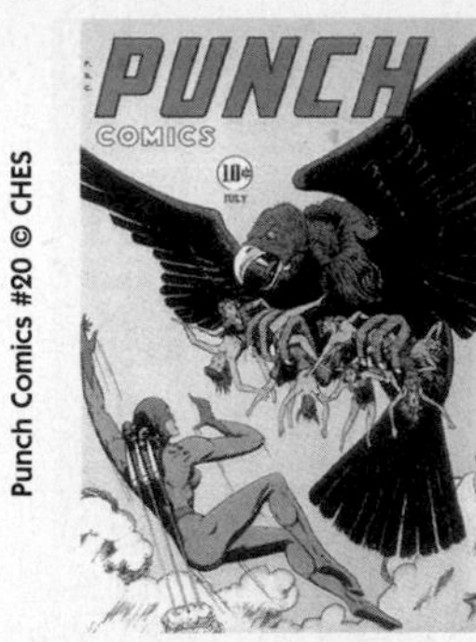
Punch Comics #20 © CHES

The Punisher #1 © MAR

	GD 2.0	VG 4.0	FN 6.0	VF 8.0	VF/NM 9.0	NM- 9.2

a-5.

PSYCHO, THE
DC Comics: 1991 - No. 3, 1991 ($4.95, squarebound, limited series)

1-3-Hudnall-s/Brereton painted-a/c 5.00
TPB (Image Comics, 2006, $17.99) r/series; Brereton sketch pages; Hudnall afterword 18.00

PSYCHOANALYSIS
E. C. Comics: Mar-Apr, 1955 - No. 4, Sept-Oct, 1955

	GD	VG	FN	VF	VF/NM	NM-
1-All Kamen-c/a; not approved by code	19	38	57	152	246	340
2-4-Kamen-c/a in all	13	26	39	104	167	230

PSYCHOANALYSIS
Gemstone Publishing: Oct, 1999 - No. 4, Jan, 2000 ($2.50)

1-4-Reprints E.C. series 2.50
Annual 1 (2000, $10.95) r/#1-4 11.00

PSYCHOBLAST
First Comics: Nov, 1987 - No. 9, July, 1988 ($1.75)

1-9 2.50

PSYCHONAUTS
Marvel Comics (Epic Comics): Oct, 1993 - No. 4, Jan, 1994 ($4.95, lim. series)

1-4: American/Japanese co-produced comic 5.00

PSYLOCKE & ARCHANGEL CRIMSON DAWN
Marvel Comics: Aug, 1997 - No. 4, Nov, 1997 ($2.50, limited series)

1-4-Raab-s/Larroca-a(p) 2.50

PTOLUS: CITY BY THE SPIRE
Dabel Brothers Productions/Marvel Comics (Dabel Brothers) #2 on: June, 2006 - No. 6, Mar, 2007 ($2.99)

1-(1st printing, Dabel) Adaptation of the Monte Cook novel; Cook-s 3.00
1-(2nd printing, Marvel), 2-6 3.00
Monte Cooke's Ptolus: City By the Spire TPB (2007, $14.99) r/#1-6 15.00

P.T. 109 (See Movie Comics)

PUBLIC DEFENDER IN ACTION (Formerly Police Trap)
Charlton Comics: No. 7, Mar, 1956 - No. 12, Oct, 1957

	GD	VG	FN	VF	VF/NM	NM-
7	10	20	30	58	79	100
8-12	8	16	24	40	50	60

PUBLIC ENEMIES
D. S. Publishing Co.: 1948 - No. 9, June-July, 1949

	GD	VG	FN	VF	VF/NM	NM-
1-True Crime Stories	26	52	78	152	244	335
2-Used in **SOTI**, pg. 95	22	44	66	127	204	280
3-5: 5-Arrival date of 10/1/48	15	30	45	85	130	175
6,8,9	15	30	45	83	124	165
7-McWilliams-a; injury to eye panel	15	30	45	85	130	175

PUBO
Dark Horse Comics: Dec, 2002 - No. 3, Mar, 2003 ($3.50, B&W, limited series)

1-3-Leland Purvis-s/a 3.50

PUDGY PIG
Charlton Comics: Sept, 1958 - No. 2, Nov, 1958

	GD	VG	FN	VF	VF/NM	NM-
1,2	3	6	9	17	25	32

PUFFED
Image Comics: Jul, 2003 - No. 3, Sept, 2003 ($2.95, B&W)

1-3-Layman-s/Crosland-a. 1-Two covers by Crosland & Quitely 3.00

PULP FANTASTIC (Vertigo V2K)
DC Comics (Vertigo): Feb, 2000 - No. 3, Apr, 2000 ($2.50, limited series)

1-3-Chaykin & Tischman-s/Burchett-a 2.50

PULP FICTION LIBRARY: MYSTERY IN SPACE
DC Comics: 1999 ($19.95, TPB)

nn-Reprints classic sci-fi stories from Mystery in Space, Strange Adventures, Real Fact Comics and My Greatest Adventure 20.00

PULSE, THE (Also see Alias and Deadline)
Marvel Comics: Apr, 2004 - No. 14, May, 2006 ($2.99)

1-14: 1-5-Bendis-s/Bagley-a; Jessica Jones, Ben Urich, Kat Farrell app. 3-5-Green Goblin app. 6,7-Brent Anderson-a 9-Wolverine app. 10-House of M. 11-14-Gaydos-a 3.00
...: House of M Special (9/05, 50¢) tabloid newspaper format; Mayhew- "photos" 2.50
Vol. 1: Thin Air (2004, $13.99) r/#1-5, gallery of cover layouts and sketches 14.00
Vol. 2: Secret War (2005, $11.99) r/#6-9 12.00
Vol. 3: Fear (2006, $14.99) r/#11-14 and New Avengers Annual #1 15.00

PUMA BLUES
Aardvark One International/Mirage Studios #21 on: 1986 - No. 26, 1990 ($1.70-$1.75, B&W)

1-19, 21-26: 1-1st & 2nd printings. 25,26-$1.75-c 2.50
20 ($2.25)-By Alan Moore, Miller, Grell, others 3.00
Trade Paperback (12/88, $14.95) 15.00

PUMPKINHEAD: THE RITES OF EXORCISM (Movie)
Dark Horse Comics: 1993 - No. 2, 1993 ($2.50, limited series)

1,2: Based on movie; painted-c by McManus 2.50

PUNCH & JUDY COMICS
Hillman Per.: 1944; No. 2, Fall, 1944 - V3#2, 12/47; V3#3, 6/51 - V3#9, 12/51

	GD	VG	FN	VF	VF/NM	NM-
V1#1-(60 pgs.)	23	46	69	133	214	295
2	14	28	42	78	112	145
3-12(7/46)	11	22	33	62	86	110
V2#1(8/49),3-9	9	18	27	47	61	75
V2#2,10-12, V3#1-Kirby-a(2) each	21	42	63	123	197	270
V3#2-Kirby-a	19	38	57	112	176	240
3-9	8	16	24	44	57	70

PUNCH COMICS
Harry 'A' Chesler: 12/41; #2, 2/42; #9, 7/44 - #19, 10/46; #20, 7/47 - #23, 1/48

	GD	VG	FN	VF	VF/NM	NM-
1-Mr. E, The Sky Chief, Hale the Magician, Kitty Kelly begin	147	294	441	926	1563	2200
2-Captain Glory app.	90	180	270	567	959	1350
9-Rocketman & Rocket Girl & The Master Key begin	87	174	261	548	924	1300
10-Sky Chief app.; J. Cole-a; Master Key-r/Scoop #3	62	124	186	391	663	935
11-Origin Master Key-r/Scoop #1; Sky Chief, Little Nemo app.; Jack Cole-a; Fine-*ish* art by Sultan	57	114	171	359	605	850
12-Rocket Boy & Capt. Glory app; classic Skull-c	267	534	801	1682	2841	4000
13-Cover has list of 4 Chesler artists' names on tombstone	62	124	186	391	663	935
14,15,19,21: 21-Hypo needle story	54	108	162	340	575	810
16,17-Gag-c	42	84	126	260	435	610
18-Bondage-c; hypodermic panels	67	134	201	422	711	1000
20-Unique cover with bare-breasted women. Rocket Girl-c	105	201	315	662	1119	1575
22,23-Little Nemo-not by McCay. 22-Intro Baxter (teenage)(68 pgs.)	23	46	69	133	214	295

PUNCHY AND THE BLACK CROW
Charlton Comics: No. 10, Oct, 1985 - No. 12, Feb, 1906

10-12: Al Fago funny animal-r; low print run 6.00

PUNISHER (See Amazing Spider-Man #129, Blood and Glory, Born, Captain America #241, Classic Punisher, Daredevil #182-184, 257, Daredevil and the..., Ghost Rider V2#5, 6, Marc Spector #8 & 9, Marvel Preview #2, Marvel Super Action, Marvel Tales, Power Pack #46, Spectacular Spider-Man #81-83, 140, 141, 143 & new Strange Tales #13 & 14)

PUNISHER (The...)
Marvel Comics Group: Jan, 1986 - No. 5, May, 1986 (Limited series)

	GD	VG	FN	VF	VF/NM	NM-
1-Double size	2	4	6	13	18	22
2-5	2	4	6	8	10	12

Trade Paperback (1988)-r/#1-5 11.00
Circle of Blood TPB (8/01, $15.95) Zeck-c 16.00
Circle of Blood HC (2008, $19.99) two covers 20.00
NOTE: ***Zeck*** *a-1-4; c-1-5.*

PUNISHER (The...) (Volume 2)
Marvel Comics: July, 1987 - No. 104, July, 1995

	GD	VG	FN	VF	VF/NM	NM-
1	1	3	4	6	0	10

2-9: 8-Portacio/Williams-c/a begins, ends #18. 9-Scarcer, low dist. 6.00

	GD	VG	FN	VF	VF/NM	NM-
10-Daredevil app; ties in w/Daredevil #257	1	3	4	6	8	10

11-74,76-85,87-89: 13-18-Kingpin app. 19-Stroman-c/a. 20-Portacio-c(p). 24-1st app. Shadowmasters. 25,50:($1.50,52 pgs.). 25-Shadowmasters app. 57-Photo-c; came w/outer-c (newsstand ed. w/o outer-c). 59-Punisher is severely cut & has skin grafts (has black skin). 60-62-Luke Cage app. 62-Punisher back to white skin. 68-Tarantula-c/story. 85-Prequel to Suicide Run Pt. 0. 87,88-Suicide Run Pt. 6 & 9 2.50
75-($2.75, 52 pgs.)-Embossed silver foil-c 3.00
86-($2.95, 52 pgs.)-Embossed & foil stamped-c; Suicide Run part 3 3.00
90-99: 90-bound-in cards. 99-Cringe app. 2.50
100,104: 100-($2.95, 68 pgs.). 104-Last issue 4.00
100-($3.95, 68 pgs.)-Foil cover 5.00
101-103: 102-Bullseye 3.50
"Ashcan" edition (75¢)-Joe Kubert-c 3.00

The Punisher (1998 series) #1 © MAR

The Punisher (2004 series) #54 © MAR

Punisher Magazine #4 © MAR

GD VG FN VF VF/NM NM-
2.0 4.0 6.0 8.0 9.0 9.2

Annual 1-7 ('88-'94, 68 pgs.) 1-Evolutionary War x-over. 2-Atlantis Attacks x-over; Jim Lee-a(p) (back-up story, 6 pgs.); Moon Knight app. 4-Golden-c(p). 6-Bagged w/card. 3.00
...: A Man Named Frank (1994, $6.95, TPB) 7.00
...and Wolverine in African Saga nn (1989, $5.95, 52 pgs.)-Reprints Punisher War Journal #6 & 7; Jim Lee-c/a(r) 6.00
... Assassin Guild ('88, $6.95, graphic novel) 10.00
Back to School Special 1-3 (11/92-10/94, $2.95, 68 pgs.) 3.00
.../Batman: Deadly Knights (10/94, $4.95) 5.00
.../Black Widow: Spinning Doomsday's Web (1992, $9.95, graphic novel) 12.00
...Bloodlines nn (1991, $5.95, 68 pgs.) 6.00
...: Die Hard in the Big Easy nn ('92, $4.95, 52 pgs.) 5.00
...: Empty Quarter nn ('94, $6.95) 7.00
...G-Force nn (1992, $4.95, 52 pgs.)-Painted-c 5.00
...Holiday Special 1-3 (1/93-1/95,, 52 pgs.,68pgs.)-1-Foil-c 3.00
...Intruder Graphic Novel (1989, $14.95, hardcover) 20.00
...Intruder Graphic Novel (1991, $9.95, softcover) 12.00
...Invades the 'Nam: Final Invasion nn (2/94, $6.95)-J. Kubert-c & chapter break art; reprints The 'Nam #84 & unpublished #85,86 7.00
...Kingdom Gone Graphic Novel (1990, $16.95, hardcover) 20.00
...Meets Archie (8/94, $3.95, 52 pgs.)-Die cut-c; no ads; same contents as Archie Meets The Punisher 5.00
...Movie Special 1 (6/90, $5.95, squarebound, 68 pgs.) painted-c; Brent Anderson-a; contents intended for a 3 issue series which was advertised but not published 6.00
...: No Escape nn (1990, $4.95, 52 pgs.)-New-a 5.00
...Return to Big Nothing Graphic Novel (Epic, 1989, $16.95, hardcover) 25.00
...Return to Big Nothing Graphic Novel (Marvel, 1989, $12.95, softcover) 15.00
...The Prize nn (1990, $4.95, 68 pgs.)-New-a 5.00
Summer Special 1-4(8/91-7/94, 52 pgs.):1-No ads. 2-Bisley-c; Austin-a(i). 3-No ads 3.00

NOTE: ***Austin** c(i)-47, 48. **Cowan** c-39. **Golden** c-50, 85, 86, 100. **Heath** a-26, 27, 89, 90, 91; c-26, 27. **Quesada** c-56p, 62p. **Sienkiewicz** c-Back to School 1.**Stroman** a-76p(9 pgs.). **Williamson** a(i)-25, 60-62i, 64-70, 74, Annual 5; c(i)-62, 65-68.*

PUNISHER (Also see Double Edge)
Marvel Comics: Nov, 1995 - No. 18, Apr, 1997 ($2.95/$1.95/$1.50)

1 ($2.95)-Ostrander scripts begin; foil-c. 3.00
2-18. 7-Vs. S.H.I.E.L.D. 11-"Onslaught." 12-17-X-Cutioner-c/app. 17-Daredevil, Spider-Man-c/app. 2.50

PUNISHER (Marvel Knights)
Marvel Comics: Nov, 1998 - No. 4, Feb, 1999 ($2.99, limited series)

1-4: 1-Wrightson-a; Wrightson & Jusko-c 3.00
1-($6.95) DF Edition; Jae Lee variant-c 7.00

PUNISHER (Marvel Knights) (Volume 3)
Marvel Comics: Apr, 2000 - No. 12, Mar, 2001 ($2.99, limited series)

1-Ennis-s/Dillon & Palmiotti-a/Bradstreet-c 5.00
1-Bradstreet white variant-c 10.00
1-($6.95) DF Edition; Jurgens & Ordway variant-c 7.00
2-Two covers by Bradstreet & Dillon 3.00
3-($3.99) Bagged with Marvel Knights Genesis Edition; Daredevil app. 4.00
4-12: 9-11-The Russian app. 3.00
HC (6/02, $34.95) r/#1-12, Punisher Kills the Marvel Universe, and Marvel Knights Double Shot #1 35.00
... By Garth Ennis Omnibus (2008, $99.99) oversized r/#1-12, #1-7 & #13-37 of 2001 series, Punisher Kills the Marvel Universe, and Marvel Knights Double Shot #1; extras 100.00
.../Painkiller Jane (1/01, $3.50) Jusko-c; Ennis-s/Jusko and Dave Ross-a(p) 3.50
...: Welcome Back Frank TPB (4/01, $19.95) r/#1-12 20.00

PUNISHER (Marvel Knights) (Volume 4)
Marvel Comics: Aug, 2001 - No. 37, Feb, 2004 ($2.99)

1-Ennis-s/Dillon & Palmiotti-a/Bradstreet-c; The Russian app. 4.00
2-Two covers (Dillon & Bradstreet) Spider-Man-c/app. 3.00
3-37: 3-7-Ennis-s/Dillon-a. 9-12-Peyer-s/Gutierrez-a. 13,14-Ennis-s/Dilllon-a. 16,17-Wolverine app.; Robertson-a. 18-23,32-Dillon-a. 24-27-Mandrake-a. 27-Elektra app. 33-37-Spider-Man, Daredevil, & Wolverine app. 36,37-Hulk app. 3.00
...Army of One TPB (2/02, $15.95) r/#1-7; Bradstreet-c 16.00
Vol. 2 HC (2003, $29.95) r/#1-7,13-18; intro. by Mike Millar 30.00
Vol. 3 HC (2004, $29.95) r/#19-27; script pages for #19 30.00
Vol. 3: Business as Usual TPB (2003, $14.99) r/#13-18; Bradstreet-c 15.00
Vol. 4: Full Auto TPB (2003, $17.99) r/#20-26; Bradstreet-c 18.00
Vol. 5: Streets of Laredo TPB (2003, $17.99) r/#19,27-32 18.00
Vol. 6: Confederacy of Dunces TPB (2004, $13.99) r/#33-37 14.00

PUNISHER (Marvel MAX)
Marvel Comics: Mar, 2004 - Present ($2.99)

1-49,51-60: 1-Ennis-s/LaRosa-a/Bradstreet-c; flashback to his family's murder; Micro app. 6-Micro killed. 7-12,19-25-Fernandez-a. 13-18-Braithwaite-a. 31-36-Barracuda. 43-49-Medina-a. 51-54-Barracuda app. 60-Last Ennis-s/Bradstreet-c 3.00
50-($3.99) Barracuda returns; Chaykin-a 4.00
61,62-Gregg Hurwitz-s/Dave Johnson-c/Laurence Campbell-a 3.00
Annual (11/07, $3.99) Mike Benson-s/Laurence Campbell-a 4.00
...: Bloody Valentine (4/06, $3.99) Palmiotti & Gray-s/Gulacy & Palmiotti-a; Gulacy-c 4.00
...: Force of Nature (4/08, $3.99) Swierczynski-s/Lacombe-a/Deodato-c 4.00
...: MAX Special: Little Black Book (8/08, $3.99) Gischler-s/Palo-a/Johnson-c 4.00
...: Red X-Mas (2/05, $3.99) Palmiotti & Gray-s/Texeira & Palmiotti-a; Texeira-c 4.00
...: Silent Night (2/06, $3.99) Diggle-s/Hotz-a/Deodato-c 4.00
...: The Cell (7/05, $4.99) Ennis-s/LaRosa-a/Bradstreet-c 5.00
.... The Tyger (2/00, $4.99) Ennis-s/Severin-a/Bradstreet-c, Castle's childhood 5.00
...: Very Special Holidays TPB ('06, $12.99) r/Red X-Mas, Bloody Valentine and Silent Night 13.00
...: X-Mas Special (1/07, $3.99) Stuart Moore-s/CP Smith-a 4.00
... MAX: From First to Last HC (2006, $19.99) r/The Tyger, The Cell and The End 1-shots 20.00
... MAX Vol. 1 (2005, $29.99) oversized r/#1-12; gallery of Fernandez art from #7 shown from layout to colored pages 30.00
... MAX Vol. 2 (2006, $29.99) oversized r/#13-24, gallery of Fernandez pencil art 30.00
... MAX Vol. 3 (2007, $29.99) oversized r/#25-36; gallery of Fernandez & Parlov art 30.00
... MAX Vol. 4 (2008, $29.99) oversized r/#37-49; gallery of Fernandez & Medina art 30.00
Vol. 1: In the Beginning TPB (2004, $14.99) r/#1-6 15.00
Vol. 2: Kitchen Irish TPB (2004, $14.99) r/#7-12 15.00
Vol. 3: Mother Russia TPB (2005, $14.99) r/#13-18 15.00
Vol. 4: Up is Down and Black is White TPB (2005, $14.99) r/#19-24 15.00
Vol. 5: The Slavers TPB (2006, $15.99) r/#25-30; Fernandez pencil pages 16.00
Vol. 6: Barracuda TPB (2006, $15.99) r/#31-36; Parlov sketch page 16.00
Vol. 7: Man of Stone TPB (2007, $15.99) r/#37-42 16.00
Vol. 8: Widowmaker TPB (2007, $17.99) r/#43-49 18.00
Vol. 9: Long Cold Dark TPB (2008, $15.99) r/#50-54 16.00

PUNISHER AND WOLVERINE: DAMAGING EVIDENCE (See Wolverine and...)

PUNISHER ARMORY, THE
Marvel Comics: 7/90 ($1.50); No. 2, 6/91; No. 3, 4/92 - 10/94($1.75/$2.00)

1-10: 1-r/weapons pgs. from War Journal. 1,2-Jim Lee-c. 3-10- All new material. 3-Jusko painted-c 2.50

PUNISHER KILLS THE MARVEL UNIVERSE
Marvel Comics: Nov, 1995 ($5.95, one-shot)

1-Garth Ennis script/Doug Braithwaite-a 7.00
1-2nd printing (3/00) Steve Dillon-c 6.00
1-3rd printing (2008, $4.99) original 1995 cover 5.00

PUNISHER MAGAZINE, THE
Marvel Comics: Oct, 1989 - No. 16, Nov, 1990 ($2.25, B&W, Magazine, 52 pgs.)

1-16: 1-r/Punisher #1('86). 2,3-r/Punisher 2-5. 4-16: 4-7-r/Punisher V2#1-8. 4-Chiodo-c. 8-r/Punisher #10 & Daredevil #257; Portacio & Lee-r. 14-r/Punisher War Journal #1,2 w/new Lee-c. 16-r/Punisher W. J. #3,8 3.00

NOTE: ***Chiodo** painted c-4, 7, 16. **Jusko** painted c-6, 8. **Jim Lee** r-8, 14-16; c-14. **Portacio/Williams** r-7-12.*

PUNISHER: OFFICIAL MOVIE ADAPTATION
Marvel Comics: May, 2004 - No. 3, May, 2004 ($2.99, limited series)

1-3-Photo-c of Thomas Jane; Milligan-s/Olliffe-a 3.00

PUNISHER: ORIGIN OF MICRO CHIP, THE
Marvel Comics: July, 1993 - No. 2, Aug, 1993 ($1.75, limited series)

1,2 2.50

PUNISHER: P.O.V.
Marvel Comics: 1991 - No. 4, 1991 ($4.95, painted, limited series, 52 pgs.)

1-4: Starlin scripts & Wrightson painted-c/a in all. 2-Nick Fury app. 5.00

PUNISHER PRESENTS: BARRACUDA MAX
Marvel Comics (MAX): Apr, 2007 - No. 5, Aug, 2007 ($3.99, limited series)

1-5-Ennis-s/Parlov-a/c 4.00
SC (2007, $17.99) r/series; sketch pages 18.00

PUNISHER: THE END
Marvel Comics: June, 2004 ($4.50, one-shot)

1-Ennis-s/Corben-a/c 4.50

PUNISHER: THE GHOSTS OF INNOCENTS
Marvel Comics: Jan, 1993 - No. 2, Jan, 1993 ($5.95, 52 pgs.)

1,2-Starlin scripts 6.00

PUNISHER: THE MOVIE
Marvel Comics: 2004 ($12.99,TPB)

nn-Reprints Amazing Spider-Man #129; Official Movie Adaptation and Punisher V3 #1 13.00

Punisher War Journal (2007 series) #10 © MAR

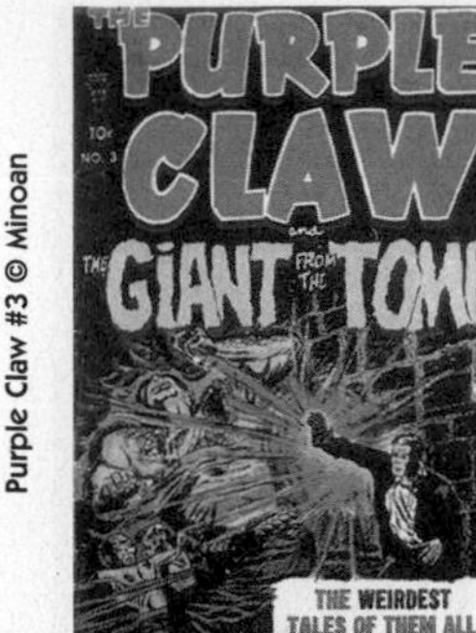

Purple Claw #3 © Minoan

PvP V2 #36 © Scott R. Kurtz

GD VG FN VF VF/NM NM-
2.0 4.0 6.0 8.0 9.0 9.2

GD VG FN VF VF/NM NM-
2.0 4.0 6.0 8.0 9.0 9.2

PUNISHER 2099 (See Punisher War Journal #50)
Marvel Comics: Feb, 1993 - No. 34, Nov, 1995 ($1.25/$1.50/$1.95)
1-24,26-34: 1-Foil stamped-c. 1-Second printing. 13-Spider-Man 2099 x-over; Ron Lim-c(p). 16-bound-in card sheet 2.50
25 ($2.95, 52 pgs.)-Deluxe edition; embossed foil-cover 3.00
25 ($2.25, 52 pgs.) 2.50
(Marvel Knights) #1 (11/04, $2.99) Kirkman-s/Mhan-a/Pat Lee-c 3.00

PUNISHER VS. BULLSEYE
Marvel Comics: Jan, 2006 - No. 5, May, 2006 ($2.99, limited series)
1-5-Daniel Way-s/Steve Dillon-a 3.00
TPB (2006, $13.99) r/#1-5; cover sketch pages 14.00

PUNISHER VS. DAREDEVIL
Marvel Comics: Jun, 2000 ($3.50, one-shot)
1-Reprints Daredevil #183,#184 & #257 3.50

PUNISHER WAR JOURNAL, THE
Marvel Comics: Nov, 1988 - No. 80, July, 1995 ($1.50/$1.75/$1.95)
1-Origin The Punisher; Matt Murdock cameo; Jim Lee inks begin 5.00
2-7: 2,3-Daredevil x-over; Jim Lee-c(i). 4-Jim Lee c/a begins. 6-Two part Wolverine story begins. 7-Wolverine-c, story ends 4.00
8-49,51-60,62,63,65: 13-16,20-22: No Jim Lee-a. 13-Lee-c only. 13-15-Heath-i. 14,15-Spider-Man x-over. 19-Last Jim Lee-c/a.29,30-Ghost Rider app. 31-Andy & Joe Kubert art. 36-Photo-c. 47,48-Nomad/Daredevil-c/stories; see Nomad. 57,58-Daredevil & Ghost Rider-c/stories. 62,63-Suicide Run Pt. 4 & 7 3.00
50,61,64($2.95, 52 pgs.): 50-Preview of Punisher 2099 (1st app.); embossed-c. 61-Embossed foil cover; Suicide Run Pt. 1. 64-Die-cut-c; Suicide Run Pt. 10 3.00
64-($2.25, 52 pgs.)-Regular cover edition 2.50
66-74,76-80: 66-Bound-in card sheet 2.50
75 ($2.50, 52 pgs.) 2.75
NOTE: ***Golden*** *c-25-30, 40, 61, 62.* ***Jusko*** *painted c-31, 32.* ***Jim Lee*** *a-1i-3i, 4p-13p, 17p-19p; c-2i, 3i, 4p-15p, 17p, 18p, 19p. Painted c-40.*

PUNISHER WAR JOURNAL (Frank Castle back in the regular Marvel Universe)
Marvel Comics: Jan, 2007 - Present ($2.99)
1-Civil War tie-in; Spider-Man app; Fraction-s/Olivetti-a 5.00
1-B&W edition (11/06) 5.00
2-5: 2,3-Civil War tie-in. 4-Deodato-a 4.00
6-11,13-23: 6-10-Punisher dons Captain America-*esque* outfit. 7-Two covers. 11-Winter Soldier app. 16-23-Chaykin-a. 18-23-Jigsaw app. 3.00
12-($3.99) World War Hulk x-over; Fraction-s/Olivetti-a 4.00
... Vol. 1: Civil War HC (2007, $19.99) r/#1-4 and #1 B&W edition; Olivetti sketch pages 20.00
... Vol. 1: Civil War SC (2007, $14.99) r/#1-4 and #1 B&W edition; Olivetti sketch pages 15.00
... Vol. 2: Goin' Out West HC (2007, $24.99) r/#5-11; Olivetti sketch page 25.00
... Vol. 2: Goin' Out West SC (2008, $17.99) r/#5-11; Olivetti sketch page 18.00
... Vol. 3: Hunter Hunted HC (2008, $19.99) r/#12-17 20.00

PUNISHER: WAR ZONE, THE
Marvel Comics: Mar, 1992 - No. 41, July, 1995 ($1.75/$1.95)
1-($2.25, 40 pgs.)-Die cut-c; Romita, Jr.-c/a begins 3.00
2-22,24,26,27-41: 8-Last Romita, Jr.-c/a. 19-Wolverine app. 24-Suicide Run Pt. 5. 27-Bound-in card sheet. 31-36-Joe Kubert-a 2.50
23-($2.95, 52 pgs.)-Embossed foil-c; Suicide Run part 2; Buscema-a(part) 3.00
25-($2.25, 52 pgs.)-Suicide Run part 8; painted-c 2.50
Annual 1,2 ('93, 94, $2.95, 68 pgs.)-1-Bagged w/card; John Buscema-a 3.00
...: River Of Blood TPB (2006, $15.99) r/#31-36; Joe Kubert-a 16.00
NOTE: ***Golden*** *c-23.* ***Romita, Jr.*** *c/a-1-8.*

PUNISHER: YEAR ONE
Marvel Comics: Dec, 1994 - No. 4, Apr, 1995 ($2.50, limited series)
1-4 2.50

PUNX
Acclaim (Valiant): Nov, 1995 - No. 3, Jan, 1996 ($2.50, unfinished lim. series)
1-3: Giffen story & art in all. 2-Satirizes Scott McCloud's Understanding Comics 2.50
(Manga) Special 1 (3/96, $2.50)-Giffen scripts 2.50

PUPPET COMICS
George W. Dougherty Co.: Spring, 1946 - No. 2, Summer, 1946
1-Funny animal in both 14 28 42 76 108 140
2 11 22 33 60 83 105

PUPPETOONS (See George Pal's...)

PUREHEART (See Archie as...)

PURGATORI
Chaos! Comics: Prelude #-1, 5/96 ($1.50, 16 pgs.); 1996 - No. 3 Dec, 1996 ($3.50/$2.95, limited series)
Prelude #-1-Pulido story; Balent-c/a; contains sketches & interviews 2.25
0-(2/01, $2.99) Prelude to "Love Bites"; Rio-c/a 3.00
1/2 (12/00, $2.95) Al Rio-c/a 3.00
1-($3.50)-Wraparound cover; red foil embossed-c; Jim Balent-a 5.00
1-($19.95)-Premium Edition (1000 print run) 20.00
2-($3.00)-Wraparound-c 3.00
2-Variant-c 5.00
..: Heartbreaker 1 (3/02, $2.99) Jolley-s 3.00
..: Love Bites 1 (3/01, $2.99) Turnbull-a/Kaminski-s 3.00
..: Mischief Night 1 (11/01, $2.99) 3.00
..: Re-Imagined 1 (7/02, $2.99) Jolley-s/Neves-a 3.00
...The Dracula Gambit-($2.95) 3.00
...The Dracula Gambit Sketchbook-($2.95) 3.00
...The Vampire's Myth 1-($19.95) Premium Ed. (10,000) 20.00
...Vs. Chastity (7/00, $2.95) Two versions (Alpha and Omega) with different endings; Rio-a 3.00
...Vs. Lady Death (1/01, $2.95) Kaminski-s 3.00
...Vs. Vampirella (4/00, $2.95) Zanier-a; Chastity app. 3.00

PURGATORI
Chaos! Comics: Oct, 1998 - No. 7, Apr, 1999 ($2.95)
1-7-Quinn-s/Rio-c/a. 2-Lady Death-c 3.00

PURGATORI: DARKEST HOUR
Chaos! Comics: Sept, 2001 - No. 2, Oct, 2001 ($2.99, limited series)
1,2 3.00

PURGATORI: EMPIRE
Chaos! Comics: May, 2000 - No. 3, July, 2000 ($2.95, limited series)
1-3-Cleavenger-c 3.00

PURGATORI: GODDESS RISING
Chaos! Comics: July, 1999 - No. 4, Oct, 1999 ($2.95, limited series)
1-4-Deodato-c/a 3.00

PURGATORI: GOD HUNTER
Chaos! Comics: Apr, 2002 - No. 2, May, 2002 ($2.99, limited series)
1,2-Molenaar-a/Jolley-s 3.00

PURGATORI: GOD KILLER
Chaos! Comics: Jun, 2002 - No. 2, July, 2002 ($2.99, limited series)
1,2-Molenaar-a/Jolley-s 3.00

PURGATORI: THE HUNTED
Chaos! Comics: Jun, 2001 - No. 2, Aug, 2001 ($2.99, limited series)
1,2 3.00

PURPLE CLAW, THE (Also see Tales of Horror)
Minoan Publishing Co./Toby Press: Jan, 1953 - No. 3, May, 1953
1-Origin; horror/weird stories in all 32 64 96 186 298 410
2,3: 1-3 r-in Tales of Horror #9-11 23 46 69 133 214 295
I.W. Reprint #8-Reprints #1 3 6 9 16 23 30

PUSSYCAT (Magazine)
Marvel Comics Group: Oct, 1968 (B&W reprints from Men's magazines)
1-(Scarce)-Ward, Everett, Wood-a; Everett-c 17 34 51 120 223 325

PUZZLE FUN COMICS (Also see Jingle Jangle)
George W. Dougherty Co.: Spring, 1946 - No. 2, Summer, 1946 (52 pgs.)
1-Gustavson-a 23 46 69 133 214 295
2 15 30 45 88 137 185
NOTE: *#1 & 2('46) each contain a* ***George Carlson*** *cover plus a 6 pg. story "Alec in Fumbleland"; also many puzzles in each.*

PvP (Player vs. Player)
Image Comics: Mar, 2003 - Present ($2.95/$2.99/$3.50, B&W, reads sideways)
1-34,36-Scott Kurtz-s/a in all. 1,16-Frank Cho-c. 11-Savage Dragon-c/app. 14-Invincible app. 19-Jonathan Luna-c. 25-Cho-a (2 pgs.) 3.00
35,37-40 ($3.50) 3.50
#0 (7/05, 50¢) Secret Origin of Skull 2.25
...: At Large TPB (7/04, $11.95) r/#1-6 12.00
... Vol. 2: Reloaded TPB (12/04, $11.95) r/#7-12 12.00
... Vol. 3: Rides Again TPB (2005, $11.99) r/#13-18 12.00
... Vol. 4: PVP Goes Bananas TPB (2007, $12.99) r/#19-24 13.00
... Vol. 5: PVP Treks On TPB (2008, $14.99) r/#25-31 15.00
...: The Dork Ages TPB (2/04, $11.95) r/#1-6 from Dork Storm Press 12.00

QUACK!
Star Reach Productions: July, 1976 - No. 6, 1977? ($1.25, B&W)

Quasar #15 © MAR

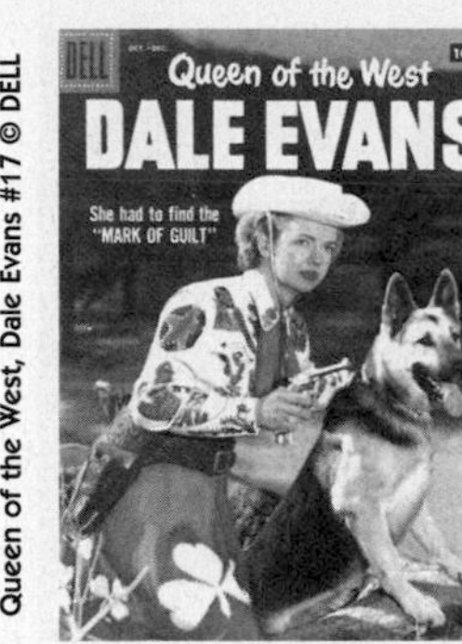

Queen of the West, Dale Evans #17 © DELL

Quick Draw McGraw #3 © H-B

GD VG FN VF VF/NM NM-
2.0 4.0 6.0 8.0 9.0 9.2

1-Brunner-c/a on Duckaneer (Howard the Duck clone); Dave Stevens, Gilbert, Shaw-a
2 4 6 8 11 14
1-2nd printing (10/76) 5.00
2-6: 2-Newton the Rabbit Wonder by Aragonés/Leialoha; Gilbert, Shaw-a; Leialoha-c. 3-The Beavers by Dave Sim begin, end #5; Gilbert, Shaw-a; Sim/Leialoha-c. 6-Brunner-a (Duckeneer); Gilbert-a 1 2 3 5 7 9

QUADRANT
Quadrant Publications: 1983 - No. 8, 1986 (B&W, nudity, adults)

1-Peter Hsu-c/a in all 2 4 6 8 11 14
2-8 1 2 3 5 6 8

QUANTUM & WOODY
Acclaim Comics: June, 1997 - No. 17, No. 32 (9/99), No. 18 - No. 21, Feb, 2000 ($2.50)

1-17: 1-1st app.; two covers. 6-Copycat-c. 9-Troublemakers app. 2.50
32-(9/99); 18-(10/99),19-21 2.50
The Director's Cut TPB ('97, $7.95) r/#1-4 plus extra pages 8.00

QUANTUM LEAP (TV) (See A Nightmare on Elm Street)
Innovation Publishing: Sept, 1991 - No. 12, Jun, 1993 ($2.50, painted-c)

1-12: Based on TV show; all have painted-c. 8-Has photo gallery 3.00
Special Edition 1 (10/92)-r/#1 w/8 extra pgs. of photos & articles 3.00
Time and Space Special 1 (#13) ($2.95)-Foil logo 3.00

QUANTUM TUNNELER, THE
Revolution Studio: Oct, 2001 (no cover price, one-shot)

1-Prequel to "The One" movie; Clayton Henry-a 2.50

QUASAR (See Avengers #302, Captain America #217, Incredible Hulk #234, Marvel Team-Up #113 & Marvel Two-in-One #53)
Marvel Comics: Oct, 1989 - No. 60, Jul, 1994 ($1.00/$1.25, Direct sales #17 on)

1-Origin; formerly Marvel Boy/Marvel Man 3.00
2-49,51-60: 3-Human Torch app. 6-Venom cameo (2 pgs.). 7-Cosmic Spidey. 11-Excalibur x-over. 14-McFarlane-c. 16-($1.50, 52 pgs.). 17-Flash parody (Buried Alien). 20-Fantastic Four app. 23-Ghost Rider x-over. 25-($1.50, 52 pgs.)-New costume Quasar. 26-Infinity Gauntlet x-over, Thanos-c/story. 27-Infinity Gauntlet x over. 30-Thanos cameo in flashback; last $1.00-c. 31-Begin $1.25-c; D.P. 7 guest stars. 38-40-Infinity War x-overs. 38-Battles Warlock. 39-Thanos c & cameo. 40-Thanos app. 42-Punisher-c/story. 53-Warlock & Moondragon app. 58-w/bound-in card sheet 2.50
50-($2.95, 52 pgs.)-Holo-grafx foil-c; Silver Surfer, Man-Thing, Ren & Stimpy app. 3.00
Special #1-3 ($1.25, newsstand)-Same as #32-34 2.50

QUEEN & COUNTRY (See Whiteout)
Oni Press: Mar, 2001 - No. 32, Aug, 2007 ($2.95/$2.99, B&W)

1-Rucka-s in all. Rolston-a/Sale-c 1 2 3 4 5 7
2-5: 2-4-Rolston-a/Sale-c. 5-Snyder-c/Hurtt-a 4.00
6-24,26-32: 6,7-Snyder-c/Hurtt-a. 13-15-Alexander-a. 16-20-McNeil-a. 21-24-Hawthorne-a 26-28-Norton-a 3.00
25-($5.99) Rolston-a 6.00
Free Comic Book Day giveaway (5/02) r/#1 with "Free Comic Book Day" banner on-c 2.25
Operation: Blackwall (10/03, $8.95, TPB) r/#13-15; John Rogers intro. 9.00
Operation: Broken Ground (2002, $11.95, TPB) r/#1-4; Ellis intro. 12.00
Operation: Crystal Ball (1/03, $14.95, TPB) r/#8-12; Judd Winick intro. 15.00
Operation: Dandelion HC (8/04, $25.00) r/#21-24; Jamie S. Rich intro. 25.00
Operation: Dandelion (8/04, $11.95, TPB) r/#21-24; Jamie S. Rich intro. 12.00
Operation: Morningstar (9/02, $8.95, TPB) r/#5-7; Stuart Moore intro. 9.00
Operation: Storm Front (3/04, $14.95, TPB) r/#16-20; Geoff Johns intro. 15.00

QUEEN & COUNTRY: DECLASSIFIED
Oni Press: Nov, 2002 - No. 3, Jan, 2003 ($2.95, B&W, limited series)

1-3-Rucka-s/Hurtt-a/Morse-c 3.00
TPB (7/03, $8.95) r/#1-3; intro. by Micah Wright 9.00

QUEEN & COUNTRY: DECLASSIFIED (Volume 2)
Oni Press: Jan, 2005 - No. 3, Feb, 2006 ($2.95/$2.99, B&W, limited series)

1-3-Rucka-s/Burchett-a/c 3.00
TPB (3/06, $8.95) r/#1-3 9.00

QUEEN & COUNTRY: DECLASSIFIED (Volume 3)
Oni Press: Jun, 2005 - No. 3, Aug, 2005 ($2.95, B&W, limited series)

1-3- "Sons & Daughters;" Johnston-s/Mitten-a/c 3.00
TPB (3/06, $8.95) r/#1-3 9.00

QUEEN OF THE WEST, DALE EVANS (TV)(See Dale Evans Comics, Roy Rogers & Western Roundup under Dell Giants)
Dell Publ. Co.: No. 479, 7/53 - No. 22, 1-3/59 (All photo-c; photo back c-4-8,15)

Four Color 479(#1, '53) 19 38 57 135 250 365
Four Color 528(#2, '54) 10 20 30 70 123 175
3,4: 3(4-6/54)-Toth-a. 4-Toth, Manning-a 8 16 24 54 90 125
5-10-Manning-a. 5-Marsh-a 7 14 21 47 76 105
11,19,21-No Manning 21-Tufts-a 5 10 15 34 55 75
12-18,20,22-Manning-a 6 12 18 39 62 85

QUENTIN DURWARD
Dell Publishing Co.: No. 672, Jan, 1956

Four Color 672-Movie, photo-c 7 14 21 45 73 100

QUESTAR ILLUSTRATED SCIENCE FICTION CLASSICS
Golden Press: 1977 (224 pgs.) ($1.95)

11197-Stories by Asimov, Sturgeon, Silverberg & Niven; Starstream-r
3 6 9 20 30 40

QUEST FOR CAMELOT
DC Comics: July, 1998 ($4.95)

1-Movie adaption 5.00

QUEST FOR DREAMS LOST (Also see Word Warriors)
Literacy Volunteers of Chicago: July 4, 1987 ($2.00, B&W, 52 pgs.)(Proceeds donated to help fight illiteracy)

1-Teenage Mutant Ninja Turtles by Eastman/Laird, Trollords, Silent Invasion, The Realm, Wordsmith, Reacto Man, Eb'nn, Aniverse 2.50

QUESTION, THE (See Americomics, Blue Beetle (1967), Charlton Bullseye & Mysterious Suspense)

QUESTION, THE (Also see Showcase '95 #3)
DC Comics: Feb, 1987 - No. 36, Mar, 1990 ($1.50)

1-36: Denny O'Neil scripts in all 2.50
Annual 1 (1988, $2.50) 2.50
Annual 2 (1989, $3.50) 3.50
...: Poisoned Ground (2008, $19.99) r/#7-12 20.00
...: Zen and Violence (2007, $19.99) r/#1-6 20.00

QUESTION, THE (Also see Crime Bible and 52)
DC Comics: Jan, 2005 - No. 6, Jun, 2005 ($2.95, limited series)

1-6-Rick Veitch-s/Tommy Lee Edwards-a. 4,6-Superman app. 3.00

QUESTION QUARTERLY, THE
DC Comics: Summer, 1990 - No. 5, Spring, 1992 ($2.50, 52pgs.)

1-5 2.50
NOTE: *Cowan a-1, 2, 4, 5; c-1-3, 5.* ***Mignola*** *a-5i.* ***Quesada*** *a-3-5.*

QUESTION RETURNS, THE
DC Comics: Feb, 1997 ($3.50, one-shot)

1-Brereton-c 3.50

QUESTPROBE
Marvel Comics: 8/84; No. 2, 1/85; No. 3, 11/85 (lim. series)

1-3: 1-The Hulk app. by Romita. 2-Spider-Man; Mooney-a(i). 3-Human Torch & Thing 3.00

QUICK DRAW McGRAW (TV) (Hanna-Barbera)(See Whitman Comic Books)
Dell Publishing Co./Gold Key No. 12 on: No. 1040, 12-2/59-60 - No. 11, 7-9/62; No. 12, 11/62; No. 13, 2/63; No. 14, 4/63; No. 15, 6/69 (1st show aired 9/29/59)

Four Color 1040(#1) 1st app. Quick Draw & Baba Looey, Augie Doggie & Doggie Daddy and Snooper & Blabber 13 26 39 95 168 240
2(4-6/60) 4,6: 2-Augie Doggie & Snooper & Blabber stories (8 pgs. each); pre-dates both of their #1 issues. 4-Augie Doggie & Snooper & Blabber stories.
6 12 18 41 66 90
5-1st Snagglepuss app.; last 10¢ issue 7 14 21 45 73 100
7-11 5 10 15 32 51 70
12,13-Title change to ...Fun-Type Roundup (84pgs.) 7 14 21 45 73 100
14,15: 15-Reprints 4 8 12 28 44 60

QUICK DRAW McGRAW (TV)(See Spotlight #2)
Charlton Comics: Nov, 1970 - No. 8, Jan, 1972 (Hanna-Barbera)

1 5 10 15 32 51 70
2-8 3 6 9 19 29 38

QUICKSILVER (See Avengers)
Marvel Comics: Nov, 1997 - No. 13, Nov, 1998 ($2.99/$1.99)

1-($2.99)-Peyer-s/Casey Jones-a; wraparound-c 3.00
2-11: 2-Two covers-variant by Golden. 4-6-Inhumans app. 2.50
12-($2.99) Siege of Wundagore pt. 4 3.00
13-Magneto-c/app.; last issue 2.50

QUICK-TRIGGER WESTERN (...Action #12; Cowboy Action #5-11)
Atlas Comics (ACI #12/WPI #13-19): No. 12, May, 1956 - No. 19, Sept, 1957

12-Baker-a 15 30 45 90 140 190

Racer X #3 © Speed Racer Ents.

Radioactive Man #100 © Bongo

Raggedy Ann & Andy #7 © Bobbs & Merrill

	GD 2.0	VG 4.0	FN 6.0	VF 8.0	VF/NM 9.0	NM- 9.2
13-Williamson-a, 5 pgs.	15	30	45	84	127	170
14-Everett, Crandall, Torres-a; Heath-c	14	28	42	81	118	155
15,16: 15-Torres, Crandall-a. 16-Orlando, Kirby-a	12	24	36	69	97	125
17,18: 18-Baker-a	12	24	36	67	94	120
19	10	20	30	54	72	90

NOTE: ***Ayers** a-17. **Colan** a-16. **Maneely** a-15, 17; c-15, 18. **Morrow** a-18. **Powell** a-14. **Severin** a-19; c-12, 13, 16, 17, 19. **Shores** a-16. **Tuska** a-17.*

QUINCY (See Comics Reading Libraries in the Promotional Comics section)

QUITTER, THE
DC Comics (Vertigo): 2005 ($19.99, B&W graphic novel)

HC ($19.99) Autobiography of Harvey Pekar; Pekar-s/Daen Haspiel-a						20.00
SC (2006, $12.99)						13.00

RACCOON KIDS, THE (Formerly Movietown Animal Antics)
National Periodical Publications (Arleigh No. 63,64): No. 52, Sept-Oct, 1954 - No. 62, Oct-Nov, 1956; No. 63, Sept, 1957; No. 64, Nov, 1957

52-Doodles Duck by Mayer	15	30	45	83	124	165
53-64: 53-62-Doodles Duck by Mayer	11	22	33	62	86	110

NOTE: ***Otto Feuer**-a most issues. **Rube Grossman**-a most issues.*

RACE FOR THE MOON
Harvey Publications: Mar, 1958 - No. 3, Nov, 1958

1-Powell-a(5); 1/2-pg. S&K-a; cover redrawn from Galaxy Science Fiction pulp (5/53)	15	30	45	94	147	200
2-Kirby/Williamson-c(r)/a(3); Kirby-p 7 more stys	26	52	78	152	244	335
3-Kirby/Williamson-c/a(4); Kirby-p 6 more stys	28	56	84	162	261	360

RACER-X
Now Comics: 8/88 - No. 11, 8/89; V2#1, 9/89 - V2#10, 1990 ($1.75)

0-Deluxe ($3.50)						3.50
1 (9/88) - 11, V2#1-10						2.50

RACER X (See Speed Racer)
DC Comics (WildStorm): Oct, 2000 - No. 3, Dec, 2000 ($2.95, limited series)

1-3: 1-Tommy Yune-s/Jo Chen-a; 2 covers by Yune. 2,3-Kabala app.						3.50

RACING PETTYS
STP Corp.: 1980 ($2.50, 68 pgs., 10 1/8" x 13 1/4")

1-Bob Kane-a. Kane bio on inside back-c.						10.00

RACK & PAIN
Dark Horse Comics: Mar, 1994 - No. 4, June, 1994 ($2.50, limited series)

1-4: Brian Pulido scripts in all. 1-Greg Capullo-c						3.00

RACK & PAIN: KILLERS
Chaos! Comics: Sept, 1996 - No. 4, Jan, 1997 ($2.95, limited series)

1-4: Reprints Dark Horse series; Jae Lee-c						3.00

RACKET SQUAD IN ACTION
Capitol Stories/Charlton Comics: May-June, 1952 - No. 29, Mar, 1958

1	28	56	84	162	261	360
2-4,6: 3,4,6-Dr. Neff, Ghost Breaker app.	15	30	45	85	130	175
5-Dr. Neff, Ghost Breaker app; headlights-c	21	42	63	123	197	270
7-10: 10-Explosion-c	14	28	42	80	115	150
11-Ditko-c/a	30	60	90	174	280	385
12-Ditko explosion-c (classic); Shuster-a(2)	52	104	156	322	536	750
13-Shuster-c(p)/a.	12	24	36	69	97	125
14-Marijuana story "Shakedown"; Giordano-c	15	30	45	83	124	165
15-28: 15,20,22,23-Giordano-c	11	22	33	60	83	105
29-(15¢, 68 pgs.)	14	28	42	76	108	140

RADIANT LOVE (Formerly Daring Love #1)
Gilmor Magazines: No. 2, Dec, 1953 - No. 6, Aug, 1954

2	12	24	36	67	94	120
3-6	8	16	24	44	57	70

RADICAL DREAMER
Blackball Comics: No. 0, May, 1994 - No. 4, Nov, 1994 ($1.99, bi-monthly) (1st poster format comic)

0-4: 0-2-($1.99, poster format): 0-1st app. Max Wrighter. 3,4-($2.50-c)						3.00

RADICAL DREAMER
Mark's Giant Economy Size Comics: V2#1, June, 1995 - V2#6, Feb, 1996 ($2.95, B&W, limited series)

V2#1-6						3.00
Prime (5/96, $2.95)						3.00
Dreams Cannot Die!-(1996, $20.00, softcover)-Collects V1#0-4 & V2#1-6; intro by Kurt Busiek; afterward by Mark Waid						20.00
Dreams Cannot Die!-(1996, $60.00, hardcover)-Signed & limited edition; collects V1#0-4 & V2#1-6; intro by Kurt Busiek; afterward by Mark Waid						60.00

RADIOACTIVE MAN (Simpsons TV show)
Bongo Comics: 1993 - No. 6, 1994 ($1.95/$2.25, limited series)

1-($2.95)-Glow-in-the-dark-c; bound-in jumbo poster; origin Radioactive Man; (cover dated Nov. 1952)						5.00
2-6: 2-Says #88 on-c & inside & dated May 1962; cover parody of Atlas Kirby monster-c; Superior Squad app.; origin Fallout Boy. 3-($1.95)-Cover "dated" Aug 1972 #216. 4-($2.25)-Cover "dated" Oct 1980 #412; w/trading card. 5-Cover "dated" Jan 1986 #679; w/trading card. 6-(Jan 1995 #1000)						4.00
Colossal #1-($4.95)						7.00
#4 (2001, $2.50) Faux 1953 issue; Murphy Anderson-i (6 pgs.)						2.50
#100 (2000, $2.50) Comic Book Guy-c/app.; faux 1963 issue inside						2.50
#136 (2001, $2.50) Dan DeCarlo-c/a						2.50
#222 (2001, $2.50) Batton Lash-s; Radioactive Man in 1972-style						2.50
#575 (2002, $2.50) Chaykin-c; Radioactive Man in 1984-style						2.50
1963-106 (2002, $2.50) Radioactive Man in 1960s Gold Key-style; Groening-c						2.50
#7 Bongo Super Heroes Starring... (2003, $2.50) Marvel Silver Age-style Superior Squad						2.50
#8 Official Movie Adaptation (2004, $2.99) starring Rainier Wolfcastle and Milhouse						3.00
#9 (#197 on-c) (2004, $2.50) Kirby-esque New Gods spoof; Golden Age Radio Man app.						2.50

RADIO FUNNIES
DC Comics: Mar. 1931

nn - Ashcan comic, not distributed to newsstands, only for in-house use. Cover art is Adventure Comics #39 with interior being Detective Comics #19						(no known sales)

RAGAMUFFINS
Eclipse Comics: Jan, 1985 ($1.75, one shot)

1-Eclipse Magazine-r, w/color; Colan-a						2.50

RAGGEDY ANN AND ANDY (See Dell Giants, March of Comics #23 & New Funnies)
Dell Publishing Co.: No. 5, 1942 - No. 533, 2/54; 10-12/64 - No. 4, 3/66

Four Color 5(1942)	45	90	135	360	680	1000
Four Color 23(1943)	34	68	102	256	483	710
Four Color 45(1943)	29	58	87	213	394	575
Four Color 72(1945)	24	48	72	172	319	465
1(6/46)-Billy & Bonnie Bee by Frank Thomas	32	64	96	246	461	675
2,3: 3-Egbert Elephant by Dan Noonan begins	17	34	51	120	223	325
4-Kelly-a, 16 pgs.	18	36	54	128	237	345
5,6,8-10	14	28	42	99	175	250
7-Little Black Sambo, Black Mumbo & Black Jumbo only app; Christmas-c	16	32	48	112	209	305
11-20	11	22	33	79	140	200
21-Alice In Wonderland cover/story	14	28	42	99	175	250
22-27,29-39(8/49), Four Color 262(1/50): 34-"...In Candyland"	10	20	30	67	116	165
28-Kelly-c	10	20	30	70	123	175
Four Color 306,354,380,452,533	7	14	21	50	83	115
1(10-12/64-Dell)	4	8	12	24	37	50
2,3(10-12/65), 4(3/66)	3	6	9	16	23	30

NOTE: ***Kelly** art ("Animal Mother Goose")-#1-34, 36, 37; c-28. Peterkin Pottle by **John Stanley** in 32-38.*

RAGGEDY ANN AND ANDY
Gold Key: Dec, 1971 - No. 6, Sept, 1973

1	3	6	9	19	29	38
2-6	3	6	9	15	21	26

RAGGEDY ANN & THE CAMEL WITH THE WRINKLED KNEES (See Dell Jr. Treasury #8)

RAGMAN (See Batman Family #20, The Brave & The Bold #196 & Cancelled Comic Cavalcade)
National Per. Publ./DC Comics No. 5: Aug-Sept, 1976 - No. 5, Jun-Jul, 1977

1-Origin & 1st app.	2	4	6	9	12	15
2-5: 2-Origin ends; Kubert-c. 4-Drug use story	1	2	3	5	7	9

NOTE: ***Kubert** a-4, 5; c-1-5. **Redondo** studios a-1-4.*

RAGMAN (2nd Series)
DC Comics: Oct, 1991 - No. 8, May, 1992 ($1.50, limited series)

1-8: 1-Giffen plots/breakdowns. 3-Origin. 8-Batman-c/story						3.00

RAGMAN: CRY OF THE DEAD
DC Comics: Aug, 1993 - No. 6, Jan, 1994 ($1.75, limited series)

1-6: Joe Kubert-c						3.00

RAGS RABBIT (Formerly Babe Ruth Sports #10 or Little Max #10?; also see Harvey Hits #2, Harvey Wiseguys & Tastee Freez)
Harvey Publications: No. 11, June, 1951 - No. 18, March, 1954 (Written & drawn for little folks)

Rampaging Hulk #6 © MAR

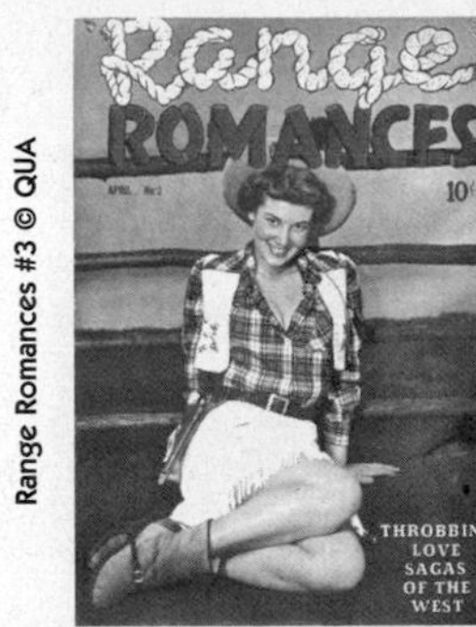

Range Romances #3 © QUA

Rangers Comics #22 © FH

	GD	VG	FN	VF	VF/NM	NM-
	2.0	4.0	6.0	8.0	9.0	9.2

11-(See Nutty Comics #5 for 1st app.) 6 12 18 31 38 45
12-18 5 10 15 24 30 35

RAI (Rai and the Future Force #9-23) (See Magnus #5-8)
Valiant: Mar, 1992 - No. 0, Oct, 1992; No. 9, May, 1993 - No. 33, Jun, 1995 ($1.95/$2.25)

1-Valiant's 1st original character 2 4 6 8 11 14
2-4,0: 4-Low print run. 0-(11/92)-Origin/1st app. new Rai (Rising Spirit) & 1st full app. & partial origin Bloodshot; also see Eternal Warrior #4; tells future of all characters
1 3 4 6 8 10
5-10: 6,7-Unity x-overs. 7-Death of Rai. 9-($2.50)-Gatefold-c; story cont'd from Magnus #24; Magnus, Eternal Warrior & X-O app. 5.00
11-33: 15-Manowar Armor app. 17-19-Magnus x-over. 21-1st app. The Starwatchers (cameo); trading card. 22-Death of Rai. 26-Chaos Effect Epsilon Pt. 3 2.50
NOTE: *Layton c-2i, 9i. Miller c-6. Simonson c-7.*

RAIDERS OF THE LOST ARK (Movie)
Marvel Comics Group: Sept, 1981 - No. 3, Nov, 1981 (Movie adaptation)

1-3: 1-r/Marvel Comics Super Special #18 3.00
NOTE: *Buscema a(p)-1-3; c(p)-1. Simonson a-3i; scripts-1-3.*

RAINBOW BRITE AND THE STAR STEALER
DC Comics: 1985

nn-Movie adaptation 2 4 6 8 10 12

RAISE THE DEAD
Dynamite Entertainment: 2007 - Present ($3.50)

1-3-Arthur Suydam-c/Leah Moore & John Reppion-s/Hugo Petrus-a. 3-Phillips var-c 3.50
... Vol. 1 HC (2007, $19.99) r/#1-4; script, interview & sketch pages; cover gallery 20.00

RALPH KINER, HOME RUN KING
Fawcett Publications: 1950 (Pittsburgh Pirates)

nn-Photo-c; life story 59 118 177 372 629 885

RALPH SNART ADVENTURES
Now Comics: June, 1986 - V2#9, 1987; V3#1 - #26, Feb, 1991; V4#1, 1992 - #4, 1992

1-3, V2#1-7,V3#1-23,25,26:1-($1.00, B&W)-1(B&W),V2#1(11/86), B&W), 8,9-color. V3#1(9/88)-Color begins 2.50
V3#24-($2.50)-3-D issue, V4#1-3-Direct sale versions w/cards 2.50
V4#1-3-Newsstand versions w/random cards 2.50
Book 1 1 2 3 5 6 8
3-D Special (11/92, $3.50)-Complete 12-card set w/3-D glasses 3.50

RAMAR OF THE JUNGLE (TV)
Toby Press No. 1/Charlton No. 2 on: 1954 (no month); No. 2, Sept, 1955 - No. 5, Sept, 1956

1-Jon Hall photo-c; last pre-code issue 21 42 63 123 197 270
2-5: 2-Jon Hall photo-c 15 30 45 85 130 175

RAMAYAN 3392 A.D.
Virgin Comics: Sept, 2006 - Present ($2.99)

1-8: 1-Alex Ross-c; re-imagining of the Indian myth of Ramayana; poster of cover inside 3.00
... Reloaded (8/07 - No. 7, 7/08, $2.99) 1-7: 1-Two covers by Kang and Oeming 3.00
... Reloaded Guidebook (4/08, $2.99) Profiles of characters and weapons 3.00

RAMM
Megaton Comics: May, 1987 - No. 2, Sept, 1987 ($1.50, B&W)

1,2-Both have 1 pg. Youngblood ad by Liefeld 2.50

RAMPAGING HULK (The Hulk #10 on; also see Marvel Treasury Edition)
Marvel Comics Group: Jan, 1977 - No. 9, June, 1978 ($1.00, B&W magazine)

1-Bloodstone story w/Buscema & Nebres-a. Origin re-cap w/Simonson-a; Gargoyle, UFO story; Ken Barr-c 3 6 9 18 27 35
2-Old X-Men app; origin old w/Simonson-a & new X-Men in text w/Cockrum illos; Bloodstone story w/Brown & Nebres-a 3 6 9 14 20 26
3-9: 3-Iron Man app.; Norem-c. 4-Gallery of villains w/Giffen-a. 5,6-Hulk vs. Sub-Mariner. 7-Man-Thing story. 8-Original Avengers app. 9-Thor vs. Hulk battle; Shanna the She-Devil story w/DeZuniga-a 2 4 6 11 16 20
NOTE: *Alcala a-1-3i, 5i, 8i. Buscema a-1. Giffen a-4. Nino a-4i. Simonson a-1-3p. Starlin a-4(w/Nino), 7; c-4, 5, 7.*

RAMPAGING HULK
Marvel Comics: Aug, 1998 - No. 6, Jan, 1999 ($2.99/$1.99)

1-($2.99) Flashback stories of Savage Hulk; Leonardi-a 3.00
2-6-($1.99): 2-Two covers 2.50

RANDOLPH SCOTT (Movie star)(See Crack Western #67, Prize Comics Western #76, Western Hearts #8, Western Love #1 & Western Winners #7)

RANGE BUSTERS
Fox Features Syndicate: Sept, 1950 (One shot)

1 (Exist?) 20 40 60 114 180 245

	GD	VG	FN	VF	VF/NM	NM-
	2.0	4.0	6.0	8.0	9.0	9.2

RANGE BUSTERS (Formerly Cowboy Love?; Wyatt Earp, Frontier Marshall #11 on)
Charlton Comics: No. 8, May, 1955 - No. 10, Sept, 1955

8 8 16 24 42 54 65
9,10 6 12 18 28 34 40

RANGELAND LOVE
Atlas Comics (CDS): Dec, 1949 - No. 2, Mar, 1950 (52 pgs.)

1-Robert Taylor & Arlene Dahl photo-c 17 34 51 98 154 210
2-Photo-c 14 28 42 80 115 150

RANGER, THE (See Zane Grey, Four Color #255)

RANGE RIDER, THE (TV)(See Flying A's...)

RANGE ROMANCES
Comic Magazines (Quality Comics): Dec, 1949 - No. 5, Aug, 1950 (#5: 52 pg)

1-Gustavson-c/a 26 52 78 152 244 335
2-Crandall-c/a 26 52 78 152 244 335
3-Crandall, Gustavson-a; photo-c 22 44 66 127 204 280
4-Crandall-a; photo-c 19 38 57 112 176 240
5-Gustavson-a; Crandall-a(p); photo-c 19 38 57 112 176 240

RANGERS COMICS (...of Freedom #1-7)
Fiction House Magazines: 10/41 - No. 67, 10/52; No. 68, Fall, 1952; No. 69, Winter, 1952-53 (Flying stories)

1-Intro. Ranger Girl & The Rangers of Freedom; ends #7, cover app. only #5
318 636 954 2162 3781 5400
2 95 190 285 599 1012 1425
3 69 138 207 435 738 1040
4,5 62 124 186 391 663 935
6-10: 8-U.S. Rangers begin 50 100 150 310 518 725
11,12-Commando Rangers app. 47 94 141 291 483 675
13-Commando Ranger begins-not same as Commando Rangers
45 90 135 279 465 650
14-20 40 80 120 244 397 550
21-Intro/origin Firehair (begins, 2/45) 41 82 123 253 419 585
22-30: 23-Kazanda begins, ends #28. 28-Tiger Man begins (origin/1st app., 4/46), ends #46. 30-Crusoe Island begins, ends #40 31 62 93 181 291 400
31-40: 33-Hypodermic panels 26 52 78 154 247 340
41-46: 41-Last Werewolf Hunter 22 44 66 127 204 280
47-56- "Eisnerish" Dr. Drew by Grandenetti. 48-Last Glory Forbes. 53-Last 52 pg. issue. 55-Last Sky Rangers 21 42 63 123 197 270
57-60-Straight run of Dr. Drew by Grandenetti 15 30 45 92 144 195
61-69: 64-Suicide Smith begins. 63-Used in **POP**, pgs. 85, 99. 67-Space Rangers begin, end #69 14 28 42 82 121 160
NOTE: *Bondage, discipline covers, lingerie panels are common. Crusoe Island by **Larsen**-#30-36. Firehair by **Lubbers**-#30-49. Glory Forbes by **Baker**-#36-45, 47; by **Whitman**-#34, 35. I Confess in #41-53. Jan of the Jungle in #42-58. King of the Congo in #49-53. Tiger Man by **Celardo**-#30-39. **M. Anderson** a-30? **Baker** a-36-38, 42, 44. **John Celardo** a-34, 36-39. **Lee Elias** a-21-28. **Evans** a-19, 38-46, 48-52. **Hopper** a-25, 26. **Ingels** a-13-16. **Larsen** a-34. **Bob Lubbers** a-30-38, 40-44; c-40-45. **Moreira** a-41-47. **Tuska** a-16, 17, 19, 22. **M. Whitman** c-61-66. **Zolnerwich** c-1-17.*

RANGO (TV)
Dell Publishing Co.: Aug, 1967

1-Photo-c of comedian Tim Conway 4 8 12 24 37 50

RANN-THANAGAR HOLY WAR (Also see Hawkman Special #1)
DC Comics: July, 2008 - No. 8 ($3.50, limited series)

1-3-Adam Strange & Hawkman app.; Starlin-s/Lim-a. 1-Two covers by Starlin & Lim 3.50

RANN-THANAGAR WAR (See Adam Strange 2004 mini-series)(Prelude to Infinite Crisis)
DC Comics: July, 2005 - No. 6, Dec, 2005 ($2.50, limited series)

1-6-Adam Strange, Hawkman and Green Lantern (Kyle Rayner) app.; Gibbons-s/Reis-a 2.50
...: Infinite Crisis Special (4/06, $4.99) Kyle Rayner becomes Ion again; Jade dies 5.00
TPB (2005, $12.99) r/#1-6; cover gallery; new Bolland-c 13.00

RAPHAEL (See Teenage Mutant Ninja Turtles)
Mirage Studios: 1985 ($1.50, 7-1/2x11", B&W w/2 color cover, one-shot)

1-1st Turtles one-shot spin-off; contains 1st drawing of the Turtles as a group from 1983 6.00
1-2nd printing (11/87); new-c & 8 pgs. art 2.50

RAPHAEL BAD MOON RISING (See Teenage Mutant Ninja Turtles)
Mirage Publishing: July, 2007 - No. 4, Oct, 2007 ($3.25, B&W, limited series)

1-4-Continued from Tales of the TMNT #7; Lawson-a 3.25

RASCALS IN PARADISE
Dark Horse Comics: Aug, 1994 - No. 3, Dec, 1994 ($3.95, magazine size)

1-3-Jim Silke-a/story 4.00
Trade paperback-($16.95)-r/#1-3 17.00

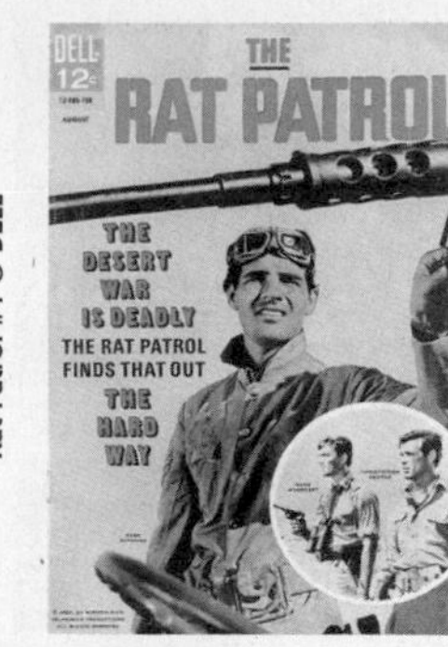

Rat Patrol #4 © DELL

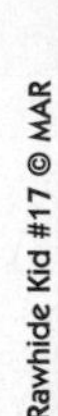
Rawhide Kid #17 © MAR

Real Clue Crime Stories V2 #2 © HILL

GD VG FN VF VF/NM NM-
2.0 4.0 6.0 8.0 9.0 9.2

RASL
Cartoon Books: Mar, 2008 - Present ($3.50, B&W)
1,2-Jeff Smith-s/a/c 3.50

RATFINK (See Frantic, Zany, & Ed "Big Daddy" Roth's Ratfink Comix)
Canrom, Inc.: Oct, 1964
1-Woodbridge-a 7 14 21 45 73 100

RAT PATROL, THE (TV)
Dell Publishing Co.: Mar, 1967 - No. 5, Nov, 1967; No. 6, Oct, 1969
1-Christopher George photo-c 7 14 21 47 76 105
2-6: 3-6-Photo-c 4 8 12 28 44 60

RAVAGE 2099 (See Marvel Comics Presents #117)
Marvel Comics: Dec, 1992 - No. 33, Aug, 1995($1.25/$1.50)
1-($1.75)-Gold foil stamped-c; Stan Lee scripts 3.00
1-($1.75)-2nd printing 2.50
2-24,26-33: 5-Last Ryan-c. 6-Last Ryan-a. 14-Punisher 2099 x-over. 15-Ron Lim-c(p). 18-Bound-in card sheet 2.50
25 ($2.25, 52 pgs.) 2.50
25 ($2.95, 52 pgs.)-Silver foil embossed-c 3.00

RAVEN (See DC Special: Raven and Teen Titans titles)

RAVEN, THE (See Movie Classics)

RAVEN CHRONICLES
Caliber (New Worlds): 1995 - No. 16 ($2.95, B&W)
1-16: 10-Flip book w/Wordsmith #6. 15-Flip book w/High Caliber #4 3.00

RAVENS AND RAINBOWS
Pacific Comics: Dec, 1983 (Baxter paper)(Reprints fanzine work in color)
1-Jeff Jones-c/a(r); nudity scenes 3.00

RAWHIDE (TV)
Dell Publishing Co./Gold Key: Sept-Nov, 1959 - June-Aug, 1962; July, 1963 - No. 2, Jan, 1964
Four Color 1028 (#1) 22 44 66 157 291 425
Four Color 1097,1160,1202,1261,1269 14 28 42 102 181 260
01-684-208 (8/62, Dell) 12 24 36 87 156 225
1(10071-307) (7/63, Gold Key) 12 24 36 87 156 225
2-(12¢) 11 22 33 79 140 200
NOTE: *All have Clint Eastwood photo-c.* ***Tufts*** *a-1028.*

RAWHIDE KID
Atlas/Marvel Comics (CnPC No. 1-16/AMI No. 17-30): Mar, 1955 - No. 16, Sept, 1957; No. 17, Aug, 1960 - No. 151, May, 1979
1-Rawhide Kid, his horse Apache & sidekick Randy begin; Wyatt Earp app.; #1 was not code approved; Maneely splash pg. 92 184 276 580 978 1375
2 40 80 120 235 380 525
3-5 30 60 90 174 280 385
6-10: 7-Williamson-a (4 pgs.) 23 46 69 133 214 295
11-16: 16-Torres-a 18 36 54 105 165 225
17-Origin by Jack Kirby; Kirby-a begins 42 84 126 261 436 610
18-21,24-30 11 22 33 79 140 200
22-Monster-c/story by Kirby/Ayers 14 28 42 103 184 265
23-Origin retold by Jack Kirby 17 34 51 120 223 335
31-35,40: 31,32-Kirby-a. 33-35-Davis-a. 34-Kirby-a. 35-Intro & death of The Raven. 40-Two-Gun Kid x-over. 10 20 30 68 119 170
36,37,39,41,42-No Kirby. 42-1st Larry Lieber issue 9 18 27 60 100 140
38-Red Raven-c/story; Kirby-c (2/64). 11 22 33 75 133 190
43-Kirby-a (beware: pin-up often missing) 11 22 33 75 133 190
44,46: 46-Toth-a. 46-Doc Holliday-c/s 8 16 24 56 93 130
45-Origin retold, 17 pgs. 10 20 30 68 119 170
47-49,51-60 6 12 18 37 59 80
50-Kid Colt x-over; vs. Rawhide Kid 6 12 18 41 66 90
61-70: 64-Kid Colt story. 66-Two-Gun Kid story. 67-Kid Colt story. 70-Last 12¢ issue 4 8 12 28 44 60
71-78,80-83,85 3 6 9 17 25 32
79,84,86,95: 79-Williamson-a(r). 84,86: Kirby-a. 86-Origin-r; Williamson-r/Ringo Kid #13 (4 pgs.) 3 6 9 18 27 35
87-91: 90-Kid Colt app. 91-Last 15¢ issue 3 6 9 16 22 28
92,93 (52 pg.Giants). 92-Kirby-a 3 6 9 21 32 42
94,96-99 3 6 9 14 19 24
100 (6/72)-Origin retold & expanded 3 6 9 18 27 35
101-120: 115-Last new story 2 4 6 10 14 18
121-151 2 4 6 8 10 12
133,134-(30¢-c variants, limited distribution)(5,7/76) 4 8 12 26 41 55
140,141-(35¢-c variants, limited distribution)(7,9/77) 6 12 18 39 62 85

GD VG FN VF VF/NM NM-
2.0 4.0 6.0 8.0 9.0 9.2

Special 1(9/71, 25¢, 68 pgs.)-All Kirby/Ayers-r 4 8 12 26 41 55
NOTE: ***Ayers*** *a-13, 14, 16.* ***Colan*** *a-5, 35, 37; c-145p, 148p, 149p.* ***Davis*** *a-125r.* ***Everett*** *a-54i, 65, 66, 88, 96i, 148i(r).* ***Gulacy*** *c-147.* ***Heath*** *c-4.* ***G. Kane*** *c-101, 144.* ***Keller*** *a-5, 144r.* ***Kirby*** *a-17-32, 34, 42, 43, 84, 86, 92, 109r, 112r, 116r, 117r, 137r, Spec. 1; c-17-35, 37, 38, 40, 41, 43-47, 137r.* ***Maneely*** *c-1, 2, 5, 6, 14.* ***Morisi*** *a-13.* ***Morrow/Williamson*** *r-111.* ***Roussos*** *r-146i, 147i, 149-151i.* ***Severin*** *a-16; c-8, 13.* ***Sutton*** *a-93.* ***Torres*** *a-99r.* ***Tuska*** *a-14.* ***Wildey*** *r-146-151(Outlaw Kid).* ***Williamson*** *r-79, 86, 95.*

RAWHIDE KID
Marvel Comics Group: Aug, 1985 - No. 4, Nov, 1985 (Mini-series)
1-4 5.00

RAWHIDE KID
Marvel Comics (MAX): Apr, 2003 - No. 5, June, 2003 ($2.99, limited series)
1-John Severin-a/Ron Zimmerman-s; Dave Johnson-c 3.00
2-5: 3-Dodson-c. 4-Darwyn Cooke-c. 5-J. Scott Campbell-c 3.00
Vol. 1: Slap Leather TPB (2003, $12.99) r/#1-5 13.00

RAY, THE (See Freedom Fighters & Smash Comics #14)
DC Comics: Feb, 1992 - No. 6, July, 1992 ($1.00, mini-series)
1-Sienkiewicz-c; Joe Quesada-a(p) in 1-5 5.00
2-6: 3-6-Quesada-c(p). 6-Quesada layouts only 3.00
...In a Blaze of Power (1994, $12.95)-r/#1-6 w/new Quesada-c 13.00

RAY, THE
DC Comics: May, 1994 - No. 28, Oct, 1996 ($1.75/$1.95/$2.25)
1-Quesada-c(p); Superboy app. 3.00
1-($2.95)-Collectors Edition w/diff. Quesada-c; embossed foil-c 4.00
2-5,0,6-24,26-28: 2-Quesada-c(p); Superboy app. 5-(9/94). 0-(10/94) 2.50
25-($3.50)-Future Flash (Bart Allen)-c/app; double size 3.50
Annual 1 ($3.95, 68 pgs.)-Superman app. 4.00

RAY BRADBURY COMICS
Topps Comics: Feb, 1993 - V4#1, June, 1994 ($2.95)
1-5-Polybagged w/3 trading cards each. 1-All dinosaur issue; Corben-a; Williamson/Torres/Krenkel-r/Weird Science-Fantasy #25. 3-All dinosaur issue; Steacy painted-c; Stout-a 3.00
Special Edition 1 (1994, $2.95)-The Illustrated Man 3.00
...Special: Tales of Horror #1 ($2.50), ...Trilogy of Terror V3#1 (5/94, $2.50), ...Martian Chronicles V4#1 (6/94, $2.50)-Steranko-c 2.50
NOTE: ***Kelley Jones*** *a-Trilogy of Terror V3#1.* ***Kaluta*** *a-Martian Chronicles V4#1.* ***Kurtzman/Matt Wagner*** *c-2.* ***McKean*** *c-4.* ***Mignola*** *a-4.* ***Wood*** *a-Trilogy of Terror V3#1r.*

RAZORLINE
Marvel Comics: Sept, 1993 (75¢, one-shot)
1-Clive Barker super-heroes: Ectokid, Hokum & Hex, Hyperkind & Saint Sinner 2.50

RAZOR'S EDGE, THE
DC Comics (WildStorm): Dec, 2004 - No. 5, Apr, 2005 ($2.95)
1-5-Warblade; Bisley-c/a; Ridley-s 3.00

REAL ADVENTURE COMICS (Action Adventure #2 on)
Gillmor Magazines: Apr, 1955
1 9 18 27 47 61 75

REAL ADVENTURES OF JONNY QUEST, THE
Dark Horse Comics: Sept, 1996 - No. 12, Sept, 1997 ($2.95)
1-12 3.00

REAL CLUE CRIME STORIES (Formerly Clue Comics)
Hillman Periodicals: V2#4, June, 1947 - V8#3, May, 1953
V2#4(#1)-S&K c/a(3); Dan Barry-a 48 96 144 298 499 700
5-7-S&K c/a(3-4). 7-Iron Lady app. 40 80 120 235 380 525
8-12 14 28 42 76 108 140
V3#1-8,10-12, V4#1-3,5-8,11,12 11 22 33 64 90 115
V3#9-Used in **SOTI**, pg. 102 14 28 42 78 112 145
V4#4-S&K-a 14 28 42 81 118 155
V4#9,10-Krigstein-a 12 24 36 67 94 120
V5#1-5,7,8,10,12 10 20 30 54 72 90
6,9,11(1/54)-Krigstein-a 10 20 30 58 79 100
V6#1-5,8,9,11 9 18 27 50 65 80
6,7,10,12-Krigstein-a. 10-Bondage-c 10 20 30 58 79 100
V7#1-3,5-11, V8#1-3: V7#6-1 pg. Frazetta ad "Prayer" - 1st app.? 9 18 27 50 65 90
4,12-Krigstein-a 10 20 30 58 79 100
NOTE: ***Barry*** *a-9, 10; c-V2#8.* ***Briefer*** *a-V6#6.* ***Fuje*** *a- V2#7(2), 8, 11.* ***Infantino*** *a-V2#8; c-V2#11.* ***Lawrence*** *a-V3#8, V5#7.* ***Powell*** *a-V4#11, 12. V5#4, 5, 7 are 68 pgs.*

REAL EXPERIENCES (Formerly Tiny Tessie)
Atlas Comics (20CC): No. 25, Jan, 1950
25-Virginia Mayo photo-c from movie "Red Light" 10 20 30 56 76 95

Real Fact Comics #18 © DC

Real Life Comics #7 © Nedor

Real Screen Comics #14 © DC

	GD	VG	FN	VF	VF/NM	NM-
	2.0	4.0	6.0	8.0	9.0	9.2

REAL FACT COMICS
National Periodical Publications: Mar-Apr, 1946 - No. 21, July-Aug, 1949

	GD	VG	FN	VF	VF/NM	NM-
1-S&K-c/a; Harry Houdini story; Just Imagine begins (not by Finlay); Fred Ray-a	54	108	162	338	562	785
2-S&K-a; Rin-Tin-Tin & P. T. Barnum stories	34	68	102	197	311	425
3-H.G. Wells, Lon Chaney stories; early DC letter column (New Fun Comics #3 from 1935 may be the 1st)	32	64	96	186	293	400
4-Virgil Finlay-a on 'Just Imagine' begins, ends #12 (2 pgs. each); Jimmy Stewart & Jack London stories; Joe DiMaggio 1 pg. biography	35	70	105	204	322	440
5-Batman/Robin-c taken from cover of Batman #9; 5 pg. story about creation of Batman & Robin; Tom Mix story	179	358	537	1119	1860	2600
6-Origin & 1st app. Tommy Tomorrow by Weisinger and Sherman (1-2/47); Flag-c; 1st writing by Harlan Ellison (letter column, non-professional); "First Man to Reach Mars" epic-c/story	103	206	309	644	1072	1500
7-(No. 6 on inside)-Roussos-a; D. Fairbanks sty.	18	36	54	105	165	225
8-2nd app. Tommy Tomorrow by Finlay (5-6/47)	59	118	177	369	610	850
9-S&K-a; Glenn Miller, Indianapolis 500 stories	25	50	75	145	228	310
10-Vigilante by Meskin (based on movie serial); 4 pg. Finlay s/f story	24	48	72	139	220	300
11,12: 11-Annie Oakley, G-Men stories; Kinstler-a	15	30	45	86	133	180
13-Dale Evans and Tommy Tomorrow-c/stories	43	86	129	262	431	600
14,17,18: 14-Will Rogers story	15	30	45	83	124	165
15-Nuclear explosion part-c ("Last War on Earth" story); Clyde Beatty story	18	36	54	105	165	225
16-Tommy Tomorrow app.; 1st Planeteers?	41	82	123	250	400	550
19-Sir Arthur Conan Doyle story	15	30	45	88	137	185
20-Kubert-a, 4 pgs; Daniel Boone story	17	34	51	98	154	210
21-Kubert-a, 2 pgs; Kit Carson story	15	30	45	83	124	165

Ashcan (2/46) nn-Not distributed to newsstands, only for in house use. Covers were produced, but not the rest of the book. A copy sold in 2008 for $500.
NOTE: *Barry c-16. Virgil Finlay c-6, 8. Meskin c-10. Roussos a-1-4, 6.*

REAL FUNNIES
Nedor Publishing Co.: Jan, 1943 - No. 3, June, 1943

	GD	VG	FN	VF	VF/NM	NM-
1-Funny animal, humor; Black Terrier app. (clone of The Black Terror)	32	64	96	186	298	410
2,3	15	30	45	94	147	200

REAL GHOSTBUSTERS, THE (Also see Slimer)
Now Comics: Aug, 1988 - No. 32, 1991 ($1.75/$1.95)

1-32: 1-Based on Ghostbusters movie. #29-32 exist? 3.00

REAL HEROES COMICS
Parents' Magazine Institute: Sept, 1941 - No. 16, Oct, 1946

	GD	VG	FN	VF	VF/NM	NM-
1-Roosevelt-c/story	32	64	96	186	298	410
2-J. Edgar Hoover-c/story	15	30	45	83	124	165
3-5,7-10: 4-Churchill, Roosevelt stories	14	28	42	76	108	140
6-Lou Gehrig-c/story	20	40	60	115	180	245
11-16: 13-Kiefer-a	10	20	30	54	72	90

REALISTIC ROMANCES
Realistic Comics/Avon Periodicals: July-Aug, 1951 - No. 17, Aug-Sept, 1954 (No #9-14)

	GD	VG	FN	VF	VF/NM	NM-
1-Kinstler-a; c-/Avon paperback #211	27	54	81	158	254	350
2	14	28	42	82	121	160
3,4	14	28	42	80	115	150
5,8-Kinstler-a	14	28	42	81	118	155
6-c-/Diversey Prize Novels #6; Kinstler-a	14	28	42	82	121	160
7-Evans-a?; c-/Avon paperback #360	14	28	42	82	121	160
15,17: 17-Kinstler-c	14	28	42	76	108	140
16-Kinstler marijuana story-r/Romantic Love #6	14	28	42	81	118	155
I.W. Reprint #1,8,9: #1-r/Realistic Romances #4; Astarita-a. 9-r/Women To Love #1	2	4	6	9	13	16

NOTE: *Astarita a-2-4, 7, 8, 17. Photo c-1, 2. Painted c-3, 4.*

REAL LIFE COMICS
Nedor/Better/Standard Publ./Pictorial Magazine No. 13: Sept, 1941 - No. 59, Sept, 1952

	GD	VG	FN	VF	VF/NM	NM-
1-Uncle Sam-c/story; Daniel Boone story	58	116	174	365	620	875
2	30	60	90	174	280	385
3-Hitler cover	133	266	399	838	1419	2000
4,5: 4-Story of American flag "Old Glory"	19	38	57	109	172	235
6-10: 6-Wild Bill Hickok story	18	36	54	105	165	225
11-20: 17-Albert Einstein story	15	30	45	94	147	200
21-23,25,26,28-30: 29-A-Bomb story	15	30	45	84	127	170
24-Story of Baseball (Babe Ruth)	21	42	63	123	197	270
27-Schomburg A-Bomb-c; story of A-Bomb	20	40	60	117	186	255
31-33,35,36,42-44,48,49: 49-Baseball issue	14	28	42	80	115	150
34,37-41,45-47: 34-Jimmy Stewart story. 37-Story of motion pictures; Bing Crosby story. 38-Jane Froman story. 39- "1,000,000 A.D." story. 40-Bob Feller. 41-Jimmie Foxx story ("Jimmy" on-c); "Home Run" Baker story. 45-Story of Olympic games; Burl Ives & Kit Carson story. 46-Douglas Fairbanks Jr. & Sr. story. 47-George Gershwin story	15	30	45	84	127	170
50-Frazetta-a (5 pgs.)	30	60	90	174	280	385
51-Jules Verne "Journey to the Moon" by Evans; Severin/Elder-a	20	40	60	117	186	255
52-Frazetta-a (4 pgs.); Severin/Elder-a(2); Evans-a	33	66	99	192	309	425
53-57-Severin/Elder-a. 54-Bat Masterson-c/story	15	30	45	92	144	195
58-Severin/Elder-a(2)	15	30	45	94	147	200
59-1 pg. Frazetta; Severin/Elder-a	15	30	45	92	144	195

NOTE: *Some issues had two titles. **Guardineer** a-40(2), 44. **Meskin** a-52. **Roussos** a-50. **Schomburg** c-1, 2, 4, 5, 7, 11, 13-21, 23, 24, 26, 28, 30-32, 34-40, 42, 44-47, 55. **Tuska** a-53. Photo-c 5, 6.*

REAL LIFE SECRETS (Real Secrets #2 on)
Ace Periodicals: Sept, 1949 (one-shot)

	GD	VG	FN	VF	VF/NM	NM-
1-Painted-c	14	28	42	76	108	140

REAL LIFE STORY OF FESS PARKER (Magazine)
Dell Publishing Co.: 1955

	GD	VG	FN	VF	VF/NM	NM-
1	9	18	27	61	103	145

REAL LIFE TALES OF SUSPENSE (See Suspense)

REAL LOVE (Formerly Hap Hazard)
Ace Periodicals (A. A. Wyn): No. 25, April, 1949 - No. 76, Nov, 1956

	GD	VG	FN	VF	VF/NM	NM-
25	14	28	42	76	108	140
26	10	20	30	56	76	95
27-L. B. Cole-a	12	24	36	67	94	120
28-35	9	18	27	50	65	80
36-66: 66-Last pre-code (2/55)	8	16	24	44	57	70
67-76	7	14	21	37	46	55

NOTE: *Photo c-50-76. Painted c-46.*

REALM, THE
Arrow Comics/WeeBee Comics #13/Caliber Press #14 on: Feb, 1986 - No. 21, 1991 ($1.50/$1.95/$2.50, B&W)

1-21: 4-1st app. Deadworld (9/86) 2.50
Book 1 ($4.95, B&W) 5.00

REAL McCOYS, THE (TV)
Dell Publ. Co.: No. 1071, 1-3/60 - 5-7/1962 (All have Walter Brennan photo-c)

	GD	VG	FN	VF	VF/NM	NM-
Four Color 1071,1134-Toth-a in both	9	18	27	60	100	140
Four Color 1193,1265	8	16	24	56	93	130
01-689-207 (5-7/62)	7	14	21	50	83	115

REALM OF THE CLAW (Also see Mutant Earth as part of a flipbook)
Image Comics: Oct, 2003 - No. 2 ($2.95)

0-(7/03, $5.95) Convention Special; cover has gold-foil title logo 6.00
1,2-Two covers by Yardin 3.00
Vol. 1 TPB (2006, $16.99) r/series; concept art & sketch pages 17.00

REAL SCREEN COMICS (#1 titled Real Screen Funnies; TV Screen Cartoons #129-138)
National Periodical Publications: Spring, 1945 - No. 128, May-June, 1959 (#1-40: 52 pgs.)

	GD	VG	FN	VF	VF/NM	NM-
1-The Fox & the Crow, Flippity & Flop, Tito & His Burrito begin	98	196	294	617	1046	1475
2	47	94	141	291	483	675
3-5	32	64	96	186	298	410
6-10 (2-3/47)	21	42	63	123	197	270
11-20 (10-11/48): 13-The Crow x-over in Flippity & Flop	16	32	48	92	144	195
21-30 (6-7/50)	13	26	39	74	105	135
31-50	11	22	33	60	83	105
51-99	10	20	30	54	72	90
100	10	20	30	56	76	95
101-128	8	16	24	44	57	70

REAL SCREEN FUNNIES
DC Comics: Spring 1945

1-Ashcan comic, not distributed to newsstands, only for in-house use. Cover art is Real Screen Funnies #1 with interior being Detective Comics #92. Only ashcan cover to be produced using the regular production first issue art and only using the color yellow. A copy sold in 2008 for $3,000.

REAL SECRETS (Formerly Real Life Secrets)
Ace Periodicals: No. 2, Nov, 1950 - No. 5, May, 1950

	GD	VG	FN	VF	VF/NM	NM-
2-Painted-c	10	20	30	56	76	95

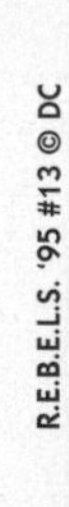

Realworlds: Wonder Woman © DC

R.E.B.E.L.S. '95 #13 © DC

Red Dragon Comics (2nd series) #1 © CN

	GD 2.0	VG 4.0	FN 6.0	VF 8.0	VF/NM 9.0	NM- 9.2
3-5: 3-Photo-c	8	16	24	42	54	65

REAL SPORTS COMICS (All Sports Comics #2 on)
Hillman Periodicals: Oct-Nov, 1948 (52 pgs.)

	GD 2.0	VG 4.0	FN 6.0	VF 8.0	VF/NM 9.0	NM- 9.2
1-Powell-a (12 pgs.)	40	80	120	235	380	525

REAL WAR STORIES
Eclipse Comics: July, 1987; No. 2, Jan, 1991 ($2.00, 52 pgs.)

	GD 2.0	VG 4.0	FN 6.0	VF 8.0	VF/NM 9.0	NM- 9.2
1-Bolland-a(p), Bissette-a, Totleben-a(i); Alan Moore scripts (2nd printing exists, 2/88)						3.00
2-($4.95)						5.00

REAL WESTERN HERO (Formerly Wow #1-69; Western Hero #76 on)
Fawcett Publications: No. 70, Sept, 1948 - No. 75, Feb, 1949 (All 52 pgs.)

	GD 2.0	VG 4.0	FN 6.0	VF 8.0	VF/NM 9.0	NM- 9.2
70(#1)-Tom Mix, Monte Hale, Hopalong Cassidy, Young Falcon begin	28	56	84	162	256	350
71-75: 71-Gabby Hayes begins. 71,72-Captain Tootsie by Beck. 75-Big Bow and Little Arrow app.	17	34	51	98	154	210

NOTE: *Painted/photo c-70-73; painted c-74, 75.*

REAL WEST ROMANCES
Crestwood Publishing Co./Prize Publ.: 4-5/49 - V1#6, 3/50; V2#1, Apr-May, 1950 (All 52 pgs. & photo-c)

	GD 2.0	VG 4.0	FN 6.0	VF 8.0	VF/NM 9.0	NM- 9.2
V1#1-S&K-a(p)	26	52	78	152	244	335
2	14	28	42	80	115	150
3-Kirby-a(p) only	14	28	42	82	121	160
4-S&K-a; Whip Wilson, Reno Browne photo-c	19	38	57	112	176	240
5-Audie Murphy, Gale Storm photo-c; S&K-a	17	34	51	98	154	210
6-Produced by S&K, no S&K-a; Robert Preston & Cathy Downs photo-c	14	28	42	78	112	145
V2#1-Kirby-a(p)	12	24	36	69	97	125

NOTE: ***Meskin** a-V1#5, 6. **Severin/Elder** a-V1#3-6, V2#1. **Meskin** a-V1#6. **Leonard Starr** a-1-3. Photo-c V1#1-6, V2#1.*

REALWORLDS :...
DC Comics: 2000 ($5.95, one-shots, prestige format)

	GD 2.0	VG 4.0	FN 6.0	VF 8.0	VF/NM 9.0	NM- 9.2
Batman - Marshall Rogers-a/Golden & Sniegoski-s; Justice League of America -Dematteis-s/Barr-painted art; Superman - Vance-s/García-López & Rubenstein-a; Wonder Woman - Hanson & Neuwirth-s/Sam-a						6.00

RE-ANIMATOR IN FULL COLOR
Adventure Comics: Oct, 1991 - No. 3, 1992 ($2.95, mini-series)

	GD 2.0	VG 4.0	FN 6.0	VF 8.0	VF/NM 9.0	NM- 9.2
1-3: Adapts horror movie. 1-Dorman painted-c						3.00

REAP THE WILD WIND (See Cinema Comics Herald)

REBEL, THE (TV)
Dell Publishing Co.: No. 1076, Feb-Apr, 1960 - No. 1262, Dec-Feb, 1961-62

	GD 2.0	VG 4.0	FN 6.0	VF 8.0	VF/NM 9.0	NM- 9.2
Four Color 1076 (#1)-Sekowsky-a, photo-c	9	18	27	65	113	160
Four Color 1138 (9-11/60), 1207 (9-11/61), 1262-Photo-c	8	16	24	56	93	130

R.E.B.E.L.S. '94 (Becomes R.E.B.E.L.S. '95 & R.E.B.E.L.S. '96)
DC Comics: No. 0, Oct, 1994 - No. 17, Mar, 1996 ($1.95/$2.25)

	GD 2.0	VG 4.0	FN 6.0	VF 8.0	VF/NM 9.0	NM- 9.2
0-17: 8-$2.25-c begins. 15-R.E.B.E.L.S '96 begins.						2.50

RECORD BOOK OF FAMOUS POLICE CASES
St. John Publishing Co.: 1949 (25¢, 132 pgs.)

	GD 2.0	VG 4.0	FN 6.0	VF 8.0	VF/NM 9.0	NM- 9.2
nn-Kubert-a(3); r/Son of Sinbad; Baker-c	40	80	120	240	390	540

RED
DC Comics (Homage): Sept, 2003 - No. 3, Feb, 2004 ($2.95, limited series)

	GD 2.0	VG 4.0	FN 6.0	VF 8.0	VF/NM 9.0	NM- 9.2
1-3-Warren Ellis-s/Cully Hamner-a/c						3.00
Red/Tokyo Storm Warning TPB (2004, $14.95) Flip book r/both series						15.00

RED ARROW
P. L. Publishing Co.: May-June, 1951 - No. 3, Oct, 1951

	GD 2.0	VG 4.0	FN 6.0	VF 8.0	VF/NM 9.0	NM- 9.2
1	11	22	33	60	83	105
2,3	9	18	27	47	61	75

RED BAND COMICS
Enwil Associates: Nov, 1944 - No. 4, May, 1945

	GD 2.0	VG 4.0	FN 6.0	VF 8.0	VF/NM 9.0	NM- 9.2
1	40	80	120	235	380	525
2-Origin Bogeyman & Santanas; c-reprint/#1	28	56	84	162	261	360
3,4-Captain Wizard app. in both (1st app.); each has identical contents/cover	26	52	78	152	244	335

REDBLADE
Dark Horse Comics: Apr, 1993 - No. 3, July, 1993 ($2.50, mini-series)

	GD 2.0	VG 4.0	FN 6.0	VF 8.0	VF/NM 9.0	NM- 9.2
1-3: 1-Double gatefold-c						3.00

RED CIRCLE COMICS (Also see Blazing Comics & Blue Circle Comics)
Rural Home Publications (Enwil): Jan, 1945 - No. 4, April, 1945

	GD 2.0	VG 4.0	FN 6.0	VF 8.0	VF/NM 9.0	NM- 9.2
1-The Prankster & Red Riot begin	40	80	120	244	397	550
2-Starr-a; The Judge (costumed hero) app.	29	58	87	169	272	375
3,4-Starr-c/a. 3-The Prankster not in costume	23	46	69	135	218	300
4-(Dated 4/45)-Leftover covers to #4 were later restapled over early 1950s coverless comics; variations in the coverless comics used are endless; Woman Outlaws, Dorothy Lamour, Crime Does Not Pay, Sabu, Diary Loves, Love Confessions & Young Love V3#3 known	17	34	51	98	154	210

RED CIRCLE SORCERY (Chilling Adventures in Sorcery #1-5)
Red Circle Prod. (Archie): No. 6, Apr, 1974 - No. 11, Feb, 1975 (All 25¢ iss.)

	GD 2.0	VG 4.0	FN 6.0	VF 8.0	VF/NM 9.0	NM- 9.2
6,8,9,11: 6-Early Chaykin-a. 7-Pino-a. 8-Only app. The Cobra	2	4	6	8	10	12
7-Bruce Jones-a with Wrightson, Kaluta, Jeff Jones	2	4	6	10	14	18
10-Wood-a(i)	2	4	6	8	11	14

NOTE: ***Chaykin** a-6, 10. **McWilliams** a-10(2 & 3 pgs.). **Mooney** a-11p. **Morrow** a-6-8, 9(text illos), 10, 11i; c-6-11. **Thorne** a-8, 10. **Toth** a-8, 9.*

RED DOG (See Night Music #7)

RED DRAGON
Comico: June, 1996 ($2.95)

	GD 2.0	VG 4.0	FN 6.0	VF 8.0	VF/NM 9.0	NM- 9.2
1-Bisley-c						3.00

RED DRAGON COMICS (1st Series) (Formerly Trail Blazers; see Super Magician V5#7, 8)
Street & Smith Publications: No. 5, Jan, 1943 - No. 9, Jan, 1944

	GD 2.0	VG 4.0	FN 6.0	VF 8.0	VF/NM 9.0	NM- 9.2
5-Origin Red Rover, the Crimson Crimebuster; Rex King, Man of Adventure, Captain Jack Commando, & The Minute Man begin; text origin Red Dragon; Binder-c	97	194	291	611	1031	1450
6-Origin The Black Crusader & Red Dragon (3/43); 1st story app. Red Dragon & 1st cover (classic-c)	257	514	771	1619	2735	3850
7-Classic-c	207	414	621	1304	2202	3100
8-The Red Knight app.	76	152	228	479	810	1140
9-Origin Chuck Magnon, Immortal Man	76	152	228	479	810	1140

RED DRAGON COMICS (2nd Series)(See Super Magician V2#8)
Street & Smith Publications: Nov, 1947 - No. 6, Jan, 1949; No. 7, July, 1949

	GD 2.0	VG 4.0	FN 6.0	VF 8.0	VF/NM 9.0	NM- 9.2
1-Red Dragon begins; Elliman, Nigel app.; Edd Cartier-c/a	93	186	279	586	993	1400
2-Cartier-c	65	130	195	410	693	975
3-1st app. Dr. Neff Ghost Breaker by Powell; Elliman, Nigel app.	53	106	159	334	567	800
4-Cartier c/a	77	154	231	481	816	1150
5-7	40	80	120	244	397	550

NOTE: ***Maneely** a-5, 7. **Powell** a-2-7; c-3, 5, 7.*

RED EAGLE
David McKay Publications: No. 16, Aug, 1938

	GD 2.0	VG 4.0	FN 6.0	VF 8.0	VF/NM 9.0	NM- 9.2
Feature Books 16	26	52	78	152	244	335

REDEYE (See Comics Reading Libraries in the Promotional Comics section)

RED FOX (Formerly Manhunt! #1-14; also see Extra Comics)
Magazine Enterprises: No. 15, 1954

	GD 2.0	VG 4.0	FN 6.0	VF 8.0	VF/NM 9.0	NM- 9.2
15(A-1 #108)-Undercover Girl story; L.B. Cole-c/a (Red Fox); r-from Manhunt; Powell-a	19	38	57	109	172	235

RED GOOSE COMIC SELECTIONS (See Comic Selections)

RED HAWK (See A-1 Comics, Bobby Benson's ..#14-16 & Straight Arrow #2)
Magazine Enterprises: No. 90, 1953

	GD 2.0	VG 4.0	FN 6.0	VF 8.0	VF/NM 9.0	NM- 9.2
A-1 90-Powell-c/a	13	26	39	72	101	130

RED MASK (Formerly Tim Holt; see Best Comics, Blazing Six-Guns)
Magazine Enterprises No. 42-53/Sussex No. 54 (M.E. on-c): No. 42, June-July, 1954 - No. 53, May, 1956; No. 54, Sept, 1957

	GD 2.0	VG 4.0	FN 6.0	VF 8.0	VF/NM 9.0	NM- 9.2
42-Ghost Rider by Ayers continues, ends #50; Black Phantom continues; 3-D effect c/stories begin	21	42	63	123	197	270
43- 3-D effect-c/stories	19	38	57	109	172	235
44-52: 3-D effect stories only. 47-Last pre-code issue. 50-Last Ghost Rider. 51-The Presto Kid begins by Ayers (1st app.); Presto Kid-c begins; last 3-D effect story. 52-Origin The Presto Kid	17	34	51	98	154	210
53,54-Last Black Phantom; last Presto Kid-c	15	30	45	83	124	165
I.W. Reprint #1 (r-/#52). 2 (nd, r/#51 w/diff.-c). 3, 8 (nd; Kinstler-c); 8-r/Red Mask #52	3	6	9	16	22	28

NOTE: ***Ayers** art on Ghost Rider & Presto Kid. **Bolle** art in all (Red Mask); c-43, 44, 49. **Guardineer** a-52. Black Phantom in #42-44, 47-50, 53, 54.*

REDMASK OF THE RIO GRANDE

Red Prophet: The Tales of Alvin Maker #12 © Orson Scott Card

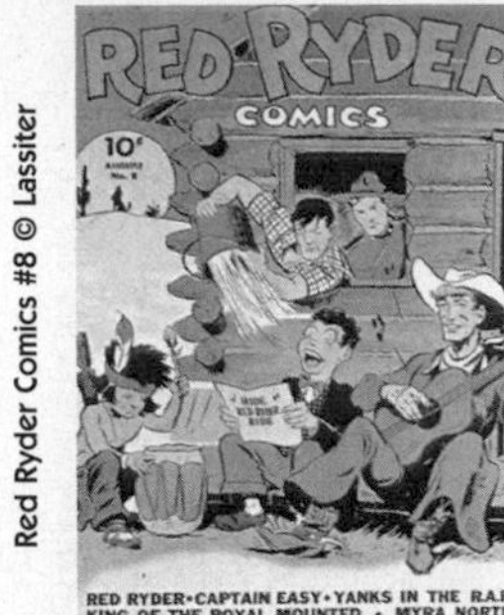

Red Ryder Comics #8 © Lassiter

Red Sonja #26 © Red Sonja LLC

	GD	VG	FN	VF	VF/NM	NM-
	2.0	4.0	6.0	8.0	9.0	9.2

AC Comics: 1990 ($2.50, 28pgs.)(Has photos of movie posters)
1-Bolle-c/a(r); photo inside-c 2.50

RED MENACE
DC Comics (WildStorm): Jan, 2007 - No. 6, Jun, 2007 ($2.99, limited series)
1-6-Ordway-a/c; Bilson, DeMeo & Brody-s 3.00
TPB (2007, $17.99) r/series, sketch pages & variant covers 18.00

RED MOUNTAIN FEATURING QUANTRELL'S RAIDERS (Movie)(Also see Jesse James #28)
Avon Periodicals: 1952
nn-Alan Ladd; Kinstler-c 27 54 81 158 254 350

RED PROPHET: THE TALES OF ALVIN MAKER
Dabel Brothers Prods./Marvel Comics (Dabel Brothers): Mar, 2006 - No. 12, Mar, 2008 ($2.99)
1-12-Adaptation of Orson Scott Card novel. 1-Miguel Montenegro-a 3.00
... Vol. 1 HC (2007, $19.99, dustjacket) r/#1-6 20.00
... Vol. 1 SC (2007, $15.99) r/#1-6 16.00
... Vol. 2 HC (2008, $19.99, dustjacket) r/#7-12 20.00

"RED" RABBIT COMICS
Dearfield Comic/J. Charles Laue Publ. Co.: Jan, 1947 - No. 22, Aug-Sep, 1951
1 14 28 42 76 108 140
2 8 16 24 44 57 70
3-10 7 14 21 37 46 55
11-17,19-22 7 14 21 35 43 50
18-Flying Saucer-c (1/51) 8 16 24 44 57 70

RED RAVEN COMICS (Human Torch #2 on)(Also see X-Men #44 & Sub-Mariner #26, 2nd series)
Timely Comics: August, 1940
1-Origin & 1st app. Red Raven; Comet Pierce & Mercury by Kirby, The Human Top & The Eternal Brain; intro. Magar, the Mystic & only app.; Kirby-c (his 1st signed work)
1185 2370 3555 8900 15,700 22,500

RED ROCKET 7
Dark Horse Comics: Aug, 1997 - No. 7, June, 1998 ($3.95, square format, limited series)
1-7-Mike Allred-c/s/a 4.00

RED RYDER COMICS (Hi Spot #2)(Movies, radio)(See Crackajack Funnies & Super Book of Comics)
Hawley Publ. No. 1/Dell Publishing Co.(K.K.) No. 3 on: 9/40; No. 3, 8/41 - No. 5, 12/41; No. 6, 4/42 - No. 151, 4-6/57
1-Red Ryder, his horse Thunder, Little Beaver & his horse Papoose strip reprints begin by Fred Harman; 1st meeting of Red & Little Beaver; Harman line-drawn-c #1-85
276 552 828 1725 2863 4000
3-(Scarce)-Alley Oop, Capt. Easy, Dan Dunn, Freckles & His Friends, King of the Royal Mtd., Myra North strip-r begin 70 140 210 595 1098 1600
4-6: 6-1st Dell issue (4/42) 35 70 105 263 482 700
7-10 30 60 90 220 398 575
11-20 21 42 63 156 278 400
21-32-Last Alley Oop, Dan Dunn, Capt. Easy, Freckles
15 30 45 107 191 275
33-40 (52 pgs.): 40-Photo back-c begin, end #57 11 22 33 75 133 190
41 (52 pgs.)-Rocky Lane photo back-c 11 22 33 79 140 200
42-46 (52 pgs.): 46-Last Red Ryder strip-r 9 18 27 64 110 155
47-53 (52 pgs.): 47-New stories on Red Ryder begin. 49,52-Harmon photo back-c
8 16 24 56 93 130
54-92: 54-73 (36 pgs.). 59-Harmon photo back-c. 73-Last King of the Royal Mtd; strip-r by Jim Gary. 74-85 (52 pgs.)-Harman line-drawn-c. 86-92 (52 pgs.)-Harman painted-c
7 14 21 47 76 105
93-99,101-106: 94-96 (36 pgs.)-Harman painted-c. 97,98,(36 pgs.)-Harman line-drawn-c. 99,101-106 (36 pgs.)-Jim Bannon Photo-c 6 12 18 41 66 90
100 (36 pgs.)-Bannon photo-c 6 12 18 43 69 95
107-118 (52 pgs.)-Harman line-drawn-c 6 12 18 39 62 85
119-129 (52 pgs.): 119-Painted-c begin, not by Harman, end #151
6 12 18 37 59 80
130-151 (36 pgs.): 145-Title change to Red Ryder Ranch Magazine
149-Title change to Red Ryder Ranch Comics 5 10 15 35 55 75
Four Color 916 (7/58) 5 10 15 35 55 75
NOTE: *Fred Harman a-1-99; c-1-98, 107-118. Don Red Barry, Allan Rocky Lane, Wild Bill Elliott & Jim Bannon starred as Red Ryder in the movies. Robert Blake starred as Little Beaver.*

RED RYDER PAINT BOOK
Whitman Publishing Co.: 1941 (8-1/2x11-1/2", 148 pgs.)
nn-Reprints 1940 daily strips 76 152 228 475 788 1100

RED SEAL COMICS (Formerly Carnival Comics, and/or Spotlight Comics?)
Harry 'A' Chesler/Superior Publ. No. 19 on: No. 14, 10/45 - No. 18, 10/46; No. 19, 6/47 - No. 22, 12/47
14-The Black Dwarf begins (continued from Spotlight?); Little Nemo app; bondage/hypo-c; Tuska-a 77 154 231 485 818 1150
15-Torture story; funny-c 41 82 123 250 413 575
16-Used in **SOTI**, pg. 181, illo "Outside the forbidden pages of de Sade, you find draining a girl's blood only in children's comics;" drug club story r-later in Crime Reporter #1, Veiled Avenger & Barry Kuda app; Tuska-a; funny-c 62 124 186 391 663 935
17,18,20: Lady Satan, Yankee Girl & Sky Chief app; 17-Tuska-a
49 98 147 302 506 710
19-No Black Dwarf (on-c only); Zor, El Tigre app. 43 86 129 267 446 625
21-Lady Satan & Black Dwarf app. 32 64 96 186 298 410
22-Zor, Rocketman app. (68 pgs.) 32 64 96 186 298 410

REDSKIN (Thrilling Indian Stories)(Famous Western Badmen #13 on)
Youthful Magazines: Sept, 1950 - No. 12, Oct, 1952
1-Walter Johnson-a (7 pgs.) 17 34 51 98 154 210
2 11 22 33 62 86 110
3-12: 3-Daniel Boone story. 6-Geronimo story 10 20 30 54 72 90
NOTE: *Walter Johnson c-3, 4. Palais a-11. Wildey a-5, 11. Bondage c-6, 12.*

RED SONJA (Also see Conan #23, Kull & The Barbarians, Marvel Feature & Savage Sword Of Conan #1)
Marvel Comics Group: 1/77 - No. 15, 5/79; V1#1, 2/83 - V2#2, 3/83; V3#1, 8/83 - V3#4, 2/84; V3#5, 1/85 - V3#13, 5/86
1-Created by Robert E. Howard 2 4 6 9 12 15
2-10: 5-Last 30¢ issue 1 2 3 4 5 7
4,5-(35¢-c variants, limited distribution)(7,9/77) 3 6 9 20 30 40
11-15, V1#1,V2#2: 14-Last 35¢ issue 6.00
V3#1-13: #1-4 ($1.00, 52 pgs.) 3.50
NOTE: *Brunner c-12-14. J. Buscema a(p)-12, 13, 15; c-V#1. Nebres a-V3#3i(part). N. Redondo a-8i, V3#2i, 3i. Simonson a-V3#1. Thorne c/a-1-11.*

RED SONJA
Dynamite Entertainment: No. 0, Apr, 2005 - Present (25¢/$2.99)
0-(4/05, 25¢) Greg Land-c/Mel Rubi-a/Oeming & Carey-s 2.25
1 (6/05, $2.99) Five covers by Ross, Linsner, Cassaday, Turner, Rivera; Rubi-a 3.00
2-37-Multiple covers on all. 29-Sonja dies. 34-Sonja reborn 3.00
5-RRP Edition with Red Foil logo and Isonove-a 10.00
Annual #1 (2007, $3.50) Oeming-s/Sadowski-a; Red Sonja Comics Chronology 3.50
... Cover Showcase Vol. 1 (2007, $5.99) gallery of variant covers; Cho sketches 6.00
Giant Size Red Sonja #1 (2007, $4.99) Chaykin-c; new story and reprints and pin-ups 5.00
... Goes East ($4.99) three covers; Joe Ng-a 5.00
...: Monster Isle ($4.99) two covers; Pablo Marcos-a/Roy Thomas-s 5.00
... One More Day ($4.99) two covers; Liam Sharp-a 5.00
... Vacant Shell ($4.99) two covers; Remender-a/Renaud-a 5.00
The Adventures of Red Sonja TPB (2005, $19.99) r/Marvel Feature #1-7 20.00
The Adventures of Red Sonja Vol. 2 TPB (2007, $19.99) r/#1-7 of '77 Marvel series 20.00
... Vol. 1 TPB (2006, $19.99) r/#0-6; gallery of covers and variants; creators interview 20.00
... Vol. 2 Arrowsmith TPB (2007, $19.99) r/#7-12; gallery of covers and variants 20.00
... Vol. 3 The Rise of Gath TPB (2007, $19.99) r/#13-18; gallery of covers and variants 20.00
... Vol. 4 Animals & More TPB (2007, $24.99) r/#19-24; gallery of covers and variants 25.00

RED SONJA/CLAW: THE DEVIL'S HANDS (See Claw the Unconquered)
DC Comics (WildStorm)/Dynamite Ent.: May, 2006 - No. 4, Aug, 2006 ($2.99, limited series)
1-4-Covers by Jim Lee & Dell'Otto.; Andy Smith-a 1-Alex Ross var-c. 2-Dell'Otto var-c. 3-Bermejo var-c. 4-Andy Smith var-c 3.00
TPB (2007, $12.99) r/#1-4; cover gallery 13.00

RED SONJA: SCAVENGER HUNT
Marvel Comics: Dec, 1995 ($2.95, one-shot)
1 3.00

RED SONJA: THE MOVIE
Marvel Comics Group: Nov, 1985 - No. 2, Dec, 1985 (Limited series)
1,2-Movie adapt-r/Marvel Super Spec. #38 3.00

RED SONJA VS. THULSA DOOM
Dynamite Entertainment: 2005 - No. 4, 2006 ($3.50)
1-4-Conrad-a; Conrad & Dell'Otto covers 3.50
..., Volume 1 TPB (2006, $14.99) r/series; cover gallery 15.00

RED STAR, THE
Image Comics/Archangel Studios: June, 2000 - No. 9, June, 2002 ($2.95)
1-Christian Gossett-s/a(p) 4.00
2-9: 9-Beck-c 3.00
#(7.5) Reprints Wizard #1/2 story with new pages 3.00
Annual 1 (Archangel Studios, 11/02, $3.50) "Run Makita Run" 3.50

Reform School Girl! © AVON

Reggie's Revenge #2 © AP

Remember Pearl Harbor © S&S

	GD 2.0	VG 4.0	FN 6.0	VF 8.0	VF/NM 9.0	NM- 9.2
TPB (4/01, $24.95, 9x12") oversized r/#1-4; intro. by Bendis						25.00
Nokgorka TPB (8/02, $24.95, 9x12") oversized r/#6-9; w/sketch pages						25.00
Wizard 1/2 (mail order)						10.00

RED STAR, THE (Volume 2)
CrossGen #1,2/Archangel Studios #3 on: Feb, 2003 - No. 5, July, 2004 ($2.95/$2.99)

1-5-Christian Gossett-s/a(p) 3.00
Prison of Souls TPB (8/04, $24.95, 9x12") oversized r/#1-5; w/sketch pages 25.00

RED STAR, THE: SWORD OF LIES
Archangel Studios: Aug, 2006 ($4.50)

1-Christian Gossett-s/a(p); origin of the Red Star team 4.50

RED TORNADO (See All-American #20 & Justice League of America #64)
DC Comics: July, 1985 - No. 4, Oct, 1985 (Limited series)

1-4: Kurt Busiek scripts in all. 1-3-Superman & Batman cameos 3.00

RED WARRIOR
Marvel/Atlas Comics (TCI): Jan, 1951 - No. 6, Dec, 1951

	GD 2.0	VG 4.0	FN 6.0	VF 8.0	VF/NM 9.0	NM- 9.2
1-Red Warrior & his horse White Wing; Tuska-a	16	32	48	92	144	195
2-Tuska-c	10	20	30	56	76	95
3-6: 4-Origin White Wing. 6-Maneely-c	9	18	27	47	61	75

RED, WHITE & BLUE COMICS
DC Comics: 1941

nn - Ashcan comic, not distributed to newsstands, only for in-house use. Cover art is All-American Comics #20 with interior being Flash Comics #17 (no known sales)

RED WOLF (See Avengers #80 & Marvel Spotlight #1)
Marvel Comics Group: May, 1972 - No. 9, Sept, 1973

	GD 2.0	VG 4.0	FN 6.0	VF 8.0	VF/NM 9.0	NM- 9.2
1-(Western hero); Gil Kane/Severin-c; Shores-a	3	6	9	17	25	32
2-9: 2-Kane-c; Shores-a. 6-Tuska-r in back-up. 7-Red Wolf as super hero begins. 9-Origin sidekick, Lobo (wolf)	2	4	6	11	16	20

REESE'S PIECES
Eclipse Comics: Oct, 1985 - No.2, Oct, 1985 ($1.75, Baxter paper)

1,2-B&W-r in color 2.50

REFORM SCHOOL GIRL!
Realistic Comics: 1951

	GD 2.0	VG 4.0	FN 6.0	VF 8.0	VF/NM 9.0	NM- 9.2
nn-Used in **SOTI**, pg. 358, & cover ill. with caption "Comic books are supposed to be like fairy tales"	324	648	972	2203	3852	5500

(Prices vary widely on this book)

NOTE: *The cover and title originated from a digest-sized book published by Diversey Publishing Co. of Chicago in 1948. The original book "House of Fury", Doubleday, came out in 1941. The girl's real name which appears on the cover of the digest and comic is Marty Collins, Canadian model and ice skating star who posed for this special color photograph for the Diversey novel.*

REGENTS ILLUSTRATED CLASSICS
Prentice Hall Regents, Englewood Cliffs, NJ 07632: 1981 (Plus more recent reprintings) (48 pgs., B&W-a with 14 pgs. of teaching helps)

NOTE: *This series contains Classics Ill. art, and was produced from the same illegal source as* ***Cassette Books.*** *But when Twin Circle sued to stop the sale of the Cassette Books, they decided to permit this series to continue. This series was produced as a teaching aid. The 20 title series is divided into four levels based upon number of basic words used therein. There is also a teacher's manual for each level. All of the titles are still available from the publisher for about $5 each retail. The number to call for mail order purchases is (201)767-5937. Almost all of the issues have new covers taken from some interior art panel. Here is a list of the series by Regents ident. no. and the Classics Ill. counterpart.*

16770(Cl#24-A2)18333(Cl#3-A2)21668(Cl#13-A2)32224(Cl#21)33051(Cl#26)35788(Cl#84)37153(Cl#16)44460(Cl#19-A2)44808(Cl#18-A2)52395(Cl#4-A2)58627(Cl#5-A2)60067(Cl#30)68405(Cl#23A1)70302(Cl#29)78192(Cl#7-A2)78193(Cl#10-A2)79679(Cl#85)92046(Cl#1-A2)93062(Cl#64)93512(Cl#25)

RE: GEX
Awesome-Hyperwerks: Jul, 1998 - No. 0, Dec, 1998; ($2.50)

Preview (7/98) Wizard Con Edition 3.00
0-(12/98) Loeb-s/Liefeld-a/Pat Lee-c, 1-(9/98) Loeb-s/Liefeld-a/c 2.50

REGGIE (Formerly Archie's Rival...; Reggie & Me #19 on)
Archie Publications: No. 15, Sept, 1963 - No. 18, Nov, 1965

	GD 2.0	VG 4.0	FN 6.0	VF 8.0	VF/NM 9.0	NM- 9.2
15(9/63), 16(10/64), 17(8/65), 18(11/65)	5	10	15	30	48	65

NOTE: *Cover title No. 15 & 16 is Archie's Rival Reggie.*

REGGIE AND ME (Formerly Reggie)
Archie Publ.: No. 19, Aug, 1966 - No. 126, Sept, 1980 (No. 50-68: 52 pgs.)

	GD 2.0	VG 4.0	FN 6.0	VF 8.0	VF/NM 9.0	NM- 9.2
19-Evilheart app.	4	8	12	23	36	48
20-23-Evilheart app.; with Pureheart #22	3	6	9	19	29	38
24-40(3/70)	3	6	9	14	19	24
41-49(7/71)	2	4	6	10	14	18
50(9/71)-68 (1/74, 52 pgs.)	2	4	6	13	18	22
69-99	1	3	4	6	8	10
100(10/77)	2	4	6	8	11	14
101-126	1	2	3	5	6	8

REGGIE'S JOKES (See Reggie's Wise Guy Jokes)

REGGIE'S REVENGE!
Archie Comic Publications, Inc.: Spring, 1994 - No. 3 ($2.00, 52 pgs.) (Published semi-annually)

1-Bound-in pull-out poster 3.00
2,3 2.50

REGGIE'S WISE GUY JOKES
Archie Publications: Aug, 1968 - No. 55, 1980 (#5-28 are Giants)

	GD 2.0	VG 4.0	FN 6.0	VF 8.0	VF/NM 9.0	NM- 9.2
1	4	8	12	28	44	60
2-4	3	6	9	14	20	26
5-16 (1/71)(68 pg. Giants)	3	6	9	17	25	32
17-28 (52 pg. Giants)	2	4	6	13	18	22
29-40(1/77)	1	3	4	6	8	10
41-55						6.00

REGISTERED NURSE
Charlton Comics: Summer, 1963

	GD 2.0	VG 4.0	FN 6.0	VF 8.0	VF/NM 9.0	NM- 9.2
1-r/Nurse Betsy Crane & Cynthia Doyle	3	6	9	16	23	30

REG'LAR FELLERS
Visual Editions (Standard): No. 5, Nov, 1947 - No. 6, Mar, 1948

	GD 2.0	VG 4.0	FN 6.0	VF 8.0	VF/NM 9.0	NM- 9.2
5,6	9	18	27	47	61	75

REG'LAR FELLERS HEROIC (See Heroic Comics)

REID FLEMING, WORLD'S TOUGHEST MILKMAN
Eclipse Comics/ Deep Sea Comics: 8/86; V2#1, 12/86 - V2#3, 12/88; V2#4, 11/89; V2#5, 11/90 (B&W)

1 (3rd print, large size, 8/86, $2.50), 1-4th & 5th printings ($2.50) 3.00
V2#1 (10/86, regular size, $2.00), 1-2nd print, 3rd print ($2.00, 2/89) 2.50
2-8 , V2#2-2nd & 3rd printings, V2#4-2nd printing, V2#5 ($2.00) 2.50

REIGN IN HELL
DC Comics: Sept, 2008 - No. 8, ($3.50, limited series)

1-Neron, Shadowpact app.; Giffen-s; Dr. Occult back-up w/Segovia-a; two covers 3.50

REIGN OF THE ZODIAC
DC Comics: Oct, 2003 - No. 8, May, 2004 ($2.75)

1-8: 1-6,8-Giffen-s/Doran-a/Harris-c. 7-Byrd-a 2.75

RELATIVE HEROES
DC Comics: Mar, 2000 - No. 6, Aug, 2000 ($2.50, limited series)

1-6-Grayson-s/Guichet & Sowd-a. 6-Superman-c/app. 2.50

RELOAD
DC Comics (Homage): May, 2003 - No. 3, Sept, 2003 ($2.95, limited series)

1-3-Warren Ellis-s/Paul Gulacy & Jimmy Palmiotti-a 3.00
.../Mek TPB (2004, $14.95, flip book) r/Reload #1-3 & Mek #1-3 15.00

RELUCTANT DRAGON, THE (Walt Disney's...)
Dell Publishing Co.: No. 13, 1940

	GD 2.0	VG 4.0	FN 6.0	VF 8.0	VF/NM 9.0	NM- 9.2
Four Color 13-Contains 2 pgs. of photos from film; 2 pg. foreword to Fantasia by Leopold Stokowski; Donald Duck, Goofy, Baby Weems & Mickey Mouse (as the Sorcerer's Apprentice) app.	217	434	651	1367	2309	3250

REMAINS
IDW Publishing: May, 2004 - No. 5, Sept, 2004 ($3.99)

1-5-Steve Niles-s/Kieron Dwyer-a 4.00

REMARKABLE WORLDS OF PROFESSOR PHINEAS B. FUDDLE, THE
DC Comics (Paradox Press): 2000 - No. 4, 2000 ($5.95, limited series)

1-4-Boaz Yakin-s/Erez Yakin-a 6.00
TPB (2001, $19.95) r/series 20.00

REMEMBER PEARL HARBOR
Street & Smith Publications: 1942 (68 pgs.) (Illustrated story of the battle)

	GD 2.0	VG 4.0	FN 6.0	VF 8.0	VF/NM 9.0	NM- 9.2
nn-Uncle Sam-c; Jack Binder-a	47	94	141	291	483	675

REN & STIMPY SHOW, THE (TV) (Nicklodeon cartoon characters)
Marvel Comics: Dec, 1992 - No. 44, July, 1996 ($1.75/$1.95)

1-($2.25)-Polybagged w/scratch & sniff Ren or Stimpy air fowler (equal numbers of each were made) 6.00
1-2nd & 3rd printing; different dialogue on-c 2.50
2-6: 4-Muddy Mudskipper back-up. 5-Bill Wray painted-c. 6-Spider-Man vs. Powdered Toast Man 4.00

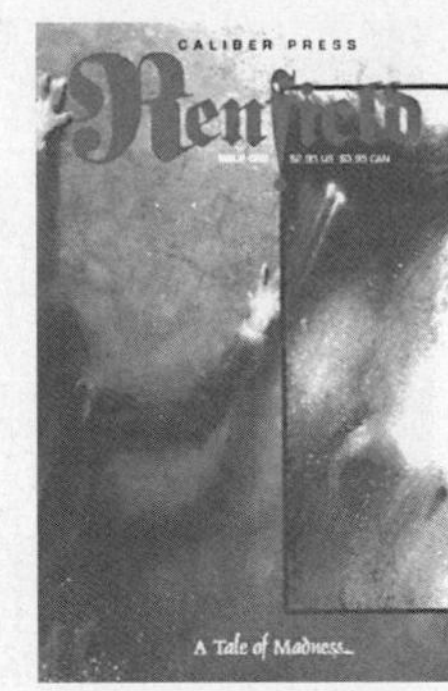

Renfield #1 © Caliber

Resurrection Man #25 © DC

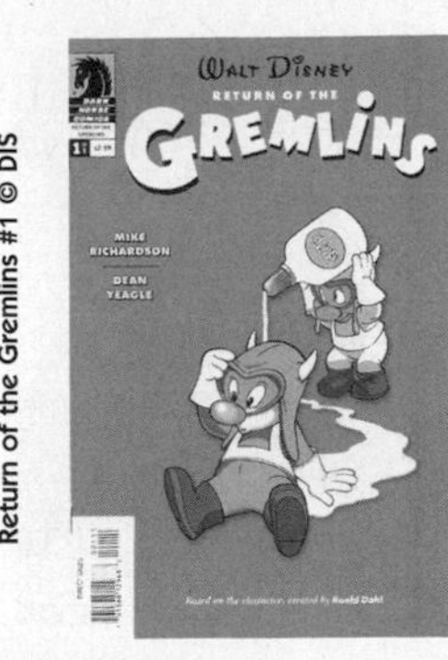

Return of the Gremlins #1 © DIS

	GD	VG	FN	VF	VF/NM	NM-
	2.0	4.0	6.0	8.0	9.0	9.2

7-17: 12-1st solo back-up story w/Tank & Brenner 2.50
18-44: 18-Powered Toast Man app. 2.50
25 ($2.95) Deluxe edition w/die cut cover 3.00
...Don't Try This at Home (3/94, $12.95, TPB)-r/#9-12 13.00
...Eenteractive Special ('95, $2.95) 3.00
...Holiday Special 1994 (2/95, $2.95, 52 pgs.) 3.00
...Mini Comic (1995) 5.00
...Pick of the Litter nn (1993, $12.95, TPB)-r/#1-4 13.00
...Radio Daze (11/95, $1.95) 2.50
...Running Joke nn (1993, $12.95, TPB)-r/#1-4 plus new-a 13.00
...Seeck Little Monkeys (1/95, $12.95)-r/#17-20 13.00
...Special 2 (7/94, $2.95, 52 pgs.), ...Special 3 (10/94, $2.95, 52 pgs.)-Choose adventure, ...Special: Around the World in a Daze ($2.95), ...Special: Four Swerks (1/95, $2.95, 52 pgs.)-FF #1 cover swipe; cover reads "Four Swerks w/5 pg. coloring book.", ...Special: Powdered Toast Man 1 (4/94, $2.95, 52 pgs.), ...Special: Powdered Toast Man's Cereal Serial (4/95, $2.95), ...Special: Sports (10/95, $2.95) 3.00
...Tastes Like Chicken nn (11/93,$12.95,TPB)-r/#5-8 13.00
...Your Pals (1994, $12.95, TPB)-r/#13-16 13.00

RENFIELD
Caliber Press:1994 - No. 3, 1995 ($2.95, B&W, limited series)

1-3 3.00

RENO BROWNE, HOLLYWOOD'S GREATEST COWGIRL (Formerly Margie Comics; Apache Kid #53 on; also see Western Hearts, Western Life Romances & Western Love)
Marvel Comics (MPC): No. 50, April, 1950 - No. 52, Sept, 1950 (52 pgs.)

50-Reno Browne photo-c on all 31 62 93 178 282 385
51,52 26 52 78 152 239 325

REPLACEMENT GOD
Amaze Ink: June, 1995 - No. 8 ($2.95, B&W)

1-8-Zander Cannon-s/a 3.00

REPLACEMENT GOD
Image Comics: May, 1997 - No. 5 ($2.95, B&W)

1-5: 1-Flip book w/"Knute's Escapes", r/original series. 2-Flip book w/"Harris Thermidor". 3-5: 3-Flip book w/"Myth and Legend" 3.00

REPTILICUS (Becomes Reptisaurus #3 on)
Charlton Comics: Aug, 1961 - No. 2, Oct, 1961

1 (Movie) 19 38 57 135 250 365
2 10 20 30 71 126 180

REPTISAURUS (Reptilicus #1,2)
Charlton Comics: V2#3, Jan, 1962 - No. 8, Dec, 1962; Summer, 1963

V2#3-8: 3-Flying saucer-c/s. 8-Montes/Bache-c/a 6 12 18 41 66 90
Special Edition 1 (Summer, 1963) 6 12 18 39 62 85

REQUIEM FOR DRACULA
Marvel Comics: Feb, 1993 ($2.00, 52 pgs.)

nn-r/Tomb of Dracula #69,70 by Gene Colan 2.50

RESCUERS, THE (See Walt Disney Showcase #40)

RESIDENT EVIL (Based on video game)
Image Comics (WildStorm): Mar, 1998 - No. 5 ($4.95, quarterly magazine)

1 7.00
2-5 5.00
...Code: Veronica 1-4 (2002, $14.95) English reprint of Japanese comics 15.00
...Collection One ('99, $14.95, TPB) r/#1-4 15.00

RESIDENT EVIL: FIRE AND ICE
DC Comics (WildStorm): Dec, 2000 - No. 4, May, 2001 ($2.50, limited series)

1-4-Bermejo-c 2.50

RESISTANCE, THE
DC Comics (WildStorm): Nov, 2002 - No. 8, June, 2003 ($2.95)

1-8-Palmiotti & Gray-s/Santacruz-a 3.00

RESTAURANT AT THE END OF THE UNIVERSE, THE (See Hitchhiker's Guide to the Galaxy & Life, the Universe & Everything)
DC Comics: 1994 - No. 3, 1994 ($6.95, limited series)

1-3 7.00

RESTLESS GUN (TV)
Dell Publishing Co.: No. 934, Sept, 1958 - No. 1146, Nov-Jan, 1960-61

Four Color 934 (#1)-Photo-c 10 20 30 71 126 180
Four Color 986 (5/59), 1045 (11-1/60), 1089 (3/60), 1146-Wildey-a; all photo-c 8 16 24 52 86 120

RESURRECTION MAN
DC Comics: May, 1997 - No. 27, Aug, 1999 ($2.50)

1-Lenticular disc on cover 5.00
2-5: 2-JLA app. 4.00
6-10: 6-Genesis-x-over. 7-Batman app. 10-Hitman-c/app. 3.00
11-27: 16,17-Supergirl x-over. 18-Deadman & Phantom Stranger-c/app. 21-JLA-c/app. 2.50
#1,000,000 (11/98) 853rd Century x-over 2.50

RETIEF (Keith Laumer's)
Adventure Comics (Malibu): Dec, 1989 - Vol. 2, No.6, ($2.25, B&W)

1-6,Vol. 2, #1-6,Vol. 3 (...of The CDT) #1-6 2.50
...and The Warlords #1-6, ...: Diplomatic Immunity #1 (4/91), ...: Giant Killer #1 (9/91), ...: Crime & Punishment #1 (11/91) 2.50

RETURN FROM WITCH MOUNTAIN (See Walt Disney Showcase #44)

RETURN OF ALISON DARE: LITTLE MISS ADVENTURES, THE (Also see Alison Dare: Little Miss Adventures)
Oni Press: Apr, 2001 - No. 3, Sept, 2001 ($2.95, B&W, limited series)

1-3-J. Torres-s/J.Bone-c/a 3.00

RETURN OF GORGO, THE (Formerly Gorgo's Revenge)
Charlton Comics: No. 2, Aug, 1963; No. 3, Fall, 1964 (12¢)

2,3-Ditko-c/a; based on M.G.M. movie 7 14 21 49 80 110

RETURN OF KONGA, THE (Konga's Revenge #2 on)
Charlton Comics: 1962

nn 7 14 21 49 80 110

RETURN OF MEGATON MAN
Kitchen Sink Press: July, 1988 - No. 3, 1988 ($2.00, limited series)

1-3: Simpson-c/a 2.50

RETURN OF THE GREMLINS (The Roald Dahl characters)
Dark Horse Comics: Mar, 2008 - No. 3, May, 2008 ($2.99, limited series)

1-3-Richardson-s/Yeagle-a. 1-Back-up reprint of intro. from 1943. 2-Back-up reprints of three Gremlin Gus 2-pagers from 1943. 3-Back-up reprints 3.00

RETURN OF THE OUTLAW
Toby Press (Minoan): Feb, 1953 - No. 11, 1955

1-Billy the Kid 10 20 30 54 72 90
2 7 14 21 35 43 50
3-11 6 12 18 31 38 45

RETURN TO JURASSIC PARK
Topps Comics: Apr, 1995 - No. 9, Feb, 1996 ($2.50/$2.95)

1-9: 3-Begin $2.95-c. 9-Artist's Jam issue 3.00

RETURN TO THE AMALGAM AGE OF COMICS: THE MARVEL COMICS COLLECTION
Marvel Comics: 1997 ($12.95, TPB)

nn-Reprints Amalgam one-shots: Challengers of the Fantastic #1, The Exciting X-Patrol #1, Iron Lantern #1, The Magnetic Men Featuring Magneto #1, Spider-Boy Team-Up #1 & Thorion of the New Asgods #1 13.00

REVEAL
Dark Horse Comics: Nov, 2002 ($6.95, squarebound)

1-Short stories of Dark Horse characters by various; Lone Wolf 2100, Buffy, Spyboy app. 7.00

REVEALING LOVE STORIES (See Fox Giants)

REVEALING ROMANCES
Ace Magazines: Sept, 1949 - No. 6, Aug, 1950

1 14 28 42 80 115 150
2 9 18 27 47 61 75
3-6 8 16 24 42 54 65

REVELATIONS
Dark Horse Comics: Aug, 2005 - No. 6, Jan, 2006 ($2.99, limited series)

1-6-Paul Jenkins-s/Humberto Ramos-a/c 3.00

REVENGE OF THE PROWLER (Also see The Prowler)
Eclipse Comics: Feb, 1988 - No. 4, June, 1988 ($1.75/$1.95)

1,3,4: 1-$1.75. 3,4-$1.95-c; Snyder III-a(p) 2.50
2 ($2.50)-Contains flexi-disc 2.75

REVOLUTION ON THE PLANET OF THE APES
Mr. Comics: Dec, 2005 - No. 6, Aug, 2006 ($3.95)

1-6: 1,2-Salgood Sam-a 4.00

REX ALLEN COMICS (Movie star)(Also see Four Color #877 & Western Roundup under Dell Giants)

Rex Allen Comics #9 © DELL

Rex Mundi V2 #1 © Arvid Nelson

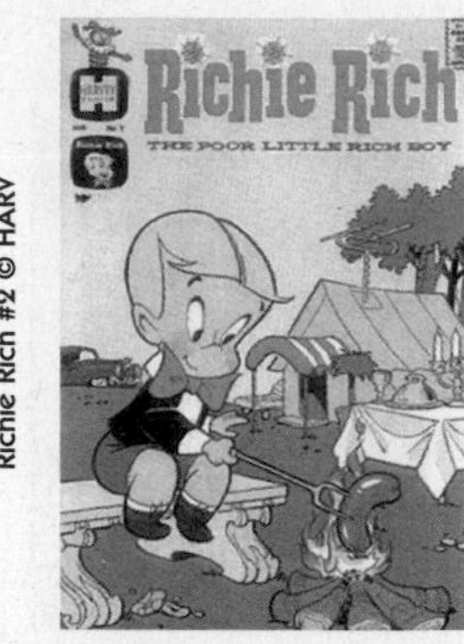

Richie Rich #2 © HARV

	GD 2.0	VG 4.0	FN 6.0	VF 8.0	VF/NM 9.0	NM- 9.2

Dell Publ. Co.: No. 316, Feb, 1951 - No. 31, Dec-Feb, 1958-59 (All-photo-c)

	GD	VG	FN	VF	VF/NM	NM-
Four Color 316(#1)(52 pgs.)-Rex Allen & his horse Koko begin; Marsh-a	14	28	42	102	181	260
2 (9-11/51, 36 pgs.)	9	18	27	63	107	150
3-10	7	14	21	45	73	100
11-20	6	12	18	39	62	85
21-23,25-31	5	10	15	35	55	75
24-Toth-a	6	12	18	39	62	85

NOTE: *Manning a-20, 27-30. Photo back-c F.C. #316, 2-12, 20, 21.*

REX DEXTER OF MARS (See Mystery Men Comics)
Fox Features Syndicate: Fall, 1940 (68 pgs.)

	GD	VG	FN	VF	VF/NM	NM-
1-Rex Dexter, Patty O'Day, & Zanzibar (Tuska-a) app.; Briefer-c/a	193	386	579	1216	2058	2900

REX HART (Formerly Blaze Carson; Whip Wilson #9 on)
Timely/Marvel Comics (USA): No. 6, Aug, 1949 - No. 8, Feb, 1950 (All photo-c)

	GD	VG	FN	VF	VF/NM	NM-
6-Rex Hart & his horse Warrior begin; Black Rider app; Captain Tootsie by Beck	26	52	78	152	244	335
7,8: 18 pg. Thriller in each. 8-Blaze the Wonder Collie app. in text	18	36	54	103	162	220

REX MORGAN, M.D. (Also see Harvey Comics Library)
Argo Publ.: Dec, 1955 - No. 3, Apr?, 1956

	GD	VG	FN	VF	VF/NM	NM-
1-r/Rex Morgan daily newspaper strips & daily panel-r of "These Women" by D'Alessio & "Timeout" by Jeff Keate	14	28	42	76	108	140
2,3	10	20	30	54	72	90

REX MUNDI (Latin for "King of the World")
Image Comics: No. 0, Aug, 2002 - No. 18, Apr, 2006 ($2.95/$2.99)

0-18-Arvid Nelson-s. 0-13-Eric Johnson-a. 14,15-Jim DiBartolo-a. 18-Ramos-c 3.00
Vol. 1: The Guardian of the Temple TPB (1/04, $14.95) r/#0-5 15.00
Book 1: The Guardian of the Temple TPB (Dark Horse, 11/06, $16.95) r/#0-5 & Brother Matthew web comic; Dysart intro. 17.00
Vol. 2: The River Underground TPB (4/05, $14.95) r/#6-11 15.00
Book 2: The River Underground (Dark Horse, 2006, $16.95) r/#6-11 17.00
Vol. 3: The Lost Kings TPB (Dark Horse, 9/06, $16.95) r/#12-17 17.00
Book Four: Crowd and Sword TPB (Dark Horse, 12/07, $16.95) r/#18 plus V2 #1-5 and story from Dark Horse Book of Monsters 17.00

REX MUNDI (Volume 2)
Dark Horse Comics: July, 2006 - Present ($2.99)

1-13-Arvid Nelson-s. 1-JH Williams-c 3.00

REX THE WONDER DOG (See The Adventures of...)

RHUBARB, THE MILLIONAIRE CAT
Dell Publishing Co.: No. 423, Sept-Oct, 1952 - No. 563, June, 1954

	GD	VG	FN	VF	VF/NM	NM-
Four Color 423 (#1)	6	12	18	39	62	85
Four Color 466(5/53),563	5	10	15	34	55	75

RIB
Dilemma Productions: Oct, 1995 - April, 1996 ($1.95, B&W)

Ashcan, 1 3.00

RIB
Bookmark Productions: 1996 ($2.95, B&W)

1-Sakai-c; Andrew Ford-s/a 3.00

RIB
Caliber Comics: May, 1997 - No. 5, 1998 ($2.95, B&W)

1-5: 1-"Beginnings" pts. 1 & 2 3.00

RIBIT! (Red Sonja imitation)
Comico: Jan, 1989 - No. 4, April?, 1989 ($1.95, limited series)

1-4: Frank Thorne-c/a/scripts 3.00

RIBTICKLER (Also see Fox Giants)
Fox Feature Synd./Green Publ. (1957)/Norlen (1959): 1945 - No. 9, Aug, 1947; 1957; 1959

	GD	VG	FN	VF	VF/NM	NM-
1-Funny animal	15	30	45	90	140	190
2-(1946)	10	20	30	54	72	90
3-9: 3,7-Cosmo Cat app.	9	18	27	47	61	75
3,7,8 (Green Publ.-1957), 3,7,8 (Norlen Mag.-1959)	3	6	9	16	23	30

RICHARD DRAGON
DC Comics: July, 2004 - No. 12, Jun, 2005 ($2.50)

1-12: 1-Dixon-s/McDaniel-a/c; Ben Turner app. 2,3-Nightwing app. 4-6,11,12-Lady Shiva 2.50

RICHARD DRAGON, KUNG-FU FIGHTER (See The Batman Chronicles #5, Brave & the Bold, & The Question)
National Periodical Publ./DC Comics: Apr-May, 1975 - No. 18, Nov-Dec, 1977

	GD	VG	FN	VF	VF/NM	NM-
1-Intro Richard Dragon, Ben Stanley & O-Sensei; 1st app. Barney Ling; adaptation of Jim Dennis novel "Dragon's Fists" begins, ends #4	2	4	6	11	16	20
2,3: 2-Intro Carolyn Woosan; Starlin/Weiss-c/a; bondage-c. 3-Kirby-a(p); Giordano bondage-c	2	4	6	8	10	12
4-8-Wood inks. 4-Carolyn Woosan dies. 5-1st app. Lady Shiva	1	2	3	5	7	9
9-13,15-18: 9-Ben Stanley becomes Ben Turner; intro Preying Mantis. 16-1st app. Prof Ojo. 18-1st app. Ben Turner as The Bronze Tiger	1	2	3	5	6	8
14-"Spirit of Bruce Lee"	2	4	6	11	16	20

NOTE: ***Buckler** a-14. c-15, 18. **Chua** c-13. **Estrada** a-9, 13-18. **Estrada/Abel** a-10-12. **Estrada/Wood** a-4-8. **Giordano** c-1, 3-11. **Weiss** a-2(partial) c-2i.*

RICHARD THE LION-HEARTED (See Ideal a Classical Comic)

RICHIE RICH (See Harvey Collectors Comics, Harvey Hits, Little Dot, Little Lotta, Little Sad Sack, Million Dollar Digest, Mutt & Jeff, Super Richie & 3-D Dolly; also Tastee-Freez Comics in the Promotional Comics section)

RICHIE RICH (...the Poor Little Rich Boy) (See Harvey Hits #3, 9)
Harvey Publ.: Nov, 1960 - #218, Oct, 1982; #219, Oct, 1986 - #254, Jan, 1991

	GD	VG	FN	VF	VF/NM	NM-
1-(See Little Dot #1 for 1st app.)	220	440	660	1925	3713	5500
2	69	138	207	587	1119	1650
3-5	44	88	132	352	664	975
6-10: 8-Christmas-c	26	52	78	192	359	525
11-20	17	34	51	120	223	325
21-30	12	24	36	82	146	210
31-40	10	20	30	67	116	165
41-50: 42(2/66)-X-mas-c	8	16	24	52	86	120
51-55,57-60: 59-Buck, prototype of Dollar the Dog	6	12	18	37	59	80
56-1st app. Super Richie	7	14	21	45	73	100
61-64,66-80: 71-Nixon & Robert Kennedy caricatures; outer space-c	4	8	12	28	44	60
65-Buck the Dog (Dollar prototype) on cover	6	12	18	41	66	90
81-99	3	6	9	20	30	40
100(12/70)-1st app. Irona the robot maid	4	8	12	24	37	50
101-111,117-120	3	6	9	14	19	24
112-116: All 52 pg. Giants	3	6	9	16	23	30
121-140: 137-1st app. Mr. Cheepers and Professor Keenbean	2	4	6	9	13	16
141-160: 145-Infinity-c. 155-3rd app. The Money Monster	2	4	6	8	10	12
161-180	1	3	4	6	8	10
181-199	1	2	3	5	6	8
200	1	3	4	6	8	10
201-218: 210-Stone-Age Riches app	1	2	3	4	5	7

219-254: 237-Last original material 6.00
Harvey Comics Classics Vol. 2 TPB (Dark Horse Books, 10/07, $19.95) Reprints Richie Rich's early appearances in this title, Little Dot and Richie Rich Success Stories, mostly B&W with some color stories; history and interview with Ernie Colón 20.00

RICHIE RICH
Harvey Comics: Mar, 1991 - No. 28, Nov, 1994 ($1.00, bi-monthly)

1-28: Reprints best of Richie Rich 2.50
Giant Size 1-4 (10/91-10/93, $2.25, 68 pgs.) 3.00

RICHIE RICH ADVENTURE DIGEST MAGAZINE
Harvey Comics: 1992 - No. 7, Sept, 1994 ($1.25, quarterly, digest-size)

1-7 4.00

RICHIE RICH AND...
Harvey Comics: Oct, 1987 - No. 11, May, 1990 ($1.00)

1-Professor Keenbean 4.00
2-11: 2-Casper. 3-Dollar the Dog. 4-Cadbury. 5 Mayda Munny. 6-Irona. 7-Little Dot. 8-Professor Keenbean. 9-Little Audrey. 10-Mayda Munny. 11-Cadbury 3.00

RICHIE RICH AND BILLY BELLHOPS
Harvey Publications: Oct, 1977 (52 pgs., one-shot)

	GD	VG	FN	VF	VF/NM	NM-
1	2	4	6	9	12	15

RICHIE RICH AND CADBURY
Harvey Publ.: 10/77; #2, 9/78 - #23, 7/82; #24, 7/90 - #29, 1/91 (1-10: 52pgs.)

	GD	VG	FN	VF	VF/NM	NM-
1-(52 pg. Giant)	2	4	6	11	16	20
2-10-(52 pg. Giant)	2	4	6	8	10	12

11-23 6.00
24-29: 24-Begin $1.00-c 4.00

RICHIE RICH AND CASPER

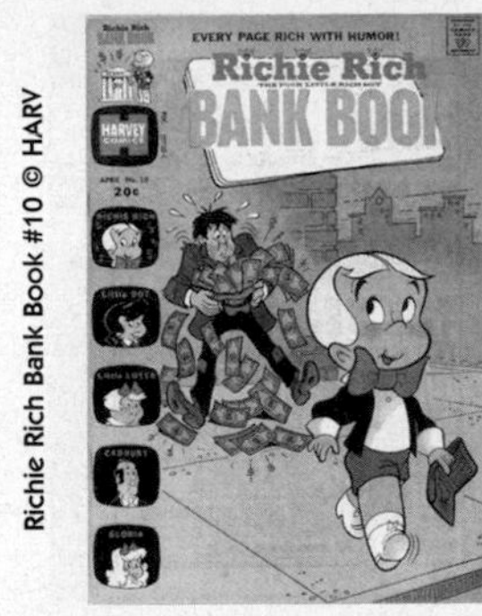

Richie Rich Bank Book #10 © HARV

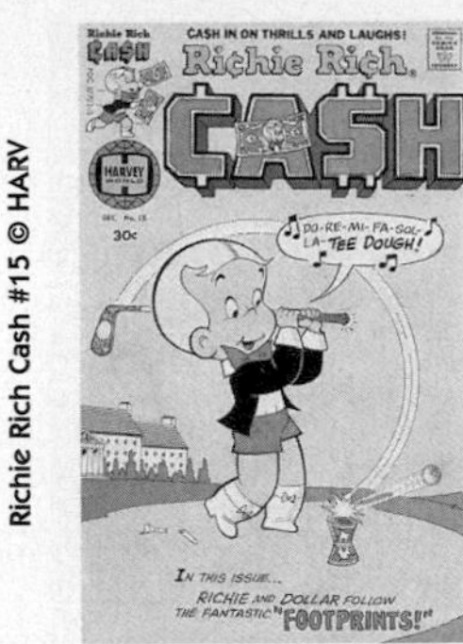

Richie Rich Cash #15 © HARV

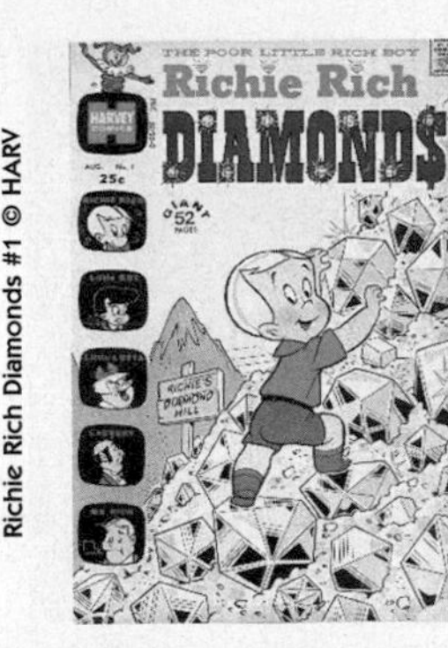

Richie Rich Diamonds #1 © HARV

Harvey Publications: Aug, 1974 - No. 45, Sept, 1982

	GD 2.0	VG 4.0	FN 6.0	VF 8.0	VF/NM 9.0	NM- 9.2
1	3	6	9	20	30	40
2-5	2	4	6	13	18	22
6-10: 10-Xmas-c	2	4	6	9	13	16
11-20	1	3	4	6	8	10
21-45: 22-Xmas-c						6.00

RICHIE RICH AND DOLLAR THE DOG (See Richie Rich #65)
Harvey Publications: Sept, 1977 - No. 24, Aug, 1982 (#1-10: 52 pgs.)

	GD 2.0	VG 4.0	FN 6.0	VF 8.0	VF/NM 9.0	NM- 9.2
1-(52 pg. Giant)	2	4	6	11	16	20
2-10-(52 pg. Giant)	2	4	6	8	10	12
11-24						6.00

RICHIE RICH AND DOT
Harvey Publications: Oct, 1974 (one-shot)

	GD 2.0	VG 4.0	FN 6.0	VF 8.0	VF/NM 9.0	NM- 9.2
1	3	6	9	16	22	28

RICHIE RICH AND GLORIA
Harvey Publications: Sept, 1977 - No. 25, Sept, 1982 (#1-11: 52 pgs.)

	GD 2.0	VG 4.0	FN 6.0	VF 8.0	VF/NM 9.0	NM- 9.2
1-(52 pg. Giant)	2	4	6	11	16	20
2-11 (52 pg. Giant)	2	4	6	8	10	12
12-25						6.00

RICHIE RICH AND HIS GIRLFRIENDS
Harvey Publications: April, 1979 - No. 16, Dec, 1982

	GD 2.0	VG 4.0	FN 6.0	VF 8.0	VF/NM 9.0	NM- 9.2
1-(52 pg. Giant)	2	4	6	9	13	16
2-(52 pg. Giant)	1	3	4	6	8	10
3-10	1	2	3	5	6	8
11-16						6.00

RICHIE RICH AND HIS MEAN COUSIN REGGIE
Harvey Publications: April, 1979 - No. 3, 1980 (50¢) (#1,2: 52 pgs.)

	GD 2.0	VG 4.0	FN 6.0	VF 8.0	VF/NM 9.0	NM- 9.2
1	2	4	6	9	13	16
2-3:	1	3	4	6	8	10

NOTE: *No. 4 was advertised, but never released.*

RICHIE RICH AND JACKIE JOKERS (Also see Jackie Jokers)
Harvey Publications: Nov, 1973 - No. 48, Dec, 1982

	GD 2.0	VG 4.0	FN 6.0	VF 8.0	VF/NM 9.0	NM- 9.2
1: 52 pg. Giant; contains material from unpublished Jackie Jokers #5	4	8	12	24	37	50
2,3-(52 pg. Giants). 2-R.R. & Jackie 1st meet	3	6	9	16	22	28
4,5	2	4	6	13	18	22
6-10	2	4	6	9	13	16
11-20,26: 11-1st app. Kool Katz. 26-Star Wars parody	1	3	4	6	8	10
21-25,27-40	1	2	3	4	5	7
41-48						6.00

RICHIE RICH AND PROFESSOR KEENBEAN
Harvey Comics: Sept, 1990 - No. 2, Nov, 1990 ($1.00)

	GD 2.0	VG 4.0	FN 6.0	VF 8.0	VF/NM 9.0	NM- 9.2
1,2						3.00

RICHIE RICH AND THE NEW KIDS ON THE BLOCK
Harvey Publications: Feb, 1991 - No. 3, June, 1991 ($1.25, bi-monthly)

	GD 2.0	VG 4.0	FN 6.0	VF 8.0	VF/NM 9.0	NM- 9.2
1-3: 1,2-New Richie Rich stories						3.00

RICHIE RICH AND TIMMY TIME
Harvey Publications: Sept, 1977 (50¢, 52 pgs, one-shot)

	GD 2.0	VG 4.0	FN 6.0	VF 8.0	VF/NM 9.0	NM- 9.2
1	2	4	6	9	12	15

RICHIE RICH BANK BOOK
Harvey Publications: Oct, 1972 - No. 59, Sept, 1982

	GD 2.0	VG 4.0	FN 6.0	VF 8.0	VF/NM 9.0	NM- 9.2
1	5	10	15	30	48	65
2-5: 2-2nd app. The Money Monster	3	6	9	16	23	30
6-10	2	4	6	11	16	20
11-20: 18-Super Richie app.	2	4	6	8	10	12
21-30	1	2	3	5	7	9
31-40	1	2	3	4	5	7
41-59						6.00

RICHIE RICH BEST OF THE YEARS
Harvey Publications: Oct, 1977 - No. 6, June, 1980 (128 pgs., digest-size)

	GD 2.0	VG 4.0	FN 6.0	VF 8.0	VF/NM 9.0	NM- 9.2
1(10/77)-Reprints	2	4	6	9	12	15
2-6(11/79-6/80, 95¢). #2(10/78)-Rep.. #3(6/79, 75¢)	1	2	3	5	7	9

RICHIE RICH BIG BOOK
Harvey Publications: Nov, 1992 - No. 2, May, 1993 ($1.50, 52 pgs.)

	GD 2.0	VG 4.0	FN 6.0	VF 8.0	VF/NM 9.0	NM- 9.2
1,2						3.00

RICHIE RICH BIG BUCKS
Harvey Publications: Apr, 1991 - No. 8, July, 1992 ($1.00, bi-monthly)

	GD 2.0	VG 4.0	FN 6.0	VF 8.0	VF/NM 9.0	NM- 9.2
1-8						3.00

RICHIE RICH BILLIONS
Harvey Publications: Oct, 1974 - No. 48, Oct, 1982 (#1-33: 52 pgs.)

	GD 2.0	VG 4.0	FN 6.0	VF 8.0	VF/NM 9.0	NM- 9.2
1	4	8	12	22	34	45
2-5: 2-Christmas issue	3	6	9	14	20	25
6-10	2	4	6	10	14	18
11-20	2	4	6	8	10	12
21-33	1	2	3	5	6	8
34-48: 35-Onion app.						6.00

RICHIE RICH CASH
Harvey Publications: Sept, 1974 - No. 47, Aug, 1982

	GD 2.0	VG 4.0	FN 6.0	VF 8.0	VF/NM 9.0	NM- 9.2
1-1st app. Dr. N-R-Gee	3	6	9	20	30	40
2-5	2	4	6	13	18	22
6-10	2	4	6	9	13	16
11-20	1	3	4	6	8	10
21-30	1	2	3	4	5	7
31-47: 33-Dr. Blemish app.						6.00

RICHIE RICH CASH MONEY
Harvey Comics: May, 1992 - No. 2, Aug, 1992 ($1.25)

	GD 2.0	VG 4.0	FN 6.0	VF 8.0	VF/NM 9.0	NM- 9.2
1,2						3.00

RICHIE RICH, CASPER AND WENDY - NATIONAL LEAGUE
Harvey Comics: June, 1976 (50¢)

	GD 2.0	VG 4.0	FN 6.0	VF 8.0	VF/NM 9.0	NM- 9.2
1-Newsstand version of the baseball giveaway	2	4	6	13	18	22

RICHIE RICH COLLECTORS COMICS (See Harvey Collectors Comics)

RICHIE RICH DIAMONDS
Harvey Publications: Aug, 1972 - No. 59, Aug, 1982 (#1, 23-45: 52 pgs.)

	GD 2.0	VG 4.0	FN 6.0	VF 8.0	VF/NM 9.0	NM- 9.2
1-(52 pg. Giant)	5	10	15	32	51	70
2-5	3	6	9	16	23	30
6-10	2	4	6	11	16	20
11-22	2	4	6	8	10	12
23-30-(52 pg. Giants)	2	4	6	8	11	14
31-45: 39-r/Origin Little Dot	1	2	3	5	7	9
46-50	1	2	3	4	5	7
51-59						6.00

RICHIE RICH DIGEST
Harvey Publications: Oct, 1986 - No. 42, Oct, 1994 ($1.25/$1.75, digest-size)

	GD 2.0	VG 4.0	FN 6.0	VF 8.0	VF/NM 9.0	NM- 9.2
1	1	3	4	6	8	10
2-10						6.00
11-20						5.00
21-42						4.00

RICHIE RICH DIGEST STORIES (...Magazine #?-on)
Harvey Publications: Oct, 1977 - No., 17, Oct, 1982 (75¢/95¢, digest-size)

	GD 2.0	VG 4.0	FN 6.0	VF 8.0	VF/NM 9.0	NM- 9.2
1-Reprints	2	4	6	9	12	15
2-10: Reprints	1	2	3	5	7	9
11-17: Reprints						6.00

RICHIE RICH DIGEST WINNERS
Harvey Publications: Dec, 1977 - No. 16, Sept, 1982 (75¢/95¢, 132 pgs., digest-size)

	GD 2.0	VG 4.0	FN 6.0	VF 8.0	VF/NM 9.0	NM- 9.2
1	2	4	6	9	12	15
2-5	1	2	3	5	7	9
6-16						6.00

RICHIE RICH DOLLARS & CENTS
Harvey Publications: Aug, 1963 - No. 109, Aug, 1982 (#1-43: 68 pgs.; 44-60, 71-94: 52 pgs.)

	GD 2.0	VG 4.0	FN 6.0	VF 8.0	VF/NM 9.0	NM- 9.2
1: (#1-64 are all reprint issues)	18	36	54	130	240	350
2	10	20	30	70	123	175
3-5: 5-r/1st app. of R.R. from Little Dot #1	9	18	27	63	107	150
6-10	7	14	21	47	76	105
11-20	5	10	15	30	48	65
21-30: 25-r/1st app. Nurse Jenny (Little Lotta #62)	4	8	12	22	34	45
31-43: 43-Last 68 pg. issue	3	6	9	18	27	35
44-60: All 52 pgs.	3	6	9	14	19	25
61-71	1	3	4	6	8	10
72-94: All 52 pgs.	2	4	6	8	10	12
95-99,101-109						6.00
100-Anniversary issue	1	2	3	5	7	9

RICHIE RICH FORTUNES
Harvey Publications: Sept, 1971 - No. 63, July, 1982 (#1-15: 52 pgs.)

Richie Rich Gems #2 © HARV

Richie Rich Millions #14 © HARV

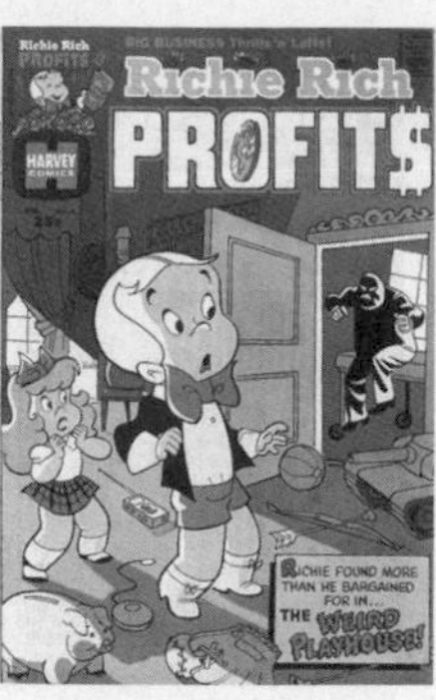
Richie Rich Profits #2 © HARV

	GD 2.0	VG 4.0	FN 6.0	VF 8.0	VF/NM 9.0	NM- 9.2
1	6	12	18	39	62	85
2-5	3	6	9	20	30	40
6-10	2	4	6	13	18	22
11-15: 11-r/1st app. The Onion	2	4	6	9	12	15
16-30	1	2	3	5	7	9
31-40	1	2	3	4	5	7
41-63: 62-Onion app.						6.00

RICHIE RICH GEMS
Harvey Publications: Sept, 1974 - No. 43, Sept, 1982

	GD 2.0	VG 4.0	FN 6.0	VF 8.0	VF/NM 9.0	NM- 9.2
1	3	6	9	20	30	40
2-5	2	4	6	13	18	22
6-10	2	4	6	9	13	16
11-20	1	3	4	6	8	10
21-30	1	2	3	4	5	7
31-43: 36-Dr. Blemish, Onion app. 38-1st app. Stone-Age Riches						6.00

RICHIE RICH GOLD AND SILVER
Harvey Publications: Sept, 1975 - No. 42, Oct, 1982 (#1-27: 52 pgs.)

	GD 2.0	VG 4.0	FN 6.0	VF 8.0	VF/NM 9.0	NM- 9.2
1	3	6	9	18	27	35
2-5	2	4	6	11	16	20
6-10	2	4	6	8	11	14
11-27	1	2	3	5	7	9
28-42: 34-Stone-Age Riches app.						6.00

RICHIE RICH GOLD NUGGETS DIGEST
Harvey Publications: Dec., 1990 - No. 4, June, 1991 ($1.75, digest-size)

	GD 2.0	VG 4.0	FN 6.0	VF 8.0	VF/NM 9.0	NM- 9.2
1-4						3.00

RICHIE RICH HOLIDAY DIGEST MAGAZINE (...Digest #4)
Harvey Publications: Jan, 1980 - #3, Jan, 1982; #4, 3/88; #5, 2/89 (annual)

	GD 2.0	VG 4.0	FN 6.0	VF 8.0	VF/NM 9.0	NM- 9.2
1-X-Mas-c	1	3	4	6	8	10
2-5: 2,3: All X-Mas-c. 4-(3/88, $1.25), 5-(2/89, $1.75)	1	2	3	4	5	7

RICHIE RICH INVENTIONS
Harvey Publications: Oct, 1977 - No. 26, Oct, 1982 (#1-11: 52 pgs.)

	GD 2.0	VG 4.0	FN 6.0	VF 8.0	VF/NM 9.0	NM- 9.2
1	2	4	6	11	16	20
2-5	2	4	6	8	10	12
6-11	1	2	3	5	6	8
12-26						6.00

RICHIE RICH JACKPOTS
Harvey Publications: Oct, 1972 - No. 58, Aug, 1982 (#41-43: 52 pgs.)

	GD 2.0	VG 4.0	FN 6.0	VF 8.0	VF/NM 9.0	NM- 9.2
1-Debut of Cousin Jackpots	5	10	15	30	48	65
2-5	3	6	9	16	23	30
6-10	2	4	6	11	16	20
11-15,17-20	2	4	6	8	10	12
16-Super Richie app.	2	4	6	9	12	15
21-30	1	2	3	5	7	9
31-40,44-50: 37-Caricatures of Frank Sinatra, Dean Martin, Sammy Davis, Jr. 45-Dr. Blemish app.	1	2	3	4	5	7
41-43 (52 pgs.)	1	3	4	6	8	10
51-58						6.00

RICHIE RICH MILLION DOLLAR DIGEST (...Magazine #?-on)(See Million Dollar Digest)
Harvey Publications: Oct, 1980 - No. 10, Oct, 1982 ($1.50)

	GD 2.0	VG 4.0	FN 6.0	VF 8.0	VF/NM 9.0	NM- 9.2
1	1	3	4	6	8	10
2-10						6.00

RICHIE RICH MILLIONS
Harvey Publ.: 9/61; #2, 9/62 - #113, 10/82 (#1-48: 68 pgs.; 49-64, 85-97: 52 pgs.)

	GD 2.0	VG 4.0	FN 6.0	VF 8.0	VF/NM 9.0	NM- 9.2
1: (#1-3 are all reprint issues)	21	42	63	152	281	410
2	11	22	33	79	140	200
3-5: All other giants are new & reprints. 5-1st 15 pg. Richie Rich story	9	18	27	65	113	160
6-10	8	16	24	58	97	135
11-20	6	12	18	41	66	90
21-30	4	8	12	28	44	60
31-48: 31-1st app. The Onion. 48-Last 68 pg. Giant	3	6	9	20	30	40
49-64: 52 pg. Giants	3	6	9	14	20	25
65-67,69-73,75-84	2	4	6	8	10	12
68-1st Super Richie-c (11/74)	2	4	6	13	18	22
74-1st app. Mr. Woody; Super Richie app.	2	4	6	8	11	14
85-97: 52 pg. Giants	2	4	6	8	11	14
98,99	1	2	3	4	5	7
100	1	2	3	5	7	9
101-113						6.00

RICHIE RICH MONEY WORLD
Harvey Publications: Sept, 1972 - No. 59, Sept, 1982

	GD 2.0	VG 4.0	FN 6.0	VF 8.0	VF/NM 9.0	NM- 9.2
1-(52 pg. Giant)-1st app. Mayda Munny	6	12	18	37	59	80
2-Super Richie app.	3	6	9	18	27	35
3-5	3	6	9	16	23	30
6-10: 9,10-Richie Rich mistakenly named Little Lotta on covers	2	4	6	11	16	20
11-20: 16,20-Dr. N-R-Gee	2	4	6	8	10	12
21-30	1	2	3	5	7	9
31-50	1	2	3	4	5	7
51-59						6.00
Digest 1 (2/91, $1.75)						5.00
2-8 (12/93, $1.75)						3.00

RICHIE RICH PROFITS
Harvey Publications: Oct, 1974 - No. 47, Sept, 1982

	GD 2.0	VG 4.0	FN 6.0	VF 8.0	VF/NM 9.0	NM- 9.2
1	3	6	9	20	30	40
2-5	2	4	6	13	18	22
6-10: 10-Origin of Dr. N-R-Gee	2	4	6	9	13	16
11-20: 15-Christmas-c	1	3	4	6	8	10
21-30	1	2	3	4	5	7
31-47						6.00

RICHIE RICH RELICS
Harvey Comics: Jan, 1988 - No.4, Feb, 1989 (75¢/$1.00, reprints)

	GD 2.0	VG 4.0	FN 6.0	VF 8.0	VF/NM 9.0	NM- 9.2
1-4						3.00

RICHIE RICH RICHES
Harvey Publications: July, 1972 - No. 59, Aug, 1982 (#1, 2, 41-45: 52 pgs.)

	GD 2.0	VG 4.0	FN 6.0	VF 8.0	VF/NM 9.0	NM- 9.2
1-(52 pg. Giant)-1st app. The Money Monster	6	12	18	37	59	80
2-(52 pg. Giant)	3	6	9	20	30	40
3-5	3	6	9	16	23	30
6-10: 7-1st app. Aunt Novo	2	4	6	11	16	20
11-20: 17-Super Richie app. (3/75)	2	4	6	8	10	12
21-40	1	2	3	5	6	8
41-45: 52 pg. Giants	1	3	4	6	8	10
46-59: 56-Dr. Blemish app.						6.00

RICHIE RICH SUCCESS STORIES
Harvey Publications: Nov, 1964 - No. 105, Sept, 1982 (#1-38: 68 pgs., 39-55, 67-90: 52 pgs.)

	GD 2.0	VG 4.0	FN 6.0	VF 8.0	VF/NM 9.0	NM- 9.2
1	17	34	51	120	223	325
2	9	18	27	65	113	160
3-5	8	16	24	58	97	135
6-10	6	12	18	39	62	85
11-20	5	10	15	32	51	70
21-30: 27-1st Penny Van Dough (8/69)	4	8	12	24	37	50
31-38: 38-Last 68 pg. Giant	3	6	9	20	30	40
39-55-(52 pgs.): 44-Super Richie app.	3	6	9	14	20	25
56-66	2	4	6	8	10	12
67-90: 52 pgs.	2	4	6	8	11	14
91-99,101-105: 91-Onion app. 101-Dr. Blemish app.						6.00
100	1	2	3	5	7	9

RICHIE RICH SUMMER BONANZA
Harvey Comics: Oct, 1991 ($1.95, one-shot, 68 pgs.)

	GD 2.0	VG 4.0	FN 6.0	VF 8.0	VF/NM 9.0	NM- 9.2
1-Richie Rich, Little Dot, Little Lotta						3.00

RICHIE RICH TREASURE CHEST DIGEST (...Magazine #3)
Harvey Publications: Apr, 1982 - No. 3, Aug, 1982 (95¢, Digest Mag.)
(#4 advertised but not publ.)

	GD 2.0	VG 4.0	FN 6.0	VF 8.0	VF/NM 9.0	NM- 9.2
1	1	2	3	5	7	9
2,3	1	2	3	4	5	7

RICHIE RICH VACATION DIGEST
Harvey Comics: Oct, 1991; Oct, 1992; Oct, 1993 ($1.75, digest-size)

	GD 2.0	VG 4.0	FN 6.0	VF 8.0	VF/NM 9.0	NM- 9.2
1-(10/91), 1-(10/92), 1-(10/93)						4.00

RICHIE RICH VACATIONS DIGEST
Harvey Publ.: 11/77; No. 2, 10/78 - No. 7, 10/81; No. 8, 8/82; No. 9, 10/82 (Digest, 132 pgs.)

	GD 2.0	VG 4.0	FN 6.0	VF 8.0	VF/NM 9.0	NM- 9.2
1-Reprints	2	4	6	9	12	15
2-6	1	2	3	5	7	9
7-9						6.00

RICHIE RICH VAULT OF MYSTERY
Harvey Publications: Nov, 1974 - No. 47, Sept, 1982

	GD 2.0	VG 4.0	FN 6.0	VF 8.0	VF/NM 9.0	NM- 9.2
1	3	6	9	20	30	40
2-5: 5-The Condor app.	2	4	6	13	18	22

Rima, The Jungle Girl #6 © DC

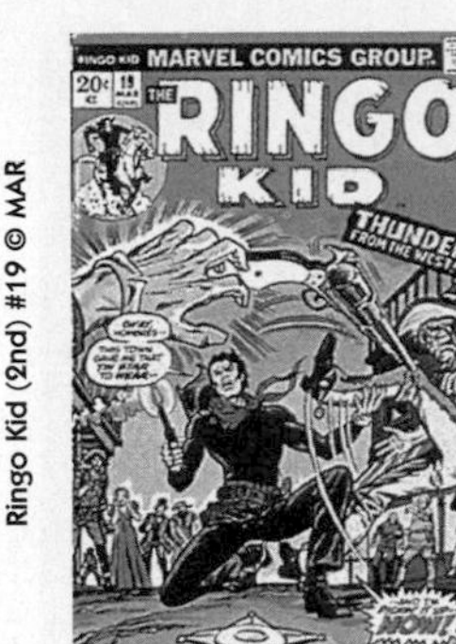

Ringo Kid (2nd) #19 © MAR

Ripclaw V2 #2 © TCOW

	GD 2.0	VG 4.0	FN 6.0	VF 8.0	VF/NM 9.0	NM- 9.2
6-10	2	4	6	9	13	16
11-20	1	3	4	6	8	10
21-30	1	2	3	4	5	7
31-47						6.00

RICHIE RICH ZILLIONZ
Harvey Publ.: Oct, 1976 - No. 33, Sept, 1982 (#1-4: 68 pgs.; #5-18: 52 pgs.)

	GD 2.0	VG 4.0	FN 6.0	VF 8.0	VF/NM 9.0	NM- 9.2
1	3	6	9	18	27	35
2-4: 4-Last 68 pg. Giant	2	4	6	11	16	20
5-10	2	4	6	8	10	12
11-18: 18-Last 52 pg. Giant	1	2	3	5	6	8
19-33						6.00

RICKY
Standard Comics (Visual Editions): No. 5, Sept, 1953

	GD 2.0	VG 4.0	FN 6.0	VF 8.0	VF/NM 9.0	NM- 9.2
5-Teenage humor	6	12	18	28	34	40

RICKY NELSON (TV)(See Sweethearts V2#42)
Dell Publishing Co.: No. 956, Dec, 1958 - No. 1192, June, 1961 (All photo-c)

	GD 2.0	VG 4.0	FN 6.0	VF 8.0	VF/NM 9.0	NM- 9.2
Four Color 956,998	17	34	51	120	223	325
Four Color 1115,1192: 1192-Manning-a	14	28	42	102	181	260

RIDE, THE (Also see Gun Candy flip-book)
Image Comics: June, 2004 - No. 2, July, 2004 ($2.95, B&W, anthology)

	GD 2.0	VG 4.0	FN 6.0	VF 8.0	VF/NM 9.0	NM- 9.2
1,2: Hughes-c/Wagner-s. 1-Hamner & Stelfreeze-a. 2-Jeanty & Pearson-a						3.00
... Die Valkyrie 1-3 (6/07 - No. 3, 2/08, $2.99) Stelfreeze-a/Wagner-s/Pearson-c						3.00
... Foreign Parts 1 (1/05, $2.95) Dixon-s/Haynes-a; Marz-s/Brunner-a; Pearson-c						3.00
... Halloween Special: The Key to Survival (10/07, $3.50) Tomm Coker-s/a						3.50
... Savannah 1 (4/07, $4.99) s/a by students of Savannah College of Art						5.00
... 2 For the Road 1 (10/04, $2.95) Dixon-s/Hamner & Gregory-a/Johnson-c						3.00
Vol. 1 TPB (2005, $9.99) r/#1,2, Foreign Parts, 2 For the Road; Chaykin intro.						10.00
Vol. 2 TPB (2005, $15.99) r/Gun Candy #1,2 & Die Valkyrie #1-3; sketch pages						16.00

RIDER, THE (Frontier Trail #6; also see Blazing Sixguns I.W. Reprint #10, 11)
Ajax/Farrell Publ. (Four Star Comic Corp.): Mar, 1957 - No. 5, 1958

	GD 2.0	VG 4.0	FN 6.0	VF 8.0	VF/NM 9.0	NM- 9.2
1-Swift Arrow, Lone Rider begin	13	26	39	72	101	130
2-5	8	16	24	42	54	65

RIDERS OF THE PURPLE SAGE (See Zane Grey & Four Color #372)

RIFLEMAN, THE (TV)
Dell Publ. Co./Gold Key No. 13 on: No. 1009, 7-9/59 - No. 12, 7-9/62; No. 13, 11/62 - No. 20, 10/64

	GD 2.0	VG 4.0	FN 6.0	VF 8.0	VF/NM 9.0	NM- 9.2
Four Color 1009 (#1)	21	42	63	152	281	410
2 (1-3/60)	11	22	33	79	140	200
3-Toth-a (4 pgs.)	11	22	33	79	140	200
4-10: 6-Toth-a (4 pgs.)	10	20	30	70	123	175
11-20	8	16	24	54	90	125

NOTE: ***Warren Tufts** a-2-9. All have Chuck Connors photo-c. Photo back c-13-15.*

RIMA, THE JUNGLE GIRL
National Periodical Publications: Apr-May, 1974 - No. 7, Apr-May, 1975

	GD 2.0	VG 4.0	FN 6.0	VF 8.0	VF/NM 9.0	NM- 9.2
1-Origin, part 1 (#1-5: 20¢; 6,7: 25¢)	2	4	6	10	14	18
2-7: 2-4-Origin, parts 2-4. 7-Origin & only app. Space Marshal	1	2	3	5	7	9

NOTE: ***Kubert** c-1-7. **Nino** a-1-7. **Redondo** a-1-7.*

RING OF BRIGHT WATER (See Movie Classics)

RING OF THE NIBELUNG, THE
DC Comics: 1989 - No. 4, 1990 ($4.95, squarebound, 52 pgs., mature readers)

	GD 2.0	VG 4.0	FN 6.0	VF 8.0	VF/NM 9.0	NM- 9.2
1-4: Adapts Wagner cycle of operas, Gil Kane-c/a						5.00

RING OF THE NIBELUNG, THE
Dark Horse Comics: Feb, 2000 - Sept, 2001 ($2.95/$2.99/$5.99, limited series)

	GD 2.0	VG 4.0	FN 6.0	VF 8.0	VF/NM 9.0	NM- 9.2
Vol. 1 (The Rhinegold) 1-4: Adapts Wagner; P. Craig Russell-s/a						3.00
Vol. 2,3: Vol. 2 (The Valkyrie) 1-3: 1-(8/00). Vol. 3 (Siegfried) 1-3: 1-(12/00)						3.00
Vol. 4 (The Twilight of the Gods) 1-3: 1-(6/01)						3.00
4-(9/01, $5.99, 64 pgs.) Conclusion with sketch pages						6.00

RINGO KID, THE (2nd Series)
Marvel Comics Group: Jan, 1970 - No. 23, Nov, 1973; No. 24, Nov, 1975 - No. 30, Nov, 1976

	GD 2.0	VG 4.0	FN 6.0	VF 8.0	VF/NM 9.0	NM- 9.2
1-Williamson-a r-from #10, 1956.	3	6	9	16	23	30
2-11: 2-Severin-c. 11-Last 15¢ issue	2	4	6	9	13	16
12 (52 pg. Giant)	3	6	9	14	19	24
13-20: 13-Wildey-r. 20-Williamson-r/#1	2	4	6	8	10	12
21-30	1	2	3	5	7	9
27,28-(30¢-c variant, limited distribution)(5,7/76)	3	6	9	20	30	40

RINGO KID WESTERN, THE (1st Series) (See Wild Western & Western Trails)
Atlas Comics (HPC)/Marvel Comics: Aug, 1954 - No. 21, Sept, 1957

	GD 2.0	VG 4.0	FN 6.0	VF 8.0	VF/NM 9.0	NM- 9.2
1-Origin; The Ringo Kid begins	30	60	90	174	280	385
2-Black Rider app.; origin/1st app. Ringo's Horse Arab	15	30	45	88	137	185
3-5	12	24	36	67	94	120
6-8-Severin-a(3) each	13	26	39	72	101	130
9,11,12,14-21: 12-Orlando-a (4 pgs.)	10	20	30	54	72	90
10,13-Williamson-a (4 pgs.)	10	20	30	58	79	100

NOTE: ***Berg** a-8. **Maneely** a-1-5, 15, 16(text illos only), 17(4), 18, 20, 21; c-1-6, 8, 13, 15-18, 20. **J. Severin** c-10, 11. **Sinnott** a-1. **Wildey** a-16-18.*

RIN TIN TIN (See March of Comics #163,180,195)

RIN TIN TIN (TV) (...& Rusty #21 on; see Western Roundup under Dell Giants)
Dell Publishing Co./Gold Key: Nov, 1952 - No. 38, May-July, 1961; Nov, 1963 (All Photo-c)

	GD 2.0	VG 4.0	FN 6.0	VF 8.0	VF/NM 9.0	NM- 9.2
Four Color 434 (#1)	14	28	42	102	181	260
Four Color 476,523	8	16	24	56	93	130
4(3-5/54)-10	7	14	21	45	73	100
11-17,19,20	6	12	18	43	69	95
18-(4-5/57) 1st app. of Rusty and the Cavalry of Fort Apache; photo-c	7	14	21	50	83	115
21-38: 36-Toth-a (4 pgs.)	5	10	15	34	55	75
... & Rusty 1 (11/63-Gold Key)	6	12	18	37	59	80

RIO (Also see Eclipse Monthly)
Comico: June, 1987 ($8.95, 64 pgs.)

	GD 2.0	VG 4.0	FN 6.0	VF 8.0	VF/NM 9.0	NM- 9.2
1-Wildey-c/a						9.00

RIO AT BAY
Dark Horse Comics: July, 1992 - No. 2, Aug, 1992 ($2.95, limited series)

	GD 2.0	VG 4.0	FN 6.0	VF 8.0	VF/NM 9.0	NM- 9.2
1,2-Wildey-c/a						3.00

RIO BRAVO (Movie) (See 4 Color #1018)
Dell Publishing Co.: June, 1959

	GD 2.0	VG 4.0	FN 6.0	VF 8.0	VF/NM 9.0	NM- 9.2
Four Color 1018-Toth-a; John Wayne, Dean Martin, & Ricky Nelson photo-c.	22	44	66	157	291	425

RIO CONCHOS (See Movie Comics)

RIOT (Satire)
Atlas Comics (ACI No. 1-5/WPI No. 6): Apr, 1954 - No. 3, Aug, 1954; No. 4, Feb, 1956 - No. 6, June, 1956

	GD 2.0	VG 4.0	FN 6.0	VF 8.0	VF/NM 9.0	NM- 9.2
1-Russ Heath-a	32	64	96	190	305	420
2-Li'l Abner satire by Post	23	46	69	133	214	295
3-Last precode (8/54)	20	40	60	117	186	255
4-Infinity-c; Marilyn Monroe "7 Year Itch" movie satire; Mad Rip-off ads	26	52	78	152	244	335
5-Marilyn Monroe, John Wayne parody; part photo-c	26	52	78	154	247	340
6-Lorna of the Jungle satire by Everett; Dennis the Menace satire-c/story; part photo-c	20	40	60	117	186	255

NOTE: ***Berg** a-3. **Burgos** c-1, 2. **Colan** a-1. **Everett** a-1, 4, 6. **Heath** a-1. **Maneely** a-1, 2, 4-6; c-3, 4, 6. **Post** a-1-4. **Reinman** a-2. **Severin** a-4-6.*

RIOT GEAR
Triumphant Comics: Sept, 1993 - No. 11, July, 1994 ($2.50, serially numbered)

	GD 2.0	VG 4.0	FN 6.0	VF 8.0	VF/NM 9.0	NM- 9.2
1-11: 1-2nd app. Riot Gear. 2-1st app. Rabin. 3,4-Triumphant Unleashed x-over. 3-1st app. Surzar. 4-Death of Captain Tich						2.50
Violent Past 1,2: 1-(2/94, $2.50)						2.50

R.I.P.
TSR, Inc.: 1990 - No. 8, 1991 ($2.95, 44 pgs.)

	GD 2.0	VG 4.0	FN 6.0	VF 8.0	VF/NM 9.0	NM- 9.2
1-8-Based on TSR game						3.00

RIPCLAW (See Cyberforce)
Image Comics (Top Cow Prod.): Apr, 1995 - No. 3, June, 1995 (Limited series)

	GD 2.0	VG 4.0	FN 6.0	VF 8.0	VF/NM 9.0	NM- 9.2
1/2-Gold, 1/2-San Diego ed., 1/2-Chicago ed.	1	3	4	6	8	10
1-3: Brandon Peterson-a(p)						3.00
Special 1 (10/95, $2.50)						2.50

RIPCLAW
Image Comics (Top Cow Prod.): V2#1, Dec, 1995 - No. 6, June, 1996 ($2.50)

	GD 2.0	VG 4.0	FN 6.0	VF 8.0	VF/NM 9.0	NM- 9.2
V2#1-6: 5-Medieval Spawn/Witchblade Preview						2.50
...: Pilot Season 1 (2007, $2.99) Jason Aaron-s/Jorge Lucas-a/Tony Moore-c						3.00

RIPCORD (TV)
Dell Publishing Co.: Mar-May, 1962

	GD 2.0	VG 4.0	FN 6.0	VF 8.0	VF/NM 9.0	NM- 9.2
Four Color 1294	7	14	21	47	76	105

R.I.P.D.

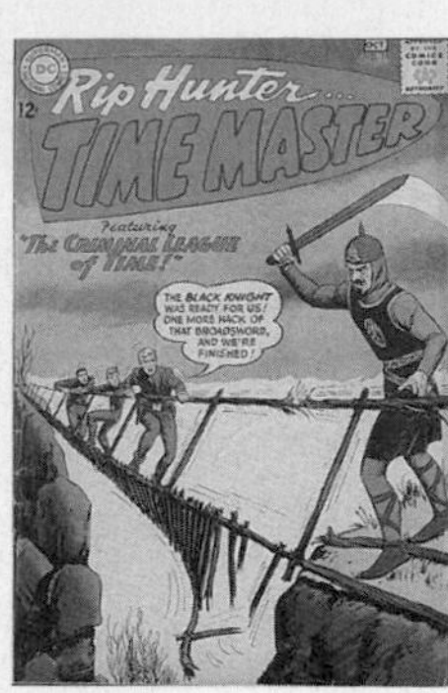

Rip Hunter Time Master #16 © DC

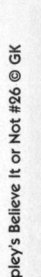

Ripley's Believe It or Not #26 © GK

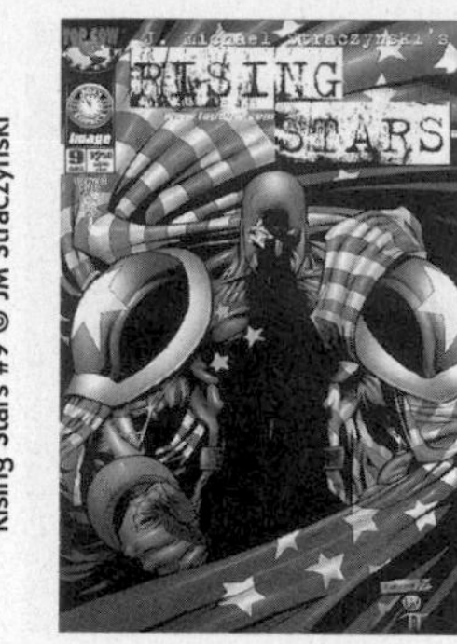

Rising Stars #9 © JM Straczynski

	GD 2.0	VG 4.0	FN 6.0	VF 8.0	VF/NM 9.0	NM- 9.2

Dark Horse Comics: Oct, 1999 - No. 4, Jan, 2000 ($2.95, limited series)

	GD	VG	FN	VF	VF/NM	NM-
1-4						3.00
TPB (2003, $12.95) r/#1-4						13.00

RIP HUNTER TIME MASTER (See Showcase #20, 21, 25, 26 & Time Masters)
National Periodical Publications: Mar-Apr, 1961 - No. 29, Nov-Dec, 1965

	GD	VG	FN	VF	VF/NM	NM-
1-(3-4/61)	50	100	150	413	782	1150
2	24	48	72	185	343	500
3-5: 5-Last 10¢ issue	15	30	45	111	206	300
6,7-Toth-a in each	11	22	33	75	133	190
8-15	9	18	27	60	100	140
16-20: 20-Hitler c/s	7	14	21	47	76	105
21-29: 29-Gil Kane-c	6	12	18	41	66	90

RIP IN TIME (Also see Teenage Mutant Ninja Turtles #5-7)
Fantagor Press: Aug, 1986 - No.5, 1987 ($1.50, B&W)

	GD	VG	FN	VF	VF/NM	NM-
1-5: Corben-c/a in all						3.00

RIP KIRBY (Also see Harvey Comics Hits #57, & Street Comix)
David McKay Publications: 1948

	GD	VG	FN	VF	VF/NM	NM-
Feature Books 51,54: Raymond-c; 51-Origin	35	70	105	203	327	450

RIPLEY'S BELIEVE IT OR NOT! (See Ace Comics, All-American Comics, Mystery Comics Digest #1, 4, 7, 10, 13, 16, 19, 22, 25)

RIPLEY'S BELIEVE IT OR NOT!
Harvey Publications: Sept, 1953 - No. 4, March, 1954

	GD	VG	FN	VF	VF/NM	NM-
1-Powell-a	14	28	42	76	108	140
2-4	10	20	30	54	72	90

RIPLEY'S BELIEVE IT OR NOT! (Continuation of Ripleys'...True Ghost Stories & Ripley's...True War Stories)
Gold Key: No. 4, April, 1967 - No. 94, Feb, 1980

	GD	VG	FN	VF	VF/NM	NM-
4-Photo-c; McWilliams-a	4	8	12	24	37	50
5-Subtitled "True War Stories"; Evans-a; 1st Jeff Jones-a in comics? (2 pgs.)	4	8	12	24	37	50
6-10: 6-McWilliams-a. 10-Evans-a(2)	3	6	9	20	30	40
11-20: 15-Evans-a	3	6	9	16	23	30
21-30	2	4	6	13	18	22
31-38,40-60	2	4	6	9	13	16
39-Crandall-a	2	4	6	10	14	18
61-73	1	3	4	6	8	10
74,77-83-(52 pgs.)	2	4	6	9	13	16
75,76,84-94	1	2	3	5	6	8
Story Digest Mag. 1(6/70)-4-3/4x6-1/2", 148pp.	5	10	15	34	55	75

NOTE: ***Evanish** art by **Luiz Dominguez** #22-25, 27, 30, 31, 40. **Jeff Jones** a-5(2 pgs.). **McWilliams** a-65, 66, 70, 89. **Orlando** a-8. **Sparling** c-68. Reprints-74, 77-84, 87 (part); 91, 93 (all). **Williamson, Wood** a-80r/#1.*

RIPLEY'S BELIEVE IT OR NOT!
Dark Horse Comics: May, 2002 - No. 4 ($2.99, B&W, limited series)

	GD	VG	FN	VF	VF/NM	NM-
1-3-Nord-c/a. 1-Stories of Amelia Earhart & D.B. Cooper						3.00

RIPLEY'S BELIEVE IT OR NOT! TRUE GHOST STORIES (Along with Ripley's...True War Stories, the three issues together precede the 1967 series that starts its numbering with #4) (Also see Dan Curtis)
Gold Key: June, 1965 - No. 2, Oct, 1966

	GD	VG	FN	VF	VF/NM	NM-
1-Williamson, Wood & Evans-a; photo-c	7	14	21	49	80	110
2-Orlando, McWilliams-a; photo-c	4	8	12	26	41	55
Mini-Comic 1(1976-3-1/4x6-1/2")	2	4	6	8	11	14
11186(1977)-Golden Press; ($1.95, 224 pgs.)-All-r	4	8	12	24	37	50
11401(3/79)-Golden Press; ($1.00, 96 pgs.)-All-r	3	6	9	15	21	26

RIPLEY'S BELIEVE IT OR NOT! TRUE WAR STORIES (Along with Ripley's...True Ghost Stories, the three issues together precede the 1967 series that starts its numbering with #4)
Gold Key: Nov, 1965 (Aug, 1965 in indicia)

	GD	VG	FN	VF	VF/NM	NM-
1-No Williamson-a	4	8	12	26	41	55

RIPLEY'S BELIEVE IT OR NOT! TRUE WEIRD
Ripley Enterprises: June, 1966 - No. 2, Aug, 1966 (B&W Magazine)

	GD	VG	FN	VF	VF/NM	NM-
1,2-Comic stories & text	3	6	9	18	27	35

RISE OF APOCALYPSE
Marvel Comics: Oct, 1996 - No. 4, Jan, 1997 ($1.95, limited series)

	GD	VG	FN	VF	VF/NM	NM-
1-4: Adam Pollina-c/a						2.50

RISING STARS
Image Comics (Top Cow): Mar, 1999 - No. 24, Mar, 2005 ($2.50/$2.99)

	GD	VG	FN	VF	VF/NM	NM-
Preview-(3/99, $5.00) Straczynski-s						6.00
0-(6/00, $2.50) Gary Frank-a/c						2.50
1/2-(8/01, $2.95) Anderson-c; art & sketch pages by Zanier						3.00
1-Four covers; Keu Cha-c/a	1	2	3	5	7	9
1-($10.00) Gold Editions-four covers						10.00
1-($50.00) Holofoil-c						50.00
2-7: 5-7-Zanier & Lashley-a(p)	1	2	3	5	7	9
8-23: 8-13-Zanier & Lashley-a(p). 14-Immonen-a. 15-Flip book B&W preview of Universe. 15-23-Brent Anderson-a						3.00
24-($3.99) Series finale; Anderson-a/c						4.00
Born In Fire TPB (11/00, $19.95) r/#1-8; foreword by Neil Gaiman						20.00
Power TPB (2002, $19.95) r/#9-16						20.00
Prelude-(10/00, $2.95) Cha-a/Lashley-c						3.00
...: Visitations (2002, $8.99) r/#0, 1/2, Preview; new Anderson-c; cover gallery						9.00
Vol. 3: Fire and Ash TPB (2005, $19.99) r/#17-24; design pages & cover gallery						20.00
Vol. 4 TPB (2006, $19.99) r/Rising Stars Bright #1-3 and Voices of the Dead #1-6						20.00
Vol. 5 TPB (2007, $16.99) r/Rising Stars: Untouchable #1-5 and ...: Visitations						17.00
Wizard #0-(3/99) Wizard supplement; Straczynski-s						2.50
Wizard #1/2						10.00

RISING STARS BRIGHT
Image Comics (Top Cow): Mar, 2003 - No. 3, May, 2003 ($2.99, limited series)

	GD	VG	FN	VF	VF/NM	NM-
1-3-Avery-s/Jurgens & Gorder-a/Beck-c						3.00

RISING STARS: UNTOUCHABLE
Image Comics (Top Cow): Mar, 2006 - No. 5, July, 2006 ($2.99, limited series)

	GD	VG	FN	VF	VF/NM	NM-
1-5-Avery-s/Anderson-a						3.00

RISING STARS: VOICES OF THE DEAD
Image Comics (Top Cow): June, 2005 - No. 6, Dec, 2005 ($2.99, limited series)

	GD	VG	FN	VF	VF/NM	NM-
1-6-Avery-s/Staz Johnson-a						3.00

RIVERDALE HIGH (Archie's... #7,8)
Archie Comics: Aug, 1990 - No. 8, Oct, 1991 ($1.00, bi-monthly)

	GD	VG	FN	VF	VF/NM	NM-
1						4.00
2-8						3.00

RIVER FEUD (See Zane Grey & Four Color #484)

RIVETS
Dell Publishing Co.: No. 518, Nov, 1953

	GD	VG	FN	VF	VF/NM	NM-
Four Color 518	4	8	12	24	37	50

RIVETS (A dog)
Argo Publ.: Jan, 1956 - No. 3, May, 1956

	GD	VG	FN	VF	VF/NM	NM-
1-Reprints Sunday & daily newspaper strips	6	12	18	31	38	45
2,3	5	10	15	22	26	30

ROACHMILL
Blackthorne Publ.: Dec, 1986 - No. 6, Oct, 1987 ($1.75, B&W)

	GD	VG	FN	VF	VF/NM	NM-
1-6						2.50

ROACHMILL
Dark Horse Comics: May, 1988 - No. 10, Dec, 1990 ($1.75, B&W)

	GD	VG	FN	VF	VF/NM	NM-
1-10: 10-Contains trading cards						2.50

ROAD RUNNER (See Beep Beep, the...)

ROAD TO PERDITION (Inspired the 2002 Tom Hanks/Paul Newman movie) (Also see On the Road to Perdition)
DC Comics/Paradox Press: 1998, 2002 ($13.95, B&W paperback graphic novel)

	GD	VG	FN	VF	VF/NM	NM-
nn-(1st printing) Max Allan Collins-s/Richard Piers Rayner-a						30.00
2nd & 3rd printings (2002, $13.95)						14.00
Movie photo cover edition (2002)						14.00

ROADTRIP
Oni Press: Aug, 2000 ($2.95, B&W, one-shot)

	GD	VG	FN	VF	VF/NM	NM-
1-Reprints Judd Winick's back-up stories from Oni Double Feature #9,10						3.00

ROADWAYS
Cult Press: May, 1994 ($2.75, B&W, limited series)

	GD	VG	FN	VF	VF/NM	NM-
1						2.75

ROARIN' RICK'S RARE BIT FIENDS
King Hell Press: July, 1994 - No. 21, Aug, 1996 ($2.95, B&W, mature)

	GD	VG	FN	VF	VF/NM	NM-
1-21: Rick Veitch-c/a/scripts in all. 20-(5/96). 21-(8/96)-Reads Subtleman #1 on cover						3.00
Rabid Eye: The Dream Art of Rick Veitch ($14.95, B&W, TPB)-r/#1-8 & the appendix from #12						15.00
Pocket Universe (6/96, $14.95, B&W, TPB)-Reprints						15.00

ROBERT E. HOWARD'S CONAN THE BARBARIAN
Marvel Comics: 1983 ($2.50, 68 pgs., Baxter paper)

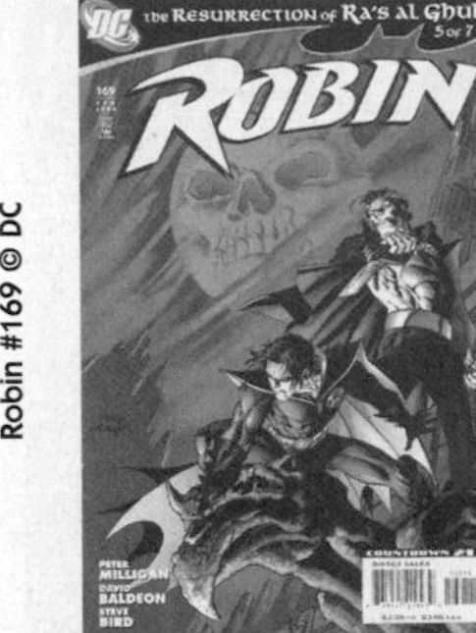

Robin #169 © DC

Robin Hood Tales #11 © DC

Robin: Year One #2 © DC

GD 2.0 | VG 4.0 | FN 6.0 | VF 8.0 | VF/NM 9.0 | NM- 9.2

1-r/Savage Tales #2,3 by Smith, c-r/Conan #21 by Smith. 4.00

ROBERT LOUIS STEVENSON'S KIDNAPPED (See Kidnapped)

ROBIN (See Aurora, Birds of Prey, Detective Comics #38, New Teen Titans, Robin II, Robin III, Robin 3000, Star Spangled Comics #65, Teen Titans & Young Justice)

ROBIN (See Batman #457)
DC Comics: Jan, 1991 - No. 5, May, 1991 ($1.00, limited series)

1-Free poster by N. Adams; Bolland-c on all 4.00
1-2nd & 3rd printings (without poster) 2.50
2-5 3.00
2-2nd printing 2.50
Annual 1,2 (1992-93, $2.50, 68 pgs.): 1-Grant/Wagner scripts; Sam Kieth-c.
2-Intro Razorsharp; Jim Balent-c(p) 3.00

ROBIN (See Detective #668)
DC Comics: Nov, 1993 - Present ($1.50/$1.95/$1.99/$2.25)

1-($2.95)-Collector's edition w/foil embossed-c; 1st app. Robin's car, The Redbird; Azrael as Batman app. 4.00
1-Newsstand ed. 2.50
0,2-49,51-66-Regular editions: 3-5-The Spoiler app. 6-The Huntress-c/story cont'd from Showcase '94 #5. 7-Knightquest: The Conclusion w/new Batman (Azrael) vs. Bruce Wayne. 8-KnightsEnd Pt. 5. 9-KnightsEnd Aftermath; Batman-c & app. 10-(9/94)-Zero Hour. 0-(10/94). 11-(11/94). 25-Green Arrow-c/app. 26-Batman app. 27-Contagion Pt. 3; Catwoman-c/app; Penguin & Azrael app. 28-Contagion Pt. 11. 29-Penguin app. 31-Wildcat-c/app. 32-Legacy Pt. 3. 33-Legacy Pt. 7. 35-Final Night. 46-Genesis. 52,53-Cataclysm pt. 7, conclusion. 55-Green Arrow app. 62-64-Flash-c/app. 2.50
14 ($2.50)-Embossed-c; Troika Pt. 4 3.00
50-($2.95)-Lady Shiva & King Snake app. 3.00
67-74,76-78: 67-72-No Man's Land 2.50
75-($2.95) 3.00
79-97: 79-Begin $2.25-c, Green Arrow app. 86-Pander Bros.-a 2.50
98,99-Bruce Wayne: Murderer x-over pt. 6, 11 2.50
100-($3.50) Last Dixon-s 3.50
101-147: 101-Young Justice x-over. 106-Kevin Lau c. 121,122-Willingham-s/Mays-a. 125-Tim Drake quits. 126-Spoiler becomes the new Robin. 129-131-War Games. 132-Robin moves to Bludhaven, Batgirl app. 138-Begin $2.50-c. 139-McDaniel-a begins. 146-147-Teen Titans app. 2.50
148-174: 148-One Year Later; new costume. 150-Begin $2.99-c. 152,153-Boomerang app. 168,169-Resurrection of Ra's al Ghul x-over. 174 Spoiler unmasked 3.00
175,176-Batman R.I.P. x-over 3.00
#1,000,000 (11/98) 853rd Century x-over 2.50
Annual 3-5: 3-(1994, $2.95)-Elseworlds story. 4-(1995, $2.95)-Year One story. 5-(1996, $2.95)-Legends of the Dead Earth story 3.00
Annual 6 (1997, $3.95)-Pulp Heroes story. 4.00
Annual 7 (12/07, $3.99)-Pearson-c/a; prelude to Resurrection of Ra's al Ghul x-over 4.00
.../Argent 1 (2/98, $1.95) Argent (Teen Titans) app. 2.50
.../Batgirl: Fresh Blood TPB (2005, $12.99) r/#132,133 & Batgirl #58,59 13.00
...: Days of Fire and Madness (2006, $12.99, TPB) r/#140-145 13.00
...Eighty-Page Giant 1 (9/00, $5.95) Chuck Dixon-s/Diego Barreto-a 6.00
...: Flying Solo (2000, $12.95, TPB) r/#1-6, Showcase '94 #5,6 13.00
...Plus 1 (12/96, $2.95) Impulse-c/app.; Waid-s 3.00
...Plus 2 (12/97, $2.95) Fang (Scare Tactics) app. 3.00
.../Spoiler Special 1 (8/08, $3.99) Follows Spoiler's return in Robin #174; Dixon-s 4.00
...: Teenage Wasteland (2007, $17.99, TPB) r/#154-162 18.00
...: The Big Leagues (2008, $12.99, TPB) r/#163-167 13.00
...: Unmasked (2004, $12.95, TPB) r/#121-125; Pearson-c 13.00
...: Wanted (2007, $12.99, TPB) r/#148-153 13.00

ROBIN: A HERO REBORN
DC Comics: 1991 ($4.95, squarebound, trade paperback)

nn-r/Batman #455-457 & Robin #1-5; Bolland-c 5.00

ROBIN HOOD (See The Advs. of..., Brave and the Bold, Four Color #413, 669, King Classics, Movie Comics & Power Record Comics)

ROBIN HOOD (...& His Merry Men, The Illustrated Story of...) (See Classic Comics #7 & Classics Giveaways, 12/44)

ROBIN HOOD (Disney)
Dell Publishing Co.: No. 413, Aug, 1952; No. 669, Dec, 1955

	GD	VG	FN	VF	VF/NM	NM-
Four Color 413-(1st Disney movie Four Color book)(8/52)-Photo-c	9	18	27	65	113	160
Four Color 669 (12/55)-Reprints #413 plus photo-c	6	12	18	37	59	80

ROBIN HOOD (Adventures of... #7, 8)
Magazine Enterprises (Sussex Pub. Co.): No. 52, Nov, 1955 - No. 6, Jun, 1957

	GD	VG	FN	VF	VF/NM	NM-
52 (#1)-Origin Robin Hood & Sir Gallant of the Round Table	15	30	45	85	130	175
53 (#2), 3-6: 6-Richard Greene photo-c (TV)	12	24	36	67	94	120
I.W. Reprint #1,2,9: 1-r/#3. 2-r/#4. 9-r/#52 (1963)	2	4	6	9	13	16
Super Reprint #10,15: 10-r/#53. 15-r/#5	2	4	6	9	13	16

NOTE: *Bolle a-in all; c-52. Powell a-6.*

ROBIN HOOD (Not Disney)
Dell Publishing Co.: May-July, 1963 (one-shot)

	GD	VG	FN	VF	VF/NM	NM-
1	3	6	9	16	23	30

ROBIN HOOD (Disney) (Also see Best of Walt Disney)
Western Publishing Co.: 1973 ($1.50, 8-1/2x11", 52 pgs., cardboard-c)

	GD	VG	FN	VF	VF/NM	NM-
96151- "Robin Hood", based on movie, 96152- "The Mystery of Sherwood Forest", 96153- "In King Richard's Service", 96154- "The Wizard's Ring" each....	3	6	9	16	22	28

ROBIN HOOD
Eclipse Comics: July, 1991 - No. 3, Dec, 1991 ($2.50, limited series)

1-3: Timothy Truman layouts 2.50

ROBIN HOOD AND HIS MERRY MEN (Formerly Danger & Adventure)
Charlton Comics: No. 28, Apr, 1956 - No. 38, Aug, 1958

	GD	VG	FN	VF	VF/NM	NM-
28	10	20	30	54	72	90
29-37	8	16	24	42	54	65
38-Ditko-a (5 pgs.); Rocke-c	14	28	42	76	108	140

ROBIN HOOD TALES (Published by National Periodical #7 on)
Quality Comics Group (Comic Magazines): Feb, 1956 - No. 6, Nov-Dec, 1956

	GD	VG	FN	VF	VF/NM	NM-
1-All have Baker/Cuidera-c	32	64	96	186	298	410
2-6-Matt Baker-a	30	60	90	174	280	385

ROBIN HOOD TALES (Cont'd from Quality series)(See Brave & the Bold #5)
National Periodical Publ.: No. 7, Jan-Feb, 1957 - No. 14, Mar-Apr, 1958

	GD	VG	FN	VF	VF/NM	NM-
7-All have Andru/Esposito-c	36	72	108	212	341	470
8-14	30	60	90	174	280	385

ROBINSON CRUSOE (See King Classics & Power Record Comics)
Dell Publishing Co.: Nov-Jan, 1963-64

	GD	VG	FN	VF	VF/NM	NM-
1	3	6	9	15	21	26

ROBIN II (The Joker's Wild)
DC Comics: Oct, 1991 - No. 4, Dec, 1991 ($1.50, mini-series)

1-(Direct sales, $1.50)-With 4 diff.-c; same hologram on each 3.00
1-(Newsstand, $1.00)-No hologram; 1 version 2.50
1-Collector's set ($10.00)-Contains all 5 versions bagged with hologram trading card inside 12.00
2-(Direct sales, $1.50)-With 3 different-c 2.50
2-4-(Newsstand, $1.00)-1 version of each 2.50
2-Collector's set ($8.00)-Contains all 4 versions bagged with hologram trading card inside 9.00
3-(Direct sale, $1.50)-With 2 different-c 2.50
3-Collector's set ($6.00)-Contains all 3 versions bagged with hologram trading card inside 7.00
4-(Direct sales, $1.50)-Only one version 2.50
4-Collector's set ($4.00)-Contains both versions bagged with Bat-Signal hologram trading card 5.00
Multi-pack (All four issues w/hologram sticker) 8.00
Deluxe Complete Set ($30.00)-Contains all 14 versions of #1-4 plus a new hologram trading card; numbered & limited to 25,000; comes with slipcase & 2 acid free backing boards 35.00

ROBIN III: CRY OF THE HUNTRESS
DC Comics: Dec, 1992 - No. 6, Mar, 1993 (Limited series)

1-6 ($2.50, collector's ed.)-Polybagged w/movement enhanced-c plus mini-poster of newsstand-c by Zeck 3.00
1-6 ($1.25, newsstand ed.): All have Zeck-c 2.50

ROBIN 3000
DC Comics (Elseworlds): 1992 - No. 2, 1992 ($4.95, mini-series, 52 pgs.)

1,2-Foil logo; Russell-c/a 5.00

ROBIN: YEAR ONE
DC Comics: 2000 - No. 4, 2001 ($4.95, square-bound, limited series)

1-4: Earliest days of Robin's career; Javier Pulido-c/a. 2,4-Two-Face app. 5.00
TPB (2002, $14.95) r/#1-4 15.00

ROBOCOP
Marvel Comics: Oct, 1987 ($2.00, B&W, magazine, one-shot)

R.O.B.O.T. Battalion 2050 #1 © ECL

Robotech The Macross Saga #4 © Comico

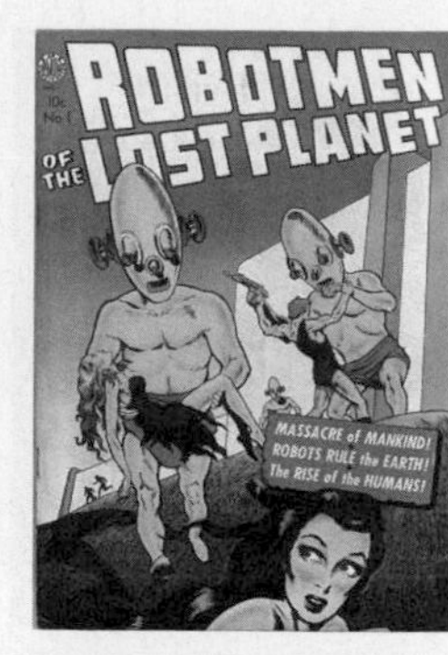

Robotmen of the Lost Planet #1 © AVON

GD 2.0 | VG 4.0 | FN 6.0 | VF 8.0 | VF/NM 9.0 | NM- 9.2

1-Movie adaptation 4.00

ROBOCOP (Also see Dark Horse Comics)
Marvel Comics: Mar, 1990 - No. 23, Jan, 1992 ($1.50)
1-Based on movie 3.00
2-23 2.50
nn (7/90, $4.95, 52 pgs.)-r/B&W magazine in color; adapts 1st movie 5.00

ROBOCOP (FRANK MILLER'S...) (Also see Promotional Comics section for FCBD Ed.)
Avatar Press: July, 2003 - No. 9, Jan, 2006 ($3.50/$3.99, limited series)
1-9-Frank Miller-s/Juan Ryp-a. 1-Three covers by Miller, Ryp, and Barrows. 2-Two covers 4.00

ROBOCOP: MORTAL COILS
Dark Horse Comics: Sept, 1993 - No. 4, Dec, 1993 ($2.50, limited series)
1-4: 1,2-Cago painted-c 2.50

ROBOCOP: PRIME SUSPECT
Dark Horse Comics: Oct, 1992 - No. 4, Jan, 1993 ($2.50, limited series)
1-4: 1,3-Nelson painted-c. 2,4-Bolton painted-c 2.50

ROBOCOP: ROULETTE
Dark Horse Comics: Dec, 1993 - No. 4, 1994 ($2.50, limited series)
1-4: 1,3-Nelson painted-c. 2,4-Bolton painted-c 2.50

ROBOCOP 2
Marvel Comics: Aug, 1990 ($2.25, B&W, magazine, 68 pgs.)
1-Adapts movie sequel 2.50

ROBOCOP 2
Marvel Comics: Aug, 1990; Late Aug, 1990 - #3, Late Sept, 1990 ($1.00, limited series)
nn-(8/90, $4.95, 68 pgs., color)-Same contents as B&W magazine 5.00
1: #1-3 reprint no number issue 3.00
2,3: 2-Guice-c(i) 2.50

ROBOCOP 3
Dark Horse Comics: July, 1993 - No. 3, Nov, 1993 ($2.50, limited series)
1-3: Nelson painted-c; Nguyen-a(p) 2.50

ROBOCOP VERSUS THE TERMINATOR
Dark Horse Comics: Sept, 1992 - No. 4, 1992 (Dec.) ($2.50, limited series)
1-4: Miller scripts & Simonson-c/a in all 3.00
1-Platinum Edition 6.00
NOTE: *All contain a different Robocop cardboard cut-out stand-up.*

ROBO DOJO
DC Comics (WildStorm): Apr, 2002 - No. 6, Sept, 2002 ($2.95, limited series)
1-6-Wolfman-s 3.00

ROBO-HUNTER (Also see Sam Slade...)
Eagle Comics: Apr, 1984 - No. 5, 1984 ($1.00)
1-5-2000 A.D. 2.50

R.O.B.O.T. BATTALION 2050
Eclipse Comics: Mar, 1988 ($2.00, B&W, one-shot)
1 2.50

ROBOT COMICS
Renegade Press: No. 0, June, 1987 ($2.00, B&W, one-shot)
0-Bob Burden story & art 2.50

ROBOTECH
Antarctic Press: Mar, 1997 - No. 11, Nov, 1998 ($2.95)
1-11, Annual 1 (4/98, $2.95) 3.00
...Class Reunion (12/98, $3.95, B&W) 4.00
...Escape (5/98, $2.95, B&W), ...Final Fire (12/98, $2.95, B&W) 3.00

ROBOTECH
DC Comics (WildStorm): No. 0, Feb, 2003 - No. 6, Jul, 2003 ($2.50/$2.95, limited series)
0-Tommy Yune-s; art by Jim Lee, Garza, Bermejo and others; pin-up pages by various 2.50
1-6 ($2.95)-Long Vo-a 3.00
...: From the Stars (2003, $9.95, digest-size) r/#0-6 & Sourcebook 10.00
... Sourcebook (3/03, $2.95) pin-ups and info on characters and mecha; art by various 3.00

ROBOTECH: COVERT-OPS
Antarctic Press: Aug, 1998 - No. 2, Sept, 1998 ($2.95, B&W, limited series)
1,2-Gregory Lane-s/a 3.00

ROBOTECH DEFENDERS
DC Comics: Mar, 1985 - No. 2, Apr, 1985 (Mini-series)
1,2 3.00

GD 2.0 | VG 4.0 | FN 6.0 | VF 8.0 | VF/NM 9.0 | NM- 9.2

ROBOTECH IN 3-D (TV)
Comico: Aug, 1987 ($2.50)
1-Steacy painted-c 4.00

ROBOTECH: INVASION
DC Comics (WildStorm): Feb, 2004 - No. 5, July, 2004 ($2.95, limited series)
1-5-Faerber & Yune-s/Miyazawa & Dogan-a 3.00

ROBOTECH: LOVE AND WAR
DC Comics (WildStorm): Aug, 2003 - No. 6, Jan, 2004 ($2.95, limited series)
1-6-Long Vo & Charles Park-a/Faerber & Yune-s. 2-Variant-c by Warren 3.00

ROBOTECH MASTERS (TV)
Comico: July, 1985 - No. 23, Apr, 1988 ($1.50)
1-23 3.00

ROBOTECH: PRELUDE TO THE SHADOW CHRONICLES
DC Comics (WildStorm): Dec, 2005 - No. 5, Mar, 2006 ($3.50, limited series)
1-5-Yune-s/Dogan & Udon Studios-a 3.50

ROBOTECH: SENTINELS - RUBICON
Antarctic Press: July, 1998 ($2.95, B&W)
1 3.00

ROBOTECH SPECIAL
Comico: May, 1988 ($2.50, one-shot, 44 pgs.)
1-Steacy wraparound-c; partial photo-c 4.00

ROBOTECH THE GRAPHIC NOVEL
Comico: Aug, 1986 ($5.95, 8-1/2x11", 52 pgs.)
1-Origin SDF-1; intro T.R. Edwards, Steacy-c/a; 2nd printing also exists (12/86) 7.00

ROBOTECH: THE MACROSS SAGA (TV)(Formerly Macross)
Comico: No. 2, Feb, 1985 - No. 36, Feb, 1989 ($1.50)
2-10 4.00
11-36: 12,17-Ken Steacy painted-c. 26-Begin $1.75-c. 35,36-($1.95) 3.00
Volume 1-4 TPB (WildStorm, 2003, $14.95, 5-3/4" x 8-1/4")1-Reprints #2-6 & Macross #1. 2- r/#7-12. 3-r/#13-18. 4-r/#19-24 15.00

ROBOTECH: THE NEW GENERATION
Comico: July, 1985 - No. 25, July, 1988
1-25 3.00

ROBOTECH: VERMILION
Antarctic Press: Mar, 1997 - No. 4, ($2.95, B&W, limited series)
1-4 3.00

ROBOTECH: WINGS OF GIBRALTAR
Antarctic Press: Aug, 1998 - No. 2, Sept, 1998 ($2.95, B&W, limited series)
1,2-Lee Duhig-s/a 3.00

ROBOTIX
Marvel Comics: Feb, 1986 (75¢, one-shot)
1-Based on toy 3.00

ROBOTMEN OF THE LOST PLANET (Also see Space Thrillers)
Avon Periodicals: 1952 (Also see Strange Worlds #19)
1-McCann-a (3 pgs.); Fawcette-a 113 226 339 712 1206 1700

ROB ROY
Dell Publishing Co.: 1954 (Disney-Movie)
Four Color 544-Manning-a, photo-c 7 14 21 50 83 115

ROCK, THE (WWF Wrestling)
Chaos! Comics: June, 2001 ($2.99, one-shot)
1-Photo-c; Grant-s/Neves-a 3.00

ROCK & ROLL HIGH SCHOOL
Roger Corman's Cosmic Comics: Oct, 1995 ($2.50)
1-Bob Fingerman scripts 2.50

ROCK AND ROLLO (Formerly TV Teens)
Charlton Comics: V2#14, Oct, 1957 - No. 19, Sept, 1958
V2#14-19 6 12 18 31 38 45

ROCK COMICS
Landgraphic Publ.: Jul/Aug, 1979 ($1.25, tabloid size, 28 pgs.)
1-N. Adams-c; Thor(not Marvel's) story by Adams 3 6 9 14 19 24

ROCKET COMICS
Hillman Periodicals: Mar, 1940 - No. 3, May, 1940

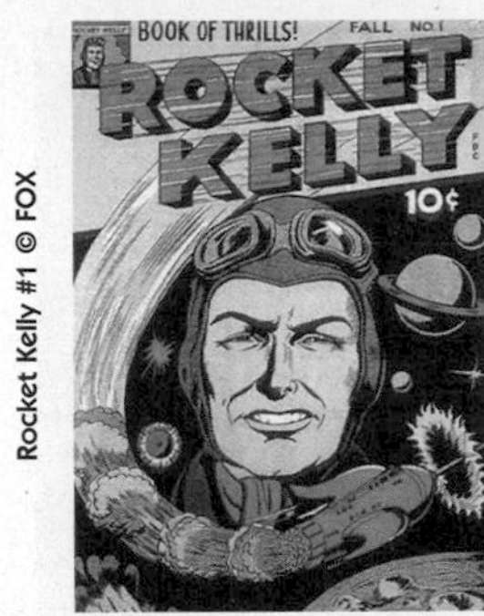

Rocket Kelly #1 © FOX

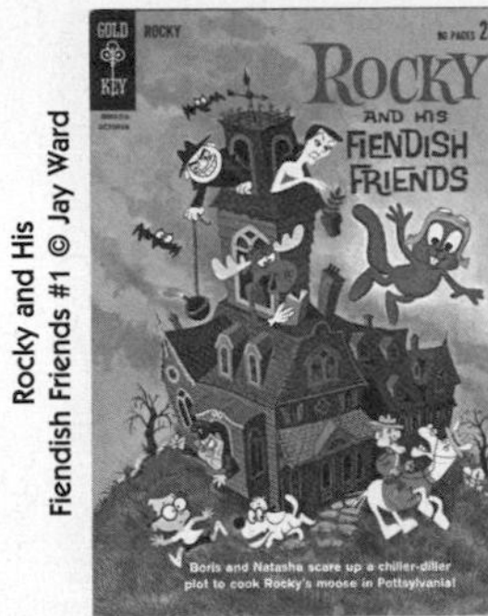

Rocky and His Fiendish Friends #1 © Jay Ward

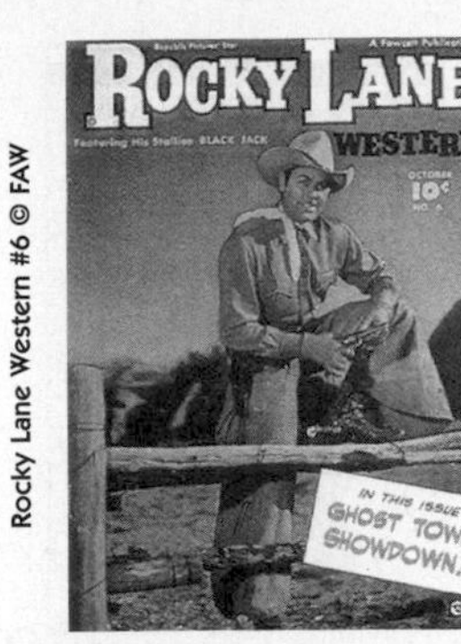

Rocky Lane Western #6 © FAW

GD 2.0 VG 4.0 FN 6.0 VF 8.0 VF/NM 9.0 NM- 9.2

1-Rocket Riley, Red Roberts the Electro Man (origin), The Phantom Ranger, The Steel Shark, The Defender, Buzzard Barnes and his Sky Devils, Lefty Larson, & The Defender, the Man with a Thousand Faces begin (1st app. of each); all have Rocket Riley-c 257 514 771 1619 2735 3850
2,3 125 250 345 788 1332 1875

ROCKETEER, THE (See Eclipse Graphic Album Series, Pacific Presents & Starslayer)

ROCKETEER ADVENTURE MAGAZINE, THE
Comico/Dark Horse Comics No. 3: July, 1988 ($2.00); No. 2, July, 1989 ($2.75); No. 3, Jan, 1995 ($2.95)
1-(7/88, $2.00)-Dave Stevens-c/a in all; Kaluta back-up-a; 1st app. Jonas (character based on The Shadow) 1 2 3 5 7 9
2-(7/89, $2.75)-Stevens/Dorman painted-c 6.00
3-(1/95, $2.95)-Includes pinups by Stevens, Gulacy, Plunkett, & Mignola 3.50
Volume 2-(9/96, $9.95, magazine size TPB)-Reprints #1-3 10.00

ROCKETEER SPECIAL EDITION, THE
Eclipse Comics: Nov, 1984 ($1.50, Baxter paper)(Chapter 5 of Rocketeer serial)
1-Stevens-c/a; Kaluta back-c; pin-ups inside 2 4 6 8 10 12
NOTE: *Originally intended to be published in Pacific Presents.*

ROCKETEER: THE OFFICIAL MOVIE ADAPTATION, THE
W. D. Publications (Disney): 1991
nn-($5.95, 68 pgs.)-Squarebound deluxe edition 6.00
nn-($2.95, 68 pgs.)-Stapled regular edition 3.00
3-D Comic Book (1991, $7.98, 52 pgs.) 8.00

ROCKET KELLY (See The Bouncer, Green Mask #10); becomes Li'l Pan #6)
Fox Feature Syndicate: 1944; Fall, 1945 - No. 5, Oct-Nov, 1946
nn (1944), 1 35 70 105 203 327 450
2-The Puppeteer app. (costumed hero) 24 48 72 140 225 310
3-5: 5-(#5 on cover, #4 inside) 21 42 63 125 200 275

ROCKETMAN (Strange Fantasy #2 on) (See Hello Pal & Scoop Comics)
Ajax/Farrell Publications: June, 1952 (Strange Stories of the Future)
1-Rocketman & Cosmo 40 80 120 240 390 540

ROCKET RACCOON (Also see Incredible Hulk #271)
Marvel Comics: May, 1985 - No. 4, Aug, 1985 (color, limited series)
1-4: Mignola-a 2.50

ROCKET SHIP X
Fox Features Syndicate: September, 1951; 1952
1 62 124 186 391 658 925
1952 (nn, nd, no publ.)-Edited 1951-c (exist?) 39 78 117 230 370 510

ROCKET TO ADVENTURE LAND (See Pixie Puzzle...)

ROCKET TO THE MOON
Avon Periodicals: 1951
nn-Orlando-c/a; adapts Otis Adelbert Kline's "Maza of the Moon" 113 226 339 712 1206 1700

ROCK FANTASY COMICS
Rock Fantasy Comics: Dec, 1989 - No. 16?, 1991 ($2.25/$3.00, B&W)(No cover price)
1-Pink Floyd part 1 5.00
1-2nd printing ($3.00-c) 3.00
2,3: 2-Rolling Stones #1. 3-Led Zeppelin #1 4.00
2,3: 2nd printings ($3.00-c, 1/90 & 2/90) 3.00
4-Stevie Nicks Not published
5-Monstrosities of Rock #1; photo back-c 4.00
5-2nd printing ($3.00, 3/90 indicia, 2/90-c) 3.00
6-9,11-15,17,18: 6-Guns n' Roses #1 (1st & 2nd printings, 3/90)-Begin $3.00-c. 7-Sex Pistols #1. 8-Alice Cooper; not published. 9-Van Halen #1; photo back-c. 11-Jimi Hendrix #1; wraparound-c 3.00
10-Kiss #1; photo back-c 2 4 6 8 10 12
16-($5.00, 68 pgs.)-The Great Gig in the Sky(Floyd) 5.00

ROCK HAPPENING (See Bunny and Harvey Pop Comics:...)

ROCK N' ROLL COMICS
DC Comics: Dec./Jan 1956 (ashcan)
nn-Ashcan comic, not distributed to newsstands, only for in house use (no known sales)

ROCK N' ROLL COMICS
Revolutionary Comics: Jun, 1989 - No. 65 ($1.50/$1.95/$2.50, B&W/col. #15 on)
1-Guns N' Roses 1 2 3 5 6 8
1-2nd thru 7th printings. 7th printing (full color w/new-c/a) 2.50
2-Metallica 1 3 4 6 8 10
2-2nd thru 6th printings (6th in color) 2.50
3-Bon Jovi (no reprints) 1 2 3 5 6 8
4-8,10-65: 4-Motley Crue(2nd printing only, 1st destroyed). 5-Def Leppard (2 printings). 6-Rolling Stones(4 printings). 7-The Who (3 printings). 8-Skid Row; not published. 10-Warrant/Whitesnake(2 printings; 1st has 2 diff.-c). 11-Aerosmith (2 printings?). 12-New Kids on the Block(2 printings). 12-3rd printing; rewritten & titled NKOTB Hate Book. 13-Led Zeppelin. 14-Sex Pistols. 15-Poison; 1st color issue. 16-Van Halen. 17-Madonna. 18-Alice Cooper. 19-Public Enemy/2 Live Crew. 20-Queensryche/Tesla. 21-Prince? 22-AC/DC; begin $2.50-c. 23-Living Colour. 24-Anthrax. 29-Ozzy. 45,46-Grateful Dead. 49-Rush. 50,51-Bob Dylan. 56-David Bowie 5.00
9-Kiss 2 4 6 8 10 12
9-2nd & 3rd printings 2.50
NOTE: *Most issues were reprinted except #3. Later reprints are in color. #8 was not released.*

ROCKO'S MODERN LIFE (TV)
Marvel Comics: June, 1994 - No. 7, Dec, 1994 ($1.95) (Nickelodeon cartoon)
1-7 2.50

ROCKY AND HIS FIENDISH FRIENDS (TV)(Bullwinkle)
Gold Key: Oct, 1962 - No. 5, Sept, 1963 (Jay Ward)
1 (25¢, 80 pgs.) 15 30 45 105 190 275
2,3 (25¢, 80 pgs.) 10 20 30 73 129 185
4,5 (Regular size, 12¢) 8 16 24 52 86 120

ROCKY AND HIS FRIENDS (See Kite Fun Book & March of Comics #216 in the Promotional Comics section)

ROCKY AND HIS FRIENDS (TV)
Dell Publishing Co.: No. 1128, 8-10/60 - No.1311,1962 (Jay Ward)
Four Color #1128 (#1) (8-10/60) 29 58 87 213 394 575
Four Color #1152 (12-2/61), 1166, 1208, 1275, 1311('62) 18 36 54 133 247 360

ROCKY HORROR PICTURE SHOW THE COMIC BOOK, THE
Caliber Press: Jul, 1990 - No. 3, Jan, 1991 ($2.95, mini-series, 52 pgs.)
1-3: 1-Adapts cult film plus photos, etc., 1-2nd printing 3.00
...Collection ($4.95) 5.00

ROCKY JONES SPACE RANGER (See Space Adventures #15-18)

ROCKY JORDEN PRIVATE EYE (See Private Eye)

ROCKY LANE WESTERN (Allan Rocky Lane starred in Republic movies & TV for a short time as Allan Lane, Red Ryder & Rocky Lane) (See Black Jack Fawcett Movie Comics, Motion Picture Comics & Six Gun Heroes)
Fawcett Publications/Charlton No. 56 on: May, 1949 - No. 87, Nov, 1959
1 (36 pgs.)-Rocky, his stallion Black Jack, & Slim Pickens begin; photo-c begin, end #57; photo back-c 83 166 249 519 860 1200
2 (36 pgs.)-Last photo back-c 34 68 102 197 311 425
3-5 (52 pgs.): 4-Captain Tootsie by Beck 24 48 72 139 220 300
6,10 (36 pgs.): 10-Complete western novelette "Badman's Reward" 16 32 48 94 147 200
7-9 (52 pgs.) 18 36 54 105 165 225
11-13,15-17,19,20 (52 pgs.): 15-Black Jack's Hitching Post begins, ends #25. 20-Last Slim Pickens 14 28 42 82 121 160
14,18 (36 pgs.) 13 26 39 74 105 135
21,23,24 (52 pgs.): 21-Dee Dickens begins, ends #55,57,65-68 13 26 39 74 105 135
22,25-28,30 (36 pgs. begin) 12 24 36 69 97 125
29-Classic complete novel "The Land of Missing Men" with hidden land of ancient temple ruins (r-in #65) 16 32 48 94 147 200
31-40 12 24 36 67 94 120
41-54 10 20 30 58 79 100
55-Last Fawcett issue (1/54) 12 24 36 67 94 120
56-1st Charlton issue (2/54)-Photo-c 18 36 54 103 162 220
57,60-Photo-c 12 24 36 67 94 120
58,59,61-64,66-78,80-86: 59-61-Young Falcon app. 64-Slim Pickens app. 66-68: Reprints #30,31,32 10 20 30 56 76 95
65-r/#29, "The Land of Missing Men" 11 22 33 62 86 110
79-Giant Edition (68 pgs.) 12 24 36 69 97 125
87-Last issue 11 22 33 64 90 115
NOTE: *Complete novels in #10, 14, 18, 22, 25, 30-32, 36, 38, 39, 49. Captain Tootsie in #4, 12, 20. Big Bow and Little Arrow in #11, 28, 63. Black Jack's Hitching Post in #15-25, 64, 73.*

ROCKY LANE WESTERN
AC Comics: 1989 ($2.50, B&W, one-shot?)
1-Photo-c; Giordano reprints 4.00
Annual 1 (1991, $2.95, B&W, 44 pgs.)-photo front/back & inside-c; reprints 4.00

ROD CAMERON WESTERN (Movie star)

Rogue V2 #4 © MAR

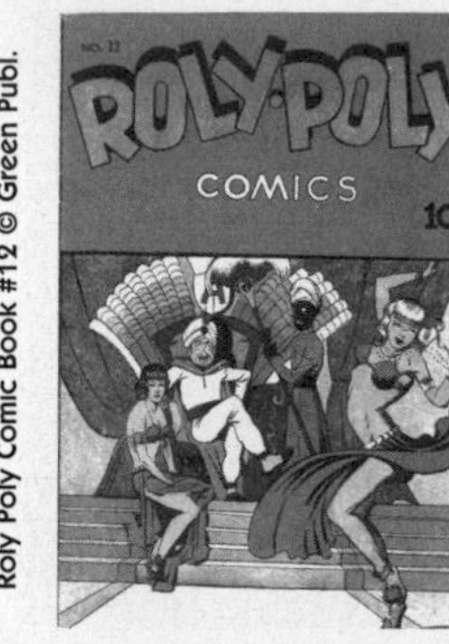

Roly Poly Comic Book #12 © Green Publ.

Romance Trail #3 © DC

	GD	VG	FN	VF	VF/NM	NM-
	2.0	4.0	6.0	8.0	9.0	9.2

Fawcett Publications: Feb, 1950 - No. 20, Apr, 1953
1-Rod Cameron, his horse War Paint, & Sam The Sheriff begin; photo front/back-c begin
41 82 123 256 416 575
2 21 42 63 124 195 265
3-Novel length story "The Mystery of the Seven Cities of Cibola"
19 38 57 109 172 235
4-10: 9-Last photo back-c 15 30 45 88 137 185
11-19 14 28 42 80 115 150
20-Last issue & photo-c 14 28 42 82 121 160
NOTE: *Novel length stories in No. 1-8, 12-14.*

RODEO RYAN (See A-1 Comics #8)

ROGAN GOSH
DC Comics (Vertigo): 1994 ($6.95, one-shot)
nn-Peter Milligan scripts 7.00

ROGER DODGER (Also in Exciting Comics #57 on)
Standard Comics: No. 5, Aug, 1952
5-Teen-age 6 12 18 28 34 40

ROGER RABBIT (Also see Marvel Graphic Novel)
Disney Comics: June, 1990 - No. 18, Nov, 1991 ($1.50)
1-18-All new stories 3.00
In 3-D 1 (1992, $2.50)-Sold at Wal-Mart?; w/glasses 4.00

ROGER RABBIT'S TOONTOWN
Disney Comics: Aug, 1991 - No. 5, Dec, 1991 ($1.50)
1-5 2.50

ROGER ZELAZNY'S AMBER: THE GUNS OF AVALON
DC Comics: 1996 - No. 3, 1996 ($6.95, limited series)
1-3: Based on novel 7.00

ROG 2000
Pacific Comics: June, 1982 ($2.95, 44 pgs., B&W, one-shot, magazine)
nn-Byrne-c/a (r) 2 4 6 8 10 12
2nd printing (7/82) 1 2 3 4 5 7

ROG 2000
Fantagraphics Books: 1987 - No. 2, 1987 ($2.00, limited series)
1,2-Byrne-r 3.00

ROGUE (From X-Men)
Marvel Comics: Jan, 1995 - No. 4, Apr, 1995 ($2.95, limited series)
1-4: 1-Gold foil logo 4.00
TPB-($12.95) r/#1-4 13.00

ROGUE (Volume 2)
Marvel Comics: Sept, 2001 - No. 4, Dec, 2001 ($2.50, limited series)
1-4-Julie Bell painted-c/Lopresti-a; Rogue's early days with X-Men 2.50

ROGUE (From X-Men)
Marvel Comics: Sept, 2004 - No. 12, Aug, 2005 ($2.99)
1-12: 1-Richards-a. 4-Gambit app. 11-Sunfire dies, Rogue absorbs his powers 3.00
...: Going Rogue TPB (2005, $14.99) r/#1-6 15.00
...: Forget-Me-Not TPB (2006, $14.99) r/#7-12 15.00

ROGUE ANGEL: TELLER OF TALL TALES (Based on the Alex Archer novels)
IDW Publishing: Feb, 2008 - No. 5, Jun, 2008 ($3.99)
1-5-Annja Creed adventures; Barbara-Kesel-s/Renae De Liz-a 4.00

ROGUES GALLERY
DC Comics: 1996 ($3.50, one-shot)
1-Pinups of DC villains by various artists 3.50

ROGUES, THE (VILLAINS) (See The Flash)
DC Comics: Feb, 1998 ($1.95, one-shot)
1-Augustyn-s/Pearson-c 2.50

ROKKIN
DC Comics (WildStorm): Sept, 2006 - No. 6, Feb, 2007 ($2.99, limited series)
1-6-Hartnell-s/Bradshaw-a 3.00

ROLLING STONES: VOODOO LOUNGE
Marvel Comics: 1995 ($6.95, Prestige format, one-shot)
nn-Dave McKean-script/design/art 7.00

ROLY POLY COMIC BOOK
Green Publishing Co.: 1945 - No. 15, 1946 (MLJ reprints)
1-Red Rube & Steel Sterling begin; Sahle-c 31 62 93 181 291 400
6-The Blue Circle & The Steel Fist app. 19 38 57 112 176 240
10-Origin Red Rube retold; Steel Sterling story (Zip #41)
27 54 81 158 254 350
11,12: The Black Hood app. in both 19 38 57 109 172 235
14-Classic decapitation-c; the Black Hood app. 45 90 135 279 465 650
15-The Blue Circle & The Steel Fist app.; cover exact swipe from Fox Blue Beetle #1
32 64 96 186 298 410

ROM (Based on the Parker Brothers toy)
Marvel Comics Group: Dec, 1979 - No. 75, Feb, 1986
1-Origin/1st app. 2 4 6 10 14 18
2-16,19-23,28-30: 5-Dr. Strange. 13-Saga of the Space Knights begins. 19-X-Men cameo. 23-Powerman & Iron Fist app. 6.00
17,18-X-Men app. 2 4 6 8 10 12
24-27: 24-F.F. cameo; Skrulls, Nova & The New Champions app. 25-Double size. 26,27-Galactus app. 1 2 3 4 5 7
31-49,51-60: 31,32-Brotherhood of Evil Mutants app. 32-X-Men cameo. 34,35-Sub-Mariner app. 41,42-Dr. Strange app. 56,57-Alpha Flight app. 58,59-Ant-Man app. 4.00
50-Skrulls app. (52 pgs.) Pin-ups by Konkle, Austin 5.00
61-74: 65-West Coast Avengers & Beta Ray Bill app. 65,66-X-Men app. 4.00
75-Last issue 1 3 4 6 8 10
Annual 1-4: (1982-85, 52 pgs.) 4.00
NOTE: ***Austin** c-3i, 18i, 61i. **Byrne** a-74i; c-56, 57, 74. **Ditko** a-59-75p, Annual 4. **Golden** c-7-12, 19. **Guice** a-61i; c-55, 58, 60p, 70p. **Layton** a-59i, 72i; c-15, 59i, 69. **Miller** c-2p?, 3p, 17p, 18p. **Russell** a(i)-64, 65, 67, 69, 71, 75; c-64, 65i, 66, 71i, 75. **Severin** c-41p. **Sienkiewicz** a-53i; c-46, 47, 52-54, 68, 71p, Annual 2. **Simonson** c-18. **P. Smith** c-59p. **Starlin** c-67. **Zeck** c-50.*

ROMANCE (See True Stories of...)

ROMANCE AND CONFESSION STORIES (See Giant Comics Edition)
St. John Publishing Co.: No date (1949) (25¢, 100 pgs.)
1-Baker-c/a; remaindered St. John love comics 45 90 135 279 465 650

ROMANCE DIARY
Marvel Comics (CDS)(CLDS): Dec, 1949 - No. 2, Mar, 1950
1,2 15 30 45 85 130 175

ROMANCE OF FLYING, THE
David McKay Publications: 1942
Feature Books 33 (nn)-WW II photos 15 30 45 85 130 175

ROMANCES OF MOLLY MANTON (See Molly Manton)

ROMANCES OF NURSE HELEN GRANT, THE
Atlas Comics (VPI): Aug, 1957
1 9 18 27 47 61 75

ROMANCES OF THE WEST (Becomes Romantic Affairs #3?)
Marvel Comics (SPC): Nov, 1949 - No. 2, Mar, 1950 (52 pgs.)
1-Movie photo-c of Yvonne DeCarlo & Howard Duff (Calamity Jane & Sam Bass)
23 46 69 133 214 295
2-Photo-c 15 30 45 85 130 175

ROMANCE STORIES OF TRUE LOVE (Formerly True Love Problems & Advice Illustrated)
Harvey Publications: No. 45, 5/57 - No. 50, 3/58; No. 51, 9/58 - No. 52, 11/58
45-51: 45,46,48-50-Powell-a 6 12 18 31 38 45
52-Matt Baker-a 9 18 27 47 61 75

ROMANCE TALES (Formerly Western Winners #6?)
Marvel Comics (CDS): No. 7, Oct, 1949 - No. 9, Mar, 1950 (7,8: photo-c)
7 14 28 42 80 115 150
8,9: 8-Everett-a 10 20 30 54 72 90

ROMANCE TRAIL
National Periodical Publications: July-Aug, 1949 - No. 6, May-June, 1950
(All photo-c & 52 pgs.)
1-Kinstler, Toth-a; Jimmy Wakely photo-c 59 118 177 369 610 850
2-Kinstler-a; Jim Bannon photo-c 33 66 99 190 300 410
3-Photo-c; Kinstler, Toth-a 35 70 105 201 318 435
4-Photo-c; Toth-a 26 52 78 150 235 320
5,6: Photo-c on both. 5-Kinstler-a 23 46 69 135 213 290

ROMAN HOLIDAYS, THE (TV)
Gold Key: Feb, 1973 - No. 4, Nov, 1973 (Hanna-Barbera)
1 4 8 12 28 44 60
2-4 3 6 9 18 27 35

ROMANTIC ADVENTURES (My... #49-67, covers only)
American Comics Group (B&I Publ. Co.): Mar-Apr, 1949 - No. 67, July, 1956 (Becomes

Romantic Hearts #8 © Story

Romantic Marriage #2 © Z-D

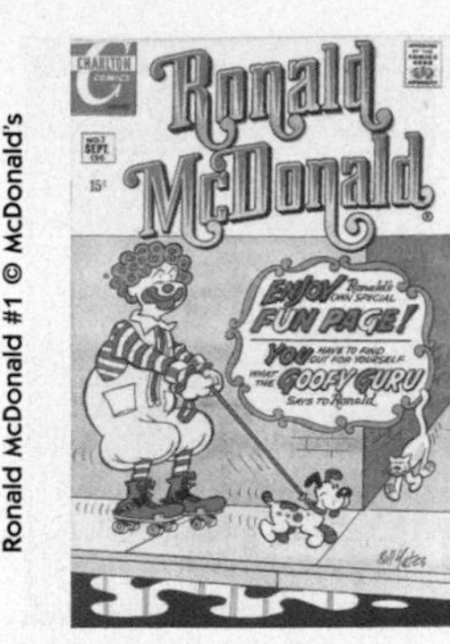

Ronald McDonald #1 © McDonald's

My... #68 on)

	GD 2.0	VG 4.0	FN 6.0	VF 8.0	VF/NM 9.0	NM- 9.2
1	18	36	54	103	162	220
2	11	22	33	62	86	110
3-10	9	18	27	50	65	80
11-20 (4/52)	8	16	24	42	54	65
21-45,51,52: 52-Last Pre-code (2/55)	7	14	21	37	46	55
46-49-3-D effect-c/stories (TrueVision)	12	24	36	69	97	125
50-Classic cover/story "Love of A Lunatic"	11	22	33	62	86	110
53-67	7	14	21	35	43	50

NOTE: *#1-23, 52 pgs.* ***Shelly*** *a-40. Whitney c/art in many issues.*

ROMANTIC AFFAIRS (Formerly Molly Manton's Romances #2 and/or Romances of the West #2 and/or Our Love #2?)
Marvel Comics (SPC): No. 3, Mar, 1950

	GD 2.0	VG 4.0	FN 6.0	VF 8.0	VF/NM 9.0	NM- 9.2
3-Photo-c from Molly Manton's Romances #2	10	20	30	54	72	90

ROMANTIC CONFESSIONS
Hillman Periodicals: Oct, 1949 - V3#1, Apr-May, 1953

	GD 2.0	VG 4.0	FN 6.0	VF 8.0	VF/NM 9.0	NM- 9.2
V1#1-McWilliams-a	15	30	45	94	147	200
2-Briefer-a; negligee panels	10	20	30	58	79	100
3-12	9	18	27	50	65	80
V2#1,2,4-8,10-12: 2-McWilliams-a	8	16	24	44	57	70
3-Krigstein-a	9	18	27	52	69	85
9-One pg. Frazetta ad	8	16	24	44	57	70
V3#1	8	16	24	42	54	65

ROMANTIC HEARTS
Story Comics/Master/Merit Pubs.: Mar, 1951 - No. 10, Oct, 1952; July, 1953 - No. 12, July, 1955

	GD 2.0	VG 4.0	FN 6.0	VF 8.0	VF/NM 9.0	NM- 9.2
1(3/51) (1st Series)	14	28	42	80	115	150
2	9	18	27	47	61	75
3-10: Cameron-a	8	16	24	42	54	65
1(7/53) (2nd Series)-Some say #11 on-c	9	18	27	52	69	85
2	8	16	24	40	50	60
3-12	7	14	21	36	43	50

ROMANTIC LOVE
Avon Periodicals/Realistic (No #14-19): 9-10/49 - #3, 1-2/50; #4, 2-3/51 - #13, 10/52; #20, 3-4/54 - #23, 9-10/54

	GD 2.0	VG 4.0	FN 6.0	VF 8.0	VF/NM 9.0	NM- 9.2
1-c-/Avon paperback #252	28	56	84	162	261	360
2-5: 3-c-/paperback Novel Library #12. 4-c-/paperback Diversey Prize Novel #5. 5-c-/paperback Novel Library #34	17	34	51	98	154	210
6- "Thrill Crazy" marijuana story; c-/Avon paperback #207; Kinstler-a	23	46	69	135	218	300
7,8: 8-Astarita-a(2)	15	30	45	94	147	200
9-12: 9-c-/paperback Novel Library #41; Kinstler-a. 10-c-/Avon paperback #212. 11-c-/paperback Novel Library #17; Kinstler-a. 12-c-/paperback Novel Library #13	17	34	51	98	154	210
13,21-23: 22,23-Kinstler-c	15	30	45	92	144	195
20-Kinstler-c/a	15	30	45	94	147	200
nn(1-3/53)(Realistic-r)	11	22	33	62	86	110

NOTE: ***Astarita*** *a-7, 10, 11, 21. Painted c-1-3, 5, 7-11, 13. Photo c-4, 6.*

ROMANTIC LOVE
Quality Comics Group: 1963-1964

	GD 2.0	VG 4.0	FN 6.0	VF 8.0	VF/NM 9.0	NM- 9.2
I.W. Reprint #2,3,8,11: 2-r/Romantic Love #2	2	4	6	9	12	15

ROMANTIC MARRIAGE (Cinderella Love #25 on)
Ziff-Davis/St. John No. 18 on (#1-8: 52 pgs.): #1-3 (1950, no months); #4, 5-6/51 - #17, 9/52; #18, 9/53 - #24, 9/54

	GD 2.0	VG 4.0	FN 6.0	VF 8.0	VF/NM 9.0	NM- 9.2
1-Photo-c; Cary Grant/Betsy Drake photo back-c.	21	42	63	123	197	270
2-Painted-c; Anderson-a (also #15)	15	30	45	83	124	165
3-9: 3,4,8,9-Painted-c; 5-7-Photo-c	14	28	42	78	112	145
10-Unusual format; front-c is a painted-c; back-c is a photo-c complete with logo, price, etc.	20	40	60	114	180	245
11-17 13-Photo-c. 15-Signed story by Anderson. 17-(9/52)-Last Z-D issue	13	26	39	72	101	130
18-22,24: 20-Photo-c	13	26	39	72	101	130
23-Baker-c; all stories are reprinted from #15	14	28	42	81	118	155

ROMANTIC PICTURE NOVELETTES
Magazine Enterprises: 1946

	GD 2.0	VG 4.0	FN 6.0	VF 8.0	VF/NM 9.0	NM- 9.2
1-Mary Worth-r; Creig Flessel-c	16	32	48	92	144	195

ROMANTIC SECRETS (Becomes Time For Love)
Fawcett/Charlton Comics No. 5 (10/55) on: Sept, 1949 - No. 39, 4/53; No. 5, 10/55 - No. 52, 11/64 (#1-5: photo-c)

	GD 2.0	VG 4.0	FN 6.0	VF 8.0	VF/NM 9.0	NM- 9.2
1-(52 pg. issues begin, end #?)	16	32	48	92	144	195
2,3	10	20	30	58	79	100
4,9-Evans-a	11	22	33	62	86	110
5-8,10	9	18	27	47	61	75
11-23	8	16	24	42	54	65
24-Evans-a	9	18	27	47	61	75
25-39('53)	8	16	24	40	50	60
5 (Charlton, 2nd Series)(10/55, formerly Negro Romances #4)	10	20	30	54	72	90
6-10	8	16	24	42	54	65
11-20	3	6	9	21	32	42
21-35: Last 10¢ issue?	3	6	9	18	27	35
36-52('64)	3	6	9	16	22	28

NOTE: ***Bailey*** *a-20.* ***Powell*** *a(1st series)-5, 7, 10, 12, 16, 17, 20, 26, 29, 33, 34, 36, 37.* ***Sekowsky*** *a-26. Photo c(1st series)-1-5, 16, 25, 27, 33.* ***Swayze*** *a(1st series)-16, 18, 19, 23, 26-28, 31, 32, 39.*

ROMANTIC STORY (Cowboy Love #28 on)
Fawcett/Charlton Comics No. 23 on: 11/49 - #22, Sum, 1953; #23, 5/54 - #27, 12/54; #28, 8/55 - #130, 11/73

	GD 2.0	VG 4.0	FN 6.0	VF 8.0	VF/NM 9.0	NM- 9.2
1-Photo-c begin, end #24; 52 pgs. begins	18	36	54	103	162	220
2	11	22	33	62	86	110
3-5	10	20	30	54	72	90
6-14	9	18	27	50	65	80
15-Evans-a	10	20	30	54	72	90
16-22(Sum, '53; last Fawcett issue). 21-Toth-a?	8	16	24	42	54	65
23-39: 26,29-Wood swipes	7	14	21	37	46	55
40-(100 pgs.)	11	22	33	64	90	115
41-50	3	6	9	21	32	42
51-80: 57-Hypo needle story	3	6	9	16	23	30
81-99	2	4	6	10	14	18
100	2	4	6	13	28	22
101-130: 120-Bobby Sherman pin-up	2	4	6	9	12	15

NOTE: ***Jim Aparo*** *a-94.* ***Powell*** *a-7, 8, 16, 20, 30.* ***Marcus Swayze*** *a-2, 12, 20, 32.*

ROMANTIC THRILLS (See Fox Giants)

ROMANTIC WESTERN
Fawcett Publications: Winter, 1949 - No. 3, June, 1950 (All Photo-c)

	GD 2.0	VG 4.0	FN 6.0	VF 8.0	VF/NM 9.0	NM- 9.2
1	22	44	66	127	204	280
2-(Spr/50)-Williamson, McWilliams-a	20	40	60	115	183	250
3	15	30	45	85	130	175

ROMEO TUBBS (...That Lovable Teenager; formerly My Secret Life)
Fox Feature Syndicate/Green Publ. Co. No. 27: No. 26, 5/50 - No. 28, 7/50; No. 1, 1950; No. 27, 12/52

	GD 2.0	VG 4.0	FN 6.0	VF 8.0	VF/NM 9.0	NM- 9.2
26-Teen-age	11	22	33	64	90	115
28 (7/50)	10	20	30	58	79	100
27 (12/52)-Contains Pedro on inside; Wood-a (exist?)	15	30	45	84	127	170

RONALD McDONALD (TV)
Charlton Press (King Features Synd.): Sept, 1970 - No. 4, March, 1971

	GD 2.0	VG 4.0	FN 6.0	VF 8.0	VF/NM 9.0	NM- 9.2
1	8	16	24	56	93	130
2-4	5	10	15	32	51	70
V2#1,3-Special reprint for McDonald systems; "Not for resale" on cover	6	12	18	39	62	85

RONIN
DC Comics: July, 1983 - No. 6, Aug, 1984 ($2.50, limited series, 52 pgs.)

	GD 2.0	VG 4.0	FN 6.0	VF 8.0	VF/NM 9.0	NM- 9.2
1-5-Frank Miller-c/a/scripts in all	1	2	3	5	6	8
6-Scarcer; has fold-out poster.	1	3	4	6	8	10
Trade paperback (1987, $12.95)-Reprints #1-6						13.00

RONNA
Knight Press: Apr, 1997 ($2.95, B&W, one-shot)

	GD 2.0	VG 4.0	FN 6.0	VF 8.0	VF/NM 9.0	NM- 9.2
1-Beau Smith-s						3.00

ROOK (See Eerie Magazine & Warren Presents: The Rook)
Warren Publications: Oct, 1979 - No. 14, April, 1982 (B&W magazine)

	GD 2.0	VG 4.0	FN 6.0	VF 8.0	VF/NM 9.0	NM- 9.2
1-Nino-a/Corben-c; with 8 pg. color insert	3	6	9	16	23	30
2-4,6,7: 2-Voltar by Alcala begins. 3,4-Toth-a	2	4	6	9	13	16
5,8-14: 11-Zorro-s. 12-14-Eagle by Severin	2	4	6	9	13	16

ROOK
Harris Comics: No. 0, Jun, 1995 - No. 4, 1995 ($2.95)

	GD 2.0	VG 4.0	FN 6.0	VF 8.0	VF/NM 9.0	NM- 9.2
0-4: 0-short stories (3) w/preview. 4-Brereton-c.						3.00

ROOKIE COP (Formerly Crime and Justice?)
Charlton Comics: No. 27, Nov, 1955 - No. 33, Aug, 1957

Room 222 #1 © 20th Century Fox

Roy Rogers Comics #19 © Roy Rogers

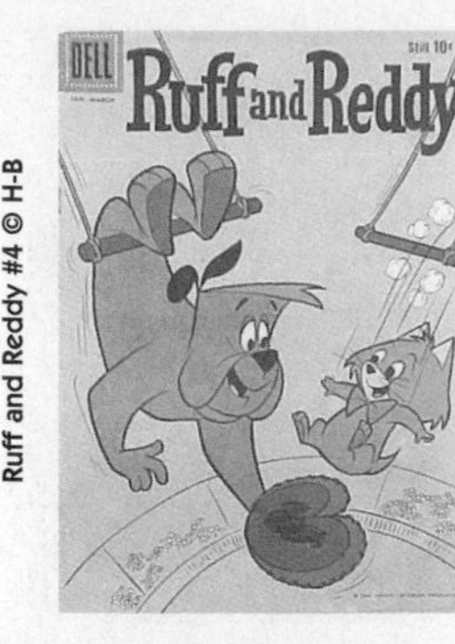

Ruff and Reddy #4 © H-B

	GD 2.0	VG 4.0	FN 6.0	VF 8.0	VF/NM 9.0	NM- 9.2
27	9	18	27	47	61	75
28-33	6	12	18	31	38	45

ROOM 222 (TV)
Dell Publishing Co.: Jan, 1970; No. 2, May, 1970 - No. 4, Jan, 1971

1	5	10	15	34	55	75
2-4: 2,4-Photo-c. 3-Marijuana story. 4 r/#1	4	8	12	22	34	45

ROOTIE KAZOOTIE (TV)(See 3-D-ell)
Dell Publishing Co.: No. 415, Aug, 1952 - No. 6, Oct-Dec, 1954

Four Color 415 (#1)	9	18	27	65	113	160
Four Color 459,502(#2,3), 4(4-6/54)-6	7	14	21	47	76	105

ROOTS OF THE SWAMP THING
DC Comics: July, 1986 - No.5, Nov, 1986 ($2.00, Baxter paper, 52 pgs.)

1-5: r/Swamp Thing #1-10 by Wrightson & House of Mystery-r. 1-new Wrightson-c (2-5 reprinted covers). 4.00

ROSE (See Bone)
Cartoon Books: Nov, 2000 - No. 3, Feb, 2002 ($5.95, lim. series, square-bound)

1-3-Prequel to Bone; Jeff Smith-s/Charles Vess painted-a/c 6.00
HC (2001, $29.95) r/#1-3; new Vess cover painting 30.00
SC (2002, $19.95) r/#1-3; new Vess cover painting 20.00
1-($6.00)-Blood & Glory Edition 6.00

ROSE AND THORN
DC Comics: Feb, 2004 - No. 6, July, 2004 ($2.95, limited series)

1-6-Simone-sMelo-a/Hughes-c 3.00

ROSWELL: LITTLE GREEN MAN (See Simpsons Comics #19-22)
Bongo Comics: 1996 - No. 6 ($2.95, quarterly)

1-6 3.50
...Walks Among Us ('97, $12.95, TPB) r/ #1-3 & Simpsons flip books 13.00

ROUND TABLE OF AMERICA: PERSONALITY CRISIS (See Big Bang Comics)
Image Comics: Aug, 2005 ($3.50, one-shot)

1-Carlos Rodriguez-a/Pedro Angosto-s 3.50

ROUNDUP (...Western Crime Stories)
D. S. Publishing Co.: July-Aug, 1948 - No. 5, Mar-Apr, 1949 (All 52 pgs.)

1-Kiefer-a	18	36	54	107	169	230
2-5: 2-Marijuana drug mention story	14	28	42	82	121	160

ROUTE 666
CrossGeneration Comics: July, 2002 - No. 22, Jun, 2004 ($2.95)

1-22-Bedard-s/Moline-a in most. 5-Richards-a. 15-McCrea-a 3.00
...: Highway to Horror (4/03, $15.95, TPB) r/#1-6 16.00
Vol. 2: Three-Ring Circus (2003, $15.95) r/#7-12 16.00

ROYAL ROY
Marvel Comics (Star Comics): May, 1985 - No.6, Mar, 1986 (Children's book)

1-6 4.00

ROY CAMPANELLA, BASEBALL HERO
Fawcett Publications: 1950 (Brooklyn Dodgers)

nn-Photo-c; life story	59	118	177	372	629	885

ROY ROGERS (See March of Comics #17, 35, 47, 62, 68, 73, 77, 86, 91, 100, 105, 116, 121, 131, 136, 146, 151, 161, 167, 176, 191, 206, 221, 236, 250)

ROY ROGERS AND TRIGGER
Gold Key: Apr, 1967

1-Photo-c; reprints	4	8	12	28	44	60

ROY ROGERS ANNUAL
Wilson Publ. Co., Toronto/Dell: 1947 ("Giant Edition" on-c)(132 pgs., 50¢)

nn-Less than 5 known copies. Front and back cover art are from Roy Rogers #2. Stories reprinted from Roy Rogers #2, Four Color #137 and Four Color #153. (A copy in VG/FN was sold in 1986 for $400, in 1996 for $1200 & in 2000 for $1500; a FN+ sold for $1,650.)

ROY ROGERS COMICS (See Western Roundup under Dell Giants)
Dell Publishing Co.: No. 38, 4/44 - No. 177, 12/47 (#38-166: 52 pgs.)

Four Color 38 (1944)-49 pg. story; photo front/back-c on all 4-Color issues (1st western comic with photo-c)	167	334	501	1461	2731	4000
Four Color 63 (1945)-Color photos on all four-c	41	82	123	328	589	850
Four Color 86,95 (1945)	31	62	93	222	404	585
Four Color 109 (1946)	23	46	69	171	306	440
Four Color 117,124,137,144	19	38	57	138	244	350
Four Color 153,160,166: 166-48 pg. story	17	34	51	124	220	315
Four Color 177 (36 pgs.)-32 pg. story	16	32	48	118	209	300

ROY ROGERS COMICS (...& Trigger #92(8/55)-on)(Roy starred in Republic movies, radio & TV) (Singing cowboy) (Also see Dale Evans, It Really Happened #8, Queen of the West Dale Evans, & Roy Rogers' Trigger)
Dell Publishing Co.: Jan, 1948 - No. 145, Sept-Oct, 1961 (#1-19: 36 pgs.)

	GD 2.0	VG 4.0	FN 6.0	VF 8.0	VF/NM 9.0	NM- 9.2
1-Roy, his horse Trigger, & Chuck Wagon Charley's Tales begin; photo-c begin, end #145	67	134	201	570	1060	1550
2	24	48	72	180	323	465
3-5	17	34	51	128	227	325
6-10	14	28	42	103	184	265
11-19: 19-Chuck Wagon Charley's Tales ends	12	24	36	86	153	220
20 (52 pgs.)-Trigger feature begins, ends #46	12	24	36	87	156	225
21-30 (52 pgs.)	10	20	30	71	126	180
31-46 (52 pgs.): 37-X-Mas-c	9	18	27	60	100	140
47-56 (36 pgs.): 47-Chuck Wagon Charley's Tales returns, ends #133. 49-X-mas-c. 55-Last photo back-c	7	14	21	47	76	105
57 (52 pgs.)-Heroin drug propaganda story	7	14	21	49	80	110
58-70 (52 pgs.): 58-Heroin drug use/dealing story. 61-X-Mas-c	7	14	21	47	76	105
71-80 (52 pgs.): 73-X-Mas-c	6	12	18	41	66	90
81-91 (36 pgs. #81-on): 85-X-Mas-c	6	12	18	39	62	85
92-99,101-110,112-118: 92-Title changed to Roy Rogers and Trigger (8/55)	6	12	18	37	59	80
100-Trigger feature returns, ends #131	6	12	18	43	69	95
111,119-124-Toth-a	7	14	21	45	73	100
125-131: 125-Toth-a (1 pg.)	5	10	15	35	55	75
132-144-Manning-a. 132-1st Dale Evans-sty by Russ Manning. 138,144-Dale Evans featured	6	12	18	39	62	85
145-Last issue	7	14	21	47	76	105

NOTE: ***Buscema** a-74-108(2 stories each). **Manning** a-123, 124, 132-144. **Marsh** a-110. Photo back-c No. 1-9, 11-35, 38-55.*

ROY ROGERS' TRIGGER
Dell Publishing Co.: No. 329, May, 1951 - No. 17, June-Aug, 1955

Four Color 329 (#1)-Painted-c	14	28	42	103	184	265
2 (9-11/51)-Photo-c	11	22	33	77	136	195
3-5: 3-Painted-c begin, end #17, most by S. Savitt	6	12	18	43	69	95
6-17: Title merges with Roy Rogers after #17	5	10	15	35	55	75

ROY ROGERS WESTERN CLASSICS
AC Comics: 1989 -No. 4 ($2.95/$3.95, 44pgs.) (24 pgs. color, 16 pgs. B&W)

1-4: 1-Dale Evans-r by Manning, Trigger-r by Buscema; photo covers & interior photos by Roy & Dale. 2-Buscema-r (3); photo-c & B&W photos inside. 3-Dale Evans-r by Manning; Trigger-r by Buscema plus other Buscema-r; photo-c 4.00

RUDOLPH, THE RED-NOSED REINDEER
National Per. Publ.: 1950 - No. 13, Winter, 1962-63 (Issues are not numbered)

1950 issue (#1); Grossman-c/a in all	21	42	63	123	197	270
1951-53 issues (3 total)	13	26	39	74	105	135
1954/55, 55/56, 56/57	11	22	33	64	90	115
1957/58, 58/59, 59/60, 60/61, 61/62	7	14	21	45	73	100
1962/63 (rare)(84 pgs.)(shows "Annual" in indicia)	10	20	30	73	129	185

NOTE: *13 total issues published. Has games & puzzles also.*

RUDOLPH, THE RED-NOSED REINDEER (Also see Limited Collectors' Edition C-20, C-24, C-33, C-42, C-50; and All-New Collectors' Edition C-53 & C-60)
National Per. Publ.: Christmas 1972 (Treasury-size)

nn-Precursor to Limited Collectors' Edition title (scarce) (implied to be Lim. Coll .Ed. C-20)	20	40	60	143	264	385

RUFF AND REDDY (TV)
Dell Publ. Co.: No. 937, 9/58 - No. 12, 1-3/62 (Hanna-Barbera)(#9 on: 15¢)

Four Color 937(#1)(1st Hanna-Barbera comic book)	12	24	36	84	150	215
Four Color 981,1038	8	16	24	52	86	120
4(1-3/60)-12: 8-Last 10¢ issue	7	14	21	45	73	100

RUGGED ACTION (Strange Stories of Suspense #5 on)
Atlas Comics (CSI): Dec, 1954 - No. 4, June, 1955

1-Brodsky-c	14	28	42	76	108	140
2-4: 2-Last precode (2/55)	10	20	30	54	72	90

NOTE: ***Ayers** a-2, 3. **Maneely** c-2, 3. **Severin** a-2.*

RUINS
Marvel Comics (Alterniverse): July, 1995 - No. 2, Sept, 1995 ($5.00, painted, limited series)

1,2: Phil Sheldon from Marvels; Warren Ellis scripts; acetate-c 5.00

RULAH JUNGLE GODDESS (Formerly Zoot; I Loved #28 on) (Also see All Top Comics & Terrors of the Jungle)
Fox Features Syndicate: No. 17, Aug, 1948 - No. 27, June, 1949

Runaways V2 #30 © MAR

Ruse #2 © CRO

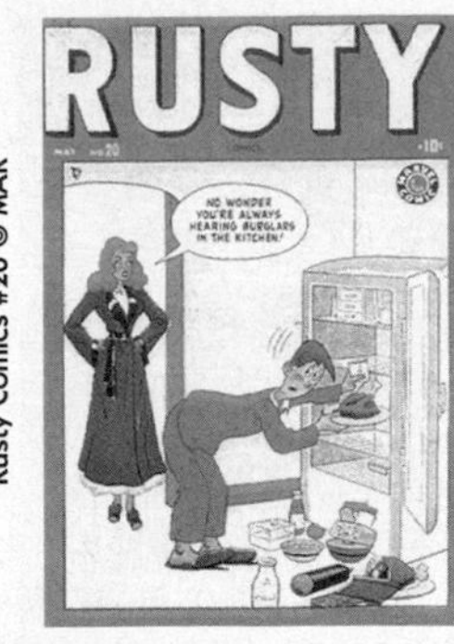

Rusty Comics #20 © MAR

	GD 2.0	VG 4.0	FN 6.0	VF 8.0	VF/NM 9.0	NM- 9.2
17	103	206	309	649	1100	1550
18-Classic girl-fight interior splash	70	140	210	441	746	1050
19,20	67	134	201	422	711	1000
21-Used in **SOTI**, pg. 388,389	68	136	204	428	727	1025
22-Used in **SOTI**, pg. 22,23	67	134	201	422	711	1000
23-27	52	104	156	322	536	750

NOTE: ***Kamen*** *c-17-19, 21, 22.*

RUNAWAY, THE (See Movie Classics)

RUNAWAYS
Marvel Comics: July, 2003 - No. 18, Nov, 2004 ($2.95/$2.25/$2.99)

1-($2.95) Vaughan-s/Alphona-a/Jo Chen-c 3.00
2-9-($2.50) 2.50
10-18-($2.99) 11,12-Miyazawa-a; Cloak and Dagger app. 16-The mole revealed 3.00
Hardcover (2005, $34.99) oversized r/#1-18; proposal & sketch pages; Vaughan intro. 35.00
Marvel Age Runaways Vol. 1: Pride and Joy (2004, $7.99, digest size) r/#1-6 8.00
...Vol. 2: Teenage Wasteland (2004, $7.99, digest size) r/#7-12 8.00
...Vol. 3: The Good Die Young (2004, $7.99, digest size) r/#13-18 8.00

RUNAWAYS (Also see X-Men/Runaways 2006 FCBD Edition in the Promotional Section)
Marvel Comics: Apr, 2005 - No. 30, Aug, 2008 ($2.99)

1-24: 1-6-Vaughan-s/Alphona-a/Jo Chen-c. 7,8-Miyazawa-a/Bachalo-c. 11-Spider-Man app. 12-New Avengers app. 18-Gert killed 3.00
25-30-Joss Whedon-s/Michael Ryan-a. 25-Punisher app. 3.00
... Saga (2007, $3.99) re-caps the 2 series thru #24; 4 new pages w/Ramos-a; Ramos-c 4.00
Hardcover (2006, $24.99) oversized r/#1-12 & X-Men/Runaways; script & sketch pages 25.00
Hardcover Vol. 3 (2007, $24.99) oversized r/#13-24; sketch pages 25.00
...Vol. 4: True Believers (2006, $7.99, digest size) r/#1-6 8.00
...Vol. 5: Escape To New York (2006, $7.99, digest size) r/#7-12 8.00
...Vol. 6: Parental Guidance (2006, $7.99, digest size) r/#13-18 8.00

RUNAWAYS (3rd series)
Marvel Comics: Oct, 2008 - Present ($2.99)

1,2-Terry Moore-s/Humberto Ramos-a/c 3.00

RUN BABY RUN
Logos International: 1974 (39¢, Christian religious)

	GD	VG	FN	VF	VF/NM	NM-
nn-By Tony Tallarico from Nicky Cruz's book	2	4	6	8	11	14

RUN, BUDDY, RUN (TV)
Gold Key: June, 1967 (Photo-c)

	GD	VG	FN	VF	VF/NM	NM-
1 (10204-706)	3	6	9	18	27	35

RUNE (See Curse of Rune, Sludge & all other Ultraverse titles for previews)
Malibu Comics (Ultraverse): 1994 - No. 9, Apr, 1995 ($1.95)

	GD	VG	FN	VF	VF/NM	NM-
0-Obtained by sending coupons from 11 comics; came w/Solution #0, poster, temporary tattoo, card	1	2	3	5	6	8

1,2,4-9: 1-Barry Windsor-Smith-c/a/stories begin, ends #6. 5-1st app. of Gemini. 6-Prime & Mantra app. 2.50
1-(1/94)-"Ashcan" edition flip book w/Wrath #1 2.50
1-Ultra 5000 Limited silver foil edition 4.00
3-(3/94, $3.50, 68 pgs.)-Flip book w/Ultraverse Premiere #1 3.50
Giant Size 1 ($2.50, 44 pgs.)-B.Smith story & art. 2.50

RUNE (2nd Series)(Formerly Curse of Rune)(See Ultraverse Unlimited #1)
Malibu Comics (Ultraverse): Infinity, Sept, 1995 - V2#7, Apr, 1996 ($1.50)

Infinity, V2#1-7: Infinity-Black September tie-in; black-c & painted-c exist. 1,3-7-Marvel's Adam Warlock app; regular & painted-c exist. 2-Flip book w/ "Phoenix Resurrection" Pt. 6 2.50
...Vs. Venom 1 (12/95, $3.95) 4.00

RUNE: HEARTS OF DARKNESS
Malibu Comics (Ultraverse): Sept, 1996 - No. 3, Nov, 1996 ($1.50, lim. series)

1-3: Moench scripts & Kyle Hotz-c/a; flip books w/6 pg. Rune story by the Pander Bros. 2.50

RUNE/SILVER SURFER
Marvel Comics/Malibu Comics (Ultraverse): Apr, 1995 ($5.95/$2.95, one-shot)

1 ($5.95, direct market)-BWS-c 6.00
1 ($2.95, newstand)-BWS-c 3.00
1-Collector's limited edition 6.00

RUSE (Also see Archard's Agents)
CrossGeneration Comics: Nov, 2001 - No. 26, Jan, 2004 ($2.95)

1-Waid-s/Guice & Perkins-a 5.00
2-26: 6-Jeff Johnson-a. 11,15-Paul Ryan-a. 12-Last Waid-s 3.00
Enter the Detective Vol. 1 TPB (2002, $15.95) r/#1-6; Guice-c 16.00
...: The Silent Partner Vol. 2 (3/03, $15.95, TPB) r/#7-12 16.00
...: Criminal Intent Vol. 3 ('03, $15.95, TPB) r/#13-18 16.00
Traveler 1,2 ($9.95): Digest-size editions of the TPBs 10.00

RUSH CITY
DC Comics: Sept, 2006 - No. 6, May, 2007 ($2.99, limited series)

1-6: 1-Dixon-s/Green-a/Jock-c. 2,3-Black Canary app. 3.00

RUSTLERS, THE (See Zane Grey Four Color 532)

RUSTY, BOY DETECTIVE
Good Comics/Lev Gleason: Mar-April, 1955 - No. 5, Nov, 1955

	GD	VG	FN	VF	VF/NM	NM-
1-Bob Wood, Carl Hubbell-a begins	9	18	27	47	61	75
2-5	6	12	18	31	38	45

RUSTY COMICS (Formerly Kid Movie Comics; Rusty and Her Family #21, 22; The Kelleys #23 on; see Millie The Model)
Marvel Comics (HPC): No. 12, Apr, 1947 - No. 22, Sept, 1949

	GD	VG	FN	VF	VF/NM	NM-
12-Mitzi app.	21	42	63	123	197	270
13	14	28	42	76	108	140
14-Wolverton's Powerhouse Pepper (4 pgs.) plus Kurtzman's "Hey Look"	22	44	66	129	207	285
15-17-Kurtzman's "Hey Look"	15	30	45	92	144	195
18,19	12	24	36	69	97	125
20-Kurtzman-a (5 pgs.)	16	32	48	96	151	205
21,22-Kurtzman-a (17 & 22 pgs.)	21	42	63	125	200	275

RUSTY DUGAN (See Holyoke One-Shot #2)

RUSTY RILEY
Dell Publishing Co.: No. 418, Aug, 1952 - No. 554, April, 1954 (Frank Godwin strip reprints)

	GD	VG	FN	VF	VF/NM	NM-
Four Color 418 (...a Boy, a Horse, and a Dog #1)	5	10	15	32	51	70
Four Color 451(2/53), 486 ('53), 554	4	8	12	26	41	50

RUULE
Beckett Comics: Dec, 2003 - No. 5, Apr, 2004 ($2.99)

1-5-David Mack-c/Mike Hawthorne-a 3.00

RUULE: KISS & TELL
Beckett Comics: Jun, 2004 - No. 8 ($1.99)

1-7: 1-Amano-s/c; Rousseau-a. 4-Maleev-c 2.00
TPB (2005, $19.99) r/#1-8 20.00

SAARI ("The Jungle Goddess")
P. L. Publishing Co.: November, 1951

	GD	VG	FN	VF	VF/NM	NM-
1	45	90	135	279	465	650

SABAN POWERHOUSE (TV)
Acclaim Books: 1997 ($4.50, digest size)

1,2-Power Rangers, BeetleBorgs, and others 4.50

SABAN PRESENTS POWER RANGERS TURBO VS. BEETLEBORGS METALLIX (TV)
Acclaim Books: 1997 ($4.50, digest size, one-shot)

nn 4.50

SABAN'S MIGHTY MORPHIN POWER RANGERS
Hamilton Comics: Dec, 1994 - No. 6, May, 1995 ($1.95, limited series)

1-6: 1-w/bound-in Power Ranger Barcode Card 2.50

SABAN'S MIGHTY MORPHIN POWER RANGERS (TV)
Marvel Comics: 1995 - No. 8, 1996 ($1.75)

1-8 2.50

SABLE (Formerly Jon Sable, Freelance; also see Mike Grell's...)
First Comics: Mar, 1988 - No. 27, May, 1990 ($1.75/$1.95)

1-27: 10-Begin $1.95-c 2.50

SABLE & FORTUNE (Also see Silver Sable and the Wild Pack)
Marvel Comics: Mar, 2006 - No. 4, June, 2006 ($2.99, limited series)

1-4-John Burns-a/Brendan Cahill-s 3.00

SABRE (See Eclipse Graphic Album Series)
Eclipse Comics: Aug, 1982 - No. 14, Aug, 1985 (Baxter paper #4 on)

1-14: 1-Sabre & Morrigan Tales begin. 4-6-Incredible Seven origin 2.50

SABRETOOTH (See Iron Fist, Power Man, X-Factor #10 & X-Men)
Marvel Comics: Aug, 1993 - No. 4, Nov, 1993 ($2.95, lim. series, coated paper)

1-4: 1-Die-cut-c. 3-Wolverine app. 4.00
...Special 1 "In the Red Zone" (1995, $4.95) Chromium wraparound-c 6.00
V2 #1 (1/98, $5.95, one-shot) Wildchild app. 6.00
Trade paperback (12/94, $12.95) r/#1-4 13.00

SABRETOOTH

Sabrina V2 #24 © AP

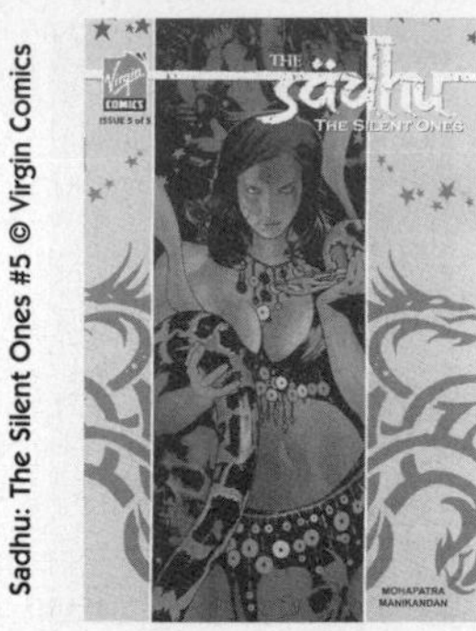
Sadhu: The Silent Ones #5 © Virgin Comics

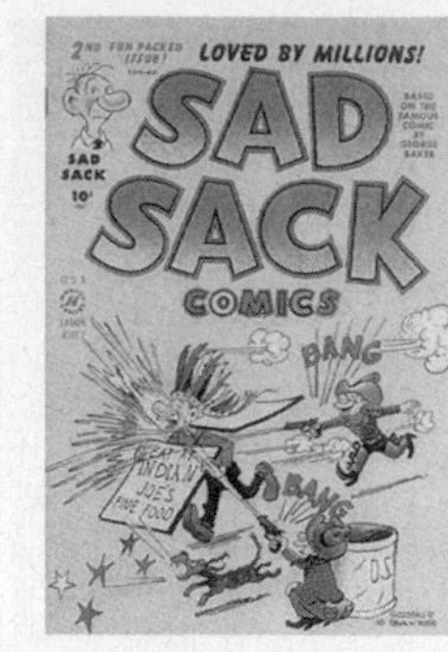

Sad Sack Comics #2 © HARV

Marvel Comics: Dec, 2004 - No. 4, Feb, 2005 ($2.99, limited series)

	GD 2.0	VG 4.0	FN 6.0	VF 8.0	VF/NM 9.0	NM- 9.2
1-4-Sears-a. 3,4-Wendigo app.						3.00
...: Open Season TPB (2005, $9.99) r/#1-4						10.00

SABRETOOTH AND MYSTIQUE (See Mystique and Sabretooth)

SABRETOOTH CLASSIC
Marvel Comics: May, 1994 - No. 15, July, 1995 ($1.50)

	GD 2.0	VG 4.0	FN 6.0	VF 8.0	VF/NM 9.0	NM- 9.2
1-15: 1-3-r/Power Man & Iron Fist #66,78,84. 4-r/Spec. S-M #116. 9-Uncanny X-Men #212, 10-r/Uncanny X-Men #213. 11-r/ Daredevil #238. 12-r/Classic X-Men #10						3.00

SABRETOOTH: MARY SHELLEY OVERDRIVE
Marvel Comics: Aug, 2002 - No. 4, Nov, 2002 ($2.99, limited series)

	GD 2.0	VG 4.0	FN 6.0	VF 8.0	VF/NM 9.0	NM- 9.2
1-4-Jolley-s; Harris-c						3.00

SABRINA (Volume 2) (Based on animated series)
Archie Publications: Jan, 2000 - Present ($1.79/$1.99/$2.19/$2.25)

	GD 2.0	VG 4.0	FN 6.0	VF 8.0	VF/NM 9.0	NM- 9.2
1-Teen-age Witch magically reverted to 12 years old						4.00
2-10: 4-Begin $1.99-c						3.00
11-99: 38-Sabrina aged back to 16 years old. 39-Begin $2.19-c. 58-Manga-style begins; Tania Del Rio-a. 67-Josie and the Pussycats app.						2.50

SABRINA'S CHRISTMAS MAGIC (See Archie Giant Series Magazine #196, 207, 220, 231, 243, 455, 467, 479, 491, 503, 515)

SABRINA'S HALLOWEEN SPOOOKTACULAR
Archie Publications: 1993 - 1995 ($2.00, 52 pgs.)

	GD 2.0	VG 4.0	FN 6.0	VF 8.0	VF/NM 9.0	NM- 9.2
1-Neon orange ink-c; bound-in poster	1	2	3	5	6	8
2,3-Titled "Sabrina's Holiday Spectacular"						5.00

SABRINA, THE TEEN-AGE WITCH (TV)(See Archie Giant Series, Archie's Madhouse 22, Archie's TV..., Chilling Advs. In Sorcery, Little Archie #59)
Archie Publications: April, 1971 - No. 77, Jan, 1983 (52 pg.Giants No. 1-17)

	GD 2.0	VG 4.0	FN 6.0	VF 8.0	VF/NM 9.0	NM- 9.2
1-52 pgs. begin, end #17	14	28	42	104	187	270
2-Archie's group x-over	8	16	24	56	93	130
3-5: 3,4-Archie's Group x-over	6	12	18	39	62	85
6-10	5	10	15	34	55	75
11-17(2/74)	4	8	12	26	41	55
18-30	3	6	9	19	29	38
31-40(8/77)	3	6	9	14	20	26
41-60(6/80)	2	4	6	10	14	18
61-70	2	4	6	8	11	14
71-76-low print run	2	4	6	10	14	18
77-Last issue; low print run	3	6	9	14	19	24

SABRINA, THE TEEN-AGE WITCH
Archie Publications: 1996 ($1.50, 32 pgs., one-shot)

	GD 2.0	VG 4.0	FN 6.0	VF 8.0	VF/NM 9.0	NM- 9.2
1-Updated origin						5.00

SABRINA, THE TEEN-AGE WITCH (Continues in Sabrina, Vol. 2)
Archie Publications: May, 1997 - No. 32, Dec, 1999 ($1.50/$1.75/$1.79)

	GD 2.0	VG 4.0	FN 6.0	VF 8.0	VF/NM 9.0	NM- 9.2
1-Photo-c with Melissa Joan Hart	1	2	3	5	6	8
2-10: 9-Begin $1.75-c						5.00
11-20						4.00
21-32: 24-Begin $1.79-c. 28-Sonic the Hedgehog-c/app.						3.00

SABU, "ELEPHANT BOY" (Movie; formerly My Secret Story)
Fox Features Syndicate: No. 30, June, 1950 - No. 2, Aug, 1950

	GD 2.0	VG 4.0	FN 6.0	VF 8.0	VF/NM 9.0	NM- 9.2
30(#1)-Wood-a; photo-c from movie	26	52	78	152	244	335
2-Photo-c from movie; Kamen-a	19	38	57	112	176	240

SACHS & VIOLENS
Marvel Comics (Epic Comics): Nov, 1993 - No. 4, July, 1994 ($2.25, limited series, mature)

	GD 2.0	VG 4.0	FN 6.0	VF 8.0	VF/NM 9.0	NM- 9.2
1-($2.75)-Embossed-c w/bound-in trading card						2.75
1-($3.50)-Platinum edition (1 for each 10 ordered)						4.00
2-4: Perez-c/a; bound-in trading card: 2-(5/94)						2.50
TPB (DC, 2006, $14.99) r/series; intro. by Peter David; creator bios.						15.00

SACRAMENTS, THE
Catechetical Guild Educational Society: Oct, 1955 (25¢)

	GD 2.0	VG 4.0	FN 6.0	VF 8.0	VF/NM 9.0	NM- 9.2
304	5	10	15	24	30	35

SACRED AND THE PROFANE, THE (See Eclipse Graphic Album Series #9 & Epic Illustrated #20)

SADDLE JUSTICE (Happy Houlihans #1,2) (Saddle Romances #9 on)
E. C. Comics: No. 3, Spring, 1948 - No. 8, Sept-Oct, 1949

	GD 2.0	VG 4.0	FN 6.0	VF 8.0	VF/NM 9.0	NM- 9.2
3-The 1st E.C. by Bill Gaines to break away from M. C. Gaines' old Educational Comics format. Craig, Feldstein, H. C. Kiefer, & Stan Asch-a; mentioned in Love and Death	52	104	156	322	536	750
4-1st Graham Ingels-a for E.C.	45	90	135	279	465	650
5-8-Ingels-a in all	41	82	123	250	413	575

NOTE: *Craig* and *Feldstein* art in most issues. Canadian reprints known; see Table of Contents. *Craig* c-3, 4. *Ingels* c-5-8. #4 contains a biography of *Craig*.

SADDLE ROMANCES (Saddle Justice #3-8; Weird Science #12 on)
E. C. Comics: No. 9, Nov-Dec, 1949 - No. 11, Mar-Apr, 1950

	GD 2.0	VG 4.0	FN 6.0	VF 8.0	VF/NM 9.0	NM- 9.2
9,11: 9-Ingels-c/a. 11-Ingels-a; Feldstein-c	46	92	138	285	473	660
10-Wally Wood's 1st work at E. C.; Ingels-a; Feldstein-c	46	92	138	290	480	670

NOTE: Canadian reprints known; see Table of Contents. *Wood/Harrison* a-10, 11.

SADHU
Virgin Comics: July, 2006 - No. 8, June, 2007 ($2.99)

	GD 2.0	VG 4.0	FN 6.0	VF 8.0	VF/NM 9.0	NM- 9.2
1-8: 1,2-Gotham Chopra-s/Jeevan Kang-a						3.00
...: The Silent Ones (8/07 - No. 5, 2/08, $2.99) 1-5						3.00
...: Wheel of Destiny (4/08 - No. 5, $2.99) 1,2						3.00

SADIE SACK (See Harvey Hits #93)

SAD SACK AND THE SARGE
Harvey Publications: Sept, 1957 - No. 155, June, 1982

	GD 2.0	VG 4.0	FN 6.0	VF 8.0	VF/NM 9.0	NM- 9.2
1	14	28	42	99	175	250
2	8	16	24	52	86	120
3-10	6	12	18	41	66	90
11-20	5	10	15	32	51	70
21-30	3	6	9	20	30	40
31-50	3	6	9	14	20	25
51-70	2	4	6	9	13	16
71-90,97-99	1	3	4	6	8	10
91-96: All 52 pg. Giants	2	4	6	9	13	16
100	2	4	6	8	10	12
101-120	1	2	3	4	5	7
121-155						5.00

SAD SACK COMICS (See Harvey Collector's Comics #16, Little Sad Sack, Tastee Freez Comics #4 & True Comics #55)
Harvey Publications/Lorne-Harvey Publications (Recollections) #288 On: Sept, 1949 - No. 287, Oct, 1982; No. 288, 1992 - No. 291, 1993

	GD 2.0	VG 4.0	FN 6.0	VF 8.0	VF/NM 9.0	NM- 9.2
1-Infinity-c; Little Dot begins (1st app.); civilian issues begin, end #21; based on comic strip	71	142	213	604	1152	1700
2-Flying Fool by Powell	28	56	84	203	377	550
3	15	30	45	111	206	300
4-10	12	24	36	82	146	210
11-21	8	16	24	56	93	130
22-("Back In The Army Again" on covers #22-36); "The Specialist" story about Sad Sack's return to Army	9	18	27	65	113	160
23-30	6	12	18	37	59	80
31-50	4	8	12	28	44	60
51-80,100: 62-"The Specialist" reprinted	3	6	9	20	30	40
81-99	3	6	9	16	23	30
101-140	3	6	9	14	19	24
141-170,200	2	4	6	11	16	20
171-199	2	4	6	9	13	16
201-207: 207-Last 12¢ issue	2	4	6	8	11	14
208-222	1	2	3	5	6	8
223-228 (25¢ Giants, 52 pgs.)	2	4	6	8	11	14
229-250	1	3	4	6	8	10
251-285						6.00
286,287-Limited distribution	1	2	3	5	7	9
288,289 ($2.75, 1992): 289-50th anniversary issue						6.00
290,291 ($1.00, 1993, B&W)						3.00
3-D 1 (1/54, 25¢)-Came with 2 pairs of glasses; titled "Harvey 3-D Hits"	16	32	48	112	209	305
...At Home for the Holidays 1 (1993, no-c price)-Publ. by Lorne-Harvey' X-Mas issue						4.00

NOTE: *The Sad Sack Comics comic book was a spin-off from a Sunday Newspaper strip launched through John Wheeler's Bell Syndicate. The previous Sunday page and the first 21 comics depicted the Sad Sack in civvies. Unpopularity caused the Sunday page to be discontinued in the early '50s. Meanwhile Sad Sack returned to the Army, by popular demand, in issue No. 22, remaining there ever since. Incidentally, relatively few of the first 21 issues were ever collected and remain scarce due to this.*

SAD SACK FUN AROUND THE WORLD
Harvey Publications: 1974 (no month)

	GD 2.0	VG 4.0	FN 6.0	VF 8.0	VF/NM 9.0	NM- 9.2
1-About Great Britain	2	4	6	11	16	20

SAD SACK GOES HOME
Harvey Publications: 1951 (16 pgs. in color, no cover price)

	GD 2.0	VG 4.0	FN 6.0	VF 8.0	VF/NM 9.0	NM- 9.2
nn-By George Baker	5	10	15	34	55	75

SAD SACK LAUGH SPECIAL

Sad Sack Laugh Special #92 © HARV

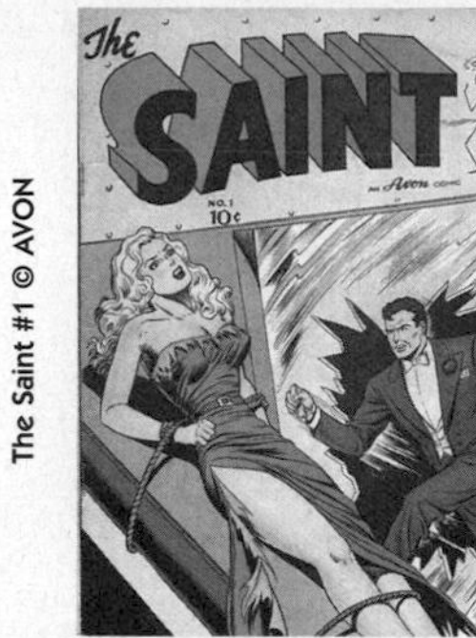

The Saint #1 © AVON

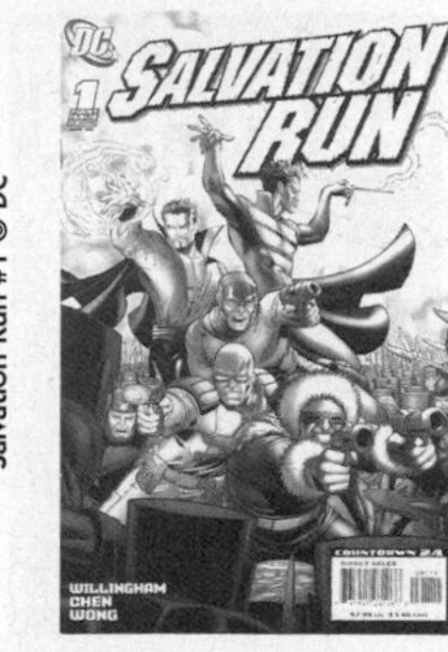

Salvation Run #1 © DC

Harvey Publications: Winter, 1958-59 - No. 93, Feb, 1977 (#1-9: 84 pgs.; #10-60: 68 pgs.; #61-76: 52 pgs.)

	GD 2.0	VG 4.0	FN 6.0	VF 8.0	VF/NM 9.0	NM- 9.2
1-Giant 25¢ issues begin	10	20	30	71	126	180
2	6	12	18	41	66	90
3-10	5	10	15	32	51	70
11-30	4	8	12	26	41	55
31-60: 31-Hi-Fi Tweeter app. 60-Last 68 pg. Giant	3	6	9	16	23	30
61-76-(All 52 pg. issues)	2	4	6	10	14	18
77-93	1	2	3	5	6	8

SAD SACK NAVY, GOBS 'N' GALS
Harvey Publications: Aug, 1972 - No. 8, Oct, 1973

	GD 2.0	VG 4.0	FN 6.0	VF 8.0	VF/NM 9.0	NM- 9.2
1: 52 pg. Giant	3	6	9	16	23	30
2-8	2	4	6	9	12	15

SAD SACK'S ARMY LIFE (See Harvey Hits #8, 17, 22, 28, 32, 39, 43, 47, 51, 55, 58, 61, 64, 67, 70)

SAD SACK'S ARMY LIFE (...Parade #1-57, ...Today #58 on)
Harvey Publications: Oct, 1963 - No. 60, Nov, 1975; No. 61, May, 1976

	GD 2.0	VG 4.0	FN 6.0	VF 8.0	VF/NM 9.0	NM- 9.2
1-(68 pg. issues begin)	8	16	24	52	86	120
2-10	4	8	12	28	44	60
11-20	3	6	9	20	30	40
21-34: Last 68 pg. issue	3	6	9	16	23	30
35-51: All 52 pgs.	2	4	6	10	14	18
52-61	1	3	4	6	8	10

SAD SACK'S FUNNY FRIENDS (See Harvey Hits #75)
Harvey Publications: Dec, 1955 - No. 75, Oct, 1969

	GD 2.0	VG 4.0	FN 6.0	VF 8.0	VF/NM 9.0	NM- 9.2
1	10	20	30	71	126	180
2-10	6	12	18	41	66	90
11-20	4	8	12	24	37	50
21-30	3	6	9	18	27	35
31-50	3	6	9	14	20	25
51-75	2	4	6	9	13	16

SAD SACK'S MUTTSY (See Harvey Hits #74, 77, 80, 82, 84, 87, 89, 92, 90, 99, 102, 105, 108, 111, 113, 115, 117, 119, 121)

SAD SACK USA (...Vacation #8)
Harvey Publications: Nov, 1972 - No. 7, Nov, 1973; No. 8, Oct, 1974

	GD 2.0	VG 4.0	FN 6.0	VF 8.0	VF/NM 9.0	NM- 9.2
1	3	6	9	14	20	25
2-8	2	4	6	8	10	12

SAD SACK WITH SARGE & SADIE
Harvey Publications: Sept, 1972 - No. 8, Nov, 1973

	GD 2.0	VG 4.0	FN 6.0	VF 8.0	VF/NM 9.0	NM- 9.2
1-(52 pg. Giant)	3	6	9	14	20	25
2-8	2	4	6	8	10	12

SAD SAD SACK WORLD
Harvey Publ.: Oct, 1964 - No. 46, Dec, 1973 (#1-31: 68 pgs.; #32-38: 52 pgs.)

	GD 2.0	VG 4.0	FN 6.0	VF 8.0	VF/NM 9.0	NM- 9.2
1	7	14	21	49	80	110
2-10	4	8	12	26	41	55
11-20	3	6	9	20	30	40
21-31: 31-Last 68 pg. issue	3	6	9	16	23	30
32-39-(All 52 pgs)	2	4	6	10	14	18
40-46	1	3	4	6	8	10

SAFEST PLACE IN THE WORLD, THE
Dark Horse Comics: 1993 ($2.50, one-shot)

1-Steve Ditko-c/a/scripts — 2.50

SAFETY-BELT MAN
Sirius Entertainment: June, 1994 - No. 6, 1995 ($2.50, B&W)

1-6: 1-Horan-s/Dark One-a/Sprouse-c. 2,3-Warren-c. 4-Linsner back-up story. 5,6-Crilley-a — 3.00

SAFETY-BELT MAN ALL HELL
Sirius Entertainment: June, 1996 - No. 6, Mar, 1997 ($2.95, color)

1-6-Horan-s/Fillbach Bros.-a — 3.00

SAGA OF BIG RED, THE
Omaha World-Herald: Sept, 1976 ($1.25) (In color)

nn-by Win Mumma; story of the Nebraska Cornhuskers (sports) — 6.00

SAGA OF CRYSTAR, CRYSTAL WARRIOR, THE
Marvel Comics: May, 1983 - No. 11, Feb, 1985 (Remco toy tie-in)

1,6: 1-(Baxter paper). 6-Nightcrawler app; Golden-c — 4.00
2-5,7-11: 3-Dr. Strange app. 3-11-Golden-c (painted-4,5). 11-Alpha Flight app. — 3.00

SAGA OF RA'S AL GHUL, THE
DC Comics: Jan, 1988 - No. 4, Apr, 1988 ($2.50, limited series)

1-4-r/N. Adams Batman — 6.00

SAGA OF SABAN'S MIGHTY MORPHIN POWER RANGERS (Also see Saban's Mighty Morphin Power Rangers)
Hamilton Comics: 1995 - No. 4, 1995 ($1.95, limited series)

1-4 — 2.50

SAGA OF SEVEN SUNS, THE : VEILED ALLIANCES
DC Comics (WildStorm): 2004 ($24.95, hardcover graphic novel with dustjacket)

HC-Kevin J. Anderson-s/Robert Teranishi-a — 25.00
SC-(2004, $17.95) — 18.00

SAGA OF THE SWAMP THING, THE (See Swamp Thing)

SAGA OF THE ORIGINAL HUMAN TORCH
Marvel Comics: Apr, 1990 - No. 4, July, 1990 ($1.50, limited series)

1-4: 1-Origin; Buckler-c/a(p). 3-Hitler-c — 2.50

SAGA OF THE SUB-MARINER, THE
Marvel Comics: Nov, 1988 - No. 12, Oct, 1989 ($1.25/$1.50 #5 on, maxi-series)

1-12: 9-Original X-Men app. — 3.00

SAILOR MOON (Manga)
Mixx Entertainment Inc.: 1998 - Present ($2.95)

	GD 2.0	VG 4.0	FN 6.0	VF 8.0	VF/NM 9.0	NM- 9.2
1	2	4	6	10	14	18
1-(San Diego edition)	2	4	6	11	16	20
2-5	2	4	6	8	10	12
6-25						5.00
26-35						3.00
... Rini's Moon Stick 1						15.00

SAILOR ON THE SEA OF FATE (See First Comics Graphic Novel #11)

SAILOR SWEENEY (Navy Action #1-11, 15 on)
Atlas Comics (CDS): No. 12, July, 1956 - No. 14, Nov, 1956

	GD 2.0	VG 4.0	FN 6.0	VF 8.0	VF/NM 9.0	NM- 9.2
12-14: 12-Shores-a. 13,14-Severin-c	9	18	27	52	69	85

SAINT, THE (Also see Movie Comics(DC) #2 & Silver Streak #18)
Avon Periodicals: Aug, 1947 - No. 12, Mar, 1952

	GD 2.0	VG 4.0	FN 6.0	VF 8.0	VF/NM 9.0	NM- 9.2
1-Kamen bondage-c/a	85	170	255	536	906	1275
2	40	80	120	246	403	560
3-5: 4-Lingerie panels	37	74	111	215	345	475
6-Miss Fury app. by Tarpe Mills (14 pgs.)	48	96	144	298	499	700
7-c-/Avon paperback #118	29	58	87	169	272	375
8,9(12/50): Saint strip-r in #8-12; 9-Kinstler-c	26	52	78	152	244	335
10-Wood-a, 1 pg; c-/Avon paperback #289	26	52	78	152	244	335
11	20	40	60	115	183	250
12-c-/Avon paperback #123	22	44	66	127	204	280

NOTE: *Lucky Dale, Girl Detective in #1,2,4,6.* **Hollingsworth** *a-4, 6. Painted-c 7, 8, 10-12.*

SAINT ANGEL
Image Comics: Mar, 2000 - No. 4, Mar, 2001 ($2.95/$3.95)

0-Altstaetter & Napton-s/Altstaetter-a — 3.00
1-4-($3.95) Flip book w/Deity. 1-(6/00). 2-(10/00) — 4.00

ST. GEORGE
Marvel Comics (Epic Comics): June, 1988 - No.8, Oct, 1989 ($1.25,/$1.50)

1-8: Sienkiewicz-c. 3-begin $1.50-c — 2.50

SAINT GERMAINE
Caliber Comics: 1997 - No. 8, 1998 ($2.95)

1-8: 1,5-Alternate covers — 3.00

ST. SWITHIN'S DAY
Trident Comics: Apr, 1990 ($2.50, one-shot)

1-Grant Morrison scripts — 3.00

ST. SWITHIN'S DAY
Oni Press: Mar, 1998 ($2.95, B&W, one-shot)

1-Grant Morrison-s/Paul Grist-a — 3.00

SALOMÉ (See Night Music #6)

SALVATION RUN
DC Comics: Jan, 2008 - No. 7, Jul, 2008 ($2.99, limited series)

1-7-DC villains banished to an alien planet; Willingham-s/Chen-a/c. 1-Var-c by Corroney — 3.00

SAM AND MAX, FREELANCE POLICE SPECIAL
Fishwrap Prod./Comico: 1987 ($1.75, B&W); Jan, 1989 ($2.75, 44 pgs.)

1 ($1.75, B&W, Fishwrap) — 3.00

Samson #13 © AJAX

Sandman #5 © DC

Sandman (2nd series) #40 © DC

GD VG FN VF VF/NM NM-
2.0 4.0 6.0 8.0 9.0 9.2

2 ($2.75, color, Comico) 2.75

SAM AND TWITCH (See Spawn and Case Files:...)
Image Comics (Todd McFarlane Prod.): Aug, 1999 - No. 26, Feb, 2004 ($2.50)

1-26: 1-19-Bendis-s. 1-14-Medina-a. 15-19-Maleev-a. 20-24-McFarlane-s/Maleev-a 2.50
Book One: Udaku (2000, $21.95, TPB) B&W reprint of #1-8 22.00
...: The Brian Michael Bendis Collection Vol. 1 (2/06, $24.95) r/#1-9 in color; sketch pages 25.00
...: The Brian Michael Bendis Collection Vol. 2 (6/07, $24.95) r/#10-19; cover gallery 25.00

SAM HILL PRIVATE EYE
Close-Up (Archie): 1950 - No. 7, 1951

1 16 32 48 92 144 195
2 10 20 30 56 76 95
3-7 10 20 30 54 72 90

SAMSON (1st Series) (Captain Aero #7 on; see Big 3 Comics)
Fox Features Syndicate: Fall, 1940 - No. 6, Sept, 1941 (See Fantastic Comics)

1-Samson begins, ends #6; Powell-a, signed 'Rensie;' Wing Turner by Tuska app; Fine-c?
220 440 660 1386 2343 3300
2-Dr. Fung by Powell; Fine-c? 80 160 240 504 852 1200
3-Navy Jones app.; Joe Simon-c 60 120 180 378 639 900
4-Yarko the Great, Master Magician begins 53 106 159 330 553 775
5,6: 6-Origin The Topper 43 86 129 267 446 625

SAMSON (2nd Series) (Formerly Fantastic Comics #10, 11)
Ajax/Farrell Publications (Four Star): No. 12, April, 1955 - No. 14, Aug, 1955

12-Wonder Boy 30 60 90 174 280 385
13,14: 13-Wonder Boy, Rocket Man 26 52 78 152 244 335

SAMSON (See Mighty Samson)

SAMSON & DELILAH (See A Spectacular Feature Magazine)

SAMUEL BRONSTON'S CIRCUS WORLD (See Circus World under Movie Classics)

SAMURAI (Also see Eclipse Graphic Album Series #14)
Aircel Publications: 1985 - No. 23, 1987 ($1.70, B&W)

1, 14-16-Dale Keown-a 3.00
1-(reprinted),2-12,17-23: 2 (reprinted issue exists) 2.50
13-Dale Keown's 1st published artwork (1987) 5.00

SAMURAI
Warp Graphics: May, 1997 ($2.95, B&W)

1 3.00

SAMURAI CAT
Marvel Comics (Epic Comics): June, 1991 - No. 3, Sept, 1991 ($2.25, limited series)

1-3: 3-Darth Vader-c/story parody 2.50

SAMURAI: HEAVEN & EARTH
Dark Horse Comics: Dec, 2004 - No. 5, Dec, 2005 ($2.99)

1-5-Luke Ross-a/Ron Marz-s 3.00
TPB (4/06, $14.95) r/#1-5; sketch pages and cover and pin-up gallery 15.00

SAMURAI: HEAVEN & EARTH (Volume 2)
Dark Horse Comics: Nov, 2006 - No. 5, June, 2007 ($2.99)

1-5-Luke Ross-a/Ron Marz-s 3.00
TPB (10/07, $14.95) r/#1-5; sketch pages and cover and pin-up gallery 15.00

SAMURAI JACK SPECIAL (TV)
DC Comics: Sept, 2002 ($3.95, one-shot)

1-Adaptation of pilot episode with origin story; Tartakovsky-s 4.00

SAMURAI: LEGEND
Marvel Comics (Soleil): 2008 - No. 4, 2009 ($5.99)

1-Genet-a/DiGiorgio-s; English version of French comic; preview of other titles 6.00

SAMUREE
Continuity Comics: May, 1987 - No. 9, Jan, 1991

1-9 3.00

SAMUREE
Continuity Comics: V2#1, May, 1993 - V2#4, Jan,1994 ($2.50)

V2#1-4-Embossed-c: 2,4-Adams plot, Nebres-i. 3-Nino-c(i) 2.50

SAMUREE
Acclaim Comics (Windjammer): Oct, 1995 - No. 2, Nov,1995 ($2.50, lim. series)

1,2 2.50

SAN DIEGO COMIC CON COMICS
Dark Horse Comics: 1992 - No.4, 1995 (B&W, promo comic for the San Diego Comic Con)

GD VG FN VF VF/NM NM-
2.0 4.0 6.0 8.0 9.0 9.2

1-(1992)-Includes various characters published from Dark Horse including Concrete, The Mask, RoboCop and others; 1st app. of Sprint from John Byrne's Next Men; art by Quesada, Byrne, Rude, Burden, Moebius & others; pin-ups by Rude, Dorkin, Allred & others; Chadwick-c 1 2 3 5 7 9
2-(1993)-Intro of Legend imprint; 1st app. of John Byrne's Danger Unlimited, Mike Mignola's Hellboy, Art Adams' Monkeyman & O'Brien; contains stories featuring Concrete, Sin City, Martha Washington & others; Grendel, Madman, & Big Guy pin-ups; Don Martin-c.
2 4 6 8 10 12
3-(1994)-Contains stories featuring Barb Wire, The Mask, The Dirty Pair, & Grendel by Matt Wagner; contains pin-ups of Ghost, Predator & Rascals In Paradise; The Mask-c. 6.00
4-(1995)-Contains Sin City story by Miller (3pg.), Star Wars, The Mask, Tarzan, Foot Soldiers; Sin City & Star Wars flip-c 6.00

SANDMAN, THE (1st Series) (Also see Adventure Comics #40, New York World's Fair & World's Finest #3)
National Periodical Publ.: Winter, 1974; No. 2, Apr-May, 1975 - No. 6, Dec-Jan, 1975-76

1-1st app. Bronze Age Sandman by Simon & Kirby (last S&K collaboration)
6 12 18 41 66 90
2-6: 6-Kirby/Wood-c/a 3 6 9 20 30 40

NOTE: *Kirby a-1p, 4-6p; c-1-5, 6p.*

SANDMAN (2nd Series) (See Books of Magic, Vertigo Jam & Vertigo Preview)
DC Comics (Vertigo imprint #47 on): Jan, 1989 - No. 75, Mar, 1996 ($1.50-$2.50, mature)

1 ($2.00, 52 pgs.)-1st app. Modern Age Sandman (Morpheus); Neil Gaiman scripts begin; Sam Kieth-a(p) in #1-5; Wesley Dodds (G.A. Sandman) cameo.
4 8 12 22 34 45
2-Cain & Abel app. (from HOM & HOS) 2 4 6 11 16 20
3-5: 3-John Constantine app. 2 4 6 9 13 16
6,7 2 4 6 8 10 12
8-Death-c/story (1st app.)-Regular ed. has Jeanette Kahn publishorial & American Cancer Society ad w/no indicia on inside front-c
3 6 9 14 19 24
8-Limited ed. (600+ copies?); has Karen Berger editorial and next issue teaser on inside covers (has indicia) 5 10 15 30 48 65
9-14: 10-Has explaination about #8 mixup; has bound-in Shocker movie poster.
14-(52 pgs.)-Bound-in Nightbreed fold-out 1 3 4 6 8 10
15-20: 16-Photo-c. 17,18-Kelley Jones-a. 19-Vess-a. 6.00
18-Error version w/1st 3 panels on pg. 1 in blue ink 3 6 9 16 22 28
19-Error version w/pages 18 & 20 facing each other 2 4 6 13 18 22
21,23-27: Seasons of Mist storyline. 22-World Without End preview. 24-Kelley Jones/Russell-a 6.00
22-1st Daniel (Later becomes new Sandman) 2 4 6 8 10 12
28-30 5.00
31-49,51-74: 36-(52 pgs.). 41,44-48-Metallic ink on-c. 48-Cerebus appears as a doll. 54-Re-intro Prez; Death app.; Belushi, Nixon & Wildcat cameos. 57-Metallic ink on c. 65-w/bound-in trading card. 69-Death of Sandman. 70-73-Zulli-a. 74-Jon J. Muth-a. 4.00
50-($2.95, 52 pgs.)-Black-c w/metallic ink by McKean; Russell-a; McFarlane pin-up 5.00
50-($2.95)-Signed & limited (5,000) Treasury Edition with sketch of Neil Gaiman
1 2 3 5 6 8
50-Platinum 20.00
75-($3.95)-Vess-a. 5.00
Special 1 (1991, $3.50, 68 pgs.)-Glow-in-the-dark-c 5.00
Absolute Sandman Special Edition #1 (2006, 50¢) sampling from HC; recolored r/#1 2.50
Absolute Sandman Volume One (2006, $99.00, slipcased hardcover) recolored r/#1-20; Gaiman's original proposal; script and pencils from #19; character sketch gallery 100.00
Absolute Sandman Volume Two (2007, $99.00, slipcased hardcover) recolored r/#21-39; r/A Gallery of Dreams one-shot; bonus stories, scripts and pencil art 100.00
Absolute Sandman Volume Three (2008, $99.00, slipcased hardcover) recolored r/#40-56; & Special #1; bonus galleries, scripts and pencil art; Jill Thompson intro. 100.00
...: A Gallery of Dreams ($2.95)-Intro by N. Gaiman 3.00
...: Preludes & Nocturnes ($29.95, HC)-r/#1-8. 30.00
...: The Doll's House (1990, $29.95, HC)-r/#8-16. 30.00
...: Dream Country ($29.95, HC)-r/#17-20. 30.00
...: Season of Mists ($29.95, Leatherbound HC)-r/#21-28. 50.00
...: A Game of You ($29.95, HC)-r/32-37, ...: Fables and Reflections ($29.95, HC)-r/Vertigo Preview #1, Sandman Special #1, #29-31, #38-40 & #50. ...: Brief Lives ($29.95, HC)-r/#41-49. ...: World's End ($29.95, HC)-r/#51-56 30.00
...: The Kindly Ones (1996, $34.95, HC)-r/#57-69 & Vertigo Jam #1 35.00
...: The Wake ($29.95, HC)-r/#70-75. 30.00

NOTE: *A new set of hardcover printings with new covers was introduced in 1998-99. Multiple printings exist of softcover collections.* **Bachalo** *a-12;* **Kelley Jones** *a-17, 18, 22, 23, 26, 27.* **Vess** *a-19, 75.*

SANDMAN: ENDLESS NIGHTS
DC Comics (Vertigo): 2003 ($24.95, hardcover, with dust jacket)

HC-Neil Gaiman stories of Morpheus and the Endless illustrated by Fabry, Manara, Prado, Quitely, Russell, Sienkiewicz, and Storey; McKean-c 25.00

Sandman Mystery Theater #5 © DC

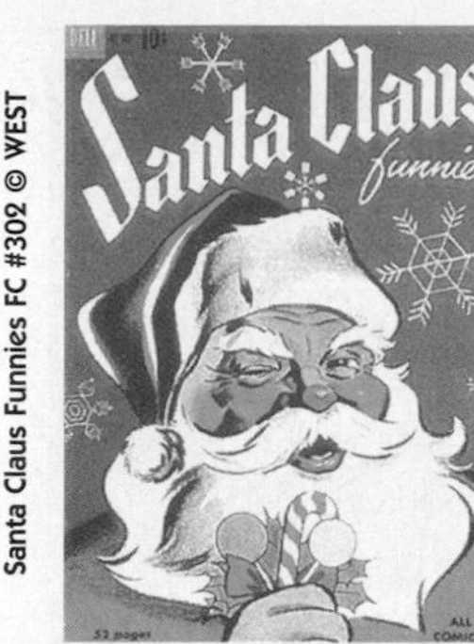

Santa Claus Funnies FC #302 © WEST

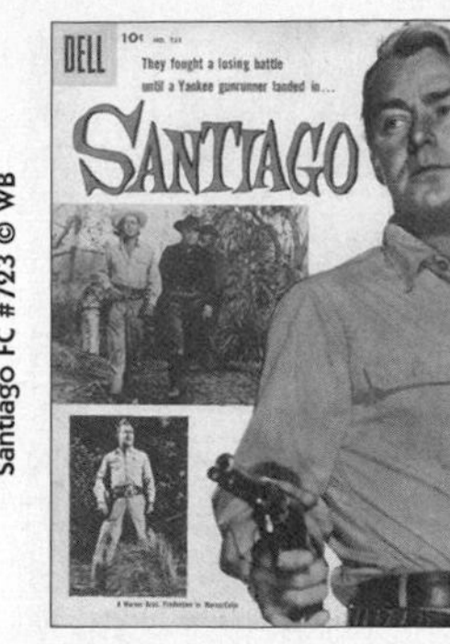

Santiago FC #723 © WB

GD 2.0 | VG 4.0 | FN 6.0 | VF 8.0 | VF/NM 9.0 | NM- 9.2

...Special (11/03, $2.95) Previews hardcover; Dream story w/Prado-a; McKean-c 3.00
SC (2004, $17.95) 18.00

SANDMAN MIDNIGHT THEATRE
DC Comics (Vertigo): Sept, 1995 ($6.95, squarebound, one-shot)

nn-Modern Age Sandman (Morpheus) meets G.A. Sandman; Gaiman & Wagner story; McKean-c; Kristiansen-a 7.00

SANDMAN MYSTERY THEATRE (Also see Sandman (2nd Series) #1)
DC Comics (Vertigo): Apr, 1993 - No. 70, Feb, 1999 ($1.95/$2.25/$2.50)

1-G.A. Sandman advs. begin; Matt Wagner scripts begin 4.50
2-49: 5-Neon ink logo. 29-32-Hourman app. 38-Ted Knight (G.A. Starman) app. 42-Jim Corrigan (Spectre) app. 45-48-Blackhawk app. 2.50
50-($3.50, 48 pgs.) w/bonus story of S.A. Sandman, Torres-a 3.50
51-70 2.50
Annual 1 (10/94, $3.95, 68 pgs.)-Alex Ross, Bolton & others-a 5.00
...: Dr. Death and the Night of the Butcher (2007, $19.99) r/#21-28 20.00
...: The Face and the Brute (2004, $19.95) r/#5-12 20.00
...: The Hourman and The Python (2008, $19.99) r/#29-36 20.00
...: The Scorpion (2006, $12.99) r/#17-20 13.00
...: The Tarantula (1995, $14.95) r/#1-4 15.00
...: The Vamp (2005, $12.99) r/#13-16 13.00

SANDMAN MYSTERY THEATRE (2nd Series)
DC Comics (Vertigo): Feb, 2007 - No. 5, Jun, 2007 ($2.99, limited series)

1-5-Wesley Dodds and Dian in 1997; Rieber-s/Nguyen-a 3.00

SANDMAN PRESENTS...
DC Comics (Vertigo)

Taller Tales TPB (2003, $19.95) r/S.P: The Thessaliad #1-4; Merv Pumpkinhead, Agent...; The Dreaming #55; S.P. Everything You Always...; new McKean-c; intro by Willingham 20.00

SANDMAN PRESENTS: BAST
DC Comics (Vertigo): Mar, 2003 - No. 3, May, 2003 ($2.95, limited series)

1-3-Kiernan-s/Bennett-a/McKean-c 3.00

SANDMAN PRESENTS: DEADBOY DETECTIVES (See Sandman #21-28)
DC Comics (Vertigo): Aug, 2001 - No. 4, Nov, 2001 ($2.50, limited series)

1-4:Talbot-a/McKean-c/Brubaker-s 2.50

SANDMAN PRESENTS: EVERYTHING YOU ALWAYS WANTED TO KNOW ABOUT DREAMS...BUT WERE AFRAID TO ASK
DC Comics (Vertigo): Jul, 2001 ($3.95, one-shot)

1-Short stories by Willingham; art by various; McKean-c 4.00

SANDMAN PRESENTS: LOVE STREET
DC Comics (Vertigo): Jul, 1999 - No. 3, Sept, 1999 ($2.95, limited series)

1-3: Teenage Hellblazer in 1968 London; Zulli-a 3.00

SANDMAN PRESENTS: LUCIFER
DC Comics (Vertigo): Mar, 1999 - No. 3, May, 1999 ($2.95, limited series)

1-3: Scott Hampton painted-c/a 3.00

SANDMAN PRESENTS: PETREFAX
DC Comics (Vertigo): Mar, 2000 - No. 4, Jun, 2000 ($2.95, limited series)

1-4-Carey-s/Leialoha-a 3.00

SANDMAN PRESENTS: THE CORINTHIAN
DC Comics (Vertigo): Dec, 2001 - No. 3, Feb, 2002 ($2.95, limited series)

1-3-Macan-s/Zezelj-a/McKean-c 3.00

SANDMAN PRESENTS, THE: THE FURIES
DC Comics (Vertigo): 2002 ($24.95, one-shot)

Hardcover-Mike Carey-s/John Bolton-painted art; Lyta Hall's reunion with Daniel 30.00
Softcover-(2003, $17.95) 18.00

SANDMAN PRESENTS, THE: THESSALY: WITCH FOR HIRE
DC Comics (Vertigo): Apr, 2004 - No. 4, July, 2004 ($2.95, limited series)

1-4-Willingham-s/McManus-a/McPherson-c 3.00
TPB-(2005, $12.99) r/#1-4 13.00

SANDMAN PRESENTS, THE: THE THESSALIAD
DC Comics (Vertigo): Mar, 2002 - No. 4, Jun, 2002 ($2.95, limited series)

1-4-Willingham-s/McManus-a/McKean-c 3.00

SANDMAN, THE: THE DREAM HUNTERS
DC Comics (Vertigo): Oct, 1999 ($29.95/$19.95, one-shot)

Hardcover-Neil Gaiman-s/Yoshitaka Amano-painted art 30.00
Softcover-(2000, $19.95) new Amano-c 20.00

GD 2.0 | VG 4.0 | FN 6.0 | VF 8.0 | VF/NM 9.0 | NM- 9.2

SANDS OF THE SOUTH PACIFIC
Toby Press: Jan, 1953

	GD	VG	FN	VF	VF/NM	NM-
1	20	40	60	117	186	255

SANTA AND HIS REINDEER (See March of Comics #166)

SANTA AND THE ANGEL (See Dell Junior Treasury #7)
Dell Publishing Co.: Dec, 1949 (Combined w/Santa at the Zoo) (Gollub-a condensed from FC#128)

	GD	VG	FN	VF	VF/NM	NM-
Four Color 259	5	10	15	35	55	75

SANTA AT THE ZOO (See Santa And The Angel)

SANTA CLAUS AROUND THE WORLD (See March of Comics #241 in Promotional Comics section)

SANTA CLAUS CONQUERS THE MARTIANS (See Movie Classics)

SANTA CLAUS FUNNIES (Also see Dell Giants)
Dell Publishing Co.: Dec?, 1942 - No. 1274, Dec, 1961

	GD	VG	FN	VF	VF/NM	NM-
nn(#1)(1942)-Kelly-a	35	70	105	270	498	725
2(12/43)-Kelly-a	23	46	60	167	309	450
Four Color 61(1944)-Kelly-a	22	44	66	163	302	440
Four Color 91(1945)-Kelly-a	17	34	51	120	223	325
Four Color 128('46),175('47)-Kelly-a	14	28	42	102	181	260
Four Color 205,254-Kelly-a	13	26	39	93	164	235
Four Color 302,361,525,607,666,756,867	7	14	21	45	73	100
Four Color 958,1063,1154,1274	6	12	18	41	66	90

NOTE: *Most issues contain only one Kelly story.*

SANTA CLAUS PARADE
Ziff-Davis (Approved Comics)/St. John Publishing Co.: 1951; No. 2, Dec, 1952; No. 3, Jan, 1955 (25¢)

	GD	VG	FN	VF	VF/NM	NM-
nn(1951-Ziff-Davis)-116 pgs. (Xmas Special 1,2)	29	58	87	169	272	375
2(12/52-Ziff-Davis)-100 pgs.; Dave Berg-a	22	44	66	127	204	280
V1#3(1/55-St. John)-100 pgs.; reprints-c/#1	19	38	57	112	176	240

SANTA CLAUS' WORKSHOP (See March of Comics #50,168 in Promotional Comics section)

SANTA IS COMING (See March of Comics #197 in Promotional Comics section)

SANTA IS HERE (See March of Comics #49 in Promotional Comics section)

SANTA'S BUSY CORNER (See March of Comics #31 in Promotional Comics section)

SANTA'S CANDY KITCHEN (See March of Comics #14 in Promotional Comics section)

SANTA'S CHRISTMAS BOOK (See March of Comics #123 in Promotional Comics section)

SANTA'S CHRISTMAS COMICS
Standard Comics (Best Books): Dec, 1952 (100 pgs.)

	GD	VG	FN	VF	VF/NM	NM-
nn-Supermouse, Dizzy Duck, Happy Rabbit, etc.	18	36	54	105	165	225

SANTA'S CHRISTMAS LIST (See March of Comics #255 in Promotional Comics section)

SANTA'S HELPERS (See March of Comics #64, 106, 198 in Promotional Comics section)

SANTA'S LITTLE HELPERS (See March of Comics #270 in Promotional Comics section)

SANTA'S SHOW (See March of Comics #311 in Promotional Comics section)

SANTA'S SLEIGH (See March of Comics #298 in Promotional Comics section)

SANTA'S SURPRISE (See March of Comics #13 in Promotional Comics section)

SANTA'S TINKER TOTS
Charlton Comics: 1958

	GD	VG	FN	VF	VF/NM	NM-
1-Based on "The Tinker Tots Keep Christmas"	4	8	12	22	34	45

SANTA'S TOYLAND (See March of Comics #242 in Promotional Comics section)

SANTA'S TOYS (See March of Comics #12 in Promotional Comics section)

SANTA'S VISIT (See March of Comics #283 in Promotional Comics section)

SANTA THE BARBARIAN
Maximum Press: Dec, 1996 ($2.99, one-shot)

1-Fraga/Mhan-s/a 3.00

SANTIAGO (Movie)
Dell Publishing Co.: Sept, 1956 (Alan Ladd photo-c)

	GD	VG	FN	VF	VF/NM	NM-
Four Color 723-Kinstler-a	9	18	27	63	107	150

SARGE SNORKEL (Beetle Bailey)
Charlton Comics: Oct, 1973 - No. 17, Dec, 1976

	GD	VG	FN	VF	VF/NM	NM-
1	2	4	6	11	16	20
2-10	2	4	6	8	10	12
11-17	1	2	3	5	7	9

SARGE STEEL (Becomes Secret Agent #9 on; also see Judomaster)
Charlton Comics: Dec, 1964 - No. 8, Mar-Apr, 1966 (All 12¢ issues)

Satan's Six: Hellspawn #3 © Topps

Savage Dragon #134 © Erik Larsen

Savage She-Hulk #25 © MAR

	GD	VG	FN	VF	VF/NM	NM-
	2.0	4.0	6.0	8.0	9.0	9.2

	GD 2.0	VG 4.0	FN 6.0	VF 8.0	VF/NM 9.0	NM- 9.2
1-Origin & 1st app.	4	8	12	24	37	50
2-5,7,8	3	6	9	16	23	30
6-2nd app. Judomaster	3	6	9	20	30	40

SATAN'S SIX
Topps Comics (Kirbyverse): Apr, 1993 - No. 4, July, 1993 ($2.95, lim. series)

1-4: 1-Polybagged w/Kirbychrome trading card; Kirby/McFarlane-c plus 8 pgs. Kirby-a(p); has coupon for Kirbychrome ed. of Secret City Saga #0. 2-4-Polybagged w/3 cards. 4-Teenagents preview 3.00
NOTE: *Ditko a-1. Miller a-1.*

SATAN'S SIX: HELLSPAWN
Topps Comics (Kirbyverse): June, 1994 - No. 3, July, 1994 ($2.50, limited series)

1-3: 1-(6/94)-Indicia incorrectly shows "Vol 1 #2". 2-(6/94) 2.50

SAURIANS: UNNATURAL SELECTION (See Sigil)
CrossGeneration Comics: Feb, 2002 - No. 2, Mar, 2002 ($2.95, limited series)

1,2-Waid-s/DiVito-a 3.00

SAVAGE COMBAT TALES
Atlas/Seaboard Publ.: Feb, 1975 - No. 3, July, 1975

	GD	VG	FN	VF	VF/NM	NM-
1,3: 1-Sgt. Stryker's Death Squad begins (origin); Goodwin-s	1	2	3	5	7	9
2-Toth-a; only app. War Hawk; Goodwin-s	2	4	6	8	10	12

NOTE: *Buckler c-3. McWilliams a-1-3; c-1. Sparling a-1, 3.*

SAVAGE DRAGON, THE (See Megaton #3 & 4)
Image Comics (Highbrow Entertainment): July, 1992 - No. 3, Dec, 1992 ($1.95, lim. series)

1-Erik Larsen-c/a/scripts & bound-in poster in all; 4 cover color variations w/4 different posters; 1st Highbrow Entertainment title 4.00
2-Intro SuperPatriot-c/story (10/92) 3.00
3-Contains coupon for Image Comics #0 3.00
3-With coupon missing 2.50
...Vs. Savage Megaton Man 1 (3/93, $1.95)-Larsen & Simpson-c/a. 3.00
TPB-('93, $9.95) r/#1-3 10.00

SAVAGE DRAGON, THE
Image Comics (Highbrow Entertainment): June, 1993 - Present ($1.95/$2.50/$2.99)

1-Erik Larsen-c/a/scripts 4.00
2-30: 2-(Wondercon Exclusive): 2-($2.95, 52 pgs.)-Teenage Mutant Ninja Turtles-c/story; flip book features Vanguard #0 (See Megaton for 1st app.). 3-7: Erik Larsen-c/a/scripts. 3-Mighty Man back-up story w/Austin-a(i). 4-Flip book w/Ricochet. 5-Mighty Man flip-c & back-up plus poster. 6-Jae Lee poster. 7-Vanguard poster. 8-Deadly Duo poster by Larsen. 13A (10/94)-Jim Lee-c/a; 1st app. Max Cash (Condition Red). 13B (6/95)-Larsen story. 15-Dragon poster by Larsen. 22-TMNT-c/a; Bisley pin-up. 27-"Wondercon Exclusive" new-c. 28-Maxx-c/app. 29-Wildstar-c/app. 30-Spawn app. 3.00
25 ($3.95)-variant-c exists. 4.00
31-49,51-71: 31-God vs. The Devil; alternate version exists w/o expletives (has "God Is Good" inside Image logo) 33-Birth of Dragon/Rapture's baby. 34,35-Hellboy-c/app. 51-Origin of She-Dragon. 70-Ann Stevens killed 2.50
50-($5.95, 100 pgs.) Kaboom and Mighty Man app.; Matsuda back-c; pin-ups by McFarlane, Simonson, Capullo and others 6.00
72-74: 72-Begin $2.95-c 3.00
75-($5.95) 6.00
76-99,101-106,108-114,116-124,126-127,129-131,133-136: 76-New direction starts. 83,84-Madman-c/app. 84-Atomics app. 97-Dragon returns home; Mighty Man app. 134-Bomb Queen app. 3.00
100-($8.95) Larsen-s/a; inked by various incl. Sienkiewicz, Timm, Austin, Simonson, Royer; plus pin-ups by Timm, Silvestri, Miller, Cho, Art Adams, Pacheco 9.00
107-($3.95) Firebreather, Invincible, Major Damage-c/app.; flip book w/Major Damage 4.00
115-($7.95, 100 pgs.) Wraparound-c; Freak Force app.; Larsen & Englert-a 8.00
125-($4.99, 64 pgs.) new story, The Fly, & various Mr. Glum reprints 5.00
128-Wesley and the villains from Wanted app.; J.G. Jones-c 4.00
132-($6.99, 80 pgs.) new story with Larsen-a; back-up story with Fosco-a 7.00
137-(8/08) Madman and Amazing Joy Buzzards-c/app. 3.00
137-(8/08) Variant cover with Barack Obama endorsed by Savage Dragon; yellow bkgrd 10.00
137-(8/08) 2nd printing of variant cover with Barack Obama and red background 4.00
#0-(7/06, $1.95) reprints origin story from 2005 Image Comics Hardcover 2.50
...Archives Vol. 1 (12/06, $19.99) B&W rep. 1st mini-series #1-3 & #1-21 20.00
...Archives Vol. 2 (2007, $19.99) B&W rep. #22-50; roster pages of Dragon's fellow cops 20.00
...Companion (7/02, $2.95) guide to issues #1-100, character backgrounds 3.00
...Endgame (2/04, $15.95, TPB) r/#47-52 16.00
The Fallen (11/97, $12.95, TPB) r/#7-11, ...Possessed (9/98, $12.95, TPB) r/#12-16, ...Revenge (1998, $12.95, TPB) r/#17-21 13.00
...Gang War (4/00, $16.95, TPB) r/#22-26 17.00
.../Hellboy (10/02, $5.95) r/#34 & #35; Mignola-c 6.00
...Team-Ups (10/98, $19.95, TPB) r/team-ups 20.00
...: Terminated HC (2/03, $28.95) r/#34-40 & #1/2 29.00
...: This Savage World HC (2002, $24.95) r/#76-81; intro. by Larsen 25.00
...: This Savage World SC (2003, $15.95) r/#76-81; intro. by Larsen 16.00
...: Worlds at War SC (2004, $16.95) r/#41-46; intro. by Larsen; sketch pages 17.00

SAVAGE DRAGON ARCHIVES (Also see Dragon Archives, The)

SAVAGE DRAGONBERT: FULL FRONTAL NERDITY
Image Comics: Oct, 2002 ($5.95, B&W, one-shot)

1-Reprints of the Savage Dragon/Dilbert spoof strips 6.00

SAVAGE DRAGON/DESTROYER DUCK, THE
Image Comics/ Highbrow Entertainment: Nov, 1996 ($3.95, one-shot)

1 4.00

SAVAGE DRAGON: GOD WAR
Image Comics: July, 2004 - No. 4, Oct, 2005 ($2.95, limited series)

1-4-Kirkman-s/Englert-a 3.00

SAVAGE DRAGON/MARSHALL LAW
Image Comics: July, 1997 - No. 2, Aug, 1997 ($2.95, B&W, limited series)

1,2-Pat Mills-s, Kevin O'Neill-a 3.00

SAVAGE DRAGON: SEX & VIOLENCE
Image Comics: Aug, 1997 - No. 2, Sept, 1997 ($2.50, limited series)

1,2-T&M Bierbaum-s, Mays, Lupka, Adam Hughes-a 3.00

SAVAGE DRAGON/TEENAGE MUTANT NINJA TURTLES CROSSOVER
Mirage Studios: Sept, 1993 ($2.75, one-shot)

1-Erik Larsen-c(i) only 3.00

SAVAGE DRAGON: THE RED HORIZON
Image Comics/ Highbrow Entertainment: Feb, 1997 - No. 3 ($2.50, lim. series)

1-3 3.00

SAVAGE FISTS OF KUNG FU
Marvel Comics Group: 1975 (Marvel Treasury)

	GD	VG	FN	VF	VF/NM	NM-
1-Iron Fist, Shang Chi, Sons of Tiger; Adams, Starlin-a	3	6	9	17	25	32

SAVAGE HULK, THE (Also see Incredible Hulk)
Marvel Comics: Jan, 1996 ($6.95, one-shot)

1-Bisley-c; David, Lobdell, Wagner, Loeb, Gibbons, Messner-Loebs scripts; McKone, Kieth, Ramos & Sale-a. 7.00

SAVAGE RAIDS OF GERONIMO (See Geronimo #4)

SAVAGE RANGE (See Luke Short, Four Color 807)

SAVAGE RED SONJA: QUEEN OF THE FROZEN WASTES
Dynamite Entertainment: 2006 - No. 4, 2006 ($3.50, limited series)

1-4: 1-Three covers by Cho, Texeira & Homs; Cho & Murray-s/Homs-a 3.50
TPB (2007, $14.99) r/series; cover gallery and sketch pages 15.00

SAVAGE RETURN OF DRACULA
Marvel Comics: 1992 ($2.00, 52 pgs.)

1-r/Tomb of Dracula #1,2 by Gene Colan 3.00

SAVAGE SHE-HULK, THE (See The Avengers, Marvel Graphic Novel #18 & The Sensational She-Hulk)
Marvel Comics Group: Feb, 1980 - No. 25, Feb, 1982

	GD	VG	FN	VF	VF/NM	NM-
1-Origin & 1st app. She-Hulk	2	4	6	8	10	12
2-5,25: 25-(52 pgs.)						6.00
6-24: 6-She-Hulk vs. Iron Man. 8-Vs. Man-Thing						5.00

NOTE: *Austin a-25i; c-23i-25i. J. Buscema a-1p; c-1, 2p. Golden c-8-11.*

SAVAGE SWORD OF CONAN (The... #41 on; ...The Barbarian #175 on)
Marvel Comics Group: Aug, 1974 - No. 235, July, 1995 ($1.00/$1.25/$2.25, B&W magazine, mature)

	GD	VG	FN	VF	VF/NM	NM-
1-Smith-r; J. Buscema/N. Adams/Krenkel-a; origin Blackmark by Gil Kane (part 1, ends #3); Blackmark's 1st app. in magazine form-r/from paperback) & Red Sonja (3rd app.)	10	20	30	68	119	170
2-Neal Adams-c; Chaykin/N. Adams-a	5	10	15	34	55	75
3-Severin/B. Smith-a; N. Adams-a	4	8	12	26	41	55
4-Neal Adams/Kane-a(r)	3	6	9	21	32	42
5-10: 5-Jeff Jones frontispiece (r)	3	6	9	17	25	32
11-20	2	4	6	11	16	20
21-30	2	4	6	9	13	16
31-50: 34-3 pg. preview of Conan newspaper strip. 35-Cover similar to Savage Tales #1. 45-Red Sonja returns; begin $1.25-c	2	4	6	8	11	14

51-99: 63-Toth frontispiece. 65-Kane-a w/Chaykin/Miller/Simonson/Sherman finishes.

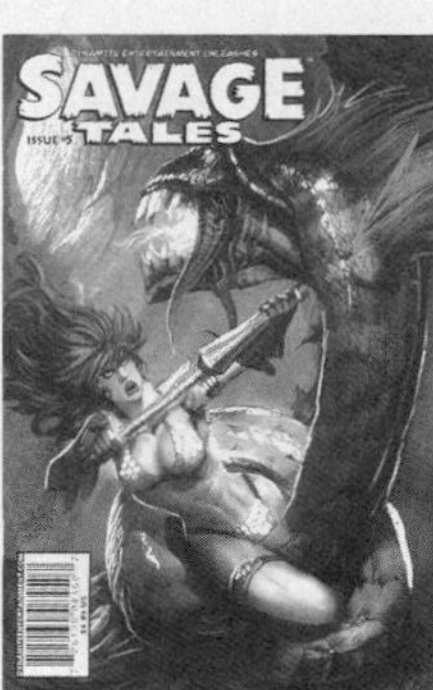
Savage Tales #5 © DFI

Scalped #12 © Aaron & Milosevic

Scary Godmother #1 © Jill Thompson

	GD 2.0	VG 4.0	FN 6.0	VF 8.0	VF/NM 9.0	NM- 9.2
70-Article on movie. 83-Red Sonja-r by Neal Adams from #1	1	2	3	5	7	9
100	1	3	4	6	8	10
101-176: 163-Begin $2.25-c. 169-King Kull story. 171-Soloman Kane by Williamson (i). 172-Red Sonja story						6.00
177-199: 179,187,192-Red Sonja app. 190-193-4 part King Kull story. 196-King Kull story						5.00
200-220: 200-New Buscema-a; Robert E. Howard app. with Conan in story. 202-King Kull story. 204-60th anniversary (1932-92). 211-Rafael Kayanan's 1st Conan-a. 214-Sequel to Red Nails by Howard						6.00
221-230	1	2	3	5	7	9
231-234	2	4	6	8	11	14
235-Last issue	3	6	9	14	19	24
Special 1(1975, B&W)-B. Smith-r/Conan #10,13	3	6	9	17	25	32
Volume 1 TPB (Dark Horse Books, 12/07, $17.95, B&W) r/#1-10 and selected stories from Savage Tales #1-5 with covers						18.00
Volume 2 TPB (Dark Horse Books, 3/08, $17.95, B&W) r/#11-24						18.00
Volume 3 TPB (Dark Horse Books, 5/08, $19.95, B&W) r/#25-36 and selected pin-ups						20.00

NOTE: ***N. Adams** a-14p, 60, 83p(r). **Alcala** a-2 ,4, 7, 12, 15-20, 23, 24, 28, 59, 67, 69, 75, 76i, 80i, 82i, 83i, 89, 180i, 184i, 187i, 189i, 216p. **Austin** a-78i. **Boris** painted c-1, 4, 5, 7, 9, 10, 12, 15. **Brunner** a-30; c-8, 30. **Buscema** a-1-5, 7, 10-12, 15-24, 26-28, 31, 32, 36-43, 45, 47-58p, 60-67p, 70, 71-74p, 76-81p, 87-96p, 98, 99-101p, 190-204p; painted c-40. **Chaykin** c-31. **Chiodo** painted c-71, 76, 79, 81, 84, 85, 178. **Conrad** c-215, 217. **Corben** a-4, 16, 29. **Finlay** a-16. **Golden** a-98, 101; c-98, 101, 105, 106, 117, 124, 150. **Kaluta** a-11, 18; c-3, 91, 93. **Gil Kane** a-2, 3, 8, 13r, 29, 47, 64, 65, 67, 85p, 86p. **Rafael Kayanan** a-211-213, 215, 217. **Krenkel** a-9, 11, 14, 16, 24. **Morrow** a-7. **Nebres** a-93i, 101i, 107, 114. **Newton** a-6. **Nino** c/a-6. **Redondo** painted c-48-50, 52, 56, 57, 85i, 90, 96i. **Marie & John Severin** a-Special 1. **Simonson** a-7, 8, 12, 15-17. **Barry Smith** a-7, 16, 24, 82r, Special 1r. **Starlin** c-26. **Toth** a-64. **Williamson** a(i)-162, 171, 186. No. 8 , 10 & 16 contain a Robert E. Howard Conan adaptation.*

SAVAGE TALES (...Featuring Conan #4 on)(Magazine)
Marvel Comics Group: May, 1971; No. 2, 10/73; No. 3, 2/74 - No. 12, Summer, 1975 (B&W)

	GD 2.0	VG 4.0	FN 6.0	VF 8.0	VF/NM 9.0	NM- 9.2
1-Origin/1st app. The Man-Thing by Morrow; Conan the Barbarian by Barry Smith (1st Conan x-over outside his own title); Femizons by Romita-r/in #3; Ka-Zar story by Buscema	16	32	48	118	219	320
2-B. Smith, Brunner, Morrow, Williamson-a; Wrightson King Kull reprint/ Creatures on the Loose #10	6	12	18	39	62	85
3-B. Smith, Brunner, Steranko, Williamson-a	5	10	15	30	48	65
4,5-N. Adams-c; last Conan (Smith-r/#4) plus Kane/N. Adams-a. 5-Brak the Barbarian begins, ends #8	4	8	12	26	41	55
6-Ka-Zar begins; Williamson-r; N. Adams-c	3	6	9	18	27	35
7-N. Adams-i	3	6	9	14	19	24
8,9,11: 8-Shanna, the She-Devil app. thru #10; Williamson-r	2	4	6	13	18	22
10-Neal Adams-a(i), Williamson-r	3	6	9	14	19	24
...Featuring Ka-Zar Annual 1 (Summer, '75, B&W)(#12 on inside)-Ka-Zar origin by Gil Kane; B. Smith-r/Astonishing Tales	3	6	9	16	22	28

NOTE: ***Boris** c-7, 10. **Buscema** a-5r, 6p, 8p; c-2. **Colan** a-1p. **Fabian** c-8. **Golden** a-1, 4; c-1. **Heath** a-10p, 11p. **Kaluta** c-9. **Maneely** r-2, 4(The Crusader in both). **Morrow** a-1, 2, Annual 1. **Reese** a-2. **Severin** a-1-7. **Starlin** a-5. Robert E. Howard adaptations-1-4.*

SAVAGE TALES
Marvel Comics Group: Nov, 1985 - No. 8, Dec, 1986 ($1.50, B&W, magazine, mature)

	NM- 9.2
1-1st app. The Nam; Golden, Morrow-a	5.00
2-8: 2,7-Morrow-a. 4-2nd Nam story; Golden-a	3.00

SAVAGE TALES
Dynamite Entertainment: 2007 - Present ($4.99)

	NM- 9.2
1-9: 1-Anthology; Red Sonja app.; three covers	5.00

SAVANT GARDE (Also see WildC.A.T.S...)
Image Comics/WildStorm Productions: Mar, 1997 - No. 7, Sept, 1997 ($2.50)

	NM- 9.2
1-7	2.50

SAVED BY THE BELL (TV)
Harvey Comics: Mar, 1992 - No. 5, May, 1993 ($1.25, limited series)

	NM- 9.2
1-5, Holiday Special (3/92), Special 1 (9/92, $1.50)-photo-c, Summer Break 1 (10/92)	2.50

SAW: REBIRTH (Based on 2004 movie Saw)
IDW Publ.: Oct, 2005 ($3.99, one-shot)

	NM- 9.2
1-Guedes-a	4.00

SCALPED
DC Comics (Vertigo): Mar, 2007 - Present ($2.99, limited series)

	NM- 9.2
1-19-Aaron-s/Guera-a/Jock-c. 12-Leon-a	3.00
...: Casino Blood TPB (2008, $14.99) r/#6-11; intro. by Garth Ennis	15.00
...: Indian Country TPB (2007, $9.99) r/#1-5; intro. by Brian K. Vaughan	10.00

SCAMP (Walt Disney)(See Walt Disney's Comics & Stories #204)
Dell Publ. Co./Gold Key: No. 703, 5/56 - No. 1204, 8-10/61; 11/67 - No. 45, 1/79

	GD 2.0	VG 4.0	FN 6.0	VF 8.0	VF/NM 9.0	NM- 9.2
Four Color 703(#1)	8	16	24	58	97	135
Four Color 777,806('57),833	6	12	18	43	69	95
5(3-5/58)-10(6-8/59)	5	10	15	34	55	75
11-16(12-2/60-61), Four Color 1204(1961)	4	8	12	28	44	60
1(12/67-Gold Key)-Reprints begin	4	8	12	26	41	55
2(3/69)-10	2	4	6	13	18	22
11-20	2	4	6	8	11	14
21-45	1	2	3	4	5	7

NOTE: *New stories-#20(in part), 22-25, 27, 29-31, 34, 36-40, 42-45. New covers-#11, 12, 14, 15, 17-25, 27, 29-31, 34, 36-38.*

SCARAB
DC Comics (Vertigo): Nov, 1993 - No. 8, June, 1994 ($1.95, limited series)

	NM- 9.2
1-8-Glenn Fabry painted-c: 1-Silver ink-c. 2-Phantom Stranger app.	2.50

SCARECROW OF ROMNEY MARSH, THE (See W. Disney Showcase #53)
Gold Key: April, 1964 - No. 3, Oct, 1965 (Disney TV Show)

	GD 2.0	VG 4.0	FN 6.0	VF 8.0	VF/NM 9.0	NM- 9.2
10112-404 (#1)	4	8	12	28	44	60
2,3	3	6	9	20	30	40

SCARECROW (VILLAINS) (See Batman)
DC Comics: Feb, 1998 ($1.95, one-shot)

	NM- 9.2
1-Fegredo-a/Milligan-s/Pearson-c	2.50

SCARE TACTICS
DC Comics: Dec, 1996 - No. 12, Mar, 1998 ($2.25)

	NM- 9.2
1-12: 1-1st app.	2.50

SCAR FACE (See The Crusaders)

SCARFACE: SCARRED FOR LIFE (Based on the 1983 movie)
IDW Publishing: Dec, 2006 - No. 5, Apr, 2007 ($3.99, limited series)

	NM- 9.2
1-5-Tony Montana survives his shooting; Layman-s/Crosland-a	4.00
Scarface: Devil in Disguise (7/07 - No. 4, 10/07, $3.99) Alberto Dose-a	4.00

SCARLET O'NEIL (See Harvey Comics Hits #59 & Invisible...)

SCARLET SPIDER
Marvel Comics: Nov, 1995 - No. 2, Jan, 1996 ($1.95, limited series)

	NM- 9.2
1,2: Replaces Spider-Man	2.50

SCARLET SPIDER UNLIMITED
Marvel Comics: Nov, 1995 ($3.95, one-shot)

	NM- 9.2
1-Replaces Spider-Man Unlimited	4.00

SCARLET WITCH (See Avengers #16, Vision &... & X-Men #4)
Marvel Comics: Jan, 1994 - No. 4, Apr, 1994 ($1.75, limited series)

	NM- 9.2
1-4	2.50

SCARY GODMOTHER (Hardcover story books)
Sirius: 1997 - Present ($19.95, HC with dust jackets, one-shots)

	NM- 9.2
Volume 1 (9/97) Jill Thompson-s/a; first app. of Scary Godmother	20.00
Vol. 2 - The Revenge of Jimmy (9/98, $19.95)	20.00
Vol. 3 - The Mystery Date (10/99, $19.95)	20.00
Vol. 4 - The Boo Flu (9/02, $19.95)	20.00

SCARY GODMOTHER
Sirius: 2001 - No. 6, 2002 ($2.95, B&W, limited series)

	NM- 9.2
1-6-Jill Thompson-s/a	3.00
...: Activity Book (12/00, $2.95, B&W) Jill Thompson-s/a	3.00
...: Bloody Valentine Special (2/98, $3.95, B&W) Jill Thompson-s/a; pin-ups by Ross, Mignola, Russell	4.00
.... Ghoul's Out For Summer (2002,$14.95, B&W) r/#1-6	15.00
...: Holiday Spooktakular (11/98, $2.95, B&W) Jill Thompson-s/a; pin-ups by Brereton, LaBan, Dorkin, Fingerman	3.00

SCARY GODMOTHER: WILD ABOUT HARRY
Sirius: 2000 - No. 3 ($2.95, B&W, limited series)

	NM- 9.2
1-3-Jill Thompson-s/a	3.00
TPB (2001, $9.95) r/series	10.00

SCARY TALES
Charlton Comics: 8/75 - #9, 1/77; #10, 9/77 - #20, 6/79; #21, 8/80 - #46, 10/84

	GD 2.0	VG 4.0	FN 6.0	VF 8.0	VF/NM 9.0	NM- 9.2
1-Origin/1st app. Countess Von Bludd, not in #2	3	6	9	16	23	30
2,4,6,9,10: 4,9-Sutton-c/a. 4-Man-Thing copy	2	4	6	8	10	12
3-Sutton painted-c; Ditko-a	2	4	6	9	13	16
5,11-Ditko-c/a.	2	4	6	10	14	18
7,8-Ditko-a	2	4	6	8	11	14
12,15,16,19,21,39-Ditko-a	2	4	6	8	10	12
13,17,20	1	2	3	5	7	9
14,18,30,32-Ditko-c/a	2	4	6	9	12	15

Science Comics #1 © FOX

Scion #19 © CRO

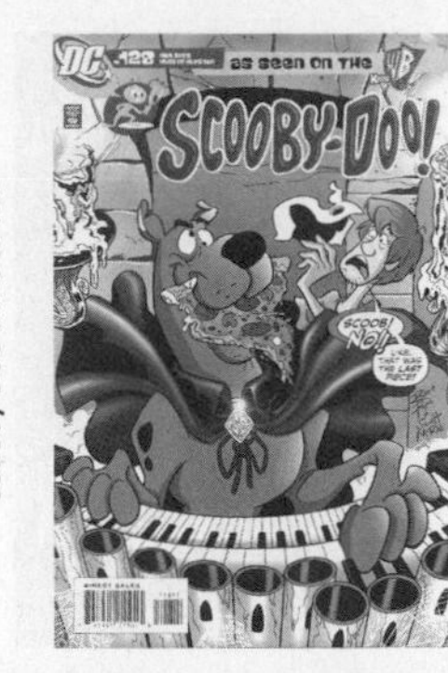

Scooby-Doo #128 © H-B

	GD 2.0	VG 4.0	FN 6.0	VF 8.0	VF/NM 9.0	NM- 9.2
22-29,33-37,39,40: 37,38,40-New-a. 39-Reprints	1	2	3	5	6	8
31,38: 31-Newton-c/a. 38-Mr. Jigsaw app.	1	2	3	5	6	8
41-45-New-a. 41-Ditko-a(3). 42-45-(Low print)	1	2	3	5	7	9
46-Reprints (Low print)	2	4	6	8	11	14
1(Modern Comics reprint, 1977)						4.00

NOTE: *Adkins a-31i; c-31i. Ditko a-3, 5, 7, 8(2), 11, 12, 14-16r, 18(3)r, 19r, 21r, 30r, 32, 39r, 41(3); c-5, 11, 14, 18, 30, 32. Newton a-31p; c-31p. Powell a-18r. Staton a-1(2 pgs.), 4, 20r; c-1, 20. Sutton a-4, 9; c-4, 9. Zeck a-9.*

SCATTERBRAIN
Dark Horse Comics: Jun, 1998 - No. 4, Sept, 1998 ($2.95, limited series)

	GD	VG	FN	VF	VF/NM	NM-
1-4-Humor anthology by Aragonés, Dorkin, Stevens and others						3.00

SCAVENGERS
Quality Comics: Feb, 1988 - No. 14, 1989 ($1.25/$1.50)

	GD	VG	FN	VF	VF/NM	NM-
1-14: 9-13-Guice-c						2.50

SCAVENGERS
Triumphant Comics: 1993(nd, July) - No. 11, May, 1994 ($2.50, serially numbered)

	GD	VG	FN	VF	VF/NM	NM-
1-9,0,10,11: 5,6-Triumphant Unleashed x-over. 9-(3/94). 0-Retail ed. (3/94, $2.50, 36 pgs.). 0-Giveaway edition (3/94, 20 pgs.). 0-Coupon redemption edition. 10-(4/94)						2.50

SCENE OF THE CRIME (Also see Vertigo: Winter's Edge #2)
DC Comics (Vertigo): May, 1999 - No. 4, Aug, 1999 ($2.50, limited series)

	GD	VG	FN	VF	VF/NM	NM-
1-4-Brubaker-s/Lark-a						2.50
...: A Little Piece of Goodnight TPB ('00, $12.95) r/#1-4; Winter's Edge #2						13.00

SCHOOL DAY ROMANCES (...of Teen-Agers #4; Popular Teen-Agers #5 on)
Star Publications: Nov-Dec, 1949 - No. 4, May-June, 1950 (Teenage)

	GD	VG	FN	VF	VF/NM	NM-
1-Toni Gayle (later Toni Gay), Ginger Snapp, Midge Martin & Eve Adams begin	28	56	84	162	261	360
2,3: 3-Jane Powell photo on-c & true life story	20	40	60	117	186	255
4-Ronald Reagan photo on-c; L.B. Cole-c	31	62	93	181	291	400

NOTE: *All have **L. B. Cole** covers.*

SCHWINN BICYCLE BOOK (...Bike Thrills, 1959)
Schwinn Bicycle Co.: 1949; 1952; 1959 (10¢)

	GD	VG	FN	VF	VF/NM	NM-
1949	6	12	18	28	34	40
1952-Believe It or Not facts; comic format; 36 pgs.	5	10	14	20	24	28
1959	3	6	8	11	13	15

SCIENCE COMICS (1st Series)
Fox Features Syndicate: Feb, 1940 - No. 8, Sept, 1940

	GD	VG	FN	VF	VF/NM	NM-
1-Origin Dynamo (1st app., called Electro in #1), The Eagle (1st app.), & Navy Jones; Marga, The Panther Woman (1st app.), Cosmic Carson & Perisphere Payne, Dr. Doom begin; bondage/hypo-c; Electro-c	423	846	1269	3000	5250	7500
2-Classic Lou Fine Dynamo-c	230	460	690	1449	2450	3450
3-Classic Lou Fine Dynamo-c	187	374	561	1178	1989	2800
4-Kirby-a; Cosmic Carson-c by Joe Simon	167	334	501	1052	1776	2500
5-8: 5,8-Eagle-c. 6,7-Dynamo-c	100	200	300	630	1065	1500

NOTE: *Cosmic Carson by **Tuska**-#1-3; by **Kirby**-#4. **Lou Fine** c-1-3 only.*

SCIENCE COMICS (2nd Series)
Humor Publications (Ace Magazines?): Jan, 1946 - No. 5, 1946

	GD	VG	FN	VF	VF/NM	NM-
1-Palais-c/a in #1-3; A-Bomb-c	19	38	57	109	172	235
2	11	22	33	62	86	110
3-Feldstein-a (6 pgs.)	15	30	45	88	137	185
4,5: 4-Palais-c	9	18	27	50	65	80

SCIENCE COMICS
Ziff-Davis Publ. Co.: May, 1947 (8 pgs. in color)

	GD	VG	FN	VF	VF/NM	NM-
nn-Could be ordered by mail for 10¢; like the nn Amazing Adventures (1950) & Boy Cowboy (1950); used to test the market	40	80	120	235	380	525

SCIENCE COMICS (True Science Illustrated)
Export Publication Ent., Toronto, Canada: Mar, 1951 (Distr. in U.S. by Kable News Co.)

	GD	VG	FN	VF	VF/NM	NM-
1-Science Adventure stories plus some true science features; man on moon story	13	26	39	72	101	130

SCIENCE FICTION SPACE ADVENTURES (See Space Adventures)

SCION (Also see CrossGen Chronicles)
CrossGeneration Comics: July, 2000 - No. 43, Apr, 2004 ($2.95)

	GD	VG	FN	VF	VF/NM	NM-
1-43: 1-Marz-s/Cheung-a						3.00
...: Conflict of Conscience Vol. 1 TPB (5/01, $19.95) r/#1-7; Adam Hughes-c						20.00
...: Blood For Blood Vol. 2 TPB (2002, $19.95) r/#8-14 & CrossGen Chronicles #2						20.00
...: Divided Loyalties Vol. 3 TPB (2002, $15.95) r/#15-21						16.00
...: Sanctuary Vol. 4 TPB (2003, $15.95) r/#22-27						16.00
Vol. 5: The Far Kingdom (2003, $15.95) r/#28-33						16.00
Vol. 6: The Royal Wedding (2004, $15.95) r/#34-39						16.00
Traveler Vol. 1-3 ($9.95) Digest-sized reprints of TPBs						10.00

SCI-SPY
DC Comics (Vertigo): Apr, 2002 - No. 6, Sept, 2002 ($2.50, limited series)

	GD	VG	FN	VF	VF/NM	NM-
1-6-Moench-s/Gulacy-c/a						2.50

SCI-TECH
DC Comics (WildStorm): Sept, 1999 - No. 4, Dec, 1999 ($2.50, limited series)

	GD	VG	FN	VF	VF/NM	NM-
1-4-Benes-a/Choi & Peterson-s						2.50

SCOOBY DOO (TV)(...Where are you? #1-16,26; ...Mystery Comics #17-25, 27 on) (See March Of Comics #356, 368, 382, 391 in the Promotional Comics section)
Gold Key: Mar, 1970 - No. 30, Feb, 1975 (Hanna-Barbera)

	GD	VG	FN	VF	VF/NM	NM-
1	14	28	42	99	175	250
2-5	7	14	21	50	83	115
6-10	6	12	18	43	69	95
11-20: 11-Tufts-a	5	10	15	34	55	75
21-30	4	8	12	26	41	55

SCOOBY DOO (TV)
Charlton Comics: Apr, 1975 - No. 11, Dec, 1976 (Hanna-Barbera)

	GD	VG	FN	VF	VF/NM	NM-
1	6	12	18	39	62	85
2-5	4	8	12	24	37	50
6-11	3	6	9	20	30	40
nn-(1976, digest, 68 pgs., B&W)	4	8	12	24	37	50

SCOOBY-DOO (TV)(Newsstand sales only) (See Dynamutt & Laff-A-Lympics)
Marvel Comics Group: Oct, 1977 - No. 9, Feb, 1979 (Hanna-Barbera)

	GD	VG	FN	VF	VF/NM	NM-
1,6-9: 1-Dyno-Mutt begins	3	6	9	17	25	32
1-(35¢-c variant, limited distribution)(10/77)	8	16	24	54	90	125
2-5	3	6	9	14	19	24

SCOOBY-DOO (TV)
Harvey Comics: Sept, 1992 - No. 3, May, 1993 ($1.25)

	GD	VG	FN	VF	VF/NM	NM-
V2#1,2						6.00
Big Book 1,2 (11/92, 4/93, $1.95, 52 pgs.)	1	2	3	5	6	8
Giant Size 1,2 (10/92, 3/93, $2.25, 68 pgs.)	1	2	3	5	6	8

SCOOBY DOO (TV)
Archie Comics: Oct, 1995 -No. 21, June, 1997 ($1.50)

	GD	VG	FN	VF	VF/NM	NM-
1						6.00
2-21: 12-Cover by Scooby Doo creative designer Iwao Takamoto						4.00

SCOOBY DOO (TV)
DC Comics: Aug, 1997 - Present ($1.75/$1.95/$1.99/$2.25)

	GD	VG	FN	VF	VF/NM	NM-
1						6.00
2-10: 5-Begin-$1.95-c						4.00
11-45: 14-Begin $1.99-c						2.50
46-89,91-134: 63-Begin $2.25-c. 75-With 2 Garbage Pail Kids stickers. 100-Wray-c						2.50
90-($2.95) Bonus stories						3.00
...Spooky Spectacular 1 (10/99, $3.95) Comic Convention story						4.00
...Spooky Spectacular 2000 (10/00, $3.95)						4.00
...Spooky Summer Special 2001 (8/01, $3.95) Staton-a						4.00
...Super Scarefest (8/02, $3.95) r/#20,25,30-32						4.00
Vol. 1: You Meddling Kids (2003, $6.95, digest-size) r/#1-5						7.00
Vol. 2: Ruh-Roh! (2003, $6.95, digest-size) r/#6-10						7.00
Vol. 3: All Wrapped Up! (2005, $6.95, digest-size) r/#11-15						7.00
Vol. 4: The Big Squeeze! (2005, $6.95, digest-size) r/#16-20						7.00
Vol. 5: Surf's Up! (2006, $6.99, digest-size) r/#21-25						7.00
Vol. 5: Space Fright! (2006, $6.99, digest-size) r/#26-30						7.00

SCOOP COMICS (Becomes Yankee Comics #4-7, a digest sized cartoon book; then after #8 it becomes Snap #9)
Harry 'A' Chesler (Holyoke): November, 1941 - No. 3, Mar, 1943; No. 8, 1944

	GD	VG	FN	VF	VF/NM	NM-
1-Intro. Rocketman & Rocketgirl & begins; origin The Master Key & begins; Dan Hastings begins; Charles Sultan-c/a	153	306	459	964	1632	2300
2-Rocket Boy begins; injury to eye story (reprinted in Spotlight #3); classic-c	167	334	501	1052	1776	2500
3-Injury to eye story-r from #2; Rocket Boy	73	116	219	460	780	1100
8-Formerly Yankee Comics; becomes Snap	45	90	135	279	465	650

SCOOTER (See Swing With...)

SCOOTER COMICS
Rucker Publ. Ltd. (Canadian): Apr, 1946

	GD	VG	FN	VF	VF/NM	NM-
1-Teen-age/funny animal	11	22	33	60	83	105

SCOOTER GIRL

Scout: War Shaman #7 © ECL

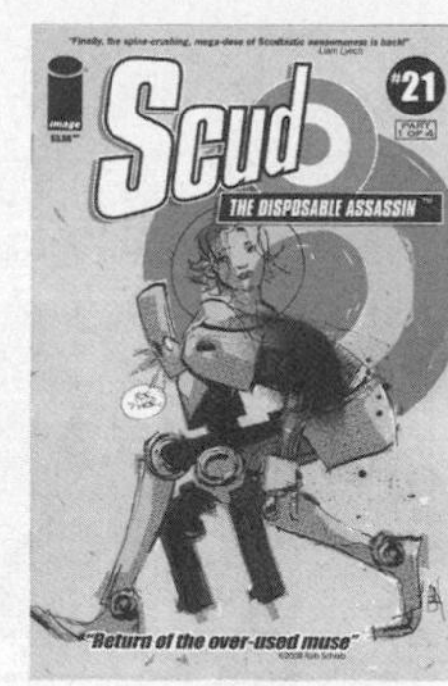

Scud, The Disposable Assassin #21 © Rob Schaub

Sea Devils #7 © DC

	GD 2.0	VG 4.0	FN 6.0	VF 8.0	VF/NM 9.0	NM- 9.2

Oni Press: May, 2003 - No. 6, Feb, 2004 ($2.99, B&W, limited series)
1-6-Chynna Clugston-Major-s/a 3.00
TPB (5/04, $14.95, digest size) r/series; sketch pages 15.00

SCORPION
Atlas/Seaboard Publ.: Feb, 1975 - No. 3, July, 1975
1-Intro.; bondage-c by Chaykin 2 4 6 8 11 14
2-Chaykin-a w/Wrightson, Kaluta, Simonson assists(p) 2 4 6 8 11 14
3-Jim Craig-c/a 1 3 4 6 8 10
NOTE: ***Chaykin** a-1, 2; c-1. **Colon** c-2. **Craig** c/a-3.*

SCORPION KING, THE (Movie)
Dark Horse Comics: March, 2002 - No. 2, Apr, 2002 ($2.99, limited series)
1,2-Photo-c of the Rock; Richards-a 3.00

SCORPIO ROSE
Eclipse Comics: Jan, 1983 - No. 2, Oct, 1983 ($1.25, Baxter paper)
1,2: Dr. Orient back-up story begins. 2-origin. 4.00

SCOTLAND YARD (Inspector Farnsworth of)(Texas Rangers in Action #5 on?)
Charlton Comics Group: June, 1955 - No. 4, Mar, 1956
1-Tothish-a 14 28 42 80 115 150
2-4: 2-Tothish-a 10 20 30 54 72 90

SCOUT (See Eclipse Graphic Album #16, New America & Swords of Texas) (Becomes Scout: War Shaman)
Eclipse Comics: Dec, 1985 - No. 24, Oct, 1987($1.75/$1.25, Baxter paper)
1-15,17,18,20-24: 19-Airboy preview. 10-Bissette-a. 11-Monday, the Eliminator begins. 15-Swords of Texas 2.50
16,19: 16-Scout 3-D Special ($2.50), 16-Scout 2-D Limited Edition, 19-contains flexidisk ($2.50) 3.00
...Handbook 1 (8/87, $1.75, B&W) 2.50
Mount Fire (1989, $14.95, TPB) r/#8-14 15.00

SCOUT: WAR SHAMAN (Formerly Scout)
Eclipse Comics: Mar, 1988 - No. 16, Dec, 1989 ($1.95)
1-16 2.50

SCRATCH
DC Comics: Aug, 2004 - No. 5, Dec, 2004 ($2.50, limited series)
1-5-Sam Kieth-s/a/c; Batman app. 2.50

SCREAM (...Comics) (Andy Comics #20 on)
Humor Publications/Current Books(Ace Magazines): Autumn, 1944 - No. 19, Apr, 1948
1-Teenage humor 16 32 48 92 144 195
2 10 20 30 56 76 95
3-16: 11-Racist humor (Indians). 16-Intro. Lily-Belle 9 18 27 47 61 75
17,19 8 16 24 42 54 65
18-Hypo needle story 9 18 27 47 61 75

SCREAM (Magazine)
Skywald Publ. Corp.: Aug, 1973 - No. 11, Feb, 1975 (68 pgs., B&W) (Painted-c on all)
1-Nosferatu-c/1st app. (series thru #11); Morrow-a. Cthulhu/Necronomicon-s 7 14 21 45 73 100
2,3: 2-(10/73) Lady Satan 1st app. & series begins; Edgar Allan Poe adaptations begin (thru #11); Phantom of the Opera-s. 3-(12/73) Origin Lady Satan 5 10 15 30 48 65
4-1st Cannibal Werewolf and 1st Lunatic Mummy 4 8 12 26 41 55
5,7,8: 5,7-Frankenstein app. 8-Buckler-a; Werewolf-s; Slither-Slime Man-s 4 8 12 26 41 55
6, 9,10: 6-(6/74) Saga of The Victims/ I Am Horror, classic GGA Hewetson series begins (thru #11); Frankenstein 2073-s. 9-Severed head-c; Marcos-a. 9,10-Werewolf-s. 10-Dracula-c/s 4 8 12 28 44 60
11- (1975 Winter Special) "Mr. Poe and the Raven" story 5 10 15 30 48 65
NOTE: ***Buckler** a-8. **Hewetson** s-1-11. **Marcos** a-9. **Miralles** c-2. **Morrow** a-1. **Poe** s-2-11. **Segrelles** a-7; c-1.*

SCREEN CARTOONS
DC Comics: Dec, 1944 (cover only ashcan)
nn-Ashcan comic, not distributed to newsstands, only for in house use. Covers were produced, but not the rest of the book. A copy sold in 2006 for $400 and in 2008 for $500.

SCREEN COMICS
DC Comics: Dec, 1944 (cover only ashcan)
nn-Ashcan comic, not distributed to newsstands, only for in house use. Covers were produced, but not the rest of the book. A copy sold in 2006 for $400 and in 2008 for $500.

SCREEN FABLES
DC Comics: Dec, 1944 (cover only ashcan)
nn-Ashcan comic, not distributed to newsstands, only for in house use. Covers were produced, but not the rest of the book. A copy sold in 2006 for $400 and in 2008 for $500.

SCREEN FUNNIES
DC Comics: Dec, 1944 (cover only ashcan)
nn-Ashcan comic, not distributed to newsstands, only for in house use. Covers were produced, but not the rest of the book. A copy sold in 2006 for $400 and in 2008 for $500.

SCREEN GEMS
DC Comics: Dec, 1944 (cover only ashcan)
nn-Ashcan comic, not distributed to newsstands, only for in house use. Covers were produced, but not the rest of the book. A copy sold in 2006 for $400 and in 2008 for $500.

SCREWBALL SQUIRREL
Dark Horse Comics: July, 1995 - No. 3, Sept, 1995 ($2.50, limited series)
1-3: Characters created by Tex Avery 2.50

SCRIBBLY (See All-American Comics, Buzzy, The Funnies, Leave It To Binky & Popular Comics)
National Periodical Publ.: 8-9/48 - No. 13, 8-9/50; No. 14, 10-11/51 - No. 15, 12-1/51-52
1-Sheldon Mayer-c/a in all; 52 pgs. begin 93 186 279 581 966 1350
2 59 118 177 369 610 850
3-5 48 96 144 293 484 675
6-10 39 78 117 225 355 485
11-15: 13-Last 52 pgs. 33 66 99 192 304 415

SCUD: TALES FROM THE VENDING MACHINE
Fireman Press: 1998 - No. 5 ($2.50, B&W)
1-5: 1-Kaniuga-a. 2-Ruben Martinez-a 2.50

SCUD: THE DISPOSABLE ASSASSIN
Fireman Press: Feb, 1994 - No. 20, 1997 ($2.95, B&W)
Image Comics: No. 21, Feb, 2008 - No. 24, May, 2008 ($3.50, B&W)
1 6.00
1-2nd printing in color 2.50
2,3 4.00
4-20 3.00
21-24: 21-(2/08, $3.50) Ashley Wood-c. 22-Mahfood-c 3.50
Heavy 3PO ($12.95, TPB) r/#1-4 13.00
Programmed For Damage ($14.95, TPB) r/#5-9 15.00
Solid Gold Bomb ($17.95, TPB) r/#10-15 18.00

SEA DEVILS (See Limited Collectors' Edition #39,45, & Showcase #27-29)
National Periodical Publications: Sept-Oct, 1961 - No. 35, May-June, 1967
1-(9-10/61) 54 108 162 459 880 1300
2-Last 10¢ issue 30 60 90 222 411 600
3-Begin 12¢ issues thru #35 19 38 57 139 257 375
4,5 17 34 51 120 223 325
6-10 12 24 36 82 146 210
11,12,14-20 9 18 27 60 100 140
13-Kubert, Colan-a; Joe Kubert app. in story 9 18 27 61 103 145
21-35: 22-Intro. International Sea Devils; origin & 1st app. Capt. X & Man Fish 6 12 18 43 69 95
NOTE: ***Heath** a-Showcase 27-29, 1-10; c-Showcase 27-29, 1-10, 14-16. **Moldoff** a-16i.*

SEA DEVILS (See Tangent Comics/ Sea Devils)

SEADRAGON (Also see the Epsilion Wave)
Elite Comics: May, 1986 - No. 8, 1987 ($1.75)
1-8: 1-1st & 2nd printings exist 2.50

SEAGUY
DC Comics (Vertigo): July, 2004 - No. 3, Sept, 2004 ($2.95, limited series)
1-3-Grant Morrison-s/Cameron Stewart-a/c 3.00
TPB (2005, $9.95) r/#1-3 10.00

SEA HOUND, THE (Captain Silver's Log Of The...)
Avon Periodicals: 1945 (no month) - No. 2, Sept-Oct, 1945
nn (#1)-29 pg. novel length sty-"The Esmeralda's Treasure" 18 36 54 105 165 225
2 13 26 39 74 105 135

SEA HOUND, THE (Radio)
Capt. Silver Syndicate: No. 3, July, 1949 - No. 4, Sept, 1949
3,4 10 20 30 54 72 90

SEA HUNT (TV)
Dell Publishing Co.: No. 928, 8/58 - No. 1041, 10-12/59; No. 4, 1-3/60 - No. 13, 4-6/62 (All have Lloyd Bridges photo-c)
Four Color 928(#1) 11 22 33 79 140 200

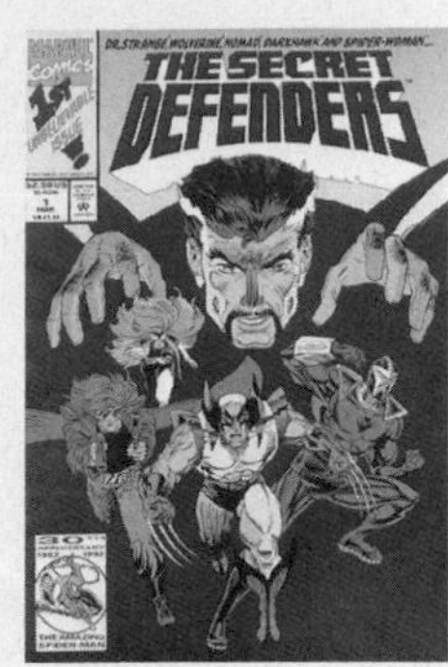

Secret Defenders #1 © MAR

Secret Hearts #10 © DC

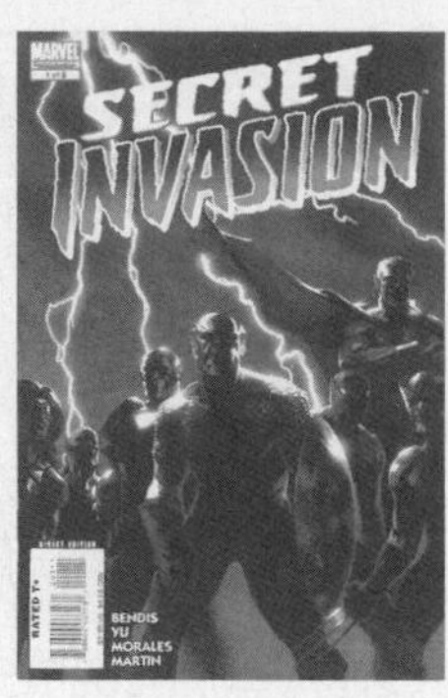

Secret Invasion #1 © MAR

GD VG FN VF VF/NM NM-
2.0 4.0 6.0 8.0 9.0 9.2

Four Color 994(#2), 4-13: Manning-a #4-6,8-11,13 8 16 24 54 90 125
Four Color 1041(#3)-Toth-a 8 16 24 54 90 125

SEA OF RED
Image Comics: Mar, 2005 - No. 13, Nov, 2006 ($2.95/$2.99/$3.50)
1-12-Vampirates at sea; Remender & Dwyer-s/Dwyer & Sam-a 3.00
13-($3.50) 3.50
Vol. 1: No Grave But The Sea (9/05, $8.95) r/#1-4 9.00
Vol. 2: No Quarter (2006, $11.99) r/#5-8 12.00
Vol. 3: The Deadlights (2006, $14.99) r/#9-13 15.00

SEAQUEST (TV)
Nemesis Comics: Mar, 1994 ($2.25)
1-Has 2 diff-c stocks (slick & cardboard); Alcala-i 2.50

SEARCH FOR LOVE
American Comics Group: Feb-Mar, 1950 - No. 2, Apr-May, 1950 (52 pgs.)
1 12 24 36 69 97 125
2 9 18 27 47 61 75

SEARCHERS, THE (Movie)
Dell Publishing Co.: No. 709, 1956
Four Color 709-John Wayne photo-c 23 46 69 167 309 450

SEARCHERS, THE
Caliber Comics: 1996 - No. 4, 1996 ($2.95, B&W)
1-4 3.00

SEARCHERS, THE : APOSTLE OF MERCY
Caliber Comics: 1997 - No. 2, 1997 ($2.95/$3.95, B&W)
1-($2.95) 3.00
2-($3.95) 4.00

SEARS (See Merry Christmas From...)

SEASON'S GREETINGS
Hallmark (King Features): 1935 (6-1/4x5-1/4", 32 pgs. in color)
nn-Cover features Mickey Mouse, Popeye, Jiggs & Skippy. "The Night Before Christmas" told one panel per page, each panel by a famous artist featuring their character. Art by Alex Raymond, Gottfredson, Swinnerton, Segar, Chic Young, Milt Gross, Sullivan (Messmer), Herriman, McManus, Percy Crosby & others (22 artists in all)
Estimated value... 950.00

SEBASTIAN O
DC Comics (Vertigo): May, 1993 - No. 3, July, 1993 ($1.95, limited series)
1-3-Grant Morrison scripts; Steve Yeowell-a 2.50
TPB (2004, $9.95) r/#1-3; intro. chronology by Morrison 10.00

SECOND LIFE OF DOCTOR MIRAGE, THE (See Shadowman #16)
Valiant: Nov, 1993 - No. 18, May, 1995 ($2.50)
1-18: 1-With bound-in poster. 5-Shadowman x-over. 7-Bound-in trading card 2.50
1-Gold ink logo edition; no price on-c 3.00

SECRET AGENT (Formerly Sarge Steel)
Charlton Comics: V2#9, Oct, 1966; V2#10, Oct, 1967
V2#9-Sarge Steel part-r begins 3 6 9 17 25 32
10-Tiffany Sinn, CIA app. (from Career Girl Romances #39); Aparo-a
3 6 9 14 19 24

SECRET AGENT (TV) (See Four Color #1231)
Gold Key: Nov, 1966; No. 2, Jan, 1968
1-Photo-c 8 16 24 58 97 135
2-Photo-c 6 12 18 41 66 90

SECRET AGENT X-9 (See Flash Gordon #4 by King)
David McKay Publ.: 1934 (Book 1: 84 pgs.; Book 2: 124 pgs.) (8x7-1/2")
Book 1-Contains reprints of the first 13 weeks of the strip by Alex Raymond; complete except for 2 dailies 43 86 129 267 446 625
Book 2-Contains reprints immediately following contents of Book 1, for 20 weeks by Alex Raymond; complete except for two dailies. Note: Raymond mis-dated the last five strips from 6/34, and while the dating sequence is confusing, the continuity is correct
39 78 117 230 370 510

SECRET AGENT X-9 (See Magic Comics)
Dell Publishing Co.: Dec, 1937 (Not by Raymond)
Feature Books 8 47 94 141 291 483 675

SECRET AGENT Z-2 (See Holyoke One-Shot No. 7)

SECRET CITY SAGA (See Jack Kirby's Secret City Saga)

GD VG FN VF VF/NM NM-
2.0 4.0 6.0 8.0 9.0 9.2

SECRET DEFENDERS (Also see The Defenders & Fantastic Four #374)
Marvel Comics: Mar, 1993 - No. 25, Mar, 1995 ($1.75/$1.95)
1-($2.50)-Red foil stamped-c; Dr. Strange, Nomad, Wolverine, Spider Woman & Darkhawk begin 3.00
2-11,13-24: 9-New team w/Silver Surfer, Thunderstrike, Dr. Strange & War Machine. 13-Thanos replaces Dr. Strange as leader; leads into Cosmic Powers limited series; 14-Dr. Druid. 15-Bound in card sheet. 18-Giant Man & Iron Fist app. 2.50
12,25: 12-($2.50)-Prismatic foil-c. 25 ($2.50, 52 pgs.) 2.75

SECRET DIARY OF EERIE ADVENTURES
Avon Periodicals: 1953 (25¢ giant, 100 pgs., one-shot)
nn-(Rare)-Kubert-a; Hollingsworth-c; Sid Check back-c
207 414 621 1304 2202 3100

SECRET FILES & ORIGINS GUIDE TO THE DC UNIVERSE
DC Comics: Mar, 2000; Feb, 2002 ($6.95/$4.95)
2000 (3/00, $6.95)-Overview of DC characters; profile pages by various 7.00
2001-2002 (2/02, $4.95) Olivetti-c 5.00

SECRET FILES PRESIDENT LUTHOR
DC Comics: Mar, 2001 ($4.95, one-shot)
1-Short stories & profile pages by various; Harris-c 5.00

SECRET HEARTS
National Periodical Publications (Beverly)(Arleigh No. 50-113):
9-10/49 - No. 6, 7-8/50; No. 7, 12-1/51-52 - No. 153, 7/71
1-Kinstler-a; photo-c begin, end #6 55 110 165 347 586 825
2-Toth-a (1 pg.); Kinstler-a 30 60 90 174 280 385
3,6 (1950) 26 52 78 152 244 335
4,5-Toth-a 26 52 78 154 247 340
7(12-1/51-52) (Rare) 40 80 120 244 397 550
8-10 (1952) 19 38 57 112 176 240
11-20 15 30 45 86 133 180
21-26: 26-Last precode (2-3/55) 14 28 42 80 115 150
27-40 7 14 21 47 76 105
41-50 5 10 15 34 55 75
51-60 5 10 15 30 48 65
61-75,100: 75-Last 10¢ issue 4 8 12 28 44 60
76-99,101-109 4 8 12 22 34 45
110- "Reach for Happiness" serial begins, ends #138 4 8 12 24 37 50
111-119,121-126 3 6 9 17 25 32
120,134-Neal Adams-c 4 8 12 24 37 50
127 (4/68)-Beatles cameo 4 8 12 24 37 50
128-133,135 142: 141,142- "20 Miles to Heartbreak", Chapter 2 & 3 (see Young Love for Chapters 1 & 4); Toth, Colletta-a 3 6 9 16 23 30
143-148,150-152: 144-Morrow-a 3 6 9 14 19 24
149,153: 149-Toth-a. 153-Kirby-i 3 6 9 15 21 26

SECRET HISTORY OF THE AUTHORITY: HAWKSMOOR
DC Comics (WildStorm): May, 2008 - No. 6 ($2.99, limited series)
1-5-Costa-s/Staples-a/Hamner-c 3.00

SECRET INVASION (Also see Mighty Avengers, New Avengers, and Skrulls!)
Marvel Comics: June, 2008 - No. 8 ($3.99, limited series)
1-Skrull invasion; Bendis-s/Yu-a/Dell'Otto-c 4.00
1-Variant cover with blank area for sketches 4.00
1-McNiven variant-c 12.00
1-Yu variant-c 30.00
1-2nd printing with old Avengers variant-c by Yu 4.00
1 Director's Cut (2008, $4.99) r/#1 with script; concept and promo art; cover gallery 5.00
2-6-Dell'Otto-c 4.00
2-4-McNiven variant-c. 2-Avengers. 3-Nick Fury. 4 Tony Stark, Spider-Woman, Black Widow 6.00
2-6-Yu variant-c. 2-Hawkeye & Mockingbird. 3-Spider-Woman. 4-Nick Fury 10.00
5-Rubi variant-c 5.00
6-Cho Spider-Woman variant-c 8.00
... Saga (2008, giveaway) history of the Skrulls told through reprint panels and text 2.25
...: Who Do You Trust? (8/08, $3.99) short tie-in stories by various; Jimenez-c 4.00
...: The Infiltration TPB (2008, $19.99) r/FF #2; New Avengers #31,32,38,39; New Avengers: Illuminati #1,5; Mighty Avengers #7; and Avengers: The Initiative Annual #1 20.00

SECRET INVASION: AMAZING SPIDER-MAN
Marvel Comics: Oct, 2008 - No. 3, Dec, 2008 ($2.99, limited series)
1,2-Jackpot battles a Super-Skrull; Santucci-a. 2-Menace app. 3.00

SECRET INVASION: FANTASTIC FOUR
Marvel Comics: July, 2008 - No. 3, Sept, 2008 ($2.99, limited series)

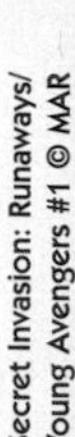

EXCITING LOVE STORIES!
SECRET Romances
"Dear Miss Martin..." OPEN HEART FORUM

Secret Romances #2 © SUPR

	GD 2.0	VG 4.0	FN 6.0	VF 8.0	VF/NM 9.0	NM- 9.2

1-3-Skrulls and Lyja invade; Kitson-a/Davis-c 3.00
1-Variant Skrull cover by McKone 5.00

SECRET INVASION: FRONT LINE
Marvel Comics: Sept, 2008 - No. 5 ($2.99, limited series)

1-3-Ben Urich covering the Skrull invasion; Reed-s/Castiello-a 3.00

SECRET INVASION: INHUMANS
Marvel Comics: Oct, 2008 - No. 4 ($2.99, limited series)

1-Raney-a/Sejic-c/Pokasky-s; search for Black Bolt 3.00

SECRET INVASION: RUNAWAYS/YOUNG AVENGERS (Follows Runaways #30)
Marvel Comics: Aug, 2008 - No. 3, Nov, 2008 ($2.99, limited series)

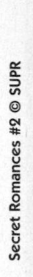

1-3-Miyazawa-a/Ryan-c 3.00

SECRET INVASION: THOR
Marvel Comics: Oct, 2008 - No. 3 ($2.99, limited series)

1,2-Fraction-s/Braithwaite-a; Skrulls invade Asgard; Beta Ray Bill app. 3.00
1-2nd printing with Beta Ray Bill cover 3.00

SECRET INVASION: X-MEN
Marvel Comics: Oct, 2008 - No. 4 ($2.99, limited series)

1,2-Carey-s/Nord-a/Dodson-c; Skrulls invade San Francisco 3.00
1-2nd printing with variant Nord-c 3.00

SECRET ISLAND OF OZ, THE (See First Comics Graphic Novel)

SECRET LOVE (See Fox Giants & Sinister House of...)

SECRET LOVE
Ajax-Farrell/Four Star Comic Corp. No. 2 on: 12/55 - No. 3, 8/56; 4/57 - No. 5, 2/58; No. 6, 6/58

	GD	VG	FN	VF	VF/NM	NM-
1(12/55-Ajax, 1st series)	10	20	30	54	72	90
2,3	7	14	21	35	40	50
1(4/57-Ajax, 2nd series)	8	16	24	44	57	70
2-6: 5-Bakerish-a	6	12	18	31	38	45

SECRET LOVES
Comic Magazines/Quality Comics Group: Nov, 1949 - No. 6, Sept, 1950

	GD	VG	FN	VF	VF/NM	NM-
1-Ward-c	25	50	75	147	236	325
2-Ward-c	21	42	63	123	197	270
3-Crandall-a	14	28	42	82	121	160
4,6	12	24	36	67	94	120
5-Suggestive art "Boom Town Babe"; photo-c	14	28	42	82	121	160

SECRET LOVE STORIES (See Fox Giants)

SECRET MISSIONS (Admiral Zacharia's...)
St. John Publishing Co.: February, 1950

	GD	VG	FN	VF	VF/NM	NM-
1-Joe Kubert-c; stories of U.S. foreign agents	20	40	60	115	183	250

SECRET MYSTERIES (Formerly Crime Mysteries & Crime Smashers)
Ribage/Merit Publications No. 17 on: No. 16, Nov, 1954 - No. 19, July, 1955

	GD	VG	FN	VF	VF/NM	NM-
16-Horror, Palais-a; Myron Fass-c	28	56	84	162	261	360
17-19-Horror. 17-Fass-c; mis-dated 3/54?	20	40	60	115	183	250

SECRET ORIGINS (1st Series) (See 80 Page Giant #8)
National Periodical Publications: Aug-Oct, 1961 (Annual) (Reprints)

	GD	VG	FN	VF	VF/NM	NM-
1-Origin Adam Strange (Showcase #17), Green Lantern (Green Lantern #1), Challengers (partial-r/Showcase #6, 6 pgs. Kirby-a), J'onn J'onzz (Det. #225), The Flash (Showcase #4), Green Arrow (1 pg. text), Superman-Batman team (World's Finest #94), Wonder Woman (Wonder Woman #105)	45	90	135	360	680	1000

Replica Edition (1998, $4.95) r/entire book and house ads 5.00
Even More Secret Origins (2003, $6.95) reprints origins of Hawkman, Eclipso, Kid Flash, Blackhawks, Green Lantern's oath, and Jimmy Olsen-Robin team in 80 pg. Giant style 7.00

SECRET ORIGINS (2nd Series)
National Periodical Publications: Feb-Mar, 1973 - No. 6, Jan-Feb, 1974; No. 7, Oct-Nov, 1974 (All 20¢ issues) (All origin reprints)

	GD	VG	FN	VF	VF/NM	NM-
1-Superman(r/1 pg. origin/Action #1, 1st time since G.A.), Batman(Detective #33), Ghost(Flash #88), The Flash(Showcase #4)	4	8	12	28	44	60
2-7: 2-Green Lantern & The Atom(Showcase #22 & 34), Supergirl(Action #252). 3-Wonder Woman(W.W. #1), Wildcat(Sensation #1). 4-Vigilante (Action #42) by Meskin, Kid Eternity(Hit #25). 5-The Spectre by Baily (More Fun #52,53). 6-Blackhawk(Military #1) & Legion of Super-Heroes(Superboy #147). 7-Robin (Detective #38), Aquaman (More Fun #73)	3	6	9	17	25	32

NOTE: *Infantino a-1. Kane a-2. Kubert a-1.*

SECRET ORIGINS (3rd Series)
DC Comics: 4/86 - No. 50, 8/90 (All origins)(52 pgs. #6 on)(#27 on: $1.50)

1-Origin Superman 6.00
2-6: 2-Blue Beetle. 3-Shazam. 4-Firestorm. 5-Crimson Avenger. 6-Halo/G.A. Batman 3.00
7-9,11,12,14-20,22-26: 7-Green Lantern(Guy Gardner)/G.A. Sandman. 8-Shadow Lass/Doll Man. 9-G.A. Flash/Skyman.11-G.A. Hawkman/Power Girl. 12-Challengers of Unknown/G.A. Fury (2nd modern app.). 14-Suicide Squad; Legends spin-off. 15-Spectre/Deadman. 16-G.A. Hourman/Warlord. 17-Adam Strange story by Carmine Infantino; Dr. Occult. 18-G.A. Gr. Lantern/The Creeper. 19-Uncle Sam/The Guardian. 20-Batgirl/G.A. Dr. Mid-Nite. 22-Manhunters. 23-Floronic Man/Guardians of the Universe. 24-Blue Devil/Dr. Fate. 25-LSH/Atom. 26-Black Lightning/Miss America 2.50
10-Phantom Stranger w/Alan Moore scripts; Legends spin-off 2.50
13-Origin Nightwing; Johnny Thunder app. 2.50
21-Jonah Hex/Black Condor 2.50
27-30,36-38,40-49: 27-Zatara/Zatanna. 28-Midnight/Nightshade. 29-Power of the Atom/Mr. America; new 3 pg. Red Tornado story by Mayer (last app. of Scribbly, 8/88). 30-Plastic Man/Elongated Man. 36-Poison Ivy by Neil Gaiman & Mark Buckingham/Green Lantern. 37-Legion Of Substitute Heroes/Doctor Light. 38-Green Arrow/Speedy; Grell scripts. 40-All Ape issue. 41-Rogues Gallery of Flash. 42-Phantom Girl/GrimGhost. 43-Original Hawk & Dove/Cave Carson/Chris KL-99. 44-Batman app.; story based on Det. #40. 45-Blackhawk/El Diablo. 46-JLA/LSH/New Titans. 47-LSH. 48-Ambush Bug/Stanley & His Monster/Rex the Wonder Dog/Trigger Twins. 49-Newsboy Legion/Silent Knight/Bouncing Boy 2.50
31-35,39: 31-JSA. 32-JLA. 33-35-JLI. 39-Animal Man-c/story continued in Animal Man #10; Grant Morrison scripts; Batman app. 3.00
50-($3.95, 100 pgs.)-Batman & Robin in text, Flash of Two Worlds, Johnny Thunder, Dolphin, Black Canary & Space Museum 5.00
Annual 1 (8/87)-Capt. Comet/Doom Patrol 3.00
Annual 2 ('88, $2.00)-Origin Flash II & Flash III 3.00
Annual 3 ('89, $2.95, 84 pgs.)-Teen Titans; 1st app. new Flamebird who replaces original Bat-Girl 3.00
Special 1 (10/89, $2.00)-Batman villains: Penguin, Riddler, & Two-Face; Bolland-c; Sam Kieth-a; Neil Gaiman scripts(2) 3.00

NOTE. ***Art Adams** a-33i(part). **M. Anderson** 8, 10, 21, 26i; c-19(part). **Aparo** c/a-10. **Bissette** c-23. **Bolland** c-7. **Byrne** c/a-Annual 1. **Colan** c/a-5p. **Forte** a-37. **Giffen** a-18p, 44p, 48. **Infantino** a-17, 50p. **Kaluta** c-39. **Gil Kane** a-2, 28; c-2p. **Kirby** c-19(part). **Erik Larsen** a-13. **Mayer** a-29. **Morrow** a-21. **Orlando** a-10. **Perez** a-50i, Annual 3i; c- Annual 3. **Rogers** a-6p. **Russell** a-27i. **Simonson** c-22. **Staton** a-36, 50p. **Steacy** a-35. **Tuska** a-4p, 9p.*

SECRET ORIGINS 80 PAGE GIANT (Young Justice)
DC Comics: Dec, 1998 ($4.95, one-shot)

1-Origin-s of Young Justice members; Ramos-a (Impulse) 5.00

SECRET ORIGINS FEATURING THE JLA
DC Comics: 1999 ($14.95, TPB)

1-Reprints recent origin-s of JLA members; Cassaday-c 15.00

SECRET ORIGINS OF SUPER-HEROES (See DC Special Series #10, 19)

SECRET ORIGINS OF SUPER-VILLAINS 80 PAGE GIANT
DC Comics: Dec, 1999 ($4.95, one-shot)

1-Origin-s of Sinestro, Amazo and others; Gibbons-c 5.00

SECRET ORIGINS OF THE WORLD'S GREATEST SUPER-HEROES
DC Comics: 1989 ($4.95, 148 pgs.)

	GD	VG	FN	VF	VF/NM	NM-
nn-Reprints Superman, JLA origins; new Batman origin-s; Bolland-c	1	2	3	4	5	7

SECRET ROMANCE
Charlton Comics: Oct, 1968 - No. 41, Nov, 1976; No. 42, Mar, 1979 - No. 48, Feb, 1980

	GD	VG	FN	VF	VF/NM	NM-
1-Begin 12¢ issues, ends #?	3	6	9	16	22	28
2-10: 9-Reese-a	2	4	6	9	13	16
11-16,18,19,21-30	2	4	6	8	10	12
17,20: 17-Susan Dey poster. 20-David Cassidy pin-up	2	4	6	9	12	15
31-48	1	2	3	5	7	9

NOTE: *Beyond the Stars app.-No. 9, 11, 12, 14.*

SECRET ROMANCES (Exciting Love Stories)
Superior Publications Ltd.: Apr, 1951 - No. 27, July, 1955

	GD	VG	FN	VF	VF/NM	NM-
1	15	30	45	85	130	175
2	11	22	33	60	83	105
3-10	9	18	27	47	61	75
11-13,15-18,20-27	8	16	24	40	50	60
14,19-Lingerie panels	8	16	24	42	54	65

SECRET SERVICE (See Kent Blake of the...)

SECRET SIX (See Action Comics Weekly)
National Periodical Publications: Apr-May, 1968 - No. 7, Apr-May, 1969 (12¢)

	GD	VG	FN	VF	VF/NM	NM-
1-Origin/1st app.	6	12	18	41	66	90
2-7	4	8	12	22	34	45

SECRET SIX (See Tangent Comics/ Secret Six)

Secrets of Haunted House #19 © DC

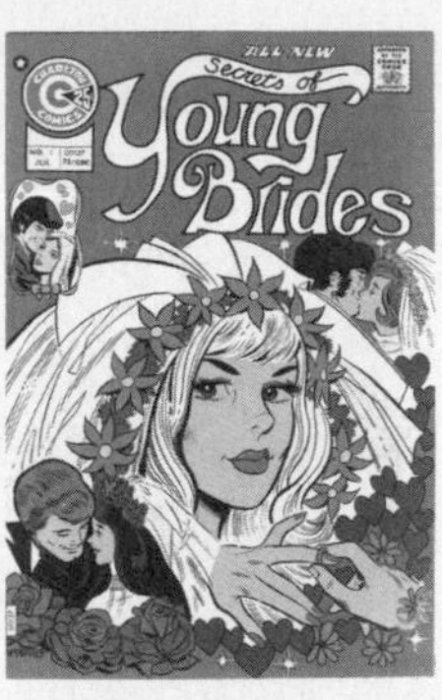

Secrets of Young Brides #2 © CC

Secret Weapons #6 © Voyager Comm.

GD VG FN VF VF/NM NM-
2.0 4.0 6.0 8.0 9.0 9.2

GD VG FN VF VF/NM NM-
2.0 4.0 6.0 8.0 9.0 9.2

SECRET SIX (See Villains United)
DC Comics: Jul, 2006 - No. 6, Jan, 2007 ($2.99, limited series)
1-6-Gail Simone-s/Brad Walker-a. 4-Doom Patrol app. 3.00
...: Six Degrees of Devastation TPB (2007, $14.99) r/#1-6 15.00

SECRET SKULL
IDW Publ.: Aug, 2004 - No. 4, Nov, 2004 ($3.99)
1-4-Steve Niles-s/Chuck BB-a 4.00

SECRET SOCIETY OF SUPER-VILLAINS
National Per. Publ./DC Comics: May-June, 1976 - No. 15, June-July, 1978
1-Origin; JLA cameo & Capt. Cold app. 2 4 6 11 16 20
2-5,15: 2-Re-intro/origin Capt. Comet; Green Lantern x-over. 5-Green Lantern, Hawkman x-over; Darkseid app. 15-G.A. Atom, Dr. Midnite, & JSA app. 2 4 6 8 10 12
6-14: 9,10-Creeper x-over. 11-Capt. Comet; Orlando-i 1 2 3 5 7 9

SECRET SOCIETY OF SUPER-VILLAINS SPECIAL (See DC Special Series #6)

SECRETS OF HAUNTED HOUSE
National Periodical Publications/DC Comics: 4-5/75 - #5, 12-1/75-76; #6, 6-7/77 - #14, 10-11/78; #15, 8/79 - #46, 3/82
1 5 10 15 32 51 70
2-4 3 6 9 16 23 30
5-Wrightson-c 3 6 9 20 30 40
6-14 2 4 6 9 13 16
15-30 1 3 4 6 8 10
31,44: 31-(12/80) Mr. E series begins (1st app.), ends #41. 44-Wrightson-c 2 4 6 8 10 12
32-(1/81) Origin of Mr. E 1 3 4 6 8 10
33-43,45,46: 34,35-Frankenstein Monster app. 1 2 3 4 5 7
NOTE: ***Aparo** c-7. **Aragones** a-1. **B. Bailey** a-8. **Bissette** a-46. **Buckler** c-32-40p. **Ditko** a-9, 12, 41, 45. **Golden** a-10. **Howard** a-13i. **Kaluta** c-8, 10, 11, 14, 16, 29. **Kubert** c-41, 42. **Sheldon Mayer** a-43p. **McWilliams** a-35. **Nasser** a-24. **Newton** a-30p. **Nino** a-1, 13, 19. **Orlando** c-13, 30, 43, 45i. **N. Redondo** a-4, 5, 29. **Rogers** c-26. **Spiegle** a-31-41. **Wrightson** c-5, 44.*

SECRETS OF HAUNTED HOUSE SPECIAL (See DC Special Series #12)

SECRETS OF LIFE (Movie)
Dell Publishing Co.: 1956 (Disney)
Four Color 749-Photo-c 5 10 15 32 51 70

SECRETS OF LOVE (See Popular Teen-Agers...)

SECRETS OF LOVE AND MARRIAGE
Charlton Comics: V2#1, Aug, 1956 - V2#25, June, 1961
V2#1 4 8 12 26 41 55
V2#2-6 3 6 9 18 27 35
V2#7-9-(All 68 pgs.) 4 8 12 28 44 60
10-25 3 6 9 16 22 28

SECRETS OF MAGIC (See Wisco)

SECRETS OF SINISTER HOUSE (Sinister House of Secret Love #1-4)
National Periodical Publ.: No. 5, June-July, 1972 - No. 18, June-July, 1974
5-(52 pgs.). 5 10 15 34 55 75
6-9: 7-Redondo-a 3 6 9 20 30 40
10-Neal Adams-a(i) 4 8 12 22 34 45
11-18: 15-Redondo-a. 17-Barry-a; early Chaykin 1 pg. strip 3 6 9 14 20 25
NOTE: ***Alcala** a-6, 13, 14. **Glanzman** a-7. **Kaluta** c-6, 7. **Nino** a-8, 11-13. Ambrose Bierce adapt.-#14.*

SECRETS OF THE LEGION OF SUPER-HEROES
DC Comics: Jan, 1981 - No. 3, Mar, 1981 (Limited series)
1-3: 1-Origin of the Legion. 2-Retells origins of Brainiac 5, Shrinking Violet, Sun-Boy, Bouncing Boy, Ultra-Boy, Matter-Eater Lad, Mon-El, Karate Kid & Dream Girl 4.00

SECRETS OF TRUE LOVE
St. John Publishing Co.: Feb, 1958
1 7 14 21 37 46 55

SECRETS OF YOUNG BRIDES
Charlton Comics: No. 5, Sept, 1957 - No. 44, Oct, 1964; July, 1975 - No. 9, Nov, 1976
5 4 8 12 28 44 60
6-10: 8-Negligee panel 3 6 9 20 30 40
11-20 3 6 9 18 27 35
21-30: Last 10¢ issue? 3 6 9 16 23 30
31-44(10/64) 2 4 6 11 16 20
1-(2nd series) (7/75) 2 4 6 13 18 22
2-9 2 4 6 8 10 12

SECRET SQUIRREL (TV)(See Kite Fun Book)
Gold Key: Oct, 1966 (12¢) (Hanna-Barbera)
1-1st Secret Squirrel and Morocco Mole, Squiddly Diddly, Winsome Witch 10 20 30 73 129 185

SECRET STORY ROMANCES (Becomes True Tales of Love)
Atlas Comics (TCI): Nov, 1953 - No. 21, Mar, 1956
1-Everett-a; Jay Scott Pike-c 15 30 45 86 133 180
2 10 20 30 54 72 90
3-11: 11-Last pre-code (2/55) 9 18 27 47 61 75
12-21 8 16 24 42 54 65
NOTE: ***Colletta** a-10, 14, 15, 17, 21; c-10, 14, 17.*

SECRET VOICE, THE (See Great American Comics Presents...)

SECRET WAR
Marvel Comics: Apr, 2004 - No. 5, Dec, 2005 ($3.99, limited series)
1-Bendis-s/Dell'Otto painted-a/c; 5.00
1-2nd printing with gold logo on white cover and full-color Spider-Man 4.00
1-3rd printing with white cover and B&W sketched Spider-Man 4.00
2-5: 2-Wolverine-c. 3-Capt. America-c. 4-Black Widow-c. 5-Daredevil-c 4.00
2-2nd printing with white cover and B&W sketched Wolverine 4.00
... : From the Files of Nick Fury (2005, $3.99) Fury's journal entries; profiles of characters 4.00
HC (2005, $29.99, dust jacket) r/#1-5 & ...From the Files of Nick Fury; additional art 30.00
SC (2006, $24.99) r/#1-5 & ...From the Files of Nick Fury; additional art 25.00

SECRET WARS II (Also see Marvel Super Heroes...)
Marvel Comics Group: July, 1985 - No. 9, Mar, 1986 (Maxi-series)
1,9: 9-(52 pgs.) X-Men app., Spider-Man app. 4.00
2-8: 2,8-X-Men app. 5-1st app. Boom Boom. 5,8-Spider-Man app. 3.00

SECRET WEAPONS
Valiant: Sept, 1993 - No. 21, May, 1995 ($2.25)
1-10,12-21: 3-Reese-a(i). 5-Ninjak app. 9-Bound-in trading card. 12-Bloodshot app. 2.50
11-(Sept. on envelope, Aug on-c, $2.50)-Enclosed in manilla envelope; Bloodshot app; intro new team. 2.50

SECTAURS
Marvel Comics: June, 1985 - No. 8, Sept, 1986 (75¢) (Based on Coleco Toys)
1-8, 1-Giveaway; same-c with "Coleco 1985 Toy Fair Collectors' Edition" 3.00

SECTION ZERO
Image Comics (Gorilla): June, 2000 - No. 3, Sept, 2000 ($2.50)
1-3-Kesel-s/Grummett-a 2.50

SEDUCTION OF THE INNOCENT (Also see New York State Joint Legislative Committee to Study...)
Rinehart & Co., Inc., N. Y.: 1953, 1954 (400 pgs.) (Hardback, $4.00)(Written by Fredric Wertham, M.D.)(Also printed in Canada by Clarke, Irwin & Co. Ltd.)
(1st Version)-with bibliographical note intact (pages 399 & 400)(several copies got out before the comic publishers forced the removal of this page) 57 114 171 359 605 850
Dust jacket only 35 70 105 203 327 450
(1st Version)-without bibliographical note 35 70 105 203 327 450
Dust jacket only 17 34 51 98 154 210
(2nd Version)-Published in England by Kennikat Press, 1954, 399 pgs. has bibliographical page; "Second print" listed on inside flap of the dust jacket; publication page has no "R" colophon; unlike 1st version 14 28 42 80 115 150
1972 r-/of 2nd version; 400 pgs. w/bibliography page; Kennikat Press 4 8 12 24 37 50
NOTE: *Material from this book appeared in the November, 1953 (Vol.70, pp50-53,214) issue of the **Ladies' Home Journal** under the title "What Parents Don't Know About Comic Books". With the release of this book, Dr. Wertham reveals seven years of research attempting to link juvenile delinquency to comic books. Many illustrations showing excessive violence, sex, sadism, and torture are shown. This book was used at the Kefauver Senate hearings which led to the Comics Code Authority. Because of the influence this book had on the comic industry and the collector's interest in it, we feel this listing is justified. Modern printings exist in limited editions. Also see **Parade of Pleasure.***

SEDUCTION OF THE INNOCENT! (Also see Halloween Horror)
Eclipse Comics: Nov, 1985 - 3-D#2, Apr, 1986 ($1.75)
1-6: Double listed under cover title from #7 on 3.00
3-D 1 (10/85, $2.25, 36 pgs.)-contains unpublished Advs. Into Darkness #15 (pre-code); Dave Stevens-c 4.00
2-D 1 (100 copy limited signed & #ed edition)(B&W) 1 2 3 5 6 8
3-D 2 (4/86)-Baker, Toth, Wrightson-c 5.00
2-D 2 (100 copy limited signed & #ed edition)(B&W) 1 2 3 5 7 9
NOTE: ***Anderson** r-2, 3. **Crandall** c/a(r)-1. **Meskin** c/a(r)-3, 3-D 1. **Moreira** r-2. **Toth** a-1-6r; c-4r. **Tuska** r-6.*

SEEKER
Sky Comics: Apr, 1994 ($2.50, one-shot)

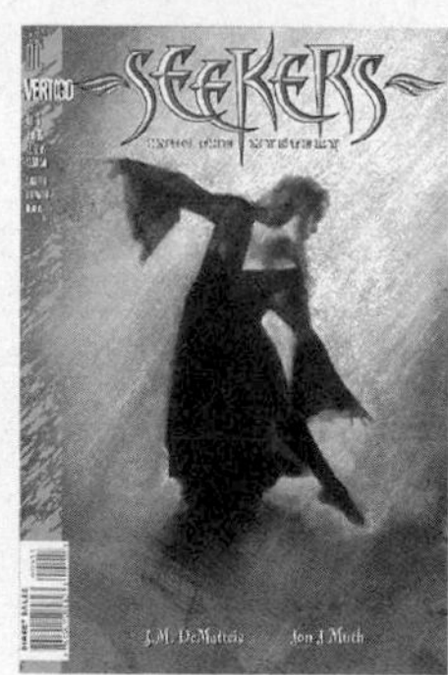
Seekers Into the Mystery #6 © JM DeMatteis

Sensational Spider-Man #41 © MAR

Sensation Comics #3 © DC

	GD 2.0	VG 4.0	FN 6.0	VF 8.0	VF/NM 9.0	NM- 9.2
1						2.50

SEEKERS INTO THE MYSTERY
DC Comics (Vertigo): Jan, 1996 - No. 15, Apr, 1997 ($2.50)

1-14: J.M. DeMatteis scripts in all. 1-4-Glenn Barr-a. 5,10-Muth-c/a. 6-9-Zulli-c/a. 11-14-Bolton-c; Jill Thompson-a						2.50
15-($2.95)-Muth-c/a						3.00

SEEKER 3000 (See Marvel Premiere #41)
Marvel Comics: Jun, 1998 - No. 4, Sept, 1998 ($2.99/$2.50, limited series)

1-($2.99)-Set 25 years after 1st app.; wraparound-c						3.00
2-4-($2.50)						2.50
...Premiere 1 (6/98, $1.50) Reprints 1st app. from Marvel Premiere #41; wraparound-c						2.50

SELECT DETECTIVE (Exciting New Mystery Cases)
D. S. Publishing Co.: Aug-Sept, 1948 - No. 3, Dec-Jan, 1948-49

1-Matt Baker-a	29	58	87	169	272	375
2-Baker, McWilliams-a	19	38	57	112	176	240
3	15	30	45	88	137	185

SEMPER FI (Tales of the Marine Corp)
Marvel Comics: Dec, 1988- No.9, Aug, 1989 (75¢)

1-9: Severin-c/a						2.50

SENSATIONAL POLICE CASES (Becomes Captain Steve Savage, 2nd Series)
Avon Periodicals: 1952; No. 2, 1954 - No. 4, July-Aug, 1954

nn-(1952, 25¢, 100 pgs.)-Kubert-a?; Check, Larsen, Lawrence & McCann-a; Kinstler-c	40	80	120	235	380	525
2-4: 2-Kirbyish-a (3-4/54). 4-Reprint/Saint #5	15	30	45	85	130	175
I.W. Reprint #5-(1963?, nd)-Reprints Prison Break #5(1952-Realistic); Infantino-a	3	6	9	16	23	30

SENSATIONAL SHE-HULK, THE (She-Hulk #21-23) (See Savage She-Hulk)
Marvel Comics: V2#1, 5/89 - No. 60, Feb, 1994 ($1.50/$1.75, deluxe format)

V2#1-Byrne-c/a(p)/scripts begin, end #8						3.00
2,3,5-8: 3-Spider-Man app.						2.50
4,14-17,21-23: 4-Reintro G.A. Blonde Phantom. 14-17-Howard the Duck app. 21-23-Return of the Blonde Phantom. 22-All Winners Squad app.						2.50
9-13,18-20,24-49,51-60: 25-Thor app. 26-Excalibur app.; Guice-c. 29-Wolverine app. (3 pgs.). 30-Hobgoblin-c & cameo. 31-Byrne-c/a/scripts begin again. 35-Last $1.50-c. 37-Wolverine/Punisher/Spidey-c, but no app. 39-Thing app. 56-War Zone app.; Hulk cameo. 57-Vs. Hulk-c/story. 58-Electro-c/story. 59-Jack O'Lantern app.						2.50
50-($2.95, 52 pgs.)-Embossed green foil-c; Byrne app.; last Byrne-c/a; Austin, Chaykin, Simonson-a; Miller-a(2 pgs.)						3.00

NOTE: *Dale Keown a(p)-13, 15-22.*

SENSATIONAL SHE-HULK IN CEREMONY, THE
Marvel Comics: 1989 - No. 2, 1989 ($3.95, squarebound, 52 pgs.)

nn-Part 1, nn-Part 2						4.00

SENSATIONAL SPIDER-MAN
Marvel Comics: Apr, 1989 ($5.95, squarebound, 80 pgs.)

1-r/Amazing Spider-Man Annual #14,15 by Miller & Annual #8 by Kirby & Ditko						6.00

SENSATIONAL SPIDER-MAN, THE
Marvel Comics: Jan, 1996 - No. 33, Nov, 1998 ($1.95/$1.99)

0 ($4.95)-Lenticular-c; Jurgens-a/scripts						5.00
1						5.00
1-($2.95) variant-c; polybagged w/cassette	1	2	3	5	6	8
2-5: 2-Kaine & Rhino app. 3-Giant-Man app.						4.00
6-18: 9-Onslaught tie-in; revealed that Peter & Mary Jane's unborn baby is a girl. 11-Revelations. 13-15-Ka-Zar app. 14,15-Hulk app.						3.00
19-24: Living Pharoah app. 22,23-Dr. Strange app.						2.50
25-($2.99) Spiderhunt pt. 1; Normie Osborne kidnapped						4.00
25-Variant-c	1	2	3	5	6	8
26-33: 26-Nauck-a. 27-Double-c with "The Sensational Hornet #1"; Vulture app. 28-Hornet vs. Vulture. 29,30-Black Cat-c/app. 33-Last issue; Gathering of Five concludes						2.50
#(-1) Flashback(7/97) Dezago-s/Wieringo-a						3.00
'96 Annual ($2.95)						3.00

SENSATIONAL SPIDER-MAN, THE (Previously Marvel Knights Spider-Man #1-22)
Marvel Comics: No. 23, Apr, 2006 - No. 41, Dec, 2007 ($2.99)

23-40: 23-25-Aguirre-Sacasa-s/Medina-a. 23-Wraparound-c. 24,34,37-Black Cat app. 26-New costume. 28-Unmasked; Dr. Octopus app.; Crain-a. 35-Black costume resumes						3.00
41-($3.99) One More Day pt. 3; Straczynski-s/Quesada-a/c						4.00
... Annual 1 (2007, $3.99) Flashbacks of Peter & MJ's relationship; Larroca-a/Fraction-s						4.00
... Feral HC (2006, $19.99, dustjacket) r/#23-27; sketch pages						20.00
Civil War: Peter Parker, Spider-Man TPB (2007, $17.99) r/#28-34; Crain cover concepts						18.00

SENSATION COMICS (Sensation Mystery #110 on)
National Per. Publ./All-American: Jan, 1942 - No. 109, May-June, 1952

	GD 2.0	VG 4.0	FN 6.0	VF 8.0	VF/NM 9.0	NM- 9.2
1-Origin Mr. Terrific(1st app.), Wildcat(1st app.), The Gay Ghost, & Little Boy Blue; Wonder Woman (cont'd from All Star #8), The Black Pirate begin; intro. Justice & Fair Play Club	3100	6200	9300	23,000	44,000	65,000

1-Reprint, Oversize 13-1/2x10". WARNING: This comic is an exact duplicate reprint of the original except for its size. DC published it in 1974 with a second cover titling it as a Famous First Edition. There have been many reported cases of the outer cover being removed and the interior sold as the original edition. The reprint with the new outer cover removed is practically worthless. See Famous First Edition for value.

2-Etta Candy begins	467	934	1401	3362	5881	8400
3-W. Woman gets secretary's job	293	500	079	1046	3123	4400
4-1st app. Stretch Skinner in Wildcat	200	400	600	1260	2130	3000
5-Intro. Justin, Black Pirate's son	160	320	480	1008	1704	2400
6-Origin/1st app. Wonder Woman's magic lasso	163	326	489	1027	1739	2450
7-10	117	234	351	737	1244	1750
11,12,14-20	100	200	300	630	1065	1500
13-Hitler, Tojo, Mussolini-c (as bowling pins)	150	300	450	945	1508	2260
21-30	80	160	240	504	852	1200
31-33	60	120	180	378	639	900
34-Sargon, the Sorcerer begins (10/44), ends #36; begins again #52	63	126	189	397	674	950
35-40: 38-X-Mas-c	55	110	165	347	586	825
41-50: 43-The Whip app.	53	106	159	330	553	775
51-60: 51-Last Black Pirate. 56,57-Sargon by Kubert	52	104	156	322	536	750
61-67,69-80: 63-Last Mr. Terrific. 66-Wildcat by Kubert	43	86	129	267	446	625
68-Origin & 1st app. Huntress (8/47)	50	100	150	310	518	725
81-Used in **SOTI**, pg. 33,34; Krigstein-a	48	96	144	298	499	700
82-90: 88-Last Sargon. 86-The Atom app. 90-Last Wildcat. 91-Streak begins by Alex Toth. 92-Toth-a (2 pgs.)	41	82	123	256	428	600
94-1st all girl issue	60	120	180	378	639	900
95-99,101-106: 95-Unmasking of Wonder Woman-c/story. 99-1st app. Astra, Girl of the Future, ends #106. 103-Robot-c. 105-Last 52 pgs. 106-Wonder Woman ends	53	106	159	330	553	775
100-(11-12/50)	63	126	189	397	674	950
107-(Scarce, 1-2/52)-1st mystery issue; Johnny Peril by Toth(p), 8 pgs. & begins; continues from Danger Trail #5 (3-4/51)(see Comic Cavalcade #15 for 1st app.)	71	142	213	447	754	1060
108-(Scarce)-Johnny Peril by Toth(p)	60	120	180	378	639	900
109-(Scarce)-Johnny Peril by Toth(p)	71	142	213	447	754	1060

NOTE: ***Krigstein** a-(Wildcat)-81, 83, 84. **Moldoff** Black Pirate-1-25; Black Pirate not in 34-36, 43-48. **Oskner** c(i)-89-91, 94-106. Wonder Woman by **H. G. Peter**, all issues except #8, 17-19, 21; c-4-7, 9-18, 20-88, 92, 93. **Toth** a-91, 98; c-107. Wonder Woman c-1-106.*

SENSATION COMICS (Also see All Star Comics 1999 crossover titles)
DC Comics: May, 1999 ($1.99, one-shot)

1-Golden Age Wonder Woman and Hawkgirl; Robinson-s						2.50

SENSATION MYSTERY (Formerly Sensation Comics #1-109)
National Periodical Publ.: No. 110, July-Aug, 1952 - No. 116, July-Aug, 1953

110-Johnny Peril continues	47	94	141	291	483	675
111-116-Johnny Peril in all. 116-M. Anderson-a	47	94	141	291	483	675

NOTE: ***M. Anderson** c-110. **Colan** a-114p. **Giunta** a-112. **G. Kane** c(p)-108, 109, 111-115.*

SENSUOUS STREAKER
Marvel Publ.: 1974 (B&W magazine, 68pgs.)

1	4	8	12	2	34	45

SENTENCES: THE LIFE OF M.F. GRIMM
DC Comics (Vertigo): 2007 ($19.99, B&W graphic novel)

HC-Autobiography of Percy Carey (M.F. Grimm); Ronald Wimberly-a						20.00

SENTINEL
Marvel Comics: June, 2003 - No. 12, April, 2004 ($2.99/$2.50)

1-Sean McKeever-s/Udon Studios-a						3.00
2-12						3.00
Marvel Age Sentinel Vol. 1: Salvage (2004, $7.99, digest size) r/#1-6						8.00
Vol. 2: No Hero (2004, $7.99, digest size) r/#7-12; sketch pages						8.00

SENTINEL (2nd series)
Marvel Comics: Jan, 2006 - No. 5, May, 2006 ($2.99, limited series)

1-5-Sean McKeever-s/Joe Vriens-a						3.00
Vol. 3: Past Imperfect (2006, $7.99, digest size) r/#1-5						8.00

SENTINELS OF JUSTICE, THE (See Americomics & Captain Paragon &...)

SENTINEL SQUAD O*N*E

Serenity: Better Days #1 © Universal

Sgt. Bilko #12 © DC

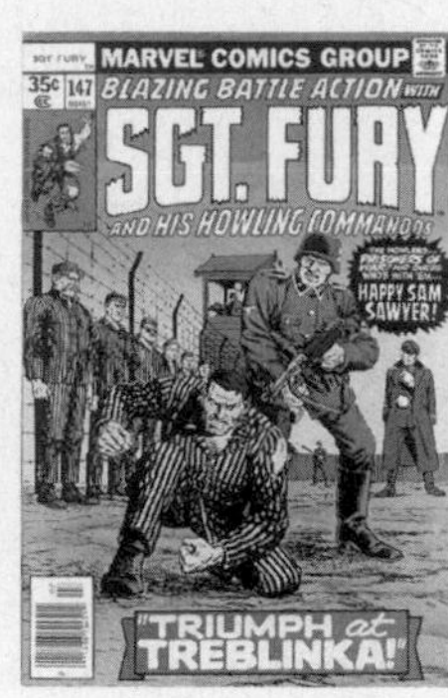

Sgt. Fury #147 © MAR

Marvel Comics: Mar, 2006 - No. 5, July, 2006 ($2.99, limited series)

	GD 2.0	VG 4.0	FN 6.0	VF 8.0	VF/NM 9.0	NM- 9.2
1-5-Lopresti-a/Layman-s						3.00
Decimation: Sentinel Squad O*N*E (2006, $13.99, TPB) r/series; sketch pg. by Caliafore						14.00

SENTRY (Also see New Avengers)
Marvel Comics: Sept, 2000 - No. 5, Jan, 2001 ($2.99, limited series)

	GD 2.0	VG 4.0	FN 6.0	VF 8.0	VF/NM 9.0	NM- 9.2
1-5-Paul Jenkins-s/Jae Lee-a. 3-Spider-Man-c/app. 4-X-Men, FF app.						3.00
.../Fantastic Four (2/01, $2.99) Continues story from #5; Winslade-a						3.00
.../Hulk (2/01, $2.99) Sienkiewicz-c/a						3.00
.../Spider-Man (2/01, $2.99) back story of the Sentry; Leonardi-a						3.00
.../The Void (2/01, $2.99) Conclusion of story; Jae Lee-a						3.00
.../X-Men (2/01, $2.99) Sentry and Archangel; Texeira-a						3.00
TPB (10/01, $24.95) r/#1-5 & all one-shots; Stan Lee interview						25.00
TPB (2nd edition, 2005, $24.99)						25.00

SENTRY (Follows return in New Avengers #10)
Marvel Comics: Nov, 2005 - No. 8, Jun, 2006 ($2.99, limited series)

	GD 2.0	VG 4.0	FN 6.0	VF 8.0	VF/NM 9.0	NM- 9.2
1-8-Paul Jenkins-s/John Romita Jr.-a. 1-New Avengers app. 3-Hulk app.						3.00
1-(Rough Cut) (12/05, $3.99) Romita sketch art and Jenkins script; cover sketches						4.00
...: Reborn TPB (2006, $21.99) r/#1-8						22.00

SENTRY SPECIAL
Innovation Publishing: 1991 ($2.75, one-shot)(Hero Alliance spin-off)

	GD 2.0	VG 4.0	FN 6.0	VF 8.0	VF/NM 9.0	NM- 9.2
1-Lost in Space preview (3 pgs.)						2.75

SERAPHIM
Innovation Publishing: May, 1990 ($2.50, mature readers)

	GD 2.0	VG 4.0	FN 6.0	VF 8.0	VF/NM 9.0	NM- 9.2
1						2.50

SERENITY (Based on 2005 movie Serenity and 2003 TV series Firefly)
Dark Horse Comics: July, 2005 - No. 3, Sept, 2005 ($2.99, limited series)

	GD 2.0	VG 4.0	FN 6.0	VF 8.0	VF/NM 9.0	NM- 9.2
1-3: Whedon & Matthews-s/Conrad-a. Three covers for each issue by various						4.00
...: Those Left Behind HC (11/07, $19.95, dustjacket) r/series; intro. by Nathan Fillion; pre-production art for the movie; Hughes-c						20.00
...: Those Left Behind TPB (1/06, $9.95) r/series; intro. by Nathan Fillion; Hughes-c						10.00

SERENITY BETTER DAYS (Firefly)
Dark Horse Comics: Mar, 2008 - No. 3, May, 2008 ($2.99, limited series)

	GD 2.0	VG 4.0	FN 6.0	VF 8.0	VF/NM 9.0	NM- 9.2
1-3: Whedon & Matthews-s/Conrad-a; Adam Hughes-c						3.00

SERGEANT BARNEY BARKER (Becomes G. I. Tales #4 on)
Atlas Comics (MCI): Aug, 1956 - No. 3, Dec, 1956

	GD 2.0	VG 4.0	FN 6.0	VF 8.0	VF/NM 9.0	NM- 9.2
1-Severin-c/a(4)	18	36	54	105	165	225
2,3: 2-Severin-c/a(4). 3-Severin-c/a(5)	14	28	42	76	108	140

SERGEANT BILKO (Phil Silvers Starring as...) (TV)
National Periodical Publications: May-June, 1957 - No. 18, Mar-Apr, 1960

	GD 2.0	VG 4.0	FN 6.0	VF 8.0	VF/NM 9.0	NM- 9.2
1-All have Bob Oskner-c	62	124	186	388	644	900
2	34	68	102	195	308	420
3-5	28	56	84	162	256	350
6-18: 11,12,15,17-Photo-c	23	46	69	130	205	280

SGT. BILKO'S PVT. DOBERMAN (TV)
National Periodical Publications: June-July, 1958 - No. 11, Feb-Mar, 1960

	GD 2.0	VG 4.0	FN 6.0	VF 8.0	VF/NM 9.0	NM- 9.2
1-Bob Oskner c-1-4,7,11	26	52	78	195	348	500
2	14	28	42	102	181	260
3-5: 5-Photo-c	10	20	30	71	126	180
6-11: 6,9-Photo-c	8	16	24	52	86	120

SGT. DICK CARTER OF THE U.S. BORDER PATROL (See Holyoke One-Shot)

SGT. FURY (& His Howling Commandos)(See Fury & Special Marvel Edition)
Marvel Comics Group (BPC earlier issues): May, 1963 - No. 167, Dec, 1981

	GD 2.0	VG 4.0	FN 6.0	VF 8.0	VF/NM 9.0	NM- 9.2
1-1st app. Sgt. Nick Fury (becomes agent of Shield in Strange Tales #135); Kirby/Ayers-c/a; 1st Dum-Dum Dugan & the Howlers	160	320	480	1400	2700	4000
2-Kirby-a	40	80	120	319	597	875
3-5: 3-Reed Richards x-over. 4-Death of Junior Juniper. 5-1st Baron Strucker app.; Kirby-a	24	48	72	176	326	475
6-10: 8-Baron Zemo, 1st Percival Pinkerton app. 9-Hitler-c & app. 10-1st app. Capt. Savage (the Skipper)(9/64)	14	28	42	102	181	260
11,12,14-20: 14-1st Blitz Squad. 18-Death of Pamela Hawley	8	16	24	58	97	135
13-Captain America & Bucky app.(12/64); 2nd solo Capt. America x-over outside The Avengers; Kirby-a	35	70	105	270	498	725
13-2nd printing (1994)	2	4	6	8	10	12
21-24,26,28-30	6	12	18	37	59	80
25,27: 25-Red Skull app. 27-1st app. Eric Koenig; origin Fury's eye patch	6	12	18	39	62	85
31-33,35-50: 35-Eric Koenig joins Howlers. 43-Bob Hope, Glen Miller app. 44-Flashback on Howlers' 1st mission	4	8	12	22	34	45
34-Origin Howling Commandos	4	8	12	23	36	48
51-60	3	6	9	19	29	38
61-67: 64-Capt. Savage & Raiders x-over; peace symbol-c. 67-Last 12¢ issue; flag-c	3	6	9	16	23	30
68-80: 76-Fury's Father app. in WWI story	3	6	9	14	20	26
81-91: 91-Last 15¢ issue	2	4	6	11	16	20
92-(52 pgs.)	3	6	9	15	21	26
93-99: 98-Deadly Dozen x-over	2	4	6	10	14	18
100-Capt. America, Fantastic 4 cameos; Stan Lee, Martin Goodman & others app.	3	6	9	15	21	26
101-120: 101-Origin retold	2	4	6	9	12	15
121-130: 121-123-r/#19-21	1	3	4	6	8	10
131-167: 167-Reprints (from 1963)	1	2	3	5	6	8
133,134-(30¢-c variants, limited dist.)(5,7/76)	3	6	9	16	22	28
141,142-(35¢-c variants, limited dist.)(7,9/77)	4	8	12	22	34	45
Annual 1(1965, 25¢, 72 pgs.)-r/#4,5 & new-a	14	28	42	99	175	250
Special 2(1966)	6	12	18	39	62	85
Special 3(1967) All new material	4	8	12	24	37	50
Special 4(1968)	3	6	9	18	27	35
Special 5-7(1969-11/71)	3	6	9	15	21	26

NOTE: ***Ayers*** *a-8, Annual 1.* ***Ditko*** *a-15i.* ***Gil Kane*** *c-37, 96.* ***Kirby*** *a-1-7, 13p, 167p(r). Special 5; c-1-8, 10-20, 25, 167p.* ***Severin*** *a-44-46, 48, 162, 164; inks-49-79, Special 4, 6; c-4i, 5, 6, 44, 46, 110, 149i, 155i, 162-166.* ***Sutton*** *a-57p. Reprints in #80, 82, 85, 87, 89, 91, 93, 95, 99, 101, 103, 105, 107, 109, 111, 121-123, 145-155, 167.*

SGT. FURY AND HIS HOWLING DEFENDERS (See The Defenders #147)

SERGEANT PRESTON OF THE YUKON (TV)
Dell Publishing Co.: No. 344, Aug, 1951 - No. 29, Nov-Jan, 1958-59

	GD 2.0	VG 4.0	FN 6.0	VF 8.0	VF/NM 9.0	NM- 9.2
Four Color 344(#1)-Sergeant Preston & his dog Yukon King begin; painted-c begin, end #18	12	24	36	82	146	210
Four Color 373,397,419('52)	8	16	24	52	86	120
5(11-1/52-53)-10(2-4/54): 6-Bondage-c.	6	12	18	41	66	90
11,12,14-17	6	12	18	37	59	80
13-Origin Sgt. Preston	6	12	18	41	66	90
18-Origin Yukon King; last painted-c	6	12	18	41	66	90
19-29: All photo-c	7	14	21	49	80	110

SGT. ROCK (Formerly Our Army at War; see Brave & the Bold #52 & Showcase #45)
National Periodical Publications/DC Comics: No. 302, Mar, 1977 - No. 422, July, 1988

	GD 2.0	VG 4.0	FN 6.0	VF 8.0	VF/NM 9.0	NM- 9.2
302	4	8	12	22	34	45
303-310	2	4	6	13	18	22
311-320: 318-Reprints	2	4	6	8	11	14
321-350	1	3	4	6	8	10
329-Whitman variant (scarce)	2	4	6	10	14	18
351-399,401-421						6.00
400,422: 422-1st Joe, Adam, Andy Kubert-a team	1	3	4	6	8	10
Annual 2-4: 2(1982)-Formerly Sgt. Rock's Prize Battle Tales #1. 3(1983). 4(1984)	1	3	4	6	8	10

NOTE: ***Estrada*** *a-322, 327, 331, 336, 337, 341, 342i.* ***Glanzman*** *a-384, 421.* ***Kubert*** *a-302, 303, 305r, 306, 328, 351, 356, 368, 373, 422; c-317, 318r, 319-323, 325-333-on, Annual 2, 3.* ***Severin*** *a-347.* ***Spiegle*** *a-382, Annual 2, 3.* ***Thorne*** *a-384.* ***Toth*** *a-385r.* ***Wildey*** *a-307, 311, 313, 314.*

SGT. ROCK: BETWEEN HELL AND A HARD PLACE
DC Comics (Vertigo): 2003 ($24.95, hardcover one-shot)

	GD 2.0	VG 4.0	FN 6.0	VF 8.0	VF/NM 9.0	NM- 9.2
HC-Joe Kubert-a/c; Brian Azzarello-s						25.00
SC (2004, $17.95)						18.00

SGT. ROCK'S COMBAT TALES
DC Comics: 2005 - Present ($9.99, digest)

	GD 2.0	VG 4.0	FN 6.0	VF 8.0	VF/NM 9.0	NM- 9.2
Vol. 1-Reprints early app. in Our Army at War, G.I. Combat, Star Spangled War Stories						10.00

SGT. ROCK SPECIAL (Sgt. Rock #14 on; see DC Special Series #3)
DC Comics: Oct, 1988 - No. 21, Feb, 1992; No. 1, 1992; No. 2, 1994
($2.00, quarterly/monthly, 52 pgs)

	GD 2.0	VG 4.0	FN 6.0	VF 8.0	VF/NM 9.0	NM- 9.2
1-Reprint begin	1	3	4	6	8	10
2-21: All-r; 5-r/early Sgt. Rock/Our Army at War #81. 7-Tomahawk-r by Thorne. 9-Enemy Ace-r by Kubert. 10-All Rock issue. 11-r/1st Haunted Tank story. 12-All Kubert issue; begins monthly. 13-Dinosaur story by Heath(r). 14-Enemy Ace-r (22 pgs.) by Adams/Kubert. 15-Enemy Ace (22 pgs.) by Kubert. 16-Iron Major-c/story. 16,17-Enemy Ace-r. 19-r/Batman/Sgt. Rock team-up/B&B #108 by Aparo						6.00
1 (1992, $2.95, 68 pgs.)-Simonson-c; unpubbed Kubert-a; Glanzman, Russell, Pratt, & Wagner-a						5.00
2 (1994, $2.95) Brereton painted-c						4.00

NOTE: ***Neal Adams*** *r-1, 8, 14p.* ***Chaykin*** *a-2; r-3, 9(2pgs.); c-3.* ***Drucker*** *r-6.* ***Glanzman*** *r-20.* ***Golden*** *a-1.* ***Heath*** *a-2; r-5, 9-13, 16, 19, 21.* ***Krigstein*** *r-4, 8.* ***Kubert*** *r-1-17, 20, 21; c-1p, 2, 8, 14-21.* ***Miller*** *r-6p.* ***Severin*** *r-3, 6, 10.*

Sgt. Rock: The Prophecy #1 © DC

Seven Brothers V2 #5 © Virgin

Seven Soldiers: Mister Miracle #1 © DC

GD 2.0 | VG 4.0 | FN 6.0 | VF 8.0 | VF/NM 9.0 | NM- 9.2

Simonson r-2, 4; c-4. Thorne r-7. Toth r-2, 8, 11. Wood r-4.

SGT. ROCK SPECTACULAR (See DC Special Series #13)

SGT. ROCK'S PRIZE BATTLE TALES (Becomes Sgt. Rock Annual #2 on; see DC Special Series #18 & 80 Page Giant #7)
National Periodical Publications: Winter, 1964 (Giant - 80 pgs., one-shot)

1-Kubert, Heath-r; new Kubert-c 30 60 90 222 411 600
... Replica Edition (2000, $5.95) Reprints entire issue 6.00

SGT. ROCK: THE PROPHECY
DC Comics: Mar, 2006 - No. 6, Aug, 2006 ($2.99, limited series)

1-6-Joe Kubert-s/a/c. 1-Variant covers by Andy and Adam Kubert 3.00
TPB (2007, $17.99) r/#1-6 18.00

SGT. STRYKER'S DEATH SQUAD (See Savage Combat Tales)

SERGIO ARAGONÉS' ACTIONS SPEAK
Dark Horse Comics: Jan, 2001 - No. 6, Jun, 2001 ($2.99, B&W, limited series)

1-6-Aragonés-c/a; wordless one-page cartoons 3.00

SERGIO ARAGONÉS' BLAIR WHICH?
Dark Horse Comics: Dec, 1999 ($2.95, B&W, one-shot)

nn-Aragonés-c/a; Evanier-s. Parody of "Blair Witch Project" movie 3.00

SERGIO ARAGONÉS' BOOGEYMAN
Dark Horse Comics: June, 1998 - No. 4, Sept, 1998 ($2.95, B&W, lim. series)

1-4-Aragonés-c/a 3.00

SERGIO ARAGONÉS DESTROYS DC
DC Comics: June, 1996 ($3.50, one-shot)

1-DC Superhero parody book; Aragonés-c/a; Evanier scripts 3.50

SERGIO ARAGONÉS' DIA DE LOS MUERTOS
Dark Horse Comics: Oct, 1998 ($2.95, one-shot)

1-Aragonés-c/a; Evanier scripts 3.00

SERGIO ARAGONÉS' GROO & RUFFERTO
Dark Horse Comics: Dec, 1998 - No. 4, Mar, 1999 ($2.95, lim. series)

1-3-Aragonés-c/a 3.00

SERGIO ARAGONÉS' GROO: DEATH AND TAXES
Dark Horse Comics: Dec, 2001 - No. 4, Apr, 2002 ($2.99, lim. series)

1-4-Aragonés-c/a; Evanier-s 3.00

SERGIO ARAGONÉS' GROO: HELL ON EARTH
Dark Horse Comics: Nov, 2007 - No. 4, Apr, 2008 ($2.99, lim. series)

1-4-Aragonés-c/a; Evanier-s 3.00

SERGIO ARAGONÉS' GROO: MIGHTIER THAN THE SWORD
Dark Horse Comics: Jan, 2000 - No. 4, Apr, 2000 ($2.95, lim. series)

1-4-Aragonés-c/a; Evanier-s 3.00

SERGIO ARAGONÉS' GROO THE WANDERER (See Groo...)

SERGIO ARAGONÉS' GROO: 25TH ANNIVERSARY SPECIAL
Dark Horse Comics: Aug, 2007 ($5.99, one-shot)

nn-Aragonés-c/a; Evanier scripts; wraparound cover 6.00

SERGIO ARAGONÉS' LOUDER THAN WORDS
Dark Horse Comics: July, 1997 - No. 6, Dec, 1997 ($2.95, B&W, limited series)

1-6-Aragonés-c/a 3.00

SERGIO ARAGONÉS MASSACRES MARVEL
Marvel Comics: June, 1996 ($3.50, one-shot)

1-Marvel Superhero parody book; Aragonés-c/a; Evanier scripts 3.50

SERGIO ARAGONÉS STOMPS STAR WARS
Marvel Comics: Jan, 2000 ($2.95, one-shot)

1-Star Wars parody; Aragonés-c/a; Evanier scripts 3.00

SEVEN
Intrinsic Comics: July, 2007 ($3.00)

1-Jim Shooter-s/Paul Creddick-a 3.00

SEVEN BLOCK
Marvel Comics (Epic Comics): 1990 ($4.50, one-shot, 52 pgs.)

1-Dixon-s/Zaffino-a 4.50
nn-(IDW Publ., 2004, $5.99) reprints #1 6.00

SEVEN BROTHERS (John Woo's...)
Virgin Comics: Oct, 2006 - No. 5, Feb, 2007 ($2.99)

GD 2.0 | VG 4.0 | FN 6.0 | VF 8.0 | VF/NM 9.0 | NM- 9.2

1-5-Garth Ennis-s/Jeevan Kang-a. 1-Two covers by Amano & Horn. 2-Kang var-c 3.00
TPB (6/07, $14.99) r/#1-5; cover gallery, deleted scenes and concept art 15.00
Volume 2 (9/07 - No. 5, 2/08) 1-Edison George-a. 4,5-David Mack-c 3.00

SEVEN DEAD MEN (See Complete Mystery #1)

SEVEN DWARFS (Also see Snow White)
Dell Publishing Co.: No. 227, 1949 (Disney-Movie)

Four Color 227 9 18 27 65 113 160

SEVEN MILES A SECOND
DC Comics (Vertigo Verité): 1996 ($7.95, one-shot)

nn-Wojnarowicz-s/Romberg-a 8.00

SEVEN SAMUROID, THE (See Image Graphic Novel)

SEVEN SEAS COMICS
Universal Phoenix Features/Leader No. 6: Apr, 1946 - No. 6, 1947(no month)

1-South Sea Girl by Matt Baker, Capt. Cutlass begin; Tugboat Tessie by Baker app.
90 180 270 567 959 1350
2-Swashbuckler-c 68 136 204 428 727 1025
3,5,6: 3-Six pg. Feldstein-a 67 134 201 422 711 1000
4-Classic Baker-c 87 174 261 548 924 1300
NOTE: *Baker a-1-6; c-3-6.*

SEVEN SOLDIERS OF VICTORY (Book-ends for seven related mini-series)
DC Comics: No. 0, Apr, 2005; No. 1; Dec, 2006 ($2.95/$3.99)

0-Grant Morrison-s/J.H. Williams-a 3.00
1-($3.99) Series conclusion; Grant Morrison-s/J.H. Williams-a 4.00
... Volume One (2006, $14.99) r/#0, Shining Knight #1,2; Zatanna #1,2; Guardian #1,2; and Klarion the Witch Boy #1; intro. by Morrison; character design sketches 15.00
... Volume Two (2006, $14.99) r/Shining Knight #3,4; Zatanna #3; Guardian #3,4; and Klarion the Witch Boy #2,3 15.00
... Volume Three ('06, $14.99) r/Zatanna #4; Mister Miracle #1,2; Bulleteer #1,2; Frankenstein #1 and Klarion the Witch Boy #4; 15.00
... Volume Four ('07, $14.99) r/Mister Miracle #3,4; Bulleteer #3,4; Frankenstein #2-4 and Seven Soldiers of Victory #1; script pages 15.00

SEVEN SOLDIERS: BULLETEER
DC Comics: Jan, 2006 - No. 4, May, 2006 ($2.99, limited series)

1-4-Grant Morrison-s/Yanick Paquette-a/c 3.00

SEVEN SOLDIERS: FRANKENSTEIN
DC Comics: Jan, 2006 - No. 4, May, 2006 ($2.99, limited series)

1-4-Grant Morrison-s/Doug Mahnke-a/c 3.00

SEVEN SOLDIERS: GUARDIAN
DC Comics: May, 2005 - No. 4, Nov, 2005 ($2.99, limited series)

1-4-Grant Morrison-s/Cameron Stewart-a; Newsboy Army app. 3.00

SEVEN SOLDIERS: KLARION THE WITCH BOY
DC Comics: June, 2005 - No. 4, Dec, 2005 ($2.99, limited series)

1-4-Grant Morrison-s/Frazer Irving-a 3.00

SEVEN SOLDIERS: MISTER MIRACLE
DC Comics: Nov, 2005 - No. 4, May, 2006 ($2.99, limited series)

1-4: 1-Grant Morrison-s/Pasqual Ferry-a/c. 3,4-Freddie Williams II-a/c 3.00

SEVEN SOLDIERS: SHINING KNIGHT
DC Comics: May, 2005 - No. 4, Oct, 2005 ($2.99, limited series)

1-4-Grant Morrison-s/Simone Bianchi-a 3.00

SEVEN SOLDIERS: ZATANNA
DC Comics: June, 2005 - No. 4, Dec, 2005 ($2.99, limited series)

1-4-Grant Morrison-s/Ryan Sook-a 3.00

1776 (See Charlton Classic Library)

7TH VOYAGE OF SINBAD, THE (Movie)
Dell Publishing Co.: Sept, 1958 (photo-c)

Four Color 944-Buscema-a 12 24 36 87 156 225

77 SUNSET STRIP (TV)
Dell Publ. Co./Gold Key: No. 1066, Jan-Mar, 1960 - No. 2, Feb, 1963 (All photo-c)

Four Color 1066-Toth-a 10 20 30 71 126 180
Four Color 1106,1159-Toth-a 8 16 24 58 97 135
Four Color 1211,1263,1291, 01-742-209(7-9/62)-Manning-a in all
8 16 24 54 90 125
1,2: Manning-a. 1(11/62-G.K.) 8 16 24 54 90 125

77TH BENGAL LANCERS, THE (TV)

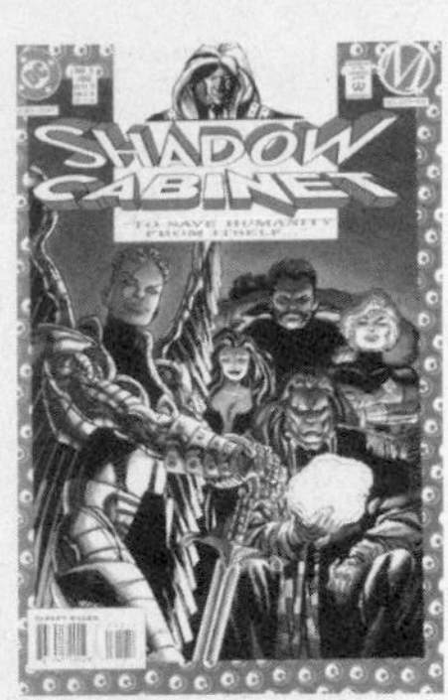

Shadow Cabinet #1 © Milestone Media

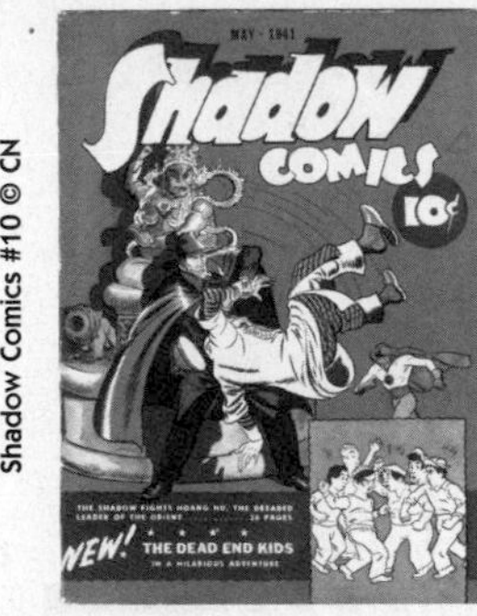

Shadow Comics #10 © CN

Shadowhawk #12 © Jim Valentino

GD 2.0 | VG 4.0 | FN 6.0 | VF 8.0 | VF/NM 9.0 | NM- 9.2

Dell Publishing Co.: May, 1957
Four Color 791-Photo-c 7 14 21 47 76 105

SEYMOUR, MY SON (See More Seymour)
Archie Publications (Radio Comics): Sept, 1963
1-DeCarlo-a? 3 6 9 20 30 40

SHADE, THE (See Starman)
DC Comics: Apr, 1997 - No. 4, July, 1997 ($2.25, limited series)
1-4-Robinson-s/Harris-c: 1-Gene Ha-a. 2-Williams/Gray-a 3-Blevins-a. 4-Zulli-a 3.00

SHADE, THE CHANGING MAN (See Cancelled Comic Cavalcade)
National Per. Publ./DC Comics: June-July, 1977 - No. 8, Aug-Sept, 1978
1-1st app. Shade; Ditko-c/a in all 2 4 6 9 12 15
2-8 1 2 3 5 7 9

SHADE, THE CHANGING MAN (2nd series) (Also see Suicide Squad #16)
DC Comics (Vertigo imprint #33 on): July, 1990 - No. 70, Apr, 1996 ($1.50-$2.25, mature)
1-($2.50, 52 pgs.)-Peter Milligan scripts in all 4.00
2-41,45-49,51-59: 6-Preview of World Without End. 17-Begin $1.75-c. 33-Metallic ink on-c. 41-Begin $1.95-c 2.50
42-44-John Constantine app. 3.00
50-($2.95, 52 pgs.) 3.50
60-70: 60-begin $2.25-c 2.50
...: The American Scream (2003, $17.95) r/#1-6 18.00
NOTE: ***Bachalo** a-1-9, 11-13, 15-21, 23-26, 33-39, 42-45, 47, 49, 50; c-30, 33-41.*

SHADO: SONG OF THE DRAGON (See Green Arrow #63-66)
DC Comics: 1992 - No. 4, 1992 ($4.95, limited series, 52 pgs.)
Book One - Four: Grell scripts; Morrow-a(i) 5.00

SHADOW, THE (See Batman #253, 259 & Marvel Graphic Novel #35)

SHADOW, THE (Pulp, radio)
Archie Comics (Radio Comics): Aug, 1964 - No. 8, Sept, 1965 (All 12¢)
1-Jerrry Siegel scripts in all; Shadow-c. 8 16 24 52 86 120
2-8: 2-App. in super-hero costume on-c only; Reinman-a(backup). 3-Superhero begins; Reinman-a (book-length novel). 3,4,6,7-The Fly 1 pg. strips. 4-8-Reinman-a. 5-8-Siegel scripts. 7-Shield app. 5 10 15 30 48 65

SHADOW, THE
National Periodical Publications: Oct-Nov, 1973 - No. 12, Aug-Sept, 1975
1-Kaluta-a begins 5 10 15 34 55 75
2 3 6 9 18 27 35
3-Kaluta/Wrightson-a 3 6 9 20 30 40
4,6-Kaluta-a ends. 4-Chaykin, Wrightson part-i 3 6 9 16 23 30
5,7-12: 11-The Avenger (pulp character) x-over 2 4 6 9 13 16
NOTE: ***Craig** a-10. **Cruz** a-10-12. **Kaluta** a-1, 2, 3p, 4, 6; c-1-4, 6, 10-12. **Kubert** c-9. **Robbins** a-5, 7-9; c-5, 7, 8.*

SHADOW, THE
DC Comics: May, 1986 - No. 4, Aug, 1986 (limited series)
1-4: Howard Chaykin art in all 3.00
Blood & Judgement ($12.95)-r/1-4 13.00

SHADOW, THE
DC Comics: Aug, 1987 - No. 19, Jan, 1989 ($1.50)
1-19: Andrew Helfer scripts in all. 3.00
Annual 1,2 (12/87, '88,)-2-The Shadow dies; origin retold (story inspired by the movie "Citizen Kane"). 4.00
NOTE: ***Kyle Baker** a-7i, 8-19, Annual 2. **Chaykin** c-Annual 1. **Helfer** scripts in all. **Orlando** a-Annual 1. **Rogers** c/a-7. **Sienkiewicz** c/a-1-6.*

SHADOW, THE (Movie)
Dark Horse Comics: June, 1994 - No. 2, July, 1994 ($2.50, limited series)
1,2-Adaptation from Universal Pictures film 3.00
NOTE: ***Kaluta** c/a-1, 2.*

SHADOW AND DOC SAVAGE, THE
Dark Horse Comics: July, 1995 - No. 2, Aug, 1995 ($2.95, limited series)
1,2 3.50

SHADOW AND THE MYSTERIOUS 3, THE
Dark Horse Comics: Sept, 1994 ($2.95, one-shot)
1-Kaluta co-scripts. 3.00
NOTE: ***Stevens** c-1.*

SHADOW CABINET (See Heroes)
DC Comics (Milestone): Jan, 1994 - No. 17, Oct, 1995 ($1.75/$2.50)
0,1-17: 0-($2.50, 52 pgs.)-Silver ink-c; Simonson-c. 1-Byrne-c 2.50

SHADOW COMICS (Pulp, radio)
Street & Smith Publications: Mar, 1940 - V9#5, Aug-Sept, 1949
NOTE: *The Shadow first appeared on radio in 1929 and was featured in pulps beginning in April, 1931, written by Walter Gibson. The early covers of this series were reprinted from the pulp covers.*
V1#1-Shadow, Doc Savage, Bill Barnes, Nick Carter (radio), Frank Merriwell, Iron Munro, the Astonishing Man begin 461 922 1383 3319 5810 8300
2-The Avenger begins, ends #6; Capt. Fury only app. 207 414 621 1304 2202 3100
3(nn-5/40)-Norgil the Magician app.; cover is exact swipe of Shadow pulp from 1/33 147 294 441 926 1563 2200
4,5: 4-The Three Musketeers begins, ends #8. 5-Doc Savage ends 110 220 330 693 1172 1650
6,8,9: 9-Norgil the Magician app. 93 186 279 586 993 1400
7-Origin/1st app. The Hooded Wasp & Wasplet (11/40); series ends V3#8; Hooded Wasp/Wasplet app. on-c thru #9 98 196 294 617 1046 1475
10-Origin The Iron Ghost, ends #11; The Dead End Kids begins, ends #14 93 184 279 586 993 1400
11-Origin Hooded Wasp & Wasplet retold 93 184 279 586 993 1400
12-Dead End Kids app. 87 174 261 548 924 1300
V2#1(11/41, Vol.II#2 in indicia) Dead End Kids -s 83 166 249 523 887 1250
2-(Rare, Vol.II#3 in indicia) Giant ant-c 160 320 480 1008 1704 2400
3-Origin & 1st app. Supersnipe (3/42); series begins; Little Nemo story (Vol.II#4 in indicia) 137 274 411 863 1457 2050
4,5: 4,8-Little Nemo story 73 146 219 460 780 1100
6-9: 6-Blackstone the Magician story 70 140 210 441 746 1050
10,12: 10-Supersnipe app.' Skull-c 68 136 204 428 727 1025
11-Classic Devil Kyoti World War 2 sunburst-c 78 156 234 491 833 1175
V3#1-5,7-12: 10-Doc Savage begins, not in V5#5, V6#10-12, V8#4 67 134 201 422 711 1000
6-Classic underwater-c 77 154 231 481 816 1150
V4#1-12 47 94 141 291 488 685
V5#1-12 41 82 123 256 428 600
V6#1-11: 9-Intro. Shadow, Jr. (12/46) 40 80 120 235 380 525
12-Powell-c/a; atom bomb panels 41 82 123 256 428 600
V7#1,2,5,7-9,12: 2,5-Shadow, Jr. app.; Powell-a 40 80 120 235 380 525
3,6,11-Powell-c/a 43 86 129 269 446 625
4-Powell-c/a; Atom bomb panels 45 90 135 279 465 650
10(1/48)-Flying Saucer-c/story (2nd of this theme; see The Spirit 9/28/47); Powell-c/a 57 114 171 359 605 850
V8#1-12-Powell-a. 8-Powell Spider-c/a 43 86 129 267 446 625
V9#1,5-Powell-a 41 82 123 256 428 600
2-4-Powell-c/a 43 86 129 267 446 625
NOTE: ***Binder** c-V3#1. **Powell** art in most issues beginning V6#12. Painted c-1-6.*

SHADOWDRAGON
DC Comics: 1995 ($3.50, annual)
Annual 1-Year One story 3.50

SHADOW EMPIRES: FAITH CONQUERS
Dark Horse Comics: Aug, 1994 - No. 4, Nov, 1994 ($2.95, limited series)
1-4 3.00

SHADOWHAWK (See Images of Shadowhawk, New Shadowhawk, Shadowhawk II, Shadowhawk III & Youngblood #2)
Image Comics (Shadowline Ink): Aug, 1992 - No. 4, Mar, 1993; No. 12, Aug, 1994 - No. 18, May, 1995 ($1.95/$2.50)
1-($2.50)-Embossed silver foil stamped-c; Valentino/Liefeld-c; Valentino-c/a/scripts in all; has coupon for Image #0; 1st Shadowline Ink title 4.00
1-With coupon missing 2.00
1-($1.95)-Newsstand version w/o foil stamp 2.50
2-13,0,1418: 2-Shadowhawk poster w/McFarlane-i; brief Spawn app.; wraparound-c w/silver ink highlights. 3-($2.50)-Glow-in-the-dark-c. 4-Savage Dragon-c/story; Valentino/Larsen-c. 5-11-(See Shadowhawk II and III). 12-Cont'd from Shadowhawk III; pull-out poster by Texeira.13-w/ShadowBone poster; WildC.A.T.s app. 0 (10/94)-Liefeld c/a/story; ShadowBart poster. 14-(10/94, $2.50)-The Others app. 16-Supreme app. 17-Spawn app.; story cont'd from Badrock & Co. #6. 18-Shadowhawk dies; Savage Dragon & Brigade app. 2.50
Special 1(12/94, $3.50, 52 pgs.)-Silver Age Shadowhawk flip book 3.50
Gallery (4/94, $1.95) 2.50
Out of the Shadows ($19.95)-r/Youngblood #2, Shadowhawk #1-4, Image Zero #0, Operation: Urban Storm (Never published) 20.00
.../Vampirella (2/95, $4.95)-Pt.2 of x-over (See Vampirella/Shadowhawk for Pt. 1) 5.00
NOTE: *Shadowhawk was originally a four issue limited series. The story continued in Shadowhawk II, Shadowhawk III & then became Shadowhawk again with issue #12.*

SHADOWHAWK II (Follows Shadowhawk #4)
Image Comics (Shadowline Ink): V2#1, May, 1993 - V2#3, Aug, 1993 ($3.50/$1.95/$2.95, limited series)

Shadow Hunter #2 © Virgin

Shadowpact #21 © DC

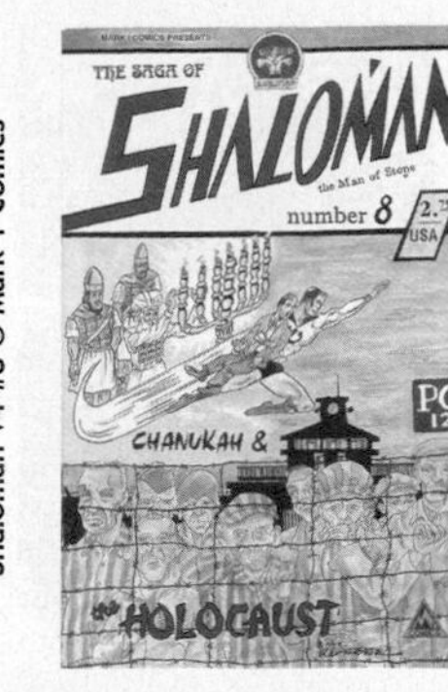

Shaloman V4 #8 © Mark 1 Comics

GD 2.0 | VG 4.0 | FN 6.0 | VF 8.0 | VF/NM 9.0 | NM- 9.2

V2#1 ($3.50)-Cont'd from Shadowhawk #4; die-cut mirricard-c 3.50
2 ($1.95)-Foil embossed logo; reveals identity; gold-c variant exists 2.50
3 ($2.95)-Pop-up-c w/Pact ashcan insert 3.00

SHADOWHAWK III (Follows Shadowhawk II #3)
Image Comics (Shadowline Ink): V3#1, Nov, 1993 - V3#4, Mar, 1994 ($1.95, limited series)

V3#1-4: 1-Cont'd from Shadowhawk II; intro Valentine; gold foil & red foil stamped-c variations. 2-(52 pgs.)-Shadowhawk contracts HIV virus; U.S. Male by M. Anderson (p) in free 16 pg.insert. 4-Continues in Shadowhawk #12 2.50

SHADOWHAWK (Volume 2) (Also see New Man #4)
Image Comics: May, 2005 - Present ($2.99/$3.50)

1-4-Eddie Collins as Shadowhawk; Rodríguez-a; Valentino-co-plotter 3.00
5-15-($3.50) 5-Cover swipe of Superman Vs. Spider-Man treasury edition 3.50
...One Shot #1 (7/06, $1.99) r/Return of Shadowhawk 2.50
Return of Shadowhawk (12/04, $2.99) Valentino-s/a/c; Eddie Collins origin retold 3.00

SHADOWHAWKS OF LEGEND
Image Comics (Shadowline Ink): Nov, 1995 ($4.95, one-shot)

nn-Stories of past Shadowhawks by Kurt Busiek, Beau Smith & Alan Moore 5.00

SHADOW, THE: HELL'S HEAT WAVE (Movie, pulp, radio)
Dark Horse Comics: Apr, 1995 - No. 3, June, 1995 ($2.95, limited series)

1-3: Kaluta story 3.00

SHADOW HUNTER (Jenna Jameson's...)
Virgin Comics: No. 0, Dec, 2007 - Present ($2.99)

0-Preview issue; creator interviews; gallery of covers for upcoming issues; Greg Horn-c 3.00
1-3: 1-Two covers by Horn & Land; Jameson & Christina Z-s/Singh-a. 2-Three covers 3.00

SHADOWHUNT SPECIAL
Image Comics (Extreme Studios): Apr, 1996 ($2.50)

1-Retells origin of past Shadowhawks; Valentino script; Chapel app. 2.50

SHADOW, THE: IN THE COILS OF THE LEVIATHAN (Movie, pulp, radio)
Dark Horse Comics: Oct, 1993 - No. 4, Apr, 1994 ($2.95, limited series)

1-4-Kaluta-c & co-scripter 3.00
Trade paperback (10/94, $13.95)-r/1-4 14.00

SHADOWLINE SAGA: CRITICAL MASS, A
Marvel Comics (Epic): Jan, 1990 - No. 7, July, 1990 ($4.95, lim. series, 68 pgs)

1-6: Dr. Zero, Powerline, St. George 5.00
7 ($5.95, 84 pgs.)-Morrow-a, Williamson-c(i) 6.00

SHADOWMAN (See X-O Manowar #4)
Valiant/Acclaim Comics (Valiant): May, 1992 - No. 43, Dec, 1995 ($2.50)

1-Partial origin 5.00
2-5: 3-1st app. Sousa the Soul Eater 4.00
6-43: 8-1st app. Master Darque. 16-1st app. Dr. Mirage (8/93). 15-Minor Turok app. 17,18-Archer & Armstrong x-over. 19-Aerosmith-c/story. 23-Dr. Mirage x-over. 24-(4/94). 25-Bound-in trading card. 29-Chaos Effect. 43-Shadowman jumps to his death 2.50
0-($2.50, 4/94)-Regular edition 2.50
0-($3.50)-Wraparound chromium-c edition 3.50
0-Gold 15.00
Yearbook 1 (12/94, $3.95) 4.00

SHADOWMAN (Volume 2)
Acclaim Comics (Valiant Heroes): Mar, 1997 - No. 20 ($2.50, mature)

1-20: 1-1st app. Zero; Garth Ennis scripts begin, end #4. 2-Zero becomes new Shadowman. 4-Origin; Jack Boniface (original Shadowman) rises from the grave. 5-Jamie Delano scripts begin. 9-Copycat-c 2.50
1-Variant painted cover 2.50
#0 Gold 5.00

SHADOWMAN (Volume 3)
Acclaim Comics: July, 1999 - No. 5, Nov, 1999 ($3.95/$2.50)

1-($3.95)-Abnett & Lanning-s/Broome & Benjamin-a 4.00
2-5-($2.50): 3,4-Flip book with Unity 2000 2.50

SHADOWMASTERS
Marvel Comics: Oct, 1989 - No.4, Jan, 1990 ($3.95, squarebound, 52 pgs.)

1-4: Heath-a(i). 1-Jim Lee-c; story cont'd from Punisher 4.00

SHADOW OF THE BATMAN
DC Comics: Dec, 1985 - No. 5, Apr, 1986 ($1.75, limited series)

1-Detective-r (all have wraparound-c) 1 2 3 4 5 7
2,3,5: 3-Penguin-c & cameo. 5-Clayface app. 5.00
4-Joker-c/story 6.00
NOTE: ***Austin*** *a(new)-2i, 3i; r-2-4i.* ***Rogers*** *a(new)-1, 2p, 3p, 4, 5; r-1-5p; c-1-5.* ***Simonson*** *a-1r.*

SHADOW OF THE TORTURER, THE
Innovation: July, 1991 - No. 3, 1992 ($2.50, limited series)

1-3: Based on Pocket Books novel 2.50

SHADOW ON THE TRAIL (See Zane Grey & Four Color #604)

SHADOWPACT (See Day of Vengeance)
DC Comics: Jul, 2006 - No. 25, Jul, 2008 ($2.99)

1-25: 1-Bill Willingham-s; Detective Chimp, Ragman, Blue Devil, Nightshade, Enchantress and Nightmaster app. 1-Superman app. 13-Zauriel app.; S. Hampton-a 3.00
...: Cursed TPB (2007, $14.99) r/#4,9-13 15.00
...: Darkness and Light TPB (2008, $14.99) r/#14-19 15.00
...: The Pentacle Plot TPB (2007, $14.99) r/#1-3,5-8 15.00

SHADOW PLAY (Tales of the Supernatural)
Whitman Publications: June, 1982

1-Painted-c 1 2 3 4 5 7

SHADOWPLAY
IDW Publ.: Sept, 2005 - No. 4, Dec, 2005 ($3.99)

1-4-Benson-s/Templesmith-a; Christina Z-s/Wood-a; 2 covers by Templesmith & Wood 4.00
TPB (3/06, $17.99) r/series; flip book format 18.00

SHADOW REAVERS
Black Bull Ent.: Oct, 2001 - No. 5, Mar, 2002 ($2.99)

1-5-Nelson-a; two covers for each issue 3.00
Limited Preview Edition (5/01, no cover price) 2.50

SHADOW RIDERS
Marvel Comics UK, Ltd.: June, 1993 - No. 4, Sept, 1993 ($1.75, limited series)

1-($2.50)-Embossed-c; Cable-c/story 2.75
2-4-Cable app. 2-Ghost Rider app. 2.50

SHADOWS
Image Comics: Feb, 2003 - No. 4, Nov, 2003 ($2.95)

1-4-Jade Dodge-s/Matt Camp-a/c 3.00

SHADOWS & LIGHT
Marvel Comics: Feb, 1998 - No. 3, July, 1998 ($2.99, B&W, quarterly)

1-3: 1-B&W anthology of Marvel characters; Black Widow art by Gene Ha, Hulk by Wrightson, Iron Man by Ditko & Daredevil by Stelfreeze; Stelfreeze painted-c. 2-Weeks, Sharp, Starlin, Thompson-a. 3-Buscema, Grindberg, Giffen, Layton-a 3.00

SHADOW'S FALL
DC Comics (Vertigo): Nov, 1994 - No. 6, Apr, 1995 ($2.95, limited series)

1-6: Van Fleet-c/a in all. 3.00

SHADOWS FROM BEYOND (Formerly Unusual Tales)
Charlton Comics: V2#50, October, 1966

V2#50-Ditko-c 3 6 9 20 30 40

SHADOW STATE
Broadway Comics: Dec, 1995 - No. 5, Apr, 1996 ($2.50)

1-5: 1,2-Fatale back-up story; Cockrum-a(p) 2.50
Preview Edition 1,2 (10-11/95, $2.50, B&W) 2.50

SHADOW STRIKES!, THE (Pulp, radio)
DC Comics: Sept, 1989 - No.31, May, 1992 ($1.75)

1-4,7-31: 31-Mignola-c 2.50
5,6-Doc Savage x-over 4.00
Annual 1 (1989, $3.50, 68 pgs.)-Spiegle a; Kaluta-c 3.50

SHADOW WAR OF HAWKMAN
DC Comics: May, 1985 - No. 4, Aug, 1985 (limited series)

1-4 2.50

SHAGGY DOG & THE ABSENT-MINDED PROFESSOR (See Four Color #1199, Movie Comics & Walt Disney Showcase #46)(Disney-Movie)
Dell Publ. Co.: No. 985, May, 1959

Four Color 985 7 14 21 50 83 115

SHALOMAN (Jewish-themed stories and history)
Al Wiesner/ Mark 1 Comics: 1989 - Present (B&W)

V1#1-Al Wiesner-s/a in all 4.50
2-9 2.50
V2 #1(The New Adventures)-4,6-10, V3 (The Legend of...) #1-12 2.75
V2 #5 (Color)-Shows Vol 2, No. 4 in indicia 3.00
V4 (The Saga of ...) #1(2004), 2-8: 8-Chanukah & The Holocaust 2.75
The Saga of Shaloman (20th Anniversary Edition) TPB (10/08, $15.99) r/V4 #1-8 16.00

Shaman's Tears #2 © Mike Grell

Shazam! #11 © DC

Sheena, Queen of the Jungle #7 © FH

	GD	VG	FN	VF	VF/NM	NM-
	2.0	4.0	6.0	8.0	9.0	9.2

SHAMAN'S TEARS (Also see Maggie the Cat)
Image Comics (Creative Fire Studio): 5/93 - No. 2, 8/93; No. 3, 11/94 - No. 0, 1/96 ($2.50/$1.95)

0-2: 0-(DEC-c, 1/96)-Last Issue. 1-(5/93)-Embossed red foil-c; Grell-c/a & scripts in all. 2-Cover unfolds into poster (8/93-c, 7/93 inside) 2.50
3-12: 3-Begin $1.95-c. 5-Re-intro Jon Sable. 12-Re-intro Maggie the Cat (1 pg.) 2.50

SHANG-CHI: MASTER OF KUNG-FU ("Master of Kung Fu" on cover for #1&2)
Marvel Comics: Nov, 2002 - No. 6, Apr, 2003 ($2.99, limited series)

1-6-Moench-s/Gulacy-c/a 3.00
... Vol. 1: The Hellfire Apocalypse TPB (2003, $14.99) r/#1-6 15.00

SHANGRI-LA
Image Comics: Jan, 2004 ($7.95, B&W, square-bound graphic novel)

1-Marc Bryant-s/Shepherd Hendrix-a 8.00

SHANNA, THE SHE-DEVIL (See Savage Tales #8)
Marvel Comics Group: Dec, 1972 - No. 5, Aug, 1973 (All are 20¢ issues)

1-1st app. Shanna; Steranko-c; Tuska-a(p) 3 6 9 18 27 35
2-Steranko-c; heroin drug story 3 6 9 14 20 26
3-5 2 4 6 9 13 16

SHANNA, THE SHE-DEVIL
Marvel Comics: Apr, 2005 - No. 7, Oct, 2005 ($3.50, limited series)

1-7-Reintro of Shanna; Frank Cho-s/a/c in all 3.50
HC (2005, $24.99, dust jacket) r/#1-7 25.00
SC (2006, $16.99) r/#1-7 17.00

SHANNA, THE SHE-DEVIL: SURVIVAL OF THE FITTEST
Marvel Comics: Oct, 2007 - No. 4, Jan, 2008 ($2.99, limited series)

1-4-Khari Evans-a/c; Gray & Palmiotti-s 3.00
SC (2008, $10.99) r/#1-4 11.00

SHAOLIN COWBOY
Burlyman Entertainment: Dec, 2004 - Present ($3.50)

1-7-Geof Darrow-s/a. 3-Moebius-c 3.50

SHARK FIGHTERS, THE (Movie)
Dell Publishing Co.: Jan, 1957

Four Color 762-Buscema-a; photo-c 7 14 21 50 83 115

SHARK-MAN
Thrill House/Image Comics: Jul, 2006; Jul, 2007; Jan, 2008 - No. 3, Jun, 2008 ($3.99/$3.50)

1,2: 1-(Thrill House, 7/06, $3.99)-Steve Pugh-s/a. 2-(Image Comics, 7/07) 4.00
1-3: 1-(Image, 1/08, $3.50) reprints Thrill House #1 3.50

SHARKY
Image Comics: Feb, 1998 - No. 4, 1998 ($2.50, bi-monthly)

1-4: 1-Mask app.; Elliot-s/a. Horley painted-c. 3-Three covers by Horley, Bisley, & Horley/Elliot. 4-Two covers (swipe of Avengers #4 and wraparound) 2.50
1-($2.95) "$1,000,000" variant 3.00
2-($2.50) Savage Dragon variant-c 2.50

SHARP COMICS (Slightly large size)
H. C. Blackerby: Winter, 1945-46 - V1#2, Spring, 1946 (52 pgs.)

V1#1-Origin Dick Royce Planetarian 40 80 120 244 397 550
2-Origin The Pioneer; Michael Morgan, Dick Royce, Sir Gallagher, Planetarian, Steve Hagen, Weeny and Pop app. 36 72 108 212 341 470

SHARPY FOX (See Comic Capers & Funny Frolics)
I. W. Enterprises/Super Comics: 1958; 1963

1,2-I.W. Reprint (1958): 2-r/Kiddie Kapers #1 2 4 6 8 10 12
14-Super Reprint (1963) 2 4 6 8 10 12

SHATTER (See Jon Sable #25-30)
First Comics: June, 1985; Dec, 1985 - No. 14, Apr, 1988. ($1.75, Baxter paper/deluxe paper)

1 (6/85)-1st computer generated-a in a comic book (1st printing) 3.00
1-(2nd print.); 1(12/85)-14: computer generated-a & lettering in all 2.50
Special 1 (1988) 2.50

SHATTERED IMAGE
Image Comics (WildStorm Productions): Aug, 1996 - No. 4, Dec, 1996 ($2.50, lim. series)

1-4: 1st Image company-wide x-over; Kurt Busiek scripts in all. 1-Tony Daniel-c/a(p). 2-Alex Ross-c/swipe (Kingdom Come) by Ryan Benjamin & Travis Charest 2.50

SHAUN OF THE DEAD (Movie)
IDW Publishing: June, 2005 - No. 4, Sept, 2005 ($3.99, limited series)

1-4-Adaptation of 2004 movie; Zach Howard-a 4.00
TPB (12/05, $17.99) r/series; sketch pages and cover gallery 18.00

	GD	VG	FN	VF	VF/NM	NM-
	2.0	4.0	6.0	8.0	9.0	9.2

SHAZAM (See Billy Batson and the Magic of Shazam!, Giant Comics to Color, Limited Collectors' Edition, Power Of Shazam! and Trials of Shazam!)

SHAZAM! (TV)(See World's Finest #253 for story from unpublished #36)
National Periodical Publ./DC Comics: Feb, 1973 - No. 35, May-June, 1978

1-1st revival of original Captain Marvel since G.A. (origin retold), by C.C. Beck; Mary Marvel & Captain Marvel Jr. app.; Superman-c 5 10 15 34 55 75
2-5: 2-Infinity photo-c.; re-intro Mr. Mind & Tawny. 3-Capt. Marvel-r. (10/46). 4-Origin retold; Capt. Marvel-r. (1949). 5-Capt. Marvel Jr. origin retold; Capt. Marvel-r. (1948, 7 pgs.) 3 6 9 14 20 25
6,7,9-11: 6-photo-c.; Capt. Marvel-r (1950, 6 pgs.). 9-Mr. Mind app. 10-Last C.C. Beck issue. 11-Schaffenberger-a begins. 2 4 6 11 16 20
8 (100 pgs.) 8-r/Capt. Marvel Jr. by Raboy; origin/C.M. #80; origin Mary Marvel/C.M.A. #18; origin Mr. Tawny/C.M.A. #79 5 10 15 34 55 75
12-17-(All 100 pgs.). 15-vs. Lex Luthor & Mr. Mind 4 8 12 22 37 55
18-24,26-30: 21-24-All reprints. 26-Sivana app. (10/76). 27-Kid Eternity teams up w/Capt. Marvel. 28-1st S.A. app. of Black Adam. 30-1st DC app. 3 Lt. Marvels 2 4 6 8 11 14
25-1st app. Isis 2 4 6 10 14 18
31-35: 31-1st DC app. Minuteman. 34-Origin Capt. Nazi & Capt. Marvel Jr. retold 2 4 6 10 14 18
...: The Greatest Stories Ever Told TPB (2008, $24.99) reprints; Alex Ross-c 25.00
NOTE: *Reprints in #1-8, 10, 12-17, 21-24.* ***Beck*** *a-1-10, 12-17r, 21-24r; c-1, 3-9.* ***Nasser*** *c-35p.* ***Newton*** *a-35p.* ***Raboy*** *a-5r, 8r, 17r.* ***Schaffenberger*** *a-11, 14-20, 25, 26, 27p, 28, 29-31p, 33i, 35i; c-20, 22, 23, 25, 26i, 27i, 28-33.*

SHAZAM! AND THE SHAZAM FAMILY! ANNUAL
DC Comics: 2002 ($5.95, squarebound, one-shot)

1-Reprints Golden Age stories including 1st Mary Marvel and 1st Black Adam 6.00

SHAZAM!: POWER OF HOPE
DC Comics: Nov, 2000 ($9.95, treasury size, one-shot)

nn-Painted art by Alex Ross; story by Alex Ross and Paul Dini 10.00

SHAZAM!: THE MONSTER SOCIETY OF EVIL
DC Comics: 2007 - No. 4, 2007 ($5.99, square-bound, limited series)

1-4: Jeff Smith-s/a/c in all. 1-Retelling of origin. 2-Mary Marvel & Dr. Sivana app. 6.00
HC (2007, $29.99, over-sized with dust jacket that unfolds to a poster) r/#1-4; Alex Ross intro.; Smith afterword; sketch pages, script pages and production notes 30.00

SHAZAM: THE NEW BEGINNING
DC Comics: Apr, 1987 - No. 4, July, 1987 (Legends spin-off) (Limited series)

1-4: 1-New origin & 1st modern app. Captain Marvel; Marvel Family cameo. 2-4-Sivana & Black Adam app. 3.00

SHEA THEATRE COMICS
Shea Theatre: No date (1940's) (32 pgs.)

nn-Contains Rocket Comics; MLJ cover in one color 10 20 30 56 76 95

SHE-BAT (See Murcielaga, She-Bat & Valeria the She-Bat)

SHE-DRAGON (See Savage Dragon #117)
Image Comics: July, 2006 ($5.99, one-shot)

nn- She-Dragon in Dimension-X; origin retold; Franchesco-a/Larsen-s; sketch pages 6.00

SHEENA (Movie)
Marvel Comics: Dec, 1984 - No. 2, Feb, 1985 (limited series)

1,2-r/Marvel Comics Super Special #34; Tanya Roberts movie 3.00

SHEENA, QUEEN OF THE JUNGLE (See Jerry Iger's Classic..., Jumbo Comics, & 3-D Sheena)
Fiction House Magazines: Spr, 1942; No. 2, Wint, 1942-43; No. 3, Spr, 1943; No. 4, Fall, 1948; No. 5, Sum, 1949; No. 6, Spr, 1950; No. 7-10, 1950(nd); No. 11, Spr, 1951 - No. 18, Wint, 1952-53 (#1-3: 68 pgs.; #4-7: 52 pgs.)

1-Sheena begins 273 546 819 1720 2910 4100
2 (Winter, 1942-43) 117 234 351 737 1244 1750
3 (Spring, 1943) 83 166 249 523 887 1250
4,5 (Fall, 1948, Sum, 1949): 4-New logo; cover swipe from Jumbo #20 52 104 156 322 536 750
6,7 (Spring, 1950, 1950) 44 88 132 272 454 635
8-10(1950 - Win/50, 36 pgs.) 40 80 120 244 397 550
11-18: 15-Cover swipe from Jumbo #43. 18-Used in **POP**, pg. 98 35 70 105 203 327 450
I.W. Reprint #9-r/#18; c-r/White Princess #3 4 8 12 28 44 60
NOTE: ***Baker*** *c-5-10?* ***Whitman*** *c-11-18(most).*

SHEENA, QUEEN OF THE JUNGLE
Devil's Due Publishing: Mar, 2007 - Present (99¢/$3.50)

1-5: 1-Rodi-s/Merhoff-a; 5 covers 3.50

She-Hulk (2005 series) #26 © MAR

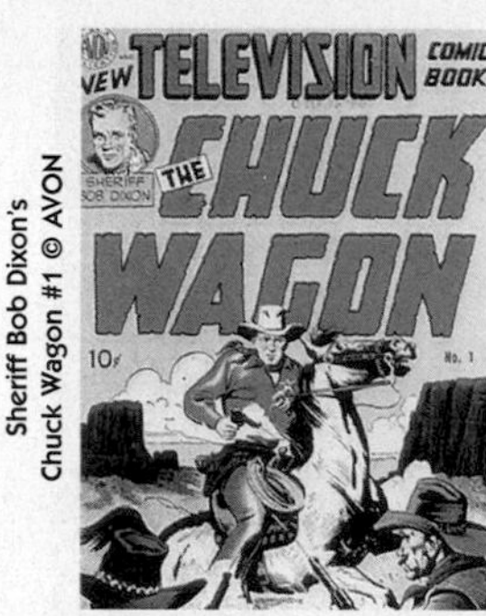

Sheriff Bob Dixon's Chuck Wagon #1 © AVON

Shield-Wizard Comics #2 © MLJ

	GD	VG	FN	VF	VF/NM	NM-
	2.0	4.0	6.0	8.0	9.0	9.2

... 99¢ Special (3/07) Revival of the character; Rodi-s/Cummings-a; sketch pages; history 2.25
... Trail of the Mapinguari (4/08, $5.50) Two covers 5.50

SHEENA 3-D SPECIAL (Also see Blackthorne 3-D Series #1)
Eclipse Comics: Jan, 1985 ($2.00)
1-Dave Stevens-c 5.00

SHE-HULK (Also see The Savage She-Hulk & The Sensational She-Hulk)
Marvel Comics: May, 2004 - No. 12, Apr, 2005 ($2.99)
1-4-Bobillo-a/Slott-s/Granov-c. 1-Avengers app. 4-Spider-Man-c/app. 3.00
5-12: Mayhew-c. 9,12-Pelletier-a. 10-Origin of Titania 3.00
Vol. 1: Single Green Female TPB (2004, $14.99) r/#1-6 15.00
Vol. 2: Superhuman Law TPB (2005, $14.99) r/#7-12 15.00

SHE-HULK (2nd series)
Marvel Comics: Dec, 2005 - Present ($2.99)
1,2,4-7,9-24: 1-Bobillo-a/Slott-s/Horn-c. 1-New Avengers app. 2-Hawkeye-c/app. 9-Jen marries John Jameson. 12-Thanos app. 16-Wolverine app. 3.00
3-($3.99) 100th She-Hulk issue; new story w/art by various incl. Bobillo, Conner, Mayhew & Powell; r/Savage She-Hulk #1 and r/Sensational She-Hulk #1 4.00
8-Civil War 15.00
8-2nd printing with variant Bobillo-c 3.00
25-($3.99) Intro. the Behemoth; Juggernaut cameo; Handbook bio pages of She-Hulk 4.00
26-33: 27-Iron Man app. 30-Hercules app. 31-X-Factor app. 32,33-Secret Invasion 3.00
Vol. 3: Time Trials (2006, $14.99) r/#1-5; Bobillo sketch page 15.00
Vol. 4: Laws of Attraction (2007, $19.99) r/#6-12; Paul Smith sketch page 20.00
Vol. 5: Planet Without a Hulk (2007, $19.99) r/#14-21; Slott's original series pitch 20.00
...: Jaded HC (2008, $19.99) r/#22-27; cover gallery 20.00

SHERIFF BOB DIXON'S CHUCK WAGON (TV) (See Wild Bill Hickok #22)
Avon Periodicals: Nov, 1950
1-Kinstler c/a(3) 14 28 42 76 108 140

SHERIFF OF TOMBSTONE
Charlton Comics: Nov, 1958 - No. 17, Sept, 1961
V1#1-Giordano-c; Severin-a 6 12 18 41 66 90
2 4 8 12 22 34 45
3-10 3 6 9 17 25 32
11-17 3 6 9 14 20 25

SHERLOCK HOLMES (See Marvel Preview, New Adventures of..., & Spectacular Stories)

SHERLOCK HOLMES (All New Baffling Adventures of...)(Young Eagle #3 on?)
Charlton Comics: Oct, 1955 - No. 2, Mar, 1956
1-Dr. Neff, Ghost Breaker app. 40 80 120 243 389 535
2 36 72 108 208 329 450

SHERLOCK HOLMES (Also see The Joker)
National Periodical Publications: Sept-Oct, 1975
1-Cruz-a; Simonson-c 3 6 9 16 22 28

SHERRY THE SHOWGIRL (Showgirls #4)
Atlas Comics: July, 1956 - No. 3, Dec, 1956; No. 5, Apr, 1957 - No. 7, Aug, 1957
1-Dan DeCarlo-c/a in all 18 36 54 103 162 220
2 13 26 39 72 101 130
3,5-7 11 22 33 62 86 110

SHE'S JOSIE (See Josie)

SHEVA'S WAR
DC Comics (Helix): Oct, 1998 - No. 5, Feb, 1999 ($2.95, mini-series)
1-5-Christopher Moeller-s/painted-a/c 3.00

SHI (one-shots and TPBs)
Crusade Comics
...: Akai (2001, $2.99)-Intro. Victoria Cross; Tucci-a/c; J.C. Vaughn-s 3.00
...: Akai Victoria Cross Ed. ($5.95, edition of 2000) variant Tucci-c 6.00
...: C.G.I. (2001, $4.99) preview of unpublished series 5.00
.../ Cyblade: The Battle for the Independents (9/95, $2.95) Tucci-c; Hellboy, Bone app. 3.00
.../ Cyblade: The Battle for the Independents (9/95, $2.95) Silvestri variant-c 3.00
.../ Daredevil: Honor Thy Mother (1/97, $2.95) Flip book 3.00
...: Judgment Night (200, $3.99) Wolverine app.; Battlebook card and pages; Tucci-a 4.00
...: Kaidan (10/96, $2.95) Two covers; Tucci-c; Jae Lee wraparound-c 3.00
...: Masquerade (3/98, $3.50) Painted art by Lago, Texeira, and others 3.50
...: Nightstalkers (9/97, $3.50) Painted art by Val Mayerik 3.50
...: Rekishi (1/97, $2.95) Character bios and story summaries of Shi: The Way of the Warrior told in Detective Joe Labianca's point of view; Christopher Golden script; Tucci-c; J.G. Jones-a; flip book w/Shi: East Wind Rain preview 3.00
...: The Art of War Tourbook (1998, $4.95) Blank cover for sketches; early Tucci-a inside 5.00
.../ Vampirella (10/97, $2.95) Ellis-s/Lau-a 3.00
... Vs. Tomoe (8/96, $3.95) Tucci-a/scripts; wraparound foil-c 4.00
... Vs. Tomoe (6/96, $5.00, B&W)-Preview Ed.; sold at San Diego Comic Con 5.00
The Definitive Shi Vol. 1 (2006-2007, $24.99, TPB) B&W r/Way of the Warrior, Tomoe, Rekishi, and Senryaku series; cover gallery with sketches; Tucci & Sparacio-c 25.00

SHI: BLACK, WHITE AND RED
Crusade Comics: Mar, 1998 - No. 2, May, 1998 ($2.95, B&W&Red, mini-series)
1,2-J.G. Jones-painted art 3.00
...- Year of the Dragon Collected Edition (2000, $5.95) r/#1&2 6.00

SHIDIMA
Image Comics: Jan, 2001 - No. 7, Nov, 2002 ($2.95, limited series)
1-7-Prequel to Warlands 3.00
#0-(10/01, $2.25) Short story and sketch pages 2.50

SHI: EAST WIND RAIN
Crusade Comics: Nov, 1997 - No. 2, Feb, 1998 ($3.50, limited series)
1,2-Shi at WW2 Pearl Harbor 3.50

S.H.I.E.L.D. (Nick Fury & His Agents of...) (Also see Nick Fury)
Marvel Comics Group: Feb, 1973 - No. 5, Oct, 1973 (All 20¢ issues)
1-All contain reprint stories from Strange Tales #146-155; new Steranko-c 2 4 6 10 14 18
2-New Steranko flag-c 2 4 6 8 11 14
3-5: 3-Kirby/Steranko-c(r). 4-Steranko-c(r) 1 2 3 5 7 9
NOTE: *Buscema a-3p(r). Kirby layouts 1-5; c-3 (w/Steranko). Steranko a-3r, 4r(2).*

SHIELD, THE (Becomes Shield-Steel Sterling #3; #1 titled Lancelot Strong; also see Advs. of the Fly, Double Life of Private Strong, Fly Man, Mighty Comics, The Mighty Crusaders, The Original... & Pep Comics #1)
Archie Enterprises, Inc.: June, 1983 - No. 2, Aug, 1983
1,2: Steel Sterling app. 2-Kanigher-s 4.00
America's 1st Patriotic Comic Book Hero, The Shield (2002, $12.95, TPB) r/Pep Comics #1-5, Shield-Wizard Comics #1; foreward by Robert M. Overstreet 13.00

SHIELD, THE: SPOTLIGHT (TV)
IDW Publishing: Jan, 2004 - No. 5, May, 2004 ($3.99)
1-5-Jeff Marriote-s/Jean Diaz-a/Tommy Lee Edwards-c 4.00
TPB (7/04, $19.99) r/#1-5; Michael Chiklis photo-c 20.00

SHIELD-STEEL STERLING (Formerly The Shield)
Archie Enterprises, Inc.: No. 3, Dec, 1983 (Becomes Steel Sterling No. 4)
3-Nino-a; Steel Sterling by Kanigher & Barreto 3.00

SHIELD WIZARD COMICS (Also see Pep Comics & Top-Notch Comics)
MLJ Magazines: Summer, 1940 - No. 13, Spring, 1944
1-(V1#5 on inside)-Origin The Shield by Irving Novick & The Wizard by Ed Ashe, Jr; Flag-c 500 1000 1500 3600 6300 9000
2-(Winter/40)-Origin The Shield retold; Wizard's sidekick, Roy the Super Boy begins (see Top-Notch #8 for 1st app.) 260 520 780 1638 2769 3900
3,4 163 326 489 1027 1739 2450
5-Dusty, the Boy Detective begins 137 274 411 863 1457 2050
6,7: 6-Roy the Super Boy app. 7-Shield dons new costume (Summer, 1942); S & K-c? 133 266 399 838 1419 2000
8-Bondage-c; Hitler photo on-c 137 274 411 863 1457 2050
9-13: 9,13-Bondage-c 92 184 276 580 978 1375
NOTE: *Bob Montana c-13. Novick c-1-6,8-11. Harry Sahle c-12.*

SHI: FAN EDITIONS
Crusade Comics: 1997
1-3-Two covers polybagged in FAN #19-21 3.00
1-3-Gold editions 4.00

SHI: HEAVEN AND EARTH
Crusade Comics: June, 1997 - No. 4, Apr, 1998 ($2.95)
1-4 3.00
4-($4.95) Pencil-c variant 5.00
Rising Sun Edition-signed by Tucci in FanClub Starter Pack 4.00
"Tora No Shi" variant-c 3.00

SHI: JU-NEN
Dark Horse Comics: July, 2004 - No. 4, May, 2005 ($2.99, mini-series)
1-4-Tucci-a/Tucci & Vaughn-s; origin retold 3.00
TPB (2/06, $12.95) r/#1-4; Tucci and Sparacio-c 13.00

SHINING KNIGHT (See Adventure Comics #66)

SHINOBI (Based on Sega video game)

Shi: The Series #7 © William Tucci

Shocking Mystery Cases #60 © STAR

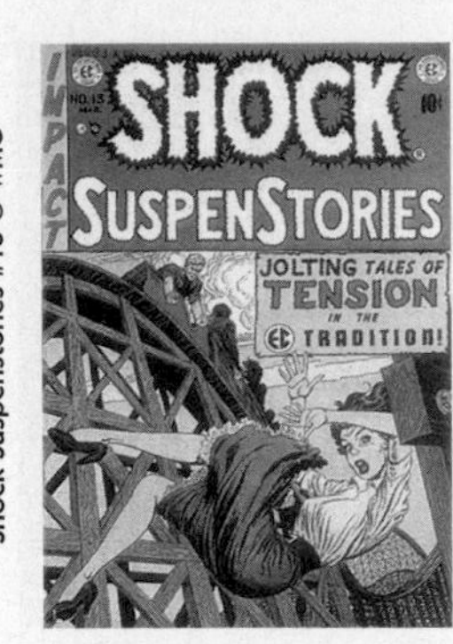

Shock Suspenstories #13 © WMG

GD VG FN VF VF/NM NM-
2.0 4.0 6.0 8.0 9.0 9.2

Dark Horse Comics: Aug, 2002 ($2.99, one-shot)
1-Medina-a/c 3.00

SHIP AHOY
Spotlight Publishers: Nov, 1944 (52 pgs.)
1-L. B. Cole-c 19 38 57 109 172 235

SHIP OF FOOLS
Image Comics: Aug, 1997 - No. 3 ($2.95, B&W)
0-3-Glass-s/Oeming-a 3.00

SHI: POISONED PARADISE
Avatar Press: July, 2002 - No. 2, Aug, 2002 ($3.50, limited series)
1,2-Vaughn and Tucci-s/Waller-a; 1-Four covers 3.50

SHIPWRECKED! (Disney-Movie)
Disney Comics: 1990 ($5.95, graphic novel, 68 pgs.)
nn-adaptation; Spiegle-a 6.00

SHI: SEMPO
Avatar Press: Aug, 2003 - No. 2, ($3.50, B&W, limited series)
1,2-Vaughn and Tucci-s/Alves-a; 1-Four covers 3.50

SHI: SENRYAKU
Crusade Comics: Aug, 1995 - No. 3, Nov, 1995 ($2.95, limited series)
1-3: 1-Tucci-c; Quesada, Darrow, Sim, Lee, Smith-a. 2-Tucci-c; Silvestri, Balent, Perez, Mack-a. 3-Jusko-c; Hughes, Ramos, Bell, Moore-a 3.00
1-variant-c (no logo) 4.00
Hardcover ($24.95)-r/#1-3; Frazetta-c. 25.00
Trade Paperback ($13.95)-r/#1-3; Frazetta-c. 14.00

SHI: THE ILLUSTRATED WARRIOR
Crusade Comics: 2002 - No. 7, 2003 ($2.99, B&W)
1-7-Story text with Tucci full page art 3.00

SHI: THE SERIES
Crusade Comics: Aug, 1997 - No. 13 ($2.95, color #1-10, B&W #11)
1-10 3.00
11-13: 11-B&W. 12-Color; Lau-a 3.00
#0 Convention Edition 5.00

SHI: THE WAY OF THE WARRIOR
Crusade Comics: Mar, 1994 - No. 12, Apr, 1997 ($2.50/$2.95)
1/2 4.00
1 2 4 6 8 10 12
1-Commemorative ed., B&W, new-c; given out at 1994 San Diego Comic Con
2 4 6 10 14 18
1-Fan appreciation edition -r/#1 2.50
1-Fan appreciation edition (variant) 6.00
1- 10th Anniversary Edition (2004, $2.99) 3.00
2 5.00
2-Commemorative edition (3,000) 2 4 6 9 13 16
2-Fan appreciation edition -r/#2 2.50
3 4.00
4-7: 4-Silvestri poster. 7-Tomoe app. 2.50
5,6: 5-Silvestri variant-c. 6-Tomoe #1 variant-c 3.00
5-Gold edition 12.00
6,8-12: 6-Fan appreciation edition 2.50
8-Combo Gold edition 6.00
8-Signed Edition-(5000) 3.00
Trade paperback (1995, $12.95)-r/#1-4 13.00
Trade paperback (1995, $14.95)-r/#1-4 revised; Julie Bell-c 15.00

SHI: YEAR OF THE DRAGON
Crusade Comics: 2000 - No. 3, 2000 ($2.99, limited series)
1-3: 1-Two covers; Tucci-a/c; flashback to teen-aged Ana 3.00

SHMOO (See Al Capp's... & Washable Jones &...)

SHOCK (Magazine)
Stanley Publ.: May, 1969 - V3#4, Sept, 1971 (B&W reprints from horror comics, including some pre-code) (No V2#1,3)
V1#1-Cover-r/Weird Tales of the Future #7 by Bernard Baily; r/Weird Chills #1
7 14 21 45 73 100
2-Wolverton-r/Weird Mysteries 5; r-Weird Mysteries #7 used in **SOTI**; cover reprints cover to Weird Chills #1 5 10 15 34 55 75
3,5,6 4 8 12 24 37 50
4-Harrison/Williamson-r/Forbid. Worlds #6 4 8 12 26 41 55
V2#2(5/70), V1#8(7/70), V2#4(9/70)-6(1/71), V3#1-4: V2#4-Cover swipe from Weird Mysteries #6 4 8 12 22 34 45
NOTE: *Disbrow r-V2#4; Bondage c-V1#4, V2#6, V3#1.*

SHOCK DETECTIVE CASES (Formerly Crime Fighting Detective)
(Becomes Spook Detective Cases No. 22)
Star Publications: No. 20, Sept, 1952 - No. 21, Nov, 1952
20,21-L.B. Cole-c; based on true crime cases 23 46 69 133 214 295
NOTE: *Palais a-20. No. 21-Fox-r.*

SHOCK ILLUSTRATED (...Adult Crime Stories; Magazine format)
E. C. Comics: Sept-Oct, 1955 - No. 3, Spring, 1956 (Adult Entertainment on-c #1,2)(All 25¢)
1-All by Kamen; drugs, prostitution, wife swapping 18 36 54 103 162 220
2-Williamson-a redrawn from Crime SuspenStories #13 plus Ingels, Crandall, Evans & part Torres-i; painted-c 18 36 54 107 169 230
3-Only 100 known copies bound & given away at E.C. office; Crandall, Evans-a; painted-c; shows May, 1956 on-c 113 226 339 712 1206 1700

SHOCKING MYSTERY CASES (Formerly Thrilling Crime Cases)
Star Publications: No. 50, Sept, 1952 - No. 60, Oct, 1954 (All crime reprints?)
50-Disbrow "Frankenstein" story 42 84 126 261 436 610
51-Disbrow-a 27 54 81 156 251 345
52-60: 56-Drug use story 25 50 75 147 236 325
NOTE: *L. B. Cole covers on all; a-60(2 pgs.). Hollingsworth a-52. Morisi a-55.*

SHOCKING TALES DIGEST MAGAZINE
Harvey Publications: Oct, 1981 (95¢)
1-1957-58-r; Powell, Kirby, Nostrand-a 2 4 6 9 13 16

SHOCK ROCKETS
Image Comics (Gorilla): Apr, 2000 - No. 6, Oct, 2000 ($2.50)
1-6-Busiek-s/Immonen & Grawbadger-a. 6-Flip book w/Superstar preview 2.50
...: We Have Ignition TPB (Dark Horse, 8/04, $14.95, 6" x 9") r/#1-6 15.00

SHOCK SUSPENSTORIES (Also see EC Archives • Shock SuspenStories)
E. C. Comics: Feb-Mar, 1952 - No. 18, Dec-Jan, 1954-55
1-Classic Feldstein electrocution-c 82 164 246 656 1046 1435
2 45 90 135 360 573 785
3,4: 4-Used in **SOTI**, pg. 387,388 33 66 99 264 425 585
5-Hanging-c 39 78 117 312 494 675
6-Classic hooded vigilante bondage-c 51 102 153 408 654 900
7-Classic face melting-c 50 100 150 400 638 875
8-Williamson-a 33 66 99 264 420 575
9-11: 9-Injury to eye panel. 10-Junkie story 28 56 84 224 357 490
12- "The Monkey" classic junkie cover/story; anti-drug propaganda issue
36 72 108 288 457 625
13-Frazetta's only solo story for E.C., 7 pgs. 39 78 117 312 494 675
14-Used in Senate Investigation hearings 23 46 69 184 292 400
15-Used in 1954 Reader's Digest article, "For the Kiddies to Read"
21 42 63 168 264 360
16-18: 16- "Red Dupe" editorial; rape story 19 38 57 152 246 340
NOTE: ***Ray Bradbury** adaptations-1, 7, 9. **Craig** a-11; c-11. **Crandall** a-9-13, 15-18. **Davis** a-1-5. **Evans** a-7, 8, 14-18; c-16-18. **Feldstein** c-1, 7-9, 12. **Ingels** a-1, 2, 6. **Kamen** a-in all; c-10, 13, 15. **Krigstein** a-14, 18. **Orlando** a-1, 3-7, 9, 10, 12, 16, 17. **Wood** a-2-15; c-2-6, 14.*

SHOCK SUSPENSTORIES (Also see EC Archives • Shock SuspenStories)
Russ Cochran/Gemstone Publishing: Sept, 1992 - No. 18, Dec, 1996 ($1.50/$2.00/$2.50, quarterly)
1-18: 1-3: Reprints with original-c. 17-r/HOF #17 2.50

SHOGUN WARRIORS
Marvel Comics Group: Feb, 1979 - No. 20, Sept, 1980 (Based on Mattel toys of the classic Japanese animation characters) (1-3: 35¢; 4-19: 40¢; 20: 50¢)
1-Raydeen, Combatra, & Dangard Ace begin; Trimpe-a
2 4 6 8 10 12
2-20: 2-Lord Maurkon & Elementals of Evil app.; Rok-Korr app. 6-Shogun vs. Shogun. 7,8-Cerberus. 9-Starchild. 11-Austin-c. 12-Simonson-c. 14-16-Doctor Demonicus. 17-Juggernaut. 19,20-FF x-over 1 2 3 5 6 8

SHOOK UP (Magazine) (Satire)
Dodsworth Publ. Co.: Nov, 1958
V1#1 4 8 12 26 41 55

SHORT RIBS
Dell Publishing Co.: No. 1333, Apr - June, 1962
Four Color 1333 5 10 15 34 55 75

SHORTSTOP SQUAD (Baseball)
Ultimate Sports Ent. Inc.: 1999 ($3.95, one-shot)

Showcase #25 © DC

Showcase #54 © DC

Showcase '93 #9 © DC

GD	VG	FN	VF	VF/NM	NM-
2.0	4.0	6.0	8.0	9.0	9.2

1-Ripken Jr., Larkin, Jeter, Rodriguez app.; Edwards-c/a 4.00

SHORT STORY COMICS (See Hello Pal,...)

SHORTY SHINER (The Five-Foot Fighter in the Ten Gallon Hat)
Dandy Magazine (Charles Biro): June, 1956 - No. 3, Oct, 1956

1 7 14 21 37 46 55
2,3 5 10 15 24 30 35

SHOTGUN SLADE (TV)
Dell Publishing Co.: No. 1111, July-Sept, 1960

Four Color 1111-Photo-c 6 12 18 41 66 90

SHOWCASE (See Cancelled Comic Cavalcade & New Talent...)
National Per. Publ./DC Comics: 3-4/56 - No. 93, 9/70; No. 94, 8-9/77 - No. 104, 9/78

1-Fire Fighters; w/Fireman Farrell 272 544 816 2380 4590 6800
2-Kings of the Wild; Kubert-a (animal stories) 83 166 249 706 1353 2000
3-The Frogmen by Russ Heath; Heath greytone-c (early DC example, 7-8/56)
88 176 264 748 1424 2100
4-Origin/1st app. The Flash (1st DC Silver Age hero, Sept-Oct, 1956); Kanigher-s; Infantino & Kubert-c/a; 1st app. Iris West and The Turtle; r/in Secret Origins #1 ('61 & '73); Flash shown reading G.A. Flash Comics #13; back-up story w/Broome-s/Infantino & Kubert-a
1500 3000 4500 16,000 32,000 48,000
5-Manhunters; Meskin-a 81 162 243 689 1320 1950
6-Origin/1st app. Challengers of the Unknown by Kirby, partly r/in Secret Origins #1 & Challengers #64,65 (1st S.A. hero team & 1st original concept S.A. series)(1-2/57)
300 600 900 2642 5121 7600
7-Challengers of the Unknown by Kirby (2nd app.) reprinted in Challengers of the Unknown #75 152 304 456 1301 2500 3700
8-The Flash (5-6/57, 2nd app.); origin & 1st app. Captain Cold
820 1640 2460 7500 12,750 18,000
9-Lois Lane (Pre-#1, 7-8/57) (1st Showcase character to win own series)
Superman app. on-c 650 1300 1950 5200 9350 13,500
10-Lois Lane; Jor-El cameo; Superman app. on-c 240 480 720 2100 4050 6000
11-Challengers of the Unknown by Kirby (3rd) 142 284 426 1207 2304 3400
12-Challengers of the Unknown by Kirby (4th) 142 284 426 1207 2304 3400
13-The Flash (3rd app.); origin Mr. Element 320 640 960 2880 5440 8000
14-The Flash (4th app.); origin Dr. Alchemy, former Mr. Element (rare in NM)
335 670 1005 3015 5858 8700
15-Space Ranger (7-8/58, 1st app.) 152 304 456 1320 2532 3750
16-Space Ranger (9-10/58, 2nd app.) 75 150 225 638 1219 1800
17-(11-12/58)-Adventures on Other Worlds; origin/1st app. Adam Strange by Gardner Fox & Mike Sekowsky 188 376 564 1645 3173 4700
18-Adventures on Other Worlds (2nd A. Strange) 94 188 282 799 1525 2250
19-Adam Strange; 1st Adam Strange logo 102 204 306 867 1659 2450
20-Rip Hunter; origin & 1st app. (5-6/59); Moreira-a 81 162 243 689 1320 1950
21-Rip Hunter (7-8/59, 2nd app.); Sekowsky-c/a 44 88 132 352 664 975
22-Origin & 1st app. Silver Age Green Lantern by Gil Kane and John Broome (9-10/59); reprinted in Secret Origins #2 385 770 1155 3465 6733 10,000
23-Green Lantern (11-12/59, 2nd app.); nuclear explosion-c
133 266 399 1131 2166 3200
24-Green Lantern (1-2/60, 3rd app.) 133 266 399 1131 2166 3200
25,26-Rip Hunter by Kubert. 25-Grey tone-c 37 74 111 283 529 775
27-Sea Devils (7-8/60, 1st app.); Heath-c/a 73 146 219 621 1186 1750
28-Sea Devils (9-10/60, 2nd app.); Heath-c/a 39 78 117 302 564 825
29-Sea Devils; Heath-c/a; grey tone c-27-29 42 84 126 336 631 925
30-Origin Silver Age Aquaman (1-2/61) (see Adventure #260 for 1st S.A. origin)
75 150 225 638 1219 1800
31,32-Aquaman 40 80 120 312 581 850
33-Aquaman 40 80 120 312 581 850
34-Origin & 1st app. Silver Age Atom by Gil Kane & Murphy Anderson (9-10/61); reprinted in Secret Origins #2 117 234 351 995 1898 2800
35-The Atom by Gil Kane (2nd); last 10¢ issue 54 108 162 459 880 1300
36-The Atom by Gil Kane (1-2/62, 3rd app.) 44 88 132 352 664 975
37-Metal Men (3-4/62, 1st app.) 57 114 171 485 930 1375
38-Metal Men (5-6/62, 2nd app.) 35 70 105 270 498 725
39-Metal Men (7-8/62, 3rd app.) 27 54 81 197 366 535
40-Metal Men (9-10/62, 4th app.) 24 48 72 176 326 475
41,42-Tommy Tomorrow (parts 1 & 2). 42-Origin 15 30 45 107 196 285
43-Dr. No (James Bond); Nodel-a; originally published as British Classics Illustrated #158A & as #6 in a European Detective series, all with diff. painted-c. This Showcase #43 version is actually censored, deleting all racial skin color and dialogue thought to be racially demeaning (1st DC S.A. movie adaptation)(based on Ian Fleming novel & movie)
43 86 129 344 647 950
44-Tommy Tomorrow 11 22 33 75 133 190
45-Sgt. Rock (7-8/63); pre-dates B&B #52; origin retold; Heath-c

GD	VG	FN	VF	VF/NM	NM-
2.0	4.0	6.0	8.0	9.0	9.2

31 62 93 239 445 650
46,47-Tommy Tomorrow 10 20 30 67 116 165
48,49-Cave Carson (3rd tryout series; see B&B) 8 16 24 58 97 135
50,51-I Spy (Danger Trail-r by Infantino), King Farady story (#50 has new 4 pg. story)
8 16 24 52 86 120
52-Cave Carson 8 16 24 52 86 120
53,54-G.I. Joe (11-12/64, 1-2/65); Heath-a 11 22 33 75 133 190
55-Dr. Fate & Hourman (3-4/65); origin of each in text; 1st solo app. G.A. Green Lantern in Silver Age (pre-dates Gr. Lantern #40); 1st S.A. app. Solomon Grundy
24 48 72 172 319 465
56-Dr. Fate & Hourman 14 28 42 104 187 270
57-Enemy Ace by Kubert (7-8/65, 4th app. after Our Army at War #155)
20 40 60 143 264 385
58-Enemy Ace by Kubert (5th app.) 17 34 51 120 223 325
59-Teen Titans (11-12/65, 3rd app.) 15 30 45 105 190 275
60-1st S. A. app. The Spectre; Anderson-a (1-2/66); origin in text
27 54 81 197 369 540
61-The Spectre by Anderson (2nd app.) 14 28 42 102 181 260
62-Origin & 1st app. Inferior Five (5-6/66) 9 18 27 63 107 150
63,65-Inferior Five. 63-Hulk parody. 65-X-Men parody (11-12/66)
6 12 18 41 66 90
64-The Spectre by Anderson (5th app.) 14 28 42 99 175 250
66,67-B'wana Beast 5 10 15 32 51 70
68-Maniaks (1st app., spoof of The Monkees) 5 10 15 34 55 75
69,71-Maniaks. 71-Woody Allen-c/app. 5 10 15 32 51 70
70-Binky (9-10/67)-Tryout issue; 1950's Leave It To Binky reprints with art changes
6 12 18 39 62 85
72-Top Gun (Johnny Thunder-r)-Toth-a 5 10 15 32 51 70
73-Origin/1st app. Creeper; Ditko-c/a (3-4/68) 12 24 36 87 156 225
74-Intro/1st app. Anthro; Post-c/a (5/68) 8 16 24 56 93 130
75-Origin/1st app. Hawk & the Dove; Ditko-c/a 11 22 33 79 140 200
76-1st app. Bat Lash (8/68) 7 14 21 50 83 115
77-1st app. Angel & The Ape (9/68) 7 14 21 45 73 100
78-1st app. Jonny Double (11/68) 5 10 15 30 48 65
79-1st app. Dolphin (12/68); Aqualad origin-r 6 12 18 41 66 90
80-1st S.A. app. Phantom Stranger (1/69); Neal Adams-c
9 18 27 65 113 160
81-Windy & Willy; r/Many Loves of Dobie Gillis #26 with art changes
5 10 15 34 55 75
82-1st app. Nightmaster (5/69) by Grandenetti & Giordano; Kubert-c
7 14 21 45 73 100
83,84-Nightmaster by Wrightson w/Jones/Kaluta ink assist in each; Kubert-c.
83-Last 12¢ issue 84-Origin retold; begin 15¢ 6 12 18 43 69 95
85-87-Firehair; Kubert-a 3 6 9 16 23 30
88-90-Jason's Quest: 90-Manhunter 2070 app. 3 6 9 14 20 25
91-93-Manhunter 2070: 92-Origin. 93-(9/70) Last 15¢ issue
3 6 9 14 20 25
94-Intro/origin new Doom Patrol & Robotman(8-9/77) 2 4 6 10 14 18
95,96-The Doom Patrol. 95-Origin Celsius 1 2 3 5 7 9
97-99-Power Girl; origin-97,98; JSA cameos 1 2 3 5 7 9
100-(52 pgs.)-Most Showcase characters featured 2 4 6 9 12 15
101-103-Hawkman; Adam Strange x-over 1 2 3 5 7 9
104-(52 pgs.)-O.S.S. Spies at War 1 2 3 5 7 9

NOTE: ***Anderson*** *a-22-24i, 34-36i, 55, 56, 60, 61, 64, 101-103i; c-50i, 51i, 55, 56, 60, 61, 64.* ***Aparo*** *c-94-96.* ***Boring*** *c-10.* ***Estrada*** *a-104.* ***Fraden*** *c(p)-30, 31, 33.* ***Heath*** *c-3, 27-29.* ***Infantino*** *c/a(p)-4, 8, 13, 14; c-50p, 51p.* ***Gil Kane*** *a-22-24p, 34-36p; c-17-19, 22-24p(w/**Giella**), 31.* ***Kane/Anderson*** *c-34-36.* ***Kirby*** *c-11, 12.* ***Kirby/Stein*** *c-6, 7.* ***Kubert*** *a-2, 4i, 25, 26, 45, 53, 54, 72; c-25, 26, 53, 54, 57, 58, 82-87, 101-104; c-2, 4i.* ***Moreira*** *c-5.* ***Orlando*** *a-62p, 63p, 97i; c-62, 63, 97i.* ***Sekowsky*** *a-65p.* ***Sparling*** *a-78.* ***Staton*** *a-94, 95-99p, 100; c-97-100p.*

SHOWCASE '93
DC Comics: Jan, 1993 - No. 12, Dec, 1993 ($1.95, limited series, 52 pgs.)

1-12: 1-Begin 4 part Catwoman story & 6 part Blue Devil story; begin Cyborg story; Art Adams/Austin-c. 3-Flash by Charest (p). 6-Azrael in Bat-costume (2 pgs.). 7,8-Knightfall parts 13 & 14. 6-10-Deathstroke app. (6,10-cameo). 9,10-Austin-i. 10-Azrael as Batman in new costume app.; Gulacy-c. 11-Perez-c. 12-Creeper app.; Alan Grant scripts 3.00

NOTE: ***Chaykin*** *c-9.* ***Fabry*** *c-8.* ***Giffen*** *a-12.* ***Golden*** *c-3.* ***Zeck*** *c-6.*

SHOWCASE '94
DC Comics: Jan, 1994 - No. 12, Dec, 1994 ($1.95, limited series, 52 pgs.)

1-12: 1,2-Joker & Gunfire stories. 1-New Gods. 4-Riddler story. 5-Huntress-c/story w/app. new Batman. 6-Huntress-c/story w/app. Robin; Atom story. 7-Penguin story by Peter David, P. Craig Russell, & Michael T. Gilbert; Penguin-c by Jae Lee. 8,9-Scarface origin story by Alan Grant, John Wagner,& Teddy Kristiansen; Prelude to Zero Hour. 10-Zero Hour tie-in story. 11-Man-Bat. 3.00

NOTE: ***Alan Grant*** *scripts-3, 4.* ***Kelley Jones*** *c-12.* ***Mignola*** *c-3.* ***Nebres*** *a(i)-2.* ***Quesada*** *c-10.* ***Russell*** *a-7p.* ***Simonson*** *c-5.*

Showcase Presents Brave and the Bold Vol.#2 © DC

Shrugged #1 © Aspen MLT

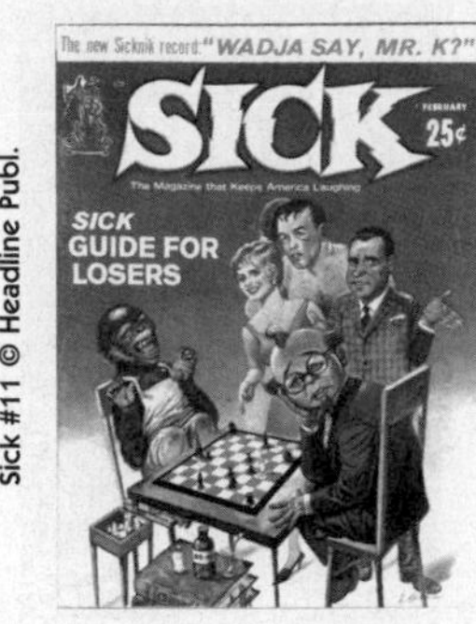

Sick #11 © Headline Publ.

	GD	VG	FN	VF	VF/NM	NM-
	2.0	4.0	6.0	8.0	9.0	9.2

SHOWCASE '95
DC Comics: Jan, 1995 - No. 12, Dec, 1995 ($2.50/$2.95, limited series)

1-4-Supergirl story. 3-Eradicator-c.; The Question story. 4-Thorn c/story 3.00
5-12: 5-Thorn-c/story; begin $2.95-c. 8-Spectre story. 12-The Shade story by James Robinson & Wade Von Grawbadger; Maitresse story by Claremont & Alan Davis 3.00

SHOWCASE '96
DC Comics: Jan, 1996 - No. 12, Dec, 1996 ($2.95, limited series)

1-12: 1-Steve Geppi cameo. 3-Black Canary & Lois Lane-c/story; Deadman story by Jamie Delano & Wade Von Grawbadger, Gary Frank-c. 4-Firebrand & Guardian-c/story; The Shade & Dr. Fate "Times Past" story by James Robinson & Matt Smith begins, ends #5. 6-Superboy-c/app.; Atom app.; Capt. Marvel (Mary Marvel)-c/app. 8-Supergirl by David & Dodson. 11-Scare Tactics app. 11,12-Legion of Super-Heroes vs. Brainiac. 12-Jesse Quick app. 3.00

SHOWCASE PRESENTS... (B&W archive reprints of DC Silver Age stories)
DC Comics: 2005 - Present ($9.99/$16.99, B&W, over 500 pgs., squarebound)

Adam Strange Vol. 1 (2007, $16.99) r/Showcase #17-19 & Mystery in Space #53-84 17.00
Aquaman Vol. 1 (2007, $16.99) r/Aquaman #1-6 & other early app. 17.00
Aquaman Vol. 2 (2008, $16.99) r/Aquaman #7-23 & other early app. 17.00
The Atom Vol. 1 (2007, $16.99) r/Showcase #34-36 & The Atom #1-17 17.00
Batgirl Vol. 1 (2007, $16.99) r/early apps. from Detective #359 (1967) thru 1975 17.00
Batman Vol. 1 (2006, $16.99) r/"new look" from Detective #327-342, Batman #164-174 17.00
Batman Vol. 2 (2007, $16.99) r/"new look" from Detective #343-358, Batman #175-188 17.00
Batman Vol. 3 (2008, $16.99) r/"new look" from Detective #359-375, Batman #189, 190-192,194-197,199-202 17.00
Batman and the Outsiders Vol. 1 (2007, $16.99) r/#1-19, Annual #1; Brave and the Bold #200; and New Teen Titans #37 17.00
Booster Gold Vol. 1 (2008, $16.99) r/#1-25 & Action Comics #594 17.00
The Brave and the Bold Batman Team-ups Vol. 1 (2007, $16.99) r/#59,64,67-71,74-87 17.00
The Brave and the Bold Batman Team-ups Vol. 2 (2007, $16.99) r/#88-108 17.00
Challengers of the Unknown Vol. 1 (2006, $16.99) r/#1-17 & Showcase #6,7,11,12 17.00
Challengers of the Unknown Vol. 2 (2008, $16.99) r/#18-37 17.00
The Elongated Man Vol. 1 ('06, $16.99) r/early apps. in Flash & Detective ('60-'68) 17.00
Enemy Ace Vol. 1 (2008, $16.99) r/Our Army at War #151 & other early app. 17.00
The Flash Vol. 1 (2007, $16.99) r/Flash Comics #104 (last G.A. issue), Showcase #4,8,13,14 & The Flash #105-119 17.00
The Flash Vol. 2 (2008, $16.99) r/The Flash #120-140 17.00
The Great Disaster Featuring The Atomic Knights and Hercules Vol. 1 (2007, $16.99) 17.00
Green Arrow Vol. 1 (2006, $16.99) r/Adventure #250-269, Brave and the Bold #50,71,85; Justice League of America #4; World's Finest #95-134,136,138,140 17.00
Green Lantern Vol. 1 (2005, $9.99) r/Showcase #22-24 & Green Lantern #1-17 10.00
Green Lantern Vol. 2 (2007, $16.99) r/Green Lantern #18-38 17.00
Green Lantern Vol. 3 (2008, $16.99) r/Green Lantern #39-59 17.00
Haunted Tank Vol. 1 ('06, $16.99) r/G.I. Combat #87-119, Brave & The Bold #52 and Our Army at War #155; Russ Heath-c 17.00
Haunted Tank Vol. 2 ('08, $16.99) r/G.I. Combat #120-156 17.00
Hawkman Vol. 1 ('07, $16.99) r/Brave&Bold #34-36,42-44, Mystery in Space #87-90, Hawkman #1-11, and The Atom #7 17.00
The House of Mystery Vol. 1 ('06, $16.99) r/House of Mystery #174-194 ('68-'71) 17.00
The House of Mystery Vol. 2 ('07, $16.99) r/House of Mystery #195-211 ('71-'73) 17.00
Jonah Hex Vol. 1 (2005, $16.99) r/All Star Western #10-12, Weird Western Tales #13,14, 16-33; plus the complete adventures of Outlaw from All Star Western #2-8 17.00
Justice League of America Vol. 1 ('05, $16.99) r/Brave & the Bold #28-30, J.L. of A. #1-16 and Mystery in Space #75 17.00
Justice League of America Vol. 2 ('07, $16.99) r/Justice League of America #17-36 17.00
Justice League of America Vol. 3 ('07, $16.99) r/Justice League of America #37-60 17.00
Legion of Super-Heroes Vol. 1 ('07, $16.99) r/Adventure #247 & early app. thru 1964 17.00
Legion of Super-Heroes Vol. 2 ('08, $16.99) r/app. in Adventure & Superboy 1964-66 17.00
Martian Manhunter Vol. 1 (2007, $16.99) r/Detective #225-304 & Batman #78 (prototype) 17.00
Metal Men Vol. 1 (2007, $16.99) r/#1-16; Brave & Bold #55, Showcase #37-40 17.00
Metamorpho Vol. 1 ('05, $16.99) r/Brave&Bold #57,58,66,68; Metamorpho #1-17;JLA #42 17.00
Phantom Stranger Vol. 1 (2006, $16.99) r/#1-21 (2nd series) & Showcase #80 17.00
Phantom Stranger Vol. 2 (2008, $16.99) r/#22-41 and various 1970-1978 appearances 17.00
Robin The Boy Wonder Vol. 1 (2007, $16.99) r/back-ups from Batman, Detective, WF 17.00
Sgt. Rock Vol. 1 ('07, $16.99) r/G.I. Combat #68, Our Army at War #81-117 17.00
Shazam! Vol. 1 ('06, $16.99) r/#1-33 17.00
Supergirl Vol. 1 ('07, $16.99) r/prototype from Superman #123 (8/58); 1st app. Action #252 (5/59) and early appearances thru Nov. 1961 17.00
Superman Vol. 1 ('05, $9.99) r/Action #241-257 & Superman #122-134 (1958-59) 10.00
Superman Vol. 2 ('06, $16.99) r/Action #258-275 & Superman #134-145 (1959-61) 17.00
Superman Vol. 3 ('07, $16.99) r/Action #279-292 & Superman #146-156 & Annual #3,4 17.00
Superman Family Vol. 1 ('06, $16.99) Superman's Pal, Jimmy Olsen #1-22; Showcase #9 and Superman #22 17.00
Superman Family Vol. 2 ('08, $16.99) Superman's Pal, Jimmy Olsen #23-34; Showcase #10 and Superman's Girl Friend, Lois Lane #1-7 17.00
Teen Titans Vol. 1 ('06, $16.99) r/#1-18; Brave & the Bold #54,60; Showcase #59 17.00
Teen Titans Vol. 2 ('07, $16.99) r/#19-37, World's Finest #205 and Brave & Bold #83,94 17.00
The Unknown Soldier Vol. 1 ('06, $16.99) r/Star Spangled War Stories #158-188 17.00
The War That Time Forgot Vol. 1 ('07, $16.99) r/S.S.W.S. #90,92,94-125,127,128 17.00
Wonder Woman Vol. 1 ('07, $16.99) r/#98-117 17.00
World's Finest Vol. 1 ('07, $16.99) r/#71-111 & Superman #76 17.00

SHOWGIRLS (Formerly Sherry the Showgirl #3)
Atlas Comics (MPC No. 2): No. 4, 2/57; June, 1957 - No. 2, Aug, 1957

	GD	VG	FN	VF	VF/NM	NM-
4-(2/57) Dan DeCarlo-c/a begins	10	20	30	58	79	100
1-(6/57) Millie, Sherry, Chili, Pearl & Hazel begin	13	26	39	74	105	135
2	10	20	30	58	79	100

SHREK (Movie)
Dark Horse Comics: Sept, 2003 - No. 3, Dec, 2003 ($2.99, limited series)

1-3-Takes place after 1st movie; Evanier-s/Bachs-a; CGI cover 3.00

SHROUD, THE (See Super-Villain Team-Up #5)
Marvel Comics: Mar, 1994 - No. 4, June, 1994 ($1.75, mini-series)

1-4: 1,2,4-Spider-Man & Scorpion app. 2.50

SHROUD OF MYSTERY
Whitman Publications: June, 1982

	GD	VG	FN	VF	VF/NM	NM-
1	1	2	3	4	5	7

SHRUGGED
Aspen MLT, Inc.: No. 0, June, 2006 - Present ($2.50/$2.99)

0-($2.50) Turner & Mastromauro-s/Gunnell-a; intro. story and character profiles 2.50
1-7-($2.99) 1-Six covers. 2-Three covers 3.00
... : Beginnings (5/06, $1.99) Prequel intro. to Ange and Dev; Gunnell-a; development art 2.50

SHUT UP AND DIE
Image Comics/Halloween: 1998 - No. 3, 1998 ($2.95,B&W, bi-monthly)

1-3: Hudnall-s 3.00

SICK (Sick Special #131) (Magazine) (Satire)
Feature Publ./Headline Publ./Crestwood Publ. Co./Hewfred Publ./ Pyramid Comm./Charlton Publ. No. 109 (4/76) on: Aug, 1960 - No. 134, Fall, 1980

	GD	VG	FN	VF	VF/NM	NM-
V1#1-Jack Paar photo on-c; Torres-a; Untouchables-s; Ben Hur movie photo-s	16	32	48	114	212	310
2-Torres-a; Elvis app.; Lenny Bruce app.	10	20	30	71	126	180
3-5-Torres-a in all. 3-Khruschev-c; Hitler-s. 4-Newhart-s; Castro-s; John Wayne. 5-JFK/Castro-c; Elvis pin-up; Hitler.	9	18	27	63	107	150
6-Photo-s of Ricky Nelson & Marilyn Monroe; JFK	9	18	27	65	113	160
V2#1,2,4-8 (#7,8,10-14): 1-(#7) Hitler-s; Brando photo-s. 2-(#8) Dick Clark-s. 4-(#10) Untouchables-c; Candid Camera-s. 5-(#11) Nixon-c; Lone Ranger-s; JFK-s. 6-(#12) Beatnik-c/s. 8-(#14) Liz Taylor pin-up, JFK-s; Dobie Gillis-s; Sinatra & Dean Martin photo-s	8	16	24	58	97	135
3-(#9) Marilyn Monroe/JFK-c; Kingston Trio-s	9	18	27	63	107	150
V3#1-7(#15-21): 1-(#15) JFK app.; Liz Tayor/Richard Burton-s. 2-(#16) Ben Casey/ Frankenstein-c/s; Hitler photo-s. 5-(#19) Nixon back-c/s; Sinatra photo-s. 6-(#20) 1st Huckleberry Fink-c	5	10	15	34	55	75
8-(#22) Cassius Clay vs. Liston-s; 1st Civil War Blackouts-/Pvt. Bo Reargard w/ Jack Davis-a	6	12	18	39	62	85
V4#1-5 (#23-27): Civil War Blackouts-/Pvt. Bo Reargard w/ Jack Davis-a in all. 1-(#23) Smokey Bear-c; Tarzan-s. 2-(#24) Goldwater & Paar-s; Castro-s. 3-(#25) Frankenstein-c; Cleopatra/Liz Taylor-s; Steve Reeves photo-s. 4-(#26) James Bond-s; Hitler-s. 5-(#27) Taylor/Burton pin-up; Sinatra, Martin, Andress, Ekberg photo-s	4	8	12	28	44	60
28,31,36,39: 31-Pink Panther movie photo-s; Burke's Law-s. 39-Westerns; Elizabeth Montgomery photo-s; Beat mag-s	4	8	12	24	37	50
29,34,37,38: 29-Beatles-c by Jack Davis. 34-Two pg. Beatles-s & photo pin-up. 37-Playboy parody issue. 38-Addams Family-s	4	8	12	28	44	60
30,32,35,40: 30-Beatles photo pin-up; James Bond photo-s. 32-Ian Fleming-s; LBJ-s; Tarzan-s. 35-Beatles cameo; Three Stooges parody. 40-Tarzan-s; Crosby/Hope-s; Beatles parody	5	10	15	30	48	65
33-Ringo Starr photo-c & spoof on "A Hard Day's Night"; inside-c has Beatles photos	6	12	18	41	66	90
41,50,51,53,54,60: 41-Sports Illustrated parody-c/s. 50-Mod issue; flip-c w/1967 calendar w/Bob Taylor-a. 51-Get Smart-s. 53-Beatles cameo; nudity panels. 54-Monkees-c. 60-TV Daniel Boone-s	3	6	9	20	30	40
42-Fighting American-c revised from Simon/Kirby-c; "Good girl" art by Sparling; profile on Bob Powell; superhero parodies	6	12	18	37	59	80

43-49,52,55-59: 43-Sneaker set begins by Sparling. 45-Has #44 on-c & #45 on inside;

Silke #1 © F5 Ent.

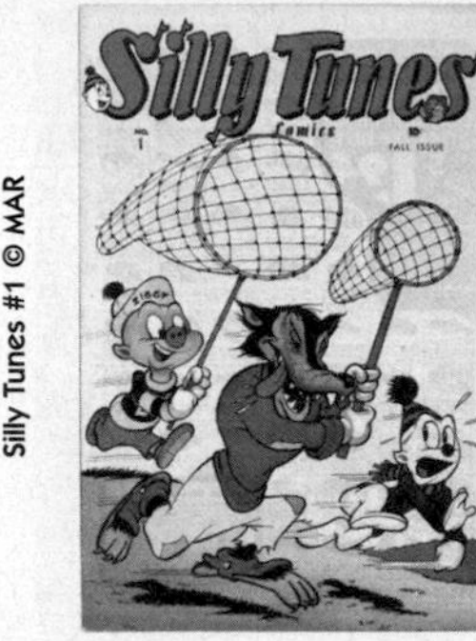

Silly Tunes #1 © MAR

Silver Age #1 © DC

GD VG FN VF VF/NM NM-
2.0 4.0 6.0 8.0 9.0 9.2

TV Westerns-s; Beatles cameo. 46-Hell's Angels-s; NY Mets-s. 47-UFO/Space-c. 49-Men's Adventure mag. parody issue; nudity. 52-LBJ-s. 55-Underground culture special. 56-Alfred E. Neuman-c; inventors issue. 58-Hippie issue-c/s. 59-Hippie-s 3 6 9 17 25 32

61-64,66-69,71,73,75-80: 63-Tiny Tim-c & poster; Monkees-s. 64-Flip-c. 66-Flip-c; Mod Squad-s. 69-Beatles cameo; Peter Sellers photo-s. 71-Flip-c; Clint Eastwood-s. 76-Nixon-s; Marcus Welby-s. 78-Ma Barker-s; Courtship of Eddie's Father-s; Abbie Hoffman-s 3 6 9 16 22 28

65,70,74: 65-Cassius Clay/Brando/J. Wayne-c; Johnny Carson-s. 70-(9/69) John & Yoko-c, 1/2 pg. story. 74-Clay, Agnew, Namath & others as superheroes-c/s; Easy Rider-c; Ghost and Mrs. Muir-s 3 6 9 17 25 32

72-(84 pgs.) Xmas issue w/2 pg. slick color poster; Tarzan-s; 2 pg. Superman & superheroes-s 4 8 12 22 34 45

81-85,87-95,98,99: 81-(2/71) Woody Allen photo-s. 85 Monster Mag. parody-s; Nixon-s w/Ringo & John cameo. 88-Klute photo-s; Nixon paper dolls page. 92-Lily Tomlin; Archie Bunker pin-up. 93-Woody Allen 2 4 6 13 18 22

86,96,97,100: 86-John & Yoko, Tiny Tim-c; Love Story movie photo-s. 96-Kung Fu-c; Mummy-s, Dracula & Frankenstein app. 97-Superman-s; 1974 Calendar; Charlie Brown & Snoopy pin-up. 100-Serpico-s; Cosell-s; Jacques Cousteau-s 3 6 9 14 19 24

101-103,105-114,116,119,120: 101-Three Musketeers-s; Dick Tracy-s. 102-Young Frankenstein-s. 103-Kojak-s; Evel Knievel-s. 105-Towering Inferno-s; Peanuts/Snoopy-s. 106-Cher-c/s. 10 7-Jaws-c/s. 108-Pink Panther-c/s; Archie-s. 109-Adam & Eve-s(nudity). 110-Welcome Back Kotter-s. 111 Sonny & Cher-s. 112-King Kong-c/s. 120-Star Trek-s 2 4 6 9 13 16

104,115,117,118: 104-Muhammad Ali-c/s. 115-Charlie's Angels-s. 117-Bionic Woman & Six Million $ Man-c/s; Cher D'Flower begins by Sparling (nudity). 118-Star Wars-s; Popeye-s 2 4 6 11 16 20

121-125,128-130: 122-Darth Vador-c. 123-Jaws II-s. 128-Superman-c/movie parody. 130-Alien movie-s 2 4 6 10 14 18

126,127: 126-(68 pgs.) Battlestar Galactica-c/s; Star Wars-s; Wonder Woman-s. 127-Mork & Mindy-s; Lord of the Rings-s 2 4 6 13 18 22

131-(1980 Special) Star Wars/Star Trek/Flash Gordon wraparound-c/s; Superman parody; Battlestar Galactica-s 3 6 9 14 19 24

132,133: 132-1980 Election-c/s; Apocalypse Now-s. 133-Star Trek-s; Chips-s; Superheroes page 2 4 6 13 18 22

134 (scarce)(68 pg. Giant)-Star Wars-c; Alien-s; WKRP-s; Mork & Mindy-s; Taxi-s; MASH-s 4 8 12 21 30 40

Annual 1- Birthday Annual (1966)-3 pg. Huckleberry Fink fold out 4 8 12 23 34 50

Annual 2- 7th Annual Yearbook (1967)-Davis-c, 2 pg. glossy poster insert 4 8 12 23 34 50

Annual 3 (1968) "Big Sick Laff-in" on-c (84 pgs.)-w/psychedelic posters; Frankenstein poster 3 6 9 18 27 35

Annual 1969 "Great Big Fat Annual Sick", 1969 "9th Year Annual Sick", 1970, 1971 3 6 9 17 25 32

Annual 12,13-(1972,1973, 84 pgs.) 13-Monster-c 3 6 9 17 25 32
Annual 14,15-(1974,1975, 84 pgs.) 14-Hitler photo-s 3 6 9 17 25 32
Annual 2-4 (1980) 2 4 6 9 13 16
Special 1 (1980) Buck Rogers-c/s; MASH-s 3 6 9 14 19 24
Special 2 (1980) Wraparound Star Wars:Empire Strikes Back-c; Charlie's Angels/Farrah-s; Rocky-s; plus reprints 3 6 9 14 19 24
Yearbook 15(1975, 84 pgs.) Paul Revere-c 3 6 9 16 23 30

NOTE: ***Davis*** *a-42, 87; c-22, 23, 25, 29, 31, 32.* ***Powell*** *a-7, 31, 57.* ***Simon*** *a-1-3, 10, 41, 42, 87, 99; c-1, 47, 57, 59, 69, 91, 95-97, 99, 100, 102, 107, 112.* ***Torres*** *a-1-3, 29, 31, 47, 49.* ***Tuska*** *a-14, 41-43. Civil War Blackouts-23, 24. #42 has biography of Bob Powell.*

SIDEKICK (Paul Jenkins'...)
Image Comics (Desperado): June, 2006 - No. 5, May, 2007 ($3.50, limited series)

1-5-Paul Jenkins-s/Chris Moreno-a 3.50
... Super Summer Sidekick Spectacular 1 (7/07, $2.99) 3.00
... Super Summer Sidekick Spectacular 2 (9/07, $3.50) 3.50

SIDEKICKS
Fanboy Ent., Inc.: Jun, 2000 - No. 3, Apr, 2001 ($2.75, B&W, lim. series)

1-3-J.Torres-s/Takesi Miyazawa-a. 3-Variant-c by Wieringo 2.75
...: Super Fun Summer Special (Oni Press, 7/03, $2.99) art by various incl. Wieringo 3.00
...: The Substitute (Oni Press, 7/02, $2.95) 3.00
...: The Transfer Student TPB (Oni Press, 6/02, $8.95, 9" x 6") r/#1-3 9.00
...: The Transfer Student TPB 2nd Ed. (10/03, $11.95, 9" x 6") r/#1-3; The Substitute 12.00

SIDESHOW
Avon Periodicals: 1949 (one-shot)

1-(Rare)-Similar to Bachelor's Diary 38 76 114 226 363 500

SIEGEL AND SHUSTER: DATELINE 1930s
Eclipse Comics: Nov, 1984 - No. 2, Sept, 1985 ($1.50/$1.75, Baxter paper #1)

1,2: 1-Unpublished samples of strips from the '30s; includes 'Interplanetary Police'; Shuster-c. 2 ($1.75, B&W)-unpublished strips; Shuster-c 2.50

SIGIL (Also see CrossGen Chronicles)
CrossGeneration Comics: Jul, 2000 - No. 43, Jan, 2004 ($2.95)

1-43: 1-Barbara Kesel-s/Ben & Ray Lai-a. 12-Waid-s begin. 21-Chuck Dixon-s begin 3.00
...: Mark of Power TPB (5/01, $19.95) r/#1-7; Moeller painted-c 20.00
...: The Marked Man Vol. 2 TPB (2002, $19.95) r/#8-14 20.00
...: The Lizard God Vol. 3 TPB (2002, $15.95) r/#15-20 16.00
Vol. 4: Hostage Planet (4/03, $15.95) r/#21-26 16.00
Vol. 5: Death Match (2003, $15.95) r/#27-32 10.00

SIGMA
Image Comics (WildStorm): March, 1996 - No. 3, June, 1996 ($2.50, limited series)

1-3: 1-"Fire From Heaven" prelude #2; Coker-a. 2-"Fire From Heaven" pt. 6. 3 "Fire From Heaven" pt. 14. 2.50

SILENT DRAGON
DC Comics (WildStorm): Sept, 2005 - No. 6, Feb, 2006 ($2.99, limited series)

1-6-Tokyo 2066 A.D.; Leinil Yu-a/c; Andy Diggle-s 3.00
TPB (2006, $19.99) r/series; sketch page 20.00

SILENT HILL: DEAD/ALIVE
IDW Publishing: Dec, 2005 - No. 5, Apr, 2006 ($3.99, limited series)

1-5-Stakal-a/Ciencin-s. 1-Four covers. 2-5-Two covers 4.00

SILENT HILL: DYING INSIDE
IDW Publishing: Feb, 2004 - No. 5, June, 2004 ($3.99, limited series)

1-5-Based on the Konami computer game. 1-Templesmith-a; Ashley Wood-c 4.00
...: Paint It Black (2/05, $7.49) Ciencin-s/Thomas-a 7.50
...: The Grinning Man 5/05, $7.49) Ciencin-s/Stakal-a 7.50
TPB (8/04, $19.99) r/#1-5; Ashley Wood-c 20.00

SILENT HILL: SINNER'S REWARD
IDW Publishing: Feb, 2008 - No. 4, Apr, 2008 ($3.99, limited series)

1-4-Waltz-s/Stamb-a 4.00

SILENT INVASION, THE
Rengade Press: Apr, 1986 - No.12, Mar, 1988 ($1.70/$2.00, B&W)

1-12-UFO sightings of the '50's 3.00
Book 1- reprints ($7.95) 8.00

SILENT MOBIUS
Viz Select Comics: 1991 - No. 5, 1992 ($4.95, color, squarebound, 44 pgs.)

1-5: Japanese stories translated to English 5.00

SILENT SCREAMERS (Based on the Aztech Toys figures)
Image Comics: Oct, 2000 ($4.95)

Nosferatu Issue - Alex Ross front & back-c 5.00

SILENT WAR
Marvel Comics: Mar, 2007 - No. 6, Aug, 2007 ($2.99, limited series)

1-6-Inhumans, Black Bolt and Fantastic Four app.; Hine-s/Irving-a/Watson-c 3.00
TPB (2007, $14.99) r/series 15.00

SILKE
Dark Horse Comics: Jan, 2001 - No. 4, Sept, 2001 ($2.95)

1-4-Tony Daniel-s/a 3.00

SILKEN GHOST
CrossGen Comics: June, 2003 - No. 5, Oct, 2003 ($2.95, limited series)

1-5-Dixon-s/Rosado-a 3.00
Traveler Vol. 1 (2003, $9.95) digest-sized reprint #1-5 10.00

SILLY PILLY (See Frank Luther's...)

SILLY SYMPHONIES (See Dell Giants)

SILLY TUNES
Timely Comics: Fall, 1945 - No. 7, June, 1947

1-Silly Seal, Ziggy Pig begin 22 44 66 127 204 280
2-(2/46) 14 28 42 76 108 140
3-7: 6-New logo 11 22 33 62 86 110

SILVER (See Lone Ranger's Famous Horse...)

SILVER AGE
DC Comics: July, 2000 ($3.95, limited series)

1-Waid-s/Dodson-a; "Silver Age" style x-over; JLA & villains switch bodies 4.00
...: Challengers of the Unknown ($2.50) Joe Kubert-c; vs. Chronos 2.50

Silver Kid Western #2 © Stanmor Pub.

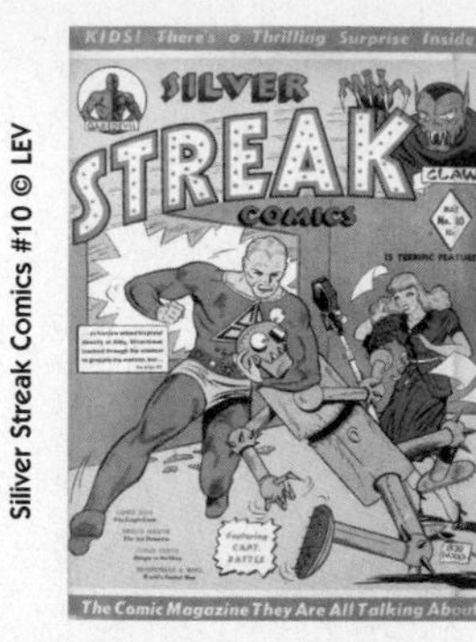

Silver Streak Comics #10 © LEV

Silver Surfer #142 © MAR

GD 2.0 | VG 4.0 | FN 6.0 | VF 8.0 | VF/NM 9.0 | NM- 9.2

...: Dial H For Hero ($2.50) Jim Mooney-c; vs. Martian Manhunter 2.50
...: Doom Patrol ($2.50) Ramona Fradon-c/Peyer-s 2.50
...: Flash ($2.50) Carmine Infantino-c; Kid Flash and Elongated Man app. 2.50
...: Green Lantern ($2.50) Gil Kane-c/Busiek-s/Anderson-a; vs. Sinestro 2.50
...: Justice League of America ($2.50) Ty Templeton-c 2.50
...: Showcase ($2.50) Dick Giordano-c/a; Batgirl, Adam Strange app. 2.50
... Secret Files ($4.95) Intro. Agamemno; short stories & profile pages 5.00
...: Teen Titans ($2.50) Nick Cardy-c; vs. Penguin, Mr. Element, Black Manta 2.50
...: The Brave and the Bold ($2.50) Jim Aparo-c; Batman & Metal Men 2.50
... 80-Page Giant ($5.95) Conclusion of x-over; "lost" Silver Age stories 6.00

SILVERBACK
Comico: 1989 - No. 3, 1990 ($2.50, color, limited series, mature readers)
1-3: Character from Grendel: Matt Wagner-a 3.00

SILVERBLADE
DC Comics: Sept, 1987 - No. 12, Sept, 1988
1-12: Colan-c/a in all 2.50

SILVERHAWKS
Star Comics/Marvel Comics #6: Aug, 1987 - No. 6, June, 1988 ($1.00)
1-6 3.00

SILVERHEELS
Pacific Comics: Dec, 1983 - No. 3, May, 1984 ($1.50)
1-3 2.50

SILVER KID WESTERN
Key/Stanmor Publications: Oct, 1954 - No. 5, July, 1955
1 10 20 30 54 72 90
2 6 12 18 31 38 45
3-5 6 12 18 28 34 40
I.W. Reprint #1,2-Severin-c: 1-r/#? 2-r/#1 2 4 6 8 11 14

SILVER SABLE AND THE WILD PACK (See Amazing Spider-Man #265 and Sable & Fortune)
Marvel Comics: June, 1992 - No. 35, Apr, 1995 ($1.25/$1.50)
1-($2.00)-Embossed & foil stamped-c; Spider-Man app. 3.00
2-35: 4,5-Dr. Doom-c/story. 6,7-Deathlok-c/story. 9-Origin Silver Sable. 10-Punisher-c/s. 15-Capt. America-c/s. 16,17-Intruders app. 18,19-Venom-c/s. 19-Siege of Darkness x-over. 23-Daredevil (in new costume) & Deadpool app. 24-Bound-in card sheet. Li'l Sylvie backup story. 25-($2.00, 52 pgs.)-Li'l Sylvie backup story 2.50

SILVER STAR (Also see Jack Kirby's...)
Pacific Comics: Feb, 1983 - No. 6, Jan, 1984 ($1.00)
1-6: 1-1st app. Last of the Viking Heroes. 1-5-Kirby-c/a. 2-Ditko-a 5.00
...: Graphite Edition TPB (TwoMorrows Publ., 3/06, $19.95) r/series in B&W including Kirby's original pencils; sketch pages; original screenplay 20.00
Jack Kirby's Silver Star, Volume 1 HC (Image Comics, 2007, $34.99) r/series in color; sketch pages; original screenplay 35.00

SILVER STREAK COMICS (Crime Does Not Pay #22 on)
Your Guide Publs. No. 1-7/New Friday Publs. No. 8-17/Comic House Publ./ Newsbook Publ.: Dec, 1939 - No. 21, May, 1942; No. 23, 1946; No # 22 (Silver logo-#1-5)
1-(Scarce)-Intro The Claw by Cole (r-/in Daredevil #21), Red Reeves, Boy Magician, & Captain Fearless; The Wasp, Mister Midnight begin; Spirit Man app. Silver metallic-c begin, end #5; Claw c-1,2,6-8 1075 2150 3225 7600 13,050 18,500
2-The Claw by Cole; Simon-c/a 388 776 1164 2638 4619 6600
3-1st app. & origin Silver Streak (2nd with lightning speed); Dickie Dean the Boy Inventor, Lance Hale, Ace Powers, Bill Wayne, & The Planet Patrol begin 329 658 987 2237 3919 5600
4-Sky Wolf begins; Silver Streak by Jack Cole (new costume); 1st app. Jackie, Lance Hale's sidekick 167 334 501 1052 1776 2500
5-Jack Cole c/a(2) 193 386 579 1216 2058 2900
6-(Scarce, 9/40)-Origin & 1st app. Daredevil (blue & yellow costume) by Jack Binder; The Claw returns; classic Cole Claw-c 1285 2570 3855 9600 17,300 25,000
7-Claw vs. Daredevil (new costume-blue & red) by Jack Cole & 3 other Cole stories (38 pgs.) 2nd app. Daredevil & 1st Daredevil-c 733 1466 2199 5278 9239 13,200
8-Claw vs. Daredevil by Cole; last Cole Silver Streak 329 658 987 2237 3919 5600
9-Claw vs. Daredevil by Cole 190 380 570 1197 2024 2850
10-Origin & 1st app. Captain Battle (5/41); Claw vs. Daredevil by Cole; Robot-c 170 340 510 1071 1811 2550
11-Intro. Mercury by Bob Wood, Silver Streak's sidekick; conclusion Claw vs. Daredevil by Rico; in 'Presto Martin,' 2nd pg., newspaper says 'Roussos does it again' 118 236 354 743 1259 1775
12-14: 13-Origin Thun-Dohr 85 170 255 536 906 1275
15, 17-Last Daredevil issue. 80 160 240 504 852 1200
16-Hitler-c 97 194 291 611 1031 1450
18-The Saint begins (2/42, 1st app.) by Leslie Charteris (see Movie Comics #2 by DC); The Saint-c 67 134 201 422 711 1000
19-21(1942): 20,21 have Wolverton's Scoop Scuttle. 21-Hitler app. in strip on cover 48 96 144 298 499 700
23(1946(An Atomic Comic)-Reprints; bondage-c 50 100 150 310 518 725
nn(11/46)(Newsbook Publ.)-R-/S.S. story from #4-7 plus 2 Captain Fearless stories, all in color; bondage/torture-c (scarce) 57 114 171 359 605 850
NOTE: ***Binder*** *c-3, 4, 13-15, 17.* ***Jack Cole*** *a-(Daredevil)-#6-10, (Dickie Dean)-#3-10, (Pirate Prince)-#7, (Silver Streak)-#4-8, nn; c-5 (Silver Streak), 6 (Claw), 7, 8 (Daredevil).* ***Everett*** *Red Reed begins #20.* ***Guardineer*** *a-#8-13.* ***Don Rico*** *a-11-17 (Daredevil); c-11, 12, 16.* ***Simon*** *a-3 (Silver Streak).* ***Bob Wood*** *a-9 (Silver Streak); c-9, 10. Captain Battle c-11, 13-15, 17. Claw c-#1, 2, 6-8. Daredevil c-7, 8, 12. Dickie Dean c-19. Ned of the Navy c-20 (war). The Saint c-18. Silver Streak c-5, 9, 10, 16, 23.*

SILVER SURFER (See Fantastic Four, Fantasy Masterpieces V2#1, Fireside Book Series, Marvel Graphic Novel, Marvel Presents #8, Marvel's Greatest Comics & Tales To Astonish #92)

SILVER SURFER, THE (Also see Essential Silver Surfer)
Marvel Comics Group: Aug, 1968 - No. 18, Sept, 1970; June, 1982
1-More detailed origin by John Buscema (p); The Watcher back-up stories begin (origin), end #7; (No. 1-7: 25¢, 68 pgs.) 40 80 120 319 597 875
2 17 34 51 126 233 340
3-1st app. Mephisto 15 30 45 111 206 300
4-Lower distribution; Thor & Loki app. 37 74 111 283 529 775
5-7-Last giant size. 5-The Stranger app.; Fantastic Four app. 6-Brunner inks. 7-(8/69)-Early cameo Frankenstein's monster (see X-Men #40) 11 22 33 79 140 200
8-10: 8-18-(15¢ issues) 9 18 27 63 107 150
11-13,15-18: 15-Silver Surfer vs. Human Torch; Fantastic Four app. 17-Nick Fury app. 18-Vs. The Inhumans; Kirby-c/a 8 16 24 56 93 130
14-Spider-Man x-over 12 24 36 87 156 225
... Omnibus Vol. 1 Hardcover (2007, $74.99, dustjacket) r/#1-18 re-colored with original letter pages, Fantastic Four Annual #5 & Not Brand Echh #13; Lee and Buscema bios 75.00
V2#1 (6/82, 52 pgs.)-Byrne-c/a 1 3 4 6 8 10
NOTE: ***Adkins*** *a-8-15i.* ***Brunner*** *a-6i.* ***J. Buscema*** *a-1-17p.* ***Colan*** *a-1-3p.* ***Reinman*** *a-1-4i. #1-14 were reprinted in Fantasy Masterpieces V2#1-14.*

SILVER SURFER (Volume 3) (See Marvel Graphic Novel #38)
Marvel Comics Group: V3#1, July, 1987 - No. 146, Nov, 1998
1-Double size ($1.25) 1 2 3 5 7 9
2-17: 15-Ron Lim-c/a begins (9/88) 4.00
18-33,39-43: 25,31 ($1.50, 52 pgs.). 25-Skrulls app. 32,39-No Ron Lim-c/a. 39-Alan Grant scripts 3.00
34-Thanos returns (cameo); Starlin scripts begin 5.00
35-38: 35-1st full Thanos app. in Silver Surfer (3/90); reintro Drax the Destroyer on last pg. (cameo). 36-Recaps history of Thanos; Capt. Marvel & Warlock app. in recap. 37-1st full app. Drax the Destroyer; Drax-c. 38-Silver Surfer battles Thanos 6.00
44,45,49-Thanos stories (c-44,45) 4.00
46-48: 46-Return of Adam Warlock (2/91); re-intro Gamora & Pip the Troll. 47-Warlock battles Drax. 48-Last Starlin scripts (also #50) 4.00
50-($1.50, 52 pgs.)-Embossed & silver foil-c; Silver Surfer has brief battle w/Thanos; story cont'd in Infinity Gauntlet #1 1 2 3 4 5 7
50-2nd & 3rd printings 2.50
51-59: 51-53: Infinity Gauntlet x-over . 54-57: Infinity Gauntlet x-overs. 54-Rhino app. 55,56-Thanos-c & app. 57-Thanos-c & cameo. 58,59-Infinity Gauntlet x-overs; 58-Lim-c only. 59-Thanos battles Silver Surfer-c/story; Thanos joins 3.00
60-74,76-99,101-124,126-139: 63-Capt. Marvel app. 67-69-Infinity War x-overs. 76-78-Jack of Hearts-c/s. 83-85-Infinity Crusade x-over; 83,84-Thanos cameo. 85-Storm, Wonder Man x-over. 86-Thor-c/s. 87-Dr. Strange & Warlock app. 88-Thanos-c/s. 82 (52 pgs.). 95-FF app. 96-Hulk & FF app. 97-Terrax & Nova app. 101-Bound in card sheet. 106-Doc Doom app. 121-Quasar & Beta Ray Bill app. 123-w/card insert; begin Garney-a. 126-Dr. Strange-c/app. 128-Spider-Man & Daredevil-c/app. 138-Thing-c 2.50
75-($2.50, 52 pgs.)-Embossed foil-c; Lim-c/a 3.00
100 ($2.25, 52 pgs.)-Wraparound-c 2.50
100 ($3.95, 52 pgs.)-Enhanced-c 4.00
125 ($2.95)-Wraparound-c; Vs. Hulk-c/app. 3.00
140-146: 140-142,144,145-Muth-c/a. 143,146-Cowan-a. 146-Last issue 2.50
#(-1) Flashback (7/97) 2.50
Annual 1 (1988, $1.75)-Evolutionary War app.; 1st Ron Lim-a on Silver Surfer (20 pg. back-up story & pin-ups) 5.00
Annual 2-7 ('89-'94, 68 pgs.): 2-Atlantis Attacks. 4-3 pg. origin story; Silver Surfer battles Guardians of the Galaxy. 5-Return of the Defenders, part 3; Lim-c/a (3 pgs. of pin-ups only). 6-Polybagged w/trading card; 1st app. Legacy; card is by Lim/Austin 3.00
Annual '97 ($2.99), .../Thor Annual '98 ($2.99) 3.00
Ashcan (1995, 75¢) reprints part of V1#3; Lim-c 2.50
...Dangerous Artifacts-(1996, $3.95)-Ron Marz scripts; Galactus-c/app. 4.00
Graphic Novel (1988, HC, $14.95) Judgment Day; Lee-s/Buscema-a 15.00
The Enslavers Graphic Novel (1990, $16.95) 17.00

Simon Dark #7 © DC

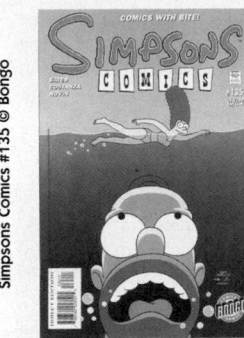

Simpsons Comics #135 © Bongo

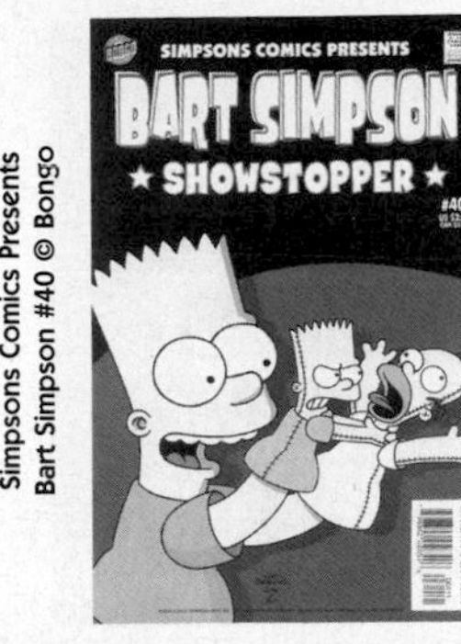

Simpsons Comics Presents Bart Simpson #40 © Bongo

	GD	VG	FN	VF	VF/NM	NM-
	2.0	4.0	6.0	8.0	9.0	9.2

Homecoming Graphic Novel (1991, $12.95, softcover) Starlin-s 15.00
Inner Demons TPB (4/98, $3.50)r/#123,125,126 3.50
...: Rebirth of Thanos TPB (2006, $24.99) r/#34-38, Thanos Quest #1,2; Logan's Run #6 25.00
...: The First Coming of Galactus nn (11/92, $5.95, 68 pgs.)-Reprints Fantastic Four #48-50 with new Lim-c 6.00
Wizard 1/2 2 4 6 9 12 15
NOTE: *Austin c(i)-7, 8, 71, 73, 74, 76, 79. Cowan a-143,146. Cully Hamner a-83p. Ron Lim a(p)-15-31, 33-38, 40-55, (56, 57-part-p), 60-65, 73-82, Annual 2, 4; c(p)-15-31, 32-38, 40-84, 86-92, Annual 2, 4-6. Muth c/a-140-142,144,145. M. Rogers a-1-10, 12, 19, 21; c-1-9, 11, 12, 21.*

SILVER SURFER (Volume 4)
Marvel Comics: Sept, 2003 - No. 14, Dec, 2004 ($2.25/$2.99)
1-6: 1-Milx-a; Jusko-c. 2-Jae Lee-c 2.50
7-14-($2.99) 3.00
...Vol. 1: Communion (2004, $14.99) r/#1-6 15.00

SILVER SURFER, THE
Marvel Comics (Epic): Dec, 1988 - No. 2, Jan, 1989 ($1.00, lim. series)
1,2: By Stan Lee scripts & Moebius-c/a 4.00
HC (1988, $19.95, dust jacket) r/#1,2; "Making Of" text section and sketch pages 30.00
....: Parable ('98, $5.99) r/#1&2 6.00

SILVER SURFER: IN THY NAME
Marvel Comics: Jan, 2008 - No. 4, Apr, 2008 ($2.99, limited series)
1-4-Spurrier-s/Huat-a. 1-Turner-c. 2-Dell'Otto-c. 3-Paul Pope-c. 4-Galactus app. 3.00

SILVER SURFER: LOFTIER THAN MORTALS
Marvel Comics: Oct, 1999 - No. 2, Oct, 1999 ($2.50, limited series)
1,2-Remix of Fantastic Four #57-60; Velluto-a 2.50

SILVER SURFER: REQUIEM
Marvel Comics: July, 2007 - No. 4, Oct, 2007 ($3.99, limited series)
1-4-Straczynski-s/Ribic-a. 1-Origin retold; Fantastic Four app. 4.00
HC (2007, $19.99) r/#1-4, Ribic cover sketches 20.00

SILVER SURFER/SUPERMAN
Marvel Comics: 1996 ($5.95,one-shot)
1-Perez-s/Lim-c/a(p) 6.00

SILVER SURFER VS. DRACULA
Marvel Comics: Feb, 1994 ($1.75, one-shot)
1-r/Tomb of Dracula #50; Everett Vampire-r/Venus #19; Howard the Duck back-up by Brunner; Lim-c(p) 2.50

SILVER SURFER/WARLOCK: RESURRECTION
Marvel Comics: Mar, 1993 - No. 4, June, 1993 ($2.50, limited series)
1-4: Starlin-c/a & scripts 2.50

SILVER SURFER/WEAPON ZERO
Marvel Comics: Apr, 1997 ($2.95, one-shot)
1-"Devil's Reign" pt. 8 3.00

SILVERTIP (Max Brand)
Dell Publishing Co.: No. 491, Aug, 1953 - No. 898, May, 1958

	GD	VG	FN	VF	VF/NM	NM-
Four Color 491 (#1); all painted-c	8	16	24	52	86	120
Four Color 572,608,637,667,731,789,898-Kinstler-a	5	10	15	30	48	65
Four Color 835	5	10	15	30	48	65

SIMON DARK
DC Comics: Dec, 2007 - Present ($2.99)
1-Intro. Simon Dark; Steve Niles-s/Scott Hampton-a/c 4.00
1-Second printing with full face variant cover 3.00
2-10 3.00

SIMPSONS COMICS (See Bartman, Futurama, Itchy & Scratchy & Radioactive Man)
Bongo Comics Group: 1993 - Present ($1.95/$2.50/$2.99)
1-($2.25)-FF#1-c swipe; pull-out poster; flip book 1 2 3 5 6 8
2-5: 2-Patty & Selma flip-c/sty. 3-Krusty, Agent of K.L.O.W.N. flip-c/story. 4-Infinity-c; flip-c of Busman #1; w/trading card. 5-Wraparound-c w/trading card 5.00
6-40: All Flip books. 6-w/Chief Wiggum's "Crime Comics". 7-w/"McBain Comics". 8-w/"Edna, Queen of the Congo". 9-w/"Barney Gumble". 10-w/"Apu". 11-w/"Homer". 12-w/"White Knuckled War Stories". 13-w/"Jimbo Jones' Wedgie Comics". 14-w/"Grampa". 15-w/"Itchy & Scratchy". 16-w/"Bongo Grab Bag". 17-w/"Headlight Comics". 18-w/"Milhouse". 19,20-w/"Roswell". 21,22-w/"Roswell". 23-w/"Hellfire Comics". 24-w/"Lil' Homey". 36-39-Flip book w/Radioactive Man 4.00
41-49,51-99: 43-Flip book w/Poochie. 52-Dini-s. 77-Dixon-s. 85-Begin $2.99-c 3.00
50-($5.95) Wraparound-c; 80 pgs.; square-bound 1 2 3 4 5 7
100-($6.99) 100 pgs.; square-bound; clip issue of past highlights 7.00
101-146: 102-Barks Ducks homage. 117-Hank Scorpio app. 122-Archie spoof. 132-Movie poster enclosed. 132-133-Two-parter. 144-Flying Hellfish flashback 3.00
... A Go-Go (1999, $11.95)-r/#32-35; ...Big Bonanza (1998, $11.95)-r/#28-31, ...Extravaganza (1994, $10.00)-r/#1-4; infinity-c, ...On Parade (1998, $11.95)-r/#24-27, ...Simpsorama (1996, $10.95)-r/#11-14 12.00
Simpsons Classics 1-17 (2004-Present, $3.99, magazine-size, quarterly) reprints 4.00
Simpsons Comics Barn Burner ('04, $14.95) r/#57-61,63 15.00
Simpsons Comics Beach Blanket Bongo ('07, $14.95) r/#71-75,77 15.00
Simpsons Comics Belly Buster ('04, $14.95) r/#49,51,53-56 15.00
Simpsons Comics Jam-Packed Jamboree ('06, $14.95) r/#64-69 15.00
Simpsons Comics Madness ('03, $14.95) r/#43-48 15.00
Simpsons Comics Royale ('01, $14.95) r/various Bongo issues 15.00
Simpsons Comics Treasure Trove ('08, $3.99, 6" x 8") r/various Bongo issues 4.00
Simpsons Summer Shindig ('07, '08, $4.99) 1,2-Anthology. 1-Batman/Ripken insert 5.00
Simpsons Winter Wing Ding ('06, '08 $4.99) 1,2-Holiday anthology. 1-Dini-s 5.00

SIMPSONS COMICS AND STORIES
Welsh Publishing Group: 1993 ($2.95, one-shot)
1-(Direct Sale)-Polybagged w/Bartman poster 6.00
1-(Newsstand Edition)-Without poster 4.00

SIMPSONS COMICS PRESENTS BART SIMPSON
Bongo Comics Group: 2000 - Present ($2.50/$2.99, quarterly)
1-43: 7-9-Dan DeCarlo-layouts. 13-Begin $2.99-c. 17,37-Bartman app. 3.00
The Big Book of Bart Simpson TPB (2002, $12.95) r/#1-4 13.00
The Big Bad Book of Bart Simpson TPB (2003, $12.95) r/#5-8 13.00
The Big Bratty Book of Bart Simpson TPB (2004, $12.95) r/#9-12 13.00
The Big Beefy Book of Bart Simpson TPB (2005, $13.95) r/#13-16 14.00
The Big Bouncy Book of Bart Simpson TPB (2006, $13.95) r/#17-20 14.00
The Big Beastly Book of Bart Simpson TPB (2007, $14.95) r/#21-24 15.00
The Big Brilliant Book of Bart Simpson TPB (2008, $14.95) r/#25-28 15.00

SIMPSONS FUTURAMA CROSSOVER CRISIS II (TV) (Also see Futurama/Simpsons Infinitely Secret Crossover Crisis)
Bongo Comics: 2005 - No. 2, 2005 ($3.00, limited series)
1,2-The Professor brings the Simpsons' Springfield crew to the 31st century 3.00

SIMPSONS SUPER SPECTACULAR (TV)
Bongo Comics: 2006 - Present ($2.99)
1-7: 2-Bartman, Stretch Dude and The Cupcake Kid team up; back-up story Brereton-a. 5-Ramona Fradon-a on Metamorpho spoof 3.00

SIMULATORS, THE
Neatly Chiseled Features: 1991 ($2.50, stiff-c)
1-Super hero group 2.50

SINBAD, JR (TV Cartoon)
Dell Publishing Co.: Sept-Nov, 1965 - No. 3, May, 1966

	GD	VG	FN	VF	VF/NM	NM-
1	4	8	12	24	37	50
2,3	3	6	9	18	27	35

SIN CITY (See Dark Horse Presents, A Decade of Dark Horse, & San Diego Comic Con Comics #2,4)
Dark Horse Comics (Legend)
TPB ($15.00) Reprints early DHP stories 15.00
Booze, Broads & Bullets TPB ($15.00) 15.00

SIN CITY (FRANK MILLER'S...) (Reissued TPBs to coincide with the April 2005 movie)
Dark Horse Books: Feb, 2005 ($17.00/$19.00, 6" x 9" format with new Miller covers)
Volume 1: The Hard Goodbye ($17.00) reprints stories from Dark Horse Presents #51-62 and DHP Fifth Anniv. Special; covers and publicity pieces 17.00
Volume 2: A Dame to Kill For ($17.00) r/Sin City: A Dame to Kill For #1-6 17.00
Volume 3: The Big Fat Kill ($17.00) r/Sin City: The Big Fat Kill #1-5; pin-up gallery 17.00
Volume 4: That Yellow Bastard ($19.00) r/Sin City: That Yellow Bastard #1-6; pin-up gallery by Mike Allred, Kyle Baker, Jeff Smith and Bruce Timm; cover gallery 19.00
Volume 5: Family Values ($12.00) r/Sin City: Family Values GN 12.00
Volume 6: Booze, Broads & Bullets ($15.00) r/Sin City: The Babe Wore Red and Other Stories; Silent Night; story from A Decade of Dark Horse; Lost Lonely & Lethal; Sex & Violence; and Just Another Saturday Night 15.00
Volume 7: Hell and Back ($28.00) r/Sin City: Hell and Back #1-9; pin-up gallery 28.00

SIN CITY: A DAME TO KILL FOR
Dark Horse Comics (Legend): Nov, 1993 - No. 6, May, 1994 ($2.95, B&W, limited series)
1-6: Frank Miller-c/a & story in all. 1-1st app. Dwight. 6.00
Limited Edition Hardcover 85.00
Hardcover 25.00
TPB ($15.00) 15.00

SIN CITY: FAMILY VALUES

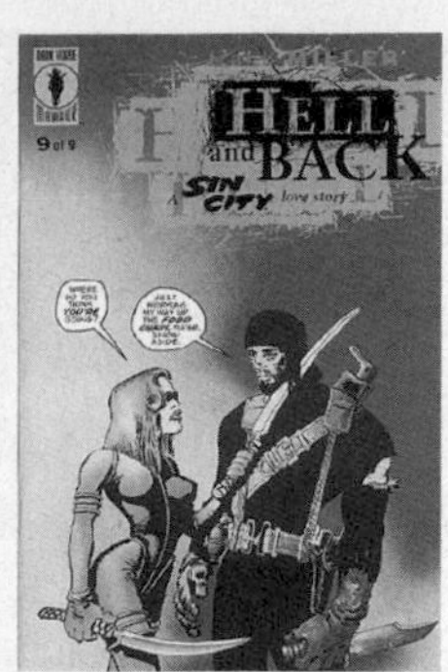

Sin City: Hell and Back #9 © Frank Miller

Single Series #5 © UFS

Six Gun Heroes #4 © FAW

	GD	VG	FN	VF	VF/NM	NM-
	2.0	4.0	6.0	8.0	9.0	9.2

Dark Horse Comics (Legend): Oct, 1997 ($10.00, B&W, squarebound, one-shot)
nn-Miller-c/a & story 10.00
Limited Edition Hardcover 75.00

SIN CITY: HELL AND BACK
Dark Horse (Maverick): Jul, 1999 - No. 9 ($2.95/$4.95, B&W, limited series)
1-8-Miller-c/a & story. 7-Color 4.00
9-($4.95) 6.00

SIN CITY: JUST ANOTHER SATURDAY NIGHT
Dark Horse Comics (Legend): Aug, 1997 (Wizard 1/2 offer, B&W, one-shot)

	GD	VG	FN	VF	VF/NM	NM-
1/2-Miller-c/a & story	1	2	3	5	6	8

nn (10/98, $2.50) r/#1/2 2.50

SIN CITY: LOST, LONELY & LETHAL
Dark Horse Comics (Legend): Dec, 1996 ($2.95, B&W and blue, one-shot)
nn-Miller-c/s/a; w/pin-ups 5.00

SIN CITY: SEX AND VIOLENCE
Dark Horse Comics (Legend): Mar, 1997 ($2.95, B&W and blue, one-shot)
nn-Miller-c/a & story 5.00

SIN CITY: SILENT NIGHT
Dark Horse Comics (Legend): Dec, 1995 ($2.95, B&W, one-shot)
1-Miller-c/a & story; Marv app. 5.00

SIN CITY: THAT YELLOW BASTARD (Second Ed. TPB listed under Sin City (Frank Miller's...)
Dark Horse Comics (Legend): Feb, 1996 - No. 6, July, 1996 ($2.95/$3.50, B&W and yellow, limited series)
1-5: Miller-c/a & story in all. 1-1st app. Hartigan. 5.00
6-($3.50) Error & corrected 5.00
Limited Edition Hardcover 25.00
TPB ($15.00) 15.00

SIN CITY: THE BABE WORE RED AND OTHER STORIES
Dark Horse Comics (Legend): Nov, 1994 ($2.95, B&W and red, one-shot)
1-r/serial run in Previews as well as other stories; Miller-c/a & scripts; Dwight app. 4.00

SIN CITY: THE BIG FAT KILL (Second Edition TPB listed under Sin City (Frank Miller's...)
Dark Horse Comics (Legend): Nov, 1994 - No. 5, Mar, 1995 ($2.95, B&W, limited series)
1-5-Miller story & art in all; Dwight app. 5.00
Hardcover 25.00
TPB ($15.00) 15.00

SIN CITY: THE FRANK MILLER LIBRARY
Dark Horse Books: Set 1, Nov, 2005; Set 2, Mar, 2006 ($150, slipcased hardcover, 8" x 12")
Set 1 - Individual hardcovers for Volume 1: The Hard Goodbye, Volume 2: A Dame to Kill For, Volume 3: The Big Fat Kill, Volume 4: That Yellow Bastard; new red foil stamped covers; slipcase box is black with red foil graphics 150.00
Set 2 - Individual hardcovers for Volume 5: Family Values, Volume 6: Booze, Broads & Bullets, Volume 7: Hell and Back, new red foil stamped covers; The Art of Sin City red hardcover; slipcase box is black with red foil graphics 150.00

SINDBAD (See Capt. Sindbad under Movie Comics, and Fantastic Voyages of Sindbad)

SINGING GUNS (See Fawcett Movie Comics)

SINGLE SERIES (Comics on Parade #30 on)(Also see John Hix...)
United Features Syndicate: 1938 - No. 28, 1942 (All 68 pgs.)

Note: See Individual Alphabetical Listings for prices

1-Captain and the Kids (#1)
2-Broncho Bill (1939) (#1)
3-Ella Cinders (1939)
4-Li'l Abner (1939) (#1)
5-Fritzi Ritz (#1)
6-Jim Hardy by Dick Moores (#1)
7-Frankie Doodle
8-Peter Pat (On sale 7/14/39)
9-Strange As It Seems
10-Little Mary Mixup
11-Mr. and Mrs. Beans
12-Joe Jinks
13-Looy Dot Dope
14-Billy Make Believe
15-How It Began (1939)
16-Illustrated Gags (1940)-Has ad for Captain and the Kids #1 reprint listed below
17-Danny Dingle
18-Li'l Abner (#2 on-c)
19-Broncho Bill (#2 on-c)
20-Tarzan by Hal Foster
21-Ella Cinders (#2 on-c; on sale 3/19/40)
22-Iron Vic
23-Tailspin Tommy by Hal Forrest (#1)
24-Alice in Wonderland (#1)
25-Abbie and Slats
26-Little Mary Mixup (#2 on-c, 1940)
27-Jim Hardy by Dick Moores (1942)
28-Ella Cinders & Abbie and Slats (1942)
1-Captain and the Kids (1939 reprint)-2nd Edition
1-Fritzi Ritz (1939 reprint)-2nd ed.

NOTE: *Some issues given away at the 1939-40 New York World's Fair (#6).*

	GD	VG	FN	VF	VF/NM	NM-
	2.0	4.0	6.0	8.0	9.0	9.2

SINGULARITY 7
IDW Publ.: July, 2004 - No. 4, Oct, 2004 ($3.99, limited series)
1-4-Templesmith-s/a 4.00

SINISTER HOUSE OF SECRET LOVE, THE (Becomes Secrets of Sinister House No. 5 on)
National Periodical Publ.: Oct-Nov, 1971 - No. 4, Apr-May, 1972

	GD	VG	FN	VF	VF/NM	NM-
1 (all 52 pgs.)	15	30	45	111	206	300
2,4: 2-Jeff Jones-c	8	16	24	56	93	130
3-Toth-a; greytone-c	8	16	24	58	97	135

SINS OF YOUTH... (Also see Young Justice: Sins of Youth)
DC Comics: May 2000 ($4.95/$2.50, limited crossover series)
Secret Files 1 ($4.95) Short stories and profile pages; Nauck-c 5.00
...Aquaboy/Lagoon Man; Batboy and Robin; JLA Jr.; Kid Flash/Impulse; Starwoman and the JSA, Superman, Jr./Superboy, Sr.; The Secret/ Deadboy, Wonder Girls ($2.50-c) Old and young heroes switch ages 2.50

SIR CHARLES BARKLEY AND THE REFEREE MURDERS
Hamilton Comics: 1993 ($9.95, 8-1/2" x 11", 52 pgs.)

	GD	VG	FN	VF	VF/NM	NM-
nn-Photo-c; Sports fantasy comic book fiction (uses real names of NBA superstars). Script by Alan Dean Foster, art by Joe Staton. Comes with bound-in sheet of 35 gummed "Moods of Charles Barkley" stamps. Photo/story on Barkley	2	4	6	8	10	12
Special Edition of 100 copies for charity signed on an affixed book plate by Barkley, Foster & Staton						150.00
Ashcan edition given away to dealers, distributors & promoters (low distribution). Four pages in color, balance of story in b&w	2	4	6	8	10	12

SIREN (Also see Eliminator & Ultraforce)
Malibu Comics (Ultraverse): Sept, 1995 - No. 3, Dec, 1995 ($1.50)
Infinity, 1-3: Infinity-Black-c & painted-c exists. 1-Regular-c & painted-c; War Machine app. 2-Flip book w/Phoenix Resurrection Pt. 3 2.50
Special 1-(2/96, $1.95, 28 pgs.)-Origin Siren; Marvel Comic's Juggernaut-c/app. 2.50

SIREN: SHAPES
Image Comics: May, 1998 - No. 3, Nov, 1998 ($2.95, B&W, limited series)
1-3-J. Torres -s 3.00

SIR LANCELOT (TV)
Dell Publishing Co.: No. 606, Dec, 1954 - No. 775, Mar, 1957

	GD	VG	FN	VF	VF/NM	NM-
Four Color 606 (not TV)	7	14	21	49	80	110
Four Color 775(...and Brian)-Buscema-a; photo-c	9	18	27	65	113	160

SIR WALTER RALEIGH (Movie)
Dell Publishing Co.: May, 1955 (Based on movie "The Virgin Queen")

	GD	VG	FN	VF	VF/NM	NM-
Four Color 644-Photo-c	7	14	21	45	73	100

SISTERHOOD OF STEEL (See Eclipse Graphic Adventure Novel #13)
Marvel Comics (Epic Comics): Dec, 1984 -No. 8, Feb, 1986 ($1.50, Baxter paper, mature)
1-8 3.00

SIX
Image Comics: Aug, 2004 ($5.95, B&W)
1-Oeming-s/c; Beavers-a 6.00

6 BLACK HORSES (See Movie Classics)

SIX FROM SIRIUS
Marvel Comics (Epic Comics): July, 1984 - No. 4, Oct, 1984 ($1.50, limited series, mature)
1-4: Moench scripts; Gulacy-c/a in all 2.50

SIX FROM SIRIUS II
Marvel Comics (Epic Comics): Feb, 1986 - No. 4, May, 1986 ($1.50, limited series, mature)
1-4: Moench scripts; Gulacy-c/a in all 2.50

SIX-GUN HEROES
Fawcett Publications: March, 1950 - No. 23, Nov, 1953 (Photo-c #1-23)

	GD	VG	FN	VF	VF/NM	NM-
1-Rocky Lane, Hopalong Cassidy, Smiley Burnette begin (same date as Smiley Burnette #1)	41	82	123	256	416	575
2	23	46	69	132	209	285
3-5: 5-Lash LaRue begins	16	32	48	94	147	200
6-15	14	28	42	80	115	150
16-22: 17-Last Smiley Burnette. 18-Monte Hale begins	12	24	36	67	94	120
23-Last Fawcett issue	13	26	39	72	101	130

NOTE: *Hopalong Cassidy photo c-1-3. Monte Hale photo c-18. Rocky Lane photo c-4, 5, 7, 9, 11, 13, 15, 17, 20, 21, 23. Lash LaRue photo c-6, 8, 10, 12, 14, 16, 19, 22.*

SIX-GUN HEROES (Cont'd from Fawcett; Gunmasters #84 on) (See Blue Bird)
Charlton Comics: No. 24, Jan, 1954 - No. 83, Mar-Apr, 1965 (All Vol. 4)

Six Million Dollar Man #1 © CC

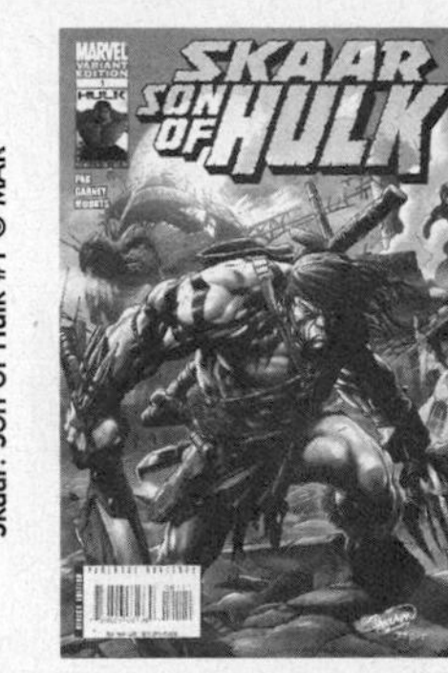

Skaar: Son of Hulk #1 © MAR

Skrulls! #1 © MAR

	GD 2.0	VG 4.0	FN 6.0	VF 8.0	VF/NM 9.0	NM- 9.2
24-Lash LaRue, Hopalong Cassidy, Rocky Lane & Tex Ritter begin; photo-c	19	38	57	109	172	235
25	11	22	33	64	90	115
26-30: 26-Rod Cameron story. 28-Tom Mix begins?	10	20	30	56	76	95
31-40: 38-Jingles & Wild Bill Hickok (TV)	9	18	27	50	65	80
41-46,48,50	9	18	27	47	61	75
47-Williamson-a, 2 pgs; Torres-a	9	18	27	50	65	80
49-Williamson-a (5 pgs.)	10	20	30	56	76	95
51-56,58-60: 58-Gunmaster app.	4	8	12	24	37	50
57-Origin & 1st app. Gunmaster	5	10	15	30	48	65
61,63-70	3	6	9	18	27	35
62-Origin Gunmaster	4	8	12	22	34	45
71-75,77,78,80-83	3	6	9	14	19	24
76,79: 76-Gunmaster begins. 79-1st app. & origin of Bullet, the Gun-Boy	3	6	9	16	22	28

SIXGUN RANCH (See Luke Short & Four Color #580)

SIX-GUN WESTERN
Atlas Comics (CDS): Jan, 1957 - No. 4, July, 1957

	GD	VG	FN	VF	VF/NM	NM-
1-Crandall-a; two Williamson text illos	18	36	54	105	165	225
2,3-Williamson-a in both	14	28	42	80	115	150
4-Woodbridge-a	10	20	30	58	79	100

NOTE: ***Ayers** a-2, 3. **Maneely** a-1; c-2, 3. **Orlando** a-2. **Pakula** a-2. **Powell** a-3. **Romita** a-1, 4. **Severin** c-1, 4. **Shores** a-2.*

SIX MILLION DOLLAR MAN, THE (TV)
Charlton Comics: 6/76 - No. 4, 12/76; No. 5, 10/77; No. 6, 2/78 - No. 9, 6/78

	GD	VG	FN	VF	VF/NM	NM-
1-Staton-c/a; Lee Majors photo on-c	3	6	9	14	20	25
2-9: 2-Neal Adams-c; Staton-a	2	4	6	10	14	18

SIX MILLION DOLLAR MAN, THE (TV)(Magazine)
Charlton Comics: July, 1976 - No. 7, Nov, 1977 (B&W)

	GD	VG	FN	VF	VF/NM	NM-
1-Neal Adams-c/a	3	6	9	18	27	35
2-Neal Adams-c	3	6	9	14	20	25
3-N. Adams part inks; Chaykin-a	2	4	6	11	16	20
4-7	2	4	6	9	13	16

SIX STRING SAMURAI
Awesome-Hyperwerks: Sept, 1998 ($2.95)

	GD	VG	FN	VF	VF/NM	NM-
1-Stinsman & Fraga-a						3.00

67 SECONDS
Marvel Comics (Epic Comics): 1992 ($15.95, 54 pgs., graphic novel)

	GD	VG	FN	VF	VF/NM	NM-
nn-James Robinson scripts; Steve Yeowell-c/a	2	4	6	11	14	18

SKAAR: SON OF HULK (Also see World War Hulk crossover)
Marvel Comics: Aug, 2008 - Present ($2.99)

	GD	VG	FN	VF	VF/NM	NM-
1-Garney-a/Pak-s; 2 covers by Pagulayan and Julie Bell; origin						4.00
1-Second printing - 2 covers by Garney and Hulk movie image						3.00
1-Third printing - Garney sketch variant-c						3.00
2,3-Back-up story with Guice-a						3.00
... Presents - Savage World of Sakaar (11/08, $3.99) Pak-s/art by various; Garney-c						4.00

SKATEMAN
Pacific Comics: Nov, 1983 (Baxter paper, one-shot)

	GD	VG	FN	VF	VF/NM	NM-
1-Adams-c/a						4.00

SKELETON HAND (...In Secrets of the Supernatural)
American Comics Gr. (B&M Dist. Co.): Sept-Oct, 1952 - No. 6, Jul-Aug, 1953

	GD	VG	FN	VF	VF/NM	NM-
1	45	90	135	279	465	650
2	33	66	99	192	309	425
3-6	26	52	78	152	244	335

SKELETON KEY
Amaze Ink: July, 1995 - No. 30, Jan, 1998 ($1.25/$1.50/$1.75, B&W)

	GD	VG	FN	VF	VF/NM	NM-
1-30						3.00
Special #1 (2/98, $4.95) Unpublished short stories						5.00
Sugar Kat Special (10/98, $2.95) Halloween stories						3.00
Beyond The Threshold TPB (6/96. $11.95)-r/#1-6						12.00
Cats and Dogs TPB ($12.95)-r/#25-30						13.00
The Celestial Calendar TPB ($19.95)-r/#7-18						20.00
Telling Tales TPB ($12.95)-r/#19-24						13.00

SKELETON KEY (Volume 2)
Amaze Ink: 1999 - No. 4, 1999 ($2.95, B&W)

	GD	VG	FN	VF	VF/NM	NM-
1-4-Andrew Watson-s/a						3.00

SKELETON WARRIORS
Marvel Comics: Apr, 1995 - No. 4, July, 1995 ($1.50)

	GD	VG	FN	VF	VF/NM	NM-
1-4: Based on animated series.						2.50

SKIN GRAFT: THE ADVENTURES OF A TATTOOED MAN
DC Comics (Vertigo): July, 1993 - No. 4, Oct, 1993 ($2.50, lim. series, mature)

	GD	VG	FN	VF	VF/NM	NM-
1-4						2.50

SKINWALKER
Oni Press: May, 2002 - No. 4, Sept, 2002 ($2.95, limited series)

	GD	VG	FN	VF	VF/NM	NM-
1-4-Hurtt & Dela Cruz-a; Talon-c						3.00
1-(5/05) Free Comic Book Day Edition						2.50

SKI PARTY (See Movie Classics)

SKREEMER
DC Comics: May, 1989 - No. 6, Oct, 1989 ($2.00, limited series, mature)

	GD	VG	FN	VF	VF/NM	NM-
1-6: Contains graphic violence; Milligan-s						2.50
TPB (2002, $19.95) r/#1-6						20.00

SKRULL KILL KREW
Marvel Comics: Sept, 1995 - No. 5, Dec, 1995 ($2.95, limited series)

	GD	VG	FN	VF	VF/NM	NM-
1-5: Grant Morrison & Mark Millar scripts; Steve Yeowell-a. 2,3-Cap America app.						3.00
TPB (2006, $16.99) r/#1-5						17.00

SKRULLS! (Tie-in to Secret Invasion crossover)
Marvel Comics: 2008 ($4.99, one-shot)

	GD	VG	FN	VF	VF/NM	NM-
1-Skrull history, profiles of Skrulls, their allies & foes; checklist of appearances; Horn-c						5.00

SKRULLS VS. POWER PACK (Tie-in to Secret Invasion crossover)
Marvel Comics: Sept, 2008 - No. 4 ($2.99, limited series)

	GD	VG	FN	VF	VF/NM	NM-
1,2-Van Lente-s/Hamscher-a; Franklin Richards app.						3.00

SKUL, THE
Virtual Comics (Byron Preiss Multimedia): Oct, 1996 - No. 3, Dec, 1996 ($2.50, lim. series)

	GD	VG	FN	VF	VF/NM	NM-
1-3: Ron Lim & Jimmy Palmiotti-a						2.50

SKULL & BONES
DC Comics: 1992 - No. 3, 1992 ($4.95, limited series, 52 pgs.)

	GD	VG	FN	VF	VF/NM	NM-
Book 1-3: 1-1st app.						5.00

SKULL, THE SLAYER
Marvel Comics Group: Aug, 1975 - No. 8, Nov, 1976 (20¢/25¢)

	GD	VG	FN	VF	VF/NM	NM-
1-Origin & 1st app.; Gil Kane-c	2	4	6	8	10	12
2-8: 2-Gil Kane-c. 5,6-(Regular 25¢-c). 8-Kirby-c	1	2	3	4	5	7
5,6-(30¢-c variants, limited distribution)(5,7/76)	3	6	9	18	27	35

SKY BLAZERS (CBS Radio)
Hawley Publications: Sept, 1940 - No. 2, Nov, 1940

	GD	VG	FN	VF	VF/NM	NM-
1-Sky Pirates, Ace Archer, Flying Aces begin	60	120	180	378	639	900
2-WWII aerial battle-c	39	78	117	230	370	510

SKY DOLL
Marvel Comics (Soleil): 2008 - No. 3, 2008 ($5.99)

	GD	VG	FN	VF	VF/NM	NM-
1-3-Barbucci & Canepa-s/a; English version of French comic; preview of other titles						6.00

SKYE RUNNER
DC Comics (WildStorm): June, 2006 - No. 6, Mar, 2007 ($2.99)

	GD	VG	FN	VF	VF/NM	NM-
1-6: 1-Three covers; Warner-s/Garza-a. 2-Three covers, incl. Campbell						3.00

SKYMAN (See Big Shot Comics & Sparky Watts)
Columbia Comics Gr.: Fall?, 1941 - No. 2, Fall?, 1942; No. 3, 1948 - No. 4, 1948

	GD	VG	FN	VF	VF/NM	NM-
1-Origin Skyman, The Face, Sparky Watts app.; Whitney-c/a; 3rd story-r from Big Shot #1; Whitney c-1-4	123	246	369	775	1313	1850
2 (1942)-Yankee Doodle	59	118	177	372	629	885
3,4 (1948)	40	80	120	235	380	525

SKYPILOT
Ziff-Davis Publ. Co.: No. 10, 1950(nd) - No. 11, Apr-May, 1951

	GD	VG	FN	VF	VF/NM	NM-
10,11-Frank Borth-a; Saunders painted-c	15	30	45	83	124	165

SKY RANGER (See Johnny Law...)

SKYROCKET
Harry 'A' Chesler: 1944

	GD	VG	FN	VF	VF/NM	NM-
nn-Alias the Dragon, Dr. Vampire, Skyrocket & The Desperado app.; WWII Japan zero-c	32	64	96	186	298	410

SKY SHERIFF (Breeze Lawson...) (Also see Exposed & Outlaws)
D. S. Publishing Co.: Summer, 1948

	GD	VG	FN	VF	VF/NM	NM-
1-Edmond Good-c/a	14	28	42	76	108	140

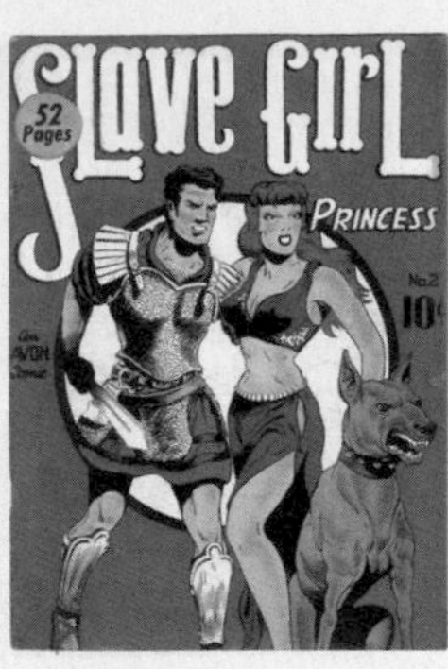

Slave Girl Comics #2 © AVON

Slingers #2 © MAR

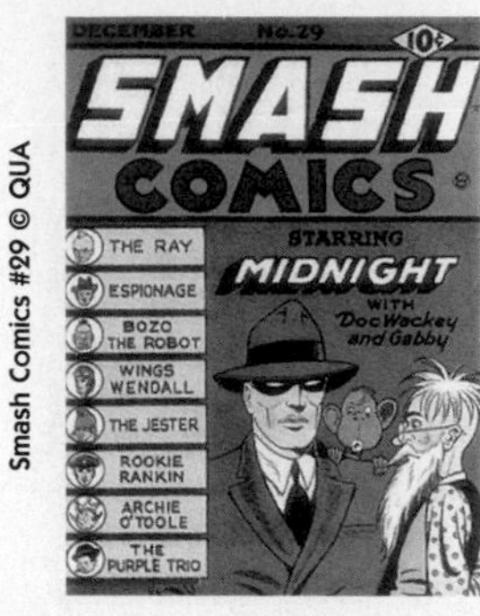

Smash Comics #29 © QUA

GD VG FN VF VF/NM NM-
2.0 4.0 6.0 8.0 9.0 9.2

GD VG FN VF VF/NM NM-
2.0 4.0 6.0 8.0 9.0 9.2

SKY WOLF (Also see Airboy)
Eclipse Comics: Mar, 1988 - No. 3, Oct, 1988 ($1.25/$1.50/$1.95, lim. series)
1-3 2.50

SLAINE, THE BERSERKER (Slaine the King #21 on)
Quality: July, 1987 - No. 28, 1989 ($1.25/$1.50)
1-28 2.50

SLAINE, THE HORNED GOD
Fleetway: 1998 - No. 3 ($6.99)
1-3-Reprints series from 2000 A.D.; Bisley-a 7.00

SLAM BANG COMICS (Western Desperado #8)
Fawcett Publications: Mar, 1940 - No. 7, Sept, 1940 (Combined with Master Comics #7)
1-Diamond Jack, Mark Swift & The Time Retarder, Lee Granger, Jungle King begin & continue in Master 207 414 621 1304 2202 3100
2 83 166 249 523 887 1250
3-Classic-c 157 314 471 989 1670 2350
4-7: 6-Intro Zoro, the Mystery Man (also in #7) 66 132 198 416 701 985
Ashcan (1940) Not distributed to newsstands, only for in house use. A copy sold in 2006 for $4,500.

SLAPSTICK
Marvel Comics: Nov, 1992 - No. 4, Feb, 1993 ($1.25, limited series)
1-4: Fry/Austin-c/a. 4-Ghost Rider, D.D., F.F. app. 2.50

SLAPSTICK COMICS
Comic Magazines Distributors: nd (1946?) (36 pgs.)
nn-Firetop feature; Post-a(2) 25 50 75 145 233 320

SLASH-D DOUBLECROSS
St. John Publishing Co.: 1950 (Pocket-size, 132 pgs.)
nn-Western comics 21 42 63 123 197 270

SLAUGHTERMAN
Comico: Feb, 1983 - No. 2, 1983 ($1.50, B&W)
1,2 3.00

SLAVE GIRL COMICS (See Malu... & White Princess of the Jungle #2)
Avon Periodicals/Eternity Comics (1989): Feb, 1949 - No. 2, Apr, 1949 (52 pgs.); Mar, 1989 (B&W, 44 pgs)
1-Larsen-c/a 97 194 291 611 1031 1450
2-Larsen-a 70 140 210 441 746 1050
1-(3/89, $2.25, B&W, 44 pgs.)-r/#1 3.00

SLEDGE HAMMER (TV)
Marvel Comics: Feb, 1988 - No. 2, Mar,1988 ($1.00, limited series)
1,2 3.00

SLEEPER
DC Comics (WildStorm): Mar, 2003 - No. 12, Mar, 2004 ($2.95)
1-12-Brubaker-s/Phillips-c/a. 3-Back-up preview of The Authority: High Stakes pt. 2 3.00
...: All False Moves TPB (2004, $17.95) r/#7-12 18.00
...: Out in the Cold TPB (2004, $17.95) r/#1-6 18.00

SLEEPER: SEASON TWO
DC Comics (WildStorm): Aug, 2004 - No. 12, July, 2005 ($2.95/$2.99)
1-12-Brubaker-s/Phillips-c/a. 3.00
...: A Crooked Line TPB (2005, $17.99) r/#1-6 18.00
...: The Long Way Home TPB (2005, $14.99) r/#7-12 15.00

SLEEPING BEAUTY (See Dell Giants & Movie Comics)
Dell Publishing Co.: No. 973, May, 1959 - No. 984, June, 1959 (Disney)
Four Color 973 (...and the Prince) 11 22 33 75 133 190
Four Color 984 (...Fairy Godmother's) 9 18 27 61 103 145

SLEEPWALKER
Marvel Comics: June, 1991 - No. 33, Feb, 1994 ($1.00/$1.25)
1-1st app. Sleepwalker 3.00
2-33: 4-Williamson-i. 5-Spider-Man-c/stor. 7-Infinity Gauntlet x-over. 8-Vs. Deathlok-c/story. 11-Ghost Rider-c/story. 12-Quesada-c/a(p) 14-Intro Spectra. 15-F.F.-c/story. 17-Darkhawk & Spider-Man x-over. 18-Infinity War x-over; Quesada/Williamson-c. 21,22-Hobgoblin app. 19-($2.00)-Die-cut Sleepwalker mask-c 2.50
25-($2.95, 52 pgs.)-Holo-grafx foil-c; origin 3.00
Holiday Special 1 (1/93, $2.00, 52 pgs.)-Quesada-c(p) 2.50

SLEEPWALKING
Hall of Heroes: Jan, 1996 ($2.50, B&W)
1-Kelley Jones-c 2.50

SLEEPY HOLLOW (Movie Adaption)
DC Comics (Vertigo): 2000 ($7.95, one-shot)
1-Kelley Jones-a/Seagle-s 8.00

SLEEZE BROTHERS, THE
Marvel Comics (Epic Comics): Aug, 1989 - No. 6, Jan, 1990 ($1.75, mature)
1-6: 4-6 (9/89 - 11/89 indicia dates) 2.50
nn-(1991, $3.95, 52 pgs.) 4.00

SLICK CHICK COMICS
Leader Enterprises: 1947(nd) - No. 3, 1947(nd)
1-Teenage humor 14 28 42 76 108 140
2,3 10 20 30 54 72 90

SLIDERS (TV)
Acclaim Comics (Armada): June, 1996 - No. 2, July, 1996 ($2.50, lim. series)
1,2: D.G. Chichester scripts; Dick Giordano-a. 2.50

SLIDERS: DARKEST HOUR (TV)
Acclaim Comics (Armada): Oct, 1996 - No. 3, Dec, 1996 ($2.50, limited series)
1-3 2.50

SLIDERS SPECIAL
Acclaim Comics (Armada): Nov, 1996 - No 3, Mar, 1997 ($3.95, limited series)
1-3: 1-Narcotica-Jerry O'Connell-s. 2-Blood and Splendor. 3-Deadly Secrets 4.00

SLIDERS: ULTIMATUM (TV)
Acclaim Comics (Armada): Sept, 1996 - No. 2, Sept, 1996 ($2.50, lim. series)
1,2 2.50

SLIMER! (TV cartoon) (Also see the Real Ghostbusters)
Now Comics: 1989 - No. 19, Feb?, 1991 ($1.75)
1-19: Based on animated cartoon 3.00

SLIM MORGAN (See Wisco)

SLINGERS (See Spider-Man: Identity Crisis issues)
Marvel Comics: Dec, 1998 - No. 12, Nov, 1999 ($2.99/$1.99)
0-(Wizard #88 supplement) Prelude story 2.50
1-($2.99) Four editions w/different covers for each hero, 16 pages common to all, the other pages from each hero's perspective 3.00
2-12: 2-Two-c. 12-Saltares-a 2.50

SLUDGE
Malibu Comics (Ultraverse): Oct, 1993 - No. 12, Dec, 1994 ($2.50/$1.95)
1-($2.50, 48 pgs.)-Intro/1st app. Sludge; Rune flip-c/story Pt. 1 (1st app., 3 pgs.) by Barry Smith; The Night Man app. (3 pg. preview); The Mighty Magnor 1 pg strip begins by Aragonés (cont. in other titles) 3.00
1-Ultra 5000 Limited silver foil 4.00
2-11: 3-Break-Thru x-over. 4-2 pg. Mantra origin. 8-Bloodstorm app. 2.50
12 ($3.50)-Ultraverse Premiere #8 flip book; Alex Ross poster 3.50
...:Red Xmas (12/94, $2.50, 44 pgs.) 2.50

SLUGGER (Little Wise Guys Starring...)(Also see Daredevil Comics)
Lev Gleason Publications: April, 1956
1-Biro-c 7 14 21 35 43 50

SMALL GODS
Image Comics: Jun, 2004 - No. 12, Nov, 2005 ($2.95/$2.99, B&W)
1-12-Rand-s/Ferreyna-a 3.00
... Special #1 (6/05, $2.95) flip cover 3.00
Vol. 1: Killing Grin (1/05, $9.95, TPB) r/#1-4; sketch pages, cover gallery & script page 10.00

SMALLVILLE (Based on TV series)
DC Comics: May, 2003 - No. 11 ($3.50/$3.95, bi-monthly)
1-6-Photo-c. 1-Plunkett-a; interviews with cast; season 1 episode guide begins 3.50
7-11-($3.95) 7-Chloe Chronicles begin; season 2 episode guide begins 4.00
Vol. 1 TPB (2004, $9.95) r/#1-4 & Smallville: The Comic; photo-c 10.00

SMALLVILLE: THE COMIC (Based on TV series)
DC Comics: Nov, 2002 ($3.95, 64 pages, one-shot)
1-Photo-c; art by Martinez and Leon; interviews with cast; season 2 preview 4.00

SMASH COMICS (Becomes Lady Luck #86 on)
Quality Comics Group: Aug, 1939 - No. 85, Oct, 1949
1-Origin Hugh Hazard & His Iron Man, Bozo the Robot, Espionage, Starring Black X by Eisner, & Hooded Justice (Invisible Justice #2 on); Chic Carter & Wings Wendall begin; 1st Robot on the cover of a comic book (Bozo) 318 636 954 2162 3781 5400
2-The Lone Star Rider app; Invisible Hood gains power of invisibility; bondage/torture-c

Smokey Bear #6 © GK

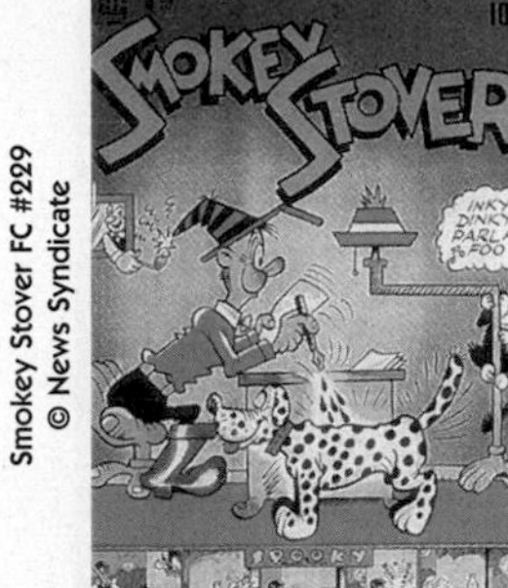

Smokey Stover FC #229 © News Syndicate

Snakes on a Plane #1 © New Line

	GD 2.0	VG 4.0	FN 6.0	VF 8.0	VF/NM 9.0	NM- 9.2
	133	266	399	838	1419	2000
3-Captain Cook & Eisner's John Law begin	68	136	204	428	727	1025
4,5: 4-Flash Fulton begins	65	130	195	410	693	975
6-12: 12-One pg. Fine-a	58	116	174	365	615	865
13-Magno begins (8/40); last Eisner issue; The Ray app. in full page ad; The Purple Trio begins	58	116	174	365	620	875
14-Intro. The Ray (9/40) by Lou Fine & others	300	600	900	1930	3315	4700
15,16: 16-The Scarlet Seal begins	124	248	372	781	1323	1865
17-Wun Cloo becomes plastic super-hero by Jack Cole (9-months before Plastic Man)	128	256	384	806	1366	1925
18-Midnight by Jack Cole begins (origin & 1st app., 1/41)	163	326	489	1027	1739	2450
19-22: Last Ray by Fine; The Jester begins-#22	87	174	261	548	924	1300
23,24: 24-The Sword app.; last Chic Carter; Wings Wendall dons new costume #24,25	67	134	201	422	711	1000
25-Origin/1st app. Wildfire; Rookie Rankin begins	75	150	225	473	799	1125
26-30: 28-Midnight-c begin, end #85	64	128	192	403	682	900
31,32,34: The Ray by Rudy Palais; also #33	54	108	162	340	575	810
33-Origin The Marksman	62	124	186	391	663	935
35-37	49	98	147	304	507	710
38-The Yankee Eagle begins; last Midnight by Jack Cole; classic-c by Cole	98	196	294	617	1046	1475
39,40-Last Ray issue	50	100	150	310	518	725
41,44-50	40	80	120	244	397	550
42-Lady Luck begins by Klaus Nordling	102	264	306	832	1404	1975
43-Lady Luck-c (1st & only in Smash)	63	126	189	397	674	950
51-60	30	60	90	174	280	385
61-70	23	46	69	133	214	295
71-85: 79-Midnight battles the Men from Mars-c/s	21	42	63	123	197	270

NOTE: ***Al Bryant** c-54, 63-68. **Cole** a-17-00, 00, 60, 72, 73, 78, 80, 83, 85; c-38, 60-62, 69-84. **Crandall** a-(Ray)-23-29, 35-38; c-36, 39, 40, 42-44, 46. **Fine** a(Ray)-14, 15, 16(w/**Tuska**), 17-22. **Fox** c-24-35. **Fuje** Ray-30. **Gil Fox** a-6-7, 9, 11-13. **Guardineer** a-(The Marksman)-39-?, 49, 52. **Gustavson** a-4-7, 9, 11-13 (The Jester)-22-46; (Magno)-13-21; (Midnight)-39(Cole inks), 49, 52, 63-65. **Kotzky** a-(Espionage)-33-38; c-45, 47-53. **Nordling** a-49, 52, 63-65. **Powell** a-11, 12, (Abdul the Arab)-13-24.Black X c-2, 6, 9, 11, 13, 16. Bozo the Robot c-1, 3, 5, 8, 10, 12, 14, 18, 20, 22, 24, 26. Midnight c-28-85. The Ray c-15, 17, 19, 21, 23, 25, 27. Wings Wendall c-4, 7.*

SMASH COMICS (Also see All Star Comics 1999 crossover titles)
DC Comics: May, 1999 ($1.99, one-shot)

1-Golden Age Doctor Mid-nite and Hourman						2.50

SMASH HIT SPORTS COMICS
Essankay Publications: V2#1, Jan, 1949

V2#1-L.B. Cole-c/a	28	56	84	162	261	360

SMAX (Also see Top Ten)
America's Best Comics: Oct, 2003 - No. 5, May, 2004 ($2.95, limited series)

1-5-Alan Moore-s/Zander Cannon-a						3.00
... Collected Edition (2004, $19.95, HC with dustjacket) r/#1-5						20.00
... Collected Edition SC (2005, $12.99) r/#1-5						13.00

SMILE COMICS (Also see Gay Comics, Tickle, & Whee)
Modern Store Publ.: 1955 (52 pgs.; 5x7-1/4") (7¢)

1	6	12	18	31	38	45

SMILEY BURNETTE WESTERN (Also see Patches #8 & Six-Gun Heroes)
Fawcett Publ.: March, 1950 - No. 4, Oct, 1950 (All photo front & back-c)

1-Red Eagle begins	36	72	108	208	329	450
2-4	24	48	72	139	220	300

SMILEY (THE PSYCHOTIC BUTTON) (See Evil Ernie)
Chaos! Comics: July, 1998 - Present ($2.95, one-shots)

1-Ivan Reis-a						3.00
... Holiday Special (1/99), ...'s Spring Break (4/99), ...Wrestling Special (5/99)						3.00

SMILIN' JACK (See Famous Feature Stories and Popular Comics) (Also see Super Book of Comics #1&2 and Super-Book of Comics #7&19 in the Promotional Comics section)
Dell Publishing Co.: No. 5, 1940 - No. 8, Oct-Dec, 1949

Four Color 5	71	142	213	447	754	1060
Four Color 10 (1940)	61	122	183	384	647	910
Large Feature Comic 12,14,25 (1941)	58	116	174	365	615	865
Four Color 4 (1942)	38	76	114	286	536	785
Four Color 14 (1943)	30	60	90	222	411	600
Four Color 36,58 (1943-44)	22	44	66	157	291	425
Four Color 80 (1945)	14	28	42	103	184	265
Four Color 149 (1947)	10	20	30	68	119	170
1 (1-3/48)	10	20	30	70	123	175
2	6	12	18	41	66	90
3-8 (10-12/49)	5	10	15	32	51	70

SMILING SPOOK SPUNKY (See Spunky)

SMITTY (See Popular Comics, Super Book #2, 4 & Super Comics)
Dell Publishing Co.: No. 11, 1940 - No. 7, Aug-Oct, 1949; No. 909, Apr, 1958

	GD 2.0	VG 4.0	FN 6.0	VF 8.0	VF/NM 9.0	NM- 9.2
Four Color 11 (1940)	45	90	135	279	465	650
Large Feature Comic 26 (1941)	36	72	108	212	341	470
Four Color 6 (1942)	21	42	63	152	281	410
Four Color 32 (1943)	15	30	45	107	196	285
Four Color 65 (1945)	13	26	39	90	160	230
Four Color 99 (1946)	10	20	30	73	129	185
Four Color 138 (1947)	9	18	27	64	110	155
1 (2-4/48)	9	18	27	63	107	150
2-(5-7/48)	5	10	15	32	51	70
3,4: 3-(8-10/48), 4-(11-1/48-49)	4	8	12	28	44	60
5-7, Four Color 909 (4/58)	4	8	12	24	37	50

SMOKEY BEAR (TV) (See March Of Comics #234, 362, 372, 383, 407)
Gold Key: Feb, 1970 - No. 13, Mar, 1973

1	3	6	9	19	29	38
2-5	2	4	6	10	14	18
6-13	2	4	6	8	10	12

SMOKEY STOVER (See Popular Comics, Super Book #5,17,29 & Super Comics)
Dell Publishing Co.: No. 7, 1942 - No. 827, Aug, 1957

Four Color 7 (1942)-Reprints	28	56	84	203	377	550
Four Color 35 (1943)	16	32	48	114	212	310
Four Color 64 (1944)	13	26	39	93	164	235
Four Color 229 (1949)	6	12	18	41	66	90
Four Color 730,827	5	10	15	32	51	70

SMOKEY THE BEAR (See Forest Fire for 1st app.)
Dell Publ. Co.: No. 653, 10/55 - No. 1214, 8/61 (See March of Comics #234)

Four Color 653 (#1)	10	20	30	71	126	180
Four Color 708,754,818,932	6	12	18	41	66	90
Four Color 1016,1119,1214	4	8	12	28	44	60

SMOKY (See Movie Classics)

SMURFS (TV)
Marvel Comics: 1982 (Dec) - No. 3, 1983

1-3	1	3	4	6	8	10
...Treasury Edition 1 (64 pgs.)-r/#1-3	3	6	9	16	23	30

SNAFU (Magazine)
Atlas Comics (RCM): Nov, 1955 - V2#2, Mar, 1956 (B&W)

V1#1-Heath/Severin-a; Everett, Maneely-a	14	28	42	82	121	160
V2#1,2-Severin-a	11	22	33	62	86	110

SNAGGLEPUSS (TV)(See Hanna-Barbera Band Wagon, Quick Draw McGraw #5 & Spotlight #4)
Gold Key: Oct, 1962 - No. 4, Sept, 1963 (Hanna-Barbera)

1	8	16	24	58	97	135
2-4	6	12	18	43	69	95

SNAKE EYES (G.I. Joe)
Devil's Due Publ.: Aug, 2005 - No. 6, Jan, 2006 ($2.95)

1-6-Santalucia-a						3.00
...: Declassified TPB (4/06, $18.95) r/series; source guide						19.00

SNAKE PLISSKEN CHRONICLES, (John Carpenter's...)
Hurricane Entertainment: June, 2003 - No. 4 ($2.99)

Preview Issue (8/02, no cover price) B&W preview; John Carpenter interview						2.50
1-4: 1-Three covers; Rodriguez-a						3.00

SNAKES AND LADDERS
Eddie Campbell Comics: 2001 ($5.95, B&W, one-shot)

nn-Alan Moore-s/Eddie Campbell-a						6.00

SNAKES ON A PLANE (Adaptation of the 2006 movie)
Virgin Comics: Oct, 2006 - No. 2, Nov, 2006 ($2.99, limited series)

1,2: 1-Dixon-s/Purcell-a. JG Jones and photo-c. 2-Klebs, Jr.-a; Moore & photo-c						3.00

SNAKE WOMAN (Shekhar Kapur's...)
Virgin Comics: July, 2006 - Present ($2.99)

1-10: 1-6-Michael Gaydos-a/Zeb Wells-s. 1-Two covers by Gaydos & Singh						3.00
#0 (5/07, 99¢) origin of the Snake Goddess; background info; Gaydos-a/c						2.25
... Curse of the 68 (3/08 - No. 4, 5/08, $2.99) 1-4: 1-Ingale-a. 2-Manu-a						3.00
... Tale of the Snake Charmer 1-6 (6/07-12/07, $2.99) Vivek Shinde-a						3.00
... Vol. 1 TPB (6/07, $14.99) r/#1-5; Gaydos sketch pages; creator commentary						15.00

Snooper and Blabber Detectives #3 © H-B

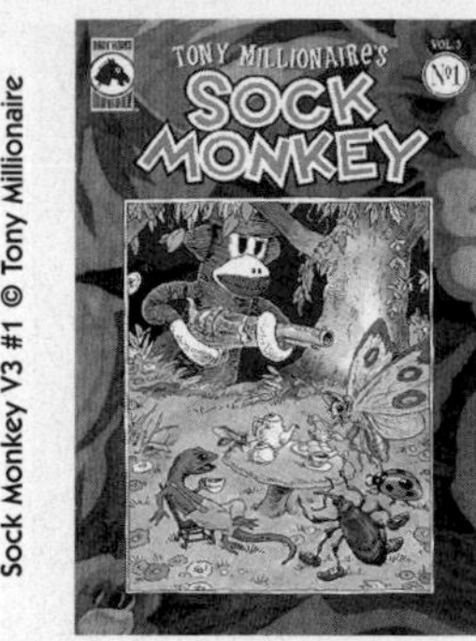

Sock Monkey V3 #1 © Tony Millionaire

Solar #3 © Voyager Comm.

GD VG FN VF VF/NM NM-
2.0 4.0 6.0 8.0 9.0 9.2

... Vol. 2 TPB (9/07, $14.99) r/#6-10; Cebulski intro. 15.00

SNAP (Formerly Scoop #8; becomes Jest #10,11 & Komik Pages #10)
Harry 'A' Chesler: No. 9, 1944
9-Manhunter, The Voice 22 44 66 127 204 280

SNAPPY COMICS
Cima Publ. Co. (Prize Publ.): 1945
1-Airmale app.; 9 pg. Sorcerer's Apprentice adapt; Kiefer-a
33 66 99 192 309 425

SNARKY PARKER (See Life With...)

SNIFFY THE PUP
Standard Publ. (Animated Cartoons): No. 5, Nov, 1949 - No. 18, Sept, 1953
5-Two Frazetta text illos 10 20 30 58 79 100
6-10 7 14 21 35 43 50
11-18 6 12 18 28 34 40

SNOOPER AND BLABBER DETECTIVES (TV) (See Whitman Comic Books)
Gold Key: Nov, 1962 - No. 3, May, 1963 (Hanna-Barbera)
1 7 14 21 49 80 110
2,3 6 12 18 37 59 80

SNOW WHITE (See Christmas With... (in Promotional Comics section), Mickey Mouse Magazine, Movie Comics & Seven Dwarfs)
Dell Publishing Co.: No. 49, July, 1944 - No. 382, Mar, 1952 (Disney-Movie)
Four Color 49 (...& the Seven Dwarfs) 50 100 150 400 750 1100
Four Color 382 (1952)-origin; partial reprint of Four Color 49
9 18 27 65 113 160

SNOW WHITE
Marvel Comics: Jan, 1995 ($1.95, one-shot)
1-r/1937 Sunday newspaper pages 2.50

SNOW WHITE AND THE SEVEN DWARFS
Whitman Publications: April, 1982 (60¢)
nn-r/Four Color 49 1 2 3 5 6 8

SNOW WHITE AND THE SEVEN DWARFS GOLDEN ANNIVERSARY
Gladstone: Fall, 1987 ($2.95, magazine size, 52 pgs.)
1-Contains poster 2 4 6 8 11 14

SOAP OPERA LOVE
Charlton Comics: Feb, 1983 - No. 3, June, 1983
1-3-Low print run 3 6 9 18 27 35

SOAP OPERA ROMANCES
Charlton Comics: July, 1982 - No. 5, March, 1983
1-5-Nurse Betsy Crane-r; low print run 3 6 9 18 27 35

SOCK MONKEY
Dark Horse Comics: Sept, 1998 - No. 2, Oct, 1998 ($2.95/$2.99, B&W)
1,2-Tony Millionaire-s/a 4.00
Vol. 2 -(Tony Millionaire's Sock Monkey) July, 1999 - No. 2, Aug, 1999
1,2 3.00
Vol. 3 -(Tony Millionaire's Sock Monkey) Nov, 2000 - No. 2, Dec, 2000
1,2 3.00
Vol. 4 -(Tony Millionaire's Sock Monkey) May, 2003 - No. 2, Aug, 2003
1,2 3.00
...The Inches Incident (Sept, 2006 - No. 4, Apr, 2007) 1-4-Tony Millionaire-s/a 3.00

SOJOURN
White Cliffs Publ. Co.: Sept, 1977 - No. 2, 1978 ($1.50, B&W & color, tabloid size)
1,2: 1-Tor by Kubert, Eagle by Severin, E. V. Race, Private Investigator by Doug Wildey, T. C. Mars by Aragonés begin plus other strips 2 4 6 8 10 12
NOTE: Most copies came folded. Unfolded copies are worth 50% more.

SOJOURN
CrossGeneration Comics: July, 2001 - No. 34, May, 2004 ($2.95)
Prequel -Ron Marz-s/Greg Land-c/a; preview pages 3.00
1-Ron Marz-s/Greg Land-c/a in most 6.00
2,3 5.00
4-24: 7-Immonen-a. 12-Brigman-a. 17-Lopresti-a. 21-Luke Ross-a 3.25
25-34: 25-$1.00-c. 34-Cariello-a 3.00
...: From the Ashes TPB (2001, $19.95) r/#1-6; Land painted-c 20.00
...: The Dragon's Tale TPB (2002, $15.95) r/#7-12; Jusko painted-c 16.00
...: The Warrior's Tale TPB (2003, $15.95) r/#13-18 16.00
Vol. 4: The Thief's Tale (2003, $15.95) r/#19-24 16.00
Vol. 5: The Sorcerer's Tale (Checker Book Publ.,2007, $17.95) r/#25-30 18.00

GD VG FN VF VF/NM NM-
2.0 4.0 6.0 8.0 9.0 9.2

Vol. 6: The Berzerker's Tale (Checker Book Publ.,2007, $17.95) r/#31-34, Prequel 18.00
Traveler Vol.1,2 ($9.95) digest-sized reprints of TPBs 10.00

SOLAR (...Man of the Atom) (Also see Doctor Solar)
Valiant/Acclaim Comics (Valiant): Sept, 1991 - No. 60, Apr, 1996 ($1.75-$2.50, 44 pgs.)
1-Layton-a(i) on Solar; Barry Windsor-Smith-c/a 1 3 4 6 8 10
2-9: 2-Layton-a(i) on Solar, B. Smith-a. 3-1st app. Harada (11/91). 7-vs. X-O Armor 6.00
10-(6/92, $3.95)-1st app. Eternal Warrior (6 pgs.); black embossed-c; origin & 1st app. Geoff McHenry (Geomancer) 1 3 4 6 8 11
10-($3.95)-2nd printing 4.00
11-15: 11-1st full app. Eternal Warrior. 12,13-Unity x-overs. 14-1st app. Fred Bender (becomes Dr. Eclipse). 15-2nd Dr. Eclipse 3.00
16-60: 17-X-O Manowar app. 23-Solar splits. 29-1st Valiant Vision book. 33-Valiant Vision; bound-in trading card. 38-Chaos Effect Epsilion Pt.1. 46-52-Dan Jurgens-a(p)/scripts w/Giordano-i. 53,54-Jurgens scripts only. 60-Giffen scripts; Jeff Johnson-a(p) 2.50
0-($9.95, trade paperback)-r/Alpha and Omega origin story; polybagged w/poster 10.00
...:Second Death (1994, $9.95)-r/issues #1-4. 10.00
NOTE: *#1-10 all have free 8 pg. insert "Alpha and Omega" which is a 10 chapter Solar origin story. All 10 centerfolds can pieced together to show climax of story.* ***Ditko*** *a-11p, 14p.* ***Giordano*** *a-46, 47, 48, 49, 50, 51, 52i.* ***Johnson*** *a-60p.* ***Jurgens*** *a-46, 47, 48, 49, 50 , 51, 52p.* ***Layton*** *a-1-3i; c-2i, 11i, 17i, 25i.* ***Miller*** *c-12.* ***Quesada*** *c-17p, 20-23p, 29p.* ***Simonson*** *c-13.* ***B. Smith*** *a-1-10; c-1, 3, 5, 7, 19i.* ***Thibert*** *c-22i, 23i.*

SOLAR LORD
Image Comics: Mar, 1999 - No. 7, Sept, 1999 ($2.50)
1-7-Khoo Fuk Lung-s/a 2.50

SOLARMAN (See Pendulum Ill. Originals)
Marvel Comics: Jan, 1989 - No. 2, May, 1990 ($1.00, limited series)
1,2 2.50

SOLAR, MAN OF THE ATOM (Man of the Atom on cover)
Acclaim Comics (Valiant Heroes): Vol. 2, May, 1997 ($3.95, one-shot, 46 pgs)
(1st Valiant Heroes Special Event)
Vol. 2-Reintro Solar; Ninjak cameo; Warren Ellis scripts; Darick Robertson-a 4.00

SOLAR, MAN OF THE ATOM: HELL ON EARTH
Acclaim Comics (Valiant Heroes): Jan, 1998 - No. 4 ($2.50, limited series)
1-4-Priest-s/ Zircher-a(p) 2.50

SOLAR, MAN OF THE ATOM: REVELATIONS
Acclaim Comics (Valiant Heroes): Nov, 1997 ($3.95, one-shot, 46 pgs.)
1-Krueger-s/ Zircher-a(p) 4.00

SOLDIER & MARINE COMICS (Fightin' Army #16 on)
Charlton Comics (Toby Press of Conn. V1#11): No. 11, Dec, 1954 - No. 15, Aug, 1955; V2#9, Dec, 1956
V1#11 (12/54)-Bob Powell-a 9 18 27 50 65 80
V1#12(2/55)-15: 12-Photo-c. 14-Photo-c; Colan-a 6 12 18 31 38 45
V2#9(Formerly Never Again; Jerry Drummer V2#10 on)
6 12 18 28 34 40

SOLDIER COMICS
Fawcett Publications: Jan, 1952 - No. 11, Sept, 1953
1 14 28 42 76 108 140
2 8 16 24 44 57 70
3-5 8 16 24 42 54 65
6-11: 8-Illo. in **POP** 8 16 24 40 50 60

SOLDIERS OF FORTUNE
American Comics Group (Creston Publ. Corp.): Mar-Apr, 1951 - No. 13, Feb-Mar, 1953
1-Capt. Crossbones by Shelly, Ace Carter, Lance Larson begin
23 46 69 133 214 295
2 14 28 42 80 115 150
3-10: 6 Bondage-c 12 24 36 69 97 125
11-13 (War format) 9 18 27 47 61 75
NOTE: ***Shelly*** *a-1-3, 5.* ***Whitney*** *a-6, 8-11, 13; c-1-3, 5, 6.*

SOLDIERS OF FREEDOM
Americomics: 1987 - No. 2, 1987 ($1.75)
1,2 3.00

SOLDIER X (Continued from Cable)
Marvel Comics: Sept, 2002 - No. 12, Aug, 2003 ($2.99/$2.25)
1,10,11,12-($2.99) 1-Kordey-a/Macan-s. 10-Bollers-s/Ranson-a 3.00
2-9-($2.25) 2.50

SOLITAIRE (Also See Prime V2#6-8)
Malibu Comics (Ultraverse): Nov, 1993 - No. 12, Dec, 1994 ($1.95)
1-($2.50)-Collector's edition bagged w/playing card 3.00

Solution #10 © MAL

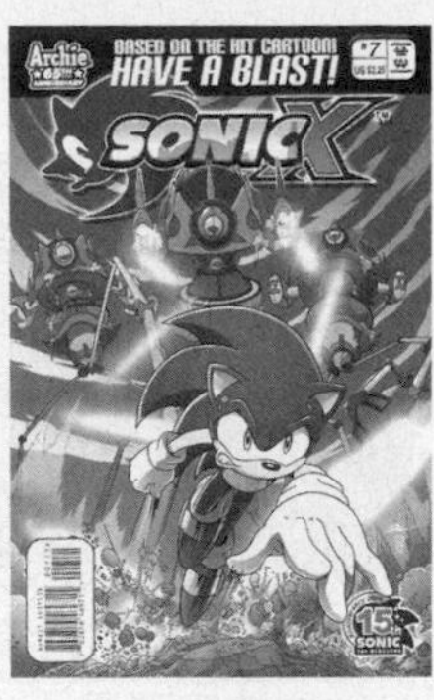

Sonic X #7 © Sonic Project

(Michael Turner Presents) Soulfire #1 © Aspen MLT

GD VG FN VF VF/NM NM-
2.0 4.0 6.0 8.0 9.0 9.2

GD VG FN VF VF/NM NM-
2.0 4.0 6.0 8.0 9.0 9.2

1-12: 1-Regular edition w/o playing card. 2,4-Break-Thru x-over. 3-2 pg. origin The Night Man. 4-Gatefold-c. 5-Two pg. origin the Strangers 2.50

SOLO
Marvel Comics: Sept, 1994 - No. 4, Dec, 1994 ($1.75, limited series)
1-4: Spider-Man app. 2.50

SOLO (Movie)
Dark Horse Comics: July, 1996 - No. 2, Aug, 1996 ($2.50, limited series)
1,2: Adaptation of film: photo-c 2.50

SOLO (Anthology showcasing individual artists)
DC Comics: Dec, 2004 - No. 12, Oct, 2006 ($4.95/$4.99)
1-11: 1-Tim Sale-a; stories by Sale and various. 2-Richard Corben-a; stories by Corben and Arcudi. 3-Paul Pope. 4-Howard Chaykin. 5-Darwyn Cooke. 6-Jordi Bernet. 7-Michael Allred; Teen Titans & Doom Patrol app. 8-Teddy Kristiansen. 9-Scott Hampton. 10-Damion Scott. 11-Sergio Aragonés. 12-Brendan McCarthy 5.00

SOLO AVENGERS (Becomes Avenger Spotlight #21 on)
Marvel Comics: Dec, 1987 - No. 20, July, 1989 (75¢/$1.00)
1-Jim Lee-a on back-up story 3.00
2-20: 11-Intro Bobcat 2.50

SOLOMON AND SHEBA (Movie)
Dell Publishing Co.: No. 1070, Jan-Mar, 1960
Four Color 1070-Sekowsky-a; photo-c 8 16 24 58 97 135

SOLOMON KANE (Based on the Robert E. Howard character. Also see Blackthorne 3-D Series #60 & Marvel Premiere)
Marvel Comics: Sept, 1985 - No. 6, July, 1986 (Limited series)
1-6: 1-Double size. 3-6 Williamson-a(i) 3.00

SOLUS
CG Entertainment, Inc.: Apr, 2003 - No. 8, Jan, 2004 ($2.95)
1-8: 1-4,6,7-George Pérez-a/c; Barbara Kesel-s. 5-Ryan-a. 8-Kirk-a 3.00
Vol. 1: Genesis (1/04, $15.95) r/#1-6 16.00

SOLUTION, THE
Malibu Comics (Ultraverse): Sept, 1993 - No. 17, Feb, 1995 ($1.95)
1,3-15: 1-Intro Meathook, Deathdance, Black Tiger, Tech. 4-Break-Thru x-over; gatefold-c. 5-2 pg. origin The Strangers. 11-Brereton-c 2.50
1-($2.50)-Newsstand ed. polybagged w/trading card 2.50
1-Ultra 5000 Limited silver foil 4.00
0-Obtained w/Rune #0 by sending coupons from 11 comics 3.00
2-($2.50, 48 pgs.)-Rune flip-c/story by B. Smith; The Mighty Magnor 1 pg. strip by Aragonés 2.50
16 ($3.50)-Flip-c Ultraverse Premiere #10 3.50
17 ($2.50) 2.50

SOMERSET HOLMES (See Eclipse Graphic Novel Series)
Pacific Comics/ Eclipse Comics No. 5, 6: Sept, 1983 - No. 6, Dec, 1984 ($1.50, Baxter paper)
1-6: 1-Brent Anderson-c/a. Cliff Hanger by Williamson in all 3.00

SONG OF THE SOUTH (See Brer Rabbit)

SONIC & KNUCKLES
Archie Comics: Aug, 1995 ($2.00)
1 6.00

SONIC DISRUPTORS
DC Comics: Dec, 1987 - No. 7, July, 1988 ($1.75, unfinished limited series)
1-7 3.00

SONIC'S FRIENDLY NEMESIS KNUCKLES
Archie Publications: July, 1996 - No. 3, Sept, 1996 ($1.50, limited series)
1-3 4.00

SONIC SUPER SPECIAL
Archie Publications: 1997 - Present ($2.00/$2.25/$2.29, 48 pgs)
1-3 4.00
4-6,8-15: 10-Sabrina-c/app. 15-Sin City spoof 3.00
7-(w/Image) Spawn, Maxx, Savage Dragon-c/app.; Valentino-a 3.00

SONIC THE HEDGEHOG (TV, video game)
Archie Comics: No. 0, Feb, 1993 - No. 3, May, 1993 ($1.25, mini-series)
0(2/93),1: Shaw-a(p) & covers on all 3 6 9 16 22 28
2,3 2 4 6 10 14 18
Beginnings TPB (2003, $10.95) r/#0-3 11.00
...: The Beginning TPB (2006, $10.95) r/#0-3 11.00

SONIC THE HEDGEHOG (TV, video game) (Also see Promotional Comics section for Free Comic Book Day edition)
Archie Comics: July, 1993 - Present ($1.25/$1.50/$1.75/$1.79/$1.99/$2.19/$2.25)
1 3 6 9 18 27 35
2,3 2 4 6 13 18 22
4-10: 8-Neon ink-c. 2 4 6 10 14 18
11-20 2 4 6 9 12 15
21-30 ($1.50): 25-Silver ink-c 1 3 4 6 8 10
31-50 1 2 3 4 5 7
51-93 3.50
94-195: 117-Begin $2.19-c. 152-Begin $2.25-c. 157-Shadow app. 2.25
Triple Trouble Special (10/95, $2.00, 48 pgs.) 4.50

SONIC VS. KNUCKLES "BATTLE ROYAL" SPECIAL
Archie Publications: 1997 ($2.00, one-shot)
1 4.00

SONIC X (Sonic the Hedgehog)
Archie Publications: Nov, 2005 - Present ($2.25)
1-40: 1-Sam Speed app. 2.25

SON OF AMBUSH BUG (See Ambush Bug)
DC Comics: July, 1986 - No. 6, Dec, 1986 (75¢)
1-6: Giffen-c/a in all. 5-Bissette-a. 2.50

SON OF BLACK BEAUTY (Also see Black Beauty)
Dell Publishing Co.: No. 510, Oct, 1953 - No. 566, June, 1954
Four Color 510, 566 4 8 12 26 41 55

SON OF FLUBBER (See Movie Comics)

SON OF M (Also see House of M series)
Marvel Comics: Feb, 2006 - No. 6, July, 2006 ($2.99, limited series)
1-6: 1-Powerless Quicksilver; Martinez-a. 2-Quicksilver regains powers; Inhumans app. 3.00
Decimation: Son of M (2006, $13.99, TPB) r/series; Martinez sketch pages 14.00

SON OF MUTANT WORLD
Fantagor Press: 1990 - No. 5, 1990? ($2.00, bi-monthly)
1-5: 1-3: Corben-c/a. 4,5 ($1.75, B&W) 3.00

SON OF ORIGINS OF MARVEL COMICS (See Fireside Book Series)

SON OF SATAN (Also see Ghost Rider #1 & Marvel Spotlight #12)
Marvel Comics Group: Dec, 1975 - No. 8, Feb, 1977 (25¢)
1-Mooney-a; Kane-c(p), Starlin splash(p) 3 6 9 16 23 32
2,6-8: 2-Origin The Possessor. 8-Heath-a 2 4 6 9 12 16
3-5-(Regular 25¢ editions)(4-8/76): 5-Russell-p 2 4 6 9 12 16
3-5-(30¢-c variants, limited distribution) 4 8 12 20 30 40

SON OF SINBAD (Also see Abbott & Costello & Daring Adventures)
St. John Publishing Co.: Feb, 1950
1-Kubert-c/a 40 80 120 235 380 525

SON OF SUPERMAN (Elseworlds)
DC Comics: 1999 ($14.95, prestige format, one-shot)
nn-Chaykin & Tischman-s/Williams III & Gray-a 15.00

SON OF TOMAHAWK (See Tomahawk)

SON OF VULCAN (Formerly Mysteries of Unexplored Worlds #1-48; Thunderbolt V3#51 on)
Charlton Comics: V2#49, Nov, 1965 - V2#50, Jan, 1966
V2#49,50: 50-Roy Thomas scripts (1st pro work) 3 6 9 17 25 32

SONS OF KATIE ELDER (See Movie Classics)

SORCERY (See Chilling Adventures in... & Red Circle...)

SORORITY SECRETS
Toby Press: July, 1954
1 9 18 27 52 69 85

SOULFIRE (MICHAEL TURNER PRESENTS:...)
Aspen MLT, Inc.: No. 0, 2004 - Present ($2.50/$2.99)
0-($2.50) Turner-a/c; Loeb-s; intro. to characters & development sketches 2.50
1-($2.99) Two covers 3.00
1-Diamond Previews Exclusive 5.00
2-7: 2,3-Two covers. 4-Four covers 3.00
...: The Collected Edition Vol. 1 (5/05, $6.99) r/#1,2; cover gallery 7.00
HardcoverVolume 1 (12/05, $24.99) r/#0-5 & preview from Wizard Magazine; Johns intro. 25.00

SOULFIRE: CHAOS REIGN

Sovereign Seven #32 © Chris Claremont

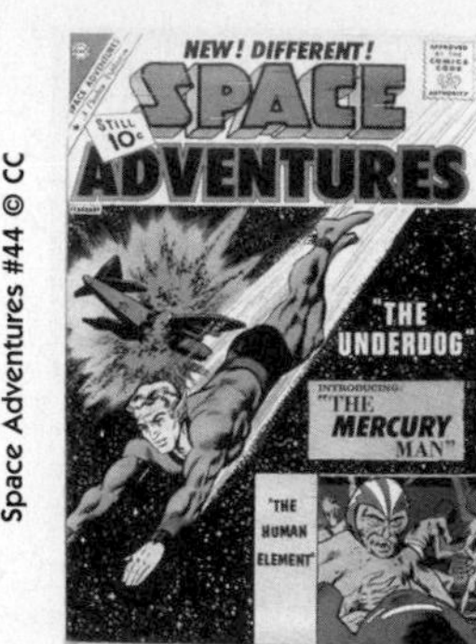

Space Adventures #44 © CC

Space Detective #2 © AVON

	GD 2.0	VG 4.0	FN 6.0	VF 8.0	VF/NM 9.0	NM- 9.2

Aspen MLT, Inc.: No. 0, June, 2006 - No. 3, Jan, 2007 ($2.50/$2.99)
0-($2.50) Three covers; Marcus To-a; J.T. Krul-s 2.50
1-3-($2.99) 1-Three covers 3.00
...: Beginnings (7/06, $1.99) Marcus To-a; J.T. Krul-s 2.25

SOULFIRE: DYING OF THE LIGHT
Aspen MLT, Inc.: No. 0, 2004 - Present ($2.50/$2.99)
0-($2.50) Three covers; Gunnell-a; Krul-s; back-story to the Soulfire universe 2.50
1-5-($2.99) 1-Five covers 3.00
... Vol. 1 TPB (2007, $14.99) r/#0-5; Gunnell sketch pages, cover gallery 15.00

SOULFIRE: NEW WORLD ORDER
Aspen MLT, Inc.: No. 0, July, 2007 - Present ($2.50/$2.99)
0-($2.50) Two covers; Herrera-a/Krul-s 2.50

SOULQUEST
Innovation: Apr, 1989 ($3.95, squarebound, 52 pgs.)
1-Blackshard app. 4.00

SOUL SAGA
Image Comics (Top Cow): Feb, 2000 - No. 5, Apr, 2001 ($2.50)
1-5: 1-Madureira-c; Platt & Batt-a 2.50

SOULSEARCHERS AND COMPANY
Claypool Comics: June, 1995 - No. 82, Jan, 2007 ($2.50, B&W)
1-10: Peter David scripts 5.00
11-25 3.00
26-82 2.50

SOULWIND
Image Comics: Mar, 1997 - No. 8 ($2.95, B&W, limited series)
1-8: 5-"The Day I Tried To Live" pt. 1 3.00
Book Five; The August Ones (Oni Press, 3/01, $8.50) 8.50
...The Kid From Planet Earth (1997, $9.95, TPB) 10.00
...The Kid From Planet Earth (Oni Press, 1/00, $8.50, TPB) 8.50
...The Day I Tried to Live (Oni Press, 4/00, $8.50, TPB) 8.50
The Complete Soulwind TPB ($29.95, 11/03, 8" x 5 1/2") r/Oni Books #1-5 30.00

SOUPY SALES COMIC BOOK (TV)(The Official...)
Archie Publications: 1965
1 9 18 27 60 100 140

SOUTHERN KNIGHTS, THE (See Crusaders #1)
Guild Publ/Fictioneer Books: No. 2, 1983 - No. 41, 1993 (B&W)
2-Magazine size 1 2 3 5 6 8
3-35, 37-41 3.00
36-($3.50-c) 3.50
Dread Halloween Special 1, Primer Special 1 (Spring, 1989, $2.25) 2.50
Graphic Novels #1-4 4.00

SOVEREIGN SEVEN (Also see Showcase '95 #12)
DC Comics: July, 1995 - No. 36, July, 1998 ($1.95) (1st creator-owned mainstream DC comic)
1-1st app. Sovereign Seven (Reflex, Indigo, Cascade, Finale, Cruiser, Network & Rampart); 1st app. Maitresse; Darkseid app.; Chris Claremont-s & Dwayne Turner-c/a begins 3.00
1-Gold 8.00
1-Platinum 40.00
2-25: 2-Wolverine cameo. 4-Neil Gaiman cameo. 5,8-Batman app. 7-Ramirez cameo (from the movie Highlander). 9-Humphrey Bogart cameo from Casablanca. 10-Impulse app; Manoli Wetherell & Neal Conan cameo from Uncanny X-Men #226. 11-Robin app. 16-Final Night. 24-Superman app. 25-Power Girl app. 2.50
26-36: 26-Begin $2.25-c. 28-Impulse-c/app. 2.50
Annual 1 (1995, $3.95)-Year One story; Big Barda & Lobo app.; Jeff Johnson-c/a 4.00
Annual 2 (1996, $2.95)-Legends of the Dead Earth; Leonardi-c/a 3.50
...Plus 1(2/97, $2.95)-Legion-c/app. 3.50
TPB-($12.95) r/#1-5, Annual #1 & Showcase '95 #12 13.00

SPACE: ABOVE AND BEYOND (TV)
Topps Comics: Jan, 1996 - No. 3, Mar, 1996 ($2.95, limited series)
1-3: Adaptation of pilot episode; Steacy-c. 3.00

SPACE: ABOVE AND BEYOND--THE GAUNTLET (TV)
Topps Comics: May, 1996 -No. 2, June, 1996 ($2.95, limited series)
1,2 3.00

SPACE ACE (Also see Manhunt!)
Magazine Enterprises: No. 5, 1952
5(A-1 #61)-Guardineer-a 53 106 159 334 567 800

SPACE ACE: DEFENDER OF THE UNIVERSE (Based on the Don Bluth video game)
CrossGen Comics: Oct, 2003 - No. 6 ($2.95, limited series)
1,2-Kirkman-s/Borges-a 3.00

SPACE ACTION
Ace Magazines (Junior Books): June, 1952 - No. 3, Oct, 1952
1-Cameron-a in all (1 story) 75 150 225 473 799 1125
2,3 53 106 159 330 553 775

SPACE ADVENTURES (War At Sea #22 on)
Capitol Stories/Charlton Comics: 7/52 - No. 21, 8/56; No. 23, 5/58 - No. 59, 11/64; V3#60, 10/67; V1#2, 7/68 - V1#8, 7/69; No. 9, 5/78 - No. 13, 3/79
1 53 106 159 331 558 785
2 27 54 81 158 254 350
3-5: 4,6-Flying saucer-c/stories 22 44 66 127 204 280
6-9: 7-Sex change story "Transformation". 8-Robot-c. 9-A-Bomb panel
20 40 60 115 183 250
10,11-Ditko-c/a. 10-Robot-c. 11-Two Ditko stories 52 104 156 322 536 750
12-Ditko-c (classic) 70 140 210 441 746 1050
13-(Fox-r, 10-11/54); Blue Beetle-c/story 16 32 48 92 144 195
14,15,17,18: 14-Blue Beetle-c/story; Fox-r (12-1/54-55, last pre-code).
15,17,18-Rocky Jones-c/s.(TV); 15-Part photo-c 20 40 60 115 183 250
16-Krigstein-a; Rocky Jones-c/story (TV) 22 44 66 127 204 280
19 15 30 45 85 130 175
20-Reprints Fawcett's "Destination Moon" 26 52 78 152 244 335
21-(8/56) (no #22)(Becomes War At Sea) 15 30 45 85 130 175
23-(5/58; formerly Nyoka, The Jungle Girl)-Reprints Fawcett's "Destination Moon"
23 46 69 133 214 295
24,25,31,32-Ditko-a. 24-Severin-a(signed "LePoer") 20 40 60 115 183 250
26,27-Ditko-a(4) each. 26,28-Flying saucer-c 21 42 63 123 197 270
28-30 11 22 33 60 83 105
33-Origin/1st app. Capt. Atom by Ditko (3/60) 50 100 150 310 518 725
34-40,42-All Captain Atom by Ditko 21 42 63 123 197 270
41,43,45-59: 45-Mercury Man app. 5 10 15 30 48 65
44-1st app. Mercury Man 5 10 15 32 51 70
V3#60(#1, 10/67)-Origin & 1st app. Paul Mann & The Saucers From the Future
5 10 15 30 48 65
2,5,6,8 (1968-69)-Ditko-a: 2-Aparo-c/a 3 6 9 19 29 38
3,4,7: 4-Aparo-c/a 3 6 9 16 22 28
9-13(1978-79)-Capt. Atom-r/Space Adventures by Ditko; 9-Reprints origin/1st app. Capt. Atom from #33 6.00
NOTE: ***Aparo** a-V3#60. c-V3#8. **Ditko** c-12, 31-42. **Giordano** c-3, 4, 7-9, 18p. **Krigstein** c-15. **Shuster** a-11. Issues 13 & 14 have Blue Beetle logos; #15-18 have Rocky Jones logos.*

SPACE ARK
Americomics (AC Comics)/ Apple Comics #3 on: June, 1985 - No. 5, Sept, 1987 ($1.75)
1-5: Funny animal (#1,2-color; #3-5-B&W) 2.50

SPACE BUSTERS
Ziff-Davis Publ. Co.: Spring, 1952 - No. 2, Fall, 1952
1-Krigstein-a(3); Painted-c by Norman Saunders 80 160 240 504 852 1200
2-Kinstler-a(2 pgs.); Saunders painted-c 61 122 183 384 647 910
NOTE: ***Anderson** a-2. Bondage c-2.*

SPACE CADET (See Tom Corbett,...)

SPACE CIRCUS
Dark Horse Comics: July, 2000 - No. 4, Oct, 2000 ($2.95, limited series)
1-4-Aragonés-a/Evanier-s 3.00

SPACE COMICS (Formerly Funny Tunes)
Avon Periodicals: No. 4, Mar-Apr, 1954 - No. 5, May-June, 1954
4,5-Space Mouse, Peter Rabbit, Super Pup (formerly Spotty the Pup), & Merry Mouse continue from Funny Tunes 8 16 24 40 50 60
I.W. Reprint #8 (nd)-Space Mouse-r 2 4 6 8 10 12

SPACED
Anthony Smith Publ. #1,2/Unbridled Ambition/Eclipse Comics #10 on: 1982 - No. 13, 1988 ($1.25/$1.50, B&W, quarterly)
1-($1.25-c) 3.00
2-13, Special Edition (1983, Mimeo) 2.50

SPACE DETECTIVE
Avon Periodicals: July, 1951 - No. 4, July, 1952
1-Rod Hathway, Space Detective begins, ends #4; Wood-c/a(3)-23 pgs.; "Opium Smugglers of Venus" drug story; Lucky Dale-r/Saint #4 112 224 336 706 1191 1675
2-Tales from the Shadow Squad story; Wood/Orlando-c; Wood inside layouts; "Slave Ship of Saturn" story 87 174 261 548 924 1300
3,4: 3-Kinstler-c. 4-Kinstlerish-a by McCann 42 84 123 260 435 610

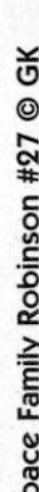
Space Family Robinson #27 © GK

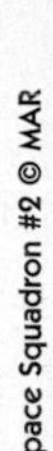
Space Squadron #2 © MAR

Space Western Comics #45 © CC

	GD 2.0	VG 4.0	FN 6.0	VF 8.0	VF/NM 9.0	NM- 9.2

I.W. Reprint #1(Reprints #2), 8(Reprints cover #1 & part Famous Funnies #191) 4 8 12 22 34 45
I.W. Reprint #9-Exist? 4 8 12 22 34 45

SPACE EXPLORER (See March of Comics #202)

SPACE FAMILY ROBINSON (TV)(...Lost in Space #15-37, ...Lost in Space On Space Station One #38 on)(See Gold Key Champion)
Gold Key: Dec, 1962 - No. 36, Oct, 1969; No. 37, 10/73 - No. 54, 11/78; No. 55, 3/81 - No. 59, 5/82 (All painted covers)

1-(Low distribution); Spiegle-a in all 21 42 63 152 281 410
2(3/63)-Family becomes lost in space 11 22 33 70 140 200
3-5 8 16 24 52 86 120
6-10: 6-Captain Venture back-up stories begin 6 12 18 43 69 95
11-20: 14-(10/65). 15-Title change (1/66) 5 10 15 30 48 65
21-36: 28-Last 12¢ issue. 36-Captain Venture ends 4 8 12 23 36 45
37-48: 37-Origin retold 2 4 6 10 14 18
49-59: Reprints #49,50,55-59 2 4 6 8 10 12
NOTE: *The TV show first aired on 9/15/65. Title changed after TV show debuted.*

SPACE FAMILY ROBINSON (See March of Comics #320, 328, 352, 404, 414)

SPACE GHOST (TV) (Also see Golden Comics Digest #2 & Hanna-Barbera Super TV Heroes #3-7)
Gold Key: March, 1967 (Hanna-Barbera) (TV debut was 9/10/66)

1 (10199-703)-Spiegle-a 29 58 87 213 394 575

SPACE GHOST (TV cartoon)
Comico: Mar, 1987 ($3.50, deluxe format, one-shot) (Hanna-Barbera)

1-Steve Rude-c/a 1 2 3 5 6 8

SPACE GHOST (TV cartoon)
DC Comics: Jan, 2005 - No. 6, June, 2005 ($2.95/$2.99, limited series)

1-6-Alex Ross-c/Ariel Olivetti-a/Joe Kelly-s; origin of Space Ghost 3.00
TPB (2005, $14.99) r/series; cover gallery 15.00

SPACE GIANTS, THE (TV cartoon)
FBN Publications: 1979 ($1.00, B&W, one-shots)

1-Based on Japanese TV series 2 4 6 9 12 15

SPACEHAWK
Dark Horse Comics: 1989 - No. 3, 1990 ($2.00, B&W)

1-3-Wolverton-c/a(r) plus new stories by others. 4.00

SPACE JAM
DC Comics: 1996 ($5.95, one-shot, movie adaption)

1-Wraparound photo cover of Michael Jordan 1 2 3 5 6 8

SPACE KAT-ETS (...in 3-D)
Power Publishing Co.: Dec, 1953 (25¢, came w/glasses)

1 30 60 90 174 280 385

SPACEKNIGHTS
Marvel Comics: Oct, 2000 - No. 5, Feb, 2001 ($2.99, limited series)

1-5-Starlin-s/Batista-a 3.00

SPACEMAN (Speed Carter...)
Atlas Comics (CnPC): Sept, 1953 - No. 6, July, 1954

1-Grey tone-c 68 136 204 428 727 1025
2 43 86 129 267 446 625
3-6: 4-A-Bomb explosion-c 40 80 120 235 380 525
NOTE: ***Everett** c-1, 3. **Heath** a-1. **Maneely** a-1(3), 2(4), 3(3), 4-6; c-5, 6. **Romita** a-1. **Sekowsky** c-4. **Sekowsky/Abel** a-4(3). **Tuska** a-5(3).*

SPACE MAN
Dell Publ. Co.: No. 1253, 1-3/62 - No. 8, 3-5/64; No. 9, 7/72 - No. 10, 10/72

Four Color 1253 (#1)(1-3/62)(15¢-c) 7 14 21 49 80 110
2,3: 2-(15¢-c). 3-(12¢-c) 4 8 12 28 44 60
4-8-(12¢-c) 4 8 12 22 34 45
9,10-(15¢-c): 9-Reprints #1253. 10-Reprints #2 2 4 6 9 12 15

SPACEMAN (From the Atomics)
Oni Press: July, 2002 ($2.95, one-shot)

1-Mike Allred-s/a; Lawrence Marvit additional art 3.00

SPACE MOUSE (Also see Funny Tunes & Space Comics)
Avon Periodicals: April, 1953 - No. 5, Apr-May, 1954

1 10 20 30 54 72 90
2 7 14 21 35 43 50
3-5 6 12 18 28 34 40

SPACE MOUSE (Walter Lantz...#1; see Comic Album #17)
Dell Publishing Co./Gold Key: No. 1132, Aug-Oct, 1960 - No. 5, Nov, 1963 (Walter Lantz)

Four Color 1132,1244, 1(11/62)(G.K.) 4 8 12 28 44 60
2-5 4 8 12 24 37 50

SPACE MYSTERIES
I.W. Enterprises: 1964 (Reprints)

1-r/Journey Into Unknown Worlds #4 w/new-c 3 6 9 16 22 28
8,9: 9-r/Planet Comics #73 3 6 9 16 22 28

SPACE: 1999 (TV) (Also see Power Record Comics)
Charlton Comics: Nov, 1975 - No. 7, Nov, 1976

1-Origin Moonbase Alpha; Staton-c/a 3 6 9 14 19 24
2,7: 2-Staton-a 2 4 6 10 14 18
3-6: All Byrne-a; c-3,5,6 3 6 9 14 19 24
nn (Charlton Press, digest, 100 pgs., B&W, no cover price) new stories & art 4 8 12 22 34 45

SPACE: 1999 (TV)(Magazine)
Charlton Comics: Nov, 1975 - No. 8, Nov, 1976 (B&W) (#7 shows #6 inside)

1-Origin Moonbase Alpha; Morrow-c/a 3 6 9 14 19 24
2-8: 2,3-Morrow-c/a. 4-6-Morrow-c. 5,8-Morrow-a 2 4 6 10 14 18

SPACE PATROL (TV)
Ziff-Davis Publishing Co. (Approved Comics): Summer, 1952 - No. 2, Oct-Nov, 1952 (Painted-c by Norman Saunders)

1-Krigstein-a 90 180 270 567 959 1350
2-Krigstein-a(3) 65 130 195 410 693 975

SPACE PIRATES (See Archie Giant Series #533)

SPACE RANGER (See Mystery in Space #92, Showcase #15 & Tales of the Unexpected)

SPACE SQUADRON (In the Days of the Rockets)(Becomes Space Worlds #6)
Marvel/Atlas Comics (ACI): June, 1951 - No. 5, Feb, 1952

1-Space team; Brodsky c-1,5 68 136 204 428 727 1025
2. Tuska c-2-4 54 108 162 340 575 810
3-5: 3-Capt. Jet Dixon by Tuska(3). 4-Weird advs. begin 47 94 141 291 483 675

SPACE THRILLERS
Avon Periodicals: 1954 (25¢ Giant)

nn-(Scarce)-Robotmen of the Lost Planet; contains 3 rebound comics of The Saint & Strange Worlds. Contents could vary 120 240 360 756 1278 1800

SPACE TRIP TO THE MOON (See Space Adventures #23)

SPACE USAGI
Mirage Studios: June, 1992 - No. 3, 1992 ($2.00, B&W, mini-series)
V2#1, Nov, 1993 - V2#3, Jan, 1994 ($2.75)

1-3: Stan Sakai-c/a/scripts, V2#1-3 3.00

SPACE USAGI
Dark Horse Comics: Jan, 1996 - No. 3, Mar, 1996 ($2.95, B&W, limited series)

1-3: Stan Sakai-c/a/scripts 3.00

SPACE WAR (Fightin' Five #28 on)
Charlton Comics: Oct, 1959 - No. 27, Mar, 1964; No. 28, Mar, 1978 - No. 34, 3/79

V1#1-Giordano-c begin, end #3 13 26 39 93 164 235
2,3 7 14 21 50 83 115
4-6,8,10-Ditko-c/a 13 26 39 93 164 235
7,9,11-15: Last 10¢ issue? 6 12 18 37 59 80
16-27 (3/64): 18,19-Robot-c 5 10 15 30 48 65
28(3/78),29-31,33,34-Ditko-c/a(r): 30-Staton, Sutton/Wood-a. 31-Ditko-c/a(3); same-c as Strange Suspense Stories #2 (1968); atom blast-c 1 3 4 6 8 10
32-r/Charlton Premiere V2#2; Sutton-a 5.00

SPACE WESTERN (Formerly Cowboy Western Comics; becomes Cowboy Western Comics #46 on)
Charlton Comics (Capitol Stories): No. 40, Oct, 1952 - No. 45, Aug, 1953

40-Intro Spurs Jackson & His Space Vigilantes; flying saucer story 55 110 135 347 586 825
41,43-45: 41-Flying saucer-c. 45-Hitler app. 41 82 123 253 419 585
42-Atom bomb explosion-c 43 86 129 267 446 625

SPACE WORLDS (Formerly Space Squadron #1-5)
Atlas Comics (Male): No. 6, April, 1952

6-Sol Brodsky-c 43 86 129 267 446 625

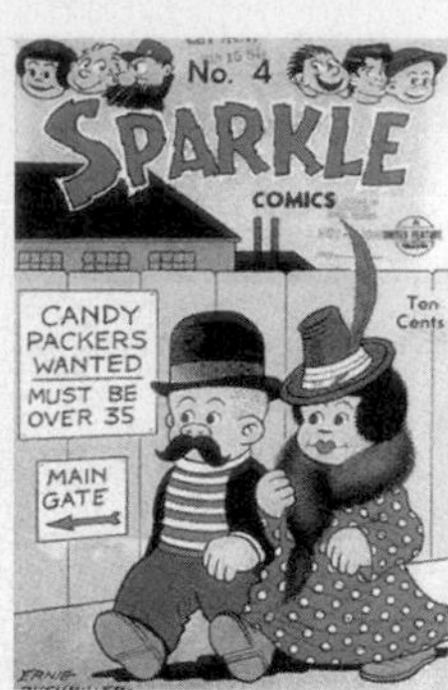

Sparkle Comics #4 © UFS

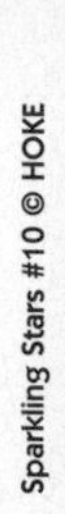
Sparkling Stars #10 © HOKE

Spawn #156 © TMP

SPAGHETTI WESTERN
Oni Press: June, 2004 ($11.95, digest-size, widescreen, sepia & white)

	GD 2.0	VG 4.0	FN 6.0	VF 8.0	VF/NM 9.0	NM- 9.2
nn-Scott Morse-s/a; outer wraparound-c						12.00

SPANKY & ALFALFA & THE LITTLE RASCALS (See The Little Rascals)

SPANNER'S GALAXY
DC Comics: Dec, 1984 - No. 6, May, 1985 (limited series)

	GD 2.0	VG 4.0	FN 6.0	VF 8.0	VF/NM 9.0	NM- 9.2
1-6: Mandrake-c/a in all.						2.50

SPARKIE, RADIO PIXIE (Radio)(Becomes Big Jon & Sparkie #4)
Ziff-Davis Publ. Co.: Winter, 1951 - No. 3, July-Aug, 1952 (Painted-c)(Sparkie #2,3; #1?)

	GD 2.0	VG 4.0	FN 6.0	VF 8.0	VF/NM 9.0	NM- 9.2
1-Based on children's radio program	27	54	81	156	251	345
2,3: 3-Big Jon and Sparkie on-c only	18	36	54	105	165	225

SPARKLE COMICS
United Features Synd.: Oct-Nov, 1948 - No. 33, Dec-Jan, 1953-54

	GD 2.0	VG 4.0	FN 6.0	VF 8.0	VF/NM 9.0	NM- 9.2
1-Li'l Abner, Nancy, Captain & the Kids, Ella Cinders (#1-3: 52 pgs.)	15	30	45	83	124	165
2	9	18	27	50	65	80
3-10	8	16	24	40	50	60
11-20	7	14	21	35	43	50
21-32	6	12	18	28	34	40
33-(2-3/54) 2 pgs. early Peanuts by Schulz	9	18	27	47	61	75

SPARKLE PLENTY (See Harvey Comics Library #2 & Dick Tracy)

SPARKLER COMICS (1st series)
United Feature Comic Group: July, 1940 - No. 2, 1940

	GD 2.0	VG 4.0	FN 6.0	VF 8.0	VF/NM 9.0	NM- 9.2
1-Jim Hardy	40	80	120	235	380	525
2-Frankie Doodle	29	58	87	169	272	375

SPARKLER COMICS (2nd series)(Nancy & Sluggo #121 on)(Cover title becomes Nancy and Sluggo #101? on)
United Features Syndicate: July, 1941 - No. 120, Jan, 1955

	GD 2.0	VG 4.0	FN 6.0	VF 8.0	VF/NM 9.0	NM- 9.2
1-Origin 1st app. Sparkman; Tarzan (by Hogarth in all issues), Captain & the Kids, Ella Cinders, Danny Dingle, Dynamite Dunn, Nancy, Abbie & Slats, Broncho Bill, Frankie Doodle, begin; Spark Man c-1-9,11,12; Hap Hopper c-10,13	238	476	714	1488	2469	3450
2	78	156	234	488	812	1135
3,4	59	118	177	369	615	860
5-9: 9-Spark Man's new costume	54	108	162	338	562	785
10-Spark Man's secret ID revealed	54	108	162	338	562	785
11,12-Spark Man war-c. 12-Spark Man's new costume (color change)	43	86	129	262	431	600
13-Hap Hopper war-c	41	82	123	250	400	550
14-Tarzan-c by Hogarth	53	106	159	323	537	750
15,17: 15-Capt & Kids-c. 17-Nancy & Sluggo-c	36	72	108	208	329	450
16,18-Spark Man war-c	41	82	123	256	416	575
19-1st Race Riley and the Commandos-c/s	41	82	123	250	400	550
20-Nancy war-c	36	72	108	208	329	450
21,25,28,31,34,37,39-Tarzan-c by Hogarth	45	90	135	275	455	635
22-24,26,27,29,30: 22-Race Riley & the Commandos strips begin, ends #44	31	62	93	178	282	385
32,33,35,36,38,40	18	36	54	105	165	225
41,43,45,46,48,49	14	28	42	80	115	150
42,44,47,50-Tarzan-c (42,47,50 by Hogarth)	28	56	84	164	260	355
51,52,54-70: 57-Li'l Abner begins (not in #58); Fearless Fosdick app. in #58	14	28	42	76	108	140
53-Tarzan-c by Hogarth	24	48	72	139	220	300
71-80	10	20	30	54	72	90
81,82,84-86: 86 Last Tarzan; lingerie panels	9	18	27	47	61	75
83-Tarzan-c; Li'l Abner ends	13	26	39	74	105	135
87-96,98-99	8	16	24	44	57	70
97-Origin Casey Ruggles by Warren Tufts	13	26	39	72	101	130
100	9	18	27	50	65	80
101-107,109-112,114-119	7	14	21	37	46	55
108,113-Toth-a	9	18	27	50	65	80
120-(10-11/54) 2 pgs. early Peanuts by Schulz	9	18	27	50	65	80

SPARKLING LOVE
Avon Periodicals/Realistic (1953): June, 1950; 1953

	GD 2.0	VG 4.0	FN 6.0	VF 8.0	VF/NM 9.0	NM- 9.2
1(Avon)-Kubert-a; photo-c	23	46	69	135	218	300
nn(1953)-Reprint; Kubert-a	10	20	30	54	72	90

SPARKLING STARS
Holyoke Publishing Co.: June, 1944 - No. 33, March, 1948

	GD 2.0	VG 4.0	FN 6.0	VF 8.0	VF/NM 9.0	NM- 9.2
1-Hell's Angels, FBI, Boxie Weaver, Petey & Pop, & Ali Baba begin	20	40	60	114	180	245
2-Speed Spaulding story	12	24	36	67	94	120
3-Actual FBI case photos & war photos	10	20	30	54	72	90
4-10: 7-X-Mas-c	9	18	27	50	65	80
11-19: 13-Origin/1st app. Jungo the Man-Beast-c/s	8	16	24	44	57	70
20-Intro Fangs the Wolf Boy	9	18	27	50	65	80
21-33: 29-Bondage-c. 31-Sid Greene-a	8	16	24	42	54	65

SPARK MAN (See Sparkler Comics)
Frances M. McQueeny: 1945 (36 pgs., one-shot)

	GD 2.0	VG 4.0	FN 6.0	VF 8.0	VF/NM 9.0	NM- 9.2
1-Origin Spark Man r/Sparkler #1-3; female torture story; cover redrawn from Sparkler #1	32	64	96	186	298	410

SPARKS (William Katt Presents...)
Catastrophic Comics: June, 2008 - Present ($2.99)

	GD 2.0	VG 4.0	FN 6.0	VF 8.0	VF/NM 9.0	NM- 9.2
1,2: 1-Folino-s/Ringuet-a; origin of Sparks						3.00

SPARKY WATTS (Also see Big Shot Comics & Columbia Comics)
Columbia Comic Corp.: Nov?, 1942 - No. 10, 1949

	GD 2.0	VG 4.0	FN 6.0	VF 8.0	VF/NM 9.0	NM- 9.2
1(1942)-Skyman & The Face app; Hitler-c	73	146	219	460	780	1100
2(1943)	29	58	87	169	272	375
3(1944)	21	42	63	123	197	270
4(1944)-Origin	18	36	54	105	165	225
5(1947)-Skyman app.; Boody Rogers-c/a	15	30	45	88	137	185
6,7,9,10: 6(1947),10(1949)	11	22	33	60	83	105
8(1948)-Surrealistic-c	14	28	42	76	108	140

NOTE: ***Boody Rogers*** *c-1-8.*

SPARTACUS (Movie)
Dell Publishing Co.: No. 1139, Nov, 1960 (Kirk Douglas photo-c)

	GD 2.0	VG 4.0	FN 6.0	VF 8.0	VF/NM 9.0	NM- 9.2
Four Color 1139-Buscema-a	12	24	36	87	156	225

SPARTAN: WARRIOR SPIRIT (Also see WildC.A.T.S: Covert Action Teams)
Image Comics (WildStorm Productions): July, 1995 - No. 4, Nov, 1995 ($2.50, lim. series)

	GD 2.0	VG 4.0	FN 6.0	VF 8.0	VF/NM 9.0	NM- 9.2
1-4: Kurt Busiek scripts; Mike McKone-c/a						2.50

SPAWN (Also see Curse of the Spawn and Sam & Twitch)
Image Comics (Todd McFarlane Prods.): May, 1992 - Present ($1.95/$2.50)

	GD 2.0	VG 4.0	FN 6.0	VF 8.0	VF/NM 9.0	NM- 9.2
1-1st app. Spawn; McFarlane-c/a begins; McFarlane/Steacy-c; 1st Todd McFarlane Productions title.	1	3	4	6	8	10
1-Black & white edition	2	4	6	11	16	20
2,3: 2-1st app. Violator; McFarlane/Steacy-c	1	2	3	5	7	9
4-Contains coupon for Image Comics #0	1	2	3	5	7	9
4-With coupon missing						3.00
4-Newsstand edition w/o poster or coupon						3.00
5-Cerebus cameo (1 pg.) as stuffed animal; Spawn mobile poster #1						6.00
6-8,10: 7-Spawn Mobile poster #2. 8-Alan Moore scripts; Miller poster. 10-Cerebus app.; Dave Sim scripts; 1 pg. cameo app. by Superman						4.00
9-Neil Gaiman scripts; Jim Lee poster; 1st Angela.						6.00
11-17,19,20,22-30: 11-Miller script; Darrow poster. 12-Bloodwulf poster by Liefeld. 14,15-Violator app. 16,17-Grant Morrison scripts; Capullo-c/a(p). 23,24-McFarlane-a/stories. 25-(10/94). 19-(10/94). 20-(11/94)						3.00
18-Grant Morrison script, Capullo-c/a(p); low distr.	1	2	3	5	7	9
21-low distribution	1	2	3	5	7	9
31-49: 31-1st app. The Redeemer; new costume (brief). 32-1st full app. new costume. 38-40,42,44,46,48-Tony Daniel-c/a(p). 38-1st app. Cy-Gor. 40,41-Cy-Gor & Curse app.						4.00
50-($3.95, 48 pgs.)						3.00
51-66: 52-Savage Dragon app. 56-w/ Darkchylde preview. 57-Cy-Gor-c/app. 64-Polybagged w/McFarlane Toys catalog. 65-Photo-c of movie Spawn and McFarlane						3.00
67-97: 81-Billy Kincaid returns. 97-Angela-c/app.						2.50
98,99,101-149-($2.50): 98,99-Angela app.						2.50
100-($4.95) Angela dies; 6 covers by McFarlane, Ross, Miller, Capullo, Wood, Mignola						5.00
150-($4.95) 4 covers by McFarlane, Capullo, Tan, Jim Lee						5.00
151-183: 151-($2.95) Wraparound-c by Tan. 167-Clown app. 179-Mayhew-a						3.00
Annual 1-Blood & Shadows ('99, $4.95) Ashley Wood-c/a; Jenkins-s						5.00
....: Armegeddon Complete Collection TPB ('07, $29.95) r/#150-163						30.00
....: Armegeddon, Part 1 TPB (10/06, $14.99) r/#150-155						15.00
....: Armegeddon, Part 2 TPB (2/07, $15.95) r/#156-164						16.00
...Bible-(8/96, $1.95)-Character bios						4.00
Book 1 TPB($9.95) r/#1-5; Book 2-r/#6-9,11; Book 3 -r/#12-15, Book 4- r/#16-20; Book 5-r/#21-25; Book 6- r/#26-30; Book 7-r/#31-34; Book 8-r/#35-38; Book 9-r/#39-42; Book 10-r/#43-47						11.00
Book 11 TPB ($10.95) r/#48-50; Book 12-r/#51-54						11.00
... Collection Vol. 1 (10/05, $19.95) r/#1-8,11,12; intro. by Frank Miller						20.00
... Collection Vol. 2 HC (7/07, $49.95) r/#13-33						50.00
... Collection Vol. 2 SC (9/06, $29.95) r/#13-33						30.00

Spawn: Godslayer #7 © TMP

Special Forces #1 © Kyle Baker

Spectacular Spider-Man #29 © MAR

GD 2.0 | VG 4.0 | FN 6.0 | VF 8.0 | VF/NM 9.0 | NM- 9.2

... Collection Vol. 3 (3/07, $29.95) r/#34-54 30.00
... Collection Vol. 4 (9/07, $29.95) r/#55-75 30.00
... Collection Vol. 5 ('08, $29.95) r/#76-95 30.00
... Collection Vol. 6 ('08, $29.95) r/#96-114 30.00
... Godslayer Vol. 1 (9/06, $6.99) Anacleto-c/a; Holguin-s; sketch pages 7.00
...: New Flesh TPB ('07, $14.95) r/#166-169 15.00
...Simony (5/04, $7.95) English translation of French Spawn story; Briclot-a 8.00

NOTE: *Capullo a-16p-18p; c-16p-18p. Daniel a-38-40, 42, 44, 46. McFarlane a-1-15; c-1-15p. Thibert a-16i(part). Posters come with issues 1, 4, 7-9, 11, 12. #25 was released before #19 & 20.*

SPAWN-BATMAN (Also see Batman/Spawn: War Devil under Batman One-Shots)
Image Comics (Todd McFarlane Productions): 1994 ($3.95, one-shot)
1-Miller scripts; McFarlane-c/a 6.00

SPAWN: BLOOD FEUD
Image Comics (Todd McFarlane Prods.): June, 1995 - No. 4, Sept, 1995 ($2.25, lim. series)
1-4-Alan Moore scripts, Tony Daniel-a 3.50

SPAWN FAN EDITION
Image Comics (Todd McFarlane Productions): Aug, 1996 - No. 3, Oct, 1996 (Giveaway, 12 pgs.) (Polybagged w/Overstreet's FAN)
1-3: Beau Smith scripts; Brad Gorby-a(p). 1-1st app. Nordik, the Norse Hellspawn. 2-1st app. McFallon. 3-1st app. Mercy 1 2 3 5 6 8
1-3-(Gold): All retailer incentives 16.00
1-3-Variant-c 1 2 3 5 6 8
2-(Platinum)-Retailer incentive 25.00

SPAWN GODSLAYER
Image Comics (Todd McFarlane Prods.): May, 2007 - No. 8, Apr, 2008 ($2.99)
1-8: 1-Holguin-s/Tan-a/Anacleto-c 3.00

SPAWN: THE DARK AGES
Image Comics (Todd McFarlane Productions): Mar, 1999 - No. 28, Oct, 2001 ($2.50)
1-Fabry-c; Holguin-s/Sharp-a; variant-c by McFarlane 2.50
2-28 2.50

SPAWN THE IMPALER
Image Comics (Todd McFarlane Prods.): Oct, 1996 - No. 3, Dec, 1996 ($2.95, limited series)
1-3-Mike Grell scripts, painted-a 3.00

SPAWN: THE UNDEAD
Image Comics (Todd McFarlane Prod.): Jun, 1999 - No. 9, Feb, 2000 ($1.95/$2.25)
1-9-Dwayne Turner-c/a; Jenkins-s. 7-9-($2.25-c) 2.50
TPB (6/08, $24.99) r/#1-9 25.00

SPAWN/WILDC.A.T.S
Image Comics (WildStorm): Jan, 1996 - No. 4, Apr, 1996 ($2.50, lim. series)
1-4: Alan Moore scripts in all. 3.00

SPECIAL AGENT (Steve Saunders...)(Also see True Comics #68)
Parents' Magazine Institute (Commended Comics No. 2): Dec, 1947 - No. 8, Sept, 1949 (Based on true FBI cases)
1-J. Edgar Hoover photo on-c 12 24 36 67 94 120
2 8 16 24 40 50 60
3-8 7 14 21 35 43 50

SPECIAL COLLECTORS' EDITION (See Savage Fists of Kung-Fu)

SPECIAL COMICS (Becomes Hangman #2 on)
MLJ Magazines: Winter, 1941-42
1-Origin The Boy Buddies (Shield & Wizard x-over); death of The Comet retold (see Pep #17); origin The Hangman retold; Hangman-c 300 600 900 2010 3505 5000

SPECIAL EDITION (See Gorgo and Reptisaurus)

SPECIAL EDITION COMICS
Fawcett Publications: 1940 (August) (68 pgs., one-shot)
1-1st book devoted entirely to Captain Marvel; C.C. Beck-c/a; only app. of Captain Marvel with belt buckle; Capt. Marvel appears with button-down flap; 1st story (came out before Captain Marvel #1) 744 1488 2232 5357 9379 13,400

NOTE: *Prices vary widely on this book. Since this book is all Captain Marvel stories, it is actually a pre-Captain Marvel #1. There is speculation that this book almost became **Captain Marvel** #1. After **Special Edition** was published, there was an editor change at Fawcett. The new editor commissioned Kirby to do a nn **Captain Marvel** book early in 1941. This book was followed by a 2nd book several months later. This 2nd book was advertised as a #3 (making Special Edition the #1, & the nn issue the #2). However, the 2nd book did come out as a #2.*

SPECIAL EDITION: SPIDER-MAN VS. THE HULK (See listing under The Amazing Spider-Man)

SPECIAL EDITION X-MEN
Marvel Comics Group: Feb, 1983 ($2.00, one-shot, Baxter paper)
1-r/Giant-Size X-Men #1 plus one new story 2 4 6 8 10 12

GD 2.0 | VG 4.0 | FN 6.0 | VF 8.0 | VF/NM 9.0 | NM- 9.2

SPECIAL FORCES
Image Comics: Oct, 2007 - No. 4 ($2.99)
1-3-Iraq war combat; Kyle Baker-s/a/c 3.00

SPECIAL MARVEL EDITION (Master of Kung Fu #17 on)
Marvel Comics Group: Jan, 1971 - No. 16, Feb, 1974 (#1-3: 25¢, 68 pgs.; #4: 52 pgs.; #5-16: 20¢, regular ed.)
1-Thor-r by Kirby; 68 pgs. 3 6 9 18 27 35
2-4: Thor-r by Kirby; 2,3-68 pg. Giant. 4-(52 pgs.) 2 4 6 11 16 20
5-14: Sgt. Fury-r; 11-r/Sgt. Fury #13 (Capt. America) 1 3 4 6 8 10
15-Master of Kung Fu (Shang Chi) begins (1st app., 12/73); Starlin-a; origin/1st app. Nayland Smith & Dr. Petrie 10 20 30 73 129 185
16-1st app. Midnight; Starlin-a (2nd Shang-Chi) 5 10 15 34 55 75

NOTE: *Kirby c-10-14.*

SPECIAL MISSIONS (See G.I. Joe...)

SPECIAL WAR SERIES (Attack V4#3 on?)
Charlton Comics: Aug, 1965 - No. 4, Nov, 1965
V4#1-D-Day (also see D-Day listing) 4 8 12 22 34 45
2-Attack! 3 6 9 14 20 25
3-War & Attack (also see War & Attack) 2 4 6 11 16 20
4-Judomaster (intro/1st app.; see Sarge Steel) 7 14 21 49 80 110

SPECIES (Movie)
Dark Horse Comics: June, 1995 - No. 4, Sept, 1995 ($2.50, limited series)
1-4: Adaptation of film 3.00

SPECIES: HUMAN RACE (Movie)
Dark Horse Comics: Nov, 1996 - No. 4, Feb, 1997 ($2.95, limited series)
1-4 3.00

SPECTACULAR ADVENTURES (See Adventures)

SPECTACULAR FEATURE MAGAZINE, A (Formerly My Confessions) (Spectacular Features Magazine #12)
Fox Feature Syndicate: No. 11, April, 1950
11 (#1)-Samson and Delilah 27 54 81 158 254 350

SPECTACULAR FEATURES MAGAZINE (Formerly A Spectacular Feature Magazine)
Fox Feature Syndicate: No. 12, June, 1950 - No. 3, Aug, 1950
12 (#2)-Iwo Jima; photo flag-c 27 54 81 156 251 345
3-True Crime Cases From Police Files 22 44 66 127 204 280

SPECTACULAR SCARLET SPIDER
Marvel Comics: Nov, 1995 - No. 2, Dec, 1995 ($1.95, limited series)
1,2: Replaces Spectacular Spider-Man 2.50

SPECTACULAR SPIDER-MAN, THE (See Marvel Special Edition and Marvel Treasury Edition)

SPECTACULAR SPIDER-MAN, THE (Magazine)
Marvel Comics Group: July, 1968 - No. 2, Nov, 1968 (35¢)
1-(B&W)-Romita/Mooney 52 pg. story plus updated origin story with Everett-a(i) 11 22 33 79 140 200
1-Variation w/single c-price of 40¢ 11 22 33 79 140 200
2-(Color)-Green Goblin-c & 58 pg. story; Romita painted-c (story reprinted in King Size Spider-Man #9); Romita/Mooney-a 12 24 36 86 153 220

SPECTACULAR SPIDER-MAN, THE (Peter Parker...#54-132, 134)
Marvel Comics Group: Dec, 1976 - No. 263, Nov, 1998
1-Origin recap in text; return of Tarantula 6 12 18 37 59 80
2-Kraven the Hunter app. 3 6 9 16 23 30
3-5: 3-Intro Lightmaster. 4-Vulture app. 2 4 6 13 18 22
6-8-Morbius app.; 6-r/Marvel Team-Up #3 w/Morbius 3 6 9 14 19 24
7,8-(35¢-c variants, limited distribution)(6,7/77) 5 10 15 34 55 75
9-20: 9,10-White Tiger app. 11-Last 30¢-c. 17,18-Angel & Iceman app. (from Champions); Ghost Rider cameo. 18-Gil Kane-c 2 4 6 8 10 12
9-11-(35¢-c variants, limited distribution)(8-10/77) 3 6 9 20 30 40
21,24-26: 21-Scorpion app. 26-Daredevil app. 1 2 3 5 7 9
22,23-Moon Knight app. 1 3 4 6 8 10
27-Miller's 1st art on Daredevil (2/79); also see Captain America #235 4 8 12 28 44 60
28-Miller Daredevil (p) 4 8 12 24 37 50
29-55,57,59: 33-Origin Iguana. 38-Morbius app. 5.00
56-2nd app. Jack O'Lantern (Macendale) & 1st Spidey/Jack O'Lantern battle (7/81) 6.00
58-Byrne-a(p) 6.00
60-Double size; origin retold with new facts revealed 6.00
61-63,65-68,71-74: 65-Kraven the Hunter app. 4.00

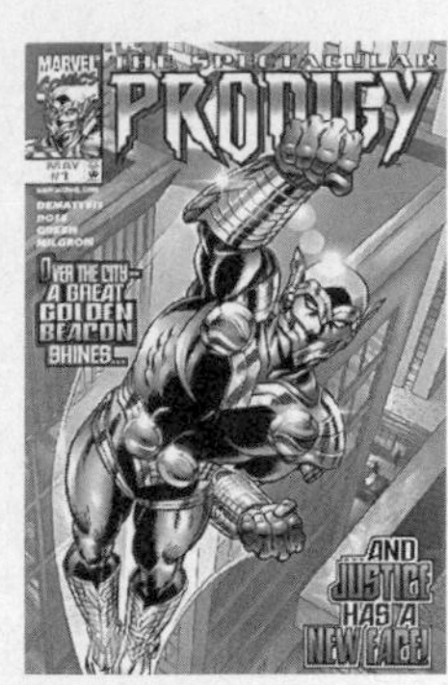

Spectacular Spider-Man #257 © MAR

The Spectre (4th series) #2 © DC

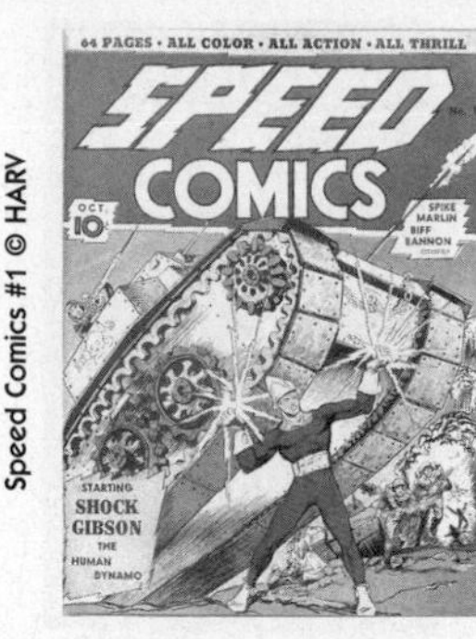

Speed Comics #1 © HARV

	GD 2.0	VG 4.0	FN 6.0	VF 8.0	VF/NM 9.0	NM- 9.2
64-1st app. Cloak & Dagger (3/82)	2	4	6	9	12	15
69,70-Cloak & Dagger app.	1	2	3	5	6	8
75-Double size						5.00
76-80: 78,79-Punisher cameo						4.00
81,82-Punisher, Cloak & Dagger app.						6.00
83-Origin Punisher retold (10/83)	1	3	4	6	8	10
84,86-89,91-99: 94-96-Cloak & Dagger app. 98-Intro The Spot						4.00
85-Hobgoblin (Ned Leeds) app. (12/83); gains powers of original Green Goblin (see Amazing Spider-Man #238)	1	3	4	6	8	10
90-Spider-Man's new black costume, last panel (ties w/Amazing Spider-Man #252 & Marvel Team-Up #141 for 1st app.)						5.00
100-(3/85)-Double size						5.00
101-115,117,118,120-129: 107-110-Death of Jean DeWolff. 111-Secret Wars II tie-in. 128-Black Cat new costume						3.00
116,119-Sabretooth-c/story	1	3	4	5	6	8
130-132: 30-Hobgoblin app. 131-Six part Kraven tie-in. 132-Kraven tie-in	1	2	3	4	5	7
133-140: 138-1st full app. Tombstone (origin #139). 140-Punisher cameo						3.00
141-143-Punisher app.						5.00
144-146,148-157: 151-Tombstone returns						3.00
147-1st brief app. new Hobgoblin (Macendale), 1 page; continued in Web of Spider-Man #48	2	4	6	8	10	12
158-Spider-Man gets new powers (1st Cosmic Spidey, cont'd in Web of Spider-Man #59)	1	2	3	4	5	7
159-Cosmic Spider-Man app.						6.00
160-170: 161-163-Hobgoblin app. 168-170-Avengers x-over. 169-1st app. The Outlaws						2.50
171-188,190-199: 180,181,183,184-Green Goblin app. 197-199-Original X-Men-c/story						2.50
189-($2.95, 52 pgs.)-Silver hologram on-c; battles Green Goblin; origin Spidey retold; Vess poster w/Spidey & Hobgoblin						4.00
189-(2nd printing)-Gold hologram on-c						3.00
195-(Deluxe ed.)-Polybagged w/"Dirt" magazine #2 & Beastie Boys/Smithereens music cassette						4.00
200-($2.95)-Holo-grafx foil-c; Green Goblin-c/story						3.00
201-219,221,222,224,226-228,230-247: 212-w/card sheet. 203-Maximum Carnage x-over. 204-Begin 4 part death of Tombstone story. 207,208-The Shroud-c/story. 208-Siege of Darkness x-over (#207 is a tie-in). 209-Black Cat back-up. 215,216-Scorpion app. 217-Power & Responsibility Pt. 4. 231-Return of Kaine; Spider-Man corpse discovered. 232-New Doc Octopus app. 233-Carnage-c/app. 235-Dragon Man cameo. 236-Dragon Man-c/app; Lizard app.; Peter Parker regains powers. 238,239-Lizard app. 239-w/card insert. 240-Revelations storyline begins. 241-Flashback						2.50
213-Collectors ed. polybagged w/16 pg. preview & animation cel; foil-c; 1st meeting Spidey & Typhoid Mary						3.00
213-Version polybagged w/Gamepro #7; no-c date, price						2.50
217,219 ($2.95)-Deluxe edition foil-c: flip book						3.00
220 ($2.25, 52 pgs.)-Flip book, Mary Jane reveals pregnancy						3.00
223,229: ($2.50) 229-Spidey quits						3.00
223,225: ($2.95)-223-Die Cut-c. 225-Newsstand ed.						3.00
225,229: ($3.95) 225-Direct Market Holodisk-c (Green Goblin). 229-Acetate-c, Spidey quits						4.00
240-Variant-c						3.00
248,249,251-254,256: 249-Return of Norman Osborn 256-1st app. Prodigy						2.50
250-($3.25) Double gatefold-c						3.25
255-($2.99) Spiderhunt pt. 4						3.00
257-262: 257-Double cover with "Spectacular Prodigy #1"; battles Jack O'Lantern. 258-Spidey is cleared. 259,260-Green Goblin & Hobgoblin app. 262-Byrne-s						2.50
263-Final issue; Byrne-c; Aunt May returns						4.00
#(-1) Flashback (7/97)						2.50
Annual 1 (1979)-Doc Octopus-c & 46 pg. story	2	4	6	8	10	12
Annual 2 (1980)-Origin/1st app. Rapier	1	2	3	4	5	7
Annual 3-5: ('81-'83) 3-Last Man-Wolf						4.00
Annual 6 14: 8 ('88,$ 1.75)-Evolutionary War x-over; Daydreamer returns Gwen Stacy "clone" back to real self (not Gwen Stacy). 9 ('89, $2.00, 68 pgs.)-Atlantis Attacks. 10 ('90, $2.00, 68 pgs.)-McFarlane-a. 11 ('91, $2.00, 68 pgs.)-Iron Man app. 12 ('92, $2.25, 68 pgs.)-Venom solo story cont'd from Amazing Spider-Man Annual #26. 13 ('93, $2.95, 68 pgs.)-Polybagged w/trading card; John Romita, Sr. back-up-a						3.00
Special 1 (1995, $3.95)-Flip book						4.00

NOTE: ***Austin*** *c-21i, Annual 11i.* ***Buckler*** *a-103, 107-111, 116, 117, 119, 122, Annual 1, Annual 10; c-103, 107-111, 113, 116-119, 122, Annual 1.* ***Buscema*** *a-121.* ***Byrne*** *c(p)-17, 43, 58, 101, 102.* ***Giffen*** *a-120p.* ***Hembeck*** *c/a-86p.* ***Larsen*** *c-Annual 11p.* ***Miller*** *c-46p, 48p, 50, 51p, 52p, 54p, 55, 56p, 57, 60.* ***Mooney*** *a-7i, 11i, 21p, 23p, 25p, 26p, 29-34p, 36p, 37p, 39i, 41, 42i, 49p, 50i, 51i, 53p, 54-57i, 59-66i, 68i, 71i, 73-79i, 81-83i, 85i, 87-99i, 102i, 125p, Annual 1i, 2p.* ***Nasser*** *c-37p.* ***Perez*** *c-10.* ***Simonson*** *c-54i.* ***Zeck*** *a-22, 118, 131, 132; c-131, 132.*

SPECTACULAR SPIDER-MAN (2nd series)
Marvel Comics: Sept, 2003 - No. 27, June, 2005 ($2.25/$2.99)

	GD 2.0	VG 4.0	FN 6.0	VF 8.0	VF/NM 9.0	NM- 9.2
1-Jenkins-s/Ramos-a/c; Venom-c/app.						3.00
2-22: 2-5-Venom app. 6-9-Dr. Octopus app. 11-13-The Lizard app. 14-Rivera painted-a. 15,16-Capt. America app. 17,18-Ramos-a. 20-Spider-Man gets organic webshooters 21,22-Caldwell-a. 23-26-Sarah & Gabriel app.; Land-c						2.25
27-($2.99) Last issue; Uncle Ben app. in flashback; Buckingham-a						3.00
... Vol. 1: The Hunger TPB (2003, $11.99) r/#1-5						12.00
... Vol. 2: Countdown TPB (2004, $11.99) r/#6-10						12.00
... Vol. 3: Here There Be Monsters TPB (2004, $9.99) r/#11-14						10.00
... Vol. 4: Disassembled TPB (2004, $14.99) r/#15-20						15.00
... Vol. 5: Sins Remembered (2005, $9.99) r/#23-26						10.00
... Vol. 6: The Final Curtain (2005, $14.99) r/#21,22,27 & Peter Parker: Spider-Man #39-41						15.00

SPECTACULAR STORIES MAGAZINE (Formerly A Star Presentation)
Fox Feature Syndicate (Hero Books): No. 4, July, 1950; No. 3, Sept, 1950

	GD 2.0	VG 4.0	FN 6.0	VF 8.0	VF/NM 9.0	NM- 9.2
4-Sherlock Holmes (true crime stories)	36	72	108	212	341	470
3-The St. Valentine's Day Massacre (true crime)	24	48	72	140	225	310

SPECTRE, THE (1st Series) (See Adventure Comics #431-440, More Fun & Showcase)
National Periodical Publ.: Nov-Dec, 1967 - No. 10, May-June, 1969 (All 12¢)

	GD 2.0	VG 4.0	FN 6.0	VF 8.0	VF/NM 9.0	NM- 9.2
1-(11-12/67)-Anderson-c/a	14	28	42	99	175	250
2-5-Neal Adams-c/a; 3-Wildcat x-over	9	18	27	63	107	150
6-8,10: 6-8-Anderson inks. 7-Hourman app.	7	14	21	45	73	100
9-Wrightson-a	7	14	21	47	76	105

SPECTRE, THE (2nd Series) (See Saga of the Swamp Thing #58, Showcase '95 #8 & Wrath of the...)
DC Comics: Apr, 1987 - No. 31, Oct, 1989 ($1.00, new format)

	GD 2.0	VG 4.0	FN 6.0	VF 8.0	VF/NM 9.0	NM- 9.2
1-Colan-a begins						4.00
2-32: 9-Nudity panels. 10-Batman cameo. 10,11-Millennium tie-ins						3.00
Annual 1 (1988, $2.00)-Deadman app.						3.00

NOTE: ***Art Adams*** *c-Annual 1.* ***Colan*** *a-1-6.* ***Kaluta*** *c-1-3.* ***Mignola*** *c-7-9.* ***Morrow*** *a-9-15.* ***Sears*** *c/a-22.* ***Vess*** *c-13-15.*

SPECTRE, THE (3rd Series) (Also see Brave and the Bold #72, 75, 116, 180, 199 & Showcase '95 #8)
DC Comics: Dec, 1992 - No. 62, Feb, 1998 ($1.75/$1.95/$2.25/$2.50)

	GD 2.0	VG 4.0	FN 6.0	VF 8.0	VF/NM 9.0	NM- 9.2
1-($1.95)-Glow-in-the-dark-c; Mandrake-a begins						5.00
2,3						3.00
4-7,9-12,14-20: 10-Kaluta-c. 11-Hildebrandt painted-c. 16-Aparo/K. Jones-a. 19-Snyder III-c. 20-Sienkiewicz-c						2.50
8,13-($2.50)-Glow-in-the-dark-c						3.00
21-62: 22-(9/94)-Superman-c & app. 23-(11/94). 43-Kent Williams-c. 44-Kaluta-c. 47-Final Night x-over. 49-Begin Bolton-c. 51-Batman-c/app. 52-Gianni-c. 54-Corben-c. 60-Harris-c						2.50
#0 (10/94) Released between #22 & #23						2.50
Annual 1 (1995, $3.95)-Year One story						4.00

NOTE: ***Bisley*** *c-27.* ***Fabry*** *c-2.* ***Kelley Jones*** *c-31.* ***Vess*** *c-5.*

SPECTRE, THE (4th Series) (Hal Jordan; also see Day of Judgment #5 and Legends of the DC Universe #33-36)
DC Comics: Mar, 2001 - No. 27, May, 2003 ($2.50/$2.75)

	GD 2.0	VG 4.0	FN 6.0	VF 8.0	VF/NM 9.0	NM- 9.2
1-DeMatteis-s/Ryan Sook-c/a						3.00
2-27: 3,4-Superman & Batman-c/app. 5-Two-Face-c/app. 20-Begin $2.75-c. 21-Sinestro returns. 24-JLA app.						2.75

SPECTRE, THE (See Crisis Aftermath: The Spectre)

SPEEDBALL (See Amazing Spider-Man Annual #12, Marvel Super-Heroes & The New Warriors)
Marvel Comics: Sept, 1988(10/88-inside) - No. 11, July, 1989 (75¢)

	GD 2.0	VG 4.0	FN 6.0	VF 8.0	VF/NM 9.0	NM- 9.2
1-11: Ditko/Guice a-1-4, c-1; Ditko a-1-10; c-1-11p						2.25

SPEED BUGGY (TV)(Also see Fun-In #12, 15)
Charlton Comics: July, 1975 - No. 9, Nov, 1976 (Hanna-Barbera)

	GD 2.0	VG 4.0	FN 6.0	VF 8.0	VF/NM 9.0	NM- 9.2
1	3	6	9	16	22	28
2-9	2	4	6	10	14	18

SPEED CARTER SPACEMAN (See Spaceman)

SPEED COMICS (New Speed)(Also see Double Up)
Brookwood Publ./Speed Publ./Harvey Publications No. 14 on:
10/39 - #11, 8/40; #12, 3/41 - #44, 1-2/47 (#14-16: pocket size, 100 pgs.)

	GD 2.0	VG 4.0	FN 6.0	VF 8.0	VF/NM 9.0	NM- 9.2
1-Origin & 1st app. Shock Gibson; Ted Parrish, the Man with 1000 Faces begins; Powell-a; becomes Champion #2 on?; has earliest? full page panel in comics	341	682	1023	2319	4060	5800
2-Powell-a	117	234	351	737	1244	1750
3	67	134	201	422	711	1000
4,5: 4-Powell-a? 5-Dinosaur-c	54	108	162	340	575	810
6-11: 7-Mars Mason begins, ends #11	50	100	150	310	518	725
12 (3/41; shows #11 in indicia)-The Wasp begins; Major Colt app. (Capt. Colt #12)						

Speed Racer #1 © Speed Racer Ent.

Spellbound #13 © MAR

Spider-Girl #50 © MAR

53 106 159 330 553 775
13-Intro. Captain Freedom & Young Defenders; Girl Commandos, Pat Parker (costumed heroine), War Nurse begins; Major Colt app. 59 118 177 372 629 885
14-16 (100 pg. pocket size, 1941): 14-2nd Harvey comic (See Pocket); Shock Gibson dons new costume. 15-Pat Parker dons costume, last in costume #23; no Girl Commandos
80 160 240 504 852 1200
17-Black Cat begins (4/42, early app.; see Pocket #1); origin Black Cat-r/Pocket #1; not in #40,41; S&K-c 78 156 234 491 833 1175
18-20-S&K-c 63 126 189 397 674 950
21-Hitler, Tojo-c; Kirby-c 87 174 261 548 924 1300
22-Kirby-c 63 126 189 397 674 950
23-Origin Girl Commandos; Kirby-c 63 126 189 397 674 950
24-Pat Parker team-up with Girl Commandos; Hitler, Tojo, & Mussolini-c
70 140 210 441 746 1050
25-30: 26-Flag-c 50 100 150 310 518 725
31-Schomburg Hitler & Hirohito-c 83 166 249 523 887 1250
32-36-Schomburg-c 53 106 159 332 559 785
37,39-42, 44 41 82 123 253 419 585
38-Iwo-Jima Flag-c 43 86 129 267 446 625
43-Robot-c 45 90 135 279 465 650

NOTE: ***Al Avison*** *c-14-16, 30, 43.* ***Briefer*** *a-6, 7.* ***Jon Henri*** *(Kirbyesque) c-17-20.* ***Kubert*** *a-37, 38, 42-44.* ***Kirby/Caseneuve*** *c-21-23.* ***Cecelia Munson*** *a-7-11(Mars Mason).* ***Palais*** *c-37, 39-42.* ***Powell*** *a-1, 2, 4-7, 28, 31, 44.* ***Schomburg*** *c-31-36.* ***Tuska*** *a-3, 6, 7. Bondage c-18, 35. Captain Freedom c-16-24, 25(part), 26-44(w/Black Cat #27, 29, 31, 32-40). Shock Gibson c-1-15.*

SPEED DEMON (Also see Marvel Versus DC #3 & DC Versus Marvel #4)
Marvel Comics (Amalgam): Apr, 1996 ($1.95, one-shot)
1 2.50

SPEED DEMONS (Formerly Frank Merriwell at Yale #1-4?; Submarine Attack #11 on)
Charlton Comics: No. 5, Feb, 1957 - No. 10, 1958
5-10 7 14 21 35 43 50

SPEED FORCE (See The Flash 2nd Series #143-Cobalt Blue)
DC Comics: Nov, 1997 ($3.95, one-shot)
1-Flash & Kid Flash vs. Cobalt Blue; Waid-s/Aparo & Sienkiewicz-a; Flash family stories and pin-ups by various 4.00

SPEED RACER (Also see The New Adventures of...)
Now Comics: July, 1987 - No. 38, Nov, 1990 ($1.75)
1-38, 1-2nd printing 2.50
Special 1 (1988, $2.00) 2.50
Special 2 (1988, $3.50) 3.50

SPEED RACER (Also see Racer X)
DC Comics (WildStorm): Oct, 1999 - No. 3, Dec, 1999 ($2.50, limited series)
1-3-Tommy Yune-s/a; origin of Racer X; debut of the Mach 5 2.50
...: Born To Race (2000, $9.95, TPB) r/series & conceptual art 10.00
...: The Original Manga Vol. 1 ('00, $9.95, TPB) r/1950s B&W manga 10.00

SPEED RACER: CHRONICLES OF THE RACER
IDW Publishing: 2007 - No. 4, Apr, 2008 ($3.99)
1-4-Multiple covers for each 4.00

SPEED RACER FEATURING NINJA HIGH SCHOOL
Now Comics: Aug, 1993 - No. 2, 1993 ($2.50, mini-series)
1,2: 1-Polybagged w/card. 2-Exists? 2.50

SPEED RACER: RETURN OF THE GRX
Now Comics: Mar, 1994 - No. 2, Apr, 1994 ($1.95, limited series)
1,2 2.50

SPEED SMITH-THE HOT ROD KING (Also see Hot Rod King)
Ziff-Davis Publishing Co.: Spring, 1952
1-Saunders painted-c 23 46 69 133 214 295

SPEEDY GONZALES
Dell Publishing Co.: No. 1084, Mar, 1960
Four Color 1084 5 10 15 34 55 75

SPEEDY RABBIT (See Television Puppet Show)
Realistic/I. W. Enterprises/Super Comics: nd (1953); 1963
nn (1953)-Realistic Reprint? 2 4 6 9 13 16
I.W. Reprint #1 (2 versions w/diff. c/stories exist)-Peter Cottontail #?
Super Reprint #14(1963) 2 4 6 8 10 12

SPELLBINDERS
Quality: Dec, 1986 - No. 12, Jan, 1988 ($1.25)
1-12: Nemesis the Warlock, Amadeus Wolf 2.50

SPELLBINDERS
Marvel Comics: May, 2005 - No. 6, Oct, 2005 ($2.99, limited series)
1-6-Carey-s/Perkins-a 3.00
...: Signs and Wonders TPB (2006, $7.99, digest) r/#1-6 8.00

SPELLBOUND (See The Crusaders)

SPELLBOUND (Tales to Hold You... #1, Stories to Hold You...)
Atlas Comics (ACI 1-15/Male 16-23/BPC 24-34): Mar, 1952 - #23, June, 1954; #24, Oct, 1955 - #34, June, 1957
1-Horror/weird stories in all 70 140 210 441 746 1050
2-Edgar A. Poe app. 40 80 120 239 387 535
3-5: 3-Whitney-a; cannibalism story 35 70 105 203 327 450
6-Krigstein-a 35 70 105 203 327 450
7-10: 8-Ayers-a 30 60 90 174 280 385
11-16,18-20: 14-Ed Win-a 25 50 75 147 236 325
17-Krigstein-a 25 50 75 149 240 330
21-23: 23-Last precode (6/54) 20 40 60 118 189 260
24-28,30,31,34: 25-Orlando-a 19 38 57 109 172 235
29-Ditko-a (4 pgs.) 20 40 60 118 189 260
32,33-Torres-a 19 38 57 109 172 235

NOTE: ***Brodsky*** *a-5; c-1, 5-7, 10, 11, 13, 15, 25-27, 32.* ***Colan*** *a-17.* ***Everett*** *a-2, 5, 7, 10, 16, 28, 31; c-2, 8, 9, 14, 17-19, 28, 30.* ***Forgione/Abel*** *a-29.* ***Forte/Fox*** *a-16.* ***Al Hartley*** *a-2.* ***Heath*** *a-2, 4, 8, 9, 12, 14, 16; c-3, 4, 12, 16, 20, 21.* ***Infantino*** *a-15.* ***Keller*** *a-5.* ***Kida*** *a-2, 14.* ***Maneely*** *a-7, 14, 27; c-24, 29, 31.* ***Mooney*** *a-5, 13, 18.* ***Mac Pakula*** *a-22, 32.* ***Post*** *a-8.* ***Powell*** *a-19, 20, 32.* ***Robinson*** *a-1.* ***Romita*** *a-24, 26, 27.* ***R.Q. Sale*** *a-29.* ***Sekowsky*** *a-5.* ***Severin*** *c-29.* ***Sinnott*** *a-8, 16, 17.*

SPELLBOUND
Marvel Comics: Jan, 1988 - Apr, 1988 ($1.50, bi-weekly, Baxter paper)
1-5 2.50
6 ($2.25, 52 pgs.) 2.50

SPELLJAMMER (Also see TSR Worlds Comics Annual)
DC Comics: Sept, 1990 - No. 15, Nov, 1991 ($1.75)
1-15: Based on TSR game. 11-Heck-a. 2.50

SPENCER SPOOK (Formerly Giggle Comics; see Adventures of...)
American Comics Group: No. 100, Mar-Apr, 1955 - No. 101, May-June, 1955
100,101 7 14 21 37 46 55

SPIDER, THE
Eclipse Books: 1991 - Book 3, 1991 ($4.95, 52 pgs., limited series)
Book 1-3-Truman-c/a 5.00

SPIDER-BOY (Also see Marvel Versus DC #3)
Marvel Comics (Amalgam): Apr, 1996 ($1.95)
1-Mike Wieringo-c/a; Karl Kesel story; 1st app. of Bizarnage, Insect Queen, Challengers of the Fantastic, Sue Storm: Agent of S.H.I.E.L. D., & King Lizard 2.50

SPIDER-BOY TEAM-UP
Marvel Comics (Amalgam): June, 1997 ($1.95, one-shot)
1-Karl Kesel & Roger Stern-s/Jo Ladronn-a(p) 2.50

SPIDER-GIRL (See What If... #105)
Marvel Comics: Oct, 1998 - No. 100, Sept, 2006 ($1.99/$2.25/$2.99)
0-($2.99)-r/1st app. Peter Parker's daughter from What If #105; previews regular series, Avengers-Next and J2 1 2 3 4 5 7
1-DeFalco-s/Olliffe & Williamson-s 1 2 3 4 5 7
2-Two covers 4.00
3-16,18-20: 3-Fantastic Five-c/app. 10,11-Spider-Girl time-travels to meet teenaged Spider-Man 2.50
17-($2.99) Peter Parker suits up 3.00
21-24,26-49,51-59: 21-Begin $2.25-c. 31-Avengers app. 2.50
25-($2.99) Spider-Girl vs. the Savage Six 3.00
50-($3.50) 3.50
59-99-($2.99) 59-Avengers app.; Ben Parker born. 75-May in Black costume. 82-84-Venom bonds with Normie Osborn. 93-Venom-c. 95-Tony Stark app. 3.00
100-($3.99) Last issue; story plus Rogues Gallery, profile pages; r/#27,53 4.00
1999 Annual ($3.99) 4.00
Wizard #1/2 (1999) 3.00
... A Fresh Start (1/99,$5.99, TPB) r/#1&2 6.00
... Presents The Buzz and Darkdevil (2007, $7.99, digest) r/mini-series 8.00
TPB (10/01, $19.95) r/#0-8; new Olliffe-c 20.00
Marvel Age Spider-Girl Vol. 1: Legacy (2004, $7.99, digest size) r/#0-5 8.00
Marvel Age Spider-Girl Vol. 2: Like Father, Like Daughter (2004, $7.99, digest) r/#6-11 8.00
Spider-Girl Vol. 3: Avenging Allies (2005, $7.99, digest) r/#12-16 & 1999 Annual 8.00
Spider-Girl Vol. 4: Turning Point (2005, $7.99, digest) r/#17-21 & #1/2 8.00
Spider-Girl Vol. 5: Endgame (2006, $7.99, digest) r/#22-27 8.00

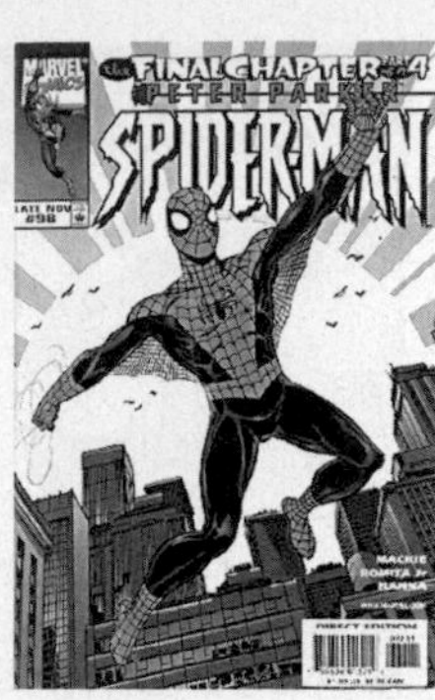

Spider-Man #98 © MAR

Spider-Man: Back in Black TPB © MAR

Spider-Man and His Amazing Friends #1 © MAR

GD VG FN VF VF/NM NM-
2.0 4.0 6.0 8.0 9.0 9.2

Spider-Girl Vol. 6: Too Many Spiders! (2006, $7.99, digest) r/#28-33 8.00
Spider-Girl Vol. 7: Betrayed (2006, $7.99, digest) r/#34-38 & #51 8.00
Spider-Girl Vol. 8: Duty Calls (2007, $7.99, digest) r/#39-44 8.00
Spider-Girl Vol. 9: Secret Lives (2007, $7.99, digest) r/#45-50 8.00

SPIDER-MAN (See Amazing..., Friendly Neighborhood..., Giant-Size..., Marvel Age..., Marvel Knights..., Marvel Tales, Marvel Team-Up, Spectacular..., Spidey Super Stories, Ultimate Marvel Team-Up, Ultimate..., Venom, & Web Of...)

SPIDER-MAN (Peter Parker Spider-Man on cover but not indicia #75-on)
Marvel Comics: Aug, 1990 - No. 98, Nov, 1998 ($1.75/$1.95/ $1.99)

1-Silver edition, direct sale only (unbagged) 1 2 3 5 6 8
1-Silver bagged edition; direct sale, no price on comic, but $2.00 on plastic bag (125,000 print run) 20.00
1-Regular edition w/Spidey face in UPC area (unbagged); green-c 6.00
1-Regular bagged edition w/Spidey face in UPC area; green cover (125,000) 12.00
1-Newsstand bagged w/UPC code 8.00
1-Gold edition, 2nd printing (unbagged) with Spider-Man in box (400,000-450,000) 5.00
1-Gold 2nd printing w/UPC code; (less than 10,000 print run) intended for Wal-Mart; much scarcer than originally believed 120.00
1-Platinum ed. mailed to retailers only (10,000 print run); has new McFarlane-a & editorial material instead of ads; stiff-c, no cover price 130.00
2-26: 2-McFarlane-c/a/scripts continue. 6,7-Ghost Rider & Hobgoblin app. 8-Wolverine cameo; Wolverine storyline begins. 12-Wolverine storyline ends. 13-Spidey's black costume returns; Morbius app. 14-Morbius app. 15-Erik Larsen-c/a; Beast c/s. 16-X-Force-c/story w/Liefeld assists; continues in X-Force #4; reads sideways; last McFarlane issue. 17-Thanos-c/story; Leonardi/Williamson-c/a. 13,14-Spidey in black costume. 18-Ghost Rider-c/story. 18-23-Sinister Six storyline w/Erik Larsen-c/a/scripts. 19-Hulk & Hobgoblin-c & app. 20-22-Deathlok app. 22,23-Ghost Rider, Hulk, Hobgoblin app. 23-Wrap-around gatefold-c. 24-Infinity War x-over w/Demogoblin & Hobgoblin-c/story. 24-Demogoblin dons new costume & battles Hobgoblin-c/story. 26-($3.50, 52 pgs.)-Silver hologram on-c w/gatefold poster by Ron Lim; Spidey retells his origin. 4.00
26-2nd printing; gold hologram on-c 3.50
27-45: 32-34-Punisher-c/story. 37-Maximum Carnage x-over. 39,40-Electro-c/s (cameo #38). 41-43-Iron Fist-c/stories w/Jae Lee-c/a. 42-Intro Platoon. 44-Hobgoblin app. 3.00
46-49,51-53, 55, 56,58-74,76-81: 46-Begin $1.95-c; bound-in card sheet. 51-Power & Responsibility Pt. 3. 52,53-Venom app. 60-Kaine revealed. 61-Origin Kaine. 65-Mysterio app. 66-Kaine-c/app.; Peter Parker app. 67-Carnage-c/app. 68,69-Hobgoblin-c/app. 72-Onslaught x-over; Spidey vs. Sentinels. 74-Daredevil-c/app. 77-80-Morbius-c/app. 2.50
46-($2.95)-Polybagged; silver ink-c w/16 pg. preview of cartoon series & animation style print; bound-in trading card sheet 3.00
50-($2.50)-Newsstand edition 2.50
50-($3.95)-Collectors edition w/holographic-c 4.00
51-($2.95)-Deluxe edition foil-c; flip book 3.00
54-($2.75, 52 pgs.)-Flip book 2.75
57-($2.50) 2.50
57-($2.95)-Die cut-c 3.00
65-($2.95)-Variant-c; polybagged w/cassette 3.00
75-($2.95)-Wraparound-c; Green Goblin returns; death of Ben Reilly (who was the clone) 4.00
82-97: 84-Juggernaut app. 91-Double cover with "Dusk #1"; battles the Shocker. 93-Ghost Rider app. 2.50
98-Double cover; final issue 3.00
#(-1) Flashback (7/97) 2.50
Annual '97 ($2.99), '98 ($2.99)-Devil Dinosaur-c/app. 3.00
NOTE: ***Erik Larsen** c/a-15, 18-23. **M. Rogers/Keith Williams** c/a-27, 28.*

SPIDER-MAN (one-shots, hardcovers and TPBs)
...& Arana Special: The Hunter Revealed (5/06, $3.99) Del Rio-s; art by Del Rio & various 3.00
...and Batman ('95, $5.95) DeMatteis-s; Joker, Carnage app. 6.00
...and Daredevil ('84, $2.00) 1-r/Spectacular Spider-Man #26-28 by Miller 3.00
...: Back in Black HC (2007, $34.99, dustjacket) oversized r/Amaz. S-M #539-543, Friendly Neighborhood S-M #17-23 & Annual #1; cover pencils and sketch pages 35.00
...: Back in Black SC (2008, $24.99) same contents as HC 25.00
...: Back in Black Handbook (2007, $3.99) Official Handbook format; Lopresti-c 4.00
...: Birth of Venom TPB (2007, $29.99) r/Secret Wars #8, AS-M #252-259,298-300,315-317, AS-M Annual #25, Fantastic Four #274 and Web of Spider-Man #1 30.00
...: Carnage nn (6/93, $6.95, TPB)-r/Amazing S-M #344,345,359-363; spot varnish-c 7.00
.../Daredevil (10/02, $2.99) Vatche Mavlian-c/a; Brett Matthews-s 3.00
...: Dead Man's Hand 1 (4/97, $2.99) 3.00
...: Death of the Stacys HC (2007, $19.99, dustjacket) r/Amazing Spider-Man #88-92 and #121,122; intro. by Gerry Conway; afterword by Romita; cover gallery incl. reprints 20.00
.../Dr. Strange: "The Way to Dusty Death" nn (1992, $6.95, 68 pgs.) 7.00
.../Elektra '98-($2.99) vs. The Silencer 3.00
... Family (2005, $4.99, 100 pgs.) new story and reprints; Spider-Ham app. 5.00
... Fear Itself Graphic Novel (2/92, $12.95) 18.00
Giant-Sized Spider-Man (12/98, $3.99) r/team-ups 4.00
Holiday Special 1995 ($2.95) 3.00
...: Hot Shots nn (1/96, $2.95) fold out posters by various, inc. Vess and Ross 3.00
Identity Crisis (9/98, $19.95, TPB) 20.00
...: Kraven's Last Hunt HC (2006, $19.99) r/Amaz. S-M #293,294; Web of S-M #31,32 and Spect. S-M #131-132; intro. by DeMatteis; Zeck-a; cover pencils and interior pencils 20.00
...: Legacy of Evil 1 (6/96, $3.95) Kurt Busiek script & Mark Texeira-c/a 4.00
...Legends Vol. 1: Todd McFarlane ('03, $19.95, TPB)-r/Amaz. S-M #298-305 20.00
...Legends Vol. 2: Todd McFarlane ('03, $19.99, TPB)-r/Amaz. S-M #306-314, & Spec. Spider-Man Annual #10 20.00
...Legends Vol. 3: Todd McFarlane ('04, $24.99, TPB)-r/Amaz. S-M #315-323,325,328 25.00
...Legends Vol. 4: Spider-Man & Wolverine ('03, $13.95, TPB) r/Spider-Man & Wolverine #1-4 and Spider-Man/Daredevil #1 14.00
.../Marrow (2/01, $2.99) Garza-a 3.00
...: One More Day HC (2008. $24.99, dustjacket) r/Amaz. S-M #544-545, Friendly N.S-M #24, Sensational S-M #41 and Marvel Spotlight: Spider-Man-One More Day 25.00
..., Peter Parker: Back in Black HC (2007, $34.99) oversized r/Sensational Spider-Man #35-40 & Annual #1, Spider-Man Family #1,2; Marvel Spotlight: Spider-Man and Spider-Man Back in Black Handbook; cover sketches 35.00
..., Punisher, Sabretooth: Designer Genes (1993, $8.95) 9.00
...Return of the Goblin TPB (See Peter Parker: Spider-Man)
...Revelations ('97, $14.99, TPB) r/end of Clone Saga plus 14 new pages by Romita Jr. 15.00
...: Saga of the Sandman TPB (2007, $19.99) r/1st app. Amazing S-M #4 and other app. 20.00
...: Son of the Goblin (2004, $15.99, TPB) r/AS-M#136-137,312 & Spec. S-M #189,200 16.00
... Special: Black and Blue and Read All Over 1 (11/06, $3.99) new story and r/ASM #12 4.00
Special Edition 1 (12/92-c, 11/92 inside)-The Trial of Venom; ordered thru mail with $5.00 donation or more to UNICEF; embossed metallic ink; came bagged w/bound-in poster; Daredevil app. 1 3 4 6 8 10
Super Special (7/95, $3.95)-Planet of the Symbiotes 4.00
The Best of Spider-Man Vol. 2 (2003, $29.99, HC with dust jacket) r/AS-M V2 #37-45, Peter Parker: S-M #44-47, and S-M's Tangled Web #10,11; Pearson-c 30.00
The Best of Spider-Man Vol. 3 (2004, $29.99, HC with d.j.) r/AS-M V2 #46-58, 500 30.00
The Best of Spider-Man Vol. 4 (2005, $29.99, HC with d.j.) r/#501-514; sketch pages 30.00
The Best of Spider-Man Vol. 5 (2006, $29.99, HC with d.j.) r/#515-524; sketch pages 30.00
The Complete Frank Miller Spider-Man (2002, $29.95, HC) r/Miller-s/a 30.00
The Death of Captain Stacy ($3.50) r/AS-M#88-90 3.50
The Death of Gwen Stacy ($14.95) r/AS-M#96-98,121,122 15.00
...: The Movie ($12.95) adaptation by Stan Lee-s/Alan Davis-a; plus r/Ultimate Spider-Man #8, Peter Parker #35, Tangled Web #10; photo-c 13.00
...: The Official Movie Adaptation ($5.95) Stan Lee-s/Alan Davis-a 6.00
...: The Other HC (2006, $29.99, dust jacket) r/Amazing S-M #525-528, Friendly Neighborhood S-M #1-4 and Marvel Knights S-M #19-22; gallery of variant covers 30.00
...: The Other SC (2006, $24.99) r/crossover; gallery of variant covers 25.00
...: The Other Sketchbook (2005, $2.99) sketch page preview of 2005-6 x-over 3.00
Torment TPB (5/01$15.95) r/#1-5, Spec. S-M #10 16.00
... Vs. Doctor Octopus ($17.95) reprints early battles; Sean Chen-c 18.00
... Vs. Punisher (7/00, $2.99) Michael Lopez-c/a 3.00
...Vs. Silver Sable (2006, $15.99, TPB)-r/Amazing Spider-Man #265,279-281 & Peter Parker, The Spectacular Spider-Man #128,129 16.00
...Vs. The Black Cat (2005, $14.99, TPB)-r/Amaz. S-M #194,195,204,205,226,227 15.00
...Vs. Venom (1990, $8.95, TPB)-r/Amaz. S-M #300,315-317 w/new McFarlane-c 9.00
...Visionaries (10/01, $19.95, TPB)-r/Amaz. S-M #298-305; McFarlane-a 20.00
...Visionaries: John Romita (8/01, $19.95, TPB)-r/Amaz. S-M #39-42, 50,68,69,108,109; new Romita-c 20.00
...Visionaries: Kurt Busiek (2006, $19.99, TPB)-r/Untold Tales of Spider-Man #1-8 20.00
...Visionaries: Roger Stern (2007, $24.99, TPB)-r/Amazing Spider-Man #206 & Spectacular Spider-Man #43-52,54; Stern interview 25.00
Wizard 1/2 ($10.00) Leonardi-a; Green Goblin app. 10.00

SPIDER-MAN ADVENTURES
Marvel Comics: Dec, 1994 - No. 15, Mar, 1996 ($1.50)

1-15 ($1.50)-Based on animated series 2.50
1-($2.95)-Foil embossed-c 3.00

SPIDER-MAN AND HIS AMAZING FRIENDS (See Marvel Action Universe)
Marvel Comics Group: Dec, 1981 (one-shot)

1-Adapted from NBC TV cartoon show; Green Goblin-c/story; 1st Spidey, Firestar, Iceman team-up; Spiegle-p 5.00

SPIDER-MAN AND POWER PACK
Marvel Comics: Jan, 2007 - No. 4, Apr, 2007 ($2.99, limited series)

1-4-Sumerak-s/Gurihiru-a; Sandman app. 3,4-Venom app. 3.00
...: Big City Heroes (2007, $6.99, digest) r/#1-4 7.00

SPIDER-MAN AND THE FANTASTIC FOUR
Marvel Comics: Jun, 2007 - No. 4, Sept, 2007 ($2.99, limited series)

1-4-Mike Wieringo-a/c; Jeff Parker-s. 1,4-Impossible Man app. 3.00

Spider-Man: Blue #3 © MAR

Spider-Man Family #5 © MAR

Spider-Man Loves Mary Jane Season 2 #1 © MAR

	GD 2.0	VG 4.0	FN 6.0	VF 8.0	VF/NM 9.0	NM- 9.2

...: Silver Rage TPB (2007, $10.99) r/#1-4; series outline and cover sketches 11.00

SPIDER-MAN AND THE INCREDIBLE HULK (See listing under Amazing...)

SPIDER-MAN AND THE UNCANNY X-MEN
Marvel Comics: Mar, 1996 ($16.95, trade paperback)

nn-r/Uncanny X-Men #27, Uncanny X-men #35, Amazing Spider-Man #92, Marvel Team-Up Annual #1, Marvel Team-Up #150, & Spectacular Spider-Man #197-199 17.00

SPIDER-MAN & WOLVERINE (See Spider-Man Legends Vol. 4 for TPB reprint)
Marvel Comics: Aug, 2003 - No. 4, Nov, 2003 ($2.99, limited series)

1-4-Matthews-s/Mavlian-a 3.00

SPIDER-MAN AND X-FACTOR
Marvel Comics: May, 1994 - No. 3, July, 1994 ($1.95, limited series)

1-3 2.50

SPIDER-MAN /BADROCK
Maximum Press: Mar, 1997 ($2.99, mini-series)

1A, 1B(#2)-Jurgens-s 3.00

SPIDER-MAN/BLACK CAT: THE EVIL THAT MEN DO (Also see Marvel Must Haves)
Marvel Comics: Aug, 2002 - No. 6, Mar, 2006 ($2.99, limited series)

1-6-Kevin Smith-s/Terry Dodson-c/a 3.00
HC (2006, $19.99, dust jacket) r/#1-6; script to #6 with sketches 20.00

SPIDER-MAN: BLUE
Marvel Comics: July, 2002 - No. 6, Apr, 2003 ($3.50, limited series)

1-6: Jeph Loeb-s/Tim Sale-a/c; flashback to early MJ and Gwen Stacy 3.50
HC (2003, $21.99, with dust jacket) over-sized r/#1-6; intro. by John Romita 22.00
SC (2004, $14.99) r/#1-6; cover gallery 15.00

SPIDER-MAN: BREAKOUT (See New Avengers #1)
Marvel Comics: June, 2005 - No. 5, Oct, 2005 ($2.99, limited series)

1-5-Bedard-s/Garcia-a. 1-U-Foes app. 5-New Avengers app. 3.00
TPB (2006, $13.99) r/#1-5 14.00

SPIDER-MAN: CHAPTER ONE
Marvel Comics: Dec, 1998 - No. 12, Oct, 1999 ($2.50, limited series)

1-Retelling/updating of origin; John Byrne-s/c/a 2.50
1-($6.95) DF Edition w/variant-c by Jae Lee 7.00
2-11: 2-Two covers (one is swipe of ASM #1); Fantastic Four app. 9-Daredevil. 11-Giant-Man-c/app. 2.50
12-($3.50) Battles the Sandman 3.50
0-(5/99) Origins of Vulture, Lizard and Sandman 2.50

SPIDER-MAN CLASSICS
Marvel Comics: Apr, 1993 - No. 16, July, 1994 ($1.25)

1-14,16: 1-r/Amaz. Fantasy #15 & Strange Tales #115. 2-16-r/Amaz. Spider-Man #1-15. 6-Austin-c(i) 2.50
15-($2.95)-Polybagged w/16 pg. insert & animation style print; r/Amazing Spider-Man #14 (1st Green Goblin) 3.00

SPIDER-MAN COLLECTOR'S PREVIEW
Marvel Comics: Dec, 1994 ($1.50, 100 pgs., one-shot)

1-wraparound-c; no comics 3.00

SPIDER-MAN COMICS MAGAZINE
Marvel Comics Group: Jan, 1987 - No. 13, 1988 ($1.50, digest-size)

1-13-Reprints 6.00

SPIDER-MAN: DEATH AND DESTINY
Marvel Comics: Aug, 2000 - No. 3, Oct, 2000 ($2.99, limited series)

1-3-Aftermath of the death of Capt. Stacy 3.00

SPIDER-MAN/ DOCTOR OCTOPUS: OUT OF REACH
Marvel Comics: Jan, 2004 - No. 5, May, 2004 ($2.99, limited series)

1-5: 1-Keron Grant-a/Colin Mitchell-s 3.00
Marvel Age... TPB (2004, $5.99, digest size) r/#1-5 6.00

SPIDER-MAN/ DOCTOR OCTOPUS: YEAR ONE
Marvel Comics: Aug, 2004 - No. 5, Dec, 2004 ($2.99, limited series)

1-5-Kaare Andrews-a/Zeb Wells-s 3.00

SPIDER-MAN FAIRY TALES
Marvel Comics: July, 2007 - No. 4, Oct, 2007 ($2.99, limited series)

1-4: 1-Cebulski-s/Tercio-a. 2-Henrichon-a. 3-Kobayashi-a. 4-Dragotta-p/Allred-i 3.00
TPB (2007, $10.99) r/#1-4 11.00

SPIDER-MAN FAMILY (Also see Amazing Spider-Man Family)
Marvel Comics: Apr, 2007 - No. 9, Aug, 2008 ($4.99, anthology)

1-9-New tales and reprints. 1-Black costume, Sandman, Black Cat app. 4-Agents of Atlas app., Kirk-a; Puppet Master by Eliopoulos. 8-Iron Man app. 9-Hulk app. 5.00
... Featuring Spider-Clan 1 (1/07, $4.99) new Spider-Clan story; reprints w/Spider-Man 2099 and Amazing Spider-Man #252 (black costume) 5.00
... Featuring Spider-Man's Amazing Friends 1 (10/06, $4.99) new story with Iceman and Firestar; Mini Marvels w/Giarrusso-a; reprints w/Spider-Man 2099 5.00
...: Back In Black (2007, $7.99, digest) r/new content from #1-3 8.00
...: Untold Team-Ups (2008, $9.99, digest) r/new content from #4-6 10.00

SPIDER-MAN: FRIENDS AND ENEMIES
Marvel Comics: Jan, 1995 - No. 4, Apr, 1995 ($1.95, limited series)

1-4-Darkhawk, Nova & Speedball app. 2.50

SPIDER-MAN: FUNERAL FOR AN OCTOPUS
Marvel Comics: Mar, 1995 - No. 3, May, 1995 ($1.50, limited series)

1-3 2.50

SPIDER-MAN/ GEN 13
Marvel Comics: Nov, 1996 ($4.95, one-shot)

nn-Peter David-s/Stuart Immonen-a 5.00

SPIDER-MAN: GET KRAVEN
Marvel Comics: Aug, 2002 - No. 6, Jan, 2003 ($2.99/$2.25, limited series)

1-($2.99) McCrea-a/Quesada-c; back-up story w/Rio-a 3.00
2-6-($2.25) 2-Sub-Mariner app. 2.50

SPIDER-MAN: HOBGOBLIN LIVES
Marvel Comics: Jan, 1997 - No. 3, Mar, 1997 ($2.50, limited series)

1-3-Wraparound-c 2.50
TPB (1/98, $14.99) r/#1-3 plus timeline 15.00

SPIDER-MAN: HOUSE OF M (Also see House of M and related x-overs)
Marvel Comics: Aug, 2005 - No. 5, Dec, 2005 ($2.99, limited series)

1-5-Waid & Peyer-s/Larroca-a; rich and famous Peter Parker in mutant-ruled world 3.00
House of M: Spider-Man TPB (2006, $13.99) r/series 14.00

SPIDER-MAN/ HUMAN TORCH
Marvel Comics: Mar, 2005 - No. 5, July, 2005 ($2.99, limited series)

1-5-Ty Templeton-a/Dan Slott-s; team-ups from early days to the present 3.00
...: I'm With Stupid (2006, $7.99, digest) r/#1-5 8.00

SPIDER-MAN: INDIA
Marvel Comics: Jan, 2005 - No. 4, Apr, 2005 ($2.99, limited series)

1-4-Pavitr Prabhakar gains spider powers; Kang-a/Seetharaman-s 3.00

SPIDER-MAN: LEGEND OF THE SPIDER-CLAN (See Marvel Mangaverse for TPB)
Marvel Comics: Dec, 2002 - No. 5, Apr, 2003 ($2.25, limited series)

1-5-Marvel Mangaverse Spider-Man; Kaare Andrews-s/Skottie Young-c/a 2.50

SPIDER-MAN: LIFELINE
Marvel Comics: Apr, 2001 - No. 3, June, 2001 ($2.99, limited series)

1-3-Nicieza-s/Rude-c/a; The Lizard app. 3.00

SPIDER-MAN LOVES MARY JANE (Also see Mary Jane limited series)
Marvel Comics: Feb, 2006 - No. 20, Sept, 2007 ($2.99)

1-20-Mary Jane & Peter in high school; McKeever-s/Miyazawa-a/c. 5-Gwen Stacy app. 16-18,20-Firestar app. 17-Felecia Hardy app. 3.00
... Vol. 1: Super Crush (2006, $7.99, digest) r/#1-5; cover concepts page 8.00
... Vol. 2: The New Girl (2006, $7.99, digest) r/#6-10; sketch pages 8.00
... Vol. 3: My Secret Life (2007, $7.99, digest) r/#11-15; sketch pages 8.00
... Vol. 4: Still Friends (2007, $7.99, digest) r/#16-20 8.00
Hardcover Vol. 1 (2007, $24.99) oversized reprints of #1-5, Mary Jane #1-4 and Mary Jane: Homecoming #1-4; series proposals, sketch pages and covers; coloring process 25.00
Hardcover Vol. 2 (2008, $39.99) oversized reprints of #6-20, sketch & layout pages 40.00

SPIDER-MAN LOVES MARY JANE SEASON 2
Marvel Comics: Oct, 2008 - Present ($2.99)

1,2-Terry Moore-s/c; Craig Rousseau-a 3.00
1-Variant-c by Alphona 8.00

SPIDER-MAN: MADE MEN
Marvel Comics: Aug, 1998 ($5.99, one-shot)

1-Spider-Man & Daredevil vs. Kingpin 6.00

SPIDER-MAN MAGAZINE
Marvel Comics: 1994 - No. 3, 1994 ($1.95, magazine)

1-3: 1-Contains 4 S-M promo cards & 4 X-Men Ultra Fleer cards; Spider-Man story by Romita, Sr.; X-Men story; puzzles & games. 2-Doc Octopus & X-Men stories 3.00

SPIDER-MAN: MAXIMUM CLONAGE

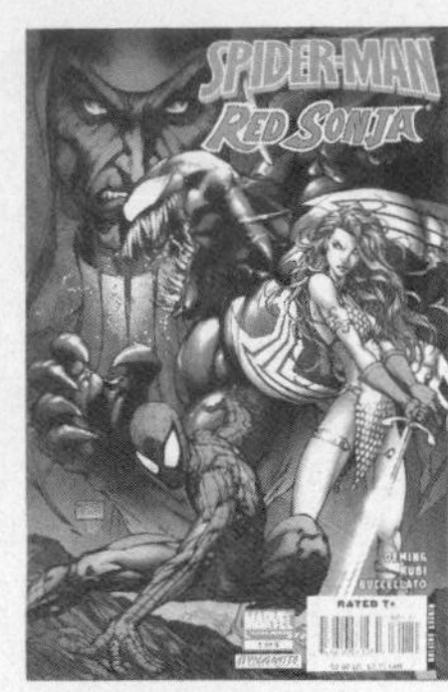
Spider-Man / Red Sonja #1 © MAR

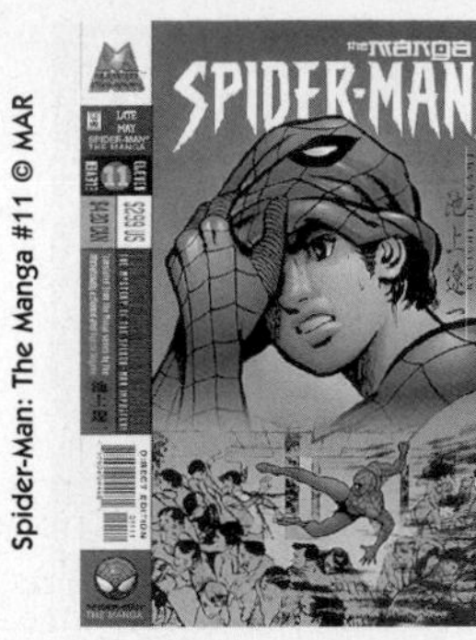

Spider-Man: The Manga #11 © MAR

Spider-Man 2099 Annual #1 © MAR

	GD 2.0	VG 4.0	FN 6.0	VF 8.0	VF/NM 9.0	NM- 9.2

Marvel Comics: 1995 ($4.95)
Alpha #1-Acetate-c, Omega #1-Chromium-c. 5.00

SPIDER-MAN MEGAZINE
Marvel Comics: Oct, 1994 - No. 6, Mar, 1995 ($2.95, 100 pgs.)
1-6: 1-r/ASM #16,224,225, Marvel Team-Up #1 3.00

SPIDER-MAN: POWER OF TERROR
Marvel Comics: Jan, 1995 - No. 4, Apr, 1995 ($1.95, limited series)
1-4-Silvermane & Deathlok app. 2.50

SPIDER-MAN/PUNISHER: FAMILY PLOT
Marvel Comics: Feb, 1996 - No. 2, Mar, 1996 ($2.95, limited series)
1,2 3.00

SPIDER-MAN: QUALITY OF LIFE
Marvel Comics: Jul, 2002 - No. 4, Oct, 2002 ($2.99, limited series)
1-4-All CGI art by Scott Sava; Rucka-s; Lizard app. 3.00
TPB (2002, $12.99) r/#1-4; a "Making of..." section detailing the CGI process 13.00

SPIDER-MAN: REDEMPTION
Marvel Comics: Sept, 1996 - No. 4, Dec, 1996 ($1.50, limited series)
1-4: DeMatteis scripts; Zeck-a 2.50

SPIDER-MAN/ RED SONJA
Marvel Comics: Oct, 2007 - No. 5, Feb, 2008 ($2.99, limited series)
1-5-Rubi-a/Oeming-s/Turner-c; Venom & Kulan Gath app. 3.00
HC (2008, $19.99, dustjacket) r/#1-5 and Marvel Team-Up #79; sketch pages 20.00

SPIDER-MAN: REIGN
Marvel Comics: Feb, 2007 - No. 4, May, 2007 ($3.99, limited series)
1-Kaare Andrews-s/a; red costume on cover 4.00
1-Variant cover with black costume 10.00
2-4 4.00
HC (2007, $19.99, dustjacket) r/#1-4; sketch pages and cover variant gallery 20.00
HC 2nd printing (2007, $19.99, dustjacket) with variant black cover 20.00
SC (2008, $14.99) r/#1-4; sketch pages and cover variant gallery 15.00

SPIDER-MAN: REVENGE OF THE GREEN GOBLIN
Marvel Comics: Oct, 2000 - No. 3, Dec, 2000 ($2.99, limited series)
1-3-Frenz & Olliffe-a; continues in AS-M #25 & PP:S-M #25 3.00

SPIDER-MAN SAGA
Marvel Comics: Nov, 1991 - No. 4, Feb, 1992 ($2.95, limited series)
1-4: Gives history of Spider-Man: text & illustrations 3.00

SPIDER-MAN: SWEET CHARITY
Marvel Comics: Aug, 2002 ($4.95, one-shot)
1-The Scorpion-c/app.; Campbell-c/Zimmerman-s/Robertson-a 5.00

SPIDER-MAN'S TANGLED WEB (Titled **"Tangled Web"** in indicia for #1-4)
Marvel Comics: Jun, 2001 - No. 22, Mar, 2003 ($2.99)
1-3: "The Thousand" on-c; Ennis-s/McCrea-a/Fabry-c 4.00
4-"Severance Package" on-c; Rucka-s/Risso-a; Kingpin-c/app. 5.00
5,6-Flowers for Rhino; Milligan-s/Fegredo-a 3.00
7-10,12,15-20,22: 7-9-Gentlemen's Agreement; Bruce Jones-s/Lee Weeks-a. 10-Andrews-s/a. 12-Fegredo-a. 15-Paul Pope-s/a. 18-Ted McKeever-s/a. 19-Mahfood-a. 20-Haspiel-a 3.00
11,13,21-($3.50) 11-Darwyn Cooke-s/a. 13-Phillips-a. 21-Christmas-s by Cooke & Bone 3.50
14-Azzarello & Scott Levy (WWE's Raven)-s about Crusher Hogan 4.00
TPB (10/01, $15.95) r/#1-6 16.00
Volume 2 TPB (4/02, $14.95) r/#7-11 15.00
Volume 3 TPB (2002, $15.99) r/#12-17; Jason Pearson-c 16.00
Volume 4 TPB (2003, $15.99) r/#18-22; Frank Cho-c 16.00

SPIDER-MAN TEAM-UP
Marvel Comics: Dec, 1995 - No. 7, June, 1996 ($2.95)
1-7: 1-w/ X-Men. 2-w/Silver Surfer. 3-w/Fantastic Four. 4-w/Avengers. 5-Gambit & Howard the Duck-c/app. 7-Thunderbolts-c/app. 3.00
... Special 1 (5/05, $2.99) Fantastic Four app.; Todd Dezago-s/Shane Davis-a 3.00

SPIDER-MAN: THE ARACHNIS PROJECT
Marvel Comics: Aug, 1994 - No. 6, Jan, 1995 ($1.75, limited series)
1-6-Venom, Styx, Stone & Jury app. 2.50

SPIDER-MAN: THE CLONE JOURNAL
Marvel Comics: Mar, 1995 ($2.95, one-shot)
1 3.00

SPIDER-MAN: THE FINAL ADVENTURE
Marvel Comics: Nov, 1995 - No. 4, Feb, 1996 ($2.95, limited series)
1-4: 1-Nicieza scripts; foil-c 3.00

SPIDER-MAN: THE JACKAL FILES
Marvel Comics: Aug, 1995 ($1.95, one-shot)
1 2.50

SPIDER-MAN: THE LOST YEARS
Marvel Comics: Aug, 1995-No. 3, Oct, 1995; No. 0, 1996 ($2.95/$3.95,lim. series)
0-(1/96, $3.95)-Reprints. 4.00
1-3-DeMatteis scripts, Romita, Jr.-c/a 3.00
NOTE: ***Romita** c-0i. **Romita, Jr.** a-0r, 1-3p. c-0-3p. **Sharp** a-0r.*

SPIDER-MAN: THE MANGA
Marvel Comics: Dec, 1997 - No. 31, June, 1999 ($3.99/$2.99, B&W, bi-weekly)
1-($3.99)-English translation of Japanese Spider-Man 4.00
2-31-($2.99) 3.00

SPIDER-MAN: THE MUTANT AGENDA
Marvel Comics: No. 0, Feb, 1994; No. 1, Mar, 1994 - No. 3, May, 1994 ($1.75, limited series)
0-(2/94, $1.25, 52 pgs.)-Crosses over w/newspaper strip; has empty pages to paste in newspaper strips; gives origin of Spidey 2.50
1-3: Beast & Hobgoblin app. 1-X-Men app. 2.50

SPIDER-MAN: THE MYSTERIO MANIFESTO (Listed as "Spider-Man and Mysterio" in indicia)
Marvel Comics: Jan, 2001 - No. 3, Mar, 2001 ($2.99, limited series)
1-3-Daredevil-c/app.; Weeks & McLeod-a 3.00

SPIDER-MAN: THE PARKER YEARS
Marvel Comics: Nov, 1995 ($2.50, one-shot)
1 2.50

SPIDER-MAN 2: THE MOVIE
Marvel Comics: Aug, 2004 ($3.50/$12.99, one-shot)
1-($3.50) Movie adaptation; Johnson, Lim & Olliffe-a 3.50
TPB-($12.99) Movie adaptation; r/Amazing Spider-Man #50, Ultimate Spider-Man #14,15 13.00

SPIDER-MAN 2099 (See Amazing Spider-Man #365)
Marvel Comics: Nov, 1992 - No. 46, Aug, 1996 ($1.25/$1.50/$1.95)
1-(stiff-c)-Red foil stamped-c; begins origin of Miguel O'Hara (Spider-Man 2099); Leonardi/Williamson-c/a begins 3.00
1-2nd printing, 2-24,26-40: 2-Origin continued, ends #3. 4-Doom 2099 app. 13-Extra 16 pg. insert on Midnight Sons. 19-Bound-in trading cards. 35-Variant-c. 36-Two-c; Jae Lee-a. 37,38-Two-c 2.50
25-($2.25, 52 pgs.)-Newsstand edition 2.50
25-($2.95, 52 pgs.)-Deluxe edition w/embossed foil-c 3.00
41-46: 46-The Vulture app; Mike McKone-a(p) 3.00
Annual 1 (1994, $2.95, 68 pgs.) 3.00
Special 1 (1995, $3.95) 4.00
NOTE: ***Chaykin** c-37. **Ron Lim** a(p)-18; c(p)-13, 16, 18. **Kelley Jones** c/a-9. **Leonardi/Williamson** a-1-8, 10-13, 15-17, 19, 20, 22-25; c-1-13, 15, 17-19, 20, 22-25, 35.*

SPIDER-MAN 2099 MEETS SPIDER-MAN
Marvel Comics: 1995 ($5.95, one-shot)
nn-Peter David script; Leonardi/Williamson-c/a. 6.00

SPIDER-MAN UNIVERSE
Marvel Comics: Mar, 2000 - No. 7, Oct, 2000 ($4.95/$3.99, reprints)
1-5-Reprints recent issues from the various Spider-Man titles 5.00
6,7-($3.99) 4.00

SPIDER-MAN UNLIMITED
Marvel Comics: May, 1993 - No. 22, Nov, 1998 ($3.95, quarterly, 68 pgs.)
1-Begin Maximum Carnage storyline, ends; Carnage-c/story 5.00
2-12: 2-Venom & Carnage-c/story; Lim-c/a(p) in #2-6. 10-Vulture app. 4.00
13-22: 13-Begin $2.99-c; Scorpion-c/app. 15-Daniel-c; Puma-c/app. 19-Lizard-c/app. 20-Hannibal King and Lilith app. 21,22-Deodato-a 3.00

SPIDER-MAN UNLIMITED (Based on the TV animated series)
Marvel Comics: Dec, 1999 - No. 5, Apr, 2000 ($2.99/$1.99)
1-($2.99) Venom and Carnage app. 3.00
2-5: 2-($1.99) Green Goblin app. 2.50

SPIDER-MAN UNLIMITED (3rd series)
Marvel Comics: Mar, 2004 - No. 15, July, 2006 ($2.99)
1-16: 1-Short stories by various incl. Miyazawa & Chen-a. 2-Mays-a. 6-Allred-c. 14-Finch-c/a; Black Cat app. 3.00

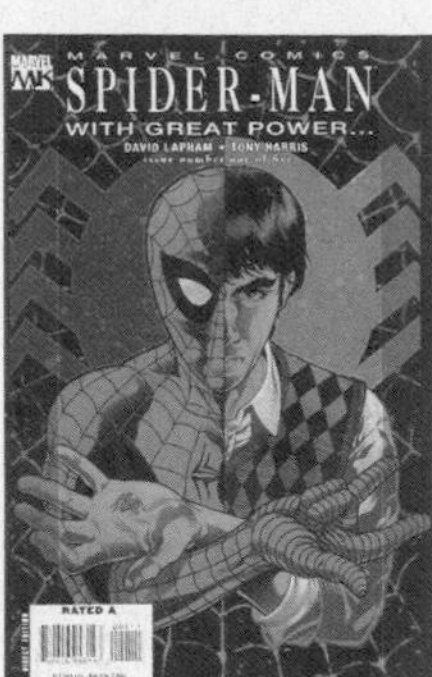

Spider-Man: With Great Power #1 © MAR

Spike: After the Fall #1 © 20th Century Fox

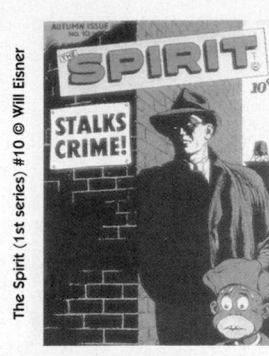

The Spirit (1st series) #10 © Will Eisner

	GD 2.0	VG 4.0	FN 6.0	VF 8.0	VF/NM 9.0	NM- 9.2

SPIDER-MAN UNMASKED
Marvel Comics: Nov, 1996 ($5.95, one-shot)

nn-Art w/text 6.00

SPIDER-MAN: VENOM AGENDA
Marvel Comics: Jan, 1998 ($2.99, one-shot)

1-Hama-s/Lyle-c/a 3.00

SPIDER-MAN VS. DRACULA
Marvel Comics: Jan, 1994 ($1.75, 52 pgs., one-shot)

1-r/Giant-Size Spider-Man #1 plus new Matt Fox-a 2.50

SPIDER-MAN VS. WOLVERINE
Marvel Comics Group: Feb, 1987; V2#1, 1990 (68 pgs.)

	GD	VG	FN	VF	VF/NM	NM-
1-Williamson-c/a(i); intro Charlemagne; death of Ned Leeds (old Hobgoblin)	2	4	6	12	16	20
V2#1 (1990, $4.95)-Reprints #1 (2/87)						5.00

SPIDER-MAN: WEB OF DOOM
Marvel Comics: Aug, 1994 - No. 3, Oct, 1994 ($1.75, limited series)

1-3 2.50

SPIDER-MAN: WITH GREAT POWER...
Marvel Comics: Mar, 2008 - No. 5, Sept, 2008 ($3.99, limited series)

1-5-Origin and early days re-told; Lapham-s/Harris-a/c 4.00

SPIDER-MAN: YEAR IN REVIEW
Marvel Comics: Feb, 2000 ($2.99)

1-Text recaps of 1999 issues 3.00

SPIDER REIGN OF THE VAMPIRE KING, THE (Also see The Spider)
Eclipse Books: 1992 - No. 3, 1992 ($4.95, limited series, coated stock, 52 pgs.)

Book One - Three: Truman scripts & painted-c 5.00

SPIDER'S WEB, THE (See G-8 and His Battle Aces)

SPIDER-WOMAN (Also see The Avengers #240, Marvel Spotlight #32, Marvel Super Heroes Secret Wars #7, Marvel Two-In-One #29 and New Avengers)
Marvel Comics Group: April, 1978 - No. 50, June, 1983 (New logo #47 on)

	GD	VG	FN	VF	VF/NM	NM-
1-New complete origin & mask added	2	4	6	11	14	18
2-5,7-18: 2-Excalibur app. 3,11,12-Brother Grimm app. 13,15-The Shroud-c/s. 16-Sienkiewicz-c						5.00
6,19,20,28,29,32: 6-Morgan LeFay app. 6,19,32-Werewolf by Night-c/s. 20,28,29-Spider-Man app. 32-Universal Monsters photo/Miller-c						6.00
21-27,30,31,33-36						5.00
37,38-X-Men x-over: 37-1st app. Siryn of X-Force; origin retold	1	3	4	6	8	10
39-49: 46-Kingpin app. 49-Tigra-c/story						4.00
50-(52 pgs.)-Death of Spider-Woman; photo-c	2	4	6	8	11	14

NOTE: *Austin a-37i. Byrne c-26p. Infantino a-1-19. Layton c-19. Miller c-32p.*

SPIDER-WOMAN
Marvel Comics: Nov, 1993 - No. 4, Feb, 1994 ($1.75, mini-series)

V2#1-4: 1,2-Origin; U.S. Agent app. 2.50

SPIDER-WOMAN
Marvel Comics: July, 1999 - No. 18, Dec, 2000 ($2.99/$1.99/$2.25)

1-($2.99) Byrne-s/Sears-a 3.00
2-18: 2-11-($1.99). 2-Two covers. 12-Begin $2.25-c. 15-Capt. America-c/app. 2.50

SPIDER-WOMAN: ORIGIN (Also see New Avengers)
Marvel Comics: Feb, 2006 - No. 5, June, 2006 ($2.99, limited series)

1-5-Bendis & Reed-s/Jonathan & Joshua Luna-a/c 3.00
1-Variant cover by Olivier Coipel 3.00
HC (2006, $19.99) r/series 20.00
SC (2007, $13.99) r/series 14.00

SPIDEY SUPER STORIES (Spider-Man) (Also see Fireside Books)
Marvel/Children's TV Workshop: Oct, 1974 - No. 57, Mar, 1982 (35¢, no ads)

	GD	VG	FN	VF	VF/NM	NM-
1-Origin (stories simplified for younger readers)	4	8	12	26	41	55
2-Kraven	3	6	9	16	23	30
3-10,15: 6-Iceman. 15-Storm-c/sty	2	4	6	13	18	22
11-14,16-20: 19,20-Kirby-c	2	4	6	11	16	20
21-30: 24-Kirby-c	2	4	6	10	14	18
31-53: 31-Moondragon-c/app.; Dr. Doom app. 33-Hulk. 34-Sub-Mariner. 38-F.F. 39-Thanos-c/story. 44-Vision. 45-Silver Surfer & Dr. Doom app.	2	4	6	9	13	16
54-57: 56-Battles Jack O'Lantern-c/sty (exactly one year after 1st app. in Machine Man #19)	2	4	6	13	18	22

SPIKE AND TYKE (See M.G.M.'s...)

SPIKE... (Also see Buffy the Vampire Slayer and related titles)
IDW Publ.: Aug, 2005; Jan, 2006; Apr, 2006 ($7.49, squarebound, one-shots)

...: Lost & Found (4/06, $7.49) Scott Tipton-s/Fernando Goni-a 8.00
...: Old Times (8/05, $7.49) Peter David-s/Fernando Goni-a; Cecily/Halfrek app. 8.00
...: Old Wounds (1/06, $7.49) Tipton-s/Goni-a; flashback to Black Dahlia murder case 8.00
TPB (7/06, $19.99) r/one-shots 20.00

SPIKE: AFTER THE FALL (Also see Angel: After the Fall) (Follows the last Angel TV episode)
IDW Publ.: July, 2008 - Present ($3.99, limited series)

1,2-Lynch-s/Urru-a; multiple covers on each 4.00

SPIKE: ASYLUM (Buffy the Vampire Slayer)
IDW Publ.: Sept, 2006 - No. 5, Jan, 2007 ($3.99, limited series)

1-5-Lynch-s/Urru-a; multiple covers on each 4.00

SPIKE: SHADOW PUPPETS (Buffy the Vampire Slayer)
IDW Publ.: June, 2007 - No. 4, Sept, 2007 ($3.99, limited series)

1-4-Lynch-s/Urru-a; multiple covers on each 4.00

SPIKE VS. DRACULA (Buffy the Vampire Slayer)
IDW Publ.: Feb, 2006 - No. 5, Mar, 2006 ($3.99, limited series)

1-5: 1-Peter David-s/Joe Corroney-a; Dru and Bela Lugosi app. 4.00

SPIN & MARTY (TV) (Walt Disney's)(See Walt Disney Showcase #32)
Dell Publishing Co. (Mickey Mouse Club): No. 714, June, 1956 - No. 1082, Mar-May, 1960 (All photo-c)

	GD	VG	FN	VF	VF/NM	NM-
Four Color 714 (#1)	12	24	36	87	156	225
Four Color 767,808 (#2,3)	9	18	27	63	107	150
Four Color 826 (#4)-Annette Funicello photo-c	22	44	66	157	291	425
5(3-5/58) - 9(6-8/59)	8	16	24	52	86	120
Four Color 1026,1082	8	16	24	52	86	120

SPINE-TINGLING TALES (Doctor Spektor Presents...)
Gold Key: May, 1975 - No. 4, Jan, 1976 (All 25¢ issues)

	GD	VG	FN	VF	VF/NM	NM-
1-1st Tragg-r/Mystery Comics Digest #3	2	4	6	9	12	15
2-4: 2-Origin Ra-Ka-Tep-r/Mystery Comics Digest #1; Dr. Spektor #12. 3-All Durak-r issue; 4-Baron Tibor's 1st app.-r/Mystery Comics Digest #4; painted-c	1	2	3	5	6	8

SPINWORLD
Amaze Ink (Slave Labor Graphics): July, 1997 - No. 4, Jan, 1998 ($2.95/$3.95, B&W, mini-series)

1-3-Brent Anderson-a(p) 3.00
4-($3.95) 4.00

SPIRAL PATH, THE
Eclipse Comics: July, 1986 - No. 2 ($1.75, Baxter paper, limited series)

1,2 2.50

SPIRAL ZONE
DC Comics: Feb, 1988 - No. 4, May, 1988 ($1.00, mini-series)

1-4-Based on Tonka toys 2.50

SPIRIT, THE (Newspaper comics - see Promotional Comics section)

SPIRIT, THE (1st Series)(Also see Police Comics #11 and The Best of the Spirit TPB)
Quality Comics Group (Vital): 1944 - No. 22, Aug, 1950

	GD	VG	FN	VF	VF/NM	NM-
nn(#1)- "Wanted Dead or Alive"	100	200	300	630	1065	1500
nn(#2)- "Crime Doesn't Pay"	50	100	150	310	518	725
nn(#3)- "Murder Runs Wild"	41	82	123	252	419	585
4,5: 4-Flatfoot Burns begins, ends #22. 5-Wertham app.	35	70	105	203	327	450
6-10	29	58	87	169	272	375
11-Crandall-c	27	54	81	158	254	350
12-17-Eisner-c. 19-Honeybun app.	38	76	114	226	363	500
18-21-Strip-r by Eisner; Eisner-c	43	86	129	267	446	625
22-Used by N.Y. Legis. Comm; classic Eisner-c	93	186	279	586	993	1400
Super Reprint #11-r/Quality Spirit #19 by Eisner	3	6	9	18	27	35
Super Reprint #12-r/Spirit #17 by Fine; Sol Brodsky-c	3	6	9	18	27	35

SPIRIT, THE (2nd Series)
Fiction House Magazines: Spring, 1952 - No. 5, 1954

	GD	VG	FN	VF	VF/NM	NM-
1-Not Eisner	41	82	123	256	428	600
2-Eisner-c/a(2)	41	82	123	252	419	585
3-Eisner/Grandenetti-c	37	74	111	219	352	485
4-Eisner/Grandenetti-c; Eisner-a	38	76	114	226	363	500
5-Eisner-c/a(4)	42	84	126	248	404	560

The Spirit (2007 series) #14 © Will Eisner

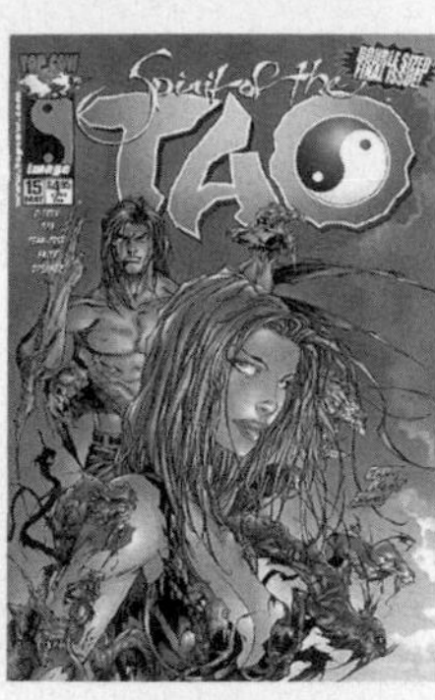

Spirit of the Tao #15 © TCOW

Spooky #35 © HARV

GD 2.0 VG 4.0 FN 6.0 VF 8.0 VF/NM 9.0 NM- 9.2

SPIRIT, THE
Harvey Publications: Oct, 1966 - No. 2, Mar, 1967 (Giant Size, 25¢, 68 pgs.)

1-Eisner-r plus 9 new pgs.(origin Denny Colt, Take 3, plus 2 filler pgs.) (#3 was advertised, but never published) 9 18 27 63 107 150
2-Eisner-r plus 9 new pgs.(origin of the Octopus) 8 16 24 52 86 120

SPIRIT, THE (Underground)
Kitchen Sink Enterprises (Krupp Comics): Jan, 1973 - No. 2, Sept, 1973 (Black & White)

1-New Eisner-c & 4 pgs. new Eisner-a plus-r (titled Crime Convention) 3 6 9 18 27 35
2-New Eisner-c & 4 pgs. new Eisner-a plus-r (titled Meets P'Gell) 3 6 9 20 30 40

SPIRIT, THE (Magazine)
Warren Publ. Co./Krupp Comic Works No. 17 on: 4/74 - No. 16, 10/76; No. 17, Winter, 1977 - No. 41, 6/83 (B&W w/color) (#6-14,16 are squarebound)

1-Eisner-r begin; 8 pg. color insert 6 12 18 41 66 90
2-5: 2-Powder Pouf-s; UFO-s. 4-Silk Satin-s 4 8 12 23 36 48
6-9,11-15: 7-All Ebony issue. 8-Female Foes issue. 8,12-Sand Seref-s. 9-P'Gell & Octupus-s. 12-X-Mas issue 3 6 9 21 32 42
10-Giant Summer Special ($1.50)-Origin 4 8 12 24 37 50
16-Giant Summer Special ($1.50)-Olga Bustle-c/s 4 8 12 22 34 45
17,18(8/78): 17-Lady Luck-r 3 6 9 14 20 25
19-21-New Eisner-a. 20,21-Wood-r (#21-r/A DP on the Moon by Wood). 20-Outer Space-r 3 6 9 14 20 25
22-41: 22,23-Wood-r (#22-r/Mission the Moon by Wood). 28-r/last story (10/5/52). 30-(7/81)-Special Spirit Jam issue w/Caniff, Corben, Bolland, Byrne, Miller, Kurtzman, Rogers, Sienkiewicz-a & 40 others. 36-Begin Spirit Section-r; r/1st story (6/2/40) in color; new Eisner-c/a(18 pgs.)($2.95). 37-r/2nd story in color plus 18 pgs. new Eisner-a. 38-41: r/3rd - 6th stories in color. 41-Lady Luck Mr. Mystic in color 2 4 6 13 18 22
Special 1(1975)-All Eisner-a (mail only, 1500 printed, full color) 9 18 27 63 107 150

NOTE: *Covers pencilled/inked by* **Eisner** *only #1-9,12-16; painted by Eisner & Ken Kelly #10 & 11; painted by Eisner #17-up; one color story reprinted in #1-10.* **Austin** *a-30i.* **Byrne** *a-30p.* **Miller** *a-30p.*

SPIRIT, THE
Kitchen Sink Enterprises: Oct, 1983 - No. 87, Jan, 1992 ($2.00, Baxter paper)

1-60: 1-Origin-r/12/23/45 Spirit Section. 2-r/ 1/20/46-2/10/46. 3-r/2/17/46-3/10/46. 4-r/3/17/46-4/7/46. 11-Last color issue. 54-r/section 2/19/50 4.00
61-87: 85-87-Reprint the Outer Space Spirit stories by Wood. 86-r/A DP on the Moon by Wood from 1952 4.00

SPIRIT, THE (Also see Batman/The Spirit in Batman one-shots)
DC Comics: Feb, 2007 - Present ($2.99)

1-19: 1-6,8 12-Darwyn Cooke-s/a/c. 2-P'Gell app. 3-Origin re-told. 7-Short stories by Baker, Bernet, Palmiotti, Simonson & Sprouse; Cooke-c. 13-Short stories by various 3.00
... Book One HC (2007, $24.99, die-cut dust jacket) r/#1-6 and Batman/The Spirit 25.00

SPIRIT JAM
Kitchen Sink Press: Aug, 1998 ($5.95, B&W, oversized, square-bound)

nn-Reprints Spirit (Magazine) #30 by Eisner & 50 others; and "Cerebus Vs. The Spirit" from Cerebus Jam #1 6.00

SPIRIT, THE: THE NEW ADVENTURES
Kitchen Sink Press: 1997 - No. 8, Nov, 1998 ($3.50, anthology)

1-Moore-s/Gibbons-c/a 4.00
2-8: 2-Gaiman-s/Eisner-c. 3-Moore-s/Bolland-c/Moebius back-c. 4-Allred-s/a; Busiek-s/Anderson-a. 5-Chadwick-s/c/a(p); Nyberg-i. 6-S.Hampton & Mandrake-a 3.50

SPIRIT: THE ORIGIN YEARS
Kitchen Sink Press: May, 1992 - No. 10, Dec, 1993 ($2.95, B&W)

1-10: 1-r/sections 6/2/40(origin)-6/23/40 (all 1940s) 3.00

SPIRITMAN (Also see Three Comics)
No publisher listed: No date (1944) (10¢)
(Triangle Sales Co. ad on back cover)

1-Three 16pg. Spirit sections bound together, (1944, 10¢, 52 pgs.) 21 42 63 123 197 270
2-Two Spirit sections (3/26/44, 4/2/44) bound together; by Lou Fine 19 38 57 109 172 235

SPIRIT OF THE BORDER (See Zane Grey & Four Color #197)

SPIRIT OF THE TAO
Image Comics (Top Cow): Jun, 1998 - No. 15, May, 2000 ($2.50)

Preview 5.00
1-14: 1-D-Tron-s/Tan & D-Tron-a 2.50
15-($4.95) 5.00

SPIRIT WORLD (Magazine)
National Periodical Publications: Fall, 1971 (B&W)

1-New Kirby-a; Neal Adams-c; poster inside 7 14 21 45 73 100
(1/2 price without poster)

SPITFIRE (Female undercover agent)
Malverne Herald (Elliot)(J. R. Mahon): No. 132, 1944 (Aug) - No. 133, 1945

132,133: Both have Classics Gift Box ads on b/c with checklist to #20 25 50 75 147 236 325

SPITFIRE AND THE TROUBLESHOOTERS
Marvel Comics: Oct, 1986 - No. 9, June, 1987 (Codename: Spitfire #10 on)

1-3,5-9 2.50
4-McFarlane-a 3.00

SPITFIRE COMICS (Also see Double Up)
Harvey Publications: Aug, 1941 - No. 2, Oct, 1941 (Pocket size; 100 pgs.)

1-Origin The Clown, The Fly-Man, The Spitfire & The Magician From Bagdad 76 152 228 479 810 1140
2-(Scarce) 69 138 207 435 738 1040

SPLITTING IMAGE
Image Comics: Mar, 1993 - No. 2, 1993 ($1.95)

1,2-Simpson-c/a; parody comic 2.50

SPOOF
Marvel Comics Group: Oct, 1970; No. 2, Nov, 1972 - No. 5, May, 1973

1-Infinity-c; Dark Shadows-c & parody 3 6 9 20 30 40
2-5: 2-All in the Family. 3-Beatles, Osmond's, Jackson 5, David Cassidy, Nixon & Agnew-c. 5-Rod Serling, Woody Allen, Ted Kennedy-c 3 6 9 16 22 28

SPOOK (Formerly Shock Detective Cases)
Star Publications: No. 22, Jan, 1953 - No. 30, Oct, 1954

22-Sgt. Spook-r; acid in face story; hanging-c 40 80 120 235 380 525
23,25,27: 25-Jungle Lil-r. 27-Two Sgt. Spook-r 28 56 84 164 265 365
24-Used in **SOTI**, pgs. 182,183-r/Inside Crime #2; Transvestism story 29 58 87 169 272 375
26,28-30: 26-Disbrow-a. 28,29-Rulah app. 29-Jo-Jo app. 30-Disbrow-c/a(2); only Star-c 28 56 84 164 265 365

NOTE: **L. B. Cole** *covers-all issues except #30; a-28(1 pg.).* **Disbrow** *a-26(2), 28, 29(2), 30(2); No. 30 r/Blue Bolt Weird Tales #114.*

SPOOK COMICS
Baily Publications/Star: 1946

1-Mr. Lucifer story 30 60 90 174 280 385

SPOOKY (The Tuff Little Ghost; see Casper The Friendly Ghost)
Harvey Publications: 11/55 - 139, 11/73; No. 140, 7/74 - No. 155, 3/77; No. 156, 12/77 - No. 158, 4/78; No. 159, 9/78; No. 160, 10/79; No. 161, 9/80

	GD 2.0	VG 4.0	FN 6.0	VF 8.0	VF/NM 9.0	NM- 9.2
1-Nightmare begins (see Casper #19)	43	86	129	344	647	950
2	20	40	60	148	274	400
3-10(1956-57)	12	24	36	87	156	225
11-20(1957-58)	8	16	24	52	86	120
21-40(1958-59)	6	12	18	37	59	80
41-60	4	8	12	28	44	60
61-80,100	3	6	9	20	30	40
81-99	3	6	9	17	25	32
101-120	2	4	6	11	16	20
121-126,133-140	2	4	6	8	11	14
127-132: All 52 pg. Giants	2	4	6	11	16	20
141-161	1	2	3	5	7	9

SPOOKY
Harvey Comics: Nov, 1991 - No. 4, Sept, 1992 ($1.00/$1.25)

1 4.00
2-4: 3-Begin $1.25-c 3.00
...Digest 1-3 (10/92, 6/93, 10/93, $1.75, 100 pgs.)-Casper, Wendy, etc. 4.00

SPOOKY HAUNTED HOUSE
Harvey Publications: Oct, 1972 - No. 15, Feb, 1975

	GD 2.0	VG 4.0	FN 6.0	VF 8.0	VF/NM 9.0	NM- 9.2
1	3	6	9	18	27	35
2-5	2	4	6	10	14	18
6-10	2	4	6	8	10	12
11-15	1	2	3	5	7	9

SPOOKY MYSTERIES
Your Guide Publ. Co.: No date (1946) (10¢)

Sports Action #4 © MAR

Spotty the Pup #2 © AVON

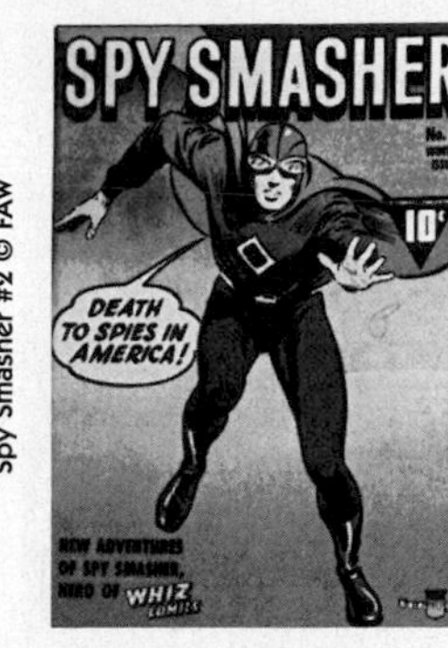

Spy Smasher #2 © FAW

	GD 2.0	VG 4.0	FN 6.0	VF 8.0	VF/NM 9.0	NM- 9.2
1-Mr. Spooky, Super Snooper, Pinky, Girl Detective app.	20	40	60	115	180	245

SPOOKY SPOOKTOWN
Harvey Publ.: 9/61; No. 2, 9/62 - No. 52, 12/73; No. 53, 10/74 - No. 66, 12/76

	GD 2.0	VG 4.0	FN 6.0	VF 8.0	VF/NM 9.0	NM- 9.2
1-Casper, Spooky; 68 pgs. begin	16	32	48	114	212	310
2	9	18	27	63	107	150
3-5	7	14	21	45	73	100
6-10	5	10	15	34	55	75
11-20	4	8	12	24	37	50
21-39: 39-Last 68 pg. issue	3	6	9	20	30	40
40-45: All 52 pgs.	2	4	6	11	16	20
46-66: 61-Hot Stuff/Spooky team-up story	1	2	3	5	7	9

SPORT COMICS (Becomes True Sport Picture Stories #5 on)
Street & Smith Publications: Oct, 1940 (No mo.) - No. 4, Nov, 1941

	GD 2.0	VG 4.0	FN 6.0	VF 8.0	VF/NM 9.0	NM- 9.2
1-Life story of Lou Gehrig	54	108	162	340	575	810
2	31	62	93	181	291	400
3,4	27	54	81	156	251	345

SPORT LIBRARY (See Charlton Sport Library)

SPORTS ACTION (Formerly Sport Stars)
Marvel/Atlas Comics (ACI No. 2,3/SAI No. 4-14): No. 2, Feb, 1950 - No. 14, Sept, 1952

	GD 2.0	VG 4.0	FN 6.0	VF 8.0	VF/NM 9.0	NM- 9.2
2-Powell painted-c; George Gipp life story	43	86	129	267	446	625
1-(nd,no price, no publ., 52pgs, #1 on-c; has same-c as #2; blank inside-c (giveaway?)	22	44	66	129	207	285
3-Everett-a	24	48	72	140	225	310
4-11,14: Weiss-a	21	42	63	125	200	275
12,13: 12-Everett-c. 13-Krigstein-a	23	46	69	133	214	295

NOTE: *Title may have changed after No. 3, to Crime Must Lose No. 4 on, due to publisher change.* ***Sol Brodsky*** *c-4-7, 13, 14.* ***Maneely*** *c-3, 8-11.*

SPORT STARS
Parents' Magazine Institute (Sport Stars): Feb-Mar, 1946 - No. 4, Aug-Sept, 1946 (Half comic, half photo magazine)

	GD 2.0	VG 4.0	FN 6.0	VF 8.0	VF/NM 9.0	NM- 9.2
1- "How Tarzan Got That Way" story of Johnny Weissmuller	40	80	120	240	390	540
2-Baseball greats	26	52	78	152	244	335
3,4	23	46	69	133	214	295

SPORT STARS (Becomes Sports Action #2 on)
Marvel Comics (ACI): Nov, 1949 (52 pgs.)

	GD 2.0	VG 4.0	FN 6.0	VF 8.0	VF/NM 9.0	NM- 9.2
1-Knute Rockne; painted-c	45	90	135	279	465	650

SPORT THRILLS (Formerly Dick Cole; becomes Jungle Thrills #16)
Star Publications: No. 11, Nov, 1950 - No. 15, Nov, 1951

	GD 2.0	VG 4.0	FN 6.0	VF 8.0	VF/NM 9.0	NM- 9.2
11-Dick Cole begins; Ted Williams & Ty Cobb life stories	29	58	87	170	268	365
12-Joe DiMaggio, Phil Rizzuto stories & photos on-c; L.B. Cole-c/a	24	48	72	137	216	295
13-15-All L. B. Cole-c. 13-Jackie Robinson, Pee Wee Reese stories & photo on-c. 14-Johnny Weissmuller life story	24	48	72	137	216	295
Accepted Reprint #11 (#15 on-c, nd); L.B. Cole-c	10	20	30	54	72	90
Accepted Reprint #12 (nd); L.B. Cole-c; Joe DiMaggio & Phil Rizzuto life stories-r/#12	10	20	30	54	72	90

SPOTLIGHT (TV) (newsstand sales only)
Marvel Comics Group: Sept, 1978 - No. 4, Mar, 1979 (Hanna-Barbera)

	GD 2.0	VG 4.0	FN 6.0	VF 8.0	VF/NM 9.0	NM- 9.2
1-Huckleberry Hound, Yogi Bear; Shaw-a	3	6	9	20	30	40
2,4: 2-Quick Draw McGraw, Augie Doggie, Snooper & Blabber. 4-Magilla Gorilla, Snagglepuss	3	6	9	18	23	30
3-The Jetsons; Yakky Doodle	3	6	9	20	30	40

SPOTLIGHT COMICS
Country Press Inc.: Sept, 1940

nn-Ashcan, not distributed to newsstands, only for in house use. A copy sold in 2006 for $2,225.

SPOTLIGHT COMICS (Becomes Red Seal Comics #14 on?)
Harry 'A' Chesler (Our Army, Inc.): Nov, 1944 - No. 3, 1945

	GD 2.0	VG 4.0	FN 6.0	VF 8.0	VF/NM 9.0	NM- 9.2
1-The Black Dwarf (cont'd in Red Seal?), The Veiled Avenger, & Barry Kuda begin; Tuska-c	87	174	261	548	924	1300
2	56	112	168	353	594	835
3-Injury to eye story (reprinted from Scoop #3)	58	116	174	365	620	875

SPOTTY THE PUP (Becomes Super Pup #4, see Television Puppet Show)
Avon Periodicals/Realistic Comics: No. 2, Oct-Nov, 1953 - No. 3, Dec-Jan, 1953-54 (Also see Funny Tunes)

	GD 2.0	VG 4.0	FN 6.0	VF 8.0	VF/NM 9.0	NM- 9.2
2,3	7	14	21	35	43	50
nn (1953, Realistic-r)	4	7	9	14	16	18

SPUNKY (...Junior Cowboy)(...Comics #2 on)
Standard Comics: April, 1949 - No. 7, Nov, 1951

	GD 2.0	VG 4.0	FN 6.0	VF 8.0	VF/NM 9.0	NM- 9.2
1-Text illos by Frazetta	11	22	33	62	86	110
2-Text illos by Frazetta	9	18	27	47	61	75
3-7	6	12	18	31	38	45

SPUNKY THE SMILING SPOOK
Ajax/Farrell (World Famous Comics/Four Star Comic Corp.): Aug, 1957 - No. 4, May, 1958

	GD 2.0	VG 4.0	FN 6.0	VF 8.0	VF/NM 9.0	NM- 9.2
1-Reprints from Frisky Fables	10	20	30	54	72	90
2-4	6	12	18	31	38	45

SPY AND COUNTERSPY (Becomes Spy Hunters #3 on)
American Comics Group: Aug-Sept, 1949 - No. 2, Oct-Nov, 1949 (52 pgs.)

	GD 2.0	VG 4.0	FN 6.0	VF 8.0	VF/NM 9.0	NM- 9.2
1-Origin, 1st app. Jonathan Kent, Counterspy	27	54	81	156	251	345
2	17	34	51	98	154	210

SPYBOY
Dark Horse Comics: Oct, 1999 - No. 17, May, 2001 ($2.50/$2.95/$2.99)

	GD 2.0	VG 4.0	FN 6.0	VF 8.0	VF/NM 9.0	NM- 9.2
1-17: 1-6-Peter David-s/Pop Mhan-a. 7,8-Meglia-a. 9-17-Mhan-a						3.00
13.1-13.3 (4/03-8/03, $2.99), 13.2,13.3-Mhan-a						3.00
... Special (5/02, $4.99) David-s/Mhan-a						5.00

SPYBOY: FINAL EXAM
Dark Horse Comics: May, 2004 - No. 4, Aug, 2004 ($2.99, limited series)

	GD 2.0	VG 4.0	FN 6.0	VF 8.0	VF/NM 9.0	NM- 9.2
1-4-Peter David-s/Pop Mhan-a/c						3.00
TPB (2005, $12.95) r/series						13.00

SPYBOY/ YOUNG JUSTICE
Dark Horse Comics: Feb, 2002 - No. 3, Apr, 2002 ($2.99, limited series)

	GD 2.0	VG 4.0	FN 6.0	VF 8.0	VF/NM 9.0	NM- 9.2
1-3: 1-Peter David-s/Todd Nauck-a/Pop Mhan-c. 2-Mhan-a						3.00

SPY CASES (Formerly The Kellys)
Marvel/Atlas Comics (Hercules Publ.): No. 26, Sept, 1950 - No. 19, Oct, 1953

	GD 2.0	VG 4.0	FN 6.0	VF 8.0	VF/NM 9.0	NM- 9.2
26 (#1)	23	46	69	133	214	295
27(#2),28(#3, 2/51): 27-Everett-a; bondage-c	14	28	42	80	115	150
4(4/51) - 7,9,10	12	24	36	69	97	125
8-A-Bomb-c/story	14	28	42	80	115	150
11-19: 10-14-War format	10	20	30	56	76	95

NOTE: ***Sol Brodsky*** *c-1-5, 8, 9, 11-14, 17, 18.* ***Maneely*** *a-8; c-7, 10.* ***Tuska*** *a-7.*

SPY FIGHTERS
Marvel/Atlas Comics (CSI): March, 1951 - No. 15, July, 1953 (Cases from official records)

	GD 2.0	VG 4.0	FN 6.0	VF 8.0	VF/NM 9.0	NM- 9.2
1-Clark Mason begins; Tuska-a; Brodsky-c	25	50	75	145	233	320
2-Tuska-a	14	28	42	81	118	155
3-13: 3-5-Brodsky-c. 7-Heath-c	14	28	42	76	108	140
14,15-Pakula-a(3), Ed Win-a. 15-Brodsky-c	14	28	42	78	112	145

SPY-HUNTERS (Formerly Spy & Counterspy)
American Comics Group: No. 3, Dec-Jan, 1949-50 - No. 24, June-July, 1953 (#3-14: 52 pgs.)

	GD 2.0	VG 4.0	FN 6.0	VF 8.0	VF/NM 9.0	NM- 9.2
3-Jonathan Kent continues, ends #10	23	46	69	133	214	295
4-10: 4,8,10-Starr-a	14	28	42	80	115	150
11-15,17-22,24: 18-War-c begin. 21-War c/stories begin	10	20	30	56	76	95
16-Williamson-a (9 pgs.)	15	30	45	88	137	185
23-Graphic torture, injury to eye panel	20	40	60	115	183	250

NOTE: ***Drucker*** *a-12.* ***Whitney*** *a-many issues; c-7, 8, 10-12, 15, 16.*

SPYMAN (Top Secret Adventures on cover)
Harvey Publications (Illustrated Humor): Sept, 1966 - No. 3, Feb, 1967 (12¢)

	GD 2.0	VG 4.0	FN 6.0	VF 8.0	VF/NM 9.0	NM- 9.2
1-Origin and 1st app. of Spyman. Steranko-a(p)-1st pro work; 1 pg. Neal Adams ad; Tuska-c/a, Crandall-a(i)	7	14	21	45	73	100
2-Simon-c; Steranko-a(p)	4	8	12	28	44	60
3-Simon-c	4	8	12	26	41	55

SPY SMASHER (See Mighty Midget, Whiz & Xmas Comics) (Also see Crime Smasher)
Fawcett Publications: Fall, 1941 - No. 11, Feb, 1943

	GD 2.0	VG 4.0	FN 6.0	VF 8.0	VF/NM 9.0	NM- 9.2
1-Spy Smasher begins; silver metallic-c	329	658	987	2237	3919	5600
2-Raboy-c	152	304	456	958	1617	2275
3,4: 3-Bondage-c. 4-Irvin Steinberg-c	102	204	306	643	1084	1525
5-7: Raboy-a; 6-Raboy-c/a. 7-Part photo-c (movie)	87	174	261	548	924	1300
8,11: War-c	72	144	216	454	770	1085
9-Hitler, Tojo, Mussolini-c.	103	206	309	649	1100	1550
10-Hitler-c	93	186	279	586	993	1400

SPY THRILLERS (Police Badge No. 479 #5)

Squadron Supreme (2008 series) #1 © MAR

Stamps Comics #2 © YM

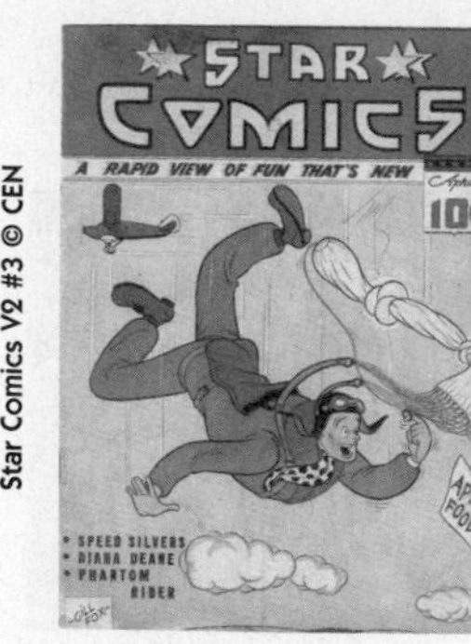

Star Comics V2 #3 © CEN

	GD 2.0	VG 4.0	FN 6.0	VF 8.0	VF/NM 9.0	NM- 9.2

Atlas Comics (PrPl): Nov, 1954 - No. 4, May, 1955

1-Brodsky c-1,2	21	42	63	122	191	260
2-Last precode (1/55)	14	28	42	76	108	140
3,4	11	22	33	60	83	105

SQUADRON SUPREME (Also see Marvel Graphic Novel - ...: Death of a Universe)
Marvel Comics Group: Aug, 1985 - No. 12, Aug, 1986 (Maxi-series)

1-Double size						3.00
2-12						2.50
TPB ($24.99) r/#1-12; Alex Ross painted-c; printing inks contain some of the cremated remains of late writer Mark Gruenwald						25.00
TPB-2nd printing ($24.99): Inks contain no ashes						25.00
...Death of a Universe TPB (2006, $24.99) r/Marvel Graphic Novel, Thor #280, Avengers #5,6; Avengers/Squadron Supreme Annual and Squadron Supreme: New World Order						25.00

SQUADRON SUPREME (Also see Supreme Power)
Marvel Comics: May, 2006 - No. 7, Nov, 2006 ($2.99)

1-7-Straczynski-s/Frank-a/c						3.00
Saga of Squadron Supreme (2006, $3.99) summary of Supreme Power #1-18; plus Hyperion and Nighthawk limited series; wraparound-c; preview of Squadron Supreme #1						4.00
... Vol. 1: The Pre-War Years (2006, $20.99, dustjacket) r/#1-5 & Saga of S.S.						21.00

SQUADRON SUPREME
Marvel Comics: Sept, 2008 - Present ($2.99)

1-3-Set 5 years after Ultimate Power; Nick Fury app.; Chaykin-s/Turini-a/Land-c						3.00

SQUADRON SUPREME: HYPERION VS. NIGHTHAWK
Marvel Comics: Mar, 2007 - No. 4, June, 2007 ($2.99, limited series)

1-4-Hyperion and Nighthawk in Darfur; Gulacy-a/c; Guggenheim-s						3.00
TPB (2007, $10.99) r/#1-4						11.00

SQUADRON SUPREME: NEW WORLD ORDER
Marvel Comics: Sept, 1998 ($5.99, one-shot)

1-Wraparound-c; Kaminski-s						6.00

SQUALOR
First Comics: Dec, 1989 - Aug, 1990 ($2.75, limited series)

1-4: Sutton-a						2.75

SQUEE (Also see JohnnyThe Homicidal Maniac)
Slave Labor Graphics: Apr, 1997 - No. 4, May, 1998 ($2.95, B&W)

1-4: Jhonen Vasquez-s/a in all						3.00

SQUEEKS (Also see Boy Comics)
Lev Gleason Publications: Oct, 1953 - No. 5, June, 1954

1-Funny animal; Biro-c; Crimebuster's pet monkey "Squeeks" begins	10	20	30	54	72	90
2-Biro-c	6	12	18	31	38	45
3-5: 3-Biro-c	6	12	18	28	34	40

S.R. BISSETTE'S SPIDERBABY COMIX
SpiderBaby Grafix: Aug, 1996 - No. 2 ($3.95, B&W, magazine size)

Preview-(8/96, $3.95)-Graphic violence & nudity; Laurel & Hardy app.						4.00
1,2						4.00

S.R. BISSETTE'S TYRANT
SpiderBaby Grafix: Sept, 1994 - No. 4 ($2.95, B&W)

1-4						4.00

STAINLESS STEEL RAT
Eagle Comics: Oct, 1985 - No. 6, Mar, 1986 (Limited series)

1 (52 pgs.; $2.25-c)						3.00
2-6 ($1.50)						2.50

STALKER (Also see All Star Comics 1999 and crossover issues)
National Periodical Publications: June-July, 1975 - No. 4, Dec-Jan, 1975-76

1-Origin & 1st app; Ditko/Wood-c/a	2	4	6	8	11	14
2-4-Ditko/Wood-c/a	1	2	3	5	6	8

STALKERS
Marvel Comics (Epic Comics): Apr, 1990 - No. 12, Mar, 1991 ($1.50)

1-12: 1-Chadwick-c						2.50

STAMP COMICS (Stamps... on-c; Thrilling Adventures In...#8)
Youthful Magazines/Stamp Comics, Inc.: Oct, 1951 - No. 7, Oct, 1952

1-(15¢) ('Stamps' on indicia No. 1-3,5,7)	27	54	81	156	251	345
2	15	30	45	86	133	180
3-6: 3,4-Kiefer, Wildey-a	14	28	42	81	118	155
7-Roy Krenkel (4 pgs.)	17	34	51	98	154	210

NOTE: *Promotes stamp collecting; gives stories behind various commemorative stamps. No. 2, 10¢ printed over 15¢ c-price.* ***Kiefer*** *a-1-7.* ***Kirkel*** *a-1-6.* ***Napoli*** *a-2-7.* ***Palais*** *a-2-4, 7.*

STAND, THE : CAPTAIN TRIPS
Marvel Comics: Dec, 2008 - No. 4 ($3.99, limited series)

1-Based on the Stephen King novel; Aguirre-Sacasa-s/Perkins-a						4.00

STAN LEE MEETS...
Marvel Comics: Nov, 2006 - Jan, 2007 ($3.99, series of one-shots)

Doctor Doom 1 (12/06) Lee-s/Larroca-a/c; Loeb-s/McGuinness-a; r/Fantastic Four #87						4.00
Doctor Strange 1 (11/06) Lee-s/Davis-a/c; Bendis-s/Bagley-a; r/Marvel Premiere #3						4.00
Silver Surfer 1 (1/07) Lee-s/Wieringo-a/c; Jenkins-s/Buckinham-a; r/S.S. #14						4.00
Spider-Man 1 (11/06) Lee-s/Coipel-a/c; Whedon-s/Gaydos-a; Hembeck-s/a; r/AS-M #87						4.00
The Thing 1 (12/06) Lee-s/Weeks-a/c; Thomas-s/Kolins-a; r/FF #79; FF #51 cover swipe						4.00
HC (2007, $24.99, dustjacket) r/one-shots; interviews and features						25.00

STANLEY & HIS MONSTER (Formerly The Fox & the Crow)
National Periodical Publ.: No. 109, Apr-May, 1968 - No. 112, Oct-Nov, 1968

109-112	4	8	12	20	30	40

STANLEY & HIS MONSTER
DC Comics: Feb, 1993 - No. 4, May, 1993 ($1.50, limited series)

1-4						2.50

STAN SHAW'S BEAUTY & THE BEAST
Dark Horse Comics: Nov, 1993 ($4.95, one-shot)

1						5.00

STAR
Image Comics (Highbrow Entertainment): June, 1995 - No. 4, Oct, 1995 ($2.50, lim. series)

1-4						2.50

STARBLAST
Marvel Comics: Jan, 1994 - No. 4, Apr, 1994 ($1.75, limited series)

1-4: 1-($2.00, 52 pgs.)-Nova, Quasar, Black Bolt; painted-c						2.50

STAR BLAZERS
Comico: Apr, 1987 - No. 4, July, 1987 ($1.75, limited series)

1-4						3.00

STAR BLAZERS
Comico: 1989 ($1.95/$2.50, limited series)

1-5- Steacy wraparound painted-c on all						3.00

STAR BLAZERS (The Magazine of Space Battleship Yamato)
Argo Press: No. 0, Aug, 1995 - No. 3, Dec, 1995 ($2.95)

0-3						3.00

STAR BRAND
Marvel Comics (New Universe): Oct, 1986 - No. 19, May, 1989 (75¢/$1.25)

1-15: 14-begin $1.25-c						2.50
16-19-Byrne story & art; low print run						4.00
Annual 1 (10/87)						2.50
... Classic Vol. 1 TPB (2006, $19.99) r/#1-7						20.00

STARCHILD
Tailspin Press: 1992 - No. 12($2.25/$2.50, B&W)

1,2-('92),0(4/93),3-12: 0-Illos by Chadwick, Eisner, Sim, M. Wagner. 3-(7/93). 4-(11/93). 6-(2/94)						3.00

STARCHILD: MYTHOPOLIS
Image Comics: No. 0, July, 1997 - No. 4, Apr, 1998 ($2.95, B&W, limited series)

0-4-James Owen-s/a						3.00

STAR COMICS
Ultem Publ. (Harry `A' Chesler)/Centaur Publications: Feb, 1937 - V2#7 (No. 23), Aug, 1939 (#1-6: large size)

V1#1-Dan Hastings (s/f) begins	213	426	639	1342	2271	3200
2	93	186	279	586	993	1400
3-Classic Black Americana cover (rare)	160	320	480	1008	1704	2400
4-6 (#6, 9/37): 4,5-Little Nemo-c/stories	78	156	234	491	833	1175
7-9: 8-Severed head centerspread; Impy & Little Nemo by Winsor McCay Jr, Popeye app. by Bob Wood; Mickey Mouse & Popeye app. as toys in Santa's bag on-c; X-Mas-c	70	140	210	441	746	1050
10 (1st Centaur; 3/38)-Impy by Winsor McCay Jr; Don Marlow by Guardineer begins	90	180	270	567	959	1350
11-1st Jack Cole comic-a, 1 pg. (4/38)	68	136	204	428	727	1025
12-15: 12-Riders of the Golden West begins; Little Nemo app. 15-Speed Silvers by Gustavson & The Last Pirate by Burgos begins						

Starfire #8 © DC

Starman (2nd series) #45 © DC

Star Ranger #1 © CHES

GD VG FN VF VF/NM NM-
2.0 4.0 6.0 8.0 9.0 9.2

55 110 165 347 586 825
16 (12/38)-The Phantom Rider & his horse Thunder begins, ends V2#6
57 114 171 359 610 860
V2#1(#17, 2/39)-Phantom Rider-c (only non-funny-c)
62 124 186 391 658 925
2-7(#18-23): 2-Diana Deane by Tarpe Mills app. 3-Drama of Hollywood by Mills begins. 7-Jungle Queen app. 49 98 147 304 507 710

NOTE: ***Biro** c-6, 9, 10. **Burgos** a-15, 16, V2#1-7. **Ken Ernst** a-10, 12, 14. **Filchock** c-15, 18, 22. **Gill Fox** c-14, 19. **Guardineer** a-6, 8-14. **Gustavson** a-13-16, V2#1-7. **Winsor McCay** c-4, 5. **Tarpe Mills** a-15, V2#1-7. **Schwab** c-20, 23. **Bob Wood** a-10, 12, 13; c-7, 8.*

STAR COMICS MAGAZINE
Marvel Comics (Star Comics): Dec, 1986 - No. 13, 1988 ($1.50, digest-size)
1,9-Spider-Man-c/s 2 4 6 8 11 14
2-8-Heathcliff, Ewoks, Top Dog, Madballs-r in #1-13 1 2 3 5 7 9
10-13 2 4 6 8 10 12

S.T.A.R. CORPS
DC Comics: Nov, 1993 - No. 6, Apr, 1994 ($1.50, limited series)
1-6: 1,2-Austin-c(i). 1-Superman app. 2.50

STAR CROSSED
DC Comics (Helix): June, 1997 - No. 3, Aug, 1997 ($2.50, limited series)
1-3-Matt Howarth-s/a 2.50

STARDUST (See Neil Gaiman and Charles Vess' Stardust)

STARDUST KID, THE
Image Comics/Boom! Studios #4-on: May, 2005 - Present ($3.50)
1-4-J.M. DeMatteis-s/Mike Ploog-a 3.50

STAR FEATURE COMICS
I. W. Enterprises: 1963
Reprint #9-Stunt Man Stetson-r/Feat. Comics #141 2 4 6 10 13 16

STARFIRE (Not the Teen Titans character)
National Periodical Publ./DC Comics: Aug-Sept, 1976 - No. 8, Oct-Nov, 1977
1-Origin (CCA stamp fell off cover art; so it was approved by code)
2 4 6 8 10 12
2-8 1 2 3 4 5 7

STAR HUNTERS (See DC Super Stars #16)
National Periodical Publ./DC Comics: Oct-Nov, 1977 - No. 7, Oct-Nov, 1978
1,7: 1-Newton-a(p). 7-44 pgs. 1 3 4 6 8 10
2-6 6.00

NOTE: ***Buckler** a-4-7p; c-1-7p. **Layton** a-1-5i; c-1-6i. **Nasser** a-3p. **Sutton** a-6i.*

STARJAMMERS (See X-Men Spotlight on Starjammers)

STARJAMMERS (Also see Uncanny X-Men)
Marvel Comics: Oct, 1995 - No. 4, Jan, 1996 ($2.95, limited series)
1-4: Foil-c; Ellis scripts 3.00

STARJAMMERS
Marvel Comics: Sept, 2004 - No. 6, Jan, 2005 ($2.99, limited series)
1-6-Kevin J. Anderson-s. 1-Garza-a. 2-6-Lucas-a 3.00

STARK TERROR
Stanley Publications: Dec, 1970 - No. 5, Aug, 1971 (B&W, magazine, 52 pgs.)
(1950s Horror reprints, including pre-code)
1-Bondage, torture-c 6 12 18 41 66 90
2-4 (Gillmor/Aragon-r) 4 8 12 24 37 50
5 (ACG-r) 3 6 9 20 30 40

STARLET O'HARA IN HOLLYWOOD (Teen-age) (Also see Cookie)
Standard Comics: Dec, 1948 - No. 4, Sept, 1949
1-Owen Fitzgerald-a in all 26 52 78 152 244 335
2 15 30 45 85 130 175
3,4 14 28 42 76 108 140

STAR-LORD THE SPECIAL EDITION (Also see Marvel Comics Super Special #10, Marvel Premiere & Preview & Marvel Spotlight V2#6,7)
Marvel Comics Group: Feb, 1982 (one-shot, direct sales) (1st Baxter paper comic)
1-Byrne/Austin-a; Austin-c; 8 pgs. of new-a by Golden (p); Dr. Who story by Dave Gibbons; 1st deluxe format comic 6.00

STARLORD
Marvel Comics: Dec, 1996 - No. 3, Feb, 1997 ($2.50, limited series)
1-3-Timothy Zahn-s 2.50

STARLORD MEGAZINE
Marvel Comics: Nov, 1996 ($2.95, one-shot)
1-Reprints w/preview of new series 3.00

STARMAN (1st Series) (Also see Justice League & War of the Gods)
DC Comics: Oct, 1988 - No. 45, Apr, 1992 ($1.00)
1-25,29-45: 1-Origin. 4-Intro The Power Elite. 9,10,34-Batman app. 14-Superman app. 17-Power Girl app. 38-War of the Gods x-over. 42-45-Eclipso-c/stories 2.50
26-1st app. David Knight (G.A.Starman's son). 5.00
27,28: 27-Starman (David Knight) app. 28-Starman disguised as Superman; leads into Superman #50 4.00

STARMAN (2nd Series) (Also see The Golden Age, Showcase 95 #12, Showcase 96 #4,5)
DC Comics : No. 0, Oct, 1994 - No. 80, Aug, 2001 ($1.95/$2.25/$2.50)
0,1: 0-James Robinson scripts, Tony Harris-c/a(p) & Wade Von Grawbadger-a(i) begins; Sins of the Father storyline begins, ends #3; 1st app. new Starman (Jack Knight); reintro of the G.A. Mist & G.A. Shade; 1st app. Nash; David Knight dies
1 2 3 4 5 7
2-7: 2-Reintro Charity from Forbidden Tales of Dark Mansion. 3-Reintro/2nd app. "Blue" Starman (1st app. in 1st Issue Special #12); Will Payton app. (both cameos). 5-David Knight app. 6-The Shade "Times Past" story; Kristiansen-a. 7-The Black Pirate cameo 5.00
8-17: 8-Begin $2.25-c. 10-1st app. new Mist (Nash). 11-JSA "Times Past" story; Matt Smith-a. 12-16-Sins of the Child. 17-The Black Pirate app. 4.00
18-37: 18-G.A. Starman "Times Past" story; Watkiss-a. 19-David Knight app. 20-23-G.A. Sandman app. 24-26-Demon Quest; all 3 covers make-up triptych. 33-36-Batman-c/app. 37-David Knight and deceased JSA members app. 3.00
38-49,51-56: 38-Nash vs. Justice League Europe. 39,40-Crossover w/ Power of Shazam! #35,36; Bulletman app. 42-Demon-c/app. 43 JLA c/app. 44-Phantom Lady-c/app. 46-Gene Ha-a. 51-Jor-el app. 52,53-Adam Strange-c/app. 2.50
50-($3.95) Gold foil logo on-c; Star Boy (LSH) app. 4.00
57-79: 57-62-Painted covers by Harris and Alex Ross. 72-Death of Ted Knight 2.50
80-($3.95) Final issue; cover by Harris & Robinson 4.00
#1,000,000 (11/98) 853rd Century x-over; Snejbjerg-a 2.50
Annual 1 (1996, $3.50)-Legends of the Dead Earth story; Prince Gavyn & G.A. Starman stories; J.H. Williams III, Bret Blevins, Craig Hamilton-c/a(p) 4.00
Annual 2 (1997, $3.95)-Pulp Heroes story; 4.00
...80 Page Giant (1/99, $4.95) Harris-c 5.00
...Secret Files 1 (4/98, $4.95)-Origin stories and profile pages 5.00
...The Mist (6/98, $1.95) Girlfrenzy; Mary Marvel app. 2.50
A Starry Knight-($17.95, TPB) r/#47-53 18.00
Grand Guingnol-(2004, $19.95, TPB)-r/#61-73 20.00
Infernal Devices-($17.95, TPB) r/#29-35,37,38 18.00
Night and Day-($14.95, TPB)-r/#7-10,12-16 15.00
Sins of the Father-($12.95, TPB)-r/#0-5 13.00
Sons of the Father-($14.99, TPB)-r/#75-80 15.00
Stars My Destination-(2003, $14.95, TPB)-r/#55-60 15.00
Times Past-($17.95, TPB)-r/stories of other Starmen 18.00
The Starman Omnibus Vol. One (2008, $49.99, HC with dj) r/#0,1-16; Robinson intro. 50.00

STARMASTERS
Marvel Comics: Dec, 1995 - No. 3, Feb, 1996 ($1.95, limited series)
1-3-Continues in Cosmic Powers Unlimited #4 2.50

STAR PRESENTATION, A (Formerly My Secret Romance #1,2; Spectacular Stories #4 on) (Also see This Is Suspense)
Fox Features Syndicate (Hero Books): No. 3, May, 1950
3-Dr. Jekyll & Mr. Hyde by Wood & Harrison (reprinted in Startling Terror Tales #10); "The Repulsing Dwarf" by Wood; Wood-c 55 110 165 347 586 825

STAR QUEST COMIX (Warren Presents... on cover)
Warren Publications: Oct, 1978 ($1.50, B&W magazine, 84 pgs., square-bound)
1-Corben, Maroto, Neary-a; Ken Kelly-c; Star Wars 2 4 6 9 12 15

STAR RAIDERS (See DC Graphic Novel #1)

STAR RANGER (Cowboy Comics #13 on)
Chesler Publ./Centaur Publ.: Feb, 1937 - No. 12, May, 1938 (Large size: No. 1-6)
1-(1st Western comic)-Ace & Deuce, Air Plunder; Creig Flessel-a
213 426 639 1342 2271 3200
2 92 184 276 580 978 1375
3-6 80 160 240 504 852 1200
7-9: 8(12/37)-Christmas-c; Air Patrol, Gold coast app.; Guardineer centerfold
57 114 171 359 605 850
V2#10 (1st Centaur; 3/38) 90 180 270 567 959 1350
11,12 66 132 198 416 701 985

NOTE: ***J. Cole** a-10, 12; c-12. **Ken Ernst** a-11. **Gill Fox** a-8(illo), 9, 10. **Guardineer** a-1, 3, 6, 7, 8(illos), 9, 10, 12. **Gustavson** a-8-10, 12. **Fred Schwab** c-2-11. **Bob Wood** a-8-10.*

STAR RANGER FUNNIES (Formerly Cowboy Comics)

Star Reach #1 © Star Reach

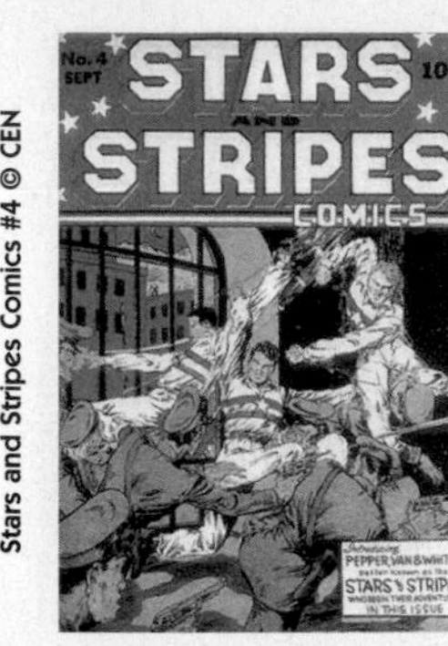

Stars and Stripes Comics #4 © CEN

Star Spangled Comics #8 © DC

GD VG FN VF VF/NM NM-
2.0 4.0 6.0 8.0 9.0 9.2

GD VG FN VF VF/NM NM-
2.0 4.0 6.0 8.0 9.0 9.2

Centaur Publications: V1#15, Oct, 1938 - V2#5, Oct, 1939

V1#15-Lyin Lou, Ermine, Wild West Junior, The Law of Caribou County by Eisner, Cowboy Jake, The Plugged Dummy, Spurs by Gustavson, Red Coat, Two Buckaroos & Trouble Hunters begin 97 194 291 611 1031 1450

V2#1 (1/39) 72 144 216 454 770 1085

2-5: 2-Night Hawk by Gustavson. 4-Kit Carson app. 60 120 180 378 639 900

NOTE: ***Jack Cole** a-V2#1, 3; c-V2#1. **Filchock** c-V2#2, 3. **Guardineer** a-V2#3. **Gustavson** a-V2#2. **Pinajian** c/a-V2#5.*

STAR REACH (Mature content)
Star Reach Publ.: Apr, 1974 - No. 18, Oct, 1979 (B&W, #12-15 w/color)

1-(75¢, 52 pgs.) Art by Starlin, Simonson. Chaykin-c/a; origin Death. Cody Starbuck-sty 2 4 6 13 18 22

1-2nd, 3th, and 4th printings ($1.00-$1.50-c) 6.00

2-11: 2-Adams, Giordano-a; 1st Stephanie Starr-c/s. 3-1st Linda Lovecraft. 4-1st Sherlock Duck. 5-1st Gideon Faust by Chaykin. 6-Elric-c. 7-BWS-c. 9-14-Sacred & Profane-c/s by Steacy. 11-Samurai 1 3 4 6 8 10

2-2nd printing 4.00

12-15 (44 pgs.): 12-Zelazny-s. Nasser-a, Brunner-c 2 4 6 8 10 12

16-18-Magazine size: 17-Poe's Raven-c/s 2 4 6 8 10 12

NOTE: ***Adams** c-2. **Bonivert** a-17. **Brunner** a-3,5; c-3,10,12. **Chaykin** a-1,4,5; c-1(1st ed),4,5; back-c-1(2nd,3rd,4th ed). **Gene Day** a-6,8,9,11,15. **Friedrich** s-2,3,8,10. **Gasbarri** a-7. **Gilbert** a-9,12. **Giordano** a-2. **Gould** a-6. **Hirota/Mukaide** s/a-7. **Jones** c-6. **Konz** a-17. **Leialoha** a-3,4,6-i, 13,15; c-13,15. **Lyda** a-6,12-15. **Marrs** a-2-5,7,10,14,15,16,18; c-18; back-c-2. **Mukaide** a-18. **Nasser** a-12. **Nino** a-6; **Russell** a-8,10; c-8. **Dave Sim** s-7; lettering-9. **Simonson** a-1. **Skeates** a-1,2. **Starlin** a-1(x2), 2(x2); back-c-1(1st ed); c-1(2nd,3rd,4th ed). **Barry Smith** c-7. **Staton** a-5,6,7. **Steacy** a-8-14; c-9,11,14,16. **Vosburg** a-2-5,7,10. **Workman** a-2-5,8. Nudity panels in most. Wraparound-c: 3-5,7-11,13-16,18.*

STAR REACH CLASSICS
Eclipse Comics: Mar, 1984 - No. 6, Aug, 1984 ($1.50, Baxter paper)

1-6: 1-Neal Adams-r/Star Reach #1 3.00

NOTE: ***Dave Sim** a-1. **Starlin** a-1.*

STARR FLAGG, UNDERCOVER GIRL (See Undercover...)

STARRIORS
Marvel Comics: Aug, 1984 - Feb, 1985 (Limited series) (Based on Tomy toys)

1-4 3.00

STARS AND S.T.R.I.P.E. (Also see JSA)
DC Comics: July, 1999 - No. 14, Sept, 2000 ($2.95/$2.50)

0-($2.95) Moder and Weston-a; Starman app. 3.00

1-Johns and Robinson-s/Moder-a; origin new Star Spangled Kid 2.50

2-14: 4-Marvel Family app. 9-Seven Soldiers of Victory-c/app. 2.50

JSA Presents: Stars and S.T.R.I.P.E. Vol. 1 TPB (2007, $17.99) r/#1-8; Johns intro. 18.00

JSA Presents: Stars and S.T.R.I.P.E. Vol. 2 TPB (2008, $17.99) r/#0,9-14 18.00

STARS AND STRIPES COMICS
Centaur Publications: No. 2, May, 1941 - No. 6, Dec, 1941

2(#1)-The Shark, The Iron Skull, A-Man, The Amazing Man, Mighty Man, Minimidget begin; The Voice & Dash Dartwell, the Human Meteor, Reef Kinkaid app.; Gustavson Flag-c 222 444 666 1399 2362 3325

3-Origin Dr. Synthe; The Black Panther app. 122 244 366 769 1297 1825

4-Origin/1st app. The Stars and Stripes; injury to eye-c 103 206 309 649 1100 1550

5(#5 on cover & inside) 72 144 216 454 765 1075

5(#6)-(#5 on cover, #6 on inside) 72 144 216 454 765 1075

NOTE: ***Gustavson** c/a-3. **Myron Strauss** c-4, 5(#5), 5(#6).*

STAR SEED (Formerly Powers That Be)
Broadway Comics: No. 7, 1996 - No. 9 ($2.95)

7-9 3.00

STARSHIP TROOPERS
Dark Horse Comics: 1997 - No. 2, 1997 ($2.95, limited series)

1,2-Movie adaption 3.00

STARSHIP TROOPERS: BRUTE CREATIONS
Dark Horse Comics: 1997 ($2.95, one-shot)

1 3.00

STARSHIP TROOPERS: DOMINANT SPECIES
Dark Horse Comics: Aug, 1998 - No. 4, Nov, 1998 ($2.95, limited series)

1-4-Strnad-s/Bolton-c 3.00

STARSHIP TROOPERS: INSECT TOUCH
Dark Horse Comics: 1997 - No. 3, 1997 ($2.95, limited series)

1-3 3.00

STAR SLAMMERS (See Marvel Graphic Novel #6)
Malibu Comics (Bravura): May, 1994 - No. 4, Aug, 1994 ($2.50, unfinished limited series)

1-4: W. Simonson-a/stories; contain Bravura stamps 2.50

STAR SLAMMERS SPECIAL
Dark Horse Comics (Legend): June, 1996 ($2.95, one-shot)

nn-Simonson-c/a/scripts; concludes Bravura limited series. 3.00

STARSLAYER
Pacific Comics/First Comics No. 7 on: Feb, 1982 - No. 6, Apr, 1983; No. 7, Aug, 1983 - No. 34, Nov, 1985

1-Origin & 1st app.; excessive blood & gore; 1 pg. Rocketeer brief app. which continues in #2 5.00

2-Origin/1st full app. the Rocketeer (4/82) by Dave Stevens (Chapter 1 of Rocketeer saga; see Pacific Presents #1,2) 1 2 3 5 6 8

3-Chapter 2 of Rocketeer saga by Stevens 6.00

4,6,7: 7-Grell-a ends 3.00

5-2nd app. Groo the Wanderer by Aragones 1 2 3 4 5 7

8-34: 10-1st app. Grimjack (11/83, ends #17). 18-Starslayer meets Grimjack. 20-The Black Flame begins (9/84, 1st app.), ends #33. 27-Book length Black Flame story 2.50

NOTE: ***Grell** a-1-7; c-1-8. **Stevens** back c-2, 3. **Sutton** a-17p, 20-22p, 24-27p, 29-33p.*

STARSLAYER (The Director's Cut)
Acclaim Comics (Windjammer): June, 1994 - No. 8, Dec, 1995 ($2.50)

1-8: Mike Grell-c/a/scripts 2.50

STAR SPANGLED COMICS (Star Spangled War Stories #131 on)
National Periodical Publications: Oct, 1941 - No. 130, July, 1952

1-Origin/1st app. Tarantula; Captain X of the R.A.F., Star Spangled Kid (see Action #40), Armstrong of the Army begin; Robot-c 489 978 1467 3521 6161 8800

2 162 324 486 1021 1723 2425

3-5 102 204 306 643 1084 1525

6-Last Armstrong/Army; Penniless Palmer begins 62 124 186 391 663 935

7-(4/42)-Origin/1st app. The Guardian by S&K, & Robotman (by Paul Cassidy & created by Siegel);The Newsboy Legion (1st app.), Robotman & TNT begin; last Captain X 667 1334 2001 4802 8401 12,000

8-Origin TNT & Dan the Dyna-Mite 232 464 696 1670 2573 3475

9,10 165 330 495 1188 1832 2475

11-17 120 240 360 756 1278 1800

18-Origin Star Spangled Kid 150 300 450 945 1598 2250

19-Last Tarantula 120 240 360 756 1278 1800

20-Liberty Belle begins (5/43) 135 270 405 851 1438 2025

21-29-Last S&K issue; 23-Last TNT. 25-Robotman by Jimmy Thompson begins. 29-Intro Robbie the Robotdog 102 204 306 643 1084 1525

30-40: 31-S&K-c 59 118 177 372 629 885

41-51: 41,49-Kirby-c. 51-Robot-c by Kirby 53 106 159 330 558 785

52-64: 53 by S&K. 64-Last Newsboy Legion & The Guardian 48 96 144 298 499 700

65-Robin begins with c/app. (2/47); Batman cameo in 1 panel; Robin-c begins, end #95 167 334 501 1052 1776 2500

66-Batman cameo in Robin story 82 164 246 517 871 1225

67,68,70-80: 68-Last Liberty Belle? 72-Burnley Robin-c 67 134 201 422 711 1000

69-Origin/1st app. Tomahawk by F. Ray; atom bomb story & splash (6/47) 140 280 420 882 1491 2100

81-Origin Merry, Girl of 1000 Gimmicks in Star Spangled Kid story 57 114 171 359 605 850

82,85: 82-Last Robotman? 85-Last Star Spangled Kid? 52 104 156 322 536 750

83-Tomahawk enters the lost valley, a land of dinosaurs; Capt. Compass begins, ends #130 52 104 156 326 543 760

84,87 (Rare): 87-Batman cameo in Robin 83 166 249 523 887 1250

86-Batman cameo in Robin story 58 116 174 365 615 865

88(1/49)-94: Batman-c/stories in all. 91-Federal Men begin, end #93. 94-Manhunters Around the World begin, end #121 59 118 177 372 629 885

95-Batman story; last Robin-c 53 106 159 332 554 775

96,98-Batman cameo in Robin stories. 96-1st Tomahawk-c (also #97-121) 40 80 120 235 380 525

97,99 34 68 102 198 319 440

100 (1/50)-Pre-Bat-Hound tryout in Robin story (pre-dates Batman #92). 40 80 120 244 397 550

101-109,118,119,121: 121-Last Tomahawk-c 32 64 96 190 305 420

110,111,120-Batman cameo in Robin stories. 120-Last 52 pg. issue 34 68 102 198 319 440

Star Spangled War Stories #38 © DC

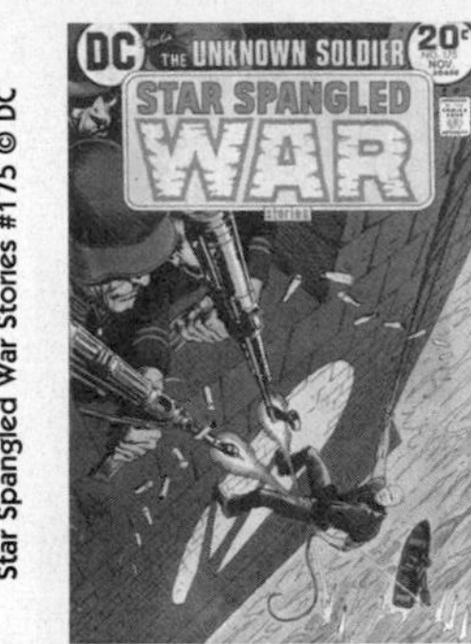

Star Spangled War Stories #175 © DC

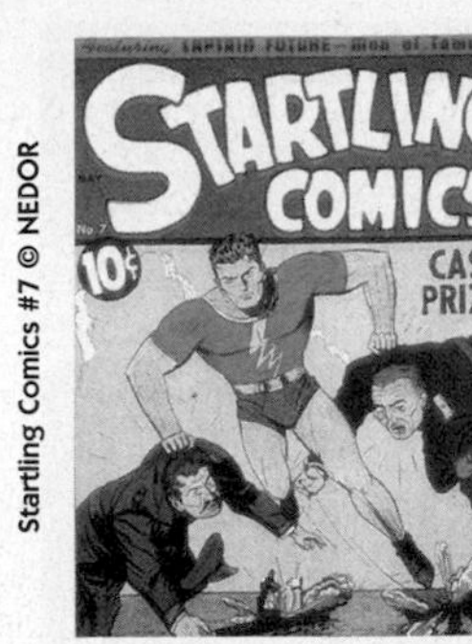

Startling Comics #7 © NEDOR

GD VG FN VF VF/NM NM-
2.0 4.0 6.0 8.0 9.0 9.2

112-Batman & Robin story 36 72 108 212 341 470
113-Frazetta-a (10 pgs.) 41 82 123 256 428 600
114-Retells Robin's origin (3/51); Batman & Robin story
43 86 129 267 446 625
115,117-Batman app. in Robin stories 35 70 105 208 334 460
116-Flag-c 35 70 105 208 334 460
122-(11/51)-Ghost Breaker-c/stories begin (origin/1st app.), ends #130 (Ghost Breaker covers #122-130) 43 86 129 267 446 625
123-126,128,129 31 62 93 181 291 400
127-Batman app. 33 66 99 192 309 425
130-Batman cameo in Robin story 35 70 105 200 327 450

NOTE: *Most all issues after #29 signed by Simon & Kirby are not by them.* ***Bill Ely*** *c-122-130.* ***Mortimer*** *c-65-74(most), 76-95(most).* ***Fred Ray*** *c-96-106, 109, 110, 112, 113, 115-120.* ***S&K*** *c-7-31, 33, 34, 36, 37, 39, 40, 48, 49, 50-54, 56-58.* ***Hal Sherman*** *c-1-6.* ***Dick Sprang*** *c-75.*

STAR SPANGLED COMICS (Also see All Star Comics 1999 crossover titles)
DC Comics: May, 1999 ($1.99, one-shot)

1-Golden Age Sandman and the Star Spangled Kid 2.50

STAR SPANGLED KID (See Action #40, Leading Comics & Star Spangled Comics)

STAR SPANGLED WAR STORIES
DC Comics: Aug/Sept 1952

nn - Ashcan comic, not distributed to newsstands, only for in-house use. Cover art is Western Comics #28 with interior being Western Comics #13 (no known sales)

STAR SPANGLED WAR STORIES (Formerly Star Spangled Comics #1-130; Becomes The Unknown Soldier #205 on) (See Showcase)
National Periodical Publications: No. 131, 8/52 - No. 133, 10/52; No. 3, 11/52 - No. 204, 2-3/77

131(#1) 110 220 330 693 1172 1650
132 68 136 204 428 727 1025
133-Used in **POP**, pg. 94 58 116 174 365 620 875
3-6: 4-Devil Dog Dugan app. 6-Evans-a 41 82 123 256 428 600
7-10 24 48 72 176 326 475
11-20 20 40 60 143 264 385
21-30: 30 Last precode (2/55) 17 34 51 126 233 340
31-33,35-40 14 28 42 99 175 250
34-Krigstein-a 14 28 42 102 181 260
41-44,46-50: 50-1st S.A. issue 13 26 39 95 168 240
45-1st DC grey tone war-c (5/56) 25 50 75 185 343 500
51,52,54-63,65,66, 68-83 11 22 33 75 133 190
53-"Rock Sergeant," 3rd Sgt. Rock prototype; inspired "P.I. & The Sand Fleas" in G.I. Combat #56 (1/57) 17 34 51 120 223 325
64-Pre-Sgt. Rock Easy Co. story (12/57) 13 26 39 95 168 240
67-Two Easy Co. stories without Sgt. Rock 14 28 42 99 175 250
84-Origin Mlle. Marie 17 34 51 126 233 340
85-89-Mlle. Marie in all 12 24 36 86 153 220
90-1st app. "War That Time Forgot" series; dinosaur issue-c/story (4-5/60) (also see Weird War Tales #94 & #99) 38 76 114 293 547 800
91,93-No dinosaur stories 11 22 33 79 140 200
92-2nd dinosaur-c/s 17 34 51 120 223 325
94 (12/60)- "Ghost Ace" story; Baron Von Richter as The Enemy Ace (predates Our Army at War #151) 20 40 60 148 274 400
95-99: Dinosaur-c/s 14 28 42 104 187 270
100-Dinosaur-c/story. 15 30 45 111 206 300
101-115: All dinosaur issues 12 24 36 82 146 210
116-125,127-133,135-137-Last dinosaur story; Heath Birdman-#129,131
10 20 30 70 123 175
126-No dinosaur story 9 18 27 63 107 150
134-Dinosaur story; Neal Adams-a 12 24 36 82 146 210
138-New Enemy Ace-c/stories begin by Joe Kubert (4-5/68), end #150 (also see Our Army at War #151 and Showcase #57) 12 24 36 86 153 220
139-Origin Enemy Ace (7/68) 9 18 27 63 107 150
140-143,145: 145-Last 12¢ issue (6-7/69) 7 14 21 47 76 105
144-Neal Adams/Kubert-a 8 16 24 52 86 120
146-Enemy Ace-c/app. 5 10 15 34 55 75
147,148-New Enemy Ace stories 6 12 18 41 66 90
149,150-Last new Enemy Ace by Kubert. Viking Prince by Kubert
6 12 18 39 62 85
151-1st solo app. Unknown Soldier (6-7/70); Enemy Ace-r begin (from Our Army at War, Showcase & SSWS); end #161 14 28 42 104 187 270
152-Reprints 2nd Enemy Ace app. 5 10 15 30 48 65
153,155-Enemy Ace reprints; early Unknown Soldier stories
4 8 12 26 41 55
154-Origin Unknown Soldier 10 20 30 73 129 185

GD VG FN VF VF/NM NM-
2.0 4.0 6.0 8.0 9.0 9.2

156-1st Battle Album; Unknown Soldier story; Kubert-c/a
4 8 12 24 37 50
157-Sgt. Rock x-over in Unknown Soldier story. 4 8 12 22 34 45
158-163-(52 pgs.): New Unknown Soldier stories; Kubert-c/a. 161-Last Enemy Ace-r
3 6 9 17 25 32
164-183,200: 181-183-Enemy Ace vs. Balloon Buster serial app; Frank Thorne-a. 200-Enemy Ace back-up 2 4 6 10 14 18
184-199,201-204 2 4 6 8 11 14

NOTE: ***Anderson*** *a-28.* ***Chaykin*** *a-167.* ***Drucker*** *a-59, 61, 64, 66, 67, 73-84.* ***Estrada*** *a-149.* ***John Giunta*** *a-72.* ***Glanzman*** *a-167, 171, 172, 174.* ***Heath*** *a-122, 132, 133; c-67, 122, 132-134.* ***Kaluta*** *a-197i; c-167.* ***G. Kane*** *a-169.* ***Kubert*** *a-6-163(most later issues), 200.* ***Maurer*** *a-160, 165.* ***Severin*** *a-65, 162.* ***S&K*** *c-7-31, 33, 34, 37, 40.* ***Simonson*** *a-170, 172, 174, 180.* ***Sutton*** *a-168.* ***Thorne*** *a-183.* ***Toth*** *a-164.* ***Wildey*** *a-161. Suicide Squad in 110, 116-118, 120, 121, 127.*

STARSTREAM (Adventures in Science Fiction)(See Questar illustrated)
Whitman/Western Publishing Co.: 1976 (79¢, 68 pgs, cardboard-c)

1-4: 1-Bolle-a. 2-4-McWilliams & Bolle-a 2 4 6 9 13 16

STARSTRUCK
Marvel Comics (Epic Comics): Feb, 1985 - No. 6, Feb, 1986 ($1.50, mature)

1-6: Kaluta-a 3.00

STARSTRUCK
Dark Horse Comics: Aug, 1990 - No. 4, Nov?, 1990 ($2.95, B&W, 52pgs.)

1-3:Kaluta-r/Epic series plus new-c/a in all 3.00
4 (68, pgs.)-contains 2 trading cards 3.00

STAR STUDDED
Cambridge House/Superior Publishers: 1945 (25¢, 132 pgs.); 1945 (196 pgs.)

nn-Captain Combat by Giunta, Ghost Woman, Commandette, & Red Rogue app.; Infantino-a
34 68 102 198 319 440
nn-The Cadet, Edison Bell, Hoot Gibson, Jungle Lil (196 pgs.); copies vary; Blue Beetle in some 28 56 84 162 261 360

STARTLING COMICS
Better Publications (Nedor): June, 1940 - No. 53, Sept, 1948

1-Origin Captain Future-Man Of Tomorrow, Mystico (By Sansone), The Wonder Man; The Masked Rider & his horse Pinto begins; Masked Rider formerly in pulps; drug use story 280 560 840 1764 2982 4200
2 -Don Davis, Espionage Ace begins 100 200 300 630 1065 1500
3 83 166 249 523 887 1250
4 60 120 180 378 639 900
5-9 52 104 156 322 536 750
10-The Fighting Yank begins (9/41, origin/1st app.)
394 788 1182 2679 4690 6700
11-2nd app. Fighting Yank 120 240 360 756 1278 1800
12-Hitler, Hirohito, Mussolini-c 113 226 339 712 1206 1700
13-15 64 128 192 403 682 960
16-Origin The Four Comrades; not in #32,35 66 132 198 416 701 985
17-Last Masked Rider & Mystico 49 98 147 304 507 710
18-Pyroman begins (12/42, origin)(also see America's Best Comics #3 for 1st app., 11/42)
102 204 306 643 1084 1525
19 49 98 147 304 507 710
20,21: 20-The Oracle begins (3/43); not in issues 26,28,33,34. 21-Origin The Ape, Oracle's enemy 52 104 156 322 536 750
22-34: 34-Origin The Scarab & only app. 50 100 150 310 518 725
35-Hypodermic syringe attacks Fighting Yank in drug story
52 104 156 322 536 750
36-43: 36-Last Four Comrades. 38-Bondage/torture-c. 40-Last Capt. Future & Oracle. 41-Front Page Peggy begins; A-Bomb-c. 43-Last Pyroman
44 88 132 273 454 635
44,45: 44-Lance Lewis, Space Detective begins; Ingels-c; sci/fi-c begin. 45-Tygra begins (intro/origin, 5/47); Ingels-c/a (splash pg. & inside f/c B&W ad)
70 140 210 441 746 1050
46-Classic Ingels-c; Ingels-a 113 226 339 712 1206 1700
47,48,50-53: 50,51-Sea-Eagle app. 65 130 195 410 693 975
49-Classic Schomburg Robot-c; last Fighting Yank 423 846 1269 3000 5250 7500

NOTE: ***Ingels*** *a-44, 45; c-44, 45, 46(wash).* ***Schomburg (Xela)*** *c-21-43; 47-53 (airbrush).* ***Tuska*** *c-45? Bondage c-16, 21, 37, 46-49. Captain Future c-1-9, 13, 14. Fighting Yank c-10-12, 15-17, 21, 22, 24, 26, 28, 30, 32, 34, 36, 38, 40, 42. Pyroman c-18-20, 23, 25, 27, 29, 31, 33, 35, 37, 39, 41, 43.*

STARTLING STORIES: BANNER
Marvel Comics: July, 2001 - No. 4, Oct, 2001 ($2.99, limited series)

1-4-Hulk story by Azzarello; Corben-c/a 3.00
TPB (11/01, $12.95) r/1-4 13.00

STARTLING STORIES: FANTASTIC FOUR - UNSTABLE MOLECULES (See Fantastic Four - ...)

STARTLING STORIES: THE MEGALOMANIACAL SPIDER-MAN

Startling Terror Tales #13 © STAR

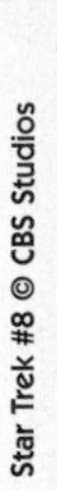
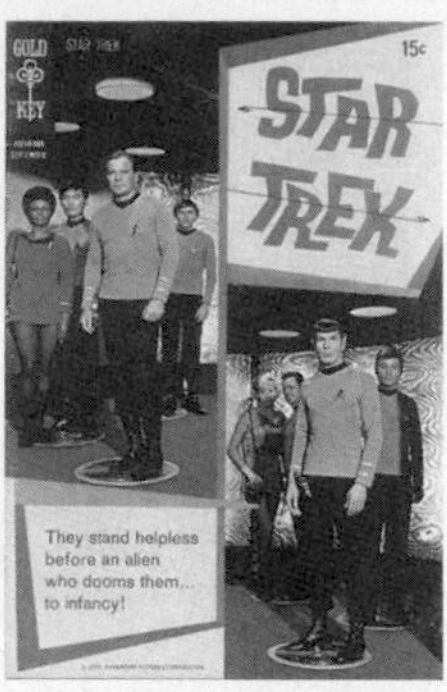
Star Trek #8 © CBS Studios

Star Trek: Alien Spotlight Orions © CBS Studios

	GD 2.0	VG 4.0	FN 6.0	VF 8.0	VF/NM 9.0	NM- 9.2

Marvel Comics: Jun, 2002 ($2.99, one-shot)

1-Spider-Man spoof; Peter Bagge-s/a 3.00

STARTLING STORIES: THE THING
Marvel Comics: 2003 ($3.50, one-shot)

1-Zimmerman-s/Kramer-a; Inhumans and the Hulk app. 3.50

STARTLING STORIES: THE THING - NIGHT FALLS ON YANCY STREET
Marvel Comics: Jun, 2003 - No. 4, Sept, 2003 ($3.50, limited series)

1-4-Dorkin-s/Haspiel-a. 2,3-Frightful Four app. 3.50

STARTLING TERROR TALES
Star Publications: No. 10, May, 1952 - No. 14, Feb, 1953; No. 4, Apr, 1953 - No. 11, 1954

	GD	VG	FN	VF	VF/NM	NM-
10-(1st Series)-Wood/Harrison-a (r/A Star Presentation #3) Disbrow/Cole-c; becomes 4 different titles after #10; becomes Confessions of Love #11 on, The Horrors #11 on, Terrifying Tales #11 on, Terrors of the Jungle #11 on & continues w/Startling Terror #11	75	150	225	473	799	1125
11-(8/52)-L. B. Cole Spider-c; r-Fox's "A Feature Presentation" #5 (blue-c)	160	320	480	1008	1704	2400
11-Black-c (variant; believed to be a pressrun change) (Unique)	167	334	501	1052	1776	2500
12,14	32	64	96	190	305	420
13-Jo-Jo-r; Disbrow-a	34	68	102	198	319	440
4-9,11(1953-54) (2nd Series): 11-New logo	29	58	87	169	272	375
10-Disbrow-a	35	70	105	203	327	450

NOTE: *L. B. Cole covers-all issues. Palais a-V2#8r, V2#11r.*

STAR TREK (TV) (See Dan Curtis Giveaways, Dynabrite Comics & Power Record Comics)
Gold Key: 7/67; No. 2, 6/68; No. 3, 12/68; No. 4, 6/69 - No. 61, 3/79

	GD	VG	FN	VF	VF/NM	NM-
1-Photo-c begin, end #9	41	82	123	328	614	900
1 (rare variation w/photo back-c)	50	100	150	413	782	1150
2	22	44	66	157	291	425
2 (rare variation w/photo back-c)	31	62	93	239	445	650
3-5	15	30	45	105	190	275
3 (rare variation w/photo back-c)	23	46	69	167	309	450
6-9	12	24	36	82	146	210
10-20	6	12	18	43	69	95
21-30	6	12	18	37	59	80
31-40	4	8	12	28	44	60
41-61: 52-Drug propaganda story	4	8	12	22	34	45
...the Enterprise Logs nn (8/76)-Golden Press, ($1.95, 224 pgs.)-r/#1-8 plus 7 pgs. by McWilliams (#11185)-Photo-c	6	12	18	37	59	80
...the Enterprise Logs Vol. 2 ('76)-r/#9-17 (#11187)-Photo-c	5	10	15	32	51	70
...the Enterprise Logs Vol. 3 ('77)-r/#18-26 (#11188); McWilliams-a (4 pgs.)-Photo-c	5	10	15	32	51	70
Star Trek Vol. 4 (Winter '77)-Reprints #27,28,30-34,36,38 (#11189) plus 3 pgs. new art	5	10	15	32	51	70

... : The Key Collection (Checker Book Publ. Group, 2004, $22.95) r/#1-8 23.00
... : The Key Collection Volume 2 (Checker, 2004, $22.95) r/#9-16 23.00
... : The Key Collection Volume 3 (Checker, 2005, $22.95) r/#17-24 23.00
... : The Key Collection Volume 4 (Checker, 2005, $22.95) r/#25-33 23.00
... : The Key Collection Volume 5 (Checker, 2006, $22.95) r/#34,36,38,39,40-43 23.00

NOTE: *McWilliams a-38, 40-44, 46-61. #29 reprints #1; #35 reprints #4; #37 reprints #5; #45 reprints #7. The tabloids all have photo covers and blank inside covers. Painted covers #10-44, 46-59.*

STAR TREK
Marvel Comics Group: April, 1980 - No. 18, Feb, 1982

	GD	VG	FN	VF	VF/NM	NM-
1: 1-3-r/Marvel Super Special; movie adapt.	2	4	6	9	12	15
2-16: 5-Miller-c	1	2	3	5	6	8
17-Low print run	2	4	6	8	10	12
18-Last issue; low print run	2	4	6	10	14	18

NOTE: *Austin c-18i. Buscema a-13. Gil Kane a-15. Nasser c/a-7. Simonson c-17.*

STAR TREK (Also see Who's Who In Star Trek)
DC Comics: Feb, 1984 - No. 56, Nov, 1988 (75¢, Mando paper)

	GD	VG	FN	VF	VF/NM	NM-
1-Sutton-a(p) begins	1	3	4	6	8	10

2-5 6.00
6-10: 7-Origin Saavik 5.00
11-20: 19-Walter Koenig story 4.00
21-32 3.50
33-($1.25, 52 pgs.)-20th anniversary issue 4.00
34-49: 37-Painted-c 3.00
50-($1.50, 52 pgs.) 4.00
51-56, Annual 1-3: 1(1985). 2(1986). 3(1988, $1.50) 3.00
...: To Boldly Go TPB (Titan Books, 7/05, $19.95) r/#1-6; Koenig foreward; cast interviews 20.00
...: The Trial of James T. Kirk TPB (Titan Books, 6/06, $19.95) r/#7-12; cast interviews 20.00
...: The Return of the Worthy TPB (Titan Books, 12/06, $19.95) r/#13-18; cast interviews 20.00

NOTE: *Morrow a-28, 35, 36, 56. Orlando c-8i. Perez c-1-3. Spiegle a-19. Starlin c-24, 25. Sutton a-1-6p, 8-18p, 20-27p, 29p, 31-34p, 39-52p, 55p; c-4-6p, 8-22p, 46p.*

STAR TREK
DC Comics: Oct, 1989 - No. 80, Jan, 1996 ($1.50/$1.75/$1.95/$2.50)

1-Capt. Kirk and crew 6.00
2,3 4.00
4-23,25-30: 10-12-The Trial of James T. Kirk. 21-Begin $1.75-c 3.00
24-($2.95, 68 pgs.)-40 pg. epic w/pin-ups 3.50
31-49,51-60 2.50
50-($3.50, 68 pgs.)-Painted-c 3.50
61-74,76-80 2.50
75 ($3.95) 4.00
Annual 1-6('90-'95, 68 pgs.): 1-Morrow-a. 3-Painted-c 4.00
Special 1-3 ('9-'95, 68 pgs.)-1-Sutton-a. 4.00
...: The Ashes of Eden (1995, $14.95, 100 pgs.)-Shatner story 15.00
...Generations (1994, $3.95, 68 pgs.)-Movie adaptation 4.00
...Generations (1994, $5.95, 68 pgs.)-Squarebound 6.00

STAR TREK...(TV)
DC Comics (WildStorm): one-shots

All of Me (4/00, $5.95, prestige format) Lopresti-a 6.00
Enemy Unseen TPB (2001, $17.95) r/Perchance to Dream, Embrace the Wolf, The Killing Shadows; Struzan-c 18.00
Enter the Wolves (2001, $5.95) Crispin & Weinstein-s; Mota-a/c 6.00
New Frontier - Double Time (11/00, $5.95)-Captain Calhoun's USS Excalibur; Peter David-s; Stelfreeze-c 6.00
Other Realities TPB (2001, $14.95) r/All of Me, New Frontier - Double Time, and DS9-N-Vector; Van Fleet-c 15.00
Special (2001, $6.95) Stories from all 4 series by various; Van Fleet-c 7.00

STAR TREK: ALIEN SPOTLIGHT
IDW Publishing: Sept, 2007 - Feb, 2008 ($3.99, series of one-shots)

... Andorians (11/07) Storrie-s/O'Grady-a; Counselor Troi app.; two art & one photo-c 4.00
... Borg (1/08) Harris-s/Murphy-a; Janeway & Next Gen crew app.; two art & one photo-c 4.00
... The Gorn (9/07) Messina-a; Chekov app.; two art & one photo-c 4.00
... Orions (12/07) Casagrande-a; Capt. Pike app.; two art & one photo-c 4.00
... Romulans (2/08) John Byrne-s/a; Kirk era; two art & one photo-c 4.00
... Vulcans (10/07) Spock's early Enterprise days with Capt. Pike; two art & one photo-c 4.00

STAR TREK: ASSIGNMENT EARTH
IDW Publishing: May, 2008 - No. 5, Sept, 2008 ($3.99, limited series)

1-4-Further adventures of Gary Seven and Roberta; John Byrne-s/a/c 4.00

STAR TREK: DEBT OF HONOR
DC Comics: 1992 ($24.95/$14.95, graphic novel)

Hardcover ($24.95) Claremont-s/Hughes-a(p) 25.00
Softcover ($14.95) 15.00

STAR TREK: DEEP SPACE NINE (TV)
Malibu Comics: Aug, 1993 - No. 32, Jan, 1996 ($2.50)

1-Direct Sale Edition w/line drawn-c 4.00
1-Newsstand Edition with photo-c 3.00
0-(1/95, $2.95)-Terok Nor 3.00
2-30: 2-Polybagged w/trading card. 9-4 pg. prelude to Hearts & Minds 2.50
31-($3.95) 4.00
32-($3.50) 3.50
Annual 1 (1/95, $3.95, 68 pgs.) 4.00
Special 1 (1995, $3.50) 3.50
Ultimate Annual 1 (12/95, $5.95) 6.00
...:Lightstorm (12/94, $3.50) 3.50

STAR TREK: DEEP SPACE NINE (TV)
Marvel Comics (Paramount Comics): Nov, 1996 - No. 15, Mar, 1998 ($1.95/$1.99)

1-15: 12,13-"Telepathy War" pt. 2,3 2.50

STAR TREK: DEEP SPACE NINE -- N-VECTOR (TV)
DC Comics (WildStorm): Aug, 2000 - No. 4, Nov, 2000 ($2.50, limited series)

1-4-Cypress-a 2.50

STAR TREK DEEP SPACE NINE-THE CELEBRITY SERIES
Malibu Comics: May, 1995 ($2.95)

1-Blood and Honor; Mark Lenard script 3.00
1-Rules of Diplomacy; Aron Eisenberg script 3.00

STAR TREK: DEEP SPACE NINE HEARTS AND MINDS
Malibu Comics: June, 1994 - No. 4, Sept, 1994 ($2.50, limited series)

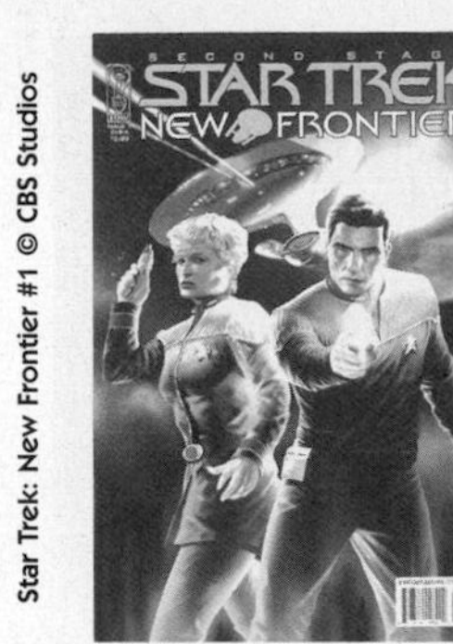

Star Trek: New Frontier #1 © CBS Studios

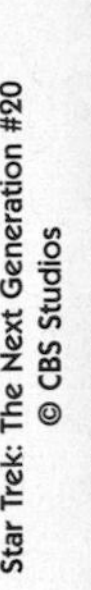

Star Trek: The Next Generation #20 © CBS Studios

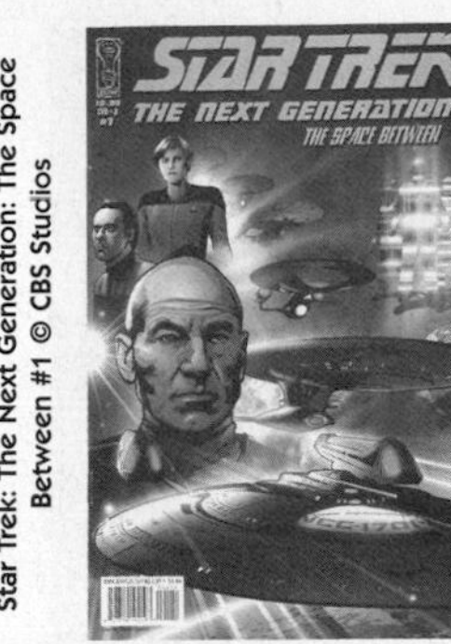

Star Trek: The Next Generation: The Space Between #1 © CBS Studios

GD VG FN VF VF/NM NM-
2.0 4.0 6.0 8.0 9.0 9.2

1-4 2.50
1-Holographic-c 4.00

STAR TREK: DEEP SPACE NINE, THE MAQUIS
Malibu Comics: Feb, 1995 - No. 3, Apr, 1995 ($2.50, limited series)
1-3-Newsstand-c, 1-Photo-c 2.50

STAR TREK: DEEP SPACE NINE/THE NEXT GENERATION
Malibu Comics: Oct, 1994 - No. 2, Nov, 1994 ($2.50, limited series)
1,2: Parts 2 & 4 of x-over with Star Trek: TNG/DS9 from DC Comics 2.50

STAR TREK: DEEP SPACE NINE WORF SPECIAL
Malibu Comics: Dec, 1995 ($3.95, one-shot)
1-Includes pinups 4.00

STAR TREK: DIVIDED WE FALL
DC Comics (WildStorm): July, 2001 - No. 4, Oct, 2001 ($2.95, limited series)
1-4: Ordover & Mack-s; Lenara Kahn, Verad and Odan app. 3.00

STAR TREK EARLY VOYAGES (TV)
Marvel Comics (Paramount Comics): Feb, 1997 - No. 17, Jun, 1998 ($2.95/$1.95/$1.99)
1-($2.95) 3.00
2-17 2.50

STAR TREK: ENTERPRISE EXPERIMENT
IDW Publishing: Apr, 2008 - No. 5, Aug, 2008 ($3.99, limited series)
1-5-Year Four story; D.C. Fontana & Derek Chester-s; Purcell-a 4.00

STAR TREK: FIRST CONTACT (Movie)
Marvel Comics (Paramount Comics): Nov, 1996 ($5.95, one-shot)
nn-Movie adaption 6.00

STAR TREK: KLINGONS: BLOOD WILL TELL
IDW Publishing: Apr, 2007 - No. 5 ($3.99, limited series)
1-5-Star Trek TOS episodes from the Klingon viewpoint; Messina-a. 2-Tribbles 4.00
1-($4.99) Klingon Language Variant; comic with Kliingon text; English script 5.00

STAR TREK: MIRROR IMAGES
IDW Publishing: June, 2008 - No. 5 ($3.99, limited series)
1-3-Further adventures in the Mirror Universe. 3-Mirror-Picard app. 4.00

STAR TREK: MIRROR MIRROR
Marvel Comics (Paramount Comics): Feb, 1997 ($3.95, one-shot)
1-DeFalco-s 4.00

STAR TREK MOVIE SPECIAL
DC Comics: 1984 (June) - No. 2, 1987 ($1.50); No. 1, 1989 ($2.00, 52 pgs)
nn-(#1)-Adapts Star Trek III; Sutton-p (68 pgs.) 3.00
2-Adapts Star Trek IV; Sutton-a; Chaykin-c. (68 pgs.) 3.00
1 (1989)-Adapts Star Trek V; painted-c 3.00

STAR TREK: NEW FRONTIER
IDW Publishing: Mar, 2008 - No. 5, July, 2008 ($3.99, limited series)
1-5-Capt. Calhoun & Adm. Shelby app.; Peter David-s 4.00

STAR TREK: OPERATION ASSIMILATION
Marvel Comics (Paramount Comics): Dec, 1996 ($2.95, one-shot)
1 3.00

STAR TREK: ROMULANS THE HOLLOW CROWN
IDW Publishing: Sept, 2008 - Present ($3.99, limited series)
1-John Byrne-s/a/c 4.00

STAR TREK VI: THE UNDISCOVERED COUNTRY (Movie)
DC Comics: 1992
1-($2.95, regular edition, 68 pgs.)-Adaptation of film 3.00
nn-($5.95, prestige edition)-Has photos of movie not included in regular edition; painted-c by Palmer; photo back-c 6.00

STAR TREK: STARFLEET ACADEMY
Marvel Comics (Paramount Comics): Dec, 1996 - No. 19, Jun, 1998 ($1.95/$1.99)
1-19: Begin new series. 12-"Telepathy War" pt. 1. 18-English and Klingon language editions 2.50

STAR TREK: TELEPATHY WAR
Marvel Comics (Paramount Comics): Nov, 1997 ($2.99, 48 pgs., one-shot)
1-"Telepathy War" x-over pt. 6 3.00

STAR TREK - THE MODALA IMPERATIVE
DC Comics: Late July, 1991 - No. 4, Late Sept, 1991 ($1.75, limited series)
1-4 2.50
TPB ($19.95) r/series and ST:TNG - The Modala Imperative 20.00

STAR TREK: THE NEXT GENERATION (TV)
DC Comics: Feb, 1988 - No. 6, July, 1988 (limited series)
1 ($1.50, 52 pgs.)-Sienkiewicz painted-c 6.00
2-6 ($1.00) 4.00

STAR TREK: THE NEXT GENERATION (TV)
DC Comics: Oct, 1989 -No. 80, 1995 ($1.50/$1.75/$1.95)
1-Capt. Picard and crew from TV show 1 2 3 5 7 9
2,3 5.00
4-10 4.00
11-23,25-49,51-60 3.00
24,50: 24-($2.50, 52 pgs.). 50-($3.50, 68 pgs.)-Painted-c 5.00
61-74,76-80 2.50
75-($3.95, 50 pgs.) 4.00
Annual 1-6 ('90-'95, 68 pgs.) 4.00
Special 1 -3('93-'95, 68 pgs.)-1-Contains 3 stories 4.00
...-The Series Finale (1994, $3.95, 68 pgs.) 4.00

STAR TREK: THE NEXT GENERATION (TV)
DC Comics (WildStorm): one-shots
Embrace the Wolf (6/00, $5.95, prestige format) Golden & Sniegoski-s 6.00
Forgiveness (2001, $24.95, HC) David Brin-s/Scott Hampton painted-a; dust jacket-c 30.00
Forgiveness (2002, $17.95, SC) 18.00
The Gorn Crisis (1/01, $29.95, HC) Kordey painted-a/dust jacket-c 30.00
The Gorn Crisis (1/01, $17.95, SC) Kordey painted-a 18.00

STAR TREK: THE NEXT GENERATION/DEEP SPACE NINE (TV)
DC Comics: Dec, 1994 - No. 2, Jan, 1995 ($2.50, limited series)
1,2-Parts 1 & 3 of x-over with Star Trek: DS9/TNG from Malibu Comics 2.50

STAR TREK: THE NEXT GENERATION - ILL WIND
DC Comics: Nov, 1995 - No. 4, Feb, 1996 ($2.50, limited series)
1-4: Hugh Fleming painted-c on all 2.50

STAR TREK: THE NEXT GENERATION: INTELLIGENCE GATHERING
IDW Publishing: Jan, 2008 - No. 5, May, 2008 ($3.99)
1-5-Messina-a/Scott & David Tipton-s; two covers on each 4.00

STAR TREK: THE NEXT GENERATION - PERCHANCE TO DREAM
DC Comics/WildStorm: Feb, 2000 - No. 4, May, 2000 ($2.50, limited series)
1-4-Bradstreet-c 2.50

STAR TREK: THE NEXT GENERATION - RIKER
Marvel Comics (Paramount Comics): July, 1998 ($3.50, one-shot)
1-Riker joins the Maquis 3.50

STAR TREK: THE NEXT GENERATION - SHADOWHEART
DC Comics: Dec, 1994 - No. 4, Mar, 1995 ($1.95, limited series)
1-4 2.50

STAR TREK: THE NEXT GENERATION - THE KILLING SHADOWS
DC Comics/WildStorm: Nov, 2000 - No. 4, Feb, 2001 ($2.50, limited series)
1-4-Scott Ciencin-s; Sela app. 2.50

STAR TREK: THE NEXT GENERATION - THE MODALA IMPERATIVE
DC Comics: Early Sept, 1991 - No. 4, Late Oct, 1991 ($1.75, limited series)
1-4 2.50

STAR TREK: THE NEXT GENERATION: THE SPACE BETWEEN
IDW Publishing: Jan, 2007 - No. 6, June, 2007 ($3.99)
1-6-Single issue stories from various seasons; photo & art covers 4.00

STAR TREK UNLIMITED
Marvel Comics (Paramount Comics): Nov, 1996 - No. 10, July, 1998 ($2.95/$2.99)
1,2-Stories from original series and Next Generation 4.00
3-10: 3-Begin $2.99-c. 6-"Telepathy War" pt. 4. 7-Q & Trelane swap Kirk & Picard 3.50

STAR TREK UNTOLD VOYAGES
Marvel Comics (Paramount Comics): May, 1998 - No. 5, July, 1998 ($2.50)
1-5-Kirk's crew after the 1st movie 2.50

STAR TREK: VOYAGER
Marvel Comics (Paramount Comics): Nov, 1996 - No. 15, Mar, 1998 ($1.95/$1.99)
1-15: 13-"Telepathy War" pt. 5. 14-Seven of Nine joins crew 3.00

STAR TREK: VOYAGER
DC Comics/WildStorm: one-shots and trade paperbacks

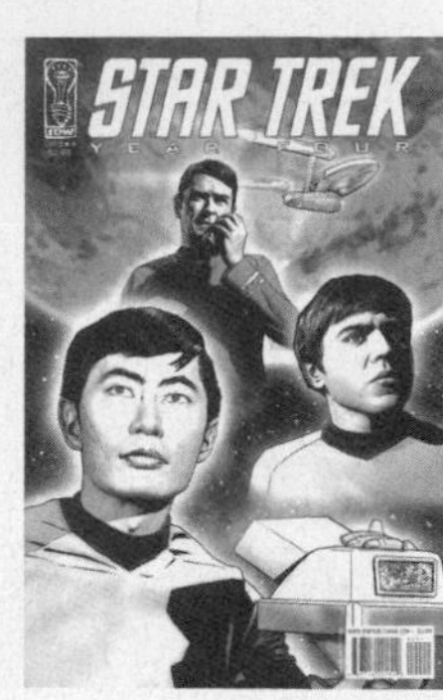

Star Trek: Year Four #4 © CBS Studios

Star Wars #40 © Lucasfilm

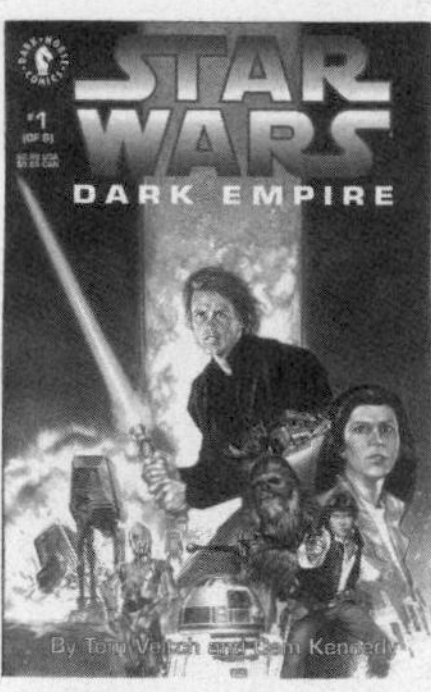

Star Wars: Dark Empire #1 © Lucasfilm

GD VG FN VF VF/NM NM-
2.0 4.0 6.0 8.0 9.0 9.2

GD VG FN VF VF/NM NM-
2.0 4.0 6.0 8.0 9.0 9.2

- Elite Force (7/00, $5.95) The Borg app.; Abnett & Lanning-s 6.00
... Encounters With the Unknown TPB (2001, $19.95) reprints 20.00
- False Colors (1/00, $5.95) Photo-c and Jim Lee-c; Jeff Moy-a 6.00

STAR TREK: VOYAGER-- THE PLANET KILLER
DC Comics/WildStorm: Mar, 2001 - No. 3, May, 2001 ($2.95, limited series)
1-3-Voyager vs. the Planet Killer from the ST:TOS episode; Teranishi-a 3.00

STAR TREK: VOYAGER SPLASHDOWN
Marvel Comics (Paramount Comics): Apr, 1998 - No. 4, July, 1998 ($2.50, limited series)
1-4-Voyager crashes on a water planet 3.00

STAR TREK/ X-MEN
Marvel Comics (Paramount Comics): Dec, 1996 ($4.99, one-shot)
1-Kirk's crew & X-Men; art by Silvestri, Tan, Winn & Finch; Lobdell-s 5.00

STAR TREK/ X-MEN: 2ND CONTACT
Marvel Comics (Paramount Comics): May, 1998 ($4.99, 64 pgs., one-shot)
1-Next Gen. crew & X-Men battle Kang, Sentinels & Borg following First Contact movie 5.00
1-Painted wraparound variant cover 5.00

STAR TREK: YEAR FOUR (Also see Star Trek: Enterprise Experiment)
IDW Publishing: July, 2007 - No. 5, Nov, 2007 ($3.99, limited series)
1-5: 1-Original series crew; Tischman-s/Conley-a; three covers on each 4.00

STAR WARS (Movie) (See Classic..., Contemporary Motivators, Dark Horse Comics, The Droids, The Ewoks, Marvel Movie Showcase, Marvel Special Ed.)
Marvel Comics Group: July, 1977 - No. 107, Sept, 1986
1-(Regular 30¢ edition)-Price in square w/UPC code; #1-6 adapt first movie; first issue on sale before movie debuted 6 12 18 39 62 95
1-(35¢-c; limited distribution - 1500 copies?)- Price in square w/UPC code (Prices vary widely on this book. In 2005 a CGC certified 9.4 sold for $6,500, a CGC certified 9.2 sold for $3,403, and a CGC certified 6.0 sold for $610)
96 192 288 816 1558 2300
NOTE: *The rare 35¢ edition has the cover price in a square box, and the UPC box in the lower left hand corner has the UPC code lines running through it.*
2-4-(30¢ issues). 4-Battle with Darth Vader 4 8 12 22 34 45
2-4-(35¢ with UPC code; not reprints) 9 18 27 63 107 150
5,6: 5-Begin 35¢-c on all editions. 6-Stevens-a(i).
2 4 6 13 18 22
7-20 2 4 6 8 10 12
21-70: 39-44-The Empire Strikes Back-r by Al Williamson in all. 50-Giant.
68-Reintro Boba Fett. 1 2 3 5 7 9
71-80 1 3 4 6 8 10
81-90: 81-Boba Fett app. 2 4 6 8 10 12
91,93-99: 98-Williamson-a. 2 4 6 9 12 15
92,100-106: 92,100-($1.00, 52 pgs.). 2 4 6 11 16 20
107(low dist.); Portacio-a(i) 5 10 15 35 55 75
1-9: Reprints; has "reprint" in upper lefthand corner of cover or on inside or price and number inside a diamond with no date or UPC on cover; 30¢ and 35¢ issues published 4.00
Annual 1 (12/79, 52 pgs.)-Simonson-c 2 4 6 8 10 12
Annual 2 (11/82, 52 pgs.), 3(12/83, 52 pgs.) 1 3 4 6 8 10
... A Long Time Ago...Vol. 1 TPB (Dark Horse Comics, 6/02, $29.95) r/#1-14 30.00
... A Long Time Ago...Vol. 2 TPB (Dark Horse Comics, 7/02, $29.95) r/#15-28 30.00
... A Long Time Ago...Vol. 3 TPB (Dark Horse Comics, 11/02, $29.95) r/#39-53 30.00
... A Long Time Ago...Vol. 4 TPB (Dark Horse Comics, 1/03, $29.95) r/#54-67 & Ann. 2 30.00
... A Long Time Ago...Vol. 5 TPB (Dark Horse Comics, 3/03, $29.95) r/#68-81 & Ann. 3 30.00
... A Long Time Ago...Vol. 6 TPB (Dark Horse Comics, 5/03, $29.95) r/#82-93 30.00
... A Long Time Ago...Vol. 7 TPB (Dark Horse Comics, 6/03, $29.95) r/#96-107 30.00
***Austin** a-11-15i, 21i, 38; c-12-15i, 21i. **Byrne** c-13p. **Chaykin** a-1-10p; c-1. **Golden** c/a-38. **Miller** c-47p; pin-up-43. **Nebres** c/a-Annual 2i. **Portacio** a-107i. **Sienkiewicz** c-92i, 98. **Simonson** a-16p, 49p, 51-63p, 65p, 66p; c-16, 49-51, 52p, 53-62, Annual 1. **Steacy** painted a-105i, 106i; c-105. **Williamson** a-39-44p, 50p, 98; c-39, 40, 41-44p. Painted c-81, 87, 92, 95, 98, 100, 105.*

STAR WARS (Monthly series) (Becomes Star Wars Republic #46-on)
Dark Horse Comics: Dec, 1998 - No. 45, Aug, 2005 ($2.50/$2.95/$2.99)
1-12: 1-6-Prelude To Rebellion; Strnad-s. 4-Brereton-c. 7-12-Outlander 3.00
5,6 (Holochrome-c variants) 6.00
13, 17-18-($2.95): 13-18-Emissaries to Malastare; Truman-s 3.00
14-16-($2.50) Schultz-c 3.00
19-45: 19-22-Twilight; Duursema-a. 23-26-Infinity's End. 42-45-Rite of Passage 3.00
#0 Another Universe.com Ed.($10.00) r/serialized pages from Pizzazz Magazine; new Dorman painted-c 10.00
... A Valentine Story (2/03, $3.50) Leia & Han Solo on Hoth; Winick-s/Chadwick-a/c 3.50
...: Rite of Passage (2004, $12.95) r/#42-45 13.00
...: The Stark Hyperspace War (903, $12.95) r/#36-39 13.00

STAR WARS: A NEW HOPE- THE SPECIAL EDITION
Dark Horse Comics: Jan, 1997 - No. 4, Apr, 1997 ($2.95, limited series)
1-4-Dorman-c 4.00

STAR WARS: BOBA FETT
Dark Horse Comics: Dec, 1995 - No. 3 ($3.95) (Originally intended as a one-shot)
1-Kennedy-c/a 6.00
2,3 5.00
Death, Lies, & Treachery TPB (1/98, $12.95) r/#1-3 13.00
... - Agent of Doom (11/00, $2.99) Ostrander-s/Cam Kennedy-a 3.00
... - Overkill (3/06, $2.99) Hughes-c/Andrews-s/Velasco-a 3.00
Twin Engines of Destruction (1/97, $2.95) 3.00

STAR WARS: BOBA FETT: ENEMY OF THE EMPIRE
Dark Horse Comics: Jan, 1999 - No. 4, Apr, 1999 ($2.95, limited series)
1-4-Recalls 1st meeting of Fett and Vader 3.00

STAR WARS: CHEWBACCA
Dark Horse Comics: Jan, 2000 - No. 4, Apr, 2000 ($2.95, limited series)
1-4-Macan-s/art by various incl. Anderson, Kordey, Gibbons; Phillips-c 3.00

STAR WARS: CLONE WARS ADVENTURES
Dark Horse Comics: 2004 - Present ($6.95, digest-sized)
1-9-Short stories inspired by Clone Wars animated series 7.00

STAR WARS: CRIMSON EMPIRE
Dark Horse Comics: Dec, 1997 - No. 6, May, 1998 ($2.95, limited series)
1-Richardson-s/Gulacy-a 1 2 3 4 5 7
2-6 5.00

STAR WARS: CRIMSON EMPIRE II: COUNCIL OF BLOOD
Dark Horse Comics: Nov, 1998 - No. 6, Apr, 1999 ($2.95, limited series)
1-6-Richardson & Stradley-s/Gulacy-a 3.00

STAR WARS: DARK EMPIRE
Dark Horse Comics: Dec, 1991 - No. 6, Oct, 1992 ($2.95, limited series)
Preview-(99¢) 3.00
1-All have Dorman painted-c 1 2 3 5 7 9
1-3-2nd printing 4.00
2-Low print run 2 4 6 8 10 12
3 6.00
4-6 4.00
Gold Embossed Set (#1-6)-With gold embossed foil logo (price is for set) 90.00
Platinum Embossed Set (#1-6) 120.00
Trade paperback (4/93, 16.95) 17.00
Dark Empire 1 - TPB 3rd printing (2003, $16.95) 17.00
Ltd. Ed. Hardcover ($99.95) Signed & numbered 100.00

STAR WARS: DARK EMPIRE II
Dark Horse Comics: Dec, 1994 - No. 6, May, 1995 ($2.95, limited series)
1-Dave Dorman painted-c 5.00
2-6: Dorman-c in all. 4.00
Platinum Embossed Set (#1-6) 35.00
Trade paperback ($17.95) 18.00
TPB Second Edition (9/06, $19.95) r/#1-6 and Star Wars: Empire's End #1,2 20.00

STAR WARS: DARK FORCE RISING
Dark Horse Comics: May, 1997 - No. 6, Oct, 1997 ($2.95, limited series)
1-6 4.00
TPB (2/98, $17.95) r/#1-6 18.00

STAR WARS: DARK TIMES (Continued from Star Wars Republic #84)(Continues in Star Wars: Rebellion #15)
Dark Horse Comics: Oct, 2006 - No. 12, Jun, 2008 ($2.99)
1-12-Nineteen years before Episode IV; Doug Wheatley-a. 11-Celeste Morne awakens 3.00
... Volume 1: The Path To Nowhere (1/08, $17.95, TPB) r/#1-5 18.00

STAR WARS: DARTH MAUL
Dark Horse Comics: Sept, 2000 - No. 4, Dec, 2000 ($2.95, limited series)
1-4-Photo-c and Struzan painted-c; takes place 6 months before Ep. 1 3.00

STAR WARS: DROIDS (See Dark Horse Comics #17-19)
Dark Horse Comics: Apr, 1994 - #6, Sept, 1994; V2#1, Apr, 1995 - V2#8, Dec, 1995 ($2.50, limited series)
1-($2.95)-Embossed-c 4.00
2-6 , Special 1 (1/95, $2.50), V2#1-8 3.00
Star Wars Omnibus: Droids One TPB (6/08, $24.95) r/#1-6, Special 1, V2#1-8, Star Wars: The Protocol Offensive and "Artoo's Day Out" story from Star Wars Galaxy Magazine #1 25.00

STAR WARS: EMPIRE

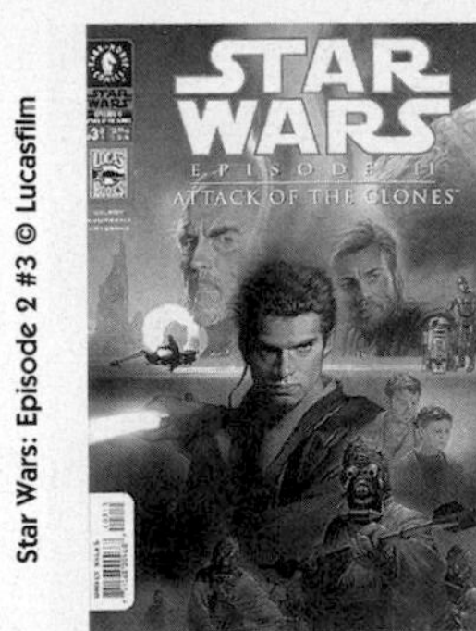

Star Wars: Episode 2 #3 © Lucasfilm

Star Wars: Legacy #16 © Lucasfilm

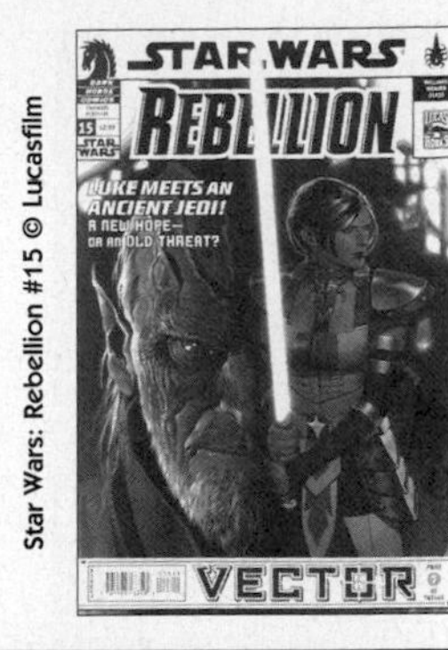

Star Wars: Rebellion #15 © Lucasfilm

GD VG FN VF VF/NM NM-
2.0 4.0 6.0 8.0 9.0 9.2

Dark Horse Comics: Sept, 2002 - No. 40, Feb, 2006 ($2.99)

1-40: 1-Benjamin-a; takes place weeks before SW: A New Hope. 7,28-Boba Fett-c. 14-Vader after the destruction of the Death Star. 15-Death of Biggs; Wheatley-a 3.00
... Volume 1 (2003, $12.95, TPB) r/#1-4 13.00
... Volume 2 (2004, $17.95, TPB) r/#8-12,15 18.00
... Volume 3: The Imperial Perspective (2004, $17.95, TPB) r/#13,14,16-19 18.00
... Volume 4: The Heart of the Rebellion (2005, $17.95, TPB) r/#5,6,20-22 & Star Wars: A Valentine Story 18.00
... Volume 5 (2006, $14.95, TPB) r/#23-27 18.00
... Volume 6: In the Shadows of Their Fathers (10/06, $17.95, TPB) r/#29-34 18.00
... Volume 7: The Wrong Side of the War (1/07, $17.95, TPB) r/#34-40 18.00

STAR WARS: EMPIRE'S END
Dark Horse Comics: Oct, 1995 - No. 2, Nov, 1995 ($2.95, limited series)

1,2-Dorman-c 3.00

STAR WARS: EPISODE 1 THE PHANTOM MENACE
Dark Horse Comics: May, 1999 - No. 4 ($2.95, movie adaptation)

1-4-Regular and photo-c; Damaggio & Williamson-a 3.00
TPB ($12.95) r/#1-4 13.00
...Anakin Skywalker-Photo-c & Bradstreet-c, ...Obi-Wan Kenobi-Photo-c & Egeland-c, ...Queen Amidala-Photo-c & Bradstreet-c, ...Qui-Gon Jinn-Photo-c & Bradstreet-c 3.00
Gold foil covers; Wizard 1/2 10.00

STAR WARS: EPISODE II - ATTACK OF THE CLONES
Dark Horse Comics: Apr, 2002 - No. 4, May, 2002 ($3.99, movie adaptation)

1-4-Regular and photo-c; Duursema-a 4.00
TPB ($17.95) r/#1-4; Struzan-c 18.00

STAR WARS: EPISODE III - REVENGE OF THE SITH
Dark Horse Comics: May, 2005 - No. 4, May, 2005 ($2.99, movie adaptation)

1-4-Wheatley-a/Dorman-c 3.00
TPB ($12.95) r/#1-4; Dorman-c 13.00

STAR WARS: GENERAL GRIEVOUS
Dark Horse Comics: Mar, 2005 - No. 4, June, 2005 ($2.99, limited series)

1-4-Leonardi-a/Dixon-s 3.00
TPB (2005, $12.95) r/#1-4 13.00

STAR WARS HANDBOOK
Dark Horse Comics: July, 1998 - Present ($2.95, one-shots)

...X-Wing Rogue Squadron (7/98)-Guidebook to characters and spacecraft 3.00
...Crimson Empire (7/99) Dorman-c 3.00
...Dark Empire (3/00) Dorman-c 3.00

STAR WARS: HEIR TO THE EMPIRE
Dark Horse Comics: Oct, 1995 - No.6, Apr, 1996 ($2.95, limited series)

1-6: Adaptation of Zahn novel 3.00

STAR WARS: INFINITIES - A NEW HOPE
Dark Horse Comics: May, 2001 - No. 4, Oct, 2001 ($2.99, limited series)

1-4: "What If..." the Death Star wasn't destroyed in Episode 4 3.00
TPB (2002, $12.95) r/ #1-4 13.00

STAR WARS: INFINITIES - THE EMPIRE STRIKES BACK
Dark Horse Comics: July, 2002 - No. 4, Oct, 2002 ($2.99, limited series)

1-4: "What If..." Luke died on the ice planet Hoth; Bachalo-c 3.00
TPB (2/03, $12.95) r/ #1-4 13.00

STAR WARS: INFINITIES - RETURN OF THE JEDI
Dark Horse Comics: Nov, 2003 - No. 4, Mar, 2004 ($2.99, limited series)

1- 4:"What If..." ; Benjamin-a 3.00

STAR WARS: JABBA THE HUTT
Dark Horse Comics: Apr, 1995 ($2.50, one-shots)

nn, ...The Betrayal, ...The Dynasty Trap, ...The Hunger of Princess Nampi 3.00

STAR WARS: JANGO FETT - OPEN SEASONS
Dark Horse Comics: Apr, 2002 - No. 4, July, 2002 ($2.99, limited series)

1-4: 1-Bachs & Fernandez-a 3.00

STAR WARS: JEDI
Dark Horse Comics: Feb, 2003 - Jun, 2004 ($4.99, one-shots)

... - Aayla Secura (8/03) Ostrander-s/Duursema-a 5.00
... - Count Dooku (11/03) Duursema-a 5.00
... - Mace Windu (2/03) Duursema-a 5.00
... - Shaak Ti (5/03) Ostrander-s/Duursema-a 5.00
... - Yoda (6/04) Barlow-s/Hoon-a 5.00

GD VG FN VF VF/NM NM-
2.0 4.0 6.0 8.0 9.0 9.2

STAR WARS: JEDI ACADEMY - LEVIATHAN
Dark Horse Comics: Oct, 1998 - No. 4, Jan, 1999 ($2.95, limited series)

1-4: 1-Lago-c. 2-4-Chadwick-c 3.00

STAR WARS: JEDI COUNCIL: ACTS OF WAR
Dark Horse Comics: Jun, 2000 - No. 4, Sept, 2000 ($2.95, limited series)

1-4-Stradley-s; set one year before Episode 1 3.00

STAR WARS: JEDI QUEST
Dark Horse Comics: Sept, 2001 - No. 4, Dec, 2001 ($2.99, limited series)

1-4-Anakin's Jedi training; Windham-s/Mhan-a 3.00

STAR WARS: JEDI VS. SITH
Dark Horse Comics: Apr, 2001 - No. 6, Sept, 2001 ($2.99, limited series)

1-6: Macan-s/Bachs-a/Robinson-c 3.00

STAR WARS: KNIGHTS OF THE OLD REPUBLIC
Dark Horse Comics: Jan, 2006 - Present ($2.99)

1-32-Takes place 3,964 years before Episode IV. 1-6-Brian Ching-a/Travis Charest-c 3.00
... Handbook (11/07, $2.99) profiles of characters, ships, locales 3.00
.../Rebellion #0 (3/06, 25¢) flip book preview of both series 2.50
... Vol. 1 Commencement TPB (11/06, $18.95) r/#0-6 19.00
... Vol. 2 Flashpoint TPB (5/07, $18.95) r/#17-12 19.00
... Vol. 3 Days of Fear, Nights of Anger TPB (1/08, $18.95) r/#13-18 19.00

STAR WARS: LEGACY
Dark Horse Comics: No. 0, June, 2006 - Present ($2.99)

0-(25¢) Dossier of characters, settings, ships and weapons; Duursema-c 2.50
0 1/2-(1/08, $2.99) Updated dossier of characters, settings, ships, and history 3.00
1-27: 1-Takes place 130 years after Episode IV; Hughes-c/Duursema-a. 4-Duursema-c 7-Luke Skywalker on-c. 16-Obi-Wan Kenobi app. 3.00
...: Broken Vol. 1 TPB (4/07, $17.95) r/#1-3,5,6 18.00

STAR WARS: MARA JADE
Dark Horse Comics: Aug, 1998 - No. 6, Jan, 1999 ($2.95, limited series)

1-6-Ezquerra-a 3.00

STAR WARS: OBSESSION (Clone Wars)
Dark Horse Comics: Nov, 2004 - No. 5, Apr, 2005 ($2.99, limited series)

1-5-Blackman-s/Ching-a/c; Anakin & Obi-Wan 5 months before Episode III 3.00
...: Clone Wars Vol. 7 (2005, $17.95) r/#1-5 and 2005 Free Comic Book Day edition 18.00

STAR WARS: PURGE
Dark Horse Comics: Dec, 2005 ($2.99, one-shot)

nn-Vader vs. remaining Jedi one month after Episode III; Hughes-c/Wheatley-a 5.00

STAR WARS: QUI-GON & OBI-WAN - LAST STAND ON ORD MANTELL
Dark Horse Comics: Dec, 2000 - No. 3, Mar, 2001 ($2.99, limited series)

1-3: 1-Three covers (photo, Tony Daniel, Bachs) Windham-s 3.00

STAR WARS: QUI-GON & OBI-WAN - THE AURORIENT EXPRESS
Dark Horse Comics: Feb, 2002 - No. 2, Mar, 2002 ($2.99, limited series)

1,2-Six years prior to Phantom Menace; Marangon-a 3.00

STAR WARS: REBELLION (Also see Star Wars: Knights of the Old Republic flip book)
Dark Horse Comics: Apr, 2006 - Present ($2.99)

1-16-Takes place 9 months after Episode IV; Luke Skywalker app. 1-Badeaux-a/c 3.00
Vol. 1 TPB (2/07, $14.95) r/#0 (flip book) & #1-5 15.00

STAR WARS: REPUBLIC (Formerly Star Wars monthly series)
Dark Horse Comics: No. 46, Sept, 2002 - No. 83, Feb, 2006 ($2.99)

46-83-Events of the Clone Wars 3.00
...: Clone Wars Vol. 1 (2003, $14.95) r/#46-50 15.00
...: Clone Wars Vol. 2 (2003, $14.95) r/#51-53 & Star Wars: Jedi - Shaak Ti 15.00
...: Clone Wars Vol. 3 (2004, $14.95) r/#55-59 15.00
...: Clone Wars Vol. 4 (2004, $16.95) r/#54, 63 & Star Wars: Jedi - Aayla Secura & Dooku 17.00
...: Clone Wars Vol. 5 (2004, $17.95) r/#60-62, 64 & Star Wars: Jedi - Yoda 17.00
...: Clone Wars Vol. 6 (2005, $17.95) r/#65-71 18.00
(Clone Wars Vol. 7 - see Star Wars: Obsession)
...: Clone Wars Vol. 8 (2006, $17.95) r/#72-78 18.00
...: Clone Wars Vol. 9 (2006, $17.95) r/#79-83 & Star Wars: Purge 18.00
...: Honor and Duty TPB (5/06, $12.95) r/#46-48,78 13.00

STAR WARS: RETURN OF THE JEDI (Movie)
Marvel Comics Group: Oct, 1983 - No. 4, Jan, 1984 (limited series)

1-4-Williamson-p in all; r/Marvel Super Special #27 1 3 4 6 8 10
Oversized issue (1983, $2.95, 10-3/4x8-1/4", 68 pgs., cardboard-c)-r/#1-4 2 4 6 10 13 16

Star Wars: Tales of the Jedi - Dark Lords of the Sith #6 © Lucasfilm

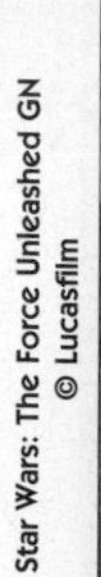
Star Wars: The Force Unleashed GN © Lucasfilm

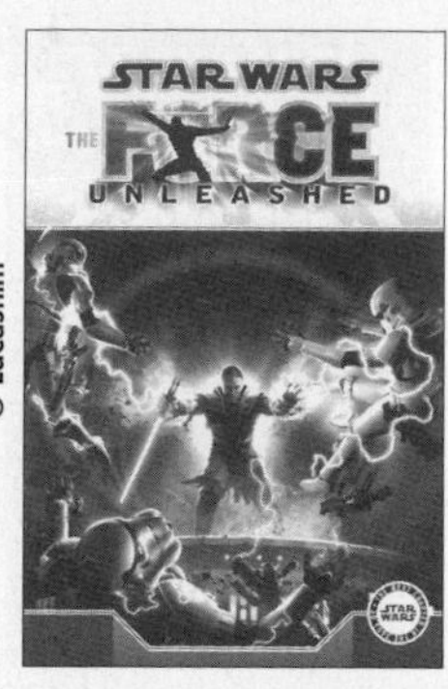

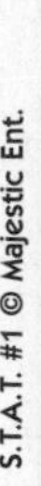
S.T.A.T. #1 © Majestic Ent.

GD 2.0 | VG 4.0 | FN 6.0 | VF 8.0 | VF/NM 9.0 | NM- 9.2

GD 2.0 | VG 4.0 | FN 6.0 | VF 8.0 | VF/NM 9.0 | NM- 9.2

STAR WARS: RIVER OF CHAOS
Dark Horse Comics: June, 1995 - No. 4, Sept, 1995 ($2.95, limited series)
1-4: Louise Simonson scripts 3.00

STAR WARS: SHADOWS OF THE EMPIRE
Dark Horse Comics: May, 1996 - No. 6, Oct, 1996 ($2.95, limited series)
1-6: Story details events between The Empire Strikes Back & Return of the Jedi; Russell-a(i). 3.00

STAR WARS: SHADOWS OF THE EMPIRE - EVOLUTION
Dark Horse Comics: Feb, 1998 - No. 5, June, 1998 ($2.95, limited series)
1-5: Perry-s/Fegredo-c. 3.00

STAR WARS: SHADOW STALKER
Dark Horse Comics: Sept, 1997 ($2.95, one-shot)
nn-Windham-a. 3.00

STAR WARS: SPLINTER OF THE MIND'S EYE
Dark Horse Comics: Dec, 1995 - No. 4, June, 1996 ($2.50, limited series)
1-4: Adaption of Alan Dean Foster novel 3.00

STAR WARS: STARFIGHTER
Dark Horse Comics: Jan, 2002 - No. 3, March, 2002 ($2.99, limited series)
1-3-Williams & Gray-c 3.00

STAR WARS: TAG & BINK ARE DEAD
Dark Horse Comics: Oct, 2001 - No. 2, Nov, 2001($2.99, limited series)
1,2-Rubio-s 3.00
Star Wars: Tag & Bink Were Here TPB (11/06, $14.95) r/both SW: Tag & Bink series 15.00

STAR WARS: TAG & BINK II
Dark Horse Comics: Mar, 2006 - No. 2, Apr, 2006($2.99, limited series)
1-Tag & Bink invade Return of the Jedi; Rubio-s. 2-T&B as Jedi younglings during Ep II 3.00

STAR WARS TALES
Dark Horse Comics: Sept, 1999 - No. 24, Jun, 2005 ($4.95/$5.95/$5.99, anthology)
1-4-Short stories by various 5.00
5-24 ($5.95/$5.99-c) Art and photo-c on each 6.00
Volume 1-6 ($19.95) 1-(1/02) r/#1-4. 2-('02) r/#5-8. 3-(1/03) r/#9-12. 4-(1/04) r/#13-16 5-(1/05) r/#17-20; introduction pages from #1-20. 6-(1/06) r/#21-24 20.00

STAR WARS: TALES - A JEDI'S WEAPON (See Promotional Comics section)

STAR WARS: TALES FROM MOS EISLEY
Dark Horse Comics: Mar, 1996 ($2.95, one-shot)
nn-Bret Blevins-a. 3.00

STAR WARS: TALES OF THE JEDI (See Dark Horse Comics #7)
Dark Horse Comics: Oct, 1993 - No. 5, Feb, 1994 ($2.50, limited series)
1-5: All have Dave Dorman painted-c. 3-r/Dark Horse Comics #7-9 w/new coloring & some panels redrawn 3.00
1-5-Gold foil embossed logo; limited # printed-7500 (set) 50.00
Star Wars Omnibus: Tales of the Jedi Volume One TPB (11/07, $24.95) r/#1-5, ... - The Golden Age of the Sith #0-5 and ... - The Fall of the Sith Empire #1-5 25.00

STAR WARS: TALES OF THE JEDI-DARK LORDS OF THE SITH
Dark Horse Comics: Oct, 1994 - No. 6, Mar, 1995 ($2.50, limited series)
1-6: 1-Polybagged w/trading card 3.00

STAR WARS: TALES OF THE JEDI-REDEMPTION
Dark Horse Comics: July, 1998 - No. 5, Nov, 1998 ($2.95, limited series)
1-5: 1-Kevin J. Anderson-s/Kordey-c 3.00

STAR WARS: TALES OF THE JEDI-THE FALL OF THE SITH EMPIRE
Dark Horse Comics: June, 1997 - No. 5, Oct, 1997 ($2.95, limited series)
1-5 3.00

STAR WARS: TALES OF THE JEDI-THE FREEDON NADD UPRISING
Dark Horse Comics: Aug, 1994 - No. 2, Nov, 1994 ($2.50, limited series)
1,2 3.00

STAR WARS: TALES OF THE JEDI-THE GOLDEN AGE OF THE SITH
Dark Horse Comics: July, 1996 - No. 5, Feb, 1997 (99¢/$2.95, limited series)
0-(99¢)-Anderson-s 3.00
1-5-Anderson-s 3.00

STAR WARS: TALES OF THE JEDI-THE SITH WAR
Dark Horse Comics: Aug, 1995 - No. 6, Jan, 1996 ($2.50, limited series)
1-6: Anderson scripts 3.00

STAR WARS: THE BOUNTY HUNTERS
Dark Horse Comics: July, 1999 - Oct, 1999 ($2.95, one-shots)
...Aurra Sing (7/99), ...Kenix Kil (10/99), ...Scoundrel's Wages (8/99) Lando Calrissian app. 3.00

STAR WARS: THE CLONE WARS (Based on the Cartoon Network series)
Dark Horse Comics: Sept, 2008 - Present ($2.99)
1-Gilroy-s/Hepburn-a/Filoni-c 3.00

STAR WARS: THE FORCE UNLEASHED (Based on the LucasArts video game)
Dark Horse Comics: Aug, 2008 ($15.95, one-shot graphic novel)
GN-Intro. Starkiller, Vader's apprentice; takes place 2 years before Battle of Yavin 16.00

STAR WARS: THE JABBA TAPE
Dark Horse Comics: Dec, 1998 ($2.95, one-shot)
nn-Wagner-s/Plunkett-a 3.00

STAR WARS: THE LAST COMMAND
Dark Horse Comics: Nov, 1997 - No. 6, July, 1998 ($2.95, limited series)
1-6:Based on the Timothy Zaun novel 4.00

STAR WARS: THE PROTOCOL OFFENSIVE
Dark Horse Comics: Sept, 1997 ($4.95, one-shot)
nn-Anthony Daniels & Ryder Windham-s 5.00

STAR WARS: UNDERWORLD - THE YAVIN VASSILIKA
Dark Horse Comics: Dec, 2000 - No. 5, June, 2001 ($2.99, limited series)
1-5-(Photo and Robinson covers) 3.00

STAR WARS: UNION
Dark Horse Comics: Nov, 1999 - No. 4, Feb, 2000 ($2.95, limited series)
1-4-Wedding of Luke and Mara Jade; Teranishi-a/Stackpole-s 3.00

STAR WARS: VADER'S QUEST
Dark Horse Comics: Feb, 1999 - No. 4, May, 1999 ($2.95, limited series)
1-4-Follows destruction of 1st Death Star; Gibbons-a 3.00

STAR WARS: VISIONARIES
Dark Horse Comics: Apr, 2005 ($17.95, TPB)
nn-Short stories from the concept artists for Revenge of the Sith movie 18.00

STAR WARS: X-WING ROGUE SQUADRON (Star Wars: X-Wing Rogue Squadron-The Phantom Affair #5-8 appears on cover only)
Dark Horse Comics: July, 1995 - No. 35, Nov, 1998 ($2.95)
1/2 8.00
1-24,26-35: 1-4-Baron scripts. 5-20-Stackpole scripts 3.00
25-($3.95) 4.00
The Phantom Affair TPB ($12.95) r/#5-8 13.00

STAR WARS: X-WING ROGUE SQUADRON: ROGUE LEADER
Dark Horse Comics: Sept, 2005 - No. 3, Nov, 2005 ($2.99)
1-3-Takes place one week after the Batttle of Endor 3.00

S.T.A.T.
Majestic Entertainment: Dec, 1993 ($2.25)
1 2.50

STATIC (Also see Eclipse Monthly)
Charlton Comics: No, 11, Oct, 1985 - No. 12, Dec, 1985
11,12-Ditko-c/a; low print run 6.00

STATIC (See Heroes)
DC Comics (Milestone): June, 1993 - No. 45, Mar, 1997 ($1.50/$1.75/$2.50)
1-($2.95)-Collector's Edition; polybagged w/poster & trading card & backing board (direct sales only) 4.00
1-24,26-45: 2-Origin. 8-Shadow War; Simonson silver ink-c. 14-($2.50, 52 pgs.)-Worlds Collide Pt. 14. 27-Kent Williams-c 2.50
25 ($3.95) 4.00
...: Trial by Fire (2000, $9.95) r/#1-4; Leon-c 10.00

STATIC SHOCK!: REBIRTH OF THE COOL (TV)
DC Comics: Jan, 2001 - No. 4, Sept, 2001 ($2.50, limited series)
1-4: McDuffie-s/Leon-c/a 2.50

STATIC-X
Chaos! Comics: Aug, 2002 ($5.99)
1-Polybagged with music CD; metal band as super-heroes; Pulido-s 6.00

STEAMPUNK
DC/WildStorm (Cliffhanger): Apr, 2000 - No. 12, Aug, 2002 ($2.50/$3.50)
Catechism (1/00) Prologue -Kelly-s/Bachalo-a 2.50
1-4,6-11: 4-Four covers by Bachalo, Madureira, Ramos, Campbell 2.50

Steampunk #6 © Kelly & Bachalo

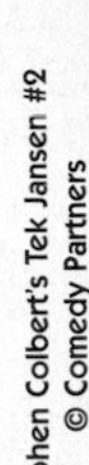

Stephen Colbert's Tek Jansen #2 © Comedy Partners

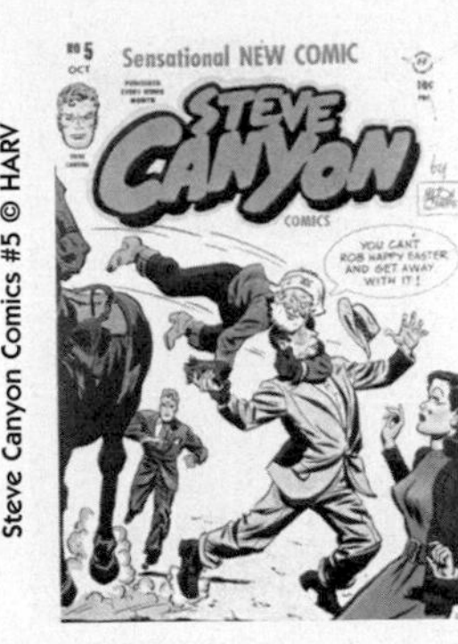

Steve Canyon Comics #5 © HARV

GD 2.0 | VG 4.0 | FN 6.0 | VF 8.0 | VF/NM 9.0 | NM- 9.2

5,12-($3.50) 3.50
...: Drama Obscura ('03, $14.95) r/#6-12 15.00
...: Manimatron ('01, $14.95) r/#1-5, Catechism, Idiosincratica 15.00

STEED AND MRS. PEEL (TV)(Also see The Avengers)
Eclipse Books/ ACME Press: 1990 - No. 3, 1991 ($4.95, limited series)

Books One - Three: Grant Morrison scripts 5.00

STEEL (Also see JLA)
DC Comics: Feb, 1994 - No. 52, July, 1998 ($1.50/$1.95/$2.50)

1-0,0,0 [illegible] 1 From Reign of the Supermen storyline. 6,7-Worlds Collide Pt. 5 &12.
8-(9/94). 0-(10/94). 9-(11/94). 46-Superboy-c/app. 50-Millennium Giants x-over 2.60
Annual 1 (1994, $2.95)-Elseworlds story 3.00
Annual 2 (1995, $3.95)-Year One story 4.00
...Forging of a Hero TPB (1997, $19.95) r/ early app. 20.00

STEEL: THE OFFICIAL COMIC ADAPTION OF THE WARNER BROS. MOTION PICTURE
DC Comics: 1997 ($4.95, Prestige format, one-shot)

nn-Movie adaption; Bogdanove & Giordano-a 5.00

STEELGRIP STARKEY
Marvel Comics (Epic Comics): June, 1986 - No. 6, July, 1987 ($1.50, limited series, Baxter paper)

1-6 2.50

STEEL STERLING (Formerly Shield-Steel Sterling; see Blue Ribbon, Jackpot, Mighty Comics, Mighty Crusaders, Roly Poly & Zip Comics)
Archie Enterprises, Inc.: No. 4, Jan, 1984 - No. 7, July, 1984

4-7: 4-6-Kanigher-s; Barreto-a. 5,6-Infantino-a. 6-McWilliams-a 4.00

STEEL, THE INDESTRUCTIBLE MAN (See All-Star Squadron #8 and J.L. of A. Annual #2)
DC Comics: Mar, 1978 - No. 5, Oct-Nov, 1978

1 1 3 4 6 8 10
2-5: 5-44 pgs. 6.00

STEELTOWN ROCKERS
Marvel Comics: Apr, 1987 - No. 6, Sept, 1990 ($1.00, limited series)

1-6: Small town teens form rock band 2.50

STEPHEN COLBERT'S TEK JANSEN (From the animated shorts on The Colbert Report)
Oni Press: July, 2007 - No. 5 ($3.99, limited series)

1-Chantier-a/Layman & Peyer-s; back-up story by Massey-s/Rodriguez-a; Chantier-c 4.00
1-Variant-c by John Cassaday 6.00
1-Second printing with flip book of Cassaday & Chantier covers 4.00
2-(6/08) Flip book with covers by Rodriguez & Wagner 4.00

STEVE AUSTIN (See Stone Cold Steve Austin)

STEVE CANYON (See Harvey Comics Hits #52)
Dell Publishing Co.: No. 519, 11/53 - No. No. 1033, 9/59 (All Milton Caniff-a except #519, 939, 1033)

Four Color 519 (1, '53) 8 16 24 56 93 130
Four Color 578 (8/54), 641 (7/55), 737 (10/56), 804 (5/57), 939 (10/58),
1033 (9/59) (photo-c) 5 10 15 34 55 75

STEVE CANYON
Grosset & Dunlap: 1959 (6-3/4x9", 96 pgs., B&W, no text, hardcover)

100100-Reprints 2 stories from strip (1953, 1957) 6 12 18 31 38 45
100100 (softcover edition) 5 10 15 24 30 35

STEVE CANYON COMICS
Harvey Publ.: Feb, 1948 - No. 6, Dec, 1948 (Strip reprints, No. 4,5: 52pgs.)

1-Origin; has biography of Milton Caniff; Powell-a, 2 pgs.; Caniff-a
21 42 63 120 188 255
2-Caniff, Powell-a in #2-6 14 28 42 80 115 150
3-6: 6-Intro Madame Lynx-c/story 14 28 42 76 108 140

STEVE CANYON IN 3-D
Kitchen Sink Press: June, 1986 ($2.25, one-shot)

1-Contains unpublished story from 1954 5.00

STEVE DITKO'S STRANGE AVENGING TALES
Fantagraphics Books: Feb, 1997 ($2.95, B&W)

1-Ditko-c/s/a 3.00

STEVE DONOVAN, WESTERN MARSHAL (TV)
Dell Publishing Co.: No. 675, Feb, 1956 - No. 880, Feb, 1958 (All photo-c)

Four Color 675-Kinstler-a 8 16 24 52 86 120
Four Color 768-Kinstler-a 6 12 18 43 69 95
Four Color 880 5 10 15 30 48 65

STEVE ROPER
Famous Funnies: Apr, 1948 - No. 5, Dec, 1948

1-Contains 1944 daily newspaper-r 12 24 36 69 97 125
2 9 18 27 47 61 75
3-5 8 16 24 40 50 60

STEVE SAUNDERS SPECIAL AGENT (See Special Agent)

STEVE SAVAGE (See Captain...)

STEVE ZODIAC & THE FIRE BALL XL-5 (TV)
Gold Key: Jan, 1964

10108-401 (#1) 8 16 24 52 86 120

STEVIE (Mazie's boy friend)(Also see Flat-Top, Mazie & Mortie)
Mazie (Magazine Publ.): Nov, 1952 - No. 6, Apr, 1954

1-Teenage humor; Stevie, Mortie & Mazie begin 8 16 24 44 57 70
2-6 6 12 18 28 34 40

STEVIE MAZIE'S BOY FRIEND (See Harvey Hits #5)

STEWART THE RAT (See Eclipse Graphic Album Series)

ST. GEORGE (See listing under Saint...)

STIG'S INFERNO
Vortex/Eclipse: 1985 - No. 7, Mar, 1987 ($1.95, B&W)

1-7 ($1.95) 2.50
Graphic Album (1988, $6.95, B&W, 100 pgs.) 7.00

STING OF THE GREEN HORNET (See The Green Hornet)
Now Comics: June, 1992 - No. 4, 1992 ($2.50, limited series)

1-4: Butler-c/a 2.50
1-4 ($2.75)-Collectors Ed.; polybagged w/poster 3.00

STOKER'S DRACULA (Reprints unfinished Dracula story from 1974-75 with new ending)
Marvel Comics: 2004 - No. 4, May, 2005 ($3.99, B&W)

1-4. 1-Reprints from Dracula Lives! #5-8; Roy Thomas-s/Dick Giordano-a. 2-R/#10,11 & Legion of Monsters #1. 3,4-New story/artwork to finish story. 4-Giordano afterword 4.00
HC (2005, $24.99) r/#1-4; foreward by Thomas; Giordano afterword; bonus art & covers 25.00

STONE
Avalon Studios: Aug, 1998 - No. 4, Apr, 1999 ($2.50, limited series)

1-4-Portacio-a/Haberlin-s 2.50
1-Alternate-c 5.00
2-($14.95) DF Stonechrome Edition 15.00

STONE (Volume 2)
Avalon Studios: Aug, 1999 - No. 4, May, 2000 ($2.50)

1-4-Portacio-a/Haberlin-s 2.50
1-Chrome-c 5.00

STONE COLD STEVE AUSTIN (WWF Wrestling)
Chaos! Comics: Oct, 1999 - No. 4, Feb, 2000 ($2.95)

1-4-Reg. & photo-c; Steven Grant-s 3.00
1-Premium Ed. ($10.00) 10.00
Preview ($5.00) 5.00

STONE PROTECTORS
Harvey Pubications: May, 1994 - No. 3, Sept, 1994

nn (1993, giveaway)(limited distribution, scarce) 6.00
1-3-Ace Novelty action figures 4.00

STONEY BURKE (TV)
Dell Publishing Co.: June-Aug, 1963 - No. 2, Sept-Nov, 1963

1,2-Jack Lord photo-c on both 3 6 9 17 25 32

STONY CRAIG
Pentagon Publishing Co.: 1946 (No #)

nn-Reprints Bell Syndicate's "Sgt. Stony Craig" newspaper strips
8 16 24 40 50 60

STORIES BY FAMOUS AUTHORS ILLUSTRATED (Fast Fiction #1-5)
Seaboard Publ./Famous Authors Ill.: No. 6, Aug, 1950 - No. 13, Mar, 1951

1-Scarlet Pimpernel-Baroness Orczy 29 58 87 170 268 365
2-Capt. Blood-Raphael Sabatini 28 56 84 162 256 350
3-She, by Haggard 32 64 96 186 293 400
4-The 39 Steps-John Buchan 18 36 54 107 169 230
5-Beau Geste-P. C. Wren 18 36 54 107 169 230

NOTE: *The above five issues are exact reprints of Fast Fiction #1-5 except for the title change and new Kiefer*

Stories of Romance #13 © ATL

Storming Paradise #1 © Dixon & Guice

StormWatch: P.H.D. #1 © WSP

covers on #1 and 2. Kiefer c(r)-3-5. The above 5 issues were released before Famous Authors #6.
6-Macbeth, by Shakespeare; Kiefer art (8/50); used in **SOTI**, pg. 22,143;
Kiefer-c; 36 pgs. 26 52 78 152 239 325
7-The Window; Kiefer-c/a; 52 pgs. 18 36 54 107 169 230
8-Hamlet, by Shakespeare; Kiefer-c/a; 36 pgs. 23 46 69 132 209 285
9,10: 9-Nicholas Nickleby, by Dickens; G. Schrotter-a; 52 pgs. 10-Romeo & Juliet,
by Shakespeare; Kiefer-c/a; 36 pgs. 18 36 54 107 169 230
11-13: 11-Ben-Hur; Schrotter-a; 52 pgs. 12-La Svengali; Schrotter-a; 36 pgs.
13-Scaramouche; Kiefer-c/a; 36 pgs. 18 36 54 103 162 220
NOTE: *Artwork was prepared/advertised for #14, The Red Badge Of Courage. Gilberton bought out Famous Authors, Ltd. and used that story as C.I. #98. Famous Authors, Ltd. then published the Classics Junior series. The Famous Authors titles were published as part of the regular Classics Ill. Series in Brazil starting in 1952.*

STORIES FROM THE TWILIGHT ZONE
Skylark Pub: Mar, 1979, 68pgs. (B&W comic digest, 5-1/4x7-5/8")
15405-2: Pfevfer-a, 56 pgs, new comics 3 6 9 18 27 35

STORIES OF ROMANCE (Formerly Meet Miss Bliss)
Atlas Comics (LMC): No. 5, Mar, 1956 - No. 13, Aug, 1957
5-Baker-a? 10 20 30 56 76 95
6-10,12,13 7 14 21 37 46 55
11-Baker, Romita-a; Colletta-c/a 9 18 27 52 69 85
NOTE: *Ann Brewster a-13. Colletta a-9(2), 11; c-5, 11.*

STORM
Marvel Comics: Feb, 1996 - No. 4, May, 1996 ($2.95, limited series)
1-4-Foil-c; Dodson-a(p); Ellis-s: 2-4-Callisto app. 3.50

STORM
Marvel Comics: Apr, 2006 - No. 6, Sept, 2006 ($2.99, limited series)
1-6: Ororo and T'Challa meet as teens; Eric Jerome Dickey-s 3.00
HC (2007, $19.99, dustjacket) r/#1-6 20.00
SC (2008, $14.99) r/#1-6 15.00

STORMBREAKER: THE SAGA OF BETA RAY BILL (Also see Thor)
Marvel Comics: Mar, 2005 - No. 6, Aug, 2005 ($2.99, limited series)
1-6-Oeming & Berman-s/DiVito-a; Galactus app. 6-Spider-Man app. 3.00
TPB (2006, $16.99) r/#1-6 17.00

STORMING PARADISE
DC Comics (WildStorm): Sept, 2008 - No. 6 ($2.99, limited series)
1,2-WW2 invasion of Japan; Dixon-s/Guice-a/c 3.00

STORM SHADOW (G.I. Joe character)
Devil's Due Publishing: May, 2007 - No. 7, Nov, 2007 ($3.50)
1-7-Larry Hama-s 3.50

STORMWATCH (Also see The Authority)
Image Comics (WildStorm Prod.): May, 1993 - No. 50, Jul, 1997 ($1.95/$2.50)
1-8,0,9-36: 1-Intro StormWatch (Battalion, Diva, Winter, Fuji, & Hellstrike); 1st app. Weatherman; Jim Lee-c & part scripts; Lee plots in all. 1-Gold edition.1-3-Includes coupon for limited edition StormWatch trading card #00 by Lee. 3-1st brief app. Backlash. 0-($2.50)-Polybagged w/card; 1st full app. Backlash. 9-(4/94, $2.50)-Intro Defile. 10-(6/94),11,12-Both (8/94). 13,14-(9/94). 15-(10/94). 21-Reads #1 on-c. 22-Direct Market; Wildstorm Rising Pt. 9, bound-in card. 23-Spartan joins team. 25-(6/94, June 1995 on-c, $2.50). 35-Fire From Heaven Pt. 5. 36-Fire From Heaven Pt. 12 2.50
10-Alternate Portacio-c, see Deathblow #5 2.50
22-($1.95)-Newsstand, Wildstorm Rising Pt. 9 2.50
37-(7/96, $3.50, 38 pgs.)-Weatherman forms new team; 1st app. Jenny Sparks, Jack Hawksmoor & Rose Tattoo; Warren Ellis scripts begin; Justice League #1-c/swipe 3.50
38-49: 44-Three covers. 2.50
50-($4.50) 4.50
Special 1 ,2(1/94, 5/95, $3.50, 52 pgs.) 3.50
Sourcebook 1 (1/94, $2.50) 2.50
Forces of Nature ('99, $14.95, TPB) r/V1 #37-42 15.00
Lightning Strikes ('00, $14.95, TPB) r/V1 #43-47 15.00

STORMWATCH (Also see The Authority)
Image Comics (WildStorm): Oct, 1997 - No. 11, Sept, 1998 ($2.50)
1-Ellis-s/Jimenez-a(p); two covers by Bennett 2.50
1-($3.50)-Voyager Pack bagged w/Gen 13 preview 3.50
2-4: 4-1st app. Midnighter and Apollo 2.50
5-11: 7,8-Freefall app. 9-Gen13 & DV8 app. 2.50
A Finer World ('99, $14.95, TPB) r/V2 #4-9 15.00
Change or Die ('99, $14.95, TPB) r/V1 #48-50 & V2 #1-3 15.00
Final Orbit ('01, $9.95, TPB) r/V2 #10,11 & WildC.A.T.S./Aliens; Hitch-c 10.00

STORMWATCHER
Eclipse Comics (Acme Press): Apr, 1989 - No. 4, Dec, 1989 ($2.00, B&W)
1-4 2.50

STORMWATCH: P.H.D. (Post Human Division)
DC Comics (WildStorm): Jan, 2007 - No. 12, Dec, 2008 ($2.99)
1-12: 1-Two covers by Mahnke & Hairsine; Gage-s/Mahnke-a. 2-Var-c by Dell'Otto 3.00
...: Armageddon 1 (2/08, $2.99) Gage-s/Fernández-a/McKone-c 3.00
TPB (2007, $17.99) r/#1-4,6,7 & story from Worldstorm #1 18.00
... Book Two TPB (2008, $17.99) r/#5,8-12; sketch pages and concept art 18.00

STORMWATCH: TEAM ACHILLES
DC Comics (WildStorm): Sept, 2002 - No. 23, Aug, 2004 ($2.95)
1-8: 1-Two covers by Portacio; Portacio-a/Wright-s. 5,6-The Authority app. 3.00
9-23: 9-Back-up preview of The Authority: High Stakes pt. 1 3.00
TPB (2003, $14.95) r/Wizard Preview and #1-6; Portacio art pages 15.00
Book 2 (2004, $14.95) r/#7-11 & short story from Eye of the Storm Annual 15.00

STORMY (Disney) (Movie)
Dell Publishing Co.: No. 537, Feb, 1954
Four Color 537 (...the Thoroughbred)-on top 2/3 of each page; Pluto story on bottom 1/3
5 10 15 30 48 65

STORY OF JESUS (See Classics Illustrated Special Issue)

STORY OF MANKIND, THE (Movie)
Dell Publishing Co.: No. 851, Jan, 1958
Four Color 851-Vincent Price/Hedy Lamarr photo-c 7 14 21 47 76 105

STORY OF MARTHA WAYNE, THE
Argo Publ.: April, 1956
1-Newspaper strip-r 6 12 18 29 36 42

STORY OF RUTH, THE
Dell Publishing Co.: No. 1144, Nov-Jan, 1961 (Movie)
Four Color 1144-Photo-c 8 16 24 58 97 135

STORY OF THE COMMANDOS, THE (Combined Operations)
Long Island Independent: 1943 (15¢, B&W, 68 pgs.) (Distr. by Gilberton)
nn-All text (no comics); photos & illustrations; ad for Classic Comics on back cover (Rare)
32 64 96 186 298 410

STORY OF THE GLOOMY BUNNY, THE (See March of Comics #9)

STRAIGHT ARROW (Radio)(See Best of the West & Great Western)
Magazine Enterprises: Feb-Mar, 1950 - No. 55, Mar, 1956 (All 36 pgs.)
1-Straight Arrow (alias Steve Adams) & his palomino Fury begin; 1st mention of Sundown Valley & the Secret Cave 46 92 138 285 475 665
2-Red Hawk begins (1st app?) by Powell (origin), ends #55
23 46 69 135 218 300
3-Frazetta-c 31 62 93 181 291 400
4,5: 4-Secret Cave-c 21 42 63 123 197 270
6-10 17 34 51 98 154 210
11-Classic story "The Valley of Time", with an ancient civilization made of gold
22 44 66 129 207 285
12-19 14 28 42 82 121 160
20-Origin Straight Arrow's Shield 16 32 48 92 144 195
21-Origin Fury 19 38 57 109 172 235
22-Frazetta-c 25 50 75 145 233 320
23,25-30: 25-Secret Cave-c. 28-Red Hawk meets The Vikings
11 22 33 60 83 105
24-Classic story "The Dragons of Doom!" with prehistoric pteradactyls
14 28 42 80 115 150
31-38: 36-Red Hawk drug story by Powell 9 18 27 52 69 85
39-Classic story "The Canyon Beast", with a dinosaur egg hatching a Tyranosaurus Rex
13 26 39 74 105 135
40-Classic story "Secret of The Spanish Specters", with Conquistadors' lost treasure
11 22 33 64 90 115
41,42,44-54: 45-Secret Cave-c 9 18 27 47 61 75
43-Intro & 1st app. Blaze, S. Arrow's Warrior dog 10 20 30 56 76 95
55-Last issue 11 22 33 60 83 105
NOTE: *Fred Meagher a 1-55; c-1, 2, 4-21, 23-55. Powell a 2-55. Whitney a-1. Many issues advertise the radio premiums associated with Straight Arrow.*

STRAIGHT ARROW'S FURY (Also see A-1 Comics)
Magazine Enterprises: No. 119, 1954 (one-shot)
A-1 119-Origin; Fred Meagher-c/a 15 30 45 85 130 175

STRANDED
Virgin Comics: Dec, 2007 - No. 5, June, 2008 ($2.99)
1-5-Carey-s/Kotian-a. 1-Silvestri-c. 2-5-Moeller-c 3.00

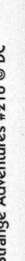

Strange Adventures #10 © DC

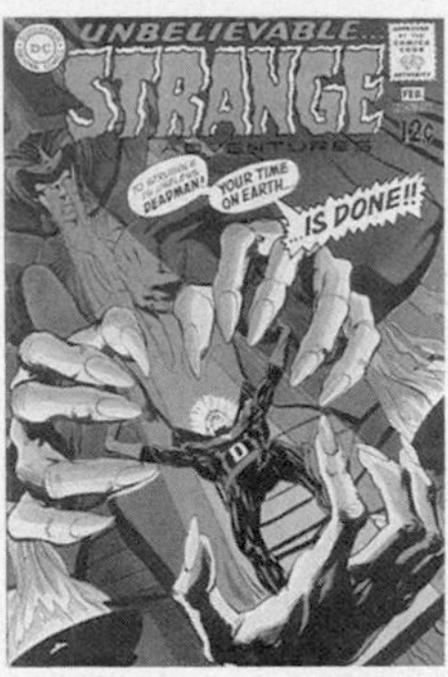

Strange Adventures #216 © DC

Strange Fantasy #4 © AJAX

	GD 2.0	VG 4.0	FN 6.0	VF 8.0	VF/NM 9.0	NM- 9.2

GD VG FN VF VF/NM NM- 2.0 4.0 6.0 8.0 9.0 9.2

STRANGE (Tales You'll Never Forget)
Ajax-Farrell Publ. (Four Star Comic Corp.): March, 1957 - No. 6, May, 1958

1	21	42	63	123	197	270
2-Censored r/Haunted Thrills	13	26	39	74	105	135
3-6	10	20	30	56	76	95

STRANGE (Dr. Strange)
Marvel Comics (Marvel Knghts): Nov, 2004 - No. 6, July, 2005 ($3.50)

1-6-Straczynski & Darnoc c/Peterson a; Dr. Strange's origin retold 3.50
...: Beginnings and Endings TPB (2006, $17.99) r/#1-6 18.00

STRANGE ADVENTURES
DC Comics: July/Aug 1950

nn - Ashcan comic, not distributed to newsstands, only for in-house use. Cover art is All Star Comics #47 with interior being Detective Comics #140. A second example has the interior of Detective Comics #146. A third example has an unidentified issue of Detective Comics as the interior. This is the only ashcan with multiple interiors. A FN+ copy sold for $1,000 in 2007.

STRANGE ADVENTURES
National Periodical Publ.: Aug-Sept, 1950 - No. 244, Oct-Nov, 1973 (No. 1-12: 52 pgs.)

1-Adaptation of "Destination Moon"; preview of movie w/photo-c from movie (also see Fawcett Movie Comic #2); adapt. of Edmond Hamilton's "Chris KL-99" in #1-3; Darwin Jones begins	228	456	684	1995	3848	5700
2	102	204	306	867	1659	2450
3,4	71	142	213	604	1152	1700
5-8,10: 7-Origin Kris KL-99	61	122	183	519	990	1460
9-(6/51)-Origin/1st app. Captain Comet (c/story)	142	284	426	1207	2304	3400
11-20: 12,13,17,18-Toth-a. 14-Robot-c	41	82	123	328	614	900
21-30: 28-Atomic explosion panel. 30-Robot-c	33	66	99	254	477	700
31,34-38	30	60	90	235	438	640
32,33-Krigstein-a	31	62	93	239	445	650
39-Ill. in **SOTI** "Treating police contemptuously" (top right)	35	70	105	273	507	740
40-49-Last Capt. Comet; not in 45,47,48	30	60	90	229	427	625
50-53-Last precode issue (2/55)	22	44	66	161	298	435
54-70	17	34	51	120	223	325
71-99	14	28	42	99	175	250
100	15	30	45	106	193	280
101-110: 104-Space Museum begins by Sekowsky	10	20	30	73	129	185
111-116,118,119: 114-Star Hawkins begins, ends #185; Heath-a in Wood E.C. style	10	20	30	70	123	175
117-(6/60)-Origin/1st app. Atomic Knights.	47	94	141	376	701	1025
120-2nd app. Atomic Knights	22	44	66	163	302	440
121,122,125,127,128,130,131,133,134: 134-Last 10¢ issue	9	18	27	63	107	150
123,126-3rd & 4th app. Atomic Knights	13	26	39	93	164	235
124-Intro/origin Faceless Creature	10	20	30	67	116	165
129,132,135,138,141,147-Atomic Knights app.	10	20	30	68	119	170
136,137,139,140,143,145,146,148,149,151,152,154,155,157-159: 159-Star Rovers app.; Gil Kane/Anderson-a.	7	14	21	47	76	105
142-2nd app. Faceless Creature	8	16	24	54	90	125
144-Only Atomic Knights-c (by M. Anderson)	10	20	30	73	129	185
150,153,156,160: Atomic Knights in each. 153-(6/63)-3rd app. Faceless Creature; atomic explosion-c. 160-Last Atomic Knights	8	16	24	52	86	120
161-179: 161-Last Space Museum. 163-Star Rovers app. 170-Infinity-c. 177-Intro/origin Immortal Man	6	12	18	39	62	85
180-Origin/1st app. Animal Man	16	32	48	114	212	310
181-183,185-189: 187-Intro/origin The Enchantress	5	10	15	32	51	70
184-2nd app. Animal Man by Gil Kane	10	20	30	70	123	175
190-1st app. Animal Man in costume	13	26	39	90	160	230
191-194,196-200,202-204	4	8	12	28	44	60
195-1st full app. Animal Man	7	14	21	47	76	105
201-Last Animal Man; 2nd full app.	6	12	18	37	59	80
205-(10/67)-Intro/origin Deadman by Infantino & begin series, ends #216	13	26	39	95	168	240
206-Neal Adams-a begins	10	20	30	67	116	165
207-210	9	18	27	60	100	140
211-216: 211-Space Museum-r. 216-(1-2/69)-Deadman story finally concludes in Brave & the Bold #86 (10-11/69); secret message panel by Neal Adams (pg. 13); tribute to Steranko	8	16	24	52	86	120
217-r/origin & 1st app. Adam Strange from Showcase #17, begin-r; Atomic Knights-r begin	3	6	9	14	19	24
218-221,223-225: 218-Last 12¢ issue. 225-Last 15¢ issue	2	4	6	13	18	22
222-New Adam Strange story; Kane/Anderson-a	3	6	9	18	27	36
226,227,230-236-(68-52 pgs.): 226, 227-New Adam Strange text story w/illos by Anderson (8,6 pgs.) 231-Last Atomic Knights-r. 235-JLA-c/s	2	4	6	13	18	22
228,229 (68 pgs.)	3	6	9	16	22	28
237-243	2	4	6	8	11	14
244-Last Issue	2	4	6	9	13	16

NOTE: ***Neal Adams*** *a-206-216; c-207-218, 228, 235.* ***Anderson*** *a-8-52, 94, 96, 99, 115, 117, 119-163, 217r, 218r, 222, 223-225r, 226, 229r, 242i(r); c-18, 19, 21, 23, 24, 27, 30, 32-44(most); c/r-157i, 190i, 217-224, 228-231, 233, 235-239, 241-243.* ***Ditko*** *a-188, 189.* ***Drucker*** *a-42, 43, 45.* ***Elias*** *a-212.* ***Finlay*** *a-2, 3, 6, 7, 210r, 229r.* ***Giunta*** *a-237r.* ***Heath*** *a-116.* ***Infantino*** *a-10-101, 106-151, 154, 157-163, 180, 190, 218-221r, 223-244p(r); c-50; c(r)-190p, 197, 199-211, 218-221, 223-244.* ***Kaluta*** *c-238, 240.* ***Gil Kane*** *a-8-116, 124, 125, 130, 138, 146-157, 173-186, 204r, 222r, 227-231r; c(p)-11-17, 25, 154, 157.* ***Kubert*** *a-55(2 pgs.), 226; c-219, 220, 225-227, 232, 234.* ***Moreira*** *a-26, 28, 29, 71.* ***Morrow*** *c-230.* ***Mortimer*** *c-8.* ***Powell*** *a-4.* ***Sekowsky*** *a-71p, 97-162p, 217p(r), 218p(r); c-206, 217-219r.* ***Simon & Kirby*** *a-2r (2 pgs).* ***Sparling*** *a-201.* ***Toth*** *a-8, 12, 13, 17-19.* ***Wood*** *a-154i. Atomic Knights in #117, 120, 123, 126, 129, 132, 135, 138, 141, 144, 147, 150, 153, 156, 160. Atomic Knights reprints by* ***Anderson*** *in 217-221, 223-231. Chris KL99 in 1-3, 5, 7, 9, 11, 15. Capt. Comet covers-9-14, 17-19, 24, 26, 27, 32-44.*

STRANGE ADVENTURES
DC Comics (Vertigo): Nov, 1999 - No. 4 ($2.50, limited series)

1-3: 1-Bolland-c; art by Bolland, Gibbons, Quitely 2.50

STRANGE AS IT SEEMS (See Famous Funnies-A Carnival of Comics, Feature Funnies #1, The John Hix Scrap Book & Peanuts)

STRANGE AS IT SEEMS
United Features Syndicate: 1939

Single Series 9, 1, 2	35	70	105	203	327	450

STRANGE ATTRACTORS
RetroGraphix: 1993 - No. 15, Feb, 1997 ($2.50, B&W)

1-15: 1-(5/93), 2-(8/93), 3-(11/93), 4-(2/94) 2.50
Volume One-($14.95, trade paperback)-r/#1-7 15.00

STRANGE ATTRACTORS: MOON FEVER
Caliber Comics: Feb, 1997 - No. 3, June, 1997 ($2.95, B&W, mini-series)

1-3 3.00

STRANGE COMBAT TALES
Marvel Comics (Epic Comics): Oct, 1993 - No. 4, Jan, 1994 ($2.50, limited series)

1-4 2.50

STRANGE CONFESSIONS
Ziff-Davis Publ. Co.: Jan-Mar (Spring on-c), 1952 - No. 4, Fall, 1952 (All have photo-c)

1(Scarce)-Kinstler-a	53	106	159	329	550	770
2(Scarce, 7-8/52)	38	76	114	222	356	490
3(Scarce, 9-10/52)-#3 on-c, #2 on inside; Reformatory girl story; photo-c	37	74	111	215	345	475
4(Scarce)	35	70	105	203	327	450

STRANGE DAYS
Eclipse Comics: Oct, 1984 - No. 3, Apr, 1985 ($1.75, Baxter paper)

1-3: Freakwave, Johnny Nemo, & Paradax from Vanguard Illustrated; nudity, violence & strong language 2.50

STRANGE DAYS (Movie)
Marvel Comics: Dec, 1995 ($5.95, squarebound, one-shot)

1-Adaptation of film 6.00

STRANGE FANTASY (Eerie Tales of Suspense!)(Formerly Rocketman #1)
Ajax-Farrell: Aug, 1952 - No. 14, Oct-Nov, 1954

2(#1, 8/52)-Jungle Princess story; Kamenish-a; reprinted from Ellery Queen #1	47	94	141	291	483	675
2(10/52)-No Black Cat or Rulah; Bakerish, Kamenish-a; hypo/meathook-c	40	80	120	240	390	540
3-Rulah story, called Pulah	40	80	120	235	380	525
4-Rocket Man app. (2/53)	38	76	114	222	356	490
5,6,8,10,12,14	27	54	81	158	254	350
7-Madam Satan/Slave story	38	76	114	222	356	490
9(w/Black Cat), 9(w/Boy's Ranch; S&K-a), 9(w/War)(A rebinding of Harvey interiors; not publ. by Ajax)	34	68	102	198	319	440
9-Regular issue; Steve Ditko's 3rd published work (tied with Captain 3D)	45	90	135	279	465	650
11-Jungle story	35	70	105	203	327	450
13-Bondage-c; Rulah (Kolah) story	35	70	105	203	327	450

STRANGE GALAXY
Eerie Publications: V1#8, Feb, 1971 - No. 11, Aug, 1971 (B&W, magazine)

V1#8-Reprints-c/Fantastic V19#3 (2/70) (a pulp)	3	6	9	20	30	40
9-11	3	6	9	16	23	30

STRANGE GIRL

Strange Mysteries #5 © SUPR

Strangers in Paradise #90 © Terry Moore

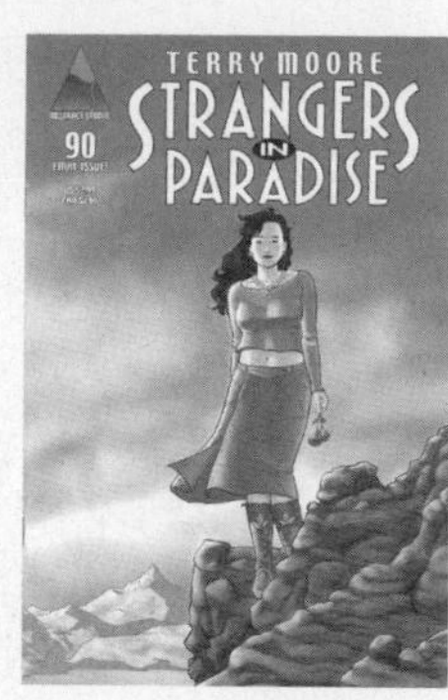

Strange Stories of Suspense #7 © MAR

Image Comics: June, 2005 - No. 18, Sept, 2007 ($2.95/$2.99/$3.50)

	GD 2.0	VG 4.0	FN 6.0	VF 8.0	VF/NM 9.0	NM- 9.2
1-12: 1-Rick Remender-s/Eric Nguyen-a						3.00
13-18-($3.50)						3.50
... Vol. 1: Girl Afraid TPB (2005, $12.99) r/#1-4; sketch pages and pin-ups						13.00

STRANGE JOURNEY

America's Best (Steinway Publ.) (Ajax/Farrell): Sept, 1957 - No. 4, Jun, 1958 (Farrell reprints)

	GD 2.0	VG 4.0	FN 6.0	VF 8.0	VF/NM 9.0	NM- 9.2
1	20	40	60	115	183	250
2-4: 2-Flying saucer-c. 3-Titanic-c	15	30	45	83	124	165

STRANGE LOVE (See Fox Giants)

STRANGE MYSTERIES

Superior/Dynamic Publications: Sept, 1951 - No. 21, Jan, 1955

	GD 2.0	VG 4.0	FN 6.0	VF 8.0	VF/NM 9.0	NM- 9.2
1-Kamenish-a & horror stories begin	66	132	198	416	701	985
2	38	76	114	222	356	490
3-5	35	70	105	203	327	450
6-8	30	60	90	176	283	390
9-Bondage 3-D effect-c	36	72	108	212	341	470
10-Used in **SOTI**, pg. 181	26	52	78	154	247	340
11-18	23	46	69	135	218	300
19-r/Journey Into Fear #1; cover is a splash from one story; Baker-r(2)	24	48	72	143	229	315
20,21-Reprints; 20-r/#1 with new-c	17	34	51	100	158	215

STRANGE MYSTERIES

I. W. Enterprises/Super Comics: 1963 - 1964

	GD 2.0	VG 4.0	FN 6.0	VF 8.0	VF/NM 9.0	NM- 9.2
I.W. Reprint #9; Rulah-r/Spook #28; Disbrow-a	3	6	9	20	30	40
Super Reprint #10-12,15-17(1963-64): 10,11-r/Strange #2,1. 12-r/Tales of Horror #5 (3/53) less-c. 15-r/Dark Mysteries #23. 16-r/The Dead Who Walk. 17-r/Dark Mysteries #22	3	6	9	20	30	40
Super Reprint #18-r/Witchcraft #1; Kubert-a	3	6	9	20	30	40

STRANGE PLANETS

I. W. Enterprises/Super Comics: 1958; 1963-64

	GD 2.0	VG 4.0	FN 6.0	VF 8.0	VF/NM 9.0	NM- 9.2
I.W. Reprint #1(nd)-Reprints E. C. Incredible S/F #30 plus-c/Strange Worlds #3	6	12	18	39	62	85
I.W. Reprint #9-Orlando/Wood-r/Strange Worlds #4; cover-r from Flying Saucers #1	7	14	21	49	80	110
Super Reprint #10-Wood-r (22 pg.) from Space Detective #1; cover-r/Attack on Planet Mars	7	14	21	49	80	110
Super Reprint #11-Wood-r (25 pg.) from An Earthman on Venus	8	16	24	54	90	125
Super Reprint #12-Orlando-r/Rocket to the Moon	7	14	21	49	80	110
Super Reprint #15-Reprints Journey Into Unknown Worlds #8; Heath, Colan-r	4	8	12	28	44	60
Super Reprint #16-Reprints Avon's Strange Worlds #6; Kinstler, Check-a	5	10	15	30	48	65
Super Reprint #18-r/Great Exploits #1 (Daring Adventures #6); Space Busters, Explorer Joe, The Son of Robin Hood; Krigstein-a	4	8	12	24	37	50

STRANGERS

Image Comics: Mar, 2003 - No. 6, Sept, 2003 ($2.95)

	GD 2.0	VG 4.0	FN 6.0	VF 8.0	VF/NM 9.0	NM- 9.2
1-6-Randy & Jean-Marc Lofficier-s; two covers. 2-Nexus back-up story						3.00

STRANGERS, THE

Malibu Comics (Ultraverse): June, 1993 - No. 24, May, 1995 ($1.95/$2.50)

	GD 2.0	VG 4.0	FN 6.0	VF 8.0	VF/NM 9.0	NM- 9.2
1-4,6-12,14-20: 1-1st app. The Strangers; has coupon for Ultraverse Premiere #0; 1st app. the Night Man (not in costume). 2-Polybagged w/trading card. 7-Break-Thru x-over. 8-2 pg. origin Solution. 12-Silver foil logo; wraparound-c. 17-Rafferty app.						2.50
1-With coupon missing						2.50
1-Full cover holographic edition, 1st of kind w/Hardcase #1 & Prime #1						6.00
1-Ultra 5000 limited silver foil						4.00
4-($2.50)-Newsstand edition bagged w/card						2.50
5-($2.50, 52 pgs.)-Rune flip-c/story by B. Smith (3 pgs.); The Mighty Magnor 1 pg. strip by Aragones; 3-pg. Night Man preview						2.50
13-($3.50, 68 pgs.)-Mantra app.; flip book w/Ultraverse Premiere #4						3.50
21-24 ($2.50)						2.50
...:The Pilgrim Conundrum Saga (1/95, $3.95, 68pgs.)						4.00

STRANGERS IN PARADISE

Antarctic Press: Nov, 1993 - No. 3, Feb, 1994 ($2.75, B&W, limited series)

	GD 2.0	VG 4.0	FN 6.0	VF 8.0	VF/NM 9.0	NM- 9.2
1	5	10	15	30	48	65
1-2nd/3rd prints	1	2	3	5	6	8
2 (2300 printed)	4	8	12	22	34	45
3	3	6	9	16	23	30
Trade paperback (Antarctic Press, $6.95)-Red -c (5000 print run)						10.00
Trade paperback (Abstract Studios, $6.95)-Red-c (2000 print run)						15.00
Trade paperback (Abstract Studios, $6.95, 1st-4th printing)-Blue-						7.00
Hardcover ('98, $29.95) includes first draft pages						30.00
Gold Reprint Series ($2.75) 1-3-r/#1-3						2.75

STRANGERS IN PARADISE

Abstract Studios: Sept, 1994 - No. 14, July, 1996 ($2.75, B&W)

	GD 2.0	VG 4.0	FN 6.0	VF 8.0	VF/NM 9.0	NM- 9.2
1	2	4	6	9	13	16
1,3- 2nd printings						4.00
2,3: 2-Color dream sequence	1	2	3	5	6	8
4-10						4.00
4-6-2nd printings						2.75
11-14: 14-The Letters of Molly & Poo						3.00
Gold Reprint Series ($2.75) 1-13-r/#1-13						2.75
I Dream Of You ($16.95, TPB) r/#1-9						17.00
It's a Good Life ($8.95, TPB) r/#10-13						9.00

STRANGERS IN PARADISE (Volume Three)

Homage Comics #1-8/Abstract Studios #9-on: Oct, 1996 - No. 90, May, 2007 ($2.75-$2.99, color #1-5, B&W #6-on)

	GD 2.0	VG 4.0	FN 6.0	VF 8.0	VF/NM 9.0	NM- 9.2
1-Terry Moore-c/s/a in all; dream seq. by Jim Lee-a						4.00
1-Jim Lee variant-c	1	2	3	6	7	8
2-5						3.50
6-16: 6-Return to B&W. 13-15-High school flashback. 16-Xena Warrior Princess parody; two covers						3.00
17-89: 33-Color issue. 46-Molly Lane. 49-Molly & Poo. 86-David dies						3.00
90-Last issue; 3 covers of Katchoo, Francine and David forming a triptych						3.00
...Lyrics and Poems (2/99)						2.75
...Source Book (2003, $2.95) Background on characters & story arcs, checklists						3.00
Brave New World ('02, $8.95, TPB) r/#44,45,47,48						9.00
Child of Rage ($15.95, TPB) r/#31-38						16.00
David's Story (6/04, $8.95, TPB) r/#61-63						9.00
Ever After ('07, $15.95, TPB) r/#83-90						16.00
Flower to Flame ('03, $15.95, TPB) r/#55-60						16.00
Heart in Hand ('03, $12.95, TPB) r/#50-54						13.00
High School ('98, $8.95, TPB) r/#13-16						9.00
Immortal Enemies ('98, $14.95, TPB) r/#6-12						15.00
Love & Lies (2006, $14.95, TPB)r/#77-82						15.00
Love Me Tender ($12.95, TPB) r/#1-5 in B&W w/ color Lee seq.						13.00
Molly & Poo (2005, $8.95, TPB)r/#46,49,73						9.00
My Other Life ($14.95, TPB) r/#25-30						15.00
Pocket Book 1-5 ($17.95, 5 1/2" x 8", TPB) 1-r/Vol.1 & 2. 2-r/#1-17 in B&W. 3-r/#18-24,26-32,34-38. 4-r/#41-45,47,48,50-60. 5-r/#46,49,61-76						18.00
Sanctuary ($15.95, TPB) r/#17-24						16.00
Tattoo ($14.95, TPB) r/#70-76; sketch pages and fan tattoo photos						15.00
Tomorrow Now (11/04, $14.95, TPB) r/#64-69						15.00
Tropic of Desire ($12.95, TPB) r/#39-43						13.00
The Complete... : Volume 3 Part 1 HC ($49.95) r/#1-12						50.00
The Complete... : Volume 3 Part 2 HC ($49.95) r/#13-15,17-25						50.00
The Complete... : Volume 3 Part 3 HC ('01, $49.95) r/#26-38						50.00
The Complete... : Volume 3 Part 4 HC ('02, $39.95) r/#39-46,49						40.00
The Complete... : Volume 3 Part 5 HC ('03, $49.95) r/#47,48,50-57						50.00
The Complete... : Volume 3 Part 6 HC ('04, $49.95) r/#58-69						50.00
The Complete... : Volume 3 Part 7 HC ('06, $49.95) r/#70-80						50.00

STRANGE SPORTS STORIES (See Brave & the Bold #45-49, DC Special, and DC Super Stars #10)

National Periodical Publications: Sept-Oct, 1973 - No. 6, July-Aug, 1974

	GD 2.0	VG 4.0	FN 6.0	VF 8.0	VF/NM 9.0	NM- 9.2
1	3	6	9	16	23	30
2-6: 2-Swan/Anderson-a	2	4	6	9	13	16

STRANGE STORIES FROM ANOTHER WORLD (Unknown World #1)

Fawcett Publications: No. 2, Aug, 1952 - No. 5, Feb, 1953

	GD 2.0	VG 4.0	FN 6.0	VF 8.0	VF/NM 9.0	NM- 9.2
2-Saunders painted-c	50	100	150	310	518	725
3-5-Saunders painted-c	40	80	120	235	380	525

STRANGE STORIES OF SUSPENSE (Rugged Action #1-4)

Atlas Comics (CSI): No. 5, Oct, 1955 - No. 16, Aug, 1957

	GD 2.0	VG 4.0	FN 6.0	VF 8.0	VF/NM 9.0	NM- 9.2
5(#1)	40	80	120	244	397	550
6,9	25	50	75	147	236	325
7-E. C. swipe cover/Vault of Horror #32	26	52	78	152	244	335
8-Morrow/Williamson-a; Pakula-a	27	54	81	158	254	350
10-Crandall, Torres, Meskin-a	26	52	78	152	244	335
11-13: 12-Torres, Pakula-a. 13-E.C. art swipes	21	42	63	125	200	275
14-16: 14-Williamson/Mayo-a. 15-Krigstein-a. 16-Fox, Powell-a						

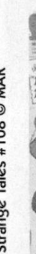

Strange Suspense Stories #7 © CC

Strange Tales #7 © MAR

Strange Tales #108 © MAR

	GD 2.0	VG 4.0	FN 6.0	VF 8.0	VF/NM 9.0	NM- 9.2

23 46 69 135 218 300

NOTE: **Everett** a-6, 7, 13; c-8, 9, 11-14. **Heath** a-5. **Maneely** c-5. **Morisi** a-11. **Morrow** a-13. **Powell** a-8. **Severin** c-7. **Wildey** a-14.

STRANGE STORY (Also see Front Page)
Harvey Publications: June-July, 1946 (52 pgs.)

1-The Man in Black Called Fate by Powell 32 64 96 186 298 410

STRANGE SUSPENSE STORIES (Lawbreakers Suspense Stories #10-15; This Is Suspense #23-26; Captain Atom V1#78 on)
Fawcett Publications/Charlton Comics No. 16 on: 6/52 - No. 5, 2/53; No. 16, 1/54 - No. 22, 11/54; No. 27, 10/55 - No. 77, 10/65; V3#1, 10/67 - V1#9, 9/69

1-(Fawcett)-Powell, Sekowsky-a 82 164 246 517 871 1225
2-George Evans horror story 48 96 144 298 499 700
3-5 (2/53)-George Evans horror stories 40 80 120 244 397 550
16(1-2/54) Formerly Lawbreakers S.S. 29 58 87 169 272 375
17,21: 21-Shuster-a 23 46 69 135 218 300
18-E.C. swipe/HOF 7; Ditko-c/a(2) 40 80 120 235 380 525
19-Ditko electric chair-c; Ditko-a 52 104 156 322 536 750
20-Ditko-c/a(2) 40 80 120 235 380 525
22(11/54)-Ditko-c, Shuster-a; last pre-code issue; becomes This Is Suspense
35 70 105 203 327 450
27(10/55)-(Formerly This Is Suspense #26) 15 30 45 85 130 175
28-30,38 12 24 36 67 94 120
31-33,35,37,40-Ditko-c/a(2-3 each) 21 42 63 125 200 275
34-Story of ruthless business man, Wm. B. Gaines; Ditko-c/a
47 94 141 291 483 675
36-(15¢, 68 pgs.); Ditko-a(4) 26 52 78 152 244 335
39,41,52,53-Ditko-a 18 36 54 107 169 230
42-44,46,49,54-60 6 12 18 37 59 80
45,47,48,50,51-Ditko-c/a 14 28 42 99 175 250
61-74 4 8 12 28 44 60
75(6/65) Reprints origin/1st app. Captain Atom by Ditko from Space Advs. #33;
r/Severin-a/Space Advs. #24 (75-77: 12¢ issues) 12 24 36 82 146 210
76,77-Captain Atom-r by Ditko/Space Advs. 6 12 18 43 69 95
V3#1(10/67): 12¢ issues begin 3 6 9 20 30 40
V1#2-Ditko-c/a; atom bomb-c 3 6 9 20 30 40
V1#3-9: All 12¢ issues 2 4 6 13 18 22

NOTE: **Alascia** a-19. **Aparo** a-60, V3#1, 2, 4; c-V1#4, 8, 9. **Daily** a-1-3; c-2, 5. **Evans** c-3, 4. **Giordano** c-16, 17p, 24p, 25p. **Montes/Bache** c-66. **Powell** a-4. **Shuster** a-19, 21. **Marcus Swayze** a-27.

STRANGE TALES (...Featuring Warlock #178-181; Doctor Strange #169 on)
Atlas (CCPC #1-67/ZPC #68-79/VPI #80-85)/Marvel #86(7/61) on:
June, 1951 - No. 168, May, 1968; No. 169, Sept, 1973 - No. 188, Nov, 1976

1-Horror/weird stories begin 300 600 900 2040 3570 5100
2 105 210 315 662 1119 1575
3,5: 3-Atom bomb panels 80 160 240 504 852 1200
4-Cosmic eyeball story "The Evil Eye" 83 166 249 523 887 1250
6-9: 6-Heath-c/a. 7-Colan-a 57 114 171 359 605 850
10-Krigstein-a 60 120 180 378 639 900
11-14,16-20 41 82 123 253 419 585
15-Krigstein-a 41 82 123 256 428 600
21,23-27,29-34: 27-Atom bomb panels. 33-Davis-a. 34-Last pre-code issue (2/55)
37 74 111 215 345 475
22-Krigstein, Forte/Fox-a 37 74 111 219 352 485
28-Jack Katz story used in Senate Investigation report, pgs. 7 & 169
37 74 111 219 352 485
35-41,43,44: 37-Vampire story by Colan 19 38 57 139 257 375
42,45,59,61-Krigstein-a; #61 (2/58) 20 40 60 145 268 390
46-57,60: 51-(10/56) 1st S.A. issue. 53,56-Crandall-a. 60-(8/57)
18 36 54 130 240 350
58,64-Williamson-a in each, with Mayo-#58 18 36 54 133 247 360
62,63,65,66: 62-Torres-a. 66-Crandall-a 17 34 51 126 233 340
67-Prototype ish. (Quicksilver) 19 38 57 135 250 365
68,71,72,74,77,80: Ditko/Kirby-a in #67-80 18 36 54 130 240 350
69,70,73,75,76,78,79: 69-Prototype ish. (Prof. X). 70-Prototype ish. (Giant Man). 73-Prototype ish. (Ant-Man). 75-Prototype ish. (Iron Man). 76-Prototype ish. (Human Torch). 78-Prototype ish. (Ant-Man). 79-Prototype ish. (Dr. Strange) (12/60)
22 44 66 157 291 425
81-83,85-88,90,91-Ditko/Kirby-a in all: 86-Robot-c. 90-(11/61)-Atom bomb blast panel
17 34 51 120 223 325
84-Prototype ish. (Magneto)(5/61); has powers like Magneto of X-Men, but two years earlier; Ditko/Kirby-a 20 40 60 148 274 400
89-1st app. Fin Fang Foom (10/61) by Kirby 44 88 132 352 664 975
92-Prototype ish. (Ancient One & Ant-Man); last 10¢ issue
18 36 54 130 240 350

	GD 2.0	VG 4.0	FN 6.0	VF 8.0	VF/NM 9.0	NM- 9.2

93,95,96,98-100: Kirby-a 15 30 45 111 206 300
94-Creature similar to The Thing; Kirby-a 18 36 54 130 240 350
97-1st app. Aunt May & Uncle Ben by Ditko (6/62), before Amazing Fantasy #15; (see Tales Of Suspense #7); Kirby-a 37 74 111 283 529 775
101-Human Torch begins by Kirby (10/62); origin recap Fantastic Four & Human Torch; Human Torch-c begin 104 208 312 884 1692 2500
102-1st app. Wizard; robot-c 39 78 117 301 563 825
103-105: 104-1st app. Trapster. 105-2nd Wizard 31 62 93 239 445 650
106,108,109: 106-Fantastic Four guests (3/63) 24 48 72 176 326 475
107-(4/63)-Human Torch/Sub-Mariner battle; 4th S.A. Sub-Mariner app. & 1st x-over outside of Fantastic Four 32 64 96 246 461 675
110-(7/63)-Intro Doctor Strange, Ancient One & Wong by Ditko
129 258 387 1097 2099 3100
111-2nd Dr. Strange 33 66 99 254 477 700
112,113 17 34 51 120 223 325
114-Acrobat disguised as Captain America, 1st app. since the G.A.; intro. & 1st app. Victoria Bentley; 3rd Dr. Strange app. & begin series (11/63)
39 78 117 301 563 825
115-Origin Dr. Strange; Human Torch vs. Sandman (Spidey villain; 2nd app. & brief origin), early Spider-Man x-over, 12/63 45 90 135 360 680 1000
116-(1/64)-Human Torch battles The Thing; 1st Thing x-over
15 30 45 105 190 275
117,118,120: 120-1st Iceman x-over (from X-Men) 11 22 33 79 140 200
119-Spider-Man x-over (2 panel cameo) 13 26 39 95 168 240
121,122,124,126-134: Thing/Torch team-up in 121-134. 126-Intro Clea. 128-Quicksilver & Scarlet Witch app. (1/65). 130-The Beatles cameo. 134-Last Human Torch; The Watcher-c/story; Wood-a(i) 9 18 27 63 107 150
123-1st app. The Beetle (see Amazing Spider-Man #21 for next app.); 1st Thor x-over (8/64); Loki app. 10 20 30 70 123 175
125-Torch & Thing battle Sub-Mariner (10/64) 10 20 30 73 129 185
135-Col. (formerly Sgt.) Nick Fury becomes Nick Fury Agent of Shield (origin/1st app.) by Kirby (8/65); series begins 15 30 45 105 190 275
136-140: 138-Intro Eternity 7 14 21 45 73 100
141-147,149: 145-Begins alternating-c features w/Nick Fury (odd #'s) & Dr. Strange (even #'s). 146-Last Ditko Dr. Strange who is in consecutive stories since #113; only full Ditko Dr. Strange-c this title. 147-Dr. Strange (by Everett #147-152) continues thru #168, then Dr. Strange #169 5 10 15 34 55 75
148-Origin Ancient One 7 14 21 49 80 110
150(11/66)-John Buscema's 1st work at Marvel 6 12 18 39 62 85
151-Kirby/Steranko-c/a; 1st Marvel work by Steranko 8 16 24 56 93 130
152,153-Kirby/Steranko-a 6 12 18 39 62 85
154-158-Steranko-a/script 6 12 18 39 62 85
159-Origin Nick Fury retold; Intro Val; Captain America-c/story; Steranko-a
7 14 21 45 73 100
160-162-Steranko-a/scripts; Capt. America app. 6 12 18 39 62 85
163-166,168-Steranko-a(p). 168-Last Nick Fury (gets own book next month) & last Dr. Strange who also gets own book 6 12 18 37 59 80
167-Steranko pen/script; classic flag-c 7 14 21 45 73 100
169-1st app. Brother Voodoo(origin in #169,170) & begin series, ends #173. 3 6 9 14 20 25
170-174: 174-Origin Golem 2 4 6 9 13 16
175-177: 177-Brunner-c 2 4 6 8 11 14
178-(2/75)-Warlock by Starlin begins; origin Warlock & Him retold; 1st app. Magus; Starlin-c/a/scripts in #178-181 (all before Warlock #9)
3 6 9 18 27 35
179-181-All Warlock. 179-Intro/1st app. Pip the Troll. 180-Intro Gamora. 181-(8/75)-Warlock story continued in Warlock #9 3 6 9 14 20 25
182-188: 185,186-(Regular 25¢ editions) 6.00
185,186-(30¢-c variants, limited distribution)(5,7/76) 2 4 6 11 16 20
Annual 1(1962)-Reprints from Strange Tales #73,76,78, Tales of Suspense #7,9, Tales to Astonish #1,6,7, & Journey Into Mystery #53,55,59; (1st Marvel annual?)
48 96 144 384 717 1050
Annual 2(7/63)-Reprints from Strange Tales #67, Strange Worlds (Atlas) #1-3, World of Fantasy #16; new Human Torch vs. Spider-Man story by Kirby/Ditko (1st Spidey x-over; 4th app.); Kirby-c 71 142 213 604 1152 1700

NOTE: **Briefer** a-17. **Burgos** a-123p. **J. Buscema** a-174p. **Colan** a-7, 11, 20, 37, 53, 169-173p, 188p. **Davis** c-71. **Ditko** a-46, 50, 67-122, 123-125p, 126-146, 175r, 182-188r; c-51, 93, 115, 121, 146. **Everett** a-4, 21, 40-42, 73, 147-152, 164i; c-8, 10, 11, 13, 15, 24, 45, 49-54, 56, 58, 60, 61, 63, 148, 150, 152, 158i. **Forte** a-27, 43, 50, 53, 54, 60. **Heath** a-2, 6; c-6, 18-20. **Kamen** a-45. **G. Kane** c-170-173, 182p. **Kirby** Human Torch-101-105, 108, 109, 114, 120; Nick Fury-135p, 141-143p; (Layouts)-135-153; other **Kirby** a-67-100p; c-68-70, 72-74, 76-92, 94, 95, 101-114, 116-123, 125-130, 132-135, 136p, 138-145, 147, 149, 151p. **Kirby/Ayers** c-101-106, 108-110. **Kirby/Ditko** a-80, 88, 121; c-75, 93, 97, 100, 139. **Lawrence** a-29. **Leiber/ Fox** a-110-113. **Maneely** a-3, 7, 37, 42; c-33, 40. **Moldoff** a-20. **Mooney** a-174i. **Morisi** a-53, 56. **Morrow** a-54. **Orlando** a-41, 44, 46, 49, 52. **Powell** a-42, 44, 49, 54, 130-134p; c-131p. **Reinman** a-11, 50, 74, 88, 91, 95, 104, 106, 112i, 124-127i. **Robinson** a-17. **Romita** c-169. **Roussos** c-201i. **R.Q. Sale** a-56; c-16. **Sekowski** a-3, 11. **Severin** a(i)-136-138; c-137. **Starlin** a-178, 179, 180p, 181p; c-178-180, 181p. **Steranko** a-151-161, 162-168p; c-151i, 153, 155, 157, 159, 161, 163,

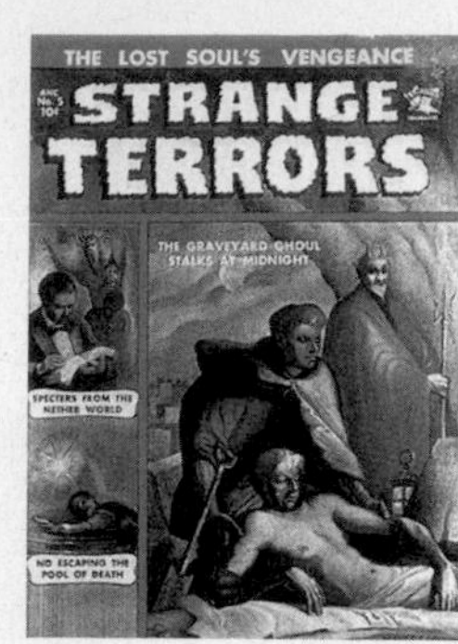

Strange Terrors #5 © STJ

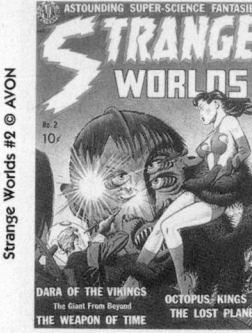

Strange Worlds #2 © AVON

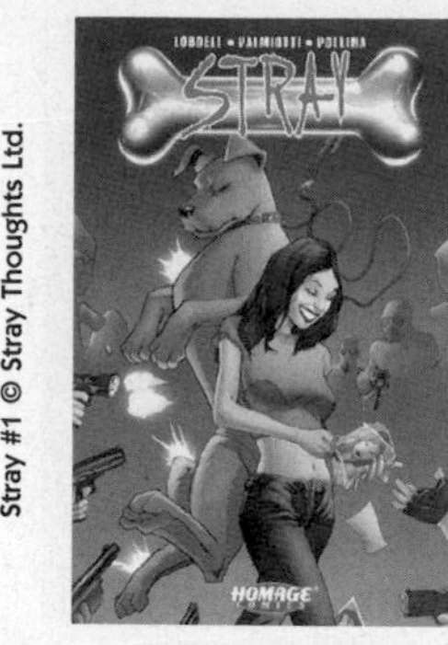

Stray #1 © Stray Thoughts Ltd.

165, 167. **Torres** a-53, 62. **Tuska** a-14, 166p. **Whitney** a-149. **Wildey** a-42, 56. **Woodbridge** a-59. Fantastic Four cameos #101-134. Jack Katz app.-26.

STRANGE TALES
Marvel Comics Group: Apr, 1987 - No. 19, Oct, 1988

	GD 2.0	VG 4.0	FN 6.0	VF 8.0	VF/NM 9.0	NM- 9.2
V2#1-19						2.50

STRANGE TALES
Marvel Comics: Nov, 1994 ($6.95, one-shot)

	GD 2.0	VG 4.0	FN 6.0	VF 8.0	VF/NM 9.0	NM- 9.2
V3#1-acetate-c						7.00

STRANGE TALES (Anthology; continues stories from Man-Thing #8 and Werewolf By Night #6)
Marvel Comics: Sept, 1998 - No. 2, Oct, 1998 ($4.99)

	GD 2.0	VG 4.0	FN 6.0	VF 8.0	VF/NM 9.0	NM- 9.2
1,2: 1-Silver Surfer app. 2-Two covers						5.00

STRANGE TALES: DARK CORNERS
Marvel Comics: May, 1998 ($3.99, one-shot)

	GD 2.0	VG 4.0	FN 6.0	VF 8.0	VF/NM 9.0	NM- 9.2
1-Anthology; stories by Baron & Maleev, McGregor & Dringenberg, DeMatteis & Badger; Estes painted-c						4.00

STRANGE TALES OF THE UNUSUAL
Atlas Comics (ACI No. 1-4/WPI No. 5-11): Dec, 1955 - No. 11, Aug, 1957

	GD 2.0	VG 4.0	FN 6.0	VF 8.0	VF/NM 9.0	NM- 9.2
1-Powell-a	45	90	135	279	465	650
2	28	56	84	166	268	370
3-Williamson-a (4 pgs.)	30	60	90	174	280	385
4,6,8,11	21	42	63	125	200	275
5-Crandall, Ditko-a	26	52	78	152	244	335
7,9: 7-Kirby, Orlando-a. 9-Krigstein-a	23	46	69	135	218	300
10-Torres, Morrow-a	21	42	63	125	200	275

NOTE: **Baily** a-6. **Brodsky** c-2-4. **Everett** a-2, 6; c-6, 9, 11. **Heck** a-1. **Maneely** c-1. **Orlando** a-7. **Pakula** a-10. **Romita** a-1. **R.Q. Sale** a-3. **Wildey** a-3.

STRANGE TERRORS
St. John Publishing Co.: June, 1952 - No. 7, Mar, 1953

	GD 2.0	VG 4.0	FN 6.0	VF 8.0	VF/NM 9.0	NM- 9.2
1-Bondage-c; Zombies spelled Zoombies on-c; Fine-*esque* -a	57	114	171	359	605	850
2	35	70	105	203	327	450
3-Kubert-a; painted-c	41	82	123	250	413	575
4-Kubert-a (reprinted in Mystery Tales #18); Ekgren painted-c; Fine-*esque* -a; Jerry Iger caricature	52	104	156	322	536	750
5-Kubert-a; painted-c	41	82	123	250	413	575
6-Giant (25¢, 100 pgs.)(1/53); bondage-c	53	106	159	330	553	775
7-Giant (25¢, 100 pgs.); Kubert-c/a	54	108	162	340	575	810

NOTE: *Cameron a-6, 7. Morisi a-6.*

STRANGE WORLD OF YOUR DREAMS
Prize Publications: Aug, 1952 - No. 4, Jan-Feb, 1953

	GD 2.0	VG 4.0	FN 6.0	VF 8.0	VF/NM 9.0	NM- 9.2
1-Simon & Kirby-a	64	128	192	403	682	960
2,3-Simon & Kirby-c/a. 2-Meskin-a	50	100	150	310	518	725
4-S&K-c; Meskin-a	41	82	123	250	413	575

STRANGE WORLDS (#18 continued from Avon's Eerie #1-17)
Avon Periodicals: 11/50 - No. 9, 11/52; No. 18, 10-11/54 - No. 22, 9-10/55 (No #11-17)

	GD 2.0	VG 4.0	FN 6.0	VF 8.0	VF/NM 9.0	NM- 9.2
1-Kenton of the Star Patrol by Kubert (r/Eerie #1 from 1947); Crom the Barbarian by John Giunta	133	266	399	838	1419	2000
2-Wood-a; Crom the Barbarian by Giunta; Dara of the Vikings app.; used in **SOTI**, pg. 112; injury to eye panel	120	240	360	756	1278	1800
3-Wood/Orlando-a (Kenton), Wood/Williamson/Frazetta/Krenkel/Orlando-a (7 pgs.); Malu Slave Girl Princess app.; Kinstler-c	233	466	699	1468	2484	3500
4-Wood-c/a (Kenton); Orlando-a; origin The Enchanted Daggar; Sultan-a; classic cover	130	260	390	819	1385	1950
5-Orlando/Wood-a (Kenton); Wood-c	70	140	210	441	746	1050
6-Kinstler-a(2); Orlando/Wood-c; Check-a	47	94	141	291	483	675
7-Fawcette & Becker/Alascia-a	40	80	120	246	403	560
8-Kubert, Kinstler, Hollingsworth & Lazarus-a; Lazarus Robot-c	40	80	120	246	403	560
9-Kinstler, Fawcette, Alascia-a	40	80	120	237	376	515
18-(Formerly Eerie #17)-Reprints "Attack on Planet Mars" by Kubert	32	64	96	186	298	410
19-r/Avon's "Robotmen of the Lost Planet"; last pre-code issue; Robot-c	32	64	96	186	298	410
20-War-c/story; Wood-c(r)/U.S. Paratroops #1	10	20	30	56	76	95
21,22-War-c/stories. 22-New logo	9	18	27	47	61	75
I.W. Reprint #5-Kinstler-a(r)/Avon's #9	4	8	12	24	37	50

STRANGE WORLDS
Marvel Comics (MPI No. 1,2/Male No. 3,5): Dec, 1958 - No. 5, Aug, 1959

	GD 2.0	VG 4.0	FN 6.0	VF 8.0	VF/NM 9.0	NM- 9.2
1-Kirby & Ditko-a; flying saucer issue	88	176	264	554	940	1325
2-Ditko-c/a	50	100	150	310	518	725
3-Kirby-a(2)	41	82	123	250	413	575
4-Williamson-a	40	80	120	244	397	550
5-Ditko-a	35	70	105	210	338	465

NOTE: ***Buscema** a-3, 4. **Ditko** a-1-5; c-2.. **Heck** a-2. **Kirby** a-1, 3. **Kirby/Brodsky** c-1, 3-5.*

STRAWBERRY SHORTCAKE
Marvel Comics (Star Comics): Jun, 1985 - No. 6, Feb, 1986 (Children's comic)

	GD 2.0	VG 4.0	FN 6.0	VF 8.0	VF/NM 9.0	NM- 9.2
1-6: Howie Post-a	1	2	3	5	6	8

STRAY
DC Comics (Homage Comics): 2001 ($5.95, prestige format, one-shot)

	GD 2.0	VG 4.0	FN 6.0	VF 8.0	VF/NM 9.0	NM- 9.2
1-Pollina-c/a; Lobdell & Palmiotti-s						6.00

STRAY BULLETS (Also see Promotional Comics section for Free Comic Book Day edition)
El Capitan Books: 1995 - Present ($2.95/$3.50, B&W, mature readers)

	GD 2.0	VG 4.0	FN 6.0	VF 8.0	VF/NM 9.0	NM- 9.2
1-David Lapham-c/a/scripts	2	4	6	8	10	12
2,3						6.00
4-8						3.50
9-21,31,32-($2.95)						3.00
22-30,33-40-($3.50) 22-Includes preview to Murder Me Dead						3.50
Innocence of Nihilism Volume 1 HC ($29.95, hardcover) r/#1-7						30.00
Somewhere Out West Volume 2 HC ($34.95, hardcover) r/#8-14						35.00
Other People Volume 3 HC ($34.95, hardcover) r/#15-22						35.00
Volume 1-3 TPB ($11.95, softcover) 1-r/#1-4. 2-r/#5-8. 3-r/ #9-12						12.00
Volume 4-7 TPB ($14.95) 4- r/#13-16. 5- r/#17-20. 6- r/#21-24. 7-r/#25-28						15.00

NOTE: *Multiple printings of most issues exist & are worth cover price.*

STRAY TOASTERS
Marvel Comics (Epic Comics): Jan, 1988 - No. 4, April, 1989 ($3.50, squarebound, limited series)

	GD 2.0	VG 4.0	FN 6.0	VF 8.0	VF/NM 9.0	NM- 9.2
1-4: Sienkiewicz-c/a/scripts						3.50

STREET COMIX
Street Enterprises/King Features: 1973 (50¢, B&W, 36 pgs.)(20,000 print run)

	GD 2.0	VG 4.0	FN 6.0	VF 8.0	VF/NM 9.0	NM- 9.2
1-Rip Kirby	2	4	6	8	11	14
2-Flash Gordon	2	4	6	10	14	18

STREETFIGHTER
Ocean Comics: Aug, 1986 - No. 4, Spr, 1987 ($1.75, limited series)

	GD 2.0	VG 4.0	FN 6.0	VF 8.0	VF/NM 9.0	NM- 9.2
1-4: 2-Origin begins						3.00

STREET FIGHTER
Malibu Comics: Sept, 1993 - No. 3, Nov, 1993 ($2.95)

	GD 2.0	VG 4.0	FN 6.0	VF 8.0	VF/NM 9.0	NM- 9.2
1-3: 3-Includes poster; Ferret x-over						3.00

STREET FIGHTER
Image Comics: Sept, 2003 - No. 14, Feb, 2005 ($2.95)

	GD 2.0	VG 4.0	FN 6.0	VF 8.0	VF/NM 9.0	NM- 9.2
1-Back-up story w/Madureira-a; covers by Madureira and Tsang						3.00
2-6,8-14: 2-Two covers by Campbell and Warren; back-up story w/Warren-a						3.00
7-($4.50) Larocca-c						4.50
... Vol. 1 (3/04, $9.99, digest-size) r/main stories from #1-6						10.00

STREET FIGHTER: THE BATTLE FOR SHADALOO
DC Comics/CAP Co. Ltd.: 1995 ($3.95, one-shot)

	GD 2.0	VG 4.0	FN 6.0	VF 8.0	VF/NM 9.0	NM- 9.2
1-Polybagged w/trading card & Tattoo						4.00

STREET FIGHTER II
Tokuma Comics (Viz): Apr, 1994 - No. 8, Nov, 1994 ($2.95, limited series)

	GD 2.0	VG 4.0	FN 6.0	VF 8.0	VF/NM 9.0	NM- 9.2
1-8						3.00

STREET FIGHTER II
UDON Comics: No. 0, Oct, 2005 - Present ($1.99/$3.95/$2.95)

	GD 2.0	VG 4.0	FN 6.0	VF 8.0	VF/NM 9.0	NM- 9.2
0-(10/05, $1.99) prelude to series; Alvin Lee-a						2.50
1-($3.95) Two covers by Alvin Lee & Ed McGuinness						4.00
2-5-($2.95)						3.00

STREET FIGHTER LEGENDS
UDON Comics: Aug, 2006 - Present ($3.95)

	GD 2.0	VG 4.0	FN 6.0	VF 8.0	VF/NM 9.0	NM- 9.2
1-Spotlight on Sakura; two covers						4.00

STREETS
DC Comics: 1993 - No. 3, 1993 ($4.95, limited series, 52 pgs.)

	GD 2.0	VG 4.0	FN 6.0	VF 8.0	VF/NM 9.0	NM- 9.2
Book 1-3-Estes painted-c						5.00

STREET SHARKS
Archie Publications: Jan, 1996 - No. 3, Mar, 1996 ($1.50, limited series)

	GD 2.0	VG 4.0	FN 6.0	VF 8.0	VF/NM 9.0	NM- 9.2
1-3						2.50

Stumbo Tinytown #9 © HARV

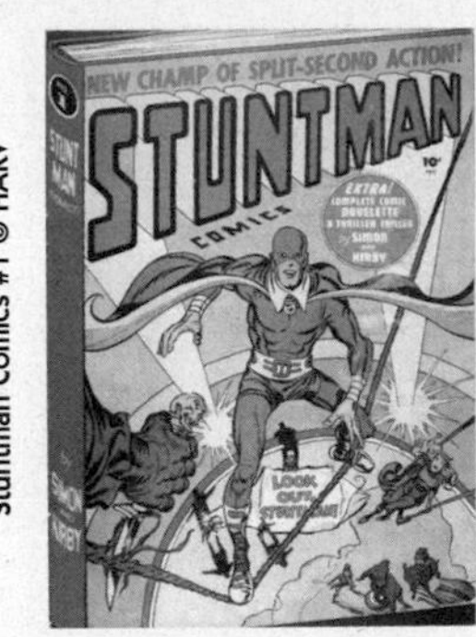

Stuntman Comics #1 © HARV

Sub-Mariner #46 © MAR

GD VG FN VF VF/NM NM-
2.0 4.0 6.0 8.0 9.0 9.2

STREET SHARKS
Archie Publications: May, 1996 - No. 6 ($1.50, published 8 times a year)
1-6 2.50

STRICTLY PRIVATE (You're in the Army Now)
Eastern Color Printing Co.: July, 1942 (#1 on sale 6/15/42)
1,2: Private Peter Plink. 2-Says 128 pgs. on-c 23 46 69 133 214 295

STRIKE!
Eclipse Comics: Aug, 1987 - No. 6, Jan, 1988 ($1.75)
1-6, ...Vs. Sgt. Strike Special 1 (5/88, $1.95) 2.50

STRIKEBACK! (The Hunt For Nikita)
Malibu Comics (Bravura): Oct, 1994 - No. 3, Jan, 1995 ($2.95, unfinished limited series)
1-3: Jonathon Peterson script, Kevin Maguire-c/a 3.00
1-Gold foil embossed-c 5.00

STRIKEBACK!
Image Comics (WildStorm Productions): Jan, 1996 - No. 5, May, 1996 ($2.50, limited series)
1-5: Reprints original Bravura series w/additional story & art by Kevin Maguire & Jonathon Peterson; new Maguire-c in all. 4,5-New story & art 2.50

STRIKEFORCE: AMERICA
Comico: Dec, 1995 ($2.95)
V2#1-Polybagged w/gaming card; S. Clark-a(p) 3.00

STRIKEFORCE: MORITURI
Marvel Comics Group: Dec, 1986 - No. 31, July, 1989
1-31: 14-Williamson-i. 13-Double size. 25-Heath-c 2.50

STRIKEFORCE MORITURI: ELECTRIC UNDERTOW
Marvel Comics: Dec, 1989 - No. 5, Mar, 1990 ($3.95, 52 pgs., limited series)
1-5 Squarebound 4.00

STRONG GUY REBORN (See X-Factor)
Marvel Comics: Sept, 1997 ($2.99, one-shot)
1-Dezago-s/Andy Smith, Art Thibert-a 3.00

STRONG MAN (Also see Complimentary Comics & Power of...)
Magazine Enterprises: Mar-Apr, 1955 - No. 4, Sept-Oct, 1955
1(A-1 #130)-Powell-c/a 23 46 69 133 214 295
2-4: (A-1 #132,134,139)-Powell-a. 2-Powell-c 18 36 54 105 165 225

STRONTIUM DOG
Eagle Comics: Dec, 1985 - No. 4, Mar, 1986 ($1.25, limited series)
1-4, Special 1: 4-Moore script. Special 1 (1986)-Moore script 2.50

STRYFE'S STRIKE FILE
Marvel Comics: Jan, 1993 ($1.75, one-shot, no ads)
1-Stroman, Capullo, Andy Kubert, Brandon Peterson-a; silver metallic ink-c; X-Men tie-in to X-Cutioner's Song 3.00
1-Gold metallic ink 2nd printing 2.50

STRYKEFORCE
Image Comics (Top Cow): May, 2004 - No. 5, Oct, 2004 ($2.99)
1-5-Faerber-s/Kirkham-a. 4,5-Preview of HumanKind 3.00
Vol. 1 TPB (2005, $16.99) r/#1-5 & Codename: Strykeforce #0-3; sketch pages 17.00

STUMBO THE GIANT (See Harvey Hits #49,54,57,60,63,66,69,72,78,88 & Hot Stuff #2)

STUMBO TINYTOWN
Harvey Publications: Oct, 1963 - No. 13, Nov, 1966 (All 25¢ giants)
1-Stumbo, Hot Stuff & others begin 15 30 45 105 190 275
2 9 18 27 61 103 145
3-5 7 14 21 45 73 100
6-13 6 12 18 37 59 80

STUNT DAWGS
Harvey Comics: Mar, 1993 ($1.25, one-shot)
1 2.50

STUNTMAN COMICS (Also see Thrills Of Tomorrow)
Harvey Publ.: Apr-May, 1946 - No. 2, June-July, 1946; No. 3, Oct-Nov, 1946
1-Origin Stuntman by S&K reprinted in Black Cat #9; S&K-c 115 230 345 725 1225 1725
2-S&K-c/a; The Duke of Broadway story 68 136 204 428 727 1025
3-Small size (5-1/2x8-1/2"; B&W; 32 pgs.); distributed to mail subscribers only; S&K-a; Kid Adonis by S&K reprinted in Green Hornet #37 83 166 249 523 887 1250
(Also see All-New #15, Boy Explorers #2, Flash Gordon #5 & Thrills of Tomorrow)

STUPID COMICS (Also see 40 oz. Collected)
Oni Press/Image Comics: July, 2000; Sept, 2002 - Present ($2.95, B&W)
1-(Oni Press, 7/00) Jim Mahfood 1 page satire strips reprinted from JAVA magazine 3.00
1-3-(Image Comics, 9/02; 10/03) Jim Mahfood 1 page and 2 page satire strips 3.00
TPB (4/06, $12.99) r/#1(Oni) and #1-3(Image); Phoenix New Times strips 13.00

STUPID HEROES
Mirage Studios: Sept, 1993 - No. 3, Dec, 1994 ($2.75, unfinished limited series)
1-3-Laird-c/a & scripts; 2 trading cards bound in 2.75

STUPID, STUPID RAT TAILS (See Bone)
Cartoon Books: Dec, 1999 - No. 3, Feb, 2000 ($2.95, limited series)
1-3-Jeff Smith-a/Tom Sniegoski-s 3.00

SUBHUMAN
Dark Horse Comics: Nov, 1998 - No. 4, Feb, 1999 ($2.95, limited series)
1-4-Mark Schultz-c 3.00

SUBMARINE ATTACK (Formerly Speed Demons)
Charlton Comics: No. 11, May, 1958 - No. 54, Feb-Mar, 1966
11 4 8 12 24 37 50
12-20 3 6 9 18 27 35
21-30 3 6 9 16 23 30
31-54 3 6 9 14 19 24
NOTE: ***Glanzman** c/a-25. **Montes/Bache** a-38, 40, 41.*

SUB-MARINER (See All-Select, All-Winners, Blonde Phantom, Daring, The Defenders, Fantastic Four #4, Human Torch, The Invaders, Iron Man &..., Marvel Mystery, Marvel Spotlight #27, Men's Adventures, Motion Picture Funnies Weekly, Namora, Namor, The..., Prince Namor, The Sub-Mariner, Saga Of The..., Tales to Astonish #70 & 2nd series, USA & Young Men)

SUB-MARINER, THE (2nd Series)(Sub-Mariner #31 on)
Marvel Comics Group: May, 1968 - No. 72, Sept, 1974 (No. 43: 52 pgs.)
1-Origin Sub-Mariner; story continued from Iron Man & Sub-Mariner #1 17 34 51 120 223 325
2-Triton app. 8 16 24 56 93 130
3-5: 5-1st Tiger Shark (9/68) 6 12 18 41 66 90
6,7,9,10: 6-Tiger Shark-c & 2nd app., cont'd from #5. 7-Photo-c. (1968). 9-1st app. Serpent Crown (origin in #10 & 12) 5 10 15 30 48 65
8-Sub-Mariner vs. Thing 8 16 24 58 97 135
8-2nd printing (1994) 2 4 6 8 10 12
11-13,15: 15-Last 12¢ issue 4 8 12 24 37 50
14-Sub-Mariner vs. G.A. Human Torch; death of Toro (1st modern app. & only app. Toro, 6/69) 5 10 15 34 55 75
16-20: 19-1st Sting Ray (11/69); Stan Lee, Romita, Heck, Thomas, Everett & Kirby cameos. 20-Dr. Doom app. 3 6 9 17 25 32
21,23-33,37-39,41,42: 25-Origin Atlantis. 30-Capt. Marvel x-over. 37-Death of Lady Dorma. 38-Origin retold. 42-Last 15¢ issue. 3 6 9 14 20 26
22,40: 22-Dr. Strange x-over. 40-Spider-Man x-over 3 6 9 16 22 28
34-Prelude (w/#35) to 1st Defenders story; Hulk & Silver Surfer x-over 7 14 21 49 80 110
35-Namor/Hulk/Silver Surfer team-up to battle The Avengers-c/story (3/71); hints at teaming up again 6 12 18 39 62 85
36 Wrightson-a(i) 3 6 9 18 27 35
43-King Size Special (52 pgs.) 3 6 9 18 27 35
44,45-Sub-Mariner vs. Human Torch 3 6 9 16 23 30
46-49,56,62,64-72: 47,48-Dr. Doom app. 49-Cosmic Cube story. 62-1st Tales of Atlantis, ends #66. 64-Hitler cameo. 67-New costume; F.F. x-over. 69-Spider-Man x-over (6 panels) 2 4 6 8 10 12
50-1st app. Nita, Namor's niece (later Namorita in New Warriors) 2 4 6 9 13 16
51-55,57,58,60,61,63-Everett issues: 61-Last artwork by Everett; 1st 4 pgs. completed by Mortimer; pgs. 5-20 by Mooney 2 4 6 9 12 15
59-1st battle with Thor; Everett-a 3 6 9 18 27 35
Special 1 (1/71)-r/Tales to Astonish #70-73 3 6 9 17 25 32
Special 2 (1/72)-(52 pgs.)-r/T.T.A. #74-76; Everett-a 3 6 9 14 19 24
NOTE: ***Bolle** a-67i. **Buscema** a(p)-1-8, 20, 24. **Colan** a(p)-10, 11, 40, 43, 46-49, Special 1, 2; c(p)-10, 11, 40. **Craig** a-17i, 19-23i. **Everett** a-45r, 50-55, 57, 58, 59-61(plot), 63(plot); c-47, 48i, 55, 57-59i, 61, Spec. 2. **G. Kane** c(p)-42-52, 58, 66, 70, 71. **Mooney** a-24i, 25i, 32-35i, 39i, 42i, 44i, 45i, 60i, 61i, 65p, 66p, 68i. **Severin** c/a-38i. **Starlin** c-59p. **Tuska** a-41p, 42p, 69-71p. **Wrightson** a-36i. #53, 54-r/stories Sub-Mariner Comics #41 & 39.*

SUB-MARINER (The Initiative, follows Civil War series)
Marvel Comics: Aug, 2007 - No. 6, Jan, 2008 ($2.99, limited series)
1-6: 1-Turner-c/Briones-a/Cherniss & Johnson-s; Iron Man app. 3-Yu-c; Venom app. 3.00
...: Revolution TPB (208, $14.99) r/#1-6 15.00

SUB-MARINER COMICS (1st Series) (The Sub-Mariner #1, 2, 33-42)(Official True Crime

Sub-Mariner Comics #18 © MAR

Sugar & Spike #90 © DC

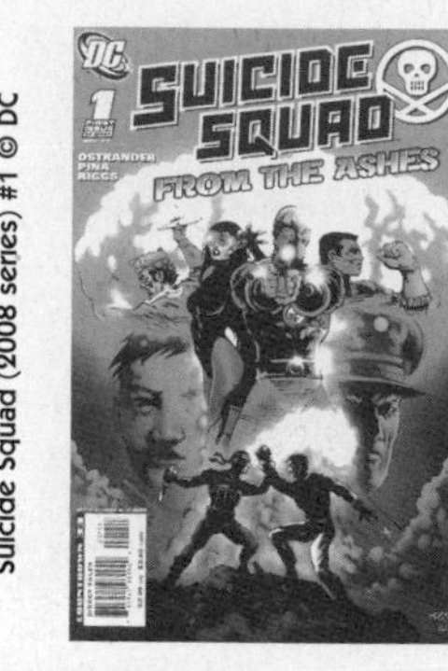

Suicide Squad (2008 series) #1 © DC

GD VG FN VF VF/NM NM-
2.0 4.0 6.0 8.0 9.0 9.2

Cases #24 on; Amazing Mysteries #32 on; Best Love #33 on)
Timely/Marvel Comics (TCI 1-7/SePI 8/MPI 9-32/Atlas Comics (CCC 33-42)): Spring, 1941 - No. 23, Sum, 1947; No. 24, Wint, 1947 - No. 31, 4/49; No. 32, 7/49; No. 33, 4/54 - No. 42, 10/55

1-The Sub-Mariner by Everett & The Angel begin
2950 5900 8850 22,800 42,400 62,000
2-Everett-a 543 1086 1629 3800 6650 10,000
3-Churchill assassination-c; 40 pg. S-M story 472 944 1416 3398 5949 8500
4-Everett-a, 40 pgs.; 1 pg. Wolverton-a 377 754 1131 2564 4482 6400
5-Gabrielle/Klein-c 300 600 900 1950 3375 4800
6-10: 9-Wolverton-a, 3 pgs.; flag-c 287 574 861 1808 3054 4300
11-Classic Schomburg-c 293 586 879 1846 3123 4400
12-15 200 400 600 1260 2130 3000
16-20 163 326 489 1027 1739 2450
21-Last Angel; Everett-a 123 246 369 775 1313 1850
22-Young Allies app. 123 246 369 775 1313 1850
23-The Human Torch, Namora x-over (Sum/47); 2nd app. Namora after Marvel Mystery #82 147 294 441 926 1563 2200
24-Namora x-over (3rd app.) 125 250 375 788 1332 1875
25-The Blonde Phantom begins (Spr/48), ends No. 31; Kurtzman-a; Namora x-over; last quarterly issue 143 286 429 901 1526 2150
26-28: 28-Namora cover; Everett-a 123 246 369 775 1313 1850
29-31 (4/49): 29-The Human Torch app. 31-Capt. America app.
123 246 369 775 1313 1850
32 (7/49, Scarce)-Origin Sub-Mariner 187 374 561 1178 1989 2800
33 (4/54)-Origin Sub-Mariner; The Human Torch app.; Namora x-over in Sub-Mariner #33-42
107 214 321 674 1137 1600
34,35-Human Torch in each 83 166 249 523 887 1250
36,37,39-41: 36,39-41-Namora app. 82 164 246 517 871 1225
38-Origin Sub-Mariner's wings; Namora app.; last pre-code (2/55)
90 180 270 567 959 1350
42-Last issue 88 176 264 554 935 1315

NOTE: *Angel by* **Gustavson**-*#1, 8.* **Brodsky** *c-34-36, 42.* **Everett** *a-1-4, 22-24, 26-42; c-32, 33, 40.* **Maneely** *a-38; c-37, 39-41.* **Rico** *c-27-31.* **Schomburg** *c-1-4, 6, 8-18, 20.* **Sekowsky** *c-24. 25, 26(w/***Rico***).* **Shores** *c-21-23, 38. Bondage c-13, 22, 24, 25, 34.*

SUB-MARINER: THE DEPTHS
Marvel Comics: Nov, 2008 - No. 5 ($3.99, limited series)
1-Peter Milligan-s/Esad Ribic-a/c 4.00

SUBSPECIES
Eternity Comics: May, 1991 - No. 4, Aug, 1991 ($2.50, limited series)
1-4: New stories based on horror movie 2.50

SUBTLE VIOLENTS
CFD Productions: 1991 ($2.50, B&W, mature)
1-Linsner-c & story 1 3 4 8 10 12
San Diego Limited Edition 4 8 12 24 37 50

SUE & SALLY SMITH (Formerly My Secret Life)
Charlton Comics: V2#48, Nov, 1962 - No. 54, Nov, 1963 (Flying Nurses)
V2#48 3 6 9 17 25 32
49-54 2 4 6 13 18 22

SUGAR & SPIKE (Also see The Best of DC & DC Silver Age Classics)
National Periodical Publications: Apr-May, 1956 - No. 98, Oct-Nov, 1971
1 (Scarce) 300 600 900 2010 3505 5000
2 117 234 351 737 1244 1750
3-5: 3-Letter column begins 73 146 219 460 780 1100
6-10 45 90 135 279 465 650
11-20 37 74 111 220 353 485
21-29: 26-Christmas-c 26 52 78 152 244 335
30-Scribbly & Scribbly, Jr. x-over 27 54 81 156 251 345
31-40 20 40 60 115 183 250
41-60 9 18 27 60 100 140
61-80: 69-1st app. Tornado-Tot-c/story. 72-Origin & 1st app. Bernie the Brain
7 14 21 47 76 105
81-84,86-95: 84-Bernie the Brain apps. as Superman in 1 panel (9/69)
6 12 18 37 59 80
85 (68 pgs.)-r/#72 6 12 18 41 66 90
96 (68 pgs.) 7 14 21 45 73 100
97,98 (52 pgs.) 6 12 18 41 66 90
No. 1 Replica Edition (2002, $2.95) reprint of #1 3.00
NOTE: *All written and drawn by* **Sheldon Mayer.** *Issues with Paper Doll pages cut or missing are common.*

SUGAR BOWL COMICS (Teen-age)
Famous Funnies: May, 1948 - No. 5, Jan, 1949

GD VG FN VF VF/NM NM-
2.0 4.0 6.0 8.0 9.0 9.2

1-Toth-c/a 15 30 45 83 124 165
2,4,5 9 18 27 50 65 80
3-Toth-a 10 20 30 56 76 95

SUGARFOOT (TV)
Dell Publishing Co.: No. 907, May, 1958 - No. 1209, Oct-Dec, 1961
Four Color 907 (#1)-Toth-a, photo-c 12 24 36 84 150 215
Four Color 992 (5-7/59), Toth-a, photo-c 11 22 33 77 136 195
Four Color 1059 (11-1/60), 1098 (5-7/60), 1147 (11-1/61), 1209-all photo-c
8 16 24 58 97 135

SUICIDE SQUAD (See Brave & the Bold and Doom Patrol & Suicide Squad Spec., Legends #3 & note under Star Spangled War stories)
DC Comics: May, 1987 - No. 66, June, 1992 (Direct sales only #32 on)
1-66: 9-Millennium x-over. 10-Batman-c/story. 13-JLI app. (Batman). 16-Re-intro Shade The Changing Man. 23-1st Oracle. 27-34,36,37-Snyder-a. 40-43-"The Phoenix Gambit" Batman storyline. 40-Free Batman/Suicide Squad poster 2.50
Annual 1 (1988, $1.50)-Manhunter x-over 2.50
NOTE: *Chaykin c-1.*

SUICIDE SQUAD (2nd series)
DC Comics: Nov, 2001 - No. 12, Oct, 2002 ($2.50)
1-12-Giffen-s/Medina-a; Sgt. Rock app. 4-Heath-a. 10-J. Severin-a. 12-JSA app. 2.50

SUICIDE SQUAD (3rd series)
DC Comics: Nov, 2007 - No. 8, Jun, 2008 ($2.99, limited series)
1-8-Ostrander-s/Pina-a/Snyder III-c 3.00

SUMMER FUN (See Dell Giants)

SUMMER FUN (Formerly Li'l Genius; Holiday Surprise #55)
Charlton Comics: No. 54, Oct, 1966 (Giant)
54 4 8 12 22 34 45

SUMMER FUN (Walt Disney's...)
Disney Comics: Summer, 1991 ($2.95, annual, 68 pgs.)
1-D. Duck, M. Mouse, Brer Rabbit, Chip 'n' Dale & Pluto, Li'l Bad Wolf, Super Goof, Scamp stories 4.00

SUMMER LOVE (Formerly Brides in Love?)
Charlton Comics: V2#46, Oct, 1965; V2#47, Oct, 1966; V2#48, Nov, 1968
V2#46-Beatles-c & 8 pg. story 13 26 39 95 168 240
47-(68 pgs.) Beatles-c & 12 pg. story 10 20 30 70 123 175
48 3 6 9 15 21 26

SUMMER MAGIC (See Movie Comics)

SUNDANCE (See Hotel Deparee...)

SUNDANCE KID (Also see Blazing Six-Guns)
Skywald Publications: June, 1971 - No. 3, Sept, 1971 (52 pgs.)(Pre-code reprints & new-s)
1-Durango Kid; Two Kirby Bullseye-r 3 6 9 14 20 26
2,3: 2-Swift Arrow, Durango Kid, Bullseye by S&K; Meskin plus 1 pg. origin. 3-Durango Kid, Billy the Kid, Red Hawk-r 2 4 6 10 14 18

SUNDAY PIX (Christian religious)
David C. Cook Pub/USA Weekly Newsprint Color Comics: V1#1, Mar,1949 - V16#26, July 19, 1964 (7x10", 12 pgs., mail subscription only)
V1#1 8 16 24 40 50 60
V1#2-up 5 10 15 24 30 35
V2#1-52 (1950) 5 10 15 22 26 30
V3-V6 (1951-1953) 4 8 12 17 21 24
V7-V11#1-7,23-52 (1954-1959) 2 4 6 11 16 20
V11#8-22 (2/22-5/31/59) H.G. Wells First Men in the Moon serial
2 4 6 13 18 22
V12#1-19,21-52; V13-V15#1,2,9-52; V16#1-26(7/19/64)
2 4 6 9 13 16
V12#20 (5/15/60) 2 page interview with Peanuts' Charles Schulz
4 8 12 22 34 45
V15#3-8 (2/24/63) John Glenn, Christian astronaut 2 4 6 13 18 22

SUN DEVILS
DC Comics: July, 1984 - No. 12, June, 1985 ($1.25, maxi series)
1-12: 6-Death of Sun Devil 2.50

SUNDIATA: A LEGEND OF AFRICA
NBM Publishing Inc.: 2002 ($15.95, hardcover with dustjacket)
nn-Will Eisner-s/a; adaptation of an African folk tale 16.00

SUN FUN KOMIKS
Sun Publications: 1939 (15¢, B&W & red)

Sunset Carson #3 © CC

Superboy #76 © DC

Superboy #219 © DC

	GD	VG	FN	VF	VF/NM	NM-
	2.0	4.0	6.0	8.0	9.0	9.2

1-Satire on comics (rare) 80 160 240 504 852 1200

SUNFIRE & BIG HERO SIX (See Alpha Flight)
Marvel Comics: Sept, 1998 - No. 3, Nov, 1998 ($2.50, limited series)
1-3-Lobdell-s 2.50

SUN GIRL (See The Human Torch & Marvel Mystery Comics #88)
Marvel Comics (CCC): Aug, 1948 - No. 3, Dec, 1948
1-Sun Girl begins; Miss America app. 173 346 519 1090 1845 2600
2,3: 2-The Blonde Phantom begins 117 234 351 737 1244 1750

SUNNY, AMERICA'S SWEETHEART (Formerly Cosmo Cat #1-10)
Fox Features Syndicate: No. 11, Dec, 1947 - No. 14, June, 1948
11-Feldstein-c/a 110 220 330 693 1172 1650
12-14-Feldstein-c/a; 13,14-Lingerie panels. 13-L.B. Cole-a
80 160 240 504 852 1200
I.W. Reprint #8-Feldstein-a; r/Fox issue 10 20 30 73 129 185

SUN-RUNNERS (Also see Tales of the...)
Pacific Comics/Eclipse Comics/Amazing Comics: 2/84 - No. 3, 5/84; No. 4, 11/84 - No. 7, 1986 (Baxter paper)
1-7: P. Smith-a in #2-4 2.50
Christmas Special 1 (1987, $1.95)-By Amazing 2.50

SUNSET CARSON (Also see Cowboy Western)
Charlton Comics: Feb, 1951 - No. 4, 1951 (No month) (Photo-c on each)
1-Photo/retouched-c (Scarce, all issues) 72 144 216 450 750 1050
2-Kit Carson story; adapts "Kansas Raiders" w/Brian Donlevy, Audie Murphy & Margaret Chapman 53 106 159 323 537 750
3,4 41 82 123 250 400 550

SUNSET PASS (See Zane Grey & 4-Color #230)

SUPER ANIMALS PRESENTS PIDGY & THE MAGIC GLASSES
Star Publications: Dec, 1953 (25¢, came w/glasses)
1-(3-D Comics)-L. B. Cole-c 41 82 123 250 413 575

SUPER BAD JAMES DYNOMITE
5-D Comics: Dec, 2005 - No. 5, Feb, 2007 ($3.99)
1-5-Created by the Wayans brothers 4.00

SUPERBOY
DC Comics: Jan, 1942
nn-Ashcan comic, not distributed to newsstands, only for in house use. Covers were produced, but not the rest of the book. A CGC certified 9.2 copy sold in 2003 for $6,600.

SUPERBOY (See Adventure, Aurora, DC Comics Presents, DC 100 Page Super Spectacular #15, DC Super Stars, 80 Page Giant #10, More Fun Comics, The New Advs. of... & Superman Family #191, Young Justice)

SUPERBOY (1st Series)(...& the Legion of Super-Heroes with #231)
(Becomes The Legion of Super-Heroes No. 259 on)
National Periodical Publ./DC Comics: Mar-Apr, 1949 - No. 258, Dec, 1979 (#1-16: 52 pgs.)
1-Superman cover; intro in More Fun #101 (1-2/45)
833 1666 2499 5998 10,499 15,000
2-Used in **SOTI**, pg. 35-36,226 233 466 699 1468 2484 3500
3 180 360 540 1134 1917 2700
4,5: 5-1st pre-Supergirl tryout (c/story, 11-12/49) 123 246 369 775 1313 1850
6-9: 8-1st Superbaby 107 214 321 674 1137 1600
10-1st app. Lana Lang 117 234 351 737 1244 1750
11-15: 2nd Lana Lang app.; 1st Lana cover 80 160 240 504 852 1200
16-20: 20-2nd Jor-El cover 55 110 165 347 586 825
21-26,28-30: 21-Lana Lang app. 45 90 135 279 465 650
27-Low distribution 47 94 141 291 483 675
31-38: 38-Last pre-code issue (1/55) 40 80 120 235 380 525
39-48,50 (7/56) 35 70 105 208 334 460
49 (6/56)-1st app. Metallo (Jor-El's robot) 38 76 114 226 363 500
51-60: 52-1st S.A. issue. 56-Krypto-c 26 52 78 154 247 340
61-67 21 42 63 125 200 275
68-Origin/1st app. original Bizarro (10-11/58) 62 124 186 391 658 925
69-77,79: 76-1st Supermonkey 18 36 54 105 165 225
78-Origin Mr. Mxyzptlk & Superboy's costume 25 50 75 147 236 325
80-1st meeting Superboy/Supergirl (4/60) 23 46 69 135 218 300
81,83-85,87,88: 83-Origin/1st app. Kryptonite Kid 11 22 33 79 140 200
82-1st Bizarro Krypto 12 24 36 82 146 210
86-(1/61)-4th Legion app; Intro Pete Ross 18 36 54 133 247 360
89-(6/61)-1st app. Mon-el; 2nd Phantom Zone 26 52 78 192 359 525
90-92: 90-Pete Ross learns Superboy's I.D. 92-Last 10¢ issue
11 22 33 75 133 190
93-10th Legion app.(12/61); Chameleon Boy app. 11 22 33 79 140 200
94-97,99: 94-1st app. Superboy Revenge Squad 9 18 27 65 113 160
98-(7/62)-18th Legion app; origin & 1st app. Ultra Boy; Pete Ross joins Legion
12 24 36 86 153 220
100-(10/62)-Ultra Boy app; 1st app. Phantom Zone villains, Dr. Xadu & Erndine. 2 pg. map of Krypton; origin Superboy retold; r-cover of Superman #1
18 36 54 133 247 360
101-120: 104-Origin Phantom Zone. 115-Atomic bomb-c. 117-Legion app.
9 18 27 60 100 140
121-128: 124-(10/65)-1st app. Insect Queen (Lana Lang). 125-Legion cameo. 126-Origin Krypto the Super Dog retold with new facts 8 16 24 52 86 120
129-(80-pg. Giant G-22)-Reprints origin Mon-El 9 18 27 63 107 150
130-137,139,140: 131-Legion statues cameo in Dog Legionnaires story. 132-1st app Supremo. 133-Superboy meets Robin 6 12 18 43 69 95
138 (80-pg. Giant G-35) 7 14 21 49 80 110
141-146,148-155,157: 145-Superboy's parents regain their youth. 148-Legion app. 157-Last 12¢ issue 5 10 15 34 55 75
147(6/68)-Giant G-47; 1st origin of L.S.H. (Saturn Girl, Lightning Lad, Cosmic Boy); origin Legion of Super-Pets-r/Adv. #293 6 12 18 43 69 95
147 Replica Edition (2003, $6.95) reprints entire issue; cover recreation by Ordway 7.00
156,165,174 (Giants G-59,71,83): 165-r/1st app. Krypto the Superdog from Adventure Comics #210 5 10 15 32 51 70
158-164,166-171,175: 171-1st app. Aquaboy 3 6 9 17 25 32
172,173,176-Legion app.: 172-1st app. & origin Yango (The Super Ape). 176-Partial photo-c; last 15¢ issue 3 6 9 18 27 35
177-184,186,187 (All 52 pgs.): 182-All new origin of the classic World's Finest team (Superman & Batman) as teenagers (2/72, 22pgs). 184-Origin Dial H for Hero-r
3 6 9 19 29 38
185-Also listed as DC 100 Pg. Super Spectacular #12; Legion-c/story; Teen Titans, Kid Eternity(r/Hit #46), Star Spangled Kid-r(S.S. #55)
(see DC 100 Pg. Super Spectacular #12 for price)
188-190,192,194,196: 188-Origin Karkan. 196-Last Superboy solo story
2 4 6 11 16 20
191,193,195: 191-Origin Sunboy retold; Legion app. 193-Chameleon Boy & Shrinking Violet get new costumes. 195-1st app. Erg-1/Wildfire; Phantom Girl gets new costume
2 4 6 13 18 22
197-Legion series begins; Lightning Lad's new costume
3 6 9 19 29 38
198,199: 198-Element Lad & Princess Projectra get new costumes
3 6 9 14 19 24
200-Bouncing Boy & Duo Damsel marry; J'onn J'onzz cameo
3 6 9 16 22 28
201,204,206,207,209: 201-Re-intro Erg-1 as Wildfire. 204-Supergirl resigns from Legion. 206-Ferro Lad & Invisible Kid app. 209-Karate Kid gets new costume
2 4 6 10 14 18
202,205-(100 pgs.): 202-Light Lass gets new costume; Mike Grell's 1st comic work-i (5-6/74)
4 8 12 28 44 60
203-Invisible Kid killed by Validus 3 6 9 15 21 26
208,210: 208-(68 pgs.). 208-Legion of Super-Villains app. 210-Origin Karate Kid
3 6 9 14 19 24
211-220: 212-Matter-Eater Lad resigns. 216-1st app. Tyroc, who joins the Legion in #218
2 4 6 8 11 14
221-230,246-249: 226-Intro. Dawnstar. 228-Death of Chemical King
1 3 4 6 8 10
231-245: (Giants). 240-Origin Dawnstar. 242-(52 pgs.). 243-Legion of Substitute Heroes app. 243-245-(44 pgs.). 2 4 6 9 13 16
244,245-(Whitman variants; low print run, no issue# shown on cover)
3 6 9 14 19 24
246-248-(Whitman variants; low ...) 2 4 6 10 14 18
250-258: 253-Intro Blok. 257-Return of Bouncing Boy & Duo Damsel by Ditko
1 2 3 5 6 8
251-258-(Whitman variants; low print run) 2 4 6 9 13 16
Annual 1 (Sum/64, 84 pgs.)-Origin Krypto-r 17 34 51 128 227 325
Spectacular 1 (1980, Giant)-1st comic distributed only through comic stores; mostly-r
1 3 4 6 8 10

NOTE: ***Neal Adams** c-143, 145, 146, 148-155, 157-161, 163, 164, 166-168, 172, 173, 175, 176, 178. **M. Anderson** a-178,179, 245i. **Ditko** a-257p. **Grell** a-202i, 203-219, 220-224p, 235p; c-207-232, 235, 236p, 237, 239p, 240p, 243p, 246, 258. **Nasser** a(p)-222, 225, 226, 230, 231, 233, 236. **Simonson** a-237p. **Starlin** a(p)-239, 250, 251; c-238. **Staton** a-227p, 243-249p, 252-258p; c-247-251p. **Swan/Moldoff** c-109. **Tuska** a-172, 173, 176, 183, 235p. **Wood** inks-153-155, 157-161. Legion app.-172, 173, 176, 177, 183, 184, 188, 190, 191, 193, 195, 197-258.*

SUPERBOY (TV)(2nd Series)(The Adventures of...#19 on)
DC Comics: Feb, 1990 - No. 22, Dec, 1991 ($1.00/$1.25)
1-22: Mooney-a(p) in 1-8,18-20; 1-Photo-c from TV show. 8-Bizarro-c/story; Arthur Adams-a(i). 9-12,14-17-Swan-p 3.00
...Special 1 (1992, $1.75) Swan-a 3.00

Superboy (3rd series) #52 © DC

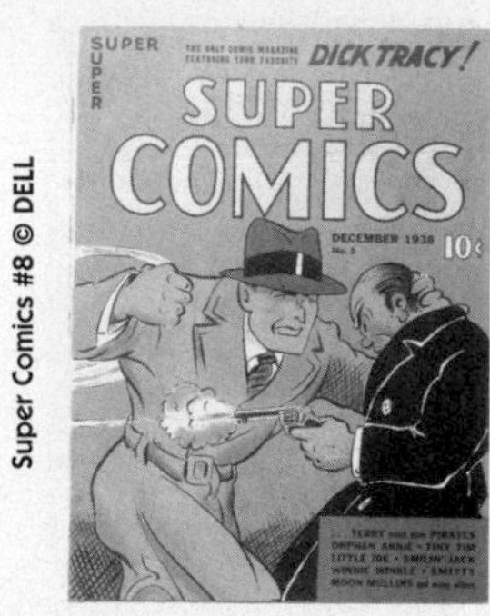

Super Comics #8 © DELL

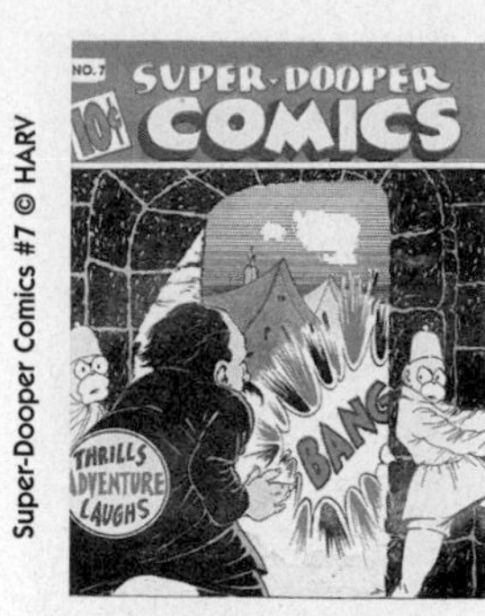

Super-Dooper Comics #7 © HARV

GD VG FN VF VF/NM NM-
2.0 4.0 6.0 8.0 9.0 9.2

SUPERBOY (3rd Series)
DC Comics: Feb, 1994 - No. 100, Jul, 2002 ($1.50/$1.95/$1.99/$2.25)

1-Metropolis Kid from Reign of the Supermen 4.00
2-8,0,9-24,26-76: 6,7-Worlds Collide Pts. 3 & 8. 8-(9/94)-Zero Hour x-over. 0-(10/94). 9-(11/94)-King Shark app. 21-Legion app. 28-Supergirl-c/app. 33-Final Night. 38-41-"Meltdown". 45-Legion-c/app. 47-Green Lantern-c/app. 50-Last Boy on Earth begins. 60-Crosses Hypertime. 68-Demon-c/app. 2.50
25-($2.95)-New Gods & Female Furies app.; w/pin-ups 3.50
77-99: 77-Begin $2.25-c. 79-Superboy's powers return. 80,81-Titans app. 83-New costume. 85-Batgirl app. 90,91-Our Worlds at War x-over 2.50
100-($3.50) Sienkiewicz-c; Grummett & McCrea-a; Superman cameo 3.50
#1,000,000 (11/98) 853rd Century x-over 2.50
Annual 1 (1994, $2.95, 68 pgs.)-Elseworlds story, Pt. 2 of The Super Seven (see Adventures Of Superman Annual #6) 3.00
Annual 2 (1995, $3.95)-Year One story 4.00
Annual 3 (1996, $2.95)-Legends of the Dead Earth 3.00
Annual 4 (1997, $3.95)-Pulp Heroes story 4.00
...Plus 1 (Jan, 1997, $2.95) w/Capt. Marvel Jr. 3.00
...Plus 2 (Fall, 1997, $2.95) w/Slither (Scare Tactics) 3.00
.../Risk Double-Shot 1 (Feb, 1998, $1.95) w/Risk (Teen Titans) 2.50

SUPERBOY & THE RAVERS
DC Comics: Sept, 1996 - No. 19, March, 1998 ($1.95)

1-19: 4-Adam Strange app. 7-Impulse-c/app. 9-Superman-c/app. 2.50

SUPERBOY COMICS
DC Comics: Jan. 1942

nn - Ashcan comic, not distributed to newsstands, only for in-house use. Cover art is Detective Comics #57 with interior being Action Comics #38. A CGC certified 9.2 copy sold for $6,600 in 2003 and for $15,750 in 2008.

SUPERBOY/ROBIN: WORLD'S FINEST THREE
DC Comics: 1996 - No. 2, 1996 ($4.95, squarebound, limited series)

1,2: Superboy & Robin vs. Metallo & Poison Ivy; Karl Kesel & Chuck Dixon scripts; Tom Grummett-c(p)/a(p) 5.00

SUPERBOY'S LEGION (Elseworlds)
DC Comics: 2001 - No. 2, 2001 ($5.95, squarebound, limited series)

1,2-31st century Superboy forms Legion; Farmer-s/i; Davis-a(p)/c 6.00

SUPER BRAT (Li'l Genius #5 on)
Toby Press: Jan, 1954 - No. 4, July, 1954

	GD	VG	FN	VF	VF/NM	NM-
1	8	16	24	42	54	65
2-4: 4-Li'l Teevy by Mel Lazarus	5	10	15	24	30	35
I.W. Reprint #1,2,3,7,8('58): 1-r/#1	2	4	6	8	10	12
I.W. (Super) Reprint #10('63)	2	4	6	8	10	12

SUPERCAR (TV)
Gold Key: Nov, 1962 - No. 4, Aug, 1963 (All painted-c)

	GD	VG	FN	VF	VF/NM	NM-
1	16	32	48	112	209	305
2,3	9	18	27	63	107	150
4-Last issue	10	20	30	73	129	185

SUPER CAT (Formerly Frisky Animals; also see Animal Crackers)
Star Publications #56-58/Ajax/Farrell Publ. (Four Star Comic Corp.): No. 56, Nov, 1953 - No. 58, May, 1954; Aug, 1957 - No. 4, May, 1958

	GD	VG	FN	VF	VF/NM	NM-
56-58-L.B. Cole-c on all	20	40	60	115	180	245
1(1957-Ajax)- "The Adventures of..." c-only	10	20	30	54	72	90
2-4	7	14	21	35	43	50

SUPER CIRCUS (TV)
Cross Publishing Co.: Jan, 1951 - No. 5, Sept, 1951 (Mary Hartline)

	GD	VG	FN	VF	VF/NM	NM-
1-(52 pgs.)-Cast photos on-c	15	30	45	85	130	175
2-Cast photos on-c	10	20	30	58	79	100
3-5	9	18	27	50	65	80

SUPER CIRCUS (TV)
Dell Publ. Co.: No. 542, Mar, 1954 - No. 694, Mar, 1956 (Mary Hartline)

	GD	VG	FN	VF	VF/NM	NM-
Four Color 542: Mary Hartline photo-c	7	14	21	47	76	105
Four Color 592,694: Mary Hartline photo-c	6	12	18	43	69	95

SUPER COMICS
Dell Publishing Co.: May, 1938 - No. 121, Feb-Mar, 1949

	GD	VG	FN	VF	VF/NM	NM-
1-Terry & The Pirates, The Gumps, Dick Tracy, Little Orphan Annie, Little Joe, Gasoline Alley, Smilin' Jack, Smokey Stover, Smitty, Tiny Tim, Moon Mullins, Harold Teen, Winnie Winkle begin	292	584	876	1679	2590	3500
2	106	212	318	610	943	1275

GD VG FN VF VF/NM NM-
2.0 4.0 6.0 8.0 9.0 9.2

	GD	VG	FN	VF	VF/NM	NM-
3	94	188	282	541	833	1125
4,5: 4-Dick Tracy-c; also #8-10,17,26(part),31	73	146	219	420	648	875
6-10	58	116	174	334	517	700
11-20: 20-Smilin' Jack-c (also #29,32)	46	92	138	265	408	550
21-29: 21-Magic Morro begins (origin & 1st app., 2/40). 22,27-Ken Ernst-c (also #25?); Magic Morro c-22,25,27,34	36	72	108	208	329	450
30- "Sea Hawk" movie adaptation-c/story with Errol Flynn	38	76	114	216	343	470
31-40: 34-Ken Ernst-c	30	60	90	174	275	375
41-50: 41-Intro Lightning Jim. 43-Terry & The Pirates ends	25	50	75	148	232	315
51-60	19	38	57	109	172	235
61-70: 62-Flag-c. 65-Brenda Starr-r begin? 67-X-Mas-c	17	34	51	98	154	210
71-80	14	28	42	80	115	150
81-99	13	26	39	74	105	135
100	14	28	42	78	112	145
101-115-Last Dick Tracy (moves to own title)	10	20	30	56	76	95
116-121: 116,118-All Smokey Stover. 117-All Gasoline Alley. 119-121-Terry & The Pirates app. in all	9	18	27	50	65	80

SUPER COPS, THE
Red Circle Productions (Archie): July, 1974 (one-shot)

	GD	VG	FN	VF	VF/NM	NM-
1-Morrow-c/a; art by Pino, Hack, Thorne	1	3	4	6	8	10

SUPER COPS
Now Comics: Sept, 1990 - No. 4, Dec?, 1990 ($1.75)

1-($2.75, 52 pgs.)-Dave Dorman painted-c (both printings) 2.75
2-4 2.50

SUPER CRACKED (See Cracked)

SUPER DC GIANT (25-50¢, all 68-52 pg. Giants)
National Per. Publ.: No. 13, 9-10/70 - No. 26, 7-8/71; V3#27, Summer, 1976 (No #1-12)

	GD	VG	FN	VF	VF/NM	NM-
S-13-Binky	10	20	30	73	129	185
S-14-Top Guns of the West; Kubert-c; Trigger Twins, Johnny Thunder, Wyoming Kid-r; Moreira-r (9-10/70)	5	10	15	32	51	70
S-15-Western Comics; Kubert-c; Pow Wow Smith, Vigilante, Buffalo Bill-r; new Gil Kane-a (9-10/70)	5	10	15	32	51	70
S-16-Best of the Brave & the Bold; Batman-r & Metamorpho origin-r from Brave & the Bold; Spectre pin-up.	4	8	12	24	37	50
S-17-Love 1970 (scarce)	24	48	72	176	326	475
S-18-Three Mouseketeers; Dizzy Dog, Doodles Duck, Bo Bunny-r; Sheldon Mayer-a	9	18	27	61	103	145
S-19-Jerry Lewis; Neal Adams pin-up	9	18	27	65	113	160
S-20-House of Mystery; N. Adams-c; Kirby-r(3)	6	12	18	43	69	95
S-21-Love 1971 (scarce)	29	58	87	217	401	585
S-22-Top Guns of the West; Kubert-c	4	8	12	22	34	45
S-23-The Unexpected	4	8	12	26	41	55
S-24-Supergirl	4	8	12	22	34	45
S-25-Challengers of the Unknown; all Kirby/Wood-r	3	6	9	21	32	42
S-26-Aquaman (1971)-r/S.A. Aquaman origin story from Showcase #30	3	6	9	21	32	42
27-Strange Flying Saucers Adventures (Sum, 1976)	3	6	9	17	25	32

NOTE: ***Sid Greene** r-27p(2), **Heath** r-27. **G. Kane** a-14r(2), 15, 27r(p). **Kubert** r-16.*

SUPER-DOOPER COMICS
Able Mfg. Co./Harvey: 1946 - No. 8, 1946 (10¢, 32 pgs., paper-c)

	GD	VG	FN	VF	VF/NM	NM-
1-The Clock, Gangbuster app.	21	42	63	123	197	270
2	14	28	42	80	115	150
3,4,6	13	26	39	72	101	130
5-Capt. Freedom	14	28	42	80	115	150
7,8-Shock Gibson. 7-Where's Theres A Will by Ed Wheelan, Steve Case Crime Rover, Penny & Ullysses Jr. 8-Sam Hill app.	14	28	42	80	115	150

SUPER DUCK COMICS (The Cockeyed Wonder) (See Jolly Jingles)
MLJ Mag. No. 1-4(9/45)/Close-Up No. 5 on (Archie): Fall, 1944 - No. 94, Dec, 1960 (Also see Laugh #24)(#1-5 are quarterly)

	GD	VG	FN	VF	VF/NM	NM-
1-Origin; Hitler & Hirohito-c	63	126	189	397	674	950
2-Bill Vigoda-c	27	54	81	158	254	350
3-5: 4-20-Al Fagaly-c (most)	18	36	54	105	165	225
6-10	14	28	42	82	121	160
11-20(6/48)	11	22	33	60	83	105
21,23-40 (10/51)	10	20	30	54	72	90
22-Used in **SOTI**, pg. 35,307,308	10	20	30	58	79	100
41-60 (2/55)	8	16	24	44	57	70
61-94	7	14	21	35	43	50

Super Friends (2008 series) #1 © DC

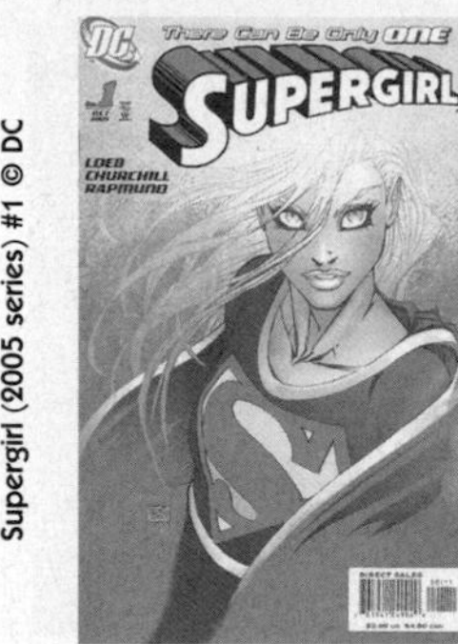

Supergirl (2005 series) #1 © DC

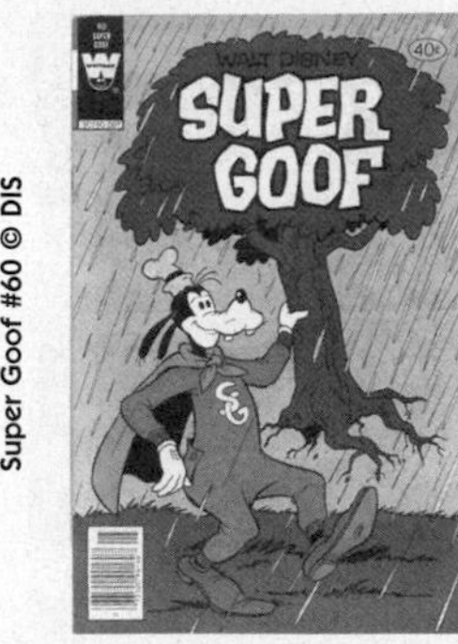

Super Goof #60 © DIS

GD VG FN VF VF/NM NM-
2.0 4.0 6.0 8.0 9.0 9.2

GD VG FN VF VF/NM NM-
2.0 4.0 6.0 8.0 9.0 9.2

SUPER DUPER (Formerly Pocket Comics #1-4?)
Harvey Publications: No. 5, 1941 - No. 11, 1941

5-Captain Freedom & Shock Gibson app. 32 64 96 186 298 410
8,11 20 40 60 115 183 250

SUPER DUPER COMICS (Formerly Latest Comics?)
F. E. Howard Publ.: No. 3, May-June, 1947

3-1st app. Mr. Monster 15 30 45 94 147 200

SUPER FRIENDS (TV) (Also see Best of DC & Limited Collectors' Edition)
National Periodical Publications/DC Comics: Nov, 1976 - No. 47, Aug, 1981 (#14 is 44 pgs.)

1-Superman, Batman, Robin, Wonder Woman, Aquaman, Atom, Wendy, Marvin & Wonder Dog begin (1st Super Friends) 4 8 12 28 44 60
2-Penguin-c/sty 3 6 9 14 20 25
3-5 2 4 6 13 18 22
6-10,14: 7-1st app. Wonder Twins & The Seraph. 8-1st app. Jack O'Lantern. 9-1st app. Icemaiden. 14-Origin Wonder Twins 2 4 6 10 14 18
11-13,15-30: 13-1st app. Dr. Mist. 25-1st app. Fire as Green Fury. 28-Bizarro app. 2 4 6 8 10 12
13-16,20-23,25,32-(Whitman variants; low print run, no issue# on cover) 2 4 6 9 12 15
31,47: 31-Black Orchid app. 47-Origin Fire & Green Fury 2 4 6 9 12 15
32-46: 36,43 Plastic Man app 1 3 4 6 8 10
TBP (2001, $14.95) r/#1,6-9,14,21,27 & L.C.E. C-41; Alex Ross-c 15.00
...: Truth, Justice and Peace TPB (2003, $14.95) r/#10,12,13,25,28,29,31,36,37 15.00
NOTE: *Estrada a-1p, 2p. Orlando a-1p. Staton a-43, 45.*

SUPER FRIENDS (All ages stories with puzzles and games)(Based on Mattel toy line)
DC Comics: May, 2008 - Present ($2.25)

1-5-Superman, Batman, Wonder Woman, Aquaman, Flash & Green Lantern 2.50

SUPER FUN
Gillmor Magazines: Jan, 1956 (By A.W. Nugent)

1-Comics, puzzles, cut-outs by A.W. Nugent 7 14 21 35 43 50

SUPER FUNNIES (...Western Funnies #3,4)
Superior Comics Publishers Ltd. (Canada): Dec, 1953 - No. 4, Sept, 1954

1-(3-D, 10¢)-...Presents Dopey Duck; make your own 3-D glasses cut-out inside front-c; did not come w/glasses 35 70 105 208 334 460
2-Horror & crime satire 14 28 42 82 121 160
3-Phantom Ranger-c/s; Geronimo, Billy the Kid app. 10 20 30 54 72 90
4-Phantom Ranger-c/story 10 20 30 54 72 90

SUPERGIRL
DC Comics: Feb. 1944

nn - Ashcan comic, not distributed to newsstands, only for in-house use. Cover art is Boy Commandos #1 with interior being Action Comics #80. A copy sold for $15,750 in 2008.

SUPERGIRL (See Action, Adventure #281, Brave & the Bold, Crisis on Infinite Earths #7, Daring New Advs. of..., Super DC Giant, Superman Family, & Super-Team Family)

SUPERGIRL
National Periodical Publ.: Nov, 1972 - No. 9, Dec-Jan, 1973-74; No. 10, Sept-Oct, 1974 (1st solo title)(20¢)

1-Zatanna back-up stories begin, end #5 6 12 18 43 69 95
2-4,6,7,9 4 8 12 22 34 45
5,8,10: 5-Zatanna origin-r. 8-JLA x-over; Batman cameo. 10-Prez 4 8 12 23 36 48
NOTE: *Zatanna in #1-5, 7(Guest); Prez app. in #10. #1-10 are 20¢ issues.*

SUPERGIRL (Formerly Daring New Adventures of...)
DC Comics: No. 14, Dec, 1983 - No. 23, Sept, 1984

14-23: 16-Ambush Bug app. 20-JLA & New Teen Titans app. 3.00
...Movie Special (1985)-Adapts movie; Morrow-a; photo back-c 4.00

SUPERGIRL
DC Comics: Feb, 1994 - No. 4, May, 1994 ($1.50, limited series)

1-4: Guice-a(i) 3.00

SUPERGIRL (See Showcase '96 #8)
DC Comics: Sept, 1996 - No. 80, May, 2003 ($1.95/$1.99/$2.25/$2.50)

1-Peter David scripts & Gary Frank-c/a 1 2 3 5 6 8
1-2nd printing 3.00
2,4-9: 4-Gorilla Grodd-c/app. 6-Superman-c/app. 9-Last Frank-a 4.00
3-Final Night, Gorilla Grodd app. 5.00
10-19: 14-Genesis x-over. 16-Power Girl app. 3.50
20-35: 20-Millennium Giants x-over; Superman app. 23-Steel-c/app. 24-Resurrection Man x-over. 25-Comet ID revealed; begin $1.99-c 3.00
36-46: 36,37-Young Justice x-over 2.50
47-49,51-74: 47-Begin $2.25-c. 51-Adopts costume from animated series. 54-Green Lantern app. 59-61-Our Worlds at War x-over. 62-Two-Face-c/app. 66,67-Demon-c/app. 68-74-Mary Marvel app. 70-Nauck-a. 73-Begin $2.50-c 2.50
50-($3.95) Supergirl's final battle with the Carnivore 4.00
75-80: 75-Re-intro. Kara Zor-El; cover swipe of Action Comics #252 by Haynes; Benes-a. 78-Spectre app. 80-Last issue; Romita-c 2.50
#1,000,000 (11/98) 853rd Century x-over 3.00
Annual 1 (1996, $2.95)-Legends of the Dead Earth 3.00
Annual 2 (1997, $3.95)-Pulp Heroes; LSH app.; Chiodo-c 4.00
...: Many Happy Returns TPB (2003, $14.95) r/#75-80; intro. by Peter David 15.00
...Plus (2/97, $2.95) Capt.(Mary) Marvel-c/app.; David-s/Frank-a 3.00
.../Prysm Double-Shot 1 (Feb, 1998, $1.95) w/Prysm (Teen Titans) 2.50
...: Wings (2001, $5.95) Elseworlds; DeMatteis-s/Tolagson-a 6.00
TPB-('98, $14.95) r/Showcase '96 #8 & Supergirl #1-9 15.00

SUPERGIRL (See Superman/Batman #8 & #19)
DC Comics: No. 0, Oct, 2005 - Present ($2.99)

0-Reprints Superman/Batman #19 with white variant of that cover 3.00
1-Loeb-s/Churchill-a; two covers by Churchill & Turner; Power Girl app. 5.00
1-2nd printing with B&W sketch variant of Turner-c 3.00
1-3rd printing with variant-c homage to Action Comics #252 by Churchill 3.00
2-4: 2-Teen Titans app. 3-Outsiders app.; covers by Turner & Churchill 3.00
5-($3.99) Supergirl vs. Supergirl; Churchill & Turner-c 4.00
6-32: 6-9-One Year Later; Power Girl app. 11-Intro. Powerboy. 12-Terra debut; Conner-a 20-Amazons Attack x-over. 21,22-Karate Kid app. 28-31-Resurrection Man app. 3.00
...: Candor TPB (2007, $14.99) r/#6-9; and pages from JSA Classified #2, Superman #223, Superman/Batman #27 and JLA #122,123 15.00
...: Identity TPB (2007, $19.99) r/#10-16 and story from DCU Infinite Holiday Special 20.00
...: Power TPB (2006, $14.99) r/#1-5 and Superman/Batman #19; variant-c gallery 15.00

SUPERGIRL AND THE LEGION OF SUPER-HEROES (Continues from Legion of Super-Heroes #15, Apr, 2006)(Continues as Legion of Super-Heroes #37)
DC Comics: No. 16, May, 2006 - No. 36, Jan, 2008 ($2.99)

16-Supergirl appears in the 31st century 4.00
16-2nd printing 3.00
17-36: 23-Mon-el cameo. 24,25-Mon-el returns 3.00
...: Adult Education TPB (2007, $14.99) r/#20-25 & LSH #6,9,13-15 15.00
...: Dominator War TPB (2007, $14.99) r/#26-30 15.00
...: Strange Visitor From Another Century TPB (2006, $14.99) r/#16-19 & LSH #11,12,15 15.00
...: The Quest For Cosmic Boy TPB (2008, $14.99) r/#31-36 15.00

SUPERGIRL/LEX LUTHOR SPECIAL (Supergirl and Team Luthor on-c)
DC Comics: 1993 ($2.50, 68 pgs., one-shot)

1-Pin-ups by Byrne & Thibert 2.50

SUPER GOOF (Walt Disney) (See Dynabrite & The Phantom Blot)
Gold Key No. 1-57/Whitman No. 58 on: Oct, 1965 - No. 74, July, 1984

1 4 8 12 28 44 60
2-5 3 6 9 16 23 30
6-10 3 6 9 14 19 24
11-20 2 4 6 8 11 14
21-30 1 3 4 6 8 10
31-50 1 2 3 4 5 7
51-57 6.00
58,59 (Whitman) 1 2 3 5 6 8
60(8/80), 62(11/80) 3-pack only (scarce) 4 8 12 24 37 50
61(9-10/80) 3-pack only (rare) 4 8 12 26 41 55
63-66('81) 1 2 3 5 6 8
63 (1/81, 40¢-c) Cover price error variant (scarce) 2 4 6 10 14 18
67-69: 67(2/82), 68(2-3/82), 69(3/82) 6.00
70-74 (#90180 on-c; pre-pack, nd, nd code): 70(5/83), 71(8/83), 72(5/84), 73(6/84), 74(7/84) 3 6 9 16 22 28
NOTE: *Reprints in #16, 24, 28, 29, 37, 38, 43, 45, 46, 54(1/2), 56-58, 65(1/2), 72(r-#2).*

SUPER GREEN BERET (Tod Holton...)
Lightning Comics (Milson Publ. Co.): Apr, 1967 - No. 2, Jun, 1967

1-(25¢, 68 pgs) 5 10 15 32 51 70
2-(25¢, 68 pgs) 4 8 12 22 34 45

SUPER HEROES (See Giant-Size... & Marvel...)

SUPER HEROES
Dell Publishing Co.: Jan, 1967 - No. 4, June, 1967

1-Origin & 1st app. Fab 4 4 8 12 24 37 50
2-4 3 6 9 17 25 32

Superior Stories #1 © Nesbit

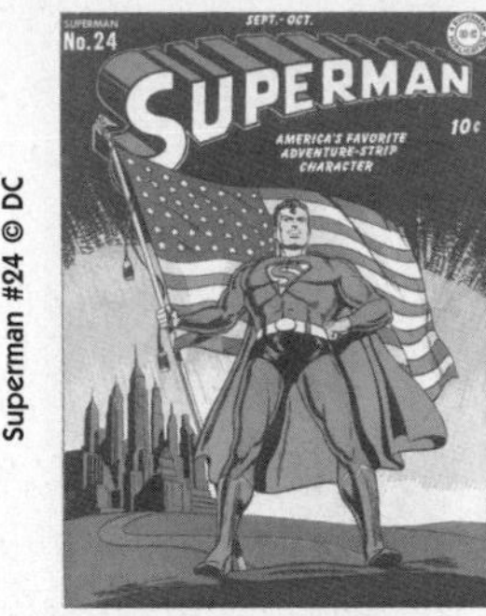

Superman #24 © DC

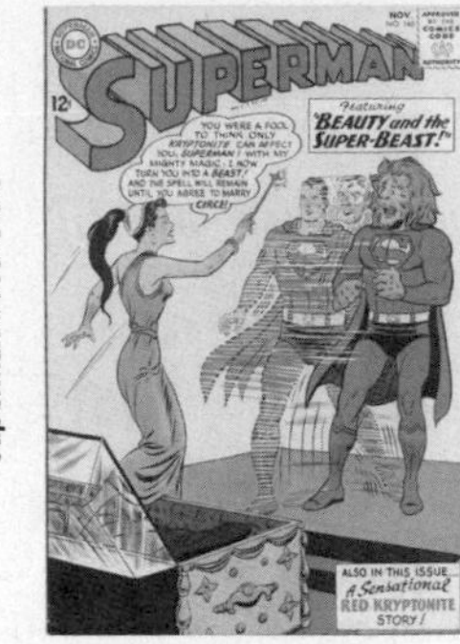

Superman #165 © DC

	GD 2.0	VG 4.0	FN 6.0	VF 8.0	VF/NM 9.0	NM- 9.2

SUPER-HEROES BATTLE SUPER-GORILLAS (See DC Special #16)
National Periodical Publications: Winter, 1976 (52 pgs., all reprints, one-shot)

1-Superman, Batman, Flash stories; Infantino-a(p) 2 4 6 10 14 18

SUPER HEROES VERSUS SUPER VILLAINS
Archie Publications (Radio Comics): July, 1966 (no month given)(68 pgs.)

1-Flyman, Black Hood, Web, Shield-r; Reinman-a 6 12 18 41 66 90

SUPERHERO WOMEN, THE - FEATURING THE FABULOUS FEMALES OF MARVEL COMICS (See Fireside Book Series)

SUPERICHIE (Formerly Super Richie)
Harvey Publications: No. 5, Oct, 1976 - No. 18, Jan, 1979 (52 pgs. giants)

5-Origin/1st app. new costumes for Rippy & Crashman 2 4 6 9 13 16
6-18 2 4 6 8 10 12

SUPERIOR STORIES
Nesbit Publishers, Inc.: May-June, 1955 - No. 4, Nov-Dec, 1955

1-The Invisible Man by H.G. Wells 23 46 69 133 214 295
2-4: 2-The Pirate of the Gulf by J.H. Ingrahams. 3-Wreck of the Grosvenor by William Clark Russell. 4-The Texas Rangers by O'Henry 11 22 33 62 86 110
NOTE: *Morisi c/a in all. Kiwanis stories in #3 & 4. #4 has photo of Gene Autry on-c.*

SUPER MAGIC (Super Magician Comics #2 on)
Street & Smith Publications: May, 1941

V1#1-Blackstone the Magician-c/story; origin/1st app. Rex King (Black Fury); Charles Sultan-c; Blackstone-c begin 167 334 501 1052 1776 2500

SUPER MAGICIAN COMICS (Super Magic #1)
Street & Smith Publications: No. 2, Sept, 1941 - V5#8, Feb-Mar, 1947

V1#2-Blackstone the Magician continues; Rex King, Man of Adventure app. 64 128 192 403 682 960
3-Tao-Anwar, Boy Magician begins 41 82 123 247 406 565
4-7,9-12: 4-Origin Transo. 11-Supersnipe app. 39 78 117 230 370 510
8-Abbott & Costello story (1st app?, 11/42) 40 80 120 238 387 535
V2#1-The Shadow app. 41 82 123 246 403 560
2-12: 5-Origin Tigerman. 8-Red Dragon begins 20 40 60 118 189 260
V3#1-12: 5-Origin Mr. Twilight 20 40 60 118 189 260
V4#1-12: 5-KKK-c/sty. 11-Nigel Elliman Ace of Magic begins (3/46) 16 32 48 92 144 195
V5#1-6 16 32 48 92 144 195
7,8-Red Dragon by Edd Cartier-c/a 39 78 117 230 370 510
NOTE: *Jack Binder c-1-14(most). Red Dragon c-V5#7, 8.*

SUPERMAN (See Action Comics, Advs. of..., All-New Coll. Ed., All-Star Comics, Best of DC, Brave & the Bold, Cosmic Odyssey, DC Comics Presents, Heroes Against Hunger, JLA, The Kents, Krypton Chronicles, Limited Coll. Ed., Man of Steel, Phantom Zone, Power Record Comics, Special Edition, Steel, Super Friends, Superman: The Man of Steel, Superman: The Man of Tomorrow, Taylor's Christmas Tabloid, Three-Dimension Advs., World Of Krypton, World Of Metropolis, World Of Smallville & World's Finest)

SUPERMAN (Becomes Adventures of...#424 on)
National Periodical Publ./DC Comics: Summer, 1939 - No. 423, Sept, 1986
(#1-5 are quarterly)

1(nn)-1st four Action stories reprinted; origin Superman by Siegel & Shuster; has a new 2 pg. origin plus 4 pgs. omitted in Action story; see The Comics Magazine #1 & More Fun #14-17 for Superman prototype app.; cover r/splash page from Action #10; 1st pin-up Superman on back-c - 1st pin-up in comics 25,000 50,000 75,000 190,000 315,000 440,000
1-Reprint, Oversize 13-1/2x10". **WARNING:** This comic is an exact duplicate reprint of the original except for its size. DC published it in 1978 with a second cover titling it as a Famous First Edition. There have been many reported cases of the outer cover being removed and the interior sold as the original edition. The reprint with the new outer cover removed is practically worthless. See Famous First Edition for value.
2-All daily strip-r; full pg. ad for N.Y. World's Fair 1550 3100 4650 11,800 21,400 31,000
3-2nd story-r from Action #5; 3rd story-r from Action #6 944 1888 2832 6797 11,899 17,000
4-2nd mention of Daily Planet (Spr/40); also see Action #23; 2nd & 3rd app. Luthor (red-headed; also see Action #23) 667 1334 2001 4802 8401 12,000
5-4th Luthor app. (red hair) 528 1056 1584 3802 6651 9500
6,7: 6-1st splash pg. in a Superman comic. 7-1st Perry White? (11-12/40) 353 706 1059 2400 4200 6000
8-10: 10-5th app. Luthor (1st bald Luthor, 5-6/41) 329 658 987 2237 3919 5600
11-13,15: 13-Jimmy Olsen & Luthor app. 273 546 819 1720 2910 4100
14-Patriotic Shield-c classic by Fred Ray 423 846 1269 3000 5250 7500
16,18-20: 16-1st Lois Lane-c this title (5-6/42); 2nd Lois-c after Action #29 220 440 660 1386 2343 3300
17-Hitler, Hirohito-c 312 624 936 2122 3711 5300
21,22,25: 25-Clark Kent's only military service; Fred Ray's only super-hero story 157 314 471 989 1670 2350
23-Classic periscope-c 183 366 549 1153 1952 2750
24-Classic Jack Burnley flag-c 267 534 801 1682 2841 4000
26-Classic war-c 247 494 741 1556 2628 3700
27-29: 27,29-Lois Lane-c. 28-Lois Lane Girl Reporter series begins, ends #40,42 140 280 420 882 1491 2100
28-Overseas edition for Armed Forces; same as reg. #28 140 280 420 882 1491 2100
30-Origin & 1st app. Mr. Mxyztplk (9-10/44)(pronounced "Mix-it-plk") in comic books; name later became Mxyzptlk ("Mix-yez-pit-l-ick"); the character was inspired by a combination of the name of Al Capp's Joe Blyfstyk (the little man with the black cloud over his head) & the devilish antics of Bugs Bunny; he 1st app. in newspapers 3/7/44; Superman flies for the first time 267 534 801 1682 2841 4000
31-40: 33-(3-4/45)-3rd app. Mxyztplk. 35,36-Lois Lane-c. 38-Atomic bomb story (1-2/46); delayed because of gov't censorship; Superman shown reading Batman #32 on cover. 40-Mxyztplk-c 118 236 354 743 1259 1775
41-50: 42-Lois Lane-c. 45-Lois Lane as Superwoman (see Action #60 for 1st app.). 46-(5-6/47)-1st app. Superboy this title? 48-1st time Superman travels thru time 97 194 291 611 1031 1450
51,52: 51-Lois Lane-c 82 164 246 517 871 1225
53-Third telling of Superman origin; 10th anniversary issue ('48); classic origin-c by Boring 317 634 951 1981 3391 4800
54,56-60: 57-Lois Lane as Superwoman-c. 58-Intro Tiny Trix 82 164 246 517 871 1225
55-Used in **SOTI**, pg. 33 83 166 249 523 887 1250
61-Origin Superman retold; origin Green Kryptonite (1st Kryptonite story); Superman returns to Krypton for 1st time & sees his parents for 1st time since infancy, discovers he's not an Earth man 153 206 459 964 1632 2300
62-70: 62-Orson Welles-c/story. 65-1st Krypton Foes: Mala, Kizo, & U-Ban. 66-2nd Superbaby story. 67-Perry Como-c/story. 68-1st Luthor-c this title (see Action Comics) 80 160 240 504 852 1200
71-75: 74-2nd Luthor-c this title. 75-Some have #74 on-c 77 154 231 481 816 1150
76-Batman x-over; Superman & Batman learn each other's I.D. for the 1st time (5-6/52) (also see World's Finest #71) 227 454 681 1430 2415 3400
77-81: 78-Last 52 pg. issue. 81-Used in **POP**, pg. 88 68 136 204 428 727 1025
82-87,89,90: 89-1st Curt Swan-c in title 62 124 186 391 658 925
88-Prankster, Toyman & Luthor team-up 67 134 201 422 711 1000
91-95: 95-Last precode issue (2/55) 53 106 159 334 567 800
96-99: 96-Mr. Mxyztplk-c/story 48 96 144 298 499 700
100 (9-10/55)-Shows cover to #1 on-c 223 446 669 1383 2367 3350
101-105,107-110: 109-1st S.A. issue 45 90 135 279 465 650
106 (7/56)-Retells origin 47 94 141 291 483 675
111-120 41 82 123 250 413 575
121,122,124-127,129: 127-Origin/1st app. Titano. 129-Intro/origin Lori Lemaris, The Mermaid 37 74 111 215 345 475
123-Pre-Supergirl tryout-c/story (8/58). 45 90 135 279 465 650
128-(4/59)-Red Kryptonite used. Bruce Wayne x-over who protects Superman's i.d. (3rd story) 38 76 114 226 363 500
130-(7/59)-2nd app, Krypto, the Superdog with Superman (see Sup.'s Pal Jimmy Olsen #29) (all other previous app. w/Superboy) 38 76 114 226 363 500
131-139: 135-2nd Lori Lemaris app. 139-Lori Lemaris app.; 28 56 84 164 265 365
140-1st Blue Kryptonite & Bizarro Supergirl; origin Bizarro Jr. #1 29 58 87 169 272 375
141-145,148: 142-2nd Batman x-over 24 48 72 140 225 310
146-(7/61)-Superman's life story; back-up hints at Earth II. Classic-c 33 66 99 192 309 425
147(8/61)-7th Legion app; 1st app. Legion of Super-Villains; 1st app. Adult Legion; swipes-c to Adv. #247 30 60 90 174 280 385
149(11/61)-8th Legion app. (cameo); "The Death of Superman" imaginary story; last 10¢ issue 27 54 81 158 254 350
150,151,153,154,157,159,160: 157-Gold Kryptonite used (see Adv. #299); Mon-el app.; Lightning Lad cameo (11/62) 11 22 33 79 140 200
152,155,156,158,162: 152(4/62)-15th Legion app. 155-(8/62)-Legion app; Lightning Man & Cosmic Man, & Adult Legion app. 156,162-Legion app. 158-1st app. Flamebird & Nightwing & Nor-Kan of Kandor (12/62) 12 24 36 82 146 210
161-1st told death of Ma and Pa Kent 12 24 36 82 146 210
161-2nd printing (1987, $1.25)-New DC logo; sold thru So Much Fun Toy Stores (cover title: Superman Classic) 4.00
163-166,168-180: 166-XMas-c. 168-All Luthor issue; JFK tribute/memorial. 169-Bizarro Invasion of Earth-c/story; last Sally Selwyn. 170-Pres. Kennedy story is finally published after delay from #168 due to assassination. 172,173-Legion cameos. 174-Super-Mxyzptlk; Bizarro app. 10 20 30 67 116 165
167-New origin Brainiac, text reference of Brainiac 5 descending from adopted human son

Superman #330 © DC

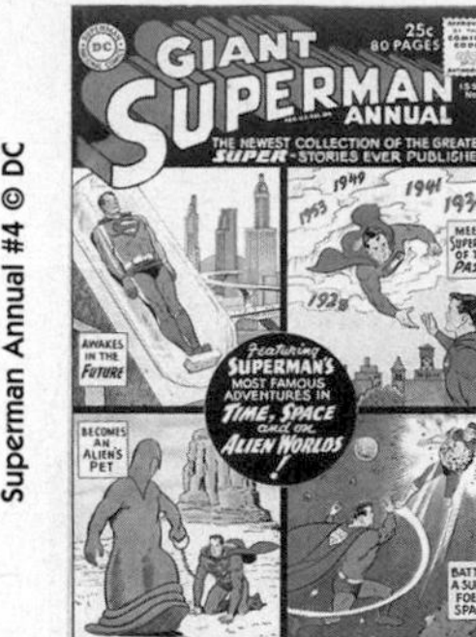

Superman Annual #4 © DC

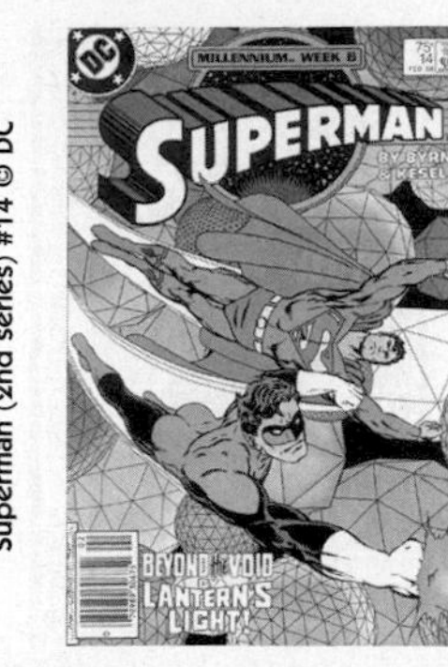

Superman (2nd series) #14 © DC

GD VG FN VF VF/NM NM-
2.0 4.0 6.0 8.0 9.0 9.2

Brainiac II; intro Tharla (later Luthor's wife) 11 22 33 79 140 200
181,182,184-186,188-192,194-196,198,200: 181-1st 2465 story/series. 182-1st S.A. app. of The Toyman (1/66). 189-Origin/destruction of Krypton II.
8 16 24 54 90 125
183 (Giant G-18) 10 20 30 70 123 175
187,193,197 (Giants G-23,G-31,G-36) 9 18 27 60 100 140
199-1st Superman/Flash race (8/67): also see Flash #175 & World's Finest #198,199 (r-in Limited Coll. Ed. C-48) 26 52 78 192 359 525
201,203-206,208-211,213-216: 213-Brainiac-5 app. 216-Last 12¢ issue
5 10 15 32 51 70
202 (80-pg. Giant G-42)-All Bizarro issue 6 12 18 41 66 90
207,212,217 (Giants G-48,G-54,G-60): 207-30th anniversary Superman (6/68)
6 12 18 41 66 90
218-221,223-226,228-231 4 8 12 28 44 60
222,239(Giants, G-66,G-84) 6 12 18 39 62 85
227,232(Giants, G-72,G-78)-All Krypton issues 6 12 18 39 62 85
233-2nd app. Morgan Edge; Clark Kent switches from newspaper reporter to TV newscaster; all Kryptonite on earth destroyed; classic Neal Adams-c
7 14 21 50 83 115
234-238 4 8 12 28 44 60
240-Kaluta-a; last 15¢ issue 4 8 12 22 34 45
241-244 (All 52 pgs.): 241-New Wonder Woman app. 243-G.A.-r/#38
4 8 12 24 37 50
245-Also listed as DC 100 Pg. Super Spectacular #7; Air Wave, Kid Eternity, Hawkman-r; Atom-r/Atom #3 (see DC 100 Pg. Super Spectacular #7 for price)
246-248,250,251,253 (All 52 pgs.): 246-G.A.-r/#40. 248-World of Krypton story. 251-G.A.-r/#45. 253-Finlay-a, 2 pgs., G.A.-r/#1 4 8 12 24 37 50
249,254-Neal Adams-a. 249-(52 pgs.); 1st app. Terra-Man (Swan-a) & origin-s by Dick Dillin (p) & Neal Adams (inks) 5 10 15 34 55 75
252-Also listed as DC 100 Pg. Super Spectacular #13; Ray(r/Smash #17), Black Condor, (r/Crack #18), Hawkman(r/Flash #24); Starman-r/Adv. #67; Dr. Fate & Spectre-r/More Fun #57; N. Adams-c (see DC 100 Pg. Super Spectacular #13 for price)
255-271,273-277,279-283: 263-Photo-c. 264-1st app. Steve Lombard. 276-Intro Capt. Thunder. 279-Batman, Batgirl app. 282-Luthor battlesuit 2 4 6 10 14 18
272,278,284-All 100 pgs. G.A.-r in all. 272-r/2nd app. Mr. Mxyztplk from Action #80
4 8 12 28 44 60
285-299: 289-Partial photo-c. 292-Origin Lex Luthor retold
2 4 6 8 10 12
300-(6/76) Superman in the year 2001 3 6 9 18 27 35
301-350: 301,320-Solomon Grundy app. 323-Intro. Atomic Skull. 327-329-(44 pgs.). 327-Kobra app. 330-More facts revealed about I.D. 338-The bottled city of Kandor enlarged. 344-Frankenstein & Dracula app. 6.00
321-323,325-327,329-332,335-345,348,350 (Whitman variants; low print run; no issue # on cover) 2 4 6 8 10 12
351-399: 353-Brief origin. 354,355,357-Superman 2020 stories (354-Debut of Superman III). 356-World of Krypton story (also #360,367,375). 366-Fan letter by Todd McFarlane. 372-Superman 2021 story. 376-Free 16 pg. preview Daring New Advs. of Supergirl. 377-Free 16 pg. preview Masters of the Universe 5.00
400 (10/84, $1.50, 68 pgs.)-Many top artists featured; Chaykin painted cover, Miller back-c; Steranko-s/a (10 pages) 6.00
401-422: 405-Super-Batman story. 408-Nuclear Holocaust-c/story. 411-Special Julius Schwartz tribute issue. 414,415-Crisis x-over. 422-Horror-c 4.00
409-(7/85) Variant-c with Superman/Superhombre logo (no reported sales)
423-Alan Moore scripts; Perez-a(i); last Earth I Superman story, cont'd in Action #583
1 3 4 6 8 10
Annual 1(10/60, 84 pgs.)-Reprints 1st Supergirl story/Action #252; r/Lois Lane #1; Krypto-r (1st Silver Age DC annual) 83 166 249 706 1353 2000
Annual 2(Win, 1960-61)-Super-villain issue; Brainiac, Titano, Metallo, Bizarro origin-r
38 76 114 293 547 800
Annual 3(Sum, 1961)-Strange Lives of Superman 25 50 75 185 343 500
Annual 4(Win, 1961-62)-11th Legion app; 1st Legion origins (text & pictures); advs. in time, space & on alien worlds 21 42 63 155 288 420
Annual 5(Sum, 1962)-All Krypton issue 17 34 51 126 233 340
Annual 6(Win, 1962-63)-Legion-r/Adv. #247 15 30 45 111 206 300
Annual 7(Sum, 1963)-Origin-r/Superman-Batman team/Adv. 275; r/1955 Superman dailies
12 24 36 87 156 225
Annual 8(Win, 1963-64)-All origins issue 11 22 33 79 140 200
Annual 9(8/64)-Was advertised but came out as 80 Page Giant #1 instead
Annual 9(1983)-Toth/Austin-a 6.00
Annuals 10-13: 10(1984, $1.25)-M. Anderson inks. 11(1985)-Moore scripts. 12(1986)-Bolland-c. 13-(1/08, $3.99) Camelot Falls finale 4.00
Special 1-3('83-'85): 1-G. Kane-c/a; contains German-r 4.00
The Amazing World of Superman "Official Metropolis Edition" (1973, $2.00, treasury-size)-Origin retold; Wood-r(i) from Superboy #153,161; poster incl. (half price if poster missing)
4 8 12 26 41 55
11195 (2/79, $1.95, 224 pgs.)-Golden Press 4 8 12 22 34 45

NOTE: ***N. Adams** a-249i, 254p; c-204-206, 210, 212-215, 219, 231i, 233-237, 240-243, 249-252, 254, 263, 307, 308, 313, 314, 317. **Adkins** a-323i. **Austin** c-368i. **Wayne Boring** art-late 1940's to early 1960's. **Buckler** a(p)-352, 363, 364, 369; c(p)-324-327, 356, 363, 368, 369, 373, 376, 378. **Burnley** a-252r; c-19-25, 30, 33, 34, 35p, 38p, 39p, 45p. **Fine** a-252r. **Kaluta** a-400. **Gil Kane** a-272r, 367, 372, 375, Special 2; c-374p, 375p, 377, 381, 382, 384-390, 392, Annual 9, Special 2. **Joe Kubert** c-216. **Morrow** a-238. **Mortimer** a-250r. **Perez** c-364p. **Fred Ray** a-25; c-6, 8-18. **Starlin** c-355. **Staton** a-354i, 355i. **Swan/Moldoff** c-149. **Williamson** a(i)-408-410, 412-416; c-408i, 409i. **Wrightson** a-400, 416.*

SUPERMAN (2nd Series) (Title continues numbering from Adventures of Superman #649)
DC Comics: Jan, 1987 - No. 226, Apr, 2006; No. 650, May, 2006 - Present (75¢-$2.99)

0-(10/94) Zero Hour; released between #93 & #94 2.50
1-Byrne-c/a begins; intro new Metallo 5.00
2-8,10: 3-Legends x-over; Darkseid-c & app. 7-Origin/1st app. Rampage. 8-Legion app. 3.00
9-Joker-c 4.50
11-15,17-20,22-49,51,52,54-56,58-67: 11-1st new Mr. Mxyzptlk. 12-Lori Lemaris revived. 13-1st app. new Toyman. 13,14-Millennium x-over. 20-Doom Patrol app.; Supergirl cameo. 31-Mr. Mxyzptlk app. 37-Newsboy Legion app. 41 Lobo app. 44-Batman storyline, part 1. 45-Free extra 8 pgs. 54-Newsboy Legion story. 63-Aquaman x-over. 67-Last $1.00-c 2.50
16,21: 16-1st app. new Supergirl (4/88). 21-Supergirl-c/story; 1st app. Matrix who becomes new Supergirl 4.00
50-($1.50, 52 pgs.)-Clark Kent proposes to Lois 5.00
50-2nd printing 2.50
53-Clark reveals i.d. to Lois (Cont'd from Action #662) 3.00
53-2nd printing 2.50
57-($1.75, 52 pgs.) 3.00
68-72: 65,66,68-Deathstroke-c/stories. 70-Superman & Robin team-up 2.50
73-Doomsday cameo 5.00
74-Doomsday Pt. 2 (Cont'd from Justice League #69); Superman battles Doomsday 6.00
73,74-2nd printings 2.50
75-($2.50)-Collector's Ed.; Doomsday Pt. 6; Superman dies; polybagged w/poster of funeral, obituary from Daily Planet, postage stamp & armband premiums (direct sales only)
2 4 6 10 14 18
75-Direct sales copy (no upc code, 1st print) 1 2 3 5 6 8
75-Direct sales copy (no upc code, 2nd-4th prints) 2.50
75-Newsstand copy w/upc code 1 2 3 5 6 8
75-Platinum Edition; given away to retailers 60.00
76,77-Funeral For a Friend parts 4 & 8 3.00
78-($1.95)-Collector's Edition with die-cut outer-c & mini poster; Doomsday cameo 3.00
78-($1.50)-Newsstand Edition w/poster and different-c; Doomsday-c & cameo 2.50
79-81,83-89: 83-Funeral for a Friend epilogue; new Batman (Azrael) cameo. 87,88-Bizarro-c/story 2.50
82-($3.50)-Collector's Edition w/all chromium-c; real Superman revealed; Green Lantern x-over from G.L. #46; no ads 6.00
82-($2.00, 44 pgs.)-Regular Edition w/different-c 2.50
90-99: 93-(9/94)-Zero Hour. 94-(11/94). 95-Atom app. 96-Brainiac returns 2.50
100-Death of Clark Kent foil-c 4.00
100-Newsstand 3.00
101-122: 101-Begin $1.95-c; Black Adam app. 105-Green Lantern app. 110-Plastic Man-c/app. 114-Brainiac app; Dwyer-c. 115-Lois leaves Metropolis. 116-(10/96)-1st app. Teen Titans by Jurgens & Perez in 8 pg. preview. 117-Final Night. 118-Wonder Woman app. 119-Legion app. 122-New powers 2.50
123-Collector's Edition w/glow in the dark-c, new costume 6.00
123-Standard ed., new costume 4.00
124-149: 128-Cyborg-c/app. 131-Birth of Lena Luthor. 132-Superman Red/Superman Blue. 134-Millennium Giants. 136,137-Superman 2999. 139-Starlin-a. 140-Grindberg-a 2.50
150-($2.95) Standard Ed.; Brainiac 2.0 app.; Jurgens-s 3.00
150-($3.95) Collector's Ed. w/holo-foil enhanced variant-c 4.00
151-158: 151-Loeb-s begins; Daily Planet reopens 2.50
159-174: 159-$2.25-c begin. 161-Joker-c/app. 162-Aquaman-c/app. 163-Young Justice app. 165-JLA app.; Ramos; Madureira, Liefeld, A. Adams, Wieringo, Churchill-a. 166-Collector's and reg. editions. 167-Return to Krypton. 168-Batman-c/app.(cont'd in Detective #756). 171-173-Our Worlds at War. 173-Sienkiewicz-a (2 pgs.). 174-Adopts black & red "S" logo 2.50
175-($3.50) Joker: Last Laugh x-over; Doomsday-c/app. 3.50
176-189,191-199: 176,180-Churchill-a. 180-Dracula app. 181-Bizarro-c/app. 184-Return to Krypton II. 189-Van Fleet-c. 192,193,195,197-199-New Supergirl app. 2.50
190-($2.25) Regular edition 2.50
190-($3.95) Double-Feature Issue; included reprint of Superman: The 10¢ Adventure 4.00
200-($3.50) Gene Ha-c/art by various; preview art by Yu & Bermejo 3.50
201-Mr Majestic-c/app.; cover swipe of Action #1 2.50
202,203-Godfall parts 3,6; Turner-c; Caldwell-a(p). 203-Jim Lee sketch pages 2.50
204-Jim Lee-c/a begins; Azzarello-s 3.00
204-Diamond Retailer Summit edition with sketch cover 125.00
205-214: 205-Two covers by Jim Lee and Michael Turner. 208-JLA app. 211-Battles Wonder

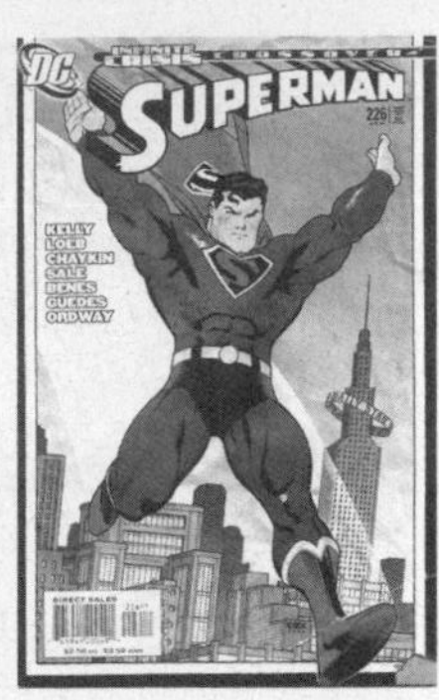

Superman (2nd series) #226 © DC

Superman #675 © DC

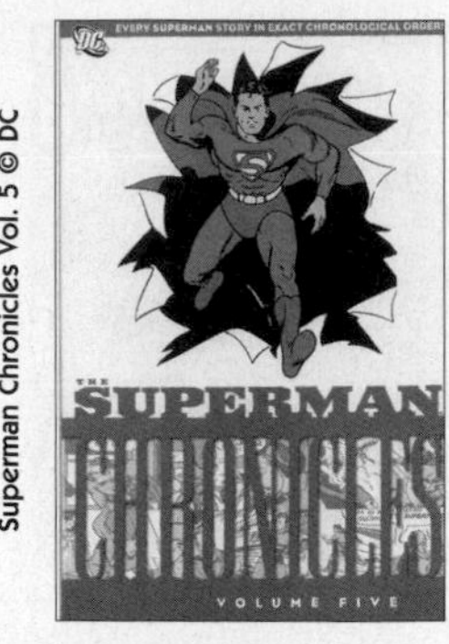

Superman Chronicles Vol. 5 © DC

GD 2.0 | VG 4.0 | FN 6.0 | VF 8.0 | VF/NM 9.0 | NM- 9.2

Woman 2.50
215-($2.99) Conclusion to Azzarello/Lee arc 3.00
216-218,220-226: 216-Captain Marvel app. 221-Bizarro & Zoom app. 226-Earth-2 Superman story; Chaykin,Sale, Benes, Ordway-a 2.50
219-Omac/Sacrifice pt. 1; JLA app. 3.00
219-2nd printing with red background variant-c 2.50
(Title continues numbering from Adventures of Superman #649)
650-(5/06) One Year Later; Clark powerless after Infinite Crisis 3.00
651-665,667-669,671-674.676-678: 652-Begin $2.99-c. 654-658,662-664,667-Pacheco-a. 665-Origin of Jimmy Olsen. 671-673-Insect Queen. 676,677-Ross-c 3.00
666, 670,675-($3.99) 666-Simonson-a. 670-The Third Kryptonian. 675-Ross-c 4.00
#1,000,000 (11/98) 853rd Century x-over; Gene Ha-c 2.50
Annual 1,2: 1 (1987)-No Byrne-a. 2 (1988)-Byrne-a; Newsboy Legion; Guardian returns 4.00
Annual 3-6 ('91-'94 68 pgs.): 1-Armageddon 2001 x-over; Batman app.; Austin-c(i) & part inks. 4-Eclipso app. 6-Elseworlds sty 3.00
Annual 3-2nd & 3rd printings; 3rd has silver ink 2.50
Annual 7 (1995, $3.95, 69 pgs.)-Year One story 4.00
Annual 8 (1996, $2.95)-Legends of the Dead Earth story 3.00
Annual 9 (1997, $3.95)-Pulp Heroes story 4.00
Annual 10 (1998, $2.95)-Ghosts; Wrightson-c 3.00
Annual 11 (1999, $2.95)-JLApe; Art Adams-c 3.00
Annual 12 (2000, $3.50)-Planet DC 3.50
...: 80 Page Giant (2/99, $4.95) Jurgens-c 5.00
...: 80 Page Giant 2 (6/99, $4.95) Harris-c 5.00
...: 80 Page Giant 3 (11/00, $5.95) Nowlan-c; art by various 6.00
Special 1 (1992, $3.50, 68 pgs.)-Simonson-c/a 5.00

SUPERMAN (Hardcovers and Trade Paperbacks)
... and the Legion of Super-Heroes HC (2008, $24.99) r/Action Comics #858-863, covers and variants; intro. by Giffen; Gary Frank design sketch pages 25.00
...: Back in Action TPB (2007, $14.99) r/Action Comics #841-843 and DC Comics Presents #4,17,24; commentary by Busiek 15.00
.../Batman: Saga of the Super Sons TPB (2007, $19.99) r/Super Sons stories from '70s World's Finest #215,216,221,222,224,228,230,231,233,242,263 & Elseworlds 80-Page Giant 20.00
...: Camelot Falls HC (2007, $19.99, dustjacket) r/Superman #654-658 20.00
...: Camelot Falls SC (2008, $12.99) r/Superman #654-658 13.00
...: Camelot Falls Vol. 2 HC (2008, $19.99, dj) r/Superman #662-664,667 & Ann. #13 20.00
...: Chronicles Vol. 1 ('06, $14.99, TPB) r/early Superman app. in Action Comics #1-13, New York World's Fair 1939 and Superman #1 15.00
...: Chronicles Vol. 2 ('07, $14.99, TPB) r/early Superman app. in Action Comics #14-20 and Superman #2,3 15.00
...: Chronicles Vol. 3 ('07, $14.99, TPB) r/early Superman app. in Action Comics #21-25, Superman #3,4 and New York World's Fair 1940 15.00
...: Chronicles Vol. 4 ('08, $14.99, TPB) r/early Superman app. in Action Comics #26-31, Superman #6,7 15.00
...: Chronicles Vol. 5 ('08, $14.99, TPB) r/early Superman app. in Action Comics #32-36, Superman #8,9 and World's Best Comics #1 15.00
...: Critical Condition ('03, $14.95, TPB) r/2000 Kryptonite poisoning storyline 15.00
.../ Doomsday: The Collection Edition (2006, $19.99) r/Superman/Doomsday: Hunter/Prey #1-3, Doomsday Ann. #1, Superman: The Doomsday Wars #1-3, Advs. of Superman #594 and Superman #175; intro. by Dan Jurgens 20.00
...: Daily Planet (2006, $19.99, TPB)-Reprints stories of Daily Planet staff 20.00
...: Emperor Joker TPB (2007, $14.99) reprints 2000 x-over from Superman titles 15.00
...: Endgame (2000, $14.95, TPB)-Reprints Y2K and Brainiac story line 15.00
...: Eradication! The Origin of the Eradicator (1996, $12.95, TPB) 13.00
...: Escape From Bizarro World (2008, $24.99, dustjacket) r/Action #855-857; early apps. in Superman #140, DC Comics Presents #71 and Man of Steel #5; Vaughan intro. 25.00
...: Exile (1998, $14.95, TPB)-Reprints space exile following execution of Kryptonian criminals; 1st Eradicator 15.00
...: For Tomorrow Volume 1 HC (2005, $24.99, dustjacket) r/#204-209; intro by Azzarello; new cover and sketch section by Lee 25.00
...: For Tomorrow Volume 1 SC (2005, $14.99) r/#204-209; foil-stamped S emblem-c 15.00
...: For Tomorrow Volume 2 HC (2005, $24.99, dustjacket) r/#210-215; afterword and sketch section by Lee; new Lee-c with foil-stamped S emblem 25.00
...: For Tomorrow Volume 2 SC (2005, $14.99) r/#210-215; foil-stamped S emblem-c 15.00
...: Godfall HC (2004, $19.95, dustjacket) r/Action #812-813, Advs. of Superman #625-626, Superman #202-203; Caldwell sketch pages; Turner cover gallery; new Turner-c 20.00
...: Godfall SC (2004, $9.99) r/Action #812-813, Advs. of Superman #625-626, Superman #202-203; Caldwell sketch pages; Turner cover gallery; new Turner-c 10.00
...: Infinite Crisis TPB (2006, $12.99) r/Infinite Crisis #5, I.C. Secret Files and Origins 2006, Action Comics #836, Superman #226 and Advs. of Superman #649 13.00
... In the Forties ('05, $19.99, TPB) Intro. by Bob Hughes 20.00
... In the Fifties ('02, $19.95, TPB) Intro. by Mark Waid 20.00
... In the Sixties ('01, $19.95, TPB) Intro. by Mark Waid 20.00
... In the Seventies ('00, $19.95, TPB) Intro. by Christopher Reeve 20.00
... In the Eighties ('06, $19.99, TPB) Intro. by Jerry Ordway 20.00
... In the Name of Gog ('05, $17.99, TPB) r/Action Comics #820-825 18.00
...: Last Son HC (2008, $19.99) r/Action Comics #844-846,851 and Annual #11; sketch pages and variant covers; Marc McClure intro. 20.00
... No Limits ('00, $14.95, TPB) Reprints early 2000 stories 15.00
...: Our Worlds at War Book 1 ('02, $19.95, TPB) r/1st half of x-over 20.00
...: Our Worlds at War Book 2 ('02, $19.95, TPB) r/2nd half of x-over 20.00
...: Our Worlds at War - The Complete Collection ('06, $24.99, TPB) r/entire x-over 25.00
...: President Lex TPB (2003, $17.95) r/Luthor's run for the White House; Harris-c 18.00
...: Redemption TPB (2007, $12.99) r/Superman #659,666 & Action Comics #848,849 13.00
...: Return to Krypton (2004, $17.95, TPB) r/2001-2002 x-over 18.00
...: Sacrifice (2005, $14.99, TPB) prelude x-over to Infinite Crisis; r/Superman #218-220, Advs. of Superman #642,643; Action #829, Wonder Woman #219,220 15.00
... : Strange Attractors (2006, $14.99, TPB) r/Action Comics #827,828,830-835 15.00
...: That Healing Touch TPB (2005, $14.99) r/Advs. of Superman #633-638 & Superman Secret Files 2004 15.00
The Bottle City of Kandor TPB (2007, $14.99)-Reprints 1st app. in Action #242 and other stories; Nightwing and Flamebird app. 15.00
The Death of Clark Kent (1997, $19.95, TPB)-Reprints Man of Steel #43 (1 page), Superman #99 (1 page),#100-102, Action #709 (1 page), #710,711, Advs. of Superman #523-525, Superman:The Man of Tomorrow #1 20.00
The Death of Superman (1993, $4.95, TPB)-Reprints Man of Steel #17-19, Superman #73-75, Advs. of Superman #496,497, Action #683,684, & Justice League #69 1 2 3 5 6 8
The Death of Superman, 2nd & 3rd printings 5.00
The Death of Superman Platinum Edition 15.00
...: The Greatest Stories Ever Told ('04, $19.95, TPB) Ross-c, Uslan intro. 20.00
...: The Greatest Stories Ever Told Vol. 2 ('06, $19.99, TPB) Ross-c, Greenberger intro. 20.00
...: The Journey ('06, $14.99, TPB) r/Action Comics #831 & Superman #217,221-225 15.00
...: The Man of Steel Vol. 2 ('03, $19.95, TPB) r/Superman #1-3, Action #584-586, Advs. of Superman #424-426 & Who's Who Update '87 20.00
...: The Man of Steel Vol. 3 ('04, $19.95, TPB) r/Superman #4-6, Action #587-589, Advs. of Superman #427-429; intro. by Ordway; new Ordway-c 20.00
...: The Man of Steel Vol. 4 ('05, $19.99, TPB) r/Superman #7,8; Action #590,591; Advs. of Superman #430,431; Legion of Super-Heroes #37,38; new Ordway-c 20.00
...: The Man of Steel Vol. 5 ('06, $19.99, TPB) r/Superman #9-11, Action #592-593, Advs. of Superman #432-435; intro. by Mike Carlin; new Ordway-c 20.00
...: The Man of Steel Vol. 6 ('08, $19.99, TPB) r/Superman #12 & Ann. #1, Action #594-595 & Ann. #1, Advs. of Superman Ann.#1; Booster Gold #23; new Ordway-c 20.00
The Trial of Superman ('97, $14.95, TPB) reprints story arc 15.00
The World of Krypton ('08, $14.99, TPB) r/World of Krypton Vol. 2 #1-4 and various tales of Krypton and its history; Kupperberg intro. 15.00
The Wrath of Gog ('05, $14.99, TPB) reprints Action Comics #812-819 15.00
...: They Saved Luthor's Brain ('00, $14.95) r/ "death" and return of Luthor 15.00
...: 3-2-1 Action! ('08, $14.99) Jimmy Olsen super-powered stories; Steve Rude-c 15.00
...: 'Til Death Do Us Part ('01, $17.95) reprints; Mahnke-c 18.00
...: Time and Time Again (1994, $7.50, TPB)-Reprints 8.00
...: Transformed ('98, $12.95, TPB) r/post Final Night powerless Superman to Electric Superman 13.00
...: Unconventional Warfare (2005, $14.95, TPB) r/Adventures of Superman #625-632 and pages from Superman Secret Files 2004 15.00
...: Up, Up and Away! (2006, $14.99, TPB) r/Superman #650-653 and Action #837-840 15.00
... Vs. Lex Luthor (2006, $19.99, TPB) reprints 1st meeting in Action #23 and 11 other classic duels 1940-2001 20.00
... Vs. The Flash (2005, $19.99, TPB) reprints their races from Superman #199, Flash #175, World's Finest #198, DC Comics Presents #1&2, Advs. of Superman #463 & DC First: Flash/Superman; new Alex Ross-c 20.00
... Vs. The Revenge Squad (1999, $12.95, TPB) 13.00

NOTE: ***Austin** a(i)-1-3. **Byrne** a-1-16p, 17, 19-21p, 22; c-1-17, 20-22; scripts-1-22. **Guice** c/a-64. **Kirby** c-37p. **Joe Quesada** c-Annual 4. **Russell** c/a-23i. **Simonson** c-69i. #19-21 2nd printings sold in multi-packs.*

SUPERMAN (one-shots)
Daily News Magazine Presents DC Comics' Superman nn-(1987, 8 pgs.)-Supplement to New York Daily News; Perez-c/a 5.00
...: A Nation Divided (1999, $4.95)-Elseworlds Civil War story 5.00
... & Savage Dragon: Chicago (2002, $5.95) Larsen-a; Ross-c 6.00
... & Savage Dragon: Metropolis (11/99, $4.95) Bogdanove-a 5.00
...: At Earth's End (1995, $4.95)-Elseworlds story 5.00
...: Blood of My Ancestors (2003, $6.95)-Gil Kane & John Buscema-a 7.00
...: Distant Fires (1998, $5.95)-Elseworlds; Chaykin-s 6.00
...: Emperor Joker (10/00, $3.50)-Follows Action #769 3.50
...: End of the Century (2/00, $24.95, HC)-Immonen-s/a 25.00
...: End of the Century (2003, $17.95, SC)-Immonen-s/a 18.00
... For Earth (1991, $4.95, 52 pgs, printed on recycled paper)-Ordway wraparound-c 5.00
...IV Movie Special (1987, $2.00)-Movie adaptation; Heck-a 3.00

Superman Adventures #26 © DC

Superman/Batman #8 © DC

Superman: Confidential #11 © DC

GD VG FN VF VF/NM NM-
2.0 4.0 6.0 8.0 9.0 9.2

...Gallery, The 1 (1993, $2.95)-Poster-a 3.00
..., Inc. (1999, $6.95)-Elseworlds Clark as a sports hero; Garcia-Lopez-a 7.00
...: Infinite City HC (2005, $24.99, dustjacket) Mike Kennedy-s/Carlos Meglia-a 25.00
...: Infinite City SC (2006, $17.99) Mike Kennedy-s/Carlos Meglia-a 18.00
...: Kal (1995, $5.95)-Elseworlds story 6.00
...: Lex 2000 (1/01, $3.50)-Election night for the Luthor Presidency 3.50
...: Monster (1999, $5.95)-Elseworlds story; Anthony Williams-a 6.00
... Movie Special-(9/83)-Adaptation of Superman III; other versions exist with store logos on bottom 1/3 of-c 4.00
...: Our Worlds at War Secret Files 1-(8/01, $5.95)-Stories & profile pages 6.00
... Plus 1(2/97, $2.95)-Legion of Super-Heroes-c/app. 3.00
...'s Metropolis-(1996, $5.95, prestige format)-Elseworlds; McKeever-c/a 6.00
...: Speeding Bullets-(1993, $4.95, 52 pgs.)-Elseworlds 5.00
.../Spider-Man-(1995, $3.95)-r/DC and Marvel Presents... 4.00
... 10-Cent Adventure 1 (3/02, 10¢) McDaniel-a; intro. Cir-El Supergirl 2.25
...: The Earth Stealers 1-(1988, $2.95, 52 pgs, prestige format) Byrne script; painted-c 4.00
...: The Earth Stealers 1-2nd printing 3.00
...: The Legacy of Superman #1 (3/93, $2.50, 68 pgs.)-Art Adams-c; Simonson-a 4.00
...: The Last God of Krypton ('99,$4.95) Hildebrandt Bros.-a/Simonson-s 5.00
...: The Odyssey ('99, $4.95) Clark Kent's post-Smallville journey 5.00
...: 3-D (12/98, $3.95)-with glasses 4.00
.../Thundercats (1/04, $5.95) Winick-s/Garza-a; two covers by Garza & McGuinness 6.00
.../Through the Ages (2006, $3.99) r/Action #1, Superman ('87) #7; origins and pin-ups 4.00
.../Toyman-(1996, $1.95) 2.50
...: True Brit (2004, $24.95, HC w/dust jacket) Elseworlds; Kal-El's rocket lands in England; co-written by John Cleese and Kim Howard Johnson; John Byrne-a 25.00
...: True Brit (2005, $17.99, TPB) Elseworlds; Kal-El's rocket lands in England 18.00
...: Under A Yellow Sun (1994, $5.95, 68 pgs.)-A Novel by Clark Kent; embossed-c 6.00
... Vs. Darkseid: Apokolips Now! 1 (3/03, $2.95) McKone-a; Kara (Supergirl #75) app. 3.00
...: War of the Worlds (1999, $5.95)-Battles Martians 0.00
...: Where is thy Sting? (2001, $6.95)-McCormack-Sharp-c/a 7.00
...: Y2K (2/00, $4.95)-1st Brainiac 13 app.; Guice-c/a 5.00

SUPERMAN ADVENTURES, THE (Based on animated series)
DC Comics: Oct, 1996 - No. 66, Apr, 2002 ($1.75/$1.95/$1.99)

1-Rick Burchett-c/a begins; Paul Dini script; Lex Luthor app.; silver ink, wraparound-c 3.00
2-20,22: 2-McCloud scripts begin; Metallo-c/app. 3-Brainiac-c/app. 6-Mxyzptlk-c/app. 2.50
21-($3.95) 1st animated Supergirl 5.00
23-66: 23-Begin $1.99-c; Livewire app. 25-Batgirl-c/app. 28-Manley-a. 54-Retells Superman #233 "Kryptonite Nevermore" 58-Ross-c 2.25
Annual 1 (1997, $3.95)-Zatanna and Bruce Wayne app. 4.00
Special 1 (2/98, $2.95) Superman vs. Lobo 3.00
TPB (1998, $7.95) r/#1-6 8.00
... Vol 1: Up, Up and Away (2004, $6.95, digest) r/#16,19,22-24; Amancio-a 7.00
... Vol 2: The Never-Ending Battle (2004, $6.95) r/#25-29 7.00
... Vol 3: Last Son of Krypton (2006, $6.99) r/#30-34 7.00
... Vol 4: The Man of Steel (2006, $6.99) r/#35-39 7.00

SUPERMAN ALIENS 2: GOD WAR (Also see Superman Vs. Aliens)
DC Comics/Dark Horse Comics: May, 2002 - No. 4, Nov, 2002 ($2.99, limited series)

1-4-Bogdanove & Nowlan-a; Darkseid & New Gods app. 3.00
TPB (6/03, $12.95) r/#1-4 13.00

SUPERMAN & BATMAN: GENERATIONS (Elseworlds)
DC Comics: 1999 - No. 4, 1999 ($4.95, limited series)

1-4-Superman & Batman team-up from 1939 to the future; Byrne-c/s/a 5.00
TPB (2000, $14.95) r/series 15.00

SUPERMAN & BATMAN: GENERATIONS II (Elseworlds)
DC Comics: 2001 - No. 4, 2001 ($5.95, limited series)

1-4-Superman, Batman & others team-up from 1942-future; Byrne-c/s/a 6.00
TPB (2003, $19.95) r/series 20.00

SUPERMAN & BATMAN: GENERATIONS III (Elseworlds)
DC Comics: Mar, 2003 - No. 12, Feb, 2004 ($2.95, limited series)

1-12-Superman & Batman through the centuries; Byrne-c/s/a 3.00

SUPERMAN & BATMAN VS. ALIENS AND PREDATOR
DC Comics: 2007 - No. 2, 2007 ($5.99, squarebound, limited series)

1,2-Schultz-s/Olivetti-a 6.00
TPB (2007, $12.99) r/#1,2; pencil breakdown pages 13.00

SUPERMAN & BATMAN: WORLD'S FUNNEST (Elseworlds)
DC Comics: 2000 ($6.95, square-bound, one-shot)

nn-Mr. Mxyzptlk and Bat-Mite destroy each DC Universe; Dorkin-s; art by various incl. Ross, Timm, Miller, Allred, Moldoff, Gibbons, Cho, Jimenez 7.00

GD VG FN VF VF/NM NM-
2.0 4.0 6.0 8.0 9.0 9.2

SUPERMAN & BUGS BUNNY
DC Comics: Jul, 2000 - No. 4, Oct, 2000 ($2.50, limited series)

1-4-JLA & Looney Tunes characters meet 2.50

SUPERMAN/BATMAN
DC Comics: Oct, 2003 - Present ($2.95/$2.99)

1-Two covers (Superman or Batman in foreground) Loeb-s/McGuinness-a; Metallo app. 5.00
1-2nd printing (Batman cover) 3.00
1-3rd printing; new McGuinness cover 3.00
1-Diamond/Alliance Retailer Summit Edition-variant cover 100.00
2-6: 2,5-Future Superman app. 6-Luthor in battlesuit 3.00
7-Pat Lee-c/a; Superboy & Robin app. 3.00
8-Michael Turner-c/a; intro. new Kara Zor-El 5.00
8-Second printing with sketch cover 3.00
8-Third printing with new Turner cover 3.00
9-13-Michael Turner-c/a; Wonder Woman app. 10,13-Variant-c by Jim Lee 3.00
14-25: 14-18-Pacheco-a; Lightning Lord, Saturn Queen & Cosmic King app. 19-Supergirl app.; leads into Supergirl #1. 21-25-Bizarro app. 25-Superman & Batman covers; 2nd printing with white bkgrd cover 3.00
26-($3.99) Sam Loeb tribute issue; 2 covers by Turner; story & art by 26 various; back-up by Loeb & Sale 5.00
27-49: 27-Flashback to Earth-2 Power Girl & Huntress; Maguire-a. 34-36-Metal Men app. 3.00
50-($3.99) Thomas Wayne meets Jor-El; Justice League app. 4.00
Annual #1 (12/06, $3.99) Re-imaging of 1st meeting from World's Finest #71 4.00
Annual #2 (5/08, $3.99) Kolins-a; re-imaging of Superman as Supernova story 4.00
...Absolute Power HC (2005, $19.99) r/#14-18 20.00
...Absolute Power SC (2006, $12.99) r/#14-18 13.00
...Public Enemies HC (2004, $19.95) r/#1-6 & Secret Files 2003 20.00
...Public Enemies SC (2005, $12.99) r/#1-6 & Secret Files 2003 13.00
...Secret Files 2003 (11/03, $4.95) Reis-a; pin-ups by various; Loeb/Sale short-s 5.00
... : Supergirl HC (2004, $19.95) r/#8-13; intro by Loeb, cover gallery, sketch pages 20.00
... : Supergirl SC (2005, $12.99) r/#8-13; intro by Loeb, cover gallery, sketch pages 13.00
... : Torment HC (2008, $19.99) r/#37-42; cover gallery, Nguyen sketch pages 20.00
... : Vengeance HC (2006, $19.99) r/#20-25; sketch pages 20.00

SUPERMAN/BATMAN: ALTERNATE HISTORIES
DC Comics: 1996 ($14.95, trade paperback)

nn-Reprints Detective Comics Annual #7, Action Comics Annual #6, Steel Annual #1, Legends of the Dark Knight Annual #4 15.00

SUPERMAN: BIRTHRIGHT
DC Comics: Sept, 2003 - No. 12, Sept, 2004 ($2.95, limited series)

1-12-Waid-s/Leinil Yu-a; retelling of origin and early Superman years 3.00
HC (2004, $29.95, dustjacket) r/series; cover gallery; Waid proposal with Yu concept art 30.00
SC (2005, $19.99) r/series; cover gallery; Waid proposal with Yu concept art 20.00

SUPERMAN COMICS
DC Comics: 1939

nn - Ashcan comic, not distributed to newsstands, only for in-house use. Cover art is Action Comics #7 with interior being Action Comics #8. A CGC certified 9.0 copy sold for $37,375 in 2005 and for $90,000 in 2007.

SUPERMAN CONFIDENTIAL
DC Comics: Jan, 2007 - Present ($2.99)

1-14: 1-5,9-Darwyn Cooke-s/Tim Sale-a/c; origin of Kryptonite re-told. 8-10-New Gods and Darkside app. 3.00

SUPERMAN: DAY OF DOOM
DC Comics: Jan, 2003 - No. 4, Feb, 2003 ($2.95, weekly limited series)

1-4-Jurgens-s/Jurgens & Sienkiewicz-a 3.00
TPB (2003, $9.95) r/#1-4 10.00

SUPERMAN/DOOMSDAY: HUNTER/PREY
DC Comics: 1994 - No. 3, 1994 ($4.95, limited series, 52 pgs.)

1-3 5.00

SUPERMAN FAMILY, THE (Formerly Superman's Pal Jimmy Olsen)
National Per. Publ./DC Comics: No. 164, Apr-May, 1974 - No. 222, Sept, 1982

	GD 2.0	VG 4.0	FN 6.0	VF 8.0	VF/NM 9.0	NM- 9.2
164-(100 pgs.) Jimmy Olsen, Supergirl, Lois Lane begin	4	8	12	28	44	60
165-169 (100 pgs.)	3	6	9	18	27	35
170-176 (68 pgs.)	2	4	6	13	18	22
177-190 (52 pgs.): 177-181-52 pgs. 182-Marshall Rogers-a; $1.00 issues begin; Krypto begins, ends #192. 183-Nightwing-Flamebird begins, ends #194. 189-Brainiac 5, Mon-el app.	2	4	6	9	12	15
191-193,195-199: 191-Superboy begins, ends #198	1	2	3	5	7	9
194,200: 194-Rogers-a. 200-Book length sty	1	3	4	6	8	10

Superman/Gen13 #1 © DC

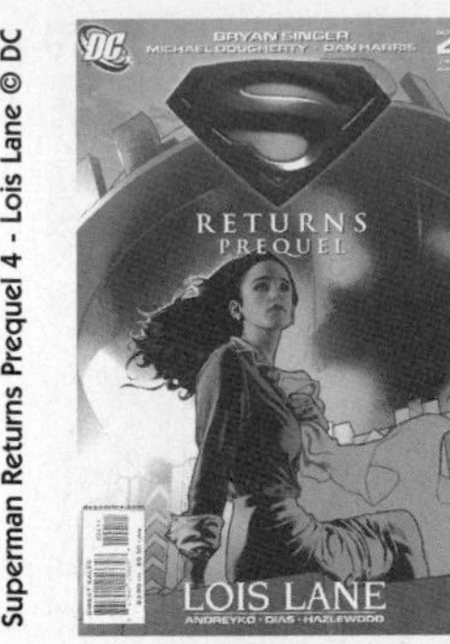

Superman Returns Prequel 4 - Lois Lane © DC

Superman's Girlfriend Lois Lane #136 © DC

	GD	VG	FN	VF	VF/NM	NM-
	2.0	4.0	6.0	8.0	9.0	9.2
201-222: 211-Earth II Batman & Catwoman marry	1	2	3	4	5	7

NOTE: *N. Adams c-182-185. Anderson a-186i. Buckler c(p)-190, 191, 209, 210, 215, 217, 220. Jones a-191-193. Gil Kane c(p)-221, 222. Mortimer a(p)-191-193, 199, 201-222. Orlando a(i)-186, 187. Rogers a-182, 194. Staton a-191-194, 196p. Tuska a(p)-203, 207-209.*

SUPERMAN/FANTASTIC FOUR
DC Comics/Marvel Comics: 1999 ($9.95, tabloid size, one-shot)
1-Battle Galactus and the Cyborg; wraparound-c by Alex Ross and Dan Jurgens; Jurgens-s/a; Thibert-a 10.00

SUPERMAN FOR ALL SEASONS
DC Comics: 1998 - No, 4, 1998 ($4.95, limited series, prestige format)
1-Loeb-s/Sale-a/c; Superman's first year in Metropolis 6.00
2-4 5.00
Hardcover (1999, $24.95) r/#1-4 25.00

SUPERMAN FOR EARTH (See Superman one-shots)

SUPERMAN FOREVER
DC Comics: Jun, 1998 ($5.95, one-shot)
1-($5.95)-Collector's Edition with a 7-image lenticular-c by Alex Ross; Superman returns to normal; s/a by various 7.00
1-($4.95) Standard Edition with single image Ross-c 5.00

SUPERMAN/GEN13
DC Comics (WildStorm): Jun, 2000 - No. 3, Aug, 2000 ($2.50, limited series)
1-3-Hughes-s/ Bermejo-a; Campbell variant-c for each 2.50
TPB (2001, $9.95) new Bermejo-c; cover gallery 10.00

SUPERMAN: KING OF THE WORLD
DC Comics: June, 1999 ($3.95/$4.95, one-shot)
1-($3.95) Regular Ed. 4.00
1-($4.95) Collectors' Ed. with gold foil enhanced-c 5.00

SUPERMAN: LAST SON OF EARTH
DC Comics: 2000 - No. 2, 2000 ($5.95, limited series, prestige format)
1,2-Elseworlds; baby Clark rockets to Krypton; Gerber-s/Wheatley-a 6.00

SUPERMAN: LAST STAND ON KRYPTON
DC Comics: 2003 ($6.95, one-shot, prestige format)
1-Sequel to Superman: Last Son of Earth; Gerber-s/Wheatley-a 7.00

SUPERMAN: LOIS LANE (Girlfrenzy)
DC Comics: Jun, 1998 ($1.95, one shot)
1-Connor & Palmiotti-a 2.50

SUPERMAN/MADMAN HULLABALOO!
Dark Horse Comics: June, 1997 - No. 3, Aug, 1997 ($2.95, limited series)
1-3-Mike Allred-c/s/a 3.00
TPB (1997, $8.95) 9.00

SUPERMAN: METROPOLIS
DC Comics: Apr, 2003 - No. 12, Mar, 2004 ($2.95, limited series)
1-12-Focus on Jimmy Olsen; Austen-s. 1-6-Zezelj-a. 7-12-Kristiansen-a. 8,9-Creeper app. 3.00

SUPERMAN METROPOLIS SECRET FILES
DC Comics: Jun, 2000 ($4.95, one shot)
1-Short stories, pin-ups and profile pages; Hitch and Neary-c 5.00

SUPERMAN: PEACE ON EARTH
DC Comics: Jan, 1999 ($9.95, Treasury-sized, one-shot)
1-Alex Ross painted-c/a; Paul Dini-s 12.00

SUPERMAN: RED SON
DC Comics: 2003 - No. 3, 2003 ($5.95, limited series, prestige format)
1-Elseworlds; Superman's rocket lands in Russia; Mark Millar-s/Dave Johnson-c/a 10.00
2,3 6.00
TPB (2004, $17.95) r/#1-3; intro. by Tom DeSanto; sketch pages 18.00

SUPERMAN RED/ SUPERMAN BLUE
DC Comics: Feb, 1998 ($4.95, one shot)
1-Polybagged w/3-D glasses and reprint of Superman 3-D (1955); Jurgens-plot/3-D cover; script and art by various 5.00
1-($3.95)-Standard Ed.; comic only, non 3-D cover 4.00

SUPERMAN RETURNS... (2006 movie)
DC Comics: Aug, 2006 ($3.99, movie tie-in stories by Singer, Dougherty and Harris)
Prequel 1 - Krypton to Earth; Olivetti-a/Hughes-c; retells Jor-el's story 6.00
Prequel 2 - Ma Kent; Kerschl-a/Hughes-c; Ma Kent during Clark childhood and absence 4.00
Prequel 3 - Lex Luthor; Leonardi-a/Hughes-c; Luthor's 5 years in prison 4.00

GD VG FN VF VF/NM NM-
2.0 4.0 6.0 8.0 9.0 9.2

Prequel 4 - Lois Lane; Dias-a/Hughes-c; Lois during Superman's absence 4.00
The Movie and Other Tales of the Man of Steel (2006, $12.99, TPB) adaptation; origin from Amazing World of Superman; Action #810, Superman #185; Advs. of Superman #575 13.00
The Official Movie Adaptation (2006, $6.99) Pasko-s/Haley-a; photo-c 7.00
...: The Prequels TPB (2006, $12.99) r/the 4 prequels

SUPERMAN: SAVE THE PLANET
DC Comics: Oct, 1998 ($2.95, one-shot)
1-($2.95) Regular Ed.; Luthor buys the Daily Planet 3.00
1-($3.95) Collector's Ed. with acetate cover 4.00

SUPERMAN SCRAPBOOK (Has blank pages; contains no comics)

SUPERMAN: SECRET FILES
DC Comics: Jan, 1998; May 1999 ($4.95)
1,2: 1-Retold origin story, "lost" pages & pin-ups 5.00
... & Origins 2004 (8/04) pin-ups by Lee, Turner and others 5.00
... & Origins 2005 (1/06) short stories and pin-ups by various 5.00

SUPERMAN: SECRET IDENTITY
DC Comics: 2004 - No. 4, 2004 ($5.95, squarebound, mini-series)
1-4-Busiek-s/Immonen-a/c 6.00

SUPERMAN'S GIRLFRIEND LOIS LANE (See Action Comics #1, 80 Page Giant #3, 14, Lois Lane, Showcase #9, 10, Superman #28 & Superman Family)

SUPERMAN'S GIRLFRIEND LOIS LANE (See Showcase #9,10)
National Periodical Publ.: Mar-Apr, 1958 - No. 136, Jan-Feb, 1974; No. 137, Sept-Oct, 1974

	GD	VG	FN	VF	VF/NM	NM-
1-(3-4/58)	323	646	969	2907	5654	8400
2	83	166	249	706	1353	2000
3	53	106	159	451	863	1275
4,5	43	86	129	344	647	950
6,7	35	70	105	270	498	725
8-10: 9-Pat Boone-c/story	30	60	90	222	411	600
11-13,15-19: 12-(10/59)-Aquaman app. 17-(5/60) 2nd app. Brainiac.	18	36	54	133	247	360
14-Supergirl x-over; Batman app. on-c only	19	38	57	139	257	375
20-Supergirl-c/sty	19	38	57	135	250	365
21-28: 23-1st app. Lena Thorul, Lex Luthor's sister; 1st Lois as Elastic Lass. 27-Bizarro-c/story	14	28	42	104	187	270
29-Aquaman, Batman, Green Arrow cover app. and cameo; last 10¢ issue	15	30	45	107	196	285
30-32,34-46,48,49	9	18	27	63	107	150
33(5/62)-Mon-el app.	9	18	27	65	113	160
47-Legion app.	9	18	27	65	113	160
50(7/64)-Triplicate Girl, Phantom Girl & Shrinking Violet app.	9	18	27	65	113	160
51-55,57-67,69: 59-Jor-el app.; Batman back-up sty	7	14	21	47	76	105
56-Saturn Girl app.	7	14	21	49	80	110
68-(Giant G-26)	8	16	24	58	97	135
70-Penguin & Catwoman app. (1st S.A. Catwoman, 11/66; also see Detective #369 for 3rd app.); Batman & Robin cameo	24	48	72	176	326	475
71-Batman & Robin cameo (3 panels); Catwoman story cont'd from #70 (2nd app.); see Detective #369 for 3rd app	14	28	42	103	184	265
72,73,75,76,78	6	12	18	37	59	80
74-1st Bizarro Flash (5/67); JLA cameo	6	12	18	39	62	85
77-(Giant G-39)	7	14	21	49	80	110
79-Neal Adams-c or c(i) begin, end #95,108	6	12	18	39	62	85
80-85,87,88,90-92: 92-Last 12¢ issue	4	8	12	26	41	55
86,95 (Giants G-51,G-63)-Both have Neal Adams-c	6	12	18	41	66	90
89,93: 89-Batman x-over; all N. Adams-c. 93-Wonder Woman-c/story	4	8	12	28	44	60
94,96-99,101-103,107-110	4	8	12	22	34	45
100	4	8	12	24	37	50
104-(Giant G-75)	6	12	18	37	59	80
105-Origin/1st app. The Rose & the Thorn.	6	12	18	37	59	80
106-"Black Like Me" story; Lois changes her skin color to black	7	14	21	45	73	100
111-Justice League-c/s; Morrow-a; last 15¢ issue	4	8	12	24	37	50
112,114-123 (52 pgs.): 122-G.A. Lois Lane-r/Superman #30. 123-G.A. Batman-r/Batman #35 (w/Catwoman)	4	8	12	22	34	45
113-(Giant G-87) Kubert-a (previously unpublished G.A. story)(scarce in NM)	6	12	18	39	66	90
124-135: 130-Last Rose & the Thorn. 132-New Zatanna story	3	6	9	16	22	28
136,137: 136-Wonder Woman x-over	3	6	9	17	25	32
Annual 1(Sum, 1962)-r/L. Lane #12; Aquaman app.	20	40	60	148	274	400

Superman's Pal Jimmy Olsen #53 © DC

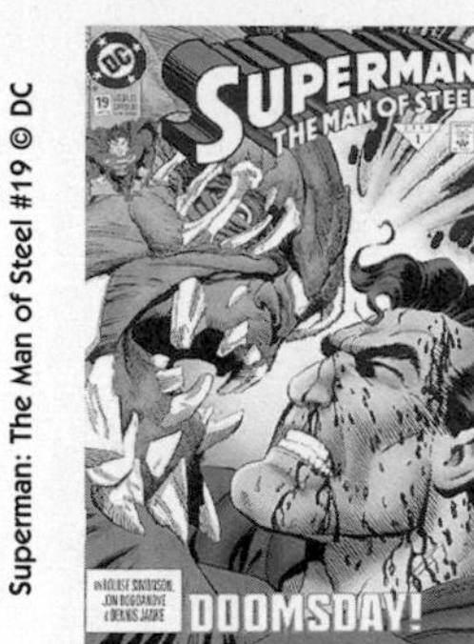

Superman: The Man of Steel #19 © DC

Superman: The Man of Tomorrow #7 © DC

	GD 2.0	VG 4.0	FN 6.0	VF 8.0	VF/NM 9.0	NM- 9.2

Annual 2(Sum, 1963) 14 28 42 103 184 265
NOTE: *Buckler a-117-121p.* ***Curt Swan or Kurt Schaffenberger*** *a-1-81(most); c(p)-1-15.*

SUPERMAN/SHAZAM: FIRST THUNDER
DC Comics: Nov, 2005 - No. 4, Feb, 2006 ($3.50, limited series)
1-4-Retells first meeting; Winick-s/Middleton-a. Dr. Sivana app. 3.50

SUPERMAN: SILVER BANSHEE
DC Comics: Dec, 1998 - No. 2, Jan, 1999 ($2.25, mini-series)
1,2-Brereton-s/c; Chin-a 2.50

SUPERMAN'S NEMESIS: LEX LUTHOR
DC Comics: Mar, 1999 - No. 4, Jun, 1999 ($2.50, mini-series)
1-4-Semeiks-a 2.50

SUPERMAN'S PAL JIMMY OLSEN (Superman Family #164 on)
(See Action Comics #6 for 1st app. & 80 Page Giant)
National Periodical Publ.: Sept-Oct, 1954 - No. 163, Feb-Mar, 1974 (Fourth World #133-148)

	GD 2.0	VG 4.0	FN 6.0	VF 8.0	VF/NM 9.0	NM- 9.2
1	500	1000	1500	4500	8500	12,500
2	138	276	414	1173	2237	3300
3-Last pre-code issue	79	158	237	672	1286	1900
4,5	52	104	156	442	846	1250
6-10	39	78	117	301	563	825
11-20: 15-1st S.A. issue	27	54	81	197	366	535
21-30: 29-(6/58) 1st app. Krypto with Superman	17	34	51	124	230	335
31-Origin & 1st app. Elastic Lad (Jimmy Olsen)	15	30	45	111	206	300
32-40: 33-One pg. biography of Jack Larson (TV Jimmy Olsen). 36-Intro Lucy Lane. 37-2nd app. Elastic Lad & 1st cover app.	12	24	36	87	156	225
41-50: 41-1st J.O. Robot. 48-Intro/origin Superman Emergency Squad	10	20	30	70	123	175
51-56: 56-Last 10¢ issue	8	16	24	58	97	135
57-62,64-70: 57-Olsen marries Supergirl. 62-Mon-El & Elastic Lad app. but not as Legionnaires. 70-Element Boy (Lad) app.	6	12	18	43	69	95
63(9/62)-Legion of Super-Villains app.	7	14	21	45	73	100
71,74,75,78,80-84,86,89,90: 86-Jimmy Olsen Robot becomes Congorilla	5	10	15	34	55	75
72,73,76,77,79,85,87,88: 72(10/63)-Legion app; Elastic Lad (Olsen) joins. 73-Ultra Boy app. 76,85-Legion app. 76-Legion app. 77-Olsen with Colossal Boy's powers & costume; origin Titano retold. 79-(9/64)-Titled The Red-headed Beatle of 1000 B.C. 85-Legion app. 87-Legion of Super-Villains app. 88-Star Boy app.	6	12	18	37	59	80
91-94,96-98	4	8	12	28	44	60
95 (Giant G-25)	7	14	21	45	73	100
99-Olsen w/powers & costumes of Lightning Lad, Sun Boy & Element Lad	5	10	15	30	48	65
100-Legion cameo	5	10	15	32	51	70
101-103,105-112,114-120: 106-Legion app. 110-Infinity-c. 117-Batman & Legion cameo. 120-Last 12¢ issue	4	8	12	22	34	45
104 (Giant G-38)	6	12	18	37	59	80
113,122,131,140 (Giants G-50,G-62,G-74,G-86)	5	10	15	32	51	70
121,123-130,132	3	6	9	20	30	40
133-(10/70)-Jack Kirby story & art begins; re-intro Newsboy Legion; 1st app. Morgan Edge	6	12	18	39	62	85
134-1st app. Darkseid (1 panel, 12/70)	7	14	21	45	73	100
135-2nd app. Darkseid (1 pg. cameo; see New Gods & Forever People); G.A. Guardian app.	4	8	12	28	44	60
136-139: 136-Origin new Guardian. 138-Partial photo-c. 139-Last 15¢ issue	4	8	12	22	34	45
141-150: (25¢,52 pgs.). 141-Photo-c; Newsboy Legion-r by S&K begin; full pg. self-portrait of Jack Kirby; Don Rickles cameo. 149,150-G.A. Plastic Man-r in both; 150-Newsboy Legion app.	3	6	9	20	30	40
151-163	3	6	9	14	19	24

Superman: The Amazing Transformations of Jimmy Olsen TPB (2007, $14.99) reprints Olsen's transformations into Wolf-Man, Elastic Lad, Turtle Boy and others; new Bolland-c 15.00
NOTE: *Issues #141-148 contain* ***Simon & Kirby*** *Newsboy Legion reprints from Star Spangled #7, 8, 9, 10, 11, 12, 13, 14 in that order.* ***N. Adams*** *c-109-112, 115, 117, 118, 120, 121, 132, 134-136, 147, 148.* ***Kirby*** *a-133-139p, 141-148p; c-133, 137, 139, 142, 145p.* ***Kirby/N. Adams*** *c-137, 138, 141-144, 146.* ***Curt Swan*** *c-1-14(most)., 140.*

SUPERMAN SPECTACULAR (Also see DC Special Series #5)
DC Comics: 1982 (Magazine size, 52 pgs., square binding)
1-Saga of Superman Red/ Superman Blue; Luthor and Terra-Man app.; Gonzales & Colletta-a 1 3 4 6 8 10

SUPERMAN: STRENGTH
DC Comics: 2005 - No. 3, 2005 ($5.95, limited series)
1-3: Alex Ross-c/Scott McCloud-s/Aluir Amancio-a 6.00

SUPERMAN / SUPERHOMBRE
DC Comics: Apr, 1945
nn - Ashcan comic, not distributed to newsstands, only for in-house use (no known sales)

SUPERMAN / TARZAN: SONS OF THE JUNGLE
Dark Horse Comics: Oct, 2001 - No. 3, May, 2002 ($2.99, limited series)
1-3-Elseworlds; Kal-El lands in the jungle; Dixon-s/Meglia-a/Ramos-c 3.00

SUPERMAN: THE DARK SIDE
DC Comics: 1998 - No. 3, 1998 ($4.95, squarebound, mini-series)
1-3: Elseworlds; Kal-El lands on Apokolips 5.00

SUPERMAN: THE DOOMSDAY WARS
DC Comics: 1998 - No. 3, 1999 ($4.95, squarebound, mini-series)
1-3: Superman & JLA vs. Doomsday; Jurgens-s/a(p) 5.00

SUPERMAN: THE KANSAS SIGHTING
DC Comics: 2003 - No. 2, 2003 ($6.95, squarebound, mini-series)
1,2-DeMatteis-s/Tolagson-a 7.00

SUPERMAN: THE MAN OF STEEL (Also see Man of Steel, The)
DC Comics: July, 1991 - No. 134, Mar, 2003 ($1.00/$1.25/$1.50/$1.95/$2.25)
0-(10/94) Zero Hour; released between #37 & #38 2.50
1-($1.75, 52 pgs.)-Painted-c 5.00
2-16: 3-War of the Gods x-over. 5-Reads sideways. 10-Last $1.00-c. 14-Superman & Robin team-up 3.00
17-1st brief app. Doomsday 1 2 3 4 5 7
17,18: 17-2nd printing. 18 2nd & 3rd printings 2.50
18-1st full app. Doomsday 1 2 3 5 7 9
19-Doomsday battle issue (c/story) 6.00
20-22: 20,21-Funeral for a Friend. 22-($1.95)-Collector's Edition w/die-cut outer-c & bound-in poster; Steel-c/story 2.50
22-($1.50)-Newsstand Ed. w/poster & different-c 2.50
23-49,51-99: 30-Regular edition. 32-Bizarro-c/story. 35,36-Worlds Collide Pt. 1 & 10. 37-(9/94)-Zero Hour x-over. 38-(11/94). 48-Aquaman app. 54-Spectre-c/app; Lex Luthor app. 56-Mxyzptlk-c/app. 57-G.A. Flash app. 58-Supergirl app. 59-Parasite-c/app.; Steel app. 60-Heintro Bottled City of Kandor. 62-Final Night. 64-New Gods app. 67-New powers. 75-"Death" of Mxyzptlk. 78,79-Millennium Giants. 80-Golden Age style. 92-JLA app. 98-Metal Men app. 2.50
30-($2.50)-Collector's Edition; polybagged with Superman & Lobo vinyl clings that stick to wraparound-c; Lobo-c/story 3.00
50 ($2.95)-The Trial of Superman 4.00
100-($2.99) New Fortress of Solitude revealed 3.00
100-($3.99) Special edition with fold out cardboard-c 4.00
101,102-101-Batman app. 2.50
103-133: 103-Begin $2.25. 105-Batman-c/app. 111-Return to Krypton. 115-117-Our Worlds at War. 117-Maxima killed. 121-Royal Flush Gang app. 128-Return to Krypton II. 2.50
134-($2.75) Last issue; Steel app.; Bogdanove-c 2.75
#1,000,000 (11/98) 853rd Century x-over; Gene Ha-c 2.50
Annual 1-5 ('92-'96,68 pgs.): 1-Eclipso app.; Joe Quesada-c(p). 2-Intro Edge. 3 -Elseworlds; Mignola-c; Batman app. 4-Year One story. 5-Legends of the Dead Earth story 3.00
Annual 6 (1997, $3.95)-Pulp Heroes story 4.00
...Gallery (1995, $3.50) Pin-ups by various 3.50

SUPERMAN: THE MAN OF TOMORROW
DC Comics: 1995 - No. 15, Fall, 1999 ($1.95, quarterly)
1-15: 1-Lex Luthor app. 3-Lex Luthor-c/app; Joker app. 4-Shazam! app. 5-Wedding of Lex Luthor. 10-Maxima-c/app. 13-JLA-c/app. 2.50
#1,000,000 (11/98) 853rd Century x-over; Gene Ha-c 2.50

SUPERMAN: THE SECRET YEARS
DC Comics: Feb, 1985 - No. 4, May, 1985 (limited series)
1-4-Miller-c on all 3.00

SUPERMAN: THE WEDDING ALBUM
DC Comics: Dec, 1996 ($4.95, 96 pgs, one-shot)
1-Standard Edition-Story & art by past and present Superman creators; gatefold back-c. Byrne-c 5.00
1-Collector's Edition-Embossed cardstock variant-c w/ metallic silver ink and matte and gloss varnishes 5.00
Retailer Rep. Program Edition (#'d to 250, signed by Bob Rozakis on back-c) 50.00
TPB ('97, $14.95) r/Wedding and honeymoon stories 15.00

SUPERMAN 3-D (See Three-Dimension Adventures)

SUPERMAN-TIM (See Promotional Comics section)

SUPERMAN VILLAINS SECRET FILES
DC Comics: Jun, 1998 ($4.95, one shot)

Supermouse #1 © STD

Super-Mystery Comics V7 #2 © ACE

Supernatural: Origins #6 © WB

GD VG FN VF VF/NM NM-
2.0 4.0 6.0 8.0 9.0 9.2

1-Origin stories, "lost" pages & pin-ups 5.00

SUPERMAN VS. ALIENS (Also see Superman Aliens 2: God War)
DC Comics/Dark Horse Comics: July, 1995 - No. 3, Sept, 1995 ($4.95, limited series)
1-3: Jurgens/Nowlan-a 5.00

SUPERMAN VS. MUHAMMAD ALI (See All-New Collectors' Edition C-56)

SUPERMAN VS. PREDATOR
DC Comics/Dark Horse Comics: 2000 - No. 3, 2000 ($4.95, limited series)
1-3-Micheline-s/Maleev-a 5.00
TPB (2001, $14.95) r/series 15.00

SUPERMAN VS. THE AMAZING SPIDER-MAN (Also see Marvel Treasury Edition No. 28)
National Periodical Publications/Marvel Comics Group: 1976
($2.00, Treasury sized, 100 pgs.)
1-Superman and Spider-Man battle Lex Luthor and Dr. Octopus; Andru/Giordano-a; 1st Marvel/DC x-over. 7 14 21 50 83 115
1-2nd printing; 5000 numbered copies signed by Stan Lee & Carmine Infantino on front cover & sold through mail 13 26 39 95 168 240
nn-(1995, $5.95)-r/#1 6.00

SUPERMAN VS. THE TERMINATOR: DEATH TO THE FUTURE
Dark Horse/DC Comics: Dec, 1999 - No. 4, Mar, 2000 ($2.95, limited series)
1-4-Grant-s/Pugh-a/c: Steel and Supergirl app. 3.00

SUPERMAN/WONDER WOMAN: WHOM GODS DESTROY
DC Comics: 1997 ($4.95, prestige format, limited series)
1-4-Elseworlds; Claremont-s 5.00

SUPERMAN WORKBOOK
National Periodical Publ./Juvenile Group Foundation: 1945 (B&W, reprints, 68 pgs)
nn-Cover-r/Superman #14 167 334 501 1052 1776 2500

SUPER MARIO BROS. (Also see Adventures of the..., Blip, Gameboy, and Nintendo Comics System)
Valiant Comics: 1990 - No. 5?, 1991 ($1.95, slick-c) V2#1, 1991 - No. 5, 1991
1-Wildman-a 4.00
2-5, V2#1-5-($1.50) 3.00
Special Edition 1 (1990, $1.95)-Wildman-a 3.00

SUPER MARKET COMICS
Fawcett Publications: No date (1950s)
nn - Ashcan comic, not distributed to newsstands, only for in-house use (no known sales)

SUPER MARKET VARIETIES
Fawcett Publications: No date (1950s)
nn - Ashcan comic, not distributed to newsstands, only for in-house use (no known sales)

SUPERMEN OF AMERICA
DC Comics: Mar, 1999 ($3.95/$4.95, one-shot)
1-($3.95) Regular Ed.; Immonen-s/art by various 4.00
1-($4.95) Collectors' Ed. with membership kit 5.00

SUPERMEN OF AMERICA (Mini-series)
DC Comics: Mar, 2000 - No. 6, Aug, 2000 ($2.50)
1-6-Nicieza-s/Braithwaite-a 2.50

SUPERMOUSE (...the Big Cheese; see Coo Coo Comics)
Standard Comics/Pines No. 35 on (Literary Ent.): Dec, 1948 - No. 34, Sept, 1955; No. 35, Apr, 1956 - No. 45, Fall, 1958
1-Frazetta text illos (3) 28 56 84 162 261 360
2-Frazetta text illos 15 30 45 84 127 170
3,5,6-Text illos by Frazetta in all 13 26 39 74 105 135
4-Two pg. text illos by Frazetta 14 28 42 78 112 145
7-10 9 18 27 47 61 75
11-20: 13-Racist humor (Indians) 7 14 21 37 46 55
21-45 6 12 18 31 38 45
1-Summer Holiday issue (Summer, 1957, 25¢, 100 pgs.)-Pines 14 28 42 78 112 145
2-Giant Summer issue (Summer, 1958, 25¢, 100 pgs.)-Pines; has games, puzzles & stories 10 20 30 56 76 95

SUPER-MYSTERY COMICS
Ace Magazines (Periodical House): July, 1940 - V8#6, July, 1949
V1#1-Magno, the Magnetic Man & Vulcan begins (1st app.); Q-13, Corp. Flint, & Sky Smith begin 306 612 918 2081 3641 5200
2 102 204 306 643 1084 1525
3-The Black Spider begins (1st app.) 80 160 240 504 852 1200

GD VG FN VF VF/NM NM-
2.0 4.0 6.0 8.0 9.0 9.2

4-Origin Davy 56 112 168 359 605 840
5-Intro. The Clown & begin series (12/40) 60 120 180 378 639 900
6(2/41) 52 104 156 322 536 750
V2#1(4/41)-Origin Buckskin 50 100 150 310 518 725
2-6(2/42): 6-Vulcan begins again 47 94 141 291 488 685
V3#1(4/42),2: 1-Black Ace begins 41 82 123 256 428 600
3-Intro. The Lancer; Dr. Nemesis & The Sword begin; Kurtzman-c/a(2) (Mr. Risk & Paul Revere Jr.); Robot-c 53 106 159 329 550 770
4-Kurtzman-c/a; classic-c 85 170 255 536 906 1275
5-Kurtzman-a(2); L.B. Cole-a; Mr. Risk app. 51 102 153 316 526 735
6(10/43)-Mr. Risk app.; Kurtzman's Paul Revere Jr.; L.B. Cole-a 51 102 153 316 526 735
V4#1(1/44)-L.B. Cole-a 45 90 135 279 465 650
2-6(4/45): 2,5,6-Mr. Risk app. 32 64 96 186 298 410
V5#1(7/45)-6 32 64 96 186 298 410
V6#1,2,4,5,6: 4-Last Magno. Mr. Risk app. in #2,4-6. 6-New logo 26 52 78 152 244 335
3-Torture c-story 35 70 105 203 327 450
V7#1-6, V8#1-4,6 24 48 72 140 225 310
V8#5-Meskin, Tuska, Sid Greene-a 23 46 69 133 214 295
NOTE: ***Sid Greene** a-V7#4. **Mooney** c-V1#5, 6, V2#1-6. **Palais** a-V5#3, 4; c-V4#6-V5#4, V6#2, V8#4. Bondage c-V2#5, 6, V3#2, 5. Magno c-V1#1-V3#6, V4#2-V5#5, V6#2. The Sword c-V4#1, 6(w/Magno).*

SUPERNATURAL FREAK MACHINE: A CAL MCDONALD MYSTERY
IDW Publishing: Mar, 2005 - No. 3 ($3.99)
1-3-Steve Niles-s/Kelley Jones-a 4.00

SUPERNATURAL LAW (Formerly Wolff & Byrd, Counselors of the Macabre)
Exhibit A Press: No. 24, Oct, 1999 - Present ($2.50/$2.95/$3.50, B&W)
24-35-Batton Lash-s/a. 29-Marie Severin-c. 33-Cerebus spoof 2.50
36-40-($2.95). 37-Frank Cho pin-up and story panels 3.00
(#41) ...First Amendment Issue (2005, $3.50) anti-censorship story; CBLDF info 3.50
(#42) With a Silver Bullet (2006, $3.50) new stories and pin-ups 3.50
(#43) At the Box Office (2006, $3.50) new stories and pin-ups 3.50
(#44) Wolff & Byrd: The Movie (2007, $3.50) new stories and pin-ups 3.50
45-($3.50) Toxic Avenger and Lloyd Kaufman app. 3.50
#1 (2005, $2.95) r/Wolff & Byrd with redrawn and re-toned art; relettered 3.00

SUPERNATURAL LAW SECRETARY MAVIS
Exhibit A Press: 2001 - Present ($2.95/$3.50, B&W)
1-3: 3-DeCarlo-c 3.00
4,5-($3.50) Jaime Hernandez-c 3.50

SUPERNATURAL: ORIGINS (Based on the CW television series)
DC Comics (WildStorm): July, 2007 - No. 6, Dec, 2007 ($2.99, limited series)
1-6: 1-Bradstreet-c; Johnson-s/Smith-a; back-up w/Johns-s/Hester-a 3.00
TPB (2008, $14.99) r/#1-6; sketch pages 15.00

SUPERNATURAL: RISING SON (Based on the CW television series)
DC Comics (WildStorm): Jun, 2008 - No. 6, ($2.99, limited series)
1-4-Johnson & Dessertine-s/Olmos-a. 1-Oliver-c 3.00
1-Variant-c by Nguyen 6.00

SUPERNATURALS
Marvel Comics: Dec, 1998 - No. 4, Dec, 1998 ($3.99, weekly limited series)
1-4-Pulido-s/Balent-c; bound-in Halloween masks 4.00
1-4-With bound-in Ghost Rider mask (1 in 10) 4.00

SUPERNATURAL THRILLERS
Marvel Comics Group: Dec, 1972 - No. 6, Nov, 1973; No. 7, Jun, 1974 - No. 15, Oct, 1975
1-It!; Sturgeon adap. (see Astonishing Tales #21) 3 6 9 18 27 35
2-4,6: 2-The Invisible Man; H.G. Wells adapt. 3-The Valley of the Worm; R.E. Howard adapt. 4-Dr. Jekyll & Mr. Hyde; R.L. Stevenson adapt.. 6-The Headless Horseman; last 20¢ issue 2 4 6 13 18 22
5-1st app. The Living Mummy 6 12 18 41 66 90
7-15: 7-The Living Mummy begins 3 6 9 16 23 30
NOTE: ***Brunner** c-11. **Buckler** a-5p. **Ditko** a-8r, 9r. **G. Kane** a-3p; c-3, 9p, 15p. **Mayerik** a-2p, 7, 8, 9p, 10p, 11. **McWilliams** a-14i. **Mortimer** a-4. **Steranko** c-1, 2. **Sutton** a-15. **Tuska** a-6p.*

SUPERPATRIOT (Also see Freak Force & Savage Dragon #2)
Image Comics (Highbrow Entertainment): July, 1993 - No. 4, Dec, 1993 ($1.95, lim. series)
1-4: Dave Johnson-c/a; Larsen scripts; Giffen plots 2.50

SUPERPATRIOT: AMERICA'S FIGHTING FORCE
Image Comics: July, 2002 - No. 4, Oct, 2002 ($2.95, limited series)
1-4-Cory Walker-a/c; Savage Dragon app. 3.00

SUPERPATRIOT: LIBERTY & JUSTICE
Image Comics (Highbrow Entertainment): July, 1995 - No. 4, Oct, 1995 ($2.50, lim. series)

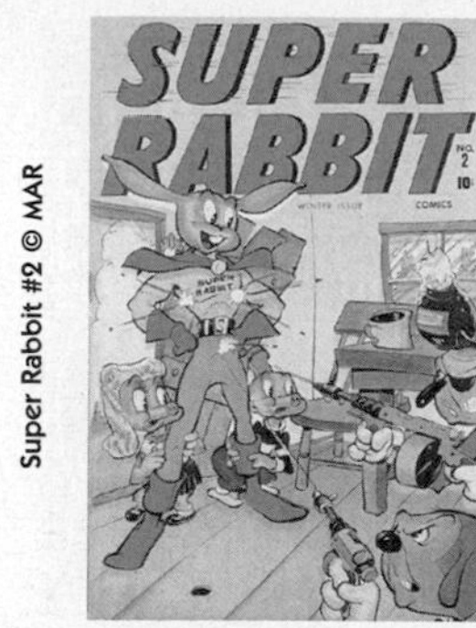

Super Rabbit #2 © MAR

Super Spy #2 © CEN

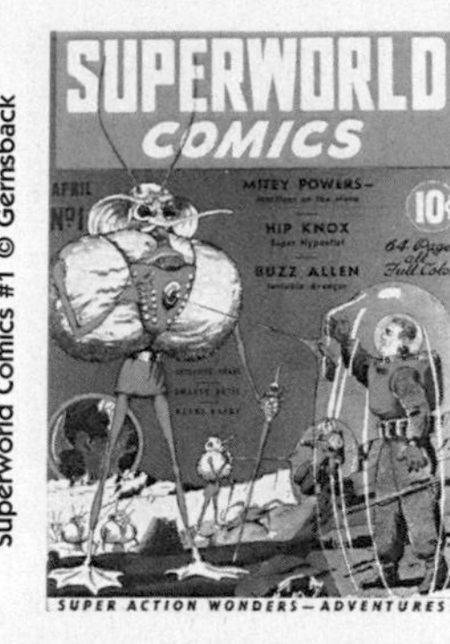

Superworld Comics #1 © Gernsback

GD 2.0 | VG 4.0 | FN 6.0 | VF 8.0 | VF/NM 9.0 | NM- 9.2

1-4: Dave Johnson-c/a. 1-1st app. Liberty & Justice 2.50
TPB (2002, $12.95) r/#1-4; new cover by Dave Johnson; sketch pages 13.00

SUPERPATRIOT: WAR ON TERROR
Image Comics: July, 2004 - No. 4, May, 2007 ($2.95/$2.99, limited series)
1-4-Kirkman-s/Su-a 3.00

SUPER POWERS (1st Series)
DC Comics: July, 1984 - No. 5, Nov, 1984
1-5: 1-Joker/Penguin-c/story; Batman app.; all Kirby-c. 5-Kirby c/a 5.00

SUPER POWERS (2nd Series)
DC Comics: Sept, 1985 - No. 6, Feb, 1986
1-6: Kirby-c/a; Capt. Marvel & Firestorm join; Batman cameo; Darkseid storyline in all. 4-Batman cameo. 5,6-Batman app. 5.00

SUPER POWERS (3rd Series)
DC Comics: Sept, 1986 - No. 4, Dec, 1986
1-4: 1-Cyborg joins; 1st app. Samurai from Super Friends TV show. 1-4-Batman cameos; Darkseid storyline in #1-4 4.00

SUPER PUP (Formerly Spotty The Pup) (See Space Comics)
Avon Periodicals: No. 4, Mar-Apr, 1954 - No. 5, 1954
4,5: 4-Atom bomb-c. 5-Robot-c 6 12 18 31 38 45

SUPER RABBIT (See All Surprise, Animated Movie Tunes, Comedy Comics, Comic Capers, Ideal Comics, It's A Duck's Life, Movie Tunes & Wisco)
Timely Comics (CmPI): Fall, 1944 - No. 14, Nov, 1948
1-Hitler & Hirohito-c; war effort paper recycling PSA by S&K; Ziggy Pig & Silly begin? 93 186 279 586 993 1400
2 40 80 120 235 380 525
3-5 25 50 75 147 236 325
6-Origin 27 54 81 158 254 350
7-10: 9-Infinity-c 15 30 45 94 147 200
11-Kurtzman's "Hey Look" 17 34 51 98 154 210
12-14 15 30 45 94 147 200
I.W. Reprint #1,2('58),7,10('63): 1-r/#13. 2-r/#10. 2 4 6 9 13 16

SUPER RICHIE (Superichie #5 on) (See Richie Rich Millions #68)
Harvey Publications: Sept, 1975 - No. 4, Mar, 1976 (All 52 pg. Giants)
1 3 6 9 16 23 30
2-4 2 4 6 11 16 20

SUPER SLUGGERS (Baseball)
Ultimate Sports Ent. Inc.: 1999 ($3.95, one-shot)
1-Bonds, Piazza, Caminiti, Griffey Jr. app.; Martinbrough-c/a 4.00

SUPERSNIPE COMICS (Formerly Army & Navy #1-5)
Street & Smith Publications: V1#6, Oct, 1942 - V5#1, Aug-Sept, 1949
(See Shadow Comics V2#3)
V1#6-Rex King - Man of Adventure (costumed hero, see Super Magic/Magician) by Jack Binder begins; Supersnipe by George Marcoux continues from Army & Navy #5; Bill Ward-a 113 226 339 712 1206 1700
7,10-12: 10,11-Little Nemo app. 53 106 159 330 553 775
8-Hitler, Tojo, Mussolini in Hell with Devil-c 93 186 279 586 993 1400
9-Doc Savage x-over in Supersnipe; Hitler-c 103 206 309 649 1100 1550
V2 #1: Both V2#1(2/44) & V2#2(4/44) have V2#1 on outside-c; Huck Finn by Clare Dwiggins begins, ends V3#5 (rare) 77 154 231 481 816 1150
V2#2 (4/44) has V2#1 on outside-c; classic shark-c 45 90 135 279 465 650
3-12 39 78 117 230 370 510
V3#1-12: 8-Bobby Crusoe by Dwiggins begins, ends V3#12. 9-X-Mas-c 32 64 96 186 298 410
V4#1-12, V5#1: V4#10-X-Mas-c 23 46 69 133 214 295
NOTE: *George Marcoux c-V1#6-V3#4. Doc Savage app. in some issues.*

SUPER SOLDIER (See Marvel Versus DC #3)
DC Comics (Amalgam): Apr, 1996 ($1.95, one-shot)
1-Mark Waid script & Dave Gibbons-c/a. 2.50

SUPER SOLDIER: MAN OF WAR
DC Comics (Amalgam): June, 1997 ($1.95, one-shot)
1-Waid & Gibbons-s/Gibbons & Palmiotti-c/a. 2.50

SUPER SOLDIERS
Marvel Comics UK: Apr, 1993 - No. 8, Nov, 1993 ($1.75)
1-($2.50)-Embossed silver foil logo 2.50
2-8: 5-Capt. America app. 6-Origin; Nick Fury app.; neon ink-c 2.50

SUPERSPOOK (Formerly Frisky Animals on Parade)
Ajax/Farrell Publications: No. 4, June, 1958
4 8 16 24 44 57 70

SUPER SPY (See Wham Comics)
Centaur Publications: Oct, 1940 - No. 2, Nov, 1940 (Reprints)
1-Origin The Sparkler 90 180 270 563 932 1300
2-The Inner Circle, Dean Denton, Tim Blain, The Drew Ghost, The Night Hawk by Gustavson, & S.S. Swanson by Glanz app. 54 108 162 338 562 785

SUPERSTAR: AS SEEN ON TV
Image Comics (Gorilla): 2001 ($5.95)
1-Busiek-s/Immonen-a 6.00

SUPER STAR HOLIDAY SPECIAL (See DC Special Series #21)

SUPER-TEAM FAMILY
National Periodical Publ./DC Comics: Oct-Nov, 1975 - No. 15, Mar-Apr, 1978
1-Reprints by Neal Adams & Kane/Wood; 68 pgs. begin, ends #4. New Gods app. 3 6 9 14 19 24
2,3: New stories 2 4 6 10 14 18
4-7: Reprints. 4-G.A. JSA-r & Superman/Batman/Robin-r from World's Finest. 5-52 pgs. begin 2 4 6 8 11 14
8-14: 8-10-New Challengers of the Unknown stories. 9-Kirby-a. 11-14: New stories 2 4 6 10 14 18
15-New Gods app. New stories 2 4 6 11 16 20
NOTE: *Neal Adams r-1-3. Brunner c-3. Buckler c-8p. Tuska a-7r. Wood a-1i(r), 3.*

SUPER TV HEROES (See Hanna-Barbera...)

SUPER-VILLAIN CLASSICS
Marvel Comics Group: May, 1983
1-Galactus -The Origin; Kirby-a 6.00

SUPER-VILLAIN TEAM-UP (See Fantastic Four #0 & Giant Size...)
Marvel Comics Group: 8/75 - No. 14, 10/77; No. 15, 11/78; No. 16, 5/79, No. 17, 6/80
1-Giant-Size Super-Villain Team-Up #2; Sub-Mariner & Dr. Doom begin, end #10 4 8 12 22 34 45
2-5: 5-1st app. The Shroud 2 4 6 9 13 16
5-(30¢-c variant, limited distribution)(4/76) 4 8 12 22 34 45
6,7-(25¢ editions) 6-(6/76)-F.F., Shroud app. 7-Origin Shroud 1 2 3 5 7 9
6,7-(30¢-c, limited distribution)(6,8/76) 3 6 9 20 30 40
8-17: 9-Avengers app. 11-15-Dr. Doom & Red Skull app. 1 2 3 5 7 9
12-14-(35¢-c variants, limited distribution)(6,8,10/77) 4 8 12 24 37 50
NOTE: *Buckler c-4p, 5p, 7p. Buscema c-1. Byrne/Austin c-14. Evans a-1p, 3p. Everett a-1p. Giffen a-8p, 13p; c-13p. Kane c-2p, 9p. Mooney a-4i. Starlin c-6. Tuska r-1p, 15p. Wood r-15p.*

SUPER-VILLAIN TEAM-UP/ MODOK'S 11
Marvel Comics: Sept, 2007 - No. 5, Jan, 2008 ($2.99, limited series)
1-5: 1-MODOK's origin re-told; Portela-a/Powell-c; Purple Man & Mentallo app. 3.00
... TPB (2008, $13.99) r/#1-5 14.00

SUPER WESTERN COMICS (Also see Buffalo Bill)
Youthful Magazines: Aug, 1950 (One shot)
1-Buffalo Bill begins; Wyatt Earp, Calamity Jane & Sam Slade app; Powell-c/a 14 28 42 82 121 160

SUPER WESTERN FUNNIES (See Super Funnies)

SUPERWOMAN
DC Comics: Jan 1942
nn - Ashcan comic, not distributed to newsstands, only for in-house use. Cover art is More Fun Comics #73 with interior being Action Comics #38 (no known sales)

SUPERWORLD COMICS
Hugo Gernsback (Komos Publ.): Apr, 1940 - No. 3, Aug, 1940 (68 pgs.)
1-Origin & 1st app. Hip Knox, Super Hypnotist; Mitey Powers & Buzz Allen, the Invisible Avenger, Little Nemo begin; cover by Frank R. Paul (all have sci/fi-c) (Scarce) 750 1500 2250 5400 9450 13,500
2-Marvo 1-2 Go+, the Super Boy of the Year 2680 (1st app.); Paul-c (Scarce) 423 846 1269 2958 5179 7400
3 (Scarce) 341 682 1023 2319 4060 5800

SUPREME (Becomes ...The New Adventures #43-48)(See Youngblood #3)
(Also see Bloodwulf Special, Legend of Supreme, & Trencher #3)
Image Comics (Extreme Studios)/ Awesome Entertainment #49 on:
V2#1, Nov, 1992 - V2#42, Sept, 1996; V3#49 - No. 56, Feb, 1998
V2#1-Liefeld-a(i) & scripts; embossed foil logo 4.00
1-Gold Edition 6.00

Surf N' Wheels #1 © CC

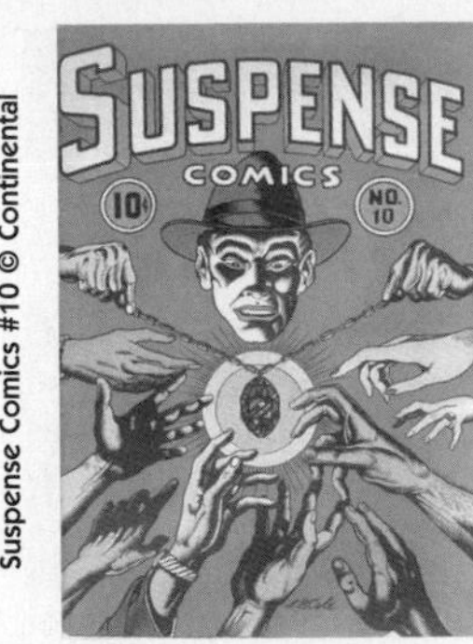

Suspense Comics #10 © Continental

Suzie Comics #76 © AP

2-(3/93)-Liefeld co-plots & inks; 1st app. Grizlock 3.00
3-42: 3-Intro Bloodstrike; 1st app. Khrome. 5-1st app. Thor. 6-1st brief app. The Starguard. 7-1st full app. The Starguard. 10-Black and White Pt 1 (1st app.) by Art Thibert (2 pgs. ea. installment). 25-(5/94)-Platt-c. 11-Coupon #4 for Extreme Prejudice #0; Black and White Pt. 7 by Thibert. 12-(4/94)-Platt-c. 13,14-(6/94). 15 (7/94). 16 (7/94)-Stormwatch app. 18-Kid Supreme Sneak Preview; Pitt app.19,20-Polybagged w/trading card. 20-1st app. Woden & Loki (as a dog); Overtkill app. 21-1st app. Loki (in true form). 21-23-Poly-bagged trading card. 32-Lady Supreme cameo. 33-Origin & 1st full app. of Lady Supreme (Probe from the Starguard); Babewatch! tie-in. 37-Intro Loki; Fraga-c. 40-Retells Supreme's past advs. 41-Alan Moore scripts begin; Supreme revised; intro The Supremacy; Jerry Ordway-c (Joe Bennett variant-c exists). 42-New origin w/Rick Veitch-a; intro Radar, The Hound Supreme & The League of Infinity 3.00
28-Variant-c by Quesada & Palmiotti 3.00
(#43-48-**See Supreme: The New Adventures**)
V3#49,51: 49-Begin $2.99-c 3.00
50-($3.95)-Double sized, 2 covers, pin-up gallery 4.00
52a,52b-($3.50) 3.50
53-56: 53-Sprouse-a begins. 56-McGuinness-c 3.00
Annual 1-(1995, $2.95) 3.00
...: Supreme Sacrifice (3/06, $3.99) Flip book with Suprema; Kirkman-s/Malin-a 4.00
...: The Return TPB (Checker Book Publ., 2003, $24.95) r/#53-56 & Supreme; The Return #1-6; Ross-c; additional sketch pages by Ross 25.00
...: The Story of the Year TPB (Checker Book Publ., 2002, $26.95) r/#41-52; Ross-c 27.00
NOTE: ***Rob Liefeld*** *a(i)-1, 2; co-plots-2-4; scripts-1, 5, 6.* ***Ordway*** *c-41.* ***Platt*** *c-12, 25.* ***Thibert*** *c(i)-7-9.*

SUPREME: GLORY DAYS
Image Comics (Extreme Studios): Oct, 1994 - No. 2, Dec, 1994 ($2.95/$2.50, limited series)
1,2: 2-Diehard, Roman, Superpatriot, & Glory app. 3.00

SUPREME POWER (Also see Squadron Supreme 2006 series)
Marvel Comics (MAX): Oct, 2003 - No. 18, Oct, 2005 ($2.99)
1-($2.99) Straczynski-s/Frank-a; Frank-c 3.00
1-($4.99) Special Edition with variant Quesada-c; includes r/early Squadron Supreme apps. 5.00
2-18: 4-Intro. Nighthawk. 6-The Blur debuts. 10-Princess Zarda returns. 17-Hyperion revealed as alien. 18-Continues in mini-series 3.00
Vol. 1: Contact TPB (2004, $14.99) r/#1-6 15.00
Vol. 2: Powers & Principalities TPB (2004, $14.99) r/#7-12 15.00
Vol. 3: High Command TPB (2005, $14.99) r/#13-18 15.00
Vol. 1 HC (2005, $29.99, 7 1/2" x 11" with dustjacket) r/#1-12; Avengers #85 & 86, Straczynski intro., Frank cover sketches and character design pages 30.00
Vol. 2 HC (2006, $29.99, 7 1/2" x 11" with dustjacket) r/#13-18; ...: Hyperion #1-5; character design pages 30.00

SUPREME POWER: HYPERION
Marvel Comics (MAX): Nov, 2005 - No. 5, Mar, 2006 ($2.99, limited series)
1-5: 1-Straczynski-s/Jurgens-a/Dodson-c 3.00
TPB (2006, $14.99) r/#1-5 15.00

SUPREME POWER: NIGHTHAWK
Marvel Comics (MAX): Nov, 2005 - No. 6, Apr, 2006 ($2.99, limited series)
1-6-Daniel Way-s/Steve Dillon-a; origin of Whiteface 3.00
TPB (2006, $16.99) r/#1-6; cover concept art 17.00

SUPREME: THE NEW ADVENTURES (Formerly Supreme)
Maximum Press: V3#43, Oct, 1996 - V3#48, May, 1997 ($2.50)
V3#43-48: 43-Alan Moore scripts begin; Joe Bennett-a; Rick Veitch-a (8 pgs.); Dan Jurgens-a (1 pg.); intro Citadel Supreme & Suprematons; 1st Allied Supermen of America 3.00

SUPREME: THE RETURN
Awesome Entertainment: May, 1999 - No. 6, June, 2000 ($2.99)
1-6: Alan Moore-s. 1,2-Sprouse & Gordon-a/c. 2,4-Liefeld-c. 6-Kirby app. 3.00

SURE-FIRE COMICS (Lightning Comics #4 on)
Ace Magazines: June, 1940 - No. 4, Oct, 1940 (Two No. 3's)
V1#1-Origin Flash Lightning & begins; X-The Phantom Fed, Ace McCoy, Buck Steele, Marvo the Magician, The Raven, Whiz Wilson (Time Traveler) begin (all 1st app.); Flash Lightning c-1-4 180 360 540 1134 1917 2700
2 82 164 246 517 871 1225
3(9/40), 3(#4)(10/40)-nn on-c, #3 on inside 60 120 180 378 639 900

SURF 'N' WHEELS
Charlton Comics: Nov, 1969 - No. 6, Sept, 1970
1 3 6 9 20 30 40
2-6 3 6 9 14 19 24

SURGE
Eclipse Comics: July, 1984 - No. 4, Jan, 1985 ($1.50, lim. series, Baxter paper)
1-4 Ties into DNAgents series 2.50

SURPRISE ADVENTURES (Formerly Tormented)
Sterling Comic Group: No. 3, Mar, 1955 - No. 5, July, 1955
3-5: 3,5-Sekowsky-a 9 18 27 47 61 75

SUSIE Q. SMITH
Dell Publishing Co.: No. 323, Mar, 1951 - No. 553, Apr, 1954
Four Color 323 (#1) 5 10 15 32 51 70
Four Color 377, 453 (2/53), 553 4 8 12 26 41 55

SUSPENSE (Radio/TV issues #1-11; Real Life Tales of... #1-4) (Amazing Detective Cases #3 on?)
Marvel/Atlas Comics (CnPC No. 1-10/BFP No. 11-29): Dec, 1949 - No. 29, Apr, 1953 (#1-8, 17-23: 52 pgs.)
1-Powell-a; Peter Lorre, Sidney Greenstreet photo-c from Hammett's "The Verdict" 59 118 177 372 629 885
2-Crime stories; Dennis O'Keefe & Gale Storm photo-c from Universal movie "Abandoned" 35 70 105 203 327 450
3-Change to horror 40 80 120 244 397 550
4,7-10: 7-Dracula-sty 32 64 96 186 298 410
5-Krigstein, Tuska, Everett-a 33 66 99 196 316 435
6-Tuska, Everett, Morisi-a 33 66 99 192 309 425
11-13,15-17,19,20 25 50 75 147 236 325
14-Clasic Heath Hypo-c; A-Bomb panels 37 74 111 215 345 475
18,22-Krigstein-a 26 52 78 152 244 335
21,23,24,26-29: 24-Tuska-a 22 44 66 129 207 285
25-Electric chair-c/story 31 62 93 181 291 400
NOTE: ***Ayers*** *a-20.* ***Briefer*** *a-5, 7, 27.* ***Brodsky*** *c-4, 6-9, 11, 16, 17, 25.* ***Colan*** *a-8(2), 9.* ***Everett*** *a-5, 6(2), 19, 23, 28; c-21-23, 26.* ***Fuje*** *a-29.* ***Heath*** *a-5, 6, 8, 10, 12, 14; c-14, 19, 24.* ***Maneely*** *a-12, 23, 24, 28, 29; c-5, 6p, 10, 13, 15, 18.* ***Mooney*** *a-24, 28.* ***Morisi*** *a-6, 12.* ***Palais*** *a-10.* ***Rico*** *a-7-9.* ***Robinson*** *a-29.* ***Romita*** *a-20(2), 25.* ***Sekowsky*** *a-11, 13, 14.* ***Sinnott*** *a-23, 25.* ***Tuska*** *a-5, 6(2), 12; c-12.* ***Whitney*** *a-15, 16, 22.* ***Ed Win*** *a-27.*

SUSPENSE COMICS
Continental Magazines: Dec, 1943 - No. 12, Sept, 1946
1-The Grey Mask begins; bondage/torture-c; L. B. Cole-a (7 pgs.) 411 822 1233 2795 4898 7000
2-Intro. The Mask; Rico, Giunta, L. B. Cole-a (7 pgs.) 276 552 828 1725 2863 4000
3-L.B. Cole-a; classic Schomburg-c (Scarce) 3000 6000 9000 18,000 27,000 36,000
4-6: 4-L. B. Cole-c begin 207 414 621 1304 2202 3100
7,9,10,12: 9-L.B. Cole eyeball-c 160 320 480 1008 1704 2400
8-Classic L. B. Cole spider-c 400 800 1200 2720 4760 6800
11-Classic Devil-c 306 612 918 2081 3641 5200
NOTE: ***L. B. Cole*** *c-4-12.* ***Fuje*** *a-8.* ***Larsen*** *a-11.* ***Palais*** *a-10, 11. Bondage c-1, 3, 4.*

SUSPENSE DETECTIVE
Fawcett Publications: June, 1952 - No. 5, Mar, 1953
1-Evans-a (11 pgs); Baily-c/a 45 90 135 279 465 650
2-Evans-a (10 pgs.) 27 54 81 158 254 350
3-5 23 46 69 133 214 295
NOTE: ***Baily*** *a-4, 5; c-1-3.* ***Sekowsky*** *a-2, 4, 5; c-5.*

SUSPENSE STORIES (See Strange Suspense Stories)

SUSSEX VAMPIRE, THE (Sherlock Holmes)
Caliber Comics: 1996 ($2.95, 32 pgs., B&W, one-shot)
nn-Adapts Sir Arthur Conan Doyle's story; Warren Ellis scripts 3.00

SUZIE COMICS (Formerly Laugh Comix; see Laugh Comics, Liberty Comics #10, Pep Comics & Top-Notch Comics #28)
Close-Up No. 49,50/MLJ Mag./Archie No. 51 on: No. 49, Spring, 1945 - No. 100, Aug, 1954
49-Ginger begins 24 48 72 140 225 310
50-55: 54-Transvestism story. 55-Woggon-a 15 30 45 88 137 180
56-Katy Keene begins by Woggon 15 30 45 90 140 190
57-65 12 24 36 69 97 125
66-80 11 22 33 64 90 115
81-87,89-99 10 20 30 56 76 95
88,100: 88-Used in **POP**, pgs. 76,77; Bill Woggon draws himself in story. 100-Last Katy Keene 11 22 33 64 90 115
NOTE: ***Al Fagaly*** *c-49-67. Katy Keene app. in 53-82, 85-100.*

SWAMP FOX, THE (TV, Disney)(See Walt Disney Presents #2)
Dell Publishing Co.: No. 1179, Dec, 1960
Four Color 1179-Leslie Nielsen photo-c 8 16 24 56 93 130

SWAMP THING (See Brave & the Bold, Challengers of the Unknown #82, DC Comics Presents #8 & 85, DC Special Series #2, 14, 17, 20, House of Secrets #92, Limited Collectors' Edition C-59, & Roots of the...)

SWAMP THING
National Per. Publ./DC Comics: Oct-Nov, 1972 - No. 24, Aug-Sept, 1976

Swamp Thing #155 © DC

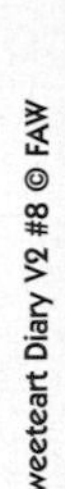
Sweeteart Diary V2 #8 © FAW

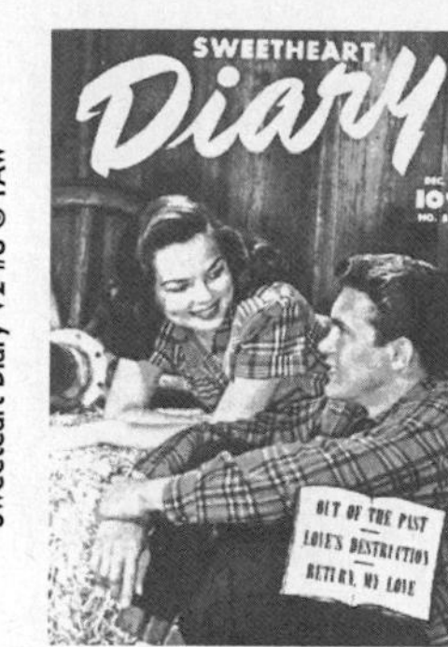

Sweethearts #80 © FAW

	GD 2.0	VG 4.0	FN 6.0	VF 8.0	VF/NM 9.0	NM- 9.2
1-Wrightson-c/a begins; origin	15	30	45	105	190	275
2-1st brief app. Patchwork Man (1 panel)	8	16	24	52	86	120
3-1st full app. Patchwork Man (see House of Secrets #140)	6	12	18	39	62	85
4-6,	5	10	15	32	51	70
7-Batman-c/story	5	10	15	34	55	75
8-10: 10-Last Wrightson issue	4	8	12	28	44	60
11-20: 11-19-Redondo-a. 13-Origin retold (1 pg.)	3	6	9	16	23	30
21-24: 23,24-Swamp Thing reverts back to Dr. Holland. 23-New logo	3	6	9	16	23	30
Secret of the Swamp Thing (2005, $9.99, digest) r/#1-10						10.00

NOTE: ***J. Jones*** *a-9i(assist).* ***Kaluta*** *a-9i.* ***Redondo*** *c-12-19, 21.* ***Wrightson*** *issues (#1-10) reprinted in DC Special Series #2, 14, 17, 20 & Roots of the Swamp Thing.*

SWAMP THING (Saga Of The... #1-38,42-45) (See Essential Vertigo:...)
DC Comics (Vertigo imprint #129 on): May, 1982 - No. 171, Oct, 1996 (Direct sales #65 on)

	GD 2.0	VG 4.0	FN 6.0	VF 8.0	VF/NM 9.0	NM- 9.2
1-Origin retold; Phantom Stranger series begins; ends #13; Yeates-c/a begins						6.00
2-15: 2-Photo-c from movie. 13-Last Yeates-a						4.00
16-19: Bissette-a.						5.00
20-1st Alan Moore issue	3	6	9	14	19	24
21-New origin	2	4	6	11	16	20
22,23,25: 25-John Constantine 1-panel cameo	2	4	6	8	11	14
24-JLA x-over; Last Yeates-c.	2	4	6	9	12	15
26-30	1	2	3	4	5	7
31-33,35,36: 33-r/1st app. from House of Secrets #92						5.00
34	1	2	3	5	6	8
37-1st app. John Constantine (Hellblazer) (6/85)	2	4	6	9	12	15
38-40: John Constantine app.	1	2	3	5	6	8
41-52,54-64: 44 Batman cameo. 44-51-John Constantine app. 46 Crisis x-over; Batman cameo. 49-Spectre app. 50-($1.25, 52 pgs.)-Deadman, Dr. Fate, Demon. 52-Arkham Asylum-c/story; Joker-c/cameo. 58-Spectre preview. 64-Last Moore issue						3.50
53-($1.25, 52 pgs.) Arkham Asylum; Batman-c/story						4.50
65-83,85-99,101-124,126-149,151-153: 65-Direct sales only begins. 66-Batman & Arkham Asylum story. 70,76-John Constantine x-over; 76-X-over w/Hellblazer #9. 79-Superman-c/story. 85-Jonah Hex app. 102-Preview of World Without End. 116-Photo-c. 129-Metallic ink on-c. 140-Millar scripts begin, end #171						3.00
84-Sandman (Morpheus) cameo.						4.00
100,125,150: 100 ($2.50, 52 pgs.). 125-($2.95, 52 pgs.)-20th anniversary issue. 150 (52 pgs.)-Anniversary issue						3.00
154-171: 154-$2.25-c begins. 165-Curt Swan-a(p). 166,169,171-John Constantine & Phantom Stranger app. 168-Arcane returns						2.50
Annual 1,3-6('82-91): 1-Movie Adaptation; painted-c. 3-New format; Bolland-c. 4-Batman-c/story. 5-Batman cameo; re-intro Brother Power (Geek),1st app. since 1968						4.00
Annual 2 (1985)-Moore scripts; Bissette-a(p); Deadman, Spectre app.						7.00
Annual 7(1993, $3.95)-Children's Crusade						4.00
...A Murder of Crows (2001, $19.95)-r/#43-50; Moore-s						20.00
...: Earth To Earth (2002, $17.95)-r/#51-56; Batman app.						18.00
...: Infernal Triangles (2006, $19.99, TPB) r/#77-81 & Annual #3; cover gallery						20.00
...Love and Death (1990, $17.95)-r/#28-34 & Annual #2; Totleben painted-c						18.00
...: Regenesis (2004, $17.95, TPB) r/#65-70; Veitch-s						18.00
...: Reunion (2003, $19.95, TPB) r/#57-64; Moore-s						20.00
...: Roots (1998, $7.95) Jon J Muth-s/painted-a/c						8.00
Saga of the Swamp Thing ('87, '89)-r/#21-27 (1st & 2nd print)						13.00
...: Spontaneous Generation (2005, $19.99) r/#71-76						20.00
...: The Curse (2000, $19.95, TPB) r/#35-42; Bisley-c						20.00

NOTE: ***Bissette*** *a(p)-16-19, 21-27, 29, 30, 34-36, 39-42, 44, 46, 50, 64; c-17i, 24-32p, 35-37p, 40p, 44p, 46-50p, 51-58, 61, 62, 63p.* ***Kaluta*** *c/a-74.* ***Spiegle*** *a-1-3, 6.* ***Sutton*** *a-98p.* ***Totleben*** *a(i)-10, 16-27, 29, 31, 34-40, 42, 44, 46, 48, 50, 53, 55i; c-25-32i, 33, 35-40i, 42i, 44i, 46-50i, 53, 55i, 59p, 64, 65, 68, 73, 76, 80, 82, 84, 89, 91-100, Annual 4, 5.* ***Vess*** *painted c-121, 129-139, Annual 7.* ***Williamson*** *86i.* ***Wrightson*** *a-18i(r), 33r. John Constantine appears in #37-40, 44-51, 65-67, 70-77, 80-90, 99, 114, 115, 130, 134-138.*

SWAMP THING
DC Comics (Vertigo): May, 2000 - No. 20, Dec, 2001 ($2.50)

	GD 2.0	VG 4.0	FN 6.0	VF 8.0	VF/NM 9.0	NM- 9.2
1-3-Tefé Holland's return; Vaughan-s/Petersen-a; Hale painted-c.						3.00
4-20: 7-9-Bisley-c. 10-John Constantine-c/app. 10-12-Fabry-c. 13-15-Mack-c 18-Swamp Thing app.						2.50
Preview-16 pg. flip book w/Lucifer Preview						2.25

SWAMP THING
DC Comics (Vertigo): May, 2004 - No. 29, Sept, 2006 ($2.95/$2.99)

	GD 2.0	VG 4.0	FN 6.0	VF 8.0	VF/NM 9.0	NM- 9.2
1-29: 1-Diggle-s/Breccia-a; Constantine app. 2-6-Sargon app. 7,8,20-Corben-c/a. 21-29-Eric Powell-c						3.00
...: Bad Seed (2004, $9.95) r/#1-6						10.00
...: Healing the Breach (2006, $17.99) r/#15-20						18.00
...: Love in Vain (2005, $14.99) r/#9-14						15.00

SWAT MALONE (America's Home Run King)
Swat Malone Enterprises: Sept, 1955

	GD 2.0	VG 4.0	FN 6.0	VF 8.0	VF/NM 9.0	NM- 9.2
V1#1-Hy Fleishman-a	11	22	33	62	86	110

SWEATSHOP
DC Comics: Jun, 2003 - No. 6, Nov, 2003 ($2.95)

	GD 2.0	VG 4.0	FN 6.0	VF 8.0	VF/NM 9.0	NM- 9.2
1-6-Peter Bagge-s/a; Destefano-a						3.00

SWEENEY (Formerly Buz Sawyer)
Standard Comics: No. 4, June, 1949 - No. 5, Sept, 1949

	GD 2.0	VG 4.0	FN 6.0	VF 8.0	VF/NM 9.0	NM- 9.2
4,5: 5-Crano-a	9	18	27	47	61	75

SWEE'PEA (Also see Popeye #46)
Dell Publishing Co.: No. 219, Mar, 1949

	GD 2.0	VG 4.0	FN 6.0	VF 8.0	VF/NM 9.0	NM- 9.2
Four Color 219	8	16	24	56	93	130

SWEET CHILDE
Advantage Graphics Press: 1995 - No. 2, 1995 ($2.95, B&W, mature)

	GD 2.0	VG 4.0	FN 6.0	VF 8.0	VF/NM 9.0	NM- 9.2
1,2						3.00

SWEETHEART DIARY (Cynthia Doyle #66-on)
Fawcett Publications/Charlton Comics No. 32 on: Wint, 1949; #2, Spr, 1950; #3, 6/50 - #5, 10/50; #6, 1951(nd); #7, 9/51 - #14, 1/53; #32, 10/55; #33, 4/56 - #65, 8/62 (#1-14: photo-c)

	GD 2.0	VG 4.0	FN 6.0	VF 8.0	VF/NM 9.0	NM- 9.2
1	19	38	57	112	176	240
2	12	24	36	67	94	120
3,4-Wood-a	15	30	45	85	130	175
5-10: 8-Bailey-a	10	20	30	54	72	90
11-14: 13-Swayze-a. 14-Last Fawcett issue	8	16	24	44	57	70
32 (10/55; 1st Charlton issue)(Formerly Cowboy Love #31)	9	18	27	50	65	80
33-40: 34-Swayze-a	7	14	21	35	43	50
41-(68 pgs.)	7	14	21	37	46	55
42-60	3	6	9	20	30	40
61-65	3	6	9	18	27	35

SWEETHEARTS (Formerly Captain Midnight)
Fawcett Publications/Charlton No. 122 on: #68, 10/48 - #121, 5/53; #122, 3/54; V2#23, 5/54 - #137, 12/73

	GD 2.0	VG 4.0	FN 6.0	VF 8.0	VF/NM 9.0	NM- 9.2
68-Photo-c begin	17	34	51	98	154	210
69,70	11	22	33	60	83	105
71-80	9	18	27	50	65	80
81-84,86-93,95-99,105	8	16	24	44	57	70
85,94,103,110,117-George Evans-a	9	18	27	52	69	85
100	9	18	27	50	65	80
101,107-Powell-a	9	18	27	47	61	75
102,104,106,108,109,112-116,118	8	16	24	42	54	65
111-1 pg. Ronald Reagan biography	10	20	30	54	72	90
119-Marilyn Monroe & Richard Widmark photo-c (1/54?); also appears in story; part Wood-a	57	114	171	359	605	850
120-Atom Bomb story	11	22	33	64	90	115
121-Liz Taylor/Fernanado Lamas photo-c	27	54	81	158	254	350
122-(1st Charlton? 3/54)-Marijuana story	12	24	36	69	97	125
V2#23 (5/54)-28: 28-Last precode issue (2/55)	8	16	24	40	50	60
29-39,41,43-45,47-50	4	8	12	24	37	50
40-Photo-c; Tommy Sands story	4	8	12	26	41	55
42-Ricky Nelson photo-c/story	8	16	24	56	93	130
46-Jimmy Rodgers photo-c/story	4	8	12	26	41	55
51-60	3	6	9	20	30	40
61-80,100	3	6	9	18	27	35
81-99	3	6	9	17	25	32
101-110	2	4	6	13	18	22
111-137: 121,125-David Cassidy pin-ups	2	4	6	10	14	18

NOTE: *Photo c-68-121(Fawcett), 40, 42, 46(Charlton).* ***Swayze*** *a(Fawcett)-70-118(most).*

SWEETHEART SCANDALS (See Fox Giants)

SWEETIE PIE
Dell Publishing Co.: No. 1185, May-July, 1961 - No. 1241, Nov-Jan, 1961/62

	GD 2.0	VG 4.0	FN 6.0	VF 8.0	VF/NM 9.0	NM- 9.2
Four Color 1185 (#1)	5	10	15	30	48	65
Four Color 1241	4	8	12	24	37	50

SWEETIE PIE
Ajax-Farrell/Pines (Literary Ent.): Dec, 1955 - No. 15, Fall, 1957

	GD 2.0	VG 4.0	FN 6.0	VF 8.0	VF/NM 9.0	NM- 9.2
1-By Nadine Seltzer	10	20	30	54	72	90
2 (5/56; last Ajax?)	7	14	21	35	43	50
3-15	6	12	18	28	34	40

SWEET LOVE

Sweet XVI #1 © MAR

The Sword #1 © Luna Bros.

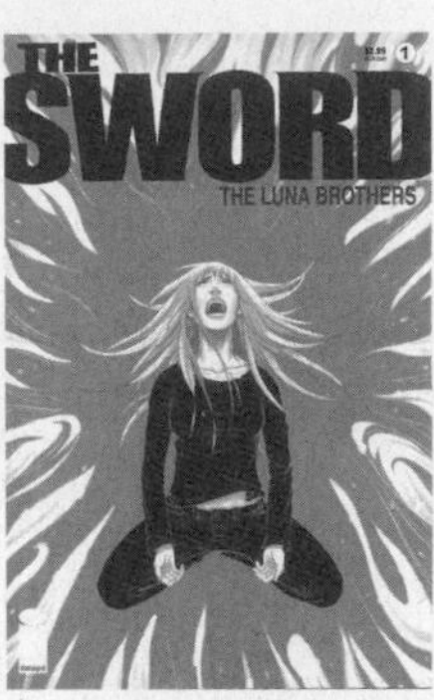

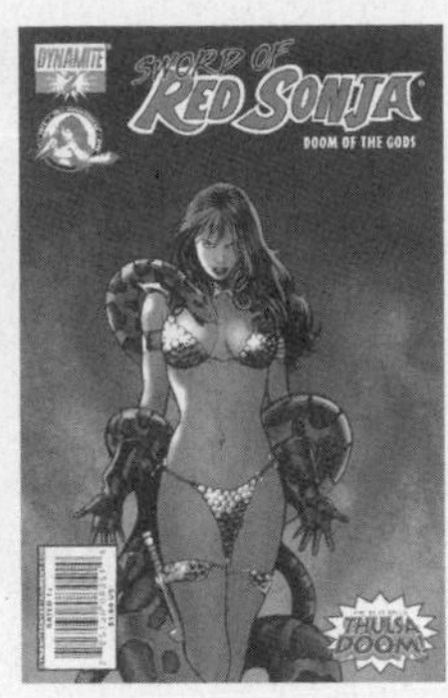

Sword of Red Sonja: Doom of the Gods #2 © Red Sonja Prop.

GD VG FN VF VF/NM NM-
2.0 4.0 6.0 8.0 9.0 9.2

GD VG FN VF VF/NM NM-
2.0 4.0 6.0 8.0 9.0 9.2

Home Comics (Harvey): Sept, 1949 - No. 5, May, 1950 (All photo-c)

1 10 20 30 58 79 100
2 7 14 21 37 46 55
3,4: 3-Powell-a 6 12 18 31 38 45
5-Kamen, Powell-a 9 18 27 47 61 75

SWEET ROMANCE
Charlton Comics: Oct, 1968

1 3 6 9 14 20 25

SWEET SIXTEEN (...Comics and Stories for Girls)
Parents' Magazine Institute: Aug-Sept, 1946 - No. 13, Jan, 1948 (All have movie stars photos on covers)

1-Van Johnson's life story; Dorothy Dare, Queen of Hollywood Stunt Artists begins (in all issues); part photo-c 22 44 66 129 207 285
2-Jane Powell, Roddy McDowall "Holiday in Mexico" photo on-c; Alan Ladd story 15 30 45 86 133 180
3,5,6,8-11: 5-Ann Francis photo on-c; Gregory Peck story. 6-Dick Haymes story. 8-Shirley Jones photo on-c. 10-Jean Simmons photo on-c; James Stewart story 12 24 36 69 97 125
4-Elizabeth Taylor photo on-c 25 50 75 147 236 325
7-Ronald Reagan's life story 22 44 66 129 207 285
12-Bob Cummings, Vic Damone story 13 26 39 74 105 135
13-Robert Mitchum's life story 14 28 42 76 108 140

SWEET XVI
Marvel Comics: May, 1991 - No. 5, Sept, 1991($1.00, color)

1-5: Barbara Slate story & art 3.00

SWIFT ARROW (Also see Lone Rider & The Rider)
Ajax/Farrell Publications: Feb-Mar, 1954 - No. 5, Oct-Nov, 1954; Apr, 1957 - No. 3, Sept, 1957

1(1954) (1st Series) 16 32 48 92 144 195
2 10 20 30 56 76 95
3-5: 5-Lone Rider story 9 18 27 50 65 80
1 (2nd Series) (Swift Arrow's Gunfighters #4) 9 18 27 50 65 80
2,3: 2-Lone Rider begins 8 16 24 40 50 60

SWIFT ARROW'S GUNFIGHTERS (Formerly Swift Arrow)
Ajax/Farrell Publ. (Four Star Comic Corp.): No. 4, Nov, 1957

4 8 16 24 40 50 60

SWING WITH SCOOTER
National Periodical Publ.: June-July, 1966 - No. 35, Aug-Sept, 1971; No. 36, Oct-Nov, 1972

1 8 16 24 56 93 130
2,6-10: 9-Alfred E. Newman swipe in last panel 5 10 15 30 48 65
3-5: 3-Batman cameo on-c. 4-Batman cameo inside. 5-JLA cameo 5 10 15 32 51 70
11-13,15-19: 18-Wildcat of JSA 1pg. text. 19-Last 12¢-c 3 6 9 19 29 38
14-Alfred E. Neuman cameo 3 6 9 20 30 40
20 (68 pgs.) 4 8 12 28 44 60
21-23,25-31 3 6 9 16 23 30
24-Frankenstein-c. 3 6 9 19 29 38
32-34 (68 pgs.). 32-Batman cameo. 33-Interview with David Cassidy. 34-Interview with Rick Ely (The Rebels) 4 8 12 26 41 55
35-(52 pgs.). 1 pg. app. Clark Kent and 4 full pgs. of Superman 7 14 21 47 76 105
36-Bat-signal refererence to Batman 3 6 9 19 29 38

NOTE: *Aragonés* a-13 (1pg.), 18(1pg.), 30(2pgs.) *Orlando* a-1-11; c-1-11, 13. #20, 33, 34: 68 pgs.; #35: 52 pgs.

SWISS FAMILY ROBINSON (Walt Disney's..; see King Classics & Movie Comics)
Dell Publishing Co.: No. 1156, Dec, 1960

Four Color 1156-Movie-photo-c 7 14 21 49 80 110

SWORD, THE
Image Comics: Oct, 2007 - Present ($2.99)

1-Luna Brothers-s/a 4.00
1-(2nd printing) 3.00
2-11 3.00
..., Vol. 1: Fire (TPB, 2008, $14.99) r/#1-8 15.00

SWORD & THE DRAGON, THE
Dell Publishing Co.: No. 1118, June, 1960

Four Color 1118-Movie, photo-c 7 14 21 50 83 115

SWORD & THE ROSE, THE (Disney)
Dell Publishing Co.: No. 505, Oct, 1953 - No. 682, Feb, 1956

Four Color 505-Movie, photo-c 8 16 24 56 93 130
Four Color 682-When Knighthood Was in Flower-Movie, reprint of #505; Renamed the Sword & the Rose for the novel; photo-c 7 14 21 47 76 105

SWORD IN THE STONE, THE (See March of Comics #258 & Movie Comics & Wart and the Wizard)

SWORD OF DAMOCLES
Image Comics (WildStorm Productions): Mar, 1996 - No. 2, Apr, 1996 ($2.50, limited series)

1,2: Warren Ellis scripts. 1-Prelude to "Fire From Heaven" x-over; 1st app. Sword 2.50

SWORD OF DRACULA
Image Comics: Oct, 2003 - No. 6, Sept, 2004 ($2.95, B&W, limited series)

1-6-Tony Harris-c. 1,2-Greg Scott-a 3.00
TPB (IDW, 2/05, $14.99) r/series 15.00

SWORD OF RED SONJA: DOOM OF THE GODS
Dynamite Entertainment: 2007 - No. 4, 2007 ($3.50, limited series)

1-4-Lui Antonio-a; multiple covers on each 3.50

SWORD OF SORCERY
National Periodical Publications: Feb-Mar, 1973 - No. 5, Nov-Dec, 1973 (20¢)

1-Leiber Fafhrd & The Grey Mouser; Chaykin/Neal Adams (Crusty Bunkers) art; Kaluta-c 2 4 6 13 18 22
2,3: 2-Wrightson-c(i); Adams-a(i). 3-Wrightson-i(5 pgs.) 2 4 6 8 10 12
4,5: 5-Starlin-a(p); Conan cameo 1 2 3 5 7 9

NOTE: *Chaykin* a-1-4p; c-2p, 3-5. *Kaluta* a-3i. *Simonson* a-3i, 4i, 5p; c-5.

SWORD OF THE ATOM
DC Comics: Sept, 1983 - No. 4, Dec, 1983 (Limited series)

1-4: Gil Kane-c/a in all 3.00
Special 1-3('84, '85, '88): 1,2-Kane-c/a each 3.00
TPB (2007, $19.99) r/#1-4 and Special #1-3 20.00

SWORDS OF TEXAS (See Scout #15)
Eclipse Comics: Oct, 1987 - No. 4, Jan, 1988 ($1.75, color, Baxter paper)

1-4: Scout app. 2.50

SWORDS OF THE SWASHBUCKLERS (See Marvel Graphic Novel)
Marvel Comics (Epic Comics): May, 1985 - No. 12, Jun, 1987 ($1.50; mature)

1-12-Butch Guice-c/a (Cont'd from Marvel G.N.) 2.50

SWORN TO PROTECT
Marvel Comics: Sept, 1995 ($1.95) (Based on card game)

nn-Overpower Game Guide; Jubilee story 2.50

SYN
Dark Horse Comics: Aug, 2003 - No. 5, Feb, 2004 ($2.99, limited series)

1-5-Giffen-s/Titus-a 3.00

SYPHONS
Now Comics: V2#1, May, 1994 - V2#3, 1994 ($2.50, limited series)

V2#1-3: 1-Stardancer, Knightfire, Raze & Brigade begin 2.50
TPB (9/04, $15.95) B&W reprints #1-3; intro. by Tony Caputo 16.00

SYSTEM, THE
DC Comics (Vertigo Verite): May, 1996 - No. 3, July, 1996 ($2.95, lim. series)

1-3: Kuper-c/a 3.00
TPB (1997, $12.95) r/#1-3 13.00

TAFFY COMICS
Rural Home/Orbit Publ.: Mar-Apr, 1945 - No. 12, 1948

1-L.B. Cole-c; origin & 1st app. of Wiggles The Wonderworm plus 7 chapter WWII funny animal adventures 60 120 180 378 639 900
2-L.B. Cole-c with funny animal Hitler; Wiggles-c/stories in #1-4 32 64 96 186 298 410
3,4,6-12: 6-Perry Como-c/story. 7-Duke Ellington, 2 pgs. 8-Glenn Ford-c/story. 9-Lon McCallister part photo-c & story. 10-Mort Leav-c. 11-Mickey Rooney-c/story 15 30 45 83 124 165
5-L.B. Cole-c; Van Johnson-c/story 22 44 66 127 204 280

TAILGUNNER JO
DC Comics: Sept, 1988 - No. 6, Jan, 1989 ($1.25)

1-6 2.50

TAILS
Archie Publications; Dec, 1995 - No. 3, Feb, 1996 ($1.50, limited series)

1-3: Based on Sonic, the Hedgehog video game 4.00

TAILSPIN
Spotlight Publishers: November, 1944

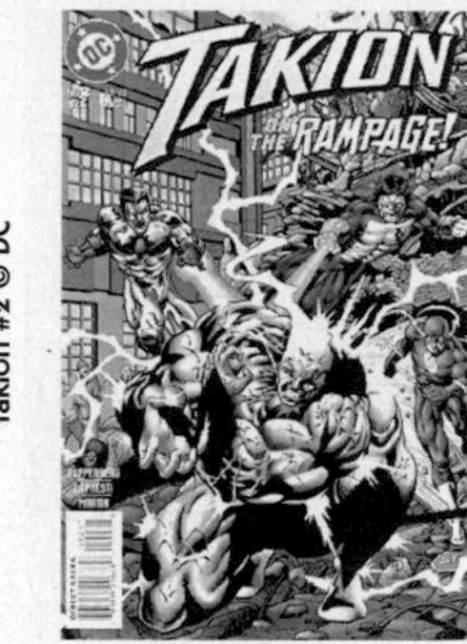

Takion #2 © DC

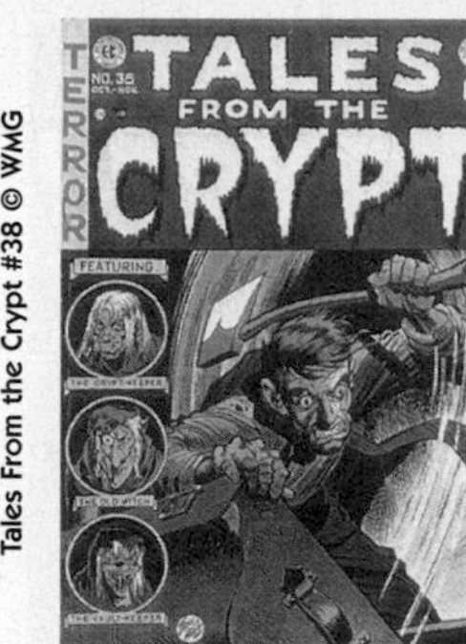

Tales From the Crypt #38 © WMG

Tales From the Tomb V6 #3 © Eerie Pub.

	GD 2.0	VG 4.0	FN 6.0	VF 8.0	VF/NM 9.0	NM- 9.2
nn-Firebird app.; L.B. Cole-c	28	56	84	162	261	360

TAILSPIN TOMMY (Also see Popular Comics)
United Features Syndicate/Service Publ. Co.: 1940; 1946

	GD 2.0	VG 4.0	FN 6.0	VF 8.0	VF/NM 9.0	NM- 9.2
Single Series 23(1940)	40	80	120	235	380	525
Best Seller (nd, 1946)-Service Publ. Co.	15	30	45	86	133	180

TAINTED
DC Comics (Vertigo): Jan, 1995 ($4.95, one-shot)

1-Jamie Delano scripts; Al Davison-c/a; reads February '95 on-c 5.00

TAKION
DC Comics: June, 1996 - No. 7, Dec, 1996 ($1.75)

1-7: Lopresti-c/a(p). 1-Origin; Green Lantern app. 6-Final Night x-over 2.50

TALENT SHOWCASE (See New Talent Showcase)

TALE OF ONE BAD RAT, THE
Dark Horse Comics: Oct, 1994 - No. 4, Jan, 1995 ($2.95, limited series)

1-4: Bryan Talbot-c/a/scripts 3.00
HC ($69.95, signed and numbered) R/#1-4 70.00

TALES CALCULATED TO DRIVE YOU BATS
Archie Publications: Nov, 1961 - No. 7, Nov, 1962; 1966 (Satire)

	GD 2.0	VG 4.0	FN 6.0	VF 8.0	VF/NM 9.0	NM- 9.2
1-Only 10¢ issue; has cut-out Werewolf mask (price includes mask)	12	24	36	90	160	230
2-Begin 12¢ issues	7	14	21	50	83	115
3-6: 3-UFO cover	6	12	18	39	62	85
7-Storyline change	6	12	18	37	59	80
1(1966, 25¢, 44 pg. Giant)-r/#1; UFO cover	6	12	18	37	59	80

TALES CALCULATED TO DRIVE YOU MAD
E.C. Publications: Summer, 1997 - No. 8, Winter, 1999 ($3.99/$4.99, satire)

1-6-Full color reprints of Mad: 1-(#1-3), 2-(#4-6), 3-(#7-9), 4-(#10-12) 5-(#13-15), 6-(#16-18) 5.00
7,8-($4.99-c): 7-(#19-21), 8-(#22,23) 5.00

TALES FROM RIVERDALE DIGEST
Archie Publ.: June, 2005 - Present ($2.39/$2.49, digest-size)

1-31: 1-Sabrina and Josie & the Pussycats app. 11-Begin $2.49-c 2.50

TALES FROM THE AGE OF APOCALYPSE
Marvel Comics: 1996 ($5.95, prestige format, one-shots)

1, ...: Sinister Bloodlines (1997, $5.95) 6.00

TALES FROM THE BOG
Aberration Press: Nov, 1995 - No. 7, Nov, 1997 ($2.95/$3.95, B&W)

1-7 4.00
Alternate #1 (Director's Cut) (1998, $2.95) 3.00

TALES FROM THE BULLY PULPIT
Image Comics: Aug, 2004 ($6.95, square-bound)

1-Teddy Roosevelt and Edison's ghost with a time machine; Cereno-s/MacDonald-a 7.00

TALES FROM THE CLERKS (See Jay and Silent Bob, Clerks and Oni Double Feature)
Graphitti Designs, Inc.: 2006 ($29.95, TPB)

nn-Reprints all the Kevin Smith Clerks and Jay and Silent Bob stories; new Clerks II story with Mahfood-a; cover gallery, sketch pages, Mallrats credits covers; Smith intro. 30.00

TALES FROM THE CRYPT (Formerly The Crypt Of Terror; see Three Dimensional...) (Also see EC Archives • Tales From the Crypt)
E.C. Comics: No. 20, Oct-Nov, 1950 - No. 46, Feb-Mar, 1955

	GD 2.0	VG 4.0	FN 6.0	VF 8.0	VF/NM 9.0	NM- 9.2
20-See Crime Patrol #15 for 1st Crypt Keeper	116	232	348	928	1477	2025
21-Kurtzman-r/Haunt of Fear #15(#1)	96	192	288	768	1222	1675
22-Moon Girl costume at costume party, one panel	76	152	228	608	969	1325
23-25: 24-E. A. Poe adaptation	59	118	177	472	754	1035
26-30: 26-Wood's 2nd EC-c	47	94	141	376	596	815
31-Williamson-a(1st at E.C.); B&W and color illos. in **POP**; Kamen draws himself, Gaines & Feldstein; Ingels, Craig & Davis draw themselves in his story	48	96	144	384	607	830
32,35-39: 38-Censored-c	42	84	126	336	533	730
33-Origin The Crypt Keeper	65	130	195	520	825	1130
34-Used in **POP**, pg. 83; lingerie panels	43	86	129	344	545	745
40-Used in Senate hearings & in Hartford Cournat anti-comics editorials-1954	42	84	126	336	533	730
41-45: 45-2 pgs. showing E.C. staff	41	82	123	328	519	710
46-Low distribution; pre-advertised cover for unpublished 4th horror title "Crypt of Terror" used on this book	48	96	144	384	442	835

NOTE: ***Ray Bradbury** adaptations-34, 36. **Craig** a-20, 22-24; c-20. **Crandall** a-38, 44. **Davis** a-24-46; c-29-46. **Elder** a-37, 38. **Evans** a-32-34, 36, 40, 41, 43, 46. **Feldstein** a-20-23; c-21-25, 28. **Ingels** a-in all. **Kamen** a-20, 22, 25, 27-31, 33-36, 39, 41-45. **Krigstein** a-40, 42, 45. **Kurtzman** a-21. **Orlando** a-27-30, 35, 37, 39, 41-45. **Wood** a-21, 24, 25; c-26, 27. Canadian reprints known; see Table of Contents.*

TALES FROM THE CRYPT (Magazine)
Eerie Publications: No. 10, July, 1968 (35¢, B&W)

	GD 2.0	VG 4.0	FN 6.0	VF 8.0	VF/NM 9.0	NM- 9.2
10-Contains Farrell reprints from 1950s	5	10	15	30	48	65

TALES FROM THE CRYPT
Gladstone Publishing: July, 1990 - No. 6, May, 1991 ($1.95/$2.00, 68 pgs.)

1-r/TFTC #33 & Crime S.S. #17; Davis-c(r) 3.00
2-6: 2,3,5,6-Davis-c(r). 4-Begin $2.00-c; Craig-c(r) 3.00

TALES FROM THE CRYPT
Extra-Large Comics (Russ Cochran)/Gemstone Publishing: Jul, 1991 - No. 6 ($3.95, 10 1/4 x13 1/4", 68 pgs.)

1-Davis-c(r); Craig back-c(r); E.C. reprints 4.00
2-6 ($2.00, comic sized) 3.00

TALES FROM THE CRYPT
Russ Cochran: Sept, 1991 - No. 7, July, 1992 ($2.00, 64 pgs.)

1-7 3.00

TALES FROM THE CRYPT (Also see EC Archives • Tales From the Crypt)
Russ Cochran/Gemstone: Sept, 1992 - No. 30, Dec, 1999 ($1.50, quarterly)

1-4-r/Crypt of Terror #17-19, TFTC #20 w/original-c 3.00
5-30: 5-15 ($2.00)-r/TFTC #21-23 w/original-c. 16-30 ($2.50) 3.00
Annual 1-6('93-'99) 1-r/#1-5. 2- r/#6-10. 3- r/#11-15. 4- r/#16-20. 5-r/#21-25. 6- r/#26-30 14.00

TALES FROM THE CRYPT
Papercutz: July, 2007 - Present ($3.95)

1-6: 1-New stories in the same vein as the originals; Cryptkeeper app. Kyle Baker-c 4.00

TALES FROM THE GREAT BOOK
Famous Funnies: Feb, 1955 - No. 4, Jan, 1956 (Religious themes)

	GD 2.0	VG 4.0	FN 6.0	VF 8.0	VF/NM 9.0	NM- 9.2
1-Story of Samson; John Lehti-a in all	9	18	27	50	65	80
2-4. 2-Joshua. 3-Jonah the Boy King. 4-David	7	14	21	35	43	50

TALES FROM THE HEART OF AFRICA (The Temporary Natives)
Marvel Comics (Epic Comics): Aug, 1990 ($3.95, 52 pgs.)

1 4.00

TALES FROM THE TOMB (Also see Dell Giants)
Dell Publishing Co.: Oct, 1962 (25¢ giant)

	GD 2.0	VG 4.0	FN 6.0	VF 8.0	VF/NM 9.0	NM- 9.2
1(02-810-210)-All stories written by John Stanley	15	30	45	108	199	290

TALES FROM THE TOMB (Magazine)
Eerie Publications: V1#6, July, 1969 - V7#3, 1975 (52 pgs.)

	GD 2.0	VG 4.0	FN 6.0	VF 8.0	VF/NM 9.0	NM- 9.2
V1#6	7	14	21	45	73	100
V1#7,8	6	12	18	37	59	80
V2#1-6: 4-LSD story-r/Weird V3#5. 6-Rulah-r	5	10	15	30	48	65
V3#1-Rulah-r	5	10	15	30	48	65
2-6('71),V4#1-5('72),V5#1-6('73),V6#1-6('74),V7#1-3('75)	4	8	12	28	44	60

TALES OF ASGARD
Marvel Comics Group: Oct, 1968 (25¢, 68 pgs.); Feb, 1984 ($1.25, 52 pgs.)

	GD 2.0	VG 4.0	FN 6.0	VF 8.0	VF/NM 9.0	NM- 9.2
1-Reprints Tales of Asgard (Thor) back-up stories from Journey into Mystery #97-106; new Kirby-c; Kirby-a	5	10	15	32	51	70
V2#1 (2/84)-Thor-r; Simonson-c						5.00

TALES OF ARMY OF DARKNESS
Dynamite Entertainment: 2006 ($5.95, one-shot)

1-Short stories by Kuhoric, Kirkman, Bradshaw, Sablik, Ottley, Acs, O'Hare and others 6.00

TALES OF EVIL
Atlas/Seaboard Publ.: Feb, 1975 - No. 3, July, 1975 (All 25¢ issues)

	GD 2.0	VG 4.0	FN 6.0	VF 8.0	VF/NM 9.0	NM- 9.2
1-3: 1-Werewolf w/Sekowsky-a. 2-Intro. The Bog Beast; Sparling-a. 3-Origin The Man-Monster; Buckler-a(p)	1	2	3	6	8	10

NOTE: ***Grandenetti** a-1, 2. **Lieber** c-1. **Sekowsky** a-1. **Sutton** a-2. **Thorne** c-2.*

TALES OF GHOST CASTLE
National Periodical Publications: May-June, 1975 - No. 3, Sept-Oct, 1975 (All 25¢ issues)

	GD 2.0	VG 4.0	FN 6.0	VF 8.0	VF/NM 9.0	NM- 9.2
1-Redondo-a; 1st app. Lucien the Librarian from Sandman (1989 series)	3	6	9	14	20	25
2,3: 2-Nino-a. 3-Redondo-a.	2	4	6	8	11	14

TALES OF G.I. JOE
Marvel Comics: Jan, 1988 - No. 15, Mar, 1989

1 ($2.25, 52 pgs.) 3.00

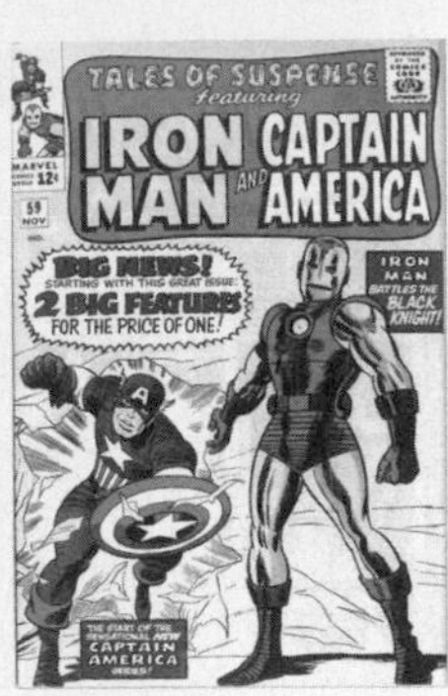
Tales of Suspense #59 © MAR

Tales of Terror Annual #3 © WMG

Tales of the Darkness #1 © TCOW

GD VG FN VF VF/NM NM-
2.0 4.0 6.0 8.0 9.0 9.2

GD VG FN VF VF/NM NM-
2.0 4.0 6.0 8.0 9.0 9.2

2-15 ($1.50): 1-15-r/G.I. Joe #1-15 2.50

TALES OF HORROR
Toby Press/Minoan Publ. Corp.: June, 1952 - No. 13, Oct, 1954

1 40 80 120 244 397 550
2-Torture scenes 32 64 96 186 298 410
3-13: 9-11-Reprints Purple Claw #1-3 22 44 66 127 204 280
12-Myron Fass-c/a; torture scenes 23 46 69 133 214 295
NOTE: ***Andru** a-5. **Baily** a-5. **Myron Fass** a-2, 3, 12; c-1-3, 12. **Hollingsworth** a-2. **Sparling** a-6, 9; c-9.*

TALES OF JUSTICE
Atlas Comics(MjMC No. 53-66/Male No. 67): No. 53, May, 1955 - No. 67, Aug, 1957

53 15 30 45 83 124 165
54-57: 54-Powell-a 11 22 33 60 83 105
58,59-Krigstein-a 12 24 36 67 94 120
60-63,65: 60-Powell-a 10 20 30 54 72 90
64,66,67: 64,67-Crandall-a. 66-Torres, Orlando-a 10 20 30 56 76 95
NOTE: ***Everett** a-53, 60. **Orlando** a-65, 66. **Severin** a-64; c-58, 60, 65. **Wildey** a-64, 67.*

TALES OF LEONARDO BLIND SIGHT (See Tales of the TMNT Vol. 2 #5)
Mirage Publishing: June, 2006 - No. 4, Sept, 2006 ($3.25, B&W, limited series)

1-4-Jim Lawson-s/a 3.25

TALES OF SUSPENSE (Becomes Captain America #100 on)
Atlas (WPI No. 1,2/Male No. 3-12/VPI No. 13-18)/Marvel No. 19 on:
Jan, 1959 - No. 99, Mar, 1968

1-Williamson-a (5 pgs.); Heck-c; #1-4 have sci/fi-c 150 300 450 1275 2438 3600
2,3: 2-Robot-c. 3-Flying saucer-c/story 52 104 156 442 846 1250
4-Williamson-a (4 pgs.); Kirby/Everett-c/a 43 86 129 344 647 950
5,6,8,10: 5-Kirby monster-c begin 33 66 99 254 477 700
7-Prototype ish. (Lava Man); 1 panel app. Aunt May (see Str. Tales #97)
36 72 108 280 520 760
9-Prototype ish. (Iron Man) 37 74 111 286 536 785
11,12,15,17-19: 12-Crandall-a. 27 54 81 196 368 540
13-Elektro-c/story 28 56 84 203 377 550
14-Intro/1st app. Colossus-c/sty 36 72 108 277 514 750
16-1st Metallo-c/story (4/61, Iron Man prototype) 32 64 96 246 461 675
20-Colossus-c/story (2nd app.) 29 58 87 213 394 575
21-25: 25-Last 10¢ issue 22 44 66 157 291 425
26,27,29,30,33,34,36-38: 33-(9/62)-Hulk 1st x-over cameo (picture on wall)
20 40 60 148 274 400
28-Prototype ish. (Stone Men) 21 42 63 152 281 410
31-Prototype ish. (Dr. Doom) 23 46 69 167 309 450
32-Prototype ish. (Dr. Strange)(8/62)-Sazzik The Sorcerer app.; "The Man and the Beehive" story, 1 month before TTA #35 (2nd Antman), came out after "The Man in the Ant Hill" in TTA #27 (1/62) (1st Antman)-Characters from both stories were tested to see which got best fan response 31 62 93 239 445 650
35-Prototype issue (The Watcher) 23 46 69 167 309 450
39 (3/63)-Origin/1st app. Iron Man & begin series; 1st Iron Man story has Kirby layouts
600 1200 1800 5400 10,200 15,000
40-2nd app. Iron Man (in new armor) 152 304 456 1317 2509 3700
41-3rd app. Iron Man; Dr. Strange (villain) app. 88 176 264 748 1424 2100
42-45: 45-Intro. & 1st app. Happy & Pepper 52 104 156 442 846 1250
46,47: 46-1st app. Crimson Dynamo 41 82 123 328 614 900
48-New Iron Man armor by Ditko 48 96 144 384 717 1050
49-1st X-Men x-over (same date as X-Men #3, 1/64); also 1st Avengers x-over (w/o Captain America); 1st Tales of the Watcher back-up story & begins (2nd app. Watcher; see F.F. #13) 58 116 174 493 947 1400
50-1st app. Mandarin 30 60 90 222 411 600
51-1st Scarecrow 23 46 69 167 309 450
52-1st app. The Black Widow (4/64) 32 64 96 246 461 675
53-Origin The Watcher; 2nd Black Widow app. 23 46 69 167 309 450
54-56: 56-1st app. Unicorn 17 34 51 120 223 325
57-Origin/1st app. Hawkeye (9/64) 33 66 99 254 477 700
58-Captain America battles Iron Man (10/64)-Classic-c; 2nd Kraven app. (Cap's 1st app. in this title) 36 72 108 277 514 750
59-Iron Man plus Captain America double feature begins (11/64); 1st S.A. Captain America solo story; intro Jarvis, Avenger's butler; classic-c 36 72 108 277 514 750
60-2nd app. Hawkeye (#64 is 3rd app.) 20 40 60 143 264 385
61,62,64: 62-Origin Mandarin (2/65) 12 24 36 87 156 225
63-1st Silver Age origin Captain America (3/65) 26 52 78 192 359 525
65-G.A. Red Skull in WWII stories(also in #66);-1st Silver-Age Red Skull (5/65).
19 38 57 139 257 375
66-Origin Red Skull 15 30 45 107 196 285
67-70: 69-1st app. Titanium Man. 70-Begin alternating-c features w/Capt. America (even #'s) & Iron Man (odd #'s) 8 16 24 58 97 135
71-75, 77,78,81-98: 75-1st app. Agent 13 later named Sharon Carter. 78-Col. Nick Fury app. 82-Intro the Adaptoid by Kirby (also in #83,84). 88-Mole Man app. in Iron Man story. 92-1st Nick Fury x-over (cameo, as Agent of S.H.I.E.L.D., 8/67). 94-Intro Modok. 95-Capt. America's i.d. revealed. 97-1st Whiplash. 98-1st brief app. new Zemo (son?); #99 is 1st full app. 6 12 18 41 66 90
76-Intro Batroc & Sharon Carter, Agent 13 of S.H.I.E.L.D.
7 14 21 45 73 100
79-Begin 3 part Iron Man Sub-Mariner battle story; Sub-Mariner-c & cameo; 1st app. Cosmic Cube; 1st modern Red Skull 8 16 24 52 86 120
80-Iron Man battles Sub-Mariner story cont'd in Tales to Astonish #82; classic Red Skull-c
8 16 24 52 86 120
99-Captain America story cont'd in Captain America #100; Iron Man story cont'd in Iron Man & Sub-Mariner #1 8 16 24 52 86 120
Onmibus (See Iron Man Omnibus for reprints of #39-83)
NOTE: ***Abel** a-73-81i(as Gary Michaels), **J. Buscema** a-1; c-3. **Colan** a-39, 73-99p; c(p)-73, 75, 77, 79, 81, 83, 85-87, 89, 91, 93, 95, 97, 99. **Crandall** a-12. **Davis** a-38. **Ditko** a-1-15, 17-44, 46, 47-49p; c-2, 10i, 13i, 23i. **Kirby/Ditko** a-7; c-10, 13, 22, 28, 34. **Everett** a-8. **Forte** a-5, 9. **Giacoia** a-82. **Heath** a-2, 10. **Gil Kane** a-88p, 89-91; c-88, 89-91p. **Kirby** a(p)-2-4, 6-35, 40, 41, 43, 59-75, 77-86, 92-99; layouts-69-75, 77; c(p)4-28(most), 29-56, 58-72, 74, 76, 78, 80, 82, 84, 86, 92, 94, 96, 98. **Leiber/Fox** a-42, 43, 45, 51. **Reinman** a-26, 44i, 49i, 52i, 53i. **Tuska** a-58, 70-74. **Wood** c/a-71i.*

TALES OF SUSPENSE
Marvel Comics: V2#1, Jan, 1995 ($6.95, one-shot)

V2#1-James Robinson script; acetate-c. 7.00

TALES OF SUSPENSE: CAPTAIN AMERICA & IRON MAN #1 COMMEMORATIVE EDITION
Marvel Comics: 2004 ($3.99, one-shot)

nn-Reprints Captain America (2004) #1 and Iron Man (2004) #1 4.00

TALES OF SWORD & SORCERY (See Dagar)

TALES OF TELLOS (See Tellos)
Image Comics: Oct, 2004 - No. 3, ($3.50, anthology)

1-3: 1-Dezago-s; art by Yates & Rousseau; Wieringo-c. 3-Porter-a 3.50

TALES OF TERROR
Toby Press Publications: 1952 (no month)

1-Fawcette-c; Ravielli-a 26 52 78 154 247 340
NOTE: *This title was cancelled due to similarity to the E.C. title.*

TALES OF TERROR (See Movie Classics)

TALES OF TERROR (Magazine)
Eerie Publications: Summer, 1964

1 6 12 18 37 59 80

TALES OF TERROR
Eclipse Comics: July, 1985 - No. 13, July, 1987 ($2.00, Baxter paper, mature)

1-13: 5-1st Lee Weeks-a. 7-Sam Kieth-a. 10-Snyder-a. 12-Vampire story 3.00

TALES OF TERROR (IDW's...)
IDW Publishing: Sept, 2004 ($16.99, hardcover)

1-Anthology of short graphic stories and text stories; incl. 30 Days of Night 17.00

TALES OF TERROR ANNUAL
E.C. Comics: 1951 - No. 3, 1953 (25¢, 132 pgs., 16 stories each)

nn(1951)(Scarce)-Feldstein infinity-c 750 1500 2250 6000 - -
2(1952)-Feldstein-c 253 506 759 1594 2697 3800
3(1953)-Feldstein bondage/torture-c 200 400 600 1260 2130 3000
NOTE: *No. 1 contains three horror and one science fiction comic which came out in 1950. No. 2 contains a horror, crime, and science fiction book which generally had cover dates in 1951, and No. 3 had horror, crime, and shock books that generally appeared in 1952. All E.C. annuals contain four complete books that did not sell on the stands which were rebound in the annual format, minus the covers, and sold from the E.C. office and on the stands in key cities. The contents of each annual may vary in the same year. Crypt Keeper, Vault Keeper, Old Witch app. on all-c.*

TALES OF TERROR ILLUSTRATED (See Terror Illustrated)

TALES OF TEXAS JOHN SLAUGHTER (See Walt Disney Presents, 4-Color #997)

TALES OF THE BEANWORLD
Beanworld Press/Eclipse Comics: Feb, 1985 - No. 19, 1991; No. 20, 1993 - No. 21, 1993 ($1.50/$2.00, B&W)

1-21 3.00

TALES OF THE BIZARRO WORLD
DC Comics: 2000 ($14.95, TPB)

nn-Reprints early Bizarro stories; new Jaime Hernandez-c 15.00

TALES OF THE DARKNESS
Image Comics (Top Cow): Apr, 1998 - No. 4, Dec, 1998 ($2.95)

1-4: 1,2-Portacio-c/a(p). 3,4-Lansing & Nocon-a(p) 3.00
1-American Entertainment Ed. 3.00

Tales of the Mysterious Traveller #9 © CC

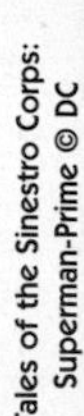
Tales of the Sinestro Corps: Superman-Prime © DC

Tales of the Unexpected #13 © DC

	GD 2.0	VG 4.0	FN 6.0	VF 8.0	VF/NM 9.0	NM- 9.2
#1/2 (1/01, $2.95)						3.00

TALES OF THE GREEN BERET
Dell Publishing Co.: Jan, 1967 - No. 5, Oct, 1969

	GD	VG	FN	VF	VF/NM	NM-
1-Glanzman-a in 1-4 & 5r	4	8	12	20	30	40
2-5: 5-Reprints #1	3	6	9	16	23	30

TALES OF THE GREEN HORNET
Now Comics: Sept, 1990 - No. 2, 1990; V2#1, Jan, 1992 - No.4, Apr, 1992; V3#1, Sept, 1992 - No. 3, Nov, 1992

	GD	VG	FN	VF	VF/NM	NM-
1,2						2.50
V2#1-4 ($1.95)						2.50
V3#1 ($2.75)-Polybagged w/hologram trading card						3.00
V3#2,3 ($2.50)						2.50

TALES OF THE GREEN LANTERN CORPS (See Green Lantern #107)
DC Comics: May, 1981 - No. 3, July, 1981 (Limited series)

	GD	VG	FN	VF	VF/NM	NM-
1-3: 1-Origin of G.L. & the Guardians, Annual 1 (1/85)-Gil Kane c/a						3.50

TALES OF THE INVISIBLE SCARLET O'NEIL (See Harvey Comics Hits #59)

TALES OF THE KILLERS (Magazine)
World Famous Periodicals: V1#10, Dec, 1970 - V1#11, Feb, 1971 (B&W, 52 pg)

	GD	VG	FN	VF	VF/NM	NM-
V1#10-One pg. Frazetta; r/Crime Does Not Pay	4	8	12	28	44	60
11-similar-c to Crime Does Not Pay #47; contains r/Crime Does Not Pay	4	8	12	24	37	50

TALES OF THE LEGION (Formerly Legion of Super-Heroes)
DC Comics: No. 314, Aug, 1984 - No. 354, Dec, 1987

	GD	VG	FN	VF	VF/NM	NM-
314-354: 326-r-begin						2.50
Annual 4,5 (1986, 1987)-Formerly LSH Annual						3.50

TALES OF THE MARINES (Formerly Devil-Dog Dugan #1-3)
Atlas Comics (OPI): No. 4, Feb, 1957 (Marines At War #5 on)

	GD	VG	FN	VF	VF/NM	NM-
4-Powell-a; Severin-c	10	20	30	54	72	90

TALES OF THE MARVELS
Marvel Comics: 1995/1996 (all acetate, painted-c)

	GD	VG	FN	VF	VF/NM	NM-
...Blockbuster 1 (1995, $5.95, one-shot), ...Inner Demons 1 (1996, $5.95, one shot), ...Wonder Years 1,2 (1995, $4.95, limited series)						6.00

TALES OF THE MARVEL UNIVERSE
Marvel Comics: Feb, 1997 ($2.95, one-shot)

	GD	VG	FN	VF	VF/NM	NM-
1-Anthology; wraparound-c; Thunderbolts, Ka-Zar app.						3.00

TALES OF THE MYSTERIOUS TRAVELER (See Mysterious...)
Charlton Comics: Aug, 1956 - No. 13, June, 1959; V2#14, Oct, 1985 - No. 15, Dec, 1985

	GD	VG	FN	VF	VF/NM	NM-
1-No Ditko-a; Giordano/Alascia-c	50	100	150	310	518	725
2-Ditko-a(1)	41	82	123	250	413	575
3-Ditko-c/a(1)	41	82	123	256	428	600
4-7-Ditko-c/a(3-4 stories each)	48	96	144	298	499	700
8,9-Ditko-a(1-3 each). 8-Rocke-c	40	80	120	246	403	560
10,11-Ditko-c/a(3-4 each)	44	88	132	273	454	635
12	18	36	54	103	162	220
13-Baker-a (r?)	19	38	57	109	172	235
V2#14,15 (1985)-Ditko-c/a-low print run	1	2	3	5	7	9

TALES OF THE NEW GODS
DC Comics: 2008 ($19.99, TPB)

	GD	VG	FN	VF	VF/NM	NM-
SC-Reprints from Jack Kirby's Fourth World, Orion and Mister Miracle Special						20.00

TALES OF THE NEW TEEN TITANS
DC Comics: June, 1982 - No. 4, Sept, 1982 (Limited series)

	GD	VG	FN	VF	VF/NM	NM-
1-4						4.00

TALES OF THE PONY EXPRESS (TV)
Dell Publishing Co.: No. 829, Aug, 1957 - No. 942, Oct, 1958

	GD	VG	FN	VF	VF/NM	NM-
Four Color 829 (#1)--Painted-c	5	10	15	30	48	65
Four Color 942-Title -Pony Express	5	10	15	30	48	65

TALES OF THE REALM
CrossGen Comics/MVCreations #4-on: Oct, 2003 - No. 5, May, 2004 ($2.95, limited series)

	GD	VG	FN	VF	VF/NM	NM-
1-5-Robert Kirkman-s/Matt Tyree-a						3.00
Volume 1 HC (8/04, $39.95, dust jacket) r/#1-5; sketch pages and concept art						40.00

TALES OF THE SINESTRO CORPS (See Green Lantern and Green Lantern Corps x-over)
DC Comics: Nov, 2007 - Jan, 2008 ($2.99/$3.99, one-shots)

	GD	VG	FN	VF	VF/NM	NM-
...: Cyborg-Superman (12/07, $2.99) Burnett-s/Blaine-a/VanSciver-c; JLA app.						3.00
...: Ion (1/08, $2.99) Marz-s/Lacombe-a/Benes-c; Sodam Yat app.						3.00
...: Parallax (11/07, $2.99) Marz-s/Melo-a; Kyle Rayner vs. Parallax						3.00
...: Superman-Prime (12/07, $3.99) Johns-s/VanSciver-c; origin re-told w/Ordway-a						4.00

TALES OF THE TEENAGE MUTANT NINJA TURTLES (See Teenage Mutant...)
Mirage Studios: May, 1987 - No. 7, Aug (Apr-c), 1989 (B&W, $1.50)

	GD	VG	FN	VF	VF/NM	NM-
1-7: 2-Title merges w/Teenage Mutant Ninja...						2.50

TALES OF THE TEEN TITANS (Formerly The New Teen Titans)
DC Comics: No. 41, Apr, 1984 - No. 91, July, 1988 (75¢)

	GD	VG	FN	VF	VF/NM	NM-
41,45-49: 46-Aqualad & Aquagirl join						3.00
42-44: The Judas Contract part 1-3 with Deathstroke the Terminator in all; concludes in Annual #3. 44-Dick Grayson becomes Nightwing (3rd to be Nightwing) & joins Titans; Jericho (Deathstroke's son) joins; origin Deathstroke						3.50
50,53-55: 50-Double size; app. Betty Kane (Bat-Girl) out of costume. 53-1st full app. Azrael; Deathstroke cameo. 54,55-Deathstroke-c/stories						3.50
51,52,56-91: 52-1st brief app. Azrael (not same as newer character). 56-Intro Jinx. 57-Neutron app. 59-r/DC Comics Presents #26. 60-91-r/New Teen Titans Baxter series. 68-B. Smith-c. 70-Origin Kole						2.50
Annual 3(1984, $1.25)-Part 4 of The Judas Contract; Deathstroke-c/story; Death of Terra; indicia says Teen Titans Annual; previous annuals listed as New Teen Titans Annual #1,2						4.00
Annual 4-(1986, $1.25)						2.50

TALES OF THE TEXAS RANGERS (See Jace Pearson...)

TALES OF THE THING (Fantastic Four)
Marvel Comics: May, 2005 - No. 3, July, 2005 ($2.50, limited series)

	GD	VG	FN	VF	VF/NM	NM-
1-3-Dr. Strange app; Randy Green-c						2.50

TALES OF THE TMNT (Also see Teenage Mutant Ninja Turtles)
Mirage Studios: Jan, 2004 - Present ($2.95/$3.25, B&W)

	GD	VG	FN	VF	VF/NM	NM-
1-7: 1-Brizuela-a						3.00
8-50: 8-Begin $3.25-c. 47-Origin of the Super Turtles						3.25

TALES OF THE UNEXPECTED (Becomes The Unexpected #105 on)(See Adventure #75, Super DC Giant)
National Periodical Publications: Feb-Mar, 1956 - No. 104, Dec-Jan, 1967-68

	GD	VG	FN	VF	VF/NM	NM-
1	100	200	300	850	1625	2400
2	43	86	129	344	647	950
3-5	32	64	96	246	461	675
6-10: 6-1st Silver Age issue	26	52	78	192	359	525
11,14,19,20	18	36	54	130	240	350
12,13,15-18,21-24: All have Kirby-a. 15,17-Grey tone-c. 16-Characters named 'Thor' (with a magic hammer) and Loki by Kirby (8/57, characters do not look like Marvel's Thor & Loki)	22	44	66	157	291	425
25-30	15	30	45	111	206	300
31-39	14	28	42	99	175	250
40-Space Ranger begins (8/59, 3rd ap.), ends #82	100	200	300	850	1625	2400
41,42-Space Ranger stories	37	74	111	283	529	775
43-1st Space Ranger-c this title; grey tone-c	65	130	195	553	1052	1550
44-46	24	48	72	180	335	485
47-50	19	38	57	139	257	375
51-60: 54-Dinosaur-c/story	15	30	45	111	206	300
61-67: 67-Last 10¢ issue	14	28	42	99	175	250
68-82: 82-Last Space Ranger	8	16	24	58	97	135
83,90,92-99	6	12	18	41	66	90
91,100: 91-1st Automan (also in #94,97)	6	12	18	43	69	95
101-104	6	12	18	37	59	80

NOTE: ***Neal Adams** c-104. **Anderson** a-50. **Brown** a-50-82(Space Ranger); c-19, 40, & many Space Ranger-c. **Cameron** a-24, 27, 29; c-24. **Heath** a-49. **Bob Kane** a-24, 48. **Kirby** a-12, 13, 15-18, 21-24; c-13, 18, 22. **Meskin** a-15, 18, 26, 27, 35, 66. **Moreira** a-16, 20, 29, 38, 44, 62, 71; c-38. **Roussos** c-10. **Wildey** a-31.*

TALES OF THE UNEXPECTED (See Crisis Aftermath: The Spectre)
DC Comics: Dec, 2006 - No. 8, Jul, 2007 ($3.99, limited series)

	GD	VG	FN	VF	VF/NM	NM-
1-8-The Spectre, Lapham-s/Battle-a; Dr. 13, Azzarello-s/Chiang-a. 4-Wrightson-c						4.00
1-Variant Spectre cover by Neal Adams						5.00
The Spectre: Tales of the Unexpected TPB (2007, $14.99) r/#4-8						15.00

TALES OF THE VAMPIRES (Also see Buffy the Vampire Slayer and related titles)
Dark Horse Comics: 2003 - No. 5, Apr, 2004 ($2.99, limited series)

	GD	VG	FN	VF	VF/NM	NM-
1-Short stories by Joss Whedon and others. 1-Totleben-c. 3-Powell-c. 4-Edlund-c						3.00
TPB (11/04, $15.95) r/#1-5; afterword by Marv Wolfman						16.00

TALES OF THE WEST (See 3-D...)

TALES OF THE WITCHBLADE
Image Comics (Top Cow Productions): Nov, 1996 - No. 9 ($2.95)

	GD	VG	FN	VF	VF/NM	NM-
1/2	1	2	3	5	7	9
1/2 Gold						15.00
1-Daniel-c/a(p)	1	3	4	6	8	10

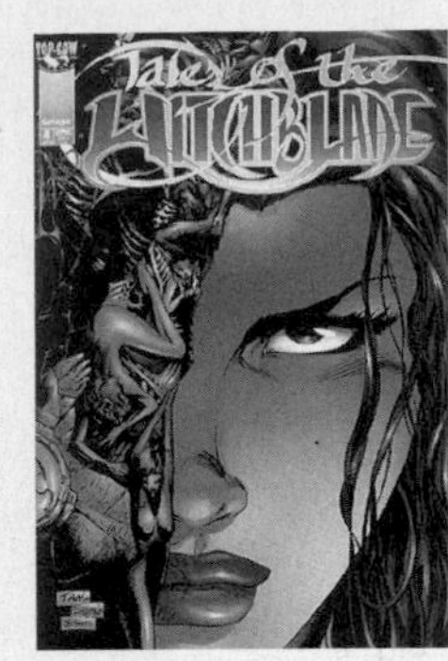

Tales of the Witchblade #4 © TCOW

Tales to Astonish #7 © MAR

Tangent Comics / Flash #1 © DC

	GD	VG	FN	VF	VF/NM	NM-
	2.0	4.0	6.0	8.0	9.0	9.2

1-Variant-c by Turner 2 4 6 9 12 15
1-Platinum Edition 30.00
2,3 6.00
4-6: 6-Green-c 5.00
7-9: 9-Lara Croft-c 3.00
7-Variant-c by Turner 1 2 3 5 6 8
Witchblade: Distinctions (4/01, $14.95, TPB) r/#1-6; Green-c 15.00

TALES OF THE WITCHBLADE COLLECTED EDITION
Image Comics (Top Cow): May, 1998 - No. 2 ($4.95/$5.95, square-bound)

1,2: 1-r/#1,2. 2-($5.95) r/#3,4 6.00

TALES OF THE WIZARD OF OZ (See Wizard of OZ, 4-Color #1308)

TALES OF THE ZOMBIE (Magazine)
Marvel Comics Group: Aug, 1973 - No. 10, Mar, 1975 (75¢, B&W)

V1#1-Reprint/Menace #5; origin 5 10 15 30 48 65
2,3: 2-Everett biog. & memorial 4 8 12 24 37 50
V2#1(#4)-Photos & text of James Bond movie "Live & Let Die"
3 6 9 20 30 40
5-10: 8-Kaluta-a 3 6 9 18 27 35
Annual 1(Summer,'75)(#11)-B&W; Everett, Buscema-a
3 6 9 20 30 40

NOTE: Brother Voodoo app. 2, 5, 6, 10. ***Alcala** a-7-9. **Boris** c-1-4. **Colan** a-2r, 6. **Heath** a-5r. **Reese** a-2. **Tuska** a-2r.*

TALES OF THUNDER
Deluxe Comics: Mar, 1985

1-Dynamo, Iron Maiden, Menthor app.; Giffen-a 2.50

TALES OF VOODOO
Eerie Publications: V1#11, Nov, 1968 - V7#6, Nov, 1974 (Magazine)

V1#11 6 12 18 41 66 90
V2#1(3/69)-V2#4(9/69) 4 8 12 28 44 60
V3#1-6('70): 4- "Claws of the Cat" redrawn from Climax #1
4 8 12 22 34 45
V4#1-6('71), V5#1-7('72), V6#1-6('73), V7#1-6('74) 4 8 12 22 34 45
Annual 1 4 8 12 24 37 50

NOTE: *Bondage-c-V1#10, V2#4, V3#4.*

TALES OF WELLS FARGO (TV)(See Western Roundup under Dell Giants)
Dell Publishing Co.: No. 876, Feb, 1958 - No. 1215, Oct-Dec, 1961

Four Color 876 (#1)-Photo-c 9 18 27 60 100 140
Four Color 968 (2/59), 1023, 1075 (3/60), 1113 (7-9/60)-All photo-c
8 16 24 56 93 130
Four Color 1167 (3-5/61), 1215-Photo-c 8 16 24 52 86 120

TALESPIN (Also see Cartoon Tales & Disney's Talespin Limited Series)
Disney Comics: June, 1991 - No. 7, Dec, 1991 ($1.50)

1-7 2.50

TALES TO ASTONISH (Becomes The Incredible Hulk #102 on)
Atlas (MAP No. 1/ZPC No. 2-14/VPI No. 15-21/Marvel No. 22 on: Jan, 1959 - No. 101, Mar, 1968

1-Jack Davis-a; monster-c. 150 300 450 1275 2438 3600
2-Ditko flying saucer-c (Martians); #2-4 have sci/fi-c.
58 116 174 493 947 1400
3,4 43 86 129 344 647 950
5-Prototype issue (Stone Men); Williamson-a (4 pgs.); Kirby monster-c begin
45 90 135 360 673 985
6-Prototype issue (Stone Men) 36 72 108 277 514 750
7-Prototype issue (Toad Men) 36 72 108 277 514 750
8-10 32 64 96 248 467 685
11-14,17-20: 13-Swipes story from Menace #8 27 54 81 196 366 535
15-Prototype issue (Electro) 32 64 96 250 468 685
16-Prototype issue (Stone Men) 29 58 87 213 394 575
21-(7/61)-Hulk prototype 29 58 87 213 394 575
22-26,28-34: 32-Sandman prototype 22 44 66 157 291 425
27-1st Ant-Man app. (1/62); last 10¢ issue (see Strange Tales #73,78 & Tales of Suspense #32) 385 770 1155 3465 6733 10,000
35-(9/62)-2nd app. Ant-Man, 1st in costume; begin series & Ant-Man-c
160 320 480 1400 2700 4000
36-3rd app. Ant-Man 71 142 213 604 1152 1700
37-40: 38-1st app. Egghead 41 82 123 328 614 900
41-43 33 66 99 254 477 700
44-Origin & 1st app. The Wasp (6/63) 43 86 129 344 647 950
45-48: 48-Origin & 1st app. The Porcupine. 22 44 66 157 291 425
49-Ant-Man becomes Giant Man (11/63) 26 52 78 192 359 525

	GD	VG	FN	VF	VF/NM	NM-
	2.0	4.0	6.0	8.0	9.0	9.2

50,51,53-56,58: 50-Origin/1st app. Human Top (alias Whirlwind). 53-Origin Colossus
15 30 45 105 190 275
52-Origin/1st app. Black Knight (2/64) 17 34 51 120 223 325
57-Early Spider-Man app. (7/64) 31 62 93 239 445 650
59-Giant Man vs. Hulk feature story (9/64); Hulk's 1st app. this title
29 58 87 216 401 585
60-Giant Man & Hulk double feature begins 20 40 60 148 274 400
61-69: 61-All Ditko issue; 1st mailbag. 62-1st app./origin The Leader; new Wasp costume; Hulk pin-up page missing from many copies. 63-Origin Leader; 65-New Giant Man costume. 68-New Human Top costume. 69-Last Giant Man 10 20 30 73 129 185
70-Sub-Mariner & Incredible Hulk begins (8/65) 12 24 36 82 146 210
71-81,83-91,94-99: 72-Begin alternating-c features w/Sub-Mariner (even #'s) & Hulk (odd #'s). 79-Hulk vs. Hercules-c/story. 81-1st app. Boomerang. 90-1st app. The Abomination. 97-X-Men cameo (brief) 6 12 18 39 62 85
82-Iron Man battles Sub-Mariner (1st Iron Man x-over outside The Avengers & TOS); story cont'd from Tales of Suspense #80 7 14 21 49 80 110
92-1st Silver Surfer x-over (outside of Fantastic Four, 6/67); 1 panel cameo only
7 14 21 47 76 105
93-Hulk battles Silver Surfer-c/story (1st full x-over) 13 26 39 95 168 240
100-Hulk battles Sub-Mariner full-length story 7 14 21 49 80 110
101-Hulk story cont'd in Incredible Hulk #102; Sub-Mariner story continued in Iron Man & Sub-Mariner #1 8 16 24 52 86 120

NOTE: ***Ayers** c(i)-9-12, 16, 18, 19. **Berg** a-1. **Burgos** a-62-64p. **Buscema** a-85-87p. **Colan** a(p)-70-76, 78-82, 84, 85, 101; c(p)-71-76, 78, 80, 82, 84, 86, 88, 90. **Ditko** a-1, 3-48, 50i, 60-67p; c-2, 7i, 8i, 14i, 17i. **Everett** a-78, 79i, 80-84, 85-90i, 94i, 95, 96; c(i)-79-81, 83, 86, 88. **Forte** a-6. **Kane** a-76, 88-91; c-89, 91. **Kirby** a(p)-1, 5-34-40, 44, 49-51, 68-70, 82, 83; layouts-71-84; c(p)-1, 3-48, 50-70, 72, 73, 75, 77, 78, 79, 81, 85, 90. **Kirby/Ditko** a-7, 8, 12, 13, 50; c-7, 8, 10, 13. **Leiber/Fox** a-47, 48, 50, 51. **Powell** a-65-69p, 73, 74. **Reinman** a-6, 36, 45, 46, 54i, 56-60i.*

TALES TO ASTONISH (2nd Series)
Marvel Comics Group: Dec, 1979 - No. 14, Jan, 1981

V1#1-Reprints Sub-Mariner #1 by Buscema 6.00
2-14: Reprints Sub-Mariner #2-14 4.00

TALES TO ASTONISH
Marvel Comics: V3#1, Oct, 1994 ($6.95, one-shot)

V3#1-Peter David scripts; acetate, painted-c 7.00

TALES TO HOLD YOU SPELLBOUND (See Spellbound)

TALES TO OFFEND
Dark Horse Comics: July, 1997 ($2.95, one-shot)

1-Frank Miller-s/a, EC-style cover 3.50

TALES TOO TERRIBLE TO TELL (Becomes Terrology #10, 11)
New England Comics: Wint, 1989-90 - No. 11, Nov-Dec.1993 ($2.95/$3.50, B&W with card-stock covers)

1-($2.95) Reprints of non-EC pre-code horror; EC-style cover by Bissette 4.00
1-($3.50, 5-6/93) Second printing with alternate cover not by Bissette 4.00
2-8-($3.50) Story reprints, history of the pre-code titles and creators; cover galleries (B&W) inside & on back-c (color) 4.00
9-11-($2.95) 10,11-"Terrology" on cover 4.00

TALEWEAVER
DC Comics (WildStorm): Nov, 2001 - No. 6, Apr, 2002 ($3.50, limited series)

1-6-Philip Tan-a/Leonard Banaag-s. 2-Variant-c by Anacleto 3.50

TALKING KOMICS
Belda Record & Publ. Co.: 1947 (20 pgs, slick-c)

Each comic contained a record that followed the story.- much like the Golden Record sets. Known titles: Chirpy Cricket, Lonesome Octopus, Sleepy Santa, Grumpy Shark, Flying Turtle, Happy Grasshopper
with records... 3 6 9 16 23 30

TALLY-HO COMICS
Swappers Quarterly (Baily Publ. Co.): Dec, 1944

nn-Frazetta's 1st work as Giunta's assistant; Man in Black horror story; violence; Giunta-c 47 94 141 291 483 675

TALULLAH (See Comic Books Series I)

TAMMY, TELL ME TRUE
Dell Publishing Co.: No. 1233, 1961

Four Color 1233-Movie 6 12 18 43 69 95

TANGENT COMICS
../ THE ATOM, DC Comics: Dec, 1997 ($2.95, one-shot)
1-Dan Jurgens-s/Jurgens & Paul Ryan-a 3.00
../ THE BATMAN, DC Comics: Sept, 1998 ($1.95, one-shot)
1-Dan Jurgens-s/Klaus Janson-a 3.00

Tank Girl - The Odyssey #3 © Deadline

Target Comics V9#6 © NOVP

Targitt #2 © Seaboard

GD 2.0 | VG 4.0 | FN 6.0 | VF 8.0 | VF/NM 9.0 | NM- 9.2

.../ DOOM PATROL, DC Comics: Dec, 1997 ($2.95, one-shot)
1- Dan Jurgens-s/Sean Chen & Kevin Conrad-a 3.00

.../ THE FLASH, DC Comics: Dec, 1997 ($2.95, one-shot)
1-Todd Dezago-s/Gary Frank & Cam Smith-a 3.00

.../ GREEN LANTERN, DC Comics: Dec, '97 ($2.95, one-shot)
1-James Robinson-s/J.H. Williams III & Mick Gray-a 3.00

.../ JLA, DC Comics: Sept, 1998 ($1.95, one-shot)
1-Dan Jurgens-s/Banks & Rapmund-a 3.00

.../ THE JOKER, DC Comics: Dec, 1997 ($2.95, one-shot)
1-Karl Kesel-s/Matt Haley & Tom Simmons-a 3.00

.../ THE JOKER'S WILD, DC Comics: Sept, 1998 ($1.95, one-shot)
1-Kesel & Simmons-s/Phillips & Rodriguez-a 2.25

.../ METAL MEN, DC Comics: Dec, 1997 ($2.95, one-shot)
1-Ron Marz-s/Mike McKone & Mark McKenna-a 3.00

.../ NIGHTWING, DC Comics: Dec, 1997 ($2.95, one-shot)
1-John Ostrander-s/Jan Duursema-a 3.00

.../ NIGHTWING: NIGHTFORCE, DC Comics: Sept, 1998 ($1.95, one-shot)
1-John Ostrander-s/Jan Duursema-a 2.50

.../ POWERGIRL, DC Comics: Sept, 1998 ($1.95, one-shot)
1-Marz-s/Abell & Vines-a 2.50

.../ SEA DEVILS, DC Comics: Dec, 1997 ($2.95, one-shot)
1-Kurt Busiek-s/Vince Giarrano & Tom Palmer-a 3.00

.../ SECRET SIX, DC Comics: Dec, 1997 ($2.95, one-shot)
1-Chuck Dixon-s/Tom Grummett & Lary Stucker-a 3.00

.../ THE SUPERMAN, DC Comics: Sept, 1998 ($1.95, one-shot)
1-Millar-s/Guice-a 3.00

.../ TALES OF THE GREEN LANTERN, DC Comics: Sept, 1998 ($1.95, one-shot)
1-Story & art by various 3.00

.../ THE TRIALS OF THE FLASH, DC Comics: Sept, 1998 ($1.95, one-shot)
1-Dezago-s/Pelletier & Lanning-a 2.50

.../ WONDER WOMAN DC Comics: Sept, 1998 ($1.95, one-shot),
1-Peter David-s/Unzueta & Mendoza-a 3.00
... Volume One TPB (2007, $19.99) r/The Atom, Metal Men, Green Lantern, The Flash, Sea Devils one-shots; intro and new cover by Jurgens 20.00
... Volume Two TPB (2008, $19.99) r/Batman, Doom Patrol, Joker, Nightwing and Secret Six one-shots; new cover by Jurgens 20.00
... Volume Three TPB (2008, $19.99) r/The Superman, Wonder Woman, Nightwing: Nightforce, The Joker's Wild, The Trials of the Flash, Tales of the Green Lantern, Powergirl, and JLA one-shots; new cover by Jurgens 20.00

TANGENT: SUPERMAN'S REIGN
DC Comics: May, 2008 - No. 12 ($2.99, limited series)
1-5-Jurgens-s; Flash & Green Lantern app.; back-up histories of Tangent heroes 3.00

TANGLED WEB (See Spider-Man's Tangled Web)

TANK GIRL
Dark Horse Comics: May, 1991 - No. 4, Aug, 1991 ($2.25, B&W, mini-series)
1-Contains Dark Horse trading cards 6.00
2-4 4.00

TANK GIRL: APOCALYPSE
DC Comics: Nov, 1995 - No. 4, Feb, 1996 ($2.25, limited series)
1-4 3.00

TANK GIRL: MOVIE ADAPTATION
DC Comics: 1995 ($5.95, 68 pgs., one-shot)
nn-Peter Milligan scripts 6.00

TANK GIRL: THE GIFTING
IDW Publishing: May, 2007 - No. 4, Aug, 2007 ($3.99)
1-4: 1-Ashley Wood-a/c; Alan Martin-s; 3 covers 4.00

TANK GIRL: THE ODYSSEY
DC Comics: May, 1995 - No.4, Oct, 1995 ($2.25, limited series)
1-4: Peter Milligan scripts; Hewlett-a 3.00

TANK GIRL 2
Dark Horse Comics: June, 1993 - No. 4, Sept, 1993 ($2.50, lim. series, mature)
1-4: Jamie Hewlett & Alan Martin-s/a 3.00
TPB (2/95, $17.95) r/#1-4 18.00

TAPPAN'S BURRO (See Zane Grey & 4-Color #449)

TAPPING THE VEIN (Clive Barker's...)
Eclipse Comics: 1989 - No. 5, 1992 ($6.95, squarebound, mature, 68 pgs.)
Book 1-5: 1-Russell-a, Bolton-c. 2-Bolton-a. 4-Die-cut-c 7.00
TPB (2002, $24.95, Checker Book Publ. Group) r/#1-5 25.00

TARANTULA (See Weird Suspense)

TARGET: AIRBOY
Eclipse Comics: Mar, 1988 ($1.95)
1 2.50

TARGET COMICS (...Western Romances #106 on)
Funnies, Inc./Novelty Publications/Star Publ.: Feb, 1940 - V10#3 (#105), Aug-Sept, 1949

	GD 2.0	VG 4.0	FN 6.0	VF 8.0	VF/NM 9.0	NM- 9.2
V1#1-Origin & 1st app. Manowar, The White Streak by Burgos, & Bulls-Eye Bill by Everett; City Editor (ends #5), High Grass Twins by Jack Cole (ends #4), T-Men by Joe Simon (ends #9), Rip Rory (ends #4), Fantastic Feature Films by Tarpe Mills (ends #39), & Calling 2-R (ends #14) begin; marijuana use story	500	1000	1500	3600	6300	9000
2-Everett-c/a	253	506	759	1594	2697	3800
3,4-Everett, Jack Cole-a	152	304	456	958	1617	2275
5-Origin The White Streak in text; Space Hawk by Wolverton begins (6/40) (see Blue Bolt & Circus)	423	846	1269	3046	5323	7600
6-The Chameleon by Everett begins (7/40, 1st app.); White Streak origin cont'd. in text; early mention of comic collecting in letter column; 1st letter column in comics? (7/40)	215	430	645	1355	2290	3225
7-Wolverton Spacehawk-c/story (Scarce)	667	1334	2001	4802	8401	12,000
8-Classic sci-fi cover	183	366	549	1153	1952	2750
9,12: 12-(1/41)	142	284	426	895	1510	2125
10-Intro/1st app. The Target (11/40); Simon-c; Spacehawk-s; text piece by Wolverton	233	466	699	1468	2484	3500
11-Origin The Target & The Targeteers	178	356	534	1121	1898	2675
V2#1-Target by Bob Wood; Uncle Sam flag-c	87	174	261	548	924	1300
2-Ten part Treasure Island serial begins; Harold Delay-a; reprinted in Catholic Comics V3#1-10 (see Key Comics #5)	78	156	234	491	828	1165
3-5: 4-Kit Carter, The Cadet begins	61	122	183	384	647	910
6-9: Red Seal with White Streak in #6-10	58	116	174	365	615	865
10-Classic-c	102	204	306	643	1084	1525
11,12: 12-10-part Last of the Mohicans serial begins; Delay-a	57	114	171	359	605	850
V3#1-3,5-7,9,10: 10-Last Wolverton issue	54	108	162	340	575	810
4-V for Victory-c	60	120	180	378	639	900
8-Hitler, Tojo, Flag-c; 6-part Gulliver Travels serial begins; Delay-a.	77	154	231	481	816	1150
11,12	18	36	54	105	165	225
V4#1-4,7-12: 8-X-Mas-c	14	28	42	76	108	140
5-Classic Statue of Liberty-c	15	30	45	83	124	165
6-Targetoons by Wolverton	15	30	45	83	124	165
V5#1-8	12	24	36	67	94	120
V6#1-4,6-10	11	22	33	64	90	115
5-Tojo-c	15	30	45	88	137	185
V7#1-12	10	20	30	58	79	100
V8#1,3-5,8,9,11,12	10	20	30	56	76	95
2,6,7-Krigstein-a	11	22	33	62	86	110
10-L.B. Cole-c	34	68	102	198	319	440
V9#1,4,6,8,10-L.B. Cole-c	33	66	99	192	309	425
2,3,5,7,9,11, V10#1	10	20	30	56	76	95
12-Classic L.B. Cole-c	38	76	114	222	356	490
V10#2,3-L.B. Cole-c	32	64	96	186	298	410

NOTE: ***Certa** c-V8#9, 11, 12, V9#5, 9, 11, V10#1. **Jack Cole** a-1-8. **Everett** a-1-9; c(signed Blake)-1, 2. **Al Fago** c-V6#8. **Sid Greene** c-V2#9, 12, V3#3. **Walter Johnson** c-V5#6, V6#4. **Tarpe Mills** a-1-4, 6, 8, 11, V3#1. **Rico** a-V7#4, 10, V8#5, 6, V9#3; c-V7#6, 8, 10, V8#2, 4, 6, 7. **Simon** a-1, 2. **Bob Wood** c-V2#2, 3, 5, 6.*

TARGET: THE CORRUPTORS (TV)
Dell Publishing Co.: No. 1306, Mar-May, 1962 - No. 3, Oct-Dec, 1962
(All have photo-c)

	GD 2.0	VG 4.0	FN 6.0	VF 8.0	VF/NM 9.0	NM- 9.2
Four Color 1306(#1), #2,3	6	12	18	37	59	80

TARGET WESTERN ROMANCES (Formerly Target Comics; becomes Flaming Western Romances #3)
Star Publications: No. 106, Oct-Nov, 1949 - No. 107, Dec-Jan, 1949-50

	GD 2.0	VG 4.0	FN 6.0	VF 8.0	VF/NM 9.0	NM- 9.2
106(#1)-Silhouette nudity panel; L.B. Cole-c	36	72	108	208	329	450
107(#2)-L.B. Cole-c; lingerie panels	30	60	90	174	275	375

TARGITT
Atlas/Seaboard Publ.: March, 1975 - No. 3, July, 1975

	GD 2.0	VG 4.0	FN 6.0	VF 8.0	VF/NM 9.0	NM- 9.2
1-3: 1-Origin; Nostrand-a in all. 2-1st in costume. 3-Becomes Man-Stalker	1	2	3	5	7	9

Tarzan #70 © ERB

Tarzan #210 © ERB

Tarzan #1 © ERB

GD VG FN VF VF/NM NM-
2.0 4.0 6.0 8.0 9.0 9.2

GD VG FN VF VF/NM NM-
2.0 4.0 6.0 8.0 9.0 9.2

TARZAN (See Aurora, Comics on Parade, Crackajack, DC 100-Page Super Spec., Edgar Rice Burroughs'..., Famous Feature Stories #1, Golden Comics Digest #4, 9, Jeep Comics #1-29, Jungle Tales of..., Limited Collectors' Edition, Popular, Sparkler, Sport Stars #1, Tip Top & Top Comics)

TARZAN
Dell Publishing Co./United Features Synd.: No. 5, 1939 - No. 161, Aug, 1947

Large Feature Comic 5('39)-(Scarce)-By Hal Foster; reprints 1st dailies from 1929 173 346 519 1090 1845 2600
Single Series 20(:40)-By Hal Foster 117 234 351 737 1244 1750
Four Color 134(2/47)-Marsh-c/a 52 104 156 442 846 1250
Four Color 161(8/47)-Marsh-c/a 48 96 144 384 717 1050

TARZAN (...of the Apes #138 on)
Dell Publishing Co./Gold Key No. 132 on: 1-2/48 - No. 131, 7-8/62; No. 132, 11/62 - No. 206, 2/72

1-Jesse Marsh-a begins 96 192 288 816 1558 2300
2 43 86 129 344 647 950
3-5 31 62 93 239 445 650
6-10: 6-1st Tantor the Elephant. 7-1st Valley of the Monsters 26 52 78 192 359 525
11-15: 11-Two Against the Jungle begins, ends #24. 13-Lex Barker photo-c begin 21 42 63 155 288 420
16-20 17 34 51 126 233 340
21-24,26-30 15 30 45 105 190 275
25-1st "Brothers of the Spear" episode; series ends #156,160,161,196-206 16 32 48 114 212 310
31-40 11 22 33 79 140 200
41-54: Last Barker photo-c 9 18 27 63 107 150
55-60: 56-Eight pg. Boy story 8 16 24 54 90 125
61,62,64-70 7 14 21 47 76 105
63-Two Tarzan stories, 1 by Manning 7 14 21 49 80 110
71-79 6 12 18 43 69 95
80-99: 80-Gordon Scott photo-c begin 6 12 18 39 62 85
100 6 12 18 43 69 95
101-109 6 12 18 37 59 80
110 (Scarce)-Last photo-c 6 12 18 43 69 95
111-120 5 10 15 34 55 75
121-131: Last Dell issue 5 10 15 32 51 70
132-1st Gold Key issue 5 10 15 34 55 75
133-138,140-154 4 8 12 26 41 55
139-(12/63)-1st app. Korak (Boy); leaves Tarzan & gets own book (1/64) 6 12 18 43 69 95
155-Origin Tarzan 5 10 15 32 51 70
156-161: 157-Banlu, Dog of the Arande begins, ends #159, 195. 169-Leopard Girl app. 4 8 12 22 34 45
162,165,168,171 (TV)-Ron Ely photo covers 4 8 12 23 36 48
163,164,166,167,169,170: 169-Leopard Girl app. 3 6 9 21 32 42
172-199,201-206: 178-Tarzan origin-r/#155; Leopard Girl app., also in #179, 190-193 3 6 9 19 29 38
200 4 8 12 22 34 45
Story Digest 1-(6/70, G.K., 148pp.)(scarce) 7 14 21 49 80 110

NOTE: *#162, 165, 168, 171 are TV issues. #1-153 all have* ***Marsh*** *art on Tarzan. #154-161, 163, 164, 166, 167, 172-177 all have* ***Manning*** *art on Tarzan. #178, 202 have* ***Manning*** *Tarzan reprints. No "Brothers of the Spear" in #1-24, 157-159, 162-195. #39-126, 128-156 all have* ***Russ Manning*** *art on "Brothers of the Spear". #196-201, 203-205 all have* ***Manning*** *B.O.T.S. reprints; #25-38, 127 all have Jesse* ***Marsh*** *art on B.O.T.S. #206 has a Marsh B.O.T.S. reprint.* ***Gollub*** *c-8-12.* ***Marsh*** *c-1-7.* ***Doug Wildey*** *a-162, 179-187. Many issues have front and back photo covers.*

TARZAN (Continuation of Gold Key series)
National Periodical Publications: No. 207, Apr, 1972 - No. 258, Feb, 1977

207-Origin Tarzan by Joe Kubert, part 1; John Carter begins (origin); 52 pg. issues thru #209 5 10 15 32 51 70
208,209-(52 pgs.): 208-210-Parts 2-4 of origin. 209-Last John Carter 3 6 9 18 27 35
210-220: 210-Kubert-a. 211-Hogarth, Kubert-a. 212-214: Adaptations from "Jungle Tales of Tarzan". 213-Beyond the Farthest Star begins, ends #218. 215-218,224,225-All by Kubert. 215-part Foster-r. 219-223: Adapts "The Return of Tarzan" by Kubert 2 4 6 13 18 22
221-229: 221-223-Continues adaptation of "The Return of Tarzan". 226-Manning-a 2 4 6 9 13 16
230-DC 100 Page Super Spectacular; Kubert, Kaluta-a(p); Korak begins, ends #234; Carson of Venus app. 4 8 12 23 36 48
231-235-New Kubert-a.: 231-234-(All 100 pgs.)-Adapts "Tarzan and the Lion Man"; Rex, the Wonder Dog r-#232, 233. 235-(100 pgs.)-Last Kubert issue. 4 8 12 22 34 45
236,237,239-258: 240-243 adapts "Tarzan & the Castaways". 250-256 adapts "Tarzan the Untamed." 252,253-r/#213 1 3 4 6 8 10
238-(68 pgs.) 2 4 6 11 16 20
Comic Digest 1-(Fall, 1972, 50¢, 164 pgs.)(DC)-Digest size; Kubert-c; Manning-a 4 8 12 26 41 55
Edgar Rice Burroughs' Tarzan The Joe Kubert Years - Volume One HC (Dark Horse Books, 10/05, $49.95, dust jacket) recolored r/#207-214; intro. by Joe Kubert 50.00
Edgar Rice Burroughs' Tarzan The Joe Kubert Years - Volume Two HC (Dark Horse Books, 2/06, $49.95, dust jacket) recolored r/#215-224; intro. by Joe Kubert 50.00
Edgar Rice Burroughs' Tarzan The Joe Kubert Years - Volume Three HC (Dark Horse Books, 6/06, $49.95, dust jacket) recolored r/#225,227-235; Kubert intro. and sketch pages 50.00

NOTE: ***Anderson*** *a-207, 209, 217, 218.* ***Chaykin*** *a-216.* ***Finlay*** *a(r)-212.* ***Foster*** *strip-r #207-209, 211, 212, 221.* ***Heath*** *a-230i.* ***G. Kane*** *a(r)-232p, 233p.* ***Kubert*** *a-207-225, 227-235, 257r, 258r; c-207-249, 253.* ***Lopez*** *a-250-255p; c-250p, 251, 252, 254.* ***Manning*** *strip-r 230-235, 238.* ***Morrow*** *a-208.* ***Nino*** *a-231-234.* ***Sparling*** *a-230, 231.* ***Starr*** *a-233r.*

TARZAN (Lord of the Jungle)
Marvel Comics Group: June, 1977 - No. 29, Oct, 1979

1-New adaptions of Burroughs stories; Buscema-a 1 3 4 6 8 10
1-(35¢-c variant, limited distribution)(6/77) 4 8 12 24 37 50
2-29: 2-Origin by John Buscema. 9-Young Tarzan. 12-14-Jungle Tales of Tarzan. 25-29-New stories 5.00
2-5-(35¢-c variants, limited distribution)(7-10/77) 3 6 9 16 23 30
Annual 1-3: 1-(1977). 2-(1978). 3-(1979) 6.00

NOTE: ***N. Adams*** *c-11i, 12i.* ***Alcala*** *a-9i, 10i; c-8i, 9i.* ***Buckler*** *c-25-27p, Annual 3p.* ***John Buscema*** *a-1-3, 4-18p, Annual 1; c-1-7, 8p, 9p, 10, 11p, 12p, 13, 14-19p, 21p, 22, 23p, 24p, 28p, Annual 1.* ***Mooney*** *a-22i.* ***Nebres*** *a-22i.* ***Russell*** *a-29i.*

TARZAN
Dark Horse Comics: July, 1996 - No. 20, Mar, 1998 ($2.95)

1-20: 1-6-Suydam-c 3.00

TARZAN / CARSON OF VENUS
Dark Horse Comics: May, 1998 - No. 4, Aug, 1998 ($2.95, limited series)

1-4-Darko Macan-s/Igor Korday-a 3.00

TARZAN FAMILY, THE (Formerly Korak, Son of Tarzan)
National Periodical Publications: No. 60, Nov-Dec, 1975 - No. 66, Nov-Dec, 1976

60-62-(68 pgs.): 60-Korak begins; Kaluta-r 2 4 6 9 13 16
63-66 (52 pgs.) 2 4 6 8 10 12

NOTE: *Carson of Venus-r 60-65. New John Carter-62-64, 65r, 66r. New Korak-60-66. Pellucidar feature-66. Foster strip r-60(9/4/32-10/16/32), 62(6/29/32-7/31/32), 63(10/11/31-12/13/31).* ***Kaluta*** *Carson of Venus-60-65.* ***Kubert*** *a-61, 64; c-60-64.* ***Manning*** *strip-r 60-62, 64.* ***Morrow*** *a-66r.*

TARZAN/JOHN CARTER: WARLORDS OF MARS
Dark Horse Comics: Jan, 1996 - No. 4, June, 1996 ($2.50, limited series)

1-4: Bruce Jones scripts in all. 1,2,4-Bret Blevins-c/a. 2-(4/96)-Indicia reads #3 3.00

TARZAN KING OF THE JUNGLE (See Dell Giant #37, 51)

TARZAN, LORD OF THE JUNGLE
Gold Key: Sept, 1965 (Giant) (25¢, soft paper-c)

1-Marsh-r 8 16 24 56 93 130

TARZAN: LOVE, LIES AND THE LOST CITY (See Tarzan the Warrior)
Malibu Comics: Aug. 10, 1992 - No. 3, Sept, 1992 ($2.50, limited series)

1-($3.95, 68 pgs.)-Flip book format; Simonson & Wagner scripts 4.00
2,3-No Simonson or Wagner scripts 3.00

TARZAN MARCH OF COMICS (See March of Comics #82, 98, 114, 125, 144, 155, 172, 185, 204, 223, 240, 252, 262, 272, 286, 300, 332, 342, 354, 366)

TARZAN OF THE APES
Metropolitan Newspaper Service: 1934? (Hardcover, 4x12", 68 pgs.)

1-Strip reprints 25 50 75 145 233 320

TARZAN OF THE APES
Marvel Comics Group: July, 1984 - No. 2, Aug, 1984 (Movie adaptation)

1,2: Origin-r/Marvel Super Spec. 3.00

TARZAN'S JUNGLE ANNUAL (See Dell Giants)

TARZAN'S JUNGLE WORLD (See Dell Giant #25)

TARZAN: THE BECKONING
Malibu Comics: 1992 - No. 7, 1993 ($2.50, limited series)

1-7 3.00

TARZAN: THE LOST ADVENTURE (See Edgar Rice Burroughs' ...)

TARZAN-THE RIVERS OF BLOOD
Dark Horse Comics: Nov, 1999 - No. 8 ($2.95, limited series)

1-4: Korday-c/a 3.00

TARZAN THE SAVAGE HEART
Dark Horse Comics: Apr, 1999 - No. 4, July, 1999 ($2.95, limited series)

Team 7 #2 © WSP

Team Zero #1 © WSP

Teen-Age Diary Secrets #6 © STJ

GD 2.0 | VG 4.0 | FN 6.0 | VF 8.0 | VF/NM 9.0 | NM- 9.2

1-4: Grell-c/a 3.00

TARZAN THE WARRIOR (Also see Tarzan: Love, Lies and the Lost City)
Malibu Comics: Mar, 19, 1992 - No. 5, 1992 ($2.50, limited series)

1-5: 1-Bisley painted pack-c (flip book format-c) 3.00
1 2nd printing w/o flip-c by Bisley 2.50

TARZAN VS. PREDATOR AT THE EARTH'S CORE
Dark Horse Comics: Jan, 1996 - No. 4, June, 1996 ($2.50, limited series)

1-4: Lee Weeks-c/a; Walt Simonson scripts 3.00

TASKMASTER
Marvel Comics: Apr, 2002 - No. 4, July, 2002 ($2.99, limited series)

1-4-Udon Studio-s/a. 1-Iron Man app. 3.00

TASMANIAN DEVIL & HIS TASTY FRIENDS
Gold Key: Nov, 1962 (12¢)

1-Bugs Bunny & Elmer Fudd x-over 14 28 42 102 181 260

TATTERED BANNERS
DC Comics (Vertigo): Nov, 1998 - No. 4, Feb, 1999 ($2.95, limited series)

1-4-Grant & Giffen-s/McMahon-a 3.00

TEAM AMERICA (See Captain America #269)
Marvel Comics Group: June, 1982 - No. 12, May, 1983

1-12:1-Origin; Ideal Toy motorcycle characters. 9-Iron Man app. 11-Ghost Rider app. 12-Double size 2.50

NOTE: *There are 16 pg. variants known for most issues, possibly all. The only ad is on the inside front cover.*

TEAM HELIX
Marvel Comics: Jan, 1993 - No. 4, Apr, 1993 ($1.75, limited series)

1-4: Teen Super Group. 1,2-Wolverine app. 2.50

TEAM ONE: STORMWATCH (Also see StormWatch)
Image Comics (WildStorm Productions): June, 1995 - No. 2, Aug, 1995 ($2.50, lim. series)

1,2: Steven T. Seagle scripts 2.50

TEAM ONE: WILDC.A.T.S (Also see WildC.A.T.S)
Image Comics (WildStorm Productions): July, 1995 - No. 2, Aug, 1995 ($2.50, lim. series)

1,2: James Robinson scripts 2.50

TEAM 7
Image Comics (WildStorm): Oct, 1994 - No.4, Feb, 1995 ($2.50, limited series)

1-4: Dixon scripts in all, 1-Portacio variant-c 2.50

TEAM 7-DEAD RECKONING
Image Comics (WildStorm): Jan, 1996 - No. 4, Apr, 1996 ($2.50, limited series)

1-4: Dixon scripts in all 2.50

TEAM 7-OBJECTIVE HELL
Image Comics (WildStorm): May, 1995 - No. 3, July, 1995 ($1.95/$2.50, limited series)

1-($1.95)-Newstand; Dixon scripts in all; Barry Smith-c 2.50
1-3: 1-($2.50)-Direct Market; Barry Smith-c, bound-in card 2.50

TEAM SUPERMAN
DC Comics: July, 1999 ($2.95, one-shot)

1-Jeanty-a/Stelfreeze-c 3.00
...Secret Files 1 (5/98, $4.95)Origin-s and pin-ups of Superboy, Supergirl and Steel 5.00

TEAM TITANS (See Deathstroke & New Titans Annual #7)
DC Comics: Sept, 1992 - No. 24, Sept, 1994 ($1.75/$1.95)

1-Five different #1s exist w/origins in 1st half & the same 2nd story in each: Kilowat, Mirage, Nightrider w/Netzer/Perez-a, Redwing, & Terra w/part Perez-p; Total Chaos Pt. 3 3.00
2-24: 2-Total Chaos Pt 6. 11-Metallik app. 24-Zero Hour x-over 2.50
Annual 1,2 ('93, '94, $3.50, 68 pgs.): 2-Elseworlds tory 3.50

TEAM X/TEAM 7
Marvel Comics: Nov, 1996 ($4.95, one-shot)

1 5.00

TEAM X 2000
Marvel Comics: Feb, 1999 ($3.50, one-shot)

1-Kevin Lau-a; Bishop vs. Shi'ar Empire 3.50

TEAM YANKEE
First Comics: Jan, 1989 - No. 6, Feb, 1989 ($1.95, weekly limited series)

1-6 2.50

TEAM YOUNGBLOOD (Also see Youngblood)
Image Comics (Extreme Studios): Sept, 1993 - No. 22, Sept, 1995 ($1.95/$2.50)

1-22: 1-9-Liefeld scripts in all: 1,2,4-6,8-Thibert-c(i). 1-1st app. Dutch & Masada. 3-Spawn cameo. 5-1st app. Lynx. 7,8-Coupons 1 & 4 for Extreme Prejudice #0; Black and White Pt. 4 & 8 by Thibert. 8-Coupon #4 for E. P. #0. 9-Liefeld wraparound-c &(p)/a(p) on Pt. I. 16,17-Bagged w/trading card. 21-Angela & Glory-app. 2.50

TEAM ZERO
DC Comics (WildStorm Productions): Feb, 2006 - No. 6, Jul, 2006 ($2.99, limited series)

1-6-Dixon-s/Mahnke-a 3.00
TPB (2008, $17.99) r/#1-6 18.00

TECH JACKET
Image Comics: Nov, 2002 - No. 6, Apr, 2003 ($2.95)

1-6-Kirkman-s/Su-a 3.00
Vol. 1: Lost and Found TPB (7/03, $12.95, 7-3/4" x 5-1/4") B&W r/#1-6; Valentino intro. 13.00

TEDDY ROOSEVELT & HIS ROUGH RIDERS (See Real Heroes #1)
Avon Periodicals: 1950

1-Kinstler-c; Palais-a; Flag-c 18 36 54 105 165 225

TEDDY ROOSEVELT ROUGH RIDER (See Battlefield #22 & Classics Illustrated Special Issue)

TED MCKEEVER'S METROPOL (See Transit)
Marvel Comics (Epic Comics): Mar, 1991 - No. 12, Mar, 1992 ($2.95, limited series)

V1#1-12: Ted McKeever-c/a/scripts 3.50

TED MCKEEVER'S METROPOL A.D.
Marvel Comics (Epic Comics): Oct, 1992 - No. 3, Dec, 1992 ($3.50, limited series)

V2#1-3: Ted McKeever-c/a/scripts 3.50

TEENA
Magazine Enterprises/Standard Comics No. 20 on: No. 11, 1948 - No. 15, 1948; No. 20, Aug, 1949 - No. 22, Oct, 1950

A-1 #11-Teen-age; Ogden Whitney-c 10 20 30 54 72 90
A-1 #12, 15 9 18 27 47 61 75
20-22 (Standard) 7 14 21 35 43 50

TEEN-AGE BRIDES (True Bride's Experiences #8 on)
Harvey/Home Comics: Aug, 1953 - No. 7, Aug, 1954

1-Powell-a 11 22 33 62 86 110
2-Powell-a 8 16 24 44 57 70
3-7: 3,6-Powell-a 8 16 24 40 50 60

TEEN-AGE CONFESSIONS (See Teen Confessions)

TEEN-AGE CONFIDENTIAL CONFESSIONS
Charlton Comics: July, 1960 - No. 22, 1964

1 4 8 12 24 37 50
2-10 3 6 9 16 23 30
11-22 2 4 6 13 18 22

TEEN-AGE DIARY SECRETS (Formerly Blue Ribbon Comics; becomes Diary Secrets #10 on)
St. John Publishing Co.: No. 4, 9/49; nn (#5), 9/49 - No. 7, 11/49; No. 8, 2/50; No. 9, 8/50

4(9/49)-Oversized; part mag., part comic 31 62 93 181 291 400
nn(#5)(no indicia)-Oversized, all comics; contains sty "I Gave Boys the Green Light." 29 58 87 169 272 375
6,8: (Reg. size) -Photo-c; Baker-a(2-3) in each 31 63 93 181 291 400
7,9-Digest size (Pocket Comics); Baker-a(5); both have same contents; diff.-c 35 70 105 203 327 450

TEEN-AGE DOPE SLAVES (See Harvey Comics Library #1)

TEENAGE HOTRODDERS (Top Eliminator #25 on; see Blue Bird)
Charlton Comics: Apr, 1963 - No. 24, July, 1967

1 6 12 18 37 59 80
2-10 3 6 9 20 30 40
11-24 3 6 9 17 25 32

TEEN-AGE LOVE (See Fox Giants)

TEEN-AGE LOVE (Formerly Intimate)
Charlton Comics: V2#4, July, 1958 - No. 96, Dec, 1973

V2#4 4 8 12 28 44 60
5-9 3 6 9 20 30 40
10(9/59)-20 3 6 9 17 25 32
21-35 3 6 9 16 22 28
36-70 2 4 6 13 18 22
71-96: 61&62-Jonnie Love begins (origin). 80,84,88-David Cassidy pin-ups. 83-Bobby Sherman pin-up. 89-Danny Bonaduce pin-up 2 4 6 10 14 18

TEENAGE MUTANT NINJA TURTLES (Also see Anything Goes, Donatello, First Comics Graphic Novel, Gobbledygook, Grimjack #26, Leonardo, Michaelangelo, Raphael & Tales Of The...)

Teenage Mutant Ninja Turtles #6 © MS

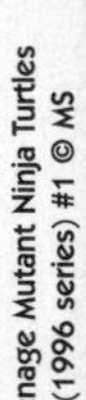
Teenage Mutant Ninja Turtles (1996 series) #1 © MS

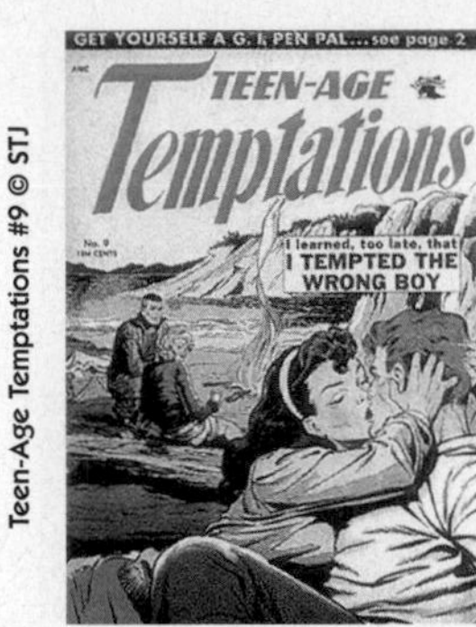

Teen-Age Temptations #9 © STJ

	GD 2.0	VG 4.0	FN 6.0	VF 8.0	VF/NM 9.0	NM- 9.2

Mirage Studios: 1984 - No. 62, Aug, 1993 ($1.50/$1.75, B&W; all 44-52 pgs.)

1-1st printing (3000 copies)-Origin and 1st app. of the Turtles and Splinter. Only printing to have ad for Gobbledygook #1 & 2; Shredder app. (#1-4: 7-1/2x11") (Prices vary widely on this book. In 2005 a CGC certified 9.4 sold for $8,300, a CGC certified 9.2 sold for $2,850, and a CGC certified 6.0 sold for $1,300)

1-2nd printing (6/84)(15,000 copies) 2 4 6 11 16 20
1-3rd printing (2/85)(36,000 copies) 2 4 6 8 10 12
1-4th printing, new-c (50,000 copies) 5.00
1-5th printing, new-c (8/88-c, 11/88 inside) 4.00
1-Counterfeit. **Note**: Most counterfeit copies have a half inch wide white streak or scratch marks across the center of back cover. Black part of cover is a bluish black instead of a deep black. Inside paper is very white & inside cover is bright white (no value)
2-1st printing (1984; 15,000 copies) 9 18 27 63 107 150
2-2nd printing 1 3 4 6 8 10
2-3rd printing; new Corben-c/a (2/85) 5.00
2-Counterfeit with glossy cover stock (no value).
3-1st printing (1985, 44 pgs.) 7 14 21 45 73 100
3-Variant, 500 copies, given away in NYC. Has 'Laird's Photo' in white rather than light blue 9 18 27 63 107 150
3-2nd printing; contains new back-up story 3.00
4-1st printing (1985, 44 pgs.) 4 8 12 28 44 60
4,5-2nd printing (5/87, 11/87) 2.50
5-Fugitoid begins, ends #7; 1st full color-c (1985) 3 6 9 16 23 30
6-1st printing (1986) 2 4 6 10 14 18
6-2nd printing (4/88-c, 5/88 inside) 2.50
7-4 pg. Eastman/Corben color insert; 1st color TMNT (1986, $1.75-c); Bade Biker back-up story 2 4 6 8 10 12
7-2nd printing (1/89) w/o color insert 2.50
8-Cerebus-c/story with Dave Sim-a (1986) 1 2 3 5 7 9
9,10: 9 (9/86)-Rip In Time by Corben 6.00
11-15 4.00
16-18: 18-Mark Bode'-a 3.00
18-2nd printing ($2.25, color, 44 pgs.)-New-c 2.50
19-34: 19-Begin $1.75-c. 24-26-Veitch-c/a. 2.50
32-2nd printing ($2.75, 52 pgs., full color) 3.00
35-49,51: 35-Begin $2.00-c. 2.50
50-Features pin-ups by Larsen, McFarlane, Simonson, etc. 3.00
52-62: 52-Begin $2.25-c 2.50
nn (1990, $5.95, B&W)-Movie adaptation 6.00
Book 1,2($1.50, B&W): 2-Corben-c 2.50
...Christmas Special 1 (12/90, $1.75, B&W, 52 pgs.)-Cover title: Michaelangelo Christmas Special; r/Michaelangelo one-shot plus new Raphael story 2.50
...Special (The Maltese Turtle) nn (1/93, $2.95, color, 44 pgs.) 3.00
...Special: "Times" Pipeline nn (9/92, $2.95, color, 44 pgs.)-Mark Bode-c/a 3.00
Hardcover ($100)-r/#1-10 plus one-shots w/dust jackets - limited to 1000 w/letter of authenticity 100.00
Softcover ($40)-r/#1-10 40.00

TEENAGE MUTANT NINJA TURTLES
Mirage Studios: V2#1, Oct, 1993 - V2#13, Oct, 1995 ($2.75)

V2#1-13: 1-Wraparound-c 2.75

TEENAGE MUTANT NINJA TURTLES
Image Comics (Highbrow Ent.): June, 1996 - No. 23, Oct, 1999 ($1.95-$2.95)

1-23: 1-8: Eric Larsen-c(i) on all. 10-Savage Dragon-c/app. 3.00

TEENAGE MUTANT NINJA TURTLES
Mirage Publishing: V4#1, Dec, 2001 - Present ($2.95, B&W)

V4#1-9,11-28-Laird-s/a(i)/Lawson-a(p). 3.00
10-($3.95) Splinter dies 4.00

TEENAGE MUTANT NINJA TURTLES
Dreamwave Productions: June 2003 - Present ($2.95, color)

1-7-Animated style; Peter David-s/Lesean-a 3.00
Vol. 1 TPB (2003, $9.95) r/#1-4; cover gallery and sketch pages 10.00

TEENAGE MUTANT NINJA TURTLES (Adventures)
Archie Publications: Jan, 1996 - No. 3, Mar, 1996 ($1.50, limited series)

1-3 2.50

TEENAGE MUTANT NINJA TURTLES ADVENTURES (TV)
Archie Comics: 8/88 - No. 3, 12/88; 3/89 - No. 72, Oct, 1995 ($1.00/$1.25/$1.50/$1.75)

1-Adapts TV cartoon; not by Eastman/Laird 4.00
2,3 (Mini-series), 1 (2nd on-going series), 1-2nd printing 2.50
2-18,20-30: 5-Begins original stories not based on TV. 14-Simpson-a(p). 22-Colan-c/a 3.00
2-11: 2nd printings 2.50
19-1st Mighty Mutanimals (also in #20, 51-54) 1 2 3 5 6 8
31-49 4.50
50-Poster by Eastman/Laird 1 2 3 5 6 8
51-54: Mighty Mutanimals 1 3 4 6 8 10
55-60 6.00
61-70: 62-w/poster 1 2 3 5 7 9
71 1 3 4 6 8 10
72- Last issue 2 4 6 9 12 15
nn (1990, $2.50)-Movie adaptation 2.50
nn (Spring, 1991, $2.50, 68 pgs.)-(Meet Archie) 2.50
nn (Sum, 1991, $2.50, 68 pgs.)-(Movie II)-Adapts movie sequel 2.50
...Meet the Conservation Corps 1 (1992, $2.50, 68 pgs.) 2.50
...III The Movie: The Turtles are Back...In Time (1993, $2.50, 68 pgs.) 2.50
Special 1,4,5 (Sum/92, Spr/93, Sum/93, 68 pgs.)-1-Bill Wray-c 2.50
Giant Size Special 6 (Fall/93, $1.95, 52 pgs.) 2.50
Special 7-10 (Win/93-Fall//94, 52 pgs.): 9-Jeff Smith-c 2.50
NOTE: *There are 2nd printings of #1-11 w/B&W inside covers. Originals are color.*

TEENAGE MUTANT NINJA TURTLES CLASSICS DIGEST (TV)
Archie Comics: Aug, 1993 - No. 8, Mar, 1995? ($1.75)

1-8: Reprints TMNT Advs. 4.00

TEENAGE MUTANT NINJA TURTLES/FLAMING CARROT CROSSOVER
Mirage Publishing: Nov, 1993 - No. 4, Feb, 1994 ($2.75, limited series)

1-4: Bob Burden story 3.00

TEENAGE MUTANT NINJA TURTLES PRESENTS: APRIL O'NEIL
Archie Comics: Mar, 1993 - No. 3, June, 1993 ($1.25, limited series)

1-3 3.00

TEENAGE MUTANT NINJA TURTLES PRESENTS: DONATELLO AND LEATHERHEAD
Archie Comics: July, 1993 - No. 3, Sept, 1993 ($1.25, limited series)

1-3 3.00

TEENAGE MUTANT NINJA TURTLES PRESENTS: MERDUDE
Archie Comics: Oct, 1993 - No. 3, Dec, 1993 ($1.25, limited series)

1-3-See Mighty Mutanimals #7 for 1st app. Merdude 3.00

TEENAGE MUTANT NINJA TURTLES/SAVAGE DRAGON CROSSOVER
Mirage Studios: Aug, 1995 ($2.75, one-shot)

1 3.00

TEEN-AGE ROMANCE (Formerly My Own Romance)
Marvel Comics (ZPC): No. 77, Sept, 1960 - No. 86, Mar, 1962

77-83 4 8 12 24 37 50
84-86-Kirby c. 84 Kirby a(2 pgs.). 85,86 (3 pgs.) 5 10 15 30 48 65

TEEN-AGE ROMANCES
St. John Publ. Co. (Approved Comics): Jan, 1949 - No. 45, Dec, 1955 (#3,7,10-18,21 are 1/2 inch taller than other issues)

1-Baker-c/a(1) 48 96 144 298 499 700
2,3: 2-Baker-c/a. 3-Baker-c/a(3) 35 70 105 203 327 450
4,5,7,8-Photo-c; Baker-a(2-3) each 26 52 78 154 247 340
6-Photo-c; part magazine; Baker-a (10/49) 28 56 84 162 261 360
9-Baker-c/a; Kubert-a 35 70 105 203 327 450
10-12,20-Baker-c/a(2-3) each 28 56 84 166 268 370
13-19,21,22-Complete issues by Baker 35 70 105 203 327 450
23-25-Baker-c/a(2-3) each 27 54 81 158 254 350
26,27,33,34,36-40,42: Baker-c/a. 33,40-Signed story by Estrada. 38-Suggestive-c. 42-r/Cinderella Love #9; Last pre-code (3/55) 20 40 60 115 183 250
28-30-No Baker-a 11 22 33 62 86 110
31,32-Baker-c. 31-Estrada-s 15 30 45 94 147 200
35-Baker-c/a (16 pgs.) 20 40 60 115 183 250
41-Baker-c; Infantino-a(r); all stories are Ziff-Davis-r 15 30 45 94 147 200
43-45-Baker-c/a 20 40 60 115 183 250

TEEN-AGE TALK
I.W. Enterprises: 1964

Reprint #1 2 4 6 10 14 18
Reprint #5,8,9: 5-r/Hector #? 9-Punch Comics #?; L.B. Cole-c reprint from School Day Romances #1 2 4 6 9 13 16

TEEN-AGE TEMPTATIONS (Going Steady #10 on)(See True Love Pictorial)
St. John Publishing Co.: Oct, 1952 - No. 9, Aug, 1954

1-Baker-c/a; has story "Reform School Girl" by Estrada 60 120 180 378 639 900
2,4-Baker-c 25 50 75 147 236 325
3,5-7,9-Baker-c/a 33 66 99 192 309 425

Teen Love Stories #1 © WP

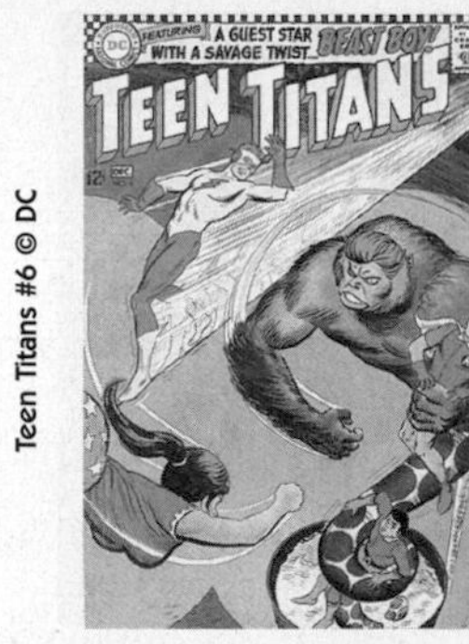

Teen Titans #6 © DC

Teen Titans (2003 series) #17 © DC

GD VG FN VF VF/NM NM-
2.0 4.0 6.0 8.0 9.0 9.2

8-Teenagers smoke reefer; Baker-c/a 38 76 114 226 363 500
NOTE: *Estrada a-1, 3-5.*

TEEN BEAM (Formerly Teen Beat #1)
National Periodical Publications: No. 2, Jan-Feb, 1968

2-Superman cameo; Herman's Hermits, Yardbirds, Simon & Garfunkel, Lovin Spoonful, Young Rascals app.; Orlando, Drucker-a(r); Monkees photo-c; 15 30 45 105 190 275

TEEN BEAT (Becomes Teen Beam #2)
National Periodical Publications: Nov-Dec, 1967

1-Photos & text only; Monkees photo-c; Beatles, Herman's Hermits, Animals, Supremes, Byrds app. 15 30 45 111 206 300

TEEN COMICS (Formerly All Teen; Journey Into Unknown Worlds #36 on)
Marvel Comics (WFP): No. 21, Apr, 1947 - No. 35, May, 1950

21-Kurtzman's "Hey Look"; Patsy Walker, Cindy (1st app.?), Georgie, Margie app.; Syd Shores-a begins, end #23 15 30 45 94 147 200
22,23,25,27,29,31-35: 22-(6/47)-Becomes Hedy Devine #22 (8/47) on? 14 28 42 80 115 150
24,26,28,30-Kurtzman's "Hey Look" 14 28 42 82 121 160

TEEN CONFESSIONS
Charlton Comics: Aug, 1959 - No. 97, Nov, 1976

1 8 16 24 52 86 120
2 4 8 12 28 44 60
3-10 4 8 12 22 34 45
11-30 3 6 9 18 27 35
31-Beatles-c 11 22 33 79 140 200
32-36,38-55 3 6 9 15 21 26
37 (1/66)-Beatles Fan Club story; Beatles-c 11 22 33 79 140 200
56-58,60-97: 77-Partridge Family poster. 89,90-Newton-c 2 4 6 10 14 18
59-Kaluta's 1st pro work? (12/69) 3 6 9 19 29 38

TEENIE WEENIES, THE (America's Favorite Kiddie Comic)
Ziff-Davis Publishing Co.: No. 10, 1950 - No. 11, Apr-May, 1951 (Newspaper reprints)

10,11-Painted-c 20 40 60 115 180 245

TEEN-IN (Tippy Teen)
Tower Comics: Summer, 1968 - No. 4, Fall, 1969

nn(#1, Summer, 1968)(25¢) Has 3 full pg. B&W photos of Sonny & Cher, Donovan and Herman's Hermits; interviews and photos of Eric Clapton, Jim Morrison and others 9 18 27 63 107 150
nn(#2, Spring, 1969),3,4 6 12 18 37 59 80

TEEN LIFE (Formerly Young Life)
New Age/Quality Comics Group: No. 3, Winter, 1945 - No. 5, Fall, 1945 (Teenage magazine)

3-June Allyson photo on-c & story 14 28 42 76 108 140
4-Duke Ellington photo on-c & story 11 22 33 64 90 115
5-Van Johnson, Woody Herman & Jackie Robinson articles; Van Johnson & Woody Herman photos on-c 14 28 42 78 112 145

TEEN LOVE STORIES (Magazine)
Warren Publ. Co.: Sept, 1969 - No. 3, Jan, 1970 (68 pgs., photo covers, B&W)

1-Photos & articles plus 36-42 pgs. new comic stories in all; Frazetta-a 7 14 21 45 73 100
2,3: 2-Anti-marijuana story 5 10 15 30 48 65

TEEN ROMANCES
Super Comics: 1964

10,11,15-17-Reprints 2 4 6 8 11 14

TEEN SECRET DIARY (Nurse Betsy Crane #12 on)
Charlton Comics: Oct, 1959 - No. 11, June, 1961; No. 1, 1972

1 5 10 15 32 51 70
2 3 6 9 21 32 42
3-11 3 6 9 18 27 35
1 (1972)(exist?) 3 6 9 15 21 26

TEEN TALK (See Teen)

TEEN TITANS (See Brave & the Bold #54,60, DC Super-Stars #1, Marvel & DC Present, New Teen Titans, New Titans, Official...Index and Showcase #59)
National Periodical Publications/DC Comics: 1-2/66 - No. 43, 1-2/73; No. 44, 11/76 - No. 53, 2/78

1-(1-2/66)-Titans join Peace Corps; Batman, Flash, Aquaman, Wonder Woman cameos 30 60 90 222 411 600
2 14 28 42 102 181 260

GD VG FN VF VF/NM NM-
2.0 4.0 6.0 8.0 9.0 9.2

3-5: 4-Speedy app. 9 18 27 63 107 150
6-10: 6-Doom Patrol app.; Beast Boy x-over; readers polled on him joining Titans 7 14 21 50 83 115
11-18: 11-Speedy app. 13-X-Mas-c 6 12 18 41 66 90
19-Wood-i; Speedy begins as regular 6 12 18 43 69 95
20-22: All Neal Adams-a. 21-Hawk & Dove app.; last 12¢ issue. 22-Origin Wonder Girl 8 16 24 54 90 125
23-Wonder Girl dons new costume 5 10 15 32 51 70
24-31: 25-Flash, Aquaman, Batman, Green Arrow, Green Lantern, Superman, & Hawk & Dove guests; 1st app. Lilith who joins T.T. West in #50. 29-Hawk & Dove & Ocean Master app. 30-Aquagirl app. 31-Hawk & Dove app.; last 15¢ issue 4 8 12 28 44 60
32-34,40-43 3 6 9 18 27 35
35-39-(52 pgs.): 36,37-Superboy-r. 38-Green Arrow/Speedy-r; Aquaman/Aqualad story. 39-Hawk & Dove-r. 3 6 9 20 30 40
44-(11/76) Dr. Light app.; Mal becomes the Guardian 2 4 6 13 18 22
45,47,49,51,52 2 4 6 11 16 20
46,48: 46-Joker's daughter begins (see Batman Family). 48-Intro Bumblebee; Joker's daughter becomes Harlequin 3 6 9 16 22 28
50-1st revival original Bat-Girl; intro. Teen Titans West 3 6 9 16 23 30
53-Origin retold 3 6 9 14 19 24
... Lost Annual 1 (3/08, $4.99) Sixties-era story by Bob Haney; Jay Stephens & Mike Allred-a; President Kennedy app.; Nick Cardy-c a nd sketch pages 5.00
NOTE: *Aparo a-36.* ***Buckler*** *c-46-53.* ***Cardy*** *c-1-16.* ***Kane*** *a(p)-19, 22-24, 39r.* ***Tuska*** *a(p)-31, 36, 38, 39. DC Super-Stars #1 (3/76) was released before #44.*

TEEN TITANS (Also see Titans Beat in the Promotional Comics section)
DC Comics: Oct, 1996 - No. 24, Sept, 1998 ($1.95)

1-Dan Jurgens-c/a(p)/scripts & George Pérez-c/a(i) begin; Atom forms new team (Risk, Argent, Prysm, & Joto); 1st app. Loren Jupiter & Omen; no indicia. 1-3-Origin. 4.00
2-24: 4,5-Robin, Nightwing, Supergirl, Capt. Marvel Jr. app. 12-"Then and Now" begins w/original Teen Titans-c/app. 15-Death of Joto. 17-Capt. Marvel Jr. and Fringe join. 19-Millennium Giants x-over. 23,24-Superman app. 3.00
Annual 1 (1997, $3.95)-Pulp Heroes story 4.00

TEEN TITANS (Also see Titans/Young Justice: Graduation Day)
DC Comics: Sept, 2003 - Present ($2.50/$2.99)

1-McKone-c/a;Johns-s 4.00
1-Variant-c by Michael Turner 5.00
1-2nd and 3rd printings 2.50
2-Deathstroke app. 5.00
2-2nd printing 2.50
3-15: 4-Impulse becomes Kid Flash. 5-Raven returns. 6-JLA app. 2.50
16-33: 16-Titans go to 31st Century; Legion and Fatal Five app. 17-19-Future Titans app. 21-23-Dr. Light. 24,25-Outsiders #24,25 x-over. 27,28-Liefeld-a. 32,33-Infinite Crisis 2.50
34-49,51-61: 34-One Year Later begins; two covers by Daniel and Benes. 36-Begin $2.99-c. 40-Jericho returns. 42-Kid Devil origin; Snejbjerg-a. 43-Titans East. 48,49-Amazons Attack x-over; Supergirl app. 51-54-Future Titans app. 3.00
50-($3.99) Art by Pérez (4 pgs.), McKone (6 pgs.), Nauck and Green; future Titans app. 4.00
Annual 1 (4/06, $4.99) Infinite Crisis x-over; Benes-c 5.00
... And Outsiders Secret Files and Origins 2005 (10/05, $4.99) Daniel-c 5.00
.../Legion Special (11/04, $3.50) (cont'd from #16) Reis-a; leads into 2005 Legion of Super-Heroes series; LSH preview by Waid & Kitson 3.50
#1/2 (Wizard mail offer) origin of Ravager; Reis-a 8.00
.../Outsiders Secret Files 2003 (12/03, $5.95) Reis & Jimenez-a; pin-ups by various 6.00
...: A Kid's Game TPB (2004, $9.95) r/#1-7; Turner-c from #1; McKone sketch pages 10.00
...: Beast Boys and Girls TPB (2005, $9.99) r/#13-15 and Beast Boy #1-4 10.00
...: Family Lost TPB (2004, $9.95) r/#8-12 & #1/2 10.00
...: Life and Death TPB (2006, $14.99) r/#29-33 and pages from Infinite Crisis x-over 15.00
.../ Outsiders: The Death and Return of Donna Troy (2006, $14.99) r/Titans/Young Justice: Graduation Day #1-3, Teen Titans/Outsiders Secret Files 2003 and DC Special: The Return of Donna Troy #1-4; cover gallery 15.00
.../ Outsiders: The Insiders (2006, $14.99) r/Teen Titans/ #24-26 & Outsiders #24,25,28 15.00
...: The Future is Now (2005, $9.99) r/#15-23 & Teen Titans/Legion Special 10.00
...: Titans Around the World TPB (2007, $14.99) r/#34-41 15.00
...: Titans of Tomorrow TPB (2008, $14.99) r/#50-54 15.00

TEEN TITANS GO! (Based on Cartoon Network series) (Also see Free Comic Book Day Edition in the Promotional Comics section)
DC Comics: Jan, 2004 - No. 55, Jul, 2008 ($2.25)

1-12,14-55: 1,2-Nauck-a/Bullock-c/J. Torres-s. 8-Mad Mod app. 14-Speedy-c. 28-Doom Patrol app. 31-Nightwing app. 36-Wonder Girl. 38-Mad Mod app.; Clugston-a 2.25
13-($2.95) Bonus pages with Shazam! reprint 3.00
Jam Packed Action (2005, $7.99, digest) adaptations of two TV episodes 8.00
... Vol 1: Truth, Justice, Pizza! (2004, $6.95, digest-size) r/#1-5 7.00

Teen Titans Spotlight #21 © DC

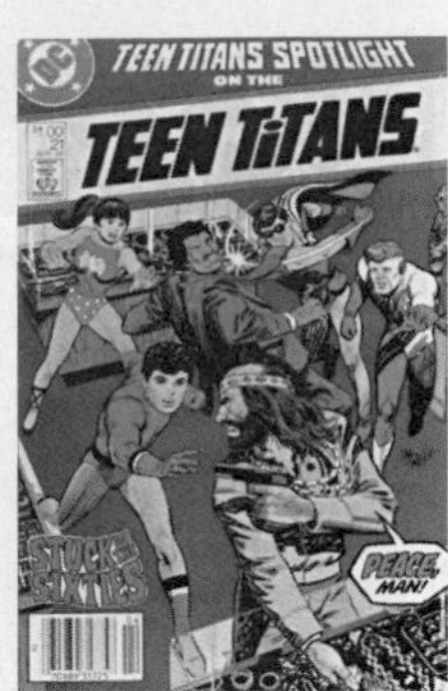

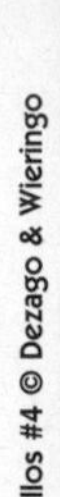
Tellos #4 © Dezago & Wieringo

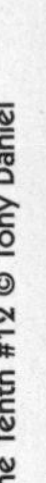
The Tenth #12 © Tony Daniel

GD VG FN VF VF/NM NM-
2.0 4.0 6.0 8.0 9.0 9.2

GD VG FN VF VF/NM NM-
2.0 4.0 6.0 8.0 9.0 9.2

... Vol 2: Heroes on Patrol (2005, $6.99, digest-size) r/#6-10 7.00
... Vol 3: Bring It On! (2005, $6.99, digest-size) r/#11-15 7.00
... Vol 4: Ready For Action! (2006, $6.99, digest-size) r/#16-20 7.00
... Vol 5: On The Move! (2006, $6.99, digest-size) r/#21-25 7.00
... Titans Together TPB (2007, $12.99) r/#26-32 13.00

TEEN TITANS SPOTLIGHT
DC Comics: Aug, 1986 - No. 21, Apr, 1988
1-21: 7-Guice's 1st work at DC. 14-Nightwing; Batman app. 15-Austin-c(i). 18,19-Millennium x-over. 21-($1.00-c)-Original Teen Titans; Spiegle-a 3.00
*Note: **Guice** a-7p, 8p; c-7,8. **Orlando** c/a-11p. **Perez** c-1, 17i, 19. **Sienkiewicz** c-10*

TEEN TITANS YEAR ONE
DC Comics: Mar, 2008 - No. 6 ($2.99, limited series)
1-5-The original five form a team; Wolfram-s/Kerschl-a 3.00

TEEPEE TIM (...Heap Funny Indian Boy)(Formerly Ha Ha Comics)
American Comics Group: No. 100, Feb-Mar, 1955 - No. 102, June-July, 1955
100-102 6 12 18 31 38 45

TEGRA JUNGLE EMPRESS (Zegra Jungle Empress #2 on)
Fox Features Syndicate: August, 1948
1-Blue Beetle, Rocket Kelly app.; used in **SOTI**, pg. 31 60 120 180 378 639 900

TEK JANSEN (See Stephen Colbert's...)

TEKNO COMIX HANDBOOK
Tekno Comix: May, 1996 ($3.95, one-shot)
1-Guide to the Tekno Universe 4.00

TEKNOPHAGE (See Neil Gaiman's...)

TEKNOPHAGE VERSUS ZEERUS
BIG Entertainment: July, 1996 ($3.25, one-shot)
1-Paul Jenkins script 3.25

TEKWORLD (William Shatner's... on-c only)
Epic Comics (Marvel): Sept, 1992 - Aug, 1994 ($1.75)
1-Based on Shatner's novel, TekWar, set in L.A. in the year 2120 3.00
2-24 2.50

TELEVISION (See TV)

TELEVISION COMICS (Early TV comic)
Standard Comics (Animated Cartoons): No. 5, Feb, 1950 - No. 8, Nov, 1950
5-1st app. Willy Nilly 10 20 30 54 72 90
6-8: #6 on inside has #2 on cover 8 16 24 42 54 65

TELEVISION PUPPET SHOW (Early TV comic) (See Spotty the Pup)
Avon Periodicals: 1950 - No. 2, Nov, 1950
1-1st app. Speedy Rabbit, Spotty The Pup 19 38 57 112 176 240
2 14 28 42 80 115 150

TELEVISION TEENS MOPSY (See TV Teens)

TELL IT TO THE MARINES
Toby Press Publications: Mar, 1952 - No. 15, July, 1955
1-Lover O'Leary and His Liberty Belles (with pin-ups), ends #6; Spike & Bat begin, end #6 19 38 57 112 176 240
2-Madame Cobra-c/story 12 24 36 67 94 120
3-5 10 20 30 54 72 90
6-12,14,15: 7-9,14,15-Photo-c 8 16 24 42 54 65
13-John Wayne photo-c 15 30 45 83 124 165
I.W. Reprint #9-r/#1 above 2 4 6 8 10 12
Super Reprint #16(1964)-r/#4 above 2 4 6 8 10 12

TELLOS
Image Comics: May, 1999 - No. 10, Nov, 2000 ($2.50)
1-Dezago-s/Wieringo-a 3.00
1-Variant-c ($7.95) 8.00
2-10: 4-Four covers 2.50
...: Maiden Voyage (3/01, $5.95) Didier Crispeels-a/c 6.00
...: Sons & Moons (2002, $5.95) Nick Cardy-c 6.00
...: The Last Heist (2001, $5.95) Rousseau-a/c 6.00
Prelude ($5.00, AnotherUniverse.com) 5.00
Prologue ($3.95, Dynamic Forces) 4.00
...Collected Edition 1 (12/99, $8.95) r/#1-3 9.00
... Colossal, Vol. 1 TPB (2008, $17.99) r/#1-10, Prelude, Prologue, Scatterjack-s from Section Zero #1, cover gallery, Wieringo sketch pages; Dezago afterword 18.00
...: Kindred Spirits (2/01, $17.95) r/#6-10, Section Zero #1 (Scatterjack-s) 18.00
...: Reluctant Heroes (2/01, $17.95) r/#1-5, Prelude, Prologue; sketchbook 18.00

TEMPEST (See Aquaman, 3rd Series)
DC Comics: Nov, 1996 - No. 4, Feb, 1997 ($1.75, limited series)
1-4: Formerly Aqualad; Phil Jimenez-c/a/scripts in all 2.50

TEMPUS FUGITIVE
DC Comics: 1990 - No. 4, 1991 ($4.95, squarebound, 52 pgs.)
Book 1,2: Ken Steacy painted-c/a & scripts 6.00
Book 3,4-($5.95-c) 6.00
TPB (Dark Horse Comics, 1/97, $17.95) 18.00

TEN COMMANDMENTS (See Moses & the... and Classics Illustrated Special)

TENDER LOVE STORIES
Skywald Publ. Corp.: Feb, 1971 - No. 4, July, 1971 (Pre-code reprints and new stories)
1 (All 25¢, 52 pgs.) 4 8 12 22 34 45
2-4 3 6 9 18 27 35

TENDER ROMANCE (Ideal Romance #3 on)
Key Publications (Gilmour Magazines): Dec, 1953 - No. 2, Feb, 1954
1-Headlight & lingerie panels; B. Baily-c 18 36 54 103 162 220
2-Bernard Baily-c 11 22 33 62 86 110

TENSE SUSPENSE
Fago Publications: Dec, 1958 - No. 2, Feb, 1959
1 10 20 30 54 72 90
2 8 16 24 40 50 60

TEN STORY LOVE (Formerly a pulp magazine with same title)
Ace Periodicals: V29#3, June-July, 1951 - V36#5(#209), Sept, 1956 (#3-6: 52 pgs.)
V29#3(#177)-Part comic, part text; painted-c 14 28 42 82 121 160
4-6(1/52) 9 18 27 52 69 85
V30#1(3/52)-6(1/53) 9 18 27 50 65 80
V31#1(2/53),V32#2(4/53)-6(12/53) 9 18 27 47 61 75
V33#1(1/54)-3(5#54, #195), V34#4(7/54, #196)-6(10/54, #198) 8 16 24 44 57 70
V35#1(12/54, #199)-3(4/55, #201)-Last precode 8 16 24 42 54 65
V35#4-6(9/55, #201-204), V36#1(11/55, #205)-3, 5(9/56, #209) 8 16 24 40 50 60
V36#4-L.B. Cole-a 10 20 30 56 76 95

TENTH, THE
Image Comics: Jan, 1997 - No. 4, June, 1997 ($2.50, limited series)
1-4-Tony Daniel-c/a, Beau Smith-s 5.00
Abuse of Humanity TPB ($10.95) r/#1-4 11.00
Abuse of Humanity TPB (10/98, $11.95) r/#1-4 & 0(8/97) 12.00

TENTH, THE
Image Comics: Sept, 1997 - No. 14, Jan, 1999 ($2.50)
0-(8/97, $5.00) American Ent. Ed. 6.00
1-Tony Daniel-c/a, Beau Smith-s 6.00
2-9: 3,7-Variant-c 4.00
10-14 3.00
...Configuration (8/98) Re-cap and pin-ups 2.50
...Collected Edition 1 ('98, $4.95, square-bound) r/#1,2 5.00
...Special (4/00, $2.95) r/#0 and Wizard #1/2 3.00
Wizard #1/2-Daniel-s/Steve Scott-a 10.00

TENTH, THE (Volume 3) (The Black Embrace)
Image Comics: Mar, 1999 - No. 4, June, 1999 ($2.95)
1-4-Daniel-c/a 3.00
TPB (1/00, $12.95) r/#1-4 13.00

TENTH, THE (Volume 4) (Evil's Child)
Image Comics: Sept, 1999 - No. 4, Mar, 2000 ($2.95, limited series)
1-4-Daniel-c/a 3.00

TENTH, THE (Darkk Dawn)
Image Comics: July, 2005 ($4.99, one-shot)
1-Kirkham-a/Bonny-s 5.00

TENTH, THE : RESURRECTED
Dark Horse Comics: July, 2001 - No. 4, Feb, 2002 ($2.99, limited series)
1-4: 1-Two covers; Daniel-s/c; Romano-a 3.00

10th MUSE
Image Comics (TidalWave Studios): Nov, 2000 - No. 9, Jan, 2002 ($2.95)
1-Character based on wrestling's Rena Mero; regular & photo covers 3.00

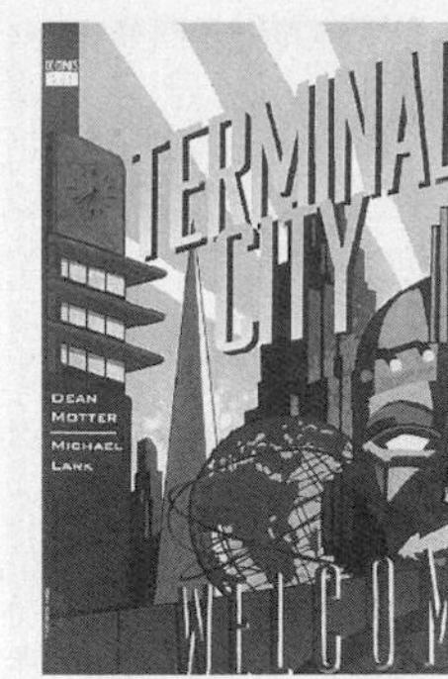

Terminal City TPB © DC

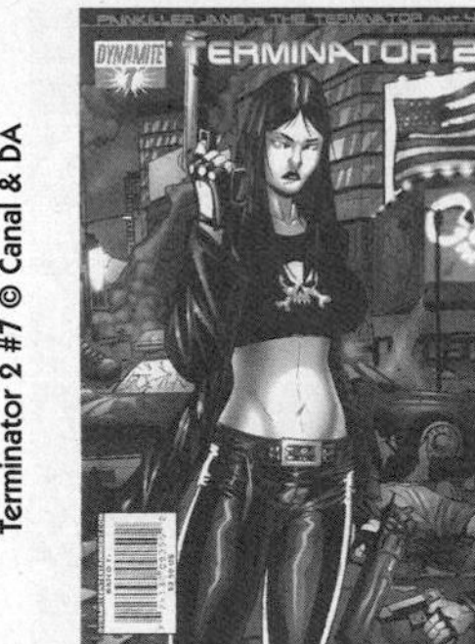

Terminator 2 #7 © Canal & DA

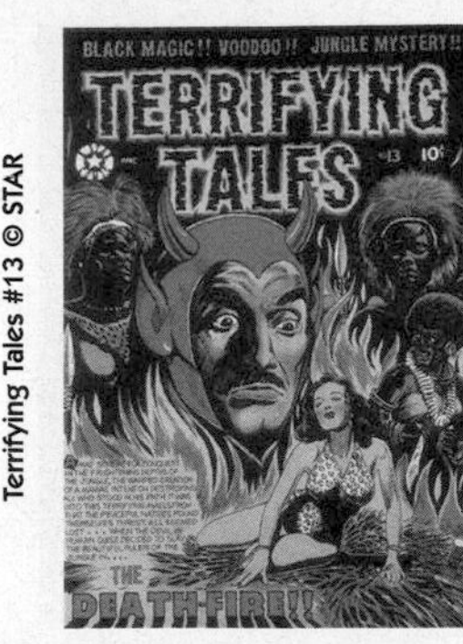

Terrifying Tales #13 © STAR

GD VG FN VF VF/NM NM-
2.0 4.0 6.0 8.0 9.0 9.2

GD VG FN VF VF/NM NM-
2.0 4.0 6.0 8.0 9.0 9.2

2-9: 2-Photo and 2 Lashley covers; flip book Dollz preview. 5-Savage Dragon app.; 2 covers by Lashley and Larsen. 6-Tellos x-over 3.00

10th MUSE (Volume 2)
Avatar Press: July, 2002 ($3.50)
1-Wolfman-s; Cruz-a. 1-Five homage covers by various 3.50

TENTH MUSE
Alias Enterprises: Apr, 2005 - Present ($2.99)
1,2-Amezcua-a. 1-Four covers. 2-Two covers plus Cindy Margolis photo-c 3.00

TEN WHO DARED (Disney)
Dell Publishing Co.: No. 1178, Dec, 1960
Four Color 1178-Movie, painted-c; cast member photo on back-c 7 14 21 49 80 110

TERMINAL CITY
DC Comics (Vertigo): July, 1996 - No. 9, Mar, 1997 ($2.50, limited series)
1-9: Dean Motter scripts, 7,8-Matt Wagner-c 2.50
TPB ('97, $19.95) r/series 20.00

TERMINAL CITY: AERIAL GRAFFITI
DC Comics (Vertigo): Nov, 1997 - No. 5, Mar, 1998 ($2.50, limited series)
1-5: Dean Motter-s/Lark-a/Chiarello-c 2.50

TERMINATOR, THE (See Robocop vs. ... & Rust #12 for 1st app.)
Now Comics: Sept, 1988 - No. 17, 1989 ($1.75, Baxter paper)
1-Based on movie 1 3 4 6 8 10
2-5 6.00
6-17: 12-($2.95, 52 pgs.)-Intro. John Connor 3.00
Trade paperback (1989, $9.95) 10.00

TERMINATOR, THE
Dark Horse Comics: Aug, 1990 - No. 4, Nov, 1990 ($2.50, limited series)
1-Set 39 years later than the movie 4.00
2-4 3.00

TERMINATOR, THE
Dark Horse Comics: 1998 - No. 4, Dec, 1998 ($2.95, limited series)
1-4-Alan Grant-s/Steve Pugh-a/c 3.00
...Special (1998, $2.95) Darrow-c/Grant-s 3.00

TERMINATOR, THE: ALL MY FUTURES PAST
Now Comics: V3#1, Aug, 1990 - V3#2, Sept, 1990 ($1.75, limited series)
V3#1,2 3.00

TERMINATOR, THE: ENDGAME
Dark Horse Comics: Sept, 1992 - No. 3, Nov, 1992 ($2.50, limited series)
1-3: Guice-a(p); painted-c 3.00

TERMINATOR, THE: HUNTERS AND KILLERS
Dark Horse Comics: Mar, 1992 - No. 3, May, 1992 ($2.50, limited series)
1-3 3.00

TERMINATOR, THE: ONE SHOT
Dark Horse Comics: July, 1991 ($5.95, 56 pgs.)
nn-Matt Wagner-a; contains stiff pop-up inside 6.00

TERMINATOR, THE: SECONDARY OBJECTIVES
Dark Horse Comics: July, 1991 - No. 4, Oct, 1991 ($2.50, limited series)
1-4: Gulacy-c/a(p) in all 3.00

TERMINATOR, THE: THE BURNING EARTH
Now Comics: V2#1, Mar, 1990 - V2#5, July, 1990 ($1.75, limited series)
V2#1: Alex Ross painted art (1st published work) 2 4 6 9 12 15
2-5: Ross-c/a in all 1 3 4 6 8 10
Trade paperback (1990, $9.95)-Reprints V2#1-5 12.00
Trade paperback (ibooks, 2003, $17.95)-Digitally remastered reprint 18.00

TERMINATOR, THE: THE DARK YEARS
Dark Horse Comics: Aug, 1999 - No. 4, Dec, 1999 ($2.95, limited series)
1-4-Alan Grant-s/Mel Rubi-a; Jae Lee-c 3.00

TERMINATOR: THE ENEMY FROM WITHIN, THE
Dark Horse Comics: Nov, 1991 - No. 4, Feb, 1992 ($2.50, limited series)
1-4: All have Simon Bisley painted-c 3.00

TERMINATOR 2: CYBERNETIC DAWN
Malibu: Nov, 1995 - No.4, Feb, 1996; No. 0. Apr, 1996 ($2.50, lim. series)
0 (4/96, $2.95)-Erskine-c/a; flip book w/Terminator 2: Nuclear Twilight 3.00
1-4: Continuation of film. 3.00

TERMINATOR 2: INFINITY
Dynamite Entertainment: 2007 - No. 7 ($3.50)
1-7: 1-Furman-s/Raynor-a; 3 covers. 6,7-Painkiller Jane x-over 3.50

TERMINATOR 2: JUDGEMENT DAY
Marvel Comics: Early Sept, 1991 - No. 3, Early Oct, 1991 ($1.00, lim. series)
1-3: Based on movie sequel; 1-3-Same as nn issues 3.00
nn (1991, $4.95, squarebound, 68 pgs.)-Photo-c 5.00
nn (1991, $2.25, B&W, magazine, 68 pgs.) 3.00

TERMINATOR 2: NUCLEAR TWILIGHT
Malibu: Nov, 1995 - No.4, Feb, 1996; No. 0, Apr, 1996 ($2.50, lim. series)
0 (4/96, $2.95)-Erskine-c/a; flip book w/Terminator 2: Cybernetic Dawn 3.00
1-4:Continuation of film. 3.00

TERMINATOR 3: RISE OF THE MACHINES (... BEFORE THE RISE on cover)
Beckett Comics: July, 2003 - No. 6, Jan, 2004 ($5.95, limited series)
1-6: 1,2-Leads into movie; 2 covers on each. 3-6-Movie adaptation 6.00

TERRAFORMERS
Wonder Color Comics: April, 1987 - No. 2, 1987 ($1.95, limited series)
1,2-Kelley Jones-a 2.50

TERRANAUTS
Fantasy General Comics: Aug, 1986 - No. 2, 1986 ($1.75, limited series)
1,2 2.50

TERRA OBSCURA (See Tom Strong)
America's Best Comics: Aug, 2003 - No. 6, Feb, 2004 ($2.95)
1-6-Alan Moore & Peter Hogan-s/Paquette-a 3.00
TPB (2004, $14.95) r/#1-6 15.00

TERRA OBSCURA VOLUME 2 (See Tom Strong)
America's Best Comics: Oct, 2004 - No. 6, May, 2005 ($2.95)
1-6-Alan Moore & Peter Hogan-s/Paquette-a; Tom Strange app. 3.00
TPB (2005, $14.99) r/#1-6 15.00

TERRARISTS
Marvel Comics (Epic): Nov, 1993 - No. 4, Feb, 1994 ($2.50, limited series)
1-4-Bound-in trading cards in all 2.50

TERRIFIC COMICS (Also see Suspense Comics)
Continental Magazines: Jan, 1944 - No. 6, Nov, 1944
1-Kid Terrific; opium story 318 636 954 2162 3781 5400
2-1st app. The Boomerang by L.B. Cole & Ed Wheelan's "Comics" McCormick, called the world's #1 comic book fan begins 228 456 684 1436 2431 3425
3-Diana becomes Boomerang's costumed aide; L.B. Cole-c 228 456 684 1436 2431 3425
4-Classic war-c (Scarce) 411 822 1233 2795 4898 7000
5-The Reckoner begins; Boomerang & Diana by L.B. Cole; Classic Schomburg bondage & hooded vigilante-c (Scarce) 750 1500 2250 4500 7250 10,000
6-L.B. Cole-c/a 207 414 621 1304 2202 3100
NOTE: *L.B. Cole a-1, 2(2), 3-6. Fuje a-5, 6. Rico a-2; c-1. Schomburg c-2, 5.*

TERRIFIC COMICS (Formerly Horrific; Wonder Boy #17 on)
Mystery Publ.(Comic Media)/(Ajax/Farrell): No. 14, Dec, 1954; No. 16, Mar, 1955 (No #15)
14-Art swipe/Advs. into the Unknown #37; injury-to-eye-c; pg. 2, panel 5 swiped from Phantom Stranger #4; surrealistic Palais-a; Human Cross story; classic-c 62 124 186 391 658 925
16-Wonder Boy-c/story (last pre-code) 27 54 81 158 254 350

TERRIFYING TALES (Formerly Startling Terror Tales #10)
Star Publications: No. 11, Jan, 1953 - No. 15, Apr, 1954
11-Used in **POP**, pgs. 99,100; all Jo-Jo-r 49 98 147 304 507 710
12-Reprints Jo-Jo #19 entirely; L.B. Cole splash 47 94 141 291 488 685
13-All Rulah-r; classic devil-c 53 106 159 330 553 775
14-All Rulah reprints 44 88 132 273 454 635
15-Rulah, Zago-r; used in **SOTI**-r/Rulah #22 44 88 132 273 454 635
NOTE: *All issues have L.B. Cole covers; bondage covers-No. 12-14.*

TERROR ILLUSTRATED (Adult Tales of...)
E.C. Comics: Nov-Dec, 1955 - No. 2, Spring (April on-c), 1956 (Magazine, 25¢)
1-Adult Entertainment on-c 21 42 63 123 197 270
2-Charles Sultan-a 15 30 45 88 137 185
NOTE: *Craig, Evans, Ingels, Orlando art in each. Crandall c-1, 2.*

TERROR INC. (See A Shadowline Saga #3)
Marvel Comics: July, 1992 - No. 13, July, 1993 ($1.75)

Terror, Inc. #4 © MAR

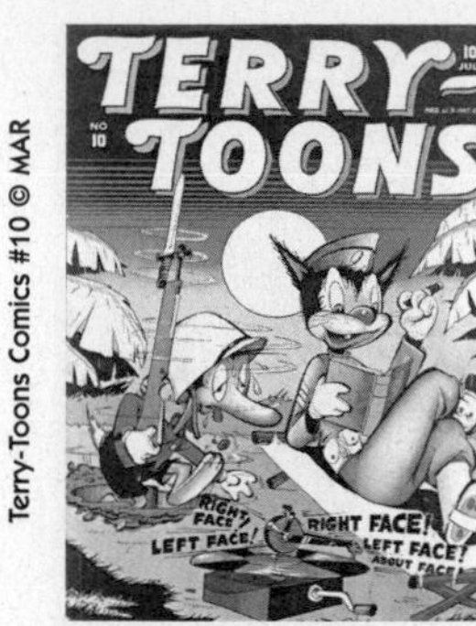

Terry-Toons Comics #10 © MAR

Testament #22 © Rushkoff & Sharp

GD VG FN VF VF/NM NM-
2.0 4.0 6.0 8.0 9.0 9.2

GD VG FN VF VF/NM NM-
2.0 4.0 6.0 8.0 9.0 9.2

1-8,11-13: 6,7-Punisher-c/story. 13-Ghost Rider app. 2.50
9,10-Wolverine-c/story 3.00

TERROR INC.
Marvel Comics (MAX): Oct, 2007 - No. 5, Apr, 2008 ($3.99, limited series)
1-5: 1-Lapham-s/Zircher-a; origin of Mr. Terror retold 4.00

TERRORS OF DRACULA (Magazine)
Modern Day Periodical/Eerie Publ.: Vol. 1 #3, May, 1979 - Vol. 3 #2, Sept, 1981 (B&W)
Vol. 1 #3 (5/79, 1st issue) 4 8 12 24 37 50
#4(8/79), #5(11/79) 3 6 9 19 29 38
Vol. 2 #1-3: 1-(2/80). 2-(5/80). 3-(8/80) 3 6 9 16 23 30
Vol. 3 #1 (5/81), #2 (9/81) 3 6 9 18 27 35

TERRORS OF THE JUNGLE (Formerly Jungle Thrills)
Star Publications: No. 17, 5/52 - No. 21, 2/53; No. 4, 4/53 - No. 10, 9/54
17-Reprints Rulah #21, used in **SOTI**; L.B. Cole bondage-c
47 94 141 291 483 675
18-Jo-Jo-r 36 72 108 212 341 470
19,20(1952)-Jo-Jo-r; Disbrow-a 34 68 102 198 319 440
21-Jungle Jo, Tangi-r; used in **POP**, pg. 100 & color illos.
38 76 114 222 356 490
4-10: All Disbrow-a. 5-Jo-Jo-r. 8-Rulah, Jo-Jo-r. 9-Jo-Jo-r; Disbrow-a; Tangi by Orlando10-Rulah-r 38 76 114 222 356 490
NOTE: ***L.B. Cole** c-all; bondage c-17, 19, 21, 5, 7.*

TERROR TALES (See Beware Terror Tales)

TERROR TALES (Magazine)
Eerie Publications: V1#7, 1969 - V6#6, Dec, 1974; V7#1, Apr, 1976 - V10, 1979? (V1-V6: 52 pgs.; V7 on: 68 pgs.)
V1#7 6 12 18 43 69 95
V1#8-11('69): 9-Bondage-c 4 8 12 28 44 60
V2#1-6('70), V3#1-6('71), V4#1-7('72), V5#1-6('73), V6#1-6('74), V7#1,4('76) (no V7#2), V8#1-3('77) 4 8 12 24 37 50
V7#3-(7/76) LSD story-r/Weird V3#5 4 8 12 24 37 50
V9#2-4, V10#1(1/79) 4 8 12 26 41 55

TERRY AND THE PIRATES (See Famous Feature Stories, Merry Christmas From Sears Toyland, Popular Comics, Super Book #3,5,9,16,28, & Super Comics)

TERRY AND THE PIRATES
Dell Publishing Co.: 1939 - 1953 (By Milton Caniff)
Large Feature Comic 2(1939) 87 174 261 548 924 1300
Large Feature Comic 6(1938)-r/1936 dailies 71 142 213 447 754 1060
Four Color 9(1940) 67 134 201 422 711 1000
Large Feature Comic 27('41), 6('42) 57 114 171 359 605 850
Four Color 44('43) 34 68 102 256 483 710
Four Color 101('45) 22 44 66 157 291 425
Family Album(1942) 19 38 57 112 176 240

TERRY AND THE PIRATES (Formerly Boy Explorers; Long John Silver & the Pirates #30 on) (Daily strip-r) (Two #26's)
Harvey Publications/Charlton No. 26-28: No. 3, 4/47 - No. 26, 4/51; No. 26, 6/55 - No. 28, 10/55
3(#1)-Boy Explorers by S&K; Terry & the Pirates begin by Caniff; 1st app. The Dragon Lady 40 80 120 235 380 525
4-S&K Boy Explorers 23 46 69 133 214 295
5-11: 11-Man in Black app. by Powell 13 26 39 72 101 130
12-20: 16-Girl threatened with red hot poker 10 20 30 56 76 95
21-26(4/51)-Last Caniff issue & last pre-code issue 10 20 30 54 72 90
26-28('55)(Formerly This Is Suspense)-No Caniff-a 9 18 27 47 61 75
NOTE: ***Powell** a (Tommy Tween)-5-10, 12, 14; 15-17(1/2 to 2 pgs. each).*

TERRY BEARS COMICS (TerryToons, The... #4)
St. John Publishing Co.: June, 1952 - No. 3, Mar, 1953
1-By Paul Terry 10 20 30 54 72 90
2,3 7 14 21 35 43 50

TERRY-TOONS ALBUM (See Giant Comics Edition)

TERRY-TOONS COMICS (1st Series) (Becomes Paul Terry's Comics #85 on; later issues titled "Paul Terry's...")
Timely/Marvel No. 1-59 (8/47)(Becomes Best Western No. 58 on?, Marvel)/ St. John No. 60 (9/47) on: Oct, 1942 - No. 86, May, 1951
1 (Scarce)-Features characters that 1st app. on movie screen; Gandy Goose & Sourpuss begin; war-c; Gandy Goose c-1-37 193 386 579 1216 2058 2900
2 67 134 201 422 711 1000
3-5 47 94 141 291 488 685
6,8-10: 9,10-World War II gag-c 37 74 111 215 345 475
7-Hitler, Hirohito, Mussolini-c 57 114 171 359 605 850
11-20 23 46 69 135 218 300
21-37 15 30 45 94 147 200
38-Mighty Mouse begins (1st app., 11/45); Mighty Mouse-c begin, end #86; Gandy, Sourpuss welcome Mighty Mouse on-c 160 320 480 1008 1704 2400
39-2nd app. Mighty Mouse 50 100 150 310 518 725
40-49: 43-Infinity-c 25 50 75 147 236 325
50-1st app. Heckle & Jeckle (11/46) 43 86 129 267 446 625
51-60: 55-Infinity-c. 60-(9/47)-Atomic explosion panel; 1st St. John issue
15 30 45 88 137 185
61-86: 85,86-Same book as Paul Terry's Comics #85,86 with only a title change; published at same time? 14 28 42 80 115 150

TERRY-TOONS COMICS (2nd Series)
St. John Publishing Co./Pines: June, 1952 - No. 9, Nov, 1953; 1957; 1958
1-Gandy Goose & Sourpuss begin by Paul Terry 18 36 54 105 165 225
2 10 20 30 56 76 95
3-9 9 18 27 52 69 85
Giant Summer Fun Book 101,102-(Sum, 1957, Sum, 1958, 25¢, Pines)(TV) CBS Television Presents...; Tom Terrific, Mighty Mouse, Heckle & Jeckle Gandy Goose app. 14 28 42 80 115 150

TERRYTOONS, THE TERRY BEARS (Formerly Terry Bears Comics)
Pines Comics: No. 4, Summer, 1958 (CBS Television Presents...)
4 7 14 21 35 43 50

TESSIE THE TYPIST (Tiny Tessie #24; see Comedy Comics, Gay Comics & Joker Comics)
Timely/Marvel Comics (20CC): Summer, 1944 - No. 23, Aug, 1949
1-Doc Rockblock & others by Wolverton 73 146 219 460 780 1100
2-Wolverton's Powerhouse Pepper 40 80 120 238 387 535
3-(3/45)-No Wolverton 17 34 51 100 158 215
4,5,7,8-Wolverton-a. 4-(Fall/45) 30 60 90 176 283 390
6-Kurtzman's "Hey Look", 2 pgs. Wolverton-a 30 60 90 176 283 390
9-Wolverton's Powerhouse Pepper (8 pgs.) & 1 pg. Kurtzman's "Hey Look"
33 66 99 192 309 425
10-Wolverton's Powerhouse Pepper (4 pgs.) 31 62 93 181 291 400
11-Wolverton's Powerhouse Pepper (8 pgs.) 33 66 99 192 309 425
12-Wolverton's Powerhouse Pepper (4 pgs.) & 1 pg. Kurtzman's "Hey Look"
31 62 93 181 291 400
13-Wolverton's Powerhouse Pepper (4 pgs.) 31 62 93 181 291 400
14,15: 14-Wolverton's Dr. Whackyhack (1 pg.); 1-1/2 pgs. Kurtzman's "Hey Look". 15-Kurtzman's "Hey Look" (3 pgs.) & 3 pgs. Giggles 'n' Grins
23 46 69 135 218 300
16-18-Kurtzman's "Hey Look" (?, 2 & 1 pg.) 17 34 51 98 154 210
19-Annie Oakley story (8 pgs.) 14 28 42 80 115 150
20-23: 20-Anti-Wertham editorial (2/49) 13 26 39 74 105 135
NOTE: *Lana app.-21. Millie The Model app.-13, 15, 17, 21. Rusty app.-10, 11, 13, 15, 17.*

TESTAMENT
DC Comics (Vertigo): Feb, 2006 - No. 22, Mar, 2008 ($2.99)
1-22: 1-5-Rushkoff-s/Sharp-a. 6,7-Gross & Erskine-a 3.00
...: Akedah TPB (2006, $9.99) r/#1-5; Rushkoff intro. 10.00
...: Babel TPB (2007, $12.99) r/#11-16 13.00
...: West of Eden TPB (2007, $12.99) r/#6-10; Rushkoff commentary 13.00

TEXAN, THE (Fightin' Marines #15 on; Fightin' Texan #16 on)
St. John Publishing Co.: Aug, 1948 - No. 15, Oct, 1951
1-Buckskin Belle 16 32 48 94 147 200
2 10 20 30 58 79 100
3,10: 10-Oversized issue 10 20 30 54 72 90
4,5,7,15-Baker-c/a 20 40 60 115 183 250
6,9-Baker-c 15 30 45 83 124 165
8,11,13,14-Baker-c/a(2-3) each 21 42 63 125 200 275
12-All Matt Baker-c/a; Peyote story 28 56 84 162 261 360
NOTE: ***Matt Baker** c-4-9, 11-15. **Larsen** a-4-6, 8-10, 15. **Tuska** a-1, 2, 7-9.*

TEXAN, THE (TV)
Dell Publishing Co.: No. 1027, Sept-Nov, 1959 - No. 1096, May-July, 1960
Four Color 1027 (#1)-Photo-c 8 16 24 56 93 130
Four Color 1096-Rory Calhoun photo-c 8 16 24 52 86 120

TEXAS CHAINSAW MASSACRE
DC Comics (WildStorm): Jan, 2007 - No. 6, Jun, 2007 ($2.99, limited series)
1-6: 1-Two covers by Bermejo & Bradstreet; Abnett & Lanning-s 3.00
...: About a Boy #1 (9/07, $2.99) Abnett & Lanning-s/Gomez-a/Robertson-c 3.00
...: By Himself #1 (10/07, $2.99) Abnett & Lanning-s/Craig-a/Robertson-c 3.00

Texas Kid #7 © MAR

Tex Taylor #3 © MAR

That Wilkin Boy #1 © AP

	GD 2.0	VG 4.0	FN 6.0	VF 8.0	VF/NM 9.0	NM- 9.2
...: Cut! #1 (8/07, $2.99) Pfeiffer-s/Raffaele-a/Robertson-c						3.00
...: Raising Cain 1-3 (7/08 - No. 3, 9/08, $3.50) Bruce Jones-s/Chris Gugliotti-a						3.50

TEXAS JOHN SLAUGHTER (See Walt Disney Presents, 4-Color #997, 1181 & #2)

TEXAS KID (See Two-Gun Western, Wild Western)
Marvel/Atlas Comics (LMC): Jan, 1951 - No. 10, July, 1952

	GD 2.0	VG 4.0	FN 6.0	VF 8.0	VF/NM 9.0	NM- 9.2
1-Origin; Texas Kid (alias Lance Temple) & his horse Thunder begin; Tuska-a	23	46	69	133	214	295
2	13	26	39	74	105	135
3-10	10	20	30	56	76	95

NOTE: *Maneely a-1-4, c-1, 3, 5-10.*

TEXAS RANGERS, THE (See Jace Pearson of... and Superior Stories #4)

TEXAS RANGERS IN ACTION (Formerly Captain Gallant or Scotland Yard?)
Charlton Comics: No. 5, Jul, 1956 - No. 79, Aug, 1970 (See Blue Bird Comics)

	GD 2.0	VG 4.0	FN 6.0	VF 8.0	VF/NM 9.0	NM- 9.2
5	8	16	24	44	57	70
6,7,9,10	6	12	18	28	34	40
8-Ditko-a (signed)	10	20	30	54	72	90
11-Williamson-a(5&8 pgs.); Torres/Williamson-a (5 pgs.)	10	20	30	54	72	90
12,14-20	5	10	15	23	28	32
13-Williamson-a (5 pgs); Torres, Morisi-a	8	16	24	42	54	65
21-30	3	6	9	16	22	28
31-59: 32-Both 10¢-c & 15¢-c exist	2	4	6	13	18	22
60 Riley's Rangers begin	3	6	9	14	19	24
61-65,68-70	2	4	6	8	11	14
66,67: 66-1st app. The Man Called Loco. 67-Origin	2	4	6	9	13	16
71-79: 77-(4/70) Ditko-c & a (8 pgs.)	1	3	4	6	8	10
76 (Modern Comics-r, 1977)						4.00

TEXAS SLIM (See A-1 Comics)

TEX DAWSON, GUN-SLINGER (Gunslinger #2 on)
Marvel Comics Group: Jan, 1973 (20¢)(Also see Western Kid, 1st series)

	GD 2.0	VG 4.0	FN 6.0	VF 8.0	VF/NM 9.0	NM- 9.2
1-Steranko-c; Williamson-r (4 pgs.); Tex Dawson-r by Romita(3) from 1955; Tuska-r	3	6	9	14	20	25

TEX FARNUM (See Wisco)

TEX FARRELL (...Pride of the Wild West)
D. S. Publishing Co.: Mar-Apr, 1948

	GD 2.0	VG 4.0	FN 6.0	VF 8.0	VF/NM 9.0	NM- 9.2
1-Tex Farrell & his horse Lightning; Shelly-c	15	30	45	88	137	185

TEX GRANGER (Formerly Calling All Boys; see True Comics)
Parents' Magazine Inst./Commended: No. 18, Jun, 1948 - No. 24, Sept, 1949

	GD 2.0	VG 4.0	FN 6.0	VF 8.0	VF/NM 9.0	NM- 9.2
18-Tex Granger & his horse Bullet begin	12	24	36	67	94	120
19	10	20	30	54	72	90
20-24: 22-Wild Bill Hickok story. 23-Vs. Billy the Kid; Tim Holt app.	8	16	24	44	57	70

TEX MORGAN (See Blaze Carson and Wild Western)
Marvel Comics (CCC): Aug, 1948 - No. 9, Feb, 1950

	GD 2.0	VG 4.0	FN 6.0	VF 8.0	VF/NM 9.0	NM- 9.2
1-Tex Morgan, his horse Lightning & sidekick Lobo begin	28	56	84	162	261	360
2	18	36	54	103	162	220
3-6: 3,4-Arizona Annie app.	13	26	39	74	105	135
7-9: All photo-c. 7-Captain Tootsie by Beck. 8-18 pg. story "The Terror of Rimrock Valley"; Diablo app.	18	36	54	103	162	220

NOTE: *Tex Taylor app.-6, 7, 9.* ***Brodsky*** *c-6.* ***Syd Shores*** *c-2, 5.*

TEX RITTER WESTERN (Movie star; singing cowboy; see Six-Gun Heroes and Western Hero)
Fawcett No. 1-20 (1/54)/Charlton No. 21 on: Oct, 1950 - No. 46, May, 1959 (Photo-c: 1-21)

	GD 2.0	VG 4.0	FN 6.0	VF 8.0	VF/NM 9.0	NM- 9.2
1-Tex Ritter, his stallion White Flash & dog Fury begin; photo front/back-c begin	55	110	165	344	572	800
2	28	56	84	162	256	350
3-5: 5-Last photo back-c	20	40	60	117	184	250
6-10	16	32	48	89	137	185
11-19	12	24	36	69	97	125
20-Last Fawcett issue (1/54)	13	26	39	74	105	135
21-1st Charlton issue; photo-c (3/54)	16	32	48	89	137	185
22-B&W photo back-c begin, end #32	11	22	33	60	83	105
23-30: 23-25-Young Falcon app.	10	20	30	56	76	95
31-38,40-45	9	18	27	50	65	80
39-Williamson-a; Whitman-c (1/58)	10	20	30	56	76	95
46-Last issue	10	20	30	54	72	90

TEX TAYLOR (...The Fighting Cowboy on-c #1, 2)(See Blaze Carson, Kid Colt, Tex Morgan, Wild West, Wild Western, & Wisco)
Marvel Comics (HPC): Sept, 1948 - No. 9, March, 1950

	GD 2.0	VG 4.0	FN 6.0	VF 8.0	VF/NM 9.0	NM- 9.2
1-Tex Taylor & his horse Fury begin	29	58	87	169	272	375
2	15	30	45	88	137	185
3	14	28	42	82	121	160
4-6: All photo-c. 4 Anti Wortham editorial. 5,6-Blaze Carson app.	15	30	45	92	144	195
7-9: 7-Photo-c;18 pg. Movie-Length Thriller "Trapped in Time's Lost Land!" with sabretoothed tigers, dinosaurs; Diablo app. 8-Photo-c; 18 pg. Movie-Length Thriller "The Mystery of Devil-Tree Plateau!" with dwarf horses, dwarf people & a lost miniature Inca type village; Diablo app. 9-Photo-c; 18 pg. Movie-Length Thriller "Guns Along the Border!" Captain Tootsie by Schreiber; Nimo the Mountain Lion app.	19	38	57	109	172	235

NOTE: ***Syd Shores*** *c-1-3.*

THANE OF BAGARTH (Also see Hercules, 1967 series)
Charlton Comics: No. 24, Oct, 1985 - No. 25, Dec, 1985

	GD 2.0	VG 4.0	FN 6.0	VF 8.0	VF/NM 9.0	NM- 9.2
24,25-Low print run						5.00

THANOS
Marvel Comics: Dec, 2003 - No. 12, Sept, 2004 ($2.99)

	GD 2.0	VG 4.0	FN 6.0	VF 8.0	VF/NM 9.0	NM- 9.2
1-12: 1-6-Starlin-s/a(p)/Milgrom-i; Galactus app. 7-12-Giffen-s/Lim-a						3.00
Vol. 4: Epiphany TPB (2004, $14.99) r/#1-6						15.00
Vol. 5: Samaritan TPB (2004, $14.99) r/#7-12						15.00

THANOS QUEST, THE (See Capt. Marvel #25, Infinity Gauntlet, Iron Man #55, Logan's Run, Marvel Feature #12, Marvel Universe: The End, Silver Surfer #34 & Warlock #9)
Marvel Comics: 1990 - No. 2, 1990 ($4.95, squarebound, 52 pgs.)

	GD 2.0	VG 4.0	FN 6.0	VF 8.0	VF/NM 9.0	NM- 9.2
1,2-Both have Starlin scripts & covers (both printings)	1	2	3	4	5	7
1-(3/2000, $3.99) r/material from #1&2						4.00

THAT DARN CAT (See Movie Comics & Walt Disney Showcase #19)

THAT'S MY POP! GOES NUTS FOR FAIR
Bystander Press: 1939 (76 pgs., B&W)

	GD 2.0	VG 4.0	FN 6.0	VF 8.0	VF/NM 9.0	NM- 9.2
nn-by Milt Gross	30	60	90	174	280	385

THAT WILKIN BOY (Meet Bingo...)
Archie Publications: Jan, 1969 - No. 52, Oct, 1982

	GD 2.0	VG 4.0	FN 6.0	VF 8.0	VF/NM 9.0	NM- 9.2
1-1st app. Bingo's Band, Samantha & Tough Teddy	4	8	12	28	44	60
2-5	3	6	9	16	23	30
6-11	2	4	6	13	18	22
12-26-Giants. 12-No # on-c	3	6	9	14	20	26
27-40(1/77)	2	4	6	8	10	12
41-49						6.00
50-52 (low print)	1	3	4	6	8	10

THB
Horse Press: Oct, 1994 - Present ($5.50/$2.50/$2.95, B&W)

	GD 2.0	VG 4.0	FN 6.0	VF 8.0	VF/NM 9.0	NM- 9.2
1 ($5.50) Paul Pope-s/a in all	1	2	3	5	6	8
1 (2nd Printing)-r/#1 w/new material						3.00
2 ($2.50)						5.00
3-5						4.00
69 (1995, no price, low distribution, 12 pgs.)-story reprinted in #1 (2nd Printing)						3.00
Giant THB-($4.95)						5.00
Giant THB 1 V2-(2003, $6.95)						7.00
...M3/THB: Mars' Mightiest Mek #1 (2000, $3.95)						4.00
...6A: Mek-Power #1, 6B: Mek-Power #2, 6C: Mek-Power #3 (2000, $3.95)						4.00
... 6D: Mek-Power #4 (2002, $4.95)						5.00

T.H.E. CAT (TV)
Dell Publishing Co.: Mar, 1967 - No. 4, Oct, 1967 (All have photo-c)

	GD 2.0	VG 4.0	FN 6.0	VF 8.0	VF/NM 9.0	NM- 9.2
1	4	8	12	22	34	45
2-4	3	6	9	17	25	32

THERE'S A NEW WORLD COMING
Spire Christian Comics/Fleming H. Revell Co.: 1973 (35/49¢)

	GD 2.0	VG 4.0	FN 6.0	VF 8.0	VF/NM 9.0	NM- 9.2
nn	2	4	6	8	10	12

THEY ALL KISSED THE BRIDE (See Cinema Comics Herald)

THIEF OF BAGHDAD
Dell Publishing Co.: No. 1229, Oct-Dec, 1961 (one-shot)

	GD 2.0	VG 4.0	FN 6.0	VF 8.0	VF/NM 9.0	NM- 9.2
Four Color 1229-Movie, Crandall/Evans-a, photo-c	7	14	21	45	73	100

THIMK (Magazine) (Satire)
Counterpoint: May, 1958 - No. 6, May, 1959

	GD 2.0	VG 4.0	FN 6.0	VF 8.0	VF/NM 9.0	NM- 9.2
1	10	20	30	54	72	90
2-6	7	14	21	37	46	55

The Thing! #2 © CC

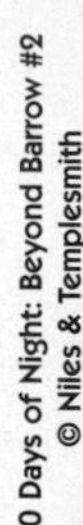
30 Days of Night: Beyond Barrow #2 © Niles & Templesmith

This Magazine is Haunted #7 © FAW

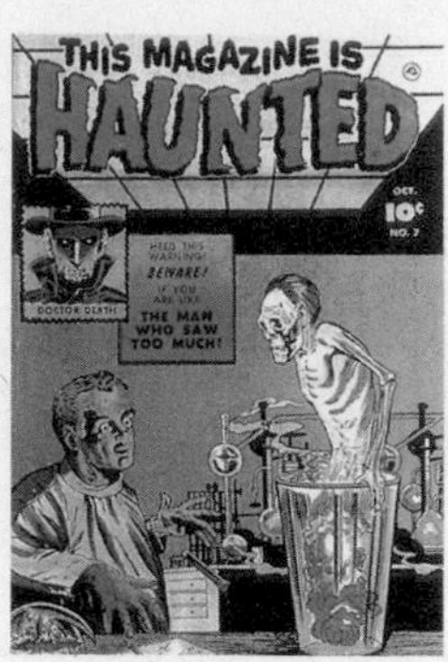

	GD 2.0	VG 4.0	FN 6.0	VF 8.0	VF/NM 9.0	NM- 9.2

THING!, THE (Blue Beetle #18 on)
Song Hits No. 1,2/Capitol Stories/Charlton: Feb, 1952 - No. 17, Nov, 1954

	GD	VG	FN	VF	VF/NM	NM-
1-Weird/horror stories in all; shrunken head-c	90	180	270	567	959	1350
2,3	58	116	174	365	620	875
4-6,8,10: 5-Severed head-c; headlights	53	106	159	330	553	775
7-Injury to eye-c & inside panel	70	140	210	441	746	1050
9-Used in **SOTI**, pg. 388 & illo "Stomping on the face is a form of brutality which modern children learn early"	82	164	246	517	871	1225
11-Necronomicon story; Hansel & Gretel parody; Injury-to-eye panel; Check-a	64	128	192	403	682	960
12-1st published Ditko-c; "Cinderella" parody; lingerie panels. Ditko-a	90	180	270	567	959	1350
13,15-Ditko-c/a(3 & 5)	90	180	270	567	959	1350
14-Extreme violence/torture; Rumpelstiltskin story; Ditko-c/a(4)	92	184	276	580	978	1375
16-Injury to eye panel	33	66	99	192	309	425
17-Ditko-c; classic parody "Through the Looking Glass"; Powell-r/Beware Terror Tales #1 & recolored	80	160	240	504	852	1200

NOTE: *Excessive violence, severed heads, injury to eye are common No. 5 on.* ***Al Fago*** *c-4.* ***Forgione*** *c-1i, 2, 6, 8, 9. All* ***Ditko*** *issues #14, 15.* ***Giordano*** *a-6.*

THING, THE (See Fantastic Four, Marvel Fanfare, Marvel Feature #11,12, Marvel Two-In-One and Startling Stories:...- Night Falls on Yancy Street)
Marvel Comics Group: July, 1983 - No. 36, June, 1986

1-Life story of Ben Grimm; Byrne scripts begin — 3.00
2-36: 5-Spider-Man, She-Hulk app. — 2.50

NOTE: ***Byrne*** *a-2i, 7; c-1, 7, 36i; scripts-1-13, 19-22.* ***Sienkiewicz*** *c-13i.*

THING, THE (Fantastic Four)
Marvel Comics: Jan, 2006 - No. 8 ($2.99)

1-8: 1-DiVito-a/Slott-s. 4-Lockjaw app. 6-Spider-Man app. 8-Super-Hero poker game — 3.00
...: Idol of Millions TPB (2006, $20.99) r/#1-8; Divito sketch page — 21.00

THING & SHE-HULK: THE LONG NIGHT (Fantastic Four)
Marvel Comics: May, 2002 ($2.99, one-shot)

1-Hitch-c/a(pg. 1-25); Reis-a(pg. 26-39); Dezago-s — 3.00

THING, THE (From Another World)
Dark Horse Comics: 1991 - No. 2, 1992 ($2.95, mini-series, stiff-c)

1,2-Based on Universal movie; painted-c/a — 3.00

THING, THE: FREAKSHOW (Fantastic Four)
Marvel Comics: Aug, 2002 - No. 4, Nov, 2002 ($2.99, limited series)

1-4-Geoff Johns-s/Scott Kolins-a — 3.00
TPB (2005, $17.99) r/#1-4 & Thing & She-Hulk: The Long Night one-shot — 18.00

THING FROM ANOTHER WORLD: CLIMATE OF FEAR, THE
Dark Horse Comics: July, 1992 - No. 4, Dec, 1992 ($2.50, mini-series)

1-4: Painted-c — 3.00

THING FROM ANOTHER WORLD: ETERNAL VOWS
Dark Horse Comics: Dec, 1993 - No. 4, 1994 ($2.50, mini-series)

1-4-Gulacy-c/a — 3.00

THIRD WORLD WAR
Fleetway Publ. (Quality): 1990 - No. 6, 1991 ($2.50, thick-c, mature)

1-6 — 2.50

THIRTEEN (...Going on 18)
Dell Publishing Co.: 11-1/61-62 - No. 25, 12/67; No. 26, 7/69 - No. 29, 1/71

	GD	VG	FN	VF	VF/NM	NM-
1	6	12	18	41	66	90
2-10	5	10	15	30	48	65
11-25	4	8	12	24	37	50
26-29-r	3	6	9	18	27	35

NOTE: ***John Stanley*** *script-No. 3-29; art?*

13: ASSASSIN
TSR, Inc.: 1990 - No. 8, 1991 ($2.95, 44 pgs.)

1-8: Agent 13; Alcala-a(i); Springer back-up-a — 3.00

13th SON, THE
Dark Horse Comics: Nov, 2005 - No. 4, Feb, 2006 ($2.99, limited series)

1-4-Kelley Jones-s/a/c — 3.00

30 DAYS OF NIGHT
Idea + Design Works: June, 2002 - No. 3, Oct, 2002 ($3.99, limited series)

1-Vampires in Alaska; Steve Niles-s/Ben Templesmith-a/Ashley Wood-c — 30.00
1-2nd printing — 10.00
2 — 12.00
3 — 6.00
Annual 2004 (1/04, $4.99) Niles-s/art by Templesmith and others — 5.00
Annual 2005 (12/05, $7.49) Niles-s/art by Nat Jones — 7.50
... 5th Anniversary (10/07 - No. 3, $2.99) reprints original series — 3.00
... Sourcebook (10/07, $7.49) Illustrated guide to the 30 Days world — 7.50
... Three Tales TPB (7/06, $19.99) r/Annual 2005, ...: Dead Space #1-3, and short story from Tales of Terror (IDW's...) — 20.00
TPB (2003, $17.99) r/#1-3, foreward by Clive Barker; script for #1 — 18.00
The Complete 30 Days of Night (2004, $75.00, oversized hardcover with slipcase) r/#1-3; prequel; script pages for #1-3; original cover and promotional materials — 75.00

30 DAYS OF NIGHT: BEYOND BARROW
IDW Publishing: Sept, 2007 - No. 3, Dec, 2007 ($3.99, limited series)

1-3-Niles-s/Sienkiewicz-a/c — 4.00

30 DAYS OF NIGHT: BLOODSUCKER TALES
IDW Publishing: Oct, 2004 - No. 8, May, 2005 ($3.99, limited series)

1-8-Niles-s/Chamberlain-a; Fraction-s/Templesmith-a/c — 4.00
HC (8/05, $49.99) r/#1-8; cover gallery — 50.00
SC (8/05, $24.99) r/#1-8; cover gallery — 25.00

30 DAYS OF NIGHT: DEAD SPACE
IDW Publishing: Jan, 2006 - No. 3, Mar, 2006 ($3.99, limited series)

1-3-Niles and Wickline-s/Milx-a/c — 4.00

30 DAYS OF NIGHT: EBEN & STELLA
IDW Publishing: May, 2007 - No. 3, July, 2007 ($3.99, limited series)

1-3-Niles and DeConnick-s/Randall-a/c — 4.00

30 DAYS OF NIGHT: RED SNOW
IDW Publishing: Aug, 2007 - No. 3, Oct, 2007 ($3.99, limited series)

1-3-Ben Templesmith-s/a/c — 4.00

30 DAYS OF NIGHT: RETURN TO BARROW
IDW Publishing: Mar, 2004 - No. 6, Aug, 2004 ($3.99, limited series)

1-6-Steve Niles-s/Ben Templesmith-a/c — 4.00
TPB (2004, $19.99) r/#1-6; cover gallery — 20.00

30 DAYS OF NIGHT: SPREADING THE DISEASE
IDW Publishing: Dec, 2006 - No. 5, Apr, 2007 ($3.99, limited series)

1-5: 1-Wickline-s/Sanchez-a. 3-5-Sandoval-a — 4.00

THIRTY SECONDS OVER TOKYO (See American Library)

THIS IS SUSPENSE! (Formerly Strange Suspense Stories; Strange Suspense Stories #27 on)
Charlton Comics: No. 23, Feb, 1955 - No. 26, Aug, 1955

	GD	VG	FN	VF	VF/NM	NM-
23-Wood-a(r)/A Star Presentation #3 "Dr. Jekyll & Mr. Hyde"; last pre-code issue	24	48	72	140	225	310
24-Censored Fawcett-r; Evans-a (r/Suspense Detective #1)	14	28	42	80	115	150
25,26: 26-Marcus Swayze-a	10	20	30	56	76	95

THIS IS THE PAYOFF (See Pay-Off)

THIS IS WAR
Standard Comics: No. 5, July, 1952 - No. 9, May, 1953

	GD	VG	FN	VF	VF/NM	NM-
5-Toth-a	14	28	42	76	108	140
6,9-Toth-a	11	22	33	60	83	105
7,8: 8-Ross Andru-c	8	16	24	44	57	70

THIS IS YOUR LIFE, DONALD DUCK (See Donald Duck..., Four Color #1109)

THIS MAGAZINE IS CRAZY (Crazy #? on)
Charlton Publ. (Humor Magazines): V3#2, July, 1957 - V4#8, Feb, 1959 (25¢, magazine, 68 pgs.)

	GD	VG	FN	VF	VF/NM	NM-
V3#2-V4#7: V4#5-Russian Sputnik-c parody	10	20	30	54	72	90
V4#8-Davis-a (8 pgs.)	10	20	30	58	79	100

THIS MAGAZINE IS HAUNTED (Danger and Adventure #22 on)
Fawcett Publications/Charlton No. 15(2/54) on: Oct, 1951 - No. 14, 12/53; No. 15, 2/54 - V3#21, Nov, 1954

	GD	VG	FN	VF	VF/NM	NM-
1-Evans-a; Dr. Death as host begins	64	128	192	403	682	960
2,5-Evans-a	44	88	132	273	454	635
3,4: 3-Vampire-c/story	35	70	105	203	327	450
6-9,11,12,14	26	52	78	152	244	335
10-Severed head-c	41	82	123	256	428	600
13-Severed head-c/story	41	82	123	249	410	570
15,20: 15-Dick Giordano-c. 20-Cover is swiped from panel in The Thing #16	21	42	63	125	200	275

Thor #287 © MAR

Thor #500 © MAR

Thor V2 #25 © MAR

GD VG FN VF VF/NM NM-
2.0 4.0 6.0 8.0 9.0 9.2

16,19-Ditko-c. 19-Injury-to-eye panel; story-r/#1 40 80 120 244 397 550
17-Ditko-c/a(4); blood drainage story 47 94 141 291 483 675
18-Ditko-c/a(1 story); E.C. swipe/Haunt of Fear #5; injury-to-eye panel; reprints "Caretaker of the Dead" from Beware Terror Tales & recolored 41 82 123 253 419 585
21-Ditko-c, Evans-r/This Magazine Is Haunted #1 38 76 114 222 356 490
NOTE: ***Baily** a-1, 3, 4, 21r/#1. **Moldoff** c/a-1-13. **Powell** a-3-5, 11, 12, 17. **Shuster** a-18-20. Issues 19-21 have reprints which have been recolored from This Magazine is Haunted #1.*

THIS MAGAZINE IS HAUNTED (2nd Series) (Formerly Zaza the Mystic; Outer Space #17 on)
Charlton Comics: V2#12, July, 1957 - V2#16, May, 1958

V2#12-14-Ditko-c/a in all 40 80 120 236 383 530
15-No Ditko-c/a 12 24 36 69 97 125
16-Ditko-a(4). 27 54 81 158 254 350

THIS MAGAZINE IS WILD (See Wild)

THIS WAS YOUR LIFE (Religious)
Jack T. Chick Publ.: 1964 (3 1/2 x 5 1/2", 40 pgs., B&W and red)

nn, Another version (5x2 3/4", 26 pgs.) 2 4 6 10 14 18

THOR (See Avengers #1, Giant-Size..., Marvel Collectors Item Classics, Marvel Graphic Novel #33, Marvel Preview, Marvel Spectacular, Marvel Treasury Edition, Special Marvel Edition & Tales of Asgard)

THOR (Journey Into Mystery #1-125, 503-on)(The Mighty Thor #413-490)
Marvel Comics Group: No. 126, Mar, 1966 - No. 502, Sept, 1996

126-Thor continues (#125-130 Thor vs. Hercules) 19 38 57 139 257 375
127-130: 127-1st app. Pluto 9 18 27 63 107 150
131-133,135-140: 132-1st app. Ego. 136- Intro. Sif 8 16 24 52 86 120
134-Intro High Evolutionary 8 16 24 54 90 125
141-150: 146-Inhumans begin (early app.), end #151 (see Fantastic Four #45 for 1st app.). 146,147-Origin The Inhumans. 148,149-Origin Black Bolt in each. 149-Origin Medusa, Crystal, Maximus, Gorgon, Karnak 7 14 21 45 73 100
151-157,159,160: 159-Origin Dr. Blake (Thor) concl. 6 12 18 39 62 85
158-Origin-r/#83; origin Dr. Blake 8 16 24 58 97 135
161,167,170-179: 179-Last Kirby issue 5 10 15 30 48 65
162,168,169-Origin Galactus; Kirby-a 6 12 18 37 59 80
163,164-2nd & 3th brief app. Warlock (Him) 5 10 15 30 48 65
165-1st full app. Warlock (Him) (6/69, see Fantastic Four #67); last 12¢ issue; Kirby-a 7 14 21 47 76 105
166-2nd full app. Warlock (Him); battles Thor 6 12 18 41 66 90
180,181-Neal Adams-a 5 10 15 34 55 75
182-192: 192-Last 15¢ issue 3 6 9 20 30 40
193-(25¢, 52 pgs.); Silver Surfer x-over 8 16 24 52 86 120
194-199 3 6 9 16 23 30
200 3 6 9 20 30 40
201-206,208-224 2 4 6 9 13 16
207-Rutland, Vermont Halloween x-over 2 4 6 11 16 20
225-Intro. Firelord 3 6 9 14 20 26
226-245: 226-Galactus app. 2 4 6 8 10 12
246-250-(Regular 25¢ editions)(4-8/76) 2 4 6 8 10 12
246-250-(30¢-c variants, limited distribution) 4 8 12 22 34 45
251-280: 271-Iron Man x-over. 274-Death of Balder the Brave 1 2 3 4 5 7
260-264-(35¢-c variants, limited distribution)(6-10/77) 4 8 12 22 34 45
281-299: 294-Origin Asgard & Odin 6.00
300-(12/80)-End of Asgard; origin of Odin & The Destroyer 1 2 3 5 7 9
301-336,338-373,375-381,383: 316-Iron Man x-over. 332,333-Dracula app. 340-Donald Blake returns as Thor. 341-Clark Kent & Lois Lane cameo. 373-X-Factor tie-in 4.00
337-Simonson-c/a begins, ends #382; Beta Ray Bill becomes new Thor 1 3 4 6 8 10
374-Mutant Massacre; X-Factor app. 5.00
382-($1.25)-Anniversary issue; last Simonson-a 5.00
384-Intro. new Thor 5.00
385-399,401-410,413-428: 385-Hulk x-over. 391-Spider-Man x-over; 1st Eric Masterson. 395-Intro Earth Force. 408-Eric Masterson becomes Thor. 427,428-Excalibur x-over 3.00
400,411: 400-($1.75, 68 pgs.)-Origin Loki. 411-Intro New Warriors (appears in costume in last panel); Juggernaut-c/story 5.00
412-1st full app. New Warriors (Marvel Boy, Kid Nova, Namorita, Night Thrasher, Firestar & Speedball) 6.00
429-431,434-443: 429,430-Ghost Rider x-over. 434-Capt. America x-over. 437-Thor vs. Quasar; Hercules app.;Tales of Asgard back-up stories begin. 443-Dr. Strange & Silver Surfer x-over; last $1.00-c 2.50
432,433: 432-(52 pgs.)-Thor's 300th app. (vs. Loki); reprints origin & 1st app. from Journey into Mystery #83. 433-Intro new Thor 3.00
444-449,451-473: 448-Spider-Man-c/story. 455,456-Dr. Strange back-up. 457-Old Thor returns (3 pgs.). 459-Intro Thunderstrike. 460-Starlin scripts begin. 465-Super Skrull app. 466-Drax app. 469,470-Infinity Watch x-over. 472-Intro the Godlings 2.50
450-($2.50, 68 pgs.)-Flip-book format; r/story JIM #87 (1st Loki) plus-c plus a gallery of past-c; gatefold-c 3.00
474,476-481,483-499: 474-Begin $1.50-c; bound-in trading cards. 459-Intro Thunderstrike, 460-Starlin scripts begin. 472-Intro the Godlings. 490-The Absorbing Man app. 491-Warren Ellis scripts begins, ends #494; Deodato-c/a begins. 492-Reintro The Enchantress; Beta Ray Bill dies. 495-Wm. Messner-Loebs scripts begin; Isherwood-c/a. 2.50
475 ($2.00, 52 pgs.)-Regular edition 2.50
475 ($2.50, 52 pgs.)-Collectors edition w/foil embossed-c 3.00
482 ($2.95, 84 pgs.)-400th issue 3.00
500 ($2.50)-Double-size; wraparound-c; Deodato-c/a; Dr. Strange app. 5.00
501-Reintro Red Norvell 3.00
502-Onslaught tie-in; Red Norvell, Jane Foster & Hela app. 4.00
Special 2(9/66)-(See Journey Into Mystery for 1st annual) 8 16 24 56 93 130
Special 2 (2nd printing, 1994) 2 4 6 8 10 12
King Size Special 3(1/71) 3 6 9 20 30 40
Special 4(12/71)-r/Thor #131,132 & JIM #113 3 6 9 16 23 30
Annual 5,6: 5(11/76). 6(10/77)-Guardians of the Galaxy app. 2 4 6 9 13 16
Annual 7,8: 7(1978). 8(1979)-Thor vs. Zeus-c/story 1 3 4 6 8 10
Annual 9-12: 9('81). 10('82). 11('83). 12('84) 6.00
Annual 13-19('85-'94, 68 pgs.):14-Atlantis Attacks. 16-3 pg. origin; Guardians of the Galaxy x-over.18-Polybagged w/card 3.00
...Alone Against the Celestials nn (6/92, $5.95)-r/Thor #387-389 6.00
...Legends Vol. 2: Walter Simonson Book 2 TPB (2003, $24.99) r/#349-355,357-359 25.00
...Legends Vol. 3: Walter Simonson Book 3 TPB (2004, $24.99) r/#360-369 25.00
...: The Eternals Saga TPB (2006, $24.99) r/#283-291 & Annual #7; profile pages 25.00
...: The Eternals Saga Vol. 2 TPB ('07, $24.99) r/#292-301; Thomas & Gruenwald essays 25.00
... Visionaries: Mike Deodato Jr. TPB (2004, $19.99) r/#491-494,498-500 20.00
... Visionaries: Walter Simonson (Vol. 1) TPB (5/01, $24.95) r/#337-348 25.00
... Visionaries: Walter Simonson Vol. 4 TPB (2007, $24.99) r/#371-373 & Balder the Brave #1-4 25.00
... Visionaries: Walter Simonson Vol. 5 TPB (2008, $24.95) r/#375-382 25.00
....: Worldengine (8/96, $9.95)-r/#491-494; Deodato-c/a; story & new intermission by Warren Ellis 10.00
NOTE: ***Neal Adams** a-180,181; c-179-181. **Austin** a-342i, 346i; c-312i. **Buscema** a(p)-178, 182-213, 215-226, 231-238, 241-253, 254r, 256-259, 272-278, 283-285, 370, Annual 6, 8, 11i; c(p)-175, 182-196, 198-200, 202-204, 206, 211, 212, 215, 219, 221, 226, 256, 259, 261, 262, 272-278, 283, 289, 370, Annual 6. **Everett** a(i)-143, 170-175; c(i)-171, 172, 174, 176, 241. **Gil Kane** a-318p; c(p)-201, 205, 207-210, 216, 220, 222, 223, 231, 233-240, 242, 243, 318. **Kirby** a(p)-126-177, 179, 194r, 254r; c(p)-126-169, 171-174, 176-178, 249-253, 255, 257, 258, Annual 5, Special 2-4. **Mooney** a(i)-201, 204, 214-216, 218, 322i, 324i, 325i, 327i. **Sienkiewicz** c-332, 333, 335. **Simonson** a-260-271p, 337-354, 357-367, 380, Annual 7p; c-260, 263-271, 337-355, 357-369, 371, 373-382, Annual 7. **Starlin** c-213.*

THOR (Volume 2)
Marvel Comics: July, 1998 - No. 85, Dec, 2004 ($2.99/$1.99/$2.25)

1-($2.99)-Follows Heroes Return; Jurgens-s/Romita Jr. & Janson-a; wraparound-c; battles the Destroyer 5.00
1-Variant-c 1 2 3 5 6 8
1-Rough Cut-($2.99) Features original script and pencil pages 3.00
1-Sketch cover 20.00
2-($1.99) Two covers; Avengers app 3.00
3-11,13-23: 3-Assumes Jake Olson ID. 4-Namor-c/app. 8-Spider-Man-c/app. 14-Iron Man c/app. 17-Juggernaut-c 2.50
12-($2.99) Wraparound-c; Hercules appears 3.00
12-($10.00) Variant-c by Jusko 10.00
24,26-31,33,34: 24-Begin $2.25-c. 26-Mignola-c/Larsen-a. 29-Andy Kubert-a. 30-Maximum Security x-over; Beta Ray Bill-c/app. 33-Intro. Thor Girl 2.50
25-($2.99) Regular edition 3.00
25-($3.99) Gold foil enhanced cover 4.00
32-($3.50, 100 pgs.) new story plus reprints w/Kirby-a; Simonson-a 3.50
35-($2.99) Thor battles The Gladiator; Andy Kubert-a 3.00
36-49,51-61: 37-Starlin-a. 38,39-BWS-c. 38-42-Immonen-a. 40-Odin killed. 41-Orbik-c. 44-'Nuff Said silent issue. 51-Spider-Man app. 57-Art by various. 58-Davis-a; x-over with Iron Man #64. 60-Brereton-c 2.50
50-($4.95) Raney-c/a; back-ups w/Nuckols-a & Armenta-s/Bennett-a 5.00
62-84: 62-Begin $2.99-c. 64-Loki-c/app. 80-Oeming-s begins; Avengers app. 3.00
85-Last issue; Thor dies; Oeming-s/DiVito-a/Epting-c 3.00
...1999 Annual ($3.50) Jurgens-s/a(p) 3.50
...2000 Annual ($3.50) Jurgens-s/Ordway-a(p); back-up stories 3.50
...2001 Annual ($3.50) Jurgens-s/Grummett-a(p); Lightle-c 3.50
...Across All Worlds (9/01, $19.95, TPB) r/#28-35 20.00
Avengers Disassembled: Thor TPB (2004, $16.99) r/#80-85; afterword by Oeming 17.00
...Resurrection ($5.99, TPB) r/#1,2 6.00

Thor (2007 series) #6 © MAR

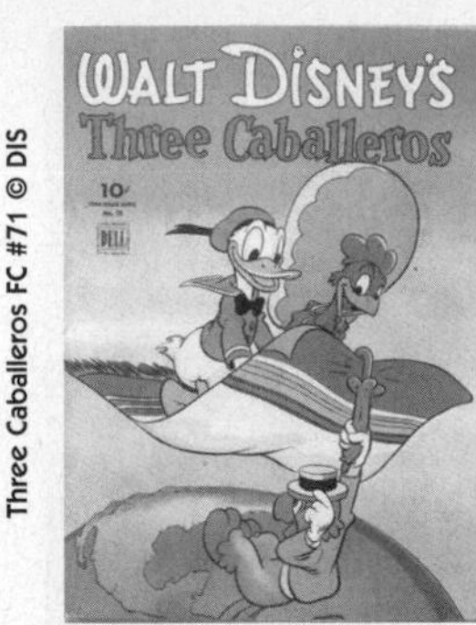

Three Caballeros FC #71 © DIS

3-D Tales From the Crypt of Terror #2 © WMG

GD VG FN VF VF/NM NM-
2.0 4.0 6.0 8.0 9.0 9.2

...: The Dark Gods (7/00, $15.95, TPB) r/#9-13 16.00
...Vol. 1: The Death of Odin (7/02, $12.99, TPB) r/#39-44 13.00
...Vol. 2: Lord of Asgard (9/02, $15.99, TPB) r/#45-50 16.00
...Vol. 3: Gods on Earth (2003, $21.99, TPB) r/#51-58, Avengers #63, Iron Man #64, Marvel Double-Shot #1; Beck-c 22.00
...Vol. 4: Spiral (2003, $19.99, TPB) r/#59-67; Brereton-c 20.00
...Vol. 5: The Reigning (2004, $17.99, TPB) r/#68-74 18.00
...Vol. 6: Gods and Men (2004, $13.99, TPB) r/#75-79 14.00

THOR (Also see Fantastic Four #538)
Marvel Comics: Sept, 2007 - Present ($2.99)

1-Straczynski-s/Coipel-a/c 4.00
1-Variant-c by Michael Turner 5.00
1-Zombie variant-c by Suydam 5.00
1-Non-zombie variant-c by Suydam 5.00
2-10: 2-Two covers by Dell'Otto and Coipel. 3-Iron Man app.; McGuinness var-c. 4-Bermejo var-c. 5-Campbell var-c. 6-Art Adams var-c. 7,8-Djurdjevic-a/c; Coipel var-c 3.00
2-2nd printing with wraparound-c 3.00
...: Ages of Thunder (6/08, $3.99) Fraction-s/Zircher-a/Djurdjevic-c 4.00
...: Reign of Blood (8/08, $3.99) Fraction-s/Evans & Zircher-a/Djurdjevic-c 4.00
... By J. Michael Straczynski Vol. 1 HC (2008, $19.99) r/#1-6; variant cover gallery 20.00

THOR: BLOOD OATH
Marvel Comics: Nov, 2005 - No. 6, Feb, 2006 ($2.99, limited series)

1-6-Oeming-s/Kolins-a/c 3.00
HC (2006, $19.99, dust jacket) r/series; afterword by Oeming 20.00
SC (2006, $14.99) r/series; afterword by Oeming 15.00

THOR CORPS
Marvel Comics: Sept, 1993 - No. 4, Jan, 1994 ($1.75, limited series)

1-4: 1-Invaders cameo. 2-Invaders app. 3-Spider-Man 2099, Rawhide Kid, Two-Gun Kid & Kid Colt app. 4-Painted-c 2.50

THOR: GODSTORM
Marvel Comics: Nov, 2001 - No. 3, Jan, 2002 ($3.50, limited series)

1-3-Steve Rude-c/a; Busiek-s; Avengers app. 3.50

THORION OF THE NEW ASGODS
Marvel Comics (Amalgam): June, 1997 ($1.95, one-shot)

1-Keith Giffen-s/John Romita Jr.-c/a 2.50

THOR: SON OF ASGARD
Marvel Comics: May, 2004 - No. 12, Mar, 2005 ($2.99, limited series)

1-12: Teenaged Thor, Sif, and Balder; Tocchini-a. 1-6-Granov-c. 7-12-Jo Chen-c 3.00
... Vol. 1: The Warriors Teen (2004, $7.99, digest) r/#1-6 8.00
... Vol. 2: Worthy (2005, $7.99, digest) r/#7-12 8.00

THOR: THE LEGEND
Marvel Comics: Sept, 1996 ($3.95, one-shot)

nn-Tribute issue 4.00

THOR: VIKINGS
Marvel Comics (MAX): Sept, 2003 - No. 5, Jan, 2004 ($3.50, limited series)

1-5-Garth Ennis-s/Glenn Fabry-a/c 3.50
TPB (2004, $13.99) r/series 14.00

THOSE MAGNIFICENT MEN IN THEIR FLYING MACHINES (See Movie Comics)

THRAX
Event Comics: Nov, 1996 ($2.95, one-shot)

1 3.00

THREE CABALLEROS (Walt Disney's...)
Dell Publishing Co.: No. 71, 1945

Four Color 71-by Walt Kelly, c/a 62 124 186 527 1006 1485

THREE CHIPMUNKS, THE (TV) (Also see Alvin)
Dell Publishing Co.: No. 1042, Oct-Dec, 1959

Four Color 1042 (#1)-(Alvin, Simon & Theodore) 8 16 24 52 86 120

THREE COMICS (Also see Spiritman)
The Penny King Co.: 1944 (10¢, 52 pgs.) (2 different covers exist)

1,3,4-Lady Luck, Mr. Mystic, The Spirit app. (3 Spirit sections bound together); Lou Fine-a 26 52 78 154 247 340

NOTE: *No. 1 contains Spirit Sections 4/9/44 - 4/23/44, and No. 4 is also from 4/44.*

3-D (NOTE: The prices of all the 3-D comics listed include glasses. Deduct 40-50 percent if glasses are missing, and reduce slightly if glasses are loose.)

3-D ACTION
Atlas Comics (ACI): Jan, 1954 (Oversized, 15¢)(2 pairs of glasses included)

GD VG FN VF VF/NM NM-
2.0 4.0 6.0 8.0 9.0 9.2

1-Battle Brady; Sol Brodsky-c 38 76 114 226 363 500

3-D ADVENTURE COMICS
Stats, Etc.: Aug, 1986 (one shot)

1-Promo material 4.00

3-D ALIEN TERROR
Eclipse Comics: June, 1986 ($2.50)

1-Old Witch, Crypt-Keeper, Vault Keeper cameo; Morrow, John Pound-a, Yeates-c 6.00
...in 2-D: 100 copies signed, numbered(B&W) 1 3 4 8 10 12

3-D ANIMAL FUN (See Animal Fun)

THREE DAYS IN EUROPE
Oni Press: Nov, 2002 - No. 5, Apr, 2003 ($2.95, B&W, limited series)

1-5-Johnston-s/Hawthorne-a 3.00
TPB (11/03, $14.95, digest-sized) r/#1-5 15.00

3-D BATMAN (Also see Batman 3-D)
National Periodical Publications: 1953 (Reprinted in 1966)

1953-(25¢)-Reprints Batman #42 & 48 (Penguin-c/story); Tommy Tomorrow story; came with pair of 3-D Bat glasses 103 206 309 649 1100 1550
1966-Reprints 1953 issue; new cover by Infantino/Anderson; has inside-c photos of Batman & Robin from TV show (50¢) 22 44 66 157 291 425

3-D CIRCUS
Fiction House Magazines (Real Adventures Publ.): 1953 (25¢, w/glasses)

1 32 64 96 186 298 410

3-D COMICS (See Mighty Mouse, Tor and Western Fighters)

3-D DOLLY
Harvey Publications: December, 1953 (25¢, came with 2 pairs of glasses)

1-Richie Rich story redrawn from his 1st app. in Little Dot #1; shows cover in 3-D on inside 70 140 210 441 746 1050

3-D-ELL
Dell Publishing Co.: No. 1, 1953; No. 3, 1953 (3-D comics) (25¢, came w/glasses)

1-Rootie Kazootie (#2 does not exist) 34 68 102 198 319 440
3-Flukey Luke 32 64 96 186 298 410

3-D EXOTIC BEAUTIES
The 3-D Zone: Nov, 1990 ($2.95, 28 pgs.)

1-L.B. Cole-c 1 2 3 5 7 9

3-D FEATURES PRESENTS JET PUP
Dimensions Publications: Oct-Dec (Winter on-c), 1953 (25¢, came w/glasses)

1-Irving Spector-a(2) 34 68 102 198 319 440

3-D FUNNY MOVIES
Comic Media: 1953 (25¢, came w/glasses)

1-Bugsey Bear & Paddy Pelican 34 68 102 198 319 440

THREE-DIMENSION ADVENTURES (Superman)
National Periodical Publications: 1953 (25¢, large size, came w/glasses)

nn-Origin Superman (new art) 103 206 309 649 1100 1550

THREE DIMENSIONAL ALIEN WORLDS (See Alien Worlds)
Pacific Comics: July, 1984 (1st Ray Zone 3-D book)(one-shot)

1-Bolton-a(p); Stevens-a(i); Art Adams 1st published-a(p) 6.00

THREE DIMENSIONAL DNAGENTS (See New DNAgents)

THREE DIMENSIONAL E. C. CLASSICS (Three Dimensional Tales From the Crypt No. 2)
E. C. Comics: Spring, 1954 (Prices include glasses; came with 2 pair)

1-Stories by Wood (Mad #3), Krigstein (W.S. #7), Evans (F.C. #13), & Ingels (CSS #5); Kurtzman-c (rare in high grade due to unstable paper) 93 186 279 586 993 1400

NOTE: *Stories redrawn to 3-D format. Original stories not necessarily by artists listed. CSS: Crime SuspenStories; F.C.: Frontline Combat; W.S.: Weird Science.*

THREE DIMENSIONAL TALES FROM THE CRYPT (Formerly Three Dimensional E. C. Classics)(Cover title: ...From the Crypt of Terror)
E. C. Comics: No. 2, Spring, 1954 (Prices include glasses; came with 2 pair)

2-Davis (TFTC #25), Elder (VOH #14), Craig (TFTC #24), & Orlando (TFTC #22) stories; Feldstein-c (rare in high grade) 92 184 276 580 978 1375

NOTE: *Stories redrawn to 3-D format. Original stories not necessarily by artists listed. TFTC: Tales From the Crypt; VOH: Vault of Horror.*

3-D LOVE
Steriographic Publ. (Mikeross Publ.): Dec, 1953 (25¢, came w/glasses)

1 34 68 102 198 319 440

3-D Sheena, Jungle Queen #1 © FH

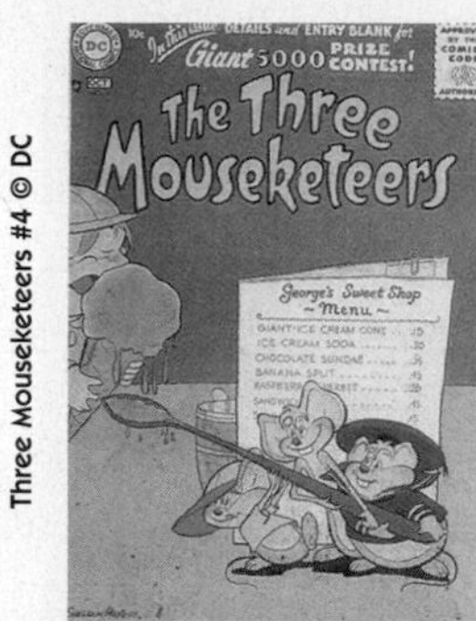

Three Mouseketeers #4 © DC

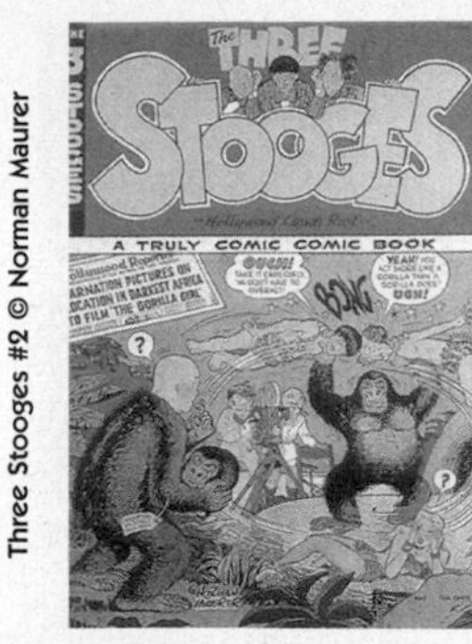

Three Stooges #2 © Norman Maurer

GD VG FN VF VF/NM NM-
2.0 4.0 6.0 8.0 9.0 9.2

3-D NOODNICK (See Noodnick)

3-D ROMANCE
Steriographic Publ. (Mikeross Publ.): Jan, 1954 (25¢, came w/glasses)
1 34 68 102 198 319 440

3-D SHEENA, JUNGLE QUEEN (Also see Sheena 3-D)
Fiction House Magazines: 1953 (25¢, came w/glasses)
1-Maurice Whitman-c 68 136 204 428 727 1025

3-D SUBSTANCE
The 3-D Zone: July, 1990 ($2.95, 28 pgs.)
1-Ditko-c/a(r) 5.00

3-D TALES OF THE WEST
Atlas Comics (CPS): Jan, 1954 (Oversized) (15¢, came with 2 pair of glasses)
1 (3-D)-Sol Brodsky-c 38 76 114 226 363 500

3-D THREE STOOGES (Also see Three Stooges)
Eclipse Comics: Sept, 1986 - No. 2, Nov, 1986; No. 3, Oct, 1987; No. 4, 1989 ($2.50)
1-4: 3-Maurer-r. 4-r-/"Three Missing Links" 5.00
1-3 (2-D) 5.00

3-D WHACK (See Whack)

3-D ZONE, THE
The 3-D Zone (Renegade Press)/Ray Zone: Feb, 1987 - No. 20, 1989 ($2.50)
1,3,4,7-9,11,12,14,15,17,19,20: 1-r/A Star Presentation. 3-Picture Scope Jungle Advs. 4-Electric Fear. 7-Hollywood 3-D Jayne Mansfield photo-c. 8-High Seas 3-D, 9-Redmask-r. 11-Danse Macabre; Matt Fox c/a(r). 12-3-D Presidents. 14-Tyranostar. 15-3-Dementia Comics; Kurtzman-c, Kubert, Maurer-a. 17-Thrilling Love. 19-Cracked Classics. 20-Commander Battle and His Atomic Submarine 1 2 3 4 5 7
2,5,6,10,13,16,18: 2-Wolverton-r. 5-Krazy Kat-r. 6-Ratfink. 10-Jet 3-D; Powell & Williamson-r. 13-Flash Gordon. 16-Space Vixens; Dave Stevens c/a. 18-Spacehawk; Wolverton-r 1 2 3 5 6 8

NOTE: *Davis r-19. Ditko r-19. Elder r-19. Everett r-19. Feldstein r-17. Frazetta r-17. Heath r-19. Kamen r-17. Severin r-10. Ward r-17,19. Wolverton r-2,18,19. Wood r-1,17. Photo c-12*

3 GEEKS, THE (Also see Geeksville)
3 Finger Prints: 1996 - No. 11, Jun, 1999 (B&W)
1,2 -Rich Koslowski-s/a in all 1 2 3 5 6 8
1-(2nd printing) 2.50
3-7, 9-11 2.50
8-(48 pgs.) 4.00
10-Variant-c 3.50
...48 Page Super-Sized Summer Spectacular (7/04, $4.95) 5.00
...Full Circle (7/03, $4.95) Origin story of the 3 Geeks; "Buck Rodinski" app. 5.00
How to Pick Up Girls If You're a Comic Book Geek (color)(7/97) 4.00
When the Hammer Fallls TPB (2001, $14.95) r/#8-11 15.00

300 (Adapted for 2007 movie)
Dark Horse Comics: May, 1998 - No. 5, Sept, 1998 ($2.95/$3.95, limited series)
1-Frank Miller-s/c/a; Spartans vs. Persians war 15.00
1-Second printing 5.00
2-4 8.00
5-($3.95-c) 12.00
HC ($30.00) -oversized reprint of series 30.00

3 LITTLE KITTENS
BroadSword Comics: Aug, 2002 - No. 3, Dec, 2002 ($2.95, limited series)
1-3-Jim Balent-s/a; two covers 3.00

3 LITTLE PIGS (Disney)(...and the Wonderful Magic Lamp)
Dell Publishing Co.: No. 218, Mar, 1949
Four Color 218 (#1) 10 20 30 71 126 180

3 LITTLE PIGS, THE (See Walt Disney Showcase #15 & 21)
Gold Key: May, 1964; No. 2, Sept, 1968 (Walt Disney)
1-Reprints Four Color #218 3 6 9 20 30 40
2 3 6 9 15 21 26

THREE MOUSEKETEERS, THE (1st Series)(See Funny Stuff #1)
National Per. Publ.: 3-4/56 - No. 24, 9-10/59; No. 25, 8-9/60 - No. 26, 10-12/60
1 16 32 48 114 212 310
2 9 18 27 64 110 155
3-5,7,9,10 7 14 21 49 80 110
6,8-Grey tone-c 8 16 24 56 93 130
11-26: 24-Cover says 11/59, inside says 9-10/59 6 12 18 43 69 95

NOTE: *Rube Grossman a-1-26. Sheldon Mayer a-1-8; c-1-7.*

THREE MOUSEKETEERS, THE (2nd Series) (See Super DC Giant)
National Periodical Publications: May-June, 1970 - No. 7, May-June, 1971 (#5-7: 68 pgs.)
1-Mayer-r in all 5 10 15 34 55 75
2-4: 4-Doodles Duck begins (1st app.) 4 8 12 22 34 45
5-7:(68 pgs.). 5-Dodo & the Frog, Bo Bunny begin 5 10 15 32 51 70

THREE MUSKETEERS, THE (Also see Disney's The Three Musketeers)
Gemstone Publishing: 2004 ($3.95, squarebound, one-shot)
nn-Adaptation of the 2004 DVD movie; Petrossi-c/a 4.00

THREE NURSES (Confidential Diary #12-17; Career Girl Romances #24 on)
Charlton Comics: V3#18, May, 1963 - V3#23, Mar, 1964
V3#18-23 3 6 9 17 25 32

THREE RASCALS
I. W. Enterprises: 1958; 1963
I.W. Reprint #1,2,10: 1-(Says Super Comics on inside)-(M.E.'s Clubhouse Rascals) DeCarlo-a. #2-(1958). 10-(1963)-r/#1 2 4 6 8 10 12

THREE RING COMICS
Spotlight Publishers: March, 1945
1-Funny animal 16 32 48 92 144 195

THREE RING COMICS (Also see Captain Wizard & Meteor Comics)
Century Publications: April, 1946
1-Prankster-c; Captain Wizard, Impossible Man, Race Wilkins, King O'Leary, & Dr. Mercy app. 35 70 105 203 327 450

THREE ROCKETEERS (See Blast-Off)

THREE STOOGES (See Comic Album #18, Top Comics, The Little Stooges, March of Comics #232, 248, 268, 280, 292, 304, 316, 336, 373, Movie Classics & Comics & 3-D Three Stooges)

THREE STOOGES
Jubilee No. 1/St. John No. 1 (9/53) on: Feb, 1949 - No. 2, May, 1949; Sept, 1953 - No. 7, Oct, 1954
1-(Scarce, 1949)-Kubert-a; infinity-c 115 230 345 725 1225 1725
2-(Scarce)-Kubert, Maurer-a 80 160 240 504 852 1200
1(9/53)-Hollywood Stunt Girl by Kubert (7 pgs.) 68 136 204 428 727 1025
2(3-D, 10/53, 25¢)-Came w/glasses; Stunt Girl story by Kubert 48 96 144 298 499 700
3(3-D, 10/53, 25¢)-Came w/glasses; has 3-D-c 45 90 135 279 465 650
4(3/54)-7(10/54): 4-1st app. Li'l Stooge? 40 80 120 238 387 535

NOTE: *All issues have **Kubert-Maurer** art & **Maurer** covers. 6, 7-Partial photo-c.*

THREE STOOGES
Dell Publishing Co./Gold Key No. 10 (10/62) on: No. 1043, Oct-Dec, 1959 - No. 55, June, 1972
Four Color 1043 (#1) 25 50 75 185 343 500
Four Color 1078,1127,1170,1187 14 28 42 99 175 250
6(9-11/61) - 10: 6-Professor Putter begins; ends #16 10 20 30 73 129 185
11-14,16,18-20 9 18 27 63 107 150
15-Go Around the World in a Daze (movie scenes) 9 18 27 65 113 160
17-The Little Monsters begin (5/64)(1st app.?) 9 18 27 65 113 160
21,23-30 8 16 24 54 90 125
22-Movie scenes from "The Outlaws Is Coming" 8 16 24 58 97 135
31-55 6 12 18 41 66 90

NOTE: *All Four Colors, 6-50, 52-55 have photo-c.*

THREE STOOGES IN 3-D, THE
Eternity Comics: 1991 ($3.95, high quality paper, w/glasses)
1-Reprints Three Stooges by Gold Key; photo-c 5.00

THREE STRIKES
Oni Press: Apr, 2003 - No. 5, Oct, 2003 ($2.99, B&W, limited series)
1-5-Brian Hurtt-a/DeFilippis & Weir-s 3.00
TPB (3/04, $14.95, digest-size) r/#1-5; Ed Brubaker intro. 15.00

3 WORLDS OF GULLIVER
Dell Publishing Co.: No. 1158, July, 1961 (2 issues exist with diff. covers)
Four Color 1158-Movie, photo-c 7 14 21 45 73 100

THRILL COMICS (See Flash Comics, Fawcett)

THRILLER
DC Comics: Nov, 1983 - No. 12, Nov, 1984 ($1.25, Baxter paper)
1-12: 1-Intro Seven Seconds; Von Eeden-c/a begins. 2-Origin. 5,6-Elvis satire 2.50

THRILLING ADVENTURES IN STAMPS COMICS (Formerly Stamp Comics)
Stamp Comics, Inc. (Very Rare): V1#8, Jan, 1953 (25¢, 100 pgs.)

Thrilling Comics #70 © BP

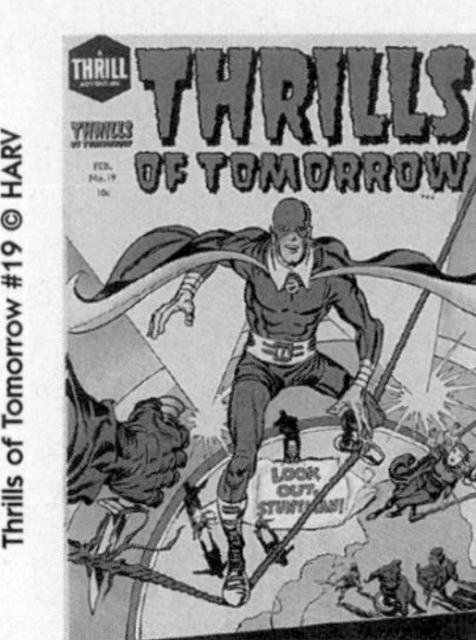

Thrills of Tomorrow #19 © HARV

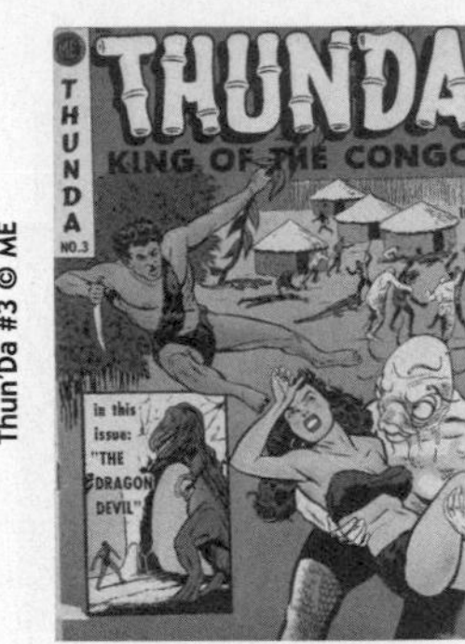

Thun'Da #3 © ME

	GD	VG	FN	VF	VF/NM	NM-
	2.0	4.0	6.0	8.0	9.0	9.2
V1#8-Harrison, Wildey, Kiefer, Napoli-a	75	150	225	473	799	1125

THRILLING ADVENTURE STORIES (See Tigerman)
Atlas/Seaboard Publ.: Feb, 1975 - No. 2, Aug, 1975 (B&W, 68 pgs.)

1-Tigerman, Kromag the Killer begin; Heath, Thorne-a; Doc Savage movie photos of Ron Ely	3	6	9	14	20	25
2-Heath, Toth, Severin, Simonson-a; Adams-c	3	6	9	18	27	35

THRILLING COMICS
Better Publ./Nedor/Standard Comics: Feb, 1940 - No. 80, April, 1951

1-Origin & 1st app. Dr. Strange (37 pgs.), ends #?; Nickie Norton of the Secret Service begins	317	634	951	1981	3391	4800
2-The Rio Kid, The Woman in Red, Pinocchio begins	132	264	396	832	1404	1975
3-The Ghost & Lone Eagle begin	85	170	255	536	906	1275
4-6,8-10 (11/40): 5-Dr. Strange changed to Doc Strange. 10-1st WWII-c (Nazi)	66	132	198	416	701	985
7-Classic-c	87	174	261	548	924	1300
11-18,20	57	114	171	359	610	860
19-Origin & 1st app. The American Crusader (8/41), ends #39,41	64	128	192	403	682	960
21-30: 24-Intro. Mike, Doc Strange's sidekick (1/42). 27-Robot-c. 29-Last Rio Kid	52	104	156	322	536	750
31-40: 36-Commando Cubs begin (7/43, 1st app.)	47	94	141	291	483	675
41-Classic Hitler & Mussolin WWII-c	113	226	339	712	1206	1700
42,43,45-51: 45-Hitler pict. on-c. 51(12/45)-Last WWII-c (Japanese)	40	80	120	244	397	550
44-Hitler WWII-c	103	206	309	649	1100	1550
52-Classic Schomburg hooded bondage-c; the Ghost ends	60	120	180	378	639	900
53,54: 53-The Phantom Detective begins. The Cavalier app. in both; no Commando Cubs in either	40	80	120	235	380	525
55-The Lone Eagle ends	37	74	111	220	353	485
56 (10/46)-Princess Pantha begins (not on-c), 1st app.	48	96	144	298	499	700
57-Doc Strange-c; 2nd Princess Pantha	41	82	123	256	428	600
58-66: All Princess Pantha jungle-c, w/Doc Strange #59, his last-c. 61-Ingels-a; The Lone Eagle app. 65-Last Phantom Detective & Commando Cubs. 66-Frazetta text illo	40	80	120	244	397	550
67,70,71-Last jungle-c; Frazetta-a(5-7 pgs.) in each	47	94	141	291	483	675
68,69-Frazetta-a(2), 8 & 6 pgs.; 9 & 7 pgs.	50	100	150	310	518	725
72,73: 72-Buck Ranger, Cowboy Detective c/stys begin (western theme), end #80; Frazetta-a(5-7 ps.) in each	43	86	129	267	446	625
74-Last Princess Pantha; Tara app.	34	68	102	198	319	440
75-78: 75-All western format begins	14	28	42	81	118	155
79-Krigstein-a	15	30	45	83	124	165
80-Severin & Elder, Celardo, Moreira-a	15	30	45	83	124	165

NOTE: *Bondage c-5, 9, 13, 20, 22, 27-30, 38, 41, 52, 54, 70.* ***Kinstler*** *a-45.* ***Leo Morey*** *a-7.* ***Schomburg*** *(sometimes signed as* ***Xela****) c-7, 9-19, 36-80 (airbrush 62-71).* ***Tuska*** *a-62, 63. Woman in Red not in #19, 23, 31-33, 39-45. No. 45 exists as a Canadian reprint but numbered #48. No. 72 exists as a Canadian reprint with no* ***Frazetta*** *story. American Crusader c-20-24. Buck Ranger c-72-80. Commando Cubs c-37, 39, 41, 43, 45, 47, 49, 51. Doc Strange c-1-19, 25-36, 38, 40, 42, 44, 46, 48, 50, 52-57, 59. Princess Pantha c-58, 60-71.*

THRILLING COMICS (Also see All Star Comics 1999 crossover titles)
DC Comics: May, 1999 ($1.99, one-shot)

1-Golden Age Hawkman and Wildcat; Russ Heath-a 2.50

THRILLING CRIME CASES (Formerly 4Most; becomes Shocking Mystery Cases #50 on)
Star Publications: No. 41, June-July, 1950 - No. 49, July, 1952

41	28	56	84	162	261	360
42-45: 42-L. B. Cole-c/a (1); Chameleon story (Fox-r)	25	50	75	145	233	320
46-48: 47-Used in **POP**, pg. 84	24	48	72	140	225	310
49-(7/52)-Classic L. B. Cole-c	45	90	135	279	465	650

NOTE: ***L. B. Cole*** *c-all; a-43p, 45p, 46p, 49(2 pgs.).* ***Disbrow*** *a-48.* ***Hollingsworth*** *a-48.*

THRILLING ROMANCES
Standard Comics: No. 5, Dec, 1949 - No. 26, June, 1954

5	14	28	42	82	121	160
6,8	10	20	30	54	72	90
7-Severin/Elder-a (7 pgs.)	11	22	33	64	90	115
9,10-Severin/Elder-a; photo-c	11	22	33	60	83	105
11,14-21,26: 12-Tyrone Power/ Susan Hayward photo-c.14-Gene Tierney & Danny Kaye photo-c from movie "On the Riviera". 15-Tony Martin/Janet Leigh photo-c	9	18	27	50	65	80
12-Wood-a (2 pgs.)	12	24	36	67	94	120
13-Severin-a	10	20	30	54	72	90

	GD	VG	FN	VF	VF/NM	NM-
	2.0	4.0	6.0	8.0	9.0	9.2
22-25-Toth-a	11	22	33	60	83	105

NOTE: *All photo-c.* ***Celardo*** *a-9, 16.* ***Colletta*** *a-23, 24(2).* ***Toth*** *text illos-19.* ***Tuska*** *a-9.*

THRILLING SCIENCE TALES
AC Comics: 1989 - No. 2 ($3.50, 2/3 color, 52 pgs.)

1,2: 1-r/Bob Colt #6(saucer); Frazetta, Guardineer (Space Ace), Wood, Krenkel, Orlando, WIlliamson-r; Kaluta-c. 2-Capt. Video-r by Evans, Capt. Science-r by Wood, Star Pirate-r by Whitman & Mysta of the Moon-r by Moreira 4.00

THRILLING TRUE STORY OF THE BASEBALL...
Fawcett Publications: 1952 (Photo-c, each)

...Giants-photo-c; has Willie Mays rookie photo-biography; Willie Mays, Eddie Stanky & others photos on-c	68	136	204	428	727	1025
...Yankees-photo-c; Yogi Berra, Joe DiMaggio, Mickey Mantle & others photos on-c	66	132	198	416	701	985

THRILLING WONDER TALES
AC Comics : 1991 ($2.95, B&W)

1-Includes a Bob Powell Thun'da story 3.00

THRILLKILLER
DC Comics : Jan, 1997 - No. 3, Mar, 1997($2.50, limited series)

1-3-Elseworlds Robin & Batgirl; Chaykin-s/Brereton-c/a 3.00
...'62 ('98, $4.95, one-shot) Sequel; Chaykin-s/Brereton-c/a 5.00
TPB-(See Batman: Thrillkiller)

THRILLOGY
Pacific Comics: Jan, 1984 (One-shot, color)

1-Conrad-c/a 3.00

THRILL-O-RAMA
Harvey Publications (Fun Films): Oct, 1965 - No. 3, Dec, 1966

1-Fate (Man in Black) by Powell app.; Doug Wildey-a(2); Simon-c	5	10	15	34	55	75
2-Pirana begins (see Phantom #46); Williamson 2 pgs.; Fate (Man in Black) app.; Tuska/Simon-c	4	8	12	22	34	45
3-Fate (Man in Black) app.; Sparling-c	3	6	9	19	29	38

THRILLS OF TOMORROW (Formerly Tomb of Terror)
Harvey Publications: No. 17, Oct, 1954 - No. 20, April, 1955

17-Powell-a (horror); r/Witches Tales #7	15	30	45	85	130	175
18-Powell-a (horror); r/Tomb of Terror #1	14	28	42	80	115	150
19,20-Stuntman-c/stories by S&K (r/from Stuntman #1 & 2); 19 has origin & is last pre-code (2/55)	31	62	93	181	291	400

NOTE: ***Kirby*** *c-19, 20.* ***Palais*** *a-17.* ***Simon*** *c-18?*

THROBBING LOVE (See Fox Giants)

THROUGH GATES OF SPLENDOR
Spire Christian Comics (Flemming H. Revell Co.): 1973, 1974 (36 pages) (39-49 cents)

nn-1973 Edition	2	4	6	8	11	14
nn-1974 Edition	1	3	4	6	8	10

THUMPER (Disney)
Dell Publishing Co.: No, 19, 1942 - No. 243, Sept, 1949

Four Color 19-Walt Disney's...Meets the Seven Dwarfs; reprinted in Silly Symphonies	47	94	141	376	701	1025
Four Color 243-...Follows His Nose	11	22	33	79	140	200

THUN'DA (...King of the Congo)
Magazine Enterprises: 1952 - No. 6, 1953

1(A-1 #47)-Origin; Frazetta c/a; only comic done entirely by Frazetta; all Thun'da stories, no Cave Girl	150	300	450	945	1598	2250
2(A-1 #56)-Powell-c/a begins, ends #6; Intro/1st app. Cave Girl in filler strip (also app. in 3-6)	23	46	69	135	218	300
3(A-1 #73), 4(A-1 #78)	17	34	51	98	154	210
5(A-1 #83), 6(A-1 #86)	15	30	45	94	147	200

THUN'DA TALES (See Frank Frazetta's...)

THUNDER AGENTS (See Dynamo, Noman & Tales Of Thunder)
Tower Comics: 11/65 - No. 17, 12/67; No. 18, 9/68, No. 19, 11/68, No. 20, 11/69 (No. 1-16: 68 pgs.; No. 17 on: 52 pgs.)(All are 25¢)

1-Origin & 1st app. Dynamo, Noman, Menthor, & The Thunder Squad; 1st app. The Iron Maiden	18	36	54	130	240	350
2-Death of Egghead; A-bomb blast panel	10	20	30	70	123	175
3-5: 4-Guy Gilbert becomes Lightning who joins Thunder Squad; Iron Maiden app.	8	16	24	54	90	125

6-10: 7-Death of Menthor. 8-Origin & 1st app. The Raven

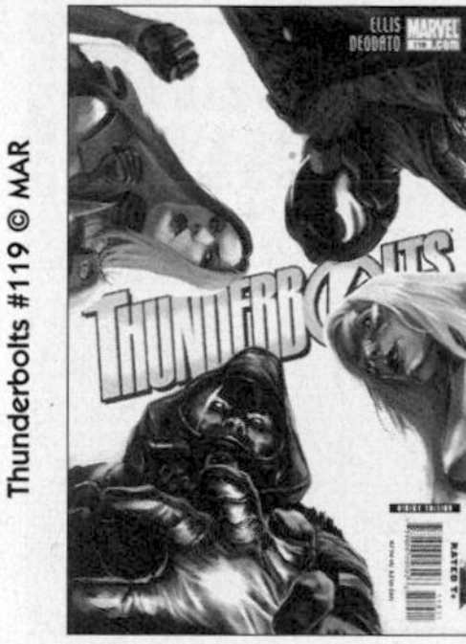

Thunderbolts #119 © MAR

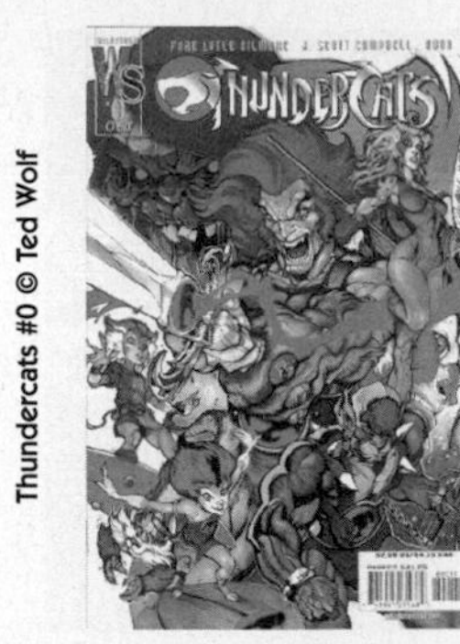

Thundercats #0 © Ted Wolf

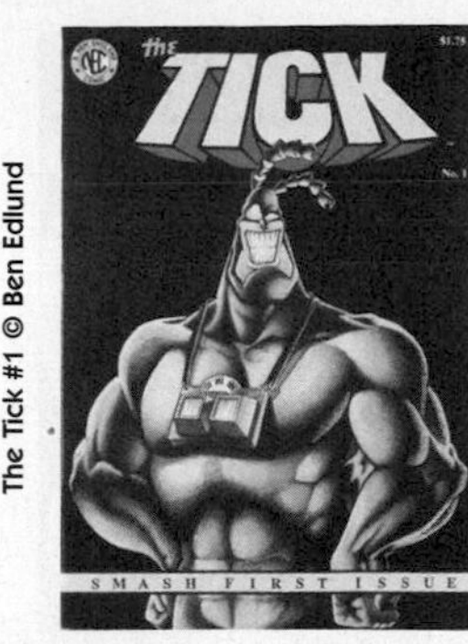

The Tick #1 © Ben Edlund

GD VG FN VF VF/NM NM-
2.0 4.0 6.0 8.0 9.0 9.2

GD VG FN VF VF/NM NM-
2.0 4.0 6.0 8.0 9.0 9.2

6 12 18 43 69 95
11-15: 13-Undersea Agent app.; no Raven story 6 12 18 39 62 85
16-19 6 12 18 37 59 80
20-Special Collectors Edition; all reprints 4 8 12 26 41 55
...Archives Vol. 1 (DC Comics, 2003, $49.95, HC) r/#1-4, restored and recolored 50.00
...Archives Vol. 2 (DC Comics, 2003, $49.95, HC) r/#5-7, Dynamo #1 50.00
...Archives Vol. 3 (DC Comics, 2003, $49.95, HC) r/#8-10, Dynamo #2 50.00
...Archives Vol. 4 (DC Comics, 2004, $49.95, HC) r/#11, Noman #1,2 & Dynamo #3 50.00
NOTE: *Crandall a-1, 4p, 5p, 18, 20r; c-18. **Ditko** a-6, 7p, 12p, 13?, 14p, 16, 18. **Giunta** a-6. **Kane** a-1, 5p, 6p?, 14, 16p; c-14, 15. **Reinman** a-13. **Sekowsky** a-6. **Tuska** a-1p, 7, 8, 10, 13-17, 19. **Whitney** a-9p, 10, 13, 15, 17, 18; c-17. **Wood** a-1-11, 15(w/**Ditko**-12, 18), (inks-#9, 13, 14, 16, 17), 19i, 20r; c-1-8, 9i, 10-13(#10 w/**Williamson**(p)), 16.*

T.H.U.N.D.E.R. AGENTS (See Blue Ribbon Comics, Hall of Fame Featuring the..., JCP Features & Wally Wood's...)
JC Comics (Archie Publications): May, 1983 - No. 2, Jan, 1984
1,2: 1-New Manna/Blyberg-c/a. 2-Blyberg-c 6.00

THUNDER BIRDS (See Cinema Comics Herald)

THUNDERBOLT (See The Atomic...)

THUNDERBOLT (Peter Cannon...; see Crisis on Infinite Earths & Peter...)
Charlton Comics: Jan, 1966; No. 51, Mar-Apr, 1966 - No. 60, Nov, 1967
1-Origin & 1st app. Thunderbolt 4 8 12 28 44 60
51-(Formerly Son of Vulcan #50) 3 6 9 20 30 40
52-59: 54-Sentinels begin. 59-Last Thunderbolt & Sentinels (back-up story)
3 6 9 14 19 24
60-Prankster app. 3 6 9 15 21 26
57,58 ('77)-Modern Comics-r 4.00
NOTE: *Aparo a-60. **Morisi** a-1, 51-56, 58; c-1, 51-56, 58, 59.*

THUNDERBOLT JAXON (Revival of 1940s British comics character)
DC Comics (WildStorm): Apr, 2006 - No. 5, Sept, 2006 ($2.99, limited series)
1-5-Dave Gibbons-s/John Higgins-a 3.00
TPB (2007, $19.99) r/#1-5; intro. by Gibbons; cover gallery 20.00

THUNDERBOLTS (Also see New Thunderbolts and Incredible Hulk #449)
Marvel Comics: Apr, 1997 - No. 81, Sept, 2003; No. 100, May, 2006 - Present ($1.95-$2.99)
1-($2.99)-Busiek-s/Bagley-c/a 1 2 3 5 7 9
1-2nd printing; new cover colors 2.50
2-4: 2-Two covers. 4-Intro. Jolt 6.00
5-11: 9-Avengers app. 3.50
12-($2.99)-Avengers and Fantastic Four-c/app. 4.00
13-24: 14-Thunderbolts return to Earth. 21-Hawkeye app. 2.50
25-($2.99) Wraparound-c 3.00
26-38: 26-Manco-a 2.50
39-($2.99) 100 Page Monster; Iron Man reprints 3.00
40-49: 40-Begin $2.25-c; Sandman-c/app. 44-Avengers app. 47-Captain Marvel app. 49-Zircher-a 2.50
50-($2.99) Last Bagley-a; Captain America becomes leader 3.00
51-74,76,77,80,81: 51,52-Zircher-a; Dr. Doom app. 80,81-Spider-Man app. 2.50
75-($3.50) Hawkeye leaves the team; Garcia-a 3.50
78,79-($2.99-c) Velasco-a begins 3.00
(See New Thunderbolts for #82-99)
100 (5/06, $3.99) resumes from New Thunderbolts #18; back-up origin stories 4.00
101-109: 103-105-Civil War x-over 3.00
110-New team begins including Bullseye, Venom and Norman Osborn; Ellis-s/Deodato-a 5.00
111-124: 111-121-Ellis-s/Deodato-a. 112-Stan Lee cameo. 122-Gage-s. 123-124-Secret Invasion x-over 3.00
Annual '97 ($2.99)-Wraparound-c 3.00
Annual 2000 ($3.50) Breyfogle-a 3.50
...: Breaking Point (1/08, $2.99, one-shot) Gage-s/Denham-a/Djurdjevic-c 3.00
... By Warren Ellis Vol. 1 HC (2007, $24.99, dustjacket) r/#150-154, ...: Desperate Measures and stories from Civil War: Choosing Sides and The Initiative 25.00
... By Warren Ellis Vol. 1: Faith in Monsters SC (2008, $19.99) same contents as HC 20.00
Civil War: Thunderbolts TPB (2007, $13.99) r/#101-105 14.00
...: Desperate Measures (9/07, $2.99, one-shot) Jenkins-s/Steve Lieber-a 3.00
...: Distant Rumblings (#-1) (7/97, $1.95) Busiek-s 5.00
First Strikes (1997, $4.99,TPB) r/#1,2 5.00
...: Guardian Protocols (2007, $10.99) r/#106-109 11.00
...: International Incident (4/08, $2.99, one-shot) Gage-s/Oliver-a/Djurdjevic-c 3.00
...: Life Sentences (7/01, $3.50) Adlard-a 3.50
...: Marvel's Most Wanted TPB ('98, $16.99) r/origin stories of original Masters of Evil 17.00
...: Reason in Madness (7/08, $2.99, one-shot) Gage-s/Oliver-a/Djurdjevic-c 3.00
Wizard #0 (bagged with Wizard #89) 2.50

THUNDERBOLTS PRESENTS: ZEMO - BORN BETTER
Marvel Comics: Apr, 2007 - No. 4, July, 2007 ($2.99, limited series)
1-4-History of Baron Zemo; Nicieza-s/Grummett-a/c 3.00
TPB (2007, $10.99) r/#1-4 11.00

THUNDERBUNNY (See Blue Ribbon Comics #13, Charlton Bullseye & Pep Comics #393)
Red Circle Comics: Jan, 1984 (Direct sale only)
WaRP Graphics: Second series No. 1, 1985 - No. 6, 1985
Apple Comics: No. 7, 1986 - No. 12, 1987
1-Humor/parody; origin Thunderbunny; 2 page pin-up by Anderson 5.00
(2nd series) 1,2-Magazine size 3.00
3-12-Comic size 2.50

THUNDERCATS (TV)
Marvel Comics (Star Comics)/Marvel #22 on: Dec, 1985 - No. 24, June, 1988 (75¢)
1-Mooney-c/a begins 2 4 6 8 11 14
2-20: 2-(65¢ & 75¢ cover exists). 12-Begin $1.00-c. 18-20-Williamson-i
1 2 3 5 7 9
21-24: 23-Williamson-c(i) 1 3 4 6 8 10

THUNDERCATS (TV)
DC Comics (WildStorm): No. 0, Oct, 2002 - No. 5, Feb, 2003 ($2.50/$2.95, limited series)
0-($2.50) J. Scott Campbell-c/a 3.00
1-5-($2.95) 1-McGuinness-a/c; variant cover by Art Adams; rebirth of Mumm-Ra 3.00
.../ Battle of the Planets (7/03, $4.95) Kaare Andrews-s/a; 2 covers by Campbell & Ross 5.00
...: Origins-Heroes & Villains (2/04, $3.50) short stories by various 3.50
...Reclaiming Thundera TPB (2003, $12.95) r/#0-5 13.00
... Sourcebook (1/03, $2.95) pin-ups and info on characters; art by various; A. Adams-c 3.00

THUNDERCATS: DOGS OF WAR
DC Comics (WildStorm): Aug, 2003 - No. 5, Dec, 2003 ($2.95, limited series)
1-5: 1-Two covers by Booth & Pearson; Booth-a/Layman-s. 2-4-Two covers 3.00
TPB (2004, $14.95) r/#1-5 15.00

THUNDERCATS: ENEMY'S PRIDE
DC Comics (WildStorm): Aug, 2004 - No. 5 ($2.95, limited series)
1-5-Vriens-a/Layman-s 3.00
TPB (2005, $14.99) r/#1-5 15.00

THUNDERCATS: HAMMERHAND'S REVENGE
DC Comics (WildStorm): Dec, 2003 - No. 5, Apr, 2004 ($2.95, limited series)
1-5-Avery-s/D'Anda-a. 2-Variant-c by Warren 3.00
TPB (2004, $14.95) r/#1-5 15.00

THUNDERCATS: THE RETURN
DC Comics (WildStorm): Apr, 2003 - No. 5, Aug, 2003 ($2.95, limited series)
1-5: 1-Two covers by Benes & Cassaday; Gilmore-s 3.00
TPB (2004, $12.95) r/series 13.00

THUNDER MOUNTAIN (See Zane Grey, Four Color #246)

THUNDERSTRIKE (See Thor #459)
Marvel Comics: June, 1993 - No. 24, July, 1995 ($1.25)
1-($2.95, 52 pgs.)-Holo-grafx lightning patterned foil-c; Bloodaxe returns 3.00
2-24: 2-Juggernaut-c/s. 4-Capt. America app. 4-6-Spider-Man app. 8-bound-in trading card sheet. 18-Bloodaxe app. 24-Death of Thunderstrike 2.50
Marvel Double Feature...Thunderstrike/Code Blue #13 ($2.50)-Same as Thunderstrike #13 w/Code Blue flip book 2.50

TICK, THE (Also see The Chroma-Tick)
New England Comics Press: Jun, 1988 - No. 12, May, 1993
($1.75/$1.95/$2.25; B&W, over-sized)
Special Edition 1-1st comic book app. serially numbered & limited to 5,000 copies
5 10 15 34 55 75
Special Edition 1-(5/96, $5.95)-Double-c; foil-c; serially numbered (5,001 thru 14,000) & limited to 9,000 copies 6.00
Special Edition 2-Serially numbered and limited to 3000 copies
5 10 15 30 48 65
Special Edition 2-(8/96, $5.95)-Double-c; foil-c; serially numbered (5,001 thru 14,000) & limited to 9,000 copies 1 2 3 5 6 8
1-Regular Edition 1st printing; reprints Special Ed. 1 w/minor changes
4 8 12 24 37 50
1-2nd printing 6.00
1-3rd-5th printing 3.00
2-Reprints Special Ed. 2 w/minor changes 2 4 6 13 18 22
2-8-All reprints 3.00
3-5 ($1.95): 4-1st app. Paul the Samurai 1 3 4 6 8 10
6,8 ($2.25) 5.00
7-1st app. Man-Eating Cow 6.00

The Tick Karma Tornado #5 © Ben Edlund

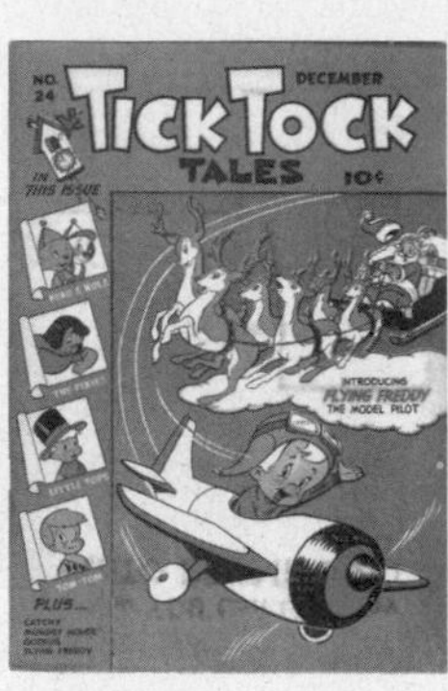
Tick Tock Tales #24 © ME

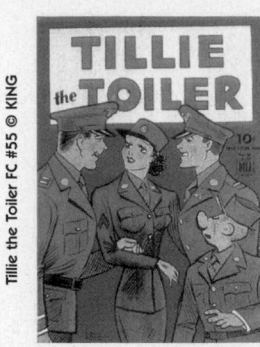

Tillie the Toiler FC #55 © KING

GD 2.0 | VG 4.0 | FN 6.0 | VF 8.0 | VF/NM 9.0 | NM- 9.2

8-Variant with no logo, price, issue number or company logos.
2 4 6 10 14 18
9-12 ($2.75) 4.00
12-Special Edition; card-stock, virgin foil-c; numbered edition
2 4 6 13 18 22
Pseudo-Tick #13 (11/00, $3.50) Continues story from #12 (1993) 4.00
Promo Sampler-(1990)-Tick-c/story 1 2 3 5 6 8

TICK, THE (One shots)
... Big Back to School Special 1-(10/98, $3.50, B&W) Tick & Arthur undercover in H.S. 3.50
... Big Cruise Ship Vacation Special 1-(9/00, $3.50, B&W) 3.50
... Big Father's Day Special 1-(6/00, $3.50, B&W) 3.50
... Big Halloween Special 1-(10/99, $3.50, B&W) 3.50
... Big Halloween Special 2000 (10/00, $3.50) 3.50
... Big Halloween Special 2001 (9/01, $3.95) 4.00
... Big Mother's Day Special 1-(4/00, $3.50, B&W) 3.50
... Big Red-N-Green Christmas Spectacle 1-(12/01, $3.95) 4.00
... Big Romantic Adventure 1-(2/98, $2.95, B&W) Candy box-c with candy map on back 3.50
... Big Summer Annual 1-(7/99, $3.50, B&W) Chainsaw Vigilante vs. Barry 3.50
... Big Summer Fun Special 1-(8/98, $3.50, B&W) Tick and Arthur at summer camp 3.50
... Big Tax Time Terror 1-(4/00, $3.50, B&W) 3.50
... Big Year 2000 Spectacle 1-(3/00, $3.50, B&W) 3.50
... Incredible Internet Comic 1-(7/01, $3.95, color) r/New England Comics website story 4.00
Introducing the Tick 1-(4/02, $3.95, color) summary of Tick's life and adventures 4.00
The Tick's Back #0 -(8/97, $2.95, B&W) 3.00
The Tick's Comic Con Extravaganza -(6/07, $3.95, color) Wang-c 4.00
The Tick's 20th Anniversary Special Edition #1 (5/07, $5.95) short stories by various; history of the character; creator profiles; 2 covers by Suydam & Bisley 6.00

--MASSIVE SUMMER DOUBLE SPECTACLE
1,2-(7,8/00, $3.50, B&W) 3.50

TICK & ARTIE
1-(6/02, $3.50, color) prints strips from Internet comic 3.50
2-(10/02, $3.95) 4.00

TICK AND ARTHUR, THE
New England Comics: Feb, 1999 - No. 6 ($3.50, B&W)
1-6-Sean Wang-s/a 3.50

TICK BIG BLUE DESTINY, THE
New England Comics: Oct, 1997 - No. 9 ($2.95)
1-4: 1-"Keen" Ed. 2-Two covers 3.50
1-($4.95) "Wicked Keen" Ed. w/die cut-c 5.00
5-($3.50) 3.50
6-Luny Bin Trilogy Proview #0 (7/98, $1.50) 3.50
7-9: 7-Luny Bin Trilogy begins 3.50

TICK BIG BLUE YULE LOG SPECIAL, THE
New England Comics: Dec, 1997; 1999 ($2.95, B&W)
1-"Jolly" and "Traditional" covers; flip book w/"Arthur Teaches the Tick About Hanukkah" 3.50
...1999 ($3.50) 3.50
Tick Big Yule Log Special 2001-(12/00, $3.50, B&W) 3.50

TICK, THE : CIRCUS MAXIMUS
New England Comics: Mar, 2000 - No. 4, Jun, 2000 ($3.50, B&W)
1-4-Encyclopedia of characters from Tick comics 3.50
Giant No. 1 (8/03, $14.95) r/#1-4, Redux 15.00
Redux No. 1 (4/01, $3.50) 3.50

TICK, THE - COLOR
New England Comics: Jan, 2001 - Present ($3.95)
1-6: 1-Marc Sandroni-a 4.00

TICK, THE : DAYS OF DRAMA
New England Comics: July, 2005 - No. 6, June, 2006 ($4.95/$3.95, limited series)
1-($4.95) Dave Garcia-a; has a mini-comic attached to cover 5.00
2-6-($3.95) 4.00

TICK, THE - HEROES OF THE CITY
New England Comics: Feb, 1999 - Present ($3.50, B&W)
1-6-Short stories by various 3.50

TICK KARMA TORNADO (The...)
New England Comics Press: Oct, 1993 - No. 9, Mar, 1995 ($2.75, B&W)
1-($3.25) 4.00
2-9: 2-$2.75-c begins 3.50

TICK'S BIG XMAS TRILOGY, THE
New England Comics: Dec, 2002 - No. 3, Dec, 2002 ($3.95, limited series)
1-3 4.00

TICK'S GOLDEN AGE COMIC, THE
New England Comics: May, 2002 - No. 3, Feb, 2003 ($4.95, Golden Age size)
1-3-Facsimile 1940s-style Tick issue; 2 covers 5.00
Giant Edition TPB (9/03, $12.95) r/#1-3 13.00

TICK'S GIANT CIRCUS OF THE MIGHTY, THE
New England Comics: Summer, 1992 - No. 3, Fall, 1993 ($2.75, B&W, magazine size)
1-(A-O). 2-(P-Z). 3-1993 Update 4.00

TICKLE COMICS (Also see Gay, Smile, & Whee Comics)
Modern Store Publ.: 1955 (7¢, 5x7-1/4", 52 pgs)
1 6 12 18 28 34 40

TICK TOCK TALES
Magazine Enterprises: Jan, 1946 - V3#33, Jan-Feb, 1951
1-Koko & Kola begin 15 30 45 86 133 180
2 10 20 30 54 72 90
3-10 9 18 27 50 65 80
11-33: 19-Flag-c. 23-Muggsy Mouse, The Pixies & Tom-Tom the Jungle Boy app. 24-X-mas-c. 25-The Pixies & Tom-Tom app. 8 16 24 44 57 70

TIGER (Also see Comics Reading Libraries in the Promotional Comics section)
Charlton Press (King Features): Mar, 1970 - No. 6, Jan, 1971 (15¢)
1 3 6 9 14 19 24
2-6 2 4 6 8 11 14

TIGER BOY (See Unearthly Spectaculars)

TIGER GIRL
Gold Key: Sept, 1968 (15¢)
1(10227-809)-Sparling-c/a; Jerry Siegel scripts. Some issues have a pin-up on back cover instead of advertising 4 8 12 24 37 50

TIGERMAN (Also see Thrilling Adventure Stories)
Seaboard Periodicals (Atlas): Apr, 1975 - No. 3, Sept, 1975 (All 25¢ issues)
1-3: 1-Origin; Colan-c. 2,3-Ditko-p in each 2 4 6 8 10 12

TIGER WALKS, A (See Movie Comics)

TIGRA (The Avengers)
Marvel Comics: May, 2002 - No. 4, Aug, 2002 ($2.99, limited series)
1-4-Christina Z-s/Deodato-c/a 3.00

TIGRESS, THE
Hero Graphics: Aug, 1992 - No. 6?, June, 1993 ($3.95/$2.95/$3.95, B&W)
1,6: 1-Tigress vs. Flare. 6-44 pgs. 4.00
2-5: 2-$2.95-c begins 3.00

TILLIE THE TOILER (See Comic Monthly)
Dell Publishing Co.: No. 15, 1941 - No. 237, July, 1949
Four Color 15(1941) 45 90 135 279 465 650
Large Feature Comic 30(1941) 34 68 102 198 319 440
Four Color 8(1942) 23 46 69 167 309 450
Four Color 22(1943) 17 34 51 120 223 325
Four Color 55(1944), 89(1945) 13 26 39 97 171 245
Four Color 106('45),132('46): 132-New stories begin 10 20 30 68 119 170
Four Color 150,176,184 9 18 27 63 107 150
Four Color 195,213,237 7 14 21 50 83 115

TIMBER WOLF (See Action Comics #372, & Legion of Super-Heroes)
DC Comics: Nov, 1992 - No. 5, Mar, 1993 ($1.25, limited series)
1-5 2.50

TIME BANDITS
Marvel Comics Group: Feb, 1982 (one-shot, Giant)
1-Movie adaptation 4.00

TIME BEAVERS (See First Comics Graphic Novel #2)

TIME BREAKERS
DC Comics (Helix): Jan, 1997 - No. 5, May, 1997 ($2.25, limited series)
1-5-Pollack-s 2.50

TIMECOP (Movie)
Dark Horse Comics: Sept, 1994 - No. 2, Nov, 1994 ($2.50, limited series)
1,2-Adaptation of film 2.50

TIME FOR LOVE (Formerly Romantic Secrets)
Charlton Comics: V2#53, Oct, 1966; Oct, 1967 - No. 47, May, 1976

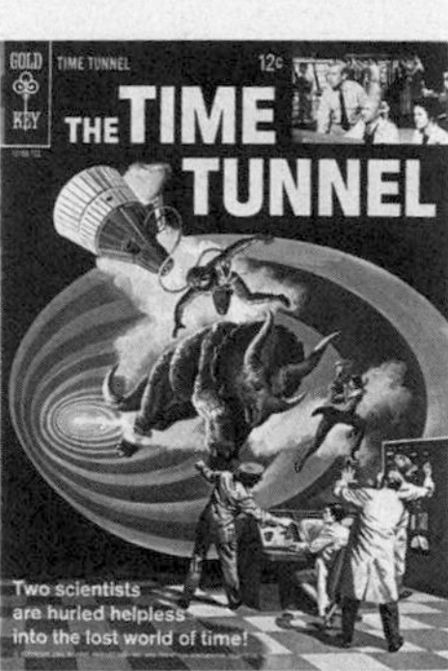

Time Tunnel #1 © 20th Century Fox

Tim Holt #30 © ME

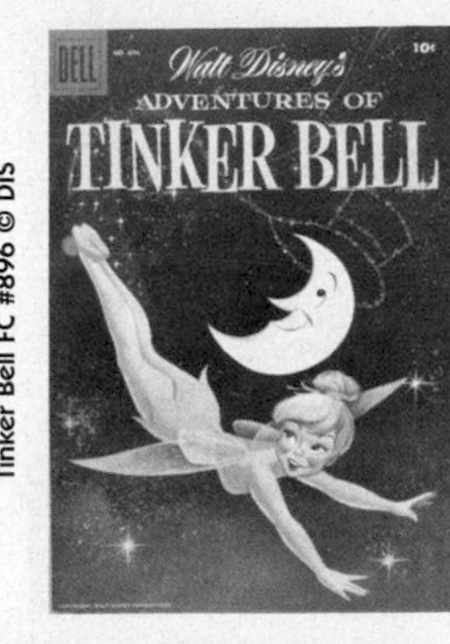

Tinker Bell FC #896 © DIS

	GD 2.0	VG 4.0	FN 6.0	VF 8.0	VF/NM 9.0	NM- 9.2
V2#53(10/66) Herman-s Hermits app.	3	6	9	20	30	40
1(10/67)	4	8	12	22	34	45
2(12/67)-10	3	6	9	15	21	26
11-20	2	4	6	11	16	20
21-29: 28-Shirley Jones poster. 29-Bobby Sherman pin-up	2	4	6	9	13	16
30-(10/72)-David Cassidy full page poster	3	6	9	17	25	32
31-47: 31 Bobby Sherman pin-up	2	4	6	8	11	14

TIMELESS TOPIX (See Topix)

TIMELY PRESENTS: ALL WINNERS
Marvel Comics: Dec, 1999 ($3.99)

1-Reprints All Winners Comics #19 (Fall 1946); new Lago-c — 4.00

TIMELY PRESENTS: HUMAN TORCH
Marvel Comics: Feb, 1999 ($3.99)

1-Reprints Human Torch Comics #5 (Fall 1941); new Lago-c — 4.00

TIME MACHINE, THE
Dell Publishing Co.: No. 1085, Mar, 1960 (H.G. Wells)

	GD	VG	FN	VF	VF/NM	NM-
Four Color 1085-Movie, Alex Toth-a; Rod Taylor photo-c	14	28	42	100	178	255

TIME MASTERS
DC Comics: Feb, 1990 - No. 8, Sept, 1990 ($1.75, mini-series)

1-8: New Rip Hunter series. 5-Cave Carson, Viking Prince app. 6-Dr. Fate app. — 2.50
TPB (2008, $19.99) r/#1-8 and Secret Origins #43; intro. by Geoff Johns — 20.00

TIMESLIP COLLECTION
Marvel Comics: Nov, 1998 ($2.99, one-shot)

1-Pin-ups reprinted from Marvel Vision magazine — 3.00

TIMESLIP SPECIAL (The Coming of the Avengers)
Marvel Comics: Oct, 1998 ($5.99, one-shot)

1-Alternate world Avengers vs. Odin — 6.00

TIME TO RUN (Based on 1973 Billy Graham movie)
Spire Christian Comics (Fleming H. Revell Co.): 1975 (39¢)

	GD	VG	FN	VF	VF/NM	NM-
nn-By Al Hartley	2	4	6	8	11	14

TIME TUNNEL, THE (TV)
Gold Key: Feb, 1967 - No. 2, July, 1967 (12¢)

	GD	VG	FN	VF	VF/NM	NM-
1-Photo back-c on both issues	7	14	21	47	76	105
2	5	10	15	34	55	75

TIME TWISTERS
Quality Comics: Sept, 1987 - No. 21, 1989 ($1.25/$1.50)

1-21: Alan Moore scripts in 1-4, 6-9, 14 (2 pg.). 14-Bolland-a (2 pg.). 15,16-Guice-c — 2.50

TIME 2: THE EPIPHANY (See First Comics Graphic Novel #9)

TIMEWALKER (Also see Archer & Armstrong)
Valiant: Jan, 1994 - No. 15, Oct, 1995 ($2.50)

1-15,0(3/96): 2-"JAN" on-c, February, 1995 in indicia. — 2.50
Yearbook 1 (5/95, $2.95) — 3.00

TIME WARP (See The Unexpected #210)
DC Comics, Inc.: Oct-Nov, 1979 - No. 5, June-July, 1980 ($1.00, 68 pgs.)

	GD	VG	FN	VF	VF/NM	NM-
1	2	4	6	8	11	14
2-5	1	3	4	6	8	10

NOTE: ***Aparo** a-1. **Buckler** a-1p. **Chaykin** a-2. **Ditko** a-1-4. **Kaluta** c-1-5. **G. Kane** a-2. **Nasser** a-4. **Newton** a-1-5p. **Orlando** a-2. **Sutton** a-1-3.*

TIME WARRIORS: THE BEGINNING
Fantasy General Comics: 1986 (Aug) - No. 2, 1986? ($1.50)

1,2-Alpha Track/Skellon Empire — 2.50

TIM HOLT (Movie star) (Becomes Red Mask #42 on; also see Crack Western #72, & Great Western)
Magazine Enterprises: 1948 - No. 41, April-May, 1954 (All 36 pgs.)

	GD	VG	FN	VF	VF/NM	NM-
1-(A-1 #14)-Line drawn-c w/Tim Holt photo on-c; Tim Holt, His horse Lightning & sidekick Chito begin	59	118	177	369	610	850
2-(A-1 #17)(9-10/48)-Photo-c begin, end #18	32	64	96	186	293	400
3-(A-1 #19)-Photo back-c	24	48	72	139	220	300
4(1-2/49),5: 5-Photo front/back-c	17	34	51	98	154	210
6-(5/49)-1st app. The Calico Kid (alias Rex Fury), his horse Ebony & Sidekick Sing-Song (begin series); photo back-c	29	58	87	167	264	360
7-10: 7-Calico Kid by Ayers. 8-Calico Kid by Guardineer (r-in/Great Western #10). 9-Map of Tim's Home Range	16	32	48	89	137	185
11-The Calico Kid becomes The Ghost Rider (origin & 1st app.) by Dick Ayers (r-in/Great Western I.W. #8); his horse Spectre & sidekick Sing-Song begin series	45	90	135	275	455	635
12-16,18-Last photo-c	14	28	42	80	115	150
17-Frazetta Ghost Rider-c	40	80	120	242	389	535
19,22,24: 19-Last Tim Holt-c; Bolle line-drawn-c begin; Tim Holt photo on covers #19-28, 30-41. 22-interior photo-c	12	24	36	69	97	125
20-Tim Holt becomes Redmask (origin); begin series; Redmask-c #20-on	16	32	48	94	147	200
21-Frazetta Ghost Rider/Redmask-c	38	76	114	224	355	485
23-Frazetta Redmask-c	30	60	90	174	275	375
25-1st app. Black Phantom	20	40	60	117	184	250
26-30: 28-Wild Bill Hickok, Bat Masterson team up with Redmask. 29-B&W photo-c	11	22	33	62	86	110
31-33-Ghost Rider ends	10	20	30	58	79	100
34-Tales of the Ghost Rider begins (horror)-Classic "The Flower Women" & "Hard Boiled Harry!"	14	28	42	82	121	160
35-Last Tales of the Ghost Rider	11	22	33	62	86	110
36-The Ghost Rider returns, ends #41; liquid hallucinogenic drug story	13	26	39	74	105	135
37-Ghost Rider classic "To Touch Is to Die!", about Inca treasure	13	26	39	74	105	135
38-The Black Phantom begins (not in #39); classic Ghost Rider "The Phantom Guns of Feather Gap!"	13	26	39	74	105	135
39-41: All 3-D effect c/stories	14	28	42	81	118	155

NOTE: ***Dick Ayers** a-7, 9-41. **Bolle** a-1-41; c-19, 20, 22, 24-28, 30-41.*

TIM McCOY (Formerly Zoo Funnies; Pictorial Love Stories #22 on)
Charlton Comics: No. 16, Oct, 1948 - No. 21, Aug, 1949 (Western Movie Stories)

	GD	VG	FN	VF	VF/NM	NM-
16-John Wayne, Montgomery Clift app. in "Red River"; photo back-c	41	82	123	250	400	550
17-21: 17-Allan "Rocky" Lane guest stars. 18-Rod Cameron guest stars. 19-Whip Wilson, Andy Clyde guest star; Jesse James story. 20-Jimmy Wakely guest stars. 21-Johnny Mack Brown guest stars	35	70	105	201	318	435

TIMMY
Dell Publishing Co.: No. 715, Aug, 1956 - No. 1022, Aug-Oct, 1959

	GD	VG	FN	VF	VF/NM	NM-
Four Color 715 (#1)	5	10	15	30	48	65
Four Color 823 (8/57), 923 (8/58), 1022	4	8	12	26	41	55

TIMMY THE TIMID GHOST (Formerly Win-A-Prize?; see Blue Bird)
Charlton Comics: No. 3, 2/56 - No. 44, 10/64; No. 45, 9/66; 10/67 - No. 23, 7/71; V4#24, 9/85 - No. 26, 1/86

	GD	VG	FN	VF	VF/NM	NM-
3(1956) (1st Series)	12	24	36	69	97	125
4,5	8	16	24	42	54	65
6-10	3	6	9	20	30	40
11,12(4/58,10/58)-(100 pgs.)	6	12	18	43	69	95
13-20	3	6	9	18	27	35
21-45(1966)	3	6	9	14	19	24
1(10/67, 2nd series)	3	6	9	16	22	28
2-10	2	4	6	10	14	18
11-23: 23 (7/71)	1	3	4	8	10	12
24-26 (1985-86): Fago-r (low print run)						6.00

TIM TYLER (See Harvey Comics Hits #54)

TIM TYLER (Also see Comics Reading Libraries in the Promotional Comics section)
Better Publications: 1942

	GD	VG	FN	VF	VF/NM	NM-
1	15	30	45	85	130	175

TIM TYLER COWBOY
Standard Comics (King Features Synd.): No. 11, Nov, 1948 - No. 18, 1950

	GD	VG	FN	VF	VF/NM	NM-
11-By Lyman Young	9	18	27	50	65	80
12-18: 13-15-Full length western adventures	7	14	21	35	43	50

TINKER BELL (Disney, TV)(See Walt Disney Showcase #37)
Dell Publishing Co.: No. 896, Mar, 1958 - No. 982, Apr-June, 1959

	GD	VG	FN	VF	VF/NM	NM-
Four Color 896 (#1)-The Adventures of...	8	16	24	56	93	130
Four Color 982-The New Advs. of...	8	16	24	52	86	120

TINY FOLKS FUNNIES
Dell Publishing Co.: No. 60, 1944

	GD	VG	FN	VF	VF/NM	NM-
Four Color 60	15	30	45	107	196	285

TINY TESSIE (Tessie #1-23; Real Experiences #25)
Marvel Comics (20CC): No. 24, Oct, 1949 (52 pgs.)

	GD	VG	FN	VF	VF/NM	NM-
24	12	24	36	69	97	125

Tiny Titans #4 © DC

Tip Top Comics #34 © UFS

Titans (2008 series) #1 © DC

TINY TIM (Also see Super Comics)
Dell Publishing Co.: No. 4, 1941 - No. 235, July, 1949

	GD 2.0	VG 4.0	FN 6.0	VF 8.0	VF/NM 9.0	NM- 9.2
Large Feature Comic 4('41)	40	80	120	244	397	550
Four Color 20(1941)	37	74	111	215	345	475
Four Color 42(1943)	16	32	48	114	212	310
Four Color 235	6	12	18	37	59	80

TINY TITANS (Teen Titans)(See Promotional Comics section for Free Comic Book Day edition)
DC Comics: Apr, 2008 - Present ($2.25)

	GD 2.0	VG 4.0	FN 6.0	VF 8.0	VF/NM 9.0	NM- 9.2
1-6-All ages stories of Teen Titans in Elementary school; Baltazar & Franco-s/a						2.25

TINY TOT COMICS
E. C. Comics: Mar, 1946 - No. 10, Nov-Dec, 1947 (For younger readers)

	GD 2.0	VG 4.0	FN 6.0	VF 8.0	VF/NM 9.0	NM- 9.2
1(nn)-52 pg. issues begin, end #4	40	80	120	235	380	525
2 (5/46)	22	44	66	129	207	285
3-10: 10-Christmas-c	20	40	60	118	189	260

TINY TOT FUNNIES (Formerly Family Funnies; becomes Junior Funnies)
Harvey Publ. (King Features Synd.): No. 9, June, 1951

	GD 2.0	VG 4.0	FN 6.0	VF 8.0	VF/NM 9.0	NM- 9.2
9-Flash Gordon, Mandrake, Dagwood, Daisy, etc.	8	16	24	42	54	65

TINY TOTS COMICS
Dell Publishing Co.: 1943 (Not reprints)

	GD 2.0	VG 4.0	FN 6.0	VF 8.0	VF/NM 9.0	NM- 9.2
1-Kelly-a(2); fairy tales	40	80	120	235	380	525

TIPPY & CAP STUBBS (See Popular Comics)
Dell Publishing Co.: No. 210, Jan, 1949 - No. 242, Aug, 1949

	GD 2.0	VG 4.0	FN 6.0	VF 8.0	VF/NM 9.0	NM- 9.2
Four Color 210 (#1)	5	10	15	32	51	70
Four Color 242	4	8	12	26	41	55

TIPPY'S FRIENDS GO-GO & ANIMAL
Tower Comics: July, 1966 - No. 15, Oct, 1969 (25¢)

	GD 2.0	VG 4.0	FN 6.0	VF 8.0	VF/NM 9.0	NM- 9.2
1	9	18	27	63	107	150
2-5,7,9-15: 12-15 titled "Tippy's Friend Go-Go"	5	10	15	34	55	75
6-The Monkees photo-c	8	16	24	58	97	135
8-Beatles app. on front/back-c	10	20	30	73	129	185

TIPPY TEEN (See Vicki)
Tower Comics: Nov, 1965 - No. 25, Oct, 1969 (25¢)

	GD 2.0	VG 4.0	FN 6.0	VF 8.0	VF/NM 9.0	NM- 9.2
1	10	20	30	71	126	180
2-4,6-10	6	12	18	41	66	90
5-1 pg. Beatles pin-up	7	14	21	45	73	100
11-20: 16-Twiggy photo-c	6	12	18	39	62	85
21-25	5	10	15	34	55	75
Special Collectors' Editions nn-(1969, 25¢)	6	12	18	39	62	85

TIPPY TERRY
Super/I. W. Enterprises: 1963

	GD 2.0	VG 4.0	FN 6.0	VF 8.0	VF/NM 9.0	NM- 9.2
Super Reprint #14('63)-r/Little Groucho #1	2	4	6	8	10	12
I.W. Reprint #1 (nd)-r/Little Groucho #1	2	4	6	8	10	12

TIP TOP COMICS
United Features #1-188/St. John #189-210/Dell Publishing Co. #211 on:
4/36 - No. 210, 1957; No. 211, 11-1/57-58 - No. 225, 5-7/61

	GD 2.0	VG 4.0	FN 6.0	VF 8.0	VF/NM 9.0	NM- 9.2
1-Tarzan by Hal Foster, Li'l Abner, Broncho Bill, Fritzi Ritz, Ella Cinders, Capt. & The Kids begin; strip-r (1st comic book app. of each)	958	1916	2874	5461	8581	11,700
2	229	458	687	1305	2053	2800
3-Tarzan-c	204	408	612	1163	1832	2500
4	119	238	357	678	1064	1450
5-8,10: 7-Photo & biography of Edgar Rice Burroughs. 8-Christmas-c	83	166	249	473	749	1025
9-Tarzan-c	104	208	312	593	947	1300
11,13,16,18-Tarzan-c: 11-Has Tarzan pin-up	79	158	237	450	713	975
12,14,15,17,19,20: 20-Christmas-c	60	120	180	342	539	735
21,24,27,30-(10/38)-Tarzan-c	63	126	189	359	567	775
22,23,25,26,28,29	43	86	129	245	383	520
31,35,38,40	37	74	111	215	345	475
32,36-Tarzan-c: 32-1st published Jack Davis-a (cartoon). 36-Kurtzman panel (1st published comic work)	53	106	159	334	567	800
33,34,37,39-Tarzan-c	50	100	150	310	518	725
41-Reprints 1st Tarzan Sunday; Tarzan-c	53	106	159	334	567	800
42,44,46,48,49	31	62	93	181	291	400
43,45,47,50,52-Tarzan-c. 43-Mort Walker panel	40	80	120	240	390	540
51,53	30	60	90	174	280	385
54-Origin Mirror Man & Triple Terror, also featured on cover	38	76	114	222	356	490
55,56,58,60: Last Tarzan by Foster	25	50	75	147	236	325
57,59,61,62-Tarzan by Hogarth	32	64	96	186	298	410
63-80: 65,67-70,72-74,77,78-No Tarzan	15	30	45	88	137	185
81-90	14	28	42	80	115	150
91-99	13	26	39	72	101	130
100	14	28	42	76	108	140
101-140: 110-Gordo story. 111-Li'l Abner app. 118, 132-No Tarzan. 137-Sadie Hawkins Day story	10	20	30	54	72	90
141-170: 145,151-Gordo stories. 157-Last Li'l Abner; lingerie panels	8	16	24	44	57	70
171-188-Tarzan reprints by B. Lubbers in all. 173-Peanuts by Schulz begins; no Peanuts in #174-183	9	18	27	47	61	75
189-225-Peanuts (8 pgs.) in most	8	16	24	40	50	60
Bound Volumes (Very Rare) sold at 1939 World's Fair; bound by publisher in pictorial comic boards (also see Comics on Parade)						
Bound issues 1-12	306	612	918	2081	3641	5200
Bound issues 13-24	173	346	519	1090	1845	2600
Bound issues 25-36	153	306	459	964	1632	2300

NOTE: *Tarzan by* **Foster**-*#1-40, 44-50; by* **Rex Maxon**-*#41-43; by* **Burne Hogarth**-*#57, 59, 62.*

TIP TOPPER COMICS
United Features Syndicate: Oct-Nov, 1949 - No. 28, 1954

	GD 2.0	VG 4.0	FN 6.0	VF 8.0	VF/NM 9.0	NM- 9.2
1-Li'l Abner, Abbie & Slats	12	24	36	67	94	120
2	8	16	24	44	57	70
3-5: 5-Fearless Fosdick app.	8	16	24	40	50	60
6-10: 6-Fearless Fosdick app.	7	14	21	37	46	55
11-16	6	12	18	31	38	45
17(6-7/52) (2nd app. of Peanuts by Schulz in comics?) (see United Comics #22 for 5-6/52 app.)	10	20	30	58	79	100
18-26: 18-24,26-Early Peanuts (2 pgs.). 25-Early Peanuts (3 pgs.) 26-Twin Earths	9	18	27	52	69	85
27,28-Twin Earths	8	16	24	40	50	60

NOTE: *Many lingerie panels in Fritzi Ritz stories.*

TITAN A.E.
Dark Horse Comics: May, 2000 - No. 3, July, 2000 ($2.95, limited series)

	GD 2.0	VG 4.0	FN 6.0	VF 8.0	VF/NM 9.0	NM- 9.2
1-3-Movie prequel; Al Rio-a						3.00

TITANS (Also see Teen Titans, New Teen Titans and New Titans)
DC Comics: Mar, 1999 - No. 50, Apr, 2003 ($2.50/$2.75)

	GD 2.0	VG 4.0	FN 6.0	VF 8.0	VF/NM 9.0	NM- 9.2
1-Titans re-form; Grayson-s; 2 covers						3.00
2-11,13-24,26-50: 2-Superman-c/app. 9,10,21,22-Deathstroke app. 24-Titans from "Kingdom Come" app. 32-36-Asamiya-c. 44-Begin $2.75-c						2.75
12-($3.50, 48 pages)						3.50
25-($3.95) Titans from "Kingdom Come" app.; Wolfman & Faerber-s; art by Pérez, Cardy, Grumment, Jimenez, Dodson, Pelletier						4.00
Annual 1 ('00, $3.50) Planet DC; intro Bushido						3.50
... East Special 1 (1/08, $3.99) Winick-s/Churchill-a; continues in Titans #1 (2008)						4.00
...Secret Files 1,2 (3/99, 10/00; $4.95) Profile pages & short stories						5.00

TITANS (Also see Teen Titans)
DC Comics: Jun, 2008 - Present ($3.50/$2.99)

	GD 2.0	VG 4.0	FN 6.0	VF 8.0	VF/NM 9.0	NM- 9.2
1-Titans re-form again; Winick-s/Churchill-a; covers by Churchill & Van Sciver						3.50
2,3-($2.99) Trigon returns						3.00

TITANS/ LEGION OF SUPER-HEROES: UNIVERSE ABLAZE
DC Comics: 2000 - No. 4, 2000 ($4.95, prestige format, limited series)

	GD 2.0	VG 4.0	FN 6.0	VF 8.0	VF/NM 9.0	NM- 9.2
1-4-Jurgens-s/a; P. Jimenez-a; teams battle Universo						5.00

TITAN SPECIAL
Dark Horse Comics: June, 1994 ($3.95, one-shot)

	GD 2.0	VG 4.0	FN 6.0	VF 8.0	VF/NM 9.0	NM- 9.2
1-($3.95, 52 pgs.)						4.00

TITANS: SCISSORS, PAPER, STONE
DC Comics: 1997 ($4.95, one-shot)

	GD 2.0	VG 4.0	FN 6.0	VF 8.0	VF/NM 9.0	NM- 9.2
1-Manga style Elseworlds; Adam Warren-s/a(p)						5.00

TITANS SELL-OUT SPECIAL
DC Comics: Nov, 1992 ($3.50, 52 pgs., one-shot)

	GD 2.0	VG 4.0	FN 6.0	VF 8.0	VF/NM 9.0	NM- 9.2
1-Fold-out Nightwing poster; 1st Teeny Titans						3.50

TITANS/ YOUNG JUSTICE: GRADUATION DAY
DC Comics: Early July, 2003 - No. 3, Aug, 2003 ($2.50, limited series)

	GD 2.0	VG 4.0	FN 6.0	VF 8.0	VF/NM 9.0	NM- 9.2
1,2-Winick-s/Garza-a; leads into Teen Titans and The Outsiders series. 2-Lilith dies						2.50
3-Death of Donna Troy (Wonder Girl)						2.50
TPB (2003, $6.95) r/#1-3; plus previews of Teen Titans and The Outsiders series						7.00

T-MAN (Also see Police Comics #103)
Quality Comics Group: Sept, 1951 - No. 38, Dec, 1956

Toka #4 © DELL

Tomahawk #7 © DC

Tom & Jerry #1 © Turner Ent.

GD VG FN VF VF/NM NM-
2.0 4.0 6.0 8.0 9.0 9.2

1-Pete Trask, T-Man begins; Jack Cole-a 40 80 120 244 397 550
2-Crandall-c 22 44 66 127 204 280
3,7,8: All Crandall-c 20 40 60 117 186 255
4,5-Crandall-c/a each 21 42 63 123 197 270
6-"The Man Who Could Be Hitler" c/story; Crandall-c.
23 46 69 135 218 300
9,10-Crandall-c 17 34 51 100 158 215
11-Used in **POP**, pg. 95 & color illo. 14 28 42 82 121 160
12,13,15-19,21,22-26: 21- "The Return of Mussolini" c/story. 23-H-Bomb panel.
24-Last pre-code issue (4/55). 25 Not Crandall-a 12 24 36 69 97 125
14-Hitler-c 15 30 45 94 147 200
20-H-Bomb explosion-c/story 15 30 45 86 133 180
27-33,35-38 12 24 36 69 97 125
34-Hitler-c 15 30 45 83 124 160
NOTE: *Anti-communist stories common.* **Crandall** *c-2-10p.* **Cuidera** *c(i)-1-38. Bondage c-15.*

TMNT... (Also see Teenage Mutant Ninja Turtles and related titles)
Mirage Publishing: March 2007 ($3.25/$4.95, B&W, one-shots)
...: Raphael Movie Prequel 1; ...: Michelangelo Movie Prequel 2; ...: Donatello Movie Prequel 3; ...: April Movie Prequel 4; ...: Leonardo Movie Prequel 5; back-story for movie 3.25
...: The Official Movie Adaptation ($4.95) adapts 2007 movie; Munroe-c 5.00

TMNT MUTANT UNIVERSE SOURCEBOOK
Archie Comics: 1992 - No. 3, 1992? ($1.95, 52 pgs.)(Lists characters from A-Z)
1-3: 3-New characters; fold-out poster 2.50

TNT COMICS
Charles Publishing Co.: Feb, 1946 (36 pgs.)
1-Yellowjacket app. 31 62 93 181 291 400

TOBY TYLER (Disney, see Movie Comics)
Dell Publishing Co.: No. 1092, Apr-June, 1960
Four Color 1092-Movie, photo-c 6 12 18 43 69 95

TODAY'S BRIDES
Ajax/Farrell Publishing Co.: Nov, 1955; No. 2, Feb, 1956; No. 3, Sept, 1956; No. 4, Nov, 1956
1 9 18 27 47 61 75
2-4 6 12 18 31 38 45

TODAY'S ROMANCE
Standard Comics: No. 5, March, 1952 - No. 8, Sept, 1952 (All photo-c?)
5-Photo-c 10 20 30 56 76 95
6-Photo-c; Toth-a 10 20 30 58 79 100
7,8 8 16 24 44 57 70

TOE TAGS FEATURING GEORGE A. ROMARO
DC Comics: Dec, 2004 - No. 6, May, 2005 ($2.95/$2.99)
1-6-Zombie story by George Romaro; Wrightson-c/Castillo-a 3.00

TOKA (Jungle King)
Dell Publishing Co.: Aug-Oct, 1964 - No. 10, Jan, 1967 (Painted-c #1,2)
1 4 8 12 28 44 60
2 3 6 9 17 25 32
3-10 3 6 9 14 20 26

TOKYO STORM WARNING (See Red/Tokyo Storm Warning for TPB)
DC Comics (Cliffhanger): Aug, 2003 - No. 3, Dec, 2003 ($2.95, limited series)
1-3-Warren Ellis-s/James Raiz-a 3.00

TOMAHAWK (Son of... on-c of #131-140; see Star Spangled Comics #69 & World's Finest Comics #65)
National Periodical Publications: Sept-Oct, 1950 - No. 140, May-June, 1972
1-Tomahawk & boy sidekick Dan Hunter begin by Fred Ray
173 346 519 1090 1845 2600
2-Frazetta/Williamson-a (4 pgs.) 66 132 198 416 701 985
3-5 41 82 123 250 413 575
6-10: 7-Last 52 pg. issue 35 70 105 203 327 450
11-20 24 48 72 140 225 310
21-27,30: 30-Last precode (2/55) 21 42 63 123 197 270
28-1st app. Lord Shilling (arch-foe) 22 44 66 127 204 280
29-Frazetta-r/Jimmy Wakely #3 (3 pgs.) 27 54 81 156 251 345
31-40 17 34 51 100 158 215
41-50 10 20 30 68 119 170
51-56,58-60 9 18 27 60 100 140
57-Frazetta-r/Jimmy Wakely #6 (3 pgs.) 10 20 30 70 123 175
61-77: 77-Last 10¢ issue 8 16 24 54 90 125
78-85: 81-1st app. Miss Liberty. 83-Origin Tomahawk's Rangers
7 14 21 45 73 100

GD VG FN VF VF/NM NM-
2.0 4.0 6.0 8.0 9.0 9.2

86-99: 96-Origin/1st app. The Hood, alias Lady Shilling
5 10 15 32 51 70
100 5 10 15 34 55 75
101-110: 107-Origin/1st app. Thunder-Man 4 8 12 26 41 55
111-115,120,122: 122-Last 12¢ issue 4 8 12 24 37 50
116-1st Neal Adams cover 6 12 18 39 62 85
117-119,121,123-130-Neal Adams-c 4 8 12 26 41 55
131-Frazetta-r/Jimmy Wakely #7 (3 pgs.); origin Firehair retold
3 6 9 20 30 40
132-135: 135-Last 15¢ issue 3 6 9 16 22 28
136-138,140 (52 pg. Giants) 3 6 9 18 27 35
139-Frazetta-r/Star Spangled #113 3 6 9 20 30 40
NOTE: **Fred Ray** *c-1, 2, 8, 11, 30, 34, 35, 40-43, 45, 46, 82. Firehair by* **Kubert**-*131-134, 136.* **Maurer** *a-138.* **Severin** *a-135.* **Starr** *a-5.* **Thorne** *a-137, 140.*

TOM AND JERRY (See Comic Album #4, 8, 12, Dell Giant #21, Dell Giants, Golden Comics Digest #1, 5, 8, 13, 15, 18, 22, 25, 28, 35, Kite fun Book & March of Comics #21, 46, 61, 70, 88, 103, 119, 128, 145, 154, 173, 190, 207, 224, 281, 295, 305, 321,333, 345, 361, 365, 388, 400, 444, 451, 463, 480)

TOM AND JERRY (...Comics, early issues) (M.G.M.)
(Formerly Our Gang No. 1-59) (See Dell Giants for annuals)
Dell Publishing Co./Gold Key No. 213-327/Whitman No. 328 on: No. 193, 6/48; No. 60, 7/49 - No. 212, 7-9/62; No. 213, 11/62 - No. 291, 2/75; No. 292, 3/77 - No. 342, 5/82 - No. 344, 6/84
Four Color 193 (#1)-Titled "M.G.M. Presents..." 22 44 66 161 298 435
60-Barney Bear, Benny Burro cont. from Our Gang; Droopy begins
12 24 36 82 146 210
61 10 20 30 67 116 165
62-70: 66-X-Mas-c 8 16 24 56 93 130
71-80: 77,90-X-Mas-c. 79-Spike & Tyke begin 7 14 21 45 73 100
81-99 6 12 18 41 66 90
100 6 12 18 43 69 95
101-120 5 10 15 34 55 75
121-140: 126-X-Mas-c 5 10 15 30 48 65
141-160 4 8 12 26 41 55
161-200 4 8 12 24 37 50
201-212(7-9/62)(Last Dell issue) 4 8 12 22 34 45
213,214-(84 pgs.)-Titled "...Funhouse" 6 12 18 41 66 90
215-240: 215-Titled "...Funhouse" 3 6 9 17 25 32
241-270 2 4 6 11 16 20
271-300: 286- "Tom & Jerry" 2 4 6 8 11 14
301-327 (Gold Key) 1 3 4 6 8 10
328,329 (Whitman) 2 4 6 8 11 14
330(8/80),331(10/80), 332-(3-pack only) 3 6 9 20 30 40
333-341: 339(2/82), 340(2-3/82), 341(4/82) 2 4 6 8 10 12
342-344 (All #90058, no date, date code, 3-pack): 342(6/83), 343(8/83), 344(6/84)
3 6 9 14 19 24
Mouse From T.R.A.P. 1(7/66)-Giant, G. K. 5 10 15 30 48 65
Summer Fun 1(7/67, 68 pgs.)(Gold Key)-Reprints Barks' Droopy from Summer Fun #1
5 10 15 30 48 65
NOTE: *#60-87, 98-121, 268, 277, 289, 302 are 52 pgs.. Reprints-#225, 241, 245, 247, 252, 254, 266, 268, 270, 292-327, 329-342, 344.*

TOM & JERRY
Harvey Comics: Sept, 1991 - No. 18, Aug, 1994 ($1.25)
1-18: 1-Tom & Jerry, Barney Bear-r by Carl Barks 3.00
50th Anniversary Special 1 (10/91, $2.50, 68 pgs.)-Benny the Lonesome Burro-r by Barks (story/a)/Our Gang #9 4.00

TOMB OF DARKNESS (Formerly Beware)
Marvel Comics Group: No. 9, July, 1974 - No. 23, Nov, 1976
9 3 6 9 16 22 28
10-23: 11,16,18-21-Kirby-a. 15,19-Ditko-r. 17-Woodbridge-r/Astonishing #62; Powell-r. 20-Everett Venus-r/Venus #19. 22-r/Tales To Astonish #27; 1st Hank Pym. 23-Everett-r
2 4 6 9 12 15
20,21-(30¢-c variants, limited distribution)(5,7/76) 4 8 12 24 37 50

TOMB OF DRACULA (See Giant-Size Dracula, Dracula Lives, Nightstalkers, Power Record Comics & Requiem for Dracula)
Marvel Comics Group: Apr, 1972 - No. 70, Aug, 1979
1-1st app. Dracula & Frank Drake; Colan-p in all; Neal Adams-c
15 30 45 105 190 275
2 7 14 21 49 80 110
3-6: 3-Intro. Dr. Rachel Van Helsing & Inspector Chelm. 6-Neal Adams-c
6 12 18 39 62 85
7-9 5 10 15 32 51 70
10-1st app. Blade the Vampire Slayer (who app. in 1998 and 2002 movies)

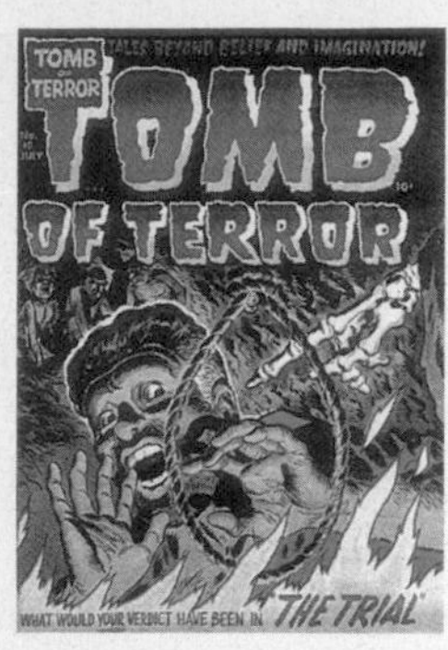

Tomb of Terror #10 © HARV

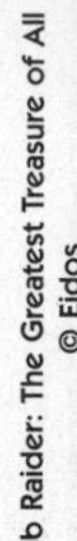

Tomb Raider: The Greatest Treasure of All © Eidos

Tom Mix Western #3 © FAW

	GD 2.0	VG 4.0	FN 6.0	VF 8.0	VF/NM 9.0	NM- 9.2
	18	36	54	130	240	350
11,14-16,20:	4	8	12	24	37	50
12-2nd app. Blade; Brunner-c(p)	7	14	21	49	80	110
13-Origin Blade	9	18	27	60	100	140
17,19: 17-Blade bitten by Dracula. 19-Blade discovers he is immune to vampire's bite. 1st mention of Blade having vampire blood in him	5	10	15	34	55	75
18-Two-part x-over cont'd in Werewolf by Night #15	5	10	15	30	48	65
21,24-Blade app.	4	8	12	24	37	50
22,23,26,27,29	3	6	9	16	23	30
25-1st app. & origin Hannibal King	3	6	9	20	30	40
25-2nd printing (1994)	2	4	6	8	10	12
28-Blade app. on-c & inside as an illusion	3	6	9	20	30	40
30,41,42-45-Blade app. 45-Intro. Deacon Frost, the vampire who bit Blade's mother	3	6	9	20	30	35
31-40	3	6	9	14	20	26
43-45-(30¢-c variants, limited distribution)	5	10	15	32	51	70
46,47-(Regular 25¢ editions)(4-8/76)	2	4	6	10	14	18
46,47-(30¢-c variants, limited distribution)	3	6	9	20	30	40
48,49,51-57,59,60: 57,59,60-(30¢-c)	2	4	6	10	14	18
50-Silver Surfer app.	3	6	9	18	27	35
57,59,60-(35¢-c variants)(6-9/77)	4	8	12	24	37	50
58-All Blade issue (Regular 30¢ edition)	4	8	12	22	34	45
58-(35¢-c variant)(7/77)	7	14	21	45	73	100
61-69	2	4	6	10	14	18
70-Double size	3	6	9	18	27	35

NOTE: ***N. Adams** c-1, 6. **Colan** a-1-70p; c(p)-8, 38-42, 44-56, 58-70. **Wrightson** c-43.*

TOMB OF DRACULA, THE (Magazine)
Marvel Comics Group: Oct, 1979 - No. 6, Aug, 1980 (B&W)

	GD 2.0	VG 4.0	FN 6.0	VF 8.0	VF/NM 9.0	NM- 9.2
1,3: 1-Colan-a; features on movies "Dracula" and "Love at First Bite" w/photos. 3-Good girl cover-a; Miller-a (2 pg. sketch)	2	4	6	10	14	18
2,6: 2-Ditko-a (36 pgs.); Nosferatu movie feature. 6-Lilith story w/Sienkiewicz-a	2	4	6	8	10	12
4,5: Stephen King interview	2	4	6	11	16	20

NOTE: ***Buscema** a-4p, 5p. **Chaykin** c-5, 6. **Colan** a(p)-1, 3-6. **Miller** a-3. **Romita** a-2p.*

TOMB OF DRACULA
Marvel Comics (Epic Comics): 1991 - No. 4, 1992 ($4.95, 52 pgs., squarebound, mini-series)

	NM- 9.2
Book 1-4: Colan/Williamson-a; Colan painted-c	5.00

TOMB OF DRACULA
Marvel Comics: Dec, 2004 - No. 4, Mar, 2005 ($2.99, limited series)

	NM- 9.2
1-4-Blade app.; Tolagson-a/Sienkiewicz-c	3.00

TOMB OF LEGEIA (See Movie Classics)

TOMB OF TERROR (Thrills of Tomorrow #17 on)
Harvey Publications: June, 1952 - No. 16, July, 1954

	GD 2.0	VG 4.0	FN 6.0	VF 8.0	VF/NM 9.0	NM- 9.2
1	45	90	135	279	465	650
2	29	58	87	169	272	375
3-Bondage-c; atomic disaster story	30	60	90	174	280	385
4-12: 4-Heart ripped out. 8-12-Nostrand-a	28	56	84	162	261	360
13-Special S/F issue	38	76	114	226	363	500
14-Classic S/F-c; Check-a	53	106	159	334	567	800
15-S/F issue; c-shows face exploding	100	200	300	630	1065	1500
16-Special S/F issue; Nostrand-a	35	70	105	203	327	450

NOTE: ***Edd Cartier** a-13? **Elias** c-2, 5-16. **Kremer** a-1, 7; c-1. **Nostrand** a-8-12, 15r 16. **Palais** a-2, 3, 5-7. **Powell** a-1, 3, 5, 9-16. **Sparling** a-12, 13, 15.*

TOMB RAIDER (one-shots)
Image Comics (Top Cow Prod.)

	NM- 9.2
...: Arabian Nights (8/04, $5.99) Avery-s/Tan-a/c	6.00
... Cover Gallery 2006 (4/06, $2.99) artist galleries and series gallery; pin-ups	3.00
.../The Darkness Special 1 (2001, TopCowStore.com)-Wohl-s/Tan-a	3.00
Epiphany 1 (8/03, $4.99)-Jurgens-s/Banks-a/Haley-c; preview of Witchblade Animated	5.00
Takeover 1 (1/04, $2.99)-Benefiel-a/Daniel-c	3.00
... Vs. The Wolf-Men: Monster War 2005 (7/05, $2.99) 2nd part of Monster War x-over	3.00
.../Witchblade/Magdalena/Vampirella #1 (8/05, $2.99, B&W) three covers; Chin-a	3.00

TOMB RAIDER: JOURNEYS
Image Comics (Top Cow Prod.): Jan, 2002 - No. 12, May, 2003 ($2.50/$2.99)

	NM- 9.2
1-12: 1-Avery-s/Drew Johnson-a. 1-Two covers by Johnson & Hughes	3.00

TOMB RAIDER: THE GREATEST TREASURE OF ALL
Image Comics (Top Cow Prod.): 2002; Oct, 2005 ($6.99)

	NM- 9.2
Prelude (2002, 16 pgs., no cover price) Jusko-c/a	3.00
1-(10/05, $6.99) Jusko-a/Jurgens-s; sketch pages, reference photos, art in progress	7.00

TOMB RAIDER: THE SERIES (Also see Witchblade/Tomb Raider)(Also see Promotional Comics section for Free Comic Book Day edition)
Image Comics (Top Cow Prod.): Dec, 1999 - No. 50, Mar, 2005 ($2.50/$2.99)

	NM- 9.2
1-Jurgens-s/Park-a; 3 covers by Park, Finch, Turner	4.00
2-24,26-29,31-50: 21-Black-c w/foil. 31-Mhan-a. 37-Flip book preview of Stryke Force	3.00
25-Michael Turner-c/a; Witchblade app.; Endgame x-over with Witchblade #60 & Evo #1	3.00
30-($4.99) Tony Daniel-a	5.00
#0 (6/01, $2.50) Avery-s/Ching-a/c	2.50
#1/2 (10/01, $2.95) Early days of Lara Croft; Jurgens-s/Lopez-a	3.00
...: Chasing Shangri-La (2002, $12.95, TPB) r/#11-15	13.00
... Gallery (12/00, $2.95) Pin-ups & previous covers by various	3.00
... Magazine (6/01, $4.95) Hughes-c; r/#1,2; Jurgens interview	5.00
...: Mystic Artifacts (2001, $14.95, TPB) r/#5-10	15.00
...: Saga of the Medusa Mask (9/00, $9.95, TPB) r/#1-4; new Park-c	10.00
... Vol. 1 Compendium (11/06, $59.99) r/#1-50; variant covers and pin-up art	60.00

TOMB RAIDER/WITCHBLADE SPECIAL (Also see Witchblade/Tomb Raider)
Top Cow Prod.: Dec, 1997 (mail-in offer, one-shot)

	GD 2.0	VG 4.0	FN 6.0	VF 8.0	VF/NM 9.0	NM- 9.2
1-Turner-s/a(p); green background cover	1	3	4	6	8	10
1-Variant-c with orange sun background	1	3	4	6	8	10
1-Variant-c with black sides	1	3	4	6	8	10
1-Revisited (12/98, $2.95) reprints #1, Turner-c						3.00
...: Trouble Seekers TPB (2002, $7.95) rep. T.R./W & W/T.R. & W/T.R. 1/2; new Turner-c						8.00

TOMBSTONE TERRITORY
Dell Publishing Co.: No. 1123, Aug, 1960

	GD 2.0	VG 4.0	FN 6.0	VF 8.0	VF/NM 9.0	NM- 9.2
Four Color 1123	8	16	24	56	93	130

TOM CAT (Formerly Bo; Atom The Cat #9 on)
Charlton Comics: No. 4, Apr, 1956 - No. 8, July, 1957

	GD 2.0	VG 4.0	FN 6.0	VF 8.0	VF/NM 9.0	NM- 9.2
4-Al Fago-c/a	8	16	24	44	57	70
5-8	6	12	18	31	38	45

TOM CORBETT, SPACE CADET (TV)
Dell Publishing Co.: No. 378, Jan-Feb, 1952 - No. 11, Sept-Nov, 1954 (All painted covers)

	GD 2.0	VG 4.0	FN 6.0	VF 8.0	VF/NM 9.0	NM- 9.2
Four Color 378 (#1)-McWilliams-a	16	32	48	114	212	310
Four Color 400,421-McWilliams-a	10	20	30	68	119	170
4(11-1/53) - 11	8	16	24	54	90	125

TOM CORBETT SPACE CADET (See March of Comics #102)

TOM CORBETT SPACE CADET (TV)
Prize Publications: V2#1, May-June, 1955 - V2#3, Sept-Oct, 1955

	GD 2.0	VG 4.0	FN 6.0	VF 8.0	VF/NM 9.0	NM- 9.2
V2#1-Robot-c	32	64	96	186	298	410
2,3-Meskin-c	24	48	72	140	225	310

TOM, DICK & HARRIET (See Gold Key Spotlight)

TOM LANDRY AND THE DALLAS COWBOYS
Spire Christian Comics/Fleming H. Revell Co.: 1973 (35/49¢)

	GD 2.0	VG 4.0	FN 6.0	VF 8.0	VF/NM 9.0	NM- 9.2
nn-35¢ edition	2	4	6	13	18	22
nn-49¢ edition	2	4	6	9	12	15

TOM MIX WESTERN (Movie, radio star) (Also see The Comics, Crackajack Funnies, Master Comics, 100 Pages Of Comics, Popular Comics, Real Western Hero, Six Gun Heroes, Western Hero & XMas Comics)
Fawcett Publications: Jan, 1948 - No. 61, May, 1953 (1-17: 52 pgs.)

	GD 2.0	VG 4.0	FN 6.0	VF 8.0	VF/NM 9.0	NM- 9.2
1 (Photo-c, 52 pgs.)-Tom Mix & his horse Tony begin; Tumbleweed Jr. begins, ends #52,54,55	76	152	228	475	788	1100
2 (Photo-c)	37	74	111	213	337	460
3-5 (Painted/photo-c): 5-Billy the Kid & Oscar app.	26	52	78	152	239	325
6-8: 6,7 (Painted/photo-c). 8-Kinstler tempera-c	22	44	66	128	202	275
9,10 (Paint/photo-c) 9-Used in **SOTI**, pgs. 323-325	21	42	63	124	195	265
11-Kinstler oil-c	18	36	54	105	165	225
12 (Painted/photo-c)	16	32	48	94	147	200
13-17 (Painted-c, 52 pgs.)	16	32	48	94	147	200
18,22 (Painted-c, 36 pgs.)	15	30	45	84	127	170
19 (Photo-c, 52 pgs.)	15	30	45	86	133	180
20,21,23 (Painted-c, 52 pgs.)	15	30	45	84	127	170
24,25,27-29 (52 pgs.): 24-Photo-c begin, end #61. 29-Slim Pickens app.	14	28	42	78	112	145
26,30 (36 pgs.)	13	26	39	74	105	135
31-33,35-37,39,40,42 (52 pgs.): 39-Red Eagle app.	13	26	39	72	101	130
34,38 (36 pgs. begin)	12	24	36	67	94	120
41,43-60: 57-(9/52)-Dope smuggling story	9	18	27	52	69	85
61-Last issue	11	22	33	60	83	105

NOTE: *Photo-c from 1930s Tom Mix movies (he died in 1940). Many issues contain ads for Tom Mix, Rocky Lane, Space Patrol and other premiums. Captain Tootsie by **C.C. Beck** in #6-11, 20.*

TOM MIX WESTERN

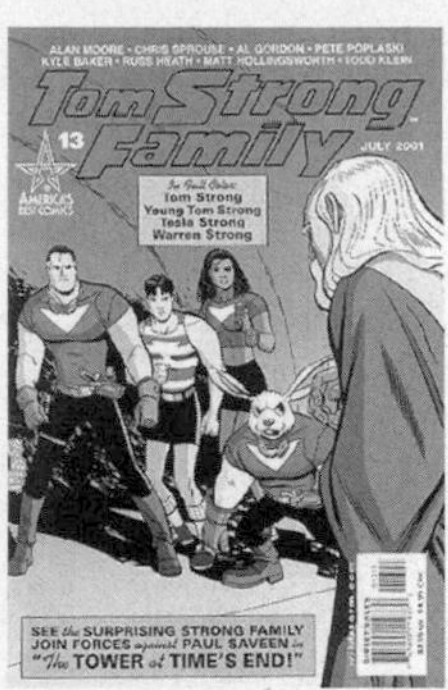

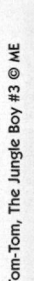

Tom Strong #13 © ABC

Tom-Tom, The Jungle Boy #3 © ME

Too Much Coffee Man #5 © Wheeler

GD 2.0 | VG 4.0 | FN 6.0 | VF 8.0 | VF/NM 9.0 | NM- 9.2

AC Comics: 1988 - No. 2, 1989? ($2.95, B&W w/16 pgs. color, 44 pgs.)
1-Tom Mix-r/Master #124,128,131,102 plus Billy the Kid-r by Severin; photo front/back/inside-c 3.50
2-($2.50, B&W)-Gabby Hayes-r; photo covers 3.00
...Holiday Album 1 (1990, $3.50, B&W, one-shot, 44 pgs.)-Contains photos & 1950s Tom Mix-r; photo inside-c 4.00

TOMMY OF THE BIG TOP (Thrilling Circus Adventures)
King Features Synd./Standard Comics: No. 10, Sep, 1948 - No. 12, Mar, 1949
10-By John Lehti 9 18 27 50 65 80
11,12 6 12 18 31 38 45

TOMMYSAURUS REX
Image Comics: Aug, 2004 ($11.95, B&W, graphic novel)
Vol. 1 - Doug TenNapel-s/a 12.00

TOMMY TOMORROW (See Action Comics #127, Real Fact #6, Showcase #41,42,44,46,47 & World's Finest #102)

TOMOE (Also see Shi: The Way Of the Warrior #6)
Crusade Comics: July, 1995 - No. 3, June, 1996($2.95)
0-3: 2-B&W Dogs o' War preview. 3-B&W Demon Gun preview 3.00
0 (3/96, $2.95)-variant-c. 3.00
0-Commemorative edition (5,000) 2 4 6 8 10 12
1-Commemorative edition (5,000) 2 4 6 9 12 15
1-($2.95)-FAN Appreciation edition 3.00
TPB (1997, $14.95) r/#0-3 15.00

TOMOE: UNFORGETTABLE FIRE
Crusade Comics: June, 1997 ($2.95, one-shot)
1-Prequel to Shi: The Series 3.00

TOMOE-WITCHBLADE/FIRE SERMON
Crusade Comics: Sept, 1996 ($3.95, one-shot)
1-Tucci-c 5.00
1-($9.95)-Avalon Ed. w/gold foil-c 10.00

TOMOE-WITCHBLADE/MANGA SHI PREVIEW EDITION
Crusade Comics: July, 1996 ($5.00, B&W)
nn-San Diego Preview Edition 5.00

TOMORROW KNIGHTS
Marvel Comics (Epic Comics): June, 1990 - No. 6, Mar, 1991 ($1.50)
1-6: 1-($1.95, 52 pgs.) 2.50

TOMORROW STORIES
America's Best Comics: Oct, 1999 - No. 12, Aug, 2002 ($3.50/$2.95)
1-Two covers by Ross and Nowlan; Moore-s 3.50
2-12-($2.95) 3.00
... Special (1/06, $6.99) Nowlan-c; Moore-s; Greyshirt tribute to Will Eisner 7.00
... Special 2 (5/06, $6.99) Gene Ha-c; Moore-s; Promethea app. 7.00
Book 1 Hardcover (2002, $24.95) r/#1-6 25.00
Book 1 TPB (2003, $17.95) r/#1-6 18.00
Book 2 Hardcover (2004, $24.95) r/#7-12 25.00
Book 2 TPB (2005, $17.99) r/#7-12 18.00

TOM SAWYER (See Adventures of... & Famous Stories)

TOM SKINNER-UP FROM HARLEM (See Up From Harlem)

TOM STRONG (Also see Many Worlds of Tesla Strong)
America's Best Comics: June, 1999 - No. 36, May, 2006 ($3.50/$2.95/$2.99)
1-Two covers by Ross and Sprouse; Moore-s/Sprouse-a 4.00
2-36: 4-Art Adams-a (8 pgs.) 13-Fawcett homage w/art by Sprouse, Baker, Heath 20-Origin of Tom Stone. 22-Ordway-a. 31,32-Moorcock-s 3.00
...: Book One HC ('00, $24.95) r/#1-7, cover gallery and sketchbook 25.00
...: Book One TPB ('01, $14.95) r/#1-7, cover gallery and sketchbook 15.00
...: Book Two HC ('02, $24.95) r/#8-14, sketchbook 25.00
...: Book Two TPB ('03, $14.95) r/#8-14, sketchbook 15.00
...: Book Three HC ('04, $24.95) r/#15-19, sketchbook 25.00
...: Book Three TPB ('04, $17.95) r/#15-19, sketchbook 18.00
...: Book Four HC ('04, $24.95) r/#20-25, sketch pages 25.00
...: Book Four TPB ('05, $17.99) r/#20-25, sketch pages 18.00
...: Book Five HC ('05, $24.99) r/#26-30, sketch pages 25.00
...: Book Five TPB ('06, $17.99) r/#26-30, sketch pages 18.00
...: Book Six HC ('06, $24.99) r/#31-36 25.00
...: Book Six TPB ('08, $17.99) r/#31-36 18.00

TOM STRONG'S TERRIFIC TALES
America's Best Comics: Jan, 2002 - No. 12 ($3.50/$2.95)
1-Short stories; Moore-s; art by Adams, Rivoche, Hernandez, Weiss 3.50
2-12-($2.95) 2-Adams, Ordway, Weiss-a; Adams-c. 4-Rivoche-a. 5-Pearson, Aragonés-a 11-Timm-a 3.00
...: Book One HC ('04, $24.95) r/#1-6, cover gallery and sketch pages 25.00
...: Book One SC ('05, $17.99) r/#1-6, cover gallery and sketch pages 18.00
...: Book Two HC ('05, $24.95) r/#7-12, covers 25.00

TOM TERRIFIC! (TV)(See Mighty Mouse Fun Club Magazine #1)
Pines Comics (Paul Terry): Summer, 1957 - No. 6, Fall, 1958
(See Terry Toons Giant Summer Fun Book)
1-1st app.?; CBS Television Presents... 23 46 69 130 205 280
2-6-(scarce) 10 [illegible] 48 92 144 195

TOM THUMB
Dell Publishing Co.: No. 972, Jan, 1959
Four Color 972-Movie, George Pal 8 16 24 58 97 135

TOM-TOM, THE JUNGLE BOY (See A-1 Comics & Tick Tock Tales)
Magazine Enterprises: 1947 - No. 3, 1947; Nov, 1957 - No. 3, Mar, 1958
1-Funny animal 11 22 33 64 90 115
2,3(1947): 3-Christmas issue 9 18 27 47 61 75
Tom-Tom & Itchi the Monk 1(11/57) - 3(3/58) 5 10 15 24 30 35
I.W. Reprint No. 1,2,8,10: 1,2,8-r/Koko & Kola #? 2 4 6 8 10 12

TONGUE LASH
Dark Horse Comics: Aug, 1996 - No. 2, Sept, 1996 ($2.95, lim. series, mature)
1,2: Taylor-c/a 3.00

TONGUE LASH II
Dark Horse Comics: Feb, 1999 - No. 2, Mar, 1999 ($2.95, lim. series, mature)
1,2: Taylor-c/a 3.00

TONKA (Disney)
Dell Publishing Co.: No. 966, Jan, 1959
Four Color 966-Movie (Starring Sal Mineo)-photo-c 8 16 24 58 97 135

TONTO (See The Lone Ranger's Companion...)

TONY TRENT (The Face #1,2)
Big Shot/Columbia Comics Group: No. 3, 1948 - No. 4, 1949
3,4: 3-The Face app. by Mart Bailey 18 36 54 105 165 225

TOODLES, THE (The Toodle Twins with #1)
Ziff-Davis (Approved Comics)/Argo: No. 10, July-Aug, 1951; Mar, 1956 (Newspaper-r)
10-Painted-c, some newspaper-r by The Baers 12 24 36 67 94 120
...Twins 1(Argo, 3/56)-Reprints by The Baers 8 16 24 42 54 65

TOO MUCH COFFEE MAN
Adhesive Comics: July, 1993 - No. 10, Dec, 2000 ($2.50, B&W)
1-Shannon Wheeler story & art 2 4 6 9 12 15
2,3 1 2 3 5 7 9
4,5 6.00
6-10 3.00
Full Color Special-nn($2.95),2-(7/97, $3.95) 4.00

TOO MUCH COFFEE MAN SPECIAL
Dark Horse Comics: July, 1997 ($2.95, B&W)
nn-Reprints Dark Horse Presents #92-95 3.00

TOO MUCH HOPELESS SAVAGES
Oni Press: June, 2003 - No. 4, Apr, 2004 ($2.99, B&W, limited series)
1-4-Van Meter-s/Norrie-a 3.00
TPB (8/04, $11.95, digest-size) r/series 12.00

TOOTS & CASPER
Dell Publishing Co.: No. 5, 1942
Large Feature Comic 5 20 40 60 115 183 250

TOP ADVENTURE COMICS
I. W. Enterprises: 1964 (Reprints)
1-r/High Adv. (Explorer Joe #2); Krigstein-r 2 4 6 11 16 20
2-Black Dwarf-r/Red Seal #22; Kinstler-c 2 4 6 13 18 22

TOP CAT (TV) (Hanna-Barbera)(See Kite Fun Book)
Dell Publishing Co./Gold Key No. 4 on: 12-2/61-62 - No. 3, 6-8/62; No. 4, 10/62 - No. 31, 9/70
1 (TV show debuted 9/27/61) 14 28 42 100 178 255
2-Augie Doggie back-ups in #1-4 8 16 24 54 90 125
3-5: 3-Last 15¢ issue. 4-Begin 12¢ issues; Yakky Doodle app. in 1 pg. strip. 5-Touché Turtle app. 6 12 18 43 69 95

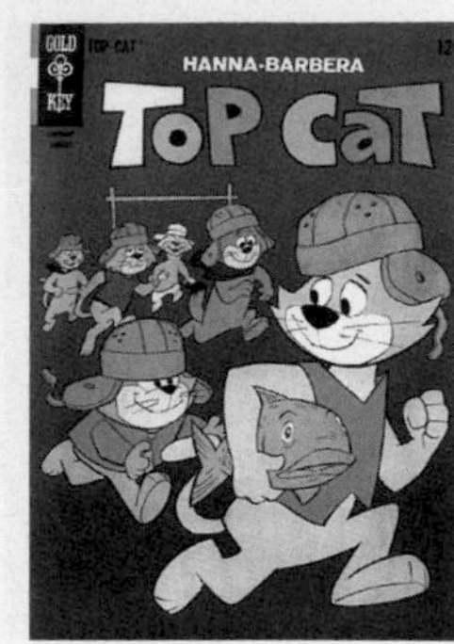

Top Cat #17 © H-B

Topix V5 #1 © CG

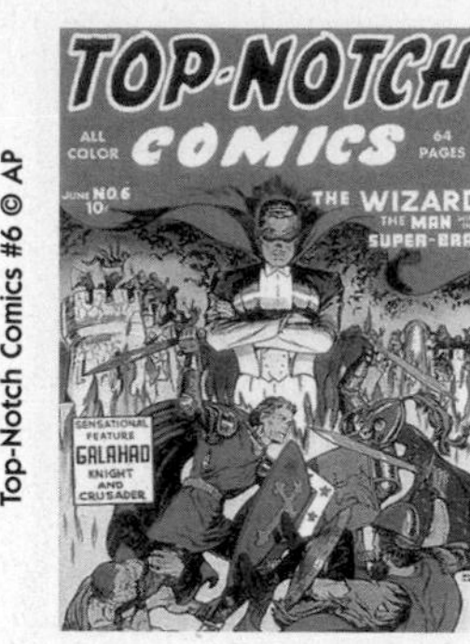

Top-Notch Comics #6 © AP

	GD 2.0	VG 4.0	FN 6.0	VF 8.0	VF/NM 9.0	NM- 9.2
6-10	5	10	15	32	51	70
11-20	4	8	12	24	37	50
21-31-Reprints	3	6	9	19	29	38

TOP CAT (TV) (Hanna-Barbera)(See TV Stars #4)
Charlton Comics: Nov, 1970 - No. 20, Nov, 1973

	GD	VG	FN	VF	VF/NM	NM-
1	6	12	18	37	59	80
2-10	3	6	9	20	30	40
11-20	3	6	9	17	25	32

NOTE: *#8 (1/72) went on sale late in 1972 between #14 and #15 with the 1/73 issues.*

TOP COMICS
K. K. Publications/Gold Key: July, 1967 (All reprints)

	GD	VG	FN	VF	VF/NM	NM-
nn-The Gnome-Mobile (Disney-movie)	2	4	6	13	18	22
1-Beagle Boys (#7), Beep Beep the Road Runner (#5), Bugs Bunny, Chip 'n' Dale, Daffy Duck (#50), Flipper, Huey, Dewey & Louie, Junior Woodchucks, Lassie, The Little Monsters (#71), Moby Duck, Porky Pig (has Gold Key label - says Top Comics on inside), Scamp, Super Goof, Tom & Jerry, Top Cat (#21), Tweety & Sylvester (#7), Walt Disney C&S (#322), Woody Woodpecker known issues; each character given own book	2	4	6	9	13	16
1-Donald Duck (not Barks), Mickey Mouse	2	4	6	13	18	22
1-Flintstones	4	8	12	22	34	45
1-Huckleberry Hound, Yogi Bear (#30)	3	6	9	14	19	24
1-The Jetsons	5	10	15	30	48	65
1-Tarzan of the Apes (#169)	3	6	9	16	22	28
1-Three Stooges (#35)	3	6	9	18	27	35
1-Uncle Scrooge (#70)	3	6	9	16	23	30
1-Zorro (r/G.K. Zorro #7 w/Toth-a; says 2nd printing)	3	6	9	14	19	24
2-Bugs Bunny, Daffy Duck, Mickey Mouse (#114), Porky Pig, Super Goof, Tom & Jerry, Tweety & Sylvester, Walt Disney's C&S (r/#325), Woody Woodpecker	2	4	6	9	12	15
2-Donald Duck (not Barks), Three Stooges, Uncle Scrooge (#71)-Barks-c, Yogi Bear (#30), Zorro (r/#8; Toth-a)	2	4	6	11	16	20
2-Snow White & 7 Dwarfs(6/67)(1944-r)	2	4	6	10	14	18
3-Donald Duck	2	4	6	11	16	20
3-Uncle Scrooge (#72)	2	4	6	13	18	22
3,4-The Flintstones	4	8	12	22	34	45
3,4: 3-Mickey Mouse (r/#115), Tom & Jerry, Woody Woodpecker, Yogi Bear. 4-Mickey Mouse, Woody Woodpecker	2	4	6	9	12	15

NOTE: *Each book in this series is identical to its counterpart except for cover, and came out at same time. The number in parentheses is the original issue it contains.*

TOP COW (Company one-shots)
Image Comics (Top Cow Productions)

	NM-
... Book of Revelations (7/03, $3.99)-Pin-ups and info; art by various; Gossett-c	4.00
... Convention Sketchbook 2004 (4/04, $3.00, B&W) art by various	3.00
... Preview Book 2005 (3/05, 99¢) Preview pages of Tomb Raider, Darkness, Rising Stars	2.50
... Productions, Inc./Ballistic Studios Swimsuit Special (5/95, $2.95)	3.00
...'s Best of: Dave Finch Vol. 1 TPB (8/06, $19.99) r/issues of Cybrforce, Aphrodite IX, Ascension and The Darkness; art & cover gallery	20.00
...'s Best of: Michael Turner Vol. 1 TPB (12/05, $24.99) r/Witchblade #1,10,12,18,19,25 & Witchblade/Tomb Raider chapters 1&3; Tomb Raider #25; art & cover gallery	25.00
... Secrets: Special Winter Lingerie Edition 1 (1/96, $2.95) Pin-ups	3.00
... 2001 Preview (no cover price) Preview pages of Tomb Raider; Jusko-a; flip cover & pages of Inferno	2.50

TOP COW CLASSICS IN BLACK AND WHITE
Image Comics (Top Cow): Feb, 2000 - Present ($2.95, B&W reprints)

	NM-
...: Aphrodite IX #1(9/00) B&W reprint	3.00
...: Ascension #1(4/00) B&W reprint plus time-line of series	3.00
...: Battle of the Planets #1(1/03) B&W reprint plus script and cover gallery	3.00
...: Darkness #1(3/00) B&W reprint plus time-line of series	3.00
...: Fathom #1(5/00) B&W reprint	3.00
...: Magdalena #1(10/02) B&W reprint plus time-line of series	3.00
...: Midnight Nation #1(9/00) B&W preview	3.00
...: Rising Stars #1(7/00) B&W reprint plus cover gallery	3.00
...: Tomb Raider #1(12/00) B&W reprint plus back-story	3.00
...: Witchblade #1(2/00) B&W reprint plus back-story	3.00
...: Witchblade #25(5/01) B&W reprint plus interview with Wohl & Haberlin	3.00

TOP DETECTIVE COMICS
I. W. Enterprises: 1964 (Reprints)

	GD	VG	FN	VF	VF/NM	NM-
9-r/Young King Cole #14; Dr. Drew (not Grandenetti)	2	4	6	10	14	18

TOP DOG (See Star Comics Magazine, 75¢)
Star Comics (Marvel): Apr, 1985 - No. 14, June, 1987 (Children's book)

	NM-
1-14: 10-Peter Parker & J. Jonah Jameson cameo	4.00

TOP ELIMINATOR (Teenage Hotrodders #1-24; Drag 'n' Wheels #30 on)
Charlton Comics: No. 25, Sept, 1967 - No. 29, July, 1968

	GD	VG	FN	VF	VF/NM	NM-
25-29	3	6	9	16	22	28

TOP FLIGHT COMICS: Four Star Publ.: 1947 (Advertised, not published)

TOP FLIGHT COMICS
St. John Publishing Co.: July, 1949

	GD	VG	FN	VF	VF/NM	NM-
1(7/49, St. John)-Hector the Inspector; funny animal	9	18	27	52	69	85

TOP GUN (See Luke Short, 4-Color #927 & Showcase #72)

TOP GUNS OF THE WEST (See Super DC Giant)

TOPIX (...Comics) (Timeless Topix-early issues) (Also see Men of Battle, Men of Courage & Treasure Chest)(V1-V5#1,V7 on-paper-c)
Catechetical Guild Educational Society: 11/42 - V10#15, 1/28/52 (Weekly - later issues)

	GD	VG	FN	VF	VF/NM	NM-
V1#1(8 pgs.,8x11")	24	48	72	140	225	310
2,3(8 pgs.,8x11")	14	28	42	80	115	150
4-8(16 pgs.,8x11")	11	22	33	64	90	115
V2#1-10(16 pgs.,8x11"): V2#8-Pope Pius XII	10	20	30	56	76	95
V3#1-10(16 pgs.,8x11"): V3#1-(9/44)	10	20	30	54	72	90
V4#1-10: V4#1-(9/45)	9	18	27	47	61	75
V5#1(10/46,52 pgs.,2(11/46),no #3),4(1/47)-9(6/47),10(7/47), no #13,4(10/47), 14(11/47),15(12/47)	8	16	24	40	50	60
11(8/47),12(9/47)-Life of Christ editions	10	20	30	54	72	90
V6#4(1/48),5(2/48),7(3/48),8(4/48),9(5/48),10(6/48),11(7/48)-14 (no #1-3,6)	7	14	21	35	43	50
V7#1(9/1/48)-20(6/15/49), 36 pgs.	6	12	18	29	36	42
V8#1(9/19/49)-3,5-11,13-30(5/15/50)	6	12	18	28	34	40
4-Dagwood Splits the Atom(10/10/49)-Magazine format	8	16	24	42	54	65
12-Ingels-a	10	20	30	54	72	90
V9#1(9/25/50)-11,13-30(5/14/51)	6	12	18	27	33	38
12-Special 36 pg. Xmas issue, text illos format	6	12	18	28	34	40
V10#1(10/1/51)-15: 14-Hollingsworth-a	6	12	18	27	33	38

TOP JUNGLE COMICS
I. W. Enterprises: 1964 (Reprint)

	GD	VG	FN	VF	VF/NM	NM-
1(nd)-Reprints White Princess of the Jungle #3, minus cover; Kintsler-a	3	6	9	16	23	30

TOP LOVE STORIES (Formerly Gasoline Alley #2)
Star Publications: No. 3, 5/51 - No. 19, 3/54

	GD	VG	FN	VF	VF/NM	NM-
3(#1)	23	46	69	132	209	285
4,5,7-9: 8-Wood story	18	36	54	105	165	225
6-Wood-a	24	48	72	139	220	300
10-16,18,19-Disbrow-a	18	36	54	105	165	225
17-Wood art (Fox-r)	19	38	57	112	176	240

NOTE: *All have* ***L. B. Cole*** *covers.*

TOP-NOTCH COMICS (...Laugh #28-45; Laugh Comix #46 on)
MLJ Magazines: Dec, 1939 - No. 45, June, 1944

	GD	VG	FN	VF	VF/NM	NM-
1-Origin/1st app. The Wizard; Kardak the Mystic Magician, Swift of the Secret Service (ends #3), Air Patrol, The Westpointer, Manhunters (by J. Cole), Mystic (ends #2) & Scott Rand (ends #3) begin; Wizard covers begin, end #8	572	1144	1716	4118	7209	10,300
2-(1/40)-Dick Storm (ends #8), Stacy Knight M.D. (ends #4) begin; Jack Cole-a; 1st app. Nazis swastika on-c	242	484	726	1524	2575	3625
3-Bob Phantom, Scott Rand on Mars begin; J. Cole-a	170	340	510	1071	1811	2550
4-Origin/1st app. Streak Chandler on Mars; Moore of the Mounted only app.; J. Cole-a	150	300	450	945	1598	2250
5-Flag-c; origin/1st app. Galahad; Shanghai Sheridan begins (ends #8); Shield cameo; Novick-a; classic-c	167	334	501	1052	1776	2500
6-Meskin-a	110	220	330	693	1172	1650
7-The Shield x-over in Wizard; The Wizard dons new costume	140	280	420	882	1491	2100
8-Origin/1st app. The Firefly & Roy, the Super Boy (9/40, 2nd costumed boy hero after Robin?; also see Toro in Human Torch #1 (Fall/40)	153	306	459	964	1632	2300
9-Origin & 1st app. The Black Hood; 1st Black Hood-c & logo (10/40); Fran Frazier begins (Scarce)	611	1222	1833	4399	7700	11,000
10-2nd app. Black Hood	200	400	600	1260	2130	3000
11-3rd Black Hood	133	266	399	838	1419	2000
12-15	110	220	330	693	1172	1650
16-18,20	95	190	285	599	1012	1425

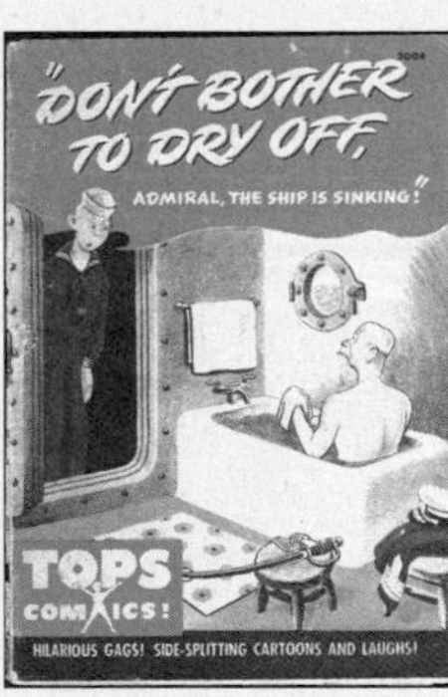

Tops Comics 2004 © LEV

Tor #1 © Tell-A-Graphics Inc.

Torchy #1 © QUA

GD VG FN VF VF/NM NM-
2.0 4.0 6.0 8.0 9.0 9.2

19-Classic bondage-c 103 206 309 649 1100 1550
21-30: 23-26-Roy app. 24-No Wizard. 25-Last Bob Phantom. 27-Last Firefly. 28-Suzie, Pokey Oakey begin. 29-Last Kardak 67 134 201 422 711 1000
31-44: 33-Dotty & Ditto by Woggon begins (2/43, 1st app.). 44-Black Hood series ends 41 82 123 256 428 600
45-Last issue 46 92 138 285 473 660

NOTE: ***J. Binder** a-1-3. **Meskin** a-2, 3, 6, 15. **Bob Montana** a-30; c-28-31. **Harry Sahle** c-42-45. **Woggon** a-33-40, 42. Bondage c-17, 19. Black Hood also appeared on radio in 1944.Black Hood app. on c-9-34, 41-44. Roy the Super Boy app. on c-8, 9, 11-27. The Wizard app. on c-1-8, 11-13, 15-22, 24, 25, 27. Pokey Oakey app. on c-28-43. Suzie app. on c-44-on.*

TOPPER & NEIL (TV)
Dell Publishing Co.: No. 859, Nov, 1957
Four Color 859 5 10 15 30 48 65

TOPPS COMICS: Four Star Publications: 1947 (Advertised, not published)

TOPS
July, 1949 - No. 2, Sept, 1949 (25¢, 10-1/4x13-1/4", 68 pgs.)
Tops Magazine, Inc. (Lev Gleason): (Large size-magazine format; for the adult reader)
1 (Rare)-Story by Dashiell Hammett; Crandall/Lubbers, Tuska, Dan Barry, Fuje-a; Biro painted-c 127 254 381 800 1350 1900
2 (Rare)-Crandall/Lubbers, Biro, Kida, Fuje, Guardineer-a 120 240 360 756 1278 1800

TOPS COMICS
Consolidated Book Publishers: 1944 (10¢, 132 pgs.)
2000-(Color-c, inside in red shade & some in full color)-Ace Kelly by Rick Yager, Black Orchid, Don on the Farm, Dinky Dinkerton (Rare) 26 52 78 152 244 335

NOTE: *This book is printed in such a way that when the staple is removed, the strips on the left side of the book correspond with the same strips on the right side. Therefore, if strips are removed from the book, each strip can be folded into a complete comic section of its own.*

TOPS COMICS (See Tops In Humor)
Consolidated Book (Lev Gleason): 1944 (7-1/4x5", 32 pgs.)
2001-The Jack of Spades (costumed hero) 16 32 48 92 144 195
2002-Rip Raider 10 20 30 56 76 95
2003-Red Birch (gag cartoons) 5 10 15 22 26 30
2004-Gag cartoons 16 32 48 92 144 195

TOP SECRET
Hillman Publ.: Jan, 1952
1 20 40 60 115 183 250

TOP SECRET ADVENTURES (See Spyman)

TOP SECRETS (...of the F.B.I.)
Street & Smith Publications: Nov, 1947 - No. 10, July-Aug, 1949
1-Powell-c/a 35 70 105 203 327 450
2-Powell-c/a 25 50 75 145 233 320
3-6,8,10-Powell-a 22 44 66 129 207 285
9-Powell-c/a 23 46 69 133 214 295
7-Used in **SOTI**, pg. 90 & illo. "How to hurt people"; used by N.Y. Legis. Comm.; Powell-c/a 34 68 102 198 319 440

NOTE: ***Powell** c-1-3, 5-10.*

TOPS IN ADVENTURE
Ziff-Davis Publishing Co.: Fall, 1952 (25¢, 132 pgs.)
1-Crusader from Mars, The Hawk, Football Thrills, He-Man; Powell-a; painted-c 47 94 141 291 483 675

TOPS IN HUMOR (See Tops Comics?)
Consolidated Book Publ. (Lev Gleason): 1944 (7-1/4x5")
2001(#1)-Origin The Jack of Spades, Ace Kelly by Rick Yager, Black Orchid (female crime fighter) app. 16 32 48 92 144 195
2 11 22 33 64 90 115

TOP SPOT COMICS
Top Spot Publ. Co.: 1945
1-The Menace, Duke of Darkness app. 35 70 105 203 327 450

TOPSY-TURVY (Teenage)
R. B. Leffingwell Publ.: Apr, 1945
1-1st app. Cookie 14 28 42 76 108 140

TOP TEN
America's Best Comics: Sept, 1999 - No. 12, Oct, 2001 ($3.50/$2.95)
1-Two covers by Ross and Ha/Cannon; Alan Moore-s/Gene Ha-a 3.50
2-11-($2.95) 3.00
12-($3.50) 3.50
Hardcover ('00, $24.95) Dust jacket with Gene Ha-a; r/#1-7 25.00
Softcover ('00, $14.95) new Gene Ha-c; r/#1-7 15.00
Book 2 HC ('02, $24.95) Dust jacket with Gene Ha-a; r/#8-12 25.00
Book 2 SC ('03, $14.95) new Gene Ha-c; r/#8-12 15.00
...: The Forty-Niners HC (2005, $24.99, dust jacket) prequel set in 1949; Moore-s/Ha-a 25.00

TOP TEN: BEYOND THE FARTHEST PRECINCT
America's Best Comics: Oct, 2005 - No. 5, Feb, 2006 ($2.99, limited series)
1-5-Jerry Ordway-a/Paul DiFilippo-s 3.00
TPB (2006, $14.99) r/series; cover sketch pages 15.00

TOR (Prehistoric Life on Earth) (Formerly One Million Years Ago)
St. John Publ. Co.: No. 2, Oct, 1953; No. 3, May, 1954 - No. 5, Oct, 1954
3-D 2(10/53)-Kubert-c/a 14 28 42 76 108 140
3-D 2(10/53)-Oversized, otherwise same contents 12 24 36 67 94 120
3-D 2(11/53)-Kubert-c/a; has 3-D cover 12 24 36 67 94 120
3-5-Kubert-c/a: 3-Danny Dreams by Toth; Kubert 1 pg. story (w/self portrait) 14 28 42 76 108 140

NOTE: *The two October 3-D's have same contents and **Powell** art; the October & November issues are titled 3-D Comics. All 3-D issues are 25¢ and came with 3-D glasses.*

TOR (See Sojourn)
National Periodical Publications: May-June, 1975 - No. 6, Mar-Apr, 1976
1-New origin by Kubert 2 4 6 8 10 12
2-6: 2-Origin-r/St. John #1 6.00

NOTE: ***Kubert** a-1, 2-6r; c-1-6. **Toth** a(p)-3r.*

TOR (3-D)
Eclipse Comics: July, 1986 - No. 2, Aug, 1987 ($2.50)
1,2: 1-r/One Million Years Ago. 2-r/Tor 3-D #2 5.00
...2-D: 1,2-Limited signed & numbered editions 1 2 3 4 5 7

TOR
Marvel Comics (Epic Comics/Heavy Hitters): June, 1993 - No. 4, 1993 ($5.95, limited series)
1-4: Joe Kubert-c/a/scripts 6.00

TOR (Joe Kubert's...)
DC Comics: Jul, 2008 - No. 6 ($2.99, limited series)
1-4-New story; Joe Kubert-c/a/scripts 3.00

TOR BY JOE KUBERT
DC Comics: 2001 - 2003 ($49.95, hardcovers with dust jacket)
Volume 1 (2001) r/One Million Years Ago #1 & 3-D Comics #1&2 in flat color; script pages, sketch pages, proposals for TV and newspapers strips; intro. by Roy Thomas 50.00
Volume 2 (2002) r/Tor (St. John) #3-5; Danny Dreams; portfolio section 50.00
Volume 3 (2003) r/Tor (DC '75) #1; (Marvel '93) #1-4; portfolio section 50.00

TORCH OF LIBERTY SPECIAL
Dark Horse Comics (Legend): Jan, 1995 ($2.50, one-shot)
1-Byrne scripts 2.50

TORCHY (...Blonde Bombshell) (See Dollman, Military, & Modern)
Quality Comics Group: Nov, 1949 - No. 6, Sept, 1950
1-Bill Ward-c, Gil Fox-a 160 320 480 1008 1704 2400
2,3-Fox-c/a 68 136 204 428 727 1025
4-Fox-c/a(3), Ward-a (9 pgs.) 85 170 255 536 906 1275
5,6-Ward-c/a, 9 pgs; Fox-a(3) each 100 200 300 630 1065 1500
Super Reprint #16(1964)-r/#4 with new-c 10 20 30 60 93 125

TO RIVERDALE AND BACK AGAIN (Archie Comics Presents...)
Archie Comics: 1990 ($2.50, 68 pgs.)
nn-Byrne-c, Colan-a(p); adapts NBC TV movie 5.00

TORMENTED, THE (Becomes Surprise Adventures #3 on)
Sterling Comics: July, 1954 - No. 2, Sept, 1954
1,2: Weird/horror stories 26 52 78 152 244 335

TORNADO TOM (See Mighty Midget Comics)

TORSO (See Jinx: Torso)

TOTAL ECLIPSE
Eclipse Comics: May, 1988 - No. 5, Apr, 1989 ($3.95, 52 pgs., deluxe size)
Book 1-5: 3-Intro/1st app. new Black Terror. 4-Many copies have upside down pages and are mis-cut 4.00

TOTAL ECLIPSE
Image Comics: July, 1998 (one-shot)
1-McFarlane-c; Eclipse Comics character pin-ups by Image artists 2.50

TOTAL ECLIPSE: THE SERAPHIM OBJECTIVE

Totems #1 © DC

Tower of Shadows #6 © MAR

Transformers #80 © Hasbro

	GD 2.0	VG 4.0	FN 6.0	VF 8.0	VF/NM 9.0	NM- 9.2

Eclipse Comics: Nov, 1988 ($1.95, one-shot, Baxter paper)
1-Airboy, Valkyrie, The Heap app. 3.00

TOTAL JUSTICE
DC Comics: Oct, 1996 - No. 3, Nov, 1996 ($2.25, bi-weekly limited series) (Based on toyline)
1-3 2.50

TOTAL RECALL (Movie)
DC Comics: 1990 ($2.95, 68 pgs., movie adaptation, one-shot)
1-Arnold Schwarzenegger photo-c 3.00

TOTAL WAR (M.A.R.S. Patrol #3 on)
Gold Key: July, 1965 - No. 2, Oct, 1965 (Painted-c)
1-Wood-a in both issues 7 14 21 45 73 100
2 5 10 15 34 55 75

TOTEMS (Vertigo V2K)
DC Comics (Vertigo): Feb, 2000 ($5.95, one-shot)
1-Swamp Thing, Animal Man, Zatanna, Shade app.; Fegredo-c 6.00

TO THE HEART OF THE STORM
Kitchen Sink Press: 1991 (B&W, graphic novel)
Softcover-Will Eisner-s/a/c 15.00
Hardcover ($24.95) 25.00
TPB-(DC Comics, 9/00, $14.95) reprints 1991 edition 15.00

TO THE LAST MAN (See Zane Grey Four Color #616)

TOUCH OF SILVER, A
Image Comics: Jan, 1997 - No. 6, Nov, 1997 ($2.95, B&W, bi-monthly)
1-6-Valentino-s/a; photo-c: 5-color pgs. w/Round Table 3.00
TPB ($12.95) r/#1-6 13.00

TOUGH KID SQUAD COMICS
Timely Comics (TCI): Mar, 1942
1-(Scarce)-Origin & 1st app.The Human Top & The Tough Kid Squad; The Flying Flame app. 939 1878 2817 6761 11,831 16,900

TOWER OF SHADOWS (Creatures on the Loose #10 on)
Marvel Comics Group: Sept, 1969 - No. 9, Jan, 1971
1-Romita-c, classic Steranko-a; Craig-a(p) 8 16 24 52 86 120
2,3: 2-Neal Adams-a. 3-Barry Smith, Tuska-a 4 8 12 28 44 60
4,6: 4-Marie Severin-c. 6-Wood-a 4 8 12 24 37 50
5-B. Smith-a(p), Wood-a; Wood draws himself (1st pg., 1st panel) 4 8 12 26 41 55
7-9: 7-B. Smith-a(p), Wood-a. 8-Wood-a; Wrightson-c. 9-Wrightson-c; Roy Thomas app. 4 8 12 28 44 60
Special 1(12/71, 52 pgs.)-Neal Adams-a; Romita-c 4 8 12 24 37 50
*NOTE: **J. Buscema** a-1p, 2p, Special 1r. **Colan** a-3p, 6p, Special 1. **J. Craig** a(r)-1p. **Ditko** a-6, 8, 9r, Special 1. **Everett** a-9(i)r; c-5i. **Kirby** a-9(p)r. **Severin** c-5p, 6. **Steranko** a-1p. **Tuska** a-3. **Wood** a-5-8. Issues 1-9 contain new stories with some pre-Marvel age reprints in 6-9. **H. P. Lovecraft** adaptation-9.*

TOXIC AVENGER (Movie)
Marvel Comics: Apr, 1991 - No. 11, Feb, 1992 ($1.50)
1-11: Based on movie character. 3,10-Photo-c 2.50

TOXIC CRUSADERS (TV)
Marvel Comics: May, 1992 - No. 8, Dec, 1992 ($1.25)
1-8: 1-3,8-Sam Kieth-c; based on USA network cartoon 2.50

TOXIC GUMBO
DC Comics (Vertigo): 1998 ($5.95, one-shot, mature)
1-McKeever-a/Lydia Lunch-s 6.00

TOXIN (Son of Carnage)
Marvel Comics: June, 2005 - No. 6, Nov, 2005 ($2.99, limited series)
1-6-Milligan-s/Robertson-a; Spider-Man app. 3.00
...: The Devil You Know TPB (2006, $17.99) r/#1-6 18.00

TOYBOY
Continuity Comics: Oct, 1986 - No. 7, Mar, 1989 ($2.00, Baxter paper)
1-7 3.00
*NOTE: **N. Adams** a-1; c-1, 2,5. **Golden** a-7p; c-6,7. **Nebres** a(i)-1,2.*

TOYLAND COMICS
Fiction House Magazines: Jan, 1947 - No. 2, Mar, 1947; No. 3, July, 1947
1-Wizard of the Moon begins 30 60 90 174 280 385
2,3-Bob Lubbers-c. 3-Tuska-a 17 34 51 98 154 210
*NOTE: All above contain strips by **Al Walker.***

TOY TOWN COMICS
Toytown/Orbit Publ./B. Antin/Swapper Quarterly: 1945 - No. 7, May, 1947
1-Mertie Mouse; L. B. Cole-c/a; funny animal 40 80 120 235 380 525
2-L. B. Cole-a 23 46 69 133 214 295
3-7-L. B. Cole-a. 5-Wiggles the Wonderworm-c 20 40 60 115 183 250

TRAGG AND THE SKY GODS (See Gold Key Spotlight, Mystery Comics Digest #3,9 & Spine Tingling Tales)
Gold Key/Whitman No. 9: June, 1975 - No. 8, Feb, 1977; No. 9, May, 1982 (Painted-c #3-8)
1-Origin 2 4 6 11 16 20
2-8: 4-Sabre-Fang app. 8-Ostellon app. 2 4 6 8 10 12
9-(Whitman, 5/82) r/#1 1 2 3 5 7 9
*NOTE: **Santos** a-1, 2, 9r; c-3-7. **Spiegel** a-3-8.*

TRAIL BLAZERS (Red Dragon #5 on)
Street & Smith Publications: 1941; No. 2, Apr, 1942 - No. 4, Oct, 1942
(True stories of American heroes)
1-Life story of Jack Dempsey & Wright Brothers 35 70 105 203 327 450
2-Brooklyn Dodgers-c/story; Ben Franklin story 22 44 66 127 204 280
3,4: 3-Fred Allen, Red Barber, Yankees stories 20 40 60 115 183 250

TRAIL COLT (Also see Extra Comics, Manhunt! & Undercover Girl)
Magazine Enterprises: 1949 - No. 2, 1949
nn(A-1 #24)-7 pg. Frazetta-a r-in Manhunt #13; Undercover Girl app.; The Red Fox by L. B. Cole; Ingels-c; Whitney-a (Scarce) 40 80 120 235 380 525
2(A-1 #26)-Undercover Girl; Ingels-c; L. B. Cole-a (6 pgs.) 31 62 93 181 291 400

TRANSFORMERS, THE (TV)(See G.I. Joe and...)
Marvel Comics Group: Sept, 1984 - No. 80, July, 1991 (75¢/$1.00)
1-Based on Hasbro Toys 3 6 9 14 20 25
2-5: 2-Golden-c. 3-(1/85) Spider-Man (black costume)-c/app. 4-Texeira-c; brief app. of Dinobots 2 4 6 9 12 15
6-10: 6-1st Josie Beller. 8-Dinobots 1st full app. 9-Circuit Breaker 1st full app. 10-Intro Constructicons 1 3 4 6 8 10
11-49: 11-1st app. Jetfire. 14-Jetfire becomes an Autobot; 1st app. of Grapple, Hoist, Smokescreen, Skids, and Tracks. 17-1st app. of Blaster, Powerglide, Cosmos, Seaspray, Warpath, Beachcomber, Preceptor, Straxus, Kickback, Bombshell, Shrapnel, Dirge, and Ramjet. 19-1st Omega Supreme. 21-1st app. of Aerialbots; 1st Slingshot; Circuit Breaker app. 22-Retells origin of Circuit Breaker, 1st Stunticons. 23-Battle at Statue of Liberty. 24-1st app. Protectobots, Combaticons; Optimus Prime killed. 25-1st Predacons. 26-Intro The Mechanic, Prime's Funeral. 27-1st Trypticon app.; Grimlock named new Autobot leader. 28-The Mechanic app. 29-Intro Scraplets, 1st app. of Triple Changers 6.00
50-60: 53-Jim Lee-c. 54-Intro Micromasters. 60-Brief 1st app. of Primus 1 2 3 5 7 9
61-70: 61-Origin of Cybertron and the Transformers, Unicron app.; app. of Primus, creator of the Transformers. 62-66 Matrix Quest 5-part series. 67-Jim Lee-c 2 4 6 9 12 15
71-77: 75-($1.50, 52 pgs.) (Low print run) 3 6 9 16 23 30
78,79 (Low print run) 3 6 9 20 30 40
80-Last issue 4 8 12 24 37 50
*NOTE: Second and third printings of most early issues (1-9?) exist and are worth less than originals. Was originally planned as a four issue mini-series. **Wrightson** a-64i(4 pgs.).*

TRANSFORMERS
IDW Publishing: No. 0, Oct, 2005 (99¢, one-shot)
0-Prelude to Transformers: Infiltration series; Furman-s/Su-a; 4 covers 2.50

TRANSFORMERS: ALL HAIL MEGATRON
IDW Publishing: Jul, 2008 - Present ($3.99, limited series)
1,2-McCarthy-s/Guidi-a; 2 covers 4.00

TRANSFORMERS ANIMATED: THE ARRIVAL
IDW Publishing: Sept, 2008 - Present ($3.99, limited series)
1,2-Brizuela-a; 2 covers 4.00

TRANSFORMERS ARMADA (Continues as Transformers Energon with #19)
(Also see Promotional Comics section for FCBD Ed.)
Dreamwave Productions: July, 2002 - No. 18, Dec, 2003 ($2.95)
1-Sarracini-s/Raiz-a; wraparound gatefold-c 3.00
2-18 3.00
Vol. 1 TPB (2003, $13.95) r/#1-5 14.00
Vol. 2 TPB (2003, $15.95) r/#6-11 16.00

TRANSFORMERS ARMADA: MORE THAN MEETS THE EYE
Dreamwave Productions: Mar, 2004 - No. 3, May, 2004 ($4.95, limited series)
1-3-Pin-ups with tech info; art by Pat Lee & various 5.00

TRANSFORMERS, BEAST WARS: THE ASCENDING

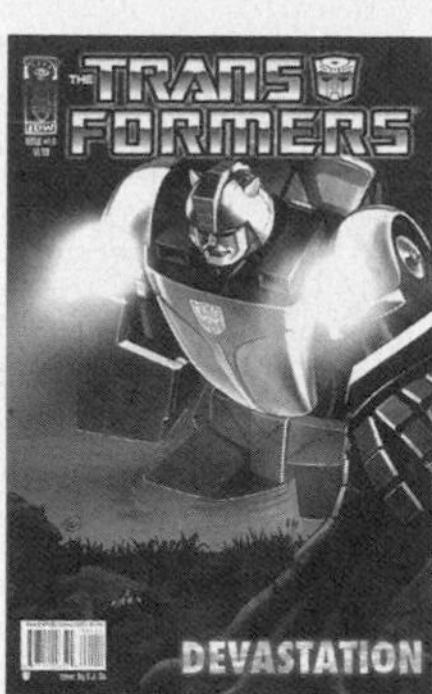

Transformers: Devastation #1 © Hasbro

Transformers: Saga of the Allspark #3 © Hasbro

Transformers Spotlight: Ramjet © Hasbro

GD 2.0 | VG 4.0 | FN 6.0 | VF 8.0 | VF/NM 9.0 | NM- 9.2

IDW Publishing: Aug, 2007 - No. 4, Nov, 2007 ($3.99, limited series)
1-4-Furman-s/Figueroa-a; mulitple covers on all 4.00

TRANSFORMERS, BEAST WARS: THE GATHERING
IDW Publishing: Feb, 2006 - No. 4, May, 2006 ($2.99, limited series)
1-4-Furman-s/Figueroa-a; mulitple covers on all 3.00
TPB (8/06, $17.99) r/series; sketch pages & gallery of covers and variants 18.00

TRANSFORMERS COMICS MAGAZINE (Digest)
Marvel Comics: Jan, 1987 - No. 10, July, 1988
1,2-Spider-Man-c/s 2 4 6 9 12 15
3-10 2 4 6 8 10 12

TRANSFORMERS: DEVASTATION
IDW Publishing: Sept, 2007 - No. 6, Feb, 2008 ($3.99, limited series)
1-6-Furman-s/Su-a; multiple covers on all 4.00

TRANSFORMERS ENERGON (Continued from Transformers Armada #18)
Dreamwave Productions: No. 19, Jan, 2004 - No. 30, Dec, 2004 ($2.95)
19-30-Furman-s 3.00

TRANSFORMERS: ESCALATION
IDW Publishing: Nov, 2006 - No. 6, Apr, 2007 ($3.99, limited series)
1-6-Furman-s/Su-a; multiple covers 4.00

TRANSFORMERS: EVOLUTIONS - HEARTS OF STEEL
IDW Publishing: June, 2006 - No. 4, Sept, 2006 ($2.99, limited series)
1-4-Bumblebee meets John Henry in 1880s railroad times 3.00

TRANSFORMERS: GENERATION 1
Dreamwave Productions: Apr, 2002 - No. 6, Oct, 2002 ($2.95)
Preview- 6 pg. story; robot sketch pages; Pat Lee-a 2.00
1-Pat Lee-a; 2 wraparound covers by Lee 4.00
2-6: 2-Optimus Prime reactivated; 2 covers by Pat Lee 3.00
...Vol. 1 HC (2003, $49.95) r/#1-6; black hardcover with red foil lettering and art 50.00
...Vol. 1 TPB (2002, $17.95) r/#1-6 plus six page preview; 8 pg. preview of future issues 18.00

TRANSFORMERS: GENERATION 1 (Volume 2)
Dreamwave Productions: Apr, 2003 - No. 6, Sept, 2003 ($2.95)
1-6: 1-Pat Lee-a; 2 wraparound gatefold covers by Lee 3.00
1-($5.95) Chrome wraparound variant-c 6.00
...Vol. 2 TPB (IDW Publ., 3/06, $19.99) r/#1-6 plus cover gallery 20.00

TRANSFORMERS: GENERATION 1 (Volume 3)
Dreamwave Productions: No. 0, Dec, 2003 - Present ($2.95)
0-10: 0-Pat Lee-a. 1-Figueroa-a; wrapaound-c 3.00

TRANSFORMERS: GENERATION 2
Marvel Comics: Nov, 1993 - No. 12, Oct, 1994 ($1.75)
1-($2.95, 68 pgs.)-Collector's ed. w/bi-fold metallic-c 1 3 4 6 8 10
1-11: 1-Newsstand edition (68 pgs.). 2-G.I. Joe app., Snake-Eyes, Scarlett, Cobra Commander app. 5-Red Alert killed, Optimus Prime gives Grimlock leadership of Autobots. 6-G.I. Joe app. 1 2 3 4 5 7
12-($2.25, 52 pgs.) 1 3 4 6 8 10

TRANSFORMERS: GENERATIONS
IDW Publishing: Mar, 2006 - No. 12, Mar, 2007 ($1.99/$2.49/$3.99)
1,2. 1-R/Transformers #7 (1985); preview of Transformers, Beast Wars. 2-R/#13 2.50
3-10-($2.49) 3-R/Transformers #14 (1986). 4-6-Reprint #16-18. 7-R/#24 2.50
11,12-($3.99) 4.00
Volume 1 (12/06, $19.99) r/#1-6; cover gallery 20.00

TRANSFORMERS/G.I. JOE
Dreamwave Productions: Aug, 2003 - No. 6, Mar, 2004 ($2.95/$5.25)
1-Art & gatefold wraparound-c by Jae Lee; Ney Rieber-s; variant-c by Pat Lee 3.00
1-($5.95) Holofoil wraparound-c by Norton 6.00
2-6-Jae Lee-a/c 3.00
TPB (8/04, $17.95) r/#1-6; cover gallery and sketch pages 18.00

TRANSFORMERS/G.I. JOE: DIVIDED FRONT
Dreamwave Productions: Oct, 2004 ($2.95)
1-Art & gatefold wraparound-c by Pat Lee 3.00

TRANSFORMERS: HEADMASTERS
Marvel Comics Group: July, 1987 - No. 4, Jan, 1988 ($1.00, limited series)
1-Springer, Akin, Garvey-a 5.00
2-4-Springer-c on all 4.00

TRANSFORMERS: INFILTRATION
IDW Publishing: Jan, 2006 - No. 6, June, 2006 ($2.99, limited series)
1-6-Furman-s/Su-a; multiple covers on all 3.00
... Cover Gallery (8/06, $5.99) 6.00

TRANSFORMERS: MEGATRON ORIGIN
IDW Publishing: May, 2007 - No. 4, Sept, 2008 ($3.99, limited series)
1-4-Alex Milne-a; 2 covers 4.00

TRANSFORMERS: MICROMASTERS
Dreamwave Productions: June, 2004 - No. 4 ($2.95, limited series)
1-4-Ruffolo-a, Pat Lee-c 3.00

TRANSFORMERS: MORE THAN MEETS THE EYE
Dreamwave Productions: Apr, 2003 - No. 8, Nov, 2003 ($5.25)
1-8-Pin-ups with tech info on Autobots and Decepticons; art by Pat Lee & various 5.25
Vol. 1,2 (2004, $24.95, TPB) 1-r/#1-4. 2-r/#5-8 25.00

TRANSFORMERS: MOVIE ADAPTATION (For the 2007 live action movie)
IDW Publishing: Jun, 2007 - No. 4, June, 2007 ($3.99, weekly limited series)
1-4: Wraparound covers on each; Milne-a 4.00

TRANSFORMERS: MOVIE PREQUEL (For the 2007 live action movie)
IDW Publishing: Feb, 2007 - No. 4, May, 2007 ($3.99, limited series)
1-4: 1-Origin of the Transformers on Cybertron; multiple covers on each 4.00
Special (6/08, $3.99) 2 covers 4.00
TPB (6/07, $19.99) r/series; gallery of covers and variants 20.00

TRANSFORMERS: SAGA OF THE ALLSPARK (From the 2007 live action movie)
IDW Publishing: Jul, 2008 - Present ($3.99, limited series)
1-3-Launch of the Allspark into outer space; Furman-s/Roche-c 4.00

TRANSFORMERS: SPOTLIGHT
IDW Publishing: Sept, 2006 - Present ($3.99, multiple covers on each)
... Arcee (2/08); ... Blaster (1/08); ... Cyclonus (6/08); Doubledealer (8/08); Grimlock (3/08); ... Hardhead (7/08); Hot Rod (11/06); ... Kup (4/07); ... Mirage (3/08); ... Nightbeat (10/06); ... Ramjet (11/07); ... Shockwave (9/06); ... Sixshot (12/06); ... Soundwave (3/07); ... Ultra Magnus (1/07) 4.00

TRANSFORMERS: STORMBRINGER
IDW Publishing: Jul, 2006 - No. 4, Oct, 2006 ($2.99, limited series)
1-4-Furman-s/Figueroa-a; multiple covers on all 3.00
TPB (2/07, $17.99) r/series; cover gallery and sketch pages 18.00

TRANSFORMERS SUMMER SPECIAL
Dreamwave Productions: May, 2004 ($4.95)
1-Pat Lee-a; Figueroa-a 5.00

TRANSFORMERS: TARGET 2006
IDW Publishing: Apr, 2007 - No. 5, Aug, 2007 ($3.99, limited series)
1-5-Reprints from 1980s series; multiple covers on all 4.00

TRANSFORMERS: THE ANIMATED MOVIE
IDW Publishing: Oct, 2006 - No. 4, Jan, 2007 ($3.99, limited series)
1-4-Adapts animated movie; Don Figueroa-a 4.00

TRANSFORMERS, THE MOVIE
Marvel Comics Group: Dec, 1986 - No. 3, Feb, 1987 (75¢, limited series)
1-3-Adapts animated movie 4.00

TRANSFORMERS: THE REIGN OF STARSCREAM
IDW Publishing: Apr, 2008 - No. 5, Aug, 2008 ($3.99, limited series)
1-5-Continuation of the 2007 movie; Milne-a; multiple covers 4.00

TRANSFORMERS: THE WAR WITHIN
Dreamwave Productions: Oct, 2002 - No. 6, Mar, 2003 ($2.95)
1-6-Furman-s/Figueroa-a. 1-Wraparound gatefold-c 3.00
TPB (2003, $15.95) r/#1-6; plus cover gallery 16.00

TRANSFORMERS UNIVERSE
Marvel Comics Group: Dec, 1986 - No. 4, Mar, 1987 ($1.25, limited series)
1-4-A guide to all characters 6.00
TPB-r/#1-4 15.00

TRANSFORMERS WAR WITHIN: THE AGE OF WRATH
Dreamwave Productions: Sept, 2004 - No. 6 ($2.95, limited series)
1-3-Furman-s/Ng-a 3.00

TRANSFORMERS WAR WITHIN: THE DARK AGES
Dreamwave Productions: Oct, 2003 - No. 6 ($2.95)
1-6: 1-Furman-s/Wildman-a; two covers by Pat Lee & Figueroa 3.00

Transmetropolitan #9 © Ellis & Robertson

Treasure Chest V3 #9 © Pflaum

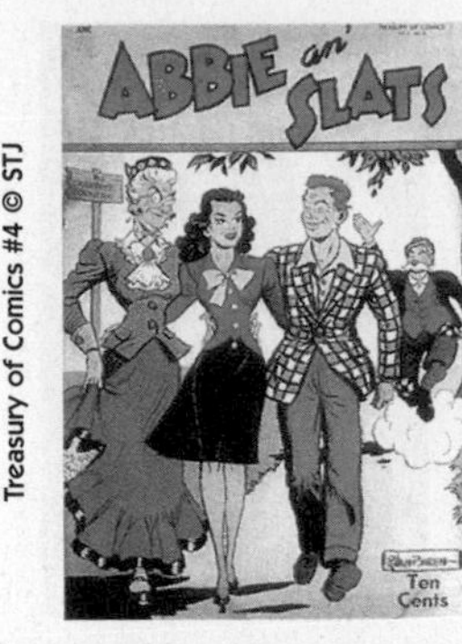

Treasury of Comics #4 © STJ

GD VG FN VF VF/NM NM-
2.0 4.0 6.0 8.0 9.0 9.2

GD VG FN VF VF/NM NM-
2.0 4.0 6.0 8.0 9.0 9.2

TPB (2004, $17.95) r/#1-6; plus cover gallery and design sketches 18.00

TRANSIT
Vortex Publ.: March, 1987 - No. 5, Nov, 1987 (B&W)

1-5-Ted McKeever-s/a 1 2 3 5 6 8

TRANSMETROPOLITAN
DC Comics (Vertigo): Sept, 1997 - No. 60, Nov, 2002 ($2.50)

1-Warren Ellis-s/Darick Robertson-a(p) 2 4 6 8 10 12
2,3 1 2 3 4 5 7
4-8 4.00
9-60: 15-Jae Lee-c. 25-27-Jim Lee-c. 37-39-Bradstreet-c 2.50
Back on the Street ('97, $7.95) r/#1-3 8.00
Dirge ('03, $14.95) r/#43-48 15.00
Filth of the City ('01, $5.95) Spider's columns with pin-up art by various 6.00
Gouge Away ('02, $14.95) r/#31-36 15.00
I Hate It Here ('00, $5.95) Spider's columns with pin-up art by various 6.00
Lonely City ('01, $14.95) r/#25-30; intro. by Patrick Stewart 15.00
Lust For Life ('98, $14.95) r/#4-12 15.00
One More Time ('04, $14.95) r/#55-60 15.00
Spider's Thrash ('02, $14.95) r/#37-42; intro. by Darren Aronofsky 15.00
Tales of Human Waste ('04, $9.95) r/Filth of the City, I Hate It Here & story from Vertigo Winter's Edge 2 10.00
The Cure ('03, $14.95) r/#49-54 15.00
The New Scum ('00, $12.95) r/#19-24 & Vertigo: Winter's Edge #3 13.00
Year of the Bastard ('99, $12.95) r/#13-18 13.00

TRANSMUTATION OF IKE GARUDA, THE
Marvel Comics (Epic Comics): July, 1991 - No. 2, 1991 ($3.95, 52 pgs.)

1,2 4.00

TRAPMAN
Phantom Comics: June, 1994 - No. 2, 1994? ($2.95, quarterly, unfinished limited series)

1,2 3.00

TRAPPED!
Periodical House Magazines (Ace): Oct, 1954 - No. 4, April, 1955

1 (All reprints) 10 20 30 54 72 90
2-4: 4-r/Men Against Crime #4 in its entirety 7 14 21 35 43 50
NOTE: *Colan a-1, 4.* ***Sekowsky*** *a-1.*

TRASH
Trash Publ. Co.: Mar, 1978 - No. 4, Oct, 1978 (B&W, magazine, 52 pgs.)

1,2: 1-Star Wars parody. 2-UFO-c 2 4 6 10 14 18
3-Parodies of KISS, the Beatles, and monsters 3 6 9 14 19 24
4-(84 pgs.)-Parodies of Happy Days, Rocky movies 3 6 9 14 20 26

TRAVELS OF JAIMIE McPHEETERS, THE (TV)
Gold Key: Dec, 1963

1-Kurt Russell photo on-c plus photo back-c 4 8 12 26 41 55

TREASURE CHEST (Catholic Guild; also see Topix)
George A. Pflaum: 3/12/46 - V27#8, July, 1972 (Educational comics)
(Not published during Summer)

V1#1 27 54 81 158 254 350
2-6 (5/21/46): 5-Dr. Styx app. by Baily 14 28 42 80 115 150
V2#1-20 (9/3/46-5/27/47) 11 22 33 60 83 105
V3#1-5,7-20 (1st slick cover) 10 20 30 54 72 90
V3#6-Jules Verne's "Voyage to the Moon" 11 22 33 64 90 115
V4#1-20 (9/9/48-5/31/49) 9 18 27 47 61 75
V5#1-20 (9/6/49-5/31/50) 8 16 24 44 57 70
V6#1-20 (9/14/50-5/31/51) 8 16 24 42 54 65
V7#1-20 (9/13/51-6/5/52) 8 16 24 40 50 60
V8#1-20 (9/11/52-6/4/53) 7 14 21 37 46 55
V9#1-20 ('53-'54), V10#1-20 ('54-'55) 7 14 21 35 43 50
V11('55-'56), V12('56-'57) 6 12 18 29 36 42
V13#1,3-5,7,9-V17#1 ('57-'63) 6 12 18 27 33 38
V13#2,6,8-Ingels-a 6 12 18 41 66 90
V17#2- "This Godless Communism" series begins(not in odd #'d issues); cover shows hammer & sickle over Statue of Liberty; 8 pg. Crandall-a of family life under communism 18 36 54 130 240 350
V17#3,5,7,9,11,13,15,17,19 3 6 9 16 23 30
V17#4,6,14- "This Godless Communism" stories 14 28 42 102 181 260
V17#8-Shows red octopus encompassing Earth, firing squad; 8 pgs. Crandall-a 15 30 45 111 206 300
V17#10- "This Godless Communism" - how Stalin came to power, part I; Crandall-a 15 30 45 107 196 285
V17#12-Stalin in WWII, forced labor, death by exhaustion; Crandall-a 15 30 45 107 196 285
V17#16-Kruschev takes over; de-Stalinization 15 30 45 107 196 285
V17#18-Kruschev's control; murder of revolters, brainwash, space race by Crandall 15 30 45 107 196 285
V17#20-End of series; Kruschev-people are puppets, firing squads hammer & sickle over Statue of Liberty, snake around communist manifesto by Crandall 17 34 51 120 223 325
V18#1-20, V19#11-20, V20#1-20(1964-65): V18#11-Crandall draws himself & 13 other artists on cover 3 6 9 16 22 28
V18#5- "What About Red China?" - describes how communists took over China 8 16 24 54 90 125
V19#1-10- "Red Victim" anti-communist series in all 8 16 24 54 90 125
V21-V25(1965-70)-(two V24#5's 11/7/68 & 11/21/68) (no V24#6) 3 6 9 14 19 24
V26, V27#1-8 (V26,27-68 pgs.) 3 6 9 16 22 28
Summer Edition V1#1-6('66), V2#1-6('67) 3 6 9 16 23 30
NOTE: ***Anderson*** *a-V18#13.* ***Borth*** *a-V7#10-19 (serial), V8#8-17 (serial), V9#1-10 (serial), V13#2, 6, 11, V14-V25 (except V22#1-3, 11-13), Summer Ed. V1#3-6.* ***Crandall*** *a-V16#7, 9, 12, 14, 16-18, 20; V17#1, 2, 4-6, 10, 12, 14, 16-18, 20; V18#1, 2, 3(2 pg.), 7, 9-20; V19#4, 11, 13, 16, 19, 20; V20#1, 2, 4, 6, 8-10, 12, 14-16, 18, 20; V21#1-5, 8-11, 13, 16-18; V22#3, 7, 9-11, 14; V23#3, 6, 9, 16, 18; V24#7, 8, 10, 13, 16; V25#8, 16; V27#1-7r, 8r(2 pg.), Summer Ed. V1#3-5, V2#3; c-V16#7, V18#2(part), 7, 11, V19#4, 19, 20, V20#15, V21#5, 9, V22#3, 7, 9, 11, V23#9, 16, V24#13, 16, V25#8, Summer Ed. V1#2 (back c-V1#2-5).* ***Powell*** *a-V10#11. V19#11, 15, V10#13, V13#6, 8 all have wraparound covers.*

TREASURE CHEST OF THE WORLD'S BEST COMICS
Superior, Toronto, Canada: 1945 (500 pgs., hard-c)

Contains Blue Beetle, Captain Combat, John Wayne, Dynamic Man, Nemo, Li'l Abner; contents can vary - represents random binding of extra books; Captain America on-c 90 180 270 567 959 1350

TREASURE COMICS
Prize Publications? (no publisher listed): No date (1943) (50¢, 324 pgs., cardboard-c)

1-(Rare)-Contains rebound Prize Comics #7-11 from 1942 (blank inside-c) 250 500 750 1575 2663 3750

TREASURE COMICS
Prize Publ. (American Boys' Comics): June-July, 1945 - No. 12, Fall, 1947

1-Paul Bunyan & Marco Polo begin; Highwayman & Carrot Topp only app.; Kiefer-a 48 96 144 298 499 700
2-Arabian Knight, Gorilla King, Dr. Styx begin 28 56 84 164 265 365
3,4,9,12: 9-Kiefer-a 22 44 66 131 211 290
5-Marco Polo-c; Krigstein-a 28 56 84 164 265 365
6,11-Krigstein-a; 11-Krigstein-c 27 54 81 158 254 350
7,8-Frazetta-a (5 pgs. each). 7-Capt. Kidd Jr. app. 41 82 123 250 413 575
10-Simon & Kirby-c/a 36 72 108 212 341 470
NOTE: ***Barry*** *a-9-11; c-12.* ***Kiefer*** *a-3, 5, 7; c-2, 6, 7.* ***Roussos*** *a-11.*

TREASURE ISLAND (See Classics Illustrated #64, Doc Savage Comics #1, King Classics, Movie Classics & Movie Comics)
Dell Publishing Co.: No. 624, Apr, 1955 (Disney)

Four Color 624-Movie, photo-c 8 16 24 54 90 125

TREASURY OF COMICS
St. John Publishing Co.: 1947; No. 2, July, 1947 - No. 4, Sept, 1947; No. 5, Jan, 1948

nn(#1)-Abbie an' Slats (nn on-c, #1 on inside) 14 28 42 80 115 150
2-Jim Hardy Comics; featuring Windy & Paddles 11 22 33 62 86 110
3-Bill Bumlin 10 20 30 54 72 90
4-Abbie an' Slats 11 22 33 62 86 110
5-Jim Hardy Comics #1 11 22 33 62 86 110

TREASURY OF COMICS
St. John Publishing Co.: Mar, 1948 - No. 5, 1948 (Reg. size); 1948-1950
(Over 500 pgs., $1.00)

1 19 38 57 112 176 240
2(#2 on-c, #1 on inside) 12 24 36 67 94 120
3-5 10 20 30 56 76 95
1-(1948, 500 pgs., hard-c)-Abbie & Slats, Abbott & Costello, Casper, Little Annie Rooney, Little Audrey, Jim Hardy, Ella Cinders (16 books bound together) (Rare) 122 244 366 769 1297 1825
1(1949, 500 pgs.)-Same format as above 110 220 330 693 1172 1650
1(1950, 500 pgs.)-Same format as above; different-c; (also see Little Audrey Yearbook) (Rare) 110 220 330 693 1172 1650

TREASURY OF DOGS, A (See Dell Giants)

TREASURY OF HORSES, A (See Dell Giants)

TREEHOUSE OF HORROR (Bart Simpson's...)
Bongo Comics: 1995 - Present ($2.95/$2.50/$3.50/$4.50/$4.99, annual)

The Trials of Shazam! #9 © DC

Trinity #1 © DC

Trinity Angels #3 © Acclaim

GD 2.0 | VG 4.0 | FN 6.0 | VF 8.0 | VF/NM 9.0 | NM- 9.2

1-(1995, $2.95)-Groening-c; Allred, Robinson & Smith stories 3.50
2-(1996, $2.50)-Stories by Dini & Bagge; infinity-c by Groening 3.00
3-(1997, $2.50)-Dorkin-s/Groening-c 3.00
4-(1998, $2.50)-Lash & Dixon-s/Groening-c 3.00
5-(1999, $3.50)-Thompson-s; Shaw & Aragonés-s/a, TenNapel-s/a 3.50
6-(2000, $4.50)-Mahfood-s/a; DeCarlo-a; Morse-s/a; Kuper-s/a 4.50
7-(2001, $4.50)-Hamill-s/Morrison-a; Ennis-s/McCrea-a; Sakai-s/a; Nixey-s/a; Brereton back-c 4.50
8-(2002, $3.50)-Templeton, Shaw, Barta, Simone, Thompson-s/a 3.50
9-(2003, $4.99)-Lord of the Rings-Brereton-a; Dini, Naifeh, Millidge, Boothby, Noto-s/a 5.00
10-(2004, $4.99)-Monsters of Rock w/Alice Cooper, Gene Simmons, Rob Zombie and Pat Boone; art by Rodriguez, Morrison, Morse, Templeton 5.00
11-(2005, $4.99)-EC style w/art by John Severin, Angelo Torres & Al Williamson and flip book with Dracula by Wolfman/Colan and Squish Thing by Wein/Wrightson 5.00
12-(2006, $4.99)-Terry Moore, Kyle Baker, Eric Powell-s/a 5.00
13-(2007, $4.99)-Oswalt, Posehn, Lennon-s; Guerra, Austin, Barta, Rodriguez-a 5.00
14-(2008, $4.99)-s/a by Niles & Fabry, Boothby & Matsumoto; Gilbert Hernandez 5.00

TREKKER (See Dark Horse Presents #6)
Dark Horse Comics: May, 1987 - No. 6, Mar,1988 ($1.50, B&W)

1-6: Sci/Fi stories 2.50
Color Special 1 (1989, $2.95, 52 pgs.) 3.00
Collection ($5.95, B&W) 6.00
Special 1 (6/99, $2.95, color) 3.00

TRENCHCOAT BRIGADE, THE
DC Comics (Vertigo): Mar, 1999 - No. 4, Jun, 1999 ($2.50, limited series)

1-4: Hellblazer, Phantom Stranger, Mister E, Dr. Occult app. 2.50

TRENCHER (See Blackball Comics)
Image Comics: May, 1993 - No. 4, Oct, 1993 ($1.95, unfinished limited series)

1-4: Keith Giffen-c/a/scripts. 3-Supreme-c/story 2.50

TRIALS OF SHAZAM!
DC Comics: Oct, 2006 - No. 12, May, 2008 ($2.99)

1-12: 1-8-Winick-s/Porter-a. 9-11-Cascioli-a. 10-Shadowpact app. 12-JLA app. 3.00
... Volume 1 TPB (2007, $14.99) r/#1-6 and story from DCU Brave New World #1 15.00

TRIB COMIC BOOK, THE
Winnipeg Tribune: Sept. 24, 1977 - Vol. 4, #36, 1980 (8-1/2"x11", 24 pgs., weekly) (155 total issues)

V1# 1-Color pages (Sunday strips)-Spiderman, Asterix, Disney's Scamp, Wizard of Id, Doonesbury, Inside Woody Allen, Mary Worth, & others (similar to Spirit sections) 2 4 6 10 14 18
V1#2-15, V2#1-52, V3#1-52, V4#1-33 1 3 4 6 8 10
V4#34-36 (not distributed) 2 4 6 11 16 20

NOTE: *All issues have Spider-Man. Later issues contain Star Trek and Star Wars. 20 strips in ea. The first newspaper to put Sunday pages into a comic book format.*

TRIBE (See WildC.A.T.S #4)
Image Comics/Axis Comics No. 2 on: Apr, 1993; No. 2, Sept, 1993 - No. 3, 1994 ($2.50/$1.95)

1-By Johnson & Stroman; gold foil & embossed on black-c 2.50
1-($2.50)-Ivory Edition; gold foil & embossed on white-c; available only through the creators 2.50
2,3: 2-1st Axis Comics issue. 3-Savage Dragon app. 2.50

TRIBUTE TO STEVEN HUGHES, A
Chaos! Comics: Sept, 2000 ($6.95)

1-Lady Death & Evil Ernie pin-ups by various artists; testimonials 7.00

TRIGGER (See Roy Rogers'...)

TRIGGER
DC Comics (Vertigo): Feb, 2005 - No. 8, Sept, 2005 ($2.95/$2.99)

1-8-Jason Hall-s/John Watkiss-a/c 3.00

TRIGGER TWINS
National Periodical Publications: Mar-Apr, 1973 (20¢, one-shot)

1-Trigger Twins & Pow Wow Smith-r/All-Star Western #94,103 & Western Comics #81; Infantino-r(p) 2 4 6 13 18 22

TRINITY (See DC Universe: Trinity)

TRINITY
DC Comics: Aug, 2008 - Present ($2.99, weekly series)

1-10-Superman, Batman & Wonder Woman star; Busiek-s/Bagley-a 3.00

TRINITY ANGELS
Acclaim Comics (Valiant Heroes): July, 1997 - No. 12, June, 1998 ($2.50)

GD 2.0 | VG 4.0 | FN 6.0 | VF 8.0 | VF/NM 9.0 | NM- 9.2

1-12-Maguire-s/a(p):4-Copycat-c 3.00

TRIPLE GIANT COMICS (See Archie All-Star Specials under Archie Comics)

TRIPLE THREAT
Special Action/Holyoke/Gerona Publ.: Winter, 1945

1-Duke of Darkness, King O'Leary 32 64 96 186 298 410

TRIPLE-X
Dark Horse Comics: Dec, 1994 - No. 7, June, 1995 ($3.95, B&W, limited series)

1-7 4.00

TRIUMPH (Also see JLA #28-30, Justice League Task Force & Zero Hour)
DC Comics: June, 1995 - No. 4, Sept, 1995 ($1.75, limited series)

1-4: 3-Hourman, JLA app. 2.50

TRIUMPHANT UNLEASHED
Triumphant Comics: No. 0, Nov, 1993 - No. 1, Nov, 1993 ($2.50, lim. series)

0-Serially numbered, 0-Red logo, 0-White logo (no cover price; giveaway), 1-Cover is negative & reverse of #0-c 2.50

TROLL (Also see Brigade)
Image Comics (Extreme Studios): Dec, 1993 ($2.50, one-shot, 44 pgs.)

1-1st app. Troll; Liefeld scripts; Matsuda-c/a(p) 2.50
Halloween Special (1994, $2.95) Maxx app. 3.00
...Once A Hero (8/94, $2.50) 2.50

TROLLORDS
Tru Studios/Comico V2#1 on: 2/86 - No. 15, 1988; V2#1, 11/88 - V2#4, 1989 (1-15: $1.50, B&W)

1-15: 1-Both printings. 6-Christmas issue; silver logo 2.50
V2#1-4 ($1.75, color, Comico) 2.50
Special 1 ($1.75, 2/87, color)-Jerry's Big Fun Bk. 2.50

TROLLORDS
Apple Comics: July, 1989 - No. 6, 1990 ($2.25, B&W, limited series)

1-6: 1-"The Big Batman Movie Parody" 2.50

TROLL PATROL
Harvey Comics: Jan, 1993 ($1.95, 52 pgs.)

1 2.50

TROLL II (Also see Brigade)
Image Comics (Extreme Studios): July, 1994 ($3.95, one-shot)

1 4.00

TRON (Based on the video game and film)
Slave Labor Graphics: Apr, 2006 - Present ($3.50/$3.95)

1-4: 1-DeMartinis-a/Walker & Jones-s 3.50
5,6-($3.95) 4.00

TROUBLE
Marvel Comics (Epic): Sept, 2003 - No. 5, Jan, 2004 ($2.99, limited series)

1-5-Photo-c; Richard and Ben meet Mary and May; Millar-s/Dodson-a 3.00
1-2nd printing with variant Frank Cho-c 5.00

TROUBLED SOULS
Fleetway: 1990 ($9.95, trade paperback)

nn-Garth Ennis scripts & John McCrea painted-c/a. 10.00

TROUBLEMAKERS
Acclaim Comics (Valiant Heroes): Apr, 1997 - No. 19, June, 1998 ($2.50)

1-19: Fabian Nicieza scripts in all. 1-1st app. XL, Rebound & Blur; 2 covers. 8-Copycat-c. 12-Shooting of Parker 2.50

TROUBLE SHOOTERS, THE (TV)
Dell Publishing Co.: No. 1108, Jun-Aug, 1960

Four Color 1108-Keenan Wynn photo-c 5 10 15 34 55 75

TROUBLE WITH GIRLS, THE
Malibu Comics (Eternity Comics) #7-14/Comico V2#1-4/Eternity V2#5 on: 8/87 - #14, 1988; V2#1, 2/89 - V2#23, 1991? ($1.95, B&W/color)

1-14 ($1.95, B&W, Eternity)-Gerard Jones scripts & Tim Hamilton-c/a in all. 2.50
V2#1-23-Jones scripts, Hamilton-c/a. 2.50
Annual 1 (1988, $2.95) 3.00
Christmas Special 1 (12/91, $2.95, B&W, Eternity)-Jones scripts, Hamilton-c/a 3.00
Graphic Novel 1,2 (7/88, B&W)-r/#1-3 & #4-6 8.00

TROUBLE WITH GIRLS, THE: NIGHT OF THE LIZARD
Marvel Comics (Epic Comics/Heavy Hitters): 1993 - No. 4, 1993 ($2.50/$1.95, lim. series)

True Believers #1 © MAR

True Comics #10 © PMI

True Life Romance #1 © AJAX

GD VG FN VF VF/NM NM-
2.0 4.0 6.0 8.0 9.0 9.2

1-Embossed-c; Gerard Jones scripts & Bret Blevins-c/a in all 2.50
2-4: 2-Begin $1.95-c. 2.50

TROUT
Oni Press: Oct, 2001 - No. 2, Feb, 2002 ($2.95, B&W, limited series)
1,2-Troy Nixey-s/a 3.00

TRUE ADVENTURES (Formerly True Western)(Men's Adventures #4 on)
Marvel Comics (CCC): No. 3, May, 1950 (52 pgs.)
3-Powell, Sekowsky-a; Brodsky-c 16 32 48 94 147 200

TRUE ANIMAL PICTURE STORIES
True Comics Press: Winter, 1947 - No. 2, Spring-Summer, 1947
1,2 10 20 30 56 76 95

TRUE AVIATION PICTURE STORIES (Becomes Aviation Adventures & Model Building #16 on)
Parents' Mag. Institute: 1942; No. 2, Jan-Feb, 1943 - No. 15, Sept-Oct, 1946
1-(#1 & 2 titled ...Aviation Comics Digest)(not digest size)
15 30 45 85 130 175
2 10 20 30 56 76 95
3-14: 3-10-Plane photos on-c. 11,13-Photo-c 9 18 27 50 65 80
15-(Titled "True Aviation Adventures & Model Building")
9 18 27 47 61 75

TRUE BELIEVERS
Marvel Comics: Sept, 2008 - No. 5 ($2.99, limited series)
1-3-Cary Bates-s/Paul Gulacy-a. 1,2-Reed Richards app. 3-Luke Cage app. 3.00

TRUE BRIDE'S EXPERIENCES (Formerly Teen-Age Brides)
(True Bride-To-Be Romances No. 17 on)
True Love (Harvey Publications): No. 8, Oct, 1954 - No. 16, Feb, 1956
8 9 18 27 50 65 80
9,10: 10-Last pre-code (2/55) 7 14 21 37 46 55
11-15 6 12 18 31 38 45
16-Last issue 7 14 21 37 46 55
NOTE: *Powell a-8-10, 12, 13.*

TRUE BRIDE-TO-BE ROMANCES (Formerly True Bride's Experiences)
Home Comics/True Love (Harvey): No. 17, Apr, 1956 - No. 30, Nov, 1958
17-S&K-c, Powell-a 10 20 30 56 76 95
18-20,22,25-28,30 6 12 18 31 38 45
21,23,24,29-Powell-a. 29-Baker-a (1 pg.) 7 14 21 35 43 50

TRUE COMICS (Also see Outstanding American War Heroes)
True Comics/Parents' Magazine Press: April, 1941 - No. 84, Aug, 1950
1-Marathon run story; life story Winston Churchill 31 62 93 181 291 400
2-Red Cross story; Everett-a 15 30 45 85 130 175
3-Baseball Hall of Fame story; Chiang Kai-Shek-c/s 17 34 51 100 158 215
4,5: 4-Story of American flag "Old Glory". 5-Life story of Joe Louis
14 28 42 80 115 150
6-Baseball World Series story 15 30 45 90 140 190
7-10: 7-Buffalo Bill story. 10,11-Teddy Roosevelt 11 22 33 62 86 110
11-14,16,18-20: 11-Thomas Edison, Douglas MacArthur stories. 13-Harry Houdini story. 14-Charlie McCarthy story. 18-Story of America begins, ends #26. 19-Eisenhower-c/s
10 20 30 54 72 90
15-Flag-c; Bob Feller story 10 20 30 58 79 100
17-Brooklyn Dodgers story 11 22 33 64 90 115
21-30: 24-Marco Polo story. 28-Origin of Uncle Sam. 29-Beethoven story. 30-Cooper Brothers baseball story 9 18 27 47 61 75
31-Red Grange "Galloping Ghost" story 8 16 24 40 50 60
32-46: 33-Origin/1st app. Steve Saunders, Special Agent of the FBI, series begins. 35-Mark Twain story. 38-General Bradley-c/s. 39-FDR story. 44-Truman story. 46-George Gershwin story 7 14 21 37 46 55
47-Atomic bomb issue (c/story, 3/46) 10 20 30 56 76 95
48-54,56-65: 49-1st app. Secret Warriors. 53-Bobby Riggs story. 58-Jim Jeffries (boxer) story; Harry Houdini story. 59-Bob Hope story; pirates-c/s. 60-Speedway Speed Demon-c/story.
7 14 21 35 43 50
55-(12/46)-1st app. Sad Sack by Baker (1/2 pg.) 9 18 27 47 61 75
66-Will Rogers-c/story 7 14 21 37 46 55
67-1st oversized issue (12/47); Steve Saunders, Special Agent begins
8 16 24 42 54 65
68-70,74-77,79: 68-70,74-77-Features Steve Sanders True FBI advs. 68-Oversized; Admiral Byrd-c/s. 69-Jack Benny story. 74-Amos 'n' Andy story
6 12 18 31 38 45
71-Joe DiMaggio-c/story. 9 18 27 47 61 75
72-Jackie Robinson story; True FBI advs. 8 16 24 40 50 60
73-Walt Disney's life story 9 18 27 47 61 75

GD VG FN VF VF/NM NM-
2.0 4.0 6.0 8.0 9.0 9.2

78-Stan Musial-c/story; True FBI advs. 8 16 24 40 50 60
80-84 (Scarce)-All distr. to subscribers through mail only; paper-c. 80-Rocket trip to the moon story. 81-Red Grange story. 84-Wyatt Earp app. (1st app. in comics?); Rube Marquard story
18 36 54 103 162 220
(Prices vary widely on issues 80-84)
NOTE: *Bob Kane a-7.* ***Palais*** *a-80.* ***Powell*** *c/a-80. #80-84 have soft covers and combined with Tex Granger, Jack Armstrong, and Calling All Kids. #68-78 featured true FBI adventures.*

TRUE COMICS AND ADVENTURE STORIES
Parents' Magazine Institute: 1965 (Giant) (25¢)
1,2: 1-Fighting Hero of Viet Nam; LBJ on-c 3 6 9 18 27 35

TRUE COMPLETE MYSTERY (Formerly Complete Mystery)
Marvel Comics (PrPI): No. 5, Apr, 1949 - No. 8, Oct, 1949
5 26 52 78 152 244 335
6-8: 6-8-Photo-c 20 40 60 117 184 250

TRUE CONFIDENCES
Fawcett Publications: 1949 (Fall) - No. 4, June, 1950 (All photo-c)
1-Has ad for Fawcett Love Adventures #1, but publ. as Love Memoirs #1 as Marvel published the title first; Swayze-a 18 36 54 103 162 220
2-4: 3-Swayze-a. 4-Powell-a 11 22 33 64 90 115

TRUE CRIME CASES (...From Official Police Files)
St. John Publishing Co.: 1944 (25¢, 100 pg. Giant)
nn-Matt Baker-c 47 94 141 291 483 675

TRUE CRIME COMICS (Also see Complete Book of...)
Magazine Village: No. 2, May, 1947; No. 3, July-Aug, 1948 - No. 6, June-July, 1949; V2#1, Aug-Sept, 1949 (52 pgs.)
2-Jack Cole-c/a; used in **SOTI**, pgs. 81,82 plus illo. "A sample of the injury-to-eye motif" & illo. "Dragging living people to death"; used in **POP**, pg. 105; "Murder, Morphine and Me" classic drug propaganda story used by N.Y. Legis. Comm.
160 320 480 1008 1704 2400
3-Classic Cole-c/a; drug story with hypo, opium den & with drawing addict
115 230 345 725 1225 1725
4-Jack Cole-c/a; c-taken from a story panel in #3 (r-(2) **SOTI** & **POP** stories/#2?) 98 196 294 617 1046 1475
5-Jack Cole-c, Marijuana racket story (Canadian ed. w/cover similar to #3 exists w/out drug story) 66 132 198 416 701 985
6-Not a reprint, original story (Canadian ed. reprints #4 w/different coloring on-c)
53 106 159 330 553 775
V2#1-Used in **SOTI**, pgs. 81,82 & illo. "Dragging living people to death"; Toth, Wood (3 pgs.), Roussos-a; Cole-r from #2 90 180 270 567 959 1350
NOTE: *V2#1 was reprinted in Canada as V2#9 (12/49); same-c & contents minus Wood-a.*

TRUE FAITH
Fleetway: 1990 ($9.95, graphic novel)
nn-Garth Ennis scripts 2 4 6 12 16 20
Reprinted by DC/Vertigo ('97, $12.95) 13.00

TRUE GHOST STORIES (See Ripley's...)

TRUE LIFE ROMANCES (...Romance on cover)
Ajax/Farrell Publications: Dec, 1955 - No. 3, Aug, 1956
1 10 20 30 58 79 100
2 8 16 24 40 50 60
3-Disbrow-a 8 16 24 44 57 70

TRUE LIFE SECRETS
Romantic Love Stories/Charlton: Mar-April, 1951 - No. 28, Sept, 1955; No. 29, Jan, 1956
1-Photo-c begin, end #3? 14 28 42 80 115 150
2 9 18 27 47 61 75
3-19: 12-"I Was An Escort Girl" story 8 16 24 40 50 60
20-29: 25-Last precode(3/55) 7 14 21 35 43 50

TRUE LIFE TALES (Formerly Mitzi's Romances #8?)
Marvel Comics (CCC): No. 8, Oct, 1949 - No. 2, Jan, 1950 (52 pgs.)
8(#1, 10/49), 2-Both have photo-c 11 22 33 62 86 110

TRUE LOVE
Eclipse Comics: Jan, 1986 - No. 2, Jan, 1986 ($2.00, Baxter paper)
1,2-Love stories reprinted from pre-code Standard Comics; Toth-a(p) in both; 1-Dave Stevens-c. 2-Mayo-a 3.00

TRUE LOVE CONFESSIONS
Premier Magazines: May, 1954 - No. 11, Jan, 1956
1-Marijuana story 14 28 42 76 108 140

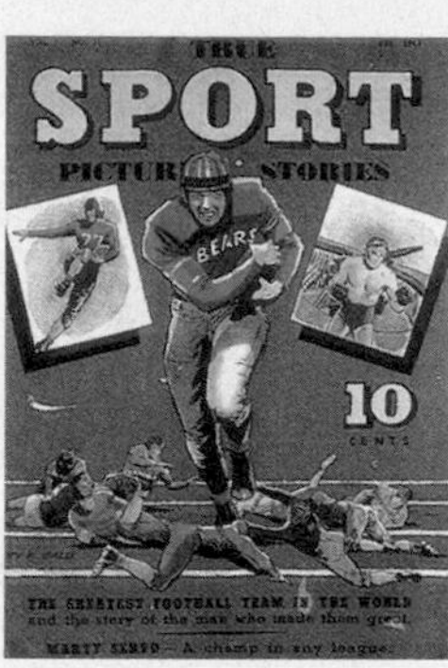

True Sport Picture Stories #11 © S&S

True-To-Life Romances #6 © STAR

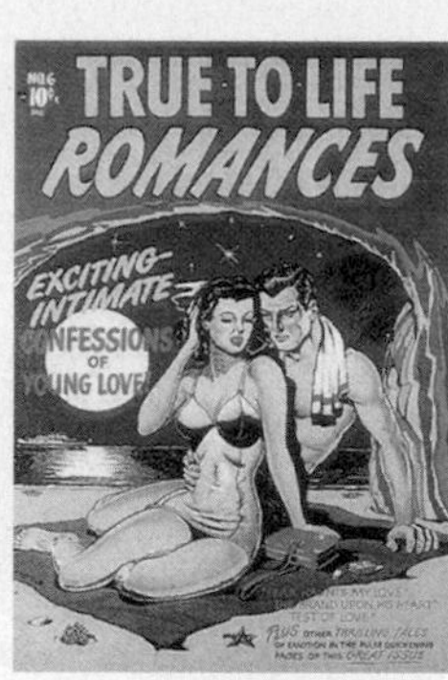

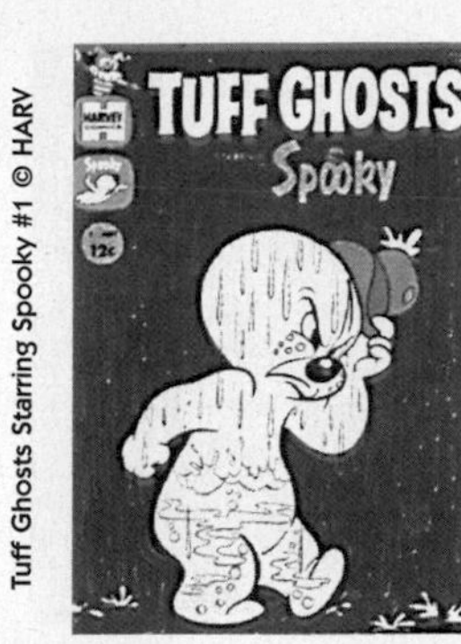

Tuff Ghosts Starring Spooky #1 © HARV

	GD 2.0	VG 4.0	FN 6.0	VF 8.0	VF/NM 9.0	NM- 9.2
2	8	16	24	44	57	70
3-11	8	16	24	40	50	60

TRUE LOVE PICTORIAL
St. John Publishing Co.: Dec, 1952 - No. 11, Aug, 1954

	GD	VG	FN	VF	VF/NM	NM-
1-Only photo-c	19	38	57	112	176	240
2-Baker-c/a	27	54	81	158	254	350
3-5(All 25¢, 100 pgs.): 4-Signed story by Estrada. 5-(4/53)-Formerly Teen-Age Temptations; Kubert-a in #3; Baker-c/a in #3-5	41	82	123	250	413	575
6,7: Baker-c/a; signed stories by Estrada	25	50	75	147	236	325
8,10,11-Baker-c/a	25	50	75	147	236	325
9-Baker-c	20	40	60	115	183	250

TRUE LOVE PROBLEMS AND ADVICE ILLUSTRATED (Becomes Romance Stories of True Love No. 45 on)
McCombs/Harvey Publ./Home Comics: June, 1949 - No. 6, Apr, 1950; No. 7, Jan, 1951 - No. 44, Mar, 1957

	GD	VG	FN	VF	VF/NM	NM-
V1#1	15	30	45	86	133	180
2-Elias-c	10	20	30	54	72	90
3-10: 3,4,7-9-Elias-c	8	16	24	42	54	65
11-13,15-23,25-31: 31-Last pre-code (1/55)	7	14	21	35	43	50
14,24-Rape scene	7	14	21	37	46	55
32-37,39-44	6	12	18	29	36	42
38-S&K-c	9	18	27	52	69	85

NOTE: *Powell a-1, 2, 7-14, 17-25, 28, 29, 33, 40, 41. #3 has True Love... on inside.*

TRUE MOVIE AND TELEVISION (Part teenage magazine)
Toby Press: Aug, 1950 - No. 3, Nov, 1950; No. 4, Mar, 1951 (52 pgs.)(1-3: 10¢)

	GD	VG	FN	VF	VF/NM	NM-
1-Elizabeth Taylor photo-c; Gene Autry, Shirley Temple app.	55	110	165	347	586	825
2-(9/50)-Janet Leigh/Liz Taylor/Ava Gardner & others photo-c; Frazetta John Wayne illo from J.Wayne Adv. Comics #2 (4/50)	41	82	123	250	413	575
3-June Allyson photo-c; Montgomery Cliff, Esther Williams, Andrews Sisters app; Li'l Abner featured; Sadie Hawkins' Day	31	62	93	181	291	400
4-Jane Powell photo-c (15¢)	20	40	60	115	183	250

NOTE: *16 pgs. in color, rest movie material in black & white.*

TRUE SECRETS (Formerly Our Love?)
Marvel (IPS)/Atlas Comics (MPI) #4 on: No. 3, Mar, 1950; No. 4, Feb, 1951 - No. 40, Sept, 1956

	GD	VG	FN	VF	VF/NM	NM-
3 (52 pgs.)(IPS one-shot)	14	28	42	82	121	160
4,5,7-10	10	20	30	54	72	90
6,22-Everett-a	11	22	33	64	90	115
11-20	9	18	27	50	65	80
21,23-28: 24-Colletta-c. 28-Last pre-code (2/55)	8	16	24	44	57	70
29-40: 34,36-Colletta-a	8	16	24	40	50	60

TRUE SPORT PICTURE STORIES (Formerly Sport Comics)
Street & Smith Publications: V1#5, Feb, 1942 - V5#2, July-Aug, 1949

	GD	VG	FN	VF	VF/NM	NM-
V1#5-Joe DiMaggio-c/story	37	74	111	215	345	475
6-12 (1942-43): 12-Jack Dempsey story	21	42	63	123	197	270
V2#1-12 (1943-45): 7-Stan Musial-c/story; photo story of the New York Yankees	20	40	60	115	183	250
V3#1-12 (1946-47): 7-Joe DiMaggio, Stan Musial, Bob Feller & others back from the armed service story. 8-Billy Conn vs. Joe Louis-c/story	19	38	57	109	172	235
V4#1-12 (1948-49), V5#1,2	18	36	54	105	165	225

NOTE: *Powell a-V3#10, V4#1-4, 6-8, 10-12; V5#1, 2; c-V3#10-12, V4#2-7, 9-12. Ravielli c-V5#2.*

TRUE STORIES OF ROMANCE
Fawcett Publications: Jan, 1950 - No. 3, May, 1950 (All photo-c)

	GD	VG	FN	VF	VF/NM	NM-
1	14	28	42	80	115	150
2,3: 3-Marcus Swayze-a	10	20	30	58	79	100

TRUE STORY OF JESSE JAMES, THE (See Jesse James, Four Color 757)

TRUE SWEETHEART SECRETS
Fawcett Publs.: 5/50; No. 2, 7/50; No. 3, 1951(nd); No. 4, 9/51 - No. 11, 1/53 (All photo-c)

	GD	VG	FN	VF	VF/NM	NM-
1-Photo-c; Debbie Reynolds?	15	30	45	88	137	185
2-Wood-a (11 pgs.)	18	36	54	105	165	225
3-11: 4,5-Powell-a. 8-Marcus Swayze-a. 11-Evans-a	11	22	33	64	90	115

TRUE TALES OF LOVE (Formerly Secret Story Romances)
Atlas Comics (TCI): No. 22, April, 1956 - No. 31, Sept, 1957

	GD	VG	FN	VF	VF/NM	NM-
22	10	20	30	54	72	90
23-24,26-31-Colletta-a in most:	8	16	24	40	50	60
25-Everett-a; Colletta-a	8	16	24	44	57	70

TRUE TALES OF ROMANCE
Fawcett Publications: No. 4, June, 1950

	GD	VG	FN	VF	VF/NM	NM-
4-Photo-c	10	20	30	54	72	90

TRUE 3-D
Harvey Publications: Dec, 1953 - No. 2, Feb, 1954 (25¢)(Both came with 2 pair of glasses)

	GD	VG	FN	VF	VF/NM	NM-
1-Nostrand, Powell-a	5	10	15	35	55	75
2-Powell-a	6	12	18	37	59	80

NOTE: *Many copies of #1 surfaced in 1984.*

TRUE-TO-LIFE ROMANCES (Formerly Guns Against Gangsters)
Star Publ.: #8, 11-12/49; #9, 1-2/50; #3, 4/50 - #5, 9/50; #6, 1/51 - #23, 10/54

	GD	VG	FN	VF	VF/NM	NM-
8(#1, 1949)	24	48	72	140	225	310
9(#2),4-10	17	34	51	100	158	215
3-Janet Leigh/Glenn Ford photo on-c plus true life story of each	19	38	57	109	172	235
11,22,23	15	30	45	86	133	180
12-14,17-21-Disbrow-a	16	32	48	94	147	200
15,16-Wood & Disbrow-a in each	19	38	57	109	172	235

NOTE: *Kamen a-13. Kamen/Feldstein a-14. All have L.B. Cole covers.*

TRUE WAR EXPERIENCES
Harvey Publications: Aug, 1952 - No. 4, Dec, 1952

	GD	VG	FN	VF	VF/NM	NM-
1	8	16	24	56	93	130
2-4	5	10	15	32	51	70

TRUE WAR ROMANCES (Becomes Exotic Romances #22 on)
Quality Comics Group: Sept, 1952 - No. 21, June, 1955

	GD	VG	FN	VF	VF/NM	NM-
1-Photo-c	14	28	42	76	108	140
2	8	16	24	44	57	70
3-10: 9-Whitney-a	8	16	24	40	50	60
11-21: 20-Last precode (4/55). 14-Whitney a	7	14	21	35	43	50

TRUE WAR STORIES (See Ripley's...)

TRUE WESTERN (True Adventures #3)
Marvel Comics (MMC): Dec, 1949 - No. 2, March, 1950

	GD	VG	FN	VF	VF/NM	NM-
1-Photo-c; Billy The Kid story	16	32	48	94	147	200
2-Alan Ladd photo-c	20	40	60	115	180	245

TRUMP
HMH Publishing Co.: Jan, 1957 - No. 2, Mar, 1957 (50¢, magazine)

	GD	VG	FN	VF	VF/NM	NM-
1-Harvey Kurtzman satire	25	50	75	145	233	320
2-Harvey Kurtzman satire	20	40	60	115	183	250

NOTE: *Davis, Elder, Heath, Jaffee art-#1,2; Wood a-1. Article by Mel Brooks in #2.*

TRUMPETS WEST (See Luke Short, Four Color #875)

TRUTH ABOUT CRIME (See Fox Giants)

TRUTH ABOUT MOTHER GOOSE (See Mother Goose, Four Color #862)

TRUTH BEHIND THE TRIAL OF CARDINAL MINDSZENTY, THE (See Cardinal Mindszenty in the Promotional Comics section))

TRUTHFUL LOVE (Formerly Youthful Love)
Youthful Magazines: No. 2, July, 1950

	GD	VG	FN	VF	VF/NM	NM-
2-Ingrid Bergman's true life story	11	22	33	64	90	115

TRUTH RED, WHITE & BLACK
Marvel Comics: Jan, 2003 - No. 6 ($3.50, limited series)

	GD	VG	FN	VF	VF/NM	NM-
1-Kyle Baker-a/Robert Morales-s; the testing of Captain America's super-soldier serum						3.50
2-7: 3-Isaiah Bradley 1st dons the Captain America costume						3.50
TPB (2004, $17.99) r/series						18.00

TRY-OUT WINNER BOOK
Marvel Comics: Mar, 1988

	GD	VG	FN	VF	VF/NM	NM-
1-Spider-Man vs. Doc Octopus						5.00

TSR WORLD (...Annual on cover only)
DC Comics: 1990 ($3.95, 84 pgs.)

	GD	VG	FN	VF	VF/NM	NM-
1-Advanced D&D, ForgottenRealms, Dragonlance & 1st app. Spelljammer						4.00

TSUNAMI GIRL
Image Comics: 1999 - No. 3, 1999 ($2.95)

	GD	VG	FN	VF	VF/NM	NM-
1-3-Sorayama-c/Paniccia-s/a						3.00

TUBBY (See Marge's...)

TUFF GHOSTS STARRING SPOOKY
Harvey Publications: July, 1962 - No. 39, Nov, 1970; No. 40, Sept, 1971 - No. 43, Oct, 1972

	GD	VG	FN	VF	VF/NM	NM-
1-12¢ issues begin	12	24	36	82	146	210
2-5	7	14	21	45	73	100

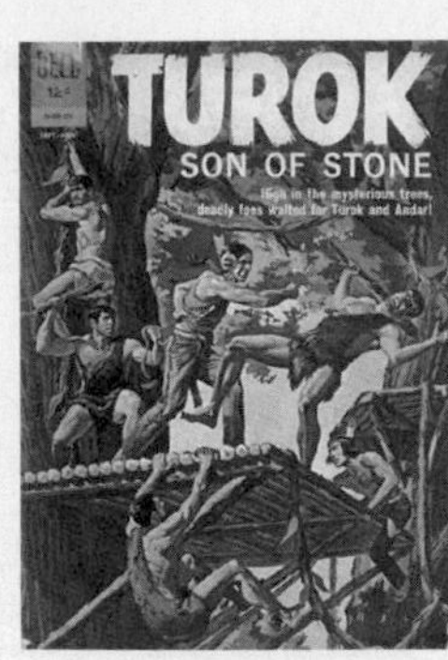

Turok, Son of Stone #29 © Acclaim

TV Stars #3 © H-B

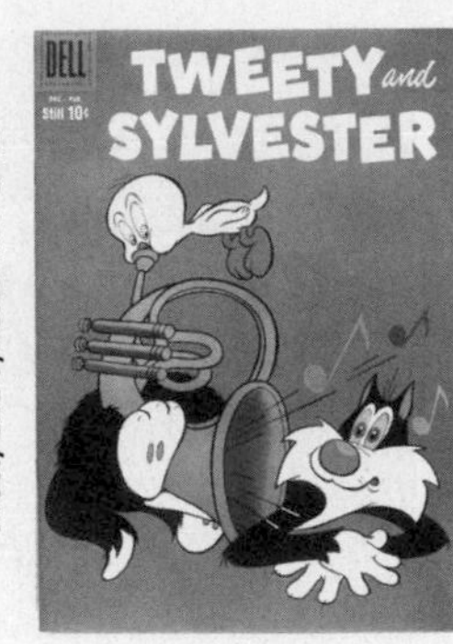

Tweety and Sylvester #31 © WB

GD VG FN VF VF/NM NM-
2.0 4.0 6.0 8.0 9.0 9.2

6-10 5 10 15 32 51 70
11-20 4 8 12 24 37 50
21-30: 29-Hot Stuff/Spooky team-up story 3 6 9 16 23 30
31-39,43 2 4 6 13 18 22
40-42: 52 pg. Giants 3 6 9 14 20 25

TUFFY
Standard Comics: No. 5, July, 1949 - No. 9, Oct, 1950
5-All by Sid Hoff 7 14 21 35 43 50
6-9 5 10 15 23 28 32

TUFFY TURTLE
I. W. Enterprises: No date
1-Reprint 2 4 6 8 11 14

TUG & BUSTER
Art & Soul Comics: Nov, 1995 - No. 7, Feb, 1998 ($2.95, B&W, bi-monthly)
1-7: Marc Hempel-c/a/scripts 3.00
1-(Image Comics, 8/98, $2.95, B&W) 3.00

TUROK
Acclaim Comics: Mar, 1998 - No. 4, Jun, 1998 ($2.50)
1-4-Nicieza-s/Kayanan-a 2.50
..., Child of Blood 1 (1/98, $3.95) Nicieza-s/Kayanan-a 4.00
... Evolution 1 (8/02, $2.50) Nicieza-s/Kayanan-a 2.50
..., Redpath 1 (10/97, $3.95) Nicieza-s/Kayanan-a 4.00
... / Shadowman 1 (2/99, $3.95) Priest-s/Broome & Jimenez-a 4.00
...: Spring Break in the Lost Land 1 (7/97, $3.95) Nicieza-s/Kayanan-a 4.00
...: Tales of the Lost Land 1 (4/98, $3.95) 4.00
...: The Empty Souls 1 (4/97, $3.95) Nicieza-s/Kayanan-a; variant-c 4.00

TUROK, DINOSAUR HUNTER (See Magnus Robot Fighter #12 & Archer & Armstrong #2)
Valiant/Acclaim Comics: June, 1993 - No. 47, Aug, 1996 ($2.50)
1-($3.50)-Chromium & foil-c 3.50
1-Gold foil-c variant 5.00
0, 2-47: 4-Andar app. 5-Death of Andar. 7-9-Truman/Glanzman-a. 11-Bound-in trading card. 16-Chaos Effect 2.50
Yearbook 1 (1994, $3.95, 52 pgs.) 4.00

TUROK, SON OF STONE (See Dan Curtis, Golden Comics Digest #31 & March of Comics #378, 399, 408)
Dell Publ. Co. #1-29(9/62)/Gold Key #30(12/62)-85(7/73)/Gold Key or Whitman #86(9/73)-125(1/80)/Whitman #126(3/81) on: No. 596, 12/54 - No. 29, 9/62; No. 30, 12/62 - No. 91, 7/74; No. 92, 9/74 - No. 125, 1/80; No. 126, 3/81 - No. 130, 4/82
Four Color 596 (12/54)(#1)-1st app./origin Turok & Andar; dinosaur-c. Created by Matthew H. Murphy; written by Alberto Giolitti 50 100 150 425 813 1200
Four Color 656 (10/55)(#2)-1st mention of Lanok 30 60 90 229 427 625
3(3-5/56)-5: 3-Cave men 20 40 60 148 274 400
6-10: 8-Dinosaur of the deep; Turok enters Lost Valley; series begins. 9-Paul S. Newman-s (most issues thru end) 15 30 45 107 196 285
11-20: 17-Prehistoric Pygmies 12 24 36 82 146 210
21-29 9 18 27 60 100 140
30-1st Gold Key. 30-33-Painted back-c. 9 18 27 61 103 145
31-Drug use story 9 18 27 60 100 140
32-40 7 14 21 47 76 105
41-50 6 12 18 39 62 85
51-57,59,60 5 10 15 34 55 75
58-Flying Saucer c/story 6 12 18 37 59 80
61-70: 62-12¢ & 15¢ covers. 63,68-Line drawn-c 4 8 12 28 44 60
71-84: 84-Origin & 1st app. Hutec 4 8 12 24 37 50
85-99: 93-r-c/#19 w/changes. 94-r-c/#28 w/changes. 97-r-c/#31 w/changes. 98-r/#58 w/o spaceship & spacemen on-c. 99-r-c/#52 w/changes. 3 6 9 19 29 38
100 4 8 12 24 37 50
101-129: 114,115-(52 pgs.). 129(2/82) 3 6 9 21 32 42
130(4/82)-Last issue 5 10 15 34 55 75
Giant 1(30031-611) (11/66)-Slick-c; r/#10-12 & 16 plus cover to #11 10 20 30 71 126 180
Giant 1-Same as above but with paper-c 11 22 33 79 140 200
NOTE: *Most painted-c; line-drawn #63 & 130.* ***Alberto Gioletti*** *a-24-27, 30-119, 123; painted-c No. 30-129.* ***Sparling*** *a-117, 120-130. Reprints-#36, 54, 57, 75, 112, 114(1/3), 115(1/3), 118, 121, 125, 127(1/3), 128, 129(1/3), 130(1/3), Giant 1. Cover r-93, 94, 97-99, 126(all different from original covers.*

TUROK THE HUNTED
Valiant/Acclaim Comics: Mar, 1995 - No. 2, Apr, 1995 ($2.50, limited series)
1,2-Mike Deodato-a(p); price omitted on #1 2.50

TUROK THE HUNTED
Acclaim Comics (Valiant): Feb, 1996 - No. 2, Mar, 1996 ($2.50, limited series)
1,2-Mike Grell story 2.50

TUROK, TIMEWALKER
Acclaim Comics (Valiant): Aug, 1997 - No. 2, Sept, 1997 ($2.50, limited series)
1,2-Nicieza story 2.50

TUROK 2 (Magazine)
Acclaim Comics: Oct, 1998 ($4.99, magazine size)
...Seeds of Evil-Nicieza-s/Broome & Benjamin-a; origin back-up story 5.00
#2 Adon's Curse -Mack painted-c/Broome & Benjamin-a; origin pt. 2 5.00

TUROK 3: SHADOW OF OBLIVION
Acclaim Comics: Sept, 2000 ($4.95, one-shot)
1-Includes pin-up gallery 5.00

TURTLE SOUP
Mirage Studios: Sept, 1987 ($2.00, 76 pgs., B&W, one-shot)
1-Featuring Teenage Mutant Ninja Turtles 5.00

TURTLE SOUP
Mirage Studios: Nov, 1991 - No. 4, 1992 ($2.50, limited series, coated paper)
1-4: Features the Teenage Mutant Ninja Turtles 2.50

TV CASPER & COMPANY
Harvey Publications: Aug, 1963 - No. 46, April, 1974 (25¢ Giants)
1- 68 pg. Giants begin; Casper, Little Audrey, Baby Huey, Herman & Catnip, Buzzy the Crow begin 12 24 36 82 146 210
2-5 6 12 18 43 69 95
6-10 5 10 15 30 48 65
11-20 4 8 12 24 37 50
21-31: 31-Last 68 pg. issue 3 6 9 18 27 35
32-46: All 52 pgs. 3 6 9 16 23 30
NOTE: *Many issues contain reprints.*

TV FUNDAY FUNNIES (See Famous TV...)

TV FUNNIES (See New Funnies)

TV FUNTIME (See Little Audrey)

TV LAUGHOUT (See Archie's...)

TV SCREEN CARTOONS (Formerly Real Screen)
National Periodical Publ.: No. 129, July-Aug, 1959 - No. 138, Jan-Feb, 1961
129-138 (Scarce) 6 12 18 43 69 95

TV STARS (TV) (Newsstand sales only)
Marvel Comics Group: Aug, 1978 - No. 4, Feb, 1979 (Hanna-Barbera)
1-Great Grape Ape app. 3 6 9 18 27 35
2,4: 4-Top Cat app. 3 6 9 16 22 28
3-Toth-c/a; Dave Stevens inks 3 6 9 17 25 32

TV TEENS (Formerly Ozzie & Babs; Rock and Rollo #14 on)
Charlton Comics: V1#14, Feb, 1954 - V2#13, July, 1956
V1#14 (#1)-Ozzie & Babs 10 20 30 54 72 90
15 (#2) 6 12 18 33 41 48
V2#3(6/54) - 6-Don Winslow 6 12 18 31 38 45
7-13-Mopsy. 8(7/55). 9-Paper dolls 6 12 18 29 36 42

TWEETY AND SYLVESTER (1st Series) (TV) (Also see Looney Tunes and Merrie Melodies)
Dell Publishing Co.: No. 406, June, 1952 - No. 37, June-Aug, 1962
Four Color 406 (#1) 10 20 30 71 126 180
Four Color 489,524 6 12 18 41 66 90
4 (3-5/54) - 20 5 10 15 32 51 70
21-37 4 8 12 28 44 60
(See March of Comics #421, 433, 445, 457, 469, 481)

TWEETY AND SYLVESTER (2nd Series)(See Kite Fun Book)
Gold Key No. 1-102/Whitman No. 103 on: Nov, 1963; No. 2, Nov, 1965 - No. 121, June, 1984
1 4 8 12 28 44 60
2-10 3 6 9 18 27 35
11-30 2 4 6 13 18 22
31-50 2 4 6 9 12 15
51-70 1 3 4 6 8 10
71-102 1 2 3 5 6 8
103,104 (Whitman) 1 3 4 6 8 10
105(9/80),106(10/80),107(12/80) 3-pack only 3 6 9 20 30 40
108-116: 113(2/82),114(2-3/82),115(3/82),116(4/82) 2 4 6 8 10 12
117-121 (All # 90094 on-c; nd, nd code): 117(6/83). 118(7/83). 119(2/84)-r(1/3). 120(5/84).

The Twelve #1 © MAR

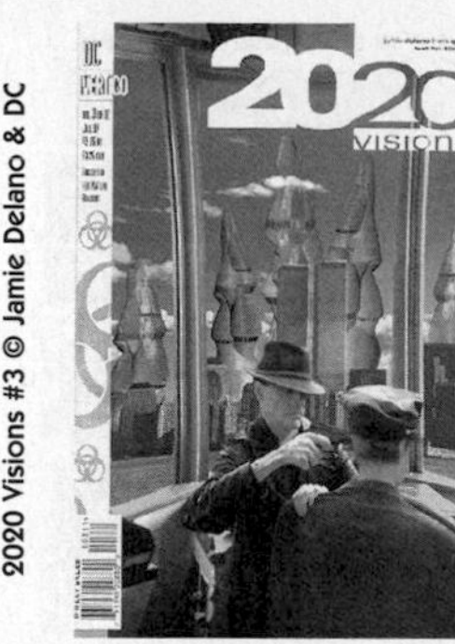

2020 Visions #3 © Jamie Delano & DC

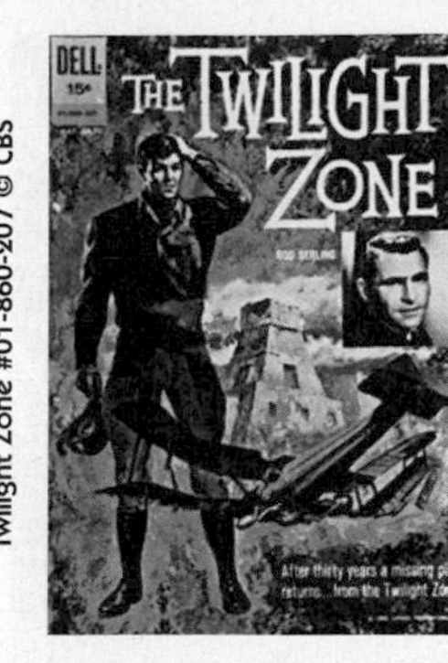

Twilight Zone #01-860-207 © CBS

	GD 2.0	VG 4.0	FN 6.0	VF 8.0	VF/NM 9.0	NM- 9.2
121(6/84)	3	6	9	14	19	24
Digest nn (Charlton/Xerox Pub., 1974) (low print run)	3	6	9	16	23	30
Mini Comic No. 1(1976, 3-1/4x6-1/2")	1	3	4	6	8	10

TWELVE, THE (Golden Age Timely heroes)
Marvel Comics: No. 0; 2008; No. 1, Mar, 2008 - No. 12 ($2.99, limited series)

	GD 2.0	VG 4.0	FN 6.0	VF 8.0	VF/NM 9.0	NM- 9.2
0-Rockman, Laughing Mask & Phantom Reporter intro. stories (1940s); series preview						3.00
1/2 (2008, $3.99) r/early app. of Fiery Mask, Mister E and Rockman; Weston-c						4.00
1-8-Straczynski-a/Weston-a; Timely heroes re-surface in the present						3.00

12 O'CLOCK HIGH (TV)
Dell Publishing Co.: Jan-Mar, 1965 - No. 2, Apr-June, 1965 (Photo-c)

	GD 2.0	VG 4.0	FN 6.0	VF 8.0	VF/NM 9.0	NM- 9.2
1- Sinnott-a	6	12	18	39	62	85
2	5	10	15	30	48	65

2099 A.D.
Marvel Comics: May, 1995 ($3.95, one-shot)

1-Acetate-c by Quesada & Palmiotti — 4.00

2099 APOCALYPSE
Marvel Comics: Dec, 1995 ($4.95, one-shot)

1-Chromium wraparound-c; Ellis script — 5.00

2099 GENESIS
Marvel Comics: Jan, 1996 ($4.95, one-shot)

1-Chromium wraparound-c; Ellis script — 5.00

2099 MANIFEST DESTINY
Marvel Comics: Mar, 1998 ($5.99, one-shot)

1-Origin of Fantastic Four 2099; intro Moon Knight 2099 — 6.00

2099 UNLIMITED
Marvel Comics: Sept, 1993 - No. 10, 1996 ($3.95, 68 pgs.)

1-10: 1-1st app. Hulk 2099 & begins. 1-3-Spider-Man 2099 app. 9-Joe Kubert-c; Len Wein & Nancy Collins scripts — 4.00

2099 WORLD OF DOOM SPECIAL
Marvel Comics: May, 1995 ($2.25, one-shot)

1-Doom's "Contract w/America" — 2.50

2099 WORLD OF TOMORROW
Marvel Comics: Sept, 1996 - No. 8, Apr, 1997 ($2.50) (Replaces 2099 titles)

1-8: 1-Wraparound-c. 2-w/bound-in card. 4,5-Phalanx — 2.50

21
Image Comics (Top Cow Productions): Feb, 1996 - No. 3, Apr, 1996 ($2.50)

1-3: Len Wein scripts — 2.50
1-Variant-c — 2.50

21 DOWN
DC Comics (WildStorm): Nov, 2002 - No. 12, Nov, 2003 ($2.95)

1-12: 1-Palmiotti & Gray-s/Saiz-a/Jusko-c — 3.00
...: The Conduit (2003, $19.95, TPB) r/#1-7; intro. by Garth Ennis — 20.00

24 (Based on TV series)
IDW Publishing: July, 2004 - Present ($6.99/$7.49, square-bound, one-shots)

...: Midnight Sun (7/05, $7.49) J.C. Vaughn & Mark Haynes-s; Renato Guedes-a — 7.50
...: One Shot (7/04, $6.99)-Jack Bauer's first day on the job at CTU; Vaughn & Haynes-s; Guedes-a — 7.00
...: Stories (1/05, $7.49) Manny Clark-a; Vaughn & Haynes-s — 7.50

24: NIGHTFALL (Based on TV series)
IDW Publishing: Nov, 2006 - No. 6 ($3.99, limited series)

1-5-Two years before Season One; Vaughn & Haynes-s; Diaz-a; two covers — 4.00

2020 VISIONS
DC Comics (Vertigo): May, 1997 - No. 12, Apr, 1998 ($2.25, limited series)

1-12-Delano-s: 1-3-Quitely-a. 4-"la tormenta"-Pleece-a — 2.50

20,000 LEAGUES UNDER THE SEA (Movie)(See King Classics, Movie Comics & Power Record Comics)
Dell Publishing Co.: No. 614, Feb, 1955 (Disney)

	GD 2.0	VG 4.0	FN 6.0	VF 8.0	VF/NM 9.0	NM- 9.2
Four Color 614-Movie, painted-c	8	16	24	58	97	135

TWICE TOLD TALES (See Movie Classics)

TWILIGHT
DC Comics: 1990 - No. 3, 1991 ($4.95, 52 pgs, lim. series, squarebound, mature)

1-3: Tommy Tomorrow app; Chaykin scripts, Garcia-Lopez-c/a — 5.00

TWILIGHT EXPERIMENT
DC Comics (WildStorm): Apr, 2004 - No. 6, Sept, 2005 ($2.95, limited series)

1-6-Gray & Palmiotti-s/Santacruz-a — 3.00

TWILIGHT MAN
First Publishing: June, 1989 - No. 4, Sept, 1989 ($2.75, limited series)

1-4 — 2.75

TWILIGHT ZONE, THE (TV) (See Dan Curtis & Stories From...)
Dell Publishing Co./Gold Key/Whitman No. 92: No. 1173, 3-5/61 - No. 91, 4/79; No. 92, 5/82

	GD 2.0	VG 4.0	FN 6.0	VF 8.0	VF/NM 9.0	NM- 9.2
Four Color 1173 (#1)-Crandall-c/a	21	42	63	152	281	410
Four Color 1288-Crandall/Evans-c/a	12	24	36	87	156	225
01-860-207 (5-7/62-Dell, 15¢)	9	18	27	63	107	150
12-860-210 on-c; 01-860-210 on inside(8-10/62-Dell)-Evans-c/a (3 stories)	9	18	27	63	107	150
1(11/62-Gold Key)-Crandall/Frazetta-a (10 & 11 pgs.); Evans-a	14	28	42	99	175	250
2	8	16	24	58	97	135
3-11: 3(11 pgs.),4(10 pgs.),9-Toth-a	6	12	18	43	69	95
12-15: 12-Williamson-a. 13,15-Crandall-a. 14-Orlando/Crandall/Torres-a	5	10	15	35	55	75
16-20	4	8	12	26	41	55
21-25: 21-Crandall-a(r). 25-Evans/Crandall-a(r); Toth-r/#4; last 12¢ issue	3	6	9	20	30	40
26,27: 26-Flying Saucer-c/story; Crandall, Evans-a(r). 27-Evans-r(2)	3	6	9	19	29	38
28-32: 32-Evans-a(r)	3	6	9	17	25	32
33-51: 43-Celardo-a. 51-Williamson-a	2	4	6	13	18	22
52-70	2	4	6	10	14	18
71-82,86-91: 71-Reprint	2	4	6	8	11	14
83-(52 pgs.)	2	4	6	13	18	22
84-(52 pgs.) Frank Miller's 1st comic book work	4	8	12	28	44	60
85-Frank Miller-a (2nd)	3	6	9	16	23	30
92-(Whitman, 5/82) Last issue; r/#1.	2	4	6	9	13	16
Mini Comic #1(1976, 3-1/4x6-1/2")	2	4	6	8	10	12

NOTE: ***Bolle** a-13(w/**McWilliams**), 50, 55, 57, 59, 77, 78, 80, 83, 84. **McWilliams** a-59, 78, 80, 82, 84. **Miller** a-84, 85. **Orlando** a-15, 19, 20, 22, 23. **Sekowsky** a-3. **Simonson** a-50, 54, 55, 83r. **Weiss** a-39, 79r(#39). (See Mystery Comics Digest 3, 6, 9, 12, 15, 18, 21, 24). Reprints-26(1/3), 71, 73, 79, 83, 84, 86, 92. Painted c-1-91.*

TWILIGHT ZONE, THE (TV)
Now Comics: Nov, 1990 ($2.95); Oct, 1991; V2#1, Nov, 1991 - No. 11, Oct, 1992 ($1.95); V3#1, 1993 - No. 4, 1993 ($2.50)

1-(11/90, $2.95, 52 pgs.)-Direct sale edition; Neal Adams-a, Sienkiewicz-c; Harlan Ellison scripts — 3.00
1-(11/90, $1.75)-Newsstand ed. w/N. Adams-c — 2.50
1-Prestige Format (10/91, $4.95)-Reprints above with extra Harlan Ellison short story — 5.00
1-Collector's Edition (10/91, $2.50)-Non-code approved and polybagged; reprints 11/90 issue; gold logo, 1-Reprint ($2.50)-r/direct sale 11/90 version, 1-Reprint ($2.50)-r/newsstand 11/90 version each... — 2.50
V2#1-Direct sale & newsstand ed. w/different-c — 2.50
V2#2-8,10-11 — 2.50
V2#9-($2.95)-3-D Special; polybagged w/glasses & hologram on-c — 3.00
V2#9-($4.95)-Prestige Edition; contains 2 extra stories & a different hologram on-c; polybagged w/glasses — 5.00
V3#1-4, Anniversary Special 1 (1992, $2.50) — 2.50
Annual 1 (4/93, $2.50)-No ads — 2.50
...Science Fiction Special (3/93, $3.50) — 3.50

TWINKLE COMICS
Spotlight Publishers: May, 1945

	GD 2.0	VG 4.0	FN 6.0	VF 8.0	VF/NM 9.0	NM- 9.2
1	24	48	72	140	225	310

TWIST, THE
Dell Publishing Co.: July-Sept, 1962

	GD 2.0	VG 4.0	FN 6.0	VF 8.0	VF/NM 9.0	NM- 9.2
01-864-209-Painted-c	4	8	12	24	37	50

TWISTED TALES (See Eclipse Graphic Album Series #15)
Pacific Comics/Independent Comics Group (Eclipse) #9,10: 11/82 - No. 8, 5/84; No. 9, 11/84; No. 10, 12/84 (Baxter paper)

1-9: 1-B. Jones/Corben-c; Alcala-a; nudity/violence in al. 2-Wrightson-c; Ploog-a — 4.00
10-Wrightson painted art; Morrow-a — 6.00

NOTE: ***Bolton** painted c-4, 6, 7; a-7. **Conrad** a-1, 3, 5; c-1i, 3, 5. **Guice** a-8. **Wildey** a-3.*

TWO BIT THE WACKY WOODPECKER (See Wacky...)
Toby Press: 1951 - No. 3, May, 1953

	GD 2.0	VG 4.0	FN 6.0	VF 8.0	VF/NM 9.0	NM- 9.2
1	10	20	30	54	72	90
2,3	6	12	18	31	38	45

TWO FACE: YEAR ONE

Two-Fisted Tales #27 © WMG

Two-Gun Kid #19 © MAR

2001: A Space Odyssey #1 © MAR

DC Comics: 2008 - No. 2, 2008 ($5.99, squarebound, limited series)

	GD 2.0	VG 4.0	FN 6.0	VF 8.0	VF/NM 9.0	NM- 9.2
1-Origin re-told; Sable-s/Saiz & Haun-a						6.00

TWO-FISTED TALES (Formerly Haunt of Fear #15-17)
(Also see EC Archives • Two-Fisted Tales)
E. C. Comics: No. 18, Nov-Dec, 1950 - No. 41, Feb-Mar, 1955

	GD 2.0	VG 4.0	FN 6.0	VF 8.0	VF/NM 9.0	NM- 9.2
18(#1)-Kurtzman-c	89	178	267	712	1131	1550
19-Kurtzman-c	66	132	198	528	839	1150
20-Kurtzman-c	42	84	126	336	536	735
21,22-Kurtzman-c	34	68	102	272	436	600
23-25-Kurtzman-c	27	54	81	216	341	465
26-35: 33- "Atom Bomb" by Wood	19	38	57	152	246	340
36-41	15	30	45	120	195	270
Two-Fisted Annual (1952, 25¢, 132 pgs.)	100	200	300	750	1125	1500
Two-Fisted Annual (1953, 25¢, 132 pgs.)	77	154	231	578	864	1150

NOTE: ***Berg** a-29. **Colan** a-39p. **Craig** a-18, 19, 32. **Crandall** a-35, 36. **Davis** a-20-36, 40; c-30, 34, 35, 41, Annual 2. **Evans** a-34, 40, 41; c-40. **Feldstein** a-18. **Krigstein** a-41. **Kubert** a-32, 33. **Kurtzman** a-18-25; c-18-29, 31, Annual 1. **Severin** a-26, 28, 29, 31, 34-41 (No. 37-39 are all-**Severin** issues); c-36-39. **Severin/Elder** a-19-29, 31, 33, 36. **Wood** a-18-28, 30-35, 41; c-32, 33. Special issues: #26 (ChanJin Reservoir), 31 (Civil War), 35 (Civil War). Canadian reprints known; see Table of Contents. #25-Davis biog. #27-Wood biog. #28-Kurtzman biog.*

TWO-FISTED TALES
Russ Cochran/Gemstone Publishing: Oct, 1992 - No. 24, May, 1998 ($1.50/$2.00/$2.50)

	GD 2.0	VG 4.0	FN 6.0	VF 8.0	VF/NM 9.0	NM- 9.2
1-24: 1-4r/Two-Fisted Tales #18-21 w/original-c						2.50

TWO-GUN KID (Also see All Western Winners, Best Western, Black Rider, Blaze Carson, Kid Colt, Western Winners, Wild West, & Wild Western)
Marvel/Atlas (MCI No. 1-10/HPC No. 11-59/Marvel No. 60 on): 3/48(No mo.) - No. 10, 11/49; No. 11, 12/53 - No. 59, 4/61; No. 60, 11/62 - No. 92, 3/68; No. 93, 7/70 - No. 136, 4/77

	GD 2.0	VG 4.0	FN 6.0	VF 8.0	VF/NM 9.0	NM- 9.2
1-Two-Gun Kid & his horse Cyclone begin; The Sheriff begins	110	220	330	693	1172	1650
2	45	90	135	279	465	650
3,4: 3-Annie Oakley app.	37	74	111	215	345	475
5-Pre-Black Rider app. (Wint. 48/49); Anti-Wertham editorial (1st?)	39	78	117	230	370	510
6-10(11/49): 8-Blaze Carson app. 9-Black Rider app.	28	56	84	162	261	360
11(12/53)-Black Rider app.; 1st to have Atlas globe on-c; explains how Kid Colt became an outlaw	22	44	66	129	207	285
12-Black Rider app.	21	42	63	123	197	270
13-20: 14-Opium story	15	30	45	94	147	200
21-24,26-29	15	30	45	90	140	190
25,30: 25 Williamson-a (5 pgs.). 30-Williamson/Torres-a (4 pgs.)	15	30	45	94	147	200
31-33,35,37-40	8	16	24	56	93	130
34-Crandall-a	8	16	24	58	97	135
36,41,42,48-Origin in all	8	16	24	58	97	135
43,44,47	7	14	21	47	76	105
45,46-Davis-a	7	14	21	50	83	115
49,50,52,53-Severin-a(2/3) in each	6	12	18	43	69	95
51-Williamson-a (5 pgs.)	7	14	21	50	83	115
54,55,57,59-Severin-a(3) in each. 59-Kirby-a; last 10¢ issue (4/61)	6	12	18	43	69	95
56	6	12	18	39	62	85
58,60-New origin. 58-Kirby/Ayers-c/a "The Monster of Hidden Valley" cover/story (Kirby monster-c)	7	14	21	49	80	110
60-Edition w/handwritten issue number on cover	8	16	24	58	97	135
61,62-Kirby-a	6	12	18	39	62	85
63-74: 64-Intro. Boom-Boom	4	8	12	28	44	60
75-77-Kirby-a	5	10	15	32	51	70
78-89	3	6	9	20	30	40
90,95-Kirby-a	4	8	12	22	34	45
91,92: 92-Last new story; last 12¢ issue	3	6	9	18	27	35
93,94,96-99	2	4	6	13	18	22
100-Last 15¢-c	3	6	9	14	19	24
101-Origin retold/#58; Kirby-a	3	6	9	14	19	24
102-120-reprints	2	4	6	8	10	12
121-136-reprints. 129-131-(Regular 25¢ editions)	2	4	6	8	10	12
129-131-(30¢-c variants, limited distribution)(4-8/76)	4	8	12	26	41	55

NOTE: ***Ayers** a-26, 27. **Davis** c-45-47. **Drucker** a-23. **Everett** a-82, 91. **Fuje** a-13. **Heath** a-3(2), 4(3), 5(2), 7; c-13, 21, 23, 53. **Keller** a-16, 19, 28. **Kirby** a-54, 55, 57-62, 75-77, 90, 95, 101, 119, 120, 129; c-10, 52, 54-65, 67-72, 74-76, 116. **Maneely** a-20; c-11, 12, 16, 19, 20, 25-28, 30, 35, 49. **Powell** a-38, 102, 104. **Severin** a-9, 29, 51, 55, 57, 99r(3); c-9, 51. **Shores** c-1-8, 11. **Trimpe** c-99. **Tuska** a-11, 12. **Whitney** a-87, 89-91, 98-113, 124, 129; c-87, 89, 91, 113. **Wildey** a-21. **Williamson** a-110r. Kid Colt in #13, 14, 16-21.*

TWO GUN KID: SUNSET RIDERS
Marvel Comics: Nov, 1995 - No. 2, Dec, 1995 ($6.95, squarebound, lim. series)

	GD 2.0	VG 4.0	FN 6.0	VF 8.0	VF/NM 9.0	NM- 9.2
1,2: Fabian Nicieza scripts in all. 1-Painted-c.						7.00

TWO GUN WESTERN (1st Series) (Formerly Casey Crime Photographer #1-4? or My Love #1-4?)
Marvel/Atlas Comics (MPC): No. 5, Nov, 1950 - No. 14, June, 1952

	GD 2.0	VG 4.0	FN 6.0	VF 8.0	VF/NM 9.0	NM- 9.2
5-The Apache Kid (Intro & origin) & his horse Nightwind begin by Buscema	26	52	78	152	244	335
6-10: 8-Kid Colt, The Texas Kid & his horse Thunder begin?	19	38	57	112	176	240
11-14: 13-Black Rider app.	14	28	42	80	115	150

NOTE: ***Maneely** a-6, 7, 9; c-6, 11-13. **Morrow** a-9. **Romita** a-8. **Wildey** a-8.*

2-GUN WESTERN (2nd Series) (Formerly Billy Buckskin #1-3; Two-Gun Western #5 on)
Atlas Comics (MgPC): No. 4, May, 1956

	GD 2.0	VG 4.0	FN 6.0	VF 8.0	VF/NM 9.0	NM- 9.2
4-Colan, Ditko, Severin, Sinnott-a; Maneely-c	15	30	45	88	137	185

TWO-GUN WESTERN (Formerly 2-Gun Western)
Atlas Comics (MgPC): No. 5, July, 1956 - No. 12, Sept, 1957

	GD 2.0	VG 4.0	FN 6.0	VF 8.0	VF/NM 9.0	NM- 9.2
5-Return of the Gun-Hawk-c/story; Black Rider app.	15	30	45	85	130	175
6,7	12	24	36	67	94	120
8,10,12-Crandall-a	13	26	39	72	101	130
9,11-Williamson-a in both (5 pgs. each)	14	28	42	76	108	140

NOTE: ***Ayers** a-9. **Colan** a-5. **Everett** c-12. **Forgione** a-5, 6. **Kirby** a-12. **Maneely** a-6, 8, 12; c-5, 6, 8, 11. **Morrow** a-9, 10. **Powell** a-7, 11. **Severin** c-10. **Sinnott** a-5. **Wildey** a-9.*

TWO MINUTE WARNING
Ultimate Sports Ent.: 2000 - No. 2 ($3.95, cardstock covers)

	GD 2.0	VG 4.0	FN 6.0	VF 8.0	VF/NM 9.0	NM- 9.2
1,2-NFL players & Teddy Roosevelt battle evil						4.00

TWO MOUSEKETEERS, THE (See 4-Color #475, 603, 642 under M.G.M.'s...;

TWO ON A GUILLOTINE (See Movie Classics)

TWO-STEP
DC Comics (Cliffhanger): Dec, 2003 - No. 3, Jul, 2004 ($2.95, limited series)

	GD 2.0	VG 4.0	FN 6.0	VF 8.0	VF/NM 9.0	NM- 9.2
1-3-Warren Ellis-s/Amanda Conner-a						3.00

2000 A.D. MONTHLY/PRESENTS (Showcase #25 on)
Eagle Comics/Quality Comics No. 5 on: 4/85 - #6, 9/85; 4/86 - #54, 1991 ($1.25-$1.50, Mando paper)

	GD 2.0	VG 4.0	FN 6.0	VF 8.0	VF/NM 9.0	NM- 9.2
1-6,1-25:1-4 r/British series featuring Judge Dredd; Alan Moore scripts begin. 1-25 ($1.25)-Reprints from British 2000 AD						2.50
26,27/28, 29/30, 31-54: 27/28, 29/30,31-Guice-c						2.50

2001, A SPACE ODYSSEY (Movie) (See adaptation in Treasury edition)
Marvel Comics Group: Dec, 1976 - No. 10, Sept, 1977 (30¢)

	GD 2.0	VG 4.0	FN 6.0	VF 8.0	VF/NM 9.0	NM- 9.2
1-Kirby-c/a in all	2	4	6	11	16	20
2-7,9,10	1	3	4	6	8	10
7,9,10-(35¢-c variants, limited distribution)(6-9/77)	3	6	9	16	23	30
8-Origin/1st app. Machine Man (called Mr. Machine)	2	4	6	11	16	20
8-(35¢-c variant, limited distribution)(6,8/77)	4	8	12	28	44	60
...Treasury 1 ('76, 84 pgs.)-All new Kirby-a	3	6	9	15	21	26

2001 NIGHTS
Viz Premiere Comics: 1990 - No. 10, 1991 ($3.75, B&W, lim. series, mature readers, 84 pgs.)

	GD 2.0	VG 4.0	FN 6.0	VF 8.0	VF/NM 9.0	NM- 9.2
1-10: Japanese sci-fi. 1-Wraparound-c						4.25

2010 (Movie)
Marvel Comics Group: Apr, 1985 - No. 2, May, 1985

	GD 2.0	VG 4.0	FN 6.0	VF 8.0	VF/NM 9.0	NM- 9.2
1,2-r/Marvel Super Special movie adaptation.						2.50

TYPHOID (Also see Daredevil)
Marvel Comics: Nov, 1995 - No. 4, Feb, 1996 ($3.95, squarebound, lim. series)

	GD 2.0	VG 4.0	FN 6.0	VF 8.0	VF/NM 9.0	NM- 9.2
1-4: Van Fleet-c/a						4.00

UFO & ALIEN COMIX
Warren Publishing Co.: Jan, 1978 (B&W magazine, 84 pgs., one-shot)

	GD 2.0	VG 4.0	FN 6.0	VF 8.0	VF/NM 9.0	NM- 9.2
nn-Toth-a, J. Severin-a(r); Pie-s	2	4	6	10	14	18

UFO & OUTER SPACE (Formerly UFO Flying Saucers)
Gold Key: No. 14, June, 1978 - No. 25, Feb, 1980 (All painted covers)

	GD 2.0	VG 4.0	FN 6.0	VF 8.0	VF/NM 9.0	NM- 9.2
14-Reprints UFO Flying Saucers #3	1	3	4	6	8	10
15,16-Reprints	1	3	4	6	8	10
17-25: 17-20-New material. 23-McWilliams-a. 24-(3 pg.-r). 25-Reprints UFO Flying Saucers #2 w/cover	1	3	4	6	8	10

UFO ENCOUNTERS
Western Publishing Co.: May, 1978 ($1.95, 228 pgs.)

	GD 2.0	VG 4.0	FN 6.0	VF 8.0	VF/NM 9.0	NM- 9.2
11192-Reprints UFO Flying Saucers	3	6	9	20	30	40

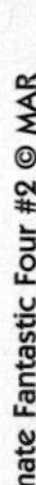
Ultimate Fantastic Four #2 © MAR

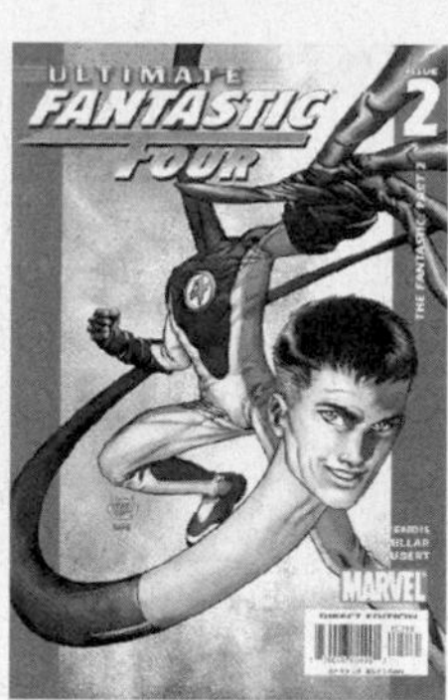

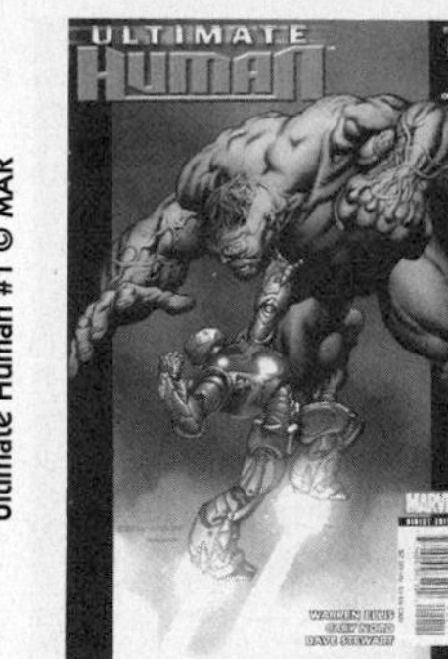

Ultimate Human #1 © MAR

Ultimate Iron Man 2 #3 © MAR

GD 2.0 | VG 4.0 | FN 6.0 | VF 8.0 | VF/NM 9.0 | NM- 9.2

11404-Vol.1 (128 pgs.)-See UFO Mysteries for Vol.2 3 6 9 17 25 32

UFO FLYING SAUCERS (UFO & Outer Space #14 on)
Gold Key: Oct, 1968 - No. 13, Jan, 1977 (No. 2 on, 36 pgs.)

1(30035-810) (68 pgs.) 4 8 12 26 41 55
2(11/70), 3(11/72), 4(11/74) 2 4 6 13 18 22
5(2/75)-13: Bolle-a #4 on 2 4 6 9 12 15

UFO MYSTERIES
Western Publishing Co.: 1978 ($1.00, reprints, 96 pgs.)

11400-(Vol.2)-Cont'd from UFO Encounters, pgs. 129-224 3 6 9 17 25 32

ULTIMAN GIANT ANNUAL (See Big Bang Comics)
Image Comics: Nov, 2001 ($4.95, B&W, one-shot)

1-Homage to DC 1960's annuals 5.00

ULTIMATE... (Collects 4-issue alternate titles from X-Men Age of Apocalypse crossovers)
Marvel Comics: May, 1995 ($8.95, trade paperbacks, gold foil covers)

Amazing X-Men, Astonishing X-Men, Factor-X, Gambit & the X-Ternals, Generation Next, X-Calibre, X-Man 9.00
Weapon X 10.00

ULTIMATE ADVENTURES
Marvel Comics: Nov, 2002 - No. 6, Dec, 2003 ($2.25)

1-6: 1-Intro. Hawk-Owl; Zimmerman-s/Fogrodo-a. 3-Ultimates app. 2.50
One Tin Soldier TPB (2005, $12.99) r/#1-6 13.00

ULTIMATE ANNUALS
Marvel Comics: 2006; 2007 ($13.99, SC)

Vol. 1 (2006, $13.99) r/Ult. FF Ann. #1, Ult. X-Men Ann. #1, Ult S-M #1, Ultimates Ann #1 14.00
Vol. 2 (2007, $13.99) r/Ult. FF Ann. #2, Ult. X-Men Ann. #2, Ult S-M #2, Ultimates Ann #2 14.00

ULTIMATE CIVIL WAR: SPIDER-HAM (See Civil War and related titles)
Marvel Comics: March, 2007 ($2.99, one-shot)

1-Spoof of Civil War series featuring Spider-Ham; art by various incl. Olivetti, Severin 3.00

ULTIMATE DAREDEVIL AND ELEKTRA
Marvel Comics: Jan, 2003 - No. 4, Mar, 2003 ($2.25, limited series)

1-4-Rucka-s/Larroca-c/a; 1st meeting of Elektra and Matt Murdock 2.50
... Vol.1 TPB (2003, $11.99) r/#1-4, Daredevil Vol. 2 #9; Larroca sketch pages 12.00

ULTIMATE ELEKTRA
Marvel Comics: Oct, 2004 - No. 5, Feb, 2005 ($2.25, limited series)

1-5-Carey-s/Larroca-c/a. 2-Bullseye app. 2.50
... : Devil's Due TPB (2005, $11.99) r/#1-5 12.00

ULTIMATE EXTINCTION (See Ultimate Nightmare and Ultimate Secret limited series)
Marvel Comics: Mar, 2006 - No. 5, July, 2006 ($2.99, limited series)

1-5-The coming of Gah Lak Tus; Ellis-s/Peterson-a 3.00
TPB (2006, $12.99) r/#1-5 13.00

ULTIMATE FANTASTIC FOUR
Marvel Comics: Feb, 2004 - Present ($2.25/$2.50/$2.99)

1-Bendis & Millar-s/Adam Kubert-a/Hitch-c 5.00
2-20: 2-Adam Kubert-a/c; intro. Moleman 7-Ellis-s/Immonen-a begin; Dr. Doom app. 13-18-Kubert-a. 19,20-Jae Lee-a. 20-Begin $2.50-c 3.00
21-Marvel Zombies; begin Greg Land-c/a; Mark Millar-s; variant-c by Land 4.00
22-29,33-57: 24-26-Namor app. 28-President Thor. 33-38-Ferry-a. 42-46-Silver Surfer 3.00
30-32-Marvel Zombies; Millar-s/Land-a; Dr. Doom app. 4.00
30-32-Zombie variant-c by Suydam 5.00
50-White variant-c by Kirkham 5.00
Annual 1 (10/05, $3.99) The Inhumans app.; Jae Lee-a/Mark Millar-s/Greg Land-c 4.00
Annual 2 (10/06, $3.99) Mole Man app.; Immonen & Irving-a/Carey-s 4.00
.../Ult. X-Men Annual 1 (11/08, $3.99) Continued from Ult. X-Men/Ult. F.F. Annual #1 4.00
.../X-Men 1 (3/06, $2.99) Carey-s/Ferry-a; continued from Ult. X-Men/Fantastic Four #1 3.00
... Vol. 1: The Fantastic (2004, $12.99, TPB) r/#1-6; cover gallery 13.00
... Vol. 2: Doom (2004, $12.99, TPB) r/#7-12 13.00
... Vol. 3: N-Zone (2005, $12.99, TPB) r/#13-18 13.00
... Vol. 4: Inhuman (2005, $12.99, TPB) r/#19,20 & Annual #1 13.00
... Vol. 5: Crossover (2006, $12.99, TPB) r/#21-26 13.00
... Vol. 6: Frightful (2006, $14.99, TPB) r/#27-32; gallery of cover sketches & variants 15.00
... Vol. 7: God War (2007, $16.99, TPB) r/#33-38 17.00
... Vol. 8: Devils (2007, $12.99, TPB) r/#39-41 & Annual #2 13.00
... Vol. 9: Silver Surfer (2007, $13.99, TPB) r/#42-46 14.00
Volume 1 HC (2005, $29.99, 7x11", dust jacket) r/#1-12; introduction, proposals and scripts by Millar and Bendis; character design pages by Hitch 30.00
Volume 2 HC (2006, $29.99, 7x11", dust jacket) r/#13-20; Jae Lee sketch page 30.00
Volume 3 HC (2007, $29.99, 7x11", dust jacket) r/#21-32; Greg Land sketch pages 30.00
Volume 4 HC (2007, $29.99, 7x11", dust jacket) r/#33-41, Annual #2, Ultimate FF/X-Men and Ultimate X-Men/FF; character design pages 30.00
Volume 5 HC (2008, $34.99, 7x11", dust jacket) r/#42-53 35.00

ULTIMATE GALACTUS TRILOGY
Marvel Comics: 2007 ($34.99, hardcover, dustjacket)

HC-Oversized reprint of Ultimate Nightmare #1-5, Ultimate Secret #1-4, Ultimate Vision #0, and Ultimate Extinction #1-5; sketch pages and cover galery 35.00

ULTIMATE HUMAN
Marvel Comics: Mar, 2008 - No. 4, Jun, 2008 ($2.99, limited series)

1-4-Iron Man vs. The Hulk; The Leader app.; Ellis-s/Nord-a 3.00
HC (2008, $19.99) r/#1-4 20.00

ULTIMATE IRON MAN
Marvel Comics: May, 2005 - No. 5, Feb, 2006 ($2.99, limited series)

1-Origin of Iron Man; Orson Scott Card-s/Andy Kubert-a; two covers 3.00
1-2nd & 3rd printings; each with B&W variant-c 3.00
2-5-Kubert-c 3.00
Volume 1 HC (2006, $19.99, dust jacket) r/#1-5; rough cut of script for #1, cover sketches 20.00
Volume 1 SC (2006, $14.99) r/#1-5; rough cut of script for #1, cover sketches 15.00

ULTIMATE IRON MAN II
Marvel Comics: Feb, 2008 - No. 5, July, 2008 ($2.99, limited series)

1-5-Early days of the Iron Man prototype; Orson Scott Card-s/Pasqual Ferry-a/c 3.00

ULTIMATE MARVEL FLIP MAGAZINE
Marvel Comics: July, 2005 - No. 26, Aug, 2007 ($3.99/$4.99)

1-11-Reprints Ultimate Fantastic Four and Ultimate X-Men in flip format 4.00
12-26-($4.99) 5.00

ULTIMATE MARVEL MAGAZINE
Marvel Comics: Feb, 2001 - No. 11, 2002 ($3.99, magazine size)

1-11: Reprints of recent stories from the Ultimate titles plus Marvel news and features. 1-Reprints Ultimate Spider-Man #1&2. 11-Lord of the Rings-c 4.00

ULTIMATE MARVEL SAMPLER
Marvel Comics: 2007 (no cover price, limited series)

1-Previews of 2008 Ultimate Marvel story arcs; Finch-c 3.00

ULTIMATE MARVEL TEAM-UP (Spider-Man Team-up)
Marvel Comics: Apr, 2001 - No. 16, July, 2002 ($2.99/$2.25)

1-Spider-Man & Wolverine; Bendis-s in all; Matt Wagner-a/c 5.00
2,3-Hulk; Hester-a 3.50
4,5,9-16: 4,5-Iron Man; Allred-a. 9-Fantastic Four; Mahfood-a. 10-Man-Thing; Totleben-a. 11-X-Men; Clugston-Major-a. 12,13-Dr. Strange; McKeever-a.14-Black Widow; Terry Moore-a. 15,16-Shang-Chi; Mays-a 3.00
6-8-Punisher; Sienkiewicz-a. 7,8-Daredevil app. 4.00
TPB (11/01, $14.95) r/#1-5 15.00
... Ultimate Collection TPB ('06, $29.99) r/#1-16 & Ult. Spider-Man Spec.; sketch pages 30.00
HC (8/02, $39.99) r/#1-16 & Ult. Spider-Man Special; Bendis afterword 30.00
...: Vol. 2 TPB (2003, $11.99) r/#9-13; Mahfood-c 12.00
...: Vol. 3 TPB (2003, $12.99) r/#14-16 & Ultimate Spider-Man Super Special; Moore-c 13.00

ULTIMATE NIGHTMARE (Leads into Ultimate Secret limited series)
Marvel Comics: Oct, 2004 - No. 5, Feb, 2005 ($2.25, limited series)

1-5: Ellis-s; Ultimates, X-Men, Nick Fury app. 1,2,4,5-Hairsine-a/c. 3-Epting-a 2.50
Ultimate Galactus Book 1: Nightmare TPB (2005, $12.99) r/Ultimate Nightmare #1-5 13.00

ULTIMATE ORIGINS
Marvel Comics: Aug, 2008 - No. 5 ($2.99, limited series)

1-4-Bendis-s/Guice-a. 1-Nick Fury origin in the 1940s. 2-Capt. America origin 3.00

ULTIMATE POWER
Marvel Comics: Dec, 2006 - No. 9, Feb, 2008 ($2.99, limited series)

1-9: 1-Ultimate FF meets the Squadron Supreme; Bendis-s; Land-a/c. 2-Spider-Man, X-Men and the Ultimates app. 6-Doom app. 3.00
1-Variant sketch-c 5.00
1-Director's Cut (2007, $3.99) r/#1 and B&W pencil and ink pages; covers to #2,3 4.00
HC (2008, $34.99) oversized r/series; profile pages; B&W sketch art 35.00

ULTIMATES, THE (Avengers of the Ultimate line)
Marvel Comics: Mar, 2002 - No. 13, Apr, 2004 ($2.25)

1-Intro. Capt. America; Millar-s/Hitch-a & wraparound-c 6.00
2-Intro. Giant-Man and the Wasp 4.00
3-12: 3-1st Capt. America in new costume. 4-Intro. Thor. 5-Ultimates vs. The Hulk. 8-Intro. Hawkeye 3.00

Ultimates 3 #1 © MAR

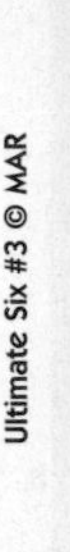
Ultimate Six #3 © MAR

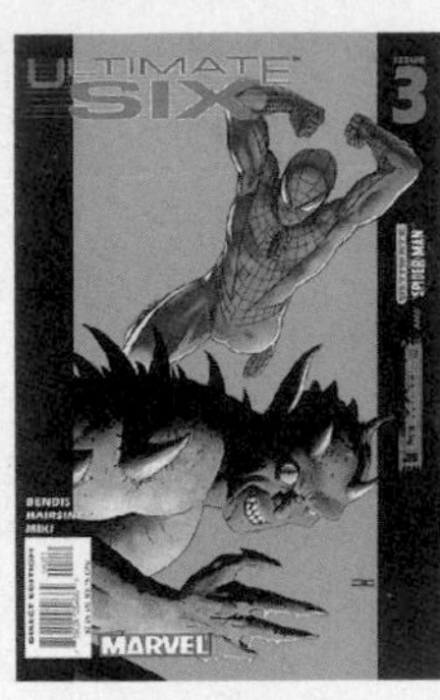

Ultimate Spider-Man #61 © MAR

	GD 2.0	VG 4.0	FN 6.0	VF 8.0	VF/NM 9.0	NM- 9.2

13-($3.50) 3.50
... Saga (2007, $3.99) Re-caps 1st 2 Ultimates series; new framing art by Charest; prelude to Ultimates 3 series; Brooks-c 4.00
... Volume 1 HC (2004, $29.99) oversized r/series; commentary pages with Millar & Hitch; cover gallery and character design pages; intro. by Joss Whedon 30.00
... Volume 1: Super-Human TPB (8/02, $12.99) r/#1-6 13.00
... Volume 2: Homeland Security TPB (2004, $17.99) r/#7-13 18.00

ULTIMATES 2
Marvel Comics: Feb, 2005 - No. 13, Feb, 2007 ($2.99/$3.99)

1-Millar-s/Hitch-a; Giant-Man becomes Ant-Man 3.00
2-11: 6-Intro. The Defenders. 7-Hawkeye shot. 8-Intro The Liberators 3.00
12,13-($3.99) Wraparound-c; X-Men, Fantastic Four, Spider-Man app. 4.00
13-Variant white cover featuring The Wasp 40.00
Annual 1 (10/05, $3.99) Millar-s/Dillon-a/Hitch-c; Defenders app. 4.00
Annual 2 (10/06, $3.99) Deodato-a; flashback to WWII with Sook-a; Falcon app. 4.00
HC (2007, $34.99) oversized r/series; commentary pages with Millar & Hitch; cover gallery, sketch and script pages; intro. by Jonathan Ross 35.00
... Volume 1: Gods & Monsters TPB (2005, $15.99) r/#1-6 16.00
... Volume 2: Grand Theft America TPB (2007, $19.99) r/#7-13; cover gallery w/sketches 20.00

ULTIMATES 3
Marvel Comics: Feb, 2008 - Present ($2.99)

1-Loeb-s/Madureira-a; two gatefold wraparound covers by Madureira; Scarlet Witch shot 3.00
1,2-Second printings: 1-Wraparound cover by Madureira. 2-Madureira-c 3.00
2-5: 2-Spider-Man app. 3-Wolverine app. 3.00
2-Variant Thor cover by Turner 8.00
3-Variant Scarlet Witch cover by Cho 8.00
4-Variant Valkyrie cover by Finch 4.00

ULTIMATE SECRET (See Ultimate Nightmare limited series)
Marvel Comics: May, 2005 - No. 4, Dec, 2005 ($2.99, limited series)

1-4-Ellis-s; Captain Marvel app. 1,2-McNiven-a. 2,3-Ultimates & FF app. 3.00
Ultimate Galactus Book 2: Secret TPB (2006, $12.99) r/#1-4 13.00

ULTIMATE SECRETS
Marvel Comics: 2008 ($3.99, one-shot)

1-Handbook-styled profiles of secondary teams and characters from Ultimate universe 4.00

ULTIMATE SIX (Reprinted in Ultimate Spider-Man Vol. 5 hardcover)
Marvel Comics: Nov, 2003 - No. 7, June, 2004 ($2.25) (See Ultimate Spider-Man for TPB)

1-The Ultimates & Spider-Man team-up; Bendis-s/Quesada & Hairsine-a; Cassaday-c 5.00
2-7-Hairsine-a; Cassaday-c 2.50

ULTIMATE SPIDER-MAN
Marvel Comics: Oct, 2000 - Present ($2.99/$2.25/$2.99)

	GD	VG	FN	VF	VF/NM	NM-
1-Bendis-s/Bagley & Thibert-a; cardstock-c; introduces revised origin and cast separate from regular Spider-continuity	6	12	18	41	66	90
1-Variant white-c (Retailer incentive)	9	18	27	60	100	140
1-DF Edition	4	8	12	28	44	60
1-Free Comic Book Day giveaway & Kay Bee Toys variant - (See Promotional Comics section)						
2-Cover with Spider-Man on car	3	6	9	18	27	35
2-Cover with Spider-Man swinging past building	3	6	9	18	27	35
3,4: 4-Uncle Ben killed	3	6	9	16	23	30
5-7: 6,7-Green Goblin app.	3	6	9	18	27	35
8-13: 13-Reveals secret to MJ	1	2	3	5	7	9

14-21: 14-Intro. Gwen Stacy & Dr. Octopus 5.00
22-($3.50) Green Goblin returns 3.50
23-32 2.50
33-1st Ultimate Venom-c; intro. Eddie Brock 3.00
34-38-Ultimate Venom 2.50
39-49,51-59: 39-Nick Fury app. 43,44-X-Men app. 46-Prelude to Ultimate Six; Sandman app. 51-53-Elektra app. 54-59-Doctor Octopus app. 2.50
50-($2.99) Intro. Black Cat 3.00
60-Intro. Ultimate Carnage on cover 3.00
61-Intro Ben Reilly; Punisher app. 2.50
62-Gwen Stacy killed by Carnage 3.00
63-92: 63,64-Carnage app. 66,67-Wolverine app. 68,69-Johnny Storm app. 78-Begin $2.50-c. 79-Debut Moon Knight. 81-85-Black Cat app. 90-Vulture app. 91-94-Deadpool 2.50
93-99: 93-Begin $2.99-c. 95-Morbius & Blade app. 97-99-Clone Saga 3.00
100-($3.99) Wraparound-c; Clone Saga; re-cap of previous issues 4.00
101-103-Clone Saga continues; Fantastic Four app. 102-Spider-Woman origin 3.00
104-($3.99) Clone Saga concludes; Fantastic Four and Dr. Octopus app. 4.00
105-126: 106-110-Daredevil app. 111-Last Bagley art; Immonen-a (6 pgs.) 112-Immonen-a; Norman Osborn app. 118-Liz Allen ignites. 123-Venom app. 3.00
Annual 1 (10/05, $3.99) Kitty Pryde app.; Bendis-s/Brooks-a/Bagley-c 4.00
Annual 2 (10/06, $3.99) Punisher, Moon Knight and Daredevil app.; Bendis-s/Brooks-a 4.00
Collected Edition (1/01, $3.99) r/#1-3 4.00
...Special (7/02, $3.50) art by Bagley and various incl. Romita,Sr., Brereton, Cho, Mack, Sienkiewicz, Phillips, Pearson, Oeming, Mahfood, Russell 3.50
Ultimate Spider-Man 100 Project (2007, $10.00, SC, charity book for the HERO Initiative) collection of 100 variant covers by Romita Sr. & Jr., Cho, Bagley, Quesada and more 10.00
...: Venom HC (2007, $19.99) r/#33-39 20.00
...(Vol. 1): Power and Responsibility TPB (4/01, $14.95) r/#1-7 15.00
...(Vol. 2): Learning Curve TPB (12/01, $14.95) r/#8-13 15.00
...(Vol. 3): Double Trouble TPB (6/02, $17.95) r/#14-21 18.00
Vol. 4: Legacy TPB (2002, $14.99) r/#22-27 15.00
Vol. 5: Public Scrutiny TPB (2003, $11.99) r/#28-32 12.00
Vol. 6: Venom TPB (2003, $15.99) r/#33-39 16.00
Vol. 7: Irresponsible TPB (2003, $12.99) r/#40-45 13.00
Vol. 8: Cats & Kings TPB (2004, $17.99) r/#47-53 18.00
Vol. 9: Ultimate Six TPB (2004, $17.99) r/#46 & Ultimate Six #1-7 18.00
Vol. 10: Hollywood TPB (2004, $12.99) r/#54-59 13.00
Vol. 11: Carnage TPB (2004, $12.99) r/#60-65 13.00
Vol. 12: Superstars TPB (2005, $12.99) r/#66-71 13.00
Vol. 13: Hobgoblin TPB (2005, $15.99) r/#72-78 16.00
Vol. 14: Warriors TPB (2005, $17.99) r/#79-85 18.00
Vol. 15: Silver Sable TPB (2006, $15.99) r/#86-90 & Annual #1 16.00
Vol. 16: Deadpool TPB (2006, $19.99) r/#91-96 & Annual #2 20.00
Vol. 17: Clone Saga TPB (2007, $24.99) r/#97-105 25.00
Vol. 18: Ultimate Knights TPB (2007, $13.99) r/#106-111 14.00
Vol. 19: Death of a Goblin TPB (2008, $14.99) r/#112-117 18.00
Hardcover (3/02, $34.95, 7x11", dust jacket) r/#1-13 & Amazing Fantasy #15; sketch pages and Bill Jemas' initial plot and character outlines 35.00
Volume 2 HC (2003, $29.99, 7x11", dust jacket) r/#14-27; pin-ups & sketch pages 30.00
Volume 3 HC (2003, $29.99, 7x11", dust jacket) r/#28-39 & #1/2; script pages 30.00
Volume 4 HC (2004, $29.99, 7x11", dust jacket) r/#40-45, 47-53; sketch pages 30.00
Volume 5 HC (2004, $29.99, 7x11", dust jacket) r/#46,54-59, Ultimate Six #1-7 30.00
Volume 6 HC (2005, $29.99, 7x11", dust jacket) r/#60-71; sketch page 30.00
Volume 7 HC (2006, $29.99, 7x11", dust jacket) r/#72-85; sketch & profile pages 30.00
Volume 8 HC (2007, $29.99, 7x11", dust jacket) r/#86-96 & Annual #1&2; sketch page 30.00
Volume 9 HC (2008, $39.99, 7x11", dust jacket) r/#97-111; sketch pages 40.00

	GD	VG	FN	VF	VF/NM	NM-
Wizard #1/2	1	3	4	6	8	10

ULTIMATE TALES FLIP MAGAZINE
Marvel Comics: July, 2005 - No. 26, Aug, 2007 ($3.99/$4.99)

1-11-Each reprints 2 issues of Ultimate Spider-Man in flip format 4.00
12-26-($4.99) 5.00

ULTIMATE VISION
Marvel Comics: No. 0, Jan, 2007 - No. 5, Jan, 2008 ($2.99, limited series)

0-Reprints back-up serial from Ultimate Extinction and related series; pin-ups 3.00
1-5: 1-(2/07) Carey-s/Peterson-a/c 3.00
TPB (2007, $14.99) r/#0-5; design pages and cover gallery 15.00

ULTIMATE WAR
Marvel Comics: Feb, 2003 - No. 4, Apr, 2003 ($2.25, limited series)

1-4-Millar-s/Bachalo-c/a; The Ultimates vs. Ultimate X-Men 2.50
Ultimate X-Men Vol. 5: Ultimate War TPB (2003, $10.99) r/#1-4 11.00

ULTIMATE WOLVERINE VS. HULK
Marvel Comics: Feb, 2006 - No. 6 ($2.99, limited series)

1,2-Leinil Yu-a/c; Damon Lindelof-s 3.00

ULTIMATE X-MEN (Also see Promotional Comics section for FCBD Ed.)
Marvel Comics: Feb, 2001 - Present ($2.99/$2.25/$2.50)

	GD	VG	FN	VF	VF/NM	NM-
1-Millar-s/Adam Kubert & Thibert-a; cardstock-c; introduces revised origin and cast separate from regular X-Men continuity	3	6	9	14	20	25
1-DF Edition						30.00
1-DF Sketch Cover Edition						45.00
2	2	4	6	11	16	20
3-6	2	4	6	8	11	14

7-10 6.00
11-24,26-33: 13-Intro. Gambit. 18,19-Bachalo-a. 23,24-Andrews-a 3.00
25-($3.50) leads into the Ultimate War mini-series; Kubert-a 3.50
34-Spider-Man-c/app.; Bendis-s begin; Finch-a 4.00
35-74: 35-Spider-Man app. 36,37-Daredevil-c/app. 40-Intro. Angel. 42-Intro. Dazzler. 44-Beast dies. 46-Intro. Mr. Sinister. 50-53-Kubert-a; Gambit app. 54-57,59-63-Immonen-a. 60-Begin $2.50-c. 61-Variant Coipel-c. 66-Kirkman-s begin. 69-Begin $2.99-c 3.00
61-Retailer Edition with variant Coipel B&W sketch-c 10.00
75-($3.99) Turner-c; intro. Cable; back-up story with Emma Frost's students 4.00
76-97: 76-Intro. Bishop. 91-Fantastic Four app. 92-96-Phoenix app. 96-Spider-Man app. 3.00

Ultimate X-Men #89 © MAR

Ultraforce #3 © MAL

Umbrella Academy: Apocalypse Suite #1 © Gerald Way

GD	VG	FN	VF	VF/NM	NM-
2.0	4.0	6.0	8.0	9.0	9.2

Annual 1 (10/05, $3.99) Vaughan-s/Raney-a; Gambit & Rogue in Vegas 4.00
Annual 2 (10/06, $3.99) Kirkman-s/Larroca-a; Nightcrawler & Dazzler 4.00
.../Fantastic Four 1 (2/06, $2.99) Carey-s/Ferry-a; concluded in Ult. Fantastic Four/X-Men 3.00
.../Ult. Fantastic Four Ann. 1 (11/08, $3.99) Continues in Ult. F.F./Ult. X-Men Annual #1 4.00
.../Fantastic Four TPB (2006, $12.99) reprints Ult X-Men/Ult. FF x-over and Official Handbook of the Ultimate Marvel Universe #1-2 13.00
... Ultimate Collection Vol. 1 (2006, $24.99) r/#1-12 & #1/2; unused Bendis script for #1 25.00
... Ultimate Collection Vol. 2 (2007, $24.99) r/#13-25; Kubert cover sketch pages 25.00
...: (Vol. 1) The Tomorrow People TPB (7/01, $14.95) r/#1-6 15.00
...: (Vol. 2) Return to Weapon X TPB (4/02, $14.95) r/#7-12 15.00
Vol. 3: World Tour TPB (2002, $17.99) r/#13-20 18.00
Vol. 4: Hellfire and Brimstone TPB (2003, $12.99) r/#21-25 13.00
Vol. 5 (See Ultimate War)
Vol. 6: Return of the King TPB (2003, $16.99) r/#26-33 17.00
Vol. 7: Blockbuster TPB (2004, $12.99) r/#34-39 13.00
Vol. 8: New Mutants TPB (2004, $12.99) r/#40-45 13.00
Vol. 9: The Tempest TPB (2004, $10.99) r/#46-49 11.00
Vol. 10: Cry Wolf TPB (2005, $8.99) r/#50-53 9.00
Vol. 11: The Most Dangerous Game TPB (2005, $9.99) r/#54-57 10.00
Vol. 12: Hard Lessons TPB (2005, $12.99) r/#58-60 & Annual #1 13.00
Vol. 13: Magnetic North TPB (2006, $12.99) r/#61-65 13.00
Vol. 14: Phoenix? TPB (2006, $14.99) r/#66-71 15.00
Vol. 15: Magical TPB (2007, $11.99) r/#72-74 & Annual #2 12.00
Vol. 16: Cable TPB (2007, $14.99) r/#75-80; sketch pages 15.00
Vol. 17: Sentinels TPB (2008, $17.99) r/#81-88 18.00
Volume 1 HC (8/02, $34.99, 7x11", dust jacket) r/#1-12 & Giant-Size X-Men #1; sketch pages and Millar and Bendis' initial plot and character outlines 35.00
Volume 2 HC (2003, $29.99, 7x11", dust jacket) r/#13-25; script for #20 30.00
Volume 3 HC (2003, $29.99, 7x11", dust jacket) r/#26-33 & Ultimate War #1-4 30.00
Volume 4 HC (2005, $29.99, 7x11", dust jacket) r/#34-45 30.00
Volume 5 HC (2006, $29.99, 7x11", dust jacket) r/#46-57; Vaughan intro.; sketch pages 30.00
Volume 6 HC (2006, $29.99, 7x11", dust jacket) r/#58-65, Annual #1 & Wizard #1/2 30.00
Volume 7 HC (2007, $29.99, 7x11", dust jacket) r/#66-74, Annual #2 30.00
Wizard #1/2 2 4 6 9 12 15

ULTRA
Image Comics: Aug, 2004 - No. 8, Mar, 2005 ($2.95, limited series)
1-8: 1-Intro. Ultra/Pearl Penalosa; Luna Brothers-s/a 3.00
Vol. 1: Seven Days TPB (4/05, $17.95) r/#1-8; sketch pages 18.00

ULTRAFORCE (1st Series) (Also see Avengers/Ultraforce #1)
Malibu Comics (Ultraverse): Aug, 1994 - No. 10, Aug, 1995 ($1.95/$2.50)
0 (9/94, $2.50)-Perez-c/a. 2.50
1-($2.50, 44 pgs.)-Bound-in trading card; team consisting of Prime, Prototype, Hardcase, Pixx, Ghoul, Contrary & Topaz; Gerard Jones scripts begin, ends #6; Perez-c/a begins. 2.50
1-Ultra 5000 Limited Silver Foil Edition 4.00
1-Holographic-c, no price 6.00
2-5: Perez-c/a in all. 2 (10/94, $1.95)-Prime quits, Strangers cameo. 3-Origin of Topaz; Prime rejoins. 5-Pixx dies. 2.50
2 ($2.50)-Florescent logo; limited edition stamp on-c 3.00
6-10: 6-Begin $2.50-c, Perez-c/a. 7-Ghoul story, Steve Erwin-a. 8-Marvel's Black Knight enters the Ultraverse (last seen in Avengers #375); Perez-c/a. 9,10-Black Knight app.; Perez-c. 10-Leads into Ultraforce/Avengers Prelude 2.50
Malibu "Ashcan ": Ultraforce #0A (6/94) 2.50
.../Avengers Prelude 1 (8/95, $2.50)-Perez-c. 2.50
.../Avengers 1 (8/95, $3.95)-Warren Ellis script; Perez-c/a; foil-c 4.00

ULTRAFORCE (2nd Series)(Also see Black September)
Malibu Comics (Ultraverse): Infinity, Sept, 1995 - V2#15, Dec, 1996 ($1.50)
Infinity, V2#1-15: Infinity-Team consists of Marvel's Black Knight, Ghoul, Topaz, Prime & redesigned Prototype; Warren Ellis scripts begin, ends #3; variant-c exists. 1-1st app.Cromwell, Lament & Wreckage. 2-Contains free encore presentation of Ultraforce #1; flip book "Phoenix Resurrection" Pt. 7. 7-Darick Robertson, Jeff Johnson & others-a. 8,9-Intro. Future Ultraforce (Prime, Hellblade, Angel of Destruction, Painkiller & Whipslash); Gary Erskine-c/a. 9-Foxfire app. 10-Len Wein scripts & Deodato Studios-c/a begin. 10-Lament back-up story. 11-Ghoul back-up story by Pander Bros. 12-Ultraforce vs. Maxis (cont'd in Ultraverse Unlimited #2); Exiles & Iron Clad app. 13-Prime leaves; Hardcase returns 2.50
Infinity (2000 signed) 4.00
.../Spider-Man ($3.95)-Marv Wolfman script; Green Goblin app; 2 covers exist. 4.00

ULTRAGIRL
Marvel Comics: Nov, 1996 - No. 3 Mar, 1997($1.50, limited series)
1-3: 1-1st app. 2.50

ULTRA KLUTZ
Onward Comics: 1981; 6/86 - #27, 1/89, #28, 4/90 - #31, 1990? ($1.50/$1.75/$2.00, B&W)
1 (1981)-Re-released after 2nd #1 2.50
1-30: 1-(6/86). 27-Photo back-c 2.50
31-($2.95, 52 pgs.) 3.00

ULTRAMAN
Nemesis Comics: Mar, 1994 - No. 4, Sept, 1994 ($1.75/$1.95)
1-($2.25)-Collector's edition; foil-c; special 3/4 wraparound-c 3.00
1-($1.75)-Newsstand edition 2.50
2-4: 3-$1.95-c begins 2.50
#(-1) (3/93) 2.50

ULTRAMAN TIGA
Dark Horse Comics: Aug, 2003 - No. 10, June, 2004 ($3.99)
1-10-Khoo Fuk Lung-a/Tony Wong-s 4.00

ULTRAVERSE DOUBLE FEATURE
Malibu Comics (Ultraverse): Jan, 1995 ($3.95, one-shot, 68 pgs.)
1-Flip-c featuring Prime & Solitaire. 4.00

ULTRAVERSE ORIGINS
Malibu Comics (Ultraverse): Jan, 1994 (99¢, one-shot)
1-Gatefold-c; 2 pg. origins all characters 2.50
1-Newsstand edition; different-c, no gatefold 2.50

ULTRAVERSE PREMIERE
Malibu Comics (Ultraverse): 1994 (one-shot)
0-Ordered thru mail w/coupons 5.00

ULTRAVERSE UNLIMITED
Malibu Comics (Ultraverse): June, 1996; No. 2, Sept, 1996 ($2.50)
1,2: 1-Adam Warlock returns to the Marvel Universe; Rune-c/app. 2-Black Knight, Reaper & Sierra Blaze return to the Marvel Universe 2.50

ULTRAVERSE YEAR ONE
Malibu Comics (Ultraverse): 1994 ($4.95, one-shot)
nn-In-depth synopsis of the first year's titles & stories. 5.00

ULTRAVERSE YEAR TWO
Malibu Comics (Ultraverse): Aug, 1995 ($4.95, one-shot)
nn-In-depth synopsis of second year's titles & stories 5.00

ULTRAVERSE YEAR ZERO: THE DEATH OF THE SQUAD
Malibu Comics (Ultraverse): Apr, 1995 - No. 4, July, 1995 ($2.95, lim. series)
1-4: 3-Codename: Firearm back-up story. 3.00

UMBRELLA ACADEMY: APOCALYPSE SUITE (See FCBD edition in Promotional Section)
Dark Horse Comics: Sept, 2007 - No. 6, Feb, 2008 ($2.99, limited series)
1-Origin of the Umbrella Aademy; Gerald Way-s/Gabriel Bá-a/James Jean-c 5.00
1-White variant-c by Bá 15.00
1-Variant-c by Gerald Way 10.00
1-2nd printing with variant-c by Bá 3.00
2-6 3.00
Vol.1: Apocalypse Suite TPB (7/08, $17.95) r/#1-6, FCBD story and web shorts; design art; Grant Morrison intro.; cover gallery 18.00

UNBIRTHDAY PARTY WITH ALICE IN WONDERLAND (See Alice In Wonderland, Four Color #341)

UNBOUND
Image Comics (Desperado): Jan, 1998 ($2.95, B&W)
1-Pruett-s/Peters-a 3.00

UNCANNY ORIGINS
Marvel Comics: Sept, 1996 - No. 14, Oct, 1997 (99¢)
1-14: 1-Cyclops. 2-Quicksilver. 3-Archangel. 4-Firelord. 5-Hulk. 6-Beast. 7-Venom. 8-Nightcrawler. 9-Storm. 10-Black Cat. 11-Black Knight. 12-Dr. Strange. 13-Daredevil. 14-Iron Fist 2.50

UNCANNY TALES
Atlas Comics (PrPl/PPI): June, 1952 - No. 56, Sept, 1957
1-Heath-a; horror/weird stories begin 90 180 270 567 959 1350
2 48 96 144 298 499 700
3-5 41 82 123 256 428 600
6-Wolvertonish-a by Matt Fox 43 86 129 267 446 625
7-10: 8-Atom bomb story; Tothish-a (by Sekowsky?). 9-Crandall-a 38 76 114 226 363 500
11-20: 17-Atom bomb panels; anti-communist story; Hitler story. 19-Krenkel-a. 20-Robert Q. Sale-c 28 56 84 166 268 370
21-25,27: 25-Nostrand-a? 25 50 75 147 236 325

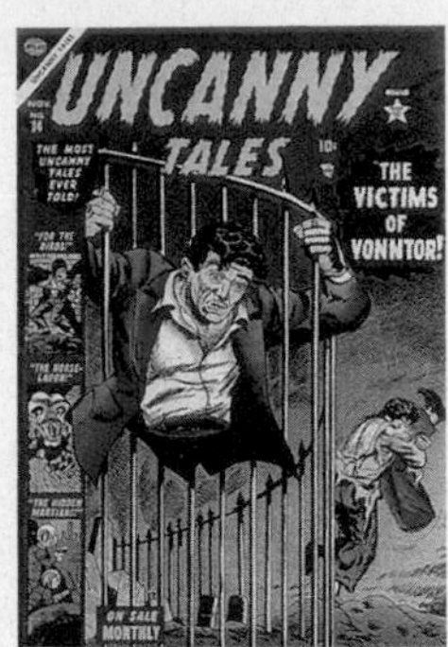

Uncanny Tales #14 © MAR

Uncle Sam and the Freedom Fighters #2 © DC

Uncle Scrooge #27 © DIS

26-Spider-Man prototype c/story 35 70 105 203 327 450
28-Last precode issue (1/55); Kubert-a; #1-28 contain 2-3 sci/fi stories each
26 52 78 152 244 335
29-41,43-49,51 18 36 54 107 169 230
42,54,56-Krigstein-a 20 40 60 114 180 245
50,53,55-Torres-a 18 36 54 107 169 230
52-Oldest Iron Man prototype (2/57) 20 40 60 117 186 255

NOTE: ***Andru*** *a-15, 27.* ***Ayers*** *a-22.* ***Bailey*** *a-51.* ***Briefer*** *a-19, 20.* ***Brodsky*** *c-1, 3, 4, 6, 8, 12-16, 19.* ***Brodsky/Everett*** *c-9.* ***Cameron*** *a-47.* ***Colan*** *a-11, 16, 17, 52.* ***Drucker*** *a-37, 42, 45.* ***Everett*** *a-2, 9, 12, 32, 36, 39, 48; c-7, 11, 17, 39, 41, 50, 52, 53.* ***Fass*** *a-9, 10, 15, 24. Forte a-18, 27, 34, 52, 53.* ***Heath*** *a-13, 14; c-5, 10, 18.* ***Keller*** *a-3.* ***Lawrence*** *a-14, 17, 19, 23, 27, 28, 35.* ***Maneely*** *a-4, 8, 10, 16, 29, 35; c-2, 22, 26, 33, 38.* ***Moldoff*** *a-23.* ***Morisi*** *a-48, 52.* ***Morrow*** *a-46, 51.* ***Orlando*** *a-49, 50, 53.* ***Powell*** *a-12, 18, 34, 36, 38, 43, 50, 56.* ***Robinson*** *a-3, 13.* ***Reinman*** *a-12.* ***Romita*** *a-10.* ***Roussos*** *a-8.* ***Sale*** *a-47, 53; c-20.* ***Sekowsky*** *a-25.* ***Sinnott*** *a-15, 52.* ***Torres*** *a-53.* ***Tothish****-a by* ***Andru****-27.* ***Wildey*** *a-22, 48.*

UNCANNY TALES
Marvel Comics Group: Dec, 1973 - No. 12, Oct, 1975

1-Crandall-r/Uncanny Tales #9('50s) 3 6 9 16 23 30
2-12: 7,12-Kirby-a 2 4 6 10 14 18

NOTE: ***Ditko*** *reprints-#4, 6-8, 10-12.*

UNCANNY X-MEN, THE (See **X-Men, The**, 1st series, #142-on)

UNCANNY X-MEN AND THE NEW TEEN TITANS (See Marvel and DC Present...)

UNCENSORED MOUSE, THE
Eternity Comics: Apr, 1989 - No. 2, Apr, 1989 ($1.95, B&W)(Came sealed in plastic bag) (Both contain racial stereotyping & violence)

1,2-Early Gottfredson strip-r in each 2 4 6 9 12 15

NOTE: *Both issues contain unauthorized reprints. Series was cancelled.* ***Win Smith*** *r-1, 2.*

UNCLE CHARLIE'S FABLES
Lev Gleason Publ.: Jan, 1952 - No. 5, Sept, 1952 (All have Biro painted-c)

1-Norman Maurer-a; has Biro's picture 15 30 45 88 137 185
2-Fuje-a; Biro photo 10 20 30 54 72 90
3-5 9 18 27 47 61 75

UNCLE DONALD & HIS NEPHEWS DUDE RANCH (See Dell Giant #52)

UNCLE DONALD & HIS NEPHEWS FAMILY FUN (See Dell Giant #38)

UNCLE JOE'S FUNNIES
Centaur Publications: 1938 (B&W)

1-Games, puzzles & magic tricks, some interior art; Bill Everett-c
58 116 174 365 620 875

UNCLE MILTY (TV)
Victoria Publications/True Cross: Dec, 1950 - No. 4, July, 1951 (52 pgs.)(Early TV comic)

1-Milton Berle photo on-c of #1,2 53 106 159 334 567 800
2 35 70 105 203 327 450
3,4 29 58 87 169 272 375

UNCLE REMUS & HIS TALES OF BRER RABBIT (See Brer Rabbit, 4-Color #129, 208, 693)

UNCLE SAM
DC Comics (Vertigo): 1997 - No. 2, 1997 ($4.95, limited series)

1,2-Alex Ross painted c/a. Story by Ross and Steve Darnell 5.00
Hardcover (1998, $17.95) 18.00
Softcover (2000, $9.95) 10.00

UNCLE SAM AND THE FREEDOM FIGHTERS
DC Comics: Sept, 2006 - No. 8, Apr, 2007 ($2.99, limited series)

1-8-Acuña-a/c; Gray & Palmiotti-s. 3-Intro. Black Condor 3.00
TPB (2007, $14.99) r/#1-8 and story from DCU Brave New World #1 15.00

UNCLE SAM AND THE FREEDOM FIGHTERS
DC Comics: Nov, 2007 - No. 8, Jun, 2008 ($2.99, limited series)

1-8-Gray & Palmiotti-s/Arlem-a/Johnson-c 3.00

UNCLE SAM QUARTERLY (Blackhawk #9 on)(See Freedom Fighters)
Quality Comics Group: Autumn, 1941 - No. 8, Fall, 1943 (see National Comics)

1-Origin Uncle Sam; Fine/Eisner-c, chapter headings, 2 pgs. by Eisner; (2 versions: dark cover, no price; light cover with price sticker); Jack Cole-a
376 752 1128 2557 4479 6400
2-Cameos by The Ray, Black Condor, Quicksilver, The Red Bee, Alias the Spider, Hercules & Neon the Unknown; Eisner, Fine-c/a 132 264 396 832 1404 1975
3-Tuska-c/a; Eisner-a(2) 97 194 291 611 1031 1450
4 87 174 261 548 924 1300
5,7-Hitler, Mussolini & Tojo-c 110 220 330 693 1172 1650
6,8 67 134 201 422 711 1000

NOTE: ***Kotzky*** *(or* ***Tuska****) a-3-8.*

GD VG FN VF VF/NM NM-
2.0 4.0 6.0 8.0 9.0 9.2

UNCLE SCROOGE (Disney) (Becomes Walt Disney's... #210 on) (See Cartoon Tales, Dell Giants #33, 55, Disney Comic Album, Donald and Scrooge, Dynabrite, Four Color #178, Gladstone Comic Album, Walt Disney's Comics & Stories #98, Walt Disney's ...)
Dell #1-39/Gold Key #40-173/Whitman #174-209: No. 386, 3/52 - No. 39, 8-10/62; No. 40, 12/62 - No. 209, 7/84

Four Color 386(#1)-in "Only a Poor Old Man" by Carl Barks; r-in Uncle Scrooge & Donald Duck #1('65) & The Best of Walt Disney Comics (1974). The very 1st cover app. of Uncle Scrooge
168 336 504 1470 2835 4200
1-(1986)-Reprints F.C. #386; given away with lithograph "Dam Disaster at Money Lake" & as a subscription offer giveaway to Gladstone subscribers
3 6 9 15 20 24
Four Color 456(#2)-in "Back to the Klondike" by Carl Barks; r-in Best of U.S. & D.D. #1('66) & Gladstone C.A. #4 88 176 264 748 1424 2100
Four Color 495(#3)-r-in #105 58 116 174 493 947 1400
4(12-2/53-54)-r-in Gladstone Comic Album #11 43 86 129 344 647 950
5-r-in Gladstone Special #2 & Walt Disney Digest #1
38 76 114 293 547 800
6-r-in U.S. #106,165,233 & Best of U.S. & D.D. #1('66)
31 62 93 239 445 650
7-The Seven Cities of Cibola by Barks; r-in #217 & Best of D.D. & U.S. #2 ('67)
29 58 87 213 394 575
8-10: 8-r-in #111,222. 9-r-in #104,214. 10-r-in #67 25 50 75 185 343 500
11-20: 11-r-in #237. 17-r-in #215. 19-r-in Gladstone C.A. #1. 20-r-in #213
20 40 60 148 274 400
21-30: 24-X-Mas-c. 26-r-in #211 17 34 51 120 223 325
31-35,37-40: 34-r-in #228. 40-X-Mas-c 14 28 42 102 181 260
36-1st app. Magica De Spell; Number one dime 1st identified by name
15 30 45 111 206 300
41-60: 48-Magica De Spell-c/story (3/64). 49-Sci/fi-c. 51-Beagle Boys-c/story (8/64) 12 24 36 82 146 210
61-63,65,66,68-71:71-Last Barks issue w/original story (#71-he only storyboarded the script)
10 20 30 73 129 185
64-(7/66) Barks Vietnam War story "Treasure of Marco Polo" banned for reprints by Disney from 1977-1989 because of its Third World revolutionary war theme. It later appeared in the hardcover Carl Barks Library set (4/89) and Walt Disney's Uncle Scrooge Adventures #42 (1/97) 15 30 45 107 196 285
67,72,73: 67,72,73-Barks-r 10 20 30 67 116 165
74-84: 74-Barks-r(1pg.). 75-81,83-Not by Barks. 82,84-Barks-r begin
7 14 21 49 80 110
85-100 6 12 18 41 66 90
101-110 5 10 15 34 55 75
111-120 4 8 12 26 41 55
121-141,143-152,154-157 3 6 9 20 30 40
142-Reprints Four Color #456 with-c 3 6 9 21 32 42
153,158,162-164,166,168-170,178,180: No Barks 3 6 9 14 19 24
159-160,165,167 3 6 9 14 20 26
161(r/#14), 171(r/#11), 177(r/#16),183(r/#6)-Barks-r 3 6 9 14 20 26
172(1/80),173(2/80)-Gold Key. Barks-a 3 6 9 17 25 32
174(3/80),175(4/80),176(5/80)-Whitman. Barks-a 4 8 12 22 34 45
177(6/80),178(7/80) 4 8 12 23 36 48
179(9/80)(r/#9)-(Very low distribution) 36 72 108 277 514 750
180(11/80),181(12/80, r/4-Color #495), pre-pack? 5 10 15 34 55 75
182-195: 182-(50¢-c). 184,185,187,188-Barks-a. 182,186,191-194-No Barks. 189(r/#5), 190(r/#4), 195(r/4-Color #386) 3 6 9 16 22 28
182(1/81, 40¢-c) Cover price error variant 4 8 12 22 34 45
196(4/82),197(5/82): 196(r/#13) 3 6 9 17 25 32
198-209 (All #90038 on-c; pre-pack; no date or date code): 198(4/83), 199(5/83), 200(6/83), 201(6/83), 202(7/83), 203(7/83), 204(8/83), 205(8/83), 206(4/84), 207(5/83), 208(6/84), 209(7/84). 198-202,204-206: No Barks. 203(r/#12), 207(r/#93,92), 208(r/U.S. #18), 209(r/U.S. #21)-Barks-r 3 6 9 19 29 38
Uncle Scrooge & Money(G.K.)-Barks-r/from WDC&S #130 (3/67)
5 10 15 34 55 75
Mini Comic #1(1976)(3-1/4x6-1/2")-r/U.S. #115; Barks-c
2 4 6 8 10 12

NOTE: ***Barks*** *c-Four Color 386, 456, 495, #4-37, 39, 40, 43-71.*

UNCLE SCROOGE & DONALD DUCK
Gold Key: June, 1965 (25¢, paper cover)

1-Reprint of Four Color #386(#1) & lead story from Four Color #29
8 16 24 54 90 125

UNCLE SCROOGE COMICS DIGEST
Gladstone Publishing: Dec, 1986 - No. 5, Aug, 1987 ($1.25, Digest-size)

1,3 1 2 3 5 6 8
2,4 6.00

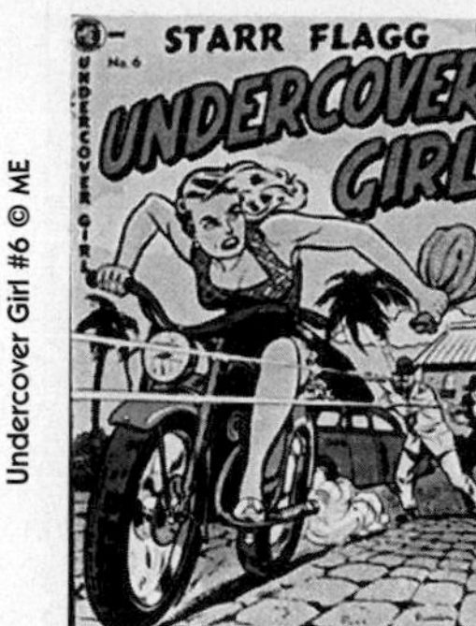

Undercover Girl #6 © ME

Underworld Crime #7 © FAW

The Unexpected #186 © DC

	GD 2.0	VG 4.0	FN 6.0	VF 8.0	VF/NM 9.0	NM- 9.2
5 (low print run)	1	2	3	5	7	9

UNCLE SCROOGE GOES TO DISNEYLAND (See Dell Giants)
Gladstone Publishing Ltd.: Aug, 1985 ($2.50)

1-Reprints Dell Giant w/new-c by Mel Crawford, based on old cover 2 4 6 8 10 12
...Comics Digest 1 ($1.50, digest size) 2 4 6 8 11 14

UNCLE SCROOGE IN COLOR
Gladstone Publishing: 1987 ($29.95, Hardcover, 9-1/4"X12-1/4", 96 pgs.)

nn-Reprints "Christmas on Bear Mountain" from Four Color 178 by Barks; Uncle Scrooge's Christmas Carol (published as Donald Duck & the Christmas Carol, A Little Golden Book), reproduced from the original art as adapted by Norman McGary from pencils by Barks; and Uncle Scrooge the Lemonade King, reproduced from the original art, plus Barks' original pencils 4 8 12 24 37 50
nn-Slipcase edition of 750, signed by Barks, issued at $79.95 300.00

UNCLE SCROOGE THE LEMONADE KING
Whitman Publishing Co.: 1960 (A Top Top Tales Book, 6-3/8"x7-5/8", 32 pgs.)

2465-Storybook pencilled by Carl Barks, finished art adapted by Norman McGary 36 72 108 277 514 750

UNCLE WIGGILY (See March of Comics #19) (Also see Animal Comics)
Dell Publishing Co.: No. 179, Dec, 1947 - No. 543, Mar, 1954

Four Color 179 (#1)-Walt Kelly-c 15 30 45 107 196 285
Four Color 221 (3/40) Part Kelly-c 9 18 27 63 107 150
Four Color 276 (5/50), 320 (#1, 3/51) 8 16 24 52 86 120
Four Color 349 (9-10/51), 391 (4-5/52) 6 12 18 43 69 95
Four Color 428 (10/52), 503 (10/53), 543 5 10 15 34 55 75

UNDEAD, THE
Chaos! Comics (Black Label): Feb, 2002 ($4.99, B&W)

1-Pulido-s/Denham-a 5.00

UNDERCOVER GIRL (Starr Flagg) (See Extra Comics, Manhunt! & Trail Colt)
Magazine Enterprises: No. 5, 1952 - No. 7, 1954

5(#1)(A-1 #62)-Fallon of the F.B.I. in all 38 76 114 222 351 480
6(A-1 #98), 7(A-1 #118)-All have Starr Flagg 36 72 108 208 329 450
NOTE: *Powell c-6, 7. Whitney a-5-7.*

UNDERDOG (TV)(See Kite Fun Book, March of Comics #426, 438, 467, 479)
Charlton Comics/Gold Key: July, 1970 - No. 10, Jan, 1972; Mar, 1975 - No. 23, Feb, 1979

1 (1st series, Charlton)-1st app. Underdog 9 18 27 63 107 150
2-10 5 10 15 34 55 75
1 (2nd series, Gold Key) 6 12 18 41 66 90
2-10 4 8 12 22 34 45
11-20: 13-1st app. Shack of Solitude 3 6 9 18 27 35
21-23 3 6 9 19 29 38

UNDERDOG
Spotlight Comics: 1987 - No. 3?, 1987 ($1.50)

1-3 4.00

UNDERDOG (Volume 2)
Harvey Comics: Nov, 1993 - No. 5, July, 1994 ($2.25)

1-5 4.00
Summer Special (10/93, $2.25, 68 pgs.) 4.00

UNDERSEA AGENT
Tower Comics: Jan, 1966 - No. 6, Mar, 1967 (25¢, 68 pgs.)

1-Davy Jones, Undersea Agent begins 8 16 24 58 97 135
2-6: 2-Jones gains magnetic powers. 5-Origin & 1st app. of Merman. 6-Kane/Wood-c(r) 6 12 18 37 59 80
NOTE: *Gil Kane a-3-6; c-4, 5. Moldoff a-2i.*

UNDERSEA FIGHTING COMMANDOS (See Fighting Undersea...)
I.W. Enterprises: 1964

I.W. Reprint #1,2('64): 1-r/#? 2-r/#1; Severin-c 2 4 6 9 13 16

UNDERTAKER (World Wrestling Federation)
Chaos! Comics: Feb, 1999 - No. 10, Jan, 2000 ($2.50/$2.95)

Preview (2/99) 2.50
1-10: Reg. and photo covers for each. 1-(4/99) 3.00
1-($6.95) DF Ed.; Brereton painted-c 7.00
...Halloween Special (10/99, $2.95) Reg. & photo-c 3.00
Wizard #0 2.50

UNDERWATER CITY, THE
Dell Publishing Co.: No. 1328, 1961

Four Color 1328-Movie, Evans-a 7 14 21 47 76 105

UNDERWORLD (...True Crime Stories)
D. S. Publishing Co.: Feb-Mar, 1948 - No. 9, June-July, 1949 (52 pgs.)

1-Moldoff (Shelly)-c; excessive violence 45 90 135 279 465 650
2-Moldoff (Shelly)-c; Ma Barker story used in **SOTI**, pg. 95; female electrocution panel; lingerie art 41 82 123 253 422 590
3-McWilliams-c/a; extreme violence, mutilation 40 80 120 235 380 525
4-Used in Love and Death by Legman; Ingels-a 34 68 102 198 319 440
5-Ingels-a 24 48 72 140 225 310
6-9: 8-Ravielli-a 20 40 60 114 180 245

UNDERWORLD
DC Comics: Dec, 1987 - No. 4, Mar, 1988 ($1.00, limited series, mature)

1-4 2.50

UNDERWORLD (Movie)
IDW Publishing: Sept, 2003; Dec, 2005 ($6.99)

1-Movie adaptation; photo-c 7.00
... Evolution (12/05, $7.49) adaptation of movie sequel; Vazquez-a 7.50
TPB (7/04, $19.99) r/#1 and Underworld:Red in Tooth and Claw #1-3 20.00

UNDERWORLD
Marvel Comics: Apr, 2006 - No. 5, Aug, 2006 ($2.99, limited series)

1-5: Staz Johnson-a. 2-Spider-Man app. 3,4-Punisher app. 3.00

UNDERWORLD CRIME
Fawcett Publications: June, 1952 - No. 9, Oct, 1953

1 34 68 102 198 319 440
2 21 42 63 123 197 270
3-6,8,9 (8,9-exist?) 19 38 57 112 176 240
7-(6/53)-Bondage/torture-c 45 90 135 279 465 650

UNDERWORLD: RED IN TOOTH AND CLAW (Movie)
IDW Publishing: Feb, 2004 - No. 3, Apr, 2004 ($3.99, limited series)

1-3-The early days of the Vampire and Lycan war; Postic & Marinkovich-a 4.00

UNDERWORLD STORY, THE (Movie)
Avon Periodicals: 1950

nn-(Scarce)-Ravielli-c 29 58 87 169 272 375

UNDERWORLD UNLEASHED
DC Comics: Nov, 1995 - No. 3, Jan, 1996 ($2.95, limited series)

1-3: Mark Waid scripts & Howard Porter-c/a(p) 3.50
...: Abyss: Hell's Sentinel 1-($2.95)-Alan Scott, Phantom Stranger, Zatanna app. 3.00
...: Apokolips-Dark Uprising 1 ($1.95) 2.50
...: Batman-Devil's Asylum 1-($2.95)-Batman app. 3.00
...: Patterns of Fear-($2.95) 3.00
TPB (1998, $17.95) r/#1-3 & Abyss-Hell's Sentinel 18.00

UNEARTHLY SPECTACULARS
Harvey Publications: Oct, 1965 - No. 3, Mar, 1967

1-(12¢)-Tiger Boy; Simon-c 4 8 12 26 41 55
2-(25¢ giants)-Jack Q. Frost, Tiger Boy & Three Rocketeers app.; Williamson, Wood, Kane-a; r-1 story/Thrill-O-Rama #2 5 10 15 30 48 65
3-(25¢ giants)-Jack Q. Frost app.; Williamson/Crandall-a; r-from Alarming Advs. #1,1962 5 10 15 30 48 65
NOTE: *Crandall a-3r. G. Kane a-2. Orlando a-3. Simon, Sparling, Wood c-2. Simon/Kirby a-3r. Torres a-1?. Wildey a-1(3). Williamson a-2, 3r. Wood a-2(2).*

UNEXPECTED, THE (Formerly Tales of the...)
National Per. Publ./DC Comics: No. 105, Feb-Mar, 1968 - No. 222, May, 1982

105-Begin 12¢ cover price 6 12 18 41 66 90
106-113: 113-Last 12¢ issue (6-7/69) 4 8 12 28 44 60
114,115,117,118,120-125 3 6 9 21 32 42
116 (36 pgs.)-Wrightson-a? 4 8 12 22 34 45
119-Wrightson-a, 8pgs.(36 pgs.) 5 10 15 30 48 65
126,127,129-136-(52 pgs.) 3 6 9 21 32 42
128(52 pgs.)-Wrightson-a 5 10 15 30 48 65
137-156 2 4 6 13 18 22
157-162-(100 pgs.) 4 8 12 26 41 55
163-188: 187,188-(44 pgs.) 2 4 6 9 12 15
189,190,192-195 ($1.00, 68 pgs.): 189 on are combined with House of Secrets & The Witching Hour 2 4 6 9 13 16
191-Rogers-a(p) ($1.00, 68 pgs.) 2 4 6 10 14 18
196-222: 200-Return of Johhny Peril by Tuska. 205-213-Johnny Peril app. 210-Time Warp story. 222-Giffen-a 1 2 3 5 7 9
NOTE: *Neal Adams c-110, 112-115, 118, 121, 124. J. Craig a-195. Ditko a-189, 221p, 222p; c-222. Drucker a-*

United States Fighting Air Force #2 © SUPR

Universe #1 © TCOW

Unknown Soldier #206 © DC

GD VG FN VF VF/NM NM-
2.0 4.0 6.0 8.0 9.0 9.2

107r, 132r. ***Giffen*** *a-219, 222.* ***Kaluta*** *c-203, 212.* ***Kirby*** *a-127r, 162.* ***Kubert*** *c-204, 214-216, 219-221.* ***Mayer*** *a-217p, 220, 221p.* ***Moldoff*** *a-136r.* ***Moreira*** *a-133.* ***Mortimer*** *a-212p.* ***Newton*** *a-204p.* ***Orlando*** *a-202; c-191.* ***Perez*** *a-217p.* ***Redondo*** *a-155, 166, 195.* ***Reese*** *a-145.* ***Sparling*** *a-107, 205-209p, 212p.* ***Spiegle*** *a-217.* ***Starlin*** *c-198.* ***Toth*** *a-126r, 127r.* ***Tuska*** *a-127, 132, 134, 136, 139, 152, 180, 200p.* ***Wildey*** *a-128r, 193.* ***Wood*** *a-122i, 133i, 137i, 138i.* ***Wrightson*** *a-161r(2 pgs.). Johnny Peril in #106-114, 116, 117, 200, 205-213.*

UNEXPECTED ANNUAL, THE (See DC Special Series #4)

UNHOLY UNION
Image Comics (Top Cow): July, 2007 ($3.99, one-shot)

1-Witchblade & The Darkness meet Hulk, Ghost Rider & Doctor Strange; Silvestri-c 4.00

UNIDENTIFIED FLYING ODDBALL (See Walt Disney Showcase #52)

UNION
Image Comics (WildStorm Productions): June, 1993 - No. 0, July, 1994 ($1.95, lim. series)

0-(7/94, $2.50) 2.50
0-Alternate Portacio-c (See Deathblow #5) 5.00
1-($2.50)-Embossed foil-c; Texeira-c/a in all 2.50
1-($1.95)-Newsstand edition w/o foil-c 2.50
2-4: 4-(7/94) 2.50

UNION
Image Comics (WildStorm Prod.): Feb, 1995 - No. 9, Dec, 1995 ($2.50)

1-3,5-9: 3-Savage Dragon app. 6-Fairchild from Gen 13 app. 2.50
4-($1.95, Newsstand)-WildStorm Rising Pt. 3 2.50
4-($2.50, Direct Market)-WildStorm Rising Pt. 3, bound-in card 2.50

UNION: FINAL VENGEANCE
Image Comics (WildStorm Productions): Oct, 1997 ($2.50)

1-Golden-c/Heisler-s 2.50

UNION JACK
Marvel Comics: Dec, 1998 - No. 3, Feb, 1999 ($2.99, limited series)

1-3-Raab-s/Cassaday-s/a 3.00

UNION JACK
Marvel Comics: Nov, 2006 - No. 4, Feb, 2007 ($2.99, limited series)

1-4-Gage-s/Perkins-c/a 3.00
...: London Falling TPB (2007, $10.99) r/#1-4; Perkins sketch page 11.00

UNITED COMICS (Formerly Fritzi Ritz #7; has Fritzi Ritz logo)
United Features Syndicate: Aug, 1940; No. 8, 1950 - No. 26, Jan-Feb, 1953

1(68 pgs.)-Fritzi Ritz & Phil Fumble 23 46 69 133 214 295
8-Fritzi Ritz, Abbie & Slats 8 16 24 44 57 70
9-21: 20-Strange As It Seems; Russell Patterson Cheesecake-a
8 16 24 40 50 60
22-(5-6/52) 2 pgs. early Peanuts by Schulz (1st in comics?)
12 24 36 67 94 120
23-26: 23-(7-8/52). 24-(9-10/52). 25-(11-12/52). 26-(1-2/53). All have 2 pgs. early Peanuts by Schulz 10 20 30 54 72 90
NOTE: *Abbie & Slats reprinted from Tip Top.*

UNITED NATIONS, THE (See Classics Illustrated Special Issue)

UNITED STATES AIR FORCE PRESENTS: THE HIDDEN CREW
U.S. Air Force: 1964 (36 pgs.)

nn-Schaffenberger-a 2 4 6 10 14 18

UNITED STATES FIGHTING AIR FORCE (Also see U.S. Fighting Air Force)
Superior Comics Ltd.: Sept, 1952 - No. 29, Oct, 1956

1 13 26 39 72 101 130
2 8 16 24 42 54 65
3-10 7 14 21 37 46 55
11-29 7 14 21 35 43 50

UNITED STATES MARINES
William H. Wise/Life's Romances Publ. Co./Magazine Ent. #5-8/Toby Press #7-11: 1943 - No. 4, 1944; No. 5, 1952 - No. 8, 1952; No. 7 - No. 11, 1953

nn-Mart Bailey-a 20 40 60 115 183 250
2-Bailey-a; Tojo classic-c 45 90 135 279 465 650
3-Tojo-c 40 80 120 244 397 550
4 13 26 39 74 105 135
5(A-1 #55)-Bailey-a, 6(A-1 #60), 7(A-1 #68), 8(A-1 #72)
10 20 30 56 76 95
7-11 (Toby) 9 18 27 47 61 75
NOTE: ***Powell*** *a-5-7.*

UNITY
Valiant: No. 0, Aug, 1992 - No. 1, 1992 (Free comics w/limited dist., 20 pgs.)

0 (Blue)-Prequel to Unity x-overs in all Valiant titles; B. Smith-c/a. (Free to everyone that bought all 8 titles that month.) 2.50
0 (Red)-Same as above, but w/red logo (5,000). 3.00
1-Epilogue to Unity x-overs; B. Smith-c/a. (1 copy available for every 8 Valiant books ordered by dealers.) 2.50
1 (Gold), 1-(Platinum)-Promotional copy. 6.00
... : The Lost Chapter 1 (Yearbook) (2/95, $3.95)-"1994" in indicia 4.00

UNITY 2000 (See preludes in Shadowman #3,4 flipbooks)
Acclaim Comics: Nov, 1999 - No. 3, Jan, 2000 ($2.50, unfinished limited series planned for 6 issues)

Preview -B&W plot preview and cover art; paper cover 2.50
1-3-Starlin-a/Shooter-s 2.50

UNIVERSAL MONSTERS
Dark Horse Comics: 1993 ($4.95/$5.95, 52 pgs.)(All adapt original movies)

Creature From the Black Lagoon nn-($4.95)-Art Adams/Austin-c/a, Dracula nn-($4.95), Frankenstein nn-($3.95)-Painted-c/a, The Mummy nn-($4.95)-Painted-c
1 2 3 4 5 7
...: Cavalcade of Horror TPB (1/06, $19.95) r/one-shots; Eric Powell intro. & cover 20.00

UNIVERSAL PRESENTS DRACULA-THE MUMMY& OTHER STORIES
Dell Publishing Co.: Sept-Nov, 1963 (one-shot, 84 pgs.) (Also see Dell Giants)

02-530-311-r/Dracula 12-231-212, The Mummy 12-437-211 & part of Ghost Stories No. 1
17 34 51 120 223 325

UNIVERSAL SOLDIER (Movie)
Now Comics: Sept, 1992 - No. 3, Nov, 1992 (Limited series, polybagged, mature)

1-3 ($2.50, Direct Sales) 1-Movie adapatation; hologram on-c (all direct sales editions have painted-c) 2.50
1-3 ($1.95, Newsstand)-Rewritten & redrawn code approved version; all newsstand editions have photo-c 2.50

UNIVERSAL WAR ONE
Marvel Comics (Soleil): 2008 - No. 3, 2008 ($5.99, limited series)

1-3-Denis Bajram-s/a; English version of French comic. 1-Bajram interview 6.00

UNIVERSE
Image Comics (Top Cow): Sept, 2001 - No. 8, July, 2002 ($2.50)

1-7-Jenkins-s 2.50
8-($4.95) extra short-s by Jenkins; pin-up pages 5.00

UNIVERSE X (See Earth X)
Marvel Comics: Sept, 2000 - No. 12, Sept, 2001 ($3.99/$3.50, limited series)

0-Ross-c/Braithwaite-a/Ross & Krueger-s 4.00
1-12: 5-Funeral of Captain America 3.50
... Beasts (6/00, $3.99) Yeates-a/Ross-c 4.00
... Cap (Capt. America) (2/01, $3.99) Yeates & Totleben-a/Ross-c; Cap dies 4.00
... 4 (Fantastic 4) (10/00, $3.99) Brent Anderson-a/Ross-c 4.00
... Iron Men (9/01, $3.99) Anderson-a/Ross-c; leads into #12 4.00
... Omnibus (6/01, $3.99) Ross B&W sketchbook and character bios 4.00
Sketchbook- Wizard supplement; B&W character sketches and bios 2.50
...Spidey (1/01, $3.99) Romita Sr. flashback-a/Guice-a/Ross-c 4.00
...X (11/01, $3.99) Series conclusion; Braithwaith-a/Ross wraparound-c 4.00
Volume 1 TPB (1/02, $24.95) r/#0-7 & Spidey, 4, & Cap; new Ross-c 25.00
Volume 2 TPB (6/02, $24.95) r/#8-12 &X, Beasts, Iron Men and Omnibus 25.00

UNKNOWN MAN, THE (Movie)
Avon Periodicals: 1951

nn-Kinstler-c 28 56 84 162 261 360

UNKNOWN SOLDIER (Formerly Star-Spangled War Stories)
National Periodical Publications/DC Comics: No. 205, Apr-May, 1977 - No. 268, Oct, 1982 (See Our Army at War #168 for 1st app.)

205 3 6 9 14 19 24
206-210,220,221,251: 220,221 (44pgs.). 251-Enemy Ace begins
2 4 6 10 14 18
211-218,222-247,250,252-264 2 4 6 8 11 14
219-Miller-a (44 pgs.) 2 4 6 13 18 22
248,249,265-267: 248,249-Origin. 265-267-Enemy Ace vs. Balloon Buster.
2 4 6 8 11 14
268-Death of Unknown Soldier 3 6 9 14 20 26
NOTE: ***Chaykin*** *a-234.* ***Evans*** *a-265-267; c-235.* ***Kubert*** *c-Most.* ***Miller*** *a-219p.* ***Severin*** *a-251-253, 260, 261, 265-267.* ***Simonson*** *a-254-256.* ***Spiegle*** *a-258, 259, 262-264.*

UNKNOWN SOLDIER, THE (Also see Brave &the Bold #146)
DC Comics: Winter, 1988-'89 - No. 12, Dec, 1989 ($1.50, maxi-series, mature)

1-12: 8-Begin $1.75-c 3.00

UNKNOWN SOLDIER

The Un-Men #1 © DC

The Unseen #6 © STD

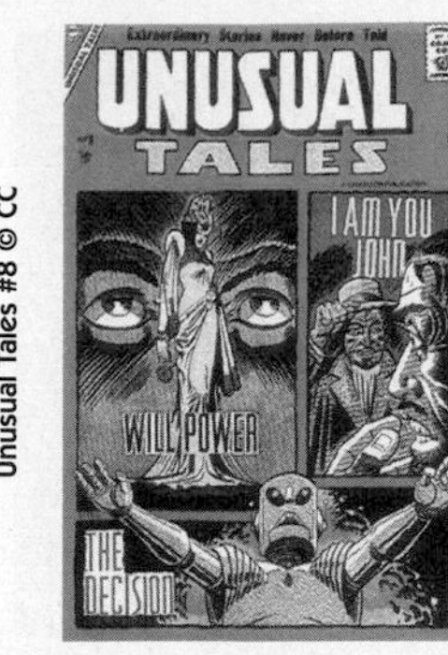

Unusual Tales #8 © CC

	GD 2.0	VG 4.0	FN 6.0	VF 8.0	VF/NM 9.0	NM- 9.2

DC Comics (Vertigo): Apr, 1997 - No 4, July, 1997 ($2.50, mini-series)

1-Ennis-s/Plunkett-a/Bradstreet-c in all 6.00
2-4 4.00
TPB (1998, $12.95) r/#1-4 13.00

UNKNOWN WORLD (Strange Stories From Another World #2 on)
Fawcett Publications: June, 1952

	GD	VG	FN	VF	VF/NM	NM-
1-Norman Saunders painted-c	45	90	135	279	465	650

UNKNOWN WORLDS (See Journey Into...)

UNKNOWN WORLDS
American Comics Group/Best Synd. Features: Aug, 1960 - No. 57, Aug, 1967

	GD	VG	FN	VF	VF/NM	NM-
1-Schaffenberger-c	19	38	57	135	250	365
2-Dinosaur-c/story	11	22	33	79	140	200
3-5	9	18	27	65	113	160
6-11: 9-Dinosaur-c/story. 11-Last 10¢ issue	8	16	24	54	90	125
12-19: 12-Begin 12¢ issues?; ends #57	6	12	18	43	69	95
20-Herbie cameo (12-1/62-63)	7	14	21	45	73	100
21-35: 31-Herbie one pagers thru #39	5	10	15	32	51	70
36- "The People vs. Hendricks" by Craig; most popular ACG story ever	5	10	15	34	55	75
37-46	4	8	12	28	44	60
47-Williamson-a r-from Adventures Into the Unknown #96, 3 pgs.; Craig-a	5	10	15	30	48	65
48-57: 53-Frankenstein app.	4	8	12	26	41	55

NOTE: ***Ditko** a-49, 50p, 54. **Forte** a-3, 6, 11. **Landau** a-56(2). **Reinman** a-3, 9, 13, 20, 22, 23, 36, 38, 54. **Whitney** c/a-most issues. John Force, Magic Agent app.-35, 36, 48, 50, 52, 54, 56.*

UNKNOWN WORLDS OF FRANK BRUNNER
Eclipse Comics: Aug, 1985 - No. 2, Aug, 1985 ($1.75)

1,2-B&W-r in color 3.50

UNKNOWN WORLDS OF SCIENCE FICTION
Marvel Comics: Jan, 1975 - No. 6, Nov, 1975; 1976 ($1.00, B&W Magazine)

	GD	VG	FN	VF	VF/NM	NM-
1-Williamson/Krenkel/Torres/Frazetta-r/Witzend #1, Neal Adams-r/Phase 1; Brunner & Kaluta-r; Freas/Romita-c	3	6	9	14	20	26
2-6: 5-Kaluta text illos	2	4	6	13	18	22
Special 1(1976,100 pgs.)-Newton painted-c	3	6	9	14	20	26

NOTE: ***Brunner** a-2; c-4, 6. **Buscema** a-Special 1p. **Chaykin** a-5. **Colan** a(p)-1, 3, 5, 6. **Corben** a-4. **Kaluta** a-2, Special 1(ext illos); c-2. **Morrow** a-3, 5. **Nino** a-3, 6, Special 1. **Perez** a-2, 3. Ray Bradbury interview in #1.*

UNLIMITED ACCESS (Also see Marvel Vs. DC))
Marvel Comics: Dec, 1997 - No. 4, Mar, 1998 ($2.99/$1.99, limited series)

1-Spider-Man, Wonder Woman, Green Lantern & Hulk app. 3.50
2,3-($1.99): 2-X-Men, Legion of Super-Heroes app. 3-Original Avengers vs. original Justice League 2.50
4-($2.99) Amalgam Legion vs. Darkseid & Magneto 3.00

UN-MEN, THE
DC Comics (Vertigo): Oct, 2007 - Present ($2.99)

1-12-Whalen-s/Hawthorne-a/Hanuka-c 3.00
...: Get Your Freak On! TPB (2008, $9.99) r/#1-5; cover gallery 10.00

UNSANE (Formerly Mighty Bear #13, 14? or The Outlaws #10-14?)(Satire)
Star Publications: No. 15, June, 1954

	GD	VG	FN	VF	VF/NM	NM-
15-Disbrow-a(2); L. B. Cole-c	34	68	102	198	319	440

UNSEEN, THE
Visual Editions/Standard Comics: No. 5, 1952 - No. 15, July, 1954

	GD	VG	FN	VF	VF/NM	NM-
5-Horror stories in all; Toth-a	41	82	123	252	419	585
6,7,9,10-Jack Katz-a	30	60	90	176	283	390
8,11,13,14	23	46	69	135	218	300
12,15-Toth-a. 12-Tuska-a	30	60	90	176	283	390

NOTE: ***Nick Cardy** c-12. **Fawcette** a-13, 14. **Sekowsky** a-7, 8(2), 10, 13, 15.*

UNTAMED
Marvel Comics (Epic Comics/Heavy Hitters): June, 1993 - No. 3, Aug, 1993 ($1.95, lim. series)

1-($2.50)-Embossed-c 2.75
2,3 2.50

UNTAMED LOVE (Also see Frank Frazetta's Untamed Love)
Quality Comics Group (Comic Magazines): Jan, 1950 - No. 5, Sept, 1950

	GD	VG	FN	VF	VF/NM	NM-
1-Ward-c, Gustavson-a	26	52	78	152	244	335
2,4: 2-5-Photo-c	16	32	48	94	147	200
3,5-Gustavson-a	17	34	51	100	158	215

UNTOLD LEGEND OF CAPTAIN MARVEL, THE
Marvel Comics: Apr, 1997 - No. 3, June, 1997 ($2.50, limited series)

1-3 2.50

UNTOLD LEGEND OF THE BATMAN, THE (Also see Promotional section)
DC Comics: July, 1980 - No. 3, Sept, 1980 (Limited series)

1-Origin; Joker-c; Byrne's 1st work at DC 6.00
2,3 4.50

NOTE: ***Aparo** a-1i, 2, 3. **Byrne** a-1p.*

UNTOLD ORIGIN OF THE FEMFORCE, THE (Also see Femforce)
AC Comics: 1989 ($4.95, 68 pgs.)

1-Origin Femforce; Bill Black-a(i) & scripts 6.00

UNTOLD TALES OF CHASTITY
Chaos! Comics: Nov, 2000 ($2.95, one-shot)

1-Origin; Steven Grant-s/Peter Vale-c/a 3.00
1-Premium Edition with glow in the dark cover 13.00

UNTOLD TALES OF LADY DEATH
Chaos! Comics: Nov, 2000 ($2.95, one-shot)

1-Origin of Lady Death; Cremator app.; Kaminski-s 3.00
1-Premium Edition with glow in the dark cover by Steven Hughes 13.00

UNTOLD TALES OF PURGATORI
Chaos! Comics: Nov, 2000 ($2.95, one-shot)

1-Purgatori in 57 B.C.; Rio-a/Grant-s 3.00
1-Premium Edition with glow in the dark cover 13.00

UNTOLD TALES OF SPIDER-MAN (Also see Amazing Fantasy #16-18)
Marvel Comics: Sept, 1995 - No. 25, Sept, 1997 (99¢)

1-Kurt Busiek scripts begin; Pat Olliffe-c/a in all (except #9). 3.00
2-22, -1(7/97), 23-25: 2-1st app. Batwing. 4-1st app. The Spacemen (Gantry, Orbit, Satellite & Vacuum). 8-1st app. The Headsman; The Enforcers (The Big Man, Montana, The Ox & Fancy Dan) app. 9-Ron Frenz-a. 10-1st app. Commanda. 16-Reintro Mary Jane Watson. 21-X-Men-c/app. 25-Green Goblin 2.50
...'96-(1996, $1.95, 46 pgs.)-Kurt Busiek scripts; Mike Allred-c/a; Kurt Busiek & Pat Olliffe app. in back-up story; contains pin-ups 2.50
...'97-(1997, $1.95)-Wraparound-c 2.50
...: Strange Encounters ('98, $5.99) Dr. Strange app. 6.00

UNTOLD TALES OF THE NEW UNIVERSE (Based on Marvel's 1986 New Universe titles)
Marvel Comics: May, 2006 ($2.99, series of one-shots)

...: D. P. 7 - Takes place between issues #4 & 5 of D. P. 7 series; Bright-a/Cebulski-s 3.00
...: Justice - Peter David-s/Carmine Di Giandomenico-a 3.00
...: Nightmask - Takes place between issues #4 & 5 of Nightmask series; The Gnome app. 3.00
...: Psi-Force - Tony Bedard-s/Russ Braun-a 3.00
...: Star Brand - Romita & Romita Jr.-c/Pulido-a 3.00
TPB (2006, $15.99) r/one-shots & stories from Amaz. Fantasy #18,19 & New Avengers #16 16.00

UNTOUCHABLES, THE (TV)
Dell Publishing Co.: No. 1237, 10-12/61 - No. 4, 8-10/62 (All have Robert Stack photo-c)

	GD	VG	FN	VF	VF/NM	NM-
Four Color 1237(#1)	20	40	60	143	264	385
Four Color 1286	14	28	42	102	181	260
01-879-207, 12-879-210(01879-210 on inside)	9	18	27	63	107	150

UNTOUCHABLES
Caliber Comics: Aug, 1997 - No. 4 ($2.95, B&W)

1-4: 1-Pruett-s; variant covers by Kaluta & Showman 3.00

UNUSUAL TALES (Blue Beetle & Shadows From Beyond #50 on)
Charlton Comics: Nov, 1955 - No. 49, Mar-Apr, 1965

	GD	VG	FN	VF	VF/NM	NM-
1	30	60	90	174	280	385
2	15	30	45	88	137	185
3-5	13	26	39	74	105	135
6-Ditko-c only	15	30	45	88	137	185
7,8-Ditko-c/a. 8-Robot-c	27	54	81	158	254	350
9-Ditko-c/a (20 pgs.)	30	60	90	174	280	385
10-Ditko-c/a(4)	31	62	93	181	291	400
11-(3/58, 68 pgs.)-Ditko-a(4)	30	60	90	174	280	385
12,14-Ditko-a	18	36	54	107	169	230
13,16-20	6	12	18	43	69	95
15-Ditko-c/a	23	46	69	133	214	295
21,24,28	5	10	15	35	55	75
22,23,25-27,29-Ditko-a	10	20	30	67	116	165
30-49	4	8	12	26	41	55

NOTE: ***Colan** a-11. **Ditko** c-22, 23, 25-27, 31(part).*

UP FROM HARLEM (Tom Skinner...)
Spire Christian Comics (Fleming H. Revell Co.): 1973 (35/49¢)

USA Comics #9 © MAR

Usagi Yojimbo #106 © Stan Sakai

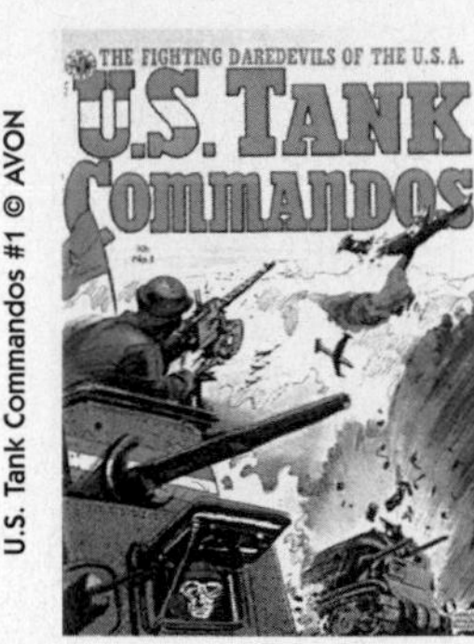

U.S. Tank Commandos #1 © AVON

GD VG FN VF VF/NM NM-
2.0 4.0 6.0 8.0 9.0 9.2

nn 2 4 6 8 10 12

UP-TO-DATE COMICS
King Features Syndicate: No date (1938) (36 pgs.; B&W cover) (10¢)
nn-Popeye & Henry cover; The Phantom, Jungle Jim & Flash Gordon by Raymond, The Katzenjammer Kids, Curley Harper & others. Note: Variations in content exist. 25 50 75 145 233 320

UP YOUR NOSE AND OUT YOUR EAR (Satire)
Klevart Enterprises: Apr, 1972 - No. 2, June, 1972 (52 pgs., magazine)
V1#1,2 2 4 6 10 14 18

URTH 4 (Also see Earth 4)
Continuity Comics: May, 1989 - No. 4, Dec, 1990 ($2.00, deluxe format)
1-4: Ms. Mystic characters. 2-Neal Adams-c(i) 2.50

URZA-MISHRA WAR ON THE WORLD OF MAGIC THE GATHERING
Acclaim Comics (Armada): 1996 - No. 2, 1996 ($5.95, limited series)
1,2 6.00

U.S. (See Uncle Sam)

USA COMICS
Timely Comics (USA): Aug, 1941 - No. 17, Fall, 1945
1-Origin Major Liberty (called Mr. Liberty #1), Rockman by Wolverton; 1st app. The Whizzer by Avison; The Defender with sidekick Rusty & Jack Frost begin; The Young Avenger only app.; S&K-c plus 1 pg. art 1167 2334 3500 8600 15,550 22,500
2-Origin Captain Terror & The Vagabond; last Wolverton Rockman; Hitler-c 394 788 1182 2679 4690 6700
3-No Whizzer 300 600 900 2010 3505 5000
4-Last Rockman, Major Liberty, Defender, Jack Frost, & Capt. Terror; Corporal Dix app. 293 586 879 1846 3123 4400
5-Origin American Avenger & Roko the Amazing; The Blue Blade, The Black Widow & Victory Boys, Gypo the Gypsy Giant & Hills of Horror only app.; Sergeant Dix begins; no Whizzer; Hitler, Mussolini & Tojo-c 273 546 819 1720 2910 4100
6-Captain America (ends #17), The Destroyer, Jap Buster Johnson, Jeep Jones begin; Terror Squad only app. 353 706 1059 2400 4200 6000
7-Captain Daring, Disk-Eyes the Detective by Wolverton app.; origin & only app. Marvel Boy (3/43); Secret Stamp begins; no Whizzer, Sergeant Dix; classic Schomburg-c 353 706 1059 2400 4200 6000
8,10: 10-The Thunderbird only app. 267 534 801 1682 2841 4000
9-Last Secret Stamp; Hitler-c; classic-c 293 586 879 1846 3123 4400
11,12: 11-No Jeep Jones 187 374 561 1178 1989 2800
13-17: 13-No Whizzer; Jeep Jones ends. 15-No Destroyer; Jap Buster Johnson ends 140 280 420 882 1491 2100
NOTE. ***Brodsky*** *c-14.* ***Gabrielle*** *c-4.* ***Schomburg*** *c-6, 7, 10, 12, 13, 15-17.* ***Shores*** *a-1, 4; c-9, 11.* ***Ed Win*** *a-4. Cover features: 1-The Defender; 2, 3-Captain Terror; 4-Major Liberty; 5-Victory Boys; 6-17-Captain America & Bucky.*

U.S. AGENT (See Jeff Jordan...)

U.S. AGENT (See Captain America #354)
Marvel Comics: June, 1993 - No. 4, Sept, 1993 ($1.75, limited series)
1-4 2.50

U.S. AGENT
Marvel Comics: Aug, 2001 - No. 3, Oct, 2001 ($2.99, limited series)
1-3: Ordway-s/a(p)/c. 2,3-Captain America app. 3.00

USAGI YOJIMBO (See Albedo, Doomsday Squad #3 & Space Usagi)
Fantagraphics Books: July, 1987 - No. 38 ($2.00/$2.25, B&W)
1 1 2 3 5 7 9
1,8,10-2nd printings 2.50
2-9 4.00
10,11: 10-Leonardo app. (TMNT). 11-Aragonés-a 6.00
12-29 3.00
30-38: 30-Begin $2.25-c 3.00
Color Special 1 (11/89, $2.95, 68 pgs.)-new & r 3.50
Color Special 2 (10/91, $3.50) 3.50
Color Special #3 (10/92, $3.50)-Jeff Smith's Bone promo on inside-c 3.50
Summer Special 1 (1986, B&W, $2.75)-r/early Albedo issues 3.00

USAGI YOJIMBO
Mirage Studios: V2#1, Mar, 1993 - No. 16, 1994 ($2.75)
V2#1-16: 1-Teenage Mutant Ninja Turtles app. 3.00

USAGI YOJIMBO
Dark Horse Comics: V3#1, Apr, 1996 - Present ($2.95/$2.99, B&W)
V3#1-99,101-113: Stan Sakai-c/a 3.00
100-(1/07, $3.50) Stan Sakai roast by various incl. Aragonés, Wagner, Miller, Geary 3.50
Color Special #4 (7/97, $2.95) "Green Persimmon" 3.00
Daisho TPB ('98, $14.95) r/Mirage series #7-14 15.00
Demon Mask TPB ('01, $15.95) 16.00
Glimpses of Death TPB (7/06, $15.95) r/#76-82 16.00
Grasscutter TPB ('99, $16.95) r/#13-22 17.00
Gray Shadows TPB ('00, $14.95) r/#23-30 15.00
Seasons TPB ('99, $14.95) r/#7-12 15.00
Shades of Death TPB ('97, $14.95) r/Mirage series #1-6 15.00
The Brink of Life and Death TPB ('98, $14.95) r/Mirage series #13,15,16 & Dark Horse series #1-6 15.00
The Shrouded Moon TPB (1/03, $15.95) r/#46-52 16.00

U.S. AIR FORCE COMICS (Army Attack #38 on)
Charlton Comics: Oct, 1958 - No. 37, Mar-Apr, 1965
1 6 12 18 41 66 90
2 4 8 12 22 34 45
3-10 3 6 9 19 29 38
11-20 3 6 9 18 27 35
21-37 3 6 9 16 22 28
NOTE: ***Glanzman*** *c/a-9, 10, 12.* ***Montes/Bache*** *a-33.*

USA IS READY
Dell Publishing Co.: 1941 (68 pgs., one-shot)
1-War propaganda 40 80 120 244 397 550

U.S. BORDER PATROL COMICS (Sgt. Dick Carter of the...) (See Holyoke One Shot)

USER
DC Comics (Vertigo): 2001 - No. 3, 2001 ($5.95, limited series)
1-3-Devin Grayson-s; Sean Phillips & John Bolton-a 6.00

U.S. FIGHTING AIR FORCE (Also see United States Fighting Air Force)
I. W. Enterprises: No date (1960s?)
1,9(nd): 1-r/United States Fighting...#?. 9-r/#1 2 4 6 8 11 14

U.S. FIGHTING MEN
Super Comics: 1963 - 1964 (Reprints)
10-r/With the U.S. Paratroops #4(Avon) 2 4 6 9 13 16
11,12,15-18: 11-r/Monty Hall #10. 12,16,17,18-r/U.S. Fighting Air Force #10,3,?&? 15-r/Man Comics #11 2 4 6 9 13 16

U.S. JONES (Also see Wonderworld Comics #28)
Fox Features Syndicate: Nov, 1941 - No. 2, Jan, 1942
1-U.S. Jones & The Topper begin; Nazi-c 125 250 375 788 1332 1875
2-Nazi-c 83 166 249 523 887 1250

U.S. MARINES
Charlton Comics: Fall, 1964 (12¢, one-shot)
1-1st app. Capt. Dude; Glanzman-a 3 6 9 20 30 40

U.S. MARINES IN ACTION
Avon Periodicals: Aug, 1952 - No. 3, Dec, 1952
1-Louis Ravielli-c/a 10 20 30 54 72 90
2,3: 3-Kinstler-c 8 16 24 40 50 60

U.S. 1
Marvel Comics Group: May, 1983 - No. 12, Oct, 1984 (7,8: painted-c)
1-12: 2-Sienkiewicz-c. 3-12-Michael Golden-c 2.50

U.S. PARATROOPS (See With the...)

U.S. PARATROOPS
I. W. Enterprises: 1964?
1,8: 1-r/With the U.S. Paratroops #1; Wood-c. 8-r/With the U.S. Paratroops #6; Kinstler-c 2 4 6 9 13 16

U.S. TANK COMMANDOS
Avon Periodicals: June, 1952 - No. 4, Mar, 1953
1-Kinstler-c 11 22 33 60 83 105
2-4: Kinstler-c 8 16 24 44 57 70
I.W. Reprint #1,8: 1-r/#1. 8-r/#3 2 4 6 9 13 16
NOTE: ***Kinstler*** *a-I.W. #1; c-1-4, I.W. #1, 8.*

U.S. WAR MACHINE (Also see Iron Man and War Machine)
Marvel Comics (MAX): Nov, 2001 - No. 12, Jan, 2002 ($1.50, B&W, weekly limited series)
1-12-Chuck Austen-s/a/c 2.50
TPB (12/01, $14.95) r/#1-12 15.00

U.S. WAR MACHINE 2.0
Marvel Comics (MAX): Sept, 2003 - No. 3, Sept, 2003 ($2.99, weekly, limited series)

Valor #21 © DC

Vampi #3 © Harris

Vampirella #12 © WP

GD VG FN VF VF/NM NM-
2.0 4.0 6.0 8.0 9.0 9.2

GD VG FN VF VF/NM NM-
2.0 4.0 6.0 8.0 9.0 9.2

1-3-Austen-s/Christian Moore-CGI art 3.00

"V" (TV)
DC Comics: Feb, 1985 - No. 18, July, 1986
1-Based on TV movie & series (Sci/Fi) 3.00
2-18: 17,18-Denys Cowan-c/a 2.50

VACATION COMICS (Also see A-1 Comics)
Magazine Enterprises: No. 16, 1948 (one-shot)
A-1 16-The Pixies, Tom Tom, Flying Fredd & Koko & Kola
6 12 18 31 38 45

VACATION DIGEST
Harvey Comics: Sept, 1987 ($1.25, digest size)
1 1 2 3 5 6 8

VACATION IN DISNEYLAND (Also see Dell Giants)
Dell Publishing Co./Gold Key (1965): Aug-Oct, 1959; May, 1965 (Walt Disney)
Four Color 1025-Barks-a 16 32 48 112 209 305
1(30024-508)(G.K., 5/65, 25¢)-r/Dell Giant #30 & cover to #1 ('58); celebrates Disneyland's 10th anniversary 5 10 15 35 55 75

VACATION PARADE (See Dell Giants)

VALERIA THE SHE BAT
Continuity Comics: May, 1993 - No. 5, Nov, 1993
1-Premium; acetate-c; N. Adams-a/scripts; given as gift to retailers
1 2 3 5 6 8
5 (11/93)-Embossed-c; N. Adams-a/scripts 3.00
NOTE: *Due to lack of continuity, #2-4 do not exist.*

VALERIA THE SHE BAT
Acclaim Comics (Windjammer): Sept, 1995 - No.2, Oct, 1995 ($2.50, limited series)
1,2 2.50

VALKYRIE (See Airboy)
Eclipse Comics: May,1987 - No. 3, July, 1987 ($1.75, limited series)
1-3: 2-Holly becomes new Black Angel 2.50

VALKYRIE
Marvel Comics: Jan, 1997 ($2.95, one-shot)
1-w/pin-ups 3.00

VALKYRIE!
Eclipse Comics: July, 1988 - No. 3, Sept, 1988 ($1.95, limited series)
1-3 2.50

VALLEY OF THE DINOSAURS (TV)
Charlton Comics: Apr, 1975 - No. 11, Dec, 1976 (Hanna-Barbara)
1-W. Howard-i 3 6 9 14 19 24
2,4-11: 2-W. Howard-i 2 4 6 8 11 14
3-Byrne text illos (early work, 7/75) 2 4 6 10 14 18

VALLEY OF THE DINOSAURS (Volume 2)
Harvey Comics: Oct, 1993 ($1.50, giant-sized)
1-Reprints 5.00

VALLEY OF GWANGI (See Movie Classics)

VALOR
E. C. Comics: Mar-Apr, 1955 - No. 5, Nov-Dec, 1955
1-Williamson/Torres-a; Wood-c/a 27 54 81 216 346 475
2-Williamson-c/a; Wood-a 21 42 63 168 272 375
3,4: 3-Williamson, Crandall-a. 4-Wood-c 16 32 48 128 207 285
5-Wood-c/a; Williamson/Evans-a 15 30 45 120 190 260
NOTE: ***Crandall** a-3, 4. **Ingels** a-1, 2, 4, 5. **Krigstein** a-1-5. **Orlando** a-3, 4; c-3. **Wood** a-1, 2, 5; c-1, 4, 5.*

VALOR
Gemstone Publishing: Oct, 1998 - No. 5, Feb, 1999 ($2.50)
1-5-Reprints 2.50

VALOR (Also see Legion of Super-Heroes & Legionnaires)
DC Comics: Nov, 1992 - No. 23, Sept, 1994 ($1.25/$1.50)
1-22: 1-Eclipso The Darkness Within aftermath. 2-Vs. Supergirl. 4-Vs. Lobo. 12-Lobo cameo. 14-Legionnaires, JLA app. 17-Austin-c(i); death of Valor. 18-22-Build-up to Zero Hour 2.50
23-Zero Hour tie-in 3.00

VALOR THUNDERSTAR AND HIS FIREFLIES
Now Comics: Dec, 1986 ($1.50)
1-Ordway-c(p) 2.50

VAMPI (Vampirella's...)
Harris Publications (Anarchy Studios): Aug, 2000 - No. 25, Feb, 2003 ($2.95/$2.99)
Limited Edition Preview Book (5/00) Preview pages & sketchbook 3.00
1-(8/00, $2.95) Lau-a(p)/Conway-s 3.00
1-Platinum Edition 20.00
2-25: 17-Barberi-a 3.00
2-25-Deluxe Edition variants ($9.95): 4-Finch-c. 5-Wieringo-c. 6-Cha-c 10.00
...Digital 1 (11/01, $2.95) CGI art; Haberlin-s 3.00
...Digital Preview (Anarchy Studios, 7/01, $2.95) preview of CGI art 3.00
Switchblade Kiss HC (2001, $24.95) r/#1-6 25.00
Vicious Preview Ed. (Apr, 2003, $1.99) Flip book w/ Xin: Journey of the Monkey King Preview Ed. 2.50
Wizard #1/2 (mail order, $9.95) includes sketch pages 10.00

VAMPIRE BITES
Brainstorm Comics: May, 1995 - No. 2, Sept, 1996 ($2.95, B&W)
1,2:1-Color pin-up 3.00

VAMPIRE LESTAT, THE
Innovation Publishing: Jan, 1990 - No. 12, 1991 ($2.50, painted limited series)
1-Adapts novel; Bolton painted-c on all 2 4 6 10 14 18
1-2nd printing (has UPC code, 1st prints don't) 3.00
1-3rd & 4th printings 2.50
2-1st printing 1 2 3 5 6 8
2-2nd & 3rd printings 2.50
3-5 5.00
3-6,9-2nd printings 2.50
6-12 3.00

VAMPIRELLA (Magazine)(See Warren Presents)
Warren Publishing Co./Harris Publications #113: Sept, 1969 - No. 112, Feb, 1983; No. 113, Jan, 1988? (B&W)
1-Intro. Vampirella in original costume & wings; Frazetta-c/intro. page; Adams-a; Crandall-a 40 80 120 312 581 850
2-1st app. Vampirella's cousin Evily-c/s; 1st/only app. Draculina, Vampirella's blonde twin sister 15 30 45 105 190 275
3 (Low distribution) 36 72 108 277 514 750
4,6 11 22 33 77 136 195
5,7,9: 5,7-Frazetta-c. 9-Barry Smith-a; Boris/Wood-c 11 22 33 79 140 200
8-Vampirella begins by Tom Sutton as serious strip (early issues-gag line)
12 24 36 82 146 210
10-No Vampi story; Brunner, Adams, Wood-a 7 14 21 49 80 110
11-Origin & 1st app. Pendragon; Frazetta-c 8 16 24 54 90 125
12-Vampi by Gonzales begins 8 16 24 54 90 125
13-15: 14-1st Maroto-a; Ploog-a 8 16 24 54 90 125
16,22,25: 16-1st full Dracula-c/app. 22-Color insert preview of Maroto's Dracula. 25-Vampi on cocaine-s 7 14 21 50 83 115
17,18,20,21,23,24: 17-Tomb of the Gods begins by Maroto, ends #22. 18-22-Dracula-s 7 14 21 49 80 110
19 (1973 Annual) Creation of Vampi text bio 8 16 24 58 97 135
26,28,34,35,39,40: All have 8 pg. color inserts. 28-Board game inside covers. 34,35-1st Fleur the Witch Woman. 39,40-Color Dracula-s. 40-Wrightson bio
5 10 15 34 55 75
27 (1974 Annual) New color Vampi-s; mostly-r 6 12 18 39 62 85
29,38,45: 38-2nd Vampi as Cleopatra/Blood Red Queen of Hearts; 1st Mayo-a.
5 10 15 34 55 75
30-32: 30-Intro. Pantha; Corben-a(color). 31-Origin Luana, the Beast Girl. 32-Jones-a 5 10 15 34 55 75
33-Wrightson-a; Pantha ends 5 10 15 34 55 75
36,37: 36-1st Vampi as Cleopatra/Blood Red Queen of Hearts; issue has 8 pg. color insert. 37-(1975 Annual) 6 12 18 37 59 80
41-44,47,48: 41-Dracula-s 5 10 15 30 48 65
46-(10/75) Origin-r from Annual 1 5 10 15 32 51 70
49-1st Blind Priestess; The Blood Red Queen of Hearts storyline begins; Poe-s
5 10 15 30 48 65
50-Spirit cameo by Eisner; 40 pg. Vampi-s; Pantha & Fleur app.; Jones-a
5 10 15 30 48 65
51-53,56,57,59-62,65,66,68,75,79,80,82-86,88,89: 60-62,65,66-The Blood Red Queen of Hearts app. 60-1st Blind Priestess-c 4 8 12 22 34 45
54,55,63,81,87: 54-Vampi-s (42 pgs.); 8 pg. color Corben-a. 55-All Gonzales-a(r). 63-10 pgs. Wrightson-a 4 8 12 22 34 45
58,70,72: 58-(92 pgs.) 70-Rook app. 4 8 12 26 41 55
64,73: 64-(100 pg. Giant) All Mayo-a; 70 pg. Vampi-s. 73-69 pg. Vampi-s; Mayo-a
4 8 12 28 44 60
67,69,71,74,76-78-All Barbara Leigh photo-c 4 8 12 26 41 55
90-99: 90-Toth-a. 91-All-r; Gonzales-a. 93-Cassandra St. Knight begins, ends #103;

Vampirella #102 © WP

Vampirella (Monthly) #10 © Harris

Vampirella & the Blood Red Queen of Hearts © Harris

GD VG FN VF VF/NM NM-
2.0 4.0 6.0 8.0 9.0 9.2

new Pantha series begins, ends #108 4 8 12 22 34 45
100 (96 pg. r-special)-Origin reprinted from Ann. 1; mostly reprints; Vampirella appears topless in new 21 pg. story 8 16 24 54 90 125
101-104,106,107: All lower print run. 101,102-The Blood Red Queen of Hearts app. 107-All Maroto reprint-a issue 6 12 18 39 62 85
105,108-110: 108-Torpedo series by Toth begins; Vampi nudity splash page. 110-(100 pg. Summer Spectacular) 6 12 18 39 62 85
111,112: Low print run. 111-Giant Collector's Edition ($2.50) 112-(84 pgs.) last Warren issue 7 14 21 50 83 115
113 (1988)-1st Harris Issue; very low print run 26 52 78 188 349 510
Annual 1(1972)-New definitive origin of Vampirella by Gonzales; reprints by Neal Adams (from #1), Wood (from #9) 25 50 75 185 343 500
Special 1 (1977) Softcover (color, large-square bound)-Only available thru mail order 15 30 45 107 196 285
Special 1 (1977) Hardcover (color, large-square bound)-Only available through mail order (scarce)(500 produced, signed & #'d) 32 64 96 246 461 675
#1 1969 Commemorative Edition (2001, $4.95) reprints entire #1 5.00
...Crimson Chronicles Vol. 1 (2004, $19.95, TPB) reprints stories from #1-10 20.00
...Crimson Chronicles Vol. 2 (2005, $19.95, TPB) reprints stories from #11-18 20.00
...Crimson Chronicles Vol. 3 (2005, $19.95, TPB) reprints stories from #19-28 20.00
...Crimson Chronicles Vol. 4 (2006, $19.95, TPB) reprints stories from #29-41 20.00

NOTE: *Ackerman s-1-3.* ***Neal Adams*** *a-1, 10p, 19p(r/#10), 44(1 pg.), Annual 1.* ***Alcala*** *a-78, 90, 93i.* ***Bodé/Todd*** *c-3.* ***Bodé/Jones*** *c-4.* ***Boris/Wood*** *c-9.* ***Brunner*** *a-10, 12(1 pg.).* ***Corben*** *a-30, 31, 33, 36, 54; c-30, 31, 33, 54.* ***Crandall*** *a-1, 19(r/#1).* ***Frazetta*** *c-1, 5, 7, 11, 31.* ***Heath*** *a-58, 61, 67, 76-78, 83.* ***Infantino*** *a-57-62.* ***Jones*** *a-5, 9, 12, 27, 32 (color), 33(2 pg.), 34, 50i, 83r.* ***Ken Kelly*** *c-6, 38, 39, 40(back-c), 46, 70, 95.* ***Nebres*** *a-84, 88-90, 92-96.* ***Nino*** *a-59i, 61i, 67, 76, 85, 90.* ***Ploog*** *a-14.* ***Barry Smith*** *a-9.* ***Starlin*** *a-78.* ***Sutton*** *a-1-5, 7-11, Annual 1.* ***Toth*** *a-90i, 108, 110.* ***Wood*** *a-9, 10, 12, 19(r/#12), 27r, Annual 1; c-9(partial).* ***Wrightson*** *a-33(w/Jones), 40(Bio cameo) 63r. All reprint issues-19, 74, 83, 91, 105, 107, 109, 111. Annuals from 1973 on are included in regular numbering. Later annuals are same format as regular issues. Color inserts (8 pgs.) in 22, 25-28, 30-35, 39, 40, 45, 46, 49, 54, 55, 67, 72. 16 pg color insert in #36.*

VAMPIRELLA (Also see Cain/... & Vengeance of...)
Harris Publications: Nov, 1992 - No. 5, Nov, 1993 ($2.95)

0-Bagged 5.00
0-Gold 3 6 9 16 23 30
1-Jim Balent inks in #1-3; Adam Hughes c-1-3 2 4 6 11 16 20
1-2nd printing 5.00
1-(11/97) Commemorative Edition 3.00
2 2 4 6 9 12 15
3-5: 4-Snyder III-c. 5-Brereton painted-c 1 2 3 5 6 8
Trade paperback nn (10/93, $5.95)-r/#1-4; Jusko-c 1 2 3 4 5 7
NOTE: *Issues 1-5 contain certificates for free* ***Dave Stevens*** *Vampirella poster.*

VAMPIRELLA (THE NEW MONTHLY)
Harris Publications: Nov, 1997 - No. 26, Apr, 2000 ($2.95)

1-3-"Ascending Evil" -Morrison & Millar-s/Conner & Palmiotti-a. 1-Three covers by Quesada/Palmiotti, Conner, and Conner/Palmiotti 3.00
1-3-($9.95) Jae Lee variant covers 10.00
1-($24.95) Platinum Ed.w/Quesada-c 25.00
4-6-"Holy War"-Small & Stull-a, 4-Linsner variant-c 3.00
7-9-"Queen's Gambit"-Shi app. 7-Two covers. 8-Pantha-c/app. 3.00
7-($9.95) Conner variant-c 10.00
10-12-"Hell on Earth"; Small-a/Coney-s. 12-New costume 3.00
10-Jae Lee variant-c 1 3 4 6 8 10
13-15-"World's End" Zircher-p; Pantha back-up, Texeira-a 3.00
16,17: 16-Pantha-c;Texeira-a; Vampi back-up story. 17-(Pantha #2) 3.00
18-20-"Rebirth": Jae Lee-c on all. 18-Loeb-s/Sale-a. 19-Alan Davis-a. 20-Bruce Timm-a 3.00
18-20-($9.95) Variant covers: 18-Sale. 19-Davis. 20-Timm 12.00
21-26: 21,22-Dangerous Games; Small-a. 23-Lady Death-c/app.; Cleavenger-a. 24,25-Lau-a. 26-Lady Death & Pantha-c/app.; Cleavenger-a. 3.00
0-(1/99) also variant-c with Pantha #0; same contents 3.00
TPB ($7.50) r/#1-3 "Ascending Evil" 8.00
Ascending Evil Ashcan (8/97, $1.00) 2.50
...: Grant Morrison/Mark Millar Collection TPB (2006, $24.95) r/#1-6; interviews 25.00
Hell on Earth Ashcan (7/98, $1.00) 2.50
... Presents: Tales of Pantha TPB (2006, $19.95) r/stories from #13-17 & one-shots 20.00
The End Ashcan (3/00, $6.00) 6.00
...30th Anniversary Celebration Preview (7/99) B&W preview of #18-20 10.00

VAMPIRELLA
Harris Publications: June, 2001 - No. 22, Aug, 2003 ($2.95/$2.99)

1-Four covers (Mayhew w/foil logo, Campbell, Anacleto, Jae Lee) Mayhew-a; Mark Millar-s 3.00
2-22: 2-Two covers (Mayhew & Chiodo). 3-Timm var-c. 4-Horn var-c. 7-10-Dawn Brown-a; Pantha back-up w/Texeira-a. 15-22-Conner-c 3.00
Giant-Size Ashcan (5/01, $5.95) B&W preview art and Mayhew interview 6.00
...: Halloween Trick & Treat (10/04, $4.95) stories & art by various; three covers 5.00
... : Nowheresville Preview Edition (3/01, $2.95)- previews Mayhew art and photo models 3.00
...Nowheresville TPB (1/02, $12.95) r/#1-3 with cover gallery 13.00
... Summer Special #1 (2005, $5.95) Batman Begins photo-c and 2 variant-c 6.00
...: 2006 Halloween Special (2006, $2.95) Conner-c; Hester-s/Segovia-a; 4 covers 3.00

VAMPIRELLA & PANTHA SHOWCASE
Harris Publications: Jan, 1997 ($1.50, one-shot)

1-Millar-s/Texeira-c/a; flip book w/"Blood Lust"; Robinson-s/Jusko-c/a 3.00

VAMPIRELLA & THE BLOOD RED QUEEN OF HEARTS
Harris Publications: Sept, 1996 ($9.95, 96 pgs., B&W, squarebound, one-shot)

nn-r/Vampirella #49,60-62,65,66,101,102; John Bolton-c; Michael Bair back-c 1 3 4 6 8 10

VAMPIRELLA: BLOODLUST
Harris Publications: July, 1997 - No. 2, Aug, 1997 ($4.95, limited series)

1,2-Robinson-s/Jusko-painted c/a 5.00

VAMPIRELLA CLASSIC
Harris Publications: Feb, 1995 - No. 5, Nov, 1995 ($2.95, limited series)

1-5: Reprints Archie Goodwin stories. 3.00

VAMPIRELLA COMICS MAGAZINE
Harris Publications: Oct, 2003 - Present ($3.95/$9.95, magazine-sized)

1-9-($3.95) 1-Texiera-c; b&w and color stories, Alan Moore interview; reviews. 2-KISS interview. 4-Chiodo-c. 6-Brereton-c 4.00
1-9-($9.95) 1-Three covers (Model Photo cover, Palmiotti-c, Wheatley Frankenstein-c) 10.00

VAMPIRELLA: CROSSOVER GALLERY
Harris Publications: Sept, 1997 ($2.95, one-shot)

1-Wraparound-c by Campbell, pinups by Jae Lee, Mack, Allred, Art Adams, Quesada & Palmiotti and others 3.00

VAMPIRELLA: DEATH & DESTRUCTION
Harris Publications: July, 1996 - No. 3, Sept, 1996 ($2.95, limited series)

1-3: Amanda Conner-a(p) in all. 1-Tucci-c. 2-Hughes-c. 3-Jusko-c 3.00
1-($9.95)-Limited Edition; Beachum-c 10.00

VAMPIRELLA/DRACULA & PANTHA SHOWCASE
Harris Publications: Aug, 1997 ($1.50, one-shot)

1-Ellis, Robinson, and Moore-s; flip book w/"Pantha" 3.00

VAMPIRELLA/DRACULA: THE CENTENNIAL
Harris Publications: Oct, 1997 ($5.95, one-shot)

1-Ellis, Robinson, and Moore-s; Beachum, Frank/Smith, and Mack/Mays-a Bolton-painted-c 6.00

VAMPIRELLA: INTIMATE VISIONS
Harris Publications: 2006 ($3.95, one-shots)

..., Amanda Conner 1 - r/Vampirella Monthly #1 with commentary; interview; 2 covers 4.00
..., Joe Jusko 1 - r/Vampirella; Blood Lust #1 with commentary; interview; 2 covers 4.00

VAMPIRELLA: JULIE STRAIN SPECIAL
Harris Publications: Sept, 2000 ($3.95, one-shot)

1-Photo-c w/yellow background; interview and photo gallery 4.00
1-Limited Edition ($9.95); cover photo w/black background 10.00

VAMPIRELLA/LADY DEATH (Also see Lady Death/Vampirella)
Harris Publications: Feb, 1999 ($3.50, one-shot)

1-Small-a/Nelson painted-c 3.50
1-Valentine Edition ($9.95); pencil-c by Small 10.00

VAMPIRELLA: LEGENDARY TALES
Harris Publications: May, 2000 - No. 2, June, 2000 ($2.95, B&W)

1,2-Reprints from magazine; Cleavenger painted-c 3.00
1,2-($9.95) Variant painted-c by Mike Mayhew 10.00

VAMPIRELLA LIVES
Harris Publications: Dec, 1996 - No. 3, Feb, 1997 ($3.50/$2.95, limited series)

1-Die cut-c; Quesada & Palmiotti-c, Ellis-s/Conner-a 3.50
1-Deluxe Ed.-photo-c 3.50
2,3-($2.95)-Two editions (1 photo-c): 3-J. Scott Campbell-c 3.00

VAMPIRELLA: MORNING IN AMERICA
Harris Publications/Dark Horse Comics: 1991 - No. 4, 1992 ($3.95, B&W, lim. series, 52 pgs.)

1,2-All have Kaluta painted-c 1 2 3 5 6 8
3,4 1 3 4 6 8 10

VAMPIRELLA OF DRAKULON
Harris Publications: Jan, 1996 - No. 5, Sept, 1996 ($2.95)

Vampirella: Sad Wings of Destiny #1 © Harris

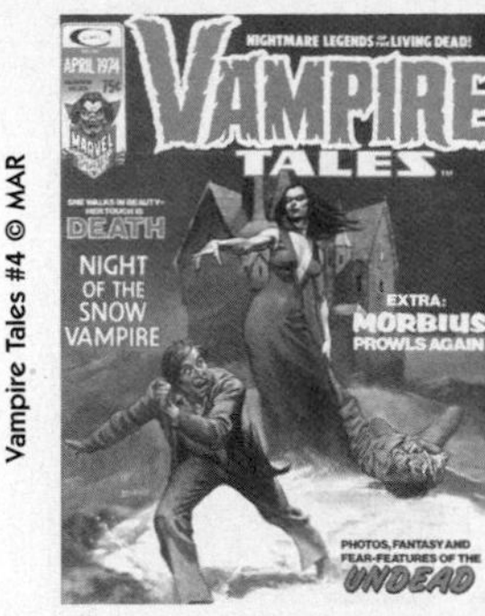

Vampire Tales #4 © MAR

Vamps #2 © Lee & Simpson

	GD 2.0	VG 4.0	FN 6.0	VF 8.0	VF/NM 9.0	NM- 9.2

0-5: All reprints. 0-Jim Silke-c. 3-Polybagged w/card. 4-Texeira-c 3.00

VAMPIRELLA/PAINKILLER JANE
Harris Publications: May, 1998 ($3.50, one-shot)
1-Waid & Augustyn-s/Leonardi & Palmiotti-a 3.50
1-($9.95) Variant-c 10.00

VAMPIRELLA PIN-UP SPECIAL
Harris Publications: Oct, 1995 ($2.95, one-shot)
1-Hughes-c, pin-ups by various 5.00
1-Variant-c 5.00

VAMPIRELLA QUARTERLY
Harris Publications: Spring, 2007 - Present ($4.95/$4.99, quarterly)
Spring, 2007 - Summer 2008-New stories and re-colored reprints; five or six covers 5.00

VAMPIRELLA: RETRO
Harris Publications: Mar, 1998 - No. 3, May, 1998 ($2.50, B&W, limited series)
1-3: Reprints; Silke painted covers 3.00

VAMPIRELLA: REVELATIONS
Harris Publications: No. 0, Oct, 2005 - No. 3, Feb, 2006 ($2.99, limited series)
0-3-Vampirella's origin retold, Lilith app.; Carey-s/Lilly-a; two covers on each 4.00
... Book 1 TPB (2006, $12.95) r/series; Carey interview, script for #1, Lilly sketch pages 13.00

VAMPIRELLA: SAD WINGS OF DESTINY
Harris Publications: Sept, 1996 ($3.95, one-shot)
1-Jusko-c 4.00

VAMPIRELLA/SHADOWHAWK: CREATURES OF THE NIGHT (Also see Shadowhawk)
Harris Publications: 1995 ($4.95, one-shot)
1 5.00

VAMPIRELLA/SHI (See Shi/Vampirella)
Harris Publications: Oct, 1997 ($2.95, one-shot)
1-Ellis-s 3.00
1-Chromium-c 6.00

VAMPIRELLA: SILVER ANNIVERSARY COLLECTION
Harris Publications: Jan, 1997 - No. 4 Apr, 1997 ($2.50, limited series)
1-4: Two editions: Bad Girl by Beachum, Good Girl by Silke 3.00

VAMPIRELLA'S SUMMER NIGHTS
Harris Publications: 1992 (one-shot)
1-Art Adams infinity cover; centerfold by Stelfreeze 3 7 10 19 27 35

VAMPIRELLA STRIKES
Harris Publications: Sept, 1995 - No. 8, Dec, 1996 ($2.95, limited series)
1-8: 1-Photo-c. 2-Deodato-c; polybagged w/card. 5-Eudaemon-c/app; wraparound-c; alternate-c exists. 6-(6/96)-Mark Millar script; Texeira-c; alternate-c exists. 7-Flip book 3.00
1-Newsstand Edition; diff. photo-c., 1-Limited Ed.; diff. photo-c 3.00
Annual 1-(12/96, $2.95) Delano-s; two covers 3.00

VAMPIRELLA: 25TH ANNIVERSARY SPECIAL
Harris Publications: Oct, 1996 ($5.95, squarebound, one-shot)
nn-Reintro The Blood Red Queen of Hearts; James Robinson, Grant Morrison & Warren Ellis scripts; Mark Texeira, Michael Bair & Amanda Conner-a(p); Frank Frazetta-c 6.00
nn-($6.95)-Silver Edition 7.00

VAMPIRELLA VS. HEMORRHAGE
Harris Publications: Apr, 1997($3.50)
1 3.50

VAMPIRELLA VS. PANTHA
Harris Publications: Mar, 1997 ($3.50)
1-Two covers; Millar-s/Texeira-c/a 3.50

VAMPIRELLA/WETWORKS (See Wetworks/Vampirella)
Harris Publications: June, 1997 ($2.95, one-shot)
1 3.00
1-($9.95) Alternate Edition; cardstock-c 10.00

VAMPIRELLA/WITCHBLADE
Harris Publications: 2003; Oct, 2004; Oct, 2005 ($2.99, one-shots)
1-Brian Wood-s/Steve Pugh-a; 3 covers by Texeira, Conner and Pugh 3.00
...: The Feast (10/05, $2.99) Joyce Chin-a; covers by Chin, Conner, Rodriguez 3.00
...: Union of the Damned (10/04, $2.99, one-shot) Sharp-a; three covers 3.00
Trilogy TPB (2006, $12.95) r/one-shots; art gallery and gallery of multiple covers 13.00

VAMPIRE'S CHRISTMAS, THE (Also see Dark Ivory)
Image Comics: Oct, 2003 ($5.95, over-sized graphic novel)
nn-Linsner-s/a; Dubisch-painted-a 6.00

VAMPIRE TALES
Marvel Comics Group: Aug, 1973 - No. 11, June, 1975 (75¢, B&W, magazine)

	GD	VG	FN	VF	VF/NM	NM-
1-Morbius, the Living Vampire begins by Pablo Marcos (1st solo Morbius series & 5th Morbius app.)	7	14	21	45	73	100
2-Intro. Satana; Steranko-r	5	10	15	30	48	65
3,5,6: 3-Satana app. 5-Origin Morbius. 6-1st Lilith app. in this title (see Giant-Size Chillers #1 for debut)	4	8	12	26	41	55
4,7	3	6	9	20	30	40
8-1st solo Blade story (see Tomb of Dracula)	5	10	15	30	48	65
9-Blade app.	4	8	12	26	41	55
10,11	3	6	9	20	30	40
Annual 1(10/75)-Heath-r/#9	3	6	9	20	30	40

NOTE: ***Alcala** a-6, 8, 9i. **Boris** c-4, 6. **Chaykin** a-7. **Everett** a-1r. **Gulacy** a-7p. **Heath** a-9. **Infantino** a-3r. **Gil Kane** a-4, 5r.*

VAMPIRE VERSES, THE
CFD Productions: Aug, 1995 - No. 4, 1995 ($2.95, B&W, mature)
1-4 3.00

VAMPI VICIOUS
Harris Publications (Anarchy Studios): Aug, 2003 - No. 3, Nov, 2003 ($2.99)
1-3: 1-McKeever-s/Dogan-a; 3 covers by Dogan, Lau & Noto. 3-Kau-a 3.00

VAMPI VICIOUS CIRCLE
Harris Publications (Anarchy Studios): Jun, 2004 - No. 3, Sept, 2004 ($2.99/$9.95)
1-3: B. Clay Moore-s 3.00
1-3-($9.95) Limited Edition w/variant-c. 1-Noto-c. 2-Norton-c. 3-Lucas-c 10.00

VAMPI VICIOUS RAMPAGE
Harris Publications (Anarchy Studios): Feb, 2005 - No. 2, Apr, 2005 ($2.99)
1,2: Raab-s/Lau-a; two covers on each 3.00

VAMPI VS. XIN
Harris Publications (Anarchy Studios): Oct, 2004 - No. 2, Jan, 2005 ($2.99)
1,2-Faerber-s/Lau-a; two covers 3.00

VAMPS
DC Comics (Vertigo): Aug, 1994 - No. 6, Jan, 1995 ($1.95, lim. series, mature)
1-6-Bolland-c 3.00
Trade paperback ($9.95)-r/#1-6 10.00

VAMPS: HOLLYWOOD & VEIN
DC Comics (Vertigo): Feb, 1996 - No. 6, July, 1996 ($2.25, lim. series, mature)
1-6: Winslade-c 2.50

VAMPS: PUMPKIN TIME
DC Comics (Vertigo): Dec, 1998 - No. 3, Feb, 1999 ($2.50, lim. series, mature)
1-3: Quitely-c 2.50

VANGUARD (...Outpost: Earth) (See Megaton)
Megaton Comics: 1987 ($1.50)
1-Erik Larsen-c(p) 3.00

VANGUARD (See Savage Dragon #2)
Image Comics (Highbrow Entertainment): Oct, 1993 - No. 6, 1994 ($1.95)
1-6: 1-Wraparound gatefold-c; Erik Larsen back-up-a; Supreme x-over. 3-(12/93)-Indicia says December 1994. 4-Berzerker back-up. 5-Angel Medina-a(p) 3.00

VANGUARD (See Savage Dragon #2)
Image Comics: Aug, 1996 - No. 4, Feb, 1997 ($2.95, B&W, limited series)
1-4 3.00

VANGUARD: ETHEREAL WARRIORS
Image Comics: Aug, 2000 ($5.95, B&W)
1-Fosco & Larsen-a 6.00

VANGUARD ILLUSTRATED
Pacific Comics: Nov, 1983 - No. 11, Oct, 1984 (Baxter paper)(Direct sales only)
1-6,8-11: 1,7-Nudity scenes. 2-1st app. Stargrazers (see Legends of the Stargrazers; Dave Stevens-c 3.00
7-1st app. Mr. Monster (r-in Mr. Monster #1) 5.00
NOTE: ***Evans** a-7. **Kaluta** c-5, 7p. **Perez** a-6; c-6. **Rude** a-1-4; c-4. **Williamson** c-3.*

VANGUARD: STRANGE VISITORS
Image Comics: Oct, 1996 - No.4, Feb, 1997 ($2.95, B&W, limited series)
1-4: 3-Supreme-c/app. 3.00

Vault of Horror #25 © WMG

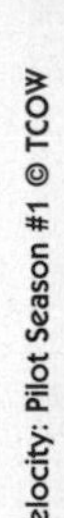

Velocity: Pilot Season #1 © TCOW

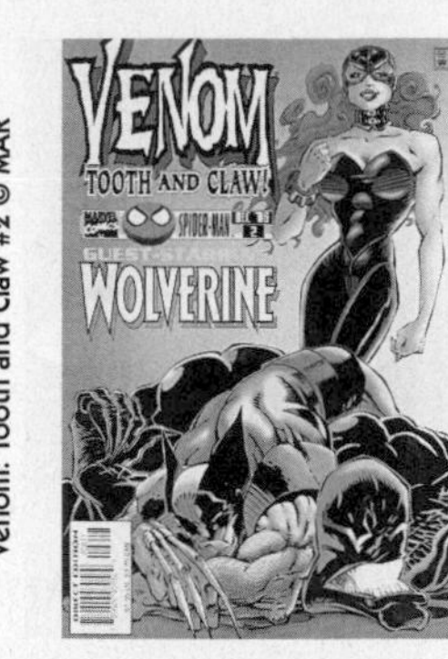

Venom: Tooth and Claw #2 © MAR

VAN HELSING: FROM BENEATH THE RUE MORGUE (Based on the 2004 movie)
Dark Horse Comics: Apr, 2004 ($2.99, one-shot)
1-Hugh Jackman photo-c; Dysart-s/Alexander-a 3.00

VANITY (See Pacific Presents #3)
Pacific Comics: Jun, 1984 - No. 2, Aug, 1984 ($1.50, direct sales)
1,2: Origin 2.50

VARIETY COMICS (The Spice of Comics)
Rural Home Publ./Croyden Publ. Co.: 1944 - No. 2, 1945; No. 3, 1946
1-Origin Captain Valiant 21 42 63 125 200 275
2-Captain Valiant 14 28 42 80 115 150
3(1946-Croyden)-Captain Valiant 12 24 36 69 97 125

VARIETY COMICS (See Fox Giants)

VARSITY
Parents' Magazine Institute: 1945
1 8 16 24 44 57 70

VAULT OF EVIL
Marvel Comics Group: Feb, 1973 - No. 23, Nov, 1975
1 (1950s reprints begin) 3 6 9 16 23 30
2-23: 3,4-Brunner-c. 11-Kirby-a 2 4 6 10 14 18
NOTE: ***Ditko** a-14r, 15r, 20-22r. **Drucker** a-10r(Mystic #52), 13r(Uncanny Tales #42). **Everett** a-11r(Menace #2), 13r(Menace #4); c-10. **Heath** a-5r. **Gil Kane** c-1, 6. **Kirby** a-11. **Krigstein** a-20r(Uncanny Tales #54). **Reinman** r-1. **Tuska** a-6r.*

VAULT OF HORROR (Formerly War Against Crime #1-11) (Also see EC Archives)
E. C. Comics: No. 12, Apr-May, 1950 - No. 40, Dec-Jan, 1954-55
12 (Scarce)-ties w/Crypt Of Terror as 1st horror comic
474 948 1422 3792 6046 8300
13-Morphine story 100 200 300 800 1273 1745
14 89 178 267 712 1131 1550
15- "Terror in the Swamp" is same story w/minor changes as "The Thing in the Swamp" from Haunt of Fear #15 76 152 228 608 967 1325
16, 59 118 177 472 749 1025
17-Classic werewolf-c 66 132 198 528 839 1150
18,19 47 94 141 376 596 815
20-25: 22-Frankenstein-c & adaptation. 23-Used in **POP**, pg. 84; Davis-a(2); Ingels bio. 24-Craig bio. 39 78 117 312 494 675
26-B&W & color illos in **POP** 39 78 117 312 494 675
27-36: 30-Dismemberment-c. 31-Ray Bradbury biog. 32-Censored-c. 35-X-Mas-c. 36- "Pipe Dream" classic opium addict story by Krigstein; "Twin Bill" cited in articles by T.E. Murphy, Wertham 32 64 96 256 408 560
37-1st app. Drusilla, a Vampirella look alike; Williamson-a
33 66 99 264 394 570
38-39: 39-Bondage-c 31 62 93 248 384 540
40-Low distribution 39 78 117 312 494 675
NOTE: ***Craig** art in all but No. 13 & 33; c-12-40. **Crandall** a-33, 34, 39. **Davis** a-17-38. **Evans** a-27, 28, 30, 32, 33. **Feldstein** a-12-16. **Ingels** a-13-20, 22-40. **Kamen** a-15-22, 25, 29, 35. **Krigstein** a-36, 38-40. **Kurtzman** a-12, 13. **Orlando** a-24, 31, 40. **Wood** a-12-14. #22, 29 & 31 have Ray Bradbury adaptations. #16 & 17 have H. P. Lovecraft adaptations.*

VAULT OF HORROR, THE
Gladstone Publ.: Aug, 1990 - No. 6, June, 1991 ($1.95, 68 pgs.)(#4 on: $2.00)
1-Craig-c(r); all contain EC reprints 4.00
2-6: 2,4-6-Craig-c(r). 3-Ingels-c(r) 3.00

VAULT OF HORROR
Russ Cochran/Gemstone Publishing: Sept, 1991 - No. 5, May, 1992 ($2.00); Oct, 1992 - No. 29, Oct, 1999 ($1.50/$2.00/$2.50)
1-29: E.C reprints. 1-4r/VOH #12-15 w/original-c 3.00

V...-COMICS (Morse code for "V" - 3 dots, 1 dash)
Fox Features Syndicate: Jan, 1942 - No. 2, Mar-Apr, 1942
1-Origin V-Man & the Boys; The Banshee & The Black Fury, The Queen of Evil, & V-Agents begin; Nazi-c 128 256 384 806 1366 1925
2-Nazi bondage/torture-c 90 180 270 567 959 1350

VECTOR
Now Comics: 1986 - No. 4, 1986? ($1.50, 1st color comic by Now Comics)
1-4: Computer-generated art 2.50

VEILS
DC Comics (Vertigo): 1999 ($24.95, one-shot)
Hardcover-($24.95) Painted art and photography; McGreal-s 25.00
Softcover ($14.95) 15.00

VELOCITY (Also see Cyberforce)
Image Comics (Top Cow Productions): Nov, 1995 - No. 3, Jan, 1996 ($2.50, limited series)
1-3: Kurt Busiek scripts in all. 2-Savage Dragon-c/app. 3.00
...: Pilot Season 1 (10/07, $2.99) Casey-s/Maguire-a 3.00

VENGEANCE OF VAMPIRELLA (Becomes Vampirella: Death & Destruction)
Harris Comics: Apr, 1994 - No. 25, Apr, 1996 ($2.95)
1-($3.50)-Quesada/Palmiotti "bloodfoil" wraparound cover 6.00
1-2nd printing; blue foil-c 3.00
1-Gold 18.00
2-8: 8-Polybagged w/trading card 4.00
9-25: 10-w/coupon for Hyde -25 poster. 11,19-Polybagged w/ trading card. 25-Quesada & Palmiotti red foil-c 3.00
...: Bloodshed (1995, $6.95) 7.00

VENGEANCE OF VAMPIRELLA: THE MYSTERY WALK
Harris Comics: Nov, 1995 ($2.95, one-shot)
0 3.00

VENGEANCE SQUAD
Charlton Comics: July, 1975 - No. 6, May, 1976 (#1-3 are 25¢ issues)
1-Mike Mauser, Private Eye begins by Staton 2 4 6 8 10 12
2-6: Morisi-a in all 1 2 3 4 5 7
5,6 (Modern Comics-r, 1977) 4.00

VENOM
Marvel Comics: June, 2003 - No. 18, Nov, 2004 ($2.25)
1-7-Herrera-a/Way-s. 6,7-Wolverine app. 2.50
8-18-($2.99): 8-10-Wolverine-c/app.; Kieth-c. 11-Fantastic Four app. 3.00
... Vol. 1: Shiver (2004, $13.99, TPB) r/#1-5 14.00
... Vol. 2: Run (2004, $19.99, TPB) r/#6-13 20.00
... Vol. 3: Twist (2004, $13.99, TPB) r/#14-18 14.00

VENOM: Marvel Comics (Also see Amazing Spider-Man #298-300)
... ALONG CAME A SPIDER, 1/96 - No. 4, 4/96 ($2.95)-Spider-Man & Carnage app. 3.00
... CARNAGE UNLEASHED, 4/95 - No. 4, 7/95 ($2.95) 3.00
... DARK ORIGIN, 10/08 - No. 5, ($2.99) 1,2-Medina-a 3.00
... DEATHTRAP: THE VAULT, 3/93 ($6.95) r/Avengers: Deathtrap: The Vault 7.00
... FUNERAL PYRE, 8/93- No. 3, 10/93 ($2.95)-#1-Holo-grafx foil-c; Punisher app. in all 3.00

VENOM: LETHAL PROTECTOR
Marvel Comics: Feb, 1993 - No. 6, July, 1993 ($2.95, limited series)
1-Red holo-grafx foil-c; Bagley-c/a in all 5.00
1-Gold variant sold to retailers 15.00
1-Black-c (at least 58 copies have been authenticated by CGC since 2000)
9 18 27 63 107 150
NOTE: Counterfeit copies of the black-c exist and are valueless
2-6: Spider-Man app. in all 3.00
... LICENSE TO KILL,6/97 - No. 3, 8/97 ($1.95) 2.50
... NIGHTS OF VENGEANCE, 8/94 - No. 4, 11/94 ($2.95), #1-Red foil-c 3.00
... ON TRIAL, 3/97 - No. 3, 5/97 ($1.95) 2.50
... SEED OF DARKNESS, 7/97 ($1.95) #(-1) Flashback 2.50
... SEPARATION ANXIETY,12/94- No. 4, 3/95 ($2.95) #1-Embossed-c 3.00
... SIGN OF THE BOSS,3/97 - No. 2, 10/97 ($1.99) 2.50
... SINNER TAKES ALL, 8/95 - No. 5, 10/95 ($2.95) 3.00
... SUPER SPECIAL, 8/95($3.95) #1-Flip book 4.00
... THE ENEMY WITHIN, 2/94 - No. 3, 4/94 ($2.95)-Demogoblin & Morbius app. 1-Glow-in-the-dark-c 3.00
... THE FINALE, 11/97 - No. 3, 1/98 ($1.99) 2.50
... THE HUNGER, 8/96- No. 4, 11/96 ($1.95) 2.50
... THE HUNTED, 5/96-No. 3, 7/96 ($2.95) 3.00
... THE MACE, 5/94 - No. 3, 7/94 ($2.95)-#1-Embossed-c 3.00
... THE MADNESS, 11/93- No. 3, 1/94 ($2.95)-Kelley Jones-c/a(p). 1-Embossed-c; Juggernaut app. 3.00
... TOOTH AND CLAW, 12/96 - No. 3, 2/97 ($1.95)-Wolverine-c/app. 2.50
... VS. CARNAGE, 9/04 - No. 4, 12/04 ($2.99)-Milligan-s/Crain-a; Spider-Man app. 3.00
TPB (2004, $9.99) r/#1-4 10.00

VENTURE
AC Comics (Americomics): Aug, 1986 - No. 3, 1986? ($1.75)
1-3: 1-3-Bolt. 1-Astron. 2-Femforce. 3-Fazers 2.50

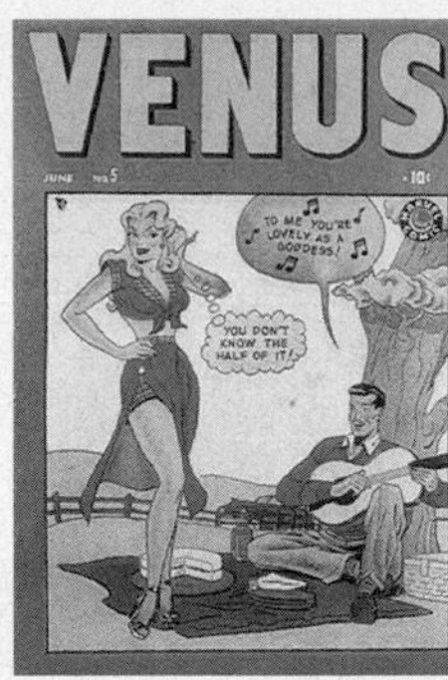

Venus #5 © MAR

Veronica #41 © AP

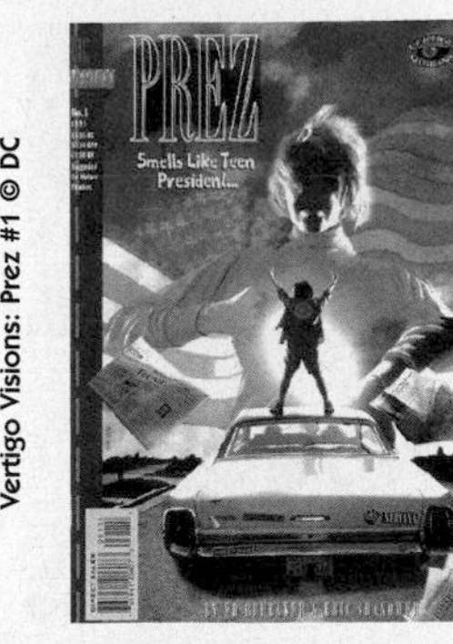

Vertigo Visions: Prez #1 © DC

GD VG FN VF VF/NM NM-
2.0 4.0 6.0 8.0 9.0 9.2

VENTURE
Image Comics: Jan, 2003 - No. 4, Sept, 2003 ($2.95)

1-4-Faerber-s/Igle-a 3.00

VENUS (See Agents of Atlas, Marvel Spotlight #2 & Weird Wonder Tales)
Marvel/Atlas Comics (CMC 1-9/LCC 10-19): Aug, 1948 - No. 19, Apr, 1952 (Also see Marvel Mystery #91)

1-Venus & Hedy Devine begin; 1st app. Venus; Kurtzman's "Hey Look"
147 294 441 926 1563 2200
2 80 160 240 504 852 1200
3,5 60 120 180 378 639 900
4-Kurtzman's "Hey Look" 61 122 183 384 647 910
6-9: 6-Loki app. 7,8-Painted-c. 9-Begin 52 pgs.; book-length feature "Whom the Gods Destroy!" 53 106 159 330 553 775
10-S/F-horror issues begin (7/50) 75 150 225 473 799 1125
11-S/F end of the world (11/50) 87 174 261 548 924 1300
12-Colan-a 50 100 150 310 518 725
13-16-Venus by Everett, 2-3 stories each; covers-#13,15,16; 14-Everett part cover (Venus).
85 170 255 536 906 1275
17-19-Classic Everett horror & skull covers; Venus app. 17-Bondage-c
133 266 399 838 1419 2000

NOTE: ***Berg** s/f story-13. **Everett** c-13, 14(part; Venus only), 15-19. **Heath** s/f story-11. **Maneely** s/f story 10(3pg.), 16. **Morisi** a-19. **Syd Shores** c-6.*

VERI BEST SURE FIRE COMICS
Holyoke Publishing Co.: No date (circa 1945) (Reprints Holyoke one-shots)

1-Captain Aero, Alias X, Miss Victory, Commandos of the Devil Dogs, Red Cross, Hammerhead Hawley, Capt. Aero's Sky Scouts, Flagman app.; same-c as Veri Best Sure Shot #1 39 78 117 230 370 510

VERI BEST SURE SHOT COMICS
Holyoke Publishing Co.: No date (circa 1945) (Reprints Holyoke one-shots)

1-Capt. Aero, Miss Victory by Quinlan, Alias X, The Red Cross, Flagman, Commandos of the Devil Dogs, Hammerhead Hawley, Capt. Aero's Sky Scouts; same-c as Veri Best Sure Fire #1 39 78 117 230 370 510

VERMILLION
DC Comics (Helix): Oct, 1996 - No. 12, Sept, 1997 ($2.25/$2.50)

1-12: 1-4: Lucius Shepard scripts. 4,12-Kaluta-c 2.50

VERONICA (Also see Archie's Girls, Betty &...)
Archie Comics: Apr, 1989 - Present

1-(75¢-c) 6.00
2-10: 2-(75¢-c) 4.00
11-38 3.00
39-Love Showdown pt. 4, Cheryl Blossom 5.00
40-70: 34-Neon ink-c 3.00
71-192: 134-Begin $2.19-c. 152,155-Cheryl Blossom app. 163-Begin $2.25-c 2.50

VERONICA'S PASSPORT DIGEST MAGAZINE (Becomes Veronica's Digest Magazine #3 on)
Archie Comics: Nov, 1992 - No. 6 ($1.50/$1.79, digest size)

1 5.00
2-6 3.00

VERONICA'S SUMMER SPECIAL (See Archie Giant Series Magazine #615, 625)

VERTICAL
DC Comics (Vertigo): 2003 ($4.95, 3-1/4" wide pages, one-shot)

1-Seagle-s/Allred & Bond-a; odd format 1/2 width pages with some 20" long spreads 5.00

VERTIGO DOUBLE SHOT
DC Comics (Vertigo): 2008 ($2.99)

1-Reprints House of Mystery (2008) #1 and Young Liars #1 in flip-book format 3.00

VERTIGO: FIRST CUT
DC Comics (Vertigo): 2008 ($4.99, TPB)

TPB-Reprints first issues of DMZ, Army@Love, Jack of Fables, Exterminators, Scalped, Crossing Midnight, and Loveless; preview of Air 5.00

VERTIGO: FIRST OFFENSES
DC Comics (Vertigo): 2005 ($4.99, TPB)

TPB-Reprints first issues of The Invisibles, Preacher, Fables, Sandman Mystery Theater, and Lucifer 5.00

VERTIGO: FIRST TASTE
DC Comics (Vertigo): 2005 ($4.99, TPB)

TPB-Reprints first issues of Y: The Last Man, 100 Bullets, Transmetropolitan, Books of Magick: Life During Wartime, Death: The High Cost of Living, and Saga of the Swamp Thing #21 (Alan Moore's first story on that title) 5.00

GD VG FN VF VF/NM NM-
2.0 4.0 6.0 8.0 9.0 9.2

VERTIGO GALLERY, THE: DREAMS AND NIGHTMARES
DC Comics (Vertigo): 1995 ($3.50, one-shot)

1-Pin-ups of Vertigo characters by Sienkiewicz, Toth, Van Fleet & others; McKean-c 4.00

VERTIGO JAM
DC Comics (Vertigo): Aug, 1993 ($3.95, one-shot, 68 pgs.)(Painted-c by Fabry)

1-Sandman by Neil Gaiman, Hellblazer, Animal Man, Doom Patrol, Swamp Thing, Kid Eternity & Shade the Changing Man 5.00

VERTIGO POP! BANGKOK
DC Comics (Vertigo): July, 2003 - No. 4, Oct, 2003 ($2.95, limited series)

1-4-Camuncoli-c/a; Jonathan Vankin-s 3.00

VERTIGO POP! LONDON
DC Comics (Vertigo): Jan, 2003 - No. 4, Apr, 2003 ($2.95, limited series)

1-4-Philip Bond-c/a; Peter Milligan-s 3.00

VERTIGO POP! TOKYO
DC Comics (Vertigo): Sept, 2002 - No. 4, Dec, 2002 ($2.95, limited series)

1-4-Seth Fisher-c/a; Jonathan Vankin-s 3.00

VERTIGO PREVIEW
DC Comics (Vertigo): 1992 (75¢, one-shot, 36 pgs.)

1-Vertigo previews; Sandman story by Neil Gaiman 2.50

VERTIGO RAVE
DC Comics (Vertigo): Fall, 1994 (99¢, one-shot)

1-Vertigo previews 2.50

VERTIGO SECRET FILES
DC Comics (Vertigo): Aug, 2000 ($4.95)

...: Hellblazer 1 (8/00, $4.95) Background info and story summaries 5.00
...: Swamp Thing 1 (11/00, $4.95) Backstories and origins; Hale-c 5.00

VERTIGO VERITE: THE UNSEEN HAND
DC Comics (Vertigo): Sept, 1996 - No. 4, Dec, 1996 ($2.50, limited series)

1-4: Terry LaBan scripts in all 2.50

VERTIGO VISIONS
DC Comics (Vertigo): June, 1993 - Present (one-shots)

Dr. Occult 1 (7/94, $3.95) 4.00
Dr. Thirteen 1 (9/98, $5.95) Howarth-s 6.00
Prez 1 (7/95, $3.95) 4.00
The Geek 1 (6/93, $3.95) 4.00
The Eaters ($4.95, 1995)-Milligan story. 5.00
The Phantom Stranger 1 (10/93, $3.50) 3.50
Tomahawk 1 (7/98, $4.95) Pollack-s 5.00

VERTIGO WINTER'S EDGE
DC Comics (Vertigo): 1998, 1999 ($7.95/$6.95, square-bound, annual)

1-Winter stories by Vertigo creators; Desire story by Gaiman/Bolton; Bolland wraparound-c 8.00
2,3-($6.95)-Winter stories: 2-Allred-c. 3-Bond-c; Desire by Gaiman/Zulli 7.00

VERTIGO X ANNIVERSARY PREVIEW
DC Comics (Vertigo): 2003 (99¢, one-shot, 48 pgs.)

1-Previews of upcoming titles and interviews; Endless Nights, Shade, The Originals 2.25

VERY BEST OF DENNIS THE MENACE, THE
Fawcett Publ.: July, 1979 - No. 2, Apr, 1980 (95¢/$1.00, digest-size, 132 pgs.)

1,2-Reprints 1 3 4 6 8 10

VERY BEST OF DENNIS THE MENACE, THE
Marvel Comics Group: Apr, 1982 - No. 3, Aug, 1982 ($1.25, digest-size)

1-3: Reprints 1 2 3 5 7 9
1,2-Mistakenly printed with DC logo on cover 2 4 6 8 11 14

NOTE: ***Hank Ketcham** c-all. A few thousand of #1 & 2 were printed with DC emblem.*

VERY VICKY
Meet Danny Ocean: 1993? - No. 8, 1995 ($2.50, B&W)

1-8, ...: Calling All Hillbillies (1995, $2.50) 2.50

VEXT
DC Comics: Mar, 1999 - No. 6, Aug, 1999 ($2.50, limited series)

1-6-Giffen-s. 1-Superman app. 2.50

V FOR VENDETTA
DC Comics: Sept, 1988 - No. 10, May, 1989 ($2.00, maxi-series)

1-Alan Moore scripts in all; David Lloyd-a 5.00

Vic Flint #2 © STJ

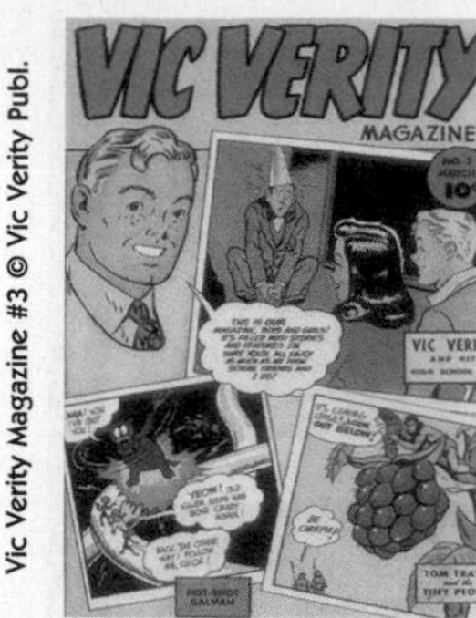

Vic Verity Magazine #3 © Vic Verity Publ.

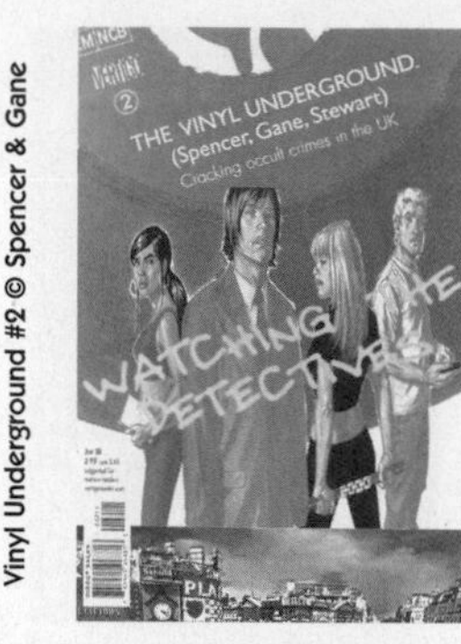

Vinyl Underground #2 © Spencer & Gane

GD VG FN VF VF/NM NM-
2.0 4.0 6.0 8.0 9.0 9.2

2-10 4.00
HC (1990) Limited edition 60.00
HC (2005, $29.99, dustjacket) r/series; foreward by Lloyd; promo art and sketches 30.00
Trade paperback (1990, $14.95) 15.00

VIC BRIDGES FAZERS SKETCHBOOK AND FACT FILE
AC Comics: Nov, 1986 ($1.75)
1 3.00

VICE
Image Comics (Top Cow): Nov, 2005 - Present ($2.99)
1-5-Coleite-s/Kirkham-a. 1-Three covers 3.00
1-Code Red Edition; variant Benitez-c 3.00

VIC FLINT(Crime Buster...)(See Authentic Police Cases #10-14 & Fugitives From Justice #2)
St. John Publ. Co.: Aug, 1948 - No. 5, Apr, 1949 (Newspaper reprints; NEA Service)
1 14 28 42 76 108 140
2 10 20 30 54 72 90
3-5 9 18 27 47 61 75

VIC FLINT (Crime Buster...)
Argo Publ.: Feb, 1956 - No. 2, May, 1956 (Newspaper reprints)
1,2 9 18 27 47 61 75

VIC JORDAN (Also see Big Shot Comics #32)
Civil Service Publ.: April, 1945
1-1944 daily newspaper-r 14 28 42 76 108 140

VICKI (Humor)
Atlas/Seaboard Publ.: Feb, 1975 - No. 4, Aug, 1975 (No. 1,2: 68 pgs.)
1,2-(68 pgs.)-Reprints Tippy Teen; Good Girl art 4 8 12 22 34 45
3,4 (Low print) 4 8 12 22 34 45

VICKI VALENTINE (...Summer Special #1)
Renegade Press: July, 1985 - No. 4, July, 1986 ($1.70, B&W)
1-4: Woggon, Rausch-a; all have paper dolls. 2-Christmas issue 3.00

VICKY
Ace Magazine: Oct, 1948 - No. 5, June, 1949
nn(10/48)-Teenage humor 8 16 24 40 50 60
4(12/48), nn(2/49), 4(4/49), 5(6/49): 5-Dotty app. 7 14 21 35 43 50

VIC TORRY & HIS FLYING SAUCER (Also see Mr. Monster's...#5)
Fawcett Publications: 1950 (one-shot)
nn-Book-length saucer story by Powell; photo/painted-c
68 136 204 428 727 1025

VICTORY
Topps Comics: June, 1994 ($2.50, unfinished limited series)
1-Kurt Busiek script; Giffen-c/a; Rob Liefeld variant-c exists 2.50

VICTORY
Image Comics: May, 2003 - No. 4, Feb, 2004 ($2.95, limited series)
1-4: 1-Two covers; Francisco-a. 4-Two covers 3.00

VICTORY (Volume 2)
Image Comics: Aug, 2004 - No. 4, Jan, 2005 ($2.95, limited series)
1-4: 1-Three covers; Francisco-a 3.00

VICTORY COMICS
Hillman Periodicals: Aug, 1941 - No. 4, Dec, 1941 (#1 by Funnies, Inc.)
1-The Conqueror by Bill Everett, The Crusader, & Bomber Burns begin; Conqueror's origin in text; Everett-c 300 600 900 1930 3315 4700
2-Everett-c/a 128 256 384 806 1366 1925
3,4 83 166 249 523 887 1250

VIC VERITY MAGAZINE
Vic Verity Publ: 1945; No. 2, Jan?, 1947 - No. 7, Sept, 1946 (A comic book)
1-C. C. Beck-c/a 23 46 69 135 218 300
2-Beck-c 14 28 42 82 121 160
3-7: 6-Beck-a. 7-Beck-c 13 26 39 74 105 135

VIDEO JACK
Marvel Comics (Epic Comics): Nov, 1987 - No. 6, Nov, 1988 ($1.25)
1-5 2.50
6-Neal Adams, Keith Giffen, Wrightson, others-a 4.00

VIETNAM JOURNAL
Apple Comics: Nov, 1987 - No. 16, Apr, 1991 ($1.75/$1.95, B&W)
1-16: Don Lomax-c/a/scripts in all, 1-2nd print 3.00

GD VG FN VF VF/NM NM-
2.0 4.0 6.0 8.0 9.0 9.2

...: Indian Country Vol. 1 (1990, $12.95)-r/#1-4 plus one new story 13.00

VIETNAM JOURNAL: VALLEY OF DEATH
Apple Comics: June, 1994 - No. 2, Aug, 1994 ($2.75, B&W, limited series)
1,2: By Don Lomax 4.00

VIGILANTE, THE (Also see New Teen Titans #23 & Annual V2#2)
DC Comics: Oct, 1983 - No. 50, Feb, 1988 ($1.25, Baxter paper)
1-Origin 3.00
2-16,19-49: 3-Cyborg app. 4-1st app. The Exterminator; Newton-a(p). 6,7-Origin. 20,21-Nightwing app. 35-Origin Mad Bomber. 47-Batman-c/s 2.50
17,18-Alan Moore scripts 4.00
50-Ken Steacy painted-c 3.00
Annual nn, 2 ('85, '86) 2.50

VIGILANTE
DC Comics: Nov, 2005 - No. 6, Apr, 2006 ($2.99, limited series)
1-6-Bruce Jones-s. 1,2,4-6-Ben Oliver-a 3.00

VIGILANTE: CITY LIGHTS, PRAIRIE JUSTICE (Also see Action Comics #42, Justice League of America #78, Leading Comics & World's Finest #244)
DC Comics: Nov, 1995 - No. 4, Feb, 1996 ($2.50, limited series)
1-4: James Robinson scripts in all 2.50

VIGILANTES, THE
Dell Publishing Co.: No. 839, Sept, 1957
Four Color 839-Movie 7 14 21 47 76 105

VIGILANTE 8: SECOND OFFENSE
Chaos! Comics: Dec, 1999 ($2.95, one-shot)
1-Based on video game 3.00

VIKINGS, THE (Movie)
Dell Publishing Co.: No. 910, May, 1958
Four Color 910-Buscema-a, Kirk Douglas photo-c 8 16 24 54 90 125

VILLAINS AND VIGILANTES
Eclipse Comics: Dec, 1986 - No. 4, May, 1987 ($1.50/$1.75, limited series, Baxter paper)
1-4: Based on role-playing game. 2-4 ($1.75-c) 2.50

VILLAINS UNITED (Leads into Infinite Crisis)
DC Comics: July, 2005 - No. 6, Dec, 2005 ($2.95/$2.50, limited series)
1-6-Simone-s/JG Jones-c. 1-The Secret Six and the "Society" form 3.00
...: Infinite Crisis Special 1 (6/06, $4.99) Simone-s/Eaglesham-a 5.00
TPB (2005, $12.99) r/#1-6; background info on villains 13.00

VILLAINY OF DOCTOR DOOM, THE
Marvel Comics: 1999 ($17.95, TPB)
nn-Reprints early battle with the Fantastic Four 18.00

VIMANARAMA
DC Comics (Vertigo): Apr, 2005 - No. 3, June, 2005 ($2.95, limited series)
1-3-Grant Morrison-s/Philip Bond-a 3.00
TPB (2005, $12.99) r/#1-3 13.00

VINTAGE MAGNUS (...Robot Fighter)
Valiant: Jan, 1992 - No. 4, Apr, 1992 ($2.25, limited series)
1-4: 1-Layton-c; r/origin from Magnus R.F. #22 2.50

VINYL UNDERGROUND
DC Comics (Vertigo): Dec, 2007 - Present ($2.99)
1-11: 1-Spencer-s/Gane & Stewart-a/Phillips-c 3.00
...: Watching the Detectives TPB ('08, $9.99) r/#1-5; David Laphan intro. 10.00

VIOLATOR (Also see Spawn #2)
Image Comics (Todd McFarlane Prods.): May, 1994 - No. 3, Aug, 1994 ($1.95, lim. series)
1-Alan Moore scripts in all 5.00
2,3: Bart Sears-c(p)/a(p) 4.00

VIOLATOR VS. BADROCK
Image Comics (Extreme Studios): May, 1995 - No. 4, Aug, 1995 ($2.50, limited series)
1-4: Alan Moore scripts in all. 1-1st app Celestine; variant-c (3?) 2.50

VIOLENT MESSIAHS (...: Lamenting Pain on cover for #9-12, numbered as #1-4)
Image Comics: June, 2000 - Present ($2.95)
1-Two covers by Travis Smith and Medina 4.00
1-Tower Records variant edition 5.00
2-8: 5-Flip book sketchbook 3.00
9-12-Lamenting Pain; 2 covers on each 3.00
...: Genesis (12/01, $5.95) r/'97 B&W issue, Wizard 1/2 prologue 6.00

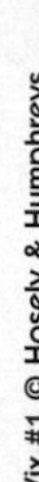
Vix #1 © Hosely & Humphreys

Voodoo #8 © AJAX

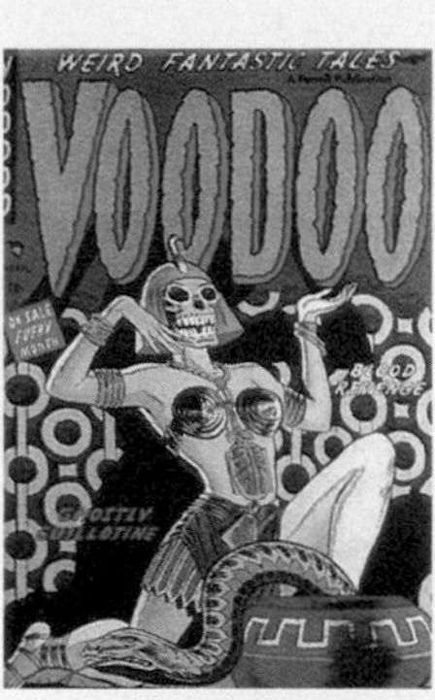

Voyage to the Bottom of the Sea #4 © DELL

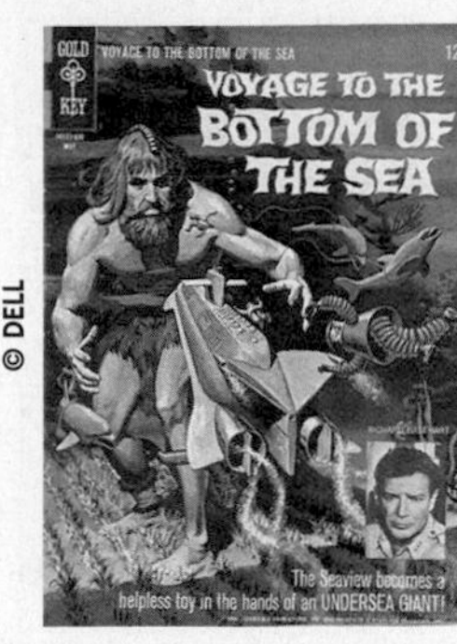

	GD	VG	FN	VF	VF/NM	NM-
	2.0	4.0	6.0	8.0	9.0	9.2

...: The Book of Job TPB (7/02, $24.95) r/#1-8; Foreward by Gossett 25.00

VIP (TV)
TV Comics: 2000 ($2.95, unfinished series)
1-Based on the Pamela Lee TV show; photo-c 3.00

VIPER (TV)
DC Comics: Aug, 1994 - No. 4, Nov, 1994 ($1.95, limited series)
1-4-Adaptation of television show 2.50

VIRGINIAN, THE (TV)
Gold Key: June, 1963
1(10060-306)-Part photo-c of James Drury plus photo back-c
4 8 12 28 44 60

VIRTUA FIGHTER (Video Game)
Marvel Comics: Aug, 1995 (2.95, one-shot)
1-Sega Saturn game 3.00

VIRUS
Dark Horse Comics: 1993 - No. 4, 1993 ($2.50, limited series)
1-4: Ploog-c 2.50

VISION, THE
Marvel Comics: Nov, 1994 - No. 4, Feb, 1995 ($1.75, limited series)
1-4 2.50

VISION, THE (AVENGERS ICONS: ...)
Marvel Comics: Oct, 2002 - No. 4, Jan, 2003 ($2.99, limited series)
1-4-Geoff Johns-s/Ivan Reis-a 3.00
...: Yesterday and Tomorrow TPB (2005, $14.99) r/#1-4 & Avengers #57 (1st app.) 15.00

VISION AND THE SCARLET WITCH, THE (See Marvel Fanfare)
Marvel Comics Group: Nov, 1982 - No. 4, Feb, 1983 (Limited series)
1-4: 2-Nuklo & Future Man app. 3.00

VISION AND THE SCARLET WITCH, THE
Marvel Comics Group: Oct, 1985 - No. 12, Sept, 1986 (Maxi-series)
V2#1-12: 1-Origin; 1st app. in Avengers #57. 2-West Coast Avengers x-over 2.50

VISIONS
Vision Publications: 1979 - No. 5, 1983 (B&W, fanzine)
1-Flaming Carrot begins(1st app?); N. Adams-c 4 8 12 28 44 60
2-N. Adams, Rogers-a; Gulacy back-c; signed & numbered to 2000
4 8 12 24 37 50
3-Williamson-c(p); Steranko back-c 3 6 9 16 23 30
4-Flaming Carrot-c & info. 3 6 9 16 23 30
5-1 pg. Flaming Carrot 2 4 6 11 16 20
NOTE: *Eisner a-4. Miller a-4. Starlin a-3. Williamson a-5. After #4, Visions became an annual publication of The Atlanta Fantasy Fair.*

VISITOR, THE
Valiant/Acclaim Comics (Valiant): Apr, 1995 - No. 13, Nov, 1995 ($2.50)
1-13: 8-Harbinger revealed. 13-Visitor revealed to be Sting from Harbinger 2.50

VISITOR VS. THE VALIANT UNIVERSE, THE
Valiant: Feb, 1995 - No. 2, Mar, 1995 ($2.95, limited series)
1,2 3.00

VIX
Image Comics: Jun, 2008 - Present ($3.50)
1-Hosely-s/Humphreys-a 3.50

VOGUE (Also see Youngblood)
Image Comics (Extreme Studios): Oct, 1995 - No.3, Jan, 1996 ($2.50, limited series)
1-3: 1-Liefeld-c, 1-Variant-c 2.50

VOID INDIGO (Also see Marvel Graphic Novel)
Marvel Comics (Epic Comics): 11/84 - No. 2, 3/85 ($1.50, direct sales, unfinished series, mature)
1,2: Cont'd from Marvel G.N.; graphic sex & violence 2.50

VOLCANIC REVOLVER
Oni Press: Dec, 1998 - No. 3, Mar, 1999 ($2.95, B&W, limited series)
1-3: Scott Morse-s/a 3.00
TPB (12/99, $9.95, digest size) r/#1-3 and Oni Double Feature #7 prologue 10.00

VOLTRON (TV)
Modern Publishing: 1985 - No. 3, 1985 (75¢, limited series)
1-3: Ayers-a in all 4.00

VOLTRON: A LEGEND FORGED (TV)
Devils Due Publishing: Jul, 2008 - Present ($3.50)
1,2-Blaylock-s/Bear-a; 4 covers 3.50

VOLTRON: DEFENDER OF THE UNIVERSE (TV)
Image Comics: No. 0, May, 2003 - No. 5, Sept, 2003 ($2.50)
0-Jolley-s/Brooks-a; character pin-ups with background info 2.50
1-5-($2.95) 1-Three covers by Norton, Brooks and Andrews; Norton-a 3.00
...: Revelations TPB (2004, $11.95, digest-sized) r/#1-5; cover gallery 12.00

VOLTRON: DEFENDER OF THE UNIVERSE (TV)
Image Comics: Jan, 2004 - No. 11, Dec, 2004 ($2.95)
1-11: 1-Jolley-s; wraparound-c 3.00

VOODA (Jungle Princess) (Formerly Voodoo) (See Crown Comics)
Ajax-Farrell (Four Star Publications): No. 20, April, 1955 - No. 22, Aug, 1955
20-Baker-c/a (r/Seven Seas #6) 40 80 120 235 380 525
21,22-Baker-a plus Kamen/Baker story, Kimbo Boy of Jungle, & Baker-c(p) in all. 22-Censored Jo-Jo-r (name Powaa) 35 70 105 203 327 450
NOTE: *#20-22 each contain one heavily censored-r of South Sea Girl by* **Baker** *from Seven Seas Comics with name changed to Vooda. #20-r/Seven Seas #6; #21-r/#4; #22-r/#3.*

VOODOO (Weird Fantastic Tales) (Vooda #20 on)
Ajax-Farrell (Four Star Publ.): May, 1952 - No. 19, Jan-Feb, 1955
1-South Sea Girl-r by Baker 60 120 180 378 639 900
2-Rulah story-r plus South Sea Girl from Seven Seas #2 by Baker (name changed from Alani to El'nee) 49 98 147 304 507 710
3-Bakerish-a; man stabbed in face 40 80 120 244 397 550
4,8-Baker-r. 8-Severed head panels 40 80 120 244 397 550
5-7,9,10: 5-Nazi death camp story (flaying alive). 6-Severed head panels
35 70 105 203 327 450
11-18: 14-Zombies take over America. 15-Opium drug story-r/Ellery Queen #3. 16-Post nuclear world story.17-Electric chair panels
30 60 90 176 283 390
19-Bondage-c; Baker-r(2)/Seven Seas #5 w/minor changes & #1, heavily modified; last pre-code; contents & covers change to jungle theme
38 76 114 226 363 500
Annual 1(1952, 25¢, 100 pgs.)-Baker-a (scarce) 127 254 381 800 1350 1900

VOODOO
Image Comics (WildStorm): Nov, 1997 - No. 4, Mar, 1998 ($2.50, lim. series)
1-4:Alan Moore-s in all; Hughes-c. 2-4-Rio-a 2.50
1-Platinum Ed 10.00
Dancing on the Dark TPB ('99, $9.95) r/#1-4 10.00
...-Zealot: Skin Trade (8/95, $4.95) 5.00

VOODOO (See Tales of...)

VOODOO CHILD (Weston Cage & Nicolas Cage's...)
Virgin Comics: July, 2007 - No. 6, Dec, 2007 ($2.99)
1-6: 1-Mike Carey-s/Dean Hyrapiet-a; covers by Hyrapiet & Templesmith 3.00
Vol. 1 TPB (1/08, $14.99) r/#1-6; variant covers; intro by Weston Cage & Nicolas Cage 15.00

VOODOOM
Oni Press: June, 2000 ($4.95, B&W)
1-Scott Morse-s/Jim Mahfood-a 5.00

VORTEX
Vortex Publs.: Nov, 1982 - No. 15, 1988 (No month) ($1.50/$1.75, B&W)
1 ($1.95)-Peter Hsu-a; Ken Steacy-c; nudity 1 2 3 5 7 9
2,12: 2-1st app. Mister X (on-c only). 12-Sam Kieth-a 6.00
3-11,13-15 3.00

VORTEX
Comico: 1991 - No. 2? ($2.50, limited series)
1,2: Heroes from The Elementals 2.50

VOYAGE TO THE BOTTOM OF THE SEA (Movie, TV)
Dell Publishing Co./Gold Key: No. 1230, Sept-Nov, 1961; Dec, 1964 - #16, Apr, 1970 (Painted-c)
Four Color 1230 (1961) 10 20 30 71 126 180
10133-412(#1, 12/64)(Gold Key) 8 16 24 52 86 120
2(7/65) - 5: Photo back-c, 1-5 5 10 15 34 55 75
6-14 4 8 12 28 44 60
15,16-Reprints 3 6 9 18 27 35

VOYAGE TO THE DEEP
Dell Publishing Co.: Sept-Nov, 1962 - No. 4, Nov-Jan, 1964 (Painted-c)

Wacky Duck #2 © MAR

The Walking Dead #27 © Robert Kirkman

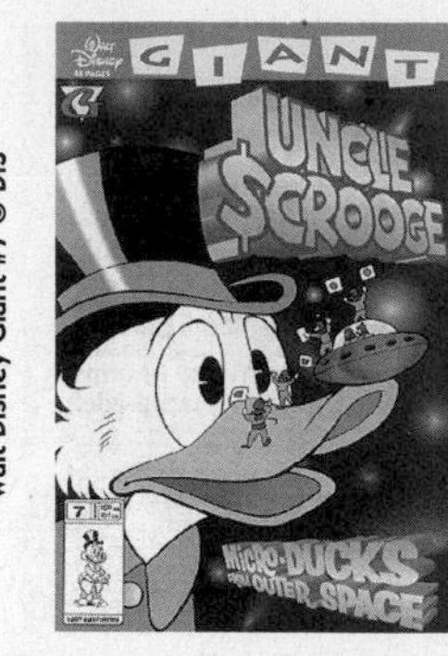

Walt Disney Giant #7 © DIS

	GD 2.0	VG 4.0	FN 6.0	VF 8.0	VF/NM 9.0	NM- 9.2
1	5	10	15	34	55	75
2-4	4	8	12	24	37	50

WACKO
Ideal Publ. Corp.: Sept, 1980 - No. 3, Oct, 1981 (84 pgs., B&W, magazine)

	GD	VG	FN	VF	VF/NM	NM-
1-3	2	4	6	8	10	12

WACKY ADVENTURES OF CRACKY (Also see Gold Key Spotlight)
Gold Key: Dec, 1972 - No. 12, Sept, 1975

	GD	VG	FN	VF	VF/NM	NM-
1	3	6	9	14	20	26
2	2	4	6	10	14	18
3-12	2	4	6	8	10	12

(See March of Comics #405, 424, 436, 448)

WACKY DUCK (...Comics #3-6; formerly Dopey Duck; Justice Comics #7 on)
(See Film Funnies)
Marvel Comics (NPP): No. 3, Fall, 1946 - No. 6, Summer, 1947; Aug, 1948 - No. 2, Oct, 1948

	GD	VG	FN	VF	VF/NM	NM-
3	23	46	69	135	218	300
4-Infinity-c	20	40	60	118	189	260
5,6(1947)-Becomes Justice comics	18	36	54	103	162	220
1(1948)	17	34	51	98	154	210
2(1948)	14	28	42	80	115	150
I.W. Reprint #1,2,7('58): 1-r/Wacky Duck #6	2	4	6	9	13	16
Super Reprint #10(I.W. on-c, Super-inside)	2	4	6	9	13	16

WACKY QUACKY (See Wisco)

WACKY RACES (TV)
Gold Key: Aug, 1969 - No. 7, Apr, 1972 (Hanna-Barbera)

	GD	VG	FN	VF	VF/NM	NM-
1	5	10	15	34	55	75
2-7	4	8	12	22	34	45

WACKY SQUIRREL (Also see Dark Horse Presents)
Dark Horse Comics: Oct, 1987 - No. 4, 1988 ($1.75, B&W)

	NM-
1-4: 4-Superman parody	2.50
Halloween Adventure Special 1 (1987, $2.00)	2.50
Summer Fun Special 1 (1988, $2.00)	2.50

WACKY WITCH (Also see Gold Key Spotlight)
Gold Key: March, 1971 - No. 21, Dec, 1975

	GD	VG	FN	VF	VF/NM	NM-
1	4	8	12	24	37	50
2	3	6	9	14	20	26
3-10	2	4	6	10	14	18
11-21	2	4	6	8	10	12

(See March of Comics #374, 398, 410, 422, 434, 446, 458, 470, 482)

WACKY WOODPECKER (See Two Bit the...)
I. W. Enterprises/Super Comics: 1958; 1963

	GD	VG	FN	VF	VF/NM	NM-
I.W. Reprint #1,2,7 (nd-reprints Two Bit...): 7-r/Two-Bit, the Wacky Woodpecker #1.	2	4	6	8	11	14
Super Reprint #10('63): 10-r/Two-Bit, The Wacky Woodpecker #?	2	4	6	8	11	14

WAGON TRAIN (1st Series) (TV) (See Western Roundup under Dell Giants)
Dell Publishing Co.: No. 895, Mar, 1958 - No. 13, Apr-June, 1962 (All photo-c)

	GD	VG	FN	VF	VF/NM	NM-
Four Color 895 (#1)	10	20	30	71	126	180
Four Color 971(#2),1019(#3)	7	14	21	45	73	100
4(1-3/60),6-13	6	12	18	39	62	85
5-Toth-a	6	12	18	43	69	95

WAGON TRAIN (2nd Series)(TV)
Gold Key: Jan, 1964 - No. 4, Oct, 1964 (All front & back photo-c)

	GD	VG	FN	VF	VF/NM	NM-
1-Tufts-a in all	5	10	15	32	51	70
2-4	4	8	12	24	37	50

WAITING PLACE, THE
Slave Labor Graphics: Apr, 1997 - No. 6, Sept, 1997 ($2.95)

	NM-
1-6-Sean McKeever-s	3.00
Vol. 2 - 1(11/99), 2-11	3.00
12-($4.95)	5.00

WAITING ROOM WILLIE (See Sad Case of...)

WAKE THE DEAD
IDW Publ.: Sept, 2003 - No. 5, Mar, 2004 ($3.99, limited series)

	NM-
1-5-Steve Niles-s/Chee-a	4.00
TPB (6/04, $19.99) r/series; intro. by Michael Dougherty; embossed die cut cover	20.00

WALK IN (Dave Stewart's ...)
Virgin Comics: Dec, 2006 - No. 6, May, 2007 ($2.99)

	NM-
1-6: 1-5-Parker-s/Padlekar-a. 6-Parker-a	3.00

WALKING DEAD, THE
Image Comics: Oct, 2003 - Present ($2.95/$2.99, B&W)

	NM-
1-Robert Kirkman-s in all/Tony Moore-a	40.00
1 Special Edition (5/08, $3.99) r/#1; Kirkman afterword; original script and proposal	4.00
2	15.00
3-10: 3-6-Tony Moore-a. 7-Charlie Adlard-a begins	5.00
11-53	3.00
... Book 1 HC (2006, $29.99) r/#1-12; sketch pages, cover gallery; Kirkman afterword	30.00
... Book 2 HC (2006, $29.99) r/#13-24; sketch pages, cover gallery	30.00
... Book 3 HC (2007, $29.99) r/#25-36; sketch pages, cover gallery	30.00
...Vol. 1: Days Gone Bye (5/04, $9.95, TPB) r/#1-4	10.00
...Vol. 2: Miles Behind Us (10/04, $12.95, TPB) r/#7-12	13.00
...Vol. 3: Safety Behind Bars (2005, $12.95, TPB) r/#13-18	13.00
...Vol. 4: The Heart's Desire (2005, $12.99, TPB) r/#19-24	13.00
...Vol. 5: The Best Defense (2006, $12.99, TPB) r/#25-30	13.00
...Vol. 6: This Sorrowful Life (2007, $12.99, TPB) r/#31-36	13.00
...Vol. 7: The Calm Before (2007, $12.99, TPB) r/#37-42	13.00

WALLY (Teen-age)
Gold Key: Dec, 1962 - No. 4, Sept, 1963

	GD	VG	FN	VF	VF/NM	NM-
1	3	6	9	21	32	42
2-4	3	6	9	17	25	32

WALLY THE WIZARD
Marvel Comics (Star Comics): Apr, 1985 - No. 12, Mar, 1986 (Children's comic)

	NM-
1-12: Bob Bolling a-1,3; c-1,9,11,12	4.00
1-Variant with "Star Chase" game on last page and inside back-c	8.00

WALLY WOOD'S T.H.U.N.D.E.R. AGENTS (See Thunder Agents)
Deluxe Comics: Nov, 1984 - No. 5, Oct, 1986 ($2.00, 52 pgs.)

	NM-
1-5: 5-Jerry Ordway-c/a in Wood style	5.00

NOTE: ***Anderson** a-2i, 3i. **Buckler** a-4. **Ditko** a-3, 4. **Giffen** a-1p-4p. **Perez** a-1p, 2, 4; c-1-4.*

WALT DISNEY CHRISTMAS PARADE (Also see Christmas Parade)
Whitman Publ. Co. (Golden Press): Wint, 1977 ($1.95, cardboard-c, 224 pgs.)

	GD	VG	FN	VF	VF/NM	NM-
11191-Barks-r/Christmas in Disneyland #1, Dell Christmas Parade #9 & Dell Giant #53	4	8	12	26	41	55

WALT DISNEY COMICS DIGEST
Gold Key: June, 1968 - No. 57, Feb, 1976 (50¢, digest size)

	GD	VG	FN	VF	VF/NM	NM-
1-Reprints Uncle Scrooge #5; 192 pgs.	7	14	21	50	83	115
2-4-Barks-r	5	10	15	34	55	75
5-Daisy Duck by Barks (8 pgs.); last published story by Barks (art only) plus 21 pg. Scrooge-r by Barks	8	16	24	52	86	120
6-13-All Barks-r	4	8	12	22	34	45
14,15	3	6	9	16	23	30
16-Reprints Donald Duck #26 by Barks	3	6	9	21	32	42
17-20-Barks-r	3	6	9	18	27	35
21-31,33,35-37-Barks-r; 24-Toth Zorro	3	6	9	16	23	30
32,41,45,47-49	2	4	6	11	16	20
34,38,39: 34-Reprints 4-Color #318. 38-Reprints Christmas in Disneyland #1. 39-Two Barks-r/WDC&S #272, 4-Color #1073 plus Toth Zorro-r	3	6	9	16	23	30
40-Mickey Mouse-r by Gottfredson	2	4	6	13	18	22
42,43-Barks-r	2	4	6	13	18	22
44-(Has Gold Key emblem, 50¢)-Reprints 1st story of 4-Color #29,256,275,282	5	10	15	32	51	70
44-Republished in 1976 by Whitman; not identical to original; a bit smaller, blank back-c, 69¢	3	6	9	16	23	30
46,50,52-Barks-r. 52-Barks-r/WDC&S #161,132	2	4	6	11	16	20
51-Reprints 4-Color #71	3	6	9	16	23	30
53-55: 53-Reprints Dell Giant #30. 54-Reprints Donald Duck Beach Party #2. 55-Reprints Dell Giant #49	2	4	6	10	14	18
56-r/Uncle Scrooge #32 (Barks)	2	4	6	13	18	22
57-r/Mickey Mouse Almanac('57) & two Barks stories	2	4	6	11	16	20

NOTE: ***Toth** a-52r. #1-10, 196 pgs.; #11-41, 164 pgs.; #42 on, 132 pgs. Old issues were being reprinted & distributed by Whitman in 1976.*

WALT DISNEY GIANT (Disney)
Bruce Hamilton Co. (Gladstone): Sept, 1995 - No. 7, Sept, 1996 ($2.25, bi-monthly, 48 pgs.)

1-7: 1-Scrooge McDuck in the Yukon; Rosa-c/a/scripts plus r/F.C. #218. 2-Uncle Scrooge-r by Barks plus 17 pg. text story. 3-Donald the Mighty Duck; Rosa-c; Barks & Rosa-r. 4-Mickey and Goofy; new-a (story actually stars Goofy. Mickey Mouse by Caesar Ferioli; Donald Duck by Giorgio Cavazzano (1st in U.S.). 6-Uncle Scrooge & the Jr. Woodchucks; new-a and

Walt Disney's Christmas Parade #4 © DIS

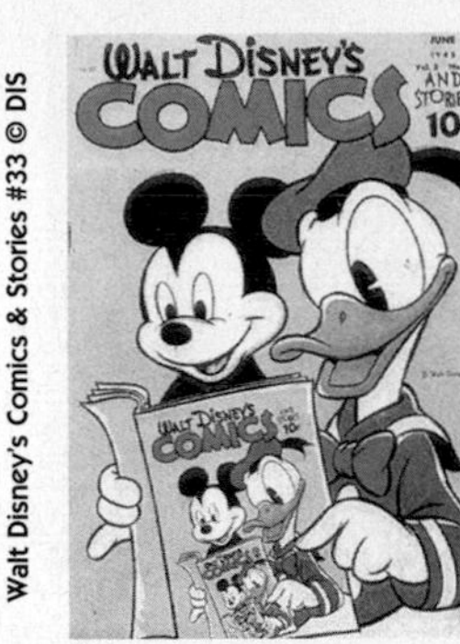

Walt Disney's Comics & Stories #33 © DIS

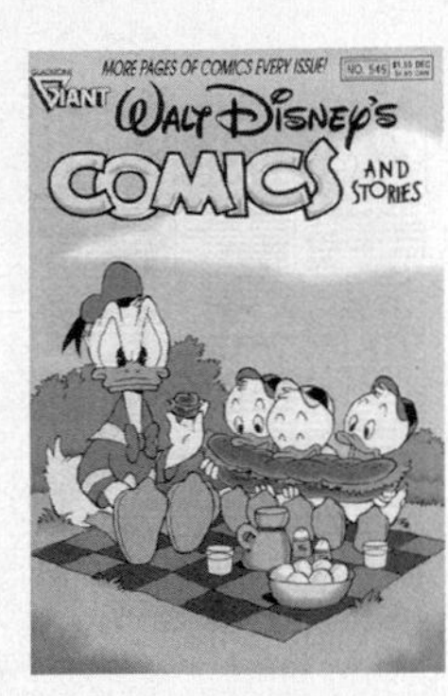

Walt Disney's Comics & Stories #545 © DIS

	GD 2.0	VG 4.0	FN 6.0	VF 8.0	VF/NM 9.0	NM- 9.2

Barks-r. 7-Uncle Scrooge-r by Barks plus new-a 3.00

NOTE: *Series was initially solicited as Uncle Walt's Collectory. Issue #8 was advertised, but later cancelled.*

WALT DISNEY PAINT BOOK SERIES

Whitman Publ. Co.: No dates; circa 1975 (Beware! Has 1930s copyright dates) (79¢-c, 52 pgs. B&W, treasury-sized) (Coloring books, text stories & comics-r)

#2052 (Whitman #886-r) Mickey Mouse & Donald Duck Gag Book
3 6 9 21 32 42
#2053 (Whitman #677-r) 3 6 9 21 32 42
#2054 (Whitman #670-r) Donald-c 4 8 12 23 36 48
#2055 (Whitman #627-r) Mickey-c 3 6 9 21 32 42
#2056 (Whitman #660-r) Buckey Bug-c 3 6 9 19 29 38
#2057 (Whitman #887-r) Mickey & Donald-c 3 6 9 21 32 42

WALT DISNEY PRESENTS (TV)(Disney)

Dell Publishing Co.: No. 997, 6-8/59 - No. 6, 12-2/1960-61; No. 1181, 4-5/61 (All photo-c)

Four Color 997 (#1) 7 14 21 49 80 110
2(12-2/60)-The Swamp Fox(origin), Elfego Baca, Texas John Slaughter (Disney TV show) begin 5 10 15 32 51 70
3-6: 5-Swamp Fox by Warren Tufts 5 10 15 30 48 65
Four Color 1181-Texas John Slaughter 7 14 21 47 76 105

WALT DISNEY'S CHRISTMAS PARADE (Also see Christmas Parade)

Gladstone: Winter, 1988; No. 2, Winter, 1989 ($2.95, 100 pgs.)

1-Barks-r/painted-c 2 4 6 8 10 12
2-Barks-r 1 2 3 5 7 9

WALT DISNEY'S CHRISTMAS PARADE

Gemstone Publishing: Dec, 2003; 2004, 2005, 2006 ($8.95, prestige format)

1-4: 1-Reprints and 3 new European holiday stories. 2-All reprints. 3-Reprints and 2 new stories, 4-Reprints and 5 new stories 9.00

WALT DISNEY'S COMICS AND STORIES (Cont. of Mickey Mouse Magazine) (#1-30 contain Donald Duck newspaper reprints) (Titled "Comics And Stories" #264 to #?; titled "Walt Disney's Comics And Stories" #511 on)

Dell Publishing Co./Gold Key #264-473/Whitman #474-510/Gladstone #511-547/ Disney Comics #548-585/Gladstone #586-633/Gemstone Publishing #634 on: 10/40 - #263, 8/62; #264, 10/62 - #510, 7/84; #511, 10/86 - #633, 2/99; #634, 7/03 - Present

NOTE: The whole number can always be found at the bottom of the title page in the lower left-hand or right hand panel.

1(V1#1-c; V2#1-indicia)-Donald Duck strip-r by Al Taliaferro & Gottfredson's Mickey Mouse begin 2000 4000 6000 14,000 25,000 36,000
2 778 1556 2334 5602 9801 14,000
3 324 648 972 2203 3852 5500
4-X-Mas-c; 1st Huey, Dewey & Louie-c this title (See Mickey Mouse Magazine V4#2 for 1st-c ever) 247 494 741 1556 2628 3700
4-Special promotional, complimentary issue; cover same except one corner was blanked out & boxed in to identify the giveaway (not a paste-over). This special pressing was probably sent out to former subscribers to Mickey Mouse Mag. whose subscriptions had expired. (Very rare-5 known copies) 353 706 1059 2400 4200 6000
5-Goofy-c 200 400 600 1260 2130 3000
6-10: 8-Only Clarabelle Cow-c. 9-Taliaferro-c (1st)167 334 501 1052 1776 2500
11-14: 11-Huey, Dewey & Louie-c/app. 127 254 381 800 1350 1900
15-17: 15-The 3 Little Kittens (17 pgs.). 16-The 3 Little Pigs (29 pgs.); X-Mas-c. 17-The Ugly Duckling (4 pgs.) 110 220 330 693 1172 1650
18-21 100 200 300 630 1065 1500
22-30: 22-Flag-c. 24-The Flying Gauchito (1st original comic book story done for WDC&S). 27-Jose Carioca by Carl Buettner (2nd original story in WDC&S)
83 166 249 523 887 1250
31-New Donald Duck stories by Carl Barks begin (See F.C. #9 for 1st Barks Donald Duck)
365 730 1095 2482 4341 6200
32-Barks-a 213 426 639 1342 2271 3200
33-Barks-a; infinity-c 150 300 450 945 1598 2250
34-Gremlins by Walt Kelly begin, end #41; Barks-a 117 234 351 737 1244 1750
35,36-Barks-a 110 220 330 693 1172 1650
37-Donald Duck by Jack Hannah 63 126 189 397 674 950
38-40-Barks-a. 39-X-Mas-c. 40,41-Gremlins by Kelly
73 146 219 460 780 1100
41-50-Barks-a. 43-Seven Dwarfs-c app. (4/44). 45-50-Nazis in Gottfredson's Mickey Mouse Stories 60 120 180 378 639 900
51-60-Barks-a. 51-X-Mas-c. 52-Li'l Bad Wolf begins, ends #203 (not in #55). 58-Kelly flag-c
31 62 93 239 445 650
61-70: Barks-a. 61-Dumbo story. 63,64-Pinocchio stories. 63-Cover swipe from New Funnies #94. 64-X-Mas-c. 65-Pluto story. 66-Infinity-c. 67,68-Mickey Mouse Sunday-r by Bill Wright 28 56 84 203 377 550
71-80: Barks-a. 75-77-Brer Rabbit stories, no Mickey Mouse. 76-X-Mas-c
21 42 63 155 288 420
81-87,89,90: Barks-a. 82-Goofy-c. 82-84-Bongo stories. 86-90-Goofy & Agnes app. 89-Chip 'n' Dale story 18 36 54 130 240 350
88-1st app. Gladstone Gander by Barks (1/48) 22 44 66 161 298 435
91-97,99: Barks-a. 95-1st WDC&S Barks-c. 96-No Mickey Mouse; Little Toot begins, ends #97. 99-X-Mas-c 17 34 51 120 223 325
98-1st Uncle Scrooge app. in WDC&S (11/48) 30 60 90 222 411 600
100-(1/49)-Barks-a 19 38 57 139 257 375
101-110-Barks-a. 107-Taliaferro-c; Donald acquires super powers
15 30 45 105 190 275
111,114,117-All Barks-a 13 26 39 90 160 230
112-Drug (ether) issue (Donald Duck) 13 26 39 90 160 230
113,115,116,118-123: No Barks. 116-Dumbo x-over. 121-Grandma Duck begins, ends #168; not in #135,142,146,155 9 18 27 64 110 155
124,126-130-All Barks-a. 124-X-Mas-c 11 22 33 75 133 190
125-1st app. Junior Woodchucks (2/51); Barks-a 15 30 45 107 196 285
131,133,135-137,139-All Barks-a 10 20 30 71 126 180
132-Barks-a(2) (D. Duck & Grandma Duck) 11 22 33 75 133 190
134-Intro. & 1st app. The Beagle Boys (11/51) 18 36 54 133 247 360
138-Classic Scrooge money story 15 30 45 107 196 285
140-(5/52)-1st app. Gyro Gearloose by Barks; 2nd Barks Uncle Scrooge-c; 3rd Uncle Scrooge cover app. 18 36 54 133 247 360
141-150-All Barks-a. 143-Little Hiawatha begins, ends #151,159
9 18 27 60 100 140
151-170-All Barks-a 8 16 24 52 86 120
171-199-All Barks-a 7 14 21 47 76 105
200 7 14 21 50 83 115
201-240: All Barks-a. 204-Chip 'n' Dale & Scamp begin
6 12 18 41 66 90
241-283: Barks-a. 241-Dumbo x-over. 247-Gyro Gearloose begins, ends #274. 256-Ludwig Von Drake begins, ends #274 5 10 15 34 55 75
284,285,287,290,295,296,309-311-Not by Barks 3 6 9 17 26 32
286,288,291-294,297,298,308-All Barks stories; 293-Grandma Duck's Farm Friends. 297-Gyro Gearloose. 298-Daisy Duck's Diary-r 3 6 9 21 32 42
289-Annette-c & back-c & story; Barks-s 4 8 12 24 37 50
299-307-All contain early Barks-r (#43-117). 305-Gyro Gearloose
4 8 12 22 34 45
312-Last Barks issue with original story 4 8 12 22 34 45
313-315,317-327,329-334,336-341 3 6 9 14 19 24
316-Last issue published during life of Walt Disney 3 6 9 14 19 24
328,335,342-350-Barks-r 3 6 9 14 19 24
351-360-With posters inside; Barks reprints (2 versions of each with & without posters)
4 8 12 23 36 48
351-360-Without posters... 3 6 9 14 19 24
361-400-Barks-r 3 6 9 14 19 24
401-429-Barks-r 2 4 6 13 18 22
430,433,437,438,441,444,445,466-No Barks 2 4 6 8 10 12
431,432,434-436,439,440,442,443-Barks-r 2 4 6 9 13 16
446-465,467-473-Barks-r 2 4 6 8 11 14
474(3/80),475-478 (Whitman) 2 4 6 13 18 22
479(8/80),481(10/80)-484(1/81) pre-pack only 4 8 12 28 44 60
480 (8-12/80)-(Very low distribution) 9 18 27 65 113 160
484 (1/81, 40¢-c) Cover price error variant (scarce) 5 10 15 32 51 70
485-499: 494-r/WDC&S #98 2 4 6 10 14 18
500-510 (All #90011 on-c; pre-packs): 500(4/83), 501(5/83), 502&503(7/83), 504-506(all 8/83), 507(4/84), 508(5/84), 509(6/84), 510(7/84). 506-No Barks
2 4 6 11 16 20
511-Donald Duck by Daan Jippes (1st in U.S.; in all through #518); Gyro Gearloose Barks-r begins (in most through #547); Wuzzles by Disney Studio (1st by Gladstone)
3 6 9 16 23 30
512,513 2 4 6 9 13 16
514-516,520 1 2 3 5 7 9
517-519,521,522,525,527,529,530,532-546: 518-Infinity-c. 522-r/1st app. Huey, Dewey & Louie from D. Duck Sunday. 535-546-Barks-r. 537-1st Donald Duck by William Van Horn in WDC&S. 541-545-52 pgs. 546,547-68 pgs. 546-Kelly-r. 547-Rosa-a 5.00
523,524,526,528,531,547: Rosa-s/a in all. 523-1st Rosa 10 pager
2 4 6 8 11 14
548-($1.50, 6/90)-1st Disney issue; new-a; no M. Mouse 6.00
549,551-570,572,573,577-579,581,584 ($1.50): 549-Barks-r begin, ends #585, not in #555, 556, & 564. 551-r/1 story from F.C. #29. 556,578-r/Mickey Mouse Cheerios Premium by Dick Moores. 562,563,568-570, 572, 581-Gottfredson strip-r. 570-Valentine issue; has Mickey/Minnie centerfold. 584-Taliaferro strip-r 4.00
550 ($2.25, 52 pgs.)-Donald Duck by Barks; previously printed only in The Netherlands (1st time in U.S.); r/Chip 'n Dale & Scamp from #204 5.00

Walt Disney's Comics & Stories #691 © DIS

Walt Disney's Donald and Mickey #28 © DIS

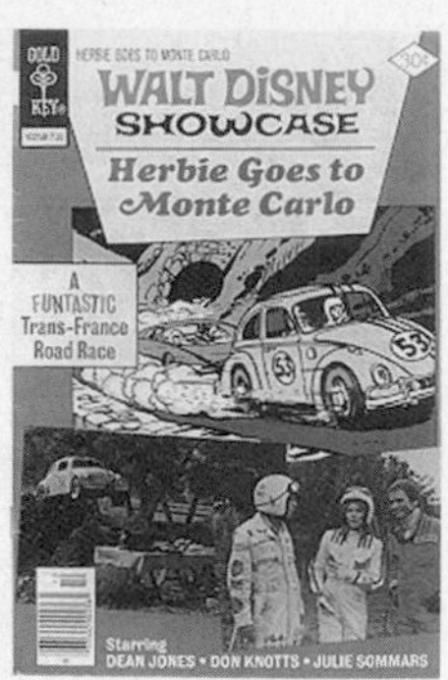

Walt Disney Showcase #41 © DIS

GD VG FN VF VF/NM NM-
2.0 4.0 6.0 8.0 9.0 9.2

571-($2.95, 68 pgs)-r/Donald Duck's Atom Bomb by Barks from 1947 Cheerios premium 6.00
574-576,580,582,583 ($2.95, 68 pgs.): 574-r/1st Pinocchio Sunday strip (1939-40). 575-Gottfredson-r, Pinocchio-r/WDC&S #64. 580-r/Donald Duck's 1st app. from Silly Symphony strip 12/16/34 by Taliaferro; Gottfredson strip-r begin; not in #584 & 600. 582,583-r/Mickey Mouse on Sky Island from WDC&S #1,2 5.00
585 ($2.50, 52 pgs.)-r/#140; Barks-r/WDC&S #140 5.00
586,587: 586-Gladstone issues begin again; begin $1.50-c; Gottfredson-r begins (not in #600). 587-Donald Duck by William Van Horn begins 4.00
588-597: 588,591-599-Donald Duck by William Van Horn 3.00
598,599 ($1.95, 36 pgs.): 598-r/1st drawings of Mickey Mouse by Ub Iwerks 3.00
600 ($2.95, 48 pgs.)-L.B. Cole-c(r)/WDC&S #1; Barks-r/WDC&S #32 plus Rosa, Jippes, Van Horn-r and new Rosa centerspread 4.00
601-611 ($5.95, 64 pgs., squarebound, bi-monthly): 601-Barks-c, r/Mickey Mouse V1#1, Rosa-a/scripts. 602-Rosa-c. 604-Taliaferro strip-r/1st Silly Symphony Sundays from 1932. 604,605-Jippes-a. 605-Walt Kelly-c; Gottfredson "Mickey Mouse Outwits the Phantom Blot" r/F.C. #16 6.00
612-633 ($6.95): 633-(2/99) Last Gladstone issue 7.00
634-675: 634-(7/03) First Gemstone issue; William Van Horn-c. 666-Mickey's Inferno 7.00
676-681: 676-Begin $7.50-c. 677-Bucky Bug's 75th Anniversary 7.50
682-695-($7.99) 8.00

NOTE: *(#1-38, 68 pgs.; #39-42, 60 pgs.; #43-57, 61-134, 143-168, 446, 447, 52 pgs.; #58-60, 135-142, 169-540, 36 pgs.)*

NOTE: **Barks** *art in all issues #31 on, except where noted; c-95, 96, 104, 108, 109, 130-172, 174-178, 183, 198-200, 204, 206-209, 212-216, 218, 220, 226, 228-233, 235-238, 240-243, 247, 250, 253, 256, 260, 261, 276-283, 288-292, 295-298, 301, 303, 304, 306, 307, 309, 310, 313-316, 319, 321, 322, 324, 326, 328, 329, 331, 332, 334, 341, 342, 350, 351, 527r, 530r, 540(never before published), 546r, 557-586r(most), 596p, 601p.* **Kelly** *a-24p, 34-41, 43; r-522-524, 546, 547, 582, 583; covers(most)-34-118, 531r, 537r, 541r-543r, 562r, 571r, 605r. Walt Disney's Comics & Stories featured Mickey Mouse serials which were in practically every issue from #1 through #394 and #511 to date. The titles of the serials, along with the issues they are in, are listed in previous editions of this price guide.* **Floyd Gottfredson** *Mickey Mouse serials in issues #1-14, 18-66, 69-74, 78-100, 128, 562, 563, 568-572, 582, 583, 586-599 , 601-603 , 605-present , plus "Service with a Smile" in #13; "Mickey Mouse in a Warplant" (3 pgs.), and "Pluto Catches a Nazi Spy" (4 pgs.) in #62; "Mystery Next Door", #93; "Sunken Treasure", #94; "Aunt Marissa", #95 (r in #575); "Gangland", #98 (r in #562); "Thanksgiving Dinner", #99 (r in #567); and "The Talking Dog", #100 (r in #563); "Morty's Escapade," #128. "The Brave Little Tailor", #580; "Introducing Mickey Mouse Movies ", #581; Circus Roustabout, #585; "Rumplewatt the Giant", #604. Mickey Mouse by* **Paul Murry** *#152-547 except 155-57 (***Dick Moore***), 327-29 (***Tony Strobl***), 348-50 (***Jack Manning***), 533 (***Bill Wright***).* **Don Rosa** *story/a-523, 524, 526, 528, 531, 547, 601-present.* **Al Taliaferro** *Silly Symphonies in #5-"Three Little Pigs"; #13-"Birds of a Feather"; #14-"The Boarding School Mystery"; #15-"Cookieland" and "Three Little Kittens"; #16-"The Practical Pig"; #17-"The Ugly Duckling"; "The Wise Little Hen" in #580; and "Ambrose the Robber Kitten"; #19-"Penguin Isle"; and "Bucky Bug" in #20-23, 25, 26, 28 (one continuous story from 1932-34; first 2 pgs. not Taliaferro).* **Gottfredson** *strip r-562, 563, 568-572, 581, 585, 586, 590.* **Taliaferro** *strip r-584, 580.* **Van Horn** *a-537, 545, 561, 574, 587, 588, 591-present.*

WALT DISNEY'S COMICS DIGEST
Gladstone: Dec, 1986 - No. 7, Sept, 1987

	GD	VG	FN	VF	VF/NM	NM-
1	1	2	3	5	6	8
2-7						6.00

WALT DISNEY'S COMICS PENNY PINCHER
Gladstone: May, 1997 - No. 4, Aug, 1997 (99¢, limited series)

1-4 2.50

WALT DISNEY'S DONALD AND MICKEY (Formerly Walt Disney's Mickey and Donald)
Gladstone (Bruce Hamilton Co.): No. 19, Sept, 1993 - No. 30, 1995 ($1.50, 36 & 68 pgs.)

19,21-24,26-30: New & reprints. 19,21,23,24-Barks-r. 19,26-Murry-r. 22-Barks "Omelet" story r/WDC&S #146. 27-Mickey Mouse story by Caesar Ferioli (1st U.S work). 29-Rosa-c; Mickey Mouse story actually starring Goofy (does not include Mickey except on title page.) 4.00
20,25-($2.95, 68 pgs.): 20-Barks, Gottfredson-r 5.00

NOTE: *Donald Duck stories were all reprints.*

WALT DISNEY'S DONALD DUCK ADVENTURES (D.D. Adv. #1-3)
Gladstone: 11/87-No. 20, 4/90 (1st Series); No. 21,8/93-No. 48, 2/98(3rd Series)

	GD	VG	FN	VF	VF/NM	NM-
1	1	2	3	4	5	7

2-r/F.C. #308 3.00
3,4,6,7,9-11,13,15-18: 3-r/F.C. #223. 4-r/F.C. #62. 9-r/F.C. #159, "Ghost of the Grotto". 11-r/F.C. #159, "Adventure Down Under." 16-r/F.C. #291; Rosa-c. 18-r/FC #318; Rosa-c 3.00
5,8-Don Rosa-c/a 5.00
12($1.50, 52pgs)-Rosa-c/a w/Barks poster 6.00
14-r/F.C. #29, "Mummy's Ring" 4.00
19($1.95, 68 pgs.)-Barks-r/F.C. #199 (1 pg.) 3.00
20($1.95, 68 pgs.)-Barks-r/F.C. #189 & cover-r; William Van Horn-a 3.00
21,22: 21-r/D.D. #46. 22-r/F.C. #282 3.00
23-25,27,29,31,32-($1.50, 36 pgs.): 21,23,29-Rosa-c. 23-Intro/1st app. Andold Wild Duck by Marco Rota. 24-Van Horn-a. 27-1st Pat Block-a, "Mystery of Widow's Gap." 31,32-Block-c 2.50
26,28($2.95, 68 pgs.): 26-Barks-r/F.C. #108, "Terror of the River". 28-Barks-r/F.C. #199, "Sheriff of Bullet Valley" 4.00
30($2.95, 68 pgs.)-r/F.C. #367, Barks' "Christmas for Shacktown" 4.00
33($1.95, 68 pgs.)-r/F.C. #408, Barks' "The Golden Helmet;"Van Horn-c 3.00
34-43: 34-Resume $1.50-c. 34,35,37-Block-a/scripts. 38-Van Horn-c/a 2.50
44-48-($1.95-c) 2.50

NOTE: **Barks** *a-1-22r, 26r, 28r, 33r, 36r; c-3r, 8r, 10r, 14r, 20r.* **Block** *a-27, 30, 34, 35, 37; c-27, 30-32, 34, 35, 37; c-27, 30, 31, 32, 34, 35, 37.* **Rosa** *a-5, 8, 12, 43; c-13, 16, 18, 21, 23, 43.*

WALT DISNEY'S DONALD DUCK ADVENTURES (2nd Series)
Disney Comics: June, 1990 - No. 38, July, 1993 ($1.50)

1-Rosa-a & scripts 5.00
2-21,23,25,27-33,35,36,38: 2-Barks-r/WDC&S #35; William Van Horn-a begins, ends #20. 9-Barks-r/F.C. #178. 9,11,14,17-No Van Horn-a. 11-Mad #1 cover parody. 14-Barks-r. 17-Barks-r. 21-r/FC #203 by Barks. 29-r/MOC #20 by Barks 3.00
22,24,26,34,37: 22-Rosa-a (10 pgs.) & scripts. 24-Rosa-a & scripts. 26-r/March of Comics #41 by Barks. 34-Rosa-c/a. 37-Rosa-a; Barks-r 4.00

NOTE: **Barks** *r-2, 4, 9(F.C. #178), 14(D.D. #45), 17, 21, 26, 27, 29 , 35, 36(D.D #60)-38.* **Taliaferro** *a-34r, 36r.*

WALT DISNEY'S DONALD DUCK ADVENTURES (Take-Along Comic)
Gemstone Publishing: July, 2003 - No. 21, Nov, 2006 ($7.95, 5" x 7-1/2")

1-21-Mickey Mouse & Uncle Scrooge app. 9-Christmas-c 8.00
... , The Barks/Rosa Collection Vol. 2 (3/08, $8.99) reprints Donald Duck's Atom Bomb, Super Snooper & The Trouble With Dimes by Barks; The Duck Who Fell to Earth, Super Snooper Strikes Again & The Money Pit by Rosa 9.00

WALT DISNEY'S DONALD DUCK AND FRIENDS
Gemstone Publishing: No. 308, Oct, 2003 - No. 346, Dec, 2006 ($2.95)

308-346: 308-Numbering resumes from Gladstone Donald Duck series; Halloween-c. 332-Halloween-c; r/#26 by Carl Barks 3.00

WALT DISNEY'S DONALD DUCK AND MICKEY MOUSE (Formerly Walt Disney's Donald and Mickey)
Gladstone (Bruce Hamilton Company): Sept, 1995 - No. 7, Sept, 1996 ($1.50, 32 pgs.)

1-7: 1-Barks-r and new Mickey Mouse stories in all. 5,6-Mickey Mouse stories by Caesar Ferioli. 7-New Donald Duck and Mickey Mouse x-over story; Barks-r/WDC&S #51 2.50

NOTE: *Issue #8 was advertised, but cancelled.*

WALT DISNEY'S DONALD DUCK AND UNCLE SCROOGE
Gemstone Publishing: Nov, 2005 ($6.95, square-bound one-shot)

nn-New story by John Lustig and Pat Block and r/Uncle Scrooge #59 7.00

WALT DISNEY'S DONALD DUCK FAMILY
Gemstone Publishing: Jun, 2008 ($8.99, square-bound)

... The Daan Jippes Collection Vol. 1 - R/Barks-s re-drawn by Jippes for Dutch comics 9.00

WALT DISNEY'S DONALD DUCK IN THE CASE OF THE MISSING MUMMY
Gemstone Publishing: Oct, 2007 ($8.99, square-bound one-shot)

nn-New story by Shelley and Pat Block and r/Donald Duck FC #29 9.00

WALT DISNEY SHOWCASE
Gold Key: Oct, 1970 - No. 54, Jan, 1980 (No. 44-48: 68pgs., 49-54: 52pgs.)

	GD	VG	FN	VF	VF/NM	NM-
1-Boatniks (Movie)-Photo-c	3	6	9	18	27	35
2-Moby Duck	3	6	9	14	19	24
3,4,7: 3-Bongo & Lumpjaw-r. 4,7-Pluto-r	2	4	6	10	14	18
5-$1,000,000 Duck (Movie)-Photo-c	3	6	9	16	22	28
6-Bedknobs & Broomsticks (Movie)	3	6	9	16	22	28
8-Daisy & Donald	2	4	6	11	16	20
9- 101 Dalmatians (cartoon feat.); r/F.C. #1183	3	6	9	17	25	32
10-Napoleon & Samantha (Movie)-Photo-c	3	6	9	17	22	28
11-Moby Duck-r	2	4	6	10	14	18
12-Dumbo-r/Four Color #668	2	4	6	11	16	20
13-Pluto-r	2	4	6	10	14	18
14-World's Greatest Athlete (Movie)-Photo-c	3	6	9	16	22	28
15- 3 Little Pigs-r	2	4	6	11	16	20
16-Aristocats (cartoon feature); r/Aristocats #1	3	6	9	16	22	28
17-Mary Poppins; r/M.P. #10136-501-Photo-c	3	6	9	16	22	28
18-Gyro Gearloose; Barks-r/F.C. #1047,1184	3	6	9	18	27	35
19-That Darn Cat; r/That Darn Cat #10171-602-Hayley Mills photo-c	3	6	9	16	22	28
20,23-Pluto-r	2	4	6	11	16	20
21-Li'l Bad Wolf & The Three Little Pigs	2	4	6	10	14	18
22-Unbirthday Party with Alice in Wonderland; r/Four Color #341	3	6	9	14	19	24
24-26: 24-Herbie Rides Again (Movie); sequel to "The Love Bug"; photo-c. 25-Old Yeller (Movie); r/F.C. #869; Photo-c. 26-Lt. Robin Crusoe USN (Movie); r/Lt. Robin Crusoe USN #10191-601; photo-c	2	4	6	11	16	20
27-Island at the Top of the World (Movie)-Photo-c	3	6	9	14	19	24
28-Brer Rabbit, Bucky Bug-r/WDC&S #58	2	4	6	11	16	20
29-Escape to Witch Mountain (Movie)-Photo-c	3	6	9	14	19	24
30-Magica De Spell; Barks-r/Uncle Scrooge #36 & WDC&S #258						

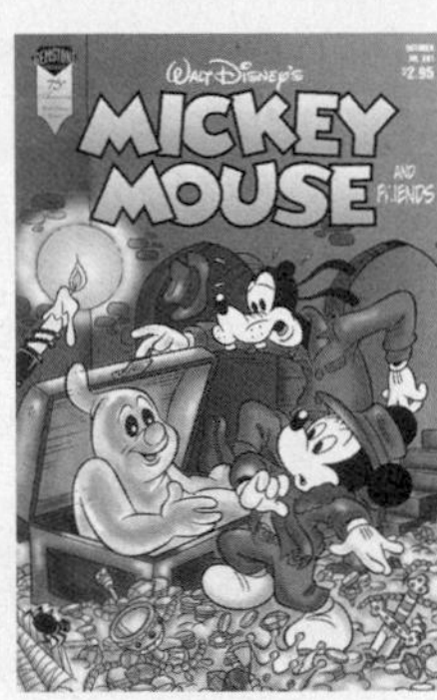

Walt Disney's Mickey Mouse and Friends #281 © DIS

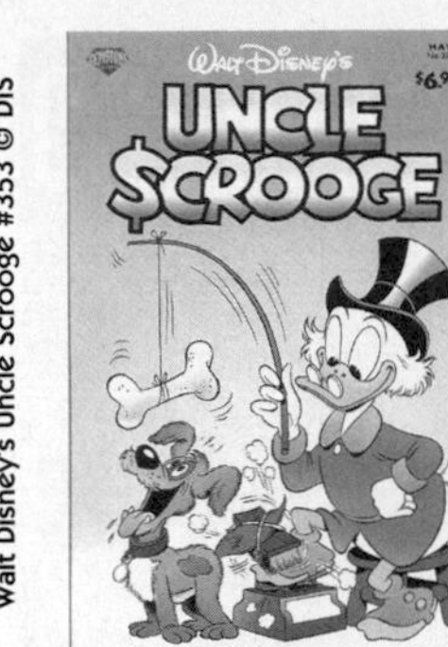

Walt Disney's Uncle Scrooge #353 © DIS

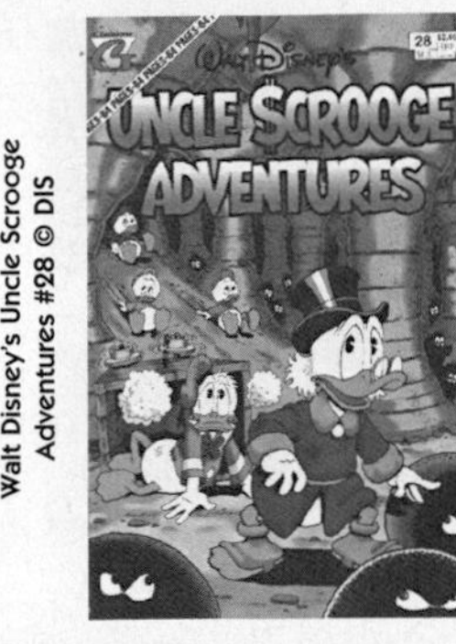

Walt Disney's Uncle Scrooge Adventures #28 © DIS

GD 2.0 | VG 4.0 | FN 6.0 | VF 8.0 | VF/NM 9.0 | NM- 9.2

3 6 9 21 32 42
31-Bambi (cartoon feature); r/Four Color #186 2 4 6 13 18 22
32-Spin & Marty-r/F.C. #1026; Mickey Mouse Club (TV)-Photo-c
3 6 9 14 19 24
33-40: 33-Pluto-r/F.C. #1143. 34-Paul Revere's Ride with Johnny Tremain (TV); r/F.C. #822. 35-Goofy-r/F.C. #952. 36-Peter Pan-r/F.C. #442. 37-Tinker Bell & Jiminy Cricket-r/F.C. #982,989. 38,39-Mickey & the Sleuth, Parts 1 & 2. 40-The Rescuers (cartoon feature)
2 4 6 9 13 16
41-Herbie Goes to Monte Carlo (Movie); sequel to "Herbie Rides Again"; photo-c
2 4 6 10 14 18
42-Mickey & the Sleuth 2 4 6 9 13 16
43-Pete's Dragon (Movie)-Photo-c 2 4 8 13 18 22
44-Return From Witch Mountain (new) & In Search of the Castaways-r (Movies)-Photo-c; 68 pg. giants begin 3 6 9 14 19 24
45-The Jungle Book (Movie); r/#30033-803 3 6 9 17 25 32
46-48: 46-The Cat From Outer Space (Movie)(new), & The Shaggy Dog (Movie)-r/F.C. #985; photo-c. 47-Mickey Mouse Surprise Party-r. 48-The Wonderful Advs. of Pinocchio-r/F.C. #1203; last 68 pg. issue 2 4 6 10 14 18
49-54: 49-North Avenue Irregulars (Movie); Zorro-r/Zorro #11; 52 pgs. begin; photo-c. 50-Bedknobs & Broomsticks-r/#6; Mooncussers-r/World of Adv. #1; photo-c. 51-101 Dalmatians-r. 52-Unidentified Flying Oddball (Movie); r/Picnic Party #8; photo-c. 53-The Scarecrow-r (TV). 54-The Black Hole (Movie)-Photo-c (predates Black Hole #1)
2 4 6 9 13 16

WALT DISNEY'S MAGAZINE (TV)(Formerly Walt Disney's Mickey Mouse Club Magazine) (50¢, bi-monthly)
Western Publishing Co.: V2#4, June, 1957 - V4#6, Oct, 1959

V2#4-Stories & articles on the Mouseketeers, Zorro, & Goofy and other Disney characters & people 7 14 21 45 73 100
V2#5, V2#6(10/57) 6 12 18 41 66 90
V3#1(12/57), V3#3-5 6 12 18 37 59 80
V3#2-Annette Funicello photo-c 11 22 33 77 136 195
V3#6(10/58)-TV Zorro photo-c 8 16 24 52 86 120
V4#1(12/58) - V4#2-4,6(10/59) 6 12 18 37 59 80
V4#5-Annette Funicello photo-c, w/ 2-photo articles 11 22 33 77 130 195
NOTE: *V2#4-V3#6 were 11-1/2x8-1/2", 48 pgs.; V4#1 on were 10x8", 52 pgs. (Peak circulation of 400,000).*

WALT DISNEY'S MERRY CHRISTMAS (See Dell Giant #39)

WALT DISNEY'S MICKEY AND DONALD (M & D #1,2)(Becomes Walt Disney's Donald & Mickey #19 on)
Gladstone: Mar, 1988 - No. 18, May, 1990 (95¢)

1-Don Rosa-a; r/1949 Firestone giveaway 6.00
2-8: 3-Infinity-c. 4-8-Barks-r 3.00
9-15: 9-r/1948 Firestone giveaway; X-Mas-c 3.00
16($1.50, 52 pgs.)-r/FC #157 5.00
17-(68 pgs.) Barks M.M.-r/FC #79 plus Barks D.D.-r; Rosa-a; x-mas-c 6.00
18($1.95, 68 pgs.)-Gottfredson-r/WDC&S #13,72-74; Kelly-c(r); Barks-r 5.00
NOTE: ***Barks** reprints in 1-15, 17, 18. **Kelly** c-13r, 14 (r/Walt Disney's C&S #58), 18r.*

WALT DISNEY'S MICKEY MOUSE ADVENTURES (Take-Along Comic)
Gemstone Publishing: Aug, 2004 - No. 12 ($7.95, 5" x 7-1/2")

1-12-Goofy, Donald Duck & Uncle Scrooge app. 8.00

WALT DISNEY'S MICKEY MOUSE AND BLOTMAN IN BLOTMAN RETURNS
Gemstone Publishing: Dec, 2006 ($5.99, squarebound, one-shot)

nn-Wraparound-c by Noel Van Horn; Super Goof back-up story 6.00

WALT DISNEY'S MICKEY MOUSE AND FRIENDS
Gemstone Publishing: No. 257, Oct, 2003 - No. 295, Dec, 2006 ($2.95)

257-295: 257-Numbering resumes from Gladstone Mickey Mouse series; Halloween-c. 285-Return of the Phantom Blot 3.00

WALT DISNEY'S MICKEY MOUSE CLUB MAGAZINE (TV)(Becomes Walt Disney's Magazine)
Western Publishing Co.: Winter, 1956 - V2#3, Apr, 1957 (11-1/2x8-1/2", quarterly, 48 pgs.)

V1#1 14 28 42 102 181 260
2-4 8 16 24 56 93 130
V2#1,2 7 14 21 45 73 100
3-Annette photo-c 13 26 39 90 160 230
Annual(1956)-Two different issues; ($1.50-Whitman); 120 pgs., cardboard covers, 11-3/4x8-3/4"; reprints 14 28 42 102 181 260
Annual(1957)-Same as above 12 24 36 82 146 210

WALT DISNEY'S MICKEY MOUSE MEETS BLOTMAN
Gemstone Publishing: Aug, 2005 ($5.99, squarebound, one-shot)

nn-Wraparound-c by Noel Van Horn; Super Goof back-up story 6.00

WALT DISNEY'S PINOCCHIO SPECIAL
Gladstone: Spring, 1990 ($1.00)

1-50th anniversary edition; Kelly-r/F.C. #92 3.00

WALT DISNEY'S SPRING FEVER
Gemstone Publishing: Apr, 2007; Apr, 2008 ($9.50, squarebound)

1,2: 1-New stories and reprints incl. "Mystery of the Swamp" by Carl Barks 9.50

WALT DISNEY'S THE ADVENTUROUS UNCLE SCROOGE MCDUCK
Gladstone: Jan, 1998 - No. 2, Mar, 1998 ($1.95)

1,2: 1-Barks-a(r). 2-Rosa-a(r) 2.50

WALT DISNEY'S THE JUNGLE BOOK
W.D. Publications (Disney Comics): 1990 ($5.95, graphic novel, 68 pgs.)

nn-Movie adaptation; movie rereleased in 1990 6.00
nn-($2.95, 68 pgs.)-Comic edition; wraparound-c 3.00

WALT DISNEY'S UNCLE SCROOGE (Formerly Uncle Scrooge #1-209)
Gladstone #210-242/Disney Comics #243-280/Gladstone #281-318/Gemstone #319 on:
No. 210, 10/86 - No. 242, 4/00; No. 243, 6/90 - No. 318, 2/99; No. 319, 7/03 - Present

210-1st Gladstone issue; r/WDC&S #134 (1st Beagle Boys)
2 4 6 9 13 16
211-218: 216-New story ("Go Slowly Sands of Time") plotted and partly scripted by Barks. 217-r/U.S. #7, "Seven Cities of Cibola" 2 4 6 9 12 15
219-"Son Of The Sun" by Rosa (his 1st pro work) 3 6 9 14 20 25
220-Don Rosa-a/scripts 1 2 3 5 6 8
221-223,225,228-234,236-240 4.00
224,226,227,235: 224-Rosa c/a. 226,227-Rosa-a. 235-Rosa-a/scripts 5.00
241-($1.95, 68 pgs.)-Rosa finishes over Barks-r 6.00
242-($1.95, 68 pgs.)-Barks-r; Rosa-a(1 pg.) 6.00
243-249,251-260,264-275,277-280,282-284-($1.50): 243-1st by Disney Comics. 274-All Barks issue. 275-Contains centerspread by Rosa. 279-All Barks issue; Rosa-c. 283-r/WDC&S #98 3.00
250-($2.25, 52 pgs.)-Barks-r; wraparound-c 4.00
261-263,276-Don Rosa-c/a 5.00
281-Gladstone issues start again; Rosa-c 6.00
285-The Life and Times of Scrooge McDuck Pt. 1; Rosa-c/a/scripts
1 3 4 6 8 10
286-293: The Life and Times of Scrooge McDuck Pt. 2-8; Rosa-c/a/scripts. 293-($1.95, 36 pgs.)-The Life and Times of Scrooge McDuck Pt. 9 6.00
294-299, 301-308-($1.50, 32 pgs.): 294-296-The Life and Times of Scrooge McDuck Pt. 10-12. 297-The Life and Times of Uncle Scrooge Pt. 0; Rosa-c/a/scripts 3.00
300-($2.25, 48 pgs.)-Rosa-c; Barks-r/WDC&S #104 and U.S. #216; r/U.S. #220; includes new centerfold. 4.00
309-318-($6.95) 318-(2/99) Last Gladstone issue 7.00
319-360: 319-(7/03) First Gemstone issue; The Dutchman's Secret by Don Rosa 7.00
361-366: 361-Begin $7.50-c 7.50
367-380-($7.99) 8.00
... Adventures, The Barks/Rosa Collection Vol. 1 (Gemstone, 7/07, $8.50) reprints Pygmy Indians appearances in U.S. #18 by Barks and WDC&S #633 by Rosa 8.50
Walt Disney's The Life and Times of Scrooge McDuck by Don Rosa TPB (Gemstone, 2005, $16.99) Reprints #285-296, with foreword, commentaries & sketch pages by Rosa 17.00
Walt Disney's The Life and Times of Scrooge McDuck Companion by Don Rosa TPB (Gemstone, 2006, $16.99) additional chapters, with foreword & commentaries 17.00
NOTE: ***Barks** r-210-218, 220-223, 224(2pg.), 225-234, 236-242, 245, 246, 250-253, 255, 256, 258, 261(2 pg.), 265, 267, 268, 270(2), 272-284, 299-present; c(r)-210, 212, 221, 228, 229, 232, 233, 284. scripts-287, 293. **Rosa** a-219, 220, 224, 226, 227, 235, 261-263, 268, 275-277, 285-289; c-219, 224, 231, 261-263, 276, 278-281, 285-296; scripts-219, 220, 224, 235, 261-263, 268, 276, 285-296.*

WALT DISNEY'S UNCLE SCROOGE ADVENTURES (U. Scrooge Advs. #1-3)
Gladstone Publishing: Nov, 1987 - No. 21, May, 1990; No. 22, Sept, 1993 - No. 54, Feb, 1998

1-Barks-r begin, ends #26 1 2 3 5 6 8
2-4 4.00
5,9,14: 5-Rosa-c/a; no Barks-r. 9,14-Rosa-a 5.00
6-8,10-13,15-19: 10-r/U.S. #18(all Barks) 3.00
20,21 ($1.95, 68 pgs.) 20-Rosa-c/a. 21-Rosa-a 5.00
22 ($1.50)-Rosa-c; r/U.S. #26 5.00
23-($2.95, 68 pgs.)-Vs. The Phantom Blot-r/P.B. #3; Barks-r 4.00
24-26,29,31,32,34-36: 24,25,29,31,32-Rosa-c. 25-r/U.S. #21 2.50
27-Guardians of the Lost Library - Rosa-c/a/story; origin of Junior Woodchuck Guidebook 3.00
28-($2.95, 68 pgs.)-r/U.S. #13 w/restored missing panels 4.00
30-($2.95, 68 pgs.)-r/U.S. #12; Rosa-c 4.00
33-($2.95, 64 pgs.)-New Barks story 3.00
37-54 2.50
NOTE: ***Barks** r-1-4, 6-8, 10-13, 15-21, 23, 22, 24; c(r)-15, 16, 17, 21. **Rosa** a-5, 9, 14, 20, 21, 27, 51; c-5, 13, 14, 17(finishes), 20, 22, 24, 25, 27, 28, 51; scripts-5, 9, 14, 27.*

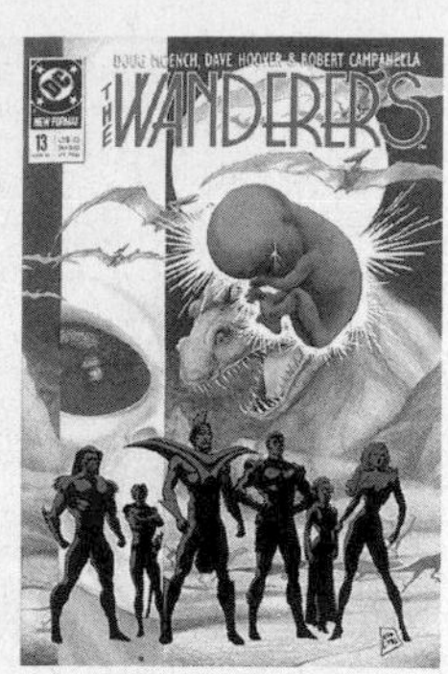

Wanderers #13 © DC

Wanted Comics #34 © Toytown

War Action #1 © MAR

GD VG FN VF VF/NM NM-
2.0 4.0 6.0 8.0 9.0 9.2

WALT DISNEY'S UNCLE SCROOGE AND DONALD DUCK
Gladstone: Jan, 1998 - No. 2, Mar, 1998 ($1.95)
1,2: 1-Rosa-a(r) 2.50

WALT DISNEY'S UNCLE SCROOGE ADVENTURES IN COLOR
Gladstone Publ.: Dec, 1995 - Present ($8.95/$9.95, squarebound, 56 issue limited series) (Polybagged w/card) (Series chronologically reprints all the stories written & drawn by Carl Barks)
1-56: 1-(12/95)-r/FC #386. 15-(12/96)-r/US #15. 16-(12/96)-r/US #16. 18-(1/97)-r/US #18 10.00

WALT DISNEY'S VACATION PARADE
Gemstone Publishing: 2004 - Present ($8.95/$9.95, squarebound, annual)
1-3: 1-Reprints stories from Dell Giant Comics Vacation Parade 1 (July 1950) 9.00
4,5-($9.95): 4-(5/07). 5-(7/08) 10.00

WALT DISNEY'S WHEATIES PREMIUMS (See Wheaties in the Promotional section)

WALT DISNEY'S WORLD OF THE DRAGONLORDS
Gemstone Publishing: 2005 ($12.99, squarebound, graphic novel)
SC-Uncle Scrooge, Donald & nephews app.; Byron Erickson-s/Giorgio Cavazzano-a 13.00

WALT DISNEY TREASURES - DISNEY COMICS: 75 YEARS OF INNOVATION
Gemstone Publishing: 2006 ($12.99, TPB)
SC-Reprints from 1930-2004, including debut of Mickey Mouse newspaper strip 13.00

WALT DISNEY TREASURES - UNCLE SCROOGE: A LITTLE SOMETHING SPECIAL
Gemstone Publishing: 2008 ($16.99, TPB)
SC-Uncle Scrooge classics from 1954-2006, including "The Seven Cities of Cibola" 17.00

WALTER LANTZ ANDY PANDA (Also see Andy Panda)
Gold Key: Aug, 1973 - No. 23, Jan, 1978 (Walter Lantz)

	GD	VG	FN	VF	VF/NM	NM-
1-Reprints	3	6	9	14	19	24
2-10-All reprints	2	4	6	9	12	15
11-23: 15,17-19,22-Reprints	1	2	3	5	7	9

WALT KELLY'S...
Eclipse Comics: Dec, 1987; Apr, 1988 ($1.75/$2.50, Baxter paper)
...Christmas Classics 1 (12/87)-Kelly-r/Peter Wheat & Santa Claus Funnies, ...Springtime Tales 1 (4/88, $2.50)-Kelly-r 2.50

WALTONS, THE (See Kite Fun Book)

WALT SCOTT (See Little People)

WALT SCOTT'S CHRISTMAS STORIES (See Christmas Stories, 4-Color #959, 1062)

WAMBI, JUNGLE BOY (See Jungle Comics)
Fiction House Magazines: Spr, 1942; No. 2, Win, 1942-43; No. 3, Spr, 1943; No. 4, Fall, 1948; No. 5, Sum, 1949; No. 6, Spr, 1950; No. 7-10, 1950(nd); No. 11, Spr, 1951 - No. 18, Win, 1952-53 (#1-3: 68 pgs.)

	GD	VG	FN	VF	VF/NM	NM-
1-Wambi, the Jungle Boy begins	93	186	279	586	993	1400
2 (1942)-Kiefer-c	50	100	150	310	518	725
3 (1943)-Kiefer-c/a	40	80	120	235	380	525
4 (1948)-Origin in text	26	52	78	154	247	340
5 (Fall, 1949, 36 pgs.)-Kiefer-c/a	23	46	69	135	218	300
6-10: 7-(52 pgs.)-New logo	19	38	57	112	176	240
11-18	14	28	42	82	121	160
I.W. Reprint #8('64)-r/#12 with new-c	3	6	9	14	20	25

NOTE: ***Alex Blum*** *c-8.* ***Kiefer*** *c-1-5.* ***Whitman*** *c-11-18.*

WANDERERS (See Adventure Comics #375, 376)
DC Comics: June, 1988 - No. 13, Apr, 1989 ($1.25) (Legion of Super-Heroes spin off)
1-13: 1,2-Steacy-c. 3-Legion app. 2.50

WANDERING STAR
Pen & Ink Comics/Sirius Entertainment No. 12 on: 1993 - No. 21, Mar, 1997 ($2.50/$2.75, B&W)

	GD	VG	FN	VF	VF/NM	NM-
1-1st printing; Teri Sue Wood c/a/scripts in all	1	2	3	5	6	8
1-2nd and 3rd printings						2.75
2-1st printing.						4.00
2-21: 2-2nd printing. 12-(1/96)-1st Sirius issue						2.75
Trade paperback ($11.95)-r/1-7; 1st printing of 1000, signed and #'d						18.00
Trade paperback-2nd printing, 2000 signed						15.00
TPB Volume 2,3 (11/98, 12/98, $14.95) 2-r/#8-14, 3-r/#15-21						15.00

WANTED
Image Comics (Top Cow): Dec, 2003 - No. 6, Feb, 2004 ($2.99)
1-Three covers; Mark Millar-s/J.G. Jones-a; intro Wesley Gibson 3.00
1-4-Death Row Edition; r/#1-4 with extra sketch pages and deleted panels 3.00
2-6: 2-Cameos of DC villains. 6-Giordano-a in flashback scenes 3.00
...Dossier (5/04, $2.99) Pin-ups and character info; art by Jones, Romita Jr. & others 3.00
HC (2005, $29.99) r/#1-6 & Dossier; intro by Vaughan, sketch pages & Cover gallery 30.00

GD VG FN VF VF/NM NM-
2.0 4.0 6.0 8.0 9.0 9.2

WANTED COMICS
Toytown Publications/Patches/Orbit Publ.: No. 9, Sept-Oct, 1947 - No. 53, April, 1953 (#9-33: 52 pgs.)

	GD	VG	FN	VF	VF/NM	NM-
9-True crime cases; radio's Mr. D. A. app.	25	50	75	145	233	320
10,11: 10-Giunta-a; radio's Mr. D. A. app.	15	30	45	86	133	180
12-Used in **SOTI**, pg. 277	15	30	45	94	147	200
13-Heroin drug propaganda story	15	30	45	84	127	170
14-Marijuana drug mention story (2 pgs.)	14	28	42	81	118	155
15-17,19,20	13	26	39	72	101	130
18-Marijuana story, "Satan's Cigarettes"; r-in #45 & retitled	25	50	75	145	233	320
21,22: 21-Krigstein-a. 22-Extreme violence	13	26	39	74	105	135
23,25-34,36-38,40-44,46-48,53	11	22	33	60	83	105
24-Krigstein-a; "The Dope King", marijuana mention story	14	28	42	82	121	160
35-Used in **SOTI**, pg. 160	14	28	42	80	115	150
39-Drug propaganda story "The Horror Weed"	15	30	45	94	147	200
45-Marijuana story from #18	13	26	39	72	101	130
49-Has unstable pink-c that fades easily; rare in mint condition	12	24	36	69	97	125
50-Has unstable pink-c like #49; surrealist-c by Buscema; horror stories	14	28	42	76	108	140
51- "Holiday of Horror" junkie story; drug-c	14	28	42	82	121	160
52-Classic "Cult of Killers" opium use story	14	28	42	82	121	160

NOTE: ***Buscema*** *c-50, 51.* ***Lawrence*** *and* ***Leav*** *c/a most issues.* ***Syd Shores*** *c/a-48; c-37. Issues 9-46 have wanted criminals with their descriptions & drawn picture on cover.*

WANTED: DEAD OR ALIVE (TV)
Dell Publishing Co.: No. 1102, May-July, 1960 - No. 1164, Mar-May, 1961

	GD	VG	FN	VF	VF/NM	NM-
Four Color 1102 (#1)-Steve McQueen photo-c	12	24	36	87	156	225
Four Color 1164-Steve McQueen photo-c	9	18	27	63	107	150

WANTED, THE WORLD'S MOST DANGEROUS VILLAINS (See DC Special)
National Periodical Publ.: July-Aug, 1972 - No. 9, Aug-Sept, 1973 (All reprints & 20¢ issues)

	GD	VG	FN	VF	VF/NM	NM-
1-Batman, Green Lantern (story r-from G.L. #1), & Green Arrow	3	6	9	20	30	40
2-Batman/Joker/Penguin-c/story r-from Batman #25; plus Flash story (r-from Flash #121)	3	6	9	16	23	30
3-9: 3-Dr. Fate(r/More Fun #65), Hawkman(r/Flash #100), & Vigilante(r/Action #69). 4-Green Lantern(r/All-American #61) & Kid Eternity(r/Kid Eternity #15). 5-Dollman/Green Lantern. 6-Burnley Starman; Wildcat/Sargon. 7-Johnny Quick(r/More Fun #76), Hawkman(r/Flash #90), Hourman by Baily(r/Adv. #72). 8-Dr. Fate/Flash(r/Flash #114). 9-S&K Sandman/Superman	3	6	9	14	19	24

NOTE: ***B. Bailey*** *a-7r.* ***Infantino*** *a-2r.* ***Kane*** *r-1, 5.* ***Kubert*** *r-3i, 6, 7.* ***Meskin*** *r-3, 7.* ***Reinman*** *r-4, 6.*

WAR (See Fightin' Marines #122)
Charlton Comics: Jul, 1975 - No. 9, Nov, 1976; No. 10, Sept, 1978 - No. 47, 1984

	GD	VG	FN	VF	VF/NM	NM-
1-Boyette painted-c	2	4	6	11	16	20
2-10: 3-Sutton painted-c	1	3	4	6	8	10
11-20	1	2	3	4	5	7
21-40						6.00
41-47 (lower print run): 47-Reprints	1	2	3	4	5	7
7,9 (Modern Comics-r, 1977)						4.00

WAR, THE (See The Draft & The Pitt)
Marvel Comics: 1989 - No. 4, 1990 ($3.50, squarebound, 52 pgs.)
1-4: Characters from New Universe 3.50

WAR ACTION (Korean War)
Atlas Comics (CPS): April, 1952 - No. 14, June, 1953

	GD	VG	FN	VF	VF/NM	NM-
1	20	40	60	115	183	250
2	12	24	36	69	97	125
3-10,14: 7-Pakula-a. 14-Colan-a	10	20	30	54	72	90
11-13-Krigstein-a. 11-Romita-a	10	20	30	58	79	100

NOTE: ***Berg*** *c-11.* ***Brodsky*** *c-1-4.* ***Heath*** *a-1; c-7, 14.* ***Keller*** *a-6.* ***Maneely*** *a-1; c-12.* ***Tuska*** *a-2, 8.*

WAR ADVENTURES
Atlas Comics (HPC): Jan, 1952 - No. 13, Feb, 1953

	GD	VG	FN	VF	VF/NM	NM-
1-Tuska-a	18	36	54	103	162	220
2	11	22	33	60	83	105
3-7,9-13: 3-Pakula-a. 7-Maneely-c. 9-Romita-a	9	18	27	52	69	85
8-Krigstein-a	10	20	30	58	79	100

NOTE: ***Brodsky*** *c-1-3, 6, 8, 11, 12.* ***Heath*** *a-2, 5, 7, 10; c-4, 5, 9, 13.* ***Reinman*** *a-13.* ***Robinson*** *a-3; c-10.*

War Against Crime! #1 © WMG

War Comics #6 © MAR

War Heroes #1 © Millar & Harris

	GD	VG	FN	VF	VF/NM	NM-
	2.0	4.0	6.0	8.0	9.0	9.2

WAR ADVENTURES ON THE BATTLEFIELD (See Battlefield)

WAR AGAINST CRIME! (Becomes Vault of Horror #12 on)
E. C. Comics: Spring, 1948 - No. 11, Feb-Mar, 1950

1-Real Stories From Police Records on-c #1-9	77	154	231	481	816	1150
2,3	45	90	135	279	465	650
4-9	41	82	123	250	413	575
10-1st Vault Keeper app. & 1st Vault of Horror	211	422	633	1688	2694	3700
11-2nd Vault Keeper app.; 1st horror-c	131	262	393	1048	1674	2300

NOTE: *All have* ***Johnny Craig*** *covers.* ***Feldstein*** *a-4, 7-9.* ***Harrison/Wood*** *a-11.* ***Ingels*** *a-1, 2, 8.* ***Palais*** *a-8. Changes to horror with #10.*

WAR AGAINST CRIME
Gemstone Publishing: Apr, 2000 - No. 11, Feb, 2001 ($2.50)

1-11: E.C. reprints 2.50

WAR AND ATTACK (Also see Special War Series #3)
Charlton Comics: Fall, 1964; V2#54, June, 1966 - V2#63, Dec, 1967

1-Wood-a (25 pgs.)	4	8	12	28	44	60
V2#54(6/66)-#63 (Formerly Fightin' Air Force)	3	6	9	14	20	25

NOTE: ***Montes/Bache*** *a-55, 56, 60, 63.*

WAR AT SEA (Formerly Space Adventures)
Charlton Comics: No. 22, Nov, 1957 - No. 42, June, 1961

22	7	14	21	35	43	50
23-30	5	10	15	24	30	35
31-42	3	6	9	16	23	30

WAR BATTLES
Harvey Publications: Feb, 1952 - No. 9, Dec, 1953

1-Powell-a; Elias-c	9	18	27	63	107	150
2-Powell-a	5	10	15	34	55	75
3-5,7-9: 3,7-Powell-a. 5-Flamethrower cover	5	10	15	32	51	70
6-Nostrand-a	6	12	18	39	62	85

WAR BIRDS
Fiction House Magazines: 1952(nd) - No. 3, Winter, 1952-53

1	16	32	48	94	147	200
2,3	11	22	33	62	86	110

WARBLADE: ENDANGERED SPECIES (Also see WildC.A.T.S: Covert Action Teams)
Image Comics (WildStorm Productions): Jan, 1995 - No. 4, Apr, 1995 ($2.50, limited series)

1-4: 1-Gatefold wraparound-c 2.50

WAR COMBAT (Becomes Combat Casey #6 on)
Atlas Comics (LBI No. 1/SAI No. 2-5): March, 1952 - No. 5, Nov, 1952

1	15	30	45	90	140	190
2	10	20	30	56	76	95
3-5	9	18	27	50	65	80

NOTE: ***Berg*** *a-2, 4, 5.* ***Brodsky*** *c-1, 2, 4, 5.* ***Henkel*** *a-5.* ***Maneely*** *a-1, 4; c-3.* ***Reinman*** *a-2.*

WAR COMICS (War Stories #5 on)(See Key Ring Comics)
Dell Publishing Co.: May, 1940 (No month given) - No. 4, Sept, 1941

1-Sikandur the Robot Master, Sky Hawk, Scoop Mason, War Correspondent begin; McWilliams-c; 1st war comic	58	116	174	365	620	875
2-Origin Greg Gilday (5/41)	34	68	102	198	319	440
3-Joan becomes Greg Gilday's aide	23	46	69	133	214	295
4-Origin Night Devils	24	48	72	140	225	310

WAR COMICS
Marvel/Atlas (USA No. 1-41/JPI No. 42-49): Dec, 1950 - No. 49, Sept, 1957

1	26	52	78	154	247	340
2	15	30	45	84	127	170
3-10	13	26	39	72	101	130
11-Flame thrower w/burning bodies on-c	14	28	42	82	121	160
12-20: 16-Romita-a	11	22	33	60	83	105
21,23-32: 26-Valley Forge story. 32-Last pre-code issue (2/55)	9	18	27	52	69	85
22-Krigstein-a	10	20	30	58	79	100
33-37,39-42,44,45,47,48	9	18	27	52	69	85
38-Kubert/Moskowitz-a	10	20	30	56	76	95
43,49-Torres-a. 43-Severin/Elder E.C. swipe from Two-Fisted Tales #31	10	20	30	56	76	95
46-Crandall-a	10	20	30	56	76	95

NOTE: ***Berg*** *a-13.* ***Colan*** *a-4, 36, 48, 49; c-17.* ***Drucker*** *a-37, 43, 48.* ***Everett*** *a-17.* ***Heath*** *a-6-9, 16, 19, 25, 36; c-11, 16, 19, 23, 25, 26, 29-32, 36.* ***G. Kane*** *a-19.* ***Lawrence*** *a-36.* ***Maneely*** *a-7, 9, 13, 14, 20; c-6, 27, 37.* ***Orlando*** *a-42, 48.* ***Pakula*** *a-26.* ***Ravielli*** *a-27.* ***Reinman*** *a-11, 16, 26.* ***Robinson*** *a-15; c-13.* ***Severin*** *a-26, 27; c-48.*

WAR DANCER (Also see Charlemagne, Doctor Chaos #2 & Warriors of Plasm)
Defiant: Feb, 1994 - No. 6, July, 1994 ($2.50)

1-3,5,6: 1-Intro War Dancer; Weiss-c/a begins. 1-3-Weiss-a(p). 6-Pre-Schism issue 2.50
4-($3.25, 52 pgs.)-Charlemagne app. 3.25

WAR DOGS OF THE U.S. ARMY
Avon Periodicals: 1952

1-Kinstler-c/a	15	30	45	83	124	165

WARFRONT
Harvey Publications: 9/51 - #35, 11/58; #36, 10/65; #39, 2/67

1-Korean War	10	20	30	70	123	175
2	6	12	18	39	62	85
3-10	5	10	15	32	51	70
11,12,14,16-20	4	8	12	28	44	60
13,15,22-Nostrand-a	6	12	18	39	62	85
21,23-27,31-33,35	4	8	12	28	44	60
28-30,34-Kirby-c	6	12	18	41	66	90
36-(12/66)-Dynamite Joe begins, ends #39; Williamson-a	5	10	15	32	51	70
37-Wood-a (17 pgs.)	5	10	15	32	51	70
38,39-Wood-a, 2-3 pgs.; Lone Tiger app.	4	8	12	28	44	60

NOTE: ***Powell*** *a-1-6, 9-11, 14, 17, 20, 23, 25-28, 30, 31, 34, 36.* ***Powell/Nostrand*** *a-12, 13, 15.* ***Simon*** *c-36?, 38.*

WAR FURY
Comic Media/Harwell (Allen Hardy Assoc.): Sept, 1952 - No. 4, Mar, 1953

1-Heck-c/a in all; Palais-a; bullet hole in forehead-c; all issues are very violent; soldier using flame thrower on enemy	31	62	93	181	291	400
2-4: 4-Morisi-a	15	30	45	94	147	200

WAR GODS OF THE DEEP (See Movie Classics)

WARHAWKS
TSR, Inc.: 1990 - No. 10, 1991 ($2.95, 44 pgs.)

1-10-Based on TSR game, Spiegle a-1-6 3.00

WARHEADS
Marvel Comics UK: June, 1992 - No. 14, Aug, 1993 ($1.75)

1-Wolverine-c/story; indicia says #2 by mistake 3.00
2-14: 2-Nick Fury app. 3-Iron Man-c/story. 4,5-X-Force. 5-Liger vs. Cable. 6,7-Death's Head II app. (#6 is cameo) 2.50

WAR HEROES (See Marine War Heroes)

WAR HEROES
Dell Publishing Co.: 7-9/42 (no month); No. 2, 10-12/42 - No. 11, 3/45 (Published quarterly)

1-General Douglas MacArthur-c	26	52	78	152	244	335
2	15	30	45	84	127	170
3,5: 3-Pro-Russian back-c	13	26	39	72	101	130
4-Disney's Gremlins app.	18	36	54	105	165	225
6-11: 6-Tothish-a by Discount	10	20	30	56	76	95

NOTE: *No. 1 was to be released in July, but was delayed. Painted c-4, 6-9.*

WAR HEROES
Ace Magazines: May, 1952 - No. 8, Apr, 1953

1	11	22	33	62	86	110
2-Lou Cameron-a	8	16	24	42	54	65
3-8: 6,7-Cameron-a	7	14	21	37	46	55

WAR HEROES (Also see Blue Bird Comics)
Charlton Comics: Feb, 1963 - No. 27, Nov, 1967

1,2: 2-John F. Kennedy story	4	8	12	24	37	50
3-10	3	6	9	17	25	32
11-26	3	6	9	14	19	24
27-1st Devils Brigade by Glanzman	3	6	9	17	25	32

NOTE: ***Montes/Bache*** *a-3-7, 21, 25, 27; c-3-7.*

WAR HEROES
Image Comics: July, 2008 - No. 6 ($2.99, limited series)

1,2-Soldiers given super powers; Mark Millar-s/Tony Harris-a/c; four covers 3.00

WAR IS HELL
Marvel Comics Group: Jan, 1973 - No. 15, Oct, 1975

1-Williamson-a(r), 5 pgs.; Ayers-a	3	6	9	16	22	28
2-8-Reprints. 6-(11/73). 7-(6/74). 7,8-Kirby-a	2	4	6	8	11	14
9-Intro Death	4	8	12	28	44	60
10-15-Death app.	3	6	9	16	22	28

NOTE: ***Bolle*** *a-3r.* ***Powell*** *a-1.* ***Woodbridge*** *a-1. Sgt. Fury reprints-7, 8.*

WAR IS HELL: THE FIRST FLIGHT OF THE PHANTOM EAGLE

Warlands #7 © Dreamwave

Warlock V2#1 © MAR

War Machine #3 © MAR

GD 2.0 | VG 4.0 | FN 6.0 | VF 8.0 | VF/NM 9.0 | NM- 9.2

Marvel Comics (MAX): May, 2008 - No. 5, Sept, 2008 ($3.99, limited series)
1-5-World War I fighter pilots; Ennis-s/Chaykin-a/Cassaday-c 4.00

WARLANDS
Image Comics: Aug, 1999 - No. 12, Feb, 2001 ($2.50)
1-9,11,12-Pat Lee-a(p)/Adrian Tsang-s 2.50
10-($2.95) Flip book w/Shidima preview 3.00
... Chronicles 1,2 (2/00, 7/00; $7.95) 1-r/#1-3. 2-r/#4-6 8.00
...Darklyte TPB (8/01, $14.95) r/#0,1/2,1-6 w/cover gallery; new Lee-c 15.00
...Epilogue: Three Stories (3/01, $5.95) includes r/Wizard #1/2 & AE #0 6.00
Another Universe #0 3.00
Wizard #1/2 5.00

WARLANDS: THE AGE OF ICE (Volume 2)
Image Comics: July, 2001 - No. 9, Nov, 2002 ($2.95)
#0-(2/02, $2.25) 2.50
#1/2 (4/02, $2.25) 2.50
1-9: 2-Flip book preview of Banished Knights 3.00
TPB (2003, $15.95) r/#1-9 16.00

WARLANDS: DARK TIDE RISING (Volume 3)
Image Comics: Dec, 2002 - No. 6, May, 2003 ($2.95)
1-6: 1-Wraparound gatefold-c 3.00

WARLOCK (The Power of...)(Also see Avengers Annual #7, Fantastic Four #66, 67, Incredible Hulk #178, Infinity Crusade, Infinity Gauntlet, Infinity War, Marvel Premiere #1, Marvel Two-In-One Annual #2, Silver Surfer V3#46, Strange Tales #178-181 & Thor #165)
Marvel Comics Group: Aug, 1972 - No. 8, Oct, 1973; No. 9, Oct, 1975 - No. 15, Nov, 1976
1-Origin by Kane 6 12 18 43 69 95
2,3 4 8 12 22 34 45
4-8: 4-Death of Eddie Roberts 3 6 9 14 20 26
9-Starlin's 2nd Thanos saga begins, ends #15; new costume Warlock; Thanos cameo only; story cont'd from Strange Tales #178-181; Starlin-c/a in #9-15
3 6 9 20 30 40
10-Origin Thanos & Gamora; recaps events from Capt. Marvel #25-34. Thanos vs.The Magus-c/story 4 8 12 22 34 45
11-Thanos app.; Warlock dies 3 6 9 16 23 30
12-14: (Regular 25¢ edition) 14-Origin Star Thief; last 25¢ issue
3 6 9 14 19 24
12-14-(30¢-c, limited distribution) 4 8 12 23 36 48
15-Thanos-c/story 3 6 9 14 20 26
NOTE: ***Buscema*** *a-2p; c-8p.* ***G. Kane*** *a-1p, 3-5p; c-1p, 2, 3, 4p, 5p, 7p.* ***Starlin*** *a-9-14p, 15; c-9, 10, 11p, 12p, 13-15.* ***Sutton*** *a-1-8i.*

WARLOCK (...Special Edition on-c)
Marvel Comics Group: Dec, 1982 - No. 6, May, 1983 ($2.00, slick paper, 52 pgs.)
1-Warlock-r/Strange Tales #178-180. 4.00
2-6: 2-r/Str. Tales #180,181 & Warlock #9. 3-r/Warlock #10-12(Thanos origin recap). 4-r/Warlock #12-15. 5-r/Warlock #15, Marvel Team-Up #55 & Avengers Ann. #7. 6-r/2nd half Avengers Annual #7 & Marvel Two-in-One Annual #2 4.00
Special Edition #1(12/83) 4.00
NOTE: ***Byrne*** *a-5r.* ***Starlin*** *a-1-6r; c-1-6(new). Direct sale only.*

WARLOCK
Marvel Comics: V2#1, May, 1992 - No. 6, Oct, 1992 ($2.50, limited series)
V2#1-6: 1-Reprints 1982 reprint series w/Thanos 2.50

WARLOCK
Marvel Comics: Nov, 1998 - No. 4, Feb, 1999 ($2.99, limited series)
1-4-Warlock vs. Drax 3.00

WARLOCK (M-Tech)
Marvel Comics: Oct, 1999 - No. 9, June, 2000 ($1.99/$2.50)
1-5: 1-Quesada-c. 2-Two covers 2.50
6-9: 6-Begin $2.50-c. 8-Avengers app. 2.50

WARLOCK
Marvel Comics: Nov, 2004 - No. 4, Feb, 2005 ($2.99, limited series)
1-4-Adlard-a/Williams-c 3.00

WARLOCK AND THE INFINITY WATCH (Also see Infinity Gauntlet)
Marvel Comics: Feb, 1992 - No. 42, July, 1995 ($1.75) (Sequel to Infinity Gauntlet)
1-Starlin-scripts begin; brief origin recap; sequel to Infinity Gauntlet 3.00
2,3: 2-Reintro Moondragon 2.50
4-24,26: 7-Reintro The Magus; Moondragon app.; Thanos cameo on last 2 pgs. 8,9-Thanos battles Gamora-c/story. 8-Magus & Moondragon app. 10-Thanos-c/story; Magus app. 13-Hulk x-over. 21-Drax vs. Thor 2.50
25-($2.95, 52 pgs.)-Die-cut & embossed double-c; Thor & Thanos app. 3.00

GD 2.0 | VG 4.0 | FN 6.0 | VF 8.0 | VF/NM 9.0 | NM- 9.2

28-42: 28-$1.95-c begins; bound-in card sheet 2.50
NOTE: ***Austin*** *c/a-1-4i, 7i.* ***Leonardi*** *a(p)-3, 4.* ***Medina*** *c/a(p)-1, 2, 5; 6, 9, 10, 14, 15, 20.* ***Williams*** *a(i)-8, 12, 13, 16-19.*

WARLOCK CHRONICLES
Marvel Comics: June, 1993 - No. 8, Feb, 1994 ($2.00, limited series)
1-($2.95)-Holo-grafx foil & embossed-c; origin retold; Starlin scripts begin; Keith Williams-a(i) in all 3.00
2-8: 3-Thanos & Mephisto-c/story. 4-Vs. Magus-c/s. 8-Contains free 16 pg. Razorline insert 2.50

WARLOCK 5
Aircel Pub.: 11/86 - No. 22, 5/89; V2#1, June, 1989 - V2#5, 1989 ($1.70, B&W)
1-5,7-11-Gordon Derry-s/Denis Beauvais-a thru #11. 5-Green Cyborg on-c. 5-Misnumbered as #6 (no #6); Blue Girl on-c. 2.50
12-22-Barry Blair-s/a. 18-$1.95-c begins 3.00
V2#1-5 ($2.00, B&W)-All issues by Barry Blair 2.50
Compilation 1,2: 1-r/#1-5 (1988, $5.95); 2-r/#6-9 6.00

WARLORD (See 1st Issue Special #8)
National Periodical Publications/DC Comics #123 on: 1-2/76; No.2, 3-4/76; No.3, 10-11/76 - No. 133, Win, 1988-89
1-Story cont'd. from 1st Issue Special #8 3 6 9 20 30 40
2-Intro. Machiste 2 4 6 11 16 20
3-5 2 4 6 8 10 12
6-10: 6-Intro Mariah. 7-Origin Machiste. 9-Dons new costume
1 2 3 5 6 8
11-20: 11-Origin-r. 12-Intro Aton. 15-Tara returns; Warlord has son 5.00
21-36,40,41: 27-New facts about origin. 28-1st app. Wizard World. 32-Intro Shakira. 40-Warlord gets new costume 4.00
22-Whitman variant edition 2 4 6 13 18 22
37-39: 37,38-Origin Omac by Starlin. 38-Intro Jennifer Morgan, Warlord's daughter. 39-Omac ends. 5.00
42-48: 42-47-Omac back-up series. 48-(52 pgs.)-1st app. Arak; contains free 14 pg. Arak Son of Thunder; Claw The Unconquered app. 4.00
49-62,64-99,101-132: 49-Claw The Unconquered app. 50-Death of Aton. 51-Reprints #1. 55-Arion Lord of Atlantis begins, ends #62. 91-Origin w/new facts. 114,115-Legends x-over. 125-Death of Tara. 131-1st DC work by Rob Liefeld (9/88) 3.00
63-The Barren Earth begins; free 16pg. Masters of the Universe preview 4.00
100-($1.25, 52 pgs.) 4.00
133-($1.50, 52 pgs.) 4.00
Remco Toy Giveaway (2-3/4x4") 5.00
Annual 1-6 ('82-'87): 1-Grell-c,/a(p). 6-New Gods app. 4.00
The Savage Empire TPB (1991, $19.95) r/#1-10,12 & First Issue Special #8; Grell intro. 25.00
NOTE: ***Grell*** *a-1-15, 16-50p, 51r, 52p, 59p, Annual 1p; c-1-70, 100-104, 112, 116, 117, Annual 1, 5.* ***Wayne Howard*** *a-64i.* ***Starlin*** *a-37-39p.*

WARLORD
DC Comics: Jan, 1992 - No. 6, June, 1992 ($1.75, limited series)
1-6: Grell-c & scripts in all 2.50

WARLORD
DC Comics: Apr, 2006 - No. 10, Jan, 2007 ($2.99)
1-10: 1-Bruce Jones-s/Bart Sears-a. 10-Winslade-a 3.00

WARLORDS (See DC Graphic Novel #2)

WAR MACHINE (Also see Iron Man #281,282 & Marvel Comics Presents #152)
Marvel Comics: Apr, 1994 - No. 25, Apr, 1996 ($1.50)
"Ashcan" edition (nd, 75¢, B&W, 16 pgs.) 2.50
1-($2.00, 52 pgs.)-Newsstand edition; Cable app. 2.25
1-($2.95, 52 pgs.)-Collectors ed.; embossed foil-c 3.00
2-14, 16-25: 2-Bound-in trading card sheet; Cable app. 2,3-Deathlok app. 8-red logo 2.50
8-($2.95)-Polybagged w/16 pg. Marvel Action Hour preview & acetate print; yellow logo 3.00
15 ($2.50)-Flip book 2.50

WAR MAN
Marvel Comics (Epic Comics): Nov, 1993 - No. 2, Dec, 1993 ($2.50, lim. series)
1,2 2.50

WAR OF THE GODS
DC Comics: Sept, 1991 - No. 4, Dec, 1991 ($1.75, limited series)
1-4: Perez layouts, scripts & covers. 1-Contains free mini posters (Robin, Deathstroke). 2-4-Direct sale versions include 4 pin-ups printed on cover stock plus different-c 2.50

WAR OF THE UNDEAD
IDW Publishing: Jan, 2007 - No. 3, Apr, 2007 ($3.99, limited series)
1-3-Bryan Johnson-s/Walter Flanagan-a 4.00

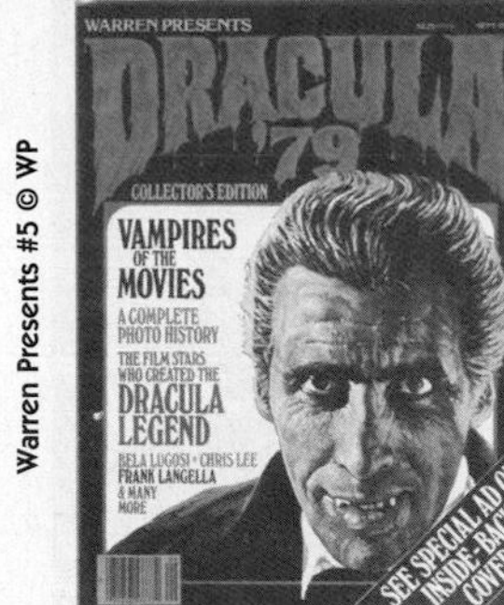

Warren Presents #5 © WP

Warstrike #1 © MAL

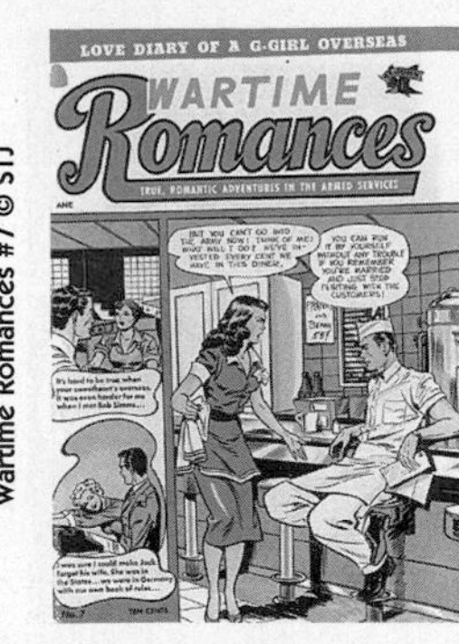

Wartime Romances #7 © STJ

GD 2.0 | VG 4.0 | FN 6.0 | VF 8.0 | VF/NM 9.0 | NM- 9.2

WAR OF THE WORLDS, THE
Caliber: 1996 - No. 5 ($2.95, B&W, 32 pgs.)(Based on H. G. Wells novel)
1-5: 1-Randy Zimmerman scripts begin 3.00

WARP
First Comics: Mar, 1983 - No. 19, Feb, 1985 ($1.00/$1.25, Mando paper)
1-Sargon-Mistress of War app.; Brunner-c/a thru #9 2.50
2-19: 2-Faceless Ones begin. 10-New Warp advs., & Outrider begin 2.50
Special 1-3: 1(7/83, 36 pgs.)-Origin Chaos-Prince of Madness; origin of Warp Universe begins, ends #3. 2(1/84)-Lord Cumulus vs. Sargon Mistress of War ($1.00). 3(6/84)-Chaos-Prince of Madness 2.50

WARPATH (Indians on the...)
Key Publications/Stanmor: Nov, 1954 - No. 3, Apr, 1955
1 11 22 33 62 86 110
2,3 8 16 24 40 50 60

WARPED
Empire Entertainment (Solson): Jun, 1990 - No. 2, Oct-Nov, 1990 (B&W mag)
1,2 2.50

WARP GRAPHICS ANNUAL
WaRP Graphics: Dec, 1985; 1988 ($2.50)
1-Elfquest, Blood of the Innocent, Thunderbunny & Myth Adventures 5.00
1 (1988) 4.00

WARREN PRESENTS
Warren Publications: Jan, 1979 - No. 14, Nov, 1981(B&W magazine)
1-Eerie, Creepy, & Vampirella-r; Ring of the Warlords; Merlin-s; Dax-s; Sanjulian-c
3 6 9 15 21 26
2-6(10/79): 2-The Rook. 3-Alien Invasions Comix. 4-Movie Aliens. 5-Dracula '79. 6-Strange Stories of Vampires Comix 2 4 6 9 13 16
8(10/80)-r/1st app. Pantha from Vamp. #30 2 4 6 11 16 20
9(11/80) Empire Encounters Comix 2 4 6 10 14 18
13(10/81),14(11/81):13-Sword and Sorcery Comix 3 6 9 14 19 24
(#7,10,11,12 may not exist, or may be a Special below)
Special-Alien Collectors Edition (1979) 3 6 9 14 19 24
Special-Close Encounters of the Third Kind (1978) 2 4 6 9 13 16
Special-Lord of the Rings (6/79) 3 6 9 19 29 38
Special-Meteor (1/80) 2 4 6 9 13 16
Special-Moonraker/James Bond (10/79) 2 4 6 9 13 16
Special-Star Wars (1977) 3 6 9 19 29 38

WAR REPORT
Ajax/Farrell Publications (Excellent Publ.): Sept, 1952 - No. 5, May, 1953
1 14 28 42 76 108 140
2-Flame thrower w/burning bodies on-c 14 28 42 80 115 150
3,5 8 16 24 44 57 70
4-Used in POP, pg. 94 9 18 27 50 65 80

WARRIOR (Wrestling star)
Ultimate Creations: May, 1996 - No. 4, 1997 ($2.95)
1-4: Warrior scripts; Callahan-c/a. 3-Wraparound-c. 4-Warrior #3 in indicia; pin-ups 3.00
1-Variant-c. 5.00
X-Mas (11/96, $3.50) listed as "No. 3" in indicia; pin-ups by various; Quesada-c 3.50

WARRIOR COMICS
H.C. Blackerby: 1945 (1930s DC reprints)
1-Wing Brady, The Iron Man, Mark Markon 22 44 66 127 204 280

WARRIOR OF WAVERLY STREET, THE
Dark Horse Comics: Nov, 1996 - No. 2, Dec, 1996 ($2.95, mini-series)
1,2-Darrow-c 3.00

WARRIORS
CFD Productions: 1993 (B&W, one-shot)
1-Linsner, Dark One-a 2 4 6 10 14 18

WARRIORS OF PLASM (Also see Plasm)
Defiant: Aug, 1993 - No. 13, Aug, 1995 ($2.95/$2.50)
1-4: Shooter-scripts; Lapham-c/a: 1-1st app. Glory. 4-Bound-in fold-out poster 3.00
5-7,10-13: 5-Begin $2.50-c. 13-Schism issue 2.50
8,9-($2.75, 44 pgs.) 2.75
The Collected Edition (2/94, $9.95)-r/Plasm #0, WOP #1-4 & Splatterball 10.00

WAR ROMANCES (See True...)

WAR SHIPS
Dell Publishing Co.: 1942 (36 pgs.)(Similar to Large Feature Comics)
nn-Cover by McWilliams; contains photos & drawings of U.S. war ships
18 36 54 103 162 220

WARSTONE
Devil's Due Publishing: Apr, 2004 ($4.95, one-shot)
1-Josh Blaylock-s/Matt & Mike Cossin-a 5.00

WAR STORIES (Formerly War Comics)
Dell Publ. Co.: No. 5, 1942(nd); No. 6, Aug-Oct, 1942 - No. 8, Feb-Apr, 1943
5-Origin The Whistler 26 52 78 152 244 335
6-8: 6-8-Night Devils app. 8-Painted-c 20 40 60 115 183 250

WAR STORIES (Korea)
Ajax/Farrell Publications (Excellent Publ.): Sept, 1952 - No. 5, May, 1953
1 12 24 36 67 94 120
2 8 16 24 40 50 60
3-5 7 14 21 37 46 55

WAR STORIES (See Star Spangled...)

WAR STORY
DC Comics (Vertigo): Nov, 2001 - Present ($4.95, series of World War II one-shots)
...: Archangel (4/03) Ennis-s/Erskine-a 5.00
...: Condors (3/03) Ennis-s/Ezquerra-a 5.00
...: D-Day Dodgers (12/01) Ennis-s/Higgins-a 5.00
...: J For Jenny (2/03) Ennis-s/Lloyd-a 5.00
...: Johann's Tiger (11/01) Ennis-s/Weston-a 5.00
...: Nightingale (2/02) Ennis-s/Lloyd-a 5.00
...: Screaming Eagles (1/02) Ennis-s/Gibbons-a 5.00
...: The Reivers (1/03) Ennis-s/Kennedy-a 5.00
Vol. 1 (2004, $19.95) r/Johann's Tiger, D-Day Dodgers, Screaming Eagles, Nightingale 20.00
Vol. 2 (2006, $19.99) r/J For Jenny, The Reivers, Condors, Archangel; Ennis afterword 20.00

WARSTRIKE
Malibu Comics (Ultraverse): May, 1994 - No. 7, Nov, 1995 ($1.95)
1-7: 1-Simonson-c 2.50
1 Ultra 5000 Limited silver foil 4.00
Giant Size 1 (12/94, 2.50, 44pgs.)-Prelude to Godwheel 2.50

WART AND THE WIZARD (See The Sword & the Stone under Movie Comics)
Gold Key: Feb, 1964 (Walt Disney)(Characters from Sword in the Stone movie)
1 (10102-402) 4 8 12 28 44 60

WAR THAT TIME FORGOT, THE
DC Comics: Jul, 2008 - No. 12 ($2.99, limited series)
1-4: 1-Bruce Jones-s/Al Barrionuevo-a/Neal Adams-c; Enemy Ace app. 3.00

WARTIME ROMANCES
St. John Publishing Co.: July, 1951 - No. 18, Nov, 1953
1-All Baker-c/a 41 82 123 256 428 600
2-All Baker-c/a 31 62 93 181 291 400
3,4-All Baker-c/a 29 58 87 169 272 375
5-8-Baker-c/a(2-3) each 27 54 81 158 254 350
9,11,12,16,18: Baker-c/a each. 9-Two signed stories by Estrada
21 42 63 125 200 275
10,13-15,17-Baker-c only 17 34 51 100 158 215

WAR VICTORY ADVENTURES (#1 titled War Victory Comics)
U.S. Treasury Dept./War Victory/Harvey Publ.: Summer, 1942 - No. 3, Winter, 1943-44 (5¢)
1-(Promotion of Savings Bonds)-Featuring America's greatest comic art by top syndicated cartoonists; Blondie, Joe Palooka, Green Hornet, Dick Tracy, Superman, Gumps, etc.; (36 pgs.); all profits were contributed to U.S.O. & Army/Navy relief funds
41 82 123 250 413 575
2-Battle of Stalingrad story; Powell-a (8/43); flag-c 22 44 66 127 204 280
3-Capt. Red Cross-c & text only; Powell-a 20 40 60 115 183 250

WAR WAGON, THE (See Movie Classics)

WAR WINGS
Charlton Comics: Oct, 1968
1 3 6 9 14 19 24

WARWORLD!
Dark Horse Comics: Feb, 1989 ($1.75, B&W, one-shot)
1-Gary Davis sci/fi art in Moebius style 2.50

WASHABLE JONES AND THE SHMOO (Also see Al Capp's Shmoo)
Toby Press: June, 1953
1- "Super-Shmoo" 19 38 57 109 172 235

Watchmen #12 © DC

Web of Mystery #1 © ACE

Web of Spider-Man #10 © MAR

WASH TUBBS (See The Comics, Crackajack Funnies)
Dell Publishing Co.: No. 11, 1942 - No. 53, 1944

	GD 2.0	VG 4.0	FN 6.0	VF 8.0	VF/NM 9.0	NM- 9.2
Four Color 11 (#1)	28	56	84	203	377	550
Four Color 28 (1943)	19	38	57	135	250	365
Four Color 53	14	28	42	102	181	260

WASTELAND
DC Comics: Dec, 1987 - No. 18, May, 1989 ($1.75-$2.00 #13 on, mature)

	GD 2.0	VG 4.0	FN 6.0	VF 8.0	VF/NM 9.0	NM- 9.2
1-5(4/88), 5(5/88), 6(5/88)-18: 13,15-Orlando-a						2.50

NOTE: ***Orlando*** *a-12, 13, 15.* ***Truman*** *a-10; c-13.*

WATCHMEN
DC Comics: Sept, 1986 - No. 12, Oct, 1987 (maxi-series)

	GD 2.0	VG 4.0	FN 6.0	VF 8.0	VF/NM 9.0	NM- 9.2
1-Alan Moore scripts & Dave Gibbons-c/a in all	2	4	6	8	10	12
2-12	1	2	3	5	6	8
Hardcover Collection-Slip-cased-r/#1-12 w/new material; produced by Graphitti Designs						90.00
Trade paperback (1987, $14.95)-r/#1-12						20.00

WATER BIRDS AND THE OLYMPIC ELK (Disney)
Dell Publishing Co.: No. 700, Apr, 1956

	GD 2.0	VG 4.0	FN 6.0	VF 8.0	VF/NM 9.0	NM- 9.2
Four Color 700-Movie	5	10	15	34	55	75

WATERWORLD: CHILDREN OF LEVIATHAN
Acclaim Comics: Aug, 1997 - No. 4, Nov, 1997 ($2.50, mini-series)

	GD 2.0	VG 4.0	FN 6.0	VF 8.0	VF/NM 9.0	NM- 9.2
1-4						2.50

WAY OF THE RAT
CrossGeneration Comics: Jun, 2002 - No. 24, June, 2004 ($2.95)

	GD 2.0	VG 4.0	FN 6.0	VF 8.0	VF/NM 9.0	NM- 9.2
1-24: 1-Dixon-s/ Jeff Johnson-a. 5-Whigham-a. 9,14-Luke Ross-a						3.00
Free Comic Book Day Special (6/03) reprints #1 w/features, interviews, CrossGen info						2.25
...: The Walls of Zhumar Vol. 1 (1/03, $15.95) r/#1-6						16.00
Vol. 2: The Dragon's Wake (2003, $15.95) r/#7-12						16.00

WEAPON X
Marvel Comics: Apr, 1994 ($12.95, one-shot)

	GD 2.0	VG 4.0	FN 6.0	VF 8.0	VF/NM 9.0	NM- 9.2
nn-r/Marvel Comics Presents #72-84						13.00

WEAPON X
Marvel Comics: Mar, 1995 - No. 4, June, 1995 ($1.95)

	GD 2.0	VG 4.0	FN 6.0	VF 8.0	VF/NM 9.0	NM- 9.2
1-Age of Apocalypse						4.00
2-4						2.50

WEAPON X
Marvel Comics: Nov, 2002 - No. 28, Nov, 2004 ($2.25/$2.99)

	GD 2.0	VG 4.0	FN 6.0	VF 8.0	VF/NM 9.0	NM- 9.2
1-7: 1-Sabretooth-c/app.; Tieri-s/Jeanty-a						2.50
8-28: 8-Begin $2.99-c. 14-Invaders app. 15-Chamber joins. 16 18,21 25 Wolverine app.						3.00
Vol. 1: The Draft TPB (2003, $21.99) r/#1-5, #1/2 & The Draft one-shots						22.00
Vol. 2: The Underground TPB (2003, $19.99) r/#6-13						20.00
Wizard #1/2 (2002)						5.00

WEAPON X: DAYS OF FUTURE NOW
Marvel Comics: Sept, 2005 - No. 5, Jan, 2006 ($2.99, limited series)

	GD 2.0	VG 4.0	FN 6.0	VF 8.0	VF/NM 9.0	NM- 9.2
1-5-Tieri-s/Sears-a; Chamber, Sauron & Fantomex app.						3.00
TPB (2006, $13.99) r/#1-5						14.00

WEAPON X: THE DRAFT (Leads into 2002 Weapon X series)
Marvel Comics: Oct, 2002 ($2.25, one-shots)

	GD 2.0	VG 4.0	FN 6.0	VF 8.0	VF/NM 9.0	NM- 9.2
...Kane 1- JH Williams-c/Raimondi-a						2.50
...Marrow 1- JH Williams-c/Badeaux-a						2.50
...Sauron 1- JH Williams-c/Kerschl-a; Emma Frost app.						2.50
...Wild Child 1- JH Williams-c/Van Sciver-a; Aurora (Alpha Flight) app.						2.50
...Zero 1- JH Williams-c/Plunkett-a; Wolverine app.						2.50

WEAPON ZERO
Image Comics (Top Cow Productions): No. T-4(#1), June, 1995 - No. T-0(#5), Dec, 1995 ($2.50, limited series)

	GD 2.0	VG 4.0	FN 6.0	VF 8.0	VF/NM 9.0	NM- 9.2
T-4(#1): Walt Simonson scripts in all.						5.00
T-3(#2) - T-1(#4)						4.00
T-0(#5)						3.00

WEAPON ZERO
Image Comics (Top Cow Productions): V2#1, Mar, 1996 - No. 15, Dec, 1997 ($2.50)

	GD 2.0	VG 4.0	FN 6.0	VF 8.0	VF/NM 9.0	NM- 9.2
V2#1-Walt Simonson scripts.						3.00
2-14: 8-Begin Top Cow. 10-Devil's Reign						2.50
15-($3.50) Benitez-a						3.50

WEAPON ZERO/SILVER SURFER
Image Comics/Marvel Comics: Jan, 1997($2.95, one-shot)

	GD 2.0	VG 4.0	FN 6.0	VF 8.0	VF/NM 9.0	NM- 9.2
1-Devil's Reign Pt. 1						3.00

WEASELGUY: ROAD TRIP
Image Comics: Sept, 1999 - No. 2 ($3.50, limited series)

	GD 2.0	VG 4.0	FN 6.0	VF 8.0	VF/NM 9.0	NM- 9.2
1,2-Steve Buccellato-s/a						3.50
1-Variant-c by Bachalo						5.00

WEASELGUY/WITCHBLADE
Hyperwerks: July, 1998 ($2.95, one-shot)

	GD 2.0	VG 4.0	FN 6.0	VF 8.0	VF/NM 9.0	NM- 9.2
1-Steve Buccellato-s/a; covers by Matsuda and Altstaetter						3.00

WEASEL PATROL SPECIAL, THE (Also see Fusion #17)
Eclipse Comics: Apr, 1989 ($2.00, B&W, one-shot)

	GD 2.0	VG 4.0	FN 6.0	VF 8.0	VF/NM 9.0	NM- 9.2
1-Funny animal						2.50

WEAVEWORLD
Marvel Comics (Epic): Dec, 1991 - No. 3, 1992 ($4.95, lim. series, 68 pgs.)

	GD 2.0	VG 4.0	FN 6.0	VF 8.0	VF/NM 9.0	NM- 9.2
1-3: Clive Barker adaptation						5.00

WEB, THE (Also see Mighty Comics & Mighty Crusaders)
DC Comics (Impact Comics): Sept, 1991 - No. 14, Oct, 1992 ($1.00)

	GD 2.0	VG 4.0	FN 6.0	VF 8.0	VF/NM 9.0	NM- 9.2
1-14: 5-The Fly x-over 9-Trading card inside						2.50
Annual 1 (1992, $2.50, 68 pgs.)-With Trading card						3.00

NOTE: ***Gil Kane*** *c-5, 9, 10, 12-14.* ***Bill Wray*** *a(i)-1-9, 10(part).*

WEB OF EVIL
Comic Magazines/Quality Comics Group: Nov, 1952 - No. 21, Dec, 1954

	GD 2.0	VG 4.0	FN 6.0	VF 8.0	VF/NM 9.0	NM- 9.2
1-Used in **SOTI**, pg. 388. Jack Cole-a; morphine use story	59	118	177	372	629	885
2-4,6,7: 2,3-Jack Cole-a. 4,6,7-Jack Cole-c/a	41	82	123	253	419	585
5-Electrocution-c/story; Jack Cole-c/a	48	96	144	298	499	700
8-11-Jack Cole-a	40	80	120	235	380	525
12,13,15,16,19-21	25	50	75	147	236	325
14-Part Crandall-c; Old Witch swipe	26	52	78	154	247	340
17-Opium drug propaganda story	26	52	78	152	244	335
18-Acid-in-face story	26	52	78	154	247	340

NOTE: ***Jack Cole*** *a(2 each)-2, 6, 8, 9.* ***Cuidera*** *c-1-21i.* ***Ravielli*** *a-13.*

WEB OF HORROR
Major Magazines: Dec, 1969 - No. 3, Apr, 1970 (Magazine)

	GD 2.0	VG 4.0	FN 6.0	VF 8.0	VF/NM 9.0	NM- 9.2
1-Jeff Jones painted-c; Wrightson-a, Kaluta-a	8	16	24	54	90	125
2-Jones painted-c; Wrightson-a(2), Kaluta-a	7	14	21	47	76	105
3-Wrightson-c/a (1st published-c); Brunner, Kaluta, Bruce Jones-a	8	16	24	52	86	120

WEB OF MYSTERY
Ace Magazines (A. A. Wyn): Feb, 1951 - No. 29, Sept, 1955

	GD 2.0	VG 4.0	FN 6.0	VF 8.0	VF/NM 9.0	NM- 9.2
1	55	110	165	347	586	825
2-Bakerish-a	32	64	96	188	302	415
3-10: 4-Colan-a	28	56	84	164	265	365
11-18,20-26: 12-John Chilly's 1st cover art. 13-Surrealistic-c. 20-r/The Beyond #1	24	48	72	143	229	315
19-Reprints Challenge of the Unknown #6 used in N.Y. Legislative Committee	24	48	72	143	229	315
27-Bakerish-a(r/The Beyond #2); last pre-code ish	22	44	66	127	204	280
28,29: 28-All-r	17	34	51	98	154	210

NOTE: *This series was to appear as "Creepy Stories", but title was changed before publication.* ***Cameron*** *a-6, 8, 11-13, 17-20, 22, 24, 25, 27; c-8, 13, 17.* ***Palais*** *a-28r.* ***Sekowsky*** *a-1-3, 7, 8, 11, 14, 21, 29.* ***Tothish*** *a-by* ***Bill Discount*** *#16. 29-all-r, 19-28-partial-r.*

WEB OF SCARLET SPIDER
Marvel Comics: Oct, 1995 - No. 4, Jan, 1996 ($1.95, limited series)

	GD 2.0	VG 4.0	FN 6.0	VF 8.0	VF/NM 9.0	NM- 9.2
1-4: Replaces "Web of Spider-Man"						2.50

WEB OF SPIDER-MAN (Replaces Marvel Team-Up)
Marvel Comics Group: Apr, 1985 - No. 129, Sept, 1995

	GD 2.0	VG 4.0	FN 6.0	VF 8.0	VF/NM 9.0	NM- 9.2
1-Painted-c (5th app. black costume?)	2	4	6	9	12	15
2,3						5.00
4-8: 7-Hulk x-over; Wolverine splash						4.00
9-13: 10-Dominic Fortune guest stars; painted-c						4.00
14-17,19-28: 19-Intro Humbug & Solo						3.00
18-1st app. Venom (behind the scenes, 9/86)						3.00
29-Wolverine, new Hobgoblin (Macendale) app.	1	2	3	5	6	8
30-Origin recap The Rose & Hobgoblin I (entire book is flashback story); Punisher & Wolverine cameo						4.00
31,32-Six part Kraven storyline begins						5.00
33-37,39-47,49: 36-1st app. Tombstone						3.00
38-Hobgoblin app.; begin $1.00-c						4.00

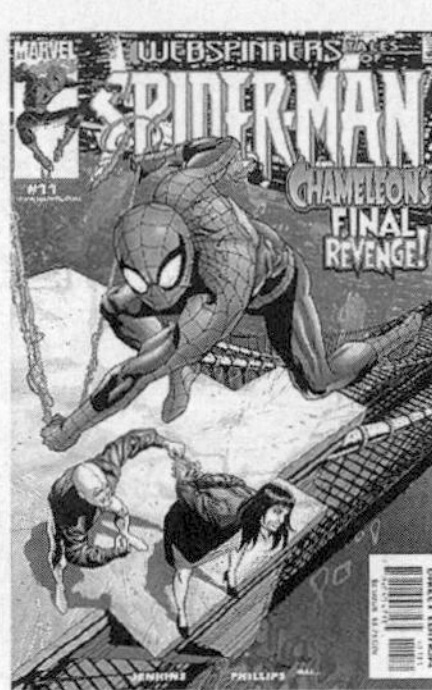

Webspinners: Tales of Spider-Man #11 © MAR

Weekender #3 © Rucker Publ.

Weird Comics #4 © FOX

	GD	VG	FN	VF	VF/NM	NM-
	2.0	4.0	6.0	8.0	9.0	9.2

48-Origin Hobgoblin II(Demogoblin) cont'd from Spectacular Spider-Man #147;
Kingpin app. 1 2 3 5 7 9
50-($1.50, 52 pgs.) 3.50
51-58 2.50
59-Cosmic Spidey cont'd from Spect. Spider-Man 3.50
60-89,91-99,101-106: 66,67-Green Goblin (Norman Osborn) app. as a super-hero. 69,70-Hulk x-over. 74-76-Austin-c(i). 76-Fantastic Four x-over. 78-Cloak & Dagger app. 81-Origin/1st app. Bloodshed. 84-Begin 6 part Rose & Hobgoblin II storyline; last $1.00-c. 86-Demon leaves Hobgoblin; 1st Demogoblin. 93-Gives brief history of Hobgoblin. 93,94-Hobgoblin (Macendale) Reborn-c/story, parts 1,2; MoonKnight app. 94-Venom cameo. 95-Begin 4 part x-over w/Spirits of Venom w/Ghost Rider/Blaze/Spidey vs. Venom & Demogoblin (cont'd in Ghost Rider/Blaze #5,6). 96-Spirits of Venom part 3; painted-c. 101,103-Maximum Carnage x-over. 103-Venom & Carnage app. 104-106-Nightwatch back-up stories 2.50
90-($2.95, 52 pgs.)-Polybagged w/silver hologram-c, gatefold poster showing Spider-Man & Spider-Man 2099 (Williamson-i) 3.50
90-2nd printing; gold hologram-c 3.00
100-($2.95, 52 pgs.)-Holo-grafx foil-c; intro new Spider-Armor 4.00
107-111: 107-Intro Sandstorm; Sand & Quicksand app. 2.50
112-116, 118, 119, 121-124, 126-128: 112-Begin $1.50-c; bound-in trading card sheet. 113-Regular Ed.; Gambit & Black Cat app. 118-1st solo clone story; Venom app. 2.50
113-($2.95)-Collector's ed. polybagged w/foil-c; 16 pg. preview of Spider-Man cartoon & animation cel 3.00
117-($1.50)-Flip book; Power & Responsibility Pt.1 2.50
117-($2.95)-Collector's edition; foil-c; flip book 3.00
119-($6.45)-Direct market edition; polybagged w/ Marvel Milestone Amazing Spider-Man #150 & coupon for Amazing Spider-Man #396, Spider-Man #53, & Spectacular Spider-Man #219. 7.00
120 ($2.25)-Flip book w/ preview of the Ultimate Spider-Man 2.50
125 ($3.95)-Holodisk-c; Gwen Stacy clone 4.00
125,129: 25 ($2.95)-Newsstand. 129-Last issue 3.00
Annual 1 (1985) 3.00
Annual 2 (1986)-New Mutants; Art Adams-a 1 2 3 5 6 8
Annual 3-10 ('87-'94, 68 pgs.): 4-Evolutionary War x-over. 5-Atlantis Attacks; Captain Universe by Ditko (p) & Silver Sable stories; F.F. app. 6-Punisher back-up plus Capt. Universe by Ditko; G. Kane-a. 7-Origins of Hobgoblin I, Hobgoblin II, Green Goblin I & II & Venom; Larsen/Austin-c. 9-Bagged w/card 3.00
Super Special 1 (1995, $3.95)-flip book 4.00

NOTE: ***Art Adams** a-Annual 2. **Byrne** c-3-6. **Chaykin** c-10. **Mignola** a-Annual 2. **Vess** c-1, 8, Annual 1, 2. **Zeck** a-6i, 31, 32; c-31, 32.*

WEBSPINNERS: TALES OF SPIDER-MAN
Marvel Comics: Jan, 1999 - No. 18, Jun, 2000 ($2.99/$2.50)

1-DeMatteis-s/Zulli-a; back-up story w/Romita Sr. art 3.00
1-($6.95) DF Edition 7.00
2,3: 2-Two covers 2.50
4-11,13-18: 4,5-Giffen-a; Silver Surfer-c/app. 7-9-Kelly-s/Sears and Smith-a. 10,11-Jenkins-s/Sean Phillips-a 2.50
12-($3.50) J.G. Jones-c/a; Jenkins-s 3.50

WEDDING BELLS
Quality Comics Group: Feb, 1954 - No. 19, Nov, 1956

1-Whitney-a 15 30 45 86 133 180
2 10 20 30 56 76 95
3-9: 8-Last precode (4/55) 8 16 24 44 57 70
10-Ward-a (9 pgs.) 14 28 42 80 115 150
11-14,17 8 16 24 40 50 60
15-Baker-c 11 22 33 62 86 110
16-Baker-c/a 14 28 42 80 115 150
18,19-Baker-a each 10 20 30 58 79 100

WEDDING OF DRACULA
Marvel Comics: Jan, 1993 ($2.00, 52 pgs.)

1-Reprints Tomb of Dracula #30,45,46 2.50

WEEKENDER, THE (Illustrated...)
Rucker Pub. Co.: V1#1, Sept, 1945? - V1#4, Nov, 1945; V2#1, Jan, 1946 - V2#3, Aug, 1946 (52 pgs.)

V1#1-4: 1-Same-c as Zip Comics #45, inside-c and back-c blank; Steel Sterling, Senor Banana, Red Rube and Ginger. 2-Capt. Victory on-c. 3-Super hero-c; Mr. E, Dan Hastings, Sky Chief and the Echo. 4-Same-c as Punch Comics #10 (9/44); r/Hale the Magician (7 pgs.) & r/Mr. E (8 pgs.-Lou Fine? or Gustavson?) plus 3 humor strips & many B&W photos & r/newspaper articles plus cheesecake photos of Hollywood stars 17 34 51 98 154 210
V2#1-Same-c as Dynamic Comics #11; 36 pgs. comics, 16 in newspaper format with photos; partial Dynamic Comics reprints; 4 pgs. of cels from the Disney film Pinocchio; Little Nemo story by Winsor McCay, Jr.; Jack Cole-a 19 38 57 109 172 235
V2#2,3: 2-Same-c as Dynamic Comics #9 by Raboy; Dan Hastings (Tuska), Rocket Boy, The Echo, Lucky Coyne. 3-Humor-c by Boddington?; Dynamic Man, Ima Slooth, Master Key, Dynamic Boy, Captain Glory 17 34 51 98 154 210

WEIRD
Eerie Publications: V1#10, 1/66 - V8#6, 12/74; V9#1, 1/75 - V14#3, Nov, 1981 (Magazine) (V1-V8: 52 pgs.; V9 on: 68 pgs.)

V1#10(#1)-Intro. Morris the Caretaker of Weird (ends V2#10); Burgos-a 8 16 24 52 86 120
11,12 5 10 15 32 51 70
V2#1-4(10/67), V3#1(1/60), V2#6(4/68) V2#7,9,10(12/68) 5 10 15 32 51 70
V2#8-r/Ditko's 1st story/Fantastic Fears #5 6 12 18 39 62 85
V3#1(2/69)-V3#4 4 8 12 28 44 60
V3#5(12/69)-Rulah reprint; "Rulah" changed to "Pulah", LSD story reprinted in Horror Tales V4#4, Tales From the Tomb V2#4, & 20 4 8 12 28 44 60
V4#1-6('70), V5#1-6('71), V6#1-7('72), V7#1-7('73), V8#1-3, V8#4(8/74), V8#4(10/74), (V8#5 does not exist), V8#6('74), V9#1-4(1/75-'76), V10#1-3('77), V11#1-4('78), V12#1(2/79)-V14#3(11/81) 4 8 12 28 44 60

NOTE: *There are two V8#4 issues (8/74 & 10/74). V9#4 (12/76) has a cover swipe from Horror Tales V5#1 (2/73). There are two V13#3 issues (6/80 & 9/80).*

WEIRD
DC Comics (Paradox Press): Sum, 1997 - Present ($2.99, B&W, magazine)

1-4: 4-Mike Tyson-c 3.00

WEIRD, THE
DC Comics: Apr, 1988 - No. 4, July, 1988 ($1.50, limited series)

1-4: Wrightson-c/a in all 3.00

WEIRD ADVENTURES
P. L. Publishing Co. (Canada): May June, 1951 - No. 3, Sept-Oct, 1951

1- "The She-Wolf Killer" by Matt Baker (6 pgs.) 58 116 174 365 620 875
2-Bondage/hypodermic panel 45 90 135 279 465 650
3-Male bondage/torture-c; severed head story 40 80 120 244 397 550

WEIRD ADVENTURES
Ziff-Davis Publishing Co.: No. 10, July-Aug, 1951

10-Painted-c 40 80 120 235 380 525

WEIRD CHILLS
Key Publications: July, 1954 - No. 3, Nov, 1954

1-Wolverton-r/Weird Mysteries No. 4; blood transfusion-c by Baily 90 180 270 567 959 1350
2-Extremely violent injury to eye-c by Baily; Hitler story 107 214 321 674 1137 1600
3-Bondage E.C. swipe-c by Baily 48 96 144 298 499 700

WEIRD COMICS
Fox Features Syndicate: Apr, 1940 - No. 20, Jan, 1942

1-The Birdman, Thor, God of Thunder (ends #5), The Sorceress of Zoom, Blast Bennett, Typhon, Voodoo Man, & Dr. Mortal begin; George Tuska bondage-c 472 944 1416 3398 5949 8500
2-Lou Fine-c 233 466 699 1468 2484 3500
3,4: 3-Simon-c. 4-Torture-c 122 244 366 769 1297 1825
5-Intro. Dart & sidekick Ace (8/40) (ends #20); bondage/hypo-c 127 254 381 800 1350 1900
6,7-Dynamite Thor app. in each. 6-Super hero covers begin 93 186 279 586 993 1400
8-Dynamo, the Eagle (11/40, early app.; see Science #1) & sidekick Buddy & Marga, the Panther Woman begin 92 184 276 580 978 1375
9,10: 10-Navy Jones app. 75 150 225 473 799 1125
11-19: 16-Flag-c. 17-Origin The Black Rider. 56 112 168 353 594 835
20-Origin The Rapier; Swoop Curtis app; Churchill & Hitler-c 73 146 219 460 780 1100

NOTE *Cover features: Sorceress of Zoom-4; Dr. Mortal-5; Dart & Ace-6-13, 15; Eagle-14, 16-20.*

WEIRD FANTASY (Formerly A Moon, A Girl, Romance; becomes Weird Science-Fantasy #23 on)
E. C. Comics: No. 13, May-June, 1950 - No. 22, Nov-Dec, 1953

13(#1) (1950) 200 400 600 1600 2550 3500
14-Necronomicon story; Cosmic Ray Bomb explosion-c/story by Feldstein; Feldstein & Gaines star 94 188 282 752 1201 1650
15,16: 16-Used in **SOTI**, pg. 144 64 128 192 512 819 1125
17 (1951) 53 106 159 424 680 935
6-10: 6-Robot-c 44 88 132 352 564 775
11-13 (1952): 11-Feldstein bio. 12-E.C. artists cameo; Orlando bio. 13-Anti-Wertham "Cosmic

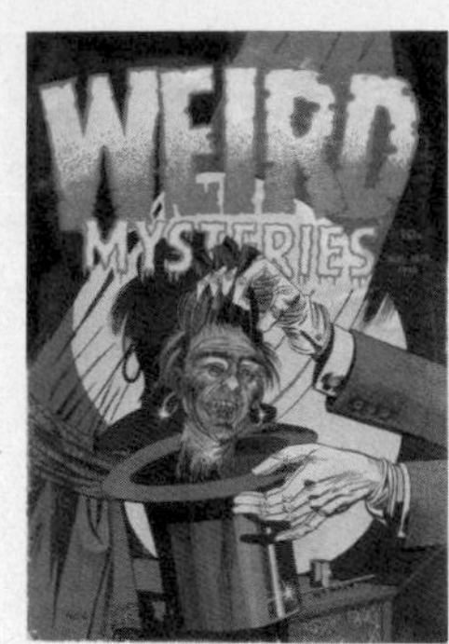

Weird Mysteries #6 © GIL

Weird Science #10 © WMG

Weird Tales of the Future #7 © Aragon

	GD 2.0	VG 4.0	FN 6.0	VF 8.0	VF/NM 9.0	NM- 9.2

Correspondence" 36 72 108 288 457 625
14-Frazetta/Williamson(1st team-up at E.C.)/Krenkel-a (7 pgs.); Orlando draws E.C. staff 49 98 147 392 621 850
15-Williamson/Evans-a(3), 4,3,&7 pgs. 36 72 108 288 457 625
16-19-Williamson/Krenkel-a in all. 18-Williamson/Feldstein-c. 19-Williamson bio. 33 66 99 264 425 585
20-Frazetta/Williamson-a (7 pgs.) 37 74 111 296 473 650
21-Frazetta/Williamson-c & Williamson/Krenkel-a 49 98 147 392 621 850
22-Bradbury adaptation 26 52 78 208 334 460

NOTE: ***Ray Bradbury*** *adaptations-13, 17-20, 22.* ***Crandall*** *a-22.* ***Elder*** *a-17.* ***Feldstein*** *a-13(#1)-8; c-13(#1)-18 (#18 w/****Williamson****), 20.* ***Harrison/Wood*** *a-13.* ***Kamen*** *a-13(#1)-16, 18-22.* ***Krigstein*** *a-22.* ***Kurtzman*** *a-13(#1)-17(#5), 6.* ***Orlando*** *a-9-22 (2 stories in #16); c-19, 22.* ***Severin/Elder*** *a-18-21.* ***Wood*** *a-13(#1)-14, 17(2 stories ea. in #10-13). Ray Bradbury adaptations in #17-19, 22. Canadian reprints exist; see Table of Contents.*

WEIRD FANTASY
Russ Cochran/Gemstone Publ.: Oct, 1992 - No. 22, Jan, 1998 ($1.50/$2.00/$2.50)

1-22: 1,2: 1,2-r/Weird Fantasy #13,14; Feldstein-c. 3-5-r/Weird Fantasy #15-17 3.00

WEIRD HORRORS (Nightmare #10 on)
St. John Publishing Co.: June, 1952 - No. 9, Oct, 1953

1-Tuska-a 58 116 174 365 620 875
2,3: 3-Hashish story 37 74 111 220 353 485
4,5 33 66 99 192 309 425
6-Ekgren-c; atomic bomb story 51 102 153 316 526 735
7-Ekgren-c; Kubert, Cameron-a 52 104 156 322 541 760
8,9-Kubert-c/a 41 82 123 250 413 575

NOTE: ***Cameron*** *a-7, 9.* ***Finesque*** *a-1-5.* ***Forgione*** *a-6.* ***Morisi*** *a-3. Bondage c-8.*

WEIRD MYSTERIES
Gillmor Publications: Oct, 1952 - No. 12, Sept, 1954

1-Partial Wolverton-c swiped from splash page "Flight to the Future" in Weird Tales of the Future #2; "Eternity" has an Ingels swipe 97 194 291 611 1031 1450
2- "Robot Woman" by Wolverton; Bernard Baily-c reprinted in Mister Mystery #18; acid in face panel 127 254 381 800 1350 1900
3,6: Both have decapitation-c 63 126 189 397 674 950
4- "The Man Who Never Smiled" (3 pgs.) by Wolverton; Classic B. Baily skull-c 123 246 369 775 1313 1850
5-Wolverton story "Swamp Monster" (6 pgs.). Classic exposed brain-c 140 280 420 882 1491 2100
7-Used in **SOTI**, illo "Indeed", illo "Sex and blood" 85 170 255 536 906 1275
8-Wolverton-c panel-r/#5; used in a '54 Readers Digest anti-comics article by T. E. Murphy entitled "For the Kiddies to Read" 58 116 174 365 620 875
9-Excessive violence, gore & torture 55 110 165 347 586 825
10-Silhouetted nudity panel 51 102 153 316 526 735
11,12: 12-r/Mr. Mystery #8(2), Weird Mysteries #3 & Weird Tales of the Future #6 47 94 141 291 488 685

NOTE: ***Baily*** *c-2-12. Anti-Wertham column in #5. #1-12 all have 'The Ghoul Teacher' (host).*

WEIRD MYSTERIES (Magazine)
Pastime Publications: Mar-Apr, 1959 (35¢, B&W, 68 pgs.)

1-Torres-a; E. C. swipe from Tales From the Crypt #46 by Tuska "The Ragman" 10 20 30 56 76 95

WEIRD MYSTERY TALES (See DC 100 Page Super Spectacular)

WEIRD MYSTERY TALES (See Cancelled Comic Cavalcade)
National Periodical Publications: July-Aug, 1972 - No. 24, Nov, 1975

1-Kirby-a; Wrightson splash pg. 5 10 15 32 51 70
2-Titanic-c/s 3 6 9 19 29 38
3,21: 21-Wrightson-c 3 6 9 16 22 28
4-10 2 4 6 11 16 20
11-20,22-24 2 4 6 9 13 16

NOTE: ***Alcala*** *a-5, 10, 13, 14.* ***Aparo*** *c-4.* ***Bailey*** *a-8.* ***Bolle*** *a-8?.* ***Howard*** *a-4.* ***Kaluta*** *a-4, 24; c-1.* ***G. Kane*** *a-10.* ***Kirby*** *a-1, 2p, 3p.* ***Nino*** *a-5, 6, 9, 13, 16, 21.* ***Redondo*** *a-9, 17.* ***Sparling*** *c-6.* ***Starlin*** *a-3?, 4.* ***Wood*** *a-23.*

WEIRD ROMANCE (Seduction of the Innocent #9)
Eclipse Comics: Feb, 1988 ($2.00, B&W)

1-Pre-code horror-r; Lou Cameron-r(2) 2.25

WEIRD SCIENCE (Formerly Saddle Romances) (Becomes Weird Science-Fantasy #23 on)
(Also see EC Archives • Weird Science)
E. C. Comics: No. 12, May-June, 1950 - No. 22, Nov-Dec, 1953

12(#1) (1950)-"Lost in the Microcosm" classic-c/story by Kurtzman; "Dream of Doom" stars Gaines & E.C. artists 200 400 600 1600 2550 3500
13-Flying saucers over Washington-c/story, 2 years before supposed UFO sighting 91 182 273 728 1164 1600
14-Robot, End of the World-c/story by Feldstein 86 172 258 688 1094 1500
15-War of Worlds-c/story (1950) 80 160 240 640 1020 1400
5-Atomic explosion-c 61 122 183 488 782 1075
6-8,10 50 100 150 400 638 875
9-Wood's 1st EC-c 53 106 159 424 675 925
11-14 (1952) 11-Kamen bio. 12-Wood bio 36 72 108 288 457 625
15-18-Williamson/Krenkel-a in each; 15-Williamson-a. 17-Used in **POP**, pgs. 81,82. 18-Bill Gaines doll app. in story 38 76 114 304 482 660
19,20-Williamson/Frazetta-a (7 pgs. each). 19-Used in **SOTI**, illo "A young girl on her wedding night stabs her sleeping husband to death with a hatpin..." 19-Bradbury bio. 47 94 141 376 601 825
21-Williamson/Frazetta-a (6 pgs.); Wood draws E.C. staff; Gaines & Feldstein app. in story 47 94 141 376 601 825
22-Williamson/Frazetta/Krenkel-a (8 pgs.); Wood draws himself in his story (last pg. & panel) 47 94 141 376 601 825

NOTE: ***Elder*** *a-14, 19.* ***Evans*** *a-22.* ***Feldstein*** *a-12(#1)-8; c-12(#1)-8, 11.* ***Ingels*** *a-15.* ***Kamen*** *a-12(#1)-13, 15-18, 20, 21.* ***Kurtzman*** *a-12(#1)-7.* ***Orlando*** *a-10-22.* ***Wood*** *a-12(#1), 13(#2), 5-22 (#9, 10, 12, 13 all have 2* ***Wood*** *stories); c-9, 10, 12-22. Canadian reprints exist; see Table of Contents. Ray Bradbury adaptations in #17-22.*

WEIRD SCIENCE
Gladstone Publishing: Sept, 1990 - No. 4, Mar, 1991 ($1.95/$2.00, 68 pgs.)

1-4: Wood-c(r); all reprints in each 3.00

WEIRD SCIENCE (Also see EC Archives • Weird Science)
Russ Cochran/Gemstone Publishing: Sept, 1992 - No. 22, Dec, 1997 ($1.50/$2.00/$2.50)

1-22: 1,2: r/Weird Science #12,13 w/original-c. ,4-r/#14,15. 5-7-w/original-c 3.00

WEIRD SCIENCE-FANTASY (Formerly Weird Science & Weird Fantasy)
(Becomes Incredible Science Fiction #30)
E. C. Comics: No. 23 Mar, 1954 - No. 29, May-June, 1955 (#23,24: 15¢)

23-Williamson, Wood-a; Bradbury adaptation 35 70 105 280 445 610
24-Williamson & Wood-a; Harlan Ellison's 1st professional story, "Upheaval!", later adapted into a short story as "Mealtime", and then into a TV episode of Voyage to the Bottom of the Sea as "The Price of Doom" 35 70 105 280 445 610
25-Williamson-c; Williamson/Torres/Krenkel-a plus Wood-a; Bradbury adaptation; cover price back to 10¢ 39 78 117 312 494 675
26-Flying Saucer Report; Wood, Crandall-a; A-bomb panels 36 72 108 288 462 635
27-Adam Link/I Robot series begins? 35 70 105 280 445 610
28-Williamson/Krenkel/Torres-a; Wood-a 36 72 108 288 457 625
29-Frazetta-c; Williamson/Krenkel & Wood-a; last pre-code issue; new logo 91 182 273 728 1164 1600

NOTE: ***Crandall*** *a-26, 27, 29.* ***Evans*** *a-26.* ***Feldstein*** *c-24, 26, 28.* ***Kamen*** *a-27, 28.* ***Krigstein*** *a-23-25.* ***Orlando*** *a-in all.* ***Wood*** *a-in all; c-23, 27. The cover to #29 was originally intended for Famous Funnies #217 (Buck Rogers), but was rejected for being "too violent."*

WEIRD SCIENCE-FANTASY
Russ Cochran/Gemstone Publishing: Nov, 1992 - No. 7, May , 1994 ($1.50/$2.00/$2.50)

1-7: 1,2: r/Weird Science-Fantasy #23,24. 3-7 r/#25-29 3.00

WEIRD SCIENCE-FANTASY ANNUAL
E. C. Comics: 1952, 1953 (Sold thru the E. C. office & on the stands in some major cities) (25¢, 132 pgs.)

1952-Feldstein-c 267 534 801 2003 3002 4000
1953-Feldstein-c 160 320 480 1200 1800 2400

NOTE: *The 1952 annual contains books cover-dated in 1951 & 1952, and the 1953 annual from 1952 & 1953. Contents of each annual may vary in same year.*

WEIRD SECRET ORIGINS
DC Comics: Oct, 2004 ($5.95, square-bound, one-shot)

nn-Reprints origins of Dr. Fate, Spectre, Congorilla, Metamorpho, Animal Man & others 6.00

WEIRD SUSPENSE
Atlas/Seaboard Publ.: Feb, 1975 - No. 3, July, 1975

1-3: 1-Tarantula begins. 3-Freidrich-s 1 2 3 5 7 9

NOTE: ***Boyette*** *a-1-3.* ***Buckler*** *c-1, 3.*

WEIRD SUSPENSE STORIES (Canadian reprints of Crime SuspenStories #1-3; see Table of Contents)

WEIRD TALES ILLUSTRATED
Millennium Publications: 1992 - No. 2, 1992 ($2.95, high quality paper)

1,2-Bolton painted-c. 1-Adapts E.A. Poe & Harlan Ellison stories. 2-E.A. Poe & H.P. Lovecraft adaptations 3.50
1-($4.95, 52 pgs.)-Deluxe edition w/Tim Vigil-a not in regular #1; stiff-c; Bolton painted-c 5.00

WEIRD TALES OF THE FUTURE
S.P.M. Publ. No. 1-4/Aragon Publ. No. 5-8: Mar, 1952 - No. 8, July-Aug, 1953

1-Andru-a(2); Wolverton partial-c 107 214 321 674 1137 1600
2,3-Wolverton-c/a(3) each. 2- "Jumpin Jupiter" satire by Wolverton begins, ends #5 147 294 441 926 1563 2200
4- "Jumpin Jupiter" satire, partial Wolverton-c 128 256 384 806 1366 1925
5-Wolverton-c/a(2); "Jumpin Jupiter" satire 147 294 441 926 1563 2200

Weird War Tales #28 © DC

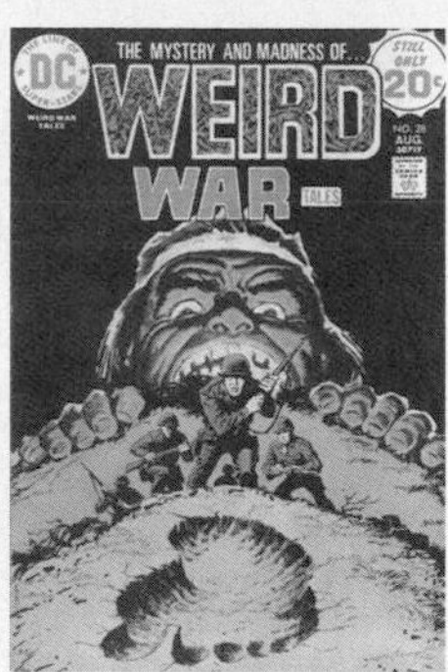

Weird Western Tales #1 © DC

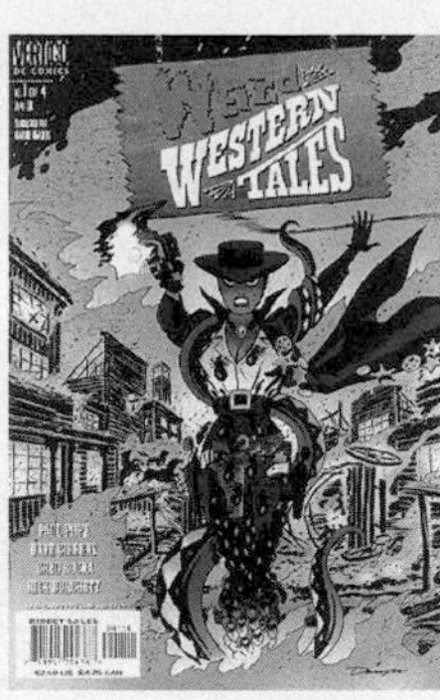

Welcome Back, Kotter #5 © Wolper Prod.

	GD 2.0	VG 4.0	FN 6.0	VF 8.0	VF/NM 9.0	NM- 9.2
6-Bernard Baily-c	55	110	165	347	586	825
7- "The Mind Movers" from the art to Wolverton's "Brain Bats of Venus" from Mr. Mystery #7 which was cut apart, pasted up, partially redrawn, and rewritten by Harry Kantor, the editor; Baily-c	127	254	381	800	1350	1900
8-Reprints Weird Mysteries #1(10/52) minus cover; gory cover showing heart ripped out, by B. Baily	82	164	246	517	871	1225

WEIRD TALES OF THE MACABRE (Magazine)
Atlas/Seaboard Publ.: Jan, 1975 - No. 2, Mar, 1975 (75¢, B&W)

	GD 2.0	VG 4.0	FN 6.0	VF 8.0	VF/NM 9.0	NM- 9.2
1-Jeff Jones painted-c; Boyette-a	3	6	9	17	25	32
2-Boris Vallejo painted-c; Severin-a	3	6	9	20	30	40

WEIRD TERROR (Also see Horrific)
Allen Hardy Associates (Comic Media): Sept, 1952 - No. 13, Sept, 1954

	GD 2.0	VG 4.0	FN 6.0	VF 8.0	VF/NM 9.0	NM- 9.2
1- "Portrait of Death", adapted from Lovecraft's "Pickman's Model"; lingerie panels, Hitler story	58	116	174	365	620	875
2,3: 2-Text on Marquis DeSade, Torture, Demonology, & St. Elmo's Fire. 3-Extreme violence, whipping, torture; article on sin eating, dowsing	48	96	144	298	499	700
4-Dismemberment, decapitation, article on human flesh for sale, Devil, whipping	48	96	144	298	499	700
5-Article on body snatching, mutilation; cannibalism story	41	82	123	256	428	600
6-Dismemberment, decapitation, man hit by lightning	45	90	135	279	465	650
7-Body burning in fireplace-c	41	82	123	260	435	610
8,11: 8-Decapitation story; Ambrose Bierce adapt. 11-End of the world story w/atomic blast panels; Tothish-a by Bill Discount	41	82	123	250	428	600
9,10,13: 13-Severed head panels	37	74	111	220	353	485
12-Discount-a	37	74	111	220	353	485

NOTE: ***Don Heck*** *a-most issues; c-1-13.* ***Landau*** *a-6.* ***Morisi*** *a-2-5, 7, 9, 12.* ***Palais*** *a-1, 5, 6, 8(2), 10, 12.* ***Powell*** *a-10.* ***Ravielli*** *a-11, 20.*

WEIRD THRILLERS
Ziff-Davis Publ. Co. (Approved Comics): Sept-Oct, 1951 - No. 5, Oct-Nov, 1952 (#2-5: painted-c)

	GD 2.0	VG 4.0	FN 6.0	VF 8.0	VF/NM 9.0	NM- 9.2
1-Rondo Hatton photo-c	88	176	264	554	940	1325
2-Toth, Anderson, Colan-a	62	124	186	391	663	935
3-Two Powell, Tuska-a; classic-c; Everett-a	87	174	261	548	924	1300
4-Kubert, Tuska-a	59	118	177	372	629	885
5-Powell-a	54	108	162	340	575	810

NOTE: ***M. Anderson*** *a-2, 3.* ***Roussos*** *a-4. #2, 3 reprinted in Nightmare #10 & 13; #4, 5 reprinted in Amazing Ghost Stories #16 & #15.*

WEIRD VAMPIRE TALES (Comic magazine)
Modern Day Periodical Pub.: V3 #1, Apr, 1979 - V5 #3, Mar, 1982 (B&W)

	GD 2.0	VG 4.0	FN 6.0	VF 8.0	VF/NM 9.0	NM- 9.2
V3 #1 (4/79) First issue, no V1 or V2	4	8	12	24	37	50
V3 #2-4	3	6	9	18	27	35
V4 #2 (4/80), V4 #3 (7/80) (no V4 #1)	3	6	9	16	23	30
V5 #1 (1/81), V5 #2 (two issues, 4/81 & 8/81)	3	6	9	16	23	30
V5 #3 (3/82) Last issue; low print	3	6	9	20	30	40

WEIRD WAR TALES
National Periodical Publ./DC Comics: Sept-Oct, 1971 - No. 124, June, 1983 (#1-5: 52 pgs.)

	GD 2.0	VG 4.0	FN 6.0	VF 8.0	VF/NM 9.0	NM- 9.2
1-Kubert-a in #1-4,7; c-1-7	22	44	66	157	291	425
2,3-Drucker-a: 2-Crandall-a. 3-Heath-a	10	20	30	68	119	170
4,5: 5-Toth-a; Heath-a	8	16	24	54	90	125
6,7,9,10: 6,10-Toth-a. 7-Heath-a	5	10	15	34	55	75
8-Neal Adams-c/a(i)	6	12	18	41	66	90
11-20	3	6	9	19	29	38
21-35	3	6	9	14	20	25
36-(68 pgs.)-Crandall & Kubert-r/#2; Heath-r/#3; Kubert-c	3	6	9	16	22	28
37-50: 38,39-Kubert-c	2	4	6	8	11	14
51-63: 58-Hitler-c/app. 60-Hindenburg-c/s	2	4	6	8	10	12
64-Frank Miller-a (1st DC work)	4	8	12	22	34	45
65-67,69-89,91,92: 89-Nazi Apes-c/s.	1	2	3	5	6	8
68-Frank Miller-a (2nd DC work)	3	6	9	16	23	30
90-Hitler app.	1	2	3	5	7	9
93-Intro/origin Creature Commandos	1	3	4	6	8	10
94-Return of War that Time Forgot; dinosaur-c/s	2	4	6	8	10	12
95,96,98,102-123: 98-Sphinx-c. 102-Creature Commandos battle Hitler. 110-Origin/1st app. Medusa. 123-1st app. Captain Spaceman	1	2	3	5	6	8
97,99,100,101,124: 99-War that Time Forgot. 100-Creature Commandos in War that Time Forgot. 101-Intro/origin G.I. Robot	1	2	3	5	7	9

NOTE: ***Chaykin*** *a-76, 82.* ***Ditko*** *a-95, 99, 104-106.* ***Evans*** *c-73, 74, 83, 85.* ***Kane*** *c-116, 118.* ***Kubert*** *c-55, 58, 60, 62, 72, 75-81, 87, 88, 90-96, 100, 103, 104, 106, 107.* ***Newton*** *a-122.* ***Starlin*** *c-89.* ***Sutton*** *a-91, 92, 103.* ***Creature Commandos*** *-93, 97, 100, 102, 105, 108-112, 114, 116-119, 121, 124.* ***G.I. Robot*** *- 101, 108, 111, 113, 116-118, 120, 122.* ***War That Time Forgot*** *- 94, 99, 100, 103, 106, 109, 120.*

WEIRD WAR TALES
DC Comics (Vertigo): June, 1997 - No. 4, Sept, 1997 ($2.50)

	GD 2.0	VG 4.0	FN 6.0	VF 8.0	VF/NM 9.0	NM- 9.2
1-4-Anthology by various						3.00

WEIRD WAR TALES
DC Comics (Vertigo): April, 2000 ($4.95, one-shot)

	GD 2.0	VG 4.0	FN 6.0	VF 8.0	VF/NM 9.0	NM- 9.2
1-Anthology by various; last Biukovic-a						5.00

WEIRD WESTERN TALES (Formerly All-Star Western)
National Per. Publ./DC Comics: No. 12, June-July, 1972 - No. 70, Aug, 1980

	GD 2.0	VG 4.0	FN 6.0	VF 8.0	VF/NM 9.0	NM- 9.2
12 (52 pgs.) 3rd app. Jonah Hex; Bat Lash, Pow Wow Smith reprints; El Diablo by Neal Adams/Wrightson	13	26	39	90	160	230
13-Jonah Hex-c & 4th app.; Neal Adams-a	8	16	24	58	97	135
14-Toth-a	6	12	18	43	69	95
15-Adams-c/a; no Jonah Hex	4	8	12	26	41	55
16,17,19,20	4	8	12	26	41	55
18,20: 18 1st all Jonah Hex issue (7-8/73) & begins. 20 Origin Jonah Hex	6	12	18	37	59	80
21-28,30: Jonah Hex in all	3	6	9	19	29	38
31-38: Jonah Hex in all. 38-Last Jonah Hex	3	6	9	16	23	30
39-Origin/1st app. Scalphunter & begins	2	4	6	10	14	18
40-47,50-69: 64-Bat Lash-c/story	1	2	3	5	6	8
48,49: (44 pgs.)-1st & 2nd app. Cinnamon	1	2	3	5	7	9
70-Last issue	2	4	6	8	10	12

NOTE: ***Alcala*** *a-16, 17.* ***Evans*** *inks-39-48; c-39i, 40, 47.* ***G. Kane*** *a-15, 20.* ***Kubert*** *c-12, 33.* ***Starlin*** *c-44, 45.* ***Wildey*** *a-26. 48 & 49 are 44 pgs.*

WEIRD WESTERN TALES
DC Comics (Vertigo): Apr, 2001 - No. 4, Jul, 2001 ($2.50, limited series)

	GD 2.0	VG 4.0	FN 6.0	VF 8.0	VF/NM 9.0	NM- 9.2
1-4-Anthology by various						2.50

WEIRD WONDER TALES
Marvel Comics Group: Dec, 1973 - No. 22, May, 1977

	GD 2.0	VG 4.0	FN 6.0	VF 8.0	VF/NM 9.0	NM- 9.2
1-Wolverton-r/Mystic #6 (Eye of Doom)	3	6	9	17	25	32
2-10	2	4	6	11	16	20
11-22: 16-18-Venus-r by Everett from Venus #19,18 & 17. 19-22-r/Dr. Droom (re-named Dr. Druid) by Kirby. 22-New art by Byrne	2	4	6	10	14	18
15-17-(30¢-c variants, limited distribution)(4-8/76)	3	6	9	15	21	27

NOTE: *All 1950s & early 1960s reprints.* ***Check*** *r-1.* ***Colan*** *r-17.* ***Ditko*** *r-4, 5, 10-13, 19-21.* ***Drucker*** *r-12, 20.* ***Everett*** *r-3(Spellbound #16), 6(Astonishing #10), 9(Adv. Into Mystery #5).* ***Heath*** *a-13r.* ***Heck*** *a-1or, 14r.* ***Gil Kane*** *c-1, 2, 10.* ***Kirby*** *r-4, 6, 10, 11, 13, 15-22; c-17, 19, 20.* ***Krigstein*** *r-19.* ***Kubert*** *r-22.* ***Maneely*** *r-8.* ***Mooney*** *r-7p.* ***Powell*** *r-3, 7.* ***Torres*** *r-7.* ***Wildey*** *r-2, 7.*

WEIRD WORLDS (See Adventures Into...)

WEIRD WORLDS (Magazine)
Eerie Publications: V1#10(12/70), V2#1(2/71) - No. 4, Aug, 1971 (52 pgs.)

	GD 2.0	VG 4.0	FN 6.0	VF 8.0	VF/NM 9.0	NM- 9.2
V1#10-Sci-fi/horror	4	8	12	28	44	60
V2#1-4	4	8	12	24	37	50

WEIRD WORLDS (Also see Ironwolf: Fires of the Revolution)
National Periodical Publications: Aug-Sept, 1972 - No. 9, Jan-Feb, 1974; No. 10, Oct-Nov, 1974 (All 20¢ issues)

	GD 2.0	VG 4.0	FN 6.0	VF 8.0	VF/NM 9.0	NM- 9.2
1-Edgar Rice Burrough's John Carter Warlord of Mars & David Innes begin (1st DC app.); Kubert-c	2	4	6	13	18	22
2-4: 2-Infantino/Orlando-c. 3-Murphy Anderson-c. 4-Kaluta-a	2	4	6	8	11	14
5-7: .5-Kaluta-c. 7-Last John Carter.	1	3	4	6	8	10
8-10: 8-Iron Wolf begins by Chaykin (1st app.)	1	3	4	6	8	10

NOTE: ***Neal Adams*** *a-2i, 3i. John Carter by* ***Andersonin*** *#1-3.* ***Chaykin*** *c-7, 8.* ***Kaluta*** *a-4; c-4-6, 10.* ***Orlando*** *a-4i; c-2, 3, 4i.* ***Wrightson*** *a-2i, 4i.*

WELCOME BACK, KOTTER (TV) (See Limited Collectors' Edition #57 for unpublished #11)
National Periodical Publ./DC Comics: Nov, 1976 - No. 10, Mar-Apr, 1978

	GD 2.0	VG 4.0	FN 6.0	VF 8.0	VF/NM 9.0	NM- 9.2
1-Sparling-a(p)	3	6	9	16	22	28
2-10: 3-Estrada-a	2	4	6	9	13	16

WELCOME SANTA (See March of Comics #63,183)

WELCOME TO HOLSOM
Gospel Publishing House: 2005 - Present (no cover price)

	GD 2.0	VG 4.0	FN 6.0	VF 8.0	VF/NM 9.0	NM- 9.2
1-12-Craig Schutt-s/Steven Butler-a						2.50

WELCOME TO THE LITTLE SHOP OF HORRORS
Roger Corman's Cosmic Comics: May, 1995 -No. 3, July, 1995 ($2.50, limited series)

	GD 2.0	VG 4.0	FN 6.0	VF 8.0	VF/NM 9.0	NM- 9.2
1-3						2.50

WELCOME TO TRANQUILITY
DC Comics (WildStorm): Feb, 2007 - No. 12, Jan, 2008 ($2.99)

Wendy, the Good Little Witch #1 © HARV

Werewolf By Night V2#6 © MAR

Western Adventures #3 © ACE

	GD 2.0	VG 4.0	FN 6.0	VF 8.0	VF/NM 9.0	NM- 9.2

1-12: 1-Simone-s/Googe-a; two covers by Googe and Campbell. 8-Pearson-a 3.00
...: Armageddon 1 (1/08, $2.99) Gage-s/Googe-a 3.00
... Book One TPB (2008, $19.99) r/#1-6 and variant cover gallery 20.00
... Book Two TPB (2008, $19.99) r/#7-12; sketch pages 20.00

WELLS FARGO (See Tales of...)

WENDY AND THE NEW KIDS ON THE BLOCK
Harvey Comics: Mar, 1991 - No. 3, July, 1991 ($1.25)
1-3 2.50

WENDY DIGEST
Harvey Comics: Oct, 1990 - No. 5, Mar, 1992 ($1.75, digest size)
1-5 4.00

WENDY PARKER COMICS
Atlas Comics (OMC): July, 1953 - No. 8, July, 1954
1 11 22 33 60 83 105
2 8 16 24 44 57 70
3-8 8 16 24 40 50 60

WENDY, THE GOOD LITTLE WITCH (TV)
Harvey Publ.: 8/60 - #82, 11/73; #83, 8/74 - #93, 4/76; #94, 9/90 - #97, 12/90
1-Wendy & Casper the Friendly Ghost begin 28 56 84 203 377 550
2 14 28 42 99 175 250
3-5 10 20 30 68 119 170
6-10 7 14 21 49 80 110
11-20 6 12 18 37 59 80
21-30 4 8 12 28 44 60
31-50 3 6 9 18 27 35
51-64,66-69 2 4 6 13 18 22
65 (2/71)-Wendy origin. 3 6 9 17 25 32
70-74: All 52 pg. Giants 3 6 9 16 23 30
75-93 2 4 6 9 13 16
94-97 (1990, $1.00-c): 94-Has #194 on-c 5.00
(See Casper the Friendly Ghost #20 & Harvey Hits #7, 16, 21, 23, 27, 30, 33)

WENDY THE GOOD LITTLE WITCH (2nd Series)
Harvey Comics: Apr, 1991 - No. 15, Aug, 1994 ($1.00/$1.25 #7-11/$1.50 #12-15)
1-15-Reprints Wendy & Casper stories. 12-Bunny app. 3.00

WENDY WITCH WORLD
Harvey Publications: 10/61; No. 2, 9/62 - No. 52, 12/73; No. 53, 9/74
1-(25¢, 68 pg. Giants begin) 14 28 42 102 181 260
2-5 8 16 24 52 86 120
6-10 6 12 18 37 59 80
11-20 4 8 12 28 44 60
21-30 4 8 12 22 34 45
31-39: 39-Last 68 pg. issue 3 6 9 17 25 32
40-45: 52 pg. issues 2 4 6 13 18 22
46-53 2 4 6 9 13 16

WEREWOLF (Super Hero) (Also see Dracula & Frankenstein)
Dell Publishing Co.: Dec, 1966 - No. 3, April, 1967
1-1st app. 4 8 12 22 34 45
2,3 3 6 9 14 19 24

WEREWOLF BY NIGHT (See Giant-Size..., Marvel Spotlight #2-4 & Power Record Comics)
Marvel Comics Group: Sept, 1972 - No. 43, Mar, 1977
1-Ploog-a cont'd. from Marvel Spotlight #4 11 22 33 79 140 200
2 6 12 18 39 62 85
3-5 4 8 12 28 44 60
6-10 4 8 12 22 34 45
11-14,16-20 3 6 9 16 23 30
15-New origin Werewolf; Dracula-c/story cont'd from Tomb of Dracula #18;
classic Ploog-c 4 8 12 24 37 50
21-31 2 4 6 11 16 20
32-Origin & 1st app. Moon Knight (8/75) 10 20 30 68 119 170
33-2nd app. Moon Knight 5 10 15 34 55 75
34,36,38-43: 35-Starlin/Wrightson-c 2 4 6 10 14 18
37-Moon Knight app; part Wrightson-c 3 6 9 18 27 35
38,39-(30¢-c variants, limited distribution)(5,7/76) 3 6 9 20 30 40
NOTE: ***Bolle** a-6i. **G. Kane** a-11p, 12p; c-21, 22, 24-30, 34p. **Mooney** a-7i. **Ploog** 1-4p, 5, 6p, 7p, 13-16p; c-5-8, 13-16. **Reinman** a-8i. **Sutton** a(i)-9, 11, 16, 35.*

WEREWOLF BY NIGHT (Vol. 2, continues in Strange Tales #1 (9/98))
Marvel Comics Group: Feb, 1998 - No. 6, July, 1998 ($2.99)
1-6-Manco-a: 2-Two covers. 6-Ghost Rider-c/app. 3.00

WEREWOLVES & VAMPIRES (Magazine)
Charlton Comics: 1962 (One Shot)
1 9 18 27 60 100 140

WEST COAST AVENGERS
Marvel Comics Group: Sept, 1984 - No. 4, Dec, 1984 (lim. series, Mando paper)
1-Origin & 1st app. W.C. Avengers (Hawkeye, Iron Man, Mockingbird & Tigra) 4.00
2-4 3.00

WEST COAST AVENGERS (Becomes Avengers West Coast #48 on)
Marvel Comics Group: Oct, 1985 - No. 47, Aug, 1989
V2#1-41 3.00
42-47: 42-Byrne-a(p)/scripts begin. 46-Byrne-c; 1st app. Great Lakes Avengers 3.00
Annual 1-3 (1986-1988): 3-Evolutionary War app. 3.00
Annual 4 (1989, $2.00)-Atlantis Attacks; Byrne/Austin-a 3.00

WESTERN ACTION
I. W. Enterprises: No. 7, 1964
7-Reprints Cow Puncher #? by Avon 2 4 6 8 11 14

WESTERN ACTION
Atlas/Seaboard Publ.: Feb, 1975
1-Kid Cody by Wildey & The Comanche Kid stories; intro. The Renegade
1 3 4 6 8 10

WESTERN ACTION THRILLERS
Dell Publishers: Apr, 1937 (10¢, square binding; 100 pgs.)
1-Buffalo Bill, The Texas Kid, Laramie Joe, Two-Gun Thompson, & Wild West Bill app.
83 166 249 523 887 1250

WESTERN ADVENTURES COMICS (Western Love Trails #7 on)
Ace Magazines: Oct, 1948 - No. 6, Aug, 1949
nn(#1)-Sheriff Sal, The Cross-Draw Kid, Sam Bass begin
21 42 63 125 200 275
nn(#2)(12/48) 13 26 39 74 105 135
nn(#3)(2/49)-Used in **SOTI**, pgs. 30,31 14 28 42 76 108 140
4-6 11 22 33 62 86 110

WESTERN BANDITS
Avon Periodicals: 1952 (Painted-c)
1-Butch Cassidy, The Daltons by Larsen; Kinstler-a; c-part-r/paperback
Avon Western Novel #1 16 32 48 92 144 195

WESTERN BANDIT TRAILS (See Approved Comics)
St. John Publishing Co.: Jan, 1949 - No. 3, July, 1949
1-Tuska-a; Baker-c; Blue Monk, Ventrilo app. 27 54 81 158 254 350
2-Baker-c 21 42 63 123 197 270
3-Baker-c/a; Tuska-a 25 50 75 147 236 325

WESTERN COMICS (See Super DC Giant #15)
National Per. Publ: Jan-Feb, 1948 - No. 85, Jan-Feb, 1961 (1-27: 52pgs.)
1-Wyoming Kid & his horse Racer, The Vigilante in "Jesse James Rides Again" (Meskin-a),
Cowboy Marshal, Rodeo Rick begin 77 154 231 481 816 1150
2 37 74 111 215 345 475
3,4-Last Vigilante 33 66 99 192 309 425
5-Nighthawk & his horse Nightwind begin (not in #6); Captain Tootsie by Beck
28 56 84 162 261 360
6,7,9,10 21 42 63 125 200 275
8-Origin Wyoming Kid; 2 pg. pin-ups of rodeo queens
35 70 105 203 327 450
11-20 18 36 54 103 162 220
21-40: 24-Starr-a. 27-Last 52 pgs. 28-Flag-c 14 28 42 82 121 160
41,42,44-49: 49-Last precode issue (2/55) 14 28 42 80 115 150
43-Pow Wow Smith begins, ends #85 14 28 42 81 118 155
50-60 12 24 36 67 94 120
61-85-Last Wyoming Kid. 77-Origin Matt Savage Trail Boss. 82-1st app. Fleetfoot,
Pow Wow's girlfriend 10 20 30 56 76 95
NOTE: ***G. Kane, Infantino** art in most. **Meskin** a-1-4. **Moreira** a-28-39. **Post** a-3-5.*

WESTERN CRIME BUSTERS
Trojan Magazines: Sept, 1950 - No. 10, Mar-Apr, 1952
1-Six-Gun Smith, Wilma West, K-Bar-Kate, & Fighting Bob Dale begin; headlight-a
36 72 108 212 341 470
2 19 38 57 109 172 235
3-5: 3-Myron Fass-c 18 36 54 103 162 220
6-Wood-a 32 64 96 186 298 410
7-Six-Gun Smith by Wood 32 64 96 186 298 410

Western Comics #7 © DC

Western Hearts #1 © STD

Western Love #1 © PRIZE

	GD 2.0	VG 4.0	FN 6.0	VF 8.0	VF/NM 9.0	NM- 9.2
8	18	36	54	103	162	220
9-Tex Gordon & Wilma West by Wood; Lariat Lucy app.	32	64	96	186	298	410
10-Wood-a	29	58	87	169	272	375

WESTERN CRIME CASES (Formerly Indian Warriors #7,8; becomes The Outlaws #10 on)
Star Publications: No. 9, Dec, 1951

	GD	VG	FN	VF	VF/NM	NM-
9-White Rider & Super Horse; L. B. Cole-c	21	42	63	123	197	270

WESTERNER, THE (Wild Bill Pecos)
"Wanted" Comic Group/Toytown/Patches: No. 14, June, 1948 - No. 41, Dec, 1951 (#14-31: 52 pgs.)

	GD	VG	FN	VF	VF/NM	NM-
14	15	30	45	85	130	175
15-17,19-21: 19-Meskin-a	9	18	27	52	69	85
18,22-25-Krigstein-a	11	22	33	60	83	105
26(4/50)-Origin & 1st app. Calamity Kate, series ends #32; Krigstein-a	14	28	42	78	112	145
27-Krigstein-a(2)	13	26	39	74	105	135
28-41: 33-Quest app. 37-Lobo, the Wolf Boy begins	8	16	24	40	50	60

NOTE: ***Mort Lawrence** a-20-27, 29, 37, 39; c-19, 22-24, 26, 27. **Leav** c-14-18, 20, 31. **Syd Shores** a-39; c-34, 35, 37-41.*

WESTERNER, THE
Super Comics: 1964

	GD	VG	FN	VF	VF/NM	NM-
Super Reprint 15-17: 15-r/Oklahoma Kid #? 16-r/Crack West. #65; Severin-c; Crandall-r. 17-r/Blazing Western #2; Severin-c	2	4	6	8	11	14

WESTERN FIGHTERS
Hillman Periodicals/Star Publ.: Apr-May, 1948 - V4#7, Mar-Apr, 1953 (#1-V3#2: 52 pgs.)

	GD	VG	FN	VF	VF/NM	NM-
V1#1-Simon & Kirby-c	36	72	108	212	341	470
2-Not Kirby-a	14	28	42	80	115	150
3-Fuje-c	12	24	36	67	94	120
4-Krigstein, Ingels, Fuje-a	13	26	39	74	105	135
5,6,8,9,12	10	20	30	54	72	90
7,10-Krigstein-a	11	22	33	62	86	110
11-Williamson/Frazetta-a	30	60	90	174	280	385
V2#1-Krigstein-a	11	22	33	62	86	110
2-12: 4-Berg-a	8	16	24	44	57	70
V3#1-11,V4#1,4-7	8	16	24	42	54	65
12,V4#2,3-Krigstein-a	11	22	33	62	86	110
3-D 1(12/53, 25¢, Star Publ.)-Came w/glasses; L. B. Cole-c	36	72	108	212	341	470

NOTE: ***Kinstlerish** a-V2#6, 8, 9, 12; V3#2, 5-7, 11, 12; V4#1(plus cover). **McWilliams** a-11. **Powell** a-V2#2. **Reinman** a-1-12, V4#3. **Rowich** c-5, 6i. **Starr** a-5.*

WESTERN FRONTIER
P. L. Publishers: Apr-May, 1951 - No. 7, 1952

	GD	VG	FN	VF	VF/NM	NM-
1	14	28	42	76	108	140
2	8	16	24	44	57	70
3-7	7	14	21	37	46	55

WESTERN GUNFIGHTERS (1st Series) (Apache Kid #11-19)
Atlas Comics (CPS): No. 20, June, 1956 - No. 27, Aug, 1957

	GD	VG	FN	VF	VF/NM	NM-
20	13	26	39	74	105	135
21-Crandall-a	13	26	39	74	105	135
22-Wood & Powell-a	18	36	54	103	162	220
23,24: 23-Williamson-a. 24-Toth-a	13	26	39	74	105	135
25-27	10	20	30	54	72	90

NOTE: ***Berg** a-20. **Colan** a-20, 26, 27. **Crandall** a-21. **Heath** a-25. **Maneely** a-24, 25; c-22, 23, 25. **Morisi** a-24. **Morrow** a-26. **Pakula** a-23. **Severin** c-20, 27. **Torres** a-26. **Woodbridge** a-27.*

WESTERN GUNFIGHTERS (2nd Series)
Marvel Comics Group: Aug, 1970 - No. 33, Nov, 1975 (#1-6: 25¢, 68 pgs.)

	GD	VG	FN	VF	VF/NM	NM-
1-Ghost Rider begins; Fort Rango, Renegades & Gunhawk app.	5	10	15	32	51	70
2,3,5,6: 2-Origin Nightwind (Apache Kid's horse)	3	6	9	18	27	35
4-Barry Smith-a	3	6	9	21	32	42
7-(52 pgs) Origin Ghost Rider retold	3	6	9	16	23	30
8-13: 10-Origin Black Rider. 12-Origin Matt Slade	2	4	6	11	16	20
14-Steranko-c	3	6	9	14	20	25
15-20	2	4	6	8	11	14
21-33	2	4	6	8	10	12

NOTE: ***Baker** r-2, 3. **Colan** r-2. **Drucker** r-3. **Everett** a-6i. **G. Kane** c-29, 31. **Kirby** a-1p(r), 5, 10-12; c-19, 21. **Kubert** r-2. **Maneely** r-2, 10. **Morrow** r-29. **Severin** c-10. **Shores** a-3, 4. **Barry Smith** a-4. **Steranko** c-14. **Sutton** a-1, 2i, 5, 4. **Torres** r-26('57). **Wildey** r-8, 9. **Williamson** r-2, 18. **Woodbridge** r-27('57). Renegades in #4, 5; Ghost Rider in #1-7.*

WESTERN HEARTS
Standard Comics: Dec, 1949 - No. 10, Mar, 1952 (All photo-c)

	GD	VG	FN	VF	VF/NM	NM-
1-Severin-a; Whip Wilson & Reno Browne photo-c	23	46	69	133	214	295
2-Beverly Tyler & Jerome Courtland photo-c from movie "Palomino"; Williamson/Frazetta-a (2 pgs.)	23	46	69	133	214	295
3-Rex Allen photo-c	14	28	42	80	115	150
4-7,10: 4-Severin & Elder, Al Carreno-a. 5-Ray Milland & Hedy Lamarr photo-c from movie "Copper Canyon". 6-Fred MacMurray & Irene Dunn photo-c from movie "Never a Dull Moment". 7-Jock Mahoney photo-c. 10-Bill Williams & Jane Nigh photo-c	14	28	42	78	112	145
8-Randolph Scott & Janis Carter photo-c from "Santa Fe"; Severin & Elder-a	14	28	42	80	115	150
9-Whip Wilson & Reno Browne photo-c; Severin & Elder-a	15	30	45	83	124	165

WESTERN HERO (Wow Comics #1-69; Real Western Hero #70-75)
Fawcett Publications: No. 76, Mar, 1949 - No. 112, Mar, 1952

	GD	VG	FN	VF	VF/NM	NM-
76(#1, 52 pgs.)-Tom Mix, Hopalong Cassidy, Monte Hale, Gabby Hayes, Young Falcon (ends #78,80), & Big Bow and Little Arrow (ends #102,105) begin; painted-c begin	23	46	69	132	209	285
77 (52 pgs.)	14	28	42	82	121	160
78,80-82 (52 pgs.): 81-Capt. Tootsie by Beck	14	28	42	80	115	150
79,83 (36 pgs.): 83-Last painted-c	13	26	39	72	101	130
84-86,88-90 (52 pgs.): 84-Photo-c begin, end #112. 86-Last Hopalong Cassidy	13	26	39	74	105	135
87,91,95,99 (36 pgs.): 87-Bill Boyd begins, ends #95	11	22	33	64	90	115
92-94,96-98,101 (52 pgs.): 96-Tex Ritter begins. 101-Red Eagle app.	12	24	36	69	97	125
100 (52 pgs.)	13	26	39	74	105	135
102-111: 102-Begin 36 pg. issues	11	22	33	64	90	115
112-Last issue	12	24	36	69	97	125

NOTE: *1/2 to 1 pg. Rocky Lane (Carnation) in 80-83, 86, 88, 97. Photo covers feature Hopalong Cassidy #84, 86, 89; Tom Mix #85, 87, 90, 92, 94, 97; Monte Hale #88, 91, 93, 95, 98, 100, 104, 107, 110; Tex Ritter #96, 99, 101, 105, 108, 111; Gabby Hayes #103.*

WESTERN KID (1st Series)
Atlas Comics (CPC): Dec, 1954 - No. 17, Aug, 1957

	GD	VG	FN	VF	VF/NM	NM-
1-Origin; The Western Kid (Tex Dawson), his stallion Whirlwind & dog Lightning begin	18	36	54	107	169	230
2 (2/55)-Last pre-code	11	22	33	62	86	110
3-8	10	20	30	54	72	90
9,10-Williamson-a in both (4 pgs. each)	10	20	30	56	76	95
11-17	8	16	24	44	57	70

NOTE: ***Ayers** a-6, 7. **Maneely** c-2-7, 10, 13-15. **Romita** a-1-17; c-1, 12. **Severin** c-16, 17.*

WESTERN KID, THE (2nd Series)
Marvel Comics Group: Dec, 1971 - No. 5, Aug, 1972 (All 20¢ issues)

	GD	VG	FN	VF	VF/NM	NM-
1-Reprints; Romita-c/a(3)	3	6	9	16	23	30
2,4,5: 2-Romita-a; Severin-c. 4-Everett-r	2	4	6	10	14	18
3-Williamson-a	2	4	6	13	18	22

WESTERN KILLERS
Fox Features Syndicate: nn, July?, 1948; No. 60, Sept, 1948 - No. 64, May, 1949; No. 6, July, 1949

	GD	VG	FN	VF	VF/NM	NM-
nn(#59?)(nd, F&J Trading Co.)-Range Busters; formerly Blue Beetle #57?	24	48	72	140	225	310
60 (#1, 9/48)-Extreme violence; lingerie panel	26	52	78	152	244	335
61-Jack Cole, Starr-a	21	42	63	123	197	270
62-64, 6 (#6-exist?)	19	38	57	112	176	240

WESTERN LIFE ROMANCES (My Friend Irma #3 on?)
Marvel Comics (IPP): Dec, 1949 - No. 2, Mar, 1950 (52 pgs.)

	GD	VG	FN	VF	VF/NM	NM-
1-Whip Wilson & Reno Browne photo-c	20	40	60	115	183	250
2-Audie Murphy & Gale Storm photo-c	16	32	48	94	147	200

WESTERN LOVE
Prize Publ.: July-Aug, 1949 - No. 5, Mar-Apr, 1950 (All photo-c & 52 pgs.)

	GD	VG	FN	VF	VF/NM	NM-
1-S&K-a; Randolph Scott photo-c from movie "Canadian Pacific" (see Prize Comics #76)	31	62	93	181	291	400
2,5-S&K-a: 2-Whip Wilson & Reno Browne photo-c. 5-Dale Robertson photo-c	23	46	69	133	214	295
3,4: 3-Pat Williams photo-c	15	30	45	85	130	175

NOTE: ***Meskin & Severin/Elder** a-2-5.*

WESTERN LOVE TRAILS (Formerly Western Adventures)
Ace Magazines (A. A. Wyn): No. 7, Nov, 1949 - No. 9, Mar, 1950

	GD	VG	FN	VF	VF/NM	NM-
7	12	24	36	67	94	120

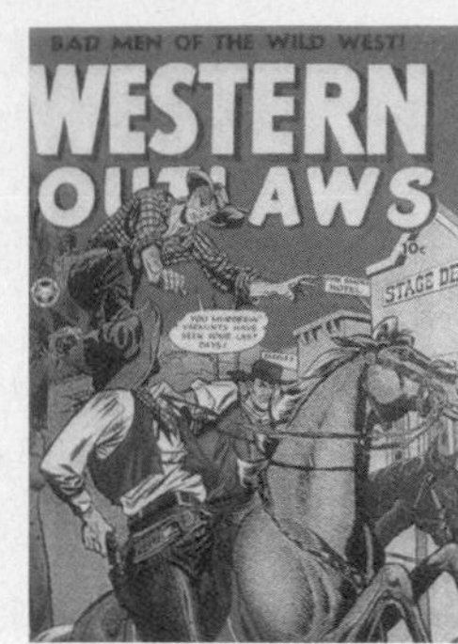

Western Outlaws #19 © FOX

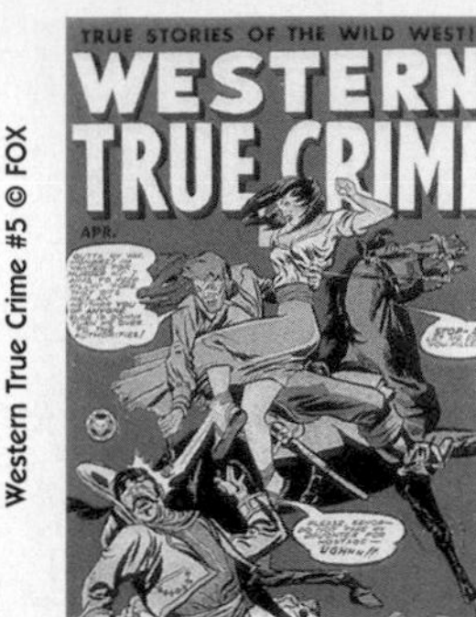

Western True Crime #5 © FOX

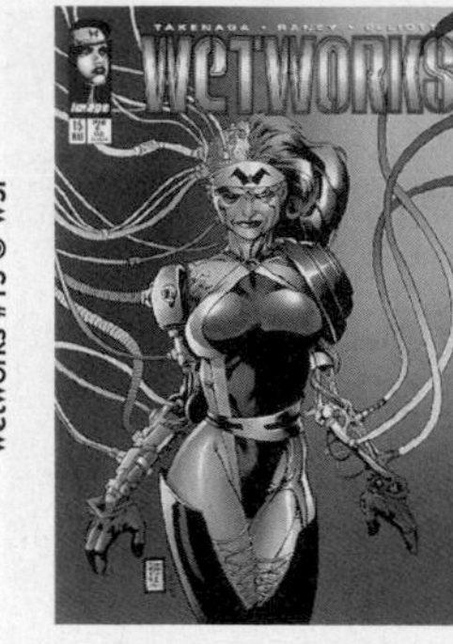

Wetworks #13 © WSP

GD 2.0 | VG 4.0 | FN 6.0 | VF 8.0 | VF/NM 9.0 | NM- 9.2

GD 2.0 | VG 4.0 | FN 6.0 | VF 8.0 | VF/NM 9.0 | NM- 9.2

8,9 10 20 30 54 72 90

WESTERN MARSHAL (See Steve Donovan...)
Dell Publishing Co.: No. 534, 2-4/54 - No. 640, 7/55 (Based on Ernest Haycox's "Trailtown")
Four Color 534 (#1)-Kinstler-a 6 12 18 39 62 85
Four Color 591 (10/54), 613 (2/55), 640-All Kinstler-a 5 10 15 34 55 75

WESTERN OUTLAWS (Junior Comics #9-16; My Secret Life #22 on)
Fox Features Syndicate: No. 17, Sept, 1948 - No. 21, May, 1949
17-Kamen-a; Iger shop-a in all; 1 pg. "Death and the Devil Pills" r-in Ghostly Weird #122
32 64 96 186 298 410
18-21 19 38 57 109 172 235

WESTERN OUTLAWS
Atlas Comics (ACI No. 1-14/WPI No. 15-21): Feb, 1954 - No. 21, Aug, 1957
1-Heath, Powell-a; Maneely hanging-c 21 42 63 123 197 270
2 12 24 36 67 94 120
3-10: 7-Violent-a by R.Q. Sale 10 20 30 54 72 90
11,14-Williamson-a in both (6 pgs. each) 11 22 33 60 83 105
12,18,20,21: Severin covers 9 18 27 50 65 80
13,15: 13-Baker-a. 15-Torres-a 10 20 30 54 72 90
16-Williamson text illo 9 18 27 50 65 80
17,19-Crandall-a. 17-Williamson text illo 10 20 30 54 72 90
NOTE: ***Ayers** a-7, 10, 18, 20. **Bolle** a-21. **Colan** a-5, 10, 11, 17. **Drucker** a-11. **Everett** a-9, 10. **Heath** a-1; c-3, 4, 8, 16. **Kubert** a-9p. **Maneely** a-13, 16, 17, 19; c-1, 5, 7, 9, 10, 12, 13. **Morisi** a-18. **Powell** a-3, 16. **Romita** a-7, 13. **Severin** a-8, 16, 19; c-17, 18, 20, 21. **Tuska** a-6, 15.*

WESTERN OUTLAWS & SHERIFFS (Formerly Best Western)
Marvel/Atlas Comics (IPC): No. 60, Dec, 1949 - No. 73, June, 1952
60 (52 pgs.) 21 42 63 123 197 270
61-65: 61-Photo-c 16 32 48 94 147 200
66-Story contains 5 hangings 16 32 48 94 147 200
68-72 14 28 42 76 108 140
67-Cannibalism story 16 32 48 94 147 200
73-Black Rider story; Everett-c 15 30 45 83 124 165
NOTE: ***Maneely** a-62, 67; c-62, 69-73. **Robinson** a-68. **Sinnott** a-70. **Tuska** a-69-71.*

WESTERN PICTURE STORIES (1st Western comic)
Comics Magazine Company: Feb, 1937 - No. 4, June, 1937
1-Will Eisner-a 193 386 579 1216 2058 2900
2-Will Eisner-a 100 200 300 630 1065 1500
3,4: 3-Eisner-a. 4-Caveman Cowboy story 83 166 249 523 887 1250

WESTERN PICTURE STORIES (See Giant Comics Edition #6, 11)

WESTERN ROMANCES (See Target...)

WESTERN ROUGH RIDERS
Gillmor Magazines No. 1,4 (Stanmor Publ.): Nov, 1954 - No. 4, May, 1955
1 9 18 27 47 61 75
2-4 7 14 21 35 43 50

WESTERN ROUNDUP (See Dell Giants & Fox Giants)

WESTERN SERENADE
DC Comics: May/June, 1949
nn - Ashcan comic, not distributed to newsstands, only for in-house use (no known sales)

WESTERN TALES (Formerly Witches...)
Harvey Publications: No. 31, Oct, 1955 - No. 33, July-Sept, 1956
31,32-All S&K-a; Davy Crockett app. in each 18 36 54 107 169 230
33-S&K-a; Jim Bowie app. 18 36 54 103 162 220
NOTE: *#32 & 33 contain Boy's Ranch reprints. **Kirby** c-31.*

WESTERN TALES OF BLACK RIDER (Formerly Black Rider; Gunsmoke Western #32 on)
Atlas Comics (CPS): No. 28, May, 1955 - No. 31, Nov, 1955
28 (#1): The Spider (a villain) dies 20 40 60 115 180 245
29-31 14 28 42 82 121 160
NOTE: ***Lawrence** a-30. **Maneely** c-28-30. **Severin** a-28. **Shores** c-31.*

WESTERN TEAM-UP
Marvel Comics Group: Nov, 1973 (20¢)
1-Origin & 1st app. The Dakota Kid; Rawhide Kid-r; Gunsmoke Kid-r by Jack Davis
4 8 12 22 34 45

WESTERN THRILLERS (My Past Confessions #7 on)
Fox Features Syndicate/M.S. Distr. No. 52: Aug, 1948 - No. 6, June, 1949; No. 52, 1954?
1- "Velvet Rose" (Kamenish-a); "Two-Gun Sal", "Striker Sisters" (all women outlaws issue); Brodsky-c 48 96 144 298 499 700
2 24 48 72 140 225 310
3-6: 4,5-Bakerish-a; 5-Butch Cassidy app. 19 38 57 112 176 240
52-(Reprint, M.S. Dist.)-1954? No date given (becomes My Love Secret #53)
9 18 27 47 61 75

WESTERN THRILLERS (Cowboy Action #5 on)
Atlas Comics (ACI): Nov, 1954 - No. 4, Feb, 1955 (All-r/Western Outlaws & Sheriffs)
1 5 30 45 88 137 185
2-4 10 20 30 54 72 90
NOTE: ***Heath** c-3. **Maneely** a-1; c-2. **Powell** a-4. **Robinson** a-4. **Romita** c-4. **Tuska** a-2.*

WESTERN TRAILS (Ringo Kid Starring in...)
Atlas Comics (SAI): May, 1957 - No. 2, July, 1957
1-Ringo Kid app.; Severin-c 14 28 42 76 108 140
2-Severin-c 9 18 27 50 65 80
NOTE: ***Bolle** a-1, 2. **Maneely** a-1, 2. **Severin** c-1, 2.*

WESTERN TRUE CRIME (Becomes My Confessions)
Fox Features Syndicate: No. 15, Aug, 1948 - No. 6, June, 1949
15(#1)-Kamen-a; formerly Zoot #14 (5/48)? 32 64 96 186 298 410
16(#2)-Kamenish-a; headlight panels, violence 23 46 69 133 214 295
3-Kamen-a 25 50 75 145 233 320
4-6: 4-Johnny Craig-a 15 30 45 90 140 190

WESTERN WINNERS (Formerly All-Western Winners; becomes Black Rider #8 on & Romance Tales #7 on?)
Marvel Comics (CDS): No. 5, June, 1949 - No. 7, Dec, 1949
5-Two-Gun Kid, Kid Colt, Black Rider; Shores-c 31 62 93 181 291 400
6-Two-Gun Kid, Black Rider, Heath Kid Colt story; Captain Tootsie by C.C. Beck
26 52 78 152 244 335
7-Randolph Scott Photo-c w/true stories about the West
26 52 78 152 244 335

WEST OF THE PECOS (See Zane Grey, 4-Color #222)

WESTWARD HO, THE WAGONS (Disney)
Dell Publishing Co.: No. 738, Sept, 1956 (Movie)
Four Color 738-Fess Parker photo-c 9 18 27 63 107 150

WE3
DC Comics (Vertigo): Oct, 2004 - No. 3, May, 2005 ($2.95, limited series)
1-3-Domestic animal cyborgs: Grant Morrison-s/Frank Quitely-a 3.00
TPB (2005, $12.99) r/series 13.00

WETWORKS (See WildC.A.T.S: Covert Action Teams #2)
Image Comics (WildStorm): June, 1994 - No. 43, Aug, 1998 ($1.95/$2.50)
1-"July" on-c; gatefold wraparound-c; Portacio/Williams-c/a 3.00
1-Chicago Comicon edition 6.00
1-(2/98, $4.95) "3-D Edition" w/glasses 5.00
2-4 2.50
2-Alternate Portacio-c, see Deathblow #5 6.00
5-7,9-24: 5-($2.50). 13-Portacio-c. 16,17-Fire From Heaven Pts. 4 & 11 2.50
8 ($1.95)-Newstand, Wildstorm Rising Pt. 7 2.25
8 ($2.50)-Direct Market, Wildstorm Rising Pt. 7 2.50
25-($3.95) 4.00
26-43: 32-Variant-c by Pat Lee & Charest. 39,40-Stormwatch app. 42-Gen 13 app. 2.50
Sourcebook 1 (10/94, $2.50)-Text & illustrations (no comics) 2.50
Voyager Pack (8/97, $3.50)- #32 w/Phantom Guard preview 3.50

WETWORKS
DC Comics (WildStorm): Nov, 2006 - No. 15, Jan, 2008 ($2.99)
1-15: 1-Carey-s/Portacio-a; two covers by Portacio and Van Sciver. 2-Golden var-c 3-Pearson var-c. 4-Powell var-c 3.00
...: Armageddon 1 (1/08, $2.99) Gage-s/Badeaux-a 3.00
... Book One (2007, $14.99) r/#1-5 and stories from Eye of the storm Annual and Coup D'Etat Afterword 15.00
... Book Two (2008, $14.99) r/#6-9,13-15 15.00

WETWORKS/VAMPIRELLA (See Vampirella/Wetworks)
Image Comics (WildStorm Productions): July, 1997 ($2.95, one-shot)
1-Gil Kane-c 3.00

WHACK (Satire)
St. John Publishing Co. (Jubilee Publ.): Oct, 1953 - No. 3, May, 1954
1-(3-D, 25¢)-Kubert-a; Maurer-c; came w/glasses 27 54 81 156 251 345
2,3-Kubert-a in each. 2-Bing Crosby on-c; Mighty Mouse & Steve Canyon parodies. 3-Li'l Orphan Annie parody; Maurer-c 15 30 45 84 127 170

WHACKY (See Wacky)

WHA...HUH?
Marvel Comics: 2005 ($3.99, one-shot)

Wham Comics #1 © CEN

What If: Captain America #1 © MAR

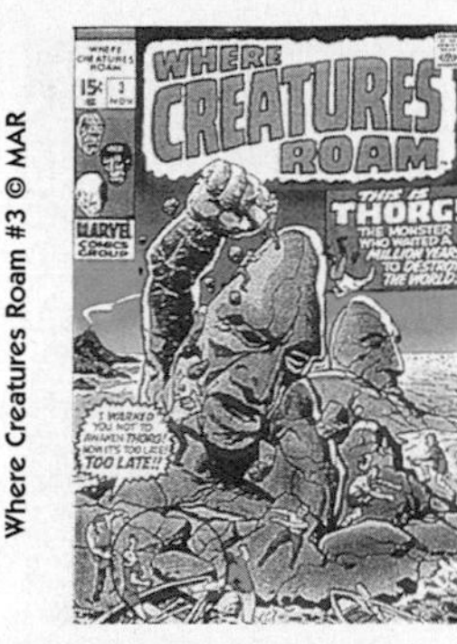

Where Creatures Roam #3 © MAR

	GD 2.0	VG 4.0	FN 6.0	VF 8.0	VF/NM 9.0	NM- 9.2

1-Humor spoofs of Marvel characters; Mahfood-a/c; Bendis, Stan Lee and others-s 4.00

WHAM COMICS (See Super Spy)
Centaur Publications: Nov, 1940 - No. 2, Dec, 1940

1-The Sparkler, The Phantom Rider, Craig Carter and his Magic Ring, Detecto, Copper Slug, Speed Silvers by Gustavson, Speed Centaur & Jon Linton (s/f) begin 160 320 480 1008 1704 2400
2-Origin Blue Fire & Solarman; The Buzzard app. 103 206 309 649 1100 1550

WHAM-O GIANT COMICS
Wham-O Mfg. Co. : April, 1967 (98¢, newspaper size, one-shot)(Six issue subscription was advertised)

1-Radian & Goody Bumpkin by Wood; 1 pg. Stanley-a; Fine, Tufts-a; flying saucer reports; wraparound-c 9 18 27 60 100 140

WHAT IF? (1st Series) (What If? Featuring... #13 & #?-33) (Also see Hero Initiative)
Marvel Comics Group: Feb, 1977 - No. 47, Oct, 1984; June, 1988 (All 52 pgs.)

1-Brief origin Spider-Man, Fantastic Four 3 6 9 16 23 30
2-Origin The Hulk retold 2 4 6 8 11 14
3-5: 3-Avengers. 4-Invaders. 5-Capt. America 1 3 4 6 8 10
6-10,13,17: 7-Betty Brant as Spider-Girl. 8-Daredevil; Spidey parody. 9-Origins Venus, Marvel Boy, Human Robot, 3-D Man. 13-Conan app.; John Buscema-c/a(p). 17-Ghost Rider & Son of Satan app. 1 2 3 5 7 9
11,12,14-16: 11-Marvel Bullpen as F.F. 6.00
18-26,29: 18-Dr. Strange. 19-Spider-Man. 22-Origin Dr. Doom retold 5.00
27-X-Men app.; Miller-c 2 4 6 12 16 20
28-Daredevil by Miller; Ghost Rider app. 2 4 6 9 11 14
30-"What If...Spider-Man's Clone Had Lived?" 1 2 3 5 7 9
31-Begin $1.00-c; featuring Wolverine & the Hulk; X-Men app.; death of Hulk, Wolverine & Magneto 2 4 6 14 18 22
32-34,36-47: 32,36-Byrne-a. 34-Marvel crew each draw themselves. 37-Old X-Men & Silver Surfer app. 39-Thor battles Conan 4.00
35 What if Elektra had lived?; Miller/Austin a. 1 2 3 5 6 8
Special 1 ($1.50, 6/88)-Iron Man, F.F., Thor app. 3.00
... Classic Vol. 1 TPB (2004, $24.99) r/#1-6; checklist 25.00
... Classic Vol. 2 TPB (2005, $24.99) r/#7-12 25.00
... Classic Vol. 3 TPB (2006, $24.99) r/#14,15,17-20 25.00
... Classic Vol. 4 TPB (2007, $24.99) r/#21-26; checklist of all What If? series/issues 25.00

NOTE: ***Austin*** *a-27p, 32i, 34, 35i; c-35i, 36i.* ***J. Buscema*** *a-13p, 15p; c-10, 13p, 23p.* ***Byrne*** *a-32i, 36; c-36p.* ***Colan*** *a-21p; c-17p, 18p, 21p.* ***Ditko*** *a-35, Special 1.* ***Golden*** *c-29, 40-42.* ***Guice*** *a-40p.* ***Gil Kane*** *a-3p, 24p; c(p)-2-4, 7, 8.* ***Kirby*** *a-11p; c-9p, 11p.* ***Layton*** *a-32i, 33i; c-30, 32p, 33i, 34.* ***Mignola*** *c-39i.* ***Miller*** *a-28p, 32i, 34(1), 35p; c-27, 28p.* ***Mooney*** *a-8i, 30i.* ***Perez*** *a-15p.* ***Robbins*** *a-4p.* ***Sienkiewicz*** *c-43-46.* ***Simonson*** *a-15p, 32i.* ***Starlin*** *a-32i.* ***Stevens*** *a-8, 16i(part).* ***Sutton*** *a-2i, 18p, 28.* ***Tuska*** *a-5p.* ***Weiss*** *a-37p.*

WHAT IF...? (2nd Series)
Marvel Comics: V2#1, July, 1989 - No. 114, Nov, 1998 ($1.25/$1.50)

V2#1-...The Avengers Had Lost the Evol. War 4.00
2-5: 2-Daredevil, Punisher app. 3.00
6-X-Men app. 4.00
7-Wolverine app.; Liefeld-c/a(1st on Wolvie?) 5.00
8,10,11,13-15,17-30: 10-Punisher app. 11-Fantastic Four app.; McFarlane-c(i).13-Prof. X; Jim Lee-c. 14-Capt. Marvel; Lim/Austin-c.15-F.F.; Capullo-c/a(p). 17-Spider-Man/Kraven. 18-F.F. 19-Vision. 20,21-Spider-Man. 22-Silver Surfer by Lim/Austin-c/a 23-X-Men. 24-Wolverine; Punisher app. 25-(52 pgs.)-Wolverine app. 26-Punisher app. 27-Namor/F.F. 28,29-Capt. America. 29-Swipes cover to Avengers #4. 30-(52 pgs.)-F.F. 3.00
9,12-X-Men 3.50
16-Wolverine battles Conan; Red Sonja app.; X-Men cameo 4.00
31-50: 31-Cosmic Spider-Man & Venom app.; Hobgoblin cameo. 32,33-Phoenix; X-Men app. 35-Fantastic Five (w/Spidey). 36-Avengers vs. Guardians of the Galaxy. 37-Wolverine; Thibert-c(i). 38-Thor; Rogers-p(part). 40-Storm; X-Men app. 41-(52 pgs.)-Avengers vs. Galactus. 42-Spider-Man. 43-Wolverine. 44-Venom/Punisher. 45-Ghost Rider. 46-Cable. 47-Magneto. 49-Infinity Gauntlet w/Silver Surfer & Thanos. 50-(52 pgs.)-Foil embossed-c; "What If Hulk Had Killed Wolverine" 3.00
51-(7/93) "What If the Punisher Became Captain America" (see it happen in 2007's Punisher War Journal #6-10) 6.00
52-104: 52-Dr. Doom. 54-Death's Head. 57-Punisher as Shield. 58-"What if Punisher Had Killed Spider-Man" w/cover similar to Amazing S-M #129. 59-...Wolverine led Alpha Flight. 60-X-Men Wedding Album. 61-Bound-in card sheet. 61,86,88-Spider-Man. 74,77,81,84,85-X-Men. 76-Last app. Watcher in title. 78-Bisley-c. 80-Hulk. 87-Sabretooth. 89-Fantastic Four. 90-Cyclops & Havok. 91-The Hulk. 93-Wolverine. 94-Juggernaut. 95-Ghost Rider. 100-($2.99, double-sized) Gambit and Rogue, Fantastic Four 3.00
105-Spider-Girl (Peter Parker's daughter) debut; Sienkiewicz-a; (Betty Brant also app. as a Spider-Girl in What If? (1st series) #7) 2 4 6 12 16 20
106-114: 106-Gambit. 108-Avengers. 111-Wolverine. 114-Secret Wars 2.50
#(-1) Flashback (7/97) 3.00

WHAT IF...? (one-shots)
Marvel Comics: Feb, 2005 ($2.99)

... Aunt May Had Died Instead of Uncle Ben? - Brubaker-s/DiVito-a/Brase-c 3.00
... Dr. Doom Had Become The Thing? - Karl Kesel-s/Paul Smith-a/c 3.00
... General Ross Had Become The Hulk? - Peter David-s/Pat Olliffe-a/Gary Frank-c 3.00
... Jessica Jones Had Joined The Avengers? - Bendis-s/Gaydos-a/McNiven-c 3.00
... Karen Page Had Lived? - Bendis-s/Lark-a/c 3.00
... Magneto and Professor X Had Formed The X-Men Together? - Claremont-s/Raney-a 3.00
What If...: Why Not? TPB (2005, $16.99) r/one-shots 17.00

WHAT IF... (one-shots)
Marvel Comics: Feb, 2006 ($2.99)

... : Captain America - Fought in the Civil War?; Bedard-s/Di Giandomenico-a 3.00
... : Daredevil - The Devil Who Dares; Daredevil in feudal Japan; Veitch-s/Edwards-a 3.00
... : Fantastic Four - Were Cosmonauts?; Marshall Rogers-a/c; Mike Carey-s 3.00
... : Submariner - Grew Up on Land?; Pak-s/Lopez-a 3.00
... : Thor - Was the Herald of Galactus?; Kirkman-s/Oeming-a/c 3.00
... : Wolverine - In the Prohibition Era; Way-s/Proctor-a/Harris-c 3.00
What If: Mirror Mirror TPB (2006, $16.99) r/one-shots; design pages and Rogers sketches 17.00

WHAT IF ?... (one-shots altering recent Marvel "event" series)
Marvel Comics: Jan, 2007 - Feb, 2007 ($3.99)

... Avengers Disassembled; Parker-s/Lopresti-a/c 4.00
... Spider-Man The Other; Peter David-s/Khoi Pham-a; Venom app. 4.00
... Wolverine Enemy of the State; Robinson-s/DiGiandomenico-a/Alexander-c 4.00
... X-Men Age of Apocalypse; Remender-s/Wilkins-a/Djurdjevic-c 4.00
... X-Men Deadly Genesis; Hine-s/Yardin-a/c 4.00
What If?: Event Horizon TPB (2007, $16.99) r/one-shots; design pages and cover sketches 17.00

WHAT IF ?... (one-shots altering recent Marvel "event" series)
Marvel Comics: Dec, 2007 - Feb, 2008 ($3.99)

... Annihilation; Nova, Iron Man and Captain America app. 4.00
... Civil War; 2 covers by Silvestri & Djurdjevic 4.00
... Planet Hulk; Pagulayan-c; Kirk, Sandoval & Hembeck-a 4.00
... Spider-Man vs. Wolverine; Romita Jr.-c; Henry-a; Nick Fury app. 4.00
... X-Men - Rise and Fall of the Shi'ar Empire; Coipel-c 4.00
What If?: Civil War TPB (2008, $16.99) r/one-shots; design pages and cover sketches 17.00

'WHAT'S NEW? - THE COLLECTED ADVENTURES OF PHIL & DIXIE'
Palliard Press: Oct, 1991 - No. 2, 1991 ($5.95, mostly color, sq.-bound, 52 pgs.)

1,2-By Phil Foglio 6.00

WHAT THE- -?!
Marvel Comics: Aug, 1988 - No. 26, 1993 ($1.25/$1.50/$2.50, semi-annual #5 on)

1-All contain parodies 3.00
2-24: 3-X-Men parody; Todd McFarlane-a. 5-Punisher/Wolverine parody; Jim Lee-a. 6-Punisher, Wolverine, Alpha Flight. 9-Wolverine. 16-EC back-c parody. 17-Wolverine/Punisher parody. 18-Star Trek parody w/Wolverine. 19-Punisher, Wolverine, Ghost Rider. 21-Weapon X parody. 22-Punisher/Wolverine parody 2.50
25-Summer Special 1 (1993, $2.50)-X-Men parody 2.50
26-Fall Special ($2.50, 68 pgs.)-Spider-Ham 2099-c/story; origin Silver Surfer; Hulk & Doomsday parody; indica reads "Winter Special." 2.50

NOTE: ***Austin*** *a-6i.* ***Byrne*** *a-2, 6, 10; c-2, 6-8, 10, 12, 13.* ***Golden*** *a-22.* ***Dale Keown*** *a-8p(8 pgs.).* ***McFarlane*** *a-3.* ***Rogers*** *c-15i, 16p.* ***Severin*** *a-2.* ***Staton*** *a-21p.* ***Williamson*** *a-2i.*

WHEE COMICS (Also see Gay, Smile & Tickle Comics)
Modern Store Publications: 1955 (7¢, 5x7-1/4", 52 pgs.)

1-Funny animal 6 12 18 28 34 40

WHEEDIES (See Panic #11 -EC Comics)

WHEELIE AND THE CHOPPER BUNCH (TV)
Charlton Comics: July, 1975 - No. 7, July, 1976 (Hanna-Barbera)

1-3: 1-Byrne text illo (see Nightmare for 1st art); Staton-a. 2-Byrne-a. 2,3-Mike Zeck text illos. 3-Staton-a; Byrne-c/a 3 6 9 16 23 30
4-7-Staton-a 2 4 6 12 16 20

WHEN KNIGHTHOOD WAS IN FLOWER (See The Sword & the Rose, 4-Color #505, 682)

WHEN SCHOOL IS OUT (See Wisco in Promotional Comics section)

WHERE CREATURES ROAM
Marvel Comics Group: July, 1970 - No. 8, Sept, 1971

1-Kirby/Ayers-c/a(r) 3 6 9 20 30 40
2-8: 2-5,7,8-Kirby-c/a(r). 6-Kirby-a(r) 3 6 9 16 22 28

NOTE: ***Ditko*** *r-1-6, 7.* ***Heck*** *r-2, 5. All contain pre super-hero reprints.*

WHERE IN THE WORLD IS CARMEN SANDIEGO (TV)
DC Comics: June, 1996 - No. 4, Dec, 1996 ($1.75)

1-4: Adaptation of TV show 2.50

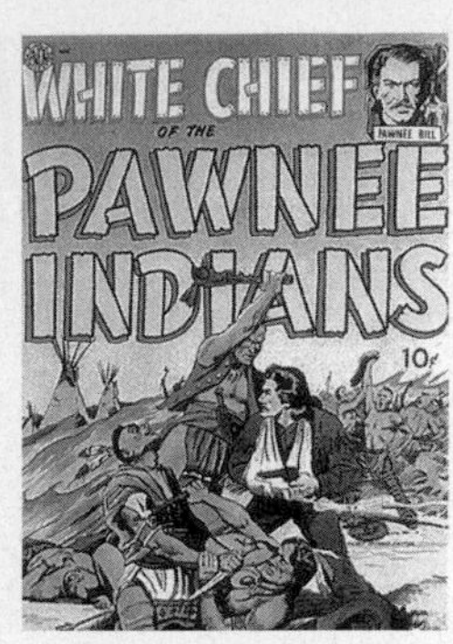

White Chief of the Pawnee Indians © AVON

Whiteout #2 © Greg Rucka

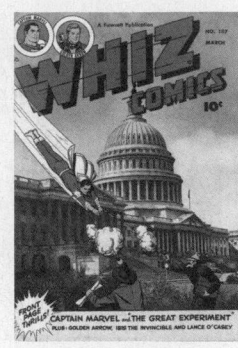

Whiz Comics #107 © FAW

GD 2.0 | VG 4.0 | FN 6.0 | VF 8.0 | VF/NM 9.0 | NM- 9.2

WHERE MONSTERS DWELL
Marvel Comics Group: Jan, 1970 - No. 38, Oct, 1975

1-Kirby/Ditko-r; all contain pre super-hero-r 4 8 12 22 34 45
2-10: 4-Crandall-a(r) 3 6 9 16 23 30
11,13-20: 11-Last 15¢ issue. 18,20-Starlin-c 3 6 9 14 19 24
12-Giant issue (52 pgs.) 3 6 9 18 27 35
21-37: 21-Reprints 1st Fin Fang Foom app. 2 4 6 10 14 18
38-Williamson-r/World of Suspense #3 2 4 6 13 18 22

NOTE: *Colan r-12. Ditko a(r)-4, 6, 8, 10, 12, 17-19, 23-25, 37. Kirby r-1-3, 5-16, 18-27, 30-32, 34-36, 38; c-12? Reinman a-3r, 4r, 12r. Severin c-15.*

WHERE'S HUDDLES? (TV) (See Fun-In #9)
Gold Key: Jan, 1971 - No. 3, Dec, 1971 (Hanna-Barbera)

1 3 6 9 19 29 38
2,3: 3-r/most #1 2 4 6 11 16 20

WHIP WILSON (Movie star) (Formerly Rex Hart; Gunhawk #12 on; see Western Hearts, Western Life Romances, Western Love)
Marvel Comics: No. 9, April, 1950 - No. 11, Sept, 1950 (#9,10: 52 pgs.)

9-Photo-c; Whip Wilson & his horse Bullet begin; origin Bullet; issue #23 listed on splash page; cover changed to #9 53 106 159 323 529 735
10,11: Both have photo-c. 11-36 pgs. 30 60 90 174 275 375
I.W. Reprint #1(1964)-Kinstler-c; r-Marvel #11 3 6 9 16 22 28

WHIRLWIND COMICS (Also see Cyclone Comics)
Nita Publication: June, 1940 - No. 3, Sept, 1940

1-Origin & 1st app. Cyclone; Cyclone-c 227 454 681 1430 2415 3400
2,3: Cyclone-c 103 206 309 649 1100 1500

WHIRLYBIRDS (TV)
Dell Publishing Co.: No. 1124, Aug, 1960 - No. 1216, Oct-Dec, 1961

Four Color 1124 (#1)-Photo-c 8 16 24 56 93 130
Four Color 1216-Photo-c 8 16 24 52 86 120

WHISKEY DICKEL, INTERNATIONAL COWGIRL
Image Comics: Aug, 2003 ($12.95, softcover, B&W)

nn-Mark Ricketts-s/Mike Hawthorne-a; pin-up by various incl. Oeming, Thompson, Mack 13.00

WHISPER (Female Ninja)
Capital Comics: Dec, 1983 - No. 2, 1984 ($1.75, Baxter paper)

1,2: 1-Origin; Golden-c, Special (11/85, $2.50) 2.50

WHISPER (Vol. 2)
First Comics: Jun, 1986 - No. 37, June, 1990 ($1.25/$1.75/$1.95)

1-37 2.50

WHISPER
Boom! Studios: Nov, 2006 ($3.99)

1-Grant-s/Dzialowski-a 4.00

WHITE CHIEF OF THE PAWNEE INDIANS
Avon Periodicals: 1951

nn-Kit West app.; Kinstler-c 16 32 48 92 144 195

WHITE EAGLE INDIAN CHIEF (See Indian Chief)

WHITE FANG
Disney Comics: 1990 ($5.95, 68 pgs.)

nn-Graphic novel adapting new Disney movie 6.00

WHITE INDIAN
Magazine Enterprises: No. 11, July, 1953 - No. 15, 1954

11(A-1 94), 12(A-1 101), 13(A-1 104)-Frazetta-r(Dan Brand) in all from Durango Kid. 11-Powell-c 23 46 69 130 205 280
14(A-1 117), 15(A-1 135)-Check-a; Torres-a-#15 14 28 42 76 108 140

NOTE: *#11 contains reprints from Durango Kid #1-4; #12 from #5, 9, 10, 11; #13 from #7, 12, 13, 16. #14 & 15 contain all new stories.*

WHITEOUT (Also see Queen & Country)
Oni Press: July, 1998 - No. 4, Nov, 1998 ($2.95, B&W, limited series)

1-4: 1-Matt Wagner-c. 2-Mignola-c. 3-Gibbons-c 3.00
TPB (5/99, $10.95) r/#1-4; Miller-c 11.00

WHITEOUT: MELT
Oni Press: Sept, 1999 - No. 4, Feb, 2000 ($2.95, B&W, limited series)

1-4-Greg Rucka-s/Steve Lieber-a 3.00
Whiteout: Melt, The Definitive Edition TPB (9/07, $13.95) r/#1-4; Rucka afterword 14.00

WHITE PRINCESS OF THE JUNGLE (Also see Jungle Adventures & Top Jungle Comics)
Avon Periodicals: July, 1951 - No. 5, Nov, 1952

GD 2.0 | VG 4.0 | FN 6.0 | VF 8.0 | VF/NM 9.0 | NM- 9.2

1-Origin of White Princess (Taanda) & Capt'n Courage (r); Kinstler-c 55 110 165 347 586 825
2-Reprints origin of Malu, Slave Girl Princess from Avon's Slave Girl Comics #1 w/Malu changed to Zora; Kinstler-c/a(2) 40 80 120 244 397 550
3-Origin Blue Gorilla; Kinstler-c/a 37 74 111 215 345 475
4-Jack Barnum, White Hunter app.; r/Sheena #9 32 64 96 186 298 410
5-Blue Gorilla by McCann?; Kinstler inside-c; Fawcette/Alascia-a(3) 34 68 102 198 319 440

WHITE RIDER AND SUPER HORSE (Formerly Humdinger V2#2; Indian Warriors #7 on; also see Blue Bolt #1, 4Most & Western Crime Cases)
Novelty-Star Publications/Accepted Publ.: No. 4, 9/50 - No. 6, 3/51

4-6-Adapts "The Last of the Mohicans". 4(#1)-(9/50)-Says #11 on inside 16 32 48 92 144 195
Accepted Reprint #5(r/#5),6 (nd); L.B. Cole-c 9 18 27 50 65 80

NOTE: *All have **L. B. Cole** covers.*

WHITE TIGER
Marvel Comics: Jan, 2007 - No. 6, Nov, 2007 ($2.99, limited series)

1-6: 1-David Mack-c; Pierce & Liebe-s/Briones-a; Spider-Man & Black Widow app. 3.00
...: A Hero's Compulsion SC (2007,$14.99) r/#1-6; re-cap art and profile page 15.00

WHITE WILDERNESS (Disney)
Dell Publishing Co.: No. 943, Oct, 1958

Four Color 943-Movie 6 12 18 43 69 95

WHITMAN COMIC BOOK, A
Whitman Publishing Co.: Sept., 1962 (136 pgs.; 7-3/4x5-3/4; hardcover) (B&W)

1-3,5,7: 1-Yogi Bear. 2-Huckleberry Hound. 3-Mr. Jinks and Pixie & Dixie. 5-Augie Doggie & Loopy de Loop. 7-Bugs Bunny-r from #47,51,53,54 & 55 6 12 18 43 69 95
4,6: 4-The Flintstones. 6-Snooper & Blabber Fearless Detectives/Quick Draw McGraw of the Wild West 7 14 21 47 76 105
8-Donald Duck-reprints most of WDC&S #209-213. Includes 5 Barks stories, 1 complete Mickey Mouse serial by Paul Murry & 1 Mickey Mouse serial missing the 1st episode 8 16 24 52 86 120

NOTE: *Hanna-Barbera #1-6(TV), reprints of British tabloid comics. Dell reprints-#7,8.*

WHIZ COMICS (Formerly Flash & Thrill Comics #1)(See 5 Cent Comics)
Fawcett Publications: No. 2, Feb, 1940 - No. 155, June, 1953

1-(nn on cover, #2 inside)-Origin & 1st newsstand app. Captain Marvel (formerly Captain Thunder) by C. C. Beck (created by Bill Parker), Spy Smasher, Golden Arrow, Ibis the Invincible, Dan Dare, Scoop Smith, Sivana, & Lance O'Casey begin 7000 14,000 21,000 40,000 67,500 95,000
(The only Mint copy sold in 1995 for $176,000 cash)

1-Reprint, oversize 13-1/2x10". **WARNING:** This comic is an exact duplicate reprint (except for dropping "Gangway for Captain Marvel" from-c) of the original except for its size. DC published it in 1974 with a second cover titling it as a Famous First Edition. There have been many reported cases of the outer cover being removed and the interior sold as the original edition. The reprint with the new outer cover removed is practically worthless. See Famous First Edition for value.

2-(3/40, nn on cover, #3 inside); cover to Flash #1 redrawn, pg. 12, panel 4; Spy Smasher reveals I.D. to Eve 461 922 1383 3319 5810 8300
3-(4/40, #3 on-c, #4 inside)-1st app. Beautia 329 658 987 2237 3919 5600
4-(5/40, #4 on cover, #5 inside)-Brief origin Capt. Marvel retold 297 594 891 1871 3161 4450
5-Captain Marvel wears button-down flap on splash page only 250 500 750 1575 2663 3750
6-10: 7-Dr. Voodoo begins (by Raboy-#9-22) 183 366 549 1153 1952 2750
11-14: 12-Capt. Marvel does not wear cape 125 250 375 788 1332 1875
15-Origin Sivana; Dr. Voodoo by Raboy 133 266 399 838 1419 2000
16-18-Spy Smasher battles Captain Marvel 128 256 384 806 1366 1925
19,20 87 174 261 548 924 1300
21-(9/41)-Origin & 1st cover app. Lt. Marvels, the 1st team in Fawcett comics. In this issue, Capt. Death similar to Ditko's later Dr. Strange 92 184 276 580 978 1375
22-24: 23-Only Dr. Voodoo by Tuska 68 134 204 428 727 1025
25-(12/41)-Captain Nazi jumps from Master Comics #21 to take on Capt. Marvel solo after being beaten by Capt. Marvel/Bulletman team, causing the creation of Capt. Marvel Jr.; 1st app./origin of Capt. Marvel Jr. (part II of trilogy origin by CC. Beck & Mac Raboy); Captain Marvel sends Jr. back to Master #22 to aid Bulletman against Capt. Nazi; origin Old Shazam in text 544 1088 1632 3917 6859 9800
26-30 60 120 180 378 639 900
31,32: 32-1st app. The Trolls; Hitler/Mussolini satire by Beck 53 106 159 330 553 775
33-Spy Smasher, Captain Marvel x-over on cover and inside 60 120 180 378 639 900
34,36-40: 37-The Trolls app. by Swayze 40 80 120 244 397 550

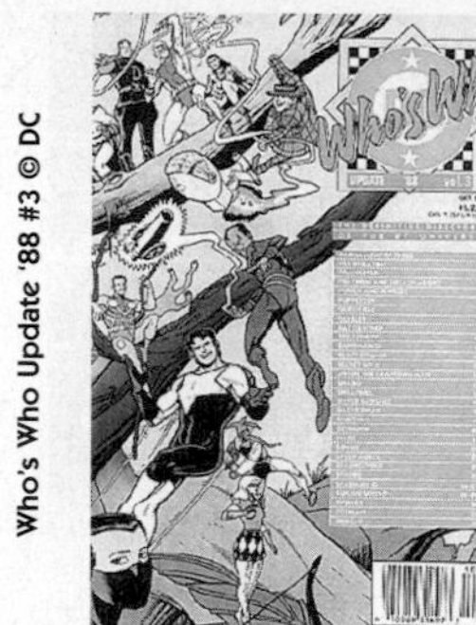
Who's Who Update '88 #3 © DC

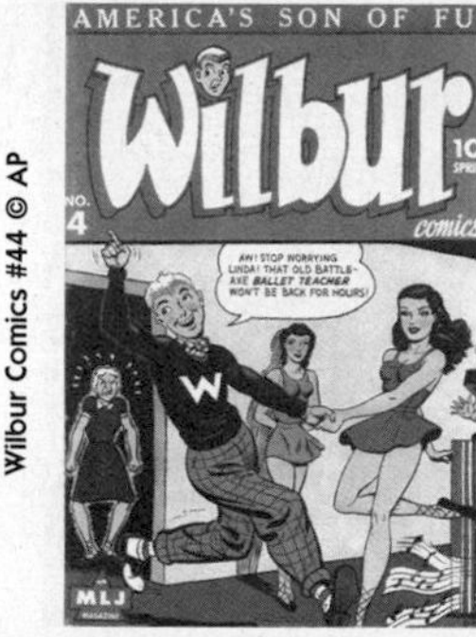

Wilbur Comics #44 © AP

Wild Bill Hickok #12 © AVON

GD 2.0 | VG 4.0 | FN 6.0 | VF 8.0 | VF/NM 9.0 | NM- 9.2

35-Captain Marvel & Spy Smasher-c 49 98 147 300 505 710
41-50: 43-Spy Smasher, Ibis, Golden Arrow x-over in Capt. Marvel. 44-Flag-c. 47-Origin recap (1 pg.) 36 72 108 212 341 470
51-60: 52-Capt. Marvel x-over in Ibis. 57-Spy Smasher, Golden Arrow, Ibis cameo 29 58 87 172 276 380
61-70 27 54 81 160 258 355
71,77-80 26 52 78 152 244 335
72-76-Two Captain Marvel stories in each; 76-Spy Smasher becomes Crime Smasher 26 52 78 154 247 340
81-99: 86-Captain Marvel battles Sivana Family; robot-c. 91-Infinity-c 26 52 78 152 244 335
100-(8/48)-Anniversary issue 29 58 87 172 276 380
101-106: 102-Commando Yank app. 106-Bulletman app. 25 50 75 147 236 325
107-149: 107-Capitol Building photo-c. 108-Brooklyn Bridge photo-c. 112-Photo-c. 139-Infinity-c. 140-Flag-c. 142-Used in **POP**, pg. 89 25 50 75 147 236 325
150-152-(Low dist.) 29 58 87 169 272 375
153-155-(Scarce):154,155-1st/2nd Dr. Death stories 38 76 114 226 363 500

NOTE: ***C.C. Beck*** *Captain Marvel-No. 25(part).* ***Krigstein*** *Golden Arrow-No. 75, 78, 91, 95, 96, 98-100.* ***Mac Raboy*** *Dr. Voodoo-No. 9-22. Captain Marvel-No. 25(part).* ***M.Swayze*** *a-37, 38, 59; c-38.* ***Schaffenberger*** *c-138-155(most).* ***Wolverton*** *1/2 pg. "Culture Corner"-No. 65-67, 68(2 1/2 pgs), 70-85, 87-96, 98-100, 102-109, 112-121, 123, 125, 126, 128-131, 133, 134, 136, 142, 143, 146.*

WHIZ KIDS (Also see Big Bang Comics)
Image Comics: Apr, 2003 ($4.95, B&W, one-shot)
1-Galahad, Cyclone, Thunder Girl and Moray app.; Jeff Austin-a 5.00

WHOA, NELLIE (Also see Love & Rockets)
Fantagraphics Books: July, 1996 - No. 3, Sept, 1996 ($2.95, B&W, lim. series)
1-3: Jamie Hernandez-c/a/scripts 3.00

WHODUNIT
D.S. Publishing Co.: Aug-Sept, 1948 - No. 3, Dec-Jan, 1948-49 (#1,2: 52 pgs.)
1-Baker-a (7 pgs.) 24 48 72 140 225 310
2,3-Detective mysteries 13 26 39 74 105 135

WHODUNNIT?
Eclipse Comics: June, 1986 - No. 3, Apr, 1987 ($2.00, limited series)
1-3: Spiegle-a. 2-Gulacy-c 2.50

WHO FRAMED ROGER RABBIT (See Marvel Graphic Novel)

WHO IS NEXT?
Standard Comics: No. 5, Jan, 1953
5-Toth, Sekowsky, Andru-a; crime stories 20 40 60 115 183 250

WHO IS THE CROOKED MAN?
Crusade: Sept, 1996 ($3.50, B&W, 40 pgs.)
1-Intro The Martyr, Scarlet 7 & Garrison 3.50

WHO'S MINDING THE MINT? (See Movie Classics)

WHO'S WHO IN STAR TREK
DC Comics: Mar, 1987 - #2, Apr, 1987 ($1.50, limited series)
1,2 6.00
NOTE: ***Byrne*** *a-1, 2.* ***Chaykin*** *c-1, 2.* ***Morrow*** *a-1, 2.* ***McFarlane*** *a-2.* ***Perez*** *a-1, 2.* ***Sutton*** *a-1, 2.*

WHO'S WHO IN THE LEGION OF SUPER-HEROES
DC Comics: Apr, 1987 - No. 7, Nov, 1988 ($1.25, limited series)
1-7 4.00

WHO'S WHO: THE DEFINITIVE DIRECTORY OF THE DC UNIVERSE
DC Comics: Mar, 1985 - No. 26, Apr, 1987 (Maxi-series, no ads)
1-DC heroes from A-Z 4.00
2-26: All have 1-2 pgs-a by most DC artists 4.00
NOTE: ***Art Adams*** *a-4, 11, 18, 20.* ***Anderson*** *a-1-5, 7-12, 14, 15, 19, 21, 23-25.* ***Aparo*** *a-2, 3, 9, 10, 12, 13, 14, 15, 17, 18, 21, 23.* ***Byrne*** *a-4, 7, 14, 16, 18i, 19, 22i, 24; c-22.* ***Cowan*** *a-3-5, 8, 10-13, 16-18, 22-25.* ***Ditko*** *a-19-22.* ***Evans*** *a-20.* ***Giffen*** *a-1, 3,-6, 8, 13, 15, 17, 18, 23.* ***Grell*** *a-6, 9, 14, 20, 23, 25, 26.* ***Infantino*** *a-1-10, 12, 15, 17-22, 24, 25.* ***Kaluta*** *a-14, 21.* ***Gil Kane*** *a-1-11, 13, 14, 16, 19, 21-23, 25.* ***Kirby*** *a-2-6, 8-18, 20, 22, 25.* ***Kubert*** *a-2, 3, 7-11, 19, 20, 25.* ***Erik Larsen*** *a-24.* ***McFarlane*** *a-10-12, 17, 19, 25, 26.* ***Morrow*** *a-4, 7, 25, 26.* ***Orlando*** *a-1, 4, 10, 11, 21i.* ***Perez*** *a-1-5, 8-19, 22-26; c-1-4, 13-18.* ***Rogers*** *a-1, 2, 5-7, 11, 12, 15, 24.* ***Starlin*** *a-13, 14, 16.* ***Stevens*** *a-4, 7, 18.*

WHO'S WHO UPDATE '87
DC Comics: Aug, 1987 - No. 5, Dec, 1987 ($1.25, limited series)
1-5: Contains art by most DC artists 3.00
NOTE: ***Giffen*** *a-1.* ***McFarlane*** *a-1-4; c-4.* ***Perez*** *a-1-4.*

WHO'S WHO UPDATE '88
DC Comics: Aug, 1988 - No. 4, Nov, 1988 ($1.25, limited series)
1-4: Contains art by most DC artists 3.00
NOTE: ***Giffen*** *a-1.* ***Erik Larsen*** *a-1.*

WICKED, THE
Avalon Studios: Dec, 1999 - No. 7, Aug, 2000 ($2.95)
Preview-(7/99, $5.00, B&W) 5.00
1-7-Anacleto-c/Martinez-a 3.00
...: Medusa's Tale (11/00, $3.95, one shot) story plus pin-up gallery 4.00
...: Vol. 1: Omnibus (2003, $19.95) r/#0-8; Drew-c 20.00

WILBUR COMICS (Teen-age) (Also see Laugh Comics, Laugh Comix, Liberty Comics #10 & Zip Comics)
MLJ Magazines/Archie Publ. No. 8, Spring, 1946 on: Sum', 1944 - No. 87, 11/59; No. 88, 9/63; No. 89, 10/64; No. 90, 10/65 (No. 1-46: 52 pgs.) (#1-11 are quarterly)
1 53 106 159 334 567 800
2(Fall, 1944) 30 60 90 174 280 385
3,4(Wint, '44-45; Spr, '45) 21 42 63 125 200 275
5-1st app. Katy Keene (Sum, '45) & begin series; Wilbur story same as Archie story in Archie #1 except Wilbur replaces Archie 103 206 309 649 1100 1550
6-10: 10-(Fall, 1946) 24 48 72 140 225 310
11-20 15 30 45 86 133 180
21-30: 30-(4/50) 11 22 33 62 86 110
31-50 9 18 27 52 69 85
51-70 8 16 24 44 57 70
71-90: 88-Last 10¢ issue (9/63) 4 8 12 26 41 55
NOTE: *Katy Keene in No. 5-56, 58-61, 63-69.* ***Al Fagaly*** *c-6-9, 12-24 at least.* ***Vigoda*** *c-2.*

WILD
Atlas Comics (IPC): Feb, 1954 - No. 5, Aug, 1954
1 26 52 78 152 244 335
2 15 30 45 90 140 190
3-5 15 30 45 83 124 165
NOTE: ***Berg*** *a-5; c-4.* ***Burgos*** *c-3.* ***Colan*** *a-4.* ***Everett*** *a-1-3.* ***Heath*** *a-2, 3, 5.* ***Maneely*** *a-1-3, 5; c-1, 5.* ***Post*** *a-2, 5.* ***Ed Win*** *a-1, 3.*

WILD (This Magazine Is...) (Satire)
Dell Publishing Co.: Jan, 1968 - No. 3, 1968 (Magazine, 52 pgs.)
1-3 3 6 9 14 19 24

WILD ANIMALS
Pacific Comics: Dec, 1982 ($1.00, one-shot, direct sales)
1-Funny animal; Sergio Aragones-a; Shaw-c/a 4.00

WILD BILL ELLIOTT (Also see Western Roundup under Dell Giants)
Dell Publishing Co.: No. 278, 5/50 - No. 643, 7/55 (No #11,12) (All photo-c)
Four Color 278(#1, 52pgs.)-Titled "Bill Elliott"; Bill & his horse Stormy begin; photo front/back-c begin 13 26 39 90 160 230
2 (11/50), 3 (52 pgs.) 8 16 24 52 86 120
4-10(10-12/52) 6 12 18 41 66 90
Four Color 472(6/53),520(12/53)-Last photo back-c 5 10 15 34 55 75
13(4-6/54) - 17(4-6/55) 5 10 15 32 51 70
Four Color 643 (7/55) 5 10 15 30 48 65

WILD BILL HICKOK (Also see Blazing Sixguns)
Avon Periodicals: Sept-Oct, 1949 - No. 28, May-June, 1956
1-Ingels-c 23 46 69 133 214 295
2-Painted-c; Kit West app. 13 26 39 74 105 135
3-5-Painted-c (4-Cover by Howard Winfield) 10 20 30 54 72 90
6-10,12: 8-10-Painted-c. 12-Kinsler-c? 10 20 30 54 72 90
11,13,14-Kinstler-c/a (#11-c & inside-f/c art only) 10 20 30 58 79 100
15,17,18,20: 18-Kit West story. 20-Kit West by Larsen 9 18 27 47 61 75
16-Kamen-a; r-3 stories/King of the Badmen of Deadwood 9 18 27 50 65 80
19-Meskin-a 9 18 27 47 61 75
21-Reprints 2 stories/Chief Crazy Horse 8 16 24 44 57 70
22-McCann-a?; r/Sheriff Bob Dixon's... 8 16 24 44 57 70
23-27: 23-Kinstler-c. 24-27-Kinstler-c/a(r) (24,25-r?) 8 16 24 44 57 70
28-Kinstler-c/a (new); r-/Last of the Comanches 9 18 27 47 61 75
I.W. Reprint #1-r/#2; Kinstler-c 2 4 6 9 13 16
Super Reprint #10-12: 10-r/#18. 11-r/#?. 12-r/#8 2 4 6 9 13 16
NOTE: *#23, 25 contain numerous editing deletions in both art and script due to code.* ***Kinstler*** *c-6, 7, 11-14, 17, 18, 20-22, 24-28.* ***Howard Larsen*** *a-1, 2, 4, 5, 6(3), 7-9, 11, 12, 17, 18, 20-24, 26.* ***Meskin*** *a-7.* ***Reinman*** *a-6, 17.*

WILD BILL HICKOK AND JINGLES (TV)(Formerly Cowboy Western) (Also see Blue Bird)
Charlton Comics: No. 68, Aug, 1958 - No. 75, Dec, 1959
68,69-Williamson-a (all are 10¢ issues) 11 22 33 60 83 105

Wild Boy of the Congo #15 © Z-D

WildC.A.T.S #50 © WSP

Wildcats V2 #18 © WSP

GD VG FN VF VF/NM NM-
2.0 4.0 6.0 8.0 9.0 9.2

70-Two pgs. Williamson-a 8 16 24 42 54 65
71-75 (#76, exist?) 6 12 18 28 34 40

WILD BILL PECOS WESTERN (Also see The Westerner)
AC Comics: 1989 ($3.50, 1/2 color/1/2 B&W, 52 pgs.)

1-Syd Shores-c/a(r)/Westerner; photo back-c 4.00

WILD BOY OF THE CONGO (Also see Approved Comics)
Ziff-Davis No. 10-12,4-8/St. John No. 9,11 on: No. 10, 2-3/51 - No. 12, 8-9/51; No. 4, 10-11/51 - No. 9, 10/53; No. 11-#15,6/55 (No #10, 1953)

10(#1)(2-3/51)-Origin; bondage-c by Saunders (painted); used in **SOTI**, pg. 189; painted-c begin thru #9 (except #7) 23 46 69 135 218 300
11(4-5/51),12(8-9/51)-Norman Saunders painted-c 14 28 42 78 112 145
4(10-11/51)-Saunders painted bondage-c 14 28 42 78 112 145
5(Winter,'51)-Saunders painted-c 12 24 36 69 97 125
6,8,9(10/53): Painted-c. 6-Saunders-c 12 24 36 69 97 125
7(8-9/52)-Kinstler-a 14 28 42 78 112 145
11-13-Baker-c. 11-r/#7 w/new Baker-c; Kinstler-a (2 pgs.) 15 30 45 84 127 170
14(4/55)-Baker-c; r-#12('51) 15 30 45 84 127 170
15(6/55) 10 20 30 58 79 100

WILDCAT (See Sensation Comics #1)

WILDC.A.T.S ADVENTURES (TV cartoon)
Image Comics (WildStorm): Sept, 1994 - No. 10, June, 1995 ($1.95/$2.50)

1-10 2.50
Sourcebook 1 (1/95, $2.95) 3.00

WILDC.A.T.S: COVERT ACTION TEAMS (Also see Alan Moore's... for TPB reprints)
Image Comics (WildStorm Productions): Aug, 1992 - No. 4, Mar, 1993; No. 5, Nov, 1993 - No. 50, June, 1998 ($1.95/$2.50)

1-1st app; Jim Lee/Williams-c/a & Lee scripts begin; contains 2 trading cards (Two diff versions of cards inside); 1st WildStorm Productions title 4.50
1-All gold foil signed edition 12.00
1-All gold foil unsigned edition 8.00
1-Newsstand edition w/o cards 3.00
1-"3-D Special"(8/97, $4.95) w/3-D glasses; variant-c by Jim Lee. 5.00
2-($2.50)-Prism foil stamped-c; contains coupon for Image Comics #0 & 4 pg. preview to Portacio's Wetworks (back-up) 4.50
2-With coupon missing 2.25
2-Direct sale misprint w/o foil-c 3.00
2-Newsstand ed., no prism or coupon 2.50
3-Lee/Liefeld-c (1/93-c, 12/92 inside) 3.50
4-($2.50)-Polybagged w/Topps trading card; 1st app. Tribe by Johnson & Stroman; Youngblood cameo 3.50
4-Variant w/red card 6.00
5-7-Jim Lee/Williams-c/a; Lee script 3.00
8-X-Men's Jean Grey & Scott Summers cameo 4.00
9-12: 10-1st app. Huntsman & Soldier; Claremont scripts begin, ends #13. 11-1st app. Savant, Tapestry & Mr. Majestic. 3.00
11-Alternate Portacio-c, see Deathblow #5 5.00
13-19,21-24: 15-James Robinson scripts begin, ends #20. 15,16-Black Razor story. 21-Alan Moore scripts begin, end #34; intro Tao & Ladytron; new WildC.A.T.S team forms (Mr. Majestic, Savant, Condition Red (Max Cash), Tao & Ladytron). 22-Maguire-a 3.00
20-($2.50)-Direct Market, WildStorm Rising Pt. 2 w/bound-in card 3.00
20-($1.95)-Newsstand, WildStorm Rising Part 2 2.50
25-($4.95)-Alan Moore script; wraparound foil-c. 5.00
26-49: 29-(5/96)-Fire From Heaven Pt 7; reads Apr on-c. 30-(6/96)-Fire From Heaven Pt. 13; Spartan revealed to have transplanted personality of John Colt (from Team One: WildC.A.T.S). 31-(9/96)-Grifter rejoins team; Ladytron dies 2.50
40-($3.50)Voyager Pack bagged w/Divine Right preview 6.00
50-($3.50) Stories by Robinson/Lee, Choi & Peterson/Benes, and Moore/Charest; Charest sketchbook; Lee wraparound-c 4.00
50-Chromium cover 6.00
Annual 1 (2/98, $2.95) Robinson-s 3.00
Compendium (1993, $9.95)-r/#1-4; bagged w/#0 10.00
Sourcebook 1 (9/93, $2.50)-Foil embossed-c 2.50
Sourcebook 1-($1.95)-Newsstand ed. w/o foil embossed-c 2.50
Sourcebook 2 (11/94, $2.50)-wraparound-c 2.50
Special 1 (11/93, $3.50, 52 pgs.)-1st Travis Charest WildC.A.T.S-a 3.50
...A Gathering of Eagles (5/97, $9.95, TPB) r/#10-12 10.00
.../ Cyberforce: Killer Instinct TPB (2004, $14.95) r/#5-7 & Cyberforce V2 #1-3 15.00
...Gang War ('98, $16.95, TPB) r/#28-34 17.00
...Homecoming (8/98, $19.95, TPB) r/#21-27 20.00

WILDCATS
DC Comics (WildStorm): Mar, 1999 - No. 28, Dec, 2001 ($2.50)

1-Charest-a; six covers by Lee, Adams, Bisley, Campbell, Madureira and Ramos; Lobdell-s 3.00
1-($6.95) DF Edition; variant cover by Ramos 7.00
2-28: 2-Voodoo cover. 3-Bachalo variant-c. 5-Hitch-a/variant-c. 7-Meglia-a. 8-Phillips-a begins. 17-J.G. Jones-c. 18,19-Jim Lee-c. 20,21-Dillon-a 2.50
Annual 2000 (12/00, $3.50) Bermejo-a; Devil's Night x-over 3.50
...: Battery Park ('03, $17.95, TPB) r/#20-28; Phillips-c 18.00
... Ladytron (10/00, $5.95) Origin; Casey-s/Canete-a 6.00
... Mosaic (2/00, $3.95) Tuska-a (10 pg. back-up story) 4.00
...: Serial Boxes ('01, $14.95, TPB) r/#14-19; Phillips-c 15.00
...: Street Smart ('00, $24.95, HC) r/#1-6; Charest-c 25.00
...: Street Smart ('02, $14.95, SC) r/#1-6; Charest-c 15.00
...: Vicious Circles ('00, $14.95, TPB) r/#8-13; Phillips-c 15.00

WILDCATS (Volume 4)
DC Comics (WildStorm): Dec, 2006 ($2.99)

1-Grant Morrison-s/Jim Lee-a; Jim Lee-c 3.00
1-Variant-c by Todd McFarlane/Jim Lee 6.00
...: Armageddon 1 (2/08, $2.99) Gage-s/Caldwell-a 3.00

WILDCATS (Volume 5) (World's End on cover)
DC Comics (WildStorm): Sept, 2008 - Present ($2.99)

1-Christos Gage-s/Neil Googe-a 3.00

WILDC.A.T.S/ ALIENS
Image Comics/Dark Horse: Aug, 1998 ($4.95, one-shot)

1-Ellis-s/Sprouse-a/c; Aliens invade Skywatch; Stormwatch app.; death of Winter; destruction of Skywatch 1 2 3 5 6 8
1-Variant-c by Gil Kane 1 3 4 6 8 10

WILDCATS: NEMESIS
DC Comics (WildStorm): Nov, 2005 - No. 9, July, 2006 ($2.99, limited series)

1-9: 1-Robbie Morrison-s/Talent Caldwell & Horacio Domingues-a/Caldwell-c 3.00
TPB (2006, $19.99) r/#1-9; cover gallery 20.00

WILDC.A.T.S: SAVANT GARDE FAN EDITION
Image Comics/WildStorm Productions: Feb, 1997 - No. 3, Apr, 1997 (Giveaway, 8 pgs.) (Polybagged w/Overstreet's FAN)

1-3: Barbara Kesel-s/Christian Uche-a(p) 3.00
1-3-(Gold): All retailer incentives 10.00

WILDC.A.T.S TRILOGY
Image Comics (WildStorm Productions): June, 1993 - No. 3, Dec, 1993 ($1.95, lim. series)

1-($2.50)-1st app. Gen 13 (Fairchild, Burnout, Grunge, Freefall) Multi-color foil-c; Jae Lee-c/a in all 5.00
1-($1.95)-Newsstand ed. w/o foil-c 2.50
2,3-($1.95)-Jae Lee-c/a 2.50

WILDCATS VERSION 3.0
DC Comics (WildStorm): Oct, 2002 - No. 24, Oct, 2004 ($2.95)

1-24: 1-Casey-s/Nguyen-a; two covers by Nguyen and Rian Hughes and Nguyen. 8-Back-up preview of The Authority: High Stakes pt. 3 3.00
...: Brand Building TPB (2003, $14.95) r/#1-6 15.00
...: Full Disclosure TPB (2004, $14.95) r/#7-12 15.00

WILDC.A.T.S/ X-MEN: THE GOLDEN AGE (See also X-Men/WildC.A.T.S.: The Dark Age)
Image Comics (WildStorm Productions): Feb, 1997 ($4.50, one-shot)

1-Lobdell-s/Charest-a; Two covers (Charest, Jim Lee) 5.00
1-"3-D" Edition ($6.50) w/glasses 7.00

WILDC.A.T.S/ X-MEN: THE MODERN AGE
Image Comics (WildStorm Productions): Aug, 1997 ($4.50, one-shot)

1-Robinson-s/Hughes-a; Two covers (Hughes, Paul Smith) 5.00
1-"3-D" Edition ($6.50) w/glasses 7.00

WILDC.A.T.S/ X-MEN: THE SILVER AGE
Image Comics (WildStorm Productions): June, 1997 ($4.50, one-shot)

1-Lobdell-s/Jim Lee-a; Two covers(Neal Adams, Jim Lee) 5.00
1-"3-D" Edition ($6.50) w/glasses 7.00

WILDCORE
Image Comics (WildStorm Prods.): Nov, 1997 - No. 10, Dec, 1998 ($2.50)

1-10: 1-Two covers (Booth/McWeeney, Charest) 2.50
1-($3.50)-Voyager Pack w/DV8 preview 3.50
1-Chromium-c 5.00

WILD DOG

Wild Stars V3 #1 © Michael Tierney

Wildstorm Revelations #5 © WSP

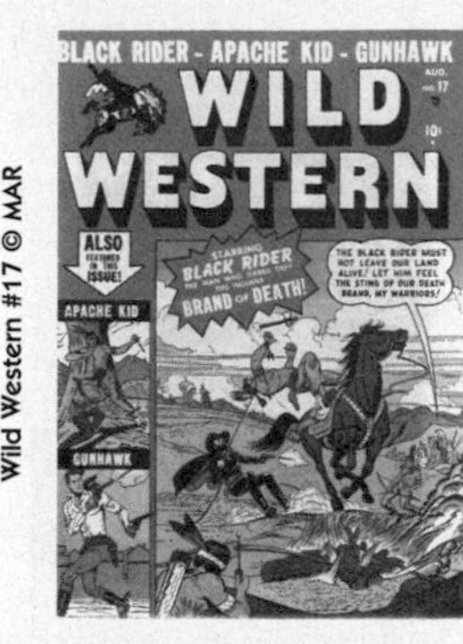

Wild Western #17 © MAR

GD VG FN VF VF/NM NM-
2.0 4.0 6.0 8.0 9.0 9.2

GD VG FN VF VF/NM NM-
2.0 4.0 6.0 8.0 9.0 9.2

DC Comics: Sept, 1987 - No. 4, Dec, 1987 (75¢, limited series)

1-4 2.50
Special 1 (1989, $2.50, 52 pgs.) 2.50

WILDERNESS TREK (See Zane Grey, Four Color 333)

WILDFIRE (See Zane Grey, FourColor 433)

WILDFLOWER
Sirius Entertainment/Neko Press: 1996 - Present (B&W)

1-5-('96, $2.50) Billy Martinez-s/a 2.50
... Beginnings TPB (Neko Press, 2003, $14.99) r/#1-5 15.00
... Dark Euphoria 1 (2004, $2.99) Klethan Jones-a/c; Martinez-s 3.00
... Dark Euphoria 1,2 (2004, $3.99) w/alternate-c by Martinez 4.00
... Tribal Screams 1-4 (12/00 - 2/03, $2.99) 3.00
... Tribal Screams 1 ($4.99) w/alternate-c by Dark One 5.00
... Y2K (16 pgs, edition of 2000) each contains an original Martinez sketch 10.00

WILD FRONTIER (Cheyenne Kid #8 on)
Charlton Comics: Oct, 1955 - No. 7, Apr, 1957

1-Davy Crockett 10 20 30 54 72 90
2-6-Davy Crockett in all 7 14 21 37 46 55
7-Origin & 1st app. Cheyenne Kid 9 18 27 47 61 75

WILD GIRL
DC Comics (WildStorm): Jan, 2005 - No. 6, Jun, 2005 ($2.95/$2.99)

1-6-Leah Moore & John Reppion-s/Shawn McManus-a/c 3.00

WILDGUARD: CASTING CALL
Image Comics: Sept, 2003 - No. 6, Feb, 2004 ($2.95)

1-6: 1-Nauck-s/a; two covers by Nauck and McGuinness. 2-Wieringo var-c. 6-Noto var-c 3.00
... Vol. 1: Casting Call (1/05, $17.95, TPB) r/#1-6; cover gallery; Todd Nauck bio 18.00
Wildguard: Fire Power 1 (12/04, $3.50) Nauck-a, two covers 3.50
Wildguard: Fool's Gold (7/05 - No. 2, 7/05, $3.50) 1,2-Todd Nauck-s/a 3.50
Wildguard: Insider (5/08 - No. 3, 7/08, $3.50) 1-3-Todd Nauck-s/a 3.50

WILDSIDERZ
DC Comics (WildStorm): No. 0, Aug, 2005 - No. 2, Jan, 2006 ($1.99/$3.50)

0-(8/05, $1.99) Series preview & character profiles; J. Scott Campbell-a 2.50
1,2: 1-(10/05, $3.50) J. Scott Campbell-s/a; Andy Hartnell-s 3.50

WILDSTAR (Also see The Dragon & The Savage Dragon)
Image Comics (Highbrow Entertainment): Sept, 1995 - No. 3, Jan, 1996 ($2.50, lim. series)

1-3: Al Gordon scripts; Jerry Ordway-c/a 2.50

WILDSTAR: SKY ZERO
Image Comics (Highbrow Entertainment): Mar, 1993 - No. 4, Nov, 1993 ($1.95, lim. series)

1-4: 1-($2.50)-Embossed-c w/silver ink; Ordway-c/a in all 2.50
1-($1.95)-Newsstand ed. w/silver ink-c, not embossed 2.50
1-Gold variant 6.00

WILD STARS
Collector's Edition/Little Rocket Productions: Summer, 1984 - Present (B&W)

Vol. 1 #1 (Summer 1984, $1.50) 5.00
Vol. 2 #1 (Winter 1988, $1.95) Foil-c; die-cut front & back-c 5.00
Vol. 3: #1-6-Brunner-c; Tierney-s. 1,2-Brewer-a. 3-6-Simons-a 3.00
7-($5.95) Simons-a 6.00
TPB (2004, $17.95) r/Vol. 1-3 18.00

WILDSTORM
Image Comics/DC Comics (WildStorm Publishing): 1994 - Present (one-shots)

...Annual 2000 (12/00, $3.50) Devil's Night x-over; Moy-a 3.50
...: Armageddon TPB (2008, $17.99) r/Armageddon one-shots in Midnighter, Welcome To Tranquility, Wetworks, Gen13, Stormwatch PHD, and Wildcats titles 18.00
...Chamber of Horrors (10/95, $3.50)-Bisley-c 3.50
...Fine Arts: Spotlight on Gen13 (2/08, $3.50) art and covers with commentary 3.50
...Fine Arts: Spotlight on Jim Lee (2/07, $3.50) art and covers by Lee with commentary 3.50
...Fine Arts: Spotlight on J. Scott Campbell (5/07, $3.50) art and covers with commentary 3.50
...Fine Arts: Spotlight on The Authority (1/08, $3.50) art and covers with commentary 3.50
...Fine Arts: Spotlight on WildCATs (3/08, $3.50) art and covers with commentary 3.50
...Fine Arts: The Gallery Collection (12/98, $19.95) Lee-c 20.00
...Halloween 1 (10/97, $2.50) Warner-c 2.50
...Rarities 1(12/94, $4.95, 52 pgs.)-r/Gen 13 1/2 & other stories 5.00
...Summer Special 1 (2001, $5.95) Short stories by various; Hughes-c 6.00
...Swimsuit Special 1 (12/94, $2.95), ...Swimsuit Special 2 (1995, $2.50) 3.00
...Swimsuit Special '97 #1 (7/97, $2.50) 2.50
...Thunderbook 1 (10/00, $6.95) Short stories by various incl. Hughes, Moy 7.00
...Ultimate Sports 1 (8/97, $2.50) 2.50
...Universe Sourcebook (5/95, $2.50) 2.50
...Universe 2008 Convention Exclusive ('08, no cover price) preview of World's End x-over 2.50

WILDSTORM!
Image Comics (WildStorm Publishing): Aug, 1995 - No. 4, Nov, 1995 ($2.50, B&W/color, anthology)

1-4: 1-Simonson-a 2.50

WILDSTORM REVELATIONS
DC Comics (WildStorm): Mar, 2008 - No. 6, May, 2008 ($2.99, limited series)

1-6-Beatty & Gage-s/Craig-a. 2-The Authority app. 3.00
TPB (2008, $17.99) r/#1-6; cover sketches 18.00

WILDSTORM RISING
Image Comics (WildStorm Publishing): May, 1995 - No.2, June, 1995 ($1.95/$2.50)

1-($2.50)-Direct Market, WildStorm Rising Pt. 1 w/bound-in card 2.50
1-($1.95)-Newstand, WildStorm Rising Pt. 1 2.50
2-($2.50)-Direct Market, WildStorm Rising Pt. 10 w/bound-in card; continues in WildC.A.T.S #21. 2.50
2-($1.95)-Newstand, WildStorm Rising Pt. 10 2.50
Trade paperback (1996, $19.95)-Collects x-over; B. Smith-c 20.00

WILDSTORM SPOTLIGHT
Image Comics (WildStorm Publishing): Feb, 1997 - No. 4 ($2.50)

1-4: 1-Alan Moore-s 2.50

WILDSTORM UNIVERSE '97
Image Comics (WildStorm Publishing): Dec, 1996 - No. 3 ($2.50, limited series)

1-3: 1-Wraparound-c. 3-Gary Frank-c 2.50

WILDTHING
Marvel Comics UK: Apr, 1993 - No. 7, Oct, 1993 ($1.75)

1-($2.50)-Embossed-c; Venom & Carnage cameo 2.50
2-7: 2-Spider-Man & Venom. 6-Mysterio app. 2.50

WILD THING (Wolverine's daughter in the M2 universe)
Marvel Comics: Oct, 1999 - No. 5, Feb, 2000 ($1.99)

1-5: 1-Lim-a in all. 2-Two covers 2.50
Wizard #0 supplement; battles the Hulk 2.50
Spider-Girl Presents Wild Thing. Crash Course (2007, $7.99, digest) r/#0-5 8.00

WILDTIMES
DC Comics (WildStorm Productions): Aug, 1999 ($2.50, one-shots)

...Deathblow #1 -set in 1899; Edwards-a; Jonah Hex app., ...DV8 #1 -set in 1944; Altieri-s/p; Sgt. Rock app., ...Gen13 #1 -set in 1969; Casey-s/Johnson-a; Teen Titans app., ...Grifter #1 -set in 1923; Paul Smith-a, ...Wetworks #1 -Waid-s/Lopresti-a; Superman app. 2.50
...WildC.A.T.s #0 -Wizard supplement; Charest-c 2.50

WILD WEST (Wild Western #3 on)
Marvel Comics (WFP): Spring, 1948 - No. 2, July, 1948

1-Two-Gun Kid, Arizona Annie, & Tex Taylor begin; Shores-c
34 68 102 198 319 440
2-Captain Tootsie by Beck; Shores-c 23 46 69 133 214 295

WILD WEST (Black Fury #1-57)
Charlton Comics: V2#58, Nov, 1966

V2#58 2 4 6 11 16 20

WILD WEST C.O.W.-BOYS OF MOO MESA (TV)
Archie Comics: Dec, 1992 - No. 3, Feb, 1993 (limited series)
V2#1, Mar, 1993 - No. 3, July, 1993 ($1.25)

1-3,V2#1-3 2.50

WILD WESTERN (Formerly Wild West #1,2)
Marvel/Atlas (WFP): No. 3, 9/48 - No. 57, 9/57 (3-11: 52 pgs, 12-on: 36 pgs)

3(#1)-Tex Morgan begins; Two-Gun Kid, Tex Taylor, & Arizona Annie continue from Wild West
27 54 81 158 254 350
4-Last Arizona Annie; Captain Tootsie by Beck; Kid Colt app.
20 40 60 115 183 250
5-2nd app. Black Rider (1/49); Blaze Carson, Captain Tootsie (by Beck) app.
23 46 69 133 214 295
6-8: 6-Blaze Carson app; anti-Wertham editorial 15 30 45 88 137 185
9-Photo-c; Black Rider begins, ends #19 19 38 57 109 172 235
10-Charles Starrett photo-c 22 44 66 127 204 280
11-(Last 52 pg. issue) 15 30 45 85 130 175
12-14,16-19: All Black Rider-c/stories. 12-14-The Prairie Kid & his horse Fury app.
15 30 45 83 124 165

Wild Wild West #3 © CBS

Win A Prize Comics #1 © CC

Wings Comics #79 © FH

GD VG FN VF VF/NM NM-
2.0 4.0 6.0 8.0 9.0 9.2

15-Red Larabee, Gunhawk (origin), his horse Blaze, & Apache Kid begin, end #22;
Black Rider-c/story 15 30 45 84 127 170
20-30: 20-Kid Colt-c begin. 24-Has 2 Kid Colt stories. 26-1st app. The Ringo Kid? (2/53);
4 pg. story. 30-Katz-a 12 24 36 69 97 125
31-40 10 20 30 54 72 90
41-47,49-51,53,57 9 18 27 47 61 75
48-Williamson/Torres-a (4 pgs); Drucker-a 10 20 30 56 76 95
52-Crandall-a 10 20 30 56 76 95
54,55-Williamson-a in both (5 & 4 pgs.), #54 with Mayo plus 2 text illos
10 20 30 56 76 95
56-Baker-a? 9 18 27 47 61 75

NOTE: *Annie Oakley in #46, 47. Apache Kid in #15-22, 39. Arizona Kid in #21, 23. Arrowhead in #34-39. Black Rider in #5, 9-19, 33-44. Fighting Texan in #17. Kid Colt in #4-6, 9-11, 20-47, 52, 54-56. Outlaw Kid in #43. Red Hawkins in #13, 14. Ringo Kid in #26, 39, 41, 43, 44, 46, 47, 50, 52-56. Tex Morgan in #3, 4, 6, 9, 11. Tex Taylor in #3-6, 9, 11. Texas Kid in #23-25. Two-Gun Kid in #3-6, 9, 11, 12, 33-39, 41. Wyatt Earp in #47.* ***Ayers*** *a-41, 42, 53, 54.* ***Berg*** *a-26; c-24.* ***Colan*** *a-49.* ***Forte*** *a-28, 30.* ***Al Hartley*** *a-16.* ***Heath*** *a-4, 5, 8; c-34, 44.* ***Keller*** *a-24, 26(2), 29-40, 44-46, 48, 52.* ***Maneely*** *a-10, 12, 15, 16, 28, 35, 38, 40-45; c-18-22, 33, 35, 36, 38, 39, 41, 42, 45, 53, 54, 56.* ***Morisi*** *a-23, 52.* ***Pakula*** *a-42, 52.* ***Powell*** *a-51.* ***Romita*** *a-24(2).* ***Severin*** *a-46, 47; c-48.* ***Shores*** *a-3, 5, 30, 31, 33, 35, 36, 38, 41; c-3-5.* ***Sinnott*** *a-34-39.* ***Wildey*** *a-43. Bondage c-19.*

WILD WESTERN ACTION (Also see The Bravados)
Skywald Publ. Corp.: Mar, 1971 - No. 3, June, 1971 (25¢, reprints, 52 pgs.)

1-Durango Kid, Straight Arrow-r; with all references to "Straight" in story relettered to
"Swift"; Bravados begin; Shores-a (new) 3 6 9 14 19 24
2,3: 2-Billy Nevada, Durango Kid. 3-Red Mask, Durango Kid
2 4 6 9 13 16

WILD WESTERN ROUNDUP
Red Top/Decker Publications/I. W. Enterprises: Oct, 1957; 1960-'61

1(1957)-Kid Cowboy-r 5 10 14 20 24 28
I.W. Reprint #1('60-61)-r/#1 by Red Top 2 4 6 8 11 14

WILD WEST RODEO
Star Publications: 1953 (15¢)

1-A comic book coloring book with regular full color cover & B&W inside
8 16 24 44 57 70

WILD WILD WEST, THE (TV)
Gold Key: June, 1966 - No. 7, Oct, 1969 (All have Robert Conrad photo-c)

1-McWilliams-a 12 24 36 84 150 215
1-Variant edition with photo back-c (scarce) 13 26 39 95 168 240
2-Robert Conrad photo-c; McWilliams-a 9 18 27 60 100 140
2-Variant edition with Conrad photo back-c (scarce) 9 18 27 65 113 160
3-7 7 14 21 50 83 115
3-Variant edition with photo back-c (scarce) 9 18 27 60 110 140

WILD, WILD WEST, THE (TV)
Millennium Publications: Oct, 1990 - No. 4, Jan?, 1991 ($2.95, limited series)

1-4-Based on TV show 3.00

WILKIN BOY (See That...)

WILL EISNER READER
Kitchen Sink Press: 1991 ($9.95, B&W, 8 1/2" x 11", TPB)

nn-Reprints stories from Will Eisner's Quarterly; Eisner-s/a/c 10.00
nn-(DC Comics, 10/00, $9.95) 10.00

WILL EISNER'S JOHN LAW: ANGELS AND ASHES, DEVILS AND DUST
IDW Publ.: Apr, 2006 - No. 4 ($3.99, B&W, limited series)

1-New stories with Will Eisner's characters; Gary Chaloner-s/a 4.00

WILLIE COMICS (Formerly Ideal #1-4; Crime Cases #24 on; Li'l Willie #20 & 21)
(See Gay Comics, Laugh, Millie The Model & Wisco)
Marvel Comics (MgPC): #5, Fall, 1946 - #19, 4/49; #22, 1/50 - #23, 5/50 (No #20 & 21)

5(#1)-George, Margie, Nellie the Nurse & Willie begin
23 46 69 135 218 300
6,8,9 14 28 42 82 121 160
7(1),10,11-Kurtzman's "Hey Look" 15 30 45 83 124 165
12,14-18,22,23 14 28 42 78 112 145
13,19-Kurtzman's "Hey Look" (#19-last by Kurtzman?)
14 28 42 80 115 150

NOTE: *Cindy app. in #17. Jeanie app. in #17. Little Lizzie app. in #22.*

WILLIE MAYS (See The Amazing...)

WILLIE THE PENGUIN
Standard Comics: Apr, 1951 - No. 6, Apr, 1952

1-Funny animal 9 18 27 47 61 75
2-6 6 12 18 28 34 40

WILLIE THE WISE-GUY (Also see Cartoon Kids)
Atlas Comics (NPP): Sept, 1957

1-Kida, Maneely-a 9 18 27 50 65 80

WILLOW
Marvel Comics: Aug, 1988 - No. 3, Oct, 1988 ($1.00)

1-3-R/Marvel Graphic Novel #36 (movie adaptation) 3.00

WILL ROGERS WESTERN (Formerly My Great Love #1-4; see Blazing & True Comics #66)
Fox Features Syndicate: No. 5, June, 1950 - No. 2, Aug, 1950

5(#1) 32 64 96 186 298 410
2: Photo-c 27 54 81 156 251 345

WILL TO POWER (Also see Comic's Greatest World)
Dark Horse Comics: June, 1994 - No. 12, Aug, 1994 ($1.00, weekly limited series, 20 pgs.)

1-12: 12-Vortex kills Titan. 2.50

NOTE: ***Mignola*** *c-10-12.* ***Sears*** *c-1-3.*

WILL-YUM!
Dell Publishing Co.: No. 676, Feb, 1956 - No. 902, May, 1958

Four Color 676 (#1), 765 (1/57), 902 4 8 12 26 41 55

WIN A PRIZE COMICS (Timmy The Timid Ghost #3 on?)
Charlton Comics: Feb, 1955 - No. 2, Apr, 1955

V1#1-S&K-a; Poe adapt; E.C. War swipe 67 134 201 422 711 1000
2-S&K-a 48 96 144 298 499 700

WINDY & WILLY
National Periodical Publications: May-June, 1969 - No. 4, Nov-Dec, 1969

1- r/Dobie Gillis with some art changes begin 4 8 12 28 44 60
2-4 3 6 9 18 27 35

WINGS COMICS
Fiction House Mag.: 9/40 - No. 109, 9/49; No. 110, Wint, 1949-50; No. 111, Spring, 1950; No. 112, 1950(nd); No. 113 - No. 115, 1950(nd); No. 116, 1952(nd); No. 117, Fall, 1952 - No. 122, Wint, 1953-54; No. 123 - No. 124, 1954(nd)

1-Skull Squad, Clipper Kirk, Suicide Smith, Jane Martin, War Nurse, Phantom Falcons,
Greasemonkey Griffin, Parachute Patrol & Powder Burns begin
267 534 801 1682 2841 4000
2 100 200 300 630 1065 1500
3-5 68 136 204 428 727 1025
6-10: 8-Indicia shows #7 (#8 on cover) 53 106 159 334 567 800
11-15 49 98 147 304 507 710
16-Origin & 1st app. Captain Wings & begin series 53 106 159 330 553 775
17-20 41 82 123 256 428 600
21-30 40 80 120 244 397 550
31-40 37 74 111 215 345 475
41-50 30 60 90 174 280 385
51-60: 60-Last Skull Squad 28 56 84 162 261 360
61-67: 66-Ghost Patrol begins (becomes Ghost Squadron #71 on), ends #112?
25 50 75 147 236 325
68,69: 68-Clipper Kirk becomes The Phantom Falcon-origin, Part 1; part 2 in #69
25 50 75 147 236 325
70-72: 70-1st app. The Phantom Falcon in costume, origin-Part 3; Capt. Wings battles
Col. Kamikaze in all 24 48 72 143 229 315
73-99: 80-Phantom Falcon by Larsen. 99-King of the Congo begins?
24 48 72 143 229 315
100-(12/48) 25 50 75 147 236 325
101-124: 111-Last Jane Martin. 112-Flying Saucer-c/story (1950). 115-Used
in POP, pg. 89 19 38 57 112 176 240

NOTE: *Bondage covers are common. Captain Wings battles Sky Hag-#75, 76; ...Mr. Atlantis-#85-92; ...Mr. Pupin(Red Agent)-#98-103. Capt. Wings by* ***Elias****-#52-64, 68, 69; by* ***Lubbers****-#29-32, 70-111; by* ***Renee****-#33-46.* ***Evans*** *a-85-106, 108-111(Jane Martin); text illos-72-84.* ***Larsen*** *a-52, 59, 64, 73-77. Jane Martin by* ***Fran Hopper****-#68-84; Suicide Smith by* ***John Celardo****-#72, 74, 76, 80-104; by* ***Hollingsworth****-#68-70, 105-109, 111; Ghost Squadron by* ***Astarita****-#67-79; by* ***Maurice Whitman****-#80-111. King of the Congo by* ***Moreira****-#99, 100. Skull Squad by* ***M. Baker****-#52-60; Clipper Kirk by* ***Baker****-#60, 61; by* ***Colan****-#53; by* ***Ingels****-(some issues?). Phantom Falcon by* ***Larsen****-#73-84.* ***Elias*** *c-58-72.* ***Fawcette*** *c-3-12, 16, 17, 19, 22-33.* ***Lubbers*** *c-74-109.* ***Tuska*** *a-5.* ***Whitman*** *c-110-124.* ***Zolnerwich*** *c-15, 21.*

WINGS OF THE EAGLES, THE
Dell Publishing Co.: No. 790, Apr, 1957 (10¢ & 15¢ editions exist)

Four Color 790-Movie; John Wayne photo-c; Toth-a 14 28 42 100 178 255

WINKY DINK (Adventures of...)
Pines Comics: No. 75, Mar, 1957 (one-shot)

75-Marv Levy-c/a 6 12 18 31 38 45

WINKY DINK (TV)
Dell Publishing Co.: No. 663, Nov, 1955

Four Color 663 (#1) 8 16 24 52 86 120

Winnie Winkle #6 © NYNS

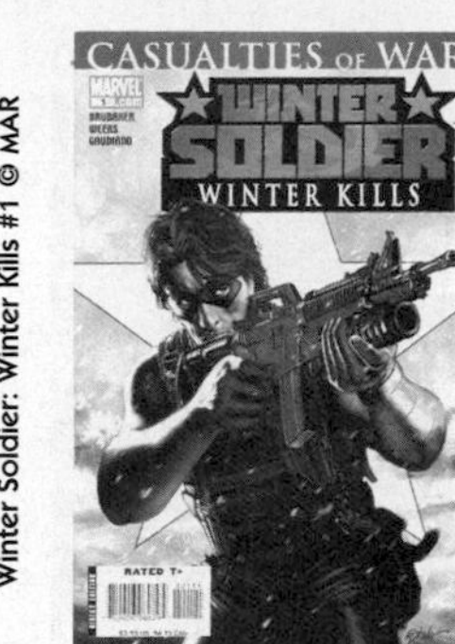

Winter Soldier: Winter Kills #1 © MAR

Witchblade #92 © TCOW

GD VG FN VF VF/NM NM-
2.0 4.0 6.0 8.0 9.0 9.2

WINNIE-THE-POOH (Also see Dynabrite Comics)
Gold Key No. 1-17/Whitman No. 18 on: January, 1977 - No. 33, July, 1984
(Walt Disney) (Winnie-The-Pooh began as Edward Bear in 1926 by Milne)

1-New art 3 6 9 16 22 28
2-5: 5-New material 2 4 6 9 13 16
6-17: 12-up-New material 2 4 6 8 10 12
18,19(Whitman) 2 4 6 9 13 16
20,21('80) pre-pack only 4 8 12 22 34 45
22('80) (scarcer) pre-pack only 4 8 12 28 44 60
23-28: 27(2/82), 28(4/82) 2 4 6 10 14 18
29-33 (#90299 on-c, no date or date code; pre-pack): 29(4/82), 30(5/83), 31(8/83), 32(4/84), 33(7/84) 3 6 9 16 23 30

WINNIE WINKLE (See Popular Comics & Super Comics)
Dell Publishing Co.: 1941 - No. 7, Sept-Nov, 1949

Large Feature Comic 2 (1941) 28 56 84 162 261 360
Four Color 94 (1945) 12 24 36 67 156 225
Four Color 174 8 16 24 58 97 135
1(3-5/48)-Contains daily & Sunday newspaper-r from 1939-1941 8 16 24 52 86 120
2 (6-8/48) 6 12 18 37 59 80
3-7 4 8 12 28 44 60

WINTER MEN, THE
DC Comics (WildStorm): Oct, 2005 - No. 5, Nov, 2006 ($2.99, limited series)

1-5-Brett Lewis-s/John Paul Leon-a 3.00

WINTER SOLDIER: WINTER KILLS (See Captain America 2005 series)
Marvel Comics: Feb, 2007 ($3.99, one-shot)

1-Flashback to Christmas Eve 1944; Toro & Sub-Mariner app.; Brubaker-s/Weeks-a 4.00

WINTERWORLD
Eclipse Comics: Sept, 1987 - No. 3, Mar, 1988 ($1.75, limited series)

1-3 2.50

WISDOM
Marvel Comics (MAX): Jan, 2007 - No. 6, July, 2007 ($3.99, limited series)

1-6: 1-Hairsine-a/c; Cornell-s. 3-6-Manuel Garcia-a 4.00
...: Rudiments of Wisdom TPB (2007, $21.99) r/#1-6; series pitch and sketch page 22.00

WISE GUYS (See Harvey...)

WISE LITTLE HEN, THE
David McKay Publ./Whitman: 1934 ,1935(48 pgs.); 1937 (Story book)

nn-(1934 edition w/dust jacket)(48 pgs. with color, 8-3/4x9-3/4") -Debut of Donald Duck (see Advs. of Mickey Mouse); Donald app. on cover with Wise Little Hen & Practical Pig; painted cover; same artist as the B&W's from Silly Symphony Cartoon, The Wise Little Hen (1934) (McKay)
Book w/dust jacket 237 474 711 1493 2522 3550
Dust jacket only 55 110 165 347 586 825
nn-(1935 edition w/dust jacket), same as 1934 ed. 138 276 414 869 1472 2075
888 (1937)(9-1/2x13", 12 pgs.)(Whitman) Donald Duck app. 34 68 102 198 319 440

WISE SON: THE WHITE WOLF
DC Comics (Milestone): Nov, 1996 - No. 4, Feb, 1997 ($2.50, limited series)

1-4: Ho Che Anderson-c/a 2.50

WIT AND WISDOM OF WATERGATE (Humor magazine)
Marvel Comics: 1973, 76 pgs., squarebound

1-Low print run 4 8 12 26 41 55

WITCHBLADE (Also see Cyblade/Shi, Tales Of The..., & Top Cow Classics)
Image Comics (Top Cow Productions): Nov, 1995 - Present ($2.50/$2.99)

0 1 2 3 5 6 8
1/2-Mike Turner/Marc Silvestri-c. 3 6 9 20 30 40
1/2 Gold Ed., 1/2 Chromium-c 3 6 9 20 30 40
1/2-(Vol. 2, 11/02, $2.99) Wohl-s/Ching-a/c 3.00
1-Mike Turner-a(p) 4 8 12 21 30 40
1,2-American Ent. Encore Ed. 1 2 3 4 5 7
2,3 2 4 6 11 16 20
4,5 2 4 6 9 13 16
6-9: 8-Wraparound-c. 9-Tony Daniel-a(p) 1 2 3 5 7 9
9-Sunset variant-c 2 4 6 8 10 12
9-DF variant-c 2 4 6 11 16 20
10-Flip book w/Darkness #0, 1st app. the Darkness 2 4 6 8 10 12
10-Variant-c 2 4 6 9 12 15
10-Gold logo 3 6 9 16 23 30
10-($3.95) Dynamic Forces alternate-c 1 2 3 5 6 8
11-15 5.00
16-19: 18,19-"Family Ties" Darkness x-over pt. 1,4 4.00
18-Face to face variant-c, 18-American Ent. Ed., 19-AE Gold Ed. 1 2 3 5 6 8
20-25: 24-Pearson, Green-a. 25-($2.95) Turner-a(p) 3.00
25 (Prism variant) 30.00
25 (Special) 15.00
26-39: 26-Green-a begins 2.50
27 (Variant) 10.00
40-49,51-53: 40-Begin Jenkins & Veitch-s/Keu Cha-a. 47-Zulli-c/a 2.50
40-Pittsburgh Convention Preview edition; B&W preview of #40 5.00
41-eWanted Chrome-c edition 5.00
49-Gold logo 1 2 3 5 6 8
50-($4.95) Darkness app.; Ching-a; B&W preview of Universe 5.00
54-59: 54-Black outer-c with gold foil logo; Wohl-s/Manapul-a 2.50
55-Variant Battle of the Planets Convention cover 3.00
60-74,76-91,93-99: 60-($2.99) Endgame x-over with Tomb Raider #25 & Evo #1. 64,65-Magdalena app. 71-Kirk-a. 77,81-85-Land-c. 80-Four covers. 87-Bachalo-a 3.00
75-($4.99) Manapul-a 5.00
92-($4.99) Origin of the Witchblade; art by various incl. Bachalo, Perez, Linsner, Cooke 5.00
100-($4.99) Five covers incl. Turner, Silvestri, Linsner; art by various; Jake dies 5.00
101-120: 103-Danielle Baptiste gets the Witchblade; Linsner variant c. 116-120-Sejic-a 3.00
... and Tomb Raider (4/05, $2.99) Jae Lee-c; art by Lee and Texiera 3.00
...: Animated (8/03, $2.99) Magdalena & Darkness app.; Dini-s/Bone, Bullock, Cooke-a/c 3.00
...: Art of the Witchblade (7/06, $2.99) pin-ups by various incl. Turner, Land, Linsner 3.00
...: Bearers of the Blade (7/06, $2.99) pin-up/profiles of bearers of the Witchblade 3.00
...: Blood Oath (8/04, $4.99) Sara teams with Phenix & Sibilla; Roux-a 5.00
...: Blood Relations TPB (2003, $12.99) r/#54-58 13.00
... Compendium Vol. 1 (2006, $59.99) r/#1-50; gallery of variant covers and art 60.00
... Compendium Vol. 2 (2007, $59.99) r/#51-100; gallery of variant covers and art 60.00
... Cover Gallery Vol. 1 (12/05, $2.99) intro. by Stan Lee 3.00
.../Darkchylde (7/00, $2.50) Green-s/a(p) 2.50
.../Dark Minds (6/04, $9.99) new story plus r/Dark Minds/Witchblade #1 10.00
.../Darkness: Family Ties Collected Edition (10/98, $9.95) r/#18,19 and Darkness #9,10 10.00
.../Darkness Special (12/99, $3.95) Green-c/a 4.00
...: Demon 1 (2003, $6.99) Mark Millar-s/Jae Lee-c/a 7.00
.../Devi (4/08, $3.99) Basaldua-a/Land-c; continues in Devi/Witchblade 4.00
...: Distinctions (See Tales of the Witchblade)
.../Elektra (3/97, $2.95) Devil's Reign Pt. 6 3.00
... Gallery (11/00, $2.95) Profile pages and pin-ups by various; Turner-c 3.00
Infinity (5/99, $3.50) Lobdell-s/Pollina-c/a 3.50
.../Lady Death (11/01, $4.95) Manapul-c/a 5.00
...: Prevailing TPB (2000, $14.95) r/#20-25; new Turner-c 15.00
...: Revelations TPB (2000, $24.95) r/#9-17; new Turner-c 25.00
.../The Punisher (6/07, $3.99) Marz-s/Melo-a/Linsner-c 4.00
.../Tomb Raider #1/2 (7/00, $2.95) Covers by Turner and Cha 3.00
...: Vol. 1 TPB (1/08, $4.99) r/#80-85; Marz intro.; cover gallery 5.00
...: Vol. 2 TPB (2/08, $14.99) r/#86-92; cover gallery 15.00
...: Vol. 3 TPB (3/08, $14.99) r/#93-100; Edginton intro.; cover gallery 15.00
... vs. Frankenstein: Monster War 2005 (8/05, $2.99) pt. 3 of x-over 3.00
...; Witch Hunt Vol. 1 TPB (2/06, $14.99) r/#80-85; Marz intro.; Choi afterward; cover gallery 15.00
Wizard #500 10.00
.../Wolverine (6/04, $2.99) Basaldua-c/a; Claremont-s 3.00

WITCHBLADE/ALIENS/THE DARKNESS/PREDATOR
Dark Horse Comics/Top Cow Productions: Nov, 2000 ($2.99)

1-3-Mel Rubi-a 3.00

WITCHBLADE COLLECTED EDITION
Image Comics (Top Cow Productions): July, 1996 - No. 8 ($4.95/$6.95, squarebound, limited series)

1-7-($4.95): Two issues reprinted in each 5.00
8-($6.95) r/#15-17 7.00
...Slipcase (10/96, $10.95)-Packaged w/ Coll. Ed. #1-4 11.00

WITCHBLADE: DESTINY'S CHILD
Image Comics (Top Cow): Jun, 2000 - No. 3, Sept, 2000 ($2.95, lim. series)

1-3: 1-Boller-a/Keu Cha-c 3.00

WITCHBLADE: MANGA (Takeru Manga)
Image Comics (Top Cow): Feb, 2007 - No. 12, Mar, 2008 ($2.99/$3.99)

1-4-Colored reprints of Japanese Witchblade manga. 1-Three covers. 2-Two covers 3.00
5-12-($3.99) 4.00

WITCHBLADE: OBAKEMONO

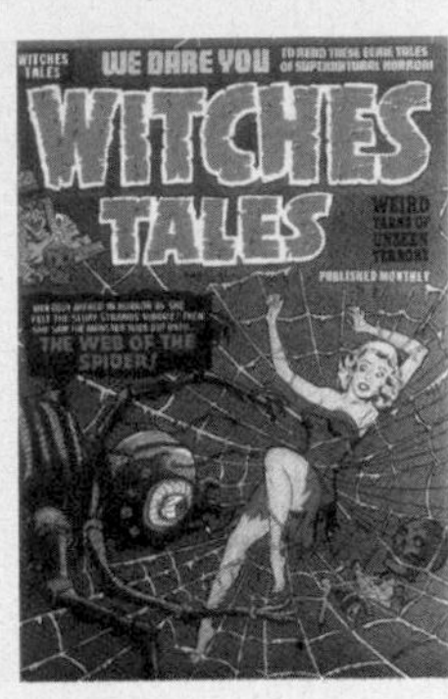

Witches Tales #12 © HARV

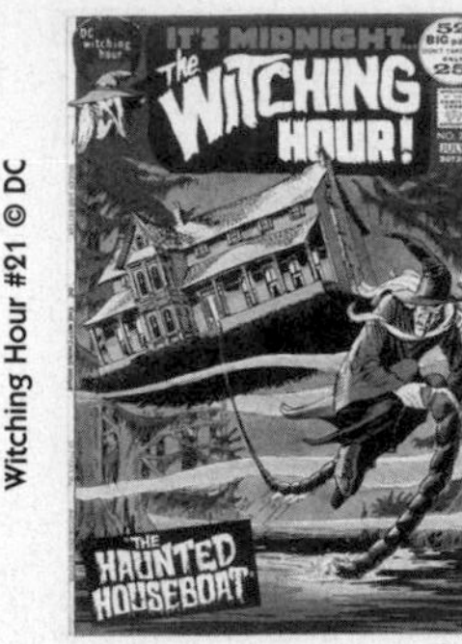

Witching Hour #21 © DC

Witching Hour (1999 series) #1 © Loeb & Bachalo

Image Comics (Top Cow Productions): 2002 ($9.95, one-shot graphic novel)

	GD 2.0	VG 4.0	FN 6.0	VF 8.0	VF/NM 9.0	NM- 9.2
1-Fiona Avery-s/Billy Tan-a; forward by Straczynski						10.00

WITCHBLADE: SHADES OF GRAY
Dynamite Ent./Top Cow: 2007 - No. 4, 2007 ($3.50, lim. series)

	GD 2.0	VG 4.0	FN 6.0	VF 8.0	VF/NM 9.0	NM- 9.2
1,2: 1-Sara Pezzini meets Dorian Gray; Segovia-a; multiple covers						3.50

WITCHBLADE/ TOMB RAIDER SPECIAL (Also see Tomb Raider/...)
Image Comics (Top Cow Productions): Dec, 1998 ($2.95)

	GD 2.0	VG 4.0	FN 6.0	VF 8.0	VF/NM 9.0	NM- 9.2
1-Based on video game character; Turner-a(p)						3.00
1-Silvestri variant-c						5.00
1-Turner bikini variant-c						10.00
1-Prism-c						12.00
Wizard 1/2 -Turner-s						10.00

WITCHCRAFT (See Strange Mysteries, Super Reprint #18)
Avon Periodicals: Mar-Apr, 1952 - No. 6, Mar, 1953

	GD 2.0	VG 4.0	FN 6.0	VF 8.0	VF/NM 9.0	NM- 9.2
1-Kubert-a; 1 pg. Check-a	72	144	216	454	765	1075
2-Kubert & Check-a	52	104	156	322	536	750
3,6: 3-Lawrence-a; Kinstler inside-c	41	82	123	256	428	600
4-People cooked alive c/story	48	96	144	298	499	700
5-Kelly Freas painted-c	53	106	159	330	553	775

NOTE: ***Hollingsworth** a-4-6; c-4, 6. **McCann** a-3?*

WITCHCRAFT
DC Comics (Vertigo): June, 1994 - No. 3, Aug, 1994 ($2.95, limited series)

	GD 2.0	VG 4.0	FN 6.0	VF 8.0	VF/NM 9.0	NM- 9.2
1-3: James Robinson scripts & Kaluta-c in all						4.00
1-Platinum Edition						8.00
Trade paperback-(1996, $14.95)-r/#1-3; Kaluta-c						15.00

WITCHCRAFT: LA TERREUR
DC Comics (Vertigo): Apr, 1998 - No. 3, Jun, 1998 ($2.50, limited series)

	GD 2.0	VG 4.0	FN 6.0	VF 8.0	VF/NM 9.0	NM- 9.2
1-3: Robinson-s/Zulli & Locke-a; interlocking cover images						2.50

WITCHES
Marvel Comics: Aug, 2004 - No. 4, Sept, 2004 ($2.99, limited series)

	GD 2.0	VG 4.0	FN 6.0	VF 8.0	VF/NM 9.0	NM- 9.2
1-4: 1,2-Deodato, Jr-a; Dr. Strange app. 3,4-Conrad-a						3.00
... Vol. 1: The Gathering (2004, $9.99) r/series						10.00

WITCHES TALES (Witches Western Tales #29,30)
Witches Tales/Harvey Publications: Jan, 1951 - No. 28, Dec, 1954 (date misprinted as 4/55)

	GD 2.0	VG 4.0	FN 6.0	VF 8.0	VF/NM 9.0	NM- 9.2
1-Powell-a (1 pg.)	55	110	165	347	586	825
2-Eye injury panel	35	70	105	208	334	460
3-7,9,10	27	54	81	158	254	350
8-Eye injury panels	28	56	84	162	261	360
11-13,15,16: 12-Acid in face story	25	50	75	145	233	320
14,17-Powell/Nostrand-a. 17-Atomic disaster story	26	52	78	154	247	340
18-Nostrand-a; E.C. swipe/Shock S.S.	26	52	78	154	247	340
19-Nostrand-a; E.C. swipe/ "Glutton"; Devil-c	28	56	84	162	261	360
20-24-Nostrand-a. 21-E.C. swipe; rape story. 23-Wood E.C. swipes/Two-Fisted Tales #34	26	52	78	154	247	340
25-Nostrand-a; E.C. swipe/Mad Barber; decapitation-c	40	80	120	244	397	550
26-28: 27-r/#6 with diff.-c. 28-r/#8 with diff.-c	19	38	57	109	172	235

NOTE: ***Check** a-24. **Elias** c-8, 10, 16-27. **Kremer** a-18; c-25. **Nostrand** a-17-25; 14, 17(w/**Powell**). **Palais** a-1, 2, 4(2), 5(2), 7-9, 12, 14, 15, 17. **Powell** a-3-7, 10, 11, 19-27. Bondage-c 1, 3, 5, 6, 8, 9.*

WITCHES TALES (Magazine)
Eerie Publications: V1#7, July, 1969 - V7#1, Feb, 1975 (B&W, 52 pgs.)

	GD 2.0	VG 4.0	FN 6.0	VF 8.0	VF/NM 9.0	NM- 9.2
V1#7(7/69)	6	12	18	41	66	90
V1#8(9/69), 9(11/69)	5	10	15	35	55	75
V2#1-6('70), V3#1-6('71)	4	8	12	28	44	60
V4#1-6('72), V5#1-6('73), V6#1-6('74), V7#1	4	8	12	24	37	50

NOTE: *Ajax/Farrell reprints in early issues.*

WITCHES' WESTERN TALES (Formerly Witches Tales)(Western Tales #31 on)
Harvey Publications: No. 29, Feb, 1955 - No. 30, Apr, 1955

	GD 2.0	VG 4.0	FN 6.0	VF 8.0	VF/NM 9.0	NM- 9.2
29,30-Featuring Clay Duncan & Boys' Ranch; S&K-r/from Boys' Ranch including-c. 29-Last pre-code	18	36	54	107	169	230

WITCHFINDER, THE
Image Comics (Liar): Sept, 1999 - No. 3, Jan, 2000 ($2.95)

	GD 2.0	VG 4.0	FN 6.0	VF 8.0	VF/NM 9.0	NM- 9.2
1-3-Romano-a/Sharon & Matthew Scott-plot						3.00

WITCH HUNTER
Malibu Comics (Ultraverse): Apr, 1996 ($2.50, one-shot)

	GD 2.0	VG 4.0	FN 6.0	VF 8.0	VF/NM 9.0	NM- 9.2
1						2.50

WITCHING, THE
DC Comics (Vertigo): Aug, 2004 - No. 10, May, 2005 ($2.95/$2.99)

	GD 2.0	VG 4.0	FN 6.0	VF 8.0	VF/NM 9.0	NM- 9.2
1-10-Vankin-s/Gallagher-a/McPherson-c. 1,2-Lucifer app.						3.00

WITCHING HOUR ("The ..." in later issues)
National Periodical Publ./DC Comics: Feb-Mar, 1969 - No. 85, Oct, 1978

	GD 2.0	VG 4.0	FN 6.0	VF 8.0	VF/NM 9.0	NM- 9.2
1-Toth-a, plus Neal Adams-a (2 pgs.)	12	24	36	87	156	225
2,6: 6-Toth-a	6	12	18	43	69	95
3,5-Wrightson-a; Toth-p. 3-Last 12¢ issue	7	14	21	45	73	100
4,12-Toth-a	4	8	12	28	44	60
7-11-Adams-c; Toth-a in all. 8-Adams-a	5	10	15	34	55	75
13-Neal Adams-c/a, 2pgs.	6	12	18	37	59	80
14-Williamson/Garzon, Jones-a; N. Adams-c	6	12	18	39	62	85
15	3	6	9	17	25	32
16-21-(52 pg. Giants)	3	6	9	20	30	40
22-37,39,40	2	4	6	11	16	20
38-(100 pgs.)	5	10	15	30	48	65
41-60	2	4	6	9	12	15
61-83,85	1	3	4	6	8	10
84-(44 pgs.)	2	4	6	8	10	12

NOTE: *Combined with The Unexpected with #189. **Neal Adams** c-7-11, 13, 14. **Alcala** a-24, 27, 33, 41, 43. **Anderson** a-9, 38. **Cardy** c-4, 5. **Kaluta** a-7. **Kane** a-12p. **Morrow** a-10, 13, 15, 16. **Nino** a-31, 40, 45, 47. **Redondo** a-20, 23, 24, 34, 65; c-53. **Reese** a-23. **Sparling** a-1. **Toth** a-1, 3-12, 38r. **Tuska** a-11, 12. **Wood** a-15.*

WITCHING HOUR, THE
DC Comics (Vertigo): 1999 - No. 3, 2000 ($5.95, limited series)

	GD 2.0	VG 4.0	FN 6.0	VF 8.0	VF/NM 9.0	NM- 9.2
1-3-Bachalo & Thibert-c/a; Loeb & Bachalo-s						6.00
Hardcover (2000, $29.95) r/#1-3; embossed cover						30.00
Softcover (2003, $19.95) r/#1-3						20.00

WITHIN OUR REACH
Star Reach Productions: 1991 ($7.95, 84 pgs.)

	GD 2.0	VG 4.0	FN 6.0	VF 8.0	VF/NM 9.0	NM- 9.2
nn-Spider-Man, Concrete by Chadwick, Gift of the Magi by Russell; X-mas stories; Chadwick-c; Spidey back-c						8.00

WITH THE MARINES ON THE BATTLEFRONTS OF THE WORLD
Toby Press: 1953 (no month) - No. 2, Mar, 1954 (Photo covers)

	GD 2.0	VG 4.0	FN 6.0	VF 8.0	VF/NM 9.0	NM- 9.2
1-John Wayne story	29	58	87	169	272	375
2-Monty Hall in #1,2	10	20	30	56	76	95

WITH THE U.S. PARATROOPS BEHIND ENEMY LINES (Also see U.S. Paratroops...; #2-6 titled U.S. Paratroops...)
Avon Periodicals: 1951 - No. 6, Dec, 1952

	GD 2.0	VG 4.0	FN 6.0	VF 8.0	VF/NM 9.0	NM- 9.2
1-Wood-c & inside f/c	17	34	51	98	154	210
2-Kinstler-c & inside f/c only	11	22	33	60	83	105
3-6: 6-Kinstler-c & inside f/c only	10	20	30	54	72	90

NOTE: ***Kinstler** c-2, 4-6.*

WITNESS, THE (Also see Amazing Mysteries, Captain America #71, Ideal #4, Marvel Mystery #92 & Mystic #7)
Marvel Comics (MjMe): Sept, 1948

	GD 2.0	VG 4.0	FN 6.0	VF 8.0	VF/NM 9.0	NM- 9.2
1(Scarce)-Rico-c?	233	466	699	1468	2484	3500

WITTY COMICS
Irwin H. Rubin Publ./Chicago Nite Life News No. 2: 1945 - No. 2, 1945

	GD 2.0	VG 4.0	FN 6.0	VF 8.0	VF/NM 9.0	NM- 9.2
1-The Pioneer, Junior Patrol; Japanese war-c	30	60	90	174	280	385
2-The Pioneer, Junior Patrol	15	30	45	86	133	180

WIZARD OF FOURTH STREET, THE
Dark Horse Comics: Dec, 1987 - No. 2, 1988 ($1.75, B&W, limited series)

	GD 2.0	VG 4.0	FN 6.0	VF 8.0	VF/NM 9.0	NM- 9.2
1,2: Adapts novel by S/F author Simon Hawke						2.50

WIZARD OF OZ (See Classics Illustrated Jr. 535, Dell Jr. Treasury No. 5, First Comics Graphic Novel, Marvelous..., & Marvel Treasury of Oz)
Dell Publishing Co.: No. 1308, Mar-May, 1962 (TV)

	GD 2.0	VG 4.0	FN 6.0	VF 8.0	VF/NM 9.0	NM- 9.2
Four Color 1308	11	22	33	79	140	200

WIZARD'S TALE, THE
Image Comics (Homage Comics): 1997 ($19.95, squarebound, one-shot)

	GD 2.0	VG 4.0	FN 6.0	VF 8.0	VF/NM 9.0	NM- 9.2
nn-Kurt Busiek-s/David Wenzel-painted-a/c						20.00

WOLF & RED
Dark Horse Comics: Apr, 1995 - No. 3, June, 1995 ($2.50, limited series)

	GD 2.0	VG 4.0	FN 6.0	VF 8.0	VF/NM 9.0	NM- 9.2
1-3: Characters created by Tex Avery						2.50

WOLFF & BYRD, COUNSELORS OF THE MACABRE (Becomes Supernatural Law with issue #24)
Exhibit A Press: May, 1994 - No. 23, Aug, 1999 ($2.50, B&W)

	GD 2.0	VG 4.0	FN 6.0	VF 8.0	VF/NM 9.0	NM- 9.2
1-23-Batton Lash-s/a						2.50

Wolverine #85 © MAR

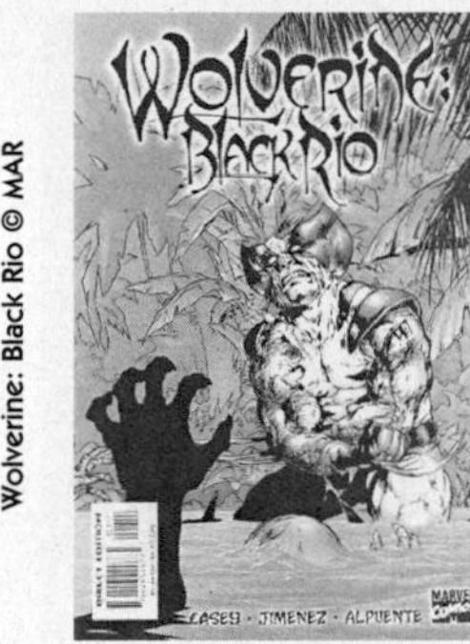

Wolverine: Black Rio © MAR

Wolverine V3 #66 © MAR

	GD 2.0	VG 4.0	FN 6.0	VF 8.0	VF/NM 9.0	NM- 9.2

WOLF GAL (See Al Capp's...)

WOLFMAN, THE (See Movie Classics)

WOLFPACK
Marvel Comics: Feb, 1988 ($7.95); Aug, 1988 - No. 12, July, 1989 (Lim. series)

	GD	VG	FN	VF	VF/NM	NM-
1-1st app./origin (Marvel Graphic Novel #31)						8.00
1-12						2.50

WOLVERINE (See Alpha Flight, Daredevil #196, 249, Ghost Rider; Wolverine; Punisher, Havok &..., Incredible Hulk #180, Incredible Hulk &..., Kitty Pryde And..., Marvel Comics Presents, New Avengers, Power Pack, Punisher and..., Spider-Man vs... & X-Men #94)

WOLVERINE (See Incredible Hulk #180 for 1st app.)
Marvel Comics Group: Sept, 1982 - No. 4, Dec, 1982 (limited series)

	GD	VG	FN	VF	VF/NM	NM-
1-Frank Miller-c/a(p) in all; Claremont-s	5	10	15	34	55	75
2-4	4	8	12	26	41	55
... By Claremont & Miller HC (2006, $19.99) r/#1-4 & Uncanny X-Men #172-173						20.00
TPB 1(7/87, $4.95)-Reprints #1-4 with new Miller-c	2	4	6	10	14	18
TPB nn (2nd printing, $9.95)-r/#1-4	2	4	6	8	10	12

WOLVERINE
Marvel Comics: Nov, 1988 - No. 189, June, 2003 ($1.50/$1.75/$1.95/$1.99/$2.25)

	GD	VG	FN	VF	VF/NM	NM-
1	4	8	12	22	34	45
2	2	4	6	13	18	22
3-5: 4-BWS back-c	2	4	6	9	13	16
6-9: 6-McFarlane back-c. 7,8-Hulk app.	1	3	4	6	8	10
10-1st battle with Sabretooth (before Wolverine had his claws)	3	6	9	16	23	30
11-16: 11-New costume	1	2	3	5	6	8
17-20: 17-Byrne-c/a(p) begins, ends #23	1	2	3	4	5	7
21-30: 24,25,27-Jim Lee-c. 26-Begin $1.75-c						5.00
31-40,44,47						4.00
41-Sabretooth claims to be Wolverine's father; Cable cameo						6.00
41-Gold 2nd printing ($1.75)						2.50
42-Sabretooth, Cable & Nick Fury app.; Sabretooth proven not to be Wolverine's father	1	2	3	5	6	8
42-Gold ink 2nd printing ($1.75)						2.50
43-Sabretooth cameo (2 panels); saga ends						5.00
45,46-Sabretooth-c/stories						5.00
48-51: 48,49-Sabretooth app. 48-Begin 3 part Weapon X sequel. 50-(64 pgs.)-Die cut-c; Wolverine back to old yellow costume; Forge, Cyclops, Jubilee, Jean Grey & Nick Fury app. 51-Sabretooth-c & app.						4.00
52-74,76-80: 54-Shatterstar (from X-Force) app. 55-Gambit, Jubilee, Sunfire-c/story. 55-57,73-Gambit app. 57-Mariko Yashida dies (Late 7/92). 58,59-Terror, Inc. x-over. 60-64-Sabretooth storyline (60,62,64-c)						4.00
75-($3.95, 68 pgs.)-Wolverine hologram on-c						5.00
81-84,86: 81-bound-in card sheet						3.00
85-($2.50)-Newsstand edition						3.00
85-($3.50)-Collectors edition						5.00
87-90 ($1.95)-Deluxe edition						3.00
87-90 ($1.50)-Regular edition						2.50
91-99,101-114: 91-Return from "Age of Apocalypse," 93-Juggernaut app. 94-Gen X app. 101-104-Elektra app. 104-Origin of Onslaught. 105-Onslaught x-over. 110-Shaman-c/app. 114-Alternate-c						3.00
100 ($3.95)-Hologram-c; Wolverine loses humanity	1	2	3	5	7	9
100 ($2.95)-Regular-c.						4.00
115-124: 115- Operation Zero Tolerance						2.50
125-($2.99) Wraparound-c; Viper secret						3.00
125-($6.95) Jae Lee variant-c						7.00
126-144: 126,127-Sabretooth-c/app. 128-Sabretooth & Shadowcat app.; Platt-a. 129-Wendigo-c/app. 131-Initial printing contained lettering error. 133-Begin Larsen-s/ Matsuda-a. 138-Galactus-c/app. 139-Cable app.; Yu-a. 142,143-Alpha Flight app.						2.50
145-($2.99) 25th Anniversary issue; Hulk and Sabretooth app.						3.00
145-($3.99) Foil enhanced cover (also see Promotional section for Nabisco mail-in ed.)						5.00
146-149: 147-Apocalypse: The Twelve; Angel-c/app. 149-Nova-c/app.						2.50
150-($2.99) Steve Skroce-s/a						3.00
151-174,176-182,184-189: 151-Begin $2.25-c. 154,155-Liefeld-s/a. 156-Churchill-a. 159-Chen-a begins. 160-Sabretooth app. 163-Texeira-a(p). 167-BWS-c. 172,173-Alpha Flight app. 176-Colossus app. 185,186-Punisher app.						2.50
175,183-($3.50) 175-Sabretooth app.						3.50
#(-1) Flashback (7/97) Logan meets Col. Fury; Nord-a						2.50
Annual nn (1990, $4.50, squarebound, 52 pgs.)-The Jungle Adventure; Simonson scripts; Mignola-c/a						5.00
Annual 2 (12/90, $4.95, squarebound, 52 pgs.)-Bloodlust						5.00
Annual nn (#3, 8/91, $5.95, 68 pgs.)-Rahne of Terror; Cable & The New Mutants app.; Andy Kubert-c/a (2nd print exists)						6.00
Annual '95 (1995, $3.95)						4.00
Annual '96 (1996, $2.95)- Wraparound-c; Silver Samurai, Yukio, and Red Ronin app.						3.00
Annual '97 ($2.99) - Wraparound-c						3.00
Annual 1999, 2000 ($3.50) : 1999-Deadpool app.						3.50
Annual 2001 ($2.99) - Tieri-s; JH Williams-c						3.00
...Battles The Incredible Hulk nn (1989, $4.95, squarebound, 52 pg.) r/Incr. Hulk #180,181						5.00
Best of Wolverine Vol. 1 HC (2004, $29.99) oversized reprints of Hulk #181, mini-series #1-4, Capt. America Ann, #8, Uncanny X-Men #205 & Marvel Comics Presents #72-84						30.00
...Black Rio (11/98, $5.99)-Casey-s/Oscar Jimenez-a						6.00
...Blood Debt TPB (7/01, $12.95)-r/#150-153; Skroce-c						13.00
...Blood Hungry nn (1993, $6.95, 68 pgs.)-Kieth-r/Marvel Comics Presents #85-92 w/ new Kieth-c						7.00
...: Bloody Choices nn (1993, $7.95, 68 pgs.)-r/Graphic Novel; Nick Fury app.						8.00
... Cable Guts and Glory (10/99, $5.99) Platt-a						6.00
... Classic Vol. 1 TPB (2005, $12.99) r/#1-5						13.00
... Classic Vol. 2 TPB (2005, $12.99) r/#6-10						13.00
... Classic Vol. 3 TPB (2006, $14.99) r/#11-16; The Gehenna Stone Affair						15.00
... Classic Vol. 4 TPB (2006, $14.99) r/#17-23						15.00
... Classic Vol. 5 TPB (2007, $14.99) r/#24-30						15.00
.../Deadpool: Weapon X TPB (7/02, $21.99)-r/#162-166 & Deadpool #57-60						22.00
... Doombringer (11/97, $5.99)-Silver Samurai-c/app.						6.00
... Evilution (9/94, $5.95)						6.00
...: Global Jeopardy 1 (12/93, $2.95, one-shot)-Embossed-c; Sub-Mariner, Zabu, Ka-Zar, Shanna & Wolverine app.; produced in cooperation with World Wildlife Fund						3.00
...:Inner Fury nn (1992, $5.95, 52 pgs.)-Sienkiewicz-c/a						6.00
...: Judgment Night (2000, $3.99) Shi app.; Battlebook						4.00
...: Killing (9/93)-Kent Williams-a						6.00
...: Knight of Terra (1995, $6.95)-Ostrander script						7.00
... Legends Vol. 2: Meltdown (2003, $19.99) r/Havok & Wolverine: Meltdown #1-4						20.00
... Legends Vol. 3 (2003, $12.99) r/#181-186						13.00
... Legends Vol. 4,5: 4 (See Wolverine: Xisle). 5 (See Wolverine: Snikt!)						
... Legends Vol. 6: Marc Silvestri Book 1 (2004, $19.99) r/#31-34, 41-42, 48-50						20.00
.../ Nick Fury: The Scorpio Connection Hardcover (1989, $16.95)						25.00
.../ Nick Fury: The Scorpio Connection Softcover(1990, $12.95)						15.00
...: Not Dead Yet (12/98, $14.95, TPB)-r/#119-122						15.00
...: Save The Tiger 1 (7/92, $2.95, 84 pgs.)-Reprints Wolverine stories from Marvel Comics Presents #1-10 w/new Kieth-c						3.00
...Scorpio Rising ($5.95, prestige format, one-shot)						6.00
.../Shi: Dark Night of Judgment (Crusade Comics, 2000, $2.99) Tucci-a						3.00
...Triumphs And Tragedies-(1995, $16.95, trade paperback)-r/Uncanny X-Men #109,172,173, Wolverine limited series #4, & Wolverine #41,42,75						17.00
...Typhoid's Kiss (6/94, $6.95)-r/Wolverine stories from Marvel Comics Presents #109-116						7.00
...Vs. Spider-Man 1 (3/95, $2.50) -r/Marvel Comics Presents #48-50						2.50
.../Witchblade 1 (3/97, $2.95) Devil's Reign Pt. 5						4.00
Wizard #1/2 (1997) Joe Phillips-a(p)						10.00

NOTE: ***Austin*** *c-3i.* ***Bolton*** *c(back)-5.* ***Buscema*** *a-1-16,25,27p; c-1-10.* ***Byrne*** *a-17-22p, 23; c-1(back), 17-22, 23p.* ***Colan*** *a-24.* ***Andy Kubert*** *c/a-51.* ***Jim Lee*** *c-24, 25, 27.* ***Silvestri*** *a(p)-31-43, 45, 46, 48-50, 52, 53, 55-57; c-31-42p, 43, 45p, 46p, 48, 49p, 50p, 52p, 53p, 55-57p.* ***Stroman*** *a-44p; c-60p.* ***Williamson*** *a-1i, 3-8i; c(i)-1, 3-6.*

WOLVERINE (Volume 3)
Marvel Comics: July, 2003 - Present ($2.25/$2.50/$2.99)

	GD	VG	FN	VF	VF/NM	NM-
1-Rucka-s/Robertson-a						4.00
2-19: 6-Nightcrawler app. 13-16-Sabretooth app.						3.00
20-Millar-s/Romita, Jr.-a begin, Elektra app.						4.00
20-B&W variant-c						5.00
21-39: 21-Elektra-c/app. 23,24-Daredevil app. 26-28-Land-c. 29-Quesada-c; begin $2.50-c. 33-35-House of M. 36,37-Decimation. 36-Quesada-c. 39-Winter Soldier app.						3.00
40,43-48: 40-Begin $2.99-c; Winter Soldier app.; Texeira-a. 43-46-Civil War, Ramos-a. 45-Sub-Mariner app.						3.00
41,49-($3.99) 41-C.P. Smith-a/Stuart Moore-s						4.00
42-Civil War						5.00
50-($3.99) Sabretooth app.; Bianchi-a/c & Loeb-s begin; wraparound-c; McGuinness-a						4.00
50-($3.99) Variant Edition; uncolored art and cover; Bianchi pencil art page						4.00
51-55-(Regular and variant uncolored editions) Bianchi-a/Loeb-s; Sabretooth app.						3.00
55-EC-style variant-c by Greg Land						5.00
56-($3.99) Howard Chaykin-a/c						4.00
57-65: 57-61-Suydam Zombie-c; Chaykin-a. 62-65-Mystique app.						3.00
66-Old Man Logan begins; Millar-s/McNiven-a; McNiven wraparound-c						3.00
66-Variant-c by Michael Turner						5.00
66-Variant sketch-c by Michael Turner						20.00
66-2nd printing with McNiven variant-c of Logan and Hulk gang member						3.00
67,68: 67-Intro. Ashley, Spider-Man's granddaughter						3.00
Annual 1 (12/07, $3.99) Hurwitz-s/Frusin-a						4.00
Annual 2 (11/08, $3.99) Swierczynski-s/Deodato-a/c						4.00
...: Blood & Sorrow TPB (2007, $13.99) r/#41,49, stories from Giant-Size Wolverine #1 and						

Wolverine: Origins #26 © MAR

Wolverine: Snikt! #1 © MAR

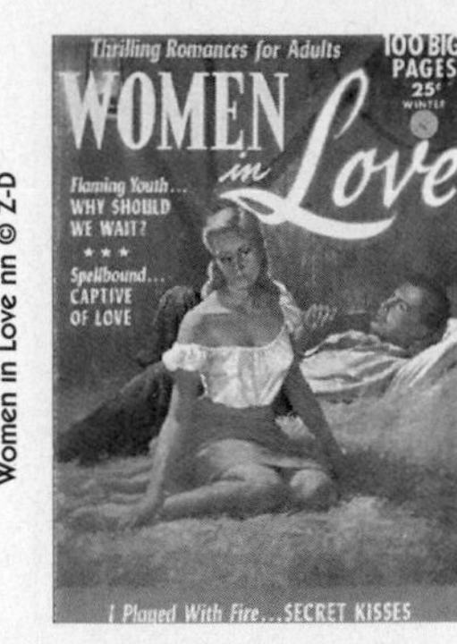

Women in Love nn © Z-D

	GD 2.0	VG 4.0	FN 6.0	VF 8.0	VF/NM 9.0	NM- 9.2
X-Men Unlimited #12						14.00
Civil War: Wolverine TPB (2007, $17.99) r/#42-48; gallery of B&W cover inks						18.00
... Dangerous Games 1 (8/08, $3.99) Spurrier-s/Oliver-a; Remender-s/Opena-a						4.00
...Enemy of the State HC Vol. 1 (2005, $19.99) r/#20-25; Ennis intro.; variant covers						20.00
...Enemy of the State HC Vol. 2 (2005, $19.99) r/#26-32						20.00
...Enemy of the State SC Vol. 1 (2005, $14.99) r/#20-25; Ennis intro.; variant covers						15.00
...Enemy of the State SC Vol. 2 (2006, $16.99) r/#26-32						17.00
...Enemy of the State - The Complete Edition (2006, $34.99) r/#20-32; Ennis intro.; sketch pages, variant covers and pin-up art						35.00
...: Evolution SC (2008, $14.99) r/#50-55						15.00
...: Killing Made Simple (10/08, $3.99) Yost-s/Turnbull-a						4.00
...Origins & Endings HC (2006, $19.99) r/#36-40						20.00
...Origins & Endings SC (2006, $13.99) r/#36-40						14.00
...: Saudade (2008, $4.99) English adaptation of Wolverine story from French comic						5.00
...Special: Firebreak (2/08, $3.99) Carey-s/Kolins-a; Lolos-a						4.00
...: The Amazing Immortal Man & Other Bloody Tales (7/08, $3.99) Lapham short stories						4.00
...: The Death of Wolverine HC (2008, $19.99) r/#56-61						20.00
...Vol. 1: The Brotherhood (2003, $12.99) r/#1-6						13.00
...Vol. 2: Coyote Crossing (2004, $11.99) r/#7-11						12.00

WOLVERINE AND THE PUNISHER: DAMAGING EVIDENCE
Marvel Comics: Oct, 1993 - No. 3, Dec, 1993 ($2.00, limited series)

1-3: 2,3-Indicia says "The Punisher and Wolverine..."						3.00

WOLVERINE/CAPTAIN AMERICA
Marvel Comics: Apr, 2004 - No. 4, Apr, 2004 ($2.99, limited series)

1-4-Derenick-a/c						3.00

WOLVERINE: DAYS OF FUTURE PAST
Marvel Comics: Dec, 1997 - No. 3, Feb, 1998 ($2.50, limited series)

1-3: J.F. Moore-s/Bennett-a						2.50

WOLVERINE/DOOP (Also see X-Force and X-Statix)(Reprinted in X-Statix Vol. 2)
Marvel Comics: July, 2003 - No. 2, July, 2003 ($2.99, limited series)

1,2-Peter Milligan-s/Darwyn Cooke & J. Bone-a						3.00

WOLVERINE: FIRST CLASS
Marvel Comics: May, 2008 - Present ($2.99)

1-7: 1-Wolverine and Kitty Pryde's first mission; DiVito-a. 2-Sabretooth app.						3.00

WOLVERINE/GAMBIT: VICTIMS
Marvel Comics: Sept, 1995 - No. 4, Dec, 1995 ($2.95, limited series)

1-4: Jeph Loeb scripts & Tim Sale-a; foil-c						4.00

WOLVERINE/HULK
Marvel Comics: Apr, 2002 - No. 4, July, 2002 ($3.50, limited series)

1-4-Sam Kieth-s/a/c						3.50
Wolverine Legends Vol. 1: Wolverine/Hulk (2003, $9.99, TPB) r/#1-4						10.00

WOLVERINE: NETSUKE
Marvel Comics: Nov, 2002 - No. 4, Feb, 2003 ($3.99, limited series)

1-4-George Pratt-s/painted-a						4.00

WOLVERINE: ORIGINS
Marvel Comics: June, 2006 - Present ($2.99)

1-15: 1-Daniel Way-s/Steve Dillon-a/Quesada-c						3.00
1-10-Variant covers. 1-Turner. 2-Quesada & Hitch. 3-Bianchi. 4-Dell'Otto. 7-Deodato						4.00
16-($3.99) Captain America WW2 app.; preview of Wolverine #56; r/X-Men #268						4.00
16-Variant-c by McGuinness						4.00
17-24: 17-20-Capt. America & Bucky app. 21-24-Deadpool app.; Bianchi-c						3.00
25-($3.99) Deadpool app.; Bianchi-c; r/Deadpool's 1st app. in New Mutants #98						4.00
26-28: 26-Origin of Dakan; Way-s/Segovia-a/Land-c. 28-Hulk & Wendigo app.						3.00
Annual 1 (9/07, $3.99) Way-s/Andrews-a; flashback to 1932						4.00
... Vol. 1 - Born in Blood HC (2006, $19.99, dustjacket) r/#1-5; variant covers						20.00
... Vol. 1 - Born in Blood SC (2007, $13.99) r/#1-5; variant covers						14.00
... Vol. 2 - Savior HC (2007, $19.99, dustjacket) r/#6-10; variant covers						20.00
... Vol. 2 - Savior SC (2007, $13.99) r/#6-10; variant covers						14.00
... Vol. 3 - Swift & Terrible HC (2007, $19.99, dustjacket) r/#11-15						20.00
... Vol. 3 - Swift & Terrible SC (2007, $13.99) r/#11-15						14.00
... Vol. 4 - Our War HC (2008, $19.99, dustjacket) r/#16-20 & Annual #1						20.00

WOLVERINE/PUNISHER
Marvel Comics: May, 2004 - No. 5, Sept, 2004 ($2.99, limited series)

1-5: Milligan-s/Weeks-a						3.00
... Vol. 1 TPB (2004, $13.99) r/series						14.00

WOLVERINE/PUNISHER REVELATIONS (Marvel Knights)
Marvel Comics: Jun, 1999 - No. 4, Sept, 1999 ($2.95, limited series)

	GD 2.0	VG 4.0	FN 6.0	VF 8.0	VF/NM 9.0	NM- 9.2
1-4: Pat Lee-a(p)						4.00
...: Revelation (4/00, $14.95, TPB) r/#1-4						15.00

WOLVERINE SAGA
Marvel Comics: Sept, 1989 - No. 4, Mid-Dec, 1989 ($3.95, lim. series, 52 pgs.)

1-Gives history; Liefeld/Austin-c (front & back)						5.00
2-4: 2-Romita, Jr./Austin-c. 4-Kaluta-c						5.00

WOLVERINE: SNIKT!
Marvel Comics: July, 2003 - No. 5, Nov, 2003 ($2.99, limited series)

1-5-Manga-style; Tsutomu Nihei-s/a						3.00
Wolverine Legends Vol. 5: Snikt! TPB (2003, $13.99) r/#1-5						14.00

WOLVERINE: SOULTAKER
Marvel Comics: May, 2005 - No. 5, Aug, 2005 ($2.99, limited series)

1-5-Yoshida-s/Nagasawa-a/Terada-c; Yukio app.						3.00
TPB (2005, $13.99) r/#1-5						14.00

WOLVERINE: THE END
Marvel Comics: Jan, 2004 - No. 6, Dec, 2004 ($2.99, limited series)

1-5-Jenkins-s/Castellini-a						3.00
1-Wizard World Texas variant-c						20.00
TPB (2005, $14.99) r/#1-5						15.00

WOLVERINE: THE ORIGIN
Marvel Comics: Nov, 2001 - No. 6, July, 2002 ($3.50, limited series)

1-Origin of Logan; Jenkins-s/Andy Kubert-a; Quesada-c						40.00
1-DF edition						60.00
2						15.00
3						9.00
4-6						5.00
HC (3/02, $34.95, 11" x 7-1/2") r/#1-6; dust jacket; sketch pages and treatments						35.00
HC (2006, $19.99) r/#1-6; dust jacket; sketch pages and treatments						20.00
SC (2002, $14.95) r/#1-6; afterwords by Jemas and Quesada						15.00

WOLVERINE: XISLE
Marvel Comics: June, 2003 - No. 5, June, 2003 ($2.50, weekly limited series)

1-5-Bruce Jones-s/Jorge Lucas-a						2.50
Wolverine Legends Vol. 4 TPB (2003, $13.99) r/ #1-5						14.00

WOMEN IN LOVE (A Feature Presentation #5)
Fox Features Synd./Hero Books: Aug, 1949 - No. 4, Feb, 1950

1	32	64	96	190	305	420
2-Kamen/Feldstein-c	27	54	81	158	254	350
3	19	38	57	109	172	235
4-Wood-a	21	42	63	125	200	275

WOMEN IN LOVE (Thrilling Romances for Adults)
Ziff-Davis Publishing Co.: Winter, 1952 (25¢, 100 pgs.)

nn-(Scarce)-Kinstler-a; painted-c	55	110	165	347	586	825

WOMEN OF MARVEL
Marvel Comics: 2006, 2007 ($24.99, TPB)

SC-Reprints 1st apps. of Dazzler, Ms. Marvel, Shanna, The Cat plus notable stories of other female Marvel characters; Mayhew-c						25.00
Vol. 2 (2007) More stories of female Marvel characters; Mayhew-c; cover process art						25.00

WOMEN OUTLAWS (My Love Memories #9 on)(Also see Red Circle)
Fox Features Syndicate: July, 1948 - No. 8, Sept, 1949

1-Used in **SOTI**, illo "Giving children an image of American womanhood"; negligee panels	78	156	234	491	833	1175
2,3: 3-Kamenish-a	59	118	177	372	629	885
4-8	47	94	141	291	483	675
nn(nd)-Contains Cody of the Pony Express; same cover as #7	32	64	96	186	298	410

WOMEN TO LOVE
Realistic: No date (1953)

nn-(Scarce)-Reprints Complete Romance #1; c-/Avon paperback #165	40	80	120	235	380	525

WONDER BOY (Formerly Terrific Comics) (See Blue Bolt, Bomber Comics & Samson)
Ajax/Farrell Publ.: No. 17, May, 1955 - No. 18, July, 1955 (Code approved)

17-Phantom Lady app. Bakerish-c/a	47	94	141	291	483	675
18-Phantom Lady app.	40	80	120	235	380	525

NOTE: *Phantom Lady not by Matt Baker.*

WONDER COMICS (Wonderworld #3 on)
Fox Features Syndicate: May, 1939 - No. 2, June, 1939 (68 pgs.)

Wonder Comics #14 © FOX

Wonder Girl #1 © DC

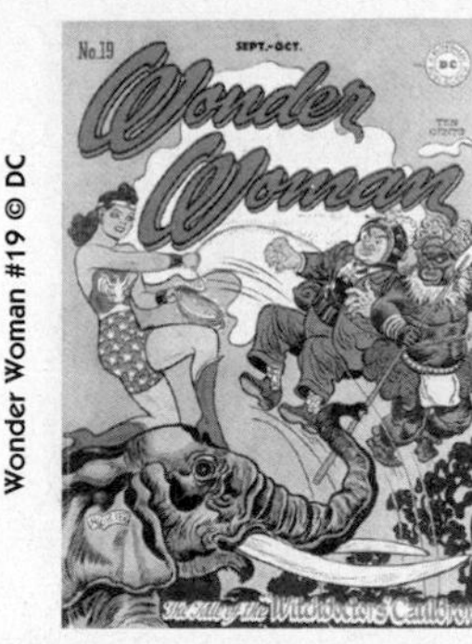
Wonder Woman #19 © DC

GD VG FN VF VF/NM NM-
2.0 4.0 6.0 8.0 9.0 9.2

1-(Scarce)-Wonder Man only app. by Will Eisner; Dr. Fung (by Powell), K-51 begins;
Bob Kane-a; Eisner-c 1420 2840 4260 10,600 18,800 27,000
2-(Scarce)-Yarko the Great, Master Magician (see Samson) by Eisner begins; 'Spark' Stevens
by Bob Kane, Patty O'Day, Tex Mason app. Lou Fine's 1st-c; Fine-a (2 pgs.);
Yarko-c (Wonder Man-c #1) 472 944 1416 3398 5949 8500

WONDER COMICS
Great/Nedor/Better Publications: May, 1944 - No. 20, Oct, 1948

1-The Grim Reaper & Spectro, the Mind Reader begin; Hitler/Hirohito bondage-c
187 374 561 1178 1989 2800
2-Origin The Grim Reaper; Super Sleuths begin, end #8,17
73 146 219 460 780 1100
3-5: 3-Indicia reads "Vol. 1, #2" 66 132 198 416 701 985
6-10: 6-Flag-c. 8-Last Spectro. 9-Wonderman begins
53 106 159 330 553 775
11-14: 11-Dick Devens, King of Futuria begins, ends #14. 11,12-Ingels-c & splash pg.
14-Bondage-c 62 124 186 391 663 935
15-Tara begins (origin), ends #20 72 144 216 454 765 1075
16,18: 16-Spectro app.; last Grim Reaper. 18-The Silver Knight begins
62 124 186 391 663 935
17-Wonderman with Frazetta panels; Jill Trent with all Frazetta inks
64 128 192 403 682 960
19-Frazetta panels 62 124 186 391 663 935
20-Most of Silver Knight by Frazetta 72 144 216 454 770 1085

NOTE: ***Ingels** c-11, 12. **Roussos** a-19. **Schomburg (Xela)** c-1-10; (airbrush)-13-20. Bondage c-12, 13, 15. Cover features: Grim Reaper #1-8; Wonder Man #9-15; Tara #16-20.*

WONDER DUCK (See Wisco)
Marvel Comics (CDS): Sept, 1949 - No. 3, Mar, 1950

1-Funny animal 16 32 48 94 147 200
2,3 12 24 36 67 94 120

WONDERFUL ADVENTURES OF PINOCCHIO, THE (See Movie Comics & Walt Disney Showcase #48)
Whitman Publishing Co.: April, 1982 (Walt Disney)

nn-(#3 Continuation of Movie Comics?); r/FC #92 6.00

WONDERFUL WORLD FOR BOYS AND GIRLS
DC Comics: May, 1964

nn - Ashcan comic, not distributed to newsstands, only for in-house use (no known sales)

WONDERFUL WORLD OF DISNEY, THE (Walt Disney)
Whitman Publishing Co.: 1978 (Digest, 116 pgs.)

1-Barks-a (reprints) 3 6 9 16 23 30
2 (no date) 2 4 6 11 16 20

WONDERFUL WORLD OF THE BROTHERS GRIMM (See Movie Comics)

WONDER GIRL (Cassandra Sandsmark)
DC Comics: Nov, 2007 - No. 6, Apr, 2008 ($2.99, limited series)

1-6-Torres-s/Greene-a; Hercules app. 2-6-Female Furies app. 5,6-Wonder Woman app. 3.00
Teen Titans Spotlight: Wonder Girl TPB (2008, $17.99) r/#1-6 18.00

WONDERLAND COMICS
Feature Publications/Prize: Summer, 1945 - No. 9, Feb-Mar, 1947

1-Alex in Wonderland begins; Howard Post-c 20 40 60 118 189 260
2-Howard Post-c/a(2) 13 26 39 72 101 130
3-9: 3,4-Post-c 10 20 30 58 79 100

WONDER MAN (See The Avengers #9, 151)
Marvel Comics Group: Mar, 1986 ($1.25, one-shot, 52 pgs.)

1 3.00

WONDER MAN
Marvel Comics Group: Sept, 1991 - No. 29, Jan, 1994 ($1.00)

1-29: 1-Free fold out poster by Johnson/Austin. 1-3-Johnson/Austin-c/a.
2-Avengers West Coast x-over. 4 Austin-c(i) 2.50
Annual 1 (1992, $2.25)-Immonen-a (10 pgs.) 3.00
Annual 2 (1993, $2.25)-Bagged w/trading card 2.50

WONDER MAN
Marvel Comics: Feb, 2007 - No. 5, June, 2007 ($2.99, limited series)

1-5: 1-Peter David-s/Andrew Currie-a; Beast app. 4-Nauck-a 3.00
...: My Fair Super Hero TPB (2007, $13.99) r/#1-5; Currie sketch page 14.00

WONDERS OF ALADDIN, THE
Dell Publishing Co.: No. 1255, Feb-Apr, 1962

Four Color 1255-Movie 6 12 18 43 69 95

GD VG FN VF VF/NM NM-
2.0 4.0 6.0 8.0 9.0 9.2

WONDER WOMAN (See Adventure Comics #459, All-Star Comics, Brave & the Bold, DC Comics Presents, JLA, Justice League of America, Legend of..., Power Record Comics, Sensation Comics, Super Friends and World's Finest Comics #244)

WONDER WOMAN
DC Comics: Jan 1942

1-Ashcan comic, not distributed to newsstands, only for in-house use. Cover art is Sensation Comics #1 with interior being Sensation Comics #2. A CGC certified 8.5 copy sold for $17,250 in 2002.

WONDER WOMAN
National Periodical Publications/All-American Publ./DC Comics:
Summer, 1942 - No. 329, Feb, 1986

1-Origin Wonder Woman retold (more detailed than All Star #8); H. G. Peter-c/a begins
2550 5100 7650 19,200 34,600 50,000
1-Reprint, Oversize 13-1/2x10". **WARNING:** This comic is an exact reprint of the original except for its size. DC published it in 1974 with a second cover titling it as a Famous First Edition. There have been many reported cases of the outer cover being removed and the interior sold as the original edition. The reprint with the new outer cover removed is practically worthless. See Famous First Edition for value.
2-Origin/1st app. Mars; Duke of Deception app. 423 846 1269 3046 5323 7600
3 253 506 759 1594 2697 3800
4,5: 5-1st Dr. Psycho app. 200 400 600 1260 2130 3000
6-9: 6-1st Cheetah app. 153 306 459 964 1632 2300
10-Invasion from Saturn classic sci-fi-c/s 160 320 480 1008 1704 2400
11-20 115 230 345 725 1225 1725
21-30: 23-Story from Wonder Woman's childhood 93 186 279 586 993 1400
31-33,35-40: 38-Last H.G. Peter-c 68 136 204 428 727 1025
34-Robot-c 72 144 216 454 765 1075
41-44,46-49: 49-Used in **SOTI**, pgs. 234,236; last 52 pg. issue
60 120 180 378 639 900
45-Origin retold 120 240 360 756 1278 1800
50-(44 pgs.)-Used in **POP**, pg. 97 62 124 186 391 658 925
51-60: 60-New logo 52 104 156 322 536 750
61-72: 62-Origin of W.W. i.d. 64-Story about 3-D movies. 70-1st Angle Man
app. 72-Last pre-code (2/55) 47 94 141 291 483 675
73-90: 80-Origin The Invisible Plane. 85-1st S.A. issue. 89-Flying
saucer-c/story 41 82 123 256 428 600
91-94,96,97,99: 97-Last H. G. Peter-a 38 76 114 220 363 500
95-A-Bomb-c 40 80 120 235 380 525
98-New origin & new art team (Andru & Esposito) begin (5/58); origin W.W. id w/new facts
40 80 120 244 397 550
100-(8/58) 41 82 123 256 428 600
101-104,106,108-110 33 66 99 192 309 425
105-(Scarce, 4/59)-W. W.'s secret origin; W. W. appears as girl (no costume yet)
(called Wonder Girl - see DC Super-Stars #1) 133 266 399 838 1419 2000
107-1st advs. of Wonder Girl; 1st Merboy; tells how Wonder Woman won her costume
41 82 123 250 413 575
111-120 25 50 75 147 236 325
121-126: 121-1st app. Wonder Woman Family. 122-1st app. Wonder Tot. 124-Wonder Woman
Family app. 126-Last 10¢ issue 20 40 60 118 189 260
127-130: 128-Origin The Invisible Plane retold. 129-3rd app. Wonder Woman Family
(#133 is 4th app.) 11 22 33 79 140 200
131-150: 132-Flying saucer-c 10 20 30 67 116 165
151-155,157,158,160-170 (1967): 151-Wonder Girl solo issue
8 16 24 52 86 120
156-(8/65)-Early mention of a comic book shop & comic collecting; mentions DCs selling
for $100 a copy 8 16 24 56 93 130
159-Origin retold (1/66); 1st S.A. origin? 9 18 27 65 113 160
171-176 6 12 18 41 66 90
177-W. Woman/Supergirl battle 8 16 24 52 86 120
178-1st new Wonder Woman on-c only; appears in old costume w/powers inside
8 16 24 54 90 125
179-Classic-c; wears no costume to issue #203 7 14 21 50 83 115
180-195: 180-Death of Steve Trevor. 195-Wood inks 5 10 15 30 48 65
196 (52 pgs.)-Origin-r/All Star #8 (6 out of 9 pgs.) 5 10 15 32 51 70
197,198 (52 pgs.)-Reprints 5 10 15 32 51 70
199-Jeff Jones painted-c; 52 pgs. 7 14 21 47 76 105
200 (5-6/72)-Jeff Jones-c; 52 pgs. 7 14 21 50 83 115
201,202-Catwoman app. 202-Fafhrd & The Grey Mouser debut.
4 8 12 22 34 45
203,205-210,212: 212-The Cavalier app. 3 6 9 16 23 30
204-Return to old costume; death of I Ching. 4 8 12 22 34 45
211,214-(100 pgs.) 7 14 21 47 76 105
213,215,216,218-220: 220-N. Adams assist 3 6 9 14 20 26
217: (68 pgs.) 3 6 9 19 29 38

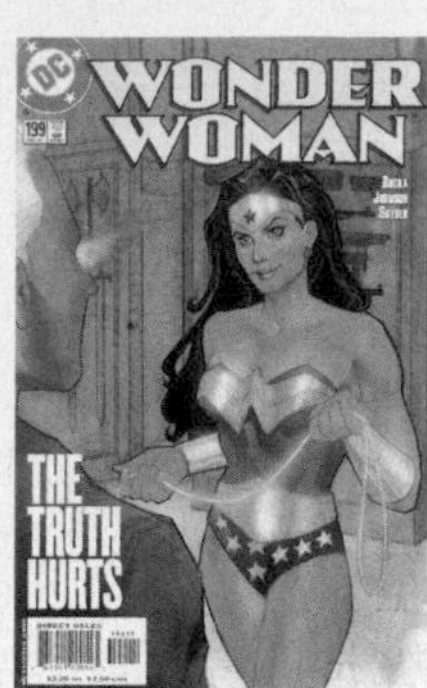

Wonder Woman (2nd series) #199 © DC

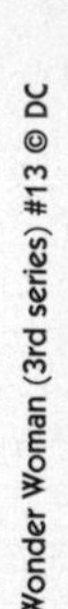

Wonder Woman (3rd series) #13 © DC

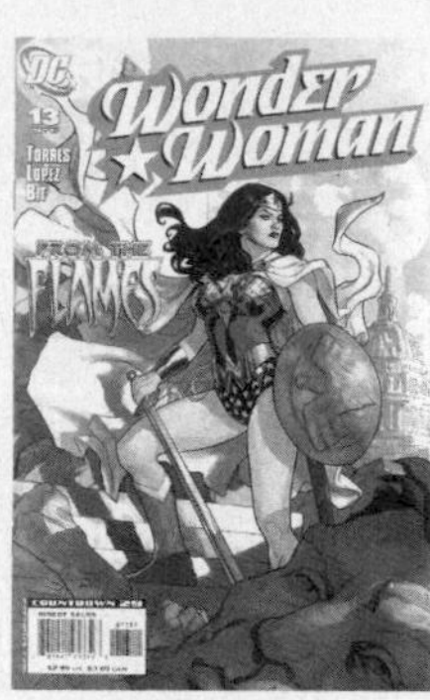

Wonderworld Comics #7 © FOX

GD VG FN VF VF/NM NM-
2.0 4.0 6.0 8.0 9.0 9.2

221,222,224-227,229,230,233-236,238-240 2 4 6 8 11 16
223,228,231,232,237,241,248: 223-Steve Trevor revived as Steve Howard & learns W.W.'s I.D. 228-Both Wonder Women team up & new World War II stories begin, end #243. 231,232: JSA app. 237-Origin retold. 241-Intro Bouncer; Spectre app. 248-Steve Trevor Howard dies (44 pgs.) 2 4 6 10 14 18
242-246,252-266,269,270: 243-Both W. Women team-up again. 269-Last Wood a(i) for DC? (7/80) 1 2 3 5 6 8
247,249-251,271: 247,249 (44 pgs.). 249-Hawkgirl app. 250-Origin/1st app. Orana, the new W. Woman. 251-Orana dies. 271-Huntress & 3rd Life of Steve Trevor begin 1 2 3 5 7 9
250-252,255-262,264-(Whitman variants, low print run, no issue # on cover) 2 4 6 10 14 18
267,268-Re-intro Animal Man (5/80 & 6/80) 1 3 4 6 8 10
272-280,284-286,289,290,294-299,301-325 5.00
281-283: Joker-c/stories in Huntress back-ups 1 2 3 5 7 9
287,288,291-293: 287-New Teen Titans x-over. 288-New costume & logo. 291-293-Three part epic with Super-Heroines 6.00
300-($1.50, 76 pgs.)-Anniv. issue; Giffen-a; New Teen Titans, Bronze Age Sandman, JLA & G.A. Wonder Woman app.; 1st app. Lyta Trevor who becomes Fury in All-Star Squadron #25; G.A. Wonder Woman & Steve Trevor revealed as married 6.00
326-328 6.00
329 (Double size)-S.A. W.W. & Steve Trevor wed 2 4 6 8 11 14
Diana Prince: Wonder Woman Vol. 1 TPB (2008, $19.99) r/#178-183 20.00
...: The Greatest Stories Ever Told TPB (2007, $19.99) intro. by Lynda Carter; Ross-c 20.00
NOTE: ***Andru/Esposito** c-66-160(most). **Buckler** a-300. **Colan** a-288-305p; c-288-290p. **Giffen** a-300p. **Grell** c-217. **Kaluta** c-297. **Gil Kane** c-294p, 303-305, 307, 312, 314. **Miller** c-298p. **Morrow** c-233. **Nasser** a-232p; c-231p, 232p. **Bob Oskner** c(i)-39-65(most). **Perez** c-283p, 284p. **Spiegle** a-312. **Staton** a(p)-241, 271-287, 289, 290, 294-299; c(p)-241, 245, 246. Huntress back-up stories 271-287, 289, 290, 294-299, 301-321.*

WONDER WOMAN
DC Comics: Feb, 1987 - No. 226, Apr, 2006 (75¢/$1.00/$1.25/$1.95/$1.99/$2.25/$2.50)

0-(10/94) Zero Hour; released between #90 & #91 1 2 3 5 6 8
1-New origin; Perez-c/a begins 1 2 3 4 5 7
2-5 5.00
6-20: 9-Origin Cheetah. 12,13-Millennium x-over. 18,26-Free 16 pg. story 4.00
21-49: 24-Last Perez-a; scripts continue thru #62 3.00
50-($1.50, 52 pgs.)-New Titans, Justice League 4.00
51-62: Perez scripts. 60-Vs. Lobo; last Perez-c. 62-Last $1.00-c 3.00
63-New direction & Bolland-c begin; Deathstroke story continued fromW. W. Special #1 4.00
64-84 2.50
85-1st Deodato-a; ends #100 2 4 6 8 10 12
86-88: 88-Superman-c & app. 5.00
89-97: 90-(9/94)-1st Artemis. 91-(11/94). 93-Hawkman app. 96-Joker-c 4.00
98,99 3.00
100 ($2.95, Newsstand)-Death of Artemis; Bolland-c ends. 4.00
100 ($3.95, Direct Market)-Death of Artemis; foil-c. 6.00
101-119, 121-125: 101-Begin $1.95-c; Byrne-c/a/scripts begin. 101-104-Darkseid app. 105-Phantom Stranger cameo. 106-108-Phantom Stranger & Demon app. 107,108-Arion app. 111-1st app. new Wonder Girl. 111,112-Vs. Doomsday. 112-Superman app. 113-Wonder Girl-c/app; Sugar & Spike app. 2.50
120 ($2.95)-Perez-c 3.00
126-149: 128-Hippolyta becomes new W.W. 130-133-Flash (Jay Garrick) & JSA app. 136-Diana returns to W.W. role; last Byrne issue. 137-Priest-s. 139-Luke-s/Paquette-a begin; Hughes-c thru #146 2.50
150-($2.95) Hughes-c/Clark-a; Zauriel app. 3.00
151-158-Hughes-c. 153-Superboy app. 2.50
159-163: 159-Begin $2.25-c. 160,161-Clayface app. 162,163-Aquaman app. 2.50
164-171: Phil Jimenez-s/a begin; Hughes-c; Batman app. 168,169-Pérez co-plot 169-Wraparound-c.170-Lois Lane-c/app. 2.50
172-Our Worlds at War; Hippolyta killed 3.00
173,174: 173-Our Worlds at War; Darkseid app. 174-Every DC heroine app. 2.50
175-($3.50) Joker: Last Laugh; JLA app.; Jim Lee-c 3.50
176-199: 177-Paradise Island returns. 179-Jimenez-c. 184,185-Hippolyta-c/app.; Hughes-c 186-Cheetah app. 189-Simonson-s/Ordway-a begin. 190-Diana's new look. 195-Rucka-s/Drew Johnson-a begin. 197-Flash-c/app. 198,199-Noto-c 2.50
200-($3.95) back-up stories in 1940s and 1960s styles; pin-ups by various 4.00
201-218,220-225: 203,204-Batman-c/app. 204-Matt Wagner-c. 212-JLA app. 214-Flash app. 215-Morales-a begins. 218-Begin $2.50-c. 220-Batman app. 2.75
219-Omac tie-in/Sacrifice pt. 4; Wonder Woman kills Max Lord; Superman app. 3.00
219-(2nd printing) Altered cover with red background 2.50
226-Last issue; flashbacks to meetings with Superman; Rucka-s/Richards-a 3.00
#1,000,000 (11/98) 853rd Century x-over; Deodato-c 3.00
Annual 1,2: 1 ('88, $1.50)-Art Adams-a. 2 ('89, $2.00, 68 pgs.)-All women artists issue; Perez-c(i)/a. 4.00
Annual 3 (1992, $2.50, 68 pgs.)-Quesada-c(p) 3.00

GD VG FN VF VF/NM NM-
2.0 4.0 6.0 8.0 9.0 9.2

Annual 4 (1995, $3.50)-Year One 3.50
Annual 5 (1996, $2.95)-Legends of the Dead Earth story; Byrne scripts; Cockrum-a 3.00
Annual 6 (1997, $3.95)-Pulp Heroes 4.00
Annual 7,8 ('98,'99, $2.95)-7-Ghosts; Wrightson-c. 8-JLApe, A.Adams-c 3.00
...: Beauty and the Beasts TPB (2005, $19.95) r/#15-19 & Action Comics #600 20.00
...: Bitter Rivals TPB (2004, $13.95) r/#200-205; Jones-c 13.00
...: Challenge of the Gods TPB ('04, $19.95) r/#8-14; Pérez-s/a 20.00
...: Destiny Calling TPB (2006, $19.99) r/#20-24 & Annual #1; Pérez-c & pin-up gallery 20.00
...Donna Troy (6/98, $1.95) Girlfrenzy; Jimenez-a 2.50
...: Down To Earth TPB (2004, $14.95) r/#195-200; Greg Land-c 15.00
... 80-Page Giant 1 (2002, $4.95) reprints in format of 1960s' 80-Page Giants 5.00
...: Eyes of the Gorgon TPB ('05, $19.99) r/#206-213 20.00
Gallery (1996, $3.50)-Bolland-c; pin-ups by various 4.00
...: Gods and Mortals TPB ('04, $19.95) r/#1-7; Pérez-a 20.00
...: Gods of Gotham TPB ('01, $5.95) r/#164-167; Jimenez-s/a 6.00
...: Land of the Dead TPB ('06, $12.99) r/#214-217 & Flash #219 13.00
Lifelines TPB ('98, $9.95) r/#106-112; Byrne-c/a 10.00
...: Mission's End TPB ('06, $19.99) r/#218-226; cover gallery 20.00
...: Our Worlds at War (10/01, $2.95) History of the Amazons; Jae Lee-c 3.00
...: Paradise Found TPB ('03, $14.95) r/#171-177, Secret Files #3; Jimenez-s/a 15.00
...: Paradise Lost TPB ('02, $14.95) r/#164-170; Jimenez-s/a 15.00
Plus 1 (1/97, $2.95)-Jesse Quick-c/app. 3.00
Second Genesis TPB (1997, $9.95)-r/#101-105 10.00
Secret Files 1-3 (3/98, 7/99, 5/02; $4.95) 5.00
Special 1 (1992, $1.75, 52 pgs.)-Deathstroke-c/story continued in Wonder Woman #63 4.00
...: The Blue Amazon (2003, $6.95) Elseworlds; McKeever-a 7.00
The Challenge Of Artemis TPB (1996, $9.95)-r/#94-100; Deodato-c/a 10.00
...: The Once and Future Story (1998, $4.95) Trina Robbins-s/Doran & Guice-a 5.00
NOTE: ***Art Adams** a-Annual 1. **Byrne** c/a 101-107. **Bolton** a-Annual 1. **Deodato** a-85-100. **Perez** a-Annual 1; c-Annual 1(i). **Quesada** c(p)-Annual 3.*

WONDER WOMAN (Also see Amazons Attack mini-series)
DC Comics: Aug, 2006 - Present ($2.99)

1-Donna Troy as Wonder Woman after Infinite Crisis; Heinberg-s/Dodson-a/c 3.00
1-Variant-c by Adam Kubert 4.00
2-22: 2-4-Giganta & Hercules app. 6-Jodi Picoult-s begins. 8-Hippolyta returns. 9-12-Amazons Attack tie-in; JLA app. 14-17-Simone-s/Dodson-a/c. 20-22-Stalker app. 3.00
14-DC Nation Convention giveaway edition 6.00
... Annual 1 (11/07, $3.99) Story cont'd from #4; Heinberg-s/Dodson-a/c; back-up Frank-a 4.00
...: Love and Murder HC (2007, $19.99) r/#6-10 20.00
...: Who is Wonder Woman? HC (2007, $19.99) r/#1-4 & Annual #1; Vaughan intro. 20.00

WONDER WOMAN: AMAZONIA
DC Comics: 1997 ($7.95, Graphic Album format, one shot)

1-Elseworlds; Messner-Loebs-s/Winslade-a 8.00

WONDER WOMAN SPECTACULAR (See DC Special Series #9)

WONDER WOMAN: SPIRIT OF TRUTH
DC Comics: Nov, 2001 ($9.95, treasury size, one-shot)

nn-Painted art by Alex Ross; story by Alex Ross and Paul Dini 10.00

WONDER WOMAN: THE HIKETEIA
DC Comics: 2002 ($24.95, hardcover, one-shot)

nn-Wonder Woman battles Batman; Greg Rucka-s/J.G. Jones-a 25.00
Softcover (2003, $17.95) 18.00

WONDERWORLD COMICS (Formerly Wonder Comics)
Fox Features Syndicate: No. 3, July, 1939 - No. 33, Jan, 1942

3-Intro The Flame by Fine; Dr. Fung (Powell-a), K-51 (Powell-a?), & Yarko the Great, Master Magician (Eisner-a) continues; Eisner/Fine-c 689 1378 2067 4961 8681 12,400
4-Lou Fine-c 324 648 972 2203 3852 5500
5,6,9,10: Lou Fine-c 187 374 561 1178 1989 2800
7-Classic Lou Fine-c 306 612 918 2081 3641 5200
8-Classic Lou Fine-c 280 560 840 1764 2982 4200
11-Origin The Flame 143 286 429 901 1526 2150
12-15:13-Dr. Fung ends; last Fine-c(p) 115 230 345 725 1225 1725
16-20 85 170 255 536 906 1275
21-Origin The Black Lion & Cub 78 156 234 491 833 1175
22-27: 22,25-Dr. Fung app. 62 124 186 391 658 925
28-Origin & 1st app. U.S. Jones (8/41); Lu-Nar, the Moon Man begins 83 166 249 523 887 1250
29,31,33 50 100 150 310 518 725
30-Intro & Origin Flame Girl 92 184 276 580 978 1375
32-Hitler-c 77 154 231 481 816 1150
NOTE: *Spies at War by **Eisner** in #13, 17. Yarko by **Eisner** in #3-11. **Eisner** text illos-3. **Lou Fine** a-3-11; c-3-13,*

Woody Woodpecker #51 © Walter Lantz

World Around Us #28 © GIL

World of Fantasy #2 © MAR

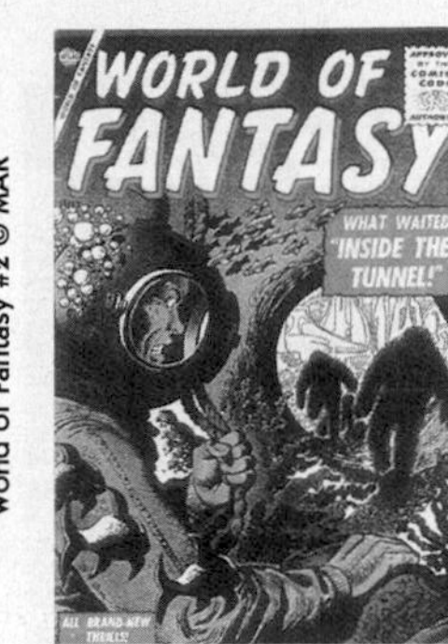

	GD	VG	FN	VF	VF/NM	NM-
	2.0	4.0	6.0	8.0	9.0	9.2

15(i); text illos-4. ***Nordling*** *a-4-14.* ***Powell*** *a-3-12.* ***Tuska*** *a-5-9. Bondage-c 14, 15, 28, 31, 32. Cover features: The Flame-#3, 5-31; U.S. Jones-#32, 33.*

WONDERWORLDS
Innovation Publishing: 1992 ($3.50, squarebound, 100 pgs.)

1-Rebound super-hero comics, contents may vary; Hero Alliance, Terraformers, etc. 3.50

WOODSY OWL (See March of Comics #395)
Gold Key: Nov, 1973 - No. 10, Feb, 1976 (Some Whitman printings exist)

	GD	VG	FN	VF	VF/NM	NM-
1	2	4	6	13	18	22
2-10	2	4	6	8	10	12

WOODY WOODPECKER (Walter Lantz... #73 on?)(See Dell Giants for annuals)
(Also see The Funnies, Jolly Jingles, Kite Fun Book, New Funnies)
Dell Publishing Co./Gold Key No. 73-187/Whitman No. 188 on:
No. 169, 10/47 - No. 72, 5-7/62; No. 73, 10/62 - No. 201, 3/84 (nn 192)

	GD	VG	FN	VF	VF/NM	NM-
Four Color 169(#1)-Drug turns Woody into a Mr. Hyde	17	34	51	120	223	325
Four Color 188	11	22	33	79	140	200
Four Color 202,232,249,264,288	8	16	24	58	97	135
Four Color 305,336,350	6	12	18	41	66	90
Four Color 364,374,390,405,416,431('52)	5	10	15	34	55	75
16 (12-1/52-53) - 30('55)	4	8	12	28	44	60
31-50	4	8	12	22	34	45
51-72 (Last Dell)	3	6	9	18	27	35
73-75 (Giants, 84 pgs., Gold Key)	5	10	15	32	51	70
76-80	3	6	9	16	22	28
81-103: 103-Last 12¢ issue	3	6	9	14	19	24
104-120	2	4	6	11	16	20
121-140	2	4	6	9	12	15
141-160	1	3	4	6	8	10
161-187	1	2	3	5	7	9
188,189 (Whitman)	2	4	6	9	13	16
190(9/80),191(11/80)-pre-pack only	4	8	12	22	34	45
(No #192)						
193-197: 196(2/82), 197(4/82)	2	4	6	11	16	20
198-201 (All #90062 on-c, no date or date code, pre-pack): 198(6/83), 199(7/83), 200(8/83), 201(3/84)	3	6	9	16	22	28
Christmas Parade 1(11/68-Giant)(G.K.)	4	8	12	26	41	55
Summer Fun 1(6/66-G.K.)(84 pgs.)	5	10	15	30	48	65
nn (1971, 60¢, 100 pgs. digest) B&W one page gags	3	6	9	17	25	32

NOTE: *15¢ Canadian editions of the 12¢ issues exist. Reprints-No. 92, 102, 103, 105, 106, 124, 125, 152, 153, 157, 162, 165, 194(1/3)-200(1/3).*

WOODY WOODPECKER (See Comic Album #5,9,13, Dell Giant #24, 40, 54, Dell Giants, The Funnies, Golden Comics Digest #1, 3, 5, 8, 15, 16, 20, 24, 32, 37, 44, March of Comics #16, 34, 85, 93, 109, 124, 139, 158, 177, 184, 203, 222, 239, 249, 261, 420, 454, 466, 478, New Funnies & Super Book #12, 24)

WOODY WOODPECKER
Harvey Comics: Sept, 1991 - No. 15, Aug, 1994 ($1.25)

1-15: 1-r/W.W. #53 2.50
50th Anniversary Special 1 (10/91, $2.50, 68 pgs.) 3.00

WOODY WOODPECKER AND FRIENDS
Harvey Comics: Dec, 1991 - No. 4, 1992 ($1.25)

1-4 2.50

WORD WARRIORS (Also see Quest for Dreams Lost)
Literacy Volunteers of Chicago: 1987 ($1.50, B&W)(Proceeds donated to help literacy)

1-Jon Sable by Grell, Ms. Tree, Streetwolf; Chaykin-c 3.00

WORLD AROUND US, THE (Illustrated Story of...)
Gilberton Publishers (Classics Illustrated): Sep, 1958 -No. 36, Oct, 1961 (25¢)

	GD	VG	FN	VF	VF/NM	NM-
1-Dogs; Evans-a	9	18	27	52	69	85
2-4: 2-Indians; Check-a. 3-Horses; L. B. Cole-c. 4-Railroads; L. B. Cole-a (5 pgs.)	9	18	27	47	61	75
5-Space; Ingels-a	10	20	30	56	76	95
6-The F.B.I.; Disbrow, Evans, Ingels-a	10	20	30	56	76	95
7-Pirates; Disbrow, Ingels, Kinstler-a	9	18	27	52	69	85
8-Flight; Evans, Ingels, Crandall-a	9	18	27	52	69	85
9-Army; Disbrow, Ingels, Orlando-a	9	18	27	47	61	75
10-13: 10-Navy; Disbrow, Kinstler-a. 11-Marine Corps. 12-Coast Guard; Ingels-a (9 pgs.). 13-Air Force; L.B. Cole-c	9	18	27	47	61	75
14-French Revolution; Crandall, Evans, Kinstler-a	10	20	30	56	76	95
15-Prehistoric Animals; Al Williamson-a, 6 & 10 pgs. plus Morrow-a	10	20	30	58	79	100
16-18: 16-Crusades; Kinstler-a. 17-Festivals; Evans, Crandall-a. 18-Great Scientists; Crandall, Evans, Torres, Williamson, Morrow-a	9	18	27	52	69	85
19-Jungle; Crandall, Williamson, Morrow-a	10	20	30	58	79	100
20-Communications; Crandall, Evans, Torres-a	10	20	30	56	76	95
21-American Presidents; Crandall/Evans, Morrow-a	10	20	30	56	76	95
22-Boating; Morrow-a	8	16	24	44	57	70
23-Great Explorers; Crandall, Evans-a	9	18	27	52	69	85
24-Ghosts; Morrow, Evans-a	10	20	30	56	76	95
25-Magic; Evans, Morrow-a	10	20	30	56	76	95
26-The Civil War	11	22	33	62	86	110
27-Mountains (High Advs.); Crandall/Evans, Morrow, Torres-a	9	18	27	52	69	85
28-Whaling; Crandall, Evans, Morrow, Torres, Wildey-a; L.B. Cole-c	9	18	27	52	69	85
29-Vikings; Crandall, Evans, Torres, Morrow-a	10	20	30	58	79	100
30-Undersea Adventure; Crandall/Evans, Kirby, Morrow, Torres-a	10	20	30	56	76	95
31-Hunting; Crandall/Evans, Ingels, Kinstler, Kirby-a	9	18	27	52	69	85
32,33: 32-For Gold & Glory; Morrow, Kirby, Crandall, Evans-a. 33-Famous Teens; Torres, Crandall, Evans-a	9	18	27	52	69	85
34-36: 34-Fishing; Crandall/Evans-a. 35-Spies; Kirby, Morrow?, Evans-a. 36-Fight for Life (Medicine); Kirby-a	9	18	27	52	69	85

NOTE: See Classics Illustrated Special Edition. Another *World Around Us* issue entitled *The Sea* had been prepared in 1962 but was never published in the U.S. It was published in the British/European *World Around Us* series. Those series then continued with seven additional WAU titles not in the U.S. series.

WORLD BELOW, THE
Dark Horse Comics: Mar, 1999 - No. 4, Jun, 1999 ($2.50, limited series)

1-4-Paul Chadwick-s/c/a 2.50
TPB (1/07, $12.95) r/#1-4; intro. by Chadwick; gallery of sketches and covers 13.00

WORLD BELOW, THE: DEEPER AND STRANGER
Dark Horse Comics: Dec, 1999 - No. 4, Mar, 2000 ($2.95, B&W)

1-4-Paul Chadwick-s/c/a 3.00

WORLD FAMOUS HEROES MAGAZINE
Comic Corp. of America (Centaur): Oct, 1941 - No. 4, Apr, 1942 (comic book)

	GD	VG	FN	VF	VF/NM	NM-
1-Gustavson-c; Lubbers, Glanzman-a; Davy Crockett, Paul Revere, Lewis & Clark, John Paul Jones stories; Flag-c	110	220	330	693	1172	1650
2-Lou Gehrig life story; Lubbers-a	47	94	141	291	483	675
3,4-Lubbers-a. 4-Wild Bill Hickok story; 2 pg. Marlene Dietrich story	43	86	129	267	446	625

WORLD FAMOUS STORIES
Croyden Publishers: 1945

	GD	VG	FN	VF	VF/NM	NM-
1-Ali Baba, Hansel & Gretel, Rip Van Winkle, Mid-Summer Night's Dream	14	28	42	76	108	140

WORLD IS HIS PARISH, THE
George A. Pflaum: 1953 (15¢)

	GD	VG	FN	VF	VF/NM	NM-
nn-The story of Pope Pius XII	6	12	18	28	34	40

WORLD OF ADVENTURE (Walt Disney's...)(TV)
Gold Key: Apr, 1963 - No. 3, Oct, 1963 (12¢)

	GD	VG	FN	VF	VF/NM	NM-
1-Disney TV characters; Savage Sam, Johnny Shiloh, Capt. Nemo, The Mooncussers	3	6	9	21	32	42
2,3	3	6	9	15	21	26

WORLD OF ARCHIE, THE (See Archie Giant Series Mag. #148, 151, 156, 160, 165, 171, 177, 182, 188, 193, 200, 208, 213, 225, 232, 237, 244, 249, 456, 461, 468, 473, 480, 485, 492, 497, 504, 509, 516, 521, 532, 543, 554, 565, 574, 587, 599, 612, 627)

WORLD OF ARCHIE
Archie Comics: Aug, 1992 - No. 22 ($1.25/$1.50)

1 4.00
2-15: 9-Neon ink-c 3.00
16-22 2.50

WORLD OF FANTASY
Atlas Comics (CPC No. 1-15/ZPC No. 16-19): May, 1956 - No. 19, Aug, 1959

	GD	VG	FN	VF	VF/NM	NM-
1	47	94	141	291	483	675
2-Williamson-a (4 pgs.)	31	62	93	181	291	400
3-Sid Check, Roussos-a	27	54	81	158	254	350
4-7	21	42	63	125	200	275
8-Matt Fox, Orlando, Berg-a	23	46	69	133	214	295
9-Krigstein-a	22	44	66	127	204	280
10-15: 11-Torres-a	18	36	54	107	169	230
16-Williamson-a (4 pgs.); Ditko, Kirby-a	25	50	75	147	236	325
17-19-Ditko, Kirby-a	25	50	75	147	236	325

NOTE: ***Ayers*** *a-3.* ***B. Baily*** *a-4.* ***Berg*** *a-5, 6, 8.* ***Brodsky*** *c-3.* ***Check*** *a-3.* ***Ditko*** *a-17, 19.* ***Everett*** *a-2; c-4-7, 9, 12, 13.* ***Forte*** *a-4.* ***Infantino*** *a-14.* ***Kirby*** *c-15, 17-19.* ***Krigstein*** *a-9.* ***Maneely*** *c-2, 14.* ***Mooney*** *a-14.* ***Morrow*** *a-7.*

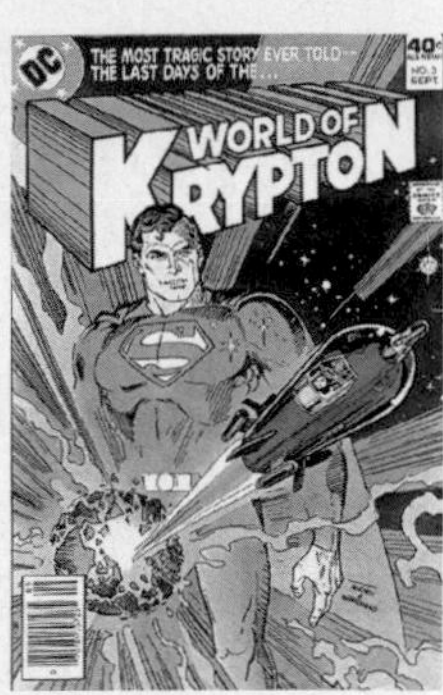

World of Krypton #3 © DC

World of Warcraft #1 © Blizzard Ent.

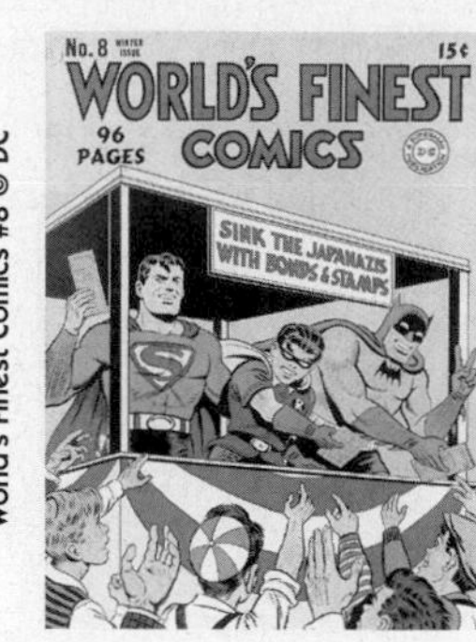

World's Finest Comics #8 © DC

	GD 2.0	VG 4.0	FN 6.0	VF 8.0	VF/NM 9.0	NM- 9.2

*Orlando a-8, 13, 14. **Pakula** a-9. **Powell** a-4, 6. **Reinman** a-10. **R.Q. Sale** a-3, 9, 10. **Severin** c-1.*

WORLD OF GIANT COMICS, THE (See Archie All-Star Specials under Archie Comics)

WORLD OF GINGER FOX, THE (Also see Ginger Fox)
Comico: Nov, 1986 ($6.95, 8 1/2 x 11", 68 pgs., mature)

Graphic Novel ($6.95) 7.00
Hardcover ($27.95) 28.00

WORLD OF JUGHEAD, THE (See Archie Giant Series Mag. #9, 14, 19, 24, 30, 136, 143, 149, 152, 157, 161, 166, 172, 178, 183, 189, 194, 202, 209, 215, 227, 233, 239, 245, 251, 457, 463, 469, 475, 481, 487, 493, 499, 505, 511, 517, 523, 531, 542, 553, 564, 577, 590, 602)

WORLD OF KRYPTON, THE (World of...#3) (See Superman #248)
DC Comics, Inc.: 7/79 - No. 3, 9/79; 12/87 - No. 4, 3/88 (Both are lim. series)

1-3 (1979, 40¢; 1st comic book mini-series): 1-Jor-El marries Lara. 3-Baby Superman sent to Earth; Krypton explodes; Mon-el app. 5.00
1-4 (75¢)-Byrne scripts; Byrne/Simonson-c 3.00

WORLD OF METROPOLIS, THE
DC Comics: Aug, 1988 - No. 4, July, 1988 ($1.00, limited series)

1-4: Byrne scripts 3.00

WORLD OF MYSTERY
Atlas Comics (GPI): June, 1956 - No. 7, July, 1957

	GD	VG	FN	VF	VF/NM	NM-
1-Torres, Orlando-a; Powell-a?	47	94	141	291	483	675
2-Woodish-a	20	40	60	118	189	260
3-Torres, Davis, Ditko-a	24	48	72	140	225	310
4-Pakula, Powell-a	24	48	72	140	225	310
5,7: 5-Orlando-a	20	40	60	115	183	250
6-Williamson/Mayo-a (4 pgs.); Ditko-a; Crandall text illo	24	48	72	140	225	310

NOTE: ***Brodsky** c-2. **Colan** a-7. **Everett** c-1, 3. **Pakula** a-4, 6. **Romita** a-2. **Severin** c-7.*

WORLD OF SMALLVILLE
DC Comics: Apr, 1988 - No. 4, July, 1988 (75¢, limited series)

1-4: Byrne scripts 3.00

WORLD OF SUSPENSE
Atlas News Co.: Apr, 1956 - No. 8, July, 1957

	GD	VG	FN	VF	VF/NM	NM-
1	40	80	120	244	397	550
2-Ditko-a (4 pgs.)	24	48	72	140	225	310
3,7-Williamson-a in both (4 pgs.); #7-with Mayo	23	46	69	135	218	300
4-6,8	20	40	60	115	183	250

NOTE: ***Berg** a-6. **Cameron** a-2. **Ditko** a-2. **Drucker** a-1. **Everett** a-1, 5; c-6. **Heck** a-5. **Maneely** a-1; c-1-3. **Orlando** a-5. **Powell** a-6. **Reinman** a-4. **Roussos** a-6. **Shores** a-1.*

WORLD OF WARCRAFT (Based on the Blizzard Entertainment video game)
DC Comics (WildStorm): Jan, 2008 - Present ($2.99)

1-Walt Simonson-s/Lullabi-a; cover by Samwise Didier 8.00
1-Variant cover by Jim Lee 12.00
1,2-Second printing with Jim Lee sketch cover 5.00
2-Two covers by Jim Lee and Samwise Didier 5.00
3-9-Two covers on each 3.00

WORLD OF WHEELS (Formerly Dragstrip Hotrodders)
Charlton Comics: No. 17, Oct, 1967 - No. 32, June, 1970

	GD	VG	FN	VF	VF/NM	NM-
17-20-Features Ken King	3	6	9	18	27	35
21-32-Features Ken King	3	6	9	16	22	28
Modern Comics Reprint 23(1978)						5.00

WORLD OF WOOD
Eclipse Comics: 1986 - No. 4, 1987; No. 5, 2/89 ($1.75, limited series)

1-4:1-Dave Stevens-c. 2-Wood/Stevens-c 4.00
5 ($2.00, B&W)-r/Avon's Flying Saucers 5.00

WORLD'S BEST COMICS
DC Comics: Feb 1940

nn - Ashcan comic, not distributed to newsstands, only for in-house use. Cover art is Action Comics #29 with interior being Action Comics #24 (no known sales)

WORLD'S BEST COMICS (World's Finest Comics #2 on)
National Per. Publications (100 pgs.): Spring, 1941 (Cardboard-c)(DC's 6th annual format comic)

	GD	VG	FN	VF	VF/NM	NM-
1-The Batman, Superman, Crimson Avenger, Johnny Thunder, The King, Young Dr. Davis, Zatara, Lando, Man of Magic, & Red, White & Blue begin; Superman, Batman & Robin covers begin (inside-c is blank); Fred Ray-c; 15¢ cover price	1475	2950	4425	10,400	17,700	25,000

WORLD'S BEST COMICS: GOLDEN AGE SAMPLER
DC Comics: 2003 (99¢, one-shot, samples from DC Archive editions)

1-Golden Age reprints from Superman #6, Batman #5, Sensation #11, Police #11 2.50

WORLD'S BEST COMICS: SILVER AGE SAMPLER
DC Comics: 2004 (99¢, one-shot, samples from DC Archive editions)

1-Silver Age reprints from Justice League #4, Adventure #247, Our Army at War #81 2.50

WORLDS BEYOND (Stories of Weird Adventure)(Worlds of Fear #2 on)
Fawcett Publications: Nov, 1951

	GD	VG	FN	VF	VF/NM	NM-
1-Powell, Bailey-a; Moldoff-c	47	94	141	291	483	675

WORLDS COLLIDE
DC Comics: July, 1994 ($2.50, one-shot)

1-($2.50, 52 pgs.)-Milestone & Superman titles x-over 2.50
1-($3.95, 52 pgs.)-Polybagged w/vinyl clings 4.00

WORLD'S FAIR COMICS (See New York...)

WORLD'S FINEST (Also see Legends of The World's Finest)
DC Comics: 1990 - No. 3, 1990 ($3.95, squarebound, limited series, 52 pgs.)

1-3: Batman & Superman team-up against The Joker and Lex Luthor; Dave Gibbons scripts & Steve Rude-c/a. 2,3-Joker/Luthor painted-c by Steve Rude 5.00
TPB-($19.95) r/#1-3 20.00

WORLD'S FINEST COMICS (Formerly World's Best Comics #1)
National Periodical Publ./DC Comics: No. 2, Sum, 1941 - No. 323, Jan, 1986 (#1-17 have cardboard covers) (#2-9 have 100 pgs.)

	GD	VG	FN	VF	VF/NM	NM-
2 (100 pgs.)-Superman, Batman & Robin covers continue from World's Best; (cover price 15¢ #2-70)	423	846	1269	2876	5188	7500
3-The Sandman begins; last Johnny Thunder; origin & 1st app. The Scarecrow	329	658	987	2237	3919	5600
4-Hop Harrigan app.; last Young Dr. Davis	253	506	759	1594	2697	3800
5-Intro. TNT & Dan the Dyna-Mite; last King & Crimson Avenger	253	506	759	1594	2697	3800
6-Star Spangled Kid begins (Sum/42); Aquaman app.; S&K Sandman with Sandy in new costume begins, ends #7	187	374	561	1178	1989	2800
7-Green Arrow begins (Fall/42); last Lando & Red, White & Blue; S&K art	187	374	561	1178	1989	2800
8-Boy Commandos begin (by Simon(p) #12); last The King; includes "Minute Man Answers the Call" promo	177	354	531	1115	1883	2650
9-Batman cameo in Star Spangled Kid; S&K-a; last 100 pg. issue; Hitler, Mussolini, Tojo-c	207	414	621	1304	2202	3100
10-S&K-a; 76 pg. issues begin	167	334	501	1052	1776	2500
11-17: 17-Last cardboard cover issue	135	270	405	851	1438	2025
18-20: 18-Paper covers begin; last Star Spangled Kid. 19-Joker story. 20-Last quarterly issue	128	256	384	806	1366	1925
21-30: 21-Begin bi-monthly. 30-Johnny Everyman app.	88	176	264	554	940	1325
31-40: 33-35-Tomahawk app. 35-Penguin app.	82	164	246	517	871	1225
41-50: 41-Boy Commandos end. 42-The Wyoming Kid begins (9-10/49), ends #63. 43-Full Steam Foley begins, ends #48. 48-Last square binding. 49-Tom Sparks, Boy Inventor begins; robot-c	65	130	195	410	693	975
51-60: 51-Zatara ends. 54-Last 76 pg. issue. 59-Manhunters Around the World begins (7-8/52), ends #62	62	124	186	391	658	925
61-64: 61-Joker story. 63-Capt. Compass app.	60	120	180	378	639	900
65-Origin Superman; Tomahawk begins (7-8/53), ends #101	90	180	270	567	959	1350
66-70-(15¢ issues, scarce)-Last 15¢, 68pg. issue	63	126	189	397	674	950
71-(10¢ issue, scarce)-Superman & Batman begin as team (7-8/54); were in separate stories until now; Superman & Batman exchange identities; 10¢ issues begin	140	280	420	882	1491	2100
72,73-(10¢ issue, scarce)	92	184	276	580	978	1375
74-Last pre-code issue	65	130	195	410	693	975
75-(1st code approved, 3-4/55)	63	126	189	397	674	950
76-80: 77-Superman loses powers & Batman obtains them	50	100	150	310	518	725
81-90: 84-1st S.A. issue. 88-1st Joker/Luthor team-up. 89-2nd Batmen of All Nations (aka Club of Heroes). 90-Batwoman's 1st app. in World's Finest (10/57, 3rd app. anywhere) plus-c app.	28	56	84	203	377	550
91-93,95-99: 96-99-Kirby Green Arrow. 99-Robot-c	20	40	60	148	274	400
94-Origin Superman/Batman team retold	51	102	153	408	767	1125
100 (3/59)	34	68	102	256	483	710
101-110: 102-Tommy Tomorrow begins, ends #124	14	28	42	102	181	260
111-121: 111-1st app. The Clock King. 113-Intro. Miss Arrowette in Green Arrow; 1st Bat-Mite/Mr. Mxyzptlk team-up (11/60). 117-Batwoman-c. 121-Last 10¢ issue	12	24	36	82	146	210
122-128: 123-2nd Bat-Mite/Mr. Mxyzptlk team-up (2/62). 125-Aquaman begins (5/62), ends #139 (Aquaman #1 is dated 1-2/62)	9	18	27	65	113	160

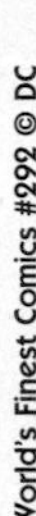

World's Finest Comics #292 © DC

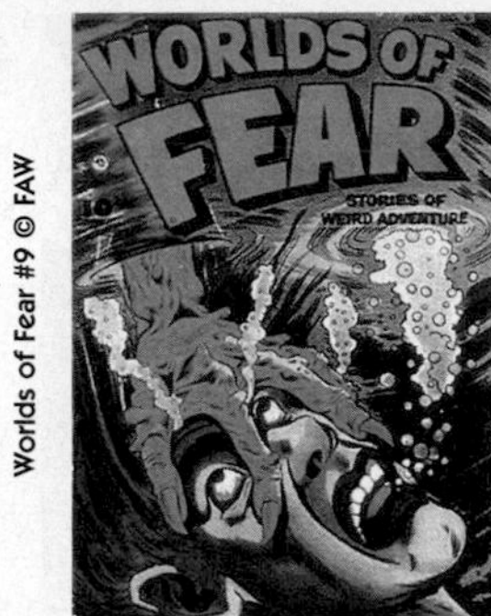

Worlds of Fear #9 © FAW

World War Hulk #4 © MAR

	GD 2.0	VG 4.0	FN 6.0	VF 8.0	VF/NM 9.0	NM- 9.2
129-Joker/Luthor team-up-c/story	11	22	33	75	133	190
130-142: 135-Last Dick Sprang story. 140-Last Green Arrow. 142-Origin The Composite Superman (villain); Legion app.	8	16	24	54	90	125
143-150: 143-1st Mailbag. 144-Clayface/Brainiac team-up; last Clayface until Action #443	7	14	21	45	73	100
151-153,155,157-160: 157-2nd Super Sons story; last app. Kathy Kane (Bat-Woman) until Batman Family #10; 1st Bat-Mite Jr.	6	12	18	37	59	80
154-1st Super Sons story; last Bat-Woman in costume until Batman Family #10.	6	12	18	41	66	90
156-1st Bizarro Batman; Joker-c/story	9	18	27	65	113	160
161,170 (80-Pg. Giants G-28,G-40)	6	12	18	43	69	95
162-165,167,168,171,172: 168,172-Adult Legion app.	5	10	15	30	48	65
166-Joker-c/story	5	10	15	34	55	75
169-3rd app. new Batgirl(9/67)(cover and 1 panel cameo); 3rd Bat-Mite/Mr. Mxyzptlk team-up	5	10	15	32	51	70
173-('68)-1st S.A. app. Two-Face as Batman becomes Two-Face in story	8	16	24	58	97	135
174-Adams-c	5	10	15	32	51	70
175,176-Neal Adams-c/a; both reprint J'onn J'onzz origin/Detective #225,226	5	10	15	34	55	75
177-Joker/Luthor team-up-c/story	5	10	15	32	51	70
178-(9/68) Intro. of Super Nova (revived in "52" weekly series); Adams-c	5	10	15	30	48	65
179-(80 Page Giant G-52) -Adams-c; r/#94	6	12	18	39	62	85
180,182,183,185,186: Adams-c on all. 182-Silent Knight-r/Brave & Bold #6. 185-Last 12¢ issue. 186-Johnny Quick-r	4	8	12	24	37	50
181,184,187: 187-Green Arrow origin-r by Kirby (Adv. #256)	4	8	12	22	34	45
188,197:(Giants G-64,G-76; 64 pages)	5	10	15	34	55	75
189-196: 190-193-Robin-r	3	6	9	18	27	36
198,199-3rd Superman/Flash race (see Flash #175 & Superman #199). 199-Adams-c	9	18	27	61	103	145
200-Adams-c	3	6	9	21	32	42
201-203: 203-Last 15¢ issue.	3	6	9	16	23	30
204,205-(52 pgs.) Adams-c: 204-Wonder Woman app. 205-Shining Knight-r (6 pgs.) by Frazetta/Adv. #153; Teen Titans x-over	3	6	9	18	27	35
206 (Giant G-88, 64 pgs.)	5	10	15	30	48	65
207,212-(52 pgs.)	3	6	9	18	27	35
208-211(25¢-c) Adams-c: 208-(52 pgs.) Origin Robotman-r/Det. #138. 209-211-(52 pgs.)	3	6	9	19	29	38
213,214,216-222,229: 217-Metamorpho begins, ends #220; Batman/Superman team-ups resume. 229-r/origin Superman-Batman team	2	4	6	10	14	18
215-(12/72-1/73) Intro. Batman Jr. & Superman Jr. (see Superman/Batman: Saga of the Super Sons TPB for all the Super Sons stories)	3	6	9	17	25	32
223-228-(100 pgs.). 223-N. Adams-r. 223-Deadman origin. 226-N. Adams, S&K, Toth-r; Manhunter part origin-r/Det. #225,226. 227-Deadman app.	4	8	12	28	44	60
230-(68 pgs.)	3	6	9	16	23	30
231-243,247,248: 242-Super Sons. 248-Last Vigilante	2	4	6	8	10	12
244-246-Adams-c: 244-$1.00, 84 pg. issues begin; Green Arrow, Black Canary, Wonder Woman, Vigilante begin; 246-Death of Stuff in Vigilante; origin Vigilante retold	2	4	6	13	18	22
249-252 (84 pgs.) Ditko-a: 249-The Creeper begins by Ditko, 84 pgs. 250-The Creeper origin retold by Ditko. 252-Last 84 pg. issue	2	4	6	11	16	20
253-257,259-265: 253-Capt. Marvel begins; 68 pgs. begin, end #265. 255-Last Creeper. 256-Hawkman begins. 257-Black Lightning begins. 263-Super Sons. 264-Clay Face app.	2	4	6	8	10	12
258-Adams-c	2	4	6	8	11	14
266-270,272-282-(52 pgs.). 267-Challengers of the Unknown app.; 3 Lt. Marvels return. 268-Capt. Marvel Jr. origin retold. 274-Zatanna begins. 279, 280-Capt. Marvel Jr. & Kid Eternity learn they are brothers	1	3	4	6	8	10
271-(52pgs.) Origin Superman/Batman team retold	2	4	6	8	10	12
283-299: 284-Legion app.	1	2	3	4	5	7
300-($1.25, 52pgs.)-Justice League of America, New Teen Titans & The Outsiders app.; Perez-a (4 pgs.)	1	2	3	5	6	8
301-322: 304-Origin Null and Void. 309,319-Free 16 pg. story in each (309-Flash Force 2000, 319-Mask preview)						3.00
323-Last issue						6.00

NOTE: ***Neal Adams** a-230ir; c-174-176, 178-180, 182, 183, 185, 186, 199-205, 208-211, 244-246, 258. **Austin** a-244-246i. **Burnley** a-8, 10; c-7-9, 11-14, 15p?, 16-18p, 20-31p. **Colan** a-274p, 297, 299. **Ditko** a-249-255. **Giffen** a-322; c-284p, 322. **G. Kane** a-38, 174r, 282, 283; c-281, 282, 289. **Kirby** a-187. **Kubert** Zatara-40-44. **Miller** c-285p. **Mooney** c-134. **Morrow** a-245-248. **Mortimer** c-16-21, 26-71. **Nasser** a(p)-244-246, 259, 260. **Newton** a-253-281p. **Orlando** a-224r. **Perez** a-300i; c-271, 276, 277p, 278p. **Fred Ray** c-1-5. **Fred Ray/Robinson** c-13-16. **Robinson** a-5, 6, 9-11, 13?, 14-16; c-6. **Rogers** a-259p. **Roussos** a-212r. **Simonson** c-291. **Spiegle** a-275-278, 284. **Staton** a-262p, 273p. **Swan/Moldoff** c-126. **Swan/Mortimer** c-79-82. **Toth** a-228r. **Tuska** a-230r, 250p, 252p, 254p, 257p, 283p, 284p, 308p. Boy Commandos by **Infantino** #39-41.*

WORLD'S FINEST COMICS DIGEST (See DC Special Series #23)

WORLD'S FINEST: OUR WORLDS AT WAR
DC Comics: Oct, 2001 ($2.95, one-shot)

	GD 2.0	VG 4.0	FN 6.0	VF 8.0	VF/NM 9.0	NM- 9.2
1-Concludes the Our Worlds at War x-over; Jae Lee-c; art by various						3.00

WORLD'S GREATEST ATHLETE (See Walt Disney Showcase #14)

WORLD'S GREATEST SONGS
Atlas Comics (Male): Sept, 1954

	GD 2.0	VG 4.0	FN 6.0	VF 8.0	VF/NM 9.0	NM- 9.2
1-(Scarce)-Heath & Harry Anderson-a; Eddie Fisher life story plus-c; gives lyrics to Frank Sinatra song "Young at Heart"	40	80	120	235	380	525

WORLD'S GREATEST STORIES
Jubilee Publications: Jan, 1949 - No. 2, May, 1949

	GD 2.0	VG 4.0	FN 6.0	VF 8.0	VF/NM 9.0	NM- 9.2
1-Alice in Wonderland; Lewis Carroll adapt.	32	64	96	186	298	410
2-Pinocchio	30	60	90	174	280	385

WORLDS OF FEAR (Stories of Weird Adventure)(Formerly Worlds Beyond #1)
Fawcett Publications: V1#2, Jan, 1952 - V2#10, June, 1953

	GD 2.0	VG 4.0	FN 6.0	VF 8.0	VF/NM 9.0	NM- 9.2
V1#2	47	94	141	291	483	675
3-Evans-a	40	80	120	244	397	550
4-6(9/52)	38	76	114	222	356	490
V2#7-9	34	68	102	198	319	440
10-Saunders painted-c, man with no eyes surrounded by eyeballs-c plus eyes ripped out story	93	186	279	586	993	1400

NOTE: ***Moldoff** c-2-8. **Powell** a-2, 4, 5. **Sekowsky** a-4, 5.*

WORLDSTORM
DC Comics (WildStorm): Nov, 2006 (Dec on cover) - Present ($2.99)

	GD 2.0	VG 4.0	FN 6.0	VF 8.0	VF/NM 9.0	NM- 9.2
1,2-Previews and pin-ups for re-launched WildStorm titles.1-Art Adams-c						3.00

WORLDS UNKNOWN
Marvel Comics Group: May, 1973 - No. 8, Aug, 1974

	GD 2.0	VG 4.0	FN 6.0	VF 8.0	VF/NM 9.0	NM- 9.2
1-r/from Astonishing #54; Torres, Reese-a	3	6	9	14	19	24
2-8	2	4	6	9	13	16

NOTE: ***Adkins/Mooney** a-5. **Buscema** c/a-4p. W. **Howard** c/a-3i. **Kane** a(p)-1,2; c(p)-5, 6, 8. **Sutton** a-2. **Tuska** a(p)-7, 8; c-7p. No. 7, 8 has Golden Voyage of Sinbad movie adaptation.*

WORLD WAR HULK (See Incredible Hulk #106)
Marvel Comics: Aug, 2007 - No. 5, Jan, 2008 ($3.99, limited series)

	GD 2.0	VG 4.0	FN 6.0	VF 8.0	VF/NM 9.0	NM- 9.2
1-Hulk returns to Earth; Iron Man and Avengers app.; Romita Jr.-a/Pak-s/Finch-c						4.00
1-Variant cover by Romita Jr.						6.00
2-5: 2-Hulk battles The Avengers and FF; Finch-c. 3,4-Dr. Strange app. 5-Sentry app.						4.00
2-5-Variant cover by Romita Jr.						6.00
...: Aftersmash 1 (1/08, $3.99) Sandoval-a/Land-c; Hercules, Iron Man app.						4.00
...: Gamma Files (2007, $3.99) profile pages of Hulk characters						4.00
...Prologue: World Breaker 1 (7/07, one-shot) Rio, Weeks, Phillips, Miyazawa-a						4.00

WORLD WAR HULK AFTERSMASH: DAMAGE CONTROL
Marvel Comics: Mar, 2008 - No. 3, May, 2008 ($2.99, limited series)

	GD 2.0	VG 4.0	FN 6.0	VF 8.0	VF/NM 9.0	NM- 9.2
1-3-The clean-up; McDuffie-s. 2-Romita- Jr.-c. 3-Romita Sr.-c						3.00

WORLD WAR HULK AFTERSMASH: WARBOUND
Marvel Comics: Feb, 2008 - No. 5, Jun, 2008 ($2.99, limited series)

	GD 2.0	VG 4.0	FN 6.0	VF 8.0	VF/NM 9.0	NM- 9.2
1-5-Kirk & Sandoval-a/Cheung-c						3.00

WORLD WAR HULK: FRONT LINE (See Incredible Hulk #106)
Marvel Comics: Aug, 2007 - No. 6, Dec, 2007 ($2.99, limited series)

	GD 2.0	VG 4.0	FN 6.0	VF 8.0	VF/NM 9.0	NM- 9.2
1-6-Ben Urich & Sally Floyd report World War Hulk; Jenkins-s/Bachs-a						3.00

WORLD WAR HULK: GAMMA CORPS
Marvel Comics: Sept, 2007 - No. 4, Jan, 2008 ($2.99, limited series)

	GD 2.0	VG 4.0	FN 6.0	VF 8.0	VF/NM 9.0	NM- 9.2
1-4-Tieri-s/Ferreira-a/Roux-c						3.00

WORLD WAR HULK: X-MEN (See New Avengers: Illuminati and Incredible Hulk #92)
Marvel Comics: Aug, 2007 - No. 3, Oct, 2007 ($2.99, limited series)

	GD 2.0	VG 4.0	FN 6.0	VF 8.0	VF/NM 9.0	NM- 9.2
1-3-Gage-s/DiVito-a/McGuinness-c; Hulk invades the Xavier Institute						3.00

WORLD WAR STORIES
Dell Publishing Co.: Apr-June, 1965 - No. 3, Dec, 1965

	GD 2.0	VG 4.0	FN 6.0	VF 8.0	VF/NM 9.0	NM- 9.2
1-Glanzman-a in all	4	8	12	26	41	55
2,3	3	6	9	17	25	32

WORLD WAR II (See Classics Illustrated Special Issue)

WORLD WAR II: 1946
Antarctic Press: Oct, 1998 - No. 2 ($3.95, B&W)

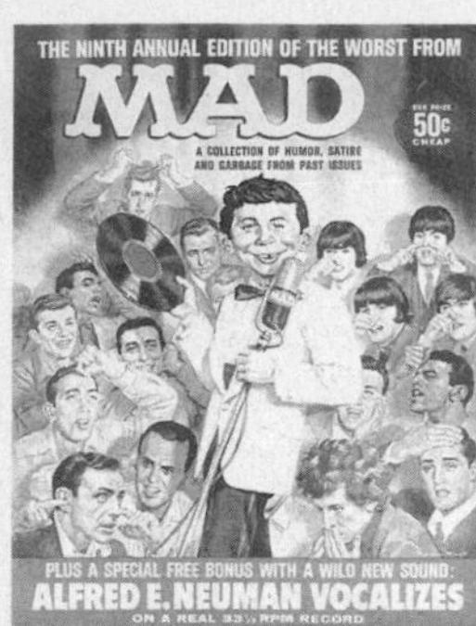

Worst From Mad #9 © EC Publ.

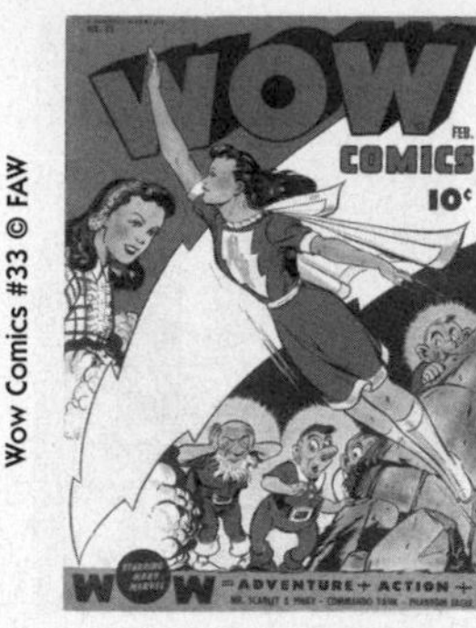

Wow Comics #33 © FAW

Wyatt Earp #4 © DELL

	GD 2.0	VG 4.0	FN 6.0	VF 8.0	VF/NM 9.0	NM- 9.2

1,2-Nomura-s/a 4.00

WORLD WAR III
Ace Periodicals: Mar, 1953 - No. 2, May, 1953

1-(Scarce)-Atomic bomb blast-c; Cameron-a 97 194 291 611 1031 1450
2-Used in **POP**, pg. 78 & B&W & color illos; Cameron-a 58 116 174 365 620 875

WORLDWATCH
Wild and Wooly Press: June, 2004 - No. 3, Dec, 2004 ($2.95)

1-3-Austen-s/Derenick-a. 1-B&W. 2,3-Color 3.00

WORLD WITHOUT END
DC Comics: 1990 - No. 6, 1991 ($2.50, limited series, mature, stiff-c)

1-6: Horror/fantasy; all painted-c/a 2.50

WORLD WRESTLING FEDERATION BATTLEMANIA
Valiant: 1991 - No. 5?, 1991 ($2.50, magazine size, 68 pgs.)

1-5: 5-Includes 2 free pull-out posters 4.00

WORST FROM MAD, THE (Annual)
E. C. Comics: 1958 - No. 12, 1969 (Each annual cover is reprinted from the cover of the Mad issues being reprinted)(Value is 1/2 if bonus is missing)

nn(1958)-Bonus; record labels & travel stickers; 1st Mad annual; r/Mad #29-34 43 86 129 267 446 625
2(1959)-Bonus is small 33 1/3 rpm record entitled "Meet the Staff of Mad"; r/Mad #35-40 41 82 123 256 428 600
3(1960)-Has 20x30" campaign poster "Alfred E. Neuman for President"; r/Mad #41-46 17 34 51 124 230 335
4(1961)-Sunday comics section; r/Mad #47-54 16 32 48 116 216 315
5(1962)-Has 33-1/3 record; r/Mad #55-62 23 46 69 167 309 450
6(1963)-Has 33-1/3 record; r/Mad #63-70 23 46 69 167 309 450
7(1964)-Mad protest signs; r/Mad #71-76 10 20 30 70 123 175
8(1965)-Build a Mad Zeppelin 11 22 33 79 140 200
9(1966)-33-1/3 rpm record; Beatles on-c 16 32 48 112 209 305
10(1967)-Mad bumper sticker 7 14 21 47 76 105
11(1968)-Mad cover window stickers 6 12 18 43 69 95
12(1969)-Mad picture postcards; Orlando-a 6 12 18 43 69 95
NOTE: *Covers:* ***Bob Clarke****-#8.* ***Mingo****-#7, 9-12.*

WOTALIFE COMICS (Formerly Nutty Life #2; Phantom Lady #13 on)
Fox Features Syndicate/Norlen Mag.: No. 3, Aug-Sept, 1946 - No. 12, July, 1947; 1959

3-Cosmo Cat, Li'l Pan, others begin 11 22 33 60 83 105
4-12-Cosmo Cat, Li'l Pan in all 9 18 27 47 61 75
1(1959-Norlen)-Atomic Rabbit, Atomic Mouse; reprints cover to #6; reprints entire book? 8 16 24 40 50 60

WOTALIFE COMICS
Green Publications: 1957 - No. 5, 1957

1 7 14 21 35 43 50
2-5 5 10 15 22 26 30

WOW COMICS ("Wow, What A Magazine!" on cover of first issue)
Henle Publishing Co.: July, 1936 - No. 4, Nov, 1936 (52 pgs., magazine size)

1-Buck Jones in "The Phantom Rider" (1st app. in comics), Fu Manchu; Capt. Scott Dalton begins; Will Eisner-a (1st in comics); Baily-a(1); Briefer-c 307 614 921 1934 3267 4600
2-Ken Maynard, Fu Manchu, Popeye by Segar plus article on Popeye; Eisner-a 203 406 609 1279 2165 3050
3-Eisner-c/a(3); Popeye by Segar, Fu Manchu, Hiram Hick by Bob Kane, Space Limited app.; Jimmy Dempsey talks about Popeye's punch; Bob Ripley Believe it or Not begins; Briefer-a 190 380 570 1197 2024 2850
4-Flash Gordon by Raymond, Mandrake, Popeye by Segar, Tillie The Toiler, Fu Manchu, Hiram Hick by Bob Kane; Eisner-a(3); Briefer-c/a 237 474 711 1493 2522 3550

WOW COMICS (Real Western Hero #70 on)(See XMas Comics)
Fawcett Publ.: Winter, 1940-41; No. 2, Summer, 1941 - No. 69, Fall, 1948

nn(#1)-Origin Mr. Scarlet by S&K; Atom Blake, Boy Wizard, Jim Dolan, & Rick O'Shay begin; Diamond Jack, The White Rajah, & Shipwreck Roberts, only app.; 1st mention of Gotham City in comics; the cover was printed on unstable paper stock and is rarely found in fine or mint condition; blank inside-c; bondage-c by Beck 1350 2700 4050 10,400 18,700 27,000
2 (Scarce)-The Hunchback begins 306 612 918 2081 3641 5200
3 (Fall, 1941) 143 286 429 901 1526 2150
4-Origin & 1st app. Pinky 150 300 450 945 1598 2250
5 83 166 249 523 887 1250

	GD 2.0	VG 4.0	FN 6.0	VF 8.0	VF/NM 9.0	NM- 9.2

6-Origin & 1st app. The Phantom Eagle (7/15/42); Commando Yank begins 83 166 249 523 887 1250
7,8,10: 10-Swayze-c/a on Mary Marvel 62 124 186 391 658 925
9 (1/6/43)-Capt. Marvel, Capt. Marvel Jr., Shazam app.; Scarlet & Pinky x-over; Mary Marvel-c/stories begin (cameo #9) 160 320 480 1008 1704 2400
11-17,19,20: 15-Flag-c 47 94 141 291 488 685
18-1st app. Uncle Marvel (10/43); infinity-c 49 98 147 304 507 710
21-30: 23-Robot-c. 28-Pinky x-over in Mary Marvel 31 62 93 181 291 400
31-40: 32-68-Phantom Eagle by Swayze 22 44 66 127 204 280
41-50 20 40 60 118 189 260
51-58: Last Mary Marvel 19 38 57 112 176 240
59-69: 59-Ozzie (teenage) begins. 62-Flying Saucer gag-c (1/48). 65-69-Tom Mix stories (cont'd in Real Western Hero) 17 34 51 100 158 215
NOTE: *Cover features: Mr. Scarlet-#1-5; Commando Yank-#6, 7, (w/Mr. Scarlet #8); Mary Marvel-#9-56, (w/Commando Yank-#46-50), (w/Mr. Scarlet & Commando Yank-#51), (w/Mr. Scarlet & Pinky #53), (w/Phantom Eagle #54, 56), (w/Commando Yank & Phantom Eagle #58); Ozzie-#59-69.*

WRAITHBORN
DC Comics (WildStorm): Nov, 2005 - No. 6, July, 2006 ($2.99, limited series)

1-6-Marcia Chen & Joe Benitez-s/a 3.00
TPB (2007, $19.99) r/series; sketch pages and unused cover sketches 20.00

WRATH (Also see Prototype #4)
Malibu Comics: Jan, 1994 - No. 9, Nov, 1995 ($1.95)

1-9: 2-Mantra x-over. 3-Intro/1st app. Slayer. 4,5-Freex app. 8-Mantra & Warstrike app. 9-Prime app. 2.50
1-Ultra 5000 Limited silver foil 4.00
Giant Size 1 (2.50, 44 pgs.) 2.50

WRATH OF THE SPECTRE, THE
DC Comics: May, 1988 - No. 4, Aug, 1988 ($2.50, limited series)

1-3: Aparo-r/Adventure #431-440 4.00
4-Three scripts intended for Adventure #441-on, but not drawn by Aparo until 1988 5.00
TPB (2005, $19.99) r/series; Peter Sanderson intro. 20.00

WRECK OF GROSVENOR (See Superior Stories #3)

WRETCH, THE
Caliber: 1996 ($2.95, B&W)

1-Phillip Hester-a/scripts 3.00

WRETCH, THE
Amaze Ink: 1997 - No. 4, 1998 ($2.95, B&W)

1-4-Phillip Hester-a/scripts 3.00
... Vol. 1: Everyday Doomsday (4/03, $13.95) 14.00

WRINGLE WRANGLE (Disney)
Dell Publishing Co.: No. 821, July, 1957

Four Color 821-Based on movie "Westward Ho, the Wagons"; Marsh-a; Fess Parker photo-c 8 16 24 52 86 120

WULF THE BARBARIAN
Atlas/Seaboard Publ.: Feb, 1975 - No. 4, Sept, 1975

1,2: 1-Origin; Janson-a. 2-Intro. Berithe the Swordswoman; Janson-a w/Neal Adams, Wood, Reese-a assists 2 4 6 8 10 12
3,4: 3-Skeates-s. 4-Friedrich-s 1 2 3 5 7 9

WYATT EARP
Atlas Comics/Marvel No. 23 on (IPC): Nov, 1955 - #29, June, 1960; #30, Oct, 1972 - #34, June, 1973

1 21 42 63 123 197 270
2-Williamson-a (4 pgs.) 14 28 42 76 108 140
3-6,8-11: 3-Black Bart app. 8-Wild Bill Hickok app. 11 22 33 60 83 105
7,12-Williamson-a, 4 pgs. ea.; #12 with Mayo 11 22 33 60 83 105
13-20: 17-1st app. Wyatt's deputy, Grizzly Grant 10 20 30 54 72 90
21-Davis-c 9 18 27 50 65 80
22-24,26-29: 22-Ringo Kid app. 23-Kid From Texas app. 29-Last 10¢ issue 8 16 24 42 54 65
25-Davis-a 8 16 24 44 57 70
30-Williamson-r (1972) 2 4 6 11 16 20
31-34-Reprints. 32-Torres-a(r) 2 4 6 9 13 16
NOTE: ***Ayers*** *a-8, 10(2), 17, 20(4).* ***Berg*** *a-9.* ***Everett*** *c-6.* ***Kirby*** *c-25, 29.* ***Maneely*** *a-1; c-1-4, 8, 12, 17, 20.* ***Maurer*** *a-2(2), 3(4), 4(4), 8(4).* ***Severin*** *a-4, 9(4), 10; c-2, 9, 10, 14.* ***Wildey*** *a-5, 17, 24, 28.*

WYATT EARP (TV) (Hugh O'Brian Famous Marshal)
Dell Publishing Co.: No. 860, Nov, 1957 - No. 13, Dec-Feb, 1960-61 (Hugh O'Brian photo-c)

Four Color 860 (#1)-Manning-a 9 18 27 65 113 160
Four Color 890,921(6/58)-All Manning-a 7 14 21 49 80 110
4 (9-11/58) - 12-Manning-a. 5-Photo back-c 6 12 18 37 59 80

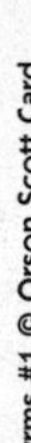

Wyrms #1 © Orson Scott Card

Xena: Warrior Princess #7 © Studio USA

X-Factor #1 © MAR

	GD 2.0	VG 4.0	FN 6.0	VF 8.0	VF/NM 9.0	NM- 9.2
13-Toth-a	6	12	18	39	62	85

WYATT EARP FRONTIER MARSHAL (Formerly Range Busters) (Also see Blue Bird)
Charlton Comics: No. 12, Jan, 1956 - No. 72, Dec, 1967

	GD	VG	FN	VF	VF/NM	NM-
12	9	18	27	47	61	75
13-19	6	12	18	31	38	45
20-(68 pgs.)-Williamson-a(4), 8,5,5,& 7 pgs.	10	20	30	54	72	90
21-(100 pgs.) Mastroserio, Maneely, Severin-a (signed LePoer)	5	10	15	32	51	70
22-30	3	6	9	16	23	30
31-50	2	4	6	12	16	20
51-72 (1967)	2	4	6	9	11	14

WYNONNA EARP
Image Comics (WildStorm Productions): Dec, 1996 - No. 5, Apr, 1997 ($2.50)

1-5-Smith-s/Chin-a 2.50

WYNONNA EARP: HOME ON THE STRANGE
IDW Publishing: Dec, 2003 - No. 3, Feb, 2004 ($3.99)

1-3-Smith-s/Ferreira-a 4.00

WYRMS
Marvel Comics (Dabel Brothers): Feb, 2007 - No. 6, Jan, 2008 ($2.99)

1-6-Orson Scott Card & Jake Black-s. 1-3-Batista-a 3.00
TPB (2008, $14.99) r/#1-6 15.00

X (Comics' Greatest World: X #1 only) (Also see Comics' Greatest World & Dark Horse Comics #8)
Dark Horse Comics: Feb, 1994 - No. 25, Apr, 1996 ($2.00/$2.50)

1-25: 3-Pit Bulls x-over. 8 -Ghost-c & app. 18-Miller-c.; Predator app. 19-22-Miller-c. 2.50
Hero Illustrated Special #1,2 (1994, $1.00, 20 pgs.) 2.50
One Shot to the Head (1994, $2.50, 36 pgs.)-Miller-c. 2.50
NOTE: *Miller c-18-22. Quesada c-6. Russell a-6.*

XANADU COLOR SPECIAL
Eclipse Comics: Dec, 1988 ($2.00, one-shot)

1-Continued from Thoughts & Images 2.50

XAVIER INSTITUTE ALUMNI YEARBOOK (See X-Men titles)
Marvel Comics: Dec, 1996 ($5.95, square-bound, one-shot)

1-Text w/art by various 6.00

X-BABIES
Marvel Comics: (one-shots)

...: Murderama (8/98, $2.95) J.J. Kirby-a 3.50
...: Reborn (1/00, $3.50) J.J. Kirby-a 3.50

X-CALIBRE
Marvel Comics: Mar, 1995 - No. 4, July, 1995 ($1.95, limited series)

1-4-Age of Apocalypse 2.50

XENA (TV)
Dynamite Entertainment: 2006 - Present ($3.50)

1-4-Three covers on each; Neves-a/Layman-s 3.50
Vol. 2 #1-4-(Dark Xena) Four covers; Salonga-a/Layman-s 3.50
Annual 1 (2007, $4.95) Three covers; Salonga-a/Champagne-s 5.00
... Vol. 2: Dark Xena TPB (2007, $14.99) r/Vol. 2 #1-4; variant cover gallery 15.00

XENA: WARRIOR PRINCESS (TV)
Topps Comics: Aug, 1997 - No. 0, Oct, 1997 ($2.95)

	GD	VG	FN	VF	VF/NM	NM-
1-Two stories by various; J. Scott Campbell-c	1	3	4	6	8	10
1,2-Photo-c	1	3	4	6	8	10
2-Stevens-c						6.00
0-(10/97)-Lopresti-c, 0-(10/97)-Photo-c	1	2	3	5	6	8
...First Appearance Collection ('97, $9.95) r/Hercules the Legendary Journeys #3-5 and 5-page story from TV Guide						10.00

XENA: WARRIOR PRINCESS (TV)
Dark Horse Comics: Sept, 1999 - No. 14, Oct, 2000 ($2.95/$2.99)

1-14: 1-Mignola-c and photo-c. 2,3-Bradstreet-c & photo-c 3.00

XENA: WARRIOR PRINCESS AND THE ORIGINAL OLYMPICS (TV)
Topps Comics: Jun, 1998 - No. 3, Aug, 1998 ($2.95, limited series)

1-3-Regular and Photo-c; Lim-a/T&M Bierbaum-s 3.00

XENA: WARRIOR PRINCESS-BLOODLINES (TV)
Topps Comics: May, 1998 - No. 2, June, 1998 ($2.95, limited series)

1,2-Lopresti-s/c/a. 2-Reg. and photo-c 3.00
1-Bath photo-c, 1-American Ent. Ed. 4.00

XENA: WARRIOR PRINCESS / JOXER: WARRIOR PRINCE (TV)
Topps Comics: Nov, 1997 - No. 3, Jan, 1998 ($2.95, limited series)

1-3-Regular and Photo-c; Lim-a/T&M Bierbaum-s 3.00

XENA: WARRIOR PRINCESS-THE DRAGON'S TEETH (TV)
Topps Comics: Dec, 1997 - No. 3, Feb, 1998 ($2.95, limited series)

1-3-Regular and Photo-c; Teranishi-a/Thomas-s 3.00

XENA: WARRIOR PRINCESS-THE ORPHEUS TRILOGY (TV)
Topps Comics: Mar, 1998 - No. 3, May, 1998 ($2.95, limited series)

1-3-Regular and Photo-c, Teranishi-a/T&M Bierbaum-s 3.00

XENA: WARRIOR PRINCESS VS. CALLISTO (TV)
Topps Comics: Feb, 1998 - No. 3, Apr, 1998 ($2.95, limited series)

1-3-Regular and Photo-c; Morgan-a/Thomas-s 3.00

XENOBROOD
DC Comics: No. 0, Oct, 1994 - No. 6, Apr, 1995 ($1.50, limited series)

0-6: 0-Indicia says "Xenobroods" 2.50

XENON
Eclipse Comics: Dec, 1987 - No. 23, Nov. 1, 1988 ($1.50, B&W, bi-weekly)

1-23 2.50

XENOZOIC TALES (Also see Cadillacs & Dinosaurs, Death Rattle #8)
Kitchen Sink Press: Feb, 1986 - No. 14, Oct, 1996

	GD	VG	FN	VF	VF/NM	NM-
1-Mark Schultz-s/a in all	1	3	4	6	8	10
1(2nd printing)(1/89)						3.00
2-14						5.00
Volume 1 ($14.95) r/#1-6 & Death Rattle #8						15.00
Volume 2 (5/03, $14.95, TPB) B&W r/#7-14; intro by Frank Cho						15.00

XENYA
Sanctuary Press: Apr, 1994 - No. 3 ($2.95)

1-3: 1-Hildebrandt-c; intro Xenya 3.00

XERO
DC Comics: May, 1997 - No. 12, Apr, 1998 ($1.75)

1-7 2.50
8-12 2.50

X-FACTOR (Also see The Avengers #263, Fantastic Four #286 and Mutant X)
Marvel Comics Group: Feb, 1986 - No. 149, Sept, 1998

	GD	VG	FN	VF	VF/NM	NM-
1-($1.25, 52 pgs)-Story recaps 1st app. from Avengers #263; story cont'd from F.F. #286; return of original X-Men (now X-Factor); Guice/Layton-a; Baby Nathan app. (2nd after X-Men #201)						6.00
2-4						4.00
5-1st brief app. Apocalypse (2 pages)						4.00
6-1st full app. Apocalypse	1	3	4	6	8	10
7-10: 10-Sabretooth app. (11/86, 3 pgs.) cont'd in X-Men #212; 1st app. in an X-Men comic book						4.00
11-22: 13-Baby Nathan app. in flashback. 14-Cyclops vs. The Master Mold. 15-Intro wingless Angel						3.00
23-1st brief app. Archangel (2 pages)	1	2	3	4	5	7
24-1st full app. Archangel (now in Uncanny X-Men); Fall Of The Mutants begins; origin Apocalypse	1	2	3	5	7	9
25,26: Fall Of The Mutants; 26-New outfits						3.00
27-39,41-83,87-91,93-99,101: 35-Origin Cyclops. 38,50-(52 pgs.): 50-Liefeld/McFarlane-c. 51-53-Sabretooth app. 52-Liefeld-c(p). 54-Intro Crimson; Silvestri-c/a(p). 60-X-Tinction Agenda x-over; New Mutants (w/Cable) x-over in #60-62; Wolverine in #62. 60-Gold ink 2nd printing. 61,62-X-Tinction Agenda. 62-Jim Lee-c. 63-Portacio/Thibert-c/a(p) begins, ends #69. 65-68-Lee co-plots. 65-The Apocalypse Files begins, ends #68. 66,67-Baby Nathan app. 67-Inhumans app. 68-Baby Nathan is sent into future to save his life. 69,70-X-Men(w/Wolverine) x-over. 71-New team begins (Havok, Polaris, Strong Guy, Wolfsbane & Madrox); Stroman-c/a begins. 71-2nd printing ($1.25). 75-(52 pgs.). 77-Cannonball (of X-Force) app. 87-Quesada-c/a(p) in monthly comic begins,ends #92. 88-1st app. Random						2.50
40-Rob Liefield-c/a (4/89, 1st at Marvel?)						3.00
84-86 -Jae Lee a(p); 85,86-Jae Lee-c. Polybagged with trading card in each; X-Cutioner's Song x-overs.						3.00
92-($3.50, 68 pgs.)-Wraparound-c by Quesada w/Havok hologram on-c; begin X-Men 30th anniversary issues; Quesada-a.						5.00
92-2nd printing						2.50
100-($2.95, 52 pgs.)-Embossed foil-c; Multiple Man dies.						5.00
100-($1.75, 52 pgs.)-Regular edition						2.50
102-105,107: 102-bound-in card sheet						2.50

X-Factor (2006 series) #26 © MAR

X-Files #0 © 20th Century Fox

X-Force (2008 series) #1 © MAR

GD VG FN VF VF/NM NM-
2.0 4.0 6.0 8.0 9.0 9.2

GD VG FN VF VF/NM NM-
2.0 4.0 6.0 8.0 9.0 9.2

106-($2.00)-Newsstand edition 2.50
106-($2.95)-Collectors edition 3.00
108-124,126-148: 112-Return from Age of Apocalypse. 115-card insert. 119-123-Sabretooth app. 123-Hound app. 124-w/Onslaught Update. 126-Onslaught x-over; Beast vs. Dark Beast. 128-w/card insert; return of Multiple Man. 130-Assassination of Grayson Creed. 146,148-Moder-a 2.50
125-($2.95)-"Onslaught"; Post app.; return of Havok 4.00
149-Last issue 3.00
#(-1) Flashback (7/97) Matsuda-a 2.50
Annual 1-9: 1-(10/86-'94, 68 pgs.) 3-Evolutionary War x-over. 4-Atlantis Attacks; Byrne/Simonson-a;Byrne-c. 5-Fantastic Four, New Mutants x-over; Keown 2 pg. pin-up. 6-New Warriors app.; 5th app. X-Force cont'd from X-Men Annual #15. 7-1st Quesada-a(p) on X-Factor plus-c(p). 8-Bagged w/trading card. 9-Austin-a(i) 3.00
...Prisoner of Love (1990, $4.95, 52 pgs.)-Starlin scripts; Guice-a 5.00
... Visionaries: Peter David Vol. 1 TPB (2005, $15.99) r/#71-75 16.00
... Visionaries: Peter David Vol. 2 TPB (2007, $15.99) r/#76-78 & Incr. Hulk #390-392 16.00
... Visionaries: Peter David Vol. 3 TPB (2007, $15.99) r/#79-83 & Annual #7 16.00
NOTE: ***Art Adams** a-41p, 42p.* ***Buckler** a-50p.* ***Liefeld** a-40; c-40, 50i, 52p.* ***McFarlane** c-50i.* ***Mignola** c-70.* ***Brandon Peterson** a-78p(part).* ***Whilce Portacio** c/a(p)-63-69.* ***Quesada** a(p)-87-92, Annual 7. c(p)-78, 79, 82, Annual 7.* ***Simonson** c/a-10, 11, 13-15, 17-19, 21, 23-31, 33, 34, 36-39; c-12, 16.* ***Paul Smith** a-44-48; c-43.* ***Stroman** a(p)-71-75, 77, 78(part), 80, 81; c(p)-71-77, 80, 81, 84.* ***Zeck** c-2.*

X-FACTOR (Volume 2)
Marvel Comics: June, 2002 - No. 4, Oct, 2002 ($2.50)
1-4: Jensen-s/Ranson-a. 1-Phillips-c. 2,3-Edwards-c 2.50

X-FACTOR
Marvel Comics: Jan, 2006 - Present ($2.99)
1-24: 1-Peter David-s/Ryan Sook-a. 8,9-Civil War. 21-24-Endangered Species back-up 3.00
25-35: 25-27-Messiah Complex x-over; Finch-c. 26-2nd printing with new Eaton-c 3.00
... Special: Layla Miller (10/08, $3.99) David-s/DeLandro-a 4.00
...: The Quick and the Dead (7/08, $2.99) Raimondi-a; Quicksilver regains powers 3.00
...: The Longest Night HC (2006, $19.99, dust jacket) r/#1-6; sketch pages by Sook 20.00
...: The Longest Night SC (2007, $14.99) r/#1-6; sketch pages by Sook 15.00
...: Life and Death Matters HC (2007, $19.99, dust jacket) r/#7-12 20.00
...: Life and Death Matters SC (2007, $14.99) r/#7-12 15.00
...: The Many Lives of Madrox SC (2007, $14.99) r/#13-17 15.00
...: Heart of Ice HC (2007, $19.99, dust jacket) r/#18-24 20.00
...: Heart of Ice SC (2008, $17.99, dust jacket) r/#18-24 18.00

X-51 (Machine Man)
Marvel Comics: Sept, 1999 - No. 12, Jul, 2000 ($1.99/$2.50)
1-7: 1-Joe Bennett-a. 2-Two covers 2.50
8-12: 8-Begin $2.50-c 2.50
Wizard #0 2.50

X-FILES, THE (TV)
Topps Comics: Jan, 1995 - No. 41, July, 1998 ($2.50)

	GD 2.0	VG 4.0	FN 6.0	VF 8.0	VF/NM 9.0	NM- 9.2
-2(9/96)-Black-c; r/X-Files Magazine #1&2	1	3	4	6	8	10
-1(9/96)-Silver-c; r/Hero Illustrated Giveaway	1	3	4	6	8	10
0-($3.95)-Adapts pilot episode						4.00
0-"Mulder" variant-c	1	2	3	5	6	8
0-"Scully" variant-c	1	2	3	5	6	8
1/2-W/certificate	3	6	9	14	20	25
1-New stories based on the TV show; direct market & newsstand editions; Miran Kim-c on all	3	6	9	16	23	30
2	2	4	6	10	14	18
3,4	1	2	3	5	6	8
5-10						4.00
11-41: 11-Begin $2.95-c. 21-W/bound-in card. 40,41-Reg. & photo-c						3.00
Annual 1,2 ($3.95)						4.00
Afterflight TPB ($5.95) Art by Thompson, Saviuk, Kim						6.00
Collection 1 TPB ($19.95)-r/#1-6.						20.00
Collection 2 TPB ($19.95)-r/#7-12, Annual #1.						20.00
...Fight the Future ('98, $5.95) Movie adaptation						6.00
Hero Illustrated Giveaway (3/95)	2	4	6	9	12	15
Special Edition 1-5 ($4.95)-r/#1-3, 4-6, 7-9, 10-12, 13, Annual 1						5.00
Star Wars Galaxy Magazine Giveaway (B&W)	1	3	4	6	8	10
Trade paperback ($19.95)						20.00
Volume 1 TPB (Checker Books, 2005, $19.95) r/#13-17, #0, Season One: Squeeze						20.00
Volume 2 TPB (Checker Books, 2005, $19.95) r/#18-24, #1/2, Comics Digest #1						20.00
Volume 3 TPB (Checker Books, 2006, $19.95) r/#23-26, Fire, Ice, Hero Ill. Giveaway						20.00

X-FILES, THE (TV)
DC Comics (WildStorm): No. 0, Sept, 2008 - Present ($3.99)
0-Spotnitz-s/Denham-a; photo-c 4.00

X-FILES COMICS DIGEST, THE
Topps Comics: Dec, 1995 - No. 3 ($3.50, quarterly, digest-size)
1-3: 1,2: New X-Files stories w/Ray Bradbury Comics-r 4.00
NOTE: ***Adlard** a-1, 2.* ***Jack Davis** a-2r.* ***Russell** a-1r.*

X-FILES, THE: GROUND ZERO (TV)
Topps Comics: Nov, 1997 - No. 4, March, 1998 ($2.95, limited series)
1-4-Adaptation of the Kevin J. Anderson novel 3.00

X-FILES, THE: SEASON ONE (TV)
Topps Comics: July, 1997 - July, 1998 ($4.95, adaptations of TV episodes)
1,2,Squeeze, Conduit, Ice, Space, Fire, Beyond the Sea, Shadows 5.00

X-FORCE (Becomes X-Statix) (Also see The New Mutants #100)
Marvel Comics: Aug, 1991 - No. 129, Aug, 2002 ($1.00-$2.25)
1-($1.50, 52 pgs.)-Polybagged with 1 of 5 diff. Marvel Universe trading cards inside (1 each); 6th app. of X-Force; Liefeld-c/a begins 4.00
1-1st printing with Cable trading card inside 5.00
1-2nd printing; metallic ink-c (no bag or card) 2.50
2-4: 2-Deadpool-c/story. 3-New Brotherhood of Evil Mutants app. 4-Spider-Man x-over; cont'd from Spider-Man #16; reads sideways 3.00
5-10: 6-Last $1.00-c. 7,9-Weapon X back-ups. 8-Intro The Wild Pack (Cable, Kane, Domino, Hammer, G.W. Bridge, & Grizzly); Liefeld-c/a (4); Mignola-a. 10-Weapon X full-length story (part 3). 11-1st Weapon Prime; Deadpool-c/story 3.00
11-15,19-24,26-33: 15-Cable leaves X-Force 2.50
16-18-Polybagged w/trading card in each; X-Cutioner's Song x-overs 3.00
25-($3.50, 52 pgs.)-Wraparound-c w/Cable hologram on-c; Cable returns 4.00
34-37,39-45: 34-bound-in card sheet 2.50
38,40-43: 38-($2.00)-Newsstand edition. 40-43 ($1.95)-Deluxe edition 2.50
38-($2.95)-Collectors edition (prismatic) 5.00
44-49,51-67: 44-Return from Age of Apocalypse. 45-Sabretooth app. 49-Sebastian Shaw app. 52-Blob app., Onslaught cameo. 55-Vs. S.H.I.E.L.D. 56-Deadpool app. 57-Mr. Sinister & X-Man-c/app. 57,58-Onslaught x-over. 59-W/card insert; return of Longshot. 60-Dr. Strange 2.50
50 ($3.95)-Gatefold wrap-around foil-c 4.00
50 ($3.95)-Liefeld variant-c 5.00
68-74: 68-Operation Zero Tolerance 2.50
75,100-($2.99): 75-Cannonball-c/app. 3.00
76-99,101,102: 81-Pollina poster. 95-Magneto-c. 102-Ellis-s/Portacio-a 2.50
103-115: 103-Begin $2.25-c; Portacio-a thru #106. 115-Death of old team 2.25
116-New team debuts; Allred-c/a; Milligan-s; no Comics Code stamp on-c 4.00
117-129: 117-Intro. Mr. Sensitive. 120-Wolverine-c/app. 123-'Nuff Said issue. 124-Darwyn Cooke-a/c. 128-Death of U-Go Girl. 129-Fegredo-a 2.50
#(-1) Flashback (7/97) story of John Proudstar; Pollina-a 2.50
Annual 1-3 ('92-'94, 68 pgs.)-1-1st Greg Capullo-a(p) on X-Force. 2-Polybagged w/trading card; intro X-Treme & Neurtap 3.00
...And Cable '95 (12/95, $3.95)-Impossible Man app. 4.00
...And Cable '96, ...'97 ('96, 7/97) -'96-Wraparound-c 3.00
...And Spider-Man: Sabotage nn (11/92, $6.95)-Reprints X-Force #3,4 & Spider-Man #16 7.00
.../ Champions '98 ($3.50) 3.50
Annual 99 ($3.50) 3.50
...: Famous, Mutant & Mortal HC (2003, $29.99) oversized r/#116-129; foreward by Milligan; gallery of covers and pin-ups; script for #123 30.00
...New Beginnings TPB (10/01, $14.95) r/#116-120 15.00
...Rough Cut ($2.99) Pencil pages and script for #102 3.00
...Youngblood (8/96, $4.95)-Platt-c 5.00
NOTE: ***Capullo** a(p)-15-25, Annual 1; c(p)-14-27.* ***Rob Liefeld** a-1-7, 9p; c-1-9, 11p; plots-1-12.* ***Mignola** a-8p.*

X-FORCE
Marvel Comics: Oct, 2004 - No. 6, Mar, 2005 ($2.99, limited series)
1-6-Liefeld-c/a; Nicieza-s. 5,6-Wolverine & The Thing app. 3.00
X-Force & Cable Vol. 1: The Legend Returns (2005, $14.99) r/#1-6 15.00

X-FORCE
Marvel Comics: Apr, 2008 - Present ($2.99)
1-Crain-a; Wolverine & X-23 app.; two covers (regular and bloody) by Crain on #1-5 4.00
2-7: 2,3-Bastion app. 4-6-Archangel app. 7-Choi-a 3.00
... Special: Ain't No Dog (8/08, $3.99) Huston-s/Palo-a; Dell'Edera-a; Hitch-c 4.00

X-FORCE MEGAZINE
Marvel Comics: Nov, 1996 ($3.95, one-shot)
1-Reprints 4.00

X-FORCE: SHATTERSTAR
Marvel Comics: Apr, 2005 - No. 4, July, 2005 ($2.99, limited series)
1-4-Liefeld-c/s; Michaels-a 3.00
TPB (2005, $15.99) r/#1-4 & New Mutants #99,100 16.00

X-Man #75 © MAR

X-Men #50 © MAR

X-Men #101 © MAR

GD VG FN VF VF/NM NM-
2.0 4.0 6.0 8.0 9.0 9.2

XIN: JOURNEY OF THE MONKEY KING
Anarchy Studios: May, 2003 - No. 3, July, 2003 ($2.99)
Preview Edition (Apr, 2003, $1.99) Flip book w/ Vampi Vicious Preview Edition 2.50
1-3-Kevin Lau-a. 1-Three covers by Lau, Park and Nauck. 2-Three covers 3.00

XIN: LEGEND OF THE MONKEY KING
Anarchy Studios: Nov, 2002 - No. 3, Jan, 2003 ($2.99)
Preview Edition (Summer 2002, Diamond Dateline supplement) 2.50
1-3-Kevin Lau-a. 1-Two covers by Lau & Madureira. 2-Two covers by Lau & Oeming 3.00
TPB (10/03, $12.95) r/#1-3; cover gallery and sketch pages 13.00

X-MAN (Also see X-Men Omega & X-Men Prime)
Marvel Comics: Mar, 1995 - No. 75, May, 2001 ($1.95/$1.99/$2.25)
1-Age of Apocalypse 5.00
1-2nd print 2.50
2-4,25: 25-($2.99)-Wraparound-c 3.00
5-24, 26-28: 5-Post Age of Apocalypse stories begin. 5-7-Madelyne Pryor app. 10-Professor X app. 12-vs. Excalibur. 13-Marauders, Cable app. 14-Vs. Cable; Onslaught app. 15-17-Vs. Holocaust. 17-w/Onslaught Update. 18-Onslaught x-over; X-Force-c/app; Marauders app. 19-Onslaught x-over. 20-Abomination-c/app.; w/card insert. 23-Bishop app. 24-Spider-Man, Morbius-c/app. 27-Re-appearance of Aurora(Alpha Flight) 2.50
29-49,51-62: 29-Operation Zero Tolerance. 37,38-Spider-Man-c/app. 56-Spider-Man app. 2.50
50-($2.99) Crossover with Generation X #50 3.00
63-74: 63-Ellis & Grant-s/Olivetti-a begins. 64-Begin $2.25-c 2.50
75 ($2.99) Final issue; Alcatena-a 3.00
#(-1) Flashback (7/97) 2.50
...'96, ...'97-($2.95)-Wraparound-c; '96-Age of Apocalypse 3.00
...: All Saints' Day ('97, $5.99) Dodson-a 6.00
.../Hulk '98 ($2.99) Wraparound-c; Thanos app. 3.00

XMAS COMICS
Fawcett Publications: 12?/1941 - No. 2, 12?/1942; (50¢, 324 pgs.)
No. 7, 12?/1947 (25¢, 132 pgs.)(#3-6 do not exist)
1-Contains Whiz #21, Capt. Marvel #3, Bulletman #2, Wow #3, & Master #18; front & back-c by Raboy. Not rebound, remaindered comics; printed at same time as originals
394 788 1182 2679 4690 6700
2-Capt. Marvel, Bulletman, Spy Smasher 160 320 480 1008 1704 2400
7-Funny animals (Hoppy, Billy the Kid & Oscar) 66 132 198 416 701 985

XMAS COMICS
Fawcett Publications: No. 4, Dec, 1949 - No. 7, Dec, 1952 (50¢, 196 pgs.)
4-Contains Whiz, Master, Tom Mix, Captain Marvel, Nyoka, Capt. Video, Bob Colt, Monte Hale, Hot Rod Comics, & Battle Stories. Not rebound, remaindered comics; printed at the same time as originals. Stocking on cover is made of green or red felt
71 142 213 447 754 1060
5-7-Same as above. 5- Red felt on-c. 7-Bill Boyd app.; stocking on cover is made of green felt (novelty cover) 55 110 165 347 586 825

X-MEN, THE (See Adventures of Cyclops and Phoenix, Amazing Adventures, Archangel, Brotherhood, Capt. America #172, Classic X-Men, Exiles, Further Adventures of Cyclops & Phoenix, Gambit, Giant-Size..., Heroes For Hope..., Kitty Pryde & Wolverine, Marvel & DC Present, Marvel Collector's Edition:..., Marvel Fanfare, Marvel Graphic Novel, Marvel Super Heroes, Marvel Team-Up, Marvel Triple Action, The Marvel X-Men Collection, New Mutants, Nightcrawler, Official Marvel Index To..., Rogue, Special Edition..., Ultimate..., Uncanny..., Wolverine, X-Factor, X-Force, X-Terminators)

X-MEN, THE (1st series)(Becomes Uncanny X-Men at #142)(The X-Men #1-93; X-Men #94-141) (The Uncanny X-Men on-c only #114-141)
Marvel Comics Group: Sept, 1963 - No. 66, Mar, 1970; No. 67, Dec, 1970 - No. 141, Jan, 1981
1-Origin/1st app. X-Men (Angel, Beast, Cyclops, Iceman & Marvel Girl); 1st app. Magneto & Professor X 775 1550 2325 7200 14,600 22,000
2-1st app. The Vanisher 152 304 456 1330 2565 3800
3-1st app. The Blob (1/64) 88 176 264 748 1424 2100
4-1st Quicksilver & Scarlet Witch & Brotherhood of the Evil Mutants (3/64); 1st app. Toad; 2nd app. Magneto 90 180 270 765 1458 2150
5-Magneto & Evil Mutants-c/story 60 120 180 510 980 1450
6,7: 6-Sub-Mariner app. 7-Magneto app. 50 100 150 413 782 1150
8,9,11: 8-1st Unus the Untouchable. 9-Early Avengers app. (1/65); 1st Lucifer. 11-1st app. The Stranger. 40 80 120 318 597 875
10-1st S.A. app. Ka-Zar & Zabu the sabertooth (3/65) 39 78 117 302 564 825
12-Origin Prof. X; Origin/1st app. Juggernaut 45 90 135 360 680 1000
13-Juggernaut and Human Torch app. 31 62 93 239 445 650
14,15: 14-1st app. Sentinels. 15-Origin Beast 32 64 96 246 461 675
16-20: 19-1st app. The Mimic (4/66) 18 36 54 133 247 360
21-27,29,30: 27-Re-enter The Mimic (r-in #75); Spider-Man cameo
14 28 42 99 175 250
28-1st app. The Banshee (1/67)(r-in #76) 19 38 57 135 250 365
28-2nd printing (1994) 2 4 6 8 10 12
31-34,36,37,39: 34-Adkins-c/a. 39-New costumes 11 22 33 75 133 190
35-Spider-Man x-over (8/67)(r-in #83); 1st app. Changeling
23 46 69 170 315 460
38,40: 38-Origins of the X-Men series begins, ends #57. 40-(1/68) 1st app. Frankenstein's monster at Marvel 11 22 33 79 140 200
41-49: 42-Death of Prof. X (Changeling disguised as). 44-1st S.A. app. G.A. Red Raven. 49-Steranko-c; 1st Polaris 10 20 30 67 116 165
50,51-Steranko-c/a 10 20 30 70 123 175
52 9 18 27 63 107 150
53-Barry Smith-c/a (his 1st comic book work) 10 20 30 70 123 175
54,55-B. Smith-c. 54-1st app. Alex Summers who later becomes Havok. 55-Summers discovers he has mutant powers 10 20 30 70 123 175
56,57,59-63,65-Neal Adams-a(p). 56-Intro Havok w/o costume. 60-1st Sauron. 65-Return of Professor X. 10 20 30 70 123 175
58-1st app. Havok in costume; N. Adams-a(p) 12 24 36 86 153 220
62,63-2nd printings (1994) 2 4 6 8 10 12
64-1st app. Sunfire 10 20 30 68 119 170
66-Last new story w/original X-Men; battles Hulk 10 20 30 73 129 185
67-70: 67-Reprints begin, end #93. 67-70: (52 pgs.) 8 16 24 54 90 125
71-93: 71-Last 15¢ issue. 72: (52 pgs.). 73-86-r/#25-38 w/new-c. 83-Spider-Man-c/story. 87-93-r/#39-45 with covers 7 14 21 49 80 110
94 (8/75)-New X-Men begin (see Giant-Size X-Men for 1st app.); Colossus, Nightcrawler, Thunderbird, Storm, Wolverine, & Banshee join; Angel, Marvel Girl & Iceman resign
65 130 195 520 835 1150
95-Death of Thunderbird 15 30 45 108 199 290
96,97 9 18 27 65 113 160
98,99-(Regular 25¢ edition)(4,6/76) 9 18 27 64 110 155
98,99-(30¢-c variants, limited distribution) 16 32 48 114 212 310
100-Old vs. New X-Men; part origin Phoenix; last 25¢ issue (8/76)
10 20 30 73 129 185
100-(30¢-c variant, limited distribution) 19 38 57 137 254 370
101-Phoenix origin concludes 12 24 36 82 146 210
102-104: 102-Origin Storm. 104-1st brief app. Starjammers; Magneto-c/story
7 14 21 50 83 115
105-107-(Regular 30¢ editions). 106-(8/77)Old vs. New X-Men. 107-1st full app. Starjammers; last 30¢ issue 7 14 21 47 76 105
105-107-(35¢-c variants, limited distribution) 12 24 36 82 146 210
108-Byrne-a begins (see Marvel Team-Up #53) 7 14 21 50 83 115
109-1st app. Weapon Alpha (becomes Vindicator) 7 14 21 47 76 105
110,111: 110-Phoenix joins 6 12 18 37 59 80
112-116 6 12 18 37 59 80
117-119: 117-Origin Professor X 5 10 15 30 48 65
120-1st app. Alpha Flight, story line begins (4/79); 1st app. Vindicator (formerly Weapon Alpha); last 35¢ issue 7 14 21 45 73 100
121-1st full Alpha Flight story 6 12 18 43 69 95
122-128: 123-Spider-Man x-over. 124-Colossus becomes Proletarian
4 8 12 28 44 60
129-Intro Kitty Pryde (1/80); last Banshee; Dark Phoenix saga begins; intro. Emma Frost (White Queen) 5 10 15 34 55 75
130-1st app. The Dazzler by Byrne (2/80) 4 8 12 28 44 60
131-135: 131-Dazzler app.; 1st White Queen-c. 133-Wolverine app. 134-Phoenix becomes Dark Phoenix 4 8 12 28 44 60
136,138: 138-Dazzler app.; Cyclops leaves 4 8 12 24 37 50
137-Giant; death of Phoenix 5 10 15 30 48 65
139-Alpha Flight app.; Kitty Pryde joins; new costume for Wolverine
4 8 12 28 44 60
140-Alpha Flight app. 4 8 12 28 44 60
141-Intro Future X-Men & The New Brotherhood of Evil Mutants; 1st app. Rachel (Phoenix II); Death of Franklin Richards 5 10 15 30 48 65

X-MEN: Titled THE UNCANNY X-MEN #142, Feb, 1981 - Present
142-Rachel app.; deaths of alt. future Wolverine, Storm & Colossus
6 12 18 37 59 80
143-Last Byrne issue 4 8 12 28 44 60
144-150: 144-Man-Thing app. 145-Old X-Men app. 148-Spider-Woman, Dazzler app. 150-Double size 2 4 6 9 12 15
151-157,159-161,163,164: 161-Origin Magneto. 163-Origin Binary. 164-1st app. Binary as Carol Danvers 1 3 4 6 8 10
158-1st app. Rogue in X-Men (6/82, see Avengers Annual #10)
3 6 9 15 21 26
162-Wolverine solo story 2 4 6 9 13 16
165-Paul Smith-c/a begins, ends #175 2 4 6 8 10 12
166-170: 166-Double size; Paul Smith-a. 167-New Mutants app. (3/83); same date as New Mutants #1; 1st meeting w/X-Men; ties into N.M. #3,4; Starjammers app.; contains skin

Uncanny X-Men #207 © MAR

Uncanny X-Men #394 © MAR

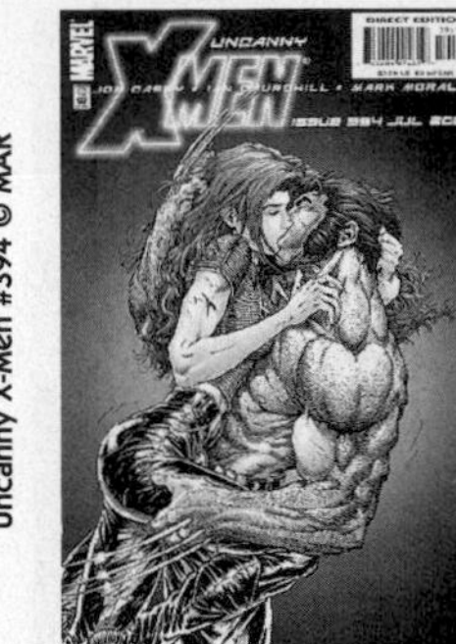

Uncanny X-Men #497 © MAR

	GD 2.0	VG 4.0	FN 6.0	VF 8.0	VF/NM 9.0	NM- 9.2

"Tattooz" decals. 168-1st brief app. Madelyne Pryor (last page) in X-Men
(see Avengers Annual #10) 1 2 3 5 7 9
171-Rogue joins X-Men; Simonson-c/a 2 4 6 11 16 20
172-174: 172,173-Two part Wolverine solo story. 173-Two cover variations, blue & black.
174-Phoenix cameo 1 2 3 5 6 8
175-(52 pgs.)-Anniversary issue; Phoenix returns 1 3 4 6 8 10
176-185,187-192,194-199: 181-Sunfire app. 182-Rogue solo story. 184-1st app. Forge (8/84).
190,191-Spider-Man & Avengers x-over. 195-Power Pack x-over
1 2 3 4 5 7
186,193: 186-Double-size; Barry Smith/Austin-a. 193-Double size; 100th app. New X-Men;
1st app. Warpath in costume (see New Mutants #16)
1 2 3 5 6 8
200-(12/85, $1.25, 52 pgs.) 1 2 3 5 6 8
201-(1/86)-1st app. Cable? (as baby Nathan; see X-Factor #1); 1st Whilce Portacio-c/a(i)
on X-Men (guest artist) 3 6 9 14 20 25
202-204,206-209: 204-Nightcrawler solo story; 2nd Portacio-a(i) on X-Men.
207-Wolverine/Phoenix story 1 2 3 4 5 7
205-Wolverine solo story by Barry Smith 2 4 6 8 11 14
210,211-Mutant Massacre begins 3 6 9 14 19 24
212,213-Wolverine vs. Sabretooth (Mutant Mass.) 3 6 9 16 22 28
214-221,223,224: 219-Havok joins (7/87); brief app. Sabretooth. 221-1st app. Mr. Sinister
1 2 3 4 5 7
222-Wolverine battles Sabretooth-c/story 3 6 9 14 19 24
225-242: 225-227: Fall Of The Mutants. 226-Double size. 240-Sabretooth app.
242-Double size, X-Factor app., Inferno tie-in 1 2 3 4 5 7
243,245-247: 245-Rob Liefeld-a(p) 1 2 3 4 5 7
244-1st app. Jubilee 3 6 9 16 23 30
248-1st Jim Lee art on X-Men (1989) 2 4 6 13 18 22
248-2nd printing (1992, $1.25) 3.00
249-252: 252-Lee-c 1 2 3 4 5 7
253-255: 253-All new X-Men begin. 254-Lee-c 1 2 3 4 5 7
256,257-Jim Lee-c/a begins 1 2 3 5 7 9
258-Wolverine solo story; Lee-c/a 1 2 3 5 7 9
259-Silvestri-c/a; no Lee-a 1 2 3 4 5 7
260-265-No Lee-a. 260,261,264-Lee-c 1 2 3 4 5 7
266-(8/90) 1st full app. Gambit (see Annual #14)-No Lee-a
4 8 12 22 34 45
267-Jim Lee-c/a resumes; 2nd full Gambit app. 2 4 6 9 13 16
268-Capt. America, Black Widow & Wolverine team-up; Lee-a
2 4 6 10 14 18
268,270: 268-2nd printing. 270-Gold 2nd printing 3.00
269,273-275: 269-Lee-a. 273-New Mutants (Cable) & X-Factor x-over; Golden, Byrne & Lee
part pencils. 275-(52 pgs.)-Tri-fold-c by Jim Lee (p); Prof. X
1 2 3 4 5 7
270-X-Tinction Agenda begins 1 2 3 5 6 8
271,272-X-Tinction Agenda 1 2 3 5 6 8
275-Gold 2nd printing 2.50
276-280: 277-Last Lee-c/a. 280-X-Factor x-over 6.00
281-(10/91)-New team begins (Storm, Archangel, Colossus, Iceman & Marvel Girl); Whilce
Portacio-c/a begins; Byrne scripts begin; wraparound-c (white logo)
1 2 3 4 5 7
281-2nd printing with red metallic ink logo w/o UPC box ($1.00-c); does not say 2nd printing
inside 3.00
282-1st brief app. Bishop (cover & 1 page) 2 4 6 8 10 12
282-Gold ink 2nd printing ($1.00-c) 3.00
283-1st full app. Bishop (12/91) 2 4 6 8 10 12
284-299: 284-Last $1.00-c. 286,287-Lee plots. 287-Bishop joins team. 288-Lee/Portacio plots.
290-Last Portacio-c/a. 294-Peterson-a(p) begins (#292 is 1st Peterson-c). 294-296 ($1.50)-
Bagged w/trading card in each; X-Cutioner's Song x-overs; Peterson/Austin-c/a on all 4.00
300-($3.95, 68 pgs.)-Holo-grafx foil-c; Magneto app. 6.00
301-303,305-309,311 3.00
303,307-Gold Edition 1 2 3 5 6 8
304-($3.95, 68 pgs.)-Wraparound-c with Magneto hologram on-c; 30th anniversary issue;
Jae Lee-a (4 pgs.) 6.00
310-($1.95)-Bound-in trading card sheet 3.00
312-$1.50-c begins; bound-in card sheet; 1st Madureira 4.00
313-321 3.00
316,317-($2.95)-Foil enhanced editions 4.00
318-321-($1.95)-Deluxe editions 3.00
322-Onslaught 5.00
323,324,326-346: 323-Return from Age of Apocalypse. 328-Sabretooth-c. 329,330-Dr. Strange
app. 331-White Queen-c/app. 334-Juggernaut app.; w/Onslaught Update. 335-Onslaught,
Avengers, Apocalypse, & X-Man app. 336-Onslaught. 338-Archangel's wings return
to normal. 339-Havok vs. Cyclops; Spider-Man app. 341-Gladiator-c/app. 342-Deathbird
cameo; two covers. 343,344-Phalanx 3.00
325-($3.95)-Anniversary issue; gatefold-c 5.00
342-Variant-c 1 3 4 6 8 10
347-349:347-Begin $1.99-c. 349-"Operation Zero Tolerance" 3.00
350-($3.99, 48 pgs.) Prismatic etched foil gatefold wraparound-c; Trial of Gambit;
Seagle-s begin 1 2 3 5 6 8
351-359: 353-Bachalo-a begins. 354-Regular-c. 355-Alpha Flight-c/app.
356-Original X-Men-c 3.00
354-Dark Phoenix variant-c 5.00
360-($2.99) 35th Anniv. issue; Pacheco-c 3.00
360-($3.99) Etched Holo-foil enhanced-c 4.00
360-($6.95) DF Edition with Jae Lee variant-c 7.00
361-374: 361-Gambit returns; Skroce-a. 362-Hunt for Xavier pt. 1; Bachelo-a. 364-Yu-a.
366-Magneto-c. 369-Juggernaut-c 3.00
375-($2.99) Autopsy of Wolverine 4.00
376-379: 376,377-Apocalypse: The Twelve 3.00
380-($2.99) Polybagged with X-Men Revolution Genesis Edition preview 4.00
381,382,384-389,391-393: 381-Begin $2.25-c; Claremont-s. 387-Maximum Security 3.00
383-($2.99) 3.50
390-Colossus dies to cure the Legacy Virus 4.00
394-New look X-Men begins; Casey-s/Churchill-c/a 3.50
395-399-Poptopia. 398-Phillips & Wood-a 3.00
400-($3.50) Art by Ashley Wood, Eddie Campbell, Hamner, Phillips, Pulido and Matt Smith;
wraparound-c by Wood 4.00
401-415: 401-'Nuff Said issue; Garney-a. 404,405,407-409,413-415-Phillips-a 3.00
416-421: 416-Asamiya-a begins. 421-Garney-a 3.00
422-($3.50) Alpha Flight app.; Garney-a 4.00
423-(25¢-c) Holy War pt. 1; Garney-a/Philip Tan-c 3.00
424-449,452-454: 425,426,429,430-Tan-a. 428-Birth of Nightcrawler. 437-Larroca-a begins.
444-New team, new costumes; Claremont-s/Davis-a begins. 448,449-Coipel-a 3.00
450,451,455-459-X-23 app.; Davis-a 3.00
460-471: 460-Begin $2.50-c; Raney-a. 462-465-House of M. 464-468-Bachalo-a 3.00
472-499: 472-Begin $2.99-c; Bachalo-a. 475-Wraparound-c. 492-494-Messiah Complex 3.00
500-($3.99) X-Men new HQ in San Francisco; Magneto app.; Land & Dodson-a; wraparound
covers by Alex Ross and Greg Land 4.00
500-Classic X-Men Dynamic Forces variant-c by Ross 8.00
500-X-Men variant-c by Michael Turner 30.00
500-X-Women variant-c by Dodson 15.00
501,502-Brubaker & Fraction-s/Land-a 3.00
#(-1) Flashback (7/97) Ladronn-c/Hitch & Neary-a 3.00
Special 1(12/70)-Kirby-c/a; origin The Stranger 9 18 27 65 113 160
Special 2(11/71, 52 pgs.) 7 14 21 49 80 110
Annual 3(1979, 52 pgs.)-New story; Miller/Austin-c; Wolverine still in old yellow costume
4 8 12 26 41 55
Annual 4(1980, 52 pgs.)-Dr. Strange guest stars 2 4 6 9 12 15
Annual 5(1981, 52 pgs.) 1 2 3 5 7 9
Annual 6-8('82-'84 52 pgs.)-6-Dracula app. 6.00
Annual 9,10('85, '86)-9-New Mutants x-over cont'd from New Mutants Special Ed. #1;
Art Adams-a. 10-Art Adams-a 1 2 3 5 7 9
Annual 11-13:('87-'89, 68 pgs.): 12-Evolutionary War; A.Adams-a(p). 13-Atlantis Attacks 4.00
Annual 14(1990, $2.00, 68 pgs.)-1st app. Gambit (minor app., 5 pgs.); Fantastic Four,
New Mutants (Cable) & X-Factor x-over; Art Adams-c/a(p)
3 6 9 14 20 25
Annual 15 (1991, $2.00, 68 pgs.)-4 pg. origin; New Mutants x-over; 4 pg. Wolverine solo
back-up story; 4th app. X-Force cont'd from New Warriors Annual #1 4.00
Annual 16-18 ('92-'94, 68 pgs.)-16-Jae Lee-c/a(p). 17-Bagged w/card 3.00
Annual '95-(11/95, $3.95)-Wraparound-c 4.00
Annual '96,'97-Wraparound-c 3.00
.../Fantastic Four Annual '98 ($2.99) Casey-s 3.00
Annual '99 ($3.50) Jubilee app. 3.50
Annual 2000 ($3.50) Cable app.; Ribic-a 3.50
Annual 2001 ($3.50, printed wide-ways) Ashley Wood-c/a; Casey-s 3.50
Annual (Vol. 2) #1 (8/06, $3.99) Storm & Black Panther wedding prelude 4.00
...At The State Fair of Texas (1983, 36 pgs., one-shot); Supplement to the Dallas Times Herald
2 4 6 9 12 15
...: The Dark Phoenix Saga TPB 1st printing (1984, $12.95) 40.00
...: The Dark Phoenix Saga TPB 2nd-5th printings 30.00
...: The Dark Phoenix Saga TPB 6th-10th printings 20.00
... Days of Future Past TPB (2004, $19.99) r/#138-143 & Annual #4 20.00
... Eve of Destruction TPB (2005, $14.99) r/#391-393 & X-Men #111-113; Churchill-c 15.00
...:Dream's End (2004, $17.99)-r/Death of Colossus story arc from Uncanny X-Men #388-390,
Cable #87, Bishop #16 and X-Men #108,110; debut pages from Giant-Size X-Men #1 18.00
...From The Ashes TPB (1990, $14.95) r/#168-176 15.00
...:God Loves, Man Kills ($6.95)-r/Marvel Graphic Novel #5 7.00

X-Men #46 © MAR

X-Men #103 © MAR

X-Men #209 © MAR

GD 2.0 | VG 4.0 | FN 6.0 | VF 8.0 | VF/NM 9.0 | NM- 9.2

...:God Loves, Man Kills - Special Edition (2003, $4.99)-reprint with new Hughes-c 5.00
...:God Loves, Man Kills HC (2007, $19.99) reprint with Claremont & Anderson interviews; original artist Neal Adams' six sketch pages and interview 20.00
House of M: Uncanny X-Men TPB (2006, $13.99) r/#462-465 and selections from Secrets Of The House of M one-shot 14.00
...In The Days of Future Past TPB (1989, $3.95, 52 pgs.) 4.00
...Old Soldiers TPB (2004, $19.99) r/#213,215 & Ann. #11; New Mutants Ann. #2&3 20.00
...Poptopia TPB (10/01, $15.95) r/#394-399 16.00
...: Rise & Fall of the Shi'Ar Empire HC (2007, $34.99, dustjacket) r/#475-486; bonus art 35.00
...: Rise & Fall of the Shi'Ar Empire SC (2008, $29.99) r/#475-486; bonus art 30.00
...: The Complete Onslaught Epic Book 1 TPB (2007, $29.99) r/X-Men #53-54, Uncanny X-Men #334-335, Fantastic Four #414-415, Avengers #400-401, Onslaught: X-Men, Cable #34 and Incredible Hulk #444 30.00
...: The Extremists TPB (2007, $13.99) r/#487-491 14.00
Uncanny X-Men Omnibus Vol. 1 HC (2006, $99.99, dust jacket) r/Giant-Size X-Men #1, (Uncanny) X-Men #94-131 & Annual #3; cover gallery, promo and sketch art 100.00
Vignettes TPB (9/01, $17.95) r/Claremont & Bolton Classic X-Men #1-13 18.00
Vignettes Vol. 2 TPB (2005, $17.99) r/Claremont & Bolton Classic X-Men #14-25 18.00
... Vol. 1: Hope TPB (2003, $12.99) r/#410-415; Harris-c 13.00
... Vol. 2: Dominant Species TPB (2003, $11.99) r/#416-420; Asamiya-c 12.00
... Vol. 3: Holy War TPB (2003, $17.99) r/#421-427 18.00
... Vol. 4: The Draco TPB (2004, $15.99) r/#428-434 16.00
... Vol. 5: She Lies with Angels TPB (2004, $11.99) r/#437-441 12.00
... Vol. 6: Bright New Mourning TPB (2004, $14.99) r/#435,436,442,443 & (New) X-Men #155,156; Larroca sketch covers 15.00
...Vs. Apocalypse Vol. 1: The Twelve TPB (2008, $29.99) r/#376-377, Cable #73-76, X-Men #96,97 and Wolverine #145-147 30.00
... - The New Age Vol. 1: The End of History (2004, $12.99) r/#444-449 13.00
... - The New Age Vol. 2: The Cruelest Cut (2005, $11.99) r/#450-454 12.00
... - The New Age Vol. 3: On Ice (2006, $15.99) r/#455-461 16.00
... - The New Age Vol. 4: End of Greys (2006, $14.99) r/#466-471 15.00
... - The New Age Vol. 5: First Foursaken (2006, $11.99) r/#472-474 & Annual #1 12.00

NOTE: ***Art Adams*** *a-Annual 9, 10p, 12p, 14p; c-218p.* ***Neal Adams*** *a-56-63p, 65p; c-56-63.* ***Adkins*** *a-34, 35p; c-31, 34, 35.* ***Austin*** *a-108i, 109i, 111-117i, 119-143i, 186i, 204i, 228i, 294-297i, Annual 3i, 7i, 9i, 13; c-109-111i, 114-122i, 123, 124-141i, 142, 143, 196i, 204i, 228i, 294-297i, Annual 3i.* ***J. Buscema*** *c-42, 43, 45.* ***Buscema/Tuska*** *a-45.* ***Byrne*** *a(p)-108, 109, 111-143, 273; c(p)-113-116, 127, 129, 131-141.* ***Capullo*** *c-14.* ***Ditko*** *r-86, 89-91, 93.* ***Everett*** *c-73.* ***Golden*** *a-273, Annual 7p.* ***Guice*** *a-216p, 217p.* ***G. Kane*** *c(p)-33, 74-76, 79, 80, 94, 95.* ***Kirby*** *a(p)-1-17 (#12-17, 67r-layouts); c(p)-1-17, 25, 30 (18, 20-parts).* ***Layton*** *a-105i, c-112i, 113i.* ***Jim Lee*** *a(p)-248, 256-258, 267-277; c(p)-252, 254, 256-261, 264, 267, 270, 275-277, 286.* ***Perez*** *a-Annual 3p; c(p)-112, 128, Annual 3.* ***Peterson*** *a(p)-294-300, 304(part); c(p)-294-299.* ***Whilce Portacio*** *a(p)-281-286, 289, 290; a(i)-267; c-281-285p, 289p, 290; c(i)-267.* ***Romita, Jr.*** *a-300; c-300.* ***Roussos*** *a-84i.* ***Simonson*** *a-171p; c-171, 217.* ***B. Smith*** *a-53, 186p, 198p, 205, 214; c-53-55, 186p, 198, 205, 212, 214, 216.* ***Paul Smith*** *a(p)-165-170, 172-175, 278; c-165-170, 172-175, 278.* ***Sparling*** *a-78p.* ***Steranko*** *a-50p, 51p; c-49-51.* ***Sutton*** *a-106i.* ***Art Thibert*** *a(i)-281-286; c(i)-281, 282, 284, 285.* ***Toth*** *a-12p, 67p(r).* ***Tuska*** *a-40-42i, 43-46p, 88i(r); c-39-41, 77p, 78p.* ***Williamson*** *a-202i, 203i, 211i; c-202i, 203i, 206i.* ***Wood*** *c-14i.*

UNCANNY X-MEN AND THE NEW TEEN TITANS (See Marvel and DC Present...)

X-MEN (2nd Series)
Marvel Comics: Oct, 1991 - Present ($1.00/$1.25/$1.95/$1.99)

1 a-d ($1.50, 52 pgs.)-Jim Lee-c/a begins, ends #11; new team begins (Cyclops, Beast, Wolverine, Gambit, Psylocke & Rogue); new Uncanny X-Men & Magneto app.; four different covers exist 4.00
1 e ($3.95)-Double gate-fold-c consisting of all four covers from 1a-d by Jim Lee; contains all pin-ups from #1a-d plus inside-c foldout poster; no ads; printed on coated stock 5.00
2-7: 4-Wolverine back to old yellow costume (same date as Wolverine #50); last $1.00-c. 5-Byrne scripts. 6-Sabretooth-c/story 5.00
8-10: 8-Gambit vs. Bishop-c/story; last Lee-a; Ghost Rider cameo cont'd in Ghost Rider #26. 9-Wolverine vs. Ghost Rider; cont'd/G.R. #26. 10-Return of Longshot 5.00
11-13,17-24,26-29,31: 12,13-Art Thibert-c/a. 28,29-Sabretooth app. 4.00
11-Silver ink 2nd printing; came with X-Men board game 2 4 6 9 12 15
14-16-($1.50)-Polybagged with trading card in each; X-Cutioner's Song x-overs; 14-Andy Kubert-c/a begins 4.00
25-($3.50, 52 pgs.)-Wraparound-c with Gambit hologram on-c; Professor X erases Magneto's mind 2 4 6 8 10 12
25-30th anniversary issue w/B&W-c with Magneto in color & Magneto hologram & no price on-c 2 4 6 9 12 15
25-Gold 30.00
30-($1.95)-Wedding issue w/bound-in trading card sheet 5.00
32-37: 32-Begin $1.50-c; bound-in card sheet. 33-Gambit & Sabretooth-c/story 3.00
36,37-($2.95)-Collectors editions (foil-c) 5.00
38-44,46-49,51-53, 55-65: 42,43- Paul Smith-a. 46,49,53-56-Onslaught app. 51-Waid scripts begin, end #56. 54-(Reg. edition)-Onslaught revealed as Professor X. 55,56-Onslaught x-over; Avengers, FF & Sentinels app. 56-Dr. Doom app. 57-Xavier taken into custody; Byrne-c/swipe (X-Men,1st Series #138). 59-Hercules-c/app. 61-Juggernaut-c/app. 62-Re-intro. Shang Chi; two covers. 63-Kingpin cameo. 64- Kingpin app. 3.00
45-($3.95)-Annual issue; gatefold-c 5.00
50-($2.95)-Vs. Onslaught, wraparound-c. 4.00
50-($3.95)-Vs. Onslaught, wraparound foil-c. 5.00
50-($2.95)-Variant gold-c. 3 6 9 20 30 40
50-($2.95)-Variant silver-c. 1 2 3 5 6 8
54-(Limited edition)-Embossed variant-c; Onslaught revealed as Professor X 3 6 9 16 23 30
66-69,71-74,76-79: 66-Operation Zero Tolerance. 76-Origin of Maggott 3.00
70-($2.99, 48 pgs.)-Joe Kelly-s begin, new members join 3.50
75-($2.99, 48 pgs.) vs. N'Garai; wraparound-c 3.50
80-($3.99) 35th Anniv. issue; holo-foil-c 5.00
80-($3.99) Regular-c 3.50
80-($6.95) Dynamic Forces Ed.; Quesada-c 7.00
81-93,95: 82-Hunt for Xavier pt. 2. 85-Davis-a. 86-Origin of Joseph. 87-Magneto War ends. 88-Juggernaut app. 3.00
94-($2.99) Contains preview of X-Men: Hidden Years 3.50
96-99: 96,97-Apocalypse: The Twelve 3.00
100-($2.99) Art Adams-c; begin Claremont-s/Yu-a 4.00
100-DF alternate-c 1 3 4 6 8 10
101-105,107,108,110-114: 101-Begin $2.25-c. 107-Maximum Security x-over; Bishop-c/app. 108-Moira MacTaggart dies; Senator Kelly shot. 111-Magneto-c. 112,113-Eve of Destruction 3.00
106-($2.99) X-Men battle Domina 3.50
109-($3.50, 100 pgs.) new and reprinted Christmas-themed stories 4.00
114-Title change to "New X-Men," Morrison-s/Quitely-c/a begins 4.00
115-Two covers (Quitely & BWS) 3.00
116-125,127-149: 116-Emma Frost joins. 117,118-Van Sciver-a. 121,122,135-Quitely-a. 127-Leon & Sienkiewicz-a. 128-Kordey-a. 132,139-141-Jimenez-a. 136-138-Quitely-a 142-Sabretooth app.; Bachalo-c/a thru #145. 146-Magneto returns; Jimenez-a 3.00
126-($3.25) Quitely-a; defeat of Cassanova 3.50
150-($3.50) Jean Grey dies again; last Jimenez-a 4.00
151-156: 151-154-Silvestri-c/a 3.00
157-169: 157-X-Men Reload begins 3.00
170-184: 171- Begin $2.50-c. 175,176-Crossover with Black Panther #8,9. 181-184-Apocalypse returns 3.00
185-199,201-216: 185-Begin $2.99-c. 188-190,192-194,197-199-Bachalo-a. 195,196,201-203-Ramos-a. 201-204-Endangered Species back-up. 205-207-Messiah Complex x-over. 208-Romita Jr.-a. 210-214-X-Men: Legacy 3.00
200-($3.99) Two wraparound covers by Bachalo & Finch; Bachalo & Ramos-a 4.00
#(-1) Flashback (7/97); origin of Magneto 3.00
Annual 1-3 ('92-'94, $2.25-$2.95, 68 pgs.) 1-Lee-c & layouts; #2-Bagged w/card 4.00
Special '95 ($3.95) 4.00
... '96,...'97-Wraparound-c 3.00
.../ Dr. Doom '98 Annual ($2.99) Lopresti-a 3.00
... Annual '99 ($3.50) Adam Kubert-c 3.50
Annual 2000 ($3.50) Art Adams-c/Claremont-s/Eaton-a 3.50
...2001 Annual ($3.50) Morrison-s/Yu-a; issue printed sideways 3.50
...2007 Annual #1 (3/07, $3.99) Casey-s/Brooks-a; Cable and Mystique app. 4.00
Animation Special Graphic Novel (12/90, $10.95) adapts animated series 11.00
Ashcan #1 (1994, 75¢) Introduces new team members 2.25
Ashcan (75¢ Ashcan Edition) (1994) 2.25
... Archives Sketchbook (12/00, $2.99) Early B&W character design sketches by various incl. Lee, Davis, Yu, Pacheco, BWS, Art Adams, Liefeld 3.00
...: Bizarre Love Triangle TPB (2005, $9.99)-r/X-Men #171-174 10.00
.../ Black Panther TPB (2006, $11.99)-r/X-Men #175,176 & Black Panther (2005) #8,9 12.00
...: Blinded By the Light (2007, $14.99)-r/X-Men #200-204 15.00
...: Blood of Apocalypse (2006, $17.99)-r/X-Men #182-187 18.00
...: Day of the Atom (2005, $19.99)-r/X-Men #157-165 20.00
Decimation: X-Men - The Day After TPB (2006, $15.99) r/#177-181 & Decimation: House of M - The Day After 16.00
...: Declassified (10/00, $3.50) Profile pin-ups by various; Jae Lee-c 3.50
...: Endangered Species (8/07, $3.99) prologue to 17-part back-up series in X-Men titles 4.00
...: Endangered Species HC (2008, $24.99, d.j.) over-sized r/prologue and 17-part series 25.00
...: Fatal Attractions ('94, $17.95)-r/x-Factor #92, X-Force #25, Uncanny X-Men #304, X-Men #25, Wolverine #75, & Excalibur #71 18.00
...: Golgotha (2005, $12.99)-r/X-Men #166-170 13.00
... Millennial Visions (8/00, $3.99) Various artists interpret future X-Men 4.00
... Millennial Visions 2 (1/02, $3.50) Various artists interpret future X-Men 3.50
...: Mutant Genesis (2006, $19.99)-r/X-Men #1-7; sketch pages and extra art 20.00
New X-Men: E is for Extinction TPB (11/01, $12.95) r/#114-117 13.00
New X-Men: Imperial TPB (7/02, $19.99) r/#118-126; Quitely-c 20.00
New X-Men: New Worlds TPB (2002, $14.99) r/#127-133; Quitely-c 15.00
New X-Men: Riot at Xavier's TPB (2003, $11.99) r/#134-138; Quitely-c 12.00
New X-Men: Vol. 5: Assault on Weapon Plus TPB (2003, $14.99) r/#139-145 15.00

X-Men/Alpha Flight #2 © MAR

X-Men and the Micronauts #2 © MAR

X-Men: Emperor Vulcan #4 © MAR

GD VG FN VF VF/NM NM-
2.0 4.0 6.0 8.0 9.0 9.2

GD VG FN VF VF/NM NM-
2.0 4.0 6.0 8.0 9.0 9.2

New X-Men: Vol. 6: Planet X TPB (2004, $12.99) r/#146-150 13.00
New X-Men: Vol. 7: Here Comes Tomorrow TPB (2004, $10.99) r/#151-154 11.00
New X-Men: Volume 1 HC (2002, $29.99) oversized r/#114-126 & 2001 Annual 30.00
New X-Men: Volume 2 HC (2003, $29.99) oversized r/#127-141; sketch & script pages 30.00
New X-Men: Volume 3 HC (2004, $29.99) oversized r/#142-154; sketch & script pages 30.00
New X-Men Omnibus HC (2006, $99.99) oversized r/#114-154 & Annual 2001; Morrison's original pitch; sketch & script pages; variant covers & promo art; Carey intro. 140.00
...: Odd Men Out (2008, $3.99) Two unpublished stories with Dave Cockrum-a 4.00
... Original Sin 1 (12/08, $3.99) Wolverine and Daken; Deodato & Eaton-a 4.00
... Origin: Colossus (7/08, $3.99) Yost-s/Hairsine-a; Piotr Rasputin before joining X-Men 4.00
... Pizza Hut Mini-comics-(See Marvel Collector's Edition: X-Men in Promotional Comics section)
... Premium Edition #1 (1993)-Cover says "Toys 'R' Us Limited Edition X-Men" 2.25
...: Rarities (1995, $5.95)-Reprints 6.00
...: Return of Magik Must Have (2008, $3.99) r/X-Men Unlimited #14, New X-Men #37 and X-Men: Divided We Stand #2; Coipel-c 4.00
...: Road Trippin' ('99, $24.95, TPB) r/X-Men road trips 25.00
...: Supernovas ('07, $34.99, oversized HC w/d.j.) r/X-Men 188-199 & Annual #1 35.00
...: Supernovas ('08, $29.99, SC) r/X-Men 188-199 & Annual #1 30.00
...: The Coming of Bishop ('95, $12.95)-r/Uncanny X-Men #282-285, 287,288 13.00
...: The Magneto War (3/99, $2.99) Davis-a 3.00
...: The Rise of Apocalypse ('98, $16.99)-r/Rise Of Apocalypse #1-4, X-Factor #5,6 17.00
... Visionaries: Chris Claremont ('98, $24.95)-r/Claremont-s; art by Byrne, BWS, Jim Lee 25.00
... Visionaries: Jim Lee ('02, $29.99)-r/Jim Lee-a from various issues between Uncanny X-Men #248 & 286; r/Classic X-Men #39 and X-Men Annual #1 30.00
... Visionaries: Joe Madureira (7/00, $17.95)-r/Uncanny X-Men #325,326,329,330,341-343; new Madureira-c 18.00
...: Zero Tolerance ('00, $24.95, TPB) r/crossover series 25.00

NOTE: ***Jim Lee** a-1-11p; c-1-6p, 7, 8, 9p, 10, 11p. **Art Thibert** a-6-9i, 12, 13; c-6i, 12, 13.*

X-MEN ADVENTURES (TV)
Marvel Comics: Nov, 1992 - No. 15, Jan, 1994 ($1.25)(Based on animated series)

1-Wolverine, Cyclops, Jubilee, Rogue, Gambit 3.50
2-15: 3-Magneto-c/story. 6-Sabretooth-c/story. 7-Cable-c/story. 10-Archangel guest star. 11-Cable-c/story. 15-($1.75, 52 pgs.) 3.00

X-MEN ADVENTURES II (TV)
Marvel Comics: Feb, 1994 - No. 13, Feb, 1995 ($1.25/$1.50)(Based on 2nd TV season)

1-13: 4-Bound-in trading card sheet. 5-Alpha Flight app. 3.00
...Captive Hearts/Slave Island (TPB, $4.95)-r/X-Men Adventures #5-8 5.00
...The Irresistible Force, The Muir Island Saga (5.95, 10/94, TPB) r/X-Men Advs. #9-12 6.00

X-MEN ADVENTURES III (TV)(See Adventures of the X-Men)
Marvel Comics: Mar, 1995 - No. 13, Mar, 1996 ($1.50) (Based on 3rd TV season)

1-13 3.00

X-MEN: AGE OF APOCALYPSE
Marvel Comics: May, 2005 - No. 6, June, 2005 ($2.99, weekly limited series)

1-6-Bachalo-c/a; Yoshida-s; follows events in the "Age of Apocalypse" storyline 3.00
... One Shot (5/05, $3.99) prequel to series; Hitch wraparound-c; pin-ups by various 4.00
X-Men: The New Age of Apocalypse TPB (2005, $20.99) r/#1-6 & one-shot 21.00

X-MEN ALPHA
Marvel Comics: 1994 ($3.95, one-shot)

nn-Age of Apocalypse; wraparound chromium-c 1 2 3 5 6 8
nn ($49.95)-Gold logo 50.00

X-MEN/ALPHA FLIGHT
Marvel Comics Group: Dec, 1985 - No. 2, Dec, 1985 ($1.50, limited series)

1,2: 1-Intro The Berserkers; Paul Smith-a 5.00

X-MEN/ALPHA FLIGHT
Marvel Comics Group: May, 1998 - No. 2, June, 1998 ($2.99, limited series)

1,2-Flashback to early meeting; Raab-s/Cassaday-s/a 3.00

X-MEN AND POWER PACK
Marvel Comics: Dec, 2005 - No. 4, Mar, 2006 ($2.99, limited series)

1-3-Sumerak-s/Gurihiru-a. 1-Wolverine & Sabretooth app. 3.00
...: The Power of X (2006, $6.99, digest size) r/#1-4 7.00

X-MEN AND THE MICRONAUTS, THE
Marvel Comics Group: Jan, 1984 - No. 4, Apr, 1984 (Limited series)

1-4: Guice-c/a(p) in all 4.00

X-MEN: APOCALYPSE/DRACULA
Marvel Comics: Apr, 2006 - No. 4, July, 2006 ($2.99, limited series)

1-4-Tieri-s/Henry-a/Jae Lee-c 3.00
TPB (2006, $10.99) r/series; cover gallery 11.00

X-MEN ARCHIVES
Marvel Comics: Jan, 1995 - No. 4, Apr, 1995 ($2.25, limited series)

1-4: Reprints Legion stories from New Mutants. 4-Magneto app. 3.00

X-MEN ARCHIVES FEATURING CAPTAIN BRITAIN
Marvel Comics: July, 1995 - No. 7, 1996 ($2.95, limited series)

1-7: Reprints early Capt. Britain stories 3.00

X-MEN BLACK SUN (See Black Sun:...)

X-MEN BOOKS OF ASKANI
Marvel Comics: 1995 ($2.95, one-shot)

1-Painted pin-ups w/text 3.00

X-MEN: CHILDREN OF THE ATOM
Marvel Comics: Nov, 1999 - No. 6 ($2.99, limited series)

1-6-Casey-s; X-Men before issue #1. 1-3-Rude-c/a. 4-Paul Smith-a/Rude-c. 5,6-Essad Ribic-c/a 3.00
TPB (11/01, $16.95) r/series; sketch pages; Casey intro. 17.00

X-MEN CHRONICLES
Marvel Comics: Mar, 1995 - No. 2, June, 1995 ($3.95, limited series)

1,2: Age of Apocalypse x-over. 1-wraparound-c 5.00

X-MEN: CLANDESTINE
Marvel Comics: Oct, 1996 - No. 2, Nov, 1996 ($2.95, limited series, 48 pgs.)

1,2: Alan Davis-c(p)/a(p)/scripts & Mark Farmer-c(i)/a(i) in all; wraparound-c 3.00

X-MEN CLASSIC (Formerly Classic X-Men)
Marvel Comics: No. 46, Apr, 1990 - No. 110, Aug, 1995 ($1.25/$1.50)

46-110: Reprints from X-Men. 54-(52 pgs.). 57,60-63,65-Russell-c(i); 62-r/X-Men #158(Rogue). 66-r/#162(Wolverine). 69-Begins-r of Paul Smith issues (#165 on). 70,79,90,97(52 pgs.). 70-r/X-Men #166. 90-r/#186. 100-($1.50). 104-r/X-Men #200 3.00

X-MEN CLASSICS
Marvel Comics Group: Dec, 1983 - No. 3, Feb, 1984 ($2.00, Baxter paper)

1-3: X-Men-r by Neal Adams 6.00

NOTE: ***Zeck** c-1-3.*

X-MEN: COLOSSUS BLOODLIINE
Marvel Comics: Nov, 2005 - No. 5, Mar, 2006 ($2.99, limited series)

1-5-Colossus returns to Russia; David Hine-s/Jorge Lucas-a; Bachalo-c 3.00
TPB (2006, $13.99) r/#1-5 14.00

X-MEN: DEADLY GENESIS (See Uncanny X-Men #475)
Marvel Comics: Jan, 2006 - No. 6, July, 2006 ($3.99/$3.50, limited series)

1-($3.99) Silvestri-c swipe of Giant-Size X-Men #1; Hairsine-a/Brubaker-s 4.00
2-6-($3.50) 2-Silvestri-c; Banshee killed. 4-Intro Kid Vulcan 3.50
HC (2006, $24.99, dust jacket) r/#1-6 25.00
SC (2006, $19.99) r/#1-6 20.00

X-MEN: DIE BY THE SWORD
Marvel Comics: Dec, 2007 - No. 5, Feb, 2008 ($2.99, limited series)

1-5-Excalibur and The Exiles app.; Claremont-s/Santacruz-a 3.00
TPB (2008, $13.99) r/#1-5; handbook pages of Merlyn, Roma and Saturne 14.00

X-MEN: DIVIDED WE STAND
Marvel Comics: June, 2008 - No. 2, July, 2008 ($3.99, limited series)

1,2-Short stories by various; Peterson-c 4.00

X-MEN: EARTHFALL
Marvel Comics: Sept, 1996 ($2.95, one-shot)

1-r/Uncanny X-Men #232-234; wraparound-c 3.00

X-MEN: EMPEROR VULCAN
Marvel Comics: Nov, 2007 - No. 5, Mar, 2008 ($2.99, limited series)

1-5: 1-Starjammers app.; Yost-s/Diaz-a/Tan-c 3.00
TPB (2008, $13.99) r/#1-5 14.00

X-MEN: EVOLUTION (Based on the animated series)
Marvel Comics: Feb, 2002 - No. 9, Sept, 2002 ($2.25)

1-9: 1-8-Grayson-s/Udon-a. 9-Farber-s/J.J.Kirby-a 3.00
TPB (7/02, $8.99) r/#1-4 9.00
Vol. 2 TPB (2003, $11.99) r/#5-9; Asamiya-c 12.00

X-MEN FAIRY TALES
Marvel Comics: July, 2006 - No. 4, Oct, 2006 ($2.99, limited series)

1-4-Re-imagining of classic stories; Cebulski-s. 2-Baker-a. 3-Sienkiewicz-a. 4-Kobayashi-a 3.00
TPB (2006, $10.99) r/#1-4 11.00

X-Men: First Class #9 © MAR

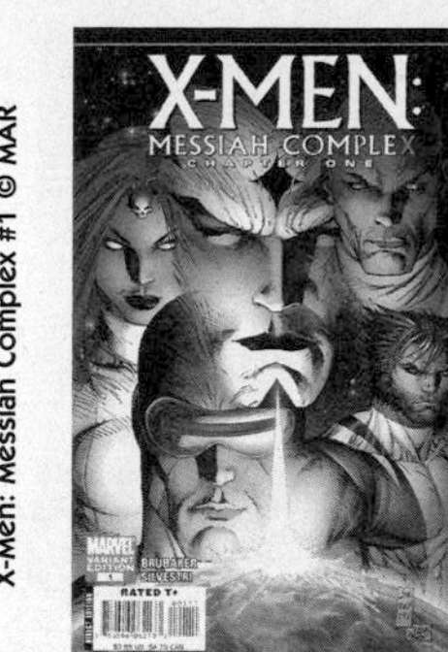

X-Men: Messiah Complex #1 © MAR

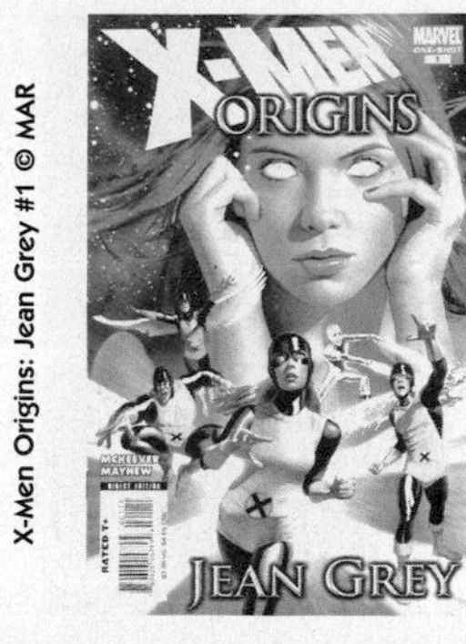

X-Men Origins: Jean Grey #1 © MAR

GD VG FN VF VF/NM NM-
2.0 4.0 6.0 8.0 9.0 9.2

X-MEN/ FANTASTIC FOUR
Marvel Comics: Feb, 2005 - No. 5, June, 2005 ($3.50, limited series)
1-5-Pat Lee-a/c; Yoshida-s; the Brood app. 3.50
HC (2005, $19.99, 7 1/2" x 11", dustjacket) oversized r/#1-5; cover gallery 20.00

X-MEN FIRST CLASS
Marvel Comics: Nov, 2006 - No. 8, Jun, 2007 ($2.99, limited series)
1-8-Xavier's first class of X-Men; Cruz-a/Parker-s. 5-Thor app. 7-Scarlet Witch app. 3.00
... Special 1 (7/07, $3.99) Nowlan-c; Nowlan, Paul Smith, Coover, Dragotta & Allred-a 4.00
... - Tomorrow's Brightest HC (2007, $24.99, d.j) r/#1-8; cover & character design art 25.00
... - Tomorrow's Brightest SC (2007, $19.99) r/#1-8; cover & character design art 20.00

X-MEN FIRST CLASS (2nd series)
Marvel Comics: Aug, 2007 - Present ($2.99)
1-16: 1-Cruz-a/Parker-s; Fantastic Four app. 8-Man-Thing app. 10-Romita Jr.-c 3.00
... - Mutant Mayhem TPB (2008, $13.99) r/#1-5 & X-Men First Class Special 14.00

X-MEN FIRSTS
Marvel Comics: Feb, 1996 ($4.95, one-shot)
1-r/Avengers Annual #10, Uncanny X-Men #266, #221; Incredible Hulk #181 5.00

X-MEN FOREVER
Marvel Comics: Jan, 2001 - No. 6, June, 2001 ($3.50, limited series)
1-6-Jean Grey, Iceman, Mystique, Toad, Juggernaut app.; Maguire-a 3.50

X-MEN: HELLFIRE CLUB
Marvel Comics: Jan, 2000 - No. 4, Apr, 2000 ($2.50, limited series)
1-4-Origin of the Hellfire Club 2.50

X-MEN: HIDDEN YEARS
Marvel Comics: Dec, 1999 - No. 22, Sept. 2001 ($3.50/$2.50)
1-New adventures from pre-#94 era; Byrne-s/a(p) 3.50
2-4,6-11,13-22-($2.50): 2-Two covers. 3-Ka-Zar app. 8,9-FF-c/app 3.00
5-($2.75) 3.00
12-($3.50) Magneto-c/app. 3.50

X-MEN: KITTY PRYDE - SHADOW & FLAME
Marvel Comics: Aug, 2005 - No. 5, Dec, 2005 ($2.99, limited series)
1-5-Akira Yoshida-s/Paul Smith-a/c; Kitty & Lockheed go to Japan 3.00
TPB (2006, $14.99) r/#1-5 15.00

X-MEN: LIBERATORS
Marvel Comics: Nov, 1998 - No. 4, Feb, 1999 ($2.99, limited series)
1-4-Wolverine, Nightcrawler & Colossus; P. Jimenez 3.00

X-MEN LOST TALES
Marvel Comics: 1997 ($2.99)
1,2-r/Classic X-Men back-up stories 3.00

X-MEN: MAGNETO TESTAMENT
Marvel Comics: Nov, 2008 - No. 5 ($3.99, limited series)
1,2-Max Eisenhardt in 1930s Nazi Germany; Pak-s/DiGiandomenico-a 4.00

X-MEN: MANIFEST DESTINY
Marvel Comics: Nov, 2008 - No. 4 ($3.99, limited series)
1,2-Short stories of X-Men re-location to San Francisco; s/a by various 4.00

X-MEN: MESSIAH COMPLEX
Marvel Comics: Dec, 2007 ($3.99)
1-Part 1 of x-over with X-Men, Uncanny X-Men, X-Factor and New X-Men; 2 covers 4.00
... - Mutant Files (2007, $3.99) Handbook pages of x-over participants; Kolins-c 4.00
HC (2008, $39.99, oversized) r/#1, Uncanny X-Men #492-494, X-Men #205-207, New X-Men #44-46 and X-Factor #25-27 40.00

X-MEN OMEGA
Marvel Comics: June, 1995 ($3.95, one-shot)
nn-Age of Apocalypse finale 1 3 4 6 8 10
nn-($49.95)-Gold edition 50.00

X-MEN: ORIGINS
Marvel Comics: Oct, 2008 - Present ($3.99, series of one-shots)
...: Beast (11/08) High school years; Carey-s; painted-a/c by Woodward 4.00
...: Jean Grey (10/08) Childhood & early X-days; McKeever-s; Mayhew painted-a/c 4.00

X-MEN: PHOENIX
Marvel Comics: Dec, 1999 - No. 3, Mar, 2000 ($2.50, limited series)
1-3: 1-Apocalypse app. 3.00

X-MEN: PHOENIX - ENDSONG
Marvel Comics: Mar, 2005 - No. 5, June, 2005 ($2.99, limited series)
1-5-The Phoenix Force returns to Earth; Greg Land-c/a; Greg Pak-s 3.00
HC (2005, $19.99, dust jacket) r/#1-5; Land sketch pages 20.00
SC (2006, $14.99) 15.00

X-MEN: PHOENIX - LEGACY OF FIRE
Marvel Comics: July, 2003 - No. 3, Sep, 2003 ($2.99, limited series)
1-3-Manga-style; Ryan Kinnard-s/a/c; intro page art by Adam Warren 3.00

X-MEN: PHOENIX - WARSONG
Marvel Comics: Nov, 2006 - No. 5, Mar, 2007 ($2.99, limited series)
1-5-Tyler Kirkham-a/Greg Pak-s/Marc Silvestri-c 3.00
HC (2007, $19.99, dustjacket) r/#1-5; variant cover gallery and Handbook pages 20.00
SC (2007, $14.99) r/#1-5; variant cover gallery and Handbook pages 15.00

X-MEN PRIME
Marvel Comics: July, 1995 ($4.95, one-shot)
nn-Post Age of Apocalyse begins 1 3 4 6 8 10

X-MEN RARITIES
Marvel Comics: 1995 ($5.95, one-shot)
nn-Reprints hard-to-find stories 6.00

X-MEN ROAD TO ONSLAUGHT
Marvel Comics: Oct, 1996 ($2.50, one-shot)
nn-Retells Onslaught Saga 3.00

X-MEN: RONIN
Marvel Comics: May, 2003 - No. 5, July, 2003 ($2.00, limited series)
1-5-Manga-style X-Men; Torres-s/Nakatsuka-a 3.00

X-MEN: SEARCH FOR CYCLOPS
Marvel Comics: Oct, 2000 - No. 4, Mar, 2001 ($2.99, limited series)
1-4-Two covers (Raney, Pollina); Raney-a 3.00

X-MEN SPOTLIGHT ON... STARJAMMERS (Also see X-Men #104)
Marvel Comics: 1990 - No. 2, 1990 ($4.50, 52 pgs.)
1,2: Features Starjammers 4.50

X-MEN SURVIVAL GUIDE TO THE MANSION
Marvel Comics: Aug, 1993 ($6.95, spiralbound)
1 7.00

X-MEN: THE COMPLETE AGE OF APOCALYPSE EPIC
Marvel Comics: 2005 - Vol. 4, 2006 ($29.99, TPB)
Book 1-4: Chronological reprintings of the crossover 30.00

X-MEN: THE EARLY YEARS
Marvel Comics: May, 1994 - No. 17, Sept, 1995 ($1.50/$2.50)
1-16: r/X-Men #1-8 w/new-c 3.00
17-$2.50-c; r/X-Men #17,18 3.00

X-MEN: THE END
Marvel Comics: Oct, 2004 - No. 6, Feb, 2005 ($2.99, limited series)
1-6-Claremont-s/Chen-a/Land-c 3.00
... Book One: Dreamers and Demons TPB (2005, $14.99) r/#1-6 15.00

X-MEN: THE END - HEROES AND MARTYRS (Volume 2)
Marvel Comics: May, 2005 - No. 6, Oct, 2005 ($2.99, limited series)
1-6-Claremont-s/Chen-a/Land-c; continued from X-Men: The End 3.00
... Vol. 2 TPB (2006, $14.99) r/#1-6 15.00

X-MEN: THE END (MEN & X-MEN) (Volume 3)
Marvel Comics: Mar, 2006 - No. 6, Aug, 2006 ($2.99, limited series)
1-6-Claremont-s/Chen-a. 1-Land-c. 2-6-Gene Ha-c 3.00
... Vol. 3 TPB (2006, $14.99) r/#1-6 15.00

X-MEN: THE MANGA
Marvel Comics: Mar, 1998 - No. 26, June, 1999 ($2.99, B&W)
1-26-English version of Japanese X-Men comics: 23,24-Randy Green-c 3.00

X-MEN: THE MOVIE
Marvel Comics: Aug, 2000; Sept, 2000
Adaptation (9/00, $5.95) Macchio-s/Williams & Lanning-a 6.00
Adaptation TPB (9/00, $14.95) Movie adaptation and key reprints of main characters; four photo covers (movie X, Magneto, Rogue, Wolverine) 15.00
Prequel: Magneto (8/00, $5.95) Texeira & Palmiotti-a; art & photo covers 6.00
Prequel: Rogue (8/00, $5.95) Evans & Nikolakakis-a; art & photo covers 6.00
Prequel: Wolverine (8/00, $5.95) Waller & McKenna-a; art & photo covers 6.00
TPB X-Men: Beginnings (8/00, $14.95) reprints 3 prequels w/photo-c 15.00

X-Men Unlimited #35 © MAR

X-O Manowar #30 © Voyager Comm.

X-Statix #1 © MAR

GD 2.0 | VG 4.0 | FN 6.0 | VF 8.0 | VF/NM 9.0 | NM- 9.2

X-MEN 2: THE MOVIE
Marvel Comics: 2003

Adaptation (6/03, $3.50) Movie adaptation; photo-c; Austen-s/Zircher-a 3.50
Adaptation TPB (2003, $12.99) Movie adaptation & r/Prequels Nightcrawler & Wolverine 13.00
Prequel: Nightcrawler (5/03, $3.50) Kerschl-a; photo cover 3.50
Prequel: Wolverine (5/03, $3.50) Mandrake-a; photo cover; Sabretooth app. 3.50

X-MEN: THE 198 (See House of M)
Marvel Comics: Mar, 2006 - No. 5, July, 2006 ($2.99, limited series)

1-5-Hine-s/Muniz-a 3.00
... Files (2006, $3.99) profiles of the 198 mutants who kept their powers after House of M 4.00
Decimation: The 198 (2006, $15.99, TPB) r/#1-5 & X-Men: The 198 Files 16.00

X-MEN: THE ULTRA COLLECTION
Marvel Comics: Dec, 1994 - No. 5, Apr, 1995 ($2.95, limited series)

1-5: Pin-ups; no scripts 3.00

X-MEN: THE WEDDING ALBUM
Marvel Comics: 1994 ($2.95, magazine size, one-shot)

1-Wedding of Scott Summers & Jean Grey 3.00

X-MEN TRUE FRIENDS
Marvel Comics: Sept, 1999 - No. 3, Nov, 1999 ($2.99, limited series)

1-3-Claremont-s/Leonardi-a 3.00

X-MEN 2099 (Also see 2099: World of Tomorrow)
Marvel Comics: Oct, 1993 - No. 35, Aug, 1996 ($1.25/$1.50/$1.95)

1-($1.75)-Foil-c; Ron Lim/Adam Kubert-a begins 3.50
1-2nd printing ($1.75) 3.00
1-Gold edition (15,000 made); sold thru Diamond for $19.40 20.00
2-24,26-35: 3-Death of Tina; Lim-c/a(p) in #1-8. 8-Bound-in trading card sheet. 35-Nostromo (from X-Nation) app; storyline cont'd in 2099: World of Tomorrow 3.00
25-($2.50)-Double sized 3.50
Special 1 ($3.95) 4.00
...: Oasis ($5.95, one-shot) -Hildebrandt Bros.-c/a 6.00

X-MEN ULTRA III PREVIEW
Marvel Comics: 1995 ($2.95)

nn-Kubert-a 3.00

X-MEN UNIVERSE
Marvel Comics: Dec, 1999 - Present ($4.99/$3.99)

1-8-Reprints stories from recent X-Men titles 5.00
9-15-($3.99) 4.00

X-MEN UNIVERSE: PAST, PRESENT AND FUTURE
Marvel Comics: Feb, 1999 ($2.99, one-shot)

1-Previews 1999 X-Men events; background info 3.00

X-MEN UNLIMITED
Marvel Comics: 1993 - No. 50, Sept, 2003 ($3.95/$2.99, 68 pgs.)

1-Chris Bachalo-c/a; Quesada-a. 5.00
2-11: 2-Origin of Magneto script. 3-Sabretooth-c/story. 10-Dark Beast vs. Beast; Mark Waid script. 11-Magneto & Rogue 4.00
12-33: 12-Begin $2.99-c; Onslaught x-over; Juggernaut-c/app. 19-Caliafore-a. 20-Generation X app. 27-Origin Thunderbird. 29-Maximum Security x-over; Bishop-c/app. 30-Mahfood-a. 31-Stelfreeze-c/a. 32-Dazzler; Thompson-c/a 33-Kaluta-c 3.00
34-37,39,40-42-($3.50) 34-Von Eeden-a. 35-Finch, Conner, Maguire-a. 36-Chiodo-c/a; Larroca, Totleben-a. 39-Bachalo-c; Pearson-a. 41-Bachalo-c; X-Statix app. 3.50
38-($2.25) Kitty Pryde; Robertson-a 3.00
43-50-($2.50) 43-Sienkiewicz-c/a; Paul Smith-a. 45-Noto-c. 46-Bisley-a. 47-Warren-s/Mays-a. 48-Wolverine story w/Isanove painted-a 3.00
X-Men Legends Vol. 4: Hated and Feared TPB (2003, $19.99) r/stories by various 20.00
NOTE: ***Bachalo** c/a-1. **Quesada** a-1. **Waid** scripts-10*

X-MEN UNLIMITED
Marvel Comics: Apr, 2004 - Present ($2.99)

1-14: 1-6-Pat Lee-c; short stories by various. 2-District X preview; Granov-a 3.00

X-MEN VS. DRACULA
Marvel Comics: Dec, 1993 ($1.75)

1-r/X-Men Annual #6; Austin-c(i) 3.00

X-MEN VS. THE AVENGERS, THE
Marvel Comics Group: Apr, 1987 - No. 4, July, 1987 ($1.50, limited series, Baxter paper)

1 4.00
2-4 3.00

X-MEN VS. THE BROOD, THE
Marvel Comics Group: Sept, 1996 - No. 2, Oct, 1996 ($2.95, limited series)

1,2-Wraparound-c; Ostrander-s/Hitch-a(p) 3.00
TPB('97, $16.99) reprints X-Men/Brood: Day of Wrath #1,2 & Uncanny X-Men #232-234 17.00

X-MEN VISIONARIES
Marvel Comics: 1995,1996,2000 (trade paperbacks)

nn-($8.95) Reprints X-Men stories; Adam & Andy Kubert-a 9.00
...2: The Neal Adams Collection (1996) r/X-Men #56-63,65 30.00
...2: The Neal Adams Col. (2nd printing, 2000, $24.95) new Adams-c 25.00

X-MEN/WILDC.A.T.S.: THE DARK AGE (See also WildC.A.T.S./X-Men...)
Marvel Comics: 1998 ($4.50, one-shot)

1-Two covers (Broome & Golden); Ellis-s 4.50

X-NATION 2099
Marvel Comics: Mar, 1996 - No. 6, Aug, 1996 ($1.95)

1-($3.95)-Humberto Ramos-a(p); wraparound, foil-c 4.00
2-6: 2,3-Ramos-a. 4-Exodus-c/app. 6-Reed Richards app 3.00

X-O MANOWAR (1st Series)
Valiant/Acclaim Comics (Valiant) No. 43 on: Feb, 1992 - No. 68, Sept, 1996 ($1.95/$2.25/$2.50, high quality)

0-(8/93, $3.50)-Wraparound embossed chromium-c by Quesada; Solar app.; origin Aric (X-O Manowar) 3.50
0-Gold variant 5.00
1-Intro/1st app. & partial origin of Aric (X-O Manowar); Barry Smith/Layton-a 1 2 3 5 6 8
2-4: 2-B. Smith/Layton-c. 3-Layton-c(i). 4-1st app. Shadowman 6.00
5-15: 5-B. Smith-c. 6-Begin $2.25-c; Ditko-a(p). 7,8-Unity x-overs. 7-Miller-c. 8-Simonson-c. 12-1st app. Randy Calder. 14,15-Turok-c/stories 3.00
15-Hot pink logo variant; came with Ultra Pro Rigid Comic Sleeves box; no price on cover 4.00
16-24,26-43: 20-Serial number contest insert. 27-29-Turok x-over. 28-Bound-in trading card. 30-1st app. new "good skin"; Solar app. 33-Chaos Effect Delta Pt. 3. 42-Shadowman app.; includes X-O Manowar Birthquake! Prequel 2.50
25-($3.50)-Has 16 pg. Armorines #0 bound-in w/origin 3.50
44-68: 44-Begin $2.50-c. 50-X, 50-O, 51, 52, 63-Bart Sears-c/a/scripts. 68-Revealed that Aric's past stories were premonitions of his future 2.50
...: Birth HC (2008, $24.95) recolored reprints #0-6; script and breakdowns for #0; cover gallery; new "The Rise of Lydia" story by Layton and Leeke 25.00
Trade paperback nn (1993, $9.95)-Polybagged with copy of X-O Database #1 inside 10.00
Yearbook 1 (4/95, $2.95) 3.00
NOTE: ***Layton** a-1i, 2i(part); c-1, 2i, 3i, 6i, 21i. **Reese** a-4i(part); c-26i.*

X-O MANOWAR (2nd Series)(Also see Iron Man/X-O Manowar: Heavy Metal)
Acclaim Comics (Valiant Heroes): V2#1, Oct, 1996 - No. 21, Jun, 1998 ($2.50)

V2#1-21: 1-Mark Waid & Brian Augustyn scripts begin; 1st app. Donavon Wylie; Rand Banion dies; painted variant-c exists. 2-Donavon Wylie becomes new X-O Manowar. 7-9-Augustyn-s. 10-Copycat-c 2.50

X-O MANOWAR FAN EDITION
Acclaim Comics (Valiant Heroes): Feb, 1997 (Overstreet's FAN giveaway)

1-Reintro the Armorines & the Hard Corps; 1st app. Citadel; Augustyn scripts; McKone-c/a 4.00

X-O MANOWAR/IRON MAN: IN HEAVY METAL (See Iron Man/X-O Manowar: Heavy Metal)
Acclaim Comics (Valiant Heroes): Sept, 1996 ($2.50, one-shot)
(1st Marvel/Valiant x-over)

1-Pt 1 of X-O Manowar/Iron Man x-over; Arnim Zola app.; Nicieza scripts; Andy Smith-a 2.50

XOMBI
DC Comics (Milestone): Jan, 1994 - No. 21, Feb, 1996 ($1.75/$2.50)

0-($1.95)-Shadow War x-over; Simonson silver ink varnish-c 2.50
1-21: 1-John Byrne-c 2.50
1-Platinum 8.00

X-PATROL
Marvel Comics (Amalgam): Apr, 1996 ($1.95, one-shot)

1-Cruz-a(p) 2.50

XSE
Marvel Comics: Nov, 1996 - No. 4, Feb, 1997 ($1.95, limited series)

1-4: 1-Bishop & Shard app. 2.50
1-Variant-c 3.00

X-STATIX
Marvel Comics: Sept, 2002 - No. 26, Oct, 2004 ($2.99/$2.25)

1-($2.99)Allred-a/c; intro. Venus Dee Milo; back-up w/Cooke-a 3.00

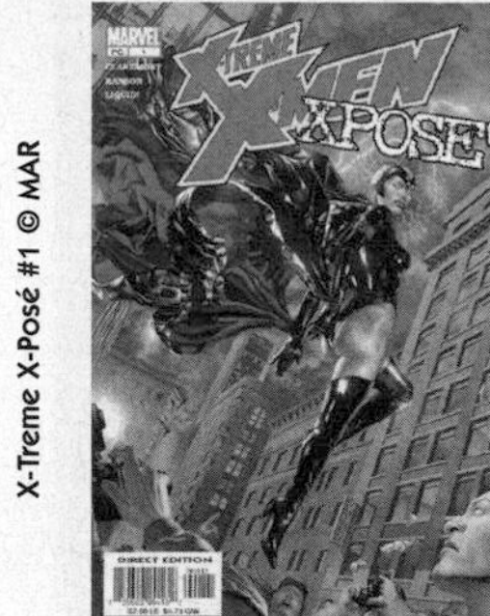

X-Treme X-Posé #1 © MAR

Yang #1 © CC

Yellowjacket Comics #10 © CC

GD VG FN VF VF/NM NM-
2.0 4.0 6.0 8.0 9.0 9.2

2-9-($2.25) 4-Quitely-c. 5-Pope-c/a 2.50
10-26: 10-Begin $2.99-c; Bond-a; U-Go Girl flashback. 13,14-Spider-Man app. 21-25-Avengers app. 26-Team dies 3.00
... Vol. 1: Good Omens TPB (2003, $11.99) r/#1-5 12.00
... Vol. 2: Good Guys & Bad Guys TPB (2003, $15.99) r/#6-10 & Wolverine/Doop #1&2 16.00
... Vol. 3: Back From the Dead TPB (2004, $19.99) r/#11-18 20.00
... Vol. 4: X-Statix Vs. the Avengers TPB (2004, $19.99) r/#19-26; pin-ups 20.00

X-STATIX PRESENTS: DEAD GIRL
Marvel Comics: Mar, 2006 - No. 5, July, 2006 ($2.99, limited series)
1-5-Dr. Strange, Dead Girl, Miss America, Tike app. Milligan-s/Dragotta & Allred-a 3.00
TPB (2006, $13.99) r/series 14.00

X-TERMINATORS
Marvel Comics: Oct, 1988 - No. 4, Jan, 1989 ($1.00, limited series)
1-1st app.; X-Men/X-Factor tie-in; Williamson-i 3.00
2-4 2.50

X, THE MAN WITH THE X-RAY EYES (See Movie Comics)

X-TREME X-MEN (Also see Mekanix)
Marvel Comics: July, 2001 - No. 46, Jun, 2004 ($2.99/$3.50)
1-Claremont-s/Larroca-c/a 4.00
2-24: 2-Two covers (Larroca & Pacheco); Psylocke killed 3.00
25-35, 40-46: 25-30-God Loves, Man Kills II; Stryker app.; Kordey-a 3.00
36-39-($3.50) 3.50
Annual 2001 ($4.95) issue opens longways 5.00
... Vol. 1: Destiny TPB (2002, $19.95) r/#1-9 20.00
... Vol. 2: Invasion TPB (2003, $19.99) r/#10-18 20.00
... Vol. 3: Schism TPB (2003, $16.99) r/#19-23; X-Treme X-Posé #1&2 17.00
... Vol. 4: Mekanix TPB (2003, $16.99) r/Mekanix #1-6 17.00
... Vol. 5: God Loves Man Kills TPB (2003, $19.99) r/#25-30 20.00
... Vol. 6: Intifada TPB (2004, $16.99) r/#24,31-35 17.00
... Vol. 7: Storm the Arena TPB (2004, $16.99) r/#36-39 17.00
... Vol. 8: Prisoner of Fire TPB (2004, $19.99) r/#40-46 and Annual 2001 20.00

X-TREME X-MEN: SAVAGE LAND
Marvel Comics: Nov, 2001 - No. 4, Feb, 2002 ($2.99, limited series)
1-4-Claremont-s/Sharpe-c/a; Beast app. 3.00

X-TREME X-POSE
Marvel Comics: Jan, 2003 - No. 2, Feb, 2003 ($2.99, limited series)
1,2-Claremont-s/Ranson-a/Migliari-c 3.00

X-23 (See debut in NYX #3)(See NYX X-23 HC for reprint)
Marvel Comics: Mar, 2005 - No. 6, July, 2005 ($2.99, limited series)
1-Origin of the Wolverine clone girl; Tan-a 4.00
1-Variant Billy Tan-c with red background 5.00
2-6-Origin continues 3.00
2-Variant B&W sketch-c 5.00
...: Innocence Lost TPB (2006, $15.99) r/#1-6 16.00

X-23: TARGET X
Marvel Comics: Feb, 2007 - No. 6, July, 2007 ($2.99, limited series)
1-6-Kyle & Yost-s/Choi & Oback-a. 6-Gallery of variant covers and sketches 3.00
TPB (2007, $15.99) r/#1-6; gallery of variant covers and sketches 16.00

X-UNIVERSE
Marvel Comics: May, 1995 - No. 2, June, 1995 ($3.50, limited series)
1,2: Age of Apocalypse 5.00

X-VENTURE (Super Heroes)
Victory Magazines Corp.: July, 1947 - No. 2, Nov, 1947
1-Atom Wizard, Mystery Shadow, Lester Trumble begin
110 220 330 693 1172 1650
2 54 108 162 340 575 810

XYR (See Eclipse Graphic Album Series #21)

YAK YAK
Dell Publishing Co.: No. 1186, May-July, 1961 - No. 1348, Apr-June, 1962
Four Color 1186 (#1)- Jack Davis-c/a; 2 versions, one minus 3 pgs.
8 16 24 58 97 135
Four Color 1348 (#2)-Davis c/a 8 16 24 52 86 120

YAKKY DOODLE & CHOPPER (TV) (See Dell Giant #44)
Gold Key: Dec, 1962 (Hanna-Barbera)
1 7 14 21 50 83 115

YANG (See House of Yang)

Charlton Comics: Nov, 1973 - No. 13, May, 1976; V14#15, Sept, 1985 - No. 17, Jan, 1986 (No V14#14, series resumes with #15)
1-Origin; Sattler-a begins; slavery-s 2 4 6 11 16 20
2-13(1976) 1 2 3 6 9 10
15-17(1986): 15-Reprints #1 (Low print run) 6.00
3,10,11(Modern Comics-r, 1977) 4.00

YANKEE COMICS
Harry 'A' Chesler: Sept, 1941 - No. 7, 1942?
1-Origin The Echo, The Enchanted Dagger, Yankee Doodle Jones, The Firebrand, & The Scarlet Sentry; Black Satan app.; Yankee Doodle Jones app. on all covers
187 374 561 1178 1989 2800
2-Origin Johnny Rebel; Major Victory app.; Barry Kuda begins
80 160 240 504 852 1200
3,4: 4-(3/42) 59 118 177 372 629 885
4 (nd, 1940s; 7-1/4x5", 68 pgs, distr. to the service)-Foxy Grandpa, Tom, Dick & Harry, Impy, Ace & Deuce, Dot & Dash, Ima Slooth by Jack Cole (Remington Morse publ.)
13 26 39 72 101 130
5-7 (nd; 10¢, 7-1/4x5", 68 pgs.)(Remington Morse publ.)-urges readers to send their copies to servicemen. 11 22 33 62 86 110

YANKEE DOODLE THE SPIRIT OF LIBERTY
Spire Publications: 1984 (no price, 36 pgs)
nn-Al Hartley-s/c/a 2 4 6 8 10 12

YANKS IN BATTLE
Quality Comics Group: Sept, 1956 - No. 4, Dec, 1956; 1963
1-Cuidera-c(i) 10 20 30 58 79 100
2-4: Cuidera-c(i) 8 16 24 40 50 60
I.W. Reprint #3(1963)-r/#?; exist? 2 4 6 9 12 15

YARDBIRDS, THE (G. I. Joe's Sidekicks)
Ziff-Davis Publishing Co.: Summer, 1952
1-By Bob Oskner 10 20 30 56 76 95

YARN MAN (See Megaton Man)
Kitchen Sink : Oct, 1989 ($2.00, B&W, one-shot)
1-Donald Simpson-c/a/scripts 2.50

YARNS OF YELLOWSTONE
World Color Press: 1972 (50¢, 36 pgs.)
nn-Illustrated by Bill Chapman 2 4 6 8 11 14

YEAH!
DC Comics (Homage): Oct, 1999 - No. 9, Jun, 2000 ($2.95)
1-Bagge-s/Hernandez-a 3.00
2-9: 2-Editorial page contains adult language 3.00

YELLOW CLAW (Also see Giant Size Master of Kung Fu)
Atlas Comics (MjMC): Oct, 1956 - No. 4, Apr, 1957
1-Origin by Joe Maneely 100 200 300 630 1065 1500
2-Kirby-a 80 160 240 504 852 1200
3,4-Kirby-a; 4-Kirby/Severin-a 77 154 231 481 816 1150
NOTE: *Everett c-3. Maneely c-1. Reinman a-2i, 3. Severin c-2, 4.*

YELLOWJACKET COMICS (Jack in the Box #11 on)(See TNT Comics)
E. Levy/Frank Comunale/Charlton: Sept, 1944 - No. 10, June, 1946
1-Intro & origin Yellowjacket; Diana, the Huntress begins; E.A. Poe's "The Black Cat" adaptation 66 132 198 416 701 985
2-Yellowjacket-c begin, end #10 41 82 123 250 413 575
3,5 40 80 120 244 397 550
4-E.A. Poe's "Fall of the House Of Usher" adaptation; Palais-a
41 82 123 250 413 575
6 48 96 144 298 499 700
7-Classic skull-c; Toth-a (1 pg. gag feature) 97 194 291 611 1031 1450
8-10: 1,3,4,6-10-Have stories narrated by old witch in "Tales of Terror" (1st horror series?)
47 94 141 291 488 685

YELLOWSTONE KELLY (Movie)
Dell Publishing Co.: No. 1056, Nov-Jan, 1959/60
Four Color 1056-Clint Walker photo-c 6 12 18 37 59 80

YELLOW SUBMARINE (See Movie Comics)

YEAR ONE: BATMAN/RA'S AL GHUL
DC Comics: 2005 - No. 2, 2005 ($5.99, squarebound, limited series)
1-Devin Grayson-s/Paul Gulacy-a 6.00
TPB (2006, $9.99) r/#1,2 10.00

Yosemite Sam #56 © WB

Young Avengers Presents #1 © MAR

Youngblood #6 © Awesome Ent.

GD VG FN VF VF/NM NM-
2.0 4.0 6.0 8.0 9.0 9.2

YEAR ONE: BATMAN SCARECROW
DC Comics: 2005 - No. 2, 2005 ($5.99, squarebound, limited series)
1-Scarecrow's origin; Bruce Jones-s/Sean Murphy-a 6.00

YIN FEI THE CHINESE NINJA
Leung's Publications: 1988 - No. 8, 1990 ($1.80/$2.00, 52 pgs.)
1-8 2.50

YOGI BEAR (See Dell Giant #41, Golden Comics Digest, Kite Fun Book, March of Comics #253, 265, 279, 291, 309, 319, 337, 344, Movie Comics under "Hey There It's..." & Whitman Comic Books)

YOGI BEAR (TV) (Hanna-Barbera) (See Four Color #990)
Dell Publishing Co./Gold Key No. 10 on: No. 1067, 12-2/59-60 - No. 9, 7-9/62; No. 10, 10/62 - No. 42, 10/70
Four Color 1067 (#1)-TV show debuted 1/30/61 10 20 30 71 126 180
Four Color 1104,1162 (5-7/61) 7 14 21 49 80 110
4(8-9/61) - 6(12-1/61-62) 6 12 18 37 59 80
Four Color 1271(11/61) 6 12 18 37 59 80
Four Color 1349(1/62)-Photo-c 8 16 24 58 97 135
7(2-3/62) - 9(7-9/62)-Last Dell 6 12 18 37 59 80
10(10/62-G.K.), 11(1/63)-titled "Yogi Bear Jellystone Jollies" (80 pgs.); 11-X-Mas-c
7 14 21 47 76 105
12(4/63), 14-20 5 10 15 30 48 65
13(7/63, 68 pgs.)-Surprise Party 7 14 21 47 76 105
21-30 3 6 9 20 30 40
31-42 3 6 9 17 25 32

YOGI BEAR (TV)
Charlton Comics: Nov, 1970 - No. 35, Jan, 1976 (Hanna-Barbera)
1 4 8 12 28 44 60
2-6,8-10 3 6 9 16 23 30
7-Summer Fun (Giant, 52 pgs.) 4 8 12 28 44 60
11-20 3 6 9 16 22 28
21-35: 28-31-partial-r 2 4 6 11 16 20
Digest (nn, 1972, 75¢-c, B&W, 100 pgs.) (scarce) 3 6 9 19 29 38

YOGI BEAR (TV)(See The Flintstones, 3rd series & Spotlight #1)
Marvel Comics Group: Nov, 1977 - No. 9, Mar, 1979 (Hanna-Barbera)
1,7-9: 1-Flintstones begin (Newsstand sales only) 3 6 9 16 23 30
2-6 2 4 6 11 16 20

YOGI BEAR (TV)
Harvey Comics: Sept, 1992 - No. 6, Mar, 1994 ($1.25/$1.50) (Hanna-Barbera)
V2#1-6 3.00
...Big Book V2#1,2 ($1.95, 52 pgs): 1-(11/92). 2-(3/93) 3.00
...Giant Size V2#1,2 ($2.25, 68 pgs.): 1-(10/92). 2-(4/93) 3.00

YOGI BEAR (TV)
Archie Publ.: May, 1997
1 3.00

YOGI BEAR'S EASTER PARADE (See The Funtastic World of Hanna-Barbera #2)

YOGI BERRA (Baseball hero)
Fawcett Publications: 1951 (Yankee catcher)
nn-Photo-c (scarce) 71 142 213 447 754 1060

YOSEMITE SAM (...& Bugs Bunny) (TV)
Gold Key/Whitman: Dec, 1970 - No. 81, Feb, 1984
1 4 8 12 28 44 60
2-10 3 6 9 16 22 28
11-20 2 4 6 10 14 18
21-30 2 4 6 8 11 14
31-50 1 3 4 6 8 10
51-65 (Gold Key) 1 2 3 5 6 8
66,67 (Whitman) 2 4 6 8 10 12
68(9/80), 69(10/80), 70(12/80) 3-pack only 3 6 9 18 27 35
71-78: 76(2/82), 77(3/82), 78(4/82) 2 4 6 8 11 14
79-81 (All #90263 on-c, no date or date code; 3-pack): 79(7/83). 80(8/83). 81(2/84)-(1/3-r)
2 4 6 13 18 22
(See March of Comics #363, 380, 392)

YOUNG ALLIES COMICS (All-Winners #21; see Kid Komics #2)
Timely Comics (USA 1-7/NPI 8,9/YAI 10-20): Sum, 1941 - No. 20, Oct, 1946
1-Origin/1st app. The Young Allies (Bucky, Toro, others); 1st meeting of Captain America & Human Torch; Red Skull-c & app.; S&K-c/splash; Hitler-c; Note: the cover was altered after its preview in Human Torch #5. Stalin was shown with Hitler but was removed due to Russia becoming an ally 1367 2734 4100 10,300 18,150 26,000
2-(Winter, 1941)-Captain America & Human Torch app.; Simon & Kirby-c
388 776 1164 2638 4619 6600
3-Fathertime, Captain America & Human Torch app.; Remember Pearl Harbor issue (Spring, 1942); Stan Lee scripts; Vs. Japenese-c/full-length story
300 600 900 1930 3315 4700
4-The Vagabond & Red Skull, Capt. America, Human Torch app. Classic Red Skull-c
418 836 1254 2842 4971 7100
5-Captain America & Human Torch app. 213 426 639 1342 2271 3200
6,7,10: 10-Origin Tommy Tyme & Clock of Ages; ends #19
153 306 459 964 1632 2300
8-Classic Schomburg WW2 bondage-c 160 320 480 1008 1704 2400
9-Hitler, Tojo, Mussolini-c. 187 374 561 1178 1989 2800
11-20: 12-Classic decapitation story 103 206 309 649 1100 1550
NOTE: ***Brodsky** c-15. **Gabrielle** a-3; c-3, 4. **S&K** c-1, 2. **Schomburg** c-5-13, 16-19. **Shores** c-20.*

YOUNG ALL-STARS
DC Comics: June, 1987 - No. 31, Nov, 1989 ($1.00, deluxe format)
1-31: 1-1st app. Iron Munro & The Flying Fox. 8,9-Millennium tie-ins 2.50
Annual 1 (1988, $2.00) 2.50

YOUNG AVENGERS
Marvel Comics: Apr, 2005 - No. 12, Aug, 2006 ($2.99)
1-Intro. Iron Lad, Patriot, Hulkling, Asgardian; Heinberg-s/Cheung-a 5.00
1-Director's Cut (2005, $3.99) r/#1 plus character sketches; original script 4.00
2-12: 3-6-Kang app. 7-DiVito-a. 9-Skrulls app. 3.00
... Special 1 (2/06, $3.99) origins of the heroes; art by various incl. Neal Adams, Jae Lee, Bill Sienkiewicz, Gene Ha, Michael Gaydos and Pasqual Ferry 4.00
... Vol. 1: Sidekicks HC (2005, $19.99, dustjacket) r/#1-6; character design sketches 20.00
... Vol. 1: Sidekicks TPB (2006, $14.99) r/#1-6; character design sketches 15.00
... Vol. 2: Family Matters HC (2006, $22.99, dustjacket) r/#7-12 & YA Special #1 23.00
... Vol. 2: Family Matters SC (2007, $17.99) r/#7-12 & YA Special #1 18.00
HC (2008, $29.99, d.j.) oversized reprint of #1-12 and Special #1; script & sketch pages 30.00

YOUNG AVENGERS PRESENTS
Marvel Comics: Mar, 2008 - No. 6, Aug, 2008 ($2.99, limited series)
1-4: 1-Patriot; Bucky app. 2-Hulkling; Captain Marvel app. 3-Wiccan & Speed. 4-Vision. 5-Stature. 6-Hawkeye; Clint Barton app.; Alan Davis-a 3.00

YOUNGBLOOD (See Brigade #4, Megaton Explosion & Team Youngblood)
Image Comics (Extreme Studios): Apr, 1992 - No. 4, Feb, 1993 ($2.50, lim. series); No. 6, June, 1994 (No #5) - No. 10, Dec, 1994 ($1.95/$2.50)
1-Liefeld-c/a/scripts in all; flip book format with 2 trading cards; 1st Image/Extreme Studios title. 5.00
1,2-2nd printing 2.50
2-(JUN-c, July 1992 indicia)-1st app. Shadowhawk in solo back-up story; 2 trading cards inside; flip book format; 1st app. Prophet, Kirby, Berzerkers, Darkthorn 2.50
3,0,4,5: 3-(OCT-c, August 1992 indicia)-Contains 2 trading cards inside (flip book); 1st app. Supreme in back-up story; 1st app. Showdown. 0-(12/92, $1.95)-Contains 2 trading cards; 2 cover variations exist, green or beige logo; w/Image #0 coupon. 4-(2/93)-Glow-in-the-dark cover w/2 trading cards; 2nd app. Dale Keown's The Pitt; Bloodstrike app. 5-Flip book w/Brigade #4 2.50
6-($3.50, 52 pgs.)-Wraparound-c 3.50
7-10: 7, 8-Liefeld-c(p)/a(p)/story. 8,9-(9/94) 9-Valentino story & art 2.50
Battlezone 1 (May-c, 4/93 inside, $1.95)-Arsenal book; Liefeld-c(p) 2.50
Battlezone 2 (7/94, $2.95)-Wraparound-c 3.00
Yearbook 1 (7/93, $2.50)-Fold out panel; 1st app. Tyrax & Kanan 2.50
...Super Special (Winter '97, $2.99) Sprouse -a 3.00
TPB (1996, $16.95)-r/Team Youngblood #8-10 & Youngblood #6-8,10 17.00

YOUNGBLOOD
Image Comics (Extreme Studios)/Maximum Press No. 14: V2#1, Sept, 1995 - No. 14, Dec, 1996 ($2.50)
V2#1-10,14: Roger Cruz-a in all. 4-Extreme Destroyer Pt. 4 w/gaming card. 5-Variant-c exists. 6-Angela & Glory. 7-Shadowhunt Pt. 3; Shadowhawk app. 8,10-Thor (from Supreme) app. 10-(7/96). 14-(12/96)-1st Maximum Press issue 2.50

YOUNGBLOOD (Volume 3)
Awesome/ Awesome-Hyperwerks #2: Feb, 1998 - No. 2, Aug, 1998 ($2.50)
1-Alan Moore-s/Skroce & Stucker-a; 12 diff. covers 2.50
2-(8/98) Skroce & Liefeld covers 2.50
...Imperial 1 (Arcade Comics, 6/04, $2.99) Kirkman-sMychaels-a 3.00

YOUNGBLOOD (Volume 4)
Image Comics: Jan, 2008 - Present ($2.99)
1-5-Casey-s/Donovan-a; two covers by Donovan & Liefeld on each 3.00

YOUNGBLOOD: STRIKEFILE
Image Comics (Extreme Studios): Apr, 1993 - No. 11, Feb, 1995 ($1.95/$2.50/$2.95)

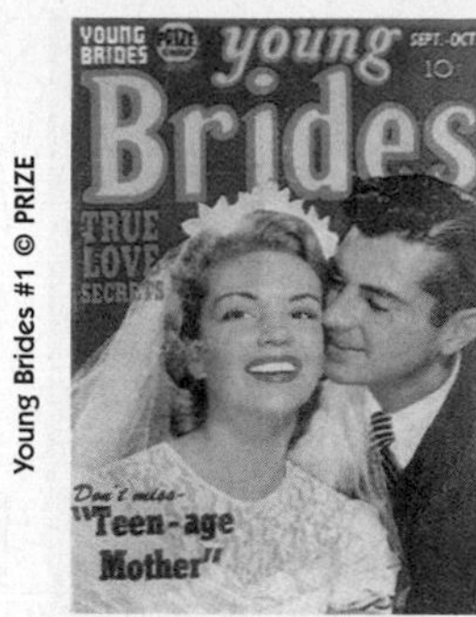

Young Brides #1 © PRIZE

Young Justice #23 © DC

Young Liars #1 © David Lapham

	GD 2.0	VG 4.0	FN 6.0	VF 8.0	VF/NM 9.0	NM- 9.2
1-10: 1-($1.95)-Flip book w/Jae Lee-c/a & Liefeld-c/a in #1-3; 1st app. The Allies,Giger, & Glory. 3-Thibert-i asisst. 4-Liefeld-c(p); no Lee-a. 5-Liefeld-c(p). 8-Platt-c						3.00

NOTE: *Youngblood: Strikefile began as a four issue limited series.*

YOUNGBLOOD/X-FORCE
Image Comics (Extreme Studios): July, 1996 ($4.95, one-shot)

	GD	VG	FN	VF	VF/NM	NM-
1-Cruz-a(p); two covers exist						5.00

YOUNG BRIDES (True Love Secrets)
Feature/Prize Publ.: Sept-Oct, 1952 - No. 30, Nov-Dec, 1956 (Photo-c: 1-4)

	GD	VG	FN	VF	VF/NM	NM-
V1#1-Simon & Kirby-a	37	74	111	215	345	475
2-S&K-a	20	40	60	115	183	250
3-6-S&K-a	18	36	54	105	165	225
V2#1-7,10-12 (#7-18)-S&K-a	17	34	51	98	154	210
8,9-No S&K-a	9	18	27	50	65	80
V3#1-3(#19-21)-Last precode (3-4/55)	9	18	27	47	61	75
4,6(#22,24), V4#1,3(#25,27)	8	16	24	42	54	65
V3#5(#23)-Meskin-c	8	16	24	44	57	70
V4#2(#26)-All S&K issue	15	30	45	90	140	190
V4#4(#28)-S&K-a	14	28	42	78	112	145
V4#5,6(#29,30)	9	18	27	47	61	75

YOUNG DR. MASTERS (See The Adventures of Young Dr. Masters)

YOUNG DOCTORS, THE
Charlton Comics: Jan, 1963 - No. 6, Nov, 1963

	GD	VG	FN	VF	VF/NM	NM-
V1#1	3	6	9	21	32	42
2-6	3	6	9	14	19	24

YOUNG EAGLE
Fawcett Publications/Charlton: 12/50 - No. 10, 6/52; No. 3, 7/56 - No. 5, 4/57 (Photo-c: 1-10)

	GD	VG	FN	VF	VF/NM	NM-
1-Intro Young Eagle	18	36	54	103	162	220
2-Complete picture novelette "The Mystery of Thunder Canyon"	10	20	30	58	79	100
3-9	9	18	27	50	65	80
10-Origin Thunder, Young Eagle's Horse	8	16	24	44	57	70
3-5(Charlton) Formerly Sherlock Holmes?	7	14	21	35	43	50

YOUNG GUNS SKETCHBOOK
Marvel Comics: Feb, 2005 ($3.99, one-shot)

	GD	VG	FN	VF	VF/NM	NM-
1-Sketch pages from 2005 Marvel projects by Coipel, Granov, McNiven, Land & others						4.00

YOUNG HEARTS
Marvel Comics (SPC): Nov, 1949 - No. 2, Feb, 1950

	GD	VG	FN	VF	VF/NM	NM-
1-Photo-c	14	28	42	82	121	160
2-Colleen Townsend photo-c from movie	10	20	30	56	76	95

YOUNG HEARTS IN LOVE
Super Comics: 1964

	GD	VG	FN	VF	VF/NM	NM-
17,18: 17-r/Young Love V5#6 (4-5/62)	2	4	6	9	13	16

YOUNG HEROES (Formerly Forbidden Worlds #34)
American Comics Group (Titan): No. 35, Feb-Mar, 1955 - No. 37, Jun-Jul, 1955

	GD	VG	FN	VF	VF/NM	NM-
35-37-Frontier Scout	10	20	30	54	72	90

YOUNG HEROES IN LOVE
DC Comics: June, 1997 - No. 17; #1,000,000, Nov, 1998 ($1.75/$1.95/$2.50)

	GD	VG	FN	VF	VF/NM	NM-
1-1st app. Young Heroes; Madan-a						3.00
2-17: 3-Superman-c/app. 7-Begin $1.95-c						2.50
#1,000,000 (11/98, $2.50) 853 Century x-over						2.50

YOUNG INDIANA JONES CHRONICLES, THE
Dark Horse Comics: Feb, 1992 - No. 12, Feb, 1993 ($2.50)

	GD	VG	FN	VF	VF/NM	NM-
1-12: Dan Barry scripts in all						2.50

NOTE: ***Dan Barry** a(p)-1, 2, 5, 6, 10; c-1-10. **Morrow** a-3, 4, 5p, 6p. **Springer** a-1i, 2i.*

YOUNG INDIANA JONES CHRONICLES, THE
Hollywood Comics (Disney): 1992 ($3.95, squarebound, 68 pgs.)

	GD	VG	FN	VF	VF/NM	NM-
1-3: 1-r/YIJC #1,2 by D. Horse. 2-r/#3,4. 3-r/#5,6						4.00

YOUNG JUSTICE (Also see Teen Titans and Titans/Young Justice)
DC Comics: Sept, 1998 - No. 55, May, 2003 ($2.50/$2.75)

	GD	VG	FN	VF	VF/NM	NM-
1-Robin, Superboy & Impulse team-up; David-s/Nauck-a						4.00
2,3: 3-Mxyzptlk app.						3.00
4-20: 4-Wonder Girl, Arrowette and the Secret join. 6-JLA app. 13-Supergirl x-over. 20-Sins of Youth aftermath						3.00
21-49: 25-Empress ID revealed. 28,29-Forever People app. 32-Empress origin. 35,36-Our Worlds at War x-over. 38-Joker: Last Laugh. 41-The Ray joins. 42-Spectre-c/app. 44,45-World Without YJ x-over pt. 1,5; Ramos-c. 48-Begin $2.75-c						2.75
50-($3.95) Wonder Twins,CM3 and other various DC teen heroes app.						4.00
51-55: 53,54-Darkseid app. 55-Last issue; leads into Titans/Young Justice mini-series						2.75
#1,000,000 (11/98) 853 Century x-over						2.50
...: A League of Their Own (2000, $14.95, TPB) r/#1-7, Secret Files #1						15.00
...: 80-Page Giant (5/99, $4.95) Ramos-c; stories and art by various						5.00
...: In No Man's Land (7/99, $3.95) McDaniel-c						4.00
...: Our Worlds at War (8/01, $2.95) Jae Lee-c; Linear Men app.						3.00
...: Secret Files (1/99, $4.95) Origin-s & pin-ups						5.00
...: The Secret (6/98, $1.95) Girlfrenzy; Nauck-a						2.50

YOUNG JUSTICE: SINS OF YOUTH (Also see Sins of Youth x-over issues and Sins of Youth: Secret Files)
DC Comics: May, 2000 - No. 2, May, 2000 ($3.95, limited series)

	GD	VG	FN	VF	VF/NM	NM-
1,2-Young Justice, JLA & JSA swap ages; David-s/Nauck-a						4.00
TPB (2000, $19.95) r/#1,2 & all x-over issues)						20.00

YOUNG KING COLE (...Detective Tales)(Becomes Criminals on the Run)
Premium Group/Novelty Press: Fall, 1945 - V3#12, July, 1948

	GD	VG	FN	VF	VF/NM	NM-
V1#1-Toni Gayle begins	32	64	96	186	298	410
2	15	30	45	90	140	190
3-4	15	30	45	84	127	170
V2#1-7(8-9/46-7/47): 6,7-Certa-c	12	24	36	67	94	120
V3#1,3-6,8,9,12: 3-Certa-c. 5-McWilliams-c/a. 8,9-Harmon-c	11	22	33	64	90	115
2-L.B. Cole-a; Certa-c	15	30	45	90	140	190
7-L.B. Cole-c/a	21	42	63	123	197	270
10,11-L.B. Cole-c	18	36	54	105	165	225

YOUNG LAWYERS, THE (TV)
Dell Publishing Co.: Jan, 1971 - No. 2, Apr, 1971

	GD	VG	FN	VF	VF/NM	NM-
1	3	6	9	16	23	30
2	2	4	6	11	16	20

YOUNG LIARS (David Lapham's...)(See Vertigo Double Shot for reprint of #1)
DC Comics (Vertigo): May, 2008 - Present ($2.99)

	GD	VG	FN	VF	VF/NM	NM-
1-5: 1-Intro. Sadie Dawkins; David Lapham-s/a/c in all						3.00

YOUNG LIFE (Teen Life #3 on)
New Age Publ./Quality Comics Group: Summer, 1945 - No. 2, Fall, 1945

	GD	VG	FN	VF	VF/NM	NM-
1-Skip Homeier, Louis Prima stories	15	30	45	86	133	180
2-Frank Sinatra photo on-c plus story	17	34	51	98	154	210

YOUNG LOVE (Sister title to Young Romance)
Prize(Feature)Publ.(Crestwood): 2-3/49 - No. 73, 12-1/56-57; V3#5, 2-3/60 - V7#1, 6-7/63

	GD	VG	FN	VF	VF/NM	NM-
V1#1-S&K-c/a(2)	48	96	144	298	499	700
2-Photo-c begin; S&K-a	27	54	81	158	254	350
3-S&K-a	19	38	57	112	176	240
4-6-Minor S&K-a	14	28	42	82	121	160
V2#1(#7)-S&K-a(2)	19	38	57	112	176	240
2-5(#8-11)-Minor S&K-a	14	28	42	76	108	140
6,8(#12,14)-S&K-c only. 14-S&K 1 pg. art	15	30	45	84	127	170
7,9-12(#13,15-18)-S&K-c/a	19	38	57	112	176	240
V3#1-4(#19-22)-S&K-c/a	18	36	54	103	162	220
5-7,9-12(#23-25,27-30)-Photo-c resume; S&K-a	15	30	45	86	133	180
8(#26)-No S&K-a	9	18	27	50	65	80
V4#1,6(#31,36)-S&K-a	14	28	42	82	121	160
2-5,7-12(#32-35,37-42)-Minor S&K-a	12	24	36	69	97	125
V5#1-12(#43-54), V6#1-9(#55-63)-Last precode; S&K-a in #1,2,4-6,8	9	18	27	47	61	75
V6#10-12(#64-66)	4	8	12	28	44	60
V7#1-7(#67-73)	4	8	12	24	37	50
V3#5(2-3/60),6(4-5/60)(Formerly All For Love)	4	8	12	23	36	48
V4#1(6-7/60)-6(4-5/61)	4	8	12	22	34	45
V5#1(6-7/61)-6(4-5/62)	4	8	12	22	34	45
V6#1(6-7/62)-6(4-5/63), V7#1	3	6	9	21	32	42

NOTE: ***Meskin** a-14(2), 27, 42. **Powell** a-V4#6. **Severin/Elder** a-V1#3. S&K art not in #53, 57, 61, 63-65. Photo-c most V3#5-V5#11.*

YOUNG LOVE
National Periodical Publ.(Arleigh Publ. Corp #49-61)/DC Comics:
#39, 9-10/63 - #120, Wint./75-76; #121, 10/76 - #126, 7/77

	GD	VG	FN	VF	VF/NM	NM-
39	6	12	18	37	59	80
40-50	4	8	12	26	41	55
51-68,70	4	8	12	24	37	50
69-(80 pg. Giant)(8-9/68)	6	12	18	41	66	90
71,72,74-77,80	3	6	9	19	29	38
73,78,79-Toth-a	3	6	9	20	30	40

Young Men #25 © MAR

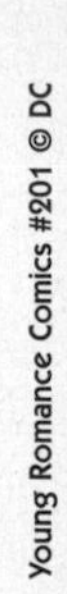

Young Romance Comics #201 © DC

Y: The Last Man #55 © Vaughan & Guerra

	GD 2.0	VG 4.0	FN 6.0	VF 8.0	VF/NM 9.0	NM- 9.2
81-99: 88-96-(52 pg. Giants)	3	6	9	18	27	35
100	3	6	9	19	29	38
101-106,115-120	3	6	9	16	22	28
107 (100 pgs.)	8	16	24	52	86	120
108-114 (100 pgs.)	7	14	21	47	76	105
121-126 (52 pgs.)	4	8	12	26	41	55

NOTE: ***Bolle** a-117. **Colan** a-107r. **Nasser** a-123, 124. **Orlando** a-122. **Simonson** c-125. **Toth** a-73, 78, 79, 122-125r. **Wood** a-109r(4 pgs.).*

YOUNG LOVER ROMANCES (Formerly & becomes Great Lover...)
Toby Press: No. 4, June, 1952 - No. 5, Aug, 1952

	GD	VG	FN	VF	VF/NM	NM-
4,5-Photo-c	9	18	27	47	61	75

YOUNG LOVERS (My Secret Life #19 on)(Formerly Brenda Starr?)
Charlton Comics: No. 16, July, 1956 - No. 18, May, 1957

	GD	VG	FN	VF	VF/NM	NM-
16,17('56): 16-Marcus Swayze-a	10	20	30	54	72	90
18-Elvis Presley picture-c, text story (biography)(Scarce)	62	124	186	391	658	925

YOUNG MARRIAGE
Fawcett Publications: June, 1950

	GD	VG	FN	VF	VF/NM	NM-
1-Powell-a; photo-c	13	26	39	74	105	135

YOUNG MEN (Formerly Cowboy Romances)(...on the Battlefield #12-20(4/53); ...In Action #21)
Marvel/Atlas Comics (IPC): No. 4, 6/50 - No. 11, 10/51; No. 12, 12/51 - No. 28, 6/54

	GD	VG	FN	VF	VF/NM	NM-
4-(52 pgs.)	20	40	60	115	183	250
5-11	14	28	42	80	115	150
12-23: 12-20-War format. 21-23-Hot Rod issues starring Flash Foster	14	28	42	76	108	140
24-(12/53)-Origin Captain America, Human Torch, & Sub-Mariner which are revived thru #28; Red Skull app.	300	600	900	1930	3315	4700
25-28: 25-Romita-c/a (see Men's Advs.). 27-Death of Golden Age Red Skull	120	240	360	756	1278	1800
25-2nd printing (1994)	2	4	6	8	10	12

NOTE: ***Berg** a-7, 14, 17, 18, 20; c-17? **Brodsky** c-4-9, 13, 14, 16, 17, 21-25. **Burgos** c-26-28. **Colan** a-14, 15, 20. **Everett** a-18-20. **Heath** a-13, 14. **Maneely** c-10-12, 15. **Pakula** a-14, 15. **Robinson** c-18. Captain America by **Romita**-#24?, 25, 26?, 27, 28. Human Torch by **Burgos**-#25, 27, 28. Sub-Mariner by **Everett**-#24-28.*

YOUNG REBELS, THE (TV)
Dell Publishing Co.: Jan, 1971

	GD	VG	FN	VF	VF/NM	NM-
1-Photo-c	3	6	9	14	19	24

YOUNG ROMANCE COMICS (The 1st romance comic)
Prize/Headline (Feature Publ.) (Crestwood): Sept-Oct, 1947 - V16#4, June-July, 1963 (#1-33: 52 pgs.)

	GD	VG	FN	VF	VF/NM	NM-
V1#1-S&K-c/a(2)	53	106	159	334	567	800
2-S&K-c/a(2-3)	35	70	105	203	327	450
3-6-S&K-c/a(2-3) each	31	62	93	181	291	400
V2#1-6(#7-12)-S&K-c/a(2-3) each	27	54	81	158	254	350
V3#1-3(#13-15): V3#1-Photo-c begin; S&K-a	18	36	54	105	165	225
4-12(#16-24)-Photo-c; S&K-a	18	36	54	105	165	225
V4#1-11(#25-35)-S&K-a	17	34	51	98	154	210
12(#36)-S&K, Toth-a	19	38	57	109	172	235
V5#1-12(#37-48), V6#4-12(#52-60)-S&K-a	17	34	51	98	154	210
V6#1-3(#49-51)-No S&K-a	10	20	30	54	72	90
V7#1-11(#61-71)-S&K-a in most	14	28	42	82	121	160
V7#12(#72), V8#1-3(#73-75)-Last precode (12-1/54-55)-No S&K-a	9	18	27	47	61	75
V8#4(#76, 4-5/55), 5(#77)-No S&K-a	8	16	24	42	54	65
V8#6-8(#78-80, 12-1/55-56)-S&K-a	12	24	36	69	97	125
V9#3,5,6(#81, 2-3/56, 83,84)-S&K-a	12	24	36	69	97	125
4, V10#1(#82,85)-All S&K-a	13	26	39	74	105	135
V10#2-6(#86-90, 10-11/57)-S&K-a	8	16	24	54	90	125
V11#1,2,5,6(#91,92,95,96)-S&K-a	8	16	24	54	90	125
3,4(#93,94), V12#2,4,5(#98,100,101)-No S&K	4	8	12	28	44	60
V12#1,3,6(#97,99,102)-S&K-a	8	16	24	54	90	125
V13#1(#103)-Powell-a; S&K's last-a for Crestwood	8	16	24	54	90	125
2,4-6(#104-108)	4	8	12	24	37	50
V13#3(#105, 4-5/60)-Elvis Presley-c app. only	6	12	18	43	69	95
V14#1-6, V15#1-6, V16#1-4(#109-124)	4	8	12	22	34	45

NOTE: ***Meskin** a-16, 24(2), 33, 47, 50. **Robinson/Meskin** a-6. **Leonard Starr** a-11. Photo c-13-32, 34-65. Issues 1-3 say "Designed for the More **Adult** Readers of **Comics**" on cover.*

YOUNG ROMANCE COMICS (Continued from Prize series)
National Periodical Publ.(Arleigh Publ. Corp. No. 127): No. 125, Aug-Sept, 1963 - No. 208, Nov-Dec, 1975

	GD	VG	FN	VF	VF/NM	NM-
125	7	14	21	47	76	105
126-140	4	8	12	28	44	60
141-153,156-162,165-169	3	6	9	21	32	42
154-Neal Adams-c	5	10	15	30	48	65
155-1st publ. Aragonés-s (no art)	4	8	12	28	44	60
163,164-Toth-a	4	8	12	24	37	50
170-172 (68 pg. Giants): 170-Michell from Young Love ends; Lily Martin, the Swinger begins	4	8	12	28	44	60
173-183 (52 pgs.)	4	8	12	22	34	45
184-196	3	6	9	16	23	30
197-204-(100 pgs.)	7	14	21	47	76	105
205-208	3	6	9	16	22	28

YOUNG X-MEN
Marvel Comics: May, 2008 - Present ($2.99)

	GD	VG	FN	VF	VF/NM	NM-
1-6: 1-Cyclops forms new team; Guggenheim-s/Paquette-a/Dodson-c						3.00

YOUR DREAMS (See Strange World of...)

YOUR UNITED STATES
Lloyd Jacquet Studios: 1946

	GD	VG	FN	VF	VF/NM	NM-
nn-Used in **SOTI**, pg. 309,310; Sid Greene-a	23	46	69	133	214	295

YOUTHFUL HEARTS (Daring Confessions #4 on)
Youthful Magazines: May, 1952 - No. 3, Sept, 1952

	GD	VG	FN	VF	VF/NM	NM-
1- "Monkey on Her Back" swipes E.C. drug story/Shock SuspenStories #12; Frankie Laine photo on-c; Doug Wildey-a in al	29	58	87	169	272	375
2,3: 2-Vic Damone photo on-c. 3-Johnny Raye photo on-c	20	40	60	115	183	250

YOUTHFUL LOVE (Truthful Love #2)
Youthful Magazines: May, 1950

	GD	VG	FN	VF	VF/NM	NM-
1	14	28	42	80	115	150

YOUTHFUL ROMANCES
Pix-Parade #1-14/Ribage #15 on: 8-9/49 - No. 5, 4/50; No. 6, 2/51; No. 7, 5/51 - #14, 10/52; #15, 1/53 - #18, 7/53; No. 5, 9/53 - No. 9, 8/54

	GD	VG	FN	VF	VF/NM	NM-
1-(1st series)-Titled Youthful Love-Romances	26	52	78	152	244	335
2-Walter Johnson c-1-4	15	30	45	90	140	190
3-5	14	28	42	80	115	150
6,7,9-14(10/52, Pix-Parade; becomes Daring Love #15). 10(1/52)-Mel Torme photo-c/story. 12-Tony Bennett photo-c, 8pg. story & text bio.13-Richard Hayes (singer) photo-c/story; Bob & Ray photo/text story.	13	26	39	74	105	135
8-Frank Sinatra photo/text story; Wood-c/a	19	38	57	109	172	235
15-18 (Ribage)-All have photos on-c. 15-Spike Jones photo-c/story. 16-Tony Bavaar photo-c	12	24	36	69	97	125
5(9/53, Ribage)-Les Paul & Mary Ford photo-c/story; Charlton Heston photo/text story	11	22	33	64	90	115
6-9: 6-Bobby Wayne (singer) photo-c/story; Debbie Reynolds photo/text story. 7(2/54)-Tony Martin photo-c/story; Cyd Charise photo/text story. 8(5/54)-Gordon McCrae photo-c/story. (8/54)-Ralph Flanagan (band leader) photo-c/story; Audrey Hepburn photo/text story	11	22	33	60	83	105

Y: THE LAST MAN
DC Comics (Vertigo): Sept, 2002 - No. 60, Mar, 2008 ($2.95/$2.99)

	GD	VG	FN	VF	VF/NM	NM-
1-Intro. Yorick Brown; Vaughan-s/Guerra-a/J.G. Jones-c	2	4	6	8	10	12
2	1	2	3	5	6	8
3-5						6.00
6-59: 16,17-Chadwick-a. 21,22-Parlov-a. 32,39-41,48,53,54-Sudzuka-a.						3.00
60-($4.99) Final issue; sixty years in the future						5.00
... Double Feature Edition (2002, $5.95) r/#1,2						6.00
... - Cycles TPB (2003, $12.95) r/#6-10; sketch pages by Guerra						13.00
... - Girl on Girl TPB (2005, $12.99) r/#32-36						13.00
... - Kimono Dragons TPB (2006, $14.99) r/#43-48						15.00
... - Motherland TPB (2007, $14.99) r/#49-54						15.00
... - One Small Step TPB (2004, $12.95) r/#11-17						13.00
... - Paper Dolls TPB (2006, $14.99) r/#37-42						15.00
... - Ring of Truth TPB (2005, $14.99) r/#24-31						15.00
... - Safeword TPB (2004, $12.95) r/#18-23						13.00
... - Unmanned TPB (2002, $12.95) r/#1-5						13.00
... - Whys and Wherefores TPB (2008, $14.99) r/#55-60						15.00

Y2K: THE COMIC
New England Comics Press: Oct, 1999 ($3.95, one-shot)

	GD	VG	FN	VF	VF/NM	NM-
1-Y2K scenarios and survival tips						4.00

YUPPIES FROM HELL (Also see Son of...)
Marvel Comics: 1989 ($2.95, B&W, one-shot, direct sales, 52 pgs.)

	GD	VG	FN	VF	VF/NM	NM-
1-Satire						3.00

Zane Grey Four Color #555 © DELL

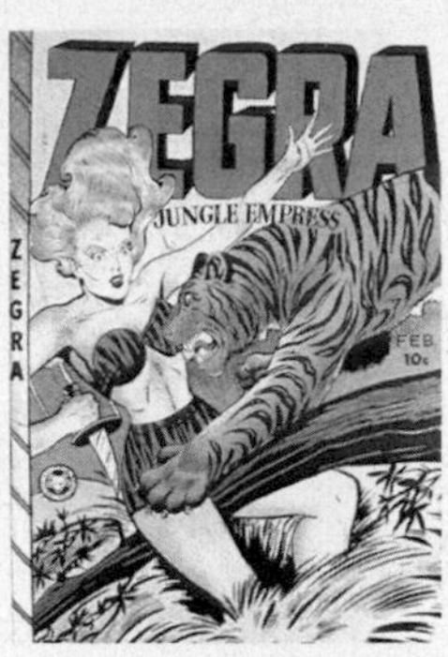

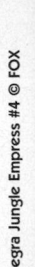

Zegra Jungle Empress #4 © FOX

Zero Killer #3 © Arvid Nelson

ZAGO, JUNGLE PRINCE (My Story #5 on)
Fox Features Syndicate: Sept, 1948 - No. 4, Mar, 1949

	GD 2.0	VG 4.0	FN 6.0	VF 8.0	VF/NM 9.0	NM- 9.2
1-Blue Beetle app.; partial-r/Atomic #4 (Toni Luck)	62	124	186	391	658	925
2,3-Kamen-a	50	100	150	310	518	725
4-Baker-c	41	82	123	256	428	600

ZANE GREY'S STORIES OF THE WEST
Dell Publishing Co./Gold Key 11/64: No. 197, 9/48 - No. 996, 5-7/59; 11/64 (All painted-c)

	GD 2.0	VG 4.0	FN 6.0	VF 8.0	VF/NM 9.0	NM- 9.2
Four Color 197(#1)(9/48)	11	22	33	79	140	200
Four Color 222,230,236('49)	7	14	21	47	76	105
Four Color 246,255,270,301,314,333,346	5	10	15	32	51	70
Four Color 357,372,395,412,433,449,467,484	4	8	12	28	44	60
Four Color 511-Kinstler-a; Kubert-a	5	10	15	32	51	70
Four Color 532,555,583,604,616,632(5/55)	4	8	12	28	44	60
27(9-11/55) - 39(9-11/58)	4	8	12	28	44	60
Four Color 996(5-7/59)	4	8	12	28	44	60
10131-411-(11/64-G.K.)-Nevada; r/4-Color #996	3	6	9	20	30	40

ZANY (Magazine)(Satire)(See Frantic & Ratfink)
Candor Publ. Co.: Sept, 1958 - No. 4, May, 1959

	GD 2.0	VG 4.0	FN 6.0	VF 8.0	VF/NM 9.0	NM- 9.2
1-Bill Everett-c	12	24	36	67	94	120
2-4: 4-Everett-c	9	18	27	47	61	75

ZATANNA (See Adv. Comics #413, JLA #161, Supergirl #1, World's Finest Comics #274)
DC Comics: July, 1993 - No. 4, Oct, 1993 ($1.95, limited series)

	GD 2.0	VG 4.0	FN 6.0	VF 8.0	VF/NM 9.0	NM- 9.2
1-4						2.50
...: Everyday Magic (2003, $5.95, one-shot) Dini-s/Mays-a/Bolland-c; Constantine app.						6.00
Special 1(1987, $2.00)-Gray Morrow-c/a						3.00

ZAZA, THE MYSTIC (Formerly Charlie Chan; This Magazine Is Haunted V2#12 on)
Charlton Comics: No. 10, Apr, 1956 - No. 11, Sept, 1956

	GD 2.0	VG 4.0	FN 6.0	VF 8.0	VF/NM 9.0	NM- 9.2
10,11	12	24	36	69	97	125

ZEALOT (Also see WildC.A.T.S. Covert Action Teams)
Image Comics: Aug, 1995 - No. 3, Nov, 1995 ($2.50, limited series)

	GD 2.0	VG 4.0	FN 6.0	VF 8.0	VF/NM 9.0	NM- 9.2
1-3						2.50

ZEGRA JUNGLE EMPRESS (Formerly Tegra)(My Love Life #6 on)
Fox Features Syndicate: No. 2, Oct, 1948 - No. 5, April, 1949

	GD 2.0	VG 4.0	FN 6.0	VF 8.0	VF/NM 9.0	NM- 9.2
2	62	124	186	391	658	925
3-5	48	96	144	298	499	700

ZEN (Intergalactic Ninja)
Zen Comics Publishing: No. 0, Apr, 2003 - No. 4, Aug, 2003 ($2.95)

	GD 2.0	VG 4.0	FN 6.0	VF 8.0	VF/NM 9.0	NM- 9.2
0-4-Bill Maus-a/Steve Stern-s. 0-Wraparound-c						3.00

ZEN INTERGALACTIC NINJA
No Publisher: 1987 -1993 ($1.75/$2.00, B&W)

	GD 2.0	VG 4.0	FN 6.0	VF 8.0	VF/NM 9.0	NM- 9.2
1	2	4	6	10	14	18
2-6: Copyright-Stern & Cote	1	3	4	6	8	10
V2#1-4-($2.00)						3.00
V3#1-5-($2.95)						3.00
... :Christmas Special 1 (1992, $2.95)						3.00
... :Earth Day Special 1 (1993, $2.95)						3.00

ZEN, INTERGALACTIC NINJA (mini-series)
Zen Comics/Archie Comics: Sept, 1992 - No. 3, 1992 ($1.25)(Formerly a B&W comic by Zen Comics)

	GD 2.0	VG 4.0	FN 6.0	VF 8.0	VF/NM 9.0	NM- 9.2
1-3: 1-Origin Zen; contains mini-poster						3.00

ZEN INTERGALACTIC NINJA
Entity Comics: No. 0, June-July, 1993 - No. 3, 1994 ($2.95, B&W, limited series)

	GD 2.0	VG 4.0	FN 6.0	VF 8.0	VF/NM 9.0	NM- 9.2
0-Gold foil stamped-c; photo-c of Zen model						3.00
1-3: Gold foil stamped-c; Bill Maus-c/a						3.00
0-(1993, $3.50, color)-Chromium-c by Jae Lee						3.50
...Sourcebook 1-(1993, $3.50)						3.50
...Sourcebook '94-(1994, $3.50)						3.50

ZEN INTERGALACTIC NINJA: APRIL FOOL'S SPECIAL
Parody Press: 1994 ($2.50, B&W)

	GD 2.0	VG 4.0	FN 6.0	VF 8.0	VF/NM 9.0	NM- 9.2
1-w/flip story of Renn Intergalactic Chihuahua						3.00

ZEN INTERGALACTIC NINJA COLOR
Entity Comics: 1994 - No. 7, 1995 ($2.25)

	GD 2.0	VG 4.0	FN 6.0	VF 8.0	VF/NM 9.0	NM- 9.2
1-($3.95)-Chromium die cut-c						4.00
1, 0-($2.25)-Newsstand; Jae Lee-c; r/...All New Color Special #0						3.00
2-($2.50)-Flip book						3.00
2-($3.50)-Flip book, polybagged w/chromium trading card						3.50
3-7						3.00
Summer Special (1994, $2.95)						3.00
Yearbook: Hazardous Duty 1 (1995)						3.00
Zen-isms 1 (1995, 2.95)						3.00
Ashcan-Tour of the Universe-(no price) w/flip cover						3.00

ZEN INTERGALACTIC NINJA COMMEMORATIVE EDITION
Zen Comics Publishing: 1997 ($5.95, color)

	GD 2.0	VG 4.0	FN 6.0	VF 8.0	VF/NM 9.0	NM- 9.2
1-Stern-s/Cote-a						6.00

ZEN INTERGALACTIC NINJA MILESTONE
Entity Comics: 1994 - No. 3, 1994 ($2.95, limited series)

	GD 2.0	VG 4.0	FN 6.0	VF 8.0	VF/NM 9.0	NM- 9.2
1-3: Gold foil logo; r/Defend the Earth						3.00

ZEN INTERGALATIC NINJA SPRING SPECTACULAR
Entity Comics: 1994 ($2.95, B&W, one-shot)

	GD 2.0	VG 4.0	FN 6.0	VF 8.0	VF/NM 9.0	NM- 9.2
1-Gold foil logo						3.00

ZEN INTERGALATIC NINJA STARQUEST
Entity Comics: 1994 - No. 6, 1995 ($2.95, B&W)

	GD 2.0	VG 4.0	FN 6.0	VF 8.0	VF/NM 9.0	NM- 9.2
1-6: Gold foil logo						3.00

ZEN, INTERGALACTIC NINJA: THE HUNTED
Entity Comics: 1993 - No. 3, 1994 ($2.95, B&W, limited series)

	GD 2.0	VG 4.0	FN 6.0	VF 8.0	VF/NM 9.0	NM- 9.2
1-3: Newsstand Edition; foil logo						3.00
1-($3.50)-Polybagged w/chromium card by Kieth; foil logo						3.50

ZERO GIRL
DC Comics (Homage): Feb, 2001 - No. 5, Jun, 2001 ($2.95, limited series)

	GD 2.0	VG 4.0	FN 6.0	VF 8.0	VF/NM 9.0	NM- 9.2
1-5-Sam Kieth-s/a						3.00
TPB (2001, $14.95) r/#1-5; intro. by Alan Moore						15.00

ZERO GIRL: FULL CIRCLE
DC Comics (Homage): Jan, 2003 - No. 5, May, 2003 ($2.95, limited series)

	GD 2.0	VG 4.0	FN 6.0	VF 8.0	VF/NM 9.0	NM- 9.2
1-5-Sam Kieth-s/a						3.00
TPB (2003, $17.95) r/#1-5						18.00

ZERO HOUR: CRISIS IN TIME (Also see Showcase '94 #8-10)
DC Comics: No. 4(#1), Sept, 1994 - No. 0(#5), Oct, 1994 ($1.50, limited series)

	GD 2.0	VG 4.0	FN 6.0	VF 8.0	VF/NM 9.0	NM- 9.2
4(#1)-0(#5)						4.00
"Ashcan"-(1994, free, B&W, 8 pgs.) several versions exist						2.25
TPB ('94, $9.95)						10.00

ZERO KILLER
Dark Horse Comics: Jul, 2007 - Present ($2.99)

	GD 2.0	VG 4.0	FN 6.0	VF 8.0	VF/NM 9.0	NM- 9.2
1-3-Arvid Nelson-s/Matt Camp-a						3.00

ZERO PATROL, THE
Continuity Comics: Nov, 1984 - No. 2 ($1.50); 1987 - No. 5, May, 1989 ($2.00)

	GD 2.0	VG 4.0	FN 6.0	VF 8.0	VF/NM 9.0	NM- 9.2
1,2: Neal Adams-c/a; Megalith begins						4.00
1-5 (#1,2-reprints above, 1987)						3.00

ZERO TOLERANCE
First Comics: Oct, 1990 - No. 4, Jan, 1991 ($2.25, limited series)

	GD 2.0	VG 4.0	FN 6.0	VF 8.0	VF/NM 9.0	NM- 9.2
1-4: Tim Vigil-c/a(p) (his 1st color limited series)						3.00

ZERO ZERO
Fantagraphics: Mar, 1995 -No. 27 ($3.95/$4.95, B&W, anthology, mature)

	GD 2.0	VG 4.0	FN 6.0	VF 8.0	VF/NM 9.0	NM- 9.2
1-7,9-15,17-25						5.00
8,16						6.00
26-($4.95) Bagge-c						5.00

ZIGGY PIG-SILLY SEAL COMICS (See Animal Fun, Animated Movie-Tunes, Comic Capers, Krazy Komics, Silly Tunes & Super Rabbit)
Timely Comics (CmPL): Fall, 1944 - No. 4, Summer, 1945; No. 5, Summer, 1946; No. 6, Sept, 1946

	GD 2.0	VG 4.0	FN 6.0	VF 8.0	VF/NM 9.0	NM- 9.2
1-Vs. the Japanese	27	54	81	158	254	350
2-(Spring, 1945)	15	30	45	83	124	165
3-5	14	28	42	78	112	145
6-Infinity-c	15	30	45	85	130	175
I.W. Reprint #1(1958)-r/Krazy Komics	2	4	6	9	13	16
I.W. Reprint #2,7,8	2	4	6	9	13	16

ZIP COMICS
MLJ Magazines: Feb, 1940 - No. 47, Summer, 1944 (#1-7?: 68 pgs.)

	GD 2.0	VG 4.0	FN 6.0	VF 8.0	VF/NM 9.0	NM- 9.2
1-Origin Kalathar the Giant Man, The Scarlet Avenger, & Steel Sterling; Mr. Satan (by Edd Ashe), Nevada Jones (masked hero) & Zambini, the Miracle Man, War Eagle, Captain Valor begins	506	1012	1518	3643	6372	9100
2-Nevada Jones adds mask & horse Blaze	243	486	729	1531	2591	3650

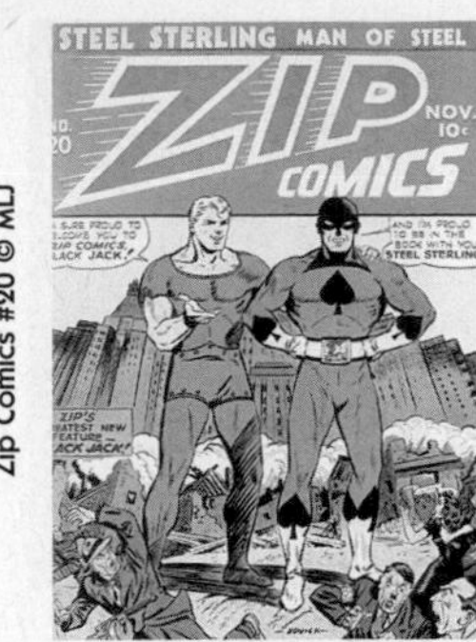

Zip Comics #20 © MLJ

Zombie Proof #3 © J.C. Vaughn & Vincent Spencer

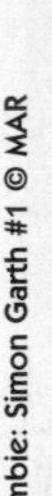
Zombie: Simon Garth #1 © MAR

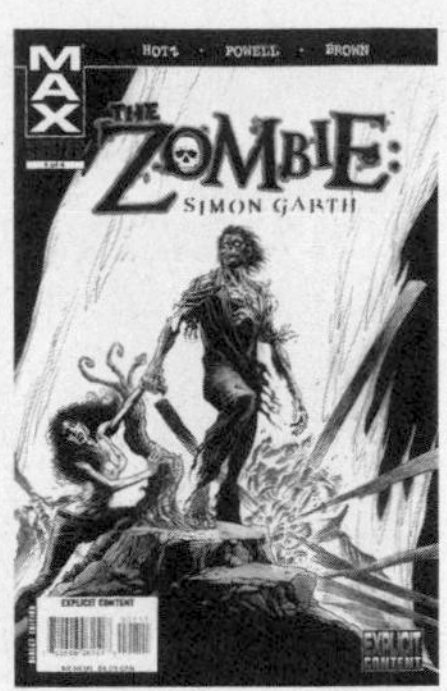

	GD 2.0	VG 4.0	FN 6.0	VF 8.0	VF/NM 9.0	NM- 9.2
3-Biro robot-c	200	400	600	1260	2130	3000
4,5-Biro WW2-c	160	320	480	1008	1704	2400
6-8-Biro-c	140	280	420	882	1491	2100
9-Last Kalathar & Mr. Satan; classic-c	158	316	474	995	1685	2375
10-Inferno, the Flame Breather begins, ends #13	150	300	450	945	1598	2250
11,12: 11-Inferno without costume	110	220	330	693	1172	1650
13-Electrocution-c	127	254	381	800	1350	1900
14,16,19	103	206	309	649	1100	1550
15-Classic spider-c	137	274	411	863	1457	2050
17-Last Scarlet Avenger; women in bondage being cooked alive-c by Biro	130	260	390	819	1385	1950
18-Wilbur begins (9/41, 1st app.)	130	260	390	819	1385	1950
20-Origin & 1st app. Black Jack (11/41); Hitler-c	177	354	531	1115	1883	2650
21,23-26: 25-Last Nevada Jones. 26-Black Witch begins; last Captain Valor; "Remember Pearl Harbor!" cover caption	93	186	279	586	993	1400
22-Classic-c	160	320	480	1008	1704	2400
27-Intro. Web (7/42) plus-c app.	180	360	540	1134	1917	2700
28-Origin Web	153	306	459	964	1632	2300
29-The Hyena app. (scarce)	80	160	240	504	852	1200
30	62	124	186	391	658	925
31,33-38: 34-1st Applejack app. 35-Last Zambini, Black Jack. 38-Last Web issue	50	100	150	310	518	725
32-Classic skeleton Nazi WW2-c	80	160	240	504	852	1200
39-Red Rube begins (origin, 8/43)	50	100	150	310	518	725
40-46: 45-Wilbur ends	45	90	135	279	465	650
47-Last issue; scarce	47	94	141	291	483	675

NOTE: ***Biro** a-5, 9, 17; c-3-17. **Meskin** a-1-3, 5-7, 9, 10, 12, 13, 15, 16 at least. **Montana** c-29, 30, 32-35. **Novick** c-18-28, 31. **Sahle** c-37, 38, 40-46. Bondage c-8, 9, 33, 34. Cover features: Steel Sterling-1-43, 47; (w/Blackjack-20-27 & Web-27-35), 28-39; (w/Red Rube-40-43); Red Rube-44-47.*

ZIP-JET (Hero)
St. John Publishing Co.: Feb, 1953 - No. 2, Apr-May, 1953

	GD 2.0	VG 4.0	FN 6.0	VF 8.0	VF/NM 9.0	NM- 9.2
1-Rocketman-r from Punch Comics; #1-c from splash in Punch #10	77	154	231	481	816	1150
2	49	98	147	304	507	710

ZIPPY THE CHIMP (CBS TV Presents...)
Pines (Literary Ent.): No. 50, March, 1957; No. 51, Aug, 1957

	GD 2.0	VG 4.0	FN 6.0	VF 8.0	VF/NM 9.0	NM- 9.2
50,51	8	16	24	40	50	60

ZODY, THE MOD ROB
Gold Key: July, 1970

	GD 2.0	VG 4.0	FN 6.0	VF 8.0	VF/NM 9.0	NM- 9.2
1	3	6	9	16	23	30

ZOMBIE
Marvel Comics: Nov, 2006 - No. 4, Feb, 2007 ($3.99, limited series)

	NM- 9.2
1-4-Kyle Hotz-a/c; Mike Raicht-s	4.00
TPB (2007, $13.99) r/#1-4	14.00
...: Simon Garth (1/08 - No. 4, 4/08) Hotz-s/a/c	4.00

ZOMBIE KING
Image Comics: No. 0, June, 2005 ($2.95, B&W, one-shot)

	NM- 9.2
0-Frank Cho-s/a	5.00

ZOMBIE PROOF
Moonstone: 2007 - Present ($3.50)

	NM- 9.2
1-3: 1-J.C. Vaughn-s/Vincent Spencer-a; two covers by Spencer and Neil Vokes	3.50
1-Baltimore Comic-Con 2007 variant-c by Vokes (ltd. ed. of 500)	5.00
2-Big Apple 2008 Convention Edition; Tucci-c (ltd. ed. of 250)	5.00
3-Convention Edition; Beck-c (ltd. ed. of 100)	5.00

ZOMBIES!: ECLIPSE OF THE UNDEAD
IDW Publ.: Nov, 2006 - No. 4, Feb, 2007 ($3.99, limited series)

	NM- 9.2
1-4-Torres-s/Herrera-a; two covers	4.00

ZOMBIES!: FEAST
IDW Publ.: May, 2006 - No. 5, Oct, 2006 ($3.99, limited series)

	NM- 9.2
1-5: 1-Chris Bolton-a/Shane McCarthy-s. 3-Lorenzana-a	4.00

ZOMBIES!: HUNTERS
IDW Publ.: May, 2008 - Present ($3.99, limited series)

	NM- 9.2
1-Don Figueroa-a/c; Dara Naraghi-s	4.00

ZOMBIE TALES THE SERIES
BOOM! Studios: Apr, 2008 - Present ($3.99)

	NM- 9.2
1-Niles-s; Lansdale-s/Barreto-a	4.00

ZOMBIE WORLD (one-shots)
Dark Horse Comics

	NM- 9.2
... :Eat Your Heart Out (4/98, $2.95) Kelley Jones-c/s/a	3.00
... :Home For The Holidays (12/97, $2.95)	3.00

ZOMBIE WORLD: CHAMPION OF THE WORMS
Dark Horse Comics: Sept, 1997 - No. 3, Nov, 1997 ($2.95, limited series)

	NM- 9.2
1-3-Mignola & McEown-c/s/a	3.00

ZOMBIE WORLD: DEAD END
Dark Horse Comics: Jan, 1998 - No. 2, Feb, 1998 ($2.95, limited series)

	NM- 9.2
1,2-Stephen Blue-c/s/a	3.00

ZOMBIE WORLD: TREE OF DEATH
Dark Horse Comics: Jun, 1999 - No. 4, Oct, 1999 ($2.95, limited series)

	NM- 9.2
1-4-Mills-s/Deadstock-a	3.00

ZOMBIE WORLD: WINTER'S DREGS
Dark Horse Comics: May, 1998 - No. 4, Aug, 1998 ($2.95, limited series)

	NM- 9.2
1-4-Fingerman-s/Edwards-a	3.00

ZONE (Also see Dark Horse Presents)
Dark Horse Comics: 1990 ($1.95, B&W)

	NM- 9.2
1-Character from Dark Horse Presents	2.50

ZONE CONTINUUM, THE
Caliber Press: 1994 ($2.95, B&W)

	NM- 9.2
1	3.00

ZOO ANIMALS
Star Publications: No. 8, 1954 (15¢, 36 pgs.)

	GD 2.0	VG 4.0	FN 6.0	VF 8.0	VF/NM 9.0	NM- 9.2
8-(B&W for coloring)	7	14	21	37	46	55

ZOO FUNNIES (Tim McCoy #16 on)
Charlton Comics/Children Comics Publ.: Nov, 1945 - No. 15, 1947

	GD 2.0	VG 4.0	FN 6.0	VF 8.0	VF/NM 9.0	NM- 9.2
101(#1)(11/45, 1st Charlton comic book)-Funny animal; Al Fago-c	21	42	63	123	197	270
2(12/45, 52 pgs.) Classic-c	15	30	45	83	124	165
3-5	11	22	33	62	86	110
6-15: 8-Diana the Huntress app.	9	18	27	52	69	85

ZOO FUNNIES (Becomes Nyoka, The Jungle Girl #14 on?)
Capitol Stories/Charlton Comics: July, 1953 - No. 13, Sept, 1955; Dec, 1984

	GD 2.0	VG 4.0	FN 6.0	VF 8.0	VF/NM 9.0	NM- 9.2
1-1st app.? Timothy The Ghost; Fago-c/a	11	22	33	64	90	115
2	8	16	24	42	54	65
3-7	7	14	21	37	46	55
8-13-Nyoka app.	9	18	27	52	69	85
1(1984) (Low print run)						6.00

ZOONIVERSE
Eclipse Comics: 8/86 - No. 6, 6/87 ($1.25/$1.75, limited series, Mando paper)

	NM- 9.2
1-6	2.50

ZOO PARADE (TV)
Dell Publishing Co.: #662, 1955 (Marlin Perkins)

	GD 2.0	VG 4.0	FN 6.0	VF 8.0	VF/NM 9.0	NM- 9.2
Four Color 662	5	10	15	32	51	70

ZOOM COMICS
Carlton Publishing Co.: Dec, 1945 (one-shot)

	GD 2.0	VG 4.0	FN 6.0	VF 8.0	VF/NM 9.0	NM- 9.2
nn-Dr. Mercy, Satannas, from Red Band Comics; Capt. Milksop origin retold	40	80	120	235	380	525

ZOOT (Rulah Jungle Goddess #17 on)
Fox Features Syndicate: nd (1946) - No. 16, July, 1948 (Two #13s & 14s)

	GD 2.0	VG 4.0	FN 6.0	VF 8.0	VF/NM 9.0	NM- 9.2
nn-Funny animal only	21	42	63	123	197	270
2-The Jaguar app.	19	38	57	109	172	235
3(Fall, 1946) - 6-Funny animals & teen-age	12	24	36	69	77	125
7-(6/47)-Rulah, Jungle Goddess (origin/1st app.)	103	206	309	649	1100	1550
8-10	70	140	210	441	746	1050
11-Kamen bondage-c	73	146	219	460	780	1100
12-Injury-to-eye panels, torture scene	52	104	156	322	541	760
13(2/48)	52	104	156	322	541	760
14(3/48)-Used in **SOTI**, pg. 104, "One picture showing a girl nailed by her wrists to trees with blood flowing from the wounds, might be taken straight from an ill. ed. of the Marquis deSade"	67	134	201	422	711	1000
13(4/48),14(5/48)-Western True Crime #15 on?	52	104	156	322	541	760
15,16	52	104	156	322	541	760

ZORRO (Walt Disney with #882)(TV)(See Eclipse Graphic Album)
Dell Publishing Co.: May, 1949 - No. 15, Sept-Nov, 1961 (Photo-c 882 on)
(Zorro first appeared in a pulp story Aug 19, 1919)

Zoot #12 © FOX

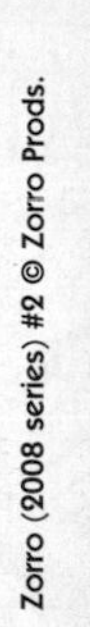

Zorro (2008 series) #2 © Zorro Prods.

Zot! #25 © Scott McCloud

	GD 2.0	VG 4.0	FN 6.0	VF 8.0	VF/NM 9.0	NM- 9.2
Four Color 228 (#1)	20	40	60	143	264	385
Four Color 425,617,732	12	24	36	82	146	210
Four Color 497,538,574-Kinstler-a	12	24	36	87	156	225
Four Color 882-Photo-c begin;1st TV Disney; Toth-a	15	30	45	105	190	275
Four Color 920,933,960,976-Toth-a in all	11	22	33	80	143	205
Four Color 1003('59)-Toth-a	11	22	33	80	140	205
Four Color 1037-Annette Funicello photo-c	14	28	42	100	178	255
8(12-2/59-60)	8	16	24	56	93	130
9-Toth-a	9	18	27	60	100	140
10,11,13-15-Last photo-c	8	16	24	54	90	125
12-Toth-a; last 10¢ issue	9	18	27	60	100	140

NOTE: ***Warren Tufts** a-4-Color 1037, 8, 9, 10, 13.*

ZORRO (Walt Disney)(TV)
Gold Key: Jan, 1966 - No. 9, Mar, 1968 (All photo-c)

	GD	VG	FN	VF	VF/NM	NM-
1-Toth-a	8	16	24	52	86	120
2,4,5,7-9-Toth-a. 5-r/F.C. #1003 by Toth	5	10	15	30	48	65
3,6-Tufts-a	4	8	12	28	44	60

NOTE: *#1-9 are reprinted from Dell issues. **Tufts** a-3, 4. #1-r/F.C. #882. #2-r/F.C. #960. #3-r/#12-c & #8 inside. #4-r/#9-c & insides. #6-r/#11(all); #7-r/#14-c. #8-r/F.C. #933 inside & back-c & #976-c. #9-r/F.C. #920.*

ZORRO (TV)
Marvel Comics: Dec, 1990 - No. 12, Nov, 1991 ($1.00)

1-12: Based on TV show. 12-Toth-c	3.00

ZORRO (Also see Mask of Zorro)
Topps Comics: Nov, 1993 - No. 11, Nov, 1994 ($2.50/$2.95)

	GD	VG	FN	VF	VF/NM	NM-
0-(11/93, $1.00, 20 pgs.)-Painted-c; collector's ed.						2.50
1,4,6-9,11: 1-Miller-c. 4-Mike Grell-c. 6-Mignola-c. 7-Lady Rawhide-c by Gulacy. 8-Perez-c. 10-Julie Bell-c. 11-Lady Rawhide-c						3.00
2-Lady Rawhide-app. (not in costume)						5.00
3-1st app. Lady Rawhide in costume, 3-Lady Rawhide-c by Adam Hughes	1	2	3	5	6	8
5-Lady Rawhide app.						4.00
10-($2.95)-Lady Rawhide-c/app.						3.00
The Lady Wears Red (12/98, $12.95, TPB) r/#1-3						13.00
Zorro's Renegades (2/99, $14.95, TPB) r/#4-8						15.00

ZORRO
Dynamite Entertainment: 2008 - Present ($3.50)

1-8-Origin retold; Wagner-s. 1-Three covers. 2-5-Two covers	3.50

ZOT!
Eclipse Comics: 4/84 - No. 10, 7/85; No. 11, 1/87 - No. 36 7/91 ($1.50, Baxter-p)

1	5.00
2,3	4.00
4-10: 4-Origin. 10-Last color issue	3.00
10 1/2 (6/86, 25¢, Not Available Comics) Ashcan; art by Feazell & Scott McCloud	4.00
11-14,15-35-($2.00-c) B&W issues	3.00
14 1/2 (Adventures of Zot! in Dimension 10 1/2)(7/87) Antisocialman app.	3.00
36-($2.95-c) B&W	4.00
... The Complete Black and White Collection TPB (2008, $24.95) r/#11-36 with commentary, interviews and bonus artwork	25.00

Z-2 COMICS (Secret Agent...)(See Holyoke One-Shot #7)

ZULU (See Movie Classics)

WALT DISNEY'S
Mickey Mouse
The POINTER
In Technicolor
RELEASED THROUGH R-K-O RADIO

No. 1
JUNE, 1938
ACTION COMICS
10¢

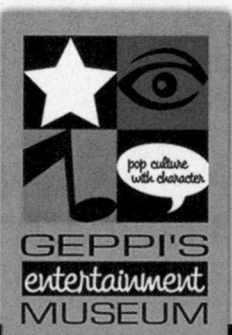

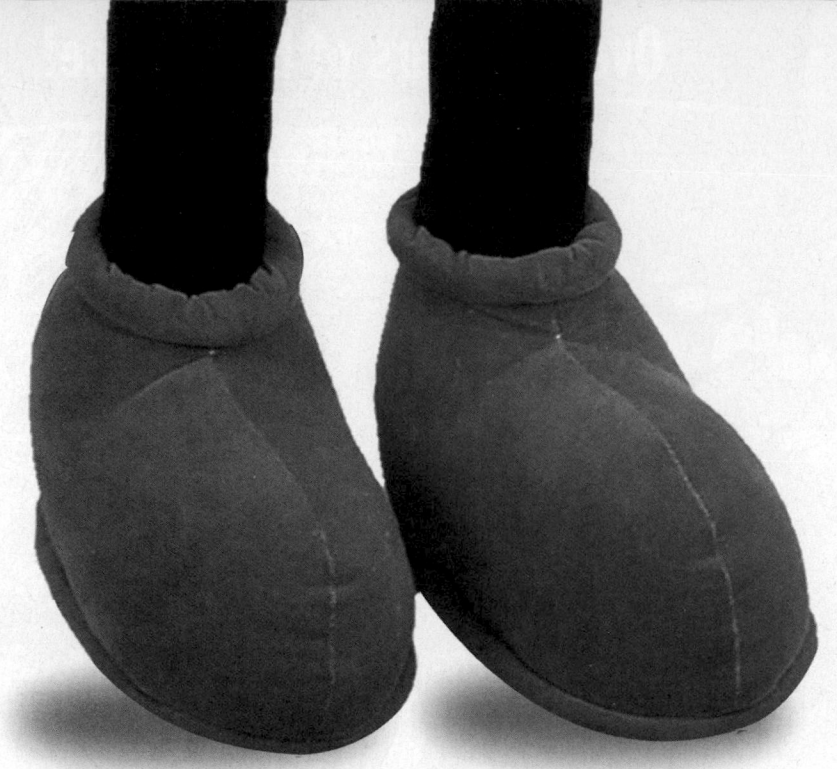

Don't Be Left Out!
Order HOGAN'S ALLEY
NOW!
Four issues only $22.95
Begin my subscription with HOGAN'S ALLEY #15!
I enclose $22.95 for four issues!
Begin my subscription with HOGAN'S ALLEY #15, and send me HOGAN'S ALLEY #14, immediately!
I enclose $29.95 for five issues!
Begin my subscription with HOGAN'S ALLEY #15, and send me both HOGAN'S ALLEY #13 and #14 immediately! I enclose $36.95 for six issues!
Limited back issues available. Please check box and remit payment. Price includes postage.
Issue #4 ($10)
Issue #5 ($10)
Issue #6 ($10)
Issue #7 ($10)
Issue #8 ($10)
Issue #9 ($10)
Issue #10 ($10)
Issue #11 ($7)
Issue #12 ($7)
Issue #13 ($7)
Issue #14 ($7)
(#1–3 SOLD OUT)
Name
Address
City
State, Zip
Send your check or money order to:
HOGAN'S ALLEY, P.O. BOX 47684, ATLANTA, GA 30362
OCBPG

WANTED
Original
Comic Art
A MARVEL MASTERWORK
YANCY ST.
THIS IS VERY EMBARRASSIN'!
THE AMAZING
SPIDER-MAN
Collector buying
any art from the
30's to the present.
Over the last 4 years I
have spent over
$1,000,000 and have
paid record prices.
Kirby, Byrne, Ditko, Perez,
Wood, Fine, Adams, Lee, Ross,
Steranko, Romita, Anderson,
Frazetta, Infantino, Wrightson,
and Miller are just some of the
artists I'm looking for.
Bechara Maalouf
PO Box 31
Marshfield MA 02059
781.910.6704
spideyslayer1@aol.com

COMICS TO ASTONISH
9400 SNOWDEN RIVER PKWY
COLUMBIA, MD 21045
MONDAY-SATURDAY 12-8PM
410-381-2732
OFFICIAL CGC SUBMISSION CENTER!
CONTACT:
KEEGAN F. CONRAD
410-381-2732
COMICS2U@AOL.COM
WE HAVE OVER 80,000 BACK ISSUES!
NOVA ROCKS!
WE BUY!
- ALL COMICS 30'S TO 80'S!
- ENTIRE COLLECTIONS!
- BRONZE TO GOLDEN AGE!
- GRADED BOOKS!
CHECK OUT OUR WEB COMIC AT:
WWW.FATGUYBLACKGUYBALDGUY.COM
WWW.COMICSTOASTONISH.COM

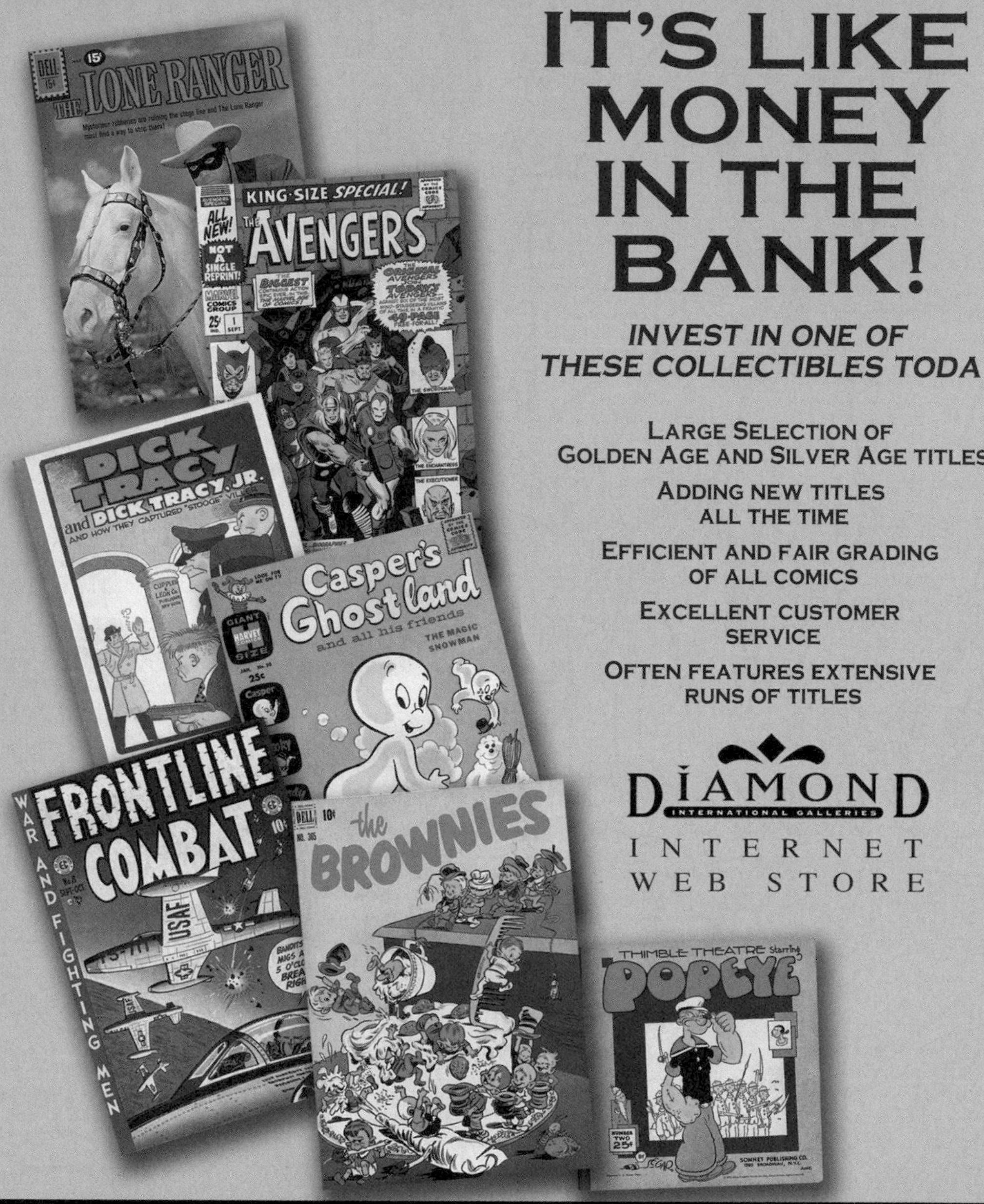
THE LONE RANGER
KING-SIZE SPECIAL!
THE AVENGERS
DICK TRACY and DICK TRACY JR.
Casper's Ghostland
FRONTLINE COMBAT
the BROWNIES
THIMBLE THEATRE starring POPEYE
IT'S LIKE MONEY IN THE BANK!
INVEST IN ONE OF THESE COLLECTIBLES TODAY
LARGE SELECTION OF GOLDEN AGE AND SILVER AGE TITLES
ADDING NEW TITLES ALL THE TIME
EFFICIENT AND FAIR GRADING OF ALL COMICS
EXCELLENT CUSTOMER SERVICE
OFTEN FEATURES EXTENSIVE RUNS OF TITLES
DIAMOND
INTERNATIONAL GALLERIES
INTERNET WEB STORE

Business Card Ads

THE OVERSTREET COMIC BOOK PRICE GUIDE BUSINESS CARD ADS are a great way to advertise in the Guide! Simply send us your business card and we'll reduce it and run it as is. Have your ad seen by thousands of serious comic book collectors for an entire year! If you are a comic book or collectible dealer, retail establishment, mail-order house, etc., you can reach potential customers throughout the United States and around the world in our **BUSINESS CARDS ADS**!

For more information, contact our Advertising Dept.
Gemstone Publishing, Inc., P.O. Box 12001, York, PA 17402
Call (888) 375-9800 Ext. 1625, or fax (717) 434-1690, or e-mail **ads@gemstonepub.com**.

BASEMENT COMICS
ALBERT M. STOLTZ, Jr.
1329 Superior Street • Havre de Grace, MD 21078
Home 410-939-8271 • Cell 443-831-2761
eMail basmntcomx@aol.com
www.basementcomix.com

Business Card Ads

We Want Your Help!

The Overstreet Comic Book Price Guide and *Hake's Price Guide To Character Toys* need your contributions! If you see something we've missed in *The Overstreet Comic Book Price Guide*, or if you have comic character collectibles not included in *Hake's Price Guide To Character Toys*, we want to know about it!

Conact us at: feedback@gemstonepub.com

Directory Listings

(PAID ADVERTISING - STORE LISTINGS)

You can have your store listed here for very reasonable rates. Send for details for next year's Guide. The following list of stores have paid to be included in this list. We cannot assume any responsibility in your dealings with these shops. This list is provided for your information only. When planning trips, it would be advisable to make appointments in advance. Remember, to get your shop included in the next edition, contact us for rates.

Gemstone Publishing, Inc., 3679 Concord Rd., York, PA 17402.
PHONE: 888-375-9800 or 717-434-1600
FAX: 717-434-1690
E-MAIL: ads@gemstonepub.com

Items stocked by these shops are noted at the end of each listing and are coded as follows:

(a) Golden Age Comics
(b) Silver Age Comics
(c) Bronze Age Comics
(d) New Comics & Magazines
(e) Back Issue magazines
(f) Comic Supplies
(g) Collectible Card Games
(h) Role Playing Games
(i) Gaming Supplies
(j) Manga
(k) Anime
(l) Underground Comics
(m) Original Comic Art
(n) Pulps
(o) Big Little Books
(p) Books - Used
(q) Books - New
(r) Comic Related Posters
(s) Movie Posters
(t) Trading Cards
(u) Statues/Mini-busts, etc.
(v) Premiums (Rings, Decoders, etc.)
(w) Action Figures
(x) Other Toys
(y) Records/CDs
(z) DVDs/VHS
(1) Doctor Who Items
(2) Simpsons Items
(3) Star Trek Items
(4) Star Wars Items
(5) HeroClix

ALABAMA

Quality Comix
Brent Moeshlin
7956 Vaughn Rd. #374
Montgomery, AL 36116
PH: (334) 300-1106
bmoeshlin@qualitycomix.com
www.qualitycomix.com

ARIZONA

Drawn To Comics
5757 W. Glendale Ave.
Glendale, AZ 85301
PH: (623) 847-9090
FAX: (623) 847-8585
drawntocomics@yahoo.com
www.drawntocomics.com
(a-d,f,r,s,w,x,z,2,4,5)

Stalking Moon Bookstore
5930 W. Greenway Rd. Ste. 23
Glendale, AZ 85306
PH/FAX: (602) 896-9992
comics@stalking-moon.com
www.stalking-moon.com
(d-k,r,t,u,w-z,1,5)

All About Books & Comics
5060 N. Central Ave.
Phoenix, AZ 85012
PH: (602) 277-0757
FAX: (602) 678-0065
alan@AllAboutComics.com
www.AllAboutComics.com
(a-j,l,n,o,r,t,u,w,x,1-5)

ARKANSAS

Alternate Worlds Cards & Comics
3812 Central Ave. Suite G
Hot Springs, AR 71913
PH: (501) 525-8999
comics@altworlds.com
www.altworlds.com
(b-i,t,u,w,1-5)

The Comic Book Store
9307 Treasure Hill
Little Rock, AR 72227
PH: (501) 227-9777
cbsrock@swbell.net
www.thewildstars.com
(a-g,i,j,q,r,t,u,w,x,1-5)

Collector's Edition
3217 John F. Kennedy Blvd.
North Little Rock, AR 72116
PH: (501) 791-4222
cbsrock@swbell.net
www.thewildstars.com
(a-g,i,j,q,r,t,u,w,x,1-5)

CALIFORNIA

A Comic City
545 E. Vine West Covina
5703 Beverly Blvd.
Arcadia, CA 91790
PH: (626) 962-0385
FAX: (323) 888-1877
acomiccity@yahoo.com
myspace.com/comiccitysgv
(a-m,r-u,w,x,y,2-5)

Gotham City Collectables
17057 Bellflower Blvd.
Suite 102
Bellflower, CA 90706
PH: (562) 461-0888
www.myspace.com/gothamcitycollectables
(d-f,j-l,q-s,u,w,x,1,3-5)

Metropolis Comics
16509 Bellflower Blvd.
Bellflower, CA 90706
PH: (562) 263-0277
FAX: (562) 461-9131
metropolis@metrohero.com
www.metrohero.com
(a-j,l,r,t,u,w,z,1-5)

LA Comic Con
Bruce Schwartz
224 East Orange Grove Ave.
Burbank, CA 91502
PH: (818) 954-8432
info@comicbookscifi.com
www.comicbookscifi.com
(a-h,j-m,s-u,w-z,1-5)

Crush Comics
2869 Castro Valley Blvd.
Castro Valley, CA 94546
PH/FAX: (510) 581-4779
mccrush@pacbell.net
www.crushcomics.com
(b-d,f,g,i,j,r,t,u,w,2-5)

BaT Comics & Games
218 Broadway
Chico, CA 95928
PH: (530) 898-0550
BaT@BaTcomics.com
www.BaTcomics.com
(b-d,f-l,r,t,u,w,x,z,2-5)

HighQualityComics.com
1106 2nd St., #110
Encinitas, CA 92024
PH: (800) 682-3936
FAX: (760) 723-7269
E-Mail: customerservice@HighQualityComics.com
Web: www.HighQualityComics.com
(a-f,j-m,p,r,s,u,w,x,2-4)

Legacy
123 W. Wilson Ave.
Glendale, CA 91203
PH: (818) 247-8803
FAX: (818) 247-2328
Legacycomics@hotmail.com
www.Legacycomics.com
(a-d,f-k,r,t,u,w,2-5)

Fantasy Books & Games
2247 First St.
Livermore, CA 94550
PH: (925) 449-5233
FAX: (925) 449-3061
FBANDG@aol.com
(a-d,f-j,o,r,t,u,w,5)

West Coast Fantasy
23901-B Sunnymead Blvd.
Moreno Valley, CA 92553
PH/FAX: (951) 924-7866
westcoastfantasy@verizon.net

Terry's Comics
Buying All 10¢ & 12¢ original priced comics
P.O. Box 2065
Orange, CA 92859
PH: (714) 288-8993 or
Hotline: (800) 938-0325
FAX: (714) 288-8992
info@terryscomics.com
www.terryscomics.com
(a,b,d-h,m,n,q)

ArchAngels
409 N. Pacific Coast Hwy.
Suite #682
Redondo Beach, CA 90277
PH: (310) 480-8105
rhughes@archangels.com
www.archangels.com

San Diego Comics
6937 El Cajon Blvd.
San Diego, CA 92115
PH: (619) 698-1177
RockofEasy@aol.com
www.san-diego-comics.com
(a-f)

Southern California Comics
8280 Clairemont Mesa Blvd.
#124
San Diego, CA 92111
PH: (858) 715-8669
SoCalCom@aol.com
www.SoCalComics.com
(a-f,m,o-r,u)

Amazing Adventures
3115 Vicente St.
San Francisco, CA 94116
PH: (415) 661-1344
FAX: (415) 661-1694
orders@amazing-adventures.com
www.amazing-adventures.com
(a-g,i,l,m,o,t-x,2,4)

Captain Nemo Games & Comics
563 Higuera St.
San Luis Obispo, CA 93401
PH: (805) 544-NEMO
FAX: (805) 543-3938
CaptainNemo@CaptainNemo.biz
www.CaptainNemo.biz
(a-l,r-u,w-z,2-5)

Lee's Comics
2222 S. El Camino Real
San Mateo, CA 94403
PH: (650) 571-1489
mark@LCOMICS.com
www.LCOMICS.com

Hi De Ho Comics & Books with Pictures
525 Santa Monica Blvd.
1st Floor, Plaza de los Comics
Santa Monica, CA 90401
PH: (310) 394-2820
info@hidehocomics.com
www.hidehocomics.com
(a-g,j-o,q-u,w,x,z,1-4)

Outerplanes
526 7th Street
Santa Rosa, CA 95401
PH: (707) 546-2000
dan@outerplanesgames.com
www.outerplanesgames.com
(c-j,u,3-5)

Comics Conspiracy
115-A E. Fremont Ave.
Sunnyvale, CA 94087
PH: (408) 245-6275
ryan@comicsconspiracy.biz
www.comicsconspiracy.biz
(b-d,f,g,l,u,w,5)

Ralph's Comic Corner
2379 E. Main St.
Ventura, CA 93003
PH: (805) 653-2732
ralph@ralphscomiccorner.com
www.ralphscomiccorner.com
(a-d,f,l,p,r,t,w)

COLORADO

All C's Collectibles
1250 S. Abilene St.
Aurora, CO 80012
PH: (303) 751-6882
FAX: (303) 695-7827
ALLCS@comcast.net
www.AllCsCollectibles.com
(a-g,i,l-n,r-u,w,x,2-5)

Time Warp Comics & Games
3105 28th Street
Boulder, CO 80301
PH: (303) 443-4500
FAX: (303) 413-7260
timewarp1@time-warp.com
www.time-warp.com
(b-g,i,j,r-u,w,x,1-5)

RTS Unlimited, Inc.
P. O. Box 150412
Lakewood, CO 80215-0412
PH: (303) 403-1840
FAX: (303) 403-1837
rtsunlimited@earthlink.net
www.RTSUnlimited.com
(a-f)

CONNECTICUT

Monkeyhead Comics
273 Greenwood Ave.
Bethel, CT 06801
PH: (203) 743-4123
MonkeyheadComics@att.net
www.MonkeyheadComics.com
(b-f,h,i,m,r,t,u,w,z)

Matt's Sportscards & Comics
169 Elm Street
Enfield, CT 06082
PH: (860) 741-2522
mattssportscardsandcomics
@cox.net
www.mattscardsandcomics.com

Ducks-R-Us
29 Markwood Lane
Manchester, CT 06040
PH: (860) 643-0453
ducksrus4u@aol.com
(a-c,e,p,3,4)

Legends of Superheros
Middlebury Edge
1655 Straits Turnpike
Middlebury, CT 06762
PH: (203) 577-2445
FAX: (203) 577-3909
legends@
legendsofsuperheros.com
www.legendsofsuperheros.com
(a-g,i,p,r,t,u,w,5)

The Eye Opener
15 Center Court
Newington, CT 06111
PH/FAX: (860) 666-5862
amassa2908@sbcglobal.net
(b-f,u,w)

Showcase New England
Dan Greenhalgh
67 Gail Drive
Northford, CT 06472
PH: (203) 484-4579
FAX: (203) 484-4837
comics@showcasene.com

Arkham Asylum
680 Boswell Ave. (Route 12)
Norwich, CT 06360
PH: (860) 859-9848
theasylum04@yahoo.com
www.arkham.cc
(b,c,d,f-k,q,t,u,w,5)

Wonderland Comics
112 Main Street Ste. 15
Putnam, CT 06260
PH: (860) 963-1027
FAX: (860) 935-0000
wonderlandcomics@aol.com
www.wonderlandcomics.com
(a-j,p-u,w,x,1-5)

FLORIDA

Emerald City Comics and Collectables, Inc.
2475 N McMullen Booth Road
Suite I (9)
Clearwater, FL 33759
PH: (727) 797-0664
E-Mail: CowardlyLion
@EmeraldCityComics.com
www.EmeraldCityComics.com
(a-j,r,t,u,w,x,1-5)

Pedigree Comics, Inc.
13678 Plaza Mayor Drive
Delray Beach, FL 33446
PH/FAX: (561) 496-7667
E-Mail: DougSchmell
@pedigreecomics.com
www.pedigreecomics.com

Samuel Frazer
11005 Lakeland Circle
Fort Myers, FL 33913
PH/FAX: (239) 768-0649
sfrazer457@aol.com
(a,b,o)

Collector's Comics
2547 S. Federal Highway
Fort Pierce, FL 34982
PH/FAX: (772) 465-5750
collectorscomics@comcast.net
www.collectorscomics.net
(a-f,h,i,m,q,r,u,w,x,1-5)

All Star Comics
4310 N.W. 23rd Ave.
Gainesville, FL 32606
PH: (352) 372-2700
ComicArtFiend@yahoo.com
www.gainesvillecomics.com
(a-d,f-i,m,t,u,w,x,5)

Greg White Comic Books
P.O. Box 45-0003
Kissimmee, FL 34745
PH: (407) 870-0400
wemisswalt@aol.com
www.gregwhitecomics.com
(a-c,e,m,o,q,t,x,4)

Paul Dyroff Comics
P.O. Box 953972
Lake Mary, FL 32795
PH: (321) 368-3993
FAX: (407) 688-2768
pdyroff@cfl.rr.com
www.paulscollectibles.com
(a-c,e,l-p,s,t,v,x)

Demolition Comics IV
1404 Seminole Blvd.
Largo, FL 33770
PH: (727) 581-7600
info@demolitioncomics.com
www.demolitioncomics.com
(a-j,r-u,w,x,2-5)

Tate's Comics + Toys + Videos + More
4566 North University Drive
Lauderhill, FL 33351
PH: (954) 748-0181
FAX: (954) 578-3949
emailus@tatescomics.com
www.tatescomics.com
(a-m,q-u,w,x,z,1-5)

Phil's Comic Shoppe
6512 West Atlantic Blvd.
Margate, FL 33063
PH: (954) 977-6947
philscomix@worldnet.att.net
(b-f,l,m,w)

Sci-Fi City
6006 E. Colonial Drive
Orlando, FL 32807
PH: (407) 282-2292
FAX: (407) 282-3361
steve@sci-fi-city.com
www.sci-fi-city.com
(a-k,m,r-x,z,1-5)

Earth 2 Comics and Collectables
Mike Prisco
7619 Pines Blvd.
Pembroke Pines, FL 33024
PH: (954) 962-3322
Mike@Earth2Comics.net
www.Earth2Comics.net
(a-l,q-u,w,x,5)

CGC
P.O. Box 4738
Sarasota, FL 34230
PH: (877) NM-Comic
FAX: (941) 360-2558
www.scgccomics.com

Emerald City Comics and Collectables, Inc.
9249 Seminole Blvd.
Seminole, FL 33772
PH: (727) 398-2665
E-Mail: CowardlyLion
@EmeraldCityComics.com
www.EmeraldCityComics.com
(a-j,o,r,t,u,v,w,x,z,1-5)

David T. Alexander Collectibles
P.O. Box 273086
Tampa, FL 33618
PH: (813) 968-1805
FAX: (813) 264-6226
davidt@cultureandthrills.com
www.dtacollectibles.com
(a-c,e,l-o,r,s)

Demolition Comics I
4049 S. Dale Mabry Hwy
Tampa, FL 33611
PH: (813) 832-2692
FAX: (813) 681-9071
info@demolitioncomics.com
www.demolitioncomics.com
(a-j,l,r-u,w,x,2-5)

Demolition Comics II
4149 West Waters Ave.
Tampa, FL 33614
PH: (813) 885-5171
FAX: (813) 681-9071
info@demolitioncomics.com
www.demolitioncomics.com
(a-j,l,r-u,w,x,2-5)

Demolition Comics III
2564 E. Fowler Ave.
Tampa, FL 33612
PH: (813) 866-1780
info@demolitioncomics.com
www.demolitioncomics.com
(a-j,r-u,w,x,2-5)

GEORGIA

Oxford Comics
2855 Piedmont Rd.
Atlanta, GA 30305
PH: (404) 233-8682

Odin's Cosmic Bookshelf
360 Killian Hill Rd.
Suite G-5
Lilburn, GA 30047
PH: (770) 923-0123
www.odins.net

Odin's Comics
2100-C Fountain Square
Snellville, GA 30078
PH: (770) 413-0123
www.odinscomics.com

ILLINOIS

The Paper Escape
205 West First Street
Dixon, IL 61021
PH: (815) 284-7567
E-Mail: paperescape
@paperescape.com
www.paperescape.com
(b-d,f-j,p-r,t,u,w,x,z,1,3,4)

GEM Comics
125 W. First St.
Elmhurst, IL 60126
PH: (630) 833-8787
(b-i,r,t,5)

Dreamland Comics
105 W. Rockland Rd.
Libertyville, IL 60048
PH: (847) 680-0727
FAX: (847) 680-4495
info@dreamland-comics.com
www.dreamland-comics.com
(b-d,f-j,r,t,u,w,4,5)

Al N' Ann's Collectibles
3819 W. Main St.
McHenry, IL 60050
PH: (815) 344-9696
al@alnanns.com
www.alnanns.com
(b-d,f-k,r,t,u,w,x,2,4,5)

Have Fun Collectibles
4327 Avenue of the Cities
Moline, IL 61265
PH: (309) 762-2474
john@havefuncollectibles.com
www.havefuncollectibles.com
(a-l,r-u,w,x,1-5)

Mellow Blue Planet
2212 5th Ave.
Rock Island, IL 61201-8908
PH: (309) 788-1653
E-Mail: mellowblueplanet
@hotmail.com
(a-f,i-l,o,r-u,w,x,z,3-5)

Dreamland Comics
1415 W. Schaumburg Rd.
Schaumburg, IL 60194
PH: (847) 524-6060
Laurie@dreamlandcomics.com
www.dreamlandcomics.com

INDIANA

Comics Ina Flash
P.O. Box 3611
Evansville, IN 47735-3611
PH: (812) 401-6127
comicflash@aol.com
www.comicsinaflash.com

Books, Comics & Things
2212 Maplecrest Rd.
Fort Wayne, IN 46815
PH: (260) 493-6116
bct@bctcomics.com
www.bctcomics.com
(a-k,r,t,u,w,x,z,1-5)

IOWA

Mayhem Comics and Games
2532 Lincoln Way
Ames, IA 50014
PH/FAX: (515) 292-3510
shop@mayhem.com
www.mayhemcomics.com
(a-k,r-u,w,x,1-5)

Majestic Comics, Ltd.
Majestic Lion Antique Center
5048 2nd Ave.
Des Moines, IA 50313
PH: (515) 480-4451
majcomic@gmail.com
www.comicsandtrains.com
(a-c,e,n-p,t,x,z,4)

KANSAS

Pop Culture Comix
9337 W. 87th Street (at Grant)
Overland Park, KS 66212
PH: (913) 341-0040
sid@popculturecomix.com
www.popculturecomix.com
(d,f,g,q,r,t,u,w,1-5)

KENTUCKY

The Great Escape
2945 Scottsville Rd.
Bowling Green, KY 42104
PH: (270) 782-8092
TGE@bellsouth.net
www.TheGreatEscapeOnline.com
(a-i,k-p,r-u,w-z,1-5)

Dale Roberts
PO Box 707
Calvert City, KY 42029
PH: (270) 395-9832
buycomics@aol.com

Comic Book World, Inc.
7130 Turfway Rd.
Florence, KY 41042
PH: (859) 371-9562
FAX: (859) 371-6925
comicbw@one.net
www.comicbookworld.com
(a-j,l,n,o,r,t,u,w,1-5)

Comic Book World, Inc.
6905 Shepherdsville Rd.
Louisville, KY 40219
PH: (502) 964-5500
FAX: (502) 964-5500
comicbw@one.net
www.comicbookworld.com
(a-j,l,r,u,w,1-5)

The Great Escape
2433 Bardstown Rd.
Louisville, KY 40205
PH: (502) 456-2216
TGE@bellsouth.net
www.TheGreatEscapeOnline.com
(a-l,p,r-u,w-z,1-5)

G's Comics
804 Coldwater Rd.
Murray, KY 42071
PH: (270) 759-4896
garrickcrump@bellsouth.net
www.gscomics.net
(b-d,f-jr,u,w,1,4,5)

Leroy Harper
P.O. Box 212
West Paducah, KY 42086
PH: (270) 748-9364
LHCOMICS@hotmail.com

MAINE

Top Shelf Coins & Comics
25 Central St.
Bangor, ME 04401
PH: (207) 947-4939
topshelf@tcomics.com
www.tcomics.com
(a-f)

MARYLAND

Doug's Comic Book Oasis
5300 East Drive
Arbutus, MD 21227
PH: (410) 242-5133
comicbookoasis@comcast.net
www.comicbookoasis.com
(b-f,j,k,u,w)

E. Gerber
1720 Belmont Ave.; Suite C
Baltimore, MD 21244

Esquire Comics.com
Mark S. Zaid, ESQ.
P.O. Box 3422492
Bethesda, MD 20827
PH: (202) 498-0011
esquirecomics@aol.com
www.esquirecomics.com
(b-k,r,u,w,4,5)

Alternate Worlds
72 Cranbrook Road
Yorktowne Plaza
Cockeysville, MD 21030
PH: (410) 666-3290
altworldstore@att.net
(b-j,r,t,u,w,1-5)

Comics To Astonish Inc.
9400 Snowden River Pkwy.
Columbia, MD 21045
PH: (410) 381-2732
comics2u@aol.com
www.comicstoastonish.com
(a-k,m,r,t,u,w,z,2,3,5)

Beyond Comics
5632 Buckeystown Pike
Frederick, MD 21704
PH: (301) 668-8202
store@beyondcomics.com
www.beyondcomics.com
(b-d,f-j,l,r,t,u,w,x,1-5)

Beyond Comics
701 Russell Ave.
Lakeforest Mall
Gaithersburg, MD 20877
PH: (301) 216-0007
store@beyondcomics.com
www.beyondcomics.com
(b-d,f-j,l,r,t,u,w,x,1-5)

Old News, Inc.
The Caren Archive and
Stephen A. Goldman
Historical Newspapers
P.O. Box 359
Parkton, MD 21120
PH: (914) 248-8038

Diamond Comic Distributors
1966 Greenspring Drive
Timonium, MD 21093
PH: (800) 45-COMIC

Diamond Select Toys
1966 Greenspring Drive
Suite 402
Timonium, MD 21093

MASSACHUSETTS

Gary Dolgoff
116 Pleasant St.
Easthampton, MA 01027
PH: (413) 529-0326
FAX: (413) 529-9824
gary@garydolgoffcomics.com
www.garydolgoffcomics.com

That's Entertainment
56 John Fitch Highway
Fitchburg, MA 01420
PH: (978) 342-8607
fitch@thatse.com
www.thatse.com
(a-x,z,1-5)

Jerry Weist
18 Edgemoor Rd.
Gloucester, MA 10930
PH: (978) 283-1419
jerryweist@adelphia.net

Main Vein Comics
74 Federal St.
Greenfield, MA 01301
PH: (413) 773-7775
info@MainVeinComics.com
www.MainVeinComics.com
(a-f,j-m,p,r,u,w,x,1-5)

Harrison's Comics
3850 Mystic Valley Parkway
Medford, MA 02155
PH: (781) 391-6111
harrisonscomics@hotmail.com
www.harrisonscomicsltd.com
(b-j,q,r,t,u,w,x,z,1-4)

Bill Cole Enterprises Inc.
P.O. Box 60, Dept. 01
Randolph, MA 02368-0060
PH: (781) 986-2653
FAX: (781) 986-2656
bcemylar@cwbusiness.com
www.bcemylar.com

Harrison's Comics
252 Essex St.
Salem, MA 01970
PH: (978) 741-0786
FAX: (978) 741-0737
harrisonscomics@hotmail.com
www.harrisonscomicsltd.com
(a-j,l,m,o,w-z,1-5)

The Outer Limits
437 Moody St.
Waltham, MA 02453
PH: (781) 891-0444
askOuterLimits@aol.com
www.myspace.com/eouterlimits
(a-j,l-x,z,1-5)

SuperWorld Comics.com
Ted Vanliew
P.O. Box 20924
Worcester, MA 01602
PH: (508) 754-0792
lvanliew@aol.com
Superworldcomics.com

That's Entertainment
244 Park Avenue (Rt. 9)
Worcester, MA 01609-1927
PH: (508) 755-4207
FAX: (508) 798-9635
ken@thatse.com
www.thatse.com
(a-z,1-5)

MICHIGAN

Amazing Book-Store
3718 Richfield Rd.
Flint, MI 48506
PH: (810) 736-3025
amazingbookstore@comcast.net
www.amazebookstore.com
(a-g,l,r,u,w,5)

Tardy's Collector's Corner, Inc.
2009 Eastern Ave. S.E.
Grand Rapids, MI 49507
PH: (616) 247-7828
tccorner@iserv.net
www.tardys.com
(a-f,l,q,r,u)

Fanfare Sports /Entertainment, Inc.
4415 S. Westnedge Ave.
Kalamazoo, MI 49008
PH: (269) 349-7918
info.fanfare@charterinternet.com
www.fanfare-se.com
(a-k,m,r,t,u,w-z,1-5)

Harley Yee Comics
P.O. Box 51758
Livonia, MI 48151-5758
PH: (800) 731-1029
FAX: (734) 421-7928
HarleyComx@aol.com
www.HarleyYeeComics.com

MINNESOTA

Midway Book & Comic
1579 University Ave.
St. Paul, MN 55104
PH: (651) 644-7605
FAX: (651) 644-8786
(a-f,n-p)

MISSISSIPPI

Ken Stribling
P.O. Box 16004
Jackson, MS 39236-6004
PH: (601) 201-2592
kenstribling@hotmail.com

MISSOURI

The Comix Strip
621 Broadway
POB 1931
Cape Girardeau, MO 63701
PH: (573) 335-9908
mobettercomics@hotmail.com
(a-f,l,m,p-s,u,w-z,5)

All American/Mo's Comics
6510 Chippewa
St. Louis, MO 63109
PH: (314) 352-7700
(a-g,i,t,u,w,x,z,1-5)

NEBRASKA

Robert Beerbohm Comic Art
P.O. Box 507
Fremont, NE 68026
PH: (402) 727-4071
Robert@BLBComics.com
www.BLBComics
(a,b,c,e,l-o,r)

Ground Zero Hobby
794 Fort Crook Rd. S
Bellevue, NE 68005
PH/FAX: (402) 292-3750
gzbellevue@cox.net
www.gzbellevue.com
(b-d,f-i,p,q,r,t,u,w,x,3-5)

Ground Zero Hobby
4601 S. 50th St. #103
Omaha, NE 68117
PH/FAX: (402) 733-7212
gzomaha@cox.net
www.gzomaha.com
(b-d,f-i,q,r,t,u,w,4,5)

Krypton Comics
2819 S. 125th Ave.
Suite 261
Omaha, NE 68144
PH: (402) 391-4131
dean@kryptoncomicsomaha.com
www.kryptoncomicsomaha.com

NEVADA

Redbeard's Book Den
P.O. Box 217
Crystal Bay, NV 89402
PH: (775) 831-4848
FAX: (775) 831-4483
www.redbeardsbookden.com
(a,b,c,l,o,p)

Alternate Reality Comics
4800 S. Maryland Pky. Suite D
Las Vegas, NV 89119
PH: (702) 736-3673
ralphcomix@lvcm.com
www.AlternateRealityComics.net
(d,f,j,q)

NEW HAMPSHIRE

Rare Books & Comics
James F. Payette
P.O. Box 750
Bethlehem, NH 03574
PH: (603) 869-2097
FAX: (603) 869-3475
JimPayette@msn.com
(a,b,c,e,n,o,p)

Jetpack Comics LLC
112 Portland Street
Rochester, NH 03867
PH: (603) 330-9636
info@jetpackcomics.com
www.jetpackcomics.com

NEW JERSEY

NeatStuffCollectibles.com
Michael Carbonaro
66 Grand Avenue
Englewood, NJ 07631
PH: (718) 326-2713
E-Mail: neatstuffcollectibles
@yahoo.com
www.NeatStuffCollectibles.com

A Time Lost.... And Found
310 East Evesham Road
Glendora, NJ 08029
PH: (856) 939-1909
famarcus@aol.com
(b-f,j,l,q,r,t,u,w,x,1)

ZAPP! Comics II
700 Tennent Road
Superfoodtown Center
Manalapan, NJ 07726
PH: (732) 866-6655
zappcomics@aol.com
www.zappcomics.com
(a-g,i,j,l,r,t,u,w,x,1-5)

Main St. Comics & Toys
74 N. Main St.
Milltown, NJ 08850
PH: (732) 828-7886
mscomics@aol.com
www.myspace.com/mscomics
(a-g,i,l,r,t,u,w,x,4)

J&S Comics
168 W. Sylvania Ave.
Neptune, NJ 07753
PH: (732) 988-5717
jandscomics@aol.com
www.jscomics.com

Fat Jack's Comicrypt
521 White Horse Pike
Oaklyn, NJ 08107
PH: (856) 858-3877
FAX: (215) 963-9361
fatjacks@comcast.net
(a-g,l,r,t,u,w,5)

J&S Comics
Jim Walsh
98 Madison Avenue
Red Bank, NJ 07701
PH: (732) 988-5717
jandscomics@aol.com
www.jscomics.com

All-Star Auctions
Nadia Mannarino
122 West End Avenue
Ridgewood, NJ 07450
PH: (201) 652-1305
FAX: (501) 325-6504
nadia@allstarauctions.net
www.allstarauctions.net

Commuter Comics
50 West South Orange Ave.
South Orange, NJ 07079
PH: (973) 762-6666
commutercomics@aol.com
www.commutercomics.com
(a-g,i-l,o,q-u,w-z,1-5)

Comic Art Showcase
42 Gerdes Avenue
Verona, NJ 07044
PH: (973) 768-6649
joe@comicartshowcase.com
www.comicartshowcase.com
(m)

ZAPP! Comics
574 Valley Road
Wayne, NJ 07470
PH: (973) 628-4500
FAX: (973) 628-1771
zappcomics@aol.com
www.zappcomics.com
(a-g,i,j,l,r,t,u,w,x,1-5)

JHV Associates
(By Appointment Only)
P. O. Box 317
Woodbury Heights, NJ 08097
PH: (856) 845-4010
FAX: (856) 845-3977
JHVassoc@hotmail.com
(a,b,n,s)

NEW MEXICO

Astro-Zombies
3108 Central Ave. SE
Albuquerque, NM 87106
PH: (505) 232-7800
info@astrozombies.com
www.astrozombies.com
(a-g,j,l,r,t,u,w,x,y,2,4,5)

NEW YORK

Silver Age Comics
22-55 31 St.
Astoria, NY 11105
PH: (718) 721-9691
PH: (800) 278-9691
FAX: (718) 728-9691
gus@silveragecomics.com
www.silveragecomics.com
(a-g,j-o,r,t,u,w,x,z,2-4)

Excellent Adventures Comics
110 Milton Ave. (Rt. #50)
Ballston Spa, NY 12020
PH: (518) 884-9498
jbelskis37@aol.com
(a-f,m-p,r,t-x,5)

HighGradeComics.com
17 Bethany Drive
Commack, NY 11725
PH: (631) 543-1917
FAX: (631) 864-1921
E-Mail: BobStorms@
HighGradeComics.com
www.HighGradeComics.com
(a,b,c)

Fantasy-Comics
P.O. Box 732
Goldens Bridge NY 10526
PH: (914) 301-5252
FAX: (914) 232-3027
buying@fantasy-comics.com
www.Fantasy-Comics.com

Comicollectors.net
Marnin Rosenberg
P.O. Box 2047
Great Neck, NY 11022
PH: (516) 466-8147
www.comiccollectors.net
www.collectorsassemble.com

The Comic Depot, LLC
2538 Route 9N
Greenfield Center, NY 12833
PH: (518) 893-2900
comicdep@comicdepotLLC.com
www.comicdepotLLC.com
(a-d,f-j,r,u,w,5)

Chautauqua Comics
214 Fairmont Ave.
Jamestown, NY 14701
PH: (716) 664-2287
comic2@alltel.net
www.chautauquacomics.com

Mahopac Cards & Comics
1000 Miller Road Plaza
P.O. Box 444
Mahopac, NY 10541
PH: (845) 621-2699
FAX: (845) 621-6719
mahopaccards@aol.com
www.mahopaccards.com
(d,f,g,i-k,r,t,u,w,5)

Ravenswood Inc.
8451 Seneca Turnpike
New Hartford, NY 13413
PH: (315) 735-3699
FAX: (315) 735-3204
E-Mail:ravenswoodcomics
@verizon.net
www.ravenswoodcomics.com
(a-k,m,q-u,w,x,1-5)

Best Comics & Jericho Comics
1300 Jericho Turnpike
New Hyde Park, NY 11040
PH: (516) 328-1900
FAX: (516) 328-1909
TommyBest@aol.com
www.bestcomics.com

Best Comics International
1300 Jericho Turnpike
New Hyde Park, NY 11040
PH: (516) 328-1900
FAX: (516) 328-1909
TommyBest2@aol.com
www.bestcomics.com
(a-d,f,r-t,w,3-5)

Metropolis
873 Broadway
Suite 201
New York, NY 10003
PH: (800) 229-6387
FAX: (212) 260-4304
E-Mail: buying@
metropoliscomics.com
www.metropoliscomics.com

Midtown Comics
459 Lexington Ave.
(Corner of 45th Street)
New York, NY 10017
PH: (212) 302-8192
info@midtowncomics.com
www.midtowncomics.com

Midtown Comics
200 West 40th Street
(Corner of 7th Ave, 2nd floor)
New York, NY 10018
PH: (212) 302-8192
info@midtowncomics.com
www.midtowncomics.com

House of Fantasy Comics & Games
1709 Pine Ave.
Niagara Falls, NY 14301-2231
PH: (716) 282-8838
(b-d,f-j,r-u,w,2-5)

The Collector's Friend
470 North Greenbush Rd.
Rensselaer, NY 12144
PH: (518) 286-2223
DialCard@nycap.rr.com
www.TCF.cc
(a-k,t,w,y,z,1-5)

Bags Unlimited, Inc.
7 Canal St.
Rochester, NY 14608
PH: (800) 767-2247
FAX. (585) 328-8526
info@bagsunlimited.com
www.bagsunlimited.com

Amazing Comics
12 Gillette Ave.
Sayville, NY 11782
PH: (631) 567-8069
info@amazingco.com
www.amazingco.com
(a-f,m,r,t,u,w)

Alternate Realities
700 Central Park Avenue
Scarsdale, NY 10583
PH: (914) 723-7950
sko@alternaterealities.com
www.alternaterealities.com
(b-g,j,r,t,u,w,x,5)

Four Color Comics
Rob Rogovin
P.O. Box 1399
Scarsdale, NY 10583
PH: (914) 722-4696
keybooks@aol.com

Fourth World Comics
33 Route 111
Smithtown, NY 11787
PH: (631) 366-4440
fourgle@aol.com
(b-l,q-u,w-z,1-5)

Krypton Comics of Staten Island
611 Midland Ave.
Staten Island, NY 10306
PH: (718) 667-7695
Krypton@KryptonSINY.com
www.KryptonSINY.com
(a-g,i,r,t,u,w)

NORTH CAROLINA

Acme Comics
2150 Lawndale Drive
Greensboro, NC 27408
PH: (336) 574-2263
AcmeLwn@bellsouth.net
www.AcmeComics.com
(a-d,f,r,u,w,1,5)

The Hobby Shop
1501 Ward Blvd.
Suite #245
Wilson, NC 27893
PH: (252) 291-3384
FAX: (252) 291-5149
info@thehobbyshopofwilson.com
www.thehobbyshopofwilson.com
(b-g,i,u,w,x,3-5)

NORTH DAKOTA

Barry's Collectors Corner
Grand Cities Mall
Grand Forks, ND 58201
PH: (701) 795-1386
UNDBKB@aol.com
(a-j,l,m,o-q,s-u,w-y,1-5)

OHIO

Up Up & Away!
4016 Harrison Avenue
Cincinnati, OH 45211
PH: (513) 661-6300
FAX: (513) 661-6312
kendall@upupandawaycomics.com
www.upupandawaycomics.com
(a-k,r,u,w,2-5)

Bookery Fantasy
16 West Main St.
Fairborn, OH 45324
PH: (937) 879-1408
FAX: (937) 879-9327
E-Mail:BookeryFan@aol.com
www.BookeryFantasy.com
(a-l,n-u,w,x,z,1-5)

Parker's Records & Comics
1222 Suite C Rt. 28
Milford, OH 45150
PH/FAX: (513) 575-3665
E-Mail: dkparker39@fuse.net
www.parkersrc.com
(a-i,y,3,4)

North Coast Nostalgia
5853 Ridge Road
Parma, OH 44129
PH: (440) 845-7040
NCNOST@wowway.com
(a-f,u)

Monarch Cards & Comics
4400 Heatherdowns
Toledo, OH 43614
PH: (419) 382-1451
(b-g,r,t,u,w,x,5)

OKLAHOMA

All Star Comics
6900 N. May Ave. #10
Oklahoma City, OK 73116
PH/FAX: (405) 842-7800
wgreenewood@cox.net
(a-f,h,n,o,s,w,x,1-5)

Comic Empire of Tulsa
3122 S. Mingo Road
Tulsa, OK 74146
PH: (918) 664-5808
(a-f,l)

Want List Comics
(Appointment Only)
P.O. Box 701932
Tulsa, OK 74170
PH: (918) 299-0440
E-Mail: wlc777@cox.net
(a,b,c,m,n,o,s,t,x,3)

OREGON

Emerald City Comics
770 E 13th
Eugene, OR 97401
PH: (541) 345-2568
(c-k,r,w,x,z,5)

Future Dreams
1847 East Burnside St.
Suite 116
Portland, OR 97214-1587
PH: (503) 231-8311
fdb@hevanet.com
www.futuredreamsbooks.com
(b-h,j,l,p-u,w,1-4)

PENNSYLVANIA

New Dimension Comics
Clear View Mall
101 Clear View Circle
Butler, PA 16001
PH: (724) 282-5283
butler@ndcomics.com
(a-z,1-5)

New Dimension Comics
20550 Route 19,
Piazza Plaza
Cranberry Township, PA
16066
PH: (724) 776-0433
cranberry@ndcomics.com
(a-z,1-5)

New Dimension Comics
516 Lawrence Ave.
Ellwood City, PA 16117
PH: (724) 758-2324
ec@ndcomics.com
(a-z,1-5)

Comic Universe
446 MacDade Blvd.
P.O. Box 246
Folsom, PA 19033
PH: (610) 461-7960
chessflink@yahoo.com
www.comicuniverse.net
(a-g,j,k,m,p-r,t,u,w,x,z,1-5)

The Comic Store
28 McGovern Ave.
Lancaster, PA 17602
PH: (717) 397-8737
FAX: (717) 397-8903
comicstore@juno.com
www.comicstorepa.com

Yukon Cards & Comics
1722 W. Market St.
Lewisburg, PA 17837
PH/FAX: (570) 522-8083
YukonCardsAndComics@
yahoo.com
(a-i,q,t,u,w,x,1-5)

New Dimension Comics
113 East McMurray Road
McMurray, PA 15317
PH: (724) 941-5445
colin@ndcomics.com
(a-z,1-5)

Fat Jack's Comicrypt
2006 Sansom St.
Philadelphia, PA 19103
PH: (215) 963-0788
FAX: (215) 963-9361
fatjacks@comcast.net
(a-l,r,t,u,w,5)

Eide's Entertainment
1121 Penn Ave.
Pittsburgh, PA 15222
PH: (412) 261-0900
FAX: (412) 261-3102
eides@eides.com
www.eides.com
(a-g,i-z,1-5)

Dave's American Comics
Buying All 10¢ & 12¢
original priced comics
P.O. Box 8198
Radnor, PA 19087-8198
PH: (610) 275-8817 or
Hotline: (800) 938-0325
FAX: (714) 288-8992
davesamerican@earthlink.net
www.terryscomics.com
(a,b,d-h,m,n,q)

New Dimension Comics
Pittsburgh Century III Mall
3075 Clairton Rd. #940
West Mifflin, PA 15213
PH: (412) 655-8661
ndccentury3@verizon.net
(a-z,1-5)

Comics World
1002 Graham Ave.
Windber, PA 15963
PH: (814) 467-4116
FAX: (814) 467-4416
pcomicon@floodcity.net
www.pittsburghcomicon.com
(b-d,f,-h,u,w,x)

Comic Store West
2111 Industrial Hwy.
York, PA 17402
PH: (717) 845-9198
Bstoner@comicstorewest.com
www.comicstorewest.com
(d,f,h,t)

Hake's Americana
3679 Concord Rd.
York, PA 17402
PH: (866) 404-9800
www.hakes.com

SOUTH CAROLINA

Planet Comics
2704 N. Main St.
Anderson, SC 29621
PH: (864) 261-3578
planetcomics@gmail.com
www.planetcomics.net
(a-d,f-l,r-u,w,z,1-5)

Heroes and Dragons
510 Bush River Rd.
Columbia, SC 29210
PH: (803) 731-4376
chris@HeroesandDragons.com
www.HeroesandDragons.com

TENNESSEE

Dewayne's World - Comics & Games
459 E. Sullivan Street
Kingsport, TN 37660
PH/FAX: (423) 247-8997
dewayne@dewaynes-world.com
www.dewaynes-world.com
(a-d,f-i,r,u,w,4,5)

Comics Universe
1869 Hwy 45 Bypass
Jackson, TN 38305
PH/FAX: (731) 664-9131
(a-f,m,r,u,w)

The Great Escape
111B N. Gallatin Rd.
Madison, TN 37115
PH: (615) 865-8052
TGE@bellsouth.net
www.TheGreatEscapeOnline.com
(a-p,r-u,w-z,1-5)

The Great Escape
1925 Broadway
Nashville, TN 37203
PH: (615) 327-0646
TGE@bellsouth.net
www.TheGreatEscapeOnline.com
(a-p,r-u,w-z,1-5)

TEXAS

Lone Star Comics
511 E. Abram St.
Arlington, TX 76010
PH: (817) 860-7827
FAX: (817) 860-2769
customerservice@
lonestarcomics.com
www.mycomicshop.com/
overstreet
(a-j,n,q,u-x,1-5)

Comic Heaven
P.O. Box 900
Big Sandy, TX 75755
PH: (903) 636-5555

Classics Incorporated
Matt Nelson
P.O. Box 600263
Dallas, TX 75360
PH: (214) 459-1866
Spectre52@aol.com

Heritage Auction Galleries
3500 Maple Avenue
17th Floor
Dallas, TX 75219-3941
PH: (800) 872-6467
www.HA.com

Titan Comics
3701 W. Northwest Hwy #125
Dallas, TX 75220
PH: (214) 350-4420
comix99999@aol.com
www.titancomics.com

Good Time Charlie's
114 W. Knox
Ennis, TX 75119
PH: (972) 875-9737
GoodtimeCharliesEnnis
@hotmail.com
(a-k,o,r,t-y,1-4)

Bill Hughes' Vintage Collectables
P.O. Box 270244
Flower Mound, TX 75027
PH: (972) 539-9190
FAX: (973) 432-4070
Whughes199@yahoo.com
www.vintagecollectables.net

Bedrock City Comic Co.
6517 Westheimer
Houston, TX 77057
PH: (713) 780-0675
www.bedrockcity.com
(a-g,j-o,r-x,z,1-5)

Bedrock City Comic Co.
4683 FM1960 West
Houston, TX 77069
PH: (281) 444-9763
www.bedrockcity.com
(a-g,j-o,r-x,z,1-5)

M&M Comic Service
3128 Hidden Haven St.
Building C
San Antonio, TX 78261
PH: (830) 438-6131
service@mmcomics.com
www.mmcomics.com
(b,c,d,j,k,l,q,u,w,z,1-4)

Ground Zero Comics
2714 East Fifth Street
Tyler, TX 75701
PH: (903) 566-1185
info@groundzerocomics.com
www.groundzerocomics.com
(b-j,r,t,u,w,3-5)

Bedrock City Comic Co.
106 W. Bay Area Blvd.
Webster, TX 77598
PH: (281) 557-2748
www.bedrockcity.com
(a-g,j-o,r-x,z,1-5)

UTAH

The Bookshelf 3.0 LLC
2671 Washington Blvd.
Ogden, UT 84401
PH: (801) 621-4752
FAX: (801) 393-2815
TheBookshelf3.0@comcast.net
www.BookshelfUtah.net
(b,d,f-l,p,q,u,w-z,2-4)

VIRGINIA

Lost Shade Games & Hobbies
625C Mt. Clinton Pike
Harrisonburg, VA 22802
PH: (540) 438-5678
lostshade@lostshade.com
www.lostshade.com
(d,f-j,4,5)

Trilogy Shop #2
700 E. Little Creek Rd.
Norfolk, VA 23518
PH: (757) 587-2540
FAX: (757) 587-5637
trilogy2@TrilogyComics.net
www.TrilogyComics.net
(d-j,w,5)

B & D Comic Shop
802 Elm Avenue SW
Roanoke, VA 24016
PH: (540) 342-6642
FAX: (540) 342-6694
bdcomics1@verizon.net
www.banddcomics.com
(b-f,r,w,5)

Trilogy Comics #1
5773 Princess Anne Rd.
Virginia Beach, VA 23462
PH: (757) 490-2205
FAX: (757) 671-7721
trilogy1@TrilogyComics.net
www.TrilogyComics.net
(a-j,p,t,u,w,3-5)

WASHINGTON

Golden Age Collectables
1501 Pike Place Market
#401 Lower Level
Seattle, WA 98101
PH: (206) 622-9799
FAX: (206) 622-9595
GACollect@Gmail.com
www.GoldenAgeCollectables.com
(a-x,1-5)

Zanadu Comics, Inc.
1923 3rd Ave.
Seattle, WA 98101-1104
PH: (206) 443-1316
Zanadu@ZanaduComics.com
www.ZanaduComics.com
(d-f,j,r,u,w,x)

WEST VIRGINIA

Comic World
1204 - 4th Avenue
Huntington, WV 25701
PH: (304) 522-3923
(a-f,l,r,t,u,w,1-5)

WISCONSIN

Nationwide Comics
Buying All 10¢ & 12¢
original priced comics
Janesville, WI 53545
Hotline: (800) 938-0325
PH: (608) 752-8128
FAX: (714) 288-8992
Bart@nationwidecomics.net
www.nationwidecomics.net
(a,b,d-h,m,n,q)

Capital City Comics
1910 Monroe St.
Madison, WI 53711
PH: (608) 251-8445
capitalcitycomics.wordpress.com
(a-f,j,l,m,o-r,t,u,w,y,z,1-4)

Jef Hinds Comics
PO Box 44803
Madison, WI 53744-4803
PH: (800) 791-3037
www.jhcomics.com
(a,b,c,f)

Westfield Comics
8608 University Green
PO Box 620470
Middleton, WI 53562-0470
www.westfieldcomics.com

CANADA

ALBERTA

Another Dimension
424B - 10 St. NW
Calgary, Alberta T2N 1V9
PH: (403) 283-7078
FAX: (403) 283-7080
E-Mail: comics@
another dimension.com
www.another-dimension.com
(a-f,j,l,m,q,r,u,w,x,z,1-4)

MANITOBA

Doug Sulipa's Comic World
Box 21986
Steinbach, MB., R5G 1B5
PH: (204) 346-3674
FAX: (204) 346-1632
E-Mail: cworld@mts.net
www.dougcomicworld.com
(a-c,e,l,n,o,p,r,s,t,y,z,1,3,4)

NEW BRUNSWICK

Mad City Comics
363 Mountain Rd.
Moncton, N.B. E1C 2M7
PH: (506) 855-0056
PH: (800) 269-7323
FAX: (506) 857-1705
MadCityMike2002@hotmail.com
www.madcitycomics.com
(b-k,p-r,t,u,w,x,z,2,3,5)

NOVA SCOTIA

Monster Comic Lounge
2091 Gottingen St.
Halifax, Nova Scotia B3K 3B2
PH: (902) 429-2398
mcrossman@ns.sympatico.ca
(b-j,r,u,w,1-5)

ONTARIO

Fantasy Realm
227 Pitt St.
Cornwall, ONT. K6J 3P8
PH/FAX: (613) 933-7997
fantasyrlm@glen-net.ca
www.fantasyrealm.ca
(b-e,q,t,w,3,4)

Big B Comics
1045 Upper James St.
Hamilton, ONT. L9C 3A6
PH: (905) 318-9636
FAX: (905) 318-9055
mailbox@bigbcomics.com
www.bigbcomics.com
(a-g,i,j,q,r,u,w,x,4,5)

B.A.'s COMICS
426 Hamilton Road
London, ONT. N5Z 1R9
PH: (519) 439-9636
ba.lm@rogers.com
(a-f,l,n)

L.A. Mood Comics and Games
350 Richmond St.
London, ONT. N6A 3C3
PH: (519) 432-3987
PH: (888) 621-7018
mailbox@lamoodcomics.com
www.lamoodcomics.com
(a-i,l-o,u,w,x,1-5)

Worlds Collide
80 Simcoe Street N
Oshawa, ONT L1G 4S2
PH: (905) 436-8999
tim@worlds-collide.com
www.worlds-collide.com
(b-d,f-k,r,u,w,1,4)

Pendragon Comics
3759 Lakeshore Boulevard West
Toronto, ONT M8W 1R1
PH: (416) 253-6974
pendragoncomics@rogers.com
www.pendragoncomics.com
(a-l,t,u,w,5)

QUEBEC

Heroes Comics
1116 Cure LaBelle
Laval, QC H7V 2V5
PH: (450) 686-9155
FAX: (450) 686-2097
E-Mail: heroes@dsuper.net
(a-i,r-u,w,x,2-5)

GERMANY

Fantastic Store
Koelner Str. 64
Kommern, NRW 53894
PH: 0049-2443-911554
FAX: 0049-2443-911966
fantasticstore@t-online.de
www.comic-heaven.de
(a-d,f,g,j,m,r,u,w,2-4)

UNITED KINGDOM

Whatever Comics
9 St. Peters Street
High Street
Canterbury, Kent CT1 2AT
PH: 01227453226
whatevercomics@hotmail.co.uk
www.whatevercomics.com

Silver Acre Comics
P.O. Box 114
Chester CH4 8WQ
England UK
PH: 01244680048
FAX: 01244680686
International phone:
+441244680048
sales@silveracre.com
www.silveracre.com

2 Tone Comics
40 Market Street
Hebden Bridge,
West Yorkshire HX7 6AA
PH: +441422 845666
amonkey21@aol.com
www.2ToneComics.com

Quicksilver Comics
2A Hilda St.
Ossett WF5 0JJ
England
PH: 01144 1132 340 111
www.QSComics.com

INTERNET

ComicLink Auctions & Exchange
PH: (718) 246-0300
buysell@ComicLink.com
www.ComicLink.com

Eric Roberts
PH: (650) 814-9196
plastered_peanuts@yahoo.com
www.triksr4kids.com

John Haines Rare Comics
PH: (216) 390-0129
E-Mail: jhrc@roadrunner.com
eBay Store: John Haines Rare Comics

M&M Comic Service
PH: (830) 438-6131
service@mmcomics.com
www.previewscatalog.com
www.mmcomics.com
(d,j,k,l,q,t,u,w,x,z,1-5)

(PAID ADVERTISING - STORE LISTINGS)

You can have your store listed here for very reasonable rates. Send for details for next year's Guide. The preceding list of stores have paid to be included in this list. We cannot assume any responsibility in your dealings with these shops. This list is provided for your information only. When planning trips, it would be advisable to make appointments in advance. Remember, to get your shop included in the next edition, contact us for rates.

Gemstone Publishing, Inc., 3679 Concord Rd., York, PA 17402.
PHONE: 888-375-9800 or 717-434-1600
FAX: 717-434-1690
E-MAIL: ads@gemstonepub.com

Items stocked by these shops are noted at the end of each listing and are coded as follows:

(a) Golden Age Comics
(b) Silver Age Comics
(c) Bronze Age Comics
(d) New Comics & Magazines
(e) Back Issue magazines
(f) Comic Supplies
(g) Collectible Card Games
(h) Role Playing Games
(i) Gaming Supplies
(j) Manga
(k) Anime
(l) Underground Comics
(m) Original Comic Art
(n) Pulps
(o) Big Little Books
(p) Books - Used
(q) Books - New
(r) Comic Related Posters
(s) Movie Posters
(t) Trading Cards
(u) Statues/Mini-busts, etc.
(v) Premiums (Rings, Decoders, etc.)
(w) Action Figures
(x) Other Toys
(y) Records/CDs
(z) DVDs/VHS
(1) Doctor Who Items
(2) Simpsons Items
(3) Star Trek Items
(4) Star Wars Items
(5) HeroClix

Glossary

a - Story art; a(i) - Story art inks; a(p) - Story art pencils;
a(r) - Story art reprint.

ADULT MATERIAL - Contains story and/or art for "mature" readers. Re: sex, violence, strong language.

ADZINE - A magazine primarily devoted to the advertising of comic books and collectibles as its first publishing priority as opposed to written articles.

ALLENTOWN COLLECTION -A collection discovered in 1987-88 just outside Allentown, Pennsylvania. The Allentown collection consisted of 135 Golden Age comics, characterized by high grade and superior paper quality.

ANNUAL - (1) A book that is published yearly; (2) Can also refer to some square bound comics.

ARRIVAL DATE - The date written (often in pencil) or stamped on the cover of comics by either the local wholesaler, newsstand owner, or distributor. The date precedes the cover date by approximately 15 to 75 days, and may vary considerably from one locale to another or from one year to another.

ASHCAN -A publisher's in-house facsimile of a proposed new title. Most ashcans have black and white covers stapled to an existing coverless comic on the inside; other ashcans are totally black and white. In modern parlance, it can also refer to promotional or sold comics, often smaller than standard comic size and usually in black and white, released by publishers to advertise the forthcoming arrival of a new title or story.

ATOM AGE - Comics published from 1946-1956.

B&W - Black and white art.

BACK-UP FEATURE -A story or character that usually appears after the main feature in a comic book; often not featured on the cover.

BAD GIRL ART - A term popularized in the early '90s to describe an attitude as well as a style of art that portrays women in a sexual and often action-oriented way.

BAXTER PAPER - A high quality, heavy, white paper used in the printing of some comics.

BC - Abbreviation for Back Cover.

BI-MONTHLY - Published every two months.

BI-WEEKLY - Published every two weeks.

BONDAGE COVER - Usually denotes a female in bondage.

BOUND COPY - A comic that has been bound into a book. The process requires that the spine be trimmed and sometimes sewn into a book-like binding.

BRITISH ISSUE - A comic printed for distribution in Great Britain; these copies sometimes have the price listed in pence or pounds instead of cents or dollars.

BRITTLENESS - A severe condition of paper deterioration where paper loses its flexibility and thus chips and/or flakes easily.

BRONZE AGE - Comics published from 1970 to 1984.

BROWNING - (1) The aging of paper characterized by the ever-increasing level of oxidation characterized by darkening; (2) The level of paper deterioration one step more severe than tanning and one step before brittleness.

c - Cover art; c(i) - Cover inks; c(p) - Cover pencils; c(r) - Cover reprint.

CAMEO - The brief appearance of one character in the strip of another.

CANADIAN ISSUE - A comic printed for distribution in Canada; these copies sometimes have no advertising.

CCA - Abbreviation for Comics Code Authority.

CCA SEAL - An emblem that was placed on the cover of all CCA approved comics beginning in April-May, 1955.

CENTER CREASE - See Subscription Copy.

CENTERFOLD or CENTER SPREAD - The two folded pages in the center of a comic book at the terminal end of the staples.

CERTIFIED GRADING - A process provided by a professional grading service that certifies a given grade for a comic and seals the book in a protective Slab.

CF - Abbreviation for Centerfold.

CFO - Abbreviation for Centerfold Out.

CGC - Abbreviation for the certified comic book grading company, Comics Guaranty, LLC.

CIRCULATION COPY - See Subscription Copy.

CIRCULATION FOLD - See Subscription Fold.

CLASSIC COVER - A cover considered by collectors to be highly desirable because of its subject matter, artwork, historical importance, etc.

CLEANING - A process in which dirt and dust is removed.

COLOR TOUCH - A restoration process by which colored ink is used to hide color flecks, color flakes, and larger areas of missing color. Short for Color Touch-Up.

COLORIST - An artist who paints the color guides for comics. Many modern colorists use computer technology.

COMIC BOOK DEALER - (1) A seller of comic books; (2) One who makes a living buying and selling comic books.

COMIC BOOK REPAIR - When a tear, loose staple or centerfold has been mended without changing or adding to the original finish of the book. Repair may involve tape, glue or nylon gossamer, and is easily detected; it is considered a defect.

COMICS CODE AUTHORITY -A voluntary organization comprised of comic book publishers formed in 1954 to review (and possibly censor) comic books before they were printed and distributed. The emblem of the CCA is a white stamp in the upper right hand corner of comics dated after February 1955. The term "post-Code" refers to the time after this practice started, or approximately 1955 to the present.

COMPLETE RUN - All issues of a given title.

CON -A convention or public gathering of fans.

CONDITION -The state of preservation of a comic book, often inaccurately used interchangeably with Grade.

CONSERVATION - The European Confederation of Conservator-Restorers' Organizations (ECCO) in its professional guidelines, defines conservation as follows: "Conservation consists mainly of direct action carried out on cultural heritage with the aim of stabilizing condition and retarding further deterioration."

COPPER AGE - Comics published from 1984 to 1992.

COSMIC AEROPLANE COLLECTION - A collection from Salt Lake City, Utah discovered by Cosmic Aeroplane Books, characterized by the moderate to high grade copies of 1930s-40s comics with pencil check marks in the margins of inside pages. It is thought that these comics were kept by a commercial illustration school and the check marks were placed beside panels that instructors wanted students to draw.

COSTUMED HERO - A costumed crime fighter with "developed" human powers instead of super powers.

COUPON CUT or COUPON MISSING - A coupon has been neatly removed with scissors or razor blade from the interior or exterior of the comic as opposed to having been ripped out.

COVER GLOSS -The reflective quality of the cover inks.

COVER TRIMMED - Cover has been reduced in size by neatly cutting away rough or damaged edges.

COVERLESS - A comic with no cover attached. There is a niche demand for coverless comics, particularly in the case of hard-to-find key books otherwise impossible to locate intact.

C/P - Abbreviation for Cleaned and Pressed. See Cleaning.

CREASE - A fold which causes ink removal, usually resulting in a white line. See Reading Crease.

CROSSOVER - A story where one character appears prominently in the story of another character. See X-Over.

CVR - Abbreviation for Cover.

DEALER - See Comic Book Dealer.

DEACIDIFICATION - Several different processes that reduce acidity in paper.

DEBUT -The first time that a character appears anywhere.

DEFECT - Any fault or flaw that detracts from perfection.

DENVER COLLECTION - A collection consisting primarily of early 1940s high grade number one issues bought at auction in Pennsylvania by a Denver, Colorado dealer.

DIE-CUT COVER - A comic book cover with areas or edges precut by a printer to a special shape or to create a desired effect.

DISTRIBUTOR STRIPES - Color brushed or sprayed on the edges of comic book stacks by the distributor/wholesaler to code them for expedient exchange at the sales racks. Typical colors are red, orange, yellow, green, blue, and purple. Distributor stripes are not a defect.

DOUBLE - A duplicate copy of the same comic book.

DOUBLE COVER - When two covers are stapled to the comic interior instead of the usual one; the exterior cover often protects the interior cover from wear and damage. This is considered a desirable situation by some collectors and may increase collector value; this is not considered a defect.

DRUG PROPAGANDA STORY - A comic that makes an editorial stand about drug use.

DRUG USE STORY - A comic that shows the actual use of drugs: needle use, tripping, harmful effects, etc.

DRY CLEANING - A process in which dirt and dust is removed.

DUOTONE - Printed with black and one other color of ink. This process was common in comics printed in the 1930s.

DUST SHADOW - Darker, usually linear area at the edge of some comics stored in stacks. Some portion of the cover was not covered by the comic immediately above it and it was exposed to settling dust particles. Also see Oxidation Shadow and Sun Shadow.

EDGAR CHURCH COLLECTION - See Mile High Collection.

EMBOSSED COVER - A comic book cover with a pattern, shape or image pressed into the cover from the inside, creating a raised area.

ENCAPSULATION - Refers to the

process of sealing certified comics in a protective plastic enclosure. Also see Slabbing.

EYE APPEAL - A term which refers to the overall look of a comic book when held at approximately arm's length. A comic may have nice eye appeal yet still possess defects which reduce grade.

FANZINE -An amateur fan publication.

FC - Abbreviation for Front Cover.

FILE COPY -A high grade comic originating from the publisher's file; contrary to what some might believe, not all file copies are in Gem Mint condition. An arrival date on the cover of a comic does not indicate that it is a file copy, though a copyright date may.

FIRST APPEARANCE - See Debut.

FLASHBACK - When a previous story is recalled.

FOIL COVER - A comic book cover that has had a thin metallic foil hot stamped on it. Many of these "gimmick" covers date from the early '90s, and might include chromium, prism and hologram covers as well.

FOUR COLOR - Series of comics produced by Dell, characterized by hundreds of different features; named after the four color process of printing. See One Shot.

FOUR COLOR PROCESS - The process of printing with the three primary colors (red, yellow, and blue) plus black.

FUMETTI - Illustration system in which individual frames of a film are colored and used for individual panels to make a comic book story. The most famous example is DC's *Movie Comics* #1-6 from 1939.

GATEFOLD COVER - A double-width fold-out cover.

GENRE - Categories of comic book subject matter; e.g. Science Fiction, Super-Hero, Romance, Funny Animal, Teenage Humor, Crime, War, Western, Mystery, Horror, etc.

GIVEAWAY - Type of comic book intended to be given away as a premium or promotional device instead of being sold.

GLASSES ATTACHED - In 3-D comics, the special blue and red cellophane and cardboard glasses are still attached to the comic.

GLASSES DETACHED - In 3-D comics, the special blue and red cellophane and cardboard glasses are not still attached to the comic; obviously less desirable than Glasses Attached.

GOLDEN AGE - Comics published from 1938 (*Action Comics* #1) to 1945.

GOOD GIRL ART - Refers to a style of art, usually from the 1930s-50s, that portrays women in a sexually implicit way.

GREY-TONE COVER - A cover art style in which pencil or charcoal underlies the normal line drawing, used to enhance the effects of light and shadow, thus producing a richer quality. These covers, prized by most collectors, are sometimes referred to as Painted Covers but are not actually painted.

HC - Abbreviation for Hardcover.

HEADLIGHTS - Forward illumation devices installed on all automobiles and many other vehicles... OK, OK, it's a euphemism for a comic book cover prominently featuring a woman's breasts in a provocative way. Also see Bondage Cover for another collecting euphemism that has long since outlived its appropriateness in these politically correct times.

HOT STAMPING - The process of pressing foil, prism paper and/or inks on cover stock.

HRN - Abbreviation for Highest Reorder Number. This refers to a method used by collectors of Gilberton's *Classic Comics* and *Classics Illustrated* series to distinguish first editions from later printings.

ILLO - Abbreviation for Illustration.

IMPAINT - Another term for Color Touch.

INDICIA - Publishing and title information usually located at the bottom of the first page or the bottom of the inside front cover. In some pre-1938 comics and many modern comics, it is located on internal pages.

INFINITY COVER - Shows a scene that repeats itself to infinity.

INKER - Artist that does the inking.

INTRO - Same as Debut.

INVESTMENT GRADE COPY - (1) Comic of sufficiently high grade and demand to be viewed by collectors as instantly liquid should the need arise to sell; (2) A comic in VF or better condition; (3) A comic purchased primarily to realize a profit.

ISSUE NUMBER - The actual edition number of a given title.

ISH - Short for Issue.

JLA - Abbreviation for Justice League of America.

JSA -Abbreviation for Justice Society of America.

KEY, KEY BOOK or KEY ISSUE - An issue that contains a first appearance, origin, or other historically or artistically important feature considered especially desirable by collectors.

LAMONT LARSON - Pedigreed collection of high grade 1940s comics with the initials or name of its original owner, Lamont Larson.

LENTICULAR COVERS or "FLICKER" COVERS -A comic book cover overlayed with a ridged plastic sheet such that the special artwork underneath appears to move when the cover is tilted at different angles perpendicular to the ridges.

LETTER COL or LETTER COLUMN - A feature in a comic book that prints and sometimes responds to letters written by its readers.

LINE DRAWN COVER -A cover published in the traditional way where pencil sketches are overdrawn with india ink and then colored. See also Grey-Tone Cover, Photo Cover, and Painted Cover.

LOGO - The title of a strip or comic book as it appears on the cover or title page.

LSH - Abbreviation for Legion of Super-Heroes.

MAGIC LIGHTNING COLLECTION - A collection of high grade 1950s comics from the San Francisco area.

MARVEL CHIPPING -A bindery (trimming/cutting) defect that results in a series of chips and tears at the top, bottom, and right edges of the cover, caused when the cutting blade of an industrial paper trimmer becomes dull. It was dubbed Marvel Chipping because it can be found quite often on Marvel comics from the late '50s and early '60s but can also occur with any company's comic books from the late 1940s through the middle 1960s.

MILE HIGH COLLECTION - High grade collection of over 22,000 comics discovered in Denver, Colorado in 1977, originally owned by Mr. Edgar Church. Comics from this collection are now famous for extremely white pages, fresh smell, and beautiful cover ink reflectivity.

MODERN AGE - A catch-all term applied to comics published since 1992.

MYLAR™ -An inert, very hard, space-age plastic used to make high quality protective bags and sleeves for comic book storage. "Mylar" is a trademark of the DuPont Co.

ND - Abbreviation for No Date.

NN - Abbreviation for No Number.

NO DATE - When there is no date given on the cover or indicia page.

NO NUMBER - No issue number is given on the cover or indicia page; these are usually first issues or one-shots.

N.Y. LEGIS. COMM. - New York Legislative Committee to Study the Publication of Comics (1951).

ONE-SHOT - When only one issue is published of a title, or when a series is published where each issue is a different title (e.g. Dell's *Four Color Comics*).

ORIGIN -When the story of a character's creation is given.

OVER GUIDE - When a comic book is priced at a value over *Guide* list.

OXIDATION SHADOW - Darker, usually linear area at the edge of some comics stored in stacks. Some portion of the cover was not covered by the comic immediately above it, and it was exposed to the air. Also see Dust Shadow and Sun Shadow.

p - Art pencils.

PAINTED COVER - (1) Cover taken from an actual painting instead of a line drawing; (2) Inaccurate name for a grey-toned cover.

PANELOLOGIST - One who researches comic books and/or comic strips.

PANNAPICTAGRAPHIST - One possible term for someone who collects comic books; can you figure out why it hasn't exactly taken off in common parlance?

PAPER COVER - Comic book cover made from the same newsprint as the interior pages. These books are extremely rare in high grade.

PARADE OF PLEASURE - A book about the censorship of comics.

PB - Abbreviation for Paperback.

PEDIGREE - A book from a famous and usually high grade collection - e.g. Allentown, Lamont Larson, Edgar Church/Mile High, Denver, San Francisco, Cosmic Aeroplane, etc. Beware of non-pedigree collections being promoted as pedigree books; only outstanding high grade collections similar to those listed qualify.

PENCILER - Artist that does the pencils...you're figuring out some of these definitions without us by now, aren't you?

PERFECT BINDING - Pages are glued to the cover as opposed to being stapled to the cover, resulting in a flat binded side. Also known as Square Back or Square Bound.

PG - Abbreviation for Page.

PHOTO COVER - Comic book cover featuring a photographic image instead of a line drawing or painting.

PIECE REPLACEMENT - A process by which pieces are added to replace areas of missing paper.

PIONEER AGE - Comics published from the 1500s to 1828.

PLATINUM AGE - Comics published from 1883 to 1938.

POLYPROPALENE - A type of plastic used in the manufacture of comic book bags; now considered harmful to paper and not recommended for long term storage of comics.

POP - Abbreviation for the anti-comic book volume, *Parade of Pleasure*.

POST-CODE - Describes comics published after February 1955 and usually displaying the CCA stamp in the upper right-hand corner.

POUGHKEEPSIE - Refers to a large collection of Dell Comics file copies believed to have originated from the warehouse of Western Publishing in Poughkeepsie, NY.

PP - Abbreviation for Pages.

PRE-CODE - Describes comics published before the Comics Code Authority seal began appearing on covers in 1955.

PRE-HERO DC - A term used to describe *More Fun* #1-51 (pre-Spectre), *Adventure* #1-39 (pre-Sandman), and *Detective* #1-26 (pre-Batman). The term is actually inaccurate because technically there were "heroes" in the above books.

PRE-HERO MARVEL - A term used to describe *Strange Tales* #1-100 (pre-Human Torch), *Journey Into Mystery* #1-82 (pre-Thor), *Tales To Astonish* #1-35 (pre-Ant Man), and *Tales Of Suspense* #1-38 (pre-Iron Man).

PRESERVATION - Another term for Conservation.

PRESSING - A term used to describe a variety of processes or procedures, professional and amateur, under which an issue is pressed to eliminate wrinkles, bends, dimples and/or other perceived defects and thus improve its appearance. Some types of pressing involve disassembling the book and performing other work on it prior to its pressing and reassembly. Some methods are generally easily discerned by professionals and amateurs. Other types of pressing, however, can pose difficulty for even experienced professionals to detect. In all cases, readers are cautioned that unintended damage can occur in some instances. Related defects will diminish an issue's grade correspondingly rather than improve it.

PROVENANCE - When the owner of a book is known and is stated for the purpose of authenticating and documenting the history of the book. Example: A book from the Stan Lee or Forrest Ackerman collection would be an example of a value-adding provenance.

PULP - Cheaply produced magazine made from low grade newsprint. The term comes from the wood pulp that was used in the paper manufacturing process.

QUARTERLY - Published every three months (four times a year).

R - Abbreviation for Reprint.

RARE - 10-20 copies estimated to exist.

RAT CHEW - Damage caused by the gnawing of rats and mice.

RBCC - Abbreviation for Rockets Blast Comic Collector, one of the first and most prominent adzines instrumental in developing the early comic book market.

READING COPY - A comic that is in FAIR to GOOD condition and is often used for research; the condition has been sufficiently reduced to the point where general handling will not degrade it further.

READING CREASE - Book-length, vertical front cover crease at staples, caused by bending the cover over the staples. Square-bounds receive these creases just by opening the cover too far to the left.

REILLY, TOM - A large high grade collection of 1939-1945 comics with 5000+ books.

REINFORCEMENT - A process by which a weak or split page or cover is reinforced with adhesive and reinforcement paper.

REPRINT COMICS - In earlier decades, comic books that contained newspaper strip reprints; modern reprint comics usually contain stories originally featured in older comic books.

RESTORATION - Any attempt, whether professional or amateur, to enhance the appearance of an aging or damaged comic book using additive procedures. These procedures may include any or all of the following techniques: recoloring, adding missing paper, trimming, re-glossing, reinforcement, glue, etc. Amateur work can lower the value of a book, and even professional restoration has now gained a negative aura in the modern marketplace from some quarters. In all cases a restored book can never be worth the same as an unrestored book in the same condition. There is no consensus on the inclusion of pressing, non-aqueous cleaning, tape removal and in some cases staple replacement in this definition. Until such time as there is consensus, we encourage continued debate and interaction among all interested parties and reflection upon the standards in other hobbies and art forms.

REVIVAL - An issue that begins republishing a comic book character after a period of dormancy.

ROCKFORD - A high grade collection of 1940s comics with 2000+ books from Rockford, IL.

ROLLED SPINE - A condition where the left edge of a comic book curves toward the front or back; a defect caused by folding back each page as the comic was read.

ROUND BOUND - Standard saddle stitch binding typical of most comics.

RUN - A group of comics of one title where most or all of the issues are present. See Complete Run.

S&K - Abbreviation for the legendary creative team of Joe Simon and Jack Kirby, creators of Marvel Comics' Captain America.

SADDLE STITCH - The staple binding of magazines and comic books.

SAN FRANCISCO COLLECTION - (see Reilly, Tom)

SCARCE - 20-100 copies estimated to exist.

SEDUCTION OF THE INNOCENT - An inflammatory book written by Dr. Frederic Wertham and published in 1953; Wertham asserted that comics were responsible for rampant juvenile deliquency in American youth.

SET - (1) A complete run of a given title; (2) A grouping of comics for sale.

SEMI-MONTHLY - Published twice a month, but not necessarily Bi-Weekly.

SEWN SPINE - A comic with many

spine perforations where binders' thread held it into a bound volume. This is considered a defect.

SF - Abbreviation for Science Fiction (the other commonly used term, "sci-fi," is often considered derogatory or indicative of more "low-brow" rather than "literary" science fiction, i.e. "sci-fi television."

SILVER AGE - Comics published from 1956 to 1970.

SILVER PROOF - A black and white actual size print on thick glossy paper hand-painted by an artist to indicate colors to the engraver.

SLAB - Colloquial term for the plastic enclosure used by grading certification companies to seal in certified comics.

SLABBING - Colloquial term for the process of encapsulating certified comics in a plastic enclosure.

SOTI - Abbreviation for Seduction of the Innocent.

SPINE - The left-hand edge of the comic that has been folded and stapled.

SPINE ROLL - A condition where the left edge of the comic book curves toward the front or back, caused by folding back each page as the comic was read.

SPINE SPLIT SEALED - A process by which a spine split is sealed using an adhesive.

SPLASH PAGE - A Splash Panel that takes up the entire page.

SPLASH PANEL - (1) The first panel of a comic book story, usually larger than other panels and usually containing the title and credits of the story; (2) An oversized interior panel.

SQUARE BACK or SQUARE BOUND - See Perfect Binding.

STORE STAMP - Store name (and sometimes address and telephone number) stamped in ink via rubber stamp and stamp pad.

SUBSCRIPTION COPY - A comic sent through the mail directly from the publisher or publisher's agent. Most are folded in half, causing a subscription crease or fold running down the center of the comic from top to bottom; this is considered a defect.

SUBSCRIPTION CREASE - See Subscription Copy.

SUBSCRIPTION FOLD - See Subscription Copy. Differs from a Subscription Crease in that no ink is missing as a result of the fold.

SUN SHADOW - Darker, usually linear area at the edge of some comics stored in stacks. Some portion of the cover was not covered by the comic immediately above it, and it suffered prolonged exposure to light. A serious defect, unlike a Dust Shadow, which can sometimes be removed. Also see Oxidation Shadow.

SUPER-HERO - A costumed crime fighter with powers beyond those of mortal man.

SUPER-VILLAIN -A costumed criminal with powers beyond those of mortal man; the antithesis of Super-Hero.

SWIPE - A panel, sequence, or story obviously borrowed from previously published material.

TEAR SEALS - A process by which a tear is sealed using an adhesive.

TEXT ILLO. - A drawing or small panel in a text story that almost never has a dialogue balloon.

TEXT PAGE - A page with no panels or drawings.

TEXT STORY - A story with few if any illustrations commonly used as filler material during the first three decades of comics.

3-D COMIC - Comic art that is drawn and printed in two color layers, producing a 3-D effect when viewed through special glasses.

3-D EFFECT COMIC - Comic art that is drawn to appear as if in 3-D but isn't.

TITLE - The name of the comic book.

TITLE PAGE - First page of a story showing the title of the story and possibly the creative credits and indicia.

TRIMMED - (1) A bindery process which separates top, right, and bottom of pages and cuts comic books to the proper size; (2) A repair process in which defects along the edges of a comic book are removed with the use of scissors, razor blades, and/or paper cutters. Comic books which have been repaired in this fashion are considered defectives.

TTA - Abbreviation for *Tales to Astonish*.

UK - Abbreviation for British edition (United Kingdom).

UNDER GUIDE - When a comic book is priced at a value less than *Guide* list.

UPGRADE - To obtain another copy of the same comic book in a higher grade.

VARIANT COVER - A different cover image used on the same issue.

VERY RARE - 1 to 10 copies estimat ed to exist.

VICTORIAN AGE - Comics published from 1828 to 1883.

WANT LIST - A listing of comics needed by a collector, or a list of comics that a collector is interested in purchasing.

WAREHOUSE COPY - Originating from a publisher's warehouse; similar to file copy.

WHITE MOUNTAIN COLLECTION - A collection of high grade 1950s and 1960s comics which originated in New England.

X-OVER - Short for Crossover.

ZINE - Short for Fanzine.

Feature Article Index

Over the years, *The Official Overstreet Comic Book Price Guide* has grown into much more than a simple catalog of values. Almost since the very beginning, Bob has worked hard to make sure that the book reflects the latest information about the hobby, and this has resulted in some fascinating in-depth articles about aspects of the industry and the rich history of comics. Sadly, many of you may never have read a lot of these articles, or even knew they existed.

These two pages contain a comprehensive index to every feature article ever published in *The Official Overstreet Comic Book Price Guide*. From interviews with legendary creators to exhaustively researched retrospectives, it's all here. Enjoy this look back at the Overstreet legacy, and remember, many of these editions are still available through Gemstone and your local comic book dealer.

Note: The first three editions of *The Guide* had no feature articles, but from #4 on, a tradition was born that has carried through to the very volume. This index begins with the 4th edition and lists all articles published up to and including last year's 38th edition of the guide.

AUTHOR (S)	TITLE	EDITION	PGS.
Adams, Weldon	Comics in the Schools - 1926: The Lost Comic Book History of the Lone Star State	#35 (2005	1001-1006
Andrae, Thomas	The Enduring Magic of Disney Comics (written with Bruce Hamilton)	#17 (1987)	A-85-90
	Of Superman and Kids With Dreams: An Interview with Jerry Siegel and Joe Shuster	#18 (1988)	A-79-98
	Origins of the Dark Knight: A Conversation with Batman Artists (with Bob Kane and Jerry Robinson)	#19 (1989)	A-72-93
	Green Lantern's Light! A History by... (with Keif Fromm)	#23 (1993)	A-71-79
Bails, Jerry	Secrets Behind All-Star Comics (More Than You May Want to Know)	#04 (1974)	26-37
Barrington, Stephen	Supergirl: Back for Justice	#36 (2006)	1048-1051
Beck, C.C.	Mr. Mind and the Monster Society of Evil	#15 (1985)	A-89-93
Beerbohm, Robert L.	The American Comic Book: 1897-1932 The Beginning: The Platinum Age	#27 (1997)	1-15
	New Discoveries Beyond the Platinum Age (with Richard D. Olsen, Ph.D.)	#30 (2000)	226-234
	The Golden Age and Beyond: Origins of the Modern Comic Book (written with Richard D. Olsen, Ph.D.)	#30 (2000)	242-249
Blumberg, Arnold T.	Gotham Knights - A Conversation with Jerry Robinson	#27 (1997)	A-25-27
	The World of Tomorrow: How Comics of the Past Portrayed the 1990s	#28 (1998)	82-88
	Invasion of the Giant (and Not So Giant) Robots!	#28 (1998)	83-87
	One For All and All for One	#29 (1999)	107-112
	History with a Twist	#30 (2000)	18-22
	The Marketing of a Medium	#30 (2000)	195-198
	Why the Fantastic Four Made it to Forty	#31 (2001)	20-24
	Brownie Points	#31 (2001)	30-32
	Re-Creations in a Flash (Murphy Anderson profile)	#31 (2001)	39-40
	Superman: Patriotic Covers Through the Years	#32 (2002)	40-43
	Spidey Goes Hollywood	#32 (2002)	44-46
	Mutant Movie Stars: The "New" X-Men Storm the Silver Screen	#33 (2003)	854-856
	Through Waves and Flames: The Elemental Entrance of the Sub-Mariner	#33 (2003)	858-860
	Comic Book Ages: Start the Discussion (with J.C. Vaughn)	#33 (2003)	866-867
	Comic Book Ages: Defining Eras (with J.C. Vaughn)	#34 (2004)	948-951
	Going Green: The Best of the Hulk	#34 (2004)	956-959
Boatner, E. B.	Carl Barks: From Burbank to Calisota	#07 (1977)	A-37-57
	Good Lord! choke...gasp...It's EC!	#09 (1979)	A-43-76
	L. B. Cole: The Man Behind the Mask	#11 (1981)	A-55-72

AUTHOR (S)	TITLE	EDITION	PGS.
Borock, Steve	Comic Book Certification: An Overview of Comic Guaranty, LLC.	#35 (2005)	1007-1011
	An Insiders Look at CGC and Comic Book Certification	#36 (2006)	1044-1047
	CGC, The Art and Science of Comic Book Certification	#37 (2007)	1036-1039
	A CGC Primer: How Professional Comic Book Certification Works	#38 (2008)	1052-1055
Braden, Scott	Strange Adventures - A Conversation with Murphy Anderson	#27 (1997)	A-30-32
	Built to Last (with J.C. Vaughan)	#28 (1998)	89-102
Calhoun, Pat S.	Living on Borrowed Time! A Nostalgic Look at the Early Years of DC's Challengers of the Unknown (with Gary M. Carter)	#24 (1994)	A-157-164
	100 Years - A Century of Comics	#25 (1995)	A-107-123
Carter, Gary M.	DC Before Superman (written with Ken Lane Carter)	#13 (1983)	A-72-86
	The Silver Age... The Beginning: A Comparative Chronology of the First Sliver Age Comic Books	#20 (1990)	A-94-107
	Journey into the Unknown World of Atlas Fantasy (written with Pat S. Calhoun)	#22 (1992)	A-87-103
	Silver Sagas of the Scarlet Speedster: Whirlwind Adventures of the Fastest Man Alive! 1956-1960	#23 (1993)	A-80-86
Chesney, Landon	The Archives of the Comic Book Price Guide	#06 (1976)	44-45
Colabuono, Gary	Golden Age Ashcans - Comics' First Editions (with Mark Zaid)	#38 (2008)	1040-1045
DeFuccio, Jerry	An Interview with Will Eisner, Creator of the Spirit	#06 (1976)	31-37
	Norman Mingo and Alfred: The World's Greatest Facelift	#12 (1982)	A-45-57
	Charles Clarence Beck: The World's Second Mightiest Mortal	#15 (1985)	A-78-88
Dempsey, "Little" Jimmy	Great Old Radio Premiums	#13 (1983)	A-62-63
Disbrow, Jay	Confessions of a Former Comic Book Artist	#08 (1978)	A-31-38
Estrada, Jackie	Friends of Lulu Sound Off on Comics	#28 (1998)	79-81
Fulop, Scoot D.	Archie Comics Publications: The Mirth of a Legend	#21 (1991)	A-77-78
Hamilton, Bruce	The Mystery of the 12 Missing EC's	#25 (1995)	A-99-106
	Special Feature: Grading - The Next Revolution for Comic Books	#29 (1999)	17-21
Hancer, Kevin B.	Edgar Rice Burroughs and the Comics	#05 (1975)	33-38
Hessee, Tim	The Pop Hollinger Story: The First Comic Book Collector/Dealer	#12 (1982)	A-58-66
Huesman, Mark	Legiondary Adventures	#29 (1999)	101-106
Irons, Christopher	The Man Behind the Cover - L. B. Cole	#18 (1988)	A-77
Kronenberg, Michael	Indelible Shadows: The Spectacular Rise of Artist Jim Lee	#36 (2006)	1052-1055
	Patriot Act!!! (Captain America profile)	#37 (2007)	1024-1029
Leavitt,Craig	Katy Keene - The Overstreet Connection	#14 (1984)	A-67-78
Lee, Stan	Twenty-Five Years? I Don't Believe It!	#16 (1986)	A-82-84
Marek, Carl, et al.	Good Girl Art - An Introduction: Why it Was and What it Was (produced by the American Comic Book Co.)	#06 (1976)	38-43
	Esoteric Comics: The Ultimate Collection (produced by the American Comic Book Co. in Consultation with Scott Shaw)	#07 (1977)	A-30-35
	Women in Comics (in collaboration with Art Amsie)	#08 (1978)	A-54-75
	For Those Who Know How to Look	#09 (1979)	A-35-42
Miller, John Jackson	From "A Long Time Ago" To Today's Galaxy	#38 (2008)	1046-1051
Moore, Dale	Comic Book Charites: Lifelines of the Industry	#34 (2004)	964-966
Murray,Will	Marvel's Hammer: The Mighty Thor	#36 (2006)	1028-1039
	The Untold Origin of Daredevil	#37 (2007)	1030-1035
Novinskie, Charles S.	Sixty Years of Wonder Woman	#31 (2001)	26-29

AUTHOR (S)	TITLE	EDITION	PGS.
Olsen, Richard D. Ph.D.	The American Comic Book: 1897-1932	#26 (1996)	1-2
	The American Comic Book: 1933-Present The Modern Comic Book	#26 (1996)	10-11
	The Golden Age and Beyond: The Modern Comic	#27 (1997) Book (Revised)	23-24
	The Golden Age and Beyond: The Modern Comic	#28 (1998) Book (Revised)	211-211
Olshevsky, George	The Origin of Marvel Comics	#10 (1980)	A-46-73
Overstreet, Robert M.	Bob's Bizarre Tales	#30 (2000)	42-63
	And When The Vault Was Opened... (with Gary M. Carter)	#38 (2008)	1036-1039
Overstreet Staff	The Man Behind the Cover - Ron Dias	#17 (1987)	A-84
Rausch, Barbara A.	Katy WHO?...Never Heard of it...	#14 (1984)	A-52-56
Ray, Benn	A Brief History of Super-Teams: Top Ten Greatest Super-Teams	#29 (1999)	108-112
Robbins, Trina	Tarpe Mills - An Appreication	#08 (1978)	A-76
Saffel, Steve	Spider-Man: An Amazing Success Story	#22 (1992)	A-77-86
Schiff, Jack	Reminiscience of a Comic Book Editor (with Gene Reed)	#13 (1983)	A-64-70
Shooter, Jim	Marvel and Me	#16 (1986)	A-85-96
Taylor, Terry	Walt Disney's Snow White and the Seven Dwarfs - Fifty Years of Collectibles	#17 (1987)	A-101-111
Thomas, Harry B.	1941: Comic Books Go To War: Those fabulous comics of World War II (with Gary M. Carter)	#21 (1991)	A-79-98
Townsend, John Ph.D.	Three Uncanny Decades of X-Men	#24 (1994)	A-146-156
Vaughn, J.C.	Built to Last (with Scott Braden)	#28 (1998)	89-102
	The American Comic Book: 1897 - 1932 In the Beginning: The Platinum Age	#28 (1998)	201-203
	Avenues of Collecting: A Walk Through the Comic Book Neighborhood	#29 (1999)	91-94
	Just Another Justice League?	#29 (1999)	95-100
	EC, MAD and Beyond: Al Feldstein	#30 (2000)	24-28
	Flights to EC and Beyond with Al Williamson	#30 (2000)	36-39
	Extraordinary! (John K. Snyder III profile)	#31 (2001)	42-44
	Bendis! (Brian Michael Bendis profile)	#31 (2001)	46-48
	Archie at 60	#32 (2002)	47-49
	A Brief History of the Justice Society	#33 (2003)	850-852
	Variant Watch: Ultimate Spider-Man #1	#33 (2003)	862-863
	Comic Book Ages: Start the Discussion (with Arnold T. Blumberg)	#33 (2003)	866-867
	Comic Book Ages: Defining Eras (with Arnold T. Blumberg)	#34 (2004)	948-951
	70 Years and Still Quacking	#34 (2004)	952-955
	(Joe) Simon Says	#34 (2004)	960-963
	Enduring Duo: Wolfman & Perez (Teen Titans at 25, Crisis at 20)	#35 (2005)	993-995
	Little Lulu at 70 (and 60)	#35 (2005)	996-997
	Iron Man: Heavy Metal	#35 (2005)	998-1000
	Publisher Spotlight: Dark Horse Comics	#35 (2005)	1012-1013
	Wonder Woman: Revisited and Renewed	#36 (2006)	1041-1043
	The Semi-Secret Origins of The Overstreet Comic Book Price Guide (Bob Overstreet interview)	#37 (2007)	1016-1023
Ward, Bill	The Man Behind Torchy	#08 (1978)	A-40-53
Weist, Jerry	The Golden Age and Beyond: A Short History of Comic Book Fandom & Comic Book Collecting in America	#26 (1996)	652-667
Zaid, Mark	Golden Age Ashcans - Comics' First Editions (with Gary Colabuono)	#38 (2008)	1040-1045
Zone, Ray	Anaglyphs - A Survey of 3-D Comic Books	#11 (1981)	A-44-53

Standing on the Shoulders of GIANTS: THE HERO INITIATIVE

by John Seals

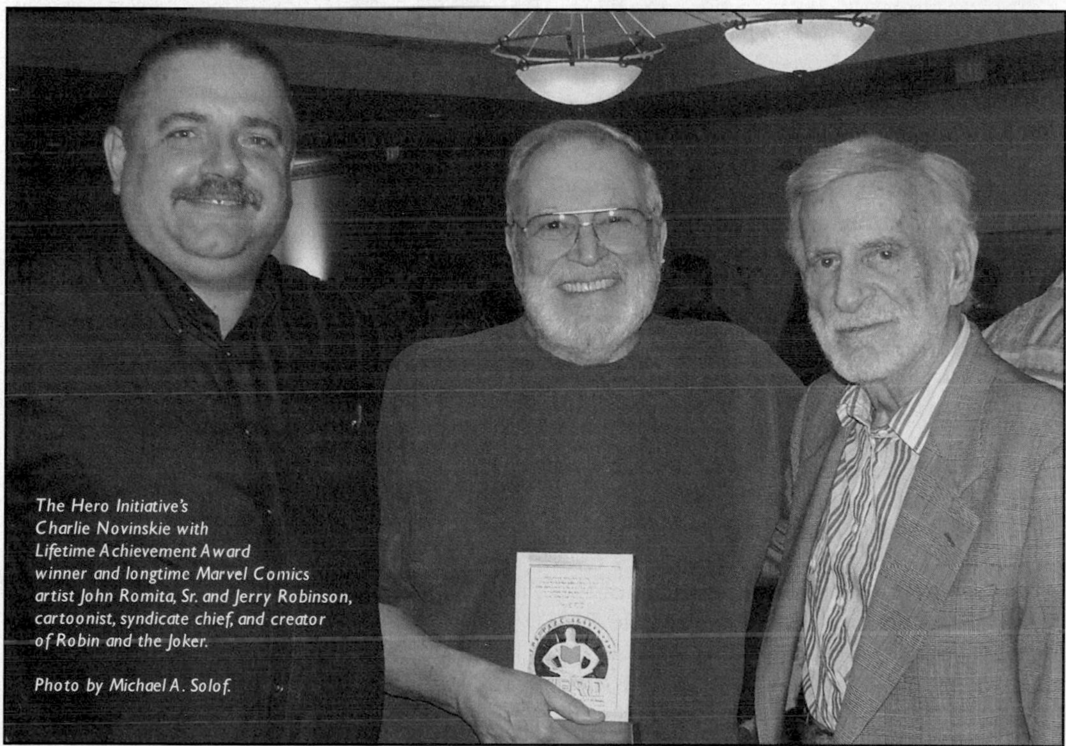

The Hero Initiative's Charlie Novinskie with Lifetime Achievement Award winner and longtime Marvel Comics artist John Romita, Sr. and Jerry Robinson, cartoonist, syndicate chief, and creator of Robin and the Joker.

Photo by Michael A. Solof.

It's November 2007 and a comic creator and his wife are counting out pennies to buy milk. After adding up their cash reserves they were also able to afford some Cheerios. This was due to a coupon they had found for a free box. They had a total of \$3.00 to their names. With winter approaching they had already resigned themselves to the fact that the heat was probably going to get turned off for at least part of the winter. With no place else to turn they looked to the Hero Initiative.

The Hero Initiative (Hero), the first-ever federally chartered not-for-profit corporation dedicated strictly to helping comic book creators in need, was able to help.

Funds totaling $3,000.00 were provided and checks were sent to creditors, like landlords for rent and a propane company to pay for heat, according to Hero President Jim McLauchlin.

On September 6, 2006 when creator Lea Hernandez lost her home, and most of the things in it, to a fire, Hero was a big help.

"Hero provided me with money to help defray costs after the fire," Hernandez said. "They also helped again a year later by granting me a significant portion of the price of a Wacom Cintiq so I could continue drawing. I have wrist problems related to Carpal Tunnel Syndrome that were making drawing with traditional media painful to the point where my output was dropping. The Cintiq has upped my production speed and given me pain relief," she added.

This experience has made Hernandez a strong supporter of the services provided by Hero.

"After the fire, Jim McLauchlin contacted me within 24 hours and simply asked if I needed help. No judgment, no strings, just help. Hero is awesome."

To be eligible for assistance from Hero, an applicant must have been a working comic book writer, penciller, inker, colorist, or letterer, who was on a work-for-hire basis for no less than 10 years at some time since January 1, 1934.

Hero has donated more than $300,000 since its inception in late 2000. It's the kind of help that seems to bring out the best in both those working in the comics industry and their fans.

"One of the most amazing things to me is that there are so many people who have given art or services so that it in turn can be given to Hero. I've been thrilled and gratified by the enthusiasm of fans as well as professionals," says comic industry legend, and Hero board member, Roy Thomas.

Famed creator Dan Jurgens adds, "We stand on the shoulders of giants. That's an old saying, often used in business to describe the work of those who came earlier. If not for the brilliant work of those who came before us, who poured their creative minds onto the page, we wouldn't have the comics we enjoy as readers and careers we enjoy as pros."

Usually Hero keeps the names of those it helps out private. But for most volunteers the names of the eventual recipients are not important.

"I see comic store owners at busy conventions giving up hours of their own time to help someone they don't even know. It's very laudable," Thomas said.

THE HERO INITIATIVE

HERO

HELPING COMIC BOOK CREATORS IN NEED

Hero is set up into 3 distinct "boards." These are the Fundraising board, the Disbursement committee, and the Regional Advisory board. Each of these is staffed by a wide variety of volunteers from the comics and entertainment industries.

For example the Fundraising board includes Joe Quesada from Marvel Comics, movie director Guillermo Del Toro, retailer Mike Malve of Atomic Comics, Steven Borock formerly of Comics Guaranty Corporation, Chaos! Comics creator Brian Pulido, and Beth Widera the owner and operator of the Orlando MegaCon.

Hero's Disbursement Committee, which votes on how to disburse the funds, consists of some of the "Elder Statesmen" of comics including Dick Giordano, Roy Thomas, John Romita Sr., Denny O'Neil and George Pérez.

These creators tend to be more of a peer group for the creators in need but they also do their part on the fundraising side.

"Pérez and Romita are hugely popular artists and they've lain in with many fundraising events, themselves," McLauchlin said.

The Regional Advisory board is made up of volunteers located all across North America who inspire others to become involved in The Hero Initiative's efforts.

Comic publishers have also provided a lot of support for Hero too.

"Marvel has been really active," Thomas says. "It's good because it shows the willingness of the companies to help out people who put them where they are today."

In terms of fund raising there are numerous ways for those interested in donating to help out. For instance last year Hero ran an eBay auction and the winners got to meet Stan Lee during the San Diego Comic Con. Lee himself is a big Hero booster.

"Its services are invaluable. As far back as I can remember there have been creative people who, after toiling for years in the comic book field, have found themselves unemployed with no pension or company plan of any sort to help them. Hero is a life jacket for those who are adrift in a sea of financial hardship," Lee said.

Those wishing to support Hero have many options. Among the many items for sale on the Hero website "http://www.heroinitiative.org/" are Hero branded merchandise, an exclusive wearable green "Excelsior!" wrist band (authorized by Stan Lee himself), and "Hero comics" created by some of the top creators working today including Terry Moore, Marv Wolfman, Matt Wagner, Ed McGuinness, and Joe Benitez.

Recently, Hero also began offering a one-of-a-kind DVD entitled "Marvel Then & Now: an Evening with Stan Lee and Joe Quesada." Hosted by Kevin Smith the production features more than 5 hours of content, "behind the scenes" footage and interviews with other top creators like Jeph Loeb.

Besides contributing financially there are other ways to help the Hero Initiative. "We encourage people who want to help to approach their local comic store and see about putting out a Hero donation jar or helping to arrange for the sale of Hero merchandise," McLauchlin said.

Repeat Hero volunteers can become members of the Regional Advisory Board. Members enjoy special discounts from Tales of Wonder.com, Comics Guaranty Corporation (CGC) and more. In addition they can qualify for invitations to special events at conventions.

"Comics is a wonderful, close-knit community. If you're into comics, you get up-close-and-personal access to the talent like you never would if you're, say, a baseball fan or a movie buff. I love seeing that, and I love seeing that the talent gives to the fans like that. I think Hero is a chance for everyone to give just a little of that back, and make the world a slightly better place," McLauchlin said.

"We're always hearing at conventions about what a thrill it is to meet people. It's time to help out the industry as a whole," Roy Thomas adds "

Stan Lee agrees.

"I feel that Hero is as deserving of a donor's support as any charity I can think of. Especially if the donor too is in the comic book field. What can be more gratifying than helping one who, but for a turn of Fate, could be you?"

Hero Initiative took white cover editions of Ultimate Spider-Man #100 and had top artists do their own one-of-a-kind sketches which were then auctioned as fund raisers.

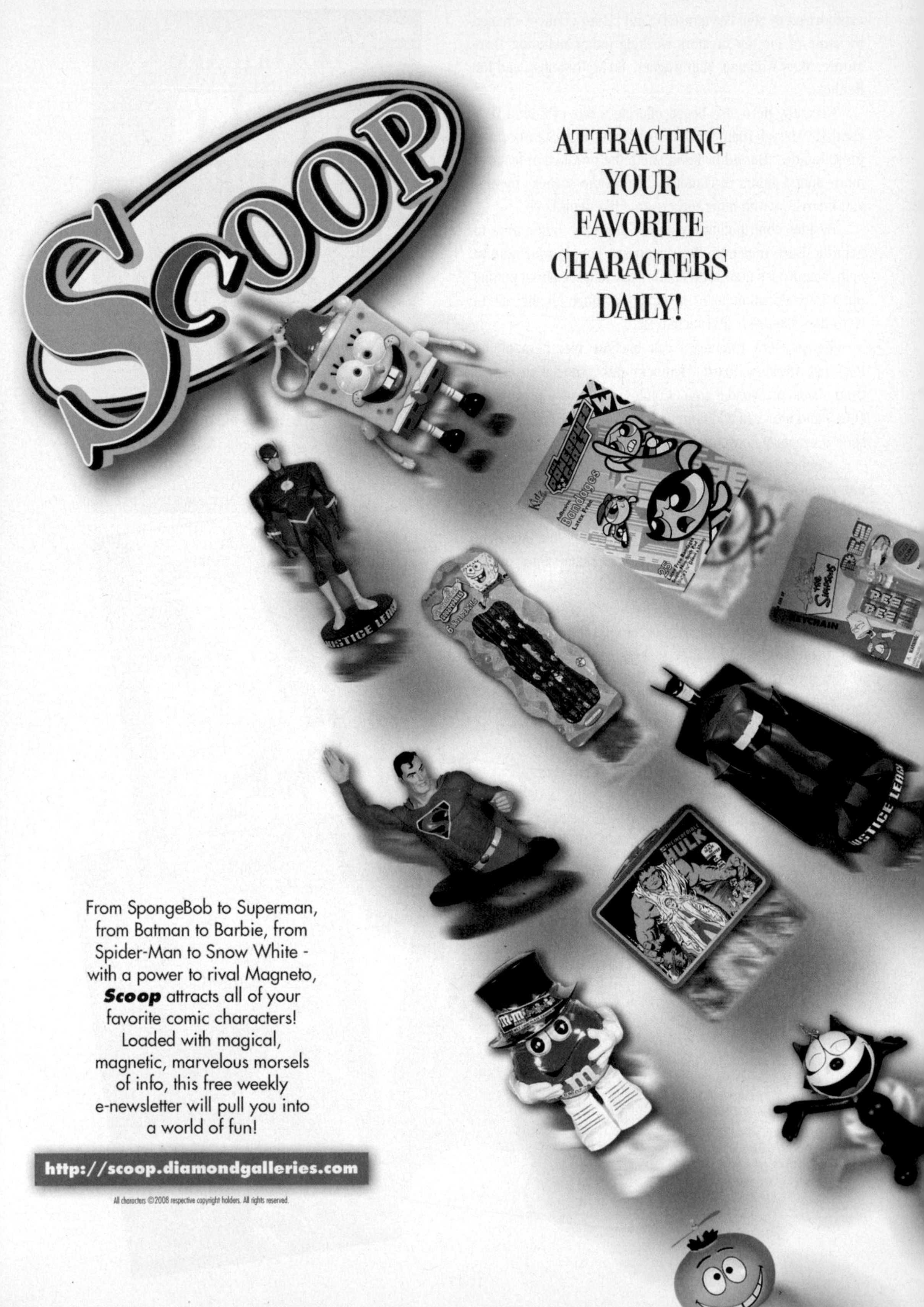
SCOOP
ATTRACTING
YOUR
FAVORITE
CHARACTERS
DAILY!
From SpongeBob to Superman,
from Batman to Barbie, from
Spider-Man to Snow White -
with a power to rival Magneto,
Scoop attracts all of your
favorite comic characters!
Loaded with magical,
magnetic, marvelous morsels
of info, this free weekly
e-newsletter will pull you into
a world of fun!
http://scoop.diamondgalleries.com
All characters ©2008 respective copyright holders. All rights reserved.

CGC EXAMINED!

A Firsthand Look at Professional Comic Book Certification

by the CGC Grading Team

You've seen CGC-certified comics at cons, offered in online auctions, and even pictured throughout the *Guide*. Expert third-party certification provides buyers confidence that a comic is accurately represented, and sellers know they are getting fair value for their comics. And it has proven popular: CGC has graded over

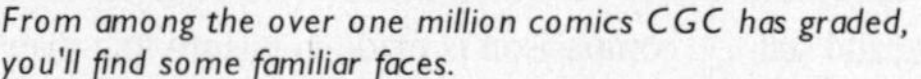

From among the over one million comics CGC has graded, you'll find some familiar faces.

1,000,000 comics! But did you ever wonder how that comic book made it into its protective holder? Or wonder how this precise grading scale came to be? Here's your chance to learn more with a firsthand look at the process of professional comic book certification at CGC.

THE FORMATION OF CGC

CGC opened in January of 2000 under the umbrella of the Certified Collectibles Group, which also includes the largest rare coin certification company in the world, Numismatic Guaranty Corporation (NGC), and the leading currency certification company, Paper Money Guaranty (PMG). To form CGC, the Collectibles Group sought out talented and ethical individuals to grade comic books. Experts needed necessary skills to verify a comic book's authenticity and to detect restoration that can affect its value. To identify these individuals, many of the most respected individuals in the hobby were consulted, and, based on their recommendations, a core grading team was selected.

The members of the CGC grading team come from diverse backgrounds, and many were comic book dealers at some time in their careers. In becoming familiar with market standards for comic book grading, experience in the commercial sector can be an essential ingredient. Once they joined CGC, these individuals immediately ceased all commercial trading. All CGC employees are prohibited from commercially buying and selling comic books. In this way CGC can remain completely impartial, having no vested interest other than a devotion to serving clients through accurate and consistent grading.

Having aided in the selection of the grading team, the hobby's leaders were again called upon to develop a uniform grading standard. Everyone seemed to agree that the *Overstreet Guide* was the foundation of this standard, but there were a number of subjective interpretations of its published definitions. It was critical to understand how these guidelines were being applied to the everyday buying and selling of comics. To accomplish this, approximately 50 of the hobby's top experts took part in a laborious grading test. Their grades were averaged and an accurate grading standard reflecting the collective experience of the hobby's most prominent figures was thus developed. CGC now had the best standard and the best team to apply it.

The next step was to develop a tamper-evident holder for the long-term storage and display of certified comics. This proved to be a significant technical challenge. Exhaustive material tests were conducted to determine that they were archival safe. To create a true first line of defense in a prudent plan for storage, it was determined that the comics book should be sealed in a soft inner well, then sealed again inside a tamper evident hard plastic case with interlocking ridges to enable compact storage. The CGC certified grade appears on a label sealed inside the holder for an additional level of security.

SUBMITTING COMICS TO CGC

Typically, comics received by CGC are submitted through one of our authorized member-dealers each of whom has passed a thorough reference check by CGC's Accounting and Customer Service departments. As well as submitting their own books, dealers are authorized to submit books on behalf of a collector and many assist in preparing submissions. Another option for individuals who wish to submit comics directly to CGC is to become a member of the Collectors Society. The Collectors Society is an online community with direct access to certification service from CGC, and submissions can be prepared online. Comics are typically sent to CGC's offices by registered mail or through an insured express company.

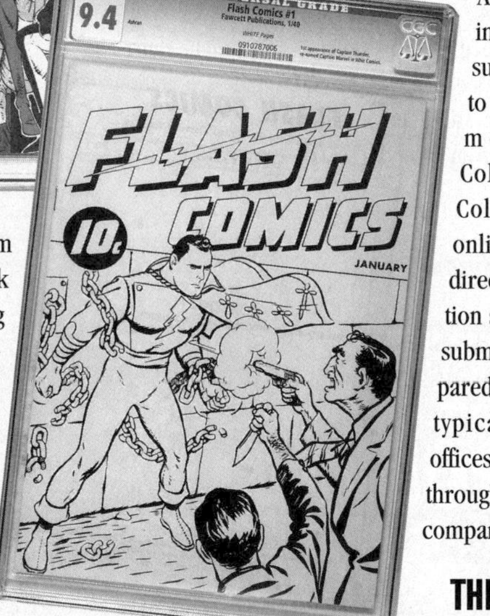

Each comic book receives a grade between 0.5 and 10.0.

THE COMICS ARE RECEIVED

CGC's Receiving Department opens the newly arrived packages each morning and immediately verifies that the number of books in each package matches the number shown on the invoice. Once this is done, a more detailed comparison is made to ensure that their invoice descriptions correspond to the actual comics. This information is entered into a computer, and the comics will henceforth be traceable at all stages of the grading process by their invoice number and their line number within that invoice. Each book is placed within protective Mylar that has affixed to it a label bearing the invoice and line item numbers, information which is duplicated on the label in a bar-coded inscription for quick reading by the computer. Before any grading is performed, each book is examined by a CGC Restoration Detection Expert. If any form of restoration work is detected, this information is entered into the computer so that it will be available to the grading team.

THE GRADING PROCESS

After being examined by a Restoration Detection Expert, a book then passes to a pre-grader. At this stage the comic books are in barcoded Mylar sleeves, and have been separated from their original invoice. This step is taken to ensure that graders do not know whose books they are grading, as a further guarantee of impartiality. The pre-grader begins the grading process by counting the book's pages and entering into the computer any peculiarities or flaws that may affect a book's grade. Some examples of this would be "a tear on third page," "a corner crease – does not break color," "a 1/2" inch spine split," and so forth. He then enters this information, if necessary, into the "Graders Notes" field and assigns his grading opinion. When the next grader examines the comic, he is not able to see the first person's assigned grade, so as to not influence his own evaluation. After determining his own grade for the comic, he can then view the Graders Notes entered by the previous grader, and he may add to this commentary if he believes more remarks are in order. This same process is repeated as the comic passes to the Grading Finalizer. He makes a final restoration check before determining his own grade, at which time he then reviews the grades and notes entered by the previous graders. If all grades are in agreement or are very close, he will then assign the book's final grade. It then is forwarded to the Encapsulation Department for sealing. If there is disagreement among the graders, a discussion will ensue until a final determination is made and the book forwarded.

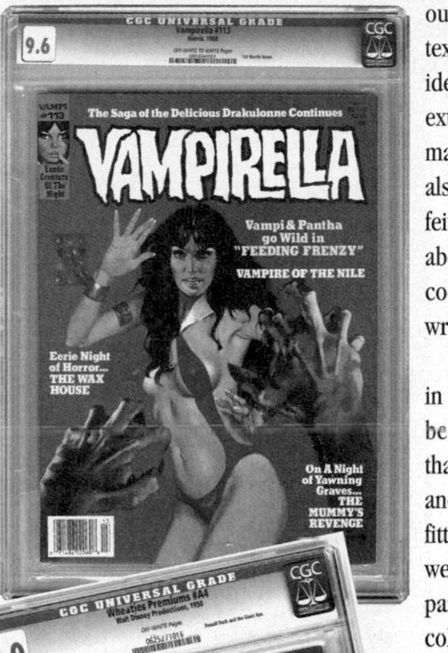

ENCAPSULATING THE COMICS

After each comic has been graded and the necessary numbers and text entered into their respective data fields, all the comics on a particular invoice are taken from the Grading Department into the Encapsulation Department. Here, appropriately color-coded labels are printed out bearing the appropriate descriptive text, including each book's grade and identification number. This last item is extremely important, as it serves to make each certified comic unique and is also an important deterrent to counterfeiting CGC's valued product. All of the above information is duplicated in a bar code, which appears underneath the written text on the comic's label.

The newly-printed labels are stacked in the same sequence as the comics to be encapsulated with them, ensuring that each book and its label match one another. The comic is now ready to be fitted inside an archival-quality interior well, which is then sealed within a transparent capsule, along with the book's color-coded label. This is accomplished through a combination of compression and ultrasonic vibration. The result is a newly-encapsulated CGC comic, ready to be shipped to its proud owner.

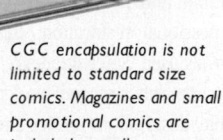

CGC encapsulation is not limited to standard size comics. Magazines and small promotional comics are included as well.

THE COMICS ARE SHIPPED

After encapsulation, all comics are returned briefly to the Grading Department for a quality control inspection. Here, they are examined to make certain that their labels are correct for both the grade and its accompanying descriptive information. The quality control person also inspects each book and holder for the quality of its presentation. CGC is careful to make certain that the comics it certifies are not only accurately graded but attractively presented, as well.

When all the comics have been inspected, they're delivered to our Shipping Department for packaging. The comics are counted and their labels checked against the original handwritten or typed invoice to make certain that no mistakes have occurred. A Shipping Department employee then verifies the method of transport as selected by the submitter on the invoice and prepares the comics for delivery.

No matter whether the US Postal Service or some private carrier is used, the method of packaging is essentially the same. The encapsulated comics are placed vertically inside boxes made of very sturdy cardboard. In 2005, CGC developed a custom shipping box to enable the highest level of stability during shipping. A copy of the submitter's invoice is included before the box is sealed and heavy tape is used to prevent accidental or unauthorized opening of the box while it's in transit.

The barcode of every comic book is scanned before it is placed into its shipping box. The status of the book is changed to "shipped" in our tracking system, and we retain an infallible record of what books were shipped in which box. This is the final critical step of our detailed internal tracking system.

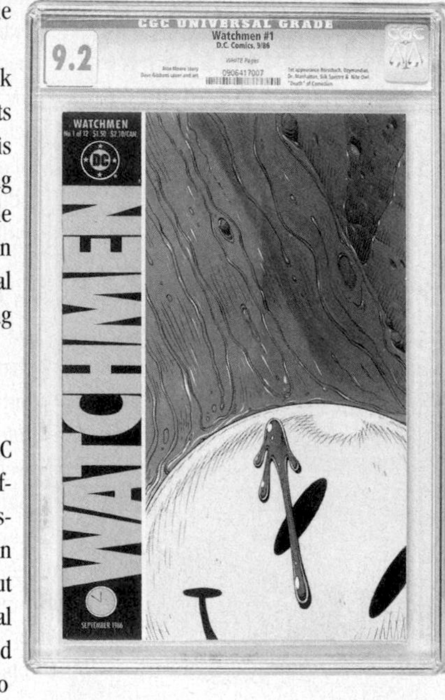

After years of sitting quietly, individual issues of Watchmen are attracting a lot of attention due to the movie.

THE CGC LABEL

Comic books certified by CGC bear color-coded labels that have different meanings. Whenever purchasing a CGC-certified comic, be certain to note not just the book's grade but also its label category. A Universal label is denoted by the color blue and indicates that a book was not found to have any qualifying defects or signs of restoration. There is one exception to this policy: At CGC's discretion, comics having a very minor amount of glue and/or color touch-up may still qualify for a Universal label provided that they were produced approximately 1950 or earlier and that such restoration is noted underneath the assigned grade.

As its name implies, the Restored label, identified by its purple color, is used for books found to have restoration work performed on them. The grade assigned is based on the book's appearance, with the restoration noted. A distinction is made between Amateur and Professional restoration, this judgment being based on the materials used. Since the degree of work performed is also significant with restored books, there are a total of seven possible descriptions under the Restored label. Each description is prefaced with word Apparent, followed by Slight, Moderate or Extensive in combination with the final descriptors Amateur or Professional. Examples of Restored labels might read Apparent Moderate Professional or Apparent Slight Amateur, both descriptions then being followed by the book's grade. Finally, comics which have had no restoration other than a trimming of their covers or edges are labeled as simply Apparent, followed by their grade.

The Qualified label is green, and this indicates that one qualifying defect is present on a book. An example of such a qualifying feature would be a missing Marvel Value Stamp that does not affect the story. While such a book technically may grade 1.5, it may appear to grade 9.6. In such instances, assigning a grade of just 1.5 does not fully represent the value of the comic to a collector. Through use of the green Qualified label, a comic buyer is able to make an informed decision as to what he is purchasing in terms of its overall desirability. Because of the complexity involved, green labels are assigned quite seldom and then only when considered absolutely necessary. In addition, comic books that have an unwitnessed signature, and therefore are not eligible for the Signature Series label (see below), get the Qualified label. This is the most common use for the Qualified label. This shows what the grade of the book would have been if the signature was not present.

CGC's Signature Series label is yellow, and this is used when a comic book has been signed or been sketched on by a creator in the presence of a CGC representative, assuring the signature's or sketch's authenticity. Only books that meet CGC's strict criteria for authenticity are eligible for the Signature Series label. In addition to the certified grade, the yellow label includes who signed it and when it was signed. If appropriate, a Signature Series label may state at which venue a book was signed. In 2007, CGC introduced a Signature Series Restored label. Similar to the CGC Signature Series label in color, it can be differentiated by a purple bar across the type. Restoration is noted in the same fashion as on the purple CGC Restored label, and, as with the regular Signature Series label, restored books must be signed in the presence of CGC representatives in order to be eligible for s ignature authentication.

In October of 2003, CGC began to certify comic book related magazines. The certification process and label system for magazines is exactly the same as for comic books. Some examples of comic book related magazines CGC certifies are *MAD Magazine*, *Vampirella*, *Creepy*, *Eerie* and *Famous Monsters of Filmland*.

For more information on comic book certification and CGC's many services, please visit our website at www.CGCcomics.com

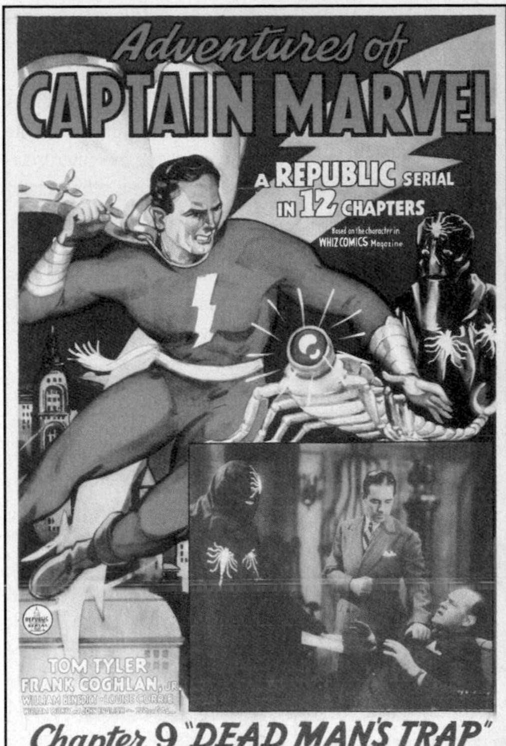

by Brandon G. DeStefano

COMICS AT THE MOVIES

A Brief History of Comic Characters on the Big Screen

From the earliest animated efforts to the modern, big budget, special effects-driven blockbusters, comic characters have always been an important part of cinema history. What was once exclusively kid's stuff, though, now seems to hold the key to box office success.

THE EARLY YEARS

Although they are not actual films based on comic properties, early animation is considered to be a cornerstone of both early film and the future of animated features. One of the first attempts at bringing illustrations to life in motion pictures came in the form of Winsor McCay's *Gertie the Dinosaur* in 1914.

Most famous for his work as a creator and illustrator on such numerous long-lived comic strips as *Tales of the Jungle Imp by Felix Fiddle*, *Little Sammy Sneeze*, *Dreams of the*

Rarebit Fiend, *A Pilgrim's Progress*, *Little Nemo in Slumberland* and *Poor Jake*, McCay's groundbreaking animation of *Gertie* is noted by many historians of film to be the first animated film to star a character that displayed a unique personality, which was not matched again until the Disney films of the 1930s.

Following the success of *Gertie the Dinosaur*, McCay created a film titled *The Sinking of the Lusitania*, which told the story of the attack on the British maritime ship and was designed to inspire America to join World War I.

Toward the end of the decade, Walt Disney, a man whose name has become synonymous with the animated feature film, created a character for Universal Pictures which skyrocketed to instant success. Oswald the Rabbit (sometimes Oswald the Lucky Rabbit) appeared in "Trolley Troubles," the first of 26 Oswald cartoons supervised by Disney and released in 1927-1928. Conflicts over the ownership of the character led to Disney's departure and his creation of Mickey Mouse.

THE MOVIE SERIALS

One of the earliest forays into adapting comic books, comic strip and pulp magazine characters to the silver screen came in the form of movie serials, short films shown in chapters generally appearing before or after the main features at local cinemas. Usually told in 12 to 15 installments, theaters would most often show a new chapter each week. The action almost always ended in a cliffhanger except for the final chapter. Interested audiences – generally kids – would then have to return the next week to find out if the hero or heroine would escape to fight another day.

(preceding page) Posters for a 1941 Captain Marvel serial and the 2002 Spider-Man movie.
(top) "Howdy Folks!" from 1927, one of the 26 Oswald, the Lucky Rabbit cartoons created by Walt Disney.
(bottom) Captain America in Chapter 9 "Triple

Many different genres including westerns, science fiction and action-adventure were represented, but superheroes in particular serials offered the first chance for live interpretations of leading characters. Studios such as Columbia, Republic and Universal all produced movie serials as early as 1912, but popularity soared to amazing heights when they began to utilize comic characters.

Superman, Batman, Captain Marvel, Blackhawk, Congo Bill, Captain America, Brick Bradford, Spy Smasher, The Green Hornet, Dick Tracy and others leaped into live-action adventures, as did Tarzan, Flash Gordon, Buck Rogers and The Spider. *Terry and the Pirates*, *Mandrake the Magician*, *The Phantom* and *Brenda Starr, Reporter* also took their bows on the silver screen.

Some of the most celebrated comic character serials of this era, noted as the Golden Age of Serials, included *Flash Gordon* (1936), *Dick Tracy* (1937), *Flash Gordon's Trip to Mars* (1938), *The Lone Ranger* (1938), *Dick Tracy's G-Men* (1939), *Mandrake the Magician* (1939), *The Drums of Fu Manchu* (1940), *The Green Hornet* (1940), *The Shadow* (1940), *Dick Tracy vs. Crime Inc.* (1941), *The Adventures of Captain Marvel* (1941), *Spy Smasher* (1942), *Batman* (1943), *The Phantom* (1943), *Captain America* (1944), *Zorro's Black Whip* (1944), *Brenda Starr, Reporter* (1945), *Superman* (1948), *Batman and Robin* (1949), and *Atom Man vs. Superman* (1950).

Animated shorts and features also grew during this period, with Fleischer Studios'

FOR THE FIRST TIME ON THE MOTION PICTURE SCREEN IN COLOR
ADAM WEST AS BATMAN AND BURT WARD AS ROBIN TOGETHER WITH ALL THEIR FANTASTIC DERRING-DO AND THEIR DASTARDLY VILLAINS, TOO!
BATMAN
ADAM WEST · BURT WARD
LEE MERIWETHER · CESAR ROMERO
BURGESS MEREDITH · FRANK GORSHIN · WILLIAM DOZIER · LESLIE H. MARTINSON · LORENZO SEMPLE JR · DELUXE

A lobby card promoting the 1966 Batman *theatrical release based on the popular television series.*

Superman cartoons leading the way. They, like their live action counterparts, were considered children's fare.

By the mid- to late-1950s, most studios had halted their production of movie serials to focus on bigger budget films. Audiences began to get their short stories fill from television and expected more when they left the house for movie theaters. This early era which brought the beloved characters from the four-color page to the big screen had ended, only to be revived decades later in a renaissance of creativity and revisited with the advent of DVD technology.

Lynda Carter as Wonder Woman embodied the beauty and strength of the Amazon Princess.

THE SMALL SCREEN

When discussing the place of comics on the big screen, it's hard to ignore the role of the small screen in their development. Television became a haven for superheroes in the 1950s. *The Adventures of Superman* ran from 1952 through 1958 with George Reeves as Clark Kent/Superman, Phyllis Coates (Season 1) and original film "Lois" Noel Neill (Seasons 2-6) as Lois Lane, Jack Larson as Jimmy Olsen, and John Hamilton as Perry White. While there were some lighthearted moments, the action was played serious.

Not so for *Batman*, which ran from 1966 to 1969 and inspired a short-lived but widely noted Bat-craze. The show starred Adam West as Bruce Wayne/Batman, Burt Ward as Dick Grayson/Robin, Alan Napier as Alfred Pennyworth, and Neil Hamilton as Commissioner Gordon. Superstar guests villains included Cesar Romero as The Joker, Frank Gorshin as The Riddler, Burgess Meredith as The Penguin, and Julie Newmar as Catwoman, among many others. The series also spawned a feature film in 1966.

Wonder Woman appeared as a pilot film which aired on ABC in 1974 and starred Cathy Lee Crosby as Wonder Woman/Diana Prince. Another, more faithful take, launched in 1976 with *The*

Nicholas Hammond as both Peter Parker and The Amazing Spider--Man in the 1977 television series.

YOU'LL BELIEVE A MAN CAN FLY.
ALEXANDER SALKIND PRESENTS MARLON BRANDO • GENE HACKMAN IN A RICHARD DONNER FILM
SUPERMAN
STARRING
ALSO STARRING
CHRISTOPHER REEVE • NED BEATTY • JACKIE COOPER • GLENN FORD • TREVOR HOWARD • MARGOT KIDDER
VALERIE PERRINE • MARIA SCHELL • TERENCE STAMP • PHYLLIS THAXTER • SUSANNAH YORK
STORY BY MARIO PUZO • SCREENPLAY BY MARIO PUZO, DAVID NEWMAN, LESLIE NEWMAN AND ROBERT BENTON
CREATIVE CONSULTANT TOM MANKIEWICZ • DIRECTOR OF PHOTOGRAPHY GEOFFREY UNSWORTH B.S.C.
PRODUCTION DESIGNER JOHN BARRY • MUSIC BY JOHN WILLIAMS • DIRECTED BY RICHARD DONNER
EXECUTIVE PRODUCER ILYA SALKIND • PRODUCED BY PIERRE SPENGLER • PANAVISION® TECHNICOLOR®
AN ALEXANDER AND ILYA SALKIND PRODUCTION
RELEASED BY WARNER BROS. A WARNER COMMUNICATIONS COMPANY TM & © DC Comics Inc. 1978
RECORDED IN
DOLBY STEREO
ORIGINAL SOUNDTRACK AVAILABLE ON WARNER BROS. RECORDS AND TAPES
WARNER SUPERMAN BOOKS AT BOOKSTORES AND NEWSSTANDS
PG PARENTAL GUIDANCE SUGGESTED

Moviegoers' belief that a man could fly led to the box office success of 1978's Superman: The Movie. *Finally comic book movies could hold their own against blockbusters of other genres, like* Jaws, The Godfather, *and* Star Wars.

New Adventures of Wonder Woman (called *The New Original Wonder Woman* in its first season). It starred Lynda Carter as Diana Prince/Wonder Woman and Lyle Waggoner is Steve Trevor. It ran for 55 episodes from 1976-1979.

Spider-Man came to live-action TV in 1977 in *The Amazing Spider-Man*, a one-hour, made-for-television movie starring Nicholas Hammond as Peter Parker/Spider-Man. Thirteen episodes followed, but the show was soon cancelled.

The Incredible Hulk debuted as a pilot film in 1978 and a series quickly followed. The show starred Bill Bixby as David Bruce Banner and Lou Ferrigno as the Hulk, transforming the tale of the title character into a version of *The Fugitive*. The show ran for four seasons and spawned three made-for-television movies.

There were other attempts at live action (including two *Captain America* tele-films and a *Doctor Strange* pilot), but other than these notable shows, success was largely confined to the world of animation.

The Justice League of America appeared on *The Superfriends*. Aquaman, Tarzan, The Lone Ranger, Spider-Man, The X-Men, The Fantastic Four, Captain America, Sub-Mariner, Iron Man and others were featured on cartoons for years with varying degrees of success. Superman and Batman particularly had a healthy number of long runs in animated form. Still, Hollywood craves the splash of the feature film.

RETURN TO THE BIG SCREEN

While the '50s, '60s and '70s offered superheroes on television, it wasn't until Superman returned to the movie theaters in 1978 with *Superman: The Movie* that the genre began to enjoy the type of box office success now expected of it. The film starred Christopher Reeve as Clark Kent/Superman, Margot Kidder as Lois Lane, Gene Hackman as Lex Luthor, and Marlon Brando as Jor-El.

The film told the origin story of the last son of Krypton, his arrival on Earth, his upbringing in Kansas, and arrival on the scene in Metropolis. It brought a modern take to the character, which was then 40 years old. With the tagline, "You'll believe a man can fly," filmmakers used then-cutting-edge special effects to make that belief possible.

Warner Brothers had from the beginning seen the potential for Superman to be a film franchise. As producers Alexander and Ilya Salkind had done with their earlier *Three Musketeers* and *Four Musketeers*, they filmed a substantial amount of the sequel during production of the first film. However, tensions lead to Donner being replaced by director Richard Lester, and much of *Superman II* was re-shot (in 2006, *Superman II: The Richard Donner Cut* was released and offered the film much as Donner had intended). Regardless of the intrigue, it was another hit.

Further films in the series, *Superman III* and *Superman IV: The Quest for Peace*, are generally considered to have lost their way. It would be 20 years before *Superman Returns* was made as an unofficial sequel to the first two, dismissing them.

Warner Brothers was not without its superhero hits, though. Tim Burton directed *Batman* (1989) and *Batman Returns* (1992).

Batman starred Michael Keaton as Bruce Wayne/Batman and Jack Nicholson as Jack Napier/The Joker. *Batman Returns* saw Keaton return with Michelle Pfeiffer as Selina Kyle/Catwoman and Danny DeVito as Oswald Cobblepot/The Penguin. Both did big business, but Burton did not return for the next sequel, *Batman Forever* (1995).

Director Joel Schumacher's film included Val Kilmer as Bruce Wayne/Batman, Chris O'Donnell as Dick Grayson/Robin, Tommy Lee Jones as Harvey Dent/Two-Face, and Jim Carrey as Edward Nygma/The Riddler.

Schumacher's *Batman & Robin* (1997) with Batman

again re-cast, this time with George Clooney, also featured Uma Thurman as Poison Ivy, Arnold Schwarzenegger as Mr. Freeze, Alicia Silverstone as Batgirl, and the returning O'Donnell was generally viewed as a franchise-killer and kept the Caped Crusader off the big screen until *Batman Begins* revived things in 2005.

During the early days of this period, Marvel's luck with feature films wasn't that great. In fact, it was just about all bad.

New World Pictures released *The Punisher* starring Dolph Lundgren in 1989. It went nowhere. Next up was *Captain America* (1990), which mercifully never made it to theaters. It featured the Red Skull as an Italian instead of a German, and starred Matt Salinger, son of author J.D Salinger, as Steve Rogers/Captain America. It eventually escaped on video.

The Fantastic Four (1994) was their next film that wasn't. According to several different sources, apparently the film was never intended for release and was just being made to keep the film rights secured for its studio. It was never released theatrically.

Stepping outside the realm of DC Comics and Marvel Comics characters, other comic book characters began to see screen time, including: *Dick Tracy* (1990) and *Teenage Mutant Ninja Turtles* (1990), which was part of a huge franchise including comic books, collected editions, cartoons, action figures and more.

The success of 2000's X-Men *opened the floodgates for a slew of Marvel big-budget movies like the* Spider-Man *trilogy and the Avengers-related movies to come.*

Walt Disney Pictures released *The Rocketeer* in 1991. The character has first appeared on the comic scene as a back-up story in 1982's *Starslayer* #2 from Pacific Comics and was a tribute to the pulp adventure characters of the 1930s and '40s. It starred Bill Campbell as Cliff Secord/The Rocketeer, Jennifer Connelly as his love interest, Jenny Blake (based on real life pin-up queen Bettie Page in the comic book version), and Timothy Dalton as the actor/Nazi spy, Neville Sinclair. It was a modest success.

Other comic book films included such hits and misses as *The Crow* (1994), *The Shadow* (1994), *The Mask* (1994), *Judge Dredd* (1995), *Tank Girl* (1995), *The Phantom* (1996), and *Barb Wire* (1996).

BIG BOX OFFICE

In 1998, Marvel's first box office hit came from a property that few in the general public knew was based on a comic book. New Line released *Blade*, with a vampire hunting title character spun out of the pages of *Tomb of Dracula* and played by Wesley Snipes. Two sequels and a short-lived TV series would eventually follow.

Twentieth Century Fox released the first *X-Men* movie in 2000. Directed by Bryan Singer, it starred Patrick Stewart as Professor Charles Xavier, Sir Ian McKellan as Magneto, Hugh Jackman as Wolverine, Famke Jannsen as Jean Grey, James Marsden at Cyclops, and Halle Berry as Storm. Its theatrical release brought in almost $300 million world wide and it spawned two sequels, *X2* (2003) and *X-Men: The Last Stand* (2006) with a third *X-Men Origins: Wolverine* due about the time this book is scheduled for release.

While the *X-Men* films were significant successes, Marvel's partnership with Sony/Columbia for *Spider-Man* was the lynchpin in the company's own Hollywood dreams. Director Sam Raimi's *Spider-Man* was the first film of which Marvel owned a sizable chunk. Starring Tobey Maguire as Peter Parker/Spider-Man, Kirsten Dunst as Mary Jane Watson, James Franco as Harry Osborn, Rosemary Harris as May Parker, J.K. Simmons as J. Jonah Jameson, Cliff Robertson as Ben Parker, William Dafoe as Norman Osborn/The Green Goblin, its $114,844,116 opening weekend in the U.S. and $821,708,551 world wide box office (both according to BoxOfficeMojo.com) were record-breakers and dominated theaters in 2002, as did its sequels in 2004 and 2007.

Not all of Marvel's characters have successfully made the transition from comic to film. In 2003, Marvel Studios released *Daredevil*, which starred Ben Affleck as Matt

Murdock/Daredevil, Jennifer Garner as Elektra Natchios, Colin Farrell as Bullseye and Michael Clark Duncan as Wilson "The Kingpin" Fisk. Its totals were respectable, but its instant sequel, *Elektra*, bombed. That same year, director Ang Lee's *Hulk* met with poor reviews from fans and critics alike. Despite underperforming, it did well enough to entice Marvel to try again in just five years.

It was also becoming clear that the term "comic book movie" didn't have to equate to "superhero movie" all of the time.

From Hell, written in comic book form by Alan Moore, was released by 20th Century Fox in 2001. *The League of Extraordinary Gentlemen*, based on the comic book series from DC's America's Best Comics (ABC) imprint and Moore, was released by Fox in 2003. The author's *V For Vendetta* was released by Warner Brothers in 2005. If all proceeds as scheduled, readers will know before this volume is released whether another adaptation of his work, *Watchmen*, was a triumph or not (regardless, anticipation of the film sold a staggering number of the collected edition of the series).

Other notable comic films, ranging from modest indy films to big budget spectaculars, and representing publishers including Dark Horse Comics, IDW Publishing, and Fantagraphics, include *Ghost World* (2001), *American Splendor* (2003), *Bulletproof Monk* (2003), *Hellboy* (2004), *Sin City* (2005), *Art School Confidential* (2006), *30 Days of Night* (2007), *300* (2007), and *Hellboy II: The Golden Army* (2008).

While Marvel experienced its share of successes, Warner Brothers had problems getting either of its Superman or Batman franchises up and running again, at least as far as films went (television was another matter, with a seemingly uninterrupted string of successful Batman cartoons and the long-running, live action *Smallville* going strong). The release of *Catwoman* in 2004 did little to help this image.

Adaptations of Road to Perdition *and* Hellboy *showed that successful comic-related movies could develop outside of standard super-hero fare.*

It is not, however, that other DC properties weren't making the grade. In addition to the aforementioned *V For Vendetta*, critical and financial successes were enjoyed by adaptations of *Road to Perdition* (2002), *A History of Violence* (2005) and *Constantine* (2005).

Proving how it's sometimes not very far from worst to first, *Batman Begins* in 2005 put the Bat-franchise back in high gear. Director Christopher Nolan cast Christian Bale as Bruce Wayne/Batman, Michael Caine as Alfred, Gary Oldman as Jim Gordon, and Morgan Freeman as Lucius Fox. He took this serious cast, treated the material seriously, and struck paydirt.

Superman Returns, with director Bryan Singer moving over from the *X-Men* franchise in 2006, brought back the feel of the earlier Richard Donner efforts. He cast Brandon Routh as Clark Kent/Superman, Kate Bosworth as Lois Lane, and Kevin Spacey as Lex Luthor.

The Dark Knight, the 2008 sequel to *Batman Begins*, returned director Nolan and the key players from the 2005 cast and added a critically praised (and sadly final) performance by Heath Ledger as The Joker. Almost nothing could have prepared audiences or theater owners for the results. With U.S. and international box office totals approaching $1 billion at press time, *The Dark Knight* quickly became not only the most successful superhero film ever, but the second highest grossing film in American box office history.

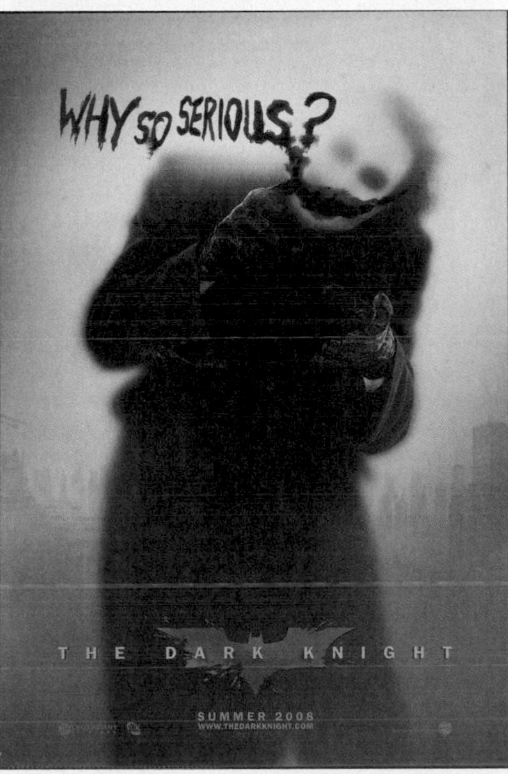

Led by the phenominal success of Iron Man *and* The Dark Knight, *2008 was a landmark year for comic book films.*

While Marvel certainly couldn't match the frenetic enthusiasm fans held for *The Dark Knight* in 2008, they reached a milestone as they released their first two self-financed films. Jon Favreau had portrayed Foggy Nelson in *Daredevil*, but now he might be best known as the director of *Iron Man*, which was a smash hit and already has a sequel in the works.

Robert Downey, Jr., who played Tony Stark/Iron Man, also made a cameo in character in their second film of the year, director Louis Leterrier's *The Incredible Hulk*, which starred Edward Norton. In addition to their financial success, it's noteworthy that the Marvel films are now clearly building a universe, just as in the comic books. More films (*Iron Man II*, *Thor*, *First Avenger: Captain America*, and *The Avengers*) are on tap, as is a fourth Spider-Man film.

Comic characters have had a rich and long lasting journey from the four-color page to the silver screen. From movie serials to summer blockbusters, these characters and their stories have provided years of entertainment for fans of all ages. The future looks bright for comic book fans as more and more properties are optioned by movie studios and even brighter for these characters that will never fade to black, even after the credits roll.

Brandon G. DeStefano, a former Editor of Gemstone Publishing, is a freelance writer.

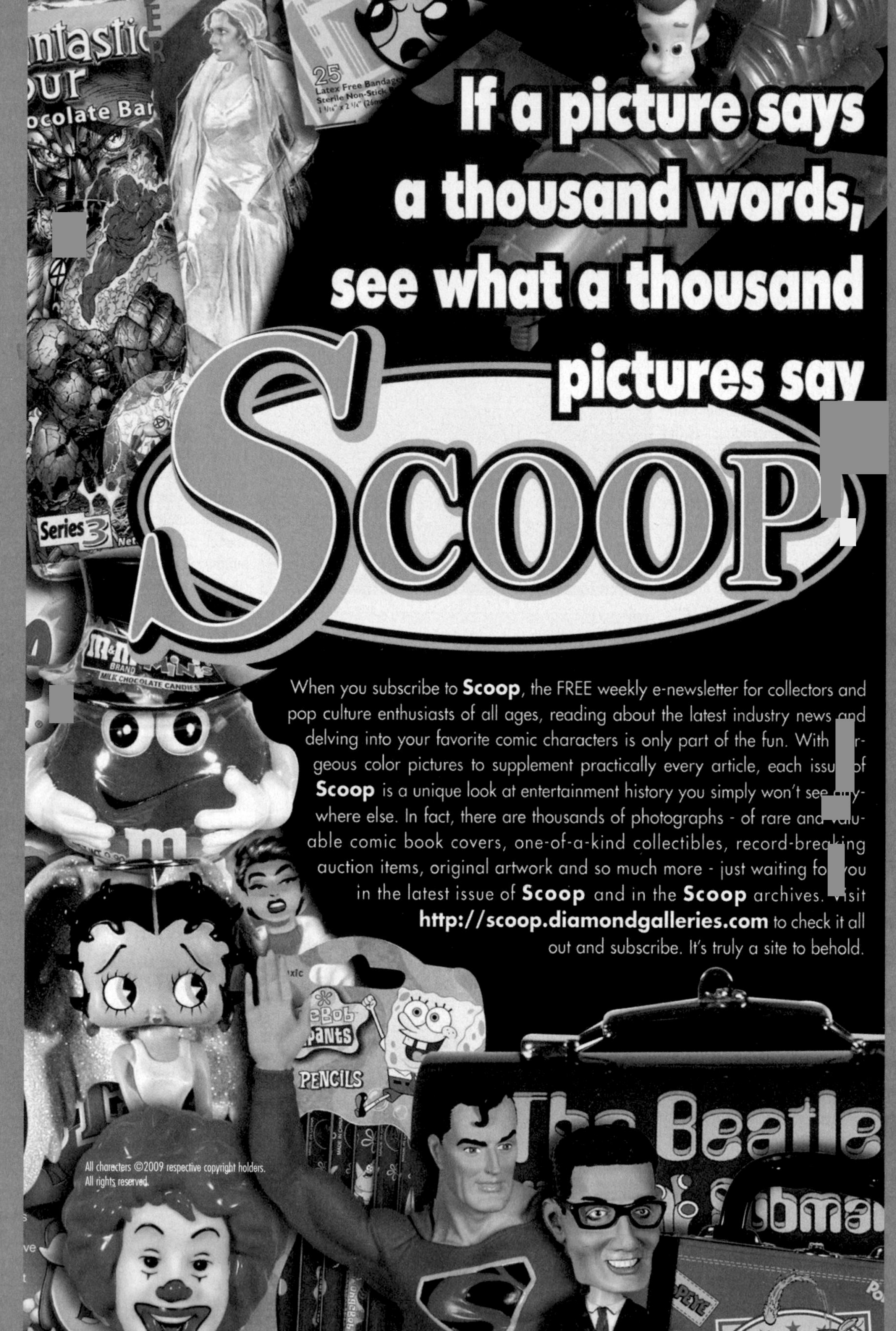

If a picture says
a thousand words,
see what a thousand
pictures say
Scoop
When you subscribe to **Scoop**, the FREE weekly e-newsletter for collectors and pop culture enthusiasts of all ages, reading about the latest industry news and delving into your favorite comic characters is only part of the fun. With gorgeous color pictures to supplement practically every article, each issue of **Scoop** is a unique look at entertainment history you simply won't see anywhere else. In fact, there are thousands of photographs - of rare and valuable comic book covers, one-of-a-kind collectibles, record-breaking auction items, original artwork and so much more - just waiting for you in the latest issue of **Scoop** and in the **Scoop** archives. Visit **http://scoop.diamondgalleries.com** to check it all out and subscribe. It's truly a site to behold.
All characters ©2009 respective copyright holders. All rights reserved.

The BAT MAN
...IN THE STRANGE LIVES OF THOSE DENIZENS OF THE HIDDEN WORLD OF CRIME, THE BATMAN...WINGED FIGURE OF VENGEANCE HAS BECOME A MENACE...

When the BAT flew ALONE!

The Bat-Man Before Robin

by Rob Hughes

Before Robin. Before the Bat-Mobile, the Bat-Cave and Gotham City. Even before the debut of such arch-foes as The Joker, The Penguin, Catwoman, Two-Face and an innumerable legion of other Bat-Baddies that would plague the shadow-warrior for seven decades...There was Police Commissioner Gordon and there was... The "Bat-Man!"

"The 'Bat-Man,' a mysterious and adventurous figure, fighting for righteousness and apprehending the wrong doer, in his lone battle against the evil forces of society...His identity remains unknown." Thus was the very first description ever printed of the Dark Avenger which appeared in the splash panel of the first page of *Detective Comics* #27: May, 1939. He appeared suddenly and magnificently by swooping down from the heavens and across rooftops (his rope and grappling hook much have been anchored to a nearby cloud) to bring swift justice to a gangster in a green pinstripe suit. Let criminals everywhere mourn, The Bat-Man had been born!

The early, pre-Robin (*Detective* #27- #37 and one story in *Batman* #1) adventures of The Bat-Man were dark, grim and quite violent. He waged an all out war against crime, and was not interested in taking prisoners, rehabilitation or giving these law-breakers a second chance. He was judge, jury and executioner all in one, meting out frightful retribution to all wrong-doers that were unfortunate enough to cross his path. Whatever the method was...sending a few thugs off rooftops to tumble to their doom via a barrage of berserk punches and kicks, breaking their neck with a fatally powerful kick, or just simply firing a few rounds into them with his .45 automatic...it made no difference (yes, in early issues of *Detective*, The Bat-Man used a gun and shot criminals dead). As long as it eliminated the filth in a reliable and effective manner. He became the true Nocturnal Nightmare to the Underworld. In his *History of Comics*; Volume #1, Jim Steranko described The Bat-Man as, "a dark, shadowy loner working outside the law, outside the public eye ruthlessly stalking his prey through rain-slick alleyways."

The whole mystique of The Bat-Man was that of the mysterious avenger of the night that struck unspeakable terror into the hearts of the Underworld and the Police Force alike. In fact, Commissioner Gordon and his department tried repeatedly to bring this urban hunter in, but to no avail. Time and time again he would stalk and capture the top criminal masterminds that had baffled the police, only to melt back into the shadows that seem to have spawned him. His name was mentioned only in whispers and in the strictest confidence. No one on either side of the law knew what to make of him, and that's the way he liked it. The Bat-Man became the enigmatic shadow which mantled and protected the city by night by preying on the vermin and criminal vampires that had sucked his city dry of goodness and decency.

The element that added the final extraordinary ingredient to the whole persona of The Bat-Man was his striking appearance…well, we will get to that shortly.

What is to follow is an exciting, in-depth and detailed journey into each of The Bat Man's pre-Robin adventures. How this lone warrior progressed and developed through the first year of his creation by writer Bill Finger and artist Bob Kane.

And now, let's embark upon our quest. Onto the dimly moon-lit rooftops. Through the cold, dark and fog-laden alleyways. To the very roots and hear of his inception. To the very beginning…

DETECTIVE COMICS #27 (MAY, 1939)

The Case of the Chemical Syndicate. The landmark issue which introduced to the world Police Commissioner Gordon and one of the most significant and famous fictional characters of all time, The "Bat-Man!" He appeared like a huge gargoyle mounted on a rooftop silhouetted against the full moon. (splash panel) This is the first of only two issues in which creator-artist Bob Kane would formally sign his name "Rob't Kane."

Panel 2, of page 3 would mark the very first time that the public would actually see The Bat-Man in the pages of a comic book (not including the cover). Here he was, in his full glory and luster. A black (with blue highlights) cape that mimicked a high pair of bat-wings when it flared out. The black cowl with the small bat-ears that seemed to protrude as much outward as they did upward. The eerie white orbs for eyes that gave the crime-fighter an almost supernatural look. His boots and trucks were the same as today's and have remained unchanged for 70 years. A metallic gray, skin-tight suit that sported the classic bat-symbol across his chest and the trusty utility belt that was fastened together with a circular belt buckle (for this issue only). And finally he wore ordinary wrist-length gloves that were light purple in color.

On this dynamic page, where the underworld first encountered The Bat-Man, he would immediately dispose of one criminal by lashing "out with a terrific right," while …"He grabs his second adversary in a deadly headlock…and with a mighty heave…sends the burly criminal flying through space…" Apparently this criminal was flung off the rooftop to his death while The Bat-Man retrieved the document that was stolen from Steven Crane's safe. After the brief rooftop battle, we would also get a glimpse of this super detective's means of transportation; A red car that he speeds "forward to a unknown destination."

The Bat-Man would soon save Paul Rogers from a gas chamber used to kill guinea pigs, subdue Alfred Stryker's assistant Jennings with a flying tackle, and rescue Rogers yet again from an enraged, knife welding Stryker. The detective explains that Stryker, Crane, Rogers, and Lambert were all partners in the Apex Chemical Corporation in which Stryker wished to be the sole owner. Due to the fact that he had no ready cash, he made secret contracts with each one of his partners, scheming to murder them and steal the contracts before paying. Panic-stricken, Stryker suddenly tears free of The Bat-Man's grasp and pulls out a gun, firing at the mysterious caped figure. The Bat-Man thunders a left hook across the madman's jaw, sending him screaming into an acid tank below and exclaiming, "A fitting end for his kind."

The next day, following a social visit with Commissioner Gordon, Bruce Wayne returns home where "a little later his door slowly opens and reveals its occupant…if the Commissioner could see his young friend now…he'd be amazed to learn that he is The Bat-Man!" And so ended *The Case of the Chemical Syndicate*, formally signed Rob't Kane!

Cover of Detective Comics No. 27, 1st appearance of Commissioner Gordon and The Bat-Man. Cover art by Bob Kane. (middle) Debut panel where the public (and underworld) first encounter The Bat-Man! (bottom) The Bat-Man's true identity is revealed as Bruce Wayne.

DETECTIVE COMICS #28 (JUNE, 1939)

The only indication that the new mysterious superhero was still employed in *Detective Comics* (without opening the comic) was a rather simple, yellow scroll rolled open at the top-middle of the book that claimed, "This month and every month The Bat-Man!" Fred Guardineer illustrated this "cops and robbers" cover which left a much less impressionable impact than did the previous issue. (Figure #4) Even today, this book seems to have been lost in obscurity and all but forgotten. Quote must frequently heard, "No Batman cover, pricy (expensive), dull story." Nevertheless, *Detective Comics* #28 kept the new costumed detective as the star and lead-off story and holds a few subtle but noteworthy additions to the history of the character.

The reader quickly discovers that Bruce Wayne, apart from his other seemingly endless talents, is a master verbal impressionist: He disguises his voice as Commissioner Gordon and intercepts, information from one of the Police Departments "stool pigeons" named Gimpy who "has access to the haunts of the underworld." Gimpy tells Wayne that Frenchy Blake is the leader of the jewel gang that just pulled off their fifth lucrative heist for over $100,000 and are planning to strike again tonight at the Vander-Smith's apartment. That night, "Gloves" and "Ricky" are in the process of making their escape to the roof when, "A mysterious figure in black watches in the darkness above them…It is 'The Bat-Man'…" A fight ensues, resulting in "Ricky" getting kicked off the roof to his premature death, and "Gloves" being knocked out cold with a crushing left hook. One notable change in The Bat-Man's uniform; He would now sport a square belt-buckle which replaced the circular one worn in the previous issue (Pg. #1, panel #7 shows our hero with a circular belt-buckle. However, panel #6 and all the other future panels have him with a square belt-buckle. (This must have been a slightly over-looked illustration error). The ears of his cowl would also begin to elongate a bit which gave the character a more unique and "bat-like" appearance. (Figure #5)

Detective #28 also introduced to the reading public The Bat-Man's amazing and death-defying acrobatic skills, perfected in the heat of combat. To escape gunfire of two police officers he, "dives off the roof…turns a complete summersault in mid-air and lands on his feet on the Penthouse roof below!" The Bat-Man's nemesis, Frenchy Blake, would be introduced on page #3, panels #6 and #7 as he barked out orders to his gang for another robbery. Our hero would soon dispose of the three gang members, call Gordon to come pick up the criminal trash and speed his car toward Frenchy's apartment, "to finish the business at hand." At Frenchy's apartment, the detective commands the gang-leader to complete and sign a written confession for all the jewel robberies while dangling him outside his high-rise apartment window and threatening to cut the supporting rope if he refused to do so. Frenchy readily agrees. After signing the confession, Frenchy makes one last dire escape by flinging himself at The Bat-Man who, "meets Frenchy's jaw and sends him flying back over the table."

Later that evening, Frenchy's unconscious body is deposited out of a car onto the sidewalk in front of Police Headquarters. Attached to the defeated adversary is a note addressed to Gordon from the Dark Avenger for the first time in their illustrious careers saying, "Dear Commissioner- I thought you might like to have the leader of the jewel gang. Am also leaving his confession and stolen jewels. Till we meet again I remain- (Bat-Symbol)." Formally signed Rob't Kane for the last time.

(top) Cover of Detective Comics #28, Cover art by Fred Guardineer. (second down) Kane giving his creation a more "bat-like" look. (third down) The Bat-Man punching into submission the leader of the jewel gang, Frenchy Blake. (fourth down) The detective leaves his first note for Commissioner Gordon, attached to his defeated foe. Signed Rob't Kane for the last time.

DETECTIVE COMICS #29 (JULY, 1939)

The quintessential Batman cover of all the early *Detectives*. This "eerie figure of the night;" Dark, grim and silent, flying in the open window from a full moonlit and bat infested sky, with his black cape unfolding to resemble a pair of gigantic bat-wings. He brings not only immediate justice and excruciating pain to Jabah, Dr. Death's assistant, by striking him square in the sternum with a powerful kick; but, also trembling fear and disdain from the doctor himself, whose thoughts betray him with sweat pouring down his brow while, at the same time, dropping one of his test-tubes (probably filled with his "Death Potion").

Detective Comics #29, "The Bat-Man meets Doctor Death," landmarks the first time a Batman saga would span over two continuing issues and introduced the hero's very first "name" villain; Doctor Karl Hellfern, alias: Dr. Death. Unexpectedly, co-creator Bill Finger was taken off the title and replaced by a young lawyer fresh out of college named Gardner Fox. Kane and Fox were given a total of 10 pages this issue to fascinate and entertain us with their newly created superhero. They also slightly modified The Bat-Man's uniform; His wrist-length gloves changed from light-purple in color to the modern day traditional blue.

The Nocturnal Knight would need every weapon in his ever-growing arsenal to battle the mad scientist, including gas pellets from his utility belt, suction gloves, and knee pads to scale the building of Beverly Apartments. His uncanny foresight and keen detective instincts shine bright when, "For a quick getaway The Bat-Man has his rope handy." The appearance of the Night-Hunter becomes even more menacing and frightening, as well as his attitude toward the evil and corrupt underworld which he utterly loathes. A stern, no-nonsense approach to getting answers from criminals can be clearly seen when he ruthlessly interrogates, at gun point, two of Dr. Death's hired assassins by coldly questioning, "And who sent you may I ask?... Your choice gentleman! Tell me! Or I'll kill you!" Without warning Jabah, Dr. Death's giant Indian assistant, opens a door and shoots The Bat-Man right in the shoulder. However, this "creature of the night" did not come unprepared. He ejects a gas pellet from his utility belt, slams it to the ground in front of Jabah, crashes though the window and dives off the roof to grab the hidden rope that he attached to the ledge earlier. With this he "swings into a projecting cornice of the roof." Another breathtaking and fantastic escape, and Hellfern's plan to trap and eliminate this elusive daredevil fails.

After a quick visit to the family doctor as Bruce Wayne to remove the lodged bullet, and later saving the life of John P. Van Smith from the doctor's deadly pollen extract, The Bat-Man prepares to engage Dr. Death in battle once again.

Jabah is quickly disposed of as The Bat-Man wraps his lasso around the giant's neck, snapping it instantly. Then, after a brief chase through the laboratory and halls of Dr. Death's house, The Bat-Man throws a fire extinguisher at Hellfern, causing him to drop a test-tube that "swiftly ignites into a blazing inferno," completely engulfing the mad scientist. Victorious, the Enigmatic-Warrior stoically watches as the house is reduced to smoldering ashes. "Death...to Dr. Death!"

"...But is it death to this arch criminal? Follow the further amazing and unique adventures of The Bat-Man...in next month's Detective Comics." Signed Bob Kane.

(top) Cover of Detective Comics #29, *1st appearance of Dr. Death. Kane cover.*
(second down) The hero's first "name" villain; Dr. Death!
(third down) Boldly accepting Dr. Death's challenge, The Bat-Man silently enters the penthouse of the Beverly Apartments.
(bottom) Questioning Dr. Death's would-be assassins.

DETECTIVE COMICS #30 (AUGUST, 1939)

The blow-torch (second non-Batman) cover, superbly illustrated by Guardineer.

The phenomenal splash panel of this tale (conclusion from issue #29) reveals a vintage Bat-Man at his ultimate zenith. Here is the absolute essence and purest visual capturing of what the "Winged Figure of Vengeance" reflects and symbolizes: A set of truly forboding bat-ears that reach their climatic pinnacle in the pages of this issue (as well as on the cover of #31) which gave The Bat-Man an exquisitely majestic appearance that radiates supernatural awesomeness as well as trembling intimidation. He became the Underworld's most loathsome and feared nightmare incarnate.

The saga beings with a brief recap of the events which took place less than one week ago as, "The Bat-Man saw his sworn enemy, the grim Doctor Death, burned to ashes in a fire that wrecked an entire house." Yet, Bruce Wayne suspects that Dr. Death is still alive after reading in the newspaper, "strange death overcomes man victim of queer disease turns purple, doctors baffled." His suspicions are confirmed by Mrs. Jones who explains to Wayne that her husband received a threatening note from Dr. Death, demanding the payment of $500,000 or else he would die. And so, that night, "The Bat-Man prepares to meet Dr. Death again," with a few gas vials tucked into his utility belt. He then drives towards the Jones's home "in his specially built high-powered auto."

Kane would excel during these next two pages as his illustrations of The Winged Warrior not only fascinates and captivates the audience, but literally addicts them to the character as well. It doesn't come any better that this.

Dr. Death, whose head is wrapped in bandages to protect his burned skin, orders his new assistant Mikhail to break into the Jones' house and steal their diamonds to "reestablish" himself. After saving Mrs. Jones from sure death at the hand of Hellfern's murderous henchman, The Bat-Man drops the bag of jewels in front of the huge Cossack and tracks his quarry to the "drop-off" point, Ivan Herd's Pawn Shop, and then to his downtown apartment. A quick shattering of a glass vial from his utility belt, and the foreigner is rendered unconscious.

The detective diligently searches through the apartment for any clue or hint of Dr. Death's whereabouts. Unexpectedly, Mikhail revives, with a gun in hand, and fires at our hero, who, once again, escapes the Grim Reaper by wheeling and diving out the nearby window to catch his silken rope. And, "as Mikhail puts his hand though the window… there is a sickening snap as the Cossack's neck breaks under the mighty pressure of Batman's foot." Chalk up another one for the ol' "Bats."

He would soon swing in through "Ivan Herd's" window and demand the diamonds back. As the quivering old man overturns a table between them, The Bat-Man lassos the fleeing thief as his wig falls to the ground. With this, a skin mask is likewise pulled off, revealing the burned and destroyed face of Dr. Death. Departing, he leaves the jewels and his calling card, "…With the compliments of The Bat-Man."

(top) Cover of Detective Comics #30, Guardineer cover. (second down) The Bat-Man at his apex. Kane could develop a deeply intense and alluring mood with his illustrations and overall layouts that they went, generally, unsurpassed throughout the Golden Age Bat-Man scripts. (third down, left) Making a silent midnight entrance through the window of the Jones' home. (third down, right) The Bat-Man breaking the neck of the villainous Mikhail. (bottom, left and right) The Bat-Man removing Dr. Death's elderly disguise.

DETECTIVE COMICS #31 (SEPTEMBER, 1939)

Likely, one of the most famous and widely renowned *Detective* covers, second only to issue #27. The classic "Batman over castle;" with The Bat-Man, Dracula-like, ominously looming over an ancient medieval castle amidst a densely fog-bound and bat-inhabited moonlit night. With his huge bat-ears towering into the heavens, all attention is focused downward at a sinister hooded and red-cloaked figure carrying a beautiful blond damsel toward the lunar-illuminated castle in the distance. This is the "terrifying master of crime known as The Monk."

Writer Gardner Fox's approach to issues #31 and #32 was darkly bizarre and rather unorthodox, infusing a spooky supernatural element into the tale. Nevertheless, he did introduce a villain that would give The Bat-Man a good run for his money, his first love interest in fiancée Julie Madison, and opened the floodgates for an inexhaustible amount of state-of-the-art equipment, weapons and gadgets that he would use to battle crime all over the world.

Detective Comics #31 opens with his "weird menace to all crime" prowling "through the dark of a New York night." There is one slight change in his costume; The short, blue, wrist length gloves were lengthened to cover his forearm which lasted though issue #35. There are two new weapons introduced: The Baterang (original spelling) and the Batgyro (first Batplane) to follow Julie in as she voyages across the Atlantic to Paris. Soon after arriving on the ship, The Night Avenger boldly attacks The Monk who immediately puts him in a paralyzing hypnotic state. However, "By tremendous effort of will, The Bat-Man leaps into action," and the powerful spell is broken. Our hero decides to take on the criminal mastermind in Paris who has kidnapped Julie by placing her under his hypnotic control and demonic will.

Locating her, The Bat-Man must first dodge a gargantuan killer gorilla, and as an encore, cut his way out of a net with a piece of broken glass while being lowered into a den of deadly poisonous snakes. Twisted and evil, the diabolical Monk traps him once again as the savage gorilla descends into the cage to tear him in pieces. But, for every perilous situation there is a way of escape, and The Bat-Man knows them all. He "makes a desperate leap for the rope that lowered the gorilla," and, while climbing hand over hand to safety, flings his Baterang toward a guard about to draw a gun which strikes true with precise accuracy that could only be achieved by years of endless practice under the most trying conditions. With no time to waste, he rescues Julie from a speeding car with his ever trusty gas pellets, climbs into the (now named) Bat-plane, "and sets his automatic controls for Hungary – home of the vicious Monk and his werewolves!"

(top) Cover of Detective Comics *#31, 1st appearance of The Monk and Julie Madison.*
(second down, left) The Arch-criminal known as The Monk!
(second down, right) Introduction of the Batgyro, now known as the Batplane.
(third down, right and left) The Bat-Man finds himself caged by The Monk!
(bottom) Rescuing Julie and planning on vengeance.

DETECTIVE COMICS #32 (OCTOBER, 1939)

By the time issue #32 was released, it becomes quite apparent that DC Comics was catching on to the fact that it was their new Super-Detective who was responsible for the increasing sales of their flag-ship title. This can be assumed since they began to place a small picture-logo of The Bat-Man at the top-center of the comic book when he was not the main cover attraction. By this time though, the hand writing was already on the wall since there would be only one more non-Batman cover after this issue. A streak that has remained unbroken for over seven decades.

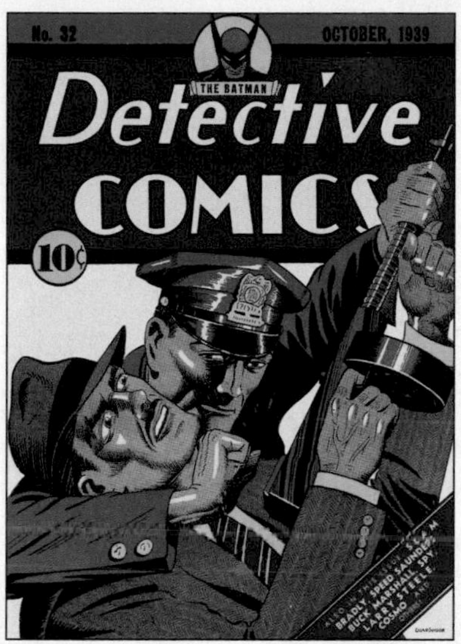

Detective #32 beings with The Bat-Man trailing the mysterious Monk into his native Hungary. Believing that he has located his strange foe, he "drops like a huge bat onto a speeding carriage," and finds Dala, the Monk's female assistant. As he returns to his hotel that is embedded deep in the Carlathan Mountains of Hungary, The Bat-Man discovers that this darkly beautiful woman is actually, a vampire who has already bitten Julie and now pleads for mercy at his feet. Furious and frustrated, the relentless man-hunter demands to know where the Monk dwells. Frightened and helpless, Dala confesses: "In the lost mountains of Cathala by the turbulent river Dess. I shall guide you." Anxious to get to the bottom of the case, he leaves Julie some money and wards her to, "fight against the power that calls you to this Monk" and departs with Dala to destroy the wicked fiend.

"A great silver net" drags the Batplane earthward, and the Monk "by his marvelous hypnotic powers, . . . slowly overpowers The Bat-Man." With his worst enemy completely subdued and harmless, the Monk then "forces his power through space" which fastens onto Julie's will to come to him and she cannot resist. Then the Monk informs the detective that he will be cast into a den of bloodthirsty wolves that will tear him asunder with their jagged fangs. Then he metamorphoses into a werewolf himself to call the wild mountain pack to dinner. Once again though, the evil mastermind has underestimated his worthy and determined foe who keeps the hungry wolves at bay with his ever-ready gas pellets. Climbing to safety, The Bat-Man melts down a silver statue into two silver bullets and slays the werewolf-vampire couple by emptying his gun into them and vowing, "Never again will you harm any mortal being." This event marks a very significant and memorable moment in the chronological evolution of the character since it is the first time in which The Bat-Man would use a gun to eliminate his adversaries.

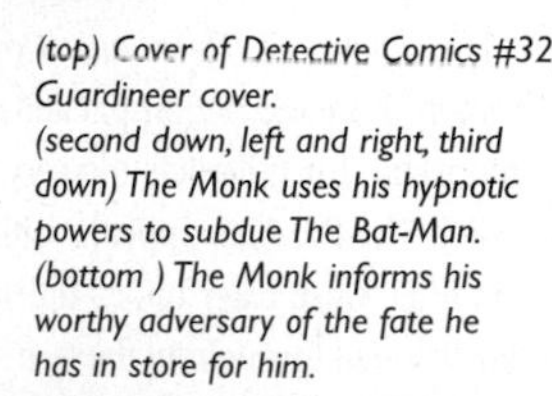

(top) Cover of Detective Comics #32, Guardineer cover.
(second down, left and right, third down) The Monk uses his hypnotic powers to subdue The Bat-Man.
(bottom) The Monk informs his worthy adversary of the fate he has in store for him.

DETECTIVE COMICS #33 (NOVEMBER, 1939)

At long last, the book that explained the legend of the cowled detective and how he came to be. The anxiously awaited origin of "this Weird Figure of the Dark. . .this Avenger of Evil, 'The Bat-Man'." (Figure #20) As a young boy, fifteen years ago, Bruce Wayne's parents were brutally and mercilessly murdered in cold blood before his terrified eyes. Some time later, a grief-stricken orphan would dedicate the rest of his life to battling crime and opposing all forms of injustice, swearing "by the spirits of [his] parents to avenge their deaths by spending the rest of [his] life warring on all criminals." For the next decade and a half, Wayne would tirelessly train and fine tune his mind to become a master scientist and his body to physical perfection for the monumental task at hand. Then, one fateful night as he sat in the study of Wayne Manor, he states one of the most famous quotes in all comic book history: "Criminals are a superstitious cowardly lot. So my disguise must be able to strike terror into their hearts. I must be a creature of the night. Black, terrible. . .A. . .A. . ." and "-As if in answer, a huge bat flies in the open window!" Wayne concludes, "A Bat! That's it! It's an omen. I shall become A Bat! And thus is born The Bat-Man." (Figure #21)

The cover of *Detective Comics* #33 is extremely dramatic, action-packed and historically important, for it depicts the very first time ever in which The Bat-Man appears with a gun holster around his waist. Later on, as the superhero grew and developed throughout the years, the use of any type of firearm became the number one no-no. Remember, it was a gun that killed his parents and these were the weapons which he utterly detested.

A full 12 pages would be given to The Bat-Man saga in issue #33 (2 page origin plus 10 page story) which was double the amount of his debut (issue #27) and second appearance (issue #28) in the title. Obviously the Nocturnal Nemesis of Crime was gaining popularity and obtaining a grander audience. Kane's artwork of his character was also becoming much more refined and authentically detailed.

The detective now faced an egotist named Dr. Carl Kruger, whose ambition was to rule the world (he suffered from Napoleon Complex), with his "Scarlet Horde" army and their Dirigible of Doom. This rocket ship carried a deadly potent Death Ray machine that shot forth a red beam of light that could completely destroy large skyscrapers and whatever else it struck. Fortunately for New York City, Batman resided there, and was not going to let this madman destroy the city which he loved so dearly.

After a quick confrontation with the demented Dr. Kruger, The Bat-Man is knocked senseless, tied up and bound with ropes and left to die as what was describe as an "incandescery bomb" ticks nearby. He slices his way free of his restraints with a secretly placed steel blade in his right boot, climbs out the nearby window and races for cover as the bomb explodes, totally demolishing the house. A miraculous escape from death with no time to spare.

Tracking Ryder (one of Kruger's lieutenants) in the Batplane to the secret hanger where the Dirigible is hidden, The Bat-Man destroys the Death Ray machine, and, as he raises an ax to strike a fatal blow to the Dirigible, is shot in the back shoulder plate by Kruger. Narrowly escaping once again, Wayne returns home and works through the whole night, developing a mysterious chemical to coat the Batplane with (to neutralize the effects of the death ray) and prepare himself for the final battle with Dr. Kruger.

The next day, The Bat-Man spots and steers his aircraft straight toward the Dirigible, ejects out with a parachute and kamikazes the scarlet rocket ship, blowing them both to smithereens. However, Kruger has likewise departed from his doomed ship in a catapult-plane. Not wanting this criminal menace to go free, the detective fastens his silken cord to a wheel of the small plane, climbs onto the wing and throws a gas pellet at Kruger, rendering him unconscious. The would-be-world-conqueror plunges to a watery death.

Final panel shows the mysterious Avenger of Evil with smoking .45 pistol in hand.

(top) Cover of Detective Comics *#33, origin of The Bat-Man. Gun holster cover. (second down) The significantly famous night in which Bruce Wayne would finally discover how to fulfill his childhood vow of "spending the rest of this life warring on all criminals." (third down, left,) Preparing for a nocturnal visit to the abode of the demented Dr. Kruger. (bottom) The Bat-Man spots and steers the Batgyro straight toward the Dirigible.*

DETECTIVE COMICS #34 (DECEMBER, 1939)

The 2nd cover appearance of The Crimson Avenger and final non-Batman cover. *Detective Comics* #34 begins exactly where issue #32 concluded. Issue #33 was substituted in at the last moment to give the readers an idea of where and how The Bat-Man came to be.

After rescuing his fiancée, Julie from the diabolically devious Monk, Bruce Wayne sees her safely aboard a ship bound for America and plans to return shortly thereafter. However, as he leaves his hotel, the wealthy socialite runs straight into a fellow with no face. And a new mystery begins in Paris, the City of Lights.

While reading the local newspaper and relaxing in a taxi cab, Wayne encounters a fair young French woman named Karel Maire. She is apparently being stalked by a group of thugs called the Apaches, who cast a dagger at her in the car. Fainting from mortal fear in Wayne's arms, the man-with-no-face suddenly appears and explains his and his sister's dire straits. The odd stranger tells Wayne that they are hiding from The Duc D'Orterre, an evil and mortally destitute individual who is the leader of the Apaches that used a "terrible ray" to burn away all the features of his face because he interfered with the Duc's enchanted infatuation with Karel.

"That night as Paris sleeps," The Bat-Man stalks the rooftops and then swoops down into the city sewer to search for the criminal's subterranean laboratory. The detective soon discovers that the lab must be nearby since he quickly defeats two attacking Apaches, who mistake the paramount expert in martial arts and combat skills for a silly masquerade ball drunk. Nevertheless, The Bat-Man is much too hasty with his flying leap to overcome the Duc and is temporarily blinded by a light that shoots forth out of the criminal's cane. Tied to a deadly "Wheel of Chance," this great escape-artist must rescue himself once again or be thrown against a concrete wall and splattered to formless paste or driven completely mad by the never ceasing whirling of the enormous wheel. Of course, our hero would not let us down. "By tensing his steel-like muscles. He breaks the leather thongs."

After freeing Charles from the "Wheel," The Bat-Man climbs in his ever-ready Batplane and tracks down the Duc who has kidnapped Karel and is speeding toward his place in Champagne.

Setting the automatic controls of the Batplane, the eerie bat-figure drops down on his rope and makes a valiant leap onto the speeding car. As Karel kicks the knife wielding Duc in his back, the Count drops his weapon, giving The Bat-Man the opportunity he needs to leap through the open window and take the offensive advantage. A fierce struggle ensues and the crime-fighter crushes the Duc's windpipe causing the runaway car to "careen crazily" off a narrow bridge. And, "Split seconds meaning life or death. The Bat-Man grasps for his rope ladder…and catches it just in time to escape sudden death." He must have studied under the great Harry Houdini.

With the mystery solved and the corrupt Duc eliminated, The Bat-Man says, "Au Revoir" to the grateful brother and sister and departs into the night.

(top) Cover of Detective Comics #34*, 2nd Crimson Avenger (and last non-Batman) cover. Cover art by Creig Flessel.*
(second down, right) Charles and Karel Maire explain their seemingly hopeless situation to Bruce Wayne.
(third down, left) Bruce leaves the Maire's company and returns as The Bat-Man.
(third down, right) Ready to do battle with a few Apaches.
(bottom) The evil Duc D'Orterre.

DETECTIVE COMICS #35 (JANUARY, 1940)

The acclaimed hypodermic (hypo) cover depicting The Bat-Man putting a strong forearm choke-hold on a villainous doctor as he is about to inject serum into a rope-tied and horror-stricken victim. Of particular note are the emphasized and fascinating bat-ears that project upward into the logo. This would be the first issue produced with a full 12 pages for one complete story and crowned the superhero as the reigning king and star of all the future covers of *Detective Comics*.

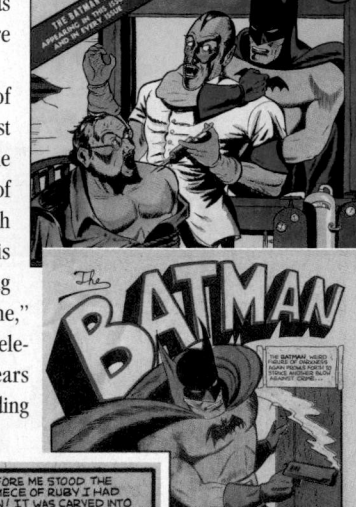

The sensational splash panel of *Detective* #35 is perhaps one of the most definitive examples of The Bat-Man's whole persona and image during his first year of crime-fighting (second only to the splash panel in *Detective* #30). Here is this "weird figure of darkness, again prowling forth to strike another blow against crime," with blazing .45 automatic in hand. The celebrated and uniquely elongated bat-ears would begin to decline, while blue shading was added to his cape and cowl, and more frequent verbal communication with allies and enemies alike took place as the character moved out from the murky shadows and into the limelight.

After purchasing a large ruby idol of the Hindu god of destruction, Kila, (usually named Kali) from its discoverer Sheldon Lenox, a globe-trotter and famous explorer, the wealthy and astute collector Weldon receives two threatening letters to return the ancient idol to the followers of Kila or he will bring "destruction" upon himself. As he discusses these letters with Commissioner Gordon and Bruce Wayne, the two long time friends race towards Lenox's house. They soon find the archaeologist being kidnapped and sped away in a car full of Hindu worshippers. Gordon and Wayne would watch in utter shock as the Hindus sacrifice Lenox by tossing his body into a river. The police search the river but never find the body.

A few weeks pass and Weldon dismisses the police protection act that Gordon had given him and his house to guard the ruby idol. After acquiring this information, Wayne plans to stakeout the rich collectors abode as his nighttime alter-ego stating, "When the police are away the rats will play." His foresights confirmed, The Bat-Man takes on a trio of gangsters who show a great interest in sculpture-art as they try to disarm the alarm-system. The shadow warrior knocks the first silly with a right hook, and performs an over-the-head judo flip with the second, breaking the gangsters arm in the process. The last gang member rushes toward the detective with knife ready, only to meet a smashing granite fist across the jaw. But, the victory is short lived as a billy club crashes down upon his head, knocking him to the ground seriously dazed. The Hindus quickly steal the idol and escape out the window as the estate's guards arrive.

The Bat-Man races his high-powered roadster to the home of the unofficial mayor of Chinatown, Wong, a wise and honest man. The Chinaman warns the superhero that the ruby idol will most likely be cut into several pieces and sold by Sin Fang who is a receiver and distributor of stolen goods. And that very night he visits the store of Sin Fang. Telling the curios dealer that the idol is stolen, Fang states that he was not aware of that fact and he will return the artifact so his reputation will not suffer.

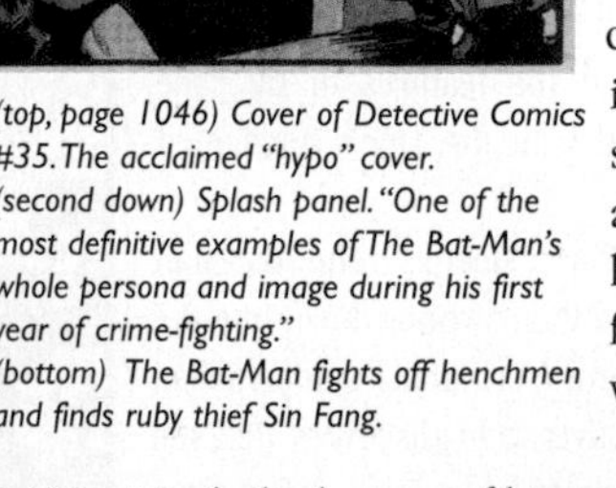

(top, page 1046) Cover of Detective Comics #35. The acclaimed "hypo" cover.
(second down) Splash panel. "One of the most definitive examples of The Bat-Man's whole persona and image during his first year of crime-fighting."
(bottom) The Bat-Man fights off henchmen and finds ruby thief Sin Fang.

Fang leads The Bat-Man into the back rooms of his store. Suddenly Fang disappears and unleashes a triad of death traps to eliminate this darkly garbed intruder. The Bat-Man disposes of two giant Mongols wielding large curved swords, renders a deadly mustard gas harmless with a gas pellet from his utility belt, escapes a watery death by catching a protruding water pipe before falling into the deep well, and climbs to safety.

Discovering that Fang is none other then Sheldon Lenox,

the detective dodges a few bullets, reaches for the small idol and hurls it at Lenox. Striking the deceitful smuggler in the head, Lenox falls through an open window to his death.

The concluding story panel has Gordon reading the newspaper and explaining to Wayne that The Bat-Man has foiled and stopped yet another criminal gang-leader and confessing that his masked vigilante is making his department look completely ridiculous. If the Commissioner only knew.

DETECTIVE COMICS #36 (FEBRUARY, 1940)

Another fantastic splash panel that perfectly sets the dark, mysterious and solemn mood for the archetype nocturnal man-hunter. This issue marked the debut of the "bat-fin" gauntlets that The Bat-Man utilizes. These became a famous traditional trademark that he has retained even to this day. These new finned gloves were an interesting surprise addition to his costume, beginning on the splash page, since they did not appear on the cover. *Detective Comics* #36 also introduced to the public the evil mastermind and notorious criminal genius known as Professor Hugo Strange.

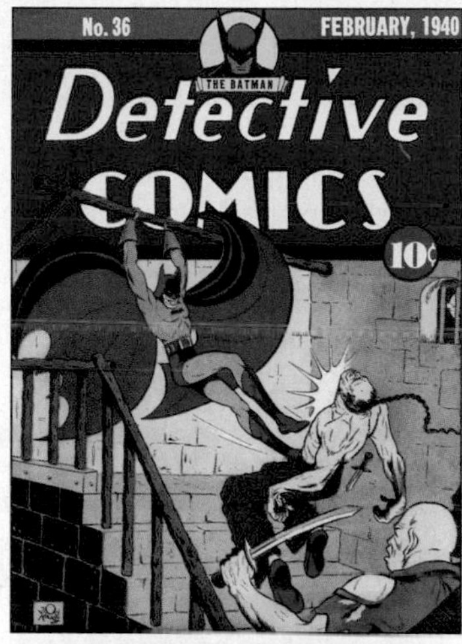

The narration of the adventures was becoming much more metaphorically sophisticated and acute. This can be seen in the introductory splash panel, "Already an almost legendary figure the cowled shadow of The Bat-Man prowls through the night preying upon the criminal parasite, like the winged creature whose name he had adopted." The crime-fighting detective was also achieving greater respect as stories and rumors of this shadow figure was bolting like wildfire throughout the underworld, making his name a by-word of terror and creating unchecked fear and anxiety for all wrong-doers. Panel #3 of page #1 quotes a thug confessing, "The Bat-Man! Let's get outa here…I don't want to fool around with him." The detective comes to the aid of a F.B.I. agent who dies in his arms after being shot with a Tommy-gun in his back. The Bat-Man quickly takes a notebook off the G-Man and hurries away into the night, escaping a barrage of screaming police bullets. His unparalleled elusiveness is complemented with a statement by one of the amazed officers, "You might as well chase a ghost."

(top) Cover of Detective Comics *#36, 1st appearance of Professor Hugo Strange.*
(second down) The first panel in Detective #36, where The Bat-Man suddenly sees a man leaping from a speeding car.
(third down, left) Professor Hugo Strange.
(third down, right) The Bat-Man engulfed in Stranges' mysterious fog.

Professor Hugo Strange appears for the very first time as "he broods over the mad evil schemes that surge through his brilliant but distorted brain." Here is this magnificent human personification of wickedness and corrupt imagination. The professor's massive muscular frame towers over his petty servants, complemented with brutally physical and verbal intimidation which is overshadowed only by his ultra-intelligent criminal plans for conquest of power and wealth.

A few nights later, Bruce Wayne figures that the unnaturally thick fog that has been blanketing the city, the disappearance of an electrical engineer, and the recent robberies of the names written in the G-Man's book must all be linked somehow with the name Hugo Strange. Thus he readies himself.

As Professor Strange's henchmen are in the process of robbing The Sterling Silver Company, The Bat-Man stuns the criminals with an expert guise and dynamically plows over the six-man gang by hurtling though the air and thundering down like a bomb-shell, leveling everyone in his path. He then alerts the police to the scene with a flare-gun. The arch-criminal Strange is outraged with The Bat-Man's interference and capture of his men. He decides to trap the detective at his next heist at The Wolf Brothers Fur Company and vows to crush him like a fragile glass.

Inside the warehouse of the Wolf Bros., The Bat-Man is now forced to engage nine of Strange's men who rush toward the darkly garbed crusader like a "feeding frenzy" of hungry sharks. The hero displays great strength, agility and fantastic speed by pouncing down on the gangsters "like a panther, crushing them with powerhouse blows," while, "keeping up a ceaseless barrage of blows upon the gunmen." However, he is only a man, and is ultimately felled by a "black jack" across the back of his head.

Transported to the professor's hideout, a warehouse near the river front, The Bat-Man is tied up and mercilessly lashed across the midsection with a bull-whip. Strange would only enjoy a single blow as the night warrior's "steel muscles suddenly surged with strength and snap his bonds." The Bat-Man renders the other men unconscious with a gas pellet and dives angrily at Strange. "With the power of a madman, the professor succeeds in securing a strangle hold on The Bat-Man's throat." But, expertly trained for years on end for such perilous situations, The Bat-Man breaks Strange's grip and sends him flying overhead with an ancient Jiu-Jitsu move. He finally conquers his foe with a dramatic leaping tackle and smashing left hook.

The hero soon discovers the huge fog-machine used to cover-up the multiple robberies throughout the city and the electrical engineer, Henry Jenkins, who had been kidnapped by Strange and forced to build his unique invention. (Figure #31) The fog is lifted from the city and the full moon is clearly viewed once again.

With Strange captured by the mysterious guardian, The Bat-Man's name and heroics begin to be greatly admired and appreciated by the citizens of his beloved city. A child asks his father who The Bat-Man is. The response, "A great man son. A great man!"

But, can the state penitentiary keep Professor Hugo Strange locked up for long? Bruce Wayne wonders.

(top, left) With a sudden and powerful surge of strength, The Bat-Man breaks free of the bonds.
(top, right) The fantastic fog-machine used by Strange to cover-up his multiple heists throughout the city.

DETECTIVE COMICS #37 (MARCH, 1940)

The final solo Bat-Man adventure in the pages of *Detective Comics*. Another darkly vivid and alluring cover drawn by Kane; The Bat-Man in brutal melee combat, Judo flipping one thug, with a .45 auto dropping to the foggy, moon illuminated dock, while racing at full velocity toward a second knife wielding adversary. A vintage scene that has never acquired the attention and acclaim it deserves. (Figure #32)

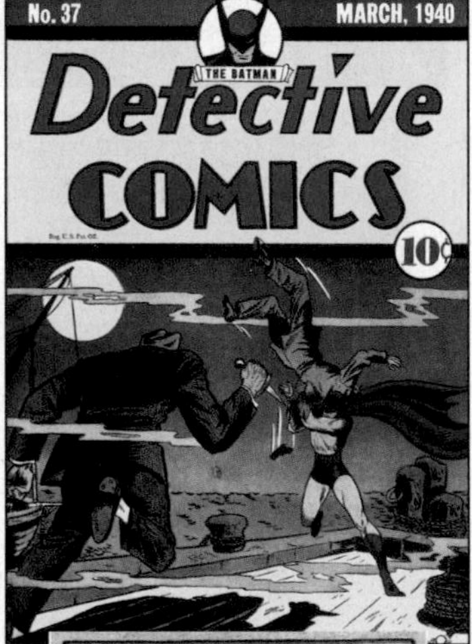

The splash panel opens with a view of The Bat-Man's high-speed roadster that will soon become widely known as The Batmobile. Cautiously stepping into a lone and remote house in the woodlands, the detective runs smack into a torturing session involving three mobsters interrogating their immobile victim, Joey, with a molten-hot iron for selling secret information. The Bat-Man materializes from out of the dense shadows and defeats the torturers in lightning quick fashion. However, Joey double-crosses his timely rescuer by knocking him cold with the handle of his gun and then murders the three gangsters in cold blood. Awakening, our hero finds the blood covered bodies and perceived that Turg, a name that was mentioned earlier that night, must be involved somehow.

Tracking his quarry to a grocery store, Bruce Wayne notices Joey walking out of the store with Elias Turg and visits the "store front" later that night as The Bat-Man. Walking in on their business meeting, the darkly garbed figure combats his five adversaries in pitch dark, inky blackness with the aid of infra-red goggles.

Discovering that these men are international spies sent on a mission to destroy the foreign ship Ronij to frame the United States and start a world wide crisis, the detective secretly follows the spies to a deserted waterfront dock. After being thrown into the ocean in a large sack and slashing free with his ever handy steel blade, The Bat-Man confronts the criminals and gains victory by kicking and heaving them all over the dock. He then foils their crafty plans by steering the small boat loaded with dynamite away from the Ocean Liner.

(middle) Cover of Detective Comics #37, *The Bat-Man's last solo (Golden Age) appearance in the title.*
(bottom) The Bat-Man freeing himself from a watery grave!

With only the leader of the spies left, the tenacious Bat-Man arrives at Turg's home, who immediately throws a razor sharp sword at the dark intruder. In a flash, the hero opens the door directly in front of the speeding blade that "sends the sharp steel hissing through the soft wood." As Turg tries to escape, The Bat-Man sends the international criminal hurling back with a stunning right hook, impaling him on his own sword. Case closed. One less vindictive vermin to plague society.

The final panel displays a "David and Goliath" scene with The Bat-Man starting up toward two "Huge, terrifying Man-Monsters" that he must confront and battle in next month's adventure of *Detective Comics*."

(top, left) Concluding panel of Detective #37. The story advertised would not appear in the following issue; the original and 1st appearance of Robin was substituted in for it This saga was postponed and published in Batman #1. (top, right) The Nocturnal Knight turning to confront international spies and terrorists.

BATMAN #1 (SPRING, 1940)

By the time of his first anniversary in the spring of 1940, The Bat-Man had become so popular and in demand that he was rewarded his own title. It would be here, in his very first issue, that this lone warrior soloed for the last time. The story was originally scheduled to appear in *Detective Comics* #38 (April 1940), but the origin and first appearance of Robin, The Boy Wonder was substituted in for it at the last minute.

The splash panel shows The Bat-Man looking skyward to a gigantic human beast, with both arms uplifted, ready to wreak immeasurable havoc and destruction upon New York City.

The story opens with the vicious Professor Hugo Strange escaping from the federal penitentiary and kidnapping several mental patients from The Metropolis Insane Asylum the following evening. A month passes and downtown Manhattan begins to be demolished by a 15 foot tall, huge Man-Monster who smashes a car with his bare hands and attacks a wave of police officers as their bullets harmlessly bounce off him. As suddenly as the raging hulk appeared, he escapes in a large truck that was idling nearby. The following day, the grotesque beast shows up again, this time wreaking the elevated subway. Even though he evades the police once again, the fleeing truck is spotted by the keen, eagle-eyes of The Bat-Man who follows the mysterious demolishers in The Batplane.

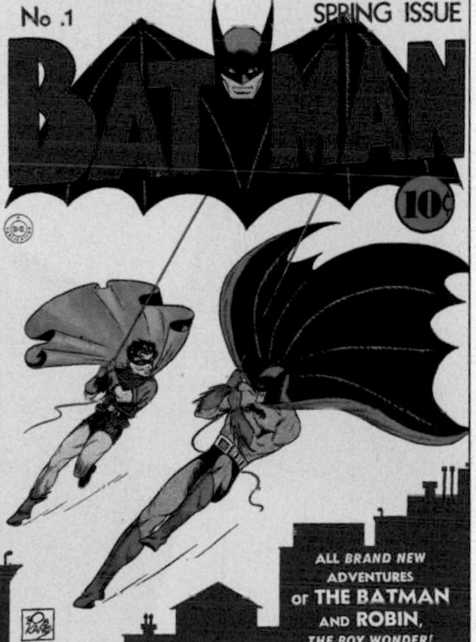

Bat-Man Comics #1. The superhero is awarded his own title.

As The Bat-Man enters cautiously into the ocean cliff warehouse, two of the angry giants grab hold of the detective and bring him before their master. The demented genius explains to the darkly garbed adversary that the giant man-beasts are the escaped lunatics which he kidnapped and injected with an extract that speeds up growth glands. The end result is a berserk gargantuan ready to do his bidding. Strange then injects The Bat-Man with the fluid which will take effect in 18 hours and instructs his men to escort a couple of the hulking beasts to the city to loot a few banks with "no slip ups!" With time running short, The Bat-Man explodes his way free out of the cell and with a powerful blow, "sends Strange out to fall to the murky waters below..." He quickly turns the raging monsters against each other who fight it out to the death while the expert chemist mixes a compound to act as an antidote to neutralize the growth gland serum.

The Bat-Man chases after the professor's hoods in his Batplane with a machine-gun mounted atop the cockpit, blazing lead death into the speeding trucks and cutting them down. "Much as I hate to take human life, I'm afraid this time it's necessary," sneers the intractable justice seeker with teeth clenched and eyes fixed on his target, burning with awesome vengeance. The bullets take their toll as the truck crashes into a nearby tree. As the monster rises from the wreckage, The Bat-Man's powerful upward lift of the Batplane, jerks the beast off the ground. His neck snaps like a dry twig as the detective grimly concludes, "He's probably better off this way."

In the concluding scene, the final giant climbs a high tower in order to attack the elusive aircraft. The Bat-Man pilots his plane for one final pass and calmly drops a gas pellet, choking the barbaric and frustrated creature who, "shakes his hands defiantly...and topples off to his doom!"

Soon this laconic loner's future would forever be changed with the introduction of his first adopted son Dick Grayson, known to the world as Robin, The Boy Wonder. The tactics of fighting his opponents were altered. The use of any kind of firearm and taking lives became totally eschewed. His attitude towards life, and preserving it at all cost, became first and foremost. He smiled more, had an ally to speak too and consult with, and most important, one to protect, nurture and set an example for, which gave the black and gray knight an even higher purpose for existing. The young boy, with his smile from ear to ear, would spring across the concrete jungle of Gotham City like a bright bolt of sunshine and provide the strip with the breath of fresh air it needed. But, this is another story...reserved for another time.

After escaping the monsters grasp, Batman vengefully attacks Strange's giant berserking Man-Monsters with his fully automatic machine gun, mounted atop the Batplane and then watches the last lunatic beast fall to his doom.

GEPPI'S ENTERTAINMENT MUSEUM PRESENTS
THE OVERSTREET HALL OF FAME

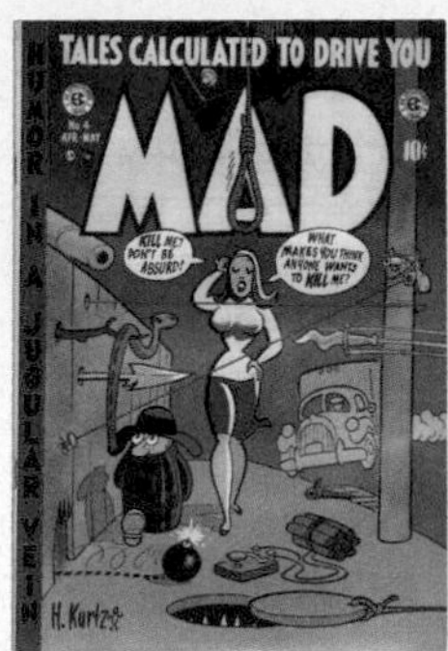

The Overstreet Hall of Fame was conceived to single out individuals who have made great contributions to the comic book arts. This includes writers, artists, editors, publishers and others who have plied their craft in insightful and meaningful ways.

While such evaluations are inherently subjective, they also serve to aid in reflecting upon those who shaped the experience of reading comic books over the years. This year's class of inductees begins on this next page. First, though, we offer a list of the previous inductees:

Class of 2006	Class of 2007	Class of 2008
Murphy Anderson	Dave Cockrum	Carl Barks
Jim Aparo	Steve Ditko	Will Eisner
Jim Lee	Bruce Hamilton	Al Feldstein
Mac Raboy	Martin Nodell	Harvey Kurtzman
	George Pérez	Stan Lee
	Jim Shooter	Marshall Rogers
	Dave Stevens	John Romita, Sr.
	Alex Toth	John Romita, Jr.
	Michael Turner	Julius Schwartz
		Mike Wieringo

"Neal Adams is one of the greatest artists our medium has ever known. He is also the single most influential artist in the history of comic book publishing. An amazing number of artists, including many whose styles are nothing like Neal's, many you'd never guess, started out trying to emulate Neal. He has personally trained a small army of artists. Not only a master of the visual, Neal writes as well, and also does, it seems, whatever else he wishes to with ease and grace. His brilliance extends beyond the printed page. He works with light, motion and sound. He creates three-dimensionally. Any medium is his medium. And, everything he does, he does with rare excellence. He brings insight to any endeavor. Most importantly, he *truly* creates. New ideas. Original thoughts. Genesis! Beyond that, he has always been a force in the industry – a righter of wrongs, a bringer of change, a leader. Neal is a genius and a giant who has lifted up us all."
- Jim Shooter

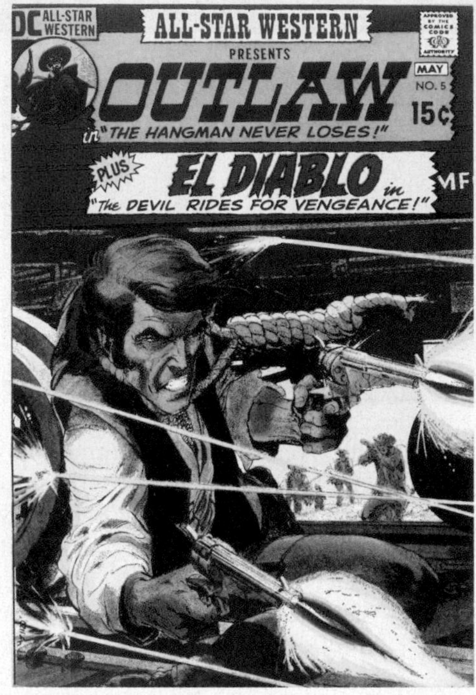

ALL-STAR WESTERN #5
April-May 1971. © DC

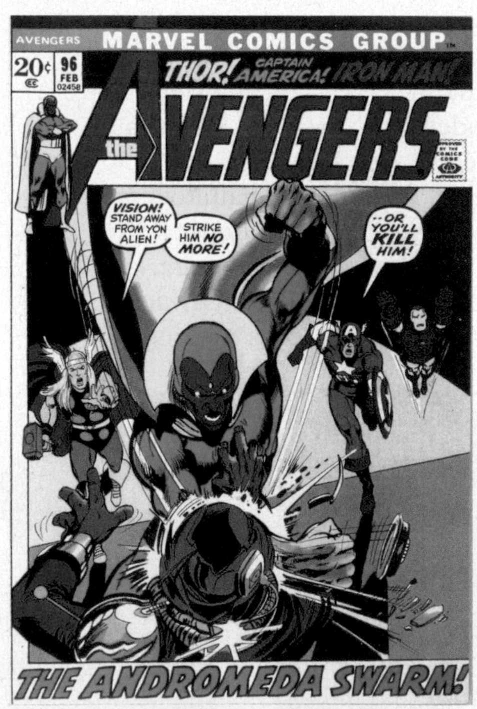

AVENGERS #96
February 1972. © MAR

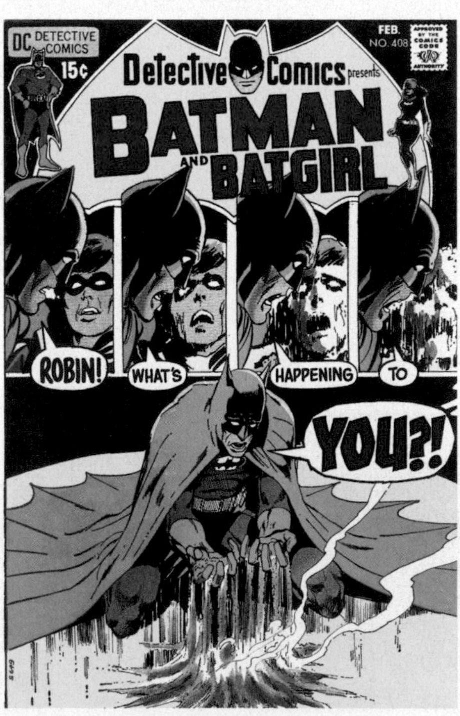

DETECTIVE COMICS #408
February 1971. © DC

GREEN LANTERN #86
October-November 1971. © DC

MS. MYSTIC #1
October 1982. © Pacific Comics

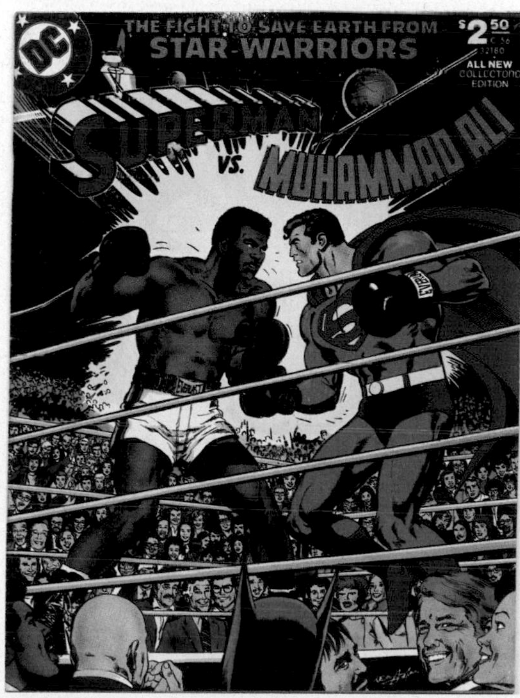

ALL-NEW COLLECTORS' EDITION C-56
1978. © DC

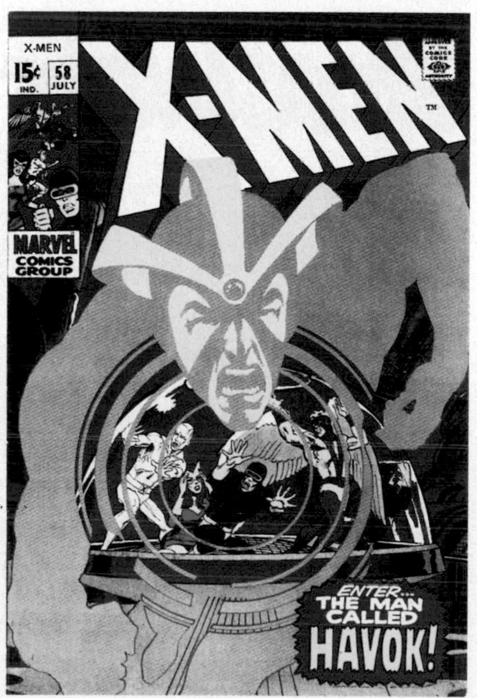

X-MEN #58
July 1969. © MAR

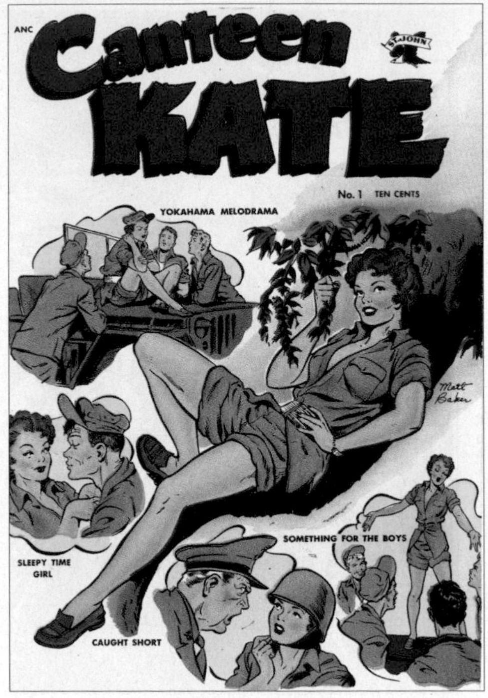

CANTEEN KATE #1
June 1952. © STJ

One of America's first major African American cartoonists, Matt Baker (1921-1959) is best known for his "good girl" comics and his romance comic work. He is considered by many to be a master in drawing the female form. He clearly adored women and enjoyed drawing them and all their beauty. Not just a pin-up artist, his attention to detail and his ability to use the background details to help set a scene was something very few of his peers were doing at the time. Educated at Cooper Union in New York City, he got his start with Iger Studios in the mid-1940s, providing art for St. John, Fox, Fiction House, Quality and Atlas. His work included the genres of Westerns, Romance, and Jungle Adventure, but he is mostly remembered for his work on the *Phantom Lady* series. So provocative for the day, one of his *Phantom Lady* covers was used in Fredrick Wertham's book on the ill effects of comic books on America's youth, *Seduction of the Innocent*.

GIANT COMICS EDITIONS #15
1950. © FOX

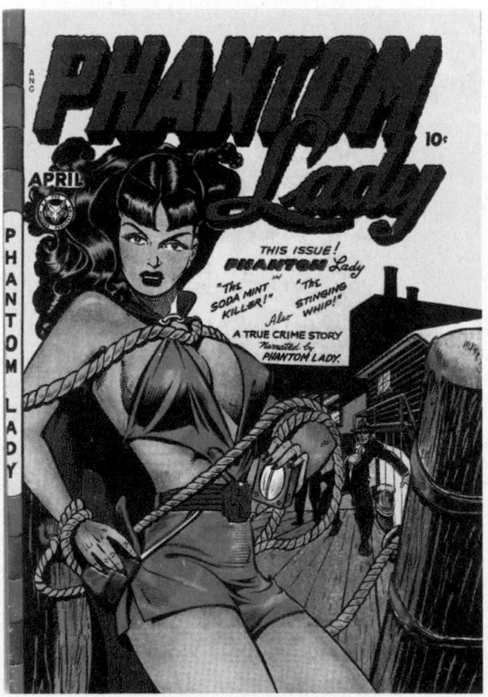

PHANTOM LADY #17
April 1948. © FOX

SEVEN SEAS COMICS #4
1947. © Universal Phoenix Feature

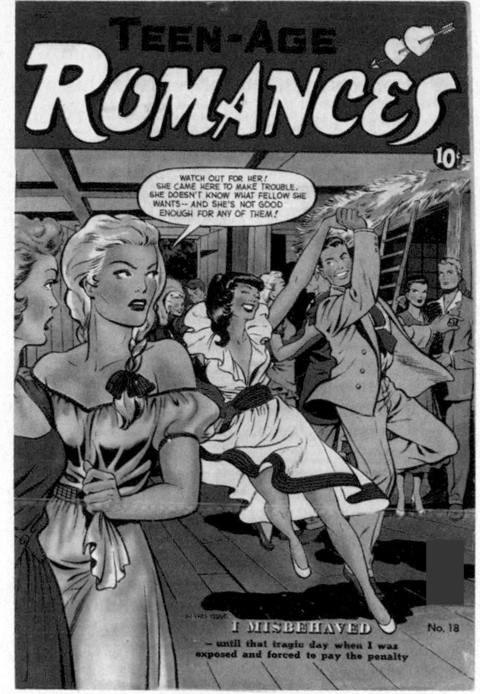

TEEN-AGE ROMANCES #18
1951. © STJ

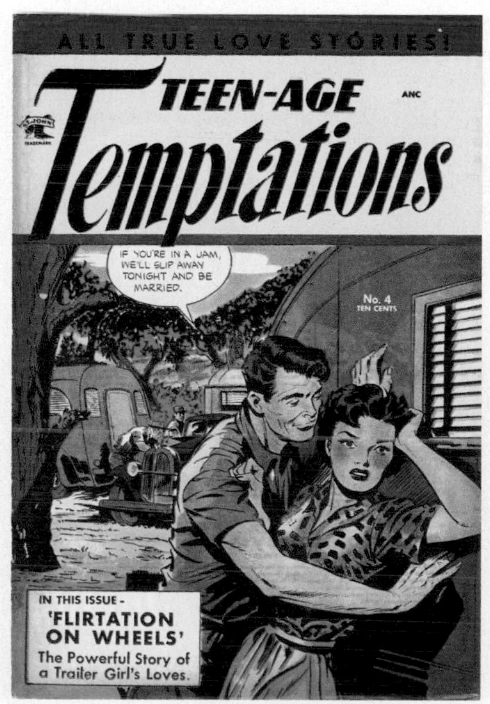

TEEN-AGE TEMPTATIONS #4
1953. © STJ

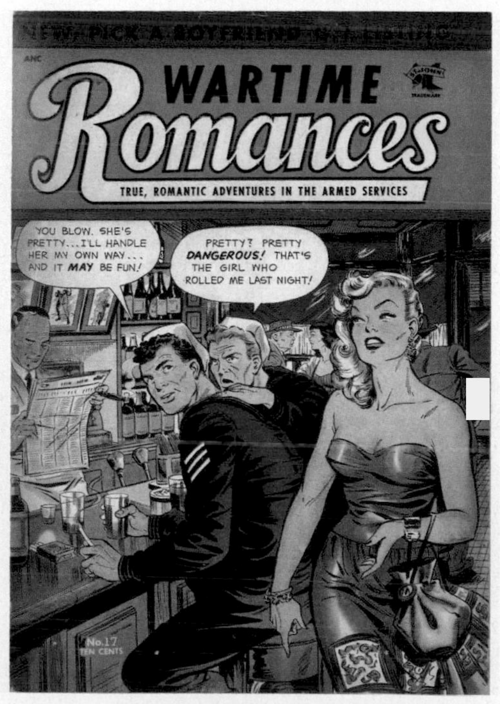

WARTIME ROMANCES #17
September 1953. © STJ

"Chris Claremont has written many wonderful things. He's passionate about everything he writes. Especially notable, of course, is his work on the X-Men. Chris gets a good deal of credit for the success of the X-Men, but not nearly as much as he deserves. Not only did he do an outstanding job as writer, he built the team that built the team. He recruited artists when needed. He made sure the lettering and coloring were consistent and top drawer. He spent time, effort and money out of his own pocket to insure the quality of the book. He sweated the details. He fought like a Wolverine to defend the integrity of his vision, his work, his words. If there's a Hall of Fame for Caring, Trying and Outworking Everyone, he should be there, too. Babe Ruth didn't create the Yankees and Chris Claremont didn't create the X-Men, but each of them built the house."
- Jim Shooter

IRON FIST #14
October 1977. © MAR

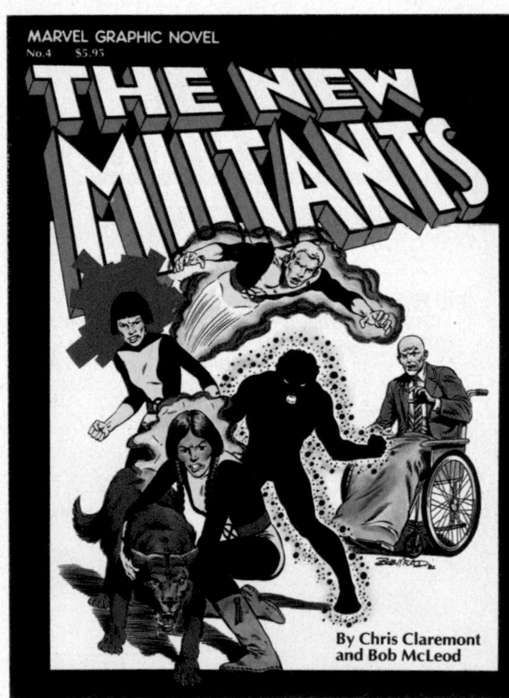

MARVEL GRAPHIC NOVEL #4
1982. © MAR

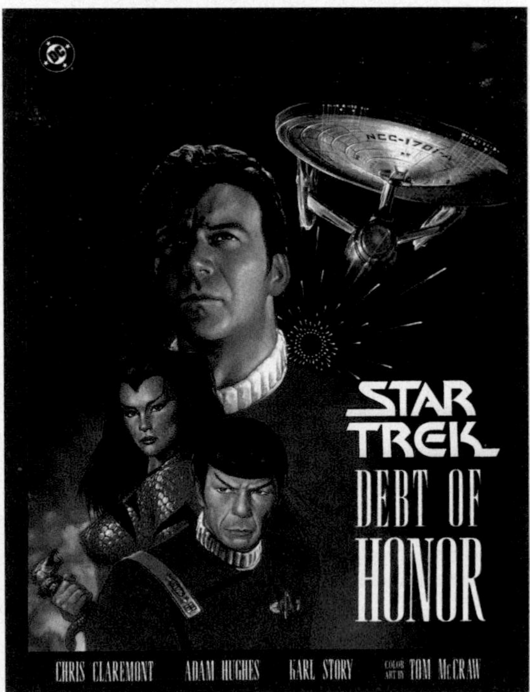

STAR TREK: DEBT OF HONOR
Graphic novel. 1992. © Paramount

X-MEN #100
August 1976. © MAR

X-MEN #136
August 1980. © MAR

UNCANNY X-MEN #142
February 1981. © MAR

UNCANNY X-MEN #222
October 1987. © MAR

PALMER COX PHOTO
Frontis page from "The Brownies and Prince Florimel" hardcover book. 1918. © The Century Co.

Palmer Cox (April 28, 1840 – July 24, 1924) was a Canadian-born cartoonist whose best known work revolutionized the world of comic characters and comic character merchandise. As the creator of The Brownies, Cox can be credited with the first successful recurring characters, the first internationally successful characters, and with developing a principled road map for producing character-themed merchandise for children. Appearing in serialized form in *St. Nicholas* magazine, the fairy- or pixie-like characters had special powers, appeared only to the virtuous, and were collected for the first time in *The Brownies, Their Book* (1887). The Kodak Brownie camera featured the characters on its box, and items ranging from sheet music to candle holders were offered, creating a road map followed regionally by The Yellow Kid and internationally by Mickey Mouse and Superman.

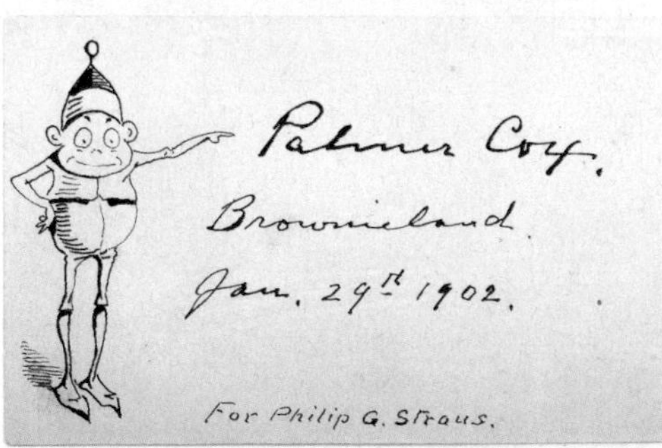

PALMER COX SIGNATURE CARD
1902.

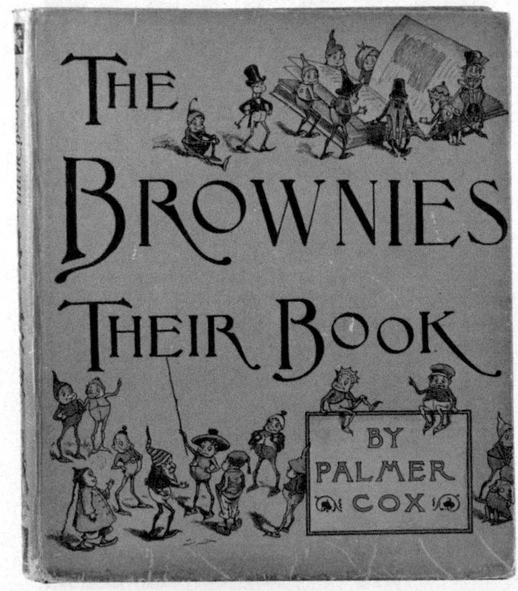

THE BROWNIES THEIR BOOK
Hardcover book. 1887. © The Century Co.

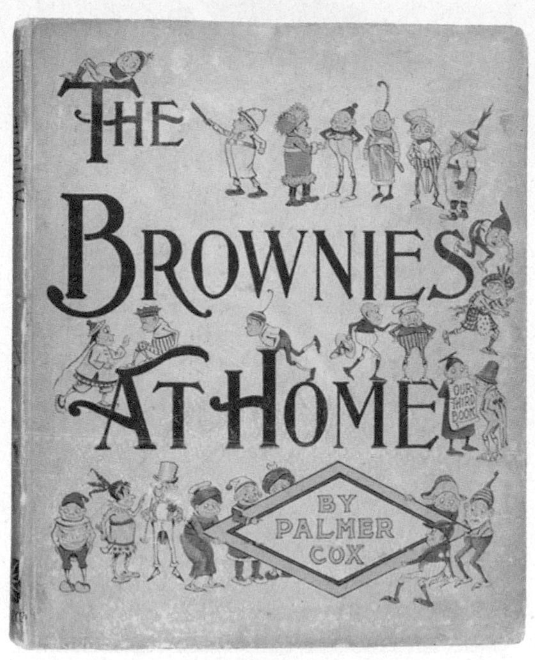

THE BROWNIES AT HOME
Hardcover book. 1893. © The Century Co.

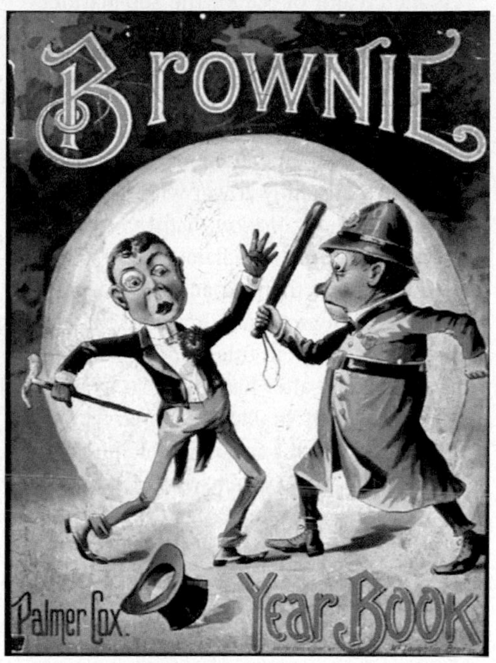

BROWNIE YEAR BOOK
1895. © McLoughlin Bros.

The judge selected for the case
Ran here and there about the place
With warning cries and gesture wide,
And seemed unable to decide.

And there they might be tugging still,
With equal strength and equal will—
But while they struggled, stars withdrew
And hints of morning broader grew,
Till arrows from the rising sun
Soon made them drop the rope and run.

Brownies.

41

THE BROWNIES THEIR BOOK
Interior page. 1893. © The Century Co.

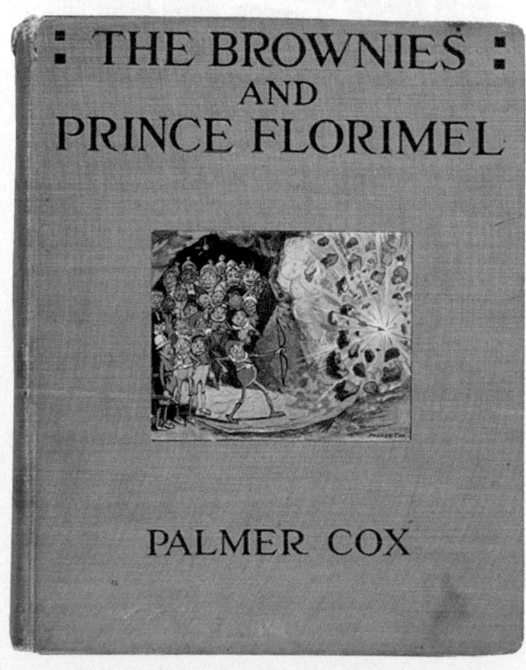

THE BROWNIES AND PRINCE FLORIMEL
Hardcover book. 1918. © The Century Co.

As the creator of Namor, the Sub-Mariner, Bill Everett (1917-1973) was responsible for one of Timely Comics' three main characters (the other two were Captain America and The Human Torch). Namor was likely the first very successful anti-hero in the comic book world, since he was nearly constantly at war with the surface-dwelling humans. *Motion Picture Funnies Weekly* #1 featured the character's first appearance, which was then expanded for *Marvel Comics* #1. He wrote and drew the character in a number of different titles for the publisher both before and after his service in World War II. During the 1950s, he illustrated Marvel Boy, Venus and the first appearance of Simon Garth, The Zombie, among other work. Timely had become Atlas and then Marvel Comics when he illustrated the first issue of *Daredevil*. His last lengthy work in comics was a 1972-1973 run on his original character, *Sub-Mariner*.

AMAZING-MAN COMICS #5
September 1939. © CEN

DAREDEVIL #1
Everett & Kirby cover. April 1964. © MAR

MYSTERY TALES #14
August 1953. © MAR

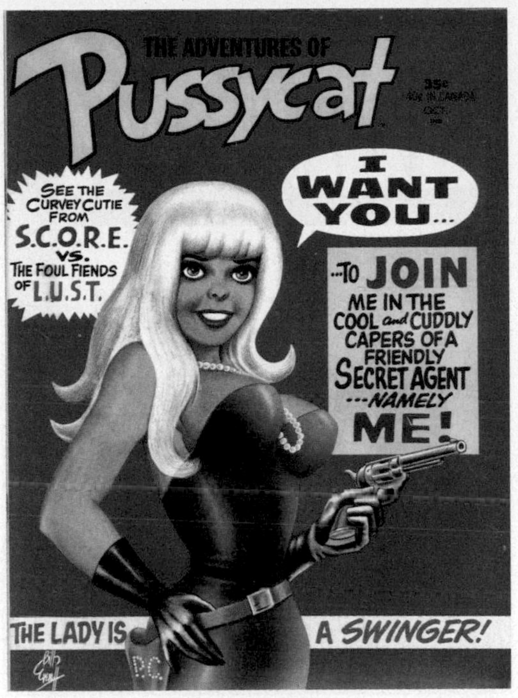

PUSSYCAT #1
October 1968. © MAR

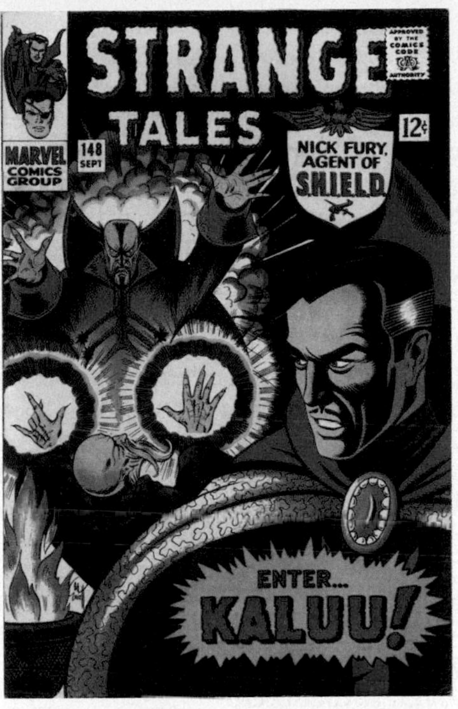

STRANGE TALES #148
September 1966. © MAR

SUB-MARINER COMICS #33
April 1954. © MAR

VENUS #13
April 1951. © MAR

"Frank Frazetta started illustrating comic books and comic strips with a wide variety of themes before becoming the almost universally lauded master fantasy illustrator he became. He worked in the western, mystery, humor, and other genres including stories for EC Comics, National's Shining Knight, Avon and other publishers (his collaborations with EC's great Al Williamson and the talented Roy Krenkel are particularly noteworthy). His work on *Buck Rogers*, *Famous Funnies*, *Li'l Abner*, *Flash Gordon* and Johnny Comet still shine, but when he turned his hand to a series of Conan book covers he found a depth and a serious connection to a legion of fans. From the 1960s to the 1990s, he illustrated more than a dozen movie posters. His own characters, such as the Death Dealer, have taken on lives of their own on posters, album covers, and in comic books. He is truly a legend whose true impact on the artists who follow him is yet to be fully felt."
-Robert M. Overstreet

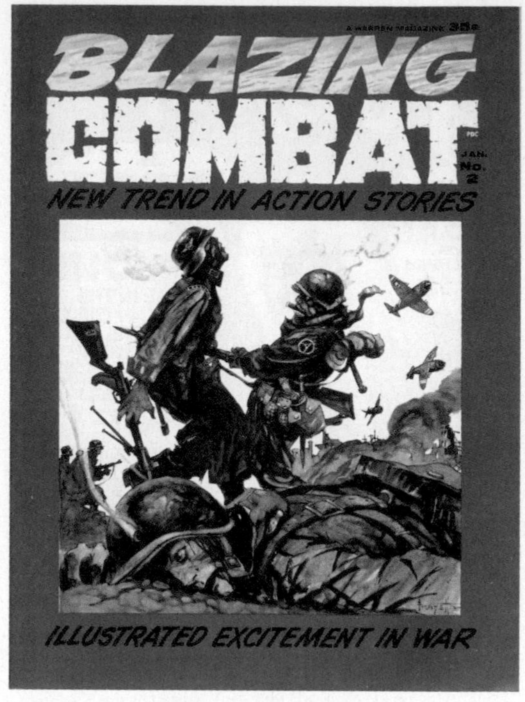

BLAZING COMBAT #2
January 1966. © WP

CREEPY#11
October 1966. © WP

EERIE #81
February 1977. © WP

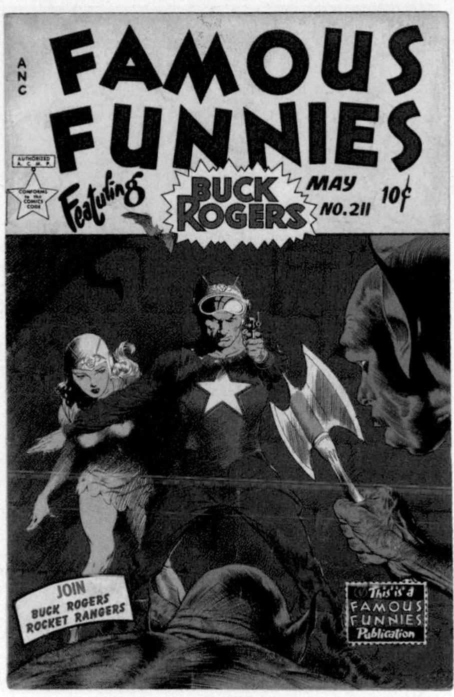

FAMOUS FUNNIES #211
May 1954. © EAS

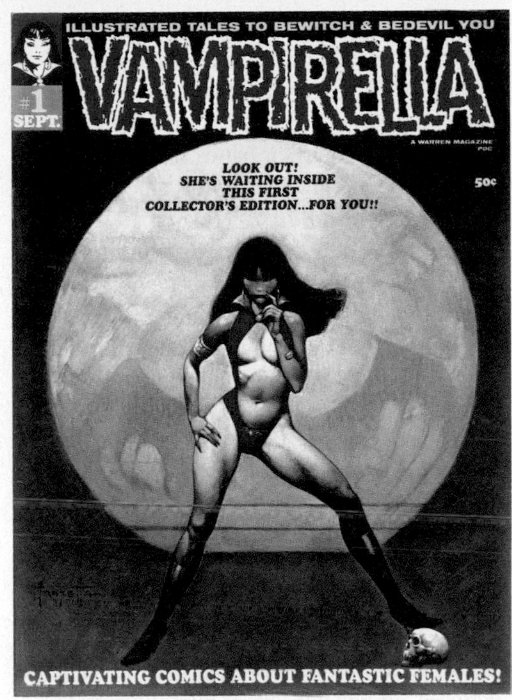

VAMPIRELLA #1
September 1969. © WP

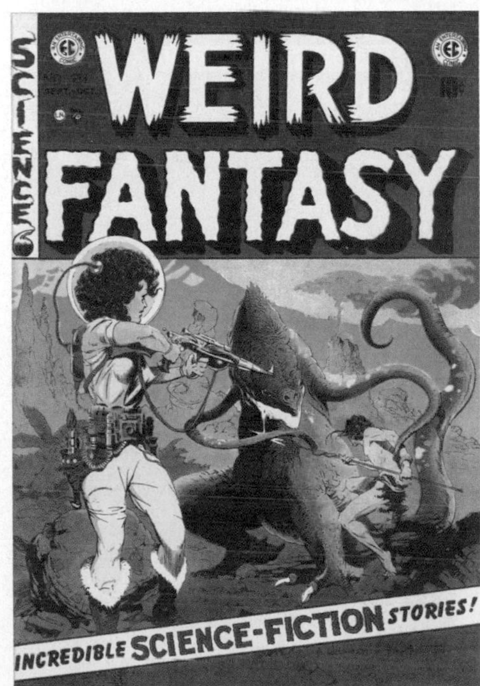

WEIRD FANTASY #21
September-October 1953. © WMG

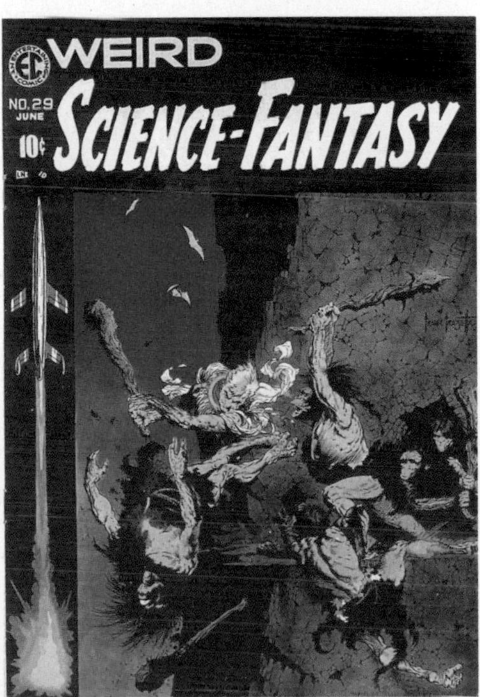

WEIRD SCIENCE-FANTASY #29
May-June 1955. © WMG

Even though they thought they had something special, when DC Comics released *Sandman* #1 (cover dated January 1989), it would have been impossible for them to know what they had on their hands since it really hadn't happened before. By the time the series ended with *Sandman* #75 (March 1996), it had given birth to DC's Vertigo imprint (*Sandman* #47), introduced or re-introduced the comic book world to a number of exceptional artists, and established Neil Gaiman as one of the medium's most distinct voices. Lyrical, moody, sensitive, and painterly, his ability to take readers to the world in which his characters lived captured and kept readers from beyond the normal fan base. With spin-offs such as *Death: The High Cost of Living*, he rounded out that world and soon began carving out others, in comics, novels, and other media. Popular world wide, his *Sandman* has never been out of print since it debuted, finding success in multiple formats.

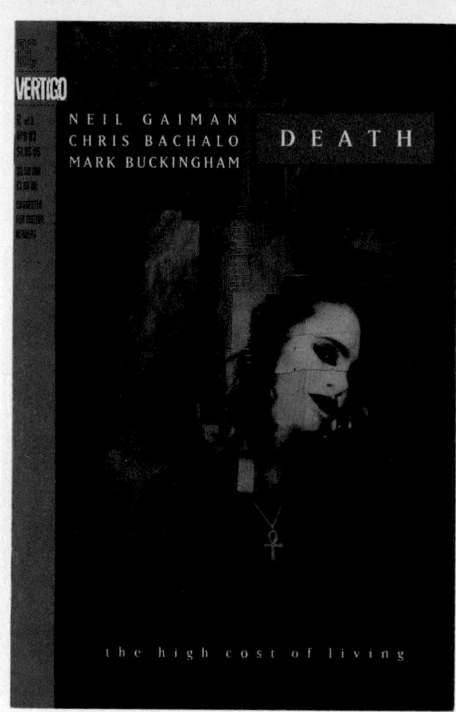

DEATH: THE HIGH COST OF LIVING #2
April 1993. © DC

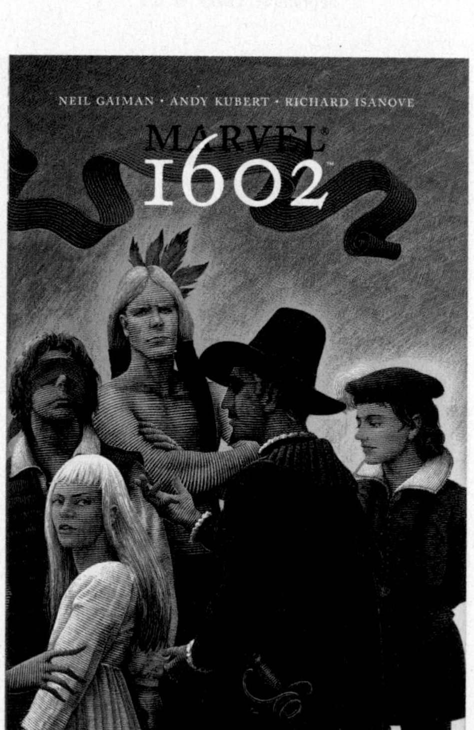

MARVEL 1602
Hardcover. 2004. © MAR

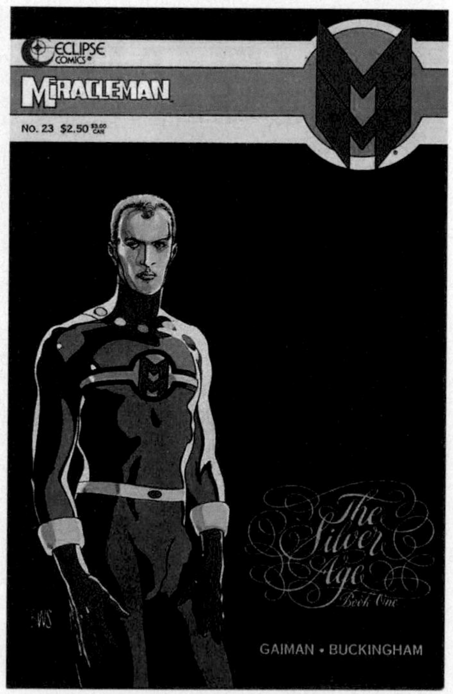

MIRACLEMAN #23
June 1992. © ECL

NEIL GAIMAN AND CHARLES VESS' STARDUST
Softcover. 1988. © Neil Gaiman & Charles Vess

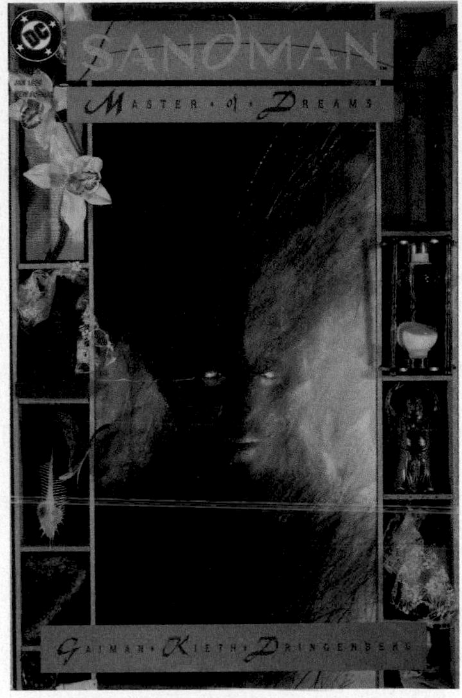

SANDMAN #1
January 1989. © DC

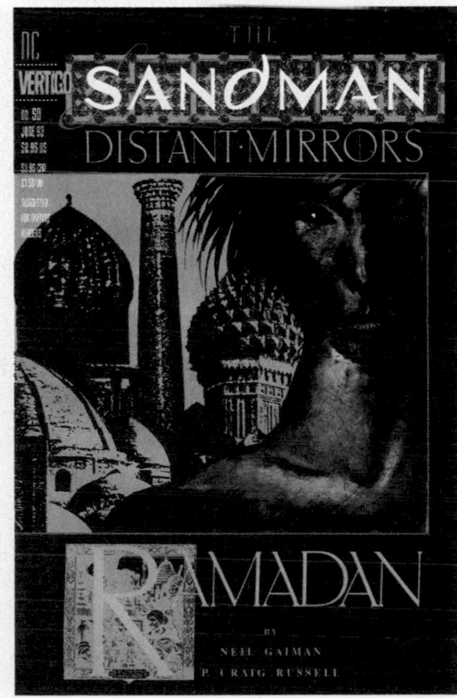

SANDMAN #50
June 1993. © DC

SANDMAN: THE DREAM HUNTERS
Softcover. October 1999. © DC

Best known on the national stage as the founder and publisher of *MAD* magazine, Bill Gaines suddenly found himself in charge of a floundering comic book company after the accidental death of his father, industry pioneer M.C. Gaines. Over the course of the next few years and in the course of trying to capture the latest trends, the younger Gaines published westerns, romances, and thrillers. Along the way, though, he began assembling an unparalleled roster of contributors, starting with writer-editor-artists Al Feldstein and Harvey Kurtzman and including Al Williamson, Jack Davis, Graham Ingles, Johnny Craig, Reed Crandall, George Evans, Wally Wood, John Severin and many others. With titles like *Tales From The Crypt*, *Weird Science*, *Two-Fisted Tales*, and *Shock SuspenStories*, in just a few years Gaines and company created titles that still influence other creators today. *MAD*, of course, became a cultural icon and did its own brand of influencing.

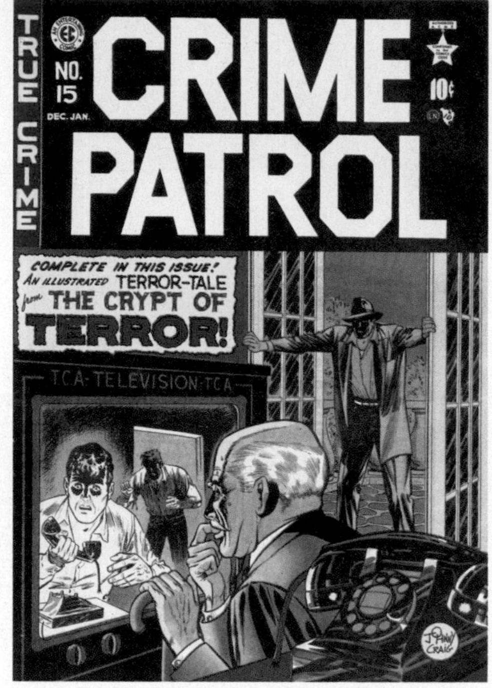

CRIME PATROL #15
1st appearance of the Crypt Keeper.
December 1949-January 1950. © WMG

CRIME SUSPENSTORIES #1
October-November 1950. © WMG

CRYPT OF TERROR #17
April-May 1950. © WMG

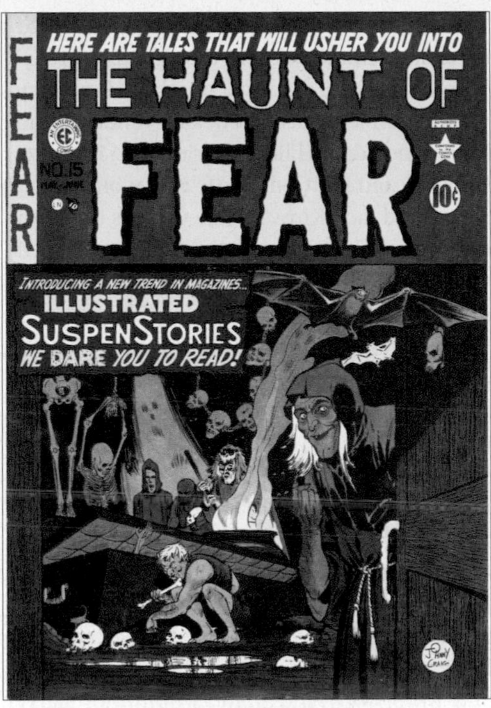

HAUNT OF FEAR #15 (#1)
1st appearance of the Old Witch.
May-June 1950. © WMG

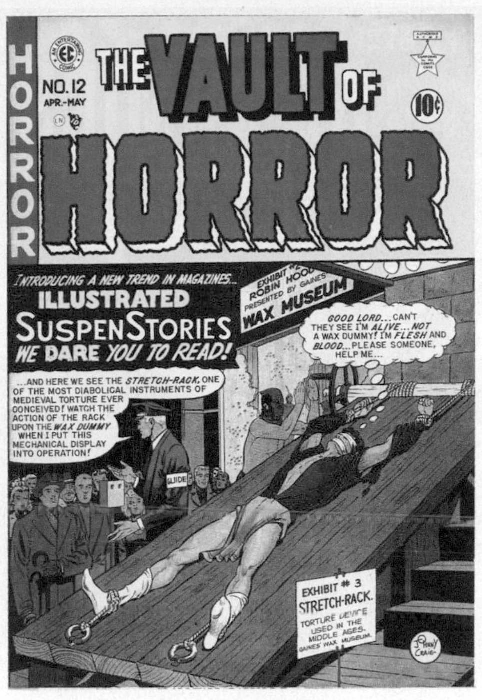

VAULT OF HORROR #12 (#1)
April-May 1950. © WMG

WAR AGAINST CRIME #10
1st appearance of the Vault Keeper.
December 1949-January 1950. © WMG

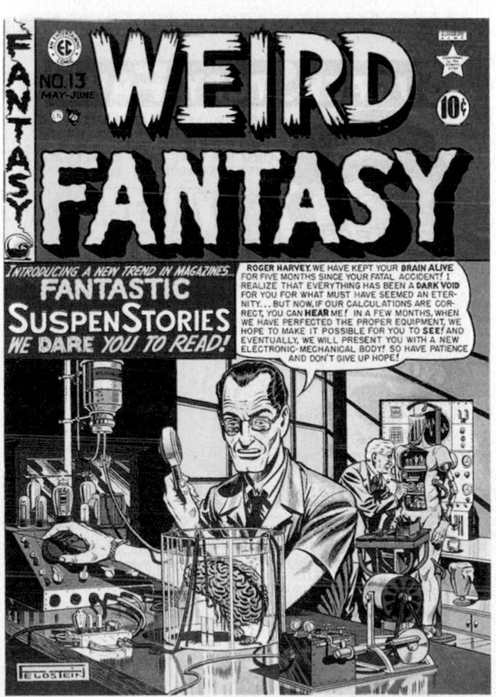

WEIRD FANTASY #13 (#1)
May-June 1950. © WMG

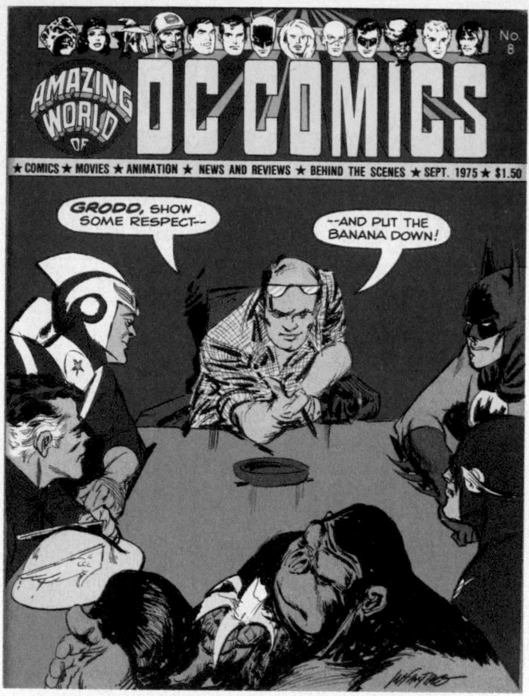

AMAZING WORLD OF DC COMICS #8
September-October 1975. © DC

As a youngster, Carmine Infantino struggled to break into comics around the demands of his school schedule, making a number of sales and working on a variety of titles for different publishers including Hillman Periodicals, Fawcett, Holyoke, and DC Comics. He also worked for Joe Simon and Jack Kirby's Prize Comics during his early days. When editor Julius Schwartz paired him with writer Robert Kanigher on a revival of the Golden Age superhero The Flash in *Showcase* #4, though, lightning struck more than just the main character. Showing his illustration and design talents on characters ranging from the science fiction adventurer Adam Strange to serious superhero Batman to somewhat silly hero Elongated Man, Infantino became DC's Art Director, Editorial Director and eventually Publisher, supervising among other things the first Marvel - DC crossover, *Superman vs. The Amazing Spider-Man*. Following his staff tenure, he returned to work as a freelancer, illustrating *Star Wars*, *Nova*, and *Spider-Woman* for Marvel and various others for DC.

BATMAN #183
August 1966. © DC

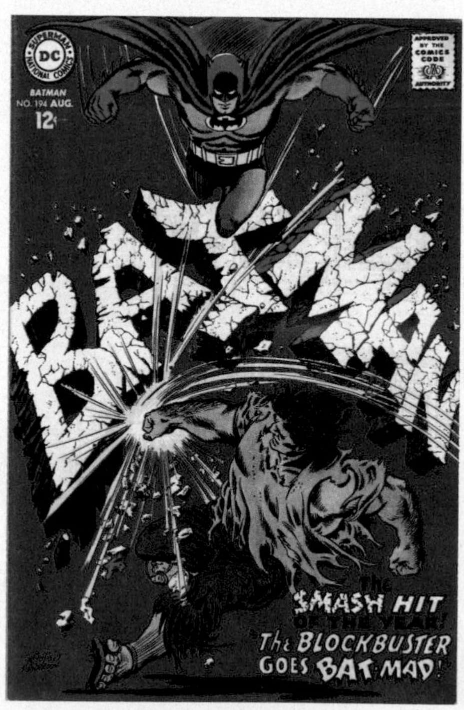

BATMAN #194
August 1967. © DC

EIGHTY PAGE GIANT #4
October 1964. © DC

MYSTERY IN SPACE #83
May 1963. © DC

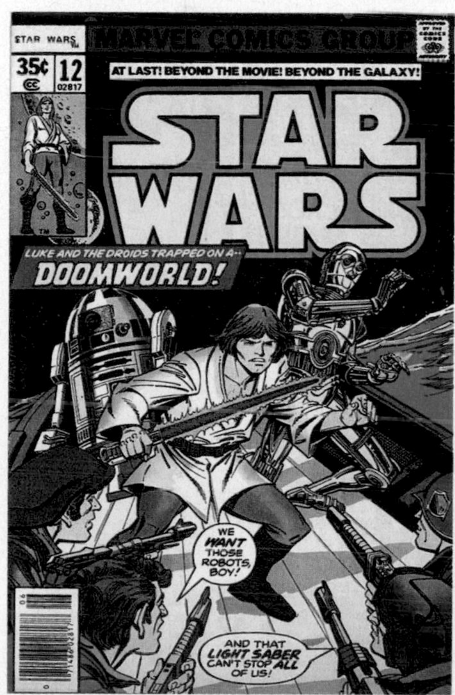

STAR WARS #12
June 1978. © Lucasfilm Ltd.

STRANGE ADVENTURES #9
June 1951. © DC

A creative dynamo given human form, for many Jack Kirby defined with his work the very idea of what comic books should be. In his art and stories, the obvious brash doses of daring design and explosive action were infused with something more unexpected in the eras in which he worked: an equally bold excitement for the cerebral, philosophical and spiritual. Whether working with partners such as Joe Simon (with whom he co-created Captain America, the Fighting American, Boys Ranch, and many would say the romance comics genre) and Stan Lee (co-creating the Fantastic Four, Thor, and the Silver Surfer, among others), or on his own (DC's "Fourth World" titles such *The New Gods*, *Mister Miracle*, *The Forever People*, or his creator-owned *Captain Victory* and *Silver Star*), Kirby worked as much in metaphor as he did in pencil. The number of creators and fans he influenced will never be known.

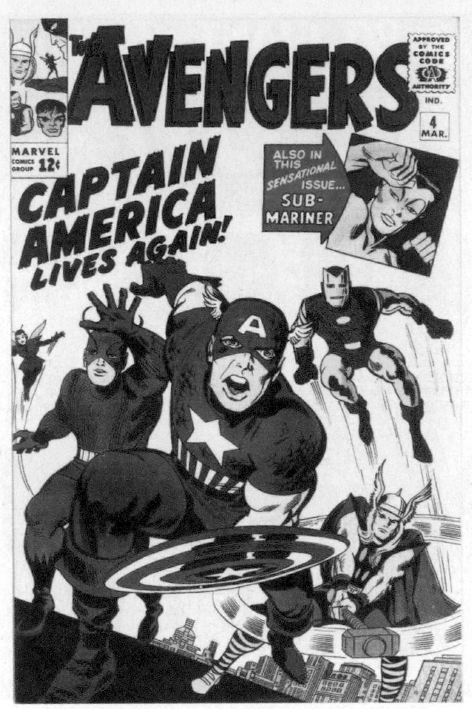

AVENGERS #4
March 1964. © MAR

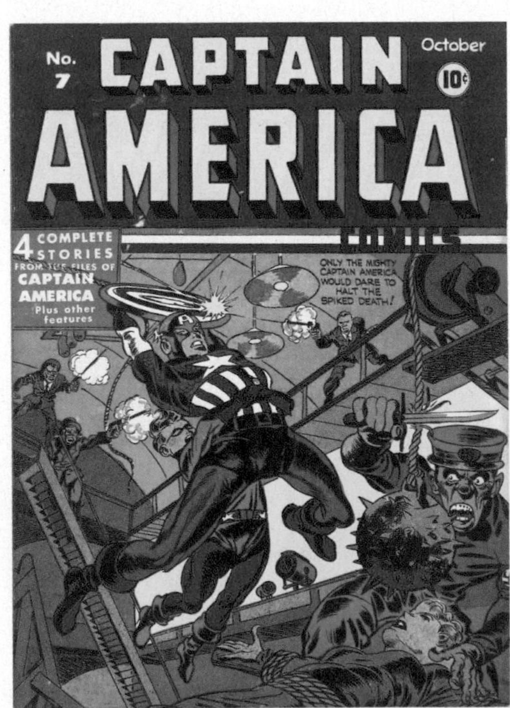

CAPTAIN AMERICA COMICS #7
October 1941. © MAR

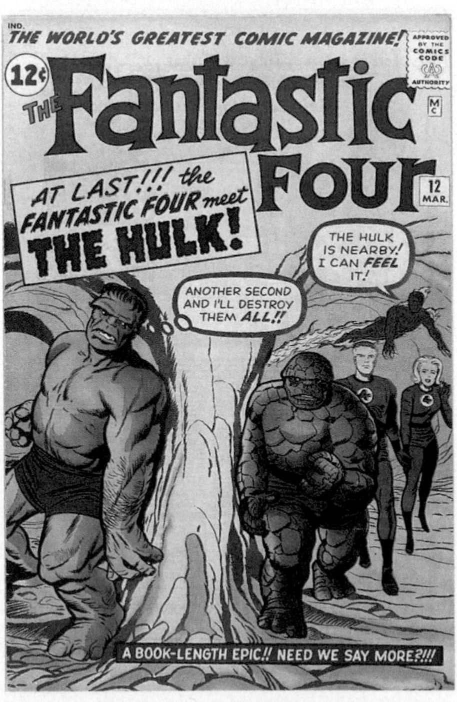

FANTASTIC FOUR #12
March 1963. © MAR

KAMANDI, THE LAST BOY ON EARTH #1
October-November 1972. © DC

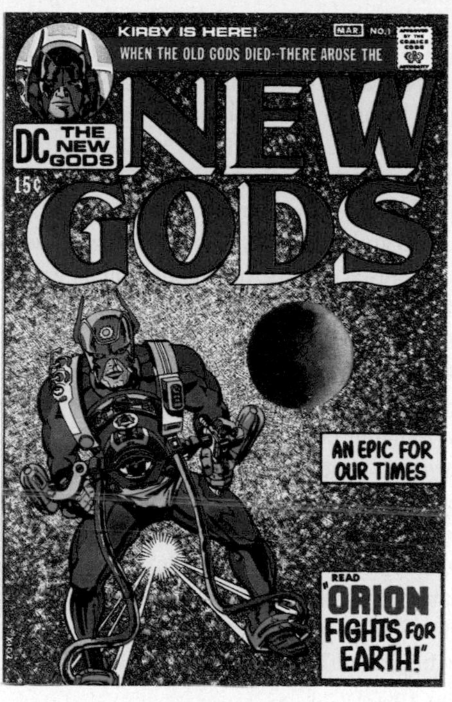

NEW GODS #1
February-March 1971. © DC

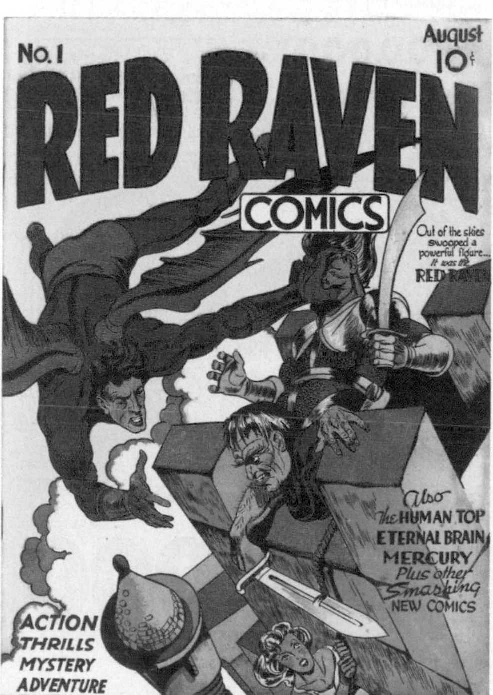

RED RAVEN COMICS #1
The cover is Kirby's first signed work.
August 1940. © MAR

STRANGE TALES #89
October 1961. © MAR

"I don't know any other words that will as quickly put a fellow artist into that zone that exists between pure fandom and the cold sweats as the mention of writer, artist, editor, and educator Joe Kubert. In an industry predisposed to overuse words like 'legend,' Mr. Kubert truly is one. He started working in the business at age 11 in 1938 and to this day is still looking for ways to push himself and the medium for all its worth. While he is no doubt best known for his work on Sgt. Rock, he also poured his efforts into DC's other iconic war titles such as *G.I. Combat*, *Our Army at War* (and characters like Enemy Ace and the Haunted Tank), his art also graced titles like *Hawkman* and *Tarzan*, all of which would be enough for any artist. Not him. He founded the Joe Kubert School of Cartoon and Graphic Art in 1976, wrote and illustrated *Tor*, *Abraham Stone*, *Fax from Sarajevo*, *Yossel: April 19, 1943*, and still has more on the way. To put it bluntly, he is my biggest influence and my comic book hero!"
-Billy Tucci

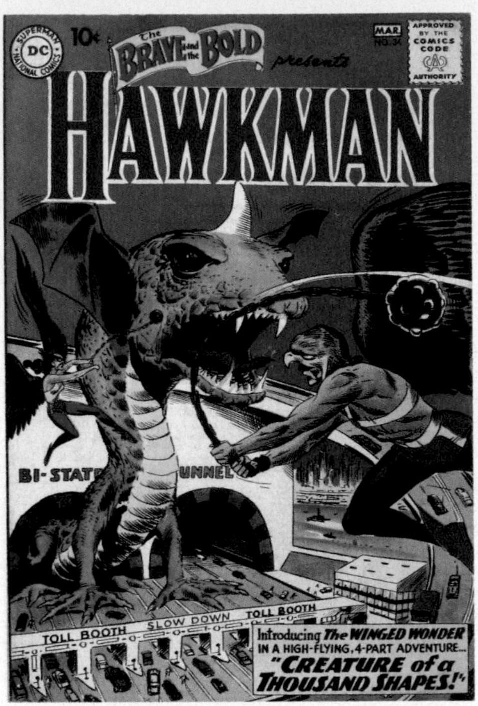

BRAVE AND THE BOLD #34
Debut of the Silver Age Hawkman and Hawkgirl.
February-March 1961. © DC

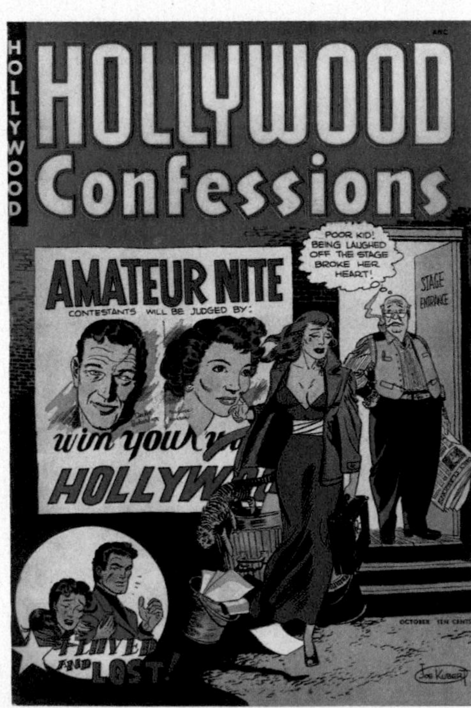

HOLLYWOOD CONFESSIONS #1
October 1949. © STJ

ONE MILLION YEARS AGO
Origin and 1st app. of Tor.
September 1953. © STJ

OUR ARMY AT WAR #112
November 1961. © DC

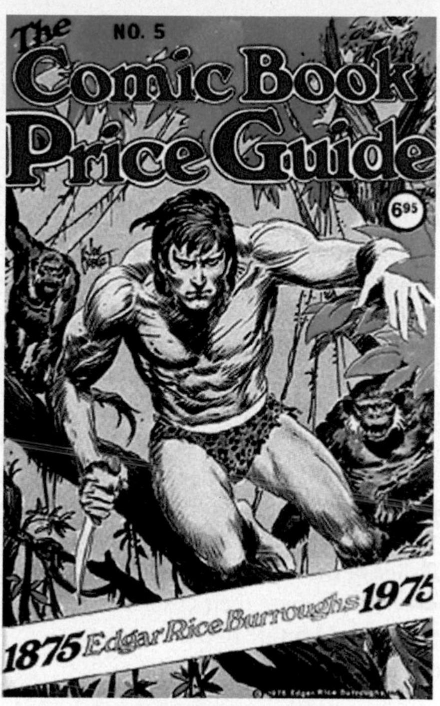

OVERSTREET COMIC BOOK PRICE GUIDE
5TH EDITION
1975. © ERB

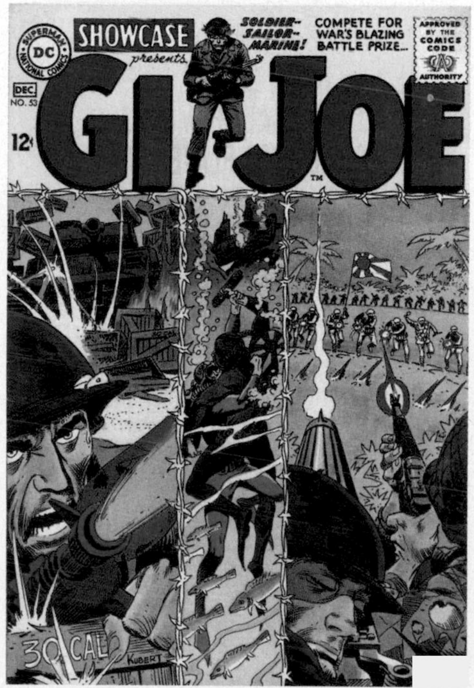

SHOWCASE #53
November-December 1964. © DC

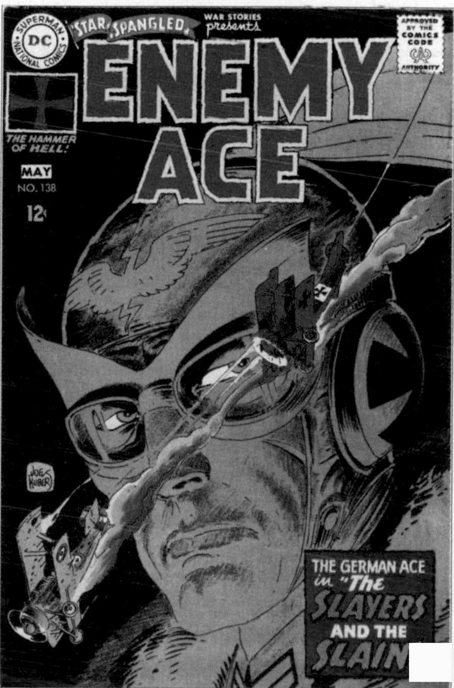

STAR SPANGLED WAR STORIES #138
April-May 1968. © DC

He started out as a fan, established a broad base of historical and contemporary knowledge about the field, developed as a writer, and eventually became the leader of one of the two biggest comic book companies. After writing and co-publishing the long-lived fanzine *The Comic Reader*, Paul Levitz could have called it a day and still been lauded for his contributions to the four color world. Good thing for us, though, he didn't stop there. As a writer, he's known for writing the Earth II adventures of the Justice Society of America in the revived *All Star Comics* in the 1970s, a period in which he co-created The Huntress. In the 1980s, he wrote a lengthy run on *Legion of Super-Heroes*, and he recently returned to scripting for a run of *JSA*. He's probably best known, though, as the President and Publisher of DC Comics, where he has worked tirelessly to promote their characters as well as the history and future of the medium.
–Steve Geppi

ADVENTURE COMICS #462
March-April 1979. © DC

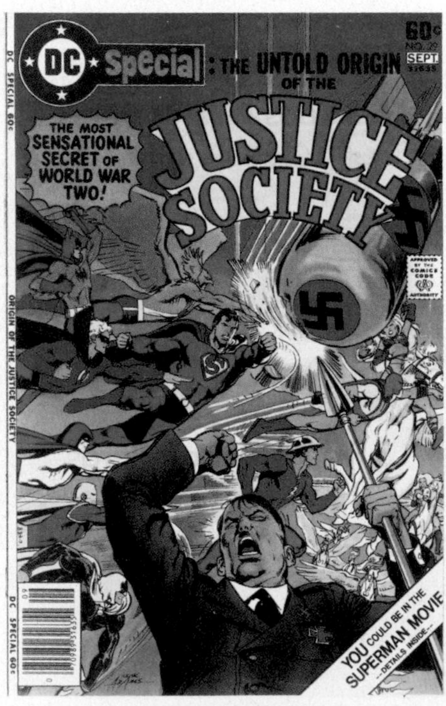

DC SPECIAL #29
August-September 1977. © DC

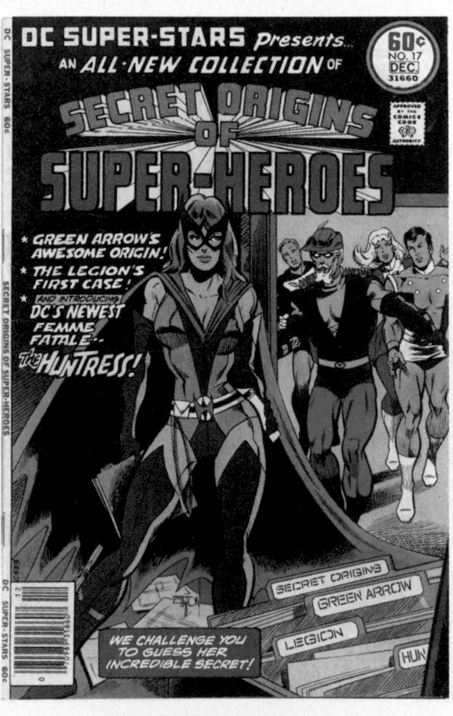

DC SUPER-STARS #17
November-December 1977. © DC

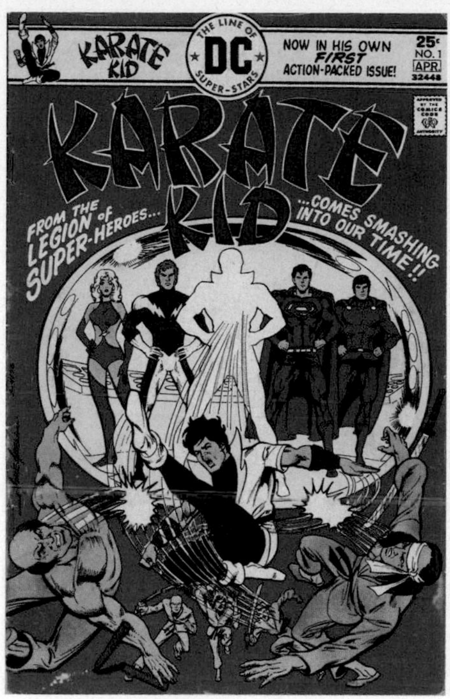

KARATE KID #1
March-April 1976. © DC

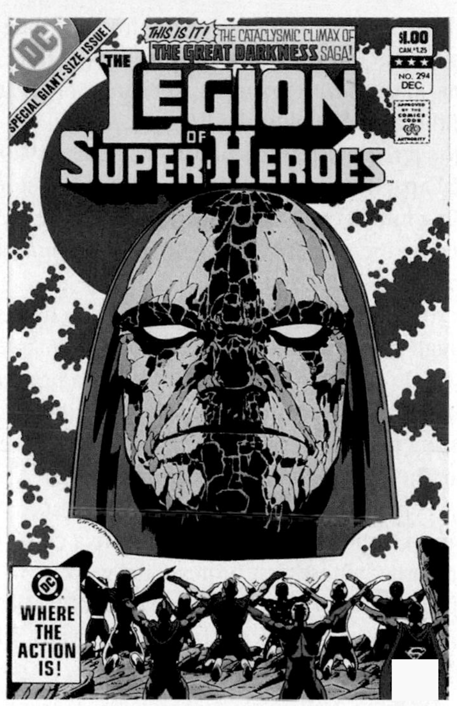

LEGION OF SUPER-HEROES #294
December 1982. © DC

SUPERBOY AND THE LEGION OF SUPER-HEROES #231
September 1977. © DC

TEEN TITANS #44
November 1976. © DC

Whether one knows his work from his long run on the *Tarzan* newspaper strip, a too-brief stint on the *Star Wars* newspaper strip, or creating the comic book series *Magnus Robot Fighter*, the illustrations of Russ Manning (1929-1981) pack clean, crisp line work and solid storytelling into every panel. With a design sense dictated by the stories (His *Star Wars* or *Magnus* are substantially different than his *Tarzan*), he became influential with comic artists, even though his work was never published by Marvel or DC. In recent years, Dark Horse has reprinted many of his Tarzan stories in collected editions, sharing them with new generations of fans. Each year The Russ Manning Most Promising Newcomer Award is an award presented at Comic-Con International: San Diego to a comic book artist whose first professional work appeared within the previous two years. In 1982 the first recipient was the late Dave Stevens, who had worked as an assistant of Manning's.

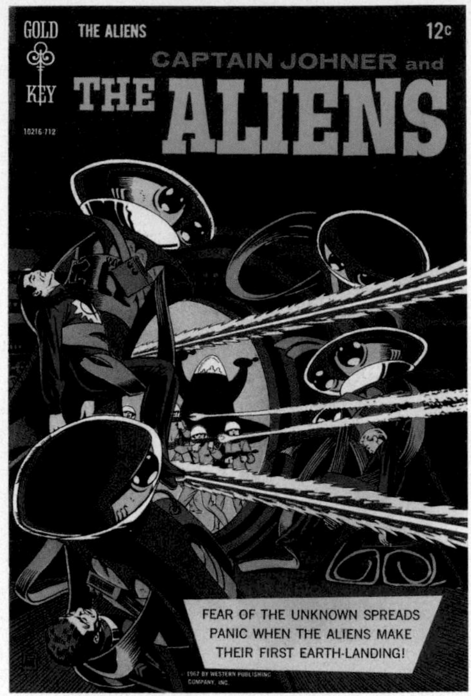

THE ALIENS #1
September-December 1967. © WEST

MAGNUS, ROBOT FIGHTER
Interior panels. © Random House

MAGNUS, ROBOT FIGHTER #5
February 1964. © Random House

MAGNUS, ROBOT FIGHTER #30
February 1972. © Random House

TARZAN #155
December 1965. © ERB

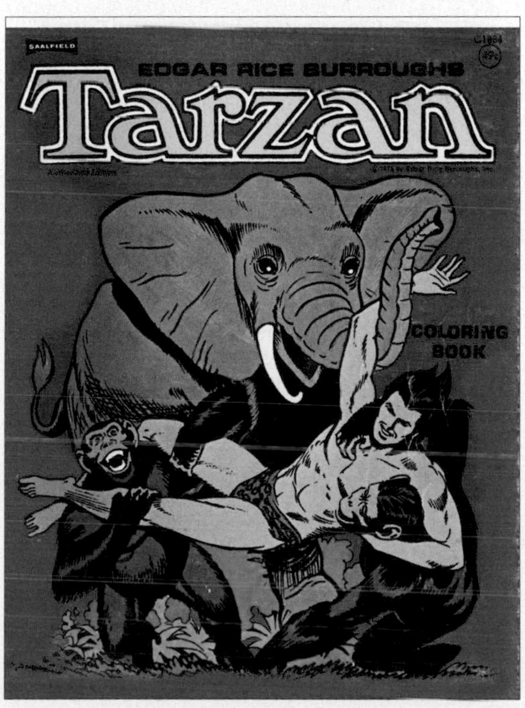

TARZAN COLORING BOOK
1975. © ERB

Writer, artist, toy designer, businessman. All of these titles and others apply to Todd McFarlane, the former Spider-Man writer-artist who capitalized on incredible sales in 1992 and co-founded Image Comics. Following a back-up story in *Coyote*, which was then published by Marvel's Epic imprint, McFarlane began quickly making a name for himself. After illustrating *Batman: Year Two* and *Infinity, Inc.* at DC Comics and *Incredible Hulk* at Marvel, he landed the art duties on *Amazing Spider-Man*. After 28 issues on that series, he launched a new one, simply *Spider-Man*, which he wrote and illustrated. He parlayed the overwhelming sales for that series into the launch of Image Comics, where he wrote and illustrated his own series, *Spawn*, and created many others. McFarlane has built his McFarlane Toys into a serious force in the toy business, and continues to work in various areas in entertainment in addition to comics.

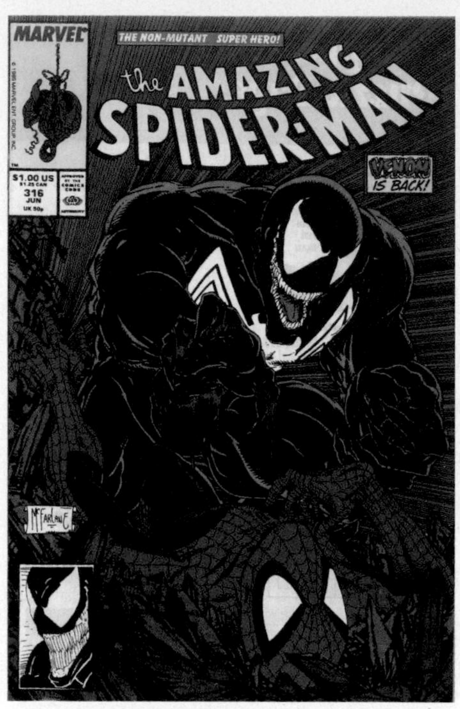

AMAZING SPIDER-MAN #316
June 1989. © MAR

AMAZING SPIDER-MAN #323
November 1989. © MAR

SPIDER-MAN #1
August 1990. © MAR

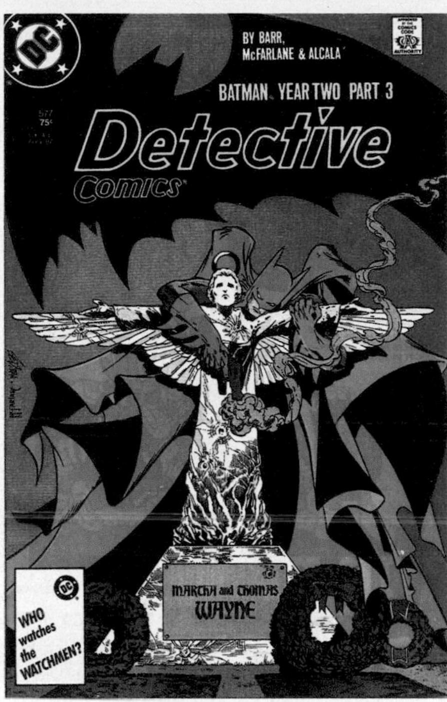

DETECTIVE COMICS #577
August 1987. © DC

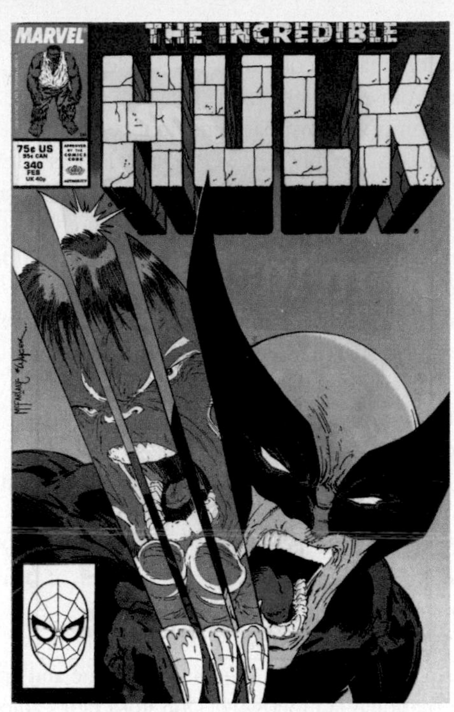

INCREDIBLE HULK #340
February 1988. © MAR

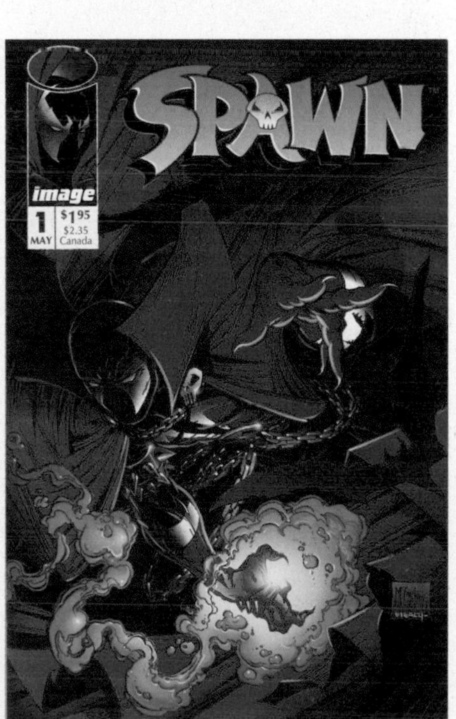

SPAWN #1
May 1992. © TMP

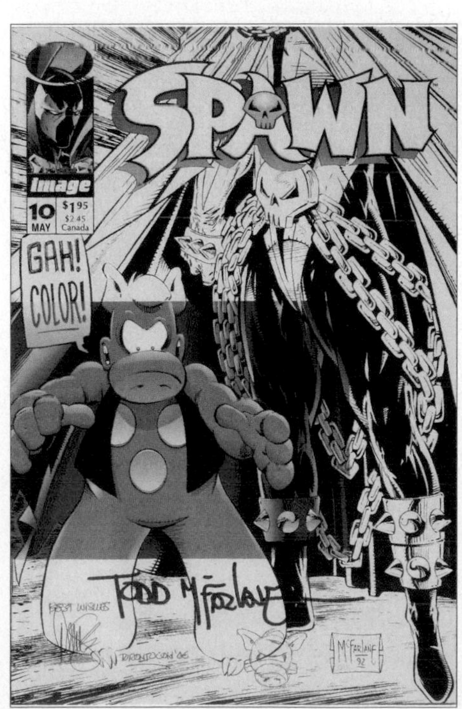

SPAWN #10
May 1993. © TMP

Born in Louisville, Kentucky in 1951, Don Rosa developed a love of Carl Barks' Uncle Scrooge tales from early childhood. That led Rosa to the creation of his own Barks-inspired comics and characters, notably "The Pertwillaby Papers" for his college newspaper. After graduation, Rosa divided his time between self-created comics, comics fanzine work, and his family's tile company. In the mid-1980s Rosa began writing and drawing his first Duck stories. "The Son of the Sun" (*Uncle Scrooge* #219) marked the start of many years' active work with Scrooge and Donald: first for Gladstone, then for Sanoma and Egmont in Europe.

Perhaps Rosa's most celebrated achievement is his 12-part epic, "The Life and Times of Scrooge McDuck," which has been repeatedly anthologized around the world and is regarded as one of Disney comics' great milestones.

With numerous beloved, highly intricate Scrooge McDuck adventures to his name and an international fan following, Don Rosa ranks among today's most significant Disney comics creators.

DON ROSA'S COMICS AND STORIES #1
1983. © Don Rosa

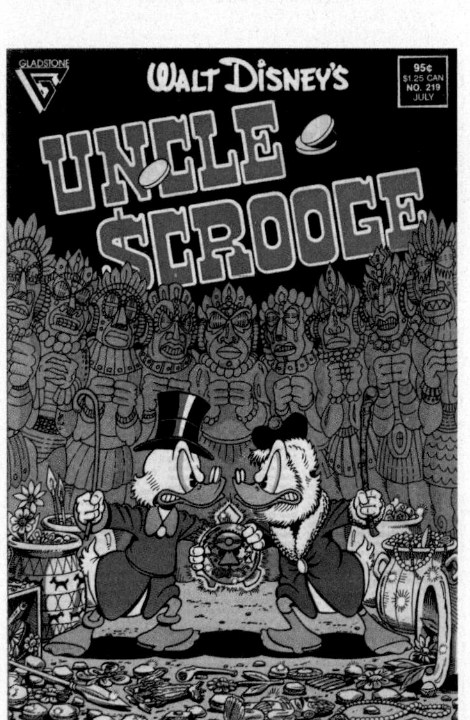

WALT DISNEY'S UNCLE SCROOGE #219
Rosa's first Duck story. July 1987. © DIS

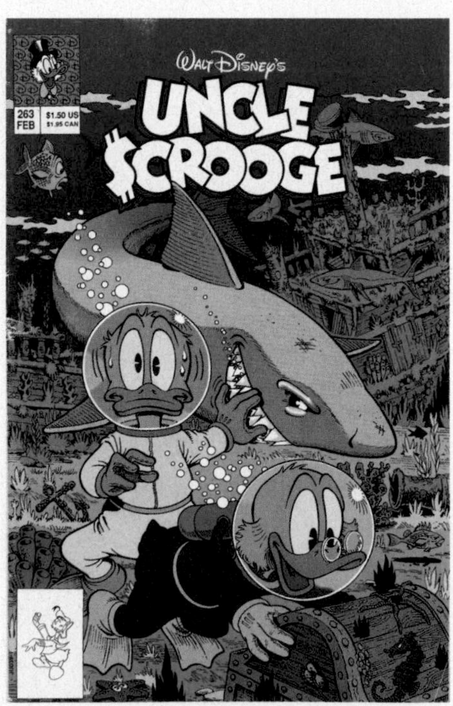

WALT DISNEY'S UNCLE SCROOGE #263
February 1992. © DIS

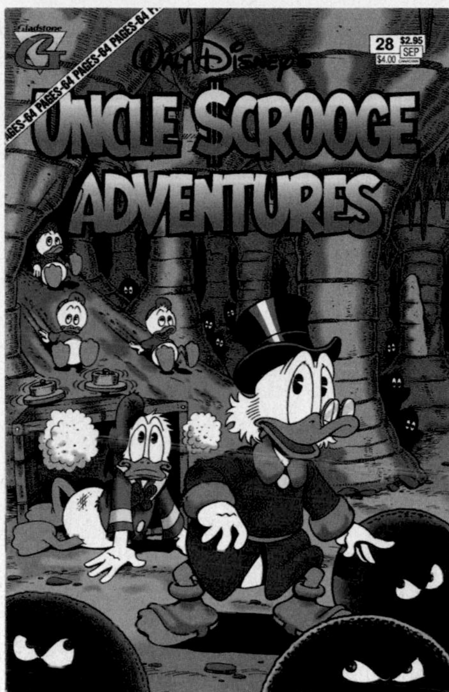

UNCLE SCROOGE ADVENTURES #28
First Rosa cover for a Barks' reprint.
September 1994. © DIS

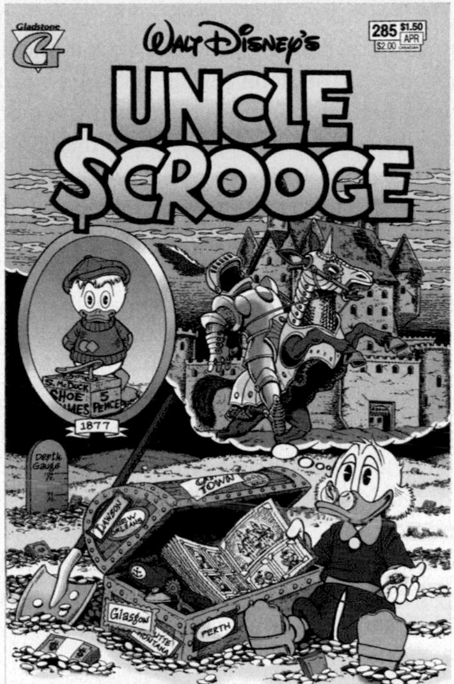

WALT DISNEY'S UNCLE SCROOGE #285
Part 1 of "The Life and Times of Scrooge McDuck".
April 1994. © DIS

WALT DISNEY'S UNCLE SCROOGE #319
July 2003. © DIS

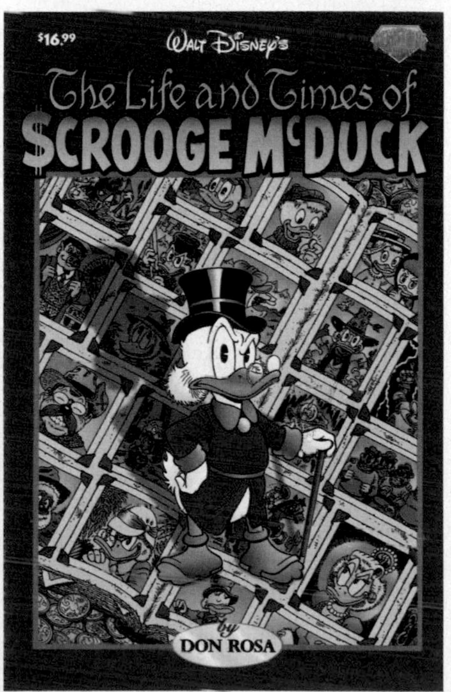

THE LIFE AND TIMES OF SCROOGE McDUCK
Trade paperback. 2005. © DIS

Rarely has an individual been known for two so distinctly different genres of work in the field of comic art, but John Severin is known equally for illustrating action-adventure tales and humorous stories. From his days as one of the original artists on EC's *MAD* (often with Will Elder providing the inking) to a lengthy run at *Cracked*, Severin became one of the prime send-up artists working in the business. Due to the wider circulation of *MAD* and *Cracked* compared to many comic books, it's safe to think that many know him for that work rather than the action-adventure genre, but comic book fans have had a deep appreciation for his westerns, war stories, horror, and other pieces in *Two-Fisted Tales*, *Blazing Combat*, *Creepy*, *King Kull*, *The 'Nam*, *Sgt. Fury*, and *Conan*, setting standards whether providing pencil art, inking, or supplying both. Most recently he has illustrated *Desperadoes: Quiet of the Grave* and *Bat Lash*.

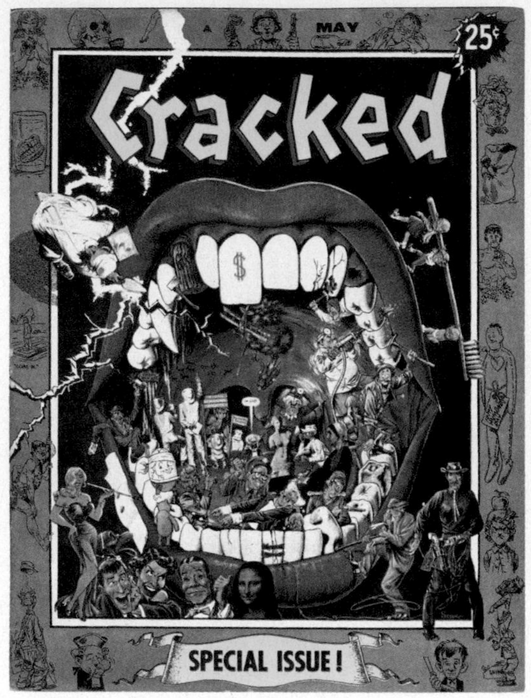

CRACKED #2
May 1958. © Major Magazines

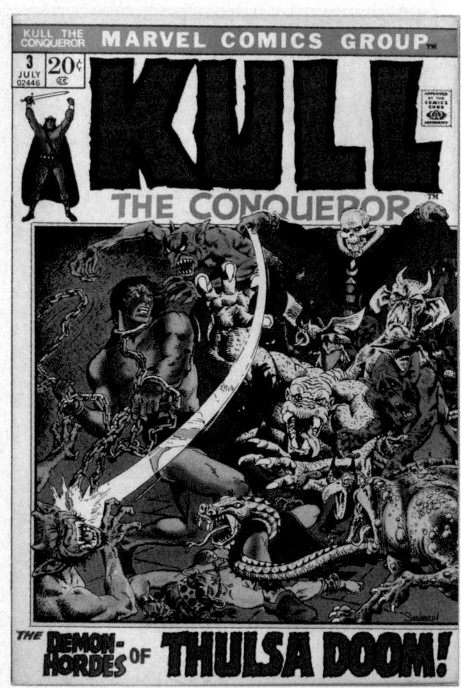

KULL THE CONQUEROR #3
July 1972. © MAR

NOT BRAND ECCH #11
December 1968. © MAR

TOMB OF DRACULA #2
May 1972. © MAR

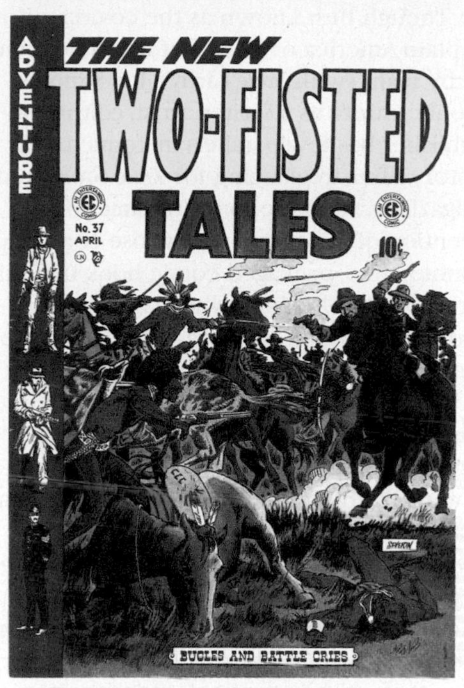

TWO-FISTED TALES #37
April 1954. © WMG

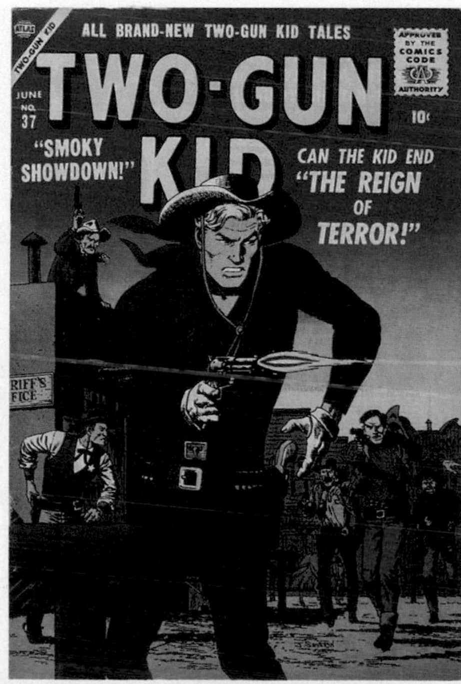

TWO-GUN KID #37
June 1957. © MAR

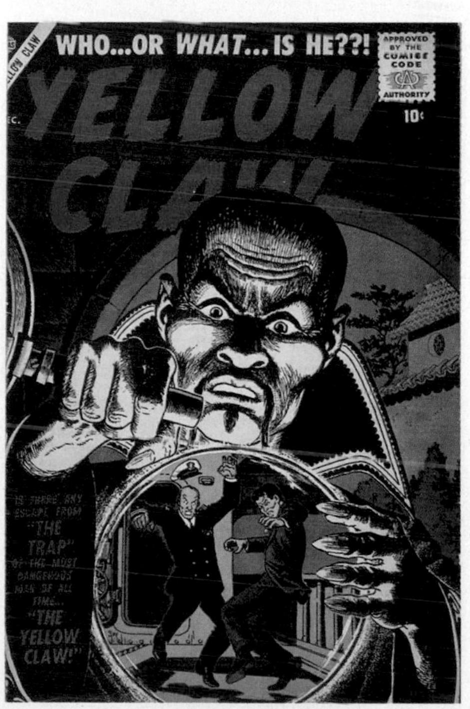

YELLOW CLAW #2
December 1956. © MAR

Though best known as the co-creator of Captain America or as half of the Simon and Kirby team (with Jack Kirby), Joe Simon's prolific career as a writer, artist, editor and publisher has few parallels in comic book history. After freelancing for *True Story* and magazines, Simon reportedly came to the attention of Lloyd Jacquet, whose company, Funnies, Inc., packaged comic book material for publishers. A short while later, he met Kirby. They began working together on the second issue of *Blue Bolt* and became one of the most influential teams in the medium's history. They worked together until 1955, when comic sales nose-dived and Simon sought work outside the field. During that time, they produced *The Fighting American*, westerns such as *Boys Ranch*, and many others. They are credited with creating the romance comics genre with *Young Romance Comics*. Among the projects he later took on, he spent a decade working with *Sick*, a *MAD*-inspired humor magazine.

ADVENTURE COMICS #76
July 1942. © DC

ADVENTURES OF THE FLY #1
August 1959. © AP

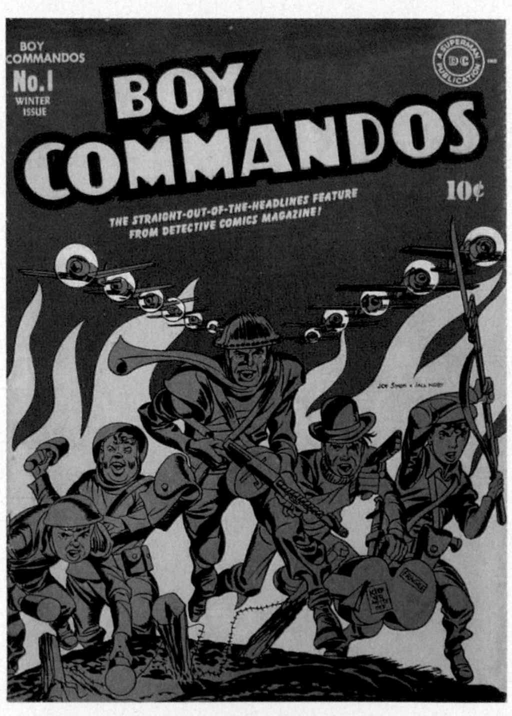

BOY COMMANDOS #1
Winter 1942. © DC

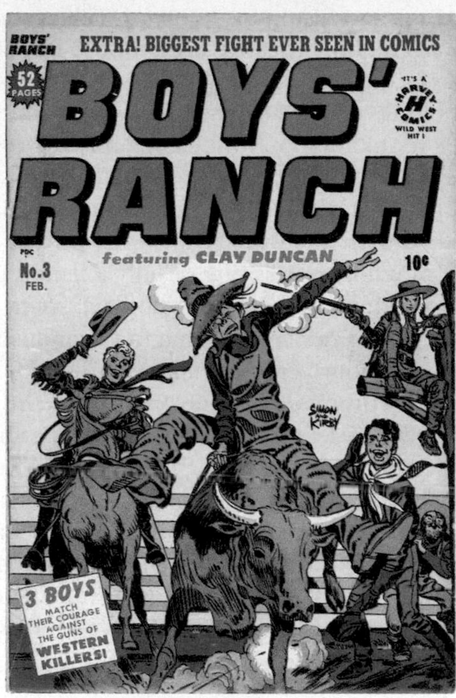

BOYS' RANCH #3
February 1951. © HARV

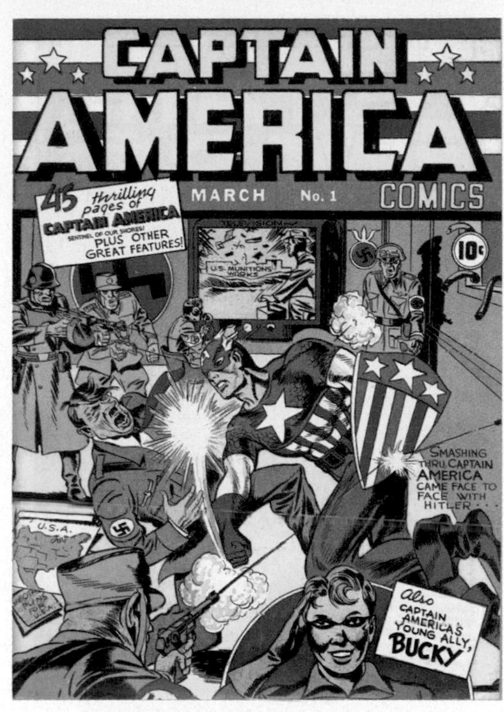

CAPTAIN AMERICA COMICS #1
March 1941. © MAR

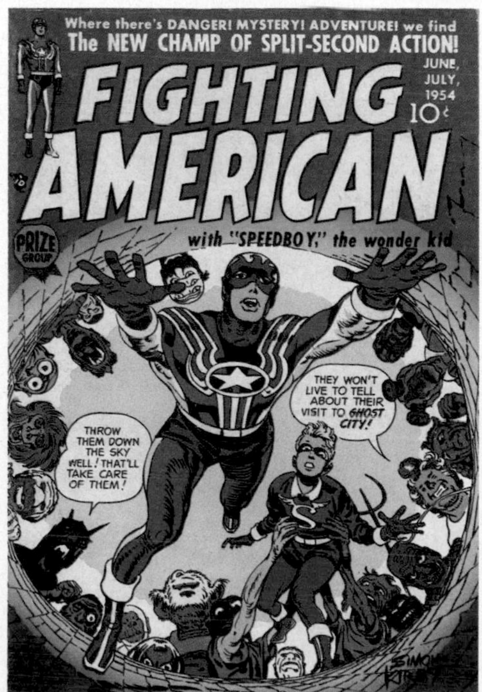

FIGHTING AMERICAN #2
July 1954. © PRIZE

YOUNG ROMANCE #11
May-June 1949. © MAR

CLASSIC STAR WARS #10
July 1993. © Lucasfilm Ltd.

Fans and historians know Al Williamson for his highly evocative art over the last fifty years, ranging from penciling and inking stories in EC's *Weird Science-Fantasy* in the '50s to inking John Romita, Jr. on *Daredevil* for Marvel in the '90s, or newspaper work including a highly respected run on the daily and Sunday *Star Wars* strip.

"Al Williamson is one of only a handful of top rated comic creators who have spent their entire careers working in our industry. Too often our very best talents are lured away by promises of fame and fortune in other venues. I think that Al stands as a shining example of the lifelong craftsman who works constantly to improve his already considerable talents; by the entire scope of his career he announces to every other person in the industry that this is a field fully worth the commitment of a lifetime of creations."
– Mark Wheatley

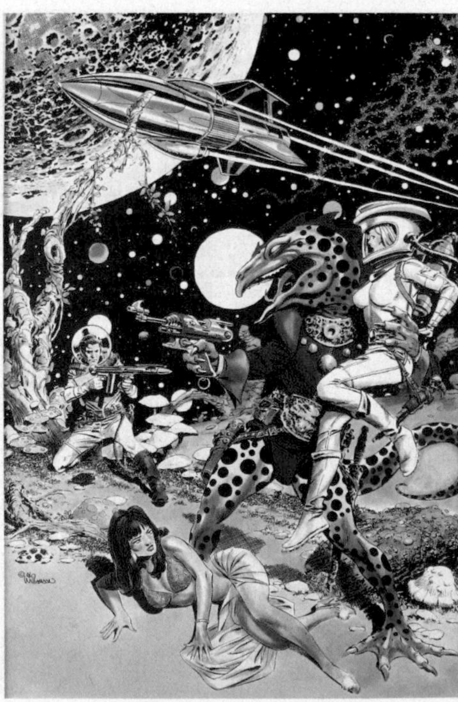

COVER ART FOR
OVERSTREET QUARTERLY #4
1994. © Gemstone Publishing

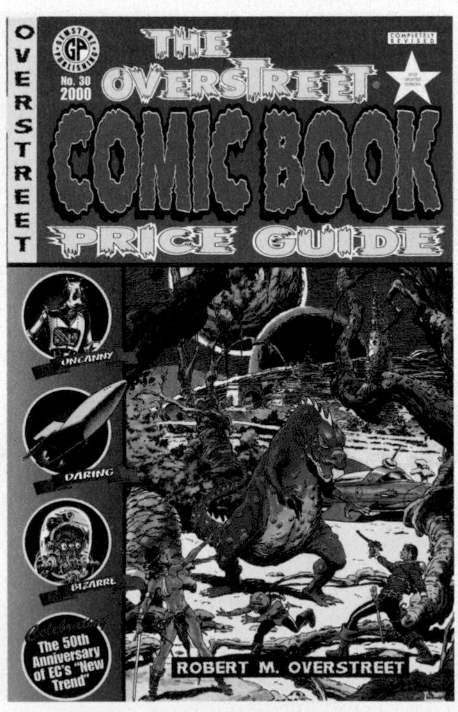

OVERSTREET COMIC BOOK PRICE GUIDE
30TH EDITION
2000. © Gemstone Publishing

FLASH GORDON #3
January 1967. © KING

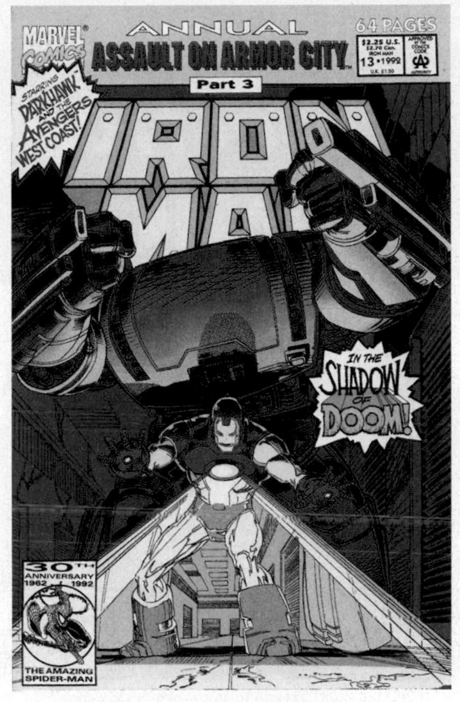

IRON MAN ANNUAL #13
1992. © MAR

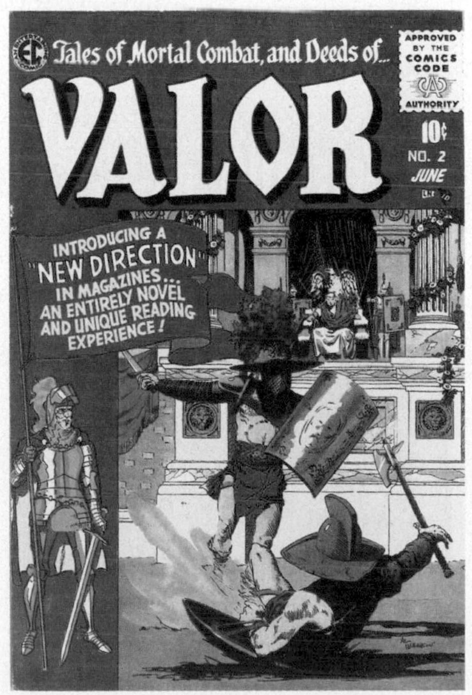

VALOR #2
May-June 1955. © WMG

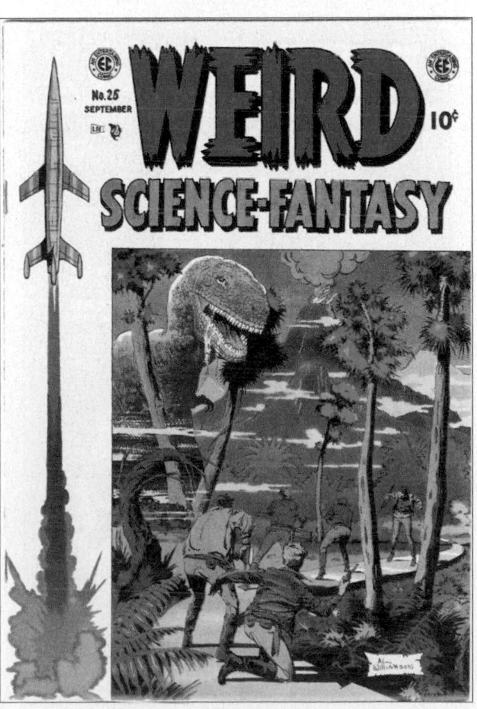

WEIRD SCIENCE-FANTASY #25
September 1954. © WMG

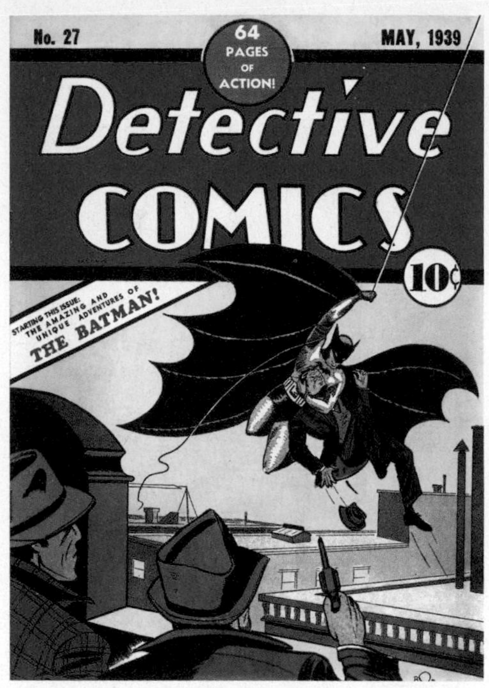

DETECTIVE COMICS #27
May 1939. Bob Kane cover. © DC

DETECTIVE COMICS #69
November 1942. Jerry Robinson cover. © DC

DETECTIVE COMICS #168
February 1951. Dick Sprang cover. © DC

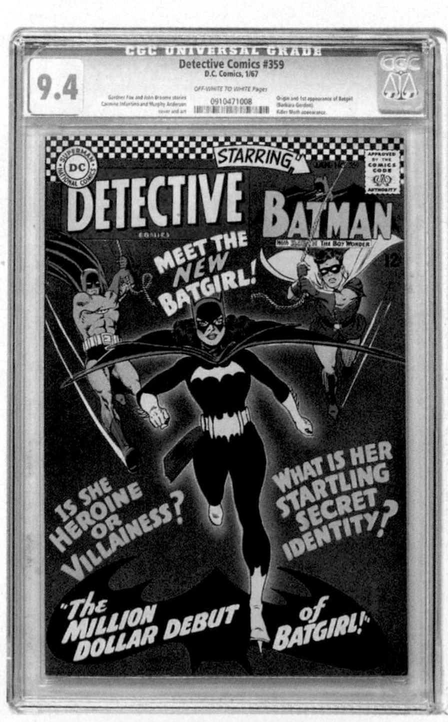

DETECTIVE COMICS #359
January 1967. Carmine Infantino cover. © DC

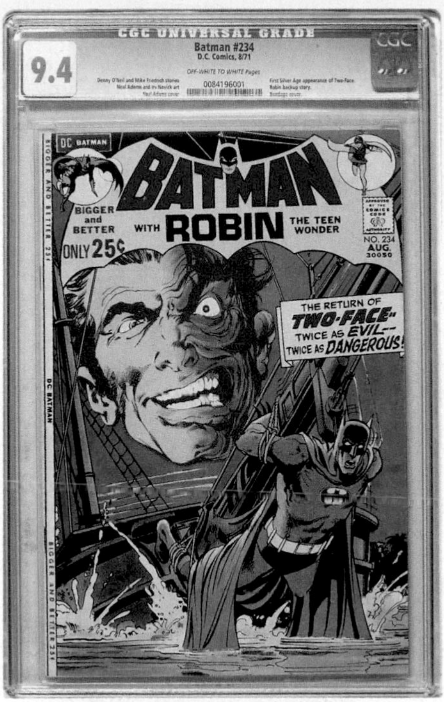

BATMAN #234
August 1971. Neal Adams cover. © DC

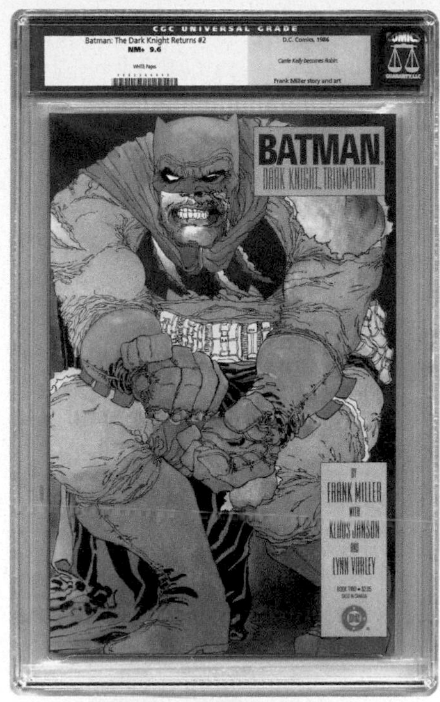

BATMAN: THE DARK KNIGHT RETURNS #2
1986. Frank Miller cover. © DC

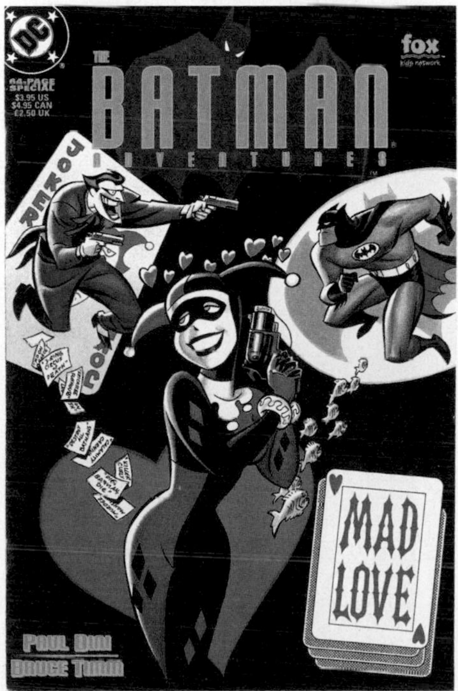

BATMAN ADVENTURES: MAD LOVE #1
February 1994. Bruce Timm cover. © DC

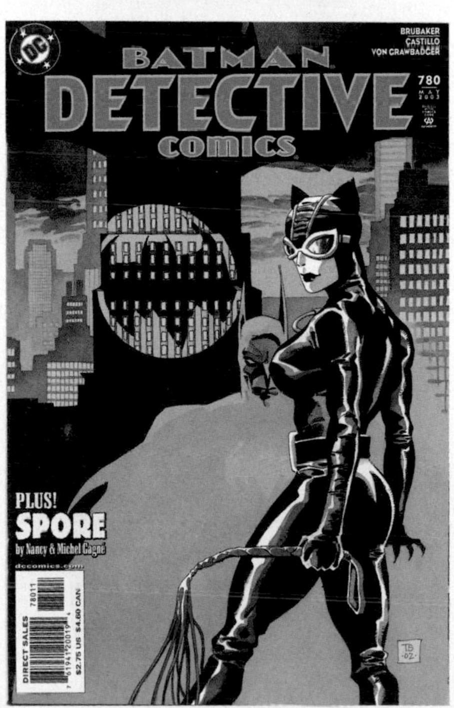

DETECTIVE COMICS #780
May 2003. Tim Sale cover. © DC

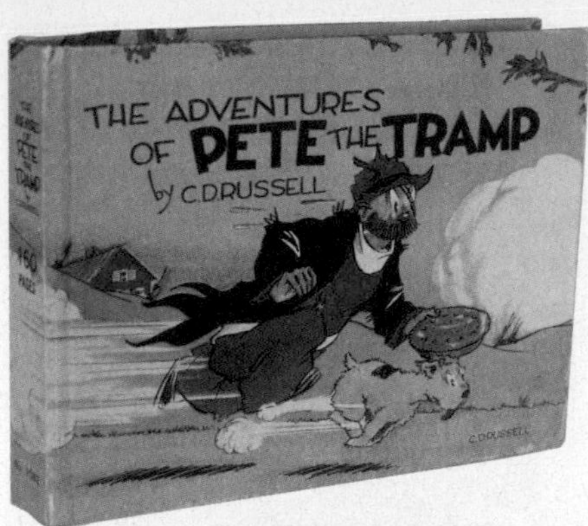

THE ADVENTURES OF PETE THE TRAMP
BLB #1082 - 1935. © Saalfield

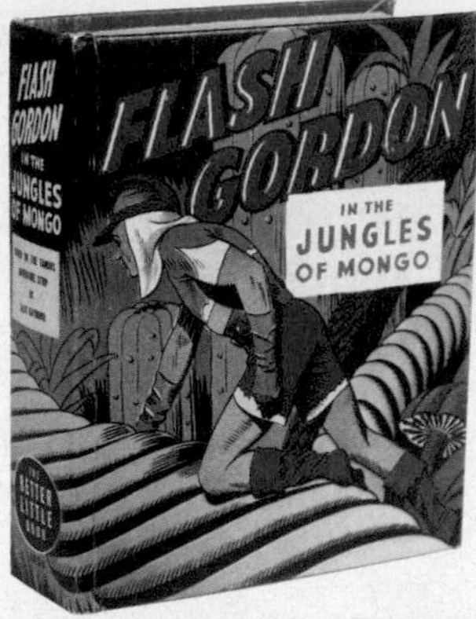

FLASH GORDON IN THE JUNGLES OF MONGO
BLB #1424 - 1947. © KING

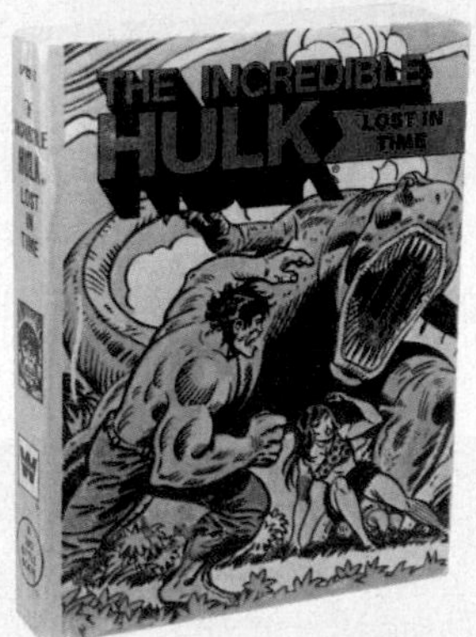

INCREDIBLE HULK LOST IN TIME
BLB #5782-2 - 1980. © MAR

"OUR GANG" ON THE MARCH
BLB #1451 - 1942. © WHIT

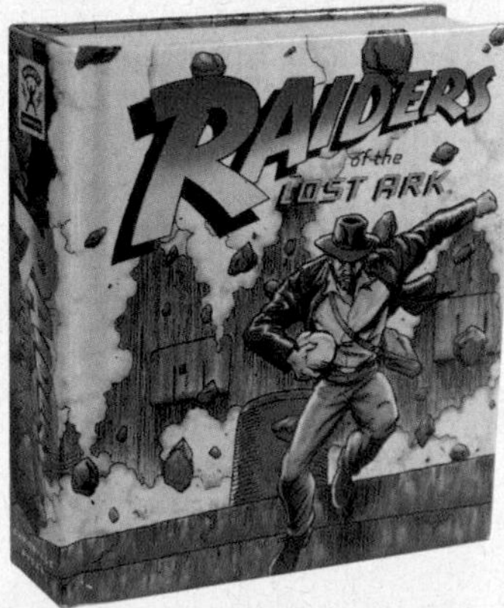

RAIDERS OF THE LOST ARK
Chronicle Books - 1998. © Lucasfilm

WALT DISNEY'S STORY OF PLUTO THE PUP
BLB #1066 - 1938. © DIS

AMAZING SPIDER-MAN
1980. Aim toothpaste giveaway. © MAR

JUGHEAD COMICS: NIGHT AT GEPPI'S ENTERTAINMENT MUSEUM
2008. Free Comic Book Day Edition. © AP

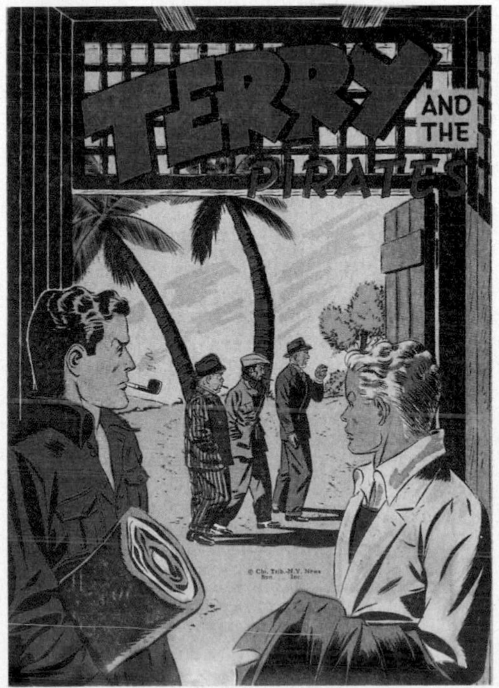

TERRY AND THE PIRATES nn
1938. Poll-Parrot Shoes giveaway © NYNS

WISCO/KLARER MINIATURE COMIC BOOKS
Blaze Carson - 1950. © Vital Pub.

Tex Taylor in "An Exciting Adventure at the Gold Mine" - 1950. © Vital Pub.

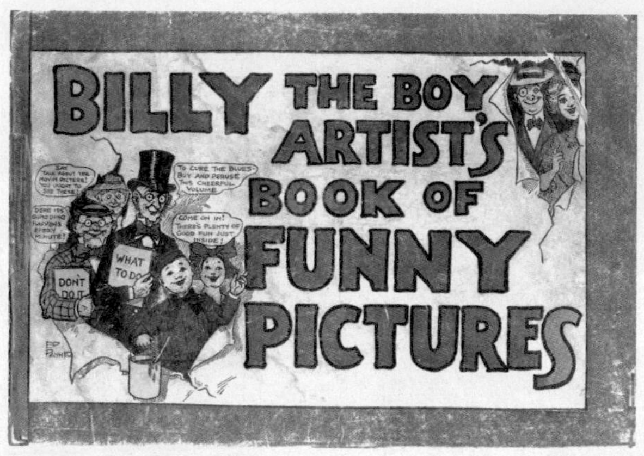

BILLY THE BOY ARTIST'S BOOK OF FUNNY PICTURES
1910. © C.M. Clark Publ.

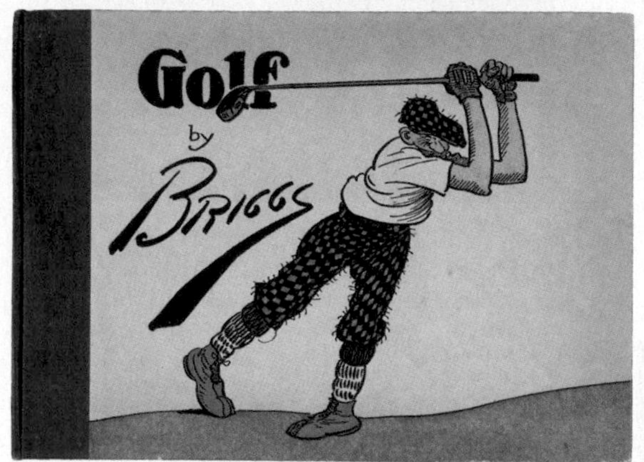

GOLF
1916. © P. F. Volland & Co.

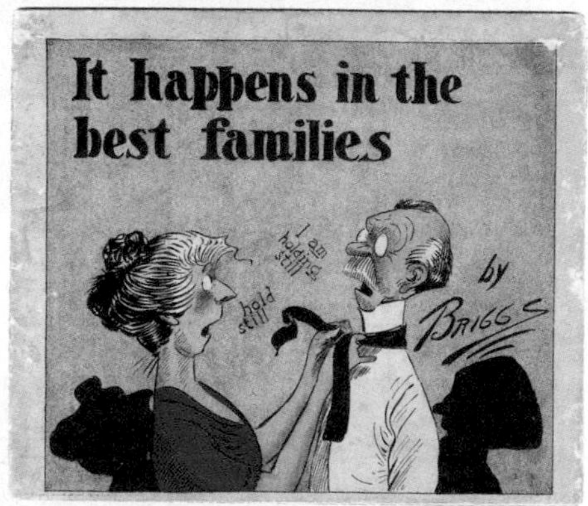

IT HAPPENS IN THE BEST FAMILIES
1920. © Powers Photo Engraving Co.

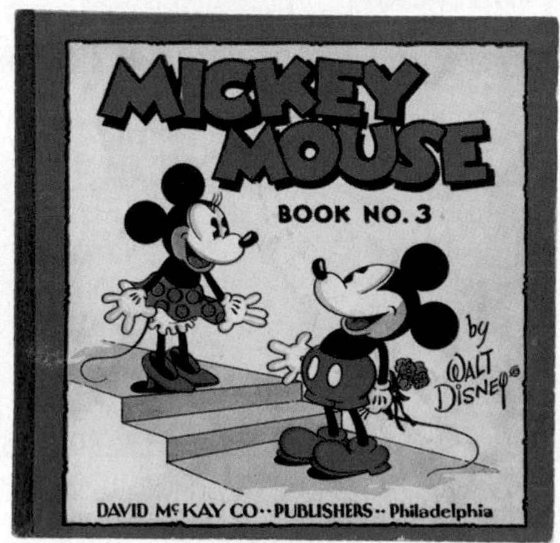

MICKEY MOUSE BOOK NO. 3
1933. © DIS

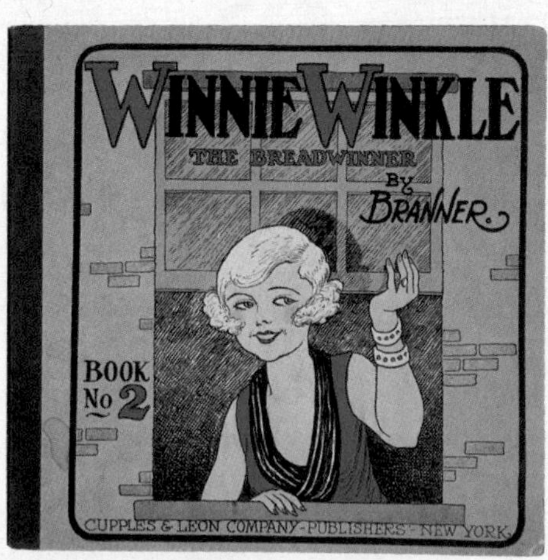

WINNIE WINKLE #2
1931. © Cupples & Leon Co.

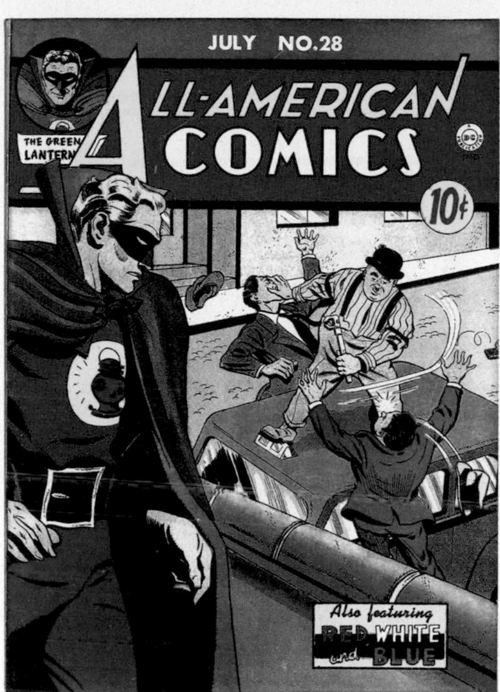

ALL-AMERICAN COMICS #28
July 1941. © DC

ARCHIE'S PAL, JUGHEAD #4
February 1951. © AP

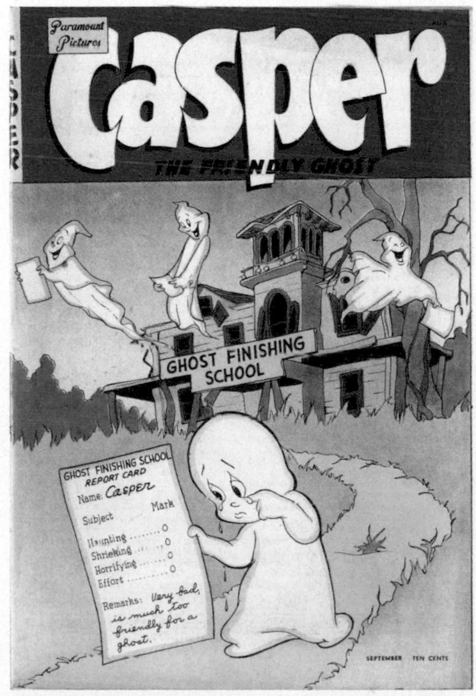

CASPER, THE FRIENDLY GHOST #1
June 1949. © Paramount Pictures

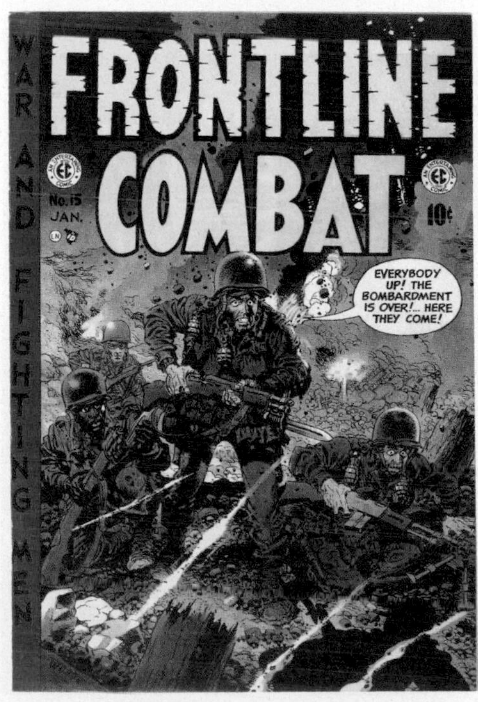

FRONTLINE COMBAT #15
January 1954. © WMG

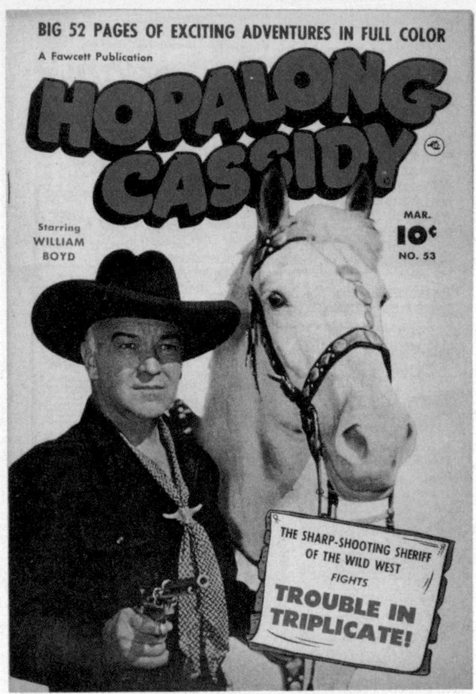

HOPALONG CASSIDY #53
March 1951. © DELL

KING COMICS #35
Mile High copy. February 1939. © KING

LONE RANGER #93
March 1956. © Lone Ranger Inc.

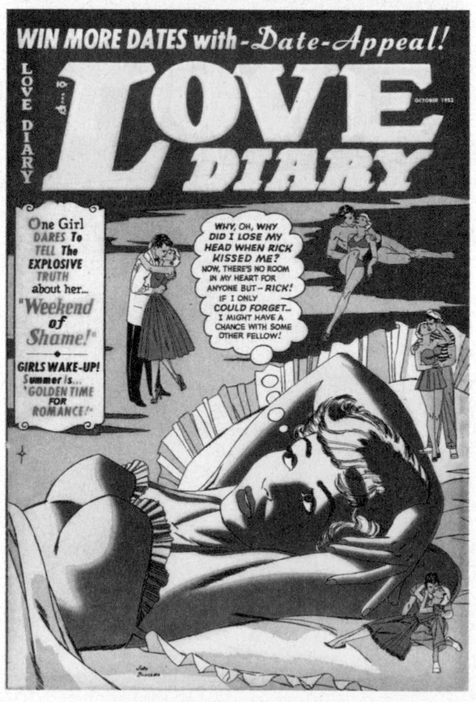

LOVE DIARY #31
October 1952. © CC

MARVEL MYSTERY COMICS #88
October 1948. © MAR

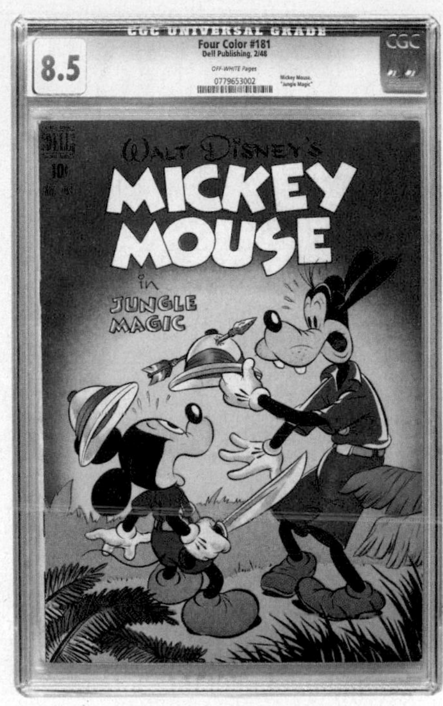

MICKEY MOUSE FOUR COLOR #181
February 1948. © DIS

TARGET COMICS Vol. 2 #1
March 1941. © NOVP

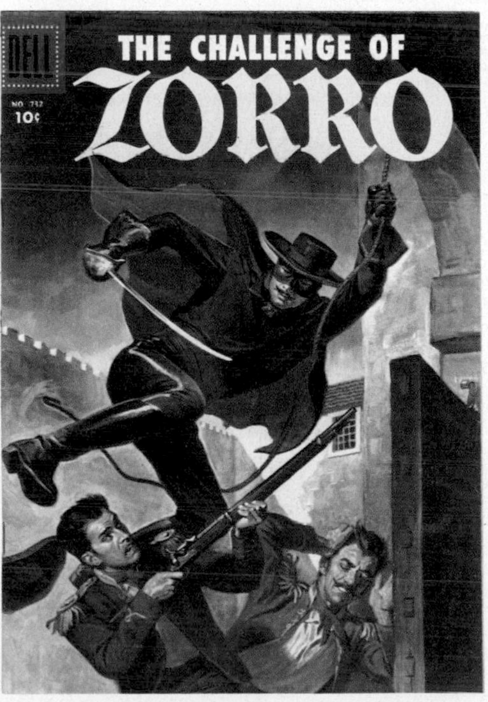

ZORRO FOUR COLOR #732
October 1956. © DIS

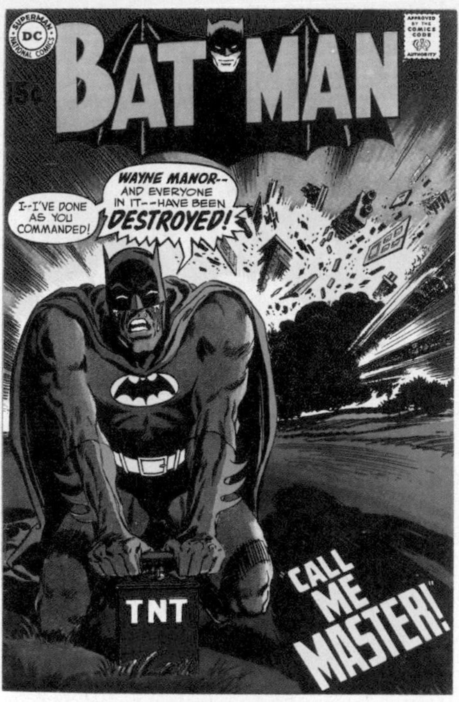

BATMAN #215
September 1969. © DC

BLUE BEETLE #2
August 1967. © CC

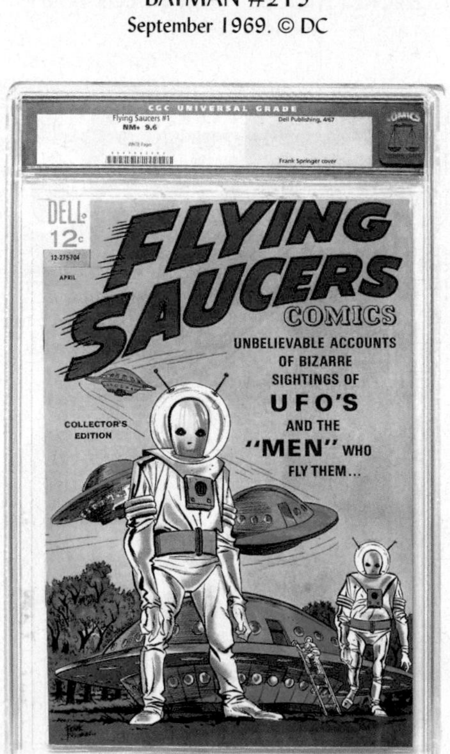

FLYING SAUCERS #1
May 1967. © DELL

GREEN LANTERN #18
January 1963. © DC

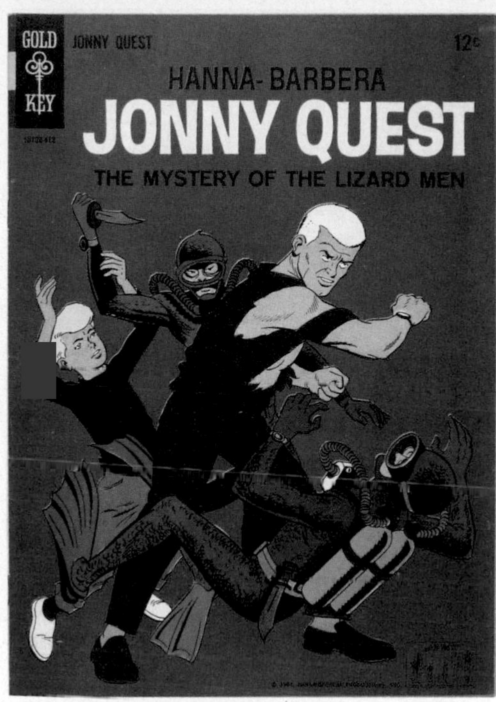

JONNY QUEST #1
December 1964. © H-B

OUR ARMY AT WAR #89
December 1959. © DC

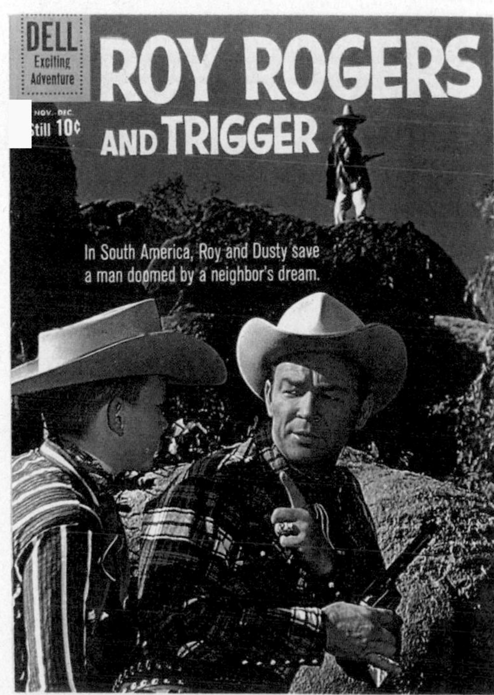

ROY ROGERS AND TRIGGER #140
November-December 1960. © Roy Rogers

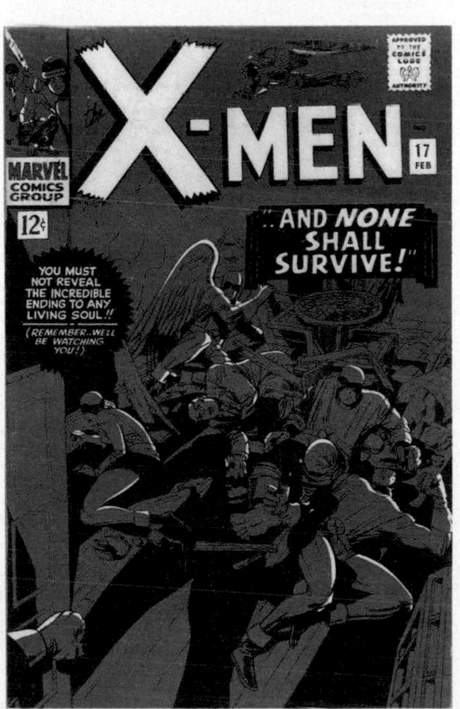

X-MEN #17
February 1966. © MAR

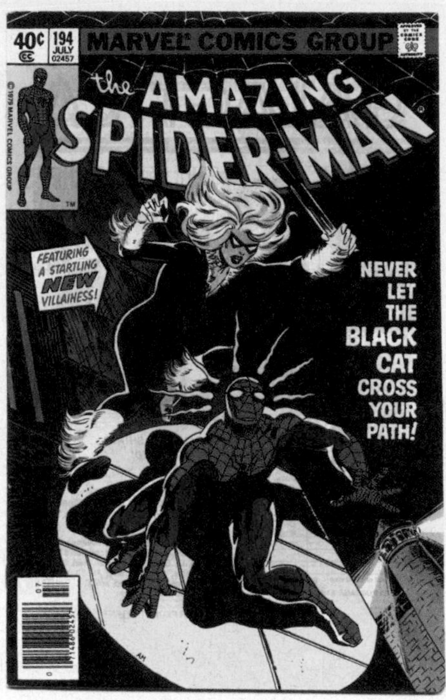

AMAZING SPIDER-MAN #194
July 1979. © MAR

CHILLING ADVENTURES IN SORCERY #5
February 1974. © AP

FOUR-STAR BATTLE TALES #1
February-March 1973. © DC

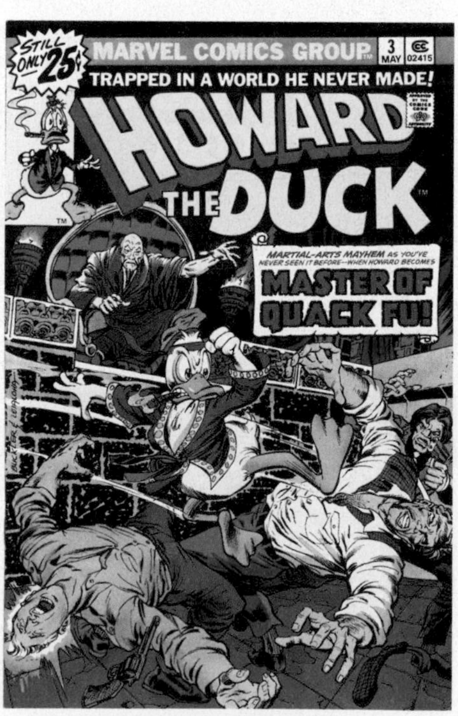

HOWARD THE DUCK #3
May 1976. © MAR

SPACE FAMILY ROBINSON #38
January 1974. © WEST

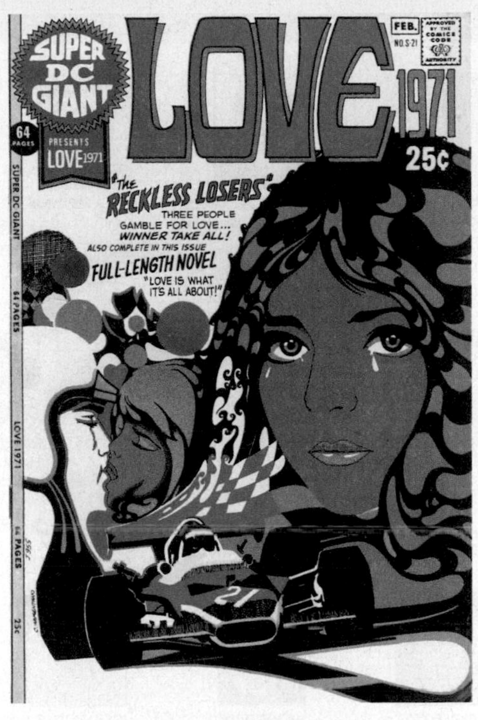

SUPER DC GIANT #21
1971. © DC

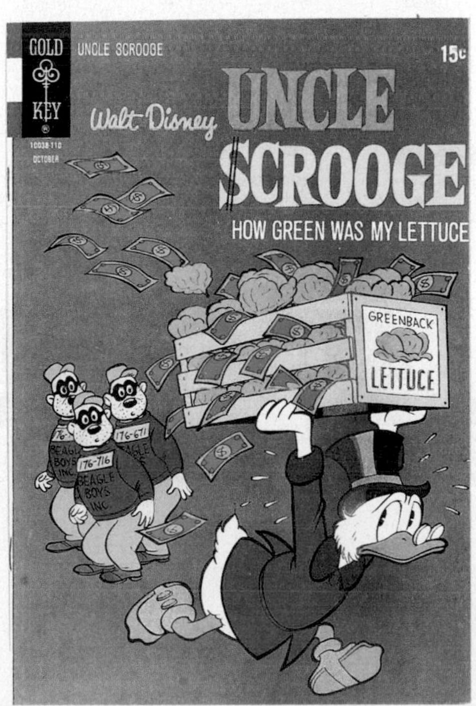

UNCLE SCROOGE #95
October 1971. © DIS

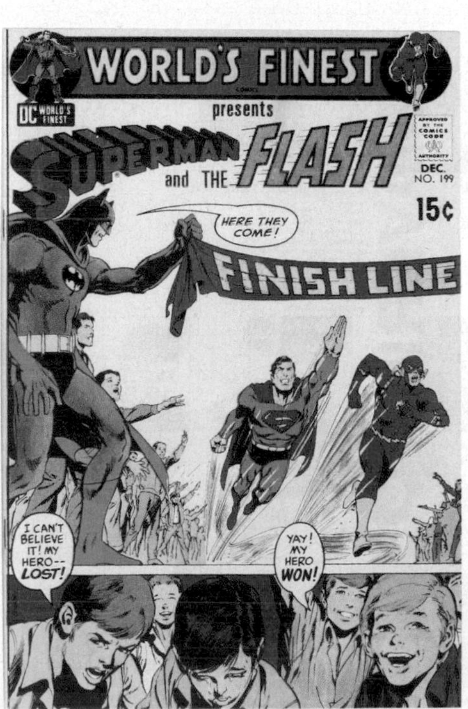

WORLD'S FINEST COMICS #199
December 1970. © DC

Overstreet Advisors

WELDON ADAMS
Comics Historian
Fort Worth, TX

DAVID T. ALEXANDER
David Alexander Comics
Tampa, FL

TYLER ALEXANDER
David Alexander Comics
Tampa, FL

LON ALLEN
Heritage Comics Auctions
Dallas, TX

DAVE ANDERSON
Want List Comics
Tulsa, OK

STEPHEN BARRINGTON
Flea Market Comics
Chickasaw, AL

LAUREN BECKER
Warp 9 Comics
Clawson, MI

ROBERT BEERBOHM
Robert Beerbohm
Comic Art
Fremont, NE

JON BERK
Collector
Hartford, CT

PETER BILELIS, ESQ.
Collector
South Windsor, CT

BRIAN BLOCK
WB Auction Services
Adamstown, PA

DR. ARNOLD T. BLUMBERG
Curator
Geppi's Entertainment Museum

STEVE BOROCK
Collector/Dealer
Sarasota, FL

KEVIN BOYD
CGC Signature Series Director
Toronto, ONT Canada

MIKE BRODER
Tropic Comics
Fort Lauderdale, FL

MICHAEL BROWNING
Collector
Danville, WV

MICHAEL CARBONARO
Neatstuffcollectibles.com
Englewood, NJ

GARY CARTER
Collector
Coronado, CA

FRANK CWIKLIK
Metropolis Comics
New York, NY

JOHN CHRUSCINSKI
Tropic Comics
Lyndora, PA

GARY COLABUONO
Dealer/Collector
Elk Grove Village, IL

BILL COLE
Bill Cole Enterprises, Inc.
Randolph, MA

TIM COLLINS
RTS Unlimited, Inc.
Lakewood, CO

JACK COPLEY
Archie Collector
Florida

DAN CUSIMANO
Flying Donut Trading Co.
Reston, VA

PETER DIXON
Paradise Comics
Toronto, ONT
Canada

GARY DOLGOFF
Gary Dolgoff Comics
Easthampton, MA

WALTER DURAJLIJA
Big B Comics
Hamilton, ONT
Canada

BRUCE ELLSWORTH
Gold Coast Comics
Nerang, QLD, Australia

CONRAD ESCHENBERG
Collector/Dealer
Cold Spring, NY

MICHAEL EURY
Author
Lake Oswego, OR

RICHARD EVANS
Bedrock City Comics
Houston, TX

D'ARCY FARRELL
Pendragon Comics
Toronto, ONT Canada

STEPHEN FISHLER
Metropolis Collectibles, Inc.
New York, NY

DAN FOGEL
Hippy Comix, Inc.
El Sobrante, CA

CHRIS FOSS
Heroes & Dragons
Columbia, SC

STEPHEN H. GENTNER
Golden Age Specialist
Portland, OR

STEVE GEPPI
Diamond Int. Galleries
Timonium, MD

Overstreet Advisors

MICHAEL GOLDMAN
Motor City Comics
Farmington Hills, MI

TOM GORDON III
ComicsPriceGuide.com
Hampstead, MD

JAMIE GRAHAM
Graham Crackers
Chicago, IL

DANIEL GREENHALGH
Showcase New England
Northford, CT

ERIC J. GROVES
Dealer/Collector
Oklahoma City, OK

JOHN HAINES
Dealer/Collector
Kirtland, OH

ROBERT HALL
Collector
Harrisburg, PA

JIM HALPERIN
Heritage Comics
Auctions
Dallas, TX

MARK HASPEL
Primary Grader
Certified Guaranty Co.,
LLC

JOHN HAUSER
Dealer/Collector
New Berlin, WI

JEF HINDS
Jef Hinds Comics
Madison, WI

GREG HOLLAND
Collector
Alexander, AR

BILL HUGHES
Dealer/Collector
Flower Mound, TX

ROB HUGHES
Arch Angels
Manhattan Beach, CA

WILLIAM INSIGNARES
Demolition Comics
Tampa, FL

ED JASTER
Heritage Comics Auctions
Dallas, TX

BRIAN KETTERER
Collector
Philadelphia, PA

DENNIS KEUM
Fantasy Comics
Goldens Bridge, NY

PHIL LEVINE
Dealer/Collector
Three Bridges, NJ

PAUL LITCH
Modern Age Specialist
Certified Guaranty Co., LLC

LARRY LOWERY
Big Little Books Specialist
Danville, CA

JOE MANNARINO
All Star Auctions
Ridgewood, NJ

NADIA MANNARINO
All Star Auctions
Ridgewood, NJ

HARRY MATETSKY
Collector
Middletown, NJ

DAVE MATTEINI
Collector
New York, NY

JON McCLURE
Dealer/Collector
Durango, CO

TODD MCDEVITT
New Dimension
Comics
Cranberry Township, PA

MIKE McKENZIE
Alternate Worlds
Cockeysville, MD

FRED McSURLEY
Dealer/Collector
Holland, Ohio

PETER MEROLO
Collector
Sedona, AZ

JOHN JACKSON MILLER
Comics Historian,
Writer
Waupaca, WI

STEVE MORTENSEN
Colossus Comics
Santa Clara, CA

MICHAEL NAIMAN
Silver Age Specialist
Chapel Hill, NC

MARC NATHAN
Cards, Comics & Collectibles
Reisterstown, MD

JOSHUA NATHANSON
ComicLink
Brooklyn, NY

MATT NELSON
Classics Incorporated
Carrolltown, TX

JAMIE NEWBOLD
Southern California Comics
San Diego, CA

CHARLIE NOVINSKIE
Silver Age Specialist
Grand Junction, CO

Overstreet Advisors

RICHARD OLSON
Collector/Academician
Poplarville, MS

TERRY O'NEILL
Terry's Comics
Orange, CA

GEORGE PANTELA
GPAnalysis for Comics
Hampton, Victoria, Australia

JIM PAYETTE
Golden Age Specialist
Bethlehem, NH

CHRIS PEDRIN
Pedrin Conservatory
Redwood City, CA

JOHN PETTY
Collector/Historian
Dallas, TX

JIM PITTS
Surf City Comix
Mountain View, CA

BILL PONSETI
Collector
Saucier, MS

RON PUSSELL
Redbeard's Book Den
Crystal Bay, NV

JO ANN REISLER
Collector
Vienna, VA

STEPHEN RITTER
Collector
Beavercreek, OH

DAVE ROBIE
Big Little Books Specialist
Lancaster, PA

ROBERT ROGOVIN
Four Color Comics
Scarsdale, NY

MARNIN ROSENBERG
Collectors Assemble
Great Neck, NY

CHUCK ROZANSKI
Mile High Comics
Denver, CO

BARRY SANDOVAL
Heritage Comics Auctions
Dallas, TX

MATT SCHIFFMAN
Bronze Age Specialist
Bend, OR

DOUG SCHMELL
Pedigree Comics, Inc.
Wellington, FL

JOHN SNYDER
Diamond Int. Galleries
York, PA

TONY STARKS
Silver Age Specialist
Evansville, IN

WEST STEPHAN
Collector
Bradenton, FL

AL STOLTZ
Basement Comics
Havre de Grace, MD

KEN STRIBLING
Action Island
Jackson, MS

DOUG SULIPA
"Everything 1960-1996"
Manitoba, Canada

MAGGIE THOMPSON
Comics Buyer's Guide
Iola, WI

MICHAEL TIERNEY
The Comic Book Store
Little Rock, AR

TED VAN LIEW
Superworld Comics
Worcester, MA

JOE VERENEAULT
JHV Associates
Woodbury Heights, NJ

BOB WAYNE
DC Comics
New York City, NY

LON WEBB
Dark Adventure Comics
Norcross, GA

JERRY WEIST
Sotheby's
Gloucester, MA

RICK WHITELOCK
New Force Comics
Lynn Haven, FL

MARK WILSON
PGC Mint
Castle Rock, WA

ALEX WINTER
Hake's Americana
York, PA

HARLEY YEE
Dealer/Collector
Detroit, MI

MARK ZAID
EsquireComics.com
Bethesda, MD

VINCENT ZURZOLO, JR.
Metropolis Collectibles, Inc.
New York, NY

Overstreet Price Guide Back Issues

The Official Overstreet® Comic Book Price Guide has held the record for being the longest running annual comic book publication. We are now celebrating our 39th anniversary, and the demand for the Overstreet® price guides is very strong. Collectors have created a legitimate market for them, and they continue to bring record prices each year. Collectors also have a record of comic book prices going back further than any other source in comic fandom. The prices listed below are for NM condition only, with GD-25% and FN-50% of the NM value. Canadian editions exist for a couple of the early issues. Abbreviations: SC-softcover, HC-hardcover, L-leather bound.

1970	1970	1972	1973
#1 White SC $1825.00	#1 Blue SC (2nd Printing) $1550.00	#2 SC $650.00 #2 HC $1100.00	#3 SC $325.00 #3 HC $950.00

1974	1975	1976	1977
#4 SC $165.00 #4 HC $475.00	#5 SC $155.00 #5 HC $260.00	#6 SC $105.00 #6 HC $155.00	#7 SC $155.00 #7 HC $230.00

1978	1979	1980	1981
#8 SC $130.00 #8 HC $180.00	#9 SC $130.00 #9 HC $180.00	#10 SC $140.00 #10 HC $190.00	#11 SC $85.00 #11 HC $115.00

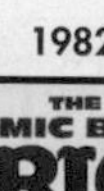

1982

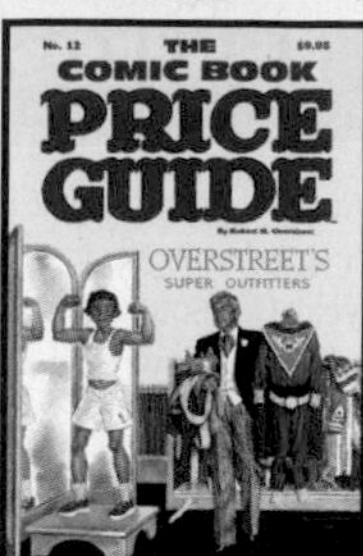

#12 SC $85.00
#12 HC $115.00

1983

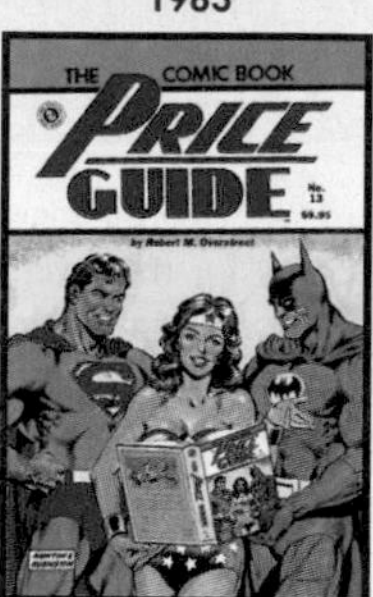

#13 SC $85.00
#13 HC $115.00

1984

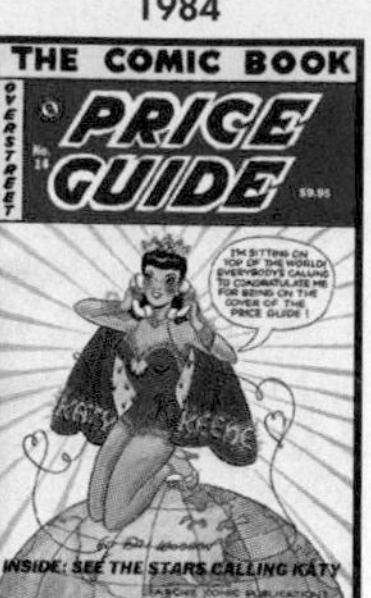

#14 SC $55.00
#14 HC $110.00
#14 L $170.00

1985

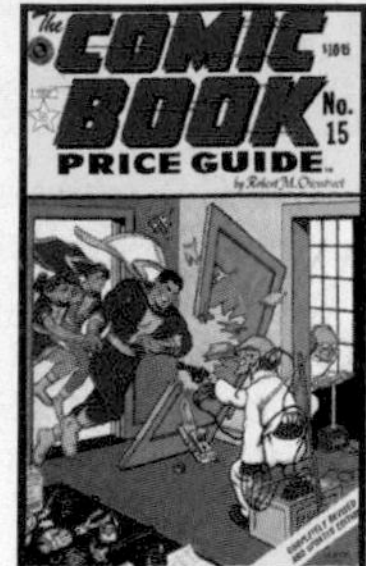

#15 SC $55.00
#15 HC $80.00
#15 L $160.00

1986

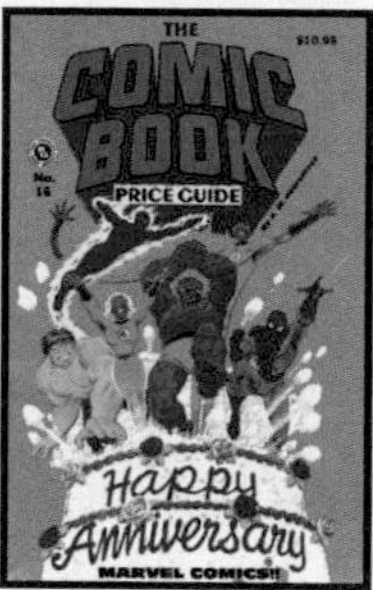

#16 SC $60.00
#16 HC $85.00
#16 L $170.00

1987

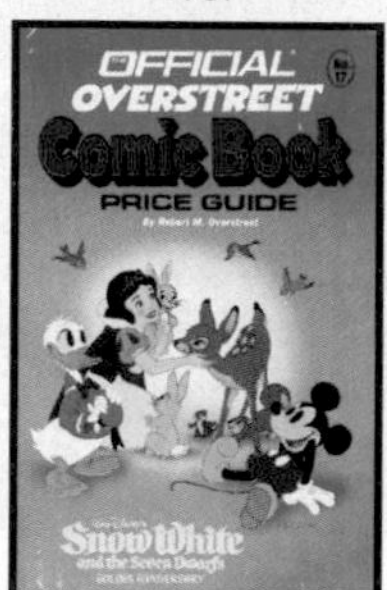

#17 SC $55.00
#17 HC $110.00
#17 L $160.00

1988

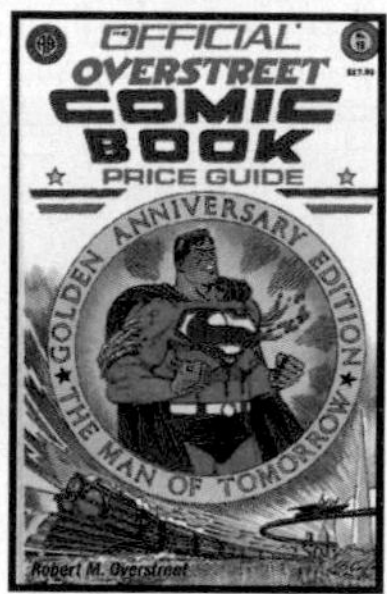

#18 SC $45.00
#18 HC $65.00
#18 L $160.00

1989

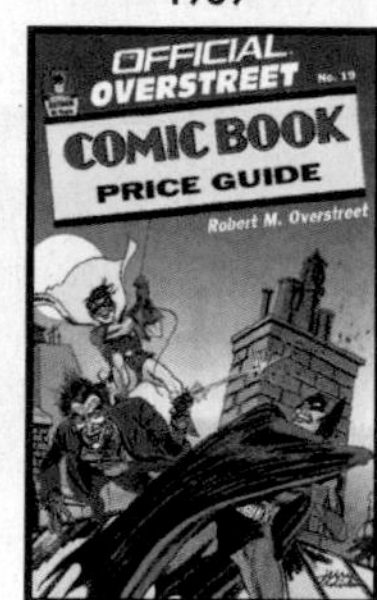

#19 SC $50.00
#19 HC $60.00
#19 L $170.00

1990

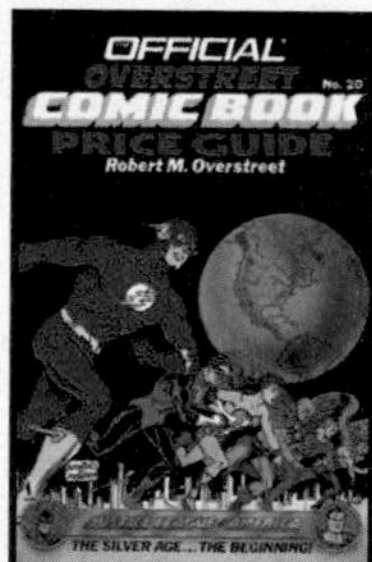

#20 SC $32.00
#20 HC $50.00
#20 L $135.00

1991

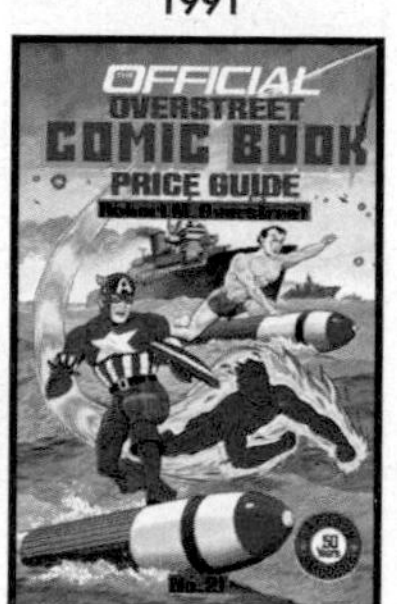

#21 SC $40.00
#21 HC $60.00
#21 L $145.00

1992

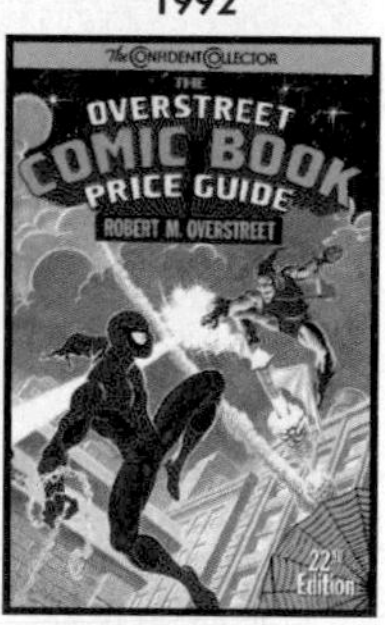

#22 SC $32.00
#22 HC $50.00

1993

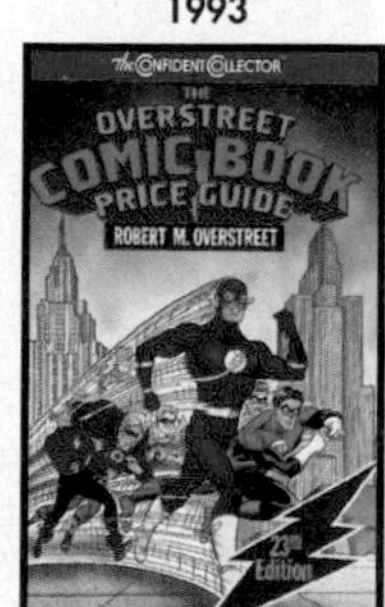

#23 SC $32.00
#23 HC $50.00

1994

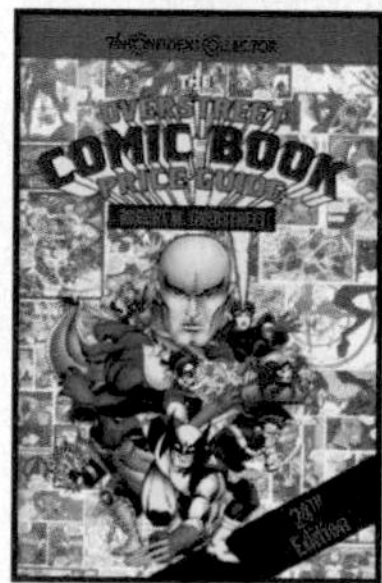

#24 SC $26.00
#24 HC $36.00

1995

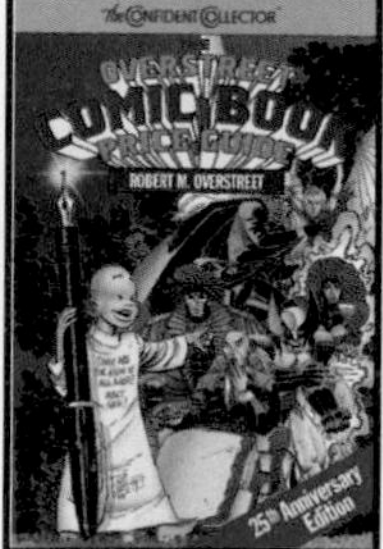

#25 SC $26.00
#25 HC $36.00
#25 L $110.00

1996

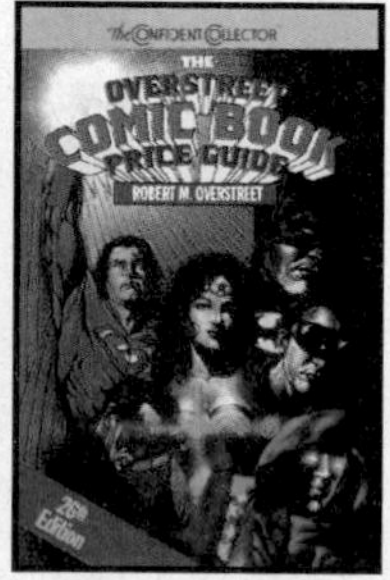

#26 SC $20.00
#26 HC $30.00
#26 L $100.00

1997

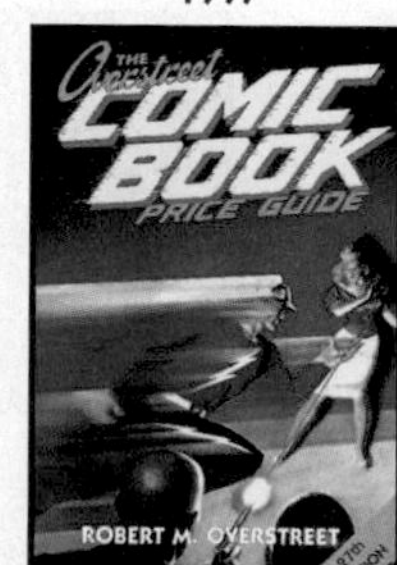

#27 SC $22.00
#27 HC $38.00
#27 L $125.00

1997

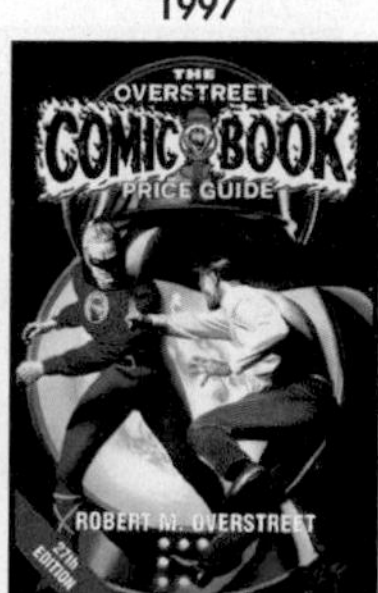

#27 SC $22.00
#27 HC $38.00
#27 L $125.00

1998

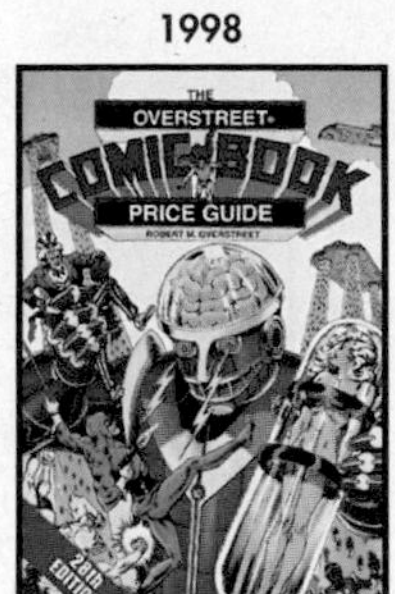

#28 SC $20.00
#28 HC $35.00

1998

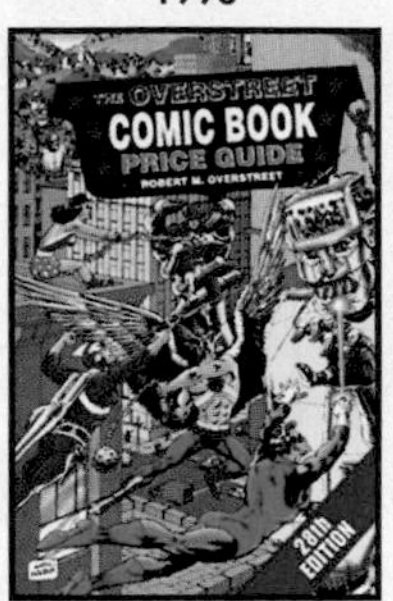

#28 SC $20.00
#28 HC $35.00

1999

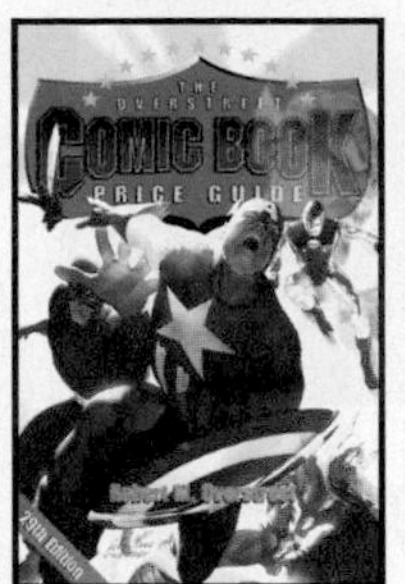

#29 SC $25.00
#29 HC $40.00

1999

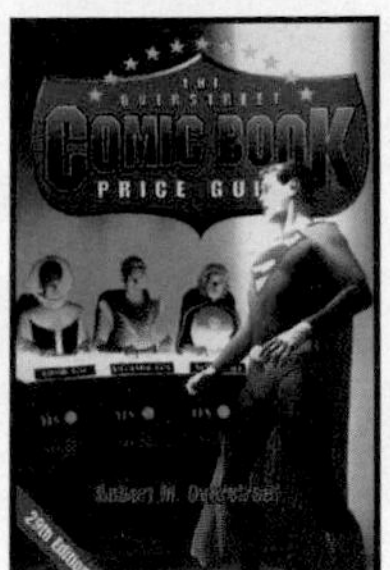

#29 SC $20.00
#29 HC $37.00

2000

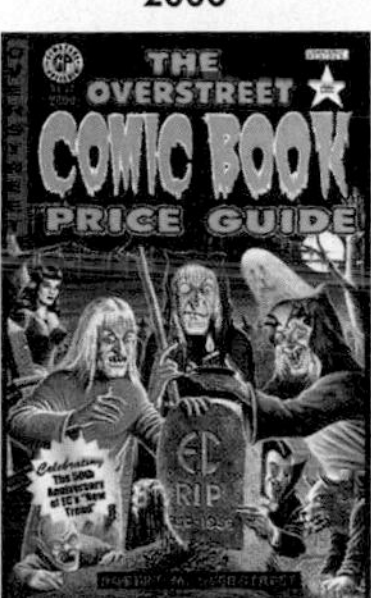

#30 SC $22.00
#30 HC $32.00

2000

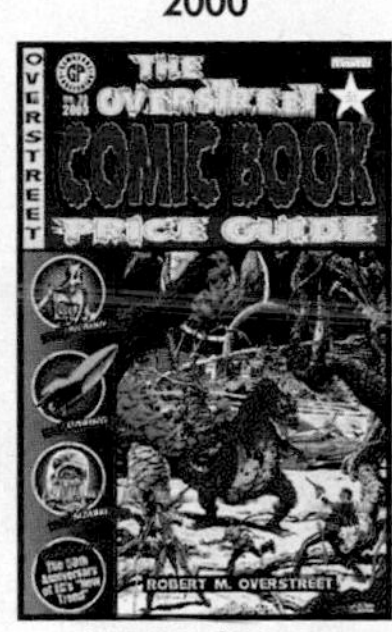

#30 SC $22.00
#30 HC $32.00

2001

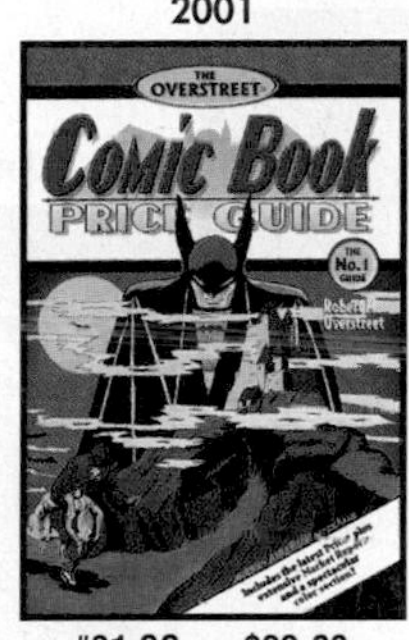

#31 SC $22.00
#31 HC $32.00

2001

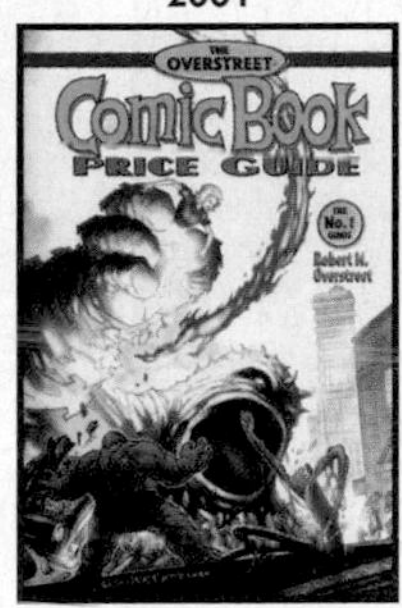

#31 SC $22.00
#31 HC $32.00

2001

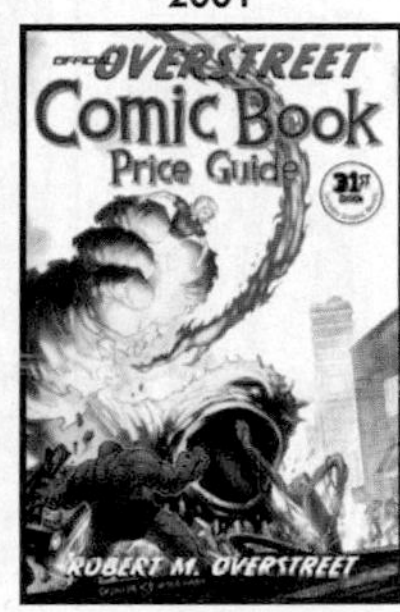

#31 Bookstore Ed.
SC only $22.00

2002

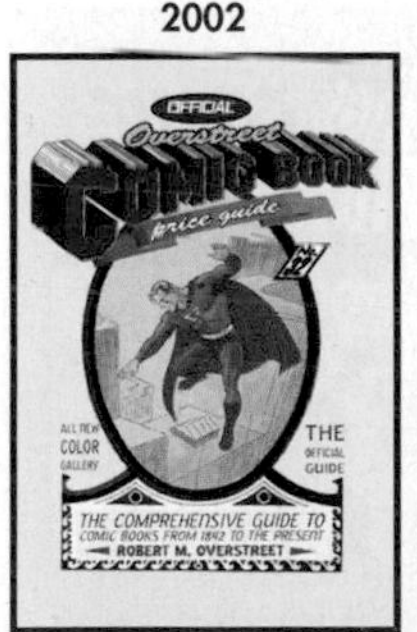

#32 SC $22.00
#32 HC $32.00

2002

#32 SC $22.00
#32 HC $32.00

2002

#32 Bookstore Ed.
SC only $22.00

2003

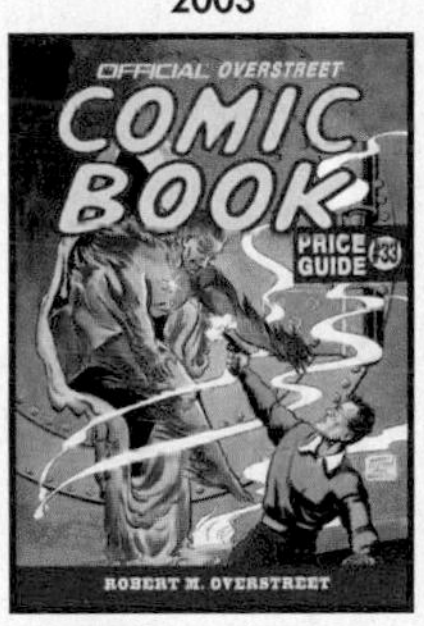

#33 SC $25.00
#33 HC $32.00

2003

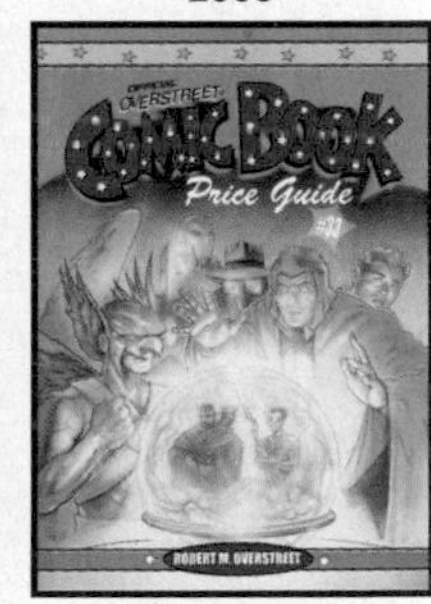

#33 SC $25.00
#33 HC $32.00

2003

#33 Bookstore Ed.
SC only $25.00

2004

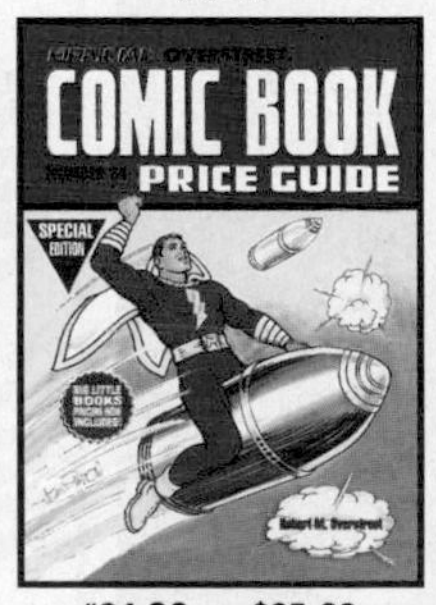

#34 SC $25.00
#34 HC $32.00

2004

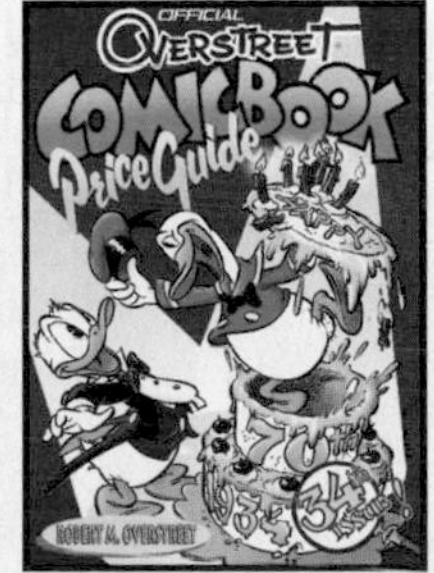

#34 SC $25.00
#34 HC $32.00

2004

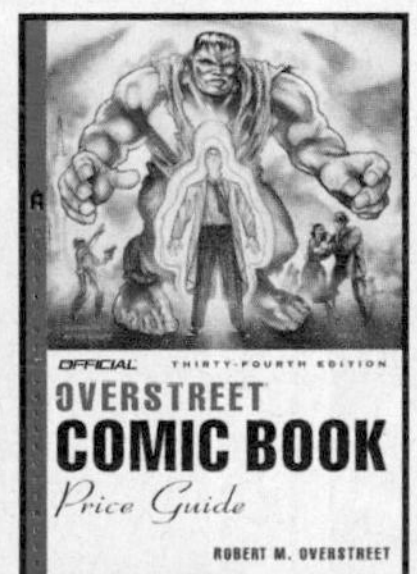

#34 Bookstore Ed.
SC only $25.00

2005

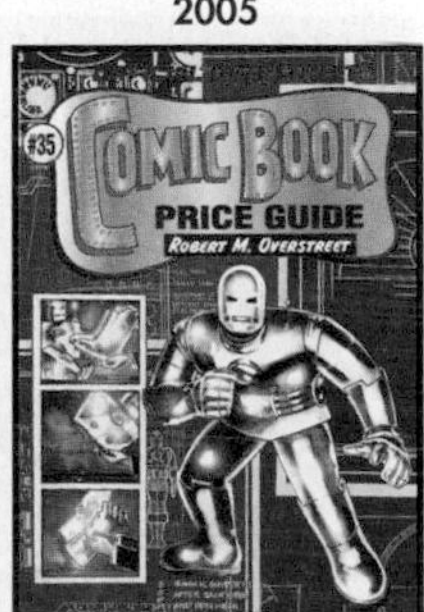

#35 SC $25.00
#35 HC $32.00

2005

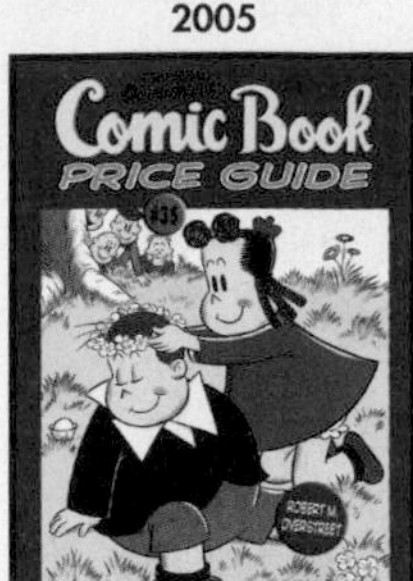

#35 SC $25.00
#35 HC $55.00

2005

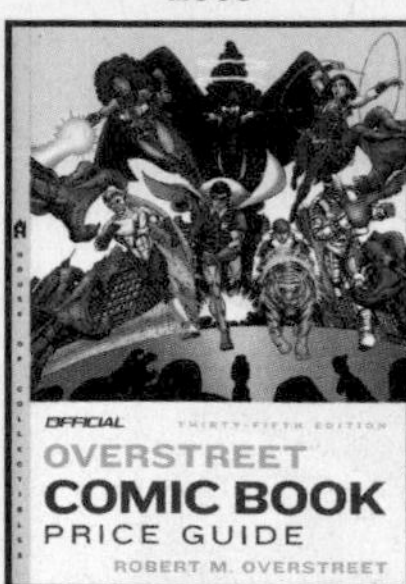

#35 Bookstore Ed.
SC only $25.00

2006

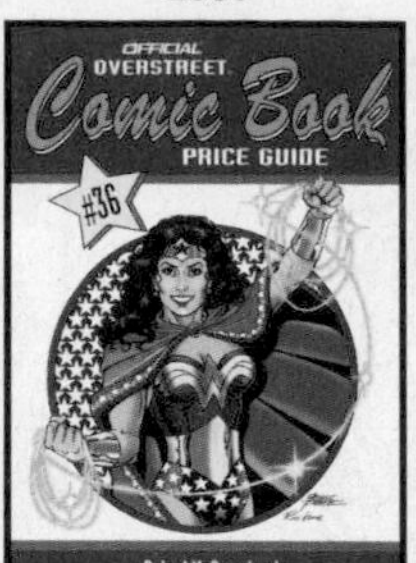

#36 SC $25.00
#36 HC $32.00

2006

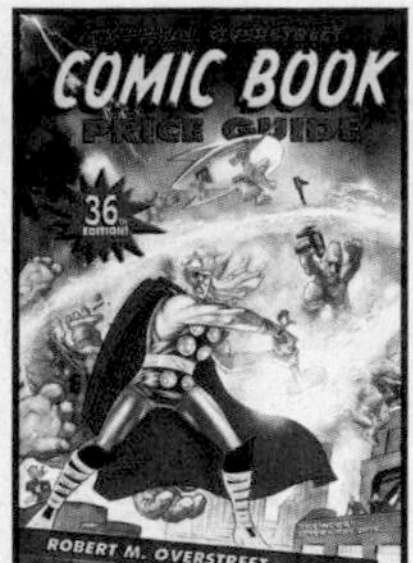

#36 SC $25.00
#36 HC $32.00

2006

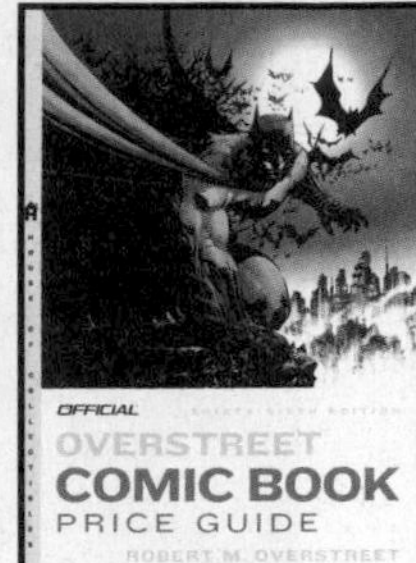

#36 Bookstore Ed.
SC only $25.00

2007

#37 SC $30.00
#37 HC $35.00

2007

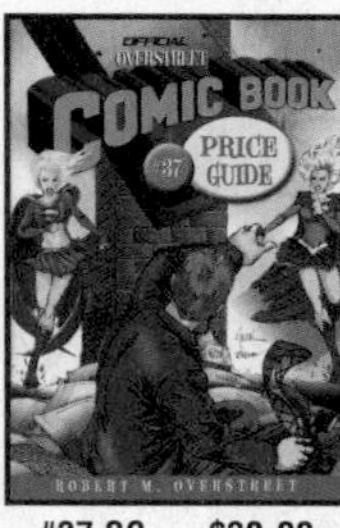

#37 SC $30.00
#37 HC $35.00

2007

#37 Bookstore Ed.
SC only $30.00

2008

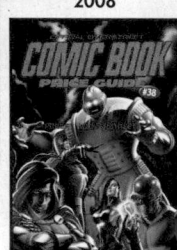

#38 SC $30.00
#38 HC $35.00

2008

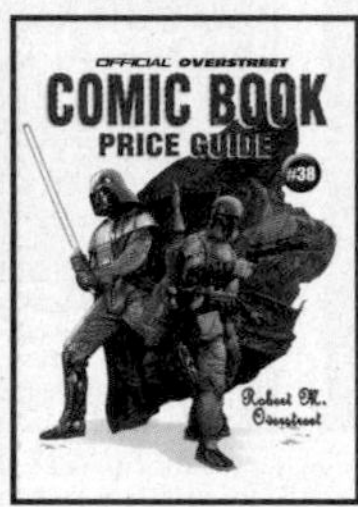

#38 SC $30.00
#38 HC $35.00

2008

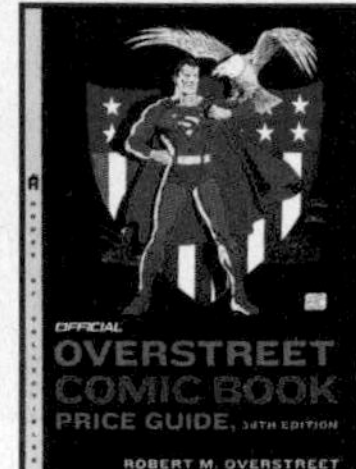

#38 Bookstore Ed.
SC only $30.00

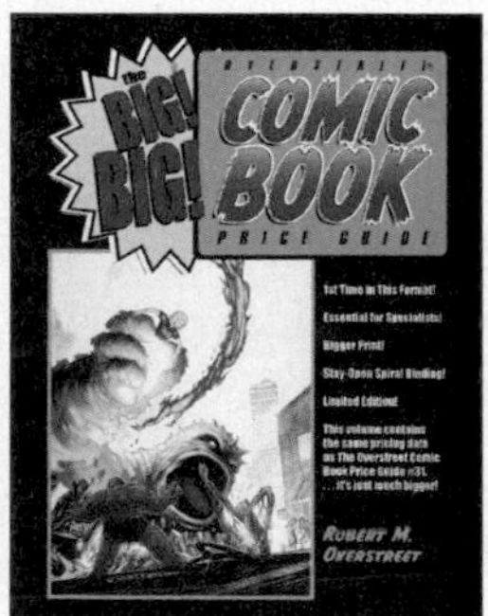

#31 Workbook - 2001
$35.00

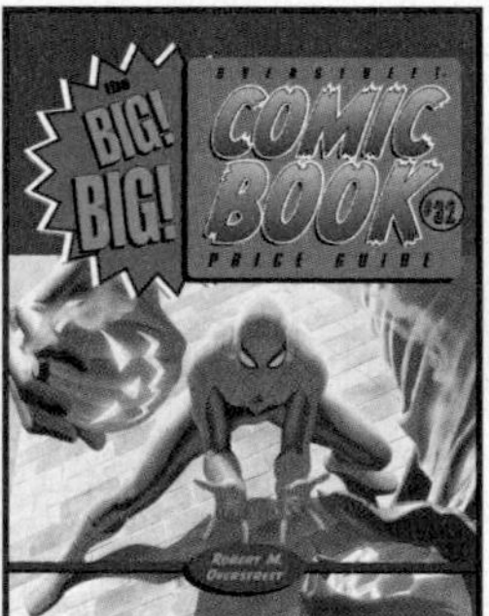

#32 Workbook - 2002
$35.00

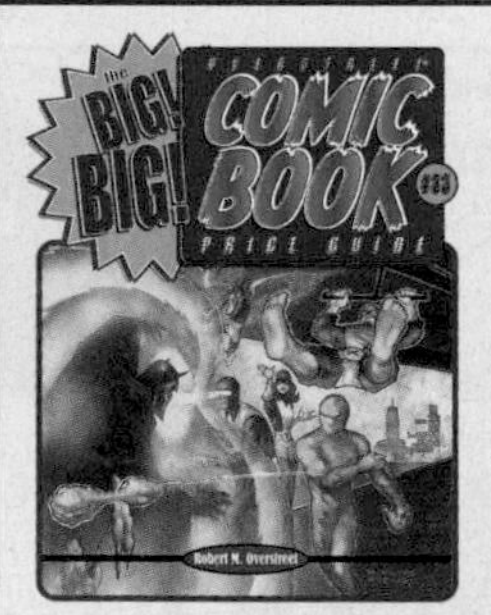

#33 Workbook - 2003
$37.00

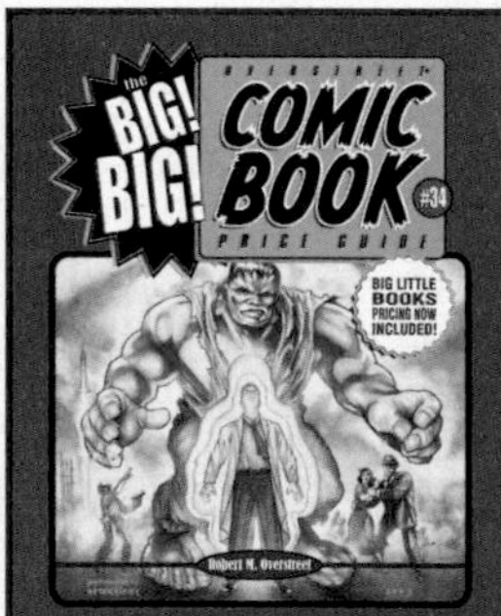

#34 Workbook - 2004
$37.00

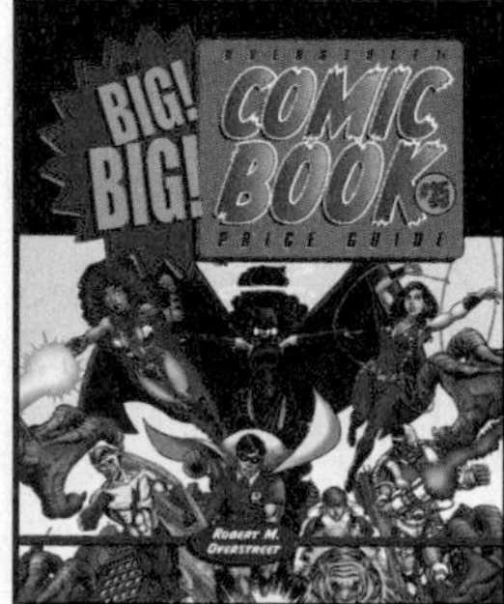

#35 Workbook - 2005
$37.00

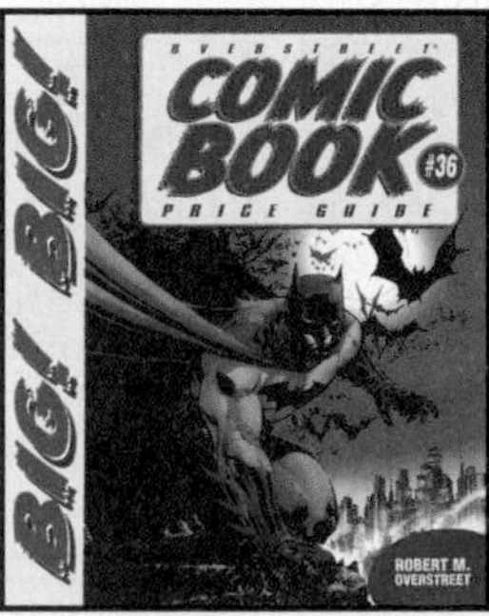

#36 Workbook - 2006
$37.00

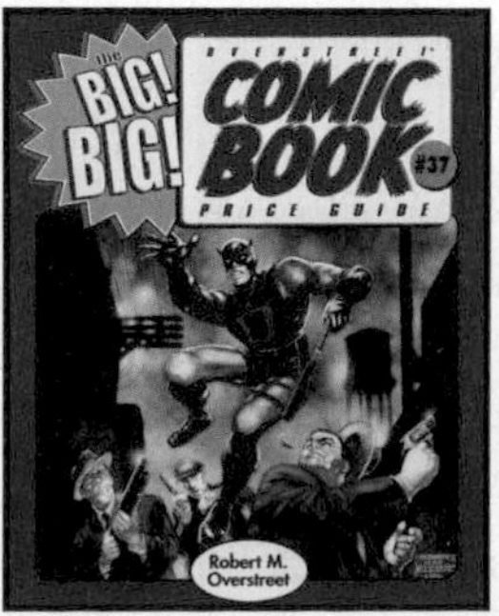

#37 Workbook - 2007
$37.00

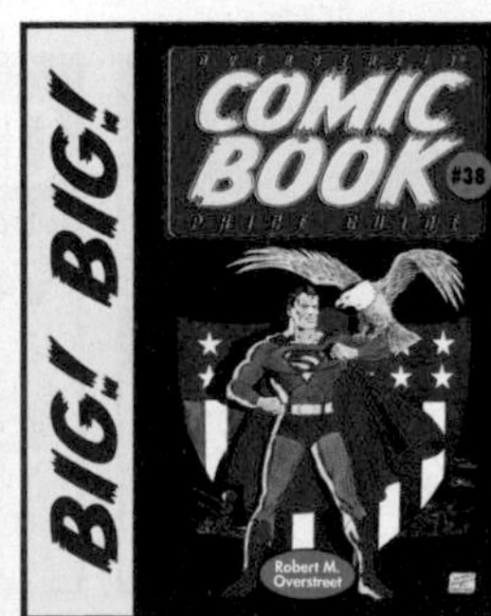

#38 Workbook - 2008
$37.00

Advertisers' Index

A

B

C

D

E

F

G

H